# SYMBOLS AND LANGUAGE ABBREVIATIONS USED IN THE ETYMOLOGIES

‡ foreign word or phrase
< derived from
? perhaps; possibly; uncertain
+ plus
& and

**Abyss.**, Abyssinian
**Afr.**, African
**Alb.**, Albanian
**Am.**, American
**Am. Ind.**, American Indian
**Am. Sp.**, American Spanish
**Anglo-Fr.**, Anglo-French
**Anglo-Ind.**, Anglo-Indian
**Anglo-Ir.**, Anglo-Irish
**Anglo-L.**, Anglo-Latin
**Anglo-N.**, Anglo-Norse
**Anglo-Norm.**, Anglo-Norman
**Ar.**, Arabic
**Aram.**, Aramaic
**AS.**, Anglo-Saxon
**Assyr.**, Assyrian

**Bab.**, Babylonian
**Beng.**, Bengali
**Bohem.**, Bohemian
**Braz.**, Brazilian
**Bret.**, Breton
**Brit.**, British
**Bulg.**, Bulgarian

**Canad.**, Canadian
**Canad. Fr.**, Canadian French
**Catal.**, Catalonian
**Celt.**, Celtic
**Ch.**, Chaldean; Chaldee
**Chin.**, Chinese
**Corn.**, Cornish
**Cym.**, Cymric

**D.**, Dutch
**Dan.**, Danish

**E.Fris.**, East Frisian
**Egypt.**, Egyptian
**E.Ind.**, East Indian
**Eng.**, English
**Esk.**, Eskimo
**Eth.**, Ethiopic

**Finn.**, Finnish
**Fl.**, Flemish
**Fr.**, French
**Frank.**, Frankish
**Fris.**, Frisian

**G.**, German
**Gael.**, Gaelic
**Gaul.**, Gaulish
**Gmc.**, Germanic
**Goth.**, Gothic
**Gr.**, Greek

**Haw.**, Hawaiian
**Heb.**, Hebrew
**Hind.**, Hindi; Hindu; Hindustani
**Hung.**, Hungarian

**Ice.**, Icelandic
**IE.**, Indo-European
**Ind.**, Indian
**Ir.**, Irish
**Iran.**, Iranian
**It.**, Italian

**Japan.**, Japanese
**Jav.**, Javanese

**Kor.**, Korean

**L.**, Latin
**LG.**, Low German
**LGr.**, Late Greek
**Lith.**, Lithuanian
**LL.**, Late Latin; Low Latin
**LWS.**, Late West Saxon

**MD.**, Middle Dutch
**ME.**, Middle English
**Med.**, Medieval
**Mex.**, Mexican
**MFl.**, Middle Flemish
**MFr.**, Middle French
**MGr.**, Medieval Greek; Middle Greek
**MHG.**, Middle High German
**MIr.**, Middle Irish
**MIt.**, Middle Italian
**ML.**, Medieval Latin
**MLG.**, Middle Low German
**MnE.**, Modern English
**Mod.**, Modern
**Mod. Gr.**, Modern Greek
**Mod. L.**, Modern Latin
**Mongol.**, Mongolian
**MScand.**, Middle Scandinavian
**MScot.**, Middle Scottish

**N.**, Norse
**Norm.**, Norman
**Norw.**, Norwegian

**O**, Old
**OAr.**, Old Arabic
**OCelt.**, Old Celtic
**OCym.**, Old Cymric
**OD.**, Old Dutch
**ODan.**, Old Danish
**OFr.**, Old French
**OFris.**, Old Frisian
**OHG.**, Old High German
**OIr.**, Old Irish
**OIt.**, Old Italian
**OLG.**, Old Low German
**ON.**, Old Norse
**ONorm.Fr.**, Old Norman French
**OPer.**, Old Persian
**OS.**, Old Saxon
**OSlav.**, Old Slavic
**OSerb.**, Old Serbian
**OSp.**, Old Spanish
**OW.**, Old Welsh

**Per.**, Persian
**Peruv.**, Peruvian
**Phoen.**, Phoenician
**Pid.Eng.**, Pidgin English
**Pol.**, Polish
**Port.**, Portuguese
**Pr.**, Provençal
**Prov. Eng.**, Provincial English
**Prov. Scot.**, Provincial Scottish

**Russ.**, Russian

**S.Afr.D.**, South African Dutch
**Sans.**, Sanskrit
**Scand.**, Scandinavian
**Scot.**, Scottish
**Sem.**, Semitic
**Serb.**, Serbian
**Singh.**, Singhalese
**Slav.**, Slavic; Slavonic
**Sp.**, Spanish
**Sw., Swed.**, Swedish
**Syr.**, Syrian; Syriac

**Tag.**, Tagalog
**Tart.**, Tartar
**Tibet.**, Tibetan
**Turk.**, Turkish

**W.**, Welsh
**W.Afr.**, West African
**W.Fl.**, West Flemish
**W.Gmc.**, West Germanic
**W.Ind.**, West Indian
**W.S.**, West Saxon

**Yid.**, Yiddish

# *Gallery of* OFFICIAL PORTRAITS *of the* PRESIDENTS *of the* UNITED STATES

George Washington
1789–1797

John Adams
1797–1801

Thomas Jefferson
1801–1809

James Madison
1809–1817

James Monroe
1817–1825

John Quincy Adams
1825–1829

Andrew Jackson
1829–1837

Martin Van Buren
1837–1841

William Henry Harrison
1841

John Tyler
1841–1845

James K. Polk
1845–1849

Zachary Taylor
1849–1850

Millard Fillmore
1850–1853

Franklin Pierce
1853–1857

James Buchanan
1857–1861

Abraham Lincoln
1861–1865

Andrew Johnson
1865–1869

Ulysses S. Grant
1869–1877

Rutherford B. Hayes
1877–1881

James A. Garfield
1881

Chester A. Arthur
1881–1885

Grover Cleveland
1885–1889, 1893–1897

Benjamin Harrison
1889–1893

William McKinley
1897–1901

Theodore Roosevelt
1901–1909

William H. Taft
1909–1913

Woodrow Wilson
1913–1921

Warren G. Harding
1921–1923

Calvin Coolidge
1923–1929

Herbert C. Hoover
1929–1933

Franklin D. Roosevelt
1933–1945

Harry S. Truman
1945–1953

Dwight D. Eisenhower
1953–1961

John F. Kennedy
1961–1963

Lyndon B. Johnson
1963–1969

Richard M. Nixon
1969–

# WEBSTER'S

## *New World*

# DICTIONARY

OF THE AMERICAN LANGUAGE

## *with Student*

# HANDBOOK

CONCISE EDITION

David B. Guralnik, *Dictionary Editor in Chief*

THE SOUTHWESTERN COMPANY

Nashville, Tennessee

PRINTED IN THE UNITED STATES OF AMERICA

# Contents

# TO USERS OF THIS DICTIONARY

## DICTIONARIES—YESTERDAY AND TODAY

A dictionary is a guide book rather than a book of rules and regulations. It presents words with their meanings, spellings, and pronunciations. Since the language is always changing and developing, the dictionary does not set down rules as to how the language ought to be used. It does report how language is being used by educated writers and speakers.

This, however, was not the thinking of Dr. Samuel Johnson. He was opposed to any deviation from what he and the scholars of the day considered good usage. In 1755, after eight years' work, he published his *Dictionary of the English Language*. It prescribed a standard for all to observe. During Dr. Johnson's lifetime, and for many years afterward, it had a tremendous effect on the English language. Indeed, with various revisions, it continued in common use until 1900. For all those years, Johnson's dictionary was the authority on the "right" and "wrong" of English usage.

However, English is a living language, and a living language is an ever-changing language. Even before the publication of Johnson's dictionary, great changes in the English language were occurring in America. New experiences in the new environment led to the creation of new words and to new meanings for old words. The mingling of peoples from many countries produced a variety of pronunciations and spellings. American English was developing. A Connecticut lawyer and schoolteacher, Noah Webster, was interested in the differences between American English and the standard English usage as prescribed in Johnson's dictionary. From 1806 to 1828 he worked on compiling a dictionary of American English. Webster regarded his dictionary as prescribing for Americans the correct pronunciation and spelling of words and the meanings attached to them.

The first dictionary to describe the way language is used, rather than to set up standards of right and wrong, was the *Oxford English Dictionary*. Started in 1879, it was finally completed, in twelve volumes, in 1928. A supplementary volume was published in 1933, and work on a second supplement is under way. Its objective—not to prescribe, but to describe—has been the objective of dictionary editors ever since. Because the language is always growing, frequent revisions of any dictionary are necessary. *Webster's New World Dictionary of the American Language*, College Edition, upon which this dictionary is based, has received updating at very frequent intervals. As a result, it presents a record of the language as it is currently used. This dictionary, the *Students Concise Webster's New World Dictionary*, is ideal for high school use. It contains over 100,000 entries, and provides a great deal of necessary information presented in a clear and concise way.

## THE ENTRIES

All entries are presented under a single listing and in alphabetical order. This listing involves not just the first letter in a word, but all the letters. When a series of words have identical beginnings, you must look for the first letter that is different. That is the letter which determines how the word will be listed within that series.

Strict alphabetical order is easy to follow, even when a listing contains compound words, inflected forms, and words formed with suffixes. Here is an example of such a listing as it appears in this dictionary. As you go down the list, notice the letters that remain the same in each succeeding entry. Notice the letters that are different, and notice especially the letter that determines the alphabetical order for each word in this series.

**mar·riage**
**mar·riage·a·ble**
**marriage portion**
**mar·ried**
**mar·row**
**mar·row·bone**
**mar·row·fat**
**mar·ry**

# To Users of This Dictionary

In locating a term, you will find the guide words, or catchwords, at the top of each page helpful. On page 758, the guide words given are *tameless* and *tap*. All main entries on this page must fall in alphabetical order between these two words. For instance, the words *tangent* and *Taoism* (but not *tame* or *tape*) are found on this page.

### Biographical and Geographical Entries

This dictionary contains approximately 2,000 geographical names, including those of countries, principal cities, mountains, rivers, lakes, and islands. There are approximately 1,600 biographical entries. Also names of Biblical, literary, and legendary significance are included. The biographical entries are listed in the form most commonly known, with pseudonym, family or maiden name, or fuller form in parentheses.

**Henry, O.,** (pseudonym of *William Sydney Porter*), 1862–1910; U.S. short story writer.

**Dick·ens, Charles** (dik′nz, -inz), (pseudonym *Boz*), 1812–1870; English novelist.

### Compound Terms

The English language contains many compound words and phrases. Sometimes they are united as a single word, the syllables separated by centered dots: **fi·ber·board.** Sometimes they appear as two separate words: **field goal.** Sometimes the parts are joined by a hyphen or hyphens: **deaf-and-dumb.** All compounds are treated as single words in determining their alphabetical order in this dictionary. Thus, *deaf-and-dumb* appears between *deaf* and *deafen.*

### Syllabification

Except for compound terms that are written as two separate words, each entry word is divided into syllables. The division of English words into syllables follows no consistent, logical pattern. In the eighteenth century, English printers for their own convenience agreed upon word divisions to be used at the ends of printed lines. This pattern has become established by usage and is followed here as in other modern dictionaries. This syllabification is used only in writing or printing, and then only at the ends of lines, where a hyphen is used to indicate word division. In this dictionary, written syllabification is shown in the entry word by a centered dot between syllables.

**hab·i·ta·tion** (hab′ə-tā′shən), *n.* 1. an inhabiting. 2. a place in which to live; dwelling; home.

### Affixes

Prefixes, suffixes, and combining forms are listed as separate entries, in alphabetical order. Since they are of great value in unlocking the meanings of thousands of words, their meaning and function are fully explained.

***Words formed by adding prefixes.*** A word made up of a base word and a prefix may appear as a main entry. In some of these entries, the meaning of the prefix may be indicated in the definition given first, as in

**non·es·sen·tial** . . . not essential; . . . (Note that *essential* is the base word.)

In others, the meaning of the prefix, no longer readily apparent in the English word, is indicated in the etymology:

**non·de·script** . . . [L. *non*, not + *descriptus*, described]

***Words formed by adding suffixes.*** Two methods are used for listing words formed by adding suffixes to a base word: (1) They are presented as separate entries in alphabetical order. Such forms (for example, *clearance* and *honorary*) usually have meanings that are not easily deduced by combining the meanings of the suffixes and of the base words: *clear* and *honor.* (2) Or they are presented as run-in entries at the close of the entry for the base word, as *circuitously*, *circuitousness*, and *circuity*, in the following entry for *circuitous.* Their meaning can easily be determined by combining the meanings of the base word with the meaning of the suffix. All such run-in forms are syllabified and accented.

**cir·cu·i·tous** (sẽr-kū′i-təs), *adj.* roundabout; indirect; devious. —**cir·cu′i·tous·ly,** *adv.* —**cir·cu′i·tous·ness, cir·cu′i·ty** [*pl.* -TIES], *n.*

# To Users of This Dictionary

***Words formed with combining forms.*** Similarly, combining forms are used to form many words in the language.

**bio-** [Gr. < *bios,* life], a combining form meaning *life, of living things, biological,* as in *biography, biochemistry*: also **bi-.**

**bi·o·de·grad·a·ble** (bī'ō-di-grā'də-b'l), *adj.* [*bio-* + *degrade* (decompose) + *-able*], capable of being readily decomposed by biological means, esp. by bacterial action, as some detergents.

**-graph** (graf, gräf), [Gr. *-graphos* < *graphein,* to write], a combining form meaning: 1. *something that writes* or *describes,* as in *telegraph.* 2. *something written,* as in *monograph.*

## Variant Spellings

Any spelling found in this dictionary is accepted usage. When a word is commonly spelled in two or more ways, each spelling is listed as an entry. If these spellings are so much alike that they would appear near each other in alphabetical order, and if they are pronounced alike, they are listed together. The more frequently used form appears first and is separated from the second by a comma.

**fi·ber, fi·bre**

When a second spelling is rarely used, it appears at the close of the entry.

## Inflected Forms

An inflection is a change in the form of a word to indicate number, case, gender, tense, etc. Inflected forms regarded as irregular or offering difficulty in spelling are entered within the main entry for the word being inflected, immediately following the part-of-speech label. Certain inflected forms are listed as main entries when they are at some distance in alphabetical order from the word being inflected, or when, as in the case of some participles of verbs, they require definition as adjectives or nouns.

When the inflected forms are not given, the user of the dictionary may assume that they are regular, involve no difficulty in pronunciation or spelling, and need only the addition of the appropriate inflectional ending to the entry word.

***Nouns.*** Most noun plurals are formed regularly by the addition of *-s* or *-es* and are usually not given. But they are given when a special problem in pronunciation or spelling or a choice of form is involved, as in the following entries:

**cloth** (klôth, kloth), *n.* [*pl.* CLOTHS (klôt*h*z, klot*h*z, "pieces of cloth"; klôths, kloths, "kinds of cloth")]

**cit·y** (sit'i), *n.* [*pl.* -IES (-iz)]

**to·ma·to** (tə-mā'tō, -mä'-), *n.* [*pl.* -TOES]

Plurals which do not end in *-s* or *-es* are always given, as are plurals of compound terms involving unusual spellings, as in these entries:

**a·lum·nus** (ə-lum'nəs), *n.* [*pl.* -NI (-nī)]

**moth·er-in-law** (mut*h*'ẽr-'n-lô'), *n.* [*pl.* MOTHERS-IN-LAW]

**mouse** (mous; *for v.,* mouz), *n.* [*pl.* MICE (mīs)]

A complete table for the formation of plurals is given in this dictionary under the entry **plural.** Occasionally, the reader is referred to this table for the explanation of an irregular form:

**fox** (foks), *n.* [*pl.* FOXES, FOX; see PLURAL, II, D, 1]

The reference following this entry is to rule 1, given under D of section II in the list of rules for plurals on pages 572 and 573.

***Adjectives and Adverbs.*** A number of adjectives and adverbs are regularly inflected to show comparative and superlative degree. If a change in spelling or pronunciation is involved, or if the inflection is irregular, the inflected forms are given immediately after the part-of-speech label. Sometimes they are given in full, sometimes they are given in abbreviated form.

**bad** (bad), *adj.* [WORSE (wũrs), WORST (wũrst)]

**fish·y** (fish'i), *adj.* [-IER, -IEST]

Some irregular inflected forms are listed also as separate entries; for example, **worse, better, less, least.**

***Verbs.*** Most English verbs are regularly inflected. The past tense and past participle are formed regularly by the addition of *-ed,* the present participle by the addition of *-ing*. Inflected forms are not given unless they involve changes in spelling or pronunciation as in these entries:

**ap·ply** (ə-plī′), *v.t.* [-PLIED, -PLYING]
**deal** (dēl), *v.t.* [DEALT, DEALING]

When only two inflected forms are given (as above), the first represents both the past tense and past participle; the second represents the present participle. When three inflected forms are given, the first represents the past tense; the second, the past participle; and the third, the present participle.

**fall** (fôl), *v.i.* [FELL, FALLEN, FALLING]
**give** (giv), *v.i.* [GAVE, GIVEN, GIVING]

## LOCATING A MEANING

When you see or hear a new word or a familiar word used in a new way, the first question that comes to mind is, "What does it mean?" With most English words in common use, a better question would be, "Which does it mean?" Relatively few words have a single meaning. The majority have several meanings, some general, some specialized. Occasionally you will find a meaning that has long since become obsolete, or a meaning so new that it has just won recognition.

### Context

Which of these several meanings serves your purpose—in reading, writing, or speaking—depends on the context. In its narrow sense, context means the words that precede or follow a particular word and determine its exact meaning. This context may be part of a sentence, a complete sentence, or several related sentences. It may be a full paragraph or several paragraphs. In its broad sense, context means the total situation in which the word is used: the time and place, the purpose of the writer or speaker, the audience with whom he is communicating.

Only if you are guided by the context of a word can you find the answer to the question, "Which does it mean?" When the meanings you know for a word do not make sense, you must look for a meaning that does. The way to look is to follow these steps:

1. Keep in mind the total situation in which the word is used.
2. Bring to the dictionary the whole sentence in which the word is used.
3. Note the part of speech of the word as it is used in the sentence.
4. Glance quickly through the entire entry to locate the part-of-speech label you have identified for the word.
5. Read all the definitions of meaning given under that label, noting any usage label or field label that signals a meaning appropriate to the particular situation in which the word is used.
6. Select the meaning that fits both the narrow context of the surrounding words and the broad context of the situation in which the word is used.

### Method of Listing

Most English words have more than one meaning. In this dictionary, each meaning is listed separately, preceded by a number. All the meanings which follow a part-of-speech label are numbered in sequence. When a new part-of-speech label appears, a new sequence of numbers also appears. Here is an example of such a listing:

**chill** (chil), *n.* [AS. *ciele*], 1. a bodily coldness with shivering. 2. a moderate coldness. 3. a checking of enthusiasm. 4. a sudden fear or discouragement. 5. coolness of manner; unfriendliness. *adj.* 1. uncomfortably cool; moderately cold. 2. depressing; deadening. 3. cool in manner; unfriendly. *v.i.* 1. to become cool. 2. to become cold; feel cold. 3. in *metallurgy*, to become hardened on the surface by rapid cooling. *v.t.* 1. to make cool. 2. to cause a chill in. 3. to check (enthusiasm, etc.). 4. to depress; dispirit. 5. in *metallurgy*, to harden (metal) by rapid cooling.

### Punctuation Marks in Definitions

Semicolons are used to separate synonyms or related parts of a single meaning. A colon is used to indicate that the following phrase or sentence is not part of the definition but is additional information applying only to the preceding definition. (See also *Examples of the Word in Use* on the next page.) A period is used to mark the end of a meaning (with information applying to it).

# To Users of This Dictionary

## Part-of-speech Labels

The meanings of many English words vary with their grammatical function in a sentence. For this reason, definitions are grouped according to part of speech: noun, verb, adjective, and so on. The definitions which apply to the use of the word as a noun follow the part-of-speech label ***n.*** The definitions which apply to the use of the word as an adjective follow the label ***adj.*** The verb group is further divided to distinguish between the meanings which apply when a word is used as a transitive verb, ***v.t.,*** and as an intransitive verb, ***v.i.*** Frequently, to pinpoint the meaning of a transitive verb, one or more direct objects are included in the definition or in the example, as shown below:

**ban·dy** (ban′di), ***v.t.*** [-DIED, -DYING], [Fr. *bander*, to bandy at tennis], 1. to toss back and forth, as a ball. 2. to pass (gossip, rumor, etc.) about carelessly. 3. to exchange: as, to *bandy* words.

## Usage Labels and Special Field Labels

In this dictionary certain words, or meanings of words, are specially identified. Some of these words or meanings are no longer in common use, though they do appear in earlier writings. Two labels are used in identifying such words: [Archaic] and [Obs.], meaning *obsolete.* When they apply to the word itself, they appear in brackets before the meaning or list of meanings. When they apply merely to a single meaning of the word, they appear in brackets between the number and the meaning, as in this entry for the word **anon.**

3. [Archaic], immediately; at once.

Other words are commonly used today in a special or restricted way. A word like *kinfolk,* for example, may be commonly used only in certain geographical areas. This use is identified by the label [Dial.], the abbreviation for the word *dialect.* A word like *perambulator* is more commonly used in England than in America. Therefore, the meaning, "a baby carriage," is labeled [Chiefly Brit.]. A limited number of words like *ere* and *evenfall* appear chiefly in poetry and are labeled [Poetic]. Two labels often used in entries are [Slang] and [Colloq.], for *colloquial.* The first identifies a word, or the meaning of a word, that is not generally regarded as standard usage but is used in highly informal situations. The second, [Colloq.], identifies a word, or the meaning of a word, that is generally considered standard usage in conversation and informal writing. The meaning and use of these labels is well illustrated in these definitions appearing under the word **pan:**

***n.*** 5. [Slang], a face.
***v.t.*** 2. [Colloq.], to criticize unfavorably, as a play or book.

In addition to special terms used in the arts and sciences, many general words are used in these fields with special meanings. For example, under the general word **order,** special meanings are given for the following fields: architecture, biology, finance, law, and theology. Each of these meanings is identified according to its field in this way:

14. in *architecture,* any of several classical styles . . .

15. in *biology,* a group of plants or animals . . .

## Examples of the Word in Use

In keeping with the concise quality of this dictionary, the examples illustrating the meaning are as brief as possible. Except where a full sentence is required, they are stated as phrases. Each example is preceded by a colon and the word *as.* Within the example, the word being illustrated is printed in italics, as in the following examples for the word **straight:**

1. having the same direction throughout its length: as, a *straight* line.

11. at a fixed price regardless of the quantity bought: as, lemons are ten cents *straight.*

## Idiomatic Phrases

Sometimes the meaning you seek is an idiomatic meaning rather than a literal one. Suppose, for example, that you couldn't figure out the meaning of the word *spirits* in this sentence: "So bitter were the accusations against him that he was quite out of spirits all day." Because the word is used as a noun you look for the meaning following that part-of-speech label. When none of these meanings "makes sense," you look for the meaning of the phrase in which the word *spirits* is used. In this dictionary, idiomatic phrases and expressions are listed near the close of the entry, just before the run-in entries. Since such expressions are printed in boldface type, you can quickly find both the phrase and its meaning: **—out of spirits,** sad; depressed.

### Synonyms and Antonyms

One of the special features of this dictionary is the manner in which synonyms are presented. Placed *within* the entry—not separately at the end—they both contribute to the meanings and become identified with them. Each synonym is, in fact, either listed with the meaning specifically related to it or is incorporated in the statement of the meaning. How this is accomplished is well illustrated in a small section of an entry from this dictionary.

**car·ry** (kar′i), ***v.t.*** [-RIED, -RYING], [< ONorm.Fr. *carier*; ult. < L. *carrus*, car], 1. to take from one place to another; transport; convey. 2. to lead or impel: as, his interests *carried* him into engineering. 3. to transmit: as, the air *carries* sounds. 4. to transfer or extend: as, *carry* the pipe to the sewer.

A total of seven synonyms is named in these few lines, each identified with a particular meaning of the verb *carry*.

In this dictionary, the antonyms are also presented within the entry, but after the definition. They are signaled by the phrases *opposed to* or *distinguished from*, or by the abbreviation *cf.*, as in this entry for the word *constant*:

2. in *mathematics & physics*, a quantity or factor that does not vary throughout a discussion or investigation: opposed to *variable*.

## PRONUNCIATION

Each entry word (with the exception of compounds written as two words) is immediately followed by its pronunciation, placed within parentheses. This pronunciation is represented by symbols that stand for the sounds used in speaking the word. The list of these symbols is called the Key to Pronunciation. This key appears on the first and last pages of this dictionary and at the bottom of each right-hand page. If the spelling syllabification of the word represents the sound patterns of spoken English, this syllabification is retained in the pronunciation. If it does not, it is changed, as in the following examples:

**stat·is·ti·cian** (stat′is-tish′ən)
**es·tate** (ə-stāt′)
**de·fend·ant** (di-fen′dənt)
**ar·te·ri·al** (är-têr′i-əl)

The term *stress* refers to the relative force given a word or syllable when it is uttered. In most words of two or more syllables, one syllable is stressed more than the others. Where *only one* is stressed, the pronunciation shows this stress by means of a heavy stroke immediately following that syllable, as in this example:

**cam·er·a** (kam′ẽr-ə)

Where more than one syllable is stressed, the second is usually pronounced with a weaker force. In the pronunciation of such words, the syllable receiving the stronger, or primary, stress is followed by a heavy stroke. The syllable receiving the weaker, or secondary, stress is followed by a lighter stroke, as in this example:

**cam·er·a·man** (kam′ẽr-ə-man′)

The pronunciations given in the *Students Concise Edition* represent General American English (now often called Midland), the standard speech for most of the country extending from New York to the Pacific. Where variant pronunciations are given, each may be regarded as standard English. No one pronunciation is preferred to another, but the one given first is usually the one heard most often among educated speakers.

### The Schwa and ŋ Symbols

Two special symbols have been borrowed from the International Phonetic Alphabet. One of them (ə) is called the *schwa*. It is used for vowels that are not stressed and represents the weakened or reduced sound of:

the *a* in **a·bout** (ə-bout′)
the *e* in **ur·gent** (ũr′jənt)
the *i* in **flex·i·ble** (flek′sə-b'l)
the *o* in **con·nect** (kə-nekt′)
the *u* in **sup·ply** (sə-plī′)

The other special symbol (ŋ) stands for the "ng" sound of

**sing** (siŋ) or **think** (thiŋk)

### Syllabic Consonants

Another symbol which needs explanation is the apostrophe in such words as:

**un·con·di·tion·al** (un'kən-dish'ən-'l)
**pa·tri·ot·ism** (pā'tri-ət-iz'm)
**sea·son** (sē'z'n)

It indicates that these consonants have become syllabic consonants; that is, they are pronounced with little or no vowel sound.

### Key Words

The key to pronunciation at the bottom of each right-hand page should help you quickly identify the sounds of the various symbols used in "sounding out" the pronunciation. Each key word illustrates the sound of one symbol. The key word "**ā**pe," for example, illustrates the sound of the symbol **ā**. The key word "h**ô**rn" illustrates the sound of the symbol **ô**.

You should refer to the key words when you are looking for the sound of one or more symbols used in "sounding out" the pronunciation of a particular word; for example, **com·mer·cial·ism** (kə-mũr'shəl-iz'm). You know how to pronounce all the symbols except **ũr**. To identify the sound of this symbol, you turn to the key words. First you find the group illustrating the sounds of the letter *u*. This brings you to the key word "**fũr**," which contains the symbol **ũr** and identifies its sound. You then go back to the pronunciation of *commercialism* and combine this sound with the sound of *m*. You can now interpret all the symbols—including the stroke indicating stress—in terms of sounds. You can pronounce the word as it is "sounded out" for you in the pronunciation.

### Foreign Terms

Many words borrowed from other languages have become completely absorbed into English. Sometimes they retain their foreign pronunciation, as in **chef** (shef) and **faux pas** (fō' pä'). Sometimes they acquire an English pronunciation, in which case both the acquired and the foreign are given.

**bas·so** (bas'ō; It. bäs'sô), ***n.*** [*pl.* -SOS; It. -SI (-sē)], [It. < LL. *bassus*, low], a bass voice, voice part, or singer.

Some foreign words and phrases used at times by American writers and speakers are not as yet considered a part of the English language. In this dictionary, a double dagger (‡) precedes the entry of such a word and indicates that that word is usually printed in italic characters or is underlined when used in an English context.

**‡fla·con** (flȧ'kōn'), ***n.*** [Fr.; see FLAGON], a small bottle with a stopper, for holding perfume, etc.

When such a word or phrase has both a foreign and an English pronunciation, both are given.

**‡con a·mo·re** (kôn'ä-mô're; Eng. kon'ə-môr'i), [It.], with love; tenderly: a direction in music.

## ETYMOLOGY

Any book devoted to the study of words would be incomplete without an account of where these words came from and how they have developed in form and meaning. Therefore, one of the essential features of a good dictionary is the etymology it provides for each word—when that etymology is known. The etymologies of most value to high school students are those in which each detail has been carefully selected for the *help* it provides. Such brief histories offer students not only an understanding of the current meanings of words but also a knowledge of foreign roots, prefixes, suffixes, and combining forms that is invaluable in determining the meaning of other words. Such brief histories are the kind of etymologies students will find in the *Students Concise Edition.*

The location of the etymologies was carefully determined. The editors believe that the same practice should be followed in this dictionary as in most of the dictionaries—abridged and unabridged—that students will be using after they leave high school. This practice is to place the etymology immediately before the definition. The advantage for students is that they can easily and quickly compare the earlier form, or forms, of the word with its present form. They can also see how the current meaning was "derived" from an earlier meaning, and to what extent the current meaning differs from it.

Each etymology is enclosed in brackets. Wherever possible, abbreviations and symbols are used in place of words. To find the languages represented by these abbreviations, the student can turn to pages xiii and xiv, where these abbreviations appear in their proper alphabetical order. A symbol common to most etymologies is <, which means "derived from." It is used only when scholars know the language or source from which the word or form was "derived." How this symbol is "read" is very important. What precedes it is "derived" from what follows it. For example, the word *chain* is derived from OFr. *chaine*, which is derived from L. *catena*, a chain.

**chain** (chān), *n.* [< OFr. *chaine* < L. *catena*, a chain]

At times, scholars are uncertain about some fact in the history of a word. In this dictionary, the degree of their uncertainty is indicated in one of three ways. The abbreviation *hyp.* indicates a guess, or hypothesis, supported by good evidence. The abbreviation *prob.* (for *probably*) indicates strong evidence in favor of the language or source given. A question mark "?" indicates uncertainty or a guess that states the most likely source but one that cannot be supported by adequate evidence.

The etymology can often give you another kind of useful information; namely, the meaning of a root word or stem that is common to a number of words. Notice, for example, the etymology of the word *biped*.

**bi·ped** . . . [< L. < *bi-* + *pes, pedis*, foot]

This root or stem is common to words like *pedal, pedestal, pedicure,* and *pedometer*; therefore, it is a key to their meaning. You will find equally helpful roots in the etymology of words like *disrupt, concede, revert, depend, propel, deduct, subscribe,* and *report*.

When you are locating the meaning of a word, always take an extra minute to gather from the etymology whatever information will help you (1) to learn about the background of the word, and (2) to unlock the meaning of other words derived from the same root or containing the same prefix, suffix, or combining form.

## WHEN SPELLING IS A PROBLEM

It's hard to find a word if you can't spell it. The English language presents us with many spelling problems. For one thing, many letters have more than one sound. Take the letter *a* for example. It has one sound in the word *ate*, another in the word *cat*, and still another in *father*. To make matters even more confusing, the same sound can have a number of different spellings. Think of the sound of *a* in the word *ate*. Now see the way the same sound is spelled in these words: a*i*d, s*ay*, br*ea*k, v*ei*n, *eigh*t, th*ey*. Learn to use the chart on the next page. It can help you whenever you are not sure of a spelling. In the left column, the sounds are identified by letters and key words. In the middle column are the letters frequently used to represent the sounds. In the right column are examples to illustrate the use of these letters to represent the sounds.

# To Users of This Dictionary

## CONSONANT SOUNDS

| SOUNDS | LETTERS | EXAMPLES |
|---|---|---|
| b as in *bat* | b, bb | rub, rubber |
| ch as in *chin* | ch, tch, te, ti, tu | chair, catch, righteous, question, nature |
| d as in *do* | d, dd, ed | nod, riddle, called |
| f as in *fine* | f, ff, gh, ph, lf | fix, differ, laugh, phrase, calf |
| g as in *go* | g, gg, gh, gu | give, egg, ghost, guard |
| h as in *high* | h, wh | her, who |
| j as in *jump* | j, g, gg, d, di, dg, dj | jig, magic, exaggerate, graduate, soldier, judgment, adjust |
| k as in *keep* | k, lk, c, cc, ch, ck, cqu, cu, qu | kite, walk, can, account, chrome, lack, lacquer, biscuit, liquor |
| l as in *let* | l, ll, sl | leave, call, isle |
| m as in *me* | m, mm, mb, mn, lm | drum, drummer, limb, hymn, calm |
| n as in *no* | n, nn, gn, kn, pn | near, dinner, gnome, kneel, pneumonia |
| ng as in *wing* | ng, n, ngue | long, think, tongue |
| p as in *pat* | p, pp | copy, dipper |
| r as in *run* | r, rr, rh, wr | river, berry, rhyme, wrong |
| s as in *sew* | s, ss, sc, c, ps, sch | sit, miss, scene, cent, psychology, schism |
| sh as in *ship* | sh, s, ss, sch, sci, si, ssi, ce, ch, ci, ti | share, sure, issue, schwa, conscience, mansion, mission, ocean, machine, facial, nation |
| t as in *top* | t, th, tt, ght, ed | tear, Thomas, better, bought, walked |
| v as in *very* | v, lv, f | dove, salve, of |
| w as in *we* | w, o, u | wail, choir, quaint |
| y as in *you* | y, i, j | yellow, union, hallelujah |
| z as in *zebra* | z, zz, s, ss, x | zone, buzzer, busy, scissors, xylophone |
| zh as in *pleasure* | z, g, s, si, zi | azure, garage, leisure, confusion, glazier |

## VOWEL SOUNDS

| SOUNDS | LETTERS | EXAMPLES |
|---|---|---|
| a as in *cat* | a, ai | lad, plaid |
| a as in *cake* | a, ai, au, ay, ea, ei, ey, et | lane, rain, gauge, ray, break, veil, obey, sachet |
| a as in *care* | a, ai, ay, e, ea, ei | dare, fair, prayer, there, wear, their |
| ah as in *father* | a, ea, o | far, hearth, stop |
| aw as in *saw* | aw, au, a, o, oa, ou | law, caught, wall, order, broad, fought |
| e as in *bed* | e, ea, eo, ie, a, ae, ai, ay, u | berry, heavy, leopard, friend, any, aerate, said, says, bury |
| e as in *we* | e, ee, ea, ei, eo, ey, i, ie, ae, oe | equal, free, lean, receive, people, key, machine, field, alumnae, phoebe |
| i as in *it* | i, ie, ee, o, u, ui, y | give, sieve, been, women, busy, build, hymn |
| i as in *kite* | i, ie, ei, ey, ai, uy, y | ice, tie, height, eye, aisle, buy, fly |
| o as in *go* | o, oa, oe, ou, ow, au, eau, ew | pole, boat, toe, soul, grow, mauve, beau, sew |
| oo as in *tool* | oo, o, oe, u, ue, ui, eu, ew, ough | moose, move, shoe, rule, blue, fruit, maneuver, threw, through |
| oo as in *book* | oo, o, ou, u | wood, wolf, would, pull |
| ow as in *now* | ow, ou, ough | crowd, out, bough |
| oy as in *boy* | oy, oi | toy, toil |
| uh as in *cuff* | u, o, oo, oe, ou | summer, son, flood, does, double |
| ur as in *hurt* | er, ear, ar, ir, or, our, ur, yr | germ, heard, forward, bird, worry, courage, turn, myrtle |
| u as in *fuse* | u, ue, ui, eau, eu, ew, iew, yu, you | use, cue, suit, beauty, feud, few, view, yule, youth |
| ə as in the first syllable of *asleep* | a, e, i, o, u, and many combinations of these letters | ago, agent, sanity, confess, focus, etc. |

# ABBREVIATIONS AND SYMBOLS USED IN THIS DICTIONARY

**abbrev.**, abbreviated; abbreviation
**abl.**, ablative
**Abyss.**, Abyssinian
**acc.**, accusative
**act.**, active
**A.D.**, anno Domini
**adj.**, adjective
**adv.**, adverb
**Afr.**, African
**Alb.**, Albanian
**alt.**, altered, alternative
**Am.**, American
**a.m., A.M.**, ante meridiem
**Am. Fr.**, American French
**Am. Ind.**, American Indian
**Am. Sp.**, American Spanish
**Anglo-Fr.**, Anglo-French
**Anglo-Ind.**, Anglo-Indian
**Anglo-Ir.**, Anglo-Irish
**Anglo-L.**, Anglo-Latin
**Anglo-N.**, Anglo-Norse
**Anglo-Norm.**, Anglo-Norman
**Ar.**, Arabic
**Aram.**, Aramaic
**art.**, article
**AS.**, Anglo-Saxon
**Assyr.**, Assyrian
**at. no.**, atomic number
**at. wt.**, atomic weight
**Bab.**, Babylonian
**B.C.**, before Christ
**Beng.**, Bengali
**Bohem.**, Bohemian
**Braz.**, Brazilian
**Bret.**, Breton
**Brit.**, British
**Bulg.**, Bulgarian
**c.**, circa (about, approximately); century
**Canad.**, Canadian
**Canad. Fr.**, Canadian French
**Catal.**, Catalonian
**caus.**, causative
**Celt.**, Celtic
**cf.**, *confer* (compare)
**Ch.**, Chaldean; Chaldee
**Chin.**, Chinese
**Chron.**, Chronicles
**coed.**, coeducational
**Col.**, Colossians
**Colloq., colloq.**, colloquial
**comb.**, combination
**comp.**, compound
**compar.**, comparative
**conj.**, conjunction
**contr.**, contracted; contraction
**Cor.**, Corinthians
**Corn.**, Cornish
**Cym.**, Cymric
**D.**, Dutch
**Dan.**, Danish; Daniel
**dat.**, dative
**def. art.**, definite article
**deriv.**, derivative
**Deut.**, Deuteronomy
**Dial., dial.**, dialect; dialectal; dialectic
**dim.**, diminutive
**E**, eastern
**Early Mod. D.**, Early Modern Dutch
**Early Mod. Eng.**, Early Modern English
**Eccles.**, Ecclesiastes
**E.Fris.**, East Frisian
**e.g.**, *exempli gratia* (for example)
**Egypt.**, Egyptian
**E.Ind.**, East Indian
**Eng.**, English
**envir.**, environment
**Eph.**, Ephesians
**equiv.**, equivalent
**Esk.**, Eskimo
**esp.**, especially
**est.**, estimated
**Esth.**, Esther
**etc.**, et cetera (and others, and so forth)
**Eth.**, Ethiopic
**etym.**, etymology
**Ex.**, Exodus
**Ez.**, Ezra
**Ezek.**, Ezekiel
**fem.**, feminine
**ff.**, following
**fig.**, figurative; figuratively
**Finn.**, Finnish
**Fl.**, Flemish
**fl.**, flourished
**Fr.**, French
**Frank.**, Frankish; Franconian
**freq.**, frequentative
**Fris.**, Frisian
**ft.**, feet
**fut.**, future
**G.**, German
**Gael.**, Gaelic
**Gal.**, Galatians
**Gaul.**, Gaulish
**Gen.**, Genesis
**genit.**, genitive
**Gmc.**, Germanic
**Goth.**, Gothic
**Gr.**, Greek
**grad.**, graduate
**Hab.**, Habakkuk
**Hag.**, Haggai
**Haw.**, Hawaiian
**Heb.**, Hebrew; Hebrews
**Hind.**, Hindi; Hindu; Hindustani
**Hos.**, Hosea
**Hung.**, Hungarian
**hyp.**, hypothetical
**Ice.**, Icelandic
**Idg.**, Indo-Germanic
**i.e.**, *id est* (that is)
**in.**, inches
**Ind.**, Indian
**indef. art.**, indefinite article
**indic.**, indicative
**inf.**, infinitive
**infl.**, influenced
**intens.**, intensified; intensifier; intensive
**interj.**, interjection
**IPA.**, International Phonetic Alphabet
**Ir.**, Irish
**Iran.**, Iranian
**irreg.**, irregular
**Isa.**, Isaiah
**It.**, Italian
**Ja.**, James
**Japan.**, Japanese
**Jav.**, Javanese
**Jer.**, Jeremiah
**Josh.**, Joshua
**Judg.**, Judges
**Kor.**, Korean
**L.**, Latin
**Lam.**, Lamentations
**Lev.**, Leviticus
**LG.**, Low German
**LGr.**, Low Greek
**LHeb.**, Late Hebrew
**lit.**, literally
**Lith.**, Lithuanian
**LL.**, Late Latin; Low Latin
**Mal.**, Malachi
**masc.**, masculine
**Matt.**, Matthew
**MD.**, Middle Dutch
**ME.**, Middle English
**Med.**, Medieval
**Mex.**, Mexican
**MFl.**, Middle Flemish
**MFr.**, Middle French
**MGr.**, Medieval Greek; Middle Greek
**MHG.**, Middle High German
**mi.**, mile; miles
**Mic.**, Micah
**MIr.**, Middle Irish
**MIt.**, Middle Italian
**ML.**, Medieval Latin
**MLG.**, Middle Low German
**Mod., mod.**, modern
**Mod. Gr.**, Modern Greek
**Mod. L.**, Modern Latin
**Mod. Pr.**, Modern Provençal
**Mongol.**, Mongolian
**MScand.**, Middle Scandinavian
**MScot.**, Middle Scottish
**N.**, Norse

# Abbreviations and Symbols Used in this Dictionary

**N**, northern
**n.**, noun
**Nah.**, Nahum
**naut.**, nautical
**NE**, northeastern
**Neh.**, Nehemiah
**neut.**, neuter
**n.fem.**, noun feminine
**nom.**, nominative
**Norm.**, Norman
**Norw.**, Norwegian
**n.pl.**, noun plural
**Numb.**, Numbers
**NW**, northwestern
**OAr.**, Old Arabic
**Ob.**, Obadiah
**Obs., obs.**, obsolete
**occas.**, occasional; occasionally
**OCelt.**, Old Celtic
**OCym.**, Old Cymric
**OD.**, Old Dutch
**ODan.**, Old Danish
**OFr.**, Old French
**OFris.**, Old Frisian
**OHG.**, Old High German
**OIr.**, Old Irish
**OIt.**, Old Italian
**OL.**, Old Latin
**OLG.**, Old Low German
**ON.**, Old Norse
**ONorm.Fr.**, Old Norman French
**OPer.**, Old Persian
**orig.**, origin; original; originally
**OS.**, Old Saxon
**OSlav.**, Old Slavic
**OSerb.**, Old Serbian
**OSp.**, Old Spanish
**OW.**, Old Welsh
**p.**, page
**pass.**, passive
**Per.**, Persic; Persian
**perf.**, perfect
**pers.**, person; personal
**Peruv.**, Peruvian
**Phil.**, Philippians; Philemon
**Phoen.**, Phoenician
**phr.**, phrase
**Pid.Eng.**, Pidgin English
**pl.**, plural
**p.m., P.M.**, post meridiem
**Pol.**, Polish
**pop.**, population
**Port.**, Portuguese
**poss.**, possessive
**pp.**, pages; past participle
**ppr.**, present participle
**Pr.**, Provençal
**prec.**, preceding
**prep.**, preposition
**pres.**, present
**prin. pts.**, principal parts
**prob.**, probable; probably
**prof.**, professional
**pron.**, pronoun
**pronun.**, pronunciation
**Prov.**, Proverbs
**prov.**, provincial
**Prov. Eng.**, Provincial English
**Prov. Scot.**, Provincial Scottish
**Ps.**, Psalms
**pt.**, past tense
**R.C.**, Roman Catholic
**redupl.**, reduplication; reduplicative
**refl.**, reflexive
**resp.**, respelling
**Rev.**, Revelation
**Rom.**, Roman; Romans
**Russ.**, Russian
**S**, southern
**S.Afr.D.**, South African Dutch
**Sam.**, Samaritan; Samuel
**Sans.**, Sanskrit
**Scand.**, Scandinavian
**Scot.**, Scottish
**SE**, southeastern
**Sem.**, Semitic
**Serb.**, Serbian
**sing.**, singular
**Singh.**, Singhalese
**Slav.**, Slavic; Slavonic
**S. of Sol.**, Song of Solomon
**Sp.**, Spanish
**sp.**, spelling; spelled
**specif.**, specifically
**sq.**, square
**subj.**, subjunctive
**superl.**, superlative
**SW**, southwestern
**Sw., Swed.**, Swedish
**Syr.**, Syrian; Syriac
**t.**, tense
**Tag.**, Tagalog
**Tart.**, Tartar
**Thess.**, Thessalonians
**Tibet.**, Tibetan
**Tim.**, Timothy
**Tit.**, Titus
**transl.**, translation
**Turk.**, Turkish
**ult.**, ultimate; ultimately
**unc.**, uncertain
**undergrad.**, undergraduate
**U.S.**, United States
**v.**, verb
**var.**, variant
**v.aux.**, verb auxiliary
**v.i.**, verb intransitive
**v.imp.**, verb impersonal
**v.t.**, verb transitive
**W**, western
**W.**, Welsh
**W.Afr.**, West African
**W.Fl.**, West Flemish
**W.Gmc.**, West Germanic
**W.Ind.**, West Indian
**Yid.**, Yiddish
**Zech.**, Zechariah
**Zeph.**, Zephaniah

‡ foreign word or phrase
< derived from; from
? perhaps; possibly; uncertain
\+ plus
& and

# A

**A, a** (ā), *n.* [*pl.* A's, a's, As, as], 1. the first letter of the English alphabet. 2. a sound of A or a. *adj.* 1. first in a sequence or group; hence, 2. first-class; A 1.

**A** (ā), *n.* 1. in *chemistry, the symbol for* argon. 2. in *music, a*) the sixth tone in the scale of C major. *b*) the scale having A as the keynote. *adj.* shaped like A.

**a** (ə; *stressed*, ā), *adj., indefinite article* [form of *an*, *adj.*], 1. one; one sort of. 2. each; any one. *A* connotes a thing not previously noted or recognized; *the*, a thing previously noted or recognized. 3. [orig. a prep. < AS. *an*, in, on, at], to each; in each; per: as, once *a* day. Before words beginning with a consonant sound or a sounded *h*, *a* is used (*a* child, *a* home, *a* uniform); before words beginning with a vowel sound or a silent *h*, *an* is used (*an* eye, *an* ultimatum, *an* honor). See also **an**.

**a** (ə), *prep.*, **a-**, *prefix* [weakened form of AS. *an, on*, in, on, at], 1. in, into, on, at, to, as in *aboard, ashore, abed.* 2. in the act or state of, as in *asleep, a-crying, a-wishing.* The prefix, hyphenated or unhyphenated, is in general use, but the preposition is now rare.

**a-**, a prefix of various origins and meanings: 1. [AS. *a-, ar-*], *up, out,* as in *awake, arise:* now generally an intensive. 2. [AS. *of-, af-*], *off, of,* as in *akin.* 3. [Gr. *a-, an-*], *not, without,* as in *agnostic*: before vowels *an-* is used, as in *anesthetic.*

**A.,** 1. Absolute. 2. Angstrom unit: also Å.

**A., a.,** [L.], 1. *anno*, in the year. 2. *ante*, before.

**a.,** 1. about. 2. acre; acres. 3. adjective. 4. alto. 5. ampere. 6. anonymous. 7. answer.

**Aa·chen** (ä′kən, ä′khən), *n.* a city in W Germany: pop., 163,000: French name, *Aix-la-Chapelle.*

**aard·vark** (ärd′värk′), *n.* [D., earth pig], a burrowing African mammal that feeds on ants and termites.

**aard·wolf** (ärd′woolf′), *n.* [*pl.* -WOLVES (-woolvz′)], [D., earth wolf], a South African flesh-eating mammal somewhat like the hyena.

**Aar·on** (âr′ən), *n.* in the *Bible*, the older brother of Moses and first high priest of the Hebrews.

**Ab** (äb, ab; Heb. ôv), *n.* [Heb.], the eleventh month of the Jewish year: see **Jewish calendar.**

**ab-**, [L.], a prefix meaning *away, from, from off, down,* as in *abdicate*: shortened to *a-* before *m, p, v;* often *abs-* before *c* or *t*, as in *abstract.*

**Ab,** in *chemistry*, alabamine.

**A.B.,** *Artium Baccalaureus*, Bachelor of Arts.

**A.B., a.b.,** able-bodied (seaman).

**a·ba** (ä′bə), *n.* [Ar.], 1. a woven fabric of camel's or goat's hair. 2. a loose robe worn by Arabs.

**a·ba·cá** (ä′bə-kä′), *n.* [Tag.], 1. a kind of hemp. 2. the Philippine plant that produces it.

**a·back** (ə-bak′), *adv. & adj.* 1. [Archaic], backward; back. 2. in *navigation*, backward against the mast, as the sails in a wind from straight ahead. **—taken aback,** surprised; startled and confused.

**ab·a·cus** (ab′ə-kəs), *n.* [*pl.* -CUSES, -CI (-sī′)], [L. < Gr. *abax*], 1. a frame with beads or balls sliding back and forth on wires or in slots, for doing arithmetic. 2. in *architecture*, a slab forming the top of the capital of a column.

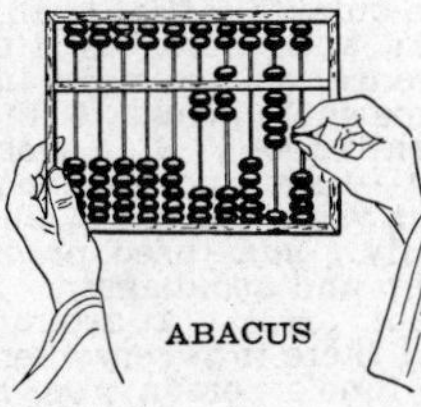

ABACUS

**a·baft** (ə-baft′), *adv.* [AS. *on-be-æftan; on*, on + *be*, by + *æftan*, behind], on or toward the stern; aft. *prep.* in *nautical usage*, behind.

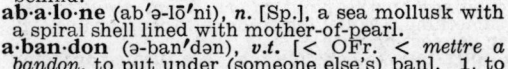

**ab·a·lo·ne** (ab′ə-lō′ni), *n.* [Sp.], a sea mollusk with a spiral shell lined with mother-of-pearl.

**a·ban·don** (ə-ban′dən), *v.t.* [< OFr. < *mettre a bandon*, to put under (someone else's) ban], 1. to give up (something) completely. 2. to forsake; desert. 3. to yield (oneself) completely, as to a feeling, etc. *n.* 1. surrender to one's impulses. 2. unrestrained freedom of activity. **—a·ban′don·ment,** *n.*

**a·ban·doned** (ə-ban′dənd), *adj.* 1. forsaken; deserted. 2. given up to wickedness; shameless. 3. unrestrained. **—a·ban′doned·ly,** *adv.*

**a·base** (ə-bās′), *v.t.* [ABASED, ABASING], [< OFr. < LL. *abassare*, to lower; see A- & BASE (low)], to humble; humiliate. **—a·base′ment,** *n.*

**a·bash** (ə-bash′), *v.t.* [OFr. *esbahir*, to astonish < L. *ex* + *bah* (interj. of surprise)], to make self-conscious and embarrassed; disconcert. **—a·bashed′,** *adj.* **—a·bash′ment,** *n.*

**a·bate** (ə-bāt′), *v.t.* [ABATED, ABATING], [OFr. *abattre*, to beat down; see A- & BATTER (to beat)], 1. to make less in amount, degree, etc. 2. to deduct. 3. in *law*, to end; quash. *v.i.* to become less; subside. **—a·bat′a·ble,** *adj.* **—a·bat′er,** *n.*

**ab·a·tis, ab·at·tis** (ab′ə-tis), *n. sing. & pl.* [Fr.; see ABATE], a barricade of felled trees with pointed branches facing the enemy.

**ab·at·toir** (ab′ə-twär′, ab′ə-twär′), *n.* [Fr.; see ABATE], a slaughterhouse.

**ab·ba·cy** (ab′ə-si), *n.* [*pl.* -CIES], an abbot's position, jurisdiction, or term of office.

**ab·bé** (ab′ā; Fr. à′bā′), *n.* [Fr. < L.; see ABBOT], in France, a title of respect for a priest or other clergyman.

**ab·bess** (ab′is), *n.* [< LL.; see ABBOT], a woman who is the superior, or head, of a nunnery.

**ab·bey** (ab′i), *n.* [*pl.* -BEYS], 1. a monastery headed by an abbot or a nunnery headed by an abbess. 2. the monks or nuns in such a place, collectively. 3. a church or building belonging to an abbey.

**ab·bot** (ab′ət), *n.* [< AS. < LL. & Gr. < Aram. *abba*, father], a man who is head of a monastery.

**abbr., abbrev.,** 1. abbreviated. 2. abbreviation.

**ab·bre·vi·ate** (ə-brē′vi-āt′), *v.t.* [-ATED, -ATING], [< L. < *ad-*, to + *brevis*, short], 1. to make shorter. 2. to shorten (a word or phrase) by leaving out or substituting letters. **—ab·bre′vi·a′tor,** *n.*

**ab·bre·vi·a·tion** (ə-brē′vi-ā′shən), *n.* 1. a making shorter. 2. the fact or state of being made shorter. 3. a shortened form of a word or phrase, as *N.Y.* for *New York*, *Mr.* for *Mister*, *lb.* for *pound.*

**A B C** (ā′ bē′ sē′), *n.* [*pl.* A B C's], 1. *usually pl.* the alphabet; hence, 2. the basic elements (*of* a subject); rudiments.

**ABC,** American Broadcasting Company.

**ab·di·cant** (ab′də-kənt), *adj.* abdicating. *n.* an abdicator.

**ab·di·cate** (ab′də-kāt′), *v.t. & v.i.* [-CATED, -CATING], [< L. < *ab-*, off + *dicare*, to proclaim], to give up formally (a high office, etc.); surrender (a power). **—ab′di·ca·ble** (-kə-b′l), *adj.* **—ab′di·ca′tion,** *n.* **—ab′di·ca′tor** (-tēr), *n.*

**ab·do·men** (ab′də-mən, ab-dō′-), *n.* [L.], 1. the part of the body between the diaphragm and the pelvis, containing the intestines, etc.; belly. 2. in insects and crustaceans, the hind part of the body. **—ab·dom·i·nal** (ab-dom′ə-n′l), *adj.* **—ab·dom′i·nal·ly,** *adv.*

**ab·duct** (ab-dukt′), *v.t.* [< L. < *ab-*, away + *ducere*, to lead], 1. to kidnap. 2. in *physiology*, to move (a part of the body) away from its normal position. **—ab·duc′tion,** *n.* **—ab·duc′tor,** *n.*

**a·beam** (ə-bēm′), *adv.* at right angles to a ship's length or keel.

**a·bed** (ə-bed′), *adv.* in bed.

**A·bel** (ā′b′l), *n.* in the *Bible*, the second son of Adam and Eve, killed by Cain, his brother: Gen. 4.

**Ab·é·lard, Pierre** (ab′ə-lärd′; Fr. à′bā′làr′), 1079–1142; French philosopher and teacher: see also **Heloise.**

---

**fat**, āpe, bâre, cär; ten, ēven, hêre, ovẽr; **is**, bīte; lot, gō, hôrn, tōōl, look; **oil**, **out**; **up**, ūse, fũr; get; joy; yet; **chin**; **she**; **thin**, *th*en; **zh**, leisure; ŋ, ring; ə for *a* in *ago*, *e* in *agent*, *i* in *sanity*, *o* in *comply*, *u* in *focus*; ′ in *able* (ā′b′l); **Fr.** bàl; **ë**, Fr. coeur; **ö**, Fr. feu; Fr. mo*n*; **ô**, Fr. coq; **ü**, Fr. duc; **H**, G. ich; **kh**, G. doch. ‡ foreign; < derived from.

**Ab·er·deen** (ab'ẽr-dēn'), *n.* a city in Scotland, on the North Sea: pop., 181,000. —**Ab'er·do'ni·an** (-dō'ni-ən), *adj. & n.*
**ab·er·rant** (ab-er'ənt), *adj.* [< L. < *ab-*, from + *errare*, to wander], deviating from what is true, normal, or typical. —**ab·er'rance, ab·er'ran·cy** [*pl.* -CIES], *n.*
**ab·er·ra·tion** (ab'ẽr-ā'shən), *n.* 1. departure from what is right, true, etc. 2. deviation from the normal or typical. 3. mental derangement or lapse. 4. in *optics*, *a*) the failure of light rays from one point to converge to a single focus. *b*) an error in a lens causing this.

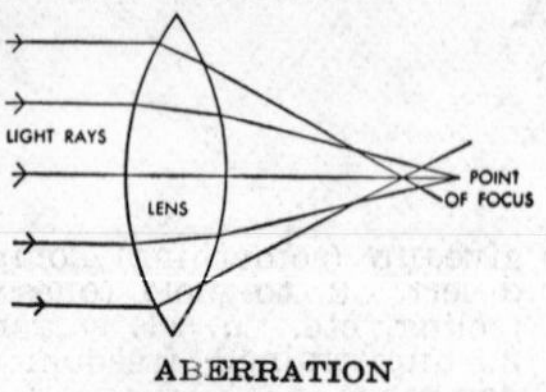

ABERRATION

**a·bet** (ə-bet'), *v.t.* [ABETTED, ABETTING], [OFr. *abeter*, to deceive; *a-*, to + *beter*, to bait], to urge on or help, especially in wrongdoing. —**a·bet'ment, a·bet'tal,** *n.* —**a·bet'tor, a·bet'ter,** *n.*
**a·bey·ance** (ə-bā'əns), *n.* [< Anglo-Fr. < OFr. *abeance*, expectation < LL. *badare*, to gape], temporary suspension, as of an activity or ruling.
**ab·hor** (əb-hôr', ab-), *v.t.* [-HORRED, -HORRING], [< L. < *ab-*, away, from + *horrere*, to shudder], to shrink from in fear, disgust, or hatred.
**ab·hor·rence** (əb-hôr'əns, ab-hor'-), *n.* 1. an abhorring; loathing. 2. something abhorred.
**ab·hor·rent** (əb-hôr'ənt, ab-hor'-), *adj.* 1. causing fear, disgust, etc.; detestable. 2. feeling abhorrence. 3. opposed (*to* one's principles, reason, etc.). —**ab·hor'rent·ly,** *adv.*
**a·bide** (ə-bīd'), *v.i.* [ABODE (-bōd') or ABIDED, ABIDING], [AS. *abidan* < *bidan*, to remain], 1. to stand fast; remain. 2. [Archaic or Poetic], to stay; reside. *v.t.* 1. to await. 2. to submit to; endure. —**abide by,** 1. to live up to (a promise, etc.). 2. to submit to and carry out: as, *abide by* the decision. —**a·bid'ance,** *n.*
**a·bid·ing** (ə-bīd'iŋ), *adj.* enduring; lasting. —**a·bid'ing·ly,** *adv.*
**Ab·i·lene** (ab'ə-lēn'), *n.* a city in central Texas: pop., 90,000.
**a·bil·i·ty** (ə-bil'ə-ti), *n.* [*pl.* -TIES], [see ABLE], 1. a being able; power to do. 2. talent. 3. *usually in pl.* special skill.
‡**ab in·i·ti·o** (ab in-ish'i-ō), [L.], from the beginning.
**ab·i·o·gen·e·sis** (ab'i-ō-jen'ə-sis), *n.* [Gr. *a-*, without; + *biogenesis*], in *biology*, spontaneous generation. —**ab'i·o·ge·net'ic** (-jə-net'ik), *adj.* —**ab'i·o·ge·net'i·cal·ly,** *adv.* —**ab'i·og'e·nist** (-oj'ə-nist), *n.*
**ab·ir·ri·tant** (ab-ir'ə-tənt), *adj.* relieving or lessening irritation; soothing. *n.* a medicine or drug that relieves or lessens irritation.
**ab·ir·ri·tate** (ab-ir'ə-tāt'), *v.t.* [-TATED, -TATING], to relieve or lessen irritation in.
**ab·ject** (ab-jekt', ab'jekt), *adj.* [< L. < *ab-*, away, from + *jacere*, to throw], 1. miserable; wretched: as, *abject* poverty. 2. lacking self-respect; degraded. —**ab·ject'ly,** *adv.* —**ab·jec'tion,** *n.*
**ab·jure** (əb-joor', ab-), *v.t.* [-JURED, -JURING], [< L. < *ab-*, away, from + *jurare*, to swear], 1. to give up (rights, allegiance, etc.) on oath; renounce. 2. to give up (opinions) publicly; recant. —**ab·ju·ra·tion** (ab'joo-rā'shən), *n.* —**ab·jur'a·to'ry** (-ə-tôr'i, -ə-tō'ri), *adj.* —**ab·jur'er,** *n.*
**abl.,** ablative.
**ab·la·tive** (ab'lə-tiv), *n.* [L. *ablativus* < *ablatus* (pp. of *auferre*), carried away], in Latin and other inflected languages, 1. the case expressing removal, deprivation, direction from, cause, and agency. 2. a word in this case. *adj.* of or in the ablative.
**ab·laut** (ab'lout; G. äp'lout), *n.* [G.; *ab-*, off, from + *laut*, sound], in *linguistics*, change of the root vowels in verbal forms, expressing change of tense, aspect, etc., as in *drink, drank, drunk:* also called *gradation*. *adj.* of or characterized by ablaut.
**a·blaze** (ə-blāz'), *adv.* on fire. *adj.* 1. flaming; gleaming. 2. greatly excited; very eager.
**a·ble** (ā'b'l), *adj.* [ABLER (-blẽr), ABLEST (-blist)], [< OFr. < L. *habilis*, handy < *habere*, to have, hold], 1. having enough power, skill, etc. (*to* do something). 2. having or showing much power of mind; skilled; talented. —**a'bly,** *adv.*
**-a·ble,** [Fr.; L. *-abilis*], a suffix meaning: 1. *able to*, as in *durable*. 2. *capable of being*, as in *drinkable*. 3. *worthy of being*, as in *laudable*. 4. *having qualities of*, as *knowledgeable*. 5. *tending* or *inclined to*, as in *perishable*. Also **-ible, -ble.**
**a·ble-bod·ied** (ā'b'l-bod'id), *adj.* healthy and strong.
**able-bodied seaman,** a trained, skilled sailor.
**a·bloom** (ə-bloom'), *adv. & adj.* in bloom; in flower.
**ab·lu·tion** (ab-loo'shən), *n.* [< L. < *ab-*, off + *luere*, to wash], 1. a washing of the body, especially as a religious ceremony. 2. the liquid used for this. —**ab·lu'tion·ar'y,** *adj.*
**-a·bly,** a suffix used to form adverbs corresponding to adjectives ending in *-able*.
**ABM,** anti-ballistic missile.
**ab·ne·gate** (ab'ni-gāt'), *v.t.* [-GATED, -GATING], [< L. < *ab-*, away, from + *negare*, to deny], to deny and refuse; give up (rights, claims, etc.); renounce. —**ab'ne·ga'tion,** *n.* —**ab'ne·ga'tor,** *n.*
**ab·nor·mal** (ab-nôr'məl), *adj.* [earlier *anormal* < Fr. < Gr. *anōmalos* (see ANOMALOUS); influenced by L. *abnormis* < *ab-*, from + *norma*, rule], not normal; not average; not typical; irregular; unnatural. —**ab·nor'mal·ly,** *adv.* —**ab·nor'mal·ness,** *n.*
**ab·nor·mal·i·ty** (ab'nôr-mal'ə-ti), *n.* 1. an abnormal condition. 2. [*pl.* -TIES], an abnormal thing. Also **ab·nor'mi·ty** (-nôr'mə-ti), [*pl.* -TIES].
**a·board** (ə-bôrd', -bōrd'), *adv.* on board; on, in, or into a train, car, etc. *prep.* 1. on board of; on; in. 2. alongside. —**all aboard!** get on! get in!: a warning that the train, car, etc. is starting.
**a·bode** (ə-bōd'), *n.* [see ABIDE], 1. a sojourn. 2. a place where one lives or stays; home; residence.
**a·bode** (ə-bōd'), alt. pt. and pp. of **abide.**
**a·bol·ish** (ə-bol'ish), *v.t.* [< Fr. < L. *abolere*, to destroy], to do away with; put an end to; annul.
**ab·o·li·tion** (ab'ə-lish'ən), *n.* 1. utter destruction; annulment. 2. [sometimes A-], the abolishing of slavery in the United States. —**ab'o·li'tion·ar'y,** *adj.* —**ab'o·li'tion·ism,** *n.*
**ab·o·li·tion·ist** (ab'ə-lish'ən-ist), *n.* 1. one who favors abolition. 2. [sometimes A-], one who favored the abolition of slavery in the United States.
**ab·o·ma·sum** (ab'ə-mā'səm), *n.* [*ab-*, from + *omasum*], the fourth, or digesting, chamber of the stomach of a cud-chewing animal, as the cow.
**A-bomb** (ā'bom'), *n.* an atomic bomb.
**a·bom·i·na·ble** (ə-bom'ə-nə-b'l), *adj.* [see ABOMINATE], 1. disgusting; vile; loathsome. 2. disagreeable; very bad. —**a·bom'i·na·bly,** *adv.*
**a·bom·i·nate** (ə-bom'ə-nāt'), *v.t.* [-NATED, -NATING], [< L. pp. of *abominari*, to regard as an ill omen], 1. to hate; loathe; abhor. 2. to dislike very much. —**a·bom'i·na'tor,** *n.*
**a·bom·i·na·tion** (ə-bom'ə-nā'shən), *n.* 1. hatred and disgust. 2. anything hateful and disgusting.
**ab·o·rig·i·nal** (ab'ə-rij'ə-n'l), *adj.* 1. existing from earliest days; first; indigenous. 2. of aborigines. *n.* an aborigine. —**ab'o·rig'i·nal·ly,** *adv.*
**ab·o·rig·i·nes** (ab ə-rij'ə-nēz'), *n.pl.* [*sing.* -NE (-nē')], [L., < *ab-*, from + *origine*, the beginning], 1. the earliest known inhabitants of a region; natives. 2. the native animals or plants of a region.
**a·bort** (ə-bôrt'), *v.i.* [< L. pp. of *aboriri*, to miscarry], 1. to have a miscarriage. 2. to fail to develop. *v.t.* to check before fully developed.
**a·bor·tion** (ə-bôr'shən), *n.* 1. expulsion of a fetus from the womb before it is viable; miscarriage. 2. an aborted fetus. 3. anything immature and incompletely developed. —**a·bor'tion·ist,** *n.*
**a·bor·tive** (ə-bôr'tiv), *adj.* 1. born too soon. 2. coming to nothing; fruitless. 3. in *biology*, rudimentary. 4. in *medicine*, causing abortion. —**a·bor'tive·ly,** *adv.* —**a·bor'tive·ness,** *n.*
**a·bound** (ə-bound'), *v.i.* [< OFr. < L. *abundare*, to overflow; *ab-* + *undare*, to rise in waves < *unda*, a wave], 1. to be plentiful. 2. to be wealthy (*in*): as, a land that *abounds* in grain. 3. to be filled (*with*): as, woods that *abound* with gm e.— **a·bound'ing,** *adj.* —**a·bound'ing·ly,** *adv.*
**a·bout** (ə-bout'), *adv.* [< AS. *onbutan*, around, on the outside (of)], 1. all around: as, look *about*. 2. here and there: as, travel *about*. 3. in circumference: as, ten miles *about*. 4. near: as standing somewhere *about*. 5. in the opposite direction: as, turn it *about*. 6. in succession or rotation: as, play fair—turn and turn *about*. 7. nearly: as, *about* four years old. 8. [Colloq.], almost: as, just *about* ready. *adj.* (used predicatively) 1. astir: as, he is up and *about* again. 2. prevalent: as, typhoid is *about*. *prep.* 1. around; on all sides of. 2. here and there in; everywhere in. 3. near to. 4. with; on (one's person): as, have your wits *about* you. 5. attending to: as, go *about* your business. 6. intending; on the point of: as, I am *about* to say something. 7. having to do with; concerning. 8. in connection with.
**a·bout-face** (ə-bout'fās'), *n.* 1. a turning or facing in the opposite direction. 2. a reversal of attitude. *v.i.* (ə-bout'fās'), [-FACED, -FACING], to turn or face in the opposite direction.
**a·bove** (ə-buv'), *adv.* [AS. *abufan*], 1. in or at a

higher place; overhead; up. 2. in heaven. 3. before or earlier (in a book or printed passage): as, *above*-mentioned. 4. higher in power, status, etc. *prep.* 1. higher than; over; on top of. 2. beyond; past: as, the road *above* the village. 3. better than: as, *above* the average. 4. more than: as, *above* fifty dollars. *adj.* placed, found, mentioned, etc. above or earlier. *n.* something that is above. —**above all,** most of all; mainly.

**a·bove·board** (ə-buv′bôrd′, -bōrd′), *adv.* & *adj.* in plain view; without dishonesty or concealment.

**‡ab o·vo** (ab ō′vō), [L.], from the egg (or origin).

**abr.,** 1. abridge. 2. abridged. 3. abridgment.

**ab·ra·ca·dab·ra** (ab′rə-kə-dab′rə), *n.* [L.], 1. a word supposed to have magic powers, used in incantations, on amulets, etc. 2. a magic spell or formula. 3. gibberish.

**ab·rade** (ə-brād′), *v.t.* [-RADED, -RADING], [< L. < *ab-*, away + *radere*, to scrape], to rub off; wear away by scraping. —**ab·rad′er,** *n.*

**A·bra·ham** (ā′brə-ham), *n.* in the *Bible*, the first patriarch and ancestor of the Hebrews.

**a·bran·chi·ate** (ā-braŋ′ki-it, -āt′), *adj.* [< Gr. *a-*, not + *branchia*, gills], in *zoology*, without gills. *n.* an animal without gills. Also **a·bran′chi·an.**

**ab·ra·sion** (ə-brā′zhən), *n.* 1. an abrading, or rubbing off. 2. an abraded spot or area.

**ab·ra·sive** (ə-brā′siv, -ziv), *adj.* causing abrasion. *n.* a substance used for grinding, polishing, etc., as sandpaper or emery.

**a·breast** (ə-brest′), *adv.* & *adj.* [*a-*, on + *breast*], side by side. —**abreast of** (or **with**), in line with.

**a·bridge** (ə-brij′), *v.t.* [ABRIDGED, ABRIDGING], [< OFr. < L. *abbreviare* < *ad-*, to + *brevis*, short], 1. to reduce in scope, extent, etc. 2. to shorten by lessening the number of words but keeping the main contents. 3. to curtail. 4. to deprive (*of* rights, privileges, etc.). —**a·bridg′a·ble, a·bridge′a·ble,** *adj.* —**a·bridg′er,** *n.*

**a·bridg·ment, a·bridge·ment** (ə-brij′mənt), *n.* 1. an abridging or being abridged. 2. an abridged form of a book, etc.

**a·broad** (ə-brôd′), *adv.* 1. broadly; far and wide. 2. current: as, a report is *abroad* that we have won. 3. outdoors: as, stroll *abroad*. 4. to or in foreign countries. *n.* a foreign land (preceded by *from*).

**ab·ro·gate** (ab′rə-gāt′), *v.t.* [-ROGATED, -ROGATING], [< L. < *ab-*, away + *rogare*, to propose], to abolish; repeal; annul; cancel. —**ab′ro·ga·ble** (-gə-b′l), *adj.* —**ab′ro·ga′tion,** *n.* —**ab′ro·ga′tive,** *adj.* —**ab′ro·ga′tor,** *n.*

**a·brupt** (ə-brupt′), *adj.* [< L. < *ab-*, off + *rumpere*, to break], 1. sudden; unexpected. 2. gruff; brusque. 3. very steep. 4. without proper transitions; disconnected: as, an *abrupt* style of writing.

**abs.,** 1. absent. 2. absolute. 3. abstract.

**Ab·sa·lom** (ab sə-ləm), *n.* in the *Bible*, David's favorite son, who rebelled against him: II Sam. 18.

**ab·scess** (ab′ses), *n.* [< L. < *abscidere* < *ab(s)-*, from + *cedere*, to go], a swollen, inflamed area in body tissues, in which pus gathers. *v.i.* to form an abscess. —**ab′scessed** (-sest), *adj.*

**ab·scis·sa** (ab-sis′ə), *n.* [*pl.* -SAS, -SAE (-ē)], [L. *abscissa* (*linea*), (a line) cut off; < *ab-*, from, off + *scindere*, to cut], in *geometry*, the line or part of a line drawn horizontally on a graph by which a point is located with reference to a system of co-ordinates: cf. *ordinate*.

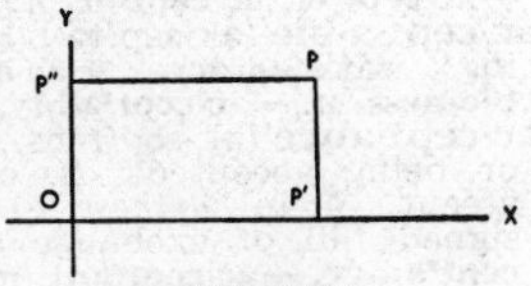


ABSCISSA

OP′, abscissa of P; OP″, ordinate of P

**ab·scond** (ab-skond′, əb-), *v.i.* [< L. < *ab(s)-*, from, away + *condere*, to hide], to go away hastily and secretly; flee. —**ab·scond′er,** *n.*

**ab·sence** (ab′s′ns), *n.* 1. a being absent. 2. the time of being absent. 3. a lack: as, in the *absence* of facts.

**ab·sent** (ab′s′nt; *for v.*, ab-sent′), *adj.* [OFr. < L. *absens* < *ab-*, away + *esse*, to be], 1. not present; away. 2. not existing; lacking. 3. not attentive; absorbed in thought. *v.t.* to take or hold (oneself) away: as, he *absents* himself from classes. —**ab′sent·ly,** *adv.*

**ab·sen·tee** (ab′s′n-tē′), *n.* a person who is absent, as from work. *adj.* of the nature of an absentee; by an absentee: as, *absentee* ownership. —**ab′sen·tee′ism,** *n.*

**ab·sent-mind·ed** (ab′s′nt-mīn′did), *adj.* 1. so lost in thought as not to pay attention to what is going on around one. 2. habitually forgetful. —**ab′sent-mind′ed·ly,** *adv.* —**ab′sent-mind′ed·ness,** *n.*

**ab·sinthe, ab·sinth** (ab sinth), *n.* [Fr. < L. < Gr. *apsinthion*], 1. wormwood. 2. a green alcoholic liquor with the flavor of wormwood and anise.

**ab·so·lute** (ab′sə-lo͞ot′), *adj.* [< L. < *absolvere;* see ABSOLVE], 1. perfect. 2. complete; whole. 3. not mixed; pure. 4. not limited; unrestricted: as, an *absolute* ruler. 5. positive; certain. 6. actual; real: as, an *absolute* truth. 7. without reference to anything else. 8. in *grammar*, *a*) forming part of a sentence, but not in the usual relations of syntax: in the sentence "The weather being good, they went," *the weather being good* is an *absolute* construction. *b*) with no expressed object: said of a verb usually transitive. *n.* something that is absolute. —**the Absolute,** in *philosophy*, that which is thought of as existing in and by itself, without relation to anything else. —**ab′so·lute′ly,** *adv.* —**ab′so·lute′ness,** *n.*

**absolute pitch,** the ability to recognize or reproduce any tone without having it sounded beforehand.

**absolute zero,** a point of temperature theoretically equal to −273.18° C. or −459.72° F.: the hypothetical point at which a substance would have no molecular motion and no heat.

**ab·so·lu·tion** (ab′sə-lo͞o′shən), *n.* [OFr. < L. < *absolvere;* see ABSOLVE], 1. a formal freeing (*from* guilt); forgiveness. 2. remission (*of* sin or its penalty); specif., in some churches, such remission formally given by a priest after penance by the sinner. 3. the formula of such remission.

**ab·so·lut·ism** (ab′sə-lo͞ot′iz′m), *n.* government in which the ruler has unlimited powers; despotism. —**ab′so·lut′ist,** *n.* & *adj.*

**ab·solve** (ab-solv′, əb-zolv′), *v.t.* [-SOLVED, -SOLVING], [< L. < *ab-*, from + *solvere*, to loose], 1. to pronounce free from guilt or blame; acquit. 2. to give absolution to (in the religious sense). 3. to free (*from* a promise, etc.). —**ab·solv′a·ble,** *adj.* —**ab·solv′er,** *n.*

**ab·sol·vent** (ab-sol′vənt, əb-zol′-), *adj.* absolving. *n.* one who absolves.

**ab·sorb** (əb-sôrb′, ab-zôrb′), *v.t.* [< L. < *ab-*, from + *sorbere*, to drink in], 1. to suck up; drink in. 2. to engulf wholly. 3. to take up fully the attention of; interest greatly. 4. to take in and incorporate; assimilate. —**ab·sorb′a·ble,** *adj.* —**ab·sorb′a·bil′i·ty,** *n.* —**ab·sorbed′,** *adj.* —**ab·sorb′ing,** *adj.* —**ab·sorb′ing·ly,** *adv.*

**ab·sorb·ent** (əb-sôrb′ənt, ab-zôrb′-), *adj.* capable of absorbing moisture, light rays, etc. *n.* a thing that absorbs moisture, etc. —**ab·sorb′en·cy,** *n.*

**ab·sorp·tion** (əb-sôrp′shən, ab-zôrp′-), *n.* 1. an absorbing or being absorbed. 2. great interest or engrossment. 3. in *biology*, the passing of nutrient material into the blood or lymph. —**ab·sorp′tive,** *adj.* —**ab′sorp·tiv′i·ty,** *n.*

**ab·stain** (əb-stān′, ab-), *v.i.* [< OFr. < L. *abstinere*, to keep from < *ab(s)-*, from + *tenere*, to hold], to voluntarily do without; refrain: as, to *abstain* from drinking. —**ab·stain′er,** *n.*

**ab·ste·mi·ous** (ab-stē′mi-əs), *adj.* [< L. < *ab(s)-*, from + *temetum*, strong drink], moderate in eating and drinking; temperate. —**ab·ste′mi·ous·ly,** *adv.* —**ab·ste′mi·ous·ness,** *n.*

**ab·sten·tion** (ab-sten′shən, əb-), *n.* an abstaining. —**ab·sten′tious,** *adj.*

**ab·sti·nence** (ab′stə-nəns), *n.* 1. an abstaining from some or all food, drink, or other pleasures. 2. the act of giving up drinking any alcoholic liquors: also called *total abstinence*. —**ab′sti·nent,** *adj.* —**ab′sti·nent·ly,** *adv.*

**abstr.,** 1. abstract. 2. abstracted.

**ab·stract** (ab-strakt′, ab′strakt), *adj.* [< L. < *ab(s)-*, from + *trahere*, to draw], 1. thought of apart from any particular instances or material objects. 2. expressing a quality so thought of: as, beauty is an *abstract* word. 3. not easy to understand; abstruse. 4. loosely, theoretical; not practical. 5. in *art*, characterized by design that is not representational. *n.* (ab′strakt), 1. a brief statement of the essential thoughts of a book, article, etc.; summary. 2. that which is abstract: as, the *abstract* fascinates him. *v.t.* (ab-strakt′), 1. to take away. 2. to think of (a quality) apart from any particular instance or material object that has it. 3. (ab strakt), to summarize. —**in the abstract,** in theory as apart from practice. —**ab·stract′er,** *n.* —**ab·stract′ly,** *adv.* —**ab′stract·ness,** *n.*

**ab·stract·ed** (ab-strak′tid), *adj.* 1. removed or separated (*from* something). 2. preoccupied; absent-minded. **—ab·stract′ed·ly,** *adv.* **—ab·stract′ed·ness,** *n.*

**ab·strac·tion** (ab-strak′shən), *n.* 1. an abstracting or being abstracted. 2. formation of an idea, as of the qualities of a thing, by mental separation from particular instances or material objects. 3. an idea so formed, or a word for it: as, "honesty" and "truth" are *abstractions.* 4. an unrealistic notion. 5. preoccupation; absent-mindedness. 6. an abstract quality; abstract character. 7. in *art,* a picture, etc. that is wholly or partly abstract. **—ab·strac′tion·ism,** *n.* **—ab·strac′tion·ist,** *n.*

**ab·struse** (ab-stro͞os′), *adj.* [< L. < *ab(s)*-, away + *trudere,* to thrust], hard to understand; recondite. **—ab·struse′ly,** *adv.* **—ab·struse′ness,** *n.*

**ab·surd** (əb-sūrd′, ab-zūrd′), *adj.* [< Fr. < L. *absurdus,* not to be heard of; *ab*-, intens. + *surdus,* dull, deaf], clearly untrue or unreasonable, and therefore ridiculous, etc. **—ab·surd′ly,** *adv.* **—ab·surd′ness,** *n.*

**ab·surd·i·ty** (əb-sūr′də-ti, ab-zūr′-), *n.* 1. the quality or state of being absurd; nonsense. 2. [*pl.* -TIES], an absurd idea or thing.

**a·bun·dance** (ə-bun′dəns), *n.* [< OFr. < L. < *abundare;* see ABOUND], 1. great plenty; more than enough. 2. wealth. **—a·bun′dant,** *adj.* **—a·bun′dant·ly,** *adv.*

**a·buse** (ə-būz′; *for n.,* ə-būs′), *v.t.* [ABUSED, ABUSING], [< Fr. < L. < *ab*-, away, from + *uti,* to use], 1. to use wrongly; misuse. 2. mistreat. 3. to use insulting language about or to; revile. 4. [Archaic exc. in the passive], to deceive. *n.* 1. wrong or excessive use. 2. mistreatment; injury. 3. a bad or corrupt custom or practice. 4. insulting language. **—a·bus′er,** *n.*

**a·bu·sive** (ə-bū′siv), *adj.* 1. abusing; mistreating. 2. insulting; scurrilous. **—a·bu′sive·ly,** *adv.* **—a·bu′sive·ness,** *n.*

**a·but** (ə-but′) *v.i.* [ABUTTED, ABUTTING], [< OFr. < *a*-, to + *bout,* end], to touch at one end; border (*on, upon,* or *against*).

**a·but·ment** (ə-but′mənt), *n.* 1. an abutting. 2. in *architecture,* a part that supports an arch, as of a bridge. 3. the point of contact between the support and the thing supported.

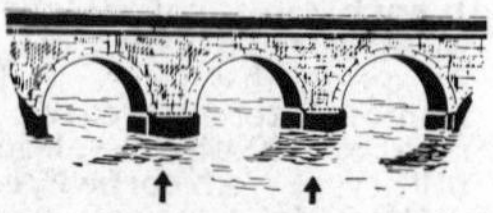
ABUTMENTS

**a·but·ter** (ə-but′ẽr), *n.* the owner of an abutting, or adjacent, piece of land.

**a·bysm** (ə-biz′'m), *n.* [Poetic], an abyss.

**a·bys·mal** (ə-biz′m'l), *adj.* of or like an abysm or abyss: unfathomable; immeasurable.

**a·bys·mal·ly** (ə-biz′m'l-i), *adv.* to an abysmal degree.

**a·byss** (ə-bis′), *n.* [< L. < Gr. < *a*-, without + *byssos,* bottom], 1. the primeval great deep. 2. a bottomless gulf; chasm. 3. anything too deep for measurement: as, an *abyss* of shame. 4. the ocean depths. **—a·byss′al,** *adj.*

**Ab·ys·sin·i·a** (ab′ə-sin′i-ə), *n.* Ethiopia. **—Ab′ys·sin′i·an,** *adj. & n.*

**-ac,** [< Fr. < L. < Gr. *-akos*], a suffix meaning: 1. *characteristic of,* as in *elegiac.* 2. *of, relating to,* as in *cardiac.* 3. *affected by* or *having,* as in *maniac.*

**Ac,** in *chemistry,* actinium.

**A C, a c,** in *bookkeeping,* account.

**A.C., a.c.,** in *electricity,* alternating current.

**a·ca·cia** (ə-kā′shə), *n.* [L. < Gr. *akakia,* thorny tree; prob. < *ake,* a point], 1. a tree or shrub of the mimosa family: some types yield gum arabic or dyes. 2. the locust tree.

**acad.,** 1. academic. 2. academy.

**ac·a·dem·ic** (ak′ə-dem′ik), *adj.* [see ACADEMY], 1. of schools or colleges; scholastic. 2. having to do with liberal rather than technical or vocational education. 3. not practical enough; too speculative. 4. formal; pedantic. Also **ac′a·dem′i·cal.** *n.* a person belonging to a college or university. **—ac′a·dem′i·cal·ly,** *adv.*

**academic freedom,** freedom of a teacher (or student) to express his beliefs (political, economic, etc.) without arbitrary interference.

**a·cad·e·mi·cian** (ə-kad′ə-mish′ən, ak′ə-də-), *n.* a member of an academy (sense 4).

**ac·a·dem·i·cism** (ak′ə-dem′ə-siz'm), *n.* formal or pedantic quality, spirit, etc. Also **a·cad′e·mism.**

**a·cad·e·my** (ə-kad′ə-mi), *n.* [*pl.* -MIES], [< Fr. < L. < Gr. *akadēmeia,* the grove of *Akadēmos,* where Plato taught], 1. a place of higher learning. 2. a private secondary or high school. 3. any school for special instruction. 4. an association of scholars, writers, artists, etc., for advancing literature, art, or science.

**A·ca·di·a** (ə-kā′di-ə), *n.* [Poetic], a French colony (1604–1713) that included what is now Nova Scotia. **—A·ca′di·an,** *adj. & n.*

**a·can·thus** (ə-kan′thəs), *n.* [*pl.* -THUSES (-iz), -THI (-thī)], [L. < Gr. *akantha,* thorn < *akis,* spine], 1. a plant with prickles and large leaves. 2. in *architecture,* a conventional representation of these leaves, especially on the capitals of Corinthian columns. **—a·can′thine** (-thin, -thīn), *adj.*

**‡a cap·pel·la** (ä′ kä-pel′lä; Eng. kə-pel′ə), [It. < L. *ad,* according to + *capella,* chapel], in chapel style; unaccompanied: said of choral singing.

**acc.,** 1. accompanied. 2. account. 3. accusative.

**ac·cede** (ak-sēd′), *v.i.* [-CEDED, -CEDING], [< L. < *ad*-, to + *cedere,* to yield], 1. to enter upon the duties (of an office); attain (with *to*). 2. to give assent; give in; agree (with *to*). **—ac·ced′ence,** *n.* **—ac·ced′er,** *n.*

**ac·cel·er·an·do** (ak-sel′ẽr-an′dō; It. ät-che′le-rän′dô), *adv. & adj.* [It.], in *music,* with gradually quickening tempo: abbrev. **accel.**

**ac·cel·er·ant** (ak-sel′ẽr-ənt), *n.* something, as a catalyst, that accelerates a process.

**ac·cel·er·ate** (ak-sel′ẽr-āt′), *v.t.* [-ATED, -ATING], [< L. < *ad*-, to + *celerare,* to hasten], 1. to increase the speed of. 2. to hasten the working of. 3. to cause to happen sooner. *v.i.* to increase in speed; go faster. **—ac·cel′er·a·ble,** *adj.* **—ac·cel′er·a·tive,** *adj.*

**ac·cel·er·a·tion** (ak-sel′ẽr-ā′shən), *n.* 1. an accelerating. 2. change in velocity (*positive* or *negative*). 3. the rate of such change.

**ac·cel·er·a·tor** (ak-sel′ẽr-ā′tẽr), *n.* 1. a person or thing, as the foot throttle of an automobile, that accelerates something. 2. in *chemistry,* a substance that speeds up a reaction.

**ac·cent** (ak′sent), *n.* [Fr. < L. < *ad*-, to + *canere,* to sing], 1. the emphasis given to a particular syllable or word in speaking it. 2. a mark used to show this emphasis, as primary (′) and secondary (′) accents. 3. a mark used to distinguish between various sounds of the same letter: as, in French there are acute (′), grave (`), and circumflex (^) *accents.* 4. a distinguishing regional or national manner of pronouncing: as, Irish *accent,* Southern *accent.* 5. *pl.* speech; words; utterance: as, *accents* mild. 6. in *music,* emphasis or stress on a note or chord. 7. in *prosody,* rhythmic stress or beat. *v.t.* (ak′sent, ak-sent′), 1. to pronounce with special stress. 2. to mark with an accent. 3. to emphasize.

**ac·cen·tu·al** (ak-sen′cho͞o-əl), *adj.* 1. of accent. 2. having rhythm based on stress, as some poetry. **—ac·cen′tu·al·ly,** *adv.*

**ac·cen·tu·ate** (ak-sen′cho͞o-āt′), *v.t.* [-ATED, -ATING], 1. to pronounce or mark with an accent or stress. 2. to emphasize. **—ac·cen′tu·a′tion,** *n.*

**ac·cept** (ək-sept′, ak-), *v.t.* [< OFr. < L. < *ad*-, to + *capere,* to take], 1. to take (what is offered or given); receive willingly. 2. to receive favorably; approve. 3. to agree to. 4. to believe in. 5. to respond to in the affirmative: as, he will *accept* an invitation. 6. in *business,* to agree to pay. 7. in *law,* to receive in person, as service of a writ. **—ac·cept′er, ac·cept′or,** *n.*

**ac·cept·a·ble** (ək-sep′tə-b'l, ak-), *adj.* worth accepting; satisfactory. **—ac·cept′a·bil′i·ty, ac·cept′a·ble·ness,** *n.* **—ac·cept′a·bly,** *adv.*

**ac·cept·ance** (ək-sep′təns, ak-), *n.* 1. an accepting or being accepted. 2. approval. 3. belief in; assent. 4. in *business, a)* a promise to pay. *b)* a signed bill of exchange showing this. Also **ac·cept′an·cy. —ac·cept′ant,** *adj.*

**ac·cep·ta·tion** (ak′sep-tā′shən), *n.* the generally accepted meaning (of a word or expression).

**ac·cept·ed** (ək-sep′tid, ak-), *adj.* generally regarded as true, proper, etc.; conventional; approved.

**ac·cess** (ak′ses), *n.* [see ACCEDE], 1. a coming toward or near to; approach. 2. a means of approach. 3. the right to enter, approach, or use (with *to*). 4. increase. 5. an outburst: as, an *access* of anger. 6. in *medicine,* the onset of a disease.

**ac·ces·sa·ry** (ak-ses′ə-ri), *adj. & n.* [*pl.* -RIES], accessory. **—ac·ces′sa·ri·ly,** *adv.* **—ac·ces′sa·ri·ness,** *n.*

**ac·ces·si·ble** (ak-ses′ə-b'l), *adj.* [see ACCEDE], 1. that can be approached or entered. 2. easy to reach. 3. obtainable. 4. open to the influence of (with *to*): as, he is not *accessible* to pity. **—ac·ces′si·bil′i·ty,** *n.* **—ac·ces′si·bly,** *adv.*

**ac·ces·sion** (ak-sesh′ən), *n.* [see ACCEDE], 1. a coming to; attaining (the throne, power, etc.). 2. assent. 3. *a)* an increase by addition. *b)* an addition. **—ac·ces′sion·al,** *adj.*

**ac·ces·so·ry** (ak-ses′ə-ri), *adj.* [see ACCEDE], 1. additional; extra; helping in a subordinate capacity. 2. in *law,* helping in an unlawful act. *n.* [*pl.* -RIES], 1. something extra added to help in a secondary way. 2. any article of clothing worn to complete one's outfit, as purse, gloves, etc. 3. equipment added for convenience, comfort, or safety: as, the *accessories* of an automobile. 4. in *law*, an accomplice. —**accessory before** (or **after**) **the fact,** one who, though absent at the commission of a felony, aids the accused before (or after) its commission. —**ac'ces·so'ri·al,** *adj.* —**ac·ces'so·ri·ly,** *adv.* —**ac·ces'so·ri·ness,** *n.*

**ac·ci·dence** (ak'sə-dəns), *n.* [see ACCIDENT], 1. the part of grammar that deals with the inflection of words: distinguished from *syntax*. 2. rudiments.

**ac·ci·dent** (ak'sə-dənt), *n.* [Fr. < L. < *ad-*, to + *cadere*, to fall], 1. a happening that is not expected, foreseen, or intended. 2. an unfortunate occurrence; sudden fall, etc. 3. fortune; chance. 4. an attribute that is not essential.

**ac·ci·den·tal** (ak'sə-den't'l), *adj.* 1. occurring by chance; fortuitous. 2. belonging but not essential; incidental. 3. in *music*, of an accidental. *n.* 1. a nonessential quality. 2. in *music*, a sign used to show a change of pitch in the note before which it is placed. —**ac'ci·den'tal·ly,** *adv.*

**ac·claim** (ə-klām'), *v.t.* [< L. < *ad-*, to + *clamare*, to cry out], 1. to greet with loud approval; applaud. 2. to announce with applause; hail: as, they *acclaimed* him president. *v.i.* to shout approval. *n.* loud applause or approval.

**ac·cla·ma·tion** (ak'lə-mā'shən), *n.* 1. an acclaiming or being acclaimed. 2. loud applause or approval. 3. a vote by voice: as, elected by *acclamation*. —**ac·clam·a·to·ry** (ə-klam'ə-tôr'i, -tō'ri), *adj.*

**ac·cli·mate** (ə-klī'mit, ak'li-māt'), *v.t.* & *v.i.* [-MATED, -MATING], [< Fr.; see AD- & CLIMATE], to accustom or become accustomed to a new climate or different environment. —**ac'cli·ma'tion,** *n.*

**ac·cli·ma·tize** (ə-klī'mə-tīz'), *v.t.* [-TIZED, -TIZING], to acclimate. —**ac·cli'ma·ti·za'tion,** *n.*

**ac·cliv·i·ty** (ə-kliv'ə-ti), *n.* [*pl.* -TIES], [< L. < *ad-*, to + *clivus*, hill], an upward slope: opposed to *declivity*. —**ac·cli·vous** (ə-klī'vəs), *adj.*

**ac·co·lade** (ak'ə-lād', ak'ə-läd'), *n.* [Fr. < It. < *accollare*, to embrace < L. *ad*, to + *collum*, neck], 1. formerly, an embrace (now, a touch on the shoulder with a sword) used in conferring knighthood. 2. an approving or praising mention; award.

**ac·com·mo·date** (ə-kom'ə-dāt'), *v.t.* [-DATED, -DATING], [< L. < *ad-*, to + *com-*, with + *modus*, a measure], 1. to adjust; adapt (often used reflexively). 2. to reconcile. 3. to supply (*with* something). 4. to do a favor for. 5. to have space for; lodge. *v.i.* to become adjusted, as the lens of the eye in focusing. —**ac·com'mo·da'tor,** *n.*

**ac·com·mo·dat·ing** (ə-kom'ə-dāt'iŋ), *adj.* obliging; complaisant: also **ac·com'mo·da'tive.** —**ac·com'mo·dat'ing·ly,** *adv.*

**ac·com·mo·da·tion** (ə-kom'ə-dā'shən), *n.* 1. adaptation (*to* a purpose); adjustment. 2. reconciliation of differences. 3. willingness to do favors. 4. a help or convenience. 5. *pl.* lodgings; room and board. 6. *pl.* traveling space, as in a train, etc. 7. in *business*, a loan. 8. in *physiology*, the self-adjustment of the lens of the eye in focusing.

**ac·com·pa·ni·ment** (ə-kum'pə-ni-mənt, ə-kump'ni-), *n.* 1. anything that accompanies something else. 2. in *music*, a part, usually instrumental, played together with the main part, as with a vocal solo.

**ac·com·pa·nist** (ə-kum'pə-nist), *n.* one who plays or sings an accompaniment.

**ac·com·pa·ny** (ə-kum'pə-ni), *v.t.* [-NIED, -NYING], [< Fr. < L.; see AD- & COMPANION], 1. to add to; supplement. 2. to go with; attend. 3. in *music*, to play or sing an accompaniment for or to.

**ac·com·plice** (ə-kom'plis), *n.* [< *a* (the article) + OFr. *complice* < L.; see COMPLEX], one who helps another in an unlawful act; partner in crime.

**ac·com·plish** (ə-kom'plish), *v.t.* [< OFr. < LL. < L. *ad*, to + *complere*, fill up], to do; succeed in doing; complete. —**ac·com'plish·a·ble,** *adj.*

**ac·com·plished** (ə-kom'plisht), *adj.* 1. done; completed. 2. trained; skilled. 3. trained in social arts.

**ac·com·plish·ment** (ə-kom'plish-mənt), *n.* 1. an accomplishing or being accomplished; completion. 2. something done successfully; work completed; achievement. 3. social art or skill.

**ac·cord** (ə-kôrd'), *v.t.* [< OFr. < LL. < L. *ad*, to + *cor, cordis*, heart], 1. to make agree or harmonize. 2. to grant. *v.i.* to agree or harmonize (usually followed by *with*). *n.* 1. mutual agreement; harmony. 2. an informal agreement between countries. 3. harmony of sound, color, etc. —**of one's own accord,** voluntarily. —**with one accord,** all agreeing.

**ac·cord·ance** (ə-kôr'd'ns), *n.* agreement; conformity. —**ac·cord'ant,** *adj.* —**ac·cord'ant·ly,** *adv.*

**ac·cord·ing** (ə-kôr'diŋ), *adj.* agreeing; in harmony. *adv.* accordingly. —**according as,** to the degree that. —**according to,** 1. in a way consistent with. 2. in proportion to. 3. as stated by.

**ac·cord·ing·ly** (ə-kôr'diŋ-li), *adv.* 1. in agreement with what has preceded. 2. therefore.

**ac·cor·di·on** (ə-kôr'di-ən), *n.* [< It. *accordare;* see ACCORD], a keyed musical instrument with a bellows, which is pressed together between the hands of the player to force air through reeds and thus produce tones. —**ac·cor'di·on·ist,** *n.*

ACCORDION

**ac·cost** (ə-kôst', -kost'), *v.t.* [< Fr. < L. < *ad-*, to + *costa*, rib, side], to approach and speak to.

**ac·couche·ment** (ə-ko͞osh'mənt; Fr. å'ko͞osh'män'), *n.* [Fr. < *à*, to + *coucher;* see COUCH], childbirth; confinement.

**ac·count** (ə-kount'), *v.t.* [< OFr. < *a-*, to + *conter*, to tell < L. *computare;* see COMPUTE], to consider or judge to be; deem. *v.i.* 1. to furnish a reckoning of money received and paid. 2. to make satisfactory amends: as, he will *account* for his crime. 3. to give satisfactory reasons (*for*); as, can he *account* for his actions? 4. put out of action: as, he *accounted* for five of the enemy. *n.* 1. a counting; calculation. 2. *often pl.* a record of business transactions. 3. a charge account. 4. worth; importance: as, a thing of small *account*. 5. an explanation. 6. a report; description; story. —**call to account,** 1. to demand an explanation of. 2. to reprimand. —**give a good account of oneself,** to acquit oneself well. —**on account,** as partial payment. —**on account of,** because of. —**on no account,** under no circumstances. —**take into account,** to take into consideration. —**turn to account,** to get use from.

**ac·count·a·ble** (ə-koun'tə-b'l), *adj.* 1. liable to be called to account; responsible. 2. explicable. —**ac·count'a·bil'i·ty,** *n.* —**ac·count'a·bly,** *adv.*

**ac·count·ant** (ə-koun't'nt), *n.* one whose work is to inspect or keep accounts: see **certified public accountant.** —**ac·count'an·cy,** *n.* —**ac·count'ant·ship',** *n.*

**ac·count·ing** (ə-koun'tiŋ), *n.* the system or science of setting up and auditing commercial accounts.

**ac·cou·ter** (ə-ko͞o'tẽr), *v.t.* [< Fr.; ? < L. *consuere*, to sew], to outfit; equip, especially for military service: also sp. **accoutre.**

**ac·cou·ter·ments** (ə-ko͞o'tẽr-mənts), *n.pl.* 1. clothes; dress. 2. all of a soldier's equipment except clothes and weapons: also sp. **accoutrements.**

**ac·cou·tre** (ə-ko͞o'tẽr), *v.t.* [-TRED (-tẽrd), -TRING], to accouter.

**ac·cred·it** (ə-kred'it), *v.t.* [< Fr.; see CREDIT], 1. to bring into credit or favor. 2. to give credentials to. 3. to believe in. 4. to certify as of a set standard. 5. to attribute. 6. to give (someone) credit for or consider as having (followed by *with*).

**ac·cre·tion** (ə-krē'shən), *n.* [< L. < *ad-*, to + *crescere*, to grow], 1. growth in size, especially by addition or accumulation. 2. a growing together of separate parts. 3. accumulated matter. 4. a whole resulting from such growth. —**ac·cre'tive,** *adj.*

**ac·crue** (ə-kro͞o'), *v.i.* [-CRUED, -CRUING], [< Fr. < L.; see ACCRETION], 1. to come as a natural growth or advantage (with *to*). 2. to be added as a natural increase: said especially of interest on money. —**ac·cru'al, ac·crue'ment,** *n.*

**acct.,** account.

**ac·cu·mu·late** (ə-kūm'yoo-lāt'), *v.t.* & *v.i.* [-LATED, -LATING], [< L. < *ad-*, to + *cumulare*, to heap], to pile up; collect; gather. —**ac·cu'mu·la·ble,** *adj.*

**ac·cu·mu·la·tion** (ə-kūm'yoo-lā'shən), *n.* 1. an accumulating; collection. 2. accumulated or collected material; heap.

**ac·cu·mu·la·tive** (ə-kūm'yoo-lā'tiv), *adj.* 1. resulting from accumulation. 2. tending to accumulate. —**ac·cu'mu·la'tive·ly,** *adv.*

**ac·cu·mu·la·tor** (ə-kūm'yoo-lā'tẽr), *n.* 1. one that accumulates. 2. [Brit.], a storage battery.

**ac·cu·ra·cy** (ak′yoo-rə-si), *n.* the quality or state of being accurate; precision.

**ac·cu·rate** (ak′yoo-rit), *adj.* [< L. < *ad-*, to + *cura*, care], 1. careful and exact. 2. free from errors; precise. —**ac′cu·rate·ly,** *adv.* —**ac′cu·rate·ness,** *n.*

**ac·curs·ed** (ə-kūr′sid, ə-kūrst′), *adj.* 1. under a curse; ill-fated. 2. damnable; abominable. Also **ac·curst** (-kūrst′). —**ac·curs′ed·ly,** *adv.* —**ac·curs′ed·ness,** *n.*

**ac·cu·sa·tion** (ak′yoo-zā′shən), *n.* 1. an accusing or being accused. 2. what one is accused of. Also **ac·cus·al** (ə-kūz′'l).

**ac·cu·sa·tive** (ə-kū′zə-tiv), *adj.* [< L. *accusativus;* see ACCUSE: the goal of an action was orig. considered to be its cause], in *linguistics,* designating or in a case (**accusative case**) expressing the goal of an action or motion, as, in *English grammar,* the objective case shown in the changed forms of the pronouns *me, us, him, her, them,* and *whom.* *n.* 1. the accusative (or objective) case. 2. a word in this case. —**ac·cu′sa·ti′val** (-tī′v'l), *adj.*

**ac·cu·sa·to·ry** (ə-kū′zə-tôr′i, -tō′ri), *adj.* accusing; making or containing an accusation.

**ac·cuse** (ə-kūz′), *v.t.* [-CUSED, -CUSING], [< OFr. < L. < *ad-*, to + *causa*, a cause or lawsuit], 1. to find at fault; blame. 2. to bring charges against (*of* breaking the law, etc.). —**ac·cus′er,** *n.*

**ac·cused** (ə-kūzd′), *n. sing. & pl.* in *law,* the person or persons accused of a crime (with *the*).

**ac·cus·tom** (ə-kus′təm), *v.t.* to make familiar by custom, habit, or use; habituate (*to* something).

**ac·cus·tomed** (ə-kus′təmd), *adj.* 1. customary; usual; characteristic. 2. wont or used (*to*).

**ace** (ās), *n.* [< L. *as,* unit], 1. a unit. 2. a playing card, domino, etc. marked with one spot. 3. a point, as in tennis, won by a single stroke. 4. a single point or particle: as, I was within an *ace* of confessing. 5. an expert, especially in combat flying. *adj.* [Colloq.], first-rate; expert: as, an *ace* salesman.

**-a·ce·a,** [L., neut. pl. of *-aceus*], a plural suffix used in forming the zoological names of classes or orders: see **-aceous.**

**-a·ce·ae,** [L., fem. pl. of *-aceus*], a plural suffix used in forming the botanical names of families: see **-aceous.**

**ace in the hole,** 1. in *stud poker,* an ace dealt and kept face down until the deal is over; hence, 2. [Slang], any advantage held in reserve.

**a·cen·tric** (ā-sen′trik, ə-), *adj.* [*a-* + *centric*], having no center; off center.

**-a·ceous,** [L. *-aceus*], a suffix meaning *of the nature of, like:* used to form adjectives corresponding to nouns ending in *-acea, -ceae.*

**ac·er·bate** (as′ēr-bāt′), *v.t.* [-BATED, -BATING], [< L. *acerbare*], 1. to make sour or bitter. 2. to irritate; exasperate.

**a·cer·bi·ty** (ə-sūr′bə-ti), *n.* [*pl.* -TIES], [< Fr. < L. < *acerbus,* sharp], 1. a sour, astringent quality. 2. sharpness or harshness of temper, etc.

**ac·e·tab·u·lum** (as′ə-tab′yoo-ləm), *n.* [*pl.* -LA (-lə)], [L., orig., vinegar cup < *acetum,* vinegar], in *anatomy,* the cup-shaped socket of the hip bone. —**ac′e·tab′u·lar,** *adj.*

**ac·e·tal** (as′ə-tal′), *n.* [< *aceto-* + *-al*], a colorless, volatile liquid, $C_6H_{14}O_2$, used as a hypnotic.

**ac·et·an·i·lide** (as′ə-tan′'l-īd′, -id), *n.* [*aceto-* + *aniline* + *-ide*], a white, crystalline organic drug, $CH_3CONHC_6H_5$, used to lessen pain and fever: also **ac′et·an′i·lid** (-id).

**ac·e·tate** (as′ə-tāt′), *n.* [< *aceto-* + *-ate*], a salt or ester of acetic acid. —**ac′e·tat′ed,** *adj.*

**a·ce·tic** (ə-sē′tik, ə-set′ik), *adj.* [< L. *acetum,* vinegar], of, like, containing, or producing acetic acid or vinegar.

**acetic acid,** a sour, colorless liquid, $CH_3COOH$, having a sharp odor: it is found in vinegar.

**a·cet·i·fy** (ə-set′ə-fī′), *v.t. & v.i.* [-FIED, -FYING], to change into vinegar or acetic acid. —**a·cet′i·fi·ca′tion,** *n.* —**a·cet′i·fi′er,** *n.*

**ac·e·to-,** [< L. *acetum,* vinegar], a combining form meaning *of acetic acid:* also, before a vowel, **acet-.**

**ac·e·tone** (as′ə-tōn′), *n.* [< *aceto-* + *-one*], a colorless, inflammable liquid, $CH_3COCH_3$, used as a solvent for certain oils, etc. —**ac′e·ton′ic** (-ton′ik), *adj.*

**a·cet·y·lene** (ə-set′'l-ēn′), *n.* [< *aceto-* + *-yl* + *-ene*], a colorless, poisonous, highly inflammable gaseous hydrocarbon, $C_2H_2$: it is used for lighting, and, with oxygen in a blowtorch, for welding, etc.

**ac·e·tyl·sal·i·cyl·ic acid** (as′ə-til-sal′ə-sil′ik, ə-sē′-t'l-), aspirin.

**ace·y-deuc·y** (ā′si-dōō′si, -dū′si), *n.* [< *ace* + *deuce*], a variation of backgammon.

**A·chae·an** (ə-kē′ən), *adj.* of Achaia or its people. *n.* 1. a native or inhabitant of Achaia. 2. a Greek: so used in Homer. Also **A·cha·ian** (-kā′ən, -kī′ən).

**A·cha·ia** (ə-kā′ə, -kī′ə), *n.* a province of ancient Greece, in the Peloponnesus. Also **A·chae·a** (-kē′ə).

**A·cha·tes** (ə-kā′tēz), *n.* [L.], 1. in Virgil's *Aeneid,* a loyal friend of Aeneas. 2. a loyal friend.

**ache** (āk), *v.i.* [ACHED (ākt), ACHING], [AS. *acan*], 1. to have or give dull, steady pain. 2. [Colloq.], to yearn (with *for* or an infinitive). *n.* a dull, continuous pain.

**a·chene** (ā-kēn′), *n.* [< Gr. *a-*, not + *chainein,* to gape], any small, dry, one-seeded fruit which ripens without bursting. —**a·che′ni·al,** *adj.*

**Ach·er·on** (ak′ēr-on′), *n.* [L.; Gr.], 1. in *Gr. & Rom. mythology,* the river in Hades across which the dead were ferried. 2. Hades; infernal regions.

**a·chieve** (ə-chēv′), *v.t.* [ACHIEVED, ACHIEVING], [< OFr. < L. *ad-*, to + *caput,* head], 1. to do; do successfully; accomplish. 2. to get by exertion; attain; gain. *v.i.* to effect a desired result. —**a·chiev′a·ble,** *adj.* —**a·chiev′er,** *n.*

**a·chieve·ment** (ə-chēv′mənt), *n.* 1. an achieving. 2. a thing achieved, as by skill, work, etc.; feat.

**A·chil·les** (ə-kil′ēz), *n.* in the *Iliad,* the Greek hero of the Trojan War, who killed Hector and was killed by Paris with an arrow that struck his vulnerable heel. —**A·chil′le·an,** *adj.*

**Achilles' heel,** (one's) vulnerable spot.

**Achilles' tendon,** the tendon connecting the heel to the muscles of the calf of the leg.

**ach·ro·mat·ic** (ak′rə-mat′ik), *adj.* [< Gr. < *a-*, without + *chrōma,* color], 1. colorless. 2. refracting white light without breaking it up into its component colors. 3. forming an image whose outline is free from prismatic colors. 4. in *music,* without accidentals: as, an *achromatic* scale. *n.* an achromatic lens. —**ach′ro·mat′i·cal·ly,** *adv.*

**a·chro·ma·tize** (ə-krō′mə-tīz′), *v.t.* [-TIZED, -TIZING], to make achromatic; rid of color.

**a·chro·mous** (ā-krō′məs, ə-), *adj.* [< Gr. < *a-*, without + *chrōma,* color], without color: also **a·chro′mic.**

**ac·id** (as′id), *adj.* [< L. *acidus,* sour < base *ac-*, sharp], 1. sour; sharp and biting to the taste; tart. 2. of or like an acid. *n.* 1. a sour substance. 2. [Slang], LSD. 3. in *chemistry,* any compound that can react with a base to form a salt: in water solution, an acid tastes sour and turns blue litmus red. —**ac′id·ly,** *adv.* —**ac′id·ness,** *n.*

**a·cid·ic** (ə-sid′ik), *adj.* forming acid.

**a·cid·i·fy** (ə-sid′ə-fī′), *v.t. & v.i.* [-FIED, -FYING], 1. to make or become sour or acid. 2. to change into an acid. —**a·cid′i·fi′a·ble,** *adj.* —**a·cid′i·fi·ca′tion,** *n.* —**a·cid′i·fi′er,** *n.*

**a·cid·i·ty** (ə-sid′ə-ti), *n.* [*pl.* -TIES], 1. acid quality or condition; sourness. 2. hyperacidity.

**ac·i·do·sis** (as′i-dō′sis), *n.* in *medicine,* a condition in which the alkali reserve of the body is lower than normal. —**ac′i·dot′ic** (-dot′ik), *adj.*

**acid test,** a crucial, final test or analysis.

**a·cid·u·late** (ə-sij′oo-lāt′), *v.t.* [-LATED, -LATING], to make somewhat acid or sour. —**a·cid′u·la′tion,** *n.*

**a·cid·u·lous** (ə-sij′oo-ləs), *adj.* [L. *acidulus*], somewhat acid or sour. —**a·cid′u·lous·ly,** *adv.* —**a·cid′u·lous·ness,** *n.*

**ac·i·er·ate** (as′i-ēr-āt′), *v.t.* [-ATED, -ATING], [Fr. *acier,* steel; + *-ate*], to change into steel.

**ac·i·nus** (as′i-nəs), *n.* [*pl.* -NI (-nī′)], [L., a grape], 1. any of the small parts composing such fruits as the raspberry, blackberry, etc. 2. a grape or any berry. —**ac′i·nous, ac′i·nose′,** *adj.*

**-a·cious,** [< L. *-ax, -acis;* + *-ous*], a suffix meaning *characterized by, inclined to, full of,* as in *tenacious.*

**-ac·i·ty,** a suffix used to form nouns corresponding to adjectives in *-acious,* as in *tenacity.*

**ack-ack** (ak′ak′), *n.* [echoic expansion of abbrev. *A.A.,* antiaircraft artillery], [Slang], 1. an antiaircraft gun. 2. its fire.

**ac·knowl·edge** (ək-nol′ij, ak-), *v.t.* [-EDGED, -EDGING], [< same base as *knowledge,* influenced by ME. *aknowen,* AS. *oncnawan,* to understand, admit], 1. to admit to be true; confess. 2. to recognize the authority or claims of. 3. to recognize and answer (a greeting or introduction). 4. to express thanks for. 5. to state that one has received (a letter, gift, etc.). 6. in *law,* to certify in legal form: as, *acknowledge* a deed. —**ac·knowl′edge·a·ble,** *adj.* —**ac·knowl′edged·ly,** *adv.* —**ac·knowl′edg·er,** *n.*

**ac·knowl·edg·ment, ac·knowl·edge·ment** (ək-nol′ij-mənt, ak-), *n.* 1. an acknowledging; admission. 2. recognition of the authority or claims of. 3. a recognizing and answering, as to a greeting. 4. an expression of thanks. 5. something given or done in return, as for a letter, a favor, etc. 6. a legal certificate.

**ac·me** (ak′mi), *n.* [Gr. *akmē*, a point, top], the highest point.

**ac·ne** (ak′ni), *n.* [? < Gr. *akmē;* see ACME], a common skin disease characterized by chronic inflammation of the sebaceous glands, usually causing pimples on the face, etc.

**ac·o·lyte** (ak′ə-līt′), *n.* [< ML. < Gr. *akolouthos*, follower], 1. in the *R. C. Church*, a member of the highest of the four minor orders, who serves at Mass. 2. an altar boy. 3. an attendant.

**ac·o·nite** (ak′ə-nīt′), *n.* [< L. < Gr. *akoniton*], 1. a poisonous plant with blue, purple, or yellow hoodlike flowers; monkshood; wolfsbane. 2. a drug made from its dried roots, used as a sedative.

**a·corn** (ā′kôrn, ā′kērn), *n.* [< AS. *æcern*, nut], the fruit of the oak tree; oak nut.

**acorn squash,** a kind of squash shaped like an acorn.

**a·cous·tic** (ə-kōōs′tik, -kous′-), *adj.* [< Fr. < Gr. < *akouein*, to hear], having to do with hearing, heard sound, or the science of heard sound: also **a·cous′ti·cal.** —**a·cous′ti·cal·ly,** *adv.*

**a·cous·tics** (ə-kōōs tiks, -kous′-), *n.pl.* 1. the qualities of a room, etc. that have to do with how clearly sounds can be heard in it. 2. [construed as sing.], the science of heard sound.

**ac·quaint** (ə-kwānt′), *v.t.* [< OFr. < ML. < L. *ad*, to + *cognitus*, pp. of *cognoscere*, to know thoroughly], 1. to familiarize (oneself *with* a thing). 2. to inform (followed by *with* or *that*).

**ac·quaint·ance** (ə-kwān′t'ns), *n.* 1. knowledge (of something or someone) got from personal experience or contact. 2. a person whom one knows only slightly. —**ac·quaint′ance·ship,** *n.*

**ac·quaint·ed** (ə-kwān′tid), *adj.* having personal knowledge of a thing, or slight personal knowledge of a person.

**ac·qui·esce** (ak′wi-es′), *v.i.* [-ESCED, -ESCING], [< Fr. < L. < *ad-*, to + *quiescere*, to be at rest], to accept quietly without protesting (with *in*); assent without enthusiasm. —**ac′qui·es′cence,** *n.* —**ac′qui·es′cent,** *adj.* —**ac′qui·es′cent·ly,** *adv.*

**ac·quire** (ə-kwīr′), *v.t.* [-QUIRED, -QUIRING], [< OFr. < L. < *ad-*, to + *quaerere*, to seek], 1. to get or gain by one's own efforts or actions. 2. to get as one's own. —**ac·quir′a·ble,** *adj.*

**acquired characteristic,** in *biology*, a modification of structure or function caused by environmental factors: now generally regarded as not inheritable: also **acquired character.**

**ac·quire·ment** (ə-kwīr′mənt), *n.* 1. an acquiring. 2. something acquired, as a skill, etc.

**ac·qui·si·tion** (ak′wə-zish′ən), *n.* 1. an acquiring or being acquired. 2. an acquired thing or person.

**ac·quis·i·tive** (ə-kwiz′ə-tiv), *adj.* eager to acquire (money, ideas, etc.); grasping. —**ac·quis′i·tive·ly,** *adv.* —**ac·quis′i·tive·ness,** *n.*

**ac·quit** (ə-kwit′), *v.t.* [-QUITTED, -QUITTING], [< OFr. < ML. < L. *ad*, to + *quietare*, to quiet], 1. to pay (a debt). 2. to release from a duty, etc. 3. to declare (a person) not guilty (*of* something); exonerate. 4. to conduct (oneself); behave. —**ac·quit′tal,** *n.* —**ac·quit′ter,** *n.*

**ac·quit·tance** (ə-kwit′'ns), *n.* 1. a settlement of, or release from, debt or liability. 2. a record of this; receipt in full.

**A·cre** (ä′kēr, ā′kēr), *n.* a seaport in W Israel, prominent during the Crusades.

**a·cre** (ā′kēr), *n.* [AS. *æcer*, field, tract plowable in a day], 1. a measure of land, 43,560 sq. ft.: abbrev. A., a. 2. *pl.* lands; estate.

**a·cre·age** (ā′kēr-ij, ā′krij), *n.* 1. acres collectively. 2. land sold or distributed by the acre.

**ac·rid** (ak′rid), *adj.* [L. *acer, acris*, sharp], 1. sharp, bitter, or irritating to the taste or smell. 2. sharp or bitter in speech, etc. —**ac′rid·ly,** *adv.*

**a·crid·i·ty** (a-krid′ə-ti, ə-), *n.* 1. the quality or state of being acrid. 2. [*pl.* -TIES], an acrid remark. Also **ac′rid·ness.**

**ac·ri·mo·ny** (ak′rə-mō′ni), *n.* [*pl.* -NIES], [< L. < *acer*, sharp], bitterness or harshness of manner or speech; asperity. —**ac′ri·mo′ni·ous,** *adj.*

**ac·ro-,** [< Gr. *akros*, at the end or top], a combining form meaning: 1. *pointed*, as in *acrocephaly*. 2. *highest, at the extremities*, as in *acromegaly*.

**ac·ro·bat** (ak′rə-bat′), *n.* [< Fr. < Gr. *akrobatos*, walking on tiptoe < *akros* (see ACRO-) + *bainein*, to walk, go], an expert performer of tricks on the trapeze, etc.; skilled gymnast or tumbler. —**ac′ro·bat′ic,** *adj.* —**ac′ro·bat′i·cal·ly,** *adv.*

**ac·ro·bat·ics** (ak′rə-bat′iks), *n.pl.* 1. an acrobat's tricks. 2. agile feats: as, mental *acrobatics*.

**ac·ro·gen** (ak′rə-jən), *n.* [*acro-* + *-gen*], a plant, such as a fern or moss, having a perennial stem with the growing point at the tip. —**ac′ro·gen′ic** (-jen′ik), **a·crog·e·nous** (ə-kroj′ə-nəs), *adj.*

**ac·ro·meg·a·ly** (ak rō-meg ə-li), *n.* [< *acro-;* + Gr. *megas, megalē*, large], a permanent enlargement of the bones of the head, hands, and feet, caused by abnormal activity of the pituitary gland. —**ac′ro·me·gal′ic** (-mi-gal′ik), *adj. & n.*

**ac·ro·nym** (ak′rə-nim), *n.* [*acro-* + homo*nym*], a word formed from the first (or first few) letters of several words, as *radar*, from *ra*dio *d*etecting *a*nd *r*anging.

**ac·ro·pho·bi·a** (ak′rə-fō′bi-ə), *n.* [*acro-* + *phobia*], a fear of high places.

**a·crop·o·lis** (ə-krop′ə-lis), *n.* [< Gr. < *akros* (see ACRO-) + *polis*, city], the fortified upper part of an ancient Greek city; esp., [A-], that of Athens, on which the Parthenon was built.

**a·cross** (ə-krôs′, ə-kros′), *adv.* 1. crossed; crosswise. 2. from one side to the other. 3. on or to the other side. *prep.* 1. from one side to the other of. 2. on or to the other side of; over. 3. into contact with: as, he came *across* an old friend.

**a·cros·tic** (ə-krôs′tik, -kros′-), *n.* [< L. < Gr. < *akros* (see ACRO-) + *stichos*, line of verse], a verse or arrangement of words in which certain letters in each line, as the first or last, when taken in order spell out a word, motto, etc. *adj.* of or like an acrostic. —**a·cros′ti·cal·ly,** *adv.*

**a·cryl·ic fiber** (ə-kril′ik), [ult. < *acr*id + *-yl* + *-ic*], any of a group of synthetic fibers derived from a compound of hydrogen cyanide and acetylene, and made into fabrics.

**act** (akt), *n.* [< Fr. < L. < *actum*, thing done < *agere*, to do], 1. a thing done; deed. 2. an action; doing. 3. a decision (of a court, legislature, etc.); law. 4. a document formally stating what has been done, etc. 5. one of the main divisions of a drama or opera. 6. a short performance on a program, as in vaudeville; hence, 7. [Colloq.], a piece of affected or feigned behavior. *v.t.* 1. to play the part of. 2. to perform in (a play). 3. to behave like: as, don't *act* the child. *v.i.* 1. to perform on the stage; play a role. 2. to behave; comport oneself. 3. to do a thing; function. 4. to have an effect: as, acids *act* on metal. 5. to appear or pretend to be: as, he *acted* angry. —**act as,** to perform the functions of. —**act for,** to act in behalf of. —**act on,** 1. to act in accord with; obey. 2. to affect. —**act one's age,** to behave in a way proper to one's age. —**act up,** [Colloq.], 1. to behave playfully. 2. to misbehave.

**act.,** active.

**act·a·ble** (ak′tə-b'l), *adj.* that can be acted: said of a play, a role, etc. —**act′a·bil′i·ty,** *n.*

**ACTH,** [< *a*drenocorti*c*o*t*ropic *h*ormone], a pituitary hormone used experimentally in the treatment of rheumatoid arthritis and certain other diseases.

**act·ing** (ak′tiŋ), *adj.* 1. adapted for performance: as, an *acting* version of a play. 2. functioning. 3. temporarily taking over the duties of someone else: as, the *acting* chairman. Abbrev. **actg.** *n.* 1. the art or occupation of an actor. 2. affected or simulated behavior.

**ac·tin·i·a** (ak-tin′i-ə), *n.* [*pl.* -AE (-ē′), -AS], [< Gr. *aktis, aktinos*, a ray], a sea anemone or any related animal. —**ac·tin′i·an,** *adj. & n.*

**ac·tin·ic** (ak-tin′ik), *adj.* of actinism. —**actinic rays,** violet or ultraviolet rays that produce chemical changes. —**ac·tin′i·cal·ly,** *adv.*

**ac·tin·ism** (ak′tin-iz'm), *n.* that property of X rays, etc. by which chemical reactions are produced.

**ac·tin·i·um** (ak-tin′i-əm), *n.* [< Gr. *aktis, aktinos*, ray], a radioactive chemical element found in pitchblende and other minerals: symbol, Ac; at. wt., 227 (?); at. no., 89.

**ac·ti·noid** (ak′ti-noid′), *adj.* having a radial form, as an actinozoan.

**ac·ti·no·zo·an** (ak′ti-nə-zō′ən), *n.* [< Gr. *aktis*, ray + *zōion*, animal], any anthozoan.

**ac·tion** (ak′shən), *n.* [OFr. < L. < *agere*, to do, drive], 1. the doing of something; motion or operation. 2. an act; thing done. 3. *pl.* behavior; habitual conduct. 4. an effect: as, the *action* of a drug. 5. the way of moving, working, etc., as of a machine. 6. the moving parts or mechanism, as of a gun, piano, etc. 7. the sequence of happenings in a story or play. 8. a legal process; lawsuit. 9. military combat. —**bring action,** to start a lawsuit. —**see action,** to participate in military combat. —**take action,** 1. to become active. 2. to start a lawsuit. —**ac'tion·less,** *adj.*

**ac·tion·a·ble** (ak'shən-ə-b'l), *adj.* in *law,* that gives cause for a lawsuit. —**ac'tion·a·bly,** *adv.*

**ac·ti·vate** (ak'tə-vāt'), *v.t.* [-VATED, -VATING], 1. to make active; hence, 2. to create or organize (a military unit, etc.). 3. to make radioactive. 4. to make capable of reacting or of accelerating a chemical reaction. 5. to aerate (sewage) in order to purify it. —**ac'ti·va'tion,** *n.* —**ac'ti·va'tor,** *n.*

**ac·tive** (ak'tiv), *adj.* [< OFr. < L. *activus;* see ACT], 1. acting; working; moving. 2. capable of acting, working, etc. 3. causing motion or change. 4. lively; busy; agile; quick: as, an *active* mind. 5. necessitating action: as, *active* sports. 6. in *grammar,* indicating the voice or form of a verb whose subject is shown as performing the action of the verb. *n.* in *grammar,* the active voice. —**ac'tive·ly,** *adv.* —**ac'tive·ness,** *n.*

**ac·tiv·i·ty** (ak-tiv'ə-ti), *n.* [*pl.* -TIES], 1. the state of being active; motion; doing. 2. energetic action; liveliness. 3. an active force. 4. any specific action or pursuit: as, student *activities.*

**ac·tiv·ize** (ak'tə-vīz'), *v.t.* [-IZED, -IZING], to make active; activate.

**act of God,** in *law,* a happening for which no one is liable, because no one could foresee or prevent it; accident due to natural causes.

**ac·tor** (ak'tēr), *n.* 1. a person who does a thing. 2. a person who acts in plays, motion pictures, etc.

**ac·tress** (ak'tris), *n.* a woman or girl who acts in plays, motion pictures, etc.

**Acts** (akts), *n.pl.* [construed as sing.], a book of the New Testament about the origins of the Christian church: full title, **Acts of the Apostles.**

**ac·tu·al** (ak'choo-əl), *adj.* [< Fr. < LL. < *agere,* to do], 1. existing in reality or in act; not merely possible, but real. 2. existing at the present moment. —**ac'tu·al·ness,** *n.*

**ac·tu·al·i·ty** (ak'choo-al'ə-ti), *n.* 1. the state of being actual; reality. 2. [*pl.* -TIES], an actual thing or condition; fact.

**ac·tu·al·ize** (ak'choo-əl-īz'), *v.t.* [-IZED, -IZING], to make actual or real. —**ac'tu·al·i·za'tion,** *n.*

**ac·tu·al·ly** (ak'choo-əl-i, -choo-li), *adv.* really; as a matter of fact.

**ac·tu·ar·y** (ak'choo-er'i), *n.* [*pl.* -IES], [L. *actuarius,* clerk; see ACT], a person who calculates risks, premiums, etc. for insurance. —**ac'tu·ar'i·al,** *adj.* —**ac'tu·ar'i·al·ly,** *adv.*

**ac·tu·ate** (ak'choo-āt'), *v.t.* [-ATED, -ATING], 1. to put into action or motion. 2. to impel to action: as, what motives *actuated* him? —**ac'tu·a'tion,** *n.* —**ac'tu·a'tor,** *n.*

**a·cu·i·ty** (ə-kū'ə-ti), *n.* [*pl.* -TIES], [< Fr. < L. *acus,* a needle], acuteness; keenness, as of thought or vision.

**a·cu·men** (ə-kū'mən), *n.* [L. < *acuere,* to sharpen], keenness and quickness of mind; sharp insight.

**a·cu·mi·nate** (ə-kū'mi-nit), *adj.* [< L. pp. of *acuminare,* to sharpen], pointed; tapering to a point: as, an *acuminate* leaf. *v.t.* (-nāt'), [-NATED, -NATING], to sharpen. —**a·cu'mi·na'tion,** *n.*

**a·cute** (ə-kūt'), *adj.* [< L. pp. of *acuere,* to sharpen; cf. ACUITY], 1. sharp-pointed. 2. keen or quick of mind; shrewd. 3. sensitive: as, *acute* hearing. 4. severe and sharp, as pain, jealousy, etc. 5. severe but of short duration; not chronic, as some diseases. 6. shrill; high in pitch. 7. less than 90°: said of angles.

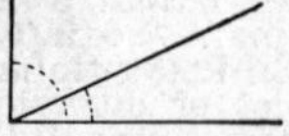

ACUTE ANGLE

**acute accent,** a mark (´) used to show: 1. the quality or length of a vowel, as in *idée.* 2. primary stress, as in *ty*pewriter.

**-a·cy,** [variously < Fr. < L. < Gr. *-ateia*], a suffix used in forming abstract nouns, meaning *quality, condition,* etc., as in *celibacy, curacy.*

**ad** (ad), *n.* [Colloq.], an advertisement.

**ad** (ad), *n.* in *tennis,* advantage: said of the first point scored after deuce. —**ad in,** server's advantage. —**ad out,** receiver's advantage.

**ad-,** [L., to, at, toward], a prefix meaning, in general, *motion toward, addition to, nearness to,* as in *admit, adjoin, adrenal:* through assimilation in Latin, it is often spelled **ac-, af-, ag, al-, an-, ap-, ar-, as-, at-,** and **a-** before certain consonants.

**A.D.,** *Anno Domini,* [L.], in the year of the Lord; of the Christian era: used with dates.

**ad·age** (ad'ij), *n.* [< Fr. < L. < *ad-,* to + *aio,* I say], an old saying or proverb; maxim.

**a·da·gio** (ə-dä'jō, -ji-ō'), *adv.* [It. *ad agio,* lit., at ease], in *music & dancing,* slowly. *adj.* slow. *n.* [*pl.* -GIOS (-jōz, -ōz)], 1. a slow movement in music. 2. a slow ballet dance.

**Ad·am** (ad'əm), *n.* in the *Bible,* the first man: Gen. 1–5. —**the old Adam,** the supposed human tendency to sin.

**ad·a·mant** (ad'ə-mant', -mənt), *n.* [OFr.; < L. < Gr. < *a-,* not + *daman,* to subdue], 1. a very hard stone or substance. 2. [Poetic], unbreakable hardness. *adj.* 1. too hard to be broken. 2. unyielding; firm. —**ad·a·man·tine** (ad'ə-man'tin, -tēn, -tīn), *adj.*

**Ad·ams, Henry Brooks** (ad'əmz), 1838–1918; American historian and writer.

**Adams, John,** 1735–1826; second president of the U.S. (1797–1801).

**Adams, John Quin·cy** (kwin'si), 1767–1848; son of *John;* sixth president of the U.S. (1825–1829).

**Adams, Samuel,** 1722–1803; American Revolutionary leader.

**Adam's apple,** the projection formed in the front of the throat by the thyroid cartilage, seen chiefly in men.

**a·dapt** (ə-dapt'), *v.t.* [< Fr. < L. < *ad-,* to + *aptare,* to fit], 1. to make suitable, especially by changing. 2. to change oneself to conform to new circumstances. —**a·dapt'er, a·dapt'or,** *n.*

**a·dapt·a·ble** (ə-dap'tə-b'l), *adj.* 1. that can be adapted or made suitable. 2. able to adapt easily to new circumstances. —**a·dapt'a·bil'i·ty,** *n.*

**ad·ap·ta·tion** (ad'əp-tā'shən), *n.* 1. an adapting or being adapted. 2. a thing resulting from adapting: as, this play is an *adaptation* of a novel. 3. in *biology,* a change in structure or function that produces better adjustment to the environment. Also **a·dap'tion.** —**ad'ap·ta'tion·al,** *adj.* —**ad'ap·ta'tion·al·ly,** *adv.*

**a·dap·tive** (ə-dap'tiv), *adj.* 1. showing adaptation. 2. able to adapt. —**a·dap'tive·ly,** *adv.* —**a·dap'tive·ness,** *n.*

**A·dar** (ə-där', ô'där), *n.* [Heb.], the sixth month of the Jewish year: see **Jewish calendar.**

**add** (ad), *v.t.* [< L. < *ad-,* to + *dare,* to give], 1. to join or unite (*to*) so as to increase the quantity, number, etc. 2. to state further. 3. to combine (numbers) into a sum. *v.i.* 1. to cause an increase of (with *to*): as, this *adds* to my income. 2. to find a sum. —**add up to,** to mean; signify. —**add'a·ble, add'i·ble,** *adj.*

**Ad·dams, Jane** (ad'əmz), 1860–1935; American social worker.

**ad·dax** (ad'aks), *n.* [L. < native Afr. word], a large antelope of N Africa and Arabia.

**ad·dend** (ad'end, ə-dend'), *n.* [< *addendum*], a number or quantity to be added to another.

**ad·den·dum** (ə-den'dəm), *n.* [*pl.* -DA (-də)], [L. < *addere,* to add], a thing added; esp., an appendix.

**ad·der** (ad'ēr), *n.* [< ME. *nadder,* by faulty separation of *a nadder,* an adder; AS. *nædre*], 1. a small, poisonous snake of Europe; common viper. 2. puff adder. 3. any of several harmless snakes of North America.

**ad·der's-tongue** (ad'ērz-tuŋ'), *n.* 1. the dogtooth violet. 2. a fern with a narrow spike.

**ad·dict** (ə-dikt'; *for n.,* ad'ikt), *v.t.* [< L. *addicere,* to give assent; *ad-,* to + *dicere,* to say], to give (oneself) up habitually (with *to*). *n.* one addicted to some habit, as to the use of a drug. —**ad·dict'ed,** *adj.* —**ad·dict'ed·ness, ad·dic'tion,** *n.*

**Ad·dis A·ba·ba** (a'dis ä'bə-bə, ä'dis), the capital of Ethiopia: pop., 443,000.

**Ad·di·son, Joseph** (ad'ə-s'n), 1672–1719; English essayist and poet. —**Ad'di·so'ni·an,** *adj.*

**ad·di·tion** (ə-dish'ən), *n.* 1. an adding of numbers to get a number called the sum. 2. a joining of a thing to another thing. 3. a thing or part added; increase: also **ad·dit'a·ment.** —**ad·di'tion·al,** *adj.* —**ad·di'tion·al·ly,** *adv.*

**ad·di·tive** (ad'ə-tiv), *adj.* 1. showing or relating to addition. 2. to be added. *n.* a substance added to another in small quantities to produce a desired effect, as a preservative added to food, an anti-knock added to gasoline, etc.

**ad·dle** (ad''l), *adj.* [< AS. *adela,* mire, filth], 1. rotten: said of an egg. 2. muddled; confused: now usually in compounds, as *addlebrained.* *v.t. & v.i.* [-DLED, -DLING], 1. to make or become rotten. 2. to make or become muddled or confused.

**ad·dle·brained** (ad''l-brānd'), *adj.* having an addle brain; stupid: also **ad'dle·head'ed, ad'dle·pat'ed.**

**ad·dress** (ə-dres'), *v.t.* [< OFr. < LL. *directiare,* to direct < *dirigere,* to lay straight], 1. to direct (spoken or written words *to*). 2. to speak to or write to. 3. to write the destination on (a letter or parcel). 4. to use a proper form in speaking to: as, *address* the judge as *Your Honor.* 5. to apply (oneself); direct (one's energies): with *to.* 6. in *golf,* to take a stance and aim the club at (the ball). *n.* (ə-dres′ *or, for 2 & 3,* ad′res), 1. a written or spoken speech. 2. the place where one lives or receives his mail. 3. the writing on an envelope, etc. showing its destination. 4. skill and tact. 5. conversational manner. 6. *pl.* wooing; attentions in courting. —**ad·dress′er, ad·dress′or,** *n.*

**ad·dress·ee** (ad res-ē′), *n.* the person to whom mail, etc. is addressed.

**ad·duce** (ə-do͞os′, ə-dūs′), *v.t.* [-DUCED, -DUCING], [< L. < *ad-*, to + *ducere*, to lead], to give as a reason or proof; cite. —**ad·duc′i·ble, ad·duce′a·ble,** *adj.*

**ad·duct** (ə-dukt′), *v.t.* [< L. pp. of *adducere;* see ADDUCE], in *physiology*, to move or pull (a part of the body) toward the median axis: opposed to *abduct.* —**ad·du′cent** (-do͞o′s′nt, -dū′-), **ad·duc′tive,** *adj.*

**ad·duc·tion** (ə-duk′shən), *n.* 1. an adducing or citing. 2. in *physiology*, an adducting.

**ad·duc·tor** (ə-duk′tẽr), *n.* a muscle that adducts.

**Ade, George** (ād), 1866–1944; American humorist.

**-ade,** [< L. *-ata,*], a suffix meaning: 1. *the act of,* as in *blockade.* 2. *the result* or *product of,* as in *pomade.* 3. *participant in an action,* as in *brigade.* 4. *drink made from,* as in *limeade.*

**Ad·e·laide** (ad′'l-ād′), *n.* the capital of South Australia: pop., 383,000.

**A·den** (ä′d'n, ā′d'n), *n.* 1. a former British colony and protectorate in SW Arabia: since 1967, part of the country of Southern Yemen. 2. a seaport in this region: pop., 99,000. 3. a gulf of the Arabian Sea, south of Arabia.

**ad·e·nec·to·my** (ad′'n-ek′tə-mi), *n.* [< *adeno-* + *-ectomy*], the surgical removal of a gland.

**ad·e·no-,** [< Gr. *aden*, gland], a combining form meaning *of a gland* or *glands:* also, before a vowel, **aden-.**

**ad·e·noid** (ad′'n-oid′), *adj.* [< *adeno-* + *-oid*], 1. glandular. 2. of or like lymphoid tissue.

**ad·e·noi·dal** (ad′'n-oi′d'l), *adj.* 1. adenoid. 2. having the characteristic mouth-breathing, nasal tone due to adenoids.

**ad·e·noids** (ad′'n-oidz′), *n.pl.* lymphoid growths in the throat behind the nose: they can swell up and obstruct nasal breathing.

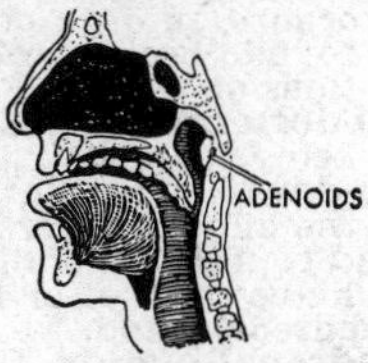

ADENOIDS

**ad·e·no·ma** (ad′'n-ō′mə), *n.* [< *adeno-* + *-oma*], a tumor of glandular origin or glandlike cell structure.

**a·dept** (ə-dept′), *adj.* [< L. < *ad-*, to + *apisci*, to pursue], highly skilled; expert. *n.* (ad′ept, ə-dept′), an expert. —**a·dept′ly,** *adv.* —**a·dept′ness,** *n.*

**ad·e·quate** (ad′ə-kwit), *adj.* [< L. < *ad-*, to + *aequare*, to make equal], 1. equal to a requirement or occasion; sufficient. 2. barely satisfactory. —**ad′e·qua·cy, ad′e·quate·ness,** *n.* —**ad′e·quate·ly,** *adv.*

**ad·here** (əd-hêr′, ad-), *v.i.* [-HERED, -HERING], [< L. < *ad-*, to + *haerere*, to stick], 1. to stick fast; become attached. 2. to give allegiance or support (with *to*).

**ad·her·ence** (əd-hêr′əns, ad-), *n.* an adhering; attachment or devotion (*to* a person, cause, etc.).

**ad·her·ent** (əd-hêr′ənt, ad-), *adj.* sticking fast; attached. *n.* a supporter or follower (*of* a cause, party, etc.). —**ad·her′ent·ly,** *adv.*

**ad·he·sion** (əd-hē′zhən, ad-), *n.* [see ADHERE], 1. a sticking (*to* something) or being stuck together. 2. adherence; devoted attachment. 3. in *medicine*, the growing together of normally separate tissues. 4. in *physics*, the force that holds together the unlike molecules of substances: distinguished from *cohesion.*

**ad·he·sive** (əd-hē′siv, ad-), *adj.* 1. sticking; clinging. 2. gummed; sticky. *n.* an adhesive substance.

**adhesive tape,** tape with a sticky substance on one side, used for holding bandages in place, etc.

**‡ad hoc** (ad′ hok′), [L., to this], for this case only.

**ad·i·a·bat·ic** (ad′i-ə-bat′ik), *adj.* [< Gr. < *a-*, not + *dia*, through + *bainein*, to go], of or denoting change in volume or pressure without loss or gain of heat.

**a·dieu** (ə-dū′, ə-do͞o′; Fr. à′dyö′), *interj. & n.* [*pl.* ADIEUS (-dūz′, -do͞oz′); Fr. ADIEUX (-dyö′)], [Fr. < OFr. < L. *ad*, to + *Deus*, God], good-by.

**ad in·fi·ni·tum** (ad in′fə-nī′təm), [L., to infinity], endlessly; forever; without limit: abbrev. **ad inf.**

**ad in·te·rim** (ad in′tə-irm), [L.], 1. in the meantime. 2. temporary. Abbrev. **ad int.**

**‡a·dios** (ä-dyôs′), *interj. & n.* [Sp. < L. *ad*, to + *Deus;* see ADIEU], good-by; farewell.

**ad·i·pose** (ad′ə-pōs′), *adj.* [< L. *adeps, adipis*, fat], of animal fat; fatty. *n.* animal fat in the connective tissue. —**ad′i·pose′ness, ad·i·pos·i·ty** (ad′ə-pos′ə-ti), *n.*

**Ad·i·ron·dacks** (ad′ə-ron′daks), *n.pl.* a mountain range in NE New York: also **Adirondack Mountains.**

**Adj.,** Adjutant.

**adj.,** 1. adjective. 2. adjourned. 3. adjudged.

**ad·ja·cen·cy** (ə-jā′s'n-si), *n.* 1. the quality or state of being adjacent; nearness. 2. [*pl.* -CIES], an adjacent thing. Also **ad·ja′cence.**

**ad·ja·cent** (ə-jā′s'nt), *adj.* [< L. < *ad-*, to + *jacere*, to lie], near or close (*to* something); adjoining. —**ad·ja′cent·ly,** *adv.*

**adjacent angles,** two angles having the same vertex and a side in common.

**ad·jec·tive** (aj′ik-tiv), *n.* [< L. < *adjicere*, to add to < *ad-*, to + *jacere*, to throw], any of a class of words used to limit or qualify a noun or other substantive: as, *good, every,* and *Aegean* are *adjectives.* *adj.* of, or having the nature or function of, an adjective. —**ad·jec·ti·val** (aj′ik-tī′v'l), *adj.* —**ad′jec·ti′val·ly,** *adv.*

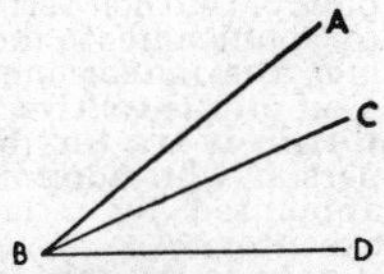

ADJACENT ANGLES (ABC, CBD)

**ad·join** (ə-join′), *v.t.* [< L. < *ad-*, to + *jungere*, to join], to be next to; be contiguous to. *v.i.* to lie close together; be in contact or proximity. —**ad·join′ing,** *adj.*

**ad·journ** (ə-jũrn′), *v.t.* [< OFr. < L. *ad*, to + *diurnus*, of a day], to put off until a future day; suspend for the day. *v.i.* 1. to suspend business (of a legislature, etc.) for a time. 2. [Colloq.], to go (*to* another place): as, let's *adjourn* to the veranda. —**ad·journ′ment,** *n.*

**Adjt.,** Adjutant.

**ad·judge** (ə-juj′), *v.t.* [-JUDGED, -JUDGING], [< OFr. < L. < *ad-*, to + *judicare*, to judge], 1. to judge or decide by law. 2. to declare or order by law. 3. to sentence by law. 4. to give or award by law, as costs, etc. —**ad·judge′a·ble** *adj.*

**ad·ju·di·cate** (ə-jo͞o′di-kāt′), *v.t.* [-CATED, -CATING], [< L. *adjudicare;* see ADJUDGE], in *law*, to hear and decide (a case); adjudge. *v.i.* to act as judge (*in* or *on* a matter). —**ad·ju′di·ca′tion,** *n.* —**ad·ju′di·ca′tive,** *adj.* —**ad·ju′di·ca′tor,** *n.*

**ad·junct** (aj′uŋkt), *n.* [< L. pp. of *adjungere;* see ADJOIN], 1. a thing added to something else, but secondary. 2. a subordinate associate. 3. in *grammar*, a modifier. 4. in *logic*, a nonessential attribute. —**ad·junc′tive,** *adj.* —**ad·junc′tive·ly,** *adv.*

**ad·jure** (ə-joor′), *v.t.* [-JURED, -JURING], [< L. < *ad-*, to + *jurare*, to swear], 1. to charge solemnly on oath or under penalty. 2. to appeal to earnestly. —**ad′ju·ra′tion,** *n.* —**ad·jur′a·to′ry** (-tôr′i, -tō′ri), *adj.* —**ad·jur′er, ad·ju′ror,** *n.*

**ad·just** (ə-just′), *v.t.* [< OFr. < L. *ad*, to + *juxta*, near; influenced by OFr. *juste* < L. *justus*, just], 1. to alter so as to make fit. 2. to regulate, as a watch. 3. to settle or arrange rightly. 4. to decide how much is to be paid in settling (an insurance claim). *v.i.* to adapt oneself; become suited or fit. —**ad·just′a·ble,** *adj.* —**ad·just′a·bly,** *adv.* —**ad·just′er, ad·just′or,** *n.*

**ad·just·ment** (ə-just′mənt), *n.* 1. an adjusting or being adjusted. 2. a means by which parts, as of a machine, are adjusted to one another. 3. the settlement of a claim.

**ad·ju·tan·cy** (aj′ə-tən-si), *n.* [*pl.* -CIES], the rank or office of a military adjutant.

**ad·ju·tant** (aj′ə-tənt), *n.* [< L. < *adjuvare*, to help], 1. an assistant. 2. an army staff officer who helps the commanding officer by handling administrative details. 3. a large stork of India and Africa: also **adjutant crane, adjutant stork.**

**adjutant general,** [*pl.* -TANTS GENERAL, -TANT GENERALS], 1. an officer who is the main assistant of a commanding general. 2. [A-G-], in the *U.S. Army*, the general in charge of the department that handles all records, orders correspondence, etc.

**ad-lib** (ad′lib′), *v.t. & v.i.* [-LIBBED, -LIBBING], [< *ad libitum*], [Colloq.], to improvise (words, gestures, etc. not in the script); extemporize.

**ad lib·i·tum** (ad lib′i-təm), [L.], 1. at pleasure.

2. in *music*, freely: a direction to change tempo, interpretation, etc. to suit the performer.

**Adm.,** 1. Admiral. 2. Admiralty.

**ad·meas·ure** (ad-mezh'ẽr), ***v.t.*** [-URED, -URING], [see MEASURE], to apportion. —**ad·meas'ure·ment,** ***n.***

**ad·min·is·ter** (əd-min'ə-stẽr, ad-), ***v.t.*** [< OFr. < L. < *ad-*, to + *ministrare*, to serve], 1. to manage; conduct; direct. 2. to give out or dispense, as punishment. 3. to give or apply (medicine, etc.). 4. to give or tender (an oath, etc.). 5. in *law*, to act as executor of (an estate). ***v.i.*** 1. to act as manager or administrator. 2. to furnish help or be of service (with *to*): as, *administer* to an invalid's needs. —**ad·min'is·tra·ble,** ***adj.*** —**ad·min'is·trant,** ***adj. & n.***

**ad·min·is·trate** (əd-min'ə-strāt', ad-), ***v.t.*** [-TRATED -TRATING], to administer.

**ad·min·is·tra·tion** (əd-min'ə-strā'shən, ad-), ***n.*** 1. management. 2. the management of governmental or institutional affairs. 3. [often A-], the executive officials of a government or institution and their policy. 4. their term of office. 5. the administering (*of* punishment, medicine, an oath, etc.). 6. in *law*, the management and settling (of an estate). —**ad·min'is·tra'tive,** ***adj.*** —**ad·min'is·tra'tive·ly,** ***adv.***

**ad·min·is·tra·tor** (əd-min'ə-strā'tẽr, ad-), ***n.*** 1. a person who administers; executive. 2. a person appointed by a law court to settle an estate; executor.

**ad·min·is·tra·trix** (əd-min'ə-strā'triks, ad-), ***n.*** [*pl.* -TRIXES, -TRICES (-tri-sēz')], a woman administrator: also **ad·min'is·tra'tress,** (-tris).

**ad·mi·ra·ble** (ad'mə-rə-b'l), ***adj.*** 1. deserving admiration. 2. excellent. —**ad'mir·a·bly,** ***adv.***

**ad·mi·ral** (ad'mə-rəl), ***n.*** [< OFr. < Ar. *amir al*, ruler of; sp. influenced by *admirable*], 1. the commanding officer of a navy or fleet. 2. a naval officer of the highest rank. 3. a flagship. 4. [orig. *admirable*], any of various colorful butterflies.

**Admiral of the Fleet,** the highest rank in the U.S. Navy, having the insigne of five stars.

**ad·mi·ral·ty** (ad'mə-rəl-ti), ***n.*** [*pl.* -TIES], 1. the rank, position, or authority of an admiral. 2. [often A-], a governmental department in charge of naval affairs. 3. maritime law or court. 4. [A-], the building in London in which British naval affairs are administered.

**ad·mi·ra·tion** (ad'mə-rā'shən), ***n.*** 1. an admiring; wonder and delight at anything fine, skillful, beautiful, etc. 2. high esteem. 3. a thing or person inspiring such feelings.

**ad·mire** (əd-mīr'), ***v.t.*** [-MIRED, -MIRING], [< OFr. < L. < *ad-*, at + *mirari*, to wonder], 1. to regard with wonder and delight. 2. to have high regard for. 3. [Dial. or Colloq.], to like or wish (*to* do something). 4. [Archaic], to marvel at.

**ad·mir·er** (əd-mīr'ẽr), ***n.*** 1. a person who admires. 2. a man who is in love with a woman; suitor.

**ad·mis·si·ble** (əd-mis'ə-b'l, ad-), ***adj.*** [see ADMIT], 1. that can be accepted or allowed: as, *admissible* evidence. 2. having the right to be admitted. —**ad·mis'si·bil'i·ty, ad·mis'si·ble·ness,** ***n.*** —**ad·mis'si·bly,** ***adv.***

**ad·mis·sion** (əd-mish'ən, ad-), ***n.*** 1. an admitting or being admitted. 2. right of entry. 3. an entrance fee. 4. a conceding; granting. 5. an acknowledging; confessing. 6. a thing conceded, acknowledged, or confessed.

**ad·mis·sive** (əd-mis'iv, ad-), ***adj.*** admitting or tending to admit.

**ad·mit** (əd-mit', ad-), ***v.t.*** [-MITTED, -MITTING], [< L. < *ad-*, to + *mittere*, to send], 1. to permit to enter or use. 2. to entitle to enter. 3. to allow; leave room for. 4. to have room for; hold: as, the hall *admits* 2,500 people. 5. to concede; grant. 6. to acknowledge; confess. 7. to permit to practice: as, he was *admitted* to the bar. ***v.i.*** 1. to give entrance (*to* a place). 2. to allow or warrant (with *of*). —**ad·mit'ter,** ***n.***

**ad·mit·tance** (əd-mit''ns, ad-), ***n.*** 1. an admitting or being admitted. 2. right of entry. 3. in *electricity*, the current divided by the voltage.

**ad·mit·ted·ly** (əd-mit'id-li, ad-), ***adv.*** by admission or general agreement; confessedly.

**ad·mix** (ad-miks'), ***v.t. & v.i.*** to mix (a thing) in; mix with something.

**ad·mix·ture** (ad-miks'chẽr, əd-), ***n.*** [< L. < *ad-*, to + *miscere*, to mix], 1. a mixture. 2. a thing added in mixing.

**ad·mon·ish** (əd-mon'ish, ad-), ***v.t.*** [< OFr. < L. < *ad-*, to + *monere*, to warn], 1. to warn; caution against specific faults. 2. to reprove mildly. 3. to advise. 4. to inform or remind, by way of a warning. —**ad·mon'ish·er,** ***n.***

**ad·mo·ni·tion** (ad'mə-nish'ən), ***n.*** 1. an admonishing 2. a mild rebuke; reprimand. Also **ad·mon'ish·ment.**

**ad·mon·i·tor** (əd-mon'ə-tẽr, ad-), ***n.*** a person who admonishes. —**ad·mon'i·to'ry** (-tôr'i, -tō'ri), ***adj.***

**‡ad nau·se·am** (ad nô'shi-am', -zi-əm), [L., to nausea], to the point of disgust.

**a·do** (ə-do͞o'), ***n.*** [< ME. *at do*, to do], fuss; stir.

**a·do·be** (ə-dō'bi), ***n.*** [Sp.], 1. unburnt, sun-dried brick. 2. the clay of which this brick is made. 3. a building made of adobe.

**ad·o·les·cence** (ad''l-es''ns), ***n.*** [see ADOLESCENT], 1. the quality of being youthful. 2. the time of life between puberty and maturity; youth. Also **ad'o·les'cen·cy.**

**ad·o·les·cent** (ad''l-es''nt), ***adj.*** [Fr. < L. < *ad-*, to + *alescere*, to increase, grow up], 1. growing up; developing from childhood to maturity. 2. of or characteristic of adolescence. ***n.*** a boy or a girl from puberty to adulthood; person in his teens.

**A·do·nis** (ə-dō'nis, ə-don'is), ***n.*** 1. in *Greek mythology*, a young man loved by Aphrodite. 2. any very handsome young man. —**A·don'ic,** ***adj.***

**a·dopt** (ə-dopt'), ***v.t.*** [< Fr. < L. < *ad-*, to + *optare*, to choose], 1. to choose and bring into a certain relationship, as into one's own family. 2. to take into one's own family by legal process and raise as one's own child. 3. to take and use as one's own: said of an idea, a word, etc. 4. to choose and follow (a course). 5. to vote to accept (a committee report, etc.). —**a·dopt'a·ble,** ***adj.*** —**a·dopt'a·bil'i·ty,** ***n.*** —**a·dopt'er,** ***n.*** —**a·dop'tion,** ***n.***

**a·dop·tive** (ə-dop'tiv), ***adj.*** 1. adopted. 2. adopting. —**a·dop'tive·ly,** ***adv.***

**a·dor·a·ble** (ə-dôr'ə-b'l, -dōr'), ***adj.*** 1. worthy of adoration or love. 2. [Colloq.], delightful; charming. —**a·dor'a·bil'i·ty,** ***n.*** —**a·dor'a·bly,** ***adv.***

**ad·o·ra·tion** (ad'ə-rā'shən), ***n.*** 1. a worshiping or paying homage. 2. great love or devotion.

**a·dore** (ə-dôr', ə-dōr'), ***v.t.*** [ADORED, ADORING], [< Fr. < L. < *ad-*, to + *orare*, to speak], 1. to worship as divine. 2. to love greatly; idolize. 3 [Colloq.], to like very much. —**a·dor'er,** ***n.*** —**a·dor'ing,** ***adj.*** —**a·dor'ing·ly,** ***adv.***

**a·dorn** (ə-dôrn'), ***v.t.*** [< OFr. < L. < *ad-*, to + *ornare*, to deck out], 1. to serve as an ornament to; add beauty or distinction to. 2. to put decorations on. —**a·dorn'er,** ***n.*** —**a·dorn'ing·ly,** ***adv.***

**a·dorn·ment** (ə-dôrn'mənt), ***n.*** 1. an adorning or being adorned. 2. a decoration or ornament.

**a·down** (ə-doun'), ***adv. & prep.*** [AS. *of dune*, from the hill, downward], [Poetic], down.

**ad·re·nal** (ad-rē'n'l), ***adj.*** [*ad-* + *renal*], 1. near the kidney. 2. of or from the adrenal glands. ***n.*** an adrenal gland.

**adrenal glands,** the two small ductless glands on the upper part of the kidneys in mammals: also called *suprarenal glands.*

**ad·ren·al·in** (ad-ren''l-in), ***n.*** [*adrenal* + *-in*], 1. a hormone produced by the adrenal glands. 2. a drug, $C_9H_{13}NO_3$, containing this hormone, used to raise blood pressure, stop bleeding, etc.: a trademark (**Adrenalin**). Also **ad·ren'al·ine** (-in, -ēn'). Also called *epinephrine.*

**A·dri·at·ic** (ā'dri-at'ik, ad'ri-), ***n.*** an arm of the Mediterranean between Italy and Yugoslavia.

**a·drift** (ə-drift'), ***adv. & adj.*** floating without mooring or direction; drifting: often figurative.

**a·droit** (ə-droit'), ***adj.*** [Fr., *a*, to + *droit*, right < L. *directus;* see DIRECT], skillful and clever. —**a·droit'ly,** ***adv.*** —**a·droit'ness,** ***n.***

**ad·sorb** (ad-sôrb', -zôrb'), ***v.t.*** [< L. *ad-*, to + *sorbere*, to drink in], to collect (a gas, liquid, or dissolved substance) in condensed form on a surface. —**ad·sorb'ent,** ***adj. & n.***

**ad·sorp·tion** (ad-sôrp'shən, -zôrp'-), ***n.*** adhesion of the molecules of a gas, liquid, or dissolved substance to a surface. —**ad·sorp'tive,** ***adj. & n.***

**ad·u·late** (aj'ə-lāt'), ***v.t.*** [-LATED, -LATING], [< L. pp. of *adulari*, to fawn upon], to praise too highly or flatter servilely. —**ad'u·la'tion,** ***n.*** —**ad'u·la'tor,** ***n.*** —**ad'u·la·to'ry** (-lə-tôr'i, -lə-tō'ri), ***adj.***

**a·dult** (ə-dult', ad'ult), ***adj.*** [< L. pp. of *adolescere;* see ADOLESCENT], 1. grown up; mature in age, size, strength, etc. 2. of or for grown men and women. ***n.*** 1. a mature person. 2. a mature animal or plant. —**a·dult'hood, a·dult'ness,** ***n.***

**a·dul·ter·ant** (ə-dul'tẽr-ənt), ***n.*** a substance that adulterates. ***adj.*** adulterating.

**a·dul·ter·ate** (ə-dul'tẽr-āt'), ***v.t.*** [-ATED, -ATING], [< L. pp. of *adulterare*, to falsify < *ad-*, to + *alter*, other], to make inferior, impure, etc. by adding a poor or improper substance. —**a·dul'ter·a'tion,** ***n.*** —**a·dul'ter·a'tor,** ***n.***

**a·dul·ter·er** (ə-dul'tẽr-ẽr), ***n.*** a person (especially a man) guilty of adultery. —**a·dul'ter·ess** (-tẽr-is, -tris), ***n. fem.***

**a·dul·ter·ous** (ə-dul′tẽr-əs), *adj.* 1. of adultery. 2. guilty of adultery. —**a·dul′ter·ous·ly,** *adv.*
**a·dul·ter·y** (ə-dul′tẽr-i), *n.* [*pl.* -IES], [L. *adulterium;* see ADULTERATE], sexual intercourse between a married person and another not the spouse.
**ad·um·brate** (ad-um′brāt, ad′əm-brāt′), *v.t.* [-BRATED, -BRATING], [< L. < *ad-*, to + *umbra*, shade], 1. to outline vaguely; foreshadow. 2. to overshadow. —**ad′um·bra′tion,** *n.* —**ad·um′bra·tive,** *adj.*
**adv.,** 1. adverb. 2. adverbial. 3. advertisement.
**ad va·lo·rem** (ad və-lôr′əm, -lō′rəm), [L.], in proportion to the value: said of duties levied on imports according to their invoiced value: abbrev. **adv., ad val.**
**ad·vance** (əd-vans′, ad-väns′), *v.t.* [-VANCED, -VANCING], [< OFr. *avancer*, to forward < L. < *ab-*, from + *ante*, before], 1. to bring or move forward. 2. to suggest. 3. to further; promote. 4. to cause to happen earlier. 5. to raise the rate of. 6. to pay (money) before due. 7. to lend. *v.i.* 1. to go forward. 2. to improve; progress; develop. 3. to rise in rank, quality, price, etc. *n.* 1. a moving forward. 2. an improvement; progress. 3. a rise in value or cost. 4. *pl.* approaches to get favor, become acquainted, etc. 5. a payment made before due, as of wages. 6. a loan. *adj.* 1. in front: as, *advance* guard. 2. beforehand: as, *advance* information. —**in advance,** 1. in front. 2. ahead of time.
**ad·vanced** (əd-vanst′, ad-vänst′), *adj.* 1. in advance; in front. 2. far on in life; old. 3. ahead of the times; progressive: as, *advanced* ideas.
**ad·vance·ment** (əd-vans′mənt, ad-väns′-), *n.* 1. an advancing or being advanced. 2. promotion; success. 3. progress; improvement; furtherance.
**ad·van·tage** (əd-van′tij, ad-vän′-), *n.* [< OFr. < *avant*, before < L. *ab ante*, from before], 1. a more favorable position; superiority (often with *of* or *over*). 2. a favorable circumstance, event, etc. 3. gain or benefit. 4. in *tennis*, the first point scored after deuce. *v.t.* [-TAGED, -TAGING], to give an advantage to. —**take advantage of,** 1. to use for one's own benefit. 2. to impose upon. —**to advantage,** to good effect.
**ad·van·ta·geous** (ad′vən-tā′jəs), *adj.* favorable; beneficial; useful; profitable.
**Ad·vent** (ad′vent), *n.* [< L. < *ad-*, to + *venire*, to come], 1. the period including the four Sundays just before Christmas. 2. Christ's birth. 3. Christ's second coming to earth, on Judgment Day. 4.[a-], a coming or arrival.
**Ad·vent·ism** (ad′ven-tiz′m), *n.* the belief that Christ's Second Advent will soon occur. —**Ad′vent·ist,** *n.* & *adj.*
**ad·ven·ti·tious** (ad′ven-tish′əs), *adj.* [< L.; see ADVENT] 1. added from outside; accidental. 2. in *botany*, occurring in unusual or abnormal places. —**ad′ven·ti′tious·ly,** *adv.* —**ad′ven·ti′tious·ness,** *n.*
**ad·ven·tive** (ad-ven′tiv), *adj.* in *botany*, not native to the environment.
**ad·ven·ture** (əd-ven′chẽr), *n.* [< OFr. < L. *adventura*, lit., a happening < *advenire*; see ADVENT] 1. the encountering of, or a liking for, danger, etc. 2. an exciting and dangerous undertaking. 3. an unusual, stirring experience, often of a romantic nature. 4. a business venture or speculation. *v.t.* & *v.i.* [-TURED, -TURING], to risk; venture; hazard.
**ad·ven·tur·er** (əd-ven′chẽr-ẽr), *n.* 1. a person who has or likes to have adventures. 2. a soldier of fortune. 3. a speculator. 4. a person who tries to become rich, socially accepted, etc. by dubious schemes. —**ad·ven′tur·ess,** *n.fem.*
**ad·ven·ture·some** (əd-ven′chẽr-səm), *adj.* adventurous.
**ad·ven·tur·ous** (əd-ven′chẽr-əs), *adj.* 1. fond of adventure; willing to take chances; daring. 2. full of danger; risky. —**ad·ven′tur·ous·ly,** *adv.* —**ad·ven′tur·ous·ness,** *n.*
**ad·verb** (ad′vẽrb), *n.* [< L. < *ad-*, to + *verbum*, a word], 1. any of a class of words used to modify a verb, adjective, or another adverb, by expressing time, place, manner, degree, cause, etc. 2. any phrase or clause similarly used. —**ad·ver′bi·al,** *adj.* —**ad·ver′bi·al·ly,** *adv.*
**ad·ver·sar·y** (ad′vẽr-ser′i), *n.* [*pl.* -IES], [see ADVERSE, ADVERT], a person who opposes or fights against another; opponent; enemy.
**ad·ver·sa·tive** (əd-vũr′sə-tiv, ad-), *adj.* [< L. < pp. of *adversari*, to be opposed to], expressing opposition or antithesis. *n.* an adversative word, such as *but, yet, however.*
**ad·verse** (əd-vũrs′, ad′vẽrs), *adj.* [< OFr. < L. < pp. of *advertere;* see ADVERT], 1. hostile; opposed. 2. unfavorable; harmful. 3. opposite in position or direction. —**ad·verse′ly,** *adv.* —**ad·verse′ness,** *n.*
**ad·ver·si·ty** (əd-vũr′sə-ti, ad-), *n.* [*pl.* -TIES (-tiz)], 1. misfortune; wretched or troubled state. 2. an instance of misfortune; calamity.
**ad·vert** (əd-vũrt′, ad-), *v.i.* [L. *advertere; ad-*, to + *vertere*, to turn], to call attention; refer (*to*).
**ad·vert·ent** (əd-vũr′t'nt, ad-), *adj.* attentive. —**ad·vert′ence, ad·vert′en·cy,** *n.*
**ad·ver·tise, ad·ver·tize** (ad′vẽr-tīz′, ad′vẽr-tīz′), *v.t.* [-TISED or -TIZED, -TISING or -TIZING], [< Fr. *advertir*, to call attention to; L. *advertere;* see ADVERT], 1. to tell people about or praise, as through newspapers, radio, etc., usually to promote sales. 2. [Archaic], to notify or warn. *v.i.* 1. to call the public's attention to things for sale, etc., as by printed notices. 2. to ask (*for*) publicly by printed notice, etc.: as, *advertise* for a servant. —**ad′ver·tis′er, ad′ver·tiz′er,** *n.*
**ad·ver·tise·ment, ad·ver·tize·ment** (ad′vẽr-tīz′mənt, əd-vũr′tiz-), *n.* a public announcement, usually paid for, as of things for sale, needs, etc.
**ad·ver·tis·ing, ad·ver·tiz·ing** (ad′vẽr-tīz′iŋ, ad′vẽr-tīz′iŋ), *n.* 1. advertisement(s). 2. the business of preparing and issuing advertisements.
**ad·vice** (əd-vīs′), *n.* [< OFr. < L. < *ad-*, at + *videre*, to look], 1. opinion given as to what to do; counsel. 2. *usually pl.* information or report.
**ad·vis·a·ble** (əd-vīz′ə-b'l), *adj.* to be advised or recommended; prudent and wise; sensible. —**ad·vis′a·bil′i·ty,** *n.* —**ad·vis′a·bly,** *adv.*
**ad·vise** (əd-vīz′), *v.t.* [-VISED, -VISING], [< OFr. < L. *ad*, at + pp. of *videre*, to look], 1. to give advice to; counsel. 2. to offer as advice; recommend. 3. to notify; inform. *v.i.* 1. to discuss or consult (*with*). 2. to give advice.
**ad·vised** (əd-vīzd′), *adj.* thought out; planned: now chiefly in *well-advised, ill-advised.*
**ad·vis·ed·ly** (əd-vīz′id-li), *adv.* with due consideration; deliberately.
**ad·vise·ment** (əd-vīz′mənt), *n.* careful consideration. —**take under advisement,** to consider carefully.
**ad·vis·er, ad·vi·sor** (əd-vīz′ẽr), *n.* one who advises. —**legal advisor,** a lawyer.
**ad·vi·so·ry** (əd-vī′zə-ri), *adj.* 1. advising or empowered to advise. 2. relating to advice. *n.* [*pl.* -RIES], a warning about weather conditions, from the Weather Bureau. —**ad·vi′so·ri·ly** (-rə-li), *adv.*
**ad·vo·ca·cy** (ad′və-kə-si), *n.* an advocating; a speaking or writing in support (*of* something).
**ad·vo·cate** (ad′və-kit, -kāt′), *n.* [< OFr. < L. < *ad-*, to + *vocare*, to call], 1. one who pleads another's cause, as a lawyer. 2. one who speaks or writes in support of something. *v.t.* (-kāt′), [-CATED, -CATING], to speak or write in support of; be in favor of. —**ad′vo·ca′tor,** *n.*
**advt.,** [*pl.* ADVTS.], advertisement.
**adz, adze** (adz), *n.* [AS. *adesa*], an axlike tool for dressing wood, etc., with a curved blade at right angles to the handle.

TYPES OF ADZ

**æ,** 1. a diphthong in some Latin words, usually written *ae* or replaced by *e* in derived English words, as in *demon* (*dæmon*). 2. an Anglo-Saxon character symbolizing a vowel like the *a* in *hat.*
**A.E.C., AEC,** Atomic Energy Commission.
**a·ë·des** (ā-ē′dēz), *n. sing.* & *pl.* [< Gr. < *a-*, not + *hēdys*, sweet], the mosquito that carries the virus of yellow fever.
**ae·dile** (ē′dīl), *n.* [< L. < *aedes*, building], in ancient Rome, an official in charge of buildings, roads, public games, etc.: also sp. **edile.**
**A.E.F.,** American Expeditionary Force (or Forces).
**Ae·ge·an** (ē-jē′ən), *n.* a sea between Greece and Asia Minor: an arm of the Mediterranean.
**Ae·gir** (ē′jir, ā′gir), *n.* [ON.], in *Norse mythology*, the god of the sea.
**ae·gis** (ē′jis), *n.* [L. < Gr. *aigis*, goatskin], 1. in *Greek mythology*, a shield or breastplate used by Zeus and, later, by Athena. 2. a protection. 3. sponsorship; auspices. Also sp. **egis.**
**Ae·ne·as** (i-nē′əs, ē-), *n.* in *Gr. & Rom. legend*, a Trojan warrior who escaped from ruined Troy and wandered for years before coming to Latium.
**Ae·ne·id** (i-nē′id, ē-), *n.* a Latin epic poem by Virgil, about Aeneas and his adventures.

**Ae·o·li·an** (ē-ō′li-ən), *adj.* 1. of Aeolus. 2. [often a-], of the wind; carried or produced by the wind.
**aeolian harp,** a boxlike stringed instrument that makes musical sounds when air blows on it.
**Ae·o·lus** (ē′ə-ləs), *n.* in *Gr. mythology*, the god of the winds.
**ae·on** (ē′ən, ē′on), *n.* [LL.; Gr. *aiōn*, an age, lifetime], an extremely long, indefinite period of time: also sp. **eon.**
**ae·o·ni·an** (ē-ō′ni-ən), *adj.* lasting forever; eternal: also sp. **eonian.**
**aer·ate** (ā′ēr-āt′, âr′-), *v.t.* [-ATED, -ATING], [*aero-* + *-ate*], 1. to expose to air; cause air to circulate through. 2. to combine oxygen with (the blood) by breathing. 3. to charge (liquid) with gas, as in making soda water. —**aer·a′tion,** *n.* —**aer′a·tor,** *n.*
**aer·i-, a·ër·i-,** aero-.
**aer·i·al** (âr′i-əl, ā-êr′i-), *adj.* [L. *aerius* < *aer* (see AIR); + *-al*], 1. of air; in the air. 2. like air; light as air. 3. not substantial; unreal; imaginary. 4. high up. 5. of or for aircraft or flying. 6. growing in the air instead of in soil or water. *n.* (âr′-), in *radio & television*, an antenna. —**aer′i·al·ly,** *adv.*
**aer·i·al·ist** (âr′i-əl-ist, ā-êr′i-), *n.* an acrobat who performs on a trapeze, high wire, etc.
**aer·ie** (âr′i, êr′i), *n.* [< ML. < OFr. < Pr. *agre;* prob. < L. *ager*, field, but infl. by L. *aer*, air & ME. *ei*, egg], 1. the nest of an eagle or other bird of prey that builds in a high place. 2. a house or stronghold on a high place. 3. the young (of an eagle, hawk, etc.) in the nest. Also sp. **aery, eyrie, eyry.**
**aer·i·fy** (ā-êr′ə-fī′, âr′ə-), *v.t.* [-FIED, -FYING], 1. to change into air or gas. 2. to put air into; aerate. —**aer′i·fi·ca′tion,** *n.*
**aer·o, a·ër·o** (âr′ō, ā′ēr-ō), *adj.* of or for flying or aircraft.
**aer·o-, a·ër·o-,** [< Gr. *aēr*, air], a combining form meaning: 1. *air, of the air*, as in *aerolite*. 2. *of aircraft* or *flying*, as in *aerostatics*. 3. *of gases*, as in *aerodynamics*.
**aer·obe** (âr′ōb, ā′ēr-ōb′), *n.* [< *aero-* + Gr. *bios*, life], a microorganism that can live and grow only where free oxygen is present. —**aer·o′bic,** *adj.*
**aer·o·drome** (âr′ə-drōm′, ā′ēr-ə-), *n.* an airdrome.
**aer·o·dy·nam·ics** (âr′ō-dī-nam′iks, ā′ēr-ō-), *n.pl.* [construed as sing.], the branch of physics dealing with the forces exerted by air or other gases in motion. —**aer′o·dy·nam′ic,** *adj.*
**aer·o·lite** (âr′ə-līt′, ā′ēr-ə-), *n.* [*aero-* + *-lite*], a meteorite of stone.
**aer·ol·o·gy** (âr-ol′ə-ji, ā′ēr-ol′-), *n.* [*aero-* + *-logy*], the study and investigation of the air or of atmospheric phenomena.
**aer·o·me·chan·ics** (âr′ō-mi-kan′iks, ā′ēr-ō-), *n.pl.* [construed as sing.], the science of air or other gases in motion or equilibrium: it has two branches, aerodynamics and aerostatics. —**aer′o·me·chan′ic, aer′o·me·chan′i·cal,** *adj.*
**aer·o·naut** (âr′ə-nôt′, ā′ēr-ə-), *n.* [< Fr. < Gr. *aēr*, air + *nautēs*, sailor], the pilot of a balloon or dirigible.
**aer·o·nau·tics** (âr′ə-nô′tiks, ā′ēr-ə-), *n.pl.* [construed as sing.], the science or art of making and flying aircraft; aviation. —**aer′o·nau′tic, aer′o·nau′ti·cal,** *adj.* —**aer′o·nau′ti·cal·ly,** *adv.*
**aer·o·pause** (âr′ō-pôz′, ā′ēr-ō-), *n.* the uppermost level of the earth's atmosphere, regarded as the boundary between the atmosphere and outer space.
**aer·o·phyte** (âr′ə-fīt′, ā′ēr-ə-), *n.* an epiphyte.
**aer·o·plane** (âr′ə-plān′, ā′ēr-ə-), *n.* an airplane.
**aer·o·pulse** (âr′ə-puls′, ā′ēr-ə-), *n.* [*aero-* + *pulse* (throb)], a jet engine in which the air-intake valves of the combustion chamber open and close in a pulselike manner; also **pulsejet.**
**aer·o·sol** (âr′ə-sōl′, ā′ēr-ə-sol′), *n.* [*aero-* + *sol* (solution)], a suspension of colloidal particles in a gas.
**aerosol bomb,** a container and atomizer for an insecticide, etc.
**aer·o·space** (âr′ə-spās′), *n.* [*aero-* + *space*], the earth's atmosphere and the space around it, considered as one continuous field.
**aer·o·stat** (âr′ə-stat′, ā′ēr-ə-), *n.* [< Fr. < Gr. *aēr*, air + *statos*, sustaining], a dirigible, balloon, or other lighter-than-air craft.
**aer·o·stat·ics** (âr′ə-stat′iks, ā′ēr-ə-), *n.pl.* [construed as sing.], the branch of physics dealing with the equilibrium of air or other gases, and with the equilibrium of solid bodies floating in air or other gases. —**aer′o·stat′ic, aer′o·stat′i·cal,** *adj.*
**aer·y** (âr′i, êr′i), *n.* an aerie.
**Aes·chy·lus** (es′kə-ləs), *n.* Greek writer of tragedies; lived 525–456 B.C.
**Aes·cu·la·pi·us** (es′kyoo-lā′pi-əs), *n.* in *Rom. mythology*, the god of medicine and of healing: identified with the Greek Asclepius. —**Aes′cu·la′pi·an,** *adj.*
**Ae·sir** (ā′sir, ē′-), *n.pl.* [ON., pl. of *ass*, a god], the principal gods of Norse mythology.
**Ae·sop** (ē′səp, ē′sop), *n.* Greek fable writer; lived c. 620–560 B.C.
**aes·thete** (es′thēt), *n.* [Gr. *aisthētēs*, one who perceives], 1. a person highly sensitive to art and beauty. 2. a person who exaggerates the value of artistic sensitivity or makes a cult of art and beauty. Also sp. **esthete.** —**aes·thet·i·cism** (es-thet′ə-siz′m), *n.*
**aes·thet·ic** (es-thet′ik), *adj.* 1. of aesthetics. 2. of beauty. 3. sensitive to art and beauty; artistic. Also sp. **esthetic.** —**aes·thet′i·cal,** *adj.* —**aes·thet′i·cal·ly,** *adv.*
**aes·thet·ics** (es-thet′iks), *n.pl.* [construed as sing.], the study or philosophy of beauty; theory of the fine arts and of people's responses to them: also sp. **esthetics.**
**aet., aetat.,** *aetatis*, [L.], at the age of.
**ae·ther** (ē′thēr), *n.* ether.
**ae·the·re·al** (i-thêr′i-əl), *adj.* ethereal.
**ae·ti·ol·o·gy** (ē′ti-ol′ə-ji), *n.* etiology.
**Aet·na** (et′nə), *n.* Etna, a volcano in Sicily.
**Af.,** 1. Africa. 2. African.
**A.F.,** 1. Air Force. 2. Anglo-French: also **AF., A.-F.**
**A.F., a.f.,** audio frequency.
**a·far** (ə-fär′), *adv.* at, to, or from a distance; far away.
**a·feard, a·feared** (ə-fêrd′), *adj.* [orig. pp. of ME. *aferen*, to frighten < AS. *a-* + *faeran*, to frighten], [Archaic or Dial.], frightened; afraid.
**af·fa·ble** (af′ə-b′l), *adj.* [Fr.; L. *affabilis* < *ad-*, to + *fari*, to speak], easy to approach and talk to; pleasant; polite. —**af′fa·bil′i·ty,** *n.* —**af′fa·bly,** *adv.*
**af·fair** (ə-fâr′), *n.* [< OFr. < *a faire*, to do < L. *ad*, to + *facere*, to do], 1. a thing to do; business. 2. *pl.* matters of business. 3. any matter, occurrence, or thing. 4. an amorous relationship or episode.
**af·fect** (ə-fekt′), *v.t.* [< L. pp. of *afficere*, to influence < *ad-*, to + *facere*, to do], 1. to have an effect on; influence. 2. to move or stir the emotions of. *n.* (af′ekt), in *psychology*, an emotion, feeling, or mood as a factor in behavior.
**af·fect** (ə-fekt′), *v.t.* [< Fr. < L. *affectare*, to strive after < *afficere;* see prec. entry], 1. to like to have, use, wear, etc.: as, she *affects* plaid coats. 2. to make a pretense of being, having, feeling, etc.; feign: as, he *affected* indifference. —**af·fect′er,** *n.*
**af·fec·ta·tion** (af′ek-tā′shən), *n.* 1. an affecting or pretending to like, have, etc. 2. artificial behavior meant to impress others.
**af·fect·ed** (ə-fek′tid), *adj.* 1. assumed for effect; artificial. 2. behaving in an artificial way to impress people. —**af·fect′ed·ly,** *adv.* —**af·fect′ed·ness,** *n.*
**af·fect·ed** (ə-fek′tid), *adj.* 1. attacked by disease. 2. influenced; acted upon. 3. emotionally moved.
**af·fect·ing** (ə-fek′tiŋ), *adj.* emotionally moving; full of pathos. —**af·fect′ing·ly,** *adv.*
**af·fec·tion** (ə-fek′shən), *n.* 1. [Archaic], a tendency; disposition. 2. *often pl.* fond or tender feeling; warm liking. 3. a disease; ailment.
**af·fec·tion·ate** (ə-fek′shən-it), *adj.* full of affection; tender and loving. —**af·fec′tion·ate·ly,** *adv.* —**af·fec′tion·ate·ness,** *n.*
**af·fec·tive** (ə-fek′tiv), *adj.* of affects, or feelings; emotional.
**af·fer·ent** (af′ēr-ənt), *adj.* [< L. < *ad-*, to + *ferre*, to bear], in *physiology*, bringing inward to a central part: as, *afferent* nerves: opposed to *efferent*.
**af·fi·ance** (ə-fī′əns), *n.* [< OFr. < ML. *affidare*, to pledge faith < L. *ad*, to + *fidare*, to trust], 1. trust or faith. 2. a plighting of faith; betrothal. *v.t.* [-ANCED (-ənst), -ANCING], to pledge, especially in marriage; betroth. —**af·fi′anc·er,** *n.*
**af·fi·da·vit** (af′ə-dā′vit), *n.* [ML., he has made oath], a written statement made on oath, as before a notary public or other authorized person.
**af·fil·i·ate** (ə-fil′i-āt′), *v.t.* [-ATED, -ATING], [< L. pp. of *affiliare*, to adopt as a son < *ad-*, to + *filius*, son], 1. to take in as a member or branch. 2. to connect or associate (oneself). 3. to trace the source and connections of. *v.i.* to associate oneself; join. *n.* (-it), an affiliated individual or organization. —**af·fil′i·a′tion,** *n.*
**af·fin·i·tive** (ə-fin′ə-tiv), *adj.* having affinity.
**af·fin·i·ty** (ə-fin′ə-ti), *n.* [*pl.* -TIES], [< L. < *affinis*, adjacent < *ad-*, to + *finis*, end], 1. relationship by marriage. 2. close relationship; connection. 3. a similarity or likeness implying common origin. 4. a spontaneous attraction to, or liking for, a person or thing. 5. a person of the opposite sex who especially attracts one. 6. the force that causes the atoms of certain elements to combine and stay combined.
**af·firm** (ə-fũrm′), *v.t.* [< OFr. < L. < *ad-*, to +

*firmare*, to make firm], 1. to declare positively; assert to be true. 2. to confirm; ratify. *v.i.* in *law*, to declare solemnly, but not under oath. —**af·firm'a·ble,** *adj.* —**af·firm'ant,** *n.* —**af·firm'er,** *n.*

**af·fir·ma·tion** (af'ẽr-mā'shən), *n.* 1. an affirming or confirming; ratification. 2. a positive declaration; assertion. 3. in *law*, a solemn declaration, but not under oath: permitted to one who has conscientious objections to taking oaths.

**af·firm·a·tive** (ə-fũr'mə-tiv), *adj.* affirming; answering "yes." *n.* 1. a word or expression indicating assent or agreement. 2. the side upholding the proposition being debated. —**af·firm'a·tive·ly,** *adv.*

**af·fix** (ə-fiks'; *for n.*, af'iks), *v.t.* [-FIXED or -FIXT, -FIXING], [< L. < *ad-*, to + *figere*, to fasten], 1. to fasten; attach. 2. to add at the end. *n.* 1. a thing affixed. 2. a prefix, suffix, or infix.

**af·fla·tus** (ə-flā'təs), *n.* [< L. < *ad-*, to + *flare*, to blow], inspiration, as of an artist, etc.

**af·flict** (ə-flikt'), *v.t.* [< OFr. < L. < *ad-*, to + *fligere*, to strike], to cause pain or suffering to; distress very much. —**af·flict'er,** *n.*

**af·flic·tion** (ə-flik'shən), *n.* 1. an afflicted condition; pain; suffering; distress. 2. anything causing pain or distress; calamity.

**af·flic·tive** (ə-flik'tiv), *adj.* causing pain or misery. —**af·flic'tive·ly,** *adv.*

**af·flu·ence** (af'lo͞o-əns), *n.* [< Fr. < L. < *ad-*, to + *fluere*, to flow], 1. great plenty; abundance. 2. riches; wealth; opulence.

**af·flu·ent** (af'lo͞o-ənt), *adj.* 1. plentiful; abundant. 2. wealthy; rich. *n.* a stream flowing into a river; tributary. —**af'flu·ent·ly,** *adv.*

**af·ford** (ə-fôrd', ə-fōrd'), *v.t.* [AS. *geforthian*, to advance, further], 1. to stand the expense of; spare (money, time, etc.) without serious inconvenience: generally preceded by *can* or *be able*. 2. to give; supply: furnish: as, music *affords* her pleasure.

**af·fray** (ə-frā'), *n.* [< OFr. < LL. < L. *ex*, out of + Gmc. base *frith-*, peace], a noisy brawl or riot.

**af·fri·cate** (af'ri-kit), *n.* [< L. < *ad-*, to + *fricare*, to rub], in *phonetics*, a sound produced when a slowly released stop consonant is followed immediately by a fricative, as the (ch) in *latch*. —**af·fric·a·tive** (ə-frik'ə-tiv), *adj. & n.*

**af·fright** (ə-frīt'), *v.t.* [Archaic], to frighten; terrify. *n.* [Archaic], terror; fright.

**af·front** (ə-frunt'), *v.t.* [< OFr. *afronter*, to encounter < ML. < *ad-*, to + *frons*, forehead], 1. to insult openly or purposely. 2. to confront defiantly. *n.* an open or intentional insult. —**af·front'er,** *n.* —**af·fron'tive,** *adj.*

**Af·ghan** (af'gən, -gan), *n.* 1. a native of Afghanistan. 2. [a-], a crocheted or knitted soft wool blanket or shawl. *adj.* of Afghanistan, its people, etc.

**Af·ghan·i·stan** (af-gan'ə-stan'), *n.* a country in SW Asia, between Iran and India: area, 245,000 sq. mi.; pop., 16,516,000; capital, Kabul.

**a·field** (ə-fēld'), *adv.* 1. in, on, or to the field. 2. away (from home); astray.

**a·fire** (ə-fīr'), *adv. & adj.* on fire.

**A.F.L., A.F. of L.,** American Federation of Labor; merged (1955) with C.I.O., as **AFL-CIO.**

**a·flame** (ə-flām'), *adv. & adj.* in flames; glowing.

**a·float** (ə-flōt'), *adj.* 1. floating. 2. on board ship; at sea. 3. flooded: said of a ship's deck, etc. 4. drifting about. 5. in circulation, as a rumor, etc.

**a·flut·ter** (ə-flut'ẽr), *adv. & adj.* in a flutter.

**a·foot** (ə-foot'), *adv. & adj.* 1. on foot. 2. in motion or operation; in progress; astir.

**a·fore** (ə-fôr', ə-fōr'), *adv., prep., conj.* [Archaic or Dial. except in compounds and nautical use], before.

**a·fore·men·tioned** (ə-fôr'men'shənd, ə-fōr'-), *adj.* mentioned before or previously.

**a·fore·said** (ə-fôr'sed', ə-fōr'-), *adj.* spoken of before; mentioned previously.

**a·fore·thought** (ə-fôr'thôt', -fōr'-), *adj.* thought out beforehand; premeditated.

**a·fore·time** (ə-fôr'tīm', -fōr'-), *adv.* in times now past; formerly. *adj.* of former times.

**a for·ti·o·ri** (ā' fôr'shi-ō'rī, fōr'-), [L., for a stronger (reason)], all the more: said of a conclusion following another with even greater certainty.

**a·foul** (ə-foul'), *adv. & adj.* in a collision or a tangle. —**run** (or **fall**) **afoul of,** to get into trouble with.

**Afr.,** 1. Africa. 2. African.

**a·fraid** (ə-frād'), *adj.* [pp. of obs. *affray*, to frighten; see AFFRAY, *n.*], feeling fear; frightened (with *of*, *that*, or an infinitive): often used colloquially to indicate regret, etc.: as, I'm *afraid* I must go.

**A-frame** (ā'frām'), *adj.* of a framework of a house, etc., with steeply angled sides meeting at the top like the sides of the letter A.

**af·reet** (af'rēt, ə-frēt'), *n.* [Ar. *'ifrīt*], in *Arabic mythology*, a strong, evil demon or giant: also sp. **afrit.**

**a·fresh** (ə-fresh'), *adv.* again; anew; once more.

**Af·ri·ca** (af'ri-kə), *n.* the second largest continent, situated south of Europe: area, 11,500,000 sq. mi.; pop., 336,000,000.

**Af·ri·can** (af'ri-kən), *adj.* 1. of Africa, its peoples, cultures, etc. 2. Negro or Negroid. *n.* 1. a native or inhabitant of Africa. 2. a member of an African race; Negro or Negroid.

**Af·ri·kaans** (af'ri-känz', -käns'), *n.* [S. Afr. D.], the Dutch dialect spoken in South Africa.

**Af·ri·ka·ner** (af'ri-kä'nẽr), *n.* [D.], a South African of European, especially Dutch, ancestry; Boer.

**Af·ro-** (af'rō), a combining form meaning: 1. *Africa*. 2. *African*: also, before a vowel, **Afr-.**

**aft** (aft, äft), *adj. & adv.* [< AS. < *afta*, behind: *aft* is now felt to be the positive of which *after* is the comparative], at, near, or toward the stern.

**af·ter** (af'tẽr, äf'-), *adv.* [AS. *æfter*; cf. AFT], 1. behind. 2. later; next. *prep.* 1. behind. 2. in search of. 3. later than. 4. as a result of: as, *after* what has happened, he won't go. 5. in spite of: as, *after* all we've done, he's still ungrateful. 6. lower in rank or order than. 7. in imitation of: as, a novel *after* Dickens' style. 8. for; in honor of: as, named *after* Lincoln. 9. concerning: as, she asked *after* you. *conj.* following the time when. *adj.* 1. next; later. 2. nearer the rear (especially of a ship).

**af·ter·birth** (af'tẽr-bũrth', äf'-), *n.* the placenta and fetal membranes expelled from the womb after childbirth.

**af·ter·burn·er** (af'tẽr-bũr'nẽr, äf'-), *n.* 1. a device for obtaining additional thrust in a jet engine by using the hot exhaust gases to burn extra fuel. 2. a device, as on an incinerator, for burning undesirable exhaust gases.

**af·ter·damp** (af'tẽr-damp', äf'-), *n.* chokedamp.

**af·ter·ef·fect** (af'tẽr-ə-fekt', äf'-), *n.* an effect coming later, or as a secondary result.

**af·ter·glow** (af'tẽr-glō', äf'-), *n.* the glow remaining after a light has gone, as in the sky after sunset.

**af·ter·im·age** (af'tẽr-im'ij, äf'-), *n.* an image or sensation that stays or comes back after the external stimulus has been withdrawn.

**af·ter·math** (af'tẽr-math', äf'-), *n.* [*after* + dial. *math* < AS. *mæth*, cutting of grass], a result or consequence, usually an unpleasant one.

**af·ter·most** (af'tẽr-mōst', äf'-), *adj.* 1. hindmost; last. 2. nearest to the stern.

**af·ter·noon** (af'tẽr-no͞on', äf'tẽr-no͞on'), *n.* the time from noon to evening. *adj.* of, in, or for the afternoon.

**af·ter·taste** (af'tẽr-tāst', äf'-), *n.* 1. a taste remaining in the mouth, as after eating. 2. the feeling remaining after an experience.

**af·ter·thought** (af'tẽr-thôt', äf'-), *n.* 1. later reflection or explanation. 2. a thought coming too late, after the time for which it was apt.

**af·ter·ward** (af'tẽr-wẽrd, äf'-), *adv.* later; subsequently: also **af'ter·wards.**

**Ag,** *argentum*, [L.], in *chemistry*, silver.

**A.G.,** 1. Adjutant General. 2. Attorney General.

**a·gain** (ə-gen', ə-gān'), *adv.* [AS. *ongegn*; *on-*, up to, toward + *gegn*, direct], 1. [Rare], in return: as, answer *again*. 2. back into a former condition. 3. once more; anew. 4. besides; further. 5. on the other hand. —**again and again,** often; repeatedly. —**as much again,** twice as much.

**a·gainst** (ə-genst', ə-gānst'), *prep.* [see AGAIN], 1. in opposition to: as, *against* my will. 2. toward so as to strike: as, throw the ball *against* a wall. 3. opposite to the direction of: as, drive *against* the traffic. 4. in contrast with: as, green *against* the gold. 5. next to; adjoining. 6. in preparation for: as, we provided *against* a poor crop. —**over against,** 1. opposite to; facing. 2. as compared with.

**Ag·a·mem·non** (ag'ə-mem'nən, -non), *n.* in *Gr. legend*, king of Mycenae and commander in chief of the Greek army in the Trojan War.

**A·ga·ña** (ä-gä'nyä), *n.* the capital of Guam: pop., 2,000.

**a·gape** (ə-gāp'), *adv. & adj.* [*a-*, on + *gape*], gaping; with the mouth wide open, as in wonder.

**a·gar-a·gar** (ā'gär-ā'gär, ā'gẽr-, ä'gär-, ag'ẽr-), *n.* [Malay], a gelatinous extract of seaweed, used for bacterial cultures, as a laxative, etc.

**a·gar·ic** (ag'ə-rik, ə-gar'ik), *n.* [< L. < Gr. < *Agaria*, a Sarmatian town], any gill fungus, as the common edible mushroom, etc.
**Ag·as·siz, Louis** (ag'ə-si), (*Jean Louis Rodolphe Agassiz*), 1807–1873; Swiss-American naturalist.
**ag·ate** (ag'it), *n.* [Fr. < L. < Gr. < *Achatēs*, Sicilian river], 1. a hard semiprecious stone with striped or clouded coloring; kind of chalcedony. 2. a playing marble made of or like this stone. 3. in *printing*, a small size of type, 5½ point.
**‡à gauche** (à' gōsh'), [Fr.], to (or on) the left.
**a·ga·ve** (ə-gā'vi), *n.* [< Gr. *Agauē*, a proper name, lit., illustrious], any of various desert plants of the amaryllis family, especially the American century plant: some agaves yield rope fiber.
**a·gaze** (ə-gāz'), *adv. & adj.* gazing.
**agcy.**, agency.
**age** (āj), *n.* [< OFr. < ML. < L. *aetas*], 1. the time that a person or a thing has existed since birth or beginning. 2. a lifetime. 3. the time of life when a person is qualified for full legal rights, etc. (preceded by *of*): as, a man comes of *age* at twenty-one. 4. a stage of life. 5. the latter part of a normal lifetime; senility. 6. a generation. 7. a historical or geological period. 8. *often pl.* [Colloq.], a long time. *v.i.* [AGED, AGING or AGEING], to grow old or mature. *v.t.* to make old or mature.
**-age,** [OFr.; LL. *-aticum*], a noun-forming suffix meaning: 1. *that which belongs or relates to the act of*, as in *passage;* hence, *a*) *amount of*, as in *drinkage*, *b*) *cost of*, as in *postage*, and *c*) *place of*, as in *steerage*. 2. *that which belongs or relates to the state or condition of*, as in *savage, voyage;* hence, *a*) *collection of*, as in *acreage, ofliage*, and *b*) *place for*, as in *orphanage*.
**a·ged** (ā'jid), *adj.* 1. old; grown old. 2. (ājd), of the age of. —**the aged** (ā'jid), old people. —**a'ged·ly,** *adv.* —**a'ged·ness,** *n.*
**age·less** (āj'lis), *adj.* 1. not growing old. 2. eternal.
**age·long** (āj'lôŋ', āj'loŋ'), *adj.* 1. lasting long. 2. lasting forever.
**a·gen·cy** (ā'jən-si), *n.* [*pl.* -CIES], [see AGENT], 1. action; power. 2. means. 3. *a*) a person, firm, etc. empowered to act for another. *b*) its business, or work. *c*) its place of business, or office.
**a·gen·da** (ə-jen'də), *n. pl.* [*sing.* -DUM (-dəm)], [< L. < *agere*, to do, act], 1. things to be done. 2. [also construed as sing.], a list of things to be dealt with (at a meeting, etc.).
**a·gent** (ā'jənt), *n.* [< L. < *agere*, to do < Gr. *agein*, to drive], 1. a person or thing that performs actions. 2. an active force or substance producing an effect: as, medical *agents*. 3. a person, firm, etc. empowered to act for another. 4. [Colloq.], a traveling salesman. —**a·gen·tial** (ā-jen'shəl), *adj.*
**‡a·gent pro·vo·ca·teur** (à'zhän' prô'vô'kà'tër'), [Fr.], a person hired to incite someone to commit unlawful acts.
**age-old** (āj'ōld'), *adj.* ages old; ancient.
**ag·er·a·tum** (aj'ēr-ā'təm, ə-jer'ə-), *n.* [< Gr. < *a-*, not + *geras*, old age], a plant of the aster family, with small, thick heads of blue or white flowers.
**ag·glom·er·ate** (ə-glom'ēr-āt'), *v.t. & v.i.* [-ATED, -ATING], [< L. < *ad-*, to + *glomerare*, to form into a ball], to gather into a mass or ball. *adj.* (-it), gathered into a mass or ball. *n.* (-it) a jumbled heap, mass, or cluster. —**ag·glom'er·a'tion,** *n.* —**ag·glom'er·a'tive** (-ā'tiv, -ə-tiv), *adj.*
**ag·glu·ti·nant** (ə-glōō't'n-ənt), *adj.* [see AGGLUTINATE], sticking together. *n.* a sticky substance.
**ag·glu·ti·nate** (ə-glōō't'n-it; *for v.* -āt'), *adj.* [< L. < *ad-*, to + *gluten*, glue], 1. stuck together, as with glue. 2. in *linguistics*, forming words by agglutination. *v.t. & v.i.* [-NATED, -NATING], 1. to stick together, as with glue. 2. in *linguistics*, to form (words) by agglutination. —**ag·glu'ti·na'tive,** *adj.*
**ag·glu·ti·na·tion** (ə-glōō't'n-ā'shən), *n.* 1. an agglutinating. 2. an agglutinated condition. 3. a mass of agglutinated parts. 4. in *linguistics*, the combining of words into compounds with no marked change of form or loss of meaning.
**ag·gran·dize** (ag'rən-dīz, ə-gran'dīz), *v.t.* [-DIZED, -DIZING], [< Fr. < L. *ad*, to + *grandis*, great], 1. to increase in power, position, riches, etc. (sometimes used reflexively). 2. to make seem greater. —**ag·gran·dize·ment** (ə-gran'diz-mənt), *n.* —**ag'gran·diz'er,** *n.*
**ag·gra·vate** (ag'rə-vāt'), *v.t.* [-VATED, -VATING], [< L. < *ad-*, to + *gravis*, heavy], 1. to make worse; make more burdensome, troublesome, etc. 2. [Colloq.], to exasperate; annoy; vex. —**ag'gra·vat'ing,** *adj.* —**ag'gra·vat'ing·ly,** *adv.* —**ag'gra·va'tion,** *n.* —**ag'gra·va'tor,** *n.*
**ag·gre·gate** (ag'ri-git; *for v.*, -gāt'), *adj.* [< L. < *ad-*, to + *grex, gregis*, a herd], gathered into a whole or mass; total. *n.* a total or whole; group or mass of distinct things gathered together. *v.t.* [-GATED, -GATING], 1. to gather into a whole or mass. 2. to amount to; total. —**in the aggregate,** taken all together; on the whole. —**ag'gre·ga'tive,** *adj.* —**ag'gre·ga·to'ry** (-gə-tôr'i, -gə-tō'ri), *adj.*
**ag·gress** (ə-gres'), *v.i.* [< L. pp. of *aggredi*, to attack < *ad-*, to + *gradus*, a step], to start a quarrel or attack.
**ag·gres·sion** (ə-gresh'ən), *n.* 1. an unprovoked attack or invasion. 2. the practice or habit of being aggressive.
**ag·gres·sive** (ə-gres'iv), *adj.* 1. aggressing or inclined to aggress; quarrelsome. 2. full of enterprise and initiative; bold and active.
**ag·gres·sor** (ə-gres'ēr), *n.* a person, nation, etc. that starts a fight or makes an unprovoked attack.
**ag·grieve** (ə-grēv'), *v.t.* [-GRIEVED, -GRIEVING], [< OFr. < L.; see AGGRAVATE], 1. to cause grief or injury to; offend. 2. to injure in one's legal rights.
**a·ghast** (ə-gast', ə-gäst'), *adj.* [< AS. *a* + *gæstan*, to terrify < *gast*, spirit, demon; cf. GHOST], terrified; horrified; showing sudden dismay or horror.
**ag·ile** (aj'əl, -il, -īl), *adj.* [Fr. < L. < *agere*, to do, act], quick and easy of movement; deft; nimble. —**ag'ile·ly,** *adv.* —**a·gil·i·ty,** (ə-jil'ə-ti), *n.*
**ag·i·tate** (aj'ə-tāt'), *v.t.* [-TATED, -TATING], [< L. < *agere*, to do, move], 1. to move violently; stir up; shake up. 2. to excite; fluster. 3. to keep discussing so as to increase dissatisfaction and produce changes. *v.i.* to stir people up so as to produce social or political changes. —**ag'i·tat'ed,** *adj.* —**ag'i·tat'ed·ly,** *adv.*
**ag·i·ta·tion** (aj'ə-tā'shən), *n.* 1. an agitating or being agitated; violent motion or stirring. 2. emotional disturbance. 3. discussion meant to arouse people so as to produce changes.
**‡a·gi·ta·to** (ä'jē-tä'tô), *adj. & adv.* [It.; see AGITATE], in *music*, fast and with excitement.
**ag·i·ta·tor** (aj'ə-tā'tēr), *n.* 1. a person or thing that agitates. 2. a person who tries to arouse others so as to produce social or political changes. 3. an apparatus for shaking or stirring.
**a·gleam** (ə-glēm'), *adv. & adj.* gleaming.
**a·gley** (ə-glī', ə-glē'), *adv.* [*a-*, on + *gley*, squint], [Scot.], awry; off to one side.
**a·glow** (ə-glō'), *adv. & adj.* in a glow (of color or emotion).
**ag·nail** (ag'nāl'), *n.* [AS. *angnægl*, a corn (on the toe); *ang-*, tight, painful + *nægl*, nail (metal): orig. in reference to the nail-head appearance], 1. a sore or swelling around a fingernail or toenail. 2. a hangnail.
**Ag·new, Spi·ro T.** (spir'ō ag'nōō), 1918– ; vice-president of the U.S. (1969– ).
**ag·no·men** (ag-nō'mən), *n.* [*pl.* -MINA (-nom'ə-nə), -MENS], [< L. *ad*, to + *nomen*, name], 1. in ancient Rome, a name added to the cognomen, especially as an epithet honoring some achievement. 2. a nickname. —**ag·nom·i nal,** (-nom'ə-nəl), *adj.*
**ag·nos·tic** (ag-nos'tik), *n.* [< Gr. < *a-*, not + base of *gignoskein*, to know], a person who thinks it is impossible to know whether there is a God or a future life, or anything beyond material phenomena. *adj.* of or characteristic of an agnostic. —**ag·nos'ti·cal·ly,** *adv.* —**ag·nos'ti·cism,** *n.*
**Ag·nus De·i** (ag'nəs dē'ī), [L., Lamb of God], 1. a representation of Christ as a lamb, often holding a cross or flag. 2. in the *R. C. Church*, *a*) a prayer in the Mass, beginning *Agnus Dei*. *b*) its music.
**a·go** (ə-gō'), *adj.* [< AS. *agan*, to pass away], gone by; past: used following the noun. *adv.* in the past: as, long *ago*.
**a·gog** (ə-gog'), *adv. & adj.* [Fr. *en gogues*, in mirth], with eager anticipation or excitement.
**-a·gogue,** [< Gr. *agogos*, leading], a combining form meaning *leading, directing, inciting*, as in *demagogue*: also sp. **-agog.**
**ag·o·nize** (ag'ə-nīz'), *v.i.* [-NIZED, -NIZING], 1. to make convulsive efforts; struggle. 2. to be in agony. *v.t.* to torture. —**ag'o·niz'ing,** *adj.* —**ag'o·niz'ing·ly,** *adv.*
**ag·o·ny** (ag'ə-ni), *n.* [*pl.* -NIES], [< L. < Gr. *agōnia*, a contest, struggle < *agōn*, an assembly < *agein*, to lead], 1. great mental or physical pain. 2. death pangs. 3. a convulsive struggle. 4. a sudden, strong emotion: as, an *agony* of joy.
**agony column,** a newspaper column for personal advertisements, as to missing relatives, etc.
**ag·o·ra** (ag'ə-rə), *n.* [*pl.* -RAE (-rē'), -RAS (-rəz)], [Gr.], 1. in ancient Greece, an assembly. 2. a place of assembly, especially a market place.
**ag·o·ra·pho·bi·a** (ag'ə-rə-fō'bi-ə), *n.* [*agora* + *-phobia*], a morbid fear of open or public places.
**a·gou·ti, a·gou·ty** (ə-gōō'ti), *n.* [*pl.* -TIS, -TIES],

[Fr. < Sp. < Tupi native name], a rodent related to the guinea pig, found in Latin America.

**A·gra** (ä′grä), ***n.*** a city in India, famous for the Taj Mahal.

**a·grar·i·an** (ə-grâr′i-ən), ***adj.*** [< L. < *ager*, a field, country], 1. relating to land; of the cultivation or ownership of land. 2. of agriculture. ***n.*** a person in favor of more equitable division of land. —**a·grar′i·an·ism, *n.***

**a·gree** (ə-grē′), ***v.i.*** [AGREED, AGREEING], [< OFr. < *a gre*, favorably < L. *ad*, to + *gratus*, pleasing], 1. to consent or accede (*to* something). 2. to be in harmony. 3. to be of the same opinion; concur (*with* someone). 4. to arrive at a satisfactory understanding (*about* prices, etc.). 5. to be suitable, healthful, etc. (followed by *with*): as, this climate does not *agree* with him. 6. in *grammar*, to have the same number, person, case, or gender. ***v.t.*** to grant or acknowledge: as, we *agreed* that it was true.

**a·gree·a·ble** (ə-grē′ə-b′l), ***adj.*** [see AGREE], 1. pleasing; pleasant; charming. 2. willing or ready to consent. 3. conformable. —**a·gree′a·bil′i·ty, a·gree′a·ble·ness, *n.*** —**a·gree′a·bly, *adv.***

**a·greed** (ə-grēd′), ***adj.*** settled by mutual consent: as, he paid the *agreed* price.

**a·gree·ment** (ə-grē′mənt), ***n.*** 1. an agreeing; being in harmony. 2. an understanding between two or more people, countries, etc. 3. a contract.

**ag·ri·cul·ture** (ag′ri-kul′chẽr), ***n.*** [< Fr. < L. < *ager*, a field + *cultura*, cultivation], the science and art of farming; work of cultivating the soil, producing crops, and raising livestock. —**ag′ri·cul′tur·al, *adj.*** —**ag′ri·cul′tur·al·ly, *adv.***

**ag·ri·cul·tur·ist** (ag′ri-kul′chẽr-ist), ***n.*** 1. an agricultural expert. 2. a farmer. Also **ag′ri·cul′tur·al·ist.**

**ag·ri·mo·ny** (ag′rə-mō′ni), ***n.*** [*pl.* -NIES], [< AS. < L. < Gr. *argemōnē*], a plant that has little yellow flowers on spiky stalks, and fruit like burs.

**ag·ro·bi·ol·o·gy** (ag′rō-bī-ol′ə-ji), ***n.*** [< Gr. *agros*, soil; + *biology*], the science of plant growth and nutrition as applied to improvement of crops and control of soil.

**ag·ro·nom·ics** (ag′rə-nom′iks), ***n.pl.*** [construed as sing.], agronomy.

**a·gron·o·my** (ə-gron′ə-mi), ***n.*** [< Fr. < Gr. < *agros*, field + *nemein*, to manage], the management of farm land; art and science of crop production. —**ag·ro·nom·ic** (ag′rə-nom′ik), ***adj.*** —**ag′ro·nom′i·cal·ly, *adv.*** —**a·gron′o·mist, *n.***

**a·ground** (ə-ground′), ***adv. & adj.*** on or onto the ground, a reef, etc., as a boat in shallow water.

**agt.,** agent.

**a·gue** (ā′gū), ***n.*** [< OFr. < ML. (*febris*) *acuta*, violent (fever)], 1. a fever, usually malarial, marked by regularly recurring chills. 2. a chill; fit of shivering. —**a′gu·ish, *adj.***

**ah** (ä, ô, an), ***interj.*** an exclamation expressing pain, delight, regret, disgust, surprise, etc.

**a·ha** (ä-hä′), ***interj.*** an exclamation expressing satisfaction, pleasure, triumph, etc., often mixed with irony or mockery.

**A·hab** (ā′hab), ***n.*** in the *Bible*, a king of Israel, led astray by his wife Jezebel: I Kings 16:22.

**a·head** (ə-hed′), ***adv. & adj.*** [*a-*, on + *head*], 1. in or to the front. 2. forward; onward. 3. in advance. —**be ahead,** [Colloq.], 1. to be winning or profiting. 2. to have as a profit or advantage. —**get ahead,** to advance socially, etc. —**get ahead of,** to outdo or excel.

**a·hem** (ə-hem′: *conventionalized pronun.*), ***interj.*** a cough or similar sound made to get attention, fill a pause, etc.

**Ah·med·a·bad, Ah·mad·a·bad** (ä′məd-ə-bäd′), ***n.*** a city in W India, in Bombay: pop., 591,000.

**a·hoy** (ə-hoi′), ***interj.*** in *nautical usage*, a call used in hailing a person or a vessel.

**A·hu·ra-Maz·da** (ä′hoo-rə-maz′də), ***n.*** Ormazd.

**a·i** (ä′i), ***n.*** [*pl.* AIS (-iz)], [Tupi; < the animal's cry], a South American sloth with three toes.

**aid** (ād), ***v.t. & v.i.*** [< OFr. < L. < *ad-*, to + *juvare*, to help], to help; assist. ***n.*** 1. help; assistance. 2. a helper; assistant. 3. an aide.

**aide** (ād), ***n.*** [Fr.; see AID], an officer in the army, navy, etc. who is assistant to a superior.

**aide-de-camp, aid-de-camp** (ād′də-kamp′; Fr. ed′də-kän′), ***n.*** [*pl.* AIDES-, AIDS- (ādz′-; Fr. ed′-)], [Fr., lit., camp assistant], an officer serving as assistant to a general, marshal, etc.

**ai·grette, ai·gret** (ā′gret, ā-gret′), ***n.*** [see EGRET], 1. a heron with long, white plumes: usually **egret.** 2. such a plume or a tuft of these plumes, used for a woman's headdress, etc. 3. any ornament resembling this.

**ail** (āl), ***v.t.*** [AS. *eglan*, to afflict with dread, trouble] to be the cause of pain to; be the trouble with. ***v.i.*** to be feeling pain; be ill.

**ai·lan·thus** (ā-lan′thəs), ***n.*** [< Malaccan *ailanto*], a tree with pointed leaflets, fine-grained wood, and clusters of small, greenish flowers with an unpleasant odor; tree of heaven.

**ai·le·ron** (ā′lə-ron′), ***n.*** [Fr. < *aile*, wing], a movable hinged section of an airplane wing, for banking in turns.

**ail·ing** (āl′iŋ), ***adj.*** sickly; ill.

**ail·ment** (āl′mənt), ***n.*** a mild illness.

**aim** (ām), ***v.i. & v.t.*** [< OFr. *aesmer* < L. < *ad-*, to + *aestimare*, to estimate], 1. to point (a weapon) or direct (a blow, remark, etc.) so as to hit. 2. to direct (one's efforts). 3. to try or purpose; intend. ***n.*** 1. the act of aiming. 2. the direction of a missile. blow, etc. 3. sighting in pointing a weapon. 4. purpose or intention. —**take aim,** to aim a weapon, blow, etc. —**aim′er, *n.***

**aim·less** (ām′lis), ***adj.*** having no aim or purpose. —**aim′less·ly, *adv.*** —**aim′less·ness, *n.***

**ain't** (ānt), [early assimilation of *amn't*, contr. of *am not;* later confused with *a'nt* (*are not*), *i'nt* (*is not*), *ha'nt* (*has not, have not*)], [Colloq.], am not: also a dialectal or substandard contraction for *is not, has not,* and *have not: ain't* was formerly standard for *am not* and is still defended by some as proper in interrogative constructions: as, I'm going too, *ain't* I?

**Ai·nu** (ī′nōō), ***n.*** [Ainu, lit., man], 1. a member of a primitive, light-skinned race of Japan. 2. its language. ***adj.*** of the Ainus, their language, etc.

**air** (âr), ***n.*** [OFr.; L *aer;* Gr. *aēr*, air, mist], 1. the elastic, invisible mixture of gases (nitrogen, oxygen, hydrogen, carbon dioxide, argon, etc.) that surrounds the earth; atmosphere. 2. space above the earth; sky. 3. a movement of air; breeze; wind. 4. an outward appearance: as, an *air* of luxury. 5. bearing or manner: as, an *air* of dignity. 6. *pl.* affected, superior manners and graces. 7. public expression: as, give *air* to your opinions. 8. a melody or tune. 9. in *radio*, the medium through which signals and broadcasts reach the audience: a figurative use. ***v.t.*** 1 to let air into or through. 2. to publicize. ***v.i.*** to become aired, dried, etc. ***adj.*** of aviation or aircraft. —**get the air,** [Slang], to be rejected. —**in the air,** 1. prevalent. 2. not decided. —**on the air,** in *radio*, broadcasting or being broadcast. —**put on airs,** to act in an affected, superior manner. —**take the air,** to go outdoors, as for a walk. —**up in the air,** 1. not settled. 2. [Colloq.], angry; highly upset, etc. —**walk on air,** to feel very happy or exalted.

**air base,** a base for aircraft, especially military aircraft.

**air bladder,** a sac with air or gas in it, found in most fishes, in other animals, and in some plants.

**air-borne** (âr′bôrn′), ***adj.*** carried by or through the air: as, *air-borne* bacteria, *air-borne* troops.

**air brake,** a brake operated by the action of compressed air on a piston, as in a railroad car.

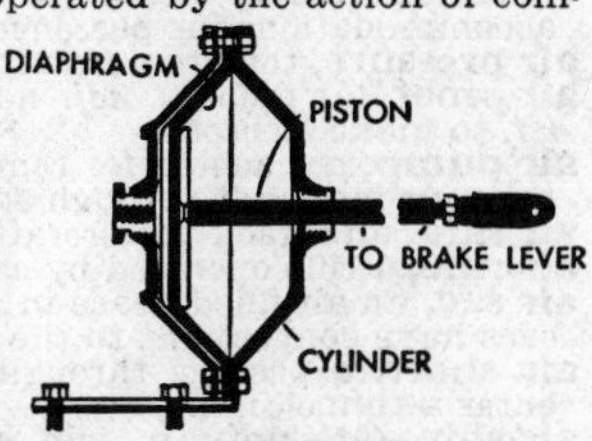

AIR BRAKE

**air·brush** (âr′-brush′), ***n.*** a kind of atomizer operated by compressed air and used for spraying on liquid paint: also **air brush.**

**air castle,** a wishful thought; daydream.

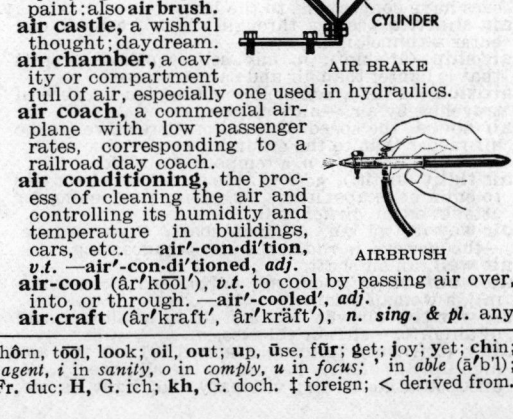

**air chamber,** a cavity or compartment full of air, especially one used in hydraulics.

**air coach,** a commercial airplane with low passenger rates, corresponding to a railroad day coach.

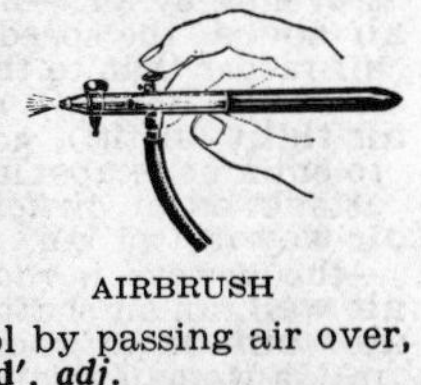
AIRBRUSH

**air conditioning,** the process of cleaning the air and controlling its humidity and temperature in buildings, cars, etc. —**air′-con·di′tion, *v.t.*** —**air′-con·di′tioned, *adj.***

**air-cool** (âr′kōōl′), ***v.t.*** to cool by passing air over, into, or through. —**air′-cooled′, *adj.***

**air·craft** (âr′kraft′, âr′kräft′), ***n. sing. & pl.*** any

fat, āpe, bâre, cär; ten, ēven, hêre, overr; is, bīte; lot, gō, hôrn, tōōl, look; oil, out; up, ūse, fũr; get; joy; yet; chin; she; thin, *th*en; zh, leisure; ŋ, ring; ə for *a* in *ago*, *e* in *agent*, *i* in *sanity*, *o* in *comply*, *u* in *focus;* ′ in *able* (ā′b′l); Fr. bál; ë, Fr. coeur; ö, Fr. feu; Fr. mon; ô, Fr. coq; ü, Fr. duc; H, G. ich; kh, G. doch. ‡ foreign; < derived from.

machine or machines for flying, whether heavier or lighter than air: airplanes, dirigibles, balloons, helicopters, etc.
**aircraft carrier,** a ship that carries aircraft, with a large, flat deck for taking off and landing.
**air·drome** (âr drōm ), *n.* [< *air;* + Gr. *dromos*, course], [Chiefly Brit.], an airport: also **aerodrome.**
**Aire·dale** (âr′dāl′), *n.* [after *Airedale* in Yorkshire, England], a large terrier having a hard, wiry, tan coat with black markings.

AIREDALE
(24 in. high at shoulder)

**air·field** (âr′fēld′), *n.* a field where aircraft can take off and land.
**air·foil** (âr′foil′), *n.* a part with a flat or curved surface used to keep an aircraft up or control its movements; wing, rudder, etc.
**air force,** 1. the aviation branch of the armed forces. 2. the largest unit of this branch.
**air gun,** a gun that shoots a projectile by means of compressed air.
**air hole,** 1. a hole that permits passage of air. 2. an unfrozen or open place in the ice on a body of water. 3. an air pocket.
**air·i·ly** (âr′ə-li), *adv.* in an airy or gay, light manner; jauntily; breezily.
**air·i·ness** (âr′i-nis), *n.* 1. the quality or state of being airy. 2. gay lightness; jauntiness.
**air·ing** (âr′iŋ), *n.* 1. exposure to the air, as for drying, etc. 2. a walk or ride outdoors.
**air lane,** a route for travel by air; airway.
**air·less** (âr′lis), *adj.* 1. without air. 2. without fresh air. 3. without a breeze; still.
**air lift,** a system of transporting troops, supplies, etc. by aircraft, as when ground routes are blocked.
**air line,** 1. a direct line; beeline. 2. a system of air transport. 3. an organization providing such transport. —**air′-line′,** *adj.*
**air liner,** a large aircraft for carrying passengers.
**air lock,** an airtight compartment, with adjustable air pressure, between places that do not have the same air pressure.
**air mail,** 1. mail transported by aircraft. 2. the system of so transporting mail. —**air′-mail′,** *adj.*
**air·man** (âr′mən), *n.* [*pl.* -MEN], an aviator.
**air mass,** in *meteorology*, a large body of air having virtually uniform conditions horizontally.
**air-mind·ed** (âr′min′did), *adj.* interested in aviation, aircraft, etc. —**air′-mind′ed·ness,** *n.*
**air·plane** (âr′plān′), *n.* an aircraft that is kept aloft by the aerodynamic forces of air upon its wings and is driven forward by a screw propeller, by jet propulsion, etc.: also **aeroplane.**
**airplane spin,** in *wrestling*, a hold in which an opponent is lifted, spun around, and thrown.
**air pocket,** an atmospheric condition that causes an aircraft to make sudden, short drops.
**air·port** (âr′pôrt′), *n.* a place where aircraft can land and take off, usually with facilities for repair, accommodations for passengers, etc.
**air pressure,** the pressure of the atmosphere.
**air·proof** (âr′prōōf′), *adj.* not penetrable by air. *v.t.* to make airproof.
**air pump,** a machine for removing air from something or forcing it through something.
**air raid,** an attack by aircraft. —**air′-raid′,** *adj.*
**air rifle,** a rifle operated by compressed air.
**air sac,** an air-filled space in a bird's body: the air sacs have connections to the lungs.
**air shaft,** a passage through which fresh air can enter a tunnel, mine, etc.
**air·ship** (âr′ship′), *n.* any self-propelled aircraft that is lighter than air and can be steered.
**air·sick** (âr′sik′), *adj.* sick or nauseated because of traveling by air. —**air′sick′ness,** *n.*
**air speed,** the speed of an aircraft relative to the air rather than to the ground.
**air·strip** (âr′strip′), *n.* a temporary airfield.
**air·tight** (âr′tīt′), *adj.* 1. too tight for air or gas to enter or escape; hence, 2. giving no opening for attack: as, an *airtight* alibi.
**air·way** (âr′wā′), *n.* 1. an air shaft. 2. an air lane. —**the airways,** in *radio*, the air; broadcasting.
**air well,** an air shaft.
**air·wom·an** (âr′woom′ən), *n.* [*pl.* -WOMEN (-wim′-in)], a woman aviator.
**air·wor·thy** (âr′wũr′thi), *adj.* fit to be flown: said of aircraft. —**air′wor′thi·ness,** *n.*
**air·y** (âr′i), *adj.* [AIRIER, AIRIEST], 1. in the air; high up. 2. of air. 3. open to the air; breezy. 4. unsubstantial as air; visionary. 5. light as air; graceful. 6. lighthearted; gay. 7. flippant. 8. [Colloq.], putting on airs; affected.
**aisle** (īl), *n.* [< OFr. < L. *ala*, a wing; Eng. *-s-* through confusion with isle], 1. a part of a church set off by a row of columns or piers. 2. a passageway, as between rows of seats. —**aisled** (īld), *adj.*
**Aisne** (ān), *n.* a river in N France: length, 170 mi.
**Aix-la-Cha·pelle** (āks′lä-sha-pel′; Fr. eks′là′shà′-pel′), *n.* Aachen: the French name.
**A·jac·cio** (ä-yä′chô), *n.* the capital of Corsica: pop., 37,000: birthplace of Napoleon.
**a·jar** (ə-jär′), *adv. & adj.* [ME. *on char;* AS. *cyrr*, a turn; see CHARE], slightly open, as a door.
**a·jar** (ə-jär′), *adv. & adj.* [*a-*, on + *jar, v.*], not in harmony.
**A·jax** (ā′jaks), *n.* in Homer's *Iliad*, a Greek hero in the Trojan war.
**a·kene** (ā-kēn′), *n.* an achene.
**a·kim·bo** (ə-kim′bō), *adv. & adj.* [ME. *in kenebowe*, lit., in keen bow; a folk etym. < ON. < *keng*, bent + *bogi*, a bow], with hands on hips and elbows bent outward: as, with arms *akimbo.*
**a·kin** (ə-kin′), *adj.* [*a-*, of + *kin*], 1. of one kin; related. 2. having similar qualities; similar.
**Ak·ron** (ak′rən), *n.* a city in NE Ohio: pop., 290,000.
**-al** (əl), [< Fr. < L. *-alis*], 1. a suffix meaning *of, like*, or *suitable for*, as in *comical, hysterical.* 2. a suffix meaning *the act or process of*, used in nouns formed from verbs, as *avowal, denial.*
**-al** (al, əl), [*al*dehyde], in *chemistry*, a suffix signifying *the presence of the aldehydes*, as in *chloral.*
**Al,** in *chemistry*, aluminum.
**a·la** (ā′lə), *n.* [*pl.* ALAE (-lē)], [L., a wing], in *biology*, a wing or winglike structure.
**à la** (ä′ lä, ä′ lə; Fr. à là), [Fr.], in the manner or style of; according to.
**Ala.,** Alabama.
**Al·a·bam·a** (al′ə-bam′ə), *n.* a Southern State of the United States: area, 51,609 sq. mi.; pop., 3,267,000; capital, Montgomery.
**Al·a·bam·i·an** (al′ə-bam′i-ən), *adj.* of Alabama. *n.* an inhabitant of Alabama. Also **Al′a·bam′an.**
**al·a·bam·ine** (al′ə-bam′ēn, -in), *n.* [< *Alabama* + *-ine*], a name given to chemical element 85: symbol, Ab: cf. **astatine.**
**al·a·bas·ter** (al′ə-bas′tẽr), *n.* [< OFr. < L. < Gr. < name of Egypt. town], 1. a translucent, whitish, fine-grained variety of gypsum. 2. a banded variety of calcite. *adj.* of or like alabaster; hard, white, etc. —**al·a·bas·trine** (al′ə-bas′trin), *adj.*
**‡à la bonne heure** (à′là′bôn′ẽr′), [Fr., lit., at the good hour], well and good; well done!
**à la carte** (ä′lə kärt′; Fr. à′là′kàrt′), [Fr.], by the bill of fare; with a separate price for each item on the menu: opposed to *table d'hôte.*
**a·lack** (ə-lak′), *interj.* [*ah* + *lack*], [Archaic], an exclamation of regret, surprise, dismay, etc.: also **a·lack′a·day′** (-ə-dā′).
**a·lac·ri·ty** (ə-lak′rə-ti), *n.* [< Fr. < L. < *alacer*, lively], 1. quick willingness; eager readiness. 2. lively action; briskness. —**a·lac′ri·tous,** *adj.*
**A·lad·din** (ə-lad′′n), *n.* a boy in *The Arabian Nights* who found a magic lamp and a magic ring.
**à la king** (ä′lä kiŋ′), [lit., in kingly style], served in a sauce containing diced mushrooms, pimientos, and green peppers.
**Al·a·me·da** (al′ə-mē′də, -mā′-), *n.* a city on San Francisco Bay, California: pop., 64,000.
**Al·a·mo** (al′ə-mō′), *n.* a Franciscan mission at San Antonio, Texas: scene of a siege and massacre of Texans by Mexican troops (1836).
**a·la·mode** (ä′lə-mōd′, al′ə-mōd′), *adj.* [Fr. *à la mode*], 1. in the fashion; stylish. 2. made or served in a certain style, as pie with ice cream, or beef braised with vegetables in sauce. Also **à la mode, a la mode.** *n.* a thin, shiny silk.
**à la New·burg** (ä′lə nōō′bẽrg, ä′lä nū′bẽrg), [Fr.; after *Newburgh*, Scotland], served in a sauce of creamed egg yolks, wine, and butter.
**a·lar** (ā′lẽr), *adj.* [< L. < *ala*, a wing], 1. of a wing. 2. having wings or alae. 3. winglike. Also **a·la·ry** (ā′lə-ri, al′ə-).
**A·lar·cón, Pe·dro An·to·ni·o de** (pe′drô an-tô′ni-ô de ä′lär-kôn′), 1833–1891; Spanish writer.
**Al·a·ric** (al′ə-rik), *n.* king of the Visigoths; lived 370?–410 A.D.; conquered Rome (410 A.D.).
**a·larm** (ə-lärm′), *n.* [< OFr. < It. *all'arme*, to arms], 1. a sudden call to arms. 2. a warning of danger. 3. a mechanism designed to warn of danger or of trespassing or to arouse from sleep. 4. fear caused by the sudden realization of danger. *v.t.* 1. to warn of approaching danger. 2. to frighten.
**alarm clock,** a clock with a mechanism that can

be set to make a sound at the desired time.

**a·larm·ing** (ə-lär′miŋ), *adj.* that alarms; frightening. —**a·larm′ing·ly,** *adv.*

**a·larm·ist** (ə-lär′mist), *n.* 1. one who habitually spreads alarming rumors, etc. 2. one likely to anticipate the worst. *adj.* of or like an alarmist.

**a·lar·um** (ə-lâr′əm, -lär′-), *n.* [Archaic], alarm.

**a·las** (ə-las′, ə-läs′), *interj.* [< OFr. < *a*, ah + *las*, wretched < L. *lassus*, weary], an exclamation expressing sorrow, pity, regret, etc.

**A·las·ka** (ə-las′kə), *n.* a State of the U.S. in NW North America: area, 586,400 sq. mi.; pop., 226,000; capital, Juneau: abbrev. **Alas.** —**A·las′kan,** *adj. & n.*

**Alaska Highway,** a highway extending from British Columbia, Canada, to Fairbanks, Alaska: length, 1,671 mi.: popular name, **Alcan Highway.**

**Alaska Range,** a mountain range in southern Alaska: highest peak, Mt. McKinley, 20,300 ft.

**a·late** (ā′lāt), *adj.* [< L. < *ala*, a wing], having wings or winglike attachments: also **a′lat·ed.**

**alb** (alb), *n.* [AS. < L. *albus*, white], a long, white linen robe with sleeves tapering to the wrist, worn by a priest at Mass.

ALB

**Alb.,** 1. Albania. 2. Albanian. 3. Albion.

**al·ba·core** (al′bə-kôr′, -kōr′), *n.* [*pl.* -CORES, -CORE; see PLURAL, II, D, 1], [Port. < Ar. *al*, the + *bukr*, young camel], any of a number of related salt-water fishes of the mackerel family, including the tuna, etc.

**Al·ba·ni·a** (al-bā′ni-ə, -bān′yə), *n.* a country in the western Balkan Peninsula: area, 10,629 sq. mi.; pop., 1,391,000; capital, Tirana. —**Al·ba′ni·an,** *adj. & n.*

**Al·ba·ny** (ôl′bə-ni), *n.* the capital of New York, on the Hudson: pop., 130,000.

**al·ba·tross** (al′bə-trôs′, -tros′), *n.* [*pl.* -TROSSES, -TROSS; see PLURAL, II, D, 1], [< Sp. < Port. < Ar. *al qādūs*, water container < Gr. *kados*, cask; prob. of Sem. origin], any of several large, web-footed sea birds related to the petrel.

ALBATROSS (30 in. long)

**al·be·it** (ôl-bē′it), *conj.* [ME. *al be it*, al(though) it be], although; even though.

**Al·bé·niz, Isaac** (äl-bā′nith; Sp. äl′be-nēth′), 1860–1909; Spanish composer and pianist.

**Albert,** Prince, 1819–1861; Prince of Saxe-Coburg-Gotha and husband of Queen Victoria of England.

**Al·ber·ta** (al-bũr′tə), *n.* a province of SW Canada: pop., 1,123,000; capital, Edmonton: abbrev. **Alta.**

**Al·ber·tus Mag·nus,** Saint (al-bũr′təs mag′nəs), (*Albert von Bollstadt*), 1193?–1280; Bavarian scholastic philosopher.

**al·bes·cent** (al-bes′'nt), *adj.* [< L. < *albus*, white], turning white. —**al·bes′cence,** *n.*

**Al·bi·gen·ses** (al′bi-jen′sēz), *n.pl.* a religious sect in France c. 1020–1250 A.D.: it was suppressed for heresy. —**Al′bi·gen′si·an** (-si-ən), *adj. & n.*

**al·bi·no** (al-bī′nō), *n.* [*pl.* -NOS], [< Port. < L. *albus*, white], 1. a person whose skin, hair, and eyes lack normal coloration: albinos have a white skin, whitish hair, and pink eyes. 2. any animal or plant abnormally lacking in color. —**al·bin′ic** (-bin′ik), *adj.* —**al·bi·nism** (al′bə-niz′m), *n.*

**Al·bi·on** (al′bi-ən), *n.* [Poetic], England.

**al·bum** (al′bəm), *n.* [L., neut. of *albus*, white], 1. a book with blank pages for mounting pictures, clippings, stamps, etc., or collecting autographs. 2. a booklike holder for phonograph records. 3. a single long-playing record with a number of musical pieces.

**al·bu·men** (al-bū′mən), *n.* [L. < *albus*, white], 1. the white of an egg. 2. the nutritive protein substance in germinating plant and animal cells. 3. [Rare], albumin.

**al·bu·men·ize** (al-bū′mən-īz′), *v.t.* [-IZED, -IZING], to cover or treat with albumen.

**al·bu·min** (al-bū′min), *n.* [Fr.; see ALBUMEN] any of a class of water-soluble proteins found in egg, milk, blood, and in many vegetable tissues and fluids: albumins consist of carbon, hydrogen, nitrogen, oxygen, and sulfur.

**al·bu·mi·nous** (al-bū′mi-nəs), *adj.* of, like, or containing albumin: also **al·bu′mi·nose′** (-nōs′).

**Al·bu·quer·que** (al′bə-kũr′ki), *n.* a city in New Mexico: pop., 201,000.

**al·bur·num** (al-bũr′nəm), *n.* [< L. < *albus*, white], sapwood.

**al·caide, al·cayde** (al-kād′; Sp. äl-kä′ē-*th*e), *n.* [Sp. < Ar. < *qāda*, to lead], 1. a governor of a Spanish fortress. 2. a warden of a Spanish prison.

**al·cal·de** (al-kal′di; Sp. äl-käl′de), *n.* [Sp. < Ar. < *qada*, to judge], the mayor of a Spanish town, who also acts as a judge.

**Al·can Highway** (al′kan), see **Alaska Highway.**

**Al·ca·traz** (al′kə-traz′, al′kə-traz′), *n.* 1. a small island in San Francisco Bay. 2. the Federal penitentiary there.

**al·caz·ar** (al′kə-zär′, al-kaz′ẽr; Sp. äl-kä′thär), *n.* [Sp. < Ar. *al-qasr*, the castle], 1. a palace of the Moors in Spain. 2. [A-], a Moorish palace in Seville, Spain, later used by the Spanish kings.

**al·che·mist** (al′kə-mist), *n.* a practitioner of alchemy. —**al′che·mis′tic,** *adj.* —**al′che·mis′ti·cal·ly,** *adv.*

**al·che·mize** (al′kə-mīz′), *v.t.* [-MIZED, -MIZING], to transmute by or as by alchemy.

**al·che·my** (al′kə-mi), *n.* [< OFr. < ML. < Ar. *al-kīmiyā*; ? ult. < Gr. *cheein*, to pour], 1. the chemistry of the Middle Ages, the chief aim of which was to change the baser metals into gold: abbrev. **alchem.** 2. a method or power of transmutation. —**al·chem·ic** (al-kem′ik), **al·chem′i·cal,** *adj.* —**al·chem′i·cal·ly,** *adv.*

**Al·ci·des** (al-sī′dēz), *n.* Hercules.

**Alc·me·ne** (alk-mē′ni), *n.* see **Amphitryon.**

**al·co·hol** (al′kə-hôl′, -hol′), *n.* [ML. < Ar. *al kohl*, powder of antimony], 1. a colorless, volatile, pungent liquid, $C_2H_5OH$; grain alcohol; ethyl alcohol: it can be burnt as fuel and is the intoxicating ingredient in whisky, gin, rum, and other fermented liquors. 2. any such intoxicating liquor. 3. any of a series of similarly constructed organic compounds, as methyl (or wood) alcohol: all alcohols contain a hydroxyl group and form esters in reactions with organic acids.

**al·co·hol·ic** (al kə-hôl′ik, -hol′-), *adj.* 1. of, containing, or caused by alcohol. 2. suffering from alcoholism. *n.* one who has chronic alcoholism. —**al′co·hol′i·cal·ly,** *adv.*

**al·co·hol·ism** (al′kə-hôl-iz′m, -hol′-), *n.* a diseased condition caused by habitually drinking too much alcoholic liquor.

**al·co·hol·ize** (al′kə-hôl-īz′, -hol-), *v.t.* [-IZED, -IZING], 1. to saturate or treat with alcohol. 2. to convert into alcohol.

**Al·co·ran** (al′kō-rän′, -ran′), *n.* the Koran.

**Al·cott, (Amos) Bron·son** (bron′sən ôl′kət), 1799–1888; U.S. philosopher and educational reformer.

**Alcott, Louisa May,** 1832–1888; daughter of *Amos Bronson;* American novelist.

**al·cove** (al′kōv), *n.* [Fr. < Sp. < Ar. < *al*, the + *qobbah*, an arch, vault], 1. a recessed section of a room. 2. a summerhouse.

**Ald., Aldm.** (as a title), Alderman.

**Al·deb·a·ran** (al-deb′ə-rən), *n.* a brilliant-red star in the constellation Taurus.

**al·de·hyde** (al′də-hīd′), *n.* [< *alcohol* + L. *de*, without; + *hydrogen*], 1. a colorless fluid $CH_3CHO$, with a strong odor, obtained from alcohol by oxidation. 2. any of a class of such organic compounds. —**al′de·hy′dic,** *adj.*

**Al·den, John** (ôl′dən), 1599?–1687; Pilgrim settler in Plymouth Colony.

**al·der** (ôl′dẽr), *n.* [AS. *alor*], any of a small group of trees and shrubs of the birch family growing in cool, moist soil in temperate climates.

**al·der·man** (ôl′dẽr-mən), *n.* [*pl.* -MEN (-mən)], [< AS. < *eald*, old + *man*], 1. in many cities, a municipal officer representing, ordinarily, a certain district or ward. 2. in England and Ireland, one of the senior members of the municipal or borough council. —**al′der·man·cy** [*pl.* -CIES], *n.* —**al′der·man′ic** (-man′ik), *adj.* —**al′der·man·ship′,** *n.*

**Al·der·ney** (ôl′dẽr-ni), *n.* 1. one of the Channel Islands of Great Britain. 2. [*pl.* -NEYS (-niz)], any of a breed of small dairy cattle originally from this island.

**ale** (āl) *n.* [AS. *ealu*], a fermented drink made from malt and hops: it is like beer but contains more alcohol and undecomposed sugar.

**a·le·a·to·ry** (ā′li-ə-tôr′i, -tō′ri), *adj.* [< L. < *alea*, chance], depending on chance or luck.

**a·lee** (ə-lē′), *adv. & adj.* [*a-*, on + *lee*], on or toward the side of a ship away from the wind.
**ale·house** (āl′hous′), *n.* a place where ale is sold and served; saloon; tavern.
**a·lem·bic** (ə-lem′bik), *n.* [< OFr. < L. < Ar. < *al*, the + *anbīq*, a still < Gr. *ambix*, a cup], 1. an apparatus of glass or metal, formerly used for distilling. 2. anything that refines or purifies.
**A·len·çon** (ä′län′sōn′), *n.* 1. a town in NW France: pop., 27,000. 2. (Eng. ə-len′sən), a needlepoint lace made there.
**a·leph** (ä′lif), *n.* [Heb., lit., ox], the first letter of the Hebrew alphabet, a neutral vowel.
**A·lep·po** (ə-lep′ō), *n.* a city in NW Syria: pop., 513,000.
**a·lert** (ə-lūrt′), *adj.* [< Fr. < It. *all' erta*, on the watch < L. *erigere*, to erect], 1. watchful; vigilantly ready. 2. active; nimble. *n.* 1. an alarm; warning signal. 2. a period of watchfulness, as before an expected air raid. *v.t.* to warn; warn to be ready: as, the troops were *alerted*. **—on the alert,** watchful; vigilant. **—a·lert′ly,** *adv.* **—a·lert′ness,** *n.*
**-a·les,** [L. pl. of *-alis*], a suffix used in forming the scientific Latin names of orders of plants.
**Al·e·ut** (al′i-ōōt′), *n.* 1. [*pl.* ALEUTS, ALEUT], a native of the Aleutian Islands. 2. the language of these natives.
**A·leu·tian** (ə-lōō′shən, -lū′-), *adj.* 1. of the Aleutian Islands. 2. of the Aleuts, their culture, etc. *n.* 1. an Aleut. 2. *pl.* the Aleutian Islands.
**Aleutian Islands,** a chain of islands extending c.1,200 mi. southwestward from Alaska: part of the State of Alaska.
**ale·wife** (āl′wif′), *n.* [*pl.* -WIVES (-wīvz)], [? Am. Ind.], an edible North American fish resembling the herring.
**Al·ex·an·der II** (al′ig-zan′dẽr), 1818–1881; czar of Russia (1855–1881); emancipated the serfs.
**Alexander Nev·ski** (nef′ski), 1220?–1263; Russian prince and hero.
**Alexander the Great,** 356–323 B.C.; military conqueror; king of Macedonia (336–323 B.C.).
**Al·ex·an·dri·a** (al′ig-zan′dri-ə), *n.* 1. a city in Egypt, on the Mediterranean: pop., 1,513,000. 2. a city in NE Virginia, near Washington, D.C.: pop., 91,000.
**Al·ex·an·dri·an** (al′ig-zan′dri-ən), *adj.* 1. of Alexander the Great. 2. of Alexandria, Egypt. 3. in *prosody*, Alexandrine.
**Al·ex·an·drine** (al′ig-zan′drin), *n.* in *prosody*, an iambic line having normally six feet; iambic hexameter. *adj.* of an Alexandrine.
**al·fal·fa** (al-fal′fə), *n.* [Sp. < Ar. *al-fachfacha*, very good fodder], a deep-rooted plant of the pea family, used extensively in the United States for fodder, pasture, and as a cover crop; lucerne.
**‡al fi·ne** (äl fē′ne), [It.], to the end.
**Al·fred the Great** (al′frid), 849–899 A.D.; king of Wessex (871–899) and of England (886–899).
**al·fres·co** (al-fres′kō), *adv.* [It.; *al*, for *a il*, in the + *fresco*, fresh, cool], in the open air; outdoors. *adj.* outdoor. Also **al fresco.**
**Alg.,** 1. Algerian. 2. Algiers.
**alg.,** algebra.
**al·gae** (al′jē), *n.pl.* [*sing.* -GA (-gə)], [pl. of L. *alga*, seaweed], a group of plants, one-celled, colonial, or many-celled, containing chlorophyll and having no true root, stem, or leaf: algae are found in water or damp places. **—al′gal** (-gəl), *adj.*
**al·ge·bra** (al′jə-brə), *n.* [It. < Ar. < *al*, the + *jebr*, reunion of broken parts], the branch of mathematics that uses positive and negative numbers, letters, etc. to express the relationship between quantities in terms of formulas, equations, etc. **—al′ge·bra′ic** (-brā′-), **al′ge·bra′i·cal,** *adj.* **—al′ge·bra′i·cal·ly,** *adv.* **—al′ge·bra′ist,** *n.*
**Al·ger, Horatio** (al′jẽr), 1834–1899; U.S. writer of boys' stories.
**Al·ger·i·a** (al-jêr′i-ə), *n.* a country in northern Africa, under French control until 1962: area, c.919,500 sq. mi.; pop., 11,300,000; capital, Algiers. **—Al·ger′i·an, Al′ge·rine′** (-jə-rēn′), *adj. & n.*
**-al·gi·a,** [< Gr. *algos*, pain], a suffix meaning *pain*, as in *neuralgia*: also **-algy.**
**al·gid** (al′jid), *adj.* [< Fr. < L. *algidus*], cold; chilly. **—al·gid′i·ty,** *n.*
**Al·giers** (al-jêrz′), *n.* the capital of Algeria; Mediterranean seaport: pop., 884,000.
**Al·gon·qui·an** (al-goŋ′ki-ən, -kwi-ən), *adj.* designating or of a widespread family of languages used by a number of North American Indian tribes, including the Cheyenne, Blackfoot, Chippewa, Fox, etc. *n.* 1. this family of languages. 2. a member of any tribe using one of these languages. Also sp. **Algonkian.**
**Al·gon·quin** (al-goŋ′kin, -kwin), *n.* 1. a member of a tribe of Algonquian Indians that lived along the Ottawa River in Canada. 2. the language of this tribe. 3. any Algonquian.
**al·go·rithm** (al′gə-rith′m), *n.* [< *algorism*, Arabic system of numerals], any special method of solving a certain kind of mathematical problem, as finding the greatest common divisor of two numbers.
**Al·ham·bra** (al-ham′brə), *n.* [Sp.; Ar. *al hamrā*, lit., the red (house)], an early palace of the Moorish kings, near Granada, Spain. **—Al′ham·bresque′** (-bresk′), *adj.*
**a·li·as** (ā′li-əs), *n.* [*pl.* ALIASES], [L., other], an assumed name. *adv.* otherwise named; called by the assumed name of: as, Bell *alias* Jones.
**A·li Ba·ba** (al′i bab′ə, ä′li bä′bə), in *The Arabian Nights*, a poor woodcutter who found the treasure of forty thieves in a cave.
**al·i·bi** (al′ə-bī′), *n.* [*pl.* -BIS], [L., contr. < *alius ibi*, elsewhere], 1. in *law*, the plea or fact that an accused person was elsewhere than at the alleged scene of the offense. 2. [Colloq.], any excuse. *v.i.* [-BIED, -BIING], [Colloq.], to offer an excuse.
**al·ien** (āl′yən, ā′li-ən), *adj.* [< OFr. < L. < *alius*, other], belonging to another country or people; foreign; strange. *n.* 1. a foreigner. 2. a foreign-born resident in a country who has not become a naturalized citizen. **—alien to,** strange to; not in harmony with.
**al·ien·a·ble** (āl′yən-ə-b'l, ā′li-ən-), *adj.* capable of being alienated or transferred to a new owner. **—al′ien·a·bil′i·ty,** *n.*
**al·ien·ate** (āl′yən-āt′, ā′li-ən-), *v.t.* [-ATED, -ATING], 1. to transfer the ownership of (property) to another. 2. to estrange, make unfriendly: as, his behavior *alienated* his friends. 3. to cause a transference of (affection). **—al′ien·a′tor,** *n.*
**al·ien·a·tion** (āl′yən-ā′shən, ā′li-ən-), *n.* 1. an alienating or being alienated. 2. insanity.
**al·ien·ee** (āl′yən-ē′, ā′li-ən-), *n.* a person to whom property is transferred.
**al·ien·ist** (āl yən-ist, ā′li-ən-), *n.* a doctor who specializes in mental diseases; psychiatrist: term used in law. **—al′ien·ism,** *n.*
**al·ien·or** (āl′yən-ẽr, ā′li-ən-ôr′), *n.* a person who transfers the ownership of property.
**al·i·form** (al′ə-fôrm′, ā′lə-), *adj.* [< L. *ala*, a wing; + *-form*], shaped like a wing.
**a·light** (ə-līt′), *v.i.* [ALIGHTED or ALIT, ALIGHTING], [< AS. < *a-*, out, off + *lihtan*, to dismount], 1. to get down or off; dismount. 2. to come down after flight. 3. to come (*upon*) accidentally.
**a·light** (ə-līt′), *adj.* lighted up; burning.
**a·lign** (ə-līn′), *v.t.* [< Fr. < *à*, to + *ligne*, line], 1. to bring into a straight line. 2. to bring into agreement, co-operation, etc.: as, he *aligned* himself with the liberals. *v.i.* to come into line; line up Also sp. **aline. —a·lign′er,** *n.*
**a·lign·ment** (ə-līn′mənt), *n.* 1. arrangement in a straight line. 2. a line or lines formed by aligning. Also sp. **alinement.**
**a·like** (ə-līk′), *adj.* [< AS. *gelic* or *onlic*; see LIKE, *adj.*], like one another; similar: usually a predicate adjective. *adv.* 1. in the same manner; similarly. 2. to the same degree; equally.
**al·i·ment** (al′ə-mənt; *for v.*, -ment′), *n.* [< L. < *alere*, to nourish] 1. anything that nourishes; food. 2. means of support. *v.t.* to nourish. **—al′i·men′tal,** *adj.* **—al′i·men′tal·ly,** *adv.*
**al·i·men·ta·ry** (al′ə-men′tə-ri), *adj.* [see ALIMENT], 1. connected with food or nutrition. 2. nourishing. 3. furnishing support or sustenance.
**limentary canal** (or **tract**), the passage in the body that food goes through: it extends from the mouth to the anus.
**al·i·men·ta·tion** (al′ə-men-tā′shən), *n.* 1. nourishment; nutrition. 2. support; sustenance. **—al′i·men′ta·tive,** *adj.*
**al·i·mo·ny** (al′ə-mō′ni), *n.* [< L. < *alere*, to nourish], money a judge orders paid to a woman by her legally separated or divorced husband.
**a·line** (ə-līn′), *v.t. & v.i.* [ALINED, ALINING], to align. **—a·line′ment,** *n.* **—a·lin′er,** *n.*
**al·i·quant** (al′ə-kwənt), *adj.* [< L. < *alius*, other + *quantus*, how much], that does not divide a number evenly but leaves a remainder: as, 8 is an *aliquant* part of 25: opposed to *aliquot*.
**al·i·quot** (al′ə-kwət), *adj.* [L. < *alius*, other + *quot*, how many], that divides a number evenly and leaves no remainder: as, 8 is an *aliquot* part of 24: opposed to *aliquant*.
**a·lit** (ə-lit′), alt. pt. and pp. of **alight.**
**a·live** (ə-līv′), *adj.* [< AS. *on*, in + *life*, life], 1. having life; living. 2. in existence, operation, etc.: as, old hatreds remain *alive*. 3. lively; alert. Alive is usually a predicate adjective. **—alive to,** awake to; aware of. **—alive with,** teeming with; full of.

—**look alive!** hurry! be alert and quick! —**a·live′ness,** *n.*

**a·liz·a·rin** (ə-liz′ə-rin), *n.* [Fr.; prob. < Ar. *al aṣārah,* the juice < *aṣara,* to press], a reddish-yellow crystalline compound, $C_{14}H_8O_4$, used in the preparation of dyes: it was originally made from madder. Also **a·liz′a·rine** (-rin, -rēn′).

**al·ka·li** (al′kə-lī′), *n.* [*pl.* -LIS, -LIES], [< OFr. < Ar. *al,* the + *qalīy,* ashes of saltwort], 1. any base or hydroxide, as soda, potash, etc., that is soluble in water and can neutralize acids: alkalis have an acrid taste and turn red litmus blue. 2. any soluble mineral salt, often found in desert soils, capable of neutralizing acids. *adj.* alkaline.

**al·ka·li·fy** (al′kə-lə-fī′, al-kal′ə-), *v.t. & v.i.* [-FIED, -FYING], to make or become alkaline.

**al·ka·line** (al′kə-līn′, -lin), *adj.* of, like, or containing an alkali. —**al′ka·lin′i·ty** (-lin′ə-ti), *n.*

**al·ka·line-earth metals** (al′kə-lin′ũrth′), the group of chemical elements comprising calcium, strontium, barium, and, sometimes, beryllium, magnesium, and radium.

**alkaline earths,** the oxides of the alkaline-earth metals.

**al·ka·lize** (al′kə-līz′), *v.t. & v.i.* [-LIZED, -LIZING], to make alkaline. —**al′ka·li·za′tion,** *n.*

**al·ka·loid** (al′kə-loid′), *n.* [< *alkali* + *-oid*], an organic alkaline substance containing nitrogen: some alkaloids taken from plants are used as drugs, as caffeine, morphine, cocaine, and quinine. *adj.* like an alkali. —**al′ka·loi′dal,** *adj.*

**Al·ko·ran** (al′kō-rän′, -ran′), *n.* the Koran.

**all** (ôl), *adj.* [AS. *eall*], 1. the whole quantity or extent of: as, *all* the gold. 2. every one of: as, *all* men must eat. 3. the greatest possible: as, in *all* sincerity. 4. any; any whatever: as, true beyond *all* question. 5. alone; only: as, life is not *all* pleasure. *pron.* 1. [construed as pl.], everyone: as, *all* are going. 2. everything: as, *all* is over between them 3. every part or bit: as, *all* of it is gone. *n.* 1. everything one has: as, give your *all.* 2. a totality; whole. *adv.* 1. wholly; quite: as, *all* worn out. 2. apiece: as, a score of thirty *all.* —**above all,** most of all. —**after all,** nevertheless; in spite of everything. —**all but,** 1. all except. 2. almost. —**all in,** [Colloq.], very tired; fatigued. —**all in all,** 1. as a whole. 2. everything. —**all the (better, worse,** etc.), so much the (better, worse, etc.). —**at all,** 1. in the least. 2. in any way. 3. under any considerations. —**for all,** in spite of. —**in all,** altogether.

**all-,** a combining form meaning: 1. *wholly, entirely,* as in *all-American.* 2. *for every,* as in *all-purpose.* 3. *of every part,* as in *all-inclusive.*

**Al·lah** (al′ə, ä′lə), *n.* [Ar. *Allāh* < *al,* the + *ilāh,* god], God: so called in the Moslem religion.

**Al·la·ha·bad** (al′ə-hä-bäd′), *n.* the former capital of the United Provinces, India: pop., 332,000.

**all-A·mer·i·can** (ôl′ə-mer′ə-kən), *adj.* 1. made up wholly of Americans or of American materials. 2. chosen as the best in the U.S. *n.* 1. an imaginary football (or other) team of the best college players of the year in the U.S. 2. a player chosen for such a team.

**all-a·round** (ôl′ə-round′), *adj.* having many abilities, talents, or uses; versatile.

**al·lay** (ə-lā′), *v.t.* [-LAYED, -LAYING], [< AS. < *a-,* down + *lecgan,* to lay], 1. to put (fears, etc.) to rest; calm. 2. to lessen or relieve (pain, etc.). —**al·lay′er** *n.* —**al·lay′ment,** *n.*

**all-clear** (ôl′klêr′), *n.* a siren or other signal that an air raid is over.

**al·le·ga·tion** (al′ə-gā′shən), *n.* 1. an alleging. 2. something alleged; assertion. 3. an assertion without proof. 4. in *law,* an assertion which its maker proposes to support with evidence.

**al·lege** (ə-lej′), *v.t.* [-LEGED, -LEGING], [ME. *alleggen,* to produce as evidence < OFr. < ML. hyp. *exlitigare* < L.; see LITIGATE], 1. to declare; affirm. 2. to assert or declare without proof. 3. to give as a plea, excuse, etc. —**al·lege′a·ble,** *adj.* —**al·leg′er,** *n.*

**al·leg·ed·ly** (ə-lej′id-li), *adv.* according to allegation.

**Al·le·ghe·ny** (al′ə-gā′ni), *n.* a river in Pennsylvania, joining the Monongahela to form the Ohio.

**Allegheny Mountains,** a mountain range of the Appalachian system in Pennsylvania, Maryland, West Virginia, and Virginia. Also **Al′le·ghe′nies** (-niz), *n.pl.*

**al·le·giance** (ə-lē′jəns), *n.* [< OFr. *a* (L. *ad*), to + *ligeance* < L. *ligare,* to bind], 1. the duty of being loyal to one's ruler, government, or country. 2. loyalty; devotion, as to a cause.

**al·le·gor·i·cal** (al′ə-gôr′i-k'l, -gor′-), *adj.* 1. of or characteristic of a legory. 2. that is or contains an allegory. Also **al′le·gor′ic.** —**al′le·gor′i·cal·ly,** *adv.* —**al′le·gor′i·cal·ness,** *n.*

**al·le·go·rist** (al′ə-gôr′ist, -gō′rist, al′ə-gẽr-ist), *n.* one who uses or writes allegories.

**al·le·go·ris·tic** (al′ə-gə-ris′tik), *adj.* allegorizing.

**al·le·go·rize** (al′ə-gə-rīz′), *v.t.* [-RIZED, -RIZING], 1. to make into or treat as an allegory. 2. to interpret in an allegorical sense. *v.i.* to make or use allegories. —**al′le·gor′i·za′tion** (-gôr′i-zā′shən, -gor′-), *n.* —**al′le·go·riz′er,** *n.*

**al·le·go·ry** (al′ə-gôr′i, -gō′ri), *n.* [*pl.* -RIES], [< L. < Gr. < *allos,* other + *agoreuein,* to speak < *agora,* place of assembly], 1. a story in which people, things, and happenings have another meaning, often morally instructive, as in a fable. 2. the presenting of ideas by means of such stories.

**al·le·gret·to** (al′ə-gret′o), *adj. & adv.* [It., dim. of *allegro*], in *music,* moderately fast. *n.* [*pl* -TOS], a moderately fast movement or passage.

**al·le·gro** (ə-lā′grō, ə-leg′rō), *adj. & adv.* [It. < L. *alacer,* brisk], in *music,* fast; faster than *allegretto* but not so fast as *presto.* *n.* [*pl.* -GROS], a fast movement or passage.

**al·le·lu·ia** (al′ə-lōō′yə), *interj.* [L. < Gr. < Heb.; see HALLELUJAH], praise ye the Lord! *n.* a song or exclamation of praise and exultation.

**Al·len·town** (al′ən-toun′), *n.* a city in eastern Pennsylvania: pop., 108,000.

**al·ler·gen** (al′ẽr-jən), *n.* [*allergy* + *-gen*], a substance inducing an allergic state or reaction. —**al′ler·gen′ic**(-jen′ik), *adj.*

**al·ler·gic** (ə-lũr′jik), *adj.* 1. of or caused by allergy. 2. having an allergy.

**al·ler·gist** (al′ẽr-jist), *n.* a doctor who specializes in treating allergies.

**al·ler·gy** (al′ẽr-ji), *n.* [*pl.* -GIES], [< Gr. *allos,* other + *ergon,* action], a hypersensitivity to a specific substance (such as a food, pollen, dust, etc.) or condition (as heat or cold).

**al·le·vi·ate** (ə-lē′vi-āt′), *v.t.* [-ATED, -ATING], [< L. < *ad-,* to + *levis,* light], to make less hard to bear; relieve (pain, etc). —**al·le′vi·a′tion,** *n.* —**al·le′vi·a′tive,** *adj.* —**al·le′vi·a′tor,** *n.* —**al·le′vi·a·to′ry** (-ə-tôr′i, -tō′ri), *adj.*

**al·ley** (al′i), *n.* [*pl.* -LEYS], [< OFr. *alee,* a going < *aler,* to go], 1. a lane in a garden or park. 2. a narrow street. 3. a long, narrow lane of polished wood for bowling. —**up one's alley,** [Slang], suited to one's tastes or abilities.

**al·ley** (al′i), *n.* [abbrev. of *alabaster*], a large marble used as the shooter in playing marbles.

**al·ley·way** (al′i-wā′), *n.* 1. an alley between buildings. 2. any narrow passageway.

**All Fools' Day,** April 1; April Fools' Day: it is a day when practical jokes are played.

**all fours,** all four limbs of an animal or human being: as, the cat landed on *all fours.*

**all hail,** all health: a greeting.

**All·hal·lows** (ôl hal′ōz, -əz), *n.* [< *all* + AS. *halga,* saint], All Saints' Day: also **All′hal′low·mas** (-ō-məs).

**al·li·ance** (ə-lī′əns), *n.* [OFr. < L. < *ad-,* to + *ligare,* to bind], 1. an allying or being allied. 2. a union, as of families by marriage. 3. a close association, as of nations, for a common objective. 4. the countries, persons, etc. in such association. 5. similarity in characteristics, structure, etc.

**al·lied** (ə-līd′, al′īd), *adj.* 1. united by kinship, treaty, etc. 2. closely related: as, *allied* sciences. 3. [A-], of the Allies.

**Al·lies** (al′īz, ə-līz′), *n.pl.* 1. in World War I, the nations allied against Germany and the other Central Powers; originally, Great Britain, France, and Russia, later joined by the U.S., Italy, Japan, etc. 2. in World War II, the nations associated against the Axis; esp., Great Britain, the Soviet Union, and the U.S.: see **United Nations.**

**al·li·ga·tor** (al′ə-gā′tẽr), *n.* [< Sp. *el lagarto* < L. *lacertus,* lizard], 1. a large lizard of the crocodile group, found in the U.S. and China: its snout is shorter and blunter than the crocodile's. 2. a leather made from its hide.

**alligator pear,** an avocado.

**all-im·por·tant** (ôl′im-pôr′t'nt), *adj.* essential.

**al·lit·er·ate** (ə-lit′ẽr-āt′), *v.i.* [-ATED, -ATING], 1. to constitute or have alliteration. 2. to use alliteration. *v.t.* to cause to have alliteration. —**al·lit′er·a′tor,** *n.*

**al·lit·er·a·tion** (ə-lit′ẽr-ā′shən), *n.* [< Fr. < L. *ad.* to + *littera,* letter], repetition of an initial sound,

usually of a consonant, in two or more words of a phrase, line of poetry, etc.
**al·lit·er·a·tive** (ə-lit'ẽr-ā'tiv, -ə-tiv), *adj.* of, showing, or using alliteration. —**al·lit'er·a'tive·ly,** *adv.* —**al·lit'er·a'tive·ness,** *n.*
**al·lo·cate** (al'ə-kāt'), *v.t.* [-CATED, -CATING], [< ML. < L. *ad*, to + *locus*, a place], 1. to set apart for a specific purpose. 2. to distribute, or allot. 3. to locate. —**al'lo·ca·ble** (-kə-b'l), *adj.* —**al'lo·ca'tion,** *n.*
**al·lom·er·ism** (ə-lom'ẽr-iz'm), *n.* [< Gr. *allos*, other + *meros*, a part; + *-ism*], variation in chemical make-up without change in crystalline form. —**al·lom'er·ous,** *adj.*
**al·lo·path** (al'ə-path'), *n.* 1. a practitioner of allopathy. 2. an advocate of allopathy. Also **al·lop·a·thist** (ə-lop'ə-thist).
**al·lop·a·thy** (ə-lop'ə-thi), *n.* [< Gr. *allos*, other; + *-pathy*], treatment of disease by remedies that produce effects different from those produced by the disease: opposed to *homeopathy*. —**al·lo·path·ic** (al'ə-path'ik), *adj.* —**al'lo·path'i·cal·ly,** *adv.*
**al·lo·phone** (al'ə-fōn'), *n.* [< Gr. *allos*, other; + *-phone*], in *linguistics*, any variant form of a phoneme as conditioned by position or adjoining sounds.
**al·lot** (ə-lot'), *v.t.* [-LOTTED, -LOTTING], [OFr. *aloter* < *a-*, to + *lot*, lot], 1. to distribute by lot or in shares; apportion. 2. to give or assign (a share): as, each speaker is *allotted* five minutes. —**al·lot'ta·ble,** *adj.* —**al·lot'ter,** *n.*
**al·lot·ment** (ə-lot'mənt), *n.* 1. an allotting or being allotted. 2. a thing allotted; portion.
**al·lo·trope** (al'ə-trōp'), *n.* an allotropic form.
**al·lo·trop·ic** (al'ə-trop'ik), *adj.* of or having allotropy: also **al'lo·trop'i·cal.** —**al'lo·trop'i·cal·ly,** *adv.* —**al'lo·tro·pic'i·ty** (-trə-pis'ə-ti), *n.*
**al·lot·ro·py** (ə-lot'rə-pi), *n.* [< Gr. *allos*, other + *tropos*, way, manner], the property that certain chemical elements have of existing in two or more different forms, as carbon in charcoal, diamonds, etc. Also **al·lot'ro·pism** (-piz'm).
**al·lot·tee** (ə-lot'ē'), *n.* one to whom something is allotted.
**all-out** (ôl'out'), *adj.* [Colloq.], complete or wholehearted: as, an *all-out* effort.
**al·low** (ə-lou'), *v.t.* [< OFr. *alouer* < ML. < L. < *ad-*, to + *locus*, a place; associated with OFr. *alouer* < L. *ad*, to + *laudare*, to praise], 1. to permit; let: as, we weren't *allowed* to go. 2. to let have: as, she *allowed* herself no sweets. 3. to let enter: as, dogs are not *allowed*. 4. to admit (a claim or the like); acknowledge as valid. 5. to provide or keep (an extra quantity) so as to have enough: as, *allow* an inch for shrinkage. 6. [Dial.], to think or say. —**allow for,** to leave room, time, etc. for. —**allow of,** to admit of; accept. —**al·low'er,** *n.*
**al·low·a·ble** (ə-lou'ə-b'l), *adj.* that can be allowed; permissible. —**al·low'a·ble·ness,** *n.* —**al·low'a·bly,** *adv.*
**al·low·ance** (ə-lou'əns), *n.* 1. an allowing. 2. something allowed. 3. an amount of money, food, etc. given regularly to a child, soldier, etc. 4. a reduction in price in consideration of a large order, a trade-in, etc. *v.t.* [-ANCED, -ANCING], 1. to put on an allowance. 2. to apportion economically. —**make allowance** (or **allowances**) **for,** to forgive or excuse because of mitigating factors.
**al·low·ed·ly** (ə-lou'id-li), *adv.* admittedly.
**al·loy** (al'oi, ə-loi'), *n.* [< Fr. < OFr. < L. < *ad-*, to + *ligare*, to bind], 1. a metal that is a mixture of two or more metals, or of a metal and something else. 2. a less valuable metal mixed with a more valuable one, often to give hardness. 3. something that lowers the value of that with which it is mixed. *v.t.* (ə-loi'), 1. to make (a metal) less valuable by mixing with a cheaper metal. 2. to mix (metals). 3. to debase with an inferior addition.
**all-right** (ôl'rit'), *adj.* [Slang], 1. honest, honorable, dependable, etc. 2. good; excellent.
**all right,** 1. satisfactory; adequate. 2. unhurt. 3. correct. 4. yes; very well. 5. certainly.
**all-round** (ôl'round'), *adj.* all-around.
**All Saints' Day,** an annual church festival (November 1) in honor of all the saints: also called *Allhallows, Allhallowmas.*
**All Souls' Day,** in the *R.C. Church*, November 2, a day of prayer for the souls in purgatory.
**all·spice** (ôl'spis'), *n.* 1. the berry of a West Indian tree of the myrtle family. 2. the spice made from this berry: so named because its flavor seems to combine the tastes of several spices.
**all-star** (ôl'stär'), *adj.* made up entirely of outstanding or star performers.
**al·lude** (ə-lōōd'), *v.i.* [-LUDED, -LUDING], [< L. *alludere*, to jest < *ad-*, to + *ludere*, to play], to mention casually; refer indirectly (*to*).
**al·lure** (ə-loor'), *v.t. & v.i.* [-LURED, -LURING], [< OFr.; see AD- & LURE], to tempt with something desirable; attract; entice. *n.* fascination; charm. —**al·lure'ment,** *n.* —**al·lur'er,** *n.*
**al·lur·ing** (ə-loor'iŋ), *adj.* tempting strongly; highly attractive. —**al·lur'ing·ly,** *adv.* —**al·lur'ing·ness,** *n.*
**al·lu·sion** (ə-lōō'zhən), *n.* 1. an alluding. 2. indirect reference; casual mention.
**al·lu·sive** (ə-lōō'siv), *adj.* 1. containing an allusion. 2. using allusion. —**al·lu'sive·ly,** *adv.* —**al·lu'sive·ness,** *n.*
**al·lu·vi·al** (ə-lōō'vi-əl), *adj.* of, composed of, or found in alluvium. *n.* alluvial soil.
**al·lu·vi·um** (ə-lōō'vi-em), *n.* [*pl.* -VIUMS, -VIA (-vi-ə)], [< L. < *ad-*, to + *luere*, to wash], sand, clay, etc. deposited by flowing water.
**al·ly** (ə-li'; *for n., usually* al'ī), *v.t.* [-LIED, -LYING], [OFr. *alier* < L. < *ad-*, to + *ligare*, to bind], 1. to unite for a specific purpose, as families by marriage or nations by treaty (with *to* or *with*). 2. to relate by similarity of structure, etc.: as, the onion is *allied* to the lily. *v.i.* to become allied. *n.* [*pl.* -LIES], 1. a country or person joined with another for a common purpose: see also **Allies.** 2. a plant, animal, or thing closely related in structure, etc. to another. 3. an associate; helper.
**Al·ma-A·ta** (äl'mə-ä'tə), *n.* the capital of the Kazak S.S.R., Asia: pop., 231,000.
**al·ma ma·ter, Al·ma Ma·ter** (al'mə mā'tẽr, äl'-, mä'-), [L., fostering mother], 1. the college, university, or school that one attended. 2. its anthem.
**al·ma·nac** (ôl'mə-nak'), *n.* [Sp. < Ar. < *al*, the + *manākh*, weather], a calendar with astronomical data, weather forecasts, etc.
**al·might·y** (ôl-mi'ti), *adj.* [< AS. < *eal*, all + *mihtig*, mighty], 1. all-powerful. 2. [Slang], great; extreme. *adv.* [Slang], extremely. —**the Almighty,** God. —**al·might'i·ly,** *adv.* —**al·might'i·ness,** *n.*
**almighty dollar** [Colloq.], money regarded figuratively as a god.
**al·mond** (ä'mənd, am'ənd), *n.* [< OFr. < L. < Gr. *amygdalē*], 1. the edible, nutlike seed of a fruit like the peach. 2. the tree that this fruit grows on. —**al'mond·like',** *adj.*
**al·mond-eyed** (ä'mənd-īd, am'ənd-), *adj.* having eyes that look almond-shaped, or oval; slant-eyed.
**al·mon·er** (al'mən-ẽr, ä'mən-), *n.* one who distributes alms, as for a church, etc.
**al·mon·ry** (al'mən-ri, ä'mən-), *n.* [*pl.* -RIES], a place where alms are given out.
**al·most** (ôl'mōst, ôl'mōst'), *adv.* [AS. *eallmæst;* see ALL & MOST], very nearly; all but.
**alms** (ämz), *n.* [*pl.* ALMS], [< AS. < L. < Gr. *eleēmosynē*, alms < *eleos*, pity], money, food, etc. given to poor people.
**alms·giv·er** (ämz'giv'ẽr), *n.* one who gives alms.
**alms·giv·ing** (ämz'giv'iŋ), *n.* the giving of alms.
**alms·house** (ämz'hous'), *n.* a home for people too poor to support themselves; poorhouse.
**al·oe** (al'ō), *n.* [*pl.* -OES], [L.; Gr. *aloē*], 1. a plant of the lily family, native to South Africa, with fleshy leaves. 2. *pl.* [construed as sing.], a laxative drug made from the juice of certain aloe leaves.
**a·loft** (ə-lôft', ə-loft'), *adv.* [*a-*, on + *loft* < ON. *lopt*, the air], 1. high up; far above the ground. 2. high above the deck of a ship.
**a·lo·ha** (ə-lō'ə, ä-lō'hä), *n. & interj.* [Haw.], love: a word used as a greeting or farewell.
**a·lone** (ə-lōn'), *adj. & adv.* [< *all* + *one* < AS. *an*, single, alone], 1. apart from anything or anyone else. 2. without any other person. 3. with nothing more; only. —**leave alone,** 1. to let be by oneself. 2. [Colloq.], to refrain from interfering with. —**let alone,** 1. to refrain from interfering with. 2. not to speak of: as, we hadn't a dime, *let alone* a dollar. —**let well enough alone,** to be content with things as they are. —**a·lone'ness,** *n.*
**a·long** (ə-lôŋ', ə-loŋ'), *prep.* [< AS. < *and*, over against + *lang*, long], on or beside the length of: as, *along* the wall is a hedge. *adv.* 1. in a line; lengthwise. 2. progressively onward: as, he walked *along* by himself. 3. together (*with* a person or thing). 4. with one: as, she took her camera *along.* —**all along,** from the beginning. —**along with,** together with. —**get along,** 1. to go forward. 2. to contrive. 3. to thrive; succeed. 4. to agree. 5. [Colloq.], to go away.
**a·long·shore** (ə-lôŋ'shôr', ə-loŋ'shōr'), *adv.* along the shore; near or beside the shore.
**a·long·side** (ə-lôŋ'sīd', ə-loŋ'-), *adv.* at or by the side; side by side. *prep.* at the side of; beside. —**alongside of,** at the side of; adjoining.
**a·loof** (ə-lōōf'), *adv.* [*a-*, on + *loof* < D. *loef*, to

windward], at a distance but in view; apart. ***adj.*** distant in sympathy, interest, etc.: as, an *aloof* manner. —**a·loof′ly,** ***adv.*** —**a·loof′ness,** ***n.***

**a·loud** (ə-loud′), ***adv.*** 1. loudly. 2. in an audible voice. 3. with the voice: as, reading *aloud.*

**alp** (alp), ***n.*** [< L. *Alpes,* the Alps], a high mountain, especially in Switzerland: see **Alps.**

**A.L.P.,** American Labor Party.

**al·pac·a** (al-pak′ə), ***n.*** [Sp. < Ar. *al,* the + Peruv. *paco,* animal], 1. a kind of llama of Bolivia and Peru. 2. its long, silky wool. 3. a thin cloth woven from this wool, often mixed with other fibers.

ALPACA (60 in. high at head)

**al·pen·horn** (al′pən-hôrn′), ***n.*** [G., horn of the Alps], a long, curved, powerful horn, used by Swiss mountaineers for signaling: also **alp′horn′.**

**al·pen·stock** (al′pən-stok′), ***n.*** [G., lit., Alps stick], a strong, iron-pointed staff used by mountain climbers.

**al·pha** (al′fə), ***n.*** [Gr. < Heb. *āleph;* see ALEPH], 1. the first letter of the Greek alphabet (A, *a*). 2. the beginning of anything.

**al·pha·bet** (al′fə-bet′), ***n.*** [< L. < Gr. *alpha* + *beta*], 1. a system of characters, or letters, used in writing a language; esp., these letters arranged in their usual order. 2. the first elements; rudiments.

**al·pha·bet·i·cal** (al′fə-bet′i-k′l), ***adj.*** 1. of or using an alphabet. 2. in the usual order of the alphabet. Also **al′pha·bet′ic.** —**al′pha·bet′i·cal·ly,** ***adv.***

**al·pha·bet·ize** (al′fə-bə-tīz′), ***v.t.*** [-IZED, -IZING], 1. to arrange in alphabetical order. 2. to express by an alphabet. —**al·pha·bet·i·za·tion** (-bet′i-zā′shən), ***n.*** —**al′pha·bet·iz′er,** ***n.***

**alpha particle,** a positively charged particle given off by certain radioactive substances: it consists of two protons and two neutrons.

**alpha rays,** rays of alpha particles: they are less penetrating than beta rays.

**Al·pine** (al′pīn, -pin), ***adj.*** 1. of the Alps or their inhabitants. 2. [a-], of or like high mountains. 3. [a-], growing in high altitudes.

**Alps** (alps), ***n.pl.*** a mountain system in southern Europe: highest peak, Mont Blanc, 15,781 ft.

**al·read·y** (ôl-red′i), ***adv.*** by or before the given or implied time; previously.

**al·right** (ôl′rīt′), ***adv.*** all right: a spelling much used but still generally considered substandard.

**Al·sace** (al-sās′, al′sas; Fr. ȧl′zȧs′), ***n.*** a former province of NE France. —**Al·sa·tian** (al-sā′shən), ***adj. & n.***

**Al·sace-Lor·raine** (al′sās′lôr-ān′, -sas-; Fr. ȧl′zȧs′-lô′ren′), ***n.*** a region in NE France seized by Germany in 1871 and again in 1940.

**al·so** (ôl′sō), ***adv.*** [< AS. < *eal,* all + *swa,* so], likewise; too; besides; in addition.

**al·so-ran** (ôl′sō-ran′), ***n.*** [Colloq.], a defeated contestant in a race, competition, election, etc.

**alt.,** 1. alternate. 2. altitude. 3. alto.

**Alta., Alberta.**

**Al·ta·ic** (al-tā′ik), ***adj.*** of the Altai Mountains or the languages spoken there: see **Ural-Altaic.**

**Al·tai Mountains** (al-tī′), a mountain range in Mongolia, Sinkiang, and south central Siberia. —**Al·tai′an,** ***adj.***

**Al·ta·ir** (al-tä′ir), ***n.*** [Ar. *al tā′ir,* the bird], a bright star in the constellation Aquila.

**al·tar** (ôl′tẽr), ***n.*** [< AS. & OFr.; both ult. < L. < *altus,* high], 1. a raised platform where sacrifices are made to a god, etc. 2. a table, stand, etc. used for sacred purposes in a place of worship, as for Communion in Christian churches. —**lead to the altar,** to marry.

**altar boy,** a boy or man who helps a priest, etc. at religious services, especially at Mass.

**al·tar·piece** (ôl′tẽr-pēs′), ***n.*** an ornamental carving, painting, etc. above and behind an altar.

**al·ter** (ôl′tẽr), ***v.t.*** [< Fr. < ML. < L. *alter,* other], 1. to change; make different; modify. 2. [Dial.], to castrate. ***v.i.*** to change; become different.

**al·ter·a·ble** (ôl′tẽr-ə-b′l), ***adj.*** that can be altered. —**al′ter·a·bil′i·ty,** ***n.*** —**al′ter·a·bly,** ***adv.***

**al·ter·ant** (ôl′tẽr-ənt), ***adj.*** causing alteration. ***n.*** a thing that causes alteration.

**al·ter·a·tion** (ôl′tẽr-ā′shən), ***n.*** 1. an altering. 2. the result of this.

**al·ter·a·tive** (ôl′tẽr-ā′tiv, -ə-tiv), ***adj.*** 1. causing alteration. 2. in *medicine,* gradually restoring to health. ***n.*** an alterative remedy.

**al·ter·cate** (ôl′tẽr-kāt′, al′-), ***v.i.*** [-CATED, -CATING], [< L. pp. of *altercari,* to dispute < *alter,* other], to dispute angrily; quarrel.

**al·ter·ca·tion** (ôl′tẽr-kā′shən, al′-), ***n.*** a quarrel; angry or heated dispute.

**al·ter e·go** (al′tẽr ē′gō, ôl′tẽr eg′ō), [L., lit., other I], 1. another self; another aspect of oneself. 2. a very close friend.

**al·ter·nate** (ôl′tẽr-nit, al′-; *for v.,* -nāt′), ***adj.*** [< L. *alternare,* to do by turns < *alternus,* one after the other < *alter,* other], 1. succeeding each other; one and then the other. 2. every other. 3. in *botany,* growing along the stem singly at intervals. ***n.*** a person selected to take the place of another if necessary; substitute. ***v.t.*** [-NATED, -NATING], to do or use by turns. ***v.i.*** 1. to act, etc. by turns; follow successively: as, good times *alternate* with bad. 2. to take turns. 3. to exchange places, etc. regularly. 4. in *electricity, a*) to reverse direction regularly, as a current. *b*) to make, or be operated by, such a current. —**al′ter·nate·ly,** ***adv.*** —**al′ter·na′tion,** ***n.***

**alternate angles,** two angles at opposite ends and on opposite sides of a line crossing two others.

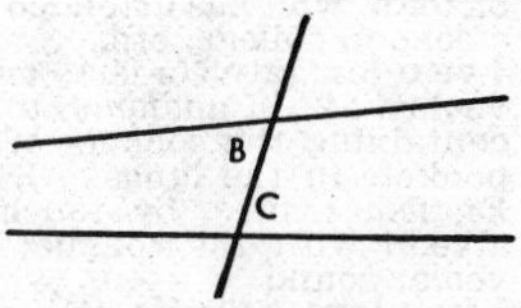


ALTERNATE ANGLES (B, C)

**alternating current,** an electric current that reverses its direction regularly and continually: abbrev. **A.C., a.c.**

**al·ter·na·tive** (ôl-tũr′nə-tiv, al-), ***adj.*** providing or necessitating a choice between two (or, loosely, more than two) things. ***n.*** 1. a choice between two or more things. 2. any one of the things to be chosen. —**al·ter′na·tive·ly,** ***adv.*** —**al·ter′na·tive·ness,** ***n.***

**al·ter·na·tor** (ôl′tẽr-nā′tẽr, al′-), ***n.*** an electric generator or dynamo producing alternating current.

**al·the·a, al·thae·a** (al-thē′ə), ***n.*** [< L. < Gr. *althaia,* wild mallows], a tall shrub of the mallow family, with showy flowers; rose of Sharon.

**alt·horn** (alt′hôrn′), ***n.*** a brass-wind instrument, the alto saxhorn, often used in place of the French horn: also **alto horn.**

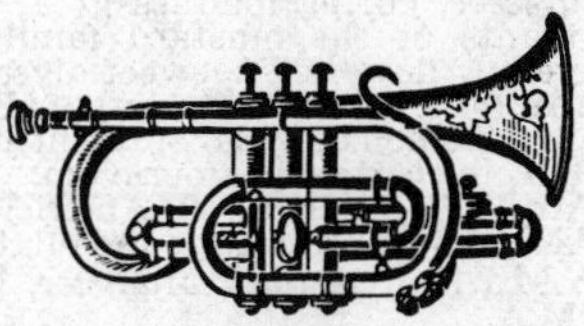

ALTHORN

**al·though** (ôl-*th*ō′), ***conj.*** [< *all* + *though*], in spite of the fact that; though: now sometimes sp. **altho.**

**al·tim·e·ter** (al-tim′ə-tẽr, al′tə-mē′-), ***n.*** [< L. *altus,* high; + *-meter*], an instrument for measuring altitude, as an aneroid barometer or a sextant or quadrant. —**al·tim′e·try,** ***n.***

**al·ti·tude** (al′tə-to͞od′, -tūd′), ***n.*** [< L. < *altus,* high], 1. the height of a thing above a certain level, especially above sea level. 2. a high place or region. 3. a high degree of rank, etc. 4. in *astronomy,* the angular height of a star, etc. above the horizon. 5. in *geometry,* the perpendicular distance from the base of a figure to its highest point. —**al′ti·tu′di·nal,** ***adj.***

**al·to** (al′tō), ***n.*** [*pl.* -TOS], [It. < L. *altus,* high], in *music,* 1. the range of the lowest female voice or the highest male voice. 2. a voice or singer with such a range. 3. an instrument having a similar range. 4. a part for such a voice or instrument. ***adj.*** of, for, or in the alto.

**al·to·geth·er** (ôl tə-geth′ẽr), ***adv.*** 1. wholly; completely. 2. on the whole. ***n.*** a whole. —**in the altogether,** [Colloq.], nude.

**Al·to·na** (äl′tô-nä), ***n.*** a former city in N Germany: now part of Hamburg.

**Al·too·na** (al-to͞o′nə), ***n.*** a city in Pennsylvania: pop., 69,000.

**al·tru·ism** (al′tro͞o-iz′m), ***n.*** [< Fr. < It. *altrui,* of or to others < L. *alter,* another], unselfish concern for the welfare of others: opposed to *egoism.* —**al′tru·ist,** ***n.***

**al·tru·is·tic** (al′tro͞o-is′tik), ***adj.*** of or motivated by altruism; unselfish. —**al′tru·is′ti·cal·ly,** ***adv.***

**al·um** (al′əm), ***n.*** [< OFr. < L. *alumen*], 1. a double sulfate as of a univalent metal and a trivalent metal; esp., a double sulfate of potassium and aluminum, used in medicine and in the manufacture of dyes, paper, etc. 2. aluminum sulfate: erroneous use.

**a·lu·mi·na** (ə-lōō′mi-nə), ***n.*** [< L. *alumen*, alum], an oxide of aluminum, $Al_2O_3$, present in bauxite and clay and found as different forms of corundum, including emery, sapphires, rubies, etc.

**al·u·min·i·um** (al′yoo-min′i-əm), ***n.*** [Brit.], aluminum.

**a·lu·mi·nize** (ə-lōō′mi-nīz′), ***v.t.*** [-NIZED, -NIZING], to cover, or treat, with aluminum.

**a·lu·mi·nous** (ə-lōō′mi-nəs), ***adj.*** of or containing alum, alumina, or aluminum.

**a·lu·mi·num** (ə-lōō′mi-nəm), ***n.*** [< L. *alumen*, alum], one of the chemical elements, a silvery, lightweight, easily worked metal that resists corrosion and is found only in combination: symbol, Al; at. wt., 26.97; at. no., 13. ***adj.*** of, containing, or made of aluminum. Abbrev. **alum.**

**aluminum oxide,** alumina.

**a·lum·na** (ə-lum′nə), ***n.*** [*pl.* -NAE (-nē)], [L., fem. of *alumnus*], a girl or woman who has attended or been graduated from a school, college, etc.

**a·lum·nus** (ə-lum′nəs), ***n.*** [*pl.* -NI (-nī)], [L., foster son < *alere*, to nourish], a person, especially a boy or man, who has attended or been graduated from a school, college, etc.

**al·ve·o·lar** (al-vē′ə-lẽr), ***adj.*** 1. of or like an alveolus. 2. in *anatomy*, *a*) of the part of the jaws containing the sockets of the teeth. *b*) of the air pockets in the lungs. 3. in *phonetics*, formed, as English *t*, *d*, *s*, by touching or approaching the alveoli with the tongue. ***n.*** in *phonetics*, an alveolar sound.

**al·ve·o·late** (al-vē′ə-lit), ***adj.*** full of many small cavities: also **al·ve′o·lat′ed** (-lāt′-). **—al·ve′o·la′tion, *n.***

**al·ve·o·lus** (al-vē′ə-ləs), ***n.*** [*pl.* -LI (-lī′)], [L., dim. of *alveus*, a cavity], 1. in *anatomy & zoology*, a small cavity or hollow, as an air cell of a lung, a tooth socket, etc. 2. *usually pl.* the ridge of the gums above and behind the upper front teeth; teethridge.

**al·way** (ôl′wā), ***adv.*** [Archaic or Poetic], always.

**al·ways** (ôl′wiz, -wāz), ***adv.*** [< *all* + *way*], 1. at all times; on all occasions: as, he's *always* late. 2. all the time; continually: as, it's *always* here.

**a·lys·sum** (ə-lis′əm), ***n.*** [Gr. *alysson*, madwort < *alyssos*, curing madness], 1. any of a number of plants of the mustard family, bearing white or yellow flowers. 2. sweet alyssum.

**am** (am; *unstressed*, əm), [AS. *eom;* see BE], the first person singular, present indicative, of **be.**

**Am,** in *chemistry*, americium.

**Am.,** 1. America. 2. American.

**AM, A.M.,** amplitude modulation.

**A.M.,** [L.], *Artium Magister*, Master of Arts: also **M.A.**

**A.M., a.m.,** *ante meridiem*, [L.], before noon: used to designate the time from midnight to noon.

**a·mah** (ä′mə), ***n.*** [Anglo-Ind. < Port. *ama*], in the Orient, a woman servant or nurse, especially one who nurses or takes care of babies.

**a·main** (ə-mān′), ***adv.*** [*a-*, on + *main*, strength], [Archaic or Poetic], 1. forcefully; vigorously. 2. at or with great speed. 3. hastily; suddenly.

**a·mal·gam** (ə-mal′gəm), ***n.*** [< Fr. < ML. prob. < Ar. < Gr. *malagma*, an emollient < *malassein*, to soften], 1. any alloy of mercury with another metal or other metals: silver amalgam is used as a dental filling. 2. a combination; mixture; blend.

**a·mal·gam·ate** (ə-mal′gə-māt′), ***v.t. & v.i.*** [-ATED, -ATING], 1. to combine in an amalgam. 2. to unite; mix; blend; combine. **—a·mal′gam·a·ble** (-gəm-ə-b'l), ***adj.*** **—a·mal′gam·a′tion, *n.*** **—a·mal′gam·a′tive, *adj.*** **—a·mal′gam·a′tor, *n.***

**a·man·u·en·sis** (ə-man′yoo-en′sis), ***n.*** [*pl.* -SES (-sēz)], [L. < *a-* (*ab*), from + *manus*, a hand + *-ensis*, relating to], one who takes dictation or copies something already written; secretary.

**am·a·ranth** (am′ə-ranth′), ***n.*** [< L. < Gr. *amarantos*, unfading < *a-*, not + *marainein*, to die away], 1. any of a number of related plants as the love-lies-bleeding, pigweed, tumbleweed, etc. 2. [Poetic], an imaginary flower that never fades or dies. 3. a dark purple. **—am′a·ran′thine** (-ran′thin), ***adj.***

**Am·a·ril·lo** (am′ə-ril′ō), ***n.*** a city in NW Texas: pop., 138,000.

**am·a·ryl·lis** (am′ə-ril′is), ***n.*** [< L. & Gr.; conventional name for a shepherdess], a bulb plant bearing several white, purple, pink, or red lilylike flowers on a single stem.

**a·mass** (ə-mas′), ***v.t.*** [< Fr. < *à*, to + *masser*, to pile up < L. *massa*, a mass], to pile up; collect together; accumulate, especially for oneself.

**am·a·teur** (am′ə-choor′, -toor′, -tyoor′; Fr. ȧ′mȧ′tẽr′), ***n.*** [Fr. < L. < *amare*, to love], 1. a person who does something for the pleasure of it rather than for money; nonprofessional. 2. a person who does something more or less unskillfully. ***adj.*** 1. of or done by or as by amateurs. 2. being an amateur. **—am′a·teur′ish, *adj.*** **—am′a·teur′ish·ly, *adv.*** **—am′a·teur′ish·ness, *n.***

**am·a·teur·ism** (am′ə-choor-iz'm, -toor-, -tyoor-), ***n.*** 1. amateurish quality. 2. nonprofessionalism.

**am·a·to·ry** (am′ə-tôr′i, -tō′ri), ***adj.*** [< L. < *amare*, to love], of, causing, or showing love, especially sexual love.

**a·maze** (ə-māz′), ***v.t.*** [AMAZED, AMAZING], [AS. *amasian;* see MAZE], to fill with great surprise or sudden wonder; astonish. ***n.*** [Poetic], amazement. **—a·mazed** (ə-māzd′), ***adj.*** **—a·maz·ed·ly** (ə-māz′id-li), ***adv.*** **—a·maz′ed·ness, *n.***

**a·maze·ment** (ə-māz′mənt), ***n.*** an amazed condition; great surprise or wonder; astonishment.

**a·maz·ing** (ə-māz′iŋ), ***adj.*** causing amazement; wonderful; astonishing. **—a·maz′ing·ly, *adv.***

**Am·a·zon** (am ə-zon , -z'n), ***n.*** [< Gr.; derived by Gr. folk etym. < *a-*, without + *mazos*, breast, because of the story that the Amazons cut off one breast to facilitate archery], 1. in *Gr. mythology*, a female warrior of a race supposed to have lived in Scythia, near the Black Sea. 2. [a-], a large, strong, masculine woman. 3. a river in South America, flowing from the Andes in Peru, across northern Brazil into the Atlantic: length, c. 4,000 mi. **—Am′a·zo′ni·an** (am′ə-zō′ni-ən), ***adj.***

**am·bas·sa·dor** (am-bas′ə-dẽr), ***n.*** [< Fr. < It. < Pr. < *ambaisat*, task, mission], 1. the highest-ranking representative appointed by one country or government to represent it in another: an **ambassador-at-large** is accredited to no particular country; an **ambassador extraordinary** is on a special diplomatic mission; an **ambassador plenipotentiary** has the power to make treaties. 2. an official messenger with a special mission. Formerly also sp. **embassador. —am·bas′sa·do′ri·al** (-dôr′i-əl, -dō′ri-əl), ***adj.*** **—am·bas′sa·dor·ship′, *n.***

**am·bas·sa·dress** (am-bas′ə-dris), ***n.*** 1. a woman ambassador. 2. the wife of an ambassador

**am·ber** (am′bẽr), ***n.*** [< Fr. < Ar. *'anbar*, ambergris], 1. a yellow or brownish-yellow translucent fossil resin used in jewelry, pipestems, etc. 2. the color of amber. ***adj.*** 1. made of or like amber. 2. having the color of amber.

**am·ber·gris** (am′bẽr-grēs′, -gris), ***n.*** [< Fr. < *ambre gris*, gray amber], a grayish, waxy substance, secreted by sperm whales and found floating in tropical seas: it is used in making perfumes.

**am·bi-** [< L. *ambo*, both], a combining form meaning *both, around*, as in *ambidextrous.*

**am·bi·dex·ter·i·ty** (am′bə-deks-ter′ə-ti), ***n.*** the quality or state of being ambidextrous.

**am·bi·dex·trous** (am′bə-dek′strəs), ***adj.*** [< L. < *ambo*, both + *dexter*, right hand], 1. able to use both hands with equal ease. 2. very skillful or versatile. 3. treacherous; deceitful. **—am′bi·dex′trous·ly, *adv.*** **—am′bi·dex′trous·ness, *n.***

**am·bi·ent** (am′bi-ənt), ***adj.*** [< L. < *ambi-*, around + ppr. of *ire*, to go], surrounding; on all sides.

**am·bi·gu·i·ty** (am′bi-gū′ə-ti), ***n.*** 1. the quality or state of being ambiguous. 2. [*pl.* -TIES], an ambiguous word or expression.

**am·big·u·ous** (am-big′ū-əs), ***adj.*** [< L. < *ambi-*, around + *agere*, to go], 1. having two or more possible meanings. 2. not clear; uncertain or vague. **—am·big′u·ous·ly, *adv.*** **—am·big′u·ous·ness, *n.***

**am·bi·tion** (am-bish′ən), ***n.*** [L. *ambitio*, a going around (to solicit votes) < pp. of *ambire;* see AMBIENT], 1. strong desire for success, fame, power, wealth, etc. 2. the thing so desired.

**am·bi·tious** (am-bish′əs), ***adj.*** 1. full of or showing ambition. 2. greatly desirous (*of* something); eager for. 3. showing great effort; aspiring. **—am·bi′tious·ly, *adv.*** **—am·bi′tious·ness, *n.***

**am·biv·a·lence** (am-biv′ə-ləns), ***n.*** [*ambi-* + *valence*], simultaneous conflicting feelings toward a person or thing, as love and hate. **—am·biv′a·lent, *adj.***

**am·bi·ver·sion** (am′bi-vũr′shən, -zhən), ***n.*** [*ambi-* + intro*version*], in *psychology*, a condition between introversion and extroversion. **—am′bi·vert, *n.***

**am·ble** (am′b'l), ***v.i.*** [-BLED, -BLING], [< OFr. < L. *ambulare*, to walk], 1. to move smoothly and easily by raising first both legs on one side, then both on the other: said of horses, etc. 2. to walk in a leisurely manner. ***n.*** 1. a horse's ambling gait. 2. a leisurely walking pace. **—am′bler, *n.***

**am·bro·sia** (am-brō′zhə), *n.* [< L. < Gr. < *a-*, not + *brotos*, mortal], 1. in *Gr. & Rom. mythology*, the food of the gods and immortals. 2. anything that tastes or smells delicious. —**am·bro′sial, am·bro′sian,** *adj.* —**am·bro′sial·ly,** *adv.*
**am·bu·lance** (am′byoo-ləns), *n.* [< Fr. (*hôpital*), *ambulant*, walking (hospital) < L. *ambulare*, to walk], 1. a mobile field hospital. 2. a specially equipped vehicle for carrying the sick or wounded.
**am·bu·lance-chas·er** (am′byoo-ləns-chās′ẽr), *n.* [Slang], a lawyer of doubtful reputation who encourages victims of accidents to sue for damages.
**am·bu·lant** (am′byoo-lənt), *adj.* moving; walking.
**am·bu·late** (am′byoo-lāt′), *v.i.* [-LATED, -LATING], [< L. pp. of *ambulare*, to walk], to move about; walk. —**am′bu·la′tion,** *n.* —**am′bu·la′tor,** *n.*
**am·bu·la·to·ry** (am′byoo-lə-tôr′i, -tō′ri), *adj.* 1. of or for walking. 2. able to walk. 3. moving from one place to another; movable. 4. in *law*, variable; changeable. *n.* [*pl.* -RIES], any covered or sheltered place for walking.
**am·bus·cade** (am′bəs-kād′), *n.* [< Fr. < It. < ML. *imboscare;* see AMBUSH], an ambush. *v.t. & v.i.* [-CADED, -CADING], to ambush. —**am′bus·cad′er,** *n.*
**am·bush** (am′boosh), *n.* [< OFr. < ML. *imboscare*, to set an ambush < *in-*, in + *boscus*, a wood, woodland], 1. an arrangement of soldiers or other persons in hiding to make a surprise attack. 2. those who are thus in hiding. 3. the place where they are hiding. *v.t. & v.i.* 1. to hide for a surprise attack. 2. to attack from hiding; waylay. —**am′bush·er,** *n.* —**am′bush·ment,** *n.*
**a·me·ba** (ə-mē′bə), *n.* [*pl.* -BAS, -BAE (-bē)], an amoeba. —**a·me′bic,** *adj.* —**a·me′boid,** *adj.*
**a·meer** (ə-mêr′), *n.* an amir.
**a·mel·io·ra·ble** (ə-mēl′yə-rə-b'l), *adj.* that can be ameliorated.
**a·mel·io·rant** (ə-mēl′yə-rənt), *n.* a thing that ameliorates.
**a·mel·io·rate** (ə-mēl′yə-rāt′), *v.t.* [-RATED, -RATING], [< Fr. < L. *ad*, to + *meliorare*, to better], to make better; improve. *v.i.* to become better. —**a·mel′io·ra′tion,** *n.* —**a·mel′io·ra′tive,** *adj.*—**a·mel′io·ra′tor,** *n.*
**A·men** (ä′mən), *n.* [Egypt., lit., hidden one], the ancient Egyptian god of life and reproduction: also sp. **Amon:** see also **Amen-Ra.**
**a·men** (ā′men′, ä′-), *interj.* [< L. < Gr. < Heb. *āmēn*, truly, certainly], may it be so!: used after a prayer or to express approval. *adv.* verily. *n.* a speaking or writing of "amen."
**a·me·na·ble** (ə-mē′nə-b'l, -men′ə-), *adj.* [< Fr. < *a-* (L. *ad*), to + *mener*, to lead < L. *minare*, to drive], 1. responsible or answerable. 2. willing to follow advice; open to suggestion; submissive. —**a·me′na·bil′i·ty,** *n.* —**a·me′na·bly,** *adv.*
**amen corner,** 1. a section of seats in certain churches, where those leading the responsive amens usually sit. 2. [Colloq.], a claque.
**a·mend** (ə-mend′), *v.t.* [< OFr. < L. *emendare*, to correct < *ex-*, from + *mendum*, fault], 1. to improve. 2. to remove the faults of; correct. 3. to change or revise, especially a legislative bill, a law, etc. *v.i.* to improve one's conduct. —**a·mend′a·ble,** *adj.* —**a·mend′er,** *n.*
**a·mend·a·to·ry** (ə-men′də-tôr′i, -tō′ri), *adj.* tending or serving to amend; corrective.
**a·mend·ment** (ə-mend′mənt), *n.* 1. improvement; betterment. 2. a correction of errors, faults, etc. 3. a revision or change proposed or made in a bill, law, constitution, etc.
**a·mends** (ə-mendz′), *n.pl.* [construed also as sing.], [< Fr. pl. of *amende*, a fine; see AMEND], payment made or satisfaction given for injury, loss, etc.
**a·men·i·ty** (ə-men′ə-ti, -mē′nə-), *n.* [*pl.* -TIES], [< Fr. < L. < *amoenus*, pleasant], 1. pleasantness; attractiveness. 2. *pl.* attractive or desirable features, as of a place, climate, etc. 3. *pl.* courteous acts; civilities.
**A·men-Ra** (ä′mən-rä′), *n.* the ancient Egyptian sun god: also sp. **Amon-Ra.**
**am·ent** (am′ənt, ā′mənt), *n.* [L. *amentum*, thong], a tassellike spike of small unisexual flowers lacking petals and sepals, as on a willow; catkin. —**am·en·ta·ceous** (am′ən-tā′shəs), *adj.*
**a·men·ti·a** (ə-men shə, ā-men′shi-ə), *n.* [L., want of reason < *a-* (*ab*), away + *mens*, mind], feeblemindedness; mental deficiency: cf. *dementia.*
**Amer.,** 1. America. 2. American.
**a·merce** (ə-mūrs′), *v.t.* [AMERCED, AMERCING], [< OFr. < *a merci*, at the mercy of], 1. to punish by imposing a fine. 2. to punish. —**a·merc′a·ble,** *adj.* —**a·merce′ment,** *n.* —**a·merc′er,** *n.*
**A·mer·i·ca** (ə-mer′ə-kə), *n.* [after *Amerigo* Vespucci], 1. North America. 2. South America. 3. North America, South America, and Central America considered together. 4. the United States. —**the Americas,** North, South, and Central America.
**A·mer·i·can** (ə-mer′ə-kən), *adj.* 1. of or in America. 2. of, in, or characteristic of the United States, its people, etc. *n.* 1. a native or inhabitant of America. 2. a citizen of the United States. 3. English as spoken in the United States.
**A·mer·i·ca·na** (ə-mer′ə-kā′nə, -kan′ə, -kä′nə), *n.pl.* a collection of books, papers, objects, etc. having to do with America, its people, and its history.
**American cheese,** a kind of fairly hard, mild Cheddar cheese, popular in the United States.
**American Expeditionary Forces,** the United States troops in Europe during World War I: abbrev. **A.E.F.**
**A·mer·i·can·ism** (ə-mer′ə-kən-iz'm), *n.* 1. a custom, characteristic, or belief of or originating in the United States. 2. a word, phrase, or idiom originating in or peculiar to American English. 3. devotion or loyalty to the United States, or to its traditions, customs, etc.
**A·mer·i·can·ize** (ə-mer′ə-kən-īz′), *v.t. & v.i.* [-IZED, -IZING], to make or become American in character, manners, methods, ideals, etc. —**A·mer′i·can·i·za′tion,** *n.*
**American plan,** a system of hotel operation in which the price charged covers room, service, and meals: distinguished from *European plan.*
**American Revolution,** 1. a sequence of actions by American colonists from 1763 to 1783 protesting British domination and culminating in the Revolutionary War. 2. the Revolutionary War (1775–1783), fought by the American colonies for independence from England.
**am·er·ic·i·um** (am′ẽr-ish′i-əm), *n.* [< *America*], a chemical element, one of the transuranium elements, produced by atomic fission: symbol, Am; at. wt., 241 (?); at. no., 95.
**Am·er·ind** (am′ə-rind′), *n.* [*Amer*ican + *Ind*ian], an American Indian or Eskimo. —**Am′er·in′di·an,** *adj. & n.* —**Am′er·in′dic,** *adj.*
**am·e·thyst** (am′ə-thist), *n.* [< OFr. < L. < Gr. < *a-*, not + *methystos*, drunken) the Greeks believed that the stone prevented intoxication)], 1. a purple or violet variety of quartz, used in jewelry. 2. a purple variety of corundum, used in jewelry: called *Oriental amethyst.* 3. purple; violet. *adj.* purple; violet. —**am′e·thys′tine** (-this′tin), *adj.*
**Am·har·ic** (am-har′ik, äm-hä′rik), *n.* the Southern Semitic language used officially in Ethiopia.
**‡a·mi** (à′mē′), *n.* [*pl.* AMIS (-mē′)], [Fr.], a (man or boy) friend.
**a·mi·a·ble** (ā′mi-ə-b'l), *adj.* [< OFr. < L. *amicabilis*, friendly < *amicus*, friend], having a pleasant disposition; good-natured; friendly. —**a′mi·a·bil′i·ty, a′mi·a·ble·ness,** *n.* —**a′mi·a·bly,** *adv.*
**am·i·ca·ble** (am′i-kə-b'l), *adj.* [L. *amicabilis;* see AMIABLE], friendly; peaceable. —**am′i·ca·bil′i·ty, am′i·ca·ble·ness,** *n.* —**am′i·ca·bly,** *adv.*
**am·ice** (am′is), *n.* [< OFr. < L. *amictus*, a cloak], an oblong white linen cloth worn about the neck and shoulders by a priest at Mass.
**a·mi·cus cu·ri·ae** (ə-mī′kəs kyoor′i-ē′), [L., friend of the court], in *law*, a person called in to advise the court on some legal matter.
**a·mid** (ə-mid′), *prep.* among; in the middle of: also **a·midst.**
**am·ide** (am′īd, -id), *n.* [*ammonia* + *-ide*], in *chemistry*, 1. any of a group of organic compounds containing the $CO \cdot NH_2$ radical or an acid radical in place of one hydrogen atom of an ammonia molecule. 2. any of the ammono bases in which one hydrogen atom of the ammonia molecule is replaced by a metal. Also **am′id** (-id). —**a·mid·ic** (ə-mid′ik), *adj.*
**am·i·dol** (am′ə-dōl′, -dol), *n.* [< *amide* + *phenol*], a colorless compound used as a developer in photography.
**a·mid·ships** (ə-mid′ships), *adv.* in or toward the middle of a ship: also **a·mid′ship.**
**a·midst** (ə-midst′), *prep.* amid; among.
**Am·i·ens** (am′i-ənz; Fr. à′myan′), *n.* a city in France, on the Somme River: pop., 85,000.
**‡a·mi·go** (ä-mē′gô; Eng. ə-mē′gō), *n.* [*pl.* -GOS (-gôs; Eng. -gōz)], [Sp.], a friend.
**a·mine** (ə-mēn′, am′in), *n.* [*ammonia* + *-ine*], an ammonia derivative in which hydrogen atoms have been replaced by radicals containing hydrogen and

carbon atoms: also **am′in.** —**a·mi·no** (am′i-nō′, ə-mē′nō), ***adj.***

**amino acids,** a group of nitrogenous organic compounds that serve as units of structure of the proteins and are essential to human metabolism.

**a·mir** (ə-mêr′), ***n.*** [Ar.], in Moslem countries, a ruler or prince: also sp. **ameer.**

**Am·ish** (am′ish, ä′mish), ***n. sing. & pl.*** [after Jacob *Ammann* (or *Amen*), the founder], Mennonites of a sect founded in the 17th c. ***adj.*** of this sect.

**a·miss** (ə-mis′), ***adv.*** [*a-*, at + *miss*], 1. astray. 2. wrongly. ***adj.*** improper; faulty: used predicatively.

**am·i·to·sis** (am′ə-tō′sis), ***n.*** [*a-*, not + *mitosis*], in *biology*, simple cell division, without structural change in the nucleus: opposed to *mitosis.* —**am′i-tot′ic** (-tot′ik), ***adj.***

**am·i·ty** (am ə-ti), ***n.*** [*pl.* -TIES], [< OFr. *amistie* < L. *amicus*, friendly < *amare*, to love], friendship; peaceful relations.

**am·me·ter** (am′mē′tẽr), ***n.*** [*ampere* + *-meter*], an instrument for measuring the strength of an electric current in amperes.

**am·mo** (am′ō), ***n.*** [Slang], ammunition.

**am·mo·ni·a** (ə-mōn′yə, ə-mō′ni-ə), ***n.*** [< *sal ammōniac*], 1. a colorless, pungent gas, $NH_3$. 2. a water solution of this gas: in full, *ammonia water.* —**am·mo·ni·a·cal** (am′ə-nī′ə-k'l), **am·mo′ni·ac′,** ***adj.***

**am·mo·ni·ac** (ə-mō′ni-ak′), ***n.*** [< L. < Gr. *ammōniakon*, gum resin said to come from near the shrine of Jupiter *Ammon* in Libya], a gum resin from an herb found in Mediterranean countries, used in medicine, etc.: also **gum ammoniac.**

**am·mo·ni·ate** (ə-mō′ni-āt′), ***v.t.*** [-ATED, -ATING], to combine with ammonia.

**am·mo·ni·um** (ə-mō′ni-əm), ***n.*** in *chemistry*, the radical $NH_4$, present in salts produced by the reaction of ammonia with an acid.

**ammonium chloride,** a white crystalline compound, $NH_4Cl$; sal ammoniac: it is used in dry cells, fertilizers, dyes, etc., and as a flux in soldering.

**ammonium hydroxide,** an alkali, $NH_4OH$, formed by dissolving ammonia in water.

**am·mo·no** (am′ə-nō′), ***adj.*** of, containing, or derived from ammonia.

**am·mu·ni·tion** (am′yoo-nish′ən), ***n.*** [L. *munitio* < *munire*, to fortify], 1. bullets, gunpowder, bombs, and other projectiles and missiles. 2. any means of attack or defense.

**am·ne·si·a** (am-nē′zhi-ə, -zhə), ***n.*** [Gr. < *a-*, not + *mnasthai*, to remember], partial or total loss of memory caused by brain injury, shock, etc.

**am·ne·sic** (am-nē′sik, -zik), ***adj.*** of amnesia. ***n.*** a person suffering from amnesia.

**am·nes·ty** (am′nəs-ti, -nes-), ***n.*** [*pl.* -TIES], [< L. < Gr. *amnēstia*, a forgetting < *a-*, not + *mnasthai*, to remember], a general pardon, especially for political offenses. ***v.t.*** [-TIED, -TYING], to pardon.

**am·ni·on** (am′ni-ən), ***n.*** [*pl.* -ONS, -A (-ə)], [Gr., dim. of *amnus*, lamb], the innermost membrane of the sac enclosing the embryo of a mammal, reptile, or bird. —**am·ni·ot·ic** (am′ni-ot′ic), ***adj.***

**amn't** (am′′nt), [Colloq.], am not: see also **ain't.**

**a·moe·ba** (ə-mē′bə), ***n.*** [*pl.* -BAS, -BAE (-bē)], [Gr. *amoibē* < *ameibein*, to change], a microscopic, one-celled animal found in stagnant water or as a parasite in other animals: it multiplies by fission: also sp. **ameba.**

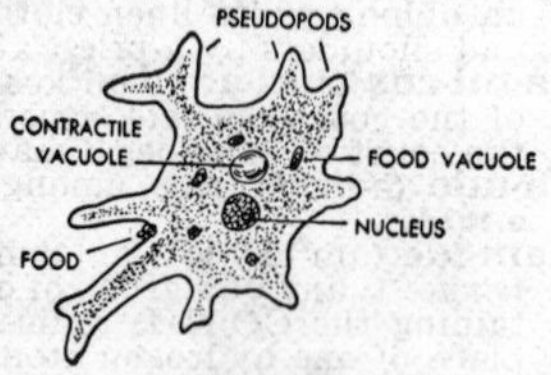

AMOEBA

**a·moe·bic** (ə-mē′bik), ***adj.*** 1. of or like an amoeba or amoebas. 2. caused by amoebas: as, *amoebic* dysentery. Also sp. **amebic.**

**a·moe·boid** (ə-mē′boid), ***adj.*** like an amoeba, as in constantly changing shape: also sp. **ameboid.**

**a·mok** (ə-muk′, -mok′), ***adj. & adv.*** amuck.

**A·mon** (ä′mən), ***n.*** Amen, the ancient Egyptian god.

**a·mong** (ə-muŋ′), ***prep.*** [AS. *on gemang*, in the company (of); *on*, in + *gemang*, a crowd, < *gemengan*, to mingle], 1. surrounded by: as, *among* friends. 2. from place to place in: as, to pass *among* the crowd. 3. in the class of: as, best *among* books. 4. with many: as, popular *among* drinkers. 5. as compared with: as, one *among* thousands. 6. with a share for each of: as, divide it *among* the relatives. 7. with one another: as, we talked *among* ourselves. 8. by the joint action of: as, we have, *among* us, made him a success.

**a·mongst** (ə-muŋst′, -muŋkst′), ***prep.*** among.

**a·mon·til·la·do** (ə-mon′ti-lä′dō; Sp. ä-môn′tē-lyä′dô), ***n.*** [Sp. < *Montilla*, a town in Spain + *-ado*, -ate], a variety of pale Spanish sherry.

**a·mor·al** (ā-môr′əl, -mor′-), ***adj.*** [*a-*, not + *moral*], not concerned with moral standards; neither moral nor immoral. —**a′mo·ral′i·ty,** ***n.*** —**a·mor′al·ly,** ***adv.***

**am·o·rist** (am′ə-rist), ***n.*** [L. *amor*, love; + *-ist*], a person much occupied with love and love-making.

**am·o·rous** (am′ə-rəs), ***adj.*** [OFr.; LL. *amorosus* < L. *amor*, love < *amare*, to love], 1. fond of making love. 2. fond (*of* a person or thing). 3. full of love or sexual desire: as, *amorous* words. 4. of sexual love or love-making.

**a·mor pa·tri·ae** (ā′môr pā′tri-ē′), [L.], patriotism.

**a·mor·phous** (ə-môr′fəs), ***adj.*** [< Gr. < *a-*, without + *morphē*, form], 1. shapeless. 2. of no definite type. 3. in *biology*, without specialized structure. 4. in *chemistry*, not crystalline. —**a·mor′phism** (-fiz'm), ***n.*** —**a·mor′phous·ly,** ***adv.*** —**a·mor′phous·ness,** ***n.***

**a·mor·ti·za·tion, a·mor·ti·sa·tion** (am′ẽr-tə-zā′shən, ə-môr′-), ***n.*** 1. an amortizing. 2. money put aside for amortizing a debt, etc. Also **a·mor·tize·ment, a·mor·tise·ment** (ə-môr′tiz-mənt).

**a·mor·tize, a·mor·tise** (am′ẽr-tīz′, ə-môr′-), ***v.t.*** [-TIZED or -TISED, -TIZING or -TISING], [< OFr. *amortir*, to deaden < L. *ad*, to + *mors*, death], 1. to put money aside at intervals for gradual payment of (a debt, etc.). 2. in *accounting*, to write off (expenditures) by prorating over a fixed period. —**a′mor·tiz′a·ble, a′mor·tis′a·ble** (-ə-b'l), ***adj.***

**A·mos** (ā′məs), [Heb. *'āmōs*, lit., borne (by God?)], ***n.*** 1. a Hebrew prophet of the 8th century B.C. 2. a book of the Old Testament.

**a·mount** (ə-mount′), ***v.i.*** [OFr. *amonter* < *amont*, upward; *a-* (L. *ad*), to + *mont* < L. *mons*, mountain], 1. to add up (*to* a sum): as, it *amounts* to $4.50. 2. to be equal (*to* something) in value or effect: as, to *amount* to much. ***n.*** 1. total. 2. a principal plus its interest. 3. the whole meaning, value, or effect. 4. a quantity. Abbrev. **amt.**

**a·mour** (ə-moor′), ***n.*** [Fr.; L. *amor*, love], a love affair, especially of an illicit or secret nature.

**a·mour-pro·pre** (a moor′prô′pr′), ***n.*** [Fr.], self-love.

**A·moy** (ə-moi′), ***n.*** 1. an island city in Fukien province, China: pop., 234,000. 2. the island.

**am·pe·lop·sis** (am′pə-lop′sis), ***n.*** [< Gr. *ampelos*, vine + *opsis*, appearance], any of a group of climbing shrubs of the grape family.

**am·per·age** (am-pêr′ij, am′pêr′-), ***n.*** [< *ampere* + *-age*], the strength of an electric current, measured in amperes: abbrev. **amp.**

**am·pere** (am′pêr, am-pêr′), ***n.*** [after A. M. *Ampère*, Fr. physicist of early 19th c.], the standard unit for measuring the strength of an electric current; amount of current sent by one volt through a resistance of one ohm: abbrev. **amp., a.**

**am·per·sand** (am′pẽr-sand′), ***n.*** [< *and per se and*, lit., (the sign) & by itself (is) *and*], a sign (& or *&*), meaning *and.*

**am·phet·a·mine** (am-fet′ə-mēn′, -min), ***n.*** a drug used as a nasal spray or inhalant.

**am·phi-,** [< Gr.], a prefix meaning: 1. *on both sides* or *ends.* 2. *of both kinds.*

**Am·phib·i·a** (am-fib′i-ə), ***n.pl.*** [see AMPHIBIOUS], a class of vertebrates, including frogs, toads, newts, and salamanders, that usually begin life in the water as tadpoles with gills, and later develop lungs: they are cold-blooded and scaleless.

**am·phib·i·an** (am-fib′i-ən), ***adj.*** 1. of the Amphibia. 2. amphibious. ***n.*** 1. one of the Amphibia. 2. any animal that lives both on land and in water. 3. any plant that grows either on land or in water. 4. an aircraft that can take off from or come down on either land or water. 5. a tank, etc. that can travel on either land or water.

**am·phib·i·ous** (am-fib′i-əs), ***adj.*** [< Gr. < *amphi-*, on both sides + *bios*, life], 1. that can operate on both land and water. 2. that can live both on land and in water. 3. having two natures. —**am·phib′i·ous·ly,** ***adv.*** —**am·phib′i·ous·ness,** ***n.***

**am·phi·bole** (am′fi-bōl′), ***n.*** [L. *amphibolus*, ambiguous < Gr. *amphiballein*, to be uncertain; *amphi-*, on both sides + *ballein*, to throw], a mineral composed largely of silica, calcium, and magnesia, as asbestos and hornblende. —**am′phi·bol′ic** (-bol′ik), ***adj.***

**am·phi·go·ry** (am′fi-gôr′i, -gō′ri), ***n.*** [*pl.* -RIES], [< Fr.], a nonsensical parody or burlesque.

**am·phi·ox·us** (am′fi-ok′səs), ***n.*** [< *amphi-* + Gr. *oxys*, sharp], the lancelet, a small sea animal.

**am·phi·pro·style** (am-fip′rə-stīl′, am′fi-prō′stīl), ***adj.*** [< L.; see AMPHI- & PROSTYLE], in *architecture*, having rows of columns only at the front and back. ***n.*** an amphiprostyle building.

**am·phi·the·a·ter, am·phi·the·a·tre** (am′fə-thē′ə-tẽr), ***n.*** [< L. < Gr. < *amphi-*, around + *theatron;* see THEATER], 1. a round or oval building with an open space (arena) surrounded by rising rows of seats. 2. a scene of contest. 3. a level place surrounded by rising ground. —**am·phi·the·at·ric,** (am′fə-thi-at′rik), **am′phi·the·at′ri·cal,** ***adj.*** —**am′phi·the·at′ri·cal·ly,** ***adv.***

**Am·phi·tri·te** (am′fi-trī′ti), ***n.*** [L. < Gr.], in *Gr. mythology,* goddess of the sea and wife of Poseidon.

**Am·phit·ry·on** (am-fit′ri-ən), ***n.*** [L. < Gr.], in *Gr. legend,* a king of Thebes: his wife, Alcmene, became the mother of Hercules by Zeus.

**am·pho·ra** (am′fə-rə), ***n.*** [*pl.* -RAE (-rē′), -RAS (-rəz)], [L. < Gr. < *amphi-,* on both sides + *pherein,* to bear], a tall jar with a narrow neck and two handles, used by the ancient Greeks and Romans.

**am·ple** (am′p'l), ***adj.*** [Fr. < L.], 1. large in size, scope, etc. 2. more than enough; abundant. 3. adequate.

**am·plex·i·caul** (am-plek′si-kôl′), ***adj.*** [< L. < *amplectari,* to twine around + *caulis,* stem], in *botany,* encircling a stem, as the base of some leaves.

**am·pli·fi·ca·tion** (am′plə-fi-kā′shən), ***n.*** 1. an amplifying or being amplified. 2. additional details. 3. a statement, etc. with something added. —**am·pli·fi·ca·to·ry** (am-pli′fi-kə-tôr′i, -tō′ri), ***adj.***

**am·pli·fi·er** (am′plə-fī′ēr), ***n.*** 1. a person or thing that amplifies. 2. in *electricity,* an electronic tube, etc. for strengthening electrical impulses.

**am·pli·fy** (am′plə-fī′), ***v.t.*** [-FIED, -FYING], [< Fr. < L. < *amplus,* large + *facere,* to make], 1. to make stronger; increase (power, authority, etc.). 2. to make fuller; expand: as, *amplify* your statement. 3. to strengthen (electrical impulses) by means of electronic tubes, etc. ***v.i.*** to expatiate.

**am·pli·tude** (am′plə-tōōd′, -tūd′), ***n.*** [< L. < *amplus,* large], 1. extent; size. 2. abundance; fullness. 3. scope or breadth, as of mind. 4. in *mathematics & physics,* the range of a fluctuating quantity from the average or mean to the extreme.

**amplitude modulation,** the changing of the amplitude of the transmitting radio wave in accordance with the sound being broadcast: abbrev. **AM, A.M.:** distinguished from *frequency modulation.*

**am·ply** (am′pli), ***adv.*** 1. in an ample manner. 2. to an ample degree.

**am·poule** (am′pōōl), ***n.*** [Fr.; L. *ampulla,* ampulla], a small, sealed glass container for one dose of a hypodermic medicine: also **am′pule** (-pūl).

**am·pul·la** (am-pul′ə, -pool′-), ***n.*** [*pl.* -LAS, -LAE (-ē)], [L.], 1. an almost round bottle used by the ancient Greeks and Romans. 2. a container used in churches for holy oil, consecrated wine, etc.

**am·pu·tate** (am′pyoo-tāt′), ***v.t.*** [-TATED, -TATING], [< L. pp. of *amputare* < *amb-,* about + *putare,* to prune], to cut off, especially by surgery. —**am′pu·ta′tion,** ***n.*** —**am′pu·ta′tor,** ***n.***

**am·pu·tee** (am′pyoo-tē′), ***n.*** [see -EE], a person who has had a limb or limbs amputated.

**Am·rit·sar** (um-rit′sēr), ***n.*** a city in northern India, Punjab state: pop., 391,000.

**Am·ster·dam** (am′stēr-dam′), ***n.*** one of the two capitals of the Netherlands: pop., 811,000.

**amt.,** amount.

**a·muck** (ə-muk′), ***adj. & adv.*** [Malay *amoq*], in a frenzy to kill: also **a·mok′.** —**run amuck,** 1. to rush about in a frenzy to kill; hence, 2. to lose control of oneself.

**am·u·let** (am′yoo-lit), ***n.*** [< Fr. < L.], something worn, as around the neck, to protect against evil.

**A·mund·sen, Ro·ald** (rō′äl ä′mən-s'n), 1872–1928; Norwegian polar explorer.

**A·mur** (ä-moor′), ***n.*** a river in eastern Asia: length, 2,900 mi.

**a·muse** (ə-mūz′), ***v.t.*** [AMUSED, AMUSING], [< Fr. < *ā* (L. *ad*), to + OFr. *muser,* to gaze at], 1. to keep agreeably occupied; entertain: as, we *amused* ourselves with games. 2. to make laugh, smile, etc. —**a·mus′a·ble,** ***adj.***

**a·mused** (ə-mūzd′), ***adj.*** [pp. of *amuse*], 1. agreeably occupied. 2. caused to laugh, smile, etc. 3. showing amusement. —**a·mus′ed·ly** (-id-li), ***adv.***

**a·muse·ment** (ə-mūz′mənt), ***n.*** 1. an amusing or being amused. 2. something that amuses.

**amusement park,** an outdoor place with devices for entertainment, as a merry-go-round, etc.

**a·mus·ing** (ə-mūz′iŋ), ***adj.*** [ppr. of *amuse*], 1. entertaining; diverting. 2. causing laughter or mirth. —**a·mus′ing·ly,** ***adv.***

**a·myg·da·la** (ə-mig′də-lə), ***n.*** [*pl.* -LAE (-lē′)], [L. < Gr. *amygdalē,* an almond], 1. [Obs.], an almond. 2. in *anatomy,* a tonsil. —**a·myg′da·late** (-lit, -lāt′), **a·myg′da·line** (-lin, -līn′), ***adj.***

**a·myg·da·lin** (ə-mig′də-lin), ***n.*** [< *amygdala* + *-in*], a glucoside, $C_{20}H_{27}NO_{11}$, present in bitter almonds.

**am·yl** (am′il, ā′mil), ***n.*** [*amylum* + *-yl*], any of the isomeric forms of the radical $C_5H_{11}$, found in certain compounds. —**a·myl·ic** (ə-mil′ik), ***adj.***

**am·y·la·ceous** (am′i-lā′shəs), ***adj.*** [< *amylum* + *-aceous*], of or like starch.

**am·yl·ase** (am′i-lās′), ***n.*** [< *amylum* + *-ase*], an enzyme that helps change starch into sugar: it is found in saliva, pancreatic juice, etc.

**am·y·loid** (am′i-loid′), ***adj.*** [< *amylum* + *-oid*], like or containing starch. ***n.*** a starchy substance.

**am·y·lum** (am′i-ləm), ***n.*** [< L. < Gr.], starch.

**am·y·tal** (am′i-tal′, -tôl′), ***n*** a colorless crystalline compound, $C_{11}H_{18}O_3N_2$, used as a sedative.

**an** (ən; *stressed,* an), ***adj., indefinite article*** [weakened variant of *one* < AS. *an,* the numeral one], 1. one; one sort of. 2. each; any one. 3. to each; in each; for each; per: as, two *an* hour. Older usage favored *an* before *h* in an unstressed initial syllable, as, *an* hotel, and before the sound (ū, yoo), as, *an* union. See also **a** (the indefinite article).

**an, an′** (an), ***conj.*** [< *and*], 1. [Dial.], and. 2. [Archaic], if.

**an-,** a- (not, without): before vowels and *h.*

**an-,** ad-: used before *n.*

**-an,** [< L. *-anus*], an adjectival and nominal suffix meaning: 1. *of, belonging to, characteristic of,* as in *diocesan.* 2. *born in, living in,* as in *American.* 3. *believing in,* as in *Mohammedan.*

**an.,** 1. *anno,* [L.], in the year. 2. anonymous.

**A.N., AN., A.-N.,** Anglo-Norman.

**an·a-** [< Gr. *ana,* up, on, etc.], a prefix meaning: 1. *up,* as in *anadromous.* 2. *back,* as in *anagram.* 3. *again,* as in *Anabaptist.* 4. *throughout,* as in *analysis.* 5. *according to, similar to,* as in *analogy.*

**-a·na,** [neut. pl. of L. *-anus*], a suffix used to form plurals from proper nouns, and meaning *sayings, writings, anecdotes,* or *facts of,* as in *Americana.*

**An·a·bap·tist** (an′ə-bap′tist), ***n.*** [< L. < Gr. < *ana-,* again + *baptizein,* to baptize], a member of a Swiss sect (c. 1522) that rejected infant baptism and practiced baptism of adults. ***adj.*** of this sect. —**An′a·bap′tism,** ***n***

**A·nab·a·sis** (ə-nab′ə-sis), ***n.*** [*pl.* -SES (-sēz′)], [Gr. < *anabainein,* to go up; *ana-,* up + *bainein,* to go], 1. the military expedition (401–400 B.C.) of Cyrus the Younger against his brother, Artaxerxes II. 2. a book about this by the Greek writer Xenophon. 3. [a-], a military expedition.

**an·a·bat·ic** (an′ə-bat′ik), ***adj.*** [Gr. *anabatikos;* see ANABASIS] rising: said of air currents.

**an·a·bi·o·sis** (an′ə-bī-ō′sis), ***n.*** [Gr. < *anabioein,* to come to life again], a bringing back to consciousness; resuscitation. —**an′a·bi·ot′ic,** ***adj.***

**a·nab·o·lism** (ə-nab′ə-liz'm), ***n.*** [Gr. *anabolē,* a rising up; + *-ism*], the process in a plant or animal by which food is changed into living tissue; constructive metabolism: opposed to *catabolism.* —**an·a·bol·ic** (an′ə-bol′ik), ***adj.***

**an·a·can·thous** (an ə-kan′thəs), ***adj.*** [< Gr. < *an-,* not + *akantha,* thorn], in *botany,* having no spines; without thorns.

**a·nach·ro·nism** (ə-nak′rə-niz'm), ***n.*** [< Fr. < L. < Gr. *anachronizein,* to refer to a wrong time < *ana-,* against + *chronos,* time], 1. the representation of something as existing or occurring at other than its proper time. 2. anything out of its proper historical time. —**a·nach′ro·nis′tic, a·nach′ro·nous** (nəs), ***adj.***

**an·a·co·lu·thon** (an′ə-kə-lōō′thon, -lū′-), ***n.*** [*pl.* -THA (-thə)], [Gr. *anakolouthos,* inconsequent; *an-,* not + *akolouthos,* following], a change from one grammatical construction to another within the same sentence, sometimes as a rhetorical device. —**an′a·co·lu′thic,** ***adj.***

**an·a·con·da** (an′ə-kon′də), ***n.*** 1. a large South American snake of the boa family. 2. any similar large snake that crushes its victim in its coils.

**a·nad·ro·mous** (ə-nad′rə-məs), ***adj.*** [< Gr. < *ana-,* upward + *dramein,* to run], going up rivers to spawn: said of the salmon, shad, etc.

**a·nae·mi·a** (ə-nē′mi-ə), ***n.*** anemia. —**a·nae′mic,** ***adj.***

**an·aer·obe** (an-âr′ōb, -ā′ēr-ōb′), ***n.*** [see AN- (not) & AEROBE], a microorganism that can live where there is no free oxygen. —**an·aer·o·bic** (an′âr-ō′bik, an-ā′ēr-ō′-), ***adj.***

**an·aer·o·bi·um** (an′âr-ō′bi-əm, -ā-ēr-ō′-), ***n.*** [*pl.* -BIA (-ə)], an anaerobe.

**an·aes·the·si·a** (an′əs-thē′zhə, -zhi-ə), ***n.*** anesthesia.

---

**an·aes·thet·ic** (an'əs-thet'ik), *adj. & n.* anesthetic.
**an·aes·the·tize** (ə-nes'thə-tīz'), *v.t.* [-TIZED, -TIZING], to anesthetize. —**an·aes'the·tist,** *n.*
**an·a·gram** (an'ə-gram'), *n.* [< Mod. L. < Gr. *anagrammatizein,* to transpose letters < *ana-,* back + *gramma,* letter < *graphein,* to write], 1. a word or phrase made from another by rearranging its letters, as *made—dame.* 2. *pl.* a game of making words by changing or adding letters.
**an·a·gram·mat·ic** (an'ə-grə-mat'ik), *adj.* of, like, or containing an anagram: also **an'a·gram·mat'i·cal.** —**an'a·gram·mat'i·cal·ly,** *adv.*
**an·a·gram·ma·tize** (an'ə-gram'ə-tīz'), *v.t.* [-TIZED, -TIZING], to make an anagram of.
**An·a·heim** (an'ə-hīm'), *n.* a city in SW California, near Los Angeles: pop., 104,000.
**a·nal** (ā'n'l), *adj.* of or near the anus.
**an·a·lects** (an'ə-lekts'), *n.pl.* [< L. < Gr. *analegein,* to collect; *ana-,* up + *legein,* to gather], collected literary excerpts; specif., [the A-], a collection of Confucius' teachings.
**an·a·lep·tic** (an'ə-lep'tik), *adj. & n.* [< Gr. < *analambanein,* to recover; *ana-,* up + *lambanein,* to take], in *medicine,* restorative.
**an·al·ge·si·a** (an'al-jē'zi-ə, -si-ə), *n.* [< Gr. *an-,* without + *algēsia,* pain], a state of not being able to feel pain.
**an·al·ge·sic** (an'al-jē'zik, -sik), *adj.* of or causing analgesia. *n.* something that produces analgesia.
**analog computer,** a computer that uses coded physical quantities, such as voltages, etc., in providing continuous solutions to complex equations.
**an·a·log·i·cal** (an'ə-loj'i-k'l), *adj.* of, using, or based upon analogy. —**an'a·log'i·cal·ly,** *adv.*
**a·nal·o·gize** (ə-nal'ə-jīz'), *v.i.* [-GIZED (-jīzd'), -GIZING], [Gr. *analogizesthai,* to calculate], to use analogy. *v.t.* to explain by analogy. —**a·nal'o·gist,** *n.*
**a·nal·o·gous** (ə-nal'ə-gəs), *adj.* [see ANALOGY], 1. similar or comparable in certain respects. 2. in *biology,* similar in function but not in origin and structure. —**a·nal'o·gous·ly,** *adv.*
**an·a·logue, an·a·log** (an'ə-lôg', -log'), *n.* a thing or part that is analogous.
**a·nal·o·gy** (ə-nal'ə-ji), *n.* [*pl.* -GIES (-jiz)], [< Fr. < L. < Gr. *analogia,* proportion < *ana-,* according to + *logos,* ratio], 1. similarity in some respects; partial resemblance. 2. a comparing of something point by point with something else. 3. in *biology,* similarity in function but not in origin and structure. 4. in *logic,* the inference that certain resemblances imply probable further similarity.
**an·a·lyse** (an'ə-līz'), *v.t.* [-LYSED, -LYSING], to analyze.
**a·nal·y·sis** (ə-nal'ə-sis), *n.* [*pl.* -SES (-sēz')], [Gr., a dissolving; *ana-,* up, throughout + *lysis,* a loosing < *lyein,* to loose], 1. a breaking up of any whole into its parts so as to find out their nature, function, etc. 2. a statement of these findings. 3. in *chemistry,* the separation of compounds and mixtures into their constituent substances to determine the nature (*qualitative analysis*) or the proportion (*quantitative analysis*) of the constituents. 4. psychoanalysis.
**an·a·lyst** (an'ə-list), *n.* 1. a person who analyzes: as, a news *analyst.* 2. a psychoanalyst.
**an·a·lyt·i·cal** (an'ə-lit'i-k'l), *adj.* 1. of analysis or analytics. 2. skilled in or using analysis. Also **an'a·lyt'ic.** —**an'a·lyt'i·cal·ly,** *adv.*
**an·a·lyt·ics** (an'ə-lit'iks), *n.pl.* [construed as sing.], 1. the part of logic having to do with analyzing. 2. mathematical analysis.
**an·a·lyze** (an'ə-līz'), *v.t.* [-LYZED, -LYZING], [< Fr. < Gr.; see ANALYSIS], 1. to separate into parts so as to find out their nature, function, etc. 2. to examine the constituents of carefully and in detail. 3. to psychoanalyze. Also sp. **analyse.** —**an'a·lyz'a·ble, an'a·lys'a·ble,** *adj.* —**an'a·lyz'er, an'a·lys'er,** *n.*
**An·a·ni·as** (an'ə-nī'əs), *n.* 1. in the *Bible,* a notorious liar who fell dead when Peter rebuked him: Acts 5:1–10. 2. [Colloq.], a liar.
**an·a·pest, an·a·paest** (an'ə-pest'), *n.* [< L. < Gr. < *ana-,* back + *paiein,* to strike], 1. a metrical foot consisting of two short (or unaccented) syllables followed by a long (or accented) one. 2. a line of verse made up of such feet. Example: "Ănd thĕ shēen / ŏf thĕir spēars / wăs ăs fōam / ŏn thĕ sēa." —**an'a·pes'tic, an'a·paes'tic,** *adj.*
**a·naph·o·ra** (ə-naf'ə-rə), *n.* [L.; Gr. < *ana-,* up, back + *pherein,* to carry], 1. the repetition of a word or phrase at the beginning of successive clauses or sentences. 2. the device of cross reference through pronouns, etc. —**an·a·phor·ic** (an'ə-fôr'ik, -for'-), *adj.*
**an·aph·ro·dis·i·ac** (an-af'rə-diz'i-ak), *adj.* [*an-* + *aphrodisiac*], that lessens sexual desire. *n.* a drug, etc. for lessening sexual desire.

**an·ar·chic** (an-är'kik), *adj.* 1. of or like anarchy. 2. advocating anarchy. 3. lawless. Also **an·ar'chi·cal.** —**an·ar'chi·cal·ly,** *adv.*
**an·arch·ism** (an'ẽr-kiz'm), *n.* [< *anarchy* + *-ism*], 1. the theory that all forms of government interfere with individual liberty and are undesirable. 2. resistance, sometimes by terrorism, to government.
**an·arch·ist** (an'ẽr-kist), *n.* 1. one who believes in or advocates anarchism. 2. one who promotes anarchy. Also **an'arch** (-ärk). *adj.* anarchistic.
**an·ar·chis·tic** (an'ẽr-kis'tik), *adj.* of or like anarchism or anarchists.
**an·arch·y** (an'ẽr-ki), *n.* [< Gr. < *an-,* without + *archos,* leader], 1. the complete absence of government and law. 2. political disorder and violence. 3. disorder in any sphere of activity.
**an·as·tig·mat·ic** (an'as-tig-mat'ik, an-as'-), *adj.* [*an-* + *astigmatic*], 1. free from astigmatism. 2. corrected for astigmatism.
**a·nas·to·mose** (ə-nas'tə-mōz'), *v.t. & v.i.* [-MOSED, -MOSING], to join by anastomosis.
**a·nas·to·mo·sis** (ə-nas'tə-mō'sis), *n.* [*pl.* -SES (-sēz)], [Gr. *anastomōsis,* opening < *ana-,* again + *stoma,* mouth], a connection between parts of a system of vessels, veins, tubes, etc.
**a·nas·tro·phe** (ə-nas'trə-fi), *n.* [Gr. < *ana-,* back + *strephein,* to turn], reversal of the usual word order of a sentence. Example: "Came the dawn."
**anat.,** 1. anatomical. 2. anatomist. 3. anatomy.
**a·nath·e·ma** (ə-nath'ə-mə), *n.* [*pl.* -MAS], [L.; Gr., thing devoted to evil < *anatithenai,* to dedicate; *ana-,* up + *tithenai,* to set], 1. a thing or person accursed; hence, 2. anything greatly detested. 3. a formal curse, as in excommunicating a person from a church. 4. any strong curse.
**a·nath·e·ma·tize** (ə-nath'ə-mə-tīz'), *v.t. & v.i.* [-TIZED, -TIZING], to utter an anathema (against); curse. —**a·nath'e·ma·ti·za'tion,** *n.* —**a·nath'e·ma·tiz'er,** *n.*
**An·a·to·li·a** (an'ə-tō'li-ə), *n.* 1. Asia Minor: ancient name. 2. the Asiatic part of modern Turkey. —**An'a·to'li·an,** *adj. & n.*
**an·a·tom·i·cal** (an'ə-tom'i-k'l), *adj.* of or connected with anatomy: also **an'a·tom'ic.** —**an'a·tom'i·cal·ly,** *adv.*
**a·nat·o·mist** (ə-nat'ə-mist), *n.* 1. one skilled in anatomy. 2. one who dissects or analyzes.
**a·nat·o·mize** (ə-nat'ə-mīz'), *v.t. & v.i.* [-MIZED, -MIZING], [see ANATOMY], 1. to dissect (animal bodies, etc.) in order to examine the structure; hence, 2. to analyze.
**a·nat·o·my** (ə-nat'ə-mi), *n.* [*pl.* -MIES], [< Fr. < L. < Gr. < *ana-,* up + *temnein,* to cut], 1. the dissecting of a plant or animal in order to study its structure. 2. the science of the structure of plants or animals. 3. the structure of an organism or body. 4. any analysis.
**An·ax·ag·o·ras** (an'ak-sag'ə-rəs), *n.* Greek philosopher; 500?–428 B.C.
**anc.,** 1. ancient. 2. anciently.
**-ance,** [< Fr. < L. *-antia, -entia*], a suffix meaning: 1. *a —ing* or *being —ed,* as in *utterance.* 2. *the quality* or *state of being —ant,* as in *vigilance.* 3. *a thing that —s,* as in *conveyance.* 4. *a thing that is —ant,* as in *dissonance.* 5. *a thing that is —ed,* as in *inheritance.* Also **-ancy, -ence, -ency.**
**an·ces·tor** (an'ses-tẽr), *n.* [< ME. & OFr. < L. *antecessor,* one who goes before < *ante-,* before + *cedere,* to go], 1. any person from whom one is descended; forebear. 2. an early type of animal from which later kinds have evolved. 3. in *law,* one from whom an estate has been inherited.
**an·ces·tral** (an-ses'trəl), *adj.* of or inherited from ancestors. —**an·ces'tral·ly,** *adv.*
**an·ces·tress** (an'ses-tris), *n.* a woman ancestor.
**an·ces·try** (an'ses-tri), *n.* [*pl.* -TRIES], 1. family descent or lineage. 2. ancestors collectively.
**an·chor** (aŋ'kẽr), *n.* [< L. < Gr. *ankyra,* a hook], 1. a heavy object, usually a hooked iron weight, lowered into the water by cable or chain to keep a ship from drifting. 2. any device that holds something else secure. 3. anything regarded as giving stability or security. *v.t.* to hold secure by or as by an anchor. *v.i.* to lower the anchor overboard; lie at anchor. —**at anchor,** anchored. —**cast** (or **drop**) **anchor,** 1. to lower the anchor overboard; hence, 2. to settle (in a place). —**weigh anchor,** 1. to raise the anchor; hence, 2. to leave; go away.

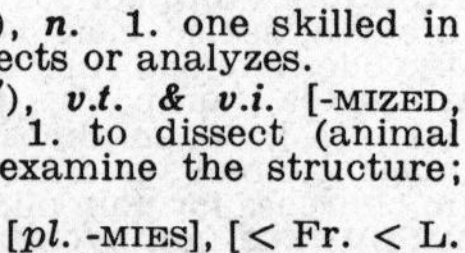

ANCHOR

**an·chor·age** (aŋ'kẽr-ij), *n.* [see -AGE], 1. money charged for the right to anchor. 2. an anchoring or being anchored. 3. a place to anchor. 4. something that can be relied on.

**an·cho·ress** (aŋ′kēr-is), *n.* a woman anchorite.

**an·cho·rite** (aŋ′kə-rīt′), *n.* [< OFr. < L. < Gr. *anachōrētes* < *ana-*, back + *chōrein*, to retire], 1. a person who lives alone for religious meditation. 2. a hermit. Also **an′cho·ret** (-kēr-it, -kə-ret′). —**an′cho·ret′ic** (-kə-ret′ik), **an′cho·rit′ic** (-kə-rit′ik), *adj.*

**an·cho·vy** (an′chə-vi, -chō′vi, an-chō′vi), *n.* [*pl.* -VIES; see PLURAL, II, D, 1], [< Port. & Sp. < Basque *anchova*], a very small fish of the herring family: anchovies are usually salted and spiced or made into a paste.

**an·chy·lose** (aŋ′ki-lōs′), *v.t. & v.i.* [-LOSED (-lōst′), -LOSING], to ankylose.

**an·chy·lo·sis** (aŋ′ki-lō′sis), *n.* ankylosis.

**‡an·cienne no·blesse** (än′syen′ nô′bles′), [Fr., old nobility], the French nobility before the Revolution of 1789.

**‡an·cien ré·gime** (än′syan′ rā′zhēm′), [Fr., old order], the former social and political system, especially that in France before the Revolution of 1789.

**an·cient** (ān′shənt), *adj.* [< OFr.; ult. < L. *ante*, before], 1. of times long past; especially, of the time before the end of the Western Roman Empire in 476 A.D. 2. antique; very old. *n.* 1. a person who lived in ancient times. 2. an aged person. —**the ancients**, the people who lived in ancient times; especially, the classical writers and artists of Graeco-Roman times.

**an·cient·ly** (ān′shənt-li), *adv.* in ancient times.

**an·cil·lar·y** (an′sə-ler′i), *adj.* [< L. *ancilla*, maidservant], 1. subordinate (*to*). 2. auxiliary.

**an·con** (aŋ′kon), *n.* [*pl.* ANCONES (aŋ-kō′nēz)], [L. < Gr. < *ankos*, a bend], 1. the elbow. 2. a bracketlike projection supporting a cornice. —**an·co·ne·al** (aŋ-kō′ni-əl), *adj.*

**and** (and; *unstressed*, ənd, ən, ′n), *conj.* [AS.], 1. also; in addition. 2. plus: as, six *and* two makes eight. 3. as a result: as, he told her *and* she wept. 4. [Obs.], if. 5. [Colloq.], to: as, try *and* get it.

**and.**, andante.

**An·da·lu·sia** (an′də-lōō′zhə, -shə), *n.* an old province of southern Spain. —**An′da·lu′sian**, *adj. & n.*

**an·dan·te** (an-dan′ti, än-dän′tā), *adj. & adv.* [It., ppr. of *andare*, to walk], in *music*, moderately slow. *n.* a moderately slow movement or passage.

**an·dan·ti·no** (an′dan-tē′nō, än′dän-), *adj & adv.* [It., dim. of *andante*], in *music*, slightly faster than andante: the current sense. *n.* [*pl.* -NOS (-nōz)], a movement or passage in this tempo.

**An·der·sen, Hans Christian** (an′dēr-s′n), 1805–1875; Danish novelist and writer of fairy stories.

**Anderson, Sher·wood** (shūr′wood an′dēr-s′n), 1876–1941; American writer.

**An·des Mountains** (an′dēz), a mountain system in western South America. —**An·de·an** (an-dē′ən, an′di-), *adj.*

**and·i·ron** (and′ī′ērn), *n.* [< OFr. *andier;* ending confused with Eng. *iron*], either of a pair of metal supports for holding logs in a fireplace: also called *firedog.*

ANDIRONS

**and/or**, either *and* or *or*, according to what is meant: as, personal *and/or* real property.

**An·dor·ra** (an-dôr′ə, -dor′-), *n.* 1. a republic in the Pyrenees Mountains, between Spain and France: area, 191 sq. mi.; pop., 6,000. 2. its capital.

**Andrea del Sarto,** see **Sarto, Andrea del.**

**An·drew** (an′drōō), *n.* in the *Bible*, one of the twelve apostles.

**An·dre·yev, Le·o·nid Ni·ko·la·ye·vich** (le′ô-nēd′ nē-kô-lä-yä′vich än-drā′yef), 1871–1919; Russian writer: also spelled **Andreév** etc.

**an·dro-**, [< Gr. *anēr, andros*, man, male], a combining form meaning: 1. *man, male, masculine.* 2. *anther, stamen.* Also, before a vowel, **andr-.**

**an·droe·ci·um** (an-drē′shi-əm, -si-), *n.* [*pl.* -CIA (-ə)], [< *andro-* + Gr. *oikos*, house], in *botany*, the stamens and the parts belonging to them, collectively.

**an·dro·gen** (an′drə-jən), *n.* [*andro-* + *-gen*], a male sex hormone or similar substance that can give rise to masculine characteristics. —**an·dro·gen·ic** (an′drə-jen′ik), *adj.*

**an·drog·y·nous** (an-droj′ə-nəs), *adj.* [< L. < Gr. < *anēr, andros*, man + *gynē*, woman], 1. hermaphroditic. 2. in *botany*, bearing both staminate and pistillate flowers in the same cluster. —**an·drog′y·ny** (-ni), *n.*

**An·drom·a·che** (an-drom′ə-ki), *n.* in *Gr. legend*, the faithful wife of Hector.

**An·drom·e·da** (an-drom′i-də), *n.* 1. in *Gr. legend*, an Ethiopian princess whom Perseus rescued from a sea monster and then married. 2. in *astronomy*, a northern constellation south of Cassiopeia.

**an·dros·ter·one** (an-dros′tēr-ōn′), *n.* [*andro-* + *sterol* + *-one*], a male sex hormone.

**-an·drous** (an′drəs), [< Gr. *anēr, andros*, man, male], a suffix meaning *having stamens.*

**-ane**, [an arbitrary coinage], a suffix denoting a hydrocarbon of the paraffin series, as in *methane.*

**a·near** (ə-nêr′), *adv. & prep.* [Dial. or Poetic], near.

**an·ec·dot·age** (an′ik-dōt′ij), *n.* [< *anecdote* + *-age;* sense 2 influenced by *dotage*], 1. a collection of anecdotes. 2. senility; a humorous usage.

**an·ec·do·tal** (an′ik-dō′t′l), *adj.* 1. of or like an anecdote. 2. full of anecdotes.

**an·ec·dote** (an′ik-dōt′), *n.* [< ML. < Gr. *anekdotos*, unpublished < *an-*, not + *ek-*, out + *didonai*, to give], a short, entertaining account of some happening, usually personal or biographical.

**an·ec·dot·ic** (an′ik-dot′ik), *adj.* 1. anecdotal. 2. fond of telling anecdotes. Also **an′ec·dot′i·cal.**

**an·ec·dot·ist** (an′ik-dōt′ist), *n.* a person who tells or collects anecdotes.

**a·ne·mi·a** (ə-nē′mi-ə), *n.* [< Gr. < *a-*, *an-*, without + *haima*, blood], a condition in which there is a reduction in the number of red blood corpuscles or of hemoglobin in the blood stream: also **anaemia.** —**a·ne′mic** (-mik), *adj.*

**a·nem·o·graph** (ə-nem′ə-graf′, -gräf′), *n.* [< Gr. *anemos*, the wind; + *-graph*], an instrument for recording the velocity or direction of the wind.

**an·e·mom·e·ter** (an′ə-mom′ə-tēr), *n.* [< Gr. *anemos*, the wind; + *-meter*], a gauge for measuring the pressure or velocity of the wind.

ANEMOMETER

**an·e·mom·e·try** (an′ə-mom′ə-tri), *n.* the act of determining the velocity of the wind by the use of an anemometer. —**an·e·mo·met·ric** (an′ə-mō-met′rik), **an′e·mo·met′ri·cal**, *adj.*

**a·nem·o·ne** (ə-nem′ə-nē′), *n.* [Gr. < *anemos*, wind], 1. any of various plants with cup-shaped flowers, usually of white, purple, or red. 2. a sea anemone.

**a·nent** (ə-nent′), *prep.* [< AS. *on efen*, lit., on even (with), in line (with)], respecting; as regards; concerning: also [Rare], **a·nenst** (-nenst′).

**an·er·oid** (an′ēr-oid′), *adj.* [< Gr. *a-*, without + *nēros*, liquid; + *-oid*], not using liquid. *n.* an aneroid barometer.

**aneroid barometer,** a barometer in which a change in atmospheric pressure causes the elastic top of a box containing no air to bend in or out, thus moving a pointer.

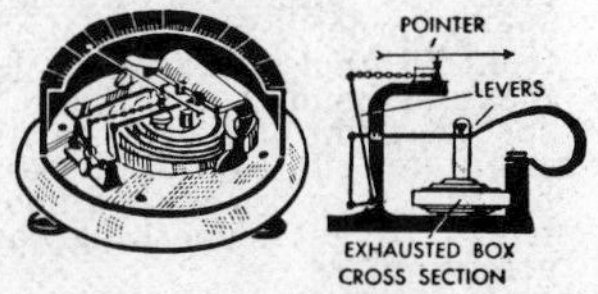


ANEROID BAROMETER, WITH CROSS SECTION

**an·es·the·si·a** (an′əs-thē′zhə, -zhi-ə), *n.* [< Gr. < *an-*, without + *aisthēsis*, feeling], a partial or total loss of the sense of pain, temperature, touch, etc., produced by disease or certain drugs: also sp. **anaesthesia.**

**an·es·thet·ic** (an′əs-thet′ik), *adj.* 1. of or with anesthesia. 2. producing anesthesia. *n.* a drug, gas, etc. that produces anesthesia. Also sp. **anaesthetic.** —**anesthetic to,** incapable of feeling; insensitive to.

**an·es·the·tist** (ə-nes′thə-tist), *n.* a person trained to administer anesthetics: also sp. **anaesthetist.**

**an·es·the·tize** (ə-nes′thə-tīz′), *v.t.* [-TIZED, -TIZING], to cause anesthesia in; give anesthetics to: also sp. **anaesthetize.** —**an·es′the·ti·za′tion** (-ti-zā′shən), *n.*

**an·eu·rysm, an·eu·rism** (an′yoor-iz′m), *n.* [< Gr. < *ana-*, up + *eurys*, broad], a sac formed by enlargement of the wall of an artery, caused by disease or injury. —**an′eu·rys′mal, an′eu·ris′mal,** *adj.*

**an·ga·ry** (aŋ′gə-ri), *n.* [L. *angaria*, enforced service < Gr. *angaros*, a dispatch bearer], in *international law*, the right of a belligerent to use or destroy a neutral's property if necessary, subject to full indemnification.

**an·gel** (ān′jəl), *n.* [< OFr. < L. < Gr. *angelos*, messenger], 1. a messenger of God. 2. a supernatural being, either good or bad, of more than human intelligence, etc. 3. a guiding spirit: as, one's good *angel*. 4. a conventionalized image of a figure in human form with wings and a halo. 5. a person regarded as beautiful, good, etc. 6. a former English coin with the archangel Michael shown on it, last issued in 1634. 7. [Slang], one who pays for the production of a play, etc. *v.t.* [Slang], to back financially.

**angel cake,** a light, spongy, white cake made without shortening or egg yolks: also **angel food (cake).**

**an·gel·fish** (ān′jəl-fish′), *n.* [*pl.* see FISH], 1. a shark with winglike pectoral fins. 2. any of a number of bright-colored tropical fishes with spiny fins.

**an·gel·ic** (an-jel′ik), *adj.* 1. of an angel or the angels. 2. like an angel in beauty, goodness, etc. Also **an·gel′i·cal** (-i-k'l). —**an·gel′i·cal·ly,** *adv.*

**an·gel·i·ca** (an-jel′i-kə), *n.* [ML. (*herba*) *angelica*, lit., the angelic (herb)], a plant of the carrot family, used in flavoring, medicine, etc.

**An·gel·i·co, Fra** (frä än-jel′i-kō′), (*Giovanni da Fiesole*), 1387–1455; Italian painter.

**An·ge·lus, an·ge·lus** (an′jə-ləs), *n.* [L.; see ANGEL], in the *R. C. Church*, 1. a prayer said at morning, noon, and night in observance of the Annunciation. 2. a bell rung to announce the time for this.

**an·ger** (aŋ′gēr), *n.* [ON. *angr*, distress, sorrow], a hostile feeling of displeasure that may result from injury, mistreatment, opposition, etc.; rage; ire. *v.t.* to make angry; enrage.

**An·ge·vin** (an′jə-vin), *adj.* 1. of Anjou. 2. of the Plantagenet line of English kings (1154–1399). *n.* 1. a native of Anjou. 2. one of the Plantagenets. Also **An′ge·vine** (-vin, -vīn′).

**an·gi·na** (an-jī′nə, an′ji-), *n.* [L., quinsy < Gr. *anchein*, to squeeze], 1. any inflammatory disease of the throat, especially one characterized by fits of suffocation, as croup. 2. angina pectoris.

**angina pec·to·ris** (pek′tə-ris), [L., angina of the breast], a heart disease in which there are chest pains with feelings of suffocation.

**an·gi·o·ma** (an′ji-ō′mə), *n.* [*pl.* -MATA (-mə-tə), -MAS (-məz)], [< Gr. *angeion*, vessel, capsule; + *-oma*], a tumor made up mainly of blood vessels and lymph vessels.

**an·gi·o·sperm** (an′ji-ō-spūrm′), *n.* [< Gr. *angeion*, vessel, capsule; + *-sperm*], any plant that has the seeds enclosed in an ovary.

**Angl.,** 1. Anglican. 2. Anglicized.

**an·gle** (aŋ′g'l), *n.* [< Fr. < L. *angulus*, a corner < Gr. *ankylos*, bent], 1. the shape made by two straight lines or plane surfaces that meet. 2. the space between such lines or surfaces. 3. the degrees of difference in direction between them. 4. a sharp corner. 5. point of view: as, consider this from all *angles*. *v.t. & v.i.* [-GLED, -GLING], 1. to move or bend at an angle. 2. [Colloq.], to give a specific point of view to (a story, report, etc.).

**an·gle** (aŋ′g'l), *v.i.* [-GLED, -GLING], [AS. *angul*, fishhook], 1. to fish with a hook and line. 2. to use tricks to get something: as, he *angled* for her attention.

**angle iron,** an angled piece of iron or steel used for joining or reinforcing two beams, etc.

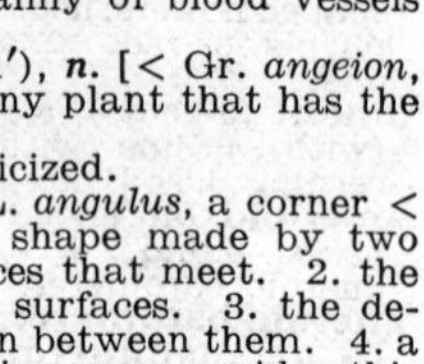

ANGLE IRON

**angle of incidence,** the angle made by a light ray with a line perpendicular to the surface on which the ray falls.

**an·gler** (aŋ′glēr), *n.* [< *angle* (to fish)], 1. a fisherman. 2. a schemer. 3. a saltwater fish that preys on other fish attracted by a filament on its head.

**An·gles** (aŋ′g'lz), *n.pl.* a Germanic people that settled in England in the 5th century A.D. —**An′gli·an** (-gli-ən), *adj. & n.*

**an·gle·worm** (aŋ′g'l-wūrm′), *n.* an earthworm: so called because used as fishing bait.

**An·gli·can** (aŋ′gli-kən), *adj.* [< L. < *Anglicus*, of the Angles], 1. of England; English. 2. of the Church of England or other church with the same faith and forms. *n.* a member of an Anglican church.

**An·gli·cism** (aŋ′glə-siz'm), *n.* 1. a word, idiom, or meaning peculiar to English, especially British English; Briticism. 2. a typically English trait, custom, etc. 3. the quality of being English.

**An·gli·cize, an·gli·cize** (aŋ′glə-sīz′), *v.t. & v.i.* [-CIZED, -CIZING], to change to English idiom, pronunciation, customs, etc. —**An′gli·ci·za′tion, an′gli·ci·za′tion** (-si-zā′shən), *n.*

**An·gli·fy** (aŋ′glə-fī′), *v.t.* [-FIED, -FYING], to Anglicize.

**an·gling** (aŋ′gliŋ), *n.* the act or art of fishing with hook and line.

**An·glo-,** a combining form meaning *English* or *English and*, as in *Anglophile, Anglo-American.*

**An·glo-A·mer·i·can** (aŋ′glō-ə-mer′ə-kən), *adj.* English and American. *n.* an American of English birth.

**An·glo-E·gyp·tian Sudan** (aŋ′glō-i-jip′shən), Sudan: the former name.

**An·glo-French** (aŋ′glō-french′), *adj.* English and French. *n* the French spoken in England by the Norman conquerors: see **Norman French.** Abbrev. **Anglo-Fr., A.-Fr., A.F., AF.**

**An·glo·ma·ni·a** (aŋ glō-mā′ni-ə), *n.* an exaggerated liking for and imitation of English customs, manners, institutions, etc.

**An·glo-Nor·man** (aŋ′glō-nôr′mən), *adj.* English and Norman. *n.* 1. a Norman settler in England after the Norman Conquest. 2. the French dialect of such settlers. Abbrev. **Anglo-Norm., A.-N., A.N., AN.**

**An·glo·phile** (aŋ′glə-fīl′), *n.* [*Anglo-* + *-phile*], one who is extremely fond of England, its people, customs, etc. *adj.* of Anglophiles.

**An·glo·phobe** (aŋ′glə-fōb′), *n.* a person who has Anglophobia. *adj.* of Anglophobes.

**An·glo·pho·bi·a** (aŋ′glə-fō′bi-ə), *n.* [*Anglo-* + *-phobia*], hatred or fear of England, its people, customs, influence, etc.

**An·glo-Sax·on** (aŋ′glō-sak′s'n), *n.* 1. a member of the Germanic peoples (Angles, Saxons, and Jutes) living in England before the Norman Conquest. 2. their language; Old English. 3. a person of English nationality or descent. *adj.* 1. of the Anglo-Saxons or their language. 2. of their descendants; English. Abbrev. **AS., A.S., A.-S., Ang.-Sax.**

**An·go·la** (aŋ-gō′lə), *n.* a Portuguese colony in southwest Africa: area, 486,079 sq. mi.; pop., 3,738,000.

**An·go·ra** (aŋ-gôr′ə, -gō′rə, aŋ′gə-rə), *n.* 1. Ankara. 2. a kind of cat with long, silky fur. 3. *a*) a kind of goat raised for its long, silky hair. *b*) a cloth made from this hair; mohair.

**an·gos·tu·ra** (aŋ′gəs-toor′ə, -tyoor′-), *n.* a bitter bark used as a tonic and as a flavoring in bitters.

**an·gry** (aŋ′gri), *adj.* [-GRIER, -GRIEST], 1. feeling, showing, or resulting from anger. 2. wild and stormy. 3. inflamed and sore. —**an′gri·ly** (-grə-li), *adv.*

**ang·strom, Ang·strom** (aŋ′strəm), *n.* [after A. J. *Angström*, 19th-c. Sw. physicist], one hundred-millionth of a centimeter, a unit used in measuring the length of light waves: symbol, λ. Also **Angstrom unit.**

**an·guish** (aŋ′gwish), *n.* [< OFr. < L. *angustia*, tightness < *angere*, to tighten, choke], great mental or physical pain; agony. *v.i. & v.t.* to feel or make feel such pain. —**an′guished** (-gwisht), *adj.*

**an·gu·lar** (aŋ′gyoo-lēr), *adj.* 1. having or forming an angle or angles; having sharp corners. 2. measured by an angle: as, *angular* distance. 3. lean; gaunt. 4. without ease or grace; stiff: as, an *angular* stride.

**an·gu·lar·i·ty** (aŋ′gyoo-lar′ə-ti), *n.* 1. the quality of being angular. 2. [*pl.* -TIES], an angular form or part.

**an·hy·dride** (an-hī′drīd, -drid), *n.* [< Gr. *anhydros* (see ANHYDROUS); + *-ide*], 1. an oxide that reacts with water to form an acid or a base. 2. any compound formed by the removal of water, usually from an acid. Also **an·hy′drid** (-drid).

**an·hy·drous** (an-hī′drəs), *adj.* [Gr. *anhydros* < *an-*, without + *hydōr*, water], 1. without water. 2. having no water of crystallization.

**an·il** (an′il), *n.* [Port. < Ar. *al*, the + *nīl*, blue], 1. a West Indian shrub from which indigo is made. 2. indigo.

**an·ile** (an′īl, ā′nīl), *adj.* [< L. < *anus*, old woman], like an old woman; mentally or physically weak.

**an·i·line** (an′'l-ēn′, -in, -īn′), *n.* [*anil* + *-ine*], a colorless, poisonous, oily liquid, $C_6H_5NH_2$, a derivative of benzene, used in making dyes. *adj.* made from aniline. Also **an′i·lin** (-in).

**aniline dye,** 1. any dye made from aniline. 2. commonly, any synthetic dye made from coal tar.
**a·nil·i·ty** (ə-nil′ə-ti), *n.* 1. the state of being anile. 2. [*pl.* -TIES], an anile act, etc.
**an·i·ma** (an′ə-mə), *n.* [L.], life principle; soul.
**an·i·mad·ver·sion** (an′ə-mad-vũr′zhən, -shən), *n.* [see ANIMADVERT], an unfavorable remark (*on* or *upon* something); blame.
**an·i·mad·vert** (an′ə-mad-vũrt′), *v.i.* [< L. < *animus*, mind + *ad-*, to + *vertere*, to turn], to comment unfavorably (*on* or *upon*); criticize.
**an·i·mal** (an′ə-m'l), *n.* [< L. < *anima*, breath, soul], 1. any living organism typically capable of moving about but not of making its own food by photosynthesis: distinguished from *plant.* 2. any four-footed creature; beast. 3. a brutish or inhuman person. *adj.* 1. of or like an animal or animals. 2. gross, bestial, etc.
**an·i·mal·cule** (an′ə-mal′kyool), *n.* [L. *animalculum*, dim. of *animal*], a very small or microscopic animal. **—an′i·mal′cu·lar,** *adj.*
**an·i·mal·cu·lum** (an′ə-mal′kyoo-ləm), *n.* [*pl.* -LA (-lə)], an animalcule.
**an·i·mal·ism** (an′ə-m'l-iz'm), *n.* 1. the activity, appetites, nature, etc. of animals. 2. the doctrine that man is a mere animal with no soul. **—an′i·mal·ist,** *n.* **—an′i·mal·is′tic,** *adj.*
**an·i·mal·i·ty** (an′ə-mal′ə-ti), *n.* 1. animal characteristics or nature. 2. the animal kingdom; animal life.
**an·i·mal·ize** (an′ə-m'l-īz′), *v.t.* [-IZED, -IZING], to make (a person) resemble a beast; make sensual; dehumanize.
**animal kingdom,** animals collectively, as distinguished from plants (vegetable kingdom).
**an·i·mal·ly** (an′ə-m'l-i), *adv.* physically, as distinguished from mentally or spiritually.
**animal magnetism,** hypnotism; mesmerism.
**an·i·mate** (an′ə-māt′; *for adj.*, -mit), *v.t.* [-MATED (-id), -MATING], [< L. pp. of *animare*, to fill with breath < *anima*, air, soul], 1. to give life to; bring to life. 2. to make gay or spirited. 3. to inspire. 4. to give motion to: as, the breeze *animated* the leaves. *adj.* 1. living; having life. 2. lively; spirited. **—an′i·mat′er, an′i·ma′tor,** *n.*
**an·i·mat·ed** (an′ə-māt′id), *adj.* 1. living; alive or seeming alive. 2. vigorous; lively.
**animated cartoon,** a kind of motion picture made by photographing a series of thousands of drawings, each slightly changed from the one before, so that the figures in them seem to move.
**an·i·ma·tion** (an′ə-mā shən), *n.* 1. an animating or being animated. 2. life. 3. vivacity. 4. the making of animated cartoons.
**‡a·ni·ma·to** (ä′nē-mä′tô), *adj.* & *adv.* [It.], in *music*, with animation: abbreviated **anim.**
**an·i·mism** (an′ə-miz'm), *n.* [< L. *anima*, air, soul; + *-ism*], 1. the belief that all life is produced by a spiritual force. 2. the belief that natural objects, as rocks, trees, etc., have souls. **—an′i·mist,** *n.* **—an′i·mis′tic,** *adj.*
**an·i·mos·i·ty** (an′ə-mos′ə-ti), *n.* [*pl.* -TIES], [< Fr. < L. *animositas*, spirit < *animus;* see ANIMUS], ill will; open or active hostility.
**an·i·mus** (an′ə-məs), *n.* [L., soul, mind, disposition, passion], 1. an animating force; intention to do something. 2. a grudge; animosity; hostility.
**an·i·on** (an′ī′ən), *n.* [< Gr. *anienai*, to go up < *ana-*, up + *ienai*, to go], a negative ion: in electrolysis, anions go toward the anode.
**an·ise** (an′is), *n.* [< Fr. < L. < Gr. *anēson*], 1. a plant of the carrot family. 2. its fragrant seed, used for flavoring and in medicine.
**an·i·seed** (an′i-sēd′), *n.* the seed of anise.
**an·i·sette** (an′i-zet′, -set′), *n.* [Fr., dim. < *anis;* see ANISE], a sweet, anise-flavored liqueur.
**An·jou** (an′jōō; Fr. än′zhōō′), *n.* an old province of western France.
**An·ka·ra** (äŋ′kə-rə, aŋ′-), *n.* the capital of Turkey: pop., 646,000: also **Angora.**
**an·kle** (aŋ′k'l), *n.* [AS. *ancleow*], 1. the joint that connects the foot and the leg. 2. the part of the leg between the foot and calf.
**an·kle·bone** (aŋ′k'l-bōn′), *n.* the bone of the ankle; talus; astragalus.
**an·klet** (aŋ klit), *n.* 1. anything worn around the ankle as a fetter or ornament. 2. a short sock.
**an·ky·lose** (aŋ′kə-lōs ), *v.t.* & *v.i.* [-LOSED (-lōst′), -LOSING], to stiffen or join by ankylosis: also sp. **anchylose.**
**an·ky·lo·sis** (aŋ′kə-lō′sis), *n.* [Gr. < *angkyloun*, to stiffen < *angkylos*, bent], 1. in *medicine*, a stiffening of a joint. 2. in *zoology*, a joining of bones or fibrous parts into a single part. Also sp. **anchylosis.** **—an′ky·lot′ic** (-lot′ik), *adj.*
**ann.,** 1. annual. 2. annuity.
**an·na** (an′ə), *n.* [Hind. *ānā*], a copper coin of India equal to 1/16 of one rupee.
**an·nal·ist** (an′'l-ist), *n.* one who writes annals. **—an′nal·is′tic,** *adj.*
**an·nals** (an′'lz), *n.pl.* [< L. < *annus*, year], 1. a written account of events year by year in chronological order. 2. historical records; history. 3. any journal containing reports of a society, etc.
**An·nam** (ə-nam′, an′am), *n.* a former state of French Indochina, now divided between North and South Vietnam.
**An·na·mese** (an′ə-mēz′), *adj.* 1. of Annam. 2. of the Annamese. *n.* 1. [*pl.* ANNAMESE], a native of Annam. 2. the language of the Annamese.
**An·nap·o·lis** (ə-nap′'l-is), *n.* the capital of Maryland, on Chesapeake Bay: pop., 23,000.
**Ann Ar·bor** (an′ är′bēr), a city in SE Michigan: pop., 67,000.
**Anne** (an), *n.* 1665–1714; queen of Great Britain and Ireland (1702–1714).
**an·neal** (ə-nēl′), *v.t.* [AS. *onælan*, to burn; *an-*, on + *ælan*, to burn < *æl*, fire], 1. to heat (glass, metals, etc.) and then cool slowly to prevent brittleness; hence, 2. to temper (the mind, will, etc.). **—an·neal′er,** *n.*
**an·ne·lid** (an′'l-id), *n.* [< Fr. < L. *annellus*, dim. of *anulus*, a ring], a worm with a body made of joined segments, as the earthworm. *adj.* of such worms.
**an·nex** (ə-neks′; *for n.*, an′eks), *v.t.* [< Fr. < L. pp. of *annectere* < *ad-*, to + *nectere*, to tie, bind], 1. to add on or attach, especially to something larger. 2. to incorporate into a state the territory of (another state). 3. to add to as a condition, consequence, etc. *n.* 1. an addition to a building. 2. an added part of a document, record, etc. **—an·nex′a·ble,** *adj.* **—an·nex′ment,** *n.*
**an·nex·a·tion** (an′ek-sā′shən), *n.* 1. an annexing or being annexed. 2. something annexed. **—an′nex·a′tion·ist,** *n.*
**An·nie Oak·ley** (an′i ōk′li), [after woman rifle expert (1860–1926) whose small targets resembled punched tickets], [Slang], a free ticket; pass.
**an·ni·hi·late** (ə-nī′ə-lāt′), *v.t.* [-LATED, -LATING], [< L. pp. of *annihilare*, to bring to nothing < *ad-*, to + *nihil*, nothing], to destroy entirely; demolish; make wholly ineffective. **—an·ni′hi·la·ble** (-lə-b'l), *adj.* **—an·ni′hi·la′tion,** *n.* **—an·ni′hi·la·tive,** *adj.* **—an·ni′hi·la′tor,** *n.*
**an·ni·ver·sa·ry** (an′ə-vũr′sẽr-i), *adj.* [< L. < *annus*, year + *vertere*, to turn], 1. occurring annually at the same date. 2. of an anniversary. *n.* [*pl.* -RIES (-iz)], 1. the yearly return of the monthly date of some event. 2. the celebration of this.
**‡an·no Do·mi·ni** (an′ō dom′ə-nī′), [L.], in the year of the Lord; in the (given) year since the beginning of the Christian era: abbrev. **A.D.**
**annot.,** 1. annotate. 2. annotation. 3. annotator.
**an·no·tate** (an′ō-tāt′), *v.t.* & *v.i.* [-TATED, -TATING], [< L. < *ad-*, to + *notare*, to mark < *nota*, a sign], to provide critical or explanatory notes for (a literary work, etc.). **—an′no·ta′tor,** *n.*
**an·nounce** (ə-nouns′), *v.t.* [-NOUNCED, -NOUNCING], [< OFr. < L. < *ad-*, to + *nuntiare*, to report < *nuntius*, messenger], 1. to give notice of formally; proclaim. 2. to say. 3. to make known the arrival of. 4. in *radio & TV*, to be an announcer for. *v.i.* to act as an announcer.**—an·nounce′ment,** *n.*
**an·nounc·er** (ə-noun′sẽr), *n.* 1. one who announces. 2. one who introduces radio or television programs, identifies the station, etc.
**an·noy** (ə-noi′), *v.t.* [< OFr. < L. < *in odio*, in aversion, at enmity], 1. to bother; vex. 2. to make angry. 3. to harm; injure; molest. **—an·noy′ing,** *adj.* **—an·noy′ing·ly,** *adv.*
**an·noy·ance** (ə-noi′əns), *n.* 1. an annoying or being annoyed. 2. a person or thing that annoys.
**an·nu·al** (an′yoo-əl), *adj.* [< OFr. < L. < *annus*, year], 1. of or measured by a year. 2. yearly. 3. for a year's time, work, etc.: as, an *annual* wage. 4. alive only one year or season. *n.* 1. a book or magazine published once a year. 2. a plant that lives only one year or season.
**an·nu·al·ly** (an′yoo-ə-li, -yool-i), *adv.* each year; every year; yearly.
**an·nu·i·tant** (ə-nōō′ə-tənt, -nū′-), *n.* a person receiving an annuity.
**an·nu·i·ty** (ə-nōō′ə-ti, -nū′-), *n.* [*pl.* -TIES], [< Fr. < ML. < L. *annus*, year], 1. a yearly payment of

---

money. 2. the right to receive such a payment. 3. an investment yielding fixed annual payments.

**an·nul** (ə-nul′), *v.t.* [-NULLED (-nuld′), -NULLING], [< Fr. < L. *annullare*, to bring to nothing < *ad-*, to + *nullum*, nothing], to do away with; nullify; cancel. —**an·nul′la·ble**, *adj.* —**an·nul′ment**, *n.*

**an·nu·lar** (an′yoo-lẽr), *adj.* [< L. < *annulus*, a ring], like or forming a ring.

**annular eclipse,** an eclipse in which a ring of sunlight can be seen around the edge of the moon.

**annular ligament,** the ligament surrounding the ankle joint or wrist joint.

**an·nu·let** (an′yoo-lit), *n.* [L. *annulus*, a ring; + *-et*], 1. a small ring. 2. in *architecture*, a ringlike molding near the top of a column.

**an·nu·lus** (an′yoo-ləs), *n.* [*pl.* -LI (-lī′), -LUSES (-ləs-iz)], [L.], any ringlike part or mark.

**an·num** (an′əm), *n.* [L.], a year.

**an·nun·ci·ate** (ə-nun′shi-āt′, -si-), *v.t.* [-ATED, -ATING], [< L. *annuntiare*], to announce.

**an·nun·ci·a·tion** (ə-nun′si-ā′shən, -shi-), *n.* 1. an announcing or being announced. 2. [A-], *a)* the angel Gabriel's announcement to Mary that she was to give birth to Jesus: Luke 1:26–38. *b)* the church festival (March 25) commemorating this.

**an·nun·ci·a·tor** (ə-nun′shi-ā′tẽr, -si-), *n.* 1. a person or thing that announces. 2. an electric indicator, as in hotels, to show the source of calls.

**an·ode** (an′ōd), *n.* [< Gr. < *ana-*, up + *hodos*, way], a positive electrode, as in a battery, radio tube, etc. —**an·od·ic** (an-od′ik), *adj.*

**an·od·ize** (an′ə-dīz′), *v.t.* [-IZED, -IZING], [< *anode* + *-ize*], to put a protective oxide film on (a light metal) by an electrolytic process.

**an·o·dyne** (an′ə-dīn′), *adj.* [< L. < Gr. < *an-*, without + *odynē*, pain], relieving or lessening pain. *n.* anything that relieves or lessens pain.

**a·noint** (ə-noint′), *v.t.* [< OFr. < L. < *in-*, on + *ungere*, to smear], 1. to pour or rub oil or ointment on. 2. to put oil on in a ceremony of consecration. —**a·noint′er**, *n.* —**a·noint′ment**, *n.*

**a·nom·a·lism** (ə-nom′′l-iz′m), *n.* 1. the state of being anomalous. 2. an anomaly. —**a·nom′a·lis′tic**, *adj.*

**a·nom·a·lous** (ə-nom′ə-ləs), *adj.* [< L. < Gr. < *an-*, not + *homalos* < *homos*, the same, common], deviating from the general rule; abnormal.

**a·nom·a·ly** (ə-nom′ə-li), *n.* [*pl.* -LIES], [< Fr. < L. < Gr. *anōmalia*, inequality; see ANOMALOUS], 1. departure from the regular arrangement or usual method; abnormality. 2. anything anomalous.

**a·non** (ə-non′), *adv.* [AS. *on an*, in one, together], 1. soon; shortly. 2. at another time. 3. [Archaic], immediately; at once. —**ever and anon,** now and then; once in a while.

**anon.,** anonymous.

**an·o·nym** (an′ə-nim), *n.* 1. a person who is anonymous. 2. a false name; pseudonym.

**an·o·nym·i·ty** (an′ə-nim′ə-ti), *n.* the quality or state of being anonymous.

**a·non·y·mous** (ə-non′ə-məs), *adj.* [< Gr. < *an-*, without + *onoma*, name], 1. with no name known or acknowledged. 2. given, written, etc. by a person whose name is withheld or unknown. —**a·non′y·mous·ly**, *adv.*

**a·noph·e·les** (ə-nof′ə-lēz′), *n.* [Gr. *anōphelēs*, harmful; *an-*, without + *ophelēs*, use], the mosquito that can transmit malaria.

**an·oth·er** (ə-nuth′ẽr), *adj.* [ME. *an other*], 1. an additional; one more. 2. a different. 3. some other: as, *another* Caesar. *pron.* 1. one additional. 2. a different one. 3. one of the same kind.

**an·ox·i·a** (an-ok′si-ə), *n.* [*an-*, not + *oxygen* + *-ia*], in *medicine*, an insufficiency of oxygen.

**ans.,** answer.

‡**An·schluss** (än′shloos), *n.* [G., < *anschliessen*, to join], a political union; especially, the annexation of Austria by Nazi Germany in 1938.

**an·swer** (an′sẽr), *n.* [< AS. < *and-*, against + *swerian*, to swear], 1. a reply to a question, letter, etc. 2. any retaliation: as, his *answer* was a well-aimed blow. 3. a solution to a problem. 4. in *law*, a defense. *v.i.* 1. to reply in words, by an action, etc. 2. to respond (with *to*): as, the horse *answered* to its rider's touch. 3. to be sufficient. 4. to be responsible (*to* a person *for* an action, etc.). 5. to agree (with *to*): as, he *answers* to the description. *v.t.* 1. to reply to in some way. 2. to comply with; serve: as, to *answer* a purpose. 3. to atone for. 4. to refute (an accusation, criticism, etc.). 5. to suit: as, he *answers* the description. —**answer back.** [Colloq.], to reply rudely or impertinently.

**an·swer·a·ble** (an′sẽr-ə-b'l), *adj.* 1. responsible; accountable. 2. that can be answered. 3. [Archaic], in proportion; corresponding. —**an′swer·a·bly**, *adv.*

**ant** (ant), *n.* [AS. *æmete*], any of a group of black or red insects, generally wingless, that live in colonies. —**ant′like′**, *adj.*

ANTS

A, pupa; B, female (after loss of wings); C, male (with wings); D, worker (3/8 in. long)

**-ant,** [Fr. < L. *-antem* or *-entem*, acc. ppr. ending], a suffix used in forming: 1. adjectives meaning *-ing*, as in *defiant, radiant.* 2. nouns meaning *a person* or *thing that —s*, as in *occupant, accountant.*

**ant.,** 1. antiquity; antiquities. 2. antonym.

**ant·ac·id** (ant-as′id), *adj.* [< *anti-* + *acid*], counteracting acidity. *n.* an antacid substance.

**An·tae·us** (an-tē′əs), *n.* in *Gr. mythology*, a giant wrestler who was invincible as long as he was touching the earth. —**An·tae′an** (-ən), *adj.*

**an·tag·o·nism** (an-tag′ə-niz′m), *n.* [see ANTAGONIZE], 1. the state of being in active opposition (*to* or *against* someone or something); hostility. 2. an opposing force, principle, etc.

**an·tag·o·nist** (an-tag′ə-nist), *n.* 1. adversary; opponent. 2. a muscle that counteracts another.

**an·tag·o·nis·tic** (an-tag′ə-nis′tik), *adj.* 1. opposing; hostile. 2. counteracting. —**an·tag′o·nis′ti·cal·ly** (-ti-k'l-i, -tik-li), *adv.*

**an·tag·o·nize** (an-tag′ə-nīz′), *v.t.* [-NIZED, -NIZING], [< Gr. < *anti-*, against + *agōn*, a contest], 1. to contend against; oppose. 2. to incur the dislike of. *v.i.* to act antagonistically.

**ant·al·ka·li** (ant-al′kə-lī′), *n.* [*pl.* -LIES, -LIS], [< *anti-* + *alkali*], a substance that counteracts alkalinity.

**ant·arc·tic** (ant-ärk′tik), *adj.* [see ANTI- & ARCTIC], of or near the South Pole or the region around it. *n.* 1. Antarctica. 2. the Antarctic Circle.

**Ant·arc·ti·ca** (ant-ärk′ti-kə), *n.* a region of ice fields (c. 5 000,000 sq. mi.) about the South Pole.

**Antarctic Circle, antarctic circle,** an imaginary circle parallel to the equator, 23°30′ from the South Pole.

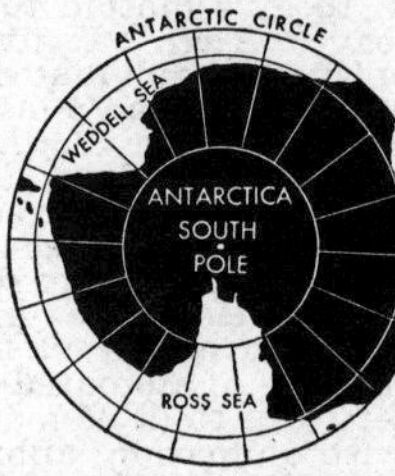


ANTARCTIC CIRCLE

**Antarctic Continent,** Antarctica.

**Antarctic Ocean,** the ocean surrounding Antarctica.

**Antarctic Zone,** all of the region south of the Antarctic Circle.

**An·tar·es** (an-târ′ēz), *n.* the brightest star in the constellation Scorpio.

**ant bear,** 1. a large South American anteater. 2. the aardvark.

**an·te** (an′ti), *n.* [L., before], 1. in *poker*, the stake that each player must put into the pool before receiving cards; hence, 2. the amount one must pay as his share. *v.t. & v.i.* [-TEED or TED (-tid), -TEING], 1. in *poker*, to put in (one's stake). 2. to pay (one's share). Also **ante up.**

**an·te-,** [< L. *ante*, before], a prefix meaning: 1. *before, prior to*, as in *antecedent, ante-Victorian.* 2. *before, in front of*, as in *anteroom.*

**ant·eat·er** (ant′ēt′ẽr), *n.* any of several mammals that feed mainly on ants: anteaters have a long sticky tongue and a long snout.

**an·te·bel·lum** (an′ti-bel′əm), *adj.* [L.], before the war; specif., before the American Civil War.

**an·te·cede** (an′tə-sēd′), *v.t. & v.i.* [-CEDED (-id), -CEDING], [< L. < *ante-*, before + *cedere*, to go], to precede.

**an·te·ced·ence** (an′tə-sēd′'ns), *n.* [see ANTECEDE], 1. priority; precedence. 2. in *astronomy*, retrograde motion. Also **an′te·ced′en·cy** (-'n-si).

**an·te·ced·ent** (an′tə-sēd′'nt), *adj.* [see ANTECEDE], prior; previous. *n.* 1. any thing prior to another. 2. anything logically preceding. 3. *pl.* one's ancestry, past life, etc. 4. in *grammar*, the word, phrase, or clause to which a pronoun refers. 5. in *mathematics*, the first term of a ratio; the first or third term of a proportion. —**an′te·ced′ent·ly**, *adv.*

**an·te·cham·ber** (an′ti-chām bẽr), *n.* [see ANTE- & CHAMBER], a smaller room leading into a larger or main room.

**an·te·date** (an′ti-dāt′, an′ti-dāt′), *v.t.* 1. to assign too early a date to. 2. to come before in time. 3. to anticipate. *n.* [Rare], a date given that is earlier than the right one.

**an·te·di·lu·vi·an** (an′ti-di-lōō′vi-ən), *adj.* [< *ante-* + L. *diluvium*, a flood], 1. of the time before the Flood; hence, 2. very old; old-fashioned. *n.* an antediluvian person or thing.

**an·te·lope** (an′t'l-ōp′), *n.* [*pl.* -LOPES, -LOPE; see PLURAL, II, D, 1], [< OFr. < ML. < Gr. *antholops*, deer], 1. a swift, cud-chewing, horned animal related to oxen and goats and resembling the deer. 2. leather made from its hide.
**‡an·te me·ri·di·em** (an′ti mə-rid′i-em), [L.], before noon: abbrev. **A.M., AM, a.m.**
**an·ten·na** (an-ten′ə), *n.* [L., sail yard], 1. [*pl.* -NAE (-ē), -NAS], either of a pair of sense organs on the head of an insect, crab, etc.; feeler. 2. [*pl.* -NAS], in *radio & television*, an arrangement of wires, metal rods, etc. used in sending and receiving the electromagnetic waves; aerial.
**an·te·pe·nult** (an′ti-pē′nəlt), *n.* [see ANTE- & PENULT], the second syllable from the last in a word, as *-lu-* in *an·te·di·lu·vi·an.*
**an·te·pe·nul·ti·mate** (an′ti-pi-nul′tə-mit), *adj.* second from the last; third from the end. *n.* 1. anything second from the last. 2. an antepenult.
**an·te·ri·or** (an-têr′i-ēr), *adj.* [L., compar. of *ante*, before], 1. forward (in space): opposed to *posterior.* 2. preceding (in time); earlier. **—an·te′ri·or·ly,** *adv.*
**an·te·room** (an′ti-rōōm′, -room′), *n.* [*ante-* + *room*], a room through which another room is entered.
**an·them** (an′thəm), *n.* [< AS. < ML. < Gr. *antiphōnos*, sounding back < *anti-*, over against + *phōnē*, voice], 1. a religious choral song usually based on words from the Bible. 2. the official national song of a country.
**an·ther** (an′thēr), *n.* [< Fr. < L. < Gr. < *anthos*, a flower], the part of a stamen that contains the pollen.
**an·ther·id·i·um** (an′thēr-id′i-əm), *n.* [*pl.* -IA (-ə)], in seedless plants, as the fern, the organ in which the male sex cells are developed. **—an′ther·id′i·al,** *adj.*
**an·thol·o·gist** (an-thol′ə-jist), *n.* a person who compiles an anthology.
**an·thol·o·gize** (an-thol′ə-jīz′), *v.i.* [-GIZED, -GIZING], to make anthologies. *v.t.* to make an anthology of.
**an·thol·o·gy** (an-thol′ə-ji), *n.* [*pl.* -GIES], [L. & Gr. *anthologia*, a garland < *anthos*, flower + *legein*, to gather], a collection of poems, stories, etc. **—an·tho·log·i·cal** (an′thə-loj′i-k'l), *adj.*
**An·tho·ny, Mark** (an′thə-ni, -tə-ni), see **Antonius, Marcus.**
**An·tho·ny, Susan Brow·nell** (brou-nel′ an′thə-ni), 1820–1906; American suffragist leader.
**an·tho·zo·an** (an′thə-zō′ən), *n.* [< Gr. *anthos*, flower + *zōion*, animal; + *-an*], any of a class of sea organisms, comprising corals, sea anemones, etc. *adj.* of the anthozoans.
**an·thra·cene** (an′thrə-sēn′), *n.* [< Gr. *anthrax*, coal; + *-ene*], a crystalline hydrocarbon, $C_{14}H_{10}$, obtained from coal tar and used in making dyes.
**an·thra·cite** (an′thrə-sīt′), *n.* [< Gr. *anthrax*, coal], hard coal, which gives much heat and little smoke. **—an′thra·cit′ic** (-sit′ik), *adj.*
**an·thrax** (an′thraks), *n.* [*pl.* -THRACES (-thrə-sēz′)], [L.; Gr., coal, carbuncle], 1. a boil or carbuncle. 2. an infectious disease of cattle, sheep, etc., which can be transmitted to man: it is characterized by malignant pustules. **—an′thra·coid′** (-thrə-koid′), *adj.*
**an·thro·po-,** [< Gr. *anthrōpos*, man], a combining form meaning *man, human*, as in *anthropology*: also, before a vowel, **anthrop-.**
**an·thro·po·cen·tric** (an′thrə-pə-sen′trik), *adj.* [*anthropo-* + *centric*], that considers man as the central fact, or final aim, of the universe.
**an·thro·po·gen·e·sis** (an′thrə-pə-jen′ə-sis), *n.* [*anthropo-* + *genesis*], the study of man's origin and development. Also **an′thro·pog′e·ny** (-poj′ə-ni).
**an·thro·poid** (an′thrə-poid′), *adj.* [*anthrop-* + *-oid*], manlike; resembling man; especially, designating or of any of the most highly developed apes, as the chimpanzee and gorilla. *n.* any anthropoid ape. **—an′thro·poid′al,** *adj.*
**an·thro·pol·o·gist** (an′thrə-pol′ə-jist), *n.* a student of or specialist in anthropology.
**an·thro·pol·o·gy** (an′thrə-pol′ə-ji), *n.* [*anthropo-* + *-logy*], the study of the races, physical and mental characteristics, distribution, customs, etc. of mankind. **—an′thro·po·log′i·cal** (-pə-loj′i-k'l), **an′thro·po·log′ic,** *adj.* **—an′thro·po·log′i·cal·ly,** *adv.*
**an·thro·pom·e·try** (an′thrə-pom′ə-tri), *n.* [*anthropo-* + *-metry*], the part of anthropology having to do with the comparative measurement of the human body. **—an′thro·po·met′ric** (-pə-met′rik), **an′thro·po·met′ri·cal,** *adj.* **—an′thro·po·met′ri·cal·ly,** *adv.*
**an·thro·po·mor·phic** (an′thrə-pə-môr′fik), *adj.* of, characterized by, or like anthropomorphism. **—an′thro·po·mor′phi·cal·ly,** *adv.*
**an·thro·po·mor·phism** (an′thrə-pə-môr′fiz'm), *n.* [*anthropomorphous* + *-ism*], the attributing of human shape or characteristics to gods, objects, animals, etc. **—an′thro·po·mor′phist,** *n.*
**an·thro·po·mor·phize** (an′thrə-pə-môr′fīz), *v.t. & v.i.* [-PHIZED, -PHIZING], to attribute human shape or characteristics to (gods, objects, etc.).
**an·thro·po·mor·phous** (an′thrə-pə-môr′fəs), *adj.* [< Gr. < *anthrōpos*, a man + *morphē*, form, shape], having human shape and appearance.
**an·thro·poph·a·gi** (an′thrə-pof′ə-jī′), *n.pl.* [*sing.* -GUS (-gəs)], [< Gr. < *anthrōpos*, man + *phagein*, to eat], cannibals. **—an′thro·po·phag′ic** (-pə-faj′ik), **an′thro·poph′a·gous** (-gəs), *adj.*
**an·ti** (an′tī, an′ti), *n.* [*pl.* -TIS], [see ANTI-], [Colloq.], a person opposed to some policy, proposal, etc. *adj.* [Colloq.], opposed; against.
**an·ti-** (an′ti; *now often* an′tī), [< Gr. < *anti*, against], a prefix meaning: 1. *against, hostile to*, as in *anti-Semitism.* 2. *that counteracts, that operates against*, as in *antiaircraft.* 3. *that prevents, cures*, or *neutralizes*, as in *antitoxin.* 4. *opposite, reverse*, as in *antiperistalsis.* 5. *rivaling*, as in *antipope.* Also, before a vowel, sometimes **ant-,** as in *antacid.*
**an·ti·air·craft** (an′ti-âr′kraft, -kräft), *adj.* used for defense against enemy aircraft: as, an *antiaircraft* gun: abbrev. **A.A.**
**an·ti·bac·te·ri·al** (an′ti-bak-têr′i-əl), *adj.* that checks the growth or effect of bacteria.
**an·ti·bal·lis·tic missile** (an′ti-bə-lis′tik), a ballistic missile intended to intercept and destroy another ballistic missile in flight.
**an·ti·bi·o·sis** (an′ti-bī-ō′sis), *n.* [*anti-* + Gr. *biōsis*, way of life], in *biology*, an association between organisms which is harmful to one of them.
**an·ti·bi·ot·ic** (an′ti-bī-ot′ik), *adj.* 1. of antibiosis. 2. destroying, or stopping the growth of, bacteria. *n.* an antibiotic substance produced by a living organism.
**an·ti·bod·y** (an′ti-bod′i), *n.* [*pl.* -IES], [*anti-* + *body*], a protein produced in the body in response to contact of the body with an antigen, serving to neutralize the antigen.
**an·tic** (an′tik), *adj.* [< It. < L. *antiquus;* see ANTIQUE], [Archaic], fantastic and queer; grotesque. *n.* 1. a ludicrous act, gesture, etc.; caper. 2. [Archaic], a clown; fool; buffoon. *v.i.* to do antics; caper.
**an·ti·christ** (an′ti-krīst′), *n.* 1. an opponent of Christ. 2. [A-], in the *Bible*, the great antagonist of Christ: I John 2:18.
**an·tic·i·pant** (an-tis ə-pənt), *adj.* expecting; anticipating (with *of*). *n.* one who anticipates.
**an·tic·i·pate** (an-tis′ə-pāt′), *v.t.* [-PATED, -PATING], [< L. < *ante-*, before + *capere*, to take], 1. to expect; look forward to. 2. to make happen earlier than due: as, to *anticipate* a reaction to a cue. 3. to forestall: as, he *anticipated* his opponent's blows. 4. to foresee (a wish) and perform in advance. 5. to use or enjoy in advance: as, to *anticipate* an inheritance. 6. to do something before (someone else). **—an·tic′i·pa′tor,** *n.*
**an·tic·i·pa·tion** (an-tis′ə-pā′shən), *n.* 1. an anticipating or being anticipated. 2. something anticipated. 3. foreknowledge; presentiment.
**an·tic·i·pa·tive** (an-tis′ə-pā′tiv), *adj.* inclined to anticipate. **—an·tic′i·pa′tive·ly,** *adv.*
**an·tic·i·pa·to·ry** (an-tis′ə-pə-tôr′i, -tō′ri), *adj.* anticipating. **—an·tic′i·pa·to′ri·ly,** *adv.*
**an·ti·cler·i·cal** (an′ti-kler′i-k'l), *adj.* opposed to the clergy or church, especially to its political influence. **—an′ti·cler′i·cal·ism,** *n.*
**an·ti·cli·max** (an′ti-klī′maks), *n.* [*anti-* + *climax*], 1. a sudden drop from the dignified or important to the commonplace or trivial. 2. a descent which is in disappointing contrast to a preceding rise. **—an′ti·cli·mac′tic** (-mak′tik), *adj.*
**an·ti·cline** (an′ti-klīn′), *n.* [< *anti-* + Gr. *klinein*, to incline], in *geology*, a fold of stratified rock in which the strata slope downward in opposite directions from the crest: opposed to *syncline.* **—an′ti·cli′nal,** *adj.*
**an·ti·cy·clone** (an′ti-sī′klōn), *n.* an atmospheric condition in which outward-spiraling winds move away from a center of high pressure. **—an′ti·cy·clon′ic** (-sī-klon′ik), *adj.*
**an·ti·dote** (an′ti-dōt′), *n.* [< L. < Gr. < *anti-*, against + *dotos*, given < *didonai*, to give], 1. a remedy to counteract a poison. 2. anything that

tends to counteract an evil. —**an'ti·dot'al,** *adj.* —**an'ti·dot'al·ly,** *adv.*

**An·tie·tam** (an-tē'təm), *n.* a creek in western Maryland: site of a Civil War battle (1862).

**an·ti·fed·er·al·ist** (an'ti-fed'ēr-əl-ist), *n.* 1. one opposed to federalism. 2. [A-], a member of the political party (**Antifederalist Party,** 1781–1789) which opposed the adoption of the Constitution of the United States.

**an·ti·freeze** (an'ti-frēz'), *n.* a substance of low freezing point, as alcohol, used, especially in automobile radiators, to prevent freezing.

**an·ti·fric·tion** (an'ti-frik'shən), *adj.* reducing friction. *n.* an antifriction lubricant, etc.

**an·ti·gen** (an'tə-jən), *n.* [*anti-* + *-gen*], a substance which causes the production of an antibody when introduced directly into the body.

**An·tig·o·ne** (an-tig'ə-nē'), *n.* in *Gr. legend,* the daughter of Oedipus: she defied her uncle by performing funeral rites for her brother.

**An·ti·gua** (an-tē'gwə, -gə), *n.* a British island in the West Indies: pop., 54,000.

**an·ti·his·ta·mine** (an ti-his'tə-mēn', -min), *n.* any of several drugs used to minimize the action of histamine in certain allergic conditions: it is variously claimed that they relieve the symptoms in asthma, hay fever, the common cold, etc.

**an·ti·knock** (an'ti-nok'), *n.* a substance added to the fuel of internal-combustion engines to do away with noise made by too rapid combustion.

**An·til·les** (an-til'ēz), *n.pl.* a group of islands in the West Indies: see **Greater Antilles, Lesser Antilles.** —**An·til·le·an** (an'ti-lē'ən, an-til'i-), *adj. & n.*

**an·ti·log·a·rithm** (an'ti-lôg'ə-rith'm, -log'-), *n.* the number corresponding to a logarithm: as, the *antilogarithm* of 1 is 10.

**an·ti·ma·cas·sar** (an'ti-mə-kas'ēr), *n.* [*anti-* + *macassar,* a former hair oil], a small cover on the back or arms of a chair, etc. to prevent soiling.

**an·ti·mat·ter** (an'ti-mat'ēr), *n.* a form of matter in which some property of the constituent particles is the reverse of that in ordinary matter.

**an·ti·mis·sile** (an'ti-mis''l), *adj.* designed as a defense against ballistic missiles.

**an·ti·mo·ny** (an'tə-mō ni), *n.* [< Fr. < ML. *antimonium*: the symbol Sb < L. name, *stibium*], a silvery-white, brittle, metallic chemical element found only in combination: used in alloys to harden them: symbol, Sb; at. wt., 121.76; at. no., 51.

**An·ti·och** (an'ti-ok'), *n.* the capital of ancient Syria: now a city in southern Turkey: pop., 46,000: Arabic name, *Antakiya.*

**an·ti·par·ti·cle** (an'ti-par'ti-k'l), *n.* any of the constituent particles of antimatter.

‡**an·ti·pas·to** (än'tē-päs'tô), *n.* [It.; *anti-* (L. *ante*), before + *pasto* < L. *pastus,* food], salted fish, meat, etc., served as an appetizer.

**an·ti·pa·thet·ic** (an'ti-pə-thet'ik), *adj.* 1. having antipathy. 2. opposed or antagonistic in character, tendency, etc. Also **an'ti·pa·thet'i·cal.** —**an'ti·pa·thet'i·cal·ly,** *adv.*

**an·tip·a·thy** (an-tip'ə-thi), *n.* [*pl.* -THIES], [< Gr. < *anti-,* against + *pathein,* to feel], 1. a definite dislike; repugnance; aversion. 2. the object of such dislike.

**an·ti·per·son·nel** (an'ti-pēr-sə-nel'), *adj.* intended to destroy people rather than material objects: as, *antipersonnel* mines.

**an·ti·phlo·gis·tic** (an'ti-flō-jis'tik), *adj.* [*anti-* + *phlogistic*], counteracting inflammation. *n.* an antiphlogistic medicine, diet, etc.

**an·ti·phon** (an'tə-fon ), *n.* [< ML. < Gr.; see ANTHEM], a hymn, psalm, etc. chanted or sung in responsive, alternating parts.

**an·tiph·o·nal** (an-tif'ə-n'l), *adj.* of or like an antiphon; sung or chanted in alternation. Also **an'ti·phon'ic** (an'ti-fon'ik). *n.* a collection of antiphons. Also **an·tiph'o·nar'y** (-ner'i), [*pl.* -IES].

**an·tip·o·dal** (an-tip'ə-d'l), *adj.* 1. of the antipodes; on the other side of the earth. 2. exactly opposite or contrary.

**an·ti·pode** (an'ti-pōd'), *n.* an exact opposite.

**an·tip·o·de·an** (an-tip'ə-dē'ən, an'ti-pə-), *adj.* 1. antipodal. 2. Australian. *n.* an Australian.

**an·tip·o·des** (an-tip'ə-dēz'), *n.pl.* [L.; Gr. pl. of *antipous; anti-,* opposite + *pous, podos,* foot], 1. any two places directly opposite each other on the earth. 2. [construed as pl. or sing.], a place on the other side of the earth: in British usage, New Zealand and Australia are usually meant. 3. two opposite or contrary things. 4. [construed as pl. or sing.], the exact opposite. 5. [A-], a group of islands southeast of New Zealand.

**an·ti·pope** (an'ti-pōp'), *n.* a pope set up against the one chosen by church laws, as in a schism.

**an·ti·py·ret·ic** (an'ti-pī-ret'ik), *adj.* [*anti-* + *pyretic*], reducing fever. *n.* anything that reduces fever.

**an·ti·quar·i·an** (an'ti-kwâr'i-ən), *adj.* 1. of antiques. 2. of antiquaries. *n.* an antiquary.

**an·ti·quar·y** (an'ti-kwer'i), *n.* [*pl.* -IES], one who collects or studies antiquities.

**an·ti·quate** (an'ti-kwāt'), *v.t.* [-QUATED, -QUATING], [see ANTIQUE], to make old or obsolete; cause to become old-fashioned. —**an'ti·quat'ed,** *adj.*

**an·tique** (an-tēk'), *adj.* [Fr. < L. *antiquus,* ancient < *ante,* before], 1. of ancient times; old. 2. out-of-date. 3. of ancient Greece or Rome; classical. 4. of or in the style of a former period. *n.* 1. an ancient relic. 2. the ancient style, especially of Greek or Roman sculpture, etc. 3. a piece of furniture, etc. of a former period. 4. in *printing,* a variety of boldface type. **This line is in antique.** *v.t.* [-TIQUED (-tēkt'), -TIQUING], to make look antique.

**an·tiq·ui·ty** (an-tik'wə-ti), *n.* [*pl.* -TIES], [see ANTIQUE], 1. the early period of history, especially before the Middle Ages. 2. great age; oldness: as, a book of great *antiquity.* 3. the people of ancient times. 4. *usually in pl.* a relic, monument, etc. of the distant past. 5. *usually pl.* ancient manners, customs, etc.

**an·ti·ra·chit·ic** (an'ti-rə-kit'ik), *adj.* [*anti-* + *rachitic*], that cures or prevents rickets. *n.* a remedy or preventive for rickets.

**an·ti·rust** (an'ti-rust'), *adj.* that prevents rust. *n.* something that prevents rust.

**an·ti·scor·bu·tic** (an'ti-skôr-bū'tik), *adj.* [*anti-* + *scorbutic*], that cures or prevents scurvy. *n.* a remedy or preventive for scurvy.

**an·ti-Sem·i·tism** (an'ti-sem'ə-tiz'm), *n.* 1. prejudice against Jews; dislike or fear of Jews and Jewish things. 2. discrimination against or persecution of Jews. —**an'ti-Sem'ite** (-īt), *n.* —**an'ti-Se·mit'ic** (-sə-mit'ik), *adj.*

**an·ti·sep·sis** (an'ti-sep'sis), *n.* [*anti-* + *sepsis*], 1. the condition of being antiseptic. 2. the use of antiseptics.

**an·ti·sep·tic** (an'ti-sep'tik), *adj.* [*anti-* + *septic*], 1. preventing infection, decay, etc.; inhibiting the action of microorganisms. 2. using antiseptics. *n.* any antiseptic substance, as alcohol, etc. —**an'ti·sep'ti·cal·ly,** *adv.*

**an·ti·slav·er·y** (an'ti-slāv'ēr-i), *adj.* against slavery.

**an·ti·so·cial** (an'ti-sō'shəl), *adj.* 1. unsociable. 2. against the welfare of the people generally.

**an·ti·spas·mod·ic** (an'ti-spaz-mod'ik), *adj.* relieving spasms. *n.* a remedy for spasms.

**an·tis·tro·phe** (an-tis'trə-fi), *n.* [Gr. < *anti-,* opposite + *strephein,* to turn], 1. the movement, left to right, made by the chorus of an ancient Greek play in answering a strophe. 2. the part of a choric song performed while making this movement. —**an·ti·stroph·ic** (an'ti-strof'ik), *adj.*

**an·ti·tank** (an'ti-taŋk'), *adj.* for use against tanks in war: abbrev. **AT** (no period).

**an·tith·e·sis** (an-tith'ə-sis), *n.* [*pl.* -SES (-sēz')], [Gr. < *anti-,* against + *tithenai,* to place], 1. a contrast of thoughts, as in the sentence "You are going; I am staying." 2. a contrast or opposition. 3. the exact opposite: as, joy is the *antithesis* of sorrow. —**an·ti·thet·ic** (an'ti-thet'ik), **an'ti·thet'i·cal,** *adj.* —**an'ti·thet'i·cal·ly,** *adv.*

**an·ti·tox·in** (an'ti-tok'sin), *n.* [*anti-* + *toxin*], 1. a substance formed in the blood to act against a specific toxin. 2. a serum, as from an infected animal, containing an antitoxin, injected into a person to prevent a disease, as tetanus. Also **an'ti·tox'ine** (-sin, -sēn). —**an'ti·tox'ic,** *adj.*

**an·ti·trades** (an'ti-trādz'), *n.pl.* winds that blow above and opposite to the trade winds.

**an·ti·trust** (an'ti-trust'), *adj.* opposed to or regulating trusts, or business monopolies.

**ant·ler** (ant'lēr), *n.* [< OFr. < L. < *ante-,* before + *ocularis,* of the eyes], 1. the branched horn of any animal of the deer family. 2. any branch of such a horn. —**ant'lered,** *adj.*

**ant lion,** 1. an insect whose larva digs a pit in which to trap and eat ants, etc. 2. its larva.

**Antoinette, Marie,** see **Marie Antoinette.**

**An·to·ni·nus, Marcus Aurelius** (an'tə-nī'nəs), see **Marcus Aurelius.**

**An·to·ni·us, Mar·cus** (mär'kəs an-tō'ni-əs), (*Mark,* or *Marc, Antony* or *Anthony*), 83?–30 B.C.; Roman general and triumvir.

**an·to·nym** (an'tə-nim'), *n.* [Gr. < *anti-,* opposite + *onyma,* name], a word whose meaning is opposite to that of another word.

**an·trum** (an'trəm), *n.* [*pl.* -TRUMS, -TRA (-trə)], [L.; Gr. *antron,* cave], 1. a cavity. 2. either of a pair of sinuses in the upper jaw.

**Ant·werp** (ant'wērp), *n.* 1. a province of northern Belgium. 2. its capital: pop., 263,000.

**A·nu·bis** (ə-nū'bis, -nōō'-), *n.* in *Egyptian religion*, a god with the head of a jackal, who led the dead to judgment.

**a·nus** (ā'nəs), *n.* [*pl.* -NUSES (-iz), -NI (-nī)], [L.], the opening at the lower end of the alimentary canal.

**an·vil** (an'vil), *n.* [AS. *onfilte* < *on-*, on + hyp. *filtan*, to beat], 1. an iron or steel block on which metal objects are hammered into shape. 2. in *anatomy*, the incus.

ANVIL

**anx·i·e·ty** (aŋ-zī'ə-ti), *n.* [*pl.* -TIES], [see ANXIOUS], 1. a state of being uneasy or worried about what may happen. 2. an eager and often slightly worried desire: as, *anxiety* to do well.

**anx·ious** (aŋk'shəs, aŋ'-), *adj.* [< L. < *angere*, to choke], 1. apprehensive; worried. 2. causing anxiety. 3. eagerly wishing. —**anx'·ious·ly,** *adv.*

**anxious seat,** at revival meetings, a bench for those with a troubled conscience who seek salvation.

**an·y** (en'i), *adj.* [AS. *ænig* < *an*, one + *-y*], 1. one (no matter which) of more than two: as, *any* boy may go. 2. some: as, do you have *any* money? 3. every: as, *any* child can tell. *pron. sing. & pl.* any person or persons (of more than two); any amount or number. *adv.* to any degree or extent; at all: as, is he *any* better?

**an·y·bod·y** (en'i-bud'i, -bod'-), *pron.* 1. any person; anyone. 2. a person of fame or importance.

**an·y·how** (en'i-hou'), *adv.* 1. in any manner or way. 2. at any rate; in any case. 3. carelessly.

**an·y·one** (en'i-wun'), *pron.* any person; anybody.

**any one,** any single (person or thing).

**an·y·thing** (en'i-thiŋ'), *pron.* any thing; any event, fact, etc. *n.* a thing, no matter of what kind. *adv.* in any way; at all. —**anything but,** not at all.

**an·y·way** (en'i-wā'), *adv.* 1. in any manner or way. 2. at any rate; at least. 3. haphazardly.

**an·y·where** (en'i-hwâr'), *adv.* 1. in, at, or to any place. 2. [Colloq.], at all; to any extent. —**get anywhere,** [Colloq.], to achieve anything.

**an·y·wise** (en'i-wīz'), *adv.* in any manner at all.

**An·zac** (an'zak), *n.* a soldier in the Australian and New Zealand Army Corps. *adj.* of the Anzacs.

**a/o, A/O.,** account of.

**A-OK** (ā'ō-kā'), *adj.* [*All OK*], [Colloq.], excellent, fine, in working order, etc.: a generalized term of commendation: also **A-Okay.**

**A one** (ā' wun'), [Colloq.], first-class; superior: also **A 1, A number 1.**

**a·o·rist** (ā'ə-rist), *n.* [< Gr. < *a-*, without + *horos*, a limit], a tense of Greek verbs expressing simple past time without further qualification. *adj.* of or in this tense. —**a'o·ris'tic,** *adj.*

**a·or·ta** (ā-ôr'tə), *n.* [*pl.* -TAS, -TAE (-tē)], [< Gr. < *aeirein*, to raise], the main artery of the body, carrying blood from the left ventricle of the heart to all parts except the lungs.

**a·ou·dad** (ä'oo-dad'), *n.* [Fr.; Moorish *audad*], a wild North African sheep with large, curved horns.

**AP, A.P., Æ,** Associated Press.

**a·pace** (ə-pās'), *adv.* at a fast pace; swiftly.

**A·pach·e** (ə-pach'i), *n.* [*pl.* -ES (-iz), APACHE], [? < Zuñi *ápachu*, enemy], a member of a tribe of fierce, nomadic Indians of the southwestern U. S.

**a·pache** (ə-päsh', -pash'; Fr. à'påsh'), *n.* [*pl.* -ES (-iz; Fr. -påsh'), APACHE], [Fr. < *Apache*], a gangster of Paris. *adj.* designating a dance which represents an apache handling his girl brutally.

**a·pa·nage** (ap'ə-nij), *n.* appanage.

**a·part** (ə-pärt'), *adv.* [< OFr. < L. *ad*, to, at + *pars*, a part, side], 1. to one side; aside. 2. away in place or time. 3. away from one another. 4. independently in use, etc.: as, viewed *apart*. 5. in or to pieces. *adj.* separated: used predicatively. —**apart from,** other than; besides. —**take apart,** to reduce (a whole) to its parts.

**a·part·heid** (ə-pärt'hīt), *n.* [S.Afr.D., apartness], in South Africa, the policy of strict racial segregation imposed on the native colored peoples.

**a·part·ment** (ə-pärt'mənt), *n.* [< Fr. < It.; see APART], 1. a suite of rooms to live in. 2. a room.

**apartment house,** a building in which the rooms are arranged and rented as apartments.

**ap·a·thet·ic** (ap'ə-thet'ik), *adj.* [< *apathy*, after *pathetic*], 1. feeling no emotion; impassive. 2. not interested; indifferent. Also **ap'a·thet'i·cal.** —**ap'a·thet'i·cal·ly,** *adv.*

**ap·a·thy** (ap'ə-thi), *n.* [*pl.* -THIES], [< Fr. < L. < Gr. < *a-*, without + *pathos*, emotion], 1. lack of emotion. 2. lack of interest; indifference.

**ape** (āp), *n.* [AS. *apa*], 1. a chimpanzee, gorilla, orangutan, or gibbon; any of the anthropoid apes. 2. any monkey. 3. one who imitates; mimic. *v.t.* [APED (āpt), APING], to imitate; mimic. —**ape'like',** *adj.*

**Ap·en·nines** (ap'ə-nīnz'), *n.pl.* a mountain range in central Italy.

**a·pe·ri·ent** (ə-pêr'i-ənt), *adj. & n.* [< L.; see APERTURE], laxative. Also **a·per'i·tive** (-per'ə-tiv).

**‡a·pé·ri·tif** (à'pā'rē'tēf'), *n.* [Fr. < L.; see APERTURE], an alcoholic drink taken before meals to stimulate the appetite.

**ap·er·ture** (ap'ēr-chēr), *n.* [< L. pp. of *aperire*, to open < *ab-*, from + *perire*, to produce], 1. an opening; hole; gap. 2. the diameter of the opening in a camera, etc., through which light passes.

**a·pet·a·lous** (ā-pet''l-əs), *adj.* without petals.

**a·pex** (ā'peks), *n.* [*pl.* -PEXES (-pek-siz), -PICES (ap'i-sēz', ā'pi-sēz')], [L.], 1. the highest point of anything; tip; peak; vertex. 2. a climax.

**a·pha·si·a** (ə-fā'zhə, -zhi-ə), *n.* [Gr. < *a-*, not + *phanai*, to speak], a total or partial loss of the power to use or understand words.

**a·pha·sic** (ə-fā'zik), *adj.* of or having aphasia. *n.* one who has aphasia: also **a·pha'si·ac'** (-zi-ak').

**a·phe·li·on** (ə-fē'li-ən), *n.* [*pl.* -ONS, -A (-ə)], [< Gr. *apo*, from + *hēlios*, sun], the point farthest from the sun in the orbit of a planet or comet: cf. **perihelion.**

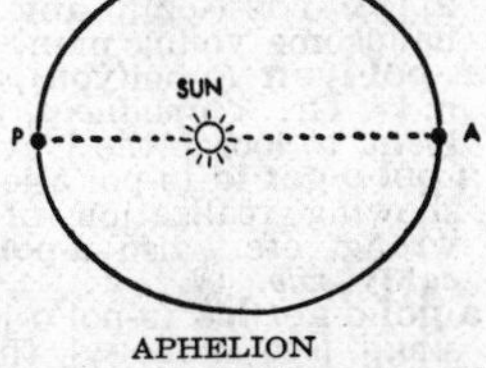


APHELION

Planet at aphelion A and at perihelion P

**a·phid** (ā'fid, af'id), *n.* [< Mod. L. *aphides*, pl. of *aphis*], an insect that lives on plants by sucking their juice; plant louse. Also **a·phis** (ā'fis, af'is), [*pl.* APHIDES (af'-i-dēz')]. —**a·phid·i·an** (ə-fid'i-ən), *adj. & n.*

**aph·o·rism** (af'ə-riz'm), *n.* [< Fr. < Gr. < *aphorizein*, to divide < *apo-*, from + *horizein*, to bound < *horos*, boundary], 1. a short, concise statement of a principle. 2. a maxim; adage. —**aph'o·rist,** *n.* —**aph'o·ris'tic,** *adj.* —**aph'o·ris'ti·cal·ly,** *adv.*

**aph·ro·dis·i·ac** (af'rə-diz'i-ak'), *adj.* [< Gr. < *Aphroditē*], arousing or increasing sexual desire. *n.* any aphrodisiac drug, food, etc.

**Aph·ro·di·te** (af'rə-dī'ti), *n.* in *Gr. mythology*, the goddess of love and beauty, identified with Venus by the Romans.

**a·pi·a·rist** (ā'pi-ə-rist), *n.* a person who keeps bees. Also **a'pi·ar'i·an** (-âr'i-ən), *adj. & n.*

**a·pi·ar·y** (ā'pi-er'i), *n.* [*pl.* -IES], [< L. < *apis*, bee], a place where bees are kept for their honey.

**ap·i·cal** (ap'i-k'l, ā'pi-), *adj.* of, at, or being the apex. —**ap'i·cal·ly,** *adv.*

**ap·i·ces** (ap'i-sēz', ā'pi-), *n.* alt. pl. of **apex.**

**a·pi·cul·ture** (ā'pi-kul'chēr), *n.* [< L. *apis*, bee; + *culture*], the raising and care of bees; beekeeping. —**a'pi·cul'tur·al,** *adj.*

**a·piece** (ə-pēs'), *adv.* [*a* + *piece*], to or for each.

**ap·ish** (āp'ish), *adj.* 1. like an ape. 2. stupidly imitative. 3. silly, affected, mischievous, etc. —**ap'ish·ly,** *adv.* —**ap'ish·ness,** *n.*

**a·plomb** (ə-plom', ə-plôm'), *n.* [< Fr.; see PLUMB], self-possession; assurance of manner; poise.

**ap·o-** (ap'ə), [< Gr. *apo*, off], a prefix meaning: 1. *off, from, away from*, as in *apogee*. 2. *detached*, as in *apocarp*. Also, before a vowel, **ap-.**

**A.P.O., APO,** Army Post Office.

**Apoc.,** 1. Apocalypse. 2. Apocrypha.

**a·poc·a·lypse** (ə-pok'ə-lips'), *n.* [< L. < Gr. < *apokalyptein*, to disclose], 1. [A-], the last book of the New Testament; book of Revelation. 2. a prophetic disclosure; revelation.

**a·poc·a·lyp·tic** (ə-pok'ə-lip'tik), *adj.* 1. of, like, or giving a revelation. 2. of the Apocalypse. Also **a·poc'a·lyp'ti·cal.** —**a·poc'a·lyp'ti·cal·ly,** *adv.*

**ap·o·carp** (ap'ə-kärp'), *n.* [*apo-* + *-carp*], a group of separate or partially joined carpels, as in the buttercup. —**ap'o·car'pous,** *adj.*

**a·poc·o·pate** (ə-pok'ə-pāt'), *v.t.* [-PATED, -PATING], to shorten by apocope. *adj.* (-pit), shortened by apocope.

**a·poc·o·pe** (ə-pok'ə-pē'), *n.* [< Gr. < *apo-*, from + *koptein*, to cut off], the dropping of the last sound, letter, or syllable of a word.

**a·poc·ry·pha** (ə-pok′rə-fə), ***n.pl.*** [< LL. < Gr. *apokryphos*, hidden, obscure < *apo-*, away + *kryptein*, to hide], 1. any writings, anecdotes, etc. of doubtful authenticity or authorship. 2. [A-], fourteen books of the Septuagint, regarded by Protestants as not canonical: they are not found in Hebrew and are entirely rejected in Judaism, but eleven of them are fully accepted in the Roman Catholic canon.

**a·poc·ry·phal** (ə-pok′rə-f'l), ***adj.*** 1. of doubtful authorship or authenticity. 2. not genuine; spurious; counterfeit. 3. [A-], of or like the Apocrypha. —**a·poc′ry·phal·ly**, ***adv.***

**a·pod·o·sis** (ə-pod′ə-sis), ***n.*** [*pl.* -SES (-sēz′)], [Gr., a giving back], the clause of result in a conditional sentence: opposed to *protasis*.

**ap·o·gee** (ap′ə-jē′), ***n.*** [< Fr. < L. < Gr. < *apo-*, from + *gē*, earth], 1. the point farthest from the earth in the orbit of the moon or of a man-made satellite: opposed to *perigee:* abbrev. **apo., apog.** 2. an apex.

**A·pol·lo** (ə-pol′ō), ***n.*** 1. in *Gr. & Rom. mythology*, god of music, poetry, prophecy, and medicine, later identified with Helios, a sun god. 2. [*pl.* -LOS (-ōz)], any handsome young man.

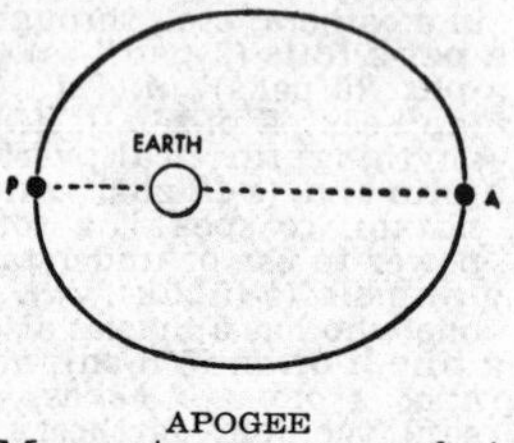


APOGEE
Moon at apogee A and at perigee P

**A·pol·lyon** (ə-pol′yən), ***n.*** [< Gr. < *apolluein*, to destroy < *apo-*, from + *lyein*, to loose], the Devil; Satan: Rev. 9:11.

**a·pol·o·get·ic** (ə-pol′ə-jet′ik), ***adj.*** that apologizes; showing realization of and regret for a fault, wrong, etc.: also **a·pol′o·get′i·cal.** —**a·pol′o·get′i·cal·ly**, ***adv.***

**a·pol·o·get·ics** (ə-pol′ə-jet′iks), ***n.pl.*** [construed as sing.], [see APOLOGY], the branch of theology dealing with the defense of Christianity.

**ap·o·lo·gi·a** (ap′ə-lō′ji-ə), ***n.*** an apology (chiefly in sense 1).

**a·pol·o·gist** (ə-pol′ə-jist), ***n.*** a person who writes or speaks in defense or justification of a doctrine, faith, action, etc.

**a·pol·o·gize** (ə-pol′ə-jīz′), ***v.i.*** [-GIZED, -GIZING], 1. to make an apology; acknowledge and express regret for a fault, wrong, etc. 2. to make a formal defense in speech or writing.

**ap·o·logue** (ap′ə-lôg′, -log′), ***n.*** [Fr. < L. < Gr.], a short allegorical story with a moral; fable.

**a·pol·o·gy** (ə-pol′ə-ji), ***n.*** [*pl.* -GIES], [< L. < Gr. *apologia*, a speaking in defense < *apo-*, from + *logos*, word], 1. a formal spoken or written defense of some idea, doctrine, etc. 2. an acknowledging and expressing regret for a fault, etc. 3. an inferior substitute: as, it is a sad *apology* for a meal.

**ap·o·phthegm** (ap′ə-them′), ***n.*** an apothegm. —**ap′o·phtheg·mat′ic** (-theg-mat′ik), **ap′o·phtheg·mat′i·cal**, ***adj.***

**ap·o·plec·tic** (ap′ə-plek′tik), ***adj.*** 1. of, like, or causing apoplexy. 2. having apoplexy. 3. likely to have apoplexy: as, *apoplectic* with rage. Also **ap′o·plec′ti·cal.** ***n.*** a person having or likely to have apoplexy. —**ap′o·plec′ti·cal·ly**, ***adv.***

**ap·o·plex·y** (ap′ə-plek′si), ***n.*** [< OFr. < L. < Gr. < *apo-*, down + *plēssein*, to strike], sudden paralysis with total or partial loss of consciousness and sensation, caused by the breaking or obstruction of a blood vessel in the brain.

**a·port** (ə-pôrt′), ***adv.*** [*a-*, on + *port*], in *nautical usage*, on or to the left, or port, side.

**a·pos·ta·sy** (ə-pos′tə-si), ***n.*** [*pl.* -SIES], [< L. < Gr. < *apo-*, away + *stasis*, a standing], an abandoning of what one believed in, as a faith, etc.

**a·pos·tate** (ə-pos′tāt, -tit), ***n.*** a person guilty of apostasy; renegade. ***adj.*** guilty of apostasy.

**a·pos·ta·tize** (ə-pos′tə-tīz′), ***v.i.*** [-TIZED, -TIZING], to be an apostate; abandon one's faith, political party, principles, etc.

**a pos·te·ri·o·ri** (ā′ pos-têr′i-ō′rī, -ôr′i), [L., from what comes later], 1. from effect to cause, or from particular instances to a generalization; inductive or inductively. 2. based on observation or experience; empirical. Opposed to *a priori*.

**a·pos·tle, A·pos·tle** (ə-pos′'l), ***n.*** [< AS. < L. < Gr. *apostolos*, a person sent forth < *apo-*, from + *stellein*, to send], 1. [usually A-], any of the twelve disciples sent out by Jesus to teach the gospel. 2. [usually a-], a person sent out on a special mission or as a preacher. 3. any early Christian missionary or leader. 4. an early advocate or leader of a new reform movement. 5. any of the twelve administrative officials of the Mormon Church. —**a·pos′tle·ship′**, ***n.***

**Apostles' Creed,** an old statement of belief in the basic Christian doctrines, formerly supposed to have been composed by the Twelve Apostles.

**ap·os·tol·ic** (ap′əs-tol′ik), ***adj.*** 1. of an apostle. 2. of the Apostles, their teachings, work, or times. 3. according to the Apostles' faith or teaching. 4. [often A-], of the Pope; papal. Also **ap′os·tol′i·cal.** —**ap′os·tol′i·cal·ly**, ***adv.*** —**ap′os·tol′i·cism, a·pos·to·lic·i·ty** (ə-pos′tə-lis′ə-ti), ***n.***

**apostolic see,** 1. a see, or bishopric, founded by an apostle. 2. [A- S-], in the *R. C. Church*, the Pope's see at Rome.

**a·pos·tro·phe** (ə-pos′trə-fi), ***n.*** [L.; Gr. *apostrophē*, a turning away to address one person < *apo-*, from + *strephein*, to turn], words addressed to a person or thing, whether absent or present.

**a·pos·tro·phe** (ə-pos′trə-fi), ***n.*** [Fr. < L. < Gr. < same base as prec. *apostrophe*], the sign (') used: 1. to show the omission of a letter or letters from a word (e.g., *it's* for *it is*). 2. to indicate the possessive case (e.g., *Mary's* dress, *one's* duty). 3. in forming some plurals, as of figures and letters (e.g., five *6's*, dot the *i's*).

**ap·os·troph·ic** (ap′ə-strof′ik), ***adj.*** of or using rhetorical apostrophe or a grammatical apostrophe.

**a·pos·tro·phize** (ə-pos′trə-fīz′), ***v.t. & v.i.*** [-PHIZED (-fīzd′), -PHIZING], to speak or write an apostrophe or apostrophes (to): as, Shelley *apostrophized* the west wind.

**apothecaries' measure,** a system of liquid measure used in pharmacy. In the U.S.: 60 minims = 1 fluid dram; 8 fluid drams = 1 fluid ounce; 16 fluid ounces = 1 pint; 8 pints = 1 gallon.

**apothecaries' weight,** a system of weights used in pharmacy: 20 grains = 1 scruple; 3 scruples = 1 dram; 8 drams = 1 ounce; 12 ounces = 1 pound.

**a·poth·e·car·y** (ə-poth′ə-ker′i), ***n.*** [*pl.* -IES], [< OFr. < LL. < L. < Gr. *apothēkē*, storehouse < *apo-*, away + *tithenai*, to put], a druggist; pharmacist: formerly, apothecaries also prescribed medicines.

**ap·o·thegm** (ap′ə-them′), ***n.*** [< Fr. < Gr. < *apo-*, from + *phthengesthai*, to cry out, utter], a short, terse saying; maxim: also **apophthegm.** —**ap·o·theg·mat·ic** (ap′ə-theg-mat′ik), **ap′o·theg·mat′i·cal,** ***adj.*** —**ap′o·theg·mat′i·cal·ly**, ***adv.***

**a·poth·e·o·sis** (ə-poth′i-ō′sis, ap′ə-thē′ə-), ***n.*** [*pl.* -SES (-sēz, -sēz′)], [L.; Gr. < *apotheoun*, to deify < *apo-*, from + *theos*, a god], 1. the act of making a god of a person; deification. 2. the glorification of a person or thing. 3. a glorified ideal.

**a·poth·e·o·size** (ə-poth′i-ə-sīz′, ap′ə-thē′-), ***v.t.*** [-SIZED, -SIZING], [< *apotheosis* + *-ize*], 1. to deify. 2. to glorify; idealize.

**app.,** 1. appended. 2. appendix. 3. appointed.

**ap·pal** (ə-pôl′), ***v.t.*** [-PALLED, -PALLING], to appall.

**Ap·pa·la·chi·an** (ap′ə-lā′chi-ən, -lach′ən), ***adj.*** of the Appalachian Mountains.

**Appalachian Mountains,** a mountain system in eastern North America, extending from Quebec to Alabama. Also **Ap′pa·la′chi·ans,** ***n.pl.***

**ap·pall** (ə-pôl′), ***v.t.*** [< OFr. *apallir*, to grow pale < *a-*, to + *pale;* see PALE, PALLID], to horrify; shock; dismay: also sp. **appal.** —**ap·pal′ling,** ***adj.*** —**ap·pal′ling·ly,** ***adv.***

**ap·pa·nage, ap·a·nage** (ap′ə-nij), ***n.*** [< Fr. < OFr. < L. *ad*, to + *panis*, bread], 1. money, land, etc. given by kings and princes for the support of their younger children. 2. a person's rightful gain; perquisite. 3. an adjunct.

**appar.,** apparently.

**ap·pa·ra·tus** (ap′ə-rā′təs, -rat′əs), ***n.*** [*pl.* -TUS, -TUSES], [L., a making ready < *ad-*, to + *parare*, to prepare], 1. the materials, tools, etc. for a specific use. 2. any complex device or machine. 3. in *physiology*, a set of organs for a specific function: as, the digestive *apparatus*.

**ap·par·el** (ə-par′əl), ***n.*** [< OFr. < *apareiller*, to prepare; *a-*, to + *pareiller*, to put like things together· ult. < L. *par*, equal], 1. clothing; attire. 2. that which adorns: as, the white *apparel* of winter. ***v.t.*** [-ELED or -ELLED, -ELING or -ELLING], to clothe; dress.

**ap·par·ent** (ə-par′ənt, ə-pâr′-), ***adj.*** [< OFr. < L. ppr. of *apparere;* see APPEAR], 1. visible; readily seen. 2. readily understood; obvious. 3. appearing to be real or true; seeming. See also **heir apparent.**

**ap·par·ent·ly** (ə-par′ənt-li, ə-pâr′-), ***adv.*** 1. plainly; clearly. 2. seemingly.

**ap·pa·ri·tion** (ap′ə-rish′ən), ***n.*** [Fr. < L. *apparere;* see APPEAR], 1. anything that appears unexpectedly. 2. a ghost; phantom. 3. an appearing or becoming apparent. —**ap′pa·ri′tion·al,** ***adj.***

**ap·peal** (ə-pēl′), ***v.t.*** [< Fr. < L. *appellare*, to accost, appeal], to make an appeal of (a law case, etc.). *v.i.* 1. to make an appeal in a law case. 2. to make an urgent request (*to* a person *for* a decision, help, etc.). 3. to be interesting; arouse a favorable response. *n.* 1. a call upon some authority for a decision, etc. 2. an urgent request for help, etc. 3. a quality that arouses sympathetic response; attraction. 4. in *law, a)* a request for the transference of a case to a higher court for rehearing. *b)* the right to this. —**ap·peal′a·ble,** *adj.* —**ap·peal′er,** *n.* —**ap·peal′ing,** *adj.* —**ap·peal′ing·ly,** *adv.* —**ap·peal′ing·ness,** *n.*

**ap·pear** (ə-pêr′), *v.i.* [< OFr. < L. *apparere* < *ad-*, to + *parere*, to become visible], 1. to come into sight or be in sight. 2. to become understood: as, it *appears* she left. 3. to seem; look. 4. to present oneself formally in court. 5. to come before the public: as, he will *appear* in *Hamlet.* 6. to be published.

**ap·pear·ance** (ə-pêr′əns), *n.* 1. an appearing. 2. the outward aspect of anything. 3. an apparition. 4. a pretense or show. —**keep up appearances,** to maintain an outward show of what is proper, etc. —**put in an appearance,** to be present for a short time, as at a party.

**ap·pease** (ə-pēz′), *v.t.* [-PEASED, -PEASING], [< OFr. < *a-*, to + *pais* < L. *pax*, peace], 1. to quiet, especially by giving in to the demands of. 2. to satisfy or relieve: as, water *appeases* thirst. —**ap·peas′a·ble,** *adj.* —**ap·peas′er,** *n.* —**ap·peas′ing·ly,** *adv.*

**ap·pease·ment** (ə-pēz′mənt), *n.* 1. an appeasing or being appeased. 2. the policy of giving in to the demands of a hostile power in an attempt to prevent trouble.

**ap·pel·lant** (ə-pel′ənt), *adj.* in *law*, relating to appeals; appealing. *n.* one who appeals, especially to a higher court.

**ap·pel·late** (ə-pel′it), *adj.* in *law*, appealed to. —**appellate court,** a court that can review appeals and reverse the decisions of lower courts.

**ap·pel·la·tion** (ap′ə-lā′shən), *n.* [< L.; see APPEAL], 1. the act of naming. 2. a name; title.

**ap·pel·la·tive** (ə-pel′ə-tiv), *adj.* of appellation; naming. *n.* 1. a name; title. 2. in *grammar*, a common noun. —**ap·pel′la·tive·ly,** *adv.*

**ap·pend** (ə-pend′), *v.t.* [< Fr. < L. < *ad-*, to + *pendere*, to suspend], to affix; add as an appendix.

**ap·pend·age** (ə-pen′dij), *n.* 1. anything appended; adjunct. 2. in *biology*, any subordinate or external organ or part, as a leg or tail.

**ap·pend·ant, ap·pend·ent** (ə-pen′dənt), *adj.* [Fr.; see APPEND], 1. attached; added. 2. attendant; consequent. *n.* an appendage.

**ap·pen·dec·to·my** (ap′ən-dek′tə-mi), *n.* [*pl.* -MIES], [see -ECTOMY], the surgical removal of the vermiform appendix.

**ap·pen·di·ci·tis** (ə-pen′də-sī′tis), *n.* [< *appendix* + *-itis*], inflammation of the vermiform appendix.

**ap·pen·dix** (ə-pen′diks), *n.* [*pl.* -DIXES, -DICES (-də-sēz′)], [< L.; see APPEND], 1. additional material at the end of a book. 2. in *anatomy*, an outgrowth of an organ; especially, the vermiform appendix.

**ap·per·cep·tion** (ap′ẽr-sep′shən), *n.* [< Fr. < L. *ad*, to + *percipere;* see PERCEIVE], 1. perception. 2. in *metaphysics*, the mind's being conscious of its consciousness. —**ap′per·cep′tive,** *adj.* —**ap′per·cep′tive·ly,** *adv.*

**ap·per·tain** (ap′ẽr-tān′), *v.i.* [< OFr. < L. < *ad-*, to + *pertinere;* see PERTAIN], to belong as a function, part, etc.; pertain; relate.

**ap·pe·ten·cy** (ap′ə-tən-si), *n.* [*pl.* -CIES], 1. a craving; appetite. 2. an instinctive tendency. 3. an affinity. Also **ap′pe·tence** (-təns).

**ap·pe·tite** (ap′ə-tīt′), *n.* [< OFr. < L. < *ad-*, to + *petere*, to seek], 1. a desire; craving. 2. a desire for food or for some specific dish.

**ap·pe·tiz·er** (ap′ə-tīz′ẽr), *n.* a tasty food that stimulates the appetite, usually served before a meal.

**ap·pe·tiz·ing** (ap′ə-tīz′iŋ), *adj.* stimulating the appetite; savory. —**ap′pe·tiz′ing·ly,** *adv.*

**ap·plaud** (ə-plôd′), *v.t. & v.i.* [< L. < *ad-*, to + *plaudere*, to strike], 1. to show approval (of) by clapping the hands, etc. 2. to praise; approve.

**ap·plause** (ə-plôz′), *n.* approval or praise, especially as shown by clapping hands, etc.

**ap·ple** (ap′'l), *n.* [AS. *æppel*], 1. a round, firm, fleshy, edible fruit. 2. the tree it grows on, widely distributed in temperate regions. 3. any of various other fruits, or fruitlike growths, as the May apple.

**ap·ple·jack** (ap′'l-jak′), *n.* a brandy distilled from apple cider.

**ap·ple-pie order** (ap′'l-pī′), [Colloq.], neat order.

**apple polisher,** [Slang], one who curries favor by gifts, flattery, etc.

**ap·ple·sauce** (ap′'l-sôs′), *n.* 1. apples sweetened and cooked to a pulp in water. 2. [Slang], hokum.

**ap·pli·ance** (ə-plī′əns), *n.* a device or machine, especially for household use.

**ap·pli·ca·ble** (ap′li-kə-b'l), *adj.* that can be applied; appropriate. —**ap′pli·ca·bil′i·ty,** *n.* —**ap′pli·ca·bly,** *adv.*

**ap·pli·cant** (ap′li-kənt), *n.* one who applies, as for employment, help, etc.

**ap·pli·ca·tion** (ap′li-kā′shən), *n.* 1. an applying or being applied. 2. anything applied, especially a remedy. 3. a method of using. 4. a request: as, an *application* for employment. 5. continued exertion; diligence. 6. relevance: as, it has no *application* to the case.

**ap·pli·ca·tive** (ap′li-kā′tiv), *adj.* applicatory.

**ap·pli·ca·tor** (ap′li-kā′tẽr), *n.* any device for applying or inserting medicine, etc.

**ap·pli·ca·to·ry** (ap′li-kə-tôr′i, -tō′ri), *adj.* applying; suitable for practical use.

**ap·plied** (ə-plīd′), *adj.* used in actual practice: as, *applied* science: distinguished from *pure, theoretical.*

**ap·pli·qué** (ap′li-kā′), *adj.* [Fr.], fastened on: said of one material attached by sewing, etc. to another. *n.* any decoration of this kind. *v.t.* [-QUÉD, -QUÉING], to decorate with appliqué.

**ap·ply** (ə-plī′), *v.t.* [-PLIED, -PLYING], [< OFr. < L. *applicare*, to attach to < *ad-*, to + *plicare*, to fold], 1. to put on: as, *apply* glue. 2. to use practically: as, *apply* your knowledge. 3. to refer to with (an epithet, etc.). 4. to concentrate (one's faculties) on. 5. to devote (oneself) diligently. *v.i.* 1. to make a request. 2. to be suitable, or relevant: as, this principle always *applies.* —**ap·pli′er,** *n.*

**ap·pog·gia·tu·ra** (ə-poj′ə-too͞′rə), *n.* [It. < LL. *appodiare*, to support < L. *ad-*, to + *podium;* see PODIUM], in *music*, a grace note.

**ap·point** (ə-point′), *v.t.* [< OFr. *apointer*, to make ready < L. *ad*, to + *punctum*, a point], 1. to ordain; set (a date, place, etc.). 2. to name for an office, etc.: as, I *appoint* him chairman. 3. to furnish and arrange: now usually in *well-appointed*, etc. —**ap·point·ee** (ə-poin′tē′) *n.* —**ap·point′er,** *n.*

**ap·poin·tive** (ə-poin′tiv), *adj.* of or filled by appointment: as, an *appointive* position.

**ap·point·ment** (ə-point′mənt), *n.* 1. an appointing or being appointed. 2. a naming for an office, etc. 3. a person thus selected. 4. a position thus filled. 5. an arrangement to meet a person; engagement. 6. *pl.* furniture.

**Ap·po·mat·tox** (ap′ə-mat′əks), *n.* a town in Virginia, where Lee surrendered to Grant (April 9, 1865).

**ap·por·tion** (ə-pôr′shən, -pōr′-), *v.t.* [see AD- & PORTION], to divide and distribute proportionally; portion out; allot. —**ap·por′tion·ment,** *n.*

**ap·pose** (ə-pōz′), *v.t.* [-POSED, -POSING], [< Fr. < L. < *ad-*, to + *ponere*, to put], 1. to put (*to* another thing). 2. to put side by side; place opposite or near. —**ap·pos′a·ble,** *adj.*

**ap·po·site** (ap′ə-zit), *adj.* [see APPOSE], fitting; apt. —**ap′po·site·ly,** *adv.* —**ap′po·site·ness,** *n.*

**ap·po·si·tion** (ap′ə-zish′ən), *n.* 1. an apposing or being apposed. 2. the position resulting from this. 3. in *grammar*, *a)* the placing of a word or expression beside another so that the second explains and has the same grammatical construction as the first. *b)* the relationship between such words, as in "*Mary*, my *cousin*, is here."

**ap·pos·i·tive** (ə-poz′ə-tiv), *adj.* of or in apposition. *n.* a word, phrase, or clause in apposition.

**ap·prais·al** (ə-prāz′'l), *n.* 1. an appraising. 2. an appraised value; estimate. Also **ap·praise′ment.**

**ap·praise** (ə-prāz′), *v.t.* [-PRAISED, -PRAISING], [< OFr. < LL. < L. *ad*, to + *pretium*, value; influenced by *praise*], 1. to set a price for. 2. to estimate the quantity or quality of. —**ap·prais′a·ble,** *adj.* —**ap·prais′er,** *n.* —**ap·prais′ing·ly,** *adv.*

**ap·pre·ci·a·ble** (ə-prē′shi-ə-b'l, -shə-b'l), *adj.* enough to be perceived; noticeable: as, an *appreciable* difference in pay. —**ap·pre′ci·a·bly,** *adv.*

**ap·pre·ci·ate** (ə-prē′shi-āt′), *v.t.* [-ATED, -ATING], [< LL. pp. of *appretiare;* see APPRAISE], 1. to think well of; value; enjoy; esteem. 2. to recognize gratefully. 3. to estimate the quality or worth of. 4. to estimate rightly. 5. to be fully or sensitively aware of. 6. to raise the price of:

**fat, āpe, bâre, cär; ten, ēven, hêre, ovẽr; is, bīte; lot, gō, hôrn, too͞l, look; oil, out; up, ūse, fũr; get; joy; yet; chin; she; thin, *th*en; zh,** leisure; **ŋ,** ring; **ə** for *a* in *ago*, *e* in *agent*, *i* in *sanity*, *o* in *comply*, *u* in *focus;* ′ in *able* (ā′b'l); **Fr. bål; ë,** Fr. coeur; **ö,** Fr. feu; Fr. mo*n*; **ô,** Fr. coq; **ü,** Fr. duc; **H,** G. ich; **kh,** G. doch. ‡ foreign; < derived from.

opposed to *depreciate*. *v.i.* to rise in value. —**ap·pre'ci·a'tor,** *n.* —**ap·pre'ci·a·to'ry** (-tôr'i, -tō'ri), *adj.*

**ap·pre·ci·a·tion** (ə-prē'shi-ā'shən), *n.* 1. grateful recognition, as of benefits. 2. an estimate, especially a correct one. 3. sensitive awareness; discriminating enjoyment, as of art. 4. a rise in value or price: opposed to *depreciation*.

**ap·pre·ci·a·tive** (ə-prē'shi-ā'tiv, -ə-tiv), *adj.* feeling or showing appreciation. —**ap·pre'ci·a'tive·ly,** *adv.* —**ap·pre'ci·a'tive·ness,** *n.*

**ap·pre·hend** (ap'ri-hend'), *v.t.* [< Fr. < L. < *ad-*, to + *prehendere*, to seize], 1. to take into custody; arrest. 2. to perceive or understand. 3. to anticipate with anxiety; fear; dread.

**ap·pre·hen·si·ble** (ap'ri-hen'sə-b'l), *adj.* that can be apprehended. —**ap'pre·hen'si·bil'i·ty,** *n.*

**ap·pre·hen·sion** (ap'ri-hen'shən), *n.* 1. arrest. 2. perception; understanding. 3. opinion. 4. foreboding; fear; dread.

**ap·pre·hen·sive** (ap'ri-hen'siv), *adj.* 1. able to apprehend; quick to understand or learn. 2. troubled by fears; anxious; uneasy. —**ap'pre·hen'sive·ly,** *adv.* —**ap'pre·hen'sive·ness,** *n.*

**ap·pren·tice** (ə-pren'tis), *n.* [< OFr. < *aprendre*, to teach < L. < *ad-*, to + *prehendere*, to seize], 1. a person under legal agreement to work a specified length of time for a master craftsman in a craft or trade in return for instruction and, formerly, support. 2. any learner or beginner. *v.t.* [-TICED, -TICING], to place or accept as an apprentice. —**ap·pren'tice·ship,** *n.*

**ap·prise, ap·prize** (ə-prīz'), *v.t.* [-PRISED or -PRIZED, -PRISING or -PRIZING], [< Fr. pp. of *apprendre*, to teach, inform < L. < *ad-*, to + *prehendere*, to seize], to inform; notify.

**ap·prize, ap·prise** (ə-prīz'), *v.t.* [-PRIZED or -PRISED, -PRIZING or -PRISING], to appraise. —**ap·prize'ment, ap·prise'ment,** *n.* —**ap·priz'er, ap·pris'er,** *n.*

**ap·proach** (ə-prōch'), *v.i.* [< OFr. < LL. < L. *ad*, to + *propius*, compar. of *prope*, near], to come or go near or nearer. *v.t.* 1. to come near or nearer to. 2. to come to resemble; approximate. 3. to bring near (*to* something). 4. to make advances, a proposal, or a request to. *n.* 1. a coming near. 2. an approximation; resemblance. 3. *often in pl.* an advance or overture (*to* someone). 4. a way of reaching a person or place; access. 5. in *golf*, a stroke from the fairway to the putting green. —**ap·proach'a·ble,** *adj.* —**ap·proach'a·bil'i·ty, ap·proach'a·ble·ness,** *n.*

**ap·pro·ba·tion** (ap'rə-bā'shən), *n.* [< L. < *approbare*; see APPROVE], 1. approval. 2. sanction. —**ap'pro·ba'tive, ap·pro·ba·to·ry** (ə-prō'bə-tôr'i, -tō'ri), *adj.*

**ap·pro·pri·ate** (ə-prō'pri-āt'; *for adj.*, -it), *v.t.* [-ATED, -ATING], [< L. < *ad-*, to + *proprius*, one's own], 1. to take for one's own use; hence, 2. to steal. 3. to set aside for a specific use: as, to *appropriate* money for schools. *adj.* suitable; fit; proper. —**ap·pro'pri·ate·ly,** *adv.* —**ap·pro'pri·ate·ness,** *n.* —**ap·pro'pri·a'tor,** *n.*

**ap·pro·pri·a·tion** (ə-prō'pri-ā'shən), *n.* 1. an appropriating or being appropriated. 2. a thing appropriated; money, etc. set aside for a specific use. —**ap·pro'pri·a'tive,** *adj.*

**ap·prov·al** (ə-prōōv''l), *n.* 1. an approving or being approved. 2. favorable opinion. 3. consent; sanction. —**on approval,** for the customer to examine and decide whether to buy or return.

**ap·prove** (ə-prōōv'), *v.t.* [-PROVED, -PROVING], [< OFr. < L. < *ad-*, to + *probare*, to try, test < *probus*, good], 1. to sanction; consent to. 2. to be favorable toward; consider to be good, satisfactory, etc. 3. to prove or show. *v.i.* to have a favorable opinion (*of*). —**ap·prov'er,** *n.* —**ap·prov'ing·ly,** *adv.*

**approx.,** 1. approximate. 2. approximately.

**ap·prox·i·mate** (ə-prok'sə-mit; *for v.*, -māt'), *adj.* [< LL. < L. *ad*, to + *proximus*, superl. of *prope*, near], 1. near in position. 2. much like; resembling. 3. more or less correct. *v.t.* [-MATED, -MATING], 1. to come near to or be almost the same as: as, this painting *approximates* reality. 2. to bring near (*to* something). *v.i.* to come near; be almost the same. —**ap·prox'i·mate·ly,** *adv.*

**ap·prox·i·ma·tion** (ə-prok'sə-mā'shən), *n.* 1. an approximating; approaching. 2. anything that approximates; close estimate; near likeness.

**ap·pur·te·nance** (ə-pûr't'n-əns), *n.* [< Anglo-Fr. < OFr.; see APPERTAIN], 1. something added to a more important thing; adjunct. 2. an additional, subordinate right or privilege.

**ap·pur·te·nant** (ə-pûr't'n-ənt), *adj.* appertaining; pertinent. *n.* an appurtenance.

**Apr.,** April.

**a·pri·cot** (ā'pri-kot', ap'ri-), *n.* [< Fr. < Port. < Ar. < MGr. < L. *praecoquus*, early matured fruit < *prae-*, beforehand + *coquere*, to cook], 1. a small, yellowish-orange, peachlike fruit. 2. the tree that it grows on. 3. yellowish orange.

**A·pril** (ā'prəl), *n.* [< OFr. < L.; prob. < hyp. *apero-*, second; orig. meaning prob. "second month"], the fourth month of the year, having 30 days.

**April fool,** a victim of jokes on April Fools' Day.

**April Fools' Day,** April 1; All Fools' Day.

**a pri·o·ri** (ā' pri-ō'rī, ä' pri-ôr'i), [L., from something prior], 1. from cause to effect; from a generalization to particular instances; deductive or deductively. 2. based on theory instead of experience or experiment. Opposed to *a posteriori*.

**a·pron** (ā'prən), *n.* [by faulty separation of *a napron* < OFr. *naperon* < *nape*, a cloth; L. *mappa*, a napkin], 1. a garment worn over the front part of the body, usually to protect one's clothes. 2. anything like an apron in appearance or use, as the paved area in front of an airplane hangar, etc. or the part of a stage in front of the curtain. *v.t.* to put an apron on.

**apron string,** a string for tying an apron on. —**tied to his mother's** (or **wife's,** etc.) **apron strings,** dominated by his mother (or wife, etc.).

**ap·ro·pos** (ap'rə-pō'), *adv.* [Fr. *à propos*, to the purpose], at the right time; opportunely. *adj.* relevant; apt. —**apropos of,** in connection with.

**apse** (aps), *n.* [< L. < Gr. *hapsis*, an arch, fastening < *haptein*, to fasten], a semicircular or polygonal projection of a church, generally at the east end and with a domed or vaulted roof.

**apt** (apt), *adj.* [< OFr. < L. < Gr. *haptein*, to fasten], 1. appropriate; fitting: as, an *apt* statement. 2. tending or inclined; likely: as, *apt* to worry. 3. quick to learn or understand: as, an *apt* student. —**apt'ly,** *adv.* —**apt ness,** *n.*

**apt.,** [*pl.* APTS.], apartment.

**ap·ter·ous** (ap'tēr-əs), *adj.* [< Gr. < *a-*, without + *pteron*, a wing], having no wings; wingless.

**ap·ter·yx** (ap'tēr-iks), *n.* [< Gr. *a-*, without + *pteryx*, wing], any of a number of related, nearly extinct, tailless birds of New Zealand, with undeveloped wings, and hairlike feathers; kiwi.

APTERYX (15 in. long)

**ap·ti·tude** (ap'tə-tōōd', -tūd'), *n.* [Fr. < LL. < L. < Gr. *haptein*, to fasten], 1. suitability; fitness. 2. a natural tendency, inclination, or ability. 3. quickness to learn or understand.

**aq·ua** (ak'wə, ä'kwə, ā'kwə), *n.* [*pl.* AQUAS, AQUAE (-wē, -kwē)], [L.], 1. water. 2. in *pharmacy*, liquid; solution, especially in water: abbrev. **Aq., aq.** *adj.* [< *aquamarine*], bluish-green.

**aqua for·tis** (fôr'tis), [L., strong water], nitric acid.

**aq·ua·ma·rine** (ak'wə-mə-rēn'), *n.* [L. *aqua marina*, sea water], 1. a transparent, pale bluish-green variety of beryl. 2. its color. *adj.* bluish-green.

**aq·ua·naut** (ak'wə-nôt'), *n.* [*aqua* + astro*naut*], a person trained to live and work in a watertight underwater chamber in and from which he can conduct oceanographic experiments.

**aq·ua·plane** (ak'wə-plān'), *n.* [coined after *airplane*], a board on which one rides standing up as it is pulled by a motorboat. *v.i.* [-PLANED, -PLANING], to ride on such a board.

AQUAPLANE

**aqua re·gi·a** (rē'ji-ə), [L., kingly water], a mixture of nitric and hydrochloric acids: so called because it can dissolve gold and platinum.

**a·quar·i·um** (ə-kwâr'i-əm), *n.* [*pl.* -IUMS, -IA (-i-ə)], [L., neut. of *aquarius*, of water], 1. a tank, usually with glass sides, or a pool, bowl, etc. for keeping live water animals and water plants. 2. a place where such collections are exhibited.

**A·quar·i·us** (ə-kwâr'i-əs), *n.* [L., the water carrier], 1. a large central constellation, supposedly outlining a man pouring water from a container. 2. the eleventh sign of the zodiac (♒).

**a·quat·ic** (ə-kwat'ik, -kwät'-), *adj.* 1. growing or living in or upon water. 2. done in or upon the water: as, *aquatic* sports. *n.* 1. an aquatic plant or animal. 2. *pl.* aquatic performances or sports. —**a·quat'i·cal·ly,** *adv.*

**aq·ua·tint** (ak'wə-tint'), *n.* 1. a process by which

spaces rather than lines are etched with acid, producing an etching like a water color. 2. such an etching. *v.t.* to etch in this way.
**aqua vi·tae** (vī'tē), [L., water of life], 1. alcohol. 2. brandy or other strong liquor.
**aq·ue·duct** (ak'wi-dukt'), *n.* [< L. < *aqua*, water + *ducere*, to lead], 1. a large pipe or conduit for bringing water from a distant source. 2. an elevated structure built to support such a pipe or conduit. 3. in *anatomy*, a passage or canal.
**a·que·ous** (ā'kwi-əs, ak wi-), *adj.* 1. of or like water; watery. 2. formed by or with water. —**a'que·ous·ly,** *adv.* —**a'que·ous·ness,** *n.*
**aqueous humor,** a watery fluid in the space between the cornea and the lens of the eye.
**aq·ui·line** (ak'wə-lin', -lin), *adj.* [< L. < *aquila*, eagle], 1. of or like an eagle. 2. like an eagle's beak, as a curved or hooked nose.
**A·qui·nas, Saint Thomas** (ə-kwī'nəs), 1225?–1274; Italian scholastic philosopher.
**A·qui·taine** (ak'wi-tān'), *n.* a former district of SW France.
**-ar** (ẽr), [< L. *-aris* or *-arius*], a suffix used in forming: 1. adjectives meaning *of, relating to, like, of the nature of*, as in *regular, singular, polar.* 2. nouns denoting *agency*, as in *bursar, vicar.* In some nouns formed after *scholar*, etc., *-ar* is equivalent to *-er*, as in *beggar, liar.*
**Ar.,** 1. Arabic. 2. Aramaic.
**Ar·ab** (ar'əb), *n.* 1. a native of Arabia. 2. any of a Semitic people originating in Arabia; commonly, a Bedouin. 3. any of a breed of swift, graceful horses native to Arabia. *adj.* Arabian.
**ar·a·besque** (ar'ə-besk'), *n.* [Fr. < It. < *Arabo*, Arab: from the designs in Moorish architecture], 1. a complex and elaborate design of intertwined flowers, foliage, geometrical patterns, etc. 2. in *ballet dancing*, a position in which one leg is extended straight backward and the arms are extended, one forward and one backward. *adj.* 1. of or done in arabesque. 2. fantastic and elaborate.
**A·ra·bi·a** (ə-rā'bi-ə), *n.* a large peninsula in SW Asia. —**A·ra'bi·an,** *adj. & n.*
**Arabian Nights,** a collection of ancient stories from Arabia, India, Persia, etc.
**Arabian Sea,** an extension of the Indian Ocean, between India and Arabia.
**Ar·a·bic** (ar'ə-bik), *adj.* 1. of Arabia. 2. of the Arabs, their language, culture, etc. *n.* the Semitic language of the Arabs, used in Arabia, Syria, Jordan, Iraq, northern Africa, etc.
**Arabic numerals,** the figures 1, 2, 3, 4, 5, 6, 7, 8, 9, and the 0 (zero).
**ar·a·ble** (ar'ə-b'l), *adj.* [Fr. < L. < *arare*, to plow], suitable for plowing. *n.* arable land.
**Arab League,** a confederation of the states of Syria, Jordan, Iraq, Saudi Arabia, Lebanon, Egypt, and Yemen, formed in 1945.
**Ar·a·by** (ar'ə-bi), *n.* [Archaic or Poetic], Arabia.
**a·rach·nid** (ə-rak'nid), *n.* [< Gr. *arachnē*, spider], any of a large group of arthropods with four pairs of legs and a body usually divided into two segments: spiders, scorpions, and mites are arachnids. —**a·rach'ni·dan** (-ni-dən), *adj. & n.*
**Ar·a·gon** (ar'ə-gon', -gən), *n.* a northeastern region in Spain, formerly a separate kingdom. —**Ar·a·go·nese** (ar'ə-gə-nēz ), *adj., n. sing. & pl.*
**Ar·al, Lake** (âr'əl), a large inland body of salt water in the Asiatic U.S.S.R., east of the Caspian Sea: also **Aral Sea.**
**Ar·am** (âr'əm), *n.* ancient Syria: the Hebrew name. —**Ar·a·mae·an, Ar·a·me·an** (ar'ə-mē'ən), *adj. & n.*
**Ar·a·ma·ic** (ar'ə-mā'ik), *n.* a group of northwest Semitic languages spoken in Biblical times, including the language used in Palestine at the time of Jesus: abbrev. **Aram., Ar.**
**A·rap·a·ho** (ə-rap'ə-hō'), *n.* [*pl.* -HO, -HOES], any member of a tribe of Algonquian Indians who lived in the area of the upper Platte and Arkansas rivers: also sp. **Arapahoe.**
**Ar·a·rat** (ar'ə-rat'), *n.* a mountain in E Turkey: supposed landing place of Noah's Ark: Gen. 8:4.
**ar·ba·lest, ar·ba·list** (är'bə-list), *n.* [< AS. or OFr.; < L. < *arcus*, a bow + *ballista* < Gr. *ballein*, to throw], a medieval crossbow with a steel bow that propelled arrows, balls, or stones. —**ar'ba·lest·er, ar'ba·list·er,** *n.*
**ar·bi·ter** (är'bi-tẽr), *n.* [L., orig., one who goes to a place, a witness < *ad-*, to + *bitere*, to go], 1. a person selected to judge a dispute; umpire; arbitrator. 2. a person fully authorized to judge or decide. —**ar'bi·tral** (-trəl), *n.* —**ar'bi·tress,** *n. fem.*
**ar·bi·tra·ble** (är'bə-trə-b'l), *adj.* that can be arbitrated; subject to arbitration.
**ar·bit·ra·ment** (är-bit'rə-mənt), *n.* 1. arbitration. 2. an arbitrator's verdict or award. 3. the power to judge; right to decide.
**ar·bi·trar·y** (är'bə-trer'i), *adj.* [< L. < *arbiter;* see ARBITER], 1. based on one's preference, notion, or whim. 2. capricious. 3. absolute; despotic. —**ar·bi·trar·i·ly** (är'bə-trer'ə-li; *emphatic, often* är'bə-trâr'ə-li), *adv.* —**ar'bi·trar'i·ness,** *n.*
**ar·bi·trate** (är'bə-trāt'), *v.t.* [-TRATED, -TRATING], [< L. < *arbitrari*, to give a decision < *arbiter;* see ARBITER], 1. to give to an arbitrator to decide. 2. to decide (a dispute) as an arbitrator. *v.i.* 1. to act as an arbitrator (*in* a dispute, *between* persons). 2. to submit a dispute to arbitration. —**ar'bi·tra'tive,** *adj.*
**ar·bi·tra·tion** (är'bə-trā'shən), *n.* settlement of a dispute by someone chosen to hear both sides and come to a decision. —**ar'bi·tra'tion·al,** *adj.*
**ar·bi·tra·tor** (är'bə-trā'tẽr), *n.* a person chosen to arbitrate a dispute. —**ar'bi·tra'tor·ship,** *n.*
**ar·bor** (är'bẽr), *n.* [< OFr. < L. < *herba*, grass, herb], a place shaded by trees or shrubs or, especially, by vines on a latticework; bower.
**ar·bor** (är'bẽr), *n.* [*pl.* ARBORES (-bə-rēz')], [L.], a tree. —**Arbor Day,** in most States, a day in late April or early May observed by planting trees.
**ar·bor** (är'bẽr), *n.* [< Fr. *arbre* < L. *arbor*, tree, beam], in *mechanics*, 1. a shaft; beam. 2. a spindle; axle. 3. a bar that holds cutting tools. *v.t.* to set in such a bar, shaft, etc.
**ar·bo·re·al** (är-bôr'i-əl, -bō'ri-), *adj.* 1. of or like a tree. 2. living in trees or adapted for living in trees. Also **ar·bo're·ous.**
**ar·bo·res·cent** (är'bə-res''nt), *adj.* treelike in shape or growth; branching.
**ar·bo·re·tum** (är'bə-rē'təm), *n.* [*pl.* -TUMS, -TA (-tə)], [L.], a place where many kinds of trees and shrubs are grown for display or study.
**ar·bor·vi·tae** (är'bẽr-vī'tē), *n.* [L., tree of life], any of a number of related trees of the pine family, having soft, scalelike leaves: also **arbor vitae.**
**ar·bour** (är'bẽr), *n.* an arbor (bower): Brit. sp.
**ar·bu·tus** (är-bū'təs), *n.* [L., wild strawberry tree], 1. a tree or shrub of the heath family, with dark-green leaves and strawberrylike berries. 2. a related trailing plant with clusters of white or pink flowers; trailing arbutus.
**arc** (ärk), *n.* [Fr. < L. *arcus*, a bow, arch], 1. a bow-like curved line or object. 2. in *astronomy*, the apparent curved path of a star or planet. 3. in *electricity*, the band of sparks or incandescent light between two closely placed electrodes when a current leaps the gap from one to the other. 4. in *geometry*, a part of a curved line, as of a circle. *v.i.* [ARCED or ARCKED (ärkt), ARCING or ARCKING], in *electricity*, to form an arc.
**Arc, Jeanne d'** (zhän' dȧrk'), see **Joan of Arc.**
**ARC, A.R.C.,** American (National) Red Cross.
**ar·cade** (är-kād'), *n.* [Fr. < ML. < L. *arcus*, a bow, arch], 1. a passage having an arched roof. 2. any covered passageway, especially one with shops along the sides. 3. a line of arches and their supporting columns. *v.t.* [ARCADED (-id), ARCADING], to make into or provide with an arcade.
**Ar·ca·di·a** (är-kā'di-ə), *n.* 1. an ancient pastoral district in. S Greece. 2. any place of rural peace and simplicity —**Ar·ca'di·an,** *adj. & n.*
**Ar·ca·dy** (är kə-di), *n.* [Poetic], Arcadia.
**ar·ca·num** (är-kā'nəm), *n.* [*pl.* -NUMS, -NA (-nə)], [L., hidden < *arca*, chest], a secret; mystery.
**arc furnace,** an electric furnace in which the heat comes from an arc between an electrode and the material being heated.
**arch** (ärch), *n.* [< OFr. < ML. < L. *arcus*, a bow, arch], 1. a curved structure, as of masonry, used as a support over an open space, as in a bridge, doorway, etc. 2. the form of an arch. 3. anything shaped like an arch: as, the *arch* of the foot, etc. *v.t.* 1. to provide with an arch or arches. 2. to form into an arch. *v.i.* 1. to form an arch. 2. to span as an arch. —**arched** (ärcht), *adj.*
**arch** (ärch), *adj.* [< *arch-*], 1. main; chief; principal. 2. gaily mischievous; pert: as, an *arch* look. —**arch'ly,** *adv.* —**arch'ness,** *n.*
**arch-,** [< AS. < L. < Gr. *archos*, ruler], a prefix meaning *main, chief, principal:* used in forming titles of rank, as *archduke, archbishop.*
**-arch** (ärk), [< Gr. *archos*, ruler], a suffix meaning *ruler*, as in *heptarch, matriarch.*
**Arch.,** Archbishop.

**arch.,** 1. archaic. 2. archipelago. 3. architect. 4. architecture.

**ar·chae·ol·o·gy** (är′ki-ol′ə-ji), *n.* [< Gr. *archaios*, ancient; + *-logy*], the scientific study of the life and culture of ancient peoples, as by excavation of ancient cities, relics, etc.: also sp. **archeology.** —**ar′chae·o·log′i·cal** (-ə-loj′i-k'l), **ar′chae·o·log′ic,** *adj.* —**ar′chae·o·log′i·cal·ly,** *adv.* —**ar′chae·ol′o·gist,** *n.*

**Ar·chae·o·zo·ic** (är′ki-ə-zō′ik), *adj.* Archeozoic.

**ar·cha·ic** (är-kā′ik), *adj.* [< Gr. < *archaios*, ancient], 1. ancient. 2. antiquated; old-fashioned. 3. that has ceased to be used except in poetry, church ritual, etc., as the word *begat.* —**ar·cha′i·cal·ly,** *adv.*

**ar·cha·ism** (är′ki-iz'm, -kā-), *n.* 1. the use or imitation of archaic words, technique, etc. 2. an archaic word, usage, technique, etc. —**ar′cha·ist,** *n.* —**ar′cha·is′tic,** *adj.*

**arch·an·gel** (ärk′ān′jəl), *n.* 1. a chief angel. 2. [A-], a seaport in the U.S.S.R. on the White Sea: pop., 194,000.

**arch·bish·op** (ärch′bish′əp), *n.* [see ARCH- & BISHOP], a chief bishop, who presides over an archbishopric or archdiocese.

**arch·bish·op·ric** (ärch′bish′əp-rik), *n.* the office, rank, term, or church district of an archbishop.

**arch·dea·con** (ärch′dē′k'n), *n.* [see ARCH- & DEACON], a chief deacon, ranking just below a bishop. —**arch′dea′con·ate** (-it), **arch′dea′con·ship,** *n.*

**arch·dea·con·ry** (ärch′dē′k'n-ri), *n.* [*pl.* -RIES], 1. the office, rank, or jurisdiction of an archdeacon. 2. an archdeacon's residence.

**arch·di·o·cese** (ärch′dī′ə-sēs′, -sis), *n.* [*arch-* + *diocese*], the diocese of an archbishop.

**arch·du·cal** (ärch′dōō′k'l, -dū′-), *adj.* of an archduke or archduchy.

**arch·duch·ess** (ärch′duch′is), *n.* 1. the wife or widow of an archduke. 2. a princess of the former royal family of Austria.

**arch·duch·y** (ärch′duch′i), *n.* [*pl.* -IES], the territory ruled by an archduke or archduchess.

**arch·duke** (ärch′dōōk′, -dūk′), *n.* a prince of the former Austrian royal family.

**ar·che·go·ni·um** (är′ki-gō′ni-əm), *n.* [*pl.* -NIA (-ni-ə)], [< Gr. < *archos*, first, chief + *gonos*, offspring], the flask-shaped female reproductive organ in mosses, ferns, etc. —**ar′che·go′ni·al,** *adj.* —**ar′che·go′ni·ate** (-it), *adj.*

**arch·en·e·my** (ärch′en′ə-mi), *n.* [*pl.* -MIES], a chief enemy. —**the archenemy,** Satan.

**ar·che·ol·o·gy** (är′ki-ol′ə-ji), *n.* archaeology. —**ar′che·o·log′i·cal** (-ə-loj′i-k'l), **ar′che·o·log′ic,** *adj.* —**ar′che·o·log′i·cal·ly,** *adv.* —**ar′che·ol′o·gist,** *n.*

**Ar·che·o·zo·ic** (är′ki-ə-zō′ik), *adj.* [< Gr. *archos*, first; + *zoo-* + *ic*], designating or of the earliest known geological era: see **geology,** chart.

**arch·er** (ärch′ẽr), *n.* [< OFr. < L. < *arcus*, a bow], 1. a person who shoots with bow and arrow; bowman. 2. [A-], the constellation Sagittarius.

**arch·er·y** (ärch′ẽr-i), *n.* 1. the practice, art, or technique of shooting with bow and arrow. 2. an archer's equipment. 3. archers collectively.

**ar·che·type** (är′kə-tīp′), *n.* [< L. < Gr. < *arche-*, first + *typos;* see TYPE, *n.*], an original pattern, or model; prototype. —**ar′che·typ′al, ar′che·typ′i·cal** (-tip′i-k'l), *adj.*

**arch·fiend** (ärch′fēnd′), *n.* a chief fiend. —**the archfiend,** Satan.

**ar·chi-,** [see ARCH-], a prefix meaning *chief, first,* as in *archiepiscopal.*

**ar·chi·di·ac·o·nal** (är′ki-dī-ak′ə-n'l), *adj.* [*archi-* + *diaconal*], of an archdeacon or an archdeaconry. —**ar′chi·di·ac′o·nate** (-nit), *n.*

**ar·chi·e·pis·co·pal** (är′ki-ə-pis′kə-p'l), *adj.* [< ML.; see ARCHI- & EPISCOPAL], of an archbishop or an archbishopric. —**ar′chi·e·pis′co·pate** (-pit, -pāt′), *n.*

**Ar·chi·me·des** (är ki-mē′dēz), *n.* Greek physicist and inventor; 287?–212 B.C. —**Ar′chi·me′de·an** (-mē′di-ən, -mi-dē′ən), *adj.*

**ar·chi·pel·a·go** (är′kə-pel′ə-gō′), *n.* [*pl.* -GOES, -GOS], [< It. < Gr. *archi-*, chief + *pelagos*, sea], 1. [A-], the Aegean Sea; hence, 2. any sea with many islands. 3. such a group of islands. —**ar′chi·pe·lag′ic** (-pə-laj′ik), *adj.*

**ar·chi·tect** (är′kə-tekt ), *n.* [< L. < Gr. < *archi-*, chief + *tektōn*, worker], 1. a person whose profession is designing buildings, drawing up plans, and generally supervising the construction. 2. any builder or creator.

**ar·chi·tec·ton·ic** (är′ki-tek-ton′ik), *adj.* 1. of an architect or architecture. 2. done as though by an architect; showing design. 3. controlling. *n.* architectonics.

**ar·chi·tec·ton·ics** (är′ki-tek-ton′iks), *n.pl.* [construed as sing.], 1. the science of architecture. 2. structural design, as of a symphony.

**ar·chi·tec·ture** (är′kə-tek′chẽr), *n.* 1. the science, art, or profession of designing and constructing buildings. 2. a building, or buildings collectively. 3. a style of construction: as, Elizabethan *architecture.* 4. design and construction. 5. any framework, system, etc. —**ar′chi·tec′tur·al,** *adj.* —**ar′chi·tec′tur·al·ly,** *adv.*

**ar·chi·trave** (är′kə-trāv′), *n.* [Fr. < It. < L. *archi-* + *trabs*, a beam], in *architecture,* 1. the lowest part of an entablature, a beam resting directly on the tops of the columns. 2. the molding around a doorway, window, etc.

**ar·chives** (är′kīvz), *n.pl.* [Fr. < L. < Gr. < *ta archeia*, public records < *archē*, the beginning, magistracy], 1. a place where public records, documents, etc. are kept. 2. the public records, etc. kept in such a place. —**ar·chi′val,** *adj.*

**ar·chi·vist** (är′kə-vist), *n.* a person having charge of archives.

**ar·chon** (är′kon), *n.* [< Gr. < *archein*, to be first, rule], one of the nine chief magistrates of ancient Athens. —**ar′chon·ship,** *n.*

**arch·priest** (ärch′prēst′), *n.* 1. formerly, a priest who acted as a bishop's chief assistant. 2. a chief priest. —**arch′priest′hood,** *n.*

**arch·way** (ärch′wā′), *n.* a passage under an arch.

**-ar·chy** (är-ki, ẽr-ki), [< Gr. < *archos*, ruler], a suffix meaning *ruling, that which is ruled,* as in *monarchy.*

**arc lamp,** a lamp in which the light is produced by an arc between electrodes. Also **arc light.**

**arc·tic** (ärk′tik, är′tik), *adj.* [< OFr. < L.; Gr. *arktikos*, lit., of the (constellation of the) Bear (Gr. *arktos*), northern], 1. of, characteristic of, or near the North Pole or the region around it; hence, 2. very cold; frigid. *n.* 1. the region around the North Pole. 2. the Arctic Circle. See also **arctics.**

**Arctic Circle, arctic circle,** 1. an imaginary circle parallel to the equator, 23°30′ from the North Pole. 2. the Arctic Zone.

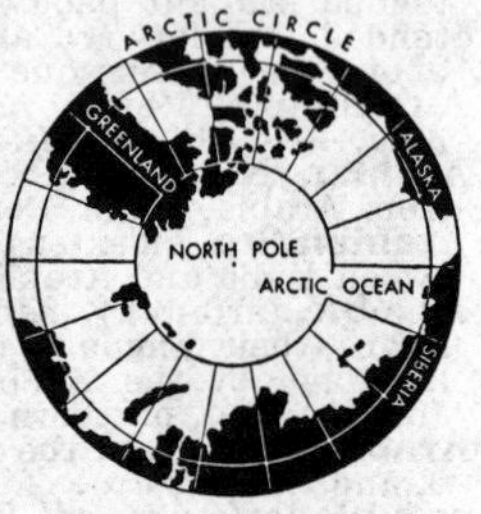

ARCTIC CIRCLE

**Arctic Ocean,** the ocean around the North Pole: area, 5,440,000 sq. mi.

**arc·tics** (ärk′tiks, är′tiks), *n.pl.* [< *arctic*], warmly lined, waterproof overshoes.

**Arctic Zone,** all the region north of the Arctic Circle.

**Arc·tu·rus** (ärk-toor′əs, -tyoor′-), *n.* [L.; Gr. *Arktouros* < *arktos*, a bear + *ouros*, a guard], the brightest star in the constellation Boötes.

**-ard** (ẽrd), [OFr. < MHG. *hart*, bold], a suffix used in forming nouns meaning *one who does* (something not admirable) *too much,* as in *sluggard, drunkard:* also **-art,** as in *braggart.*

**ar·den·cy** (är′d'n-si), *n.* a being ardent; ardor.

**ar·dent** (är′d'nt), *adj.* [< L. < *ardere*, to burn], 1. glowing; beaming. 2. passionate; vehement; eager. 3. [Obs.], burning; aflame. —**ar′dent·ly,** *adv.* —**ar′dent·ness,** *n.*

**ar·dor** (är′dẽr), *n.* [< OFr. < L. < *ardere*, to burn], 1. emotional warmth; passion; eagerness; enthusiasm; zeal. 2. intense heat; fire.

**ar·dour** (är′dẽr), *n.* ardor: Brit. sp.

**ar·du·ous** (är′jōō-əs), *adj.* [L. *arduus*, steep], 1. difficult to do; requiring exertion; laborious. 2. steep; hard to climb. 3. energetic; working hard. —**ar′du·ous·ly,** *adv.* —**ar′du·ous·ness,** *n.*

**are** (är), [AS. (Northumbrian) *aron*], pl. and second person sing., pres. indic., of **be.**

**are** (âr), *n.* [Fr. < L. *area;* see AREA], a unit of surface measure in the metric system, equal to 100 square meters or 119.6 square yards.

**ar·e·a** (âr′i-ə), *n.* [L., level piece of ground], 1. originally, a level surface. 2. a part of the earth's surface; region; tract. 3. a total outside surface, as measured in square units. 4. an areaway. 5. scope; range; extent. —**ar′e·al,** *adj.*

**ar·e·a·way** (âr′i-ə-wā′), *n.* 1. a sunken yard leading into a cellar. 2. a passage between buildings.

**a·re·na** (ə-rē′nə), *n.* [*pl.* -NAS, -NAE (-nē)], [L., sand, sandy place, arena], 1. the central part of an ancient Roman amphitheater, where gladiatorial contests took place. 2. any place like this: as, an *arena* for boxing matches. 3. any sphere of struggle or exertion.

**ar·e·na·ceous** (ar′i-nā′shəs), *adj.* sandy.

**aren't** (ärnt), are not: also occasionally used as a substitute for a contraction of *am not* in interrogative constructions: see also **ain't.**

**a·re·o·la** (ə-rē′ə-lə), *n.* [*pl.* -LAE (-lē′), -LAS], [L., small open place], 1. a small space, as between the veins of a leaf. 2. in *anatomy*, a small colored area, as around a nipple. Also **ar·e·ole** (âr′i-ōl′). —**a·re′o·lar** (-lẽr), *adj.*

**Ar·e·op·a·gus** (ar′i-op′ə-gəs), *n.* [L. < Gr. < *Areios*, of Ares + *pagos*, hill], 1. the hill west of the Acropolis in ancient Athens, where the high court of judges sat. 2. this court.

**Ar·es** (âr′ēz), *n.* in *Gr. mythology*, the god of war: identified with the Roman god Mars.

**ar·ga·li** (är′gə-li), *n.* [*pl.* -LIS, -LI; see PLURAL, II, D, 1], [Mongol.], 1. a wild sheep of Asia, with large, curved horns. 2. any of several other wild sheep, as the bighorn. Also **ar′gal** (-g'l).

**ar·gent** (är′jənt), *n.* [Fr. < L. < Gr. *argyros*, silver < *argos*, white], [Archaic or Poetic], silver. *adj.* silvery. —**ar·gen′tal** (-jen′t'l), **ar·gen′te·ous,** *adj.*

**ar·gen·tif·er·ous** (är′jən-tif′ẽr-əs), *adj.* containing silver, as ore.

**Ar·gen·ti·na** (är′jən-tē′nə), *n.* a country in S South America: area, 1,079,965 sq. mi.; pop., 20,956,000; capital, Buenos Aires: abbrev. **Arg.** —**Ar′gen·tine′** (-tēn′, -tīn′), **Ar′gen·tin′e·an** (-tin′i-ən), *adj. & n.*

**ar·gen·tine** (är′jən-tin, -tīn′). *adj.* of or like silver; silvery. *n.* silver.

**ar·gen·tum** (är-jen′təm), *n.* [L.; see ARGENT], silver: symbol, Ag: abbrev. **Ar.**

**ar·gil** (är′jil), *n.* [< Fr. < L. < Gr. < *argos*, white], clay, especially that used for pottery. —**ar′gil·la′ceous,** (-ji-lā′shəs), *adj.*

**Ar·give** (är′jīv, -gīv), *adj. & n.* Greek.

**Ar·go** (är′gō), *n.* 1. in *Gr. legend*, the ship on which Jason sailed to find the Golden Fleece. 2. a large southern constellation.

**ar·gon** (är′gon), *n.* [Gr., inert < *a-*, without + *ergon*, work], one of the chemical elements, an inert, colorless, odorless gas found in small amounts in the atmosphere: it is used in radio tubes, etc.: symbol, A; at. wt., 39.944; at. no., 18.

**Ar·go·naut** (är′gə-nôt′), *n.* [< L. < Gr. < *Argo*, Jason's ship + *nautēs*, sailor], 1. in *Gr. legend*, any of the men who sailed with Jason to search for the Golden Fleece. 2. one who took part in the California gold rush of 1848–49. —**Ar′go·nau′tic,** *adj.*

**Ar·gonne** (är′gon; Fr. år gôn′), *n.* a forest in NE France.

**ar·go·sy** (är′gə-si), *n.* [*pl.* -SIES], [earlier *ragusy* < It. *Ragusea*, vessel of *Ragusa;* sp. influenced by *Argo*], [Now Poetic], 1. a large ship; esp., a merchant ship. 2. a fleet of such ships.

**ar·got** (är′gō, -gət), *n.* [Fr.; orig. (in thieves' jargon), thievery; prob. < *argot* (now *ergot*), a claw, spur], the specialized vocabulary and idioms of a particular group, as the secret jargon of criminals or tramps: see **slang, cant.**

**ar·gue** (är′gū), *v.i.* [-GUED, -GUING], [< OFr. < L. *argutare*, to prattle, freq. of *arguere*, to prove], 1. to give reasons (*for* or *against* a proposal, etc.). 2. to dispute (*with* a person or *about* a thing). 3. to present objections. *v.t.* 1. to give reasons for and against; debate. 2. to try to prove by giving reasons; contend. 3. to indicate: as, his manners *argue* a good upbringing. 4. to persuade (*into* or *out of* an opinion, etc.) by giving reasons. —**ar′gu·a·ble,** *adj.* —**ar′gu·er,** *n.*

**ar·gu·fy** (är′gyoo-fī′), *v.t. & v.i.* [-FIED, -FYING], [< *argue* + *-fy*], [Colloq. or Dial.], to argue, especially just for the sake of arguing.

**ar·gu·ment** (är′gyoo-mənt), *n.* 1. a reason or reasons offered for or against something. 2. the offering of such reasons; reasoning. 3. discussion in which there is disagreement; dispute; debate. 4. a short statement of subject matter; summary.

**ar·gu·men·ta·tion** (är′gyoo-men-tā′shən), *n.* 1. the process of arguing. 2. debate; discussion.

**ar·gu·men·ta·tive** (är′gyoo-men′tə-tiv), *adj.* 1. controversial. 2. apt to argue. —**ar′gu·men′ta·tive·ly,** *adv.* —**ar′gu·men′ta·tive·ness,** *n.*

**Ar·gus** (är′gəs), *n.* [L. < Gr. < *argos*, bright], 1. in *Gr. mythology*, a giant with a hundred eyes, who was killed by Hermes. 2. any alert watchman.

**Ar·gus-eyed** (är′gəs-īd′), *adj.* keenly vigilant.

**ar·gy·rol** (är′jə-rôl′, -rol′), *n.* [< Gr. *argyros*, silver; + *-ol*], a compound of silver and a protein used as an antiseptic: a trade-mark (**Argyrol**).

**a·ri·a** (ä′ri-ə, âr′i-ə), *n.* [It. < L. *aer;* see AIR], an air or melody in an opera, cantata, or oratorio, especially for solo voice with accompaniment.

**-a·ri·a** (ā′ri-ə, âr′i-), [< L. *-arius*], a suffix used in botany and zoology in names of groups and genera.

**Ar·i·ad·ne** (ar′i-ad′ni), *n.* in *Gr. legend*, king Minos' daughter, who gave Theseus the thread by which he found his way out of the Minotaur's labyrinth.

**Ar·i·an** (âr′i-ən, är′yən), *n. & adj.* Aryan.

**Ar·i·an** (âr′i-ən), *adj.* of Arius or Arianism. *n.* a believer in Arianism.

**-ar·i·an** (âr′i-ən), [L. *-arius* + *-anus*], a suffix denoting variously *age, sect, social belief, occupation*, used in forming adjectives and nouns derived from adjectives, as *octogenarian*.

**Ar·i·an·ism** (âr′i-ən-iz'm), *n.* the doctrines of Arius, who taught that Jesus was not of the same substance as God.

**ar·id** (ar′id), *adj.* [< L. < *arere*, to be dry], 1. dry. 2. barren. 3. uninteresting; dull. —**a·rid·i·ty** (ə-rid′ə-ti), **ar′id·ness,** *n.* —**ar′id·ly,** *adv.*

**Ar·i·es** (âr′ēz, -i-ēz′), *n.* [L., the Ram], 1. a northern constellation, supposedly outlining a ram. 2. the first sign of the zodiac (♈).

**a·right** (ə-rīt′), *adv.* correctly; rightly.

**ar·il** (ar′il), *n.* [ML. *arillus*, dried grape], an additional covering that forms on certain seeds.

**ar·il·late** (ar′ə-lāt′), *adj.* covered with an aril.

**a·rio·so** (ä-ryō′sō), *adj.* like an aria; melodious. *adv.* in arioso style. *n.* an arioso composition.

**-ar·i·ous** (âr′i-əs), [< L. *-arius;* + *-ous*], a suffix meaning *relating to, connected with*, as in *hilarious*.

**a·rise** (ə-rīz′), *v.i.* [AROSE (-rōz′), ARISEN (-riz′'n), ARISING], [AS. < *a-*, out + *risan*, to rise], 1. to get up, as from bed. 2. to move upward; rise; ascend. 3. to come into being; originate. 4. to result or spring (*from* something).

**Ar·is·ti·des** (ar′is-tī′dēz), *n.* Athenian statesman and general: lived 530?–468? B.C.

**ar·is·toc·ra·cy** (ar′ə-stok′rə-si), *n.* [*pl.* -CIES], [< L. < Gr. < *aristos*, best + *kratein*, to rule], 1. originally, government by the best citizens. 2. government by a privileged minority, usually of inherited wealth and social position. 3. a country with this form of government. 4. a privileged ruling class; the nobility; upper class. 5. those considered the best: as, an *aristocracy* of brains.

**a·ris·to·crat** (ə-ris′tə-krat , ar′is-), *n.* 1. a member of the aristocracy; nobleman. 2. a person with the tastes, manners, beliefs, etc. of the upper class. 3. one who believes in aristocracy as a form of government.

**a·ris·to·crat·ic** (ə-ris′tə-krat′ik, ar′is-), *adj.* 1. of, characteristic of, or favoring aristocratic government. 2. of an aristocracy or upper class. 3. like an aristocrat. Also **a·ris′to·crat′i·cal.** —**a·ris′to·crat′i·cal·ly,** *adv.*

**Ar·is·toph·a·nes** (ar′is-tof′ə-nēz′), *n.* Greek writer of comedies; lived 448?–380? B.C.

**Ar·is·to·te·li·an** (ar′is-tə-tē′li-ən, ə-ris′tə-tēl′yən), *adj.* of or characteristic of Aristotle or his empirical philosophy. *n.* a follower of Aristotle. —**Ar′is·to·te′li·an·ism,** *n.*

**Ar·is·tot·le** (ar′is-tot′'l), *n.* Greek philosopher; 384–322 B.C.; pupil of Plato.

**a·rith·me·tic** (ə-rith′mə-tik′), *n.* [OFr. < L. < Gr. < *arithmos*, number], 1. the science of computing by positive, real numbers. 2. a textbook on this science. *adj.* (ar′ith-met′ik), arithmetical.

**ar·ith·met·i·cal** (ar′ith-met′i-k'l), *adj.* of or using arithmetic. —**ar′ith·met′i·cal·ly,** *adv.*

**a·rith·me·ti·cian** (ə-rith′mə-tish′ən, ar′ith-), *n.* one skilled in arithmetic.

**arithmetic mean,** the average obtained by dividing a sum by the number of its addends.

**arithmetic progression,** a sequence of terms each of which, after the first, is derived by adding to the preceding one a constant quantity: 5, 9, 13, 17, etc. are in *arithmetic progression.*

**A·ri·us** (ə-rī′əs, âr′i-əs), *n.* Greek theologian of Alexandria: lived 280?–336 A.D.: see **Arianism.**

**‡a ri·ve·der·ci** (ä rē′ve-der′chē), [It.], until we meet again; good-by.

**Ar·i·zo·na** (ar′ə-zō′nə), *n.* a SW State of the U.S.: area, 113,909 sq. mi.; pop., 1,302,000; capital, Phoenix: abbrev. **Ariz.** —**Ar′i·zo′nan, Ar′i·zo′ni·an,** *adj. & n.*

**ark** (ärk), *n.* [< AS. < L. < *arcere*, to enclose], 1. the ark of the covenant. 2. in the *Bible*, the huge boat in which Noah, his family, and two of every kind of creature survived the Flood: Gen. 6. 3. any boat like this. 4. a place of refuge.

**Ar·kan·sas** (är′kən-sô′), *n.* 1. a Southern State of the U.S.: area, 53,102 sq. mi.; pop., 1,786,000; capital, Little Rock: abbrev. **Ark.** 2. (*also* är-kan′zəs), a river flowing from Colorado into the Mississippi: length, 1,460 mi. —**Ar·kan′san** (-kan′-zən), **Ar·kan′si·an** (-zi-ən), *n. & adj.*

**ark of the covenant,** in the *Bible*, the chest in which the stone tablets inscribed with the Ten Commandments were kept.

**Ark·wright,** Sir **Richard** (ark′rīt′), 1732–1792; English inventor of a cotton-spinning machine.

**Ar·ling·ton National Cemetery** (är′liŋ-tən), a national cemetery in Virginia, near Washington, D.C.

**arm** (ärm), *n.* [AS. *earm*], 1. *a*) an upper limb of the human body. *b*) anything commonly in contact with this, as a sleeve, a support for the arm on a chair, etc. 2. anything immediately resembling this; esp., *a*) a branch of a river. *b*) the forelimb of an animal. 3. anything thought of as armlike: as, an *arm* of the sea, a yard*arm*, etc. 4. anything thought of as functioning like an arm: as, the long *arm* of the law, etc. —**arm in arm,** with arms interlocked. —**keep at arm's length,** to keep at a distance. —**with open arms,** with warm cordiality. —**arm′less,** *adj.*

**arm** (ärm), *n.* [OFr. < L. *arma*, implements, weapons], 1. any weapon: see **arms.** 2. any combatant branch of the military forces, as the infantry, etc. *v.t.* 1. to provide with weapons, etc. 2. to provide with a protective covering. *v.i.* to prepare for war.

**Arm.,** Armenian.

**ar·ma·da** (är-mä′də, -mā′), *n.* [Sp. < L. < *armare*, to arm < *arma*, weapons], 1. a fleet of warships. 2. [A-], the fleet of warships sent against England by Spain in 1588. 3. a fleet of warplanes.

**ar·ma·dil·lo** (är′mə-dil′ō), *n.* [*pl.* -LOS], [Sp., dim. of *armado;* see ARMADA], any of a number of related toothless, burrowing mammals of Texas and Central and South America, having an armorlike covering of bony plates.

ARMADILLO (30 in. long)

**Ar·ma·ged·don** (är′mə-ged′'n), *n.* 1. in the *Bible*, the place where the last, decisive battle between the forces of good and evil will be fought: Rev. 16:16. 2. any great, decisive battle.

**ar·ma·ment** (är′mə-mənt), *n.* 1. *often pl.* all the military forces and equipment of a nation. 2. all the military equipment of a warship, fortification, etc. 3. an arming or being armed for war.

**ar·ma·ture** (är′mə-chẽr), *n.* [Fr.; L. *armatura*, arms, equipment < *armare*, to arm], 1. armor. 2. an armorlike covering. 3. flat wire wound around a cable. 4. a soft iron bar placed across the poles of a magnet. 5. the part that revolves in an electric motor or dynamo: it consists of an iron core wound with wire. 6. the vibrating part in an electric relay or bell. 7. in *sculpture*, a framework for supporting the clay in modeling.

**arm·chair** (ärm′chār′), *n.* a chair with supports at the sides for one's arms or elbows.

**armd.,** armored.

**armed** (ärmd), *adj.* provided with arms (weapons), armor, etc.

**armed** (ärmd), *adj.* having arms (upper limbs): usually in compounds, as *long-armed.*

**armed forces,** all the military, naval, and air forces of a country or group of countries.

**Ar·me·ni·a** (är-mē′ni-ə, -mēn′yə), *n.* 1. a former country in SW Asia, south of the Caucasus Mountains. 2. the Armenian Soviet Socialist Republic. —**Ar·me′ni·an,** *adj. & n.*

**Armenian Soviet Socialist Republic,** a republic of the U.S.S.R., in the Transcaucasus, consisting of part of the former Armenia: area, 11,580 sq. mi.; pop., 1,282,000; capital, Erivan.

**Ar·men·tières** (år′män′tyâr′), *n.* a town in N France, near the Belgian border: pop., 23,000.

**arm·ful** (ärm′fool), *n.* [*pl.* -FULS], as much as the arms or one arm can hold.

**arm·hole** (ärm′hōl′), *n.* an opening for the arm in any garment.

**Ar·min·i·us, Ja·co·bus** (jə-kō′bəs är-min′i-əs), 1560–1609; Dutch Protestant theologian, who revised the Calvinist views of predestination. —**Ar·min′i·an,** *adj. & n.* —**Ar·min′i·an·ism,** *n.*

**ar·mi·stice** (är′mə-stis), *n.* [Fr. < L. *arma*, arms + *stare*, to stand still], a temporary stopping of warfare by mutual agreement; truce.

**Armistice Day,** the former name for November 11, the anniversary of the armistice of World War I in 1918: see **Veterans' Day.**

**arm·let** (ärm′lit), *n.* 1. a band worn for ornament around the upper arm. 2. a small arm of the sea.

**ar·moire** (är-mwär′), *n.* [Fr. < OFr. < L. *armarium*, chest for arms], a large cupboard or clothespress.

**ar·mor** (är′mẽr), *n.* [< OFr. < L. < *armare*, to arm], 1. covering worn to protect the body against weapons. 2. any defensive or protective covering, as the metal plate on warships. 3. the armored forces of an army. *v.t. & v.i.* to put armor on.

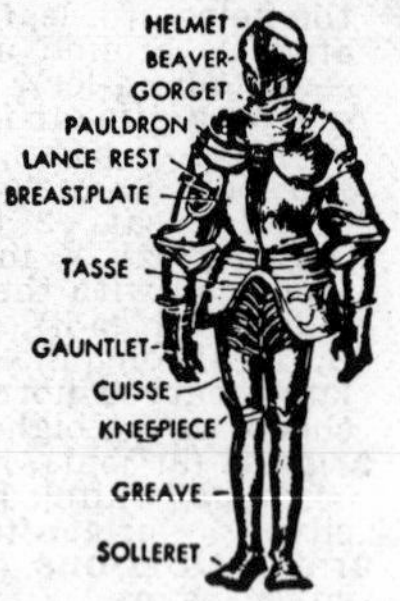

ARMOR

**ar·mor·bear·er** (är′mẽr-bâr′ẽr), *n.* one who carried the armor or weapons of a warrior.

**ar·mored** (är′mẽrd), *adj.* 1. covered with armor: as, an *armored* car. 2. equipped with armored vehicles: as, an *armored* division.

**ar·mor·er** (är′mẽr-ẽr), *n.* 1. formerly, one who made or repaired armor. 2. a maker of firearms. 3. in *military usage*, a man in charge of small arms.

**ar·mo·ri·al** (är-môr′i-əl, -mō′ri-), *adj.* of coats of arms; heraldic.

**armorial bearings,** a coat of arms.

**armor plate,** a protective covering of steel plates, as on a warship or tank. —**ar′mor-plat′ed,** *adj.*

**ar·mor·y** (är′mẽr-i), *n.* [*pl.* -IES], [< OFr. < *arme;* see ARM (weapon)], 1. an arsenal. 2. a building housing the drill hall and offices of a unit of the National Guard. 3. an armaments factory.

**ar·mour** (är′mẽr), *n., v.i. & v.t.* armor: Brit. sp.

**ar·mour·er** (är′mẽr-ẽr), *n.* armorer: Brit. sp.

**ar·mour·y** (är′mẽr-i), *n.* armory: Brit. sp.

**arm·pit** (ärm′pit′), *n.* the hollow under the arm at the shoulder; axilla.

**arms** (ärmz), *n.pl.* 1. weapons. 2. warfare; fighting. 3. heraldic symbols. 4. insignia of countries, etc. See also **small arms.** —**bear arms,** to serve in the armed forces. —**take up arms,** 1. to go to war or rise in rebellion. 2. to enter a dispute. —**to arms!** get ready to fight! —**up in arms,** 1. prepared to fight. 2. indignant.

**ar·my** (är′mi), *n.* [*pl.* -MIES], [< OFr. < L. < *armare*, to arm], 1. a large, organized body of soldiers for waging war. 2. a military unit of two or more corps. 3. [often A-], a large organization of persons for a specific cause: as, the Salvation *Army.* 4. any large number of persons, animals, etc.

**Army Air Forces,** formerly, the aviation branch of the U.S. Army: abbrev. **A.A.F.**

**army worm,** the larva of a certain moth: it travels in large groups, ruining crops.

**Arn·hem** (ärn′hem), *n.* a city in the Netherlands, on the Rhine: pop., 98,000.

**ar·ni·ca** (är′ni-kə), *n.* 1. any of a number of related plants of the aster family. 2. a medicine made from one of these plants, for treating sprains, bruises, etc.

**Ar·nold, Benedict** (är′nəld), 1741–1801; American general in the Revolutionary War who became a traitor.

**Arnold, Matthew,** 1822–1888; English poet, critic, and essayist.

**a·roint thee!** (ə-roint′), [Obs.], begone! avaunt!

**a·ro·ma** (ə-rō′mə), *n.* [< OFr. < L. < Gr. *arōma*, sweet spice], 1. a pleasant, often spicy odor; fragrance, as of a plant, cooking, etc. 2. a distinctive flavor or characteristic quality.

**ar·o·mat·ic** (ar′ə-mat′ik), *adj.* of or having an aroma: also **ar′o·mat′i·cal.** *n.* an aromatic plant, chemical, etc. —**ar′o·mat′i·cal·ly,** *adv.*

**a·ro·ma·tize** (ə-rō′mə-tīz′), *v.t.* [-TIZED, -TIZING], to make aromatic. —**a·ro′ma·ti·za′tion,** *n.*

**a·rose** (ə-rōz′), past tense of **arise.**

**a·round** (ə-round′), *adv.* 1. round; esp., *a*) in a circle; along a circular course. *b*) in or through a course or circuit. *c*) in every direction. *d*) in circumference. *e*) in or to the opposite direction, belief, etc. *f*) in various places. 2. [Colloq.], near by: as, stay *around.* 3. [Colloq.], to a (specified) place: as, come *around* to see us. *prep.* 1. round; esp., *a*) so as to encircle or envelop. *b*) on the border of. *c*) on all sides of. *d*) in various places in or on. *e*) so as to rotate about (a center). 2. [Colloq.], about: as, *around* 1890. Cf. **round.** See also phrases under **bring, come, get,** etc. —**have been around,** [Colloq.], to have had wide experience; be sophisticated.

**a·rouse** (ə-rouz′), *v.t.* [AROUSED, AROUSING], 1. to stir up, as to action; excite. 2. to wake. *v.i.* to become aroused. —**a·rous′al,** *n.* —**a·rous′er,** *n.*

**ar·peg·gio** (är-pej′ō, -i-ō′), *n.* [*pl.* -GIOS], [It. < *arpeggiare*, to play on a harp < *arpa*, a harp], 1.

the playing of the notes of a chord in quick succession instead of simultaneously. 2. a chord so played.

**ar·que·bus** (är′kwi-bəs), *n.* [< Fr. < It. < D. *haakbuse*, lit., a hook box], an early type of portable matchlock gun, supported on a hooked staff or forked rest during firing: also **harquebus.**

**arr.,** 1. arranged. 2. arrival. 3. arrives.

**ar·rack** (ar′ək), *n.* [< Fr. < Ar. < *'araq*, sweat, liquor], in the Orient, strong alcoholic drink, especially that made from rice or molasses.

**ar·raign** (ə-rān′), *v.t.* [< OFr. < ML. < L. *ad*, to + *ratio*, reason], 1. to bring before a law court to stand trial. 2. to call to account or in question; accuse. **—ar·raign′er,** *n.* **—ar·raign′ment,** *n.*

**ar·range** (ə-rānj′), *v.t.* [-RANGED, -RANGING], [< OFr. < *a-*, to + *rang*, rank; see RANGE], 1. to put in the correct order. 2. to classify. 3. to settle (a dispute); adjust (a claim, etc.). 4. in *music*, to adapt (a composition) to other instruments or voices than those for which it was written, or to a certain band or orchestra. *v.i.* 1. to come to an agreement (*with* a person, *about* a thing). 2. to make plans. 3. in *music*, to write adaptations. **—ar·range′a·ble,** *adj.* **—ar·rang′er,** *n.*

**ar·range·ment** (ə-rānj′mənt), *n.* 1. an arranging or being arranged. 2. a result or manner of arranging. 3. a combination of parts; hence, 4. loosely, a contrivance. 5. *usually in pl.* a plan: as, *arrangements* for the party. 6. a settlement or adjustment. 7. in *music*, *a*) an arranging of a composition for other instruments, voices, etc. *b*) the composition as thus arranged.

**ar·rant** (ar′ənt), *adj.* [var. of *errant*], out-and-out; unmitigated; notorious: as, an *arrant* fool.

**ar·ras** (ar′əs), *n.* [after *Arras*, city in France, where it was made], 1. a kind of tapestry. 2. a wall hanging of tapestry.

**ar·ray** (ə-rā′), *v.t.* [< OFr. < L. hyp. *arredare*, to put in order < *ad-*, to + Gmc. base *raid-*, order], 1. to place in order; marshal, as troops. 2. to dress in finery. *n.* 1. an orderly grouping, especially of troops. 2. military force. 3. an impressive display of persons or things. 4. clothes; finery.

**ar·ray·al** (ə-rā′əl), *n.* 1. the act or process of arraying. 2. something arrayed.

**ar·rear·age** (ə-rêr′ij), *n.* 1. the state of being in arrears. 2. arrears. 3. a thing kept in reserve.

**ar·rears** (ə-rêrz′), *n.pl.* [< OFr. *arere*, backward < L. *ad*, to + *retro*, behind], 1. overdue debts. 2. unfinished work, etc. **—in arrears** (or **arrear**), behind in paying a debt, in one's work, etc.

**ar·rest** (ə-rest′), *v.t.* [< OFr. < L. *ad*, to + *restare*, to stop], 1. to stop or check. 2. to seize by authority of the law. 3. to catch and keep. *n.* 1. an arresting or being arrested. 2. a thing for checking motion. **—under arrest,** in legal custody, as of the police. **—ar·rest′er, ar·rest′or,** *n.*

**ar·rest·ing** (ə-res′tiŋ), *adj.* interesting; striking; attracting attention.

**Ar·rhe·ni·us, Svan·te Au·gust** (svän′te ou′gəst är-rā′ni-əs), 1859–1927; Swedish chemist and physicist.

**ar·ris** (ar′is), *n.* the edge made by two surfaces coming together at an angle.

**ar·riv·al** (ə-rīv′'l), *n.* 1. an arriving. 2. a person or thing that arrives or has arrived.

**ar·rive** (ə-rīv′), *v.i.* [-RIVED, -RIVING], [< OFr. < L. *ad*, to + *ripa*, shore], 1. to reach one's destination. 2. to come: as, the time has *arrived*. 3. to attain fame, etc. **—arrive at,** 1. to reach by traveling. 2. to reach by thinking, etc.

**‡ar·ri·ve·der·ci** (ä-rē′ve-der′chē), *interj.* [It.], until we meet again; good-by.

**ar·ro·gance** (ar′ə-gəns), *n.* the quality of being arrogant; haughtiness: also **ar′ro·gan·cy.**

**ar·ro·gant** (ar′ə-gənt), *adj.* [OFr. < L. *arrogare*; see ARROGATE], full of or due to unwarranted pride; haughty. **—ar′ro·gant·ly,** *adv.*

**ar·ro·gate** (ar′ə-gāt′), *v.t.* [-GATED, -GATING], [< L. *arrogare* < *ad-*, for + *rogare*, to ask], 1. to claim or seize without right. 2. to ascribe or attribute without reason. **—ar′ro·ga′tion,** *n.* **—ar′ro·ga′tor,** *n.*

**‡ar·ron·disse·ment** (å′rōn′dēs′män′), *n.* [*pl.* -MENTS (-män′)], [Fr. < *arrondir*, to make round], in France, the largest subdivision of a department.

**ar·row** (ar′ō), *n.* [AS. *earh*, *arwe*], 1. a slender shaft, usually pointed at one end and feathered at the other, for shooting from a bow. 2, anything like an arrow in form, etc. 3. a sign (⟵) used to indicate direction. **—ar′row·y,** *adj.*

**ar·row·head** (ar′ō-hed′), *n.* 1. the pointed tip of an arrow. 2. anything shaped like an arrowhead, as an indicating mark. 3. any of a number of related plants with arrow-shaped leaves.

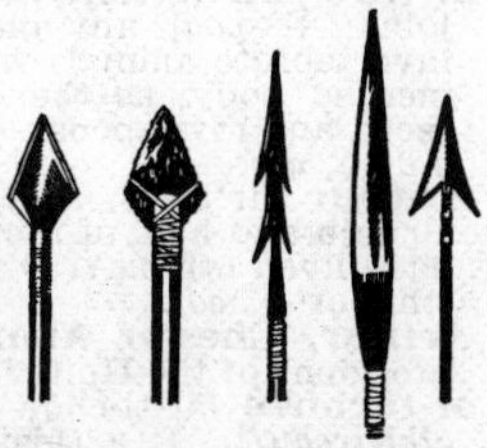

TYPES OF ARROWHEAD

**ar·row·root** (ar′ō-rōōt′, -root′), *n.* [so named from use as antidote for poisoned arrows], 1. a tropical American plant with starchy roots. 2. a starch made from its roots.

**ar·roy·o** (ə-roi′ō), *n.* [*pl.* -os], [Sp. < L. *arrugia*, mine pit], 1. a dry gully. 2. a rivulet.

**ar·se·nal** (är′s'n-əl), *n.* [It. *arsenale*, a dock; Ar. *dār aṣ-ṣināʻah*, workshop], a place for making or storing weapons and other munitions.

**ar·se·nate** (är′s'n-āt′, -it), *n.* [*arsen*ic + *-ate*], in *chemistry*, a salt or ester of arsenic acid.

**ar·se·nic** (är′s'n-ik; *for adj.*, är-sen′ik), *n.* [OFr. < L. < Gr. < Ar. *az zirnīkh* or Heb. *zarnīq*; ult. < Per. *zar*, gold], 1. a silvery-white, brittle, very poisonous chemical element, compounds of which are used in making insecticides, medicines, etc.: symbol, As; at. wt., 74.91; at. no., 33. 2. loosely, arsenic trioxide, a very poisonous compound of arsenic: it is a white, tasteless powder. *adj.* of or containing arsenic.

**ar·sen·i·cal** (är-sen′i-k'l), *adj.* of or containing arsenic. *n.* a compound that contains arsenic.

**ar·se·nous** (är′s'n-əs), *adj.* of or containing arsenic: also **ar·se·ni·ous** (är-sē′ni-əs).

**‡ars gra·ti·a ar·tis** (ärz′ grā′shi-ə är′tis), [L.], art for art's sake.

**‡ars lon·ga, vi·ta bre·vis** (ärz′ lôŋ′gə vī′tə brev′is), [L.], art (is) long, life (is) short.

**ar·son** (är′s'n), *n.* [OFr. < L. pp. of *ardere*, to burn], the crime of purposely setting fire to a building or property. **—ar′son·ist,** *n.*

**ars·phen·a·mine** (ärs′fen-ə-mēn′, -am′in), *n.* [*arse*nic + *phen*yl + *amine*], salvarsan.

**‡ars po·e·ti·ca** (ärz pō-et′i-kə), [L.], the art of poetry.

**art** (ärt), *n.* [< OFr. < L. *ars*, *artis*], 1. creativeness. 2. skill. 3. any specific skill or its application. 4. a making or doing of things that have form and beauty: see also **fine arts.** 5. any branch of this; esp., painting, drawing, or sculpture. 6. products of creative work; paintings, statues, etc. 7. *usually in pl.* any of certain branches of academic learning, as literature, music, and mathematics. 8. any craft, etc., or its principles: as, the cobbler's *art*. 9. cunning. 10. *usually in pl.* a trick; wile.

**art** (ärt), archaic second pers. sing., pres. indic., of **be**: used with *thou*.

**-art** (ẽrt), -ard, as in *braggart*.

**art.,** 1. article. 2. artificial. 3. artillery. 4. artist.

**ar·te·fact** (är′ti-fakt′), *n.* an artifact.

**Ar·te·mis** (är′tə-mis), *n.* in *Gr. mythology*, the goddess of the moon and hunting, Apollo's twin sister: identified with the Roman goddess Diana.

**ar·te·ri·al** (är-têr′i-əl), *adj.* 1. of or like an artery or arteries. 2. designating or of the bright-red, oxygenated blood in the arteries. 3. designating or of a main road with many branches.

**ar·te·ri·al·ize** (är-têr′i-əl-īz′), *v.t.* [-IZED, -IZING], to change (venous blood) into arterial blood by oxygenation. **—ar·te′ri·al·i·za′tion,** *n.*

**ar·te·ri·o·scle·ro·sis** (är-têr′i-ō-skli-rō′sis), *n.* [see ARTERY & SCLEROSIS], a thickening and hardening of the walls of the arteries, as in old age. **—ar·te′ri·o·scle·rot′ic** (-rot′ik), *adj.*

**ar·ter·y** (är′tẽr-i), *n.* [*pl.* -IES], [< L. < Gr.; prob. < *aeirein*, to raise], 1. any one of the system of tubes carrying blood from the heart to all parts of the body: cf. **vein.** 2. a main road or channel.

**ar·te·sian well** (är-tē′zhən), [Fr. *artésien*, lit., of Artois, former Fr. province], a deep well in which water is forced up by underground pressure.

**art·ful** (ärt′fəl), *adj.* 1. artificial; imitative. 2. skillful or clever; adroit. 3. crafty; cunning. **—art′ful·ly,** *adv.* **—art′ful·ness,** *n.*

**ar·thral·gi·a** (är-thral′jə), *n.* neuralgic pain in a joint or joints. **—ar·thral′gic,** *adj.*

**ar·thri·tis** (är-thrī′tis), *n.* [Gr. < *arthron*, a joint], inflammation of a joint or joints. —**ar·thrit′ic** (-thrit′ik), *adj.*

**ar·thro·pod** (är′thrə-pod′), *n.* [< Gr. *arthron*, a joint; + *-pod*], any member of a large group of invertebrate animals with jointed legs and a segmented body, as the crustaceans, arachnids, insects, and myriapods. —**ar·throp·o·dous** (är-throp′ə-dəs), *adj.*

**Ar·thur** (är′thẽr), *n.* a real or legendary king of Britain and hero of the Round Table: supposed to have lived 6th c. A. D. —**Ar·thu′ri·an** (-thoor′i-ən, -thyoor′-), *adj.*

**Arthur, Chester Alan,** 1830–1886; twenty-first president of the United States (1881–1885).

**ar·ti·choke** (är′ti-chōk′), *n.* [< It. < Sp. < Ar. *alkharshuf*], 1. a thistlelike plant. 2. its flower head, cooked as a vegetable. 3. the Jerusalem artichoke.

**ar·ti·cle** (är′ti-k'l), *n.* [OFr. < L. < *artus*, a joint], 1. one of the sections of a written document, as of a treaty, etc. 2. a complete piece of writing that is part of a newspaper, magazine, or book. 3. any one of a group of things: as, an *article* of luggage. 4. a commodity. 5. in *grammar*, any one of the words *a*, *an*, or *the* (and their equivalents in other languages), used as adjectives. *v.t.* [-CLED, -CLING], 1. to accuse. 2. to bind by the articles of an agreement. *v.i.* to bring charges (*against*).

**ar·tic·u·lar** (är-tik′yoo-lẽr), *adj.* [< L. < *artus*, a joint], of the joints: as, *articular* inflammation.

**ar·tic·u·late** (är-tik′yoo-lit; *for v.*, -lāt′), *adj.* [< L. < *articulare*, to disjoint < *artus*, a joint], 1. jointed. 2. spoken in distinct syllables or words. 3. expressing oneself clearly. 4. able to speak. 5. well formulated. *v.t.* [-LATED, -LATING], 1. to put together by joints. 2. to pronounce distinctly; enunciate. 3. to express clearly. *v.i.* 1. to speak distinctly. 2. to be jointed. —**ar·tic′u·late·ly,** *adv.* —**ar·tic′u·late·ness,** *n.* —**ar·tic′u·la′tive,** *adj.* —**ar·tic′u·la′tor,** *n.*

**ar·tic·u·la·tion** (är-tik′yoo-lā′shən), *n.* 1. a jointing or being jointed. 2. the method or manner of this. 3. enunciation. 4. a speech sound. 5. a joint between bones or similar parts. 6. in *botany*, a node or space between two nodes.

**ar·ti·fact** (är′ti-fakt′), *n.* [L. *ars*, *artis*, art + *factus*; see FACT], any object made by human work or skill: also sp. **artefact.**

**ar·ti·fice** (är′tə-fis), *n.* [< L. < *ars*, *artis*, art + *facere*, to make], 1. skill; ingenuity. 2. trickery; craft. 3. a trick; artful device.

**ar·tif·i·cer** (är-tif′ə-sẽr), *n.* 1. a maker or craftsman, especially a skillful one. 2. an inventor. 3. a military mechanic.

**ar·ti·fi·cial** (är′tə-fish′əl), *adj.* [OFr. < L.; see ARTIFICE], 1. made by human work or art: opposed to *natural*. 2. simulated: as, *artificial* teeth. 3. affected: as, an *artificial* smile. 4. in *botany*, cultivated; not native.—**ar′ti·fi′ci·al′i·ty** (-fish′i-al′ə-ti), [*pl.* -TIES], **ar′ti·fi′cial·ness,** *n.* —**ar′ti·fi′cial·ly,** *adv.*

**artificial insemination,** the insemination of a female without sexual intercourse.

**artificial respiration,** the artificial maintenance of breathing by creating and relaxing pressure on the chest cavity at regular intervals.

**ar·til·ler·y** (är-til′ẽr-i), *n.* [< OFr. < L. hyp. *apticulare*, to set aright < *aptus*, suitable], 1. mounted guns, as cannon: distinguished from *small arms*. 2. the science of guns; gunnery. —**the artillery,** the military branch specializing in the use of heavy mounted guns. —**ar·til′ler·ist, ar·til′ler·y·man** (-mən), [*pl.* -MEN (-mən)], *n.*

**ar·ti·san** (är′tə-z'n), *n.* [Fr. < It. < L. < *artire*, to instruct in arts], a skilled craftsman.

**art·ist** (är′tist), *n.* [< Fr. < It. < L. *ars*, *artis*, art], 1. one who is skilled in any of the fine, especially graphic, arts. 2. one who does anything very well, with a feeling for form, etc. 3. an artiste.

**ar·tiste** (är-tēst′), *n.* [Fr.], 1. a skilled professional entertainer. 2. one very skilled in a trade or occupation: often humorous or facetious.

**ar·tis·tic** (är-tis′tik), *adj.* 1. of art or artists. 2. done skillfully. 3. fond of the fine arts. Also **ar·tis′ti·cal.** —**ar·tis′ti·cal·ly,** *adv.*

**art·ist·ry** (är′tis-tri), *n.* artistic quality, ability, work, or workmanship.

**art·less** (ärt′lis), *adj.* 1. lacking skill or art. 2. uncultured; ignorant. 3. without artificiality; simple; natural. 4. without guile or deceit; ingenuous; naive. —**art′less·ly,** *adv.* —**art′less·ness,** *n.*

**art·y** (är′ti), *adj.* [-IER, -IEST], [Colloq.], affectedly or ostentatiously artistic. —**art′i·ness,** *n.*

**ar·um** (âr′əm), *n.* [L. < Gr. *aron*, the wake robin], any of a number of related plants bearing flowers on a fleshy spike surrounded by a hoodlike leaf.

**A.R.V.,** American Revised Version (of the Bible).

**-ar·y** (er′i, ẽr-i), 1. [L. *-arius*, *-aria*, *-arium*], a suffix meaning *relating to, connected with*, used in forming adjectives and nouns, as *auxiliary*. 2. [L. *-aris*], a suffix meaning *relating to, like*, as in *military*.

**Ar·y·an** (âr′i-ən, är′yən), *adj.* [Sans. *arya*, a tribal name], 1. formerly, Indo-European. 2. of the Aryans. *n.* 1. the hypothetical parent language of the Indo-European family. 2. a person belonging to, or supposed to be a descendant of, the prehistoric people who spoke this language. *Aryan* has no validity as a racial term, although it has been so used, notoriously by the Nazis to mean "a Caucasian of non-Jewish descent," etc. The use of the word in connection with race is due to the idea, regarded by most ethnologists as false, that peoples who spoke the same or related languages must have had a common racial origin. Misuse of *Aryan* has led to its replacement in linguistic discussion by *Indo-European*.

**Ar·y·an·ize** (âr′i-ən-īz′, är′yən-), *v.t.* [-IZED, -IZING], in *Nazi usage*, to rid of (so-called) non-Aryan elements: see **Aryan.**

**as** (az; *unstressed*, əz), *adv.* [weakened form of *also* < AS. *ealswa*, quite so, just as; see ALSO], 1. to the same amount or degree; equally: e.g., I am *as* good as he. 2. for instance; thus: e.g., some colors, *as* green and blue, seem cool. *conj.* 1. to the same amount or degree that: e.g., it flew straight *as* an arrow. 2. in the same manner that: e.g., do *as* he does. 3. at the same time that; while: e.g., she arrived *as* I was leaving. 4. because: e.g., *as* you object, we won't go. 5. that the consequence was: e.g., the question was so obvious *as* to need no reply. 6. though: e.g., tall *as* he was, he couldn't reach it. *pron.* 1. a fact that: e.g., he is tired, *as* anyone can see. 2. that (preceded by *such* or *the same*): e.g., this is the same color *as* yours (is). *prep.* in the role, function, capacity, or sense of: e.g., he poses *as* a friend. —**as . . . as,** a correlative construction used to indicate the equality or sameness of two things: *as large as, as many as*, etc. —**as for,** with reference to; concerning. —**as if,** as it (or one) would if. —**as is,** [Slang], just as it is; without any changes: said of damaged goods being sold. —**as it were,** as if it were so; so to speak. —**as though,** as if. —**as to,** 1. with reference to; concerning. 2. as if to.

**as** (as), *n.* [*pl.* ASSES (-iz; L. -ēz)], [L., a whole, integer], 1. an ancient Roman unit of weight (about 12 ozs.) and measure (about 12 in.). 2. an ancient Roman coin of copper alloy.

**As,** in *chemistry*, arsenic.

**AS.,** Anglo-Saxon: also **A.S., A.-S.**

**as·a·fet·i·da, as·a·foet·i·da** (as′ə-fet′i-də, as-fet′-), *n.* [< LL. < Per. *azā*, gum + L. *f(o)etida* < *f(o)etere*, to stink], a bad-smelling gum resin obtained from various Asiatic plants of the carrot family and used as an antispasmodic.

**as·bes·tos, as·bes·tus** (as-bes′təs, az-), *n.* [< L. < Gr. *asbestos*, inextinguishable < *a-*, not + *sbennynai*, to extinguish], a fire-resistant and heat-resistant mineral, a silicate of calcium and magnesium, which occurs in long, threadlike fibers and is used in fireproof curtains, roofing, insulation, etc.

**as·ca·rid** (as′kə-rid), *n.* [Gr. *askaris*], a nematode worm that is an intestinal parasite.

**as·cend** (ə-send′), *v.i.* [< OFr. < L. < *ad-*, to + *scandere*, to climb], 1. to go up; move upward; rise. 2. to slope or lead upward. *v.t.* to move upward along; climb. —**as·cend′a·ble, as·cend′i·ble,** *adj.* —**as·cend′er,** *n.*

**as·cend·an·cy, as·cend·en·cy** (ə-sen′dən-si), *n.* controlling influence; domination: also **as·cend′ance, as·cend′ence.**

**as·cend·ant, as·cend·ent** (ə-sen′dənt), *adj.* 1. ascending; rising. 2. controlling; predominant; superior. *n.* 1. in *astrology*, the sign of the zodiac just above the eastern horizon at any given moment. 2. a dominating position; ascendancy. —**in the ascendant,** at or heading toward the height of power, fame, etc.

**as·cen·sion** (ə-sen′shən), *n.* 1. an ascending; ascent. 2. [A-], the fortieth day after Easter (*Holy Thursday*), celebrating the Ascension: also **Ascension Day.** 3. [A-], a British island in the South Atlantic: area, 34 sq. mi. —**the Ascension,** in the *Bible*, the bodily ascent of Jesus into heaven on the fortieth day after his resurrection: Acts 1:9. —**as·cen′sion·al,** *adj.*

**as·cent** (ə-sent′), *n.* 1. an ascending or rising. 2. an advancement, as in rank, popularity, etc. 3. an upward slope. 4. the degree of upward slope. 5. a going back in time or genealogy.

**as·cer·tain** (as'ẽr-tān'), *v.t.* [< OFr. < *a-*, to + *certain* < L. *certus*, fixed], to find out with certainty. —**as'cer·tain'a·ble,** *adj.* —**as'cer·tain'a·ble·ness, as'cer·tain'a·bil'i·ty,** *n.* —**as'cer·tain'a·bly,** *adv.* —**as'cer·tain'ment,** *n.*

**as·cet·ic** (ə-set'ik), *adj.* [< Gr. < *askein*, to exercise], of or characteristic of ascetics or asceticism; self-denying; austere: also **as·cet'i·cal.** *n.* a person who leads a life of contemplation and rigorous self-denial, especially for religious purposes. —**as·cet'i·cal·ly,** *adv.*

**as·cet·i·cism** (ə-set'ə-siz'm), *n.* 1. the practices or way of life of an ascetic. 2. the religious doctrine that one can reach a higher spiritual state by rigorous self-discipline and self-denial.

**as·cid·i·an** (ə-sid'i-ən), *n.* a tunicate.

**as·cid·i·um** (ə-sid'i-əm), *n.* [*pl.* -IA (-i-ə)], [< Gr. < *askos*, a bag, bladder], a pitcherlike leaf or structure, as of the pitcher plant or bladderwort.

**As·cle·pi·us** (as-klē'pi-əs), *n.* the Greek god of medicine, corresponding to the Romans' Aesculapius.

**as·co·my·cete** (as'kə-mī-sēt'), *n.* [< Gr. *askos*, bladder + *mykēs*, fungus], any of a class of spore-reproducing fungi, including the mildews, yeasts, etc. —**as'co·my·ce'tous** (-sē'təs), *adj.*

**a·scor·bic acid** (ə-skôr'bik), [*a-*, not + *scorb*utic + *-ic*], vitamin C: see **vitamin.**

**as·cot** (as'kət), *n.* 1. [A-], a famous horse-racing meet held annually at Ascot Heath, Berkshire, England. 2. a necktie or scarf with very broad ends hanging from the knot, one upon the other.

ASCOT TIE

**as·cribe** (ə-skrīb'), *v.t.* [-CRIBED, -CRIBING], [< L. < *ad-*, to + *scribere*, to write], 1. to assign (*to* a supposed cause or source); attribute. 2. to regard as belonging (*to* something) as a quality. —**as·crib'a·ble,** *adj.*

**as·crip·tion** (ə-skrip'shən), *n.* 1. an ascribing. 2. a statement that ascribes; specifically, a prayer or text ascribing glory to God.

**ase** (ās, āz), a suffix used to form names of enzymes, usually meaning *that decomposes*, as in *amylase*.

**a·sep·sis** (ə-sep'sis, ā-), *n.* 1. the condition of being aseptic. 2. aseptic treatment or technique.

**a·sep·tic** (ə-sep'tik, ā-), *adj.* not septic; free from disease-producing microorganisms. *n.* an aseptic substance. —**a·sep'ti·cal·ly,** *adv.*

**a·sex·u·al** (ā-sek'shōō-əl), *adj.* 1. having no sex; sexless. 2. in *biology*, designating or of reproduction without the union of male and female germ cells. —**a·sex'u·al'i·ty** (-al'ə-ti), *n.* —**a·sex'u·al·ly,** *adv.*

**As·gard** (as'gärd, az'-), *n.* [< ON. < *āss*, god + *garthr*, yard], in *Norse mythology*, the home of the gods and slain heroes: also **As'garth** (-gärth).

**ash** (ash), *n.* [AS. *æsce*], 1. the white or grayish powder left of something after it has been burned. 2. the gray color of wood ash. See also **ashes.**

**ash** (ash), *n.* [AS. *æsc*], 1. a timber and shade tree of the olive family, having tough, elastic, straight-grained wood. 2. the wood.

**a·shamed** (ə-shāmd'), *adj.* 1. feeling shame. 2. reluctant because fearing shame beforehand. —**a·sham'ed·ly** (-id-li), *adv.* —**a·sham'ed·ness,** *n.*

**ash·en** (ash''n), *adj.* 1. of ashes. 2. like ashes, especially in color; pale; pallid.

**ash·en** (ash''n), *adj.* of the ash tree or its wood.

**ash·es** (ash'iz), *n.pl.* 1. the substance remaining after a thing has been burned. 2. the part of the body left after cremation. 3. a dead person; human remains. 4. fine volcanic lava.

**Ashe·ville** (ash'vil), *n.* a city in W North Carolina: pop., 60,000.

**ash·lar, ash·ler** (ash'lẽr), *n.* [< OFr. < L. < *axis*, *assis*, a plank, beam], 1. a square, hewn stone used in building. 2. a thin, dressed, square stone used for facing brick walls, etc. 3. masonry made of either kind of ashlar.

**a·shore** (ə-shôr', ə-shōr'), *adv. & adj.* 1. to or on the shore. 2. to or on land.

**Ash·to·reth** (ash'tə-rith, -reth'), *n.* Astarte.

**ash tray,** a container for smokers' tobacco ashes.

**A·shur** (ä'shoor), *n.* [Assyr.], the chief Assyrian deity, god of war and empire: also **Asshur.**

**Ash Wednesday,** the first day of Lent: from the putting of ashes on the forehead in penitence.

**ash·y** (ash'i), *adj.* [-IER, -IEST], 1. of, like, or covered with ashes. 2. of ash color; pale.

**A·sia** (ā'zhə, ā'shə), *n.* the largest continent: situated in the Eastern Hemisphere and separated from N Europe by the Ural Mountains: area, 16,990,000 sq. mi.; pop., c.1,600,000,000. —**A'sian, A·si·at·ic** (ā'zhi-at'ik, -shi-), *adj. & n.*

**Asia Minor,** a peninsula in W Asia, between the Black Sea and the Mediterranean: formerly called *Anatolia*.

**Asiatic cholera,** an acute, usually fatal, infectious disease characterized by profuse diarrhea, vomiting, intestinal pain, etc.

**a·side** (ə-sīd'), *adv.* 1. on or to one side. 2. away; on reserve: as, put this *aside* for me. 3. out of one's thoughts, etc. 4. apart; notwithstanding: as, joking *aside*, I mean it. *n.* words spoken aside; actor's words not supposed to be heard by the other actors. —**aside from,** 1. with the exception of. 2. apart from.

**as·i·nine** (as'ə-nīn'), *adj.* [< L. < *asinus*, ass], like an ass, regarded as a stupid animal; stupid; silly; unintelligent. —**as'i·nine'ly,** *adv.*

**as·i·nin·i·ty** (as'ə-nin'ə-ti), *n.* 1. the quality or state of being asinine; stupidity. 2. [*pl.* -TIES], an asinine act or remark.

**-a·sis** (ə-sis), [L. < Gr.], a suffix used in forming names of some diseases, meaning *a condition resembling, a condition characterized by*, as in *psoriasis*.

**ask** (ask, äsk), *v.t.* [AS. *ascian*], 1. to use words in seeking the answer to (a question); inquire about. 2. to put a question to (a person); inquire of. 3. to request; solicit; beg. 4. to demand or expect: as, they *ask* ten dollars for it. 5. to be in need of or call for (a thing). 6. to invite. 7. [Archaic], to publish (banns); also, to publish the banns of. *v.i.* 1. to make a request (*for* something). 2. to inquire (with *about*, *after*, or *for*). —**ask'er,** *n.*

**a·skance** (ə-skans'), *adv.* 1. with a sidewise glance; obliquely. 2. with suspicion, disapproval, etc. Also **a·skant'** (-skant').

**a·skew** (ə-skū'), *adv.* to one side; awry; crookedly. *adj.* on one side; awry.

**a·slant** (ə-slant'), *adv.* on a slant; slantingly. *prep.* slantingly across. *adj.* slanting.

**a·sleep** (ə-slēp'), *adj.* 1. in a condition of sleep; sleeping; hence, 2. inactive; dull; backward. 3. numb: as, her arm is *asleep*. 4. dead. *adv.* into a sleeping condition.

**a·slope** (ə-slōp'), *adv. & adj.* at a slant.

**a·so·cial** (ā-sō'shəl), *adj.* not social; characterized by avoidance of contact with others.

**asp** (asp), *n.* [< OFr. < L. < Gr. *aspis*], any of several small, poisonous snakes of Africa and Europe.

**asp** (asp), *n.* [Poetic], an aspen.

**as·par·a·gus** (ə-spar'ə-gəs), *n.* [L. < Gr. *asparagos*, a sprout], 1. any of a number of related plants with small, scalelike leaves and many branches. 2. the tender shoots of a certain plant of this group, used as a vegetable.

**a·spar·kle** (ə-spär'k'l), *adj.* sparkling

**as·pect** (as'pekt), *n.* [< L. < *ad-*, to, at + *specere*, to look], 1. the way one appears; looks. 2. the appearance of a thing from a specific point; view. 3. the appearance of an idea, problem, etc. regarded from a specific viewpoint. 4. a facing in a given direction. 5. a side facing in a given direction; exposure: as, the eastern *aspect* of the house. 6. in *astrology*, the position of stars in relation to each other or to the observer.

**as·pen** (as'pən), *n.* [AS. *æspe*], a kind of poplar tree with leaves that flutter in the least breeze. *adj.* of or like an aspen; fluttering; trembling.

**as·per·i·ty** (as-per'ə-ti), *n.* [*pl.* -TIES], [< OFr. < L. < *asper*, rough], 1. roughness or harshness, as of surface, sound, etc. 2. sharpness of temper.

**as·perse** (ə-spũrs'), *v.t.* [-PERSED (-spũrst'), -PERSING], [< L. < *ad-*, to + *spargere*, to sprinkle], to spread false rumors concerning, or damaging charges against; slander. —**as·pers'er,** *n.*

**as·per·sion** (ə-spũr'zhən, -shən), *n.* a damaging or disparaging remark; false rumor; slander.

**as·phalt** (as'fôlt, -falt), *n.* [< LL. < Gr.; prob. < Sem.], 1. a brown or black tarlike variety of bitumen, found in a natural state or obtained by evaporating petroleum. 2. a mixture of this with sand or gravel, for paving, roofing, etc. *v.t.* to pave, roof, etc. with asphalt. —**as·phal'tic,** *adj.*

**as·phal·tum** (as-fal'təm), *n.* asphalt.

**as·pho·del** (as'fə-del'), *n.* [< L. < Gr.; ? a narcissus; see DAFFODIL], a plant of the lily family, having fleshy roots and white or yellow flowers.

**as·phyx·i·a** (as-fik′si-ə), *n.* [Gr., a stopping of the pulse < *a-*, not + *sphyzein*, to throb], loss of consciousness as a result of too little oxygen and too much carbon dioxide in the blood: suffocation causes asphyxia. —**as·phyx′i·ant,** *adj.* & *n.*

**as·phyx·i·ate** (as-fik′si-āt′), *v.t.* [-ATED, -ATING], to cause asphyxia in, as by suffocating. —**as·phyx′i·a′tion,** *n.* —**as·phyx′i·a′tor,** *n.*

**as·pic** (as′pik), *n.* [Fr. < OFr. *aspe*], 1. [Poetic], an asp (snake). 2. a jelly of meat juice, tomato juice, etc. used as a relish or for a mold of meat, seafood, etc.

**as·pi·dis·tra** (as′pi-dis′trə), *n.* [< Gr. *aspis*, a shield + *astron*, a star], a plant of the lily family, with large evergreen leaves.

**as·pir·ant** (ə-spīr′ənt, as′pə-rənt), *adj.* aspiring. *n.* one who aspires, as after honors, etc.

**as·pi·rate** (as′pə-rāt′; *for adj.* & *n.*, -pēr-it), *v.t.* [-RATED, -RATING], [< L.; see ASPIRE], 1. to begin (a word or syllable) with the sound of English *h*. 2. to follow (a consonant) with a puff of suddenly released breath. *n.* an aspirated sound. *adj.* aspirated.

**as·pi·rat·ed** (as′pə-rāt′id), *adj.* 1. preceded by the sound of *h*. 2. followed by a puff of breath.

**as·pi·ra·tion** (as′pə-rā′shən), *n.* 1. act of breathing; breath. 2. an aspiring; strong ambition, as for honor, etc. 3. a removal by suction, as of fluid. 4. *a*) an aspirating. *b*) an aspirate.

**as·pi·ra·tor** (as′pə-rā′tēr), *n.* an apparatus using suction, as for removing air, fluids, etc.

**as·pir·a·to·ry** (ə-spīr′ə-tôr′i, -tō′ri), *adj.* of or suited for breathing or suction.

**as·pire** (ə-spīr′), *v.i.* [-PIRED, -PIRING], [< Fr. < L. < *ad-*, to + *spirare*, to breathe], 1. to be ambitious (*to* get or do something); seek (often followed by *after*). 2. [Archaic], to rise high. —**as·pir′er,** *n.* —**as·pir′ing·ly,** *adv.*

**as·pi·rin** (as′pər-in, -prin), *n.* [G. < *acetyl* + *spirsäure*, salicylic acid; + *-in*], a white crystalline powder, acetylsalicylic acid, $C_9H_8O_4$, used for reducing fever, relieving headaches, etc.

**a·squint** (ə-skwint′), *adv.* & *adj.* with a squint; out of the corner of the eye.

**ass** (as), *n.* [AS. *assa* < Celt. < L. *asinus*], 1. a donkey. 2. a stupid or silly person; fool.

**ass.,** 1. assistant. 2. association. 3. assorted.

**as·sa·fet·i·da, as·sa·foet·i·da** (as′ə-fet′i-də), *n.* asafetida.

**as·sa·gai** (as′ə-gī′), *n.* [< Sp. or Port. < Ar. < *az*, for *al*, the + *zaghāyah*, spear], a slender spear used by some South African tribes. *v.t.* to pierce with an assagai. Also sp. **assegai.**

**as·sail** (ə-sāl′), *v.t.* [< OFr. < LL. < L. *ad*, to + *salire*, to leap], 1. to attack physically and violently. 2. to attack with arguments, etc. —**as·sail′a·ble,** *adj.* —**as·sail′ment,** *n.*

**as·sail·ant** (ə-sāl′ənt), *n.* one who assails; attacker: also **as·sail′er.** *adj.* assailing.

**As·sam** (a-sam′, as′am), *n.* a state of NE India, on the borders of Burma and Tibet: area, 58,739 sq. mi.; pop., 10,418,000. —**As′sa·mese′** (-mēz′), *adj.* & *n.* [*pl.* ASSAMESE].

**as·sas·sin** (ə-sas′in), *n.* [Fr. < ML. < Ar. *hashshāshīn*, hashish eaters < *hashīsh*, hemp], 1. [A-], a member of a medieval band of hashish-eating Moslems who killed Crusaders. 2. a murderer who strikes suddenly and without warning; often, a hired killer.

**as·sas·si·nate** (ə-sas′ə-nāt′), *v.t.* [-NATED, -NATING], 1. to murder as assassins do. 2. to harm or ruin (one's reputation, etc.). —**as·sas′si·na′tion,** *n.* —**as·sas′si·na′tor,** *n.*

**as·sault** (ə-sôlt′), *n.* [< OFr. < L. *ad*, to + *saltare*, to leap], 1. a violent attack, either physical or verbal. 2. rape: a euphemism. 3. in *law*, an unlawful threat to harm another physically, or an unsuccessful attempt to do so. 4. in *military science*, the concluding stage of an attack. *v.t.* & *v.i.* to make an assault (upon). —**as·sault′a·ble,** *adj.* —**as·sault′er,** *n.*

**assault and battery,** in *law*, the carrying out of threatened physical harm or violence.

**as·say** (ə-sā′, as′ā), *n.* [OFr. *essai;* trial, test < L. *exagium*, a weighing < *ex-*, out + *agere*, to deal], 1. an examination or testing. 2. the analysis of an ore, etc. to determine the nature and proportion of the ingredients. 3. a substance to be thus analyzed. 4. the result or report of such analysis. *v.t.* (ə-sā′), 1. to make an assay of; test; analyze. 2. [Archaic], to attempt. See also **essay.** —**as·say′a·ble,** *adj.* —**as·say′er,** *n.*

**as·se·gai** (as′ə-gī′), *n.* & *v.t.* assagai.

**as·sem·blage** (ə-sem′blij), *n.* 1. an assembling or being assembled. 2. a group of persons. 3. a collection of things. 4. a fitting together of parts.

**as·sem·ble** (ə-sem′b'l), *v.t.* & *v.i.* [-BLED, -BLING], [< OFr. < L. < *ad-*, to + *simul*, together], 1. to gather together into a group; collect. 2. to put or fit together. —**as·sem′bler,** *n.*

**as·sem·bly** (ə-sem′bli), *n.* [*pl.* -BLIES], 1. an assembling or being assembled. 2. a group of persons gathered together. 3. [A-], in some States, the lower house of the legislature. 4. *a*) a fitting together of parts to form a complete unit. *b*) such parts. 5. a call, as by bugle or drum, for soldiers to form ranks.

**assembly line,** in many factories, an arrangement whereby each worker in succession performs a specialized operation on the work as it is moved along, often on a slowly moving belt.

**as·sem·bly·man** (ə-sem′bli-mən), *n.* [*pl.* -MEN (-men′, -mən)], a member of a legislative assembly, especially, [A-], of a State Assembly.

**as·sent** (ə-sent′), *v.i.* [< OFr. < L. < *ad-*, to + *sentire*, to feel], 1. to consent. 2. to agree; concur. *n.* 1. consent. 2. agreement; concurrence. —**as·sen·ta·tion** (as′en-tā′shən), *n.* —**as·sent′er,** *n.*

**as·sert** (ə-sũrt′), *v.t.* [< L. < *ad-*, to + *serere*, to join, bind], 1. to declare; affirm. 2. to maintain or defend (rights, claims, etc.). —**assert oneself,** 1. to insist on one's rights. 2. to thrust oneself forward. —**as·sert′a·ble, as·sert′i·ble,** *adj.* —**as·sert′er, as·sert′or,** *n.*

**as·ser·tion** (ə-sũr′shən), *n.* 1. an asserting. 2. a positive statement; declaration.

**as·ser·tive** (ə-sũr′tiv), *adj.* 1. positive. 2. unduly confident or insistent. —**as·ser′tive·ly,** *adv.* —**as·ser′tive·ness,** *n.*

**as·sess** (ə-ses′), *v.t.* [< OFr. < LL. *assessare*, to set a rate < L. *assidere*, to sit beside < *ad-*, to + *sedere*, to sit], 1. to set an estimated value on (property, etc.) for taxation. 2. to set the amount of (damages, a fine, etc.). 3. to impose a fine, tax, etc. on (a person or property). 4. to impose (an amount) as a fine, tax, etc.

**as·sess·ment** (ə-ses′mənt), *n.* 1. an assessing. 2. an amount assessed.

**as·ses·sor** (ə-ses′ēr), *n.* a person who assesses property for taxation. —**as·ses·so·ri·al** (as′ə-sôr′i-əl, -sō′ri-), *adj.* —**as·ses′sor·ship,** *n.*

**as·set** (as′et), *n.* [< OFr. < *asseter*, to assign, place < LL. < L. *ad-*, to + *sedere*, to sit; associated with L. *ad satis*, to sufficiency], 1. anything owned that has exchange value. 2. a valuable or desirable thing: as, charm is her chief *asset*. 3. *pl.* in *accounting*, all the entries on a balance sheet that shows the entire property or resources of a person or business, as accounts and notes receivable, cash, real estate, etc. 4. *pl.* in *law*, property usable to pay debts.

**as·sev·er·ate** (ə-sev′ə-rāt′), *v.t.* [-ATED, -ATING], [< L. < *ad-*, to + *severus*, severe], to state seriously or positively. —**as·sev′er·a′tion,** *n.*

**as·si·du·i·ty** (as′ə-dū′ə-ti), *n.* 1. the quality or condition of being assiduous; diligence. 2. [*pl.* -TIES], an instance of this.

**as·sid·u·ous** (ə-sij′oo-əs), *adj.* [< L. < *ad-*, to + *sedere*, to sit], 1. done with constant and careful attention. 2. diligent; persevering. —**as·sid′u·ous·ly,** *adv.* —**as·sid′u·ous·ness,** *n.*

**as·sign** (ə-sīn′), *v.t.* [< OFr. < L. < *ad-*, to + *signum*, a mark], 1. to set or fix for a specific purpose; designate. 2. to appoint, as to a duty or position. 3. to give out as a task; allot. 4. to ascribe, as a motive, reason, etc. 5. in *law*, to transfer, as a claim, right, property, etc. *v.i.* in *law*, to transfer a claim, property, etc. to another. *n. usually pl.* an assignee. —**as·sign′a·ble,** *adj.* —**as·sign′a·bil′i·ty,** *n.* —**as·sign′a·bly,** *adv.* —**as·sign′er,** *in law* **as·sign′or,** *n.*

**as·sig·na·tion** (as′ig-nā′shən), *n.* 1. an assigning. 2. anything assigned. 3. an appointment to meet, especially one made secretly by lovers. 4. in *law*, a transference of a claim, property, etc.

**as·sign·ee** (ə-sī′nē′, as′ə-), *n.* in *law*, a person to whom a claim, property, etc. is transferred.

**as·sign·ment** (ə-sīn′mənt), *n.* 1. an assigning or being assigned. 2. anything assigned, as a lesson, task, etc. 3. in *law*, *a*) a transfer of a claim, property, etc. *b*) a paper authorizing this.

**as·sim·i·la·ble** (ə-sim′'l-ə-b'l), *adj.* that can be assimilated. —**as·sim′i·la·bil′i·ty,** *n.*

**as·sim·i·late** (ə-sim′'l-āt′), *v.t.* [-LATED, -LATING], [< L. < *ad-*, to + *similis*, like], 1. to take up and make part of itself or oneself; absorb and incorporate. 2. to compare or liken. 3. to make like or alike. *v.i.* 1. to become like. 2. to be absorbed and incorporated. —**as·sim′i·la·tor,** *n.* —**as·sim′i·la·to′ry** (-ə-tôr′i, -ə-tō′ri), *adj.*

**as·sim·i·la·tion** (ə-sim′'l-ā′shən), *n.* 1. an assimilating or being assimilated. 2. in *phonetics*, the process whereby a sound, influenced by a neighboring sound, tends to become like it: thus, in *cupboard*, the *p* is lost by *assimilation* to *b*. 3. in *physiology*, the change of digested food into part of the living organism. —**as·sim′i·la′tive,** *adj.* —**as·sim′i·la′tive·ness,** *n.*
**as·sist** (ə-sist′), *v.t.* & *v.i.* [<Fr. < L. < *ad-*, to + *sistere*, to make stand < *stare*, to stand], to help; aid. *n.* 1. an instance or act of helping. 2. in *baseball*, a play that helps put a batter or runner out. —**assist at,** to be present at; attend. —**as·sist′er,** *in law* **as·sist′or,** *n.*
**as·sist·ance** (ə-sis′təns), *n.* help; aid.
**as·sist·ant** (ə-sis′tənt), *adj.* assisting; helping. *n.* 1. a person who assists or serves in a subordinate position; helper. 2. a thing for assisting; aid. —**as·sis′tant·ship′,** *n.*
**as·size** (ə-sīz′), *n.* [<OFr. < L. *assidere;* see ASSESS], 1. originally, an assembly or its decree. 2. *pl.* *a*) court sessions held periodically in each county of England to try civil and criminal cases. *b*) the time or place of these.
**assn.,** association.
**assoc.,** 1. associate. 2. associated. 3. association.
**as·so·ci·ate** (ə-sō′shi-āt′; *for n. & adj., usually* -it), *v.t.* [-ATED, -ATING], [< L. <*ad-*, to + *socius*, companion], 1. to connect; combine; join. 2. to bring into relationship as companion, partner, friend, etc. 3. to connect in the mind: as, she *associates* rain with grief. *v.i.* 1. to join (*with*) as a companion, partner, friend, etc. 2. to unite for a common purpose. *n.* 1. a friend, partner, fellow worker, etc. 2. a member without full status or privileges, as of a society, etc. 3. anything joined with another thing or things. *adj.* 1. united by the same interests, purposes, etc. 2. having secondary status or privileges: as, an *associate* justice. —**as·so′ci·ate·ship′,** *n.* —**as·so′ci·a′tor,** *n.*
**as·so·ci·a·tion** (ə-sō′si-ā′shən, -shi-), *n.* 1. an associating or being associated. 2. companionship; fellowship; partnership. 3. an organization of persons having common interests, purposes, etc.; society. 4. a connection between ideas, sensations, etc. —**as·so′ci·a′tion·al,** *adj.*
**association football,** soccer.
**as·so·ci·a·tive** (ə-sō′shi-ā′tiv, -ə-tiv), *adj.* of, characterized by, or causing association. —**as·so′ci·a′tive·ly,** *adv.*
**as·so·nance** (as′ə-nəns), *n.* [Fr. < L. < *ad-*, to + *sonare*, to sound], 1. likeness of sound. 2. a partial rhyme in which the stressed vowel sounds are alike but the consonant sounds are unlike, as in *late* and *make*. —**as′so·nant,** *adj.* & *n.* —**as·so·nan·tal** (as′ə-nan′t'l), *adj.*
**as·sort** (ə-sôrt′), *v.t.* [< OFr. < *a-* (L. *ad*), to + *sorte* < L. *sors*, lot], 1. to separate into classes according to sorts or kinds; classify. 2. to supply (a warehouse, etc.) with an assortment of goods. *v.i.* 1. to be of the same sort; match or harmonize (*with*). 2. to associate (*with*). —**as·sort′er,** *n.*
**as·sort·ed** (ə-sôrt′id), *adj.* 1. in an assortment; miscellaneous. 2. classified. 3. matched.
**as·sort·ment** (ə-sôrt′mənt), *n.* 1. an assorting or being assorted; classification. 2. an assorted, or miscellaneous, collection; variety.
**A.S.S.R.,** Autonomous Soviet Socialist Republic.
**asst.,** assistant.
**as·suage** (ə-swāj′), *v.t.* [-SUAGED, -SUAGING], [< OFr. < L. *ad*, to + *suavis*, sweet], 1. to lessen (pain, distress, etc.); allay. 2. to pacify; calm (passion, anger, etc.). 3. to satisfy or quench (thirst, etc.). —**as·suage′ment,** *n.* —**as·suag′er,** *n.*
**as·sume** (ə-sōōm′, ə-sūm′), *v.t.* [-SUMED, -SUMING], [< L. < *ad-*, to + *sumere*, to take], 1. to take or put on (the appearance, form, role, etc. of). 2. to seize; usurp: as, he *assumed* control. 3. to take into association: as, he was *assumed* as a partner. 4. to take upon oneself; undertake. 5. to take for granted; suppose. 6. to pretend to have; feign. —**as·sum′a·ble,** *adj.* —**as·sum′a·bly,** *adv.* —**as·sum′ed·ly,** *adv.* —**as·sum′er,** *n.*
**as·sum·ing** (ə-sōōm′iŋ, -sūm′-), *adj.* presumptuous. *n.* presumption.
**as·sump·tion** (ə-sump′shən), *n.* 1. [A-], in the *R.C. Church*, *a*) the ascent of the Virgin Mary into heaven. *b*) the church festival celebrating this (August 15). 2. an assuming or being assumed. 3. anything taken for granted; supposition. 4. presumption. —**as·sump′tive,** *adj.*
**as·sur·ance** (ə-shoor′əns), *n.* 1. an assuring or being assured. 2. sureness; confidence. 3. anything that inspires confidence, as a promise, positive statement, etc.; guarantee. 4. self-confidence. 5. impudent forwardness; presumption. 6. [British], insurance.
**as·sure** (ə-shoor′), *v.t.* [-SURED, -SURING], [< OFr. < LL. < L. *ad*, to + *securus;* see SECURE], 1. to make (a person) sure of something; convince. 2. to give confidence to: as, the news *assured* us. 3. to declare to or promise confidently. 4. to make (a doubtful thing) certain; guarantee. 5. to insure. —**as·sur′er,** *n.*
**as·sured** (ə-shoord′), *adj.* 1. sure; guaranteed. 2. confident; bold. 3. insured. *n.* an insured person. —**as·sur′ed·ly** (-shoor′id-li), *adv.* —**as·sur′ed·ness,** *n.*
**As·syr·i·a** (ə-sir′i-ə), *n.* an ancient empire in W Asia in the region of the upper Tigris River: capital, Nineveh. —**As·syr′i·an,** *adj.* & *n.*
**As·tar·te** (as-tär′ti), *n.* in *Phoenician mythology*, the goddess of fertility and sexual love.
**as·ta·tine** (as′tə-tēn′, -tin), *n.* [< Gr. *astatosi*, unstable; + *-ine*], an unstable chemical element formed from bismuth when it is bombarded by alpha particles: symbol, At; at. wt., 211 (?); at. no., 85 (formerly designated as *alabamine*).
**as·ter** (as′tēr), *n.* [L. <Gr. *astēr*, star], any of various related plants of the composite family, with spear-shaped leaves and purplish, blue, pink, or white flowers like daisies.
**-as·ter** (as′tēr), [L. dim. suffix], a suffix denoting *inferiority* or *worthlessness*, as in *poetaster.*
**as·ter·isk** (as′tēr-isk′), *n.* [< L. < Gr. dim. of *astēr*, a star], a starlike sign (*) used in printing to indicate footnote references, omissions, etc. *v.t.* to mark with this sign.
**as·ter·ism** (as′tēr-iz'm), *n.* in *astronomy*, 1. a constellation. 2. a star cluster.
**a·stern** (ə-stũrn′), *adj.* & *adv.* 1. behind a ship. 2. at or toward the rear. 3. backward.
**as·ter·oid** (as′tēr-oid′), *adj.* [< Gr. < *astēr*, star; + *-oid*], like a star or starfish. *n.* 1. any of the small planets with orbits between those of Mars and Jupiter; planetoid. 2. a starfish. —**as′ter·oid′al,** *adj.*
**asth·ma** (az′mə, as′-), *n.* [Gr., a panting < *azein*, to breathe hard], a chronic disorder characterized by wheezing, coughing, difficulty in breathing, and a suffocating feeling.
**asth·mat·ic** (az-mat′ik, as-), *adj.* of or having asthma: also **asth·mat′i·cal.** *n.* a person who has asthma. —**asth·mat′i·cal·ly,** *adv.*
**as·tig·mat·ic** (as′tig-mat′ik), *adj.* 1. of or having astigmatism. 2. correcting astigmatism. —**as′tig·mat′i·cal·ly,** *adv.*
**a·stig·ma·tism** (ə-stig′mə-tiz'm), *n.* [< Gr. *a-*, without + *stigma*, a mark; + *-ism*], a structural defect of a lens or the eyes that prevents light rays from meeting in a single focal point, so that indistinct images are formed.
**a·stir** (ə-stũr′), *adv.* & *adj.* 1. in motion; in excited activity. 2. out of bed.
**as·ton·ish** (ə-ston′ish), *v.t.* [< OFr. < L. < *ex-*, out + *tonare*, to thunder], to fill with sudden wonder or surprise; astound; amaze.
**as·ton·ish·ing** (ə-ston′ish-iŋ), *adj.* surprising; amazing. —**as·ton′ish·ing·ly,** *adv.* —**as·ton′ish·ing·ness,** *n.*
**as·ton·ish·ment** (ə-ston′ish-mənt), *n.* 1. an astonishing; amazement. 2. anything that astonishes.
**as·tound** (ə-stound′), *v.t.* [< pp. of ME. *astonien*, astound], to astonish greatly; amaze. —**as·tound′ing,** *adj.* —**as·tound′ing·ly,** *adv.*
**a·strad·dle** (ə-strad′'l), *adv.* & *adj.* astride.
**as·trag·a·lus** (as-trag′ə-ləs), *n.* [*pl.* -LI (-lī′)], [L. < Gr.], the anklebone; talus.
**As·tra·khan** (as′trə-kan′; Russ. äs′trȧ-khän′y'), *n.* a city in the SE U.S.S.R.: pop., 254,000.
**as·tra·khan** (as′trə-kən), *n.* 1. the pelt of very young lambs from Astrakhan, with tightly curled wool. 2. a woolly cloth made in imitation of this. Also sp. **astrachan.**
**as·tral** (as′trəl), *adj.* [< L. < Gr. *astron*, star], 1. of, from, or like the stars. 2. designating or of an alleged supernatural substance.
**a·stray** (ə-strā′), *adv.* & *adj.* off the right path or way.
**a·stride** (ə-strīd′), *adv.* & *adj.* 1. with a leg on either side; astraddle. 2. with legs far apart. *prep.* with a leg on either side of (a horse, etc.).
**as·trin·gent** (ə-strin′jənt), *adj.* [< L. < *ad-*, to + *stringere*, to draw, bind], 1. that contracts body tissue and blood vessels, checking the flow of

blood; styptic. 2. harsh; severe. *n.* an astringent substance. —**as·trin′gen·cy,** *n.* —**as·trin′gent·ly,** *adv.*
**as·tro-,** [< Gr. *astron,* a star], a combining form meaning *of a star* or *stars,* as in *astrophysics.*
**astrol.,** 1. astrologer. 2. astrology.
**as·tro·labe** (as′trə-lāb′), *n.* [< OFr. < LL. < Gr. < *astron,* a star + *lambanein,* to take], an instrument once used to find the altitude of stars, etc.
**as·trol·o·gy** (ə-strol′ə-ji), *n.* [< L. < Gr. < *astron,* star + *legein,* to speak], 1. a pseudo science claiming to foretell the future by studying the supposed influence of the moon, sun, and stars on human affairs. 2. [Obs.], primitive astronomy. —**as·trol′o·ger,** *n.* —**as·tro·log·i·cal** (as′trə-loj′i-k'l), **as′tro·log′ic,** *adj.* —**as′tro·log′i·cal·ly,** *adv.*
**astron.,** 1. astronomer. 2. astronomy.
**as·tro·naut** (as′trə-nôt′), *n.* [< *astronautics*], a person trained to make rocket flights in space.
**as·tro·nau·tics** (as′trō-nô′tiks), *n.pl.* [construed as sing.], [< Fr.; see ASTRO- & NAUTICAL], the science dealing with travel into or through outer space. —**as′tro·nau′ti·cal,** *adj.*
**as·tron·o·mer** (ə-stron′ə-mẽr), *n.* a student of or an authority on astronomy.
**as·tro·nom·i·cal** (as′trə-nom′i-k'l), *adj.* 1. of astronomy. 2. very large, as the numbers or quantities used in astronomy. Also **as′tro·nom′ic.** —**as′tro·nom′i·cal·ly,** *adv.*
**astronomical year,** the period in which the earth makes one revolution around the sun (365 days, 5 hours, 48 minutes, 45.51 seconds); solar year.
**as·tron·o·my** (ə-stron′ə-mi), *n.* [< L. < Gr. < *astron,* star + *nomos,* system of laws < *nemein,* to arrange], the science of the stars and other heavenly bodies, dealing with their composition, motion, relative position, size, etc.
**as·tro·phys·ics** (as′trō-fiz′iks), *n.pl.* [construed as sing.], [*astro-* + *physics*], the science of the physical properties and phenomena of the stars, planets, etc. —**as′tro·phys′i·cal,** *adj.* —**as′tro·phys′i·cist** (-fiz′ə-sist), *n.*
**as·tute** (ə-stōōt′, ə-stūt′), *adj.* [< L. < *astus,* craft, cunning], shrewd; keen; crafty. —**as·tute′ly,** *adv.* —**as·tute′ness,** *n.*
**A·sun·ción** (ä-sōōn-syôn′), *n.* the capital of Paraguay, on the Paraguay River: pop., 206,000.
**a·sun·der** (ə-sun′dẽr), *adv.* [see SUNDER], 1. into parts or pieces. 2. in different directions; apart. *adj.* separated; not close; apart.
**a·sy·lum** (ə-sī′ləm), *n.* [*pl.* -LUMS, -LA (-lə)], [L. < Gr. *asylon,* asylum < *a-,* without + *sylē,* right of seizure], 1. formerly, a sanctuary, as a temple, where criminals, debtors, etc. were safe from arrest. 2. any refuge. 3. a place for the care of the mentally ill, or of the aged, poor, etc.
**a·sym·me·try** (ā-sim′i-tri, as-im′-), *n.* lack of symmetry. —**a′sym·met′ri·cal** (-met′ri-k'l), **a′sym·met′ric,** *adj.* —**a′sym·met′ri·cal·ly,** *adv.*
**as·ymp·tote** (as′im-tōt′, -imp-tōt′), *n.* [< Gr. < *a-,* not + *syn-,* together + *piptein,* to fall], in *mathematics,* a straight line always approaching but never meeting a curve. —**as′ymp·tot′ic** (-tot′ik), **as′ymp·tot′i·cal,** *adj.*

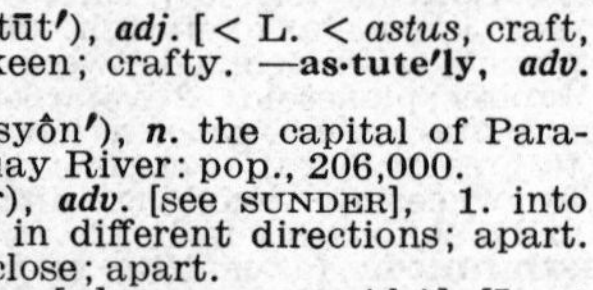

ASYMPTOTE
A, asymptote of curve *C* (PP′ becomes smaller but does not disappear)

**at** (at, ət), *prep.* [AS. *æt*], 1. on; in; near; by: as, *at* the office. 2. to or toward: as, look *at* her. 3. through: as, come in *at* the front door. 4. from: as, get the facts *at* their source. 5. attending: as, *at* the party. 6. occupied in; busy with: as, *at* work. 7. in a state of: as, *at* war. 8. in the manner of: as, *at* a trot. 9. because of: as, terrified *at* the sight. 10. according to: as, *at* his discretion. 11. in the amount, degree, price, etc. of: as, *at* five cents each. 12. on or close to the age or time of: as, *at* five o'clock.
**At,** in *chemistry,* astatine.
**at.,** 1. atmosphere. 2. atomic. 3. attorney.
**at·a·brine** (at′ə-brin, -brēn′), *n.* [G. *atebrin*], a synthetic drug used in treating malaria: a trade-mark (**Atabrine**): also **at′a·brin, at′e·brin** (-brin).
**At·a·lan·ta** (at′'l-an′tə), *n.* in *Gr. legend,* a beautiful, swift-footed maiden who offered to marry any man able to defeat her in a race.
**at·a·vism** (at′ə-viz'm), *n.* [< Fr. < L. *atavus,* ancestor < *at-,* beyond + *avus,* grandfather], 1. resemblance to a remote ancestor in some characteristic which nearer ancestors do not have. 2. reversion to a primitive type. —**at′a·vist,** *n.* —**at′a·vis′tic,** *adj.* —**at′a·vis′ti·cal·ly,** *adv.*
**a·tax·i·a** (ə-tak′si-ə), *n.* [Gr., disorder < *a-,* not + *tassein,* to arrange], inability to co-ordinate bodily, especially muscular, movements: also **a·tax′y.** —**a·tax′ic,** *adj.* & *n.*
**A·te** (ā′ti, ā′tē), *n.* 1. [a-], in ancient Greek culture, criminal folly or reckless ambition of man. 2. the goddess personifying such impulses: later she was considered the avenger of sin.
**ate** (āt; Brit. et), pt. of **eat.**
**-ate** (āt; *adj., usually* it), [< L. *-atus,* pp. ending], a suffix used: 1. to form verbs, and meaning: *a*) *to become,* as in *maturate.* *b*) *to cause to become,* as in *sublimate.* *c*) *to produce,* as in *salivate.* *d*) *to provide* or *treat with,* as in *refrigerate.* *e*) *to put in the form of,* as in *delineate.* *f*) *to arrange for,* as in *orchestrate.* *g*) *to combine with,* as in *oxygenate.* 2. to form adjectives from nouns, and meaning: *a*) *of* or *characteristic of,* as in *roseate.* *b*) *having* or *filled with,* as in *passionate.* *c*) in *botany & zoology, characterized by,* as in *spatulate.* 3. to form adjectives from verbs, as *animate* (*animated*).
**-ate** (āt, it), [L. *-atus,* a noun ending], a noun suffix denoting: 1. *a function, official,* or *agent,* as in *episcopate, potentate.* 2. [L. *-atum,* neut. of *-atus*], in *chemistry, a salt made from* (an acid with a name ending in *-ic*), as in *nitrate.*
**at·el·ier** (at′'l-yā′), *n.* [Fr.], a studio; workshop.
‡**a tem·po** (ä tem′pō), [It.], in *music,* in time: a direction to the performer to return to the preceding tempo: abbrev. **a tem.**
**ath·a·na·si·a** (ath′ə-nā′zhi-ə, -zhə), *n.* [Gr. < *a-,* not + *thanatos,* death], immortality: also **a·than·a·sy** (ə-than′ə-si).
**Ath·a·na·sius,** Saint (ath′ə-nā′shəs), 293?–373 A.D.; Greek patriarch of Alexandria, and opponent of Arianism. —**Ath′a·na′sian** (-zhən), *adj.* & *n.*
**Ath·a·pas·can** (ath′ə-pas′kən), *adj.* designating or of a widely scattered linguistic family of North American Indians, including the Navajo, Apache, and Hupa tribes. *n.* any language of this family. Also **Ath′a·bas′can** (-bas′-).
**a·the·ism** (ā′thē-iz'm), *n.* [< Fr. < Gr. < *a-,* without + *theos,* god], the belief that there is no God.
**a·the·ist** (ā′thē-ist), *n.* one who believes that there is no God: cf. *agnostic.* —**a′the·is′tic, a′the·is′ti·cal,** *adj.* —**a′the·is′ti·cal·ly,** *adv.*
**A·the·na** (ə-thē′nə), *n.* in *Gr. mythology,* the goddess of wisdom, skills, and warfare, identified with the Roman Minerva. Also **A·the′ne** (-nē).
**ath·e·nae·um, ath·e·ne·um** (ath′ə-nē′əm), *n.* 1. [A-], the temple of Athena at Athens, where writers and scholars met. 2. a literary or scientific club. 3. any library or reading room.
**Ath·ens** (ath′inz), *n.* 1. a city in Greece, in ancient times the center of Greek culture and now the capital of the country: pop., 565,000. 2. any city likened to ancient Athens as a cultural center. —**A·the·ni·an** (ə-thē′ni-ən), *adj.* & *n.*
**a·thirst** (ə-thũrst′), *adj.* 1. [Archaic], thirsty. 2. eager.
**ath·lete** (ath′lēt), *n.* [< L. < Gr. < *athlein,* to contest for a prize < *athlon,* a prize], a person trained in exercises or games requiring physical strength, skill, speed, etc.
**athlete's foot,** ringworm of the feet, a contagious skin disease caused by a tiny fungus.
**ath·let·ic** (ath-let′ik), *adj.* 1. of, like, or proper to athletes or athletics. 2. physically strong, skillful, etc. —**ath·let′i·cal·ly,** *adv.*
**ath·let·i·cism** (ath-let′ə-siz'm), *n.* 1. addiction to athletics. 2. an athletic quality.
**ath·let·ics** (ath-let′iks), *n.pl.* [sometimes construed as sing.], athletic sports, games, etc.
**ath·o·dyd** (ath′ō-did), *n.* [contr. < *aero-thermodynamic duct*], a ramjet, a type of jet engine.
**at-home** (at-hōm′), *n.* an informal reception at one's home, usually in the afternoon.
**a·thwart** (ə-thwôrt′), *prep.* 1. across; from one side to the other of. 2. against; in opposition to. 3. in *nautical usage,* across the course or length of. *adv.* 1. crosswise. 2. so as to block.
**-at·ic** (at′ik), [< Fr. or L.; Gr. *-atikos*], a suffix meaning *of, of the kind of,* as in *dramatic, chromatic.*
**a·tilt** (ə-tilt′), *adj.* & *adv.* tilted.
**a·tin·gle** (ə-tiŋ′g'l), *adj.* tingling; excited.
**-a·tion** (ā′shən), [< Fr. or L.], a suffix used to form nouns, meaning: 1. *a —ing* or *being —ed,* as in *activation.* 2. *the result of being —ed* or *a thing that is —ed,* as in *quotation.*
**-a·tive** (ā′tiv, ə-tiv), [< Fr. or L.], a suffix meaning *of the nature of, relating to,* as in *correlative.*
**At·lan·ta** (at-lan′tə), *n.* the capital of Georgia: pop., 487,000.
**At·lan·tic** (at-lan′tik), *n.* the ocean touching the Americas to the west and Europe and Africa to the east. *adj.* of, in, on, or near this ocean.
**Atlantic Charter,** a declaration of peace aims in

World War II, made by Roosevelt and Churchill at a meeting on the Atlantic, August, 1941.
**Atlantic City,** an ocean resort in S New Jersey: pop., 62,000.
**At·lan·tis** (at-lan′tis), *n.* a legendary island or continent in the Atlantic west of Gibraltar, supposed to have sunk into the ocean. —**At′lan·te′an** (-tē′ən), *adj.*
**At·las** (at′ləs), *n.* 1. in *Gr. legend,* a giant compelled to support the heavens on his shoulders. 2. [a-], a book of maps. 3. [a-], a book of tables, charts, etc. of a specific subject.
**Atlas Mountains,** a mountain system along the NW coast of Africa.
**atm.,** 1. atmosphere. 2. atmospheric.
**at·man** (ät′mən), *n.* [Sans., breath, soul], in *Hinduism,* 1. the individual soul or ego. 2. [A-], the universal soul; source of all individual souls.
**at·mos·phere** (at′məs-fêr′), *n.* [< Gr. *atmos,* vapor + *sphaira,* sphere], 1. all the air surrounding the earth. 2. the gaseous mass surrounding any star, etc. 3. the air in any given place. 4. social environment. 5. [Colloq.], the general effect produced by decoration, etc. 6. in *physics,* a unit of pressure equal to 14.69 pounds per square inch.
**at·mos·pher·ic** (at′məs-fer′ik), *adj.* 1. of or in the atmosphere. 2. caused, produced, or operated by the atmosphere. Also **at′mos·pher′i·cal.** *n. pl.* in *radio,* static. —**at′mos·pher′i·cal·ly,** *adv.*
**at. no.,** atomic number.
**at·oll** (at′ôl, -ol, ə-tol′), *n.* [? < Malayalam *adal,* uniting], a ring-shaped coral island almost or completely surrounding a lagoon.

ATOLL

**at·om** (at′əm), *n.* [< Fr. < L. < Gr. *atomos,* uncut < *a-,* not + *temnein,* to cut], 1. a tiny particle; jot. 2. in *chemistry & physics,* any of the smallest particles of an element that combine with similar particles of other elements to produce compounds: atoms consist of complex arrangements of electrons, protons, and neutrons.
**at·om·bomb** (at′əm-bom′), *n.* an atomic bomb: also **atom bomb.** *v.t.* to attack or destroy with such bombs.
**a·tom·ic** (ə-tom′ik), *adj.* 1. of an atom or atoms. 2. of atomic energy or atomic bombs. 3. tiny; minute. Also **a·tom′i·cal.** —**a·tom′i·cal·ly,** *adv.*
**Atomic Age,** the historical period since the creation of the first self-maintaining nuclear chain reaction on December 2, 1942.
**atomic bomb,** a very destructive type of bomb, the power of which results from the immense quantity of energy suddenly released when a chain reaction of nuclear fission is set off: first used in warfare in 1945.
**atomic cocktail,** [Slang], a dose of medicine to be swallowed, containing a radioactive element, used in medicine, as in diagnosing cancer.
**atomic diplomacy,** diplomacy based on the threat of atomic warfare.
**atomic energy,** the energy released from an atom in nuclear reactions, especially nuclear fission or nuclear fusion.
**atomic number,** in *chemistry,* a number representing the relative position of an element in the periodic table; number representing the positive charge in the nucleus of the atom of an element: abbrev. **at. no.**
**atomic theory,** the theory that all material objects and substances are composed of atoms.
**atomic warfare,** warfare using atomic weapons.
**atomic weapon,** any weapon whose effectiveness derives from the release of atomic energy.
**atomic weight,** in *chemistry,* a number representing the weight of one atom of an element as compared with the arbitrary weight of another element taken as the standard (now usually carbon at 12): abbrev. **at. wt.**
**at·om·ize** (at′əm-īz′), *v.t.* [-IZED, -IZING], 1. to separate into atoms. 2. to reduce a liquid to a fine spray. —**at′om·i·za′tion,** *n.*
**at·om·iz·er** (at′əm-īz′ẽr), *n.* a device for breaking a liquid, especially a medicine or perfume, into tiny particles and spraying these out.

ATOMIZER

**a·ton·al** (ā-tōn′'l), *adj.* having atonality. —**a·ton′al·ism,** *n.* —**a·ton′al·ist′ic,** *adj.* —**a·ton′al·ly,** *adv.*
**a·to·nal·i·ty** (ā′tō-nal′ə-ti), *n.* in *music,* lack of tonality through intentional disregard of key.
**a·tone** (ə-tōn′), *v.i.* [ATONED, ATONING], [< *atonement*], to make amends (*for* wrongdoing, etc.). *v.t.* to expiate. —**a·ton′a·ble,** *adj.* —**a·ton′er,** *n.*
**a·tone·ment** (ə-tōn′mənt), *n.* [*at* + obs. *onement,* physical union < *one* + *-ment*], 1. an atoning. 2. satisfaction given for wrongdoing, etc.: expiation. 3. [A-], in *theology,* the effect of Jesus' sufferings and death in bringing about the reconciliation of God to man.
**a·top** (ə-top′), *adj. & adv.* on the top; at the top. *prep.* on the top of.
**-a·to·ry** (ə-tôr′i, -tō′ri), [< L. *-atorius*], a suffix meaning *of, characterized by, produced by,* as in *accusatory.*
**at·ra·bil·i·ous** (at′rə-bil′yəs), *adj.* [< L. *atra bilis,* black bile], 1. melancholy; morose. 2. hypochondriac. Also **at′ra·bil′i·ar** (-yẽr).
**a·tri·um** (ā′tri-əm), *n.* [*pl.* ATRIA (-ə), ATRIUMS], [L.], 1. the main room of an ancient Roman house. 2. a hall or entrance court. 3. in *anatomy,* an auricle of the heart.
**a·tro·cious** (ə-trō′shəs), *adj.* [< L. *atrox,* fierce < *ater,* black; + *-ious*], 1. very cruel, evil, etc. 2. [Colloq.], very bad; in bad taste. —**a·tro′cious·ly,** *adv.* —**a·tro′cious·ness,** *n.*
**a·troc·i·ty** (ə-tros′ə-ti), *n.* [*pl.* -TIES], 1. atrocious behavior; brutality, etc. 2. an atrocious act. 3. [Colloq.], a thing in very bad taste.
**at·ro·phy** (at′rə-fi), *n.* [< Fr. < L. < Gr. < *a-,* not + *trephein,* to nourish], a wasting away or failure to grow of an organ, etc., because of insufficient nutrition. *v.i.* [-PHIED, -PHYING], to waste away or fail to grow. *v.t.* to cause atrophy in. —**a·troph′ic** (ə-trof′ik), *adj.* —**at′ro·phied,** *adj.*
**at·ro·pine** (at′rə-pēn′, -pin), *n.* [< Gr. *Atropos* (see ATROPOS); + *-ine*], a poisonous, crystalline alkaloid obtained from belladonna and similar plants, used to relieve spasms and dilate the pupil of the eye: also **at′ro·pin** (-pin).
**At·ro·pos** (at′rə-pos′), *n.* in *Gr. mythology,* that one of the three Fates who cuts the thread of life.
**att.,** attorney.
**at·tach** (ə-tach′), *v.t.* [< OFr. < *a-,* to + *tach,* a nail], 1. to fasten by tying, etc. 2. to join (often used reflexively): as, he *attached* himself to us. 3. to connect by ties of affection, etc. 4. to affix, as a signature. 5. to ascribe (with *to*). 6. to appoint by order. 7. in *law, a*) to take (property, etc.) by writ. *b*) to arrest (a person). *v.i.* to be joined; belong: as, a moral obligation *attaches* to high rank. —**at·tach′a·ble,** *adj.* —**at·tached′,** *adj.*
**at·ta·ché** (at′ə-shā′, ə-tash′ā; Fr. à′tà′shā′), *n.* [Fr.; see ATTACH], a member of a diplomatic staff, especially of an ambassador. —**at′ta·ché′ship,** *n.*
**at·tach·ment** (ə-tach′mənt), *n.* 1. an attaching or being attached. 2. anything that attaches; fastening; hence, 3. devotion. 4. anything attached. 5. an accessory for an electrical appliance, etc. 6. in *law,* a taking of a person, property, etc. into custody.
**at·tack** (ə-tak′), *v.t.* [< Fr. < It.; prob. < same source as *attach*], 1. to use force against in order to harm. 2. to speak or write against. 3. to undertake vigorously. 4. to begin acting upon harmfully. *v.i.* to make an assault. *n.* 1. an attacking; onslaught. 2. an onset or occurrence of a disease. 3. a beginning of any task, etc.
**at·tain** (ə-tān′), *v.t.* [< OFr. < L. < *ad-,* to + *tangere,* to touch], 1. to gain through effort; achieve. 2. to reach or come to; arrive at. —**attain to,** to be successful in gaining or reaching. —**at·tain′a·ble,** *adj.* —**at·tain′a·bil′i·ty, at·tain′a·ble·ness,** *n.* —**at·tain′er,** *n.*
**at·tain·der** (ə-tān′dẽr), *n.* [OFr. *ataindre,* to accuse, convict], loss of civil rights, property, etc. of one sentenced to death or outlawed.
**at·tain·ment** (ə-tān′mənt), *n.* 1. an attaining or being attained. 2. anything attained, as a skill.
**at·taint** (ə-tānt′), *v.t.* [-TAINTED, -TAINTING; *ar-*

*chaic* pp. ATTAINT], 1. to convict of crime punishable by attainder. 2. to taint or stain; disgrace; dishonor. *n.* 1. an attainder. 2. a taint; disgrace. —**at·taint′ment,** *n.*

**at·tar** (at′ẽr), *n.* [< Per. < Ar. *'itr,* perfume], a perfume made from the petals of flowers, as of roses.

**at·tempt** (ə-tempt′), *v.t.* [< OFr. < L. < *ad-*, to + *temptare,* to try], to try to do, get, etc.; endeavor. *n.* 1. a try; an endeavor. 2. an attack, as on a person's life. —**attempt the life of,** to try to kill. —**at·tempt′a·ble,** *adj.* —**at·tempt′a·bil′i·ty,** *n.* —**at·tempt′er,** *n.*

**at·tend** (ə-tend′), *v.t.* [< OFr. < L. *attendere,* to give heed to < *ad-*, to + *tendere,* to stretch], 1. to take care or charge of. 2. to go with. 3. to accompany as a result. 4. to be present at. 5. [Archaic], to listen to. *v.i.* 1. to pay attention. 2. to wait (with *on* or *upon*). —**attend to,** 1. to devote or apply oneself to. 2. to take care of. —**at·tend′er,** *n.*

**at·tend·ance** (ə-ten′dəns), *n.* 1. an attending. 2. the number of persons attending an event.

**at·tend·ant** (ə-ten′dənt), *adj.* 1. attending or serving. 2. being present. 3. accompanying: as, *attendant* difficulties. *n.* 1. one who attends or serves. 2. a person present. 3. a concomitant.

**at·ten·tion** (ə-ten′shən), *n.* 1. an attending; giving heed. 2. the ability to give heed. 3. heed; notice. 4. thoughtful consideration for others. 5. *usually in pl.* act of courtesy: as, a suitor's *attentions.* 6. in *military usage, a*) the erect, motionless posture of soldiers in readiness for a command. *b*) a command to assume this posture.

**at·ten·tive** (ə-ten′tiv), *adj.* 1. paying attention. 2. courteous, devoted, etc. —**at·ten′tive·ly,** *adv.* —**at·ten′tive·ness,** *n.*

**at·ten·u·ant** (ə-ten′ū-ənt), *adj.* in *medicine,* diluting or thinning, as liquids. *n.* any substance used for diluting liquids.

**at·ten·u·ate** (ə-ten′ū-āt′), *v.t.* [-ATED, -ATING], [< L. < *ad-*, to + *tenuis,* thin], 1. to make slender or thin. 2. to dilute; rarefy. 3. to lessen or weaken. *v.i.* to become thin, weak, etc. *adj.* (-it), attenuated. —**at·ten′u·a·ble,** *adj.* —**at·ten′u·a′tion,** *n.* —**at·ten′u·a′tor,** *n.*

**at·test** (ə-test′), *v.t.* [< Fr. < L. < *ad-*, to + *testari,* to bear witness], 1. to declare to be true or genuine. 2. to certify, as by oath. 3. to serve as proof of. *v.i.* to bear witness; certify (usually with *to*). *n.* attestation. —**at·test′ant,** *adj. & n.* —**at·test′er, at·test′or,** *n.*

**at·tes·ta·tion** (at′es-tā′shən), *n.* 1. an attesting. 2. testimony.

**At·tic** (at′ik), *adj.* 1. of Attica. 2. Athenian. 3. classical: said of a style. *n.* 1. the Greek dialect of Attica. 2. an Athenian.

**at·tic** (at′ik), *n.* [< Fr. < the prec.], in *architecture,* 1. a low story above the cornice of a classical façade. 2. the space or rooms just below the roof of a house; garret.

**At·ti·ca** (at′i-kə), *n.* a state of ancient Greece: capital, Athens.

**At·ti·cize, at·ti·cize** (at′i-sīz′), *v.t.* [-CIZED, -CIZING], to make conform to the Attic customs, style, etc. *v.i.* to use Attic dialect or literary style. —**At′ti·cism, at′ti·cism,** *n.*

**Attic salt, Attic wit,** graceful, piercing wit.

**At·ti·la** (at′'l-ə), *n.* king of the Huns (433?–453 A.D.); lived 406?–453 A.D.

**at·tire** (ə-tīr′), *v.t.* [-TIRED, -TIRING], [< OFr. < *a* (L. *ad*), to + *tire,* row, order], to clothe; dress up; array. *n.* clothes; finery. —**at·tire′ment,** *n.*

**at·ti·tude** (at′ə-to͞od′, -tūd′), *n.* [< Fr. < It. < L.; see APT], 1. a bodily posture showing a mental state or mood. 2. a manner that shows one's disposition, etc. 3. one's disposition, etc.

**at·ti·tu·di·nize** (at′ə-to͞o′d'n-īz′, -tū′-), *v.i.* [-NIZED, -NIZING], to pose to impress someone.

**at·tor·ney** (ə-tũr′ni), *n.* [*pl.* -NEYS], [< OFr. < *a-* (L. *ad*), to + *torner;* see TURN], any person legally empowered to act for another; esp., a lawyer.

**attorney at law,** a lawyer.

**attorney general,** [*pl.* ATTORNEYS GENERAL, ATTORNEY GENERALS], 1. the chief law officer of a national or State government. 2. [A- G-], the head of the U.S. Department of Justice.

**at·tract** (ə-trakt′), *v.t.* [< L. < *ad-*, to + *trahere,* to draw], 1. to draw to itself or oneself: as, a magnet *attracts* iron filings. 2. to get the admiration, attention, etc. of; allure. *v.i.* to be attractive. —**at·tract′a·ble,** *adj.* —**at·tract′a·ble·ness, at·tract′a·bil′i·ty,** *n.* —**at·trac′tor, at·tract′er,** *n.*

**at·trac·tion** (ə-trak′shən), *n.* 1. an attracting. 2. power of attracting. 3. charm; fascination. 4. anything that attracts. 5. in *physics,* the mutual action by which bodies, particles, etc. tend to cohere: opposed to *repulsion.*

**at·trac·tive** (ə-trak′tiv), *adj.* 1. that attracts. 2. pleasing, charming, pretty, etc. —**at·trac′tive·ly,** *adv.* —**at·trac′tive·ness,** *n.*

**attrib.,** 1. attribute. 2. attributive(ly).

**at·tri·bute** (ə-trib′yoot; *for n.,* at′rə-būt′), *v.t.* [-BUTED, -BUTING], [< L. < *ad-*, to + *tribuere,* to assign], to think of as belonging to or coming from; assign or ascribe (*to*): as, the play is *attributed* to Shakespeare. *n.* 1. a characteristic or quality of a thing. 2. an object used in the arts as a symbol for a person, position, etc.: as, winged feet are the *attribute* of Mercury. —**at·trib′u·ta·ble,** *adj.*—**at·trib′u·ter, at·trib′u·tor,** *n.*

**at·tri·bu·tion** (at′rə-bū′shən), *n.* 1. an attributing or being attributed. 2. an attribute.

**at·trib·u·tive** (ə-trib′yoo-tiv), *adj.* 1. attributing. 2. of or like an attribute. 3. in *grammar,* expressing a quality meant to apply to a following substantive: said of adjectives, and distinguished from *predicate* and *predicative.* *n.* an attributive word; modifier: as, in "black cat," *black* is an *attributive.* —**at·trib′u·tive·ly,** *adv.*

**at·tri·tion** (ə-trish′ən), *n.* [L. < *ad-*, to + *terere,* to rub], 1. a wearing away by friction. 2. any gradual wearing or weakening.

**at·tune** (ə-to͞on′, ə-tūn′), *v.t.* [-TUNED, -TUNING], 1. to tune. 2. to bring into harmony.

**atty.,** attorney.

**at. wt.,** atomic weight.

**a·typ·i·cal** (ā-tip′i-k'l), *adj.* not typical; not characteristic; abnormal: also **a·typ′ic.**

**Au,** *aurum,* [L.], in *chemistry,* gold.

**au·burn** (ô′bẽrn), *adj. & n.* [< OFr. < L. *alburnus* < *albus,* white; meaning influenced by association with ME. *brun,* brown], reddish brown.

**Auck·land** (ôk′lənd), *n.* a seaport in North Island, New Zealand: pop., 515,000.

‡**au cou·rant** (ō′ko͞o′rän′), [Fr.], up-to-date.

**auc·tion** (ôk′shən), *n.* [< L. < *augere,* to increase], 1. a public sale where items are sold to the highest bidders. 2. auction bridge. *v.t.* to sell at auction.

**auction bridge,** a variety of the game of bridge in which the players bid for the right to say what suit shall be trump or to declare no-trump.

**auc·tion·eer** (ôk′shən-êr′), *n.* one who auctions things, usually as a business. *v.t.* to auction.

**aud.,** auditor.

**au·da·cious** (ô-dā′shəs), *adj.* [< Fr. < L. < *audere,* to dare], 1. reckless; bold. 2. too bold; insolent. —**au·da′cious·ly,** *adv.* —**au·da′cious·ness,** *n.*

**au·dac·i·ty** (ô-das′ə-ti), *n.* 1. bold courage; daring. 2. insolence; impudence. 3. [*pl.* -TIES], an audacious act or remark.

**au·di·ble** (ô′də-b'l), *adj.* [< ML. < L. *audire,* to hear], loud enough to be heard. —**au′di·bil′i·ty, au′di·ble·ness,** *n.* —**au′di·bly,** *adv.*

**au·di·ence** (ô′di-əns, ôd′yəns), *n.* [OFr. < L. < *audire,* to hear], 1. those assembled to hear and see a play, etc. 2. all those hearing or seeing a radio or television program, reading a particular book, etc.; one's public. 3. the act or state of hearing. 4. a chance to be heard; hearing. 5. a formal interview with a person in high position.

**au·di·o** (ô′di-ō′), *adj.* [L., I hear], 1. in *electricity,* of frequencies corresponding to sound waves that are normally audible. 2. designating or of the audible portion of a telecast: opposed to *video.*

**au·di·o-fre·quen·cy** (ô′di-ō-frē′kwən-si), *adj.* of the band of audible sound frequencies or corresponding electric current frequencies, about 20 to 20,000 cycles per second.

**au·di·ol·o·gy** (ô′di-ol′ə-ji), *n.* the science of hearing, with reference to the rehabilitation of persons with hearing defects. —**au′di·ol′o·gist,** *n.*

**au·di·o-vis·u·al** (ô′di-ō-vizh′o͞o-əl), *adj.* 1. involving both sight and hearing. 2. designating or of such teaching aids as filmstrips, radio, etc.

**au·dit** (ô′dit), *n.* [< L. < *audire,* to hear], 1. a regular examination and adjustment of financial accounts. 2. an account thus examined and adjusted, or a statement of this. *v.t. & v.i.* 1. to examine and check (accounts, etc.). 2. to attend (a college class) as a listener receiving no credits.

**au·di·tion** (ô-dish′ən), *n.* 1. the act or sense of hearing. 2. a hearing to test the abilities of an actor, musician, etc. *v.t.* to give an audition to. *v.i.* to perform in an audition.

**au·di·tor** (ô′də-tẽr), *n.* 1. a hearer; listener. 2. one who audits. —**au′di·tor·ship,** *n.*

**au·di·to·ri·um** (ô′də-tôr′i-əm, -tō′ri-), *n.* [*pl.* -RIUMS, -RIA (-ə)], 1. a room where the audience sits in a church, theater, etc. 2. a building or hall for speeches, concerts, etc.

**au·di·to·ry** (ô′də-tôr′i, -tō′ri), *adj.* of hearing or the sense of hearing. *n.* [*pl.* -RIES], 1. an audience. 2. an auditorium.

**Au·du·bon, John James** (ô′də-bon′), 1785–1851; American ornithologist, painter, and naturalist.

‡**auf Wie·der·se·hen** (ouf vē′dẽr-zā′ən), [G.], till we see each other again; good-by.

**Aug.**, August.

**Au·ge·an** (ô-jē′ən), *adj.* 1. in *Gr. legend*, of King Augeas or his stable, which Hercules cleaned in one day; hence, 2. filthy.

**au·gend** (ô′jend, ô-jend′), *n.* [< L. < *augere*, to increase], a number having another number (the addend) added to it.

**au·ger** (ô′gẽr), *n.* [by faulty separation of ME. *a nauger* < AS. *nafu*, nave (of a wheel) + *gar*, a spear], a tool for boring holes in wood.

**aught** (ôt), *n.* [AS. *awiht* < *a*, one + *wiht*, a thing; see WHIT], 1. anything whatever; any little part. 2. [*a naught* (see NAUGHT), wrongly divided *an aught*], a zero. *adv.* in any way; at all.

**aug·ment** (ôg-ment′; *for n.*, ôg′ment), *v.t.* [< Fr. < L. < *augere*, to increase], to make greater; enlarge. *v.i.* to become greater; increase. *n.* an increase. —**aug·ment′a·ble,** *adj.* —**aug·ment′er,** *n.*

**aug·men·ta·tion** (ôg′men-tā′shən), *n.* 1. an augmenting or being augmented. 2. an addition.

**aug·ment·a·tive** (ôg-men′tə-tiv), *adj.* augmenting. *n.* an intensifying word or affix.

**au gra·tin** (ō grä′t'n, gra′-; Fr. ō′ grà′tan′), [Fr., lit., with scrapings], made with a lightly browned crust of bread crumbs or grated cheese.

**Augs·burg** (ôgz′bẽrg; G. ouks′boorkh), *n.* a city in S Germany, in Bavaria: pop., 204,000.

**au·gur** (ô′gẽr), *n.* [L., orig., a priest at rituals of fertility; prob. < *augere*, to increase], 1. in ancient Rome, any of certain priests who foretold events by interpreting omens. 2. a fortuneteller; soothsayer. *v.t. & v.i.* 1. to foretell; prophesy. 2. to be an omen (of). —**augur ill** (or **well**), to be a bad (or good) omen.

**au·gu·ry** (ô′gyẽr-i), *n.* [*pl.* -RIES], 1. the rite of divination. 2. an omen; indication.

**Au·gust** (ô′gəst), *n.* [L. < *Augustus* Caesar], the eighth month of the year, having 31 days: abbrev. **Aug., Ag.**

**au·gust** (ô-gust′), *adj.* [L. < *augere*, to increase], inspiring awe and reverence; imposing; majestic. —**au·gust′ly,** *adv.* —**au·gust′ness,** *n.*

**Au·gus·ta** (ô-gus′tə), *n.* 1. a city in E Georgia: pop., 71,000. 2. the capital of Maine, on the Kennebec River: pop., 22,000.

**Au·gus·tan** (ô-gus′tən), *adj.* 1. of or characteristic of Augustus Caesar, his reign (27 B.C.–14 A.D.), or his times. 2. of or like any similar age; classical; elegant. *n.* a writer living in an Augustan age.

**Augustan age,** 1. the period of Latin literature during the reign of Augustus Caesar, characterized by elegance, correctness, etc. 2. a similar period, as of English literature (early 18th c.).

**Au·gus·tine,** Saint (ô′gəs-tēn′, ô-gus′tin), 1. 354–430 A.D.; Latin church father; bishop in northern Africa. 2. ?–604 A.D.; Roman missionary among the English. —**Au′gus·tin′i·an** (-tin′i-ən), *adj. & n.*

**Au·gus·tus** (ô-gus′təs), *n.* (*Gaius Julius Caesar Octavianus*), grandnephew of Julius Caesar and first emperor of Rome (27 B.C.–14 A.D.); lived 63 B.C.–14 A.D.: also called *Octavian.*

‡**au jus** (ō′ zhü′), [Fr., with the juice], served in its natural juice or gravy: said of meat.

**auk** (ôk), *n.* [dial. *alk* < ON. *alka*], any of a number of related diving birds of northern seas, with webbed feet and short wings used as paddles.

‡**au lait** (ō′ le′), [Fr.], with milk.

**auld** (ôld), *adj.* [Dial. & Scot.], old.

**auld lang syne** (ôld′ laŋ sīn′), [Scot., lit., old long since], the good old days.

‡**au na·tu·rel** (ō′ nà′tü′rel′), [Fr.], 1. in the natural state. 2. naked. 3. prepared simply.

**aunt** (ant, änt), *n.* [< OFr. < L. *amita*, paternal aunt], 1. the sister of one's mother or father. 2. the wife of one's uncle.

**aunt·ie, aunt·y** (an′ti, än′ti), *n.* aunt: a familiar or affectionate form.

**au·ra** (ô′rə), *n.* [*pl.* -RAS, -RAE (-rē)], [L.; Gr., air, breeze], 1. an invisible emanation. 2 an invisible atmosphere supposedly arising from and surrounding a person or thing. —**au′ral,** *adj.*

**au·ral** (ô′rəl), *adj.* [< L. *auris*, ear; + *-al*], of or received through the ear or the sense of hearing. —**au′ral·ly,** *adv.*

**au·re·ate** (ô′ri-it), *adj.* [< L. < *aurum*, gold], 1. golden; gilded. 2. splendid; ornate.

**au·re·ole** (ô′ri-ōl′), *n.* [< L.; see AUREATE], 1. a halo. 2. in *astronomy*, a corona. Also **au·re·o·la** (ô-rē′ə-lə).

**au·re·o·my·cin** (ô′ri-ō-mī′sin), *n.* [< L. *aureus*, golden + Gr. *mykēs*, fungus; + *-in*], an antibiotic drug similar to penicillin, effective against certain viruses and against bacteria.

**au re·voir** (ō′ rə-vwär′), [Fr. < L. < *re-*, again + *videre*, to see], until we meet again; good-by.

**au·ri·cle** (ô′ri-k'l), *n.* [L. *auricula*, dim. of *auris*, ear], 1. the external part of the ear. 2. either of two upper chambers of the heart, into which the blood flows from the veins. 3. in *botany & zoology*, an earlike part. —**au′ri·cled,** *adj.*

**au·ric·u·lar** (ô-rik′yoo-lẽr), *adj.* 1. of or near the ear; of the sense of hearing. 2. spoken directly into the ear. 3. ear-shaped. 4. of an auricle of the heart. —**au·ric′u·lar·ly,** *adv.*

**au·rif·er·ous** (ô-rif′ẽr-əs), *adj.* [< L. < *aurum*, gold + *ferre*, to bear], bearing or yielding gold. —**au·rif′er·ous·ly,** *adv.*

**au·ri·form** (ô′ri-fôrm′), *adj.* ear-shaped.

**au·rochs** (ô′roks), *n.* [*pl.* -ROCHS], [G. *auerochs* < OHG. *urohso*], 1. originally, the wild ox of Europe, now extinct. 2. now, the European bison.

**Au·ro·ra** (ô-rôr′ə, ô-rō′rə), *n.* [*pl.* except in senses 1 & 2, -RAS, -RAE (-ē, -rē)], 1. in *Rom. mythology*, the goddess of dawn. 2. a city in NE Illinois: pop., 64,000. 3. [a-], the dawn. 4. [a-], the early period of anything. 5. [a-], the aurora australis or aurora borealis.

**aurora aus·tra·lis** (ô-strā′lis), [L. < *auster*, south wind], luminous bands or streamers sometimes appearing in the night sky of the Southern Hemisphere.

**aurora bo·re·a·lis** (bôr′i-al′is, bō′ri-ā′lis), [L., < Gr. *boreas*, north wind], luminous bands or streamers sometimes appearing in the night sky of the Northern Hemisphere; northern lights.

**au·ro·ral** (ô-rôr′əl, ô-rō′rəl), *adj.* 1. of or like the dawn; rosy; dawning. 2. of or like the aurora (borealis or australis). —**au·ro′ral·ly,** *adv.*

**au·ro·re·an** (ô-rôr′i-ən, ô-rō′ri-ən), *adj.* auroral.

**au·rum** (ô′rəm), *n.* [L.], gold: symbol, Au.

**Au·schwitz** (ou′shvits), *n.* 1. a city in SW Poland: pop., 6,700. 2. a Nazi concentration camp here, notorious as an extermination center.

**aus·cul·ta·tion** (ôs′kəl-tā′shən), *n.* [L. < *auscultare*, to listen], 1. a listening. 2. a listening to sounds in the chest, abdomen, etc. so as to determine the condition of the heart, lungs, etc. —**aus′cul·tate′,** *v.t. & v.i.* [-TATED, -TATING]. —**aus′cul·ta′tor,** *n.*

**aus·pice** (ôs′pis), *n.* [*pl.* -PICES], [L. *auspicium*, omen], 1. an omen. 2. a prophecy, especially when favorable. 3. *usually pl.* patronage: as, under the *auspices* of the mayor.

**aus·pi·cious** (ôs-pish′əs), *adj.* 1. of good omen; favorable; propitious. 2. successful; prosperous. —**aus·pi′cious·ly,** *adv.* —**aus·pi′cious·ness,** *n.*

**Aus·sie** (ôs′i), *n.* [Slang], an Australian.

**Aus·ten, Jane** (ôs′tin, -tən), 1775–1817; English novelist.

**aus·tere** (ô-stêr′), *adj.* [< OFr. < L. < Gr. *austēros* < *auos*, dry], 1. stern; harsh. 2. morally strict. 3. very simple; unadorned. 4. grave; sober: as, an *austere* face. —**aus·tere′ly,** *adv.* —**aus·tere′ness,** *n.*

**aus·ter·i·ty** (ô-ster′ə-ti), *n.* [*pl.* -TIES], 1. sternness; harshness. 2. *usually in pl.* an austere habit or practice.

**Aus·tin** (ôs′tin, -tən), *n.* the capital of Texas, on the Colorado River: pop., 187,000.

**aus·tral** (ôs′trəl), *adj.* [L. < *auster*, the south], 1. southern; southerly. 2. [A-], Australian.

**Aus·tral·a·sia** (ôs′trəl-ā′zhə, -shə), *n.* Australia, Tasmania, New Zealand, Malaysia, Melanesia, Micronesia, and Polynesia. —**Aus′tral·a′sian,** *adj. & n.*

**Aus·tral·ia** (ô-strāl′yə), *n.* 1. a continent in the Southern Hemisphere, SE of Asia. 2. a British Commonwealth comprising this continent and Tasmania: area, 2,974,581 sq. mi.; pop., 8,986,000; capital, Canberra. —**Aus·tral′ian,** *adj. & n.*

**Australian ballot,** a type of ballot listing candidates for election to public office, marked by the voter in secrecy.

**Aus·tri·a** (ôs′tri-ə), *n.* a country in central Europe: area, 32,375 sq. mi.; pop., 7,049,000; capital, Vienna: German name, *Osterreich.* —**Aus′tri·an,** *adj. & n.*

**Aus·tri·a-Hun·ga·ry** (ôs′tri-ə-huŋ gə-ri), *n.* a former monarchy in central Europe. —**Aus·tro-Hun·gar·i·an** (ôs′trō-huŋ-gâr′i-ən), *adj.*

**Aus·tro·ne·sia** (ôs′trō-nē′zhə, -shə), *n.* [< L. *auster*, the south + Gr. *nēsos*, island], the islands in the central and south Pacific.

**Aus·tro·ne·sian** (ôs′trō-nē′zhən, -shən), *adj.* 1. of Austronesia, its people, etc. 2. designating or of a family of languages spoken there, comprising the Indonesian, Melanesian, Micronesian, and Polynesian subfamilies. *n.* these languages.

**au·tarch·y** (ô′tär-ki), *n.* [*pl.* -IES], [< Gr. < *autarchos*, absolute ruler < *autos*, self + *archos*, first, ruler], 1. absolute rule; despotism. 2. a country under such rule. 3. loosely, autarky. —**au·tar′chic, au·tar′chi·cal,** *adj.*

**au·tar·ky** (ô′tär-ki), *n.* [Gr. *autarkeia* < *autos*, self + *arkeein*, to suffice], economic self-sufficiency as a national policy. —**au·tar′kic, au·tar′ki·cal,** *adj.* —**au′tar·kist,** *n.*

**au·then·tic** (ô-then′tik), *adj.* [< OFr. < L. < Gr. *authentikos* < *authentēs*, one who does things himself], 1. authoritative; trustworthy; reliable: as, an *authentic* news report. 2. genuine; real: as, an *authentic* antique. Also **au·then′ti·cal.** —**au·then′ti·cal·ly,** *adv.*

**au·then·ti·cate** (ô-then′ti-kāt′), *v.t.* [-CATED, -CATING], 1. to make authentic or valid. 2. to establish the truth of; verify; prove to be genuine. 3. to prove (a painting, book, etc.) to be the product of a certain person. —**au·then′ti·ca′tion,** *n.* —**au·then′ti·ca′tor,** *n.*

**au·then·tic·i·ty** (ô′thən-tis′ə-ti), *n.* the quality or state of being authentic; authoritativeness, reliability, or genuineness.

**au·thor** (ô′thẽr), *n.* [< OFr. < L. *auctor* < *augere*, to increase], 1. one who makes or originates something; creator. 2. the writer (*of* a book, article, etc.). 3. a person whose profession is writing books, etc. 4. an author's writings. *v.t.* to be the author of. —**au′thor·ess,** *n. fem.* —**au·tho·ri·al** (ô-thôr′i-əl, -thō′ri-), *adj.*

**au·thor·i·tar·i·an** (ə-thôr′ə-târ′i-ən, -thor′-), *adj.* believing in, relating to, or characterized by unquestioning obedience to authority rather than by individual freedom of judgment and action. *n.* a person who believes in or enforces such obedience. —**au·thor′i·tar′i·an·ism,** *n.*

**au·thor·i·ta·tive** (ə-thôr′ə-tā′tiv, -thor′-), *adj.* 1. asserting authority; dictatorial. 2. having authority; official. 3. based on competent authority; reliable because coming from recognized experts. —**au·thor′i·ta′tive·ly,** *adv.* —**au·thor′i·ta′tive·ness,** *n.*

**au·thor·i·ty** (ə-thôr′ə-ti, -thor′-), *n.* [*pl.* -TIES], [< OFr. < L. *auctoritas* < *auctor;* see AUTHOR], 1. the power or right to give commands, enforce obedience, take action, or make final decisions; jurisdiction. 2. this power as delegated to another; authorization. 3. power or influence resulting from knowledge, prestige, etc. 4. a person, writing, etc. cited in support of an opinion. 5. *usually in pl.* a government official or other person having the power or right to enforce orders, laws, etc. 6. an expert in some field whose opinion is considered reliable.

**au·thor·ize** (ô′thə-rīz′), *v.t.* [-IZED, -IZING], 1. to give official approval to or permission for: as, the city *authorized* a housing project. 2. to give power or authority to; commission: as, I *authorize* you to act for me. 3. to give authority or justification for. —**au′thor·i·za′tion,** *n.* —**au′thor·iz′er,** *n.*

**Authorized Version,** the revised English translation of the Bible published in England in 1611 with the authorization of King James I: also called *King James Version.*

**au·thor·ship** (ô′thẽr-ship′), *n.* 1. the profession of a writer. 2. the origin (of a book, idea, etc.) with reference to its author or originator: as, a plan of unknown *authorship.*

**au·to** (ô′tō), *n.* [*pl.* -TOS], [Colloq.], an automobile. *v.i.* [Colloq.], to go by automobile.

**au·to-,** [< Gr. *autos*, self], a combining form meaning: 1. *self*, as in *autobiography*: also, before a vowel, **aut-.** 2. [< *automobile*], *self-propelled.*

**au·to·bi·og·ra·phy** (ô′tə-bi-og′rə-fi, -bi-), *n.* [*pl.* -PHIES], [*auto-* + *bio-* + *-graphy*], the story of one's own life written by oneself. —**au′to·bi·og′ra·pher,** *n.* —**au′to·bi′o·graph′ic** (-bi′ə-graph′ik), **au′to·bi′o·graph′i·cal,** *adj.* —**au′to·bi′o·graph′i·cal·ly,** *adv.*

**au·to·clave** (ô′tə-klāv′), *n.* [< Fr.; *auto-* + L. *clavis*, a key], a container for sterilizing, cooking, etc. by superheated steam under pressure. *v.t.* [-CLAVED, -CLAVING], to sterilize or cook by means of such a device.

**auto court,** a motel.

**au·toc·ra·cy** (ô-tok′rə-si), *n.* [*pl.* -CIES], [< Fr. < Gr. *autokrateia;* see AUTOCRAT], 1. a government in which one person has supreme power; dictatorship. 2. unlimited power or authority over others.

**au·to·crat** (ô′tə-krat′), *n.* [< Fr. < Gr. *autokratēs* < *autos*, self + *kratos*, power], 1. a ruler with supreme power over his people; dictator. 2. anyone having unlimited power over others. 3. any domineering, self-willed person. —**au′to·crat′ic, au′to·crat′i·cal,** *adj.* —**au′to·crat′i·cal·ly,** *adv.*

**au·to-da-fé** (ô′tō-də-fā′, ou′tō-), *n.* [*pl.* AUTOS-DA-FÉ (ô′tōz-, ou′tōz-)], [Port., lit., act of the faith], 1. in the Inquisition, the ceremony connected with trying and sentencing a heretic. 2. the execution by the secular power of the sentence thus passed. 3. a public burning of a heretic.

**au·to·gi·ro** (ô′tə-jī′rō), *n.* [*pl.* -ROS], [< *auto-* + Gr. *gyros*, a circle], a kind of aircraft that moves forward by means of a propeller and is supported in the air mainly by another large propeller mounted horizontally above the fuselage and turned by air pressure: also sp. **autogyro:** a trademark (**Autogiro**).

**au·to·graph** (ô′tə-graf′, -gräf′), *n.* [< L. < Gr. *autographos* < *autos*, self + *graphein*, to write], 1. a person's own signature or handwriting. 2. a thing written in one's own handwriting. *v.t.* 1. to write (something) with one's own hand. 2. to write one's signature on or in. —**au′to·graph′ic, au′to·graph′i·cal,** *adj.* —**au′to·graph′i·cal·ly,** *adv.*

**au·to·in·tox·i·ca·tion** (ô′tō-in-tok′sə-kā′shən), *n.* [*auto-* + *intoxication*], poisoning by toxic substances formed within the body.

**au·to·ist** (ô′tō-ist), *n.* a motorist.

**au·to·mat** (ô′tə-mat′), *n.* [see AUTOMATIC], a restaurant in which patrons get food from small compartments opened by putting coins into slots.

**au·to·mat·ic** (ô′tə-mat′ik), *adj.* [Gr. *automatos*, self-moving], 1. done without conscious thought or volition, as if mechanically, or from force of habit. 2. moving, operating, etc. by itself; regulating itself: as, *automatic* machinery. *n.* 1. an automatic rifle or pistol. 2. any automatic machine. —**au′to·mat′i·cal·ly,** *adv.*

**automatic pistol** (or **rifle,** etc.), a pistol, rifle, etc. that uses the force of the explosion of a shell to eject the empty cartridge case and place the next cartridge into the breech so that shots are fired in rapid succession until the trigger is released.

**automatic tuning,** the tuning in of stations on a radio receiver by means of push buttons.

**au·to·ma·tion** (ô′tə-mā′shən), *n.* in manufacturing, a system or method in which many or all of the processes are automatically performed or controlled by machinery, electronic devices, etc.

**au·tom·a·tism** (ô-tom′ə-tiz′m), *n.* 1. the quality or condition of being automatic. 2. automatic action. 3. in *physiology*, action independent of outside stimulus or of conscious control.

**au·tom·a·ton** (ô-tom′ə-ton′, -tən), *n.* [*pl.* -TONS, -TA (-tə)], [Gr., neut. of *automatos;* see AUTOMATIC], 1. anything that can move or act of itself. 2. an apparatus with a concealed mechanism that enables it to move or work of itself. 3. a person or animal acting in an automatic or mechanical way.

**au·to·mo·bile** (ô′tə-mə-bēl′, ô′tə-mə-bēl′, ô′tə-mō′bēl), *n.* [*auto-* + *mobile*], a car, usually four-wheeled, propelled by an engine or motor that is part of it, and meant for traveling on streets or roads; motorcar. *v.i.* [-BILED, -BILING], [Rare], to go by automobile. *adj.* 1. (ô′tə-mō′bil), self-moving; self-propelled. 2. of or for an automobile. —**au·to·mo·bil·ist,** (ô′tə-mə-bēl′ist, -mō′bil-ist), *n.*

**au·to·mo·tive** (ô′tə-mō′tiv), *adj.* [*auto-* + *motive*], 1. self-propelling; self-moving. 2. having to do with automobiles.

**au·to·nom·ic** (ô′tə-nom′ik), *adj.* 1. autonomous. 2. of the autonomic nervous system. Also **au′to·nom′i·cal.** —**au′to·nom′i·cal·ly,** *adv.*

**autonomic nervous system,** the divisions of the nervous system that innervate glands as well as smooth and cardiac muscle: so called because formerly thought to function independently of the central nervous system.

**au·ton·o·mous** (ô-ton′ə-məs), *adj.* [< Gr. < *autos*, self + *nomos*, law], 1. of an autonomy. 2. having self-government. 3. in *biology*, functioning independently of other parts. —**au·ton′o·mous·ly,** *adv.*

**au·ton·o·my** (ô-ton′ə-mi), *n.* 1. self-government. 2. [*pl.* -MIES], any state that governs itself. —**au·ton′o·mist,** *n.*

**au·top·sy** (ô′top-si, -təp-), *n.* [*pl.* -SIES], [< Gr. *autopsia*, a seeing with one's own eyes < *autos*, self + *opsis*, a sight], an examination and dissection of a dead body to discover the cause of death, etc.; post-mortem.

**au·to·sug·ges·tion** (ô′tō-səg-jes′chən), *n.* suggestion to oneself arising within oneself and having effects on one's thinking and bodily functions.

**au·tumn** (ô′təm), *n.* [< OFr. < L. *autumnus;* prob. of Etruscan origin], 1. the season that comes between summer and winter. 2. any period of maturity or of beginning decline. *adj.* of, in, characteristic of, or like autumn. Also called *fall.* —**au·tum·nal** (ô-tum′n'l), *adj.* —**au·tum′nal·ly,** *adv.*

**autumnal equinox,** the equinox occurring about September 23.

**aux.,** auxiliary.

**aux·il·ia·ry** (ôg-zil′yə-ri, -ə-ri, -i-er′i), *adj.* [< L. < *auxilium,* aid < pp. of *augere,* to increase], 1. helping; assisting; giving aid. 2. subsidiary. 3. additional; supplementary. *n.* [*pl.* -RIES], 1. an auxiliary person, group, thing, etc. 2. *pl.* foreign troops aiding those of a country at war.

**auxiliary verb,** a verb that helps form tenses, aspects, moods, or voices of other verbs, as *have, be, may, can, must, do, shall, will.* Examples: *has* and *been* in "He has been working."

**Av., av.,** Avenue.

**av.,** 1. average. 2. avoirdupois.

**A.V.,** Authorized Version.

**a.v., A/V,** ad valorem.

**a·vail** (ə-vāl′), *v.i. & v.t.* [< OFr. *a* (L. *ad*), to + *valoir,* to be worth < L. *valere,* to be strong], to be of use, help, worth, or advantage (to), as in accomplishing an end. *n.* use or help; advantage; benefit; profit: as, he tried, but to no *avail.* —**avail oneself of,** to take advantage of (an opportunity, etc.); utilize.

**a·vail·a·ble** (ə-vāl′ə-b'l), *adj.* 1. that can be used. 2. that can be got, had, or reached; accessible. 3. in *law,* valid. —**a·vail′a·bil′i·ty, a·vail′a·ble·ness,** *n.* —**a·vail′a·bly,** *adv.*

**av·a·lanche** (av′ə-lanch′, -länch′), *n.* [Fr. (altered by assoc. with *avaler,* to descend) < *lavanche* < LL. < L. < *labi,* to slip, glide down], 1. a large mass of loosened snow, earth, etc. suddenly and swiftly sliding down a mountain. 2. anything regarded as like an avalanche: as, an *avalanche* of mail, of blows, etc. *v.i. & v.t.* [-LANCHED, -LANCHING], to come down (on) like an avalanche.

**‡a·vant-garde** (à′vän′gárd′), *n.* [Fr., lit., advance guard], vanguard.

**av·a·rice** (av′ə-ris), *n.* [< OFr. < L. < *avarus,* greedy < *avere,* to wish, desire], too much desire to get and keep money; greed; cupidity. —**av·a·ri·cious** (av′ə-rish′əs), *adj.* —**av′a·ri′cious·ly,** *adv.* —**av′a·ri′cious·ness,** *n.*

**a·vast** (ə-vast′, ə-väst′), *interj.* [< D. *houd vast,* hold fast], in *nautical usage,* stop! cease!

**av·a·tar** (av′ə-tär′), *n.* [Sans. *avatāra,* descent], 1. in *Hindu religion,* a god's coming down in bodily form to the earth; incarnation. 2. an embodiment; bodily manifestation.

**a·vaunt** (ə-vônt′, -vänt′), *interj.* [< OFr. < L. *ab,* from + *ante,* before], [Archaic], begone! go away!

**avdp.,** avoirdupois.

**a·ve** (ā′vi, ä′vā), *interj.* [L., imperative of *avere,* to be well], 1. hail! 2. farewell! *n.* 1. the salutation *ave.* 2. [A-], the prayer *Ave Maria.*

**Ave., ave.,** Avenue.

**A·ve Ma·ri·a** (ä′vi mə-rē′ə, ā′vi mə-rī′ə), [L.], 1. "Hail, Mary," the first words of a prayer to the Virgin Mary used in the R. C. Church. 2. this prayer.

**a·venge** (ə-venj′), *v.t. & v.i.* [AVENGED, AVENGING], [< OFr. < *a-* (L. *ad*), to + *vengier* < L. *vindicare,* to punish, avenge], 1. to get revenge for (an injury, etc.). 2. to take vengeance on behalf of, as for a wrong. —**a·venge′ment,** *n.* —**a·veng′er,** *n.* —**a·veng′ing·ly,** *adv.*

**av·e·nue** (av′ə-nōō′, -nū′), *n.* [Fr. < L. < *ad-,* to + *venire,* to come], 1. a way of approach or departure. 2. a road, path, or drive, often bordered with trees. 3. a street; esp., a wide street.

**a·ver** (ə-vũr′), *v.t.* [AVERRED, AVERRING], [< OFr. *averrer* < L. *ad,* to + *verus,* true], 1. to declare to be true; assert; affirm. 2. in *law,* to prove; justify. —**a·ver′ment,** *n.*

**av·er·age** (av′rij, -ẽr-ij), *n.* [prob. < Fr. *avarie,* damage to ship < It. < Ar. *'awar,* damaged goods; sense development from *n.* 3], 1. the numerical result obtained by dividing the sum of two or more quantities by the number of quantities; arithmetic mean. 2. the usual or normal kind, amount, quality, rate, etc.: as, his opinion is the *average.* 3. in *marine law, a*) a loss incurred by damage to a ship or its cargo. *b*) the equitable division of such loss among the interested parties. *adj.* 1. constituting a numerical average: as, the *average* speed. 2. usual; normal; ordinary. *v.i.* [-AGED, -AGING], to be or amount to on an average: as, the boys *average* six years of age. *v.t.* 1. to calculate the average or mean of. 2. to do, take, etc. on an average: as, he *averages* eight hours of work a day. 3. to divide proportionately among more than two. —**average out,** to result in an average. —**on the average,** as an average quantity, rate, etc. —**av′er·age·ly,** *adv.*

**A·ver·nus** (ə-vũr′nəs), *n.* [L.], in *Rom. mythology,* Hades; hell. —**A·ver′nal,** *adj.*

**a·verse** (ə-vũrs′), *adj.* [< L. pp. of *avertere;* see AVERT], unwilling; set against; reluctant. —**a·verse′ly,** *adv.* —**a·verse′ness,** *n.*

**a·ver·sion** (ə-vũr′zhən, -shən), *n.* 1. an averting; turning away. 2. intense or definite dislike; antipathy; repugnance. 3. the object arousing such dislike. 4. reluctance.

**a·vert** (ə-vũrt′), *v.t.* [< L. < *a-* (*ab-*), from + *vertere,* to turn], 1. to turn away or aside. 2. to prevent; ward off or avoid. —**a·vert′er,** *n.* —**a·vert′i·ble, a·vert′a·ble,** *adj.*

**A·ves** (ā′vēz), *n.pl.* [L., pl. of *avis,* bird], in *zoology,* the class of vertebrates comprising the birds.

**A·ves·ta** (ə-ves′tə), *n.* [< Per.], the sacred writings of Zoroastrianism, in an ancient Indo-European, Iranian language. —**A·ves′tan,** *adj. & n.*

**a·vi·ar·y** (ā′vi-er i), *n.* [*pl.* -IES], [< L. < *avis,* bird], a large cage for keeping many birds.

**a·vi·a·tion** (ā′vi-ā′shən, av′i-), *n.* [Fr. < L. *avis,* bird], the art or science of flying airplanes.

**a·vi·a·tor** (ā′vi-ā′tẽr, av′i-), *n.* a person who flies airplanes; airplane pilot; flier. —**a′vi·a′trix** (-triks), **a′vi·a′tress** (-tris), *n. fem.*

**av·id** (av′id), *adj.* [L. *avidus* < *avere,* to desire], very eager or greedy. —**a·vid·i·ty** (ə-vid′ə-ti), *n.* —**av′id·ly,** *adv.*

**A·vi·gnon** (à′vē′nyōn′), *n.* a city in S France: pop., 60,000: seat of the papacy (1309–1377).

**av·o·ca·do** (av′ə-kä′dō, ä′və-), *n.* [*pl.* -DOS], [< Mex. Sp. < Nahuatl *ahuacatl*], 1. a thick-skinned, pear-shaped tropical fruit, yellowish green to purplish black, with a single large seed and yellow, buttery flesh, used in salads; alligator pear. 2. the tree that it grows on.

**av·o·ca·tion** (av′ə-kā′shən), *n.* [< L. < *ab-,* away + *vocare,* to call], something one does in addition to his regular work, and usually for fun; hobby.

**av·o·cet** (av′ə-set′), *n.* [< Fr. < It.], a long-legged wading bird with webbed feet and a slender bill that curves upward: also sp. **avoset.**

**a·void** (ə-void′), *v.t.* [< Anglo-Fr. < OFr. *esvuidier,* to empty < *es-* (< L. *ex*), out + *vuidier;* see VOID], 1. to make void; annul, invalidate, or quash (a plea, etc. in law). 2. to keep away from; shun. 3. to get out of; shirk. —**a·void′a·ble,** *adj.* —**a·void′a·bly,** *adv.* —**a·void′ance,** *n.*

**av·oir·du·pois** (av′ẽr-də-poiz′, av′ẽr-də-poiz′), *n.* [< OFr. *aveir de peis,* goods having weight], 1. avoirdupois weight. 2. [Colloq.], heaviness or weight, especially of a person.

**avoirdupois weight,** an English and American system of weighing in which 16 drams = 1 ounce, 16 ounces = 1 pound, and 2,000 pounds = 1 ton: see also **apothecaries' weight, troy weight.**

**a·vouch** (ə-vouch′), *v.t.* [OFr. *avochier* < L. *advocare;* see ADVOCATE], 1. to vouch for; guarantee. 2. to declare the truth of; affirm. 3. to acknowledge openly; avow. *v.i.* to give assurance.

**a·vow** (ə-vou′), *v.t.* [OFr. *avouer* < L. *advocare;* see ADVOCATE], 1. to declare openly; admit frankly; confess. 2. to acknowledge (oneself) to be: as, he *avowed* himself a patriot. —**a·vow′er,** *n.*

**a·vow·al** (ə-vou′əl), *n.* open acknowledgment or declaration; frank admission; confession.

**a·vowed** (ə-voud′), *adj.* openly acknowledged; self-confessed. —**a·vow′ed·ly,** *adv.* —**a·vow′ed·ness,** *n.*

**a·vun·cu·lar** (ə-vuŋ′kyoo-lẽr), *adj.* [< L. *avunculus,* maternal uncle, dim. of *avus,* ancestor], of, like, or in the relationship of, an uncle.

**aw** (ô), *interj.* a sound of protest, dislike, etc.

**a·wait** (ə-wāt′), *v.t.* [< OFr. < *a-* (L. *ad*), to + *waitier,* to watch], 1. to wait for; expect. 2. to be in store for; be in readiness for.

**a·wake** (ə-wāk′), *v.t.* [AWOKE (-wōk′), or AWAKED (-wākt′), AWAKED or AWOKE, AWAKING], [< AS. *awacan* (*on-* + *wacan,* to arise, awake) & AS. *awacian* (*on-* + *wacian,* to be awake, watch)], 1. to rouse from sleep; wake. 2. to rouse from inactivity; stir up. *v.i.* 1. to come out of sleep;

wake. 2. to become active. *adj.* 1. not asleep. 2. active; alert.
**a·wak·en** (ə-wāk′ən), *v.t. & v.i.* to awake; wake up; rouse. —**a·wak′en·er,** *n.*
**a·wak·en·ing** (ə-wāk′ən-iŋ), *n. & adj.* 1. (a) waking up. 2. (a) reviving, as of religion, etc.
**a·ward** (ə-wôrd′), *v.t.* [< Anglo-Fr. < ONorm.Fr. < OFr. < *es-* (< L. *ex*) + *garder;* see GUARD], 1. to give, as by legal decision; adjudge: as, to *award* damages. 2. to give as the result of judging or considering; grant: as, to *award* a prize. *n.* 1. a decision, as by judges. 2. something awarded; prize. —**a·ward′a·ble,** *adj.* —**a·ward′er,** *n.*
**a·ware** (ə-wâr′), *adj.* [AS. *gewær* < *wær*, cautious], conscious; knowing; cognizant. —**a·ware′ness,** *n.*
**a·wash** (ə-wäsh′, ə-wôsh′), *adv. & adj.* 1. just above the surface of the water. 2. floating on the water.
**a·way** (ə-wā′), *adv.* [AS. *aweg* < *on*, on + *weg*, way], 1. from any given place: as, he ran *away*. 2. far: as, *away* behind. 3. off; aside: as, the land dropped *away*. 4. from one's possession: as, give it *away*. 5. out of existence: as, the sound faded *away*. 6. at once: as, fire *away*. 7. without stopping; continuously: as, he worked *away* all night. *adj.* 1. not present; absent; gone: as, he is *away*. 2. at a distance: as, a mile *away*. *interj.* 1. begone! 2. let's go! —**away with,** 1. take away. 2. go or come away. —**do away with,** 1. to get rid of; put an end to. 2. to kill.
**awe** (ô), *n.* [ON. *agi*], a mixed feeling of reverence, fear, and wonder, caused by something sublime, etc. *v.t.* [AWED, AWING], to inspire awe in; fill with awe. —**stand** (or **be**) **in awe of,** to respect and fear. —**awe′less, aw′less,** *adj.*
**a·weigh** (ə-wā′), *adj.* in *nautical usage*, clearing the bottom; being weighed: said of an anchor.
**awe·some** (ô′səm), *adj.* 1. inspiring awe. 2. feeling awe. —**awe′some·ly,** *adv.* —**awe′some·ness,** *n.*
**awe-struck** (ô′struk′), *adj.* filled with awe: also **awe-strick·en** (ô′strik′′n).
**aw·ful** (ô′fool), *adj.* [see AWE & -FUL], 1. inspiring awe. 2. terrifying; appalling. 3. worthy of reverence and solemn respect. 4. (ô′f′l), [Colloq.], *a*) very bad, unpleasant, etc.: as, an *awful* joke. *b*) great: as, an *awful* bore. *adv.* [Colloq.], very: as, he's *awful* happy. —**aw′ful·ness,** *n.*
**aw·ful·ly** (ô′fool-i), *adv.* 1. in a way to inspire awe. 2. (ô′f′l-i, ô′fli), [Colloq.], very; extremely: as, an *awfully* pretty dress.
**a·while** (ə-hwīl′), *adv.* for a short time.
**awk·ward** (ôk′wērd), *adj.* [< ON. *afug*, turned backward + Eng. *-ward*], 1. clumsy; bungling: as, an *awkward* person. 2. inconvenient to use; unwieldy: as, an *awkward* tool. 3. inconvenient; uncomfortable: as, an *awkward* position. 4. embarrassing; inopportune: as, an *awkward* remark. 5. not easy to manage; delicate: as, an *awkward* situation. —**awk′ward·ly,** *adv.* —**awk′ward·ness,** *n.*
**awl** (ôl), *n.* [AS. *æl*, *ealle*], a small, pointed tool for making holes in wood, leather, etc.

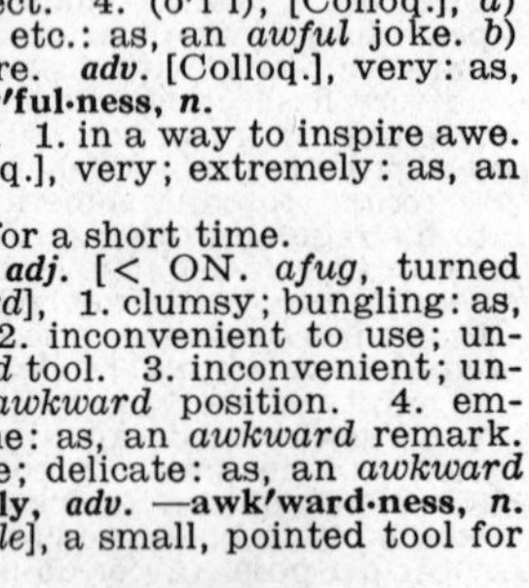

TYPES OF AWL
A, peg awl; B, sewing awl

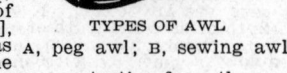

**awn** (ôn), *n.* [ON. *ögn*, chaff], the bristly fibers or beard on a head of barley, oats, etc. —**awned,** *adj.* —**awn′less,** *adj.*
**awn·ing** (ôn′iŋ), *n.* [? < MFr. *auvans*, pl. of *auvent*, window shade], a piece of canvas stretched over a frame before a window, etc. as a protection from the sun or rain.
**a·woke** (ə-wōk′), alt. pt. and occas. pp. of **awake.**
**A.W.O.L., a.w.o.l.,** absent (or absence) without leave: often pronounced (ā′wôl′).
**a·wry** (ə-rī′), *adv. & adj.* [see A- (on) & WRY], 1. with a twist to a side; askew. 2. wrong; amiss: as, our plans went *awry*.
**ax, axe** (aks), *n.* [*pl.* AXES (ak′siz)], [AS. *eax*, *æx*], 1. a tool for chopping trees and splitting wood: it has a long handle and a bladed head. 2. any similar tool or weapon, as a battle-ax. *v.t.* [AXED (akst), AXING], to trim with an ax. —**get the ax,** 1. [Colloq.], to be executed by beheading. 2. [Slang], to be discharged from one's job. —**have an ax to grind,** [Colloq.], to have a purpose of one's own to promote.
**ax·es** (ak′sēz), *n.* plural of **axis.**
**ax·es** (ak′siz), *n.* plural of **ax.**
**ax·i·al** (ak′si-əl), *adj.* 1. of, like, or forming an axis. 2. around or along an axis. —**ax′i·al·ly,** *adv.*
**ax·il** (ak′sil), *n.* [< L. *axilla;* see AXILLA], the upper angle between a leaf, twig, etc. and the stem from which it grows.
**ax·il·la** (ak-sil′ə), *n.* [*pl.* -LAE (-ē), -LAS], [L., armpit < *ala*, wing], 1. the armpit. 2. an axil.
**ax·il·la·ry** (ak′sə-ler′i), *adj.* 1. of or near the armpit. 2. of, in, or growing from an axil.
**ax·i·om** (ak′si-əm), *n.* [< L. < Gr. *axiōma*, authority < *axios*, worthy], 1. a maxim; truism. 2. an established principle or law of a science, art, etc. 3. in *logic & mathematics*, a statement that needs no proof because its truth is obvious; self-evident proposition.
**ax·i·o·mat·ic** (ak si-ə-mat′ik), *adj.* 1. of or like an axiom; self-evident. 2. full of maxims; aphoristic. Also **ax′i·o·mat′i·cal.** —**ax′i·o·mat′i·cal·ly,** *adv.*
**ax·is** (ak′sis), *n.* [*pl.* AXES (-sēz)], [L.], 1. a real or imaginary straight line on which an object supposedly or actually rotates: as, the *axis* of a planet. 2. a central line or lengthwise structure around which the parts of a thing, system, etc. are regularly arranged. 3. an alignment between countries, groups, etc. for promoting their purposes: now usually a derogatory term. —**the Axis,** the countries aligned against the United Nations in World War II: originally applied to Nazi Germany and Fascist Italy (**Rome-Berlin Axis**), later extended to include Japan (**Rome-Berlin-Tokyo Axis**).

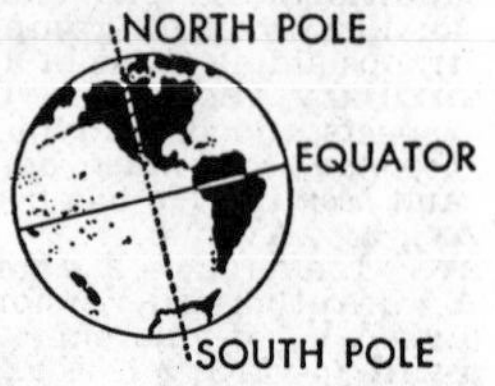

AXIS OF THE EARTH

**ax·le** (ak′s′l), *n.* [< *axletree*], 1. a rod or spindle on or with which a wheel revolves. 2. an axletree. —**ax′led,** *adj.*
**ax·le·tree** (ak′s′l-trē′), *n.* [< ON. < *öxull*, axle + *tre*, tree, beam], the bar connecting two opposite wheels of a carriage, wagon, etc.
**ax·man** (aks′mən), *n.* [*pl.* -MEN (-mən)], a person who uses an ax.
**Ax·min·ster** (aks′min-stēr), *n.* [< *Axminster*, in England], a type of carpet with a long, soft pile.
**ay** (ā), *adv.* [Archaic], always: also sp. **aye.**
**ay** (ī), *adv. & n.* yes: also sp. **aye.**
**ay** (ā), *interj.* a sound expressing sorrow, distress, etc.
**ay·ah** (ä′yə), *n.* [< Hindu < Port. *aia*, governess], a native nursemaid or lady's maid in India.
**aye** (ā) *adv.* [ON. *ei*], [Archaic], always; ever.
**aye** (ī), *adv.* [? < *aye* (always)], yes; yea. *n.* an affirmative vote or voter.
**aye-aye** (ī′ī′), *n.* [Fr. < Malagasy; origin echoic], a lemur of Madagascar, with shaggy fur, large ears, pointed claws, and a long, bushy tail.
**a·zal·ea** (ə-zāl′yə), *n.* [< Gr. fem. of *azaleos*, dry: so called because it thrives in dry soil], 1. a flowering shrub resembling the rhododendron: the flowers have various colors and are usually fragrant. 2. the flower of this plant.
**A·zer·bai·jan, Az·er·bai·dzhan** (ä′zēr-bī-jän′, az′ēr-), *n.* 1. a province of northwestern Iran. 2. the Azerbaijan Soviet Socialist Republic.
**A·zer·bai·ja·ni** (ä′zēr-bī-jä′ni, az′ēr-), *n.* [*pl.* -NIS, -NI], 1. a native or inhabitant of Azerbaijan. 2. one of a Turkic people of Azerbaijan. 3. the Turkic dialect spoken there.
**Azerbaijan Soviet Socialist Republic,** a republic of the U.S.S.R., in Transcaucasia: area, 33,200 sq. mi.; pop., 3,210,000; capital, Baku.
**az·i·muth** (az′ə-məth), *n.* [< OFr. < Ar. *as-sumūt;* *as* < *al*, the + *sumūt*, pl. of *samt*, way, path], in *astronomy*, etc., distance in angular degrees (or mils, in military usage) in a clockwise direction from the north point or, in the Southern Hemisphere, south point.

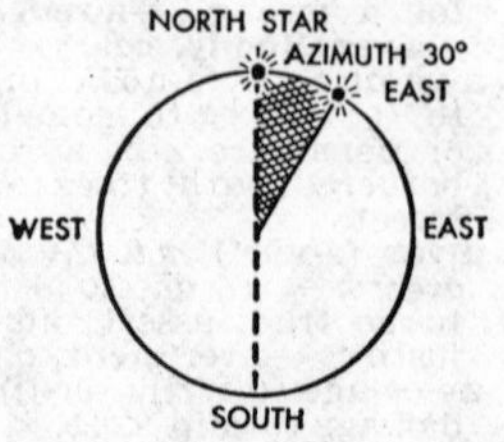

AZIMUTH

**az·o** (az′ō, ā′zō), *adj.* in *chemistry*, containing nitrogen.
**A·zores** (ə-zôrz′, ā′zôrz), *n.pl.* a group of Portuguese islands west of Portugal.
**A·zov, Sea of** (ä′zôf, ā′zov), an arm of the Black Sea, southern U.S.S.R.
**Az·tec** (az′tek), *n.* [of Aztec origin], 1. a member of a people who lived in Mexico and had an advanced civilization before the conquest of Mexico by Cortés in 1519. 2. their language, Nahuatl. *adj.* of the Aztecs, their language, culture, etc. —**Az′tec·an,** *adj.*

**az·ure** (azh'ēr, ā'zhēr), *adj.* [OFr. *azur;* (with omission of initial *l-*, as if *l'azur*) < Ar. < Per. *lāzhuward*, lapis lazuli], of or like the color of a clear sky; sky-blue; blue. *n.* 1. blue; esp., sky blue. 2. [Poetic], the blue sky.

**az·u·rite** (azh'ə-rīt'), *n.* [< *azure* + *-ite*], 1. a blue ore of copper, basic copper carbonate, $2CuCO_3 \cdot Cu(OH)_2$. 2. a semiprecious gem from this ore.

**az·y·gous** (az'i-gəs), *adj.* [Gr.], having no mate.

# B

**B, b** (bē), *n.* [*pl.* B's, b's, Bs, bs], 1. the second letter of the English alphabet. 2. the sound of B or b. *adj.* second in a sequence or group.

**B** (bē), *n.* 1. in *chemistry, the symbol for* boron. 2. in *music, a*) the seventh tone in the scale of C major. *b*) the scale having B as the keynote. *adj.* 1. shaped like B. 2. secondary; inferior to the best: as, a class *B* motion picture.

**B-**, bomber: followed by a number to designate the model of U.S. Air Force bombing airplane.

**B.**, 1. Bible. 2. British. 3. in *chess*, bishop.

**B., b.**, 1. bachelor. 2. bay. 3. book. 4. born. 5. in *baseball, a*) base. *b*) base hit. 6. in *music*, bass.

**Ba**, in *chemistry*, barium.

**B.A.**, *Baccalaureus Artium*, [L.], Bachelor of Arts: also **A.B.**

**baa** (bä), *v.i. & n.* [echoic], bleat.

**Ba·al** (bā'əl, bāl), *n.* [*pl.* BAALIM (-im), BAALS], 1. among some ancient Semitic peoples, a sun god, or a god of fertility and flocks. 2. a false god; idol. **—Ba'al·ish,** *adj.* **—Ba'al·ism,** *n.* **—Ba'al·ist, Ba'al·ite',** *n.*

**bab·bitt** (bab'it), *n.* Babbitt metal. *v.t.* to line with Babbitt metal; put Babbitt metal on.

**bab·bitt, Bab·bitt** (bab'it), *n.* [after the title character of a novel by Sinclair Lewis (1922)], a person characterized by a striving for business and social success, conventionality, smugness, and a lack of interest in cultural matters; philistine. **—bab'bitt·ry, Bab'bitt·ry,** *n.*

**Babbitt metal,** [after Isaac *Babbitt* (1799–1862), Am. inventor], a soft alloy of tin, copper, and antimony, used to reduce friction in bearings, etc.

**bab·ble** (bab''l), *v.i.* [-BLED, -BLING], [of echoic origin], 1. to make incoherent sounds, as a baby does; prattle. 2. to talk unwisely or too much. 3. to make a continuous low sound: as, the brook *babbles*. *v.t.* to say incoherently or foolishly. *n.* 1. confused, incoherent vocal sounds. 2. foolish or meaningless talk. 3. a continuous murmur. **—bab'ble·ment,** *n.* **—bab'bler,** *n.*

**babe** (bāb), *n.* 1. a baby. 2. a naive or gullible person. 3. [Slang], a girl or young woman.

**Ba·bel** (bā'b'l, bab''l), *n.* 1. in the *Bible*, a city in Babylonia, where the builders of a tower intended to reach to heaven were punished and thwarted by God, who caused them all suddenly to speak in different languages: Gen. 11:1–9. 2. [also b-], *a*) a confusion of voices, languages, etc.; tumult. *b*) a place where there is such a confusion.

**ba·bies'-breath** (bā'biz-breth'), *n.* 1. a tall plant of the pink family, with small, fragrant, white or pink flowers. 2. any similar plant, as the grape hyacinth, etc. Also **ba·by's-breath.**

**bab·i·ru·sa, bab·i·rous·sa, bab·i·rus·sa** (bab'i-rōō'sə, bä'bi-), *n.* [Malay *babi*, hog + *rusa*, deer], a wild hog of East India that has hornlike tusks curving up backward from each jaw.

**ba·boo, ba·bu** (bä'bōō), *n.* [Hind. *bābū*], 1. a Hindu title equivalent to *Mr.* 2. a Hindu clerk who can write English. 3. a Hindu who has a little English education: derogatory term.

**ba·boon** (ba-bōōn'), *n.* [OFr. *babuin*], a fierce ape of Africa and Arabia, having a doglike snout, cheek pouches, and a short tail. **—ba·boon'ish,** *adj.*

**ba·bush·ka** (bə-boosh'kə), *n.* [Russ., grandmother], a scarf worn on the head by women.

**ba·by** (bā'bi), *n.* [*pl.* -BIES], [ME. *babi*], 1. an infant; very young child. 2. one who behaves like an infant. 3. the youngest or smallest in a group. 4. [Slang], a girl or young woman. *adj.* 1. of or for an infant. 2. extremely young. 3. small of its kind 4. infantile or childish. *v.t.* [-BIED, -BYING], to treat like a baby; pamper; coddle. **—ba'by·hood',** *n.* **—ba'by·ish,** *adj.* **—ba'by·ish·ly,** *adv.* **—ba'by·ish·ness,** *n.* **—ba'by·like',** *adj.*

**Bab·y·lon** (bab''l-ən, -i-lon'), *n.* 1. the ancient capital of Babylonia, famous for wealth, luxury, and wickedness. 2. any city of great wealth, luxury, and vice.

**Bab·y·lo·ni·a** (bab''l-ō'ni-ə), *n.* an ancient empire in the lower valley of the Tigris and Euphrates rivers: it flourished c. 2700–538 B.C. **—Bab'y·lo'ni·an,** *adj. & n.*

**ba·by-sit** (bā'bi-sit'), *v.i.* [-SAT, -SITTING], to act as a baby sitter.

**baby sitter,** a person hired to take care of a child or children, as when the parents are away for the evening: also **sitter.**

**bac·ca·lau·re·ate** (bak'ə-lô'ri-it), *n.* [<ML. as if < L. *bacca laureus*, laurel berry, but actually < L. hyp. *baccalaris*; see BACHELOR], 1. the degree of bachelor of arts, bachelor of science, etc. 2. a sermon delivered to a graduating class at commencement: also **baccalaureate sermon.**

**bac·ca·rat, bac·ca·ra** (bak'ə-rä', bak'ə-rä'), *n.* [Fr.; prob. < *Baccarat*, a town in France], a gambling game played with cards.

**bac·cha·nal** (bak'ə-n'l, -nal'), *n.* 1. a worshiper of Bacchus. 2. a drunken carouser. 3. *pl.* the Bacchanalia. 4. a drunken party; orgy. *adj.* 1. of Bacchus or his worship; bacchanalian. 2. carousing.

**Bac·cha·na·li·a** (bak'ə-nā'li-ə, -nāl'yə), *n.pl.* 1. an ancient Roman festival in honor of Bacchus. 2. [b-], a drunken party; orgy. **—bac'cha·na'li·an,** *adj. & n.*

**bac·chant** (bak'ənt), *n.* [*pl.* BACCHANTS, BACCHANTES (bə-kan'tēz)], 1. a priest or worshiper of Bacchus. 2. a drunken carouser. *adj.* 1. worshiping Bacchus. 2. fond of alcoholic liquor. **—bac·chan·tic** (bə-kan'tik), *adj.*

**bac·chan·te** (bə-kan'ti, bə-kant', bak'ənt), *n.* 1. a priestess or woman votary of Bacchus. 2. a woman who carouses.

**Bac·chic** (bak'ik), *adj.* 1. of Bacchus or his worship. 2. [often b-], drunken; carousing.

**Bac·chus** (bak'əs), *n.* an ancient Greek and Roman god of wine and revelry: cf. **Dionysus.**

**Bach, Jo·hann Se·bas·tian** (yō'hän si-bäs'tyən bäkh), 1685–1750; German organist and composer.

**bach·e·lor** (bach'ə-lēr, bach'lēr), *n.* [< OFr. < L. hyp. *baccalaris* or hyp. *baccalarius*, vassal farmer < *bacca*, a cow], 1. originally, a young knight holding a farm in vassalage, who served under another's banner. 2. a person who has received the baccalaureate from a college or university: as, a *Bachelor* of Arts. 3. an unmarried man. *adj.* of or for a bachelor. **—bach'e·lor·dom,** *n.* **—bach'e·lor·hood',** *n.* **—bach'e·lor·ship',** *n.*

**Bachelor of Arts** (or **Science**, etc.), 1. a degree given by a college or university to one who has completed a four-year course in the humanities (or in science, etc.). 2. one who has this degree. Abbrev. **B.A., A.B.** (or **B.S., B.Sc.,** etc.).

**bach·e·lor's-but·ton** (bach'ə-lērz-but''n, bach'lērz-), *n.* any of several plants with flowers shaped somewhat like buttons; esp., the cornflower.

**ba·cil·lus** (bə-sil'əs), *n.* [*pl.* -LI (-ī)], [< L. dim. of *baculus*, a stick], 1. any of a genus of rod-shaped bacteria. 2. *usually pl.* loosely, any of the bacteria. **—ba·cil'lar** (-ēr), **bac·il·lar·y** (bas''l-er'i), *adj.*

**back** (bak), *n.* [AS. *bæc*, back], 1. the part of the body opposite to the front; in man and other animals, the part from the base of the neck to the end of the spine. 2. the backbone. 3. a support for the human back, as on a chair. 4. the part of a garment associated with the back. 5. the rear part of anything. 6. the reverse. 7. the part opposite the part that is used: as, the *back* of the hand. 8. physical strength. 9. in *football*, a player in a position behind the front line. *adj.* 1. at the rear; behind. 2. distant. 3. of or for a time in the past: as, *back* pay. 4. backward; reversed. 5. in *phonetics*, made at the rear of the mouth. *adv.* 1. at, to, or toward the rear. 2. to or toward a former position. 3. into or toward a previous condition. 4. to or toward an earlier time. 5. in concealment: as, to hold *back* information. 6. in return: as, to pay one *back*. *v.t.* 1. to cause to move backward (often with *up*). 2. to support (often with *up*). 3. to bet on. 4. to get on the back of; mount. 5. to provide with a back. 6. to form the back of. *v.i.* 1. to go backward (often with *up*). 2. to shift counterclockwise: said of the wind. —**back and forth,** from side to side. —**back down,** [Colloq.], to withdraw an opinion, claim, etc. —**back out,** [Colloq.], 1. to withdraw from an enterprise. 2. to break a promise. —**back water,** to retract something said. —**behind one's back,** without one's knowledge or consent. —**be on one's back,** to be ill, disabled, etc. —**get** (or **put**) **one's back up,** to be obstinate. —**go back on,** [Colloq.], 1. to back out. 2. to desert; fail. —**turn one's back on,** to desert; fail. —**with one's back to the wall,** in a desperate position.

**back·bite** (bak′bīt′), *v.t. & v.i.* [-BIT (-bit′), -BITTEN (-bit′′n) or -BIT, -BITING], to slander (an absent person or persons). —**back′bit′er,** *n.* —**back′bit′ing,** *n.*

**back·bone** (bak′bōn′), *n.* 1. the column of bones (vertebrae) along the center of the back; spine. 2. a main support. 3. courage; determination. —**back′boned′,** *adj.*

**back·break·ing** (bak′brāk′iŋ), *adj.* very tiring.

**back·court** (bak′kôrt′, -kōrt′), *n.* the back part of a tennis court, basketball court, etc.

**back·door** (bak′dôr′, -dōr′), *adj.* secret; furtive.

**back·drop** (bak′drop′), *n.* a curtain hung at the back of a stage, often part of the setting.

**backed** (bakt), *adj.* having a (specified kind of) back: as, canvas-*backed*.

**back·er** (bak′ẽr), *n.* 1. a patron; supporter. 2. one who bets on a contestant.

**back·field** (bak′fēld′), *n.* in *football*, the quarterback, two halfbacks, and fullback, whose regular position is behind the line of scrimmage.

**back·fire** (bak′fīr′), *n.* 1. a fire started to stop a prairie fire or forest fire by creating a burned area in its path. 2. a premature explosion in a cylinder of a gasoline or oil engine. 3. an explosion in an intake or exhaust pipe. *v.i.* 1. to use or set a backfire. 2. to explode as a backfire. 3. to have an unwelcome result; go awry: as, his plan *backfired*.

**back-for·ma·tion** (bak′fôr-mā′shən), *n.* a word formed from, but looking as if it were the base of, another word. Example: *burgle* (from *burglar*).

**back·gam·mon** (bak′gam′ən, bak′gam′-), *n.* [prob. *back* + *gammon*, a game], a game played on a special board by two people: each has fifteen pieces, which he moves according to the throw of dice.

**back·ground** (bak′ground′), *n.* 1. the distant part of a landscape, etc. 2. surroundings behind something, providing harmony or contrast. 3. an unimportant position: as, he stays in the *background*. 4. the whole of one's study, training, and experience. 5. events leading up to something, helping to explain it. 6. in *motion pictures, radio*, etc., music or sound effects accompanying the action.

**back·hand** (bak′hand′), *n.* 1. handwriting that slants backward, up to the left. 2. a method of stroking, as in tennis, with the back of the hand turned forward. 3. a stroke so made. *adj.* backhanded. *adv.* with a backhanded stroke.

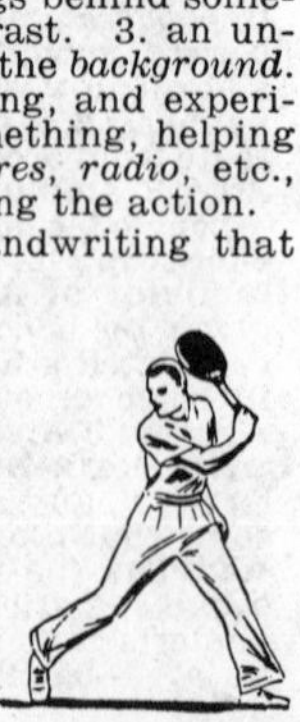

BACKHAND STROKE

**back·hand·ed** (bak′han′did), *adj.* 1. performed with the back of the hand turned forward. 2. with the letters slanting backward, up to the left. 3. not direct; equivocal; sarcastic. 4. clumsy.

**back·ing** (bak′iŋ), *n.* 1. something forming a back for support or strengthening. 2. support given to a person or cause. 3. those giving such support.

**back·lash** (bak′lash′), *n.* 1. a quick, sharp recoil. 2. a snarl in a fishing line. 3. in *mechanics*, the jarring reaction of loose or worn parts; play.

**back·log** (bak′lôg′, -log′), *n.* 1. a large log at the back of a fireplace, to support other logs. 2. an accumulation or reserve. *v.i. & v.t.* [-LOGGED, -LOGGING], to accumulate in reserve.

**back number,** 1. an old issue of a periodical. 2. [Colloq.], an old-fashioned person or thing.

**back pay,** overdue or retroactive wages.

**back seat,** 1. a seat at the back; hence, 2. [Colloq.], a secondary or inconspicuous position.

**back-seat driver** (bak′sēt′), a passenger in an automobile who offers advice and directions for driving.

**back·sheesh, back·shish** (bak′shēsh′), *n.* baksheesh.

**back·side** (bak′sīd′), *n.* 1. the back; hind part. 2. the rump; buttocks.

**back·slide** (bak′slīd′), *v.i.* [-SLID (-slid′), -SLIDDEN (-slid′′n) or -SLID, -SLIDING], to slide backward in morals or religious enthusiasm; become less virtuous, etc. —**back′slid′er,** *n.*

**back·spin** (bak′spin′), *n.* the backward rotation of a ball, etc. that is moving forward.

**back·stage** (bak′stāj′), *adv.* 1. in the wings or dressing rooms of a theater. 2. upstage. *adj.* 1. situated backstage. 2. covert; concealed.

**back·stairs** (bak′stârz′), *adj.* secret; underhanded; involving intrigue. Also **back′stair′.**

**back·stay** (bak′stā′), *n.* a rope or shroud slanting sharply aft from the top of the mast of a ship to help support the mast.

**back·stop** (bak′stop′), *n.* in *baseball*, etc. a fence or screen to stop balls that go too far.

**back·stretch** (bak′strech′), *n.* the part of a race track farthest from the grandstand.

**back·stroke** (bak′strōk′), *n.* 1. a backhanded stroke. 2. a stroke made by a swimmer lying face upward. *v.i.* to perform a backstroke. *v.t.* to hit with a backstroke.

**back talk,** [Colloq.], insolent answers or retorts.

**back·track** (bak′trak′), *v.i.* 1. to return by the same path. 2. to retreat or withdraw.

**back·ward** (bak′wẽrd), *adv.* 1. toward the back. 2. with the back foremost. 3. in reverse. 4. in a way contrary to normal. 5. into the past. 6. from a better to a worse state. Also **back′wards.** *adj.* 1. turned or directed toward the rear or in the opposite way. 2. reluctant; bashful; shy. 3. late in developing or growing; retarded; slow. —**back′ward·ly,** *adv.*—**back′ward·ness,** *n.*

**back·wash** (bak′wôsh′, -wäsh′), *n.* 1. water moved backward, as by a ship in motion, an oar, etc. 2. a backward current or flow.

**back·wa·ter** (bak′wô′tẽr, -wä′tẽr), *n.* 1. water moved backward or held back by a dam, tide, etc. 2. a place or condition regarded as stagnant, backward, etc. *adj.* stagnant; backward.

**back·woods** (bak′woodz′), *n.pl.* 1. heavily wooded areas far from centers of population. 2. [Colloq.], any remote, thinly populated place. *adj.* in, from, or like the backwoods: also **back′wood.** —**back′woods′man** [*pl.* -MEN], *n.*

**ba·con** (bā′kən), *n.* [OFr.; OHG. *bahho*, side of bacon], salted and smoked meat from the back or sides of a hog. —**bring home the bacon,** [Colloq.], 1. to earn a living. 2. to succeed or win.

**Ba·con, Francis** (bā′kən), 1561–1626; English philosopher, essayist, and statesman.

**Bacon, Roger,** 1214?–1294; English scientist and philosopher.

**Ba·co·ni·an** (bā-kō′ni-ən), *adj.* 1. of Francis Bacon or his philosophy. 2. designating or of the theory that Francis Bacon wrote Shakespeare's works. *n.* 1. a believer in the philosophy of Francis Bacon. 2. one who believes the Baconian theory.

**bac·te·ri·a** (bak-têr′i-ə), *n.pl.* [*sing.* -RIUM (-əm)], [< Gr. dim. of *baktron*, a staff], typically one-celled microorganisms which have no chlorophyll and multiply by simple division: some bacteria cause diseases, but others are necessary for fermentation, nitrogen fixation, etc. —**bac·te′ri·al,** *adj.* —**bac·te′ri·al·ly,** *adv.*

**bac·te·ri·cide** (bak-têr′ə-sīd′), *n.* [< *bacterio-* + *-cide*], an agent that destroys bacteria. —**bac·te′ri·cid′al,** *adj.*

**bac·te·ri·o-,** a combining form meaning *of bacteria*: also **bacteri-.**

**bac·te·ri·ol·o·gy** (bak′têr′i-ol′ə-ji, bak-têr′-), *n.* [*bacterio-* + *-logy*], the science that deals with bacteria: abbrev. **bacteriol., bact.** —**bac′te′ri·o·log′i·cal,** *adj.* —**bac′te′ri·o·log′i·cal·ly,** *adv.* —**bac′te′ri·ol′o·gist,** *n.*

**bac·te·ri·o·phage** (bak-têr′i-ə-fāj′), *n.* [*bacterio-* +

*-phage*], a microscopic agent that destroys disease-producing bacteria in a living organism.

**bac·te·ri·um** (bak-têr′i-əm), ***n.*** sing. of **bacteria.**

**Bac·tri·an camel** (bak′tri-ən), [< *Bactria*, ancient country in W Asia], a camel with two humps, native to SW Asia: cf. **camel.**

**bad** (bad), ***adj.*** [WORSE (wũrs), WORST (wũrst)], [ME. *badde;* ? < AS. *bæddel*, hermaphrodite], 1. not good; not as it should be; inadequate. 2. unfit; unskilled. 3. unfavorable; disagreeable: as, *bad* news. 4. rotted; spoiled. 5. incorrect; faulty: as, *bad* spelling. 6. wicked; immoral. 7. harmful; injurious. 8. severe: as, a *bad* storm. 9. ill; in pain. 10. sorry; distressed: as, he feels *bad* about it. 11. offensive: as, a *bad* smell. 12. in *law*, not valid. ***adv.*** [Colloq.], badly. ***n.*** 1. anything that is bad; bad quality or state. 2. wickedness. **—in bad,** [Colloq.], 1. in trouble. 2. in disfavor. **—not bad,** [Colloq.], good; fairly good: also **not half bad, not so bad. —bad′ness, *n.***

**bad** (bad), 1. archaic pt. of **bid.** 2. obs. pt. of **bide.**

**bad blood,** a feeling of mutual enmity.

**bade** (bad), 1. alt. pt. of **bid.** 2. alt. pt. of **bide.**

**Ba·den** (bä′d'n), ***n.*** 1. a division of SW Germany. 2. a health resort there: also **Baden-Baden.**

**badge** (baj), ***n.*** [ME. *bage*], 1. a distinctive mark or device worn to show one's rank, membership, etc. 2. any distinctive sign or symbol. ***v.t.*** [BADGED, BADGING], to mark with a badge.

**badg·er** (baj′ẽr), ***n.*** [*pl.* -ERS, -ER; see PLURAL, II, D, 1], [? < obs. n. & personal name *badger*, corn dealer], 1. a burrowing animal with thick, short legs and long claws on the forefeet. 2. its fur. ***v.t.*** to torment; nag at.

**bad·i·nage** (bad′'n-ij, bad′i-näzh′), ***n.*** [Fr. < *badiner*, to jest < Pr. < ML. *badare*, to gape], playful, teasing talk; banter. ***v.t.*** [-NAGED, -NAGING], to banter; tease with playful talk.

**bad·lands** (bad′landz′), ***n.pl.*** any section of barren land where rapid erosion has cut the loose, dry soil or soft rocks into strange shapes.

**Bad Lands,** badlands of SW South Dakota and NW Nebraska.

**bad·ly** (bad′li), ***adv.*** 1. in a bad manner. 2. [Colloq.], very much; greatly.

**bad·min·ton** (bad′min-tən), ***n.*** [after *Badminton*, estate of the Duke of Beaufort], a game in which a feathered cork (shuttlecock) is batted back and forth with light rackets across a net.

**bad-tem·pered** (bad′tem′pẽrd), ***adj.*** having a bad temper or cranky disposition; irritable.

**Bae·de·ker** (bā′di-kẽr), ***n.*** 1. any of a series of guidebooks to foreign countries first published in Germany by Karl Baedeker (1801–1859). 2. loosely, any guidebook.

**baf·fle** (baf′'l), ***v.t.*** [-FLED, -FLING], [16th-c. Scot.; prob. respelling of obs. Scot. *bauchle*], 1. to frustrate by puzzling; confound. 2. to hinder; impede. ***v.i.*** to struggle without result. ***n.*** 1. a baffling or being baffled. 2. a wall or screen to deflect the flow of liquids, gases, etc.: also **baf′fle·plate′** (-plāt′). 3. a mounting for a loud-speaker, designed to improve reproduction of low frequencies. **—baf′fle·ment, *n.* —baf′fler, *n.* —baf′fling, *adj.* —baf′fling·ly, *adv.***

**bag** (bag), ***n.*** [ON. *baggi*], 1. a container made of fabric, paper, leather, etc., with an opening that can be closed; sack. 2. a piece of hand luggage; suitcase. 3. a woman's handbag; purse. 4. game killed or captured in hunting. 5. any baglike thing or part, as an udder, a sac inside an animal to hold a fluid, etc. 6. [Slang], [< *baggage*, 3], a woman. 7. [Slang], one's special interest, talent, etc. 8. in *baseball*, a base. ***v.t.*** [BAGGED, BAGGING], 1. to make bulge. 2. to enclose within a bag. 3. to capture. 4. to kill in hunting. 5. [Slang], to get. ***v.i.*** 1. to swell. 2. to hang loosely. **—bag and baggage,** [Colloq.], 1. with all one's possessions. 2. entirely. **—be left holding the bag,** [Colloq.], to be left to suffer the bad consequences or the blame. **—in the bag,** [Colloq.], certain; assured. **—bag′like, *adj.***

**ba·gasse** (bə-gas′), ***n.*** [Fr.; Mod. Pr. *bagasso*, refuse from processing grapes or olives], the part of sugar cane or sugar beets left after the juice has been taken out.

**bag·a·telle** (bag′ə-tel′), ***n.*** [Fr.; It. *bagatella*], 1. something of little value; trifle. 2. a game played on a board with cues and balls.

**Bag·dad** (bag′dad, bäg-däd′), ***n.*** the capital of Iraq, on the Tigris River: pop., c. 1,000,000: also sp. **Baghdad.**

**ba·gel** (bā′g'l), ***n.*** [Yid.], a small, doughnut-shaped bread roll that is cooked in simmering water before it is baked.

**bag·gage** (bag′ij), ***n.*** [< OFr. < *bague*, bundle < ML. *baga*, leather bag], 1. the bags and other equipment of a traveler; luggage. 2. the supplies and gear of an army. 3. [by transference of "army baggage" to "camp follower"], formerly, a prostitute; hence, 4. a pert or lively girl.

**bag·ging** (bag′iŋ), ***n.*** sacking.

**bag·gy** (bag′i), ***adj.*** [-GIER, -GIEST], 1. puffed in a baglike way. 2. hanging loosely. **—bag′gi·ly, *adv.* —bag′gi·ness, *n.***

**bagn·io** (ban′yō, bän′-), ***n.*** [*pl.* -IOS], [< It. < L. < Gr. *balaneion*, bath], 1. in the Orient, a prison for slaves. 2. a house of prostitution; brothel.

**bag·pipe** (bag′pīp′), ***n.*** *sometimes pl.* a shrill-toned muscial instrument with a leather bag from which air is forced into reed pipes to produce the sound: now played chiefly in Scotland.

BAGPIPE

**ba·guette, ba·guet** (ba-get′), ***n.*** [< Fr. < It. < L. *baculum*, a staff], a thing with the shape of a convex oblong, as a gem, watch, etc.

**bah** (bä, ba), ***interj.*** an exclamation expressing contempt, scorn, or disgust.

**Ba·ha·ma Islands** (bə-hā′mə, -hä′-), a group of British islands in the West Indies: area, 4,404 sq. mi.; pop., 70,000; capital, Nassau: also **Ba·ha′mas** (-məz), ***n.pl.***

**Ba·hí·a** (bə-hē′ə; Port. bä-ē′ä), ***n.*** a seaport in central Brazil: pop., 388,000: also called *São Salvador*.

**Bah·rein Islands** (bä-rān′), islands in the Persian Gulf, off the Arabian coast: area, 250 sq. mi.; pop., 185,000; capital, Manama.

**Bai·kal, Lake** (bī-käl′), a lake in S Siberia: area, 13,300 sq. mi.

**bail** (bāl), ***n.*** [OFr., jurisdiction < *bailler*, keep in custody < L. *bajulare*, bear a burden], 1. money or credit deposited with the court to get an arrested person temporarily released until his trial. 2. the release thus brought about. 3. the person giving bail. ***v.t.*** 1. to set (an arrested person) free on bail (often with *out*). 2. to have (an arrested person) set free by giving bail (often with *out*). **—go bail for,** to furnish bail for. **—bail′a·ble, *adj.* —bail′ee′** (-ē′), ***n.*** **—bail′ment, *n.* —bail·or** (bāl′ôr′, bāl′ẽr), ***n.***

**bail** (bāl), ***n.*** [< OFr. < LL. hyp. *bajula*, vessel], a bucket for dipping up water from a boat. ***v.i. & v.t.*** 1. to remove water from (a boat), as with a bail. 2. to dip out (water, etc.). **—bail out,** to parachute from an aircraft. **—bail′er, *n.***

**bail** (bāl), ***n.*** [ON. *beygla*, a hoop], 1. a hoop-shaped support, as for a canopy. 2. a hoop-shaped handle for a bucket, etc.

**bail** (bāl), ***n.*** [ME. < OFr. < L. *bajulus*, porter], in *cricket*, either of two pieces of wood laid across the three stumps to form a wicket.

**bail·ie** (bāl′i), ***n.*** [Scot. < OFr. < L. *bajulus;* see BAILIFF], in Scotland, a municipal official corresponding to an alderman in England.

**bail·iff** (bāl′if), ***n.*** [OFr. *bailif* < L. *bajulus*, porter], 1. a sheriff's assistant. 2. an officer who has charge of prisoners and guards the jurors in a court. 3. in England, an administrative official of a district. 4. a steward of an estate.

**bail·i·wick** (bāl′ə-wik′), ***n.*** [ME. *bailie*, bailiff + *wick* < AS. *wic*, village], 1. a bailiff's district. 2. one's special field of interest or authority.

**bails·man** (bālz′mən), ***n.*** [*pl.* -MEN], a person who gives bail for someone.

**bairn** (bârn), ***n.*** [AS. *bearn*], [Scot.], a child.

**bait** (bāt), ***v.t.*** [ON. *beita*, to make bite; caus. < *bīta*, to bite], 1. to set dogs on for sport: as, to *bait* bears. 2. to torment or persecute, especially by verbal attacks. 3. [Rare], to feed (animals) during a break in a journey. 4. to put food, etc. on (a hook or trap) as a lure for animals or fish. 5. to lure; tempt; entice. ***v.i.*** to stop for food during a journey. ***n.*** 1. food, etc. put on a hook or trap as a lure. 2. anything used as a lure; enticement. **—bait′er, *n.***

**baize** (bāz), ***n.*** [< OFr. pl. of *baie* < L. *badius*, chestnut-brown], a coarse woolen cloth used to cover pool tables, etc.

**bake** (bāk), *v.t.* [BAKED, BAKING], [AS. *bacan*], 1. to cook (food) by dry heat, as in an oven. 2. to dry and harden by heat, as glazed stoneware. *v.i.* 1. to bake bread, etc. 2. to become baked. *n.* 1. a baking. 2. the amount baked.
**bake·house** (bāk′hous′), *n.* a bakery.
**ba·ke·lite** (bā′kə-līt′), *n.* [after L. H. *Baekeland* (1863–1944), Belgian chemist], a synthetic resin used for the same purposes as hard rubber, celluloid, etc.: a trade-mark (**Bakelite**).
**bak·er** (bāk′ēr), *n.* 1. one whose work or business is baking bread, etc. 2. a small, portable oven.
**Baker, Mount,** a mountain of the Cascade Range, in NW Washington: height, 10,750 ft.
**Baker Island,** a small island in the Pacific.
**baker's dozen,** thirteen.
**bak·er·y** (bāk′ēr-i), *n.* [*pl.* -IES], a place where bread, pastries, etc. are baked or sold.
**bak·ing** (bāk′iŋ), *n.* 1. the act of one who bakes. 2. the amount baked at a single time.
**baking powder,** a leavening agent containing baking soda and an acid substance, such as cream of tartar, which together produce carbon dioxide in the presence of water.
**baking soda,** sodium bicarbonate, $NaHCO_3$, used in baking as a leavening agent and in medicine to counteract acidity.
**bak·sheesh, bak·shish** (bak′shēsh′), *n.* [< Hind. & Per. < *bakhshidan*, to give], in Turkey, Egypt, etc. a tip; gratuity.
**Ba·ku** (bä-kōō′), *n.* the capital of the Azerbaijan S.S.R., on the Caspian Sea: pop., 809,000.
**bal.,** balance.
**Ba·laam** (bā′ləm), *n.* in the *Bible*, a prophet who was rebuked by his donkey when he beat the animal. Numb. 22–24.
**bal·a·lai·ka** (bal′ə-lī′kə), *n.* [Russ.], a Russian stringed instrument of the guitar family.

BALALAIKA

**bal·ance** (bal′əns), *n.* [OFr. < L. *bilanx*, having two scales < *bis*, twice + *lanx*, a scale], 1. an instrument for weighing, especially one with two matched scales hanging from either end of a poised lever; scales. 2. a state of equilibrium or equipoise; equality in weight, force, quantity, etc. 3. bodily equilibrium: as, he kept his *balance* on the tightrope. 4. mental or emotional equilibrium. 5. the equilibrium of elements in a design, etc.; harmonious proportion. 6. a weight, force, etc. that counteracts another or causes equilibrium. 7. *a*) equality of debits and credits in an account. *b*) the difference between credits and debits. 8. the amount still owed after a partial settlement. 9. a balancing. 10. a balance wheel. 11. [Colloq.], a remainder. *v.t.* [-ANCED, -ANCING], 1. to weigh in or as in a balance. 2. to compare as to relative importance, value, etc. 3. to counterpoise or counteract; offset. 4. to put or keep in a state of equilibrium; poise. 5. to be or cause to be equal to in weight, force, etc. 6. *a*) to find the difference (if any) between the debit and credit sides of (an account). *b*) to equalize the debit and credit sides of (an account). 7. to settle (an account). *v.i.* 1. to be in equilibrium. 2. to be equal in value, weight, etc. 3. to have the credit and debit sides equal. 4. to waver slightly; hesitate. —**in the balance,** not yet settled; undetermined. —**bal′ance·a·ble,** *adj.* —**bal′anc·er,** *n.*
**balanced diet** (or **ration**), a diet with the right amounts and variety of necessary foods.
**balance of power,** a distribution of military and economic power among nations that is sufficiently even to keep any one of them from being too strong or dangerous.
**balance of trade,** the difference in value between the imports and exports of a country.
**balance sheet,** a summarized statement showing the financial status of a business.
**balance wheel,** a wheel that regulates the movement of a mechanism, as in a watch.
**bal·a·ta** (bal′ə-tə), *n.* [Sp. < Tupi], 1. a West Indian tree of the sapodilla family. 2. its milky sap, which dries into a rubberlike gum, used commercially.
**bal·bo·a** (bäl-bō′ə), *n.* [Sp., after Vasco de *Balboa*], a silver coin, the monetary unit of Panama.
**Bal·bo·a, Vas·co Nú·ñez de** (väs′kô nōō′nyeth *the* bäl-bô′ä; Eng. bal-bō′ə), 1475–1517; Spanish explorer; discovered Pacific Ocean (1513).
**bal·brig·gan** (bal-brig′ən), *n.* [after *Balbriggan*, Ireland], a knitted cotton material used for hosiery, underwear, etc.
**bal·co·ny** (bal′kə-ni), *n.* [*pl.* -NIES], [< It. < OHG. *balcho*, a beam], 1. a platform projecting from a building and enclosed by a balustrade: balconies usually open onto an upper story. 2. in a theater, etc., a tier of seats projecting over the main floor.

BALCONY

**bald** (bôld), *adj.* [ME. *balled*: ? < W. *bal*, white spot], 1. having white on the head, as some animals and birds. 2. lacking hair on the head. 3. lacking the natural covering. 4. plain; unadorned. 5. frank; blunt. —**bald′ly,** *adv.* —**bald′ness,** *n.*
**bald eagle,** a large, strong eagle of North America, with white feathers about the head and neck.
**Bal·der** (bôl′dēr), *n.* in *Norse mythology*, the god of light, peace, virtue, and wisdom, son of Odin and Frigg: also sp. **Baldr.**
**bal·der·dash** (bôl′dēr-dash′), *n.* [< 16th-c. slang], nonsense; senseless talk or writing.
**bald·head** (bôld′hed′), *n.* 1. a person who has a bald head. 2. a bald (sense 1) bird or animal. Also **bald′pate′** (-pāt′). —**bald′head′ed, bald′pat′ed,** *adj.*
**bal·dric** (bôl′drik), *n.* [< OFr. prob. < OHG. personal name], a belt worn over one shoulder and across the chest to support a sword, etc.
**Bald·win** (bôld′win), *n.* a moderately tangy, red winter apple.
**bale** (bāl), *n.* [OFr. < OHG. *balla*, a ball], a large bundle, especially a standardized quantity of goods, as raw cotton, compressed and bound. *v.t.* [BALED, BALING], to make into bales. —**bal′er,** *n.*
**bale** (bāl), *n.* [AS. *bealu*], [Poetic], 1. evil; disaster; harm. 2. sorrow; woe.
**bale** (bāl), *n., v.i. & v.t.* bail (bucket, etc.).
**Bal·e·ar·ic Islands** (bal′i-ar′ik, bə-lêr′ik), a group of Spanish islands, including Majorca and Minorca, in the Mediterranean, east of Spain.
**ba·leen** (bə-lēn′), *n.* [< OFr. < L. *balaena*, a whale], whalebone.
**bale·ful** (bāl′fəl), *adj.* deadly; harmful; evil. —**bale′ful·ly,** *adv.* —**bale′ful·ness,** *n.*
**Ba·li** (bä′li), *n.* an island of the Republic of Indonesia, east of Java: area, 2,168 sq. mi.; pop., 1,203,000. —**Ba′li·nese′** (-nēz′), *adj. & n.* [*pl.* BALINESE].
**balk** (bôk), *n.* [AS. *balca*, a bank, ridge], 1. a ridge of unplowed land between furrows. 2. a roughly hewn piece of timber. 3. the tie beam of a house. 4. an obstruction; thwarting. 5. a blunder; error. 6. in *baseball*, an uncompleted pitch, entitling base runners to advance one base. *v.t.* 1. to miss intentionally; let slip. 2. to obstruct; thwart; foil. *v.i.* to stop and obstinately refuse to move or act. Also sp. **baulk.** —**balk′er,** *n.* —**balk′ing,** *adj. & n.* —**balk′ing·ly,** *adv.*
**Bal·kan** (bôl′kən), *adj.* 1. of the Balkan Peninsula. 2. of the Balkans, their people, etc. —**the Balkans,** the countries of the Balkan Peninsula; Yugoslavia, Romania, Bulgaria, Albania, Greece, and European Turkey: also **Balkan States.**
**Balkan Mountains,** a mountain range extending across central Bulgaria to the Black Sea.
**Balkan Peninsula,** a peninsula in S Europe, east of Italy.
**balk·y** (bôk′i), *adj.* [-IER, -IEST], balking or likely to balk: as, a *balky* mule. —**balk′i·ness,** *n.*
**ball** (bôl), *n.* [ON. *bǫllr*], 1. any round object; sphere; globe. 2. a planet or star, especially the earth. 3. a round or egg-shaped object used in various games. 4. any of several such games, especially baseball. 5. a throw, pitch, etc. of a ball: as, a slow *ball*. 6. a round, solid missile for a cannon, rifle, etc. 7. a rounded part of the body: as, the *ball* of the foot. 8. in *baseball*, a pitch that is wide of the plate or goes above the shoulder or below the knee of the batter and is not struck at by him. *v.i. & v.t.* to form into a ball —**ball up,** [Slang], to muddle; confuse. —**be on the ball,** [Slang], to be alert; be efficient. —**have something on the ball,** [Slang], to have ability. —**play ball,** 1. to begin or resume playing a ball game. 2. to begin or resume any activity. 3. [Colloq.], to co-operate.
**ball** (bôl), *n.* [Fr. *bal* < L. < Gr. *ballizein*, to dance < *ballein*, to throw], a formal social dance.
**bal·lad** (bal′əd), *n.* [Fr. *ballade*, dancing song < L.; see BALL (dance)], 1. a romantic or sentimental song with the same melody for each stanza. 2. a song or poem, usually of unknown authorship and handed down orally, that tells a story in short stanzas and simple words, with repetition, refrain, etc. —**bal′lad·eer′,** *n.* —**bal′lad·ry,** *n.*

**bal·lade** (bə-läd′), *n.* [Fr.; see BALLAD], 1. a verse form. 2. a short, romantic musical composition.

**bal·last** (bal′əst), *n.* [LG.; D. *barlast; bar*, bare + *last*, a load], 1. anything heavy carried in a ship or vehicle to give stability or in an aircraft to help control altitude. 2. anything giving stability and firmness to character, human relations, etc. 3. crushed rock or gravel, used in railroad beds, etc. *v.t.* 1. to furnish with ballast; stabilize. 2. to fill in (a railroad bed, etc.) with ballast. —**bal′last·er,** *n.*

**ball bearing,** 1. a bearing in which friction is reduced because the parts turn upon freely rolling metal balls. 2. a metal ball for such a bearing. —**ball′-bear′ing,** *adj.*

**bal·le·ri·na** (bal′ə-rē′nə), *n.* [It. < L.; see BALL (dance)], a woman ballet dancer.

**bal·let** (bal′ā, ba′lā′), *n.* [< Fr. dim. of *bal;* see BALL (dance)], 1. an intricate group dance (or dancing) using pantomime and conventionalized movements to tell a story. 2. dancers of ballet.

**bal·lis·ta** (bə-lis′tə), *n.* [*pl.* -TAE (-tē)], [L. < Gr. *ballein*, to throw], a device used in ancient warfare to hurl heavy stones, etc.

**bal·lis·tic missile** (bə-lis′tik), a long-range missile that is guided automatically in the first part of its flight, but is a free-falling object as it approaches its target.

**bal·lis·tics** (bə-lis′tiks), *n.pl.* [construed as sing.], the science dealing with the motion and impact of projectiles, especially those discharged from firearms. —**bal·lis′tic,** *adj.* —**bal·lis·ti·cian** (bal′is-tish′ən), *n.*

**bal·loon** (bə-lo͞on′), *n.* [< Fr. < It. *ballone* < *balla*, a ball], 1. a large, airtight bag which will rise above the earth when filled with a gas lighter than air. 2. a bag of this sort with an attached car for passengers or instruments. 3. a small, inflatable rubber bag, used as a toy. *v.t.* to cause to swell like a balloon. *v.i.* 1. to travel by balloon. 2. to swell; expand. *adj.* like a balloon. —**bal·loon′ist,** *n.*

**bal·lot** (bal′ət), *n.* [It. *ballotta*, dim. of *balla*, a ball], 1. originally a ball, now a ticket, paper, etc., by which a vote is registered. 2. act or method of voting, especially secret voting by the use of ballots or voting machines. 3. the total number of votes cast in an election. 4. a list of candidates for office; ticket. *v.i.* to decide by means of the ballot; vote. —**bal′lot·er,** *n.*

**ballot box,** a box into which voters put their marked ballots.

**ball·play·er** (bôl′plā′ẽr), *n.* a person who plays ball games, especially baseball.

**ball point pen,** a type of fountain pen having instead of a point a small ball bearing that rolls over an ink reservoir.

**ball·room** (bôl′ro͞om′, -room′), *n.* a large room or hall for dancing.

**ballroom dancing,** dancing in which two people dance as partners to a waltz, foxtrot, etc.

**bal·ly·hoo** (bal′i-ho͞o′), *n.* [after *Ballyhooly*, village in Ireland], [Colloq.], 1. loud talk; uproar. 2. loud or sensational advertising or propaganda. *v.t. & v.i.* (also bal′i-ho͞o′), [-HOOED, -HOOING], [Colloq.], to advertise or promote by sensational, showy methods. —**bal′ly·hoo′er,** *n.*

**balm** (bäm), *n.* [< OFr. < L. < Gr. *balsamon*], 1. an aromatic gum resin obtained from certain trees and plants and used as medicine; balsam. 2. any fragrant ointment or oil. 3. anything healing or soothing, as to the mind or temper. 4. any of various aromatic plants similar to mint. 5. pleasant odor; fragrance.

**bal·ma·caan** (bal′mə-kan′), *n.* [after *Balmacaan*, in Scotland], a loose overcoat with raglan sleeves.

**balm of Gilead,** 1. a small, Asiatic and African tree of the myrrh family. 2. an aromatic ointment prepared from its resin. 3. the balsam fir. 4. a resin-bearing American poplar.

**balm·y** (bäm′i), *adj.* [-IER, -IEST], 1. having the qualities of balm; soothing, fragrant, mild, etc. 2. [var. of *barmy*], [Brit. Slang], crazy; foolish. —**balm′i·ly,** *adv.* —**balm′i·ness,** *n.*

**ba·lo·ney** (bə-lō′ni), *n.* [altered < *bologna*, sausage], 1. bologna. 2. [Slang], nonsense. *interj.* [Slang], nonsense! Also sp. **boloney.**

**bal·sa** (bôl′sə, bäl′-), *n.* [Sp.], 1. a tropical American tree that has a very lightweight wood used for rafts, etc. 2. the wood. 3. a raft made up of a frame on cylindrical floats.

**bal·sam** (bôl′səm), *n.* [AS. < L.; see BALM], 1. any of various aromatic resins obtained from certain trees and used in some medicines and perfumes; balm. 2. any of various aromatic, resinous oils or fluids. 3. anything healing or soothing. 4. any impatiens, a kind of plant. 5. any of various trees that yield balsam; esp., the balsam fir. —**bal·sam·ic** (bôl-sam′ik, bal-), *adj.*

**balsam fir,** a North American evergreen tree, the source of balsam lumber and turpentine.

**Bal·tic** (bôl′tik), *adj.* 1. of the Baltic Sea. 2. of the Baltic States.

**Baltic Sea,** a sea northeast of Germany and west of the Baltic States, joining the North Sea.

**Baltic States,** Lithuania, Latvia, and Estonia: Finland is sometimes included.

**Bal·ti·more** (bôl′tə-môr′, -mōr′), *n.* a city in N Maryland, on Chesapeake Bay: pop., 939,000 (metropolitan area, 1,727,000).

**Baltimore,** Lord, see **Calvert, George.**

**Baltimore oriole,** [from the colors of the coat of arms of Lord *Baltimore*], a North American oriole that has an orange body with black on the head, wings, and tail: also **hang′bird′, hang′nest′, golden robin.**

**Ba·lu·chi·stan** (bə-lo͞o′chi-stän′, bə-lo͞o′ki-stan′), *n.* a former province of West Pakistan, which included a union of native states (the *Baluchistan States*).

**bal·us·ter** (bal′əs-tẽr), *n.* [< Fr. < It. < L. < Gr. *balaustion*, flower of the wild pomegranate: from the resemblance in shape], any of the small posts of a railing, as on a staircase.

**bal·us·trade** (bal′ə-strād′), *n.* a row of balusters with a rail supported on them.

**Bal·zac, Ho·no·ré de** (ô′nô′rā′ də bål′zåk′; Eng. on′ə-rā′ də bal′zak), 1799–1850; French novelist.

‡**bam·bi·no** (bäm-bē′nô; Eng. bam-bē′nō), *n.* [*pl.* -NI (-nē)], [It., dim. of *bambo*, childish], 1. a child; baby. 2. any image of the infant Jesus.

**bam·boo** (bam-bo͞o′), *n.* [Malay *bambu*], any of a number of treelike tropical grasses having a springy, hollow, jointed stem, varying greatly in circumference and height: the stems are used for furniture, canes, etc. and the young shoots for food.

**bam·boo·zle** (bam-bo͞o′z'l), *v.t.* [-ZLED, -ZLING], [? < *bombast*], [Colloq.], 1. to trick; cheat. 2. to confuse; puzzle. —**bam·boo′zle·ment,** *n.* —**bam·boo′zler,** *n.*

**ban** (ban), *v.t.* [BANNED, BANNING], [AS. *bannan*, to summon], 1. to prohibit; forbid. 2. [Archaic], to curse; condemn; place under ban. *n.* [< the *v.;* also < OFr. *ban*, decree < OHG. *bann*, prohibition], 1. an excommunication or condemnation by church authorities. 2. a curse. 3. a formal or authoritative prohibition. 4. a sentence of outlawry.

**ba·nal** (bā′n'l, bə-nal′, bə-näl′, ban′'l), *adj.* [Fr. < *ban;* see BAN, *n.*], trite; hackneyed. —**ba·nal·i·ty** (bə-nal′ə-ti), [*pl.* -TIES], *n.* —**ba′nal·ly,** *adv.*

**ba·nan·a** (bə-nan′ə), *n.* [Sp. & Port.], 1. a treelike tropical plant with long, broad leaves and large clusters of edible fruit. 2. the fruit: it is narrow and somewhat curved, and has a sweet, creamy flesh covered by a yellow or red skin.

**banana oil,** 1. a colorless liquid acetate with a bananalike odor: it is used in flavorings, as a solvent, etc. 2. [Slang], nonsense.

**Ban·croft, George** (ban′krôft, baŋ′kroft), 1800–1891; American statesman and historian.

**band** (band), *n.* [ON.; also (in meaning "thin strip") < Fr. *bande* < OFr. < OHG. < *bintan*, to bind], 1. something that binds, ties together, or encircles. 2. a strip of wood, metal, rubber, etc. fastened around something to bind or tie it together. 3. a stripe. 4. a narrow strip of cloth used for decoration or to prevent raveling: often in combination, as in *hatband*. 5. a neckband; collar. 6. *usually pl.* two strips hanging in front from the neck, as part of certain academic, legal, or clerical dress. 7. [Archaic], a fetter; bond. 8. in *radio*, a range of broadcasting frequencies or wave lengths. *v.t.* 1. to put a band on or around; tie with a band. 2. to mark with a band. —**band′ed,** *adj.*

**band** (band), *n.* [Fr. *bande*, a troupe; orig., prob., those following the same sign < Goth. *bandwa*, a sign], 1. a group of people united for a common purpose. 2. a group of musicians playing together, especially upon wind and percussion instruments: as, a dance *band*. *v.i. & v.t.* to unite for a common purpose (usually with *together*).

**band·age** (ban′dij), *n.* [Fr. < *bande*, a band], a strip of cloth or other dressing used to bind or cover an injured part of the body. *v.t.* [-AGED, -AGING], to bind with a bandage. —**band′ag·er,** *n.*

**ban·dan·na, ban·dan·a** (ban-dan′ə), *n.* [Hind. *bāndhnū*, method of dyeing], a large, colored handkerchief, usually with a figure on a bright background.

**band·box** (band′boks′), *n.* a light box of wood or pasteboard to hold hats, collars, etc.

**ban·deau** (ban-dō′, ban′dō), *n.* [*pl.* -DEAUX], [Fr.], a narrow ribbon, especially one worn around the head to confine the hair.

**ban·de·role, ban·de·rol** (ban′də-rōl′), *n.* [Fr. < It. dim. of *bandiera*, banner], a narrow flag; pennant; streamer: also **ban·ner·ol** (ban′ẽr-ōl′).

**ban·di·coot** (ban′di-ko͞ot′), *n.* [< Telugu *pandi-kokku*, pig rat], 1. a very large rat of India and Ceylon. 2. a ratlike animal of Australia that carries its young in a pouch and eats insects.

**ban·dit** (ban′dit), *n.* [*pl.* BANDITS, BANDITTI (ban-dit′i)], [It. *bandito* < *bandire*, to outlaw; ML. *bannire*, to ban; cf. BAN], a robber; brigand; highwayman. —**ban′dit·ry,** *n.*

**band·mas·ter** (band′mas′tẽr, -mäs′-), *n.* the leader or conductor of a band of musicians.

**ban·do·leer, ban·do·lier** (ban′də-lêr′), *n.* [< Fr. < It. < *banda*, a band], a broad shoulder belt with pockets for carrying ammunition, etc.

**ban·do·line** (ban′də-lēn′, -lin), *n.* [Fr. < *bandeau*, a band + L. *linere*, to smear], a sticky, perfumed dressing for the hair.

**band saw,** a saw made as an endless belt on pulleys.

**band shell,** an outdoor platform for concerts, having a concave, nearly hemispherical back serving as a sounding board.

**bands·man** (bandz′mən, banz′-), *n.* [*pl.* -MEN (-mən)], a member of a band of musicians.

**band·stand** (band′stand′, ban′-), *n.* an outdoor, usually roofed platform for a band or orchestra.

**band·wag·on** (band′wag′′n), *n.* a wagon for the band to ride in, as in a parade. —**on the bandwagon,** [Colloq.], on the winning or popular side, as in an election.

**ban·dy** (ban′di), *v.t.* [-DIED, -DYING], [Fr. *bander*, to bandy at tennis], 1. to toss back and forth, as a ball. 2. to pass (gossip, rumor, etc.) about carelessly. 3. to exchange: as, to *bandy* words.

**ban·dy** (ban′di), *n.* [*pl.* -DIES], [prob. < Fr. *bander*, to bend], 1. a hockey club. 2. a variety of field hockey. *adj.* bent or curved outward.

**ban·dy-leg·ged** (ban′di-leg′id, -legd′), *adj.* having bandy legs; bowlegged.

**bane** (bān), *n.* [AS. *bana*, slayer], 1. [Poetic], ruin. 2. the cause of harm, death, etc. 3. deadly poison: now obs. except in *ratsbane*, etc.

**bane·ber·ry** (bān′ber′i, -bẽr-i), *n.* [*pl.* -RIES], 1. any of various related plants with poisonous berries. 2. the berry of any of these plants.

**bane·ful** (bān′fəl), *adj.* full of bane; deadly; ruinous. —**bane′ful·ly,** *adj.* —**bane′ful·ness,** *n.*

**bang** (baŋ), *v.t.* [ON. *banga*, to pound], 1. to hit with a resounding blow. 2. to close (a door, etc.) noisily. 3. to handle violently. *v.i.* 1. to make a loud noise. 2. to move with a violent impact (*against* something). *n.* 1. a hard, noisy blow. 2. a loud, sudden noise. 3. [Slang], pleasure; stimulation. *adv.* 1. hard and noisily. 2. loudly and abruptly. —**bang up,** to do physical damage to.

**bang** (baŋ), *v.t.* [< dial. *bangled*, flapping < *bangle*, *v.t.*, freq. of *bang*], to cut (hair) short and straight. *n.* 1. a fringe of hair cut in this way. 2. *pl.* banged hair worn across the forehead.

**Ban·ga·lore** (baŋ′gə-lôr′, -lōr′), *n.* a city in S India: pop., 248,000: capital of Mysore state.

**Bang·ka** (bäŋ′kə), *n.* an island of the Republic of Indonesia, east of Sumatra: area, 4,611 sq. mi.; pop., 205,000: also sp. **Banka.**

**Bang·kok** (baŋ′kok), *n.* the capital of Thailand, a seaport in the southern part: pop., 827,000.

**ban·gle** (baŋ′g'l), *n.* [Hind. *bangrī*, glass bracelet], a decorative bracelet, armlet, or anklet.

**Bang's disease** (baŋz), [after B. L. F. *Bang*, Danish physician], an infectious disease of cattle, often resulting in abortion.

**bang-up** (baŋ′up′), *adj.* [Slang], excellent.

**ban·ian** (ban′yən), *n.* a banyan.

**ban·ian** (ban′yən), *n.* [Port. < Hind. *vaṇiyo*, trader; Sans. *vaṇij*, merchant], a Hindu merchant of a caste that eats no meat.

**ban·ish** (ban′ish) *v.t.* [< OFr. < ML. < *bannum*, a ban], 1. to exile. 2. to send away; dismiss. 3. to put out of one's thoughts. —**ban′ish·er,** *n.* —**ban′ish·ment,** *n.*

**ban·is·ter** (ban′is-tẽr), *n.* [altered < *baluster*], 1. a baluster. 2. *pl.* a balustrade. Also sp. **bannister.**

**ban·jo** (ban′jō), *n.* [*pl.* -JOS, -JOES], [< Sp. < L. < Gr. *pandoura*, a musical instrument], a stringed musical instrument of the guitar class, having a circular body covered with taut skin. —**ban′jo·ist,** *n.*

BANJO

**bank** (baŋk), *n.* [Fr. < It. < OHG. *bank*, a (money changer's) bench], 1. an establishment for receiving, lending, or, sometimes, issuing money. 2. the building of such an establishment. 3. a fund held, as by the dealer, in some gambling games. *v.i.* 1. to put or keep money in a bank. 2. to manage a bank. 3. to keep the bank, as in some gambling games. *v.t.* to deposit (money) in a bank. —**bank on,** [Colloq.], to depend on; rely on. —**bank′a·ble,** *adj.*

**bank** (baŋk), *n.* [< Anglo-N. hyp. *banki* (ON. *bakki*)], 1. a long mound or heap; ridge. 2. a steep slope, as of a hill. 3. a stretch of rising land at the edge of a stream or other body of water. 4. a shoal or shallow place, as in a sea. 5. the sloping of an airplane laterally to avoid slipping sideways on a turn. *v.t.* 1. to heap dirt around for protection from cold, etc. 2. to cover (a fire) with ashes and fuel so that it will burn longer. 3. to pile up so as to form a bank. 4. to slope (a curve in the road, etc.). 5. to slope (an airplane) laterally on a turn. 6. in *billiards*, to stroke (a ball) so that it recoils from a cushion. *v.i.* 1. to form a bank or banks. 2. to bank an airplane.

**bank** (baŋk), *n.* [< OFr. < OHG. *bank*, a bench], 1. a bench for rowers in a galley. 2. a row of oars. 3. a row of objects; tier. 4. a row of keys in a keyboard or console. *v.t.* to arrange in a bank. —**banked,** *adj.*

**bank account,** money deposited in a bank and subject to withdrawal by the depositor.

**bank·book** (baŋk′book′), *n.* the book in which the account of a depositor in a bank is recorded.

**bank·er** (baŋk′ẽr), *n.* 1. a person or company that owns or manages a bank. 2. the keeper of the bank in some gambling games.

**bank·ing** (baŋk′iŋ), *n.* the business of a bank.

**bank note,** a promissory note issued by a bank, payable on demand: it is a form of paper money.

**bank·rupt** (baŋk′rupt, -rəpt), *n.* [< Fr. < It. < *banca*, bench + *rotta*, broken < L. < *rumpere*, to break], a person legally declared unable to pay his debts: his property is divided among his creditors. *adj.* 1. legally declared a bankrupt. 2. lacking in some quality: as, morally *bankrupt*. *v.t.* to make bankrupt.

**bank·rupt·cy** (baŋk′rupt-si, -rəp-si), *n.* [*pl.* -CIES], state or instance of being bankrupt.

**ban·ner** (ban′ẽr), *n.* [< OFr. < LL. < Goth. *bandwa*, a sign], 1. a piece of cloth bearing an emblem, motto, etc. 2. a flag. 3. a headline extending across a newspaper page. *adj.* foremost; leading; excelling. —**ban′nered,** *adj.*

**ban·nis·ter** (ban′is-tẽr), *n.* a banister.

**banns, bans** (banz), *n.pl.* [see BAN, *n.*], the proclamation, generally made in church on three successive Sundays, of an intended marriage.

**ban·quet** (baŋ′kwit, ban′-), *n.* [Fr. < dim. of *banc*, a table], 1. a feast. 2. a formal dinner, usually with speeches. *v.t.* to honor with a banquet. *v.i.* to dine well. —**ban′quet·er,** *n.*

**ban·quette** (baŋ-ket′), *n.* [Fr., dim. of *banc*, a bench], 1. a gunners' platform along the inside of a parapet. 2. a sidewalk. 3. an upholstered bench along a wall.

**ban·shee, ban·shie** (ban′shē, ban-shē′), *n.* [< Ir. < *bean*, woman + *sith*, fairy], in *Ir. & Scot. folklore*, a female spirit believed to wail outside a house to warn of an impending death in the family.

**ban·tam** (ban′təm), *n.* [after *Bantam*, province in Java], 1. [B-], any of several breeds of small fowl. 2. a small but aggressive person. *adj.* like a bantam; small, aggressive, etc.

**ban·tam·weight** (ban′təm-wāt′), *n.* a boxer or wrestler who weighs between 113 and 118 pounds. *adj.* of bantamweights.

**ban·ter** (ban′tẽr), *v.t.* [17th-c. slang], to tease in a playful way. *v.i.* to exchange banter (*with* someone). *n.* good-natured teasing or joking. —**ban′ter·er,** *n.* —**ban′ter·ing·ly,** *adv.*

**bant·ling** (bant′liŋ), *n.* [altered < G. *bankling*, bastard < *bank*, a bench], a youngster; brat.

**Ban·tu** (ban′to͞o′), *n.* [Bantu *ba-ntu*, mankind], 1. [*pl.* -TU, -TUS], a member of a large group of Negroid tribes in central and southern Africa. 2.

the family of languages of these tribes. *adj.* of the Bantu or their languages.

**ban·yan** (ban′yən), *n.* [from a tree of this kind under which the *banians* had built a pagoda], an East Indian fig tree whose branches take root and become new trunks: also sp. **banian.**

**ban·zai** (bän′zä′i, -zī′), *interj.* a Japanese greeting or shout, meaning "May you live ten thousand years!"

**ba·o·bab** (bā′ō-bab′, bä′-), *n.* [prob. E. Afr. native name], a tall tree of Africa and India, with a thick trunk and gourdlike, edible fruit.

**bap·tism** (bap′tiz'm), *n.* [< OFr. < L. < Gr. < *baptizein*, to immerse], 1. the ceremony or rite of admitting a person into a Christian church by dipping him in water or sprinkling water on him. 2. any experience that initiates, tests, or purifies. **—bap·tis′mal,** *adj.* **—bap·tis′mal·ly,** *adv.*

**Bap·tist** (bap′tist), *n.* 1. [b-], one who baptizes; esp., 2. John the Baptist. 3. a member of a Protestant denomination holding that baptism should be given only to adult believers and only by immersion.

**bap·tis·ter·y** (bap′tis-tri, -tẽr-i), *n.* [*pl.* -IES], a place in or near a church, used for baptizing: also **bap′tist·ry** (-tri), [*pl.* -RIES].

**bap·tize** (bap-tīz′, bap′tīz), *v.t.* [-TIZED, -TIZING], 1. to administer baptism to. 2. to purify; initiate. 3. to christen. **—bap·tiz′er,** *n.*

**bar** (bär), *n.* [OFr. *barre;* LL. *barra*], 1. any piece of wood, metal, etc. longer than it is wide or thick, often used as a barrier, lever, etc. 2. an oblong piece of soap, etc. 3. anything that obstructs, hinders, or prevents. 4. a strip, band, or broad line. 5. the part of a law court, enclosed by a railing, where the judges or lawyers sit, or where prisoners are brought to trial. 6. a law court. 7. any place of judgment. 8. lawyers collectively. 9. the legal profession. 10. a counter at which alcoholic drinks are served. 11. a place with such a counter. 12. the mouthpiece of a horse's bit. 13. in *music, a*) a vertical line across a staff, dividing it into measures. *b*) a measure. *v.t.* [BARRED, BARRING], 1. to fasten with or as with a bar. 2. to obstruct; shut off; close. 3. to oppose; prevent. 4. to keep (a person) out of; exclude. *prep.* excluding: as, the best, *bar* none. **—cross the bar,** to die.

**BAR, B. A. R.,** Browning automatic rifle.

**bar.,** 1. barometer. 2. barometric. 3. barrister.

**barb** (bärb), *n.* [< OFr. < L. *barba*, a beard], 1. a beardlike growth near the mouth of certain animals. 2. a sharp point projecting backward from the main point of a fishhook, arrow, etc. 3. one of the hairlike projections from the shaft of a feather. *v.t.* to provide with a barb or barbs. **—barbed,** *adj.*

**barb** (bärb), *n.* [< Fr. < It. < Ar. *Barbar*, Berbers], a horse of a breed native to Barbary.

**Bar·ba·dos** (bär-bā′dōz, bär′bə-dōz′), *n.* a country on an island of the West Indies: a member of the British Commonwealth of Nations: area, 166 sq. mi.; pop., 245,000; capital, Bridgetown. **—Bar·ba′di·an,** *adj. & n.*

**bar·bar·i·an** (bär-bâr′i-ən), *n.* [see BARBAROUS], 1. originally, a foreigner; esp., a non-Greek or non-Roman. 2. a member of a people with a civilization regarded as primitive, etc. 3. an insensitive or coarse person; boor. 4. a savage, cruel person; brute. *adj.* of or like a barbarian; esp., uncivilized, cruel, rude, etc. **—bar·bar′i·an·ism,** *n.*

**bar·bar·ic** (bär-bar′ik), *adj.* 1. of or like barbarians; primitive or uncivilized. 2. wild, crude, and unrestrained. **—bar·bar′i·cal·ly,** *adv.*

**bar·ba·rism** (bär′bə-riz'm), *n.* 1. the use of words and expressions not standard in a language. 2. a word or expression of this sort (e.g., "youse" for "you"). 3. the state of being primitive or uncivilized. 4. a barbarous act, custom, etc.

**bar·bar·i·ty** (bär-bar′ə-ti), *n.* [*pl.* -TIES], 1. cruelty; brutality. 2. a cruel or brutal act. 3. a barbaric taste, manner, etc.

**bar·ba·rize** (bär′bə-rīz′), *v.t. & v.i.* [-RIZED, -RIZING], to make or become barbarous. **—bar′ba·ri·za′tion,** *n.*

**bar·ba·rous** (bär′bə-rəs), *adj.* [< L. < Gr. *barbaros*, foreign; prob. < echoic word describing strange tongues], 1. originally, foreign or alien; esp., in the ancient world, non-Greek or non-Roman. 2. characterized by substandard words and phrases. 3. uncivilized. 4. crude, coarse, rough, etc. 5. cruel; brutal. **—bar′ba·rous·ly,** *adv.* **—bar′ba·rous·ness,** *n.*

**Bar·ba·ry** (bär′bə-ri), *n.* the Moslem region west of Egypt, in North Africa.

**Barbary ape,** a tailless ape found in northern Africa and on the Rock of Gibraltar.

**Barbary Coast,** 1. the coastal region in northern Africa, from Tripoli to Morocco. 2. a district in San Francisco before the earthquake of 1906, known for its saloons, gambling places, etc.

**Barbary States,** the former countries of Morocco, Algiers, Tunis, and Tripoli in northern Africa.

**bar·bate** (bär′bāt), *adj.* [< L. *barba*, a beard], bearded.

**bar·be·cue** (bär′bə-kū′), *n.* [< Sp. < Haitian *barbacoa*, framework], 1. originally, a framework for smoking, drying, or broiling meat. 2. a hog, steer, etc. roasted whole over an open fire. 3. any meat roasted over an open fire. 4. an entertainment, usually outdoors, at which such meat is served. *v.t.* [-CUED, -CUING], 1. to roast (an animal) whole. 2. to prepare (meat or fish) by broiling, often in a highly seasoned sauce (**barbecue sauce**).

**barbed wire,** wire with sharp points all along it, used for barriers: also **barb′wire′.**

**bar·bel** (bär′b'l), *n.* [OFr. < L. < *barba*, a beard], 1. a threadlike growth hanging from the lips of certain fishes: it is an organ of touch. 2. a large European fresh-water fish with such growths.

**bar·bell** (bär′bel′), *n.* [*bar* + dumb*bell*], a metal bar to which disks of varying weights are attached at each end, used for weightlifting exercises.

**bar·ber** (bär′bẽr), *n.* [< OFr. *barbeor;* ult. < L. *barba*, a beard], a person whose work is cutting hair, shaving and trimming beards, etc. *v.t. & v.i.* to cut the hair (of), shave, etc.

**barber pole,** a pole with spiral stripes of red and white, a symbol of the barber's trade.

**bar·ber·ry** (bär′ber′i, -bẽr-i), *n.* [*pl.* -RIES], [< OFr. < ML. *barberis*], 1. a spiny shrub with sour, oblong, red berries. 2. the berry.

**bar·ber·shop** (bär′bẽr-shop′), *n.* a barber's place of business. *adj.* [Colloq.], designating or characterized by the close harmony of male voices: as, a *barbershop* quartet.

**bar·bi·can** (bär′bi-kən), *n.* [< OFr.; prob. < Per. *barbar-khānah*, house on a wall], a fortification at the gate or bridge of a town or castle.

**bar·bi·cel** (bär′bə-sel′), *n.* [Mod. L. < L. *barba*, a beard], any of the very small projections on the barbules of a feather.

**bar·bi·tal** (bär′bi-tal′, -tôl′), *n.* a habit-forming derivative of barbituric acid, in the form of a white powder, used to induce sleep; veronal.

**bar·bi·tu·rate** (bär′bə-tyoor′it, bär-bich′ẽr-it), *n.* any salt of barbituric acid, used as a sedative or to deaden pain.

**bar·bi·tu·ric** (bär′bə-tyoor′ik, bär′bə-toor′ik), *adj.* [Mod. L. *Usnea barbata*, lit., bearded moss (< L. *barba*, beard); + *uric* acid], designating or of a crystalline acid, $C_4H_4O_3N_2$, derivatives of which are used to induce sleep or deaden pain.

**bar·bule** (bär′būl), *n.* [< L. *barba*, a beard], a very small barb, usually forming the fringe along the barbs of a feather.

**bar·ca·role, bar·ca·rolle** (bär′kə-rōl′), *n.* [Fr. < It. < *barca*, boat], 1. a song sung by Venetian gondoliers. 2. a piece of music imitating this.

**Bar·ce·lo·na** (bär′s'l-ō′nə; Sp. bär′the-lô′nä), *n.* a seaport in NE Spain: pop., 1,696,000.

**bard** (bärd), *n.* [Gael. & Ir. *bardh*, bard], 1. an ancient Celtic poet. 2. a poet. **—bard′ic,** *adj.*

**Bard of Avon,** William Shakespeare: so called from his birthplace, Stratford-on-Avon.

**bare** (bâr), *adj.* [AS. *bær*], 1. not covered or clothed; naked. 2. exposed; revealed. 3. threadbare. 4. without equipment or furnishings; empty. 5. simple; plain. 6. mere: as, *bare* needs. *v.t.* [BARED, BARING], to make **bare**; uncover; reveal. **—lay bare,** to uncover; expose. **—bare′ness,** *n.*

**bare** (bâr), [Archaic], alt. pt. of **bear.**

**bare·back** (bâr′bak′), *adv. & adj.* on a horse with no saddle. **—bare′backed′,** *adj.*

**bare·faced** (bâr′fāst′), *adj.* 1. with the face uncovered. 2. unconcealed; open. 3. shameless; insolent. **—bare·fac·ed·ly** (bâr′fās′id-li, -fāst′li), *adv.* **—bare′fac′ed·ness,** *n.*

**bare·foot** (bâr′foot′), *adj. & adv.* without shoes and stockings: also **bare′foot′ed.**

**bare·hand·ed** (bâr′han′did), *adj. & adv.* 1. with hands uncovered. 2. [Colloq.], in the act.

**bare·head·ed** (bâr′hed′id), *adj. & adv.* without a hat, etc. on the head. **—bare′head′ed·ness,** *n.*

**bare·leg·ged** (bâr′leg′id, -legd′), *adj. & adv.* with the legs bare; without stockings on.

**bare·ly** (bâr′li), *adv.* 1. openly. 2. nakedly. 3. only just; scarcely. 4. scantily.
**bar·fly** (bär′flī′), *n.* [Slang], one who spends much time in barrooms.
**bar·gain** (bär′g'n, -gin), *n.* [< OFr. < *bargaignier*, to haggle], 1. an agreement to exchange, sell, or buy goods. 2. such an agreement in relation to one of the parties: as, a bad *bargain.* 3. any mutual agreement. 4. something sold at a price favorable to the buyer. *v.i.* 1. to haggle. 2. to make a bargain (*with* someone). *v.t.* to barter. —**bargain for,** 1. to try to get cheaply. 2. to expect; count on. —**into the bargain,** in addition; besides. —**strike a bargain,** to agree on terms. —**bar′gain·er,** *n.*
**barge** (bärj), *n.* [OFr.; LL. *barga*], 1. a large flat-bottomed boat for carrying freight on rivers, etc. 2. a large pleasure boat, used for pageants, etc. 3. the official launch of a flagship. 4. a houseboat. *v.t.* [BARGED, BARGING], to carry by barge. *v.i.* 1. to move slowly and clumsily. 2. [Colloq.], to enter in a rude, abrupt way (with *in* or *into*). 3. [Colloq.], to collide (with *into*). —**barge′man** [*pl.* -MEN], *n.*
**Ba·ri** (bä′ri), *n.* a city in SE Italy, on the Adriatic: pop., 249,000.
**bar·ite** (bâr′it), *n.* a white, crystalline mineral, barium sulfate: also **barytes.**
**bar·i·tone** (bar′ə-tōn′), *n.* [< It. < Gr. < *barys*, deep + *tonos*, tone], 1. a male voice with a range between tenor and bass. 2. a man with such a voice. 3. a brass-wind instrument with a similar range. 4. a musical part for a baritone. Also sp. **barytone.**
**bar·i·um** (bâr′i-əm), *n.* [< Gr. *barys*, heavy], a silver-white, metallic chemical element: symbol, Ba; at. wt., 137.36; at. no., 56. —**bar′ic,** *adj.*
**bark** (bärk), *n.* [ON. *bǫrkr*], the outside covering of trees and some plants. *v.t.* 1. to treat with bark. 2. to take the bark off (a tree or log). 3. [Colloq.], to take the skin off: as, he *barked* his knees. —**bark′less,** *adj.*
**bark** (bärk), *v.i.* [AS. *beorcan; echoic*], 1. to make the sharp, abrupt cry of a dog. 2. to make a similar sound: as, the cannon *barked.* 3. to speak sharply; snap. 4. [Colloq.], to cough. 5. [Slang], to work as a barker. *v.t.* to say with a bark or shout. *n.* 1. the characteristic cry of a dog. 2. any noise like this. —**bark at the moon,** to make futile protests. —**bark up the wrong tree,** to attack or pursue the wrong thing.
**bark** (bärk), *n.* [< Fr. < It. < L. *barca*], 1. [Poetic], any small sailing boat. 2. a sailing vessel with its two forward masts square-rigged and its rear mast rigged fore-and-aft. Also sp. **barque.**
**bar·keep·er** (bär′kēp′ẽr), *n.* a bartender: also **bar′keep′.**
**bark·en·tine** (bär′kən-tēn′), *n.* [< *bark* (sailboat) after *brigantine*], a sailing vessel with its foremast square-rigged and its two other masts rigged fore-and-aft: also sp. **barkantine, barquentine.**
**bark·er** (bär′kẽr), *n.* one that barks; esp., a person in front of a side show, etc. who attracts customers by loud, animated talking.
**Bark·ley, Al·ben William** (al′b'n bärk′li), 1877–1956; vice-president of the U.S. (1949–1953).
**bar·ley** (bär′li), *n.* [see PLURAL, II, D, 3], [AS. *bærlic, adj.*, < *bere*, barley] 1. a cereal grass. 2. its seed or grain, used in making liquors, soups, etc.
**bar·ley·corn** (bär′li-kôrn′), *n.* 1. barley, or a grain of barley. 2. any strong alcoholic liquor; esp., whisky: cf. **John Barleycorn.**
**barm** (bärm), *n.* [AS. *beorma*], the foamy yeast that appears on the surface of fermenting malt liquors.
**bar·maid** (bär′mād′), *n.* a woman bartender.
**bar·man** (bär′mən), *n.* [*pl.* -MEN], a bartender.
**Bar·me·cide** (bär′mə-sīd′), *n.* [Ar.], 1. in *The Arabian Nights,* a ruling prince of Bagdad who pretends to serve a feast to a beggar, but gives him no food; hence, 2. one who offers imaginary benefits. *adj.* pretended, false, deceptive, etc.
**barm·y** (bär′mi), *adj.* [-IER, -IEST], 1. full of barm; foamy. 2. [Brit. Slang], silly; idiotic.
**barn** (bärn), *n.* [< AS. *bereærn; bere*, barley + *ærn*, a building], 1. a farm building for sheltering harvested crops, livestock, etc. 2. a large building for streetcars, etc.
**bar·na·cle** (bär′nə-k'l), *n.* [< (West) Fr. *bernicle;* Bret. *bernic*], any of a number of related shell-bearing sea animals that attach themselves to rocks, ship bottoms, etc. —**bar′na·cled,** *adj.*
**barn dance,** a party, originally held in a barn, with square dances, etc.
**barn owl,** a kind of brown and gray owl commonly found in barns.
**barn·storm** (bärn′stôrm′), *v.i.* to tour in small towns and rural districts, performing plays, etc. in barns or the like. —**barn′storm′er,** *n.* —**barn′storm′ing,** *adj. & n.*
**barn swallow,** a common swallow with a long, deeply forked tail: it usually nests in barns.
**Bar·num, Phineas Taylor** (bär′nəm), 1810–1891; American showman.
**barn·yard** (bärn′yärd′), *n.* the yard or ground near a barn. *adj.* 1. of a barnyard. 2. like or fit for a barnyard; earthy, smutty, etc.
**bar·o-,** [< Gr. *baros*, weight], a prefix meaning *of atmospheric pressure*, as in *barograph.*
**Ba·ro·da** (bə-rō′də), *n.* an independent state of India, north of Bombay.
**bar·o·gram** (bar′ə-gram′), *n.* the line recorded by a barograph.
**bar·o·graph** (bar′ə-graf′, -gräf′), *n.* [*baro-* + *-graph*], a barometer that automatically records on a revolving cylinder the variations in atmospheric pressure. —**bar′o·graph′ic,** *adj.*
**ba·rom·e·ter** (bə-rom′ə-tẽr), *n.* [*baro-* + *-meter*], 1. an instrument for measuring atmospheric pressure and thus for forecasting the weather or finding height above sea level. 2. anything that indicates change. —**bar·o·met·ric** (bar′ə-met′rik), **bar′o·met′ri·cal,** *adj.* —**bar′o·met′ri·cal·ly,** *adv.* —**ba·rom′e·try,** *n.*

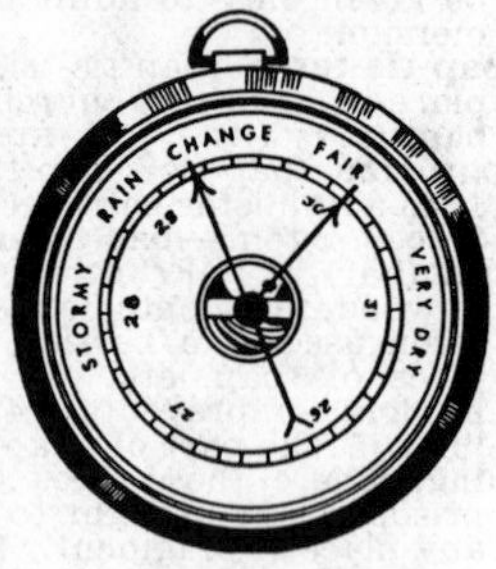

BAROMETER

**bar·on** (bar′ən), *n.* [OFr. < base of OHG. *baro*, a man], 1. a member of the lowest rank of British nobility. 2. a European or Japanese nobleman of like rank. 3. a powerful capitalist; magnate. —**ba·ro·ni·al** (bə-rō′ni-əl), *adj.*
**bar·on·age** (bar′ən-ij), *n.* 1. barons as a class; peerage. 2. the rank, title, or domain of a baron. 3. the nobility in general.
**bar·on·ess** (bar′ə-nis), *n.* 1. a baron's wife or widow. 2. a lady with a barony in her own right.
**bar·on·et** (bar′ə-nit, -net′), *n.* 1. a man holding the lowest hereditary British rank of honor, below a baron. 2. the title that shows this rank. —**bar′on·et·age, bar′on·et·cy** [*pl.* -CIES], *n.*
**bar·o·ny** (bar′ə-ni), *n.* [*pl.* -NIES], 1. a baron's domain. 2. the rank or title of a baron.
**ba·roque** (bə-rōk′; Fr. bȧ′rôk′), *adj.* [Fr.; Port. *barroco*, imperfect pearl], 1. irregular in shape: said of pearls. 2. of or like a style of art and architecture (esp. c. 1550–1750) characterized by much ornamentation and curved rather than straight lines. 3. rococo. 4. fantastically overdecorated; gaudily ornate. *n.* baroque style, baroque art, etc.
**bar·o·scope** (bar′ə-skōp′), *n.* [*baro-* + *-scope*], an instrument for indicating changes in atmospheric pressure. —**bar′o·scop′ic** (-skop′ik), **bar′o·scop′i·cal,** *adj.*
**ba·rouche** (bə-rōōsh′), *n.* [< G. < It. < L. *birotus* < *bis*, two + *rota*, a wheel], a four-wheeled carriage with a collapsible hood, two double seats opposite each other, and a driver's seat in front.
**barque** (bärk), *n.* a bark (sailing vessel).
**bar·quen·tine** (bär′kən-tēn′), *n.* a barkentine.
**bar·rack** (bar′ək), *n.* [Fr. < It. < Sp. < *barro*, clay < LL. hyp. *barrum*, clay], 1. *pl.* a building or group of buildings for housing soldiers. 2. *pl.* any large, plain building for housing many people. *v.t. & v.i.* to house in barracks.
**barracks bag,** a cloth bag to hold a soldier's equipment and personal possessions.
**bar·ra·cu·da** (bar′ə-kōō′də), *n.* [*pl.* -DA, -DAS; see PLURAL, II, D, 2], [Sp.; ? < dial. *barraco*, tooth growing over another], a ferocious, edible, pikelike fish of tropical seas.
**bar·rage** (bə-räzh′), *n.* [Fr. < *barrer*, to stop; see BAR, *n.*], 1. a curtain of artillery fire laid down to keep enemy forces from moving, or to cover one's own forces, especially in attack. 2. a prolonged attack of words, blows, etc. 3. a man-made barrier in a stream, etc.; dam. *v.t. & v.i.* [-RAGED, -RAGING], to lay down a barrage (against).
**barrage balloon,** any of a series of anchored balloons with cables or nets attached for entangling attacking airplanes.
**bar·ran·ca** (bə-raŋ′kə), *n.* [Sp.], a deep ravine.
**Bar·ran·quil·la** (bä′rän-kēl′yä), *n.* a city in NW Colombia: pop., 207,000.
**bar·ra·tor, bar·ra·ter** (bar′ə-tẽr), *n.* [OFr. < ON. *baratta*, quarrel], a person guilty of barratry.

**bar·ra·try** (bar′ə-tri), *n.* [see BARRATOR], 1. the habitual bringing about of quarrels or lawsuits. 2. negligence or fraud on the part of a ship's officers or crew resulting in loss to the owners. —**bar′ra·trous,** *adj.* —**bar′ra·trous·ly,** *adv.*
**barred** (bärd), *adj.* 1. having bars or stripes. 2. closed off with bars; hence, 3. not allowed.
**bar·rel** (bar′əl), *n.* [OFr.; ? < LL. *barra,* a stave, bar], 1. a large, wooden, cylindrical container with slightly bulging sides and flat ends, made usually of staves bound together with hoops. 2. the capacity of a standard barrel (in the U.S., usually 31½ gals.). 3. any somewhat similar cylinder, drum, etc.: as, the *barrel* of a windlass. 4. the straight tube of a gun, which directs the projectile. *v.t.* [-RELED or -RELLED, -RELING or -RELLING], to put or pack in a barrel or barrels.
**bar·rel-house** (bar′əl-hous′), *adj.* in *jazz music,* of or in the unrestrained style of playing associated with a barrel house.
**barrel house,** formerly, a small, disreputable saloon with racked barrels along the wall.
**barrel organ,** a mechanical musical instrument having a revolving cylinder studded with pins which open pipe valves, producing a tune; hand organ.
**barrel roll,** a complete revolution made by an airplane around its longitudinal axis while in flight.
**bar·ren** (bar′ən), *adj.* [< OFr. *baraigne*], 1. that cannot bear offspring; sterile. 2. without vegetation; unfruitful. 3. unproductive; unprofitable. 4. lacking interest, charm, etc.; boring; dull. 5. empty; devoid: as, *barren* of creative spirit. *n. usually pl.* an area of relatively unproductive land, with shrubs, brush, etc. and sandy soil. —**bar′ren·ly,** *adv.* —**bar′ren·ness,** *n.*
**bar·rette** (bə-ret′), *n.* a bar or clasp worn by a girl or woman for holding the hair in place.
**bar·ri·cade** (bar′ə-kād′; *also, for n.,* bar′ə-kād′), *n.* [Fr. < It. *barra,* a bar], 1. a barrier thrown up hastily for defense. 2. any barrier. *v.t.* [-CADED, -CADING], 1. to keep in or out with a barricade. 2. to block or obstruct. —**bar′ri·cad′er,** *n.*
**Bar·rie,** Sir **James Matthew** (bar′i), 1860–1937; Scottish dramatist and novelist.
**bar·ri·er** (bar′i-ēr), *n.* [< OFr. < LL. *barra,* a bar], 1. an obstruction, as a fence, wall, etc. 2. anything that holds apart: as, shyness was a *barrier* between them. 3. a boundary or limitation.
**barrier reef,** a long ridge of rock or coral near a coast line, often serving as a breakwater.
**bar·ring** (bär′iŋ), *prep.* excepting; excluding.
**bar·ris·ter** (bar′is-tēr), *n.* [< *bar* (court of justice)], in England, a counselor-at-law who presents and pleads cases in court: distinguished from *solicitor.*
**bar·room** (bär′rōōm′, -room′), *n.* a room with a bar at which alcoholic drinks are sold.
**bar·row** (bar′ō), *n.* [< AS. < *beran,* to bear], 1. a handbarrow. 2. a handcart.
**bar·row** (bar′ō), *n.* [AS. *beorg,* hill, mound], a heap of earth or rocks marking an ancient grave.
**Bar·row, Point** (bar′ō), a cape at the northernmost point of Alaska.
**bar sinister,** in *heraldry,* erroneously, a bend sinister.
**Bart.,** Baronet.
**bar·tend·er** (bär′ten′dēr), *n.* a man who mixes and serves alcoholic drinks at a bar.
**bar·ter** (bär′tēr), *v.i.* [< OFr. < ON. *baratta;* ? influenced by Bret. *barad,* trickery], to trade by exchanging goods without using money. *v.t.* to exchange (goods); trade. *n.* 1. the act or practice of bartering. 2. anything bartered. —**bar′ter·er,** *n.*
**bar·ti·zan, bar·ti·san** (bär′tə-z'n, bär′tə-zan′), *n.* [altered < ME. *bretasce,* a parapet < OFr.; prob. < OHG. *bret,* a board], a small, overhanging turret on a tower, battlement, etc.
**Bart·lett pear** (bärt′lit), [after E. *Bartlett* of Dorchester, Mass., the distributor], a variety of large, juicy pear.
**Bar·tók, Bé·la** (bā′lä bär′tôk), 1881–1945; Hungarian composer.
**Bar·ton, Clara** (bär′t'n), 1821–1912; U.S. philanthropist; organizer of the American Red Cross.
**Bar·uch** (bâr′ək), *n.* a book of the Old Testament Apocrypha.
**bar·y·on** (bar′i-än′), *n.* [< Gr. *barys,* heavy; + electr*on*], one of a class of heavy atomic particles, including the proton, neutron, etc.
**ba·ry·tes** (bə-rī′tēz), *n.* [< Gr. *barys,* heavy], barite.
**bar·y·tone** (bar′ə-tōn′), *adj.* & *n.* baritone.
**bas·al** (bā′s'l), *adj.* 1. of, at, or forming the base. 2. basic; fundamental. —**bas′al·ly,** *adv.*
**basal anesthesia,** anesthesia induced as a preliminary to further and deeper anesthesia.
**basal metabolism,** the quantity of energy used by any organism at rest, measured by the rate (**basal metabolic rate**) at which heat is given off by the organism.
**ba·salt** (bə-sôlt′, bas′ôlt), *n.* [L. *basaltes,* dark marble], a hard, heavy, dark volcanic rock. —**ba·sal′tic,** *adj.*
**bas·cule** (bas′kūl), *n.* [Fr.], a seesaw or similarly balanced apparatus.
**bascule bridge,** a drawbridge counterweighted so that it can be raised and lowered easily.

BASCULE BRIDGE

**base** (bās), *n.* [*pl.* BASES], [OFr. *bas;* L. *basis;* see BASIS], 1. the part of a thing that the thing rests on; foundation. 2. the most important element, as of a system or set of ideas. 3. a basis. 4. a goal or station in certain games, as baseball. 5. the point of attachment of an organism. 6. a center of operations or source of supply; headquarters. 7. in *chemistry,* a substance which forms a salt when it reacts with an acid. 8. in *geometry,* the line or plane upon which a figure is thought of as resting. 9. in *linguistics,* any morpheme to which prefixes, suffixes, etc. are added; stem; root. 10. in *mathematics,* a constant figure upon which a mathematical table is computed, as in logarithms. *adj.* forming a base. *v.t.* [BASED, BASING], 1. to make a base for. 2. to put (a thing) on a base: often used figuratively, as, he *based* his argument on authority. 3. to establish or found. —**get to first base,** 1. in *baseball,* to reach first base safely. 2. [Slang], to succeed in the first step of anything.
**base** (bās), *adj.* [OFr. *bas;* LL. *bassus,* low], 1. deep or low: said of sounds: see **bass.** 2. morally low; disgraceful; vile. 3. menial; servile. 4. inferior in quality; coarse. 5. comparatively worthless: as, iron is a *base* metal, gold a precious one. 6. debased; counterfeit. 7. [Archaic], of servile or humble birth. *n.* a bass voice, tone, part, etc. —**base′ly,** *adv.* —**base′ness,** *n.*
**base·ball** (bās′bôl′), *n.* 1. a game played with ball and bat by two opposing teams, properly of nine players each, on a field with four bases forming a diamond. 2. the ball used in this game.
**base·board** (bās′bôrd′, -bōrd′), *n.* 1. a board or molding covering a plaster wall where it meets the floor. 2. any board serving as a base.
**base·born** (bās′bôrn′), *adj.* 1. of humble birth or origin. 2. of illegitimate birth.
**base·burn·er, base-burn·er** (bās′būr′nēr), *n.* any stove or furnace in which more coal is fed automatically from above when that at the base is consumed.
**base hit,** in *baseball,* a hit by which the batter gets on base without benefit of an opponent's error and without forcing out a base runner.
**Ba·sel** (bä′z'l), *n.* a city in N Switzerland, on the Rhine: pop., 213,000: also **Basle.**
**base·less** (bās′lis), *adj.* having no basis in fact; unfounded. —**base′less·ness,** *n.*
**base line,** 1. a line serving as a base. 2. in *baseball,* the straight line between any two consecutive bases.
**base·man** (bās′mən), *n.* [*pl.* -MEN], in *baseball,* a player stationed at first, second, or third base.
**base·ment** (bās′mənt), *n.* [*base, v.* or *n.* + *-ment*], 1. the lower part of a wall or walls. 2. the story of a building just below the main floor, usually below the surface of the ground.
**base metal,** 1, any of the common, nonprecious metals. 2. the metal under a plating.
**base runner,** in *baseball,* any member of the team at bat who is on base.
**bas·es** (bās′iz), *n.* pl. of **base.**
**ba·ses** (bā′sēz), *n.* pl. of **basis.**
**bash** (bash), *v.t.* [echoic; akin to (? <) ON. **hyp.** *basca,* to strike; see BASK], [Colloq.], to strike with a violent blow; smash (*in*). *n.* [Colloq.], a violent blow.
**bash·ful** (bash′fəl), *adj.* [ME. *baschen,* to abash; + *-ful*], showing social timidity; shy.—**bash′ful·ly,** *adv.* —**bash′ful·ness,** *n.*
**bas·ic** (bās′ik), *adj.* 1. of or at the base; forming a

base or basis; fundamental. 2. in *chemistry*, of, having the nature of, or containing a base; alkaline. —**bas'i·cal·ly**, *adv.*

**Basic English,** a simplified form of English for international communication and for first steps into full English, invented by Charles K. Ogden (1889–1957): it consists of a selected vocabulary of 850 essential words and is copyrighted.

**bas·il** (baz''l), *n.* [< OFr. < ML. < Gr. *basilikos*, royal < *basileus*, king], a fragrant plant of the mint family, used as an herb.

**bas·i·lar** (bas'ə-lēr), *adj.* 1. of or at the base, esp. of the skull. 2. basic; basal. Also **bas'i·lar'y.**

**ba·sil·i·ca** (bə-sil'i-kə), *n.* [*pl.* -CAS], [L.; Gr. *basilikē* (*stoa*), royal (portico)], 1. in ancient times, a rectangular building with a broad nave flanked by colonnaded aisles, used as a courtroom, etc. 2. an early Christian church shaped like this. —**ba·sil'i·can,** *adj.*

**bas·i·lisk** (bas'ə-lisk'), *n.* [< L.; Gr. dim. of *basileus*, king], 1. a mythical, lizardlike monster with fatal breath and glance. 2. a tropical American lizard with a crest on its back and tail.

**ba·sin** (bā's'n), *n.* [< OFr. < LL. < *bacca*, water vessel], 1. a wide, shallow container for liquid; bowl. 2. its contents or capacity. 3. a sink. 4. a pond or other large hollow containing water. 5. a bay. 6. the area drained by a river and its branches: in full, **river basin.** 7. a great hollow in the earth's surface filled by an ocean: in full, **ocean basin.** —**ba'sined,** *adj.*—**ba'sin·like',** *adj.*

**ba·sis** (bā'sis), *n.* [*pl.* -SES (-sēz)], [L.; Gr., a step], 1. the base or foundation of anything. 2. a principal constituent. 3. the basic principle or theory, as of a system of knowledge.

**bask** (bask, bäsk), *v.i.* & *v.t.* [ME. *basken*, to beat, strike; cf. BASH], to expose (oneself) pleasantly to warmth: as, he *basked* in the sun: often figuratively, as, he *basked* in her favor.

**bas·ket** (bas'kit, bäs'-), *n.* [< OCelt. *bascauda*, crock with woven pattern], 1. a container made of interwoven cane, strips of wood, etc. 2. its contents or capacity. 3. anything used or shaped like a basket. 4. a passenger cabin hung from a balloon. 5. in *basketball*, *a*) the goal, a net shaped like a basket open at the bottom. *b*) a scoring toss of the ball through this net. —**bas'ket·like',** *adj.*

**bas·ket·ball** (bas'kit-bôl', bäs'-), *n.* 1. a game played by two teams of five players each, in a zoned floor area with a raised basket at either end through which the ball must be tossed. 2. the inflated, leather-covered ball used in this game.

**bas·ket·ry** (bas'kit-ri, bäs'-), *n.* 1. the craft of making baskets. 2. basketware.

**basket weave,** a weave of fabrics resembling the weave used in basketmaking.

**bas·ket·work** (bas'kit-wũrk', bäs'-), *n.* work that is interlaced or woven like a basket.

**Basle** (bäl), *n.* Basel.

**ba·so·phile** (bā'sə-fil', -fil), *n.* [< *basic* + *-phile*], in *biology*, a cell or tissue that is readily stained with basic dyes. —**ba'so·phil'ic,** *adj.*

**Basque** (bask), *n.* 1. any member of a certain people living in the W Pyrenees. 2. their language. *adj.* of the Basques or their language.

**basque** (bask), *n.* [Fr. < Pr. *basto* < ?], a woman's blouse or tunic with a tight-fitting waist.

**Basque Provinces,** a region in N Spain inhabited by Basques.

**bas-re·lief** (bä'ri-lēf', bä'ri-lēf', bas'-), *n.* [Fr.; It. *basso-rilievo;* see BASSO & RELIEF], sculpture in which the figures project only a little from the background: also **bas·so-re·lie·vo** (bas'ō-ri-lē'vō), [*pl.* -VOS].

**bass** (bās), *n.* [ME. *bas;* see BASE (low)], 1. the lowest male singing voice. 2. the lowest part in vocal or instrumental music. 3. a singer or instrument having a very low range; specif., a bass viol. *adj.* 1. having, or in, the range of a bass. 2. for a bass or basses.

**bass** (bas), *n.* [*pl.* BASS, BASSES (-iz); see PLURAL, II, D, 2], [< ME. *bars;* AS. *bears*], an edible perchlike fish found in fresh or salt water.

**bass** (bas), *n.* [< ME. *bast;* AS. *bæst*, inner bark of trees], 1. bast. 2. basswood.

**bass clef** (bās), in *music*, a sign on a staff indicating that the notes on the staff are below middle C: symbol, F.

**bass drum** (bās), the largest and lowest-toned of the double-headed drums.

**bas·set** (bas'it), *n.* [OFr.; orig., dim. of *bas*, low], a kind of hunting hound with a long body, short legs, and long, drooping ears: also **basset hound.**

**bass horn** (bās), a tuba.

**bas·si·net** (bas'ə-net', bas'ə-net'), *n.* [< OFr. dim. of *bacin;* see BASIN], a large basket used as a baby's bed, often hooded and on wheels.

**bas·so** (bas'ō; It. bäs'sô), *n.* [*pl.* -SOS; It. -SI (-sē)], [It. < LL. *bassus*, low], a bass voice, voice part, or singer. *adj.* bass.

**bas·soon** (ba-sōōn', bə-), *n.* [< Fr. < It. < *basso;* see BASSO], a double-reed bass musical instrument of the wood-wind class, with a long, curved mouthpiece. —**bas·soon'ist,** *n.*

BASSOON

**bass viol** (bās), the largest and deepest-toned musical instrument of the viol group, resembling a huge violin: also called *double bass, contrabass.*

**bass·wood** (bas'wood'), *n.* 1. a linden. 2. its wood. *adj.* made of basswood.

**bast** (bast), *n.* [AS. *bæst*], 1. phloem. 2. fiber obtained from phloem, used in making ropes, etc.

**bas·tard** (bas'tērd), *n.* [OFr. < Goth. *bansts*, a barn; + *-ard*], 1. an illegitimate child. 2. anything inferior, spurious, or varying from standard. *adj.* 1. of illegitimate birth or origin. 2. sham, inferior, not standard, etc. The word is widely and vulgarly used as an indiscriminate term of abuse and, sometimes, of playful affection. —**bas'tard·ly,** *adj.*—**bas'tar·dy,** *n.*

**bas·tard·ize** (bas'tēr-dīz'), *v.t.* [-IZED, -IZING], 1. to make, declare, or show to be a bastard. 2. to misuse; corrupt. *v.i.* to become inferior. —**bas'tard·i·za'tion,** *n.*

**baste** (bāst), *v.t.* [BASTED, BASTING], [< OFr. < OHG. *bastjan*, to sew with bast], to sew with long, loose stitches so as to keep the parts together until properly sewed. —**bast'er,** *n.*

**baste** (bāst), *v.t.* [BASTED, BASTING], [< OFr. < *bassiner*, to moisten < *bassin;* see BASIN], to moisten (meat) with melted butter, drippings, etc. while roasting.

**baste** (bāst), *v.t.* [BASTED, BASTING], [ON. *beysta*], 1. to strike; beat. 2. to abuse.

**bas·tille, bas·tile** (bas-tēl'; Fr. bȧs'tē'y'), *n.* [Fr. < OFr. *bastir*, to build; see BASTION], a prison. —**the Bastille,** a fortress in Paris used as a prison until destroyed (July 14, 1789) in the French Revolution.

**bas·ti·na·do** (bas'tə-nā'dō), *n.* [*pl.* -DOES], [< Sp. < *baston*, a stick], 1. a beating with a stick, usually on the bottoms of the feet: an Oriental method of punishment. 2. a stick; cudgel. *v.t.* [-DOED, -DOING], to inflict the bastinado on.

**bast·ing** (bāst'iŋ), *n.* 1. the act of sewing with loose, temporary stitches. 2. *pl.* loose, temporary stitches. 3. a thread for basting.

**bas·tion** (bas'chən, -ti-ən), *n.* [Fr. < It. < *bastire*, to build < Gmc. *bastjan*, to make with bast], 1. a projection from a fortification. 2. any strong defense. —**bas'tioned,** *adj.*

**Ba·su·to·land** (bə-sōō'tō-land'), *n.* Lesotho: the former name.

**bat** (bat), *n.* [AS. *batt*, cudgel < Celt.], 1. any stout club or stick. 2. a club used in striking the ball in baseball and cricket. 3. the process of batting. 4. a turn at batting. 5. [Brit.], a batsman at cricket. 6. [Colloq.], a blow or hit. 7. [Slang], a spree. *v.t.* [BATTED, BATTING], to strike with or as with a bat. *v.i.* to take a turn at batting. —**at bat,** having a turn at batting. —**bat around,** [Slang], 1. to travel about. 2. to discuss (an idea, plan, etc.). —**go to bat for,** [Slang], to defend; advocate.

**bat** (bat), *n.* [altered < ME. *bakke* < ON.], a mouselike mammal with a furry body and membranous wings, usually seen flying about at night. —**blind as a bat,** entirely blind. —**have bats in the belfry,** [Slang], to be insane; have crazy notions.

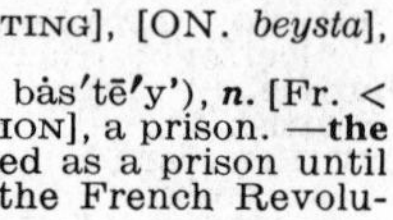

BAT (10 in. across)

**bat** (bat), *v.t.* [BATTED, BATTING], [< OFr. *batre;* see BATTER (to beat)], [Colloq.], to wink. —**not bat an eye,** [Colloq.], not show surprise.

**Ba·taan** (bə-tän', bə-tan', ba-tan'), *n.* a peninsula west of Manila Bay in the Philippines: famous for the heroic stand made by U.S. soldiers against Japanese forces in 1942.

**Ba·ta·vi·a** (bə-tā'vi-ə; D. bä-tä'vi-ä), *n.* Jakarta: the former, Dutch name.

**batch** (bach), *n.* [AS. *bacan*, to bake], 1. the amount (of bread, etc.) produced at one baking. 2. the quantity of anything needed for or made in one operation or lot. 3. a number of things or persons taken as a group.

**bate** (bāt), *v.t. & v.i.* [BATED, BATING], [< *abate*], to abate; reduce. —**with bated breath,** with the breath held in because of fear, excitement, etc.

**ba·teau** (ba-tō′), *n.* [*pl.* -TEAUX (-tōz′)], [Fr. < OFr. *batel* < AS. *bat*, boat], a lightweight, flat-bottomed river boat.

**bat·fish** (bat′fish′), *n.* [*pl.* see FISH], any of various fishes resembling a bat.

**Bath** (bath, bäth), *n.* 1. a city in SW England, known for its hot springs: pop., 81,000.

**bath** (bath, bäth), *n.* [*pl.* BATHS (bathz, bäthz)], [AS. *bæth*], 1. a washing or dipping of a thing, especially the body, in water or other liquid, etc. 2. water or other liquid for bathing, or for dipping or soaking anything. 3. a container for such liquid. 4. a bathtub. 5. a bathroom. 6. a building or set of rooms for bathing. 7. *often pl.* a resort where bathing is part of the medical treatment. *v.t. & v.i.* to soak or steep in a bath.

**bathe** (bāth), *v.t.* [BATHED (bāthd), BATHING], [AS. *bathian* < *bæth*, bath], 1. to put into a liquid; immerse. 2. to give a bath to; wash. 3. to wet; moisten. 4. to cover as if with liquid: as, trees ***bathed*** in moonlight. *v.i.* 1. to take a bath. 2. to go into or be in water so as to swim, cool oneself, etc. 3. to soak oneself in some substance or influence. *n.* [Brit.], a swim. —**bath′er,** *n.*

**bath·house** (bath′hous′, bäth′-), *n.* 1. a building equipped for bathing. 2. a building used by bathers for changing clothes.

**bath·i·nette** (bath′ə-net′, bäth′ə-net′), *n.* [< *bath*, after *bassinet*], a portable folding bathtub for babies, made of rubberized cloth, etc.: a trademark (**Bathinette**).

**bathing suit,** a garment designed for swimming.

**ba·thos** (bā′thos), *n.* [Gr., depth], 1. change from the exalted to the trite and trivial in writing or speech; anticlimax. 2. false or overdone pathos. —**ba·thet·ic** (bə-thet′ik), *adj.*

**bath·robe** (bath′rōb′, bäth′-), *n.* a long, loose-fitting garment with sleeves, for wear to and from the bath, in lounging, etc.

**bath·room** (bath′rōōm′, bäth′room′), *n.* 1. a room to bathe in, etc. 2. a toilet.

**bath·tub** (bath′tub′, bäth′-), *n.* a tub to bathe in; esp., a bathroom fixture for this purpose.

**bath·y·sphere** (bath′i-sfêr′), *n.* [< Gr. *bathys*, deep; + *-sphere*], a round, watertight chamber with windows, in which men can be lowered into the sea depths to study the plants and animals there.

**ba·tik** (bə-tēk′, bä′tēk, bat′ik), *n.* [Malay], 1. a method of dyeing designs on cloth by coating with removable wax the parts not to be dyed. 2. cloth thus decorated. 3. a design thus made. *adj.* of or like batik. *v.t.* to dye or design by means of batik.

**ba·tiste** (ba-tēst′, bə-), *n.* [Fr.; OFr. *baptiste*: so called from the supposed original maker, *Baptiste* of Cambrai], a fine, thin cotton fabric.

**ba·ton** (ba-ton′, bat′'n; Fr. bȧ′tōn′), *n.* [< Fr. < OFr. < LL. *bastum*, a stick], 1. a staff serving as a symbol of office. 2. a slender stick used by the conductor of an orchestra, etc. for directing. 3. a hollow metal rod twirled in a showy way, as by a drum majorette.

**Bat·on Rouge** (bat′'n rōōzh′), the capital of Louisiana, on the Mississippi: pop., 152,000.

**Ba·tra·chi·a** (bə-trā′ki-ə), *n.pl.* [< Gr. < *batrachos*, frog], 1. amphibians without tails, as frogs and toads. 2. loosely, all amphibians. —**ba·tra′chi·an,** *adj. & n.*

**bats·man** (bats′mən), *n.* [*pl.* -MEN], in *baseball & cricket*, the batter.

**bat·tal·ion** (bə-tal′yən), *n.* [< Fr. < It. < L. *battalia;* see BATTLE], 1. a large group of soldiers arrayed for battle. 2. a large group somewhat like this: as, a *battalion* of strikers. 3. *pl.* military forces. 4. a tactical unit now usually made up of four infantry companies and a headquarters company, or four artillery batteries and a headquarters battery: three battalions form a regiment.

**bat·ten** (bat′'n), *n.* [see BATON], 1. a sawed strip of wood, flooring, etc. 2. a strip of wood put over a seam between boards as a fastening or covering. 3. a strip used to fasten canvas over a ship's hatchways. *v.t.* to fasten or supply with battens (with *up* or *down*).

**bat·ten** (bat′'n), *v.i.* [ON. *batna*, to improve], to grow fat; thrive. *v.t.* to fatten up; overfeed.

**bat·ter** (bat′ẽr), *v.t.* [OFr. *batre, battre* < LL. <L. *battuere*, to beat; also, in part, freq. of Eng. *bat*, to strike], 1. to beat or strike with blow after blow; pound. 2. to injure by pounding, hard wear, or use. *v.i.* to pound noisily.

**bat·ter** (bat′ẽr), *n.* in *baseball & cricket*, the player whose turn it is to bat; batsman.

**bat·ter** (bat′ẽr), *n.* [< OFr.; prob. < *batre;* see BATTER (to beat)], a thin mixture of flour, milk, etc., used in making cakes, waffles, etc.

**bat·ter·ing-ram** (bat′ẽr-iŋ-ram′), *n.* 1. an ancient military machine having a heavy wooden beam for battering down gates, walls, etc. 2. anything used like this to force entrance.

**bat·ter·y** (bat′ẽr-i), *n.* [*pl.* -IES], [< Fr. < *battre;* see BATTER (to beat)], 1. a battering; beating. 2. any set of devices arranged, connected, or used together. 3. in *baseball*, the pitcher and the catcher. 4. in *electricity*, a cell or connected group of cells storing an electrical charge and capable of furnishing a current. 5. in *law*, any illegal beating of another person: see **assault and battery.** 6. in *military science, a)* an emplacement or fortification equipped with heavy guns. *b)* a set of heavy guns. *c)* the men who operate such guns: usually the basic unit of field artillery.

**bat·tik** (bat′ik), *n., adj., v.t.* batik.

**bat·ting** (bat′iŋ), *n.* [see BAT (a club)], cotton or wool fiber wadded in sheets.

**batting average,** 1. a measure of a baseball player's batting effectiveness, figured by dividing the number of safe hits by the number of times at bat. 2. [Colloq.], the average level of competence in any activity.

**bat·tle** (bat′'l), *n.* [< OFr. < L. *battalia*, < *battuere;* see BATTER (to beat)], 1. a large-scale fight between armed forces. 2. armed fighting; combat or war. 3. any fight or conflict; struggle. *v.t. & v.i.* [-TLED, -TLING], to fight. —**give** (or **do**) **battle,** to engage in battle; fight. —**bat′tler,** *n.*

**bat·tle-ax, bat·tle-axe** (bat′'l-aks′), *n.* 1. a heavy ax formerly used as a weapon of war. 2. [Slang], a woman who is harsh, domineering, etc.

**battle cruiser,** a large warship with longer range and greater speed and maneuverability than a battleship but less heavily armored.

**battle cry,** 1. a shout used by troops in battle. 2. a slogan for any struggle, contest, etc.

**bat·tle·dore** (bat′'l-dôr′, -dōr′), *n.* [? < Pr. *batedor*, beater], 1. a racket or paddle used to hit a shuttlecock back and forth in a game like badminton. 2. the game itself: in full, **battledore and shuttlecock.**

**battle fatigue,** combat fatigue.

**bat·tle·field** (bat′'l-fēld′), *n.* 1. the place where a battle takes place or took place. 2. any area of conflict. Also **bat′tle·ground′.**

**battle front,** the sector where actual combat is taking place between armed forces.

**bat·tle·ment** (bat′'l-mənt), *n.* [< OFr. < *batailler*, to fortify], 1. a low wall, as on top of a tower, with open spaces for shooting. 2. an architectural decoration like this.

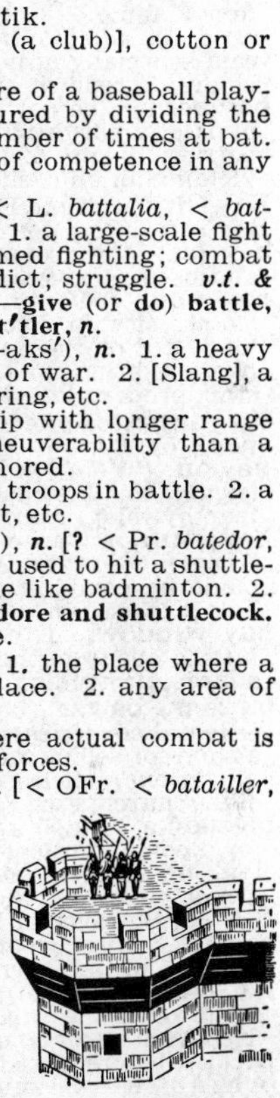
BATTLEMENT

**battle royal,** [*pl.* BATTLES ROYAL], 1. a fight involving many contestants; free-for-all. 2. a long, bitterly fought battle or dispute.

**bat·tle·ship** (bat′'l-ship′), *n.* any of a class of large warships with the biggest guns and very heavy armor: also [Slang], **bat′tle·wag′on.**

**bat·ty** (bat′i), *adj.* [-TIER, -TIEST], [< *bat* (the mammal)], [Slang], 1. insane; crazy. 2. odd; eccentric.

**bau·ble** (bô′b'l), *n.* [< OFr. redupl. of *bel* < L. *bellus*, pretty], a showy trifle; trinket; gewgaw.

**Bau·de·laire, Pierre Charles** (pyâr shȧrl bō′dlâr′), 1821–1867; French poet and essayist.

**baulk** (bôk), *n., v.t. & v.i.* balk.

**baux·ite** (bôk′sīt, bō′zīt), *n.* [Fr. < *Baux*, town near Arles], the claylike ore from which aluminum is obtained.

**Ba·var·i·a** (bə-vâr′i-ə), *n.* a division of southern Germany: capital, Munich: German name, *Bayern.* —**Ba·var′i·an,** *adj. & n.*

**bawd** (bôd), *n.* [? < OFr. *baudetrot*, pander < *baud*, gay, bold < OHG. *bald*, bold], a person, now usually a woman, who keeps a house of prostitution.

**bawd·y** (bô′di), *adj.* [-IER, -IEST], indecent; obscene. —**bawd′i·ly,** *adv.* —**bawd′i·ness,** *n.*

**bawd·y·house** (bô′di-hous′), *n.* a brothel.

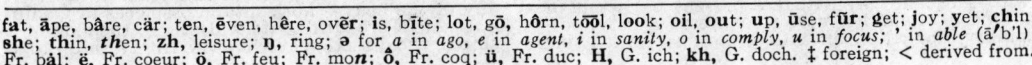

**bawl** (bôl), *v.i. & v.t.* [< ON. *baula*, to bellow], 1. to shout or call out noisily; bellow. 2. [Colloq.], to weep noisily. *n.* 1. a bellow. 2. [Colloq.], a noisy weeping. —**bawl out,** [Slang], to give a scolding to; reprimand. —**bawl′er,** *n.*

**bay** (bā), *n.* [< Fr. < LL. *baia*], a part of a sea or lake, indenting the shore line; wide inlet.

**bay** (bā), *n.* [< OFr. *baer* < LL. *badare*, to gape], 1. an opening or alcove marked off by columns, etc. 2. a part of a building projecting from the main part; wing. 3. a recess in a wall line, as for a window. 4. a bay window.

**bay** (bā), *v.i.* [< OFr. < LL. *badare*, to gape], to bark in long, deep tones. *v.t.* 1. to bark at. 2. to bring to or hold at bay. *n.* 1. a baying. 2. the situation of or as of a hunted animal forced to turn and fight. —**at bay,** 1. with escape cut off; cornered. 2. held off: as, the bear kept the hunters *at bay*. —**bring to bay,** to force into a situation that makes escape impossible.

**bay** (bā), *n.* [< OFr. < L. *baca*, berry], 1. an evergreen tree with glossy, leathery leaves; laurel tree. 2. *pl.* a wreath of bay leaves, a classical token of honor given to poets and conquerors; hence, 3. *pl.* honor; fame.

**bay** (bā), *adj.* [< Fr. < L. *badius*], reddish-brown: said especially of horses. *n.* 1. a horse, etc. of this color. 2. reddish brown.

**bay·ber·ry** (bā′ber′i), *n.* [*pl.* -RIES], 1. the wax myrtle, a shrub with clusters of wax-coated gray berries. 2. any of these berries. 3. a tropical tree yielding an oil used in bay rum.

**Bay City,** a city in E Michigan: pop., 54,000.

**Bay·ern** (bī′ẽrn), *n.* Bavaria: the German name.

**bay leaf,** the aromatic leaf of the bay tree, dried and used as a seasoning.

**bay·o·net** (bā′ə-nit, bā′ə-net′), *n.* [< Fr. < *Bayonne*, city in France], a detachable daggerlike blade put on the muzzle end of a rifle, for hand-to-hand fighting. *v.t. & v.i.* [-NETED, -NETING], to stab, prod, or kill with a bayonet.

**Ba·yonne** (bā-yōn′), *n.* a city in NE New Jersey: pop., 74,000.

**bay·ou** (bī′o͞o), *n.* [Am. Fr.; prob. < Choctaw *bayuk*, small stream], in the southern U.S., a marshy inlet or outlet of a lake, river, etc.

**bay rum,** an aromatic liquid formerly obtained from leaves of the West Indian bayberry tree, now made by combining certain oils, water, and alcohol: it is used in medicines and cosmetics.

**bay window,** 1. a window or series of windows jutting out from the wall of a building. 2. [Slang], a large, protruding belly.

**ba·zaar, ba·zar** (bə-zär′), *n.* [Per. *bāzār*], 1. in Oriental countries, a market or street of shops. 2. a shop for selling various kinds of goods. 3. a sale of various articles, usually to raise money for a club, church, etc.

**ba·zoo·ka** (bə-zo͞o′kə), *n.* [echoic term orig. coined for a comic musical horn], a weapon of metal tubing, for aiming and launching electrically fired armor-piercing rockets.

**B.B.A.,** Bachelor of Business Administration.

**B.B.C.,** British Broadcasting Corporation.

**bbl.,** [*pl.* BBLS.], barrel.

**BB (shot),** (bē′bē′), [a designation of the size], a size of shot measuring .18 of an inch in diameter, fired from an air rifle (**BB gun**).

**B.C.,** 1. before Christ. 2. British Columbia.

**bch.,** [*pl.* BCHS.], bunch.

**bd.,** [*pl.* BDS.], 1. board. 2. bond. 3. bound. 4. bundle.

**B/D,** bank draft.

**B.D.,** Bachelor of Divinity.

**bd. ft.,** board foot; board feet.

**bdl.,** [*pl.* BDLS.], bundle.

**be** (bē; *unstressed*, bi), *v.i.* [WAS (wuz, wäz, wəz) or WERE (wũr), BEEN (bin, ben, bēn), BEING (bē′iŋ)], [AS. *beon*], 1. to exist; live: as, Caesar *is* no more. 2. to happen or occur: as, when will the wedding *be*? 3. to remain or continue: as, will he *be* here long? 4. to come to; belong: as, peace *be* with you. *Note*: A. *be* is often used to link its subject to a predicate nominative, adjective, or pronoun and is sometimes equivalent to the mathematical sign (=). Examples: he *is* handsome, that coat *is* fifty dollars, let x *be* y. B. *be* is also used as an auxiliary: (1) with the past participle of a transitive verb to form the passive voice: as, he will *be* whipped. (2) with the past participle of certain intransitive verbs to form the perfect tense: as, Christ *is* risen. (3) with the present participle of another verb to express continuation: as, the player *is* running with the ball. (4) with the present participle or infinitive of another verb to express futurity, possibility, obligation, intention, etc.: as, he *is* going next week, she *is* to wash the dishes. *Be* is conjugated, in the present indicative: (I) *am*, (he, she, it) *is*, (we, you, they) *are;* in the past indicative: (I, he, she, it) *was*, (we, you, they) *were*. Archaic forms are (thou) *art*, *wert*, *wast*. The present subjunctive is *be*, the past subjunctive *were*.

**be-,** [AS. < *be*, *bi*, about, near], a prefix used variously with verbs, nouns, and adjectives to mean: 1. *around*, as in *besprinkle*, *beset*. 2. *completely, thoroughly*, as in *bedeck*, *besmear*. 3. *away*, as in *bereave*, *betake*. 4. *about*, as in *bethink*, *bemoan*. 5. *make*, as in *besot*, *bepretty*. 6. *furnish with*, *affect by*, as in *befriend*, *bedizen*, *becloud*. 7. *covered with, furnished with* (*to excess*), as in *bemedaled*, *bewhiskered*.

**Be,** in *chemistry*, beryllium.

**B.E.,** 1. Bachelor of Education. 2. Bachelor of Engineering. 3. Board of Education.

**B.E., B/E, b.e.,** bill of exchange.

**beach** (bēch), *n.* [Eng. dial., orig., pebbles, shingles], a nearly level stretch of pebbles and sand beside a sea, lake, etc.; sandy shore; strand. *v.t. & v.i.* to ground (a boat) on a beach. —**on the beach,** 1. not aboard a ship. 2. unemployed. —**beach′less,** *adj.*

**beach·comb·er** (bēch′kōm′ẽr), *n.* 1. a long wave rolling ashore; comber. 2. a man who loafs on beaches or wharves, especially on the South Sea Islands, living on what he can beg or find.

**beach·head** (bēch′hed′), *n.* a position established by invading troops on an enemy shore.

**bea·con** (bē′kən), *n.* [AS. *beacen*], 1. a fire or other light for warning or guiding. 2. a tower, as a lighthouse, from which signals are given. 3. something serving as a signal, summons, etc. 4. a guiding signal given by radio to airplanes; beam. *v.t.* 1. to provide or mark with signals or lights. 2. to guide by or as by beacons. *v.i.* 1. to shine brightly. 2. to serve as a summons or guide. —**bea′con·less,** *adj.*

**bead** (bēd), *n.* [ME. *bede*, prayer bead < AS. *biddan*, to pray], 1. a small, usually round piece of glass, wood, metal, etc., pierced for stringing. 2. *pl.* a string of beads; necklace. 3. *pl.* a rosary. 4. any small, round object, as the front sight of a rifle. 5. a drop or bubble. 6. foam, as on beer. 7. a narrow, half-round molding. *v.t.* 1. to decorate or string with beads. 2. to string like beads. *v.i.* to form a bead or beads. —**count** (or **tell** or **say**) **one's beads,** to say prayers with a rosary. —**draw a bead on,** to take careful aim at. —**bead′ed,** *adj.*

**bead·ing** (bēd′iŋ), *n.* 1. decorative work in beads. 2. a molding resembling a row of beads. 3. a narrow, half-round molding. 4. a narrow trimming. 5. a beadlike openwork.

**bea·dle** (bē′d′l), *n.* [< OFr. < Frankish *bidal*, messenger < *bieten*, to bid], formerly, a minor parish officer in the Church of England, who kept order in church, etc.

**beads·man** (bēdz′mən), *n.* [*pl.* -MEN], [see BEAD], 1. one who prays for another's soul, especially one hired to do so. 2. a person in a poorhouse. —**beads′-wom′an** [*pl.* -WOMEN], *n.fem.*

**bead·y** (bēd′i), *adj.* [-IER, -IEST], 1. small, round, and glittering like a bead. 2. decorated with beads. 3. covered with drops of sweat, etc.

**bea·gle** (bē′g′l), *n.* [? < OFr. *begueule*, wide-throat], a small hound with a smooth coat, short legs, and drooping ears.

BEAGLE
(13–15 in. high at shoulder)

**beak** (bēk), *n.* [< OFr. < L. *beccus* < Gaul.], 1. a bird's bill; esp., the large, sharp, horny bill of a bird of prey. 2. the beaklike mouth part of various insects, fishes, etc. 3. the spout of a pitcher. 4. the ram projecting from the prow of an ancient warship. 5. [Slang], the nose. —**beaked** (bēkt, bēk′id), *adj.* —**beak′-less,** *adj.* —**beak′like′,** *adj.*

**beak·er** (bēk′ẽr), *n.* [< ON. *bikarr* < LL. < Gr. *bikos*, wine jar], 1. a large wine cup; goblet. 2. its contents. 3. a jarlike container of glass or metal with a lip for pouring, used by chemists, etc.

**beam** (bēm), *n.* [< AS.; akin to G. *baum*, a tree], 1. the squared-off trunk of a tree. 2. a long, thick piece of wood, metal, or stone, used in building. 3. the part of a plow to which the handles, share, etc. are attached. 4. the crossbar of a balance. 5. the balance itself. 6. the shank of an anchor. 7. any of the heavy, horizontal crosspieces of a ship. 8. a ship's breadth at its widest. 9. the side of a ship or the direction out sidewise from a ship. 10. a slender shaft of light or other radiation. 11. a radiant look, smile, etc. 12. in *radio*, *a*) a signal sent continuously in one direction as a guide for aircraft. *b*) the angle at which a microphone receives or a loud-speaker transmits most effectively. *c*) the maximum effective range of a microphone or loud-speaker. *v.t.* 1. to give out (shafts of light); radiate. 2. to direct or aim (a radio signal, program, etc.). *v.i.* 1. to shine brightly. 2. to smile warmly. —**off the beam,** 1. not following a guiding beam, as an airplane; hence, 2. [Slang], wrong; incorrect. —**on the beam,** 1. at right angles to the ship's keel. 2. following a guiding beam, as an airplane; hence, 3. [Slang], working or functioning well; alert, keen, correct, etc.—**beamed,** *adj.* —**beam′ing,** *adj.* —**beam′ing·ly,** *adv.* —**beam′less,** *adj.* —**beam′like′,** *adj.*

**beam-ends** (bēm′endz′), *n.pl.* the ends of a ship's beams. —**on the beam-ends** (or **beam's ends**), tipping so far to the side as to almost overturn.

**beam·y** (bēm′i), *adj.* [-IER, -IEST], 1. sending out beams of light; radiant. 2. beamlike; broad.

**bean** (bēn), *n.* [AS. *bean*], 1. the edible, smooth, kidney-shaped seed of certain plants of the pea family. 2. a pod with such seeds. 3. a plant bearing such pods. 4. any of various bean-shaped seeds. 5. [Slang], the head. *v.t.* [Slang], to hit on the head.

**bean·ie** (bēn′i), *n.* [Slang], any of various kinds of skullcap worn by women and children.

**bear** (bâr), *v.t.* [BORE (bôr, bōr) or *archaic* BARE (bâr), BORNE or BORN (bôrn, bōrn), BEARING], [AS. *beran;* akin to L. *ferre*, Gr. *pherein*], 1. to carry; transport. 2. to have, show, or wear: as, the letter *bore* his signature. 3. to give birth to. 4. to support or sustain. 5. to sustain the burden of; undergo: as, *bear* the expenses. 6. to undergo successfully; withstand: as, they *bore* the torture. 7. to be capable of withstanding; permit of: as, this will *bear* investigation. 8. to carry or conduct (oneself): as, he *bears* himself well. 9. to carry over or hold (a sentiment): as, *bear* a grudge. 10. to move or push as if carrying: as, the crowd *bore* us along. 11. to give or supply: as, he will *bear* witness. *v.i.* 1. to have the strength to endure or suffer. 2. to be productive: as, the tree *bears* well. 3. to extend, lie, or move in a given direction: as, the ship *bore* west. 4. to be oppressive; weigh: as, grief *bears* heavily on her. —**bear down,** 1. to press or push down; hence, 2. to make a strong effort. —**bear down on,** 1. to exert pressure on; hence, 2. to make a strong effort toward accomplishing. 3. to move toward; approach. —**bear on,** 1. to have relation to: as, his story *bears on* the crime. 2. to be aimed in the direction of. —**bear out,** to support or confirm. —**bear up,** to endure, as under a strain. —**bear with,** to put up patiently with; tolerate.

**bear** (bâr), *n.* [*pl.* BEARS, BEAR; see PLURAL, II, D, 1], [AS. *bera*, orig. sense "the brown one"], 1. a large, heavy, clumsy mammal with shaggy fur and a very short tail, native to temperate and arctic zones. 2. [B-], either of two constellations in the northern hemisphere, the **Great Bear** and the **Little Bear.** 3. a person who is clumsy, rude, etc. 4. in the *stock exchange*, etc., a speculator who sells shares, commodities, etc. hoping to buy them back later at a lower price. *adj.* of or favorable to such speculators: as, a *bear* market. *v.t.* [-ED, -ING], to try to reduce the price of or prices in. —**be a bear for punishment,** to be able to withstand rough treatment, hardship, etc. —**bear′like′,** *adj.*

**bear·a·ble** (bâr′ə-b'l), *adj.* that can be endured. —**bear′a·ble·ness,** *n.* —**bear′a·bly,** *adv.*

**beard** (bêrd), *n.* [AS.; akin to G. *bart*], 1. the hair growing on the face, especially on the chin and cheeks, of a man; whiskers. 2. any beardlike part, as of certain animals. 3. a hairy outgrowth on the head of certain grains, etc.; awn. 4. anything that projects like a beard; barb or hook. *v.t.* 1. to grasp by the beard; hence, 2. to oppose courageously; defy. 3. to provide with a beard. —**beard′ed,** *adj.* —**beard′less,** *adj.* —**beard′like′,** *adj.*

**Beard, Daniel Carter** (bêrd), 1850–1941; U.S. naturalist; founder of Boy Scouts in the U.S.

**bear·er** (bâr′ẽr), *n.* 1. a person or thing that bears, or carries. 2. a plant or tree that bears fruit. 3. a pallbearer. 4. a person presenting for payment a check, note, money order, etc. *adj.* made out to the bearer: as, *bearer* bonds.

**bear·ing** (bâr′iŋ), *n.* 1. way of carrying and conducting oneself; carriage; manner. 2. a support or supporting part. 3. a producing; birth. 4. ability to produce. 5. anything produced, as a crop. 6. endurance. 7. *often in pl.* relative position or direction: as, the ship lost her *bearings*. 8. application; relation; relevance: as, the evidence had no *bearing* on the case. 9. in *heraldry*, any figure on the field. 10. in *mechanics*, a part of a machine on which another part revolves, slides, etc.

**bear·ish** (bâr′ish), *adj.* 1. bearlike; rude, rough, surly, etc. 2. directed toward or causing a lowering of prices in the stock exchange, etc. —**bear′ish·ly,** *adv.* —**bear′ish·ness,** *n.*

**bear·skin** (bâr′skin′), *n.* 1. the skin of a bear. 2. a rug, coat, etc. made of this.

**beast** (bēst), *n.* [< OFr. < L. *bestia*], 1. originally, any animal except man. 2. any large, four-footed animal. 3. qualities like an animal's. 4. one who is brutal, gross, stupid, etc. —**beast′like′,** *adj.*

**beast·ly** (bēst′li), *adj.* [-LIER, -LIEST], 1. of or like a beast; brutal, gross, etc. 2. [Colloq.], disagreeable; disgusting. *adv.* [British], very: as, *beastly* bad news. —**beast′li·ness,** *n.*

**beast of burden,** any animal used for carrying things.

**beast of prey,** any animal that hunts and kills other animals for food.

**beat** (bēt), *v.t.* [BEAT, BEATEN, BEATING], [AS. *beatan*], 1. to strike repeatedly; pound. 2. to punish by so striking; flog. 3. to dash repeatedly against: as, waves *beat* the shore. 4. to make flat or smooth by treading: as, we *beat* a path. 5. to shape by hammering; forge. 6. to mix by stirring or striking repeatedly with a utensil. 7. to move (wings, etc.) up and down; flap. 8. to hunt through; search: as, the posse *beat* the countryside. 9. to make or force, as by hitting or flailing: as, he *beat* his way through the crowd. 10. to outdo or defeat. 11. to mark (time) by tapping, etc. 12. to sound or signal, as by a drumbeat. 13. [Colloq.], to baffle; puzzle. 14. [Colloq.], to cheat; trick. *v.i.* 1. to strike repeatedly. 2. to sound rhythmically; throb. 3. to hunt through woods, etc. for game. 4. to take beating or stirring: as, this cream doesn't *beat* well. 5. to have a beat or rhythm; pulsate: as, the heart *beats*. 6. to make a sound by being struck, as a drum. 7. [Colloq.], to win. 8. in *nautical usage*, to progress by tacking into the wind. *n.* 1. a beating, as of the heart. 2. any of a series of blows or strokes. 3. a throb. 4. a habitual route: as, a policeman's *beat*. 5. the unit of musical rhythm: as, four *beats* to a measure. 6. a gesture of the hand, baton, etc. used to mark this. 7. in *journalism*, a publishing of news before rival newspapers; scoop. *adj.* [Slang], 1. tired; exhausted. 2. of or belonging to a group of young people in the U.S. who reject the social conventions and affect extreme slang speech, an interest in jazz, etc. —**beat about,** to hunt or look through or around. —**beat a retreat,** to retreat; withdraw. —**beat back,** to force to retreat. —**beat down,** to suppress. —**beat it!** [Slang], go away! —**beat off,** to drive back; repel. —**beat up (on),** [Slang], to give a beating to; thrash. —**beat′er,** *n.*

**beat·en** (bēt′'n), *adj.* 1. struck with repeated blows; whipped. 2. shaped by hammering. 3. flattened by treading: as, a *beaten* path. 4. defeated. 5. tired out. —**off the beaten track** (or **path**), unusual, unfamiliar, original, etc.

**be·a·tif·ic** (bē′ə-tif′ik), *adj.* [see BEATIFY], 1. making blissful or blessed. 2. very happy; blissful: as, a *beatific* smile. —**be′a·tif′i·cal·ly,** *adv.*

**be·at·i·fi·ca·tion** (bi-at′ə-fi-kā′shən), *n.* in the *R. C. Church*, the process of declaring a person who has died to be among the blessed in heaven: he is then entitled to public worship.

**be·at·i·fy** (bi-at′ə-fī′), *v.t.* [-FIED, -FYING], [< L. < *beatus*, happy + *facere*, to make], 1. to make blissfully happy. 2. in the *R. C. Church*, to pronounce the beatification of by papal decree.

**beat·ing** (bēt′iŋ), *n.* 1. the act of one that beats. 2. a whipping. 3. a throbbing. 4. a defeat.

**be·at·i·tude** (bi-at′ə-tōōd′, -tūd′), *n.* [< Fr. < L. < *beatus*, happy], 1. perfect blessedness or happiness. 2. a blessing. —**the Beatitudes,** the pronouncements in the Sermon on the Mount: Matt. 5:3–12.

**beat·nik** (bēt′nik), *n.* [Slang], a member of the beat group.

**beau** (bō), *n.* [*pl.* BEAUS, BEAUX (bōz)], [Fr. < *beau*, pretty < L. *bellus*, pretty], 1. a dandy; fop. 2. a woman's sweetheart or lover. —**beau′ish,** *adj.*

**Beau Brum·mell** (bō brum′əl), 1. (*George Bryan Brummell*), 1778–1840; Englishman famous for his fashionable dress and manners. 2. a dandy; fop.

**Beau·fort scale** (bō′fẽrt), in *meteorology*, a scale of wind velocities ranging from 0 (a calm) to 12 (a hurricane).
‡**beau geste** (bō′ zhest′), [*pl.* BEAUX GESTES (bō′ zhest′)], [Fr.], 1. a fine gesture. 2. an act that seems fine, noble, etc., but is empty.
**beau i·de·al** (bō′ ī-dē′əl), [*pl.* BEAUX or BEAUS (bōz) IDEAL], [Fr.], 1. ideal beauty. 2. a perfect type or model (*of* something).
**beau monde** (bō′ mond′; Fr. bō′mōnd′), [Fr.], fashionable society.
**Beau·mont** (bō′mont), *n.* a city in SE Texas: pop., 119,000.
**beau·te·ous** (bū′ti-əs), *adj.* beautiful. —**beau′te·ous·ly,** *adv.* —**beau′te·ous·ness,** *n.*
**beau·ti·cian** (bū-tish′ən), *n.* a person who does hairdressing, manicuring, etc. in a beauty shop.
**beau·ti·ful** (bū′tə-fəl), *adj.* having beauty. —**beau′ti·ful·ly,** *adv.* —**beau′ti·ful·ness,** *n.*
**beau·ti·fy** (bū′tə-fī′), *v.t. & v.i.* [-FIED, -FYING], to make or become beautiful or more beautiful. —**beau′ti·fi·ca′tion,** *n.* —**beau′ti·fi′er,** *n.*
**beau·ty** (bū′ti), *n.* [*pl.* -TIES], [< OFr. < L. *bellus*, pretty], 1. the quality attributed to whatever pleases in certain ways, as by line, color, form, tone, behavior, etc. 2. a thing having this quality. 3. good looks. 4. a very good-looking woman. 5. any very attractive feature.
**beauty shop** (or **salon** or **parlor**), a place where women can get a permanent wave, manicure, etc.
**beauty spot,** 1. a small black patch sometimes put on the face, etc. to emphasize the whiteness of the skin. 2. a natural mark or mole on the skin.
**beaux** (bōz; Fr. bō), *n.* alt. pl. of **beau.**
‡**beaux-arts** (bō′zȧr′), *n.pl.* [Fr.], the fine arts.
**bea·ver** (bē′vẽr), *n.* [*pl.* -VERS, -VER; see PLURAL, II, D, 1], [AS. *beofor*], 1. an animal that lives on land and in water and has soft, brown fur, webbed hind feet, and a flat, broad tail. 2. its fur. 3. a man's high silk hat. 4. [Colloq.], a hard-working conscientious person.
**bea·ver** (bē′vẽr), *n.* [OFr. *baviere;* ult. < *bave*, saliva], 1. originally, a piece of armor for protecting the mouth and chin. 2. later, the visor of a helmet.
**bea·ver·board** (bē′vẽr-bôrd′, -bōrd′), *n.* artificial board made of fiber, used for walls, partitions, etc.: a trade-mark (**Beaverboard**).
**be·bop** (bē′bop′), *n.* a modification of jazz music, characterized by much improvisation, deviation from key, and, often, meaningless lyrics.
**be·calm** (bi-käm′), *v.t.* 1. to make calm. 2. to make (a ship) motionless from lack of wind.
**be·came** (bi-kām′), past tense of **become.**
**be·cause** (bi-kôz′, bə-kuz′), *conj.* [< ME. *bi*, by + *cause*], for the reason or cause that: as, I came *because* I wanted to. —**because of,** on account of.
**be·chance** (bi-chans′, -chäns′), *v.t. & v.i.* to happen (to); befall; chance.
**be·charm** (bi-chärm′), *v.t.* to fascinate.
**Bech·u·a·na·land** (bech′o͞o-ä′nə-land′, bek′yū-), *n.* Botswana: the former name.
**beck** (bek), *n.* a beckoning gesture of the hand, head, etc. *v.t. & v.i.* [Archaic], to beckon. —**at the beck and call of,** at the service of.
**beck** (bek), *n.* [ON. *bekkr*, a brook], a little stream, especially one with a rocky bottom.
**Becket, Thomas à,** see **Thomas à Becket.**
**beck·on** (bek′'n), *v.i. & v.t.* [AS. *biecnan* < *beacen*, a sign], to summon by a silent gesture, nod, etc. *n.* a summoning gesture. —**beck′on·er,** *n.* —**beck′on·ing·ly,** *adv.*
**be·cloud** (bi-kloud′), *v.t.* to cloud over; obscure.
**be·come** (bi-kum′), *v.i.* [-CAME (-kām′), -COME, -COMING], [AS. *becuman;* see BE- & COME], to come or grow to be. *v.t.* to suit; be suitable to: as, that hat *becomes* you. —**become of,** to happen to; be the fate of.
**be·com·ing** (bi-kum′iŋ), *adj.* 1. appropriate; seemly: as, cursing is not *becoming* to a lady. 2. suitable (*to* the wearer). —**be·com′ing·ly,** *adv.* —**be·com′ing·ness,** *n.*
**Bec·que·rel, An·toine Hen·ri** (än′twȧn′ än′rē′ bek′rel′), 1852–1908; French physicist.
**Becquerel rays,** invisible rays that come from radioactive substances, as radium, uranium, etc
**bed** (bed), *n.* [AS. *bedd*], 1. a piece of furniture for sleeping or resting on, consisting usually of a bedstead, spring, mattress, and bedding. 2. a bedstead. 3. a plot of soil where plants are raised. 4. the plants growing in this. 5. the bottom of a river, lake, etc. 6. rock, etc. in which something is embedded. 7. any flat surface used as a foundation. 8. a pile or heap resembling a bed. 9. a geological layer; stratum: as, a *bed* of coal. *v.t.* [-DED, -DING], 1. to provide with a sleeping place. 2. to put to bed. 3. to embed. 4. to plant in a bed of earth. 5. to arrange in layers. *v.i.* 1. to go to bed; rest; sleep. 2. to stratify. —**be brought to bed (of),** to give birth (to a child). —**bed and board,** 1. sleeping accommodations and meals; hence, 2. the married state. —**bed down,** to prepare and use a sleeping place. —**get up on the wrong side of the bed,** to be cross or grouchy.—**take to one's bed,** to go to bed because of illness, etc. —**bed′less,** *adj.* —**bed′like′,** *adj.*
**be·daub** (bi-dôb′), *v.t.* to make daubs on; smear.
**be·daze** (bi-dāz′), *v.t.* to bewilder; stupefy.
**be·daz·zle** (bi-daz′'l), *v.t.* to bewilder; confuse.
**bed·bug** (bed′bug′), *n.* a small, wingless, reddish-brown biting insect that infests beds, etc.
**bed·cham·ber** (bed′chām′bẽr), *n.* a bedroom.
**bed·clothes** (bed′klōz′, -klōthz′), *n.pl.* sheets, pillows, blankets, bedspreads, etc.
**bed·ding** (bed′iŋ), *n.* 1. mattresses and bedclothes. 2. straw, etc. used to bed animals. 3. any foundation. 4. in *geology*, stratification.
**be·deck** (bi-dek′), *v.t.* to adorn.
**be·dev·il** (bi-dev′'l), *v.t.* [-ILED or -ILLED, -ILING or -ILLING], 1. to plague diabolically; torment. 2. to bewitch. 3. to worry; harass; bewilder. —**be·dev′il·ment,** *n.*
**be·dew** (bi-do͞o′, -dū′), *v.t.* 1. to wet with dew. 2. to make drops of liquid form on.
**bed·fast** (bed′fast′, -fäst′), *adj.* bedridden.
**bed·fel·low** (bed′fel′ō), *n.* 1. a person who shares one's bed. 2. any associate, co-worker, etc.
**bed·gown** (bed′goun′), *n.* a nightgown.
**be·dight** (bi-dīt′), *adj.* [pp. of obs. v. *bedight; be-* + AS. *dihtan*, to compose < L. *dictare;* see DICTATE], [Archaic], bedecked; arrayed.
**be·dim** (bi-dim′), *v.t.* [-DIMMED, -DIMMING], to make dim; darken or obscure.
**be·diz·en** (bi-dī′z'n, -diz′'n), *v.t.* [*be-* + *dizen*], to dress in a cheap, showy way. —**be·diz′en·ment,** *n.*
**bed jacket,** a woman's short, loose upper garment, sometimes worn over a nightgown.
**bed·lam** (bed′ləm), *n.* [altered < (St. Mary of) *Bethlehem*], 1. [B-], an old London insane asylum. 2. any insane asylum. 3. any noisy, confused place or situation. *adj.* full of confusion. —**bed′lam·ite′,** *n.*
**bed linen,** bed sheets, pillowcases, etc.
**bed of roses,** [Colloq.], 1. a life of ease and luxury. 2. an easy situation.
**Bed·ou·in** (bed′o͞o-in), *n.* [< Fr. < Ar. *badāwīn*, dwellers in the desert], 1. an Arab of any of the wandering desert tribes of Arabia, Syria, or North Africa. 2. any wanderer or nomad. *adj.* of or like the Bedouins.
**bed·pan** (bed′pan′), *n.* 1. a warming pan. 2. a shallow pan used as a toilet by one confined to bed.
**be·drag·gle** (bi-drag′'l), *v.t.* [-GLED, -GLING], to make wet, limp, and dirty, as by dragging through mire. —**be·drag′gled,** *adj.* —**be·drag′gle·ment,** *n.*
**bed·rid·den** (bed′rid′'n), *adj.* having to stay in bed, usually for a long period, because of illness, infirmity, etc.: also **bed′rid′.**
**bed·rock** (bed′rok′), *n.* 1. solid rock beneath the soil and superficial rock. 2. a secure foundation. 3. the very bottom. 4. basic principles.
**bed·roll** (bed′rōl′), *n.* a portable roll of bedding, generally for sleeping outdoors.
**bed·room** (bed′ro͞om′, -room′), *n.* a room to sleep in.
**bed·side** (bed′sīd′), *n.* the side of a bed; space beside a bed. *adj.* beside a bed.
**bed·sore** (bed′sôr′, -sōr′), *n.* a body sore on a bedridden person, caused by chafing or pressure.
**bed·spread** (bed′spred′), *n.* a cover spread over the blanket on a bed, mainly for ornament.
**bed·spring** (bed′spriŋ′), *n.* a framework of springs in a bed to support the mattress.
**bed·stead** (bed′sted′), *n.* a framework for supporting the spring and mattress of a bed.
**bed·time** (bed′tīm′), *n.* the time when one usually goes to bed.
**bed-wet·ting** (bed′wet′iŋ), *n.* urinating in bed.
**bee** (bē), *n.* [AS. *beo*], 1. a four-winged, hairy insect which feeds on the nectar of flowers. 2. a meeting of people to work together or to compete: as, a sewing *bee*, spelling *bee*. —**have a bee in one's bonnet,** to be obsessed with one notion.
**bee·bread** (bē′bred′), *n.* a yellowish-brown mixture of pollen and honey, made and eaten by some bees.
**beech** (bēch), *n.* [AS. *bece;* umlaut derivative < stem of AS. *boc;* cf. BOOK], 1. a tree with smooth, gray bark, hard wood, dark-green leaves, and edible nuts. 2. the wood of this tree. *adj.* of this tree or its wood. —**beech′en,** *adj.*

**Bee·cher, Henry Ward** (bē′chẽr), 1813–1887; American preacher and lecturer.
**beech mast,** beechnuts.
**beech·nut** (bēch′nut′), *n.* the three-cornered nut of the beech tree.
**beef** (bēf), *n.* [*pl.* BEEVES (bēvz), BEEFS], [OFr. *boef* < L. *bos, bovis,* ox], 1. a full-grown cow, bull, or steer, especially one bred for meat. 2. meat from such animals. 3. [Colloq.], human flesh or muscle. 4. [Colloq.], strength; brawn. 5. [Slang], a complaint. *v.i.* [Slang], to complain. —**beef up,** [Colloq.], to strengthen by addition, reinforcement, etc.

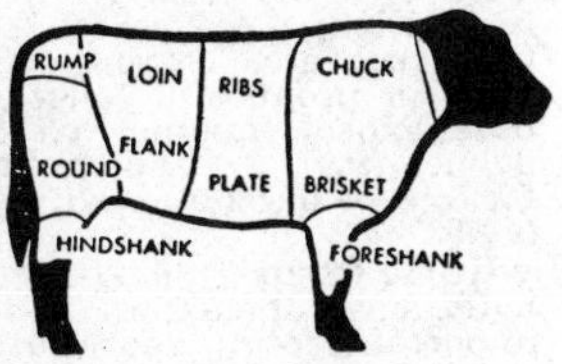

BEEF CUTS

**beef cattle,** cattle bred and fattened for meat.
**beef·eat·er** (bēf′ēt′ẽr), *n.* 1. a yeoman of the English royal guard. 2. [Slang], an Englishman.
**beef·steak** (bēf′stāk′), *n.* a slice of beef to be broiled or fried.
**beef tea,** a drink made from beef extract or by boiling lean strips of beef.
**beef·y** (bēf′i), *adj.* [-IER, -IEST], beeflike; fleshy and solid; muscular; brawny. —**beef′i·ness,** *n.*
**bee·hive** (bē′hīv′), *n.* 1. a shelter for domestic bees. 2. [Colloq.], a place of great activity.
**bee·keep·er** (bē′kēp′ẽr), *n.* a person who keeps bees for producing honey; apiarist.
**bee·line** (bē′līn′), *n.* a straight line or route from one place to another. —**make a beeline for,** [Colloq.], to go straight toward.
**Be·el·ze·bub** (bi-el′zi-bub′), *n.* 1. the chief devil; Satan. 2. any devil.
**been** (bin; *also, chiefly Brit.,* bēn &, *esp. if unstressed,* ben), pp. of **be.**
**beer** (bêr), *n.* [AS. *beor*], 1. a mildly alcoholic drink made from malt, hops, etc. 2. any of several soft drinks made from extracts of roots and plants: as, root *beer.*
**Beer·she·ba** (bêr-shē′bə, bē′ẽr-), *n.* an ancient city in SW Palestine.
**beer·y** (bêr′i), *adj.* [-IER, -IEST], 1. of or like beer. 2. resulting from drinking beer; drunken; maudlin. —**beer′i·ness,** *n.*
**beest·ings** (bēs′tiŋz), *n.* [AS. *bysting* < *beost,* beestings], the first milk of a cow after having a calf.
**bees·wax** (bēz′waks′), *n.* wax secreted by honeybees and used by them in making their honeycomb. *v.t. & v.i.* to polish, etc. with beeswax.
**beet** (bēt), *n.* [< AS. < L. *beta*], 1. a plant with edible leaves and a thick, white or red root. 2. the root of this plant: some varieties are eaten as a vegetable and some are a source of sugar.
**Bee·tho·ven, Lud·wig van** (lōōt′viH vän bā′tō-vən), 1770–1827; German composer.
**bee·tle** (bē′t'l), *n.* [AS. *bitela* < *bitan,* to bite], an insect with biting mouth parts and hard front wings used to cover the membranous hind wings when these are folded.
**bee·tle** (bē′t'l), *n.* [AS. *betel;* ult. connected with *beat*], 1. a heavy mallet, usually wooden. 2. a household mallet or pestle for mashing or beating. *v.t.* [-TLED, -TLING], to pound with a beetle.
**bee·tle** (bē′t'l), *v.i.* [-TLED, -TLING], [prob. < *beetle-browed*], to project or jut; overhang. *adj.* jutting; overhanging: also **bee′tling.**
**bee·tle-browed** (bē′t'l-broud′), *adj.* [see BEETLE (insect) & BROW], 1. having bushy or overhanging eyebrows. 2. frowning; scowling.
**beet sugar,** sugar extracted from certain beets.
**beeves** (bēvz), *n.* alt. pl. of **beef.**
**be·fall** (bi-fôl′), *v.i.* [-FELL (-fel′), -FALLEN (-fôl′ən), -FALLING], [AS. < *be-* + *feallan,* to fall], to happen; come to pass; occur. *v.t.* to happen to.
**be·fit** (bi-fit′), *v.t.* [-FITTED, -FITTING], to be suitable or fit for; be suited or becoming to. —**be·fit′ting,** *adj.* —**be·fit′ting·ly,** *adv.*
**be·fog** (bi-fôg′, -fog′), *v.t.* [-FOGGED, -FOGGING], 1. to envelop in fog. 2. to obscure; confuse.
**be·fore** (bi-fôr′, -fōr′), *adv.* [< AS. < *be-* + *foran,* before], 1. ahead; in advance; in front. 2. in the past; up to now. 3. earlier; sooner. *prep.* 1. ahead of in time, space, or order; in front of. 2. in the sight, presence, etc. of: as, he appeared *before* the court. 3. earlier than. 4. rather than: as, I'd take that book *before* this. *conj.* 1. in advance of the time that: as, drop in *before* you go. 2. sooner than; rather than: as, I'd die *before* I'd tell.
**be·fore·hand** (bi-fôr′hand′, -fōr′-), *adv. & adj.* ahead of time; early; in anticipation.
**be·foul** (bi-foul′), *v.t.* 1. to make filthy; dirty. 2. to cast aspersions on. 3. to entangle or foul.
**be·friend** (bi-frend′), *v.t.* to act as a friend to.
**be·fud·dle** (bi-fud′'l), *v.t.* [-DLED, -DLING], to stupefy, as with alcoholic liquor; fuddle.
**beg** (beg), *v.t.* [BEGGED, BEGGING], [< Anglo-Fr. < OFr. *begard*], 1. to ask for as charity: as, he *begged* a dime. 2. to ask as a favor. 3. to ask earnestly; entreat. 4. to request courteously: as, I *beg* your pardon. *v.i.* 1. to be a beggar. 2. to entreat. —**beg off,** to ask to be released from. —**beg the question,** 1. to use an argument that assumes as proved the very thing one is trying to prove. 2. loosely, to evade the issue. —**go begging,** to be unwanted.
**be·gan** (bi-gan′), pt. of **begin.**
**be·get** (bi-get′), *v.t.* [-GOT (-got′) or *archaic* -GAT (-gat′), -GOTTEN (-got′'n) or -GOT, -GETTING], [< AS. *begitan,* to acquire; see BE- & GET], 1. to become the father of; sire. 2. to cause; produce: as, tyranny *begets* rebellion. —**be·get′ter,** *n.*
**beg·gar** (beg′ẽr), *n.* 1. one who begs or lives by begging. 2. one who is very poor. 3. a rascal; scoundrel. *v.t.* 1. to make a beggar of. 2. to make appear poor or useless: as, her beauty *beggars* description. —**beg′gar·dom, beg′gar·hood′,** *n.*
**beg·gar·ly** (beg′ẽr-li), *adj.* like or fit for a beggar; very poor, mean, etc. —**beg′gar·li·ness,** *n.*
**be·gin** (bi-gin′), *v.i.* [-GAN (-gan′), -GUN (-gun′), -GINNING], [AS. *beginnan*], 1. to start. 2. to come into being. 3. to be or do in the slightest degree: as, they don't *begin* to compare. *v.t.* 1. to cause to start. 2. to originate.
**be·gin·ner** (bi-gin′ẽr), *n.* 1. one who begins anything. 2. one who is just beginning to do or learn something; inexperienced, unskilled person; novice.
**be·gin·ning** (bi-gin′iŋ), *n.* 1. a start. 2. the time or place of starting; origin; source. 3. the first part. 4. *usually pl.* an early stage.
**be·gird** (bi-gũrd′), *v.t.* [-GIRT (-gũrt′) or -GIRDED, -GIRT, -GIRDING], 1. to gird. 2. to surround.
**be·gone** (bi-gôn′, -gon′), *interj. & v.i.* (to) be gone; go away; get out.
**be·go·ni·a** (bi-gōn′yə, -gō′ni-ə), *n.* [after Michel *Bégon* (1638–1710), Fr. botanist], a plant with showy flowers and ornamental leaves.
**be·got** (bi-got′), pt. and alt. pp. of **beget.**
**be·got·ten** (bi-got′'n), alt. pp. of **beget.**
**be·grime** (bi-grīm′), *v.t.* [-GRIMED, -GRIMING], to cover with grime; make dirty; soil.
**be·grudge** (bi-gruj′), *v.t.* [-GRUDGED, -GRUDGING], [*be-* + *grudge*], 1. to envy (another) the possession of. 2. to give with ill will or reluctance: as, he *begrudges* her every cent. —**be·grudg′ing·ly,** *adv.*
**be·guile** (bi-gīl′), *v.t.* [-GUILED, -GUILING], 1. to mislead by guile; deceive. 2. to deprive (*of* or *out of*) by deceit; cheat. 3. to pass (time) pleasantly. 4. to charm or delight. —**be·guil′er,** *n.* —**be·guil′ing·ly,** *adv.* —**be·guile′ment,** *n.*
**be·gum** (bē′gəm), *n.* [Hind. *begam*], in India, a Moslem princess or lady of high rank.
**be·gun** (bi-gun′), pp. of **begin.**
**be·half** (bi-haf′, -häf′), *n.* [ME. < AS. *be,* by + *healf,* side], support, interest, side, etc. —**in behalf of,** in the interest of; for. —**on behalf of,** 1. in behalf of. 2. speaking for; representing.
**be·have** (bi-hāv′), *v.t.* [-HAVED, -HAVING], [see BE- & HAVE], to conduct (oneself), especially in a proper way. *v.i.* 1. to act in a specified way. 2. to conduct oneself well. 3. to act or react.
**be·hav·ior** (bi-hāv′yẽr), *n.* 1. manner of behaving; conduct. 2. an organism's muscular or glandular response to stimulation. —**be·hav′ior·al,** *adj.*
**behavioral science,** any of several studies, as sociology, anthropology, etc., that examine human activities in an attempt to formulate rules about man's social behavior.
**be·hav·ior·ism** (bi-hāv′yẽr-iz'm), *n.* the doctrine that observed behavior provides the only valid data of psychology: it rejects the concept of *mind.* —**be·hav′ior·ist,** *n. & adj.* —**be·hav′ior·is′tic,** *adj.*
**be·hav·iour** (bi-hāv′yẽr), *n.* behavior: Brit. sp.
**be·head** (bi-hed′), *v.t.* to cut off the head of.
**be·held** (bi-held′), pt. and pp. of **behold.**
**be·he·moth** (bi-hē′məth, bē′ə-), *n.* [Heb. *behēmōth,* intens. pl. of *behēmāh,* beast], 1. in the *Bible,* a huge animal, assumed to be the hippopotamus: Job 40:15–24. 2. any huge animal.

**be·hest** (bi-hest′), *n.* [AS. *behæs*, a vow], an order; bidding; command.
**be·hind** (bi-hīnd′), *adv.* [< AS. < *be-* + *hindan*, behind; see HIND], 1. in the rear: as, he walked *behind*. 2. in a former time, place, condition, etc.: as, the girl he left *behind*. 3. into a retarded state: as, he dropped *behind* in his studies. 4. into arrears. 5. slow; late. 6. to or toward the back: as, looking *behind*. *prep.* 1. remaining after: as, the dead leave their wealth *behind* them. 2. in the rear of; back of: as, he sat *behind* me. 3. inferior to in position, achievement, etc. 4. later than: as, *behind* schedule. 5. on the farther side of; beyond: as, *behind* the hill. 6. supporting or advocating: as, Congress is *behind* the plan. 7. hidden by; not yet revealed about: as, *behind* the news. *adj.* 1. that follows: as, the person *behind*. 2. in arrears. Used predicatively. *n.* [Colloq.], the buttocks.
**be·hind·hand** (bi-hīnd′hand′), *adv. & adj.* 1. behind in payments; in arrears. 2. behind time; late. 3. behind in progress, advancement, etc.
**be·hold** (bi-hōld′), *v.t.* [-HELD (-held′), -HELD or *archaic* -HOLDEN, -HOLDING], [AS. *bihealdan*], to hold in view or attention; see; look at. *interj.* look! see! —**be·hold′er,** *n.*
**be·hold·en** (bi-hōl′d'n), *adj.* held under obligation, as from gratitude; indebted.
**be·hoof** (bi-hōōf′), *n.* [AS. *behof*, profit, need], behalf, benefit, interest, sake, etc.
**be·hoove** (bi-hōōv′), *v.t. & v.i.* [-HOOVED, -HOOVING], [AS. *behofian*, to need], 1. to be necessary (for): as, it *behooves* me to reply. 2. to be fitting (for). Also **be·hove** (bi-hōv′, -hōōv′), *v.t. & v.i.* [-HOVED, -HOVING].
**beige** (bāzh), *n.* [Fr.], the sandy color of undyed or unbleached wool; grayish tan. *adj.* grayish-tan.
**be·ing** (bē′iŋ), *n.* [see BE], 1. existence; life. 2. one's fundamental nature: as, she responds to music with her whole *being*. 3. one that lives or exists, or is assumed to do so: as, a human *being*, a divine *being*. 4. [B], God: usually, *the Supreme Being*. *adj.* at hand; immediate: as, for the time *being*, I'll stay.
**Bei·rut** (bā′rōōt, bā-rōōt′), *n.* the capital of Lebanon: pop., 500,000: also sp. **Beyrouth.**
**be·jew·el** (bi-jōō′əl), *v.t.* [-ELED or -ELLED, -ELING or -ELLING], to adorn with jewels.
**be·la·bor** (bi-lā′bẽr), *v.t.* 1. to beat severely. 2. to attack verbally. Also, Brit. sp., **belabour.**
**be·lat·ed** (bi-lāt′id), *adj.* 1. [Archaic], overtaken by night. 2. too late; tardy. —**be·lat′ed·ly,** *adv.* —**be·lat′ed·ness,** *n.*
**be·lay** (bi-lā′), *v.t. & v.i.* [-LAYED, -LAYING], [< AS. < *be-* + *lecgan*, to lay], 1. in *nautical usage*, to make (a rope) secure by winding around a pin (**belaying pin**), cleat, etc. 2. [Colloq.], to hold; stop: as, *belay* there!
**belch** (belch), *v.i. & v.t.* [AS. *bealcian*], 1. to expel (gas) through the mouth from the stomach. 2. to throw forth violently, and often in spasms: as, the volcano *belched* flame. *n.* 1. a belching. 2. a thing belched.
**bel·dam** (bel′dəm), *n.* [*bel-* < Fr. *belle* (see BELLE); + *dame*], 1. any old woman. 2. a haggish old woman. Also **bel′dame** (-dəm, -dām′).
**be·lea·guer** (bi-lē′gẽr), *v.t.* [D. *belegeren* < *legeren*, to camp < *leger*, a camp], 1. to besiege by encircling, as with an army. 2. to surround; beset. —**be·lea′guered,** *adj.* —**be·lea′guer·er,** *n.*
**Be·lém** (be-len′), *n.* a seaport in NE Brazil: pop., 303,000: also called *Pará*.
**Bel·fast** (bel′fast, -fäst), *n.* a seaport and capital of Northern Ireland: pop., 440,000.
**bel·fry** (bel′fri), *n.* [*pl.* -FRIES], [OFr. *berfroi* < OHG < *bergen*, to protect + *frid*, peace; orig. applied to a movable tower for attacking walled positions], 1. a bell tower. 2. the part of a tower that holds the bell or bells. —**bel′fried,** *adj.*
**Belg.,** 1. Belgian. 2. Belgium.
**Belgian Congo,** a former Belgian colony in central Africa: see **Congo,** sense 2.
**Bel·gium** (bel′jəm, -ji-əm), *n.* a country in W Europe, on the North Sea: area, 11,775 sq. mi.; pop., 9,129,000; capital, Brussels. —**Bel·gian** (bel′jən, -ji-ən), *adj. & n.*
**Bel·grade** (bel-grād′, bel′grād), *n.* the capital of Yugoslavia, on the Danube: pop., 520,000.
**Be·li·al** (bē′li-əl, bēl′yəl), *n.* Satan.
**be·lie** (bi-lī′), *v.t.* [-LIED, -LYING], 1. to lie about. 2. to disguise or misrepresent: as, his words *belie* his thoughts. 3. to leave unfulfilled; disappoint: as, war *belied* their dream of victory. 4. to show to be mistaken; prove false.
**be·lief** (bə-lēf′), *n.* [ME. < *be-* + *leve* < AS. *geleafa*, belief], 1. conviction; faith, especially religious faith. 2. trust; confidence: as, I have *belief* in his ability. 3. acceptance of something as trustworthy, real, etc.: as, a claim beyond *belief*. 4. anything believed or accepted as true. 5. an opinion or expectation: as, my *belief* is that he'll come. 6. a creed or doctrine.
**be·lieve** (bə-lēv′), *v.t.* [-LIEVED, -LIEVING], [ME. < *be-* + *leven* < AS. *geliefan*, believe], 1. to take as true, real, etc. 2. to have confidence in a statement or promise of (another person). 3. to suppose; expect; assume. *v.i.* 1. to have trust or confidence (*in*). 2. to have faith, especially religious faith. —**be·liev′a·ble,** *adj.* —**be·liev′er,** *n.* —**be·liev′ing·ly,** *adv.*
**be·lit·tle** (bi-lit′'l), *v.t.* [-LITTLED, -LITTLING], 1. to make small or smaller. 2. to make seem little, less important, etc.; depreciate. —**be·lit′tle·ment,** *n.* —**be·lit′tler,** *n.*
**bell** (bel), *n.* [AS. *belle*], 1. a hollow, cuplike object, as of metal, which rings when struck. 2. the sound made by a bell. 3. anything shaped like a bell, as a flower, the flare of a horn, etc. 4. in *nautical usage*, *a*) a bell rung every half hour to mark the periods of the watch. *b*) any of these periods. *v.t.* 1. to attach a bell to. 2. to shape like a bell. *v.i.* to become bell-shaped.
**bell** (bel), *n., v.i. & v.t.* to bellow; roar.
**Bell, Alexander Gra·ham** (grā′əm bel), 1847–1922; U.S. inventor of the telephone, born in Scotland.
**bel·la·don·na** (bel′ə-don′ə), *n.* [It. *bella donna*, beautiful lady], 1. a poisonous plant with reddish bell-shaped flowers and black berries; deadly nightshade. 2. a drug obtained from this plant and used to dilate the pupil of the eye, stimulate the heart, relieve spasms, etc.: cf. **atropine.**
**bell·boy** (bel′boi′), *n.* a boy or man employed by a hotel, etc. to carry luggage and do errands.
**bell buoy,** a buoy with a warning bell rung by the motion of the waves.
**belle** (bel), *n.* [Fr., fem. of *beau;* see BEAU], a pretty woman or girl; esp., the prettiest or most popular one: as, the *belle* of the ball.
**belles-let·tres** (bel′let′rə), *n.pl.* [Fr.], literature as one of the fine arts; fiction, poetry, drama, etc. as distinguished from technical and scientific writings. —**bel·let·trist** (bel′let′rist), *n.* —**bel′le·tris′tic,** *adj.*
**bell·hop** (bel′hop′), *n.* [Slang], a bellboy.
**bel·li·cose** (bel′ə-kōs′), *adj.* [< L. < *bellicus*, of war < *bellum*, war], of a quarrelsome or hostile nature; warlike. —**bel′li·cose′ly,** *adv.* —**bel·li·cos·i·ty** (bel′ə-kos′ə-ti), *n.*
**bel·lig·er·ence** (bə-lij′ẽr-əns), *n.* 1. the state or quality of being belligerent. 2. war.
**bel·lig·er·en·cy** (bə-lij′ẽr-ən-si), *n.* 1. the state of being a belligerent. 2. belligerence.
**bel·lig·er·ent** (bə-lij′ẽr-ənt), *adj.* [Fr. < L. < *bellum*, war + *gerere*, to carry on], 1. at war. 2. of war; of fighting. 3. warlike. *n.* any person, group, or nation engaged in war or fighting. —**bel·lig′er·ent·ly,** *adv.*
**bell·man** (bel′mən), *n.* [*pl.* -MEN], a town crier.
**bel·low** (bel′ō), *v.i.* [AS. *bylgan;* see BELLY], 1. to roar with a reverberating sound, as a bull. 2. to make a sound like this. *v.t.* to utter loudly or powerfully. *n.* 1. the roar of a bull. 2. any bellowing sound. —**bel′low·er,** *n.*
**bel·lows** (bel′ōz, -əz), *n. sing. & pl.* [< AS. *belg;* see BELLY], 1. a device for producing a stream of air under pressure, used for blowing fires, in pipe organs, etc. 2. anything like a bellows, as the folding part of a camera, the lungs, etc.

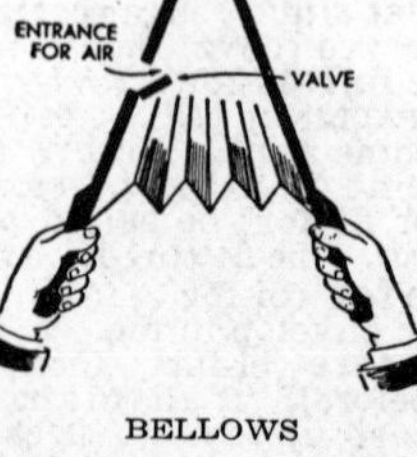

BELLOWS

**bell·weth·er** (bel′weth′ẽr), *n.* a male sheep wearing a bell, usually the leader of the flock.
**bel·ly** (bel′i), *n.* [*pl.* -LIES], [AS. *belg*, leather bag, bellows], 1. the lower front part of the human body between the chest and thighs; abdomen. 2. the underside of an animal's body. 3. the abdominal cavity. 4. the stomach. 5. the deep interior (of a thing): as, the *belly* of a ship. 6. any curved or bulging surface. *v.t. & v.i.* [-LIED, -LYING], to swell out; bulge.
**bel·ly·ache** (bel′i-āk′), *n.* [Colloq.], pain in the abdomen. *v.i.* [-ACHED, -ACHING], [Slang], to complain. —**bel′ly·ach′er,** *n.*

**bel·ly·band** (bel′i-band′), *n.* a girth around an animal's belly, for keeping a saddle, etc. in place.

**bel·ly·but·ton** (bel′i-but′′n), *n.* [Colloq.], the navel: also **belly button.**

**be·long** (bi-lôŋ′, -loŋ′), *v.i.* [ME. < *be-*, intens. + AS. *langian*, to go along with], to have a proper or suitable place; have the proper qualities to be: as, she *belongs* in the movies. **—belong to,** 1. to be part of; be connected with. 2. to be owned by. 3. to be a member of.

**be·long·ing** (bi-lôŋ′iŋ, -loŋ′-), *n.* 1. a thing that belongs to one. 2. *pl.* possessions; property.

**be·lov·ed** (bi-luv′id, -luvd′), *adj.* dearly loved. *n.* a dearly loved person.

**be·low** (bi-lō′), *adv. & adj.* [see BE- & LOW], 1. in or to a lower place; beneath. 2. in a following part (of a book, etc.). 3. in hell. 4. on earth. 5. on or to a lower floor or deck. 6. in a lesser rank, function, etc. *prep.* 1. lower than, as in position, rank, worth, price, etc. 2. not worthy of; beneath: as, it is *below* my dignity.

**Bel·shaz·zar** (bel-shaz′ẽr), *n.* in the *Bible*, the last king of Babylon: Dan. 5.

**belt** (belt), *n.* [AS.; ult. < L. *balteus*, a belt], 1. a band of leather, etc. worn around the waist to hold clothing up, support tools, etc. 2. any encircling thing like this. 3. an endless band for transferring motion from one wheel or pulley to another, or for carrying things. 4. an area distinguished from others in some way: as, the corn *belt*. 5. [Slang], a blow; cuff. *v.t.* 1. to surround or encircle as with a belt; girdle. 2. to fasten with a belt. 3. to strike hard, as with a belt. **—below the belt,** unfair(ly); foul(ly). **—tighten one's belt,** to live more thriftily. **—belt′ed,** *adj.* **—belt′less,** *adj.*

**belt·ing** (bel′tiŋ), *n.* 1. material for making belts. 2. belts collectively. 3. [Slang], a beating.

**be·lu·ga** (bə-lōō′gə), *n.* [*pl.* -GA, -GAS; see PLURAL, II, D, 2], [Russ. < *byeli*, white], a large white dolphin of the arctic seas.

**be·mire** (bi-mīr′), *v.t.* [-MIRED, -MIRING], 1. to make dirty with or as with mire, mud, etc. 2. to stick or bog down in mud.

**be·moan** (bi-mōn′), *v.t. & v.i.* to lament.

**be·muse** (bi-mūz′), *v.t.* [-MUSED, -MUSING], [*be-* + *muse*], to muddle; confuse; preoccupy.**—be·mused′,** *adj.*

**ben·a·dryl** (ben′ə-dril), *n.* a drug used in treating certain allergic conditions, as hives, hay fever, and asthma: a trade-mark (**Benadryl**).

**Be·na·res** (bə-nä′riz), *n.* a sacred city of the Hindus in the United Provinces, India, on the Ganges: pop., 263,000.

**bench** (bench), *n.* [AS. *benc;* akin to G. *bank*], 1. a long seat made of wood, stone, etc. 2. a worktable. 3. a level, narrow, high area. 4. the place where judges sit in a court; hence, 5. [sometimes B-], *a*) the status or office of a judge. *b*) judges collectively. *c*) a law court. *v.t.* 1. to provide with a bench or benches. 2. to place on a bench, especially an official one. 3. in *sports*, to take (a player) out of a game. **—on the bench,** 1. presiding in a law court; serving in court as a judge. 2. in *sports*, not taking part in the game, as a substitute player. **—bench′less,** *adj.*

**bench mark,** a surveyor's mark made on a permanent landmark for use as a reference point in determining other altitudes.

**bench warrant,** an order issued by a judge or law court for the arrest of a person.

**bend** (bend), *v.t.* [BENT or *archaic* BENDED, BENDING], [AS. *bendan*, to bind with a string; hence, to bend (a bow)], 1. to make curved or crooked. 2. to turn (one's steps, etc.) from a straight line. 3. to make submit or give in. 4. to turn or direct (one's eyes, attention, etc. *to*). 5. in *nautical usage*, to fasten (sails or ropes) into position. *v.i.* 1. to turn or be turned from a straight line; swerve; curve. 2. to yield by curving or crooking, as from pressure. 3. to crook or curve the body; stoop; bow (often with *over*). 4. to give in; yield: as, he *bent* to her wishes. 5. to direct one's attention, energy, etc. (*to* something). *n.* 1. a bending or being bent. 2. a bent or curving part. 3. any of various knots. **—the bends,** [Colloq.], decompression sickness. **—bend′a·ble,** *adj.*

**bend** (bend), *n.* [< OFr. < OHG. *bindan*, to bind], in *heraldry*, a stripe from the upper left to the lower right corner of a coat of arms.

**bend·er** (ben′dẽr), *n.* 1. a person or thing that bends. 2. [Slang], a drinking bout; spree.

**bend sinister,** a stripe from the upper right to the lower left corner of a coat of arms: a sign of bastardy in the family line: cf. **bar sinister.**

**be·neath** (bi-nēth′), *adv. & adj.* [< AS. < *be-* + *neothan*, down], 1. in a lower place; below. 2. just below something; underneath. *prep.* 1. below; lower than. 2. underneath. 3. inferior to in rank, quality, worth, etc. 4. unworthy of: as, it is *beneath* him to cheat.

**ben·e·dic·i·te** (ben′ə-dis′ə-ti), *interj.* [L.], bless you! *n.* 1. the invocation of a blessing. 2. [B-], the canticle that begins *Benedicite*, Bless (the Lord).

**ben·e·dict** (ben′ə-dikt′), *n.* [< *Benedick*, a bachelor in Shakespeare's *Much Ado About Nothing*], a recently married man, especially one who seemed to be a confirmed bachelor.

**Benedict,** Saint (ben′ə-dikt′), 480?–543? A.D.; Italian monk; founded the Benedictine order.

**Ben·e·dic·tine** (ben′ə-dik′tin; *also, and for n. 2 always*, -tēn), *adj.* 1. of Saint Benedict. 2. designating or of the monastic order based on his teachings. *n.* 1. a Benedictine monk or nun. 2. [b-], a liqueur, originally made by the Benedictine monks.

**ben·e·dic·tion** (ben′ə-dik′shən), *n.* [< L. < *bene*, well + *dicere*, to speak], 1. a blessing. 2. an invocation of divine blessing, especially at the end of a church service. **—ben′e·dic′tion·al, ben′e·dic′to·ry** (-tẽr-i), *adj.*

**ben·e·fac·tion** (ben′ə-fak′shən), *n.* [< L. < *bene*, well + *facere*, to do], 1. a benefiting, especially as an act of charity. 2. anything given as a benefit.

**ben·e·fac·tor** (ben′ə-fak′tẽr, ben′ə-fak′-), *n.* one who has given help or financial assistance; patron. **—ben′e·fac′tress** (-tris), *n.fem.*

**ben·e·fice** (ben′ə-fis), *n.* [OFr. < L. *beneficium;* see BENEFACTION], 1. an endowed church office providing a living for a vicar, rector, etc. 2. its income. *v.t.* [-FICED, -FICING], to provide with a benefice.

**be·nef·i·cence** (bə-nef′ə-s′ns), *n.* [< Fr. or L.; see BENEFACTION], 1. a being kind or doing good. 2. a kindly action or gift.

**be·nef·i·cent** (bə-nef′ə-s′nt), *adj.* showing beneficence; doing or resulting in good: also **be·nef·ic** (bə-nef′ik). **—be·nef′i·cent·ly,** *adv.*

**ben·e·fi·cial** (ben′ə-fish′əl), *adj.* productive of benefits; advantageous; favorable. **—ben′e·fi′cial·ly,** *adv.* **—ben′e·fi′cial·ness,** *n.*

**ben·e·fi·ci·ar·y** (ben′ə-fish′ẽr-i, -i-er′i), *adj.* of or holding a benefice. *n.* [*pl.* -ARIES], 1. a holder of a benefice. 2. anyone receiving benefit. 3. a person named to receive the income or inheritance from a will, insurance policy, etc.

**ben·e·fit** (ben′ə-fit), *n.* [< Anglo-Fr. < L. *benefactum;* see BENEFACTION], 1. a kindly, charitable act; favor. 2. anything contributing to an improvement in condition; advantage. 3. *often pl.* payments made by an insurance company, public agency, etc. 4. a public performance, bazaar, etc. the proceeds of which are to help a certain person, or cause. *v.t.* [-FITED, -FITING], to do good to or for; aid. *v.i.* to receive advantage; profit. **—ben′e·fit·er,** *n.*

**benefit of clergy,** 1. the exemption which the medieval clergy had from trial or punishment except in a church court. 2. the rites or approval of the church.

**Be·ne·lux** (ben′i-luks), *n.* in *political science*, Belgium, the Netherlands, and Luxemburg.

**be·nev·o·lence** (bə-nev′ə-ləns), *n.* [< OFr. < L. < *bene*, well + *volere*, to wish], 1. an inclination to do good; kindness. 2. a kindly, charitable act.

**be·nev·o·lent** (bə-nev′ə-lənt), *adj.* doing or inclined to do good; kindly; benignant; charitable. **—be·nev′o·lent·ly,** *adv.*

**Beng.,** 1. Bengal. 2. Bengali.

**Ben·gal** (ben-gôl′, beŋ-), *n.* 1. a former province of British India divided (1948) between Pakistan (**East Bengal**) and India (**West Bengal**). 2. West Bengal. *adj.* of or from Bengal.

**Bengal, Bay of,** a part of the Indian Ocean, east of India and west of Burma.

**Ben·ga·lese** (ben′gə-lēz′, beŋ′-), *adj.* of Bengal, its people, or their language. *n.* [*pl.* -LESE], a native of Bengal.

**Ben·gal·i** (ben-gôl′i, beŋ-), *n.* 1. a native of Bengal. 2. the Indo-European, Indic language of Bengal. *adj.* of Bengal or its language.

**ben·ga·line** (beŋ′gə-lēn′, beŋ′gə-lēn′), *n.* [Fr. < *Bengal*], a heavy, corded cloth of silk and either wool or cotton.

**be·night·ed** (bi-nīt′id), *adj.* 1. surrounded by darkness or night. 2. intellectually or morally backward; unenlightened. —**be·night′ed·ness,** *n.*
**be·nign** (bi-nīn′), *adj.* [< OFr. < L. < *bene,* well + *genus,* type], 1. good-natured; kindly. 2. favorable; beneficial. 3. in *medicine,* doing little or no harm; not malignant. —**be·nign′ly,** *adv.*
**be·nig·nant** (bi-nig′nənt), *adj.* [< *benign,* by analogy with *malignant*], 1. kindly or gracious, especially to inferiors. 2. benign; beneficial. —**be·nig′nan·cy** (-nən-si), *n.* —**be·nig′nant·ly,** *adv.*
**be·nig·ni·ty** (bi-nig′nə-ti), *n.* [*pl.* -TIES], 1. benignancy; kindliness. 2. a kind act; favor.
**ben·i·son** (ben′ə-z'n, -s'n), *n.* [< OFr. < L.; see BENEDICTION], a blessing; benediction.
**Ben·ja·min** (ben′jə-mən), *n.* in the *Bible,* 1. Jacob's youngest son and his favorite. 2. the tribe of Israel descended from him.
**Ben·nett, Arnold** (ben′it), (*Enoch Arnold Bennett*), 1867–1931; English novelist.
**bent** (bent), pt. and pp. of **bend.** *adj.* 1. not straight; curved; crooked. 2. strongly determined (with *on*): as, she is *bent* on going. *n.* 1. an inclining; tendency. 2. a mental leaning; propensity: as, a *bent* for music. —**to (or at) the top of one's bent,** to (or at) the limit of one's capacity or ability.
**bent** (bent), *n.* [AS. *beonot*], 1. [*pl.* BENT], the stiff flower stalk of certain grasses. 2. any of various reedy grasses: in full, **bent grass.**
**Ben·tham, Jeremy** (ben′thəm, -təm), 1748–1832; English philosopher and political scientist.
**Ben·tham·ism** (ben′thəm-iz'm, -təm-), *n.* the utilitarian philosophy of Jeremy Bentham, which holds that the greatest happiness of the greatest number should be the ultimate goal of society. —**Ben′tham·ite′,** *n.*
**Ben·ton, Thomas Hart** (ben′t'n), 1889– ; American painter.
**ben·ton·ite** (ben′t'n-īt′), *n.* a soft, porous clay formed as a weathering product from volcanic ash.
**be·numb** (bi-num′), *v.t.* 1. to make numb. 2. to deaden the mind, will, or feelings of; stupefy.
**ben·ze·drine** (ben′zə-drēn′, -drin), *n.* amphetamine, used as an inhalant to relieve nasal congestion, and as a stimulant of the central nervous system: a trade-mark (**Benzedrine**).
**ben·zene** (ben′zēn, ben-zēn′), *n.* [*benz*oin + *-ene*], a clear, inflammable liquid, $C_6H_6$, obtained from coal tar and used as a solvent for fats and in making varnishes, dyes, etc.
**ben·zine** (ben′zēn, ben-zēn′), *n.* [*benz*oin + *-ine*], a colorless, inflammable liquid obtained in the fractional distillation of petroleum and used as a motor fuel, in dry cleaning, etc.
**ben·zo·ate** (ben′zō-it, -āt′), *n.* a salt or ester of benzoic acid.
**ben·zo·caine** (ben′zō-kān′), *n.* [< *benzoin* + *cocaine*], a white, odorless powder, $C_6H_4NH_2COOC_2H_5$, used in ointments as an anesthetic and to protect against sunburn.
**ben·zo·ic** (ben-zō′ik), *adj.* of or derived from benzoin. *n.* benzoic acid.
**benzoic acid,** a white, crystalline organic acid, $C_6H_5COOH$, used as an antiseptic and preservative.
**ben·zo·in** (ben′zō-in, -zoin, ben-zō′in), *n.* [< Fr. < Sp. *benjuí* < Ar. *lubān jāwī,* incense of Java], the resin from certain trees of Sumatra and Java, used in medicine, perfumery, etc.
**ben·zol** (ben′zōl, -zol), *n.* benzene: the term sometimes denotes a mixture distilling below 100°C., 70 per cent of which is benzene.
**Be·o·wulf** (bā′ə-woolf′), *n.* the hero of the Anglo-Saxon folk epic of that name, an Anglian poem probably composed c. 700 A.D.
**be·queath** (bi-kwēth′, -kwēth′), *v.t.* [AS. < *be-* + *cwethan,* to say; see QUOTH], 1. to leave (property, etc.) to another by last will and testament. 2. to hand down; pass on. —**be·queath′a·ble,** *adj.* —**bequeath′al,** *n.* —**be·queath′ment,** *n.*
**be·quest** (bi-kwest′), *n.* [< *be-* + AS. *cwiss,* a saying < *cwethan;* see BEQUEATH], 1. a bequeathing. 2. a legacy.
**be·rate** (bi-rāt′), *v.t.* [-RATED, -RATING], [*be-* + *rate* (to scold)], to scold or rebuke severely.
**Ber·ber** (būr′bēr), *n.* 1. any of a Moslem people living in N Africa. 2. their Hamitic language. *adj.* of the Berbers or their language.
‡**ber·ceuse** (bâr′söz′), *n.* [*pl.* -CEUSES (-söz′)], [Fr. < *bercer,* to rock], a lullaby; cradlesong.
**be·reave** (bi-rēv′), *v.t.* [-REAVED or -REFT (-reft′), -REAVING], [AS. *bereafian; be-* + *reafian,* to rob], 1. to deprive or rob, as of life, hope, etc. 2. to leave destitute, as by death. —**be·reave′ment,** *n.*
**be·reft** (bi-reft′), alt. pt. and pp. of **bereave.** *adj.* 1. deprived. 2. left sad and lonely, as by a death.
**be·ret** (bə-rā′, ber′ā), *n.* [< Fr. < LL.; see BIRETTA], a flat, round cap of felt, wool, etc.

BERET

**berg** (būrg), *n.* an iceberg.
**ber·ga·mot** (būr′gə-mot′), *n.* [< Fr. < It. < Turk. *beg-armūdi,* prince's pear], 1. a kind of pear. 2. a citrus fruit whose thin, yellow rind yields an oil used in some perfumes. 3. this oil. 4. any of several plants of the mint family.
**Ber·gen** (ber′gən, būr′-), *n.* a seaport in SW Norway: pop., 117,000.
**Ber·ge·rac, Cy·ra·no de** (sir′ə-nō′ də ber′jə-rak′; Fr. sē′rä′nō′ də bâr′zhə-räk′), 1619–1655; French playwright and soldier: hero of a drama by Edmond Rostand (1897).
**Berg·son, Hen·ri** (än′rē′ bârg′sōn′; Eng. berg′s'n), 1859–1941; French philosopher. —**Berg·so·ni·an** (berg-sō′ni-ən), *adj. & n.*
**Berg·son·ism** (berg′s'n-iz'm), *n.* the philosophy of Bergson, which maintains that there is an original life force carried through all successive generations.
**be·rhyme, be·rime** (bi-rīm′), *v.t.* 1. to make rhymes about. 2. to satirize in verse.
**be·rib·boned** (bi-rib′ənd), *adj.* covered with ribbons.
**ber·i·ber·i** (ber′i-ber′i), *n.* [Singh. *beri,* weakness], a disease, occurring mainly in Asia, caused by lack of Vitamin $B_1$ in the diet: it is characterized by extreme weakness, paralysis, and anemia.
**Ber·ing Sea** (bâr′iŋ, bêr′iŋ), a sea between Siberia and Alaska, in the N Pacific.
**Bering Strait,** the strait between Siberia and Alaska: width, 36 mi.
**Berke·ley** (būrk′li), *n.* a city near San Francisco, California: pop., 111,000.
**Berke·ley, George** (būrk′li, bärk′-), 1685–1753; Irish philosopher and bishop. —**Berke·le′ian** (-lē′ən), *adj. & n.*
**berke·li·um** (būrk′li-əm), *n.* [< University of California at *Berkeley,* where first isolated], a radioactive chemical element: symbol, Bk; at. wt., 243(?); at. no., 97.
**Berk·shire** (būrk′shir), *n.* 1. a county of England. 2. any of a breed of medium-sized hogs, black with white spots.
**Berk·shire Hills** (būrk′shir), a range of hills and mountains in W Massachusetts.
**Ber·lin** (bēr-lin′), *n.* a city in eastern Germany: capital until 1945 when divided into an eastern sector under Soviet control (since 1949, cap. of East Germany) and three western sectors under British, French, and U.S. control: pop., 3,271,000.
**ber·lin** (bēr-lin′, būr′lin), *n.* [after *Berlin,* Germany], 1. a berline. 2. [sometimes B-], a fine, soft, wool yarn: in full, **Berlin wool.**
**ber·line** (bēr-lin′; Fr. ber′lēn′), *n.* an automobile with a glass partition behind the front seat.
**Ber·li·oz, Louis Hector** (ber′li-ōz′; Fr. bâr′lyôz′), 1803–1869; French composer.
**berm, berme** (būrm), *n.* [< Fr. < MD. *baerm*], a ledge, as along the edge of a paved road.
**Ber·mu·da** (bēr-mū′də), *n.* a group of British islands in the Atlantic, 677 miles SE of New York: area, 20 sq. mi.; pop., 48,000; capital, Hamilton: also **Ber·mu′das** (-dəz). —**Ber·mu′di·an,** *n. & adj.*
**Bermuda onion,** a large onion with a mild flavor grown in Bermuda, Texas, and California.
**Bermuda shorts,** knee-length tailored shorts for business or informal wear: also **walking shorts.**
**Bern** (būrn, bern), *n.* the capital of Switzerland: pop., 167,000: also sp. **Berne.**
**Ber·nard, Claude** (klōd′ bâr′när′), 1813–1878; French physiologist.
**Bernard of Clair·vaux,** Saint (klâr′vō′), 1091–1153; French founder of Cistercian order. —**Ber·nard·ine** (būr′nēr-din, -dēn′), *adj. & n.*
**Bern·hardt, Sarah** (būrn′härt′; Fr. bâr′nâr′), (born *Rosine Bernard*), 1844–1923; French actress.
**ber·ret·ta** (bə-ret′ə), *n.* a biretta.
**ber·ry** (ber′i), *n.* [*pl.* -RIES], [AS. *berie*], 1. any small, juicy, fleshy fruit with seeds, as a strawberry. 2. the dry seed or kernel of various plants, as a coffee bean. 3. in *botany,* any fleshy simple fruit with one or more seeds and a skin, as a tomato, grape, etc. *v.i.* [-RIED, -RYING], 1. to bear berries. 2. to pick berries. —**ber′ried,** *adj.*
**ber·serk** (būr′sērk, bēr-sūrk′), *n.* [ON. *berserkr,* warrior in bearskin < *ber,* a bear + *serkr,* coat], in *Norse legend,* a frenzied warrior: also **ber′serk·er.** *adj. & adv.* in or into a violent rage or frenzy.

**berth** (bũrth), ***n.*** [< base of *bear* (to carry)], 1. enough space at sea; hence, 2. space for anchoring. 3. a ship's place of anchorage. 4. a position, duty, office, etc. 5. a built-in bed, as in a ship's cabin or Pullman car. ***v.t.*** 1. to put into a berth. 2. to furnish with a berth. ***v.i.*** to have or occupy a berth. —**give a wide berth to,** to stay at a prudent distance from.

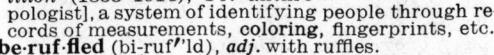

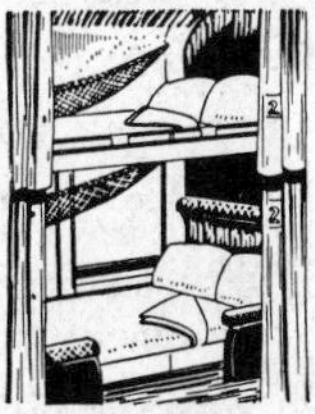
BERTHS

**ber·tha** (bũr′thə), ***n.*** [Fr. *berthe* < *Berthe,* Bertha], a woman's wide collar, often of lace.
**Ber·til·lon system** (bũr′t'l-on′; Fr. bâr′tē′yōn′), [after A. *Bertillon* (1853–1914), Fr. anthropologist], a system of identifying people through records of measurements, coloring, fingerprints, etc.
**be·ruf·fled** (bi-ruf′'ld), ***adj.*** with ruffles.
**Ber·wyn** (bũr′win), ***n.*** a city in NE Illinois, near Chicago: pop., 54,000.
**ber·yl** (ber′il), ***n.*** [< OFr. < L. < Gr. *bēryllos*], beryllium aluminum silicate, a very hard mineral: emerald and aquamarine are varieties of beryl. —**ber′yl·line** (-i-lin, -līn), ***adj.***
**be·ryl·li·um** (bə-ril′i-əm), ***n.*** [< *beryl*], a hard, rare, metallic chemical element: symbol, Be; at. wt., 9.02; at. no., 4: formerly called *glucinum.*
**be·seech** (bi-sēch′), ***v.t.*** [-SOUGHT (-sôt′) or -SEECHED, -SEECHING], [< AS. < *be-* + *secan,* to seek], to ask (for) earnestly; entreat; implore; beg. —**be·seech′er,** ***n.*** —**be·seech′ing·ly,** ***adv.***
**be·seem** (bi-sēm′), ***v.i.*** to be suitable or appropriate (to); be seemly.
**be·set** (bi-set′), ***v.t.*** [-SET, -SETTING], [< AS. < *be-* + *settan,* to set], 1. to set thickly with; stud. 2. to attack, especially from all sides; besiege; hence, 3. to surround or hem in.
**be·set·ting** (bi-set′iŋ), ***adj.*** constantly harassing or attacking: as, a *besetting* temptation.
**be·shrew** (bi-shrōō′), ***v.t.*** [< ME. < *be-* + *schrewen,* to curse], [Archaic], to curse: now used only as a literary archaism in mild oaths.
**be·side** (bi-sīd′), ***prep.*** [< ME. < *be-,* by + *side*], 1. by or at the side of; near; close to. 2. in comparison with: as, *beside* his achievement hers seemed small. 3. in addition to; besides. 4. other than; aside from: as, that's *beside* the point. ***adv.*** besides; in addition. —**beside oneself,** mad, as with fear, rage, etc.
**be·sides** (bi-sīdz′), ***adv.*** 1. in addition; as well. 2. except for that mentioned; else. 3. moreover; furthermore. ***prep.*** 1. in addition to; as well as. 2. other than; except.
**be·siege** (bi-sēj′), ***v.t.*** [-SIEGED, -SIEGING], 1. to hem in with armed forces, especially for a sustained attack; lay siege to. 2. close in on; crowd around. 3. to overwhelm: as, *besieged* with invitations. —**be·siege′ment,** ***n.*** —**be·sieg′er,** ***n.***
**be·slav·er** (bi-slav′ẽr), ***v.t.*** to slaver over.
**be·slob·ber** (bi-slob′ẽr), ***v.t.*** to slobber over.
**be·smear** (bi-smêr′), ***v.t.*** to smear over; soil.
**be·smirch** (bi-smũrch′), ***v.t.*** [*be-* + *smirch*], to make dirty; soil; sully. —**be·smirch′er,** ***n.*** —**be·smirch′ment,** ***n.***
**be·som** (bē′zəm), ***n.*** [AS. *besema,* rod; in pl., bundle of twigs], 1. a broom, especially one made of twigs tied to a handle. 2. the broom (plant).
**be·sot** (bi-sot′), ***v.t.*** [-SOTTED, -SOTTING], 1. to make a sot of; stupefy, as with alcoholic drink. 2. to make silly or foolish. —**be·sot′ted,** ***adj.*** —**be·sot′ted·ly,** ***adv.*** —**be·sot′ted·ness,** ***n.***
**be·sought** (bi-sôt′), alt. pt. and pp. of **beseech.**
**be·spake** (bi-spāk′), archaic pt. of **bespeak.**
**be·span·gle** (bi-spaŋ′g'l), ***v.t.*** to cover with spangles or something like spangles.
**be·spat·ter** (bi-spat′ẽr), ***v.t.*** 1. to spatter over, as with mud. 2. to defame.
**be·speak** (bi-spēk′), ***v.t.*** [-SPOKE (-spōk′) or *archaic* -SPAKE (-spāk′), -SPOKEN (-spōk′'n) or -SPOKE, -SPEAKING], 1. to speak for in advance; reserve: as, to *bespeak* a box at the opera. 2. to be indicative of; show: as, his charity *bespeaks* a generous nature. 3. to foreshadow. 4. [Archaic or Poetic], to speak to; address.
**be·spec·ta·cled** (bi-spek′ti-k'ld), ***adj.*** wearing spectacles; having glasses on.
**be·spread** (bi-spred′), ***v.t.*** [-SPREAD, -SPREADING], to spread over; spread thickly.
**be·sprin·kle** (bi-spriŋ′k'l), ***v.t.*** to sprinkle over (*with* something).
**Bes·sa·ra·bi·a** (bes′ə-rā′bi-ə), ***n.*** a region in the Moldavian S.S.R. —**Bes′sa·ra′bi·an,** ***adj.* & *n.***
**Bes·se·mer converter** (bes′ə-mẽr), a large, specially lined steel retort in which Bessemer steel is made.
**Bessemer process,** [after Sir Henry *Bessemer* (1813–1898), Eng. inventor], a method of making steel (**Bessemer steel**) by blasting air through molten iron to remove carbon and impurities.
**best** (best), ***adj.*** [superl. of *good*], [AS. *betst*], 1. most excellent; surpassing all others. 2. most suitable, most desirable, most favorable, etc. 3. largest: as, the *best* part of an hour. 4. most healthy. ***adv.*** [superl. of *well*], 1. in the most excellent or most suitable manner. 2. in the highest degree; most. ***n.*** 1. the most excellent person, thing, condition, etc. 2. the utmost. 3. advantage. 4. one's finest clothes. ***v.t.*** to defeat; excel. —**all for the best,** ultimately good or fortunate, despite misgivings. —**as best one can,** as well as one can. —**at best,** under the most favorable conditions. —**at one's best,** in one's best mood, form, health, etc. —**get (or have) the best of,** 1. to defeat. 2. to outwit. —**had best,** ought to. —**make the best of,** to utilize or adapt oneself to as well as possible.
**be·stead** (bi-sted′), ***adj.*** [< ME. < *bi-,* be + *stad,* placed < ON. *staddr,* ppr. of *stethja,* to place], situated; placed. ***v.t.*** to help; avail.
**bes·tial** (bes′chəl, -tyəl), ***adj.*** [OFr. < L. < *bestia,* beast], 1. of beasts. 2. like a beast; savage, brutal, vile, etc. —**bes′ti·al′i·ty** (-chi-al′ə-ti, -ti-), ***n.*** [*pl.* -TIES]. —**bes′tial·ly,** ***adv.***
**bes·tial·ize** (bes′chəl-īz′, -tyəl-), ***v.t.*** [-IZED, -IZING], to make bestial; brutalize.
**be·stir** (bi-stũr′), ***v.t.*** [-STIRRED, -STIRRING], to stir up; exert or busy (oneself).
**best man,** the principal attendant of the bridegroom at a wedding.
**be·stow** (bi-stō′), ***v.t.*** [see BE- & STOW], 1. to give or present as a gift (often with *on* or *upon*). 2. to give in marriage. 3. to apply; devote. 4. [Archaic], to put or place; store. —**be·stow′a·ble,** ***adj.*** —**be·stow′al,** ***n.*** —**be·stow′er,** ***n.*** —**be·stow′ment,** ***n.***
**be·strad·dle** (bi-strad′'l), ***v.t.*** to straddle; bestride.
**be·strew** (bi-strōō′), ***v.t.*** [-STREWED, -STREWED or -STREWN, -STREWING], 1. to cover over (a surface); strew. 2. to scatter over or about. 3. to lie scattered over or about.
**be·stride** (bi-strīd′), ***v.t.*** [-STRODE (-strōd′) or -STRID (-strid′), -STRIDDEN (-strid′'n) or -STRID, -STRIDING], 1. to sit on, mount, or stand over with a leg on each side. 2. to stride over or across.
**be·strow** (bi-strō′), ***v.t.*** [-STROWED, -STROWED or -STROWN, -STROWING], to bestrew.
**best-sell·er** (best′sel′ẽr), ***n.*** a book, phonograph record, etc. currently outselling most others.
**be·stud** (bi-stud′), ***v.t.*** [-STUDDED, -STUDDING], to cover the surface of with or as with studs.
**bet** (bet), ***n.*** [prob. < *abet*], 1. an agreement between two parties that the one proved wrong about an outcome or fact will do or pay what is stipulated; wager. 2. the thing or sum thus staked. 3. the outcome, fact, or contestant that something is staked on. ***v.t.*** [BET or BETTED, BETTING], 1. to declare in or as in a bet: as, I *bet* he'll be late. 2. to stake (money, etc.) in a bet. ***v.i.*** to make a bet. —**bet a person on,** to bet with a person about. —**you bet (you)!** [Colloq.], certainly.
**be·ta** (bā′tə, bē′-), ***n.*** [L.; Gr. *bēta;* Heb. *bēth,* lit., house; of Phoen. origin], the second letter of the Greek alphabet (Β, ***β***): often used to mark the second of a series.
**be·take** (bi-tāk′), ***v.t.*** [-TOOK (-took′), -TAKEN, -TAKING], [see BE- & TAKE], 1. to go (used reflexively): as, he *betook* himself home. 2. to apply or devote (oneself).
**beta particle,** one of the electrons of which beta rays consist.
**beta rays,** a stream of electrons given off by radioactive substances.
**be·ta·tron** (bā′tə-tron′), ***n.*** [*beta* rays + *electron*], a device used to accelerate the velocities of electrons.
**be·tel** (bē′t'l), ***n.*** [Port. < Malay *vettilai*], 1. a climbing pepper plant of Asia. 2. its leaf.
**Be·tel·geuse, Be·tel·geux** (bē′t'l-jōōz′, bet′'l-jooz′), ***n.*** [< Fr. < Ar. *bayt al jauza,* lit., house of the twins], a very large, red, first-magnitude star, largest in the constellation Orion.
**betel nut,** the fruit of the betel palm: in the Far East it is chewed together with a little lime and leaves of the betel (pepper) plant.
**betel palm,** a tropical palm with orange-colored, nutlike fruit.

**bête noire** (bāt′nwär′; Fr. bet′nwȧr′), [Fr., lit., black beast], a person or thing feared or disliked.
**Beth·a·ny** (beth′ə-ni), *n.* an ancient town near Jerusalem, on the Mount of Olives.
**Beth·el** (beth′əl), *n.* an ancient village in central Palestine, near Jerusalem.
**beth·el** (beth′əl), *n.* [Heb. *bēth 'ēl*, house of God], 1. a holy place. 2. a place of worship for seamen.
**be·think** (bi-thiŋk′), *v.t.* [-THOUGHT, -THINKING], to think of or consider; remind (oneself).
**Beth·le·hem** (beth′li-əm, -hem′), *n.* 1. an ancient town in W Jordan, near Jerusalem: birthplace of Jesus. 2. a city in E Pennsylvania: pop., 75,000.
**be·tide** (bi-tīd′), *v.i. & v.t.* [-TIDED or *obs.* -TID (-tid′), -TIDING], [ME. < *be-* + *tiden*, to happen < AS. < *tid*, time], to happen (to); befall.
**be·times** (bi-tīmz′), *adv.* [*be-* + *time*, with adv. genit. -(*e*)*s*], 1. early. 2. promptly; quickly.
**be·to·ken** (bi-tō′kən), *v.t.* 1. to be a token or sign of. 2. to indicate; denote. —**be·to′ken·er,** *n.*
**be·took** (bi-took′), pt. of **betake.**
**be·tray** (bi-trā′), *v.t.* [< ME. < *be-* + *traien*, betray < OFr. < L. *tradere*, to hand over], 1. to help the enemy of (one's country, cause, etc.). 2. to break faith with; fail to uphold: as, to *betray* a trust. 3. to deceive; lead astray. 4. to seduce and fail to marry. 5. to reveal unknowingly. 6. to reveal or show signs of. 7. to disclose (a secret, confidence, etc.). —**be·tray′al,** *n.* —**be·tray′er,** *n.*
**be·troth** (bi-trôth′, -trōth′), *v.t.* [-TROTHED, -TROTHING], [< ME. < *be-* + *treuthe* < AS. *treowth*, truth], 1. to promise in marriage. 2. [Archaic], to promise to marry.
**be·troth·al** (bi-trôth′əl, -trō′thəl), *n.* a betrothing or being betrothed; mutual pledge to marry.
**be·trothed** (bi-trôtht′, -trōthd′), *adj.* engaged to be married. *n.* a person engaged to be married.
**bet·ted** (bet′id), alt. pt. and pp. of **bet.**
**bet·ter** (bet′ẽr), *adj.* [compar. of *good*], [< AS. *betera*], 1. more excellent; surpassing another or others. 2. more suitable, more desirable, more favorable, etc. 3. larger: as, the *better* part of a day. 4. improved in health or disposition. *adv.* [compar. of *well*], 1. in a more excellent or more suitable manner. 2. in a higher degree; more. *n.* 1. a person superior in authority, position, etc.: as, obey your *betters*. 2. a more excellent thing, condition, etc. 3. advantage. *v.t.* 1. to outdo; surpass. 2. to make better; improve. *v.i.* to become better. —**better off,** in better circumstances —**for the better,** leading to a more favorable situation. —**get** (or **have**) **the better of,** 1. to defeat. 2. to outwit. —**go** (a person) **one better,** [Slang], to outdo; surpass. —**had better,** ought to; should. —**think better of,** to reconsider. —**bet′ter·ness,** *n.*
**bet·ter, bet·tor** (bet′ẽr), *n.* one who bets.
**better half,** [Colloq.], a wife or husband; spouse.
**bet·ter·ment** (bet′ẽr-mənt), *n.* 1. a bettering; improvement. 2. in *law*, an improvement, other than mere repairs, that increases the value of property.
**bet·ting** (bet′iŋ), *n.* the act or practice of making bets; wagering.
**be·tween** (bi-twēn′), *prep.* [< AS. < *be*, by + *tweon(um)* < *twegen*, *twa*, two], 1. in the space, time, amount, degree, etc. that separates (two things). 2. separating. 3. relating to; involving: as, a struggle *between* powers. 4. from one to the other of; connecting. 5. by the action of both of: as, *between* them they landed the fish. 6. in the combined possession of: as, the men had fifty dollars *between* them. 7. one or the other of: as, choose *between* love and duty. 8. as a consequence of the combined effect of: as, *between* work and study, he has no leisure time. *adv.* in an intermediate space, time, position, or function. —**between ourselves,** in confidence; as a secret: also **between you and me.** —**in between,** in an intermediate position.
**be·twixt** (bi-twikst′), *prep. & adv.* [< AS. *betweochs* < *be-* + a form related to *twegen*, *twa*, two], between: now archaic except in **betwixt and between,** neither altogether one nor altogether the other.
**bev, Bev** (bev), *n.* [*pl.* BEV, BEV], [*b*illion *e*lectron-*v*olts], a unit of energy equal to one billion electron-volts.
**bev·el** (bev′'l), *n.* [prob. < OFr. hyp. *bevel*], 1. a tool consisting of a rule with a movable arm, used in measuring or marking angles, etc.: also **bevel square.** 2. an angle other than a right angle. 3. an angled part or surface. *v.t.* [-ELED or -ELLED, -ELING or -ELLING], to cut to an angle other than a right angle. *v.i.* to slope at an angle. *adj.* sloped; beveled.

BEVEL

**bevel gear,** a gearwheel meshed with another so that their shafts are at an angle.

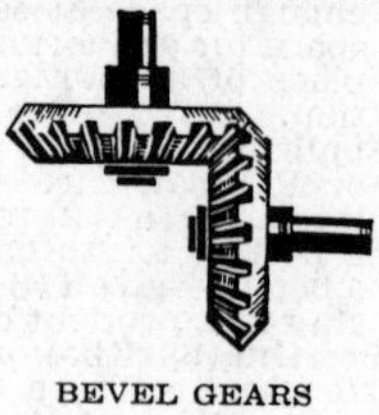
BEVEL GEARS

**bev·er·age** (bev′rij, -ẽr-ij), *n.* [< OFr. < L. *bibere;* see IMBIBE], any drink, as milk, coffee, etc.
**bev·y** (bev′i), *n.* [*pl.* -IES], [? < OFr. *bevee*, drink; ? hence, a drinking group], 1. a group, especially of girls or women. 2. a flock: now chiefly of quail.
**be·wail** (bi-wāl′), *v.t. & v.i.* to wail (over); lament; mourn; complain (about). —**be·wail′er,** *n.*
**be·ware** (bi-wâr′), *v.i. & v.t.* [-WARED, -WARING], [associated with *be* + *ware*, *v.* but prob. < AS. < *be-* + *warian*, to be wary], to be wary or careful (of); be on one's guard (against).
**be·wil·der** (bi-wil′dẽr), *v.t.* [*be-* + *wilder* < AS. *wilde*, wild], to confuse hopelessly; befuddle; puzzle. —**be·wil′dered,** *adj.* —**be·wil′dered·ly,** *adv.* —**be·wil′der·ing,** *adj.* —**be·wil′der·ing·ly,** *adv.* —**be·wil′der·ment,** *n.*
**be·witch** (bi-wich′), *v.t.* [< AS. < *wicca*, wizard, *wicce*, witch], 1. to cast a spell over. 2. to enchant; fascinate; charm. —**be·witch′er,** *n.* —**be·witch′ing,** *adj.* —**be·witch′ing·ly,** *adv.*
**be·witch·ment** (bi-wich′mənt), *n.* 1. power to bewitch. 2. a spell. Also **be·witch′er·y** [*pl.* -IES].
**be·wray** (bi-rā′), *v.t.* [< ME. < *be-* + AS. *wregan*, to inform], [Archaic], to divulge; reveal; betray.
**bey** (bā), *n.* [Turk. *bey*, *beg*], 1. the governor of a Turkish district. 2. a Turkish title of respect or rank. 3. formerly, the native ruler of Tunis.
**be·yond** (bi-yond′), *prep.* [< AS. < *be-* + *geond*, yonder], 1. on or to the far side of; farther on than; past. 2. later than. 3. outside the reach or understanding of: as, *beyond* help. 4. more or better than; in addition to: as, he says nothing *beyond* what we already know. *adv.* farther away. —**the** (**great**) **beyond,** whatever follows death.
**Bey·routh** (bā′rōōt, bā-rōōt′), *n.* Beirut.
**bez·el, bez·il** (bez′'l), *n.* [OFr. *bisel* (Fr. *biseau*), sloping edge], 1. a sloping surface, as the cutting edge of a chisel. 2. the slanting faces of a cut jewel, especially those of the upper half.
**be·zique** (bə-zēk′), *n.* [Fr. *bésique*, earlier *basseque*], a card game resembling pinochle.
**bf, bf., b.f.,** in *printing*, boldface.
**B/F,** in *bookkeeping*, brought forward.
**bg.,** [*pl.* BGS.], bag.
**Bglr.,** Bugler.
**bhang** (baŋ), *n.* [Hind. < Sans. *bhangā*, hemp], 1. the Indian hemp plant. 2. its dried leaves and seed capsules, which have narcotic and intoxicating properties. Also sp. **bang.**
**Bha·rat** (bur′ut), *n.* the Republic of India: the Hindi name.
**Bhu·tan** (bōō-tän′), *n.* a state in the Himalaya Mountains: area, 18,000 sq. mi.; pop., 750,000. —**Bhu·tan·ese** (bōō′-tən-ēz′), *adj. & n.* [*pl.* -ESE].
**bi-,** [L. *bi-* < *bis*, twice], a prefix used to form adjectives, adverbs, verbs, and nouns, and meaning: 1. *having two*, as in *biangular*. 2. *doubly*, as in *biconvex*. 3. *happening every two*, as in *biweekly*. 4. *happening twice during every*, as in *bimonthly*: in this sense, usually *semi-*. 5. *using two* or *both*, as in *bilabial*. 6. *joining* or *involving two*, as in *bilateral*. 7. in *chemistry*, *having twice as many atoms or chemical equivalents for a definite weight of the other constituent of the compound*, as in sodium *bicarbonate*: in organic compounds, equivalent to *di-*. Also, **bin-,** as in *binary*, **bis-,** as in *bissextile*.
**Bi,** in *chemistry*, bismuth.
**bi·an·gu·lar** (bī-aŋ′gyə-lẽr), *adj.* having two angles.
**bi·an·nu·al** (bī-an′yōō-əl), *adj.* coming twice a year; semiannual: see also **biennial.** —**bi·an′nu·al·ly,** *adv.*
**Biar·ritz** (byȧ′rēts′; Eng. bē′ə-rits), *n.* a resort in SW France, on the Bay of Biscay: pop., 22,000.
**bi·as** (bī′əs), *n.* [Fr. *biais*, a slant], 1. a slanting or diagonal line, cut or sewn in cloth. 2. a mental leaning; partiality; prejudice. *adj.* slanting; diagonal. *adv.* diagonally. *v.t.* [BIASED or BIASSED, BIASING or BIASSING], to cause to have a bias; prejudice. —**on the bias,** diagonally.
**bi·ax·i·al** (bi-ak′si-əl), *adj.* having two axes, as some crystals. —**bi·ax′i·al·ly,** *adv.*
**bib** (bib), *n.* [< L. *bibere*, to drink], 1. an apronlike cloth for tying around a child's neck at meals. 2. the upper part of an apron.
**Bib.,** 1. Bible. 2. Biblical.
**bib and tucker,** [Colloq.], clothes.

**bib·cock** (bib′kok′), *n.* a faucet whose nozzle is bent downward.

**‡bi·be·lot** (bēb′lō′), *n.* [Fr.; see BAUBLE], a small object whose value lies in its beauty or rarity.

**Bibl., bibl.,** 1. Biblical. 2. bibliographical.

**Bi·ble** (bī′b'l), *n.* [< OFr. < L. < Gr. *biblia*, collection of writings, pl. dim. of *biblos*, papyrus bark < Egypt.], 1. the sacred book of Christianity; Old Testament and New Testament: the Roman Catholic (Douay) Bible also includes the Apocrypha. 2. the sacred book of Judaism; Old Testament. 3. any collection of writings sacred to a religion: as, the Koran is the Moslem *Bible*. 4. [b-], any book regarded as authoritative or official. See also **Authorized Version, Douay Bible, Vulgate, Septuagint, Apocrypha.**

**Bib·li·cal, bib·li·cal** (bib′li-k'l), *adj.* 1. of or in the Bible. 2. in keeping with or according to the Bible. —**Bib′li·cal·ly, bib′li·cal·ly,** *adv.*

**Bib·li·cist** (bib′li-sist), *n.* 1. a person who takes the words of the Bible literally. 2. a specialist in Biblical literature.

**bib·li·o-,** [< Gr. *biblion*, a book], a combining form meaning: 1. *book, of books*, as in *bibliophile*. 2. *of the Bible.*

**bib·li·og·ra·phy** (bib′li-og′rə-fi), *n.* [*pl.* -PHIES], 1. the study of the editions, dates, authorship, etc. of books and other writings. 2. a list of writings on a given subject or by a given author. —**bib′li·og′ra·pher,** *n.* —**bib′li·o·graph′ic** (-ə-graf′ik), **bib′li·o·graph′i·cal,** *adj.* —**bib′li·o·graph′i·cal·ly,** *adv.*

**bib·li·o·ma·ni·a** (bib′li-ə-mā′ni-ə), *n.* [*biblio-* + *-mania*], a craze for collecting books, especially rare ones. —**bib′li·o·ma′ni·ac,** *n.* & *adj.*

**bib·li·o·phile** (bib′li-ə-fil′), *n.* a person who loves or admires books, especially for their style of binding, printing, etc.: also **bib′li·o·phil′** (-fil′). —**bib·li·oph·i·lism** (bib′li-of′ə-liz'm), *n.*

**bib·li·o·pole** (bib′li-ə-pōl′), *n.* [< L. < Gr. < *biblion*, a book + *pōlein*, to sell], a bookseller, especially one dealing in rare works. —**bib·li·o·pol·ic** (bib′-li-ə-pol′ik), *adj.*—**bib·li·op·o·lism** (bib′li-op′ə-liz'm), **bib′li·op′o·ly,** *n.*

**bib·u·lous** (bib′yoo-ləs), *adj.* [< L. < *bibere*, to drink], 1. highly absorbent. 2. addicted to alcoholic liquor.

**bi·cam·er·al** (bī-kam′ẽr-əl), *adj.* [< *bi-* + L. *camera*, a chamber], made up of or having two legislative chambers.

**bi·car·bon·ate** (bī-kär′bə-nit, -nāt′), *n.* an acid salt of carbonic acid containing the radical $HCO_3$.

**bicarbonate of soda,** sodium bicarbonate; baking soda.

**bi·cen·te·nar·y** (bī-sen′tə-ner′i, bī′sen-ten′ẽr-i), *n.* [*pl.* -NARIES], 1. a period of 200 years. 2. bicentennial. *adj.* 1. of a period of 200 years. 2. of a bicentennial.

**bi·cen·ten·ni·al** (bī′sen-ten′i-əl), *adj.* 1. happening once in a period of 200 years. 2. lasting for 200 years. *n.* 1. a 200th anniversary. 2. the celebration of this.

**bi·ceph·a·lous** (bī-sef′ə-ləs), *adj.* two-headed.

**bi·ceps** (bī′seps), *n.* [*pl.* -CEPSES], [L. < *bis*, two + *caput*, head], 1. a muscle having two heads, or points of origin; esp., the large muscle in the front of the upper arm or the corresponding muscle at the back of the thigh. 2. loosely, strength or muscular development.

**bi·chlo·ride** (bī-klôr′īd, -klō′rid), *n.* 1. a binary compound containing two atoms of chlorine for each atom of another element; dichloride. 2. bichloride of mercury. Also **bi·chlo′rid** (-id).

**bichloride of mercury,** a poisonous compound, $HgCl_2$, used as a disinfectant: also called *corrosive sublimate.*

**bi·chro·mate** (bī-krō′māt, -mit), *n.* a dichromate. *v.t.* (bī-krō′māt), [-MATED, -MATING], to treat or mix with a bichromate.

**bick·er** (bik′ẽr), *v.i.* [< ON. *bikkja* + freq. suffix *-er*], 1. to have a petty quarrel; wrangle; squabble. 2. to flicker, twinkle. *n.* a petty quarrel. —**bick′er·er,** *n.*

**bi·col·or** (bī′kul′ẽr), *adj.* of two colors: also **bi′col′ored** (-ẽrd).

**bi·con·cave** (bī-kon′kāv, -koŋ′-, bī′kon-kāv′), *adj.* concave on both surfaces.

**bi·con·vex** (bī-kon′veks, bī′kon-veks′), *adj.* convex on both surfaces.

**bi·cus·pid** (bī-kus′pid), *adj.* [< *bi-* + L. *cuspis*, pointed end], having two points: as, a *bicuspid* tooth: also **bi·cus′pi·date′** (-pi-dāt′). *n.* any of eight adult teeth with two-pointed crowns.

**bi·cy·cle** (bī′si-k'l), *n.* [Fr. < *bi-* + Gr. *kyklos*, a wheel], a vehicle consisting of a metal frame mounted on two wheels, one behind the other, and equipped with handle bars and a saddlelike seat. *v.i.* & *v.t.* [-CLED, -CLING], to ride or travel on a bicycle. —**bi′cy·cler** (-klẽr), **bi′cy·clist** (-klist), *n.*

**bid** (bid), *v.t.* [BADE (bad) or BID or *archaic* BAD, BIDDEN or BID, BIDDING], [< AS. *biddan*, to beg, ask & AS. *beodan*, offer], 1. to command or ask. 2. [pt. & pp. BID], to offer (a certain amount) as the price for. 3. to declare; say; tell: as, *bid* defiance to your enemies. 4. [Archaic or Dial.], to invite. 5. in *card games*, to state (the number of tricks one expects to take) and declare (a suit or no trump). *v.i.* [pt. & pp. BID], to make a bid. *n.* 1. a bidding; offer; proposal. 2. an amount, etc. bid. 3. an attempt or try (*for* something). 4. [Colloq.], an invitation, especially to become a member. 5. in *cards*, *a*) a bidding. *b*) the number of tricks stated. *c*) a player's turn to bid. —**bid fair,** to seem probable or likely. —**bid in,** at an auction, to bid more than the best offer in an attempt to raise the final price. —**bid up,** to raise the amount bid, as in an auction or card game.

**bid·ding** (bid′iŋ), *n.* 1. a command or request. 2. an invitation or summons. 3. the bids or the making of bids in a card game or auction.

**bid·dy** (bid′i), *n.* [*pl.* -DIES], a hen.

**bide** (bīd), *v.i.* [BODE (bōd) or BIDED or BADE (bad), BIDED, BIDING; *obs.* pt. BAD, pp. BID, BIDEN, BIDDEN], [AS. *bidan*], [Archaic or Dial.], 1. to stay; continue. 2. to dwell; reside. 3. to wait. *v.t.* to endure. —**bide one's time,** to wait patiently for an opportunity.

**bi·den·tate** (bī-den′tāt), *adj.* having two teeth.

**bi·en·ni·al** (bī-en′i-əl), *adj.* [< L. < *bis*, twice + *annus*, year], 1. happening every two years. 2. lasting for two years. *n.* 1. a biennial event. 2. in *botany*, a plant that lasts two years, usually producing flowers and seed the second year. —**bi·en′ni·al·ly,** *adv.*

**‡bien·ve·nue** (byan′və-nü′), *n.* [Fr., lit., well come], a welcome.

**bier** (bêr), *n.* [AS. *bær* < same base as *beran*, to bear], a portable framework on which a coffin or corpse is placed.

**Bierce, Ambrose** (bêrs), 1842–1914?; U.S. writer.

**biest·ings** (bēs′tiŋz), *n.pl.* beestings.

**biff** (bif), *n.* [prob. echoic], [Slang], a blow; cuff. *v.t.* to strike; hit.

**bi·fid** (bī′fid), *adj.* [< L. < *bis*, twice + *findere*, to cleave], divided into two equal parts by a cleft; forked.

**bi·fo·cal** (bī-fō′k'l, bī′fō-k'l), *adj.* adjusted or ground to two different focal lengths. *n.* a lens with one part ground for close focus, as for reading, and the other ground for distant focus.

**bi·fo·cals** (bī-fō′k'lz, bī′fō-k'lz), *n.pl.* a pair of glasses with bifocal lenses.

**bi·fur·cate** (bī′fẽr-kāt′, bī-fūr′kāt; *also, for adj.*, -kit), *adj.* [< LL. < L. < *bi-* + *furca*, two-pronged fork], having two branches; forked. *v.t.* & *v.i.* [-CATED, -CATING], to divide into two branches, as a road. —**bi′fur·ca′tion,** *n.*

**big** (big), *adj.* [BIGGER, BIGGEST], [ME.; < same base as in L. *buccae*, swollen cheeks], 1. of great size, extent, or capacity; large. 2. full-grown. 3. swollen or pregnant (*with*). 4. loud. 5. important; prominent: as, he does *big* things. 6. extravagant; pompous: as, *big* talk. 7. magnanimous; noble: as, a *big* heart. *Big* is much used in combination to form adjectives (*big*-bodied, *big*-souled, etc.) *adv.* [Colloq.], 1. pompously; boastfully: as, he talks *big*. 2. impressively. —**big′ness,** *n.*

**big·a·my** (big′ə-mi), *n.* [*pl.* -MIES], [< OFr. < LL. < *bis*, twice + Gr. *gamos*, marriage], in *law*, the criminal offense of entering into a second marriage while a previous marriage is still legally in effect. —**big′a·mist,** *n.* —**big′a·mous,** *adj.* —**big′a·mous·ly,** *adv.*

**Big Ben,** 1. the great bell in the Parliament clock in the tower in London. 2. the clock itself.

**Big Dipper,** a dipper-shaped group of stars in the constellation Ursa Major (Great Bear).

**big game,** 1. large wild animals hunted for sport, as lions, tigers, etc. 2. [Colloq.], the object of any important or dangerous undertaking.

**big-heart·ed** (big′här′tid), *adj.* generous; kind.

**big·horn** (big′hôrn′), *n.* [*pl.* -HORNS, -HORN; see

PLURAL, II, D, 1], a wild sheep with long, curved horns, found in the Rocky Mountains.

**big house,** [Slang], a penitentiary.

**bight** (bīt), *n.* [AS. *byht*], 1. a bending; corner; fork. 2. a loop in a rope. 3. a curve in a river, coast line, etc. 4. a bay.

**big·no·ni·a** (big-nō′ni-ə), *n.* [after the Abbé *Bignon*], a climbing evergreen vine with yellowish-red, trumpet-shaped flowers.

**big·ot** (big′ət), *n.* [OFr.; prob. < Sp. *hombre de bigote*, lit., man with a mustache, hence man of spirit, obstinate person], a narrow-minded person who holds blindly and intolerantly to a particular creed, opinion, etc. —**big′ot·ed,** *adj.* —**big′ot·ed·ly,** *adv.* —**big′ot·ry** (-ri) [*pl.* -RIES], *n.*

**big shot,** [Slang], an important or influential person: also [Colloq.], **big′wig′,** *n.*

**big time,** [Slang], 1. vaudeville in the larger cities, with better pay, etc. 2. the highest level in any profession, etc. —**big′-time′,** *adj.*

**big top,** [Colloq.], 1. a circus tent. 2. a circus.

**Bi·har** (bi-här′), *n.* a state of NE India: area, 70,368 sq. mi.; pop., 36,548,000: also sp. **Be·har′.**

**bi·jou** (bē′zhōō), *n.* [*pl.* -JOUX (-zhōōz)], [Fr.; prob. < Bret. *bizon*, a ring], 1. a jewel. 2. something small and exquisite; trinket.

**bi·ju·gate** (bī′joo-gāt′, bī-jōō′git), *adj.* [< *bi-* + L. pp. of *jugare*, to join < *jugum*, a yoke], having two pairs of leaflets, as some pinnate leaves: also **bi·ju·gous** (bī′joo-gəs).

**bike** (bīk), *n., v.t. & v.i.* [BIKED, BIKING], [< *bicycle*], [Colloq.], bicycle.

**Bi·ki·ni** (bi-kē′nē), *n.* an atoll in the Marshall Islands: site of atomic bomb tests in 1946.

**bi·la·bi·al** (bī-lā′bi-əl), *adj.* [*bi-* + *labial*], 1. bilabiate. 2. in *phonetics*, made by stopping or constricting the air stream between the lips, as the consonants *p*, *b*, and *m*. *n.* a bilabial sound.

**bi·la·bi·ate** (bī-lā′bi-āt′, -it), *adj.* [*bi-* + *labiate*], having two lips, as some flowers.

**bi·lat·er·al** (bī-lat′ēr-əl), *adj.* [*bi-* + *lateral*], 1. of or having two sides, factions, etc. 2. on two sides. 3. affecting both sides equally; reciprocal. 4. having bilateral symmetry. —**bi·lat′er·al·ism, bi·lat′er·al·ness,** *n.* —**bi·lat′er·al·ly,** *adv.*

**Bil·ba·o** (bil-bä′ō), *n.* a seaport in N Spain: pop., 176,000.

**bil·ber·ry** (bil′ber′i), *n.* [*pl.* -RIES], [< ON. base of Dan. *bollebær*], 1. a shrub of the heath family, with small, egg-shaped leaves and dark-blue berries. 2. its fruit. Also called *whortleberry*.

**bil·bo** (bil′bō), *n.* [*pl.* -BOES], [after *Bilbao*, Spain], 1. *pl.* a long iron bar with shackles for fettering a prisoner's feet. 2. [Archaic], a sword.

**bile** (bīl), *n.* [Fr.; L. *bilis*], 1. the bitter, greenish fluid secreted by the liver and found in the gall bladder: it helps in digestion. 2. bad temper; anger.

**bilge** (bilj), *n.* [var. of *bulge*], 1. the bulge of a cask. 2. the rounded, lower part of a ship's hold. 3. stagnant, dirty water that gathers there: also **bilge water.** 4. [Slang], nonsense. *v.t. & v.i.* [BILGED, BILGING], 1. to break open in the bilge: said of a vessel. 2. to bulge or swell out.

**bil·i·ar·y** (bil′i-er′i, -yēr-i), *adj.* [Fr. *biliaire*], 1. of the bile. 2. bile-carrying. 3. bilious.

**bi·lin·gual** (bī-liŋ′gwəl), *adj.* [< L. < *bis*, two + *lingua*, tongue], 1. of or in two languages. 2. capable of using two languages, often with equal facility. —**bi·lin′gual·ism,** *n.* —**bi·lin′gual·ly,** *adv.*

**bil·ious** (bil′yəs), *adj.* 1. of the bile. 2. having or resulting from some ailment of the bile or the liver. 3. bad-tempered; cross. —**bil′ious·ly,** *adv.* —**bil′ious·ness,** *n.*

**-bil·i·ty** (bil′ə-ti), a suffix used to form nouns from adjectives ending in *-ble*, as *capability*.

**bilk** (bilk), *v.t.* [? altered < *balk*], 1. to deceive; swindle; defraud. 2. to get away without paying (a debt, etc.). *n.* 1. a bilking or being bilked. 2. a person who cheats; swindler. —**bilk′er,** *n.*

**bill** (bil), *n.* [< Anglo-L. *billa*, altered < ML. *bulla*, sealed document; cf. BULL (edict)], 1. a statement of charges for goods or services. 2. a list of things offered, as a menu or theater program. 3. an advertising poster or handbill. 4. the entertainment offered in a theater. 5. a draft of a law proposed to a lawmaking body. 6. a bill of exchange. 7. any promissory note. 8. a bank note or piece of paper money. 9. in *law*, a written declaration of the charges against a defendant. *v.t.* 1. to make out a bill of (items); list. 2. to present a statement of charges to. 3. to advertise by bills or posters. 4. to post bills or placards throughout (a town, etc.). 5. to ship (goods). —**fill the bill,** [Colloq.], to meet the requirements. —**foot the bill,** [Colloq.], to pay the cost. —**bill′a·ble,** *adj.* —**bill′er,** *n.*

**bill** (bil), *n.* [AS. *bile*], 1. a bird's beak. 2. a beak-like mouth part, as of a turtle. *v.i.* 1. to touch bills together. 2. to caress lovingly. —**bill and coo,** to kiss, talk softly, etc., as in love-making.

**bill** (bil), *n.* [AS. *bill*], 1. an ancient spearlike weapon having a hook-shaped blade with a spike at the back. 2. a billhook.

**bill·a·bong** (bil′ə-boŋ′), *n.* [Australian native term], in Australia, a backwater channel that forms a lagoon or pool.

**bill·board** (bil′bôrd′, -bōrd′), *n.* a signboard, usually outdoors, for advertising posters, etc.

**bil·let** (bil′it), *n.* [Fr., dim. of *bille;* see BILL (an account)], 1. a written order to provide lodging for military personnel. 2. lodging; quarters. 3. a position or job. *v.t.* to assign (soldiers, etc.) to lodging by billet.

**bil·let** (bil′it), *n.* [OFr. *billette*, dim. of *bille*, tree trunk], 1. a piece of firewood. 2. a wooden club. 3. a small metal bar, often square.

**bil·let-doux** (bil′i-dōō′; Fr. bē′ye′dōō′), *n.* [*pl.* BILLETS-DOUX (-dōōz′; Fr. -dōō′)], [Fr., lit., sweet letter], a love letter.

**bill·fold** (bil′fōld′), *n.* a wallet.

**bill·head** (bil′hed′), *n.* 1. a sheet of stationery with a letterhead, used for statements of charges. 2. a letterhead.

**bill·hook** (bil′hook′), *n.* a curved or hooked tool for pruning and cutting.

**bil·liard** (bil′yērd), *adj.* of or for billiards. *n.* a point scored in billiards by a carom.

**bil·liards** (bil′yērdz), *n.* [Fr. *billard;* orig., a cue < *bille;* see BILLET (piece of wood)], 1. a game played with hard balls on an oblong table that has raised, cushioned edges: a cue is used to drive the balls. 2. any of a number of similar games, as **pocket billiards** (pool). —**bil′liard·ist,** *n.*

**bill·ing** (bil′iŋ), *n.* the listing or the order of listing of actors' names on a playbill, etc.

**bil·lings·gate** (bil′iŋz-gāt′), *n.* [after a fish market in London], foul, vulgar, abusive talk.

**bil·lion** (bil′yən), *n.* [Fr. contr. < L. *bis*, twice + *million*, million], 1. in the U.S. and France, a thousand millions (1,000,000,000). 2. in Great Britain and Germany, a million millions (1,000-000,000,000). *adj.* amounting to one billion in number. —**bil′lionth,** *adj. & n.*

**bil·lion·aire** (bil′yən-âr′), *n.* one whose wealth comes to at least a billion dollars, pounds, etc.

**bill of attainder,** a legislative bill making certain crimes, especially treason and outlawry, punishable by loss of property and civil rights: prohibited in the U.S. by the Constitution.

**bill of exchange,** a written order to pay a certain sum of money to the person named; draft.

**bill of fare,** a list of the foods served; menu.

**bill of health,** a certificate stating whether there is infectious disease aboard a ship or in a port. —**clean bill of health,** 1. a bill of health certifying the absence of infectious disease. 2. [Colloq.], a good record or recommendation.

**bill of lading,** a receipt issued to a shipper by a transportation agency, listing the goods received for shipment.

**bill of rights,** 1. a list of the rights and freedoms regarded as essential to a people. 2. [B- R-], the first ten amendments to the Constitution of the U.S. which guarantee certain rights to the people, as freedom of speech, assembly, etc.

**bill of sale,** a written statement transferring the ownership of something by sale.

**bil·low** (bil′ō), *n.* [ON. *bylgja;* cf. BELLY], 1. a large wave; great swell of water. 2. any large swelling mass or surge, as of smoke, sound, etc. *v.i.* to surge or swell like or in a billow.

**bil·low·y** (bil′ō-i), *adj.* [-IER, -IEST], swelling in or as in a billow. —**bil′low·i·ness,** *n.*

**bill·post·er** (bil′pōs′tēr), *n.* a person hired to fasten advertisements on walls, billboards, etc.

**bil·ly** (bil′i), *n.* [*pl.* -LIES], [< *billet* (wooden club)], a club or heavy stick; truncheon, especially one carried by a policeman.

**billy goat,** [Colloq.], a male goat.

**bi·lo·bate** (bī-lō′bāt), *adj.* having or divided into two lobes: also **bi·lo′bat·ed.**

**bi·man·u·al** (bī-man′ū-əl), *adj.* [*bi-* + *manual*], using both hands. —**bi·man′u·al·ly,** *adv.*

**bi·me·tal·lic** (bī′mə-tal′ik), *adj.* 1. containing or using two metals. 2. of or based on bimetallism.

**bi·met·al·lism** (bī-met′'l-iz'm), *n.* the use of two metals, usually gold and silver, as the monetary standard, with fixed values in relation to each other. —**bi·met′al·list,** *n.*

**bi·month·ly** (bī-munth′li), *adj. & adv.* 1. once every two months. 2. loosely, twice a month;

semimonthly. *n.* [*pl.* -LIES], a bimonthly publication.
**bin** (bin), *n.* [AS. *binn*, manger, crib], a box or enclosed space for storing foods, fuels, etc. *v.t.* [BINNED, BINNING], to store in a bin.
**bi·na·ry** (bī′nə-ri), *adj.* [< L. < *bini*, two by two < *bis*, double], made up of two parts; twofold; double. *n.* [*pl.* -RIES], 1. a set of two; couple; pair. 2. a binary star.
**binary star,** two stars revolving around a common center of gravity; double star.
**bi·nate** (bī′nāt), *adj.* [see BINARY], occurring in pairs: as, *binate* leaves.—**bi′nate·ly,** *adv.*
**bind** (bīnd), *v.t.* [BOUND (bound), BINDING], [AS. *bindan*], 1. to tie together; make fast, as with a rope. 2. to hold; restrain. 3. to gird or encircle with (a belt, etc.). 4. to bandage (often with *up*). 5. to make stick together. 6. to constipate. 7. to strengthen or ornament the edges of by a band, as of tape. 8. to fasten together and protect with a cover, as a book. 9. to obligate by duty, love, etc.: as, he is *bound* to help his mother. 10. to put under oath or legal restraint. 11. to unite or hold, as by a feeling of loyalty. *v.i.* 1. to do the act of binding. 2. to grow hard or stiff. 3. to be obligatory. *n.* anything that binds.
**bind·er** (bīn′dẽr), *n.* 1. a person or thing that binds. 2. a binding substance, as tar. 3. a cover for holding sheets of paper together. 4. in *agriculture*, a device attached to a reaper, for tying grain in bundles. 5. in *law*, a temporary contract, in effect pending execution of the final contract.
**bind·er·y** (bīn′dẽr-i), *n.* [*pl.* -IES], a place where books are bound.
**bind·ing** (bīn′diŋ), *n.* 1. the act of one that binds. 2. the state of being bound. 3. a band or bandage. 4. tape used in sewing for strengthening seams, edges, etc. 5. the covers and backing of a book. 6. a substance for binding a mixture. *adj.* that binds; esp., that holds one to an agreement, promise, etc.; obligatory. —**bind′ing·ly,** *adv.* —**bind′ing·ness,** *n.*
**bind·weed** (bīnd′wēd′), *n.* a trailing or twining plant with funnel-shaped flowers.
**bine** (bīn), *n.* [dial. form of *bind*], any climbing, twining stem, as of the hop.
**Bi·net-Si·mon test** (bi-nā′sī′mən), [after the Fr. psychologists who devised it, Alfred *Binet* (1857–1911) and Theodore *Simon* (1873–1964)], an intelligence test consisting of questions, problems, etc., graded in terms of mental age: also **Binet test.**
**binge** (binj), *n.* [? < dial. *binge*, to soak], [Slang], a drunken celebration or spree.
**Bing·ham·ton** (biŋ′əm-tən), *n.* a city in S New York: pop., 76,000.
**bin·go** (biŋ′gō), *n.* a gambling game resembling lotto.
**bin·na·cle** (bin′ə-k'l), *n.* [formerly *bittacle* < Port. < L. *habitaculum*, dwelling place < *habitare*, to inhabit], the case enclosing a ship's compass, usually located near the helm.
**bin·oc·u·lar** (bī-nok′yə-lẽr, bi-), *adj.* [< L. *bini*, double + *oculus*, an eye], using, or for the use of, both eyes at the same time. *n.* a binocular instrument; esp., *pl.*, field glasses or opera glasses.
**bi·no·mi·al** (bī-nō′mi-əl), *n.* [< LL. < *bi-* + Gr. *nomos*, law], a mathematical expression consisting of two terms connected by a plus or minus sign. *adj.* of or having the nature of a binomial.
**bi·o-,** [Gr. < *bios*, life], a combining form meaning *life, of living things, biological*, as in *biography, biochemistry*: also **bi-.**
**bi·o·chem·is·try** (bī′ō-kem′is-tri), *n.* the branch of chemistry that deals with plants and animals and their life processes; biological chemistry. —**bi′o·chem′i·cal, bi′o·chem′ic,** *adj.* —**bi′o·chem′i·cal·ly,** *adv.* —**bi′o·chem′ist,** *n.*
**bi·o·cide** (bī′ə-sīd′), *n.* [*bio-* + *-cide*], a poisonous chemical substance that can kill living organisms.
**bi·o·de·grad·a·ble** (bī′ō-di-grā′də-b'l), *adj.* [*bio-* + *degrade* (decompose) + *-able*], capable of being readily decomposed by biological means, esp. by bacterial action, as some detergents.
**biog.,** 1. biographical. 2. biography.
**bi·o·gen·e·sis** (bī′ō-jen′ə-sis), *n.* [*bio-* + *genesis*], the theory that living organisms come only from other living organisms, and not from non-living matter. —**bi′o·ge·net′ic** (-jə-net′ik), **bi′o·ge·net′i·cal,** *adj.* —**bi′o·ge·net′i·cal·ly,** *adv.*
**bi·og·e·ny** (bī-oj′ə-ni), *n.* biogenesis.
**bi·og·ra·phy** (bī-og′rə-fi, bi-), *n.* [< Gr. < *bios*, life + *graphein*, to write], 1. the histories of individual lives, considered as a branch of literature. 2. [*pl.* -PHIES], an account of a person's life, written or told by another. —**bi·og′ra·pher,** *n.* —**bi·o·graph·i·cal** (bī′ə-graf′i-k'l), **bi′o·graph′ic,** *adj.* —**bi′o·graph′i·cal·ly,** *adv.*
**biol.,** 1. biological. 2. biologist. 3. biology.
**bi·o·log·i·cal** (bī′ə-loj′i-k'l), *adj.* 1. of or connected with biology; of plants and animals. 2. used in or produced by practical biology. Also **bi′o·log′ic.** *n.* a biological product. —**bi′o·log′i·cal·ly,** *adv.*
**biological warfare,** the use of disease-spreading microorganisms, toxins, etc. as a weapon of war.
**bi·ol·o·gy** (bī-ol′ə-ji), *n.* [*bio-* + *-logy*], 1. the science that deals with the origin, history, physical characteristics, habits, etc. of plants and animals: it includes botany and zoology. 2. animal and plant life, as of a given area. —**bi·ol′o·gist,** *n.*
**bi·o·met·rics** (bī′ə-met′riks), *n.pl.* [construed as sing.], [< *bio-* + *metric*], that branch of biology which deals with its data statistically and by quantitative analysis. —**bi′o·met′ric, bi′o·met′ri·cal,** *adj.* —**bi′o·met′ri·cal·ly,** *adv.*
**bi·om·e·try** (bī-om′ə-tri), *n.* [*bio-* + *metry*], 1. calculation of the probable human life span. 2. biometrics.
**bi·o·phys·ics** (bī′ō-fiz′iks), *n.pl.* [construed as sing.], the branch of physics that deals with living matter. —**bi′o·phys′i·cal,** *adj.*
**bi·os·co·py** (bī-os′kə-pi), *n.* [*bio-* + *-scopy*], a medical examination to find out whether life is present.
**-bi·o·sis** (bī-ō′sis, bi-), [< Gr. *biōsis*, way of life < *bios*, life], a combining form meaning *a* (specified) *way of living*, as in *symbiosis*.
**bi·o·sphere** (bī′ə-sfêr′), *n.* [*bio-* + *sphere*], 1. the zone of the earth, from its crust out into the surrounding atmosphere, which contains living organisms. 2. all these organisms.
**bi·o·tin** (bī′ə-tin), *n.* [< Gr. *bios*, life + *-in*], a bacterial growth factor, $C_{10}H_{16}O_3N_2S$, one of the vitamin B group, found in liver, egg yolk, and yeast.
**bi·par·ti·san** (bī-pär′tə-z'n), *adj.* of or representing two parties. —**bi·par′ti·san·ship′,** *n.*
**bi·par·tite** (bī-pär′tīt), *adj.* [< L. < *bi-*, two + *partire*, to divide], 1. having two (corresponding) parts. 2. in *botany*, divided in two nearly to the base, as some leaves. —**bi·par′tite·ly,** *adv.* —**bi·par·ti·tion** (bī′pär-tish′ən), *n.*
**bi·ped** (bī′ped), *n.* [< L. < *bi-* + *pes, pedis*, foot], any animal with only two feet. *adj.* two-footed: also **bi′ped·al** (-ped-'l).
**bi·pet·al·ous** (bī-pet′'l-əs), *adj.* having two petals.
**bi·pin·nate** (bī-pin′āt), *adj.* [see BI- & PINNATE], having pinnate leaflets on stems that grow opposite each other on a main stem.

BIPINNATE LEAF (of acacia)

**bi·plane** (bī′plān′), *n.* an airplane with two wings, one above the other.
**bi·po·lar** (bī-pō′lẽr), *adj.* 1. of or having two poles. 2. of or at both of the earth's poles.
**birch** (bũrch), *n.* [AS. *beorc*], 1. a tree having slender branches, hard, close-grained wood, and smooth bark easily stripped off in layers. 2. its wood. 3. a birch rod or bunch of twigs used for whipping. *v.t.* to beat with a birch; flog. *adj.* of birch: also **birch·en** (bũr′chən).
**bird** (bũrd), *n.* [AS. *bridd*, a young bird], 1. any of a group of warm-blooded vertebrates with feathers and wings. 2. a small game bird. 3. a clay pigeon. 4. [Slang], a person: as, he's a queer *bird*. 5. [Slang], a sound of disapproval made by the lips fluttering. —**bird in the hand,** something sure because already in one's possession: opposed to **bird in the bush,** something unsure, etc. —**birds of a feather,** people with the same characteristics or tastes. —**bird′like′,** *adj.*
**bird·bath** (bũrd′bath′, -bäth′), *n.* a basinlike garden ornament for birds to bathe in.
**bird·call** (bũrd′kôl′), *n.* 1. the sound or song of a bird. 2. an imitation of this. 3. a device for imitating bird sounds. Also **bird call.**
**bird dog,** a dog trained for hunting birds, as a pointer or setter.
**bird·ie** (bũr′di), *n.* 1. a small bird: a child's word. 2. in *golf*, a score of one stroke under par for any hole.
**bird·lime** (bũrd′līm′), *n.* a sticky substance spread on twigs to catch birds.

**bird of paradise,** any of a number of brightly colored birds found in and near New Guinea.

**bird of passage,** 1. any migratory bird. 2. anyone who travels or roams about constantly.

**bird of prey,** any of a number of flesh-eating birds, as the eagle, hawk, owl, vulture, etc.

**bird·seed** (būrd′sēd′), ***n.*** small seed for feeding caged birds.

**bird's-eye** (būrdz′ī′), ***n.*** a cotton or linen cloth with a woven pattern of small diamond-shaped figures. ***adj.*** 1. seen from above or a distance; general: as, a *bird's-eye* view. 2. having markings that resemble birds' eyes: as, *bird's-eye* maple.

**bird shot,** small shot for shooting birds.

**bi·reme** (bī′rēm), ***n.*** [< L. < *bi-* + *remus*, oar], a galley having two rows of oars on each side.

**bi·ret·ta** (bi-ret′ə), ***n.*** [< It. < LL. dim. of L. *birrus*, a hood, cloak], a square cap with three projections and a tassel on top, worn by R. C. clergy: also sp. **birretta, beretta, berretta.**

BIRETTA

**Bir·ken·head** (būr′kən-hed′), ***n.*** a city in W England, at the mouth of the River Mersey: pop., 143,000.

**birl** (būrl), ***v.t.* & *v.i.*** [? echoic, after *whirl, purl,* etc.], 1. to revolve rapidly. 2. to whirr.

**birl·ing** (būr′liŋ), ***n.*** a competition among lumberjacks in which each tries to keep his balance while revolving a floating log with his feet.

**Bir·ming·ham** (būr′miŋ-ham; *also, and for 1 always,* -əm), ***n.*** 1. a city in central England: pop., 1,092,000. 2. a city in N Alabama: pop., 341,000.

**Bir·o·bi·jan, Bir·o·bi·dzhan** (bêr′ō-bi-jän′), ***n.*** 1. the Jewish National Autonomous Region in the R.S.F.S.R. 2. its capital: pop., 41,000.

**birth** (būrth), ***n.*** [AS. *byrde* < *beran*, to bear], 1. the act of bringing forth offspring. 2. a person or thing born or produced. 3. the act of being born. 4. descent or origin. 5. descent from nobility. 6. the beginning of anything: as, the *birth* of a nation. 7. an inherited or natural inclination: as, an actor by *birth*. **—give birth to,** 1. to bring forth (offspring). 2. to originate.

**birth control,** control of how many children a woman will have, as by contraception.

**birth·day** (būrth′dā′), ***n.*** 1. the day of a person's birth or a thing's beginning. 2. the anniversary of this day.

**birth·mark** (būrth′märk′), ***n.*** a skin blemish present at birth.

**birth·place** (būrth′plās′), ***n.*** 1. the place of one's birth. 2. the place of a thing's origin.

**birth rate,** the number of births per year per thousand of population in a given group: sometimes other units of time or population are used.

**birth·right** (būrth′rīt′), ***n.*** any rights that a person has by birth.

**birth·stone** (būrth′stōn′), ***n.*** a precious or semiprecious gem symbolizing the month of one's birth: as, the garnet is the *birthstone* of January.

**Bis·cay, Bay of** (bis′kā, -ki), a part of the Atlantic, north of Spain and west of France.

**bis·cuit** (bis′kit), ***n.*** [*pl.* -CUITS, -CUIT], [OFr. *bescoit* < L. *bis*, twice + *coctus*, pp. of *coquere*, to cook], 1. [Chiefly Brit.], a crisp wafer; cracker or cooky. 2. a quick bread, made light by baking powder or soda and baked in small pieces. 3. light brown; tan. 4. pottery after the first firing and before glazing.

**bi·sect** (bī-sekt′), ***v.t.*** [< *bi-* + L. *sectus*, pp. of *secare*, to cut], 1. to cut in two. 2. in *geometry*, to divide into two equal parts. ***v.i.*** to divide; fork. **—bi·sec′tion,** ***n.*** **—bi·sec′tion·al,** ***adj.*** **—bi·sec′tion·al·ly,** ***adv.*** **—bi·sec′tor,** ***n.***

**bi·sex·u·al** (bī-sek′shoo-əl), ***adj.*** 1. of both sexes. 2. having both male and female organs; hermaphroditic. ***n.*** 1. a hermaphrodite. 2. a person who is sexually attracted by both sexes.

**bish·op** (bish′əp), ***n.*** [AS. *bisc(e)op* < L. < Gr. *episkopos*, overseer < *epi-*, upon + *skopein*, to look], 1. a high-ranking clergyman with authority over a church district or diocese. 2. a chessman that can move only in a diagonal direction. **—bish′op·less,** ***adj.***

**bish·op·ric** (bish′əp-rik), ***n.*** the district, position, authority, or rank of a bishop.

**Bis·marck** (biz′märk), ***n.*** the capital of North Dakota, on the Missouri River: pop., 28,000.

**Bis·marck, Ot·to von** (ôt′ō fôn bis′märk; Eng. biz′märk), 1815–1898: Prussian chancellor.

**Bismarck Archipelago,** a group of islands northeast of New Guinea: part of the Australian trust territory of New Guinea.

**bis·muth** (biz′məth), ***n.*** [G. *bismut, wismut*], a hard, brittle, metallic element that is grayish-white with a tinge of red, used chiefly in making alloys of low melting point: symbol, Bi; at. wt., 209.00; at. no., 83. **—bis′muth·al,** ***adj.***

**bi·son** (bī′s'n, -z'n), ***n.*** [*pl.* BISON], [Fr. < L. < Gmc. hyp. *wisunt*], any of a number of related four-legged mammals with a shaggy mane, short, curved horns, and a humped back, as the American buffalo or the European aurochs.

AMERICAN BISON (10 ft. long)

**bisque** (bisk), ***n.*** [Fr.], 1. a rich meat soup made from shellfish, rabbit, fowl, etc. 2. a thick, strained, creamed vegetable soup.

**bis·sex·tile** (bi-seks′t'l, -tīl), ***adj.*** [< L. *bis*, twice + *sextus*, sixth; Feb. 24 (sixth day before the calends of March) was reckoned twice every fourth year], denoting or containing the extra day (February 29) of a leap year. ***n.*** a leap year.

**bis·ter, bis·tre** (bis′tēr), ***n.*** [Fr. *bistre*], 1. a dark-brown pigment made from soot. 2. dark brown. ***adj.*** dark-brown.

**bis·tro** (bis′trō; Fr. bē′strō′), ***n.*** [Fr. slang < dial. *bistro*, a shepherd], a small cafe or bar.

**bi·sul·fate, bi·sul·phate** (bī-sul′fāt), ***n.*** an acid sulfate, which, in water solutions, produces hydrogen ions as well as sulfate ions.

**bi·sul·fid, bi·sul·phid** (bī-sul′fid), ***n.*** bisulfide.

**bi·sul·fide, bi·sul·phide** (bī-sul′fīd, bī-sul′fid), ***n.*** 1. hydrosulfide. 2. erroneously, a disulfide.

**bit** (bit), ***n.*** [< AS. *bite*, a bite < *bitan*, to bite], 1. a metal mouthpiece on a bridle, acting as a control. 2. anything that curbs or controls. 3. the part of a key that actually turns the lock. 4. the cutting part of any tool. 5. a drilling or boring tool for use in a brace, drill press, etc. ***v.t.*** [BITTED, BITTING], 1. to put a bit into the mouth of (a horse); hence, 2. to check or curb.

**bit** (bit), ***n.*** [AS. *bita*, a piece < *bitan*, to bite], 1. a small piece or quantity. 2. somewhat: as, he's a *bit* of a bore. 3. [Colloq.], an amount equal to 12½ cents: now usually in **two bits** (a quarter) or multiples thereof. 4. [Colloq.], a short time; moment. 5. a very small role in a play. ***adj.*** very small: as, a *bit* part. **—bit by bit,** little by little; gradually. **—do one's bit,** to do one's share.

**bitch** (bich), ***n.*** [AS. *bicce*], 1. the female of the dog, wolf, fox, etc. 2. a bad or bad-tempered woman: a vulgar term of contempt. ***v.i.*** [Slang], to complain. ***v.t.*** [< *botch*], [Slang], to spoil by bungling (usually with *up*). **—bitch′y,** ***adj.***

**bite** (bīt), ***v.t.*** [BIT, BITTEN or BIT, BITING], [AS. *bitan*], 1. to seize or cut with or as with the teeth. 2. to cut into, as with a sharp weapon. 3. to sting, as a snake. 4. to cause to smart. 5. to grip; press hard into, as a car wheel. 6. to eat into; corrode. ***v.i.*** 1. to press or snap the teeth (*into, at,* etc.). 2. to cause a biting, or smarting, sensation. 3. to swallow a bait; hence, 4. to be caught, as by a trick. ***n.*** 1. a biting. 2. biting quality; sting; smart. 3. a wound or sting from biting. 4. a mouthful. 5. a tight hold or grip. 6. [Colloq.], a small lunch; snack. 7. in *dentistry*, the way the upper and lower teeth come together. **—bite off more than one can chew,** to attempt more than one is capable of. **—bite the dust,** 1. to fall dead or dying, as in combat. 2. to be humbled or defeated. **—bit′er,** ***n.***

**bit·ing** (bīt′iŋ), ***adj.*** 1. cutting; sharp. 2. sarcastic. **—bit′ing·ly,** ***adv.*** **—bit′ing·ness,** ***n.***

**bitt** (bit), ***n.*** [? < ON. *biti*, a beam], in *nautical usage*, any of the deck posts, often in pairs, to which ropes or cables are fastened. ***v.t.*** to wind (ropes or cables) around a bitt.

**bit·ter** (bit′ēr), ***adj.*** [< AS. < base of *bitan*, to bite], 1. having a sharp and disagreeable taste; acrid, as quinine. 2. causing or showing sorrow, pain, etc. 3. sharp and disagreeable; harsh: as, a *bitter* wind, *bitter* remarks. ***adv.*** bitterly. ***n.*** something bitter: as, take the *bitter* with the sweet. ***v.t.* & *v.i.*** to make or become bitter. **—bit′ter·ish,** ***adj.*** **—bit′ter·ly,** ***adv.*** **—bit′ter·ness,** ***n.***

**bit·tern** (bit′ērn), ***n.*** [*pl.* -TERNS, -TERN; see PLURAL, II, D, 1], [OFr. *butor;* ult. < L. *butio*], a heronlike wading bird with a booming cry.

**bit·ter·root** (bit′ēr-rōōt′, -root′), ***n.*** a plant of the Rocky Mountains, with clusters of narrow leaves and white or pink flowers.

**bit·ters** (bit'ẽrz), ***n.pl.*** a liquor containing bitter herbs, roots, etc. and usually alcohol, used as a medicine and for flavoring in some cocktails.
**bit·ter·sweet** (bit'ẽr-swēt'), ***n.*** 1. a poisonous vine with purple flowers and red berries that taste bitter and sweet. 2. a climbing shrub with greenish flowers, yellow fruit, and red seeds. ***adj.*** both bitter and sweet; both painful and pleasant.
**bi·tu·men** (bi-tōō'mən, -tū', bich'oo-), ***n.*** [L.], any of several substances obtained as asphaltic residue in the distillation of coal tar, petroleum, etc., or occurring as natural asphalt. —**bi·tu'mi·nize'** (-mə-nīz'), ***v.t.*** [-NIZED, -NIZING]. —**bi·tu'mi·noid** (-mə-noid), ***adj.*** —**bi·tu'mi·nous** (-mə-nəs), ***adj.***
**bituminous coal,** coal that yields pitch or tar when it burns; soft coal.
**bi·va·lent** (bī-vā'lənt, biv'ə-), ***adj.*** 1. having two valences. 2. having a valence of two. Also, esp. for 2, **divalent.** —**bi·va'lence, bi·va'len·cy,** ***n.***
**bi·valve** (bī'valv'), ***n.*** any mollusk having two valves or shells hinged together, as a mussel, clam, etc. ***adj.*** having two shells hinged together.
**biv·ou·ac** (biv'ōō-ak', biv'wak), ***n.*** [Fr. < OHG. *biwacht; bi-*, by + *wacht*, a guard], a temporary encampment (usually of soldiers) in the open, with or without shelter. ***v.i.*** [-ACKED, -ACKING], to encamp in the open.
**bi·week·ly** (bī-wēk'li), ***adj. & adv.*** 1. (occurring) once every two weeks. 2. semiweekly, ***n.*** [*pl.* -LIES], a publication that appears biweekly.
**bi·year·ly** (bī-yêr'li), ***adj. & adv.*** twice a year.
**bi·zarre** (bi-zär'), ***adj.*** [Fr. < Sp. or Port. *bizarro*, bold < Basque *bizar*, a beard], odd in manner, appearance, etc.; grotesque; queer; eccentric. —**bi-zarre'ly,** ***adv.*** —**bi·zarre'ness,** ***n.***
**Bi·zet, Georges** (zhôrzh bē'ze'; Eng. bi-zā'), 1838–1875; French composer.
**Bk,** in *chemistry*, berkelium.
**bk.,** [*pl.* BKS.], 1. bank. 2. block. 3. book.
**bkg.,** banking.
**bkt.,** 1. basket; baskets. 2. bracket.
**bl.,** 1. bale; bales. 2. barrel; barrels. 3. black.
**B/L,** [*pl.* BS/L], bill of lading.
**B.L.,** Bachelor of Laws.
**blab** (blab), ***v.t. & v.i.*** [BLABBED, BLABBING], 1. to give away (secrets). 2. to chatter; prattle. ***n.*** 1. loose chatter; gossip. 2. a person who blabs.
**blab·ber** (blab'ẽr), ***n.*** a person who blabs. ***v.t. & v.i.*** [Obs. or Dial.], to blab; babble.
**black** (blak), ***adj.*** [AS. *blæc*], 1. opposite to white: see **color.** 2. dark-complexioned. 3. Negro. 4. totally without light; in complete darkness; dark. 5. soiled; dirty. 6. wearing black clothing. 7. evil; wicked. 8. disgraceful. 9. sad; dismal. 10. sullen; angered. 11. without hope: as, a *black* future. 12. humorous or satirical in a morbid or cynical way. ***n.*** 1. black pigment: opposite of white. 2. dark clothing, as for mourning. 3. a person of dark complexion. 4. a Negro: now the term preferred by some. ***v.t. & v.i.*** 1. to blacken; soil. 2. to put blacking on (shoes, etc.). —**black out,** 1. to cover (writing, etc.) as with pencil marks. 2. to cause a blackout in. 3. to lose consciousness. —**black'er,** ***n.*** —**black'ish,** ***adj.*** —**black'ly,** ***adv.*** —**black'ness,** ***n.***
**black·a·moor** (blak'ə-moor'), ***n.*** [< *black* + *Moor*], 1. a Negro. 2. any dark-skinned person.
**black-and-blue** (blak'ən-blōō'), ***adj.*** discolored, as by a bruise.
**black and white,** writing: as, put your agreement down in *black and white.*
**black art,** black magic.
**black·ball** (blak'bôl'), ***n.*** a vote against a person or thing. ***v.t.*** 1. to vote against; hence, 2. to ostracize. —**black'ball'er,** ***n.***
**black bass** (bas), any of a number of related fresh-water game fishes of North America.
**black bear,** 1. a variety of large American bear. 2. a variety of large bear found in Asia.
**black·ber·ry** (blak'ber'i), ***n.*** [*pl.* -RIES], 1. the small, edible, dark purple or black fruit of any of a number of related brambles of the rose family. 2. a bush or vine bearing this fruit.
**black·bird** (blak'bũrd'), ***n.*** any of various birds the male of which is almost entirely black, as the red-winged blackbird, the English thrush, etc.
**black·board** (blak'bôrd', -bōrd'), ***n.*** a smooth surface, usually of slate, on which one can write or draw with chalk.
**black·cap** (blak'kap'), ***n.*** 1. a bird with a black, caplike crown, as the chickadee. 2. the black raspberry.
**black·cock** (blak'kok'), ***n.*** [*pl.* -COCKS, -COCK; see PLURAL, II, D, 1], the male of the black grouse.
**Black Death,** a deadly disease, probably bubonic plague, which greatly reduced the population of Europe and Asia in the 14th century.
**black·en** (blak''n), ***v.i.*** to become black or dark. ***v.t.*** 1. to make black; darken. 2. to slander; defame. —**black'en·er,** ***n.***
**black eye,** 1. a discoloration of the skin surrounding an eye, resulting from a sharp blow, or contusion. 2. [Colloq.], shame; dishonor.
**black-eyed Su·san** (blak'īd' sōō'z'n), a yellow, daisylike flower with a dark, cone-shaped center.
**black·face** (blak'fās'), ***adj.*** having a black face. ***n.*** 1. a Negro in a minstrel show. 2. a person made up as a Negro. 3. make-up used for Negro roles, usually exaggerated with comic intent.
**Black·feet** (blak'fēt'), ***n.pl.*** [*sing.* -FOOT (-foot')], members of three tribes of Algonquian Indians who lived in Montana and Saskatchewan, east of the Rocky Mountains.
**black flag,** the flag of piracy, usually black with a white skull and crossbones.
**Black·foot** (blak'foot'), ***n.*** [*pl.* -FEET (-fēt'); *collectively*, -FOOT], a member of the Blackfeet. ***adj.*** of the Blackfeet.
**Black Forest,** a mountainous district, about 100 miles long, in SW Germany.
**black grouse,** a large grouse of Europe and Asia, the male of which is almost entirely black.
**black·guard** (blag'ẽrd, -ärd), ***n.*** [*black* + *guard*], a scoundrel; villain. ***adj.*** vulgar, low, abusive, etc. ***v.t.*** to abuse with words; revile. ***v.i.*** to behave as a blackguard. —**black'guard·ism,** ***n.*** —**black'guard-ly,** ***adj. & adv.***
**Black Hand,** 1. a group of Sicilian immigrant blackmailers who operated in New York in the early 20th century. 2. any similar secret society.
**black·head** (blak'hed'), ***n.*** 1. a scaup duck. 2. a black-tipped plug of dried fatty matter in a pore of the skin. 3. a disease of turkeys.
**black-heart·ed** (blak'här'tid), ***adj.*** wicked; evil.
**Black Hills,** mountains of W South Dakota and NE Wyoming.
**black·ing** (blak'iŋ), ***n.*** a black polish for use on stoves, shoes, boots, etc.
**black·jack** (blak'jak'), ***n.*** [see JACK-], 1. a large mug, formerly of tar-coated leather. 2. the black flag. 3. a small, leather-covered bludgeon with a flexible handle. 4. a card game in which the object is to get cards totaling twenty-one. Also **black jack.** ***v.t.*** 1. to hit with a blackjack. 2. to coerce by threatening.
**black lead,** graphite.
**black·leg** (blak'leg'), ***n.*** 1. an infectious disease of cattle and sheep, usually fatal. 2. [British], a strikebreaker or scab. 3. [Colloq.], a gambler who cheats; crook.
**black letter,** a kind of type with thick lines. —**black'-let'ter,** ***adj.***
**black list,** a list of those to be punished, refused employment, etc. —**black'-list',** ***v.t.***
**black magic,** magic with an evil purpose; sorcery.
**black·mail** (blak'māl'), ***n.*** [lit., black rent < OFr. *maille*, a coin], 1. payment extorted to prevent disclosure of information that could bring disgrace. 2. a blackmailing. ***v.t.*** 1. to get or try to get blackmail from. 2. to coerce (*into* doing something) as by threats. —**black'mail'er,** ***n.***
**Black Ma·ri·a** (mə-rī'ə), a patrol wagon.
**black mark,** a mark of failure, criticism, etc.
**black market,** a place or system for selling goods illegally, especially in violation of rationing or price control: cf. **gray market.** —**black mar·ket·eer** (mär'kə-têr'). —**black'-mar'ket·ing,** ***n.***
**black nightshade,** a weedy plant with white flowers, poisonous leaves, and black berries.
**black·out** (blak'out'), ***n.*** 1. the extinguishing of all stage lights to end a play or scene. 2. an extinguishing or concealing of all lights that might be visible to enemy air raiders, etc. at night. 3. a momentary lapse of consciousness, such as an aviator often experiences in coming out of a steep dive. 4. suppression, censorship, concealment, etc. ***adj.*** of or for a blackout.
**black pepper,** 1. a hot seasoning made by grinding the dried, black berries of a kind of pepper plant. 2. the plant.
**Black Sea,** a sea surrounded by the U.S.S.R., Asia Minor, and the Balkan Peninsula.

**black sheep,** one regarded as undesirable, disgraceful, etc. by his family or associates.
**black shirt, Black Shirt,** [from the uniform], a member of the Italian Fascist party or of the German Nazi Elite Guard.
**black·smith** (blak′smith′), ***n.*** a man who works and repairs iron, and shoes horses.
**black·snake** (blak′snāk′), ***n.*** 1. a harmless black or dark-colored snake found in North America. 2. a long, heavy whip of braided leather or rawhide.
**Black·stone,** Sir **William** (blak′stōn′, blak′stən), 1723–1780; English jurist and legal historian.
**black·thorn** (blak′thôrn′), ***n.*** a thorny shrub with purple or black, plumlike fruit; sloe.
**black tie,** 1. a black bow tie, properly worn with a dinner jacket. 2. a dinner jacket and the proper accessories. Distinguished from *white tie.*
**black walnut,** 1. a tall walnut tree with edible, oily nuts and hard, dark-brown wood, much used in making furniture. 2. its wood. 3. its nut.
**black widow,** the female of an American spider, having a glossy black body and a very poisonous bite: so called because it eats its mate.
**blad·der** (blad′ẽr), ***n.*** [AS. *blæddre*], 1. a bag of membranous tissue in the bodies of many animals, that inflates to receive and contain liquids or gases; esp., the **urinary bladder** in the pelvic cavity, which holds urine flowing from the kidneys. 2. a thing resembling this: as, a football *bladder.* —**blad′der·like′,** ***adj.*** —**blad′der·y,** ***adj.***
**blad·der·wort** (blad′ẽr-wũrt′), ***n.*** a bog or water plant with small, bladderlike parts on its leaves for catching small organisms as food.
**blade** (blād), ***n.*** [AS. *blæd*], 1. the leaf of a grass or a cereal. 2. a broad, flat surface, as of an oar. 3. a flat bone: as, the shoulder *blade.* 4. the cutting part of a knife, tool, etc. 5. a sword. 6. a swordsman. 7. a gay, dashing young man. 8. in *botany,* the flat, expanded part of a leaf 9. in *phonetics,* the flat part of the tongue, behind the tip. ***v.i.*** [BLADED, BLADING], to grow with blades. —**blade′less,** ***adj.*** —**blade′like′,** ***adj.***
**blah** (blä), ***n. & interj.*** [Slang], nonsense.
**blain** (blān), ***n.*** [< AS. *blegen*], a pustule; blister.
**Blake, William** (blāk), 1757–1827; English poet and artist.
**blam·a·ble, blame·a·ble** (blām′ə-b'l), ***adj.*** that deserves blame; culpable. —**blam′a·ble·ness, blame′a·ble·ness,** ***n.*** —**blam′a·bly, blame′a·bly,** ***adv.***
**blame** (blām), ***v.t.*** [BLAMED, BLAMING], [< OFr. < LL. *blasphemare;* see BLASPHEME], 1. to accuse; condemn (*for* something). 2. to find fault with. 3. to put the responsibility of (an error, fault, etc. *on*). ***n.*** 1. a blaming; condemnation. 2. responsibility for a fault or wrong. 3. [Archaic], fault. —**be to blame,** to deserve blame. —**blame′ful,** ***adj.*** —**blame′ful·ly,** ***adv.*** —**blame′ful·ness,** ***n.*** —**blame′less,** ***adj.*** —**blame′less·ly,** ***adv.*** —**blame′less·ness,** ***n.***
**blame·wor·thy** (blām′wũr′thi), ***adj.*** deserving to be blamed. —**blame′wor′thi·ness,** ***n.***
**blanch** (blanch, blänch), ***v.t.*** [OFr. *blanchir* < *blanc;* see BLANK], 1. to make white; bleach. 2. to make pale. 3. in *cookery,* to remove the skin of by scalding. ***v.i.*** to whiten; turn pale.
**blanc·mange** (blə-mänzh′), ***n.*** [Fr. < *blanc,* white + *manger,* to eat], a sweet, molded, jellylike dessert made of a starchy substance and milk.
**bland** (bland), ***adj.*** [L. *blandus*], 1. pleasantly smooth; agreeable; suave. 2. mild; soothing; temperate. —**bland′ly,** ***adv.*** —**bland′ness,** ***n.***
**blan·dish** (blan′dish), ***v.t. & v.i.*** [< OFr. < L. *blandiri* < *blandus,* mild], to flatter; coax; cajole. —**blan′dish·er,** ***n.*** —**blan′dish·ment,** ***n.***
**blank** (blaŋk), ***adj.*** [OFr. *blanc* < OHG. *blanch,* white], 1. [Rare], colorless; white. 2. not written on; not marked: as, a *blank* paper. 3. having an empty or vacant look. 4. empty of thought: as, a *blank* mind. 5. utter; complete: as, a *blank* denial. 6. lacking certain elements or characteristics. ***n.*** 1. an empty space, especially one to be filled out in a printed form. 2. such a printed form. 3. an empty place or time. 4. a lottery ticket that fails to win. 5. a piece of metal, etc. to be finished by stamping or marking. 6. a powder-filled cartridge without a bullet: in full, **blank cartridge.** ***v.t.*** 1. to make blank; conceal by covering over. 2. in *games,* to hold (an opponent) scoreless. —**draw a blank,** [Colloq.], to be unsuccessful in an attempt. —**blank′ly,** ***adv.*** —**blank′ness,** ***n.***
**blank check,** a check carrying a signature only and allowing the bearer to fill in any amount.
**blan·ket** (blaŋ′kit), ***n.*** [< OFr. dim. of *blanc,* white], 1. a large, soft piece of cloth used for warmth, especially as a bed cover. 2. anything like a blanket: as, a *blanket* of leaves. ***adj.*** covering a group of conditions: as, a *blanket* insurance policy. ***v.t.*** 1. to cover, as with a blanket. 2. to apply uniformly to, as rates. 3. to overspread; overlie. 4. to suppress or obscure: as, a powerful radio station *blankets* a weaker one. —**blan′ket·less,** ***adj.***
**blank verse,** 1. [Rare], unrhymed verse. 2. unrhymed verse having five iambic feet per line.
**blare** (blâr), ***v.t. & v.i.*** [BLARED, BLARING], [ME. *bleren,* to cry noisily < LG.], 1. to sound loudly with a trumpetlike quality. 2. to exclaim loudly. ***n.*** 1. a loud, trumpetlike sound. 2. brilliance or glare, as of color.
**blar·ney** (blär′ni), ***n.*** [see BLARNEY STONE], flattery. ***v.t. & v.i.*** [-NEYED, -NEYING], to flatter; coax.
**Blarney stone,** a stone in Blarney Castle in the county of Cork, Ireland, said to impart skill in blarney to those who kiss it.
**bla·sé** (blä-zā′, blä′zā), ***adj.*** [Fr., pp. of *blaser,* to satiate], having indulged in pleasure so much as to be somewhat weary of it; satiated and bored.
**blas·pheme** (blas-fēm′), ***v.t.*** [-PHEMED, -PHEMING], [< OFr. < LL. < Gr. *blasphēmein,* to speak evil of], 1. to speak profanely of or to (God or sacred things). 2. to curse or revile (another). ***v.i.*** to utter blasphemy. —**blas·phem′er,** ***n.***
**blas·phe·my** (blas′fi-mi), ***n.*** [*pl.* -MIES], [see BLASPHEME], 1. profane or mocking abuse of God or anything regarded as sacred. 2. contempt for God. —**blas′phe·mous,** ***adj.*** —**blas′phe·mous·ly,** ***adv.***
**blast** (blast, bläst), ***n.*** [< AS. *blæst*], 1. a gust of wind; strong rush of air. 2. the sound of a sudden rush of air or gas, as through a trumpet. 3. the strong, steady current of air in a blast furnace. 4. an abrupt and damaging influence; blight. 5. an explosion, as of dynamite. 6. a charge of explosive causing this. ***v.i.*** to suffer from a blight. ***v.t.*** 1. to damage or destroy by or as by a blight; wither; ruin. 2. to blow up with an explosive; explode. —**in** (or **at**) **full blast,** at full speed or capacity. —**blast off,** [Colloq.], to take off with explosive force and begin its flight, as a rocket.
**-blast** (blast), [< Gr. *blastos,* a sprout], a combining form meaning *formative, embryonic.*
**blast·ed** (blas′tid, bläs′-), ***adj.*** 1. blighted; withered; destroyed. 2. damned; accursed.
**blast furnace,** a smelting furnace into which a blast of air is forced from below to produce intense heat.
**blast-off, blast·off** (blast′ôf′), ***n.*** [Colloq.], the launching of a rocket, ballistic missile, etc.
**blas·tu·la** (blas′choo-lə), ***n.*** [*pl.* -LAE (-lē′)], [Mod. L. dim. < Gr. *blastos,* a germ, sprout], the stage of development at which an embryo consists of one or several layers of cells around a central cavity. —**blas′tu·lar,** ***adj.***
**blat** (blat), ***v.i.*** [BLATTED, BLATTING], [var. of *bleat*], [Colloq.], to make a sound like that of a sheep or calf; bleat. ***v.t.*** to blurt out.

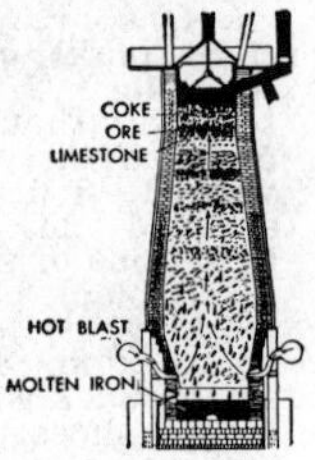

BLAST FURNACE

**bla·tant** (blā′t'nt), ***adj.*** [coined by E. Spenser; prob. < L. *blaterare,* to babble], 1. disagreeably loud; noisy. 2. obtrusive; gaudy; flashy. —**bla′tan·cy** [*pl.* -CIES], ***n.*** —**bla′tant·ly,** ***adv.***
**blath·er** (blath′ẽr), ***n.*** [ON. *blathr*], foolish talk. ***v.i. & v.t.*** to talk foolishly. Also **blether.**
**blath·er·skite** (blath′ẽr-skīt′), ***n.*** [Colloq.], 1. blather. 2. a talkative, foolish person.
**blaze** (blāz), ***n.*** [AS. *blæse*], 1. a brilliant burst of flame; fire. 2. any bright light or glare. 3. a sudden or spectacular outburst: as, a *blaze* of oratory. 4. a brightness; vivid display. ***v.i.*** [BLAZED, BLAZING], 1. to burn rapidly or brightly. 2. to give off a strong light; glare. 3. to be deeply stirred, as with anger. ***v.t.*** to cause to blaze. —**blaze away,** to shoot. —**blaz′ing·ly,** ***adv.***
**blaze** (blāz), ***n.*** [prob. < D. < ON. *blesi* < same ult. source as *blaze* (flame)], 1. a white spot on an animal's face. 2. a mark made on a tree by cutting off a piece of bark. ***v.t.*** [BLAZED, BLAZING], to mark (a tree, trail, etc.) with blazes.
**blaze** (blāz), ***v.t.*** [BLAZED, BLAZING], [ON. *blasa,* to blow], to make known publicly; proclaim.
**blaz·er** (blāz′ẽr), ***n.*** [< *blaze* (fire) + *-er*], a light, brightly colored sports jacket.
**bla·zon** (blā′z'n), ***n.*** [OFr. *blason,* a shield], 1. a coat of arms. 2. a technical description of a coat of arms. 3. showy display. ***v.t.*** 1. to make widely known; proclaim (often with *forth, out,* or *abroad*). 2. to describe or paint (coats of arms). —**bla′zon·er,** ***n.*** —**bla′zon·ment, bla′zon·ry** [*pl.* -RIES], ***n.***
**bldg.,** building.

**bleach** (blēch), *v.t. & v.i.* [AS. *blæcan* < *blac*, pale], to make or become white or colorless by means of chemicals, by exposure to sunlight, etc. *n.* 1. a bleaching. 2. any chemical used for bleaching. —**bleach'er**, *n.* —**bleach'er·y** [*pl.* -IES], *n.*

**bleach·ers** (blēch'ẽrz), *n.pl.* [< *bleach*: in reference to the effects of exposure], seats, usually roofless, for spectators at outdoor events.

**bleak** (blēk), *adj.* [prob. < ON. *bleikr*, pale], 1. exposed to wind and cold; unsheltered; bare. 2. cold; cutting; harsh. 3. cheerless; gloomy. —**bleak'ly**, *adv.* —**bleak'ness**, *n.*

**blear** (blêr), *adj.* [ME. *bleren*], 1. made dim by tears, mucous film, etc.: said of eyes. 2. blurred. *v.t.* 1. to dim with tears, film, etc. 2. to blur.

**blear-eyed** (blêr'īd'), *adj.* having blear eyes.

**blear·y** (blêr'i), *adj.* [-IER, -IEST], 1. somewhat blear or blurred. 2. having blear eyes. —**blear'i·ly**, *adv.* —**blear'i·ness**, *n.*

**bleat** (blēt), *v.i.* [AS. *blætan*], 1. to make the cry of a sheep, lamb, goat, or calf. 2. to make a sound like this cry. *v.t.* to say in a weak, trembling voice. *n.* a bleating cry or sound. —**bleat'er**, *n.* —**bleat'ing·ly**, *adv.*

**bleed** (blēd), *v.i.* [BLED (bled), BLEEDING], [AS. *bledan* < *blod*, blood], 1. to emit blood; lose blood. 2. to suffer wounds or die from loss of blood; hence, 3. to suffer; feel pain, grief, or sympathy. 4. to ooze sap, juice, etc., as bruised plants. 5. to come through a covering coat of paint. *v.t.* 1. to draw blood from. 2. to ooze (sap, juice, etc.). 3. to take sap or juice from. 4. [Colloq.], to extort money from.

**bleed·er** (blēd'ẽr), *n.* one who bleeds profusely from even a slight cut.

**bleeding heart,** a plant with fernlike leaves and drooping clusters of pink, heart-shaped flowers.

**blem·ish** (blem'ish), *v.t.* [< OFr. < *ble(s)me*, pale], to mar; injure; sully. *n.* a mark of imperfection; defect; fault; flaw. —**blem'ish·er**, *n.*

**blench** (blench), *v.t. & v.i.* to blanch.

**blench** (blench), *v.i.* [AS. *blencan*, to deceive], to shy away; shrink back; flinch. —**blench'er**, *n.*

**blend** (blend), *v.t.* [BLENDED or BLENT, BLENDING], [AS. *blendan* & ON. *blanda*, to mix], 1. to mix or mingle (varieties of tea, tobacco, etc.). 2. to mix or fuse thoroughly, so that the ingredients cannot be distinguished. *v.i.* 1. to mix; merge. 2. to shade gradually into each other, as colors. 3. to go well together; harmonize. *n.* 1. a blending. 2. a mixture of varieties: as, a *blend* of coffee.

**blende** (blend), *n.* [G. < *blenden*, to blind, dazzle], 1. sphalerite. 2. any of certain other sulfides.

**blended whisky,** whisky blended with neutral spirits, as of grain or potatoes.

**blen·ny** (blen'i), *n.* [*pl.* -NIES, -NY; see PLURAL, II, D, 1], [< L. < Gr. < *blenna*, slime], any of a number of related spiny-finned fishes covered with a slimy substance. —**blen'ni·oid'** (-oid'), *adj.*

**bless** (bles), *v.t.* [BLESSED or BLEST (blest), BLESSING], [AS. *bletsian*, orig. to consecrate with blood < *blod*, blood], 1. to make holy; hallow. 2. to ask divine favor for. 3. to wish well to. 4. to favor or endow (*with*): as, *blessed* with eloquence. 5. to make happy or prosperous. 6. to glorify; praise. 7. to make the sign of the cross upon (oneself). 8. to guard; preserve. —**bless me** (or **you, him,** etc.)! an exclamation of surprise, dismay, etc.

**bless·ed** (bles'id, blest), *adj.* 1. holy; sacred. 2. blissful; fortunate. 3. of or in eternal bliss; beatified. 4. bringing comfort. 5. cursed: a mild oath. —**bless'ed·ly**, *adv.* —**bless'ed·ness**, *n.*

**bless·ed event** (bles'id), the birth of a child: now chiefly jocular.

**Blessed Virgin,** the Virgin Mary.

**bless·ing** (bles'iŋ), *n.* [see BLESS], 1. a benediction. 2. an invoking of divine favor. 3. the gift of divine favor. 4. a wish for prosperity, success, etc. 5. approval. 6. anything that gives happiness or prevents misfortune.

**blest** (blest) alt. pt. and pp. of **bless.** *adj.* blessed.

**bleth·er** (bleth'ẽr), *n., v.i. & v.t.* blather.

**blew** (blo͞o), pt. of **blow.**

**blight** (blīt), *n.* [? < AS. *blieian* or ON. *blīkja*, to turn pale], 1. any parasite or insect that destroys or stunts plants. 2. any of several plant diseases, as mildew. 3. anything that destroys, prevents growth, frustrates, etc. *v.t* 1. to wither. 2. to destroy. *v.i.* to suffer blight.

**blimp** (blimp), *n.* [echoic coinage], [Colloq.], a small, nonrigid or semirigid airship.

**blind** (blīnd), *adj.* [AS.], 1. without the power of sight; sightless. 2. of or for sightless persons. 3. lacking insight or understanding. 4. done without adequate directions or knowledge: as, a *blind* search. 5. hard to see; hidden: as, a *blind* intersection. 6. having no opening. 7. closed at one end: as, a *blind* alley. 8. not controlled by intelligence or reason: as, *blind* destiny. 9. in *aeronautics*, by the use of instruments only: as, *blind* flying. *v.t.* 1. to make sightless. 2. to dazzle. 3. to deprive of the power of insight or judgment. 4. to make dim; obscure. 5. to hide. *n.* 1. anything that obscures or prevents sight. 2. anything that keeps out light, as a window shade. 3. a place or means of concealment. 4. a decoy. *adv.* 1. blindly. 2. recklessly. —**blind'ing**, *adj.* —**blind'ing·ly**, *adv.* —**blind'ly**, *adv.* —**blind'ness**, *n.*

**blind date,** [Slang], a social engagement arranged for a man and a woman previously unacquainted.

**blind·er** (blīn'dẽr), *n.* either of two flaps on a horse's bridle that shut out the side view.

**blind·fold** (blīnd'fōld'), *v.t.* [altered by confusion with *fold* < ME. *blindfeld*, struck blind; see FELL, *v.*], to cover the eyes of, as with a cloth. *n.* something used to cover the eyes. *adj.* 1. having the eyes covered. 2. reckless.

**blind·man's buff** (blīnd'manz' buf'), [*buff*, a blow < *buffet*], a game in which a blindfolded player has to catch and identify another.

**blind spot,** 1. the small area, insensitive to light, in the retina of the eye where the optic nerve enters. 2. a prejudice or ignorance that one has but is often unaware of.

**blink** (bliŋk), *v.i.* [? < D. *blinken*, to shine], 1. to wink rapidly. 2. to flash on and off; twinkle. 3. to look with eyes half-shut, winking, as in a glare. *v.t.* to cause (eyes, light, etc.) to wink or blink. *n.* 1. a blinking. 2. glimmer. 3. a glimpse. —**blink at,** to ignore; condone, as a mistake. —**on the blink,** [Slang], not working right; out of order.

**blink·er** (bliŋ'kẽr), *n.* 1. a blinder. 2. a flashing warning light at crossings.

**bliss** (blis), *n.* [AS. *bliths* < *blithe*, joyful], 1. great joy or happiness. 2. spiritual joy. —**bliss'ful**, *adj.* —**bliss'ful·ly**, *adv.* —**bliss'ful·ness**, *n.*

**blis·ter** (blis'tẽr), *n.* [D. *bluister* or OFr. *blestre* < ON. *blastr*], 1. a little swelling of the skin, filled with watery matter and caused by burning or rubbing. 2. anything shaped like a blister. *v.t.* 1. to raise blisters on. 2. to lash with words. *v.i.* to have or form blisters. —**blis'ter·y**, *adj.*

**blithe** (blīth), *adj.* [AS. < Gmc.], gay; joyful; cheerful. —**blithe'ly**, *adv.* —**blithe'ness**, *n.*

**blithe·some** (blīth'səm), *adj.* blithe; lighthearted. —**blithe'some·ly**, *adv.* —**blithe'some·ness**, *n.*

**B.Litt.**, *Baccalaureus Lit(t)erarum*, [L.], Bachelor of Letters; Bachelor of Literature: also **B.Lit.**

**blitz** (blits), *n.* [Colloq.], a blitzkrieg. *v.t.* to subject to a blitzkrieg; overwhelm and destroy.

**blitz·krieg** (blits'krēg'), *n.* [G. *blitz*, lightning + *krieg*, war], 1. sudden, swift, large-scale offensive warfare intended to win a quick victory. 2. swift, sudden, overwhelming attack.

**bliz·zard** (bliz'ẽrd), *n.* [dial. *bliz*, violent blow (akin to G. *blitz*, lightning) + *-ard*], a severe snowstorm with high wind.

**blk.**, 1. black. 2. block. 3. bulk.

**bloat** (blōt), *adj.* [ME. *blout*, soft; ON. *blautr*], bloated. *v.t. & v.i.* 1. to swell, as with water or air. 2. to puff up, as with pride. *n.* a bloated person or thing. —**bloat'ed**, *adj.*

**bloat** (blōt), *v.t.* [see BLOAT (to swell)], to cure (herring, etc.) by smoking. *n.* a bloater.

**bloat·er** (blōt'ẽr), *n.* a fat herring or mackerel that has been bloated (cured).

**blob** (blob), *n.* [echoic], a small drop or mass. *v.t.* [BLOBBED, BLOBBING], to splash, as with blobs.

**bloc** (blok), *n.* [Fr.; OFr.; LG. *block*, a lump], a group of persons, often of different political loyalties, combined for a common purpose.

**block** (blok), *n.* [see BLOC], 1. any large, solid piece of wood, stone, metal, etc. 2. a blocklike stand on which chopping, etc. is done: as, a headsman's *block*. 3. an auctioneer's platform. 4. a mold upon which hats, etc. are shaped. 5. an obstruction or hindrance. 6. a pulley in a frame. 7. a child's toy brick, usually wooden. 8. a group of buildings. 9. a city square. 10. one side of a city square. 11. any number of things regarded as a unit. 12. in *printing*, a piece of engraved wood, etc. with a design or picture. 13. in *railroading*, a length of track governed by signals. 14. in *sports*, an interception or thwarting of an opponent's play or movement. ***v.t.*** 1. to obstruct so as to prevent passage or progress. 2. to stand in the way of; hinder. 3. to shape or mold on a block. 4. to strengthen or support with blocks. 5. in *sports*, to hinder (an opponent or his play). ***v.i.*** to behave so as to hinder. **—block in** (or **out**), to sketch roughly; outline. **—on the block,** up for sale or auction. **—block'er,** ***n.***

**block·ade** (blo-kād'), ***n.*** [*block* + *-ade*], 1. a shutting off of a place or region by hostile troops or ships in order to prevent passage. 2. the force that maintains a blockade. 3. any strategic barrier. ***v.t.*** [-ADED, -ADING], to subject to a blockade. **—run the blockade,** to go through a blockade. **—blockad'er,** ***n.***

**blockade runner,** a ship or person that tries to go through or past a blockade.

**block and tackle,** pulley blocks and ropes or cables, used for hoisting large, heavy objects.

**block·bust·er** (blok'bus'tẽr), ***n.*** [Slang], a large aerial bomb that can demolish an entire city block.

**block·head** (blok'hed'), ***n.*** a stupid person.

**block·house** (blok'hous'), ***n.*** 1. a strong wooden fort with a projecting second story and openings in the walls for the defenders to shoot from. 2. any building of squared logs.

BLOCKHOUSE

**block·ish** (blok'ish), ***adj.*** stupid; dull. **—block'ish·ly,** ***adv.*** **—block'ish·ness,** ***n.***

**block·y** (blok'i), ***adj.*** [-IER, -IEST], 1. having contrasting blocks or patches. 2. stocky; chunky.

**bloke** (blōk), ***n.*** [Slang], a fellow; guy.

**blond** (blond), ***adj.*** [Fr., fem. *blonde* < LL. *blondus*, yellow], 1. having light-colored hair, skin, and eyes. 2. straw-colored; flaxen: said of hair. 3. light-colored: as, *blond* furniture. ***n.*** a blond man or boy. **—blond'ness,** ***n.***

**blonde** (blond), ***adj.*** blond. ***n.*** a blonde woman or girl. **—blonde'ness,** ***n.***

**blood** (blud), ***n.*** [< AS. *blod;* akin to G. *blut*], 1. the fluid, usually red, circulating in the arteries and veins of animals. 2. the spilling of blood; murder. 3. the essence of life; life: often **lifeblood.** 4. the life fluid, or sap, of a plant. 5. passion, temperament, or disposition. 6. parental heritage; family line; lineage. 7. kinship; family relation. 8. descent from nobility. 9. a dandy. **—bad blood,** anger; hatred. **—in cold blood,** 1. with cruelty; unfeelingly. 2. dispassionately; deliberately. **—make one's blood boil,** to make one angry. **—make one's blood run cold,** to terrify one. **—blood'like',** ***adj.***

**blood bank,** 1. a place where whole blood or plasma is stored for future use in transfusion. 2. any reserve of such blood.

**blood bath,** a massacre; slaughter.

**blood brother,** 1. a brother by birth. 2. a person bound to one by the ceremony of mingling his blood with one's own.

**blood count,** the number of red and white corpuscles in a given volume of a person's blood.

**blood·cur·dling** (blud'kũr'dliŋ), ***adj.*** very frightening; causing terror or horror.

**blood·ed** (blud'id), ***adj.*** 1. having (a specified kind of) blood: as, *hot-blooded.* 2. of fine stock or breed.

**blood group,** any of several (usually four) groups into which a person's blood is classified.

**blood·hound** (blud'hound'), ***n.*** 1. any of a breed of large, keen-scented dogs used to hunt escaped prisoners. 2. a person who pursues keenly or relentlessly; sleuth.

**blood·less** (blud'lis), ***adj.*** 1. without blood. 2. without bloodshed. 3. anemic or pale. 4. having little energy or vitality. 5. unfeeling; cruel. **—blood'less·ly,** ***adv.*** **—blood'less·ness,** ***n.***

**blood·let·ting** (blud'let'iŋ), ***n.*** the opening of a vein to remove blood; bleeding; leeching.

**blood money,** 1. money paid for the killing of someone. 2. money paid as compensation for a murder.

**blood plasma,** the fluid part of blood, as distinguished from the corpuscles, used in transfusions.

**blood poisoning,** a diseased condition of the blood due to certain microorganisms or other poisonous matter; septicemia.

**blood pressure,** the pressure exerted by the blood against the inner walls of the blood vessels: it varies with age, physical condition, etc.

**blood relation,** a person related by birth.

**blood·root** (blud'ro͞ot', -root'), ***n.*** a North American plant of the poppy family, with a white flower, a red root, and red sap.

**blood·shed** (blud'shed'), ***n.*** the shedding of blood; killing: also **blood'shed'ding.**

**blood·shot** (blud'shot'), ***adj.*** suffused or tinged with blood: said of the eyes.

**blood·stained** (blud'stānd'), ***adj.*** 1. soiled or discolored with blood. 2. guilty of murder.

**blood·stone** (blud'stōn'), ***n.*** a semiprecious, dark-green variety of quartz spotted with red jasper.

**blood stream,** the blood flowing through the body.

**blood·suck·er** (blud'suk'ẽr), ***n.*** 1. an animal that sucks blood; esp., a leech. 2. one who extorts or takes from others all he can get.

**blood·thirst·y** (blud'thũrs'ti), ***adj.*** murderous; cruel. **—blood'thirst'i·ly,** ***adv.*** **—blood'thirst'i·ness,** ***n.***

**blood type,** blood group.

**blood typing,** the classification of blood to determine compatible blood groups for transfusion.

**blood vessel,** a tube through which the blood circulates in the body; artery, vein, or capillary.

**blood·y** (blud'i), ***adj.*** [-IER, -IEST], 1. of, like, or containing blood. 2. covered or stained with blood. 3. involving bloodshed. 4. bloodthirsty. 5. [Brit. Slang], cursed; damned. ***adv.*** [Brit. Slang], very. ***v.t.*** [-IED, -YING], to cover or stain with blood. **—blood'i·ly,** ***adv.*** **—blood'i·ness,** ***n.***

**bloom** (blo͞om), ***n.*** [< ON. *blomi*, flowers], 1. a flower; blossom. 2. the state or time of flowering. 3. a state or time of most health, vigor, etc. 4. a youthful, healthy glow, as of the cheeks. 5. the grayish, powdery coating on certain fruits or leaves. 6. any similar coating, as on new coins. ***v.i.*** 1. to flower; blossom. 2. to be at one's prime. 3. to glow with color, health, etc. ***v.t.*** to make flower; give a bloom to; cause to flourish.

**bloom·er** (blo͞om'ẽr), ***n.*** [after Amelia Jenks *Bloomer*, Am. feminist who popularized it], 1. formerly, a woman's costume consisting of a short skirt and loose trousers gathered at the ankles; hence, 2. *pl. a*) baggy trousers gathered at the knee, worn by girls and women for athletics. *b*) a somewhat similar undergarment.

**bloom·ing** (blo͞om'iŋ), ***adj.*** 1. blossoming. 2. thriving; flourishing. 3. [Colloq.], utter; confounded: as, a *blooming* fool. **—bloom'ing·ly,** ***adv.***

**blos·som** (blos'əm), ***n.*** [AS. *blostma*], 1. a flower or bloom, especially of a fruit-bearing plant. 2. a state or time of flowering. ***v.i.*** 1. to have or open into blossoms; bloom. 2. to begin to thrive or flourish; develop. **—blos'som·y,** ***adj.***

**blot** (blot), ***n.*** [< AS. *plott*, clod], 1. a spot or stain, especially of ink. 2. an erasure. 3. a moral stain; disgrace. ***v.t.*** [BLOTTED, BLOTTING], 1. to spot; stain; blur. 2. to stain (a reputation); disgrace. 3. to erase or cancel (with *out*). 4. to darken or obscure (with *out*). 5. to dry with blotting paper. ***v.i.*** 1. to make blots. 2. to become blotted. 3. to be absorbent. **—blot'less,** ***adj.***

**blotch** (bloch), ***n.*** [extension of *blot* < OFr. *bloche*, clod], 1. a discolored patch or eruption on the skin. 2. any large, irregular blot or stain. ***v.t.*** to mark with blotches. **—blotch'y,** ***adj.***

**blot·ter** (blot'ẽr), ***n.*** 1. a piece of blotting paper. 2. a book for recording events as they occur: as, a police *blotter* is a record of arrests, etc.

**blotting paper,** a soft, absorbent paper used to dry a surface freshly written on in ink.

**blouse** (blous, blouz), ***n.*** [Fr.; workman's or peasant's smock], 1. a kind of shirtwaist worn by women and children. 2. a coat or tunic worn by soldiers, marines, etc. 3. a sailor's jumper. ***v.i.*** & ***v.t.*** [BLOUSED, BLOUSING], to gather in at the waistline. **—blouse'like',** ***adj.***

**blow** (blō), ***v.i.*** [BLEW (blo͞o), BLOWN (blōn), BLOWING], [< AS. *blawan*], 1. to stir or move: as, the wind blows. 2. to send forth air, as with the mouth. 3. to pant; be breathless. 4. to sound by blowing or being blown. 5. to spout water and air: as, whales *blow.* 6. to be carried by the wind: as, the paper *blew* away. 7. to storm. 8. to lay eggs: said of flies. 9. [Colloq.], to brag; boast. 10. [Slang], to go away. ***v.t.*** 1. to force air from (a bellows, etc.). 2. to send out (breath) from the mouth. 3. to force air onto, into, or through. 4. to drive by blowing. 5. to spread (news). 6. to sound by blowing. 7. to make (a sound) by blowing. 8. to inflate, as with anger. 9. to shape or form by air or gas. 10. to clear by blowing through. 11. to burst by an explosion (with *up* or *out*). 12. to cause (a horse) to pant. 13. to melt (a fuse, etc.). 14. [Colloq.], to spend (money) freely. 15. [Colloq.], to treat (*to* something). ***n.*** 1. a blowing or being blown. 2. a blast or gale. 3. a boast. **—blow hot**

**and cold,** to be favorable toward and then opposed to; vacillate. —**blow in,** [Slang], 1. to arrive. 2. to spend all (one's money). —**blow off,** [Colloq.], to release one's emotions, as by loud talking. —**blow out,** 1. to put out by blowing. 2. to burst suddenly, as a tire. 3. to melt, as a fuse. —**blow over,** 1. to move away, as rain clouds; hence, 2. to pass over; be forgotten. —**blow up,** 1. to fill with air or gas. 2. to explode. 3. to arise and become intense, as a storm. 4. [Colloq.], to scold severely. 5. [Colloq.], to lose one's temper. 6. to enlarge (a photograph). —**blow′er,** *n.*

**blow** (blō), *n.* [ME. *blaw;* prob. < *blow, v.i.*], 1. a hit or stroke, as with the fist. 2. a sudden attack or forcible effort. 3. a sudden calamity or misfortune; shock. —**at a** (or **one**) **blow,** with a single action. —**come to blows,** to begin fighting.

**blow** (blō), *v.i.* [BLEW (blo͞o), BLOWN (blōn), BLOWING], [AS. *blowan*], to bloom; blossom. *v.t.* to cause to bloom. *n.* a mass of blossoms.

**blow·fly** (blō′flī′), *n.* [*pl.* -FLIES], a two-winged fly that lays its eggs on meat, in wounds, etc.

**blow·gun** (blō′gun′), *n.* a long, tubelike weapon through which darts or pellets are blown.

**blow·hole** (blō′hōl′), *n.* 1. a hole in the top of the head of whales, etc., used for breathing. 2. a hole through which gas or air can escape. 3. a hole in the ice to which seals, etc. come for air.

**blown** (blōn), pp. of **blow.** *adj.* 1. swollen with gas. 2. out of breath, as with effort. 3. made by blowing or by using a blowpipe, etc.

**blow·out** (blō′out′), *n.* 1. the bursting of a tire. 2. the melting of an electric fuse. 3. [Slang], a party, banquet, etc.

**blow·pipe** (blō′pīp′), *n.* 1. a tube for forcing air or gas into a flame to intensify and concentrate its heat. 2. a blowgun.

**blow·torch** (blō′tôrch′), *n.* a small gasoline torch that shoots out a hot flame intensified by a blast of air, used to melt metal, etc.

**blow·up** (blō′up′), *n.* 1. an explosion. 2. [Colloq.], an angry or hysterical outburst.

**blow·y** (blō′i), *adj.* [-IER, -IEST], windy.

**blowz·y** (blouz′i), *adj.* [-IER, -IEST], [< obs. *blouze,* ruddy wench], 1. fat, ruddy, and coarse-looking. 2. slovenly; disheveled; frowzy.

**B.L.S.,** Bachelor of Library Science.

**blub·ber** (blub′ẽr), *n.* [ME., a bubble; prob. echoic], the fat of the whale and other sea mammals.

**blub·ber** (blub′ẽr), *v.i.* [ME. *blubren,* to bubble up; see BLUBBER (fat)], to weep loudly, like a child. *v.t.* to say while blubbering. *n.* loud weeping. *adj.* swollen from weeping. —**blub′ber·er,** *n.* —**blub′ber·ing·ly,** *adv.*

**blub·ber·y** (blub′ẽr-i), *adj.* 1. of, full, or like blubber. 2. swollen from weeping.

**blu·cher** (blo͞o′chẽr, -kẽr), *n.* [after Field Marshal von *Blücher,* Prussian general (1742–1819)], a kind of shoe in which the upper laps over the vamp, which is of one piece with the tongue.

**bludg·eon** (bluj′ən), *n.* [? altered < MFr. dim. of *bouge,* a club], a short club with a thick, heavy end. *v.t.* & *v.i.* 1. to strike with a bludgeon. 2. to threaten; coerce; bully. —**bludg′eon·er, bludg′eon·eer′** (-êr′), *n.*

**blue** (blo͞o), *adj.* [< OFr. *bleu* < OHG. *blao*], 1. of the color of the clear sky or the deep sea. 2. livid: said of the skin. 3. gloomy; depressed or depressing. 4. puritanical; rigorous: as, *blue* laws. *n.* 1. the color of the clear sky or the deep sea. 2. any blue pigment or dye. 3. anything colored blue. 4. one who wears a blue uniform, etc. *v.t.* [BLUED, BLUING or BLUEING], 1. to make blue. 2. to use bluing on or in. *v.i.* to become blue. —**like a blue streak,** [Colloq.], with great speed. —**once in a blue moon,** very seldom; almost never. —**out of the blue,** as if from the sky; unexpected. —**the blue,** 1. the sky. 2. the sea. —**the blues,** 1. [short for *blue devils*], [Colloq.], a depressed, unhappy feeling. 2. a type of Negro folk song, characterized by minor harmony, slow jazz rhythm, and melancholy words. 3. any imitation of this. —**blue′ly,** *adv.* —**blue′ness,** *n.*

**Blue·beard** (blo͞o′bêrd′), *n.* a legendary character who married and murdered one wife after another.

**blue·bell** (blo͞o′bel′), *n.* any of various plants with blue, bell-shaped flowers.

**blue·ber·ry** (blo͞o′ber′i, -bẽr-), *n.* [*pl.* -RIES], 1. a small, edible, blue-black berry with tiny seeds. 2. the shrub on which it grows.

**blue·bird** (blo͞o′bũrd′), *n.* any of a number of related small North American songbirds, the male of which usually has a blue or bluish back.

**blue blood,** 1. descent from nobility or royalty. 2. a person of such descent. —**blue′-blood′ed,** *adj.*

**blue·bon·net** (blo͞o′bon′it), *n.* 1. the cornflower. 2. a blue-flowered lupine. Also **blue bonnet.**

**blue book,** a book listing people who are socially prominent: also **blue′book′,** *n.*

**blue·bot·tle** (blo͞o′bot′'l), *n.* 1. a plant bearing blue, white, pink, or purple flowers with bottle-shaped rays; cornflower. 2. a large blowfly with a steel-blue abdomen and a hairy body.

**blue·coat** (blo͞o′kōt′), *n.* a policeman.

**blue devils,** 1. delirium tremens or its hallucinations. 2. a depressed feeling; the blues.

**blue·fish** (blo͞o′fish′), *n.* [*pl.* see FISH], a blue-and-silver food fish, common along the Atlantic coast of North America.

**blue flag,** any iris with blue flowers.

**blue·grass** (blo͞o′gras′, -gräs′), *n.* any of several related grasses with bluish-green stems; esp., **Kentucky bluegrass.**

**blue gum,** a kind of eucalyptus tree.

**blue·ing** (blo͞o′iŋ), *n.* bluing.

**blue·ish** (blo͞o′ish), *adj.* bluish. —**blue′ish·ness,** *n.*

**blue·jack·et** (blo͞o′jak′it), *n.* an enlisted man in the U.S. or British navy.

**blue·jay** (blo͞o′jā′), *n.* any of various noisy, crested birds with a blue back: also **blue jay.**

**blue laws,** puritanical laws, especially those prohibiting entertainments, sports, etc. on Sunday.

**blue·nose** (blo͞o′nōz′), *n.* [Colloq.], a puritanical person.

**blue-pen·cil** (blo͞o′pen′s'l), *v.t.* to edit, cut, or correct (a manuscript, etc.): from the blue pencils generally used by editors.

**blue·print** (blo͞o′print′), *n.* 1. a photographic reproduction in white on a blue background, as of architectural plans. 2. any exact or detailed plan or outline. *v.t.* to make a blueprint of.

**blue ribbon,** first prize in a competition.

**Blue Ridge Mountains,** a range of the Appalachians, extending from West Virginia to N Georgia.

**blue·stock·ing** (blo͞o′stok′iŋ), *n.* [from the unconventional stockings worn by such women in 18th-c. London], a learned, bookish, or pedantic woman.

**blu·et** (blo͞o′it), *n.* [< Fr. dim. of *bleu,* blue], a blue-flowered plant growing in small tufts.

**bluff** (bluf), *v.t.* & *v.i.* [prob. < D. *bluffen,* to baffle], 1. to mislead by a false, bold front. 2. to frighten by threats that cannot be made good. *n.* 1. a bluffing. 2. a person who bluffs. —**bluff′er,** *n.*

**bluff** (bluf), *adj.* [< D. *blaf,* flat], 1. ascending steeply with a broad, flat front. 2. having a rough, frank manner; brusque. *n.* a high, steep bank or cliff. —**bluff′ly,** *adv.* —**bluff′ness,** *n.*

**blu·ing** (blo͞o′iŋ), *n.* a blue liquid, powder, etc., generally of indigo, used in rinsing white fabrics to prevent yellowing: also sp. **blueing.**

**blu·ish** (blo͞o′ish), *adj.* somewhat blue: also sp. **blueish.** —**blu′ish·ness,** *n.*

**blun·der** (blun′dẽr), *v.i.* [< ON. *blunda,* to shut the eyes], 1. to move clumsily; flounder; stumble. 2. to make a foolish mistake. *v.t.* 1. to say stupidly or confusedly; blurt out. 2. to do clumsily or poorly; bungle. *n.* a foolish mistake. —**blun′der·er,** *n.* —**blun′der·ing·ly,** *adv.*

**blun·der·buss** (blun′dẽr-bus′), *n.* [D. *donderbus,* thunder box; altered after *blunder* because of the gun's random action], 1. an obsolete short gun with a broad muzzle. 2. a person who blunders.

BLUNDERBUSS

**blunt** (blunt), *adj.* [prob. < ON.], 1. slow to perceive; dull; obtuse. 2. having a dull edge or point. 3. plain-spoken; bluff. *v.t.* & *v.i.* to make or become dull or insensitive. —**blunt′ly,** *adj.* —**blunt′ness,** *n.*

**blur** (blũr), *v.t.* & *v.i.* [BLURRED, BLURRING], [? < *blear* + *blot*], 1. to smear; blot; smudge. 2. to make or become indistinct in outline or shape. 3. to dim. *n.* 1. the state of being blurred. 2. an obscuring stain or blot. 3. anything indistinct to the sight or the mind. —**blur′ry,** *adj.*

**blurb** (blũrb), *n.* [arbitrary coinage (c. 1914) by

Gelett Burgess, Am. humorist], [Colloq.], an exaggerated advertisement, as on a book jacket.

**blurt** (blũrt), *v.t.* [? < *bl*ow, *bl*ast, etc. + sp*urt*], to say thoughtlessly or impulsively (with *out*).

**blush** (blush), *v.i.* [< AS. *blyscan*, to shine], 1. to become red in the face from shame, embarrassment, etc. 2. to be ashamed (*at* or *for*). 3. to be or become rosy. *v.t.* to redden. *n.* 1. a reddening of the face from shame, etc. 2. a rosy color: as, the *blush* of youth. *adj.* rosy. —**at first blush,** at first sight; without further consideration. —**blush′er,** *n.* —**blush′ful,** *adj.* —**blush′ing·ly,** *adv.*

**blus·ter** (blus′tẽr), *v.i.* [< or akin to LG. *blüstern*], 1. to blow stormily: said of wind. 2. to speak in a noisy or swaggering manner. 3. to use empty threats. *v.t.* 1. to force by blustering; bully. 2. to say noisily and violently. *n.* 1. noisy commotion. 2. noisy, violent, or swaggering talk.—**blus′ter·er,** *n.* —**blus′ter·ing·ly,** *adv.* —**blus′ter·y, blus′ter·ous,** *adj.*

**blvd.,** boulevard.

**BM,** [Colloq.], bowel movement.

**Bn.,** 1. Baron. 2. Battalion.

**B.O.,** body odor.

**b.o.,** 1. box office. 2. branch office.

**bo·a** (bō′ə), *n.* [L.], 1. a large, nonpoisonous, tropical snake that crushes its prey in its coils, as the python, anaconda, etc. 2. a woman's long scarf of fur or feathers, worn around the neck.

**boa constrictor,** a species of boa that attains a length of 10–15 feet.

**boar** (bôr, bōr), *n.* [*pl.* BOARS, BOAR; see PLURAL, II, D, 1], [AS. *bar*], 1. an uncastrated male hog or pig. 2. a wild hog of Europe, Africa, and Asia.

**board** (bôrd, bōrd), *n.* [AS. *bord*, plank], 1. a long, thin, flat piece of sawed wood ready for use. 2. a flat piece of wood, etc. for some special use: as, a bulletin *board*. 3. pasteboard or stiff paper, often used for book covers. 4. a table for meals. 5. the food served at a table. 6. meals provided regularly for pay. 7. a council table. 8. a group of administrators; council. *v.t.* 1. to cover or close with boards (often with *up*). 2. to provide with meals, or room and meals, regularly for pay. *v.i.* to receive meals, or room and meals, regularly for pay. —**across the board,** in *horse racing*, to win, place, and show: said of betting. —**the boards,** the stage (of a theater). —**tread the boards,** to be an actor in the theater.

**board** (bôrd, bōrd), *n.* [AS. *bord*, side of a ship], 1. the side of a ship, as in *overboard*. 2. a rim or border, as in *seaboard*. *v.t.* 1. to come alongside (a ship) especially with hostile purpose. 2. to come onto the deck of (a ship). 3. to get on (a train, bus, etc.). —**go by the board,** 1. to fall overboard. 2. to be got rid of, lost, etc. —**on board,** on a ship, aircraft, bus, etc.

**board·er** (bôr′dẽr, bōr′-), *n.* a person who gets his meals, or room and meals, regularly for pay.

**board·er** (bôr′dẽr, bōr′-), *n.* one of the crew detailed to board a hostile ship.

**board foot,** [*pl.* BOARD FEET], a unit of measure of lumber, equal to a board one foot square and one inch thick: abbrev. **bd. ft.**

**board·ing** (bôrd′iŋ, bōrd′-), *n.* 1. a structure or covering of boards. 2. boards collectively.

**board·ing·house** (bôrd′iŋ-hous′, bōrd′-), *n.* a house where meals, or lodging and meals, can be had for pay: also **boarding house.**

**boarding school,** a school providing lodging and meals for the pupils.

**board measure,** measurement of lumber in board feet.

**board·walk** (bôrd′wôk′, bōrd′-), *n.* a walk made of thick boards, especially along a beach.

**boast** (bōst), *n.* [< Anglo-Fr.], 1. a bragging; boasting. 2. anything boasted of. *v.i.* 1. to talk, especially about oneself, with too much pride and satisfaction; brag. 2. to be vainly proud; exult. *v.t.* 1. to brag about. 2. to glory in having (something). —**boast′er,** *n.* —**boast′ing·ly,** *adv.*

**boast·ful** (bōst′fəl), *adj.* boasting; inclined to brag. —**boast′ful·ly,** *adv.* —**boast′ful·ness,** *n.*

**boat** (bōt), *n.* [AS. *bat*], 1. a small, open vessel or water craft. 2. a large vessel; ship: landsman's term, especially for a river steamer. 3. a boat-shaped dish: as, a gravy *boat*. *v.t.* to lay or carry in the boat: as, *boat* the oars. *v.i.* to go in a boat; row, sail, or cruise. —**in the same boat,** in the same situation.

**boat·house** (bōt′hous′), *n.* a building for storing a boat or boats.

**boat·ing** (bōt′iŋ), *n.* rowing, sailing, etc.

**boat·load** (bōt′lōd′), *n.* 1. all the freight or passengers that a boat can carry or contain. 2. the oad carried by a boat.

**boat·man** (bōt′mən), *n.* [*pl.* -MEN], a man who operates, works on, or sells boats.

**boat·swain** (bō′s′n, bōt′swān′), *n.* a ship's warrant officer or petty officer in charge of the deck crew, the rigging, etc.: also **bosun.**

**bob** (bob), *n.* [ME. *bobbe*, hanging cluster; senses 4 & 5 < the *v.*], 1. any knoblike hanging weight or pendant. 2. a docked tail, as of a horse. 3. a woman's or girl's short haircut. 4. a quick, jerky motion. 5. a float on a fishing line. *v.t.* [BOBBED, BOBBING], [ME. *bobben*, to knock against], 1. to make move with a jerky motion. 2. to cut (hair, a tail, etc.) short. *v.i.* 1. to move or act with a jerky motion. 2. to fish with a bob. —**bob up,** to appear unexpectedly or suddenly.

**bob** (bob), *n.* [*pl.* BOB], [? < *Bob*, nickname for *Robert*], [Brit. Slang], a shilling.

**bob·bin** (bob′in), *n.* [Fr. *bobine*], a reel or spool for thread, yarn, or fine wire, used in spinning, weaving, machine sewing, etc.

**bob·by** (bob′i), *n.* [*pl.* -BIES], [after Sir Robert (*Bobby*) Peel (1788–1850), who remodeled the London police force], [Brit. Slang], a policeman.

**bobby pin,** [from use with *bobbed* hair], a small metal hairpin with the ends pressing close together.

**bobby socks,** [Slang], [< *bob*, to cut short], ankle socks worn by girls.

**bobby sox·er** (sok′sẽr), [Colloq.], a girl in her teens, especially one regarded as conforming to current fads: also **bob′by·sox′er,** *n.*

**bob·cat** (bob′kat′), *n.* [*pl.* -CATS, -CAT; see PLURAL, II, D, 1], a wildcat; American lynx.

**bob·o·link** (bob′′l-iŋk′), *n.* [echoic, after its call], a migratory songbird of North America.

**bob·sled** (bob′sled′), *n.* 1. a long sled made of two short sleds joined together. 2. either of the short sleds. 3. a long toboggan, with steering apparatus and brakes, often ridden by a four-man team in races. *v.i.* [-SLEDDED, -SLEDDING], to ride on a bobsled. —**bob′sled′ding,** *n.*

**bob·sleigh** (bob′slā′), *n.* & *v.i.* bobsled.

**bob·stay** (bob′stā′), *n.* a rope or chain for tying down a bowsprit to keep it from bobbing.

**bob·tail** (bob′tāl′), *n.* 1. a tail cut short; docked tail. 2. an animal with a bobtail. *adj.* 1. having a bobtail. 2. cut short; abbreviated. *v.t.* 1. to dock the tail of. 2. to cut short; curtail.

**bob·white** (bob′hwīt′), *n.* [*pl.* -WHITES, -WHITE; see PLURAL, II, D, 1], [echoic, after its call], a small North American quail having markings of brown and white on a gray body: sometimes called *partridge*.

**Boc·cac·cio, Gio·van·ni** (jô-vän′nē bô-kät′chô; Eng. bō-kä′chi-ō′), 1313–1375; Italian writer.

**Boche, boche** (bosh, bôsh, bōsh; Fr. bôsh), *n.* [*pl.* BOCHES (-iz; Fr. bôsh)], [Fr. slang < *caboche*, hard head], a German, especially a German soldier: hostile term.

**bock** (bok), *n.* [G. *bockbier* < *Eimbecker bier* < *Eimbeck*, city where first brewed], a dark beer usually made in the spring: also **bock beer.**

**bode** (bōd), *v.t.* [BODED, BODING], [< AS. < *boda*, messenger], to be an omen of; portend. —**bode ill** (or **well**), to be a bad (or good) omen.

**bode** (bōd), alt. pt. of **bide.**

**bod·ice** (bod′is), *n.* [altered < *bodies*, pl. of *body*], 1. the close-fitting upper part of a woman's dress. 2. a woman's vest tightly laced in front, worn over a blouse or dress.

**bod·ied** (bod′id), *adj.* having a body, substance, or form.

**bod·i·less** (bod′i-lis), *adj.* 1. without a body; disembodied. 2. insubstantial.

**bod·i·ly** (bod′′l-i), *adj.* 1. physical. 2. of, in, or for the body. *adv.* 1. in person; in the flesh. 2. as a single body or group.

**bod·kin** (bod′kin), *n.* [ME. *boidekyn;* ? < Celt.], 1. a pointed instrument for making holes in cloth. 2. a long, ornamental hairpin. 3. a thick, blunt needle. 4. [Obs.], a dagger or stiletto.

**bod·y** (bod′i), *n.* [*pl.* -IES], [< AS. *bodig;* orig. sense "cask"], 1. the whole physical substance of a man, animal, or plant. 2. the trunk or torso of a man or animal. 3. the stem of a plant. 4. the main or central part of anything. 5. the part of a garment that covers the trunk. 6. a dead person; corpse. 7. a portion of matter; mass: as, a *body* of water. 8. a group of people or things regarded as a unit: as, a *body* of soldiers. 9. strength, concentration, or consistency, as of wine. 10. [Colloq.], a person. *v.t.* [BODIED, BODYING], to give a body or substance to. —**body forth,** 1. to give shape or form to. 2. to symbolize or represent. —**keep body and soul together,** to stay alive.

**bod·y·guard** (bod′i-gärd′), *n.* a person or persons, usually armed, assigned to guard someone.
**body politic,** people constituting a political unit with a government; state.
**Boe·o·ti·a** (bi-ō′shə), *n.* an ancient Greek state, northwest of Attica: capital, Thebes.
**Boe·o·tian** (bi-ō′shən), *adj.* of or like Boeotia or its people, who were reputed to be stupid. *n.* 1. a native of Boeotia. 2. a stupid person.
**Boer** (bōr, bôr, boor), *n.* [D. *boer,* peasant; see BOOR], a descendant of Dutch colonists in South Africa. *adj.* of the Boers.
**bog** (bog, bôg), *n.* [Ir. < Gael. *bog,* soft, moist], wet, spongy ground; small marsh or swamp. *v.t. & v.i.* [BOGGED, BOGGING], to sink in or as in a bog (often with *down*). **—bog′gi·ness,** *n.* **—bog′gish,** *adj.* **—bog′gy,** *adj.*
**bo·gey** (bō′gi), *n.* [*pl.* -GEYS], 1. a bogy. 2. [after Colonel *Bogey,* imaginary partner assumed to play for par], in *golf, a)* par. *b)* one stroke more than par on a hole.
**bog·gle** (bog′′l), *v.i.* [-GLED, -GLING], [<Scot. *bogle,* specter; now confused with *bungle*], 1. to be startled; shy away (with *at*). 2. to hesitate or have scruples (with *at*). 3. to equivocate (with *at*). 4. to bungle. *v.t.* to bungle or botch. *n.* 1. a boggling. 2. a scruple. 3. a botch. 4. [Dial.], a bogy: also **bogle** (bō′g'l). **—bog′gler,** *n.*
**bo·gie** (bō′gi), *n.* [*pl.* -GIES], a bogy.
**Bo·go·tá** (bō′gə-tä′), *n.* the capital of Colombia: pop., 1,125,000.
**bo·gus** (bō′gəs), *adj.* not genuine; counterfeit; spurious.
**bo·gy** (bō′gi), *n.* [*pl.* -GIES], [see BOGGLE], 1. an imaginary evil being or spirit; goblin. 2. a bogylike or frightening person or thing; bugbear. Also spelled **bogey, bogie.**
**Bo·he·mi·a** (bō-hē′mi-ə), *n.* a province of Czechoslovakia: a former kingdom: capital, Prague.
**Bo·he·mi·an** (bō-hē′mi-ən), *n.* 1. a native or inhabitant of Bohemia. 2. the West Slavic language of the Czechs: also called *Czech.* 3. a gypsy. 4. an artist, dilettante, etc. who lives unconventionally. *adj.* 1. of Bohemia, its people, or their language; Czech. 2. like a Bohemian (sense 4); unconventional, arty, etc. **—Bo·he′mi·an·ism,** *n.*
**boil** (boil), *v.i.* [< OFr. < L. < *bulla,* a bubble], 1. to bubble up and vaporize over direct heat. 2. to seethe like boiling liquids. 3. to be agitated, as with rage. 4. to cook by boiling. *v.t.* 1. to heat to the boiling point. 2. to cook, make, or clean by boiling. *n.* the act or state of boiling. **—boil away,** to evaporate as a result of boiling. **—boil down,** 1. to lessen in quantity by boiling. 2. to abridge; condense. **—boil over,** 1. to come to a boil and spill over the rim. 2. to lose one's temper; get excited.
**boil** (boil), *n.* [< AS. *byle, byl*], an inflamed, painful, pus-filled swelling on the skin, with a hard center: it is caused by infection.
**boil·er** (boil′ẽr), *n.* 1. a container in which things are boiled or heated. 2. a strong container in which water is turned to steam for heating or power. 3. a tank to hold hot water.
**boil·ing point** (boil′iŋ), the temperature at which a specified liquid boils: the usual boiling point of water is 212°F., or 100°C.
**Boi·se** (boi′si, boi′zi), *n.* the capital of Idaho: pop., 34,000.
**bois·ter·ous** (bois′tẽr-əs), *adj.* [< Anglo-Fr. *boistous,* rough (said of a road)], 1. rough; violent; turbulent. 2. loud and exuberant. **—bois′ter·ous·ly,** *adv.* **—bois′ter·ous·ness,** *n.*
**bo·la** (bō′lə), *n.* [Sp., a ball < L. *bulla,* a bubble], a throwing weapon made of a long cord with heavy balls at the end: also **bo′las** (-ləs).
**bold** (bōld), *adj.* [AS. *b(e)ald*], 1. daring; fearless; audacious. 2. very free in behavior or manner; impudent. 3. steep; abrupt. 4. prominent and clear; striking and sharp: as, he writes a *bold* hand. **—make bold,** to be so bold as (to do something); dare. **—bold′ly,** *adv.* **—bold′ness,** *n.*
**bold·face** (bōld′fās′), *n.* in *printing,* a type with a heavy face: the entry words in this dictionary are in boldface.
**bold-faced** (bōld′fāst′), *adj.* impudent; forward.
**bole** (bōl), *n.* [ON. *bolr*], a tree trunk.
**bo·le·ro** (bō-lâr′ō), *n.* [*pl.* -ROS], [Sp.], 1. a Spanish dance in ¾ time. 2. the music for this. 3. a short, open vest, with or without sleeves.
**bol·i·var** (bol′ə-vẽr; Sp. bô-lē′vär), *n.* [*pl.* -VARS; Sp. -VARES (bô′lē-vä′res)], [< Simón *Bolívar*], a silver coin and monetary unit of Venezuela.
**Bol·í·var, Simón** (bol′ə-vẽr; Am. Sp. bô-lē′vär), 1783–1830: Venezuelan general and revolutionist.
**Bo·liv·i·a** (bə-liv′i-ə), *n.* an inland country in west central South America: area, 424,000 sq. mi.; pop., 3,462,000; capitals, La Paz and Sucre. **—Bo·liv′i·an,** *adj. & n.*
**bo·li·via·no** (bô-lē′vyä′nô), *n.* [*pl.* -NOS (-nôs)], the monetary unit of Bolivia.
**boll** (bōl), *n.* [< AS. *bolla,* a bowl], the pod of a plant, especially of flax or cotton.
**boll weevil,** a small, grayish beetle whose larvae do damage to cotton bolls.
**boll·worm** (bōl′wũrm′), *n.* a kind of moth larva that feeds on cotton bolls, ears of corn, etc.
**bo·lo** (bō′lō), *n.* [*pl.* -LOS], [Sp.], a large, single-edged knife used in the Philippine Islands.
**Bo·lo·gna** (bō-lô′nyä), *n.* 1. a city in N Italy: pop., 351,000. 2. [usually b-], (bə-lō′nə, -ni), a seasoned smoked sausage of various meats: also **bologna sausage.**
**Bol·she·vik, bol·she·vik** (bol′shə-vik′, bōl′-), *n.* [*pl.* -VIKS, -VIKI (-vē′ki)], [Russ. < *bolshe,* the majority], 1. originally, a member of the majority faction of the Social Democratic Party of Russia: the Bolsheviks came into power in 1917 and formed the Communist Party. 2. a member of the Communist party of the Soviet Union. 3. loosely, any radical: hostile usage. *adj.* of or like the Bolsheviks or Bolshevism.
**Bol·she·vism, bol·she·vism** (bol′shə-viz'm, bōl′-), *n.* the policies and practices of the Bolsheviks. **—Bol′she·vist, bol′she·vist,** *n. & adj.* **—Bol′she·vis′tic, bol′she·vis′tic,** *adj.*
**Bol·she·vize, bol·she·vize** (bol′shə-vīz′, bōl′-), *v.t.* [-VIZED, -VIZING], to make Bolshevik.
**bol·ster** (bōl′stẽr), *n.* [AS.], 1. a long, narrow pillow. 2. a soft pad, cushion, or support. 3. any bolsterlike object or support. *v.t.* to prop up as with a bolster (often with *up*). **—bol′ster·er,** *n.*
**bolt** (bōlt), *n.* [AS.], 1. an arrow with a thick, blunt head, shot from a crossbow; hence, 2. a sudden, unforeseen occurrence. 3. a flash of lightning. 4. a sliding bar for locking a door, etc. 5. a similar bar in a lock, moved by a key. 6. a metal rod, threaded and used with a nut to hold parts together. 7. a roll of cloth, paper, etc. 8. a withdrawal from one's party or group. 9. in *firearms,* a sliding bar that pushes the cartridge into place and extracts the empty cartridge case after firing. *v.t.* 1. to shoot (an arrow, etc.). 2. to say suddenly or unexpectedly; blurt. 3. to swallow (food) hurriedly; gulp down. 4. to fasten as with a bolt. 5 to roll (cloth, etc.) into bolts. 6. to abandon (a party, group, etc.). *v.i.* 1. to start suddenly; spring away; dart. 2. to withdraw support from one's political party, etc. *adv.* like an arrow; suddenly; straight. **—bolt upright,** straight upright.
**bolt** (bōlt), *v.t.* [< OFr. < *bure* (L. hyp. *bura*), coarse cloth], 1. to sift (flour, grain, etc.) so as to separate and grade. 2. to inspect and separate; examine closely. **—bolt′er,** *n.*
**bo·lus** (bō′ləs), *n.* [*pl.* -LUSES], [L. < Gr. *bōlos,* a lump], 1. a small, round mass of something. 2. in *veterinary medicine,* a large pill.
**bomb** (bom), *n.* [< Fr. < Sp. < L. < Gr. *bombos,* hollow sound], 1. an explosive, incendiary, or gas-filled container, for dropping, hurling, or explosion by a timing mechanism. 2. a sudden, surprising occurrence. *v.t. & v.i.* to attack or destroy with a bomb or bombs.
**bom·bard** (bom-bärd′), *v.t.* [Fr. < *bombarde,* cannon < *bombe;* see BOMB], 1. to attack with or as with artillery or bombs. 2. to keep attacking with questions, suggestions, etc. *n.* (bom′bärd), an early type of cannon, hurling stones, etc. **—bom·bard′er,** *n.* **—bom·bard′ment,** *n.*
**bom·bard·ier** (bom′bẽr-dêr′), *n.* a person who releases the bombs in a bomber.
**bom·bast** (bom′bast), *n.* [< OFr. < LL. < *bambax-*cotton < Late Gr. < Per. *pambak,* cotton], high, sounding, pompous speech. **—bom·bas′tic, bom·bas′ti·cal,** *adj.* **—bom·bas′ti·cal·ly,** *adv.*
**Bom·bay** (bom-bā′), *n.* 1. a state of W India. 2. its capital, on the Arabian Sea: pop., 2,839,000.
**bom·ba·zine** (bom′bə-zēn′, bom′bə-zēn′), *n.* [< Fr. < L. *bombyx,* silk], a twilled cloth of silk with worsted or cotton: also sp. **bombasine.**
**bomb bay,** a compartment in a bomber, from which the bombs are dropped.

**bomb·er** (bom′ẽr), *n.* 1. an airplane designed for dropping bombs. 2. a person that bombs.
**bomb-proof** (bom′pro͞of′), *adj.* capable of withstanding bombardment.
**bomb·shell** (bom′shel′), *n.* 1. a bomb. 2. any sudden, unforeseen occurrence.
**bomb sight,** an instrument for aiming bombs dropped from aircraft.
**bo·na fi·de** (bō′nə fī′di *or* fīd′), [L.], in good faith; without dishonesty, fraud, or deceit.
**bo·nan·za** (bō-nan′zə), *n.* [Sp., prosperity < L. *bonus*, good], 1. a rich vein of ore. 2. [Colloq.], any source of wealth or high profits.
**Bo·na·parte** (bō′nə-pärt′; Fr. bô′nå′pårt′), family name of *Napoleon I*, *Napoleon II*, *Louis Napoleon*, etc.: also **Buonaparte.**
**Bo·na·part·ism** (bō′nə-pär′tiz′m), *n.* belief in and support of Napoleon Bonaparte and his methods and doctrines. —**Bo′na·part′ist,** *n.*
**bon·bon** (bon′bon′), *n.* [Fr. *bon*, good], a small piece of candy, often with a creamy filling.
**bond** (bond), *n.* [< AS. *bindan*, to bind], 1. anything that binds, fastens, or unites. 2. *pl.* fetters; shackles. 3. *pl.* imprisonment; captivity. 4. a uniting force; tie; link. 5. a binding agreement; covenant. 6. a duty or obligation imposed by a contract, promise, etc. 7. the status of goods kept in a warehouse until taxes are paid. 8. in *finance*, an interest-bearing certificate issued by a government or business, promising to pay the holder a specified sum on a specified date. 9. in *law*, *a*) a written obligation under seal to pay specified sums, or to do or not do specified things. *b*) a person acting as surety for another's action; payer of bail. *c*) the amount paid as surety or bail. *v.t.* 1. to connect with or as with a bond; bind. 2. to furnish a bond (sense 9, *a*) and thus become a surety for (another). 3. to place (goods) under bond. 4. to issue bonds (sense 8) on; mortgage. 5. to put under bonded debt. *v.i.* to hold together by or as by a bond. —**bottled in bond, bottled after having been stored in bonded warehouses for a specified length of time, as some whisky.**
**bond** (bond), *n.* [see BONDAGE], [Obs.], a serf or slave. *adj.* in bondage; in slavery.
**bond·age** (bon′dij), *n.* [< AS. *bonda*, husbandman; < ON. < *buandi* < *bua*, to dwell], 1. serfdom; slavery. 2. subjection to some force, or influence.
**bond·ed** (bon′did), *adj.* 1. subject to or secured by a bond or bonds. 2. placed in a warehouse pending payment of taxes.
**bond·hold·er** (bond′hōl′dẽr), *n.* an owner of bonds issued by a company or government.
**bond·man (bond′mən),** *n.* [*pl.* -MEN], **1. a feudal serf. 2. [Archaic], a slave. —bond′maid′,** *n.fem.* —**bond′wom′an** [*pl.* -WOMEN], *n.fem.*
**bond-ser·vant** (bond′sũr′vənt), *n.* 1. a person bound to service without pay. 2. a slave. Also **bond servant.**
**bonds·man** (bondz′mən), *n.* [*pl.* -MEN], 1. a bondman. 2. a person who takes responsibility for another by furnishing a bond; surety.
**bone** (bōn), *n.* [AS. *ban*], 1. any of the pieces of hard tissue forming the skeleton of most vertebrate animals. 2. this hard tissue. 3. *pl.* the skeleton. 4. a bonelike substance or thing. 5. a thing made of bone. 6. *pl.* flat sticks used as clappers by end men in minstrel shows. 7. *pl.* [construed as sing.], an end man in a minstrel show. 8. *pl.* [Colloq.], dice. *v.t.* [BONED, BONING], 1. to remove the bones from. 2. to put whalebone, etc. into. *v.i.* [Slang], to apply oneself diligently; esp., to study hard (often with *up*). —**feel in one's bones,** to be certain without any real reason. —**have a bone to pick,** to have something to quarrel about. —**make no bones about,** [Colloq.], to make no attempt to hide; admit freely. —**bone′less,** *adj.* —**bone′like′,** *adj.*
**bone-dry** (bōn′drī′), *adj.* dry as bone; very dry.
**bone·head** (bōn′hed′), *n.* [Slang], a stupid person; fool. —**bone′head′ed,** *adj.*
**bone meal,** crushed or finely ground bones, used as feed or fertilizer.
**bon·er** (bōn′ẽr), *n.* [Slang], a stupid blunder.
**bone·set** (bōn′set′), *n.* a plant of the composite family, with flat clusters of white or bluish-purple flowers: used as a tonic, etc.
**bon·fire** (bon′fīr′), *n.* [ME. *banfir*, bone fire, fire for burning corpses], an outdoor fire.
**bon·go** (boŋ′gō), *n.* [*pl.* BONGOS (-gōz)], either of a pair of small, tuned drums, played with the hands: in full, **bongo drum.**
**bon·ho·mie, bon·hom·mie** (bon′ə-mē′; Fr. bô′nô′mē′), *n.* [Fr. < *bon*, good + *homme*, man], good nature; pleasant, affable manner.
**bo·ni·to** (bə-nē′tō), *n.* [*pl.* -TOS, -TOES, -TO; see PLURAL, II, D, 1], [Sp.], any of several salt-water food fishes of the mackerel family.
‡**bon jour** (bōn′ zho͞or′), [Fr.], good day; hello.
**bon mot** (bōn mō′), [*pl.* BONS MOTS (bōn mōz′; Fr. mō′)], [Fr., lit., good word], a witticism; apt saying.
**bon·net** (bon′it), *n.* [< OFr. *bonet*], 1. a flat, brimless cap, worn by men and boys in Scotland. 2. a brimless hat with a chin ribbon, worn by children and women. 3. a feathered headdress, worn by some American Indians. 4. a protective covering, as an automobile hood. *v.t.* to put a bonnet on.
**bon·ny, bon·nie** (bon′i), *adj.* [-NIER, -NIEST], [Fr. *bon* (fem. *bonne*), good], 1. handsome; pretty. 2. healthy-looking; robust. 3. fine; pleasant. —**bon′ni·ly,** *adv.* —**bon′ni·ness,** *n.*
**bon·sai** (bon-sī′), *n.* [Japan., lit., tray arrangement], 1. the art of dwarfing and shaping trees, shrubs, etc. 2. such a tree or shrub.
‡**bon soir** (bōn′ swår′), [Fr.], good evening.
**bo·nus** (bō′nəs), *n.* [*pl.* -NUSES], [L., good], anything given or paid in addition to the customary or required amount.
‡**bon vi·vant** (bōn′ vē′vän′), [*pl.* BONS VIVANTS (bōn′ vē′vän′)], [Fr.], a person who enjoys good food and other pleasant things.
‡**bon voy·age** (bōn′ vwå′yåzh′), [Fr., lit., good voyage], pleasant journey.
**bon·y** (bōn′i), *adj.* [-IER, -IEST], 1. of or like bone. 2. having many bones. 3. having protruding bones; thin; emaciated. —**bon′i·ness,** *n.*
**boo** (bo͞o), *interj. & n.* [*pl.* BOOS], [echoic], a sound made to express disapproval, scorn, etc., or to startle. *v.i.* [BOOED, BOOING], to make this sound. *v.t.* to shout "boo" at.
**boob** (bo͞ob), *n.* a booby; fool.
**boo·by** (bo͞o′bi), *n.* [*pl.* -BIES], [Sp. *bobo*], 1. a stupid or foolish person. 2. a tropical seabird related to the gannet: also **booby gannet.** 3. the player who does poorest in a game, contest, etc.
**booby prize,** a prize, usually ridiculous, given to whoever has done worst in a game, race, etc.
**booby trap,** 1. any scheme or device for tricking a person unawares. 2. a mine made to be exploded by some action of the unsuspecting victim.
**boo·dle** (bo͞o′d'l), *n.* [? < D. *boedel*, property], [Slang], 1. a crowd; mob; caboodle. 2. something given as a bribe; graft. 3. the loot taken in a robbery. *v.t. & v.i.* [-DLED, -DLING], [Slang], to bribe or accept bribes. —**boo′dler,** *n.*
**boo·gie-woo·gie** (boo′gi-woo′gi), *n.* [echoic; ? suggested by the characteristic "walking bass"], jazz music in which repeated bass figures in 8/8 rhythm accompany melodic variations in the treble. *adj.* of such music.
**boo·hoo** (bo͞o′ho͞o′), *v.i.* [-HOOED, -HOOING], [echoic], to weep noisily. *n.* [*pl.* -HOOS], noisy weeping.
**book** (book), *n.* [AS. *boc* < same base as Eng. *beech:* prob. so called because runes were first carved on beech], 1. a number of printed or written sheets of paper, etc. fastened together, usually between protective covers. 2. a main division of a literary work. 3. a number of blank or ruled sheets bound together: as, an account *book*. 4. a record; account. 5. the words of an opera, etc.; libretto. 6. a booklike package, as of matches. 7. a record of bets, as on horse races. 8. in *bridge*, etc., a specified number of tricks making a set. *v.t.* 1. to record in a book; list. 2. to engage ahead of time, as lectures, rooms, etc. 3. to record charges against on a police record. *adj.* in, from, or according to a book. —**bring to book,** 1. to force to explain. 2. to reprimand. —**by the book,** according to the rules. —**close the books,** in *bookkeeping*, to make no further entries. —**keep books,** to keep a record of business transactions. —**know like a book,** to know well or fully. —**on the books,** recorded; enrolled. —**the Book,** the Bible.
**book·bind·er** (book′bīn′dẽr), *n.* a person whose trade or business is binding books. —**book′bind′er·y,** *n.* —**book′bind′ing,** *n.*
**book·case** (book′kās′), *n.* a set of shelves or a cabinet for holding books.
**book club,** an organization that sells books, usually at reduced prices, to members who undertake to buy a minimum number of them annually.
**book end,** an ornamental weight or bracket at the end of a row of books to keep them upright.
**book·ie** (book′i), *n.* [Slang], in *horse racing*, a bookmaker.
**book·ing** (book′iŋ), *n.* an engagement to perform.
**book·ish** (book′ish), *adj.* 1. of books. 2. inclined to read and study; literary. 3. having mere book learning; pedantic. —**book′ish·ness,** *n.*
**book·keep·ing** (book′kēp′iŋ), *n.* the work or prac-

tice of keeping a systematic record of business transactions. —**book′keep′er,** *n.*

**book learning,** knowledge gained from reading books rather than from practical experience.

**book·let** (book′lit), *n.* a small book; pamphlet.

**book·lore** (book′lôr′, -lōr′), *n.* book learning.

**book·mak·er** (book′māk′ẽr), *n.* 1. a maker of books. 2. a person in the business of taking bets on race horses. —**book′mak′ing,** *n.*

**book·mark** (book′märk′), *n.* anything put between the pages of a book to mark the place.

**book·plate** (book′plāt′), *n.* a label with the owner's name, etc. for pasting in a book.

**book·rack** (book′rak′), *n.* 1. a rack or shelf for books. 2. a rack for holding a reader's book open.

**book review,** an article or talk dealing with the contents, literary worth, etc. of a book.

**book·sell·er** (book′sel′ẽr), *n.* a person whose business is selling books. —**book′sell′ing,** *n.*

**book·stack** (book′stak′), *n.* a series of bookshelves, one over the other, as in a library.

**book·stall** (book′stôl′), *n.* a place, often an outdoor booth or counter, where books are sold: also **book′stand′.**

**book·store** (book′stôr′, -stōr′), *n.* a store where books, and often office supplies, etc., are sold.

**book·worm** (book′wũrm′), *n.* 1. an insect larva that harms books by feeding on the binding, paste, etc. 2. one who reads or studies much.

**boom** (bo͞om), *v.i.* [echoic], to make a deep, hollow, resonant sound. *v.t.* to say with such a sound. *n.* a deep, hollow, resonant sound, as of thunder.

**boom** (bo͞om), *n.* [D., a tree, beam, pole], 1. a spar extending from a mast to hold the bottom of a sail outstretched. 2. a long beam extending from the upright of a derrick to support and guide anything lifted. 3. a barrier, as a line of logs or a chain, to obstruct navigation or prevent floating logs from dispersing. *v.t.* to stretch out (sails) on a boom. *v.i.* to sail at top speed (usually with *along*).

**boom** (bo͞om), *v.i.* [< prec. *v.i.*; later associated with *boom* (noise)], to increase suddenly or grow swiftly; flourish. *v.t.* 1. to cause to flourish. 2. to popularize or support vigorously. *n.* a period of business prosperity, etc. *adj.* of or characteristic of a boom in business, etc.

**boom·er·ang** (bo͞om′ẽr-aŋ), *n.* [< Australian native name], 1. a flat, curved stick that can be thrown so that it will return to the thrower: used as a weapon by Australian aborigines. 2. a scheme, etc. that goes contrary to the expectation of its originator and results in his disadvantage or harm. *v.i.* to act as a boomerang.

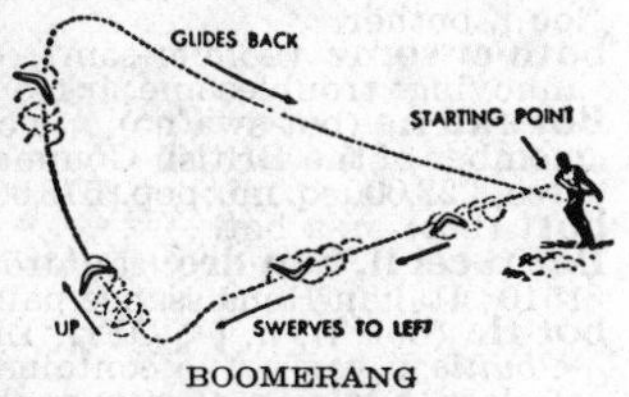

BOOMERANG

**boom town,** a town whose sudden growth or prosperity is caused by a business boom.

**boon** (bo͞on), *n.* [ON. *bon,* a petition], 1. a welcome benefit; blessing. 2. [Archaic], a favor or request.

**boon** (bo͞on), *adj.* [< OFr. < L. *bonus,* good], 1. [Archaic & Poetic], kind, generous, pleasant, etc. 2. merry; convivial: now only in *boon companion.*

**boon·docks** (bo͞on′doks′), *n.pl.* [orig. military slang < Tag. *bundok,* mountain], [Colloq.], a wild, often wooded area; wilderness.

**boon·dog·gle** (bo͞on′dôg′'l, -dog′'l), *v.i.* [-GLED, -GLING], [Slang], to do trifling, valueless work. *n.* trifling, valueless work. —**boon′dog′gler,** *n.*

**Boone, Daniel** (bo͞on), 1734–1820; American frontiersman.

**boor** (boor), *n.* [D. *boer* < *bouwen,* to cultivate], 1. originally, a peasant or farm worker. 2. a rude, awkward, ill-mannered person. —**boor′ish,** *adj.* —**boor′ish·ly,** *adv.* —**boor′ish·ness,** *n.*

**boost** (bo͞ost), *v.t.* [prob. nautical *bouse,* to haul up with tackle], [Colloq.], 1. to raise by or as by a push from behind or below. 2. to speak in favor of. *n.* [Colloq.], 1. a push to help a person or thing upward or forward. 2. a raising or increase.

**boost·er** (bo͞os′tẽr), *n.* 1. [Colloq.], one who boosts; ardent supporter. 2. an auxiliary device to increase power, thrust, etc.

**boot** (bo͞ot), *n.* [OFr. *bote*], 1. a protective covering, of leather, rubber, etc., for the foot and part of the leg. 2. a boot-shaped instrument of torture. 3. a thick patch for the inside of a tire casing. 4. a protective cover for the driver of an open vehicle. 5. a kick. 6. [Slang], a recent recruit to the navy. *v.t.* 1. to put boots on. 2. to kick. 3. [Slang], to dismiss. —**die with one's boots on,** to die in action. —**lick the boots of,** to fawn on. —**the boot,** [Slang], dismissal; discharge. —**boot′ed,** *adj.*

**boot** (bo͞ot), *n., v.t. & v.i.* [AS. *bot,* advantage], [Obs.], profit. —**to boot,** besides; in addition.

**boot·black** (bo͞ot′blak′), *n.* a person whose work is shining shoes or boots.

**boot camp,** [Colloq.], a station where navy or marine recruits receive basic training.

**boot·ee** (bo͞o-tē′), *n.* 1. a short boot worn by women. 2. (bo͞o′tē), a baby's soft, knitted shoe.

**Bo·ö·tes** (bō-ō′tēz), *n.* a northern constellation including the bright star Arcturus.

**booth** (bo͞oth, bo͞oth), *n.* [< ON. < *bua,* to dwell], 1. a temporary stall for the sale of goods, as at markets and fairs. 2. a small enclosure for voting at elections. 3. a small permanent structure to house a sentry, public telephone, etc.

**Booth, John Wilkes** (wilks bo͞oth), 1838–1865; American actor; assassin of Abraham Lincoln.

**Booth, William,** 1829–1912; English founder of Salvation Army.

**boot·jack** (bo͞ot′jak′), *n.* a device for helping a person to pull off boots.

**boot·leg** (bo͞ot′leg′), *v.t. & v.i.* [-LEGGED, -LEGGING], [in allusion to concealing liquor in the leg of a boot], to make, carry, or sell (liquor, etc.) illegally. *adj.* 1. made or sold illegally. 2. of bootlegging. *n.* bootlegged liquor. —**boot′leg′ger,** *n.*

**boot·less** (bo͞ot′lis), *adj.* [*boot* (profit) + *-less*], useless. —**boot′less·ly,** *adv.* —**boot′less·ness,** *n.*

**boot·lick** (bo͞ot′lik′), *v.t. & v.i.* [Slang], to try to gain favor with by fawning, servility, etc. —**boot′lick′er,** *n.* —**boot′lick′ing,** *n.*

**boo·ty** (bo͞o′ti), *n.* [*pl.* -TIES], [< Fr. < MLG. *bute*], 1. spoils of war. 2. pillage. 3. any prize.

**booze** (bo͞oz), *v.i.* [BOOZED, BOOZING], [D. *buizen*], [Colloq.], to drink too much liquor. *n.* [Colloq.], 1. liquor. 2. a drinking spree.

**booz·y** (bo͞oz′i), *adj.* [-IER, -IEST], [Colloq.], drunk; esp. habitually drunk. —**booz′i·ly,** *adv.*

**bop** (bop), *v.t. & n.* [echoic], [Slang], hit; punch.

**bop** (bop), *n.* [< *bebop*], a style of jazz with complex rhythms, experimental harmonies, etc.

**bo·rac·ic** (bō-ras′ik), *adj.* [< *borax* + *-ic*], boric.

**bor·age** (bũr′ij, bôr′-, bor′-), *n.* [< OFr. < ML., prob. < *burra,* coarse hair], a plant with blue flowers and hairy leaves.

**bo·rate** (bôr′āt, bō′rāt), *n.* a salt or ester of boric acid. *v.t.* [-RATED, -RATING], to treat with borax or boric acid. —**bo′rat·ed,** *adj.*

**bo·rax** (bôr′aks, bō′raks), *n.* [< OFr. < LL. < Ar. < Per. *būrah*], a white crystalline salt, $Na_2B_4O_7$, used as a flux and in glass, soaps, etc.

**Bor·deaux** (bôr-dō′), *n.* 1. a seaport in SW France: pop., 254,000. 2. white or red wine from near Bordeaux: the red is generally called *claret.*

**Bordeaux mixture,** a mixture of lime, water, and copper sulfate, used as a fungicide.

**bor·der** (bôr′dẽr), *n.* [< OFr. < OHG. *bord,* margin], 1. an edge or part near an edge; margin. 2. a dividing line between two countries, etc.; frontier. 3. a narrow, ornamental strip along an edge. *v.t.* 1. to provide with a border. 2. to bound. *adj.* of, forming, or near a border. —**border on** (or **upon**), 1. to be next to. 2. to be like; approximate.

**bor·der·land** (bôr′dẽr-land′), *n.* 1. land constituting or near a border. 2. a vague state, place, etc.

**bor·der·line** (bôr′dẽr-līn′), *n.* a boundary. *adj.* 1. on a boundary. 2. indefinite; doubtful; debatable.

**bore** (bôr, bōr), *v.t.* [BORED, BORING], [< AS. < *bor,* auger], 1. to make a hole in or through with a drill, etc. 2. to make (a hole, tunnel, etc.) by drilling, digging, etc. 3. to force (one's way), as through a crowd. 4. to weary by being dull or monotonous. *v.i.* to bore a hole or passage. *n.* 1. a hole made by or as by boring. 2. *a)* the hollow part of a tube or gun barrel. *b)* its inside diameter; caliber. 3. a tiresome, dull person or thing.

**bore** (bôr, bōr), *n.* [< ON. *bara,* a billow], 1. a high, abrupt tidal wave in a narrow channel. 2. loosely, any high, swift tidal flow.

**bore** (bôr, bōr), pt. of **bear.**

**bo·re·al** (bôr′i-əl, bō′ri-), *adj.* [LL. *borealis* < *Boreas*], 1. northern. 2. of the north wind.

**Bo·re·as** (bôr′i-əs, bō′ri-), *n.* 1. in *Gr. mythology,* the god of the north wind. 2. the north wind.

**bore·dom** (bôr′dəm, bōr′-), *n.* the condition of being bored or uninterested; ennui.
**bor·er** (bôr′ẽr, bōr′-), *n.* 1. a tool for boring. 2. an insect or worm that bores holes in fruit, etc.
**bore·some** (bôr′səm, bōr′-), *adj.* boring; tiresome.
**Bor·glum, Gut·zon** (gut′sən bôr′gləm), 1871–1941; U.S. sculptor and painter.
**bo·ric** (bô′rik, bō′rik), *adj.* of or containing boron.
**boric acid,** a white, crystalline, weakly acid compound, $H_3BO_3$, used as a mild antiseptic: also **boracic acid.**
**born** (bôrn), pp. of **bear** (to give birth): now only in passive constructions not followed by *by*. *adj.* 1. brought into life or existence. 2. by nature: as, a *born* musician.
**borne** (bôrn), pp. of **bear** (to carry): see **born.**
**Bor·ne·o** (bôr′ni-ō, bōr′-), *n.* a large island in the East Indies, southwest of the Philippines, partly in Indonesia and partly composed of Brunei and two states of Malaysia: area, 287,000 sq. mi.
**Bo·ro·din, A·lek·san·dr Por·fir·e·vich** (ä′lyek-sän′dr′ pôr′fir-ye′vich bô′rô-dēn′; Eng. bôr′ə-din), 1834–1887; Russian composer.
**bo·ron** (bôr′on, bō′-), *n.* [< *borax*], a nonmetallic, chemical element occurring only in combination, as in borax: symbol, B; at. wt., 10.82; at. no., 5: abbrev. **bor.**
**bor·ough** (bũr′ō), *n.* [AS. *burg;* akin to *beorgan*, to protect], 1. in the U.S., a self-governing, incorporated town. 2. one of the five administrative units of New York City. 3. in England, *a)* a town with a municipal corporation granted by royal charter. *b)* a town that sends representatives to Parliament. Abbrev. **bor.**
**bor·row** (bor′ō, bôr′ō), *v.t. & v.i.* [AS. *borgian* < *borh, borg*, a pledge], 1. to take or receive (something) with the understanding that one will return it. 2. to adopt (something) as one's own: as, he *borrowed* my theory. 3. in *arithmetical subtraction*, to take from one denomination in the minuend and add to the next lower. —**borrow trouble,** to worry needlessly or prematurely. —**bor′row·er,** *n.*
**borsch** (bôrsh; Russ. bôrshch), *n.* [Russ. *borshch*], a Russian beet soup, served usually with sour cream: also **borsht** (bôrsht).
**bort** (bôrt), *n.* [? < OFr. *bourt*, bastard], a poorly crystallized variety of diamond used as an abrasive.
**bor·zoi** (bôr′zoi), *n.* [Russ., swift], a Russian wolfhound.
**bos·cage** (bos′kij), *n.* [OFr. < OHG. *busk*, forest], a thicket; grove; shrubbery.
**bosh** (bosh), *n. & interj.* [Turk., empty, worthless], [Colloq.], nonsense.
**bos·kage** (bos′kij), *n.* boscage: also **bosk** (bosk).
**bosk·y** (bos′ki), *adj.* 1. covered with underbrush; wooded. 2. shady. —**bosk′i·ness,** *n.*
**bo's'n** (bō′s'n), *n.* a boatswain.
**Bos·ni·a** (boz′ni-ə), *n.* a part of Yugoslavia: a former kingdom. —**Bos′ni·an,** *adj. & n.*
**Bos·ni·a-Her·ze·go·vi·na** (boz′ni-ə-her′tsə-gō-vē′-nə), *n.* a federal republic of Yugoslavia: area, 19,678 sq. mi.; pop., 3,278,000; capital, Sarajevo.
**bos·om** (booz′əm, bōō′zəm), *n.* [AS. *bosm*], 1. the human breast. 2. a thing like this: as, the *bosom* of a hill. 3. the breast regarded as the source of feelings. 4. the enclosing space formed by the breast and arms in embracing. 5. the interior; midst: as, the *bosom* of one's family. 6. the part of a garment that covers the breast. *v.t.* 1. to embrace; cherish. 2. to conceal; hide. *adj.* 1. of the bosom. 2. close; intimate: as, a *bosom* friend.
**Bos·pho·rus** (bos′fə-rəs), *n.* the Bosporus.
**Bos·po·rus** (bos′pə-rəs), *n.* the strait between the Sea of Marmara and the Black Sea.
**boss** (bôs, bos), *n.* [D. *baas*, a master], [Colloq.], 1. one in authority over employees; employer or supervisor. 2. one who controls a political organization: often **political boss.** *v.t. & v.i.* [Colloq.], 1. to be the boss (of). 2. to exercise undue authority (over). *adj.* [Colloq.], chief.
**boss** (bôs, bos), *n.* [< OFr. *boce*, a swelling], 1. a raised part or protruding ornament on a flat surface. 2. a projecting knob or stud, as on a shield. 3. in *mechanics*, the enlarged part of a shaft. *v.t.* 1. to form raised ornaments on the surface of. 2. to decorate with studs or knobs.
**boss·ism** (bôs′iz'm, bos′iz'm), *n.* control by bosses, especially of a political machine.
**boss·y** (bôs′i, bos′i), *n.* a cow or calf.
**boss·y** (bôs′i, bos′i), *adj.* [-IER, -IEST], [Colloq.], domineering.
**Bos·ton** (bôs′t'n, bos′-), *n.* a seaport and the capital of Massachusetts: pop., 697,000 (metropolitan area, 2,589,000). —**Bos·to′ni·an** (-tō′ni-ən), *adj. & n.*
**Boston terrier,** any of a breed of small dog having a smooth coat of brindle or black with white markings: also **Boston bull.**

BOSTON TERRIER (14–20 in. high)

**bo·sun** (bō′s'n), *n.* a boatswain.
**Bos·well, James** (boz′wel, -wəl), 1740–1795; Scottish lawyer and writer; biographer of Samuel Johnson. —**Bos·well·i·an** (boz-wel′i-ən), *adj.*
**bot** (bot), *n.* [? < Gael. < *boiteag*, maggot], a botfly larva: also sp. **bott.**
**bot.,** 1. botanical. 2. botanist. 3. botany.
**bo·tan·i·cal** (bə-tan′i-k'l), *adj.* [< Fr. < LL. < Gr. < *botanē*, a plant], 1. of plants and plant life. 2. of or connected with the science of botany. Also **bo·tan′ic.** *n.* a vegetable drug prepared from bark, roots, herbs, etc. —**bo·tan′i·cal·ly,** *adv.*
**bot·a·nize** (bot′ə-nīz′), *v.i.* [-NIZED, -NIZING], 1. to gather plants for botanical study. 2. to study plants, especially in their natural environment. *v.t.* to investigate the plant life of.
**bot·a·ny** (bot′ə-ni), *n.* [< *botanical*], 1. the science that deals with plants, their structure, growth, classification, etc. 2. the plant life of an area. 3. the life cycle of a plant group. —**bot′a·nist,** *n.*
**Botany Bay,** a bay on the SE coast of Australia, near Sydney: site of a former penal colony.
**botch** (boch), *v.t.* [ME. *bocchen*, to repair; prob. < D. *botsen*, to patch], 1. to repair or patch clumsily. 2. to bungle. *n.* 1. a badly patched place or part. 2. a bungled piece of work. —**botch′er,** *n.* —**botch′er·y,** *n.* —**botch′y,** *adj.*
**bot·fly** (bot′flī′), *n.* [*pl.* -FLIES], [see BOT], any of a number of related flies whose larvae are parasitic in horses, sheep, etc.
**both** (bōth), *adj. & pron.* [< ON. *bathir* < Gmc. hyp. *ba*, two; elided onto base of Eng. *the*], the two: as, *both* (birds) sang loudly. *conj. & adv.* together; equally; as well; not only: used correlatively with *and*, as, I am *both* tired *and* hungry
**both·er** (both′ẽr), *v.t. & v.i.* [prob. Anglo-Ir. for *pother*], 1. to annoy; worry; trouble. 2. to concern or trouble (oneself). *n.* 1. worry; trouble; fuss. 2. one who gives trouble. *interj.* an expression of annoyance, etc.: as, oh, *bother!*
**both·er·a·tion** (both′ẽr-ā′shən), *n. & interj.* [Colloq.], bother.
**both·er·some** (both′ẽr-səm), *adj.* causing bother; annoying; troublesome; irksome.
**Bot·swa·na** (bot-swä′nə), *n.* a country in S Africa: a member of the British Commonwealth of Nations: area, 222,000 sq. mi.; pop., 576,000.
**bott** (bot), *n.* a bot.
**Bot·ti·cel·li, San·dro** (sän′drō bot′i-chel′i), 1444?–1510; Italian Renaissance painter.
**bot·tle** (bot′'l), *n.* [< OFr.; LL. *butticula*, a bottle < *buttis*, a vat], 1. a container for liquids, usually of glass, having a narrow neck and no handles. 2. its contents; amount that a bottle holds. *v.t.* [-TLED, -TLING], 1. to put into a bottle or bottles. 2. to hold back; restrain (with *up*). —**hit the bottle,** [Slang], to drink too much alcoholic liquor. —**bot′tler,** *n.*
**bot·tle·neck** (bot′'l-nek′), *n.* 1. a narrow passage or road. 2. any hindrance to progress.
**bot·tle·nose** (bot′'l-nōz′), *n.* a variety of dolphin with a bottle-shaped snout; porpoise.
**bot·tom** (bot′əm), *n.* [AS. *botm;* akin to G. *boden*, ground], 1. the lowest part of anything. 2. the part on which something rests. 3. the side or end that is underneath. 4. the seat of a chair. 5. the ground beneath a body of water. 6. *often pl.* low land; bottom land. 7. a ship's keel. 8. a ship. 9. basis; cause; origin; source. 10. endurance; stamina. 11. [Colloq.], the buttocks. *adj.* 1. of, at, or on the bottom. 2. lowest; last; basic. *v.t.* 1. to provide with a bottom, as a chair. 2. to understand; fathom. 3. to place on a foundation; base (*on* or *upon*). *v.i.* 1. to reach the bottom. 2. to be based (*on* or *upon*). —**at bottom,** fundamentally; actually. —**be at the bottom of,** to be the real reason for. —**bottom out,** to level off at a low point, as prices. —**bottoms up!** [Colloq.], drink deep! —**get to the bottom of,** to solve.
**bottom land,** low land through which a river flows: it is rich in alluvial deposits.
**bot·tom·less** (bot′əm-lis), *adj.* 1. having no bottom. 2. very deep, inexhaustible, etc.
**bot·tom·ry** (bot′əm-ri), *n.* [< *bottom*, a ship, after D. *bodomerij*, bottomry], a contract by which a shipowner borrows money for equipment, etc., pledging the ship as security.
**bot·u·lism** (boch′ə-liz'm), *n.* [L. *botulus*, sausage;

+ *-ism*: from early cases involving sausages], poisoning resulting from the toxin produced by a certain bacillus sometimes found in foods improperly canned or preserved.

**bou·clé** (bo͞o-klā′), *n.* [Fr., curled < *boucle;* see BUCKLE], 1. a kind of yarn that gives the cloth made from it a tufted or knotted texture. 2. cloth made from this yarn. *adj.* of such cloth.

**bou·doir** (bo͞o′dwär, bo͞o-dwär′), *n.* [Fr., lit., pouting room < *bouder*, to pout, sulk + *-oir*], a woman's private sitting room or dressing room.

**bouf·fant** (bo͞o-fänt′; Fr. bo͞o′fän′), *adj.* [Fr., ppr. of *bouffer*, to swell up], puffed out; full.

‡**bouf·fante** (bo͞o′fänt′), *adj.* [Fr., fem.], bouffant.

**bough** (bou), *n.* [AS. *boh*, shoulder, hence branch], branch of a tree; esp., a main branch.

**bought** (bôt), pt. and pp. of **buy.**

**bought·en** (bôt′'n), *adj.* [Dial.], bought; not homemade: as, *boughten* gloves.

**bouil·la·baisse** (bo͞ol′yə-bās′; Fr. bo͞o′yȧ′bes′), *n.* [Fr. < Pr. < *bouli*, to boil + *abaissa;* see ABASE], a chowder made of various kinds of fish.

**bouil·lon** (bool′yon, -yən; Fr. bo͞o′yōn′), *n.* [Fr. < *bouillir*, to boil], a clear broth.

**boul.,** boulevard.

**boul·der** (bōl′dẽr), *n.* [< *boulder stone;* ME. *bulderstan* < ON.; cf. Sw. *bullersten*, lit., noise stone], any large rock worn and rounded by weather and water: also sp. **bowlder.**

**Boulder Dam,** Hoover Dam: the former name.

**boul·e·vard** (bool′ə-värd′, bo͞o′lə-), *n.* [Fr., altered < G. *bollwerk*, bulwark], a broad street, often lined with trees, etc.: abbrev. **blvd., boul.**

**bounce** (bouns), *v.t.* [BOUNCED, BOUNCING], [< D. *bonzen* or LG. *bunsen*, to thump], 1. to bump or thump. 2. to cause to bound or rebound, as a ball. 3. [Slang], to put (a person) out by force. 4. [Slang], to discharge from employment. *v.i.* 1. to bound or rebound. 2. to move in a sudden or noisy rush. *n.* 1. a bound; rebound; jump. 2. capacity for bouncing. 3. a loud or heavy thump. 4. [Slang], spirit; dash. **—get the bounce,** [Slang], to be dismissed or discharged.

**bounc·er** (boun′sẽr), *n.* [Slang], anyone hired to remove very disorderly people from a night club, restaurant, etc.

**bounc·ing** (boun′siŋ), *adj.* [ppr. of *bounce*], 1. big; heavy; buxom. 2. healthy; strong; lusty.

**bouncing Bet** (or **Bess**), a kind of soapwort with dense clusters of white or pinkish flowers.

**bound** (bound), *v.i.* [Fr. *bondir*, to leap, orig., to echo < LL. < L. *bombus*, a humming], 1. to move with a leap or series of leaps. 2. to rebound, as a ball. *v.t.* to cause to bound or bounce. *n.* 1. a jump; leap. 2. a bounce.

**bound** (bound), pt. and pp. of **bind.** *adj.* 1. tied. 2. closely connected. 3. certain; destined: as, he's *bound* to win. 4. obliged: as, he is legally *bound* to do it. 5. provided with a binding, as a book: abbrev. **bd.** 6. [Colloq.], determined; resolved. **—bound up in (or with),** 1. deeply devoted to. 2. implicated in.

**bound** (bound) *adj.* [< ME. < *bun*, ready < ON. *buinn*, pp. of *bua*, to prepare], going; headed (often with *for* or *to*): as, *bound* for home.

**bound** (bound), *n.* [< OFr. < LL. *butina*], 1. a boundary; limit. 2. *pl.* an area near or enclosed by a boundary. *v.t.* 1. to limit; confine. 2. to be a limit or boundary to. 3. to name the boundaries of (a state, etc.). *v.i.* to have a boundary (*on*). **—out of bounds,** 1. beyond the boundaries or limits. 2. prohibited.

**-bound** (bound), a combining form meaning *going in* (a specified direction) or *to* (a specified place), as in *southbound, Chicago-bound.*

**bound·a·ry** (boun′də-ri, -dri), *n.* [*pl.* -RIES], anything marking a limit; bound; border.

**bound·en** (boun′dən), *adj.* [old pp. of *bind*], 1. obligated; indebted; obliged. 2. binding; obligatory: as, one's *bounden* duty.

**bound·er** (boun′dẽr), *n.* [*bound* (to leap) + *-er*], [Colloq.], an ill-mannered, rude person.

**bound·less** (bound′lis), *adj.* having no bounds; unlimited; vast. **—bound′less·ly,** *adv.* **—bound′less·ness,** *n.*

**boun·te·ous** (boun′ti-əs), *adj.* [< OFr. *bontif;* see BOUNTY], 1. giving without restraint; generous. 2. abundant; ample. **—boun′te·ous·ly,** *adv.* **—boun′te·ous·ness,** *n.*

**boun·ti·ful** (boun′ti-fəl), *adj.* bounteous. **—boun′ti·ful·ly,** *adv.* **—boun′ti·ful·ness,** *n.*

**boun·ty** (boun′ti), *n.* [*pl.* -TIES], [< OFr. < L. < *bonus*, good], 1. generosity. 2. generous gift. 3. a reward or premium.

**bou·quet** (bō-kā′, bo͞o-), *n.* [Fr.], 1. a bunch of flowers. 2. (bo͞o-kā′), aroma; fragrance, especially of a wine, etc.

**Bour·bon** (boor′bən), *n.* 1. the ruling family at various times of France, Spain, Naples, etc. 2. a political and social reactionary. **—Bour′bon·ism,** *n.* **—Bour′bon·ist,** *n.*

**bour·bon** (bũr′bən, boor′-), *n.* [< the corn whisky first produced in *Bourbon* County, Kentucky], a whisky made largely from corn.

**bour·geois** (boor-zhwä′, boor′zhwä), *n.* [*pl.* -GEOIS], [Fr. < OFr. < OHG. *burg*, town], 1. a shopkeeper. 2. a member of the bourgeoisie. 3. a person with the traits or viewpoint of the bourgeoisie. *adj.* of or characteristic of the bourgeoisie; middle-class: used variously to mean commonplace, respectable, smug, etc.

**bour·geoi·sie** (boor′zhwä′zē′), *n.* [construed as sing. or pl.], 1. the social class between the aristocracy or very wealthy and the working class, or proletariat; middle class. 2. in *Marxist doctrine*, capitalists as a social class antithetical to the proletariat.

**bour·geon** (bũr′jən), *n., v.t. & v.i* burgeon.

**bourn, bourne** (bôrn, bōrn, boorn), *n.* [AS. *burna*, a stream], a brook or stream: also **burn.**

**bourn, bourne** (bôrn, bōrn, boorn), *n.* [Fr. *borne;* OFr. *bodne* < LL. *bodina*, limit], [Archaic], 1. a goal; objective. 2. a domain. 3. a limit; boundary.

**bourse** (boors), *n.* [Fr., a purse < OFr. < LL. *bursa*, a bag < Gr. *bursa*, a hide], a stock exchange; esp., [B-], the stock exchange of Paris.

**bout** (bout), *n.* [for earlier *bought*, apparently a ME. pp. form < AS. *bugan*, to bend], 1. a struggle; contest or match: as, a boxing *bout.* 2. a period spent in some activity; spell or term.

**bou·tique** (bo͞o-tēk′), *n.* [Fr. < Gr. *apothēkē*, storehouse], a small shop where fashionable clothes and other articles are sold.

**bou·ton·niere, bou·ton·nière** (bo͞o′t'n-yer′), *n.* [Fr. *boutonnière*, a buttonhole], a flower or flowers worn in the buttonhole, as of a lapel.

**bo·vine** (bō′vīn, -vin), *adj.* [< LL. < L. *bos, bovis*, ox], 1. of or like an ox or cow. 2. slow, patient, stupid, stolid, etc. *n.* an ox, cow, etc.

**bow** (bou), *v.i.* [< AS. *bugan*, to bend], 1. [Dial.], to bend; stoop. 2. to bend the head or body in respect, agreement, etc. 3. to submit, as to authority. *v.t.* 1. [Dial.], to bend. 2. to bend (the head or body) in respect, agreement, etc. 3. to indicate (agreement, thanks, etc.) by bowing. 4. to weigh (*down*); overwhelm. *n.* a bending of the head or body, as in greeting, etc. **—bow and scrape,** to be too polite and ingratiating. **—make one's bow,** to make a formal entrance. **—take a bow,** to acknowledge applause, etc. **—bow′er,** *n.*

**bow** (bō), *n.* [AS. *boga* < *bugan*, to bend], 1. anything curved or bent, as a rainbow, etc. 2. a curve; bend. 3. a device for shooting arrows, a flexible, curved strip of wood, etc. with a cord connecting the two ends. 4. *pl.* archers. 5. a slender stick strung along its length with horsehairs, drawn across the strings of a violin, etc. to play it. 6. a bowknot. *adj.* curved; bent. *v.t. & v.i.* 1. to bend in the shape of a bow. 2. in *music*, to play (a violin, etc.) with a bow.

BOW AND ARROW

**bow** (bou), *n.* [< LG. or Scand.], 1. the front part of a ship, etc.; prow. 2. the oarsman nearest the bow. *adj.* of or near the bow; fore.

**bowd·ler·ize** (boud′lẽr-īz′), *v.t.* [-IZED, -IZING], [after Dr. Thomas *Bowdler*, who in 1818 published an expurgated Shakespeare], to expurgate. **—bowd′ler·ism,** *n.* **—bowd′ler·i·za′tion,** *n.*

**bow·el** (bou′əl, boul), *n.* [< OFr. < L. *botellus*, dim. of *botulus*, sausage], 1. an intestine, especially of a human being; gut; entrail. 2. *pl.* the inside: as, the *bowels* of the earth. 3. *pl.* [Archaic], tender emotions. *v.t.* [-ELED or -ELLED, -ELING or -ELLING], to disembowel. **—move one's bowels,** to pass waste matter from the large intestine.

**bow·er** (bou′ẽr), *n.* [< AS. *bur*, a dwelling], 1. a place enclosed by leafy boughs or vines; arbor. 2.

[Archaic], a bedchamber. *v.t.* to enclose in a bower. **—bow′er·like′, bow′er·y,** *adj.*

**Bow·er·y** (bou′ẽr-i), *n.* a street in New York City, a center of cheap hotels, saloons, etc.

**bow·ie knife** (bō′i, bōō′i), [after Col. J. *Bowie*, its inventor], a long, steel hunting knife with a single edge.

BOWIE KNIFE

**bow·knot** (bō′not′, bō′not′), *n.* a slipknot with one or two loops, untied by pulling the end or ends.

**bowl** (bōl), *n.* [< AS. *bolla*], 1. a deep, hollow, rounded dish. 2. a large drinking cup. 3. convivial drinking. 4. a thing or part like a bowl: as, the *bowl* of a spoon. 5. an amphitheater. 6. the contents of a bowl.

**bowl** (bōl), *n.* [< OFr. < L. *bulla*, a bubble], 1. a heavy ball used in the game of bowls. 2. a turn or a delivery of the ball in bowling. *v.i. & v.t.* 1. to roll (a ball) or participate in bowling. 2. to move swiftly and smoothly, as on wheels. 3. in *cricket*, to deliver (a ball) to the batsman. **—bowl over,** 1. to knock over. 2. [Colloq.], to astonish and confuse. **—bowl′er,** *n.*

**bow·leg** (bō′leg′), *n.* a leg with outward curvature. **—bow′leg′ged** (-leg′id, -legd′), *adj.*

**bowl·er** (bōl′ẽr), *n.* [< *bowl* (ball)], a derby hat.

**bow·line** (bō′lin, -lin′), *n.* 1. a rope used to keep the sail taut when sailing into the wind. 2. a knot used to tie off a loop: also **bowline knot.**

**bowl·ing** (bōl′iŋ), *n.* 1. a game in which a heavy ball is bowled along a wooden lane (**bowling alley**) in an attempt to knock over ten wooden pins at the far end; tenpins. 2. the game of bowls. 3. the playing of either game. *adj.* of or for bowling.

**bowls** (bōlz), *n.* 1. a game played on a smooth lawn (**bowling green**) with a weighted wooden ball which is rolled in an attempt to make it stop near a stationary ball (**jack**). 2. ninepins or tenpins.

**bow·man** (bō′mən), *n.* [*pl.* -MEN], an archer.

**bow·shot** (bō′shot′), *n.* the distance that an arrow can travel when shot from a bow.

**bow·sprit** (bou′sprit′, bō′-), *n.* [prob. < D. < *boeg*, bow of a ship + *spriet*, sprit], a large, tapered pole extending forward from the bow of a sailing vessel: the foremost stays are fastened to it.

**bow·string** (bō′striŋ′), *n.* a cord stretched from one end of a bow to the other.

**bow tie** (bō), a necktie tied in a small bowknot.

**box** (boks), *n.* [AS.; < ML. < LL. < Gr. < *pyxos*, boxwood], 1. any of many kinds of containers, usually with lids, and of various sizes, shapes, and materials; case. 2. the contents of a box. 3. the driver's seat in a vehicle. 4. a boxlike thing. 5. a small enclosed group of seats, as in a theater, stadium, etc. 6. a small booth. 7. a horse stall. 8. a space or section for a certain person or group: as, a jury *box*. 9. a short newspaper article enclosed in borders. 10. in *baseball*, the place where a player must stand while at bat: in full, **batter's box.** 11. in *mechanics*, a protective casing for a part: as, a journal *box*. *v.t.* 1. to provide with a box. 2. to put into a box. *adj.* 1. shaped or made like a box. 2. packaged in a box. **—box in** (or **up**), to shut in or keep in. **—box the compass,** 1. to name the points of the compass in order. 2. to make a complete circuit. **—box′like′,** *adj.*

**box** (boks), *n.* [? playful use of *box* (container) in sense "gift"], a blow struck with the hand or fist, especially on the ear. *v.t.* 1. to strike such a blow. 2. to fight by boxing with. *v.i.* 1. to fight with the fists. 2. to be a boxer.

**box** (boks), *n.* [AS.; < Gr. *pyxos*], 1. an evergreen shrub or small tree with small, leathery leaves. 2. the hard, close-grained wood of this plant.

**box·car** (boks′kär′), *n.* a fully enclosed railroad freight car.

**box elder,** a kind of maple tree that grows rapidly and drops its leaves early.

**Box·er** (bok′sẽr), *n.* a member of a Chinese society that led an unsuccessful uprising (the **Boxer Rebellion,** 1900) against foreigners in China.

**box·er** (bok′sẽr), *n.* 1. a man who boxes; pugilist; prize fighter. 2. a dog with a sturdy body and a smooth fawn or brindle coat.

**box·ing** (bok′siŋ), *n.* [< *box* (to hit)], the skill or occupation of fighting with the fists, especially in special padded mittens.

**boxing gloves,** padded leather mittens for boxing.

**box office,** 1. a place where admission tickets are sold, as in a theater. 2. appeal as measured by ticket sales: as, this show had a good *box office*.

**box score,** a statistical summary of a baseball game, showing in boxlike form the number of hits, runs, errors, etc.

**box seat,** a seat in a box at a theater, etc.

**box·wood** (boks′wood′), *n.* box (shrub).

**boy** (boi), *n.* [ME. *boie*], 1. a male child from birth to physical maturity. 2. any man; fellow: familiar term. 3. a male servant: term applied especially by Caucasians to native workers in India, Africa, etc. *interj.* [Slang], an exclamation of pleasure, surprise, etc.: often **oh, boy! —boy′ish,** *adj.* **—boy′ish·ly,** *adv.* **—boy′ish·ness,** *n.*

**boy·cott** (boi′kot′), *v.t.* [after Captain *Boycott*, Irish land agent so treated in 1880], 1. to join together in refusing to deal with, so as to punish, coerce, etc. 2. to refuse to buy, sell, or use (something). *n.* a boycotting. **—boy′cott′er,** *n.*

**boy friend,** [Colloq.], a boy or man who is a friend, escort, or sweetheart of a girl or woman.

**boy·hood** (boi′hood), *n.* [see -HOOD], 1. the time or state of being a boy. 2. boys collectively.

**boy scout,** a member of the Boy Scouts.

**Boy Scouts,** a boys' organization that stresses outdoor life and service to others.

**boy·sen·ber·ry** (boi′s'n-ber′i, -z'n-), *n.* [*pl.* -RIES], [after Rudolph *Boysen*, Am. horticulturist], a purple berry resulting from crossing varieties of raspberry, loganberry, and blackberry.

**bp.,** 1. birthplace. 2. bishop.

**b.p., B/P,** bills payable.

**b.p.,** boiling point.

**Br,** in *chemistry*, bromine.

**Br.,** 1. Breton. 2. Britain. 3. British.

**br.,** 1. branch. 2. brother. 3. brown.

**b.r., B/R,** bills receivable.

**bra** (brä), *n.* [Colloq.], a brassiere.

**brace** (brās), *v.t.* [BRACED, BRACING], [< OFr. < L. *brachia*, pl. of *brachium*, an arm], 1. to tie or bind on firmly. 2. to tighten, especially by stretching. 3. to strengthen or make firm by supporting the weight of, etc.; prop up. 4. to equip with braces. 5. to make ready for an impact, shock, etc. 6. to stimulate. *n.* 1. a couple; pair. 2. a thing that clamps, clasps, or connects; fastener. 3. *pl.* [Brit.], suspenders. 4. a device for setting up or maintaining tension, as a guy wire. 5. either of the signs { }, used to connect words, lines, or staves of music. 6. a device, as a beam, used to strengthen by supporting the weight of, etc.; prop. 7. *a*) any of various devices for supporting a weak part or joint of the body. *b*) *usually in pl.* a wirelike device for correcting the faulty growth of teeth. 8. a tool for holding and rotating a drilling bit. **—brace up,** [Colloq.], call forth one's courage, etc.

**brace and bit,** a boring tool consisting of a removable drill (bit) in a rotating handle (brace).

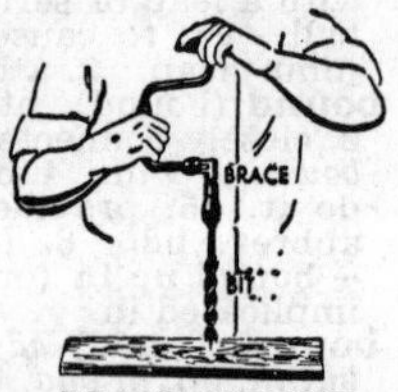

BRACE AND BIT

**brace·let** (brās′lit), *n.* [Fr. < OFr. < L. < *brachium*, an arm], 1. an ornamental band or chain worn about the wrist or arm. 2. [Colloq.], a handcuff.

**brac·er** (brās′ẽr), *n.* 1. a person or thing that braces. 2. [Slang], a drink taken as a stimulant.

**bra·ce·ro** (brə-ser′ō), *n.* [*pl.* -ROS], [Sp. < *brazo*, an arm], a Mexican farm laborer brought into the U.S. temporarily to harvest crops.

**bra·chi·o-,** [< L. < Gr. *brachiōn*, an arm], a combining form meaning *arm, connected with an arm,* as in *brachiopod*: also **brachi-.**

**bra·chi·o·pod** (brā′ki-ə-pod′, brak′i-), *n.* [*brachio-* + *-pod*], any of a number of related small, soft-bodied sea animals with upper and lower shells and two armlike parts, one on each side of the mouth.

**bra·chi·um** (brā′ki-əm, brak′i-), *n.* [*pl.* BRACHIA (-ə)], [L.], 1. the part of the arm that extends from shoulder to elbow. 2. in *biology*, any armlike limb or part. **—bra′chi·al,** *adj.*

**brach·y-,** [< Gr. *brachys*, short], a combining form meaning *short*, as in *brachycephalic*.

**brach·y·ce·phal·ic** (brak′i-sə-fal′ik), *adj.* [*brachy-* + *-cephalic*], having a relatively short or broad skull: opposed to *dolichocephalic*: see also **cephalic index:** also **brach′y·ceph′a·lous** (-sef′ə-ləs). **—brach′y·ceph′a·ly,** *n.*

**brac·ing** (brās′iŋ), *adj.* invigorating; stimulating.

**brack·en** (brak′ən), *n.* [< ON.], 1. any large, coarse fern, as the brake. 2. a growth of such ferns.

**brack·et** (brak′it), *n.* [< Fr. dim. of *brague*, kind of mortise < L. sing. of *bracae*, breeches < Gallic *braca*, pants], 1. a support or shelf projecting from a wall, etc. 2. any angle-shaped support, especially one in the form of a right triangle. 3. a gas or electric wall fixture. 4. either of the signs [ ], used to enclose a word, etc., often so as to show that it is inserted. 5. a list contained within brackets. 6. a classification: as, high income *brackets.* *v.t.* 1. to provide or support with brackets. 2. to enclose within brackets. 3. to classify together.

**brack·ish** (brak′ish), *adj.* [earlier Scot. *brack* < MD. *brac;* + *-ish*], 1. mixed with salt; briny. 2. distasteful; nauseous. —**brack′ish·ness,** *n.*

**bract** (brakt), *n.* [L. *bractea,* thin metal plate], a modified leaf, usually small and scalelike, growing at the base of a flower or on its stalk. —**brac′te·al** (-ti-əl), *adj.* —**brac′te·ate** (-ti-it), *adj.*

**bract·let** (brakt′lit), *n.* a secondary bract at the base of a flower: also **brac′te·ole′** (-ti-ōl′)

**brad** (brad), *n.* [ON. *broddr,* a spike], a thin wire nail with a small or off-center head.

**brad·awl** (brad′ôl′), *n.* a straight awl with a chisel edge, used for making holes to put brads into.

**Brad·ford, William** (brad′fẽrd), 1590–1657; second governor of Plymouth Colony.

**Bra·dy, Mat·hew B.** (math′ū brā′di), 1823?–1896; U.S. photographer.

**brae** (brā), *n.* [ON. *bra,* eyelid, brow], [Scot.], a sloping bank; hillside.

**brag** (brag), *v.t. & v.i.* [BRAGGED, BRAGGING], [prob. < OFr. *braguer;* ? < source of *bray*], to boast. *n.* 1. a boast; boasting. 2. a person or thing boasted of. 3. a braggart. —**brag′ger,** *n.*

**brag·ga·do·ci·o** (brag′ə-dō′shi-ō′), *n.* [*pl.* -CIOS], [*brag* + It. ending; coined by Spenser], 1. a braggart. 2. noisy boasting or bragging.

**brag·gart** (brag′ẽrt), *n.* [< Fr. < OFr.; see BRAG], an offensively boastful person. *adj.* boastful.

**Brah·ma** (brä′mə), *n.* in *Hindu theology,* 1. the supreme essence or spirit of the universe. 2. the chief member of the trinity (Brahma, Vishnu, and Siva): he is regarded as the creator of the universe.

**Brah·man** (brä′mən), *n.* [*pl.* -MANS (-mənz)], a member of the priestly Hindu caste, the highest. —**Brah·man·ic** (brä-man′ik), **Brah·man′i·cal,** *adj.*

**Brah·man·ism** (brä′mən-iz′m), *n.* 1. the religious doctrines and system of the Brahmans. 2. the former Hindu caste system. —**Brah′man·ist,** *n.*

**Brah·min** (brä′min), *n.* 1. a Brahman. 2. a cultured upper-class person, especially one regarded as haughty and conservative. —**Brah·min·ic** (brä-min′ik), **Brah·min′i·cal,** *adj.*

**Brah·min·ism** (brä′min-iz′m), *n.* 1. Brahmanism. 2. the characteristic spirit, attitude, etc. of Brahmins. —**Brah′min·ist,** *n.*

**Brahms, Jo·han·nes** (yō-hä′nəs brämz; G. bräms), 1833–1897; German composer.

**braid** (brād), *v.t.* [AS. *bregdan,* to move quickly, twist], 1. to interweave three or more strands of (hair, straw, etc.). 2. to tie up (the hair) in a ribbon or band. 3. to decorate or bind with braid. *n.* 1. a band or strip formed by braiding. 2. a strip of braided hair. 3. a woven band of cloth, tape, ribbon, etc., used to bind or decorate clothing. 4. a ribbon or band for tying up the hair. —**braid′er,** *n.* —**braid′ing,** *n.*

**Braille, braille** (brāl), *n.* [after Louis *Braille* (1809–1852), the originator], 1. a system of printing and writing for the blind, using raised dots felt by the fingers. 2. the symbols used in this system.

**brain** (brān), *n.* [AS. *brægen*], 1. the mass of nerve tissue in the cranium of vertebrate animals: cf. **gray matter, white matter.** 2. *often pl.* intelligence; mental ability. *v.t.* to dash out the brains of. —**beat one's brains,** to try hard to remember, understand, etc. —**have on the brain,** to be obsessed by.

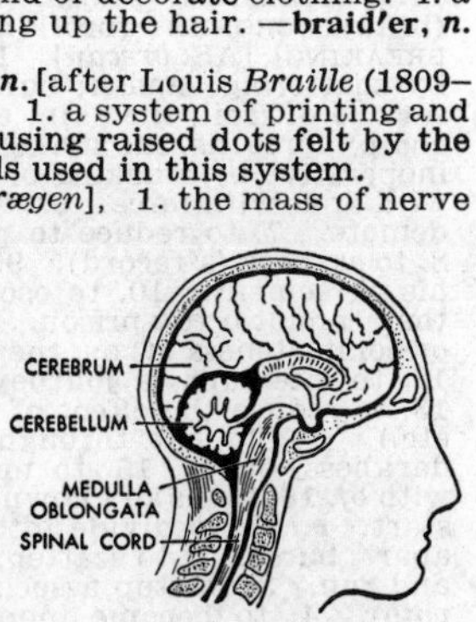

BRAIN OF MAN

**brain child,** [Colloq.], an idea, plan, etc. regarded as produced by a person's mental labor.

**brain·less** (brān′lis), *adj.* 1. having no brain. 2. foolish; stupid. —**brain′less·ly,** *adv.* —**brain′less·ness,** *n.*

**brain·pan** (brān′pan′), *n.* the cranium.

**brain·sick** (brān′sik′), *adj.* having or caused by a mental disorder. —**brain′sick′ly,** *adj. & adv.* —**brain′sick′ness,** *n.*

**brain storm,** [Colloq.], a sudden inspiration.

**brain·storm·ing** (brān′stôrm′iŋ), *n.* the unrestrained offering of ideas by all members of a group meeting as in a business planning conference.

**brain trust,** [Slang], a group of advisers with expert or special knowledge. —**brain′-trust′er,** *n.*

**brain·wash** (brān′wôsh′, -wäsh′), *v.t.* [Colloq.], to indoctrinate so intensively and thoroughly as to effect a radical transformation of beliefs. —**brain′-wash′ing,** *n.*

**brain wave,** in *physiology,* rhythmic electric impulses given off by nerve centers in the brain and spinal cord during sleep.

**brain·y** (brān′i), *adj.* [-IER, -IEST], [Colloq.], intelligent; mentally acute. —**brain′i·ness,** *n.*

**braise** (brāz), *v.t.* [BRAISED, BRAISING], [Fr. *braiser* < *braise* (< Gmc. *brasa*), live coals], to cook (meat) by browning in fat and then simmering in a covered pan with only a little liquid.

**brake** (brāk), *n.* [prob. taken as sing. of *bracken*], a large, coarse fern; bracken.

**brake** (brāk), *n.* [< MLG. or OD. < *breken,* to break], 1. a device for beating flax or hemp so that the fiber can be separated. 2. any device for slowing or stopping the motion of a vehicle or machine, as by causing a block or band to press against a moving part. *v.t.* [BRAKED, BRAKING], 1. to break up (flax or hemp) into smaller pieces. 2. to slow down or stop as with a brake. *v.i.* 1. to operate a brake. 2. to be slowed down or stopped by a brake.

**brake** (brāk), *n.* [prob. < MLG. *brake,* stumps], a clump of brushwood, briers, etc.; thicket.

**brake** (brāk), archaic pt. of **break.**

**brake·man** (brāk′mən), *n.* [*pl.* -MEN], an operator of brakes or assistant to the conductor on a railroad train.

**brake shoe,** a block curved to fit the shape of a wheel and forced against it to act as a brake.

**bram·ble** (bram′b'l), *n.* [< AS. *bræmel* < *brom,* broom], 1. any prickly shrub of the rose family, as the raspberry, blackberry, etc. 2. any prickly shrub. —**bram′bly** [-BLIER, -BLIEST], *adj.*

**bran** (bran), *n.* [OFr. *bren*], the skin or husk of grains of wheat, rye, oats, etc. separated from the flour, as by sifting.

**branch** (branch, bränch), *n.* [OFr. *branche* < LL. *branca,* a claw, paw], 1. any woody extension from the trunk, stem, or bough of a tree or shrub; bough; limb; twig. 2. anything like a branch; ramification; offshoot. 3. a tributary stream of a larger stream. 4. a division; part: as, chemistry is a *branch* of science. 5. a division of a family. 6. a separately located unit of a business, etc.: as, a suburban *branch* of a library. *v.i.* 1. to put forth branches; divide into branches; ramify. 2. to come out from the trunk or main part as a branch. *v.t.* to separate into branches. —**branch off,** 1. to separate into branches; fork. 2. to go off in another direction; diverge. —**branch out,** 1. to put forth branches. 2. to extend one's interests, activities, etc. —**branch′ing,** *adj. & n.* —**branch′less,** *adj.*

**bran·chi·ae** (braŋ′ki-ē′), *n.pl.* [sing. -CHIA (-ki-ə)], [< L. < Gr. *branchia,* gills], in *zoology,* gills. —**bran′chi·al,** *adj.* —**bran′chi·ate** (-it), *adj.*

**brand** (brand), *n.* [AS. < *biernan, v.i.,* to burn], 1. a stick that is burning or partially burned. 2. a mark made on the skin with a hot iron, formerly used to punish and identify criminals, now used on cattle to show ownership. 3. the iron thus used. 4. a mark of disgrace; stigma. 5. a mark or label of identification, grade, etc. on merchandise; trademark; hence, 6. the kind or make of a commodity: as, a *brand* of cigarettes. 7. [Archaic & Poetic], a sword. *v.t.* 1. to mark with or as with a brand. 2. to put a mark of disgrace on. —**brand′er,** *n.*

**Bran·deis, Louis Dem·bitz** (dem′bits bran′dīs), 1856–1941; U.S. Supreme Court justice.

**Bran·den·burg** (bran′dən-bũrg′; G. brän′dən-boorkh′), *n.* 1. a province of Prussia. 2. a city west of Berlin: pop., 64,000.

**bran·dish** (bran′dish), *v.t.* [< OFr. < OHG. *brand,* sword], to wave or shake menacingly, as a sword; flourish. *n.* a menacing flourish. —**bran′dish·er,** *n.*

**brand-new** (brand′nōō′, -nū′), *adj.* [orig., fresh from the fire; see BRAND], 1. entirely new; recently made. 2. loosely, recently acquired.

**bran·dy** (bran′di), *n.* [*pl.* -DIES], [earlier *brandywine* < D. *brandewijn,* lit., burnt (i.e., distilled) wine], 1. an alcoholic liquor distilled from wine. 2. a similar liquor distilled from fruit juice. *v.t.* [-DIED,

-DYING], to flavor, treat, or mix with brandy. —**bran'died,** *adj.*

**bran-new** (bran'nōō', -nū'), *adj.* brand-new.

**brant** (brant), *n.* [*pl.* BRANTS, BRANT; see PLURAL, II, D, 1], [? < *brand,* because of burnt color of the bird], any of a number of related small, dark, wild geese of Europe and North America.

**brash** (brash), *adj.* [prob. < *break* + *dash, rash,* etc.], 1. brittle or fragile, as some wood. 2. rash; too hasty. 3. insolent; impudent. *n.* a sudden shower of rain. —**brash'ness,** *n.* —**brash'y,** *adj.*

**bra·sier** (brā'zhẽr), *n.* a brazier.

**Bra·sil·i·a** (brä-sēl'yə, brə-sil'i-ə), *n.* the capital of Brazil: pop., 120,000.

**brass** (bras, bräs), *n.* [*pl.* BRASSES; see PLURAL, II, D, 3], [AS. *bræs*], 1. a yellowish metal that is essentially an alloy of copper and zinc. 2. *pl.* things made of brass. 3. *pl.* brass-wind musical instruments. 4. [Colloq.], bold impudence. 5. [Slang], military officers of high rank: see **brass hat.** *adj.* made of or containing brass.

**bras·sard** (bras'ärd, brə-särd'), *n.* [Fr. < *bras,* an arm], 1. armor for the upper arm: also **bras·sart (bras'ẽrt).** 2. an arm band worn as a badge.

**brass band,** a band in which the instruments played are mainly brass winds.

**brass hat,** [Slang], a military officer of high rank: from the gold braid on some officers' caps.

**brass·ie** (bras'i, bräs'i), *n.* [orig. made with a brass plate on the bottom of the head], a golf club with a wooden head and a loft between that of a driver and a spoon: also sp. **brassy** [*pl.* -IES].

**bras·siere, bras·sière** (brə-zêr'), *n.* [Fr. < *bras,* an arm], an undergarment worn by women to support the breasts or give a desired contour to the bust.

**brass knuckles,** linked metal rings or a metal bar with holes, worn on the hand for rough fighting.

**brass tacks,** [Colloq.], basic facts; actual details.

**brass·ware** (bras'wâr', bräs'-), *n.* articles made of brass.

**brass winds,** musical instruments made of coiled metal tubes extending from a cup-shaped mouthpiece. —**brass'-wind',** *adj.*

**brass·y** (bras'i, bräs'i), *adj.* [-IER, -IEST], 1. of or decorated with brass. 2. like **brass.** 3. cheap and showy. 4. impudent; insolent. 5. loud; blaring. —**brass'i·ly,** *adv.* —**brass'i·ness,** *n.*

**brat** (brat), *n.* [AS. *bratt,* a cloak; Gael. *bratt,* a cloth, rag; from the shabby clothes worn by poor children], a child, especially an impudent, unruly child: scornful or playful term.

**bra·va·do** (brə-vä'dō, -vā'-), *n.* [*pl.* -DOES, -DOS], [Sp. < *bravo,* brave], pretended courage or feigned confidence.

**brave** (brāv), *adj.* [Fr.; It. *bravo,* brave, orig., wild, savage < L. *barbarus;* see BARBAROUS], 1. not afraid; having courage. 2. having a fine appearance. *n.* 1. any brave man. 2. a North American Indian warrior. *v.t.* [BRAVED, BRAVING], 1. to defy; dare. 2. to meet or undergo with courage. —**brave'ly,** *adv.* —**brave'ness,** *n.*

**brav·er·y** (brāv'ẽr-i), *n.* [*pl.* -IES], 1. courage; valor. 2. fine appearance, show, or dress.

**bra·vo** (brä'vō), *interj.* [It.; see BRAVE], well done! excellent! *n.* 1. [*pl.* -VOS], a shout of "bravo!" 2. (*also* brā'vō), [*pl.* -VOES, -VOS; It. -VI (brä'vē)], an assassin or desperado.

**bra·vu·ra** (brə-vyoor'ə; It. brä-vōō'rä), *n.* [It., spirit < *bravo,* brave], 1. a display of daring; dash. 2. in *music, a)* a brilliant passage or piece that displays the performer's skill and technique. *b)* brilliant technique in performance.

**braw** (brô, brä), *adj.* [< *brave*], [Scot.], 1. finely dressed. 2. fine; excellent.

**brawl** (brôl), *v.i.* [< OFr. *brailler,* to shout < *braire,* to bray], to quarrel or fight noisily. *n.* 1. a noisy quarrel or fight; row. 2. [Slang], a noisy party.

**brawn** (brôn), *n.* [< OFr. *braon,* muscular part < OHG. *brato,* eatable flesh], 1. strong, well-developed muscles. 2. muscular strength.

**brawn·y** (brôn'i), *adj.* [-IER, -IEST], [< *brawn*], strong; muscular. —**brawn'i·ness,** *n.*

**bray** (brā), *v.i.* [< OFr. < LL. *bragire,* to cry out], to make a loud, harsh sound, as a donkey. *v.t.* to utter loudly and harshly. *n.* 1. the loud, harsh cry of a donkey. 2. a sound like this.

**Braz.,** 1. Brazil. 2. Brazilian.

**braze** (brāz), *v.t.* [BRAZED, BRAZING], [< Fr. prob. < Gmc. *brasa,* glowing coals], to solder with a high-melting metal, especially brass.

**braze** (brāz), *v.t.* [BRAZED, BRAZING], [AS. *bræsian* < *bræs,* brass], 1. to make or decorate with brass or a brasslike substance. 2. to make hard like brass.

**bra·zen** (brā'z'n), *adj.* [AS. *bræsen* < *bræs,* brass], 1. of brass. 2. like brass in color, etc. 3. shameless. 4. harsh and piercing. *v.t.* to make impudent or shameless. —**brazen out** (or **through**), to behave as if not ashamed of. —**bra'zen·ly,** *adv.* —**bra'zen·ness,** *n.*

**bra·zier** (brā'zhẽr), *n.* [< Fr.; see BRAISE], a metal container to hold burning coals or charcoal.

**bra·zier** (brā'zhẽr), *n.* [see BRASS], a person who does brasswork.

**Bra·zil** (brə-zil'), *n.* a country in central and NE South America: area, 3,275,510 sq. mi.; pop., 66,302,000: capital, Brasilia: Port. name, **Bra·sil (brä-sēl').** —**Bra·zil'ian,** *adj. & n.*

**Brazil nut,** the edible, oily, three-sided seed, or nut, of a tree growing in tropical America.

**breach** (brēch), *n.* [< AS. < *brecan,* to break], 1. a breaking or being broken. 2. a failure to observe the terms, as of a law, promise, etc. 3. an opening made by breaking something; gap. 4. an interruption in friendly relations. *v.t.* to make a breach in; break through. —**breach of faith,** a breaking of a promise. —**breach of promise,** a breaking of a promise to marry. —**breach of the peace,** a disturbance of the public peace.

**bread** (bred), *n.* [AS. *bread;* akin to G. *brot*], 1. a food made of flour or ground grain mixed with water, milk, etc., usually kneaded, and then baked. 2. a livelihood; a living: as, he earns his *bread.* 3. anything resembling bread. *v.t.* to cover with bread crumbs before cooking. —**bread and butter,** means of subsistence; livelihood. —**break bread,** 1. to eat. 2. to take Communion. —**cast one's bread upon the waters,** to do good deeds without expecting something in return. —**know which side one's bread is buttered on,** to know what is to one's economic interest. —**bread'less,** *adj.*

**bread-and-but·ter letter** (bred''n-but'ẽr), a letter of thanks sent to one's host after a visit.

**bread·bas·ket** (bred'bas'kit, -bäs'-), *n.* [Slang], the stomach or abdomen.

**bread·fruit** (bred'frōōt'), *n.* a large, round fruit with starchy, whitish pulp, breadlike when baked: found on South Pacific islands.

**bread line,** a line of people waiting to be given food as government relief or private charity.

**bread·stuff** (bred'stuf'), *n.* 1. ground grain or flour for making bread. 2. bread.

**breadth** (bredth), *n.* [AS. *brædu* < *brad,* broad; *-th* as in *length*], 1. the distance from side to side of a thing; width. 2. a piece of a given and regular width: as, a *breadth* of linoleum. 3. spaciousness; scope; extent. 4. lack of narrowness or of restriction.

**breadth·ways** (bredth'wāz'), *adv.* in the direction of the breadth: also **breadth'wise'** (-wīz').

**bread·win·ner** (bred'win'ẽr), *n.* one who supports dependents by his earnings.

**break** (brāk), *v.t.* [BROKE (brōk) or *archaic* BRAKE (brāk), BROKEN (brō'k'n) or *archaic* BROKE, BREAKING], [AS. *brecan*], 1. to separate into pieces by shattering; smash; burst. 2. to cut open the surface of (soil, the skin, etc.). 3. to bring to an end by force: as, the strike was *broken.* 4. to make inoperative by cracking or disrupting. 5. to tame with or as with force. 6. to lower in rank or grade; demote. 7. to reduce to poverty or bankruptcy. 8. to surpass (a record). 9. to violate: as, he *broke* his agreement. 10. to escape from suddenly: as, they cannot *break* prison. 11. to disrupt the order or completeness of: as, the troops *broke* formation. 12. to interrupt (a journey, electric circuit, etc.). 13. to reduce the effect of by interrupting (a fall, etc.). 14. to cut through or penetrate (silence, darkness, etc ). 15. to make give up (a habit): with *of.* 16. to make known; disclose. 17. to begin; start. *v.i.* 1. to divide into separate pieces; come apart; burst. 2. to scatter; disperse: as, let's *break* and run. 3. to stop associating (often with *up* or *with*). 4. to become inoperative. 5. to change suddenly: as, his voice *broke.* 6 to move away suddenly; escape. 7. to begin suddenly to perform, etc. (with *into,* **etc.**): as, he *broke* into song. 8. to come into being, sight, or general knowledge: as, the story *broke.* 9. to fall apart slowly; disintegrate. 10. [Colloq.], to happen in a certain way: as, things were *breaking* badly. 11. in *baseball,* to curve at or near the plate: said of a pitch. *n.* 1. a breaking; breach; fracture. 2. a breaking in, out, or forth. 3. a broken place; separation; crack. 4. a beginning to appear: as, the *break* of day. 5. an interrupting of regularity. 6. an interval; pause; omission. 7. a sudden change or deviation. 8. a lowering or drop, as of prices. 9. [Colloq.], an improper or untimely action or remark. 10. [Slang], a chance piece of luck, especially of good luck. 11. in *music*, *a*) the point where one register changes to another. *b*) a transitional solo phrase in a piece of jazz music. —**break down,** 1. to go out of working order. 2. to give way to tears or emotion. 3. to have a physical or nervous collapse. 4. to analyze. —**break in,** 1. to enter forcibly. 2. to interrupt. 3. to train (a novice, etc.). —**break off,** 1. to stop abruptly. 2. to stop being friendly. —**break out,** 1. to begin suddenly. 2. to escape. 3. to become covered with pimples or a rash.—**break up,** 1. to separate; disperse. 2. to take apart. 3. to put a stop to. 4. [Colloq.], to distress; upset. —**break with,** 1. to stop being friendly with. 2. to stop conforming to. —**break′a·ble,** *adj.*

**break·age** (brāk′ij), *n.* 1. a breaking or being broken. 2. things or quantity broken. 3. loss or damage due to breaking. 4. the sum allowed for such loss or damage.

**break·down** (brāk′doun′), *n.* 1. a breaking down; failure to work. 2. a failure of health. 3. decomposition. 4. an analysis. 5. a lively, shuffling dance.

**break·er** (brāk′ẽr), *n.* 1. a person or thing that breaks. 2. a wave that breaks into foam.

**break·fast** (brek′fəst), *n.* the first meal of the day. *v.i.* to eat breakfast. *v.t.* to give breakfast to. —**break′fast·er,** *n.*

**break·neck** (brāk′nek′), *adj.* that may cause a broken neck; dangerous to life and limb.

**break·through** (brāk′thrōō′), *n.* the act or place of breaking through against resistance.

**break·up** (brāk′up′), *n.* 1. dispersion. 2. disintegration. 3. collapse. 4. an ending.

**break·wa·ter** (brāk′wô′tẽr, -wot′ẽr), *n.* a barrier to break the impact of waves, as before a harbor.

**bream** (brēm), *n.* [*pl.* BREAM, BREAMS; see PLURAL, II, D, 2], [< OFr. *bresme* < OHG. *brahsima*], 1. a European fresh-water fish related to the carp. 2. any of various salt-water fishes, as the sea bream. 3. any of a number of fresh-water sunfishes.

**breast** (brest), *n.* [AS. *breost*], 1. either of two milk-secreting glands at the upper, front part of a woman's body. 2. a corresponding gland in other animals. 3. the upper, front part of the body; chest. 4. the part of a garment, etc. that is over the breast. 5. the breast regarded as the source of emotions. 6. one's feelings. 7. anything like the breast: as, the *breast* of the sea. *v.t.* to face; esp., to face firmly; contend with. —**make a clean breast of,** to confess fully.

**breast·bone** (brest′bōn′), *n.* the sternum.

**breast-feed** (brest′fēd′), *v.t.* [-FED (-fed′), -FEEDING], to feed (a baby) milk from the breast; suckle; nurse.

**breast·pin** (brest′pin′), *n.* an ornamental pin or brooch worn on a dress, near the throat.

**breast·plate** (brest′plāt′), *n.* a piece of armor for the breast.

**breast stroke,** a swimming stroke in which both arms are simultaneously brought out sideways from a position close to the chest.

**breast·work** (brest′wũrk′), *n.* a low, quickly constructed barrier to protect gunners.

**breath** (breth), *n.* [AS. *bræth*, odor, exhalation], 1. air taken into and let out of the lungs. 2. breathing; respiration. 3. the power to breathe easily. 4. life; spirit. 5. air carrying fragrance; odor. 6. a puff or whiff, as of air; slight breeze. 7. moisture produced by the breath and condensed, as on a mirror. 8. a whisper; murmur. 9. the time taken by a single respiration; moment. 10. a slight pause or rest. 11. in *phonetics*, a voiceless exhalation of air producing a hiss or puff, as in pronouncing *s* or *p*. —**below** (or **under**) **one's breath,** in a whisper or murmur. —**catch one's breath,** 1. to gasp or pant. 2. to pause or rest. —**in the same breath,** almost simultaneously. —**out of breath,** breathless, as from exertion. —**save one's breath,** to refrain from talking.

**breathe** (brēth), *v.i.* & *v.t.* [BREATHED, BREATHING], 1. to take (air) into the lungs and let it out again; alternately inhale and exhale. 2. to inhale. 3. to exhale. 4. to live. 5. to give out (an odor). 6. to infuse: as, he *breathed* confidence into his followers. 7. to blow softly. 8. to speak or sing softly; whisper; murmur. 9. to give or take time to breathe; rest. 10. to make breathless, as from exertion. 11. in *phonetics*, to speak without voicing. —**breathe again** (or **freely**), to have a feeling of relief or reassurance. —**breathe one's last,** to die. —**breath′a·ble,** *adj*

**breath·er** (brēth′ẽr), *n.* 1. a person who breathes. 2. [Colloq.], a pause to regain one's breath.

**breath·ing** (brēth′iŋ), *adj.* 1. that breathes; living; alive. 2. lifelike. *n.* 1. respiration. 2. *a*) a single respiration. *b*) the time needed for this; moment. 3. a light breeze. 4. aspiration; yearning. 5. utterance. 6. the sound of the letter *h* in English; aspirate.

**breath·less** (breth′lis), *adj.* 1. without breath. 2. no longer breathing; dead. 3. out of breath; gasping. 4. unable to breathe normally because of excitement, fear, etc. 5. having no breeze; stifling. —**breath′less·ly,** *adv.* —**breath′less·ness,** *n.*

**breath-tak·ing** (breth′tāk′iŋ), *adj.* 1. that takes one's breath away. 2. very exciting; thrilling.

**brec·ci·a** (brech′i-ə, bresh′-), *n.* [It.], rock consisting of sharp-cornered bits cemented together by sand, clay, or lime.

**bred** (bred), pt. and pp. of **breed.**

**breech** (brēch), *n.* [AS. *brec*, pl. of *broc*], 1. the buttocks; rump. 2. the under or back part of a thing. 3. the part of a firearm behind the barrel. *v.t.* (brēch, brich), 1. to clothe with breeches. 2. to provide with a breech, as a gun.

**breech·cloth** (brēch′klôth′, -kloth′), *n.* a loincloth: also **breech′clout′** (-klout′).

**breech·es** (brich′iz), *n.pl.* [see BREECH], 1. trousers reaching to the knees. 2. [Colloq.], any trousers.

**breeches buoy,** a device for rescuing people at sea, consisting of a pair of short canvas breeches suspended from a life preserver that is run along a rope from ship to shore or to another ship.

BREECHES BUOY

**breech·ing** (brich′iŋ, brēch′-), *n.* a harness strap put around a horse's hindquarters.

**breech·load·er** (brēch′lōd′ẽr), *n.* any breech-loading gun.

**breech-load·ing** (brēch′lōd′iŋ), *adj.* loading at the breech instead of the muzzle, as many guns.

**breed** (brēd), *v.t.* [BRED (bred), BREEDING], [< AS. *bredan* < *brod*, brood], 1. to bring forth (offspring). 2. to be the source of; produce: as, ignorance *breeds* prejudice. 3. to raise: as, he *breeds* dogs. 4. to rear; train. *v.i.* 1. to be produced; originate. 2. to reproduce. *n.* 1. a race or stock. 2. a sort; type. —**breed′er,** *n.*

**breed·ing** (brēd′iŋ), *n.* 1. the producing of young. 2. the rearing of young. 3. good manners and intelligent social behavior. 4. the producing of plants and animals, especially for the purpose of improving the stock.

**breeze** (brēz), *n.* [< Sp. & Port. *briza*, northeast wind], 1. a wind; esp., a gentle wind of up to 38 miles per hour. 2. [Colloq.], commotion. *v.i.* [BREEZED, BREEZING], [Slang], to move or go briskly or jauntily. —**breeze′less,** *adj.*

**breez·y** (brēz′i), *adj.* [-IER, -IEST], 1. having a breeze or breezes. 2. brisk; lively; carefree. —**breez′i·ly,** *adv.* —**breez′i·ness,** *n.*

**Bre·men** (brā′mən, brem′ən), *n.* a port in N Germany, on the Weser River: pop., 389,000.

**Bren·ner Pass** (bren′ẽr), a mountain pass across the Alps at the border between Austria and Italy.

**br'er** (brũr), [S. Dial.], brother: used before a name.

**Bres·lau** (bres′lô; G. -lou), *n.* a city in SW Poland, on the Oder River: formerly in Germany: pop., 203,000: Polish name, *Wroclaw.*

**Bret.,** Breton.

**breth·ren** (breth′rin), *n.pl.* [Archaic], brothers: now only of fellow members of a religious group.

**Bret·on** (bret′'n), *adj.* [ult. same word as *Briton*], of Brittany, its people, or their language. *n.* 1. a native or inhabitant of Brittany. 2. the Celtic language of the Bretons.

**Breu·ghel, Pie·ter** (pyā′tẽr broo′g'l), 1520?–1569; Flemish painter: also sp. **Brueghel, Bruegel.**

**breve** (brēv), *n.* [It. < L. *brevis*, short], 1. a curved mark (˘) put over a vowel or syllable to show that it is short. 2. in *music*, a note equal to two whole notes.

**bre·vet** (brə-vet′, brev′it), *n.* [OFr. dim. of *bref*, a letter], in *military usage*, a commission promoting an officer to a higher rank without higher pay: abbrev. **brev., bvt.** *adj.* held by brevet. *v.t.*

[-VETTED or -VETED, -VETTING or -VETING], to promote by brevet. —**bre·vet′cy** [*pl.* -CIES], *n.*

**bre·vi·ar·y** (brē′vi-er′i, brev′i-), *n.* [*pl.* -IES], [< L. *breviarium*, abridgment < *brevis*, short], a book containing daily offices and prayers, especially of the Roman Catholic Church.

**bre·vier** (brə-vêr′), *n.* [OFr.: from use in printing breviaries], a size of type, 8 point.

**brev·i·ty** (brev′ə-ti), *n.* [*pl.* -TIES], [< L. < *brevis*, short], 1. briefness of time. 2. conciseness; terseness.

**brew** (bro͞o), *v.t.* [AS. *breowan*], 1. to make (beer, ale, etc.) from malt and hops by steeping, boiling, and fermenting. 2. to make (tea, etc.) by steeping, boiling, or mixing. 3. to plot; contrive. *v.i.* 1. to brew beer, ale, etc. 2. to begin to form, as a storm. *n.* 1. a beverage brewed. 2. an amount brewed. —**brew′er,** *n.*

**brew·er·y** (bro͞o′ẽr-i), *n.* [*pl.* -IES], an establishment where beer, ale, etc. are brewed.

**brew·ing** (bro͞o′iŋ), *n.* 1. the preparation of a brew. 2. amount of brew made at any one time.

**Bri·and, A·ris·tide** (à′rē′stēd′ brē′än′), 1862–1932; French statesman.

**bri·ar** (brī′ẽr), *n.* brier. —**bri′ar·y,** *adj.*

**bri·ar·root** (brī′ẽr-ro͞ot′, -root′), *n.* brierroot.

**bri·ar·wood** (brī′ẽr-wood′), *n.* brierwood.

**bribe** (brīb), *n.* [OFr., bread given to beggars < *briber*, to beg], 1. anything given or promised to induce a person to do something illegal or wrong. 2. anything given or promised as an inducement. *v.t.* [BRIBED, BRIBING], 1. to offer or give a bribe to. 2. to influence by bribing. *v.i.* to give bribes. —**brib′a·ble,** *adj.* —**brib′er,** *n.*

**brib·er·y** (brīb′ẽr-i), *n.* [*pl.* -IES], the giving, offering, or taking of bribes.

**bric-a-brac, bric-à-brac** (brik′ə-brak′), *n.* [< Fr. < *à bric et à brac*, by hook or crook], small, rare, or artistic objects placed about a room for ornament.

**brick** (brik), *n.* [< OFr. *briche*, a fragment], 1. a substance made from clay molded into oblong blocks and baked, used in building, etc. 2. one of these blocks. 3. bricks collectively. 4. anything shaped like a brick. 5. [Colloq.], a fine fellow. *adj.* 1. built or paved with brick. 2. like brick: as, *brick* red. *v.t.* 1. to build or pave with brick. 2. to wall (*in*) with brick. —**brick′like′,** *adj.* —**brick′y,** *adj.*

**brick·bat** (brik′bat′), *n.* 1. a piece of brick, especially one used as a missile. 2. an unfavorable remark.

**brick·lay·ing** (brik′lā′iŋ), *n.* the act or work of building with bricks. —**brick′lay′er,** *n.*

**brick red,** a yellowish or brownish red. —**brick′-red′,** *adj.*

**brick·work** (brik′wũrk′), *n.* 1. anything built of bricks. 2. bricklaying.

**brick·yard** (brik′yärd′), *n.* a place where bricks are made or sold.

**brid·al** (brīd′'l), *n.* [< AS. *brydealo*, bride feast < *bryd*, bride + *ealo*, ale], a wedding. *adj.* 1. of a bride. 2. of a wedding.

**bridal wreath,** a kind of spiraea, a shrub with dark, glossy leaves and small, white flowers.

**bride** (brīd), *n.* [AS. *bryd*], a woman who has just been married or is about to be married.

**bride·groom** (brīd′gro͞om′, -groom′), *n.* [AS. *brydguma*, suitor < *bryd*, bride + *guma*, man; modern *-groom* due to folk etym.], a man who has just been married or is about to be married.

**brides·maid** (brīdz′mād′), *n.* a woman attending the bride just before and during a wedding.

**bride·well** (brīd′wel, -wəl), *n.* [after a former house of correction in London], a jail or prison

**bridge** (brij) *n.* [AS. *brycg*], 1. a structure built over a river, railroad, etc. to provide a way across for vehicles or pedestrians. 2. the bony part of the nose. 3. the curved bow of eyeglasses resting on the bridge of the nose. 4. the thin arch over which the strings are stretched on a violin, etc. 5. a raised platform on a ship for the commanding officer. 6. in *dentistry*, a fixed or removable mounting for false teeth, attached to a real tooth or teeth. 7. in *music*, a connecting passage between two subjects: also **bridge passage.** *v.t.* [BRIDGED, BRIDGING], 1. to build on or over. 2. to make a passage over; span. —**burn one's bridges,** to cut off all ways to retreat. —**bridge′a·ble,** *adj.*

**bridge** (brij), *n.* [earlier *biritch*, "Russian whist," altered after *bridge;* prob. of Russ. origin], a card game similar to whist.

**bridge·head** (brij′hed′), *n.* a fortified position established by an attacking force on the enemy's side of a bridge, etc.

**Bridge·port** (brij′pôrt′, -pōrt′), *n.* a city in Connecticut, on Long Island Sound: pop., 159,000.

**Bridg·es, Robert** (brij′əz), 1844–1930; English poet and physician; poet laureate (1913–1930).

**bridge·work** (brij′wũrk′), *n.* in *dentistry*, 1. a bridge. 2. bridges collectively. 3. the making of bridges.

**bri·dle** (brī′d'l), *n.* [< AS. < *bregdan*, to pull], 1. a head harness for guiding a horse: it consists of headstall, bit, and reins. 2. anything that controls or restrains. *v.t.* [-DLED, -DLING], 1. to put a bridle on. 2. to curb with or as with a bridle. *v.i.* to raise one's head high with the chin drawn in as an expression of scorn, pride, etc. —**bri′dler,** *n.*

**bridle path,** a path for horseback riding.

**brief** (brēf), *adj.* [OFr. *bref;* L. *brevis*], 1. of short duration. 2. terse; concise. 3. curt. *n* 1. a summary. 2. a short catalogue of the main points of a law case for use in court. *v.t.* 1. to summarize. 2. [Brit.], to furnish with a legal brief. 3. [Brit.], to hire as counsel. 4. in *military usage*, to give (a person) all the pertinent facts about a planned operation: as, the pilots were *briefed* before each flight. —**hold a brief for,** to argue in behalf of; support. —**in brief,** in short; in a few words. —**brief′ly,** *adv.* —**brief′ness,** *n.*

**brief case,** a flat case or bag, usually of leather, for carrying papers, books, etc.

**bri·er** (brī′ẽr), *n.* [AS. *brer*], 1. any thorny bush, as a bramble, wild rose, etc. 2. a growth of such bushes. Also sp. **briar.** —**bri′er·y,** *adj.*

**bri·er** (brī′ẽr), *n.* [Fr. *bruyère*, white heath], 1. the tree heath, whose root is used for making tobacco pipes. 2. this root. 3. a pipe made from this root. Also sp. **briar.**

**bri·er·root** (brī′ẽr-ro͞ot′, -root′), *n.* brierwood: also sp. **briarroot.**

**bri·er·wood** (brī′ẽr-wood′), *n.* 1. the root wood of the brier (heath tree). 2. a tobacco pipe made of this. Also sp. **briarwood.**

**brig** (brig), *n.* [< *brigantine*], 1. a two-masted ship with square sails. 2. a prison on a warship.

**Brig.,** 1. Brigade. 2. Brigadier.

**bri·gade** (bri-gād′), *n.* [Fr.; It. *brigata*, troop < *brigare*, to contend < LL. *briga*, strife], 1. a large unit of soldiers. 2. formerly, a unit of the U.S. Army comprising two or more regiments. 3. any group of people organized to do a particular thing: as, a fire *brigade.* *v.t.* [-GADED, -GADING], to gather into a brigade.

**brig·a·dier** (brig′ə-dêr′), *n.* 1. a person commanding a brigade. 2. in the U.S. armed forces, a brigadier general.

**brigadier general,** [*pl.* BRIGADIER GENERALS], a military officer ranking above a colonel and below a major general: abbrev. **Brig. Gen.**

**brig·and** (brig′ənd), *n.* [Fr.; It. *brigante* < *brigare;* see BRIGADE], a bandit, usually one of a roving band. —**brig′and·ish,** *adj.*

**brig·and·age** (brig′ən-dij), *n.* organized plundering: also **brig′and·ism.**

**brig·an·tine** (brig′ən-tēn′, -tīn′), *n.* [< Fr. < It.; see BRIGAND], a two-masted ship with a fore-and-aft-rigged mainmast and a square-rigged foremast.

**bright** (brīt), *adj.* [AS. *bryht*, earlier *beorht*], 1. shining; giving light; full of light. 2. brilliant in color or sound; vivid; clear. 3. lively; vivacious; cheerful. 4. mentally quick; clever. 5. reflecting happiness or hope. 6. famous; illustrious. 7. favorable; auspicious. *adv.* in a bright manner. —**bright′ly,** *adv.* —**bright′ness,** *n.*

**bright·en** (brīt′'n), *v.t. & v.i.* to make or become bright or brighter.

**Brigh·ton** (brī′t'n), *n.* a resort city on the southern coast of England: pop., 146,000.

**Bright's disease,** [after Dr. Richard *Bright* (1789–1858), Eng. physician], a kidney inflammation characterized by albumin in the urine; nephritis.

**bril·liance** (bril′yəns), *n.* 1. great brightness or radiance. 2. splendor; magnificence. 3. keen intelligence. Also **bril′lian·cy.**

**bril·liant** (bril′yənt), *adj.* [< Fr. ppr. of *briller* < It. *brillare*, to sparkle], 1. shining brightly; sparkling. 2. vivid. 3. splendid; magnificent. 4. very able; keenly intelligent. *n.* 1. a diamond or other gem cut with many facets to increase its sparkle. 2. in *printing*, the smallest common size of type, 3½ point. —**bril′liant·ly,** *adv.* —**bril′liant·ness,** *n.*

**bril·lian·tine** (bril′yən-tēn′), *n.* [< Fr.; see BRILLIANT & -INE], an oily hairdressing.

**brim** (brim), *n.* [AS. *brim*, sea], 1. the topmost edge of a cup, glass, etc. 2. the edge around a body of water. 3. a projecting rim, as of a hat. *v.t.* [BRIMMED, BRIMMING], to fill to the brim. *v.i.* to be full to the brim.—**brim′less,** *adj.*

**brim·ful** (brim′fool′), *adj.* full to the brim.

**brim·stone** (brim′stōn′), *n.* [ME. *brinston* < *brinnen*, to burn + *ston*, a stone], sulfur.

**brin·dle** (brin′d'l), *n.* 1. a brindled color. 2. a brindled animal. *adj.* brindled.

**brin·dled** (brin′d'ld), *adj.* [prob. < ME. *brended* < *brennen*, to burn], streaked or spotted with a darker color: said of a gray or tawny cow, dog, etc.

**brine** (brīn), *n.* [AS. *bryne*], 1. water full of salt. 2. the ocean or sea. *v.t.* [BRINED, BRINING], to put into brine, as in pickling.

**bring** (briŋ), *v.t.* [BROUGHT (brôt), BRINGING], [AS. *bringan*], 1. to cause (a person or thing) to come along together with oneself; fetch. 2. to cause to come about; make happen: as, fascism *brought* disaster. 3. to lead, persuade, or influence along a course of action or belief. 4. to sell for: as, it *brought* a good price. 5. in *law*, *a*) to present in a law court: as, *bring* charges. *b*) to advance (evidence, etc.). —**bring about,** to cause; make happen. —**bring around** (or **round**), 1. to cause to change an opinion; convince. 2. [Colloq.], to bring back to consciousness. —**bring forth,** 1. to give birth to; produce; bear. 2. to make manifest; disclose. —**bring forward,** to introduce; show. —**bring in,** 1. to import. 2. to produce, as income or revenue. —**bring off,** to accomplish. —**bring on,** to cause to begin or happen. —**bring out,** 1. to expose; reveal. 2. to offer (a play, person, book, etc.) to the public. 3. to introduce (a girl) formally to society. —**bring over,** to cause to change an opinion; convince; persuade. —**bring to,** 1. to revive (one who is unconscious, drunk, etc.). 2. to cause (a ship) to stop. —**bring up,** 1. to take care of during childhood; rear; educate. 2. to introduce, as into discussion. 3. to cough up. 4. to vomit. 5. to stop abruptly.

**brink** (briŋk), *n.* [< ON. *brekka*, hillside], the edge, especially at the top of a steep place; verge: often figurative, as, on the *brink* of disaster.

**brink·man·ship** (briŋk′mən-ship′), *n.* the policy of pursuing a course of action to the brink of catastrophe.

**brin·y** (brīn′i), *adj.* [-IER, -IEST], of or like brine; very salty. —**brin′i·ness,** *n.*

**bri·quette, bri·quet** (bri-ket′), *n.* [< Fr. dim. of *brique*, brick], a brick made of compressed coal dust, etc., used for fuel or kindling.

**Bris·bane** (briz′bān, -bən), *n.* a seaport on the E coast of Australia: pop., 664,000.

**brisk** (brisk), *adj.* [prob. < Fr. *brusque;* see BRUSQUE], 1. quick in manner; energetic. 2. sharp; nippy. —**brisk′ly,** *adv.* —**brisk′ness,** *n.*

**bris·ket** (bris′kit), *n.* [prob. < OFr. *bruschet*, of Gmc. origin], 1. the breast of an animal. 2. meat cut from this part.

**bris·tle** (bris′'l), *n.* [AS. *byrst*], any short, stiff, prickly hair; esp., any of the hairs of a hog or other animal, used in making brushes. *v.i.* [-TLED, -TLING], 1. to be stiff and erect, like bristles. 2. to have one's hair stand up. 3. to stiffen with fear, anger, etc. 4. to be thick with or as with bristles. *v.t.* 1. to cause to stand up like bristles. 2. to make bristly.

**bris·tly** (bris′li), *adj.* [-TLIER, -TLIEST], 1. having bristles; rough with bristles. 2. bristlelike; stiff; prickly. —**bris′tli·ness,** *n.*

**Bris·tol** (bris′t'l), *n.* a seaport in SW England, on the Avon River: pop., 434,000.

**Bristol board** (or **paper**), [after *Bristol*, England], a fine, smooth pasteboard.

**Bristol Channel,** an arm of the Atlantic, between Wales and SW England.

**Brit.,** 1. Britain. 2. Britannia. 3. British.

**Brit·ain** (brit′'n, -ən), *n.* England, Wales, and Scotland: see **Great Britain.**

**Bri·tan·ni·a** (bri-tan′i-ə, -tan′yə), *n.* 1. Britain: the ancient Latin name. 2. Great Britain. 3. the British Empire.

**Bri·tan·nic** (bri-tan′ik), *adj.* British.

**Brit·i·cism** (brit′ə-siz'm), *n.* a word, phrase, or idiom peculiar to the British: as, *petrol* is a *Briticism* for *gasoline*: also **Brit′ish·ism.**

**Brit·ish** (brit′ish), *adj.* [AS. *Brittisc* < *Brettas*, name of the Celt. inhabitants of Britain; of Celt. origin], 1. of Great Britain or its people. 2. of the British Commonwealth of Nations. *n.* the English language as spoken and written in England. —**the British,** the people of Great Britain (or, sometimes, of the British Commonwealth of Nations).

**British America,** 1. the British possessions in or adjacent to the Americas. 2. Canada: more properly, **British North America.**

**British Columbia,** a province of SW Canada: pop., 1,771,000; capital, Victoria.

**British Commonwealth of Nations,** the British Empire; political aggregate comprising: (1) the United Kingdom (Great Britain and Northern Ireland); the Channel Islands; the Isle of Man; the British colonies, protectorates, and dependencies; and (2) Canada, Australia, New Zealand, India, Pakistan, Ceylon, Malaysia, Sierra Leone, Tanzania, Uganda, Jamaica, Trinidad and Tobago, Ghana, Nigeria, Cyprus, Gambia, Kenya, Malawi, Malta, Barbados, Botswana, Lesotho, Mauritius, Singapore, and Zambia: capital, London.

**British East Africa,** the former British territories in E Africa.

**British Empire,** 1. the British Commonwealth of Nations. 2. occasionally, the United Kingdom and its dependencies.

**Brit·ish·er** (brit′ish-ẽr), *n.* a native of Great Britain, especially an Englishman.

**British Guiana,** Guyana: the former name.

**British Honduras,** a British colony in Central America, on the Caribbean: area, 8,867 sq. mi.; pop., 109,000; capital, Belize.

**British India,** the part of India formerly under British rule: see **India.**

**British Isles,** Great Britain, Ireland, the Isle of Man, and the Channel Islands.

**British thermal unit,** quantity of heat required to raise the temperature of one pound of water from 62°F. to 63°F.: abbrev. **B.T.U., Btu, B.t.u.**

**British West Africa,** the former British possessions in W Africa.

**British West Indies,** the British possessions in the West Indies: abbrev. **B.W.I.**

**Brit·on** (brit′'n, -ən), *n.* [< OFr. < L. *Brit(t)o;* of Celt. origin; see BRITISH], 1. a native or inhabitant of Great Britain or the British Commonwealth of Nations. 2. a member of an early Celtic people of S Britain at the time of the Roman invasion.

**Brit·ta·ny** (brit′'n-i), *n.* a former province on the NW coast of France.

**brit·tle** (brit′'l), *adj.* [< AS. *breotan*, to break], easily broken or shattered; fragile; crisp. *n.* a crisp candy: as, peanut *brittle.* —**brit′tle·ness,** *n.*

**bro.,** [*pl.* BROS.], brother: also **Bro.**

**broach** (brōch), *n.* [< OFr. < LL. *brocca*, a spike < L. *broccus*, projecting], 1. a spit or skewer. 2. a tapered bit for enlarging or shaping holes. *v.t.* 1. to make a hole in so as to let out liquid. 2. to start a discussion of; bring up. —**broach′er,** *n.*

**broad** (brôd), *adj.* [AS. *brad*], 1. wide; of large extent from side to side. 2. extending about; clear; open: as, *broad* daylight. 3. open to the sight; obvious: as, a *broad* hint. 4. strongly marked: said of dialects or accents. 5. outspoken; unreserved: as, a *broad* statement. 6. ribald: as, a *broad* joke. 7. all-inclusive; tolerant; liberal: as, a *broad* view. 8. extensive; general: as, in a *broad* sense that's true. 9. main; essential: as, in *broad* outline. 10. spoken with the tongue flat in the mouth and the oral passage wide open, as *a* in *father:* the current phonetic term is *open.* *n.* 1. the broad part of anything. 2. [Slang], a woman: a vulgar term. —**broad′ish,** *adj.* —**broad′ly,** *adv.* —**broad′ness,** *n.*

**broad·ax, broad·axe** (brôd′aks′), *n.* an ax with a broad blade, used as a weapon or tool.

**broad·cast** (brôd′kast′, -käst′), *v.t.* [-CAST or, *in radio*, -CASTED, -CASTING], 1. to scatter widely. 2. to spread (information, etc.). 3. to transmit by radio or television. *v.i.* to broadcast radio or television programs. *adj.* 1. widely scattered. 2. of or for radio or television broadcasting. *n.* 1. a broadcasting. 2. a radio or television program. *adv.* far and wide. —**broad′cast′er,** *n.*

**broad·cloth** (brôd′klôth′, -kloth′), *n.* 1. a fine, smooth woolen cloth: so called because it originally came in widths over a yard. 2. a fine, smooth cotton or silk cloth, used for shirts, etc.

**broad·en** (brôd′'n), *v.t. & v.i.* to widen; expand.

**broad gauge,** 1. a width (between the rails) of more than 56½ inches. 2. a railroad having such a gauge. —**broad′-gauge′, broad′-gauged′,** *adj.*

**broad jump,** a jump for distance made either from a stationary position (**standing broad jump**) or with a running start (**running broad jump**), now officially called *long jump* in the Olympic games.

**broad·loom** (brôd′lōōm′), *adj.* woven on a wide loom: said of rugs and carpets.

**broad·mind·ed** (brôd′mīn′did), *adj.* tolerant of unconventional opinion and behavior; not bigoted; liberal. —**broad′-mind′ed·ly,** *adv.* —**broad′-mind′-ed·ness,** *n.*

**broad·side** (brôd′sīd′), *n.* 1. the entire side of a ship above the water line. 2. all the guns that can be fired from one side of a ship. 3. their simultaneous fire. 4. a large sheet of paper printed on one side, as with advertising: also **broad′sheet′** (-shēt ). 5. [Colloq.], violent abuse. *adv.* with the length turned (*to* an object): as, the ship came *broadside* to the dock.

**broad·sword** (brôd′sôrd′, -sōrd′), *n.* a sword with a broad blade, for slashing rather than thrusting.

**broad·tail** (brôd′tāl′), *n.* karakul.

**Broad·way** (brôd′wā′), *n.* a street in New York City, known for its brightly lighted theater section, night clubs, etc.

**Brob·ding·nag** (brob′diŋ-nag′), *n.* in Swift's *Gulliver's Travels,* the land of the giants. —**Brob′ding-nag′i·an,** *adj. & n.*

**bro·cade** (brō-kād′), *n.* [Sp. *brocado* < pp. of LL. *brocare,* to embroider], a rich cloth with a raised design woven into it, as of silk, velvet, gold, or silver. *v.t.* [-CADED, -CADING], to weave a raised design into (cloth). —**bro·cad′ed,** *adj.*

**broc·co·li** (brok′ə-li), *n.* [It., pl. of *broccolo,* a sprout < LL. *brocca;* see BROACH], 1. a kind of cauliflower. 2. a related vegetable with small, loose, white or green heads: also called **sprouting broccoli.**

**bro·chure** (brō-shoor′, -shyoor′), *n.* [Fr. < *brocher,* to stitch], a pamphlet.

**Brock·ton** (brok′tən), *n.* an industrial city in E Massachusetts: pop., 73,000.

**bro·gan** (brō′gən), *n.* [Ir., dim of *brōg*], a brogue (shoe).

**brogue** (brōg), *n.* [prob. < Ir. *barrōg,* a hold, grip (especially on the tongue)], the pronunciation of the dialect of English spoken by the Irish.

**brogue** (brōg), *n.* [Gael. & Ir. *brōg,* a shoe], 1. a coarse shoe of untanned leather, formerly worn in Ireland. 2. a man's heavy, comfortable oxford shoe, usually with decorative perforations.

**broil** (broil), *v.t.* [OFr. *bruillir* < *bruir,* to burn], 1. to cook by exposing to direct heat. 2. to expose directly to intense heat. *v.i.* 1. to cook by broiling. 2. to be exposed directly to great heat. *n.* a broiling.

**broil** (broil), *n.* [Fr. *brouiller,* to mix, quarrel < OFr. *brooulier,* to dirty], a noisy quarrel; brawl. *v.i.* to take part in a broil.

**broil·er** (broil′ẽr), *n.* 1. a pan, gridiron, etc. for broiling. 2. the part of a stove designed for broiling. 3. a chicken suitable for broiling.

**broke** (brōk), pt. and archaic pp. of **break.** *adj.* [Slang], having no money; bankrupt. —**go broke,** [Slang], to become bankrupt.

**bro·ken** (brō′kən), pp. of **break.** *adj.* 1. splintered, fractured, burst, etc. 2. violated: as, a *broken* promise. 3. weak or weakened. 4. subdued in feelings. 5. bankrupt. 6. interrupted; discontinuous. 7. imperfectly spoken, especially with reference to grammar and syntax: as, *broken* English. 8. tamed; subdued and trained. 9. [Colloq.], demoted. For phrases, see **break.** —**bro′ken·ly,** *adv.* —**bro′ken·ness,** *n.*

**bro·ken·heart·ed** (brō′kən-här′tid), *adj.* crushed by grief or despair; heartbroken.

**bro·ker** (brō′kẽr), *n.* [< Anglo-Fr. < ONorm.Fr. < OFr. *brochier,* to broach, tap; orig. sense "wine dealer"], a person paid a fee for acting as agent in making contracts, selling stocks, etc.

**bro·ker·age** (brō′kẽr-ij), *n.* 1. the business of a broker. 2. a broker's fee or commission.

**bro·mide** (brō′mīd, -mid) *n.* 1. a compound of bromine with another element or radical. 2. potassium bromide, KBr, used in medicine as a sedative. 3. a trite saying or statement; platitude. Also **bro′mid** (-mid).

**bro·mid·ic** (brō-mid′ik), *adj.* [see BROMIDE], using or containing a trite remark or remarks.

**bro·mine** (brō′mēn, -min), *n.* [Fr. *brome* < Gr. *brōmos,* stench; + *-ine*], a chemical element, usually a reddish-brown, corrosive liquid volatilizing to form an irritating vapor: symbol. Br; at. wt., 79.916; at. no., 35: also **bro′min** (-min).

**bron·chi** (broŋ′kī), *n.* pl. of **bronchus.**

**bron·chi·a** (broŋ′ki-ə), *n. pl.* [LL. < Gr.], bronchial tubes smaller than the bronchi but larger than the bronchioles.

**bron·chi·al** (broŋ′ki-əl), *adj.* of the bronchi, the bronchia, or the bronchioles.

**bronchial tubes,** the bronchi and the tubes branching from them.

**bron·chi·ole** (broŋ′ki-ōl′), *n.* any of the small subdivisions of the bronchia.

**bron·chi·tis** (broŋ-kī′tis), *n.* [< *broncho-* + *-itis*], an inflammation of the mucous lining of the bronchial tubes. —**bron·chit′ic** (-kit′ik), *adj.*

**bron·cho-,** [< Gr. *bronchos,* windpipe], a combining form meaning *having to do with the bronchi,* as in *bronchoscope:* also, before a vowel, **bronch-.**

**bron·cho·scope** (broŋ′kə-skōp′), *n.* [*broncho-* + *-scope*], an instrument for examining the bronchi, or for removing foreign bodies from them.

**bron·chus** (broŋ′kəs), *n.* [*pl.* -CHI (-kī)], [< Gr. *bronchos,* windpipe], either of the two main branches of the trachea, or windpipe.

**bron·co** (broŋ′kō), *n.* [*pl.* -COS], [Sp., rough, rude], a small, wild or partially tamed horse of the western U.S.: also **bron′cho** [*pl.* -CHOS].

**bron·co·bust·er** (broŋ′kō-bus′tẽr), *n.* [Slang], a person who tames broncos: also **bron′cho·bust′er.**

**Bron·të, Charlotte** (bron′ti), 1816–1855; English novelist.

**Brontë, Emily Jane,** 1818–1848; sister of *Charlotte;* English novelist.

**bron·to·sau·rus** (bron′tə-sô′rəs), *n.* [< Gr. *brontē,* thunder + *sauros,* lizard], a huge, extinct American dinosaur of the Jurassic Period.

BRONTOSAURUS

**Bronx** (broŋks), *n.* a N borough of New York City: pop., 1,425,000.

**Bronx cheer,** [Slang], a noisy vibration of the lips to show derision or scorn.

**bronze** (bronz), *n.* [Fr. < It. *bronzo*], 1. an alloy of copper and tin. 2. anything made of bronze. 3. a reddish-brown color like that of bronze. *adj.* of or like bronze. *v.t. & v.i.* [BRONZED, BRONZING], to make or become bronze in color. —**bronz′y,** *adj.*

**Bronze Age,** a period of civilization characterized by bronze tools and weapons, usually regarded as between the Stone Age and the Iron Age.

**Bronze Star,** a U.S. Army military decoration awarded for heroic or meritorious achievement.

**brooch** (brōch, brōōch), *n.* [see BROACH], a large ornamental pin with a clasp.

**brood** (brōōd), *n.* [AS. *brod*], 1. a group of birds or fowl hatched at one time and cared for together; hence, 2. the children in a family. 3. a breed or kind. *v.t.* 1. to sit on and hatch (eggs). 2. to hover over or protect (offspring, etc.). *v.i.* 1. to brood eggs or offspring. 2. to think deeply about something, usually with unhappiness, anxiety, etc. (often with *on* or *over*). —**brood′ing·ly,** *adv.* —**brood′y,** *adj.*

**brood·er** (brōōd′ẽr), *n.* 1. one that broods. 2. a heated shelter for raising young fowl.

**brook** (brook), *n.* [AS. *broc;* prob. < base of *break*], a small stream, usually not so large as a river.

**brook** (brook), *v.t.* [AS. *brucan,* to use], to put up with; endure: as, I can't *brook* his insolence.

**brook·let** (brook′lit), *n.* a little brook.

**Brook·line** (brook′līn), *n.* a town in Massachusetts: suburb of Boston: pop., 54,000.

**Brook·lyn** (brook′lin), *n.* a borough of New York City, on W Long Island: pop., 2,627,000.

**brook trout,** the speckled trout of E North America.

**broom** (brōōm, broom), *n.* [AS. *brom,* brushwood], 1. a shrub of the pea family, with small leaves, slender branches, and yellow flowers. 2. a brush with a long handle, used for sweeping: originally made of twigs of broom. *v.t.* to sweep with a broom.

**broom·corn** (brōōm′kôrn′, broom′-), *n.* a variety of grass resembling corn: the long, stiff stems of the flower clusters are used in brooms, etc.

**broom·stick** (brōōm′stik′, broom′-), *n.* the handle of a broom.

**bros.,** brothers.

**broth** (brôth, broth), *n.* [AS.], water in which meat has been boiled; thin, watery soup.

**broth·el** (brôth′əl, broth′-, broth′-), *n.* [ME., wretched person < AS. *breothan,* to go to ruin], a house of prostitution.

**broth·er** (bruth′ẽr), *n.* [*pl.* -ERS; *archaic* BRETHREN (breth′rən) is still used in senses 3 & 4], [AS. *brothor*], 1. a male related to one by having the same parents. 2. a friend who is like a brother. 3. a lay member of a men's religious order. 4. a fellow member of the same race, creed, profession, etc. *v.t.* to treat or address as a brother.

**broth·er·hood** (bruth′ẽr-hood′), *n.* 1. the state or quality of being a brother. 2. an association of men united in a common interest, work, creed, etc., as a fraternity.

**broth·er-in-law** (bruth'ẽr-in-lô'), *n.* [*pl.* BROTHERS-IN-LAW], 1. the brother of one's husband or wife. 2. the husband of one's sister. 3. the husband of the sister of one's wife or husband.

**broth·er·ly** (bruth'ẽr-li), *adj.* 1. of or like a brother. 2. friendly, kind, loyal, etc. *adv.* as a brother should. —**broth'er·li·ness,** *n.*

**brougham** (bro͞om, bro͞o'əm, brō'əm), *n.* [after Lord *Brougham* (1778–1868)], 1. a closed carriage with the driver's seat outside. 2. a gasoline-powered limousine with the driver's seat unenclosed.

BROUGHAM

**brought** (brôt), pt. and pp. of **bring.**

**brow** (brou), *n.* [AS. *bru*], 1. the eyebrow. 2. the forehead. 3. a person's facial expression: as, an angry *brow.* 4. the edge of a cliff.

**brow·beat** (brou'bēt'), *v.t.* [-BEAT, -BEATEN, -BEATING], to intimidate with harsh, stern looks and words; bully. —**brow'beat'er,** *n.*

**brown** (broun), *adj.* [AS. *brun*], 1. having the color of chocolate or coffee, a mixture of red, black, and yellow. 2. tanned; dark-skinned. *n.* 1. brown color. 2. a brown pigment or dye. *v.t. & v.i.* to make or become brown, as by exposure to sunlight or heat. —**do up brown** [Slang], to do completely; do to perfection. —**brown'ish,** *adj.* —**brown'ness,** *n.*

**Brown, John,** 1800–1859; American abolitionist; led raid at Harper's Ferry to establish a stronghold for escaped slaves: caught and hanged.

**brown betty,** a baked apple pudding made with butter, spices, sugar, and bread crumbs.

**brown bread,** 1. any bread made of dark flour. 2. a dark, sweetened, steamed bread.

**Browne,** Sir **Thomas,** 1605–1682; English physician and author.

**Brown·i·an movement** (broun'i-ən), [after Robert *Brown* (1773–1858), who first demonstrated it], the constant zigzag movement of colloidal dispersions in a liquid, caused by collision with molecules of the liquid: also **Brownian motion.**

**brown·ie** (broun'i), *n.* [dim. of *brown,* the elf's supposed color], 1. a small, helpful elf or goblin in stories. 2. [B-], a girl scout between the ages of eight and eleven. 3. a flat chocolate cake with nuts in it, generally cut into small bars.

**Brown·ing, Elizabeth Bar·rett** (bar'it broun'iŋ), 1806–1861; wife of *Robert;* English poet.

**Browning, Robert,** 1812–1889; English poet.

**brown·out** (broun'out'), *n.* partial elimination of lights in a city as an air-raid precaution or to save fuel.

**brown rice,** unpolished grains of rice.

**brown shirt,** 1. [often B- S-], a person who belonged to the Nazi *Sturmabteilung:* so called from the uniform. 2. a Nazi; Hitlerite.

**brown·stone** (broun'stōn'), *n.* a reddish-brown sandstone, used for building.

**brown study,** [< early sense of *brown,* gloomy], deep absorption in thought; reverie.

**brown sugar,** sugar wholly or partly unrefined.

**browse** (brouz), *n.* [< OFr. < OS. *brustian,* to sprout], twigs, leaves, and young shoots of trees or shrubs, which animals feed on. *v.t.* [BROWSED, BROWSING], 1. to nibble at. 2. to graze on. *v.i.* 1. to feed on or nibble at leaves, twigs, etc. 2. to glance through a book, library, etc. in a leisurely way. —**brows'er,** *n.*

**Bruce, Robert the** (bro͞os), 1274–1329; king of Scotland (1306–1329).

**Bruegel** (or **Brueghel**), **Pieter,** see **Breughel, Pieter.**

**bru·in** (bro͞o'in), *n.* [D., brown], a bear.

**bruise** (bro͞oz), *v.t.* [BRUISED, BRUISING], [merging of AS. *brysan,* to crush & OFr. *bruser,* to break], 1. to injure the surface of (the skin) without breaking it but causing discoloration; hence, 2. to injure the surface of. 3. to crush as with mortar and pestle. 4. to hurt slightly, as feelings. *v.i.* to be or become bruised. *n.* 1. a discoloration of the skin caused by a blow. 2. an injury to the outside of fruit, plants, etc.

**bruis·er** (bro͞oz'ẽr), *n.* [< *bruise*], 1. a professional boxer. 2. a strong, pugnacious man.

**bruit** (bro͞ot), *n.* [Fr. < *bruire* (prob. < L. *rugire*), to roar], rumor. *v.t.* to noise (*about*); rumor.

**brunch** (brunch), *n.* [*b*reakfast + l*unch*], [Colloq.], a combined breakfast and lunch.

**bru·nette** (bro͞o-net'), *adj.* [Fr., dim. of *brun,* brown], 1. having a dark or olive color. 2. having black or dark-brown hair and eyes, and a dark complexion. *n.* a. woman or girl with such hair, eyes, and complexion. —**bru·net',** *adj. & n.masc.*

**Brun·hild** (bro͞on'hild; G. -hilt), *n.* in the *Nibelungenlied,* a queen of Iceland: see **Brünnehilde, Brynhild.**

**Brün·ne·hil·de** (brün'ə-hil'də; Eng. broon-hil'-), *n.* in Wagner's *Die Walküre,* a Valkyrie whom Siegfried releases from a spell: see **Brunhild, Brynhild.**

**Bruns·wick** (brunz'wik), *n.* 1. a division of central Germany. 2. its capital: pop., 181,000.

**brunt** (brunt), *n.* [< ON. *bruncer,* heat], 1. shock (of an attack); impact (of a blow). 2. the main part of the shock or impact.

**brush** (brush), *n.* [< OFr. *broce,* bush < LL.; ? < OHG. *brusta,* a bristle], 1. a device for cleaning, polishing, painting, etc., having bristles, hairs, or wires fastened into a back, with or without a handle. 2. any bushy tail, especially that of a fox. 3. the act of brushing. 4. a light touch in passing. 5. in *electricity,* a piece or bundle of carbon, copper, etc. used as a conductor between an outside circuit and a revolving part. *v.t.* 1. to clean, polish, paint, etc. with a brush. 2. to go over lightly, as with a brush. 3. to touch or graze in passing. 4. to remove as by brushing. *v.i.* to graze past something. —**brush aside**(or **away**), to dismiss from consideration. —**brush off,** to dismiss; get rid of. —**brush up,** to refresh one's memory. —**brush'y** [-IER, -IEST], *adj.*

**brush** (brush), *n.* [see prec. BRUSH], 1. brushwood. 2. sparsely settled wooded country.

**brush** (brush), *v.i.* [ME. *bruschen*], to go fast; rush. *n.* a short, quick fight or quarrel.

**brush-off** (brush'ôf'), *n.* [Slang], dismissal. —**give the brush-off,** [Slang], to dismiss.

**brush·wood** (brush'wood'), *n.* 1. chopped-off tree branches. 2. low, woody growth; underbrush.

**brush·y** (brush'i), *adj.* [-IER, -IEST], thick with bushes or shrubs; covered with underbrush.

**brusque** (brusk, broosk), *adj.* [Fr. < It. *brusco;* prob. < ML. *bruscus,* brushwood; ult. < L. *ruscus,* butcher's-broom], abrupt or blunt in manner or speech; curt. —**brusque'ly,** *adv.* —**brusque'ness,** *n.*

**Brus·sels** (brus''lz), *n.* the capital of Belgium: pop., with suburbs, 1,291,000.

**Brussels sprouts,** 1. a kind of cabbage having a stem covered with edible, small, cabbagelike heads. 2. the heads of this plant.

**bru·tal** (bro͞o't'l), *adj.* like a brute; savage, cruel, coarse, rude, etc. —**bru'tal·ly,** *adv.*

**bru·tal·i·ty** (bro͞o-tal'ə-ti), *n.* 1. the quality of being brutal. 2. [*pl.* -TIES], a brutal act.

**bru·tal·ize** (bro͞o't'l-īz'), *v.t. & v.i.* [-IZED, -IZING], to make or become brutal. —**bru'tal·i·za'tion,** *n.*

**brute** (bro͞ot), *adj.* [Fr. *brut* < L. *brutus,* irrational], 1. lacking the ability to reason: as, a *brute* beast. 2. not conscious: as, the *brute* force of nature. 3. of or like an animal. 4. brutal; cruel; stupid. *n.* 1. an animal. 2. one who is brutal.

**bru·ti·fy** (bro͞o'tə-fī'), *v.t. & v.i.* [-FIED, -FYING], to brutalize.

**brut·ish** (bro͞ot'ish), *adj.* of or like a brute; savage, gross, stupid, etc. —**brut'ish·ly,** *adv.* —**brut'ish·ness,** *n.*

**Bru·tus** (bro͞o'təs), *n.* (*Marcus Junius Brutus*), Roman statesman; 85?–42 B.C.; one of the conspirators who murdered Julius Caesar.

**Bry·an, William Jen·nings** (jen'iŋz brī'ən), 1860–1925; U.S. statesman and orator.

**Bry·ant, William Cul·len** (kul''n brī'ənt), 1794–1878; U.S. poet and journalist.

**Bryn·hild** (brin'hild, brün'-), *n.* in *Norse legend,* a Valkyrie awakened from an enchanted sleep by Sigurd: see **Brunhild, Brünnehilde.**

**bry·ol·o·gy** (brī-ol'ə-ji), *n.* [< Gr. *bryon,* moss; + *-logy*], the branch of botany dealing with mosses and liverworts (bryophytes). —**bry·o·log·i·cal** (brī'ə-loj'i-k'l), *adj.* —**bry·ol'o·gist,** *n.*

**bry·o·ny** (brī'ə-ni), *n.* [*pl.* -NIES], [< L. < Gr. < *bryein,* to swell], a vine of the gourd family, with five-lobed leaves and greenish-white flower clusters.

**bry·o·phyte** (brī'ə-fīt'), *n.* [< Gr. *bryon,* moss; + *-phyte*], any moss or liverwort. —**bry'o·phyt'ic** (-fit'ik), *adj.*

**Bry·thon·ic** (bri-thon′ik), *adj. & n.* see **Celtic.**
**B/s,** 1. bags. 2. bales.
**B.S.,** Bachelor of Science.
**b.s.,** balance sheet.
**b.s., B/S,** bill of sale.
**B.S.A.,** Boy Scouts of America.
**B.Sc.,** *Baccalaureus Scientiae,* [L.], Bachelor of Science.
**B.S.Ed.,** Bachelor of Science in Education.
**Bs/L,** bills of lading.
**Bt.,** Baronet.
**B.T., B.Th.,** *Baccalaureus Theologiae,* [L.], Bachelor of Theology.
**Btry.,** Battery.
**B.T.U., Btu, B.t.u.,** British thermal unit (or units).
**bu.,** 1. bureau. 2. bushel; bushels.
**bub·ble** (bub′'l), *n.* [prob. echoic], 1. a film of liquid enveloping air or gas: as, soap *bubbles.* 2. a globule of air or gas in a liquid or solid. 3. any plausible scheme that proves to be worthless. 4. the act or sound of bubbling. *v.i.* [-BLED, -BLING], 1. to rise in bubbles; boil; foam. 2. to make a gurgling sound. *v.t.* to form bubbles in; make bubble. **—bubble over,** 1. to overflow, as a boiling liquid. 2. to be unable to keep back one's excitement, etc. **—bub′bly,** *adj.*
**bubble bath,** 1. a bath perfumed and softened by a solution, crystals, or powder that forms surface bubbles. 2. such a solution, etc.
**bubble gum,** a kind of chewing gum that can be blown into large bubbles.
**bu·bo** (bū′bō), *n.* [*pl.* -BOES], [LL. < Gr. *boubon,* groin], an inflamed swelling of a lymph gland, especially in the groin. **—bu·bon′ic** (-bon′ik), *adj.*
**bubonic plague,** a contagious disease, usually fatal, characterized by buboes, chills, and fever: fleas from infected rats are the carriers.
**buc·cal** (buk′'l), *adj.* [L. *bucca,* cheek; + *-al*], of the cheek or cheeks. 2. of the mouth.
**buc·ca·neer** (buk′ə-nêr′), *n.* [Fr. *boucanier,* user of a *boucan* (Braz.), grill for smoking meat: orig. applied to Fr. hunters in Haiti], a pirate, or sea robber.
**Bu·chan·an James** (bū-kan′ən), 1791–1868; fifteenth president of the U.S. (1857–1861).
**Bu·cha·rest** (bū′kə-rest′, bo͞o′-), *n.* the capital of Romania: pop., 985,000.
**Buch·en·wald** (bo͞okh′ən-vält′; *often Anglicized to* book′'n-wôld′), *n.* a Nazi concentration camp near Weimar, Germany.
**buck** (buk), *n.* [AS. *bucca, buc,* he-goat], 1. [*pl.* BUCKS, BUCK; see PLURAL, II, D, 1], a male deer, goat, etc. 2. the act of bucking. 3. a dandy. 4. [Colloq.], a young man: patronizing term. 5. [Slang], a dollar. *v.i.* 1. to rear upward quickly, as in an attempt to throw off a rider: said of a horse, etc. 2. to plunge forward with lowered head, as a goat. 3. [Colloq.], to resist something as if plunging against it. 4. [Colloq.], to move jerkily. *v.t.* 1. to charge against, as in football. 2. to throw by bucking. 3. [Colloq.], to resist. *adj.* male. **—buck for,** [Military Slang], to work hard for (a promotion, etc.). **—buck up,** [Colloq.], to cheer up. **—buck′er,** *n.*
**buck** (buk), *n.* [D. *zaagbok*], 1. a sawbuck; sawhorse. 2. a somewhat similar gymnastic apparatus with a padded top, for vaulting over, etc.
**buck** (buk), *n.* in *poker,* a counter, etc. placed before a player as a reminder to deal next, etc. **—pass the buck,** [Colloq.], to evade blame, responsibility, etc. by passing it to someone else.
**buck and wing,** a complicated, fast tap dance.
**buck·a·roo** (buk′ə-ro͞o′, buk′ə-ro͞o′), *n.* [*pl.* -ROOS], [altered < Sp. *vaquero*], a cowboy.
**buck·board** (buk′bôrd′, -bōrd′), *n.* [< *buck* (to move jerkily)], a four-wheeled, open carriage with the seat carried on a flooring of long, flexible boards whose ends rest directly on the axles.

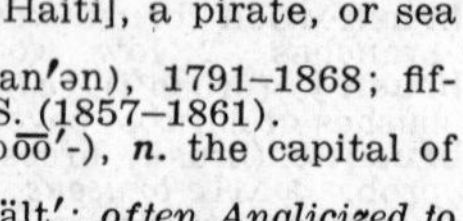

BUCKBOARD

**buck·et** (buk′it), *n.* [< dim. of AS. *buc,* pitcher], 1. a container hung from a curved handle, for carrying water, coal, etc.; pail. 2. a bucketful. 3. a thing like a bucket, as a dredge scoop. *v.t. & v.i.* to carry or lift in a bucket. **—kick the bucket,** [? < obs. *bucket,* beam on which a slaughtered pig was hung], [Slang], to die.
**buck·et·ful** (buk′it-fool′), *n.* [*pl.* -FULS], the amount that a bucket can contain.
**buck·eye** (buk′ī′), *n.* [*buck* (male deer) + *eye:* from the appearance of the seed], 1. any of several kinds of horse chestnut with showy clusters of flowers, large leaves, and burs containing large nuts. 2. the nut. 3. [B-], [Colloq.], a native or inhabitant of Ohio (the **Buckeye State**).
**Buck·ing·ham Palace** (buk′iŋ-əm), the official residence in London of British sovereigns.
**buck·le** (buk′'l), *n.* [< OFr. < LL. < L. *buccula,* cheek strap of a helmet, dim. of *bucca,* cheek], 1. a clasp for fastening a strap, belt, etc. 2. a clasplike ornament for shoes, the hair, etc. *v.t. & v.i.* [-LED, -LING], to fasten with a buckle. **—buckle down,** to apply oneself energetically.
**buck·le** (buk′'l), *v.t. & v.i.* [-LED, -LING], [D. *bukken,* to bow], to bend, warp, or crumple. *n.* a bend, bulge, kink, etc. **—buckle under,** [Colloq.], to give in; yield; submit.
**buck·ler** (buk′lẽr), *n.* [OFr. *bocler:* from the *bocle,* or boss, in its center], 1. a small, round shield worn on the arm. 2. a protection or defense.
**buck·o** (buk′ō), *n.* [*pl.* -OES], [< *buck* (he-goat)], a bully.
**buck private,** [Slang], a private.
**buck·ram** (buk′rəm), *n.* [< OFr.; ? < *Bokhara,* in Asia Minor], a coarse cloth stiffened with glue or sizing for use in bookbinding, etc. *adj.* of or like buckram. *v.t.* to stiffen with buckram.
**buck·saw** (buk′sô′), *n.* a wood-cutting saw set in a frame, held with both hands when used.

BUCKSAW

**buck·shot** (buk′shot′), *n.* a large lead shot for shooting deer and other large game.
**buck·skin** (buk′skin′), *n.* 1. a soft, strong, yellowish-gray leather made from the skins of deer or sheep. 2. a yellowish-gray horse. 3. *pl.* trousers made of buckskin. *adj.* made of buckskin.
**buck·thorn** (buk′thôrn′), *n.* [*buck* (male deer) + *thorn*], 1. a tree or shrub with black berries and thorny branches. 2. a spiny tree of the sapodilla family, found in the southern U.S.
**buck·tooth** (buk′to͞oth′), *n.* [*pl.* -TEETH (-tēth′)], [*buck* (male deer) + *tooth*], a projecting tooth. **—buck′toothed′,** *adj.*
**buck·wheat** (buk′hwēt′), *n.* [*buck,* beech < AS. *boc;* + *wheat:* from the beechnut-shaped seeds], 1. a plant with fragrant, white flowers and triangular seeds. 2. the seed of this plant, from which a dark flour is made. 3. this flour.
**bu·col·ic** (bū-kol′ik), *adj.* [< L. < Gr. < *boukolos,* herdsman < *bous,* ox], 1. of shepherds; pastoral. 2. rural; rustic. *n.* a pastoral poem. **—bu·col′i·cal·ly,** *adv.*
**bud** (bud), *n.* [AS. *budda,* beetle], 1. a small swelling on a plant, from which a shoot, cluster of leaves, or flower develops. 2. any immature person or thing. *v.i.* [BUDDED, BUDDING], 1. to put forth buds. 2. to begin to develop. 3. to be young, promising, etc. *v.t.* 1. to cause to bud. 2. to insert a bud of (a plant) into the bark of another sort of plant. **—nip in the bud,** to check at the earliest stage. **—bud′der,** *n.* **—bud′less,** *adj.* **—bud′like′,** *adj.*
**bud** (bud), *n.* [Slang], buddy; fellow: a term of direct address.
**Bu·da·pest** (bo͞o′də-pest′, bū′də-pest′), *n.* the capital of Hungary, on the Danube: pop., 1,165,000.
**Bud·dha** (bood′ə), *n.* [Sans., the enlightened one], Gautama Siddhartha, Hindu religious leader, the founder of Buddhism; lived 563?–483? B.C.
**Bud·dhism** (bood′iz'm), *n.* a religion of central and eastern Asia, founded in India by Buddha: it teaches that right living and right thinking will enable the soul to reach Nirvana, a divine state of release from earthly pain and desire. **—Bud′dhist,** *n. & adj.* **—Bud·dhis′tic,** *adj.*
**bud·dy** (bud′i), *n.* [*pl.* -DIES], [? < Brit. dial. *butty,* companion], [Colloq.], 1. a comrade; companion; pal. 2. little boy: a term of direct address.
**budge** (buj), *v.t. & v.i.* [BUDGED, BUDGING], [Fr. *bouger,* to move < LL. < L. *bullire,* to bubble < *bulla,* a bubble], to move slightly: as, the boy can't *budge* the heavy door.
**budg·et** (buj′it), *n.* [Fr. *bougette,* dim. of *bouge,* a bag < OFr. < L. *bulga,* leather bag], 1. a collection of items; stock. 2. a plan adjusting expenses during a certain period to the expected income for that period. 3. the estimated cost of living, operating, etc. *v.t.* 1. to put into or on a budget. 2. to schedule: as, *budget* your time. **—budg′et·ar′y,** *adj.* **—budg′et·er,** *n.*
**budget plan,** an installment plan.
**Bue·nos Ai·res** (bwā′nōs ī′rās, bō′nəs âr′ēz; Sp. bwe′nôs ī′res), the capital of Argentina, on the La Plata River: pop., 3,000,000.

**buff** (buf), *n.* [earlier *buffe*, buffalo < Fr. *buffle;* see BUFFALO], 1. a heavy, soft, brownish-yellow leather made from the skin of the buffalo or ox. 2. a military coat made of this leather. 3. a stick (**buff stick**) or wheel (**buffing wheel**) covered with leather, cloth, etc., used for cleaning or shining. 4. a dull brownish yellow. 5. [Colloq.], the bare skin. *adj.* 1. made of buff. 2. of the color buff. *v.t.* to clean or shine with a buff. —**buff′fer,** *n.*

**buff** (buf), *v.t.* [OFr. *buffe;* see BUFFET (a blow)], to lessen the force of. *v.i.* to serve as a buffer.

**Buf·fa·lo** (buf′′l-ō′), *n.* a city in New York, on Lake Erie: pop., 533,000.

**buf·fa·lo** (buf′′l-ō′), *n.* [*pl.* -LOES, -LOS, -LO; see PLURAL, II, D, 1], [Port. *bufalo* < L. < Gr. < *bous*, ox], 1. any of various wild oxen, sometimes domesticated, as the water buffalo of India, Cape buffalo of Africa, etc. 2. popularly, the American bison. *v.t.* [Slang], to intimidate; overawe.

**Buffalo Bill,** see **Cody, William Frederick.**

**buffalo grass,** a short grass with fine leaves, common on prairies where bison used to graze.

**buff·er** (buf′ēr), *n.* [*buff* (to lessen force) + *-er*], 1. a device to lessen the shock of collision. 2. any person or thing that lessens shock.

**buffer state,** a small country situated between two large, antagonistic powers and regarded as lessening the possibility of conflict between these.

**buf·fet** (buf′it), *n.* [OFr. < *buffe*, a blow], a blow with the hand or fist. *v.t.* 1. to punch; slap. 2. to fight against. *v.i.* to fight. —**buf′fet·er,** *n.*

**buf·fet** (bə-fā′, boo-; Brit. buf′it), *n.* [Fr.], 1. a piece of furniture with drawers and cupboards for dishes, table linen, silver, etc. 2. a counter where refreshments are served, or a restaurant with such a counter.

**buffet supper** (or **lunch**), a meal at which guests serve themselves from a buffet or table.

‡**buf·fo** (bōōf′fô; Eng. bōō′fō), *n.* [*pl.* -FI (-fē)], [It., comic; see BUFFOON], an opera singer, generally a bass, who plays a comic role. *adj.* comic.

**buf·foon** (bu-fōōn′), *n.* [< Fr. < It. < *buffare*, to jest], one who amuses by jokes and tricks; clown. —**buf·foon′er·y** [*pl.* -IES], *n.* —**buf·foon′ish,** *adj.*

**bug** (bug), *n.* [ME. *bugge*, confused form of AS. *budda*, beetle], 1. any crawling insect with sucking mouth parts and forewings thickened toward the base. 2. any insect or similar animal. 3. a bedbug. 4. [Colloq.], germ; bacterium. 5. [Slang], a defect, as in a machine. 6. [Slang], a tiny microphone hidden to record conversation secretly.

**bug·a·boo** (bug′ə-bōō′), *n.* [*pl.* -BOOS], a bugbear.

**bug·bear** (bug′bâr′), *n.* [< earlier *bug* (a bogy) + *bear* (the animal)], 1. an imaginary hobgoblin or terror. 2. anything causing seemingly needless or excessive fear or anxiety.

**bug-eyed** (bug′īd′), *adj.* [Slang], with eyes bulging.

**bug·gy** (bug′i), *n.* [*pl.* -GIES], [< *bougée*, pp. of Fr. *bouger*, to move], 1. a light, one-horse carriage with one seat. 2. a small carriage for a baby: also **baby buggy.**

**bug·gy** (bug′i), *adj.* [-GIER, -GIEST], infested or swarming with bugs.

**bug·house** (bug′hous′), *n.* [Slang], an insane asylum. *adj.* [Slang], insane; crazy.

**bu·gle** (bū′g'l), *n.* [< OFr. < L. *buculus*, young ox, dim. of *bos*, ox], a wind instrument like a trumpet but smaller, and usually without keys or valves, used chiefly for military calls. *v.i.* & *v.t.* [-GLED, -GLING], to call or signal by blowing a bugle. —**bu′gler,** *n.*

**bugs** (bugz), *adj.* [Slang], crazy; insane.

**buhl** (bōōl) *n.* [after A. C. *Boulle* (1642–1732), Fr. woodworker], 1. decoration of furniture with designs of inlaid tortoise shell, colored metals, etc. 2. furniture thus decorated.

**build** (bild), *v.t.* [BUILT or *archaic* BUILDED, BUILDING], [AS. *byldan* < base of *bold*, a house], 1. to make by putting together materials, parts, etc.; construct 2. to make a basis for; establish: as, *build* your theory on facts. 3. to create. *v.i.* 1. to put up a building or buildings; have a house, etc. built. 2. to develop a plan, etc. (with *on* or *upon*). *n.* the manner or form of construction: as, a stocky *build.* —**build up,** 1. to construct or develop gradually. 2. to make strong or healthy.

**build·er** (bil′dēr), *n.* 1. one that builds. 2. a person in the business of building houses, etc.

**build·ing** (bil′diŋ), *n.* 1. anything that is built; structure. 2. the act, art, work, or business of making houses, ships, etc.

**build-up** (bild′up′), *n.* [Slang], favorable publicity or praise.

**built-in** (bilt′in′), *adj.* made as part of the building: as, a *built-in* bathtub.

**bulb** (bulb), *n.* [< L. < Gr. *bolbos*], 1. an underground bud that sends down roots and has a very short stem covered with leafy scales, as in a lily, onion, etc. 2. a corm, tuber, or rhizome resembling a bulb, as in a crocus. 3. a plant that grows from a bulb. 4. anything shaped like a bulb. 5. an incandescent lamp. —**bulb·ar** (bul′bēr), *adj.* —**bulbed,** *adj.*

**bul·ba·ceous** (bul-bā′shəs), *adj.* 1. of or like a bulb. 2. having or growing from a bulb.

**bulb·ous** (bul′bəs), *adj.* 1. of, having, or growing from bulbs. 2. shaped like a bulb.

**Bul·gar** (bul′gēr, bool′gär), *n.* & *adj.* Bulgarian.

**Bul·gar·i·a** (bul-gâr′i-ə, bool-), *n.* a country in the Balkans, on the Black Sea: area, 42,796 sq. mi.; pop., 7,614,000; capital, Sofia.

**Bul·gar·i·an** (bul-gâr′i-ən, bool-), *adj.* of Bulgaria, its people, or their language. *n.* 1. a native or inhabitant of Bulgaria. 2. the Slavic language of the Bulgarians: abbrev. **Bulg.**

**bulge** (bulj), *n.* [< OFr. < L. *bulga*, leather bag], an outward swelling; protuberance. *v.i.* & *v.t.* [BULGED, BULGING], to swell or bend outward; protrude. —**bulg′y,** *adj.*

**bulk** (bulk), *n.* [ON. *bulki*, a heap, cargo], 1. size, mass, or volume, especially if great. 2. the main mass or body; largest part: as, the *bulk* of one's fortune. *v.i.* 1. to form into a mass. 2. to increase in size, importance, etc. 3. to have size or importance. *v.t.* to make (something) form into a mass. *adj.* 1. total; aggregate. 2. not packaged. —**in bulk,** 1. not packaged. 2. in large amounts.

**bulk·head** (bulk′hed′), *n.* [< earlier *bulk* (< ON. *balkr*, partition) + *head*], 1. an upright partition separating parts of a ship, airplane, etc. for protection against fire, leakage, etc. 2. a wall or embankment for holding back earth, fire, water, etc. 3. a boxlike structure built over an opening, as a stairway, elevator shaft, etc.

**bulk·y** (bul′ki), *adj.* [-IER, -IEST], 1. of great bulk; large; massive. 2. awkwardly large; big and clumsy. —**bulk′i·ly,** *adv.* —**bulk′i·ness,** *n.*

**bull** (bool), *n.* [< AS. *bula*, a steer], 1. the male of any bovine animal, as the ox, buffalo, etc. 2. the male of certain other large animals, as the elephant, moose, walrus, whale, etc. 3. a person who tries to raise the market price of stocks, etc. in order to sell at a profit. 4. a very large, noisy, or strong person. 5. [B-], Taurus. 6. [Slang], a policeman. 7. [Slang], insincere talk; nonsense. *adj.* 1. male. 2. like a bull in size, strength, etc. 3. rising in price: as, a *bull* market. —**shoot** (or **throw**) **the bull,** [Slang], 1. to talk nonsense. 2. to talk. —**take the bull by the horns,** to deal boldly with a danger or difficulty. —**bull′ish,** *adj.* —**bull′ish·ly,** *adv.* —**bull′ish·ness,** *n.* —**bull′-like′,** *adj.*

**bull** (bool), *n.* [< OFr. < It. < LL. < L. *bulla*, a seal], an official document or decree from the Pope.

**bull** (bool), *n.* [OFr. *boule*, a lie < L. *bulla*, a bubble], a statement that is absurdly inconsistent or self-contradictory.

**bull-** (bool), [< *bull* (ox)], a combining form meaning: 1. *of a bull* or *bulls*, as in *bullfight.* 2. *like a bull* or *bull's*, as in *bullhead.* 3. *large* or *male*, as in *bullfrog.*

**Bull, John** (bool), England, the English people, etc.: a personification.

**bull·dog** (bool′dôg′, -dog′), *n.* [*bull-* + *dog*], a short-haired, square-jawed, heavily built dog that has a strong, stubborn grip. *adj.* like or characteristic of a bulldog. *v.t.* to throw (a steer) by seizing its horns and twisting its neck.

**bull·doze** (bool′dōz′), *v.t.* [-DOZED, -DOZING], [? < *bull*-whip + *dose*, hence, lit., to give a dose of the whip], [Colloq.], to force or frighten by threatening; intimidate; bully.

**bull·doz·er** (bool′dōz′ēr), *n.* 1. a person who bulldozes. 2. a tractor with a large, shovellike blade on the front for pushing or moving earth, debris, etc.

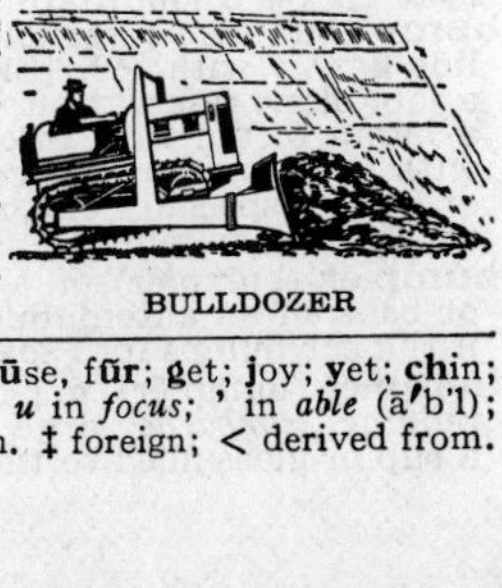

BULLDOZER

**bul·let** (bool′it), *n.* [Fr. *boulette*, dim. of *boule*, a ball], a small, shaped piece of lead, steel, etc. to be shot from a firearm.

**bul·le·tin** (bool′ə-t'n, -tin), *n.* [< It.; see BULL (papal edict)], 1. a brief statement of the latest news. 2. a regular publication, as of an organization, society, etc. *v.t.* to announce in a bulletin.
**bulletin board,** a board or wall area on which bulletins or notices are put up.
**bul·let·proof** (bool′it-pro͞of′), *adj.* that bullets cannot pierce. *v.t.* to make bulletproof.
**bull·fight** (bool′fīt′), *n.* an entertainment in which a bull is provoked by men on horseback and afoot and then killed with a sword by the matador. —**bull′fight′er,** *n.* —**bull′fight′ing,** *n.*
**bull·finch** (bool′finch′), *n.* [*bull-* + *finch*], a small European songbird with a short, rounded beak.
**bull·frog** (bool′frôg′, -frog′), *n.* [see BULL-], a large North American frog that has a deep, loud croak.
**bull·head** (bool′hed′), *n.* [see BULL-], any of various large-headed fishes, as some catfishes.
**bull·head·ed** (bool′hed′id), *adj.* blindly stubborn; headstrong. —**bull′head′ed·ness,** *n.*
**bull·horn** (bool′hôrn′), *n.* a portable electronic voice amplifier.
**bul·lion** (bool′yən), *n.* [< D. < Fr. *billon*, small coin < *bille*, a stick < Gallic hyp. *bilia*, tree trunk], 1. gold and silver regarded as raw material. 2. bars of gold or silver, as before coinage.
**bull·necked** (bool′nekt′), *adj.* having a short, thick neck.
**bull·ock** (bool′ək), *n.* [< AS. *bulluc*, young bull], a castrated bull; ox; steer.
**bull pen,** 1. a fenced enclosure for bulls. 2. [Colloq.], an enclosure where prisoners and suspects are temporarily herded. 3. in *baseball*, an area where relief pitchers practice and warm up.
**bull ring,** an enclosed arena for bullfighting.
**Bull Run,** a stream in NE Virginia: site of two Union defeats (1861, 1862) in the Civil War.
**bull's-eye** (boolz′ī′), *n.* 1. a thick, circular glass in a roof, ship's deck, etc., for admitting light. 2. the central mark of a target. 3. a direct hit. 4. a convex lens for concentrating light. 5. a lantern with such a lens.
**bull terrier,** a strong, lean, white dog developed by crossbreeding the bulldog and the terrier.
**bull-whip** (bool′hwip′), *n.* [*bull-* + *whip*], a long, heavy whip, formerly used by cattle drivers, etc.
**bul·ly** (bool′i), *n.* [*pl.* -LIES], [orig., sweetheart; < D. < MHG. *buole* (G. *buhle*), lover; later infl. by *bull* (ox)], a person who hurts, frightens, or browbeats those who are smaller or weaker. *v.t. & v.i.* [-LIED, -LYING], to act the bully (toward); intimidate (others). *adj.* 1. gallant; dashing: as, my *bully* boy. 2. [Colloq.], fine; very good. *interj.* [Colloq.], good! well done!
**bul·ly** (bool′i), *n.* [< Fr. < *bouillir*, to boil], canned or corned beef: also **bully beef.**
**bul·ly·rag** (bool′i-rag′), *v.t.* [-RAGGED, -RAGGING], [see BULLY, *v.* & RAG, *v.*], to bully or tease.
**bul·rush** (bool′rush′), *n.* [< AS. *bol*, bole of a tree + *risc*, a rush], 1. a tall plant of the sedge family, found in water and wet land. 2. [Brit.], the cattail. 3. in the *Bible*, papyrus.
**bul·wark** (bool′wẽrk), *n.* [D. & MHG. *bolwerk*, a rampart; cf. BOULEVARD], 1. an earthwork or defensive wall; rampart. 2. a defense; protection. 3. *usually pl.* a ship's side above the deck. *v.t.* 1. to provide bulwarks for. 2. to be a bulwark to.
**bum** (bum), *n.* [prob. < G. *bummler*, loafer < *bummeln*, to go slowly], 1. [Colloq.], a loafer; vagrant. 2. [Slang], a dissolute or worthless person. 3. [Slang], a spree. *v.i.* [BUMMED, BUMMING], 1. [Colloq.], to loaf. 2. [Colloq.], to live by sponging on people. 3. [Slang], to drink heavily. *v.t.* [Slang], to get by sponging on people. *adj.* [BUMMER, BUMMEST], [Slang], poor in quality. —**give (a person) the bum's rush,** [Slang], to eject (a person) forcibly. —**on the bum,** [Colloq.], 1. living the life of a vagrant. 2. out of repair; broken. —**bum′mer,** *n.*
**bum·ble·bee** (bum′b'l-bē′), *n.* [ME. *bumblen*, to buzz; + *bee*], a large, hairy, yellow-and-black bee that makes a loud, humming sound in flight.
**bump** (bump), *v.t.* [echoic], 1. to hit against; collide lightly with. 2. [Slang], to displace, as from a job, plane reservation, etc. *v.i.* 1. to collide with a bump (often with *into* or *against*). 2. to move with jolts. *n.* 1. a light collision; jolt. 2. a swelling or lump, especially one caused by a blow. —**bump off,** [Slang], to murder.
**bump·er** (bump′ẽr), *n.* a bar fastened to the front or back of an automobile to give some protection if the car bumps into something.
**bump·er** (bump′ẽr), *n.* [< *bump*, infl. by Fr. *bombé*, bulging, *bombarde*, large drinking vessel, etc.], 1. a cup or glass filled to the brim. 2. [Colloq.], anything unusually large of its kind. *adj.* [Colloq.], unusually abundant: as, a *bumper* crop.
**bump·kin** (bump′kin), *n.* [prob. < D. *boomkin*, short tree; dim. of *boom*, a tree], an awkward or loutish person from the country.
**bump·tious** (bump′shəs), *adj.* [prob. < *bump*], disagreeably conceited, arrogant, or pushing. —**bump′tious·ly,** *adv.* —**bump′tious·ness,** *n.*
**bump·y** (bump′i), *adj.* [-IER, -IEST], full of bumps; rough. —**bump′i·ly,** *adv.* —**bump′i·ness,** *n.*
**bun** (bun), *n.* [? < OFr. *bon*, good], 1. a small roll, usually somewhat sweetened and often spiced. 2. hair worn in a roll on a woman's head or neck.
**bu·na** (bo͞o′nə, bū′-), *n.* [*butadiene* + *Na*, (symbol for) sodium], a synthetic rubber made by polymerizing butadiene: a trade-mark (**Buna**).
**bunch** (bunch), *n.* [ME. *bunche;* akin to MLG. *bunk*, D. *bonk*, Norw. *bunka*, a heap, bunch], 1. a cluster of things growing together: as, a *bunch* of grapes. 2. a collection of things of the same kind fastened, grouped, or thought of together: as, a *bunch* of keys. 3. [Colloq.], a group (of people). *v.t. & v.i.* to form or collect into a bunch or bunches.
**bunch·y** (bun′chi), *adj.* [-IER, -IEST], 1. growing in bunches. 2. like or having a bunch or bunches.
**bun·co** (buŋ′kō), *n.* [*pl.* -COS], [< Sp. *banca*, card game], [Colloq.], a swindle, especially at a card game, etc.; confidence game. *v.t.* [-COED, -COING], [Colloq.], to swindle; cheat. Also sp. **bunko.**
**bun·combe** (buŋ′kəm), *n.* [< *Buncombe* county, North Carolina, represented in Congress (1819–1821) by a man who continually felt bound to "make a speech for Buncombe"], [Colloq.], talk, etc. that is empty, insincere, or merely for effect; humbug.
‡**Bund** (boont; Eng. boond), *n.* [*pl.* BÜNDE (bün′də); Eng. BUNDS], [G.], 1. a league; confederation; society. 2. the German-American Bund, a former pro-Nazi organization in the U.S.
**bun·dle** (bun′d'l), *n.* [MD. *bondel* < base of *bind*], 1. a number of things tied, wrapped, or otherwise held together. 2. a package; parcel. 3. a bunch; collection; group. *v.t.* [-DLED, -DLING], 1. to make into a bundle; wrap or tie together. 2. to put or send hastily (with *off*, *out*, *into*, etc.). *v.i.* 1. to move or go hastily; bustle. 2. to lie in the same bed with one's sweetheart without undressing, a courting custom in colonial New England. —**bundle up,** to put on plenty of warm clothing. —**bun′dler,** *n.*
**bung** (buŋ), *n.* [< MD. *bonghe*], 1. a cork or other stopper for the hole in the side or end of a barrel, cask, or keg. 2. a bunghole. *v.t.* 1. to close (a bunghole) with a stopper. 2. to stop up; close. 3. [Slang], to bruise or damage (with *up*).
**bun·ga·low** (buŋ′gə-lō′), *n.* [Hind. *bānglā*, thatched house, lit., of Bengal], a small house or cottage, usually of one story.
**bung·hole** (buŋ′hōl′), *n.* the hole in a barrel or keg through which liquid can be drawn out.
**bun·gle** (buŋ′g'l), *v.t.* [-GLED, -GLING], [echoic], to spoil by clumsy work; botch. *v.i.* to do things badly or clumsily. *n.* 1. a bungling, or clumsy, act. 2. a bungled piece of work. —**bun′gler,** *n.*
**bun·ion** (bun′yən), *n.* [17th-c. Fr. *bouillon*, lump on horse's foot (< L. *bulla*, a bubble); infl. by ME. *bunny*, a lump], an inflammation and swelling at the base of the big toe.
**bunk** (buŋk), *n.* [D. *bank*, a bench], 1. a shelflike bed or berth built into or against a wall, as in a ship. 2. any narrow bed or cot. *v.i.* 1. to sleep in a bunk. 2. [Colloq.], to go to bed or sleep.
**bunk** (buŋk), *n.* [Slang], buncombe; nonsense.
**bunk·er** (buŋ′kẽr), *n.* [Scot.; extension of *bank* (a bench); orig., a seat], 1. a large bin, especially one for coal aboard a ship. 2. a unit of an underground steel-and-concrete fortification system. 3. a mound of earth serving as an obstacle on a golf course. *v.t.* in *golf*, to hit (a ball) into a bunker.
**Bun·ker Hill** (buŋ′kẽr), a hill (in Boston, Massachusetts) near which a battle of the American Revolution was fought in 1775.
**bun·ko** (buŋ′kō), *n.* [*pl.* -KOS], & *v.t.* [-KOED, -KOING], bunco.
**bun·kum** (buŋ′kəm), *n.* buncombe.
**bun·ny** (bun′i), *n.* [*pl.* -NIES], [dim. of *bun*], a rabbit: pet name used by children.
**Bun·sen burner** (bun′s'n), [< R. W. *Bunsen*, 19th-c. German chemist], a small, tubular gas burner that produces a hot, blue flame.
**bunt** (bunt), *v.t. & v.i.* [? < base of Bret. *bounta*, to butt, via Corn.], 1. [Brit. Dial.], to strike or butt with or as with horns. 2. in *baseball*, to bat (a pitched ball) lightly so that it does not go beyond the infield: usually done as a sacrifice play. *n.* 1. a shove. 2. in *baseball*, *a*) the act of bunting. *b*) a bunted ball. —**bunt′er,** *n.*

**bun·tine** (bun′tin), *n.* bunting (cloth).
**bunt·ing** (bun′tiŋ), *n.* [? < ME. *bunten,* to sift], 1. a thin cloth used in making flags, etc. 2. flags collectively. 3. strips of cloth in patriotic colors, used as holiday decorations for halls, automobiles, etc. 4. a baby's garment of soft, warm cloth made into a kind of hooded blanket that can be closed so that only the face is exposed.
**bunt·ing** (bun′tiŋ), *n.* [< ME. < *Bunetun,* OFr. *Bonneton,* double dim. of *bon,* good], a small bird of the finch family, having a short, stout bill.
**bunt·line** (bunt′lin, -līn), *n.* [ME. *bunt,* middle part of a sail + *line,* a rope], one of the ropes attached to the foot rope of a square sail to prevent the sail from bellying when drawn up to be furled.
**Bun·yan, John** (bun′yən), 1628–1688; English author and preacher: wrote *Pilgrim's Progress.*
**Bunyan, Paul,** see **Paul Bunyan.**
**Buo·na·parte,** (bō′nə-pärt′; It. bwô′nä-pär′te), *n.* Bonaparte: Italian form of the name.
**buoy** (boi, bōō′i), *n.* [< OFr. or MD. < L. *boia,* fetter (by which the float was anchored)], 1. a floating object anchored in water to warn of rocks, shoals, etc. or to mark a channel. 2. a life preserver; life buoy. *v.t.* 1. to mark or provide with a buoy. 2. to keep afloat in a liquid. 3. to lift or hold up in mind or spirits; encourage. —**buoy up,** 1. to keep afloat. 2. to lift or hold up in mind or spirits. 3. to raise to the surface of a liquid.
**buoy·an·cy** (boi′ən-si, bōō′yən-si), *n.* [< *buoyant*] 1. the ability or tendency to float or rise in liquid or air. 2. the power to keep something afloat. 3. lightness of spirit; cheerfulness.
**buoy·ant** (boi′ənt, bōō′yənt), *adj.* [? < Sp. < *boyar,* to float], having or showing buoyancy. —**buoy′ant·ly,** *adv.*
**bur** (būr), *n.* [ME. *burre* < ON.], 1. the rough, prickly seedcase or fruit of certain plants. 2. a weed or other plant with burs. 3. a person who clings like a bur. 4. a burr. *v.t.* [BURRED, BURRING], 1. to remove burs from. 2. to burr.
**Bur·bage, Richard** (būr′bij), 1567?–1619; English actor.
**Bur·bank** (būr′baŋk), *n.* a city in California, near Los Angeles: pop., **90**,000.
**Bur·bank, Luther** (būr′baŋk), 1849–1926; American horticulturist.
**bur·ble** (būr′b'l), *v.i.* [-BLED, -BLING], [echoic], to make a gurgling or bubbling sound.
**bur·bot** (būr′bət), *n.* [*pl.* -BOT, -BOTS; see PLURAL, II, D, 2], [Fr. *bourbotte;* ult. < L. *barba,* a beard], a fresh-water fish of the cod family, having chin barbels.
**bur·den** (būr′d'n), *n.* [< AS. *byrthen* < base of *beran,* to bear], 1. anything carried or endured; load. 2. a very heavy load; whatever is hard to bear. 3. the carrying of loads: as, a beast of *burden.* 4. the carrying capacity of a ship or the weight of its cargo. *v.t.* to make bear a burden; load; oppress. Also, *archaic,* **burthen.**
**bur·den** (būr′d'n), *n.* [< OFr. *bourdon* (< ML. *burdo*), a humming; echoic], 1. a chorus or refrain of a song. 2. a repeated, central idea; theme.
**burden of proof,** the obligation to prove a statement.
**bur·den·some** (būr′d'n-səm), *adj.* hard to bear; heavy; oppressive. —**bur′den·some·ly,** *adv.* —**bur′den·some·ness,** *n.*
**bur·dock** (būr′dok′), *n.* [*bur* (seedcase) + *dock* (plant)], a plant of the composite family, with large leaves, prickly burs, and a strong smell.
**bu·reau** (byoo′rō), *n.* [*pl.* -REAUS, -REAUX (-rōz)], [Fr., desk < OFr. *burel,* coarse cloth (as covering this) < LL.; prob. < L. *burra,* coarse hair], 1. [Brit.], a desk, with drawers for papers, etc. 2. a chest of drawers, often with a mirror, for clothing, etc. 3. an office: as, an information *bureau.* 4. a government department or a subdivision of this. Abbrev. **bur., bu.**
**bu·reauc·ra·cy** (byoo-rok′rə-si, -rō′krə-si), *n.* [*pl.* -CIES], [< Fr.; see BUREAU & -CRACY], 1. the administration of government through departments managed by officials following an inflexible routine. 2. the officials collectively. 3. governmental officialism or inflexible routine. 4. the concentration of authority in administrative bureaus.
**bu·reau·crat** (byoo′rə-krat′), *n.* 1. an official in a bureaucracy. 2. an official who follows and insists on an inflexible routine, etc. —**bu′reau·crat′ic,** *adj.* —**bu′reau·crat′i·cal·ly,** *adv.*

**bu·rette, bu·ret** (byoo-ret′), *n.* [Fr., dim. of OFr. *buire,* flagon], a graduated glass tube with a stopcock at the bottom, for measuring small quantities of liquid or gas.

BURETTE

**burg** (būrg), *n.* [earlier var. of *borough*], [Colloq.], a city, town, or village.
**-burg,** a suffix meaning *burg* or *borough,* as in *Vicksburg:* also **-burgh,** as in *Pittsburgh.*
**bur·geon** (būr′jən), *v.i. & v.t.* [< OFr. < *burjon,* a bud], to put forth (buds, etc.). *n.* a bud; sprout.
**-burg·er,** [< ham*burger*], [Slang], a combining form meaning *sandwich of ground meat, etc. (and),* as in *steakburger, cheeseburger.*
**bur·gess** (būr′jis), *n.* [OFr. *burgeis;* see BOURGEOIS], 1. a citizen of a borough. 2. a member of the lower house of the legislature of Maryland or Virginia before the American Revolution.
**burgh** (būrg; Scot. bur ō, -ə), *n.* [Scot var. of *borough*], 1. [Brit.], a borough. 2. in Scotland, a chartered town. Also **burh.**
**burgh·er** (būr′gēr), *n.* a freeman of a burgh; citizen of a town.
**bur·glar** (būr′glēr), *n.* [< OFr. < Anglo-L. < LL. *burgulator;* ? < Gmc. *burg,* a dwelling + L. *latro,* robber], one who commits burglary.
**bur·glar·i·ous** (bēr-glâr′i-əs), *adj.* of, involving, constituting, or inclined to burglary. —**bur·glar′i·ous·ly,** *adv.*
**bur·glar·ize** (būr′glə-rīz′), *v.t.* [-IZED, -IZING], [Colloq.], to commit burglary in or upon.
**bur·glar·proof** (būr′glēr-prōōf′), *adj.* constructed so as to be safe against burglary.
**bur·gla·ry** (būr′glə-ri), *n.* [*pl.* -RIES], 1. the act of breaking into a house at night to commit theft or other felony. 2. the act of breaking into any building at any time to commit theft, etc.
**bur·gle** (būr′g'l), *v.i. & v.t.* [-GLED, -GLING], [< *burglar*], [Colloq.], to commit burglary (in).
**bur·go·mas·ter** (būr′gə-mas′tēr, -mäs′-), *n.* [< D. < *burg,* city + *meester,* master], the mayor or head magistrate of a city or town in the Netherlands, Flanders, Austria, or Germany.
**Bur·gun·dy** (būr′gən-di), *n.* 1. a former province of E France. 2. [*pl.* -DIES], a kind of wine, either red or white, originally made there. —**Bur·gun·di·an** (bēr-gun′di-ən), *adj. & n.*
**burh** (boorkh), *n.* a burg or burgh.
**bur·i·al** (ber′i-əl), *n.* a burying of a dead body in a grave, tomb, the sea, etc.; interment. *adj.* of or connected with burial.
**burial ground,** a cemetery; graveyard.
**bu·rin** (byoo′rin), *n.* [Fr. < It. < OHG. *boro,* borer], a pointed cutting tool used by engravers or marble workers.

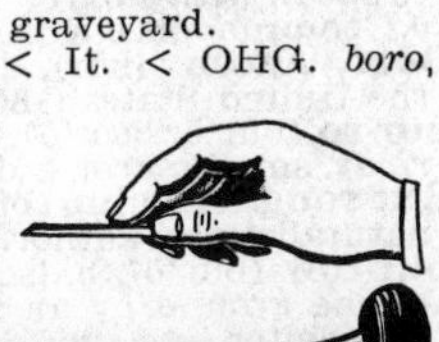

BURIN

**Burke, Edmund** (būrk), 1729–1797; English statesman and orator.
**burl** (būrl), *n.* [< OFr. < L. *burra,* coarse hair], 1. a knot in wool, thread, yarn, etc. that gives a nubby appearance to cloth. 2. a kind of knot on some tree trunks. *v.t.* to finish (cloth) by taking out the burls, etc. —**burled,** *adj.* —**burl′er,** *n.*
**bur·lap** (būr′lap), *n.* [prob. < D.; cf. D. *boer,* farmer & *boenlap,* rubbing cloth], a coarse cloth made of jute or hemp, used for making bags, etc.
**bur·lesque** (bēr-lesk′), *n.* [Fr. < It. < *burla,* a jest], 1. any broadly comic or satirical imitation; parody. 2. (*also, facetiously,* būr′li-kū′), a sort of vaudeville characterized by low comedy and display of nudity. *adj.* 1. comically imitating; parodying. 2. of or connected with burlesque (vaudeville). *v.t. & v.i.* [-LESQUED (-leskt′), -LESQUING], to imitate comically; parody.
**bur·ley, Bur·ley** (būr′li), *n.* [? < a proper name], a thin-leaved tobacco grown in Kentucky and surrounding States.
**bur·ly** (būr′li), *adj.* [-LIER, -LIEST], [prob. < ON.; akin to OHG. *burlīh,* lofty, exalted], big and strong; heavy and muscular. —**bur′li·ness,** *n.*
**Bur·ma** (būr′mə), *n.* a country in SE Asia: area, 261,610 sq. mi.; pop., 20,662,000; capital, Rangoon.

**Burma Road,** a road from N Burma to Chungking, China: an Allied supply route in World War II.
**Bur·mese** (bẽr-mēz′), *adj.* of Burma, its people, or their language. *n.* [*pl.* -MESE], 1. a native of Burma. 2. the language of the Burmese.
**burn** (bũrn), *v.t.* [BURNED or BURNT, BURNING], [AS. *bærnan, v.t., biernan, v.i.*], 1. to destroy by fire. 2. to set on fire; cause to blaze. 3. to injure by fire, friction, or acid; scorch, scald, etc. 4. to sunburn. 5. to cauterize. 6. to harden or glaze (bricks, pottery, etc.) by fire; fire. 7. to cause by fire, heat, etc.: as, he *burned* a hole in his coat. 8. to cause a sensation of heat in: as, the horseradish *burned* his throat. 9. in *chemistry,* to make undergo combustion. *v.i.* 1. to be on fire; flame; blaze. 2. to give out light or heat; shine; glow. 3. to be destroyed by fire or heat. 4. to be injured or charred by fire or heat. 5. to feel hot. 6. to be excited or inflamed. 7. in *chemistry,* to undergo combustion. *n.* 1. an injury caused by fire, heat, wind, etc. 2. a burned area. **—burn down,** to burn to the ground. **—burn oneself out,** to exhaust oneself by too much work or dissipation. **—burn up,** [Slang], to make or become angry.
**burn** (bũrn), *n.* [AS. *burna*], [Scot.], a brook.
**burn·er** (bũr′nẽr), *n.* 1. the part of a stove, lamp, etc. from which the flame comes. 2. an apparatus for burning: as, an oil *burner.* 3. one whose work consists in burning something.
**burn·ing** (bũr′niŋ), *adj.* 1. that burns; glowing. 2. intense; critical: as, a *burning* issue.
**burning glass,** a convex lens for focusing the sun's rays so as to set fire to something.
**bur·nish** (bũr′nish), *v.t. & v.i.* [OFr. *burnir,* to make brown < *brun,* brown], to make or become shiny by rubbing; polish. *n.* gloss; polish. **—bur′nish·er,** *n.* **—bur′nish·ment,** *n.*
**bur·noose, bur·nous** (bẽr-nōōs′, bũr′nōōs), *n.* [< Fr. < Ar. *burnus;* ? < Gr. *birros,* a cloak], a long cloak with a hood, worn by Arabs and Moors.
**Burns, Robert** (bũrnz), 1759–1796; Scottish poet.
**burn·sides** (bũrn′sīdz′), *n.pl.* [after A. E. *Burnside,* Union general in the Civil War], heavy growth of hair on the cheeks; side whiskers.
**burnt** (bũrnt), alt. pt. and pp. of **burn.**
**burnt sienna,** a dark brown (paint).
**burnt umber,** a reddish brown (paint).
**burp** (bũrp), *n. & v.i.* [echoic], [Slang], belch.
**burr** (bũr), *n.* 1. a bur. 2. a rough edge left on metal, etc. by cutting or drilling. 3. a dentist's drill. *v.t.* to form a rough edge on.
**burr** (bũr), *n.* [prob. echoic], 1. the trilling of *r,* with uvula or tongue. 2. any rough pronunciation: as, a Scottish *burr.* 3. a whirring sound. *v.i.* 1. to speak with a burr. 2. to make a whirring sound. *v.t.* to pronounce with a burr.
**Burr, Aaron** (bũr), 1756–1836; vice-president of the United States (1801–1805).
**bur·ro** (bũr′ō, boor′ō), *n.* [*pl.* -ROS], [< Sp.; L. *burricus,* small horse], a donkey.
**Bur·roughs, John** (bũr′ōz, -əz), 1837–1921; U.S. naturalist and author.
**bur·row** (bũr′ō), *n.* [see BOROUGH], 1. a hole dug in the ground by an animal. 2. any similar hole for shelter, etc. *v.i.* 1. to make a burrow. 2. to live or hide in or as in a burrow. 3. to search, as if by digging. 4. to dig. *v.t.* 1. to make burrows in. 2. to make by burrowing. **—bur′row·er,** *n.*
**bur·ry** (bũr′i), *adj.* [-RIER, -RIEST], 1. full of burs. 2. like a bur or burs; prickly.
**bur·sa** (bũr′sə), *n.* [*pl.* -SAE (-sē), -SAS], [LL., a bag; Gr., a hide], in *anatomy,* a sac or cavity, especially between joints. **—bur′sal,** *adj.*
**bur·sar** (bũr′sẽr), *n.* [LL. *bursarius;* see BURSA], a college treasurer. **—bur·sar·i·al** (bẽr-sâr′i-əl), *adj.* **—bur′sar·ship,** *n.*
**bur·sa·ry** (bũr′sə-ri), *n.* [*pl.* -RIES (-riz)], a treasury, especially of a college.
**bur·si·tis** (bẽr-sī′tis), *n.* [< *bursa* + *-itis*], inflammation of a bursa.
**burst** (bũrst), *v.i.* [BURST, BURSTING], [AS. *berstan*], 1. to come apart suddenly and violently; break open or out; explode. 2. to give sudden expression in some way: as, she *burst* into tears. 3. to appear, enter, etc. suddenly and violently: as, he *burst* into the room. 4. to be full beyond normal capacity; bulge. *v.t.* 1. to cause to burst or explode. 2. to make swell to the bursting point. *n.* 1. a bursting; explosion. 2. the result of a bursting; break; breach. 3. a sudden activity or spurt: as, a *burst* of speed.
**bur·then** (bũr′*th*ən), *n. & v.t.* [Archaic], burden.
**Bu·run·di** (boo-roon′di), *n.* a country in east central Africa: area, 10,745 sq. mi.; pop., 2,600,000; capital, Bujumbura.
**bur·y** (ber′i), *v.t.* [-IED, -YING], [AS. *byrgan;* akin to AS. *beorgan,* conceal], 1. to put (a dead body) into the earth, a tomb, the sea, etc.; inter. 2. to perform funeral services for. 3. to cover for, or as if for, concealment. 4. to put away: as, we *buried* our friendship. 5. to sink; immerse: as, he *buries* himself in his studies.
**burying ground,** a cemetery; graveyard.
**bus** (bus), *n.* [*pl.* BUSES, BUSSES], [< *omnibus*], 1. a large motor coach that can carry many passengers, generally following a regular route; omnibus. 2. [Colloq.], an automobile.
**bus.,** business.
**bus boy,** a waiter's assistant who clears tables, brings water, etc.
**bus·by** (buz′bi), *n.* [*pl.* -BIES (-biz)], [prob. < the name *Busby*], a tall fur hat, worn by hussars, artillerymen, and engineers in the British army.

BUSBY

**bush** (boosh), *n.* [< ON.; prob. < ML. *boscus;* ? < Frank. *busk,* forest], 1. a low-spreading, woody plant, generally smaller than a tree; shrub. 2. a thick tail or anything else resembling a bush. 3. shrubby woodland; wild or uncleared country. *v.i.* 1. to grow thickly. 2. to have the shape of a bush. *v.t.* to decorate, etc. by setting bushes. **—beat around the bush,** to talk around a subject without getting to the point.
**bush** (boosh), *n.* [D. *bos,* a box; see BOX], a bushing (metal lining). *v.t.* to put a bushing in.
**bushed** (boosht), *adj.* [Colloq.], tired; fatigued.
**bush·el** (boosh′əl), *n.* [< OFr. *boissil,* grain measure], 1. a unit of dry measure for grain, fruit, etc., equal to 4 pecks or 8 gallons: abbrev. **bu.** 2. any container with a capacity of one bushel. 3. loosely, any large quantity.
**bush·el** (boosh′əl), *v.t. & v.i.* [-ELED or -ELLED, -ELING or -ELLING], [? < G. *bosseln,* to repair], in *tailoring,* to alter or mend. **—bush′el·er, bush′el·ler, bush′el·man** [*pl.* -MEN], *n.*
**bush·el·bas·ket** (boosh′əl-bas′kit, -bäs′-), *n.* a rounded basket with a capacity of one bushel.
**bu·shi·do, Bu·shi·do** (bōō′shē-dō′), *n.* [Japan., way of the warrior], the code of conduct for the samurai of feudal Japan.
**bush·ing** (boosh′iŋ), *n.* [< *bush* (bushing)], a removable metal lining, for reducing the effect of friction on moving parts.
**bush league,** [Slang], in *baseball,* a small or second-rate minor league.
**bush leaguer,** [Slang], 1. a player in a bush league. 2. any second-rate performer.
**Bush·man** (boosh′mən), *n.* [*pl.* -MEN], [< D. *boschjesman* < *bosch* (see BUSH, 3) + *man,* man], a member of a nomadic people living in SW Africa.
**bush·man** (boosh′mən), *n.* [*pl.* -MEN], 1. one who lives in the Australian bush. 2. a backwoodsman.
**bush·mas·ter** (boosh′mas′tẽr, -mäs′-), *n.* a large, poisonous snake of Central and South America.
**bush·rang·er** (boosh′rān′jẽr), *n.* [see BUSH (wild country) & RANGE, *v.*], 1. one who lives as a wanderer in the bush. 2. in Australia, a person, especially a highwayman, who makes the bush his hide-out.
**bush·whack·er** (boosh′hwak′ẽr), *n.* [< D. *boschwachter,* forest watcher; now associated with *whack*], 1. a backwoodsman. 2. a guerrilla fighter, especially one on the Confederate side in the Civil War. **—bush′whack′ing,** *n.*
**bush·y** (boosh′i), *adj.* [-IER, -IEST], 1. covered or overgrown with bushes. 2. bushlike; thick and spreading. **—bush′i·ness,** *n.*
**bus·i·ly** (biz′'l-i), *adv.* in a busy manner.
**busi·ness** (biz′nis), *n.* [AS. *bisignes;* see BUSY], 1. one's work; occupation; profession. 2. rightful concern or responsibility. 3. a matter or affair. 4. the buying and selling of goods; commerce; trade. 5. a commercial or industrial establishment; store, factory, etc. 6. action in a drama to take up a pause in dialogue, etc. *adj.* of or for business. Abbrev. **bus. —business is business,** sentiment, friendship, etc. cannot be allowed to interfere with profit-making. **—have no business,** to have no right (to do something). **—mean business,** [Colloq.], to be in earnest.
**business college** (or **school**), a school offering instruction in stenography, office routine, etc.
**busi·ness·like** (biz′nis-līk′), *adj.* efficient, methodical, systematic, etc.
**busi·ness·man** (biz′nis-man′), *n.* [*pl.* -MEN], a man in business, especially as an owner or executive. **—busi′ness·wom′an** [*pl.* -WOMEN], *n.fem.*

**bus·kin** (bus′kin), *n.* [? < OFr. < MD. *brosekin*, small leather], 1. a boot reaching to the calf or knee, worn long ago. 2. the high, thick-soled, laced boot worn by actors in ancient Greek and Roman tragedy. 3. tragic drama. —**bus′kined,** *adj.*

BUSKINS

**bus·man** (bus′mən), *n.* [*pl.* -MEN], the driver or conductor of a bus.
**busman's holiday,** a holiday in which one does much the same thing as his daily work.
**buss** (bus), *n., v.t. & v.i.* [? akin to G. dial. (or W. & Gael.) *bus*], [Archaic or Dial.], kiss.
**bus·ses** (bus′iz), *n.* alt. pl. of **bus.**
**bust** (bust), *n.* [< Fr. < It. *busto*], 1. a piece of sculpture representing a person's head, shoulders, and upper chest. 2. a woman's bosom.
**bust** (bust), *v.t. & v.i.* [orig., dial. var. of *burst*], [Slang], 1. to burst; break. 2. to make or become bankrupt. 3. to demote or become demoted. 4. to tame: said of broncos, etc. 5. to hit or punch. *n.* [Slang], 1. a failure. 2. a blow or punch. 3. a spree.
**bus·tard** (bus′tẽrd), *n.* [OFr. *bistard, oustard* < Pr. < L. *avis tarda*, lit., slow bird], a large, long-legged game bird of Europe, Asia, and Africa.
**bus·tle** (bus′'l), *v.i. & v.t.* [-TLED, -TLING], [< ME. *busken*, to prepare < ON.], to hurry busily, fussily, and noisily. *n.* noisy, hurried activity. —**bus′tler,** *n.* —**bus′tling·ly,** *adv.*
**bus·tle** (bus′'l), *n.* [< G. *buschel*, a bunch, pad], a framework or padding worn by women to fill out the upper back of a skirt.

BUSTLE

**bus·y** (biz′i), *adj.* [-IER, -IEST], [AS. *bisig*], 1. active; at work. 2. full of activity; constantly moving. 3. being used: said especially of a telephone. 4. meddlesome. *v.t.* [-IED, -YING], to make or keep busy. —**bus′y·ness,** *n.*
**bus·y·bod·y** (biz′i-bod′i), *n.* [*pl.* -IES], one who concerns himself with other people's affairs.
**but** (but; *unstressed,* bət), *prep.* [< AS. *butan*, without < *be*, by + *utan*, out < *ut*, out], 1. except; save; as, nobody came *but* me. 2. other than; otherwise than: as, we cannot choose *but* stay. *conj.* I. *co-ordinating*: 1. only: as, nobody came *but* I (came). 2. yet; still; however: as, it's bad, *but* it could be worse. 3. on the contrary: as, I am old, *but* you are young. II. *subordinating*: 1. unless: as, it never rains *but* it pours. 2. that: as, I don't question *but* you're correct. 3. that . . . not: as, I never think of summer *but* I think of childhood. 4. otherwise than; other than: as, I cannot *but* try. 5. who . . . not; which . . . not: as, not a man *but* felt it. *adv.* 1. only: as, if I had *but* known. 2. merely: as, he is *but* a child. 3. just: as, I heard it *but* now. *But* is often indistinguishable as any one of the preceding parts of speech. —**all but,** very nearly; almost. —**but for,** if it were not for.
**bu·ta·di·ene** (bū′tə-dī′ēn, -dī-ēn′), *n.* [*butane* + *di-* + *-ene*], a hydrocarbon, $C_4H_6$, used to make buna, a synthetic rubber.
**bu·tane** (bū′tān, bū-tān′), *n.* [L. *butyrum* (see BUTTER); + *-ane*], either of two isomeric hydrocarbons in the methane series, with the formula $C_4H_{10}$.
**butch·er** (booch′ẽr), *n.* [< OFr. < *boc*, he-goat], 1. one whose work is killing animals or dressing their carcasses for meat. 2. one who sells meat. 3. any brutal or unfeeling killer. 4. a vendor of candy, magazines, etc., as in railroad cars. *v.t.* 1. to kill or dress (animals) for meat. 2. to kill brutally or in large numbers; slaughter. 3. to botch; mangle. —**butch′er·er,** *n.*
**butch·er·bird** (booch′ẽr-būrd′), *n.* a shrike.
**butch·er's-broom** (booch′ẽrz-brōōm′, -broom′), *n.* [? < former use by butchers for sweeping their shops], a plant with glossy, leaflike branches, clusters of small white flowers, and large, red berries.
**butch·er·y** (booch′ẽr-i), *n.* [*pl.* -IES], 1. a slaughterhouse. 2. the work or business of a butcher. 3. brutal bloodshed.
**but·ler** (but′lẽr), *n.* [< OFr. < *bouteille*, a bottle], a manservant, now usually the head servant of a household, in charge of wines, pantry, etc.
**But·ler, Samuel** (but′lẽr), 1. 1612–1680; English poet. 2. 1835–1902; English novelist.
**butler's pantry,** a serving pantry between the kitchen and the dining room.
**but·ler·y** (but′lẽr-i), *n.* [*pl.* -IES], the butler's pantry; buttery.
**butt** (but), *n.* [? < OFr. *bout*, end, or ? < ON. *būtr*, block of wood], 1. the thick end of anything. 2. a stub or stump, as of a partially smoked cigarette. 3. a mound of earth on a target range for receiving fired rounds. 4. *pl.* a target range. 5. an object of ridicule or criticism. 6. [Slang], a cigarette. 7. [Slang], the buttocks. *v.t. & v.i.* to join end to end.
**butt** (but), *v.t.* [OFr. *buter* (< Frank. *botan*), to thrust against < OHG. *bōzan*, to beat], 1. to ram with the head. 2. to strike against. *v.i.* 1. to make a butting motion. 2. to project. *n.* a butting. —**butt in,** [Slang], 1. to meddle. 2. to intrude. —**butt into,** [Slang], to interfere or meddle in. —**butt′er,** *n.*
**butt** (but), *n.* [< Fr. & It. *botte* < LL. *bottis*, cask], 1. a large cask for wine or beer. 2. a measure of liquid capacity equal to 126 gallons or two hogsheads.
**butte** (būt), *n.* [Fr., mound], a steep hill standing all alone in a plain; small mesa.
**but·ter** (but′ẽr), *n.* [< AS. < L. *butyrum* < Gr. *boutyron* < *bous*, ox, cow + *tyros*, cheese], 1. the thick, yellowish product that results from churning the fatty part of milk. 2. any of various substances somewhat like butter: as, peanut *butter*. *v.t.* 1. to spread with butter. 2. [Colloq.], to flatter (often with *up*). —**but′ter·like′,** *adj.*
**butter bean,** 1. the wax bean. 2. the lima bean: so called in the southern U.S.
**but·ter·cup** (but′ẽr-kup′), *n.* 1. a plant of the crowfoot family, with yellow, cup-shaped flowers. 2. its flower.
**but·ter·fat** (but′ẽr-fat′), *n.* the fatty part of milk, from which butter is made.
**but·ter·fin·gers** (but′ẽr-fiŋ′gẽrz), *n.* [Colloq.], a person who drops things easily.
**but·ter·fish** (but′ẽr-fish′), *n.* [*pl.* see FISH], any of various fishes with a slippery coating.
**but·ter·fly** (but′ẽr-flī′), *n.* [*pl.* -FLIES], [< AS. *buttorfleoge*], 1. an insect having a sucking mouth part, slender body, and four broad wings, usually bright-colored. 2. a person, especially a woman, thought of as like a butterfly in being brightly dressed, frivolous, etc.
**butter knife,** a small, dull-edged knife for cutting or spreading butter.
**but·ter·milk** (but′ẽr-milk′), *n.* the sour liquid left after the butterfat in milk has been made into butter.
**but·ter·nut** (but′ẽr-nut′), *n.* 1. the edible, oily, hard-shelled nut of the North American white walnut tree. 2. this tree.
**but·ter·scotch** (but′ẽr-skoch′), *n.* a hard, sticky candy made from brown sugar and butter. *adj.* made of, or having the flavor of, butterscotch.
**but·ter·y** (but′ri, but′ẽr-i), *n.* [*pl.* -IES], [< OFr. < LL. *bottis*, cask], 1. a storeroom for whisky, wine, etc. 2. a pantry.
**but·ter·y** (but′ẽr-i), *adj.* 1. like butter. 2. containing or spread with butter.
**but·tock** (but′ək), *n.* [< ME. *but*, thick end + dim. *-ock*], 1. either of the two fleshy, rounded parts at the back of the hips. 2. *pl.* the rump.
**but·ton** (but′'n), *n.* [OFr. *boton*, a button < *buter*; see BUTT (to ram with head)], 1. any small disk or knob used as a fastening, ornament, emblem, etc., as on a garment. 2. anything small and shaped like a button. 3. a small knob for operating a doorbell, electric lamp, etc. 4. [Slang], the point of the jaw. *v.t. & v.i.* to fasten with or as with a button or buttons. —**but′ton·er,** *n.* —**but′ton·less,** *adj.* —**but′ton·like′,** *adj.*
**but·ton·hole** (but′'n-hōl′), *n.* a hole or slit in a garment, etc. into which a button is inserted. *v.t.* [-HOLED, -HOLING], 1. to make buttonholes in. 2. to detain in conversation; compel to listen.
**but·ton·hook** (but′'n-hook′), *n.* a hook for pulling buttons through buttonholes, as in some shoes.
**but·tons** (but′'nz), *n.pl.* [construed as sing.], [Colloq.], a bellboy, hotel page, etc.
**but·ton·wood** (but′'n-wood′), *n.* 1. a plane tree with buttonlike, hanging fruit; sycamore: also called **buttonball, button tree.** 2. its wood.
**but·ton·y** (but′'n-i), *adj.* 1. of or like a button. 2. having or decorated with many buttons.

**but·tress** (but′ris), *n.* [< OFr. < *buter;* see BUTT (to ram with head)], 1. a structure built against a wall to support or reinforce it. 2. a support; prop. *v.t.* 1. to support or reinforce with a buttress. 2. to prop up; bolster.

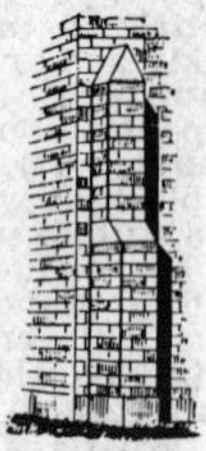
BUTTRESS

**bu·tyl** (bū′til), *n.* [L. *butyrum* (see BUTTER); + *-yl*], any of the four isomeric organic radicals $C_4H_9$.

**butyl alcohol,** any of the four isomeric alcohols $C_4H_9OH$.

**bu·tyr·ic** (bū-tir′ik), *adj.* [L. *butyrum* (see BUTTER); + *-ic*], of or obtained from butter.

**butyric acid,** colorless acid, $C_3H_7CO_2H$, with an unpleasant odor, found in rancid butter, etc.

**bux·om** (buk′səm), *adj.* [ME. *buhsum,* flexible, obedient < base of *bugan,* to bow], healthy, comely, plump, jolly, etc.: said of a woman or girl. **—bux′om·ly,** *adv.* **—bux′om·ness,** *n.*

**buy** (bī), *v.t.* [BOUGHT (bôt), BUYING], [AS. *bycgan*], 1. to get by paying money; purchase. 2. to get by a sacrifice: as, to *buy* fame with health. 3. to bribe. *v.i.* to buy things. *n.* 1. a buying. 2. anything bought or buyable. 3. [Colloq.], something bought or buyable that is worth the price. **—buy into,** [Slang], to pay money so as to get shares of, membership in, etc. **—buy off,** to bribe. **—buy out,** to buy all the stock, rights, etc. of **—buy up,** to buy all that is available of. **—buy′a·ble,** *adj.*

**buy·er** (bī′ẽr), *n.* 1. one who buys; consumer. 2. an employee whose work is to buy goods for a business firm, store, etc.

**buy·er's strike** (bī′ẽrz), an organized boycott by consumers in an attempt to bring down prices.

**buzz** (buz), *v.i.* [echoic], 1. to hum like a bee or fly. 2. to talk excitedly. 3. to gossip. *v.t.* 1. to tell (rumors, etc.) in a buzzing manner. 2. to make buzz. 3. to fly an airplane low over. 4. to signal with a buzzer. *n.* 1. a sound like a bee's hum. 2. a confused sound, as of many voices. 3. a rumor. **—buzz about** (or **around**), to scurry about. **—give (a person) a buzz,** [Slang], to telephone (a person).

**buz·zard** (buz′ẽrd), *n.* [OFr. *busart* < L. *buteo,* kind of hawk], 1. any of various hawks that are slow and heavy in flight. 2. the turkey buzzard.

**buzz bomb,** [Colloq.], a self-propelled, guided bomb, used by Nazi Germany in World War II.

**buz·zer** (buz′ẽr), *n.* an electrical device that makes a buzzing noise, used as a signal.

**buzz saw,** a circular saw driven by a motor.

**B.V.M.,** *Beata Virgo Maria,* [L.], Blessed Virgin Mary.

**B.V.Sc.,** Bachelor of Veterinary Science.

**bx.,** [*pl.* BXS.], box.

**by** (bī), *prep.* [AS. *be* (unstressed), *bi* (stressed)], 1. near; at; beside: as, stand *by* the door. 2. *a*) in or during: as, he travels *by* night. *b*) for a fixed time: as, she works *by* the hour. *c*) not later than: as, be back *by* ten o'clock. 3. *a*) through: as, we went *by* way of New York. *b*) past; beyond: as, he walked right *by* me. 4. in behalf of: as, he did well *by* me. 5. through the means, work, or operations of: as, made *by* human labor.. 6. *a*) according to: as, he fights *by* the book. *b*) in: as, it grows dark *by* degrees. 7. *a*) in or to the amount or degree of: as, apples *by* the peck, multiply six *by* ten. *b*) and in another dimension: as, a board two *by* four inches. 8. following: as, day *by* day, two *by* two. *adv.* 1. close at hand; near: as, stand *by.* 2. away; aside: as, to put money *by.* 3. past; beyond: as, he sped *by.* *adj. & n.* bye. **—by and by,** after a while. **—by and large,** in most respects. **—by the by,** incidentally.

**by-,** a prefix meaning: 1. *close by, near,* as in *bystander.* 2. *secondary,* as in *by-product.*

**by-and-by** (bī′'n-bī′), *n.* future time.

**bye** (bī), *n.* [see BY], 1. in sports in which competitors are paired, the position of the odd man, who advances to the next round without playing. 2. in *golf,* any holes left unplayed at the end of a match. *adj.* incidental. **—by the bye,** incidentally.

**bye-bye** (bī′bī′), *n. & interj.* good-by.

**by-e·lec·tion** (bī′i-lek′shən), *n.* a special election held in the interval between regular elections, generally to fill a vacancy.

**Bye·lo·rus·sia** (bye′lə-rush′ə), *n.* the Byelorussian S.S.R.: also sp. **Belorussia.**

**Bye·lo·rus·sian** (bye′lə-rush′ən), *adj.* of Byelorussia. *n.* 1. a native or inhabitant of Byelorussia. 2. the dialect of Russian spoken in Byelorussia.

**Byelorussian Soviet Socialist Republic,** a republic of the U.S.S.R., in W European Russia: area, 89,300 sq. mi.; pop., 5,568,000; capital, Minsk: also called *White Russian Soviet Socialist Republic.*

**by·gone** (bī′gôn′, -gon′), *adj.* past; gone by. *n.* anything that is gone or past. **—let bygones be bygones,** to let past offenses be forgotten.

**by·law** (bī′lô′), *n.* [*by-* < ME. *by,* town (< ON. *bȳr,* village < *būa,* to dwell); + *law*], 1. a law of local application adopted by an organization or assembly. 2. a secondary law or rule.

**by-line** (bī′lin′), *n.* a line printed above a newspaper article, etc., telling who wrote it.

**by-pass** (bī′pas′, -päs′), *n.* 1. a way, path, pipe, channel, etc. between two points that avoids or is auxiliary to the main way; detour. 2. in *electricity,* a shunt. *v.t.* 1. to detour. 2. to ignore. 3. to furnish with a by-pass. **—by′-passed′,** *adj.*

**by·path, by-path** (bī′path′, -päth′), *n.* a side path; private or little-used path.

**by·play** (bī′plā′), *n.* action going on aside from the main action, as in a play.

**by-prod·uct** (bī′prod′əkt), *n.* anything produced in the course of making another thing; secondary or incidental product or result.

**by·road** (bī′rōd′), *n.* a side road.

**By·ron, George Gordon** (bī′rən), sixth Baron Byron, 1788–1824; English poet.

**By·ron·ic** (bī-ron′ik), *adj.* like or characteristic of Byron or his writings; romantic, proud, cynical, ironic, etc. **—By·ron′i·cal·ly,** *adv.*

**by·stand·er** (bī′stand′ẽr), *n.* a person who stands near but does not participate; onlooker.

**by·way** (bī′wā′), *n.* a side path or road.

**by·word** (bī′wūrd′), *n.* 1. a familiar saying; proverb. 2. a person or thing proverbial as being contemptible or ridiculous.

**By·zan·tine** (biz′'n-tēn′, biz′'n-tīn′, bi-zan′tin), *adj.* 1. of or like Byzantium or the Byzantine Empire, its culture, etc. 2. designating or of a style of architecture developed in Byzantium, characterized by domes, round arches, mosaics, etc. *n.* a native or inhabitant of Byzantium.

**Byzantine Empire,** the eastern division of the later Roman Empire (395–1453 A.D.): capital, Byzantium: also called *Eastern Empire.*

**By·zan·ti·um** (bi-zan′shi-əm, -ti-əm), *n.* an ancient city on the Bosporus: Istanbul (Constantinople) was built on its site.

# C

**C, c** (sē), *n.* [*pl.* C's, c's, Cs, cs], 1. the third letter of the English alphabet. 2. a sound of C or c. *adj.* third in a sequence or group.

**C** (sē), *n.* 1. a Roman numeral for 100. 2. in *chemistry, the symbol for* carbon. 3. in *music,* a) the first tone in the scale of C major. b) the scale having C as the keynote. *adj.* shaped like C.

**C-,** cargo transport: followed by a number to designate the model of U.S. Army airplane designed to carry cargo or troops.

**C.,** 1. Catholic. 2. Congress. 3. Corps. 4. Court.

**C., c.,** 1. carton. 2. case. 3. cent; cents. 4. centigrade. 5. centimeter. 6. century. 7. [*pl.* CC.], chapter. 8. circa. 9. copyright. 10. cubic.

**c.,** 1. catcher. 2. center.

**Ca,** in *chemistry,* calcium.

**ca.,** 1. cathode. 2. centiare; centiares. 3. circa.
**C. A.,** 1. Central America. 2. Coast Artillery.
**CAA,** Civil Aeronautics Administration.
**Caa·ba** (kä′bə, kä′ə-bə), *n.* the Kaaba.
**cab** (kab), *n.* [< *cabriolet*], 1. an automobile or carriage for public hire; taxicab. 2. the place in a locomotive, motor truck, crane, derrick, etc. where the operator sits.
**ca·bal** (kə-bal′), *n.* [Fr., intrigue < ML. *cabbala;* see CABALA], 1. a small group of persons joined in a secret scheme; junto. 2. the intrigues of such a group; plot. *v.i.* [-BALLED, -BALLING], to join in a cabal; plot; intrigue.
**cab·a·la** (kab′ə-lə, kə-bä′lə), *n.* [< ML. < Heb. *qabbālāh*, received lore < *qābal*, to receive], 1. an occult religious philosophy developed by certain medieval rabbis, based on a mystical interpretation of the Scriptures. 2. occultism; mystical doctrine. Also sp. **cabbala, kabala. —cab′a·lism,** *n.* **—cab′a·list,** *n.*
**cab·a·lis·tic** (kab′ə-lis′tik), *adj.* 1. of the cabala. 2. secret; mystic. Also **cab′a·lis′ti·cal. —cab′a·lis′ti·cal·ly,** *adv.*
**ca·bal·le·ro** (kab′əl-yâr′ō; Sp. kä′bä-lye′rô), *n.* [*pl.* -ROS (-ōz; Sp. -rôs)], [Sp. < *caballo;* see CAVALIER], a Spanish gentleman or knight.
**ca·ba·na** (kə-bä′nə; Sp. kä-bä′nyä), *n.* [Sp. *cabaña;* LL. *capanna*, hut], 1. a cabin or hut. 2. a small shelter used as a bathhouse. Also **cabaña.**
**cab·a·ret** (kab′ə-rā′, kab′ə-rā′), *n.* [Fr. < Norm. dial.], 1. a restaurant or café with dancing and singing as entertainment. 2. such entertainment.
**cab·bage** (kab′ij), *n.* [OFr. *caboche;* dial. It. *kapocco* (< L. *caput*), the head], a common vegetable of the mustard family, with thick leaves compressed into a round head on a short stalk. *v.i.* [-BAGED, -BAGING], to form a cabbagelike head.
**cabbage palm** (or **tree**), any of several palms with terminal buds used as a vegetable; palmetto.
**cab·by** (kab′i), *n.* [*pl.* -BIES], [Colloq.], a cabman.
**cab·ette** (kab-et′), *n.* a woman taxicab driver.
**cab·in** (kab′in), *n.* [< OFr. < Pr. < LL. *capanna*, hut], 1. a small, roughly constructed house; hut. 2. any enclosed office, bedroom, etc. on a ship. 3. an enclosed space for passengers in an aircraft. *v.t.* to confine in or as in a cabin; cramp.
**cabin boy,** a boy whose work is to serve the officers and passengers aboard a ship.
**cabin cruiser,** a powerboat with a cabin and the necessary equipment for living on board: also **cruiser.**
**cab·i·net** (kab′ə-nit), *n.* [Fr., dim. of *cabine* < Eng. *cabin*], 1. a case with drawers or shelves to hold or display things. 2. formerly, a private council room. 3. [often C-], a body of official advisers to the chief executive of a nation, usually the heads of the various governmental departments. *adj.* 1. private; secret; confidential. 2. valuable or beautiful enough to keep in a case or a private room. 3. of a political cabinet.
**cab·i·net·mak·er** (kab′ə-nit-māk′ẽr), *n.* a workman who makes fine furniture or woodwork. **—cab′i·net·mak′ing,** *n.*
**cab·i·net·work** (kab′ə-nit-wũrk′), *n.* fine woodwork. **—cab′i·net·work′er,** *n.*
**ca·ble** (kā′b'l), *n.* [OFr. < LL. *capulum* < L. *capere*, to take hold], 1. a thick, heavy rope, now often of wire. 2. a cable's length. 3. a protected bundle of insulated wires through which an electric current can be passed. 4. a cablegram. *v.t.* [-BLED, -BLING], 1. to fasten with a cable. 2. to transmit by means of a cable under the sea. 3. to send a cablegram to. *v.i.* to send a cablegram.
**cable car,** a car drawn by a moving cable.
**ca·ble·gram** (kā′b'l-gram′), *n.* a message sent across the sea by telegraphic cable.
**cable railway,** a street railway on which cars are pulled by a continuously moving underground cable.
**cable's length,** a unit of nautical measure equal (in the U.S. Navy) to 720 feet (120 fathoms).
**cab·man** (kab′mən), *n.* [*pl.* -MEN], a cab driver.
**ca·boo·dle** (kə-bōō′d'l), *n.* [< *kit, kith*, family, relations + *boodle* < D. *boedel*, property], [Slang], lot; number; group: as, the whole *caboodle.*
**ca·boose** (kə-bōōs′), *n.* [MD. *kabuys*, earlier *kaban huis*, cabin house, ship's galley; see CABIN], 1. a ship's galley or kitchen. 2. the trainmen's car on a freight train, usually at the rear.
**Cab·ot, John** (kab′ət), 1450–1498; Italian navigator for England; discovered North America (1497).
**cab·ri·o·let** (kab′ri-ə-lā′), *n.* [Fr., dim. of *cabriole*, a leap < It. < L. < *caper*, he-goat], 1. a light two-wheeled carriage, usually with a hood that folds, drawn by one horse. 2. an automobile somewhat like a coupe, with a folding top.

CABRIOLET

**cab·stand** (kab′stand′), *n.* a place where cabs are stationed for hire.
**ca·ca·o** (kə-kā′ō, -kä′ō), *n.* [*pl.* -CAOS], [Sp. < Mex. *cacauatl*, cacao seed], 1. a small evergreen tree grown in tropical America for its seeds. 2. the seed, from which cocoa and chocolate are made: also **cacao bean.**
**cach·a·lot** (kash′ə-lot′, -lō′), *n.* [Fr. < Sp.; ? < Port. *cachola*, big head], the sperm whale.
**cache** (kash), *n.* [Fr. < *cacher*, to conceal < L. *coacticare*, to store up], 1. a place in which stores of food, supplies, etc. are hidden. 2. anything so stored or hidden. *v.t. & v.i.* [CACHED, CACHING], to hide or store in a cache.
**ca·chet** (ka-shā′, kash′ā), *n.* [Fr. < *cacher*, to hide], 1. originally, a seal or stamp on an official letter. 2. a distinguishing mark, as of quality. 3. a mark stamped or imprinted on mail.
**cach·in·nate** (kak′ə-nāt′), *v.i.* [-NATED, -NATING], [< L. pp. of *cachinnare;* of echoic origin], to laugh loudly or too much. **—cach′in·na′tion,** *n.*
**ca·cique** (kə-sēk′), *n.* [Sp. < Haitian word], in Latin America and the West Indies, a native chief.
**cack·le** (kak′'l), *v.i.* [-LED, -LING], [akin to D. *kakeln*, L. *cacillare;* of echoic origin], 1. to make the characteristic shrill sound of a hen. 2. to laugh or talk in a shrill manner; prattle. *v.t.* to utter in a cackling manner. *n.* 1. the act or sound of cackling. 2. silly talk; chatter.
**cac·o-,** [< Gr. *kakos*, bad, evil], a combining form meaning *bad, harsh, poor*, as in *cacography:* also, before a vowel, **cac-.**
**ca·cog·ra·phy** (ka-kog′rə-fi), *n.* [*caco-* + *-graphy*], 1. bad handwriting. 2. incorrect spelling. **—ca·cog′ra·pher,** *n.* **—cac·o·graph·ic** (kak′ə-graf′ik), **cac′o·graph′i·cal,** *adj.* **—cac′o·graph′i·cal·ly,** *adv.*
**ca·coph·o·ny** (kə-kof′ə-ni), *n.* [*pl.* -NIES], [Gr. < *kakos*, bad + *phōnē*, voice], harsh, jarring sound; discord. **—ca·coph′o·nous,** *adj.* **—ca·coph′o·nous·ly,** *adv.*
**cac·tus** (kak′təs), *n.* [*pl.* -TUSES, -TI (-tī)], [L. < Gr. *kaktos*, prickly], any of various plants with fleshy stems, spines or scales instead of leaves, and, sometimes, showy flowers: cactuses grow in hot, arid regions.
**cad** (kad), *n.* [< *cadet*], a man or boy whose behavior is not gentlemanly; ill-mannered fellow.
**ca·dav·er** (kə-dav′ẽr, -dā′vẽr), *n.* [L. < *cadere*, to fall], a dead body; corpse, as for dissection. **—ca·dav′er·ic,** *adj.*
**ca·dav·er·ous** (kə-dav′ẽr-əs), *adj.* of or like a cadaver; esp., pale, ghastly, gaunt, or haggard. **—ca·dav′er·ous·ly,** *adv.* **ca·dav′er·ous·ness,** *n.*

CACTUS
(prickly pear)

**cad·die** (kad′i), *n.* [Scot. form of Fr. *cadet;* see CADET], in *golf*, a person who attends a player, carrying his clubs, etc. *v.i.* [-DIED, -DYING], to act as a caddie. Also sp. **caddy.**
**caddis fly** (kad′is), [? < OFr. *cadas*, floss silk (with reference to the cocoon)], a small, mothlike fly: the larvae live in fresh water in cocoons covered with sand, gravel, etc.
**cad·dish** (kad′ish), *adj.* like or characteristic of a cad; ill-mannered. **—cad′dish·ly,** *adv.* **—cad′dish·ness,** *n.*
**caddis worm,** the wormlike larva of the caddis fly, used as bait by anglers.
**cad·dy** (kad′i), *n.* [*pl.* -DIES], [< Malay *kati*, weight equivalent to a little more than a pound], a small container for holding tea.
**cad·dy** (kad′i), *n.* [*pl.* -DIES] *& v.i.* [-DIED, -DYING], caddie.
**-cade** (kād), [< *cavalcade*], a suffix meaning *procession, parade*, as in *aquacade, motorcade.*
**ca·dence** (kā′d'ns), *n.* [ult. < L. ppr. of *cadere*, to fall], 1. fall of the voice in speaking. 2. flow of rhythm. 3. measured movement, as in marching, or the beat of such movement. 4. inflection or

modulation in tone. 5. in *music*, the harmonic ending, final trill, etc. of a phrase or movement. Also **ca′den·cy** [*pl.* -CIES]. —**ca′denced,** *adj.*
**ca·dent** (kā′d'nt), *adj.* having cadence; cadenced.
**ca·den·za** (kə-den′zə), *n.* [It.; see CADENCE], 1. an elaborate, often improvised musical passage played by the solo instrument in a concerto, usually near the end of the first movement. 2. any brilliant flourish in an aria or solo passage.
**ca·det** (kə-det′), *n.* [Fr. < Gascon *capdet*, lit., little chief, < L. *caput*, head + dim. suffix *-et*], 1. a younger son or brother in a gentleman's family. 2. a student in training to become an officer in the armed forces. 3. a student at a military school. —**ca·det′cy** [*pl.* -CIES], **ca·det′ship,** *n.*
**cadet teacher,** 1. an upperclass college student who does practice teaching. 2. a public school teacher assigned to a regular position but without its customary benefits, such as pension, etc., and paid at a daily rate.
**cadge** (kaj), *v.t. & v.i.* [CADGED, CADGING], [ME. *caggen*; prob. var. of *cacchen*, to catch], 1. [Dial.], to peddle. 2. [Colloq.], to beg or get by begging. —**cadg′er,** *n.*
**ca·di** (kä′di, kā′-), *n.* [Ar. *qādī*], a minor Moslem magistrate or judge.
**Cá·diz** (kā′diz, kə-diz′; Sp. kä′thēth), *n.* a seaport in SW Spain: pop., 76,000.
**Cad·me·an** (kad-mē′ən), *adj.* of or like Cadmus. —**Cadmean victory,** a victory won at great sacrifice.
**cad·mi·um** (kad′mi-əm), *n.* [Mod. L. < L. *cadmia*, zinc ore < *Cadmus*], a blue-white, malleable, ductile, metallic chemical element occurring in zinc ores: it is used in some alloys, electroplating, pigment, etc.: symbol, Cd; at. wt., 112.41; at. no., 48. —**cad′mic,** *adj.*
**Cad·mus** (kad′məs), *n.* in *Greek legend*, a Phoenician prince who killed a dragon and sowed its teeth: from these, armed men sprang up and fought until only five were left, who then helped Cadmus build Thebes.
**ca·dre** (kad′ri; Fr. kä′dr′), *n.* [Fr. < It. < L. *quadrum*, a square], 1. a framework. 2. a nucleus around which an expanded organization, as a military unit, can be built.
**ca·du·ce·us** (kə-dōō′si-əs, -dū′-), *n.* [*pl.* -CEI (-si-ī′)], [L.], 1. the staff of an ancient herald; esp., the winged staff with two serpents twined about it, carried by Mercury. 2. this staff as a symbol of the medical profession.—**ca·du′ce·an,** *adj.*

CADUCEUS

**cae·cum** (sē′kəm), *n.* [*pl.* -CA (-kə)], [L. < (*intestinum*) *caecum*, blind (intestine)], a cavity open at one end; esp., the pouch at the beginning of the large intestine: also sp. **cecum.** —**cae′cal,** *adj.*
**Caed·mon** (kad′mən), *n.* first English poet whose name is known; fl. 670 A.D.
**Cae·sar** (sē′zẽr), *n.* 1. Julius Caesar. 2. the title of the Roman emperors from Augustus to Hadrian. 3. an emperor or dictator.
**Caesar, Julius,** (*Gaius Julius Caesar*), 102?–44 B.C.; Roman statesman and general.
**Cae·sar·e·an, Cae·sar·i·an** (si-zâr′i-ən), *adj.* of Julius Caesar or the Caesars.
**Caesarean operation** (or **section**), a surgical operation for delivering a baby by cutting through the mother's abdominal and uterine walls: Julius Caesar was supposedly born in this manner.
**cae·si·um** (sē′zi-əm), *n.* cesium.
**cae·su·ra** (si-zhoor′ə, -zyoor′ə), *n.* [*pl.* -RAS, -RAE (-ē)], [L., a cutting < *caedere*, to cut], 1. a break or pause in a line of verse: in Greek and Latin verse, the caesura falls within the metrical foot; in English verse, it is usually about the middle of the line. 2. a pause showing rhythmic division of a melody. Also sp. **cesura.** —**cae·su′ral,** *adj.*
**ca·fé** (kə-fā′, ka-), *n.* [Fr.; see COFFEE], 1. a coffeehouse or restaurant. 2. coffee. 3. a barroom, sometimes providing entertainment.
‡**ca·fé au lait** (kȧ′fā′ ō′ lā′), [Fr.], 1. coffee with milk. 2. pale brown.
‡**ca·fé noir** (kȧ′fā′ nwȧr′), [Fr.], black coffee.
**café society,** a well-publicized set of habitual frequenters of cafés or night clubs.
**caf·e·te·ri·a** (kaf′ə-têr′i-ə), *n.* [Am. Sp., coffee store], a restaurant in which food is displayed on counters and patrons serve themselves.
**caf·fe·ine, caf·fe·in** (kaf′i-in, kaf′ēn′), *n.* [< Fr. < *café*, coffee], the alkaloid $C_8H_{10}N_4O_2$, present in coffee, tea, and kola: it is a stimulant to the heart and central nervous system.
**caf·tan** (kaf′tən, käf-tän′), *n.* [Turk. *qaftān*], a long-sleeved robe with a girdle, worn in eastern Mediterranean countries: also sp. **kaftan.**

CAFTAN

**cage** (kāj), *n.* [OFr.; L. *cavea*, hollow place], 1. a box or structure of wires, bars, etc. for confining birds or animals. 2. any openwork structure or frame. 3. an elevator car. 4. [Archaic], a jail. 5. in *baseball*, a backstop used for batting practice, etc. 6. in *basketball*, the basket. 7. in *hockey*, the network frame used as a goal. *v.t.* [CAGED, CAGING], to put in a cage; confine.
**cage·ling** (kāj′liŋ), *n.* a bird kept in a cage.
**cag·er** (kāj′ẽr), *n.* [Colloq.], a basketball player.
**cage·y** (kāj′i), *adj.* [prob. < *cage*, a jail], [CAGIER, CAGIEST], [Slang], sly; tricky; cunning: also sp. **cagy.** —**cag′i·ly,** *adv.* —**cag′i·ness,** *n.*
**ca·hoots** (kə-hōōts′), *n.pl.* [? < *cohort* or < Fr. *cahute*, a cabin], [Slang], partnership.—**go cahoots,** [Slang], to share alike. —**in cahoots,** [Slang], in partnership: usually applied to shady dealing.
**Cai·jan** (kā′jən), *n.* Cajun.
**cai·man** (kā′mən), *n.* a cayman.
**Cain** (kān), *n.* 1. in the *Bible*, the oldest son of Adam and Eve: he killed his brother Abel: Gen. 4; hence, 2. a murderer. —**raise Cain,** [Slang], to create a great commotion.
**ca·ique, ca·ïque** (kä-ēk′), *n.* [Fr. < It. < Turk. *qayiq*], a light rowboat used on the Bosporus.
**cairn** (kârn), *n.* [Scot. < Gael. *carn*], a conical heap of stones built as a monument or landmark. —**cairned,** *adj.*
**Cai·ro** (kī′rō), *n.* the capital of the United Arab Republic, in Egypt on the Nile: pop., 1,312,000.
**cais·son** (kā′sən), *n.* [Fr. < *caisse*, chest, box], 1. a chest for holding ammunition. 2. a two-wheeled wagon for transporting ammunition. 3. a watertight box inside which men can do construction work under water. 4. a watertight box for raising and floating sunken ships, etc.
**caisson disease,** decompression sickness.
**cai·tiff** (kā′tif), *n.* [OFr. *caitif*, a captive < L. < *capere*, to take], a mean, evil, or cowardly person. *adj.* evil; mean; cowardly.
**ca·jole** (kə-jōl′), *v.t. & v.i.* [-JOLED, -JOLING], [< Fr.; ? < OFr. *cageoler*, to use decoys to cage wild birds], to coax with false words, flattery, etc.; wheedle. —**ca·jole′ment,** *n.* —**ca·jol′er,** *n.*
**ca·jol·er·y** (kə-jōl′ẽr-i), *n.* [*pl.* -IES], a cajoling, or coaxing, wheedling, etc.
**Ca·jun** (kā′jən), *n.* [< *Acadian*], 1. a native of Louisiana supposed to have had Acadian French ancestors: sometimes used contemptuously. 2. the dialect of the Cajuns. Also sp. **Caijan.**
**cake** (kāk), *n.* [< ON; akin to Scand. *kaka*], 1. a small, flat mass of baked or fried dough or batter. 2. a mixture of flour, eggs, milk, sugar, etc. baked and often covered with icing. 3. a small, flat, fried mass of hashed meat or fish. 4. a shaped, solid mass, as of soap, ice, etc. *v.t. & v.i.* [CAKED, CAKING], to form into a hard mass. —**take the cake,** [Slang], 1. to win the prize. 2. to excel.
**cakes and ale,** the good things of life.
**cake·walk** (kāk′wôk′), *n.* a strutting dance developed by Negroes in the South competing for the prize of a cake. *v.i.* to perform a cakewalk.
**Cal.,** 1. California. 2. large calorie(s).
**cal.,** 1. calendar. 2. caliber. 3. small calorie(s).
**cal·a·bash** (kal′ə-bash′), *n.* [< Fr. < Pr.; ? < Per. *kharbuz*, melon], 1. a tropical American tree of the bignonia family. 2. its gourdlike fruit. 3. the dried, hollow shell of a gourd or calabash, used as a bowl, pipe, etc. 4. any of various gourds.
**cal·a·boose** (kal′ə-bōōs′, kal′ə-bōōs′), *n.* [Sp. *calabozo*], [Slang], a prison; jail.
**ca·la·di·um** (kə-lā′di-əm), *n.* [< Malay *kalādi*, kind of plant], a tropical American plant of the arum family, with large, brilliantly colored leaves.
**Cal·ais** (kal′ā, -is; Fr. kȧ′le′), *n.* a city in France, on the English Channel: pop., 50,000.
**cal·a·mine** (kal′ə-mīn′, -min), *n.* [Fr.; ML. *calamina* < L. *cadmia*; see CADMIUM], 1. hydrous zinc silicate, $(ZnOH)_2SiO_3$, a zinc ore. 2. native zinc carbonate, $ZnCO_3$.
**ca·lam·i·tous** (kə-lam′ə-təs), *adj.* causing or bringing calamity. —**ca·lam′i·tous·ly,** *adv.* —**ca·lam′i·tous·ness,** *n.*
**ca·lam·i·ty** (kə-lam′ə-ti), *n.* [*pl.* -TIES], [< Fr. < L. *calamitas*], 1. misery. 2. any extreme misfortune; disaster.
**cal·a·mus** (kal′ə-məs), *n.* [*pl.* -MI (-mī′)], [L. < Gr.

*kalamos*, a reed], 1. the sweet flag. 2. its aromatic root. 3. the quill of a feather.

**ca·lash** (kə-lash′), *n.* [Fr. *calèche* < Czech *kolésa*; prob. < *kolo*, a wheel], 1. a light, low-wheeled carriage, usually with a folding top: also **calèche.** 2. a folding top of a carriage. 3. a folding hood or bonnet, worn by women in the 18th century.

**cal·ca·ne·us** (kal-kā′ni-əs), *n.* [LL. < L. < *calx*, the heel], the heel bone: also **cal·ca′ne·um** (-əm).

**cal·car·e·ous** (kal-kâr′i-əs), *adj.* [< L. < *calx*, lime], of or like calcium carbonate, calcium, or lime.

**cal·ces** (kal′sēz), *n.* alt. pl. of **calx.**

**cal·ci-,** [< L. *calx*, lime], a combining form meaning calcium or lime, as in *calcify*.

**cal·cif·er·ol** (kal-sif′ẽr-ōl′, -ol′), *n.* [*calci*ferous + ergost*erol*], vitamin $D_2$: it is a crystalline alcohol, $C_{28}H_{43}OH$.

**cal·cif·er·ous** (kal-sif′ẽr-əs), *adj.* [*calci-* + *-ferous*], producing or containing calcite.

**cal·ci·fy** (kal′sə-fī′), *v.t.* & *v.i.* [-FIED, -FYING], [*calci-* + *-fy*], to change into a hard, stony substance by the deposit of lime or calcium salts. —**cal′ci·fi·ca′tion,** *n.*

**cal·ci·mine** (kal′sə-mīn′, -min), *n.* [< L. *calx*, lime], a white or colored liquid used as a wash for plastered walls, etc. *v.t.* [-MINED, -MINING], to cover with calcimine. Also sp. **kalsomine.**

**cal·cin·a·to·ry** (kal-sin′ə-tôr′i, kal′sin-ə-tō′ri), *adj.* for calcining. *n.* [*pl.* -RIES], a furnace or vessel for calcining.

**cal·cine** (kal′sīn′, -sin), *v.t.* & *v.i.* [-CINED, -CINING], [< Fr. < ML. *calcinare*], 1. to change to calx or powder by heat. 2. to burn to ashes or powder. —**cal′ci·na′tion,** *n.* —**cal′cin·er,** *n.*

**cal·cite** (kal′sīt′), *n.* calcium carbonate, $CaCO_3$, a mineral found as limestone, chalk, and marble.

**cal·ci·um** (kal′si-əm), *n.* [Mod. L. < L. *calx*, lime], a soft, silver-white metallic chemical element found combined in limestone, marble, chalk, etc.: symbol, Ca; at. wt., 40.08; at. no., 20.

**calcium carbide,** a dark-gray, crystalline compound, $CaC_2$, used in making acetylene.

**calcium carbonate,** a white powder or colorless, crystalline compound, $CaCO_3$, found mainly in limestone, marble, and chalk, and in bones, teeth, shells, and plant ash: used in making lime.

**calcium chloride,** a white, crystalline compound, $CaCl_2$, used in making ice, as a drying agent, etc.

**calcium hydroxide,** a white, crystalline compound, $Ca(OH)_2$, used in making alkalies, bleaching powder, plaster, etc.: also called *slaked lime.*

**calcium oxide,** a white, soft, caustic solid, CaO, prepared by heating calcium carbonate; quicklime.

**calcium phosphate,** any of a number of phosphates of calcium found in bones, teeth, etc.

**calc·spar, calc-spar (kalk′spär′),** *n.* **calcite.**

**cal·cu·la·ble** (kal′kyoo-lə-b'l), *adj.* that can be calculated. —**cal′cu·la·bil′i·ty,** *n.* —**cal′cu·la·bly,** *adv.*

**cal·cu·late** (kal′kyoo-lāt′), *v.t.* [-LATED, LATING], [< L. pp. of *calculare*, to reckon < *calculus*, pebble used in counting; dim. of *calx*, lime], 1. to determine by arithmetic; compute. 2. to determine by reasoning; estimate. 3. to plan; intend: used in the passive. 4. [Colloq.], to think; suppose. *v.i.* 1. to make a computation. 2. to rely (*on*).

**cal·cu·lat·ing** (kal′kyoo-lā′tiŋ), *adj.* 1. scheming; cunning. 2. shrewd; cautious.

**cal·cu·la·tion** (kal′kyoo-lā′shən), *n.* 1. a calculating. 2. something deduced by calculating. 3. forethought; prudence. —**cal′cu·la′tive,** *adj.*

**cal·cu·la·tor** (kal′kyoo-lā′tẽr), *n.* 1. a person who calculates. 2. a machine for doing rapid addition, subtraction, multiplication, and division: also **calculating machine.**

**cal·cu·lous** (kal′kyoo-ləs), *adj.* in *medicine*, caused by or having a calculus or calculi.

**cal·cu·lus** (kal′kyoo-ləs), *n.* [*pl.* -LI (-lī′), -LUSES], [L.; see CALCULATE], 1. an abnormal stony mass in the body. 2. in *higher mathematics*, a method of calculation or of analysis: see **differential calculus, integral calculus.**

**Cal·cut·ta** (kal-kut′ə), *n.* a seaport in NE India, on the Hooghly River: pop., 2,549,000.

**cal·dron** (kôl′drən), *n.* [< OFr. < L. *caldaria*, warm bath, pot < *calidus*, warm], a large kettle or boiler: also sp. **cauldron.**

‡**ca·lèche** (kȧ′lesh′), *n.* a calash.

**Cal·e·do·ni·a** (kal′ə-dō′ni-ə, -dōn′yə), *n.* [L.], [Poetic], Scotland. —**Cal′e·do′ni·an,** *adj.* & *n.*

**cal·e·fa·cient** (kal′ə-fā′shənt), *adj.* [< L. < *calere*, to be warm + *facere*, to make], making warm. *n.* a remedy that warms.

**cal·en·dar** (kal′ən-dẽr), *n.* [L. *calendarium*, account book < *calendae*, calends], 1. a system of determining the beginning, length, and divisions of a year. 2. a table, register, etc. that shows the days, weeks, and months of a given year. 3. a list or schedule, as of pending court cases. *v.t.* to enter in a calendar; schedule.

**calendar day,** the twenty-four hours from one midnight to the next midnight.

**calendar month,** any of the twelve divisions of a year.

**calendar year,** the period of 365 days (366 in a leap year) from Jan. 1 to Dec. 31.

**cal·en·der** (kal′ən-dẽr), *n.* [< Fr. < LL. < L. < Gr. *kylindros*, cylinder], a machine with rollers between which paper or cloth is run to give it a smooth or glossy finish. *v.t.* to press (paper, cloth, etc.) in a calender. —**cal′en·der·er,** *n.*

**cal·ends** (kal′əndz), *n.pl.* [L. *calendae* < *calare*, to announce solemnly < Gr. *kalein*, to proclaim], the first day of each month in the ancient Roman calendar: also sp. **kalends.**

**ca·len·du·la** (kə-len′jə-lə), *n.* [< L. *calendae*, calends: prob. because the plants flower in most months of the year], any of various plants of the daisy family, with yellow or orange flowers.

**ca·les·cent** (kə-les′'nt), *adj.* [< L. < *calescere*, to grow warm], growing warm; getting hot. —**ca·les′cence** (-'ns), *n.*

**calf** (kaf, käf), *n.* [*pl.* CALVES (kavz, kävz)], [AS. *cealf* & ON. *kalfr*], 1. a young cow or bull. 2. the young of some other large animals, as the elephant, whale, hippopotamus, seal, etc. 3. leather from the hide of a calf; calfskin. 4. [Colloq.], an awkward, callow, or silly young person. —**kill the fatted calf,** to make a feast of welcome.

**calf** (kaf, käf), *n.* [*pl.* CALVES (kavz, kävz)], [ON. *kalfi*], the fleshy back part of the leg between the knee and the ankle.

**calf love,** [Colloq.], the immature love that boys and girls may feel for each other; puppy love.

**calf·skin** (kaf′skin′, käf′skin′), *n.* 1. the skin of a calf. 2. leather made from this.

**Cal·i·ban** (kal′ə-ban′), *n.* the deformed, savage slave in Shakespeare's *The Tempest.*

**cal·i·ber** (kal′ə-bẽr), *n.* [< Fr. & Sp.; prob. < Ar. *qālib*, a mold], 1. the size of a bullet or shell as measured by its diameter. 2. the diameter of the bore of a gun. 3. the diameter of a cylindrical body or of its hollowed interior. 4. quality; ability. Also sp. **calibre.**

**cal·i·brate** (kal′ə-brāt′), *v.t.* [-BRATED, -BRATING], 1. to determine the caliber of. 2. to fix, check, or correct the graduations of (a measuring instrument, as a thermometer). —**cal′i·bra′tion,** *n.* —**cal′i·bra′tor,** *n.*

**cal·i·co** (kal′ə-kō′), *n.* [*pl.* -COES, -COS], [< *Calicut*, India, where first obtained], any of several kinds of cotton cloth, usually coarse and printed. *adj.* 1. of calico. 2. like calico; spotted.

**Cal·i·cut** (kal′ə-kut′), *n.* a seaport in S India, on the western coast: pop., 159,000.

**Cal·i·for·ni·a** (kal′ə-fôr′nyə, -ni-ə), *n.* a Western State of the U.S., on the Pacific Coast: area, 158,693 sq. mi.; pop., 15,717,000; capital, Sacramento. —**Cal′i·for′ni·an,** *adj.* & *n.*

**California, Gulf of,** an arm of the Pacific, between Lower California and the Mexican mainland.

**cal·i·for·ni·um** (kal′ə-fôr′ni-əm), *n.* [< University of *California*], a radioactive chemical element produced by the atomic bombardment of curium: symbol, Cf; at. wt., 244(?); at. no., 98.

**cal·i·per** (kal′ə-pẽr), *n.* [var. of *caliber*], *usually pl.* an instrument consisting of a pair of hinged legs, used to measure the thickness or diameter of something. *v.t.* & *v.i.* to measure with calipers. Also sp. **calliper.**

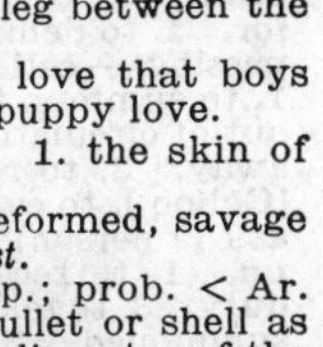

CALIPERS

**ca·liph** (kā′lif, kal′if), *n.* [< OFr. < Ar. *khalīfa*], supreme ruler; successor: the title taken by Mohammed's successors as heads of Islam: also sp. **calif, kalif, kaliph, khalif.**

**cal·iph·ate** (kal′ə-fāt′, -fit), *n.* the rank, reign, or dominion of a caliph.

**cal·is·then·ic** (kal'əs-then'ik), *adj.* relating to calisthenics: also sp. **callisthenic**: also **cal'is·then'i·cal, cal'lis·then'i·cal.**

**cal·is·then·ics** (kal'əs-then'iks), *n.pl.* [< Gr. *kallos*, beauty + *sthenos*, strength], 1. athletic exercises; simple gymnastics. 2. [construed as sing.], the art of developing bodily strength and gracefulness by such exercises. Also sp. **callisthenics.**

**calk** (kôk), *n.* [AS. *calc*, shoe < L. *calx*, a heel], 1. the part of a horseshoe that projects downward to prevent slipping. 2. a metal plate fastened to the heel or sole of a shoe to prevent slipping: also **calker.** *v.t.* to fasten calks on.

**calk** (kôk), *v.t.* [< OFr. < L. *calcare*, to tread < *calx*, a heel], 1. to make (a boat, etc.) watertight by filling the seams or cracks with oakum, tar, etc. 2. to stop up (cracks of windows, pipes, etc.) with a filler. Also sp. **caulk.** —**calk'er,** *n.*

**call** (kôl), *v.t.* [AS. *ceallian* < ON. *kalla*], 1. to say in a loud tone; shout. 2. to summon. 3. to convoke, as a court or legislative body (often with *together*). 4. to name. 5. to summon, as to a specific duty: as, he was *called* to the army. 6. to address an appeal to. 7. to awaken (a person). 8. to give a signal to. 9. to telephone. 10. to estimate or consider as being. 11. to stop (a baseball game, etc.). 12. to demand payment of, as a loan. 13. in *games*, to tell the aim of (a shot) before making it. 14. in *poker*, to require a show of cards by equaling the bet of (another player). *v.i.* 1. to speak in a loud tone; shout. 2. to visit for a short while (often with *on*). 3. to telephone. 4. in *poker*, to require a show of cards by equaling another's bet. *n.* 1. a calling. 2. a loud utterance. 3. a summons; invitation. 4. a signaling; signal. 5. a demand: as, a *call* for low-priced books. 6. the distinctive cry of an animal or bird. 7. religious vocation regarded as divinely inspired. 8. need; occasion: as, no *call* for laughter. 9. an order or demand for payment. 10. a brief, usually formal visit. —**call back,** 1. to ask or command to come back. 2. to retract. 3. to telephone again or in return. —**call down,** 1. to invoke. 2. [Slang], to scold. —**call for,** 1. to demand. 2. to come and get; stop for in passing. —**call forth,** to bring into play. —**call in,** 1. to summon for help or consultation. 2. to take out of circulation, as bonds. —**call off,** 1. to order away. 2. to read aloud in order from a list. 3. [Colloq.], to cancel a scheduled event. —**call on,** to ask (a person) to speak. —**call out,** to shout. —**call up,** 1. to recall. 2. to summon, as for military duty. 3. to telephone. —**on call,** 1. available when summoned. 2. payable when demanded.

**cal·la** (kal'ə), *n.* [< Gr. *kallaia*, wattles of a cock], 1. a plant of the arum family, with a large, white leaf surrounding a yellow flower spike. 2. its flower. Also **calla lily.**

**call·board** (kôl'bôrd', -bōrd'), *n.* in the *theater*, a bulletin board backstage for posting notices.

**call·boy** (kôl'boi'), *n.* 1. a boy who calls actors when it is time for them to go on the stage. 2. a bellboy.

**call·er** (kôl'ēr), *n.* 1. a person or thing that calls. 2. a person who makes a short visit.

**cal·lig·ra·phy** (kə-lig'rə-fi), *n.* [< Gr. < *kallos*, beauty + *graphein*, to write], 1. beautiful handwriting. 2. handwriting. —**cal·lig'ra·pher, cal·lig'ra·phist,** *n.* —**cal·li·graph·ic** (kal'ə-graf'ik), *adj.*

**call·ing** (kôl'iŋ), *n.* 1. the action of one that calls. 2. a vocation; trade; profession.

**calling card,** a small card with one's name and, sometimes, one's address, used in making visits.

**Cal·li·o·pe** (kə-lī'ə-pē'), *n.* [L. < Gr. *Kalliopē* < *kallos*, beauty + *ops*, voice], 1. in *Gr. mythology*, the Muse of eloquence and epic poetry. 2. [c-], (usually kal'i-ōp'), a musical instrument with a series of steam whistles, played like an organ.

**cal·li·per** (kal'ə-pēr), *n.*, *v.t. & v.i.* caliper.

**cal·lis·then·ic** (kal'əs-then'ik), *adj.* calisthenic.

**cal·lis·then·ics** (kal'əs-then'iks), *n.pl.* calisthenics.

**call loan,** a loan that must be repaid on demand.

**call money,** money borrowed as a call loan.

**cal·los·i·ty** (kə-los'ə-ti, ka-), *n.* 1. the quality or state of being callous or hardened. 2. [*pl.* -TIES], a hard, thickened place on the skin or on the bark of a tree; callus. 3. hardheartedness.

**cal·lous** (kal'əs), *adj.* [< L. < *callum*, hard skin], 1. having a callus or calluses; hardened. 2. unfeeling; insensitive. *v.t. & v.i.* to make or become callous. —**cal'lous·ly,** *adv.* —**cal'lous·ness,** *n.*

**cal·low** (kal'ō), *adj.* [AS. *calu*, bald], 1. without the feathers needed for flying, as a young bird. 2. undeveloped; inexperienced. —**cal'low·ness,** *n.*

**cal·lus** (kal'əs), *n.* [*pl.* -LUSES], [L. < *callum*, hard skin], 1. a hardened, thickened place on the skin. 2. a hard substance formed around the ends of a broken bone that helps them to knit. 3. a growth forming over a cut or wounded area on a plant stem; callosity. *v.i.* to develop a callus.

**calm** (käm), *n.* [< Fr. < It. <LL. < Gr. *kauma*, heat: prob. < the period of rest, at midday], lack of wind or motion; stillness; tranquillity; serenity. *adj.* undisturbed; unruffled; tranquil; still. *v.t. & v.i.* to make or become calm (often with *down*). —**calm'ly,** *adv.* —**calm'ness** *n.*

**cal·o·mel** (kal'ə-m'l, -mel'), *n.* [Fr. < Gr. *kalos*, beautiful + *melas*, black], mercurous chloride, HgCl, a white, tasteless powder, used as a cathartic, for intestinal worms, etc.

**ca·lor·ic** (kə-lôr'ik, -lor'-), *n.* [< Fr. < L. *calor*, heat], heat. *adj.* of heat. —**cal·o·ric·i·ty** (kal'ə-ris'ə-ti), *n.*

**cal·o·rie** (kal'ə-ri), *n.* [Fr. < L. *calor*, heat], 1. the amount of heat needed to raise the temperature of one gram of water one degree centigrade: called **small calorie.** 2. [usually C-], the amount of heat needed to raise the temperature of one kilogram of water one degree centigrade: called **large calorie, great calorie**: used as the unit for measuring the energy produced by food when oxidized in the body. Also sp. **calory** [*pl.* -RIES].

**cal·o·rif·ic** (kal'ə-rif'ik), *adj.* [< Fr. < L. < *calor*, heat + *facere*, to make], producing heat.

**cal·o·rim·e·ter** (kal'ə-rim'ə-tēr), *n.* [< L. *calor*, heat + *-meter*], an apparatus for measuring amounts of heat, as in chemical combination, friction, etc.

**cal·o·rim·e·try** (kal'ə-rim'ə-tri), *n.* [< L. *calor*, heat + *-metry*], the process of measuring the quantity of heat. —**cal·o·ri·met·ric** (kal'ə-ri-met'rik, kə-lôr'i-), **cal'o·ri·met'ri·cal,** *adj.*

**cal·u·met** (kal'yoo-met'), *n.* [Fr.; ult. < L. *calamus*, a reed], a long-stemmed tobacco pipe, smoked by North American Indians as a token of peace.

CALUMET

**ca·lum·ni·ate** (kə-lum'ni-āt'), *v.t. & v.i.* [-ATED, -ATING], [< L. pp. of *calumniari*, to slander < *calumnia*; see CALUMNY], to spread false and harmful statements about (a person); slander. —**ca·lum'ni·a'tion,** *n.* —**ca·lum'ni·a'tor,** *n.* —**ca·lum'ni·a·to'ry** (-ə-tôr'i, -tō'ri), *adj.*

**ca·lum·ni·ous** (kə-lum'ni-əs), *adj.* full of calumnies; slanderous. —**ca·lum'ni·ous·ly,** *adv.*

**cal·um·ny** (kal'əm-ni), *n.* [*pl.* -NIES], [< Fr. < L. *calumnia*, trickery, slander < *calvire*, to deceive], 1. a false and malicious statement meant to hurt someone's reputation. 2. slander.

**Cal·va·ry** (kal'və-ri), *n.* [L. *calvaria*, skull; transl. of Aram. *gūlgūlthā*, Golgotha, lit., skull], in the *Bible*, the place near Jerusalem where Jesus was crucified: Luke 23:33, Matt. 27:33.

**calve** (kav, käv), *v.i. & v.t.* [CALVED, CALVING], [AS. *cealfian*], to give birth to (a calf).

**Cal·vert, George** (kal'vērt), first Baron Baltimore, 1580?–1632; founder of Maryland.

**calves** (kavz, kävz), *n.* pl. of **calf.**

**Cal·vin, John** (kal'vin), (born *Jean Chauvin* or *Caulvin*), 1509–1564; French Protestant reformer.

**Cal·vin·ism** (kal'vin-iz'm), *n.* the religious system of John Calvin and his followers, which emphasizes the doctrines of predestination and salvation solely by God's grace. —**Cal'vin·ist,** *n. & adj.* —**Cal'vin·is'tic, Cal'vin·is'ti·cal,** *adj.*

**calx** (kalks), *n.* [*pl.* CALXES, CALCES (kal'sēz)], [L., small stone, lime], the ashy powder left after a metal or mineral has been calcined.

**Ca·lyp·so** (kə-lip'sō), *n.* [L. < Gr. *Kalypsō*], in Homer's *Odyssey*, a sea nymph who did not let Odysseus leave her island for seven years.

**ca·lyp·so** (kə-lip'sō), *adj.* [? < *Calypso*], designating or of lively, rhythmic, topical ballads improvised and sung by natives of Trinidad: they are characterized by wrenched syllabic stress, loose rhyme, etc. *n.* a calypso song or calypso music.

**ca·lyx** (kā'liks, kal'iks), *n.* [*pl.* CALYXES, CALYCES (kal'ə-sēz', kā'lə-)], [L., outer covering, pod], the outer whorl, or sepals, at a flower's base.

**cam** (kam), *n.* [AS. *camb*, comb; infl. by D. *cam* in this sense], a wheel, projection on a wheel, etc. which gives an eccentric, alternating, or otherwise irregular motion as to a wheel or shaft, or receives such motion from it.

**ca·ma·ra·de·rie** (kä'mə-rä'dēr-i), *n.* [Fr. < *camarade*, comrade], good spirit among comrades; comradeship.

**cam·a·ril·la** (kam'ə-ril'ə; Sp. kä'mä-rēl'yä), *n.*

[Sp., dim. of *camara*, chamber < L. *camera*, a vault], a group of secret advisers; cabal; clique.

**cam·ass, cam·as** (kam′as), *n.* [Chinook *quamash*, bulb], a North American plant of the lily family, with sweet, edible bulbs: also **quamash.**

**cam·ber** (kam′bẽr), *n.* [< Fr. < *cambrer*, to arch, ult. < L. *camur*, bent], 1. a slight convex curve of a surface, as of a road. 2. a piece of timber arched in the middle. 3. the slight arch in the surface of an airplane wing or other airfoil. *v.t. & v.i.* to arch slightly.

**cam·bi·um** (kam′bi-əm), *n.* [LL., change], the layer of tissue between the bark and wood in woody plants, from which new wood and bark develop.

**Cam·bo·di·a** (kam-bō′di-ə, -dyə), *n.* a kingdom in the S part of the Indochinese peninsula: area, 66,606 sq. mi.; pop., 6,701,000; capital, Pnom-Penh.

**Cam·bri·a** (kam′bri-ə), *n.* [Poetic], Wales.

**Cam·bri·an** (kam′bri-ən), *adj.* 1. of Cambria; Welsh. 2. designating or of the first geological period in the Paleozoic Era: see **geology**, chart. *n.* a native or inhabitant of Cambria; Welshman.

**cam·bric** (kām′brik), *n.* [< *Kamerik*, Fl. name of *Cambrai*, France], 1. a very fine, thin linen. 2. a cotton cloth like this.

**cambric tea,** a hot drink made of weak tea, milk, and sugar.

**Cam·bridge** (kām′brij), *n.* 1. a city in SE England: pop., 100,000: home of Cambridge University. 2. a city in E Massachusetts: pop., 108,000.

**Cam·den** (kam′dən), *n.* a city in New Jersey, on the Delaware River: pop., 117,000.

**came** (kām), pt. of **come.**

**cam·el** (kam′'l), *n.* [< AS. or OFr. < L. *camelus* < Gr. *kamēlos* < Heb. *gāmāl*], a large, domesticated animal with a humped back and long neck: because it can store water in its body, it is used in Asian and African deserts; the Arabian camel has one hump, the Bactrian camel has two humps.

**ca·mel·li·a** (kə-mēl′yə, -mē′li-ə), *n.* [after G. J. *Kamel* (d. 1706), missionary to the Far East], 1. an evergreen tree or shrub of the tea family, native to Asia, with shiny, dark-green leaves and white or red, rose-shaped flowers. 2. the flower.

**ca·mel·o·pard** (kə-mel′ə-pärd′, kam′'l-), *n.* [< LL. < L. < Gr. < *kamēlos*, camel + *pardalis*, leopard: from its camellike neck and leopardlike spots], 1. a giraffe. 2. [C-], a northern constellation.

**Cam·e·lot** (kam′ə-lot′), *n.* the legendary English town where King Arthur had his court.

**camel's hair,** 1. the hair of the camel. 2. cloth made of this hair, sometimes mixed with wool, etc. —**cam′el's-hair′, cam′el-hair′,** *adj.*

**Cam·em·bert (cheese)** (kam′əm-ber′), [from *Camembert*, in France], a soft, creamy kind of cheese.

**cam·e·o** (kam′i-ō′, kam′yō), *n.* [*pl.* -OS], [< It. & OFr. < ML. *camaeus*], 1. a gem with a figure carved in one layer so that it is raised on a background of another. 2. a carving so made: opposed to *intaglio*.

**cam·er·a** (kam′ẽr-ə), *n.* [L., a vault < Gr. *kamara*, vaulted chamber], 1. a chamber; specifically, the private office of a judge. 2. a device for taking photographs, consisting as of a closed box containing a sensitized plate or film on which an image is formed when light enters the box through a lens. 3. in *television*, that part of the transmitter consisting of a lens and a cathode-ray tube containing a plate on which the image to be televised is projected for transformation into a flow of electrons. —**in camera,** 1. in a judge's private office. 2. privately.

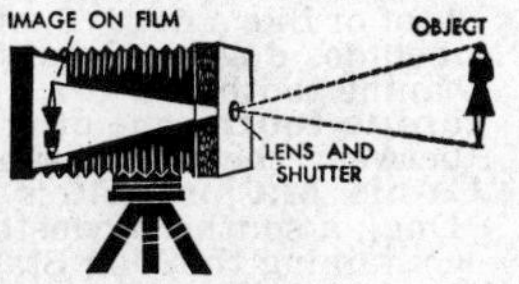

CAMERA

**cam·er·a·man** (kam′ẽr-ə-man′), *n.* [*pl.* -MEN (-men′)], an operator of a camera, especially of a motion-picture camera.

**Cam·e·roon** (kam′ə-rōōn′), *n.* Cameroun.

**Ca·me·roun** (kam-rōōn′; Fr. kȧ′m′-rōōn′), *n.* a country in west central Africa, on the Atlantic: area, 183,576 sq. mi.; pop., 5,562,000; capital, Yaoundé.

**cam·i·sole** (kam′ə-sōl′), *n.* [Fr. < Sp. dim. of *camisa*; see CHEMISE], 1. a woman's loose underwaist or corset cover. 2. a woman's loose jacket worn as a dressing gown. 3. a kind of strait jacket.

**cam·o·mile** (kam′ə-mil′), *n.* [< OFr. < L. < Gr. *chamaimēlon* < *chamai*, ground + *mēlon*, apple], a plant of the aster family, with scented leaves and daisylike flowers: the dried leaves, flowers, and buds of one variety are used in medicine.

**Ca·mor·ra** (kə-mor′ə; It. kä-môr′rä), *n.* [It., assault with violence], 1. an Italian secret society organized in Naples, c. 1820, which became politically powerful and later notorious for terror, blackmail, and violence. 2. [c-], any secret society like this. —**Ca·mor′rism,** *n.* —**Ca·mor′rist,** *n.*

**cam·ou·flage** (kam′ə-fläzh′), *n.* [Fr. < *camoufler*, to disguise], 1. the process of disguising, as ships or guns, by paint, nets, leaves, etc. to conceal them from the enemy. 2. a disguise of this sort. 3. any device used to conceal; deception. *v.t. & v.i.* [-FLAGED, -FLAGING], to conceal by changing the appearance; disguise. —**cam′ou·flag′er,** *n.*

**camp** (kamp), *n.* [< Fr. < It. < L. *campus*, a field], 1. *a*) a place where temporary tents, huts, etc. are put up, as for soldiers. *b*) those in such a place; hence, 2. *a*) a group of people who support a common opinion, cause, etc. *b*) the position taken by them. 3. a group of tents, huts, etc. for temporary lodging. 4. a place in the country for vacationers or children, with facilities for recreation, often organized and supervised. 5. the people living in a camp. 6. military life. 7. [Slang], banality, mediocrity, artifice, etc. so extreme as to amuse or have a perversely sophisticated appeal. *v.i.* 1. to set up a camp; encamp. 2. to live temporarily in a camp. 3. to live as if in a camp, without conveniences. *v.t.* to put into or as into camp. —**break camp,** to pack up camping equipment and go away. —**camp out,** to live in or as in a camp or tent.

**cam·paign** (kam-pān′), *n.* [Fr. *campagne* (It. *campagna*), open country; ult. < L. *campus*, a field], 1. a series of military operations with a particular objective. 2. a series of organized, planned actions, as for electing a candidate. *v.i.* to participate in, or go on, a campaign. —**cam·paign′er,** *n.*

**cam·pa·ni·le** (kam′pə-nē′li), *n.* [*pl.* -LES, -LI (-lē)], [It. < LL. *campana*, a bell], a bell tower, usually near a church.

**cam·pan·u·la** (kam-pan′yoo-lə), *n.* [< dim. of LL. *campana*, a bell], any of a family of plants, with showy, bell-shaped flowers of blue, pink, or white, as the harebell.

**camp chair,** a lightweight folding chair.

**camp·craft** (kamp′kraft′, -kräft′), *n.* the art or practice of camping outdoors.

**camp·er** (kamp′ẽr), *n.* 1. a person who vacations at a camp. 2. any of various motor vehicles or trailers equipped for camping out.

**camp·fire** (kamp′fīr′), *n.* 1. an outdoor fire at a camp. 2. a social gathering around such a fire.

**campfire girl,** a member of the **Camp Fire Girls of America, a girls' organization promoting a program of health and character-building activities.**

**camp·ground** (kamp′ground′), *n.* 1. a place where a camp is set up. 2. a place where a camp meeting or religious revival is held.

**cam·phor** (kam′fẽr), *n.* [< Fr. < LL. < Ar. < Malay *kāpūr*, chalk], 1. a crystalline substance, $C_{10}H_{16}O$, with a strong odor, derived chiefly from the wood of an Oriental laurel (**camphor tree**): used in moth balls, in manufacturing celluloid, in medicine as a stimulant, etc. 2. any of several derivatives of terpenes. —**cam·phor′ic** (kam-fôr′ik), *adj.*

**cam·phor·ate** (kam′fẽr-āt′), *v.t.* [-ATED, -ATING], to put camphor in or on. —**cam′phor·at′ed,** *adj.*

**camphor ball,** a moth ball.

**camphor ice,** an ointment made of white wax, camphor, spermaceti, and castor oil.

**cam·pi·on** (kam′pi-ən), *n.* [prob. ult. < Norm. < *campagne*, a field], any of various plants of the pink family, with red or white flowers.

**camp meeting,** a religious gathering held outdoors or in a tent, etc., usually lasting several days.

**camp·stool** (kamp′stōōl′), *n.* a light folding stool.

**cam·pus** (kam′pəs), *n.* [*pl.* -PUSES], [L., a field], the grounds of a school or college. *adj.* on or of the campus or student body: as, *campus* activities.

**can** (kan; *as an auxiliary, usually* kən, k'n), *v.i.* [pt. COULD (kood)], [< AS. < *cunnan*, to know, be able], 1. to know how to. 2. to be able to. 3. to have the right to. 4. [Colloq.], to be permitted to; may. —**can but,** can only.

**can** (kan), *n.* [AS. *canne*, a cup], 1. a container, usually made of metal, for liquids. 2. a container made of tinned iron or other metal, in which liquids, foods, etc. are sealed for preservation. 3. the contents of a can; canful. 4. [Slang], *a*) prison. *b*) toilet. *v.t.* [CANNED, CANNING], 1. to put into air-tight cans or jars for preservation. 2. [Slang], to dismiss; discharge. —**can′ner,** *n.*

**Can.,** 1. Canada. 2. Canadian: also **Canad.**

**Ca·naan** (kā′nən), *n.* the Promised Land of the Israelites, a region roughly corresponding to modern Palestine.

**Ca·naan·ite** (kā′nən-īt′), *n.* one of the original inhabitants of Canaan. —**Ca′naan·it′ic** (-it′ik), —**Ca′naan·it′ish** (-īt′ish), *adj.*

**Can·a·da** (kan′ə-də), *n.* a country in N North America, in the British Commonwealth of Nations: area, 3,852,000 sq. mi.; pop., 18,928,000; capital, Ottawa.

**Canada balsam,** a yellow, resinous fluid from the balsam fir tree.

**Canada goose,** a large, wild goose of Canada and the northern U.S., gray, with black head and neck.

**Ca·na·di·an** (kə-nā′di-ən), *adj.* of Canada or its people. *n.* a native or inhabitant of Canada.

**ca·naille** (kə-nāl′; Fr. kȧ′nä′y′), *n.* [Fr. < It. *canaglia* < L. *canis,* a dog], the mob; rabble.

**ca·nal** (kə-nal′), *n.* [Fr. < L. *canalis,* a channel < *canna,* a reed], 1. an artificial waterway for transportation or irrigation. 2. in *anatomy & zoology,* a tube or duct. *v.t.* [-NALLED or -NALED, -NALLING or -NALING], to build a canal through or across.

**ca·nal·boat** (kə-nal′bōt′), *n.* a long, narrow boat, used on canals to carry freight: also **canal boat.**

**can·a·lic·u·lus** (kan′ə-lik′yoo-ləs), *n.* [*pl.* -LI (-lī′)], [L., dim. of *canalis,* a pipe], in *anatomy & biology,* a very small groove. —**can′a·lic′u·lar,** *adj.*

**ca·nal·i·za·tion** (kə-nal′ə-zā′shən, kan′′l-ī-), *n.* 1. a canalizing. 2. a system or network of canals.

**ca·nal·ize** (kə-nal′īz, kan′′l-īz′), *v.t.* [-IZED, -IZING], 1. to make a canal through. 2. to change into a canal; make resemble a canal. 3. to direct into a specific channel. 4. to give an outlet to.

**Canal Zone,** a military reservation of the U.S., held in permanent lease from Panama and extending 5 miles on either side of the Panama Canal: land area, 362 sq. mi.; pop., 42,000: abbrev. **C.Z.**

**ca·na·pé** (kan′ə-pi; Fr. kȧ′nȧ′pā′), *n.* [Fr.], toasted bread or a cracker spread with spiced meat, fish, cheese, etc., served as an appetizer.

**ca·nard** (kə-närd′; Fr. kȧ′när′), *n.* [Fr., a duck], an absurd or exaggerated report spread as a hoax.

**ca·nar·y** (kə-nâr′i), *n.* [*pl.* -IES], [< *Canary* Islands], 1. a yellow songbird of the finch family: also **canary bird.** 2. a sweet wine like madeira, originally made in the Canary Islands. 3. a light yellow: also **canary yellow.** *adj.* light-yellow: also **canary-yellow.**

**Canary Islands,** a group of Spanish islands, off NW Africa: area, 2,807 sq. mi.; pop., 944,000.

**ca·nas·ta** (kə-nas′tə), *n.* [Sp., basket], a double-deck card game for two to six players.

**Ca·na·ver·al, Cape** (kə-nav′ẽr-əl), Cape Kennedy: the former name.

**Can·ber·ra** (kan′bẽr-ə), *n.* the capital of Australia, in the SE part: pop., 67,000.

**canc.,** 1. canceled. 2. cancellation.

**can·can** (kan′kan′; Fr. kän′kän′), *n.* [Fr.], a gay, wild dance, with much high kicking.

**can·cel** (kan′s′l), *v.t.* [-CELED or -CELLED, -CELING or -CELLING], [< Fr. < L. *cancellare,* to draw lattice-like lines across < *cancer,* lattice], 1. to cross out with lines or marks. 2. to annul; make invalid. 3. to do away with; abolish. 4. to neutralize; balance (often with *out*). 5. in *mathematics,* to strike out (common factors) by drawing a line through them. *v.i.* to balance (with *out*). *n.* a cancellation. —**can′cel·a·ble, can′cel·la·ble,** *adj.* —**can′cel·er, can′cel·ler,** *n.*

**can·cel·la·tion** (kan′s′l-ā′shən), *n.* 1. a canceling or being canceled. 2. something canceled. 3. the mark showing that something is canceled.

**can·cer** (kan′sẽr), *n.* [L., a crab; later, malignant tumor], 1. a malignant new growth, or tumor, anywhere in the body: cancers tend to spread and ulcerate. 2. anything harmful that spreads and destroys. 3. [C-], a northern constellation between Gemini and Leo, resembling a crab in outline. 4. [C-], the fourth sign of the zodiac (♋), entered by the sun at the summer solstice, about June 22. —**can′cer·ous,** *adj.*

**can·de·la·brum** (kan′d′l-ä′brəm, -ab′rəm), *n.* [*pl.* -BRA (-brə), -BRUMS], [L. < *candela;* see CANDLE], a large, branched candlestick: also **candelabra** (-brə), [*pl.* -BRAS].

**can·des·cent** (kan-des′′nt), *adj.* [L. *candescens* < *candere,* to shine], glowing; incandescent. —**can·des′cence,** *n.* —**can·des′cent·ly,** *adv.*

**can·did** (kan′did), *adj.* [L. *candidus,* white, sincere < *candere,* to shine], 1. unbiased; impartial. 2. honest; frank. —**can′did·ly,** *adv.* —**can′did·ness,** *n.*

**can·di·da·cy** (kan′də-də-si), *n.* [*pl.* -CIES], the fact, state, or term of being a candidate.

**can·di·date** (kan′də-dāt′, -dit), *n.* [L. *candidatus,* white-robed, as those who sought office], a person who seeks, or has been proposed for, an office, an award, etc.

**can·di·da·ture** (kan′də-dā′chẽr, -də-də-), *n.* candidacy.

**candid camera,** any small camera with a fast lens, used to take informal, unposed pictures.

**can·died** (kan′did), *adj.* [pp. of *candy*], 1. cooked in or with sugar. 2. crystallized into sugar. 3. sugary; sweetened; made pleasant.

**can·dle** (kan′d′l), *n.* [< AS. < L. *candela,* a torch < *candere,* to shine], 1. a cylinder of tallow or wax with a wick through its center, which gives light when burned. 2. anything like this in form or use. 3. a unit of luminous intensity, based on a standard candle: abbrev. **C., c.** *v.t.* [-DLED, -DLING], to examine (eggs) for freshness by holding in front of a light. —**burn the candle at both ends,** to work or play so much that one's energy is quickly dissipated. —**not hold a candle to,** not be nearly so good as. —**not worth the candle,** not worth doing. —**can′dler,** *n.*

**can·dle·ber·ry** (kan′d′l-ber′i), *n.* [*pl.* -RIES], 1. the fruit of the candlenut or of the wax myrtle tree. 2. either of these trees.

**can·dle·light** (kan′d′l-līt′), *n.* 1. the light given by a candle or candles. 2. twilight; evening.

**Can·dle·mas** (**Day**) (kan′d′l-məs), [< AS. < *candel,* a candle + *mæsse,* a Mass], 1. February 2, a church feast commemorating the purification of the Virgin Mary: candles for sacred uses are blessed then.

**candle power,** the luminous intensity of a standard candle, a unit for measuring light, as of a lamp.

**can·dle·stick** (kan′d′l-stik′), *n.* a cupped or spiked holder for a candle or candles.

**can·dor** (kan′dẽr), *n.* [L., radiance < *candere,* to shine], 1. the quality of being open-minded or fair. 2. honesty in expressing oneself; sincerity.

**can·dour** (kan′dẽr), *n.* candor: Brit. spelling.

**can·dy** (kan′di), *n.* [*pl.* -DIES], [< *sugar candy* < Fr. & It. < Ar. < Per. *qand,* cane sugar], 1. crystallized sugar made by evaporating boiled cane sugar, sirup, etc. 2. a solid confection of sugar or sirup with flavoring, nuts, fruits, etc. *v.t.* [-DIED, -DYING], 1. to preserve by cooking with sugar. 2. to crystallize into sugar. 3. to sweeten; make pleasant. *v.i.* to become candied (in sense 2).

**cane** (kān), *n.* [< OFr. < L. *canna* < Gr. *kanna*], 1. the slender, hollow, jointed stem of any of certain plants, as the bamboo. 2. a plant with such a stem. 3. a walking stick. 4. a stick used for beating. 5. sugar cane. 6. split rattan. 7. the stem of the blackberry, raspberry, etc. *v.t.* [CANED (kānd), CANING], 1. to beat with a cane. 2. to make or furnish with cane.

**cane·brake** (kān′brāk′), *n.* [*cane* + *brake* (thicket)], a dense growth of cane plants.

**cane sugar,** the sugar from sugar cane; sucrose.

**ca·nine** (kā′nīn), *adj.* [L. *caninus* < *canis,* a dog], 1. of or like a dog. 2. of the family of animals that includes dogs, wolves, jackals, and foxes. 3. of a canine tooth. *n.* 1. a dog. 2. a canine tooth.

**canine tooth,** one of the four sharp-pointed teeth between the incisors and bicuspids.

**Ca·nis Ma·jor** (kā′nis mā′jẽr), [L., the Greater Dog], a southern constellation southeast of Orion, containing the Dog Star, Sirius.

**Canis Mi·nor** (mī′nẽr), [L., the Lesser Dog], a northern constellation east of Orion, near Gemini, containing the bright star Procyon.

**can·is·ter** (kan′is-tẽr), *n.* [< L. *canistrum,* wicker basket < Gr. *kanistron* < *kanna,* a reed], 1. a box or can for coffee, tea, etc. 2. canister shot.

**canister shot,** formerly, a cannon shell consisting of pellets in a container that scattered its contents when fired: also called *case shot.*

**can·ker** (kaŋ′kẽr), *n.* [< AS. & OFr.; ult. < L. *cancer;* see CANCER], 1. an ulcerlike, spreading sore, usually in the mouth. 2. a cankerworm. 3. a plant disease that causes decay. 4. anything causing decay or rot. *v.t.* 1. to attack or infect with canker. 2. to cause to decay. *v.i.* to be attacked by canker. —**can′ker·ous,** *adj.*

**can·ker·worm** (kaŋ′kẽr-wûrm′), *n.* any of several larvae that feed on the leaves of trees.

**can·na** (kan′ə), *n.* [L., a reed], 1. a tropical plant of the banana family, with large leaves and brilliant flowers. 2. the flower of this plant.

**canned** (kand), *adj.* 1. preserved in cans or jars. 2. [Slang], discharged from a position. 3. [Slang], put on a phonograph record, as music.

**can·nel coal** (kan′'l), [< *candle coal*], a variety of bituminous coal that burns with a bright flame and has a high volatile content: also **cannel.**
**can·ner·y** (kan′ẽr-i), *n.* [*pl.* -IES], a factory where foods are canned.
**Cannes** (kanz, kan; Fr. kån), *n.* a resort on the Riviera, SE France: pop., 46,000.
**can·ni·bal** (kan′ə-b'l), *n.* [Sp. *canibal* < *Caribal*, Carib], 1. a person who eats human flesh. 2. an animal that eats its own kind. *adj.* of or like cannibals.
**can·ni·bal·ism** (kan′ə-b'l-iz'm), *n.* the act or habit of eating others of one's own kind. —**can′ni·bal·is′tic,** *adj.* —**can′ni·bal·is′ti·cal·ly,** *adv.*
**can·ni·bal·ize** (kan′ə-b'l-īz′), *v.t.* & *v.i.* [-IZED, -IZING], to salvage the useful parts of (destroyed or worn-out equipment).
**can·ni·kin** (kan′ə-kin), *n.* [< *can* + *-kin*], 1. a small can; cup. 2. a wooden bucket or pail.
**can·ning** (kan′iŋ), *n.* the act or process of putting foods in cans or jars for preservation.
**can·non** (kan′ən), *n.* [*pl.* -NONS, -NON; see PLURAL, II, D, 4], [< Fr. < It. < L. *canna*; see CANE; in *n.* 4 & *v.* 2, altered < *carom*], 1. a large mounted piece of artillery. 2. a cannon bit. 3. the cannon bone. 4. [Brit.], in *billiards*, a carom. *v.t.* 1. to attack with cannon. 2. [Brit.], to cause to carom. *v.i.* 1. to fire cannon. 2. [Brit.], to make a carom.
**can·non·ade** (kan′ən-ād′), *n.* a continuous firing of artillery. *v.t.* & *v.i.* [-ADED, -ADING], to fire artillery (at).
**cannon ball,** a heavy ball of iron or other metal, formerly used as a projectile in cannon.
**cannon bit,** a smooth, round bit for a horse: also **canon bit.**
**cannon bone,** the bone between hock or knee and fetlock in four-legged, hoofed animals.
**can·non·eer** (kan′ən-êr′), *n.* an artilleryman.
**cannon fodder,** soldiers, sailors, etc. thought of as being killed or maimed in war.
**can·non·ry** (kan′ən-ri), *n.* [*pl.* -RIES], 1. cannon collectively: artillery. 2. cannon fire.
**can·not** (kan′ot, ka-not′, kan′ət), can not. —**cannot but,** must; have no choice but to.
**can·ny** (kan′i), *adj.* [-NIER, -NIEST], [< *can* (to be able)], [Scot.], 1. cautious; wary. 2. thrifty. 3. shrewd. —**can′ni·ly,** *adv.* —**can′ni·ness,** *n.*
**ca·noe** (kə-nōō′), *n.* [< Sp. *canoa* < the Carib name], a narrow, light boat moved with paddles. *v.i.* [-NOED, -NOEING], to paddle, or go in, a canoe. *v.t.* to transport by canoe. —**ca·noe′ing,** *n.* —**ca·noe′ist,** *n.*
**can·on** (kan′ən), *n.* [AS., a rule < L. < Gr. *kanōn* < *kanē*, a reed, rod], 1. a law or body of laws of a church: as, the Anglican *canon.* 2. any law or decree. 3. a criterion. 4. a list of books of the Bible officially accepted as genuine. 5. [C-], a part of the Mass that follows the Sanctus. 6. a list of saints recognized by the R. C. Church. 7. an official list or catalogue. 8. in *music*, a round; composition in which there are exact repetitions of a preceding part in the same or related keys.
**can·on** (kan′ən), *n.* 1. a member of a clerical group living according to a canon, or rule. 2. a clergyman serving in a cathedral or collegiate church. —**can′on·ess,** *n.fem.*
**cañ·on** (kan′yən; Sp. kä-nyôn′), *n.* a canyon.
**ca·non·i·cal** (kə-non′i-k'l), *adj.* 1. of, according to, or ordered by church law. 2. authoritative; accepted. 3. belonging to the canon of the Bible. —**ca·non′i·cal·ly,** *adv.*
**canonical hour,** any of the seven periods of the day assigned to prayer and worship.
**ca·non·i·cals** (kə-non′i-k'lz), *n.pl.* the prescribed clothes for a clergyman conducting church services.
**can·on·ic·i·ty** (kan′ən-is′ə-ti), *n.* 1. the right to be included in the Biblical canon. 2. genuineness. 3. conformity to church law.
**can·on·ist** (kan′ən-ist), *n.* an expert in church canon, or law. —**can′on·is′tic, can′on·is′ti·cal,** *adj.*
**can·on·ize** (kan′ən-īz′), *v.t.* [-IZED, -IZING], 1. to declare (a dead person) a saint; add officially to the canon of saints. 2. to glorify. 3. to put in the Biblical canon. 4. to give church sanction to. —**can′on·i·za′tion,** *n.*
**canon law,** the laws governing the ecclesiastical affairs of a Christian church.
**can·on·ry** (kan′ən-ri), *n.* [*pl.* -RIES], 1. the benefice or office of a canon. 2. canons as a group.
**can·o·py** (kan′ə-pi), *n.* [*pl.* -PIES], [< OFr. < ML. < L. < Gr. *kōnōpeion*, bed with mosquito nets < *kōnōps*, gnat], 1. a drapery or other covering fastened above a bed, throne, door, etc., or held over a person or sacred thing. 2. an overhanging shelter: as, the *canopy* of the sky. *v.t.* [-PIED, -PYING], to place or form a canopy over; cover; shelter.
**canst** (kanst; *unstressed* kənst), archaic 2d person sing., present indicative, of **can:** used with *thou.*
**cant** (kant), *n.* [ONorm.Fr., singing < L. *cantus*, pp. of *canere*, to sing], 1. whining, singsong speech, especially as used by beggars. 2. the secret slang of beggars, thieves, etc.; argot. 3. the special words and phrases used by those in a certain occupation; jargon. 4. insincere, trite talk, especially when pious or moral. *v.i.* to use cant; speak in cant. *adj.* having the nature of cant.
**cant** (kant), *n.* [< OFr. < LL. < L. *cant(h)us*; prob. < Cym.], 1. a corner or outside angle. 2. a slanting surface; beveled edge. 3. a sudden movement that causes tilting, turning, or overturning. 4. the tilt, turn, or slant of position thus caused. *v.t.* 1. to slant; bevel. 2. to tilt or overturn. 3. to pitch; toss. *v.i.* 1. to tilt or turn over. 2. to slant. *adj.* 1. with oblique sides or corners. 2. slanting.
**can't** (kant, känt), cannot.
**can·ta·bi·le** (kän-tä′bi-lā′), *adj.* & *adv.* [< It. < L. < *cantare*, to sing], in *music*, in an easy, flowing manner; songlike. *n.* music in this style.
**Can·ta·brig·i·an** (kan′tə-brij′i-ən), *adj.* [< L. *Cantabrigia*, Cambridge], 1. of Cambridge, England. 2. of the University of Cambridge. —**Can′ta·brig′i·an,** *n.*
**can·ta·loupe, can·ta·loup** (kan′tə-lōp′), *n.* [< Fr. < It. < *Cantalupo*, near Rome, where first grown in Europe], 1. a melon with a hard, ribbed rind and sweet, juicy flesh. 2. any muskmelon.
**can·tan·ker·ous** (kan-taŋ′kẽr-əs), *adj.* [prob. < ME. *contac*, strife], bad-tempered; quarrelsome. —**can·tan′ker·ous·ly,** *adv.* —**can·tan′ker·ous·ness,** *n.*
**can·ta·ta** (kən-tä′tə, kan-), *n.* [< It.; see CANTABILE], a choral composition used as a setting for a story to be sung but not acted.
**can·teen** (kan-tēn′), *n.* [< Fr. < It. *cantina*, wine cellar], 1. a military shop where soldiers can buy refreshments and provisions; post exchange. 2. a recreation center for teen-agers. 3. a small flask for carrying drinking water. 4. formerly, a military kit containing cooking equipment.
**can·ter** (kan′tẽr), *n.* [contr. < *Canterbury gallop*, the riding pace of the medieval Canterbury pilgrims], an easy gallop. *v.i.* & *v.t.* to ride at this pace.
**Can·ter·bur·y** (kan′tẽr-ber′i, -bẽr-i), *n.* a city in SE England, with a famous cathedral: pop., 30,000.
**Canterbury bell,** any of a number of campanulas with bell-shaped flowers of white, pink, or blue.
**cant hook,** [see CANT (an angle)], a pole with a movable hooked arm at or near one end, for catching hold of logs and turning them over.

CANT HOOK

**can·thus** (kan′thəs), *n.* [*pl.* -THI (-thī)], [Gr. *kanthos*], the corner on either side of the eye, where the eyelids meet.
**can·ti·cle** (kan′ti-k'l), *n.* [< L. dim. of *canticum*, song < pp. of *canere*, to sing], 1. a song or chant. 2. a hymn with words from the Bible, used in certain church services.
**Can·ti·cles** (kan′ti-k'lz), *n.pl.* a book of the Old Testament, The Song of Solomon: also (in the Douay Bible) **Canticle of Canticles.**
**can·ti·le·ver** (kan′t'l-ev′ẽr, -ē′vẽr), *n.* [as if < *cant* (an angle) + *lever*], a bracket or block projecting as a support; esp., a projecting structure anchored at one end to a pier and extending over a space to be bridged: also sp. **cantalever.**
**cantilever bridge,** a bridge whose span is formed by the projecting ends of two cantilevers.

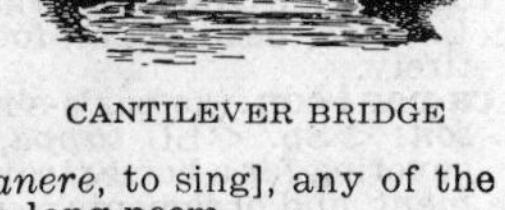

CANTILEVER BRIDGE

**can·tle** (kan′t'l), *n.* [< OFr.; ult. < L. *cantus*, an edge], the upward-curving rear part of a saddle.
**can·to** (kan′tō), *n.* [*pl.* -TOS], [It. < L. pp. of *canere*, to sing], any of the chapterlike divisions of a long poem.
**Can·ton** (kan-ton′), *n.* 1. a port in SE China: pop., 1,433,000. 2. (kan′tən, -t'n), a city in NE Ohio: pop., 116,000.

**can·ton** (kan'tən, kan-ton'), *n.* [Fr. < It.; ult. < L. *cantus*, an edge], one of the political divisions of a country: the Swiss Republic is divided into cantons. *v.t.* 1. to divide into cantons. 2. (kan-ton'), to assign quarters to. —**can'ton·al,** *adj.*
**Can·ton·ese** (kan'tən-ēz'), *adj.* of Canton, China, its people, or their Chinese dialect. *n.* 1. [*pl.* CANTONESE], a native or inhabitant of Canton. 2. the Chinese dialect spoken by the Cantonese.
**Can·ton flannel** (kan'tən), cotton flannel.
**can·ton·ment** (kan-ton'mənt, -tōn'-), *n.* [< Fr.; see CANTON], 1. the assignment of troops to temporary quarters. 2. the quarters assigned.
**can·tor** (kan'tẽr, -tôr), *n.* [L., singer < *canere*, to sing], 1. a church choir leader; precentor. 2. a singer of liturgical solos in a synagogue.
**Ca·nuck** (kə-nuk'), *n.* [Slang], [< *Canada*; ? after *Chinook*], 1. a Canadian. 2. a French Canadian.
**can·vas** (kan'vəs), *n.* [< OFr. < It. < LL. < L. *cannabis*, hemp], 1. a coarse cloth of hemp, cotton, or flax, used for tents, sails, etc. 2. a sail or set of sails. 3. *a*) a piece of canvas on which an oil painting is made. *b*) an oil painting on canvas. 4. a tent or tents. *adj.* made of canvas. —**under canvas,** 1. in tents. 2. with sails unfurled.
**can·vas·back** (kan'vəs-bak'), *n.* [*pl.* -BACKS, -BACK; see PLURAL, II, D, 1], a North American wild duck with a grayish back.
**can·vass** (kan'vəs), *v.t.* [< *canvas*: prob. because used for sifting], 1. to examine or discuss in detail. 2. to go through (places) or among (people) asking for votes, opinions, orders, etc. *v.i.* to try to get votes, orders, etc. *n.* 1. an examination or discussion. 2. the soliciting of votes, orders, etc., as in trying to predict the outcome of an election, sales campaign, etc. —**can'vass·er,** *n.*
**can·yon** (kan'yən), *n.* [Sp. *cañón*, a tube < L. *canna*, a reed], a long, narrow valley between high cliffs, often containing a stream: also sp. **cañon.**
**caou·tchouc** (kōō'chook, kou-chōōk'), *n.* [Fr. < native Carib name], 1. crude rubber obtained from latex; India rubber. 2. pure rubber.
**Cap** (kap), *n.* [Slang], captain: a term of address.
**cap** (kap), *n.* [AS. *cæppe* < LL. *cappa*], 1. any close-fitting head covering, visored or brimless. 2. a head covering worn as a mark of occupation, rank, etc. (e.g., a cardinal's cap). 3. a caplike part or thing, as a cover. 4. a percussion cap. *v.t.* [CAPPED, CAPPING], 1. to put a cap on. 2. to cover (the top or end of). 3. to match or surpass. —**cap the climax,** to exceed the limit. —**set one's cap for,** [Colloq.], to try to win (a man) as a husband. —**cap'per,** *n.*
**cap.,** 1. [*pl.* CAPS.], capital. 2. capitalize.
**ca·pa·bil·i·ty** (kā'pə-bil'ə-ti), *n.* [*pl.* -TIES], 1. practical ability or mental capacity. 2. *pl.* abilities, features, etc. not yet developed.
**ca·pa·ble** (kā'pə-b'l), *adj.* [Fr. < LL. *capabilis* < L. *capere*, to take], able; skilled; competent. —**capable of,** 1. admitting of; open to. 2. having the qualities necessary for. —**ca'pa·ble·ness,** *n.* —**ca'pa·bly,** *adv.*
**ca·pa·cious** (kə-pā'shəs), *adj.* [< L. *capax* < *capere*, to take; + *-ous*], able to contain much; roomy; spacious. —**ca·pa'cious·ly,** *adv.* —**ca·pa'cious·ness,** *n.*
**ca·pac·i·tance** (kə-pas'ə-təns), *n.* [< *capacity* reactance], that property of a condenser which determines how much electric charge can be stored in it. —**ca·pac'i·tive,** *adj.*
**ca·pac·i·tate** (kə-pas'ə-tāt'), *v.t.* [-TATED, -TATING], [< *capacity* + *-ate*], to prepare, fit, or qualify (*for* something).
**ca·pac·i·tor** (kə-pas'ə-tẽr), *n.* an electric condenser.
**ca·pac·i·ty** (kə-pas'ə-ti), *n.* [*pl.* -TIES], [< L. *capax*; see CAPACIOUS], 1. the ability to contain, absorb, or receive. 2. all that can be contained; content or volume. 3. mental ability. 4. aptitude; capability. 5. position, function, status, etc.: as, to act in the *capacity* of adviser. 6. in *law*, legal authority. 7. capacitance.
**cap and bells,** a fool's cap with little bells on it.
**cap-a-pie, cap-à-pie** (kap'ə-pē'), *adv.* [< OFr. < L. *caput*, head + *pes*, foot], from head to foot; entirely.
**ca·par·i·son** (kə-par'ə-s'n), *n.* [earlier Fr. *caparasson*; < Sp. < LL. *cappa*, cape], 1. an ornamented covering for a horse; trappings. 2. clothing, equipment, and ornaments; outfit. *v.t.* to adorn, as with trappings or rich clothing.
**cape** (kāp), *n.* [< Sp. *capa*, hood, via Fr. *cape*, hooded cloak; see next entry], a sleeveless garment, or part of a cloak, etc., fastened at the neck and hanging over the back and shoulders.
**cape** (kāp), *n.* [Fr. *cap* (It. *capo*) < L. *caput*, the head], a piece of land projecting into a body of water. —**the Cape,** 1. the Cape of Good Hope. 2. Cape Cod.
**cap·e·lin** (kap'ə-lin), *n.* [*pl.* -LIN, -LINS; see PLURAL, II, D, 2], [Fr. *caplan*], a variety of smelt used as bait for cod fishing: also **cap·lin** (kap'lin).
**ca·per** (kā'pẽr), *v.i.* [< *capriole*], to skip about in a playful manner. *n.* 1. a gay, playful jump or leap. 2. a wild, foolish action; prank. —**cut a caper** (**or capers**), 1. to caper. 2. to play silly tricks.
**ca·per** (kā'pẽr), *n.* [< OFr. < L. < Gr. *kapparis*], 1. a prickly, trailing Mediterranean bush. 2. *pl.* its green flower buds, pickled and used to flavor sauces, etc.
**cap·er·cail·lie** (kap'ẽr-kāl'yi), *n.* [< Gael. *capull coille*, lit., horse of the woods], the largest species of European grouse.
**Ca·per·na·um** (kə-pũr'ni-əm), *n.* an ancient city in Palestine, on the Sea of Galilee.
**Ca·pet, Hugh** (kā'pit, kap'it), 940?–996 A.D.; king of France (987–996 A.D.).
**Ca·pe·tian** (kə-pē'shən), *adj.* designating or of the French dynasty (987–1328 A.D.) founded by Hugh Capet.
**Cape Town,** seaport and capital of Cape of Good Hope province: legislative seat of Union of South Africa: pop., 344,000: also **Cape·town** (kāp'toun'), *n.*
**Cape Verde Islands** (vũrd), a group of Portuguese islands, 320 mi. west of Cape Verde.
**cap·ful** (kap'fool'), *n.* [*pl.* -FULS], as much as a cap can hold.
**ca·pi·as** (kā'pi-əs, kap'i-əs), *n.* [< L. < *capere*, to take], in *law*, a writ directing an officer to arrest the person named.
**cap·il·lar·i·ty** (kap''l-ar'ə-ti), *n.* 1. the property or exertion of capillary attraction or repulsion. 2. capillary attraction or repulsion.
**cap·il·lar·y** (kap''l-er'i), *adj.* [< L. < *capillus*, hair], 1. of or like a hair; very slender. 2. having a very small bore. 3. in or of capillaries. *n.* [*pl.* -IES], 1. a tube with a very small bore: also **capillary tube.** 2. any of the tiny blood vessels connecting the arteries with the veins.
**capillary attraction** (or **repulsion**), a force that is the resultant of adhesion, cohesion, and surface tension in liquids which are in contact with solids, causing the liquid surface to rise (or be depressed) in a capillary tube.
**cap·i·tal** (kap'ə-t'l), *adj.* [< OFr. < L. < *caput*, head], 1. involving or punishable by death: as, a *capital* offense. 2. chief; principal. 3. most important, as being the seat of government: as, a *capital* city. 4. of or having to do with capital. 5. first-rate; excellent. 6. see **capital letter.** *n.* 1. a capital letter. 2. a city or town that is the official seat of government of a state, nation, etc. 3. money or property owned or used in business by a person, corporation, etc. 4. an accumulation of such wealth. 5. wealth used to produce more wealth; hence, 6. any source of benefit; assets: as, energy is his only *capital.* 7. [often C-], capitalists collectively: distinguished from *labor.* —**make capital of,** to make the most of; exploit.
**cap·i·tal** (kap'ə-t'l), *n.* [< OFr. < L. dim. of *caput*, head], the top part of a column or pilaster.
**cap·i·tal·ism** (kap'ə-t'l-iz'm), *n.* 1. the economic system in which the means of production and distribution are privately owned and operated for profit, originally under fully competitive conditions. 2. the principles, power, etc. of capitalists.
**cap·i·tal·ist** (kap'ə-t'l-ist), *n.* 1. a person who has capital; owner of wealth used in business. 2. an upholder of capitalism. 3. loosely, a wealthy person. *adj.* capitalistic.
**cap·i·tal·is·tic** (kap'ə-t'l-is'tik), *adj.* 1. of or characteristic of capitalists or capitalism. 2. upholding, preferring, or practicing capitalism. —**cap'i·tal·is'ti·cal·ly,** *adv.*
**cap·i·tal·i·za·tion** (kap'ə-t'l-i-zā'shən, -ī-zā'-), *n.* 1. a capitalizing or being capitalized. 2. the total capital funds of a corporation, represented by stocks, bonds, etc.
**cap·i·tal·ize** (kap'ə-t'l-īz'), *v.t.* [-IZED, -IZING], 1. to use as capital; convert into capital. 2. to use to one's advantage or profit (often with *on*). 3. to establish the capital stock of (a business firm) at a certain figure. 4. to supply capital to or for (an enterprise). 5. to print or write (a word or words) in capital letters. 6. to begin (a word) with a capital letter.
**capital letter,** an upper-case letter, larger than, and often different from, the corresponding small letter, as A, B, C, etc.
**cap·i·tal·ly** (kap'ə-t'l-i), *adv.* in an excellent or admirable manner; very well.

**capital punishment,** the death penalty.
**capital ship,** a battleship or battle cruiser of over 10,000 tons displacement.
**capital stock,** 1. the capital of a corporation, divided into negotiable shares. 2. their face value.
**cap·i·ta·tion** (kap′ə-tā′shən), *n.* [< LL. < L. *caput*, the head], a tax or fee of so much per head.
**Cap·i·tol** (kap′ə-t′l), *n.* [< OFr. < L. *Capitolium*, the temple of Jupiter], 1. the temple of Jupiter in Rome. 2. the building in which the U.S. Congress meets, at Washington, D.C. 3. [usually c-], the building in which a State legislature meets.
**Cap·i·to·line** (kap′ə-t′l-īn′), *n.* one of the seven hills of Rome. *adj.* 1. of this hill. 2. of the temple of Jupiter which stood there.
**ca·pit·u·late** (kə-pich′ə-lāt′), *v.i.* [-LATED, -LATING], [< ML. pp. of *capitulare*, to draw up in heads or chapters], 1. to give up (*to* an enemy) on prearranged conditions. 2. to give up.
**ca·pit·u·la·tion** (kə-pich′ə-lā′shən), *n.* 1. a capitulating; conditional surrender. 2. a document containing terms of surrender; treaty; covenant. 3. a statement of the main parts of a subject.
**ca·pon** (kā′pon, -pən), *n.* [< AS. < L. < Gr. < *koptein*, to cut], a castrated rooster fattened for eating.
**ca·pote** (kə-pōt′), *n.* [Fr., dim. of *cape*, cape], 1. a long cloak, usually with a hood. 2. a woman's bonnet tying under the chin.
**Ca·pri** (kä′pri; *occas.* kə-prē′), *n.* an island in the Bay of Naples: area, 4 sq. mi.
‡**ca·pric·ci·o** (kə-prē′chi-ō; It. kȧ-prēt′chô), *n.* [*pl.* -CIOS; It. -CI (-chē)], [It.; see CAPRICE], 1. a prank; whim; caprice. 2. a lively musical composition of irregular form.
**ca·price** (kə-prēs′), *n.* [Fr.; It. *capriccio* < *capo*, head + *riccio* (< L. *ericius*), hedgehog], 1. a sudden turn of mind caused by a whim or impulse. 2. a capricious quality. 3. in *music*, a capriccio.
**ca·pri·cious** (kə-prish′əs), *adj.* subject to caprices; erratic; flighty; unpredictable. —**ca·pri′cious·ly,** *adv.* —**ca·pri′cious·ness,** *n.*
**Cap·ri·corn** (kap′ri-kôrn′), *n.* [< OFr. < L. < *caper*, goat + *cornu*, a horn], 1. a southern constellation resembling a goat in outline. 2. the tenth sign of the zodiac (♑), entered by the sun at the winter solstice, about December 22.
**cap·ri·ole** (kap′ri-ōl′), *n.* [Fr. < It.; ult. < L. *caper*, goat], 1. a caper; leap. 2. an upward leap made by a horse without going forward. *v.i.* [-OLED, -OLING], to make a capriole.
**caps.,** capitals (capital letters).
**cap·si·cum** (kap′si-kəm), *n.* [LL.; prob. < L. *capsa*, a box], 1. any of various tropical plants with many-seeded pungent pods called *chilies* or *peppers*. 2. these pods prepared as condiments or, in medicine, as a gastric stimulant.
**cap·size** (kap-sīz′), *v.t. & v.i.* [-SIZED, -SIZING], [? < Sp. *cabezar*, lit., to sink by the head], to overturn; upset: said especially of a boat.
**cap·stan** (kap′stən), *n.* [Fr. & Pr. *cabestan* < L. < *capere*, to take], an apparatus, mainly on ships, for hauling in cables and hawsers: it consists of an upright drum with the cable wound around it by poles (**capstan bars**) inserted and used as levers.

CAPSTAN

**cap·stone** (kap′stōn′), *n.* the uppermost stone of a structure.
**cap·sule** (kap′s′l, -syool), *n.* [Fr. < L. dim. of *capsa*, chest], 1. a small, soluble gelatin container for enclosing a dose of medicine. 2. a closed compartment designed to hold and protect men, instruments, etc., as in a spaceship. 3. in *anatomy*, any sac or membrane enclosing a part. 4. in *botany*, a case or pod containing seeds or spores: it usually bursts when ripe. —**cap′su·lar,** *adj.* —**cap′su·late′, cap′su·lat′ed,** *adj.*
**cap·tain** (kap′t′n), *n.* [< OFr. < LL. < L. *caput*, the head], 1. a chief or leader. 2. the head of a group or division; specif., *a*) an army officer commanding a company, battery, etc., and ranking just above a first lieutenant. *b*) a navy officer ranking just above a commander. *c*) the commander or master of a ship. *d*) the leader of a team, as in sports. *e*) a precinct commander in a police or fire department. Abbrev. **Capt.** *v.t.* to be captain of; head. —**cap′tain·cy** [*pl.* -CIES], **cap′tain·ship′,** *n.*
**cap·tion** (kap′shən), *n.* [< L. < *capere*, to take], a heading; title or subtitle, as of a newspaper article or picture. *v.t.* to supply a caption for.
**cap·tious** (kap′shəs), *adj.* [see CAPTION], 1. made for the sake of argument or faultfinding, as an objection. 2. quick to find fault. —**cap′tious·ly,** *adv.* —**cap′tious·ness,** *n.*
**cap·ti·vate** (kap′tə-vāt′), *v.t.* [-VATED, -VATING], [see CAPTIVE], 1. originally, to capture. 2. to capture the attention or affection of; charm. —**cap′ti·vat′ing,** *adj.* —**cap′ti·vat′ing·ly,** *adv.* —**cap′ti·va′tion,** *n.* —**cap′ti·va′tor,** *n.*
**cap·tive** (kap′tiv), *n.* [< L. *captivus* < pp. of *capere*, to take], 1. one held in confinement; prisoner. 2. one who is captivated. *adj.* 1. taken or held prisoner. 2 captivated. 3. of captivity.
**captive audience,** any group of people forced against their will to listen to something, as passengers on a bus having a radio loudspeaker.
**cap·tiv·i·ty** (kap-tiv′ə-ti), *n.* [*pl.* -TIES], the state of being a captive; imprisonment; bondage.
**cap·tor** (kap′tēr), *n.* [L.], a person who captures.
**cap·ture** (kap′chēr), *n.* [Fr. < L. *captura* < *capere*, to take], 1. a taking or being taken by force, surprise, etc.; seizure. 2. that which is thus taken. *v.t.* [-TURED, -TURING], to take or seize by force, surprise, etc.; make a prisoner of.
**Cap·u·chin** (kap′yoo-chin′, -shin′), *n.* [< Fr. < *capuce* (It. *cappuccio*), a cowl], 1. a monk of a certain Franciscan order whose members all wear a long, pointed hood or cowl. 2. [c-], a woman's cloak with a hood. 3. [c-], a South American monkey with a hoodlike crown of black hair.
‡**ca·put** (kā′pət, kap′ət), *n.* [*pl.* CAPITA], [L.], a head.
**car** (kär), *n.* [ONorm.Fr. < LL. < L. *carrus*, two-wheeled chariot < Gaul. *carros*], 1. any vehicle on wheels. 2. [Poetic], a chariot. 3. a vehicle that moves on tracks, as a railroad car. 4. an automobile. 5. an elevator cage. 6. the part of a balloon for carrying passengers and equipment.
**ca·ra·ba·o** (kä′rə-bä′ō), *n.* [*pl.* -BAOS, -BAO; see PLURAL, II, D, 1], [Sp. < Malay *karbau*], in the Philippines, a water buffalo.
**car·a·bi·neer, car·a·bi·nier** (kar′ə-bə-nêr′), *n.* [Fr. *carabinier*], a cavalryman armed with a carbine: also **carbineer.**
**ca·ra·ca·ra** (kä′rə-kä′rə), *n.* [< Sp. < Braz. native name], a large, vulturelike hawk of South America.
**Ca·ra·cas** (kə-rä′kəs; Sp. kä-rä′käs), *n.* the capital of Venezuela: pop., 739,000.
**car·a·cole** (kar′ə-kōl′), *n.* [Fr. < It. < Sp. *caracol*, shell of a snail], in *horsemanship*, a half turn to the right or left. *v.i.* [-COLED, -COLING], to make a caracole; move in caracoles.
**car·a·cul** (kar′ə-kəl), *n.* karakul.
**ca·rafe** (kə-raf′, -räf′), *n.* [Fr. < It. *caraffa*; prob. < Ar. *gharafa*, to draw water], a bottle made of glass or crystal; decanter.
**car·a·mel** (kar′ə-m′l, -mel′, kär′m′l), *n.* [Fr.; ? < LL. *calamellus*, tube, confused with ML. *canna mellis*, sugar cane], 1. burnt sugar used to color or flavor food. 2. chewy candy made from sugar, milk, etc. 3. a small piece of this.
**car·a·mel·ize** (kar′ə-m′l-īz′, kär′m′l-īz′), *v.t. & v.i.* [-IZED, -IZING], to turn into caramel.
**car·a·pace** (kar′ə-pās′), *n.* [Fr. < Sp. *carapacho*], an upper case or shell, as of the turtle.
**car·at** (kar′ət), *n.* [Fr. < It. < Ar. < Gr. *keration*, carat, < *keras*, a horn], 1. a unit of weight for precious stones, equal to about 3.086 grains troy or .2 of a gram. 2. one 24th part (of pure gold): 20-*carat* gold is 20 parts pure gold and 4 parts alloy. Abbrev. **car., kt.** Also sp. **karat.**
**car·a·van** (kar′ə-van′), *n.* [< Fr. < OFr. < Per. *kārwān*, caravan], 1. a company of merchants, pilgrims, etc. traveling together for safety, as through a desert. 2. a large covered vehicle for passengers, circus animals, etc.; van.
**car·a·van·sa·ry** (kar′ə-van′sə-ri), *n.* [*pl.* -RIES], [< Fr. < Per. < *kārwān*, caravan + *sarāī*, palace], 1. in the Orient, a sort of inn where caravans stop for the night. 2. a large inn or hotel. Also **car′a·van′se·rai′** (-sə-rī′, -sə-rā′).
**car·a·vel, car·a·velle** (kar′ə-vel′), *n.* [< Fr. < Sp. < LL. < Gr. *karabos*, kind of light ship], a fast, small sailing ship used in the 16th century.
**car·a·way** (kar′ə-wā′), *n.* [< Sp. < Ar. *al-karawiyā* < Gr. *karon*, caraway], 1. a plant with spicy seeds. 2. the seeds, used to flavor bread, cakes, etc.
**car·bide** (kär′bīd, -bid), *n.* [*carb-* + *-ide*], a com-

pound of an element, usually a metal, with carbon; esp., calcium carbide.
**car·bine** (kär′bīn, -bēn), *n.* [< Fr. < *scarabée*, a beetle], 1. a rifle with a short barrel: also sp. **carabin, carabine.** 2. in the *U.S. Army*, a light, semiautomatic, .30-caliber rifle.
**car·bo-**, a combining form meaning *carbon:* also, before a vowel, **carb-.**
**car·bo·hy·drate** (kär′bə-hī′drāt), *n.* [*carbo-* + *hydrate*], an organic compound composed of carbon, hydrogen, and oxygen, as a sugar, starch, or cellulose.
**car·bo·lat·ed** (kär′bə-lā′tid), *adj.* containing or treated with carbolic acid.
**car·bol·ic** (kär-bol′ik), *adj.* [< L. *carbo*, coal + *oleum*, oil; + *-ic*], designating or of a poisonous acid, $C_6H_6O$, obtained from coal or coal tar, and used in solution as an antiseptic, etc.; phenol.
**car·bo·lize** (kär′bə-līz′), *v.t.* [-LIZED, -LIZING], to treat or mix with carbolic acid.
**car·bon** (kär′bən), *n.* [< Fr. < L. *carbo*, coal], 1. a nonmetallic chemical element found in many inorganic compounds and all organic compounds: diamond and graphite are pure carbon; carbon is also present in coal, coke, etc.: symbol, C; at. wt., 12.01; at. no., 6. 2. a sheet of carbon paper. 3. a copy, as of a letter, made with carbon paper: in full, **carbon copy.** 4. in *electricity*, *a*) a stick of carbon used in an arc lamp. *b*) a carbon plate or rod used in a battery. *adj.* of or like carbon.
**car·bo·na·ceous** (kär′bə-nā′shəs), *adj.* 1. of or containing carbon. 2. containing or like coal.
**car·bon·ate** (kär′bən-it, -bə-nāt′), *n.* a salt or ester of carbonic acid. *v.t.* (-bə-nāt′), [-ATED, -ATING], 1. to burn to carbon. 2. to charge with carbon dioxide. 3. to change into a carbonate. —**car′bon·a′tion,** *n.*
**car·bon-date** (kär′bən-dāt′), *v.t.* [-DATED, -DATING], to establish the approximate age of (fossils, ancient artifacts, etc.) by measuring the amount of a radioactive isotope of carbon **(carbon 14)** remaining in them.
**carbon dioxide,** a heavy, colorless, odorless gas, $CO_2$: it passes out of the lungs in respiration, and is absorbed by plants: also **carbonic-acid gas.**
**car·bon·ic** (kär-bon′ik), *adj.* 1. of or containing carbon. 2. obtained from carbon.
**carbonic acid,** a weak, colorless acid, $H_2CO_3$, formed by the solution of carbon dioxide in water.
**car·bon·if·er·ous** (kär′bə-nif′ẽr-əs), *adj.* [< *carbon* + *-ferous*], 1. containing carbon or coal. 2. [C-], of a great coal-making period of the Paleozoic Era: the warm, damp climate produced great forests, which later formed rich coal seams. —**the Carboniferous,** 1. the Carboniferous Period. 2. the rock and coal strata formed during this period. See **geology,** chart.
**car·bon·ize** (kär′bə-nīz′), *v.t.* [-IZED, -IZING], 1. to change into carbon, as by burning incompletely. 2. to treat, cover, or combine with carbon. —**car′bon·i·za′tion,** *n.*
**carbon monoxide,** a colorless, odorless, highly poisonous gas, CO, produced by the incomplete combustion of carbon.
**carbon paper,** very thin paper coated on one side with a carbon preparation: placed between sheets of paper, it is used to make copies of letters, etc.
**carbon tet·ra·chlo·ride** (tet′rə-klôr′īd, -klō′rīd), a noninflammable, colorless liquid, $CCl_4$, used in fire extinguishers, cleaning mixtures, etc.
**car·bo·run·dum** (kär′bə-run′dəm), *n.* [*carbon* + *corundum*], a very hard abrasive substance, a compound of carbon and silicon, SiC, made into grindstones, etc.: a trade-mark (**Carborundum**).
**car·boy** (kär′boi), *n.* [< Per. *qarābah*], a large glass bottle enclosed in basketwork or in a wooden crate: used as a container for corrosive liquids.
**car·bun·cle** (kär′buŋ-k'l), *n.* [< OFr. < L. dim. of *carbo*, coal], 1. a deep-red gem, especially a smooth, convex garnet. 2. a painful, pus-bearing inflammation of the tissue beneath the skin, more severe than a boil and having several openings. —**car·bun·cu·lar** (kär-buŋ′kyoo-lẽr), *adj.*
**car·bu·ret** (kär′bə-rāt′, -byoo-ret′), *v.t.* [-RETED or -RETTED, -RETING or -RETTING], [*carb-* + *-uret*], 1. to combine chemically with carbon. 2. to mix or charge (gas or air) with volatile carbon compounds. —**car′bu·re′tion** (-bə-rā′shən, -byoo-resh′ən), *n.*
**car·bu·re·tor, car·bu·ret·tor** (kär′bə-rā′tẽr, -byoo-ret′ẽr), *n.* a device in which air is mixed with gasoline spray to make an explosive mixture in an internal-combustion engine.
**car·ca·jou** (kär′kə-jōō′, -zhōō′), *n.* [Canad.Fr. < native Ind. name], the wolverine.
**car·cass, car·case** (kär′kəs), *n.* [< Fr. < It. *carcassa*], 1. the dead body of any animal. 2. the body, living or dead, of a human being: scornful or humorous usage. 3. the worthless remains of something. 4. a framework or base structure, as of a ship or tire.
**car·cin·o·gen** (kär-sin′ə-jən), *n.* [*carcinoma* + *-gen*], any substance that produces cancer. —**car·cin′o·gen′ic** (-jen′ik), *adj.*
**car·ci·no·ma** (kär′sə-nō′mə), *n.* [*pl.* -MAS, -MATA (-mə-tə)], [L. < Gr. *karkinōma*, cancer < *karkinos*, a crab], any of several kinds of epithelial cancer. —**car′ci·nom′a·tous** (-nom′ə-təs, -nō′mə-), *adj.*
**card** (kärd), *n.* [< OFr. < L. *charta* < Gr. *chartēs*, leaf of paper], 1. a flat, stiff piece of thick paper or thin pasteboard, usually rectangular; esp., *a*) one of a pack of playing cards: see also **cards.** *b*) a compass card. *c*) a post card. *d*) a calling card. *e*) a card bearing a message or greeting: as, a birthday *card.* *f*) a card to advertise or announce: as, a window *card.* *g*) the printed program for sporting events, etc.: as, a race *card;* hence, 2. an event or attraction: as, a drawing *card.* 3. [Colloq.], a person notably funny, eccentric, etc. *v.t.* 1. to provide with a card. 2. to put or list on a card or cards. —**card up one's sleeve,** a plan or resource kept secret or in reserve. —**in** (or **on**) **the cards,** likely to occur; possible. —**put** (or **lay**) **one's cards on the table,** to reveal frankly, as one's intentions.
**card** (kärd), *n.* [< Fr. < Pr. < L. *carere*, to card; sp. affected by L. *carduus*, thistle], a metal comb or wire brush for combing the fibers of wool, cotton, flax, etc. *v.t.* to use such a tool on, as in preparing wool for spinning. —**card′er,** *n.*
**car·da·mom** (kär′də-məm), *n.* [< L. < Gr. < *kardamon*, cress + *amōmon*, spice plant], 1. an Asiatic herb of the ginger family. 2. its seed, used in medicine and as a spice. Also **car′da·mon** (-mən).
**card·board** (kärd′bôrd′, -bōrd′), *n.* stiff, thick paper, or pasteboard, used for cards, boxes, etc.
**card catalogue,** an alphabetical card index.
**car·di·ac** (kär′di-ak′), *adj.* [< Fr. < L. < Gr. < *kardia*, the heart], 1. of or near the heart. 2. relating to the upper part of the stomach. *n.* a medicine that stimulates cardiac action.
**Car·diff** (kär′dif), *n.* a city in Wales, on the Bristol Channel: pop., 261,000.
**car·di·gan** (kär′di-gən), *n.* [after 7th Earl of *Cardigan* (1797–1868)], a knitted woolen jacket or jacketlike sweater: also **cardigan jacket** (or **sweater**).
**car·di·nal** (kär′d'n-əl, -di-n'l), *adj.* [< OFr. < L. *cardinalis* < *cardo*, hinge, that on which something turns], 1. fundamental; principal; chief. 2. bright-red. *n.* 1. any of the Roman Catholic officials appointed by the Pope to his council. 2. bright red. 3. the cardinal bird. 4. a cardinal number. —**car′di·nal·ly,** *adv.* —**car′di·nal·ship′,** *n.*
**car·di·nal·ate** (kär′d'n-əl-āt′), *n.* 1. the position or rank of a cardinal. 2. the College of Cardinals.
**cardinal (bird),** a bright-red American songbird, related to the finch: also **cardinal grosbeak.**
**cardinal flower,** 1. the bright-red flower of a North American plant that grows in damp, shady places or in shallow water. 2. this plant.
**cardinal number** (or **numeral**), any number used in counting or showing how many (e.g., two, forty, 627, etc.): distinguished from *ordinal number* (e.g., second, fortieth, 627th, etc.).
**cardinal points,** the four principal points of the compass; north, south, east, and west.
**cardinal virtues,** in *theology*, the basic virtues; prudence, justice, fortitude, and temperance.
**card index,** a systematic file of data cards.
**card·ing** (kär′diŋ), *n.* the combing of wool, cotton, etc. to prepare them for spinning.
**car·di·o-** [< Gr. *kardia*, heart], a combining form meaning *of the heart;* also, before a vowel, **cardi-.**
**car·di·o·gram** (kär′di-ə-gram′), *n.* [*cardio-* + *-gram*], a record traced by a cardiograph.
**car·di·o·graph** (kär′di-ə-graf′, -gräf′), *n.* [*cardio-* + *-graph*], an instrument for making a graph of the heart's action. —**car′di·o·graph′ic,** *adj.* —**car·di·og·ra·phy** (kär′di-og′rə-fi), *n.*
**car·di·tis** (kär-dī′tis), *n.* [< Gr. *kardia*, the heart; + *-itis*], inflammation of the heart.
**cards** (kärdz), *n.pl.* 1. a game or games played with a deck of cards, as bridge, rummy, poker, etc. 2. the playing of such games; card playing.
**card·sharp** (cärd′shärp′), *n.* a professional swindler at cards: also **card′sharp′er.**
**care** (kâr), *n.* [AS. *caru*, sorrow], 1. mental pain; worry; anxiety. 2. close attention; watchfulness; heed. 3. a liking or regard (*for*); inclination (*to* do something). 4. charge; protection; custody. 5. something to worry about, watch over, or attend to.

*v.i.* [CARED, CARING], 1. to be worried or concerned; mind. 2. to wish or like (*to* do something): as, I don't *care* to answer. —**care for,** 1. to love or like. 2. to wish for; want. 3. to look after; provide for. —**care of,** at the address of. —**have a care,** to be careful: also **take care.** —**take care of,** 1. to be responsible for; attend to. 2. to provide for. —**car'er,** *n.*

**ca·reen** (kə-rēn'), *v.t.* [< Fr. < It. < L. *carina*, keel], 1. to cause (a ship) to lean or lie on one side, as for calking. 2. to cause to lean sideways; tip; tilt. *v.i.* 1. to lean sideways. 2. to lurch or toss from side to side. *n.* a careening.

**ca·reer** (kə-rêr'), *n.* [< Fr. *carrière*, racecourse < It. < L. *carrus*; see CAR], 1. full speed. 2. one's progress through life. 3. one's advancement in a particular vocation; hence, 4. a profession or occupation. *v.i.* to move at full speed; rush wildly.

**ca·reer·ist** (kə-rêr'ist), *n.* a person interested chiefly in his own professional ambitions, to the neglect of other things. —**ca·reer'ism,** *n.*

**care·free** (kâr'frē'), *adj.* without care or worry.

**care·ful** (kâr'fəl), *adj.* 1. caring (*for*) or taking care (*of*). 2. watchful; cautious; dealing cautiously (*with*). 3. accurately or thoroughly done; painstaking. 4. [Archaic], worried; anxious. —**care'ful·ly,** *adv.* —**care'ful·ness,** *n.*

**care·less** (kâr'lis), *adj.* 1. carefree; untroubled. 2. not paying enough attention; not thinking before one acts or speaks; neglectful; reckless. 3. done or made without enough attention, precision, etc. —**care'less·ly,** *adv.* —**care'less·ness,** *n.*

**ca·ress** (kə-res'), *v.t.* [-RESSED or *archaic* -REST, -RESSING], [< Fr. < It.; ult. < L. *carus*, dear], to touch or stroke lovingly or gently; also, to embrace or kiss. *n.* an affectionate touch or gesture, as a kiss, embrace, etc. —**ca·ress'a·ble,** *adj.* —**ca·ress'er,** *n.* —**ca·ress'ing·ly,** *adv.* —**ca·res'sive,** *adj.* —**ca·res'sive·ly,** *adv.*

**car·et** (kar'it, kâr'-), *n.* [L., lit., there is lacking], a mark (∧) used in writing or correcting proof, to show where something is to be added.

**care·tak·er** (kâr'tāk'ēr), *n.* a person whose work is to take care of some thing, place, or person.

**care·worn** (kâr'wôrn', -wōrn'), *adj.* showing the effects of grief and worry; haggard; weary.

**car·fare** (kär'fâr'), *n.* the price of a ride on a streetcar, bus, etc.

**car·go** (kär'gō), *n.* [*pl.* -GOES, -GOS], [< Sp. < *cargar*, to load], 1. the load of commodities carried by a ship; freight. 2. load.

**car·hop** (kär'hop'), *n.* [*car* + bell*hop*], one who serves customers in cars at a drive-in restaurant.

**Car·ib** (kar'ib), *n.* 1. a member of an Indian tribe that inhabited the S West Indies and the N coast of South America. 2. a family of South and Central American languages. —**Car'ib·an,** *adj.*

**Car·ib·be·an** (kar'ə-bē'ən, kə-rib'i-ən), *adj.* 1. of the Caribs, their language, etc. 2. of the Caribbean Sea, its islands, etc. *n.* 1. a Carib. 2. a sea bounded by Central America, the West Indies, and South America: also **Caribbean Sea.**

**car·i·bou** (kar'ə-bōō'), *n.* [*pl.* -BOUS, -BOU; see PLURAL, II, D, 1], [Canad. Fr.; prob. < Algonquian *khalibou*], a North American reindeer.

**car·i·ca·ture** (kar'i-kə-chēr, -choor'), *n.* [Fr. < It. < *caricare*, to load, exaggerate], 1. the distorted picturing or imitating of a person, literary style, etc. by exaggerating features or mannerisms for satirical effect. 2. a picture, literary work, etc. in which this is done. 3. a poor imitation. *v.t.* [-TURED, -TURING], to portray as in a caricature. —**car'i·ca·tur·al,** *adj.* —**car'i·ca·tur·ist,** *n.*

**car·ies** (kâr'ēz, -i-ēz'), *n.* [L., decay], decay of teeth, bones, or, sometimes, of tissue.

**car·il·lon** (kar'ə-lon', kə-ril'yən), *n.* [Fr., chime of (orig. four) bells < ML. < L. *quattuor*, four], 1. a set of stationary bells, each producing one tone of the chromatic scale. 2. a melody played on such bells. 3. an organ stop producing a sound like that of such bells. *v.i.* [-LONNED, -LONNING], to play a carillon.

**car·il·lon·neur** (kar'ə-lə-nũr'), *n.* [Fr.], a carillon player.

**car·i·ole** (kar'i-ōl'), *n.* [< Fr. < It. dim. of *carro*; see CAR], 1. a small carriage drawn by one horse. 2. a light, covered cart. Also sp. **carriole.**

**car·i·ous** (kâr'i-əs), *adj.* [L. *cariosus*], 1. having caries; decayed. 2. corroded. —**car·i·os·i·ty** (kâr'i-os'ə-ti), **car'i·ous·ness,** *n.*

**cark·ing** (kär'kiŋ), *adj.* [< ME. < OFr. < LL. < *carricare*, to load], [Archaic or Poetic], troublesome.

**carl, carle** (kärl), *n.* [AS. < ON. *karl*], 1. [Archaic or Obs.] a peasant or villein. 2. [Scot.] a boor.

**car·load** (kär'lōd'), *n.* a load that fills a car.

**carload lot,** a freight shipment large enough to be shipped at a special rate (**carload rate**).

**Carls·bad Caverns** (kärlz'bad), a national park in SE New Mexico, with large limestone caverns.

**Car·lyle, Thomas** (kär-līl'), 1795–1881; Scottish historian, philosopher, and essayist.

**car·ma·gnole** (kär'mən-yōl'), *n.* [Fr., altered < older *carmignole*, kind of cap], 1. the costume worn by French revolutionaries (1792). 2. a song and round dance popular during the French Revolution.

**car·man** (kär'mən), *n.* [*pl.* -MEN], a streetcar conductor or motorman.

**Car·mel·ite** (kär'm'l-īt'), *n.* a friar or nun of the order of Our Lady of Mount Carmel, founded in Syria about 1160. *adj.* of this order.

**car·min·a·tive** (kär-min'ə-tiv, kär'mi-nā'-), *adj.* [< L. pp. of *carminare*, to card, cleanse], expelling gas from the stomach and intestines. *n.* a carminative medicine.

**car·mine** (kär'min, -mīn), *n.* [< Fr. < ML. *carminus* < Ar. *qirmiz*, crimson], 1. a red or purplish-red pigment obtained mainly from cochineal. 2. its color. *adj.* red or purplish-red; crimson.

**car·nage** (kär'nij), *n.* [< Fr. < It. < LL. < L. *caro, carnis*, flesh], bloody and extensive slaughter, especially in battle; massacre; bloodshed.

**car·nal** (kär'n'l), *adj.* [< OFr. < L. *carnalis* < *caro*, flesh], 1. in or of the flesh; material or worldly, not spiritual. 2. sensual; sexual. —**car·nal·i·ty** (kär-nal'ə-ti), [*pl.* -TIES], *n.* —**car'nal·ly,** *adv.*

**car·na·tion** (kär-nā'shən), *n.* [Fr. < L. *carnatio* < *caro*, flesh], 1. formerly, rosy pink; now, deep red. 2. any cultivated variety of the clove pink. 3. its fragrant flower of pink, white, or red.

**Car·ne·gie, Andrew** (kär-nā'gi, kär'nə-), 1835–1919; U.S. industrialist and philanthropist.

**car·nel·ian** (kär-nēl'yən), *n.* [altered (after L. *caro, carnis*, flesh) < *cornelian*], a red variety of chalcedony, used in jewelry.

**car·ni·fy** (kär'nə-fī'), *v.t. & v.i.* [-FIED, -FYING], [< L. < *caro*, flesh + *facere*, to make], 1. to form into flesh. 2. to make or become fleshlike.

**car·ni·val** (kär'nə-v'l), *n.* [< Fr. or It.; < LL. < hyp. *carnem levare*, to remove meat], 1. the period of feasting and revelry just before Lent. 2. a reveling; festivity; merrymaking. 3. an entertainment with side shows, rides, and refreshments.

**Car·niv·o·ra** (kär-niv'ə-rə), *n.pl.* [see CARNIVOROUS], in *zoology*, an order of flesh-eating mammals, including the dog, cat, bear, seal, etc.

**car·ni·vore** (kär'nə-vôr', -vōr'), *n.* a carnivorous animal: opposed to *herbivore*.

**car·niv·o·rous** (kär-niv'ə-rəs), *adj.* [< L. < *caro, carnis*, flesh + *vorare*, to eat], 1. flesh-eating: opposed to *herbivorous*. 2. of the Carnivora. —**car·niv'o·rous·ly,** *adv.* —**car·niv'o·rous·ness,** *n.*

**car·ol** (kar'əl), *n.* [< OFr. < L. < Gr. < *choros*, dance + *aulein*, to play on the flute], a song of joy or praise, especially in honor of the Nativity; Christmas song. *v.i.* [-OLED or -OLLED, -OLING or -OLLING], to sing in joy; sing; warble. *v.t.* 1. to sing (a tune, etc.). 2. to praise in song. —**car'ol·er, car'ol·ler,** *n.*

**Car·o·li·na** (kar'ə-lī'nə), *n.* an American colony on the Atlantic coast, first settled in 1653. —**the Carolinas,** North Carolina and South Carolina.

**Car·o·line Islands** (kar'ə-līn', -lin), a chain of about 550 small coral islands in Micronesia, under U.S. trusteeship.

**Car·o·lin·i·an** (kar'ə-lin'i-ən), *adj.* of North Carolina or South Carolina. *n.* a native or inhabitant of North Carolina or South Carolina.

**car·om** (kar'əm), *n.* [< Fr. < Sp. *carambola*, red ball at billiards], 1. in *billiards*, any shot in which the cue ball hits two other balls in succession. 2. a hitting and rebounding. *v.i.* 1. to make a carom. 2. to hit and rebound. Also sp. **carrom.**

**car·oms** (kar'əmz), *n.pl.* [construed as sing.], a game for 2 or 4 players, played with 24 round counters on a square board with corner pockets.

**car·o·tene** (kar'ə-tēn'), *n.* [< L. *carota*, carrot; + *-ene*], a reddish-yellow compound, $C_{40}H_{56}$, found in carrots and some other vegetables, and changed into vitamin A in the body: also **car'o·tin** (-tin).

**ca·rot·e·noid** (kə-rot'ə-noid'), *n.* [< *carotene* + *-oid*], any of several red and yellow pigments related to carotene. *adj.* 1. of or like carotene. 2. of the carotenoids. Also sp. **carotinoid.**

**ca·rot·id** (kə-rot′id), *adj.* [Gr. *karōtides*, the carotids < *karoun*, to plunge into sleep: compression of these arteries causes unconsciousness], designating, of, or near either of the two main arteries, one on each side of the neck, which convey the blood to the head. *n.* a carotid artery.—**ca·rot′id·al,** *adj.*

**ca·rous·al** (kə-rouz′'l), *n.* a carouse.

**ca·rouse** (kə-rouz′), *v.i.* [-ROUSED, -ROUSING], [< OFr. < G. *gar aus(trinken)*, (to drink) quite out], to participate in a lively drinking party. *n.* a carousing; hilarious drinking party. —**ca·rous′er,** *n*

**car·ou·sel** (kar′ə-zel′, kar′oo-sel′), *n.* a carrousel.

**carp** (kärp), *n.* [*pl.* CARP, CARPS; see PLURAL, II, D, 2], [< OFr. < LL. *carpa*; prob. < Slavic], 1. any of a group of edible fresh-water fishes living in ponds. 2. any of various other similar fishes, as the goldfish, dace, etc.

**carp** (kärp), *v.i.* [< ON. *karpa*, to brag], to find fault pettily or unfairly; cavil (*at*).

**-carp** (kärp), [< Gr. *karpos*, fruit], a terminal combining form meaning *fruit*, as in *endocarp*.

**car·pal** (kär′p'l), *adj.* [Mod. L. *carpalis*], of the carpus. *n.* a bone of the carpus; carpale.

**car·pa·le** (kär-pā′li), *n.* [*pl.* -LIA (-li-ə)], [Mod. L., neut. of *carpalis*], a bone of the carpus; carpal.

**Car·pa·thi·an Mountains** (kär-pā′thi-ən), mountain ranges extending between Poland and Czechoslovakia: also **Car·pa′thi·ans,** *n.pl.*

‡**car·pe di·em** (kär′pi dī′em), [L., lit., seize the day], make the most of today.

**car·pel** (kär′p'l), *n.* [< Gr. *karpos*, fruit], 1. a simple pistil, regarded as a modified leaf. 2. any of the carpels that unite to form a compound **pistil.** —**car′·pel·lar′y, car′pel·late′,** *adj.*

CARPEL

CARPEL

**car·pen·ter** (kär′pən-tẽr), *n.* [< ONorm.Fr. < LL. *carpentarius* < L. *carpentum*, a cart], a workman who builds and repairs wooden articles, buildings, etc. *v.i.* to do a carpenter's work. *v.t.* to make or repair as by carpentry.

**car·pen·try** (kär′pən-tri), *n.* the work or trade of a carpenter.

**car·pet** (kär′pit), *n.* [< OFr. < LL. *carpita*, woolen cloth < L. *carpere*, to card], 1. a heavy fabric, or a piece of this, for covering a floor. 2. anything that covers like a carpet. *v.t.* to cover as with a carpet. —**on the carpet,** 1. under consideration. 2. in the position of being reprimanded.

**car·pet·bag** (kär′pit-bag′), *n.* an old-fashioned variety of traveling bag, made of carpeting.

**car·pet·bag·ger** (kär′pit-bag′ẽr), *n.* a Northern politician or adventurer who went South to take advantage of unsettled conditions after the Civil War: contemptuous term. —**car′pet·bag′ging,** *n.*

**carpet beetle** (or **bug**), a black beetle whose larvae feed on carpets, furs, etc.

**car·pet·ing** (kär′pit-iŋ), *n.* carpets or carpet fabric.

**carpet sweeper,** a hand-operated device with a revolving brush for sweeping carpets and rugs.

**-car·pic** (kär′pik), -carpous.

**carp·ing** (kär′piŋ), *adj.* finding fault; captious.

**car·po-** (kär′pō, -pə), [< Gr. *karpos*, fruit], a combining form meaning *fruit* or *seeds*.

**car·port** (kär′pôrt′), *n.* a shelter for an automobile, consisting of a roof extended from the side of a building, often with an additional wall.

**-car·pous** (kär′pəs), [< Gr. *karpos*, fruit], a terminal combining form meaning *fruited, having fruit.*

**car·pus** (kär′pəs), *n.* [*pl.* -PI (-pī)], [< Gr. *karpos*, wrist], 1. the wrist. 2. the wrist bones.

**car·rack** (kar′ək), *n.* [< OFr. < Sp. < Ar. pl. of *qurqūr*, merchant ship], a galleon: also sp. **carack.**

**Car·ra·ra** (kə-rä′rə), *n.* a city in NW Italy: pop., 59,000: a fine white marble is found near by.

**car·rel, car·rell** (kar′əl), *n.* [var. of *carol*, *n.*], a small enclosure in a library, for study or reading.

**car·riage** (kar′ij), *n.* [< ONorm.Fr.; ult. < L. *carrus*, cart], 1. a carrying; transportation. 2. (kar′i-ij), the cost of carrying. 3. management. 4. manner of carrying the head and body; poise; bearing. 5. a four-wheeled passenger vehicle, usually horse-drawn. 6. a wheeled support: as, a gun *carriage.* 7. a moving part (as on a typewriter) for supporting and shifting something.

**car·ri·er** (kar′i-ẽr), *n.* 1. a person or thing that carries: as, a mail *carrier.* 2. one in the business of transporting. 3. a messenger or porter. 4. something in or on which something else is carried or conducted. 5. a person or thing that carries and transmits disease germs. 6. in *electricity & radio*, the steady transmitted wave whose amplitude, frequency, or phase is modulated by the signal. 7. an aircraft carrier.

**carrier pigeon,** a homing pigeon.

**car·ri·ole** (kar′i-ōl′, -ôl′), *n.* a cariole.

**car·ri·on** (kar′i-ən), *n.* [< ONorm.Fr.; ult. < L. *caro*, flesh], the decaying flesh of a dead body: sometimes used figuratively. *adj.* 1. of or like carrion. 2. feeding on carrion.

**carrion crow,** the common crow of Europe.

**Car·roll, Lewis** (kar′əl), (pseudonym of *Charles Lutwidge Dodgson*), 1832–1898; English writer.

**car·rom** (kar′əm), *n. & v.i.* carom.

**car·rot** (kar′ət), *n.* [< Fr. < L. < Gr. *karōton*], 1. a plant of the celery family, with a fleshy, orange-red root. 2. the root, eaten as a vegetable.

**car·rot·y** (kar′ət-i), *adj.* 1. orange-red, like carrots. 2. red-haired.

**car·rou·sel** (kar′ə-zel′, kar′oo-sel′), *n.* [Fr. < It. dial. *carozello*; ult. < L. *carrus*, car], a merry-go-round: also sp. **carousel.**

**car·ry** (kar′i), *v.t.* [-RIED, -RYING], [< ONorm.Fr. *carier*; ult. < L. *carrus*, car], 1. to take from one place to another; transport; convey. 2. to lead or impel: as, his interests *carried* him into engineering. 3. to transmit: as, the air *carries* sounds. 4. to transfer or extend: as, *carry* the pipe to the sewer. 5. to transfer (a figure, entry, etc.) from one column, page, etc. to the next in order. 6. to capture (a fortress, etc.). 7. to win over or influence, as an audience. 8. to win (an election, argument, etc.). 9. [Southern Dial.], to escort. 10. to hold or support; bear the weight of. 11. to be pregnant with. 12. to involve; imply: as, his statement *carries* conviction. 13. to keep with one; have: as, he *carries* a watch. 14. to hold or poise (oneself) in a specified way. 15. in *commerce*, *a*) to keep in stock; deal in. *b*) to keep on one's account books, etc. 16. in *music*, to bear or sustain (a melody or part). *v.i.* 1. to act as a bearer, conductor, etc. 2. to have or cover a range: as, his voice doesn't *carry* well. 3. to hold the head, etc. in a specified way. *n.* [*pl.* -RIES], 1. the distance covered by a gun, golf ball, etc. 2. a portage between two navigable bodies of water. 3. a carrying. —**carry away,** to excite great emotion in. —**carry off,** 1. to kill. 2. to win (a prize, etc.). 3. to handle (a situation), especially with success. —**carry on,** 1. to do; conduct. 2. to continue as before. 3. [Colloq.], to behave in a wild or childish way. —**carry out,** 1. to put (plans, etc.) into practice. 2. to get done; accomplish. —**carry over,** 1. to have or be remaining. 2. to postpone; continue. —**carry through,** 1. to get done; accomplish. 2. to sustain.

**car·ry·all** (kar′i-ôl′), *n.* [< *cariole*], a light, covered carriage with seats for several people.

**car·ry·all** (kar′i-ôl′), *n.* a large bag, basket, etc.

**carrying charge,** interest charged by brokers, merchants, etc. on the balance owed on a purchase.

**car·ry·ings-on** (kar′i-iŋz-on′), *n.pl.* [Colloq.], wild, silly, or childish behavior.

**car·ry-o·ver** (kar′i-ō′vẽr), *n.* 1. something carried over. 2. a remainder, as of crops or goods.

**car-sick** (kär′sik′), *adj.* nauseated from riding in an automobile, train, etc. —**car′-sick′ness,** *n.*

**Car·son, Kit** (kit kär′s'n), (*Christopher Carson*), 1809–1868; U.S. frontiersman.

**Car·son City** (kär′s'n), the capital of Nevada, near Lake Tahoe: pop., 5,000.

**cart** (kärt), *n.* [< ON. *kartr*], 1. a small, often two-wheeled, wagon. 2. a small vehicle drawn or pushed by hand. *v.t. & v.i.* to carry in a cart or other vehicle. —**put the cart before the horse,** to do things backwards. —**cart′er,** *n.* —**cart′ing,** *n.*

**cart·age** (kär′tij), *n.* 1. the act or work of carting. 2. the charge made for carting.

**carte blanche** (kärt′ blänsh′; Fr. kȧrt′ blänsh′), [*pl.* CARTES BLANCHES (kärts′ blänsh′; Fr. kȧrt′ blänsh′)], [Fr., lit., white (i.e., blank) card], 1. full authority. 2. freedom to do as one thinks best.

**car·tel** (kär-tel′, kär′t'l), *n.* [Fr. < It. *cartello*, dim. of *carta* < L. *charta*, writing; see CARD (stiff paper)], 1. a written challenge, as to a duel. 2. a written agreement between nations at war, especially as to the exchange of prisoners. 3. [G. *kartell* < Fr.], an association of business firms, etc. for establishing a national or international monopoly; trust: see also **monopoly**

**Car·te·sian** (kär-tē′zhən), *adj.* [< *Cartesius*, Latinized form of (René) *Descartes*], of Descartes, his ideas, or his methods. *n.* a follower of Descartes' ideas or methods. —**Car·te′sian·ism,** *n.*

**Car·thage** (kär′thij), *n.* an ancient city and state in N Africa, founded by the Phoenicians and destroyed by the Romans (146 B.C.). —**Car′tha·gin′i·an** (-thə-jin′i-ən), *adj. & n.*

**Car·thu·sian** (kär-thōō′zhən), *n.* [< ML. < L. name of *Chartreux*, France], a monk or nun of a very strict order founded at Chartreuse, France in 1086. *adj.* of this order.
**car·ti·lage** (kär′t'l-ij), *n.* [Fr. < L. *cartilago*], 1. a tough, elastic, whitish tissue forming part of the skeleton; gristle. 2. any part of the body consisting of cartilage.
**car·ti·lag·i·nous** (kär′t'l-aj′ə-nəs), *adj.* 1. of or resembling cartilage; gristly. 2. having a skeleton made up mainly of cartilage.
**cart·load** (kärt′lōd′), *n.* as much as a cart holds.
**car·tog·ra·phy** (kär-tog′rə-fi), *n.* [< L. *carta*; see CARD (stiff paper); + *-graphy*], the art or work of making maps or charts: abbrev. **cartog.** —**car·tog′ra·pher,** *n.* —**car′to·graph′ic** (kär′tə-graf′ik), **car′to·graph′i·cal,** *adj.* —**car′to·graph′i·cal·ly,** *adv.*
**car·ton** (kär′t'n), *n.* [Fr. < It. *cartone* < *carta*; see CARD (stiff paper)], a cardboard box.
**car·toon** (kär-tōōn′), *n.* [Fr. *carton* < It. *cartone*; see CARTON], 1. a drawing that caricatures, often satirically, some situation or person. 2. a full-size sketch of a design or picture to be copied in a fresco, tapestry, etc. 3. a comic strip. 4. an animated cartoon. *v.t.* to draw a cartoon of. *v.i.* to draw cartoons. —**car·toon′ing,** *n.* —**car·toon′ist,** *n.*
**car·tridge** (kär′trij), *n.* [altered < Fr. *cartouche* < It. < *carta*; see CARD (stiff paper)], 1. a cylindrical case as of cardboard or metal, containing the charge, and usually the projectile, for a firearm. 2. any similar small container, as for razor blades, camera film, etc.

CARTRIDGE

**cartridge clip,** a metal container for cartridges, inserted in certain types of firearms.
**cart wheel,** 1. the wheel of a cart. 2. a kind of handspring performed sidewise. 3. [Slang], a large coin, especially a silver dollar.
**Ca·ru·so, En·ri·co** (en-rē′kô kä-rōō′zô; Eng. kə-rōō′sō), 1873–1921; Italian operatic tenor in U.S.
**carve** (kärv), *v.t.* [CARVED, CARVING; *archaic* pp. CARVEN (kär′vən)], [AS. *ceorfan*], 1. to make by or as by cutting: as, *carve* a design on wood, *carve* a career. 2. to shape or decorate by cutting. 3. to divide by cutting; slice. *v.i.* to carve statues or designs. 2. to carve meat. —**carv′er,** *n.*
**car·vel** (kär′v'l), *n.* a caravel.
**car·ven** (kär′vən), *adj.* [Archaic or Poetic], carved.
**carv·ing** (kär′viŋ), *n.* 1. the work or art of one who carves. 2. carved work, as a statue.
**carving knife,** a large knife for carving meat.
**car·y·at·id** (kar′i-at′id), *n.* [*pl.* -IDS (-idz), -IDES (-i-dēz′)], [< L. < Gr. *karyatides*, priestesses at Karyai, in Laconia], a supporting column that has the form of a draped female figure.

CARYATID

**car·y·o-,** karyo-.
**car·y·o·tin** (kar′i-ō′tin), *n.* karyotin; chromatin.
**ca·sa·ba** (kə-sä′bə), *n.* [< *Kassaba*, town near Smyrna, Asia Minor], a kind of muskmelon, with a yellow rind: also **casaba melon, cassaba.**
**Ca·sa·blan·ca** (kas′ə-blaŋ′kə, kä′sä-bläŋ′-), *n.* a seaport in French Morocco: pop., 257,000.
**Ca·sa·no·va, Gio·van·ni Ja·co·po** (jô-vän′nē yä′kô-pô kä′sä-nô′vä; Eng. kaz′ə-nō′və), 1725–1798; Italian adventurer; known for his *Memoirs.*
**Cas·bah** (käz′bä), *n.* the Kasbah.
**cas·cade** (kas-kād′), *n.* [Fr.; It. *cascata* < L. *cadere*, to fall], 1. a small, steep waterfall. 2. a shower, as of sparks, drapery, etc. *v.t. & v.i.* [-CADED, -CADING], to fall or drop in a cascade.
**Cascade Range,** a mountain range in W Oregon, Washington, and British Columbia.
**cas·car·a** (kas-kâr′ə), *n.* [Sp. *cáscara*, bark], 1. a buckthorn growing on the Pacific coast: also **cascara buckthorn.** 2. a mild laxative (in full, **cascara sagrada**) made from its bark.
**case** (kās), *n.* [< OFr. *cas*, a chance < L. *casus*, an accident; pp. of *cadere*, to fall], 1. an example or instance: as, a *case* of measles. 2. one in whom a disease occurs; patient. 3. a state of affairs; situation: as, state the *case* briefly. 4. a statement of the facts, as in a law court. 5. convincing arguments: as, he has no *case*. 6. a lawsuit. 7. a problem: as, this child is a difficult *case*. 8. [Slang], a peculiar person. 9. *a*) a form taken by a noun, pronoun, or adjective to show its relation to neighboring words. *b*) any such relation. *v.t.* [Slang], to examine carefully: as, the thief *cased* the house. —**in any case,** anyhow. —**in case,** if; in the event that. —**in case of,** in the event of; if there is. —**in no case,** by no means.
**case** (kās), *n.* [< ONorm.Fr. < L. *capsa*, a box < *capere*, to hold], 1. a container, as a box, sheath, etc. 2. a protective cover: as, a watch *case*. 3. a full box or its contents. 4. a set or pair: as, a *case* of pistols. 5. a frame, as for a window. 6. in *printing*, a shallow tray in which type is kept: the *upper case* is used for capitals, the *lower case* for small letters. *v.t.* [CASED, CASING], 1. to put in a container. 2. to cover or enclose.
**ca·se·fy** (kā′sə-fī′), *v.t. & v.i.* [-FIED, -FYING], [< L. *caseus*, cheese; + *-fy*], to make or become cheeselike.
**case·hard·en** (kās′här′d'n), *v.t.* 1. in *metallurgy*, to form a hard, thin surface on (iron or steel); hence, 2. to make callous or unfeeling.
**case history** (or **study**), collected information about an individual or group, for use as in sociological or medical studies.
**ca·se·in** (kā′si-in, kā′sēn), *n.* [< L. *caseus*, cheese; + *-in*], a protein that is one of the chief constituents of milk and the basis of cheese.
**case knife,** 1. a knife kept in a case; sheath knife. 2. a table knife.
**case law,** law based on previous judicial decisions, or precedents: distinguished from *statute law.*
**case·mate** (kās′māt′), *n.* [Fr. < It. < Gr. *chasmate*, pl. of *chasma* (see CHASM)], a shellproof or armored enclosure with openings for guns, as in a fortress or on a warship. —**case′mat′ed,** *adj.*
**case·ment** (kās′mənt), *n.* [< OFr. *encassement*, a frame; see CASE (box)], 1. a hinged window frame that opens outward: a **casement window** often has two such frames, opening like French doors. 2. a casing; covering. —**case′ment·ed,** *adj.*
**ca·se·ous** (kā′si-əs), *adj.* [< L. *caseus*, cheese], of or like cheese.
**ca·sern, ca·serne** (kə-zũrn′), *n.* [< Fr.; Pr. *cazerna*, small hut < LL. *quaterna*, four each < *quattuor*, four], *usually in pl.* any of a series of troop barracks near the battlements of a fortified town.
**case work,** social work in which the worker investigates a case of personal or family maladjustment, and gives advice or guidance.
**cash** (kash), *n.* [Fr. *casse*, money box < Pr. < It.; L. *capsa*; see CASE (box)], 1. money that a person actually has; esp., ready money. 2. money, a check, etc. paid at the time of purchase. *v.t.* to give or get cash for. *adj.* of, for, or requiring cash: as, a *cash* sale. —**cash in,** 1. to turn into cash. 2. [Slang], to die. —**cash in on,** 1. to make a profit from. 2. to make profitable use of.
**cash** (kash), *n.* [*pl.* CASH], [Port. *caixa* < Tamil *kāsu*], any of several East Indian or Chinese coins of small value.
**cash-and-car·ry** (kash′ən-kar′i), *adj.* with cash payments and no deliveries.
**cash·book** (kash′book′), *n.* a book in which all receipts and payments of money are entered.
**cash discount,** a discount allowed to the purchaser if he pays within a specified period.
**cash·ew** (kash′ōō, kə-shōō′), *n.* [< Fr. < Port. < Braz. (Tupi) name], 1. a tropical tree bearing kidney-shaped nuts. 2. the nut.
**cash·ier** (ka-shêr′), *n.* [Fr. *caissier*], a person in charge of the cash transactions of a bank or store.
**cash·ier** (ka-shêr′), *v.t.* [< D. < Fr. < LL. *cassare*, to destroy & L. *quassare*, to shatter], 1. to dismiss, as from a position of trust, in disgrace; discharge. 2. to discard or reject.
**Cash·mere** (kash-mêr′), *n.* Kashmir.
**cash·mere** (kash′mêr), *n.* [< *Kashmir*, India], 1. a fine carded wool from goats of Kashmir and Tibet. 2. a soft, twilled cloth of this or similar wool. 3. a cashmere shawl. *adj.* of or like such wool or cloth.
**cash register,** a device, usually with a money drawer, used by merchants, etc. for automatically recording and adding the amounts of sales.
**cas·ing** (kās′iŋ), *n.* 1. a protective covering; specif., *a*) the shoe of a tire. *b*) the skin of a sausage. 2. a frame, as of a window or door.
**ca·si·no** (kə-sē′nō), *n.* [*pl.* -NOS, -NI (-nē)], [It., dim. of *casa* (L. *casa*), a house], 1. a room or building for dancing, gambling, etc. 2. cassino.
**cask** (kask, käsk), *n.* [Sp. *casco*; ult. < L. *quassare*,

to shatter], 1. a barrel of any size, especially one for liquids. 2. a full cask or its contents; barrelful.

**cas·ket** (kas′kit, käs′-), *n.* [prob. < OFr. dim. of *casse;* see CASE (box)], 1. a small box or chest, as for valuables. 2. a coffin. *v.t.* to put into a casket.

**Cas·pi·an Sea** (kas′pi-ən), an inland sea between the Caucasus and Asia. —**Cas′pi·an,** *adj.*

**casque** (kask), *n.* [Fr. < Sp. *casco*; see CASK], a helmet. —**casqued** (kaskt), *adj.*

**cas·sa·ba** (kə-sä′bə), *n.* a casaba.

**Cas·san·dra** (kə-san′drə), *n.* 1. in *Gr. legend,* Priam's prophetic daughter, whose prophecies, Apollo decreed, should never be believed; hence, 2. one whose warnings are disregarded.

**cas·sa·va** (kə-sä′və), *n.* [< Fr. < Sp. < Haitian *kasabi*], 1. a tropical plant with edible starchy roots. 2. a starch extracted from cassava roots, used in making bread and tapioca. Also called *manioc.*

**cas·se·role** (kas′ə-rōl′), *n.* [Fr., dim. of *casse,* a bowl < Pr. < LL.; ? < Gr. dim. of *kyathos,* a bowl], 1. a covered earthenware or glass baking dish in which food can be cooked and then served. 2. food, usually in layers, baked and served in such a dish.

**cas·sette** (ka-set′, kə-), *n.* [Fr. < ONorm.Fr. *casse,* a case], 1. a case with roll film in it, for loading a camera quickly. 2. a similar case with magnetic tape, for use in a tape recorder.

**cas·sia** (kash′ə), *n.* [L. < Gr. *kasia* < Heb. < *qātsa,* to strip off bark], 1. the bark (**cassia bark**) of certain tropical evergreen trees, used like cinnamon: also called *Chinese cinnamon.* 2. a tree that it comes from. 3. any of a group of tropical herbs, shrubs, and trees of the pea family: the pods (**cassia pods**) of some of these plants have a mildly laxative pulp (**cassia pulp**); from others the cathartic drug senna is extracted. 4. cassia pods. 5. cassia pulp.

**cas·si·mere** (kas′ə-mêr′), *n.* [< *Kashmir*; cf. CASHMERE (wool)], a thin, twilled woolen cloth, used for men's suits: also sp. **casimere, casimire.**

**cas·si·no** (kə-sē′nō), *n.* [see CASINO], a card game for two to four players: also sp. **casino.**

**Cas·si·o·pe·ia** (kas′i-ə-pē′ə), *n.* 1. in *Gr. legend,* the mother of Andromeda. 2. a northern constellation near Polaris.

**Cassiopeia's Chair,** the five brightest stars in Cassiopeia: their outline suggests a chair.

**Cas·si·us** (kash′əs, -i-əs, kas′i-əs), *n.* (*Gaius Cassius Longinus*), Roman general and chief assassin of Julius Caesar; died 42 B.C.

**cas·sock** (kas′ək), *n.* [< Fr. < It. *casacca*; ? akin to LL. *casubla*; see CHASUBLE], a long, closefitting vestment, generally black, worn as an outer garment or under the surplice by clergymen. —**cas′socked,** *adj.*

**cas·so·war·y** (kas′ə-wer′i), *n.* [*pl.* -IES], [Malay *kasuārī*], a large, flightless bird of Australia and New Guinea, like the ostrich but smaller.

**cast** (kast, käst), *v.t.* [CAST, CASTING], 1. to throw; fling; hurl. 2. to deposit (a ballot or vote). 3. to cause to fall; direct: as, to *cast* a light. 4. to throw out (a fly, etc.) at the end of a fishing line. 5. to throw off; shed; slough: as, the snake *casts* its skin. 6. to add up (accounts). 7. to calculate (a horoscope, tides, etc.). 8. *a*) to shape (molten metal, etc.) by pouring or pressing into a mold. *b*) to make by such a method. 9. *a*) to choose actors for (a play). *b*) to select (an actor) for (a role). *v.i.* 1. to throw; hurl. 2. to throw out a fly, etc. on a fishing line. *n.* 1. a casting; throwing; throw; also, way of casting or distance thrown; specif., *a*) a throw of dice; also, the number thus thrown. *b*) a turn of the eye; glance; look. *c*) a throw of a fishing line, net, etc. 2. a quantity or thing cast in a certain way. 3. *a*) something formed in a mold, as a statue. *b*) the mold. 4. a plaster form for immobilizing a broken limb. 5. the set of actors in a play. 6. the form or direction in which a thing is cast. 7. an appearance or stamp, as of features. 8. kind; quality. 9. a tinge; shade. 10. a squint; strabismus. —**cast about,** 1. to search; look (*for*). 2. to make plans. —**cast aside,** to discard; abandon. —**cast away,** 1. to discard; abandon. 2. shipwrecked. —**cast down,** 1. to turn downward. 2. to sadden; depress; discourage. —**cast off,** 1. to discard; abandon; disown. 2. to free. 3. to free a ship from a dock, quay, etc., as by releasing the lines. 4. in *knitting,* to make the last row of stitches. —**cast on,** in *knitting,* to make the first row of stitches. —**cast out,** to force to get out or go away; expel. —**cast up,** 1. to turn upward. 2. to add up; total.

**cas·ta·nets** (kas′tə-nets′, kas′tə-nets′), *n.pl.* [< Fr. < Sp. *castañeta* < L. *castanea,* chestnut: from the shape], small, hollowed pieces of hard wood or ivory, held in the hand in pairs to beat time to music, especially in Spanish dances.

CASTANETS

**cast·a·way** (kast′ə-wā′, käst′-), *n.* 1. a person or thing cast out or off; esp., an outcast. 2. a shipwrecked person. *adj.* 1. thrown away; discarded. 2. shipwrecked.

**caste** (kast, käst), *n.* [Fr. < Port. *casta,* race < L. *castus,* pure], 1. any of the distinct, hereditary Hindu social classes, each formerly excluded from social dealings with the others. 2. any exclusive social or occupational class or group. 3. rigid class distinction based on birth, wealth, etc., operating as a social system or principle. —**lose caste,** to lose social status.

**cas·tel·lat·ed** (kas′tə-lā′tid), *adj.* [see CASTLE], built with turrets and battlements, like a castle. —**cas′tel·la′tion,** *n.*

**cast·er** (kas′tẽr, käs′-), *n.* 1. a person or thing that casts. 2. *a*) a small container for serving vinegar, mustard, etc. at the table. *b*) a stand for holding such containers. *c*) any of a set of small swiveled wheels for supporting and moving furniture: also sp. **castor.**

**cas·ti·gate** (kas′tə-gāt′), *v.t.* [-GATED, -GATING], [< L. pp. of *castigare,* to purify, chastise < *castus,* pure], to chastise; criticize severely; rebuke. —**cas′ti·ga′tion,** *n.* —**cas′ti·ga′tor,** *n.*

**Cas·tile** (kas-tēl′), *n.* a former kingdom of central Spain.

**Cas·tile (soap)** (kas′tēl, kas-tēl′), [< *Castile,* where first made], a fine, hard soap made from olive oil and sodium hydroxide: also **castile soap.**

**Cas·til·i·an** (kas-til′yən, -i-ən), *adj.* of Castile, its people, language, or culture. *n.* 1. a native or inhabitant of Castile. 2. the Castilian form of Spanish, now the standard form of the language.

**cast·ing** (kas′tiŋ, käs′-), *n.* 1. the action of one that casts. 2. a thing formed by pouring or pressing a substance into a mold to harden; esp., a metal piece so formed.

**casting vote** (or **voice**), the deciding vote cast by the presiding officer in the event of a tie.

**cast-i·ron** (kast′ī′ẽrn, käst′-), *adj.* 1. made of cast iron. 2. very hard, stern, rigid, strong, etc.

**cast iron,** a hard, unmalleable pig iron made by casting: it contains a high proportion of carbon.

**cas·tle** (kas′'l, käs′'l), *n.* [< AS. & ONorm.Fr. < L. *castellum,* dim. of *castrum,* fort], 1. a large building or group of buildings fortified with thick walls, battlements, etc.: castles were the strongholds of noblemen in the Middle Ages. 2. any massive dwelling like this. 3. in *chess,* a piece shaped like a castle tower: it can move only in a vertical or horizontal direction: also called *rook.* *v.t.* [-TLED, -TLING], in *chess,* to move (a king) two squares to either side and, in the same move, set the castle in the square skipped by the king. *v.i.* in *chess,* to castle a king. —**cas′tled,** *adj.*

**castle in Spain, castle in the air,** anything imagined and desired but not likely to be realized.

**cast·off** (kast′ôf′, käst′-), *adj.* discarded; abandoned. *n.* a person or thing cast off.

**Cas·tor** (kas′tẽr, käs′-), *n.* 1. in *Gr. & Rom. legend,* the mortal twin of Pollux. 2. one of the two bright stars in the constellation Gemini.

**cas·tor** (kas′tẽr, käs′-), *n.* [Fr.; L. < Gr. *kastōr,* beaver], 1. a strong-smelling, oily substance obtained from the beaver, used in medicine and in making perfumes. 2. a hat of beaver fur.

**cas·tor** (kas′tẽr, käs′-), *n.* a caster (in sense 2).

**cas·tor-oil plant** (kas′tẽr-oil′, käs′-), a tropical plant with large, beanlike seeds (**castor beans**), the source of a yellowish oil (**castor oil**) used as a cathartic and lubricant.

**cas·trate** (kas′trāt), *v.t.* [-TRATED, -TRATING], [< L. *castratus,* pp. of *castrare*], 1. to remove the testicles of; emasculate; geld; hence, 2. to mutilate, expurgate, etc. —**cas·tra′tion,** *n.*

**cas·u·al** (kazh′ōō-əl), *adj.* [< Fr. < LL. *casualis* < L. *casus,* chance], 1. happening by chance; not planned; incidental. 2. without plan or method; aimless; unpredictable. 3. working or arriving without regularity; occasional: as, a *casual* worker. 4. careless; cursory. 5. nonchalant; indifferent. 6. for informal wear: as, *casual* clothes. *n.* 1. a person who does something only occasionally; esp., a casual worker. 2. in *military usage,* a person temporarily attached to a unit. —**cas′u·al·ly,** *adv.* —**cas′u·al·ness,** *n.*

**cas·u·al·ty** (kazh'ōō-əl-ti, -ool-ti), *n.* [*pl.* -TIES], 1. an accident, especially an unfortunate or fatal one. 2. a member of the armed forces killed, wounded, or captured. 3. anyone hurt or killed in an accident.

**cas·u·ist** (kazh'ōō-ist), *n.* [< Fr. < L. *casus*, a case], one who studies or decides questions of right and wrong in conduct: used disparagingly of one who quibbles, rationalizes, or reasons falsely. —**cas'u·is'tic, cas'u·is'ti·cal,** *adj.* —**cas'u·is'ti·cal·ly,** *adv.*

**cas·u·ist·ry** (kazh'ōō-is-tri), *n.* [*pl.* -RIES], the solving of special cases of right and wrong in conduct by deciding how far circumstances alter cases: used disparagingly of subtle but false reasoning.

‡**ca·sus bel·li** (kā'səs bel'ī), [L.], an event provoking war, or used as a pretext for making war.

**cat** (kat), *n.* [*pl.* CATS, CAT; see PLURAL, II, D, 1], [AS. *catte* < LL. *cattus*], 1. a small, lithe, soft-furred animal, often kept as a pet or for killing mice. 2. any flesh-eating mammal related to this, as the lion, tiger, leopard, etc. 3. a person regarded as like a cat in some way; esp., a spiteful woman. 4. a cat-o'-nine-tails. 5. a catfish. 6. a caterpillar tractor. 7. [Slang], *a*) a jazz musician or enthusiast. *b*) any person, esp. a man. *v.t.* [CATTED, CATTING], to hoist (an anchor) to the cathead. —**let the cat out of the bag,** to let a secret be found out. —**cat'like',** *adj.*

**cat.,** 1. catalogue. 2. catechism.

**cat·a-,** [< Gr. *kata*, down], a prefix meaning: 1. *down, downward*, as in *catabolism*. 2. *away, completely*, as in *catalysis*. 3. *against*, as in *catapult*. Also, before a vowel, **cat-**, and, before an aspirate, **cath-**. Also sp. **kata-**.

**ca·tab·o·lism** (kə-tab'ə-liz'm), *n.* [< *cata-* + Gr. *ballein*, to throw; + *-ism*], the process in a plant or animal by which living tissue is changed into waste products of a simpler composition; destructive metabolism: opposed to *anabolism*. —**cat·a·bol·ic** (kat'ə-bol'ik), *adj.* —**cat'a·bol'i·cal·ly,** *adv.*

**cat·a·chre·sis** (kat'ə-krē'sis), *n.* [*pl.* -SES (-sēz)], [L. < Gr. < *kata-*, against + *chrēsthai*, to use], incorrect use of a word or words. —**cat'a·chres'tic** (-kres'tik), **cat'a·chres'ti·cal,** *adj.* —**cat'a·chres'ti·cal·ly,** *adv.*

**cat·a·clysm** (kat'ə-kliz'm), *n.* [< L. < Gr. < *kata-*, down + *klyzein*, to wash], 1. a great flood. 2. any sudden, violent change, as in a war.

**cat·a·clys·mic** (kat'ə-kliz'mik), *adj.* of, like, or caused by a cataclysm: also **cat'a·clys'mal.** —**cat'a·clys'mi·cal·ly,** *adv.*

**cat·a·comb** (kat'ə-kōm'), *n.* [< It. < LL. *catacumba* < L. < *cata*, by + *tumbas*, tombs], *usually in pl.* any of a series of galleries in an underground burial place. —**the Catacombs,** the underground cemeteries of Rome, used as a refuge by the early Christians.

**cat·a·falque** (kat'ə-falk'), *n.* [Fr. < It. < LL. <L. < *cata-*, down + *fala*, scaffolding], a framework to hold the coffin of a dead person lying in state.

**Cat·a·lan** (kat''l-an', -ən), *adj.* of Catalonia, its people, or their language. *n.* 1. a native or inhabitant of Catalonia. 2. the Romance language of Catalonia, closely akin to Provençal.

**cat·a·lep·sy** (kat'ə-lep'si), *n.* [< LL. < Gr. *katalēpsis*, a seizing < *kata-*, down + *lambanein*, to seize], a condition in which consciousness and feeling are suddenly and temporarily lost, and the muscles become rigid: it may occur in epilepsy: also **cat'a·lep'sis.** —**cat'a·lep'tic,** *adj. & n.*

**Cat·a·li·na (Island)** (kat''l-ē'nə), Santa Catalina, an island off southern California.

**cat·a·lo** (kat'ə-lō'), *n.* [*pl.* -LOES, -LOS], [*cat*tle + buf*falo*], an animal bred by crossing the American buffalo (bison) with cattle: also sp. **cattalo.**

**cat·a·logue, cat·a·log** (kat''l-ôg', -og'), *n.* [Fr. < LL. < Gr. *katalogos* < *kata-*, down + *legein*, to count], a complete list; esp., *a*) an alphabetical card file, as of the books in a library. *b*) a book or pamphlet listing titles, articles, etc., as of things exhibited or for sale. *v.t. & v.i.* [-LOGUED, -LOGUING; -LOGED, -LOGING], to enter or arrange (items) in a catalogue. —**cat'a·logu'er** or **cat'a·log'er, cat'a·logu'ist** or **cat'a·log'ist,** *n.*

**Cat·a·lo·ni·a** (kat''l-ō'ni-ə), *n.* an old province of NE Spain. —**Cat'a·lo'ni·an,** *adj. & n.*

**ca·tal·pa** (kə-tal'pə), *n.* [< Am. Ind. (Creek) *katuhlpa*], a tree with large, heart-shaped leaves, trumpet-shaped flowers, and air-borne seeds.

**ca·tal·y·sis** (kə-tal'ə-sis), *n.* [*pl.* -SES (-sēz')], [Gr. *katalysis*, dissolution < *kata-*, down + *lyein*, to loose], the causing or speeding up of a chemical reaction by the addition of a substance which itself undergoes no permanent chemical change thereby: also sp. **katalysis.** —**cat·a·lyt·ic** (kat''l-it'ik), *adj. & n.* —**cat'a·lyt'i·cal·ly,** *adv.*

**cat·a·lyst** (kat''l-ist), *n.* any substance serving as the agent in catalysis; catalyzer.

**cat·a·lyze** (kat''l-īz'), *v.t.* [-LYZED, -LYZING], to change by catalysis. —**cat'a·lyz'er,** *n.*

**cat·a·ma·ran** (kat'ə-mə-ran'), *n.* [Tamil *kaṭṭumaram*; *kaṭṭu*, tie + *maram*, log, tree], 1. a narrow log raft or float propelled by sails or paddles. 2. a boat with two parallel hulls.

**cat·a·mount** (kat'ə-mount'), *n.* [*cat* + *a*, of + *mount*], 1. a puma; cougar. 2. a lynx.

**cat·a·pult** (kat'ə-pult'), *n.* [< L. < Gr. *katapeltēs* < *kata-*, down + *pallein*, to hurl], 1. an ancient military contrivance for throwing stones, spears, etc. 2. a slingshot. 3. a device for launching an airplane from the deck of a ship. *v.t.* to shoot as from a catapult; hurl.

CATAPULT

**cat·a·ract** (kat'ə-rakt'), *n.* [< L. < Gr. *kataraktēs* < *kata-*, down + *rēgnymi*, to break], 1. a large waterfall. 2. any downpour; deluge. 3. in *medicine*, *a*) an eye disease in which the crystalline lens or its capsule becomes opaque, causing partial or total blindness. *b*) the opaque area.

**ca·tarrh** (kə-tär'), *n.* [< Fr. < L. < Gr. < *kata-*, down + *rhein*, to flow], inflammation of a mucous membrane of the nose or throat, with an increased flow of mucus. —**ca·tarrh'al, ca·tarrh'ous,** *adj.*

**ca·tas·tro·phe** (kə-tas'trə-fi), *n.* [< L. < Gr. *katastrophē* < *kata-*, down + *strephein*, to turn], 1. the culminating event of a drama, by which the plot is resolved; denouement. 2. a disastrous overthrow or ruin. 3. any great and sudden calamity or disaster. —**cat·a·stroph·ic** (kat'ə-strof'ik), *adj.* —**cat'a·stroph'i·cal·ly,** *adv.*

**Ca·taw·ba** (kə-tô'bə), *n.* 1. a reddish variety of grape. 2. a wine made from this grape.

**cat·bird** (kat'bũrd'), *n.* a slate-gray North American songbird with a black crown and tail: it makes a mewing sound like that of a cat.

**cat·boat** (kat'bōt'), *n.* a sailboat with a single sail and mast set well forward in the bow.

**cat·call** (kat'kôl'), *n.* a shrill noise or whistle expressing derision or disapproval. *v.t.* to show disapproval of with catcalls. *v.i.* to make catcalls.

**catch** (kach), *v.t.* [CAUGHT (kôt), CATCHING], [< ONorm.Fr. *cacher* < LL. < L. *captare*, to try to seize < pp. of *capere*, to take], 1. to seize and hold, as after a chase; capture. 2. to take by or as by a trap; hence, 3. to deceive; ensnare. 4. to come upon suddenly; surprise. 5. to get to in time: as, he *caught* the train. 6. to lay hold of; grab: as, *catch* the ball. 7. to take or get: as, *catch* a glimpse of her. 8. to get without intention, as by exposure: as, he *caught* cold. 9. to understand; apprehend. 10. to charm; fascinate. *v.i.* 1. to become held, fastened, or entangled. 2. to take hold or spread, as fire. 3. to take and keep hold, as a lock. 4. to act as a catcher. *n.* 1. the act of catching. 2. a thing that catches. 3. a person or thing caught. 4. an amount caught. 5. one worth catching, especially as a husband or wife. 6. a snatch, scrap, or fragment: as, *catches* of old tunes. 7. an emotional break in the voice. 8. a simple game of throwing and catching a ball. 9. [Colloq.], a hidden qualification; tricky condition: as, what's the *catch* in his offer? 10. in *music*, a round for three or more unaccompanied voices. *adj.* 1. tricky. 2. attracting attention; meant to arouse interest. —**catch as catch can,** with any hold or approach: first used of a style of wrestling. —**catch at,** to reach for eagerly; seize desperately. —**catch it,** [Colloq.], to receive a scolding or other punishment. —**catch on,** [Colloq.], 1. to understand. 2. to become fashionable, popular, etc. —**catch up,** 1. to take up suddenly; snatch. 2. to show to be in error. 3. to heckle. 4. to come up from behind; overtake. 5. to fasten in loops. —**catch'a·ble,** *adj.*

**catch·all** (kach'ôl'), *n.* a container for various sorts of things: as, most attics are *catchalls*.

**catch basin,** a sievelike device at the entrance to a sewer to catch, or stop, bulky matter.

**catch·er** (kach·ẽr), *n.* 1. one that catches. 2. in *baseball*, the player behind home plate, who catches pitched balls not hit away by the batter.
**catch·ing** (kach'iŋ), *adj.* 1. contagious; infectious. 2. attractive; catchy.
**catch·pen·ny** (kach'pen'i), *adj.* made merely to sell; cheap and flashy; worthless. *n.* [*pl.* -NIES], a catchpenny commodity.
**catch phrase,** a phrase that catches or is meant to catch the popular attention.
**catch·up** (kach'əp, kech'-), *n.* ketchup.
**catch·word** (kach'wũrd'), *n.* 1. a word placed so that it will catch attention, as either of the words at the top of this page. 2. a word or phrase repeated so often that it becomes a slogan.
**catch·y** (kach'i), *adj.* [-IER, -IEST], 1. catching attention; arousing interest. 2. easily caught up and remembered: as, a *catchy* tune. 3. tricky; deceiving. —**catch'i·ness,** *n.*
**cat·e·chet·i·cal** (kat'ə-ket'i-k'l), *adj.* 1. of or like a catechism. 2. teaching by questions and answers. Also **catechetic.** —**cat'e·chet'i·cal·ly,** *adv.*
**cat·e·chism** (kat'ə-kiz'm), *n.* [ see CATECHIZE], 1. a handbook of questions and answers for teaching the principles of a religion. 2. any similar handbook for teaching the fundamentals of a subject. 3. a formal series of questions; close questioning. —**cat'e·chis'mal,** *adj.*
**cat·e·chist** (kat'ə-kist), *n.* one who catechizes. —**cat'e·chis'tic, cat'e·chis'ti·cal,** *adj.* —**cat'e·chis'ti·cal·ly,** *adv.*
**cat·e·chize** (kat'ə-kīz'), *v.t.* [-CHIZED, -CHIZING], [< L. < Gr. *katēchizein* < *kata-*, thoroughly + *ēchein*, to sound], 1. to teach by the method of question and answer. 2. to question searchingly. Also sp. **catechise.** —**cat'e·chi·za'tion** (-ki-zā'shən), **cat'e·chi·sa'tion,** *n.* —**cat'e·chiz'er, cat'e·chis'er,** *n.*
**cat·e·chu·men** (kat'ə-kū'mən), *n.* [< L. < Gr. *katēchoumenos;* cf. CATECHIZE], a person, especially an adult, receiving instruction in the fundamentals of Christianity before confirmation.
**cat·e·gor·i·cal** (kat'ə-gôr'i-k'l, -gor'-), *adj.* 1. unqualified; unconditional; positive; explicit: said of a statement, theory, etc. 2. of, as, or in a category. —**cat'e·gor'i·cal·ly,** *adv.*
**cat·e·go·ry** (kat'ə-gôr'i, -gō'ri), *n.* [*pl.* -RIES], [< L. < Gr. < *katēgorein*, to assert < *kata-*, down + *agoreuein*, to declaim], 1. a class or division in a scheme of classification. 2. in *logic*, any of the basic concepts into which knowledge is classified.
**cat·e·nate** (kat''n-āt'), *v.t.* [-NATED, -NATING], [< LL. < L. *catena*, a chain], to form into a chain or linked series; link. —**cat'e·na'tion,** *n.*
**ca·ter** (kā'tẽr), *v.i.* [< OFr. < *acater*, to buy < LL.; ult. < L. *ad-*, to + *capere*, to take], 1. to provide food; serve as a caterer. 2. to provide what is needed, especially as a means of pleasure (with *to* or *for*). *v.t.* to serve as a caterer for, as a banquet.
**cat·er-cor·nered** (kat'ẽr-kôr'nẽrd), *adj.* [< Fr. *quatre*, four; + *cornered*], diagonal. *adv.* diagonally. Also **cater-corner.**
**ca·ter·er** (kā'tẽr-ẽr), *n.* one whose work is providing food and service, as for parties.
**cat·er·pil·lar** (kat'ẽr-pil'ẽr), *n.* [ONorm.Fr. *catepilose* < L. *catta pilosa*, hairy cat], 1. the wormlike larva of a butterfly, moth, etc. 2. a caterpillar tractor. *adj.* having an endless-track drive: as, a *caterpillar* grader.
**caterpillar tractor,** a tractor having on each side a continuous roller belt, for moving over rough ground: a trade-mark (**Caterpillar Tractor**).
**cat·er·waul** (kat'ẽr-wôl'), *v.i.* [ME. < *cater*, ? male cat + *w(r)awlen*, *v.;* prob. echoic], to make a shrill, howling sound like that of a cat; wail; scream. *n.* such a sound.
**cat·fish** (kat'fish'), *n.* [*pl.* see FISH], a scaleless fish with long feelers, like a cat's whiskers, about the mouth.
**cat·gut** (kat'gut'), *n.* a tough thread made from dried intestines, as of sheep, and used for surgical sutures, on stringed instruments, etc.
**cath-,** cata-: also sp. **kath-.**
**Cath.,** 1. Catholic. 2. [also c-], cathedral.
**ca·thar·sis** (kə-thär'sis), *n.* [Gr. *katharsis* < *katharos*, pure], 1. purgation, especially of the bowels. 2. the purifying or relieving of the emotions by art. 3. in *psychiatry*, the alleviation of fears, complexes, etc. by bringing them to consciousness and giving them expression.
**ca·thar·tic** (kə-thär'tik), *adj.* of catharsis; purging: also **cathartical.** *n.* a medicine for purging the bowels; laxative, as castor oil.
**Ca·thay** (ka-thā'), *n.* [Poetic or Archaic], China.
**cat·head** (kat'hed'), *n.* a projecting beam near the bow of a ship, to which the anchor is fastened.
**ca·the·dra** (kə-thē'drə, kath'i-), *n.* [L. < Gr. < *kata-*, down + *hedra*, a seat], 1. the bishop's throne in a cathedral. 2. the episcopal see. —**ex cathedra,** from or with official authority.
**ca·the·dral** (kə-thē'drəl), *n.* [< LL. < L.; see CATHEDRA], 1. the main church of a bishop's see, containing the cathedra. 2. loosely, any large, imposing church. *adj.* 1. of, like, or containing a cathedra. 2. official. 3. of or like a cathedral.
**Cath·er·ine II** (kath'ẽr-in), 1729–1796; empress of Russia (1762–1796): called *Catherine the Great.*
**cath·e·ter** (kath'ə-tẽr), *n.* [L. < Gr. < *kata-*, down + *hienai*, to send], a slender tube of metal or rubber, inserted into a body cavity for drawing off fluid, especially urine from the bladder.
**cath·e·ter·ize** (kath'ə-tẽr-īz'), *v.t.* [-IZED, -IZING], to insert a catheter into.
**cath·ode** (kath'ōd), *n.* [< Gr. *kathodos*, going down < *kata-*, down + *hodos*, way], a negatively charged electrode, as of a vacuum tube. —**ca·thod·ic** (kə-thod'ik), **ca·thod'i·cal,** *adj.*
**cathode rays,** streams of electrons projected from the surface of a cathode: cathode rays produce X rays when they strike solids.
**cath·o·lic** (kath'ə-lik, kath'lik), *adj.* [L. *catholicus*, universal < Gr. < *kata-*, completely + *holos*, whole], 1. universal; all-inclusive; of general interest or value. 2. having broad sympathies or understanding; liberal. 3. of the universal Christian church. 4. [C-], of the Christian church headed by the Pope; Roman Catholic. *n.* 1. a member of the universal Christian church. 2. [C ], a member of the Roman Catholic Church. —**ca·thol·i·cal·ly** (kə-thol'i-k'l-i, -ik-li), *adv.*
**Catholic Church,** the Roman Catholic Church.
**Ca·thol·i·cism** (kə-thol'ə-siz'm), *n.* 1. the doctrine, practice, and organization of the Roman Catholic Church. 2. [c-], catholicity.
**cath·o·lic·i·ty** (kath'ə-lis'ə-ti), *n.* 1. broadness of taste, sympathy, understanding, etc.; liberality. 2. universality. 3. [C-], Catholicism.
**ca·thol·i·cize** (kə-thol'ə-sīz'), *v.t. & v.i.* [-CIZED, -CIZING], 1. to make or become catholic. 2. [C-], to convert or be converted to Catholicism.
**cat·i·on** (kat'ī'ən), *n.* [coined by Faraday < Gr. *kata*, downward + *ion*, neut. ppr. of *ienai*, to go], a positively charged ion: cations move toward the cathode in an electrolyzed solution.
**cat·kin** (kat'kin), *n.* [dim. of *cat*], a spike of closely clustered, small, unisexual flowers without petals, as on a willow: also called *ament.*
**cat nap,** a short, light sleep; doze. —**cat'-nap'** [-NAPPED, -NAPPING], *v.i.*
**cat·nip** (kat'nip), *n.* [*cat* + *nip*, dial. for *nep*, catnip], a plant of the mint family, with bluish flowers: cats like its odor: also **catmint.**
**Ca·to** (kā'tō), *n.* 1. (*Marcus Porcius Cato*), Roman consul; 234–149 B.C. 2. (*Marcus Porcius Cato Uticensis*), great-grandson of *Marcus Porcius Cato;* 95–46 B.C.; Roman statesman and philosopher.
**cat-o'-nine-tails** (kat'ə-nīn'tālz'), *n.* [*pl.* CAT-O'-NINE-TAILS], 1. a whip made of nine knotted cords attached to a handle. 2. the cattail.
**cat rig,** a single large sail on a mast well forward in the bow. —**cat'rigged'** (-rigd'), *adj.*
**cat's cradle,** a child's game played with a string looped over the fingers so as to form designs.

CAT'S CRADLE

**cat's-eye** (kats'ī'), *n.* a semiprecious quartz gem that reflects light like the eye of a cat.
**Cats·kill Mountains** (kats'kil'), a group of mountains in S New York: also **Cats'kills',** *n.pl.*
**cat's-paw** (kats'pô'), *n.* 1. a person used by another to do distasteful or unlawful work; dupe; tool. 2. a light breeze that ripples water.
**cat·sup** (kat'səp, kech'əp), *n.* ketchup.
**cat·tail** (kat'tāl'), *n.* 1. a tall marsh plant with long, flat leaves and long, brown, fuzzy, round flower spikes. 2. a catkin.
**Cat·te·gat** (kat'i-gat'), *n.* Kattegat.
**cat·tish** (kat'ish), *adj.* 1. like a cat; feline. 2. catty. —**cat'tish·ly,** *adv.* —**cat'tish·ness,** *n.*
**cat·tle** (kat''l), *n.* [< ONorm.Fr. *catel* < LL. *captale*, goods < L. < *caput*, the head], 1. farm animals; livestock. 2. cows, bulls, steers, or oxen. 3. people in the mass: contemptuous term.
**cat·tle·man** (kat''l-mən), *n.* [*pl.* -MEN], a man who tends cattle or raises them for the market.
**cat·ty** (kat'i), *adj.* [-TIER, -TIEST], 1. of cats. 2. like a cat. 3. spiteful; mean; subtly malicious. —**cat'ti·ly,** *adv.* —**cat'ti·ness,** *n.*
**Ca·tul·lus** (kə-tul'əs), *n.* (*Gaius Valerius Catullus*), Roman lyric poet; lived 84?–54? B.C.

**cat·walk** (kat'wôk'), *n.* a narrow pathway, as along a bridge or over an engine room.
**Cau·ca·sia** (kô-kā'zhə, -shə), *n.* a region of the U.S.S.R., on either side of the Caucasus.
**Cau·ca·sian** (kô-kā'zhən, -kash'ən), *adj.* 1. of the Caucasus, its people, their languages, etc. 2. [so named from the erroneous notion that the original home of the hypothetical Indo-Europeans was the Caucasus], designating or of one of the main ethnic divisions of the human race: loosely called the *white race.* *n.* 1. a native of the Caucasus. 2. a member of the Caucasian division of mankind: loosely called *white person.* 3. the Caucasian languages, including Circassian, Georgian, etc.
**Cau·cas·ic** (kô-kas'ik), *adj.* Caucasian.
**Cau·ca·sus** (kô'kə-səs), *n.* 1. a mountain range in SE Europe, between the Black Sea and the Caspian. 2. Caucasia.
**cau·cus** (kô'kəs), *n.* [? < *Caucus Club,* 18th-c. social and political club; ult. < MGr. *kaukos,* drinking cup], a meeting of leaders or members of a party to decide questions of policy, candidates, etc. *v.i.* to hold a caucus.
**cau·dal** (kô'd'l), *adj.* [< L. *cauda,* tail], 1. of or like a tail. 2. at or near the tail. —**cau'dal·ly,** *adv.*
**cau·date** (kô'dāt), *adj.* [< L. *cauda,* tail], having a tail or taillike part: also **caudated.**
**cau·dle** (kô'd'l), *n.* [< OFr. < L. *caldus,* warm], a warm drink for invalids; esp., a spiced and sugared gruel with wine or ale added.
**caught** (kôt), pt. and pp. of **catch.**
**caul** (kôl), *n.* [OFr. *cale,* kind of cap; ult. < Gr. *kalyptein,* to cover], a membrane sometimes enveloping the head of a child at birth.
**caul·dron** (kôl'drən), *n.* a caldron.
**cau·li·flow·er** (kô'lə-flou'ẽr), *n.* [< Fr. *chou flori,* after L. *caulis,* cabbage], 1. a variety of cabbage with a compact white head of fleshy stalks bearing small flowers and buds. 2. this head, used as a vegetable.
**cauliflower ear,** an ear permanently deformed as a result of being injured in boxing, etc.
**cau·lis** (kô'lis), *n.* [*pl.* -LES (-lēz)], [L. < Gr. *kaulos*], in *botany,* the main stem of a plant.
**caulk** (kôk), *v.t.* to stop up (a crack or joint), as with tar or oakum: see **calk.** —**caulk'er,** *n.*
**caus·al** (kôz''l), *adj.* [L. *causalis*], 1. of, like, or being a cause. 2. relating to cause and effect. 3. expressing a cause or reason. *n.* in *grammar,* a causal connective, as *since, for.* —**caus'al·ly,** *adv.*
**cau·sal·i·ty** (kô-zal'ə-ti), *n.* [*pl.* -TIES], 1. causal quality or agency. 2. the interrelation or connection of cause and effect.
**cau·sa·tion** (kô-zā'shən), *n.* 1. a causing or being caused. 2. a causal agency; anything producing an effect. 3. causality.
**caus·a·tive** (kôz'ə-tiv), *adj.* [L. *causativus*], 1. producing an effect; causing. 2. expressing causation, as the verb *fell* (to cause to fall). *n.* a causative word or form. —**caus'a·tive·ly,** *adv.* —**caus'a·tive·ness,** *n.*
**cause** (kôz), *n.* [< OFr. < L. *causa*], 1. anything producing an effect or result. 2. a person or thing that brings about an effect or result. 3. a reason, motive, or ground for producing a given effect. 4. reason enough: as, *cause* for divorce. 5. any activity or movement that people are interested in and support. 6. in *law,* a case to be decided by the court; lawsuit. *v.t.* [CAUSED (kôzd), CAUSING], to be the cause of; bring about; effect.—**make common cause with,** to join forces with. —**caus'a·ble,** *adj.* —**cause'less,** *adj.*
‡**cause cé·lèbre** (kōz' sā'leb'r'), [Fr.], a celebrated law case, trial, or controversy.
**cau·se·rie** (kō'zə-rē'; Fr. kōz'rē'), *n.* [Fr. < Pr. < LL. < L. *causari*], 1. an informal talk; chat. 2. a short, conversational piece of writing.
**cause·way** (kôz'wā'), *n.* [< *causey* (Brit. Dial., causeway) < ONorm.Fr., ult. < L. *calx,* limestone; + *way*], 1. a raised way or road, as across wet ground. 2. a paved way or road; highway. *v.t.* to make a causeway over or through.
**caus·tic** (kôs'tik), *adj.* [< L. < Gr. *kaustikos* < *kaiein,* to burn], 1. that can burn or destroy living tissue by chemical action; corrosive. 2. biting; stinging; sarcastic. *n.* a caustic substance. —**caus'ti·cal·ly,** *adv.* —**caus·tic'i·ty** (-tis'ə-ti), *n.*
**caustic potash,** potassium hydroxide, KOH.
**caustic soda,** sodium hydroxide, NaOH.
**cau·ter·ize** (kô'tẽr-īz'), *v.t.* [-IZED, -IZING], [< LL. < Gr. *kautēriazein* < *kautēr,* branding iron < *kaiein,* to burn], to burn with a hot iron or needle, or with a caustic substance, so as to destroy dead tissue, etc. —**cau'ter·i·za'tion,** *n.*
**cau·ter·y** (kô'tẽr-i), *n.* [*pl.* -IES], 1. an instrument or substance for cauterizing: also **cau'ter·ant** (-ənt). 2. a cauterizing.
**cau·tion** (kô'shən), *n.* [L. *cautio* < same base as *cavere,* to take care], 1. a warning; admonition. 2. a word, sign, etc. by which warning is given. 3. prudence; wariness. 4. [Colloq.], an extraordinary person or thing. *v.t.* to warn; admonish.
**cau·tion·ar·y** (kô'shən-er'i), *adj.* urging caution.
**cau·tious** (kô'shəs), *adj.* full of caution; carefu to avoid danger; circumspect; wary. —**cau'tious·ly,** *adv.* —**cau'tious·ness,** *n.*
**cav·al·cade** (kav''l-kād', kav''l-kād'), *n.* [Fr. < It. < *cavalcare,* to ride < *cavallo,* horse], a procession, as of horsemen, carriages, etc.
**cav·a·lier** (kav'ə-lêr'), *n.* [Fr. < It. *cavaliere* < LL. < L. *caballus,* a horse], 1. an armed horseman; knight. 2. a gallant gentleman, especially one serving as a lady's escort. 3. [C-], a partisan of Charles I of England in his struggles with Parliament (1641–1649). *adj.* 1. free and easy; gay; offhand. 2. haughty; arrogant; supercilious. 3. [C-], of the Cavaliers. —**cav'a·lier'ly,** *adj. & adv.*
**cav·al·ry** (kav''l-ri), *n.* [*pl.* -RIES], [< Fr. < It. < *cavaliere;* see CAVALIER], combat troops mounted originally on horses but now often on motorized armored vehicles. —**cav'al·ry·man** [*pl.* -MEN], *n.*
**cave** (kāv), *n.* [< Fr. < L. < *cavus,* hollow], a hollow place inside the earth; cavern. *v.t.* [CAVED, CAVING], to make a hollow in. *v.i.* [Colloq.], to cave in. —**cave in,** 1. to collapse. 2. to make collapse. 3. [Colloq.], to submit; yield.
**ca·ve·at** (kā'vi-at'), *n.* [L., let him beware], 1. in *law,* a notice that an interested party files with the proper officers directing them to stop an action until he can be heard. 2. a warning.
‡**ca·ve·at emp·tor** (kā'vi-at' emp'tôr), [L.], let the buyer beware (i.e., buy at your own risk).
**ca·ve·a·tor** (kā'vi-ā'tẽr), *n.* a filer of a caveat.
**cave-in** (kāv'in'), *n.* 1. a caving in. 2. a place where the ground, etc. has caved in.
**cave man,** 1. a prehistoric human being of the Stone Age who lived in caves: also **cave dweller.** 2. a man who is rough and crudely direct.
**cav·ern** (kav'ẽrn), *n.* [< Fr. < L. < *cavus,* hollow], a cave, especially a large cave. *v.t.* 1. to enclose in or as in a cavern. 2. to hollow out.
**cav·ern·ous** (kav'ẽr-nəs), *adj.* 1. full of caverns. 2. of a cavern. —**cav'ern·ous·ly,** *adv.*
**cav·i·ar, cav·i·are** (kav'i-är', kä'vi-är'), *n.* [Fr. < It. < Turk. *khāvyār*], a salty relish prepared from the eggs of sturgeon, salmon, etc.
**cav·il** (kav''l), *v.i.* [-ILED or -ILLED, -ILING or -ILLING], [< OFr. < L. *cavillari* < *cavilla,* a jest], to object unnecessarily; resort to trivial faultfinding; carp. *v.t.* to cavil at. *n.* a captious criticism; quibble. —**cav'il·er, cav'il·ler,** *n.*
**cav·i·ty** (kav'ə-ti), *n.* [*pl.* -TIES], [< Fr. < LL. *cavitas* < L. *cavus,* hollow], 1. a hole; hollow place, as in a tooth. 2. a natural hollow place within the body: as, the abdominal *cavity.*
**ca·vort** (kə-vôrt'), *v.i.* [Americanism; ? blend of *curvet & gavotte*], to prance; leap about; caper.
**ca·vy** (kā'vi), *n.* [*pl.* -VIES], [< the native name in Fr. Guiana, *cabiai*], any of several short-tailed South American rodents, as the guinea pig.
**caw** (kô), *n.* [echoic], the harsh, strident cry of a crow or raven. *v.i.* to make this sound.
**Cawn·pore** (kôn-pôr', -pōr'), *n.* a city in N India, on the Ganges: pop., 487,000: also sp. **Cawnpur.**
**Cax·ton, William** (kak'stən), 1422?–1491; the first English printer.
**cay** (kā, kē), *n.* [Sp. *cayo;* see KEY (reef)], a coral reef or sand bank off a mainland.
**cay·enne** (kī-en', kā-), *n.* [< native Braz. *kynnha*], a very hot red pepper made from the dried seeds or fruit of a pepper plant, especially of the capsicum: also **cayenne pepper.**
**cay·man** (kā'mən), *n.* [*pl.* -MANS], [Sp. *caiman*], a large alligator of tropical America.
**Ca·yu·ga** (kā-ū'gə, kī-), *n.* [*pl.* -GA, -GAS], [Am. Ind.], a member of a tribe of Iroquoian Indians who lived around Cayuga Lake and Seneca Lake, in New York: see **Five Nations.**
**Cay·use** (kī-ūs'), *n.* [Am. Ind.], 1. a member of a tribe of Oregonian Indians. 2. [c-], an Indian pony.
**Cb,** in *chemistry,* columbium.

**C.B.S., CBS,** Columbia Broadcasting System.
**cc.,** chapters.
**cc., c.c.,** cubic centimeter; cubic centimeters.
**CCC,** 1. Civilian Conservation Corps. 2. Commodity Credit Corporation.
**ccm,** centimeters.
**Cd,** in *chemistry*, cadmium.
**cd.,** cord; cords.
**Ce,** in *chemistry*, cerium.
**C.E.,** 1. Church of England. 2. Civil Engineer.
**cease** (sēs), *v.t. & v.i.* [CEASED, CEASING], [< OFr. < L. *cessare* < *cedere*, to yield], to end; stop; discontinue. *n.* a ceasing: now only in *without cease*.
**cease·less** (sēs′lis), *adj.* unceasing; always going on; continual. **—cease′less·ly,** *adv.*
**Ce·cro·pi·a moth** (si-krō′pi-ə), a large silkworm moth of the U.S.
**ce·dar** (sē′dẽr), *n.* [< OFr. < L. < Gr. *kedros*], 1. an evergreen tree having durable wood with a characteristic fragrance. 2. any of various trees like this. 3. the wood of any of these. *adj.* of cedar.
**Cedar Rapids,** a city in E Iowa: pop., 92,000.
**cedar waxwing,** a brownish-gray, crested American bird with red, waxlike tips on its wing feathers: also **ce′dar·bird′,** *n.*
**cede** (sēd), *v.t.* [CEDED, CEDING], [< Fr. < L. *cedere*, to yield], 1. to give up; transfer the ownership of. 2. to admit; grant, as a point in debate.
**ce·dil·la** (si-dil′ə), *n.* [Sp. dim. of *zeda;* Gr. *zēta*, the zeta], a hooklike mark put under *c* in some French words (e.g., *garçon*), to show that it is to be sounded like a voiceless *s*.
**ceil** (sēl), *v.t.* [< Fr. *ciel*, roof, sky < L. *caelum*, heaven], 1. to build a ceiling in or over. 2. to cover the ceiling or walls of (a room).
**ceil·ing** (sēl′iŋ), *n.* [< *ceil*], 1. the inside top part or covering of a room, opposite the floor. 2. an upper limit set on anything: as, a *ceiling* on prices. 3. in *aeronautics*, *a*) the upper limit of visibility. *b*) the highest that an aircraft can go under certain conditions. **—hit the ceiling,** [Slang], to lose one's temper.
**cel·an·dine** (sel′ən-dīn′), *n.* [< OFr. < L. < Gr. < *chelidōn*, a swallow], a weedy plant of the poppy family, with yellow flowers and juice.
**Cel·a·nese** (sel′ə-nēz′, nēs′), *n.* [coined < *cel*lulose *a*cetate + *-ese*], rayon made of cellulose acetate: a trade-mark.
**-cele** (sēl), [< Gr. *kēlē*], 1. a combining form meaning *tumor* or *swelling*. 2. -coele.
**Cel·e·bes** (sel′ə-bēz′, sə-lē′bēz), *n.* an island of Indonesia, east of Borneo: area, 73,000 sq. mi.
**cel·e·brant** (sel′ə-brənt), *n.* [see CELEBRATE], 1. a person who performs a religious rite. 2. the priest officiating at Mass.
**cel·e·brate** (sel′ə-brāt′), *v.t.* [-BRATED, -BRATING], [< L. pp. of *celebrare*, to frequent, honor < *celeber*, populous, famous], 1. to perform (a ritual, etc.) publicly and formally; solemnize. 2. to commemorate (an anniversary, etc.) with ceremony or festivity. 3. to proclaim. 4. to honor or praise publicly. *v.i.* 1. to observe a holiday, etc. with festivities. 2. to perform a religious ceremony. 3. [Colloq.], to have a good time. **—cel′e·bra′tor,** *n.*
**cel·e·brat·ed** (sel′ə-brāt′id), *adj.* famous; renowned; much spoken of; well-publicized.
**cel·e·bra·tion** (sel′ə-brā′shən), *n.* 1. a celebrating; formal commemoration. 2. that which is done to celebrate.
**ce·leb·ri·ty** (sə-leb′rə-ti), *n.* [*pl.* -TIES], 1. fame; wide recognition. 2. a celebrated person.
**ce·ler·i·ty** (sə-ler′ə-ti), *n.* [< Fr. < L. < *celer*, swift, quick], swiftness; quickness; speed.
**cel·er·y** (sel′ẽr-i), *n.* [< Fr. < It. < L. < Gr. *selinon*, parsley], a plant whose crisp, blanched stalks are eaten as a vegetable.
**ce·les·ta** (sə-les′tə), *n.* [< Fr.; see CELESTIAL], a small keyboard instrument with bell-like tones produced by hammers striking against metal plates.
**ce·les·tial** (sə-les′chəl), *adj.* [< OFr. < L. < *caelum*, heaven], 1. of the heavens, or sky. 2. of heaven; heavenly; divine. 3. [C-], Chinese. *n.* 1. any being regarded as living in heaven. 2. [usually C-], a Chinese. **—ce·les′tial·ly,** *adv.*
**Celestial Empire,** the former Chinese Empire.
**celestial sphere,** the infinite sphere of the heavens as imagined from the apparent half visible by an observer on the earth.
**ce·li·ac** (sē′li-ak′), *adj.* coeliac.
**cel·i·ba·cy** (sel′ə-bə-si), *n.* [*pl.* -CIES], [see CELIBATE], the state of being unmarried, especially that of a person under a vow; single life.
**cel·i·bate** (sel′ə-bit, -bāt′), *adj.* [< L. < *caelebs*, unmarried], 1. unmarried; single. 2. bound by a vow to remain unmarried. *n.* a celibate person.
**cell** (sel), *n.* [OFr. *celle;* L. *cella*], 1. a small room; cubicle, as in a convent or prison. 2. a very small hollow, cavity, etc., as of a honeycomb. 3. in *biology*, a small unit of protoplasm, usually with a nucleus and an enclosing membrane: all plants and animals are made up of one or more cells. 4. in *botany*, any compartment of an ovary. 5. in *electricity*, a receptacle used either for generating electricity by chemical reactions or for decomposing compounds by electrolysis. 6. in *sociology*, a small organizational unit of a group whose purpose is to propagandize, proselytize, etc.
**cel·lar** (sel′ẽr), *n.* [< OFr. < L. *cellarium* < *cella*, small room], 1. a room or rooms below ground and usually under a building, often used for storing fuel, supplies, etc. 2. a cellar for wines. 3. a stock of wines. *v.t.* to store in a cellar.
**cel·lar·age** (sel′ẽr-ij), *n.* 1. a space of or in a cellar. 2. the fee for storage in a cellar.
**cel·lar·er** (sel′ẽr-ẽr), *n.* a person in charge of a cellar or provisions, as in a monastery.
**cel·lar·et** (sel′ẽr-et′), *n.* [*cellar* + *-et*], a cabinet for wine, liquor, glasses, etc.
**Cel·li·ni, Ben·ve·nu·to** (ben′ve-nōō′tô chel-lē′nē; Eng. chə-lē′ni), 1500–1571; Italian artist.
**cel·lo, ′cel·lo** (chel′ō), *n.* [*pl.* -LOS, -LI (-ē)], [< *violoncello*], an instrument of the violin family, between the viola and the double bass in size and pitch; violoncello. **—cel′list, ′cel′list,** *n.*

CELLO

**cel·lo·phane** (sel′ə-fān′), *n.* [< *cellulose* + Gr. *phanein*, to seem], a thin, transparent material made from cellulose, used as a moistureproof wrapping, as for foods: formerly a trade-mark (**Cellophane**).
**cel·lu·lar** (sel′yoo-lẽr), *adj.* of, like, or containing a cell or cells: also **cel′lu·lat′ed.**
**cel·lu·late** (sel′yoo-lāt′), *adj.* cellular. *v.t.* [-LATED, -LATING], to form into cells.
**cel·lule** (sel′ūl), *n.* a very small cell.
**cel·lu·loid** (sel′yoo-loid′), *n.* [*cellu*lose + *-oid*], a thin, inflammable substance made from pyroxylin and camphor, used for photographic films, toilet articles, etc.: a trade-mark (**Celluloid**). *adj.* made of celluloid.
**cel·lu·lose** (sel′yoo-lōs′), *n.* [< L. dim. of *cella*, cell], the chief substance composing the cell walls or woody part of plants: used in the manufacture of paper, rayon, explosives, etc.
**ce·lom** (sē′ləm), *n.* the coelom.
**cel·o·tex** (sel′ə-teks′), *n.* a composition board used for insulation: a trade-mark (**Celotex**).
**Celt** (selt, kelt), *n.* [< Fr. < L. *Celta*, pl. *Celtae* (Gr. *Keltoi*), the Gauls], 1. a Celtic-speaking person: the Bretons, Irish, Welsh, and Highland Scots are Celts. 2. an ancient Gaul or Briton. Also **Kelt.**
**Cel·tic** (sel′tik, kel′-), *adj.* of the Celts, their languages, culture, etc. *n.* a family of Indo-European languages, subdivided into *Goidelic* (Irish Gaelic, Scottish Gaelic, and Manx) and *Brythonic* (Breton, Cornish, and Welsh). **—Cel·ti·cism** (sel′tə-siz′m), *n.*
**ce·ment** (sə-ment′), *n.* [< OFr. < L. *caementum*, rough stone < *caedere*, to cut], 1. a substance of powdered lime and clay, mixed with water and used to fasten stones or bricks together, or as paving; also, the mixture (mortar), which hardens like stone when it dries. 2. any soft substance that fastens things together firmly when it hardens, as glue. 3. a cementlike substance used in filling cavities, as in teeth. 4. anything that joins or unites; bond. 5. the bony outer crust of the root of a tooth. *v.t.* 1. to join or unite as with cement. 2. to cover with cement. *v.i.* to become cemented. **—ce·men·ta·tion** (sē′mən-tā′shən, sem′ən-), *n.* **—ce·ment′er,** *n.* **—ce·ment′like′,** *adj.*
**cem·e·ter·y** (sem′ə-ter′i), *n.* [*pl.* -IES], [< LL. < Gr. *koimētērion* < *koiman*, to put to sleep], a place for the burial of the dead; graveyard.
**cen·o·bite** (sen′ə-bīt′, sē′nə-), *n.* [< LL. < Gr. *koinobion*, convent < *koinos*, common + *bios*, life], a member of a religious order in a convent or monastery: also sp. **coenobite. —cen·o·bit′ic,** (-bit′ik), **cen·o·bit′i·cal,** *adj.* **—cen′o·bit·ism,** *n.*
**cen·o·taph** (sen′ə-taf′), *n.* [< Fr. < L. < Gr. < *kenos*, empty + *taphos*, a tomb], a monument honoring a dead person whose body is somewhere else.
**Ce·no·zo·ic** (sē′nə-zō′ik, sen′ə-), *adj.* [< Gr. *kainos*, new, recent + *zōē*, life; + *-ic*], designating or of the geological era following the Mesozoic and including the present: see **geology,** chart. *n.* the Cenozoic era.

**cen·ser** (sen′sẽr), *n.* [< OFr. < *encens;* see INCENSE, *n.*], a container in which incense is burned.

**cen·sor** (sen′sẽr), *n.* [L. < *censere*, to tax, value], 1. one of two Roman magistrates appointed to take the census and, later, to supervise public morals; hence, 2. any supervisor of public morals. 3. a person whose task is to examine literature, motion pictures, mail, etc., and to remove or prohibit anything considered unsuitable. 4. a faultfinder. *v.t.* to examine, review, expurgate, or change (literature, mail, etc.) as a censor. —**cen′sor·a·ble,** *adj.* —**cen·so·ri·al** (sen-sôr′i-əl, -sō′ri-), *adj.*

**cen·so·ri·ous** (sen-sôr′i-əs, -sō′ri-), *adj.* [see CENSOR], inclined to find fault; harshly critical. —**cen·so′ri·ous·ly,** *adv.* —**cen·so′ri·ous·ness,** *n.*

**cen·sor·ship** (sen′sẽr-ship′), *n.* 1. a censoring. 2. the practice or a system of censoring. 3. the work or position of a censor.

**cen·sure** (sen′shẽr), *n.* [L. *censura* < *censere*, to tax, value], a blaming; condemnation; adverse opinion or judgment. *v.t.* [-SURED, -SURING], to blame; condemn as wrong; criticize adversely. —**cen′sur·a·ble,** *adj.* —**cen′sur·er,** *n.*

**cen·sus** (sen′səs), *n.* [L. < *censere*, to enroll, tax], 1. in *Roman history*, the act of counting the people and evaluating their property for taxation; hence, 2. any official count of population and recording of economic status, age, sex, etc.

**cent.,** 1. centigrade. 2. century.

**cent** (sent), *n.* [Fr., a hundred; L. *centum*], 1. a hundred, as in *per cent.* 2. a 100th part of a dollar or a coin having this value; penny: symbol, ¢.

**cen·tare** (sen′târ; Fr. sän′tȧr′), *n.* a centiare.

**cen·taur** (sen′tôr), *n.* [< L. < Gr. *Kentauros*], in *Gr. mythology*, a monster with a man's head, trunk, and arms, and a horse's body and legs.

CENTAUR

**cen·ta·vo** (sen-tä′vō), *n.* [*pl.* -VOS (-vōz; Sp. -vôs)], [< Sp. < L. *centum*, a hundred], 1. a small coin of the Philippines, Mexico, and certain South American countries; one 100th of a peso. 2. a coin of Portugal and Brazil; one 100th of an escudo.

**cen·te·nar·i·an** (sen′tə-nâr′i-ən), *adj.* 1. of 100 years; of a centenary. 2. of a centenarian. *n.* a person at least 100 years old.

**cen·te·nar·y** (sen′tə-ner′i, sen-ten′ə-ri), *n.* [*pl.* -IES], [< L. < *centum*, a hundred], 1. a century; period of 100 years. 2. a centennial. *adj.* 1. of a century, or period of 100 years. 2. of a centennial.

**cen·ten·ni·al** (sen-ten′i-əl), *adj.* [< L. *centum*, a hundred + *annus*, year], 1. of 100 years. 2. happening once in 100 years. 3. 100 years old. 4. lasting 100 years. 5. of a 100th anniversary. *n.* 1. a 100th year of existence; 100th anniversary. 2. the celebration of this. —**cen·ten′ni·al·ly,** *adj.*

**cen·ter** (sen′tẽr), *n.* [< OFr. < L. *centrum* < Gr. *kentron*, sharp point], 1. a point equally distant from all points on the circumference of a circle or surface of a sphere. 2. the point around which anything revolves; pivot. 3. the central, or main place of activity; headquarters. 4. the approximate middle point, place, or part of anything. 5. a thing at the middle point. 6. a place that actions, forces, people, etc. go to or come from; focal point. 7. in *biology*, a group of cells having a common function. 8. in *sports*, a player at the center of a floor, field, or line. 9. in *military usage*, that part of an army between the flanks. 10. [often C-], in *politics*, a position or party between left (radicals and liberals) and right (conservatives and reactionaries). *v.i.* to be at a center; be centered. *v.t.* 1. to place in, at, or near the center. 2. to draw or gather to one place. 3. to furnish with a center. Also sp. **centre.**

**cen·ter·board** (sen′tẽr-bôrd′, -bōrd′), *n.* a movable, keellike board lowered through a slot in the floor of a sailboat to prevent drifting to leeward.

**center field,** in *baseball*, the middle of the outfield.

**center of gravity,** that point in a thing around which its weight is evenly distributed or balanced.

**cen·ter·piece** (sen′tẽr-pēs′), *n.* an ornament, bowl of flowers, etc. for the center of a table.

**cen·tes·i·mal** (sen-tes′ə-m'l), *adj.* [< L. *centesimus* < *centum*, a hundred], 1. hundredth. 2. of or divided into hundredths. —**cen·tes′i·mal·ly,** *adv.*

**cen·ti-,** [L. < *centum*], a combining form meaning: 1. *hundred* or *hundredfold.* 2. *a 100th part of.*

**cen·ti·are** (sen′ti-âr′), *n.* [Fr.; see CENTI- & ARE, *n.*], a 100th part of an are (unit of land measure).

**cen·ti·grade** (sen′tə-grād′), *adj.* [Fr. < L. *centum*, a hundred + *gradus*, a degree], 1. consisting of or divided into 100 degrees. 2. of or by the centigrade thermometer: abbrev. **C., c.**

**centigrade thermometer,** a thermometer on which, under laboratory conditions, 0° is the freezing point and 100° is the boiling point of water.

**cen·ti·gram, cen·ti·gramme** (sen′tə-gram′), *n.* [Fr.; see CENTI- & GRAM], a unit of weight, equal to 1/100 gram: abbrev. **cg.** (*sing.* & *pl.*).

**cen·ti·li·ter, cen·ti·li·tre** (sen′tə-lē′tẽr), *n.* [Fr.; see CENTI- & LITER], a unit of capacity, equal to 1/100 liter: abbrev. **cl.** (*sing.* & *pl.*).

**cen·time** (sän′tēm; Fr. sän′tēm′), *n.* [Fr.; see CENTESIMAL], the 100th part of a franc.

**cen·ti·me·ter, cen·ti·me·tre** (sen′tə-mē′tẽr), *n.* [Fr.; see CENTI- & METER], a unit of measure, equal to 1/100 meter: abbrev. **cm., c., C.**

**cen·ti·me·ter-gram-sec·ond** (sen′tə-mē′tẽr-gram′-sek′ənd), *adj.* in *physics*, designating or of a system of measurement in which the centimeter, gram, and second are used as the units of length, mass, and time, respectively: abbrev. **C.G.S., cgs, c.g.s.**

**cen·ti·pede** (sen′tə-pēd′), *n.* [Fr. < L. < *centum*, a hundred + *pes, pedis*, a foot], a wormlike animal with a pair of legs for each body segment: the two front legs are modified into poison fangs.

**cen·tral** (sen′trəl), *adj.* [L. *centralis*], 1. in, at, or near the center. 2. of or forming the center. 3. from the center. 4. equally distant or accessible from various points. 5. main; principal; chief; basic. 6. denoting that part of the nervous system consisting of the brain and spinal cord (of a vertebrate). *n.* 1. a telephone exchange. 2. [sometimes C-], a telephone operator. —**cen′tral·ly,** *adv.*

**Central African Republic,** a country in central Africa, a member of the French Community: area, 241,700 sq. mi.; pop., 1,193,000; capital, Bangui.

**Central America,** the part of North America between Mexico and South America. —**Central American.**

**cen·tral·ism** (sen′trəl-iz'm), *n.* the principle or system of centralizing power or authority. —**cen′tral·ist,** *n.* & *adj.*

**cen·tral·ize** (sen′trə-līz′), *v.t.* [-IZED, -IZING], 1. to make central; bring to or focus on a center; gather together. 2. to organize or systematize under one control. *v.i.* to become centralized. —**cen′tral·i·za′tion,** *n.* —**cen′tral·iz′er,** *n.*

**Central Standard Time,** see **standard time.**

**cen·tre** (sen′tẽr), *n., v.t.* & *v.i.* [-RED, -RING], center: chiefly British spelling.

**cen·tri-,** centro-.

**cen·tric** (sen′trik), *adj.* 1. in, at, or near the center; central. 2. of or having a center. Also **centrical.** —**cen′tri·cal·ly,** *adv.* —**cen·tric·i·ty** (sen-tris′ə-ti), *n.*

**cen·trif·u·gal** (sen-trif′yoo-g'l), *adj.* [< *centri-* + L. *fugere*, to flee; + *-al*], 1. moving or tending to move away from the center. 2. using or acted on by centrifugal force. *n.* a centrifuge. —**cen·trif′u·gal·ly,** *adv.*

**centrifugal force,** the force tending to make rotating bodies move away from the center of rotation: it is due to inertia.

**cen·trif·u·gal·ize** (sen-trif′yoo-g'l-īz′), *v.t.* [-IZED, -IZING], to subject to the action of a centrifuge; separate by whirling in a centrifuge.

**cen·tri·fuge** (sen′trə-fūj′), *n.* a machine using centrifugal force to separate particles of varying density, as cream from milk. *v.t.* [-FUGED, -FUGING], to centrifugalize.

**cen·trip·e·tal** (sen-trip′ə-t'l), *adj.* [< *centri-* + L. *petere*, to seek; + *-al*], 1. moving or tending to move toward the center. 2. using or acted on by centripetal force. —**cen·trip′e·tal·ly,** *adv.*

**centripetal force,** the force tending to make rotating bodies move toward the center of rotation.

**cen·trist** (sen′trist), *n.* one whose political position is neither leftist nor rightist.

**cen·tro-,** [< L. < Gr. *kentron*, a point, center], a combining form meaning *center:* also **centri-** or, before a vowel, **centr-.**

**cen·tro·some** (sen′trə-sōm′), *n.* [*centro-* + *-some* (body)], a very small body near or, sometimes, in the nucleus in most animal cells and some plant cells. —**cen·tro·som·ic** (sen′trə-som′ik), *adj.*

**cen·tro·sphere** (sen′trə-sfẽr′), *n.* [*centro-* + *sphere*], in *biology*, the central mass of protoplasm about the centrosome.

**cen·tu·ple** (sen′too-p'l, sen-too͞′-, -tū′-), *adj.* [Fr. < L. *centuplus*], a hundred times as much or as many; hundredfold. *v.t.* [-PLED, -PLING], to make centuple; increase a hundredfold.

**cen·tu·pli·cate** (sen-too͞′plə-kāt′, -tū′-; *for adj. & n., usually* -kit), *v.t.* [-CATED, -CATING], to increase a hundredfold; centuple. *adj.* hundredfold; centuple. *n.* a centuple quantity.

**cen·tu·ri·on** (sen-tyoor′i-ən, -toor′-), *n.* [see CENTURY], the commanding officer of an ancient Roman military unit originally made up of 100 men.

**cen·tu·ry** (sen′chə-ri), *n.* [*pl.* -RIES], [L. *centuria* < *centum*, a hundred], 1. a series or group of 100 persons or things. 2. any period of 100 years, especially as reckoned from the beginning of the Christian Era. 3. in ancient Rome, *a)* a military unit, originally made up of 100 men. *b)* a subdivision of the people for purposes of voting. —**cen·tu·ri·al** (sen-tyoor′i-əl, -toor′-), *adj.*

**century plant,** a tropical American agave having fleshy leaves and greenish flowers: mistakenly thought to bloom only once a century.

**ce·phal·ic** (sə-fal′ik, se-), *adj.* [< L. < Gr. < *kephalē*, the head], 1. of the head, skull, or cranium. 2. in, on, near, or toward the head.

**-ce·phal·ic** (sə-fal′ik), a combining form meaning *head* or *skull*, as in *dolichocephalic*.

**cephalic index,** a measure of the human skull computed by dividing its maximum breadth by its maximum length and multiplying by 100: if an individual's index is 80 or more, he is short-headed (*brachycephalic*); if less than 80, he is long-headed (*dolichocephalic*).

**ceph·a·lo-,** [< Gr. *kephalē*, the head], a combining form meaning *the head, skull,* or *brain*: also, before a vowel, **cephal-.**

**ceph·a·lo·pod** (sef′ə-lə-pod′), *n.* [*cephalo-* + *-pod*], a class of mollusks, having a distinct head with two large eyes and muscular tentacles about the mouth: the octopus, squid, and cuttlefish are typical. —**ceph·a·lop·o·dan** (sef′ə-lop′ə-dən), *adj. & n.*

**ceph·a·lo·tho·rax** (sef′ə-lə-thôr′aks, -thō′raks), *n.* the head and thorax regarded as a single part, in certain crustaceans and arachnids.

**-ceph·a·lous** (sef′ə-ləs), [< Gr. *kephalē*], a combining form meaning *-headed.*

**ce·ram·ic** (sə-ram′ik), *adj.* [< Gr. < *keramos*, clay, pottery], 1. of pottery, earthenware, tile, porcelain, etc. 2. of ceramics.

**ce·ram·ics** (sə-ram′iks), *n.pl.* [< *ceramic*], 1. [construed as sing.], the art or work of making pottery, earthenware, etc. 2. objects made of these materials. —**cer·a·mist** (ser′ə-mist), **ce·ram′i·cist,** *n.*

**cer·a·to-** (ser′ə-tō, -ə-tə), [< Gr. *keras*, a horn], a combining form meaning *horn, hornlike*: also, before a vowel, **cerat-.**

**Cer·ber·us** (sũr′bẽr-əs), *n.* in *Gr. & Rom. mythology*, the three-headed dog guarding the gate of Hades. —**Cer·be·re·an** (sẽr-bêr′i-ən), *adj.*

**cere** (sêr), *n.* [< Fr. < L. < Gr. *kēros*, wax], a soft, waxlike membrane at the base of the beak of some birds, as the parrot, eagle, etc. *v.t.* [CERED, CERING], to wrap in a cerecloth.

**ce·re·al** (sêr′i-əl), *adj.* [< L. *Cerealis*, of Ceres], of grain or the grasses producing grain. *n.* 1. any grain used for food, as wheat, oats, etc. 2. any grass producing such grain. 3. food made from grain, especially breakfast food, as oatmeal, etc.

**cer·e·bel·lum** (ser′ə-bel′əm), *n.* [*pl.* -LUMS, -LA], [L., dim. of *cerebrum*, the brain], the section of the brain behind and below the cerebrum: it is the coordinating center for muscular movement. —**cer′e·bel′lar,** *adj.*

**cer·e·bral** (ser′ə-brəl, sə-rē′-), *adj.* of the brain or the cerebrum.

**cerebral palsy,** paralysis due to a lesion of the brain, usually one suffered at birth, and characterized chiefly by spasms: see **spastic.**

**cer·e·brate** (ser′ə-brāt′), *v.i.* [-BRATED, -BRATING], [< L. *cerebrum*, the brain; + *-ate*], to use one's brain; think. —**cer′e·bra′tion,** *n.*

**cer·e·bro-,** [< L. *cerebrum*, the brain], a combining form meaning *the brain* or *cerebrum*: also, before a vowel, **cerebr-.**

**cer·e·bro·spi·nal** (ser′ə-brō-spī′n'l), *adj.* of or affecting the brain and the spinal cord.

**cer·e·brum** (ser′ə-brəm, sə-rē′-), *n.* [*pl.* -BRUMS, -BRA], [L.], the upper, main part (the **cerebral hemispheres**) of the brain of vertebrate animals, controlling conscious and voluntary processes in man.

**cere·cloth** (sêr′klôth′), *n.* [< *cered cloth*; see CERE], cloth treated with wax or a similar substance, used to wrap a dead person for burial.

**cere·ment** (sêr′mənt), *n.* [see CERE], 1. a cerecloth; shroud. 2. *usually pl.* any clothes in which a dead person is buried.

**cer·e·mo·ni·al** (ser′ə-mō′ni-əl, -nyəl), *adj.* of or consisting of ceremony; ritual; formal. *n.* 1. an established system of rites or formal actions connected with an occasion; ritual. 2. a rite. —**cer′e·mo′ni·al·ism,** *n.* —**cer′e·mo′ni·al·ist,** *n.* —**cer′e·mo′ni·al·ly,** *adv.*

**cer·e·mo·ni·ous** (ser′ə-mō′ni-əs, -nyəs), *adj.* 1. ceremonial. 2. full of ceremony. 3. characterized by ceremony or formality; very polite. —**cer′e·mo′ni·ous·ly,** *adv.*—**cer′e·mo′ni·ous·ness,** *n.*

**cer·e·mo·ny** (ser′ə-mō′ni), *n.* [*pl.* -NIES], [L. *caerimonia*], 1. a formal act or set of formal acts established as proper to a special occasion, such as a wedding, religious rite, etc. 2. a conventional social act. 3. behavior that follows rigid etiquette. 4. formality or formalities. 5. empty or meaningless formality. —**stand on ceremony,** to behave with or insist on formality.

**Ce·res** (sêr′ēz), *n.* [L.], in *Rom. mythology*, the goddess of agriculture: identified with the Greek Demeter.

**ce·rise** (sə-rēz′, -rēs′), *n. & adj.* [Fr., a cherry; see CHERRY], bright red; cherry red.

**ce·ri·um** (sêr′i-əm), *n.* [after the asteroid *Ceres*], a gray, metallic chemical element: symbol, Ce; at. wt., 140.13; at. no., 58.

**ce·ro-,** [< L. < Gr. *kēros*, wax], a combining form meaning *wax*: also, before a vowel, **cer-.**

**ce·ro·plas·tic** (sêr′ə-plas′tik), *adj.* [< Gr. < *kēros*, wax + *plassein*, to mold], 1. having to do with wax modeling. 2. modeled in wax.

**cert.,** 1. certificate. 2. certified. Also **certif.**

**cer·tain** (sũr′t'n, -tin), *adj.* [< Fr. < L. *certus*, determined < *cernere*, to decide], 1. fixed; settled; determined. 2. inevitable. 3. not to be doubted: as, the evidence is *certain*. 4. reliable; dependable: as, a *certain* cure. 5. controlled; unerring: as, his aim was *certain*. 6. sure; positive: as, I'm *certain* he's here. 7. specific, but not described or named: as, a *certain* person is to blame. 8. some; appreciable: as, success to a *certain* extent. —**for certain,** as a certainty; without doubt. —**cer′tain·ness,** *n.*

**cer·tain·ly** (sũr′t'n-li, -tin-), *adv.* surely; beyond a doubt.

**cer·tain·ty** (sũr′t'n-ti, -tin-), *n.* 1. the quality, state, or fact of being certain. 2. [*pl.* -TIES], anything certain; definite fact. —**of a certainty,** [Archaic], without a doubt; certainly.

**cer·tes** (sũr′tēz), *adv.* [< OFr. < L. *certus*, determined], [Archaic], certainly; verily.

**cer·tif·i·cate** (sẽr-tif′ə-kit), *n.* [< Fr. < ML.; ult. < L. *certus*, certain + *facere*, to make], a written or printed statement testifying to a fact, qualification, or promise. *v.t.* (-kāt′), [-CATED, -CATING], 1. to attest by a certificate. 2. to issue a certificate to.

**cer·ti·fi·ca·tion** (sũr′tə-fi-kā′shən), *n.* 1. a certifying or being certified. 2. a certificate.

**cer·ti·fied** (sũr′tə-fīd′), *adj.* 1. vouched for; guaranteed. 2. having a certificate.

**certified public accountant,** an accountant certified by State law after meeting the requirements.

**cer·ti·fy** (sũr′tə-fī′), *v.t.* [-FIED, -FYING], [see CERTIFICATE], 1. to declare (a thing) true, accurate, certain, etc. by formal statement; verify. 2. to guarantee; vouch for: as, the bank must *certify* your check. 3. to grant a certificate to. 4. [Archaic], to assure; make certain. *v.i.* to testify (*to*). —**cer′ti·fi′a·ble,** *adj.* —**cer′ti·fi′er,** *n.*

**cer·ti·o·ra·ri** (sũr′shi-ə-râr′i, -rā′rī), *n.* [LL., to be made more certain < L. *certus*, certain], in *law*, a writ from a higher court to a lower one, requesting the record of a case for review.

**cer·ti·tude** (sũr′tə-to͞od′, -tūd′), *n.* [LL. *certitudo*], certainty; assurance.

**ce·ru·le·an** (sə-ro͞o′li-ən), *adj.* [< L., prob. < dim. of *caelum*, heaven], sky-blue; azure.

**ce·ru·men** (sə-ro͞o′mən), *n.* [< L. *cera*, wax, after *albumen*], earwax.

**Cer·van·tes, Mi·guel de** (mē-gel′ *th*e ther-vän′tes; Eng. sẽr-van′tēz), 1547–1616; Spanish writer; author of *Don Quixote*.

**cer·vi·cal** (sũr′vi-k'l), *adj.* of the neck or cervix.

**cer·vine** (sũr′vīn, -vin), *adj.* [< L. < *cervus*, deer], 1. of a deer or the deer family. 2. like a deer.

**cer·vix** (sũr′viks), *n.* [*pl.* -VICES (sẽr-vī′sēz, sũr′və-sēz′), -VIXES], [L., the neck], 1. the neck, especially the back of the neck. 2. a necklike part, as of the uterus, urinary bladder, etc.

**Ce·sar·e·an, Ce·sar·i·an** (si-zâr′i-ən), *adj. & n.* Caesarean.

**ce·si·um** (sē′zi-əm), *n.* [< L. *caesius*, bluish-gray], a soft, bluish-gray, ductile, metallic chemical element, used in photoelectric cells: symbol, Cs; at. wt., 132.91; at. no., 55: also sp. **caesium.**

**ces·sa·tion** (se-sā'shən), *n.* [< L. < pp. of *cessare*, to cease], a ceasing; stop; pause.

**ces·sion** (sesh'ən), *n.* [Fr. < L. < pp. of *cedere*, to yield], a ceding; giving up (of rights, property, etc.) to another; surrendering.

**cess·pool** (ses'pōōl'), *n.* [prob. < It. *cesso* (< L. *secessus*), privy], 1. a pool or deep hole in the ground to receive drainage or sewage from the sinks, toilets, etc. of a house. 2. a filthy place.

**ces·tus** (ses'təs), *n.* [L. *caestus* < *caedere*, to strike], a device of leather straps, sometimes weighted with lead or iron, worn on the hand by boxers in ancient Rome.

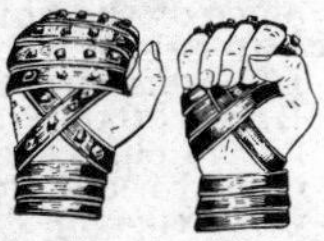

CESTUS

**ce·su·ra** (si-zhoor'ə, -zyoor'ə), *n.* [*pl.* -RAS, -RAE (-ē)], a caesura. —**ce·su'ral,** *adj.*

**ce·ta·cean** (si-tā'shən), *adj.* [L. *cetus*, whale < Gr. *kētos*], of a group of hairless, fishlike water mammals with paddlelike forelimbs, as whales, porpoises, and dolphins: also **ce·ta'ceous** (-shəs). *n.* any such animal.

**ce·vi·tam·ic acid** (sē'vi-tam'ik, -vi-), [< *C* + *vitamin* + *-ic*], vitamin C.

**Cey·lon** (si-lon'), *n.* a country on an island off the southern tip of India, a member of the British Commonwealth of Nations: area, 25,332 sq. mi.; pop., 11,964,000; capital, Colombo. —**Cey·lo·nese** (sē'lə-nēz'), *adj. & n.*

**Cé·zanne, Paul** (pôl sā'zȧn'), 1839–1906; French postimpressionist painter.

**cf.,** *confer*, [L.], compare.

**Cf,** in *chemistry*, californium.

**cg.,** centigram; centigrams.

**C.G.,** Coast Guard.

**C.G.S., cgs, c.g.s.,** centimeter-gram-second.

**Ch., ch.,** 1. chief. 2. child; children. 3. church.

**ch.,** [*pl.* CHS.], chapter.

**‡cha·conne** (shȧ'kôn'), *n.* [Fr.; Sp. *chacona*], 1. a slow, stately dance of the 18th century. 2. music for this dance, in ¾ time. 3. a similar movement in various musical compositions.

**Chad** (chad, chäd), *n.* 1. a country in central Africa, a member of the French Community: area, 495,750 sq. mi.; pop., 3,361,000; capital, Fort-Lamy. 2. a lake between Chad and Nigeria.

**chafe** (chāf), *v.t.* [CHAFED, CHAFING], [< OFr. *chaufer*, to warm < L. < *calere*, to be warm + *facere*, to make], 1. to rub so as to make warm. 2. to wear away by rubbing. 3. to make sore by rubbing. 4. to annoy; irritate. *v.i.* 1. to rub (often with *on* or *against*). 2. to be angry or irritable. *n.* 1. an injury or irritation caused by rubbing. 2. annoyance. —**chafe at the bit,** to be impatient.

**chaf·er** (chāf'ẽr), *n.* [AS. *ceafor*], any of a group of related beetles that feed on plants.

**chaff** (chaf, chäf), *n.* [AS. *ceaf*], 1. threshed or winnowed husks of wheat or other grain. 2. anything worthless. 3. teasing talk; banter. *v.t. & v.i.* to tease or ridicule in a good-natured manner. —**chaff'er,** *n.* —**chaff'y** [-IER, -IEST], *adj.*

**chaf·fer** (chaf'ẽr), *n.* [< AS. *ceap*, bargain + *faru*, journey], a haggling over price; bargaining. *v.i.* to haggle over price; bargain. —**chaf'fer·er,** *n.*

**chaf·finch** (chaf'inch), *n.* [AS. *ceaffinc;* see CHAFF & FINCH: it eats chaff], a small European songbird.

**chaf·ing dish** (chāf'iŋ), [see CHAFE], a pan with a heating apparatus beneath it, to cook food at the table or to keep food hot.

**cha·grin** (shə-grin'), *n.* [Fr.; ? < OFr. *graignier*, to sorrow < *grain*, sorrow], a feeling of disappointment, humiliation, embarrassment, etc. caused by failure or discomfiture. *v.t.* [-GRINED, -GRINING], to cause to feel chagrin.

**chain** (chān), *n.* [< OFr. *chaine* < L. *catena*, a chain], 1. a flexible series of joined links, usually of metal. 2. *pl.* bonds; fetters; hence, 3. *pl.* captivity; bondage. 4. a chainlike measuring instrument, or its measure of length: a *surveyor's chain* is 66 feet long; an *engineer's chain* is 100 feet: abbrev. **chn.** 5. a connected series of things or events. 6. in *chemistry*, a linkage of atoms in a molecule. *v.t.* 1. to fasten or shackle with chains. 2. to restrain; bind. 3. to keep in bondage or imprisonment. —**chain'like',** *adj.*

**chain gang,** a gang of prisoners chained together, as when working.

**chain letter,** a letter to be circulated among many people by being copied and passed to others.

**chain mail,** flexible armor made of metal links.

**chain reaction,** 1. in *physics & chemistry*, a series of reactions in which the products of each reaction activate additional molecules or atoms of the reactants, thus causing new reactions, as in nuclear fission. 2. any sequence of events, each of which results in the following.

**chain saw,** a portable power saw with an endless chain that carries cutting teeth.

**chain stitch,** a fancy stitch in which the loops are connected in a chainlike way, as in crocheting.

**chain store,** any of a group of retail stores owned and controlled by one company.

**chair** (châr), *n.* [< OFr. *chaiere* < L. *cathedra;* see CATHEDRA], 1. a seat for one person: it usually has four legs and a back. 2. a seat of authority or dignity. 3. an office or position of authority, as a professorship. 4. a person who presides over a meeting; chairman. 5. a sedan chair. 6. *a)* the electric chair. *b)* execution by the electric chair. *v.t.* 1. to place in a chair; seat. 2. to place in authority; choose as chairman. 3. to preside over (a meeting). —**take the chair,** 1. to preside as chairman. 2. to open a meeting.

**chair·lift** (châr'lift'), *n.* a number of seats suspended from a power-driven endless cable, used esp. to carry skiers up a mountain slope.

**chair·man** (châr'mən), *n.* [*pl.* -MEN], a person who presides at a meeting or heads a committee, board, etc. —**chair'man·ship',** *n.* —**chair'wom'an,** *n.fem.*

**chaise** (shāz), *n.* [Fr., var. of *chaire;* see CHAIR], any of certain lightweight carriages, some with a collapsible top, having two or four wheels.

**chaise longue** (shāz'lôŋg'; Fr. shez'lōng'), [*pl.* CHAISE LONGUES (lôŋgz'; Fr. lōng')], [Fr., lit., long chair], a couchlike chair with a support for the back and a seat long enough to support the outstretched legs.

**cha·la·za** (kə-lā'zə), *n.* [*pl.* -ZAS, -ZAE (-zē)], [Gr. *chalaza*, hard lump], either of the whitish spiral bands extending from the yolk to the lining membrane at each end of a bird's egg.

**chal·ced·o·ny** (kal-sed''n-i, kal'sə-dō'ni), *n.* [*pl.* -NIES], [< L. < Gr.; prob. after *Chalkēdōn*, an ancient city in Asia Minor], a kind of quartz with the luster of wax, variously colored.

**Chal·da·ic** (kal-dā'ik), *adj. & n.* Chaldean.

**Chal·de·a** (kal-dē'ə), *n.* an ancient region in SW Asia, on the Euphrates River and the Persian Gulf. —**Chal·de'an,** *adj. & n.*

**Chal·dee** (kal-dē', kal'dē), *adj. & n.* Chaldean.

**cha·let** (sha-lā', shal'i), *n.* [Swiss Fr.; ? < dim. of L. *casa*, a house], 1. a herdsman's hut or cabin in the Swiss Alps. 2. a Swiss cottage with overhanging eaves. 3. any house built in this style.

**chal·ice** (chal'is), *n.* [OFr. < L. *calix*, a cup], 1. a cup; goblet. 2. the cup for the wine in Holy Communion. 3. a cup-shaped flower. —**chal'iced,** *adj.*

**chalk** (chôk), *n.* [AS. *cealc* < L. *calx*, limestone], 1. a white or grayish limestone that is soft and easily pulverized, composed mainly of small sea shells. 2. chalklike substance. 3. a piece of chalk, often colored, used for writing on a blackboard, etc. 4. a score; reckoning, as of credit. *adj.* made or drawn with chalk. *v.t.* 1. to treat with chalk. 2. to rub or smear with chalk; hence, 3. to make pale. 4. to write, draw, or mark with chalk. —**chalk out,** 1. to mark out. 2. to outline; plan. —**chalk up,** 1. to make a record of. 2. to charge or credit to (an account). —**walk a chalk line,** [Colloq.], to behave with strict propriety. —**chalk'like',** *adj.* —**chalk'y** [-IER, -IEST], *adj.* —**chalk'i·ness,** *n.*

**chalk·board** (chôk'bôrd'), *n.* a blackboard.

**chalk talk,** a lecture accompanied with explanatory diagrams, etc. drawn in chalk on a blackboard.

**chal·lenge** (chal'ənj), *n.* [< OFr. < L. *calumnia*, false accusation], 1. a demand for identification: as, a sentry gave the *challenge*. 2. a calling into question: as, a *challenge* to an assertion. 3. a call to take part in a fight, contest, etc.; defiance. 4. a demand; claim upon. 5. an exception to a vote or to someone's right to vote. 6. in *law*, a formal objection or exception. *v.t.* [-LENGED, -LENGING], 1. to make a challenge to (a person); call to account. 2. to make objection to; question. 3. to call to take part in a fight, contest, etc.; defy. 4. to call for; claim; demand: as, this idea *challenges* attention. 5. to take exception to (a vote or voter) as not being valid or qualified. 6. in *law*, to take

formal exception to. *v.i.* to utter or issue a challenge. —**chal′lenge·a·ble,** *adj.* —**chal′leng·er,** *n.*
**chal·lis, chal·lie** (shal′i), *n.* [? < *Calais*, Fr. town], a lightweight, usually printed fabric of wool, wool mixture, or cotton and rayon.
**cha·lyb·e·ate** (kə-lib′i-āt, -it), *adj.* [< L. *chalybs* (< Gr. *chalyps*), steel], 1. containing salts of iron. 2. tasting like iron. *n.* a chalybeate liquid or medicine.
**cham** (kam), *n.* [Archaic], a khan.
**cham·ber** (chām′bēr), *n.* [< OFr. < LL. *camera;* see CAMERA], 1. a room in a house, especially a bedroom. 2. *pl.* [Brit.], a single suite of rooms. 3. *pl.* a judge's office near the courtroom. 4. an assembly hall. 5. a legislative or judicial body or division: as, the *Chamber* of Deputies. 6. a council: as, a *chamber* of commerce. 7. an enclosed space in the body. 8. the part of a gun that holds the charge or cartridge. *v.t.* to provide a chamber or chambers for. —**cham′bered** (-bērd), *adj.*
**cham·ber·lain** (chām′bēr-lin), *n.* [< OFr. < OHG. < *chamara* (L. *camera*) + dim. suffix *-linc;* see CAMERA & -LING], 1. an officer in charge of the household of a ruler or lord; steward. 2. a high official in certain royal courts. 3. a treasurer.
**cham·ber·maid** (chām′bēr-mād′), *n.* a woman whose work is taking care of bedrooms, as in hotels.
**chamber music,** music suitable for performance in a room or small hall, as trios, quartets, etc.
**chamber of commerce,** an association established to further the business interests of its community.
**chamber pot,** a portable container kept in a bedroom and used as a toilet.
**cham·bray** (sham′brā), *n.* [Fr., after *Cambrai*, France], a variety of gingham made by weaving white cotton threads across a colored warp.
**cha·me·le·on** (kə-mē′li-ən, -mēl′yən), *n.* [< L. < Gr. < *chamai*, on the ground + *leōn*, lion], 1. any of various lizards that can change the color of their skin; hence, 2. a changeable or fickle person. —**cha·me′le·on′ic,** *adj.*
**cham·fer** (cham′fēr), *n.* [< Fr. < OFr. < L. *canthum frangere;* see CANT (an angle edge) & FRAGILE], the flat surface created by slicing off the square edge or corner of a block of wood, stone, etc. *v.t.* 1. to cut a chamfer on; bevel. 2. to make a groove or fluting in.
**cham·ois** (sham′i), *n.* [*pl.* CHAMOIS], [Fr. < LL. *camox*], 1. a small, goatlike antelope of the mountains of Europe and SW Asia. 2. a soft leather made from the skin of chamois, sheep, goats, etc.: also sp. **shammy, chammy.** *adj.* 1. made of chamois. 2. fawn-colored. *v.t.* [-OISED (-id), -OISING (-i-iŋ)], to dry or polish with a chamois skin.

CHAMOIS (2 ft. high)

**cham·o·mile** (kam′ə-mil′), *n.* camomile.
**champ** (champ), *v.t. & v.i.* [earlier *cham;* prob. echoic], 1. to chew hard and noisily; munch. 2. to bite down on hard or restlessly: as, the horse *champed* at the bit. *n.* noisy chewing.
**champ** (champ), *n.* [Slang], a champion.
**cham·pagne** (sham-pān′), *n.* 1. originally, any of various wines produced in Champagne, a region in NE France. 2. now, any effervescent white wine: a symbol of luxury. 3. pale, tawny yellow. *adj.* 1. of this color. 2. of or for this wine.
**cham·paign** (sham-pān′), *n.* [< OFr. < LL. *campania* < L. *campus*, a field], a broad expanse of plain; flat, open country. *adj.* flat and open, as land.
**cham·pi·on** (cham′pi-ən), *n.* [< OFr. < LL. *campio*, gladiator < L. *campus*, a field], 1. one who fights for another or for a cause; defender; supporter. 2. a winner of first place in a competition. *adj.* winning first place; excelling over all others. *v.t.* to fight for; defend; support.
**cham·pi·on·ship** (cham′pi-ən-ship′), *n.* 1. a championing. 2. the position, title, or tenure of a champion.
**Cham·plain, Lake** (sham-plān′), a lake between N New York and Vermont.
**Champs É·ly·sées** (shän′zā′lē′zā′), [Fr., lit., Elysian fields], a famous avenue in Paris.
**Chan., Chanc.,** 1. Chancellor. 2. Chancery.
**chance** (chans, chäns), *n.* [< OFr. < LL. < L. ppr. of *cadere*, to fall], 1. the way things happen. 2. luck; fortuity. 3. a happening. 4. a risk or gamble. 5. a share in a lottery. 6. an opportunity: as, a *chance* to go. 7. a possibility or probability: as, a *chance* that he will live. *adj.* happening by chance; accidental. *v.i.* [CHANCED, CHANCING], to come about by chance; happen. *v.t.* to risk. —**by chance,** accidentally. —**chance on** (or **upon**), to find by chance. —**on the chance,** relying on the possibility.
**chan·cel** (chan′s'l, chän′-), *n.* [< OFr. < LL. < L. *cancelli, pl.*, lattices], that part of a church around the altar reserved for the clergy and the choir: it is sometimes set off by a railing.
**chan·cel·ler·y** (chan′sə-lēr-i, chän′-), *n.* [*pl.* -IES], 1. the position of a chancellor. 2. a chancellor's office or the building that houses it.
**chan·cel·lor** (chan′sə-lēr, chän′-), *n.* [< OFr. < LL. *cancellarius*, keeper of the barrier, secretary < L.; see CHANCEL], 1. a high state or church official. 2. the chief secretary of an embassy. 3. a high official secretary in the British government: the *Chancellor of the Exchequer* is the minister of finance. 4. the title of the head of some universities. 5. the prime minister in certain countries. 6. a chief judge of a court of chancery or equity in some States. —**chan′cel·lor·ship′,** *n.*
**chance-med·ley** (chans′med′li, chäns′-), *n.* [see CHANCE & MEDDLE], 1. accidental homicide. 2. haphazard action.
**chan·cer·y** (chan′sēr-i, chän′-), *n.* [*pl.* -IES], [< OFr. < LL. *cancellaria;* see CHANCELLOR], 1. a division of the High Court of Justice in Great Britain. 2. a court of equity. 3. equity law. 4. a court of record. 5. a chancellery. —**in chancery,** 1. in process of litigation in a court of equity. 2. in a helpless situation. 3. in *wrestling*, with the head held firmly between an opponent's arm and his chest.
**chan·cre** (shaŋ′kēr), *n.* [Fr.; see CANCER], a venereal sore or ulcer; primary lesion of syphilis.
**chan·croid** (shaŋ′kroid), *n.* [< *chancre* + *-oid*], a venereal ulcer not caused by syphilis: also called *soft chancre*.
**chanc·y** (chan′si, chän′-), *adj.* [-IER, -IEST], 1. [Scot.], lucky. 2. [Colloq.], risky; uncertain.
**chan·de·lier** (shan′də-lêr′), *n.* [Fr. < OFr. < L.; see CANDELABRUM], a fixture with branches for several candles, electric bulbs, etc., usually hanging from a ceiling.
**chan·dler** (chan′dlēr, chän′-), *n.* [< OFr. < L. *candela*, a candle], 1. a maker or seller of candles. 2. a retailer of supplies and groceries: a *ship chandler* sells provisions for ships. —**chan′dler·y** [*pl.* -IES], *n.*
**Chang·chun** (chäŋ′choon′), *n.* a city in S Manchuria: pop., 630,000.
**change** (chānj), *v.t.* [CHANGED, CHANGING], [< OFr. < LL. < L. *cambire*, to barter < Celt.], 1. to put or take (a thing) in place of something else; substitute: as, he *changed* his clothes. 2. to exchange: as, they *changed* places. 3. to make different; alter. 4. to give or receive the equivalent of (a coin or bank note) in currency of lower denominations. 5. to put a fresh covering, as a diaper, on. *v.i.* 1. to alter; vary: as, the scene *changes*. 2. to leave one train, bus, etc. and board another. 3. to put on other clothes. 4. to make an exchange. *n.* 1. a substitution, alteration, or variation. 2. variety. 3. something of the same kind but new or fresh. 4. another set of clothes. 5. money returned to a purchaser as the difference between the purchase price and the larger sum given in payment. 6. an equivalent sum in smaller denominations, given for a larger denomination. 7. small coins. 8. a place where merchants meet to do business; exchange: sometimes, erroneously, **'change.** 9. *usually pl.* in *bell ringing*, any order in which the bells are rung. 10. in *music*, modulation; shift of key. —**change trains** (or **buses,** etc.), to leave one train (or bus, etc.) and board another. —**ring the changes,** 1. to ring a set of bells with all possible variations. 2. to do or say a thing in many and various ways. —**change′ful,** *adj.* —**change′ful·ly,** *adv.* —**change′ful·ness,** *n.* —**chang′er,** *n.*
**change·a·ble** (chān′jə-b'l), *adj.* 1. that can change or be changed; alterable. 2. having a changing appearance or color. —**change′a·bil′i·ty,** *n.* —**change′a·ble·ness,** *n.* —**change′a·bly,** *adv.*
**change·less** (chānj′lis), *adj.* unchanging; not tending to change; constant; immutable. —**change′less·ly,** *adv.* —**change′less·ness,** *n.*
**change·ling** (chānj′liŋ), *n.* [*change* + *-ling*], a child secretly put in the place of another.
**change of life,** menopause.
**change ringing,** the ringing of a series of unrepeated changes on bells.

**chan·nel** (chan′'l), *n.* [< OFr.; see CANAL], 1. the bed of a river, etc. 2. the deeper part of a stream, harbor, etc. 3. a body of water joining two larger bodies of water. 4. a tubelike passage for liquids. 5. any means of passage. 6. the proper or official course of action: as, make your request through *channels*. 7. a long groove or furrow. 8. a frequency band assigned to a single transmitting station, as in radio or television. *v.t.* [-NELED or -NELLED, -NELING or -NELLING], 1. to make a channel in. 2. to send through a channel.

**Channel Islands,** a group of British islands in the English Channel, off the coast of Normandy, including Alderney, Jersey, and Guernsey.

**‡chan·son** (shän′sōn′; Eng. shan′sən), *n.* [*pl.* -SONS (-sōn′; Eng. -sənz)], [Fr.], a song.

**chant** (chant, chänt), *n.* [Fr.; L. *cantus* < *cantare* < *canere*, to sing], 1. a song; melody. 2. a simple song in which a number of syllables or words are sung in a monotone. 3. words, as of a psalm, to be sung in this way. 4. a singsong mode of speaking. *v.i.* 1. to speak monotonously or repetitiously. 2. to sing a chant; intone. *v.t.* 1. to sing. 2. to celebrate in song. 3. to say monotonously. 4. to intone. —**chant′er,** *n.* —**chant′ress,** *n.fem.*

**‡chan·teuse** (shän′töz′), *n.* [Fr.], a woman singer.

**chant·ey,** (shan′ti; *popularly,* chan′-), *n.* [*pl.* -TEYS], [< Fr.; see CHANT], a song that sailors sing in rhythm with their motions while working: also **chanty, shantey, shanty.**

**chan·ti·cleer** (chan′ti-klêr′), *n.* [< OFr.; see CHANT & CLEAR], a rooster.

**chan·try** (chan′tri, chän′-), *n.* [*pl.* -TRIES], [< OFr.; see CHANT], 1. an endowment to pay for the saying of special Masses and prayers. 2. a chapel or altar endowed for the same purpose.

**chant·y** (shan′ti; *popularly,* chan′-), *n.* [*pl.* -TIES], a chantey.

**Cha·nu·kah** (khä′noo-kä), *n.* [Heb.], Hanukkah.

**cha·os** (kā′os), *n.* [L. < Gr. < *chainein*, to gape], 1. the disorder of formless matter and infinite space, supposed to have existed before the ordered universe. 2. any great confusion or disorder.

**cha·ot·ic** (kā-ot′ik), *adj.* in a condition of chaos; in a completely confused or disordered condition. —**cha·ot′i·cal·ly,** *adv.*

**chap** (chap, chop), *n.* [ON. *kjaptr*], 1. a jaw. 2. a cheek: also **chop.**

**chap** (chap), *n.* [< *chapman*, in sense "one to be dealt with"], [Colloq.], a man or boy; fellow.

**chap** (chap), *v.t. & v.i.* [CHAPPED or CHAPT (chapt), CHAPPING], [ME. *chappen*, to cut], to crack open; roughen: as, her skin *chaps* easily. *n.* a chapped place in the skin.

**chap.,** 1. chaplain. 2. a chapter.

**‡cha·pa·ra·jos** (chä′pä-rä′hôs), *n.pl.* [Mex. Sp.], leather trousers worn over ordinary trousers by cowboys to protect their legs: also called *chaps.*

**‡cha·pa·re·jos** (chä′pä-re′hôs), *n.pl.* chaparajos.

**chap·ar·ral** (chap′ə-ral′), *n.* [Sp. < *chaparro*, evergreen oak], a thicket of shrubs, thorny bushes, etc.

**chap·book** (chap′book′), *n.* [*chap* < *chapman*, who often sold such books], a small book or pamphlet of poems, ballads, religious tracts, etc.

**cha·peau** (sha-pō′; Fr. shȧ′-), *n.* [*pl.* -PEAUX (-pōz′; Fr. -pō′), -PEAUS (-pōz′)], [Fr. < OFr. < LL. *capellus*, dim. of *cappa*, a hood], a hat.

**chap·el** (chap′'l), *n.* [< OFr. < LL. < *cappa*, a cope; orig., sanctuary in which the cope of St. Martin was preserved], 1. a place of Christian worship smaller than a church. 2. a private place of worship, as in a school. 3. a small room in a church, having its own altar. 4. a religious service, as in a chapel. 5. in Great Britain, any place of worship for those who are not in an established church.

**chap·er·on, chap·er·one** (shap′ə-rōn′), *n.* [Fr., hood < *chape*, a cope], a person, especially an older or married woman, who accompanies young unmarried people in public or attends their parties, etc. for propriety. *v.t.* [-ONED, -ONING], to act as chaperon to. —**chap′er·on′age,** *n.*

**chap·fall·en** (chap′fôl′ən, chop′-), *adj.* [< *chap* (jaw)], disheartened; depressed: also **chopfallen.**

**chap·lain** (chap′lin), *n.* [< OFr. < LL.; see CHAPEL], 1. a clergyman attached to a chapel, as of a prison. 2. a minister, priest, or rabbi serving in a religious capacity with the armed forces. —**chap′lain·cy** [*pl.* -CIES], **chap′lain·ship′,** *n.*

**chap·let** (chap′lit), *n.* [< OFr. < *chapel*, cap < LL. *cappa*, a cap, cape], 1. a garland for the head. 2. a string of prayer beads one third the length of a rosary. 3. the prayers told with such beads. 4. any string of beads. —**chap′let·ed,** *adj.*

**Chap·lin, Charles Spencer** (chap′lin), 1889– ; motion-picture actor and producer, born in England.

**chap·man** (chap′mən), *n.* [*pl.* -MEN], [< AS. < *ceap*, trade + *man*], [Brit.], a peddler; hawker.

**chaps** (chaps), *n.pl.* [Colloq.], chaparajos.

**chaps** (chaps, chops), *n.pl.* chops (jaws).

**chap·ter** (chap′tẽr), *n.* [< OFr. *chapitre* < L. *capitulum*, dim. of *caput*, head], 1. a main division, as of a book. 2. a thing like a chapter; part; episode. 3. a group of canons headed by a dean, or any similar church division. 4. a meeting of such a group. 5. a local branch of an organization. *v.t.* to divide into chapters.

**char** (chär), *v.t. & v.i.* [CHARRED, CHARRING], [< *charcoal*], 1. to reduce to charcoal by burning. 2. to scorch. *n.* anything charred.

**char** (chär), *n. & v.i.* [CHARRED, CHARRING], chare.

**char** (chär), *n.* [*pl.* CHARS, CHAR; see PLURAL, II, D, 1], [< Gael. *ceara*, red], a kind of trout with small scales and a red belly: also sp. **charr.**

**char·a·banc, char-à-banc** (shar′ə-baŋk′, -baŋ′; Fr. shȧ′rȧ′bän′), *n.* [*pl.* -BANCS (-baŋks′, -baŋz′; Fr. -bän′)], [Fr., lit., car with bench], a large open bus with seats facing forward.

**char·ac·ter** (kar′ik-tẽr), *n.* [< OFr. < L. < Gr. *charaktēr*, an engraving instrument < *charattein*, to engrave], 1. a distinctive mark. 2. any conventional mark, letter, or symbol, as +, 0, A, a, ?, etc. 3. a distinctive trait or quality. 4. nature; kind or sort. 5. one's pattern of behavior or personality. 6. moral strength; fortitude, etc. 7. reputation. 8. good reputation. 9. a description of the qualities of a person or type. 10. status; position: as, in his *character* as judge. 11. a person in a play, novel, etc. 12. a personage. 13. [Colloq.], a queer or eccentric person. *v.t.* to write, print, or inscribe. —**in character,** appropriate. —**out of character,** inappropriate. —**char′ac·ter·less,** *adj.*

**character actor,** an actor usually cast in the role of a person with pronounced or eccentric characteristics. —**character actress,** *fem.*

**char·ac·ter·is·tic** (kar′ik-tẽr-is′tik), *adj.* of or constituting the character; typical; distinctive. *n.* a distinguishing trait, feature, or quality. —**char′ac·ter·is′ti·cal·ly,** *adv.*

**char·ac·ter·ize** (kar′ik-tẽr-īz′), *v.t.* [-IZED, -IZING], 1. to describe the particular qualities or traits of. 2. to be the distinctive character of; mark. 3. to give character to. —**char′ac·ter·i·za′tion,** *n.* —**char′ac·ter·iz′er,** *n.*

**cha·rade** (shə-rād′; *chiefly Brit.* -räd′), *n.* [Fr. < Pr. *charrada* < *charrar*, to gossip], a game in which a word or phrase to be guessed is acted out in pantomime, syllable by syllable or as a whole.

**char·coal** (chär′kōl′), *n.* [ME. *char cole;* prob. < *charren*, to turn + *cole*, coal], 1. a black form of carbon produced by partially burning wood or other organic matter in large kilns from which air is excluded. 2. a pencil made of this substance. 3. a drawing made with such a pencil. *v.t.* to draw with charcoal.

**chard** (chärd), *n.* [Fr. *carde* < L. *carduus*, thistle], a kind of beet whose large leaves and thick stalks are used as food: also **Swiss chard.**

**chare** (châr), *n.* [AS. *cerr*, a turn, job < *cierran*, to turn], an odd job; chore. *v.i.* [CHARED, CHARING], 1. to do odd jobs or chores. 2. to do housework for pay. Also **char.**

**charge** (chärj), *v.t.* [CHARGED, CHARGING], [< OFr. < LL. *carricare*, to load < L. *carrus*, car, wagon], 1. to put a load on or in. 2. to load (a gun). 3. to fill with another substance: as, the air was *charged* with steam. 4. to add carbon dioxide to (water, etc.). 5. to add an electrical charge to (a battery, etc.); replenish. 6. to give as a task, duty, etc. to. 7. to give a command to; instruct. 8. to censure; accuse: as, he *charged* her with negligence. 9. to make liable for (a purchase, error, etc.). 10. to ask as a price: as, we *charge* a dime for this service. 11. to put down as a debt: as, *charge* the cost to me. 12. to attack vigorously. *v.i.* 1. to ask payment (*for*): as, we *charge* for this service. 2. to attack vigorously. *n.* 1. a load; burden. 2. the quantity, as of fuel, etc., that an apparatus is built to accommodate. 3. responsibility or duty (*of*). 4. care or custody (*of*). 5. a person or thing entrusted to one's care. 6. instruction; command;

fat, āpe, bâre, cär; ten, ēven, hêre, ovẽr; is, bīte; lot, gō, hôrn, tōōl, look; oil, out; up, ūse, fũr; get; joy; yet; chin; she; thin, *th*en; zh, leisure; ŋ, ring; ə for *a* in *ago*, *e* in *agent*, *i* in *sanity*, *o* in *comply*, *u* in *focus;* ′ in *able* (ā′b'l); Fr. bȧl; ë, Fr. coeur; ö, Fr. feu; Fr. mon; ô, Fr. coq; ü, Fr. duc; H, G. ich; kh, G. doch. ‡ foreign; < derived from.

injunction: as, the jury received its *charge* from the judge. 7. accusation; indictment: as, *charges* of cruelty. 8. cost; price: abbrev. **chg.** 9. a debt. 10. *a*) an onslaught; onset. *b*) the signal for this. 11. in *heraldry*, a bearing. —**charge off,** 1. to regard as a loss. 2. to ascribe. —**in charge,** having the responsibility or control.

**charge·a·ble** (chär′jə-b'l), *adj.* 1. that can be charged. 2. that may become a public charge.

**charge account,** a business arrangement by which a customer may buy things and pay for them within a specified future period.

**char·gé d'af·faires** (shär-zhā′ da-fâr′), [*pl.* CHARGÉS D'AFFAIRES (-zhāz′-)], [Fr.], 1. a temporary substitute for an ambassador or other diplomat. 2. an official of lower rank than an ambassador.

**charg·er** (chär′jẽr), *n.* 1. a person or thing that charges. 2. a war horse. 3. an apparatus used to charge storage batteries.

**charg·er** (chär′jẽr), *n.* [ME. *chargeour*], [Archaic], a large, flat dish; platter.

**char·i·ly** (châr′ə-li), *adv.* in a chary manner.

**char·i·ness** (châr′i-nis), *n.* a chary quality.

**char·i·ot** (char′i-ət), *n.* [OFr., dim. of *char*, car; see CAR], a horse-drawn, two-wheeled cart used in ancient times for war, racing, parades, etc. *v.t.* & *v.i.* to drive or ride in a chariot.

CHARIOT

**char·i·ot·eer** (char′i-ə-têr′), *n.* a chariot driver.

**cha·ris·ma** (kə-riz′mə), *n.* [*pl.* -MATA (-mə-tə)], [Gr.], 1. in *Christian theology*, a divinely inspired gift or talent, as for prophesying, healing, etc. 2. a special quality of leadership that inspires great popular allegiance. —**char·is·mat·ic** (kar′iz-mat′ik), *adj.*

**char·i·ta·ble** (char′ə-tə-b'l), *adj.* 1. kind and generous in giving help to those in need. 2. of or for charity. 3. kindly in judging others; lenient. —**char′i·ta·ble·ness,** *n.* —**char′i·ta·bly,** *adv.*

**char·i·ty** (char′ə-ti), *n.* [*pl.* -TIES], [< OFr. < L. *caritas*, affection < *carus*, dear], 1. in *Christianity*, the love of God for man or of man for his fellow men. 2. an act of good will; benevolence. 3. leniency in judging others. 4. a giving of help, as money, to those in need. 5. an institution, fund, etc. for giving help to those in need.

**cha·ri·va·ri** (shə-riv′ə-rē′, shä′ri-vä′ri, shiv′ə-ri), *n.* [Fr.], a mock serenade: see **shivaree.**

**char·la·tan** (shär′lə-t'n), *n.* [Fr. < It. *ciarlatano* < LL. *cerretanus*, seller of papal indulgences], one who pretends to have knowledge or ability that he does not have; quack; impostor. —**char′la·tan·ism,** *n.* —**char′la·tan·ry** [*pl.* -RIES], *n.*

**Char·le·magne** (shär′lə-mān′), *n.* (*Charles I*), king of the Franks (768–814 A.D.); emperor of the West (800–814 A.D.); lived 742–814 A.D.

**Charles I** (chärlz), 1. (*Charles Stuart*), 1600–1649; king of England (1625–1649). 2. Charlemagne.

**Charles II,** 1630–1685; son of Charles I; king of England (1660-1685).

**Charles V,** 1500–1558; Holy Roman emperor (1519–1556) and king of Spain (1516–1556).

**Charles's Wain** (chärl′ziz), the Big Dipper.

**Charles·ton** (chärlz′tən), *n.* 1. a seaport in South Carolina: pop., 66,000. 2. the capital of West Virginia: pop., 86,000. 3. a lively dance in 4/4 time, characterized by a twisting step.

**char·ley horse** (chär′li), [Colloq.], a cramp in the muscles of a leg or arm, caused by strain.

**char·lock** (chär′lək), *n.* [AS. *cerlic*], a weed of the mustard family, with yellow flowers.

**Char·lotte** (shär′lət), *n.* a city in S North Carolina: pop., 202,000.

**Char·lot·te A·ma·li·e** (shär-lot′ə ä-mä′li-ə), the capital of the Virgin Islands, on St. Thomas Island: pop., 13,000.

**char·lotte russe** (shär′lət rōōs), [Fr.; *charlotte*, a kind of dessert + *russe*, Russian], whipped cream or custard in a mold of sponge cake.

**charm** (chärm), *n.* [< OFr. < L. *carmen*, song, charm], 1. a chanted word or verse, an action, or an object assumed to have magic power to help or hurt. 2. a trinket worn on a bracelet, necklace, watch chain, etc. 3. the ability to fascinate, allure, or please greatly. *v.t.* 1. to act on as though by magic. 2. to attract or please greatly; fascinate; delight. *v.i.* to be charming; please greatly. —**charmed life,** a life seemingly protected from harm as though by magic. —**charm′er,** *n.*

**charm·ing** (chärm′iŋ), *adj.* attractive; enchanting; fascinating; delightful. —**charm′ing·ly,** *adv.*

**char·nel** (chär′n'l), *n.* [OFr. < LL. *carnale*, graveyard < L. *caro*, *carnis*, flesh], a charnel house. *adj.* 1. of or serving as a charnel. 2. like or fit for a charnel; deathlike; sepulchral.

**charnel house,** 1. originally, a tomb; hence, 2. any place where there are corpses, bones, etc.

**Cha·ron** (kâr′ən), *n.* in *Gr. mythology*, the boatman who ferried dead souls across the river Styx to Hades.

**char·ry** (chär′i), *adj.* [-RIER, -RIEST], like charcoal.

**chart** (chärt), *n.* [< Fr. < L. *charta;* see CARD (paper)], 1. a map of a body of water, showing coast lines, currents, a ship's course, etc. 2. a simple outline map on which special facts are given. 3. a sheet giving information in the form of diagrams, tables, etc.; also, a graph. 4. such a diagram, table, etc. *v.t.* 1. to make a chart of; map. 2. to show on or as by a chart. —**chart′less,** *adj.*

**char·ter** (chär′tẽr), *n.* [< OFr. < L. dim. of *charta;* see CARD (paper)], 1. a franchise or written grant of specified rights made by a government or ruler to a person, company, etc. 2. permission from a society for the organization of a local chapter. 3. the hire or lease of a ship, bus, airplane, etc. *v.t.* 1. to grant a charter to. 2. to hire for exclusive use. —**char′ter·age,** *n.* —**char′ter·er,** *n.*

**charter member,** any of the founders or original members of an organization.

**char·treuse** (shär-tröz′), *n.* [Fr., Carthusian], 1. a yellow, pale-green, or white liqueur made by the Carthusian monks. 2. pale, yellowish green. *adj.* of this color.

**char·wom·an** (chär′woom′ən), *n.* [*pl.* -WOMEN], [see CHARE, CHORE], a woman who does cleaning or scrubbing, as in office buildings.

**char·y** (châr′i), *adj.* [-IER, -IEST], [AS. *cearig* < *caru*, care], 1. careful; cautious: as, a burnt child is *chary* of fire. 2. shy: as, *chary* of strangers. 3. frugal; stingy.

**Cha·ryb·dis** (kə-rib′dis), *n.* a whirlpool off the coast of Sicily, opposite the rock Scylla. —**between Scylla and Charybdis,** faced with a choice of two dangers.

**chase** (chās), *v.t.* [CHASED, CHASING], [< OFr. *chacier*, *cachier* < LL.; see CATCH], 1. to follow quickly or persistently in order to catch or harm. 2. to run after; follow. 3. to make run away; drive. 4. to hunt. *v.i.* 1. to go in pursuit: as, *chase* after him. 2. [Colloq.], to go hurriedly; rush: as, I *chased* around town. *n.* 1. a chasing; pursuit. 2. the hunting of game for sport. 3. anything hunted; quarry. —**give chase,** to pursue. —**chas′er,** *n.*

**chase** (chās), *n.* [OFr. *chasse*, a frame; ult. < L. *capsa*, a box], 1. a groove; furrow. 2. a rectangular metal frame in which pages or columns of type are locked. *v.t.* [CHASED, CHASING], to make a groove or furrow in; indent.

**chase** (chās), *v.t.* [CHASED, CHASING], [< Fr. *enchâsser*, to encase], to ornament (metal) by engraving, embossing, cutting, etc. —**chas′er,** *n.*

**chas·er** (chās′ẽr), *n.* [Colloq.], a mild drink, as water, taken after or with whisky, rum, etc.

**chasm** (kaz′m), *n.* [< L. < Gr. *chasma*], 1. a deep crack in the earth's surface; abyss; gorge. 2. any break or gap; hiatus. 3. a wide divergence of feelings, sentiments, interests, etc. between people or groups; rift. —**chas′mal,** *adj.*

**chas·seur** (sha-sũr′; Fr. shȧ′sẽr′), *n.* [Fr.], 1. a hunter. 2. a soldier, especially one of certain French light infantry or cavalry troops, trained for rapid action.

**Chas·sid·im** (kas′i-dim; Heb. khä-sē′-), *n.pl.* [sing. CHASSID (kas′id; Heb. khä′sid)], a sect of Jewish mystics that originated in Poland in the 18th century. —**Chas·sid′ic,** *adj.* —**Chas′sid·ism,** *n.*

**chas·sis** (shas′i, -is, chas′i), *n.* [*pl.* CHASSIS (shas′iz, chas′-)], [< Fr. < *châsse;* see CHASE (a groove)], 1. the lower frame, including the wheels and engine parts, of a motor vehicle. 2. the frame supporting the body of an airplane. 3. *a*) the framework to which the various parts of a radio or television set are attached. *b*) the assembled frame and parts. 4. [Slang], the body; figure.

**chaste** (chāst), *adj.* [OFr. < L. *castus*, pure], 1. not indulging in unlawful sexual activity; virtuous: said especially of women. 2. not indecent; modest. 3. restrained and simple in style. —**chaste′ly,** *adv.* —**chaste′ness,** *n.*

**chas·ten** (chās′'n), *v.t.* [< OFr. < L. *castigare*, to punish < *castus*, pure + *agere*, to lead], 1. to punish in order to correct; chastise. 2. to restrain from excess; subdue. —**chas′ten·er,** *n.*

**chas·tise** (chas-tīz′), *v.t.* [-TISED, -TISING], [see CHASTEN], to punish in order to correct, usually by beating. —**chas·tise·ment** (chas′tiz-mənt, chas-tīz′-), *n.* —**chas·tis′er,** *n.*

**chas·ti·ty** (chas′tə-ti), *n.* [see CHASTE], 1. abstention from unlawful sexual activity: said especially of women. 2. celibacy or virginity. 3. decency; modesty. 4. simplicity of style.

**chas·u·ble** (chaz′yoo-b'l, chas′-), *n.* [OFr. < LL. *casubula*, hooded garment], a sleeveless outer vestment worn over the alb by priests at Mass.

**chat** (chat), *v.i.* [CHATTED, CHATTING], [< *chatter*], to talk or converse in a light, easy, informal manner. *n.* 1. light, easy, informal talk. 2. any of several birds with a chattering call.

**châ·teau** (sha-tō′; Fr. shä′tō′), *n.* [*pl.* -TEAUX (-tōz′; Fr. -tō′)], [Fr. < OFr. < L. *castellum*, a castle], 1. a French feudal castle. 2. a large country house.

**chat·e·laine** (shat′'l-ān′), *n.* [Fr.; ult. < L. *castellum*, a castle], 1. the lady of a castle; mistress of a château. 2. a woman's ornamental clasp worn at the waist, with keys, purses, watches, etc. fastened to it on a chain.

**Chat·ta·noo·ga** (chat′ə-nōō′gə), *n.* a city in SE Tennessee, on the Tennessee River: pop., 130,000.

**chat·tel** (chat′'l), *n.* [OFr. *chatel*; see CATTLE], 1. an article of movable property as distinguished from real property: furniture, automobiles, livestock, etc. are chattels. 2. [Archaic], a slave.

**chattel mortgage,** a mortgage on personal property.

**chat·ter** (chat′ẽr), *v.i.* [echoic], 1. to make short, indistinct sounds in rapid succession, as birds, apes, etc. 2. to talk fast, incessantly, and foolishly. 3. to click together rapidly, as the teeth do from fright or cold. *v.t.* to utter with a chattering sound. *n.* 1. short, rapid, indistinct sounds. 2. rapid, foolish talk. —**chat′ter·er,** *n.*

**chat·ter·box** (chat′ẽr-boks′), *n.* a person who talks incessantly.

**chat·ty** (chat′i), *adj.* [-TIER, -TIEST], 1. fond of chatting. 2. light, familiar, and informal: said of talk. —**chat′ti·ly,** *adv.* —**chat′ti·ness,** *n.*

**Chau·cer, Geoffrey** (chô′sẽr), 1340?–1400; English poet; wrote the *Canterbury Tales*, etc. —**Chau·ce·ri·an** (chô-sêr′i-ən), *adj.* & *n.*

**chauf·feur** (shō′fẽr, shō-fũr′), *n.* [Fr., lit., stoker < *chauffer*, to heat; see CHAFE], a person whose work is to drive an automobile for someone else; driver. *v.t.* to act as chauffeur to.

**chaul·moo·gra** (chôl-mōō′grə), *n.* [Beng. *cāulmugrā*], an East Indian tree whose seeds yield an oil (**chaulmoogra oil**) used in treating leprosy.

**chaunt** (chônt), *n.*, *v.t.* & *v.i.* [Archaic], chant.

**Chau·tau·qua, chau·tau·qua** (shə-tô′kwə), *n.* [< the summer schools inaugurated at Chautauqua, N. Y., in 1874], an assembly lasting several days, for educational and recreational purposes: the program includes lectures, concerts, etc. —**Chau·tau′quan, chau·tau′quan,** *n.* & *adj.*

**chau·vin·ism** (shō′vin-iz'm), *n.* [< Fr. < Nicolas *Chauvin*, Napoleonic soldier, notorious for his fanatical patriotism], 1. militant, boastful, and fanatical patriotism. 2. unreasoning devotion to one's race, sex, etc., with contempt for other races, the opposite sex, etc. —**chau′vin·ist,** *n.* & *adj.* —**chau′vin·is′tic,** *adj.* —**chau′vin·is′ti·cal·ly,** *adv.*

**chaw** (chô), *n.*, *v.t.* & *v.i.* [Colloq.], chew: now substandard or humorous.

**cheap** (chēp), *adj.* [< *good cheap*, good bargain; AS. *ceap*, bargain], 1. low in price; not expensive. 2. charging low prices: as, *cheap* jobbers. 3. worth more than the price. 4. costing little labor or trouble; easily got. 5. of little or no value. 6. held in little esteem; common. *adv.* at a low cost. —**feel cheap,** [Slang], to feel ashamed or contemptible. —**cheap′ly,** *adv.* —**cheap′ness,** *n.*

**cheap·en** (chēp′'n), *v.t.* & *v.i.* to make or become cheap or cheaper. —**cheap′en·er,** *n.*

**cheap skate,** [Slang], a miserly, ungenerous person.

**cheat** (chēt), *n.* [< ME. *eschete;* see ESCHEAT], 1. a fraud; swindle. 2. one who defrauds or tricks others; swindler. *v.t.* 1. to deceive by trickery; defraud. 2. to fool; beguile. 3. to foil; elude; escape: as, to *cheat* death. *v.i.* to practice fraud or deception. —**cheat on,** [Slang], to be sexually unfaithful to. —**cheat′er,** *n.* —**cheat′ing·ly,** *adv.*

**check** (chek), *n.* [OFr. *eschec*, a check at chess < ML. *scaccus* < Per. *shāh*, king], 1. a sudden stop. 2. any restraint or control of action. 3. a person or thing that restrains or controls. 4. a supervision of accuracy, efficiency, etc.: as, keep a *check* on his department. 5. a test of accuracy; comparison or standard of comparison; examination. 6. a mark (✓) to show verification of something, or to call attention to it. 7. an identification token showing ownership to secure against loss: as, a hat *check*. 8. one's bill at a restaurant or bar. 9. a written order to a bank to pay the amount of money stated: also sp. **cheque.** 10. *a*) a pattern of small squares like that of a chessboard. *b*) one of these squares. 11. a cloth with such a pattern. 12. a small split or crack. 13. in *chess*, the condition of a player's king that is in danger and must be put into a safe position. *interj.* 1. [Colloq.], agreed! right! 2. in *chess*, a call meaning that the opponent's king must be taken out of check. *v.t.* 1. to stop suddenly. 2. to restrain; control; curb. 3. to rebuff; repulse; rebuke. 4. to test, verify, or control by investigation or comparison: as, *check* the accounts. 5. to mark with a check (✓). 6. to mark with a crisscross pattern. 7. to deposit temporarily: as, *check* your coat. 8. to make chinks or cracks in. 9. in *chess*, to place (an opponent's king) in check. *v.i.* 1. to agree with one another item for item: as, the accounts *check*. 2. to crack in small checks. 3. in *chess*, to place an opponent's king in check. *adj.* 1. used to check or verify: as, a *check* experiment. 2. having a crisscross pattern; checked. —**check in,** 1. to register at a hotel, convention, etc. 2. [Slang], to die. —**check off,** to mark as verified, examined, etc. —**check out,** 1. to settle one's bill and leave a hotel, etc. 2. [Slang], to die. —**check up on,** to investigate or examine. —**in check,** in restraint; under control. —**check′a·ble,** *adj.* —**checked,** *adj.* —**check′er,** *n.*

**check·book** (chek′book′), *n.* a book containing blank checks, issued to a depositor by a bank.

**check·er** (chek′ẽr), *n.* [OFr. *eschequier*, a chessboard < *eschec;* see CHECK], 1. a small square like those of a chessboard. 2. a pattern of such squares. 3. one of the flat, round pieces used in playing checkers or backgammon. *v.t.* 1. to mark off in squares, as on a chessboard. 2. to break the uniformity of by color and shading.

**check·er·ber·ry** (chek′ẽr-ber′i), *n.* [*pl.* -RIES], 1. the red, berrylike fruit of the wintergreen. 2. the wintergreen.

**check·er·board** (chek′ẽr-bôrd′, -bōrd′), *n.* a board marked off into 64 squares of two alternating colors, used in the games of checkers and chess.

**check·ered** (chek′ẽrd), *adj.* 1. having a pattern of colored squares like a checkerboard. 2. varied by the use of color and shading. 3. varied; full of ups and downs: as, a *checkered* career.

**check·ers** (chek′ẽrz), *n.pl.* [construed as sing.], a game played on a checkerboard by two players, each with 12 pieces to move; draughts.

**checking account,** a bank account against which the depositor can draw checks: cf. *savings account*.

**check list,** a list of things to be checked off.

**check·mate** (chek′māt′), *n.* [OFr. *eschec mat;* ult. < Per. *shāh māt*, lit., the king is dead], 1. *a*) a move in chess that checks the opponent's king so that it cannot be put into safety, thus ending the game. *b*) the position of the king resulting from this. 2. hopeless jeopardy or defeat. *interj.* in *chess*, a call to indicate a checkmate. *v.t.* [-MATED, -MATING], 1. to place in checkmate. 2. to defeat completely; frustrate. Also **mate.**

**check·off** (chek′ôf′), *n.* an arrangement by which dues of trade-union members are withheld from wages and turned over to the union by the employers.

**check·rein** (chek′rān′), *n.* a short rein attached to the bridle to keep a horse from lowering its head: also **check line.**

**check·room** (chek′rōōm′, -room′), *n.* a room in which to check (*v.t.* 7) hats, coats, parcels, etc.

**check·up** (chek′up′), *n.* an examination; investigation; verification.

**Ched·dar** (ched′ẽr), *n.* [< *Cheddar*, Somersetshire, England, where it was first made], a variety of hard, smooth cheese: also **Cheddar cheese.**

**cheek** (chēk), *n.* [AS. *ceace*, jaw, jawbone], 1. either side of the face below the eye. 2. *usually in pl.* either of two sides of a thing suggesting this in shape or position, as the jaws of a vise. 3. [Colloq.], sauciness; impudence. —**cheek by jowl,** 1. close together. 2. familiar; intimate. —**tongue in cheek,** without sincerity; with the real meaning different from the ostensible one.

**cheek·bone** (chēk′bōn′), *n.* the bone of the upper cheek, just below the eye.

**cheek·y** (chēk′i), *adj.* [-IER, -IEST], [*cheek* + *-y*],

[Colloq.], saucy; impudent; insolent. —**cheek′i·ly,** *adv.* —**cheek′i·ness,** *n.*

**cheep** (chēp), *n.* [echoic], the short, shrill sound of a young bird; peep; chirp. *v.t.* & *v.i.* to make, or utter with, such a sound. —**cheep′er,** *n.*

**cheer** (chêr), *n.* [< OFr. *ch(i)ere* < LL. *cara,* the face < Gr. *kara,* the head; modern senses < phr. *good cheer*], 1. a mood; state of mind or of feeling. 2. gaiety; gladness; joy; encouragement. 3. food, entertainment, etc. that makes one happy. 4. a glad, excited shout to urge on, welcome, approve, etc. *v.t.* 1. to fill with joy, good spirits, and hope; gladden; comfort. 2. to urge or encourage by cheers. 3. to salute with cheers. *v.i.* 1. to be or become glad; feel encouraged: as, her heart *cheered* at the news. 2. to shout cheers. —**be of good cheer,** to be cheerful. —**cheer up,** to make or become glad; brighten up; take heart. —**cheer′er,** *n.*

**cheer·ful** (chêr′fəl), *adj.* 1. full of cheer; gay; joyful. 2. filling with cheer; bright and attractive: as, a *cheerful* room. 3. willing; hearty: as, a *cheerful* helper. —**cheer′ful·ly,** *adv.* —**cheer′ful·ness,** *n.*

**cheer·i·o** (chêr′i-ō′), *interj.* & *n.* [*pl.* -OS], [Brit. Colloq.], 1. hello. 2. good-by.

**cheer·less** (chêr′lis), *adj.* not cheerful; without cheer; unhappy; joyless; dreary. —**cheer′less·ly,** *adv.* —**cheer′less·ness,** *n.*

**cheer·y** (chêr′i), *adj.* [-IER, -IEST], cheerful; gay; lively; pleasant; bright. —**cheer′i·ly,** *adv.* —**cheer′i·ness,** *n.*

**cheese** (chēz), *n.* [AS. *ciese;* ult. < L. *caseus*], 1. a food made from the curds of milk pressed together to form a solid. 2. a shaped mass of this. —**cheese it!** [altered < *cease it*], [Slang], stop (whatever one is doing)! run!

**cheese** (chēz), *n.* [prob. < Urdu *chīz,* thing], [Slang], the important thing: as, he's the big *cheese.*

**cheese·cake** (chēz′kāk′), *n.* 1. a kind of cake made of sweetened curds, eggs, milk, sugar, etc. 2. [Slang], display of the figure, especially the legs, of a pretty girl, as in some newspaper photographs.

**cheese·cloth** (chēz′klôth′), *n.* [from its use for wrapping cheese], a thin, cotton cloth with a loose weave.

**chees·y** (chēz′i), *adj.* [-IER, -IEST], 1. like cheese in consistency or flavor. 2. [Slang], inferior; poor; inadequate. —**chees′i·ness,** *n.*

**chee·tah** (chē′tə), *n.* [Hind. *chītā* < Sans. *citra,* spotted], a leopardlike animal of Africa and S Asia, with a small head and a black-spotted, tawny coat: it can be trained to hunt: also sp. **chetah.**

**chef** (shef), *n.* [Fr. < *chef de cuisine;* see CHIEF], 1. a head cook. 2. any cook.

‡**chef-d'oeu·vre** (she′dë′vr′), *n.* [*pl.* CHEFS-D'OEUVRE (she′dë′vr′)], [Fr., principal work], a masterpiece, as in art or literature.

**Che·khov, An·ton Pa·vlo·vich** (ån-tôn′ på-vlô′-vich chekh′ôf; Eng. chek′ôf), 1860–1904; Russian writer: also sp. **Chekov, Chekoff, Tchekhov.**

**che·la** (kē′lə), *n.* [*pl.* -LAE (-lē)], [< Gr. *chēlē,* claw], a pincerlike claw of a crab, lobster, scorpion, etc. —**che′late** (-lāt), *adj.*

**chem.,** 1. chemical. 2. chemist. 3. chemistry.

**chem·i·cal** (kem′i-k'l), *adj.* 1. of chemistry: as, a *chemical* reaction. 2. made by or used in chemistry. 3. operated by the use of chemicals. *n.* any substance used in or obtained by a chemical process or processes. —**chem′i·cal·ly,** *adv.*

**chemical engineering,** the science or profession of applying chemistry to industrial uses.

**chemical warfare,** warfare using poison gases, flame throwers, incendiary bombs, etc.

**che·mise** (shə-mēz′), *n.* [Fr. < LL. *camisia,* shirt < Gaul.], an undergarment somewhat like a loose, long undershirt, worn by women and girls.

**chem·ist** (kem′ist), *n.* [< Fr. < ML. *alchimista;* see ALCHEMY], 1. a student of or specialist in chemistry. 2. [Brit.], a druggist.

**chem·is·try** (kem′is-tri), *n.* [*pl.* -TRIES], [< *chemist*], 1. the science dealing with the composition and properties of substances, and with the reactions by which substances are produced from or converted into other substances. 2. the application of this to a specified subject or field of activity. 3. the chemical properties, composition, reactions, and uses of a substance. 4. any process of synthesis or analysis similar to that used in chemistry: as, the *chemistry* of wit.

**chem·o-,** a combining form meaning: *having to do with chemicals, of chemical reactions,* as in *chemotherapy*: also, before a vowel, **chem-.**

**chem·o·ther·a·py** (kem′ō-ther′ə-pi), *n.* [*chemo-* + *therapy*], the treatment of infection by doses of chemicals, such as the sulfa drugs: also **chem′-o·ther′a·peu′tics** (-pū′tiks). —**chem′o·ther′a·pist,** *n.*

**chem·ur·gy** (kem′ēr-ji), *n.* [*chemist* + *-urgy*], the branch of chemistry dealing with the use of farm products in the manufacture of new products other than food or clothing (e.g., soy beans as a base for plastics). —**chem·ur·gic** (kem-ūr′jik), *adj.*

**che·nille** (shə-nēl′), *n.* [Fr., caterpillar < L. *canicula,* dim. of *canis,* a dog], 1. a tufted, velvety cord used for trimming, embroidery, etc. 2. a fabric filled or woven with chenille, used for rugs, bedspreads, etc.

**Che·ops** (kē′ops), *n.* (*Khufu*), king of Egypt; fl. 2900 B.C.: built the Great Pyramid near Gizeh.

**cheque** (chek), *n.* a (bank) check: Brit. spelling.

**cheq·uer** (chek′ēr), *n.* & *v.t.* checker: Brit. spelling. —**cheq′uer·board′,** *n.* —**cheq′uered,** *adj.* —**cheq′uers,** *n.pl.*

**Cher·bourg** (sher′boorg; Fr. sher′bōōr′), *n.* a seaport in NW France: pop., 34,000.

‡**cher·chez la femme** (sher′shā′ lå fåm′), [Fr.], look for the woman (as the cause of the trouble).

**cher·ish** (cher′ish), *v.t.* [< OFr. < *cher,* dear < L. *carus*], 1. to hold dear; value highly. 2. to take good care of; treat tenderly. 3. to hold in the mind; cling to: as, he *cherishes* revenge. —**cher′ish·er,** *n.* —**cher′ish·ing·ly,** *adv.*

**Cher·o·kee** (cher′ə-kē′, cher′ə-kē′), *n.* [*pl.* -KEE, -KEES], a member of a tribe of Iroquoian Indians whose original home was in the southeastern part of the U.S.: they now live in the southwestern part.

**Cherokee rose,** an evergreen climbing rose with fragrant, large, white flowers and glossy leaves.

**che·root** (shə-rōōt′), *n.* [< Fr. < Tamil *shuruttu,* a roll], a cigar with both ends cut square.

**cher·ry** (cher′i), *n.* [*pl.* -RIES], [< OFr. *cerise* < LL. <Gr. *kerasion* < *kerasos,* cherry tree], 1. a small, fleshy fruit containing a smooth, hard seed. 2. the tree that it grows on. 3. the wood of this tree. 4. a bright red. *adj.* 1. bright-red; cherry-colored. 2. made of cherry wood. 3. made with or from cherries: as, *cherry* pie.

**chert** (chūrt), *n.* [? < *shard*], a dull-colored, flintlike quartz often found in limestone. —**chert′y** [-IER, -IEST], *adj.*

**cher·ub** (cher′əb), *n.* [*pl.* -UBS; also, for 1, 2, 3, -UBIM (-ə-bim, -yoo-bim) and, in the Vulgate, -UBIN (-ə-bin, -yoo-bin)], [< LL. < Heb. *kerūbh*], 1. a winged heavenly being described in Ezekiel 1: 5–11. 2. any of the second order of angels, just below the seraphim. 3. a representation of a cherub, usually as a chubby, rosy-faced child with wings. 4. a person, especially a child, with a sweet, innocent face. 5. an innocent or lovely child. —**che·ru·bic** (chə-rōō′bik), *adj.* —**che·ru′bi·cal·ly,** *adv.*

**cher·vil** (chūr′vil), *n.* [< AS. < L. < Gr. < *chairein,* to rejoice + *phyllon,* leaf], a plant of the carrot family, with parsleylike leaves used in soups, etc.

**cher·vo·nets** (cher-vô′nits), *n.* [*pl.* -VONTSI (-vôn′-tsi)], [Russ.], a monetary unit of the Soviet Union, equal to 10 gold rubles: also sp. **tchervonetz.**

**Ches·a·peake Bay** (ches′ə-pēk′), an arm of the Atlantic, projecting into Virginia and Maryland.

**Chesh·ire** (chesh′ir, -ēr), *n.* a county of W England: also called *Chester.*

**Cheshire cat,** a proverbial grinning cat from Cheshire, England, especially one described in Lewis Carroll's *Alice's Adventures in Wonderland.*

**Chesh·van** (khesh′vən), *n.* [Heb.], the second month of the Jewish year: see **Jewish calendar.**

**chess** (ches), *n.* [< OFr. *esches,* pl. of *eschec;* see CHECK], a game of skill played on a chessboard by two players, each with 16 chessmen to move in different ways: alternate moves are made until one player wins by checkmating his opponent's king or until a stalemate occurs.

**chess·board** (ches′bôrd′, -bōrd′), *n.* a board marked off into 64 squares of two alternating colors, used in the games of chess and checkers.

**chess·man** (ches′man′, -mən), *n.* [*pl.* -MEN], any of the pieces used in the game of chess.

**chest** (chest), *n.* [< AS. < L. < Gr. *kiste,* a box], 1. a box with a lid and, sometimes, a lock: as, a tool *chest.* 2. a treasury, as of a club; treasury; hence, 3. a fund; public fund: as, the community *chest.* 4. a piece of furniture with drawers; bureau. 5. the part of the body enclosed by the ribs and breastbone; thorax. —**get (something) off one's chest,** [Colloq.], to unburden oneself of (some trouble, etc.) by talking about it.

**chest·ed** (ches′tid), *adj.* having a (specified kind of) chest (thorax): as, hollow-*chested,* etc.

**Ches·ter** (ches′tēr), [< AS. < L. *castra,* a camp], *n.* 1. the county seat of Cheshire, England: pop., 60,000. 2. Cheshire. 3. a city in Pennsylvania, near Philadelphia: pop., 64,000.

**ches·ter·field** (ches′tẽr-fēld′), *n.* [after a 19th-c. Earl of *Chesterfield*], a single-breasted topcoat, usually with a fly front and a velvet collar.

**Ches·ter·field** (ches′tẽr-fēld′), fourth Earl of, (*Philip Dormer Stanhope*), 1694–1773; English statesman, and writer on manners.

**Chester White,** [after *Chester* County, Pa.], a variety of large, white hog.

**chest·nut** (ches′nət, -nut′), *n.* [< OFr. < L. < Gr. *kastanea;* + *nut*], 1. the smooth-shelled, sweet, edible nut of a tree of the beech family. 2. this tree. 3. the wood of this tree. 4. the horse chestnut. 5. reddish brown. 6. a reddish-brown horse. 7. [Colloq.], an old, worn-out joke or phrase; cliché. *adj.* reddish-brown.

**chest·y** (ches′ti), *adj.* [-IER, -IEST], [Colloq.], boastful, proud, or conceited.

**che·tah** (chē′tə), *n.* a cheetah.

**che·val-de-frise** (shə-val′də-frēz′), *n.* [*pl.* CHEVAUX-DE-FRISE (shə-vō′-)], [Fr.; *cheval*, a horse + *de*, of + *Frise*, Friesland], a row of spikes or jagged glass set into the masonry on top of a wall to prevent escape or trespassing.

**che·val glass** (shə-val′), [Fr. *cheval*, horse, support], a full-length mirror on swivels in a frame.

**chev·a·lier** (shev′ə-lêr′), *n.* [see CAVALIER], 1. a member of the lowest rank of the French Legion of Honor. 2. a chivalrous man; gallant; cavalier. 3. [Archaic], a knight.

**Chev·i·ot** (chev′i-ət, chē′vi-), *n.* [after the *Cheviot* Hills], 1. any of a breed of sheep with short, close-set wool. 2. (shev′i-ət), [usually c-], *a*) a close-napped wool fabric in a twill weave. *b*) a cotton cloth resembling this.

**Cheviot Hills,** a range of hills forming the border between England and Scotland.

**chev·ron** (shev′rən), *n.* [Fr., rafter (∧) < L. *capra* (Fr. *chèvre*), fem. of *caper*, goat], a V-shaped bar or bars worn on one or both of the sleeves of a military or police uniform, etc., to show rank or service. **—chev′roned** (-rənd), *adj.*

CHEVRONS

**chev·y** (chev′i), *n.* [*pl.* -IES], [Brit.], 1. a hunting cry. 2. a hunt; chase. *v.t.* & *v.i.* [-IED, -YING], [Brit.], 1. to hunt; chase; run about. 2. to fret; worry.

**chew** (cho͞o), *v.t.* & *v.i.* [< AS. *ceowan*], 1. to bite and crush with the teeth; masticate. 2. to consider; cogitate. *n.* 1. the act of chewing. 2. something chewed or for chewing. **—chew′er,** *n.*

**chewing gum,** a flavored and sweetened preparation of chicle, used for chewing.

**che·wink** (chi-wiŋk′), *n.* [echoic of its note], a kind of finch with red eyes; red-eyed towhee.

**chew·y** (cho͞o′i), *adj.* [-IER, -IEST], that needs much chewing: as, *chewy* candy.

**Chey·enne** (shī-en′), *n.* 1. [*pl.* -ENNE, -ENNES], a member of a tribe of Algonquian Indians who migrated from Minnesota to the headwaters of the Platte River. 2. the capital of Wyoming: pop., 44,000.

**chg.,** [*pl.* CHGS.], charge.

**chgd.,** charged.

**chi** (kī, kē), *n.* [Gr.], the 22d letter of the Greek alphabet (Χ, χ), transliterated into English by *ch* and generally pronounced (k).

**Chiang Kai-shek** (chyäŋ′ kī′shek′), 1886– ; Chinese general and Kuomintang leader.

**Chi·an·ti** (ki-an′ti, ki-än′ti), *n.* [It.], a dry, red wine, originally made in Tuscany.

**chi·a·ro·scu·ro** (ki-är′ə-skyoor′ō), **chi·a·ro-o·scu·ro** (ki-är′ō-ə-), *n.* [*pl.* -ROS], [< It. < L. *clarus*, clear + *obscurus*, dark], 1. a style of painting, drawing, etc. using only light and shade. 2. the effect achieved by such a style. 3. a painting, etc. in which chiaroscuro is used. **—chi·a′ro·scu′rist, chi·a′ro-o·scu′rist,** *n.*

**chi·bouk, chi·bouque** (chi-bo͝ok′, chi-bo͞ok′), *n.* [< Fr. < Turk. *chibūq*], a tobacco pipe with a long stem and a clay bowl.

**chic** (shēk, shik), *n.* [Fr. < MHG. < *schicken*, to arrange, prepare], smart elegance of style and manner. *adj.* [CHICQUER, CHICQUEST], smartly stylish; clever and fashionable.

**Chi·ca·go** (shə-kä′gō, shi-kô′gō), *n.* a city in NE Illinois, on Lake Michigan: pop., 3,550,000 (metropolitan area, 6,221,000). **—Chi·ca′go·an,** *n.*

**chi·cane** (shi-kān′), *n.* [Fr. ? < Per. *chaugan*, crooked stick], 1. chicanery. 2. in *bridge*, a hand without trumps. *v.i.* [-CANED, -CANING], to use chicanery. *v.t.* 1. to trick. 2. to get by chicanery.

**chi·can·er·y** (shi-kān′ẽr-i), *n.* [*pl.* -IES], 1. trickery; sophistry; quibbling. 2. a trick.

**chic·co·ry** (chik′ẽr-i), *n.* [*pl.* -RIES], chicory.

**chick** (chik), *n.* [< *chicken*], 1. a young chicken. 2. a young bird. 3. a child.

**chick·a·dee** (chik′ə-dē′, chik′ə-dē′), *n.* [echoic of its note], a small bird of the titmouse family, with black, gray, and white feathers.

**chick·a·ree** (chik′ə-rē′), *n.* [echoic of its cry], the red squirrel, smallest of the tree squirrels.

**Chick·a·saw** (chik′ə-sô′), *n.* [*pl.* -SAW, -SAWS], a member of a tribe of Muskhogean Indians who lived in N Mississippi and part of Tennessee.

**chick·en** (chik′in, -ən), *n.* [< AS. *cycen*, lit., little cock], 1. a young hen or rooster. 2. any hen or rooster; domestic fowl. 3. the edible flesh of the chicken. 4. a young bird of some other species. 5. a young or inexperienced person. *adj.* 1. made of chicken. 2. small and tender: as, *chicken* lobster.

**chicken feed,** 1. food for chickens. 2. small coins; negligible amount of money.

**chick·en-heart·ed** (chik′in-här′tid, chik′ən-), *adj.* cowardly; timid.

**chicken pox,** an acute, infectious virus disease, usually of young children, characterized by slight fever and a skin eruption.

**chick·weed** (chik′wēd′), *n.* any of various weeds with seeds and leaves that birds eat.

**chic·le** (chik′′l, chē′k′l), *n.* [Sp.; Nahuatl *chictli*], a gumlike substance made from the milky juice of a tropical American sapodilla tree, used in making chewing gum: also **chicle gum.**

**Chic·o·pee** (chik′ə-pē′), *n.* a city in SW Massachusetts, near Springfield: pop., 62,000.

**chic·o·ry** (chik′ə-ri), *n.* [*pl.* -RIES], [< Fr. < L. < Gr. *kichora*], 1. a plant with blue flowers whose leaves are used for salad. 2. its root, ground for mixing with coffee or as a coffee substitute.

**chide** (chīd), *v.t.* & *v.i.* [CHIDED or CHID (chid), CHIDED or CHID or CHIDDEN, CHIDING], [AS. *cidan*], to scold; upbraid; blame; reprove; rebuke. **—chid′er,** *n.* **—chid′ing·ly,** *adv.*

**chief** (chēf), *n.* [< OFr. < L. *caput*, the head], 1. the head or top part of anything. 2. the head of any group or organization; leader. 3. [Archaic], the most valuable or main part of anything. 4. in *heraldry*, the upper third of a shield. *adj.* 1. foremost; highest. 2. main; most important. *adv.* [Archaic], chiefly. **—in chief,** in the position of highest authority: as, editor *in chief.* **—chief′less,** *adj.*

**chief justice,** the presiding judge of a court made up of several judges.

**chief·ly** (chēf′li), *adv.* 1. most of all; first of all. 2. mainly; principally. *adj.* of or like a chief.

**chief·tain** (chēf′tən), *n.* [< OFr. < LL. < L. *caput*, the head], 1. a chief of a clan or tribe. 2. any leader of a group. **—chief′tain·cy** [*pl.* -CIES], **chief′tain·ship′,** *n.*

**chif·fon** (shi-fon′, shif′ən), *n.* [Fr., dim. of *chiffe*, a rag], 1. *pl.* ribbons, laces, and other finery for a woman's dress. 2. a sheer silk cloth used for women's dresses, etc. *adj.* 1. made of chiffon. 2. light and fluffy from being whipped: as, a lemon *chiffon* pie filling.

**chif·fo·nier, chif·fon·nier** (shif′ə-nêr′), *n.* [Fr. < *chiffon*], a narrow, high chest of drawers, sometimes with a mirror attached.

**chig·ger** (chig′ẽr), *n.* [< *chigoe*], 1. the tiny, red larva of certain mites, whose bite causes severe itching. 2. a chigoe.

**chi·gnon** (shēn′yon; Fr. shē′nyōn′), *n.* [Fr. < OFr. < L. *catena*, a chain], a knot or coil of hair sometimes worn at the back of the neck by women.

**chig·oe, chig·o** (chig′ō), *n.* [*pl.* -OES], [Fr. *chique;* of W. Ind. origin], 1. a sand flea of South America and the West Indies: the female burrows into the skin, causing painful sores. 2. a chigger.

**Chi·hua·hua** (chi-wä′wä), *n.* 1. a state of N Mexico. 2. a very small dog with large, pointed ears, originally from Mexico.

**chil·blain** (chil′blān′), *n.* [*chill* + *blain* < AS. *blegen*, a sore], a painful swelling or inflamed sore on the feet or hands, caused by exposure to cold.

**child** (chīld), *n.* [*pl.* CHILDREN], [< AS. *cild*, pl. *cildru*], 1. an infant; baby. 2. an unborn offspring. 3. a boy or girl in the period before puberty. 4. a son or daughter. 5. a descendant. 6. a person like a child; immature or childish adult. 7. a product: as, a *child* of one's imagination. **—with**

child, pregnant. —**child′less,** *adj.* —**child′less·ness,** *n.*
**child·bear·ing** (chīld′bâr′iŋ), *n.* the act or process of giving birth to children; parturition.
**child·bed** (chīld′bed′), *n.* the state of a woman who is giving birth to a child.
**child·birth** (chīld′bũrth′), *n.* the act of giving birth to a child.
**childe** (chīld), *n.* [var. of *child*], [Archaic], a young man of noble birth: also sp. **child.**
**child·hood** (chīld′hood′), *n.* the state or time of being a child; period from infancy to puberty.
**child·ish** (chīl′dish), *adj.* 1. of or like a child. 2. immature; silly; not fit for an adult. —**child′ish·ly,** *adv.* —**child′ish·ness,** *n.*
**child·like** (chīld′līk′), *adj.* 1. of or suitable to a child. 2. like or characteristic of a child; innocent, trusting, etc. —**child′like′ness,** *n.*
**child·ly** (chīld′li), *adj.* [Rare], childlike.
**chil·dren** (chil′drən), *n.* plural of **child.**
**child's play,** any very simple task.
**Chil·e** (chil′i; Sp. chē′le), *n.* a country on the SW coast of South America: area, 286,396 sq. mi.; pop., 9,566,000; capital, Santiago. —**Chil′e·an,** *adj. & n.*
**chil·e con car·ne** (chil′i kon kär′ni), [Sp., lit., red pepper with meat], a Mexican dish made usually of red peppers, spices, beans, and meat: also sp. **chili con carne.**
**Chile saltpeter,** sodium nitrate, found in Chile and Peru.
**chil·i** (chil′i), *n.* [*pl.* -IES], [Sp. < native Mex. name], 1. the dried pod of red pepper, a very hot seasoning. 2. the tropical American plant that bears this pod. 3. chile con carne. Also sp. **chil′e** [*pl.* -ES], **chil′li** [*pl.* -LIES].
**chili sauce,** a tomato sauce spiced with chilies.
**chill** (chil), *n.* [AS. *ciele*], 1. a bodily coldness with shivering. 2. a moderate coldness. 3. a checking of enthusiasm. 4. a sudden fear or discouragement. 5. coolness of manner; unfriendliness. *adj.* 1. uncomfortably cool; moderately cold. 2. depressing; deadening. 3. cool in manner; unfriendly. *v.i.* 1. to become cool. 2. to become cold; feel cold. 3. in *metallurgy,* to become hardened on the surface by rapid cooling. *v.t.* 1. to make cool. 2. to cause a chill in. 3. to check (enthusiasm, etc.). 4. to depress; dispirit. 5. in *metallurgy,* to harden (metal) by rapid cooling. —**chill′er,** *n.* —**chill′ing·ly,** *adv.* —**chill′ness,** *n.*
**chil·ly** (chil′i), *adj.* [-LIER, -LIEST], 1. moderately cold; uncomfortably cool. 2. chilling. 3. cool in manner. 4. dispiriting. —**chill′i·ly,** *adv.* —**chill′i·ness,** *n.*
**chi·mae·ra** (kə-mêr′ə, kī-), *n.* [L.], a chimera.
**chime** (chīm), *n.* [< OFr. < L. *cymbalum;* Gr. *kymbalon,* bell], 1. *usually pl.* a set of bells tuned to the musical scale. 2. *usually pl.* the musical sounds produced by a bell or set of bells. 3. harmony; agreement. *v.i.* [CHIMED, CHIMING], 1. to sound as a chime. 2. to sound in harmony, as bells. 3. to recite in cadence. 4. to harmonize; agree. *v.t.* 1. to ring or play (a bell, set of bells, etc.). 2. to give (the hour of day) by striking bells. —**chime in,** 1. to join in or interrupt, as talk. 2. to agree. —**chim′er,** *n.*
**chime** (chīm), *n.* [AS. *cimb-* in *cimbiren,* edge iron], the extended rim at each end of a cask or barrel: also sp. **chimb.**
**chi·me·ra** (kə-mêr′ə, kī-), *n.* [< L. < Gr. *chimaira,* orig., a goat], 1. [C-], in *Gr. mythology,* a fire-breathing monster, represented as having a lion's head, a goat's body, and a serpent's tail. 2. any similar fabulous monster. 3. an impossible or foolish fancy. Also sp. **chimaera.**
**chi·mer·i·cal** (kə-mêr′i-k'l, kī-mer′-), *adj.* [< *chimera* + *-ical*], 1. imaginary; unreal. 2. absurd; impossible. 3. visionary. Also **chi·mer′ic.**
**chim·ney** (chim′ni), *n.* [*pl.* -NEYS], [< OFr. < LL. *caminata,* fireplace < L. *caminus* < Gr. *kaminos,* oven], 1. the passage through which smoke from a fire escapes; flue. 2. a structure containing the flue and extending above the roof of a building. 3. a glass tube for a lamp, placed around the flame. 4. a fissure or vent, as in a cliff or volcano.
**chimney corner,** 1. the corner or side of an open fireplace; fireside. 2. a place near the fire.
**chimney piece,** 1. a mantelpiece. 2. [Archaic], a decoration put over a fireplace.
**chimney pot,** a pipe fitted to the top of a chimney to carry the smoke away and increase the draft.
**chimney sweep,** one who cleans soot from chimneys.
**chimney swift,** a sooty-brown North American bird resembling the swallow: so called from its habit of making a nest in an unused chimney.
**chim·pan·zee** (chim′pan-zē′, chim-pan′zi), *n.* [< Fr. < Bantu *kampenzi*], an anthropoid ape of Africa, with black hair and large ears: it is smaller than a gorilla and is noted for its intelligence.

CHIMPANZEE
(4½ ft. standing)

**chin** (chin), *n.* [AS. *cin*], the part of the face below the lower lip; projecting part of the lower jaw. *v.t.* [CHINNED, CHINNING], in *gymnastics,* to pull (oneself) up, when hanging by the hands from a horizontal bar, until the chin is level with the bar. *v.i.* [Slang], to chatter; talk volubly.
**Chin.,** 1. China. 2. Chinese.
**Chi·na** (chī′nə), *n.* a country in E Asia: area, 3,760,000 sq. mi.; pop., 732,000,000; capital, Peking.
**chi·na** (chī′nə), *n.* 1. a fine porcelain made of clay specially baked, originally imported from China. 2. dishes, ornaments, etc. made of this porcelain. 3. any earthenware dishes or crockery.
**chi·na·ber·ry** (chī′nə-ber′i), *n.* [*pl.* -RIES], 1. the yellow, berrylike fruit of a widely cultivated Asian shade tree (**China tree**). 2. the orange-brown fruit of a tree that grows in Mexico, the Southwest, and the West Indies; soapberry: it is used by natives as soap. 3. either of these trees.
**Chi·na·man** (chī′nə-mən), *n.* [*pl.* -MEN], a Chinese: contemptuous or patronizing term.
**China Sea,** a part of the Pacific, divided by Taiwan into the East China Sea and South China Sea.
**Chi·na·town** (chī′nə-toun′), *n.* the Chinese quarter of any city outside of China.
**chinch** (chinch), *n.* [Sp. *chinche;* L. *cimex,* bug], 1. a bedbug. 2. a chinch bug.
**chinch bug,** a small, white-winged, black bug that damages grain plants, especially in dry weather.
**chin·chil·la** (chin-chil′ə), *n.* [Sp. dim., after *chinche* (see CHINCH) < Peruv. *sinchi,* strong], 1. a small rodent found in the Andes, South America. 2. the expensive, soft, pale-gray fur of this animal. 3. a heavy wool cloth, with a tufted, napped surface, used for making overcoats.

CHINCHILLA
(15 in. long)

**chine** (chīn), *n.* [OFr. *eschine* < OHG. *scina,* shin bone], 1. the backbone; spine. 2. a cut of meat containing part of the backbone. 3. a ridge.
**Chi·nese** (chī-nēz′), *n.* 1. [*pl.* -NESE], a native of China or a descendant of the people of China. 2. the language of the Chinese. *adj.* of China, its people, language, or culture.
**Chinese lantern,** a lantern of brightly colored paper, made so that it can be folded up.
**Chinese puzzle,** an intricate puzzle.
**chink** (chiŋk), *n.* [AS. *cinu*], a crack; fissure. *v.t.* 1. to form chinks in. 2. to close up the chinks in.
**chink** (chiŋk), *n.* [echoic], a sharp, clinking sound, as of coins striking together. *v.t. & v.i.* to make or cause to make this sound.
**chi·no** (chē′nō, shē′-), *n.* [< ?], 1. a strong, twilled cotton cloth used for work clothes, etc. 2. [*pl.*], men's pants of chino for casual wear.
**Chi·no-** (chī′nō), a combining form meaning *Chinese.*
**Chi·nook** (chi-nōōk′, -nook′), *n.* 1. [*pl.* -NOOK, -NOOKS], any of various Indian tribes formerly inhabiting the Columbia River valley. 2. their language: also **Chinuk.** 3. Chinook jargon. 4. [c-], *a*) a warm, moist southwest wind blowing from the sea onto the coast of Oregon and Washington in winter and spring. *b*) a dry wind blowing down the eastern slope of the Rocky Mountains. —**Chi·nook′an,** *adj. & n.*
**Chinook jargon,** a pidgin language consisting of Chinook with elements of English, French, etc.
**chinook salmon,** a variety of salmon found in the Pacific; quinnat salmon.
**chin·qua·pin** (chiŋ′kə-pin), *n.* [of Am. Ind. origin], 1. the dwarf chestnut tree. 2. a related evergreen tree (**Giant Chinquapin**) growing in California and Oregon. 3. the edible nut of either of these trees.
**chintz** (chints), *n.* [< pl. of *chint;* Hind. *chhīnt;* Sans. *chitra,* spotted, bright], a cotton cloth printed in various colors and usually glazed.
**chintz·y** (chint′si), *adj.* [-IER, -IEST], 1. like chintz. 2. [Colloq.], cheap, stingy, petty, etc.
**chip** (chip), *v.t.* [CHIPPED, CHIPPING], [AS. hyp. *cippian*], 1. to cut, chop, or shape with an ax or other sharp tool. 2. to break or cut off small frag-

ments from. *v.i.* to break off in small pieces. *n.* 1. a small, thin piece of wood, etc., cut or broken off. 2. a place where a small piece has been chipped off. 3. wood or Cuban palm leaf split and woven into hats, etc. 4. a fragment of dried dung used as fuel. 5. a worthless thing. 6. a small, round disk often used in gambling games in place of money; counter. 7. *pl.* thin slices of food: as, potato *chips.* —**chip in** [Colloq.], to contribute (money, help, etc.). —**chip off the old block,** a person much like his father. —**chip on one's shoulder,** [Colloq.], an inclination to fight. —**in the chips,** [Slang], wealthy; affluent. —**chip'per,** *n.*

**chip·munk** (chip'munk), *n.* [of Am. Ind. origin], a small, striped North American squirrel; ground squirrel. Also **chip'muck** (-muk).

**chipped beef** (chipt), fine shavings of dried beef.

**Chip·pen·dale** (chip'ən-dāl'), *adj.* designating or of furniture made by, or in the graceful, rococo style of, **Thomas Chippendale** (1718?–1779), an English cabinetmaker.

**chip·per** (chip'ẽr), *adj.* [< North Brit. *kipper*], [Colloq.], in good spirits; lively.

**Chip·pe·wa** (chip'ə-wä', -wə, -wā'), *n.* [*pl.* -WA, -WAS], Ojibway. *adj.* Ojibway.

**Chip·pe·way** (chip'ə-wā'), *n. & adj.* Chippewa.

**chipping sparrow,** [< *chip*, echoic of its cry], a small sparrow of eastern and central North America.

**chirk** (chũrk), *v.t. & v.i.* [ME. *chirken*, to twitter < AS. *cearcian*, to creak, gnash], [Colloq.], to make or become cheerful (with *up*). *adj.* [Colloq.], lively; cheerful.

**chi·ro-,** [< Gr. *cheir*, the hand], a combining form meaning *hand*: also **cheiro-.**

**chi·rog·ra·phy** (kī-rog'rə-fi), *n.* [*chiro-* + *-graphy*], handwriting; penmanship. —**chi·rog'ra·pher,** *n.* —**chi·ro·graph·ic** (kī'rə-graf'ik), **chi'ro·graph'i·cal,** *adj.*

**chi·ro·man·cy** (kī'rə-man'si), *n.* [*chiro-* + *-mancy*], palmistry. —**chi'ro·man'cer,** *n.*

**chi·rop·o·dist** (kī-rop'ə-dist, ki-), *n.* [*chiro-* + *-pod* + *-ist*], a person who treats foot ailments, removes corns, etc. —**chi·rop'o·dy,** *n.*

**chi·ro·prac·tic** (kī'rə-prak'tik), *n.* [< *chiro-* + Gr. *praktikos*, practical], 1. a method of treating disease by manipulation of the joints of the body, especially the spinal column. 2. a chiropractor. *adj.* of this method of treatment.

**chi·ro·prac·tor** (kī'rə-prak'tẽr), *n.* a person who treats disease by the chiropractic method.

**chirp** (chũrp), *v.i.* [echoic var. of *chirk*], 1. to make a short, shrill sound, as certain birds or insects do. 2. to speak in a lively, shrill fashion. *v.t.* to utter in a sharp, shrill tone. *n.* a short, shrill sound. —**chirp'er,** *n.*

**chirr** (chũr), *n.* [echoic], a shrill, trilled sound, as of certain insects or birds. *v.i. & v.t.* to make, or utter with, such a sound.

**chir·rup** (chir'əp), *v.i.* [-RUPED, -RUPING], [< *chirp*], to chirp repeatedly. *n.* a chirruping sound. —**chir'rup·er,** *n.* —**chir'rup·y,** *adj.*

**chis·el** (chiz''l), *n.* [< OFr. < LL. < L. *caesus*, pp. of *caedere*, to cut], a sharp-edged tool for cutting or shaping wood, stone, or metal. *v.i. & v.t.* [-ELED or -ELLED, -ELING or -ELLING], 1. to cut or engrave with a chisel. 2. [Colloq.], to cheat; swindle; also, to get by cheating or swindling. —**chis'el·er, chis'el·ler** (-'l-ẽr, -lẽr), *n.*

CHISEL

**chit** (chit), *n.* [ME. *chitte*, kitten, merged with dial. *chit*, sprout], 1. a child. 2. a pert, saucy girl.

**chit** (chit), *n.* [< Hind. < Sans. *citra*, spotted], 1. [Chiefly Brit.], a memorandum. 2. a voucher of a small sum owed for drink, food, etc.

**chit·chat** (chit'chat'), *n.* [< *chat*], 1. light, familiar, informal talk; small talk. 2. gossip.

**chi·tin** (kī'tin), *n.* [see CHITON], a horny substance forming the hard outer covering of insects, crustaceans, etc. —**chi'tin·ous,** *adj.*

**chi·ton** (kī't'n, -ton), *n.* [Gr., garment, tunic < Sem.], a loose garment similar to a tunic, worn by both men and women in ancient Greece.

**chit·ter·lings** (chit'ẽr-liŋz), *n.pl.* [ME. *chiterling*; akin to LG. *küte* (G. *kutteln*), entrails], the small intestines of pigs, used for food.

**chiv·al·ric** (shiv''l-rik, shi-val'rik), *adj.* 1. of chivalry. 2. chivalrous.

**chiv·al·rous** (shiv''l-rəs), *adj.* 1. having the attributes of an ideal knight; gallant, courteous, honorable, etc. 2. of chivalry; chivalric. —**chiv'al·rous·ly,** *adv.* —**chiv'al·rous·ness,** *n.*

**chiv·al·ry** (shiv''l-ri), *n.* [< OFr. *chevalerie* < *chevaler*, a knight; see CAVALIER], 1. a group of knights or gallant gentlemen. 2. the medieval system of knighthood. 3. the qualifications of a knight, such as courage, fairness, respect for women, protection of the poor, etc. 4. the demonstration of any of these qualities.

**chive** (chīv), *n.* [< OFr. < L. *cepa*, onion], a plant of the onion family, with small, hollow leaves used to flavor soups, stews, salads, etc.

**chiv·y, chiv·vy** (chiv'i), *n.* [*pl.* -IES; -VIES], *v.t. & v.i.* [-IED, -YING; -VIED, -VYING], chevy.

**chlo·ral** (klôr'əl, klō'rəl), *n.* [*chlor(o)-* + *al*cohol], 1. a thin, oily, colorless liquid, $CCl_3CHO$, with a pungent odor, prepared by the action of chlorine on alcohol. 2. chloral hydrate.

**chloral hydrate,** a colorless, crystalline compound, $CCl_3CH(OH)_2$, used chiefly as a sedative.

**chlo·rate** (klôr'it, klō'rāt), *n.* [*chlor(o)-* + *-ate*], a salt of chloric acid.

**chlor·dane** (klôr'dān, klōr'-), *n.* [*chlor(o)-* + *indane*, a coal-tar derivative] a poisonous volatile oil, $C_{10}H_6Cl_8$, used as an insecticide.

**chlo·ric** (klôr'ik, klō'rik), *adj.* [*chlor(o)-* + *-ic*], 1. of or containing chlorine with a higher valence than that in corresponding chlorous compounds. 2. designating or of a colorless acid, $HClO_3$, whose salts are chlorates.

**chlo·ride** (klôr'īd, klō'rid), *n.* [*chlor(o)-* + *-ide*], a compound in which chlorine is combined with another element or radical (e.g., a salt of hydrochloric acid): also **chlo'rid** (-id, -rid).

**chloride of lime,** calcium chloride, $CaOCl_2$, a white powder obtained by treating slaked lime with chlorine, used for disinfecting and bleaching.

**chlo·rin** (klôr'in, klō'rin), *n.* chlorine.

**chlo·rin·ate** (klôr'ə-nāt', klō'rə-), *v.t.* [-ATED, -ATING], to treat or combine (a substance) with chlorine; esp., to pass chlorine into (water or sewage) for purification. —**chlo'rin·a'tion,** *n.*

**chlo·rine** (klôr'ēn, klō'rin), *n.* [*chlor(o)-* + *-ine*], a greenish-yellow, poisonous, gaseous chemical element with a disagreeable odor, used in bleaching, water purification, etc.: symbol, Cl; at. wt., 35.457; at. no., 17.

**chlo·rite** (klôr'īt, klō'rīt), *n.* [*chlor(o)-* + *-ite*], a salt of chlorous acid.

**chlo·ro-,** [< Gr. *chlōros*, pale green], a combining form meaning: 1. *green*, as in *chlorophyll.* 2. *chlorine, having chlorine*, as in *chloroform.* Also, before a vowel, **chlor-.**

**chlo·ro·form** (klôr'ə-fôrm', klō'rə-), *n.* [see CHLORO- & FORMYL], a sweetish, colorless, volatile liquid, $CHCl_3$, used as an anesthetic and solvent. *v.t.* 1. to anesthetize with chloroform. 2. to kill with chloroform.

**chlo·ro·my·ce·tin** (klôr'ə-mī-sē'tin), *n.* [*chloro-* + Gr. *mykēs*, mushroom; + *-in*], an antibiotic drug effective against viruses and rickettsiae as well as against bacteria.

**chlo·ro·phyll, chlo·ro·phyl** (klôr'ə-fil', klō'rə-), *n.* [< Fr. < Gr. *chlōros*, green + *phyllon*, a leaf], the green coloring matter of plants: in the presence of sunlight it converts carbon dioxide and water into carbohydrates. —**chlo'ro·phyl'lose, chlo'ro·phyl'lous,** *adj.*

**chlo·ro·plast** (klôr'ə-plast', klō'rə-), *n.* [*chloro-* + *-plast*], an oval, chlorophyll-bearing body found outside the nucleus in a cell.

**chlo·rous** (klôr'əs, klō'rəs), *adj.* [*chlor(o)-* + *-ous*], 1. of or containing chlorine with a lower valence than that in corresponding chloric compounds. 2. designating or of an acid, $HClO_2$, whose salts are chlorites.

**chm., chmn.,** chairman.

**chock** (chok), *n.* [ONorm.Fr. *choque*, a stump, block], 1. a block or wedge placed under a wheel, barrel, etc. to prevent motion. 2. in *nautical usage*, a block with two hornlike projections curving inward, through which a rope may be run. *v.t.* 1. to provide or wedge fast as with chocks. 2. to place (a vessel) on chocks. *adv.* completely, so as to be tight or full: as, *chock* full of grain.

**chock·a·block** (chok'ə-blok'), *adj.* 1. pulled so tight as to have the blocks touching: said of a

---

fat, āpe, bâre, cär; ten, ēven, hêre, ovẽr; is, bīte; lot, gō, hôrn, tōōl, look; oil, out; up, ūse, fũr; get; joy; yet; chin; she; thin, *th*en; zh, leisure; ŋ, ring; ə for *a* in *ago*, *e* in *agent*, *i* in *sanity*, *o* in *comply*, *u* in *focus*; ' in *able* (ā'b'l); Fr. bål; ë, Fr. coeur; ö, Fr. feu; Fr. mon; ô, Fr. coq; ü, Fr. duc; H, G. ich; kh, G. doch. ‡ foreign; < derived from.

hoisting tackle. 2. crowded. *adv.* tightly together.
**chock-full** (chok′fool′), *adj.* as full as possible; filled to capacity: also **choke-full, chuck-full.**
**choc·o·late** (chôk′lit, chok′ə-), *n.* [Sp. & Port. < Mex. *chocolatl*], 1. a paste, powder, etc. made from cacao seeds that have been ground and roasted. 2. a drink made of chocolate, hot milk or water, and sugar. 3. a candy made of or containing chocolate. 4. reddish brown. *adj.* 1. made of or containing chocolate. 2. reddish-brown.
**Choc·taw** (chok′tô), *n.* 1. [*pl.* -TAW, -TAWS], a member of a tribe of Muskhogean Indians who lived originally in the Southeast. 2. the language of this tribe. *adj.* of this tribe or their language.
**choice** (chois), *n.* [< OFr. < *choisir* (< OHG. *cheosan*), to choose], 1. a choosing; selection. 2. the right or power to choose; option. 3. a person or thing chosen. 4. the best part. 5. a variety from which to choose. 6. a supply well chosen. 7. an alternative. 8. care in choosing. *adj.* 1. of special excellence. 2. carefully chosen. **—choice′ly,** *adv.* **—choice′ness,** *n.*
**choir** (kwīr), *n.* [< OFr. *cuer*; L. *chorus*; see CHORUS], 1. a group of singers in a church. 2. the part of a church where they sing. 3. any group of singers. *v.t. & v.i.* [Poetic], to sing in a chorus.
**choke** (chōk), *v.t.* [CHOKED, CHOKING], [< AS. *aceocian*], 1. to prevent from breathing by blocking the windpipe; strangle; suffocate. 2. to block up; obstruct by clogging. 3. to hinder the growth or action of. 4. to fill up. 5. to cut off air from the carburetor of (a gasoline engine) so as to make a richer gasoline mixture. *v.i.* 1. to be suffocated. 2. to be blocked up; be obstructed. *n.* 1. a choking; strangulation. 2. a sound of choking. 3. the valve that shuts off air in the carburetor of a gasoline engine. **—choke back,** to hold back (feelings, sobs, etc.). **—choke down,** to swallow with difficulty. **—choke off,** to bring to an end; end the growth of. **—choke up,** 1. to block up; clog. 2. to fill too full.
**choke·bore** (chōk′bôr′, -bōr′), *n.* 1. a shotgun bore that tapers toward the muzzle to keep the shot closely bunched. 2. a gun with such a bore.
**choke·cher·ry** (chōk′cher′i), *n.* [*pl.* -RIES], 1. a wild cherry tree of North America. 2. its astringent fruit.
**choke·damp** (chōk′damp′), *n.* a suffocating gas, chiefly carbon dioxide, found in mines and wells.
**choke-full** (chōk′fool′), *adj.* chock-full.
**chok·er** (chōk′ēr), *n.* 1. a person or thing that chokes. 2. a closely fitting necklace. 3. [Colloq.], a wide collar worn tight around the neck.
**chok·y** (chōk′i), *adj.* [-IER, -IEST], 1. inclined to choke. 2. suffocating; stifling. Also sp. **chokey.**
**chol·e-,** cholo-.
**chol·er** (kol′ēr), *n.* [< OFr. < L. < Gr. *cholera*, nausea < *cholē*, bile], 1. [Obs.], bile: in medieval times it was considered the source of anger and irritability; hence, 2. anger; wrath.
**chol·er·a** (kol′ēr-ə), *n.* [see CHOLER], any of several intestinal diseases; esp., *a*) cholera morbus. *b*) Asiatic cholera.
**cholera in·fan·tum** (in-fan′təm), [L., lit., cholera of infants], an intestinal disease of infants, characterized by vomiting and diarrhea.
**cholera mor·bus** (môr′bəs), [L., lit., cholera disease], a noninfectious, rarely fatal cholera.
**chol·er·ic** (kol′ēr-ik), *adj.* [see CHOLER], easily angered; quick-tempered.
**cho·les·ter·ol** (kə-les′tə-rōl′), *n.* [< *chole-* + Gr. *stereos*, solid; + *-ol*], a crystalline fatty alcohol, $C_{27}H_{45}OH$, found especially in animal fats, blood, gallstones, and bile.
**chol·o-,** [< Gr. *cholē*, bile], a combining form meaning *bile, gall*: also **chol-, chole-.**
**choose** (chōōz), *v.t.* [CHOSE (chōz), CHOSEN (chō′z′n) or *obs.* CHOSE, CHOOSING], [AS. *ceosan*], 1. to take as a choice; pick out; select. 2. to prefer; decide: as, I *chose* to go. *v.i.* to make a choice; select. **—cannot choose but,** cannot do otherwise than. **—choos′er,** *n.*
**choos·y** (chōōz′i), *adj.* [-IER, -IEST], [Colloq.], very particular; fussy. **—choos′i·ness,** *n.*
**chop** (chop), *v.t.* [CHOPPED, CHOPPING], [ME. *choppen*; ? < OFr. *c(h)oper*, to cut], 1. to cut by blows with an ax or other sharp tool. 2. to cut into small bits. 3. to cut short. *v.i.* 1. to make quick, cutting strokes with a sharp tool. 2. to act with a quick, jerky motion. *n.* 1. the act of chopping. 2. a short, sharp blow or stroke. 3. a piece chopped off. 4. a slice of lamb, pork, veal, etc. cut from the rib, loin, or shoulder. 5. a short, broken movement of waves. **—chop′per,** *n.*
**chop** (chop), *n.* [var. of *chap* (jaw)], 1. a jaw. 2. a cheek. See **chops.**
**chop** (chop), *v.t.* [CHOPPED, CHOPPING], [AS. *ceapian*, to bargain], [Obs.], to exchange. *v.i.* to change; shift suddenly, as the wind. *n.* an exchange. **—chop′py** [-PIER, -PIEST], *adj.*
**chop** (chop), *n.* [Hind. *chhāp*], 1. in China, a brand on or of goods. 2. [Slang], grade; brand.
**chop·fal·len** (chop′fôl′ən), *adj.* chapfallen.
**chop·house** (chop′hous′), *n.* a restaurant that specializes in chops and steaks.
**Cho·pin, Fré·dé·ric Fran·çois** (frā′dā′rēk′ frän′swȧ′ shō′pan′; Eng. shō′pan), 1810–1849; Polish pianist and composer in France.
**chop·py** (chop′i), *adj.* [-PIER, -PIEST], [< *chop* (cut)], 1. rough with short, broken waves, as the sea. 2. with sharp, abrupt movements. **—chop′pi·ly,** *adv.* **—chop′pi·ness,** *n.*
**chops** (chops), *n.pl.* [see CHAP (jaw)], 1. the jaws. 2. the mouth and lower cheeks. Also **chaps.**
**chop·sticks** (chop′stiks′), *n.pl.* [Pid.Eng. for Chin. *k′wai-tsze*, the quick ones], two small sticks held together in one hand and used by the Chinese and Japanese to lift food to the mouth.
**chop su·ey** (chop′ sōō′i), [altered < Chin. *tsa-sui*, lit., various pieces], a Chinese-American dish of meat, bean sprouts, celery, mushrooms, etc. cooked in a sauce and served with rice.
**cho·ral** (kôr′əl, kō′rəl), *adj.* [Fr.], of, for, sung by, or recited by a choir or chorus. **—cho′ral·ly,** *adv.*
**cho·ral, cho·rale** (kô-ral′, kə-, kôr′əl), *n.* [< G. *choral* (*gesang*)], a simple hymn tune sung by the choir and congregation, often in unison.
**chord** (kôrd), *n.* [Eng. *cord*; sp. revised after L. *chorda* < Gr. *chordē*, string of a musical instrument], 1. [Poetic], the string of a musical instrument. 2. a responsive emotional element: as, his speech struck a sympathetic *chord*. 3. in *anatomy*, a structure, such as a tendon, resembling a cord. 4. in *engineering*, a principal horizontal member in a rigid framework, as of a bridge. 5. in *geometry*, a straight line joining any two points on an arc or curve. **—chord′al,** *adj.*

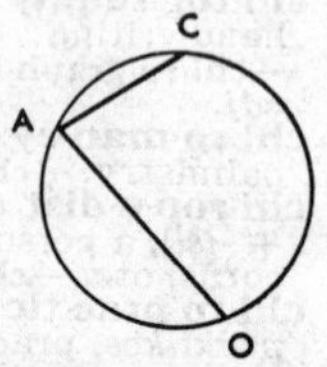

CHORDS (AC, AO)

**chord** (kôrd), *n.* [< *cord*, contr. < *accord*], in *music*, a combination of three or more tones sounded together in harmony. *v.i. & v.t.* to harmonize.
**chore** (chôr, chōr), *n.* [see CHARE], 1. a small routine task; odd job. 2. a hard or unpleasant task.
**cho·re·a** (kô-rē′ə, kō-), *n.* [L. < Gr. *choreia*, choral dance], a nervous disease in which there are jerking movements caused by involuntary muscular contractions; St. Vitus's Dance.
**chor·e·og·ra·phy** (kôr′i-og′rə-fi, kō′-), *n.* [Gr. *choreia*, dance; + *-graphy*], 1. ballet dancing. 2. the arrangement of the movements of a ballet. 3. the art of devising ballets. Also **cho·reg′ra·phy** (kə-reg′-). **—chor′e·og′ra·pher, cho·reg′ra·pher,** *n.* **—chor′e·o·graph′ic** (-ə-graf′ik), **cho′re·graph′ic** (-rə-graf′ik), *adj.*
**cho·ric** (kôr′ik, kō′rik), *adj.* of, for, or like a chorus, especially in an ancient Greek play.
**chor·is·ter** (kôr′is-tēr, kor′-), *n.* [< OFr. *cuerist(r)e*; see CHOIR], 1. a member of a choir; esp., a boy who sings in a choir. 2. the leader of a choir.
**cho·roid** (kôr′oid, kō′roid), *adj.* [< Gr. < *chorion*, leather + *eidos*, form], designating or of any of certain vascular membranes. *n.* the dark, vascular membrane between the sclera and retina of the eye. Also **cho′ri·oid** (-i-oid, -ri-oid).
**chor·tle** (chôr′t′l), *v.i. & v.t.* [-TLED, -TLING], [coined by Lewis Carroll, prob. < *chuckle* + *snort*], to make or utter with a gleeful chuckling or snorting sound. *n.* such a sound. **—chor′tler,** *n.*
**cho·rus** (kôr′əs, kō′rəs), *n.* [L. < Gr. *choros*, a dance, chorus], 1. in Greek drama, a group whose singing, dancing, and narration supplemented the main action. 2. a group of dancers and singers performing together as in an opera. 3. the part of a drama, song, etc. performed by a chorus. 4. a group singing or speaking something together simultaneously. 5. a simultaneous utterance by many: as, a *chorus* of protest. 6. music written for group singing. 7. the refrain of a song, following the verse. *v.t. & v.i.* to sing or recite all together and simultaneously. **—in chorus,** in unison.
**chorus girl** (or **boy**), a woman (or man) singing or dancing in a chorus, as of a musical comedy.
**chose** (chōz), pt. and obs. pp. of **choose.**
**Cho·sen** (chō′sen′), *n.* Korea: the Japanese name.

**cho·sen** (chō'z'n), pp. of **choose.** *adj.* picked out by preference; selected; choice.
**Chou** (jō), *n.* a Chinese dynasty (1122?–249 B.C.).
**chow** (chou), *n.* [prob. < *chowchow*], 1. any of a Chinese breed of medium-sized dog with a compact, muscular body and a thick coat of brown or black. 2. [Slang], food.
**chow·chow** (chou'chou'), *n.* [Pid.Eng. < Chin.], 1. chopped pickles in a highly seasoned mustard sauce. 2. a chow. *adj.* mixed; assorted.
**chow·der** (chou'dẽr), *n.* [Fr. *chaudière*, a pot < LL. *caldaria*; see CALDRON], a dish consisting of fresh fish, clams, etc. stewed with vegetables, often in milk.
**chow mein** (chou'mān'), [Chin. *ch'ao*, to fry + *mien*, flour], a Chinese-American dish consisting of a thick stew of meat, onions, celery, bean sprouts, etc., served with fried noodles.
**Chr.,** 1. Christ. 2. Christian.
**chrism** (kriz'm), *n.* [< AS. < LL. < Gr. *chrisma* < *chriein*, to anoint], consecrated oil used in baptism and other sacraments. **—chris'mal,** *adj.*
**Christ** (krīst), *n.* [< L. < Gr. *Christos*, lit., the Anointed < *chriein*, to anoint], Jesus of Nazareth, regarded by Christians as the Messiah prophesied in the Old Testament.
**chris·ten** (kris''n), *v.t.* [AS. *cristnian*], 1. to take into a Christian church by baptism; baptize. 2. to give a name to at baptism. 3. to give a name to. 4. [Colloq.], to make use of for the first time. **—chris'ten·ing,** *n.*
**Chris·ten·dom** (kris''n-dəm), *n.* 1. Christians collectively. 2. those parts of the world where most of the inhabitants profess Christianity.
**Chris·tian** (kris'chən), *n.* 1. a person professing belief in Jesus as the Christ, or in the religion based on the teachings of Jesus. 2. [Colloq.], a decent, respectable person. *adj.* 1. of Jesus Christ. 2. of the teachings of Jesus Christ. 3. of or professing the religion based on these teachings. 4. having the qualities demonstrated and taught by Jesus Christ, as love, kindness, etc. 5. of or representing Christians or Christianity. 6. [Colloq.], human, decent, etc. **—Chris'tian·like',** *adj.* **—Chris'tian·ly,** *adj. & adv.*
**Christian Era,** the era beginning with the year formerly thought to be that of the birth of Jesus Christ (born probably c. 4–6 B.C.).
**Chris·tia·ni·a** (kris-tyä'ni-ä), *n.* Oslo, the capital of Norway: the former name.
**Chris·ti·an·i·ty** (kris'chi-an'ə-ti), *n.* 1. Christians collectively. 2. the Christian religion. 3. [*pl.* -TIES], a particular Christian religious system. 4. the state of being a Christian. 5. Christian spirit, character, practices, etc.
**Chris·tian·ize** (kris'chən-īz'), *v.t.* [-IZED, -IZING], 1. to convert to Christianity. 2. to cause to conform with Christian character or precepts. *v.i.* to adopt Christianity. **—Chris'tian·i·za'tion,** *n.* **—Chris'tian·iz'er,** *n.*
**Christian name,** the baptismal name, as distinguished from the family name; given name.
**Christian Science,** a religion and system of healing founded by Mary Baker Eddy in 1866: official name, **Church of Christ, Scientist. —Christian Scientist.**
**Christ·like** (krīst'līk'), *adj.* like Jesus Christ, as in character or spirit. **—Christ'like'ness,** *n.*
**Christ·ly** (krīst'li), *adj.* of Jesus Christ; Christlike. **—Christ'li·ness,** *n.*
**Christ·mas** (kris'məs), *n.* [AS. *Cristesmæsse*; see CHRIST & MASS (rite)], the yearly celebration, December 25, of the birth of Jesus Christ.
**Christmas Day,** December 25.
**Christmas Eve,** the evening before Christmas Day.
**Christ·mas·tide** (kris'məs-tīd'), *n.* Christmas time; time from Christmas Eve through New Year's Day or to Epiphany (January 6).
**Chris·to·pher,** Saint (kris'tə-fẽr), 3d century A.D.: patron saint of travelers.
**chro·mate** (krō'māt), *n.* a salt of chromic acid.
**chro·mat·ic** (krō-mat'ik), *adj.* [< L. < Gr. < *chrōma*, color], 1. of or containing color or colors. 2. in *music*, using or progressing by half tones: as, a *chromatic* scale. *n.* in *music*, a tone modified by an accidental. **—chro·mat'i·cal·ly,** *adv.*
**chro·mat·ics** (krō-mat'iks), *n.pl.* [construed as sing.], the scientific study of colors: also **chro·ma·tol·o·gy** (krō'mə-tol'ə-ji). **—chro'ma·tist,** *n.*
**chromatic scale,** the musical scale made up of thirteen successive half tones to the octave.

**chro·ma·tin** (krō'mə-tin), *n.* [< Gr. *chrōma*, *chrōmatos*, a color; + *-in*], a granular substance in the nucleus of animal and plant cells that readily takes a deep stain: chromatin contains the genes.
**chro·ma·to-,** [< Gr. *chrōma*, *chrōmatos*, a color], a combining form meaning: 1. *color* or *pigmentation*. 2. *chromatin*. Also, before a vowel, **chromat-.**
**chrome** (krōm), *n.* [Fr. < Gr. *chrōma*, a color], 1. chromium. 2. chrome yellow. *adj.* designating any of various pigments (**chrome green, chrome red, chrome yellow,** etc.) made from chromium compounds. *v.t.* [CHROMED, CHROMING], to plate with chromium.
**-chrome,** [< Gr. *chrōma*, a color], a suffix meaning: 1. *color, coloring agent*. 2. *chromium*.
**chrome steel,** a very strong, hard alloy steel that contains chromium: also **chromium steel.**
**chro·mic** (krō'mik), *adj.* designating or of chromium compounds in which the valence of chromium is higher than in the corresponding chromous compounds.
**chromic acid,** an acid, $H_2CrO_4$, whose salts are chromates.
**chro·mi·um** (krō'mi-əm), *n.* [Latinized < Fr. *chrome*; see CHROME], a very hard, metallic chemical element with a high resistance to corrosion: symbol, Cr; at. wt., 52.01; at. no., 24.
**chro·mo** (krō'mō), *n.* [*pl.* -MOS], a chromolithograph.
**chro·mo-,** [< Gr. *chrōma*, a color], a combining form meaning *color, colored, pigment, pigmentation*, as in *chromosome*: also, before a vowel, **chrom-.**
**chro·mo·lith·o·graph** (krō'mō-lith'ə-graf', -gräf'), *n.* a picture in colors printed from a series of stone or zinc plates. **—chro'mo·li·thog'ra·pher** (-li-thog'rə-fẽr), *n.* **—chro'mo·lith'o·graph'ic,** *adj.* **—chro'mo·li·thog'ra·phy,** *n.*
**chro·mo·some** (krō'mə-sōm'), *n.* [*chromo-* + *-some* (body)], any of the microscopic rod-shaped bodies into which the chromatin separates during mitosis: they carry the genes that convey hereditary characteristics, and are constant in number for each species. **—chro'mo·so'mal,** *adj.*
**chro·mo·sphere** (krō'mə-sfêr'), *n.* [*chromo-* + *-sphere*], the reddish layer of incandescent gases around the sun, visible at a total eclipse. **—chro'mo·spher'ic** (-sfer'ik), *adj.*
**chro·mous** (krō'məs), *adj.* designating or of chromium compounds in which the valence of chromium is lower than in the corresponding chromic compounds.
**Chron.,** Chronicles.
**chron., chronol.,** 1. chronological. 2. chronology.
**chron·ic** (kron'ik), *adj.* [< Fr. < L. < Gr. < *chronos*, time], 1. lasting a long time; also, recurring: said of a disease: cf. *acute*. 2. having had an ailment or habit for a long time. 3. perpetual; habitual; constant. Also **chronical. —chron'i·cal·ly,** *adv.*
**chron·i·cle** (kron'i-k'l), *n.* [< Anglo-Fr. < OFr. < L. < Gr. *chronika*, annals; see CHRONIC], 1. a historical record of events in the order in which they happened. 2. a narrative; history. *v.t.* [-CLED, -CLING], to tell or write the story or history of; put into a chronicle. **—chron'i·cler,** *n.*
**Chron·i·cles** (kron'i-k'lz), *n.pl.* two books of the Old Testament, I and II Chronicles.
**chro·no-,** [Gr. < *chronos*, time], a combining form meaning *time*: also, before a vowel, **chron-.**
**chron·o·log·i·cal** (kron'ə-loj'i-k'l), *adj.* 1. arranged in the order of occurrence. 2. relating to a narrative or history. Also **chron'o·log'ic. —chron'o·log'i·cal·ly,** *adv.*
**chro·nol·o·gy** (krə-nol'ə-ji), *n.* [*pl.* -GIES], [*chrono-* + *-logy*], 1. the science of measuring time and of dating events accurately and in proper order. 2. the arrangement of events, dates, etc. in the order of occurrence. 3. a list of dates of events in their proper sequence. **—chro·nol'o·gist, chro·nol'o·ger,** *n.*
**chro·nom·e·ter** (krə-nom'ə-tẽr), *n.* [*chrono-* + *-meter*], an instrument for measuring time precisely; esp., a highly accurate kind of clock or watch. **—chron·o·met·ric** (kron'ə-met'rik), **chron'o·met'ri·cal,** *adj.* **—chron'o·met'ri·cal·ly,** *adv.*
**chro·nom·e·try** (krə-nom'ə-tri), *n.* [*chrono-* + *-metry*], scientific measurement of time.
**-chro·ous** (krə-əs, krō-), [Gr. *chrōs*, *chroos*, color], a terminal combining form meaning *colored*.
**chrys·a·lid** (kris''l-id), *n.* a chrysalis. *adj.* of a chrysalis.

**chrys·a·lis** (kris'ʼl-is), *n.* [*pl.* -LISES, CHRYSALIDES (kri-sal'ə-dēz')], [< L. < Gr. *chrysallis*, golden-colored chrysalis < *chrysos*, gold], 1. the form of an insect after the larval stage, when in a case or cocoon; pupa. 2. the case or cocoon. 3. anything in a formative or undeveloped stage.
**chrys·an·the·mum** (kris-an'thə-məm), *n.* [L. < Gr. < *chrysos*, gold + *anthemon*, a flower], 1. any of various late-blooming plants of the composite family cultivated for their showy, ball-shaped flowers, in a wide variety of colors. 2. the flower.
**chrys·o·lite** (kris'ʼl-īt'), *n.* [< OFr. < L. < Gr. < *chrysos*, gold + *lithos*, stone], a green or yellow silicate of magnesium and iron, used as a semiprecious stone.
**chrys·o·prase** (kris'ə-prāz'), *n.* [< OFr. < L. < Gr. < *chrysos*, gold + *prason*, leek], a light-green quartz, a variety of chalcedony sometimes used as a semiprecious stone.
**chub** (chub), *n.* [*pl.* CHUBS, CHUB; see PLURAL, II, D, 1], [ME. *chubbe*], 1. any of several fresh-water fishes related to the carp. 2. any of various unrelated fishes, as the large-mouthed black bass.
**chub·by** (chub'i), *adj.* [-BIER, -BIEST], [< *chub*], round and plump. —**chub'bi·ness**, *n.*
**chuck** (chuk), *v.t.* [? < Fr. *choquer*, to strike against], 1. to tap or squeeze gently, especially under the chin, as a playful gesture. 2. to throw with a quick, short movement; toss. 3. [Colloq.], to discard; get rid of. *n.* 1. a light tap or squeeze under the chin. 2. a toss; throw. 3. [Slang], food.
**chuck** (chuk), *n.* [? var. of *chock*], 1. a cut of beef including the parts around the neck and the shoulder blade. 2. a clamplike device, as on a lathe, by which the tool or work is held.
**chuck-a-luck** (chuk'ə-luk'), *n.* [< *chuck* (to throw) + *luck*], a gambling game using three dice.
**chuck-full** (chuk'fool'), *adj.* chock-full.
**chuck·hole** (chuk'hōl'), *n.* [< dial. *chock*, a bump], a rough hole in a road, made by wear and weathering.
**chuck·le** (chuk'ʼl), *v.i.* [-LED, -LING], [prob. freq. var. of *cluck*], 1. to laugh softly in a low tone, as in mild amusement. 2. to cluck, as a hen. *n.* a soft, low-toned laugh. —**chuck'ler**, *n.*
**chuck·le·head** (chuk'ʼl-hed'), *n.* [Colloq.], a stupid person; dolt. —**chuck'le·head'ed**, *adj.*
**chuck wagon**, [Slang], a portable kitchen cart for serving food to lumbermen, ranch hands, etc.
**chug** (chug), *n.* [echoic], a loud, abrupt, explosive sound, as of the exhaust from an engine. *v.i.* [CHUGGED, CHUGGING], to make, or move while making, such sounds: as, the train *chugged* along.
**chuk·ka boot** (chuk'ə), [< *chukker*], a man's ankle-high shoe, usually with two pairs of eyelets.
**chuk·ker, chuk·kar** (chuk'ēr), *n.* [Hind. *cakar* < Sans. *cakra*, wheel], one of the eight periods of play into which a polo match is divided.
**chum** (chum), *n.* [late 17th-c. slang; prob. < *chamber* in *chamber mate*], [Colloq.], 1. originally, a roommate. 2. an intimate friend. *v.i.* [CHUMMED, CHUMMING], [Colloq.], 1. originally, to share the same room. 2. to be intimate friends.
**chum·my** (chum'i), *adj.* [-MIER, -MIEST], [see CHUM], [Colloq.], intimate; friendly. —**chum'mi·ly**, *adv.* —**chum'mi·ness**, *n.*
**chump** (chump), *n.* [? < *chock* (a block) + *lump*], 1. a heavy block of wood. 2. a thick, blunt end. 3. [Colloq.], a stupid or silly person; blockhead.
**Chung·king** (choon'kin'; Chin. joon'chin'), *n.* a city in central China, on the Yangtze River: pop., 4,070,000.
**chunk** (chunk), *n.* [? var. of *chock* (a block)], [Colloq.], 1. a short, thick piece, as of meat. 2. a fair portion. 3. a stocky person or animal.
**chunk·y** (chunk'i), *adj.* [-IER, -IEST], [< *chunk*], [Colloq.], 1. short and thick. 2. stocky; thickset. —**chunk'i·ly**, *adv.* —**chunk'i·ness**, *n.*
**church** (chũrch), *n.* [< AS. < Late Gr. *kyriakon*, < *kyriakē* (*dōma*), Lord's (house) < *kyros*, power], 1. a building for public worship, especially one for Christian worship. 2. public worship; religious service. 3. all Christians. 4. [usually C-], a particular sect or denomination of Christians: as, the Methodist *Church*. 5. ecclesiastical government, or its power, as opposed to secular government. 6. the profession of the clergy. 7. a group of worshipers. *adj.* of a church or of organized Christian worship. —**church'less**, *adj.* —**church'like'**, *adj.*
**church·go·er** (chũrch'gō'ēr), *n.* a person who attends church, regularly. —**church'go'ing**, *n.* & *adj.*
**Church·ill, Win·ston** (win'st'n chũrch'il, -'l), (*Sir Winston Leonard Spencer Churchill*), 1874–1965; British prime minister (1940–1945; 1951–1955).
**church·ly** (chũrch'li), *adj.* of or fit for a church. —**church'li·ness**, *n.*
**church·man** (chũrch'mən), *n.* [*pl.* -MEN], 1. an ecclesiastic; clergyman. 2. a member of a church. —**church'man·ly**, *adj.* —**church'man·ship'**, *n.*
**Church of Christ, Scientist**, the official name of the Christian Science Church.
**Church of England**, the episcopal church of England, supported by the government and having the sovereign as its head; Anglican Church.
**Church of Jesus Christ of Latter-day Saints**, the official name of the Mormon Church.
**church·ward·en** (chũrch'wôr'd'n), *n.* 1. in the *Anglican & Episcopal churches*, a lay officer chosen annually in every parish to attend to the secular affairs of the church. 2. [Brit. Colloq.], a clay tobacco pipe with a long stem.
**church·wom·an** (chũrch'woom'ən), *n.* [*pl.* -WOMEN], a woman member of a church.
**church·yard** (chũrch'yärd'), *n.* the yard adjoining a church, often used as a place of burial.
**churl** (chũrl), *n.* [AS. *ceorl*, freeman], 1. a peasant; rustic. 2. a surly, ill-bred person; boor. —**churl'ish**, *adj.* —**churl'ish·ly**, *adv.* —**churl'ish·ness**, *n.*
**churn** (chũrn), *n.* [AS. *cyrin*], 1. a container or contrivance in which milk or cream is beaten and shaken to form butter. 2. a violent stirring; agitation. *v.t.* 1. to beat and shake (milk or cream) in a churn. 2. to make (butter) in a churn. 3. to stir up vigorously; shake violently. *v.i.* 1. to use a churn in making butter. 2. to move as if churned; seethe, as water in a whirlpool. —**churn'er**, *n.*
**churr** (chũr), *n.*, *v.i.* & *v.t.* chirr.
**chute** (shōōt), *n.* [Fr., a fall; ult. < L. *cadere*, to fall], 1. a waterfall or rapids. 2. an inclined trough or passage down which various things may slide or be sent: as, a coal *chute*.
**chute, 'chute** (shōōt), *n.* [Colloq.], a parachute.
**chut·ney** (chut'ni), *n.* [*pl.* -NEYS], [Hind. *chatnī*], a spicy relish made of fruits, spices, and herbs: also sp. **chut'nee**.
**chyle** (kīl), *n.* [< L. < Gr. *chylos* < *cheein*, to pour], a milky fluid composed of lymph and emulsified fats: it is formed from chyme in the small intestine and is passed into the blood through the thoracic duct. —**chy·la·ceous** (kī-lā'shəs), **chy'lous**, *adj.*
**chyme** (kīm), *n.* [< LL. < Gr. *chymos*, juice < *cheein*, to pour], the thick, semifluid mass resulting from gastric digestion of food: chyle is formed from it. —**chy'mous**, *adj.*
**CIA, C.I.A.**, Central Intelligence Agency.
**ci·bo·ri·um** (si-bôr'i-əm, -bō'ri-), *n.* [*pl.* -RIA (-ə)], [ML.; L., a cup < Gr. *kibōrion*, seed vessel of the Egyptian water lily, hence a cup], 1. a canopy covering an altar. 2. a covered cup for holding the consecrated wafers of the Eucharist.
**ci·ca·da** (si-kā'də, -kä'-), *n.* [*pl.* -DAS, -DAE (-dē)], [L.], a large flylike insect with transparent wings; seventeen-year locust: the male makes a loud, shrill sound by vibrating a special sound organ on its undersurface.
**cic·a·trix** (sik'ə-triks), *n.* [*pl.* CICATRICES (sik'ə-trī'sēz)], [L.], 1. in *medicine*, the contracted fibrous tissue at the place where a wound has healed; scar. 2. in *botany*, the scar left on a stem where a branch, leaf, etc. was once attached. Also **cic'a·trice** (-tris). —**cic'a·tri'cial** (-trish'əl), *adj.*
**cic·a·trize** (sik'ə-trīz'), *v.t.* & *v.i.* [-TRIZED, -TRIZING], to heal with the formation of a scar. —**cic'a·tri·za'tion**, *n.*
**Cic·er·o** (sis'ə-rō'), *n.* 1. (*Marcus Tullius Cicero*), Roman statesman, orator, and Stoic philosopher; 106–43 B.C. 2. a city in NE Illinois, near Chicago: pop., 69,000. —**Cic'e·ro'ni·an**, *adj.*
**ci·ce·ro·ne** (sis'ə-rō'ni, chich'ə-; It. chē'che-rô'ne), *n.* [*pl.* -NES; It. -NI (-nē)], [It. < L. *Cicero*, the orator: from the loquacity of guides], a guide who explains the history and chief features of a place to sightseers.
**Cid, the** (sid; Sp. thēth), [Sp. < Ar. *sayyid*, a lord], (born *Rodrigo*, or *Ruy*, *Díaz de Bivar*), 1040?–1099; Spanish hero and soldier of fortune, prominent in Spanish literature.
**-cide** (sīd), [< Fr. *-cide* or L. *-cida* < *caedere*, to kill], a suffix meaning *killer* or *killing*.
**ci·der** (sī'dēr), *n.* [< OFr. < L. < Gr. *sikera* < Heb. *shēkar*, sweet liquor], the juice pressed from apples, used as a beverage or for making vinegar: *sweet cider* is unfermented juice, *hard cider* is fermented.
**C.I.F., c.i.f.**, cost, insurance, and freight.
**ci·gar** (si-gär'), *n.* [Sp. *cigarro*; ? < *cigarra*, cicada: from resemblance to the insect's body], a compact roll of tobacco leaves for smoking.
**cig·a·rette, cig·a·ret** (sig'ə-ret', sig'ə-ret'), *n.* [Fr. dim. of *cigare*, cigar], a small cylinder of finely cut smoking tobacco rolled in thin paper.
**cil·i·a** (sil'i-ə), *n.pl.* [sing. CILIUM (-əm)], [L.], 1. the

eyelashes. 2. in *biology*, hairlike outgrowths of certain cells, capable of vibratory movement. 3. in *botany*, small hairlike processes, as on the underside of some leaves. —**cil′i·ate** (-it, -āt′), **cil′i·at′ed** (-ā′tid), *adj.*

**cil·i·ar·y** (sil′i-er′i), *adj.* of, like, or having cilia.

**Cim·me·ri·an** (si-mêr′i-ən), *n.* any of a mythical people whose land was described as a region of perpetual mist and darkness. *adj.* dark; gloomy.

**cinch** (sinch), *n.* [< Sp. < L. *cingulum*, a girdle < *cingere*, to encircle], 1. a saddle or pack girth. 2. [Colloq.], a sure grip. 3. [Slang], a thing easy to do; sure thing. *v.t.* 1. to tighten a saddle girth on. 2. [Slang], to get a firm hold on. 3. [Slang], to make sure of.

**cin·cho·na** (sin-kō′nə), *n.* [after the Countess del *Chinchon*, wife of a 17th-c. Peruv. viceroy, who was treated with the bark], 1. a tropical tree of South America, Asia, and the East Indies, from the bark of which quinine is obtained. 2. the bitter bark of this tree. —**cin·chon′ic** (-kon′ik), *adj.*

**cin·cho·nize** (sin′kə-niz′), *v.t.* [-NIZED, -NIZING], to treat with cinchona or quinine.

**Cin·cin·nat·i** (sin′sə-nat′i, -nat′ə), *n.* a city in SW Ohio, on the Ohio River: pop., 503,000.

**cinc·ture** (siŋk′chẽr), *n.* [L. *cinctura*, a girdle < *cingere*, to gird], 1. an encircling; enclosure. 2. a belt or girdle. *v.t.* [-TURED, -TURING], to encircle with or as with a cincture.

**cin·der** (sin′dẽr), *n.* [AS. *sinder*], 1. slag, as from the smelting of ores. 2. any matter, as coal or wood, burned but not reduced to ashes. 3. a minute piece of such matter. 4. a coal that is still burning but not flaming. 5. *pl.* the ashes from coal or wood. —**cin′der·y**, *adj.*

**Cin·der·el·la** (sin′dẽr-el′ə), *n.* the title character of a fairy tale, a household drudge who eventually marries a prince.

**cin·e·ma** (sin′ə-mə), *n.* [< *cinematograph*], 1. a motion picture. 2. a motion-picture theater. —**the cinema**, 1. the art or business of motion pictures. 2. motion pictures collectively. —**cin′e·mat′ic** (-mat′ik), *adj.* —**cin′e·mat′i·cal·ly**, *adv.*

**Cin·e·ma·Scope** (sin′ə-mə-skōp′), *n.* see **wide-angle.**

**cin·e·ma·tize** (sin′ə-mə-tīz′), *v.t.* & *v.i.* [-TIZED, -TIZING], to cinematograph.

**cin·e·mat·o·graph** (sin′ə-mat′ə-graf′, -gräf′), *n.* [< Fr. < Gr. *kinēma*, motion + *graphein*, to write], 1. [Brit.], a motion-picture projector. 2. a camera for taking motion pictures. *v.t.* & *v.i.* to take motion pictures (of). —**cin′e·ma·tog′ra·pher** (-mə-tog′rə-fẽr), *n.* —**cin′e·mat′o·graph′ic**, *adj.* —**cin′e·mat′o·graph′i·cal·ly**, *adv.* —**cin′e·ma·tog′ra·phy**, *n.*

**Cin·e·ra·ma** (sin′ə-ram′ə), *n.* see **wide-angle.**

**cin·e·ra·ri·a** (sin′ə-râr′i-ə), *n.* [< L. < *cinis*, ashes], a plant with heart-shaped, ash-gray leaves and daisylike, variously colored flowers.

**cin·e·ra·ri·um** (sin′ə-râr′i-əm), *n.* [*pl.* -RIA (-ə)], [L. < *cinis*, ashes], a place to keep the ashes of cremated bodies. —**cin·er·ar·y** (sin′ə-rer′i), *adj.*

**cin·er·a·tor** (sin′ə-rā′tẽr), *n.* [*cinerarium* + *-ator*], a furnace for cremation; crematory.

**Cin·ga·lese** (siŋ′gə-lēz′), *n.* & *adj.* Singhalese.

**cin·na·bar** (sin′ə-bär′), *n.* [< OFr. < L. < Gr. *kinnabari*; ult. < Per. *zinjifrah*], 1. mercuric sulfide, HgS, a heavy, bright-red mineral, the principal ore of mercury. 2. artificial mercuric sulfide, used as a red pigment. 3. vermilion; brilliant red.

**cin·na·mon** (sin′ə-mən), *n.* [< OFr. < L. < Gr. < Heb. *qinnāmōn*], 1. the yellowish-brown spice made from the dried inner bark of a laurel tree or shrub native to the East Indies. 2. this bark. 3 any tree or shrub from which it is obtained. 4. yellowish brown. *adj.* 1. yellowish-brown. 2. made or flavored with cinnamon.

**cinque·foil** (siŋk′foil′), *n.* [< It. < L. < *quinque*, five + *folium*, leaf], 1. a plant of the rose family with yellow flowers and leaves composed of five leaflets. 2. in *architecture*, a circular design made up of five converging arcs.

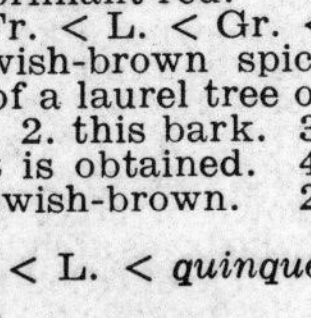
CINQUEFOIL

**C.I.O., CIO**, Congress of Industrial Organizations: see **AFL-CIO.**

**ci·on** (sī′ən), *n.* [OFr.; see SCION], a shoot or bud of a plant, used as a graft: also sp. **scion.**

**Ci·pan·go** (si-paŋ′gō), *n.* [Poetic], Japan.

**ci·pher** (sī′fẽr), *n.* [< OFr. < LL. < Ar. *ṣifr*, nothing < *ṣafara*, to be empty], 1. a naught; zero; 0. 2. a person or thing without importance or value; nonentity. 3. secret writing meant to be understood only by those who have the key to it; code. 4. the key to such a code. 5. a monogram. 6. any Arabic numeral. *v.i.* 1. to solve arithmetical problems. 2. to use secret writing. *v.t.* 1. to solve by arithmetic. 2. to express in secret writing.

**cir., circ.**, 1. circa. 2. circumference.

**cir·ca** (sũr′kə), *prep.* [L.], about: used to indicate an approximate date: as, *circa* 1650: abbrev. **c., ca., cir., circ., C.**

**Cir·cas·si·a** (sẽr-kash′i-ə, -kash′ə), *n.* a region of the U.S.S.R., north of the Caucasus Mountains.

**Cir·cas·si·an** (sẽr-kash′i-ən, -kash′ən), *n.* 1. a member of a group of Caucasian tribes of Circassia. 2. an inhabitant of Circassia. 3. the North Caucasian language of the Circassians. *adj.* of Circassia, its people, or their language.

**Cir·ce** (sũr′si), *n.* in Homer's *Odyssey*, an enchantress who turned men into swine.

**Cir·ce·an, Cir·cae·an** (sẽr-sē′ən), *adj.* of or like Circe; dangerously bewitching.

**cir·cle** (sũr′k'l), *n.* [< OFr. < L. *circulus*, dim. of *circus*; see CIRCUS], 1. a plane figure bounded by a single curved line every point of which is equally distant from the point at the center. 2. the line bounding such a figure; circumference. 3. anything shaped like a circle, as a ring, crown, etc. 4. the orbit of a planet. 5. a semicircular tier of seats in a theater. 6. a cycle; period; complete or recurring series, usually ending as it began. 7. a group of people bound together by common interests; group; coterie. 8. range; extent; scope, as of influence or interest. *v.t.* [-CLED, -CLING], 1. to form a circle around; encompass; surround. 2. to move around, as in a circle. *v.i.* to go around in a circle; revolve. —**cir′cler**, *n.*

**cir·clet** (sũr′klit), *n.* 1. a small circle. 2. a circular band worn as an ornament, esp. on the head.

**cir·cuit** (sũr′kit), *n.* [OFr. < L. *circuitus* < *circum*, around + *ire*, to go], 1. the line or the length of the line forming the boundaries of an area. 2. the area bounded. 3. a going around something; course or journey around. 4. the regular journey through a fixed district of a person performing his duties, as of a circuit court judge. 5. such a district. 6. a chain of theaters at which plays, films, etc. are shown in turn. 7. in *electricity*, a complete or partial path over which current may flow. 8. in *radio*, a hookup. *v.i.* to go in a circuit. *v.t.* to make a circuit of.

**circuit breaker**, a device that automatically interrupts the flow of an electric current.

**circuit court**, formerly, a Federal court presided over by a judge or judges who held court regularly at designated places in a district.

**cir·cu·i·tous** (sẽr-kū′i-təs), *adj.* roundabout; indirect; devious. —**cir·cu′i·tous·ly**, *adv.* —**cir·cu′i·tous·ness, cir·cu′i·ty** [*pl.* -TIES], *n.*

**circuit rider**, a Methodist minister who travels from station to station in his circuit to preach.

**cir·cuit·ry** (sũr′kit-ri), *n.* the scheme or system of an electric circuit or circuits.

**cir·cu·lar** (sũr′kyoo-lẽr), *adj.* [L. *circularis*], 1. in the shape of a circle; round. 2. relating to a circle. 3. moving in a circle. 4. roundabout; circuitous. 5. intended for circulation among a number of people, as a letter. *n.* a circular letter, advertisement, etc. —**cir·cu·lar′i·ty** (-lar′ə-ti), [*pl.* -TIES], *n.* —**cir′cu·lar·ly**, *adv.*

**cir·cu·lar·ize** (sũr′kyoo-lẽr-īz′), *v.t.* [-IZED, -IZING], 1. to make circular; make round. 2. to send circulars to. —**cir′cu·lar·i·za′tion**, *n.* —**cir′cu·lar·iz′er**, *n.*

**circular saw**, a saw in the form of a disk with a toothed edge, rotated at high speed by a motor.

**cir·cu·late** (sũr′kyoo-lāt′), *v.i.* [-LATED, -LATING], [< L. pp. of *circulari*, to form a circle], 1. to move in a circle or circuit and return to the same point, as the blood. 2. to move around from person to person or from place to place, as money, rumor, etc. *v.t.* to cause to circulate. —**cir′cu·la′tor**, *n.* —**cir′cu·la·to′ry** (-lə-tôr′i, -tō′ri), *adj.*

**circulating library**, a library from which books can be borrowed, sometimes for a small daily fee.

**cir·cu·la·tion** (sũr′kyoo-lā′shən), *n.* 1. a circulating or moving around, as water through pipes. 2. the movement of the blood in the veins and arteries throughout the body. 3. the passing of money, news, etc. from person to person or place to place. 4. the distribution of newspapers, magazines, etc.

among readers. 5. the average number of copies of a magazine or newspaper sold in a certain period. —**cir′cu·la′tive**, *adj.*

**cir·cum-**, [< L. *circum*, around, about], a prefix meaning *around, about, surrounding, on all sides.*

**cir·cum·am·bi·ent** (sũr′kəm-am′bi-ənt), *adj.* [*circum-* + *ambient*], enclosing on all sides; surrounding. —**cir′cum·am′bi·ence, cir′cum·am′bi·en·cy**, *n.*

**cir·cum·cise** (sũr′kəm-sīz′), *v.t.* [-CISED, -CISING], [< OFr. < L. < *circum-*, around + *caedere*, to cut], to cut off all or part of the foreskin of. —**cir′cum·ci′sion** (-sizh′ən), *n.*

**cir·cum·fer·ence** (sẽr-kum′fẽr-əns), *n.* [< L. < *circum-*, around + *ferre*, to carry], 1. the line bounding a circle or other rounded surface. 2. the measurement of this line; distance around. —**cir·cum′fer·en′tial** (-en′shal), *adj.*

**cir·cum·flex** (sũr′kəm-fleks′), *n.* [< L. < *circum-*, around + *flectere*, to bend], a mark (ˆ, ˄, ˜) used over a vowel in certain languages, as French, or in phonetic keys to indicate a particular pronunciation: also **circumflex accent.** *adj.* 1. of or marked by a circumflex. 2. curved; bending or twisting around. *v.t.* 1. to curve; bend or twist around. 2. to pronounce or write with a circumflex. —**cir′cum·flex′ion**, *n.*

**cir·cum·flu·ent** (sẽr-kum′flōō-ənt), *adj.* [< L.< *circum-*, around + *fluere*, to flow], flowing around; surrounding: also **cir·cum′flu·ous.**

**cir·cum·fuse** (sũr′kəm-fūz′), *v.t.* [-FUSED, -FUSING], [< L. < *circum-*, around + *fundere*, to pour], 1. to pour or spread (a fluid) around. 2. to surround (*with* a fluid); suffuse (*in*). —**cir′cum·fu′sion**, *n.*

**cir·cum·lo·cu·tion** (sũr′kəm-lō-kū′shən), *n.* [< L. < *circum-*, around + *loqui*, to speak], a roundabout, indirect, or lengthy way of expressing something. —**cir′cum·loc′u·to·ry** (-lok′yoo-tôr′i, -tō′ri), *adj.*

**cir·cum·nav·i·gate** (sũr′kəm-nav′ə-gāt′), *v.t.* [-GATED, -GATING], [< L. < *circum-*, around + *navigare*, to navigate], to sail around (the earth, etc.). —**cir′cum·nav′i·ga′tion**, *n.* —**cir′cum·nav′i·ga′tor**, *n.*

**cir·cum·scribe** (sũr′kəm-skrīb′), *v.t.* [-SCRIBED, -SCRIBING], [< L. < *circum-*, around + *scribere*, to write], 1. to trace a line around; encircle. 2. to limit; confine. 3. in *geometry*, *a*) to draw a figure around (another figure) so as to touch it at as many points as possible. *b*) to be thus drawn around. —**cir′cum·scrip′tion** (-skrip′shən), *n.*

**cir·cum·spect** (sũr′kəm-spekt′), *adj.* [< L. < *circum-*, around + *specere*, to look], carefully attentive to all circumstances; cautious; careful: also **cir′cum·spec′tive.** —**cir′cum·spec′tion, cir′cum·spect′ness**, *n.* —**cir′cum·spect′ly**, *adv.*

**cir·cum·stance** (sũr′kəm-stans′), *n.* [< OFr. < L. < *circum-*, around + *stare*, to stand], 1. a fact or event accompanying another, either incidentally or as a determining factor. 2. *pl.* conditions affecting a person, especially financial conditions: as, in comfortable *circumstances*. 3. ceremony; show: as, pomp and *circumstance*. 4. accompanying or surrounding detail, especially fullness of detail. *v.t.* [-STANCED, -STANCING], to place in certain circumstances. —**under no circumstances**, never; under no conditions. —**under the circumstances**, conditions being what they are or were. —**cir′cum·stanced′**, *adj.*

**cir·cum·stan·tial** (sũr′kəm-stan′shəl), *adj.* 1. having to do with, or depending on, circumstances. 2. incidental. 3. full of details; complete. —**cir′cum·stan′ti·al′i·ty** (-shi-al′ə-ti), *n.* —**cir′cum·stan′tial·ly**, *adv.*

**circumstantial evidence,** in *law*, proof of certain attendant circumstances which is used as evidence to infer the proof of a fact.

**cir·cum·stan·ti·ate** (sũr′kəm-stan′shi-āt′), *v.t.* [-ATED, -ATING], to give detailed proof or support of. —**cir′cum·stan′ti·a′tion**, *n.*

**cir·cum·val·late** (sũr′kəm-val′āt), *v.t.* [-LATED, -LATING], [< L. < *circum-*, around + *vallare*, a wall], to surround with a wall or trench. *adj.* surrounded by a wall or trench. —**cir′cum·val·la′tion**, *n.*

**cir·cum·vent** (sũr′kəm-vent′), *v.t.* [< L. < *circum-*, around + *venire*, to come], 1. to go around; surround. 2. to surround by trickery or craft. 3. to catch in a trap. 4. to gain superiority over; outwit. —**cir′cum·vent′er, cir′cum·ven′tor**, *n.* —**cir′cum·ven′tion**, *n.* —**cir′cum·ven′tive**, *adj.*

**cir·cus** (sũr′kəs), *n.* [L. < Gr. *kirkos*, a circle], 1. in ancient Rome, an oval or oblong arena with tiers of seats around it, used for games, races, etc. 2. a similar arena for a traveling show of acrobats, wild animals, clowns, etc. 3. such a show or the performance of such a show. 4. [Colloq.], any riotously entertaining person, thing, etc.

**cir·rho·sis** (si-rō′sis), *n.* [LL. < Gr. *kirrhos*, tawny: after the yellowish color of the diseased liver], a degenerative disease in an organ of the body, especially the liver, marked by excess formation of connective tissue and the subsequent contraction of the organ. —**cir·rhot′ic** (-rot′ik), *adj.*

**cir·ri-** (sir′i), [< L. *cirrus*], a combining form meaning *curl, ringlet*: also **cirro-, cirrhi-, cirrho-.**

CIRRO-CUMULUS

**cir·ro·cu·mu·lus** (sir′ō-kū′myoo-ləs), *n.* a high formation of small, white, fleecy clouds in rows.

**cir·ro·stra·tus** (sir′ō-strā′təs), *n.* a high, thin, delicate formation of clouds.

**cir·rus** (sir′əs), *n.* [*pl.* -RI (-ī)], [L., a curl], 1. in *biology*, *a*) a plant tendril. *b*) a flexible, threadlike appendage, as a feeler in certain organisms. 2. a formation of filmy, fleecy clouds, generally whitish. —**cir′rose** (-ōs), **cir′rous** (-əs), *adj.*

CIRRUS

**cis-** (sis), [< L. *cis*, on this side], a prefix meaning: 1. *on this side of.* 2. *subsequent to.*

**cis·al·pine** (sis-al′pīn, -pin), *adj.* on this (the Roman, or southern) side of the Alps.

**cis·co** (sis′kō), *n.* [*pl.* -COES, -COS], [< Canad. Fr. < Algonquian], a whitefish or herring found in the Great Lakes.

**Cis·ter·cian** (sis-tũr′shən, -shi-ən), *n.* [< Fr. < ML. *Cistercium* (now *Cîteaux*, France)], a monk of an order (**Cistercian Order**), a strict branch of the Benedictine Order, established in 1098 at Cîteaux, France. *adj.* of the Cistercians.

**cis·tern** (sis′tẽrn), *n.* [< OFr. < L. < *cista* (Gr. *kistē*), a chest], 1. a large tank for storing water, especially rain water. 2. in *anatomy*, a sac or cavity containing a natural fluid.

**cit·a·del** (sit′ə-d'l, -del′), *n.* [< Fr. < It. dim. of *cittade*, city < L. *civitas*, state], 1. a fortress on a commanding height for defense of a city. 2. a fortified place; stronghold. 3. a refuge; place of retreat.

**ci·ta·tion** (sī-tā′shən), *n.* [< OFr. < L. pp. of *citare*; see CITE], 1. a summons to appear before a court of law. 2. a citing; quoting. 3. a passage cited; quotation. 4. honorable mention in an official report for meritorious service, as in the armed forces. 5. a reference to a legal statute, a previous law case, etc. —**ci·ta·to·ry** (sī′tə-tôr′i, -tō′ri), *adj.*

**cite** (sīt), *v.t.* [CITED, CITING], [< Fr. < L. *citare*, to summon < *ciere*, to rouse], 1. to summon to appear before a court of law. 2. to summon; stir to action. 3. to quote (a book, passage, writer, etc.). 4. to refer to or mention by way of example, proof, etc. 5. to mention in an official report for meritorious service, as in the armed forces. —**cit·a·ble, cite·a·ble** (sīt′ə-b'l), *adj.*

**cith·a·ra** (sith′ə-rə), *n.* [L. < Gr. *kithara*], an ancient musical instrument somewhat like a lyre.

**cith·er** (sith′ẽr), *n.* [< Fr. < L. *cithara*], 1. a cithara. 2. loosely, a cithern or zither.

**cith·ern** (sith′ẽrn), *n.* [< Fr. (see CITHER)], a stringed musical instrument of the 16th century, somewhat like a guitar: also **cittern.**

**cit·i·fied** (sit′i-fīd′), *adj.* having the manners, dress, etc. of city people: also sp. **cityfied.**

**cit·i·zen** (sit′ə-z'n), *n.* [Anglo-Fr. *citizein* < OFr. < *cite*; see CITY], 1. formerly, an inhabitant of a town or city. 2. a member of a state or nation who owes allegiance to it by birth or naturalization and is entitled to full civil rights. 3. a civilian, as distinguished from a soldier, policeman, etc. —**citizen of the world**, a cosmopolitan person.

**cit·i·zen·ry** (sit′ə-z'n-ri), *n.* [*pl.* -RIES], citizens collectively.

**cit·i·zen·ship** (sit′ə-z'n-ship′), *n.* 1. the status or condition of a citizen. 2. the duties, rights, and privileges of this status.

**cit·rate** (sit′rāt, -rit, sī′trāt), *n.* [< *citrus* + *-ate*], a salt or ester of citric acid.

**cit·ric** (sit′rik), *adj.* [< *citrus* + *-ic*], 1. of or from lemons, oranges, or similar fruits. 2. designating or of an acid, $C_6H_8O_7$, obtained from such fruits, used in making dyes, citrates, etc.

**cit·rin** (sit′rin), *n.* [< *citrus* + *-in*], vitamin P, found in lemon juice and paprika.

**cit·rine** (sit′rin), *adj.* [< *citrus* + *-ine*], lemon-yellow. *n.* 1. lemon yellow. 2. a yellow quartz.

**cit·ron** (sit′rən), *n.* [< Fr. < It. *citrone* < L. *citrus*;

see CITRUS], 1. a yellow, thick-skinned fruit resembling a lemon but larger and less acid. 2. the semitropical tree or shrub bearing this fruit. 3. the candied rind of this fruit, used in fruitcake, etc. 4. a kind of watermelon (**citron melon**), with hard, white flesh.

**cit·ron·el·la** (sit′rə-nel′ə), *n.* [see CITRON], 1. a volatile, sharp-smelling oil used in perfume, soap, etc. and to keep insects away: also **citronella oil.** 2. the southern Asiatic grass from which this oil is derived.

**cit·rous** (sit′rəs), *adj.* of the trees or fruit of the citrus group.

**cit·rus** (sit′rəs), *n.* [L., citron tree; akin to Gr *kitron* (? to Gr. *kedros*, cedar)], 1. any of a group of trees and shrubs that bear oranges, lemons, limes, or other such fruit. 2. any such fruit. *adj.* of these trees and shrubs.

**cit·tern** (sit′ẽrn), *n.* a cithern.

**cit·y** (sit′i), *n.* [*pl.* -IES (-iz)], [< OFr. *cite* < L. *civitas*, orig. citizenship < *civis*, citizen], 1. a large, important town. 2. in the U.S., an incorporated municipality whose boundaries and powers of self-government are defined by a charter from its State. 3. in Canada, a municipality of the highest rank. 4. all the people of a city. *adj.* of or in a city.

**cit·y-bred** (sit′i-bred′), *adj.* raised in a city.

**city chicken,** strips of pork or veal wound on a skewer, breaded, and fried.

**city hall,** 1. a building in which are the offices of a municipal government; hence, 2. the current municipal administration.

**city manager,** an administrator appointed by a city council to act as manager of the city.

**cit·y-state** (sit′i-stāt′), *n.* a state made up of an independent city and the territory directly controlled by it, as in ancient Greece.

**Ciu·dad Tru·jil·lo** (sū-*thäth′* trōō-hē′yô), Santo Domingo, the capital of the Dominican Republic: the former name.

**civ.,** 1. civil. 2. civilian.

**civ·et** (siv′it), *n.* [< Fr. < It. *zibetto* < Ar. *zabād*], 1. a thick, yellowish, fatty secretion with a musklike scent, obtained from glands in the anal pouch of the civet cat: it is used in making some perfumes. 2. the civet cat or its fur.

**civet cat,** a catlike, flesh-eating animal of Africa and S Asia, with a spotted, yellowish fur.

**civ·ic** (siv′ik), *adj.* [< L. *civicus* < *civis*, citizen], 1. of a city. 2. of citizens. 3. of citizenship. —**civ′i·cal·ly,** *adv.*

**civ·ics** (siv′iks), *n.pl.* [construed as sing.], the branch of political science dealing with civic affairs and the duties and rights of citizenship.

**civ·il** (siv′'l, -il), *adj.* [Fr. < L. *civilis* < *civis*, citizen], 1. of a citizen or citizens. 2. of a community of citizens, their government, or their interrelations: as, *civil* affairs. 3. polite; urbane. 4. civilized. 5. not military, naval, or ecclesiastical: as, *civil* law. 6. in *law*, relating to the private rights of individuals and to legal actions involving these.

**civil disobedience,** passive resistance.

**civil engineering,** the branch of engineering dealing with the design and construction of highways, bridges, harbors, etc. —**civil engineer.**

**ci·vil·ian** (sə-vil′yən), *n.* [< OFr. < L.; see CIVIL], any person not in military or naval service. *adj.* of civilians; nonmilitary.

**ci·vil·i·ty** (sə-vil′ə-ti), *n.* [*pl.* -TIES], 1. courtesy; consideration. 2. a civil, or polite, act.

**civ·i·li·za·tion** (siv′'l-i-zā′shən, -ī-), *n.* 1. a civilizing or becoming civilized. 2. the state of being civilized; social organization of a high order. 3. the total culture of a people, nation, period, etc.: as, Aztec *civilization*. 4. the countries and peoples considered to have reached a high state of social and cultural development.

**civ·i·lize** (siv′'l-īz′), *v.t.* [-LIZED, -LIZING], [< Fr. < L.; see CIVIL], 1. to bring out of a condition of savagery or barbarism. 2. to better the habits or manners of; refine. —**civ′i·liz′a·ble,** *adj.* —**civ′i·liz′er,** *n.*

**civ·i·lized** (siv′'l-īzd′), *adj.* 1. advanced in social organization and the arts and sciences. 2. of people or countries thus advanced. 3. cultured and courteous; refined.

**civil law,** the body of law, developed from Roman law, having to do with private rights.

**civil liberties,** liberties guaranteed to the individual by law; rights of thinking, speaking, and acting as one likes without hindrance except in the interests of the public welfare.

**civ·il·ly** (siv′'l-i), *adv.* 1. with civility; politely. 2. by civil law.

**civil marriage,** a marriage performed by a public official, not by a clergyman.

**civil rights,** those rights guaranteed to the individual, especially by the 13th and 14th Amendments to the Constitution of the U.S.

**civil service,** all those employed in government administration except in the army, navy, legislature, or judiciary. —**civil servant.**

**civil war,** war between different sections or factions of the same nation. —**the Civil War,** the war between the North (the Union) and the South (the Confederacy) in the U.S. (1861–1865).

**civ·vies, civ·ies** (siv′iz), *n.pl.* [Slang], civilian clothes; mufti.

**ck.,** [*pl.* CKS.], 1. cask. 2. check.

**Cl,** in *chemistry*, chlorine.

**cl.,** 1. centiliter(s). 2. claim. 3. class. 4. clause.

**clab·ber** (klab′ẽr), *n.* [Ir. *clabar*], thick, sour milk; curdled milk. *v.i. & v.t.* to curdle.

**clack** (klak), *v.i. & v.t.* [echoic], 1. to make or cause to make an abrupt, sharp sound. 2. to chatter; prate; blab. *n.* 1. an abrupt, sharp sound. 2. chatter. —**clack′er,** *n.*

**clad** (klad), occasional pt. and pp. of **clothe.** *adj.* clothed; dressed.

**claim** (klām), *v.t.* [< OFr. < L. *clamare*, to cry out], 1. to demand as rightfully belonging to one; assert one's right to, as a title, etc. that should be recognized. 2. to call for; require; deserve: as, this problem *claims* our attention. 3. to assert; maintain. *v.i.* to assert a claim. *n.* 1. a demand for something rightfully due; assertion of a right. 2. a right or title to something. 3. something claimed, as land staked out by a settler. 4. an assertion. —**claim′a·ble,** *adv.* —**claim′er,** *n.*

**claim·ant** (klām′ənt), *n.* one who makes a claim.

**clair·voy·ance** (klâr-voi′əns), *n.* [Fr. < *clairvoyant*], 1. the ability to perceive things that are not in sight or that cannot be seen, attributed to some people. 2. keen perception; great insight.

**clair·voy·ant** (klâr-voi′ənt), *adj.* [Fr. < *clair*, clear + ppr. of *voir*, to see], of or apparently having clairvoyance. *n.* a clairvoyant person.

**clam** (klam), *n.* [*pl.* CLAMS, CLAM; see PLURAL, II, D, 1], [< earlier *clam*, a clamp], 1. a variety of hard-shelled bivalve mollusk, living in the shallows of the sea, or in fresh water. 2. the soft edible part of such a mollusk. *v.i.* [CLAMMED, CLAMMING], to dig, or go digging, for clams.

**clam·bake** (klam′bāk′), *n.* a picnic at which steamed or baked clams and other foods are served.

**clam·ber** (klam′bẽr), *v.i. & v.t.* [ME. *clamberen*], to climb by using both hands and feet; climb with difficulty or in a clumsy manner. *n.* a clumsy or hard climb. —**clam′ber·er,** *n.*

**clam·my** (klam′i), *adj.* [-MIER, -MIEST], [< AS. < *clam*, clay], moist, cold, and slightly sticky. —**clam′mi·ly,** *adv.* —**clam′mi·ness,** *n.*

**clam·or** (klam′ẽr), *n.* [< OFr. < L. < *clamare*, to cry out], 1. a loud outcry; uproar. 2. a noisy demand or complaint. 3. a loud, sustained noise. *v.i.* to make a clamor; demand or complain noisily. *v.t.* to express with clamor. —**clam′or·er,** *n.*

**clam·or·ous** (klam′ẽr-əs), *adj.* 1. noisy; vociferous. 2. loudly demanding or complaining. —**clam′or·ous·ly,** *adv.* —**clam′or·ous·ness,** *n.*

**clam·our** (klam′ẽr), *n., v.i. & v.t.* clamor: Brit. spelling.

**clamp** (klamp), *n.* [< LG. *klampe*], a device for clasping or fastening things together; esp., an appliance with two parts brought together to grip something. *v.t.* to fasten or brace with a clamp. —**clamp down (on),** [Colloq.], to become more strict (with).

CLAMP

**clan** (klan), *n.* [< Gael. *clann*, offspring < L. *planta*, offshoot], 1. a social group, as in the Scottish Highlands, composed of several families claiming descent from a common ancestor. 2. a group of people with interests in common; clique.

**clan·des·tine** (klan-des′tin), *adj.* [< Fr. < L. *clandestinus* < *clam*, secret], secret or hidden; surreptitious; underhand. —**clan·des′tine·ly,** *adv.*

**clang** (klaŋ), *v.i. & v.t.* [prob. echoic], 1. to make or cause to make a loud, sharp, ringing sound, as

by striking metal. 2. to strike together with this sound. *n.* this sound.
**clan·gor** (klaŋ′gẽr, -ẽr), *n.* [L. < *clangere*], 1. a clang. 2. a persistent clanging. *v.i.* to clang. —**clan′gor·ous,** *adj.* —**clan′gor·ous·ly,** *adv.*
**clan·gour** (klaŋ′gẽr, -ẽr), *n.* clangor: Brit. spelling.
**clank** (klaŋk), *n.* [echoic], a sharp, metallic sound, not as resonant as a clang. *v.i. & v.t.* to make or cause to make this sound.
**clan·nish** (klan′ish), *adj.* 1. of a clan. 2. tending to associate closely and exclude others; cliquish. —**clan′nish·ly,** *adv.* —**clan′nish·ness,** *n.*
**clans·man** (klanz′mən), *n.* [*pl.* -MEN], a member of a clan. —**clans′wom′an** [*pl.* -WOMEN], *n.*
**clap** (klap), *v.i.* [CLAPPED or *archaic* CLAPT, CLAPPING], [AS. *clæppan*, to beat], 1. to make a sudden, explosive sound, as of two flat surfaces being struck together. 2. to strike the hands together, as in applause. *v.t.* 1. to strike together briskly and loudly. 2. to applaud by clapping the hands. 3. to strike with an open hand. 4. to put, move, etc. swiftly and effectively: as, he was *clapped* into jail. *n.* 1. the sound of clapping. 2. the act of striking the hands together. 3. a sharp blow; slap.
**clap·board** (klab′ẽrd, klap′bôrd′, -bōrd′), *n.* [partial transl. of G. *klapholz* < *klappen*, to fit + *holz*, wood], a thin board with one edge thicker than the other, used for covering the outer walls of frame houses. *v.t.* to cover with clapboards.
**clap·per** (klap′ẽr), *n.* 1. a person who claps. 2. a thing that makes a clapping sound, as the tongue of a bell or, facetiously, that of a person.
**clapt** (klapt), archaic pt. and pp. of **clap.**
**clap·trap** (klap′trap′), *n.* [*clap* (applause) + *trap*], showy, insincere, empty talk, intended only to get applause. *adj.* showy and cheap.
**claque** (klak), *n.* [Fr. < *claquer*, to clap], 1. a group of people paid to go to a play, opera, etc. and applaud. 2. a group of fawning followers.
**clar·et** (klar′ət), *n.* [< OFr. dim. of *cler* (L. *clarus*), clear], 1. a dry red wine; esp., red Bordeaux. 2. purplish red: also **claret red.** *adj.* purplish-red.
**clar·i·fy** (klar′ə-fī′), *v.t. & v.i.* [-FIED, FYING], [< OFr. < L. < *clarus*, clear + *facere*, to make], 1. to make or become clear and free from impurities: said of liquids, etc. 2. to make or become easier to understand: as, *clarify* your meaning. —**clar′i·fi·ca′tion,** *n.* —**clar′i·fi′er,** *n.*
**clar·i·net** (klar′ə-net′, klar′ə-net′), *n.* [Fr. *clarinette*, dim. of *clarine*, little bell; ult. < L. *clarus*, clear], a single-reed, wood-wind instrument with a long wooden or metal tube and a flaring bell, played by means of holes and keys. —**clar′i·net′ist, clar′i·net′tist,** *n.*

CLARINET

**clar·i·on** (klar′i-ən), *n.* [OFr.; LL. *clario* < L. *clarus*, clear], 1. a kind of trumpet producing clear, sharp, shrill tones. 2. [Poetic], the sound of a clarion. *adj.* clear, sharp, and shrill: as, a *clarion* call. *v.t.* to announce forcefully or loudly.
**clar·i·o·net** (klar′i-ə-net′), *n.* a clarinet.
**clar·i·ty** (klar′ə-ti), *n.* [OFr. *clarte*; L. *claritas* < *clarus*, clear], clearness (in various senses).
**clash** (klash), *v.i.* [echoic], 1. to collide with a loud, harsh, metallic noise. 2. to conflict; disagree. *v.t.* to strike, shut, etc. with a loud, harsh noise. *n.* 1. the sound of clashing. 2. conflict; disagreement. —**clash′er,** *n.*
**clasp** (klasp, kläsp), *n.* [ME. *claspe*], 1. a fastening, as a hook or catch, to hold two things or parts together. 2. a grasping; embrace. 3. a grip of the hand. *v.t.* [CLASPED or *archaic* CLASPT, CLASPING], 1. to fasten with a clasp. 2. to hold tightly with the arms or hands; embrace. 3. to grip with the hand. 4. to cling to. —**clasp′er,** *n.*
**class** (klas, kläs), *n.* [< Fr. < L. *classis* < Gr. < *kalein*, to call], 1. a number of people or things grouped together because of certain likenesses; kind; sort. 2. a group of people considered as a unit; esp., a social rank: as, the working *class*. 3. high social rank or caste. 4. the division of society into ranks or castes. 5. a group of students taught together. 6. a meeting of such a group. 7. a group of students graduating together. 8. grade or quality: as, to travel first *class*. 9. in *biology*, a group of animals or plants ranking below a phylum and above an order. 10. [Slang], excellence, as of style. *v.t.* to classify. *v.i.* to be classed. —**in a class by itself** (or **oneself**), unique. —**class′a·ble,** *adj.*
**class.,** 1. classic. 2. classical. 3. classification.
**class consciousness,** an awareness of belonging to an economic class in the social order. —**class-conscious** (klas′kon′shəs, kläs′-), *adj.*
**clas·sic** (klas′ik), *adj.* [L. *classicus*, superior < *classis*, a class], 1. of the highest class; most representative of the excellence of its kind. 2. *a*) of the art, literature, and culture of the ancient Greeks and Romans. *b*) like their literary and artistic standards; hence, *c*) balanced, formal, objective, regular, simple, etc. 3. [Colloq.], famous as traditional or typical. *n.* 1. *a*) a literary or artistic work generally recognized as of the highest excellence. *b*) a creator of such works. 2. [Colloq.], a famous traditional or typical event: as, the Derby is a *classic*. —**the classics,** the literature of the ancient Greeks and Romans.
**clas·si·cal** (klas′i-k'l), *adj.* 1. classic (senses 1 & 2). 2. learned in and devoted to Greek and Roman culture, literature, etc. 3. designating or of music that conforms to certain established standards of form, complexity, musical literacy, etc.: distinguished from *popular, romantic*. 4. standard and traditionally authoritative, not new and experimental: as, an expert in *classical* economics. —**clas·si·cal·i·ty** (klas′i-kal′ə-ti), **clas′si·cal·ness,** *n.* —**clas′si·cal·ly,** *adv.*
**clas·si·cism** (klas′ə-siz'm), *n.* [*classic* + *-ism*], 1. the aesthetic principles and methods of ancient Greece and Rome: generally contrasted with *romanticism*. 2. adherence to these principles. 3. knowledge of the literature and art of ancient Greece and Rome. 4. a Greek or Latin idiom or expression. Also **clas′si·cal·ism** (-i-k'l-iz'm). —**clas′si·cist, clas′si·cal·ist,** *n.*
**clas·si·cize** (klas′ə-sīz′), *v.t.* [-CIZED, -CIZING], to make classic. *v.i.* to use a classic style.
**clas·si·fi·ca·tion** (klas′ə-fi-kā′shən), *n.* an arrangement according to some systematic division into classes or groups. —**clas′si·fi·ca′to·ry,** *adj.*
**classified advertising,** advertising under such listings as *help wanted, lost and found*, etc.
**clas·si·fy** (klas′ə-fī′), *v.t.* [-FIED, -FYING], 1. to arrange or group in classes according to some system or principle. 2. to designate (a government document) as secret or confidential. —**clas′si·fi′a·ble,** *adj.* —**clas′si·fi′er,** *n.*
**class·mate** (klas′māt′, kläs′-), *n.* a member of the same class at a school or college.
**class·room** (klas′rōōm′, kläs′room′), *n.* a room where a class is taught in a school or college.
**class·y** (klas′i), *adj.* [-IER, -IEST], [Slang], first-class, especially in style or manner.
**clat·ter** (klat′ẽr), *v.i.* [< AS. < *clatrung*, a clatter], 1. to make, or move with, a rapid succession of loud, sharp noises, as dishes rattling. 2. to chatter noisily. *v.t.* to cause to clatter. *n.* 1. a rapid succession of loud, sharp noises. 2. a tumult; hubbub. 3. noisy chatter. —**clat′ter·er,** *n.* —**clat′ter·ing,** *adj. & n.* —**clat′ter·ing·ly,** *adv.*
**clause** (klôz), *n.* [OFr. < LL. *clausa* < L. pp. of *claudere*, to close], 1. a group of words containing a subject and verb, usually forming part of a compound or complex sentence: cf. **main clause, subordinate clause.** 2. a particular article, stipulation, or provision in a formal or legal document. —**claus′al,** *adj.*
**claus·tro·pho·bi·a** (klôs′trə-fō′bi-ə), *n.* [< L. *claustrum*, enclosed place; + *-phobia*], an abnormal fear of being in enclosed or confined places.
**cla·vate** (klā′vāt), *adj.* [< L. *clava*, a club; + *-ate*], club-shaped.
**clave** (klāv), archaic pt. of **cleave.**
**clav·i·chord** (klav′ə-kôrd′), *n.* [< LL. < L. *clavis*, a key + *chorda*, a string], a stringed musical instrument with a keyboard, from which the piano developed.
**clav·i·cle** (klav′ə-k'l), *n.* [< Fr. < L. *clavicula*, dim. of *clavis*, a key], a small bone connecting the breastbone with the shoulder blade; collarbone. —**cla·vic·u·lar** (klə-vik′yoo-lẽr), *adj.*
**cla·vi·er** (klav′i-ẽr; *also, and for* 2 *always*, klə-vêr′), *n.* [Fr., keyboard < L. *clavis*, a key], 1. the keyboard of an organ, piano, etc. 2. any stringed instrument that has a keyboard; now, usually, a piano.
**claw** (klô), *n.* [AS. *clawu*], 1. a sharp, hooked nail on the foot of an animal or bird. 2. a foot with such nails. 3. the pincers (chela) of a lobster, crab, etc. 4. anything resembling or regarded as a claw, as a hammer (**claw hammer**) with one end forked and curved, used to pull nails. *v.t. & v.i.* to scratch, clutch, or tear with or as with claws.
**clay** (klā), *n.* [AS. *clæg*], 1. a firm, plastic earth, used in the manufacture of bricks, pottery, etc. 2. *a*) earth. *b*) the human body. —**clay′ey,** *adj.* —**clay′ish,** *adj.*

**Clay, Henry** (klā), 1777–1852; U.S. statesman.
**clay·more** (klā'môr', -mōr'), *n.* [Gael. *claidheamh-mor*, great sword], a large, two-edged broadsword formerly used by Scottish Highlanders.
**clay pigeon,** a disk of clay, etc. tossed into the air from the trap as a target in trapshooting.
**-cle** (k'l), [< L. dim. suffix *-culus*, *-cula*, *-culum*], a diminutive suffix, as in *particle*.
**clean** (klēn), *adj.* [AS. *clæne*], 1. free from dirt or impurities; unsoiled; unstained. 2. morally pure; sinless. 3. habitually avoiding filth. 4. shapely; well-formed. 5. clever; deft. 6. having no obstructions or flaws; clear; regular. 7. entire; complete; thorough. 8. fit for food. *adv.* 1. in a clean manner. 2. completely; wholly. *v.t.* 1. to make clean. 2. to prepare (fish, fowl, etc.) for cooking. *v.i.* 1. to be made clean. 2. to perform the act of cleaning. **—clean out,** 1. to empty. 2. [Colloq.], to use up the money, etc. of. **—clean up,** 1. to make clean or neat. 2. to get washed, combed, etc. 3. [Colloq.], to finish. 4. [Slang], to make much profit. **—come clean,** [Slang], to confess. **—with clean hands,** without guilt. **—clean'a·ble,** *adj.* **—clean'ness,** *n.*
**clean-cut** (klēn'kut'), *adj.* 1. clearly and sharply outlined. 2. well-formed. 3. distinct; clear. 4. good-looking, trim, neat, etc.
**clean·er** (klēn'ēr), *n.* 1. one whose work is cleaning up rooms, buildings, etc. 2. one who or that which dry-cleans. 3. a tool, device, or preparation for cleaning.
**clean·ly** (klen'li), *adj.* [-LIER, -LIEST], 1. clean; having clean habits. 2. always kept clean. **—clean'li·ly,** *adv.* **—clean'li·ness,** *n.*
**clean·ly** (klēn'li), *adv.* in a clean manner.
**cleanse** (klenz), *v.t.* [CLEANSED, CLEANSING], [AS. *clænsian*], 1. to make clean. 2. to free from guilt; make pure. 3. to purge. **—cleans'a·ble,** *adj.* **—cleans'er,** *n.*
**clean·up** (klēn'up'), *n.* 1. a cleaning up. 2. [Slang], profit; gain.
**clear** (klêr), *adj.* [< OFr. < L. *clarus*], 1. bright; light; free from clouds or mist. 2. transparent; not turbid. 3. easily seen; sharply defined; distinct. 4. perceptive; orderly: as, a *clear* mind. 5. not obscure; easily understood. 6. obvious. 7. certain; positive. 8. capable of being heard or understood: said of voices. 9. free from guilt; innocent. 10. free from charges or deductions; net. 11. absolute; complete. 12. free from obstruction; open. 13. emptied of freight or cargo. 14. free from debt or legal charges. *adv.* 1. in a clear manner. 2. [Colloq.], all the way: as, *clear* through the town. *v.t.* 1. to make clear or bright. 2. to free from impurities, obstructions, etc. 3. to make intelligible or lucid. 4. to open: as, to *clear* a path. 5. to remove; get rid of. 6. to unload; empty. 7. to free (a person or thing) *of* or *from* something. 8. to prove the innocence of; acquit. 9. to pass or leap over, by, etc. 10. to discharge (a debt) by paying it. 11. to free (a ship or cargo) by satisfying harbor requirements. 12. to make (a given amount) as profit; net. 13. in *banking*, to pass (a check, etc.) through a clearinghouse. *v.i.* 1. to become clear, unclouded, etc. 2. to satisfy harbor requirements in leaving a port. 3. in *banking*, to exchange checks and bills, and balance accounts, through a clearinghouse. *n.* 1. a clear space. 2. clearance. **—clear away,** 1. to remove so as to leave a cleared space. 2. to go away. **—clear off,** to clear away. **—clear out,** 1. to clear by emptying. 2. [Colloq.], to depart. **—clear the air** (or **atmosphere**), to get rid of emotional tensions, etc. **—clear up,** 1. to make or become clear. 2. to make orderly. 3. to explain. **—in the clear,** 1. in the open. 2. [Colloq.], free from guilt, etc. **—clear'a·ble,** *adj.* **—clear'er,** *n.* **—clear'ly,** *adv.* **—clear'ness,** *n.*
**clear·ance** (klêr'əns), *n.* 1. a making clear. 2. the clear space between an object and that which it passes through, by, under, etc. 3. in *banking*, the adjustment of accounts in a clearinghouse. 4. a certificate authorizing a ship to enter or leave port: also **clearance papers.**
**clear-cut** (klêr'kut'), *adj.* 1. clearly and sharply outlined. 2. distinct; plain.
**clear·head·ed** (klêr'hed'id), *adj.* having a clear mind. **—clear'head'ed·ly,** *adv.* **—clear'head'ed·ness,** *n.*
**clear·ing** (klêr'iŋ), *n.* 1. a making clear or being cleared. 2. a plot of land cleared of trees. 3. in *banking*, clearance.
**clear·ing·house** (klêr'iŋ-hous'), *n.* an office maintained by a group of banks as a center for exchanging checks, balancing accounts, etc.
**clear-sight·ed** (klêr'sīt'id), *adj.* 1. seeing clearly. 2. understanding or thinking clearly. **—clear'sight'ed·ly,** *adv.* **—clear'sight'ed·ness,** *n.*
**clear·sto·ry** (klêr'stôr'i, -stō'ri), *n.* [*pl.* -RIES], a clerestory.
**cleat** (klēt), *n.* [< AS. hyp. *cleat*, a lump], 1. a piece of wood or metal, often wedge-shaped, fastened to something to strengthen it or give secure footing. 2. in *nautical usage*, a small piece of wood or metal with projecting ends on which a rope can be fastened. *v.t.* to fasten to or with a cleat.
**cleav·age** (klēv'ij), *n.* 1. a cleaving; splitting; dividing. 2. the manner in which a thing splits. 3. a cleft; fissure; division. 4. in *biology*, cell division that transforms the fertilized ovum into the blastula.
**cleave** (klēv), *v.t.* [CLEFT (kleft) or CLEAVED or CLOVE (klōv), CLEFT or CLEAVED or CLOVEN (klō'v'n), CLEAVING; *archaic* pt. CLAVE (klāv), *poetic* pp. CLOVE], [AS. *cleofan*], 1. to divide by a blow, as of an ax; split. 2. to pierce. 3. to sever; disunite. *v.i.* 1. to split; separate. 2. to make one's way by cutting. **—cleav'a·ble,** *adj.*
**cleave** (klēv), *v.i.* [CLEAVED, CLEAVING; *archaic* pt. CLAVE (klāv), CLOVE (klōv)], [< AS. *cleofian*], 1. to adhere; cling. 2. to be faithful (*to*).
**cleav·er** (klēv'ēr), *n.* a heavy, sharp-edged cleaving tool used by butchers.

CLEAVER

**cleav·ers** (klēv'ērz), *n.* [*pl.* CLEAVERS], [< *cleave* (to cling)], a plant with stalkless leaves, clusters of small flowers, and prickly stems.
**clef** (klef), *n.* [Fr. < OFr. < L. *clavis*, a key], a symbol used in music to indicate the pitch of the notes on the staff: there are three clefs, G (treble), F (bass), and C (tenor or alto).
**cleft** (kleft), alt. pt. and pp. of **cleave** (to split). *adj.* split; divided.
**cleft** (kleft), *n.* [AS. hyp. *clyft* < *cleofan*], an opening made by cleaving; crack; fissure.
**clem·a·tis** (klem'ə-tis), *n.* [L. < Gr. < *klēma*, vine, twig], a perennial herb or woody vine of the crowfoot family, with bright-colored flowers.
**Cle·men·ceau, Georges** (zhôrzh' klā'män'sō'; Eng. klem'ən-sō'), 1841–1929; premier of France (1906–1909; 1917–1920).
**clem·en·cy** (klem'ən-si), *n.* [*pl.* -CIES], [< L. < *clemens*, merciful], 1. forbearance, leniency, or mercy. 2. mildness, as of weather.
**Clem·ens, Samuel Lang·horne** (laŋ'hôrn' klem'ənz), see **Twain, Mark.**
**clem·ent** (klem'ənt), *adj.* [L. *clemens*], 1. lenient; merciful. 2. mild, as weather. **—clem'ent·ly,** *adv.*
**clench** (klench), *v.t.* [< AS. *-clencan* (in *beclencan*), lit., to make cling], 1. to clinch, as a nail. 2. to bring together tightly; close firmly, as the teeth or fist. 3. to grip tightly. *n.* 1. a firm grip. 2. a device that clenches. **—clench'er,** *n.*
**Cle·o·pa·tra** (klē'ə-pā'trə, -pat'rə, -ō-pä'trə), *n.* queen of Egypt (51–30 B.C.); lived 69–30 B.C.
**clep·sy·dra** (klep'si-drə), *n.* [*pl.* -DRAS, -DRAE (-drē')], [L. < Gr. < *kleptein*, to steal + *hydōr*, water], a device for measuring time by marking the gradual flow of a liquid through a small opening.
**clep·to·ma·ni·a** (klep'tə-mā'ni-ə), *n.* kleptomania. **—clep'to·ma'ni·ac** (-ak), *n.*
**clere·sto·ry** (klêr'stôr'i, -stō'ri), *n.* [*pl.* -RIES], [*clere* (for *clear*) + *story* (floor)], 1. the wall of a church rising above the roofs of the flanking aisles and containing windows for lighting the central part of the structure. 2. any similar windowed wall. Also sp. **clearstory.**
**cler·gy** (klũr'ji), *n.* [*pl.* -GIES], [< OFr. < LL. *clericus;* see CLERK], men ordained for religious service, as ministers, priests, etc., collectively.
**cler·gy·man** (klũr'ji-mən), *n.* [*pl.* -MEN], a member of the clergy; minister, priest, etc.
**cler·ic** (kler'ik), *n.* [LL. *clericus;* see CLERK], a clergyman. *adj.* of a clergyman or the clergy.
**cler·i·cal** (kler'i-k'l), *adj.* [*cleric* + *-al*], 1. relating to a clergyman or the clergy. 2. relating to an office clerk or clerks; of office work. 3. favoring the influence of the clergy in political matters. *n.* 1. a clergyman. 2. one who believes in advancing

the political power of the clergy. **—cler′i·cal·ly,** *adv.*

**cler·i·cal·ism** (kler′i-k'l-iz'm), *n.* political influence or power of the clergy. **—cler′i·cal·ist,** *n.*

**clerk** (klũrk; Brit. klärk), *n.* [< OFr. & AS. < LL. *clericus;* Gr. *klērikos,* priest < *klēros,* clergy], 1. a layman who has minor duties in a church. 2. an office worker who keeps accounts and records, does filing and copying, etc.: in public service, other duties may be involved, as in the case of a city *clerk.* 3. a person employed in selling goods in a store. 4. [Archaic], *a)* a clergyman. *b)* a scholar. *v.i.* to work or be employed as a clerk. **—clerk′ing,** *n.* **—clerk′ship,** *n.*

**clerk·ly** (klũrk′li), *adj.* [-LIER, -LIEST], 1. of, like, or characteristic of a clerk. 2. of the clergy; clerical. 3. [Archaic], scholarly. *adv.* in a clerkly manner. **—clerk′li·ness,** *n.*

**Cleve·land** (klēv′lənd), *n.* a city in NE Ohio, on Lake Erie: pop., 876,000 (metropolitan area, 1,797,000).

**Cleveland, Gro·ver** (grō′vẽr), (*Stephen Grover Cleveland*), 1837–1908; 22d and 24th president of the U.S. (1885–1889; 1893–1897).

**Cleveland Heights,** a city in NE Ohio: a suburb of Cleveland: pop., 62,000.

**clev·er** (klev′ẽr), *adj.* [earlier *cliver;* ? < AS. *clifian,* to cleave], 1. skillful in doing something; adroit; dexterous. 2. intelligent; ingenious; quick-witted; bright. 3. showing ingenuity or intelligence. **—clev′er·ly,** *adv.* **—clev′er·ness,** *n.*

**clev·is** (klev′is), *n.* [akin to *cleave* (to cling)], a U-shaped piece of iron with holes in the ends through which a pin is run to attach one thing to another, as a whippletree to a wagon tongue.

CLEVIS

**clew** (klōō), *n.* [< AS. *cleowen*], 1. a ball of thread or yarn. 2. something that leads out of a maze, perplexity, etc., or helps to solve a problem: usually sp. **clue.** 3. in *nautical usage, a)* a lower corner of a square sail or the lower corner aft of a fore-and-aft sail. *b)* a metal loop in the corner of a sail. *v.t.* 1. to wind up into a ball (usually with *up*). 2. to trace, as by a clew. Also sp. **clue. —clew down,** to lower (a sail) by the clews. **—clew up,** to raise (a sail) by the clews.

**cli·ché** (klē-shā′), *n.* [*pl.* -CHÉS (-shāz′)], [Fr. < *clicher,* to stereotype], a trite or commonplace expression or idea.

**click** (klik), *n.* [echoic], 1. a slight, sharp sound like that of a door latch snapping into place. 2. a mechanical device, as a catch or pawl, that clicks into position. 3. in *phonetics,* a sound made by drawing the breath into the mouth and clicking the tongue. *v.i. & v.t.* to make or cause to make a click. **—click′er,** *n.*

**cli·ent** (klī′ənt), *n.* [< Fr. < L. *cliens,* follower], 1. a person or company in its relationship to a lawyer, accountant, etc. engaged to act in its behalf. 2. a customer. **—cli′ent·less,** *adj.*

**cli·en·tele** (klī′ən-tel′), *n.* [< Fr. < L. *clientela*], 1. the clients of a lawyer, doctor, etc., or the habitual customers of a store, hotel, etc. 2. the number of such clients, etc. Also **cli′ent·age.**

**cliff** (klif), *n.* [AS. *clif*], a high, steep rock or face of rock. **—cliff′y,** *adj.*

**Clif·ton** (klif′tən), *n.* a city in NE New Jersey: pop., 82,000.

**cli·mac·ter·ic** (klī-mak′tẽr-ik, klī′mak-ter′-), *n.* [L. < Gr. < *klimax,* ladder], 1. a period in a person's life when an important change in health or bodily function occurs, especially the menopause in women. 2. any crucial period. *adj.* of or like a climacteric; crucial: also **cli′mac·ter′i·cal.**

**cli·mac·tic** (klī-mak′tik), *adj.* of or constituting a climax: also **climactical. —cli·mac′ti·cal·ly,** *adv.*

**cli·mate** (klī′mit), *n.* [< OFr. < L. < Gr. *klima,* region], 1. the prevailing weather conditions of a place, as determined by the temperature and meteorological changes over a period of years. 2. any prevailing conditions affecting life, activity, etc. 3. a region with reference to its prevailing weather: as, he moved to a warmer *climate.* **—cli·mat·ic** (klī-mat′ik), *adj.* **—cli·mat′i·cal·ly,** *adv.*

**cli·ma·tol·o·gy** (klī′mə-tol′ə-ji), *n.* the science dealing with climate and climatic phenomena. **—cli′ma·to·log′ic** (-tə-loj′ik), **cli′ma·to·log′i·cal,** *adj.* **—cli′ma·to·log′i·cal·ly,** *adv.* **—cli′ma·tol′o·gist,** *n.*

**cli·max** (klī′maks), *n.* [L. < Gr. *klimax,* ladder], 1. a series of ideas or events arranged or occurring progressively so that the most forceful is last. 2. the final, culminating element in such a series. 3. the highest point, as of interest, excitement, etc.; culmination. *v.i. & v.t.* to reach, or bring to, a climax.

**climb** (klīm), *v.i. & v.t.* [CLIMBED or *archaic* CLOMB (klōm), CLIMBING], [< AS. *climban*], 1. to move up, especially by using the hands and feet; ascend; mount. 2. to ascend gradually or laboriously: as, he *climbed* to power. 3. in *botany,* to grow upward by winding around or adhering with tendrils. *n.* 1. a climbing; rise; ascent. 2. a thing or place to be climbed. **—climb down,** to move down, especially by using the hands and feet; descend. **—climb′a·ble,** *adj.*

**climb·er** (klīm′ẽr), *n.* 1. a person or thing that climbs. 2. a climbing iron. 3. [Colloq.], one who constantly tries to advance himself socially or in business. 4. a plant or vine that grows upward by twining about a support.

**climbing irons,** metal spikes fastened to the shoes to aid in climbing telephone poles, etc.

**clime** (klīm), *n.* [L. *clima;* see CLIMATE], [Poetic], a country; region; realm; climate.

**clinch** (klinch), *v.t.* [var. of *clench*], 1. to fasten (a nail, bolt, etc. driven through something) by bending or flattening the projecting end. 2. to fasten together by this means. 3. to settle (an argument, bargain, etc.) definitely; close conclusively. *v.i.* 1. to clinch a nail, bolt, etc. 2. in *boxing,* to grip the opponent with the arms so as to hinder his punching; hence, 3. [Slang], to embrace. *n.* 1. a clinching, as with a nail. 2. a clinched nail, bolt, etc. 3. the part clinched. 4. in *boxing,* an act of clinching. 5. [Slang], an embrace.

**clinch·er** (klin′chẽr), *n.* 1. a person who clinches. 2. a tool for clinching nails. 3. [Colloq.], a point that is decisive, as in an argument.

**cling** (kliŋ), *v.i.* [CLUNG (kluŋ), CLINGING], [AS. *clingan*], 1. to adhere; hold fast, as by embracing. 2. to be or stay near. **—cling′er,** *n.* **—cling′ing,** *adj. & n.* **—cling′ing·ly,** *adv.* **—cling′y,** *adj.*

**clinging vine,** a woman inclined to be helpless and dependent in her relationship with a man.

**cling·stone** (kliŋ′stōn′), *adj.* having a stone that clings to the fleshy part: said of some peaches. *n.* a peach of this sort.

**clin·ic** (klin′ik), *n.* [L. *clinicus,* bed-ridden person < Gr. *klinikos,* of a bed < *klinē,* a bed], 1. the teaching of medicine by examining and treating patients in the presence of students. 2. a class getting such teaching. 3. a place where patients are treated by specialists in various ailments practicing as a group: as, a cancer *clinic.* 4. an outpatient department, as of a hospital, where patients are treated free or for a small fee. 5. an organization that offers some kind of advice or treatment: as, a domestic-relations *clinic.*

**clin·i·cal** (klin′i-k'l), *adj.* 1. of or connected with a clinic or a sickbed. 2. having to do with the treatment and observation of disease in patients, as distinguished from experimental or laboratory study; hence, 3. scientifically impersonal: as, *clinical* detachment. **—clin′i·cal·ly,** *adv.*

**clinical thermometer,** a thermometer with which the body temperature is measured.

**cli·ni·cian** (kli-nish′ən), *n.* an expert in clinical medicine.

**clink** (kliŋk), *v.i. & v.t.* [origin echoic], to make or cause to make a slight, sharp sound, as of glasses striking together. *n.* 1. such a sound. 2. [< the *clink* of the fetters], [Colloq.], a jail.

**clink·er** (kliŋk′ẽr), *n.* [D. *klinker,* vitrified brick < *klinken,* to ring], 1. a very hard brick. 2. a hard mass of fused stony matter formed in a furnace, as from impurities in the coal.

**cli·nom·e·ter** (klī-nom′ə-tẽr), *n.* [< Gr. < *klinein,* to bend; + *-meter*], an instrument for measuring the angle of slope or inclination. **—cli·no·met·ric** (klī′nə-met′rik), **cli′no·met′ri·cal,** *adj.*

**Cli·o** (klī′ō), *n.* in *Gr. mythology,* the Muse of history.

**clip** (klip), *v.t.* [CLIPPED, CLIPPING], [< ON. *klippa*], 1. to cut or cut off as with shears. 2. to cut short. 3. to cut the hair of. 4. [Colloq.], to hit with a quick, sharp blow. 5. [Slang], to cheat; swindle. *v.i.* 1. to cut something. 2. to cut out newspaper or magazine clippings. 3. [Colloq.], to move rapidly. *n.* 1. a clipping; shearing. 2. a thing clipped. 3. the amount of wool clipped from a sheep. 4. [Colloq.], a quick, sharp punch or stroke. 5. [Colloq.], rapid motion or pace.

**clip** (klip), *v.i. & v.t.* [CLIPPED or *archaic* CLIPT, CLIPPING], [AS. *clyppan,* to embrace], 1. to grip tightly; fasten. 2. in *football,* to throw oneself from behind at the legs of (an opponent without the ball), so as to cause him to fall: an illegal act. *n.* 1. anything that clips or fastens: as, a paper *clip.* 2. a cartridge clip. 3. in *football*, the act of clipping.

**clipped form** (or **word**), a shortened form of a word, as *mob* (for *mobile*), *chum* (for *chamber mate*), etc.

**clip·per** (klip′ẽr), *n.* 1. a person who clips, cuts, shears, etc. 2. *often pl.* a tool for cutting or shearing. 3. a sharp-bowed, narrow-beamed sailing ship built and rigged for great speed. 4. a horse, sled, airplane, automobile, etc. regarded as especially fast.

**clip·ping** (klip′iŋ), *n.* 1. a piece cut out or off of something. 2. an item cut out of a newspaper, magazine, etc.

**clipt** (klipt), archaic pt. and pp. of **clip** (to fasten).

**clique** (klēk, klik), *n.* [Fr. < *cliquer*, to make a noise], a small, exclusive circle of people; snobbish or narrow coterie. *v.i.* [CLIQUED, CLIQUING], [Colloq.], to gather in, or act as, a clique. —**cli′quish, cli′quy, cli′quey,** *adj.* —**cli′quish·ly,** *adv.* —**cli′quish·ness,** *n.*

**cli·to·ris** (klī′tə-ris, klit′ə-), *n.* [LL. < Gr. < *kleiein*, to close], a small, sensitive, erectile organ at the upper end of the external female genital organ: it corresponds to the male's penis.

**clk.,** 1. clerk. 2. clock.

**clo·a·ca** (klō-ā′kə), *n.* [*pl.* -CAE (-sē)], [L. < *cluere*, to cleanse], 1. a sewer. 2. a water closet; privy. 3. in *zoology*, the cavity into which both the intestinal and the genitourinary tract empty in reptiles, birds, amphibians, and many fishes. —**clo·a′cal,** *adj.*

**cloak** (klōk), *n.* [< OFr. < LL. *clocca*, a bell, cloak < Celt.: so called from its bell-like appearance], 1. a loose, usually sleeveless outer garment. 2. something that covers or conceals; disguise. *v.t.* 1. to cover with or as with a cloak. 2. to conceal; hide; disguise.

**cloak·room** (klōk′rōōm′, -room′), *n.* a room where hats, coats, umbrellas, etc. can be left temporarily.

**clob·ber** (klob′ẽr), *v.t.* [? freq. of *club*, *v.t.*], [Slang], to beat or hit repeatedly; maul.

**cloche** (klōsh; Fr. klôsh), *n.* [Fr. < LL. *clocca*, bell < Celt.], a closefitting, bell-shaped hat for women.

**clock** (klok), *n.* [ME. *clocke*, orig., clock with bells < MD. < LL. *clocca*, bell; prob. < Celt.], a device for measuring time, usually by means of pointers moving over a dial: unlike a watch, a clock is not carried on one's person. *v.t.* to record the time of (a race, runner, etc.) with a stop watch. —**clock′er,** *n.* —**clock′like′,** *adj.*

**clock** (klok), *n.* [prob. < *clock* (timepiece), because orig. bell-shaped], a woven or embroidered ornament on the side of a stocking, going up from the ankle. *v.t.* to put such an ornament on.

**clock·wise** (klok′wīz′), *adv.* & *adj.* in the direction in which the hands of a clock rotate.

**clock·work** (klok′wũrk′), *n.* 1. the mechanism of a clock. 2. any similar mechanism, consisting of springs and geared wheels, as in some mechanical toys. —**like clockwork,** very regularly, precisely, and evenly.

**clod** (klod), *n.* [AS. *clott*, var. of *clot*], 1. a lump, especially of earth or clay. 2. earth; soil. 3. a dull, stupid fellow; dolt. —**clod′dish,** *adj.* —**clod′dishness,** *n.* —**clod′dy,** *adj.*

**clod·hop·per** (klod′hop′ẽr), *n.* [*clod* + *hopper*], 1. a plowman. 2. an awkward, clumsy fellow; bumpkin; boor. 3. a coarse, heavy shoe such as is worn by a plowman.

**clog** (klog), *n.* [ME. *clogge*, a lump of wood], 1. a weight fastened to an animal's leg to hinder motion. 2. anything that hinders or obstructs. 3. a heavy shoe, usually with a wooden sole: light clogs are used in clog dancing. 4. a clog dance. *v.t.* [CLOGGED, CLOGGING], 1. to hinder; impede. 2. to obstruct (a passage, etc.); block up. *v.i.* 1. to become clogged or blocked up. 2. to become thick or sticky, so as to clog. 3. to do a clog dance. —**clog′gy,** *adj.*

**clog dance,** a dance in which clogs are worn to beat out the rhythm on the floor. —**clog dancer.** —**clog dancing.**

**cloi·son·né** (kloi′zə-nā′), *adj.* [Fr., lit., partitioned], denoting a kind of enamel work in which the surface decoration is set in hollows formed by thin strips of wire welded to a metal plate in a complex pattern. *n.* cloisonné enamel.

**clois·ter** (klois′tẽr), *n.* [< OFr. < L. *claustrum*, bolt < pp. of *claudere*, to close], 1. a place of religious seclusion; monastery or nunnery. 2. monastic life. 3. any place where one may lead a secluded life. 4. a covered walk along the inside walls of a monastery, convent, etc. with a columned opening along one side. *v.t.* 1. to confine as in a cloister. 2. to furnish with a cloister. —**clois′tered,** *adj.* —**clois′tral** (-trəl), *adj.*

CLOISTER

**clomb** (klōm), archaic pt. and pp. of **climb.**

**clo·nus, clo·nos** (klō′nəs), *n.* [< Gr. *klonos*, confused motion], a series of muscle spasms. —**clon·ic** (klon′ik), *adj.* —**clo·nic·i·ty** (klə-nis′ə-ti), *n.*

**close** (klōs), *adj.* [< OFr. *clos*, pp. of *clore* (see CLOSE, *v.*)], 1. shut; not open. 2. enclosed or enclosing; shut in. 3. confined or confining: as, *close* quarters. 4. carefully guarded: as, a *close* secret. 5. hidden; secluded. 6 secretive; reserved; reticent. 7. stingy; niggardly. 8. confined to specific groups; restricted. 9. confined in circulation; oppressive; humid; stuffy. 10. hard to get; scarce: as, credit is *close*. 11. with little space between; near together. 12. compact; dense: as, a close weave. 13. fitting tightly. 14. near or down to the surface on which something grows: as, a *close* shave. 15. intimate; familiar: as, a *close* friend. 16. in strict agreement with an original: as, a *close* translation. 17. strict; thorough; careful: as, *close* attention. 18. nearly equal or alike: as, a *close* resemblance. 19. nearly equal in balance, outcome, etc.: as, a *close* contest. 20. in *phonetics*, high. *adv.* in a close manner or position. —**close to the wind,** in *nautical usage*, heading as closely as possible in the direction from which the wind blows. —**close′ly,** *adv.* —**close′ness,** *n.*

**close** (klōz), *v.t.* [CLOSED, CLOSING], [< OFr. < *clore* < L. *claudere*, to close], 1. to shut. 2. to fill up or stop (an opening). 3. to bring to a finish; conclude. 4. to bring or bind together; unite. *v.i.* 1. to become shut; shut itself. 2. to come to an end. 3. to come close, in order to attack; come to grips. 4. to come together. 5. to agree. *n.* an end; conclusion; finish. —**close down,** to shut or stop entirely. —**close in,** to draw near from various directions, cutting off escape. —**close out,** to dispose of (goods) by sale, as in ending a business. —**close up,** 1. to draw nearer together. 2. to shut or stop up entirely. —**clos′er,** *n.*

**close** (klōs), *n.* [< OFr. < L. *clausum*, neut. pp. of *claudere*, to close], 1. an enclosed place. 2. enclosed grounds around a cathedral, etc.

**close call** (klōs), [Colloq.], a narrow escape from danger or misfortune: also **close shave.**

**closed shop,** a factory, business, etc. operating under a contract with a labor union by which only members of the union may be employed.

**closed syllable,** a syllable ending in a consonant.

**close·fist·ed** (klōs′fis′tid), *adj.* stingy; miserly. —**close′fist′ed·ly,** *adv.* —**close′fist′ed·ness,** *n.*

**close·fit·ting** (klōs′fit′iŋ), *adj.* fitting tightly enough to show the contours of the body.

**close-hauled** (klōs′hôld′), *adj.* with the sails set for heading as nearly as possible into the wind.

**close-mouthed** (klōs′mouthd′, -moutht′), *adj.* not talking much; taciturn: also **close-lipped** (-lipt′).

**clos·et** (kloz′it), *n.* [OFr., dim. of *clos*; see CLOSE, *n.*], 1. a small room or cupboard for clothes, supplies, etc. 2. a small, private room for reading, consultation, etc. 3. a water closet; toilet. *adj.* 1. private; concealed. 2. for private or secluded use: as, *closet* drama is written only to be read, not acted. *v.t.* to shut up in a private room for confidential discussion.

**close-up** (klōs′up′), *n.* 1. a picture made with the camera at very close range. 2. a close view.

**clo·sure** (klō′zhẽr), *n.* [OFr. < L. *clausura* < pp. of *claudere*, to close], 1. a closing or being closed. 2. a finish; end; conclusion. 3. anything that closes. 4. the parliamentary procedure by which debate is closed and the measure brought up for an immediate vote. *v.t.* [-SURED, -SURING], to apply closure to (a debate, bill, etc.).

**clot** (klot), *n.* [AS. *clott*], a thick, coagulated mass or semisolid lump: as, a blood *clot*. *v.t.* & *v.i.* [CLOT-

TED, CLOTTING], to become or cause to become a clot; coagulate. —**clot′ty,** *adj.*

**cloth** (klôth, kloth), *n.* [*pl.* CLOTHS (klôthz, klothz, "pieces of cloth"; klôths, kloths, "kinds of cloth")], [AS. *clath*], 1. a woven, knitted, or pressed fabric of fibrous material, as cotton, wool, silk, hair, synthetic fibers, etc. 2. a piece of such fabric for a specific use: as, a table*cloth*, wash*cloth*. 3. the identifying dress of a profession. *adj.* made of cloth. —**the cloth,** the clergy.

**clothe** (klōth), *v.t.* [CLOTHED or CLAD (klad), CLOTHING], [AS. *clathian* < *clath*, cloth], 1. to put clothes on; dress. 2. to provide with clothes. 3. to cover as if with a garment; invest: as, a hero *clothed* in glory.

**clothes** (klōz, klōthz), *n.pl.* [AS. *clathas*, pl. of *clath*, cloth], 1. covering for the body; clothing; attire; raiment. 2. bedclothes.

**clothes·horse** (klōz′hôrs′), *n.* 1. a frame on which to hang clothes for airing or drying. 2. [Slang], a person regarded as paying too much attention to his clothes.

**clothes·line** (klōz′līn′), *n.* a rope or wire on which clothes are hung for drying or airing.

**clothes·pin** (klōz′pin′), *n.* a small clip of wood or plastic, for fastening clothes on a line.

**clothes·press** (klōz′pres′), *n.* a closet, wardrobe, etc. in which to keep clothes: also **clothes press.**

**clothes tree,** an upright pole with branching hooks or pegs near the top to hold coats and hats.

**cloth·ier** (klōth′yēr), *n.* 1. a person who makes or sells clothes. 2. a dealer in cloth.

**cloth·ing** (klōth′iŋ), *n.* 1. clothes; garments; wearing apparel. 2. a covering.

**Clo·tho** (klō′thō), *n.* in *Gr. mythology*, one of the three Fates, spinner of the thread of life.

**clo·ture** (klō′chēr), *n.* & *v.t.* [-TURED, -TURING], [Fr. *clôture* < OFr.; see CLOSURE], closure: applied to parliamentary debate.

**cloud** (kloud), *n.* [AS. *clud*, mass of rock], 1. a visible mass of vapor, especially one suspended in the sky. 2. a mass of smoke, dust, steam, etc. 3. a great number of moving things close together: as, a *cloud* of locusts. 4. a murkiness or dimness, as in a mirror. 5. a dark marking, as in marble. 6. anything that darkens, obscures, or makes gloomy. *v.t.* 1. to cover with clouds. 2. to darken; obscure. 3. to make gloomy or troubled. 4. to sully (a reputation, etc.). *v.i.* 1. to become cloudy. 2. to become gloomy or troubled. —**in the clouds,** 1. high up in the sky. 2. fanciful; impractical. 3. in a reverie or daydream. —**under a cloud,** 1. under suspicion of wrongdoing. 2. in a troubled state of mind. —**cloud′less,** *adj.* —**cloud′less·ness,** *n.*

**cloud·burst** (kloud′būrst′), *n.* a sudden, unusually heavy rain; violent downpour.

**cloud·land** (kloud′land′), *n.* region of dreams, myth, or imagination; visionary realm.

**cloud·y** (kloud′i), *adj.* [-IER, -IEST], 1. covered with clouds; overcast. 2. of or like clouds. 3. streaked, as marble. 4. opaque; not transparent: said of a liquid. 5 obscure; not distinct; dim. 6. gloomy; troubled. —**cloud′i·ly,** *adv.* —**cloud′i·ness,** *n.*

**clout** (klout), *n* [AS. *clut*, piece of cloth, patch], 1. [Archaic], a piece of cloth; patch. 2. [Colloq.], a blow, as with the hand; rap. 3. [Slang], a long, powerful hit in baseball. *v.t.* [Colloq.], to strike, as with the hand; hit.

**clove** (klōv), *n.* [OFr. *clou* < L. *clavus*, nail: from its shape], 1. the dried flower bud of a tropical evergreen tree. 2. a pungent, fragrant spice obtained from these buds. 3. the tree.

**clove** (klōv), *n.* [AS. *clufu*, akin to *cleofan*, to split], a segment of a bulb, as of garlic.

**clove** (klōv), 1. archaic pt. of **cleave** (to cling). 2. alt. pt. and poetic pp. of **cleave** (to split).

**clo·ven** (klō′v′n), alt. pp. of **cleave** (to split). *adj.* divided; split.

**clo·ven-hoofed** (klō′v′n-hooft′, -hōōft′), *adj.* 1. having cloven hoofs; hence, 2. satanic; devilish. Also **clo′ven-foot′ed.**

**clo·ver** (klō′vēr), *n.* [AS. *clafre*], any of a number of species of low-growing herbs with leaves in three parts and small flowers in dense heads. —**in clover,** 1. originally, in good pasture; hence, 2. living a luxurious, carefree life.

**clo·ver·leaf** (klō′vēr-lēf′), *n.* [*pl.* -LEAVES (-lēvz′)], a multiple highway intersection in the form of a four-leaf clover, which, by means of curving ramps from one level to another, permits traffic to move unhindered in any of four directions.

**clown** (kloun), *n.* [< LG. source; cf. D. *kleun*, lumpish fellow], 1. a peasant; rustic. 2. a clumsy, rude person; boor. 3. a man whose work is entertaining, as in a circus, by antics, jokes, tricks, etc.; buffoon. *v.i.* 1. to perform as a clown. 2. to play practical jokes, act silly, etc. —**clown′ish,** *adj.* —**clown′ish·ly,** *adv.* —**clown′ish·ness,** *n.*

**clown·er·y** (kloun′ēr-i), *n.* [*pl.* -IES], the actions or behavior of a clown; clowning.

**cloy** (cloi), *v.t.* [ME. *acloien*, to drive a nail into, hence stop up < OFr. < *clou* (< L. *clavus*), a nail], to surfeit by too much of anything, especially anything too sweet, rich, etc.

**club** (klub), *n.* [< ON. *klubba*, mass of something, clump], 1. a heavy stick, usually thinner at one end, used as a weapon. 2. any stick or bat used in a game, as golf, hockey, polo, etc. 3. a group of people associated for a common purpose. 4. the room, building, etc. used by such a group. 5. any of a suit of playing cards marked with a black trefoil (♣). 6. *pl.* this suit of cards. *v.t.* [CLUBBED, CLUBBING], 1. to strike as with a club. 2. to combine (something) for a common purpose; pool (resources, etc.). *v.i.* to unite for a common purpose (usually with *together*).

**club car,** a railroad car with lounge chairs and, usually, a bar.

**club·foot** (klub′foot′), *n.* 1. a congenital deformity of the foot, often with a clublike appearance: also called *talipes*. 2. [*pl.* -FEET (-fēt′)], a foot so deformed. —**club′-foot′ed,** *adj.*

**club·house** (klub′hous′), *n.* a building occupied by a club.

**club·man** (klub′mən, -man′), *n.* [*pl.* -MEN], a man who is a member of a club or clubs, especially one who spends much time at club social affairs, etc. —**club′wom′an** [*pl.* -WOMEN], *n.fem.*

**club sandwich,** a sandwich of several layers, often toasted, containing chicken, bacon, lettuce, etc.

**cluck** (kluk), *v.i.* [prob. echoic], to make the sound of a hen calling her chickens. *v.t.* to call or utter with such a sound: as, she *clucked* her disapproval. *n.* the sound of clucking.

**clue** (klōō), *n.* & *v.t.* clew: the usual spelling of *n.* 2.

**clump** (klump), *n.* [D. *klomp* or LG. *klump*], 1. a lump; mass. 2. a cluster, as of trees. 3. the sound of heavy footsteps. *v.i.* 1. to tramp heavily. 2. to form clumps. *v.t.* 1. to group together in a cluster. 2. to cause to form clumps. —**clump′ish,** *adj.* —**clump′y** [-IER, -IEST], *adj.*

**clum·sy** (klum′zi), *adj.* [-SIER, -SIEST], [ME. *clumsid*, numb with cold < ON.], 1. awkward; lacking grace or skill. 2. ill-constructed; awkwardly shaped or made. —**clum′si·ly,** *adv.* —**clum′si·ness,** *n.*

**clung** (kluŋ), pt. and pp. of **cling.**

**clus·ter** (klus′tēr), *n.* [AS. *clyster*], 1. a number of things of the same sort gathered or growing together; bunch. 2. a number of persons or animals grouped together. *v.i.* & *v.t.* to gather or grow in a cluster or clusters. —**clus′ter·y,** *adj.*

**clutch** (kluch), *v.t.* [AS. *clyccan*, to clench], 1. to grasp or snatch with a hand or claw. 2. to grasp or hold eagerly or tightly. *v.i.* to snatch or seize (with *at*). *n.* 1. a claw or hand in the act of seizing. 2. *usually pl.* power; control. 3. a grasp; grip. 4. *a*) a mechanical device, as in an automobile, for engaging and disengaging the motor or engine. *b*) the lever or pedal by which this is operated. 5. a device for gripping and holding, as in a crane.

**clutch** (kluch), *n.* [< ME. *cleken* (< ON. *klekja*), to hatch], 1. a nest of eggs. 2. a brood of chicks.

**clut·ter** (klut′ēr), *n.* [< *clot*], 1. a jumble; confusion; disorder. 2. [var. of *clatter*], a clatter. *v.t.* to put into disorder; litter; jumble (often with *up*). *v.i.* to make a clatter.

**Clydes·dale** (klīdz′dāl′), *n.* [< *Clydesdale*, Scotland, where it originated], a breed of heavy, strong draft horse.

**clyp·e·ate** (klip′i-āt′), *adj.* [< L. < *clypeus*, a shield], in *botany*, shaped like a round shield: also **clyp′e·at′ed.**

**clys·ter** (klis′tēr), *n.* [< Fr. or L. < Gr. *klystēr* < *klyzein*, to wash], an enema.

**Cly·tem·nes·tra, Cly·taem·nes·tra** (klī′təm-nes′trə), *n.* in *Gr. legend*, the wife of Agamemnon: see **Electra.**

**Cm,** in *chemistry*, curium.

**cm.,** centimeter; centimeters.

**cmdg.,** commanding.

**cml.,** commercial.

**Cnos·sus** (nos′əs), *n.* Knossos, a city in Crete.

**co-,** 1. a shortened form of *com-*, meaning: *a*) *together, with*, as in *co-operation*. *b*) *joint*, as in *co-owner*. *c*) *equally*, as in *coextensive*. 2. a prefix meaning *complement of*, as in *cosine*.

**Co,** in *chemistry*, cobalt.

**Co., co.,** [*pl.* COS.], 1. company. 2. county.

**C.O.,** 1. Commanding Officer. 2. Conscientious Objector. 3. Criminal Office.
**c/o, c.o.,** 1. care of. 2. carried over.
**coach** (kōch), *n.* [< Fr. < G. < Hung. *kocsi*, lit., of Kócs, a city in Hungary], 1. a large, covered, four-wheeled carriage with an open, raised seat in front for the driver; stagecoach. 2. a railroad passenger car furnishing the lowest-priced seating accommodations. 3. a bus. 4. an enclosed automobile, usually a two-door sedan. 5. a private tutor who prepares a student as for an examination. 6. one who instructs and trains athletes, dramatic groups, etc. *v.t.* 1. to instruct (a person), as for an examination, by private tutoring. 2. to instruct and train (athletes, actors, etc.). 3. in *baseball*, to advise (a base runner) in his movements. *v.i.* to act as a coach. —**coach′er,** *n.*
**coach-and-four** (kōch′ən-fôr′), *n.* a coach drawn by four horses.
**coach dog,** a Dalmatian dog.
**coach·man** (kōch′mən), *n.* [*pl.* -MEN], the driver of a coach or carriage.
**co·ad·ju·tor** (kō-aj′ə-tēr, kō′ə-jōō′tēr), *n.* [< OFr. < L. < *co-*, together + *adjuvare*, to help], 1. an assistant; helper. 2. a person, often another bishop, appointed to assist a bishop.
**co·ag·u·la·ble** (kō-ag′yoo-lə-b'l), *adj.* that can be coagulated. —**co·ag′u·la·bil′i·ty,** *n.*
**co·ag·u·late** (kō-ag′yoo-lāt′), *v.t.* [-LATED, -LATING], [< L. pp. of *coagulare* < *coagulum*, means of coagulation < *co-*, together + *agere*, to move], to cause (a liquid) to become a soft, semisolid mass; curdle; clot. *v.i.* to become coagulated. —**co·ag′u·la′tion,** *n.* —**co·ag′u·la′tive,** *adj.* —**co·ag′u·la′tor,** *n.*
**coal** (kōl), *n.* [AS. *col*, a live coal], 1. a black, combustible, mineral solid resulting from the partial decomposition of vegetable matter away from air and under high heat and great pressure over millions of years: used as a fuel and in the production of coke and many coal-tar compounds. 2. a piece of coal. 3. a piece of glowing or charred wood, coal, etc.; ember. 4. charcoal. *v.t.* to provide with coal. *v.i.* to take in a supply of coal. —**haul** (or **rake, drag, call) over the coals,** to criticize sharply; censure; scold. —**coal′y** [-IER, -IEST], *adj.*
**coal·er** (kōl′ēr), *n.* a ship, railroad, freight car, etc. that transports or supplies coal.
**co·a·lesce** (kō′ə-les′), *v.i.* [-LESCED, -LESCING], [< L. < *co-*, together + *alescere*, to grow up], 1. to grow together. 2. to unite or merge into a single body, group, or mass. —**co′a·les′cence,** *n.* —**co′a·les′cent,** *adj.*
**coal field,** a region where there are coal strata.
**coal gas,** 1. a gas produced by the distillation of bituminous coal: used for lighting and heating. 2. a poisonous gas given off by burning coal.
**coaling station,** a place, as a port or station, where ships or trains take on coal.
**co·a·li·tion** (kō′ə-lish′ən), *n.* [< LL. < L. < *coalescere;* see COALESCE], 1. a combination; union. 2. a temporary alliance of factions, parties, etc. for some specific purpose.
**coal measures,** 1. coal beds. 2. in geology, coal-bearing strata.
**coal oil,** 1. kerosene. 2. crude petroleum.
**coal tar,** a black, thick, opaque liquid obtained by the distillation of bituminous coal: many synthetic compounds have been developed from it, including dyes, medicines, and explosives.
**coam·ing** (kōm′iŋ), *n.* [? akin to *comb*], a raised border around a hatch on a ship, a skylight, etc., to keep out water.
**coarse** (kôrs, kōrs), *adj.* [var. of *course* in sense of "ordinary, usual," as in *of course*], 1. common; of inferior or poor quality. 2. consisting of rather large particles; not fine: as, *coarse* sand. 3. rough; harsh: as, *coarse* cloth. 4. lacking in refinement; vulgar: as, a *coarse* joke. —**coarse′ly,** *adv.* —**coarse′ness,** *n.*
**coarse-grained** (kôrs′grānd′, kōrs′-), *adj.* 1. having a coarse or rough texture. 2. crude.
**coars·en** (kôr′s'n, kōr′-), *v.t. & v.i.* to make or become coarse.
**coast** (kōst), *n.* [< OFr. < L. *costa*, a rib, side], 1. land alongside the sea; seashore. 2. [< Canad. Fr., hillside, slope], an incline down which a slide is taken; hence, 3. a slide or ride down, as on a sled. *v.i.* 1. to sail near or along the coast. 2. to make short voyages from port to port. 3. to go down an incline on a sled. 4. to continue in motion on momentum after propelling power has stopped. *v.t.* to sail along or near the coast of. —**the Coast,** [Colloq.], in the United States, the Pacific coast. —**the coast is clear,** there is no apparent danger or hindrance. —**coast′al,** *adj.*
**Coastal Eastern,** American English as typically spoken in the New England coastal area.
**coastal plain,** level land extending along a coast.
**coast·er** (kōs′tēr), *n.* 1. a person or thing that coasts. 2. a ship that travels from port to port along a coast. 3. a sled or wagon for coasting. 4. a small, round tray placed under a glass or bottle to protect a table or other surface.
**coaster brake,** a brake on the rear wheel of a bicycle, worked by reverse pressure on the pedals.
**coast guard,** 1. a group of men employed by a government to defend its coasts, prevent smuggling, aid vessels in distress, etc. 2. [C- G-], such a group in the U.S., normally under the control of the Treasury Department. 3. a member of a coast guard.
**coast·land** (kōst′land′), *n.* land along a coast.
**coast line,** the contour or outline of a coast.
**coast·ward** (kōst′wērd), *adj. & adv.* toward the coast: also **coast′wards,** *adv.*
**coast·wise** (kōst′wīz′), *adv. & adj.* along the coast: also **coast′ways′** (-wāz′), *adv.*
**coat** (kōt), *n.* [< OFr. < LL. *cot(t)a*, a tunic; prob. < Gmc.], 1. a sleeved outer garment opening down the front: as, an over*coat*, the *coat* of a suit. 2. the natural covering of an animal, as of skin, fur, wool, etc. 3. any outer covering, as of a plant. 4. a layer of some substance, as paint, over a surface. *v.t.* 1. to provide or cover with a coat. 2. to cover with a layer of something. —**coat′less,** *adj.* —**coat′like′,** *adj.*
**co·a·ti** (kō-ä′ti), *n.* [*pl.* -TIS], [Tupi < *cua*, a cincture + *tim*, the nose], a small, flesh-eating animal of Central and South America, like the raccoon but with a long, flexible snout. Also **co·a′ti-mon′di, co·a′ti-mun′di** (-mun′di), [*pl.* -DIS].
**coat·ing** (kōt′iŋ), *n.* 1. something covering or spread over a surface. 2. cloth for making coats.
**coat of arms,** [after Fr. *cotte d'armes*, light garment worn over armor, and blazoned with the heraldic arms of the wearer], 1. a shield marked with the insignia or designs of a person, family, etc. 2. a representation of such a shield.
**coat of mail,** [*pl.* COATS OF MAIL], a suit of armor made of interlinked metal rings or overlapping plates.
**coat·tail** (kōt′tāl′), *n.* the lower back part of a coat; esp., either half of the skirt of a coat that is divided in the back.
**co·au·thor** (kō-ô′thēr), *n.* a joint author.
**coax** (kōks), *v.t.* [< obs. slang *coax, cokes*, a fool], 1. to persuade or urge by soothing words, flattery, etc.; wheedle. 2. to get by coaxing. *v.i.* to use persuasion, flattery, etc. —**coax′er,** *n.* —**coax′ing,** *adj. & n.* —**coax′ing·ly,** *adv.*
**co·ax·i·al** (kō-ak′si-əl), *adj.* [< *co-* + *axis* + *-al*], 1. having a common axis. 2. designating a compound loud-speaker consisting of a smaller unit mounted within and connected with a larger one on a common axis. Also **co·ax′al.**
**coaxial cable,** a cable for sending telephone, telegraph, and television impulses: it consists of an insulated conductor tube surrounding a central core of conducting material.
**cob** (kob), *n.* [prob. < LG.], 1. a lump. 2. corncob. 3. a male swan. 4. a short, thickset horse.
**co·balt** (kō′bôlt), *n.* [G. *kobalt* < *kobold*, goblin, demon of the mines], a hard, lustrous, steel-gray metallic chemical element, used in alloys, inks, paints, etc.: symbol, Co; at. wt., 58.94; at. no., 27. —**co·bal′tic, co·bal′tous,** *adj.*
**cobalt blue,** 1. a dark-blue pigment made from cobalt. 2. dark blue.
**cob·ble** (kob′'l), *v.t.* [-BLED, -BLING], [ME.; ? < *cob* (a lump)], 1. to mend (shoes, etc.). 2. to mend or put together clumsily.
**cob·ble** (kob′'l), *n.* [prob. < *cob* (a lump)], a cobblestone. *v.t.* [-BLED, -BLING], to pave with cobblestones.
**cob·bler** (kob′lēr), *n.* [? < Hudson Valley *cobble*, stony hill], 1. an iced drink containing wine, citrus fruit, and sugar. 2. a deep-dish fruit pie.
**cob·bler** (kob′lēr), *n.* 1. one whose work is mending shoes. 2. a clumsy, bungling workman.
**cob·ble·stone** (kob′'l-stōn′), *n.* [see COBBLE, *n.*], a rounded stone formerly used for paving streets.

**cob coal,** coal in rounded lumps from about the size of a baseball to that of a basketball.
**co·bel·lig·er·ent** (kō′bə-lij′ẽr-ənt), *n.* a nation associated but not allied with another or other nations in waging war.
**co·bra** (kō′brə), *n.* [< Port. *cobra* (*de capello*), serpent (of the hood)], a very poisonous snake of Asia and Africa, having around its neck loose skin which expands into a hood when the snake is excited.

COBRA (4–17 ft. long)

**cob·web** (kob′web′), *n.* [< ME. *coppe*, spider; + *web*], 1. a web spun by a spider. 2. the substance that it is made of. 3. anything flimsy, gauzy, or ensnaring like a spider's web. *v.t.* [-WEBBED, -WEBBING], to cover as with cobwebs. —**cob′web′by,** *adj.*
**co·ca** (kō′kə), *n.* [Peruv. *cuca*], 1. a tropical shrub of South America and the West Indies whose dried leaves are the source of cocaine and certain other alkaloids. 2. its dried leaves.
**co·caine, co·cain** (kō-kān′, kō′kān), *n.* a crystalline alkaloid obtained from dried coca leaves: it is a narcotic and local anesthetic.
**-coc·cal** (kok′'l), a combining form meaning *of* or *produced by a* (specified kind of) *coccus*: also **-coc·cic** (kok′sik).
**coc·cus** (kok′əs), *n.* [*pl.* COCCI (kok′sī)], [Gr. *kokkos*, a berry], a bacterium having a spherical or oval shape. —**coc·coid** (kok′oid), *adj.*
**-coc·cus** (kok′əs), *coccus* used as a combining form in names of various bacteria, as *gonococcus*.
**coc·cyx** (kok′siks), *n.* [*pl.* COCCYGES (kok-sī′jēz)], [L. < Gr. *kokkyx*, cuckoo: so called because shaped like a cuckoo's beak], a small, triangular bone at the lower end of the vertebral column. —**coc·cyg′e·al** (-sij′i-əl), *adj.*
**co·chin** (kō′chin, koch′in), *n.* [< *Cochin-China*, place of origin], a very large domestic fowl with thickly feathered legs.
**Co·chin-Chi·na** (kō′chin-chī′nə), *n.* a former state of S French Indo-China, on the South China Sea: it is now part of South Viet-Nam.
**coch·i·neal** (koch′ə-nēl′, koch′ə-nēl′), *n.* [< Fr. < It. < L. *coccinus*, scarlet-colored < *coccum*, a berry], a red dye made from the dried bodies of the females of a scale insect that attacks cacti of tropical and subtropical America.
**coch·le·a** (kok′li-ə), *n.* [*pl.* -AE (-ē′)], [L. < Gr. *kochlias*, snail], the spiral-shaped part of the internal ear, containing the auditory nerve endings. —**coch′le·ar,** *adj.*
**coch·le·ate** (kok′li-āt′), *adj.* [< L.; see COCHLEA], shaped like the shell of a snail: also **coch′le·at′ed.**
**cock** (kok), *n.* [AS. *coc, cocc*], 1. the male of the chicken; rooster. 2. a male bird. 3. a weathercock. 4. a leader; chief. 5. a faucet or valve for regulating the flow of liquid or gas. 6. the hammer of a firearm. 7. the position of such a hammer when set for firing. 8. a jaunty, erect position: as, the *cock* of a hat. *v.t.* 1. to set (a hat, etc.) jauntily on one side. 2. to turn (the eye or ear) toward something. 3. to set the hammer of (a gun) in firing position. *v.i.* to assume an erect or tilted position.
**cock** (kok), *n.* [< Anglo-N.], a small, cone-shaped pile, as of hay. *v.t.* to pile in cocks.
**cock·ade** (kok-ād′), *n.* [Fr. *cocarde* < *coq*, a cock], a rosette, knot of ribbon, or similar device, worn on the hat as a badge. —**cock·ad′ed,** *adj.*
**cock·a·lo·rum** (kok′ə-lôr′əm, -lō′rəm), *n.* [pseudo L. < *cock* (male bird)], 1. a small rooster; bantam. 2. a little man full of exaggerated self-importance.
**cock-and-bull story** (kok′'n-bool′), [< Fr. *coq à l'âne*], an absurd, improbable story.
**cock·a·teel, cock·a·tiel** (kok′ə-tēl′), *n.* [see COCKATOO], a small parrot native to Australia.
**cock·a·too** (kok′ə-tōō′, kok′ə-tōō′), *n.* [*pl.* -TOOS], [< D. < Malay *kakatua*; prob. echoic], a large, bright-colored parrot of Australia, the East Indies, and the Philippines, often with a high crest.
**cock·a·trice** (kok′ə-tris), *n.* [< OFr. < LL. < *calcare*, to tread < *calx*, the heel], a fabulous serpent supposedly hatched from a cock's egg and having power to kill by a look.
**cock·boat** (kok′bōt′), *n.* a small boat, especially one used as a ship's tender.
**cock·chaf·er** (kok′chāf′ẽr), *n.* [*cock*, for Scot. *clock*, a beetle + *chafer*], a large European beetle whose grubs feed on the roots of plants.
**cock·crow** (kok′krō′), *n.* the time when roosters begin to crow; dawn: also **cock′crow′ing.**
**cocked hat,** 1. a three-cornered hat with a turned-up brim. 2. a peaked hat pointed in front and in back. —**knock into a cocked hat,** [Slang], to damage beyond recognition; ruin.
**cock·er·el** (kok′ẽr-əl, kok′rəl), *n.* [dim. of *cock*], a young rooster, not above a year old.
**cock·er (spaniel)** (kok′ẽr), [from its use in hunting woodcock], a small spaniel with short legs, long, silky hair, and long, drooping ears.
**cock·eye** (kok′ī′), *n.* [*cock* (to turn on one side) + *eye*], a squinting eye.
**cock·eyed** (kok′īd′), *adj.* [see COCKEYE], 1. cross-eyed. 2. [Slang], crooked; lopsided; awry. 3. [Slang], fantastically absurd. 4. [Slang], drunk.
**cock·fight** (kok′fīt′), *n.* a fight between gamecocks wearing metal spurs. —**cock′fight′ing,** *n.*
**cock·horse** (kok′hôrs′), *n.* [16th c., toy horse], a hobbyhorse; rocking horse.
**cock·le** (kok′'l), *n.* [< OFr. *coquille*, a shell < L. < Gr. < *konchē*, mussel], 1. an edible shellfish with two heart-shaped, radially ridged shells. 2. a cockleshell. 3. a small, shallow boat. 4. a wrinkle; pucker. *v.i. & v.t.* [-LED, -LING], to wrinkle; pucker. —**cockles of one's heart,** the deepest part of one's heart, or emotions.
**cock·le** (kok′'l), *n.* [< AS. *coccel*, tares], any of various weeds found in grain fields.
**cock·le·boat** (kok′'l-bōt′), *n.* a cockboat.
**cock·le·bur** (kok′'l-bũr′), *n.* 1. a ragweed plant bearing burs. 2. the common burdock.
**cock·le·shell** (kok′'l-shel′), *n.* 1. the shell of a cockle. 2. a cockboat.
**cock·ney** (kok′ni), *n.* [*pl.* -NEYS], [ME. *cokenei*, spoiled child, fop; understood as *coken-ey*, lit., cock's egg; merged with OFr. *acoquinei*, idle < *coquin*, rascal], 1. a native of the East End of London, England, speaking a characteristic dialect. 2. this dialect, characterized by loss of initial *h*, use of an intrusive *r*, etc. *adj.* of or like cockneys or their dialect. —**cock′ney·dom,** *n.*
**cock·ney·fy** (kok′ni-fī′), *v.t.* [-FIED, -FYING], to give a cockney quality to, as one's speech.
**cock·ney·ism** (kok′ni-iz'm), *n.* an idiom, pronunciation, etc. characteristic of cockneys.
**cock·pit** (kok′pit′), *n.* 1. an enclosed space for cockfighting. 2. any place regarded as like this; specif., *a*) in small decked vessels, a sunken space toward the stern used by the steersman, etc. *b*) in some small airplanes, the space where the pilot and passengers sit.
**cock·roach** (kok′rōch′), *n.* [Sp. *cucaracha*], a straight-winged insect with a flat, yellowish-brown or black body, slender legs, and long feelers: it is a common kitchen pest.
**cocks·comb** (koks′kōm′), *n.* 1. the red, fleshy growth on the head of a rooster. 2. a plant of the amaranth family, with red or yellow flower heads. 3. a coxcomb.
**cock·sure** (kok′shoor′), *adj.* [*cock* (see COCKY) + *sure*], 1. absolutely sure. 2. self-confident to an offensive degree. —**cock′sure′ness,** *n.*
**cock·swain** (kok′s'n, -swān′), *n.* a coxswain.
**cock·tail** (kok′tāl′), *n.* [etym. uncertain; ? infl. by Fr. *coquetel*, mixed drink], 1. a short mixed alcoholic drink made in various ways and usually iced. 2. an appetizer, as fruit juice, diced fruits, or sea food seasoned with a sharp sauce.
**cock·y** (kok′i), *adj.* [-IER, -IEST], [< *cock* (male bird)], [Colloq.], jauntily conceited; self-confident in a swaggering way: also **cock′ish.** —**cock′i·ly,** *adv.* —**cock′i·ness,** *n.*
**co·co** (kō′kō), *n.* [*pl.* -COS], [Sp.; Port. < L. *coccum*, a seed < Gr. *kokkos*, a berry], 1. the coconut palm. 2. its fruit; coconut. *adj.* made of the fiber from coconut husks. Also, by confusion, **cocoa.**
**co·coa** (kō′kō), *n.* [Sp. & Port. *cacao*; see CACAO], 1. powder made from cacao seeds that have been roasted and ground. 2. a drink made by adding sugar and hot water or milk to this powder. 3. reddish-yellow brown.
**co·co·nut, co·coa·nut** (kō′kə-nut′), *n.* the fruit of the coconut palm, a thick, brown, oval husk enclosing a layer of edible white meat: the hollow center is filled with a sweet, milky fluid (**coconut milk**).
**coconut oil,** oil obtained from the dried meat of coconuts, used for making soap, etc.
**coconut palm** (or **tree**), a tall tropical palm tree that bears coconuts: also **coco palm.**
**co·coon** (kə-kōōn′), *n.* [< Fr. < It. < LL. < L. *coccum*; see COCO], the silky case which the larvae of certain insects spin about themselves to shelter them during the pupa stage.
**cod** (kod), *n.* [*pl.* COD, CODS; see PLURAL, II, D, 2], [ME.], an important food fish, with firm flesh and soft fins, found in the North Atlantic.

**C.O.D., c.o.d.,** collect on delivery.
**Cod, Cape** (kod), a peninsula in SE Massachusetts.
**co·da** (kō'də), *n.* [It.; L. *cauda*, a tail], in *music*, a final passage, closing a composition or movement.
**cod·dle** (kod''l), *v.t.* [-DLED, -DLING], [? < *caudle*], 1. to cook gently, as an egg, in water not quite boiling. 2. to treat tenderly; pamper.
**code** (kōd), *n.* [Fr.; L. *codex*, tree trunk, waxed wooden tablet for writing], 1. a body of laws of a nation, state, etc., arranged systematically for easy reference. 2. any set of principles: as, a moral *code*. 3. a set of signals for sending messages, as by telegraph, flags, etc. 4. a system of secret writing in which letters, figures, etc. are given special meanings. *v.t.* [CODED, CODING], to put in a code; translate into the symbols of a code.
**co·de·ine** (kō'di-ēn', -dēn), *n.* [< Gr. *kodeia*, poppy head; + *-ine*], an alkaloid derived from opium and resembling morphine: used for the relief of pain and as a sedative: also **co'de·in** (-di-in).
**co·dex** (kō'deks), *n.* [*pl.* -DICES (kō'də-sēz', kod'ə-)], [L.; see CODE], a manuscript volume, especially of the Scriptures or of a classic text.
**cod·fish** (kod'fish'), *n.* [*pl.* see FISH], the cod.
**codg·er** (koj'ēr), *n.* [prob. var. of *cadger*], [Colloq.], a queer or peculiar person.
**cod·i·cil** (kod'ə-s'l, -sil'), *n.* [< L. dim. of *codex*; see CODE], 1. in *law*, an addition to a will, to change, explain, or add provisions. 2. an appendix or supplement. —**cod'i·cil'la·ry**, *adj.*
**cod·i·fy** (kod'ə-fī', kō'də-), *v.t.* [-FIED, -FYING], [< *code* + *-fy*], to arrange (laws, etc.) systematically. —**cod'i·fi·ca'tion**, *n.* —**cod'i·fi'er**, *n.*
**cod·ling** (kod'liŋ), *n.* [*pl.* -LING, -LINGS; see PLURAL, II, D, 2], 1. a young cod. 2. any of certain fishes allied to the cod.
**cod·ling** (kod'liŋ), *n.* [< Fr. *coeur de lion*, lit., heart of lion (a kind of apple)], 1. a variety of elongated apple. 2. an inferior or unripe apple. Also **cod'lin** (-lin).
**codling** (or **codlin**) **moth,** a small moth whose larva destroys apples, pears, and quinces.
**cod-liv·er oil** (kod'liv'ēr), oil obtained from the livers of the cod and allied fish: it contains various vitamins and is used in medicine.
**Co·dy, William Frederick** (kō'di), 1846–1917; U.S. plainsman and circus manager: called *Buffalo Bill.*
**co·ed, co-ed** (kō'ed'), *n.* [Colloq.], a girl attending a coeducational college.
**co·ed·u·ca·tion** (kō'ej-oo-kā'shən), *n.* [*co-* + *education*], the educational system in which students of both sexes attend classes together. —**co'ed·u·ca'tion·al**, *adj.* —**co'ed·u·ca'tion·al·ly**, *adv.*
**co·ef·fi·cient** (kō'ə-fish'ənt), *adj.* [< LL. < *coefficere*; see CO- & EFFECT], co-operating. *n.* 1. a factor that contributes to produce a result. 2. in *mathematics*, a number or symbol prefixed as a multiplier to a variable or unknown quantity: as, 6 is a *coefficient* in 6*ab*. 3. in *physics*, a number, constant for a given substance, used as a multiplier in measuring the change in some property of the substance under given conditions.
**-coele** (sēl), [< Gr. *koilia*, body cavity], a combining form meaning *cavity, chamber of the body*, as in *blastocoele*: also **-cele.**
**coe·len·ter·ate** (si-len'tēr-āt'), *n.* [ult. < Gr. *koilos*, hollow + *enteron*, intestine], an invertebrate saltwater animal, as the hydra, jellyfish, etc., in which the characteristic structure is a large central cavity. *adj.* of such invertebrates.
**coe·li·ac** (sē'li-ak'), *adj.* [L. *coeliacus* < Gr. < *koilia*, the belly < *koilos*, hollow], of or in the cavity of the abdomen: also sp. **celiac.**
**coe·lom** (sē'ləm), *n.* [< Gr. < *koilos*, hollow], the embryonic cavity of most multicellular animals, from which the main cavities of the body develop.
**coe·no-** (sē'nə, sen'ə), [< Gr. *koinos*, common], a combining form meaning *common*: also **coen-.**
**coe·no·bite** (sē'nə-bīt', sen'ə-), *n.* a cenobite.
**co·e·qual** (kō-ē'kwəl), *adj.* & *n.* equal.
**co·erce** (kō-ũrs'), *v.t.* [-ERCED, -ERCING], [L. *coercere* < *co-*, together + *arcere*, to confine], 1. to restrain or constrain by force; curb. 2. to force; compel. 3. to enforce. —**co·erc'er**, *n.* —**co·er'ci·ble**, *adj.*
**co·er·cion** (kō-ũr'shən), *n.* 1. a coercing or the power to coerce; compulsion; constraint. 2. government by force. —**co·er'cion·ist**, *n.*
**co·er·cive** (kō-ũr'siv), *adj.* of or characterized by coercion; tending to coerce. —**co·er'cive·ly**, *adv.* —**co·er'cive·ness**, *n.*
**co·e·val** (kō-ē'v'l), *adj.* [< LL. < L. *co-*, together + *aevum*, age], of the same age, period, or duration. *n.* a contemporary. —**co·e'val·ly**, *adv.*
**co·ex·ec·u·tor** (kō'ig-zek'yoo-tēr), *n.* a person acting as executor jointly with another.
**co·ex·ist** (kō'ig-zist'), *v.i.* to exist together, at the same time or in the same place. —**co'ex·ist'ence**, *n.* —**co'ex·ist'ent**, *adj.*
**co·ex·tend** (kō'ik-stend'), *v.t.* & *v.i.* to extend equally in space or time. —**co'ex·ten'sion**, *n.* —**co'ex·ten'sive**, *adj.*
**cof·fee** (kôf'i, kof'i), *n.* [see PLURAL, II, D, 3], [< It. < Turk. *qahveh* < Ar. *qahwah*], 1. an aromatic drink made from the roasted and ground beanlike seeds of a tall tropical shrub of the madder family. 2. the seeds, green, roasted, or ground, or the shrub. 3. the color of coffee with cream; brown. *adj.* having the flavor or color of coffee.
**coffee bean,** the seed of the coffee plant.
**coffee break,** a brief respite from work when coffee or other refreshment is usually taken.
**cof·fee·cake** (kôf'i-kāk', kof'-), *n.* a kind of cake or roll, often nut-filled, coated with sugar, etc., to be eaten with coffee or the like.
**cof·fee·pot** (kôf'i-pot', kof'-), *n.* a container in which coffee is made or served.
**coffee shop,** a restaurant, as in a hotel, where coffee, light refreshments, and now usually meals are served: also **cof'fee·room'**, *n.*
**coffee table,** a small, low table, usually in a living room, for serving refreshments.
**cof·fer** (kôf'ēr, kof'-), *n.* [< OFr. < L. *cophinus*; see COFFIN], 1. a chest or strongbox in which money or valuables are kept. 2. *pl.* a treasury; funds. 3. a decorative sunken panel in a vault, dome, etc. 4. a cofferdam. *v.t.* 1. to enclose in a coffer. 2. to furnish with coffers (*n.* 3).
**cof·fer·dam** (kôf'ēr-dam', kof'-), *n.* [*coffer* + *dam* (barrier)], 1. a watertight temporary structure in a river, lake, etc., for keeping the water from an enclosed area that has been pumped dry so that dams, etc. may be constructed. 2. a watertight box attached to the side of a ship so that repairs can be made below the water line.
**cof·fin** (kôf'in, kof'-), *n.* [< OFr. < L. *cophinus* < Gr. *kophinos*, basket], a case or box to put a dead person into for burial. *v.t.* 1. to put into a coffin. 2. to confine tightly.
**coffin nail,** [Slang], a cigarette.
**cog** (kog), *n.* [< Scand.], 1. one of a series of teeth on the rim of a wheel, for transmitting or receiving motion by fitting between the teeth of another wheel; gear tooth. 2. a wheel with such teeth on its rim. Often used figuratively. —**slip a cog,** to make an error. —**cogged** (kogd), *adj.*
**cog** (kog), *n.* [altered (after *cog*, gear tooth) < earlier *cock*, to secure], a projection on a beam that fits into a corresponding groove or notch in another beam, making a joint. *v.t.* & *v.i.* [COGGED, COGGING], to join by a cog.
**co·gent** (kō'jənt), *adj.* [< L. ppr. of *cogere*, to collect < *co-*, together + *agere*, to drive], compelling; convincing, as an argument. —**co'gen·cy**, *n.* —**co'gent·ly**, *adv.*
**cog·i·tate** (koj'ə-tāt'), *v.i.* [-TATED, -TATING], [< L. pp. of *cogitare*, to ponder], to think seriously; ponder; meditate. *v.t.* to think about; consider. —**cog'i·ta·ble** (-tə-b'l), *adj.* —**cog'i·ta'tor**, *n.*
**cog·i·ta·tion** (koj'ə-tā'shən), *n.* thought; thinking. —**cog'i·ta'tive**, *adj.* —**cog'i·ta'tive·ly**, *adv.* —**cog'i·ta'tive·ness**, *n.*
**co·gnac** (kō'nyak, kon'yak), *n.* [Fr.], a French brandy distilled from wine; loosely, any brandy.
**cog·nate** (kog'nāt), *adj.* [L. *cognatus* < *co-*, together + pp. of (*g*)*nasci*, to be born], 1. related by family. 2. derived from a common original form: as, French and Italian are *cognate* languages. 3. having the same nature or quality. *n.* 1. a person related to another by common ancestry. 2. a cognate word, language, or thing. —**cog·na'tion**, *n.*
**cog·ni·tion** (kog-nish'ən), *n.* [L. *cognito*, knowledge; ult. < *co-*, together + (*g*)*noscere*, to know], 1. the process of knowing or perceiving; perception. 2. anything that is known or perceived. —**cog·ni·tive** (kog'nə-tiv), **cog·ni'tion·al**, *adj.*
**cog·ni·za·ble** (kog'ni-zə-b'l, kon'i-), *adj.* 1. that can be recognized, known, or perceived. 2. in *law*, within the jurisdiction of a court. —**cog'ni·za·bil'i·ty**, *n.* —**cog'ni·za·bly**, *adv.*

**cog·ni·zance** (kog′ni-zəns, kon′i-), *n.* [< OFr.; see COGNITION], 1. the fact of being aware; perception; knowledge. 2. notice; heed. 3. the range of knowledge possible through observation. 4. in *heraldry*, a distinguishing device, as a crest. 5. in *law*, *a*) a hearing. *b*) the right or power of dealing with a matter judicially. —**take cognizance of,** to notice; recognize officially.

**cog·ni·zant** (kog′ni-zənt, kon′i-), *adj.* having cognizance (*of* something); aware; informed.

**cog·nize** (kog′nīz′), *v.t.* [-NIZED, -NIZING], to take cognizance of; perceive or recognize.

**cog·no·men** (kog-nō′mən), *n.* [*pl.* -NOMENS, -NOMINA (-nom′ə-nə)], [L. < *co-*, with + *nomen*, name], 1. the third or family name of an ancient Roman. 2. a family name; surname. 3. any name; esp., a nickname. —**cog·nom′i·nal** (-nom′i-n'l), *adj.*

**cog·wheel** (kog′hwēl′), *n.* a wheel with a rim notched into teeth, which mesh with those of another wheel to transmit or receive motion.

COGWHEELS

**co·hab·it** (kō-hab′it), *v.i.* [< LL. < L. *co-*, together + *habitare*, to dwell], 1. to live together as husband and wife: applied especially to those not legally married. 2. [Archaic], to live together. —**co·hab′it·ant,** *n.* —**co·hab′i·ta′tion,** *n.*

**co·heir** (kō-âr′), *n.* a person who inherits jointly with another or others. —**co·heir′ess,** *n.fem.*

**co·here** (kō-hêr′), *v.i.* [-HERED, -HERING], [< L. < *co-*, together + *haerere*, to stick], 1. to stick together, as parts of a mass. 2. to be connected naturally or logically; be in accord.

**co·her·ence** (kō-hêr′əns), *n.* 1. a sticking together; cohesion. 2. the quality of being logically connected and intelligible. Also **co·her′en·cy.**

**co·her·ent** (kō-hêr′ənt), *adj.* 1. sticking together; having cohesion. 2. logically connected and intelligible. —**co·her′ent·ly,** *adv.*

**co·her·er** (kō-hêr′ẽr), *n.* in *radio*, an early kind of detector, in use before the vacuum tube.

**co·he·sion** (kō-hē′zhən), *n.* 1. the act or condition of cohering; tendency to stick together. 2. in *physics*, the force by which the molecules of a substance are held together: cf. *adhesion*. —**co·he′sive** (-siv), *adj.* —**co·he′sive·ly** *adv.* —**co·he′sive·ness,** *n.*

**co·hort** (kō′hôrt), *n.* [< Fr. < L. *cohors*, enclosure], 1. an ancient Roman military unit, one tenth of a legion. 2. a band of soldiers. 3. a group; band. 4. now, often, an associate; colleague.

**coif** (koif), *n.* [< OFr. < LL. *cofea*, a cap, hood], a cap that fits the head closely, as that once worn under a hood of mail. *v.t.* to cover as with a coif.

‡**coif·feur** (kwȧ′fẽr′), *n.* [Fr.], a hairdresser.

**coif·fure** (kwä-fyoor′; Fr. kwȧ′für′), *n.* [< Fr.; see COIF], 1. a headdress. 2. a style of arranging the hair.

**coign, coigne** (koin), *n.* [var. of *coin*, *quoin*], a projecting corner.

**coign of vantage,** an advantageous position for observation or action.

**coil** (koil), *v.t.* [< OFr. < L. < *com-*, together + *legere*, to gather], to wind into a circular or spiral form. *v.i.* 1. to wind around and around. 2. to move in a winding course. *n.* 1. anything wound into a series of rings or spirals. 2. such a series of rings or spirals. 3. a single turn of a coiled figure. 4. a series of connected pipes in rows or coils. 5. in *electricity*, *a*) a spiral of wire. *b*) any device consisting mainly of such a spiral. —**coil′er,** *n.*

**coin** (koin), *n.* [< OFr. < L. *cuneus*, a wedge], 1. a cornerstone; wedge; quoin; coign. 2. a piece of metal with a distinctive stamp, issued by a government as money. 3. such pieces collectively. 4. [Slang], money. *v.t.* 1. *a*) to make (coins) by stamping metal. *b*) to make (metal) into coins. 2. to make up; invent, as a new word. *v.i.* to make coins. —**coin money,** [Colloq.], to earn money rapidly. —**coin′a·ble,** *adj.* —**coin′er,** *n.*

**coin·age** (koin′ij), *n.* 1. the act or process of coining. 2. a thing or things coined. 3. a system of metal currency. 4. the right to coin money. 5. an invented word or expression.

**co·in·cide** (kō′in-sīd′), *v.i.* [-CIDED, -CIDING], [< Fr. < ML. < L. *co-*, together + *in-*, upon, in + *cadere*, to fall], 1. to take up the same place in space. 2. to occur at the same time. 3. to agree; match exactly; be identical.

**co·in·ci·dence** (kō-in′sə-dəns), *n.* 1. the fact or condition of coinciding. 2. an accidental and remarkable occurrence of related or identical events, ideas, etc. at the same time with no apparent causal relationship.

**co·in·ci·dent** (kō-in′sə-dənt), *adj.* 1. coinciding; occurring at the same time. 2. taking up the same position in space at the same time. 3. in exact agreement; identical: as, a hobby *coincident* with one's vocation. —**co·in′ci·dent·ly,** *adv.*

**co·in·ci·den·tal** (kō-in′sə-den′t'l), *adj.* characterized by coincidence; coincident. —**co·in′ci·den′tal·ly,** *adv.*

**coir** (koir), *n.* [< Port.; ult. < Tamil *kayaru*, to be twisted], the prepared fiber of the husks of coconuts, used to make rope, etc.

**co·i·tus** (kō′i-təs), *n.* [< L. < *co-*, together + *ire*, to go], sexual intercourse: also **co·i·tion** (kō-ish′ən).

**coke** (kōk), *n.* [prob. < ME. *colke*, a core], coal from which most of the gases have been removed by heating: it burns with intense heat and little smoke, and is used as an industrial fuel. *v.t. & v.i* [COKED, COKING], to change into coke.

**coke** (kōk), *n.* a variety of soft drink flavored with kola: a trade-mark (**Coke**).

**col-,** com-: used before *l*.

**Col.,** 1. Colombia. 2. Colonel. 3. Colorado: officially, **Colo.** 4. Colossians.

**col.,** 1. collected. 2. collection. 3. collector. 4. college. 5. colony. 6. color(ed). 7. column.

**co·la** (kō′lə), *n.* the kola (an African tree).

**col·an·der** (kul′ən-dẽr, kol′-), *n.* [prob. < L. *colare*, to strain < *colum*, strainer], a pan with a perforated bottom to drain off liquids.

**col·chi·cum** (kol′chi-kəm, -ki-), *n.* [L. < Gr. *kolchikon*, plant with a poisonous root], 1. a plant of the lily family, with crocuslike flowers: also called **autumn crocus, meadow saffron.** 2. the seeds or corm of this plant, sometimes used in the treatment of rheumatism and gout.

**cold** (kōld), *adj.* [AS. *cald* < Gmc. base], 1. of a temperature much lower than that of the human body; very chilly; frigid. 2. lacking heat; having lost heat: as, this soup is *cold*. 3. dead. 4. feeling chilled. 5. without warmth of feeling; not cordial: as, a *cold* reception. 6. chilling; dispiriting: as, a *cold* awakening. 7. calm; detached: as, *cold* logic. 8. designatng colors that suggest cold, as tones of blue, green, or gray. 9. [Slang], completely mastered: as, the actor had his lines down *cold*. 10. [Slang], insensible: as, knocked *cold*. 11. in *hunting*, faint; not strong: said of a scent. *n.* 1. absence of heat; lack of warmth: often thought of as an active force. 2. the sensation produced by a loss or absence of heat. 3. an acute inflammation of the mucous membranes of the nose and throat, caused by a virus and characterized by sneezing, coughing, etc.; coryza. —**catch** (or **take**) **cold,** to become ill with a cold. —**cold comfort,** little or no comfort. —**have cold feet,** [Colloq.], to be timid. —**in the cold,** ignored; neglected. —**throw cold water on,** to discourage. —**cold′ish,** *adj.* —**cold′ly,** *adv.* —**cold′ness,** *n.*

**cold-blood·ed** (kōld′blud′id), *adj.* 1. having blood that varies in temperature with the surrounding air, land, or water, as fishes and reptiles. 2. easily affected by cold. 3. callous; cruel. —**cold′-blood′ed·ly,** *adv.* —**cold′blood′ed·ness,** *n.*

**cold chisel,** a hardened and tempered steel chisel for cutting or chipping cold metal.

**cold cream,** a creamy, soothing preparation for softening and cleansing the skin.

**cold front,** in *meteorology*, the forward line of a cold air mass advancing into a warmer air mass.

**cold-heart·ed** (kōld′här′tid), *adj.* not sympathetic; unfeeling; unkind. —**cold′-heart′ed·ly,** *adv.* —**cold′-heart′ed·ness,** *n.*

**cold pack,** a process of canning foodstuffs in which the raw products are placed in jars first and then subjected to heat. —**cold′-pack′,** *v.t.*

**cold shoulder,** [Colloq.], deliberate indifference; slight; rebuff; snub. —**cold′-shoul′der,** *v.t.*

**cold sore,** little blisters about the mouth during a cold or fever; fever blister: see **herpes.**

**cold steel,** a weapon of steel, as a knife, etc.

**cold war,** sharp conflict in diplomacy, economics, etc. between states, regarded as potentially leading to actual war.

**cold wave,** 1. a period of unusually cold weather. 2. a permanent wave in which the hair is set with a liquid preparation instead of heat.

**cole** (kōl), *n.* [AS. *caul* < L. *caulis*, *colis*, a cabbage], any of various plants of the mustard family, to which cabbage belongs; esp., rape.

**co·le·op·ter** (kō′li-op′tẽr, kol′i-), *n.* any coleopterous insect: also **co′le·op′ter·on′** (-on′), [*pl.* -TERA (-ə)], **co′le·op′ter·an** (-ən).

**co·le·op·ter·ous** (kō′li-op′tẽr-əs, kol′i-), *adj.* [< Gr. < *koleos*, sheath + *pteron*, wing; + *-ous*], belonging to a group of insects, including beetles and weevils, with the front wings forming a horny covering for the hind wings, which are functional.

**Cole·ridge, Samuel Taylor** (kōl′rij, kō′lə-), 1772–1834; English poet and critic.

**cole·slaw** (kōl′slô′), *n.* [< D. *kool*, a cabbage < L. *caulis* + D. *sla* for *salade*, salad], a salad made of shredded raw cabbage: also **cole slaw.**

**cole·wort** (kōl′wūrt′), *n.* [*cole* + *wort*], any cabbage whose leaves do not form a compact head.

**col·ic** (kol′ik), *n.* [< Fr. < L. < Gr. < *kōlon*, colon], acute abdominal pain caused by various abnormal conditions in the bowels. *adj.* 1. of colic. 2. of the colon. —**col′ick·y,** *adj.*

**col·i·se·um** (kol′ə-sē′əm), *n.* [< L. neut. of *colosseus*, huge], 1. [C-], the Colosseum. 2. a large building or stadium for sports events, etc.

**co·li·tis** (kō-lī′tis), *n.* [< Gr. *kōlon*, colon; + *-itis*], inflammation of the large intestine.

**coll.,** 1. collect. 2. collection. 3. college.

**col·lab·o·rate** (kə-lab′ə-rāt′), *v.i.* [-RATED, -RATING], [< L. < *com-*, with + *laborare*, to work], 1. to work together, especially in literary, artistic, or scientific work. 2. to co-operate with an enemy invader of one's country. —**col·lab′o·ra′tion,** *n.* —**col·lab′o·ra′tive,** *adj.* —**col·lab′o·ra′tor, col·lab′o·ra′tion·ist,** *n.*

**col·lapse** (kə-laps′), *v.i.* [-LAPSED, -LAPSING], [< L. < *com-*, together + *labi*, to fall], 1. to fall in or together; cave in; shrink together suddenly. 2. to break down suddenly; fail. 3. to fail suddenly in health. 4. to fold or come together compactly. 5. to fall down, as from a blow or strain. *v.t.* to cause to collapse. *n.* 1. a falling in or together; sudden caving in. 2. a failure or breakdown. 3. a sudden breakdown in health. —**col·laps′i·bil′i·ty,** *n.* —**col·laps′i·ble,** *adj.*

**col·lar** (kol′ẽr), *n.* [< OFr. < L. < *collum*, the neck], 1. the part of a dress, coat, shirt, etc. that encircles the neck. 2. a cloth band attached to the neck of a shirt, blouse, etc. 3. a band of leather or metal for a dog's neck. 4. the part of a harness that fits over the neck of a horse or other draft animal. 5. a ring or flange, as on a rod or pipe, to prevent sideward motion, connect parts, etc. *v.t.* 1. to put a collar on. 2. to seize by the collar; capture.

**col·lar·bone** (kol′ẽr-bōn′), *n.* the clavicle.

**col·lar·et, col·lar·ette** (kol′ẽr-et′), *n.* [Fr.], a small collar or cape of linen, fur, etc.

**col·late** (ko-lāt′, kol′āt), *v.t.* [-LATED, -LATING], [< L. *collatus*, pp. of *conferre* < *com-*, together + *ferre*, to bring], 1. to compare (texts, etc.) carefully. 2. to examine (the pages of a book to be bound) to see that they are in proper order. —**col·la′tor,** *n.*

**col·lat·er·al** (kə-lat′ẽr-əl), *adj.* [< LL. < L. *com-*, together + *lateralis*, lateral < *latus*, a side], 1. side by side; parallel. 2. accompanying. 3. of a similar but subordinate nature; secondary. 4. of corresponding value or importance. 5. of the same ancestors but in a different line. 6. designating or of security given as a pledge for the fulfillment of an obligation; hence, secured or guaranteed by stocks, bonds, etc.: as, a *collateral* loan. *n.* 1. a collateral relative. 2. stocks, bonds, etc. used for collateral security. —**col·lat′er·al·ly,** *adv.*

**col·la·tion** (ko-lā′shən, kə-), *n.* 1. the act, process, or result of collating. 2. a light meal.

**col·league** (kol′ēg), *n.* [< Fr. < L. *collega* < *com-*, with + *legare*, to appoint as deputy], a fellow worker in the same profession; associate in office. —**col′league·ship′,** *n.*

**col·lect** (kə-lekt′), *v.t.* [< OFr. < L. *collectus;* see COLLECT, *n.*], 1. to gather together; assemble. 2. to gather (stamps, books, etc.) for a hobby. 3. to call for and receive payment for (rent, taxes, bills, etc.). 4. to regain control of (oneself or one's wits). *v.i.* 1. to gather; assemble. 2. to accumulate. 3. to collect payments, etc. *adj. & adv.* with payment to be made by the receiver: as, he telephoned *collect.* —**col·lect′a·ble, col·lect′i·ble,** *adj.*

**col·lect** (kol′ekt), *n.* [< OFr.; ult. < L. *collectus*, pp. of *colligere* < *com-*, together + *legere*, to gather], a short prayer used in certain church services.

**col·lect·ed** (kə-lek′tid), *adj.* 1. gathered together; assembled. 2. in control of oneself; calm. —**col·lect′ed·ly,** *adv.* —**col·lect′ed·ness,** *n.*

**col·lec·tion** (kə-lek′shən), *n.* 1. the act or process of collecting. 2. things collected. 3. a mass or pile; accumulation. 4. money collected.

**col·lec·tive** (kə-lek′tiv), *adj.* 1. formed by collecting; gathered into a whole. 2. of or as a group; of or characteristic of individuals acting together: as, the *collective* effort of the students. 3. designating or of any enterprise in which people work collectively: as, *collective* farms. 4. in *grammar*, designating a noun which in the singular form denotes a collection of individuals (e.g., army, crowd). *n.* 1. any collective enterprise. 2. the people who work together in such an enterprise. 3. in *grammar*, a collective noun. —**col·lec′tive·ly,** *adv.* —**col·lec·tiv·i·ty** (kol′ek-tiv′ə-ti), *n.*

**collective bargaining,** negotiation between organized workers and their employer or employers concerning wages, hours, working conditions, etc.

**col·lec·tiv·ism** (kə-lek′tiv-iz′m), *n.* the ownership and control of the means of production and distribution by the people as a whole; socialism. —**col·lec′tiv·ist,** *n. & adj.* —**col·lec′tiv·is′tic,** *adj.* —**col·lec′tiv·is′ti·cal·ly,** *adv.*

**col·lec·tiv·ize** (kə-lek′tiv-īz′), *v.t.* [-IZED, -IZING], 1. to establish collectivism in. 2. to transfer from private to public ownership. —**col·lec′ti·vi·za′tion,** *n.*

**col·lec·tor** (kə-lek′tẽr), *n.* [LL.], 1. a person or thing that collects. 2. a person whose work is to collect money due. —**col·lec′tor·ship′,** *n.*

**col·leen** (kol′ēn, kə-lēn′), *n.* [< Ir. < *caile*, girl], [Irish], a girl.

**col·lege** (kol′ij), *n.* [< L. < *collega;* see COLLEAGUE], 1. an association of individuals having certain powers, rights, and duties: as, the electoral *college.* 2. an institution of higher education that grants degrees; university. 3. any of the schools of a university granting degrees in any of several specialized or professional courses of study. 4. that division of a university which offers a general four-year course leading to the bachelor's degree: distinguished from the graduate and professional schools. 5. a school offering specialized instruction in some profession or occupation: as, a business *college.* 6. the building or buildings of a college. —**col·le·gi·al** (kə-lē′ji-əl), *adj.*

**College of Cardinals,** the cardinals of the Roman Catholic Church, serving as a privy council to the Pope and electing his successor.

**col·le·gi·an** (kə-lē′jən, -ji-ən), *n.* [ML. *collegianus*], a college student.

**col·le·gi·ate** (kə-lē′jit, -ji-it), *adj.* of or like a college or college students. —**col·le′gi·ate·ly,** *adv.* —**col·le′gi·ate·ness,** *n.*

**col·lide** (kə-līd′), *v.i.* [-LIDED, -LIDING], [L. *collidere* < *com-*, together + *laedere*, to strike], 1. to come into violent contact; strike violently against each other; crash. 2. to conflict; clash.

**col·lie** (kol′i), *n.* [said to be < *coaly*, coal-black], a large, long-haired Scottish sheep dog with a long, narrow head.

**col·lier** (kol′yẽr), *n.* [ME. < *col*, coal; + *-ier*], 1. a coal miner. 2. a ship for carrying coal.

**col·lier·y** (kol′yẽr-i), *n.* [*pl.* -IES], a coal mine and its buildings, equipment, etc.

**col·li·mate** (kol′ə-māt′), *v.t.* [-MATED, -MATING], [< false reading of L. *collineare* < *com-*, with + *lineare*, to make straight < *linea*, a line], 1. to make parallel, as light rays. 2. to adjust the line of sight of (a telescope, etc.). —**col′li·ma′tion,** *n.*

**col·li·ma·tor** (kol′ə-mā′tẽr), *n.* [see COLLIMATE], a small telescope with cross hairs at its focus, fixed to another telescope, surveying instrument, etc. for adjusting the line of sight.

**Col·lins** (kol′inz), *n.* any of several mixed drinks made with lemon or lime juice, sugar, carbonated water, ice, and either gin (**Tom Collins**), rum (**Rum Collins**), or whisky (**John Collins**).

**col·li·sion** (kə-lizh′ən), *n.* 1. a colliding; sudden, violent contact between moving bodies. 2. a clash of opinions, interests, etc.; conflict.

**col·lo·cate** (kol′ō-kāt′), *v.t.* [-CATED, -CATING], [< L. pp. of *collocare*, < *com-*, together + *locare*, to place], 1. to arrange. 2. to place side by side. —**col′lo·ca′tion,** *n.*

**col·lo·di·on** (kə-lō′di-ən), *n.* [< Gr. < *kolla*, glue + *eidos*, form], a highly inflammable solution that dries quickly, forming a tough, elastic film: used to protect wounds, photographic plates, etc.

**col·logue** (kə-lōg′), *v.i.* [-LOGUED, -LOGUING], [< Fr. < L.; see COLLOQUY], [Dial.], to confer secretly.

**col·loid** (kol′oid), *n.* [< Gr. *kolla*, glue; + *-oid*], a gelatinous substance made up of insoluble, nondiffusible particles larger than molecules but so small that they remain suspended in a fluid medium. *adj.* colloidal.

**col·loi·dal** (kə-loi′d'l), *adj.* of, like, or containing a colloid. —**col·loid·al·i·ty** (kol′oi-dal′ə-ti), *n.*

**colloq.,** 1. colloquial(ly). 2. colloquialism.

**col·lo·qui·al** (kə-lō′kwi-əl), *adj.* [see COLLOQUY], 1. having to do with conversation. 2. belonging to the words, phrases, and idioms characteristic of conversation and informal writing; informal: the label [Colloq.] is used throughout this dictionary in this sense, and does not indicate substandard or illiterate usage. —**col·lo′qui·al·ly,** *adv.* —**col·lo′qui·al·ness,** *n.*

**col·lo·qui·al·ism** (kə-lō′kwi-əl-iz'm), *n.* 1. colloquial quality, style, or usage. 2. a colloquial word or expression.

**col·lo·quy** (kol′ə-kwi), *n.* [*pl.* -QUIES], [L. *colloquium,* conversation < *com-,* together + *loqui,* to speak], a conversation, especially a somewhat formal conversation; conference. —**col′lo·quist,** *n.*

**col·lude** (kə-lōōd′), *v.i.* [-LUDED, -LUDING], [< L. < *com-,* with + *ludere,* to play], to act in collusion; conspire in some fraud. —**col·lud′er,** *n.*

**col·lu·sion** (kə-lōō′zhən), *n.* [see COLLUDE], a secret agreement for fraudulent or illegal purpose; conspiracy. —**col·lu′sive (-siv),** *adj.* —**col·lu′sive·ly,** *adv.* —**col·lu′sive·ness,** *n.*

**Colo.,** Colorado.

**Co·logne** (kə-lōn′), *n.* a city in W Germany, on the Rhine: pop., 760,000: German name, *Köln.*

**co·logne** (kə-lōn′), *n.* [short for *eau de Cologne*], a fragrant liquid made of alcohol and various aromatic oils, used like perfume.

**Co·lom·bi·a** (kə-lum′bi-ə; Sp. kô-lôm′byä), *n.* a country in NW South America: area, 439,829 sq. mi.; pop., 14,132,000; capital, Bogotá. —**Co·lom′bi·an,** *n. & adj.*

**Co·lom·bo** (kə-lum′bō), *n.* the capital of Ceylon, on the west coast: pop., 426,000.

**Co·lón** (kō-lōn′, -lon′; Sp. kô-lôn′), *n.* a seaport in Panama, at the entrance to the Panama Canal, on the Caribbean: pop., 58,000.

**co·lon** (kō-lōn′; Sp. kô-lôn′), *n.* [*pl.* -LONS, Sp. -LONES (-lô′nes)], [< Sp. *Colón,* Columbus], the monetary unit of *a*) Costa Rica. *b*) El Salvador.

**co·lon** (kō′lən), *n.* [L. < Gr. *kōlon,* limb, clause], a mark of punctuation (:) used before an extended quotation, explanation, example, series, etc., and after the salutation of a formal letter.

**co·lon** (kō′lən), *n.* [*pl.* -LONS, -LA (-lə)], [L. < Gr. *kolon*], that part of the large intestine extending from the caecum to the rectum. —**co·lon·ic** (kə-lon′ik), *adj.*

**colo·nel** (kūr′n'l), *n.* [earlier *coronel* < Fr. < It. < *colonna,* (military) column < L. *columna*], an army officer ranking just above a lieutenant colonel: the usual commanding officer of a regiment in the army or of a group in the air force. —**colo′nel·cy** [*pl.* -CIES], **colo′nel·ship′,** *n.*

**co·lo·ni·al** (kə-lō′ni-əl), *adj.* 1. of or living in a colony or colonies. 2. of or characteristic of the thirteen British colonies in North America that became the United States. *n.* an inhabitant of a colony. —**co·lo′ni·al·ly,** *adv.*

**col·o·nist** (kol′ə-nist), *n.* 1. one of the original settlers of a colony. 2. an inhabitant of a colony.

**col·o·nize** (kol′ə-nīz′), *v.t. & v.i.* [-NIZED, -NIZING], 1. to found or establish a colony or colonies (in). 2. to place or settle in a colony. —**col′o·ni·za′tion,** *n.* —**col′o·niz′er,** *n.*

**col·on·nade** (kol′ə-nād′), *n.* [Fr. < It. < L. *columna,* column], in *architecture,* a series of columns set at regular intervals. —**col′on·nad′ed,** *adj.*

**col·o·ny** (kol′ə-ni), *n.* [*pl.* -NIES], [< Fr. < L. < *colonus,* farmer < *colere,* to cultivate], 1. a group of people who settle in a distant land but under the jurisdiction of their native land. 2. a region thus settled. 3. a territory distant from the state having jurisdiction over it. 4. [C-], *pl.* the thirteen British colonies in North America that became the United States. 5. a community of people of the same nationality or pursuits concentrated in a particular place: as, an artist's *colony.* 6. in *bacteriology,* a group of similar bacteria growing in a culture. 7. in *biology,* a group of similar plants or animals living or growing together.

**col·o·phon** (kol′ə-fon′, -fən), *n.* [LL. < Gr. *kolophōn,* summit, finishing stroke], a publisher's inscription or emblematic device, put on the last page or title page of a book.

**col·or** (kul′ēr), *n.* [< OFr. < L. < OL. *colos* < *celare,* to cover], 1. the sensation resulting from stimulation of the retina of the eye by light waves. 2. the property of reflecting light waves of a particular length: the *primary colors of the spectrum* are red, orange, yellow, green, blue, indigo, and violet. 3. any coloring matter; dye; pigment; paint: in this sense, the *primary colors* (red, yellow, and blue) and the *secondary colors* formed from these (green, orange, purple, etc.) are sometimes distinguished from black, white, and gray (*achromatic colors*). 4. color of the face, especially healthy rosiness or a blush. 5. the color of the skin of a Negro or other person not classified as Caucasian. 6. *pl.* a colored badge, costume, etc. that shows the wearer's connection with something. 7. *pl.* a flag of a country, regiment, etc. 8. *pl.* one's position or opinion: as, stick to your *colors.* 9. outward appearance; semblance; aspect. 10. appearance of truth; plausibility: as, the news lent *color* to the rumor. 11. kind; sort. 12. vivid and picturesque quality: as, there is *color* in his writing. 13. in *art,* the way of using color. *v.t.* 1. to give color to; paint; stain; dye. 2. to change the color of. 3. to alter or influence, especially by distortion: as, his experience has *colored* his views. *v.i.* 1. to become colored. 2. to change color. 3. to blush or flush. —**call to the colors,** 1. call or order to serve in the armed forces. 2. a bugle call to the daily raising of the flag at reveille and retreat. —**change color,** 1. to become pale. 2. to blush or flush. —**lose color,** to become pale. —**serve with the colors,** to serve in the armed forces. —**show one's colors,** to reveal one's true self or one's position, opinions, etc. —**under color of,** under the pretext of. —**with flying colors,** with great success.

**col·or·a·ble** (kul′ēr-ə-b'l), *adj.* 1. capable of being colored. 2. apparently plausible, but actually specious; deceptive. —**col′or·a·bil′i·ty, col′or·a·ble·ness,** *n.* —**col′or·a·bly,** *adv.*

**Col·o·rad·o** (kol′ə-rad′ō, -rä′dō), *n.* 1. a Western State of the U.S.: area, 104,247 sq. mi.; pop., 1,754,000; capital, Denver: abbrev. **Colo., Col.** 2. a river flowing from Colorado into the Gulf of California. —**Col′o·rad′an,** *n. & adj.*

**col·o·rad·o** (kol′ə-rad′ō, -rä′dō), *adj.* [Sp., red], of medium strength and color: said of cigars.

**Colorado Springs,** a city in central Colorado: pop., 70,000: site of U.S. Air Force Academy.

**col·or·a·tion** (kul′ēr-ā′shən), *n.* coloring: as, some animals have protective *coloration.*

**col·o·ra·tu·ra** (kul′ēr-ə-tyoor′ə, kol′ēr-ə-toor′ə), *n.* [It. < L. pp. of *colorare,* to color], in *music,* 1. brilliant ornamental runs, trills, etc. 2. music containing these. 3. a coloratura soprano. Also **col′or·a·ture′** (-choor′) *adj.* characterized by coloratura. *adv.* in a coloratura manner.

**coloratura soprano,** a singer or a high soprano voice capable of singing coloratura.

**col·or-bear·er** (kul′ēr-bâr′ēr), *n.* one who carries the colors (flag); standard-bearer.

**col·or-blind** (kul′ēr-blīnd′), *adj.* unable to distinguish or perceive certain colors or any colors. —**color blindness.**

**col·ored** (kul′ērd), *adj.* 1. having color. 2. of a (specified) color. 3. of a race other than the Caucasian; specif., Negro. 4. altered, influenced, distorted, or exaggerated.

**col·or·ful** (kul′ēr-fəl), *adj.* 1. full of color. 2. full of contrast or variety; picturesque, vivid, etc. —**col′or·ful·ly,** *adv.* —**col′or·ful·ness,** *n.*

**color guard,** persons escorting the colors (flag).

**col·or·ing** (kul′ēr-iŋ), *n.* 1. the act or art of applying colors. 2. anything applied to impart color; pigment, dye, stain, etc.: also **coloring matter.** 3. appearance with reference to color. 4. specious or false appearance.

**col·or·ist** (kul′ēr-ist), *n.* 1. a person who uses colors. 2. an artist skillful in using colors.

**col·or·less** (kul′ēr-lis), *adj.* 1. without color. 2. lacking variety or interest; not vivid; dull. —**col′or·less·ly,** *adv.* —**col′or·less·ness,** *n.*

**color line,** the barrier of social, political, and economic restrictions imposed on the Negroes or other colored races. —**draw the color line,** to accept and keep the color line.

**Co·los·sae** (kə-los′ē), *n.* a city in ancient Phrygia. —**Co·los′sian** (-losh′ən), *adj. & n.*

**co·los·sal** (kə-los′'l), *adj.* like a colossus in size; huge; gigantic. —**co·los′sal·ly,** *adv.*

**Col·os·se·um** (kol′ə-sē′əm), *n.* [see COLISEUM], 1. an amphitheater at Rome, begun in 75 A.D.: most of it is still standing. 2. [c-], a coliseum.

**Co·los·sians** (kə-losh′ənz), *n.pl.* [construed as sing.], a book of the New Testament: an Epistle of the Apostle Paul to the Christians of Colossae.

**co·los·sus** (kə-los′əs), *n.* [*pl.* -SI (-ī), -SUSES], [L.; Gr. *kolossos*], 1. a gigantic statue; esp., [C-], that of Apollo set at the entrance to the harbor of Rhodes c. 280 B.C.: in full, **Colossus of Rhodes.** 2. any huge or important person or thing.

**col·our** (kul′ēr), *n., v.t. & v.i.* color: Brit. spelling.

—col′our·a·ble, *adj.* —col′our·a′tion, *n.* —col′oured, *adj.* —col′our·er, *n.* —col′our·ful, *adj.* —col′our·ing, *n.* —col′our·ist, *n.* —col′our·less, *adj.*

**-co·lous** (kə-ləs), [< base of L. *colere*, to inhabit; + *-ous*], a combining form meaning *growing* (or *living*) *in* or *among*.

**colt** (kōlt), *n.* [< AS.], 1. a young horse, donkey, zebra, etc.; specif., a young male horse; hence, 2. a young, inexperienced person.

**col·ter** (kōl′tẽr), *n.* [< OFr. or AS.; both < L. *culter*, knife], a blade or disk on a plow, for making vertical cuts in the soil: also sp. **coulter.**

**colt·ish** (kōl′tish), *adj.* of or like a colt; frisky. —**colt′ish·ly,** *adv.* —**colt′ish·ness,** *n.*

**colts·foot** (kōlts′foot′), *n.* [*pl.* -FOOTS], a plant of the composite family, with yellow flowers and large, heart-shaped leaves, used medicinally.

**col·um·bar·y** (kol′əm-ber′i), *n.* [*pl.* -IES], [< L. < *columba*, dove], a house for pigeons; dovecote.

**Co·lum·bi·a** (kə-lum′bi-ə, -byə), *n.* [< Christopher *Columbus*], 1. [Poetic], the United States: feminine symbol. 2. the capital of South Carolina: pop., 97,000. 3. a river rising in British Columbia and flowing between Washington and Oregon to the Pacific: length, 1,214 mi. —**Co·lum′bi·an,** *adj.*

**col·um·bine** (kol′əm-bīn′), *n.* [< Fr. < ML. < L. *columbinus*, dovelike < *columba*, dove], a plant of the crowfoot family, with showy, spurred flowers of various colors. *adj.* of or like a dove.

**co·lum·bi·um** (kə-lum′bi-əm), *n.* [< *Columbia* (the United States)], niobium: the former name.

**Co·lum·bus** (kə-lum′bəs), *n.* 1. the capital of Ohio, in the central part of the State: pop., 471,000. 2. a city in W Georgia: pop., 117,000.

**Co·lum·bus, Christopher** (kə-lum′bəs), 1446?–1506; Italian explorer in the service of Spain; discovered America (1492).

**Columbus Day,** October 12, commemorating the discovery of America by Columbus in 1492.

**col·umn** (kol′əm), *n.* [< OFr. < L. *columna*], 1. a slender, upright structure, generally a cylindrical shaft with a base and capital; pillar: it is usually a supporting or ornamental member in a building. 2. anything like a column in shape or function: as, the **spinal** *column*. 3. any of the vertical sections of printed matter lying side by side on a page and separated by a rule or blank space. 4. a regular feature article in a newspaper or magazine, written by a special writer or devoted to a certain subject. 5. a formation in which troops or ships are placed one behind another. —**co·lum·nar** (kə-lum′nẽr), *adj.* —**col′umned,** *adj.*

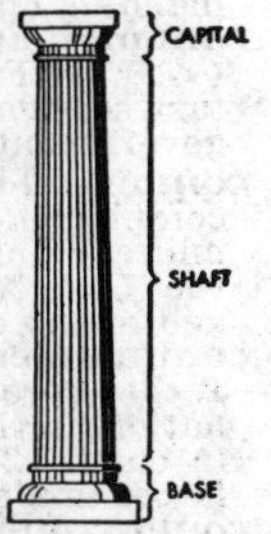

COLUMN

**co·lum·ni·a·tion** (kə-lum′ni-ā′shən), *n.* the architectural use or arrangement of columns.

**col·um·nist** (kol′əm-nist, -əm-ist), *n.* a person who writes or conducts a column (sense 4).

**col·za** (kol′zə), *n.* [Fr. < D. < *kool*, a cabbage + *zaad*, a seed], cole or its seed; esp., rapeseed, which yields an oil burned in lamps.

**com-,** [L. < *cum*, with], a prefix meaning: 1. *with, together*, as in *combine*. 2. *intensification*, as in *command*. By assimilation in Latin, *com-* becomes *col-* before *l*, *cor-* before *r*, *con-* before *c, d, g, j, n, q, s, t,* and *v*, and *co-* before *h, w,* and all vowels.

**Com.,** 1. Commander. 2. Commission(er). 3. Committee.

**com.,** 1. commerce. 2. common. 3. communication.

**co·ma** (kō′mə), *n.* [*pl.* -MAS], [< Gr. *kōma* < *koiman*, to put to sleep], a state of deep and prolonged unconsciousness; stupor: it is often caused by injury or disease.

**co·ma** (kō′mə), *n.* [*pl.* -MAE (-mē)], [< L. < Gr. *komē*, hair], 1. in *astronomy*, a globular, cloudlike mass around the nucleus of a comet. 2. in *botany*, *a*) a bunch of branches. *b*) a tuft of hairs at the end of a seed. —**co′mal,** *adj.* —**co′mate** (-māt), *adj.*

**Co·man·che** (kō-man′chi), *n.* [Mex. Sp.], 1. a member of a tribe of Shoshonean Indians who formerly ranged from the Platte River to the Mexican border. 2. their language. *adj.* of this tribe, their language, or culture.

**com·a·tose** (kom′ə-tōs′, kō′mə-), *adj.* 1. of, like, or in a coma (stupor). 2. as if in a coma; lethargic. —**com′a·tose·ly,** *adv.* —**com′a·tose·ness,** *n.*

**comb** (kōm), *n.* [AS. *camb*], 1. a thin strip of bone, plastic, metal, etc. with teeth, passed through the hair to arrange or clean it, or set in the hair to hold it in place. 2. a currycomb. 3. a thing like a comb in form or function, as a tool for cleaning and straightening wool, flax, etc. 4. the red, fleshy outgrowth on the head of certain fowls. 5. a thing like a rooster's comb in position or appearance, as the crest of a wave. 6. a honeycomb. *v.t.* 1. to clean or arrange with a comb. 2. to search thoroughly; look everywhere in. *v.i.* to roll over; break: said of waves. —**combed** (kōmd), *adj.*

**com·bat** (kom′bat, kum′-; *also, for v.*, kəm-bat′), *v.i.* [-BATED or -BATTED, -BATING or -BATTING], [< Fr. < L. *com-*, together + *batuere*, to beat], to fight; battle; contend. *v.t.* to fight against; oppose by force. *n.* 1. armed fighting; battle. 2. struggle; conflict. *adj.* in *military usage*, of or for combat. —**com′bat·a·ble,** *adj.* —**com′bat·er,** *n.*

**com·bat·ant** (kom′bə-tənt, kum′-), *adj.* 1. fighting. 2. ready or eager to fight. *n.* a person who combats; fighter.

**combat fatigue,** a psychoneurotic condition sometimes brought on by prolonged armed combat and characterized by anxiety, irritability, depression, etc.: also called *battle fatigue*.

**com·ba·tive** (kəm-bat′iv, kom′bə-tiv, kum′-), *adj.* ready or eager to fight or oppose; pugnacious. —**com·bat′ive·ly,** *adv.* —**com·bat′ive·ness,** *n.*

**comb·er** (kōm′ẽr), *n.* 1. one that combs wool, flax, etc. 2. a large wave that breaks on a beach, etc.

**com·bi·na·tion** (kom′bə-nā′shən), *n.* 1. a combining or being combined. 2. a thing made by combining. 3. an association of people for a common purpose. 4. the series of numbers or letters used in opening a combination lock. 5. a one-piece undergarment combining an undershirt and drawers. 6. in *mathematics*, any of the various groupings into which a number of units may be arranged without regard to order. —**com′bi·na′tion·al,** *adj.* —**com′bi·na′tive,** *adj.*

**combination lock,** a lock operated by a dial that is turned to a specified series of numbers or letters to work the mechanism that opens it.

**com·bine** (kəm-bīn′), *v.t. & v.i.* [-BINED, -BINING], [LL. *combinare* < L. *com-*, together + *bini*, two by two; see BI-], 1. to come or bring into union; unite; join. 2. to unite to form a chemical compound. *n.* 1. (kom′bīn), a machine for harvesting and threshing grain. 2. (kom′bīn, kəm-bīn′), [Colloq.], an association of persons, corporations, etc. for commercial or political purposes.—**com·bin′a·ble,** *adj.* —**com·bin′er,** *n.*

**comb·ings** (kōm′iŋz), *n.pl.* loose hair, wool, etc. removed in combing.

**combining form,** a word or word base used as an element in word formation, as *tele-* in *telephone*.

**com·bus·ti·ble** (kəm-bus′tə-b′l), *adj.* 1. capable of taking fire; that can be easily burned up; inflammable. 2. easily aroused; fiery. *n.* an inflammable substance. —**com·bus′ti·bil′i·ty, com·bus′ti·ble·ness,** *n.* —**com·bus′ti·bly,** *adv.*

**com·bus·tion** (kəm-bus′chən), *n.* [Fr. < LL. < L. pp. of *comburere* < *com-*, intens. + *urere*, to burn], 1. the act or process of burning. 2. rapid oxidation accompanied by heat and, usually, light. 3. slow oxidation accompanied by relatively little heat and no light. 4. violent excitement; tumult. —**com·bus′tive,** *adj.*

**comdg.,** commanding.

**Comdr.,** Commander.

**Comdt.,** Commandant.

**come** (kum), *v.i.* [CAME (kām), COME, COMING], [AS. *cuman*], 1. to move from a place thought of as "there" to a place thought of as "here." 2. to arrive or appear: as, help will *come*. 3. to extend; reach. 4. to happen; take place; occur: as, success *came* to him. 5. to exist in a certain place or order: as, 9 *comes* after 8. 6. to become actual; evolve; develop: as, peace will *come* in time. 7. to be descended. 8. to be caused; result. 9. to become; get to be: as, it *came* loose. 10. to be available: as, it *comes* in four sizes. 11. to amount: as, the bill *comes* to **$5.68.** *interj.* look! see here! stop! —**come about,** 1. to happen; occur. 2. to turn about. —**come across,** 1. to find by chance. 2. [Slang], to give or do what is wanted. —**come and get it!** [Colloq.], the meal is ready! —**come around** (or **round**), 1. to revive; recover. 2. to make a turn. 3. [Colloq.], to concede or yield. —**come at,** 1. to attain. 2. to approach angrily or swiftly. —**come back,** 1. to return. 2. [Colloq.], to recover, as in health or status. 3. [Slang], to retort. **—come between,** to estrange; divide. **—come by,** to get; gain. **—come down,** 1. to suffer loss in status, wealth, etc. 2. to be handed down. **—come down on** (or **upon**), 1. to attack swiftly. 2. [Colloq.], to scold; upbraid. **—come in,** 1. to enter. 2. to come into fashion. **—come in for,** [Colloq.], to get; acquire. **—come into,** 1. to join. 2. to get. 3. to inherit. **—come off,** 1. to become detached. 2. to occur. **—come on,** 1. to become better. 2. to find. **—come on!** [Colloq.], 1. get started! hurry! 2. stop behaving in this way! **—come out,** 1. to be disclosed. 2. to be offered for public sale, etc. 3. to make a debut. 4. to end up. **—come out with,** 1. to disclose. 2. to say; utter. 3. to offer for public sale, etc. **—come through,** 1. to complete something successfully. 2. [Slang], to do or give what is wanted. **—come to,** 1. to recover consciousness. 2. to anchor. **—come under,** 1. to pass under the control of. 2. to fall into (a category). **—come up,** to arise, as in discussion. **—come upon,** to find. **—come up to,** 1. to reach to. 2. to equal. **—come up with,** 1. to overtake. 2. to propose. **—how come?** [Colloq.], how is it that? why?

**come·back** (kum′bak′), *n.* 1. [Colloq.], a return to a previous state or position, as of power. 2. [Slang], a witty answer; retort.

**co·me·di·an** (kə-mē′di-ən), *n.* 1. an actor who plays comic parts. 2. a writer of comedy. 3. one who amuses others by clowning, joking, etc.

**co·me·di·enne** (kə-mē′di-en′), *n.* an actress in comedy; actress who plays comic parts.

**come·down** (kum′doun′), *n.* a loss of status, wealth, etc.; downfall.

**com·e·dy** (kom′ə-di), *n.* [*pl.* -DIES], [< OFr. < L. < Gr. *kōmōidia* < *kōmos*, festival + *aeidein*, to sing], 1. any of various types of play or motion picture with more or less humorous treatment of characters and situation, and a nontragic ending. 2. the branch of the drama having to do with comedies. 3. something amusing, as an incident or event. 4. a literary work with a comic theme or certain characteristics of comedy. **—cut the comedy,** [Slang], to stop joking.

**comedy of manners,** a type of comedy satirizing the manners and customs of fashionable society.

**come·ly** (kum′li), *adj.* [-LIER, -LIEST], [AS. *cymlic* < *cyme*, lit., feeble; hence, delicate + *-lic* (see -LY)], 1. of pleasing appearance; attractive. 2. seemly; proper; suitable. **—come′li·ness,** *n.*

**come-on** (kum′on′), *n.* [Slang], 1. an inviting look or gesture. 2. an inducement.

**com·er** (kum′ẽr), *n.* 1. one who comes. 2. [Slang], one who shows promise of being a success.

**co·mes·ti·ble** (kə-mes′tə-b'l), *adj.* [Fr. < L. *comestus* < *com-*, intens. + *edere*, to eat], eatable; edible. *n. usually in pl.* a thing to eat; food.

**com·et** (kom′it), *n.* [< AS. < L. < Gr. *komētēs* < *komē*, hair], a heavenly body having a starlike nucleus with a luminous mass around it, and, usually, a long, luminous tail: comets move in orbits around the sun. **—com′et·ar′y,** *adj.*

**come·up·pance** (kum′up′'ns), *n.* [< *come* + *up* + *-ance*], [Slang], deserved punishment; retribution.

**com·fit** (kum′fit, kom′-), *n.* [< OFr. < L. *conficere;* see CONFECT], a candy; candied fruit; sweetmeat.

**com·fort** (kum′fẽrt), *v.t.* [< OFr. < LL. < L. *com-*, intens. + *fortis*, strong], 1. to soothe in distress or sorrow; console. 2. in *law*, to help; aid. *n.* 1. aid; support: now only in *aid and comfort.* 2. relief from distress, grief, etc. 3. a person or thing that comforts. 4. a state of, or thing that provides, ease and quiet enjoyment. **—com′fort·ing,** *adj. & n.* **—com′fort·ing·ly,** *adv.* **—com′fort·less,** *adj.*

**com·fort·a·ble** (kum′fẽr-tə-b'l, kumf′tẽr-b'l), *adj.* 1. providing comfort: as, *comfortable* shoes. 2. at ease in body or mind; contented: as, he felt *comfortable* after his bath. 3. [Colloq.], sufficient to satisfy: as, a *comfortable* salary. **—com′fort·a·ble·ness,** *n.* **—com′fort·a·bly,** *adv.*

**com·fort·er** (kum′fẽr-tẽr), *n.* 1. a person or thing that comforts. 2. a quilted bed covering. **—the Comforter,** in *theology*, the Holy Spirit.

**comfort station,** a public toilet or rest-room.

**com·ic** (kom′ik), *adj.* [< L. < Gr. *kōmikos*], 1. of comedy. 2. amusing; humorous; funny. 3. of comic strips or cartoons. *n.* 1. a comedian. 2. the humorous part of art or life. 3. *usually in pl.* [Colloq.], a comic strip or strips.

**com·i·cal** (kom′i-k'l), *adj.* causing amusement; humorous; funny; droll. **—com′i·cal′i·ty** (-kal′-), **com′i·cal·ness,** *n.* **—com′i·cal·ly,** *adv.*

**comic opera,** opera with humorous situations, a story that ends happily, and some spoken dialogue.

**comic strip,** a series of cartoons telling a humorous or adventurous story, as in a newspaper or in a cartoon magazine (**comic book**).

**Com·in·form** (kom′in-fôrm′), *n.* [< *Com*munist *Inform*ation], the Communist Information Bureau, established in October, 1947, by various European Communist Parties.

**com·ing** (kum′iŋ), *adj.* [ppr. of *come*], 1. approaching. 2. next. 3. [Colloq.], showing promise of being a success. *n.* arrival; approach; advent.

**Com·in·tern** (kom′in-tũrn′, kom′in-tũrn′), *n.* [< *Com*munist *Intern*ational], see **International.**

**com·i·ty** (kom′ə-ti), *n.* [*pl.* -TIES], [L. *comitas* < *comis*, polite, kind], civility; courtesy.

**comity of nations,** the respect of peaceful nations for each other's laws and institutions.

**comm.,** 1. commander. 2. commission. 3. committee.

**com·ma** (kom′ə), *n.* [L. < Gr. *komma*, clause, that which is cut off < *koptein*, to cut off], 1. a mark of punctuation (,) used to indicate a slight separation of sentence elements, as in setting off nonrestrictive or parenthetical elements, quotations, items in a series, etc. 2. a slight pause.

**comma bacillus,** the bacillus that causes Asiatic cholera.

**com·mand** (kə-mand′, -mänd′), *v.t.* [< OFr. < LL. < L. *com-*, intens. + *mandare*, to commit], 1. to give an order to; direct with authority. 2. to have authority over; control. 3. to have and be able to use: as, to *command* a large vocabulary. 4. to deserve and get; require as due: as, his knowledge *commands* respect. 5. to control (a position); overlook. *v.i.* to be in authority or control; act as commander. *n.* 1. an order; direction; mandate. 2. authority to command. 3. power to control by position. 4. range of view. 5. ability to use; mastery. 6. a military or naval force, or a district, under someone's authority. 7. the post where the person in command is stationed.

**com·man·dant** (kom′ən-dant′, -dänt′), *n.* a commanding officer of a district, fort, etc.

**com·man·deer** (kom′ən-dêr′), *v.t.* [< S.Afr.D. (< D.) < Fr.; see COMMAND], 1. to force into military service. 2. to seize (property) for military or governmental use. 3. [Colloq.], to take forcibly.

**com·mand·er** (kə-man′dẽr, -män′-), *n.* 1. one who commands; leader. 2. the officer in charge of a military unit: a functional title, not a rank. 3. in the *U.S. Navy*, an officer ranking just above a lieutenant commander. **—com·man′der·ship′,** *n.*

**commander in chief,** [*pl.* COMMANDERS IN CHIEF], 1. the supreme commander of the armed forces of a nation: in the U.S. the President is the commander in chief. 2. an officer in command of all armed forces in a certain theater of war.

**com·mand·ing** (kə-man′diŋ, -män′-), *adj.* 1. in command. 2. controlling; dominating. 3. impressive. 4. controlling or dominating by position: as, a *commanding* hilltop. **—com·mand′ing·ly,** *adv.*

**com·mand·ment** (kə-mand′mənt, -mänd′-), *n.* 1. a command; order; mandate; law. 2. any of the Ten Commandments: see **Ten Commandments.**

**com·man·do** (kə-man′dō, -män′-), *n.* [*pl.* -DOS, -DOES], [D.; Port., lit., party commanded], 1. originally, in South Africa, a force of Boer troops. 2. a small raiding force trained to operate inside territory held by the enemy. 3. a member of such a group.

**command post,** the field headquarters of an army unit: abbrev. **C.P.**

**‡comme il faut** (kô′mēl′fō′), [Fr.], as it should be; proper; fitting.

**com·mem·o·rate** (kə-mem′ẽr-āt′), *v.t.* [-RATED, -RATING], [< L. < *com-*, intens. + *memorare*, to remind], 1. to honor the memory of by a ceremony, etc. 2. to serve as a memorial to. **—com·mem′o·ra·ble** (-ẽr-ə-b'l), *adj.* **—com·mem′o·ra′tion,** *n.* **—com·mem′o·ra′tion·al,** *adj.* **—com·mem′o·ra′tive,** *adj. & n.* **—com·mem′o·ra′tive·ly,** *adv.* **—com·mem′o·ra′tor,** *n.* **—com·mem′o·ra·to′ry** (-ə-tôr′i, -tō′ri), *adj.*

**com·mence** (kə-mens′), *v.i. & v.t.* [-MENCED, -MENCING], [< OFr. < LL. < L. *com-*, together + *initiare*, to begin], to begin; start; originate. **—com·menc′er,** *n.*

**com·mence·ment** (kə-mens′mənt), *n.* 1. a commencing; beginning; start. 2. the day when degrees or diplomas are conferred at a school or college. 3. the ceremonies in connection with this.

**com·mend** (kə-mend′), *v.t.* [< L. *commendare;* see COMMAND], 1. to put in the care of another; entrust. 2. to mention as worthy; recommend. 3. to praise. **—com·mend′a·ble,** *adj.* **—com·mend′a·bly,** *adv.*

**com·men·da·tion** (kom′ən-dā′shən), *n.* 1. an entrusting. 2. recommendation. 3. praise.
**com·mend·a·to·ry** (kə-men′də-tôr′i, -tō′ri), *adj.* 1. expressing praise or approval. 2. recommending.
**com·men·su·ra·ble** (kə-men′shoor-ə-b'l, -sēr-), *adj.* [LL. *commensurabilis* < L. *com-*, together + *mensurare;* see COMMENSURATE], measurable by the same standard or measure. —**com·men′su·ra·bil′i·ty, com·men′su·ra·ble·ness,** *n.* —**com·men′su·ra·bly,** *adv.*
**com·men·su·rate** (kə-men′shoor-it, -sēr-), *adj.* [< LL. < *com-* + pp. of *mensurare*, to measure < L. *mensura*, measurement], 1. equal in measure or size; coextensive. 2. proportionate; corresponding in measure. 3. measurable by the same standard or measure; commensurable. —**com·men′su·rate·ly,** *adv.* —**com·men′su·ra′tion, com·men′su·rate·ness,** *n.*
**com·ment** (kom′ent), *n.* [OFr. < L. < pp. of *comminisci*, to contrive < *com-*, intens. + base of *meminisse*, to remember], 1. a note in explanation or criticism of something written or said; annotation. 2. a remark, as in observation or criticism. 3. talk; chatter; gossip. *v.i.* (*less often*, kə-ment′), [< Fr. < LL. < L. *commentari*, to consider thoroughly], to make a comment or comments (*on* or *upon*); make remarks. —**com′ment·er,** *n.*
**com·men·tar·y** (kom′ən-ter′i), *n.* [*pl.* -IES], 1. a series of explanatory notes or annotations. 2. a series of remarks or observations. 3. a comment. 4. a memoir. —**com′men·tar′i·al,** *adj.*
**com·men·ta·tor** (kom′ən-tā′tēr), *n.* 1. one who writes a series of explanatory notes. 2. one whose profession is reporting and analyzing events, trends, etc.: as, a news *commentator.*
**com·merce** (kom′ērs), *n.* [Fr. < L. *commercium* < *com-*, together + *merx*, merchandise], 1. the buying and selling of goods on a large scale, as between cities or countries; trade. 2. social intercourse. 3. [Rare], sexual intercourse.
**com·mer·cial** (kə-mūr′shəl), *adj.* 1. of or connected with commerce. 2. designating unrefined products sold in large quantities for industrial uses. 3. made or done primarily for sale or profit. *n.* in *radio* or *television*, a paid advertisement. —**commer′cial·ly,** *adv.*
**com·mer·cial·ism** (kə-mūr′shəl-iz'm), *n.* 1. the practices and spirit of commerce or business. 2. a business practice, custom, or idiom.
**com·mer·cial·ize** (kə-mūr′shəl-īz′), *v.t.* [-IZED, -IZING], 1. to put on a business basis; apply commercial methods to. 2. to make or do mainly for profit. —**com·mer′cial·i·za′tion,** *n.*
**commercial paper,** checks, promissory notes, bills of exchange, and other negotiable paper.
**com·min·gle** (kə-miŋ′g'l), *v.t. & v.i.* [-GLED, -GLING], to mingle together; intermix; blend.
**com·mi·nute** (kom′ə-nūt′, -nōōt′), *v.t.* [-NUTED, -NUTING], [< L. < *com-*, intens. + *minuere*, to make small], to reduce to small, fine particles; make into powder; pulverize. —**com′mi·nu′tion,** *n.*
**com·mis·er·ate** (kə-miz′ēr-āt′), *v.t.* [-ATED, -ATING], [< L. < *com-*, intens. + *miserari*, to pity], to feel or show sorrow or pity for; sympathize with in distress. *v.i.* to condole (*with*). —**com·mis′er·a′tive,** *adj.*
**com·mis·er·a·tion** (kə-miz′ēr-ā′shən), *n.* pity; compassion; a commiserating.
**com·mis·sar** (kom′ə-sär′, kom′ə-sär′), *n.* [< Russ. < Fr. *commissaire* < LL.; see COMMISSARY], formerly, the head of any of the commissariats, or government departments, in the Soviet Union: now officially called *minister.*
**com·mis·sar·i·at** (kom′ə-sâr′i-ət), *n.* 1. those branches of an army which provide food and supplies for the troops. 2. a department headed by a commissar. 3. a group of commissars.
**com·mis·sar·y** (kom′ə-ser′i), *n.* [*pl.* -IES], [LL. *commissarius* < L. pp. of *committere;* see COMMIT], 1. one to whom some duty is given by authority; deputy. 2. formerly, an army officer in charge of providing food and other supplies. 3. a store in a lumber camp, army camp, etc., where food and supplies can be obtained. —**com′mis·sar′i·al,** *adj.*
**com·mis·sion** (kə-mish′ən), *n.* [< OFr. < LL. < L. pp. of *committere;* see COMMIT], 1. an authorization to perform certain duties or to take on certain powers. 2. a document giving such authorization. 3. the state of being so authorized. 4. authority to act for another. 5. that which one is authorized to do for another. 6. a group of people chosen to perform specified duties. 7. a committing; doing. 8. the thing done. 9. a percentage of the money taken in on sales, allotted to the salesclerk or agent. 10. in *military & naval usage, a*) an official certificate conferring a rank of officer. *b*) the rank thus granted. *v.t.* 1. to give a commission to. 2. to authorize; empower. 3. in *nautical usage*, to put (a vessel) into service. —**in commission,** 1. in use. 2. in fit condition to be used. —**out of commission,** 1. not in use. 2. not in fit condition to be used.
**com·mis·sion·er** (kə-mish′ən-ēr), *n.* 1. a member of a commission. 2. an official in charge of a governmental department: as, a *commissioner* of highways. 3. one of a group chosen to govern a local political unit. —**com·mis′sion·er·ship′,** *n.*
**com·mit** (kə-mit′), *v.t.* [-MITTED, -MITTING], [L. *committere* < *com-*, together + *mittere*, to send], 1. to give in charge or trust; consign: as, we *commit* his fame to posterity. 2. to put officially in custody or confinement: as, he was *committed* to prison. 3. to do or perpetrate, as an offense or crime. 4. to pledge; bind: as, he is *committed* to fight for slum clearance. 5. to refer (a bill, resolution, etc.) to a committee. —**commit to memory,** to memorize. —**commit to paper** (or **writing**), to write down; record. —**com·mit′ta·ble** *adj.*
**com·mit·ment** (kə-mit′mənt), *n.* 1. a committing or being committed. 2. official consignment of a person to prison, to a mental hospital, etc. 3. a pledge or promise. Also **com·mit′tal.**
**com·mit·tee** (kə-mit′i), *n.* [< Anglo-Fr. < L. *committere;* see COMMIT], a group of people chosen, as in a legislature or club, to act upon a certain matter. —**in committee,** under consideration by a committee, as a resolution or bill.
**com·mit·tee·man** (kə-mit′i-mən), *n.* [*pl.* -MEN], a member of a committee. —**com·mit′tee·wom′an** [*pl.* -WOMEN], *n.fem.*
**com·mode** (kə-mōd′), *n.* [Fr. < L. *commodus*, suitable; see COM- & MODE], 1. a chest of drawers. 2. a movable washstand. 3. a piece of furniture containing a chamber pot. 4. a toilet.
**com·mo·di·ous** (kə-mō′di-əs), *adj.* [ME., convenient; see COMMODE], spacious; roomy. —**com·mo′di·ous·ly,** *adv.* —**com·mo′di·ous·ness,** *n.*
**com·mod·i·ty** (kə-mod′ə-ti), *n.* [*pl.* -TIES], [< Fr. < L. < *commodus*, suitable; see COM- & MODE], 1. any useful thing. 2. anything bought and sold; any article of commerce.
**com·mo·dore** (kom′ə-dôr′, -dōr′), *n.* [prob., with Sp. or Port. influence, < Fr. *commandeur;* see COMMAND], 1. in the *U.S. Navy*, an officer ranking just above a captain: the rank was abolished in 1899 but restored in World War II. 2. in the *Brit. Navy*, a captain temporarily heading a squadron or division of a fleet. 3. a courtesy title, as of the president of a yacht club.
**com·mon** (kom′ən), *adj.* [< OFr. < L. *communis* < *com-*, with + *munus*, duties], 1. belonging equally to, or shared by, all. 2. belonging to the community at large; public. 3. of, from, by, or to all. 4. general; prevalent; widespread. 5. familiar; usual. 6. ordinary; undistinguished. 7. having no rank: as, a *common* soldier. 8. below ordinary; hence, 9. vulgar; low; coarse. 10. in *grammar, a*) designating a noun that refers to any of a group or class, as *book, apple, street*: opposed to *proper. b*) neither masculine nor feminine: as, *child* is of *common* gender. 11. in *mathematics*, belonging equally to two or more quantities: as, a *common* denominator. *n. sometimes pl.* land owned or used by all the inhabitants of a place: as, Boston *Commons.* —**in common,** equally with, or shared by, all concerned. —**com′mon·ly,** *adv.* —**com′mon·ness,** *n.*
**com·mon·al·ty** (kom′ən-əl-ti), *n.* [*pl.* -TIES], 1. the common people. 2. people in general. 3. a body corporate or its membership.
**common carrier,** a person or company in the business of transporting people or goods for a fee.
**common council,** in some cities, towns, etc., the representative lawmaking body.
**com·mon·er** (kom′ən-ēr), *n.* a person not of the nobility; member of the common people.
**common fraction,** a fraction with the numerator separated from the denominator by a diagonal or horizontal line, as $^5/_{11}$ or $\frac{3}{4}$.
**common law,** the unwritten law of a country based on custom, usage, and judicial decisions: cf. *statute law*: it is now largely codified.
**com·mon-law marriage** (kom′ən-lô′), in *law*, a marriage not solemnized by religious or civil cere-

---

mony but effected by agreement to live together as husband and wife: authorized in some States.

**common man,** one of the common people.

**Common Market,** an association formed in 1958 by Belgium, France, West Germany, Italy, Luxemburg, and the Netherlands, to effect a closer economic union: official name, **European Economic Community.**

**common people,** the people of the world, of a country, etc. who are not of the upper classes.

**com·mon·place** (kom'ən-plās'), *n.* 1. a trite remark; truism; platitude. 2. anything common or ordinary. *adj.* ordinary; neither new nor interesting; obvious and trite. —**com'mon·place'ness,** *n.*

**common pleas,** in *law*, civil suits between private parties.

**Common Prayer,** the Anglican prayer book: in full, **Book of Common Prayer.**

**com·mons** (kom'ənz), *n.pl.* 1. the common people. 2. [construed as sing.], food provided for meals in common for all members of a group, as at a college. 3. a dining room, as at a college. —**the Commons,** the House of Commons.

**common sense,** practical judgment or intelligence; ordinary good sense. —**com'mon-sense',** *adj.*

**common stock,** ordinary capital stock in a company, without a definite dividend rate or the privileges of preferred stock.

**common time,** in *music*, a rhythm of two beats to the measure or any multiple of this; esp., 4/4 time: also **common measure.**

**com·mon·weal** (kom'ən-wēl'), *n.* the public good; the general welfare: also **common weal.**

**com·mon·wealth** (kom'ən-welth'), *n.* 1. the people of a nation or state. 2. a democracy or republic. 3. loosely, any State of the United States. —**the Commonwealth,** the government in England under the Cromwells (1649–1660).

**com·mo·tion** (kə-mō'shən), *n.* [< L.; ult. < *com-*, together + *movere*, to move], violent motion; turmoil; agitation; confusion; disturbance.

**com·mu·nal** (kom'yoo-n'l, kə-mū'-), *adj.* 1. of a commune or communes. 2. of or belonging to the community; public. —**com'mu·nal·ly,** *adv.*

**com·mu·nal·ism** (kom'yoo-n'l-iz'm, kə-mū'-), *n.* a theory or system of government in which communes have virtual autonomy within a federated state. —**com'mu·nal·ist,** *n.* —**com'mu·nal·is'tic,** *adj.*

**com·mu·nal·ize** (kom'yoo-n'l-īz', kə-mū'-), *v.t.* [-IZED, -IZING], to make communal. —**com'mu·nal·i·za'tion,** *n.*

**com·mune** (kə-mūn'), *v.i.* [-MUNED, -MUNING], [< OFr. *comuner*, to share < *comun* (see COMMON)], 1. to converse intimately. 2. to receive Holy Communion. *n.* (kom'ūn), intimate conversation.

**com·mune** (kom'ūn), *n.* [Fr. < L. < *communis;* see COMMON], 1. a community. 2. the smallest administrative district of local government in France, Belgium, and some other countries in Europe. —**the Commune,** 1. the revolutionary government of Paris from 1792 to 1794. 2. the revolutionary government of Paris in 1871.

**com·mu·ni·ca·ble** (kə-mū'ni-kə-b'l), *adj.* 1. that can be communicated, as a thought. 2. that can be transmitted, as a disease. —**com·mu'ni·ca·bil'i·ty, com·mu'ni·ca·ble·ness,** *n.* —**com·mu'ni·ca·bly,** *adv.*

**com·mu·ni·cant** (kə-mū'ni-kənt), *n.* 1. a person who receives Holy Communion or belongs to a church celebrating this sacrament. 2. a person who communicates information. *adj.* communicating.

**com·mu·ni·cate** (kə-mū'nə-kāt'), *v.t.* [-CATED, -CATING], [< L. pp. of *communicare* < *communis;* see COMMON], 1. to impart; pass along; transmit. 2. to make known; give (information, etc.). *v.i.* 1. to receive Holy Communion. 2. to give, or give and receive, information, etc. as by talk, gestures, writing, etc. 3. to be connected: as, this room *communicates* with the hall. —**com·mu'ni·ca'tor,** *n.*

**com·mu·ni·ca·tion** (kə-mū'nə-kā'shən), *n.* 1. a transmitting. 2. a giving, or giving and receiving, of information, etc. by talk, gestures, writing, etc. 3. the information so given. 4. a means of communicating; specif., *a) pl.* a system for sending and receiving messages, as by telephone, radio, etc. *b) pl.* a system for moving troops and matériel. *c)* a passage for getting from one place to another.

**com·mu·ni·ca·tive** (kə-mū'nə-kā'tiv, -ni-kə-tiv), *adj.* 1. giving information readily; talkative. 2. of communication. —**com·mu'ni·ca'tive·ly,** *adv.*

**com·mun·ion** (kə-mūn'yən), *n.* [OFr. < L. < *communis;* see COMMON], 1. a sharing; possession in common. 2. a communing; sharing of one's thoughts and emotions. 3. an intimate spiritual relationship. 4. a group of people of the same religious faith. 5. [C-], a sharing in, or celebrating of, the Eucharist (*Holy Communion*).

**com·mu·ni·qué** (kə-mū'nə-kā', kə-mū'nə-kā'), *n.* [Fr.], an official communication or bulletin.

**com·mu·nism** (kom'yoo-niz'm), *n.* [< Fr. < L. *communis;* see COMMON], 1. *a)* a theory or system of the ownership of all property by the community as a whole. *b)* a theory or system of the ownership of the means of production (and distribution) by the community, with all members sharing in the work and the products. 2. [often C-], *a)* a political movement for establishing such a system. *b)* the doctrines, methods, etc. of the Communist parties. 3. loosely, communalism. See also **socialism.**

**com·mu·nist** (kom'yoo-nist), *n.* 1. an advocate or supporter of communism. 2. [C-], a member of a Communist party. *adj.* 1. of, characteristic of, or like communism or communists. 2. advocating or supporting communism. —**com'mu·nis'tic,** *adj.*

**Communist Party,** a political party based on the principles of communism.

**com·mu·ni·ty** (kə-mū'nə-ti), *n.* [*pl.* -TIES], [< OFr. < L. *communitas* < *communis;* see COMMON], 1. the people living in the same district, city, etc., under the same laws. 2. the district, city, etc. where they live. 3. a group of animals or plants living together in the same environment. 4. a group of people living together and having interests, work, etc. in common: as, a college *community.* 5. society; the public. 6. ownership or participation in common. 7. similarity; likeness: as, a *community* of spirit.

**community center,** a meeting place where people living in the same community may carry on cultural, recreational, or social activities.

**community chest** (or **fund**), a fund collected annually in many cities and towns by private contributions and used for social welfare work.

**com·mu·nize** (kom'yoo-nīz'), *v.t.* [-NIZED, -NIZING], to subject to communal ownership and control. —**com'mu·ni·za'tion,** *n.*

**com·mu·tate** (kom'yoo-tāt'), *v.t.* [-TATED, -TATING], [back-formation < *commutation*], to change the direction of (an electric current); esp., to change (alternating current) to direct current.

**com·mu·ta·tion** (kom'yoo-tā'shən), *n.* [Fr.<L. pp. of *commutare;* see COMMUTE], 1. an exchange; substitution. 2. the substitution of one kind of payment for another. 3. daily or regular travel, as by a commuter. 4. in *electricity*, change of the direction of a current by a commutator. 5. in *law*, a change of a sentence or punishment to one that is less severe. —**com·mu·ta·tive** (kə-mū'tə-tiv, kom'yoo-tā'-), *adj.*

**commutation ticket,** a ticket entitling the holder to travel back and forth, as on a railroad, a specified number of times or during a specified period at a fixed, reduced rate.

**com·mu·ta·tor** (kom'yoo-tā'tẽr), *n.* 1. a device for commutating an electric current. 2. in a dynamo or motor, a revolving part that collects the current from, or distributes it to, the brushes.

**com·mute** (kə-mūt'), *v.t.* [-MUTED, -MUTING], [< L. *commutare; com-*, intens. + *mutare*, to change], 1. to exchange; substitute. 2. to change (an obligation, punishment, etc.) to one that is less severe. *v.i.* 1. to be a substitute. 2. to travel as a commuter; use a commutation ticket. —**com·mut'a·bil'i·ty,** *n.* —**com·mut'a·ble,** *adj.*

**com·mut·er** (kə-mūt'ẽr), *n.* one who travels daily or regularly, as by train, between an outlying district and his place of work in the city.

**comp.,** 1. comparative. 2. compare. 3. compiled. 4. composition. 5. compositor. 6. compound.

**com·pact** (kəm-pakt'; *also for adj., and for n. always,* kom'pakt'), *adj.* [< L. pp. of *compingere* < *com-*, together + *pangere*, to fasten], 1. closely and firmly packed; dense; solid. 2. taking little space. 3. brief; terse. 4. composed (*of*). 5. designating or of a small, economical model of automobile. *v.t.* 1. to pack or join firmly together. 2. to make by putting together. 3. to condense. *n.* 1. a small case containing a mirror, face powder, etc. 2. a compact car. 3. [< L. pp. of *compacisci*, to agree together], an agreement; covenant. —**com·pact'ly,** *adv.* —**com·pact'ness,** *n.*

**com·pan·ion** (kəm-pan'yən), *n.* [< OFr. < hyp. LL. *companio*, messmate < L. *com-*, with + *panis*, bread], 1. one who associates with or accompanies another or others; associate; comrade. 2. a person employed to live or travel with another. 3. a thing that matches another in sort, color, etc. *v.t.* to accompany. —**com·pan'ion·ship',** *n.*

**com·pan·ion** (kəm-pan'yən), *n.* [< D. < OFr. < It. *(camera della) compagna*, (room of the) company, or crew], 1. the covering at the head of a companionway. 2. a companionway.

**com·pan·ion·a·ble** (kəm-pan′yən-ə-b'l), *adj.* having the qualities of a good companion; sociable; warm and friendly. —**com·pan′ion·a·bil′i·ty, com·pan′ion·a·ble·ness,** *n.* —**com·pan′ion·a·bly,** *adv.*

**com·pan·ion·ate** (kəm-pan′yən-it), *adj.* of or characteristic of companions.

**com·pan·ion·way** (kəm-pan′yən-wā′), *n.* the stairway leading from the deck of a ship to the cabins or space below: also **companion.**

**com·pa·ny** (kum′pə-ni), *n.* [*pl.* -NIES], [< OFr.; LL. hyp. *compania;* see COMPANION], 1. companionship; society. 2. a group of people. 3. a group of people gathered for social purposes. 4. a habitual associate or associates. 5. a group of people associated for some purpose: as, a business *company.* 6. the partners whose names are not given in the title of a firm: as, John Smith and *Company:* abbrev. **Co., co.** 7. [Colloq.], a guest or guests; visitor or visitors. 8. in *military usage,* a body of troops normally under the command of a captain. 9. in *nautical usage,* the whole crew of a ship, including officers. *v.t. & v.i.* [-NIED, -NYING], [Archaic], to accompany or keep company. —**bear company,** to accompany. —**keep company,** 1. to associate (*with*). 2. to go together, as a couple intending to marry. —**part company,** 1. to stop associating (*with*). 2. to separate and go in different directions.

**com·pa·ra·ble** (kom′pēr-ə-b'l), *adj.* 1. that can be compared. 2. worthy of comparison. —**com′pa·ra·bil′i·ty, com′pa·ra·ble·ness,** *n.* —**com′pa·ra·bly,** *adv.*

**com·par·a·tive** (kəm-par′ə-tiv), *adj.* 1. that compares; involving comparison as a method: as, *comparative* anatomy. 2. relative: as, *comparative* joy. 3. in *grammar,* designating the second degree of comparison of adjectives and adverbs. *n.* in *grammar,* 1. the comparative degree: as, *prettier* and *more beautiful* are the *comparatives* of *pretty* and *beautiful.* 2. an adjective or adverb in this degree. Abbrev. **comp., compar.** —**com·par′a·tive·ly,** *adv.*

**com·pare** (kəm-pâr′), *v.t.* [-PARED, -PARING], [< Fr. < L. < *com-,* with + *par,* equal], 1. to regard as similar; liken (*to*). 2. to examine in order to observe similarities or differences (often followed by *with*): abbrev. **cp., comp.** (see also **cf.**). 3. in *grammar,* to form the positive, comparative, and superlative degrees of (an adjective or adverb). *v.i.* to be worthy of comparison (*with*). *n.* [Poetic], comparison. —**beyond** (or **past** or **without**) **compare,** without equal. —**com·par′er,** *n.*

**com·par·i·son** (kəm-par′ə-s'n), *n.* 1. a comparing or being compared; estimation of similarities and differences. 2. similarity; likeness. 3. in *grammar,* change in an adjective or adverb to show the three degrees (positive, comparative, and superlative), as *long, longer, longest; good, better, best; slowly, more slowly, most slowly.* —**in comparison with,** compared with. —**no comparison between,** no basis for comparison between.

**com·part·ment** (kəm-pärt′mənt), *n.* [< Fr. < It. < L. *com-,* with + *partiri,* to divide < *pars,* a part], 1. any of the divisions into which a space is partitioned off. 2. a private section of a railroad car, with sleeping accommodations.

**com·pass** (kum′pəs), *v.t.* [< OFr. < LL. < L. *com-,* together + *passus,* a step], 1. to go round; make a circuit of. 2. to surround; form a circle around. 3. to achieve; gain. 4. to plot; contrive (something harmful). *n.* 1. *often pl.* an instrument consisting of two pivoted legs, used for drawing arcs or circles and taking measurements. 2. a boundary; circumference. 3. an enclosed area; hence, 4. range; extent; reach; scope. 5. an instrument for showing direction, usually consisting of a magnetic needle swinging freely and pointing to the magnetic north. 6. in *music,* the range of a voice or instrument. *adj.* round. —**com′pass·a·ble,** *adj.*

DRAWING COMPASS

**compass card,** the circular card over which the needle of a compass swings, marked with the points of direction and the degrees of the circle.

**com·pass·es** (kum′pəs-iz), *n.pl.* a compass (sense 1).

**com·pas·sion** (kəm-pash′ən), *n.* [OFr. < LL. *compassio;* ult. < L. *com-,* together + *pati,* to suffer], sorrow for the sufferings or trouble of another, with the urge to help; pity; deep sympathy.

**com·pas·sion·ate** (kəm-pash′ən-it), *adj.* feeling or showing compassion; pitying; sympathizing deeply. *v.t.* (-āt′), [-ATED, -ATING], to pity. —**com·pas′sion·ate·ly,** *adv.* —**com·pas′sion·ate·ness,** *n.*

**com·pat·i·ble** (kəm-pat′ə-b'l), *adj.* [Fr. < LL.; see COMPASSION], capable of living together harmoniously or getting along well with each other; in agreement; congruous. —**com·pat′i·bil′i·ty, com·pat′i·ble·ness,** *n.* —**com·pat′i·bly,** *adv.*

**com·pa·tri·ot** (kəm-pā′tri-ət, -pat′ri-), *n.* [< Fr. < LL. < L. *com-,* with + LL. *patriota;* see PATRIOT], a fellow countryman. *adj.* of the same country. —**com·pa′tri·ot·ism,** *n.*

**com·peer** (kəm-pêr′, kom′pêr), *n.* [< OFr. < L. < *com-,* with + *par,* equal], 1. an equal; peer. 2. a companion; comrade.

**com·pel** (kəm-pel′), *v.t.* [-PELLED, -PELLING], [< OFr. < L. < *com-,* together + *pellere,* to drive], 1. to force; constrain. 2. to get or bring about by force. 3. to overpower. —**com·pel′la·ble,** *adj.* —**com·pel′la·bly,** *adv.* —**com·pel′ler,** *n.*

**com·pen·di·ous** (kəm-pen′di-əs), *adj.* [L. *compendiosus*], containing all the essentials in a brief form; concise and comprehensive. —**com·pen′di·ous·ly,** *adv.* —**com·pen′di·ous·ness,** *n.*

**com·pen·di·um** (kəm-pen′di-əm), *n.* [*pl.* -UMS, -A (-ə)], [L., an abridgment < *com-,* together + *pendere,* to weigh], a summary containing the essential information in a brief form; concise, comprehensive treatise: also **com·pend** (kom′pend).

**com·pen·sa·ble** (kəm-pen′sə-b'l), *adj.* entitling to compensation. —**com·pen′sa·bil′i·ty,** *n.*

**com·pen·sate** (kom′pən-sāt′), *v.t.* [-SATED, -SATING], [< L. < *com-,* with + *pensare,* freq. of *pendere,* to weigh], 1. to make up for; counterbalance in weight, force, etc. 2. to make equivalent return to; recompense. *v.i.* to make compensation; make amends (often with *for*). —**com′pen·sa′tor,** *n.* —**com·pen·sa·to·ry** (kəm-pen′sə-tôr′i, -tō′ri), **com′·pen·sa′tive,** *adj.*

**com·pen·sa·tion** (kom′pən-sā′shən), *n.* 1. a compensating or being compensated. 2. an instance or means of this. 3. anything given as an equivalent, or to make amends; recompense; pay. 4. in *biology,* the counterbalancing of a defect of one part by a greater activity or development of another. —**com′pen·sa′tion·al,** *adj.*

**com·pete** (kəm-pēt′), *v.i.* [-PETED, -PETING], [< L. < *com-,* together + *petere,* to seek], 1. to be in rivalry; strive in opposition; contend; vie. 2. to participate (*in* a contest, etc.).

**com·pe·tence** (kom′pə-təns), *n.* [see COMPETENT], 1. sufficient means for one's needs. 2. ability; fitness. 3. in *law,* legal qualification, power, or jurisdiction. Also **com′pe·ten·cy** [*pl.* -CIES].

**com·pe·tent** (kom′pə-tənt), *adj.* [< Fr. < L. < *competere;* see COMPETE], 1. capable; able; fit. 2. sufficient; adequate. 3. in *law,* legally qualified or fit. —**com′pe·tent·ly,** *adv.*

**com·pe·ti·tion** (kom′pə-tish′ən), *n.* 1. a competing; rivalry. 2. a contest; match. 3. business rivalry; a competing for customers or markets.

**com·pet·i·tive** (kəm-pet′ə-tiv), *adj.* of or involving competition; based on or determined by competition: also **com·pet′i·to′ry.** —**com·pet′i·tive·ly,** *adv.* —**com·pet′i·tive·ness,** *n.*

**com·pet·i·tor** (kəm-pet′ə-tēr), *n.* a person who competes, as a business rival.

**com·pile** (kəm-pīl′), *v.t.* [-PILED, -PILING], [< OFr. < L. < *com-,* together + *pilare,* to compress], 1. to gather together (writings, facts, etc.) in an orderly form. 2. to compose (a book, etc.) by gathering materials from various sources. —**com·pi·la·tion** (kom′p'l-ā′shən), *n.* —**com·pil′er,** *n.*

**com·pla·cen·cy** (kəm-plā′s'n-si), *n.* [*pl.* -CIES], [< L. < *com-,* with + *placere,* to please], 1. quiet satisfaction; contentment. 2. self-satisfaction; smugness. Also **com·pla′cence.**

**com·pla·cent** (kəm-plā′s'nt), *adj.* 1. self-satisfied; smug. 2. complaisant. —**com·pla′cent·ly,** *adv.*

**com·plain** (kəm-plān′), *v.i.* [< OFr. < LL. < L. *com-,* with + *plangere,* to strike (the breast), complain], 1. to express pain, dissatisfaction, etc. 2. to find fault. 3. to make an accusation or a formal charge. —**com·plain′er,** *n.* —**com·plain′ing·ly,** *adv.*

**com·plain·ant** (kəm-plān′ənt), *n.* 1. a person who complains. 2. in *law,* a plaintiff.

**com·plaint** (kəm-plānt′), *n.* 1. a complaining; utterance of pain, discomfort, dissatisfaction, etc. 2. a subject or cause for complaining. 3. an illness; ailment. 4. in *law,* a formal charge.

**com·plai·sant** (kəm-plā'z'nt, -s'nt, kom'pli-zant'), *adj.* [< Fr. pp. of *complaire* < L.; see COMPLACENCY], willing to please; obliging; accommodating. —**com·plai'sance,** *n.* —**com·plai'sant·ly,** *adv.*

**com·plect·ed** (kəm-plek'tid), *adj.* [altered < *complexioned*], [Dial. or Colloq.], complexioned.

**com·ple·ment** (kom'plə-mənt), *n.* [L. *complementum* < *complere;* see COMPLETE], 1. that which completes or brings to perfection. 2. the amount needed to fill or complete. 3. an entirety; complete set. 4. either of two parts that together complete a whole. 5. in *grammar,* a word or words completing a predication. Examples: *president* in *elect him president* (*objective complement*), *pretty* in *she was pretty* (*predicate complement*). 6. in *mathematics,* the number of degrees added to an angle or arc to make it equal 90 degrees. *v.t.* (kom'plə-ment'), to make complete; be a complement to.

**com·ple·men·tal** (kom'plə-men't'l), *adj.* complementary. —**com'ple·men'tal·ly,** *adv.*

**com·ple·men·ta·ry** (kom'plə-men'tẽr-i), *adj.* 1. acting as a complement; completing. 2. mutually making up what is lacking.

**complementary colors,** any two colors of the spectrum that combine to form white light.

**com·plete** (kəm-plēt'), *adj.* [< OFr. < L. *completus* < *com-,* intens. + *plere,* to fill], 1. lacking no parts; entire. 2. ended; finished. 3. thorough; perfect. *v.t.* [-PLETED, -PLETING], 1. to end; finish. 2. to make entire, thorough, or perfect. —**complete'ly,** *adv.* —**com·plete'ness,** *n.* —**com·plet'er,** *n.*

**com·ple·tion** (kəm-plē'shən), *n.* 1. a completing; finishing. 2. the state of being completed.

**com·plex** (kəm-pleks', kom'pleks), *adj.* [LL. < L. *complexus,* a twining together < *com-,* with + *plectere,* to weave], 1. consisting of two or more related parts. 2. complicated; not simple. *n.* (kom'pleks), 1. a complex whole. 2. in *psychoanalysis,* *a*) a group of partly unconscious emotional attitudes associated with a particular object, activity, etc., strongly influencing the individual's behavior; hence, *b*) popularly, an exaggerated dislike. —**com·plex'ly,** *adv.* —**com·plex'ness,** *n.*

**complex fraction,** a fraction with a fraction in its numerator or denominator, or in both: also **compound fraction.**

**com·plex·ion** (kəm-plek'shən), *n.* [OFr. < L. < *complexus;* see COMPLEX], 1. one's temperament or disposition. 2. the color, texture, etc. of the skin, especially of the face. 3. character; nature; aspect. —**com·plex'ion·al,** *adj.*

**com·plex·ioned** (kəm-plek'shənd), *adj.* having a (specified) complexion; as, *light-complexioned.*

**com·plex·i·ty** (kəm-plek'sə-ti), *n.* 1. a complex condition or quality. 2. [*pl.* -TIES], anything complex or intricate; complication.

**complex sentence,** a sentence consisting of a main clause and one or more subordinate clauses.

**com·pli·a·ble** (kəm-plī'ə-b'l), *adj.* complying. —**com·pli'a·ble·ness,** *n.* —**com·pli'a·bly,** *adv.*

**com·pli·ance** (kəm-plī'əns), *n.* 1. a complying, or giving in to a request, demand, etc. 2. a tendency to give in to others. Also **com·pli'an·cy.** —**in compliance with,** complying with.

**com·pli·ant** (kəm-plī'ənt), *adj.* complying; yielding; submissive. —**com·pli'ant·ly,** *adv.*

**com·pli·ca·cy** (kom'plə-kə-si), *n.* 1. a complicated quality. 2. [*pl.* -CIES], complication.

**com·pli·cate** (kom'plə-kāt'), *v.t. & v.i.* [-CATED, -CATING], [< L. *complicatus* < *com-,* together + *plicare,* to fold], 1. to make or become intricate, difficult, or involved. 2. to twist together. *adj.* (-kit), [Archaic], complicated.

**com·pli·cat·ed** (kom'plə-kāt'id), *adj.* intricately involved; hard to untangle, solve, analyze, etc. —**com'pli·cat'ed·ly,** *adv.* —**com'pli·cat'ed·ness,** *n.*

**com·pli·ca·tion** (kom'plə-kā'shən), *n.* 1. a complicating. 2. a complicated condition or structure. 3. a complicating factor, as in the plot of a play. 4. in *medicine,* a disease or abnormal condition occurring during another disease.

**com·plic·i·ty** (kəm-plis'ə-ti), *n.* [*pl.* -TIES], [< Fr. < L. *complex;* see COMPLEX], 1. partnership in wrongdoing. 2. complexity.

**com·pli·ment** (kom'plə-mənt), *n.* [Fr. < It. < L.; akin to COMPLEMENT], 1. a formal act of courtesy; esp., something said in praise. 2. *pl.* respects. *v.t.* (-ment'), 1. to pay a compliment to. 2. to present something to (a person) to show respect.

**com·pli·men·ta·ry** (kom'plə-men'tẽr-i), *adj.* 1. paying or containing a compliment. 2. given free as a courtesy: as, a *complimentary* ticket. —**com'pli·men'ta·ri·ly,** *adv.* —**com'pli·men'ta·ri·ness,** *n.*

**com·plin** (kom'plin), *n.* [< OFr. < LL.; see COMPLETE], the last of the seven canonical hours: also **com'pline** (-plin, -plīn).

**com·ply** (kəm-plī'), *v.i.* [-PLIED, -PLYING], [It. *complire* < Sp. < L.; see COMPLETE], to act in accordance with a request, order, etc.: as, he *complied* with the rule. —**com·pli'er,** *n.*

**com·po·nent** (kəm-pō'nənt), *adj.* [< L. < *com-,* together + *ponere,* to put], serving as one of the parts of a whole. *n.* a part; ingredient.

**com·port** (kəm-pôrt', -pōrt'), *v.t.* [< Fr. < L. < *com-,* together + *portare,* to bring], to behave (oneself) in a specified manner. *v.i.* to agree or accord (*with*). —**com·port'ment,** *n.*

**com·pose** (kəm-pōz'), *v.t.* [-POSED, -POSING], [< Fr. < *com-,* with + *poser,* to place], 1. to make up; constitute. 2. to put in proper order or form. 3. to create (a musical or literary work). 4. to adjust; settle: as, their quarrel was *composed.* 5. to calm (oneself, one's mind, etc.); allay. 6. to set (type) for printing. *v.i.* 1. to create musical or literary works. 2. to set type.

**com·posed** (kəm-pōzd'), *adj.* calm; tranquil; self-possessed. —**com·pos'ed·ly** (-pōz'id-li), *adv.* —**com·pos'ed·ness,** *n.*

**com·pos·er** (kəm-pōz'ẽr), *n.* a person who composes, especially one who composes music.

**com·pos·ite** (kəm-poz'it), *adj.* [< L. pp. of *componere* < *com-,* together + *ponere,* to put], 1. formed of distinct parts; compound. 2. [C-], in *architecture,* designating one of the classic orders, which combines features of the Ionic and Corinthian capitals. 3. in *botany,* of a large group of plants, as the aster, sunflower, etc., having flower heads consisting of clusters of small flowers. *n.* 1. a thing of distinct parts. 2. a composite plant. —**com·pos'ite·ly,** *adv.*

**com·po·si·tion** (kom'pə-zish'ən), *n.* 1. a composing. 2. the art of writing prose or poetry. 3. the creation of musical works. 4. the make-up of a thing; constitution. 5. that which is composed. 6. a mixture of various ingredients. 7. a work of music, literature, or art. 8. an exercise in writing done as schoolwork. 9. an aesthetically unified arrangement of parts. 10. an agreement; settlement, often by compromise. 11. in *printing,* typesetting.

**com·pos·i·tor** (kəm-poz'i-tẽr), *n.* a person who sets type; typesetter.

**com·pos men·tis** (kom'pəs men'tis), [L.], in *law,* of sound mind; sane.

**com·post** (kom'pōst), *n.* [< OFr. < L.; see COMPOSITE], 1. a compound. 2. a mixture of decomposing vegetation, manure, etc. for fertilizing soil.

**com·po·sure** (kəm-pō'zhẽr), *n.* [see COMPOSE], calmness; tranquillity; self-possession.

**com·pote** (kom'pōt; Fr. kōn'pôt'), *n.* [Fr.; see COMPOST], 1. a dish of stewed fruits in sirup. 2. a long-stemmed dish for candy, fruit, etc.

**com·pound** (kom-pound', kəm-), *v.t.* [< OFr. < L. *componere;* see COMPOSITE], 1. to mix; combine. 2. to make by combining parts. 3. to compromise. 4. to settle (a debt) by a compromise payment. *v.i.* to agree; compromise. *adj.* (kom'pound, kom-pound'), made up of two or more parts or elements. *n.* (kom'pound), 1. a thing formed by the combination of parts. 2. in *chemistry,* a substance containing two or more elements combined in fixed proportions: distinguished from *mixture* in that a compound has characteristics different from those of its constituents. 3. a word composed of two or more other words. —**compound a felony** (or **crime**), to agree, for payment, not to prosecute a felony (or crime). —**com·pound'a·ble,** *adj.* —**com·pound'er,** *n.*

**com·pound** (kom'pound), *n.* [Malay *kampun*], in the Orient, an enclosed space with a building or group of buildings in it, especially if occupied by foreigners.

**compound fracture,** a fracture in which the broken bone has pierced the skin.

**compound interest,** interest paid on both the principal and the accumulated unpaid interest.

**compound number,** a quantity expressed in two or more sorts of units (e.g., 4 ft., 7 in.).

**compound sentence,** a sentence consisting of two or more independent, co-ordinate clauses (e.g., I came, I saw, I conquered.).

**com·pre·hend** (kom'pri-hend'), *v.t.* [< L. < *com-,* with + *prehendere,* to seize], 1. to grasp mentally; understand. 2. to include; comprise. —**com'pre·hend'i·ble,** *adj.* —**com'pre·hend'ing·ly,** *adv.*

**com·pre·hen·si·ble** (kom'pri-hen'sə-b'l), *adj.* that can be comprehended; intelligible; understandable.

**—com′pre·hen′si·bil′i·ty,** *n.* **—com′pre·hen′si·bly,** *adv.*
**com·pre·hen·sion** (kom′pri-hen′shən), *n.* 1. a comprehending or comprising; inclusiveness. 2. the act of or capacity for understanding.
**com·pre·hen·sive** (kom′pri-hen′siv), *adj.* 1. including much; inclusive. 2. understanding. —**com′pre·hen′sive·ly,** *adv.* **—com′pre·hen′sive·ness,** *n.*
**com·press** (kəm-pres′; *for n.,* kom′pres), *v.t.* [< OFr. < LL. < L. *compressus,* pp.; ult. < *com-,* together + *premere,* to press], to press together; make more compact as by pressure. *n.* 1. a pad of folded cloth, often wet or medicated, applied to a part of the body to exert pressure or to lessen inflammation. 2. a machine for pressing cotton into bales. **—com·pressed′,** *adj.* **—com·pres′si·bil′i·ty,** *n.* **—com·pres′si·ble,** *adj.* **—com·pres′sive,** *adj.*
**com·pres·sion** (kəm-presh′ən), *n.* a compressing or being compressed; specif., the compressing of a working fluid in an engine, as of gas in an automobile engine just before ignition.
**com·pres·sor** (kəm-pres′ẽr), *n.* one that compresses; specif., *a*) a muscle that compresses a part. *b*) a machine for compressing air, gas, etc.
**com·pris·al, com·priz·al** (kəm-prīz′'l), *n.* 1. a comprising. 2. a summary; abstract.
**com·prise, com·prize** (kəm-prīz′), *v.t.* [-PRISED, -PRISING; -PRIZED, -PRIZING], [< Fr. pp. of *comprendre;* see COMPREHEND], 1. to include; contain. 2. to consist of; be composed of. **—com·pris′a·ble, com·priz′a·ble,** *adj.*
**com·pro·mise** (kom′prə-mīz′), *n.* [< Fr. < LL. *compromissum,* < L. < *com-,* together + *promittere,* to promise], 1. a settlement in which each side makes concessions. 2. the result of such a settlement. 3. something midway between different things. 4. exposure, as of one's reputation, to danger, suspicion, or disrepute. *v.t.* [-MISED, -MISING], 1. to settle by concessions on both sides. 2. to lay open to danger, suspicion, or disrepute. 3. to surrender (one's principles, etc.). *v.i.* to make a compromise. **—com′pro·mis′er,** *n.*
**comp·tom·e·ter** (komp-tom′ə-tẽr), *n.* [< Fr. *compter* (see COMPUTE); + *-meter*], a machine for doing addition, subtraction, multiplication, and division mechanically: a trade-mark (**Comptometer**).
**Comp·ton** (komp′tən), *n.* a city in SW California, near Los Angeles: pop., 72,000.
**comp·trol·ler** (kən-trōl′ẽr), *n.* [< *controller,* after Fr. *compte,* an account], a controller (**sense 1**).
**com·pul·sion** (kəm-pul′shən), *n.* [Fr. < LL. < L. pp. of *compellere*], 1. a compelling or being compelled; force; coercion. 2. in *psychology,* an irresistible impulse to perform some irrational act. **—com·pul′sive** (-siv), *adj.* **—com·pul′sive·ly,** *adv.*
**com·pul·so·ry** (kəm-pul′sẽr-i), *adj.* 1. compelled; required. 2. compelling; coercive. **—com·pul′so·ri·ly,** *adv.* **—com·pul′so·ri·ness,** *n.*
**com·punc·tion** (kəm-puŋk′shən), *n.* [< OFr. < LL. *compunctio,* a pricking (of conscience) < L. < *com-,* intens. + *pungere,* to prick], 1. a sharp feeling of uneasiness brought on by a sense of guilt; remorse; scruple. 2. a feeling of slight regret for some wrong done. **—com·punc′tious,** *adj.*
**com·pu·ta·tion** (kom′pyoo-tā′shən), *n.* 1. a computing; reckoning; calculation. 2. a method of computing. 3. a result obtained in computing.
**com·pute** (kəm-pūt′), *v.t. & v.i.* [-PUTED, -PUTING], [< Fr. < L. < *com-,* with + *putare,* to reckon], to determine, as an amount, by reckoning; calculate. *n.* computation: as, beyond *compute.* **—com·put′a·bil′i·ty,** *n.* **—com·put′a·ble,** *adj.*
**com·put·er** (kəm-pū′tẽr), *n.* a person or thing that computes; specif., an electronic machine that performs rapid, often complex calculations or compiles, correlates, and selects data: see also **analog computer, digital computer.**
**com·put·er·ize** (kəm-pū′tẽr-īz′), *v.t.* [-IZED, -IZING], to equip with, or operate, produce, control, etc. by or as if by means of, electronic computers.
**com·rade** (kom′rad, -rid), *n.* [< Fr. < Sp. *camarada,* chamber mate < L. *camera,* a chamber], 1. a friend; close companion. 2. one who shares interests and activities in common with others; associate; fellow. **—com′rade·li·ness,** *n.* **—com′rade·ly,** *adj.* **—com′rade·ship′,** *n.*
**comrade in arms,** a fellow soldier.
‡**comte** (kōnt), *n.* [Fr.], count (a title).
**Comte, Au·guste** (ō′güst′ kōnt; Eng. kônt), 1798–1857; French philosopher; exponent of positivism. **—Com·ti·an** (kom′ti-ən, kôn′-), *adj.*
**con** (kon), *adv.* [contr. < L. *contra,* against], against; in opposition: as, to argue pro and *con.* *n.* an argument, vote, person, etc. in opposition.
**con** (kon), *v.t.* [CONNED, CONNING], [ME. *cunnen,* to be able; cf. CAN], to peruse carefully; study; fix in the memory.
**con** (kon), *v.t.* [CONNED, CONNING], [< OFr. < L. *conducere;* see CONDUCE], to direct the course of (a vessel). *n.* the act of conning. Also sp. **conn.**
**con** (kon), *adj.* [Slang], confidence: as, a *con* man. *v.t.* [CONNED, CONNING], [Slang], to swindle (a victim) by first gaining his confidence.
**con-** (kon), com-: used before *c, d, g, j, n, q, s, t,* and *v.*
**con.,** 1. concerto. 2. conclusion. 3. consolidate.
‡**con a·mo·re** (kôn′ ä-mô′re; Eng. kon′ ə-môr′i), [It.], with love; tenderly: a direction in music.
‡**con bri·o** (kôn brē′ô), [It.], in *music,* with spirit; spiritedly.
**con·cat·e·nate** (kon-kat′'n-āt′), *adj.* [< LL. < L. < *com-,* together + *catenare,* to link < *catena,* a chain], linked together; connected. *v.t.* [-NATED, -NATING], to link or join, as in a chain.
**con·cat·e·na·tion** (kon′kat-'n-ā′shən), *n.* [< LL.; see CONCATENATE], 1. a linking together or being linked together. 2. a connected series of things or events regarded as causally related.
**con·cave** (kon-kāv′, kən-, kon′kāv), *adj.* [Fr. < L. < *com-,* intens. + *cavus,* hollow], hollow and curved like a section of the inside of a sphere. *n.* (kon′kāv, koŋ′-), a concave surface, line, object, etc. *v.t.* (kon-kāv′, kən-), [-CAVED, -CAVING], to make concave. **—con·cave′ly,** *adv.* **—con·cave′ness,** *n.*

CONCAVE LENSES
A, plano-concave;
B, concavo-concave;
C, concavo-convex

**con·cav·i·ty** (kon-kav′ə-ti, kən-), *n.* 1. the quality or condition of being concave. 2. [*pl.* -TIES], a concave surface or object.
**con·ca·vo-con·cave** (kon-kā′vō-kon-kāv′), *adj.* concave on both sides, as some lenses.
**con·ca·vo-con·vex** (kon-kā′vō-kon-veks′), *adj.* having one concave side and one convex side.
**con·ceal** (kən-sēl′), *v.t.* [< OFr. < L. < *com-,* together + *celare,* to hide], 1. to hide; secrete. 2. to keep secret. **—con·ceal′a·ble,** *adj.* **—con·ceal′er,** *n.* **—con·ceal′ment,** *n.*
**con·cede** (kən-sēd′), *v.t.* [-CEDED, -CEDING], [< L. < *com-,* with + *cedere,* to cede], 1. to admit the truth of; acknowledge. 2. to grant as a right. *v.i.* to make a concession. **—con·ced′er,** *n.*
**con·ceit** (kən-sēt′), *n.* [see CONCEIVE], 1. originally, an idea. 2. an exaggerated opinion of oneself, one's merits, etc.; vanity. 3. a fanciful or witty expression or notion. 4. imagination.
**con·ceit·ed** (kən-sēt′id), *adj.* having an exaggerated opinion of oneself, one's merits, etc.; vain. **—con·ceit′ed·ly,** *adv.* **—con·ceit′ed·ness,** *n.*
**con·ceiv·a·ble** (kən-sēv′ə-b'l), *adj.* that can be conceived; that can be understood, imagined, or believed. **—con·ceiv′a·bil′i·ty, con·ceiv′a·ble·ness,** *n.* **—con·ceiv′a·bly,** *adv.*
**con·ceive** (kən-sēv′), *v.t.* [-CEIVED, -CEIVING], [< OFr. < L. *concipere,* to receive < *com-,* together + *capere,* to take], 1. to become pregnant with. 2. to form in the mind; imagine. 3. to understand. 4. to express in words. *v.i.* 1. to become pregnant. 2. to form an idea (*of*). **—con·ceiv′er,** *n.*
**con·cen·ter** (kon-sen′tẽr), *v.t.* [Fr. < L. *com-,* together + *centrum,* center], to bring to a common center; focus; concentrate. *v.i.* to come together to or at a common center; converge. Brit. spelling **concentre.**
**con·cen·trate** (kon′s'n-trāt′), *v.t.* [-TRATED, -TRATING], [< *con-* + L. *centrum,* center; + *-ate*], 1. to bring to a common center. 2. to focus (one's thoughts, efforts, etc.). 3. to increase the strength or density of. *v.i.* 1. to come to a common center. 2. to fix one's attention (*on* or *upon*). *n.* a substance that has been concentrated. *adj.* concentrated. **—con′cen·tra′tive,** *adj.* **—con′cen·tra′tor,** *n.*
**con·cen·tra·tion** (kon′s'n-trā′shən), *n.* 1. a concentrating or being concentrated. 2. close or fixed attention. 3. the strength or density, as of a solution.
**concentration camp,** 1. a place in which enemy aliens or prisoners of war are kept under guard. 2. a place of confinement for those considered dangerous to the regime, as in Nazi Germany.

**con·cen·tric** (kən-sen′trik), *adj.* [< OFr. < ML. < L. *com-*, together + *centrum*, center], having a center in common, as circles: also **concentrical.** —**con·cen′tri·cal·ly,** *adv.* —**con·cen·tric·i·ty** (kon′sen-tris′ə-ti), *n.*

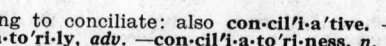

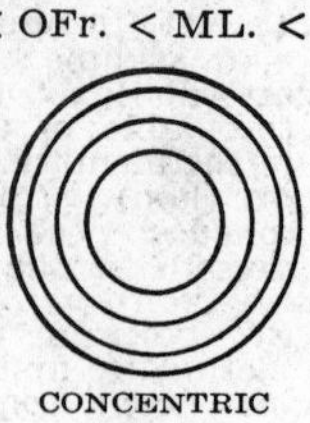
CONCENTRIC CIRCLES

**con·cept** (kon′sept), *n.* [L. *conceptus;* see CONCEIVE], an idea; idea of a class of objects; a thought; general notion.

**con·cep·tion** (kən-sep′shən), *n.* 1. a conceiving or being conceived in the womb. 2. an embryo or fetus. 3. the beginning of some process, etc. 4. the formulation of ideas. 5. a mental image; concept. 6. an original idea, design, etc. —**con·cep′tion·al,** *adj.* —**con·cep′tive,** *adj.*

**con·cep·tu·al** (kən-sep′cho͞o-əl), *adj.* of conception or concepts. —**con·cep′tu·al·ly,** *adv.*

**con·cep·tu·al·ize** (kən-sep′cho͞o-əl-īz′), *v.t.* [-IZED, -IZING], to form a concept or idea of; conceive.

**con·cern** (kən-sûrn′), *v.t.* [< Fr. < ML. < LL. < L. *com-*, with + *cernere*, to sift], 1. to have a relation to; be of interest or importance to. 2. to involve or interest (used in the passive). *n.* 1. a matter of importance to one; affair. 2. interest in or regard for a person or thing. 3. relation; reference. 4. worry; anxiety. 5. a business firm. —**as concerns,** in regard to. — **concern oneself,** 1. to busy oneself (*with, about, over, in* something). 2. to be worried or anxious.

**con·cerned** (kən-sûrnd′), *adj.* 1. involved or interested (*in* some matter). 2. uneasy or anxious.

**con·cern·ing** (kən-sûrn′iŋ), *prep.* relating to; having to do with; in regard to.

**con·cern·ment** (kən-sûrn′mənt), *n.* 1. an affair; matter. 2. importance. 3. worry; anxiety.

**con·cert** (kən-sûrt′; *for n. & adj.*, kon′sērt), *v.t. & v.i.* [< Fr. < It. < L. < *com-*, with + *certare*, to strive], to arrange by mutual understanding; plan together; devise. *n.* 1. mutual agreement; concord. 2. musical consonance. 3. a performance of vocal or instrumental music. *adj.* of or for concerts. — **in concert,** in unison.

**con·cert·ed** (kən-sûr′tid), *adj.* 1. mutually arranged or agreed upon; combined. 2. in *music*, arranged in parts. —**con·cert′ed·ly,** *adv.*

**con·cer·ti·na** (kon′sēr-tē′nə), *n.* [*concert* + *-ina*: a coinage], a small musical instrument of the accordion type, with bellows and keys.

CONCERTINA

**con·cert·mas·ter** (kon′sērt-mas′tēr, -mäs′-), *n.* the leader of the first violin section of a symphony orchestra, often an assistant to the conductor: also **con′cert·meis′ter** (-mīs′-).

**con·cer·to** (kən-cher′tō), *n.* [*pl.* -TOS, -TI (-tē)], [It.; see CONCERT], a composition in symphonic form for one or more solo instruments and an orchestra: it usually has three movements.

**con·ces·sion** (kən-sesh′ən), *n.* 1. a conceding. 2. a thing conceded; acknowledgment, as of an argument. 3. a privilege granted by a government, company, etc.; esp., *a*) the right to use land. *b*) the right to sell food, check hats, etc., as at a park. —**con·ces′sive** (-ses′iv), *adj.*

**con·ces·sion·aire** (kən-sesh′ən-âr′), *n.* [< Fr.], the holder of a concession granted by a government, company, etc.: also **con·ces′sion·er.**

**con·ces·sion·ar·y** (kən-sesh′ən-er′i), *adj.* of a concession. *n.* [*pl.* -IES], a concessionaire.

**conch** (koŋk, konch), *n.* [*pl.* CONCHS (koŋks), CONCHES (kon′chiz)], [< L. < Gr. *konchē*], the spiral, one-piece shell of certain sea mollusks.

CONCH

**con·chol·o·gy** (koŋ-kol′ə-ji), *n.* [< Gr. *konchē*, a shell; + *-logy*], the branch of zoology that deals with mollusks and shells. —**con·chol′o·gist,** *n.*

**con·ci·erge** (kon′si-ûrzh′; Fr. kōn′syârzh′), *n.* [Fr.], 1. a doorkeeper. 2. a caretaker; janitor.

**con·cil·i·ate** (kən-sil′i-āt′), *v.t.* [-ATED, -ATING], [< L. < *concilium;* see COUNCIL], 1. to win over; soothe; placate. 2. to gain (good will, esteem, etc.) by acts of friendship. 3. [Archaic], to reconcile; make consistent. —**con·cil′i·a·ble,** *adj.* —**con·cil′i·a′tion,** *n.* —**con·cil′i·a′tor,** *n.*

**con·cil·i·a·to·ry** (kən-sil′i-ə-tôr′i, -tō′ri), *adj.* tending to conciliate: also **con·cil′i·a′tive.** —**con·cil′i·a·to′ri·ly,** *adv.* —**con·cil′i·a·to′ri·ness,** *n.*

**con·cise** (kən-sīs′), *adj.* [< L. pp. of *concidere* < *com-*, intens. + *caedere*, to cut], brief and to the point; stating much in few words; terse; succinct. —**con·cise′ly,** *adv.* —**con·cise′ness,** *n.*

**con·clave** (kon′klāv, koŋ′-), *n.* [OFr.; L., a room, closet < *com-*, with + *clavis*, a key], 1. in the *R. C. Church*, *a*) the rooms in which the cardinals meet in private to elect a pope. *b*) the meeting for this purpose. 2. any private meeting.

**con·clude** (kən-klo͞od′), *v.t.* [-CLUDED, -CLUDING], [< L. < *com-*, together + *claudere*, to shut], 1. to bring to a close; end; finish. 2. to decide by reasoning; infer; deduce. 3. to decide; determine. 4. to settle; come to an agreement about. *v.i.* 1. to come to a close; end; finish. 2. to come to an agreement. —**con·clud′er,** *n.*

**con·clu·sion** (kən-klo͞o′zhən), *n.* 1. the end or last part; as, *a*) the last division of a discourse. *b*) the last part of a chain of reasoning; judgment or opinion formed after thought. *c*) the last of a chain of events; outcome. 2. a concluding (*of* a treaty, etc.). —**in conclusion,** lastly; in closing.

**con·clu·sive** (kən-klo͞o′siv), *adj.* that settles a question; decisive; final. —**con·clu′sive·ly,** *adv.* —**con·clu′sive·ness,** *n.*

**con·coct** (kon-kokt′, kən-), *v.t.* [< L. pp. of *concoquere* < *com-*, together + *coquere*, to cook], 1. to make by combining ingredients; compound. 2. to devise; plan. —**con·coct′er,** *n.* —**con·coc′tive,** *adj.*

**con·coc·tion** (kon-kok′shən, kən-), *n.* 1. a concocting. 2. something concocted.

**con·com·i·tance** (kon-kom′ə-təns, kən-), *n.* the fact of being concomitant: also **con·com′i·tan·cy.**

**con·com·i·tant** (kon-kom′ə-tənt, kən-), *adj.* [< L. < *com-*, together + *comitari*, to accompany < *comes*, companion], accompanying; attendant. *n.* an accompanying or attendant condition, circumstance, or thing. —**con·com′i·tant·ly,** *adv.*

**Con·cord** (koŋ′kērd, kon′kôrd), *n.* 1. the capital of New Hampshire: pop., 29,000. 2. a town in E Massachusetts: site of second battle of American Revolution (April 19, 1775). 3. a large, dark-blue grape of North America: also **Concord grape.**

**con·cord** (kon′kôrd, koŋ′-), *n.* [< Fr. < L. < *concors*, of the same mind < *com-*, together + *cor*, heart], 1. agreement; harmony. 2. peaceful relations, as between nations. 3. a treaty establishing this. 4. in *grammar*, agreement between words in regard to forms showing person, gender, number, and case. 5. in *music*, a combination of simultaneous and harmonious tones: opposed to *discord.*

**con·cord·ance** (kon-kôr′d'ns, kən-), *n.* [see CONCORD], 1. agreement; harmony. 2. an alphabetical list of the important words of a book, with references to the passages in which they occur.

**con·cord·ant** (kon-kôr′d'nt, kən-), *adj.* agreeing; consonant; harmonious. —**con·cord′ant·ly,** *adv.*

**con·cor·dat** (kon-kôr′dat), *n.* [Fr. < ML. < L. < *concors;* see CONCORD], 1. a compact; formal agreement; covenant. 2. an agreement between the Pope and a government on church matters.

**con·course** (kon′kôrs, koŋ′kōrs), *n.* [< Fr. < L. < *concurrere;* see CONCUR], 1. a running or flowing together. 2. a crowd; throng. 3. a place where crowds gather. 4. an open space, as in a park or railroad station. 5. a broad boulevard.

**con·crete** (kon-krēt′, kon′krēt), *adj.* [< L. *concretus* < *com-*, together + *crescere*, to grow], 1. formed into a solid mass; coalesced. 2. having a material, perceptible existence; real; actual. 3. specific, not general or abstract. 4. made of concrete. 5. in *grammar*, designating a thing or class of things that can be perceived by the senses: opposed to *abstract.* *n.* (kon′krēt, kon-krēt′), 1. anything concrete. 2. a hard, compact substance made of sand, gravel, cement, and water, used in bridges, dams, buildings, etc. *v.t.* [-CRETED, -CRETING], 1. (kon-krēt′), to form into a mass; solidify. 2. (kon′krēt), to make of, or cover with, concrete (*n.*, 2). *v.i.* to form into a mass; solidify.—**con·crete′ly,** *adv.* —**con·crete′ness,** *n.*

**con·cre·tion** (kon-krē′shən), *n.* [see CONCRETE], 1. a solidifying or being solidified. 2. a solidified mass. —**con·cre′tive,** *adj.* —**con·cre′tive·ly,** *adv.*

**con·cret·ize** (kon′kri-tīz′), *v.t.* [-IZED, -IZING], to make (something) concrete; make specific.

**con·cu·bine** (koŋ′kyoo-bīn′, kon′-), *n.* [OFr. < L. < *com-*, with + *cubare*, to lie down], 1. a woman who lives with a man although not legally married to him. 2. in certain polygamous societies, a secondary wife; wife of inferior social and legal status. —**con·cu·bi·nage** (kon-kū′bə-nij), *n.*

**con·cu·pis·cence** (kon-kū′pə-s'ns), *n.* [OFr. < LL. < L. < *com-*, together + *cupere*, to desire], strong desire or appetite; esp., sexual desire; lust. —**con·cu′pis·cent,** *adj.*

**con·cur** (kən-kūr′), *v.i.* [-CURRED, -CURRING], [< L. < *com-*, together + *currere*, to run], 1. to occur at the same time; coincide. 2. to combine in having an effect; act together. 3. to agree; be in accord; have the same opinion.

**con·cur·rence** (kən-kūr′əns), *n.* 1. a happening together in time or place. 2. a combining to produce or bring about something. 3. agreement in opinion. 4. in *geometry*, the junction of lines or surfaces. Also **con·cur′ren·cy** [*pl.* -CIES].

**con·cur·rent** (kən-kūr′ənt), *adj.* 1. occurring or existing at the same time. 2. meeting in the same point; converging. 3. acting together; co-operating. 4. in agreement. 5. in *law*, having equal jurisdiction or authority. —**con·cur′rent·ly,** *adv.*

**con·cus·sion** (kən-kush′ən), *n.* [L. *concussio* < pp. of *concutere* < *com-*, together + *quatere*, to shake], 1. a violent shaking; agitation; shock, as from impact. 2. in *medicine*, a condition of impaired functioning, especially of the brain, as a result of a violent blow or impact. —**con·cus′sion·al,** *adj.* —**con·cus′sive** (-siv), *adj.*

**con·demn** (kən-dem′), *v.t.* [< OFr. < L. < *com-*, intens. + *damnare*, to harm, condemn], 1. to disapprove of strongly; censure. 2. to declare guilty of wrongdoing; convict. 3. to inflict a penalty upon; doom. 4. to appropriate (property) for public use. 5. to declare unfit for use or service. —**con·dem′na·ble** (-nə-b'l), *adj.* —**con·demn′er,** *n.* —**con·demn′ing·ly,** *adv.*

**con·dem·na·tion** (kon′dem-nā′shən), *n.* 1. a condemning or being condemned. 2. a cause for condemning. —**con·dem·na·to·ry** (kən-dem′nə-tôr′i, -tō′ri), *adj.*

**con·den·sa·tion** (kon′den-sā′shən), *n.* 1. a condensing or being condensed. 2. anything condensed; product of condensation.

**con·dense** (kən-dens′), *v.t.* [-DENSED, -DENSING], [< Fr. < L. < *com-*, intens. + *densus*, dense], 1. to make more dense or compact; compress; concentrate. 2. to express in fewer words; make concise. 3. to change to a denser form, as from gas to a liquid. *v.i.* 1. to become more dense or compact. 2. to pass into a denser form, as a gas into a liquid. —**con·den′sa·bil′i·ty, con·den′si·bil′i·ty,** *n.* —**con·den′sa·ble, con·den′si·ble,** *adj.* —**con·densed′,** *adj.*

**condensed milk,** a thick, sweetened milk made by evaporating part of the water from cow's milk and adding sugar: cf. *evaporated milk.*

**con·dens·er** (kən-den′sēr), *n.* a person or thing that condenses; specif., *a*) an apparatus for converting gases or vapors to a liquid. *b*) a lens or lenses for concentrating light rays on an area. *c*) in *electricity*, a device for receiving and storing an electric charge.

**con·de·scend** (kon′di-send′), *v.i.* [< OFr. < LL. < *com-*, together + *descendere;* see DESCEND], 1. to descend voluntarily to the level, regarded as lower, of the person that one is dealing with; deign. 2. to deal with others in a patronizing manner. —**con′de·scen′sion, con′de·scend′ence,** *n.* —**con′de·scend′ing,** *adj.* —**con′de·scend′ing·ly,** *adv.*

**con·dign** (kən-dīn′), *adj.* [L. *condignus*, very worthy < *com-*, intens. + *dignus*, worthy], deserved; suitable: said especially of punishment.

**con·di·ment** (kon′də-mənt), *n.* [Fr. < L. *condimentum*, a spice < *condire*, to pickle], a seasoning or relish for food, as pepper, mustard, etc.

**con·di·tion** (kən-dish′ən), *n.* [< OFr. < L. *condicio*, agreement < *com-*, together + *dicere*, to speak], 1. something required before the performance, completion, or effectiveness of something else; provision; stipulation. 2. anything essential to the existence or occurrence of something else; prerequisite: as, health is a *condition* of happiness. 3. anything that modifies the nature or occurrence of something else: as, poor business *conditions.* 4. manner or state of being: as, in a critical *condition.* 5. proper or healthy state: as, athletes train to be in *condition.* 6. social position; rank; station. 7. the requirement that a student make up deficiencies in a subject in order to pass it. 8. in *law*, a clause in a contract, will, etc. that revokes or modifies a stipulation on certain contingencies. *v.i.* to make conditions. *v.t.* 1. to stipulate; make terms concerning. 2. to subject to a condition or conditions. 3. to be a condition of. 4. to bring into proper or fit condition. 5. in *psychology*, to develop a conditioned reflex or behavior pattern in; hence, 6. loosely, to accustom to. —**on condition that,** provided that; if. —**con·di′tion·er,** *n.*

**con·di·tion·al** (kən-dish′ən-'l), *adj.* 1. containing or dependent on a condition; qualified; not absolute: as, a *conditional* award. 2. expressing a condition: as, a *conditional* clause. —**con·di′tion·al′i·ty** (-al′ə-ti), *n.* —**con·di′tion·al·ly,** *adv.*

**conditioned reflex** (or **response**), a reflex in which the response (e.g., secretion of saliva in a dog) is occasioned by a secondary stimulus (e.g., a ringing bell) repeatedly associated with the primary stimulus (e.g., the sight of meat).

**con·dole** (kən-dōl′), *v.i.* [-DOLED, -DOLING], [< LL. < L. *com-*, with + *dolere*, to grieve], to express sympathy; mourn in sympathy; commiserate. —**con·do′la·to′ry** (-ə-tôr′i, -tō′ri), *adj.* —**con·dol′er,** *n.* —**con·dol′ing·ly,** *adv.*

**con·do·lence** (kən-dō′ləns), *n.* expression of sympathy with another in grief: also **con·dole′ment.**

**con·do·min·i·um** (kon′də-min′i-əm), *n.* [Mod.L. < *com-*, with + *dominium*, ownership], 1. *a*) joint rule by two or more states. *b*) the territory so ruled. 2. *a*) one of the units in a multiple-unit dwelling, each separately owned. *b*) [*pl.* -IUMS, -IA], a building or complex made up of these.

**con·done** (kən-dōn′), *v.t.* [-DONED, -DONING], [< L. < *com-*, intens. + *donare*, to give], to forgive, pardon, or overlook (an offense). —**con·do·na·tion** (kon′dō-nā′shən), *n.* —**con·don′er,** *n.*

**con·dor** (kon′dēr), *n.* [Sp. < Peruv. (Quechua) *cuntur*], 1. a large vulture of the South American Andes, with a bare head and a neck ruff of downy white feathers. 2. a similar vulture of California. 3. (Sp. kôn′dôr), [*pl.* CONDORES (kôn-dô′res)], any of various South American gold coins.

**con·duce** (kən-dōōs′, -dūs′), *v.i.* [-DUCED, -DUCING], [< L. < *com-*, together + *ducere*, to lead], to tend; contribute; lead (*to* or *toward*). —**con·duc′er,** *n.*

**con·du·cive** (kən-dōō′siv, -dū′-), *adj.* conducing; tending; contributive. —**con·du′cive·ness,** *n.*

**con·duct** (kon′dukt; *for v.*, kən-dukt′), *n.* [< L. pp. of *conducere;* see CONDUCE], 1. a leading; guidance. 2. management; handling. 3. behavior; way that one acts. *v.t.* 1. to lead; escort. 2. to manage; direct; carry on. 3. to direct (an orchestra, etc.). 4. to behave (oneself). 5. to be a channel for; transmit: as, this wire *conducts* electricity. *v.i.* 1. to lead. 2. to act as a conductor. —**con·duct′i·bil′i·ty,** *n.* —**con·duct′i·ble,** *adj.* —**con·duc′tive,** *adj.*

**con·duct·ance** (kən-duk′təns), *n.* the ability of a substance to conduct electricity, measured by the ratio of the current to the applied electromotive force: also called *reciprocal of resistance.*

**con·duc·tion** (kən-duk′shən), *n.* 1. a conveying, as of liquid through a channel. 2. in *physics*, *a*) transmission (of electricity, heat, etc.) by the passage of energy from particle to particle. *b*) conductivity. See also **convection, radiation.**

**con·duc·tiv·i·ty** (kon′duk-tiv′ə-ti), *n.* the property or power of conducting or transmitting heat, electricity, etc.

**con·duc·tor** (kən-duk′tēr), *n.* 1. one who conducts; leader; guide. 2. the director of an orchestra, choir, etc. 3. one who has charge of the passengers and collects fares, as on a streetcar or train. 4. a thing that conducts electricity, heat, etc. —**con·duc′tor·ship′,** *n.* —**con·duc′tress,** *n.fem.*

**con·duit** (kon′dit, -doo-it), *n.* [< OFr. < L. pp. of *conducere;* see CONDUCE], 1. a pipe or channel for conveying fluids. 2. a tube or protected trough for electric wires.

**cone** (kōn), *n.* [Fr. < L. < Gr. *kōnos*], 1. in *geometry*, *a*) a solid with a circle for its base and a curved surface tapering evenly to a point. *b*) a surface described by a moving straight line passing through a fixed point and tracing a fixed curve, as a circle or ellipse, at another point. 2. any object shaped like a cone, as a shell of pastry for holding a scoop of ice cream, the peak of a volcano, etc. 3. the fruit of evergreen trees, consisting of a woody axis with stiff, leaflike scales containing ovules or pollen. *v.t.* [CONED, CONING], to shape like a cone.

**Con·es·to·ga (wagon)** (kon′ə-stō′gə), [after *Conestoga*, Pennsylvania], a broad-wheeled covered wagon used by American pioneers crossing the prairies.

**co·ney** (kō′ni, kun′i), *n.* [*pl.* -NEYS], a cony.

**Co·ney Island** (kō′ni), a beach and amusement park in Brooklyn, New York.
**conf.,** conference.
**con·fab** (kon′fab), *n.* [Colloq.], a confabulation.
**con·fab·u·late** (kən-fab′yoo-lāt′), *v.i.* [-LATED, -LATING], [< L. < *com-*, together + *fabulari*, to talk; see FABLE], to talk together in an informal, familiar way; chat. —**con·fab′u·la′tion,** *n.*
**con·fect** (kən-fekt′), *v.t.* [< L. *confectus* < *com-*, with + *facere*, to make, do], to prepare, especially by mixing or combining.
**con·fec·tion** (kən-fek′shən), *n.* 1. a confecting. 2. a bonbon, candy, ice cream, preserve, etc. —**con-fec′tion·ar′y,** *adj.*
**con·fec·tion·er** (kən-fek′shən-ẽr), *n.* one who makes or sells candy and other confections.
**confectioners' sugar,** very fine powdered sugar.
**con·fec·tion·er·y** (kən-fek′shən-er′i), *n.* [*pl.* -IES], 1. candies, ice cream, and other confections. 2. the business, work, or shop of a confectioner: sometimes sp. **confectionary.**
**con·fed·er·a·cy** (kən-fed′ẽr-ə-si), *n.* [*pl.* -CIES], [see CONFEDERATE], 1. people or nations united for some common purpose. 2. a league or alliance formed by such a union; federation. 3. a conspiracy. —**the Confederacy,** the eleven Southern States that seceded from the U.S. in 1860 and 1861: also **Confederate States of America.**
**con·fed·er·ate** (kən-fed′ẽr-it), *adj.* [< LL. < L. *com-*, together + *foederare* < *foedus*, a league], 1. united in an alliance or league. 2. [C-], of the Confederacy. *n.* 1. a person, group, or state united with another or others for some common purpose; ally. 2. an associate in crime; accomplice. 3. [C-], any Southerner who supported the Confederacy. *v.t.* & *v.i* (-āt′), [-ATED, -ATING], to unite in a confederacy; join together; ally.
**con·fed·er·a·tion** (kən-fed′ẽr-ā′shən), *n.* 1. a uniting or being united in a league or alliance. 2. nations or states joined in a league for a special purpose.—**the Confederation,** the union of the American States from 1781 to 1789 under the *Articles of Confederation.* —**con·fed′er·a′tive,** *adj.*
**con·fer** (kən-fũr′), *v.t.* [-FERRED, -FERRING], [< L. < *com-*, together + *ferre*, to bring], to give; bestow. *v.i.* to have a conference; meet for discussion. —**con·fer′ment,** *n.* —**con·fer′ra·ble,** *adj.* —**con-fer′rer,** *n.*
‡**con·fer** (kən-fũr′), *v.t.* [L., imperative of *conferre;* see prec. entry], compare: abbrev. **cf.**
**con·fer·ee** (kon′fẽr-ē′), *n.* a participant in a conference: also sp. **conferree.**
**con·fer·ence** (kon′fẽr-əns), *n.* 1. a conferring or consulting. 2. a formal meeting of a number of people for discussion or consultation. 3. an association of religious bodies, schools, etc. for some common purpose. —**con′fer·en′tial** (-en′shəl), *adj.*
**con·fess** (kən-fes′), *v.t.* [< OFr. < LL. *confessare* < L. < *com-*, together + *fateri*, to acknowledge], 1. to admit or acknowledge (a fault, crime, opinion, etc.). 2. to declare one's faith in. 3. *a)* to tell (one's sins) to a priest in order to receive absolution. *b)* to hear the confession of (a person): said of a priest. *v.i.* 1. to admit one's faults or crimes. 2. to tell one's sins to a priest in order to receive absolution. —**confess to,** to admit; acknowledge; admit having. —**stand confessed as,** to be revealed as. —**con·fess′ed·ly,** *adv.*
**con·fes·sion** (kən-fesh′ən), *n.* 1. a confessing; acknowledgment; admission. 2. something confessed. 3. an admission of guilt. 4. the confessing of sins to a priest in order to receive absolution. 5. declaration of faith; creed: also **confession of faith.** 6. a group of people adhering to a certain creed; church; sect; denomination.
**con·fes·sion·al** (kən-fesh′ən-'l), *n.* a small, enclosed place in a church, where a priest hears confessions. *adj.* of or for confession.
**con·fes·sor** (kən-fes′ẽr), *n.* 1. one who confesses. 2. a priest authorized to hear confessions and give absolution. Also sp. **confesser.**
**con·fet·ti** (kən-fet′i), *n.pl.* [It., pl. of *confetto*, sweetmeat: candies were formerly used in this way], [construed as sing.], bits of colored paper scattered about at carnivals and celebrations.
**con·fi·dant** (kon′fə-dant′, kon′fə-dant′), *n.* a close, trusted friend, to whom one confides intimate affairs or secrets. —**con′fi·dante′,** *n.fem.*
**con·fide** (kən-fīd′), *v.i.* [-FIDED, -FIDING], [< L. < *com-*, intens. + *fidere*, to trust], to trust (*in* someone); share secrets or discuss private affairs. *v.t.* 1. to tell about as a secret: as, she *confided* her difficulties to me. 2. to entrust (a duty, person, etc. *to* someone).
**con·fi·dence** (kon′fə-dəns), *n.* 1. firm belief; trust; reliance. 2. assurance; certainty. 3. belief in one's own abilities; self-confidence. 4. a relationship as confidant: as, take me into your *confidence.* 5. the belief that another will keep a secret: as, told in strict *confidence.* 6. something told as a secret.
**confidence game,** a swindle effected by one (**confidence man**) who first gains the confidence of his victim.
**con·fi·dent** (kon′fə-dənt), *adj.* full of or expressing confidence; specifically, *a)* assured; certain: as, *confident* of victory. *b)* sure of oneself; self-confident; bold. *n.* a friend in whom one confides; confidant. —**con′fi·dent·ly,** *adv.*
**con·fi·den·tial** (kon′fə-den′shəl), *adj.* 1. told in confidence; secret. 2. of or showing confidence. 3. entrusted with private or secret matters; as, a *confidential* agent. —**con′fi·den′tial·ly,** *adv.*
**con·fid·ing** (kən-fīd′iŋ), *adj.* trustful or inclined to trust. —**con·fid′ing·ly,** *adv.*
**con·fig·u·ra·tion** (kən-fig′yoo-rā′shən), *n.* [< L. *configuratio* < *com-*, together + *figurare;* see FIGURE], arrangement of parts; form or figure as determined by the disposition of parts; contour; outline. —**con·fig′u·ra′tion·al,** *adj.* —**con·fig′u·ra′tion-al·ly,** *adv.*
**con·fine** (kon′fīn′; *for v.*, kən-fīn′), *n.* [< Fr. < L. *confinium*, boundary < *com-*, with + *finis*, an end, limit], *usually in pl.* a boundary or bounded region; border; limit. *v.t.* [-FINED, -FINING], 1. to keep within limits; restrict: as, *confine* your remarks to the facts. 2. to keep shut up, as in prison, in bed because of illness, indoors, etc. —**be confined,** to be undergoing childbirth. —**con·fin′a-ble, con·fine′a·ble,** *adj.* —**con·fin′er,** *n.*
**con·fine·ment** (kən-fīn′mənt), *n.* a confining or being confined; specif., *a)* imprisonment. *b)* restriction; restraint. *c)* childbirth; lying-in.
**con·firm** (kən-fũrm′), *v.t.* [< OFr. < L. < *com-*, intens. + *firmare* < *firmus*, firm], 1. to make firm; strengthen. 2. to make valid by formal approval; ratify. 3. to prove the truth or validity of; verify. 4. to admit (a person of a certain age) to full membership in a church by a special ceremony. —**con-firm′a·ble,** *adj.* —**con·firm′er, con·firm·or** (kon′fẽr-môr′, kən-fũr′mẽr), *n.*
**con·fir·ma·tion** (kon′fẽr-mā′shən), *n.* 1. a confirming or being confirmed; ratification; verification. 2. something that confirms or proves. 3. a ceremony in which a person of a certain age is admitted to full membership in a church.
**con·firm·a·to·ry** (kən-fũr′mə-tôr′i, -tō′ri), *adj.* confirming or serving to confirm: also **con·firm′a-tive.**
**con·firmed** (kən-fũrmd′), *adj.* [pp. of *confirm*], 1. firmly established, as in a habit or condition: as, a *confirmed* bachelor. 2. chronic, as a disease. 3. corroborated; proved. 4. having gone through the religious ceremony of confirmation. —**con·firm′ed-ly,** *adv.* —**con·firm′ed·ness,** *n.*
**con·fis·cate** (kon′fis-kāt′), *v.t.* [-CATED, -CATING], [< L. pp. of *confiscare*, orig., to lay up in a chest < *com-*, together + *fiscus*, money chest, treasury], 1. to seize (private property) for the public treasury, usually as a penalty. 2. to seize as by authority; appropriate. —**con′fis·ca′tion,** *n.* —**con′fis·ca′-tor,** *n.*
**con·fis·ca·to·ry** (kən-fis′kə-tôr′i, -tō′ri), *adj.* 1. of, constituting, or effecting confiscation: as, a *confiscatory* tax. 2. confiscating.
**con·fla·gra·tion** (kon′flə-grā′shən), *n.* [< L. *conflagratio;* ult. < *com-*, intens. + *flagrare*, to burn], a big, destructive fire.
**con·flict** (kən-flikt′; *for n.*, kon′flikt), *v.i.* [< L. *conflictus*, pp. < *com-*, together + *fligere*, to strike], 1. originally, to fight; contend. 2. to clash; be antagonistic, incompatible, or contradictory. *n.* 1. a fight; struggle. 2. sharp disagreement or opposition, as of interests or ideas. 3. emotional disturbance resulting from a clash of impulses in a person. —**con·flic′tion,** *n.* —**con·flic′tive,** *adj.*
**con·flu·ence** (kon′floo-əns), *n.* [< LL. < L. *confluens*, ppr. < *com-*, together + *fluere*, to flow], 1. a flowing together, as of two or more streams. 2. the place of, or a stream formed by, this. 3. a flocking together; hence, 4. a crowd; throng. —**con′flu·ent,** *adj.* —**con′flu·ent·ly,** *adv.*
**con·flux** (kon′fluks), *n.* confluence.
**con·form** (kən-fôrm′), *v.t.* [< OFr. < L. < *com-*, together + *formare*, to form], 1. to give the same form to; make similar. 2. to bring into harmony or agreement; adapt. *v.i.* 1. to have the same form; be or become similar. 2. to be in accord or agreement. 3. to act in accordance with rules customs, ritual, etc. —**con·form′er,** *n.*

**con·form·a·ble** (kən-fôr′mə-b'l), *adj.* 1. that conforms; specifically, *a*) similar. *b*) in harmony or agreement. *c*) adapted; suited. 2. quick to conform; obedient; submissive. —**con·form′a·bil′i·ty, con·form′a·ble·ness,** *n.* —**con·form′a·bly,** *adv.*

**con·form·ance** (kən-fôr′məns), *n.* conformity.

**con·for·ma·tion** (kon′fôr-mā′shən), *n.* 1. [Rare], a conforming; adaptation. 2. a symmetrical formation and arrangement of the parts of a thing. 3. the structure or form of a thing as determined by the arrangement of its parts.

**con·form·ist** (kən-fôrm′ist), *n.* one who conforms.

**con·form·i·ty** (kən-fôr′mə-ti), *n.* [*pl.* -TIES], 1. the condition or fact of being in harmony or agreement; correspondence; similarity. 2. action in accordance with rules, customs, ritual, etc.

**con·found** (kən-found′, kon-), *v.t.* [< OFr. < L. < *com-*, together + *fundere*, to pour], 1. to mix up or lump together indiscriminately; confuse. 2. to cause to become confused; bewilder. 3. [Archaic], to defeat; destroy. 4. (*usually* kon′found′), to damn: used as a mild oath. —**con·found′er,** *n.*

**con·found·ed** (kən-foun′did; *also, for 2 & 3,* kon′-foun′-), *adj.* 1. confused; bewildered. 2. damned: a mild oath. 3. detestable. —**con·found′ed·ly,** *adv.*

**con·frere** (kon′frâr; Fr. kōn′frâr′), *n.* [Fr. *confrère*], colleague; associate; fellow member.

**con·front** (kən-frunt′), *v.t.* [< OFr. < ML. < L. *com-*, together + *frons*, forehead, front], 1. to face; meet face to face. 2. to face boldly or defiantly. 3. to bring (a person) face to face (*with*): as, he *confronted* the accused with the evidence. —**con·fron·ta·tion** (kon′frun-tā′shən), **con·front′ment,** *n.* —**con·front′er,** *n.*

**Con·fu·cian·ism** (kən-fū′shən-iz'm), *n.* the ethical teachings of Confucius, emphasizing devotion to parents, ancestor worship, and the maintenance of justice and peace. —**Con·fu′cian·ist,** *n. & adj.*

**Con·fu·cius** (kən-fū′shəs), *n.* (*Kung Fu-tse*), Chinese philosopher and teacher; lived 557?–479 B.C. —**Con·fu′cian,** *adj. & n.*

**con·fuse** (kən-fūz′), *v.t.* [-FUSED, -FUSING], [< OFr. < L. *confusus*, pp. of *confundere;* see CONFOUND], 1. to mix up; jumble together; put into disorder. 2. to mix up mentally; specif., *a*) to bewilder; perplex. *b*) to embarrass; disconcert; abash. *c*) to fail to distinguish between; mistake the identity of. —**con·fus′ed·ly,** *adv.* —**con·fus′ing·ly,** *adv.*

**con·fu·sion** (kən-fū′zhən), *n.* a confusing or being confused; specif., *a*) disorder. *b*) bewilderment. *c*) embarrassment. *d*) failure to distinguish between things. —**con·fu′sion·al,** *adj.*

**con·fute** (kən-fūt′), *v.t.* [-FUTED, -FUTING], [L. *confutare*], 1. to prove (a person) to be in error; overcome by argument. 2. to prove (a statement, argument, etc.) to be false or invalid. 3. to make useless; defeat. —**con·fu·ta·tion** (kon′fyoo-tā′shən), *n.* —**con·fut′a·tive,** *adj.* —**con·fut′er,** *n.*

**Cong.,** 1. Congress. 2. Congressional.

**con·ga** (koŋ′gə), *n.* [Am. Sp.], 1. a Latin-American dance in which the dancers form a winding line. 2. music for it. *v.i.* to dance the conga.

**con·gé** (kon′zhā; Fr. kōn′zhā′), *n.* [Fr. < OFr. < L. < *com-*, intens. + *meare*, to go], 1. a curt dismissal. 2. a formal farewell.

**con·geal** (kən-jēl′), *v.t. & v.i.* [< OFr. < L. < *com-*, together + *gelare*, to freeze], 1. to solidify or thicken by cooling or freezing. 2. to thicken; coagulate; jell. —**con·geal′a·ble,** *adj.* —**con·geal′er,** *n.* —**con·geal′ment,** *n.*

**con·gen·ial** (kən-jēn′yəl), *adj.* [see COM- & GENIAL], 1. kindred; compatible. 2. having the same tastes and temperament; friendly. 3. suited to one's needs or disposition; agreeable. —**con·ge′ni·al′i·ty** (-jē′ni-al′ə-ti), *n.* —**con·gen′ial·ly,** *adv.*

**con·gen·i·tal** (kən-jen′ə-t'l), *adj.* [< L.; see COM- & GENITAL], existing as such at birth; resulting from heredity or prenatal environment: as, a *congenital* disease. —**con·gen′i·tal·ly,** *adv.*

**con·ger** (koŋ′gēr), *n.* [< OFr. < L. < Gr. *gongros*], a large, edible, salt-water eel: also **conger eel.**

**con·ge·ri·es** (kon-jêr′ēz, -i-ēz′), *n.* [*pl.* CONGERIES], [see CONGEST], a collection of things or parts massed together; heap; pile.

**con·gest** (kən-jest′), *v.t.* [< L. pp. of *congerere*, to pile up < *com-*, together + *gerere*, to carry], 1. to cause too much blood to accumulate in (a part of the body). 2. to overcrowd; fill to excess. *v.i.* to become congested. —**con·ges′tion,** *n.* —**con·ges′tive,** *adj.*

**con·glom·er·ate** (kən-glom′ēr-āt′; *for adj. & n.*, -ēr-it), *v.t. & v.i.* [-ATED, -ATING], [< L. < *com-*, together + *glomerare* < *glomus*, a ball], to form or collect into a ball or rounded mass. *adj.* 1. formed into a ball or rounded mass; clustered. 2. made up of separate substances collected into a single mass. 3. in *geology*, made up of rock fragments or pebbles cemented together in hardened clay and sand. *n.* 1. a conglomerate mass; cluster. 2. a large corporation formed by the merger of a number of companies in unrelated industries. 3. in *geology*, a conglomerate rock. —**con·glom′er·a′tion,** *n.*

**con·glom·er·at·ic** (kən-glom′ēr-at′ik), *adj.* in *geology*, conglomerate: also **con·glom′er·it′ic.**

**con·glu·ti·nate** (kən-gloo′tə-nāt′), *adj.* [< L. < *com-*, together + *glutinare* < *gluten*, glue], glued together; adhering. *v.t. & v.i.* [-NATED, -NATING], to stick together by or as by adhesion.

**Con·go** (koŋ′gō), *n.* 1. a river in Africa, flowing through the Congo (sense 2) into the Atlantic. 2. a country in central Africa: area, 905,378 sq. mi.; pop., 16,730,000; capital, Kinshasa: formerly, *Belgian Congo*. 3. a country in west central Africa, northwest of Congo (sense 2): it is a member of the French Community: area, 134,750 sq. mi.; pop., 826,000; capital, Brazzaville.

**congo snake,** an eellike amphibian with two pairs of small, weak legs, found in the swamps of the southeastern U.S.: also **congo eel.**

**con·grat·u·late** (kən-grach′ə-lāt′), *v.t.* [-LATED, -LATING], [< L. < *com-*, together + *gratulari*, to wish joy < *gratus*, agreeable], to rejoice with and express one's happiness to (a person who has been fortunate, successful, etc.); felicitate. —**con·grat′u·lant,** *adj. & n.* —**con·grat′u·la′tor,** *n.* —**con·grat′u·la·to′ry** (-lə-tôr′i, -tō′ri), *adj.*

**con·grat·u·la·tion** (kən-grach′ə-lā′shən), *n.* 1. a congratulating. 2. *pl.* expressions of pleasure over another's good fortune or success.

**con·gre·gate** (koŋ′grə-gāt′), *v.t. & v.i.* [-GATED, -GATING], [< L. < *com-*, together + *gregare*, to gather < *grex, gregis*, a flock], to gather into a mass or crowd; collect; assemble. *adj.* (*usually* -git), 1. collected; assembled. 2. collective. —**con′gre·ga′tive,** *adj.* —**con′gre·ga′tor,** *n.*

**con·gre·ga·tion** (koŋ′grə-gā′shən), *n.* 1. a congregating or being congregated. 2. a gathering of people or things; assemblage. 3. an assembly of people for religious worship. 4. the members of a particular place of worship. 5. in the *R.C. Church*, a religious order not necessarily under solemn vows but bound by a common rule.

**con·gre·ga·tion·al** (koŋ′grə-gā′shən-'l), *adj.* 1. of or like a congregation. 2. [C-], of Congregationalism or Congregationalists.

**con·gre·ga·tion·al·ism** (koŋ′grə-gā′shən-'l-iz'm), *n.* 1. a form of church organization in which each congregation is self-governing. 2. [C-], the faith and form of organization of a Protestant denomination in which each member church is self-governing. —**Con′gre·ga′tion·al·ist,** *adj. & n.*

**con·gress** (koŋ′grəs), *n.* [< L. < *com-*, together + *gradi*, to step < *gradus*, a step], 1. a coming together; meeting. 2. an assembly or conference. 3. any of various legislatures, especially the national legislature of a republic. 4. [C-], *a*) the legislature of the U.S., consisting of the Senate and the House of Representatives. *b*) its session. *c*) the body of Senators and Representatives serving together for any two-year term.

**con·gres·sion·al** (kən-gresh′ən-'l), *adj.* 1. of a congress. 2. [C-], of Congress.

**Congressional district,** any of the districts into which a State is divided for electing Congressional Representatives.

**con·gress·man** (koŋ′grəs-mən), *n.* [*pl.* -MEN], a member of Congress, especially of the House of Representatives. —**con′gress·wom′an,** *n.fem.*

**Con·greve, William** (kon′grēv, koŋ′-), 1670–1729; English writer of comedies.

**con·gru·ent** (koŋ′groo-ənt), *adj.* [< L. ppr. of *congruere*, to come together, agree], 1. agreeing; corresponding; harmonious. 2. in *geometry*, coinciding exactly in all parts: as, *congruent* figures. —**con′gru·ence, con′gru·en·cy,** *n.* —**con′gru·ent·ly,** *adv.*

**con·gru·i·ty** (kən-groo′ə-ti), *n.* [*pl.* -TIES], 1. the condition, quality, or fact of being congruous; specif., *a*) agreement; harmony. *b*) appropriateness. 2. in *geometry*, exact coincidence in all parts.

**con·gru·ous** (koŋ′groo-əs), *adj.* 1. congruent. 2.

corresponding to what is right, proper, or reasonable; fitting; suitable; appropriate. —**con′gru·ous·ly,** *adv.* —**con′gru·ous·ness,** *n.*
**con·ic** (kon′ik), *adj.* conical. *n.* a conic section.
**con·i·cal** (kon′i-k′l), *adj.* 1. of a cone. 2. resembling or shaped like a cone. —**con′i·cal·ly,** *adv.*
**conic section,** in *geometry,* a curve, as an ellipse, parabola, or hyperbola, produced by the intersection of a plane with a right circular cone.
**co·nid·i·um** (kō-nid′i-əm), *n.* [*pl.* -IA (-i-ə)], [< Gr. *konis,* dust], a small asexual spore of certain fungi. —**co·nid′i·al, co·nid′i·an,** *adj.*
**co·ni·fer** (kō′nə-fẽr, kon′ə-), *n.* [< L. *conus,* a cone + *ferre,* to bear], any of a large group of cone-bearing trees and shrubs, mostly evergreens, as the pine, spruce, fir, cedar, yew, etc. —**co·nif·er·ous** (kō-nif′ẽr-əs), *adj.*
**conj.,** 1. conjugation. 2. conjunction.
**con·jec·tur·al** (kən-jek′chẽr-əl), *adj.* 1. based on or involving conjecture. 2. inclined to make conjectures. —**con·jec′tur·al·ly,** *adv.*
**con·jec·ture** (kən-jek′chẽr), *n.* [< L. *conjectura* < pp. of *conjicere,* to guess < *com-,* together + *jacere,* to throw], 1. guesswork; inferring, theorizing, or predicting from incomplete evidence. 2. a guess; inference, theory, or prediction based on guesswork. *v.t.* [-TURED, -TURING], to guess; arrive at or predict by conjecture. *v.i.* to make a conjecture. —**con·jec′tur·a·ble,** *adj.* —**con·jec′tur·a·bly,** *adv.* —**con·jec′tur·er,** *n.*
**con·join** (kən-join′), *v.t. & v.i.* [< OFr. < L. < *com-,* together + *jungere,* to join], to join together; unite. —**con·join′er,** *n.*
**con·joint** (kən-joint′), *adj.* 1. joined together; united. 2. of or involving two or more in association; joint. —**con·joint′ly,** *adv.*
**con·ju·gal** (kon′joo-gəl), *adj.* [Fr. < L. < *conjunx,* spouse < *com-,* together + base akin to *jugum,* yoke], of marriage or the relation between husband and wife; matrimonial. —**con′ju·gal′i·ty** (-gal′ə-ti), *n.* —**con′ju·gal·ly,** *adv.*
**con·ju·gate** (kon′joo-git; *also, and for v. always,* -gāt′), *adj.* [< L. *conjugatus,* pp. < *com-,* together + *jugare,* to join < *jugum,* a yoke], 1. joined together, especially in a pair; coupled. 2. in *grammar,* derived from the same base and, usually, related in meaning. *n.* a conjugate word. *v.t.* [-GATED, -GATING], 1. to join together; couple. 2. in *grammar,* to give the different forms of (a verb) according to voice, mood, tense, number, and person. *v.i.* in *grammar, a)* to conjugate a verb. *b)* to be conjugated. —**con′ju·ga′tive,** *adj.* —**con′ju·ga′tor,** *n.*
**con·ju·ga·tion** (kon′joo-gā′shən), *n.* 1. a conjugating or being conjugated; union. 2. in *grammar, a)* a methodical presentation or arrangement of the inflectional forms of a verb. *b)* a class of verbs with similar inflectional forms. —**con′ju·ga′tion·al,** *adj.* —**con′ju·ga′tion·al·ly,** *adv.*
**con·junc·tion** (kən-juŋk′shən), *n.* [see CONJOIN], 1. a joining together or being joined together; union; combination. 2. coincidence. 3. in *astrology & astronomy, a)* the apparent closeness of two or more heavenly bodies. *b)* the condition of being in the same celestial longitude: as, planets in *conjunction.* 4. in *grammar,* an uninflected word used to connect words, phrases, clauses, or sentences; connective: conjunctions may be co-ordinating (e.g., *and, but, or*), subordinating (e.g., *if, when, as, because, though,* etc.), or correlative (*either . . .or, both . . . and,* etc.).
**con·junc·ti·va** (kon′juŋk-tī′və), *n.* [*pl.* -VAS, -VAE (-vē)], [Mod. L., in *membrana conjunctiva,* connecting membranes], the mucous membrane lining the inner surface of the eyelids and covering the front part of the eyeball. —**con′junc·ti′val,** *adj.*
**con·junc·tive** (kən-juŋk′tiv), *adj.* 1. serving to join together; connective. 2. united; combined; joint. 3. in *grammar,* used as a conjunction: as, a *conjunctive* adverb. *n.* in *grammar,* a conjunctive word, especially a conjunction. —**con·junc′tive·ly,** *adv.*
**con·junc·ti·vi·tis** (kən-juŋk′tə-vī′tis), *n.* [see -ITIS], inflammation of the conjunctiva.
**con·junc·ture** (kən-juŋk′chẽr), *n.* 1. a joining or being joined together. 2. a combination of events or circumstances. 3. a critical situation; crisis.
**con·ju·ra·tion** (kon′joo-rā′shən), *n.* 1. a conjuring; invocation. 2. a magic spell; incantation.
**con·jure** (kun′jẽr, kon′-; *for v.t. 1,* kən-joor′), *v.i.* [-JURED, -JURING], [< OFr. < L. < *com-,* together + *jurare,* to swear], 1. to summon a demon, spirit, etc. by magic. 2. to practice magic. *v.t.* 1. to appeal to or entreat solemnly. 2. to summon (a demon, etc.) by magic. 3. to cause to appear, come (*up*), or go (*away,* etc.) as by magic.
**con·jur·er, con·jur·or** (kun′jẽr-ẽr, kon′-), *n.* 1. a magician; sorcerer. 2. (kən-joor′er), one who solemnly entreats or appeals to someone.
**conk** (koŋk), *n.* [< *conch*], [Slang], a blow on the head. *v.t.* [Slang], to hit on the head. —**conk out,** [Slang], to fail suddenly in operation.
**Conn.,** Connecticut.
**con·nect** (kə-nekt′), *v.t.* [< L. < *com-,* together + *nectere,* to fasten], 1. to join (two things together, or one thing *with* or *to* another); link; couple. 2. to show or think of as related; associate. *v.i.* 1. to join or be joined. 2. to meet so that passengers can transfer promptly: said of trains, buses, etc. —**con·nec′tor, con·nect′er,** *n.*
**con·nect·ed** (kə-nek′tid), *adj.* 1. joined together; fastened. 2. joined in proper order; coherent. 3. related; affiliated. —**con·nect′ed·ly,** *adv.*
**Con·nect·i·cut** (kə-net′i-kət), *n.* a New England State of the U.S.: area, 5,009 sq. mi.; pop., 2,535,000; capital, Hartford: abbrev. **Conn.**
**con·nec·tion** (kə-nek′shən), *n.* 1. a connecting or being connected; union. 2. a thing that connects; means of joining. 3. a relation; association; coherence. 4. *usually in pl. a)* a relative, especially by marriage. *b)* an associate, friend, etc. 5. *usually in pl.* the act or means of meeting buses, trains, etc., or transferring from one to another. 6. a group of people associated in politics, business, etc. 7. a religious sect or denomination: usually **connexion** (Brit. form in all senses). —**in connection with,** 1. together with. 2. with reference to. —**con·nec′tion·al,** *adj.*
**con·nec·tive** (kə-nek′tiv), *adj.* connecting or serving to connect. *n.* something that connects; esp., a word that connects words, phrases, or clauses, as a conjunction or relative pronoun. —**con·nec′tive·ly,** *adv.* —**con·nec·tiv·i·ty** (kon′ek-tiv′ə-ti), *n.*
**connective tissue,** tissue that connects and supports other tissues and organs in the body.
**conn·ing tower** (kon′iŋ), [ppr. of *con, conn* (to direct)], 1. an armored pilothouse on the deck of a warship. 2. in submarines, a low observation tower serving also as an entrance to the interior.
**con·nip·tion (fit)** (kə-nip′shən), [pseudo-Latin], [Colloq.], a fit of anger, hysteria, etc.
**con·niv·ance** (kə-nīv′əns), *n.* a conniving; passive co-operation, as by pretended ignorance, especially in wrongdoing: also **con·niv′an·cy.**
**con·nive** (kə-nīv′), *v.i.* [-NIVED, -NIVING], [< Fr. or L; L. *connivere,* to wink, connive], 1. to pretend not to look (*at* crime, deceit, etc.), thus giving tacit consent or co-operation. 2. to co-operate secretly (*with* someone), especially in wrongdoing. —**con·niv′er,** *n.*
**con·nois·seur** (kon′ə-sũr′), *n.* [< Fr. < OFr. < L. *cognoscere,* to know; see COGNITION], one who has expert knowledge and keen discrimination in some field, especially in the fine arts.
**con·no·ta·tion** (kon′ə-tā′shən), *n.* 1. the act or process of connoting. 2. something connoted; idea suggested by or associated with a word, phrase, etc. in addition to its explicit meaning. —**con·no·ta·tive** (kon′ə-tā′tiv, kə-nō′tə-), *adj.* —**con′no·ta·tive·ly,** *adv.*
**con·note** (kə-nōt′), *v.t.* [-NOTED, -NOTING], [< ML. < L. *com-,* together + *notare,* to mark], to suggest or convey (associations, overtones, etc.) in addition to the explicit, or denoted, meaning.
**con·nu·bi·al** (kə-nōō′bi-əl, -nū′-), *adj.* [< L. < *com-,* together + *nubere,* to marry], of marriage or the state of being married; conjugal. —**con·nu′bi·al′i·ty** [*pl.* -TIES], *n.* —**con·nu′bi·al·ly,** *adv.*
**co·noid** (kō′noid), *adj.* cone-shaped. *n.* a cone-shaped thing. —**co·noi′dal,** *adj.*
**con·quer** (koŋ′kẽr), *v.t.* [< OFr. < LL. < L. *com-,* intens. + *quaerere,* to seek], 1. to get possession or control of by or as by winning a war. 2. to overcome by physical, mental, or moral force; defeat. *v.i.* to win; be victorious. —**con′quer·a·ble,** *adj.* —**con′quer·ing,** *adj.* —**con′quer·ing·ly,** *adv.* —**con′quer·or,** *n.*
**con·quest** (koŋ′kwest, kon′-), *n.* [< pp. of OFr. *conquerre*], 1. act or process of conquering. 2. something conquered. 3. *a)* a winning of someone's love. *b)* one whose love has been won.
**con·quis·ta·dor** (kon-kwis′tə-dôr′), *n.* [*pl.* -DORS, -DORES], [Sp., conqueror], any of the Spanish conquerors of Mexico, Peru, or other parts of America in the 16th century.
**Con·rad, Joseph** (kon′rad), (born *Teodor Jozef Konrad Korzeniowski*), 1857–1924; English novelist, born in Poland.
**cons.,** 1. consolidated. 2. consonant.
**cons., Cons.,** 1. constitution. 2. consul.

**con·san·guin·e·ous** (kon′saŋ-gwin′i-əs), *adj.* [see COM- & SANGUINE], having the same ancestor; related by blood. Also **con·san′guine.** —**con′san·guin′e·ous·ly,** *adv.* —**con′san·guin′i·ty,** *n.*
**con·science** (kon′shəns), *n.* [Fr. < L. < *consciens,* ppr. < *com-,* with + *scire,* to know], a knowledge or feeling of right and wrong, with a compulsion to do right; moral judgment that opposes the violation of a previously recognized ethical principle. —**in all conscience,** 1. in reason or fairness. 2. certainly. —**on 's conscience,** causing one to feel guilty. —**con science·less,** *adj.*
**con·sci·en·tious** (kon′shi-en′shəs, kon′si-), *adj.* [see CONSCIENCE], governed by, or done according to, what one kn ws is right; scrupulous. —**con′sci·en′tious·ly,** *adv.* —**con′sci·en′tious·ness,** *n.*
**conscientious objector,** one who for reasons of conscience refuses to take part in warfare.
**con·scion·a·ble** (kon′shən-ə-b'l), *adj.* [Rare], that agrees with one's ideas of right and wrong; just. —**con′scion·a·bly,** *adv.*
**con·scious** (kon′shəs), *adj.* [< L. *conscius* < *conscire;* see CONSCIENCE], 1. having a feeling or knowledge (with *of* or *that*); aware; cognizant. 2. able to feel and think; awake. 3. aware of oneself as a thinking being. 4. painfully aware of oneself; self-conscious. 5. intentional: as, *conscious* humor. 6. known to or felt by oneself: as, *conscious* guilt. —**con′scious·ly,** *adv.*
**con·scious·ness** (kon′shəs-nis), *n.* 1. the state of being conscious; awareness, especially of what is happening around one. 2. the totality of one's thoughts, feelings, and impressions; mind.
**con·script** (kən-skript′ *for v.;* kon′skript *for adj. & n.*), *v.t.* [< the *adj.*], 1. to enroll for compulsory service in the armed forces; draft. 2. to force (labor, capital, etc.) into service for the government. *adj.* [< L. *conscriptus,* enrolled < *com-,* with + *scribere,* to write], conscripted; drafted. *n.* a conscripted person; draftee. —**con·scrip′tion,** *n.*
**con·script fathers** (kon′skript), 1. the senators of ancient Rome. 2. the legislators of any nation.
**con·se·crate** (kon′sə-krāt′), *v.t.* [-CRATED, -CRATING], [< the *adj.*], 1. to set apart as holy; devote to religious use. 2. to devote; dedicate: as, he *consecrated* his life to art. 3. to cause to be revered; hallow. *adj.* [< L. *consecratus,* pp. < *com-,* together + *sacrare* < *sacer,* sacred], consecrated. —**con′se·cra′tion,** *n.* —**con′se·cra′tor,** *n.* —**con′se·cra·to′ry** (-krə-tôr′i, -tō′ri), *adj.*
**con·sec·u·tive** (kən-sek′yoo-tiv), *adj.* [Fr. < pp. of L. *consequi;* see CONSEQUENCE], 1. following in order, without interruption; successive. 2. proceeding from one part or idea to the next in logical order. —**con·sec′u·tive·ly,** *adv.* —**con·sec′u·tive·ness,** *n.*
**con·sen·sus** (kən-sen′səs), *n.* [L. < pp. of *consentire;* see CONSENT], 1. agreement, especially in opinion; hence, 2. general opinion.
**con·sent** (kən-sent′), *v.i.* [< OFr. < L. < *com-,* with + *sentire,* to feel], to agree (*to* do something); give permission or approval (*to* something). *n.* 1. permission; approval; assent. 2. agreement: as, by common *consent.* —**con·sent′er,** *n.*
**con·se·quence** (kon′si-kwens′, -kwəns), *n.* [< Fr. < L. < *consequens,* ppr. < *com-,* with + *sequi,* to follow], 1. a result; effect. 2. a logical result or conclusion; inference. 3. importance as a cause: as, a matter of slight *consequence.* 4. importance in rank; influence: as, a person of *consequence.* —**in consequence (of),** as a result (of). —**take the consequences,** to accept the results of one's actions.
**con·se·quent** (kon′si-kwent′, -kwənt), *adj.* 1. following as a result; resulting. 2. following as a logical conclusion. 3. proceeding in logical sequence. *n.* 1. anything that follows something else. 2. a result; outcome. —**consequent on** (or **upon**), 1. following as a result of. 2. inferred from.
**con·se·quen·tial** (kon′si-kwen′shəl), *adj.* 1. following as an effect. 2. feeling and acting important; pompous. 3. [Rare], important. —**con′se·quen′ti·al′i·ty** (-shi-al′ə-ti), **con′se·quen′tial·ness,** *n.* —**con′se·quen′tial·ly,** *adv.*
**con·se·quent·ly** (kon′si-kwent′li, -kwənt-li), *adv.* as a result; by logical inference; therefore.
**con·ser·va·tion** (kon′sẽr-vā′shən), *n.* 1. a conserving; protection from loss, waste, etc. 2. the official care and protection of forests, rivers, etc. 3. a forest, fishery, etc., or a part of one, under official supervision. —**con′ser·va′tion·al,** *adj.* —**con′ser·va′tion·ist,** *n.*
**conservation of energy,** the principle that energy is never consumed but only changes form, and that the total energy in the universe remains fixed.
**con·serv·a·tism** (kən-sũr′və-tiz'm), *n.* the principles and practices of a conservative person or party.
**con·serv·a·tive** (kən-sũr′və-tiv), *adj.* 1. conserving or tending to conserve; preservative. 2. tending to preserve established institutions and methods and to resist or oppose any changes in these. 3. [C-], designating or of the major right-wing political party of Great Britain or of Canada. 4. moderate; prudent; safe. *n.* 1. a preservative. 2. a conservative person. 3. [C-], a member of a Conservative party. —**con·serv′a·tive·ly,** *adv.* —**con·serv′a·tive·ness,** *n.*
**con·ser·va·toire** (kən-sũr′və-twär′, -sũr′və-twär′), *n.* [Fr.], a conservatory (sense 2).
**con·ser·va·tor** (kon′sẽr-vā′tẽr, kən-sũr′və-), *n.* [see CONSERVE], a protector; guardian; custodian.
**con·ser·va·to·ry** (kən-sũr′və-tô′ri, -tōr′i), *adj.* [see CONSERVE], preserving or tending to preserve. *n.* [*pl.* -RIES], 1. a room enclosed in glass, for growing and showing plants; greenhouse. 2. a school for teaching music, art, etc.; conservatoire.
**con·serve** (kən-sũrv′; *for n., usually* kon′sũrv), *v.t.* [-SERVED, -SERVING], [< OFr. < L. < *com-,* with + *servare,* to guard], 1. to keep from being damaged, lost, or wasted. 2. to make (fruit) into preserves. *n. often in pl.* a preserve of two or more fruits. —**con·serv′a·ble,** *adj.* —**con·serv′er,** *n.*
**con·sid·er** (kən-sid′ẽr), *v.t.* [< OFr. < L. *considerare,* to observe < *com-,* with + *sidus,* a star], 1. to think about in order to understand or decide; ponder. 2. to have or keep in mind. 3. to have regard for (others, their feelings, etc.). 4. to believe or think to be: as, I don't *consider* that important. *v.i.* to think seriously; reflect.
**con·sid·er·a·ble** (kən-sid′ẽr-ə-b'l), *adj.* 1. worth considering; important; noteworthy. 2. much or large. —**con·sid′er·a·bly,** *adv.*
**con·sid·er·ate** (kən-sid′ẽr-it), *adj.* [see CONSIDER], having or showing regard for others and their feelings; thoughtful. —**con·sid′er·ate·ly,** *adv.* —**con·sid′er·ate·ness,** *n.*
**con·sid·er·a·tion** (kən-sid′ə-rā′shən), *n.* 1. act of considering; deliberation. 2. *a*) thoughtful or sympathetic regard. *b*) esteem. 3. an opinion produced by considering; reflection. 4. something considered in making a decision. 5. claim to regard; importance. 6. a recompense, as for a service rendered; fee. —**in consideration of,** 1. because of. 2. in return for. —**take into consideration,** to keep in mind; take into account. —**under consideration,** being thought over.
**con·sid·ered** (kən-sid′ẽrd), *adj.* 1. arrived at after careful thought. 2. respected; esteemed.
**con·sid·er·ing** (kən-sid′ẽr-iŋ), *prep.* in view of; taking into account; making allowance for. *adv.* [Colloq.], all things considered.
**con·sign** (kən-sīn′), *v.t.* [< Fr. < L. *consignare,* to seal < *com-,* together + *signare* < *signum,* a sign], 1. to hand over; deliver. 2. to put in the charge of; entrust. 3. to assign; set apart. 4. to send or deliver (goods). —**con·sign′a·ble,** *adj.* —**con·sign·ee** (kon′sī-nē′, -si-), *n.* —**con·sign′or** (*also,* kon′-sī-nôr′), **con·sign′er,** *n.*
**con·sign·ment** (kən-sīn′mənt), *n.* 1. a consigning or being consigned. 2. something consigned; esp., a shipment of goods sent to an agent for sale or safekeeping.
**con·sist** (kən-sist′), *v.i.* [< L. < *com-,* together + *sistere,* to stand], 1. to be made up or composed (*of* something). 2. to be contained or inherent (*in* something). 3. to exist in harmony (*with*).
**con·sist·en·cy** (kən-sis′tən-si), *n.* [*pl.* -CIES], 1. firmness or thickness, as of a liquid. 2. degree of firmness or thickness. 3. agreement; harmony. 4. conformity with previous practice or principle. Also **con·sist′ence.**
**con·sist·ent** (kən-sis′tənt), *adj.* [see CONSIST], 1. [Rare], firm or coherent. 2. in harmony; in accord; compatible. 3. holding to the same principles or practice. —**con·sist′ent·ly,** *adv.*
**con·sis·to·ry** (kən-sis′tə-ri), *n.* [*pl.* -RIES], [ONorm. Fr. < L. *consistorium,* place of assembly < *consistere;* see CONSIST], 1. a church council or court, as the papal senate. 2. a session of such a body.

—**con·sis·to·ri·al** (kon'sis-tôr'i-əl, -tō'ri-), **con'sis·to'ri·an,** *adj.*

**con·so·la·tion** (kon'sə-lā'shən), *n.* 1. a consoling or being consoled; comfort; solace. 2. a person or thing that consoles.

**consolation prize,** a prize given to a person who does well but does not win.

**con·sol·a·to·ry** (kən-sol'ə-tôr'i, -tō'ri), *adj.* consoling or tending to console; comforting.

**con·sole** (kən-sōl'), *v.t.* [-SOLED, -SOLING], [< Fr. < L. < *com-*, with + *solari*, to solace], to comfort; cheer (a person) up, especially by making up for a loss or disappointment. —**con·sol'a·ble,** *adj.* —**con·sol'er,** *n.* —**con·sol'ing·ly,** *adv.*

**con·sole** (kon'sōl), *n.* [Fr.], 1. an ornamental bracket for supporting a shelf, bust, cornice, etc. 2. a console table. 3. the desklike frame containing the keys, stops, pedals, etc. of an organ. 4. a radio, television, or phonograph cabinet meant to stand on the floor.

**console table,** a small table with legs resembling consoles, placed against a wall.

**con·sol·i·date** (kən-sol'ə-dāt'), *v.t.* & *v.i.* [-DATED, -DATING], [< L. < *com-*, together + *solidare* < *solidus*, solid], 1. to combine into one; merge; unite. 2. to make or become solid, strong, or stable: as, the troops *consolidated* their position. —**con·sol'i·da'tion,** *n.* —**con·sol'i·da'tor,** *n.*

**con·sols** (kon'solz, kən-solz'), *n.pl.* [< *consolidated annuities*], British funded government securities.

**con·som·mé** (kon'sə-mā'), *n.* [Fr. < L. *consummare;* see CONSUMMATE], a clear soup made by boiling meat and, sometimes, grains or vegetables, in water.

**con·so·nance** (kon'sə-nəns), *n.* [OFr. < L. < *com-*, with + *sonare*, to sound < *sonus*, a sound], 1. harmony; agreement; congruity. 2. harmony of musical tones. Also **con'so·nan·cy.**

**con·so·nant** (kon'sə-nənt), *adj.* [see CONSONANCE], 1. in harmony or agreement; in accord. 2. harmonious in tone: opposed to *dissonant*. 3. consonantal. *n.* 1. any speech sound produced by obstructing the breath stream in any of various ways, as the sounds of p, t, k, m, l, etc. 2. a letter representing such a sound. —**con'so·nant·ly,** *adv.*

**con·so·nan·tal** (kon'sə-nan't'l), *adj.* of, like, or having a consonant or consonants.

**con·sort** (kon'sôrt; *for v.*, kən-sôrt'), *n.* [OFr. < L. < *com-*, with + *sors*, a share], 1. a partner; companion. 2. a wife or husband; spouse, especially of a reigning king or queen. 3. a ship that travels along with another. *v.i.* 1. to keep company; associate. 2. to agree; be in accord. *v.t.* to associate; join.

**con·sor·ti·um** (kən-sôr'shi-əm), *n.* [*pl.* -TIA (-shi-ə)], [L., community of goods; see CONSORT], an agreement among banks of two or more nations, as for giving financial aid to another nation.

**con·spec·tus** (kən-spek'təs), *n.* [L., a view < *conspicere;* see CONSPICUOUS], 1. a general view; survey. 2. a summary; synopsis; digest.

**con·spic·u·ous** (kən-spik'ū-əs), *adj.* [< L. < *conspicere*, to look at < *com-*, intens. + *specere*, to see], 1. easy to see or perceive; obvious. 2. attracting attention by being outstanding; remarkable: as, *conspicuous* bravery. —**con·spic'u·ous·ly,** *adv.* —**con·spic'u·ous·ness,** *n.*

**con·spir·a·cy** (kən-spir'ə-si), *n.* [*pl.* -CIES], 1. a conspiring, especially in an unlawful or harmful plot. 2. such a plot. 3. the group taking part in such a plot. 4. a combining or working together: as, the *conspiracy* of events.

**con·spir·a·tor** (kən-spir'ə-tēr), *n.* a person who takes part in a conspiracy; plotter. —**con·spir'a·to'ri·al** (-tôr'i-əl, -tō'ri-), *adj.*

**con·spire** (kən-spīr'), *v.i.* [-SPIRED, -SPIRING], [< OFr. < L. < *com-*, together + *spirare*, to breathe], 1. to plan and act together secretly, especially in order to commit a crime. 2. to combine or work together for any purpose or effect: as, events *conspired* to ruin him. —**con·spir'er,** *n.*

‡**con spi·ri·to** (kôn spē'rē-tô'), [It.], in *music*, with spirit; with vigor.

**con·sta·ble** (kon'stə-b'l, kun'-), *n.* [< OFr. < LL. *comes stabuli*, lit., count of the stable], 1. in the Middle Ages, the highest ranking official of a royal household, court, etc. 2. a policeman. —**con'sta·ble·ship',** *n.*

**Con·sta·ble, John** (kun'stə-b'l), 1776–1837; English landscape painter.

**con·stab·u·lar·y** (kən-stab'yoo-ler'i), *n.* [*pl.* -IES], 1. the constables of a district, collectively. 2. a police force characterized by a military organization; state police. *adj.* of constables or a constabulary: also **con·stab'u·lar** (-lēr).

**con·stant** (kon'stənt), *adj.* [Fr. < L. *constans*, ppr. < *com-*, together + *stare*, to stand], 1. not changing; remaining the same; specif., *a*) remaining firm in purpose; resolute. *b*) loyal; faithful. *c*) remaining uniform in value, extent, etc.; regular; stable. 2. going on all the time; continual; persistent: as, *constant* interruptions. *n.* 1. anything that does not change or vary. 2. in *mathematics & physics*, a quantity or factor that does not vary throughout a discussion or investigation: opposed to *variable*: symbol, C. —**con'stan·cy,** *n.* —**con'stant·ly,** *adv.*

**Con·stan·tine I** (kon'stən-tēn', -tīn'), 280?–337 A.D.; first Christian emperor of Rome (306–337 A.D.): called *the Great*.

**Con·stan·ti·no·ple** (kon'stan-tə-nō'p'l), *n.* Istanbul, a city in Turkey: the former name.

**con·stel·late** (kon'stə-lāt'), *v.i.* & *v.t.* [-LATED, -LATING], to unite in a constellation; cluster.

**con·stel·la·tion** (kon'stə-lā'shən), *n.* [< OFr. < LL. < L. < *com-*, with + pp. of *stellare*, to shine < *stella*, a star], 1. an arbitrary group of fixed stars, usually named after some mythological being that they supposedly resemble in outline. 2. the part of the heavens occupied by such a group. 3. any brilliant cluster or gathering.

**con·ster·nate** (kon'stēr-nāt'), *v.t.* [-NATED, -NATING], to fill with consternation; dismay.

**con·ster·na·tion** (kon'stēr-nā'shən), *n.* [< Fr. < L. < *consternare*, to terrify], paralyzing amazement or terror; dismay.

**con·sti·pate** (kon'stə-pāt'), *v.t.* [-PATED, -PATING], [< L. < *com-*, together + *stipare*, to cram], to cause constipation in. —**con'sti·pat'ed,** *adj.*

**con·sti·pa·tion** (kon'stə-pā'shən), *n.* a condition in which the emptying of waste matter from the bowels is infrequent and difficult.

**con·stit·u·en·cy** (kən-stich'o͞o-ən-si), *n.* [*pl.* -CIES], [< *constituent* + *-cy*], 1. the voters or, loosely, the residents in a district. 2. the district of such a group of voters, etc.

**con·stit·u·ent** (kən-stich'o͞o-ənt), *adj.* [< L. ppr. of *constituere;* see CONSTITUTE], 1. necessary in the formation of the whole; component: as, a *constituent* part. 2. that can or does appoint or elect. 3. authorized to make or revise a constitution: as, a *constituent* assembly. *n.* 1. one who helps appoint another as his representative, especially by voting in an election. 2. a necessary part or element; component.

**con·sti·tute** (kon'stə-to͞ot', -tūt'), *v.t.* [-TUTED, -TUTING], [< L. pp. of *constituere* < *com-*, together + *statuere*, to set], 1. to establish (a law, government, institution, etc.). 2. to set up (an assembly, proceeding, etc.) in a legal form. 3. to set up as; appoint: as, they *constituted* him their spokesman. 4. to make up; form; compose.

**con·sti·tu·tion** (kon'stə-to͞o'shən, -tū'-), *n.* 1. a constituting; establishment. 2. an appointing. 3. a making up; composition. 4. the way in which a person or thing is made up; structure; organization. 5. *a*) the system of fundamental laws and principles of a government, state, society, etc. *b*) a document in which these are written down. 6. [C-], the Constitution of the United States: it consists of seven articles and twenty-three amendments, and has been the supreme law of the Federal government since its adoption in 1789.

**con·sti·tu·tion·al** (kon'stə-to͞o'shən-'l, -tū'-), *adj.* 1. of or in the constitution of a person or thing; basic; essential. 2. for improving one's constitution. 3. of or in accordance with the constitution of a government, society, etc.: as, *constitutional* rights. 4. upholding the constitution. *n.* [Colloq.], a walk or other exercise taken for one's health. —**con'sti·tu'tion·al'i·ty** (-al'ə-ti), *n.* —**con'sti·tu'tion·al·ly,** *adv.*

**con·sti·tu·tive** (kon'stə-to͞o'tiv, -tū'-), *adj.* 1. having power to establish, appoint, or enact. 2. making a thing what it is; essential; basic. 3. forming a part (*of*); constituent.

**constr.,** 1. construction. 2. construed.

**con·strain** (kən-strān'), *v.t.* [< OFr. < L. < *com-*, together + *stringere*, to draw tight], 1. to force into, or hold in, close bounds; confine; restrain. 2. to force; compel: as, he was *constrained* to agree. 3. to get by force or strain, as an unnatural laugh. —**con·strain'a·ble,** *adj.* —**con·strained',** *adj.* —**con·strain'ed·ly,** *adv.* —**con·strain'er,** *n.*

**con·straint** (kən-strānt'), *n.* 1. confinement; restriction. 2. force; compulsion. 3. forced, unnatural quality of manner. 4. a constraining or being constrained.

**con·strict** (kən-strikt'), *v.t.* [< L. pp. of *constringere;* see CONSTRAIN], to make smaller or narrower by binding, squeezing, etc.; contract.

**con·stric·tion** (kən-strik′shən), *n.* 1. a constricting or being constricted; contraction. 2. a feeling of tightness or pressure, as in the chest. 3. something that constricts. 4. a constricted part. **—con·stric′tive,** *adj.*

**con·stric·tor** (kən-strik′tēr), *n.* that which constricts; specif., *a*) a muscle that contracts an opening or compresses an organ. *b*) a snake that kills by coiling around its prey and squeezing.

**con·struct** (kən-strukt′), *v.t.* [< L. *constructus*, pp. < *com-*, together + *struere*, to pile up], to put together systematically; build, frame, or devise (a bridge, theory, triangle, etc.). *n.* (kon′strukt), something built or put together systematically. **—con·struc′tor, con·struct′er,** *n.*

**con·struc·tion** (kən-struk′shən), *n.* 1. the act or process of constructing. 2. the way in which something is constructed. 3. something constructed; structure; building. 4. an explanation or interpretation, as of a statement. 5. the arrangement and relation of words in a clause, sentence, etc. **—con·struc′tion·al,** *adj.*

**con·struc·tive** (kən-struk′tiv), *adj.* 1. able or helping to construct; leading to improvements: as, *constructive* criticism. 2. relating to construction or structure. 3. not directly expressed but deduced by interpretation. **—con·struc′tive·ly,** *adv.* **—con·struc′tive·ness,** *n.*

**con·strue** (kən-stro͞o′), *v.t. & v.i.* [-STRUED, -STRUING], [< L. *construere;* see CONSTRUCT], 1. to analyze (a clause, etc.) so as to show its grammatical construction and meaning. 2. to translate. 3. to explain or deduce the meaning (of); interpret: as, her absence was *construed* as an insult. 4. in *grammar*, to combine in syntax: as, the verb *let*, unlike *permit*, is *construed* with an infinitive omitting the *to*. **—con·stru′a·ble,** *adj.* **—con·stru′er,** *n.*

**con·sul** (kon′s'l), *n.* [< OFr. < L. < *consulere*, to deliberate; akin to *counsel*], 1. either of the two chief magistrates of the ancient Roman republic. 2. any of the three highest officials of the French republic from 1799 to 1804. 3. a government official appointed to live in a foreign city and look after his country's citizens and business there. **—con′su·lar,** *adj.* **—con′sul·ship′,** *n.*

**con·su·late** (kon′s'l-it, -syoo-lit), *n.* 1. the position, powers, and duties of a consul. 2. the office or residence of a consul. 3. the term of office of a consul. 4. government by consuls; specif., [C-], the government of France from 1799 to 1804.

**consul general,** [*pl.* CONSULS GENERAL, CONSUL GENERALS], a consul in a principal commercial city, who supervises other consuls within his district.

**con·sult** (kən-sult′), *v.i.* [< Fr. < L. < pp. of *consulere*, to ask advice], to talk things over; confer in order to decide something. *v.t.* 1. to seek information or instruction from; refer to: as, *consult* your doctor. 2. to keep in mind while deciding; consider: as, *consult* your own wishes in the matter. **—con·sult′a·ble,** *adj.* **—con·sult′er,** *n.*

**con·sult·ant** (kən-sul′t'nt), *n.* 1. a person who consults another person. 2. a person who gives professional or technical advice, as a doctor.

**con·sul·ta·tion** (kon′s'l-tā′shən), *n.* 1. a consulting. 2. a meeting to discuss, decide, or plan something. **—con·sul·ta·tive** (kən-sul′tə-tiv), **con·sul′ta·to′ry** (-tôr′i, -tō′ri), *adj.*

**con·sume** (kən-so͞om′, -sūm′), *v.t.* [-SUMED, -SUMING], [< OFr. < L. < *com-*, together + *sumere*, to take < *sub-*, under + *emere*, to buy], 1. to destroy, as by fire. 2. to use up or waste (time, energy, money, etc.). 3. to drink or eat up; devour. *v.i.* to waste away; perish. **—consumed with,** filled with (grief, curiosity, etc.). **—con·sum′a·ble,** *adj.*

**con·sum·ed·ly** (kən-so͞om′id-li, -sūm′-), *adv.* extremely or excessively.

**con·sum·er** (kən-so͞om′ēr, -sūm′-), *n.* a person or thing that consumes; specif., in *economics*, one who uses goods or services to satisfy his needs rather than to resell them or produce other goods with them: opposed to *producer*.

**con·sum·mate** (kən-sum′it; *for v.*, kon′sə-māt′), *adj.* [< L. pp. of *consummare*, to sum up < *com-*, together + *summa*, a sum], complete; perfect. *v.t.* [-MATED, -MATING], 1. to bring to completion; finish. 2. to make (marriage) actual by sexual intercourse. **—con·sum′mate·ly,** *adv.* **—con′summa′tive,** *adj.* **—con′sum·ma′tor,** *n.*

**con·sum·ma·tion** (kon′sə-mā′shən), *n.* 1. a consummating or being consummated. 2. an end; outcome.

**con·sump·tion** (kən-sump′shən), *n.* 1. a consuming or being consumed; a using up, destruction, or waste. 2. a disease that causes wasting away; esp., tuberculosis of the lungs. 3. in *economics*, *a*) the using up of goods or services. *b*) the amount used up.

**con·sump·tive** (kən-sump′tiv), *adj.* 1. consuming or tending to consume; destructive; wasteful. 2. in *medicine*, of, having, or inclined to have tuberculosis of the lungs. *n.* one who has tuberculosis of the lungs. **—con·sump′tive·ly,** *adv.* **—con·sump′tive·ness,** *n.*

**cont.,** 1. containing. 2. contents. 3. continent. 4. continue. 5. continued. 6. contra.

**con·tact** (kon′takt), *n.* [< L. *contactus*, pp. < *com-*, together + *tangere*, to touch], 1. the act of touching or meeting. 2. the state of being in touch or association (*with*). 3. connection. 4. in *electricity*, *a*) a connection between two conductors in a circuit. *b*) a device for making such a connection. *v.t.* 1. to place in contact. 2. [Colloq.], to get in touch with. *v.i.* to come into contact.

**contact lenses,** small, thin lenses of glass or plastic worn next to the eyeballs, with the edges under the eyelids, used like ordinary eyeglasses.

**con·ta·gion** (kən-tā′jən), *n.* [L. *contagio*, a touching; see CONTACT], 1. the spreading of disease by contact. 2. a contagious disease. 3. a means by which disease is spread. 4. a poison. 5. the spreading of an emotion, idea, custom, etc. from person to person.

**con·ta·gious** (kən-tā′jəs), *adj.* [< OFr. < LL. *contagiosus*], 1. spread by contact: said of diseases. 2. carrying the causative agent of a contagious disease. 3. spreading from person to person. **—con·ta′gious·ly,** *adv.* **—con·ta′gious·ness,** *n.*

**con·tain** (kən-tān′), *v.t.* [< OFr. < L. < *com-*, together + *tenere*, to hold], 1. to have in it; hold; include. 2. to have the capacity for holding. 3. to hold back or within fixed limits. 4. to restrain (one's feelings, oneself, etc.). 5. to be divisible by, especially without a remainder: as, 10 *contains* 5 and 2. **—con·tain′a·ble,** *adj.*

**con·tain·er** (kən-tān′ēr), *n.* a thing for containing something, as a box, crate, can, etc.

**con·tain·ment** (kən-tān′mənt), *n.* the policy of attempting to prevent the influence of an opposing nation or political system from spreading.

**con·tam·i·nate** (kən-tam′ə-nāt′), *v.t.* [-NATED, -NATING], [< L. < *contamen*, contact < *com-*, together + base of *tangere*, to touch], to make impure, unclean, or corrupt by contact; pollute; defile; sully; taint. **—con·tam′i·na′tion,** *n.* **—con·tam′i·na′tive,** *adj.* **—con·tam′i·na′tor,** *n.*

**contd.,** continued.

**con·temn** (kən-tem′), *v.t.* [< OFr. < L. < *com-*, intens. + *temnere*, to scorn], to treat with contempt; despise; scorn. **—con·temn′er** (-ēr, -nēr), **con·tem′nor** (-nēr), *n.*

**con·tem·plate** (kon′təm-plāt′), *v.t.* [-PLATED, -PLATING], [< L. < *contemplari*, lit., to mark out a temple < *com-*, with + *templum*, temple], 1. to look at intently; gaze at. 2. to think about intently; study; consider. 3. to expect or intend. *v.i.* to meditate; muse. **—con·tem·pla·ble** (kən-tem′plə-b'l), *adj.* **—con′tem·pla′tion,** *n.* **—con′tem·pla′tor,** *n.*

**con·tem·pla·tive** (kon′təm-plā′tiv, kən-tem′plə-), *adj.* of or inclined to contemplation; thoughtful; meditative. **—con′tem·pla′tive·ly,** *adv.*

**con·tem·po·ra·ne·ous** (kən-tem′pə-rā′ni-əs), *adj.* [< L. < *com-*, with + *tempus*, time], existing or happening in the same period of time. **—con·tem′po·ra·ne′i·ty** (-pēr-ə-nē′ə-ti), **con·tem′po·ra′ne·ous·ness,** *n.* **—con·tem′po·ra′ne·ous·ly,** *adv.*

**con·tem·po·rar·y** (kən-tem′pə-rer′i), *adj.* [< L. *com-*, with + *temporarius* < *tempus*, time], 1. living or happening in the same period. 2. of about the same age. *n.* [*pl.* -RIES], 1. one living in the same period as another or others. 2. a person or thing of about the same age or date of origin.

**con·tempt** (kən-tempt′), *n.* [OFr. < L. *contemptus*; see CONTEMN], 1. the feeling of a person toward something he considers worthless or beneath notice; scorn. 2. the condition of being despised. 3. in *law*, a showing disrespect for the dignity of a court (or legislature): in full, **contempt of court** (or **congress,** etc.).

**con·tempt·i·ble** (kən-temp′tə-b'l), *adj.* deserving contempt, or scorn; despicable. **—con·tempt′i·bil′-**

i·ty, **con·tempt′i·ble·ness,** *n.* —**con·tempt′i·bly,** *adv.*

**con·temp·tu·ous** (kən-temp′cho͞o-əs) *adj.* showing contempt; scornful; disdainful. —**con·temp′tu·ous·ly,** *adv.* —**con·temp′tu·ous·ness,** *n.*

**con·tend** (kən-tend′), *v.i.* [< L. < *com-*, together + *tendere*, to stretch], 1. to strive in combat; fight. 2. to strive in debate; argue. 3. to strive in competition; compete; vie. *v.t.* to hold to be a fact; assert. —**con·tend′er,** *n.*

**con·tent** (kən-tent′), *adj.* [< OFr. < L. pp. of *continere;* see CONTAIN], 1. happy enough with what one has or is; satisfied. 2. willing; assenting. *v.t.* to satisfy. *n.* contentment; satisfaction.

**con·tent** (kon′tent), *n.* [<L. pp. of *continere;* see CONTAIN], 1. *usually pl. a)* all that is contained in something. *b)* all that is expressed in a writing or speech. 2. substance or meaning: often distinguished from *form.* 3. holding power; capacity. 4. volume or area. 5. the amount contained: as, cast iron has a high carbon *content.*

**con·tent·ed** (kən-ten′tid), *adj.* not desiring something more or different; satisfied. —**con·tent′ed·ly,** *adv.* —**con·tent′ed·ness,** *n.*

**con·ten·tion** (kən-ten′shən), *n.* [see CONTEND], 1. verbal strife; argument; controversy; dispute. 2. a statement or point that one argues for as true or valid. 3. strife; struggle; contest.

**con·ten·tious** (kən-ten′shəs), *adj.* 1. quarrelsome. 2. of or characterized by contention. —**con·ten′tious·ly,** *adv.* —**con·ten′tious·ness,** *n.*

**con·tent·ment** (kən-tent′mənt), *n.* the state, quality, or fact of being contented.

**con·ter·mi·nous** (kən-tũr′mi-nəs), *adj.* [< L. < *com-*, together + *terminus*, an end], 1. having a common boundary at some point; contiguous. 2. having the same boundaries or limits. Also **coterminous.**

**con·test** (kən-test′; *for n.*, kon′test), *v.t.* [< Fr. < L. < *com-*, together + *testari*, to bear witness < *testis*, a witness], 1. to try to disprove or invalidate (something); dispute: as, to *contest* a will. 2. to fight for; struggle to win or keep. *v.i.* to struggle (*with* or *against*). *n.* 1. strife; struggle; fight. 2. verbal strife; dispute. 3. any race, game, etc. in which there is a struggle to be the winner. —**con·test′a·ble,** *adj.* —**con·test′er,** *n.*

**con·test·ant** (kən-tes′tənt), *n.* [Fr.], a person who contests or competes in a contest.

**con·text** (kon′tekst), *n.* [< L. < *com-*, together + *texere*, to weave], the parts of a sentence, paragraph, etc. that occur just before and after a specified word or passage, and determine its exact meaning. —**con·tex·tu·al** (kən-teks′cho͞o-əl, kon-), *adj.* —**con·tex′tu·al·ly,** *adv.*

**con·ti·gu·i·ty** (kon′ti-gū′ə-ti), *n.* [*pl.* -TIES], nearness or contact; a being contiguous.

**con·tig·u·ous** (kən-tig′ū-əs), *adj.* [< L. *contiguus* < *contingere;* see CONTINGENT], 1. in physical contact; touching. 2. near; adjoining. —**con·tig′u·ous·ly,** *adv.* —**con·tig′u·ous·ness,** *n.*

**con·ti·nence** (kon′tə-nəns), *n.* [see CONTINENT], 1. self-restraint; moderation. 2. self-restraint in sexual activity; esp., complete abstinence. Also **con′ti·nen·cy** [*pl.* -CIES].

**con·ti·nent** (kon′tə-nənt), *adj.* [< OFr. < L. ppr. of *continere;* see CONTAIN], 1. self-restrained; temperate. 2. characterized by self-restraint, especially by complete abstinence, in sexual activity. *n.* any of the six (with Antarctica, seven) largest land masses of the earth; Africa, Asia, Australia, Europe, North America, and South America.—**the Continent,** the mainland of Europe. —**con′ti·nent·ly,** *adj.*

**con·ti·nen·tal** (kon′tə-nen′t'l), *adj.* 1. of a continent. 2. [sometimes C-], European. 3. [C-], of the American colonies at the time of the American Revolution. *n.* 1. [usually C-], a European. 2. [C-], a soldier of the American army during the Revolutionary period. 3. a piece of paper money issued by the Continental Congress: it became almost worthless before the end of the war, hence the phrase *not worth a continental*, worthless.

**Continental Congress,** either of two assemblies of representatives from the American colonies during the Revolutionary period: the second issued the Declaration of Independence (1776).

**con·tin·gen·cy** (kən-tin′jən-si), *n.* [*pl.* -CIES], 1. a contingent quality or condition. 2. dependence on chance or uncertain conditions. 3. a possible, accidental, or chance event. 4. something incidental to another thing. Also **con·tin′gence.**

**con·tin·gent** (kən-tin′jənt), *adj.* [< L. ppr. of *contingere* < *com-*, together + *tangere*, to touch], 1. that may or may not happen; possible. 2. happening by chance; accidental. 3. dependent (*on* or *upon* an uncertainty); conditional. *n.* 1. a chance happening. 2. a share or quota, as of troops, laborers, etc. 3. a group forming part of a larger one. —**con·tin′gent·ly,** *adv.*

**con·tin·u·al** (kən-tin′ū-əl), *adj.* 1. repeated often; going on in rapid succession. 2. continuous; going on without interruption. —**con·tin′u·al·ly,** *adv.* —**con·tin′u·al·ness,** *n.*

**con·tin·u·ance** (kən-tin′ū-əns), *n.* 1. a continuing (with *of* or *in*). 2. the time during which an action or state lasts; duration. 3. an unbroken succession. 4. a continuation; sequel. 5. in *law*, postponement or adjournment to a later date.

**con·tin·u·a·tion** (kən-tin′ū-ā′shən), *n.* 1. a continuing or being continued. 2. a beginning again after an interruption; resumption. 3. a part added to make something reach further or last longer; supplement; sequel.

**con·tin·ue** (kən-tin′ū), *v.i.* [-UED, -UING], [< OFr. < L. *continuare*, to join < *continere;* see CONTAIN], 1. to last; endure. 2. to go on in a specified condition or course of action. 3. to stay. 4. to keep on; persist. 5. to go on again after an interruption; resume. *v.t.* 1. to go on with; carry on. 2. to extend. 3. to resume. 4. to cause to remain; retain: as, they *continued* him in office. 5. in *law*, to postpone or adjourn to a later date. —**con·tin′u·a·ble,** *adj.* —**con·tin′u·er,** *n.*

**con·ti·nu·i·ty** (kon′tə-no͞o′ə-ti, -nū′-), *n.* [*pl.* -TIES], 1. a continuous state or quality. 2. an unbroken, coherent whole. 3. a written plan of scenes in a motion picture. 4. in *radio & television, a)* a series of comments connecting the parts of a program. *b)* the script of a program.

**con·tin·u·ous** (kən-tin′ū-əs), *adj.* [L. *continuus;* see CONTINUE], going on or extending without interruption or break; unbroken; connected. —**con·tin′u·ous·ly,** *adv.* —**con·tin′u·ous·ness,** *n.*

**con·tin·u·um** (kən-tin′ū-əm), *n.* [*pl.* -TINUA (-ə)], [L.], a continuous whole, quantity, or series.

**con·tort** (kən-tôrt′), *v.t.* [< L. *contortus*, pp. < *com-*, together + *torquere*, to twist], to force out of shape as by twisting, wrenching, etc.; distort. —**con·tor′tion,** *n.* —**con·tor′tive,** *adj.*

**con·tor·tion·ist** (kən-tôr′shən-ist), *n.* a person who can twist his body into unnatural positions.

**con·tour** (kon′toor), *n.* [Fr. < It. < LL. < L. *com-*, intens. + *tornare*, to turn; see TURN], the outline of a figure, land, etc. *v.t.* to represent in contour. *adj.* characterized by furrows along the natural contour lines so as to avoid erosion.

**contour map,** a map showing physical features by means of lines (**contour lines**) connecting all points of the same elevation.

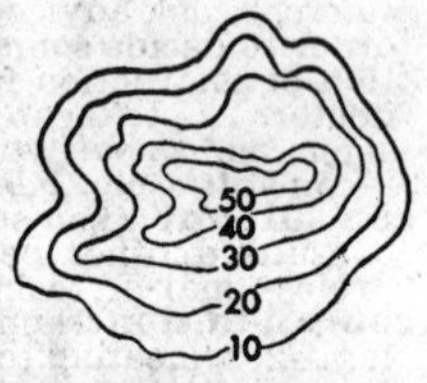

CONTOUR MAP

**contr.,** 1. contract. 2. contraction. 3. contrary.

**con·tra** (kon′trə), *adv.* [L.], to the contrary; contrariwise. *n.* something contrary or opposite.

**con·tra-,** [< L. *contra*, against], a prefix meaning *against, opposite, opposed to.*

**con·tra·band** (kon′trə-band′), *n.* [< Sp. < It. < *contra-*, against + *bando*, proclamation; see BAN], 1. unlawful or prohibited trade. 2. smuggled goods, forbidden by law to be imported and exported. 3. contraband of war. *adj.* forbidden by law to be imported or exported. —**con′tra·band′ist,** *n.*

**contraband of war,** any goods which, under international law, may be seized by either belligerent when shipped to the other by a neutral.

**con·tra·bass** (kon′trə-bās′), *adj.* [see CONTRABASSO], having its pitch an octave lower than the normal bass; double-bass. *n.* an instrument or voice having the lowest bass tone; specif., the largest and deepest-toned instrument of the viol class; double bass. —**con′tra·bass′ist,** *n.*

CONTRABASS

**con·tra·bas·so** (kon′trə-bäs′ō), *n.* [It. < L. *contra*, opposite + *bassus*, low], a contrabass.

**con·tra·bas·soon** (kon′trə-bə-so͞on′), *n.* the double bassoon, which is larger than the regular bassoon and an octave lower in pitch.

**con·tra·cep·tion** (kon′trə-sep′shən), *n.* [*contra-* + *conception*], prevention of the fertilization of the human ovum. —**con′tra·cep′tive,** *adj. & n.*

**con·tra·clock·wise** (kon'trə-klok'wīz), *adj. & adv.* counterclockwise.

**con·tract** (kon'trakt; *for v.t. 1. sometimes, and, for rest of v. always,* kən-trakt'), *n.* [OFr. < L. *contractus*, pp. < *com-*, together + *trahere*, to draw], 1. an agreement to do something, especially a written one, enforceable by law. 2. a formal agreement of marriage or betrothal. 3. a document containing the terms of an agreement. 4. in *bridge*, *a)* the number of tricks bid by the highest bidder. *b)* contract bridge. *v.t.* 1. to enter upon, or undertake, by contract. 2. to get; acquire; incur. 3. to reduce in size; draw together; shrink. 4. in *grammar*, to shorten (a word or phrase) by the omission of a letter or part. *v.i.* 1. to make a contract. 2. to become reduced in size or bulk. **—con·tract'ed,** *adj.* **—con·tract'i·bil'i·ty, con·tract'i·ble·ness,** *n.* **—con·tract'i·ble,** *adj.*

**contract bridge,** a form of auction bridge: only the tricks bid may be counted toward a game.

**con·trac·tile** (kən-trak't'l, -til), *adj.* 1. having the power of contracting. 2. producing contraction. **—con·trac·til·i·ty** (kon'trak-til'ə-ti), *n.*

**con·trac·tion** (kən-trak'shən), *n.* 1. a contracting or being contracted. 2. the drawing up and thickening of a muscle in action. 3. in *grammar*, *a)* the shortening of a word or phrase (e.g., *aren't* for *are not*). *b)* a word form resulting from this **—con·trac'tive** (-tiv), *adj.* **—con·trac'tive·ly,** *adv.* **—con·trac'tive·ness,** *n.*

**con·trac·tor** (kon'trak-tẽr, kən-trak'-), *n.* 1. one of the parties to a contract. 2. one who contracts to supply certain materials or do certain work for a stipulated sum; esp., one whose business is contracting to erect buildings.

**con·trac·tu·al** (kən-trak'cho͞o-əl), *adj.* of, or having the nature of, a contract.

**con·tra·dict** (kon'trə-dikt'), *v.t.* [< L. *contradictus*, pp. < *contra-*, against + *dicere*, to speak], 1. *a)* to assert the opposite of (a statement). *b)* to deny the statement of (a person). 2. to be contrary to; go against. *v.i.* to speak in denial; oppose verbally. **—con'tra·dict'a·ble,** *adj.* **—con'tra·dic'tor, con'tra·dict'er,** *n.*

**con·tra·dic·tion** (kon'trə-dik'shən), *n.* 1. a contradicting or being contradicted. 2. a statement in opposition to another; denial. 3. a condition in which things tend to be contrary to each other; inconsistency; discrepancy.

**con·tra·dic·to·ry** (kon'trə-dik'tẽr-i), *adj.* 1. involving a contradiction; inconsistent; contrary. 2. inclined to contradict or deny. Also **con'tra·dic'tive** (-tiv). **—con'tra·dic'to·ri·ly,** *adv.* **—con'tra·dic'to·ri·ness,** *n.*

**con·tra·dis·tinc·tion** (kon'trə-dis-tiŋk'shən), *n.* distinction by contrast: usually in *in contradistinction to*. **—con'tra·dis·tinc'tive** (-tiv), *adj.*

**con·tral·to** (kən-tral'tō), *n.* [*pl.* -TOS, -TI (-ti)], [It.; see CONTRA- & ALTO], 1. the part sung by the lowest female voice. 2. a female voice of the lowest range. 3. a woman or girl who sings in this range. *adj.* of or for a contralto.

**con·trap·tion** (kən-trap'shən), *n.* [? < *contrive*], [Colloq.], a contrivance; gadget; makeshift.

**con·tra·pun·tal** (kon'trə-pun't'l), *adj.* [< It. *contrapunto*, counterpoint; + *-al*], 1. of or characterized by counterpoint. 2. according to the principles of counterpoint. **—con'tra·pun'tist,** *n.*

**con·tra·ri·e·ty** (kon'trə-rī'ə-ti), *n.* 1. the condition or quality of being contrary. 2. [*pl.* -TIES], anything that is contrary; inconsistency.

**con·tra·ri·wise** (kon'trer-i-wīz'; *for 3, often* kən-trâr'-), *adv.* 1. on the contrary; from the opposite point of view. 2. in the opposite way, order, direction, etc. 3. perversely.

**con·tra·ry** (kon'trer-i; *for 4, often* kən-trâr'i), *adj.* [< OFr. < L. *contrarius* < *contra*, against], 1. opposed; altogether different. 2. opposite in nature, order, direction, etc. 3. unfavorable: as, *contrary* weather. 4. inclined to oppose; perverse; obstinate. *n.* [*pl.* -RIES], the opposite; thing that is the opposite of another. *adv.* in opposition; counter. **—on the contrary,** as opposed to what has been said. **—to the contrary,** to the opposite effect. **—con'tra·ri·ly,** *adv.* **—con'tra·ri·ness,** *n.*

**con·trast** (kən-trast'; *for n.,* kon'trast), *v.t.* [< Fr. < It. < LL. < L. *contra*, against + *stare*, to stand], to compare so as to point out the differences; set off against one another. *v.i.* to show differences on comparison. *n.* 1. a contrasting or being contrasted. 2. a difference, especially a striking difference, between things or parts being compared. 3. a person or thing showing differences when compared with another. **—con·trast'a·ble,** *adj.*

**con·tra·vene** (kon'trə-vēn'), *v.t.* [-VENED, -VENING], [< Fr. < LL. < L. *contra*, against + *venire*, to come], 1. to go against; oppose; violate. 2. to disagree with; contradict. **—con'tra·ven'er,** *n.* **—con'tra·ven'tion** (-ven'shən), *n.*

**‡con·tre·danse** (kōn'trə-däns'), *n.* [Fr., altered < Eng. *country-dance*], a dance in which the partners form two facing lines: also **con'tra·dance'.**

**con·tre·temps** (kōn'trə-tän'), *n.* [*pl.* -TEMPS (-tän')], [Fr. < L. *contra*, against + *tempus*, time], an inopportune happening causing embarrassment.

**con·trib·ute** (kən-trib'yoot), *v.t. & v.i* [-UTED, -UTING], [< L. *contributus*; see COM- & TRIBUTE], 1. to give jointly with others to a common fund. 2. to write (an article, poem, etc.) for a magazine, newspaper, etc. 3. to furnish (ideas, etc.). **—contribute to,** to have a share in bringing about. **—con·trib'ut·a·ble,** *adj.* **—con·trib'u·tive** (-tiv), *adj.* **—con·trib'u·tive·ly,** *adv.* **—con·trib'u·tor,** *n.*

**con·tri·bu·tion** (kon'trə-bū'shən), *n.* 1. a contributing. 2. money, aid, etc. contributed. 3. a special levy or tax. 4. something written for a magazine, newspaper, etc.

**con·trib·u·to·ry** (kən-trib'yoo-tôr'i, -tō'ri), *adj.* 1. contributing. 2. involving a contribution. *n.* [*pl.* -RIES], a person or thing that contributes.

**con·trite** (kən-trīt', kon'trīt), *adj.* [OFr. < L. < *conterere*, to grind < *com-*, together + *terere*, to rub], 1. crushed in spirit by remorse or guilt. 2. resulting from remorse or guilt. **—con·trite'ly,** *adv.* **—con·trite'ness, con·tri'tion** (-trish'ən), *n.*

**con·triv·ance** (kən-trīv'əns), *n.* 1. the act, way, or power of contriving. 2. something contrived, as an invention, mechanical device, plan, etc.

**con·trive** (kən-trīv'), *v.t.* [-TRIVED, -TRIVING], [< OFr. < *con-*, intens. + *trover*, to find], 1. to devise; plan. 2. to invent; design. 3. to bring about, as by a scheme. *v.i.* to make a contrivance. **—con·triv'a·ble,** *adj.* **—con·triv'er,** *n.*

**con·trol** (kən-trōl'), *v.t.* [-TROLLED, -TROLLING], [< Fr. < ML. *contrarotulum*, a register < L. *contra*, against + *rotulus*; see ROLL], 1. to regulate (financial affairs). 2. to exercise authority over; direct; command. 3. to curb; restrain. *n.* 1. authority to direct or regulate. 2. a holding back; restraint; curb. 3. a means of restraint; check. 4. a standard of comparison for checking the findings of an experiment. 5. *often in pl.* an apparatus to regulate a mechanism. **—con·trol'la·bil'i·ty,** *n.* **—con·trol'la·ble,** *adj.* **—con·trol'ment,** *n.*

**con·trol·ler** (kən-trōl'ẽr), *n.* 1. a person, especially a government official, in charge of expenditures or finances: also sp. **comptroller.** 2. one who controls. 3. a device for controlling speed, power, etc. of a machine. **—con·trol'ler·ship',** *n.*

**con·tro·ver·sial** (kon'trə-vũr'shəl), *adj.* 1. subject to controversy; debatable. 2. of controversy. 3. liking controversy; disputatious. **—con'tro·ver'sial·ist,** *n.* **—con'tro·ver'sial·ly,** *adv.*

**con·tro·ver·sy** (kon'trə-vũr'si), *n.* [*pl.* -SIES], [< L. < *contra*, against + pp. of *vertere*, to turn], 1. a discussion of a question in which opposing opinions clash; debate. 2. a quarrel.

**con·tro·vert** (kon'trə-vũrt', kon'trə-vũrt'), *v.t.* [< *controversy*], 1. to argue against; deny; dispute. 2. to argue about; debate. **—con'tro·vert'i·ble,** *adj.* **—con'tro·vert'i·bly,** *adv.*

**con·tu·ma·cious** (kon'too-mā'shəs, -tyoo-), *adj.* [see CONTUMACY], obstinately resisting authority; disobedient. **—con'tu·ma'cious·ly,** *adj.* **—con'tu·ma'cious·ness,** *n.*

**con·tu·ma·cy** (kon'too-mə-si, -tyoo-); *n.* [*pl.* -CIES], [< L. *contumax*, stubborn < *com-*, intens. + *tumere*, to swell up], stubborn refusal to submit to authority; disobedience.

**con·tu·me·ly** (kon'too-mə-li, -tyoo-, kən-to͞o'-, kon'too-mē'li), *n.* [*pl.* -LIES], [< L. *contumelia*, reproach < *contumax*; see CONTUMACY], 1. haughty rudeness; humiliating treatment; scornful insolence. 2. a scornful insult. **—con'tu·me'li·ous,** *adj.* **—con'tu·me'li·ous·ly,** *adv.*

**con·tuse** (kən-to͞oz', -tūz'), *v.t.* [-TUSED, -TUSING], [< L. *contusus*, pp. < *com-*, intens. + *tundere*, to beat], to bruise without breaking the skin.

**con·tu·sion** (kən-to͞o'zhən, -tū'-), *n.* a bruise.

**co·nun·drum** (kə-nun'drəm), *n.* [16th-c. university

L. slang], 1. a riddle whose answer is a pun. 2. any puzzling question or problem.

**con·ur·ba·tion** (kon'ẽr-bā'shən), *n.* [< *con-* + L. *urbs*, city; + *-ation*], a vast, densely populated urban area, usually a large city with the surrounding suburbs and smaller towns.

**con·va·lesce** (kon'və-les'), *v.i.* [-LESCED, -LESCING], [< L. < *com-*, intens. + *valere*, to be strong], to recover from illness; regain health and strength.

**con·va·les·cence** (kon'və-les''ns), *n.* 1. gradual recovery after illness. 2. the period of such recovery. **—con'va·les'cent,** *adj. & n.*

**con·vec·tion** (kən-vek'shən), *n.* [< L. < *com-*, together + *vehere*, to carry], 1. a transmitting or conveying. 2. in *physics*, the transmission of heat or electricity by the movement of the heated or electrified particles, as in gas or liquid currents. **—con·vec'tion·al,** *adj.* **—con·vec'tive,** *adj.* **—con·vec'tor,** *n.*

**con·vene** (kən-vēn'), *v.i. & v.t.* [-VENED, -VENING], [< Fr. < L. < *com-*, together + *venire*, to come], to assemble for a meeting. **—con·ven'er,** *n.*

**con·ven·ience** (kən-vēn'yəns), *n.* [< L. < *convenire;* see CONVENE], 1. the quality of being convenient; fitness. 2. personal well-being; comfort. 3. anything that adds to one's comfort or makes work less difficult. Also **con·ven'ien·cy** [*pl.* -CIES]. **—at one's convenience,** at a time or place suitable to one.

**con·ven·ient** (kən-vēn'yənt), *adj.* favorable to one's comfort; easy to do, use, or get to; handy. **—convenient to,** [Colloq.], easily accessible to; near. **—con·ven'ient·ly,** *adv.*

**con·vent** (kon'vənt, -vent), *n.* [< OFr. < ML. *conventus* < L.; see CONVENE], 1. a community of nuns or, sometimes, monks, living under strict religious vows. 2. the building or buildings occupied by such a group.

**con·ven·ti·cle** (kən-ven'ti-k'l), *n.* [< OFr. < L. dim. of *conventus*, assembly; see CONVENE], 1. a religious assembly, especially an illegal or secret one. 2. a place where such an assembly meets.

**con·ven·tion** (kən-ven'shən), *n.* 1. a convening or being convened. 2. an assembly, often periodical, or the delegates to it. 3. *a*) an agreement between persons, nations, etc. *b*) general agreement on the usages and practices of social life. *c*) custom; usage.

**con·ven·tion·al** (kən-ven'shən-'l), *adj.* 1. having to do with a convention. 2. of, sanctioned by, or growing out of custom or usage; customary. 3. formal; not natural, original, or spontaneous. 4. stylized; conventionalized. **—con·ven'tion·al·ism,** *n.* **—con·ven'tion·al·ist,** *n.* **—con·ven'tion·al·ly,** *adv.*

**con·ven·tion·al·i·ty** (kən-ven'shən-al'ə-ti), *n.* [*pl.* -TIES], 1. the quality, fact, or condition of being conventional. 2. conventional behavior or act. 3. a conventional form, usage, or rule.

**con·ven·tion·al·ize** (kən-ven'shən-'l-iz'), *v.t.* [-IZED, -IZING], 1. to make conventional. 2. in *art*, to treat in a conventional or standardized manner. **—con·ven'tion·al·i·za'tion,** *n.*

**con·ven·tu·al** (kən-ven'chōō-əl), *adj.* of or like a convent. *n.* a member of a convent.

**con·verge** (kən-vũrj'), *v.i.* [-VERGED, -VERGING], [< LL. < L. *com-*, together + *vergere*; to turn], to come together or to tend to come together at a point. *v.t.* to cause to converge.

**con·ver·gence** (kən-vũr'jəns), *n.* 1. the act, fact, or condition of converging. 2. the point at which things converge. Also **con·ver'gen·cy** [*pl.* -CIES]. **—con·ver'gent,** *adj.*

**con·vers·a·ble** (kən-vũr'sə-b'l), *adj.* 1. easy to talk to; affable. 2. liking to converse or talk.

**con·ver·sant** (kon'vẽr-s'nt, kən-vũr'-), *adj.* [see CONVERSE, *v.*], familiar or acquainted (*with*) as a result of study or experience. **—con'ver·sance, con'ver·san·cy,** *n.* **—con'ver·sant·ly,** *adv.*

**con·ver·sa·tion** (kon'vẽr-sā'shən), *n.* a conversing together; informal or familiar talk.

**con·ver·sa·tion·al** (kon'vẽr-sā'shən-'l), *adj.* 1. of or for conversation. 2. fond of or adept at conversation. **—con'ver·sa'tion·al·ist, con'ver·sa'tion·ist,** *n.* **—con'ver·sa'tion·al·ly,** *adv.*

**conversation piece,** an article of furniture, bric-a-brac, etc. that arouses comment or special interest in a room.

**con·verse** (kən-vũrs'; *for n.*, kon'vẽrs), *v.i.* [-VERSED, -VERSING], [< OFr. < L. *conversari*, to live with; ult. < *convertere;* see CONVERT], to hold a conversation; talk. *n.* familiar talk; conversation. **—con·vers'er,** *n.*

**con·verse** (kən-vũrs'; *also, and for n. always*, kon'vẽrs), *adj.* [< L. pp. of *convertere;* see CONVERT], reversed in position, order, etc.; opposite; contrary. *n.* a thing reversed in position, order, etc.; the opposite. **—con·verse'ly,** *adv.*

**con·ver·sion** (kən-vũr'zhən, -shən), *n.* a converting or being converted; specif., a change from lack of faith to religious belief or from one religion to another. **—con·ver'sion·al, con·ver'sion·ar'y,** *adj.*

**con·vert** (kən-vũrt'; *for n.*, kon'vẽrt), *v.t.* [< OFr. < L. *convertere* < *com-*, together + *vertere*, to turn], 1. to change; transform; turn: as, *convert* grain into flour. 2. to change from one religion, doctrine, opinion, etc. to another. 3. to exchange for something equal in value. 4. in *finance*, to exchange (a security, currency, etc.) into an equivalent of another form. 5. in *football*, to score (the extra point) after a touchdown. 6. in *law*, to take and use (another's property) unlawfully. *v.i.* to be converted. *n.* a person converted, as to a religion.

**con·vert·er** (kən-vũr'tẽr), *n.* 1. a person or thing that converts. 2. a furnace for converting pig iron into steel. 3. a device for transforming electrical energy. Also sp. **con·ver'tor.**

**con·vert·i·ble** (kən-vũr'tə-b'l), *adj.* that can be converted. *n.* 1. a thing that can be converted. 2. an automobile with a top that can be folded back. **—con·vert'i·bil'i·ty, con·vert'i·ble·ness,** *n.* **—con·vert'i·bly,** *adv.*

**con·vex** (kon-veks', kən-, kon'veks), *adj.* [< L. < *com-*, together + *vehere*, to bring], having a surface that curves outward, like the surface of a sphere: opposed to *concave*. *n.* (kon'veks), a convex surface, body, lens, etc. **—con·vex'i·ty** [*pl.* -TIES], *n.* **—con·vex'ly,** *adv.*

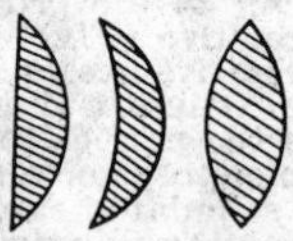

A B C

CONVEX LENSES
A, plano-convex;
B, convexo-concave;
C, convexo-convex

**con·vex·o-con·cave** (kən-vek'sō-kon-kāv'), *adj.* having one convex side and one concave side.

**con·vex·o-con·vex** (kən-vek'sō-kon-veks'), *adj.* convex on both sides, as some lenses.

**con·vex·o-plane** (kən-vek'sō-plān'), *adj.* plano-convex.

**con·vey** (kən-vā'), *v.t.* [< ONorm.Fr. *conveier*, to escort < LL. < L. *com-*, together + *via*, way], 1. to take from one place to another; transport; carry. 2. to serve as a channel or medium for; transmit. 3. to make known; communicate. 4. to transfer, as title to property, from one person to another. **—con·vey'a·ble,** *adj.*

**con·vey·ance** (kən-vā'əns), *n.* 1. a conveying. 2. means of conveying, especially a vehicle. 3. *a*) the transfer of the ownership of real property from one person to another. *b*) a deed. **—con·vey'anc·er,** *n.* **—con·vey'anc·ing,** *n.*

**con·vey·er, con·vey·or** (kən-vā'ẽr), *n.* a person or thing that conveys; esp., a mechanical contrivance, as a continuous chain or belt (**conveyer belt**), for conveying something.

**con·vict** (kən-vikt'; *for n.*, kon'vikt), *v.t.* [< L. pp. of *convincere;* see CONVINCE], 1. to prove (a person) guilty. 2. to find (a person) guilty, as a jury. *n.* 1. one found guilty of a crime and sentenced by a court. 2. one serving a sentence of confinement, as in a penitentiary.

**con·vic·tion** (kən-vik'shən), *n.* 1. a convicting or being convicted. 2. a convincing or being convinced. 3. strong belief. **—con·vic'tion·al,** *adj.* **—con·vic'tive** (-tiv), *adj.*

**con·vince** (kən-vins'), *v.t.* [-VINCED, -VINCING], [< L. < *com-*, intens. + *vincere*, to conquer], to persuade by argument or evidence; overcome the doubts of; cause to feel certain. **—con·vinc'er,** *n.* **—con·vin'ci·ble,** *adj.*

**con·vinc·ing** (kən-vin'siŋ), *adj.* persuading by argument or evidence; causing to feel certain; cogent. **—con·vinc'ing·ly,** *adv.* **—con·vinc'ing·ness,** *n.*

**con·viv·i·al** (kən-viv'i-əl), *adj.* [< L. < *convivium*, feast < *com-*, together + *vivere*, to live], 1. having to do with a feast; festive. 2. fond of eating, drinking, and good company; sociable. **—con·viv'i·al·ist,** *n.* **—con·viv'i·al'i·ty** [*pl.* -TIES], *n.* **—con·viv'i·al·ly,** *adv.*

**con·vo·ca·tion** (kon'və-kā'shən), *n.* 1. a convoking. 2. an assembly; esp., an ecclesiastical or academic assembly. **—con'vo·ca'tion·al,** *adj.* **—con'vo·ca'tor,** *n.*

**con·voke** (kən-vōk'), *v.t.* [-VOKED, -VOKING], [< Fr. < L. < *com-*, together + *vocare*, to call], to call together; assemble; convene; summon. **—con·vok'er,** *n.*

**con·vo·lute** (kon'və-lōōt'), *adj.* [< L. pp. of *convolvere;* see CONVOLVE], rolled up in a spiral with the coils falling one upon the other; coiled. *v.t. & v.i.* [-LUTED, -LUTING], to wind around; coil. **—con′vo·lut′ed,** *adj.* **—con′vo·lute′ly,** *adv.*

**con·vo·lu·tion** (kon′və-lōō′shən), *n.* 1. a twisting, coiling, or winding together. 2. a convoluted condition. 3. a fold, twist, or coil of something convoluted. 4. any of the irregular folds or ridges on the surface of the brain.

**con·volve** (kən-volv′), *v.t. & v.i.* [-VOLVED, -VOLVING], [< L. < *com-*, together + *volvere*, to roll], to roll, coil, or twist together.

**con·vol·vu·lus** (kən-vol′vyoo-ləs), *n.* [*pl.* -LUSES, -LI (-lī′)], [L., bindweed; see CONVOLVE], any of various trailing or twining plants with trumpet-shaped flowers, as the morning-glory.

**con·voy** (kən-voi′; *for n.*, kon′voi), *v.t.* [< Fr. < OFr. *convoier;* see CONVEY], to go with in order to protect; escort. *n.* 1. a convoying or being convoyed. 2. a protecting escort, as ships or troops. 3. ships, troops, etc. being convoyed.

**con·vulse** (kən-vuls′), *v.t.* [-VULSED, -VULSING], [< L. *convulsus*, pp. < *com-*, together + *vellere*, to pluck], 1. to shake or disturb violently; agitate. 2. to cause spasms in. 3. to cause to shake with laughter, rage, etc.

**con·vul·sion** (kən-vul′shən), *n.* 1. *usually in pl.* a violent, involuntary contraction or spasm of the muscles. 2. a violent fit of laughter. 3. any violent disturbance. **—con·vul′sion·ar′y,** *adj & n.* **—con·vul′sive** (-siv), *adj.* **—con·vul′sive·ly,** *adv.*

**co·ny** (kō′ni; *orig.* kun′i), *n.* [*pl.* -NIES], [< OFr. < L. *cuniculus*, rabbit], 1. a rabbit. 2. rabbit fur. 3. in the *Bible*, a hoofed, rodentlike mammal. Also sp. **coney.**

**coo** (kōō), *v.i.* [echoic], 1. to make the soft, murmuring sound of pigeons or doves or a sound like this. 2. to speak gently and lovingly: now only in *bill and coo.* *v.t.* to say gently and lovingly. *n.* the sound made in cooing. **—coo′ing·ly,** *adv.*

**cook** (kook), *n.* [AS. *coc* < LL. < L. < *coquere*, to cook], one who prepares meals. *v.t.* 1. to prepare (food) by boiling, baking, frying, etc. 2. [Colloq.], to tamper with. *v.i.* 1. to be a cook; act as cook. 2. to undergo cooking. 3. [Slang], to ruin.—**cook up,** [Colloq.], to concoct; devise; scheme.

**Cook, James** (kook), 1728–1779; English naval officer and explorer: called *Captain Cook.*

**cook·book** (kook′book′), *n.* a book with recipes and other information for preparing food.

**cook·er** (kook′ẽr), *n.* 1. a stove for cooking. 2. a container in which food is cooked.

**cook·er·y** (kook′ẽr-i), *n.* [*pl.* -IES], the art, practice, or work of cooking.

**cook·out (kook′out′), *n.* a meal prepared and eaten outdoors, as at a picnic.**

**cook·y, cook·ie** (kook′i), *n.* [*pl.* -IES], [prob. < D. *koekje*, dim. of *koek*, a cake], a small, sweet cake, usually flat.

**cool** (kōōl), *adj.* [AS. *col*], 1. moderately cold; neither warm nor very cold. 2. tending to reduce discomfort in hot weather: as, *cool* clothes. 3. not excited; composed; collected. 4. showing dislike or indifference. 5. calmly impudent or bold. 6. [Colloq.], without exaggeration: as, he lost a *cool* thousand. 7. [Slang], pleasing; excellent. *adv.* in a cool manner *n.* 1. a cool place, time, thing, etc.: as, the *cool* of the evening. 2. [Slang], cool, dispassionate attitude or manner. *v.i.* to become cool. *v.t.* to make cool. **—cool one's heels,** [Colloq.], to wait long and tediously. **—cool′ish,** *adj.* **—cool′ly,** *adv.* **—cool′ness,** *n.*

**cool·ant** (kōōl′ənt), *n.* **a substance used for cooling, as a circulating fluid in an engine.**

**cool·er** (kōōl′ẽr), *n.* 1. a device or container for cooling things or keeping them cool. 2. anything that cools. 3. [Slang], a jail.

**Coo·lidge, Calvin** (kōō′lij), (*John Calvin Coolidge*), **1872–1933; 30th president of the U.S. (1923–1929).**

**coo·lie** (kōō′li), *n.* [Hind. *qūlī*, hired servant], 1. in the Orient, an unskilled native laborer. 2. a person doing heavy labor for little pay.

**coon** (kōōn), *n.* [Colloq.], a raccoon.

**coop** (kōōp, koop), *n.* [ult. < L. *cupa*, tub, cask], 1. **a small cage or pen for poultry, etc.** 2. a place of confinement. *v.t.* to confine in or as in a coop. **—fly the coop,** [Slang], to escape.

**co-op, co·öp** (kō′op′, kō-op′), *n.* [Colloq.], a co-operative society, store, rooming house, etc.

**co-op., coöp., coop.,** co-operative.

**coop·er** (kōōp′ẽr, koop′-), *n.* [< MD. < ML. *cuparius* < L. *cupa*, a cask], a person whose work is making or repairing barrels and casks. *v.t. & v.i.* to make or repair (barrels and casks).

**Coop·er, James Fen·i·more** (fen′ə-môr′ kōōp′ẽr, koop′-), 1789–1851; U.S. novelist.

**coop·er·age** (kōōp′ẽr-ij, koop′-), *n.* 1. the work or workshop of a cooper: also **coop′er·y** [*pl.* -IES]. 2. the price for such work.

**co-op·er·ate, co·öp·er·ate, co·op·er·ate** (kō-op′ẽr-āt′), *v.i.* [-ATED, -ATING], [< LL. < L. *co-*, with + *operari*, to work < *opus*, work], to act or work together with another or others.

**co-op·er·a·tion, co·öp·er·a·tion, co·op·er·a·tion** (kō-op′ẽr-ā′shən), *n.* 1. a co-operating; joint effort or operation. 2. the joining of persons in an enterprise for mutual benefits or profits.

**co-op·er·a·tive, co·öp·er·a·tive, co·op·er·a·tive** (kō-op′ẽr-ā′tiv, -op′rə-tiv), *adj.* 1. co-operating or inclined to co-operate. 2. designating or of an organization, as for the production or marketing of goods, owned collectively by members who share in its profits and benefits. *n.* such an organization. **—co-op′er·a′tive·ly,** *adv.* **—co-op′er·a′tive·ness,** *n.*

**co-op·er·a·tor, co·öp·er·a·tor, co·op·er·a·tor** (kō-op′ẽr-ā′tẽr), *n.* a person who co-operates.

**co-or·di·nate** (kō-ôr′də-nit; *also, and for v. always,* -nāt′), *adj.* [< ML. < L. *co-*, with + *ordinare*, to arrange < *ordo*, order], 1. of equal order or importance: as, a compound sentence has two or more *co-ordinate* clauses. 2. of or involving co-ordination or co-ordinates. *n.* 1. a co-ordinate person or thing. 2. in *mathematics*, any of two or more magnitudes used to define the position of a point, line, curve, or plane. *v.t.* [-NATED, -NATING], 1. to make co-ordinate. 2. to bring into proper order or relation; adjust. *v.i.* to become co-ordinate. Also **coördinate, coordinate. —co-or′di·nate·ly,** *adv.* **—co-or′di·nate·ness,** *n.*

**co-ordinating conjunction,** a conjunction that connects co-ordinate words, phrases, or clauses (e.g., *and, but, for, or, nor, yet*).

**co-or·di·na·tion, co·ör·di·na·tion, co·or·di·na·tion** (kō-ôr′də-nā′shən), *n.* 1. a co-ordinating or being co-ordinated. 2. the harmonious adjustment or functioning, as of muscles.

**co-or·di·na·tive, co·ör·di·na·tive, co·or·di·na·tive** (kō-ôr′də-nā′tiv, -nə-), *adj.* co-ordinating.

**co-or·di·na·tor, co·ör·di·na·tor, co·or·di·na·tor** (kō-ôr′də-nā′tẽr), *n.* one that coordinates.

**coot** (kōōt), *n.* [MD. *koet*], 1. [*pl.* COOTS, COOT; see PLURAL, II, D, 1], a web-footed water bird of the rail family. 2. [Colloq.], a foolish person.

**coot·ie (kōōt′i), *n.* [Slang], a louse.**

**cop** (kop), *v.t.* [COPPED, COPPING], [< obs. *cap*, to seize; ? ult. < L. *capere*, to take], [Slang], to seize; steal. *n.* [Slang], a policeman. **—cop out,** [Slang], 1. to back down; renege. 2. to give up; quit.

**co·pal** (kō′p'l, -pal), *n.* [Sp. < Nahuatl *copalli*, **resin], a hard resin from various tropical trees.**

**co·part·ner** (kō-pärt′nẽr), *n.* an associate; fellow; partner. **—co·part′ner·ship′,** *n.*

**cope** (kōp), *v.i.* [COPED, COPING], [OFr. *couper*, to **strike < *coup*, a blow], 1. to fight or contend (*with*) successfully or on equal terms. 2. to deal with problems, troubles, etc.**

**cope** (kōp), *n.* [OFr. *cape* < L. *cappa;* see CAPE], 1. a large, capelike vestment worn by priests at certain ceremonies. 2. any cover like this, as a canopy, *v.t.* [COPED, COPING], to cover as with a cope.

**co·peck** (kō′pek), *n.* a kopeck (Russian coin).

**Co·pen·ha·gen** (kō′pən-hā′gən, -hä′-), *n.* the capital of Denmark, on the E coast of Zealand Island: pop., 1,116,000.

**Co·per·ni·can** (kō-pũr′ni-kən), *adj.* of Copernicus or his astronomical theories: the *Copernican system* **postulated the revolution of the planets around the sun and the rotation of the earth.**

**Co·per·ni·cus, Nic·o·la·us** (nik′ə-lā′əs kō-pũr′ni-kəs), 1473–1543; Polish astronomer.

**cope·stone** (kōp′stōn′), *n.* 1. the top stone of a wall; stone in a coping. 2. finishing stroke.

**cop·i·er** (kop′i-ẽr), *n.* 1. an imitator. 2. a copyist; transcriber. 3. a duplicating machine.

**co·pi·lot** (kō′pī′lət), *n.* the assistant pilot of an aircraft.

**cop·ing** (kōp′iŋ), *n.* [fig. use of *cope* (cloak)], the top layer of a masonry wall, usually sloped.

**coping saw,** a saw with a narrow blade in a U-shaped frame, for cutting curved outlines.

**co·pi·ous** (kō′pi-əs), *adj.* [< L. < *copia*, abundance],

1. abundant; plentiful. 2. wordy; profuse or diffuse. —**co′pi·ous·ly,** *adv.* —**co′pi·ous·ness,** *n.*
**cop·per** (kop′ẽr), *n.* [AS. *copor* < LL. *cuper, cuprum* < *Cyprium (aes)*, Cyprian (metal): ancient Cyprus had rich copper mines], 1. a reddish-brown, malleable, ductile, metallic element that is an excellent conductor of electricity and heat: symbol, Cu; at. wt., 63.54; at. no., 29: abbrev. **C., c., cop.** 2. a thing made of this metal. 3. a penny, etc. of copper or bronze. 4. a large container or boiler. 5. a reddish brown. *adj.* 1. of copper. 2. reddish-brown. *v.t.* to cover with copper. —**cop′per·y,** *adj.*
**cop·per** (kop′ẽr), *n.* [prob. < *cop* (to seize)], [Slang], a policeman.
**cop·per·as** (kop′ẽr-əs), *n.* [< OFr. < ML. (*aqua*) *cuprosa*, lit., copper (water)], ferrous sulfate, $FeSO_4 \cdot 7H_2O$, a green, crystalline compound used in dyeing, the making of ink, etc.
**cop·per·head** (kop′ẽr-hed′), *n.* 1. a poisonous snake of North America, related to the rattlesnake but lacking rattles. 2. [C-], a Northerner who sympathized with the South during the Civil War.
**cop·per·plate** (kop′ẽr-plāt′), *n.* 1. a flat piece of copper etched or engraved for printing. 2. a print or engraving made from this. 3. copperplate printing or engraving.
**cop·per·smith** (kop′ẽr-smith′), *n.* a man whose work is making utensils and the like out of copper.
**copper sulfate,** a blue, crystalline substance, $CuSO_4 \cdot 5H_2O$; blue vitriol: used in making pigments, electric batteries, etc.: also **cupric sulfate.**
**cop·pice** (kop′is), *n.* [< OFr. < *coper*, to cut], a thicket of small trees or shrubbery; a copse.
**cop·ra** (kop′rə), *n.* [Port. < Malayalam < Hind. *khoprā*], dried coconut meat, the source of coconut oil: also **coprah, coppra, copperah** (kop′ẽr-ə).
**copse** (kops), *n.* [< *coppice*], a thicket of small trees or shrubbery.
**Copt** (kopt), *n.* 1. a native of Egypt descended from the ancient inhabitants of that country. 2. a member of the Coptic Church.
**Cop·tic** (kop′tik), *adj.* [< L. < Ar. *Quft*, the Copts < Gr. *Aigyptios*, Egyptian], 1. of the Copts, their language, etc. 2. of the Coptic Church. *n.* the ancient Hamitic language of the Copts.
**Coptic Church,** the native Christian church of Egypt and, at one time, of Ethiopia.
**cop·u·la** (kop′yoo-lə), *n.* [*pl.* -LAS], [L., a link < *co-*, together + *apere*, to join], 1. something that links together. 2. in *grammar*, a weakened verbal form, especially a form of *be* or a similar verb, as *seem, appear*, etc., which links a subject with a predicate complement. —**cop′u·lar,** *adj.*
**cop·u·late** (kop′yoo-lāt′), *v.i.* [-LATED, -LATING], [< L. pp. of *copulare*, to couple; see COPULA], to unite in sexual intercourse. —**cop′u·la′tion,** *n.*
**cop·u·la·tive** (kop′yoo-lā′tiv, -lə-), *adj.* 1. coupling. 2. involving or comprising connected words or clauses. 3. having the nature of a copula: as, a *copulative* verb. 4. of or for copulating. *n.* a copulative word. —**cop′u·la′tive·ly,** *adv.*
**cop·y** (kop′i), *n.* [*pl.* -IES], [< OFr. < ML. *copia*, copious transcript < L. *copia*, abundance], 1. a thing made just like another; full reproduction. 2. any of a number of books, magazines, engravings, etc. having the same composition or printed matter. 3. a model or pattern to be imitated or reproduced. 4. a manuscript to be set in type. 5. subject matter for a novelist, journalist, etc. *v.t. & v.i.* [-IED, -YING], 1. to make a copy or copies of; reproduce. 2. to imitate.
**cop·y·book** (kop′i-book′), *n.* a book with models of handwriting for pupils to copy. *adj.* ordinary; trite; commonplace: as, *copybook* maxims.
**cop·y·cat** (kop′i-kat′), *n.* one who habitually imitates or mimics: a child's term.
**copy desk,** the desk in a newspaper office where copy is edited and headlines are written.
**cop·y·ist** (kop′i-ist), *n.* 1. one who makes written copies; transcriber. 2. one who imitates.
**cop·y·right** (kop′i-rīt′), *n.* [*copy* + *right*], the exclusive right to the publication, production, or sale of a literary, musical, or artistic work, granted by law for a definite period of years (in the U.S., 28 years, with the option of one renewal). *v.t.* to protect (a book, etc.) by copyright. *adj.* protected by copyright. —**cop′y·right′a·ble,** *adj.* —**cop′y·right′er,** *n.*
**cop·y·writ·er** (kop′i-rīt′ẽr), *n.* a writer of copy, especially for advertisements.
**co·quet** (kō-ket′), *v.i.* [-QUETTED, -QUETTING], [< Fr. < *coc*, a rooster; see COCK], 1. to flirt. 2. to trifle (*with*); dally. —**co·quet·ry** (kō′kə-tri, kō-ket′ri), [*pl.* -RIES], *n.*
**co·quette** (kō-ket′), *n.* [Fr.; see COQUET], a girl or woman flirt. *v.i.* [-QUETTED, -QUETTING], to flirt. —**co·quet′tish,** *adj.* —**co·quet′tish·ly,** *adv.* —**co·quet′tish·ness,** *n.*
**co·qui·na** (kə-kē′nə), *n.* [Sp., shellfish < L. *concha*; see CONCH], a soft, whitish limestone made up of broken sea shells and corals.
**Cor.,** 1. Corinthians. 2. Coroner.
**cor.,** 1. corner. 2. correct(ed). 3. correction. 4. correspondence. 5. in *music*, cornet.
**cor-,** com-: used before *r*, as in *corrupt*.
**cor·a·cle** (kôr′ə-k'l, kor′-), *n.* [< W. < *corwg*, carcass], a small boat made of a waterproof material stretched over a wooden frame.
**cor·al** (kôr′əl, kor′-), *n.* [< OFr. < L. < Gr. *korallion*; ? < Heb. *gōrāl*, pebble], 1. a hard substance made up of the skeletons of certain marine animals (called *polyps*): reefs and atolls of coral are found in tropical seas. 2. any of a number of such animals living in large colonies. 3. a piece of coral. 4. coral red. *adj.* 1. made of coral. 2. coral-red.

CORAL

**coral red,** yellowish red. —**cor′al-red′,** *adj.*
**coral reef,** a reef built up by the action of ocean waves which deposit the limestone skeletons of coral living in tropical waters.
**cor·al·root** (kôr′əl-rōōt′, kor′əl-root′), *n.* a brownish orchid with corallike rootstocks and no leaves: also **coral-root, coral root.**
**Coral Sea,** a part of the Pacific, northeast of Australia.
**coral snake,** a small, poisonous snake with coral-red, yellow, and black bands around its body, found in the southeastern U.S.
**cor·bel** (kôr′b'l), *n.* [< OFr. < L. *corvus*, raven], a bracket of stone, wood, etc. projecting from a wall and serving to support a cornice, etc. *v.t.* [-BELED or -BELLED, -BELING or -BELLING], to provide or support with a corbel or corbels.
**cor·bel·ing, cor·bel·ling** (kôr′b'l-iŋ), *n.* 1. the fashioning of corbels. 2. a series of corbels.
**cor·bie** (kôr′bi), *n.* [*pl.* -BIES], [see CORBEL], [Scot.], a crow or raven: also **corbie crow.**

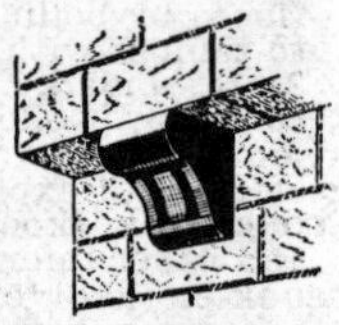
CORBEL

**cor·by** (kôr′bi), *n.* [*pl.* -BIES], a corbie.
**cord** (kôrd), *n.* [< OFr. < L. < Gr. *chordē*], 1. thick string or thin rope. 2. any force acting as a tie or bond. 3. a measure of wood cut for fuel (128 cubic feet). 4. a rib on the surface of a fabric. 5. cloth with a ribbed surface; corduroy. 6. *pl.* corduroy trousers. 7. in *anatomy*, any part like a cord: as, the spinal *cord*: also **chord.** 8. in *electricity*, a small insulated cable fitted with a plug or plugs. *v.t.* 1. to fasten or provide with a cord or cords. 2. to stack (wood) in cords.
**cord·age** (kôr′dij), *n.* 1. cords and ropes collectively, especially the ropes in a ship's rigging. 2. the amount of wood, measured in cords, in a given area.
**cor·date** (kôr′dāt), *adj.* [< L. < *cor, cordis*, heart], heart-shaped. —**cor′date·ly,** *adv.*
**cord·ed** (kôr′did), *adj.* 1. fastened with cords. 2. made of cords. 3. having a ribbed surface, as corduroy. 4. stacked in cords, as wood.
**cor·dial** (kôr′jəl), *adj.* [Fr. < ML. < L. *cor, cordis*, heart], 1. stimulating the heart. 2. hearty; sincere; warm and genuine. *n.* 1. a medicine, food, or drink that stimulates the heart. 2. an aromatic, alcoholic drink; liqueur. —**cor′dial·ly,** *adv.* —**cor′dial·ness,** *n.*
**cor·dial·i·ty** (kôr′ji-al′ə-ti, kôr-jal′-), *n.* 1. cordial quality; warm, friendly feeling. 2. [*pl.* -TIES], a cordial act or remark.
**cor·dil·le·ra** (kôr-dil′ẽr-ə, kôr′dil-yâr′ə), *n.* [Sp. < dim. of *cuerda*, rope < L. *chorda*, cord], a chain of mountains; esp., the principal mountain range of a continent. —**cor·dil′le·ran,** *adj.*
**cord·ing** (kôrd′iŋ), *n.* 1. the ribbed surface of corded cloth. 2. cordage.
**cord·ite** (kôr′dīt), *n.* [*cord* + *-ite*: from its stringiness], a smokeless explosive made of nitroglycerin, guncotton, petroleum jelly, and acetone.
**cor·don** (kôr′d'n), *n.* [Fr., dim. of *corde*, cord], 1. a line or circle of people, ships, etc. stationed around an area to guard it. 2. a cord, ribbon, or braid worn as a decoration or badge.

**cor·do·van** (kôrʹdə-vən, kôr-dōʹ-), *n.* [< Sp. < *Córdoba*, Spain, where orig. made], 1. a soft, colored leather, usually of sheepskin or split horsehide. 2. *pl.* shoes made of this leather. *adj.* made of cordovan.
**cor·du·roy** (kôrʹdə-roiʹ, kôrʹdə-roiʹ), *n.* [? < Fr. *corde du roi*, cord of the king; but prob. < *cord* + obs. *duroy*, a coarse fabric], 1. a heavy cotton fabric with a velvety surface, ribbed vertically. 2. *pl.* trousers made of this. *adj.* 1. made of corduroy. 2. ribbed like corduroy. 3. designating a road (**corduroy road**) made of logs laid crosswise.
**cord·wain·er** (kôrdʹwān-ẽr), *n.* [< OFr.; see CORDOVAN]. 1. [Archaic], a leatherworker. 2. a shoemaker.
**cord·wood** (kôrdʹwoodʹ), *n.* 1. wood stacked or sold in cords. 2. wood cut in lengths of 4 feet.
**core** (kôr, kōr), *n.* [< OFr.; prob. < L. *cor*, heart], 1. the central part of an apple, pear, etc., containing the seeds. 2. the central part of anything; hence, 3. the most important part; essence of a matter. 4. in *electricity*, a mass of ferromagnetic material placed inside a wire coil to increase the external magnetic field. 5. in *founding*, the part of a mold forming the interior of a hollow casting. *v.t.* [CORED, CORING], to remove the core of. —**coreʹless**, *adj.* —**coreʹlikeʹ**, *adj.* —**corʹer**, *n.*
**co·re·li·gion·ist** (kōʹri-lijʹən-ist), *n.* a person of the same religion: also **coʹre·liʹgion·ar·y.**
**co·re·op·sis** (kôrʹi-opʹsis, kōʹri-), *n.* [< Gr. *koris*, bug + *opsis*, appearance: from the shape of the seed], 1. any of a group of plants of the composite family, with daisylike flowers of yellow, orange, red, or brownish purple. 2. the flower.
**co·re·spond·ent** (kōʹri-sponʹdənt), *n.* [*co-* + *respondent*], in *law*, a person charged with having committed adultery with the wife or husband from whom a divorce is sought. —**coʹre·spondʹen·cy**, *n.*
**co·ri·an·der** (kôrʹi-anʹdẽr, kōʹri-), *n.* [< Fr. < L. < Gr. < *koris*, bug], 1. a European plant of the carrot family. 2. its strong-smelling, seedlike fruit, used in flavoring food and in medicine.
**Cor·inth** (kôrʹinth, korʹ-), *n.* an ancient city in S Greece.
**Co·rin·thi·an** (kə-rinʹthi-ən), *adj.* 1. of Corinth, its people, or culture. 2. dissolute and given to luxury, as the people of Corinth were reputed to be. 3. designating or of the most elaborate of the three orders of Greek architecture, distinguished by a bell-shaped capital with a design of acanthus leaves. *n.* a native or inhabitant of Corinth.

CORINTHIAN CAPITAL

**Co·rin·thi·ans** (kə-rinʹthi-ənz), *n.pl.* [construed as sing.], either of two books of the New Testament: Epistles of the Apostle Paul to the Christians of Corinth.
**Cork** (kôrk), *n.* 1. a county in S Ireland. 2. a city in this county: pop., 76,000.
**cork** (kôrk), *n.* [< Sp. < Ar. *alcorque*; ? < L. *quercus*, oak], 1. the light, thick, elastic outer bark of an oak tree (the **cork oak**) of the Mediterranean area. 2. a piece of cork, especially one used as a stopper for a bottle, cask, etc. 3. any stopper, as one made of glass, rubber, etc. 4. the outer bark of the stems of woody plants. *adj.* made of cork. *v.t.* 1. to stop with a cork. 2. to hold back; restrain; check. 3. to blacken with burnt cork. —**corkʹlikeʹ**, *adj.*
**cork·er** (kôrʹkẽr), *n.* 1. a worker or device that corks bottles. 2. [Slang], a remarkable person or thing. 3. [Slang], a preposterous lie.
**cork·ing** (kôrʹkiŋ), *adj. & interj.* [Slang], very good; excellent.
**cork·screw** (kôrkʹskrōōʹ), *n.* a spiral-shaped device for pulling corks out of bottles. *adj.* like a corkscrew in shape; spiral. *v.i. & v.t.* to move in a winding or spiral course; zigzag.
**cork·y** (kôrʹki), *adj.* [-IER, -IEST], 1. of cork. 2. like cork or a cork. —**corkʹi·ness**, *n.*
**corm** (kôrm), *n.* [< Gr. *kormos*, a lopped tree trunk < *keirein*, to cut off], the bulblike, scaly underground stem of certain plants, as the crocus.
**cor·mo·rant** (kôrʹmə-rənt), *n.* [< OFr. < L. *corvus* (raven) *marinus* (< *mare*, the sea)], 1. a large, voracious sea bird with webbed toes and a pouch of skin under its beak. 2. a greedy person; glutton. *adj.* greedy; gluttonous.
**corn** (kôrn), *n.* [< AS.], 1. a small, hard seed; esp., the seed of any cereal plant; kernel. 2. *a*) a kind of grain that grows in kernels on large ears; maize. *b*) its ears. Also called *Indian corn*. 3. in England, wheat. 4. in Scotland and Ireland, oats. 5. [Brit.], the seeds of all such cereal plants; grain. 6. [Colloq.], corn whisky. 7. [Slang], ideas, humor, etc. regarded as old-fashioned, trite, etc. *v.t.* to preserve or pickle (meat, etc.) in brine or with dry salt. —**corned**, *adj.*
**corn** (kôrn), *n.* [< OFr. < L. *cornu*, a horn], a horny thickening of the skin, especially on the toes.
**-corn** (kôrn), [< L. *cornu*, a horn], a terminal combining form meaning *horn*, as in *unicorn*.
**Corn Belt**, the region in the Middle West, from Ohio to Kansas, where much corn is grown.
**corn borer**, a moth larva that feeds on corn.
**corn bread**, bread made of corn meal.
**corn·cob** (kôrnʹkobʹ), *n.* 1. the woody core of an ear of corn. 2. a corncob pipe.
**corncob pipe**, a tobacco pipe with a bowl made of a hollowed piece of dried corncob.
**corn cockle**, a tall weed of the pink family, which often grows in grainfields.
**cor·ne·a** (kôrʹni-ə), *n.* [< L. < *cornu*, a horn], the transparent outer coat of the eyeball, covering the iris and pupil. —**corʹne·al**, *adj.*
**Cor·neille, Pierre** (pyâr kôrʹnāʹyʹ; Eng. kôr-nāʹ), 1606–1684; French dramatist and poet.
**cor·nel** (kôrʹnʹl, -nel), *n.* [< OFr. < L. < *cornum*], any of various shrubs or small trees with very hard wood, including the dogwood.
**cor·nel·ian** (kôr-nēlʹyən, kẽr-), *n.* [< OFr. *corneola*; prob. < L. *cornum*, cornel], carnelian.
**cor·ner** (kôrʹnẽr), *n.* [< OFr. < LL. < *cornu*, a horn], 1. the point or place where lines or surfaces join and form an angle. 2. the space between lines or surfaces at the point of their junction; angle. 3. the place where two streets meet. 4. a piece used to form, guard, or ornament a corner. 5. a remote or secluded place. 6. region; quarter: as, the four *corners* of the earth. 7. an awkward position, from which escape is difficult. 8. a speculative monopoly produced by buying up the available supply of some stock or commodity to raise the price. *v.t.* 1. to furnish with corners. 2. to put into a corner. 3. to force into a corner, or into an awkward position from which escape is difficult. 4. to form a corner in (some stock or commodity). *v.i.* 1. to form a corner. 2. to be on or at a corner. *adj.* 1. at or on a corner. 2. used in a corner. —**cut corners**, 1. to take a direct route by going across corners. 2. to cut down expenses, time or labor required, etc. —**corʹnered**, *adj.*
**cor·ner·stone** (kôrʹnẽr-stōnʹ), *n.* 1. a stone at the corner of a building. 2. such a stone laid at a ceremony formally beginning the erection of a building. 3. the basic or main part; foundation.
**cor·ner·ways** (kôrʹnẽr-wāzʹ), *adv.* cornerwise.
**cor·ner·wise** (kôrʹnẽr-wīzʹ), *adv.* [*corner* + *-wise*], 1. with the corner to the front. 2. diagonally.
**cor·net** (kôr-netʹ), *n.* [< OFr. < L. *cornu*, a horn], 1. a brass-wind musical instrument of the trumpet class. 2. (*usually* kôrʹnit), a piece of paper twisted like a cone, for holding sugar, candy, etc. —**cor·netʹtist**, **cor·netʹist**, *n.*

CORNET

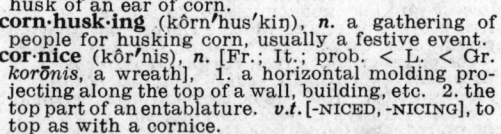

**corn·flow·er** (kôrnʹflouʹẽr), *n.* 1. the bachelor's-button. 2. the corn cockle.
**corn·husk** (kôrnʹhuskʹ), *n.* a husk of an ear of corn.
**corn·husk·ing** (kôrnʹhusʹkiŋ), *n.* a gathering of people for husking corn, usually a festive event.
**cor·nice** (kôrʹnis), *n.* [Fr.; It.; prob. < L. < Gr. *korōnis*, a wreath], 1. a horizontal molding projecting along the top of a wall, building, etc. 2. the top part of an entablature. *v.t.* [-NICED, -NICING], to top as with a cornice.
**Cor·nish** (kôrʹnish), *adj.* of Cornwall, its people, etc. *n.* the Brythonic Celtic language formerly spoken in Cornwall. —**Corʹnish·man** [*pl.* -MEN], *n.*
**corn meal**, meal made from corn; maize ground up.
**corn pone**, a kind of corn bread usually made without milk or eggs.
**corn silk**, a tassel of silky fibers growing at the end of an ear of corn.
**corn sirup**, a sweet sirup made from cornstarch.
**corn·stalk** (kôrnʹstôkʹ), *n.* a stalk of corn.

**corn·starch** (kôrn′stärch′), *n.* a starchy flour made from Indian corn, used in cooking.
**corn sugar,** a dextrose made from cornstarch.
**cor·nu·co·pi·a** (kôr′nə-kō′pi-ə, kôr′nyoo-), *n.* [L. *cornu copiae*, horn of plenty], 1. a container shaped like a horn, or a representation of this, overflowing with fruits, flowers, and grain; horn of plenty. 2. an overflowing fullness; abundance.

CORNUCOPIA

**Corn·wall** (kôrn′wôl, -wəl), *n.* a county of SW England: pop., 345,000.
**Corn·wal·lis, Charles** (kôrn-wôl′is, -wol′-), first Marquis Cornwallis 1738–1805; commanded British forces during the American Revolution.
**corn whisky,** whisky made from corn (maize).
**corn·y** (kôr′ni), *adj.* [-IER, -IEST], 1. of or producing corn. 2. [Slang], countrified; unsophisticated. 3. [Slang], old-fashioned, trite, sentimental, etc. —**corn′i·ness,** *n.*
**co·rol·la** (kə-rol′ə), *n.* [L., dim. of *corona*, a crown], the petals, or inner leaves, of a flower. —**cor·ol·la·ceous** (kôr′ə-lā′shəs, kor′-), **cor′ol·late′, cor′ol·lat′ed,** *adj.*
**cor·ol·lar·y** (kôr′ə-ler′i, kor′-), *n.* [*pl.* -IES], [< L. *corollarium*, gift < *corolla*; see COROLLA], 1. a proposition that follows from another that has been proved. 2. an inference or deduction. 3. anything that follows as a normal result.
**co·ro·na** (kə-rō′nə), *n.* [*pl.* -NAS, -NAE (-nē)], [L. < Gr. *korōnē*, wreath], 1. a crown or something like a crown. 2. in *anatomy*, the upper part of a tooth, the skull, etc. 3. in *astronomy*, a circle of light around the sun or moon; specif., the halo around the sun during a total eclipse. 4. in *botany*, the cuplike part on the inner side of the corolla of certain flowers. 5. in *electricity*, a sometimes visible electric discharge around a conductor at high potential. —**cor·o·nal** (kə-rō′n'l, kôr′ə-, kor′ə-), *adj.*
**Co·ro·na·do, Fran·cis·co Vás·quez de** (frän-thēs′kô väs′keth de kô′rô-nä′thô; Eng. kôr′ə-nä′dō), 1510–1554; Spanish explorer of SW North America.
**cor·o·nar·y** (kôr′ə-ner′i, kor′-), *adj.* [see CORONA], 1. of, or in the form of, a crown. 2. in *anatomy*, designating or of either of two arteries supplying blood directly to the heart tissues. *n.* [*pl.* -IES], a coronary thrombosis.
**coronary thrombosis,** the formation of an obstructing clot in a coronary artery.
**cor·o·na·tion** (kôr′ə-nā′shən, kor′-), *n.* [< OFr. < L. < *corona*, a crown], the act or ceremony of crowning a sovereign.
**cor·o·ner** (kôr′ə-nēr, kor′-), *n.* [ME., officer of the crown < Anglo-Fr. < L. *corona*, a crown], a public officer whose chief duty is to determine by inquest before a jury (**coroner's jury**) the causes of any deaths not obviously due to natural causes.
**cor·o·net** (kôr′ə-net′, kor′ə-nit), *n.* [< OFr. dim. of *corone*, a crown], 1. a small crown worn by princes and other nobility. 2. an ornamental band of precious metal, jewels, or flowers, worn around the head. —**cor′o·net′ed, cor′o·net′ted,** *adj.*
**Co·rot, Jean Bap·tiste Ca·mille** (zhän bȧ′tēst′ kȧ′mē′y′ kô′rō′; Eng. kə-rō′), 1796–1875; French landscape painter.
**corp., corpn.,** corporation.
**cor·po·ral** (kôr′pēr-əl), *n.* [< Fr. < It. < *capo* (< L. *caput*), the head], in the *U.S. armed forces*, the lowest-ranking noncommissioned officer in the Army, Air Force, and Marine Corps, just above a private first class: abbrev. **Corp., Cpl.** (as a title). —**cor′po·ral·cy** [*pl.* -CIES], **cor′po·ral·ship′,** *n.*
**cor·po·ral** (kôr′pēr-əl), *adj.* [< L. *corporalis* < *corpus*, body], 1. of the body; bodily. 2. personal. —**cor′po·ral′i·ty,** *n.* —**cor′po·ral·ly,** *adv.*
**cor·po·ral** (kôr′pēr-əl), *n.* [OFr.; ML. *corporalis* (*palla*), body (cloth); see CORPORAL, *adj.*], in *ecclesiastical usage*, a white linen cloth covering the altar during the sacrament of the Lord's Supper: also **cor·po·ra·le** (kôr′pə-rā′lē).
**corporal punishment,** punishment inflicted directly on the body, as flogging.
**cor·po·rate** (kôr′pēr-it), *adj.* [< L. pp. of *corporare*, to make into a body < *corpus*, body], 1. united; combined. 2. of, like, or being a corporation; incorporated. —**cor′po·rate·ly,** *adv.*
**cor·po·ra·tion** (kôr′pə-rā′shən), *n.* 1. a group of people who get a charter granting them as a body certain of the legal rights and liabilities of a single individual. 2. a group of people, as the mayor and aldermen of an incorporated town, legally authorized to act as an individual. 3. [Colloq.], a large and prominent abdomen. —**cor′po·ra′tive,** *adj.* —**cor′po·ra′tor,** *n.*
**cor·po·re·al** (kôr-pôr′i-əl, -pō′ri-), *adj.* [< L. < *corporis*, body], 1. of or for the body; bodily. 2. of a material nature; physical; tangible. —**cor·po′re·al′i·ty, cor·po′re·al·ness,** *n.* —**cor·po′re·al·ly,** *adv.*
**corps** (kôr, kōr), *n.* [*pl.* CORPS (kôrz, kōrz)], [Fr. < OFr. *corps, cors* (< L. *corpus*), body], 1. a body of people associated under common direction. 2. in *military usage*, *a*) a separate branch of the armed forces having some specialized function: as, the Medical *Corps*. *b*) a tactical subdivision of an army, composed of two or more divisions.
**corpse** (kôrps), *n.* [see CORPS], a dead body, especially of a person.
**cor·pu·lence** (kôr′pyoo-ləns), *n.* [< Fr. < L. < *corpus*, body], fatness; obesity: also **cor′pu·len·cy.** —**cor′pu·lent,** *adj.* —**cor′pu·lent·ly,** *adv.*
**cor·pus** (kôr′pəs), *n.* [*pl.* -PORA (-pēr-ə)], [L.], 1. a human or animal body, especially a dead one: now used humorously. 2. a complete collection, as of laws or writings of a specified type. 3. the main body or substance of anything.
**Cor·pus Chris·ti** (kôr′pəs kris′ti; *also, for 1,* kris′tī), [L., Body of Christ], 1. in the *R.C. Church*, a festival celebrated on the Thursday after Trinity Sunday, in honor of the Eucharist. 2. a city on the coast of SE Texas: pop., 168,000.
**cor·pus·cle** (kôr′pəs-'l, -pus-'l), *n.* [< L. dim. of *corpus*, body], 1. a very small particle. 2. in *anatomy*, a protoplasmic particle with a special function; esp., any of the red cells (*erythrocytes*) or white cells (*leucocytes*) in the blood, lymph, etc. of vertebrates. —**cor·pus′cu·lar** (-pus′kyoo-lēr), *adj.*
**corpus de·lic·ti** (di-lik′tī), [L., lit., body of the crime], 1. the facts constituting or proving a crime. 2. loosely, the body of a murder victim.
**corpus ju·ris** (joor′is), [L., body of law], a collection of all the laws of a nation or district.
**corr.,** 1. corrected. 2. correspondence.
**cor·ral** (kə-ral′), *n.* [Sp. < *corro*, ring < L. *currere*, to run], an enclosure for holding or capturing horses, cattle, etc.; pen; stockade. *v.t.* [-RALLED, -RALLING], 1. to drive into or confine in a corral. 2. to surround or capture; round up. 3. [Slang], to take possession of.
**cor·rect** (kə-rekt′), *v.t.* [< L. *correctus*, pp. of *corrigere* < *com-*, together + *regere*, to lead straight], 1. to make right; change from wrong to right. 2. to mark the errors or faults of. 3. to make conform with a standard. 4. to scold or punish for the purpose of overcoming faults. 5. to cure or counteract (a fault, disease, etc.). *adj.* 1. conforming with a conventional standard. 2. conforming with fact or logic; true; accurate; right. —**cor·rect′ly,** *adv.* —**cor·rect′ness,** *n.* —**cor·rec′tor,** *n.*
**cor·rec·tion** (kə-rek′shən), *n.* 1. a correcting or being corrected. 2. something substituted for a mistake; rectification. 3. punishment or scolding to correct faults. —**cor·rec′tion·al,** *adj.*
**cor·rec·tive** (kə-rek′tiv), *adj.* tending or intended to correct or improve; remedial. *n.* something corrective; remedy. —**cor·rec′tive·ly,** *adv.*
**Cor·reg·gio** (kôr-red′jô; Eng. kə-rej′ō, -i-ō′), *n.* (*Antonio Allegri da Correggio*), Italian painter; lived 1494–1534.
**cor·re·late** (kôr′ə-lāt′, kor′-), *n.* [*cor-* + *relate*], either of two closely related things. *adj.* closely and naturally related. *v.i.* [-LATED, -LATING], to be mutually related (*to* or *with*). *v.t.* to bring (one thing) into mutual relation (*with* another).
**cor·re·la·tion** (kôr′ə-lā′shən, kor′-), *n.* 1. a close or mutual relation. 2. a correlating or being correlated.
**cor·rel·a·tive** (kə-rel′ə-tiv), *adj.* 1. having a mutual relation; reciprocally dependent. 2. in *grammar*, expressing mutual relation and used in pairs: as, *both . . . and* and *neither . . . nor* are *correlative* conjunctions. *n.* 1. a correlate. 2. a correlative word. —**cor·rel′a·tive·ly,** *adv.* —**cor·rel′a·tiv′i·ty,** *n.*
**cor·re·spond** (kôr′ə-spond′, kor′-), *v.i.* [< Fr. < ML. < L. *com-*, together + *respondere*, to answer], 1. to be in agreement (*with* something); be congruent (*to* something); match. 2. to be similar, analogous, or equal (*to* something). 3. to communicate (*with* someone) by letters. —**cor′re·spond′ing,** *adj.* —**cor′re·spond′ing·ly,** *adv.*
**cor·re·spond·ence** (kôr′ə-spon′dəns, kor′-), *n.* 1. agreement; conformity. 2. similarity; analogy. 3. communication by exchange of letters. 4. the quantity of letters normally received or written. Also **cor′re·spond′en·cy** [*pl.* -CIES].
**correspondence school,** a school that gives in-

struction in a subject (**correspondence course**) by mail.

**cor·re·spond·ent** (kôr′ə-spon′dənt, kor′-), *adj.* corresponding. *n.* 1. a thing that corresponds. 2. one who exchanges letters with another. 3. one hired as by a newspaper to furnish news regularly from a certain place. —**cor′re·spond′ent·ly,** *adv.*

**cor·ri·dor** (kôr′ə-dēr, kor′-, -dôr′), *n.* [Fr. < It. < L. *currere,* to run], 1. a long passageway or hall. 2. a strip of land forming a passageway between two parts of a country, or between an inland country and a seaport.

**cor·ri·gen·dum** (kôr′i-jen′dəm, kor′-), *n.* [*pl.* -DA (-də)], [L., gerundive of *corrigere;* see CORRECT], an error to be corrected in a manuscript or book.

**cor·ri·gi·ble** (kôr′i-jə-b'l, kor′-), *adj.* [Fr. < L. *corrigere;* see CORRECT], 1. that can be corrected. 2. willing to be reformed. —**cor′ri·gi·bil′i·ty,** *n.* —**cor′ri·gi·bly,** *adv.*

**cor·rob·o·rate** (kə-rob′ə-rāt′), *v.t.* [-RATED, -RATING], [< L. < *com-,* intens. + *roborare* < *robur,* strength], to strengthen; confirm; support. —**cor·rob′o·ra′tion,** *n.* —**cor·rob′o·ra′tor,** *n.*

**cor·rob·o·ra·tive** (kə-rob′ə-rā′tiv, -ēr-ə-tiv), *adj.* corroborating; confirmatory: also **cor·rob′o·ra·to′·ry** (-ə-tôr′i, -tō′ri), **cor·rob′o·rant** (-rənt). —**cor·rob′o·ra′tive·ly,** *adv.*

**cor·rode** (kə-rōd′), *v.t.* [-RODED, -RODING], [< Fr. < L. < *com-,* intens. + *rodere,* to gnaw], to wear away gradually, as by the action of chemicals; rust. *v.i.* to become corroded. —**cor·rod′i·ble,** *adj.*

**cor·ro·sion** (kə-rō′zhən), *n.* 1. a corroding or being corroded. 2. a substance formed by corroding.

**cor·ro·sive** (kə-rō′siv), *adj.* [< OFr.], corroding or causing corrosion. *n.* something causing corrosion. —**cor·ro′sive·ly,** *adv.* —**cor·ro′sive·ness,** *n.*

**corrosive sublimate,** bichloride of mercury.

**cor·ru·gate** (kôr′ə-gāt′, kor′yoo-), *v.t.* & *v.i.* [-GATED, -GATING], [< L. < *com-,* intens. + *rugare,* to wrinkle], to shape or contract into folds; make wrinkles in; furrow. *adj.* (-git), corrugated.

**cor·ru·gat·ed** (kôr′ə-gāt′id, kor′yoo-), *adj.* folded or shaped into parallel ridges and furrows so as to form a wavy surface.

**cor·ru·ga·tion** (kôr′ə-gā′shən, kor′yoo-), *n.* 1. a corrugating or being corrugated. 2. any of a series of parallel folds, ridges, or furrows.

**cor·rupt** (kə-rupt′), *adj.* [OFr. < L. *corruptus,* pp. < *com-,* together + *rumpere,* to break in pieces], 1. spoiled; rotten. 2. morally debased; evil; depraved. 3. taking bribes. 4. containing alterations, foreign admixtures, or errors: as, a *corrupt* text. *v.t.* & *v.i.* to make or become corrupt. —**cor·rupt′er,** *n.* —**cor·rupt′ing·ly,** *adv.* —**cor·rupt′ive,** *adj.* —**cor·rupt′ly,** *adv.* —**cor·rupt′ness,** *n.*

**cor·rupt·i·ble** (kə-rup′tə-b'l), *adj.* that can be corrupted; specif., *a*) that can be bribed. *b*) liable to decay. —**cor·rupt′i·bil′i·ty, cor·rupt′i·ble·ness,** *n.* —**cor·rupt′i·bly,** *adv.*

**cor·rup·tion** (kə-rup′shən), *n.* 1. a making, becoming, or being corrupt. 2. depravity. 3. bribery. 4. decay. 5. a thing or influence that corrupts.

**cor·sage** (kôr-säzh′), *n.* [see CORPS & -AGE], 1. the bodice of a dress. 2. a small bouquet for a woman to wear, usually at the waist or shoulder.

**cor·sair** (kôr′sâr), *n.* [Fr. < ML. *cursarius* < *cursus,* a raid (< L., a run)], 1. a privateer. 2. a pirate. 3. a pirate ship.

**corse** (kôrs), *n.* [Archaic & Poetic], a corpse.

**corse·let** (kôrs′lit), *n.* [see CORSET], 1. armor for the body, worn in medieval times: also **cors′let.** 2. (kôr′s'l-et′), a woman's lightweight corset.

**cor·set** (kôr′sit), *n.* [Fr., dim. of OFr. *cors;* see CORPS], *sometimes pl.* a close-fitting undergarment, often reinforced with stays, worn, chiefly by women, to give support to or shape the torso. *v.t.* to dress in a corset; fit a corset on.

**Cor·si·ca** (kôr′si-kə), *n.* a French island in the Mediterranean, north of Sardinia: area, 3,367 sq. mi; capital, Ajaccio. —**Cor′si·can,** *adj.* & *n.*

**cor·tege** (kôr-tāzh′, -tezh′), *n.* [< Fr. < It. *corteggio* < *corte* < L.; see COURT], 1. a number of followers or attendants; retinue. 2. a ceremonial procession.

‡**cor·tège** (kôr′tezh′), *n.* [Fr.], a cortege.

**Cor·tés** (or **Cor·tez**), **Her·nan·do** (er-nän′dô kôr-tes′; Eng. kôr′tez), 1485–1547; Spanish soldier and explorer; conqueror of Mexico.

**cor·tex** (kôr′teks), *n.* [*pl.* -TICES (-ti-sēz′)], [L., bark of a tree], 1. in *anatomy,* the outer part of an internal organ, as of the kidney; esp., the layer of gray matter over most of the brain. 2. in *botany,* the bark or rind. —**cor′ti·cal** (-ti-k'l), *adj.* —**cor′ti·cal·ly,** *adv.*

**cor·ti·cate** (kôr′ti-kit, -kāt′), *adj.* [< LL. < L. *cortex,* bark], covered with bark. Also **cor′ti·ca′ted, cor′ti·cose′** (-kōs′), **cor′ti·cous** (-kəs).

**cor·ti·sone** (kôr′tə-sōn′, -zōn′), *n.* [< *cortico*sterone], an adrenal-gland hormone extracted from ox bile or prepared synthetically, used in the treatment of rheumatoid arthritis and certain other diseases.

**co·run·dum** (kə-run′dəm), *n.* [Tamil *kurundam* < Sans. *kuruvinda,* ruby], a very hard mineral, aluminum oxide, $Al_2O_3$, used for grinding and polishing: the ruby, sapphire, etc. are precious varieties.

**cor·us·cate** (kôr′əs-kāt′, kor′-), *v.i.* [-CATED, -CATING], [< L. < *coruscare,* to glitter < *coruscus,* vibrating], to emit flashes of light; sparkle. —**co·rus·cant** (kə-rus′kənt), *adj.* —**cor′us·ca′tion,** *n.*

**cor·vette, cor·vet** (kôr-vet′), *n.* [Fr. < Port. < L. *corbita* (*navis*), cargo (ship) < *corbis,* basket], 1. formerly, a sailing warship smaller than a frigate, with one tier of guns. 2. a small, fast warship used for anti-submarine and convoy duty.

**cor·vine** (kôr′vīn, -vin), *adj.* [< L. < *corvus,* a raven], of or like a crow or raven.

**Cor·y·bant** (kôr′ə-bant′, kor′-), *n.* [*pl.* -BANTS, -BANTES (kôr′ə-ban′tēz, kor′-)], 1. in *Gr. mythology, a*) an attendant of the goddess Cybele at her revelries. *b*) a priest of Cybele. 2. [c-], a frenzied reveler. —**Cor′y·ban′tic, Cor′y·ban′tian,** *adj.*

**cor·ymb** (kôr′imb, kor′im), *n.* [L. *corymbus,* flower cluster < Gr. *korymbos*], a broad, flat cluster of flowers in which the outer stems are long and those toward the center progressively shorter. —**co·rym·bose** (kə-rim′bōs), **co·rym′bous** (-bəs), *adj.*

CORYMB

**co·ry·za** (kə-rī′zə), *n.* [< LL. < Gr. *koryza,* catarrh], a cold in the head; acute nasal catarrh.

**cos,** cosine.

**Cos., cos.,** 1. companies. 2. counties.

**cose** (kōz), *v.i.* [COSED, COSING], & *n.* coze.

**co·se·cant** (kō-sē′kənt), *n.* in *trigonometry,* the secant of the complement of an angle or arc: abbrev. **cosec, csc** (no period).

**co·sey, co·sie** (kō′zi), *adj.* & *n.* cozy.

**co·sig·na·to·ry** (kō-sig′nə-tôr′i, -tō′ri), *adj.* signing jointly. *n.* [*pl.* -RIES], one of two or more joint signers.

**co·sine** (kō′sīn′), *n.* in *trigonometry,* the sine of the complement of an angle or arc: abbrev. **cos** (no period).

**cos·met·ic** (koz-met′ik), *adj.* [< Gr. *kosmētikos,* skilled in arranging < *kosmos,* order], beautifying or designed to beautify. *n.* any such preparation for application to the skin, hair, etc. —**cos·met′i·cal·ly,** *adv.*

**cos·mic** (koz′mik), *adj.* [Gr. *kosmikos* < *kosmos,* order], 1. of the cosmos; relating to the universe as a whole. 2. vast. —**cos′mi·cal·ly,** *adv.*

**cosmic dust,** small particles falling from interstellar space to the earth.

**cosmic rays,** rays of extremely short wave length and great penetrating power, which bombard the earth from beyond its atmosphere.

**cos·mo-,** [see COSMOS], a combining form meaning *world, universe:* also, before a vowel, **cosm-.**

**cos·mog·o·ny** (koz-mog′ə-ni), *n.* [*pl.* -NIES], [< Gr. < *kosmos,* universe + *gignesthai,* to produce], 1. the origin of the universe. 2. a theory or account of this. —**cos·mo·gon′ic** (-mə-gon′ik), **cos′mo·gon′i·cal, cos·mog′o·nal,** *adj.*

**cos·mog·ra·phy** (koz-mog′rə-fi), *n.* [< Gr.; see COSMOS & -GRAPHY], the science dealing with the structure of the universe as a whole and of its related parts. —**cos·mog′ra·pher,** *n.* —**cos′mo·graph′·ic** (-mə-graf′ik), **cos′mo·graph′i·cal,** *adj.*

**cos·mol·o·gy** (koz-mol′ə-ji), *n.* [*cosmo-* + *-logy*], theory or philosophy of the nature and principles of the universe. —**cos′mo·log′i·cal** (-mə-loj′i-k'l), *adj.* —**cos·mol′o·gist,** *n.*

**cos·mo·naut** (koz′mə-nôt), *n.* [< Russ.], an astronaut.

**cos·mo·pol·i·tan** (koz′mə-pol′ə-t'n), *adj.* [*cosmopolite* + *-an*], 1. belonging to the whole world; not local. 2. not bound by local or national prejudices; at home in all countries or places. *n.* a cosmopolitan person. —**cos′mo·pol′i·tan·ism,** *n.*

**cos·mop·o·lite** (koz-mop'ə-līt'), *n.* [< Gr. < *kosmos*, world + *politēs*, citizen < *polis*, city], 1. a cosmopolitan person. 2. a plant or animal common to all or most parts of the world.

**cos·mos** (koz'məs, -mos), *n.* [Gr. *kosmos*, world, order], 1. the universe considered as a harmonious and orderly system. 2. any complete and orderly system. 3. a tall plant of the composite family, with white, pink, or purple flowers.

**Cos·sack** (kos'ak, -ək), *n.* [Russ. *kozak*], a member of a people of the S Soviet Union, famous as horsemen. *adj.* of or characteristic of the Cossacks.

**cos·set** (kos'it), *n.* [early form *cozez* suggests AS. *cot-sæta*, cot dweller], 1. a pet lamb. 2. any pet. *v.t.* to make a pet of; pamper.

**cost** (kôst), *v.i.* [COST, COSTING], [< OFr. < LL. *costare* < L. < *com-*, together + *stare*, to stand], 1. to be obtained or obtainable for (a certain price). 2. to require the expenditure, loss, or experience of. *v.t.* in *business*, to estimate the cost of producing. *n.* 1. the amount of money, time, labor, etc. required to get a thing; price. 2. loss; sacrifice. 3. *pl.* in *law*, the court expenses of a lawsuit. —**at all costs**, by any means required: also **at any cost.**

**cos·tal** (kos't'l), *adj.* [Fr. < ML. < L. *costa*, a rib], of or near a rib or the ribs.

**Cos·ta Ri·ca** (kos'tə rē'kə, kôs'-), a country in Central America: area, 23,000 sq. mi.; pop., 1,173,000; capital, San José. —**Cos'ta Ri'can.**

**cos·ter·mon·ger** (kos'tēr-muŋ'gēr, kôs'-), *n.* [< *costard*, a kind of apple + *monger*], [Brit.], a person who sells fruit, vegetables, etc. from a cart or street stand: also **cos'ter.**

**cos·tive** (kos'tiv, kôs'-), *adj.* [< OFr. < L. *constipatus*], constipated. —**cos'tive·ly**, *adv.* —**cos'tive·ness**, *n.*

**cost·ly** (kôst'li), *adj.* [-LIER, -LIEST], 1. costing much; expensive; dear. 2. very valuable; magnificent; sumptuous. —**cost'li·ness**, *n.*

**cost of living**, the average cost of the necessities of life, as food, shelter, and clothes.

**cos·tume** (kos'to͞om, -tūm), *n.* [Fr. < OIt. < L. *consuetudo*, custom], 1. style of dress in general, including style of hair, etc. 2. the style of dress typical of a certain period, people, etc., as worn in a play. 3. a complete set of outer clothes. *v.t.* (kos-to͞om', -tūm'), [-TUMED, -TUMING], to provide with a costume.

**cos·tum·er** (kos-to͞om'ēr, -tūm'-), *n.* one whose work is making, selling, or renting costumes, as for theaters, balls, etc.: also **cos·tum'i·er** (-i-ēr).

**co·sy** (kō'zi), *adj.* [-SIER, -SIEST], & *n.* [*pl.* -SIES], cozy. —**co'si·ly**, *adv.* —**co'si·ness**, *n.*

**cot** (kot), *n.* [< Hind. *khāṭ* < Sans.], a narrow bed, especially one made of canvas on a folding frame.

**cot** (kot), *n.* [AS.], 1. [Poetic], a cottage. 2. a cote. 3. a sheath, as for a hurt finger.

**co·tan·gent** (kō-tan'jənt), *n.* in *trigonometry*, the tangent of the complement of an angle or arc: abbrev. **cot, ctn** (no period). —**co·tan·gen·tia** (kō'tan-jen'shəl), *adj.* 1

**cote** (kōt), *n.* [AS., cottage], 1. a small shelter or shed for birds, sheep, etc. 2. [Dial.], a cottage.

**co·tem·po·rar·y** (kō-tem'pə-rer'i), *adj.* & *n.* contemporary. —**co·tem'po·ra'ne·ous** (-rā'ni-əs), *adj.*

**co·ten·ant** (kō-ten'ənt), *n.* one of two or more tenants who share a place. —**co·ten'an·cy**, *n.*

**co·te·rie** (kō'tēr-i, -tə-rē'), *n.* [Fr., orig., organization of feudal tenants < *cote*, hut < MD. *kote*], a group of people who often gather for social purposes; social circle or set; clique.

**co·ter·mi·nous** (kō-tūr'mə-nəs), *adj.* conterminous.

**co·til·lion** (kō-til'yən, kə-), *n.* [Fr. *cotillon*, a petticoat < OFr. *cote*, a coat], 1. a lively dance of the 19th century, with many intricate figures and the continual changing of partners. 2. the music for this dance. Also sp. **co·til'lon.**

**cot·tage** (kot'ij), *n.* [< Anglo-Fr. < OFr. *cote*, a hut], 1. a small house. 2. a house, as at a resort, used for vacations or as a summer home.

**cottage cheese**, a soft, white cheese made by straining and seasoning the curds of sour milk.

**cottage pudding**, cake covered with a sweet sauce.

**cot·tag·er** (kot'ij-ēr), *n.* 1. a person who lives in a cottage. 2. [Brit.], a farm laborer.

**cot·ter, cot·tar** (kot'ēr), *n.* 1. a cottager. 2. [Scot.], a tenant farmer.

**cot·ter** (kot'ēr), *n.* [apparently < LG.; cf. MLG. *kote*, claw, joint, die], 1. a bolt or wedge put through a slot to hold together parts of machinery. 2. a cotter pin.

**cotter pin**, a split pin used as a cotter, fastened in place by spreading apart its ends after it is inserted.

COTTER PIN

**cot·ton** (kot''n), *n.* [< OSp. < Ar. *quṭun*], 1. the soft, white, fibrous matter around the seeds of various plants of the mallow family. 2. a plant or plants producing this material. 3. the crop of such plants. 4. thread or cloth made of cotton. *adj.* of cotton. —**cotton (up) to**, [Colloq.], 1. to agree with; be in harmony with. 2. to begin to like; become attached to. —**cot'ton·y**, *adj.*

**cotton batting**, thin, pressed layers of fluffy, absorbent cotton, for surgical dressing, etc.

**Cotton Belt**, the region in the South, from the east coast through Texas, where much cotton is grown.

**cotton flannel**, a strong cotton cloth with a long, fleecy nap: also called *Canton flannel.*

**cotton gin**, [see GIN (snare)], a machine for separating cotton fibers from the seeds.

**cot·ton·mouth** (kot''n-mouth'), *n.* [from its whitish mouth], water moccasin (sense 1).

**cot·ton·seed** (kot''n-sēd'), *n.* the seed of the cotton plant: also **cotton-seed, cotton seed.**

**cottonseed oil**, an oil pressed from cottonseed, used to make shortening, soap, etc.

**cot·ton·tail** (kot''n-tāl'), *n.* a common American rabbit with a short, fluffy tail.

**cot·ton·wood** (kot''n-wood'), *n.* 1. a poplar that has seeds covered with cottony hairs. 2. its wood.

**cotton wool**, raw cotton or cotton batting.

**cot·y·le·don** (kot''l-ē'd'n), *n.* [< L. < Gr. < *kotylē*, a cavity], a seed leaf; earliest leaf or one of the earliest leaves growing out of a seed. —**cot'y·le'don·al**, *adj.* —**cot'y·le'don·ous**, *adj.*

**couch** (kouch), *n.* [< OFr. *coucher*, to lie down < L. < *com-*, together + *locare*, to place], 1. an article of furniture on which one may lie down; sofa; divan. 2. any resting place. *v.t.* 1. to lay as on a couch. 2. to bring down; esp., to lower (a spear, etc.) to an attacking position. 3. to put in words; state. *v.i.* 1. to lie down on a bed; recline. 2. to wait in ambush to attack. —**couch'er**, *n.*

**couch·ant** (kouch'ənt), *adj.* [< Fr. ppr. of *coucher;* see COUCH], in *heraldry*, lying down or crouching, but keeping the head up: as, a lion *couchant.*

**couch grass**, any of several coarse grasses that spread rapidly by creeping stems.

**cou·gar** (ko͞o'gēr), *n.* [*pl.* -GARS, -GAR; see PLURAL, II, D, 1], [< Fr. < Tupi *suguarana* < *suusú*, deer + *rana*, false], a tawny-brown animal of the cat family, with a long, slender body: also called *puma, mountain lion, panther.*

**cough** (kôf), *v.i.* [ME. *coughen;* akin to AS. *cohhetan*], to expel air suddenly and noisily from the lungs through the glottis. *v.t.* to expel by coughing. *n.* 1. a coughing. 2. a diseased state of the lungs or throat, causing frequent coughing. —**cough up**, 1. to bring up (phlegm, etc.) by coughing. 2. [Slang], to hand over (money, etc.).

**cough drop**, a small medicated tablet for the relief of coughs, hoarseness, etc.

**could** (kood), 1. pt. of **can.** 2. an auxiliary with present or future sense, generally equivalent to *can* in meaning and use, expressing especially a shade of doubt or a smaller degree of possibility (e.g., it *could* be so).

**could·n't** (kood''nt), could not.

**couldst** (koodst), [Archaic or Poetic], 2d person sing., past indicative, of **can.**

**cou·lee** (ko͞o'li), *n.* [< Fr. < *couler*, to flow], 1. a stream or sheet of lava. 2. a deep gulch or ravine, usually dry in summer.

**cou·lomb** (ko͞o-lom'), *n.* [after C.A. de *Coulomb* (1736–1806), Fr. physicist], a unit for measuring the quantity of an electric current; amount of electricity provided by a current of one ampere flowing for one second: symbol, C (no period).

**coul·ter** (kōl'tēr), *n.* a colter.

**coun·cil** (koun's'l), *n.* [< OFr. < L. *concilium*, meeting < *com-*, with + base of *calare*, to call together], 1. a group of people called together for discussion, advice, etc. 2. a group of people chosen as an administrative or legislative assembly. 3. the legislative body of a city or town. 4. a church assembly to discuss points of doctrine, etc.

**coun·cil·man** (koun's'l-mən), *n.* [*pl.* -MEN], a member of a council, especially of a city or town.

**coun·ci·lor, coun·cil·lor** (koun's'l-ēr), *n.* [< *counselor*], a member of a council. —**coun'ci·lor·ship', coun'cil·lor·ship'**, *n.*

**coun·sel** (koun's'l), *n.* [< OFr. < L. *consilium* < *com-*, together + hyp. base *sel-*, take], 1. mutual exchange of ideas, opinions, etc.; discussion. 2. *a*) advice resulting from such an exchange. *b*) any advice. 3. a plan; resolution. 4. one giving legal advice; lawyer or group of lawyers. *v.t.* [-SELED or -SELLED, -SELING or -SELLING], 1. to give advice to; advise. 2. to recommend (an action, plan, etc.). *v.i.* to discuss and deliberate; give or take advice. —**keep one's own counsel,** to be silent. —**take counsel,** to discuss together.

**coun·se·lor, coun·sel·lor** (koun′s'l-ẽr), *n.* 1. a person who counsels; adviser. 2. a lawyer; esp., one who conducts cases in court: in full, **counselor-at-law.** —**coun′se·lor·ship′, coun′sel·lor·ship′,** *n.*

**count** (kount), *v.t.* [< OFr. < L. *computare;* see COMPUTE], 1. to name numbers in regular order to (a certain number): as, I'll *count* five. 2. to name, unit by unit, to reach a total; add. 3. to check by numbering off; inventory. 4. to take account of; include. 5. to consider; believe to be: as, I *count* him lucky. *v.i.* 1. to name numbers or things in order. 2. to be included in counting; be taken into account. 3. to have importance, weight, etc. *n.* 1. a counting, or adding up. 2. the number reached by counting; total quantity. 3. a reckoning; accounting. 4. in *boxing,* ten seconds counted to give a fallen boxer time to rise before he loses the match. 5. in *law,* any of the charges in an indictment, each of which is alone sufficient for prosecution. —**count for,** to be worth. —**count in,** to include. —**count off,** to separate into equal divisions by counting. —**count on** (or **upon**), to rely on. —**count out,** 1. to disregard; omit. 2. [Colloq.], to keep (a candidate) from office by counting the ballots incorrectly. 3. in *boxing,* to declare (a boxer) defeated when he has remained down for a count of ten. —**count′a·ble,** *adj.*

**count** (kount), *n.* [< OFr. < L. *comes,* companion < *com-,* with + *ire,* to go], a European nobleman equal in rank to an earl in England.

**count·down, count-down** (kount′doun′), *n.* the schedule for preparing to fire a rocket, detonate a nuclear blast, etc.: it is counted off in units of time going down to zero.

**coun·te·nance** (koun′tə-nəns), *n.* [< OFr. < L. *continentia,* bearing; ult. < *com-,* together + *tenere,* to hold], 1. the expression of the face. 2. the face; facial features; visage. 3. a look of approval. 4. approval; support. 5. composure; calm control. *v.t.* [-NANCED, -NANCING], to approve; give support to. —**in countenance,** calm; composed. —**keep one's countenance,** to keep calm. —**put out of countenance,** to disconcert. —**coun′te·nanc·er,** *n.*

**count·er** (koun′tẽr), *n.* [< OFr. < L. *computare;* see COMPUTE], 1. a small device of metal, wood, etc. for keeping count, especially for keeping score in some games. 2. an imitation coin. 3. a long board or table in a store, on which goods are displayed, wrapped, etc.; also, a similar table in a restaurant, etc. 4. a person or thing that counts; computer. —**under the counter,** in a surreptitious manner: said of merchandise sold illegally.

**coun·ter** (koun′tẽr), *adv.* [< Fr. < L. *contra,* against], in a contrary direction, manner, etc.; opposite to. *adj.* contrary; opposed. *n.* 1. the opposite; contrary. 2. a stiff leather piece around the heel of a shoe. 3. the part of a ship's stern between the water line and the curved part. 4. in *boxing, a*) a blow given while parrying an opponent's blow. *b*) the act of giving such a blow. *v.t. & v.i.* 1. to act, do, move, etc. counter to (a person or thing); oppose. 2. in *boxing,* to strike one's opponent while parrying (his blow).

**coun·ter** (koun′tẽr), *n. & v.t.* [Archaic], encounter.

**coun·ter-,** [see COUNTER, *adv.*], a combining form meaning: 1. *opposite, contrary to,* as in *counterclockwise.* 2. *in retaliation,* as in *counterplot.* 3. *complementary,* as in *counterpart.*

**coun·ter·act** (koun′tẽr-akt′), *v.t.* to act against; neutralize the effect of with opposing action. —**coun′ter·ac′tion,** *n.* —**coun′ter·ac′tive,** *adj. & n.*

**coun·ter·at·tack** (koun′tẽr-ə-tak′; *for v., usually* koun′tẽr-ə-tak′), *n.* an attack made in opposition to another attack. *v.t. & v.i.* to attack so as to offset the enemy's attack.

**coun·ter·bal·ance** (koun′tẽr-bal′əns; *for v.,* koun′-tẽr-bal′əns), *n.* 1. a weight used to balance another weight. 2. any force or influence that balances or offsets another. *v.t. & v.i.* [-ANCED, -ANCING], to be a counterbalance (to); offset.

**coun·ter·claim** (koun′tẽr-klām′; *for v., usually* koun′tẽr-klām′), *n.* an opposing claim to offset another. *v.t. & v.i.* to make a counterclaim (of). —**coun′ter·claim′ant** (-ənt), *n.*

**coun·ter·clock·wise** (koun′tẽr-klok′wīz′), *adj. & adv.* in a direction opposite to that in which the hands of a clock move.

**coun·ter·es·pi·on·age** (koun′tẽr-es′pi-ə-nij), *n.* actions to prevent or thwart enemy espionage.

**coun·ter·feit** (koun′tẽr-fit), *adj.* [< OFr. pp. of *contrefaire,* to imitate; *contre-,* counter + *faire* (< L. *facere*), to make], 1. made in imitation of something genuine with intention to defraud; forged: as, *counterfeit* money. 2. pretended; feigned; sham. *n.* an imitation made to deceive. *v.t. & v.i.* 1. to make an imitation of (money, pictures, etc.) in order to defraud. 2. to pretend. 3. to resemble or make resemble. —**coun′ter·feit′er,** *n.*

**coun·ter·foil** (koun′tẽr-foil′), *n.* [*counter-* + *foil* (a leaf)], the part of a check, receipt, etc. kept by the issuer as a record.

**coun·ter·ir·ri·tant** (koun′tẽr-ir′ə-tənt), *n.* anything used to produce a slight irritation to relieve more serious irritation elsewhere.

**coun·ter·man** (koun′tẽr-mən), *n.* [*pl.* -MEN], one whose work is serving customers at the counter of a lunchroom.

**coun·ter·mand** (koun′tẽr-mand′, -mänd′; *also, and for n. always,* koun′tẽr-mand′, -mänd′), *v.t.* [< Fr. < L. *contra,* opposite + *mandare,* to command], 1. to cancel or revoke (a command or order). 2. to call back or order back by a contrary order. *n.* a command or order canceling another. —**coun′ter-mand′a·ble,** *adj.*

**coun·ter·march** (koun′tẽr-märch′; *for v., usually* koun′tẽr-märch′), *n.* a march back or in the opposite direction. *v.i. & v.t.* to march back.

**coun·ter·move** (koun′tẽr-mo͞ov′; *for v.,* koun′tẽr-mo͞ov′), *n.* a move made in opposition or retaliation. *v.i. & v.t.* [-MOVED, -MOVING], to move in opposition or retaliation.

**coun·ter·of·fen·sive** (koun′tẽr-ə-fen′siv, koun′-tẽr-ə-fen′siv), *n.* an attack in force by troops who have been defending a position.

**coun·ter·pane** (koun′tẽr-pān′), *n.* [altered < *counterpoint,* quilt < OFr. < L. *culcita puncta,* pricked (i.e., embroidered) quilt], a bedspread; coverlet.

**coun·ter·part** (koun′tẽr-pärt′), *n.* 1. a person or thing that corresponds to or closely resembles another. 2. a thing that completes or complements another. 3. [Obs.], a copy; duplicate.

**coun·ter·plot** (koun′tẽr-plot′), *n.* a plot to defeat another plot. *v.t. & v.i.* (*also* koun′tẽr-plot′), [-PLOTTED, -PLOTTING], to plot against (a plot); defeat (a plot) with another plot.

**coun·ter·point** (koun′tẽr-point′), *n.* [< Fr. < It. *contrappunto,* lit., pointed against; see COUNTER- & POINT, *n.*], 1. a melody accompanying another melody note for note. 2. the art of adding related but independent melodies to a basic melody, in accordance with the fixed rules of harmony. 3. this kind of composition.

**coun·ter·poise** (koun′tẽr-poiz′), *n.* [< ONorm.Fr.; see COUNTER, *adv.* & POISE, *n.*], 1. a weight that balances another. 2. a force, influence, etc. that balances or neutralizes another. 3. a state of balance or equilibrium. *v.t. & v.i.* [-POISED, -POISING], to be a counterpoise (to).

**Counter Reformation,** the reform movement in the Roman Catholic Church in the 16th century, following the Protestant Reformation.

**coun·ter·rev·o·lu·tion** (koun′tẽr-rev′ə-lo͞o′shən), *n.* 1. a political movement or revolution against a government or social system set up by a previous revolution. 2. a movement to combat revolutionary tendencies. —**coun′ter·rev′o·lu′tion·ar·y,** *adj. & n.* —**coun′ter·rev′o·lu′tion·ist,** *n.*

**coun·ter·shaft** (koun′tẽr-shaft′, -shäft′), *n.* an intermediate shaft that transmits motion from the main shaft of a machine to a working part.

**coun·ter·sign** (koun′tẽr-sīn′; *also, for v.,* koun′-tẽr-sīn′), *n.* 1. a signature added to a previously signed piece of writing in order to confirm it. 2. in *military usage,* a secret word or signal which must be given to a sentry by someone wishing to pass. *v.t.* to confirm (a previously signed piece of writing) by signing. —**coun′ter·sig′na·ture** (-sig′nə-chẽr), *n.*

**coun·ter·sink** (koun′tẽr-siŋk′; *also, for v.,* koun′-tẽr-siŋk′), *v.t.* [-SUNK, -SINKING], 1. to enlarge the top part of (a hole in metal, wood, etc.) so that it will receive the head of a bolt, screw, etc. 2. to sink (a bolt, screw, etc.) into such a hole. *n.* 1. a tool for countersinking holes. 2. a countersunk hole.

**coun·ter·tend·en·cy** (koun'tẽr-ten'dən-si), *n.* [*pl.* -CIES], an opposing tendency.

**coun·ter·vail** (koun'tẽr-vāl', koun'tẽr-vāl'), [< OFr. < *contre* (see COUNTER, *adv.*) + *valoir*, to avail < L. *valere*, to be strong], 1. to have or use equal force against. 2. to compensate. 3. to counteract. *v.i.* to avail (*against*).

**coun·ter·weight** (koun'tẽr-wāt'), *n.* a weight equal to another. *v.t.* to counterbalance: also **coun'ter-weigh'** (-wā').

**counter word,** any word freely used as a general term of approval or disapproval without reference to its more exact meaning (e.g., *swell, nice*).

**count·ess** (koun'tis), *n.* 1. the wife or widow of a count or earl. 2. a noblewoman whose rank is equal to that of a count or earl.

**count·ing·house** (koun'tiŋ-hous'), *n.* a building or office in which a business firm keeps records, handles correspondence, etc.: also **counting room.**

**count·less** (kount'lis), *adj.* too many to count; innumerable; myriad.

**coun·tri·fied** (kun'tri-fīd'), *adj.* 1. rural; rustic. 2. having the appearance, actions, etc. attributed to country people. Also sp. **countryfied.**

**coun·try** (kun'tri), *n.* [*pl.* -TRIES], [< OFr. < LL. *contrata*, that which is beyond < L. *contra*, opposite], 1. an area; region: as, wooded *country*. 2. the whole territory of a nation. 3. the people of a nation. 4. the land of a person's birth or citizenship. 5. land with few houses; rural region. *adj.* 1. of, in, or from a rural district. 2. like the country; rustic.

**country club,** a club in the outskirts of a city equipped with a clubhouse, golf course, etc.

**coun·try-dance** (kun'tri-dans', -däns'), *n.* a folk dance, especially one in which the partners form two lines facing each other.

**coun·try·folk** (kun'tri-fōk'), *n.* rural people.

**country gentleman,** a man of some wealth who lives on a country estate.

**coun·try·man** (kun'tri-mən), *n.* [*pl.* -MEN], 1. a man who lives in the country; rustic. 2. a man of one's own country; compatriot. —**coun'try·wom'an** [*pl.* -WOMEN], *n.fem.*

**coun·try·seat** (kun'tri-sēt'), *n.* a rural estate.

**coun·try·side** (kun'tri-sīd'), *n.* 1. a rural region or district. 2. the people of such a district.

**coun·try-wide** (kun'tri-wīd'), *adj.* extending through an entire country or nation.

**coun·ty** (koun'ti), *n.* [*pl.* -TIES], [< OFr. < LL. *comitatus*, office of a count; see COUNT], 1. a small administrative district of a country; esp., *a*) a local administrative subdivision of a State. *b*) [Brit.], a shire considered as an administrative and judicial district. 2. the people living in a county. *adj.* of a county.

**county commissioner,** a member of the governing board in the counties of certain States.

**county seat,** a town or city that is the center of a county government: also **county town.**

**coup** (kōō), *n.* [*pl.* COUPS (kōōz)], [Fr. < LL. < L. *colaphus*, a blow < Gr. *kolaphos*], 1. literally, a blow. 2. a sudden, brilliant stroke or stratagem.

‡**coup de grâce** (kōō' də gräs'), [Fr., lit., stroke of mercy], 1. the blow, shot, etc. that brings death to a sufferer. 2. a finishing stroke.

‡**coup de main** (kōō' də man'), [Fr., lit., stroke of hand], a surprise attack or movement.

‡**coup d'é·tat** (kōō' dā'tȧ'), [Fr., lit., stroke of state], a sudden, forceful stroke in politics; esp., the sudden overthrow of a government.

**coupe** (kōōp; *now less often*, kōō-pā'), *n.* [see COUPÉ], a closed, two-door automobile that seats two to six people: also **coupé.**

**cou·pé** (kōō-pā'), *n.* [Fr.; pp. of *couper*, to cut], 1. a closed carriage seating two passengers, with a seat outside for the driver. 2. a coupe.

**cou·ple** (kup''l), *n.* [< OFr. < L. *copula;* see COPULA], 1. anything joining two things together; bond; link. 2. two things of the same sort that are joined together; pair. 3. a man and woman who are engaged, married, partners in a dance, etc. 4. [Colloq.], a few; several. *v.t.* [-PLED, -PLING], 1. to join together; link; connect. 2. to join in marriage. *v.i.* to pair.

**cou·pler** (kup'lẽr), *n.* a person or thing that couples; specif., *a*) a pneumatic device for coupling two railroad cars. *b*) in an organ, a device connecting two keyboards or keys an octave apart so that they can be played together.

**cou·plet** (kup'lit), *n.* [Fr. dim.; see COUPLE], 1. two successive lines of poetry, especially two of the same length that rhyme. 2. [Rare], a couple.

**cou·pling** (kup'liŋ), *n.* 1. a joining together. 2. a mechanical device for joining parts together. 3. a device for joining railroad cars. 4. a method or device for joining two electric circuits to transfer energy from one to the other.

COUPLING OF SHAFT

**cou·pon** (kōō'pon, kū'-), *n.* [Fr. < *couper*, to cut], 1. a detachable printed statement on a bond, specifying the interest due at a given time. 2. a certificate, sometimes given with a purchase, entitling one to a specified right, as redemption for cash or gifts. 3. a part of an advertisement that can be used to order goods, samples, etc.

**cour·age** (kũr'ij), *n.* [< OFr. < L. *cor*, heart], the quality of being fearless or brave; valor; pluck.

**cou·ra·geous** (kə-rā'jəs), *adj.* having or showing courage; brave. —**cou·ra'geous·ly,** *adv.*

**cou·ri·er** (koor'i-ẽr, kũr'-), *n.* [< OFr. < L. *currere*, to run], 1. a messenger sent in haste. 2. a person hired to accompany travelers and take care of hotel accommodations, luggage, etc.

**course** (kôrs, kōrs), *n.* [< Fr. *cours* < OFr. *c(o)urs;* also < Fr. *course* < It. *corsa;* both < L. *currere*], 1. an onward movement; progress. 2. a way, path, or channel: as, a race*course*, a golf *course*. 3. the direction taken: as, his *course* was due south. 4. a regular mode of action or behavior: as, the law must take its *course*. 5. a number of like things in some regular order; series. 6. natural development: as, the *course* of true love. 7. a part of a meal served at one time. 8. a continuous layer of bricks, wood, etc. on a building. 9. in *education*, *a*) a complete, progressive series of studies leading to graduation, a degree, etc. *b*) any of the studies. *v.t.* [COURSED, COURSING], 1. to pursue. 2. to cause to chase, as hounds in a hunt. 3. to traverse. *v.i.* 1. to run, chase, or race. 2. to hunt with hounds. —**a matter of course,** a regular or natural thing. —**in due course,** in the usual or proper sequence (of events). —**in the course of,** in the process of; during. —**of course,** 1. as was to be expected; naturally. 2. certainly.

**cours·er** (kôr'sẽr, kōr'-), *n.* [see COURSE], [Poetic], a swift, graceful, spirited horse.

**court** (kôrt, kōrt), *n.* [< OFr. < L. *cors, cortis*, contr. of *cohors;* see COHORT], 1. an uncovered space wholly or partly surrounded by buildings or walls. 2. a short street, often closed at one end. 3. an area for playing any of several ball games: as, a handball *court*. 4. a part of such an area. 5. formerly, a mansion with a large, uncovered entrance area. 6. a royal palace. 7. the family, advisers, etc. of a sovereign, as a group. 8. a sovereign and his councilors as a governing body. 9. any formal gathering held by a sovereign. 10. attention paid to someone in order to get something. 11. courtship; wooing. 12. in *law*, *a*) those appointed to try cases, make investigations, etc.; judge or judges. *b*) a place where trials are held, investigations made, etc. *c*) a judicial assembly. *d*) a regular session of the assembly. *v.t.* 1. to pay attention to (a person) in order to get something. 2. to try to get the love of; woo. 3. to try to get; seek: as, to *court* favor. *v.i.* to woo. *adj.* of or fit for a court. —**out of court,** without a trial. —**pay court to,** to court (*v.t.* 1 & 2).

**cour·te·ous** (kũr'ti-əs), *adj.* [OFr. *curteis* < *curt;* see COURT], polite and gracious; considerate of others. —**cour'te·ous·ly,** *adv.* —**cour'te·ous·ness,** *n.*

**cour·te·san, cour·te·zan** (kôr'tə-z'n, kōr'-, kũr'-), *n.* [< Fr. < It. *cortigiana*, court lady < *corte;* see COURT], a prostitute.

**cour·te·sy** (kũr'tə-si), *n.* [*pl.* -SIES], [< OFr. *curteisie;* see COURTEOUS], 1. courteous behavior; gracious politeness. 2. a polite or considerate act or remark. 3. favor; approval, as distinguished from legal right: as, a title of *courtesy*. 4. (kũrt'si), a curtsy.

**court·house** (kôrt'hous', kōrt'-), *n.* 1. a building in which law courts are held. 2. a building that houses the offices of a county government. Abbrev. **c.h.**

**cour·ti·er** (kôr'ti-ẽr, -tyẽr, kōr'-), *n.* 1. an attendant at a royal court. 2. a person who uses flattery to get something or to win favor.

**court·ly** (kôrt'li, kōrt'-), *adj.* [-LIER, -LIEST], 1. suitable for a king's court; dignified, elegant, etc. 2. flattering, especially in a servile way. *adv.* in a courtly manner. —**court'li·ness,** *n.*

**court-mar·tial** (kôrt′mär′shəl, kōrt′-), *n.* [*pl.* COURTS-MARTIAL], 1. a court of military or naval personnel to try offenses against military law. 2. [*pl.* now often COURT-MARTIALS], a trial by a court-martial. *v.t.* [-TIALED or -TIALLED, -TIALING or -TIALLING], to try by a court-martial.

**Court of St. James,** [< *St. James's* Palace, London], the British royal court.

**court plaster,** [from use by court ladies for beauty spots], cloth covered with an adhesive material, for protecting minor skin wounds.

**court·room** (kôrt′ro͞om′, kōrt′room′), *n.* a room in which a law court is held.

**court·ship** (kôrt′ship, kōrt′-), *n.* the act, process, or period of courting a woman.

**court tennis,** see **tennis.**

**court·yard** (kôrt′yärd′, kōrt′-), *n.* a space enclosed by walls, adjoining or in a large building.

**cous·in** (kuz′'n), *n.* [< OFr. < L. < *com-*, with + *sobrinus*, maternal cousin < *soror*, sister], 1. the son or daughter of one's uncle or aunt: also **cous′-in-ger′man** (-jũr′mən), **first** (or **full** or **own**) **cousin.** 2. loosely, any relative by blood or marriage. 3. a title of address used by one sovereign to another or to a nobleman. 4. [Slang], a rival who unwittingly advances one's interests. —**cous′in·ly,** *adj.* *& adv.* —**cous′in·ship′, cous′in·hood′,** *n.*

**cous·in·ry** (kuz′'n-ri), *n.* [*pl.* -RIES], cousins or other relatives, collectively.

‡**cou·tu·rier** (ko͞o′tü′ryā′), *n.* [Fr.], a man dressmaker. —**cou′tu′rière′** (-ryâr′), *n.fem.*

**cove** (kōv), *n.* [< AS. *cofa*, cave, cell], 1. a sheltered nook or recess, as in cliffs. 2. a small bay or inlet. *v.t. & v.i.* [COVED, COVING], to arch over or slope inward.

**cove** (kōv), *n.* [Gypsy *covo*, that man], [Brit. Slang], a boy or man; chap; fellow.

**cov·e·nant** (kuv′ə-nənt), *n.* [< OFr. < L. *convenire;* see CONVENE], 1. a binding agreement made by two or more individuals, parties, etc. to do or keep from doing a specified thing; compact. 2. [C-], the first section of the Treaty of Versailles (1919): it was the constitution of the League of Nations: in full, **Covenant of the League of Nations.** 3. in *law*, a formal, sealed contract. 4. in *theology*, the promises made by God to man, as recorded in the Bible. *v.i. & v.t.* to promise by or in a covenant. —**cov′e·nant·er, cov′e·nan·tor,** *n.*

**Cov·en·try** (kov′ən-tri, kuv′-), *n.* 1. a city in central England: pop., 286,000. 2. ostracism. —**send to Coventry,** to ostracize; refuse to speak to.

**cov·er** (kuv′ẽr), *v.t.* [< OFr. < L. < *co-*, intens. + *operire*, to hide], 1. to place something on, over, or in front of. 2. to extend over; lie upon. 3. to clothe. 4. to coat, sprinkle, etc. thickly. 5. to sit on (eggs); brood. 6. to conceal; hide. 7. to protect as by shielding. 8. to allow; provide for. 9. to protect financially: as, he will *cover* the loss with insurance. 10. to match (an opponent's stake) in a wager. 11. to travel over: as, to *cover* a distance. 12. to include; deal with: as, the book *covers* the subject thoroughly. 13. to point a firearm at. 14. in *journalism*, to get news, pictures, etc. of: as, to *cover* a train wreck. 15. in *sports*, to guard or defend (an opponent or area). *v.i.* 1. to overspread, as a liquid. 2. to put on a cap, hat, etc. *n.* 1. anything that covers, as a binding, lid, top, etc. 2. a shelter for protection, as from gunfire. 3. a tablecloth and setting for a meal, especially for one person. 4. a pretense. 5. an envelope with a newly issued stamp, postmarked with the date of issue. —**break cover,** to come out of hiding. —**cover up,** 1. to cover entirely. 2. to conceal. —**take cover,** to seek protective shelter. —**under cover,** 1. in secret. 2. by pretense. 3. hidden. —**cov′ered,** *adj.* —**cov′er·er,** *n.* —**cov′er·less,** *adj.*

**cov·er·age** (kuv′ẽr-ij), *n.* 1. the amount, extent, etc. covered by something. 2. in *insurance*, all the risks covered by an insurance policy.

**cov·er·all** (kuv′ẽr-ôl′), *n.* *usually pl.* a one-piece garment with sleeves and legs, for mechanics, etc.

**cover charge,** a charge added to the cost of food and drink at a night club or restaurant.

**cover crop,** a crop, as rye or red clover, grown to protect soil from erosion and leaching.

**covered wagon,** a large wagon with an arched cover of canvas, used by American pioneers.

**cover girl,** [Colloq.], a pretty girl whose picture is often put on magazine covers, etc.

**cov·er·ing** (kuv′ẽr-iŋ), *n.* anything that covers.

**cov·er·let** (kuv′ẽr-lit), *n.* [< Anglo-Fr. < OFr. *couvrir*, to cover + *lit* (< L. *lectus*), a bed], a bedspread; counterpane: also **cov′er·lid.**

**cov·ert** (kuv′ẽrt), *adj.* [< OFr. pp. of *couvrir;* see COVER], concealed; hidden; disguised. *n.* 1. a covered or protected place; shelter. 2. in *hunting*, a hiding place for game. 3. one of the small feathers that cover the bases of the larger feathers of a bird's wing and tail. —**cov′ert·ly,** *adv.* —**cov′ert·ness,** *n.*

**covert cloth,** a smooth, twilled cloth of wool with cotton, rayon, or silk: used for suits, etc.

**covert coat,** a short topcoat of covert cloth.

**cov·er·ture** (kuv′ẽr-chẽr), *n.* 1. a covering; refuge. 2. a concealment; disguise.

**cov·et** (kuv′it), *v.t. & v.i.* [< OFr. < LL. < L. *cupiditas;* see CUPIDITY], to desire ardently (especially, something that another person has). —**cov′et·a·ble,** *adj.* —**cov′et·er,** *n.*

**cov·et·ous** (kuv′i-təs), *adj.* greedy; avaricious. —**cov′et·ous·ly,** *adv.* —**cov′et·ous·ness,** *n.*

**cov·ey** (kuv′i), *n.* [*pl.* -EYS], [< OFr. < *cover*, to hatch < L. *cubare*, to lie down], 1. a small flock of birds, especially partridges or quail. 2. a small group of people; bevy.

**Cov·ing·ton** (kuv′iŋ-tən), *n.* a city in N Kentucky, on the Ohio River: pop., 60,000.

**cow** (kou), *n.* [*pl.* COWS; *archaic or poetic*, KINE (kīn)], [< AS. *cu*], 1. a familiar farm animal domesticated for its milk; mature female of any animal of the ox family. 2. the female of certain other animals, as the buffalo, elephant, etc. The male of such animals is called a *bull*.

**cow** (kou), *v.t.* [< ON. *kūga*, to subdue], to frighten; make timid; overawe.

**cow·ard** (kou′ẽrd), *n.* [< OFr. < *coe* (< L. *cauda*), tail], one who lacks courage; one easily or excessively frightened. *adj.* cowardly.

**cow·ard·ice** (kou′ẽr-dis), *n.* lack of courage; a being easily or excessively frightened.

**cow·ard·ly** (kou′ẽrd-li), *adj.* having or showing cowardice; of or characteristic of a coward. *adv.* in the manner of a coward. —**cow′ard·li·ness,** *n.*

**cow·bell** (kou′bel′), *n.* a bell hung from a cow's neck so she can be found by its tinkling.

**cow·ber·ry** (kou′ber′i, -bẽr-i), *n.* [pl. -RIES], 1. a shrub with white or pink flowers and red berries. 2. a plant of the rose family. 3. the fruit of either of these plants.

**cow·bird** (kou′bũrd′), *n.* a small blackbird often seen near cattle: also **cow blackbird** (or **bunting**).

**cow·boy** (kou′boi′), *n.* a ranch worker who rides horseback on his job of herding cattle: also, and in the western U.S. usually, **cowhand.**

**cow·catch·er** (kou′kach′ẽr), *n.* a metal frame on the front of a locomotive or streetcar to remove obstructions from the tracks.

**cow·er** (kou′ẽr), *v.i.* [ME. *couren;* prob. < ON.], 1. to crouch or huddle up, as from fear or cold. 2. to shrink and tremble, as from someone's anger, threats, or blows; cringe.

**cow·fish** (kou′fish′), *n.* [*pl.* see FISH], any of various marine mammals that feed on plants, as the manatee, sea cow, or dugong.

**cow·girl** (kou′gũrl′), *n.* a girl or woman who helps to herd cattle, etc. on a ranch.

**cow·hand** (kou′hand′), *n.* a cowboy: also **cow hand.**

**cow·herd** (kou′hũrd′), *n.* a person whose work is herding or tending cattle at pasture.

**cow·hide** (kou′hīd′), *n.* 1. the hide of a cow. 2. leather made from it. 3. a whip made of this. *v.t.* [-HIDED, -HIDING], to flog with a cowhide.

**cow killer,** a wasp of the southern U.S. that looks like a large ant: so called from the notion that its sting can kill cattle.

**cowl** (koul), *n.* [< AS. < LL. < L. *cucullus*, hood], 1. a monk's hood. 2. a monk's cloak with a hood. 3. something shaped like a cowl; esp., *a*) a cover for the top of a chimney, to increase the draft. *b*) the top front part of an automobile body, to which the windshield and dashboard are fastened. *c*) a cowling. *v.t.* to cover as with a cowl. —**cowled,** *adj.*

MONK'S COWL

**cow·lick** (kou′lik′), *n.* [< the notion that it looks as if it had been licked by a cow], a tuft of hair that cannot easily be combed flat.

**cowl·ing** (koul′iŋ), *n.* [see COWL], a detachable metal covering for an airplane engine.

**cow·man** (kou′mən), *n.* [*pl.* -MEN], a man who owns or operates a cattle ranch.

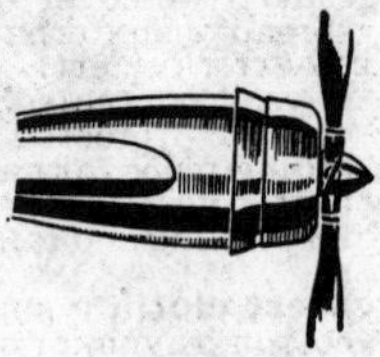

COWLING

**co-work·er** (kō-wũr′kẽr), *n.* a person who works with another or others; fellow worker.

**cow·pea** (kou′pē′), *n.* 1. a vine with very long pods, grown as fertilizer or food for animals. 2. the edible seed of this plant.

**Cow·per, William** (ko͞o′pẽr; *now occas.* kou′-), 1731–1800; English poet.

**cow pony,** a pony used in herding cattle.

**cow·pox** (kou′poks′), *n.* a disease of cows that causes pustules on the udders; vaccinia: people inoculated with a vaccine containing its virus are temporarily immune to smallpox.

**cow·punch·er** (kou′pun′chẽr), *n.* [from the prodding of animals in herding], [Colloq.], a cowboy.

**cow·rie, cow·ry** (kou′ri), *n.* [*pl.* -RIES], [< Hind. < Sans. *kaparda*], the shell of a certain sea animal, used as money in parts of Africa and S Asia.

**cow·shed** (kou′shed′), *n.* a shelter for cows.

**cow·slip** (kou′slip′), *n.* 1. the marsh marigold. 2. a wild plant of the primrose family, with yellow flowers; English primrose.

**cox** (koks), *n.* [*pl.* COXES], [Colloq.], a coxswain. *v.t. & v.i.* to act as coxswain to (a boat).

**cox·comb** (koks′kōm′), *n.* [for *cock's comb*], 1. a cap topped with a notched strip of red cloth like a cock's comb, formerly worn by jesters. 2. a silly, vain, conceited fellow; fop; dandy. 3. a cockscomb. —**cox·comb′i·cal** (-kom′-, -kō′mi-), *adj.*

**cox·comb·ry** (koks′kōm′ri), *n.* [*pl.* -RIES], see COXCOMB], silly conceit or vanity; foppery.

**cox·swain** (kok′s′n, -swān′), *n.* [*cock* (cockboat) + *swain*], the person who steers a boat or racing shell: also sp. **cockswain.**

**coy** (koi), *adj.* [< OFr. < LL. < L. *quietus;* see QUIET], 1. shy; bashful; demure. 2. pretending to be shy, often in a coquettish manner. —**coy′ly,** *adv.* —**coy′ness,** *n.*

**coy·ote** (kī′ōt, kī-ō′ti), *n.* [*pl.* -OTES, -OTE; see PLURAL, II, D, 1], [Am. Sp. < Nahuatl *coyotl*], a small wolf of the prairies of W North America.

**coy·pu** (koi′po͞o), *n.* [*pl.* -PUS, -PU; see PLURAL, II, D, 1], [< Sp. < native name], a large water rodent of South America whose fur (called *nutria*) is like that of the beaver.

**coz** (kuz), *n.* [Colloq.], cousin.

**coze** (kōz), *v.i.* [COZED, COZING], [prob. < Fr. < LL. < L. *causari*, to plead < *causa;* see CAUSE], to chat. *n.* a friendly talk.

**coz·en** (kuz′′n), *v.t. & v.i.* [Fr. *cousiner*, lit., to act as a cousin], to cheat; defraud; deceive. —**coz′en·age,** *n.* —**coz′en·er,** *n.*

**co·zy** (kō′zi), *adj.* [-ZIER, -ZIEST], [Scot.; prob. < N.], warm and comfortable; snug: also sp. **cosy, cozey, cosey, cozie, cosie.** *n.* [*pl.* -ZIES], a knitted or padded cover placed over a teapot to keep the contents hot: also sp. **cosy, cosey.** —**co′zi·ly,** *adv.* —**co′zi·ness,** *n.*

**C.P.,** 1. Command Post. 2. Common Pleas. 3. Common Prayer. 4. Communist Party. 5. Court of Probate.

**c.p.,** 1. candle power. 2. chemically pure.

**cp.,** compare.

**C.P.A., c.p.a.,** Certified Public Accountant.

**Cpl.,** Corporal.

**C.P.O.,** Chief Petty Officer.

**c.p.s.,** cycles per second.

**CQ,** a signal used by radio amateurs, inviting others to enter into communication.

**Cr,** in *chemistry*, chromium.

**cr.,** [*pl.* CRS.], 1. credit. 2. creditor.

**crab** (krab), *n.* [< AS. *crabba*, lit., the scratcher], 1. a shellfish with four pairs of legs, one pair of pincers, and a short, broad abdomen folded under its thorax. 2. a machine for hoisting heavy weights. 3. [C-], Cancer, the constellation and fourth sign of the Zodiac. *v.i.* [CRABBED, CRABBING], to fish for or catch crabs. —**catch a crab,** in *rowing*, to unbalance the boat by a faulty stroke. —**crab′ber,** *n.*

**crab** (krab), *n.* [? < prec. *crab* in lit. sense "scratcher"], 1. a crab apple. 2. one who has a sour temper or is always complaining. *adj.* of a crab apple or the tree it grows on. *v.t. & v.i.* [CRABBED, CRABBING], [Colloq.], to complain about or find fault with (a person or thing). —**crab one's act (the deal,** etc.), [Colloq.], to frustrate one's scheme (the deal, etc.). —**crab′ber,** *n.*

**crab apple,** 1. a small, very sour apple, used for making jellies and preserves. 2. a tree bearing crab apples: also **crab tree.**

**Crabbe, George** (krab), 1754–1832; English poet.

**crab·bed** (krab′id), *adj.* [< *crab* (apple)], 1. peevish; morose; ill-tempered; cross. 2. hard to understand. 3. hard to read or make out: as, *crabbed* handwriting. —**crab′bed·ness,** *n.*

**crab·by** (krab′i), *adj.* [-BIER, -BIEST], [< *crab* (apple)], peevish; morose; ill-tempered; cross. —**crab′bi·ly,** *adv.* —**crab′bi·ness,** *n.*

**crab grass,** a coarse grass that spreads quickly because of its freely rooting stems.

**crack** (krak), *v.i.* [< AS. *cracian*, to resound], 1. to make a sudden, sharp noise in breaking. 2. to make a noise like this. 3. to break or split, usually without complete separation of parts. 4. to become harsh or rasping, as the voice. 5. [Slang], to break down: as, to *crack* under a strain. 6. [Slang], to joke or retort. *v.t.* 1. to cause to make a sharp, sudden noise. 2. to break, or cause a narrow split in. 3. to damage. 4. to cause (the voice) to crack. 5. to subject (petroleum) to cracking. 6. [Colloq.], to hit with a sudden, sharp noise. 7. [Colloq.], to solve: as, to *crack* a murder case. 8. [Slang], to break into: as, to *crack* a safe. 9. [Slang], to make (a joke). *n.* 1. a sudden, sharp noise: as, the *crack* of a whip. 2. a break, usually a partial fracture; flaw. 3. a chink; crevice. 4. the cracking of the voice. 5. [Colloq.], the duration of a crack; an instant. 6. [Slang], an attempt; try. 7. [Slang], a joke, gibe, or sharp remark. *adj.* [Colloq.], excelling in skill or performance; excellent. —**crack a book,** [Slang], to open and study a book. —**crack a bottle,** to open and drink the contents of a bottle. —**crack a smile,** [Slang], to break into a smile. —**crack down (on),** [Colloq.], to become strict or stricter (with). —**cracked up to be,** [Colloq.], alleged or believed to be. —**crack up,** [Colloq.], 1. to crash. 2. to break down physically or mentally. —**crack wise,** [Slang], to wisecrack.

**crack·brain** (krak′brān′), *n.* a crazy person.

**crack·brained** (krak′brānd′), *adj.* crazy.

**cracked** (krakt), *adj.* 1. broken without complete separation into parts. 2. harsh or strident: said of a voice. 3. [Colloq.], crackbrained.

**crack·er** (krak′ẽr), *n.* 1. a person or device that cracks. 2. a firecracker. 3. a little paper roll containing candy, etc., which explodes when the ends are pulled: also **cracker bonbon.** 4. a thin, crisp wafer of unleavened dough. 5. an impoverished white person in the rural sections of Georgia, Florida, etc.: contemptuous term.

**crack·er-bar·rel** (krak′ẽr-bar′əl), *adj.* [< the large barrel of soda crackers formerly found in general stores], [Colloq.], designating, like, or characteristic of the informal discussions on all subjects by persons gathered at a country store: as, a *cracker-barrel* philosopher.

**crack·er·jack** (krak′ẽr-jak′), *adj.* [Slang], excellent; first-rate. *n.* [Slang], 1. anything excellent. 2. a person of recognized excellence or skill. Also **crack′a·jack′.**

**crack·ing** (krak′iŋ), *n.* the process of breaking down hydrocarbons, as of petroleum, by heat and pressure into lighter hydrocarbons of lower molecular weight, as those of gasoline.

**crack·le** (krak′′l), *v.i.* [-LED, -LING], [freq. of *crack*, *v.*], to make a succession of slight, sharp sounds, as of dry wood burning. *v.t.* to break with such sounds. *n.* 1. a succession of such sounds. 2. the finely cracked surface found on some pottery, porcelain, and glassware.

**crack·ling** (krak′liŋ), *n.* 1. a succession of slight, sharp, sudden sounds. 2. the browned, crisp rind of roast pork. 3. *pl.* the crisp part remaining after the lard has been removed from hog fat by frying.

**crack·ly** (krak′li), *adj.* crackling or inclined to crackle.

**crack·pot** (krak′pot′), *n.* [Colloq.], a crackbrained person. *adj.* [Colloq.], crackbrained.

**cracks·man** (kraks′mən), *n.* [*pl.* -MEN], [in reference to cracking safes], [Slang], a burglar.

**crack-up** (krak′up′), *n.* 1. a crash, as of an airplane. 2. a mental or physical breakdown.

**Cra·cow** (krak′ou, krā′kō), *n.* a city in SW Poland: pop., 348,000: Polish name, **Kraków.**

**-cra·cy** (krə-si), [< Fr. or ML. < Gr. *-kratia* < *kratos*, rule], a combining form meaning *a* (*specified*) *type of government, rule by*, as in *autocracy*.

**cra·dle** (krā′d′l), *n.* [AS. *cradol*], 1. a baby's small bed, usually on rockers; hence, 2. infancy. 3. the place of a thing's beginning. 4. a framework for support or protection. 5. a framework to support a boat, aircraft, etc. while it is being built or repaired. 6. *a*) a frame on a scythe for laying the grain evenly as it is cut. *b*) a scythe with such a frame: also **cradle scythe.** 7. in *mining*, a boxlike device on rockers, for washing gold out of gold-bearing sand. *v.t.* [-DLED, -DLING], 1. to place or rock in or as in a cradle. 2. to take care of in infancy. 3. to cut (grain) with a cradle scythe. 4. in *mining*, to wash (sand) in a cradle.

CRADLE SCYTHE

**cra·dle·song** (krā′d'l-sôŋ′), *n.* a lullaby.

**craft** (kraft, kräft), *n.* [AS. *cræfte*, orig., strength, power], 1. some special skill or art. 2. skill in deceiving; guile; slyness. 3. an occupation requiring special manual skill, as tailoring. 4. the members of a skilled trade. 5. *a*) a boat, ship, or aircraft. *b*) boats, ships, or aircraft, collectively.

**-craft,** a combining form meaning *the craft, work,* or *practice of,* as in *handicraft, witchcraft.*

**crafts·man** (krafts′mən, kräfts′-), *n.* [*pl.* -MEN], 1. a skilled workman; artisan. 2. an artist. —**crafts′man·ship′,** *n.*

**craft union,** a labor union to which only workers in a certain trade, craft, or occupation can belong: distinguished from *industrial union.*

**craft·y** (kraf′ti, kräf′-), *adj.* [-IER, -IEST], subtly deceitful; sly; cunning; artful. —**craft′i·ly,** *adv.* —**craft′i·ness,** *n.*

**crag** (krag), *n.* [< Celt.], a steep, rugged rock that rises above or projects from a rock mass.

**crag·gy** (krag′i), *adj.* [-GIER, -GIEST], having many crags: also **crag′ged.** —**crag′gi·ness,** *n.*

**crake** (krāk), *n.* [*pl.* CRAKES, CRAKE; see PLURAL, II, D, 1], [? < AS. *cracian*, to resound], a bird of the rail family with long legs and a short bill.

**cram** (kram), *v.t.* [CRAMMED, CRAMMING], [AS. *crammian*, to stuff], 1. to pack full or too full. 2. to stuff; force. 3. to stuff to excess with food. 4. [Colloq.], to prepare (a person) or review (a subject) for an examination in a hurried, intensive way. *v.i.* 1. to eat too much or too quickly. 2. [Colloq.], to stuff the mind full of a subject, as in preparation for an examination. *n.* 1. [Colloq.], a crammed condition; crush. 2. [Colloq.], the act of cramming information. —**cram′mer,** *n.*

**cramp** (kramp), *n.* [< OFr. *crampe*, bent, twisted < OLG.], 1. a sudden, painful, involuntary contraction of muscles from chill, strain, etc. 2. partial local paralysis, as from excessive use of muscles. 3. *usually in pl.* intestinal griping and pain. *v.t.* to affect with a cramp.

**cramp** (kramp), *n.* [MD. or MLG. *krampe*, lit., bent in], 1. a metal bar with both ends bent, for holding together blocks of stone, timbers, etc.: also **cramp iron.** 2. a clamp. 3. anything that confines or hampers. *v.t.* 1. to fasten as with a cramp. 2. to confine; hamper; restrain. 3. to steer. *adj.* 1. confined; restricted; narrowed. 2. hard to read or make out: also **cramped.** —**cramp one's style,** [Slang], to hamper one's usual skill, confidence, etc. in doing something.

**cramp·fish** (kramp′fish′), *n.* [*pl.* see FISH], a kind of fish that can produce an electric current: also called *electric ray, torpedo fish.*

**cram·pon** (kram′pən), *n.* [Fr. < Frank. *krampo*, iron hook], 1. either of a pair of iron hooks for raising heavy weights; grappling iron. 2. *pl.* climbing irons. Also **cram·poon′** (-po͞on′).

**cran·ber·ry** (kran′ber′i, -bẽr-i), *n.* [*pl.* -RIES], [for D. *kranebere*, G. *kranbeere*], 1. a firm, sour, edible, red berry, the fruit of a trailing shrub that grows in bogs or marshes. 2. the shrub.

**crane** (krān), *n.* [*pl.*, for 1 & 2, CRANES, CRANE; see PLURAL, II, D, 1], [AS. *cran*], 1. a large wading bird with very long legs and neck, and a long, straight bill. 2. popularly, any of various herons or storks. 3. a machine for lifting or moving heavy weights by means of a movable projecting arm or a horizontal traveling beam. 4. any device with a swinging arm fixed on a vertical axis: as, a fireplace *crane* holds a kettle. *v.t.* & *v.i.* [CRANED, CRANING], 1. to raise or move as by a crane. 2. to stretch (the neck) as a crane does.

CRANE (4 ft. tall)

**Crane, Stephen** (krān), 1871–1900; U.S. writer.

**crane fly,** any of various two-winged, slender flies with very long legs.

**crane's-bill, cranes·bill** (krānz′bil′), *n.* a geranium, especially the wild geranium.

**cra·ni·o-,** [Gr. *kranio-* < *kranion*, skull], a combining form meaning *of the head, cranial.*

**cra·ni·ol·o·gy** (krā′ni-ol′ə-ji), *n.* [*cranio-* + *-logy*], the scientific study of skulls, especially of their differences in size, shape, etc. —**cra′ni·o·log′i·cal** (-ə-loj′i-k'l), *adj.* —**cra′ni·o·log′i·cal·ly,** *adv.* —**cra′ni·ol′o·gist,** *n.*

**cra·ni·om·e·try** (krā′ni-om′ə-tri), *n.* [*cranio-* + *-metry*], the science of measuring skulls. —**cra′ni·o·met′ric** (-ə-met′rik), *adj.* —**cra′ni·o·met′ri·cal·ly,** *adv.* —**cra′ni·om′e·trist,** *n.*

**cra·ni·um** (krā′ni-əm), *n.* [*pl.* -NIUMS, -NIA (-ni-ə)], [Gr. *kranion*], the skull; esp., that part containing the brain; brainpan. —**cra′ni·al,** *adj.*

**crank** (kraŋk), *n.* [AS. *cranc*], 1. a part, as a handle, connected at right angles to a shaft of a machine in order to transmit motion. 2. a turn of speech or thought; whim; caprice. 3. a queer action or idea. 4. [Colloq.], *a*) a person given to queer actions, ideas, etc. *b*) an irritable, complaining person. *v.t.* 1. to form into the shape of a crank. 2. to start or operate by a crank. *v.i.* to turn a crank, as in starting an engine.

**crank·case** (kraŋk′kās′), *n.* the metal casing of the crankshaft of an internal-combustion engine.

**cran·kle** (kraŋ′k'l), *v.i.* [-KLED, -KLING], [freq. of *crank*, *v.*], to zigzag. *n.* a bend; twist.

**crank·shaft** (kraŋk′shaft′, -shäft′), *n.* a shaft turning a crank or turned by a crank.

**crank·y** (kraŋ′ki), *adj.* [-IER, -IEST], 1. *a*) out of order; loose. *b*) unsteady; liable to capsize: also **crank.** 2. irritable; cross. 3. queer; eccentric. —**crank′i·ly,** *adv.* —**crank′i·ness,** *n.*

**cran·ny** (kran′i), *n.* [*pl.* -NIES], [OFr. *cran* < OIt. < LL. *crena*, a notch], a small, narrow opening; crevice; crack. —**cran′nied** (-id), *adj.*

**Cran·ston** (kran′stən), *n.* a city in Rhode Island, near Providence: pop., 67,000.

**crap** (krap), *n.* [see CRAPS], 1. craps. 2. any throw that causes the thrower to lose at craps.

**crape** (krāp), *n.* [Fr. *crêpe*; see CREPE], 1. crepe. 2. a piece of black crape as a sign of mourning.

**crape·hang·er** (krāp′haŋ′ẽr), *n.* [Slang], a person with a gloomy outlook; pessimist.

**crap·pie** (krap′i), *n.* [*pl.* -PIES, -PIE; see PLURAL, II, D, 1], [ < ?], a small sunfish of the eastern U.S.

**craps** (kraps), *n.pl.* [construed as sing.], a gambling game played with two dice, in which a first throw of seven or eleven wins: also **crap′shoot′ing.** —**crap′shoot′er,** *n.*

**crap·u·lous** (krap′yoo-ləs), *adj.* [< LL. < L. *crapula*, drunkenness < Gr. *kraipalē*, drunken headache], 1. intemperate, especially in drinking; debauched. 2. sick as a result of such intemperance. Also **crap′u·lent.** —**crap′u·lous·ly, crap′u·lent·ly,** *adv.* —**crap′u·lous·ness, crap′u·lence,** *n.*

**crash** (krash), *v.i.* [ME. *crasshyn*; prob. echoic var. of *cracken* (see CRACK)], 1. to fall, collide, or break forcibly with a loud noise; smash. 2. to make a sudden, loud noise. 3. to move with such a noise. 4. to fall so as to be damaged or destroyed: said of aircraft. 5. to collapse; fail. *v.t.* 1. to cause (a car, airplane, etc.) to crash. 2. to force or impel with a crashing noise (with *in, out, through*, etc.). 3. [Colloq.], to get into (a party, theater, etc.) without an invitation or ticket. *n.* 1. a loud, sudden noise. 2. a crashing, as of a car or an airplane. 3. a sudden collapse or ruin, especially of business. *adj.* [Colloq.], characterized by the use of speed and all possible resources: as, a *crash* program.

**crash** (krash), *n.* [prob. < Russ. *krashenina*, colored linen], a coarse linen cloth, used for towels, curtains, etc.

**crass** (kras), *adj.* [L. *crassus*], 1. [Rare], gross; thick. 2. grossly stupid or dull. —**crass′ly,** *adv.* —**crass′ness,** *n.*

**-crat** (krat), [< Fr. < Gr. *-kratēs* < *kratos*, rule], a combining form meaning *participant in* or *supporter of* (a specified kind of) *government* or *ruling body*, as in *democrat, aristocrat.*

**crate** (krāt), *n.* [L. *cratis*], 1. a large basket, or a case made of slats of wood, for packing things to be shipped or stored. 2. [Slang], an old, decrepit automobile or airplane. *v.t.* [CRATED, CRATING], to pack in a crate. —**crat′er,** *n.*

**cra·ter** (krā′tẽr), *n.* [L. (< Gr. *kratēr*), a bowl], 1. the bowl-shaped cavity at the mouth of a volcano.

2. a pit resembling this, especially one made by an explosion, as of a bomb.

**cra·vat** (krə-vat′), *n.* [< Fr. < *Cravate*, Croat: referring to scarves worn by Croatian soldiers], 1. a neckcloth or scarf. 2. a necktie.

**crave** (krāv), *v.t.* [CRAVED, CRAVING], [AS. *crafian*], 1. to ask for earnestly; beg. 2. to long for eagerly; desire intensely. 3. to be in great need of. *v.i.* to have an eager longing (*for*).

**cra·ven** (krā′vən), *adj.* [< OFr. < L. < *crepare*, to creak], cowardly; abjectly afraid. *n.* a coward. —**cra′ven·ly,** *adv.* —**cra′ven·ness,** *n.*

**crav·en·ette** (krav′ə-net′, krā′və-), *n.* [after *Craven* Street, London], 1. a finish for making certain fabrics waterproof. 2. a fabric with this finish. A trade-mark (**Cravenette**).

**crav·ing** (krāv′iŋ), *n.* intense and prolonged desire; yearning, as for food, drink, etc.

**craw** (krô), *n.* [ME. *crawe*], 1. the crop of a bird or insect. 2. the stomach of any animal.—**to stick in the** (or **one's**) **craw,** to be unacceptable to one.

**craw·fish** (krô′fish′), *n.* [*pl.* see FISH], a crayfish. *v.i.* [Colloq.], to back down.

**crawl** (krôl), *v.i.* [< ON. *krafla*], 1. to move slowly by dragging the body along the ground, as a worm does. 2. to go on hands and knees; creep. 3. to move slowly or feebly. 4. to swarm with crawling things. 5. to feel as if insects were crawling on the skin. *n.* 1. the act of crawling. 2. a swimming stroke in which one lies face downward and uses alternate overarm movements. —**crawl′er,** *n.* —**crawl′ing·ly,** *adv.*

**crawl** (krôl), *n.* [W.Ind. D. *kraal* < Sp. *corral;* see CORRAL], an enclosure of vertical stakes in shallow water, for keeping fish, turtles, etc.

**crawl·y** (krôl′i), *adj.* [-IER, -IEST], [Colloq.], creepy.

**cray·fish** (krā′fish′), *n.* [*pl.* see FISH], [< OFr. *crevice* < OHG.], 1. a small, fresh-water crustacean somewhat resembling a little lobster. 2. a sea shellfish resembling a lobster but without the large pincers: also **spiny lobster.**

**cray·on** (krā′ən, -on), *n.* [Fr., < *craie*, chalk < L. < *Creta*, Crete], 1. a small stick of white or colored chalk, waxy material, etc., used for drawing or writing. 2. a drawing made with crayons. *v.t.* to draw with a crayon or crayons.

**craze** (krāz), *v.t.* [CRAZED, CRAZING], [ME. *crasen*, to crack < ON.], 1. to make insane. 2. to produce a crackled surface in the glaze of (pottery, etc.). *v.i.* 1. to become insane. 2. to become finely cracked, as the glaze of pottery. *n.* 1. a mania. 2. something that is temporarily the fashion; fad. 3. a little crack in the glaze, as of pottery. —**crazed,** *adj.*

**cra·zy** (krā′zi), *adj.* [-ZIER, -ZIEST], [< *craze*], 1. unsound; cracked; flawed. 2. unsound of mind; psychopathic; insane. 3. of or fit for an insane person. 4. temporarily unbalanced, as with great rage, etc. 5. [Colloq.], very enthusiastic; very eager. —**like crazy,** [Colloq.], with furious speed, energy, etc. —**cra′zi·ly,** *adv.* —**cra′zi·ness,** *n.*

**crazy bone,** the funny bone.

**crazy quilt,** a quilt made of pieces of cloth of various colors and irregular shapes and sizes.

**cra·zy·weed** (krā′zi-wēd′), *n.* the locoweed.

**creak** (krēk), *v.i.* & *v.t.* [ME. *creken, croken;* see CROAK], to make, cause to make, or move with a harsh, squeaking sound, as rusted hinges. *n.* such a sound.

**creak·y** (krēk′i), *adj.* [-IER, -IEST], 1. apt to creak. 2. creaking. —**creak′i·ly,** *adv.* —**creak′i·ness,** *n.*

**cream** (krēm), *n.* [OFr. *cresme* < LL. *chrisma;* see CHRISM], 1. the oily, yellowish part of milk. 2. any food made of cream or having a creamy consistency. 3. a cosmetic with a creamy consistency. 4. the finest part. 5. the color of cream; yellowish white. *adj.* 1. made of or with cream. 2. creamy. 3. yellowish-white. *v.i.* 1. to form into cream. 2. to form a foam on top. *v.t.* 1. to remove the cream from. 2. to add cream to. 3. to cook with cream. 4. to beat into a creamy consistency. —**cream of,** creamed purée of: as, *cream of* tomato soup.

**cream cheese,** a soft, white cheese made of cream or of milk enriched with cream.

**cream·er** (krēm′ēr), *n.* 1. a small pitcher for cream. 2. a device for separating cream from milk.

**cream·er·y** (krēm′ēr-i), *n.* [*pl.* -IES], 1. a place where milk and cream are pasteurized, separated, and bottled, and butter and cheese are made. 2. a shop where dairy products are sold.

**cream of tartar,** a white, acid, crystalline substance, $KHC_4H_4O_6$, used in medicine and cooking.

**cream puff,** a round shell of pastry filled with whipped cream or custard.

**cream sauce,** a sauce made of butter and flour cooked together with milk or cream.

**cream·y** (krēm′i), *adj.* [-IER, -IEST], 1. full of cream. 2. like cream in consistency or color. —**cream′i·ly,** *adv.* —**cream′i·ness,** *n.*

**crease** (krēs), *n.* [earlier *creaste*, a crest; see CREST], 1. a line or mark made by folding and pressing cloth, paper, etc. 2. a fold; wrinkle: as, a dress full of *creases. v.t.* [CREASED, CREASING], 1. to make a crease in. 2. to wrinkle; muss. 3. to graze with a bullet. *v.i.* to become creased. —**creas′er,** *n.* —**creas′y** [-IER, -IEST], *adj.*

**crease** (krēs), *n.* a creese.

**cre·ate** (krē-āt′), *v.t.* [-ATED, -ATING], [< L. pp. of *creare*], 1. to cause to come into existence; make; originate. 2. to cause; produce; bring about: as, hoarding *created* a rise in prices. 3. to invest with a new rank, function, etc. 4. to portray (a character) effectively for the first time: said of an actor.

**cre·a·tion** (krē-ā′shən), *n.* 1. a creating or being created. 2. the universe and everything in it. 3. anything created; esp., something original created by the imagination; invention. —**the Creation,** in *theology*, God's creating of the world. —**cre·a′tion·al,** *adj.*

**cre·a·tive** (krē-ā′tiv), *adj.* 1. creating or able to create. 2. productive (*of*); inventive. —**cre·a′tive·ly,** *adv.* —**cre·a′tive·ness,** *n.*

**cre·a·tor** (krē-ā′tēr), *n.* 1. one that creates. 2. [C-], God. —**cre·a′tor·ship′,** *n.*

**crea·ture** (krē′chēr), *n.* [< OFr. < L. *creatura*], 1. anything created, animate or inanimate. 2. a living being; esp., *a*) a cow, horse, or other animal. *b*) a human being: often used in a contemptuous, commiserating, or endearing sense. 3. a person completely dominated by or dependent on another. —**crea′tur·al, crea′ture·ly,** *adj.*

**crèche** (krāsh, kresh), *n.* [Fr. < Frank. hyp. *kripja*, crib; cf. CRIB], 1. a miniature representation of the Nativity. 2. a hospital for foundlings. 3. a day nursery.

**cre·dence** (krē′d'ns), *n.* [< OFr. < ML. < L. ppr. of *credere;* see CREED], belief, especially in the reports or testimony of another or others.

**cre·den·tial** (kri-den′shəl), *n.* 1. that which entitles to credit, confidence, etc. 2. *usually in pl.* a letter or certificate showing that one has a right to a certain position or authority.

**cre·den·za** (kri-den′zə), *n.* [*pl.* -ZAS], [It.], a type of buffet, or sideboard.

**cred·i·ble** (kred′ə-b'l), *adj.* [< L. < *credere;* see CREED], that can be believed; reliable. —**cred′i·bil′i·ty, cred′i·ble·ness,** *n.* —**cred′i·bly,** *adv.*

**cred·it** (kred′it), *n.* [< Fr. < It. < L. pp. of *credere;* see CREED], 1. belief; confidence; trust. 2. trustworthiness. 3. favorable reputation. 4. praise or approval; commendation: as, he deserves *credit* for telling the truth. 5. a person or thing bringing approval: as, he is a *credit* to the team. 6. *usually pl.* acknowledgment of work done, as on a motion picture. 7. the amount of money in a person's account in a bank, etc. 8. in *accounting, a*) the acknowledgment of payment on a debt by entry of the amount in an account. *b*) the right-hand side of an account, where such amounts are entered. *c*) an entry on this side. *d*) the sum of such entries. 9. in *business, a*) trust in one's integrity and in one's ability to meet payments. *b*) the time allowed for payment. 10. in *education, a*) the certification of a student's completion of a unit of study. *b*) a unit so certified. *v.t.* 1. to believe; trust. 2. to bring approval or honor to. 3. to give deserved commendation for. 4. to give credit in a bank account, etc. 5. in *accounting*, to enter on the credit side. 6. in *education*, to enter credits on the record of (a student). —**credit one with,** to ascribe to one. —**credit to one,** to believe that one has. —**do credit to,** to bring approval or honor to. —**on credit,** with the agreement to pay at a future date. —**to one's credit,** bringing approval or honor to one.

**cred·it·a·ble** (kred′it-ə-b'l), *adj.* bringing approval or honor; praiseworthy. —**cred′it·a·bil′i·ty, cred′it·a·ble·ness,** *n.* —**cred′it·a·bly,** *adv.*

**cred·i·tor** (kred′i-tēr), *n.* a person who gives credit; one to whom another is indebted.

**credit union,** a co-operative association for pooling savings of members and making loans to them at a low rate of interest.

**cre·do** (krē′dō, krā′-), *n.* [*pl.* -DOS], [L., I believe; see CREED], 1. a creed. 2. [usually C-], the Apostles' Creed or the Nicene Creed.

**cre·du·li·ty** (krə-dōō′lə-ti, -dū′-), *n.* [*pl.* -TIES], a tendency to believe too readily.

**cred·u·lous** (krej′oo-ləs), *adj.* [L. *credulus* < *credere;* see CREED], tending to believe too readily; easily convinced. —**cred′u·lous·ly,** *adv.* —**cred′u·lous·ness,** *n.*

**Cree** (krē), *n.* [*pl.* CREE, CREES], 1. a member of a tribe of Algonquian Indians who lived in central Canada. 2. the language of this tribe.

**creed** (krēd), *n.* [AS. *creda* < L. *credo* (lit., I believe), the first word of the Apostles' and Nicene Creeds], 1. a brief statement of religious belief. 2. a specific statement of this kind, accepted as authoritative by a church: as, the Apostles' *Creed.* 3. a statement of belief, principles, or opinions on any subject.

**Creek** (krēk), *n.* [*pl.* CREEK, CREEKS], an American Indian of any of several tribes, mainly Muskhogean, originally living in Georgia and Alabama, now in Oklahoma. 2. the language of the Creeks.

**creek** (krēk, krik), *n.* [ME. *creke* < ON. *kriki,* a winding], 1. a small stream, somewhat larger than a brook. 2. a narrow inlet or bay.

**creel** (krēl), *n.* [< MFr. var. of *grille,* a grill; ult. < L. *cratis,* wickerwork], a wicker basket for holding fish, often worn by fishermen.

**creep** (krēp), *v.i.* [CREPT, CREEPING], [AS. *creopan*], 1. to move along with the body close to the ground, as on hands and knees. 2. to move slowly. 3. to move stealthily, timidly, or servilely. 4. to grow along the ground or a wall, as some plants. 5. to feel as if insects were creeping on one's skin. 6. to slip slightly out of position. *n.* 1. the act of creeping. 2. a creeping movement. —**make one's flesh creep,** to cause one to feel fear, horror, or repugnance. —**the creeps,** [Colloq.], a feeling of fear, horror, or repugnance.

**creep·er** (krēp′ẽr), *n.* 1. a person, animal, or thing that creeps. 2. any plant whose stem puts out tendrils or rootlets by which it can creep along a surface. 3. *pl.* a baby's one-piece garment, combining pants and waist.

**creep·y** (krēp′i), *adj.* [-IER, -IEST], 1. creeping; moving slowly. 2. having a feeling of fear, horror, or repugnance. 3. tending to produce such a feeling. —**creep′i·ly,** *adv.* —**creep′i·ness,** *n.*

**creese** (krēs), *n.* [Malay *kris*], a dagger with a wavy blade, used by the Malays: also **crease, kris.**

**cre·mate** (krē′māt, kri-māt′), *v.t.* [-MATED, -MATING], [< L. pp. of *cremare,* to burn], to burn (a dead body) to ashes. —**cre·ma′tion,** *n.* —**cre′ma·tor,** *n.*

**cre·ma·to·ry** (krē′mə-tôr′i, krem′ə-tō′ri), *n.* [*pl.* -RIES], 1. a furnace for cremating. 2. a building with such a furnace in it. Also **cre′ma·to′ri·um.** *adj.* of or for cremation.

‡**crème** (krem), *n.* [Fr.], 1. cream. 2. a thick liqueur.

**crème de ca·ca·o** (krem′ də kə-kā′ō, -kä′ō), [Fr.], a sweet liqueur with a chocolate flavor.

**crème de menthe** (krem′də mänt′), [Fr.], a sweet greenish liqueur flavored with mint.

**Cre·mo·na** (kri-mō′nə), *n.* any of the famous violins made in Cremona, Italy, in the 17th and 18th centuries by Stradivari and certain others.

**cre·nate** (krē′nāt), *adj.* [< LL. *crena,* a notch], in *botany,* having a notched or scalloped edge, as certain leaves: also **cre′nat·ed.** —**cre′nate·ly,** *adv.* —**cre·na′tion,** *n.*

**cre·nel** (kren′'l), *n.* [OFr. < LL. *crena,* a notch], an indentation in the top of a battlement or wall: also **cre·nelle** (kri-nel′). *v.t.* [-NELED or -NELLED, -NELING or -NELLING], to crenelate.

**cren·el·ate, cren·el·late** (kren′'l-āt′), *v.t.* [-ATED, -ATING; -LATED, -LATING], to furnish with battlements or crenels. —**cren′el·a′tion, cren′el·la′tion,** *n.*

**Cre·ole** (krē′ōl), *n.* [< Fr. < Port. *crioulo* & Sp. *criollo* < *criar* (L. *creare*), to create], 1. a person of French or Spanish descent born in Latin America. 2. *a*) a person descended from the original French settlers of Louisiana. *b*) French as spoken by such people. 3. (c-), loosely, a person with both Creole and Negro ancestors. *adj.* 1. designating, of, or characteristic of the Creoles or [c-], the creoles. 2. of Creole.

**cre·o·sol** (krē′ə-sōl′, -sol′), *n.* [*creo*sote + *-ol*], a colorless, oily liquid, $C_8H_{10}O_2$, obtained from beechwood tar, etc. and used as an antiseptic.

**cre·o·sote** (krē′ə-sōt′), *n.* [< Gr. *kreas,* flesh + *sōzein,* to save], a transparent, oily liquid with a pungent odor, distilled from wood tar or coal tar: it is used as an antiseptic and as a preservative for wood. *v.t.* [-SOTED, -SOTING], to treat (wood, etc.) with creosote.

**crepe, crêpe** (krāp), *n.* [Fr. *crêpe* < L. *crispa;* see CRISP], 1. a thin, crinkled cloth of silk, rayon, cotton, wool, etc.; crape. 2. a piece of black crepe as a sign of mourning: usually sp. **crape.** 3. thin paper crinkled like crepe: also **crepe paper.**

**crêpes su·zette** (krep′ sōō-zet′), [Fr.], very thin pancakes rolled up and sprinkled with sugar, sometimes served with a flaming brandy sauce.

**crep·i·tate** (krep′ə-tāt′), *v.i.* [-TATED, -TATING], [< L. pp. of *crepitare,* freq. of *crepare,* to crack], to crackle; rattle. —**crep′i·tant,** *adj.* —**crep′i·ta′tion,** *n.*

**crept** (krept), pt. and pp. of **creep.**

**cre·pus·cu·lar** (kri-pus′kyoo-lẽr), *adj.* [< L. *crepusculum,* twilight < *creper,* dark], 1. of or like twilight; dim; obscure. 2. appearing or flying at twilight: as, *crepuscular* insects.

**cre·scen·do** (krə-shen′dō, -sen′-), *adj. & adv.* [It. < *crescere,* to increase], in *music,* gradually increasing in loudness or intensity: abbrev. **cresc., cres.**: symbol, <. *n.* *pl.* -DOS], in *music,* a gradual increase in loudness or intensity.

**cres·cent** (kres′'nt), *n.* [< OFr. < L. *crescere,* to grow], 1. the moon in its first or last quarter, when it appears concavo-convex. 2. the shape of the moon in either of these phases. 3. anything shaped like this. 4. the emblem of Turkey; hence, 5. *a*) Turkish power. *b*) Moslem power. *adj.* 1. [Poetic], increasing; growing. 2. shaped like the moon in its first or last quarter.

**cre·sol** (krē′sōl, -sol), *n.* [*creo*sote + *-ol*], a colorless, oily liquid or solid, $C_7H_8O$, distilled from coal tar and used as a disinfectant.

**cress** (kres), *n.* [AS. *cresse,* lit., creeper], a plant of the mustard family, as water cress, whose leaves are used in salads.

**cres·set** (kres′it), *n.* [< OFr.], a metal container for burning oil, wood, etc., used as a torch or lantern.

**crest** (krest), *n.* [< OFr. < L. *crista*], 1. a comb, feathered tuft, etc. on the heads of certain animals and birds. 2. a plume of feathers, or other emblem, formerly worn on a helmet. 3. a heraldic device above the shield in a coat of arms: used like a monogram on silverware, note paper, etc. 4. the top line or surface of anything; summit; ridge: as, the *crest* of a wave. *v.t.* to provide with a crest; crown. *v.i.* to form a crest or crests, as waves. —**crest′ed,** *adj.*

**crest·fall·en** (krest′fôl′'n), *adj.* 1. with drooping crest or bowed head; hence, 2. dejected; disheartened. —**crest′fall′en·ly,** *adv.* —**crest′fall′en·ness,** *n.*

**cre·ta·ceous** (kri-tā′shəs), *adj.* [< L. < *creta,* chalk], 1. containing, composed of, or having the nature of, chalk. 2. [C-], designating or of the third geological period in the Mesozoic Era: see **geology,** chart. *n.* the Cretaceous Period.

**Crete** (krēt), *n.* a Greek island in the E Mediterranean: area, 3,199 sq. mi.; pop., 438,000: also called *Candia.* —**Cre′tan,** *adj. & n.*

**cre·tin** (krē′tin), *n.* [< Fr. dial. form of *chrétien,* Christian, hence human being], a person suffering from cretinism. —**cre′tin·ous,** *adj.*

**cre·tin·ism** (krē′tin-iz'm), *n.* [see CRETIN], a congenital deficiency of thyroid secretion with resulting dwarfism, deformity, and idiocy.

**cre·tonne** (kri-ton′, krē′ton), *n.* [Fr. < *Creton,* village in Normandy], a heavy cotton or linen cloth with patterns printed in colors: used for curtains, chair covers, etc.

**cre·vasse** (krə-vas′), *n.* [Fr., a crevice], 1. a deep crack; fissure, especially in a glacier. 2. a break in the levee of a river. *v.t.* [-VASSED, -VASSING], to make crevasses in.

**crev·ice** (krev′is), *n.* [< OFr. < LL. < L. < *crepare,* to crack], a narrow opening caused by a crack or split; fissure; cleft. —**crev′iced,** *adj.*

**crew** (krōō), *n.* [< OFr. *creue,* growth; ult. < L. *crescere,* to grow], 1. a group of people associating or working together; company; gang. 2. all the men working on a ship, aircraft, etc. 3. a group; crowd; mob. 4. a rowing team.

**crew** (krōō), alt. pt. of **crow** (sense 1).

**crew·el** (krōō′əl), *n.* [prob. via MLG. or MD.], a loosely twisted, worsted yarn used in fancywork and embroidery (**crewelwork**).

**crib** (krib), *n.* [AS. *cribb*], 1. a rack, trough, or box for fodder; manger. 2. a small, crude house or room. 3. a small bed for a baby, with high sides to keep him from falling out. 4. a framework of slats or bars for support or strengthening. 5. a wooden enclosure for storing grain, salt, etc. 6.

[Colloq.], plagiarism. 7. [Colloq.], a literal translation, notes, or similar aids dishonestly used in doing schoolwork. *v.t.* [CRIBBED, CRIBBING], 1. to shut up as in a crib; confine. 2. to furnish with a crib. 3. [Colloq.], to plagiarize. *v.i.* [Colloq.], to do schoolwork dishonestly by using a crib. —**crib′ber,** *n.* —**crib′bing,** *n.*

**crib·bage** (krib′ij), *n.* [< *crib* + *-age*], a card game in which the object is to form various combinations that count for points.

**crib-bite** (krib′bīt′), *v.t.* [-BIT, -BITTEN or -BIT, -BITING], to practice crib biting.

**crib biting,** a habit, as of horses, of biting the feeding trough and at the same time swallowing air.

**crick** (krik), *n.* [prob. < ON.], a painful cramp in the neck, back, etc. *v.t.* to cause a crick in.

**crick·et** (krik′it), *n.* [< OFr. < *criquer*, to creak], a leaping insect related to the locusts and grasshoppers: the males produce a chirping noise.

**crick·et** (krik′it), *n.* [< OFr.; prob. < MD. *cricke*, a stick], 1. an outdoor game played by two teams of eleven men each, in which a ball, bats, and wickets are used. 2. [Colloq.], fair play; sportsmanship. *v.i.* to play cricket. —**crick′et·er,** *n.*

**crick·et** (krik′it), *n.* [< ?], a wooden footstool.

**cried** (krīd), pt. and pp. of **cry.**

**cri·er** (krī′ẽr), *n.* 1. one who cries. 2. one who shouts out news, proclamations, etc.

**crime** (krīm), *n.* [OFr.; L. *crimen*, verdict, offense], 1. an act committed or omitted in violation of a law. 2. extreme violation of the law, as felony or treason. 3. an offense against morality; serious offense; sin.

**Cri·me·a** (krī-mē′ə, kri-), *n.* a peninsula in Soviet Russia, extending into the Black Sea. —**Cri·me′an,** *adj.*

**crim·i·nal** (krim′ə-n′l), *adj.* 1. having the nature of crime; wrong; immoral. 2. involving or relating to crime. 3. guilty of crime. *n.* a person guilty of a crime. —**crim′i·nal′i·ty** (-ə-nal′ə-ti) [*pl.* -TIES], *n.* —**crim′i·nal·ly,** *adv.*

**criminal conversation,** adultery.

**crim·i·nate** (krim′ə-nāt′), *v.t.* [-NATED, -NATING], [see CRIME], 1. to accuse of a crime or crimes. 2. to incriminate. 3. to condemn; censure. —**crim′i·na′tion,** *n.* —**crim′i·na·to′ry** (-nə-tôr′i, -tō′ri), **crim′i·na′tive,** *adj.*

**crim·i·nol·o·gy** (krim′ə-nol′ə-ji), *n.* [< L. *crimen* (see CRIME); + *-logy*], the scientific study and investigation of crime and criminals. —**crim′i·no·log′ic** (-nə-loj′ik), **crim′i·no·log′i·cal,** *adj.* —**crim′i·no·log′i·cal·ly,** *adv.* —**crim′i·nol′o·gist,** *n.*

**crimp** (krimp) *v.t.* [< MD. *crimpen*, to contract], 1. to press into narrow, regular folds; pleat. 2. to make (hair, etc.) wavy or curly. *n.* 1. a crimping. 2. anything crimped. 3. *usually pl.* crimped hair. —**put a crimp in,** [Slang], to obstruct; hinder. —**crimp′er,** *n.*

**crimp** (krimp), *n.* [< *crimp* (to pleat)], a person who gets men to serve as sailors or soldiers by force or trickery. *v.t.* to get (men) to serve as sailors or soldiers by force or trickery.

**crimp·y** (krimp′i), *adj.* [-IER, -IEST], [< *crimp* (pleat)], having small folds; curly; wavy; frizzly. —**crimp′i·ness,** *n.*

**crim·son** (krim′z′n), *n.* [prob. via OSp. < Ar. *qirmis*, kermes < Sans. *krmi*, insect], 1. deep red. 2. deep-red coloring matter. *adj.* 1. deep-red. 2. bloody. *v.t. & v.i.* to make or become crimson.

**cringe** (krinj), *v.i.* [CRINGED, CRINGING], [< AS. *cringan*, to fall (in battle, etc.)], 1. to draw back, crouch, etc., as when afraid; cower. 2. to act in a servile manner; fawn. *n.* a cringing.

**crin·gle** (kriŋ′g′l), *n.* [< D. or LG. < *kring*, a circle], a small ring or loop of rope or metal on the edge of a sail.

**crin·kle** (kriŋ′k′l), *v.i. & v.t.* [-KLED, -KLING], [< AS. *cringan;* + freq. *-le*], 1. to be or cause to be undulated; wrinkle. 2. to rustle, as paper when crushed. *n.* an undulation; wrinkle.

**crin·kly** (kriŋ′kli), *adj.* [-KLIER, -KLIEST], full of crinkles; wrinkled; ripply; wavy.

**cri·noid** (krī′noid, krin′oid), *adj.* [< Gr. < *krinon*, lily + *-eidēs*, -oid], 1. lily-shaped. 2. designating or of a small, flower-shaped marine animal generally anchored by a stalk opposite the mouth. *n.* an animal of this kind.

**crin·o·line** (krin′'l-in, -ēn′), *n.* [Fr. < L. *crinis*, hair + *linum*, thread], 1. a coarse, stiff cloth of cotton or silk, formerly of horsehair and linen, used as a lining to stiffen garments. 2. a petticoat of this cloth, worn under a skirt to make it bulge out. 3. a hoop skirt.

**crip·ple** (krip′'l), *n.* [< AS. < base of *creopan*, to creep], a person or animal that is lame or otherwise disabled. *v.t.* [-PLED, -PLING], 1. to make a cripple of; lame. 2. to disable; damage; impair. —**crip′pler,** *n.*

**cri·sis** (krī′sis), *n.* [*pl.* -SES (-sēz)], [L. < Gr. < *krinein*, to separate], 1. the turning point in a disease, when it becomes clear whether the patient will recover or die. 2. a turning point in the course of anything. 3. a crucial situation.

**crisp** (krisp), *adj.* [AS. < L. *crispus*, curly], 1. brittle; easily broken. 2. sharp and clear: as, a *crisp* analysis. 3. lively; animated: as, *crisp* dialogue. 4. bracing; invigorating: as, *crisp* air. 5. closely curled and wiry. 6. rippled; wavy. *v.t. & v.i.* to make or become crisp. —**crisp′ly,** *adv.* —**crisp′ness,** *n.*

**crisp·y** (kris′pi), *adj.* [-IER, -IEST], crisp.

**criss·cross** (kris′krôs′), *n.* [earlier *Christ-cross*], 1. a cross (X), often used as a signature by people who cannot write. 2. a pattern made of crossed lines. *adj.* marked by crossings. *v.t.* to mark with crossing lines. *v.i.* to move crosswise. *adv.* 1. crosswise. 2. awry.

**cri·ter·i·on** (krī-têr′i-ən), *n.* [*pl.* -IA (-ə), -IONS], [< Gr. < *kritēs*, judge], a standard, rule, or test by which a judgment can be formed.

**crit·ic** (krit′ik), *n.* [< Fr. < L. < Gr. *kritikos*, orig., able to discern < *krinein*, to discern], 1. a person who forms and expresses judgments of people or things. 2. a person who writes judgments of books, plays, music, etc. professionally. 3. a person who indulges in faultfinding and censure.

**crit·i·cal** (krit′i-k′l), *adj.* 1. tending to find fault; censorious. 2. characterized by careful analysis. 3. of critics or criticism. 4. of or forming a crisis; decisive. 5. dangerous or risky; causing anxiety: as, a *critical* situation. 6. designating or of supplies subject to increased production and restricted, controlled distribution, as in wartime. 7. in *physics*, designating a point, temperature, etc. at which a change in character, property, or condition is effected. —**crit′i·cal·ly,** *adv.* —**crit′i·cal·ness,** *n.*

**crit·i·cise** (krit′ə-sīz′), *v.i. & v.t.* [-CISED, -CISING], to criticize: Brit. spelling. —**crit′i·cis′a·ble,** *adj.* —**crit′i·cis′er,** *n.*

**crit·i·cism** (krit′ə-siz′m), *n.* 1. the act of analyzing and making judgments, especially of literary or artistic work. 2. a review, article, etc. expressing such analysis and judgment. 3. a finding fault; censuring. 4. the art, principles, or methods of critics.

**crit·i·cize** (krit′ə-sīz′), *v.i. & v.t.* [-CIZED, -CIZING], 1. to analyze and judge as a critic. 2. to judge disapprovingly; censure. —**crit′i·ciz′a·ble,** *adj.* —**crit′i·ciz′er,** *n.*

**cri·tique** (kri-tēk′), *n.* [Fr.], 1. an essay or article containing an analysis of a literary or artistic work; review. 2. the art of criticism.

**crit·ter, crit·tur** (krit′ẽr), *n.* [Dial.], a creature.

**croak** (krōk), *v.i.* [< AS < *crǣcettan;* ult. echoic], 1. to make a deep, hoarse sound in the throat: as, frogs *croak.* 2. to foretell evil or misfortune; grumble. 3. [Slang], to die. *v.t.* 1. to utter in deep, hoarse tones. 2. [Slang], to kill. *n.* a croaking sound. —**croak′y** [-IER, -IEST], *adj.*

**croak·er** (krōk′ẽr), *n.* 1. an animal that croaks. 2. any of various fishes that make croaking sounds. 3. a person who foretells evil; grumbler.

**Cro·at** (krō′at, -ət), *n.* 1. a native or inhabitant of Croatia. 2. Croatian.

**Cro·a·tia** (krō-ā′shə), *n.* an ancient kingdom: now a federated republic of Yugoslavia, in the northwestern part.

**Cro·a·tian** (krō-ā′shən), *adj.* of Croatia, its people, language, or culture. *n.* 1. a Croat. 2. the South Slavic language of the Croats.

**cro·chet** (krō-shā′), *n.* [Fr., small hook; see CROTCHET], a kind of knitting done with one hooked needle. *v.t. & v.i.* [-CHETED (-shād′), -CHETING (-shā′iŋ)], to knit with such a needle.

**crock** (krok), *n.* [AS. *crocc(a)*], an earthenware pot or jar.

**crock·er·y** (krok′ẽr-i), *n.* [< *crock* (pot, jar)], earthenware; pots, jars, etc. made of baked clay.

**Crock·ett, David** (krok′it), 1786–1836; American frontiersman, killed in the defense of the Alamo.

**croc·o·dile** (krok′ə-dil′), *n.* [< OFr. < ML. < L. < Gr. *krokodilos* < *krokē*, pebble + *drilos*, worm], 1. a large, lizardlike reptile of tropical streams: crocodiles have a thick, horny skin, a long tail, and a long, narrow head with massive jaws. 2. loosely, any crocodilian.

**crocodile tears,** insincere tears or a hypocritical show of grief.

**croc·o·dil·i·an** (krok′ə-dil′i-ən), *adj.* 1. of or like a crocodile. 2. of a group of reptiles including the crocodile, alligator, cayman, and gavial. ***n.*** any reptile of this group.

**cro·cus** (krō′kəs), ***n.*** [*pl.* -CUSES, -CI (-sī)], [L. < Gr. *krokos*, saffron; of Sem. origin], any of a large group of plants of the iris family, with a bulblike stem and a yellow, purple, or white flower: it is among the earliest flowers to bloom in the spring. 2. an orange-yellow color; saffron.

**Croe·sus** (krē′səs), ***n.*** 1. a Lydian king of the 6th century B.C., whose wealth was fabulous; hence, 2. a very rich man.

**croft** (krôft), ***n.*** [AS.], [Brit.], 1. a small enclosed field. 2. a small farm, especially one worked by a renter. —**croft′er,** ***n.***

**‡croix de guerre** (krwä′ də gâr′), [Fr., cross of war], a French military decoration for bravery.

**Cro-Ma·gnon** (krō-mag′non; Fr. krō′må′nyôn′), ***adj.*** [after the *Cro-Magnon* cave in SW France, where remains were found], belonging to a prehistoric race of tall, erect men who lived on the European continent. ***n.*** a member of this race.

**crom·lech** (krom′lek), ***n.*** [W. < *crom*, bent + *llech*, flat stone], 1. a prehistoric monument consisting of a large, flat stone laid across upright stones; dolmen. 2. an ancient monument of monoliths, arranged in a circle around a mound.

**Crom·well, Oliver** (krom′wəl, -wel), 1599–1658; English general and statesman; lord protector of England (1653–1658): called *Ironsides*.

**crone** (krōn), ***n.*** [prob. < OFr. *carogne* (cf. CARRION) or via MD. *kronje*, old ewe], a withered old woman.

**Cro·nus** (krō′nəs), ***n.*** in *Gr. mythology*, a Titan who overthrew his father, Uranus, and was himself overthrown by his son Zeus: identified by the Romans with Saturn: also **Cro′nos** (-nos).

**cro·ny** (krō′ni), ***n.*** [*pl.* -NIES], [< Gr. *chronios*, contemporary], a familiar friend; close companion.

**crook** (krook), ***n.*** [< ON. *krōkr*, hook], 1. a hook; hooked, bent, or curved thing or part. 2. a shepherd's staff. 3. a crosier. 4. a bend or curve. 5. [Colloq.], a swindler; thief. ***v.t. & v.i.*** [CROOKED, CROOKING], to bend or curve.

**crook·ed** (krook′id *for 2 & 3;* krookt *for 1*), ***adj.*** 1. having a crook. 2. not straight; bent; curved. 3. dishonest; swindling. —**crook′ed·ly,** ***adv.*** —**crook′ed·ness,** ***n.***

**crook·neck** (krook′nek′), ***n.*** a squash with a long, tapering, curved neck.

**croon** (kro͞on), ***v.i. & v.t.*** [< MLG.; cf. MLG. *kronen*, to growl], 1. to sing or hum in a low, gentle tone. 2. to sing (popular songs) in a soft, sentimental manner. ***n.*** a low, gentle singing, humming, or murmuring. —**croon′er,** ***n.***

**crop** (krop), ***n.*** [AS. *cropp*, bunch, ear of corn], 1. a saclike enlargement of a bird's gullet, in which food is softened for digestion; craw. 2. any agricultural product, growing or harvested, as wheat, fruit, etc. 3. the yield of any product in one season or place. 4. a group or collection. 5. the handle or butt of a whip. 6. a short whip with a looped lash, used in horseback riding. 7. hair cut close to the head. 8. an earmark made by clipping. ***v.t.*** [CROPPED or *occas.* CROPT, CROPPING], 1. to cut off the tops or ends of; bite off. 2. to reap. 3. to cut short. ***v.i.*** 1. to bear a crop or crops. 2. to plant or grow a crop. —**crop out** (or **up**), 1. to appear unexpectedly. 2. to appear at the surface.

**crop·per** (krop′ẽr), ***n.*** 1. a person or thing that crops. 2. a farmer who works another's land for a share of the crop; sharecropper. 3. [Colloq.], a heavy fall; hence, a failure. —**come a cropper,** [Colloq.], 1. to fall heavily. 2. to fail.

**crop·pie** (krop′i), ***n.*** [*pl.* -PIES, -PIE; see PLURAL, II, D, 1], a crappie.

**crop rotation,** a system of growing successive crops of differing food requirements, to prevent soil depletion, break up a disease cycle, etc.

**cropt** (kropt), occas. pt. and pp. of **crop.**

**cro·quet** (krō-kā′), ***n.*** [Fr., dial. form of *crochet;* see CROTCHET], an outdoor game in which the players use mallets to drive a wooden ball through a series of hoops placed in the ground.

**cro·quette** (krō-ket′), ***n.*** [Fr. < *croquer*, to crunch], a small mass of chopped meat, fish, etc. fried in deep fat until browned.

**cro·sier** (krō′zhẽr), ***n.*** [< OFr. < *croce, crosse* < LL. < Frank. hyp. *krukja*, crutch], the staff carried by or before a bishop or abbot as a symbol of his office: also sp. **crozier.**

**cross** (krôs), ***n.*** [< AS. *cros* & OFr. *crois;* both < L. *crux*], 1. an upright post with another fastened horizontally near the top, on which convicted persons were executed in ancient times. 2. a representation of a cross, used as a badge, crossroad marker, etc. 3. a representation of a cross as a symbol of the crucifixion of Jesus, and hence of Christianity. 4. any trouble or affliction that tries one's patience or thwarts one. 5. any mark made by intersecting lines or surfaces. 6. such a mark (X) made as a signature by one who cannot write. 7. a crossing of varieties, breeds, or races; hybridization. 8. the result of such mixing; hybrid. ***v.t.*** 1. to make the sign of the cross over or upon. 2. to place across or crosswise: as, *cross* your fingers. 3. to cut across; intersect. 4. to draw a line or lines across. 5. to pass over; go across. 6. to carry (troops, etc.) across. 7. to extend across: as, a bridge *crosses* the river. 8. to meet (each other) in passing. 9. to thwart; oppose. 10. to interbreed (animals or plants). ***v.i.*** 1. to lie across; intersect. 2. to go or extend from one side to the other. 3. to meet in passing. 4. to interbreed. ***adj.*** 1. lying or passing across; transverse. 2. contrary; opposed; counter. 3. ill-tempered; cranky; irritable. 4. of mixed variety, breed, or race; hybrid. —**cross off** (or **out**), to cancel as by drawing crosses over or lines across. —**cross one's mind,** to suggest itself to one. —**cross one's palm,** to pay one money, especially as a bribe. —**cross one's path,** to meet one. —**the Cross,** 1. the cross on which Jesus was put to death; hence, 2. the suffering and death of Jesus. 3. Christianity or Christendom. —**cross′ly,** ***adv.*** —**cross′ness,** ***n.***

TYPES OF CROSS

**cross·bar** (krôs′bär′), ***n.*** a bar, line, or stripe placed crosswise. ***v.t.*** [-BARRED, -BARRING], to furnish with crossbars.

**cross·beam** (krôs′bēm′), ***n.*** a beam placed across another or from one wall to another.

**cross·bill** (krôs′bil′), ***n.*** a kind of finch with bill points that curve and cross each other.

**cross·bones** (krôs′bōnz′), ***n.*** a representation of two thighbones placed across each other, usually under that of a skull, used to symbolize death.

**cross·bow** (krôs′bō′), ***n.*** a medieval weapon consisting of a bow set transversely on a wooden stock: the stock is grooved to direct an arrow or stone. —**cross′bow′man** [*pl.* -MEN], ***n.***

CROSSBOW

**cross·bred** (krôs′bred′), ***adj.*** produced by crossbreeding. ***n.*** a crossbreed.

**cross·breed** (krôs′brēd′), ***v.t. & v.i.*** [-BRED, -BREEDING], to hybridize; cross. ***n.*** an individual or breed produced by crossing different varieties; hybrid.

**cross bun,** see **hot cross bun.**

**cross-coun·try** (krôs′kun′tri), ***adj. & adv.*** across open country or fields, not by roads.

**cross·cut** (krôs′kut′), ***adj.*** 1. made or used for cutting across. 2. cut across. ***n.*** 1. a cut across. 2. a crosscut saw. 3. a path that is a short cut. 4. in *mining*, a cutting made across a vein. ***v.t. & v.i.*** [-CUT, -CUTTING], to cut across.

**crosscut saw,** a saw for cutting wood across the grain.

**crosse** (krôs), ***n.*** [Fr.; see LACROSSE], the pouched racket used in playing lacrosse.

**cross-ex·am·ine** (krôs′ig-zam′in), ***v.t. & v.i.*** 1. to question closely. 2. in *law*, to question (a witness already questioned by the opposing side) to determine the validity of his testimony. —**cross′-ex·am′i·na′tion,** ***n.*** —**cross′-ex·am′in·er,** ***n.***

**cross-eye** (krôs′ī′), ***n.*** an abnormal condition in which the eyes are turned toward each other; convergent strabismus. —**cross′-eyed′,** ***adj.***

**cross-fer·ti·lize** (krôs′fũr′t'l-īz′), ***v.t. & v.i.*** [-LIZED, -LIZING], to fertilize or be fertilized by pollen from another flower. —**cross′-fer′ti·li·za′tion,** ***n.***

**cross-grained** (krôs′grānd′), ***adj.*** 1. having an irregular or transverse grain: said of wood. 2. contrary; perverse.

**cross·hatch** (krôs′hach′), ***v.t. & v.i.*** to shade with two sets of crossing parallel lines.

**cross·ing** (krôs′iŋ), ***n.*** 1. the act of passing across, thwarting, interbreeding, etc. 2. an intersection,

as of lines, streets, etc. 3. a place where a street, river, etc. may be crossed.
**cross·patch** (krôs′pach′), *n.* [*cross* + dial. *patch*, fool], [Colloq.], a cross, bad-tempered person.
**cross·piece** (krôs′pēs′), *n.* a piece lying across something else.
**cross-pol·li·nate** (krôs′pol′ə-nāt′), *v.t.* & *v.i.* [-NATED, -NATING], to transfer pollen from the anther of (one flower) to the stigma of (another). —**cross′-pol′li·na′tion,** *n.*
**cross-pur·pose** (krôs′pũr′pəs), *n.* a contrary or conflicting purpose. —**at cross-purposes,** having a misunderstanding as to each other's purposes.
**cross-ques·tion** (krôs′kwes′chən), *v.t.* to cross-examine. *n.* a question in cross-examination.
**cross-re·fer** (krôs′ri-fũr′), *v.t.* & *v.i.* [-FERRED, -FERRING], to refer from one part to another.
**cross reference,** a reference from one part of a book, catalogue, index, etc. to another part.
**cross·road** (krôs′rōd′), *n.* 1. a road that crosses another. 2. a road that connects main roads. 3. *usually pl.* the place where roads intersect: often alluded to as the gathering point for the countryside. —**at the crossroads,** at the point where one must choose between different courses of action.
**cross·ruff** (krôs′ruf′), *n.* in *card games*, a play in which each of two partners in turn leads a suit that the other can trump.
**cross section,** 1. a cutting through something, especially at right angles to its axis. 2. a piece so cut off. 3. a representative part of or selection from the whole.
**cross-stitch** (krôs′stich′), *n.* 1. a stitch made by crossing two stitches diagonally in the form of an X. 2. needlework made with this stitch. *v.t.* & *v.i.* to sew or embroider with this stitch.
**cross·tie** (krôs′tī′), *n.* a horizontal beam, post, etc. for support; specif., any of the transverse timbers supporting a railroad track.
**cross-town** (krôs′toun′), *adj.* going across the main avenues or transportation lines of a city.
**cross·trees** (krôs′trēz′), *n.pl.* two short, horizontal bars across a ship's masthead, which spread the rigging that supports the mast.
**cross·walk** (krôs′wôk′), *n.* a lane marked off for pedestrians to use in crossing a street.
**cross·way** (krôs′wā′), *n.* a crossroad.
**cross·ways** (krôs′wāz′), *adv.* crosswise.
**cross·wise** (krôs′wīz′), *adv.* 1. in the form of a cross. 2. across; so as to cross. 3. perversely.
**cross·word puzzle** (krôs′wũrd′), an arrangement of numbered squares to be filled in with words, a letter to each square: numbered synonyms, definitions, etc. are given as clues for the words.
**crotch** (kroch), *n.* [Fr. *croche* (< OFr. *croc*), a hook], 1. a pole forked on top. 2. a place where two branches fork from a tree. 3. the place where the legs fork from the human body.
**crotched** (krocht), *adj.* having a crotch; forked.
**crotch·et** (kroch′it), *n.* [OFr. *crochet*, dim. < *croc*, hook], 1. a small hook or hooklike device. 2. a peculiar whim; stubborn notion. 3. in *music*, a quarter note.
**crotch·et·y** (kroch′ə-ti), *adj.* 1. full of peculiar whims or stubborn notions. 2. having the nature of a crotchet. —**crotch′et·i·ness,** *n.*
**cro·ton** (krō′t'n), *n.* [Gr. *krotōn*, a tick], any of a large group of tropical shrubs, trees, and herbs: one species yields a thick, bitter oil (**croton oil**) used as a strong cathartic.
**croton bug, Croton bug** [< *Croton* aqueduct in New York City], a small, winged cockroach.
**crouch** (krouch), *v.i.* [< OFr. *crochir* < *croc*, a hook], 1. to stoop low with the limbs close to the body, as an animal ready to pounce or cowering. 2. to bow or cringe in a servile manner. *v.t.* to bend (the knee, etc.) low. *n.* 1. a crouching. 2. a crouching posture.
**croup** (krōōp), *n.* [< obs. or dial. *croup*, to speak hoarsely], an inflammation of the respiratory passages, with labored breathing and hoarse coughing. —**croup′y, croup′ous,** *adj.*
**croup** (krōōp), *n.* [OFr. *croupe* < Frank.; see CROP, *n.*], the rump of a horse, etc.
**crou·pi·er** (krōō′pi-ẽr; Fr. krōō′pyā′), *n.* [Fr., orig., one who rides on the croup; see CROUP (rump)], a person in charge of a gambling table, who rakes in and pays out the money.
**crou·ton** (krōō-ton′, krōō′ton; Fr. krōō′tōn′), *n.* [< Fr. < *croûte*; see CRUST], a small piece of toasted or fried bread often served in soup.
**Crow** (krō), *n.* 1. [*pl.* CROWS, CROW], a member of a tribe of Siouan Indians who lived near the Yellowstone River. 2. their Siouan language.
**crow** (krō), *n.* [AS. *crawa;* akin to *crow*, *v.*], 1. a large bird with glossy, black plumage and a typical harsh call: the raven, rook, and jackdaw are crows. 2. a crowbar. —**as the crow flies,** in a direct line. —**eat crow,** [Colloq.], to undergo the humiliation of admitting an error, etc.
**crow** (krō), *v.i.* [CROWED or, for 1, CREW (krōō), CROWED, CROWING], [AS. *crawan;* echoic], 1. to make the shrill cry of a rooster. 2. to utter a cry of pleasure or victory; exult. 3. to make a sound expressive of pleasure: said of a baby. *n.* 1. the shrill cry of a rooster. 2. a baby's sound expressive of pleasure.
**crow·bar** (krō′bär′), *n.* a long metal bar, chisellike at one end, used as a lever for prying, etc.
**crowd** (kroud), *v.i.* [AS. *crudan*], 1. to press; push; shove. 2. to push one's way forward. 3. to throng. *v.t.* 1. to press; push; shove. 2. to press closely together; cram. 3. to fill too full. 4. [Colloq.], to press (a person) urgently, especially for payment; dun. *n.* 1. a large number of people or things gathered closely together. 2. the common people; the masses. 3. [Colloq.], a set; clique. —**crowd′ed,** *adj.*
**crow·foot** (krō′foot′), *n.* [*pl.* CROWFOOTS], 1. a plant of the buttercup family, with leaves somewhat resembling a crow's foot. 2. any of several other similar plants, as the plantain.
**crown** (kroun), *n.* [< OFr. < L. *corona*, a garland < Gr. *korōnē*, wreath], 1. a garland or wreath worn on the head as a sign of honor, victory, etc. 2. a reward; honor. 3. the emblematic head covering of a monarch. 4. *a*) the power or dominion of a monarch. *b*) the monarch. Also **the crown.** 5. anything serving to adorn or honor like a crown. 6. a thing like a crown in shape, position, etc., as the top of the head, of a hat, etc. 7. originally, any coin bearing the figure of a crown. 8. a British silver coin equal to five shillings. 9. the highest point, as of an arch. 10. the highest quality, state, etc. of anything. 11. the part of a tooth projecting beyond the gum line. 12. an artificial substitute for this part. 13. the lowest point of an anchor, between the arms. *v.t.* 1. to put a crown on. 2. to make (a person) a monarch. 3. to give honor, dignity, etc. to. 4. to be the crown or highest part of. 5. to put the finishing touch on. 6. [Slang], to hit on the head. 7. in *checkers*, to make a king of. —**crown′er,** *n.*
**crown colony,** a British colony directly under the control of the home government.
**crown glass,** a very clear optical glass.
**crown prince,** the heir apparent to a throne.
**crown princess,** the wife of a crown prince.
**crow's-foot** (krōz′foot′), *n.* [*pl.* -FEET (-fēt′)], *usually in pl.* any of the wrinkles that often develop at the outer corners of the eyes.
**crow's-nest** (krōz′nest′), *n.* 1. a small, sheltered platform close to the top of a ship's mast, used by the lookout. 2. any platform like this.

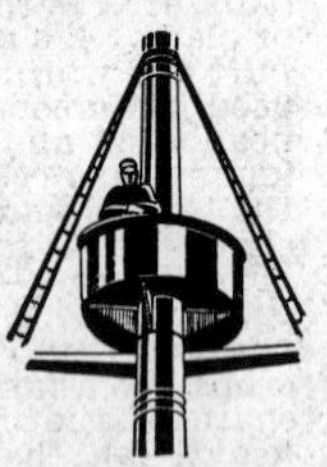
CROW'S-NEST

**Croy·don** (kroi′d'n), *n.* a city in Surrey, England, near London: pop., 249,600.
**cro·zier** (krō′zhẽr), *n.* a crosier.
**cru·ces** (krōō′sēz), *n.* alt. pl. of **crux.**
**cru·cial** (krōō′shəl), *adj.* [Fr. < L. *crux*, a cross], 1. of supreme importance; decisive; critical. 2. extremely trying; severe. —**cru′cial·ly,** *adv.*
**cru·ci·ble** (krōō′sə-b'l), *n.* [< ML. *crucibulum*, lamp], 1. a container made of a heat-resistant substance, as graphite, for melting ores, metals, etc. 2. a severe test or trial.
**cru·ci·fix** (krōō′sə-fiks′), *n.* [< OFr. < L. *crux* (see CROSS) + *fixus* (see FIX)], 1. a representation of a cross with the figure of Jesus crucified on it. 2. the cross as a religious symbol.
**cru·ci·fix·ion** (krōō′sə-fik′shən), *n.* 1. a crucifying or being crucified. 2. [C-], the crucifying of Jesus, or a representation of this in painting, statuary, etc.
**cru·ci·form** (krōō′sə-fôrm′), *adj.* [< L. *crux* (see CROSS); + *-form*], cross-shaped.
**cru·ci·fy** (krōō′sə-fī′), *v.t.* [-FIED, -FYING], [< OFr.; ult. < L. *crucifigere* < *crux* (see CROSS) + *figere* (see FIX)], 1. to execute by suspending from a cross, with the hands and feet nailed or bound to it. 2. to torment; torture. —**cru′ci·fi′er,** *n.*
**crude** (krōōd), *adj.* [L. *crudus*, raw, rough], 1. in a raw or natural condition; not refined. 2. not ripe; immature. 3. lacking grace, taste, etc.; uncultured: as, a *crude* fellow. 4. not carefully made; rough. —**crude′ly,** *adv.* —**crude′ness,** *n.*

**cru·di·ty** (krōō′də-ti), *n.* 1. a crude condition or quality. 2. [*pl.* -TIES], a crude remark, etc.

**cru·el** (krōō′əl), *adj.* [OFr. < L. *crudelis* < *crudus;* see CRUDE], 1. delighting in another's suffering; merciless. 2. causing, or of a kind to cause, pain, etc. —**cru′el·ly,** *adv.* —**cru′el·ness,** *n.*

**cru·el·ty** (krōō′əl-ti), *n.* 1. the quality of being cruel; inhumanity; hardheartedness. 2. [*pl.* -TIES], a cruel action, remark, etc.

**cru·et** (krōō′it), *n.* [< Anglo-Fr. dim. of OFr. *crue,* earthen pot < Gmc.], a small glass bottle to hold vinegar, oil, etc., for the table.

**cruise** (krōōz), *v.i.* [CRUISED, CRUISING], [< D. *kruisen,* to cross < *kruis* (< L. *crux*), cross], 1. to sail from place to place, as for pleasure, without a set destination. 2. to move about in a similar manner, as a taxi. 3. to move at a speed fit for sustained travel. *v.t.* to sail or journey over or about. *n.* a cruising voyage.

**cruis·er** (krōōz′ẽr), *n.* 1. anything that cruises, as an airplane, police car, etc. 2. a fast warship somewhat smaller than a battleship and having less armor and firepower. 3. a powerboat with a cabin and equipment for living on board.

**crul·ler** (krul′ẽr), *n.* [D. < *krullen,* to curl (see CURL)], a kind of doughnut made of sweetened dough twisted in strips and fried in deep fat.

**crumb** (krum), *n.* [AS. *cruma*], 1. a small piece broken off something, as of bread or cake. 2. any bit or scrap: as, *crumbs* of knowledge. 3. the soft, inner part of bread. *v.t.* 1. to break into crumbs. 2. in *cookery,* to cover or thicken with crumbs. 3. [Colloq.], to clear (a table, etc.) of crumbs.

**crum·ble** (krum′b'l), *v.t.* [-BLED, -BLING], [freq. of *crumb, v.*], to break into crumbs or small pieces. *v.i.* to fall to pieces; decay.

**crum·bly** (krum′bli), *adj.* [-BLIER, -BLIEST], apt to crumble; easily crumbled. —**crum′bli·ness,** *n.*

**crum·by** (krum′i), *adj.* [-BIER, -BIEST], 1. full of crumbs. 2. soft. —**crum′bi·ness,** *n.*

**crum·my** (krum′i), *adj.* [-MIER, -MIEST], [understood as *crumb* + *-y*], [Slang], of poor quality or character; inferior, shabby, contemptible, etc.

**crum·pet** (krum′pit), *n.* [< AS. *crump,* bent], a batter cake baked on a griddle: it is usually toasted before serving.

**crum·ple** (krum′p'l), *v.t.* [-PLED, -PLING], [< dial. *crump,* to curl up], to crush together into wrinkles. *v.i.* 1. to become crumpled. 2. [Colloq.], to collapse; break down. *n.* a crease or wrinkle.

**crunch** (krunch), *v.i. & v.t.* [of echoic origin], 1. to chew with a noisy, crackling sound. 2. to press, grind, or tread with a noisy, crushing sound. *n.* 1. a crunching. 2. a crunching sound. 3. [Slang], *a*) a showdown; test. *b*) a tight situation; pinch.

**crunch·y** (krun′chi), *adj.* [-IER, -IEST], making a crunching sound. —**crunch′i·ness,** *n.*

**crup·per** (krup′ẽr, kroop′-), *n.* [< OFr. *cropiere* < *crope,* rump], 1. a leather strap attached to a harness or saddle and passed under a horse's tail. 2. the rump of a horse; croup.

**cru·sade** (krōō-sād′), *n.* [< Sp. *cruzada* & Fr. *croisade;* both < ML. < *cruciare,* to mark with a cross < L. *crux,* cross], 1. [sometimes C-], any of the military expeditions which Christians undertook from the 11th to the 13th centuries to recover the Holy Land from the Moslems. 2. any war having a religious object and sanctioned by the church. 3. vigorous, concerted action for some cause or against some abuse. *v.i.* [-SADED, -SADING], to engage in a crusade. —**cru·sad′er,** *n.*

**cruse** (krōōz, krōōs), *n.* [< MD. *cruyse* or ON. *krūs*], a small container for water, oil, honey, etc.

**crush** (krush), *v.t.* [< OFr. *cruisir;* of Gmc. origin], 1. to press between opposing forces so as to break or put out of shape; crumple. 2. to grind or pound into small particles. 3. to subdue; overwhelm. 4. to extract by pressing or squeezing. *v.i.* to be or become crushed. *n.* 1. a crushing; severe pressure. 2. a crowded mass of people. 3. [Colloq.], an infatuation. —**crush′er,** *n.*

**Cru·soe, Robinson** (krōō′sō), the shipwrecked hero of Daniel Defoe's novel *Robinson Crusoe.*

**crust** (krust), *n.* [< OFr. < L. *crusta*], 1. the hard, outer part of bread. 2. a piece of this. 3. any dry, hard piece of bread. 4. the pastry shell of a pie. 5. any hard surface layer, as of snow, soil, etc. 6. [Slang], audacity; insolence. 7. in *geology,* the outer part of the earth. *v.t. & v.i.* 1. to cover or become covered with a crust. 2. to harden into a crust. —**crust′al,** *adj.* —**crust′ed,** *adj.*

**Crus·ta·ce·a** (krus-tā′shə, -shi-ə), *n.pl.* [Mod.L. < *crustaceus,* having a crust < L. *crusta,* crust], in *zoology,* a class of invertebrates, including shrimps, crabs, barnacles, and lobsters, that usually live in the water and breathe through gills: they have a hard outer shell and jointed appendages and bodies. —**crus·ta′cean** (-shən), *adj. & n.* —**crus·ta′ceous,** *adj.*

**crust·y** (krus′ti), *adj.* [-IER, -IEST], 1. having a crust. 2. hard as a crust. 3. bad-tempered; surly. —**crust′i·ly,** *adv.* —**crust′i·ness,** *n.*

**crutch** (kruch), *n.* [AS. *crycc,* staff], 1. a staff with a crosspiece on top that fits under the armpit, used by lame people as an aid in walking. 2. figuratively, a prop or support. 3. any device that resembles a crutch. *v.t.* to support as with a crutch.

**crux** (kruks), *n.* [*pl.* CRUXES (kruk′siz), CRUCES (krōō′sēz)], [L., a cross], 1. a difficult problem; puzzling thing. 2. a crucial point; critical moment. 3. the essential or most important point.

**cry** (krī), *v.i.* [CRIED, CRYING], [OFr. *crier* < L. *quiritare,* to wail], 1. to make a loud vocal sound or shout, as in pain, fright, sorrow, etc. 2. to express sorrow, pain, fear, etc. by sobbing or shedding tears; weep. 3. to utter its characteristic call: said of an animal. *v.t.* 1. to beg; implore; beseech. 2. to utter loudly; shout. 3. to call out an announcement, as of wares for sale. *n.* [*pl.* CRIES], 1. a loud vocal sound expressing pain, anger, etc. 2. any loud utterance; shout. 3. the calling out of an announcement. 4. an entreaty; appeal. 5. a popular report; rumor. 6. clamor of the people. 7. a watchword; rallying call. 8. fit of weeping. 9. the characteristic vocal sound of an animal. 10. the baying of hounds in the chase. —**a far cry,** a great distance or difference. —**cry down,** to belittle; disparage. —**cry for,** 1. to plead for. 2. to need greatly. —**cry one's eyes** (or **heart**) **out,** to weep much and bitterly. —**cry out,** 1. to shout; yell. 2. to complain loudly. —**cry up,** to praise highly. —**in full cry,** in eager pursuit.

**cry·ba·by** (krī′bā′bi), *n.* 1. a child who cries often or with little cause. 2. a person who complains constantly or accepts defeat ungraciously.

**cry·ing** (krī′iŋ), *adj.* 1. that cries. 2. demanding immediate notice: as, a *crying* shame.

**cry·o·gen·ics** (krī′ə-jen′iks), *n.* [< Gr. *kryos,* cold; + *-gen* + *-ics*], the science that deals with the production of very low temperatures and their effect on the properties of matter.

**cry·o·lite** (krī′ə-līt′), *n.* [< Gr. *kryos,* cold; + *-lite*], a fluoride of sodium and aluminum, $Na_3AlF_6$, used in the metallurgy of aluminum.

**crypt** (kript), *n.* [< L. < Gr. < *kryptein,* to hide], an underground chamber; esp., a vault under the main floor of a church, used as a burial place.

**cryp·tic** (krip′tik), *adj.* [< LL. < Gr.; see CRYPT], secret; occult; having a hidden meaning: also **cryp′ti·cal.** —**cryp′ti·cal·ly,** *adv.*

**cryp·to-,** a combining form meaning *secret, hidden*: also, before a vowel, **crypt-.**

**cryp·to·gam** (krip′tə-gam′), *n.* [< Fr. < Gr. *kryptos,* hidden + *gamos,* marriage], a plant that bears no flowers or seeds but propagates by means of special cells called spores, as algae, mosses, ferns, etc.: also **cryp′to·phyte′** (-fīt′). —**cryp′to·gam′ic, cryp·tog′am·ous** (-tog′ə-məs), *adj.*

**cryp·to·gram** (krip′tə-gram′), *n.* [*crypto-* + *-gram*], something written in code or cipher: also **cryp′to·graph′** (-graf′, -gräf′). —**cryp′to·gram′mic,** *adj.*

**cryp·tog·ra·phy** (krip-tog′rə-fi), *n.* [*crypto-* + *-graphy*], 1. the art of writing in or deciphering secret writing or code. 2. a code system. —**cryp·tog′ra·pher, cryp·tog′ra·phist,** *n.* —**cryp′to·graph′ic** (-tə-graf′ik), *adj.* —**cryp′to·graph′i·cal·ly,** *adv.*

**cryst.,** 1. crystalline. 2. crystallized.

**crys·tal** (kris′t'l), *n.* [< OFr. < L. < Gr. *krystallos,* ice < *kryos,* frost], 1. a clear, transparent quartz. 2. a piece of this cut in the form of an ornament. 3. a very clear, brilliant glass. 4. an article or articles made of such glass, as goblets, bowls, etc. 5. the transparent covering over the face of a watch. 6. anything clear and transparent like crystal. 7. a solidified form of a substance made up of plane faces in a symmetrical arrangement. 8. in *radio,* a crystal detector. *adj.* 1. of or composed of crystal. 2. like crystal; clear and transparent.

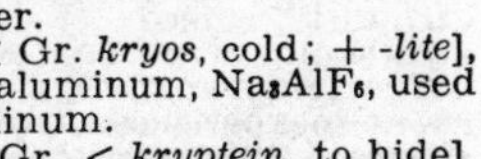

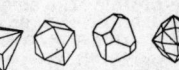

TYPES OF CRYSTAL

fat, āpe, bâre, cär; ten, ēven, hêre, ovẽr; is, bīte; lot, gō, hôrn, tōōl, look; oil, out; up, ūse, fũr; get; joy; yet; chin; she; thin, *th*en; zh, leisure; ŋ, ring; ə for *a* in *ago, e* in *agent, i* in *sanity, o* in *comply, u* in *focus;* ′ in *able* (ā′b'l); Fr. bál; ë, Fr. coeur; ö, Fr. feu; Fr. mon; ô, Fr. coq; ü, Fr. duc; H, G. ich; kh, G. doch. ‡ foreign; < derived from.

**crystal detector,** in *radio*, a rectifier consisting of a semiconductor, as silica, in contact with the sharp edge of a conductor, as tungsten.
**crystal gazing,** the practice of gazing into a large glass ball (**crystal ball**) and pretending to see images, as of future events.
**crys·tal·line** (kris′t'l-in, -īn′), *adj.* 1. made of crystal. 2. like crystal; clear and transparent. 3. having the character or structure of a crystal. 4. consisting of crystals.
**crystalline lens,** the lens of the eye, serving to focus light on the retina.
**crys·tal·lize** (kris′t'l-īz′), *v.t.* [-LIZED, -LIZING], 1. to cause to form crystals. 2. to give a definite form to: as, *crystallize* your thinking. 3. to coat with sugar. *v.i.* 1. to become crystalline in form. 2. to take on a definite form. **—crys′tal·liz′a·ble,** *adj.* **—crys′tal·li·za′tion,** *n.*
**crys·tal·lo-,** a combining form meaning *crystal*: also, before a vowel, **crystall-.**
**crys·tal·log·ra·phy** (kris′t'l-og′rə-fi), *n.* [*crystallo-* + *-graphy*], the science of the form, structure, properties, and classification of crystals. **—crys′tal-log′ra·pher,** *n.*
**crys·tal·loid** (kris′t'l-oid′), *adj.* 1. like a crystal. 2. having the nature of a crystalloid: also **crystalloidal.** *n.* a substance, usually crystallizable, which, when in solution, readily passes through vegetable and animal membranes: opposed to *colloid*.
**crys·tal·lose** (kris′t'l-ōs′), *adj.* [*crystall-* + *-ose*], the sodium salt of saccharin, used as a sugar substitute: also called *soluble saccharin.*
**crystal pickup,** a pickup with a quartz crystal, often used on electric phonographs.
**crystal set,** a simple type of radio receiver with a crystal, instead of an electron tube, detector.
**Cs,** in *chemistry*, cesium.
**cs.,** case; cases.
**C.S.,** Christian Science.
**C.S., c.s.,** 1. capital stock. 2. civil service.
**CSC,** Civil Service Commission.
**csc,** cosecant.
**C.S.T.,** Central Standard Time.
**Ct.,** 1. Connecticut. 2. Count.
**ct.,** 1. [*pl.* CTS.], cent. 2. court.
**ctn,** cotangent.
**ctr.,** center.
**cts.,** 1. centimes. 2. cents.
**Cu,** *cuprum*, [L.], in *chemistry*, copper.
**cu., cub.,** cubic.
**cub** (kub), *n.* [prob. < or via Celt.], 1. the young of certain mammals, as of the fox, bear, whale, etc. 2. an inexperienced, awkward youth.
**Cu·ba** (kū′bə), *n.* a country on an island in the West Indies, south of Florida: area, 44,206 sq. mi.; pop., 6,743,000; capital, Havana. **—Cu′ban,** *adj. & n.*
**cub·by·hole** (kub′i-hōl′), *n.* [< Brit. dial. *cub*, little shed; + *hole*], a small, enclosed space.
**cube** (kūb), *n.* [Fr. < L. < Gr. *kybos*, a cube, die], 1. a solid with six equal, square sides. 2. the product obtained by multiplying a given number or quantity by its square; third power: as, the *cube* of 3 is 27 (3 × 3 × 3). *v.t.* [CUBED, CUBING], 1. to raise to the third power. 2. to form into the shape of a cube or cubes. **—cu′bi·form′,** *adj.*
**cu·beb** (kū′beb), *n.* [< Fr. < ML.; Ar. *kabābah*], the spicy berry of an East Indian shrub of the pepper family, used medicinally, as formerly in cigarettes for treating catarrh.
**cube root,** the number or quantity of which a given number or quantity is the cube: as, the *cube root* of 8 is 2.
**cu·bic** (kū′bik), *adj.* 1. having the shape of a cube: also **cu′bi·cal.** 2. having three dimensions: a cubic foot is the volume of a cube measuring one foot in length, width, and breadth. 3. relating to the cubes of numbers or quantities. **—cu′bi·cal·ly,** *adv.*
**cu·bi·cle** (kū′bi-k'l), *n.* [L. *cubiculum* < *cubare*, to lie down], 1. a small sleeping compartment, as in a dormitory. 2. any small compartment.
**cubic measure,** a system of measuring volume in cubic units; esp., the system in which 1,728 cubic inches = 1 cubic foot and 1,000,000 cubic centimeters = 1 cubic meter.
**cub·ism** (kūb′iz'm), *n.* a school of modern art characterized by the use of cubes and other geometric forms rather than by realistic representation. **—cub′ist,** *adj. & n.* **—cu·bis′tic,** *adj.*
**cu·bit** (kū′bit), *n.* [L. *cubitum*, the elbow, cubit], an ancient measure of length, about 18–22 inches; originally, the length of the arm from the end of the middle finger to the elbow.
**cu·boid** (kū′boid), *adj.* shaped like a cube: also **cu·boi′dal.** *n.* a six-sided figure each face of which is a rectangle.
**cub reporter,** a beginning or inexperienced newspaper reporter.
**cuck·old** (kuk′'ld), *n.* [< OFr. *cucuault* < *cucu* (see CUCKOO)], a man whose wife has committed adultery. *v.t.* to make a cuckold of. **—cuck′old·ry,** *n.*
**cuck·oo** (kook′o͞o′; *also, esp. for adj.*, ko͞o′ko͞o′), *n.* [< OFr. *coucou, cucu*, echoic of its cry], 1. any of a family of grayish-brown birds with a long, slender body: the European species lays its eggs in the nests of other birds, but the American variety hatches its own young. 2. the call of a cuckoo, which sounds somewhat like its name. 3. an imitation of this. *v.i.* to utter such a call. *v.t.* to repeat continually. *adj.* [Slang], crazy; silly.
**cuckoo clock,** a clock with a toy bird that appears and cuckoos to mark intervals of time.
**cuckoo spit** (or **spittle**), a froth produced on plants by the nymphs of certain insects.
**cu. cm.,** cubic centimeter(s).
**cu·cul·late** (kū′kə-lāt′, kyoo-kul′āt), *adj.* shaped like a hood, as the leaves of violets.
**cu·cum·ber** (kū′kum-bẽr), *n.* [< OFr. < Pr. *cogombre* < L. *cucumis*], 1. a long, green-skinned vegetable with firm, white flesh, used in salads and preserved as pickles. 2. the vine on which it grows. **—cool as a cucumber,** 1. comfortably cool. 2. calm and self-possessed.
**cud** (kud), *n.* [AS. *cwudu*], a mouthful of swallowed food regurgitated from the first stomach of cattle and other ruminants and chewed slowly a second time. **—chew the cud,** to ruminate; ponder.
**cud·dle** (kud′'l), *v.t.* [-DLED, -DLING], [? < ME. hyp. *couthelen* < *couth*, known, hence comfortable with + freq. *-le*], to hold lovingly and gently in one's arms; embrace and fondle. *v.i.* to lie close and snug; nestle. *n.* 1. a cuddling. 2. an embrace; hug. **—cud′dle·some (-səm), cud′dly [-DLIER, -DLIEST],** *adj.*
**cud·dy** (kud′i), *n.* [*pl.* -DIES], [? < D. or Fris.], 1. a small room or cabin on a ship. 2. on a small ship, the cook's galley.
**cudg·el** (kuj′əl), *n.* [AS. *cycgel*], a short, thick stick or club. *v.t.* [-ELED or -ELLED, -ELING or -ELLING], to beat with a cudgel. **—cudgel one's brains,** to think hard. **—take up the cudgels for,** to defend. **—cudg′el·er, cudg′el·ler,** *n.*
**cue** (kū), *n.* [< *q*, *Q* (? for L. *quando*, when) found on 16th-c. plays to mark actors' entrances], 1. a signal in dialogue, action, etc. for an actor's entrance or speech, or for lights, music, etc. 2. any signal to begin or enter. 3. a hint; suggestion. 4. the part that an actor is to play. 5. frame of mind; mood. *v.t.* [CUED, CUING], [Colloq.], to give a cue or cues to.
**cue** (kū), *n.* [< Fr. *queue*, pigtail], 1. a queue. 2. a long, tapering rod used in billiards, pool, etc. to strike the cue ball. *v.t.* [CUED, CUING], to braid (hair, etc.).
**cue ball,** the ball, usually white, that a player strikes with his cue in billiards or pool.
**cuff** (kuf), *n.* [< ME. *cuffe*, glove], 1. a fixed or detachable band at the wrist end of the sleeve of a garment. 2. a turned-up fold at the bottom of a trouser leg. 3. a handcuff. *v.t.* to put a cuff on. **—on the cuff,** [Slang], with payment deferred.
**cuff** (kuf), *v.t.* [? < *cuff, n.*], to strike, especially with the open hand; slap. *n.* a slap.
**cuff link,** a pair of linked buttons or similar small device for keeping a shirt cuff closed.
**cu. ft.,** cubic foot; cubic feet.
**‡cui bo·no** (kwē′ bō′nō, kī′), [L., to whom for a good], 1. for whose benefit? 2. to what purpose?
**cu. in.,** cubic inch; cubic inches.
**cui·rass** (kwi-ras′), *n.* [< Fr. < It. < L. (*vestis*) *coriacea*, leather (clothing) < *corium*, leather], 1. a piece of closefitting armor for protecting the breast and back. 2. the breastplate of such armor. *v.t.* to cover as with a cuirass.
**cui·ras·sier** (kwi′rə-sêr′), *n.* [Fr.], a cavalryman wearing a cuirass.
**cui·sine** (kwi-zēn′), *n.* [Fr. < L. *coquina*, kitchen < *coquere*, to cook], 1. a kitchen. 2. a style of cooking or preparing food. 3. the food prepared, as at a restaurant.
**cuisse** (kwis), *n.* [< OFr. < L. *coxa*, hip], *usually in pl.* a piece of armor for protection of the thigh; thigh piece: also **cuish** (kwish).
**cul-de-sac** (kul′də-sak′, kool′-; Fr. kü'd'-sȧk′), *n.* [*pl.* -SACS; Fr. CULS-DE-SAC (kü'd'-)], [Fr., lit., bottom of a sack], a passage or position with only one outlet; blind alley.
**-cule** (kūl), [< Fr. or L.], a suffix added to nouns to indicate the diminutive.
**cu·lex** (kū′leks), *n.* [L., a gnat], any of a large group of mosquitoes including the most common species found in North America and Europe.

**cu·li·nar·y** (kū′lə-ner′i), *adj.* [< L. < *culina*, kitchen], 1. of the kitchen. 2. of cookery.
**cull** (kul), *v.t.* [< OFr. < L. *colligere;* see COLLECT], 1. to pick out; select and gather. 2. to pick over. *n.* something picked out, especially something rejected as not up to standard.
**cul·len·der** (kul′ən-dēr), *n.* a colander.
**cul·ly** (kul′i), *n.* [*pl.* -LIES], [17th-c. thieves' slang], 1. [Rare], a dupe. 2. [Brit. Slang], fellow; pal. *v.t.* [-LIED, -LYING], [Obs.], to trick.
**culm** (kulm), *n.* [< L. *culmus*, a stem], the jointed stem of various grasses, usually hollow. *v.i.* to grow or develop into a culm.
**culm** (culm), *n.* [< ME. *colme*], coal dust or slack; small pieces of anthracite.
**cul·mi·nate** (kul′mə-nāt′), *v.i.* [-NATED, -NATING], [< ML. *culminatus*, pp. of *culminare* < L. *culmen*, peak], to reach its highest point or climax. —**cul′mi·nant,** *adj.*
**cul·mi·na·tion** (kul′mə-nā′shən), *n.* 1. a culminating. 2. the highest point or climax.
**cu·lottes** (koo-lots′, kyoo-), *n.pl.* [Fr.], knee-length trousers made full in the legs to resemble a skirt, worn by women and girls.
**cul·pa·ble** (kul′pə-b'l), *adj.* [< OFr. < L. < *culpa*, fault, blame], deserving blame; blameworthy.—**cul′pa·bil′i·ty,** *n.* —**cul′pa·bly,** *adv.*
**cul·prit** (kul′prit), *n.* [< Anglo-Fr. *cul.*, contr. for *culpable*, guilty + *prit*, ready (i.e., to prove guilt)], 1. a person accused of a crime or offense, as in court. 2. a person guilty of a crime or offense; offender.
**cult** (kult), *n.* [< Fr. < L. *cultus*, care < *colere*, to cultivate], 1. a system of religious worship or ritual. 2. devoted attachment to, or admiration for, a person, principle, etc. 3. a group of followers; sect. —**cult′ist,** *n.*
**cul·ti·va·ble** (kul′tə-və-b'l), *adj.* that can be cultivated: also **cul′ti·vat′a·ble** (-vāt′ə-b'l). —**cul′ti·va·bil′i·ty, cul′ti·vat′a·bil′i·ty,** *n.*
**cul·ti·vate** (kul′tə-vāt′), *v.t.* [-VATED, -VATING], [< ML. < *cultivus*, tilled < L. *cultus;* see CULT], 1. to prepare and use (land) for growing crops; till. 2. to break up the surface soil around (plants) in order to aerate it, destroy weeds, etc. 3. to grow (plants or crops). 4. to develop (plants) by various horticultural techniques. 5. to develop or improve by care, training, etc.; foster or refine: as, *cultivate* your mind. 6. to seek to become familiar with. —**cul′ti·vat′ed,** *adj.*
**cul·ti·va·tion** (kul′tə-vā′shən), *n.* 1. the cultivating of land, plants, etc. 2. the giving of attention to the development or advancement of something. 3. training and development; culture.
**cul·ti·va·tor** (kul′tə-vā′tēr), *n.* 1. one who cultivates. 2. a tool or machine for loosening the earth and destroying weeds around growing plants.
**cul·tur·al** (kul′chēr-əl), *adj.* 1. of culture. 2. obtained by breeding. —**cul′tur·al·ly,** *adv.*
**cul·ture** (kul′chēr), *n.* [Fr. < L. *cultura* < *colere;* see CULT], 1. the cultivation of soil. 2. the raising or development of some plant or animal. 3. a growth of bacteria, etc. in a specially prepared nourishing substance (**culture medium**). 4. improvement or development by study or training. 5. the training and refining of the mind, manners, taste, etc. or the result of this. 6. the concepts, skills, arts, institutions, etc. of a given people in a given period; civilization. *v.t.* [-TURED, -TURING], to cultivate. —**cul′tur·ist,** *n.*
**cul·tured** (kul′chērd), *adj.* 1. produced by cultivation. 2. having culture or refinement.
**cul·tus** (kul′təs), *n.* [L.], a religious cult.
**cul·ver·in** (kul′vēr-in), *n.* [< Fr. < L. *colubra*, a snake], 1. a musket used in the Middle Ages. 2. a long cannon of the 16th and 17th centuries.
**cul·vert** (kul′vērt), *n.* [? < name of inventor], a drain or waterway under a road or embankment.

CULVERT

**cum·ber** (kum′bēr), *v.t.* [< OFr. < LL. *combrus*, barrier; prob. of Gmc. origin], 1. to hinder by obstruction or interference; hamper. 2. to burden in a troublesome way. *n.* anything that cumbers. —**cum′ber·er,** *n.*
**Cum·ber·land** (kum′bēr-lənd), *n.* a river in Kentucky and Tennessee, flowing into the Ohio.
**Cumberland Gap,** a pass through the Appalachians at the joint boundary of Virginia, Kentucky, and Tennessee.
**cum·ber·some** (kum′bēr-səm), *adj.* [*cumber* + *-some*], burdensome; unwieldy; clumsy: also **cum′brous** (-brəs). —**cum′ber·some·ly, cum′brous·ly,** *adv.* —**cum′ber·some·ness, cum′brous·ness,** *n.*
**cum·brance** (kum′brəns), *n.* an encumbrance.
**cum·in** (kum′in), *n.* [< AS. < L.; ult. < Heb. *kammōn* or Ar. *kammūn* via Gr.], 1. a small plant of the carrot family. 2. its aromatic seeds, used for flavoring pickles, soups, etc. Also sp. **cummin.**
**‡cum lau·de** (kum lô′di, koom lou′de), [L.], with praise: phrase used to signify graduation with honors from a college.
**cum·quat** (kum′kwot), *n.* a kumquat.
**cu·mu·late** (kūm′yə-lāt′; *for adj., usually* -lit), *v.t. & v.i.* [-LATED, -LATING], [< L. pp. of *cumulare*, to heap up < *cumulus*, a heap], to gather into a heap; accumulate. *adj.* gathered into a heap. —**cu′mu·la′tion,** *n.*
**cu·mu·la·tive** (kūm′yə-lā′tiv, -lə-tiv), *adj.* [see CUMULATE], increasing in effect, size, quantity, etc. by successive additions; accumulated: *cumulative interest* is interest that is added to the principal and draws additional interest. —**cu′mu·la′tive·ly,** *adv.* —**cu′mu·la′tive·ness,** *n.*
**cu·mu·lo-cir·rus** (kūm′yə-lō-sir′əs), *n.* a small cumulus that is white and filmy like a cirrus.
**cu·mu·lo-nim·bus** (kūm′yə-lō-nim′bəs), *n.* a towering cloud formation, usually producing rain.
**cu·mu·lo-stra·tus** (kūm′yə-lō-strā′təs), *n.* a cumulus with a horizontal base like a stratus.
**cu·mu·lus** (kūm′yə-ləs), *n.* [pl. -LI (-lī)], [L., a heap], 1. a heap. 2. a thick cloud formation with a horizontal base and rounded masses piled up on each other. —**cu′mu·lous,** *adj.*

CUMULUS

**cu·ne·ate** (kū′ni-it, -āt′), *adj.* [< L. < *cuneus*, a wedge], wedge-shaped; tapering, as some leaves: also **cu′ne·al, cu′ne·at′ed, cu′ne·at′ic.**
**cu·ne·i·form** (kū-nē′ə-fôrm′, kū′ni-fôrm′), *adj.* [< L. *cuneus*, a wedge; + *-form*], wedge-shaped: said especially of the characters used in ancient Assyrian, Babylonian, and Persian inscriptions. *n.* cuneiform characters or inscriptions.

CUNEIFORM CHARACTERS

**cu·ni·form** (kū′ni-fôrm′), *adj. & n.* cuneiform.
**cun·ning** (kun′iŋ), *adj.* [ME. < *cunnen*, to know], 1. skillful; clever. 2. skillful in deception; sly; crafty. 3. pretty in a delicate way, as a child. 4. created with skill or ingenuity. *n.* 1. skill in deception; slyness; craftiness. 2. [Archaic], skill. —**cun′ning·ly,** *adv.* —**cun′ning·ness,** *n.*
**cup** (kup), *n.* [AS. *cuppe* < Gmc.; prob. infl. by LL. *cuppa* < L. *cupa*, tub], 1. a small, bowl-shaped container for beverages, often with a handle. 2. the bowl of a drinking container. 3. a cup and its contents. 4. as much as a cup will hold; cupful: usually half a pint. 5. anything shaped like a cup. 6. a cup-shaped ornament given as a prize. 7. the wine chalice at Communion; also, the wine. 8. one's portion or allotment (of a given experience). 9. a drink of iced, sweetened wine: as, claret *cup*. 10. in *golf*, the hole in each putting green. *v.t.* [CUPPED, CUPPING], 1. to subject to cupping. 2. to shape like a cup. 3. to take or put in a cup. —**in one's cups,** drunk. —**cupped,** *adj.*
**cup·bear·er** (kup′bâr′ēr), *n.* a person who fills and serves the wine cups, as in a king's palace.
**cup·board** (kub′ērd), *n.* 1. a closet or cabinet fitted with shelves for holding cups, plates, food, etc. 2. [Brit.], any small closet.
**cup·cake** (kup′kāk′), *n.* a small cake, sometimes baked in a paper cup.
**cup·ful** (kup′fool′), *n.* [*pl.* -FULS], 1. as much as a cup will hold. 2. in *cookery*, half a pint.
**Cu·pid** (kū′pid), *n.* [< L. < *cupido*, desire], 1. the Roman god of love, son of Venus, identified with the Greek god Eros. 2. [c-], a representation of Cupid as a naked, winged boy with bow and arrow.
**cu·pid·i·ty** (kū-pid′ə-ti), *n.* [< Fr. < L. < *cupere*, to desire], strong desire for wealth; greed.

**cup of tea,** [Brit. Colloq.], a favorite thing, activity, etc.: as, golf isn't his *cup of tea.*
**cu·po·la** (kū′pə-lə), *n.* [It. < L. dim. of *cupa,* a tub], 1. a rounded roof or ceiling. 2. a small dome or similar structure on a roof. *v.t.* [-LAED (-ləd), -LAING], to provide with a cupola.
**cup·ping** (kup′iŋ), *n.* in *medicine,* the use of a glass cup (**cupping glass**) to draw blood to or through the skin by creating a partial vacuum.
**cu·pre·ous** (kū′pri-əs), *adj.* [< L. < *cuprum,* copper], of, like, or containing copper.
**cu·pric** (kū′prik), *adj.* in *chemistry,* of or containing copper with a valence of two.
**cu·prous** (kū′prəs), *adj.* in *chemistry,* of or containing copper with a valence of one.
**cu·prum** (kū′prəm), *n.* [L.], copper; symbol, Cu.
**cur** (kūr), *n.* [prob. < ON. *kurra* or MLG. *korren,* to growl], 1. a dog of mixed breed; mongrel. 2. a mean, contemptible, or cowardly person.
**cur.,** 1. currency. 2. current.
**cur·a·ble** (kyoor′ə-b'l), *adj.* that can be cured. **—cur′a·bil′i·ty,** *n.* **—cur′a·bly,** *adv.*
**Cu·ra·çao** (kyoor′ə-sō′, kōō′rä-sou′), *n.* a West Indian island in the Netherlands Antilles.
**cu·ra·çao, cu·ra·çoa** (kyoor′ə-sō′), *n.* [< *Curaçao*], a sweet liqueur made by flavoring distilled spirits with the peel of bitter oranges.
**cu·ra·cy** (kyoor′ə-si), *n.* [*pl.* -CIES], the position, office, or work of a curate.
**cu·ra·re** (kyoo-rä′ri), *n.* [< Port. or Sp. < native (Tupi) name], 1. a black, resinous substance prepared from the bark of certain South American plants, used as an arrow poison by some Indians and in medicine as a strong antispasmodic. 2. any of the plants from which this is prepared. Also **curari, curara, ourali, wourali, urari,** etc.
**cu·rate** (kyoor′it), *n.* [< ML. < L. *cura,* care (of souls)], a clergyman who assists a vicar or rector.
**cur·a·tive** (kyoor′ə-tiv), *adj.* curing or having the power to cure. *n.* a thing that cures; remedy.
**cu·ra·tor** (kyoo-rā′tẽr), *n.* [< Fr. or L.; ult. < L. *curare,* take care of < *cura,* care], one who has charge, as of a museum or library. **—cu·ra·to·ri·al** (kyoor′ə-tôr′i-əl, -tō′ri-), *adj.* **—cu·ra′tor·ship′,** *n.*
**curb** (kūrb), *n.* [< Fr. < L. *curvus,* bent], 1. a chain or strap passed around a horse's lower jaw and attached to the bit, used to check the horse. 2. anything that checks, restrains, or subdues. 3. a raised margin along an edge, to strengthen or confine. 4. a stone or concrete edging of a sidewalk or pavement. 5. a market dealing in stocks and bonds not listed on the stock exchange. *v.t.* 1. to restrain; check; control. 2. to provide with a curb.
**curb bit,** a horse's bit with a curb.
**curb·ing** (kūrb′iŋ), *n.* 1. material for curbstones. 2. a curb or part of a curb (sense 4).
**curb roof,** a roof with a double slope on each side, the lower one being the steeper.
**curb·stone** (kūrb′stōn′), *n.* the stone or stones making up a curb.
**cur·cu·li·o** (kẽr-kū′li-ō′), *n.* [*pl.* -OS], [L., corn weevil], any of a group of beetles with long snouts: some are harmful to fruit.
**curd** (kūrd), *n.* [< ME. *crudde* < AS. *crudan,* to press], the coagulated part of milk from which cheese is made: it is formed when milk sours, and is distinguished from whey, the watery part. *v.t. & v.i.* to curdle. **—curd′y** [-IER, -IEST], *adj.* **—curd′i·ness,** *n.*
**cur·dle** (kūr′d'l), *v.t. & v.i.* [-DLED, -DLING], [< *curd* + *-le,* freq. suffix], to form into curd; coagulate; congeal. **—curdle one's blood,** to horrify or terrify one.
**cure** (kyoor), *n.* [OFr. < L. *cura,* care], 1. a healing or being healed. 2. a thing that makes one well; remedy. 3. a method of medical treatment. 4. spiritual charge; care of souls. 5. curacy. 6. the preserving of fish, meat, etc., as by salting or smoking. *v.t.* [CURED, CURING], 1. to heal; restore to health. 2. to remedy (an ailment, evil, etc.). 3. to preserve (meat, etc.), as by salting or smoking. *v.i.* 1. to bring about a cure. 2. to be or become preserved. **—cure′less,** *adj.* **—cur′er,** *n.*
**cu·ré** (kyoo-rā′), *n.* [Fr. < ML. *curatus;* see CURATE], in France, a parish priest.
**cure-all** (kyoor′ôl′), *n.* something supposed to cure all ailments or evils; panacea.
**cur·few** (kūr′fū), *n.* [< Anglo-Fr. < OFr. *covrefeu* < *covrir* (see COVER) + *feu,* fire < L. *focus,* fireplace], 1. in the Middle Ages, a regulation that a bell be rung every evening as a signal for people to cover fires, put out lights, and retire. 2. the time at which it was rung. 3. the bell or the ringing of it. 4. a time in the evening set as a deadline beyond which children, etc. may not appear on the streets. 5. the regulation establishing this time.
**cu·ri·a** (kyoor′i-ə), *n.* [*pl.* -AE (-ē′)], [L.], 1. a medieval judicial court held in the king's name. 2. [C-], the Curia Romana. **—cu′ri·al,** *adj.*
**Cu·ri·a Ro·ma·na** (kyoor′i-ə rō-mā′nə), [L., lit., Roman Curia], the papal court, including all the officials that help the Pope in the government of the Roman Catholic Church.
**cu·rie** (kyoor′i, kyoo-rē′), *n.* [after Marie *Curie*], the unit used in measuring radioactivity.
**Cu·rie, Ma·rie** (mà′rē′ kü′rē′; Eng. kyoo-rē′, kyoor′i), 1867–1934; wife of *Pierre;* Polish chemist and physicist in France; discovered radium and polonium, in collaboration with her husband.
**Curie, Pierre** (pyâr), 1859–1906; French physicist and chemist: see **Curie, Marie.**
**cu·ri·o** (kyoor′i-ō′), *n.* [*pl.* -OS], [contr. of *curiosity*], an art object valued as a curiosity.
**cu·ri·os·i·ty** (kyoor′i-os′ə-ti), *n.* [*pl.* -TIES], 1. a desire to learn or know. 2. a meddling desire to learn about things that do not concern one. 3. anything curious, rare, or novel.
**cu·ri·ous** (kyoor′i-əs), *adj.* [OFr. < L. *curiosus,* careful], 1. eager to learn or know. 2. unnecessarily inquisitive; prying. 3. careful; accurate. 4. arousing attention or interest; strange; unusual. **—cu′ri·ous·ly,** *adv.* **—cu′ri·ous·ness,** *n.*
**cu·ri·um** (kyoor′i-əm), *n.* [after Marie *Curie*], a transuranic element produced by atomic fission: symbol, Cm; at. wt., 242 (?); at. no., 96.
**curl** (kūrl), *v.t.* [ME. *curlen* < *crull,* curly], 1. to twist (hair, etc.) into ringlets or coils. 2. to cause to bend around. *v.i.* 1. to become curled. 2. to assume a spiral or curved shape. 3. to undulate. *n.* 1. a ringlet of hair. 2. anything with a curled shape; coil. 3. a curling or being curled. **—curl up,** 1. to gather into spirals or curls. 2. to sit or lie with the legs drawn up. **—in curl,** curled. **—curl′er,** *n.*
**cur·lew** (kūr′lōō, -lū), *n.* [*pl.* -LEWS, -LEW; see PLURAL, II, D, 1], [< OFr. *corlieu;* of echoic origin], a large, brownish wading bird with long legs and a long bill that curves downward.
**curl·i·cue** (kūr′li-kū′), *n.* [< *curly* + *cue*], a fancy curve, flourish, etc.: also sp. **curlycue.**
**curl·ing** (kūr′liŋ), *n.* a game played on ice by sliding a heavy, flat, smooth stone at a mark.
**curling iron** (or **irons**), a kind of metal tongs heated for curling or waving the hair.
**curl·y** (kūr′li), *adj.* [-IER, -IEST], 1. curling or having a tendency to curl. 2. having curls. 3. having a curled or undulating grain, as certain woods. **—curl′i·ly,** *adv.* **—curl′i·ness,** *n.*
**cur·mudg·eon** (kẽr-muj′ən), *n.* [< ?], a surly, ill-mannered person; cantankerous fellow.
**cur·rant** (kūr′ənt), *n.* [< Anglo-Fr. (*raisins de*) *Corauntz,* lit., raisins of Corinth], 1. a small, seedless raisin from the Mediterranean region. 2. the sour, red, white, or black berry of a large group of hardy shrubs, used for jellies and jams. 3. the shrub bearing this fruit.
**cur·ren·cy** (kūr′ən-si), *n.* [*pl.* -CIES], [< L. *currens;* see CURRENT], 1. a continual passing from hand to hand; circulation. 2. the money in circulation in any country. 3. common acceptance; general use; prevalence.
**cur·rent** (kūr′ənt), *adj.* [< OFr. < L. *currere,* to run], 1. now in progress; of this day, week, month, or year: as, the *current* issue of a magazine. 2. passing from hand to hand; circulating. 3. commonly accepted; in general use; prevalent. *n.* 1. a body of water or air flowing in a definite direction. 2. a running or flowing. 3. a general tendency or drift; course. 4. in *electricity,* the flow or rate of flow of electric force in a conductor. **—cur′rent·ly,** *adv.*
**cur·ri·cle** (kūr′i-k'l), *n.* [L.; see CURRICULUM], a two-wheeled carriage drawn by two horses.
**cur·ric·u·lum** (kə-rik′yoo-ləm), *n.* [*pl.* -LUMS, -LA (-lə)], [L., a course, race < *currere,* to run], a specific course of study or, collectively, all the courses of study in a school, university, etc. **—cur·ric′u·lar** (-lẽr), *adj.*
**cur·rish** (kūr′ish), *adj.* like a cur; snarling; mean. **—cur′rish·ly,** *adv.* **—cur′rish·ness,** *n.*
**cur·ry** (kūr′i), *v.t.* [-RIED, -RYING], [OFr. *correier,* to put in order < L. *com-,* with + hyp. base; see ARRAY], 1. to rub down and clean the coat of (a horse, etc.) with a currycomb or brush. 2. to prepare (tanned leather) by soaking, cleaning, beating, etc. **—curry favor,** to try to get favor by flattery, fawning, etc. **—cur′ri·er,** *n.*
**cur·ry** (kūr′i), *n.* [*pl.* -RIES], [Tamil *kari*], 1. curry powder or a sauce made with this, used especially in India. 2. a kind of stew made with curry. *v.t.* [-RIED, -RYING], to flavor with curry.

**cur·ry·comb** (kũr′i-kōm′), ***n.*** a comb with metal teeth, for currying a horse's coat. ***v.t.*** to use a currycomb on.

**curry powder,** a condiment prepared from turmeric and various spices and herbs.

**curse** (kũrs), ***n.*** [Late AS. *curs, n., cursian, v.*], 1. a calling on God or the gods to send evil or injury down on some person or thing. 2. a blasphemous oath. 3. a thing cursed. 4. evil or injury that seems to come in answer to a curse. 5. any cause of evil or injury. ***v.t.*** [CURSED or CURST, CURSING], 1. to call evil or injury down on; damn. 2. to swear at. 3. to bring evil or injury on; afflict. ***v.i.*** to swear; blaspheme. **—be cursed with,** to suffer from. **—curs′er, *n.***

**curs·ed** (kũr′sid, kũrst), ***adj.*** 1. under a curse. 2. deserving to be cursed; evil; wicked; hateful. **—curs′ed·ly, *adv.* —curs′ed·ness, *n.***

**cur·sive** (kũr′siv), ***adj.*** [ML. *cursivus* < L. *cursus;* see COURSE], designating or of writing in which the letters are joined in each word. ***n.*** 1. a cursive character. 2. in *printing*, a type face that looks like writing. **—cur′sive·ly, *adv.***

**cur·so·ry** (kũr′sẽr-i), ***adj.*** [< L. < *cursor*, runner < *cursus*, course], hastily, hence often superficially, done, or doing rapidly without attention to details. **—cur′so·ri·ly, *adv.* —cur′so·ri·ness, *n.***

**curst** (kũrst), alt. pt. and pp. of **curse.** ***adj.*** cursed.

**curt** (kũrt), ***adj.*** [L. *curtus*], 1. short; shortened. 2. so brief as to be rude; terse and abrupt: as, a *curt* reply. **—curt′ly, *adv.* —curt′ness, *n.***

**cur·tail** (kẽr-tāl′), ***v.t.*** [< obs. *curtal*, shortened < L. *curtus*, short], to cut short; reduce; abridge. **—cur·tail′er, *n.* —cur·tail′ment, *n.***

**cur·tain** (kũr′t'n, -tin), ***n.*** [< OFr.; LL. *cortina*, dim. < L. *cors*, a court], 1. a piece of cloth, etc., often one that can be drawn up or sideways, hung, as at a window, to decorate, cover, or conceal. 2. anything that conceals or shuts off as a curtain. 3. in the *theater*, the drape at the front of the stage, which may be drawn up or aside to reveal the stage. 4. *pl.* [Slang], death; the end. ***v.t.*** 1. to provide or shut off as with a curtain. **—draw the curtain on,** 1. to end. 2. to conceal. **—lift the curtain on,** 1. to begin. 2. to reveal.

**curtain call,** a call, usually by continued applause, for a performer to return to the stage and acknowledge the applause.

**curtain raiser,** a short play or skit presented before a longer production.

**curt·sy** (kũrt′si), ***n.*** [*pl.* -SIES], [var. of *courtesy*], a salutation made by bending the knees and dipping the body slightly, as a mark of respect: now only of women and girls. ***v.i.*** [-SIED, -SYING], to make a curtsy. Also sp. **curtsey.**

**cur·va·ceous** (kũr-vā′shəs), ***adj.*** [< *curve* + *-aceous*], [Colloq.], having a full, shapely figure: said of a woman.

**cur·va·ture** (kũr′və-chẽr), ***n.*** 1. a curving or being curved. 2. a curve or curved part.

**curve** (kũrv), ***adj.*** [L. *curvus*, bent], curved. ***n.*** 1. a line having no straight part; bend with no angles. 2. a thing or part with the shape of a curve. 3. a curving. 4. in *baseball*, a pitched ball thrown so that it curves before crossing the plate. 5. in *mathematics*, a line whose path is traced by an equation that can be applied to every point on it. ***v.t. & v.i.*** [CURVED, CURVING], 1. to form a curve by bending. 2. to move in a curve.

**cur·vet** (kũr′vit), ***n.*** [< It. dim. < *corvo* < L. *curvus*, bent], an upward leap by a horse, in which the hind legs are raised just before the forelegs come down again. ***v.i.*** (*also* kẽr-vet′), [-VETTED or -VETED, -VETTING or -VETING], 1. to make a curvet. 2. to leap; frolic. ***v.t.*** to cause to curvet.

**cur·vi·lin·e·ar** (kũr′və-lin′i-ẽr), ***adj.*** consisting of or enclosed by a curved line or lines: also **cur′vi·lin′e·al.**

**cush·ion** (koosh′ən), ***n.*** [< Anglo-Fr. < OFr. *coussin* < LL. *coxinum* (< L. *culcita*), infl. by L. *coxa*, hip], 1. a pillow or pad for sitting or kneeling on, or reclining against. 2. a thing like this in shape or use; specif., *a*) anything serving to absorb shock, as air or steam in some machines. *b*) the elastic inner rim of a billiard table. ***v.t.*** 1. to provide with a cushion. 2. to seat or set on a cushion. 3. to protect from shock by means of a cushion, as of air or steam. **—cush′ioned, *adj.***

**Cush·it·ic** (cush-it′ik), ***adj.*** [< *Cush*, son of Ham; see HAM], designating or of a group of Hamitic languages spoken in Ethiopia and E Africa. ***n.*** this group of languages. Also sp. **Kushitic.**

**cush·y** (koosh′i), ***adj.*** [-IER, -IEST], [orig. Brit. army slang < Hind. *khush*, pleasant < Per.], [Slang], easy; pleasant; comfortable: as, a *cushy* job.

**cusp** (kusp), ***n.*** [L. *cuspis*, point], 1. a point or pointed end formed where two curves meet. 2. one of the elevations on the chewing surface of a tooth. 3. either horn of a crescent moon.**—cus·pate** (kus′pit, -pāt), **cus′pat·ed** (-pā-tid), **cusped** (kuspt), ***adj.***

**cus·pid** (kus′pid), ***n.*** a tooth with one cusp; canine tooth. ***adj.*** cuspidate. **—cus′pi·dal, *adj.***

**cus·pi·date** (kus′pi-dāt′), ***adj.*** having a cusp or cusps; pointed: also **cus′pi·dat′ed.**

**cus·pi·dor** (kus′pə-dôr′), ***n.*** [< Port. < *cuspir*, to spit < L. < *com-*, intens. + *spuere*, to spit out], a spittoon.

**cuss** (kus), ***n.*** [< *curse*], [Colloq.], 1. a curse. 2. a person or animal regarded as queer, annoying, perverse, etc. ***v.t. & v.i.*** [Colloq.], to curse. **—cuss′ed, *adj.* —cuss′ed·ly, *adv.* —cuss′ed·ness, *n.***

**cus·tard** (kus′tẽrd), ***n.*** [prob. ult. < OFr. *croustade*, dish with a crust; see CRUST], a mixture of eggs, milk, sugar, etc., boiled or baked.

**Cus·ter, George Arm·strong** (ärm′strôŋ kus′tẽr), 1836–1876; U.S. army officer and Indian fighter.

**cus·to·di·an** (kus-tō′di-ən), ***n.*** 1. one who has the custody or care of something, as of a museum; caretaker. 2. a janitor. **—cus·to′di·an·ship′, *n.***

**cus·to·dy** (kus′tə-di), ***n.*** [*pl.* -DIES], [< L. < *custos*, a guard], 1. a guarding or keeping safe; care. 2. imprisonment. **— in custody,** in the keeping of the police; in jail or prison. **—take into custody,** to arrest. **—cus·to′di·al** (-tō′di-əl), ***adj.***

**cus·tom** (kus′təm), ***n.*** [< OFr. < L. *consuetudo* < *com-*, intens. + *suere*, to be accustomed], 1. a usual practice; habit; usage. 2. established usage; social conventions carried on by tradition. 3. *pl. a*) duties or taxes imposed by a government on imported and, occasionally, exported goods. *b*) the agency in charge of collecting these duties. 4. the regular patronage of a business establishment. 5. in *law*, such usage as by common consent and long-established practice has taken on the force of law. ***adj.*** 1. made to or as if to order. 2. making things to order, or dealing in such things.

**cus·tom·ar·y** (kus′tə-mer′i), ***adj.*** 1. according to or established by custom, or usage; usual; habitual. 2. in *law*, *a*) subject to customs. *b*) holding or held by custom. ***n.*** [*pl.* -IES], a collection of laws established by custom. **—cus′tom·ar′i·ly, *adv.* —cus′tom·ar′i·ness, *n.***

**cus·tom-built** (kus′təm-bilt′), ***adj.*** built to order, according to the customer's specifications.

**cus·tom·er** (kus′təm-ẽr), ***n.*** [see CUSTOM], 1. a person who buys, especially one who buys regularly. 2. [Colloq.], a person with whom one has to deal: as, he's a rough *customer.*

**cus·tom·house** (kus′təm-hous′), ***n.*** a building or office where duties are paid on imported goods and ships are cleared for entering or leaving.

**cus·tom-made** (kus′təm-mād′), ***adj.*** made to order, according to the customer's specifications; not ready-made.

**cut** (kut), ***v.t.*** [CUT, CUTTING], [ME. *cutten*], 1. to make an opening in with a sharp-edged instrument; pierce; gash. 2. to pierce sharply so as to hurt. 3. to hurt the feelings of. 4. to get (a new tooth cutting through the gum). 5. to divide into parts with a sharp-edged instrument; sever. 6. to carve (meat). 7. to fell; hew. 8. to mow or reap. 9. to pass through or across; intersect: as, the path *cuts* the meadow. 10. to divide (a pack of cards) at random before dealing. 11. to reduce; curtail; decrease: as, salaries were *cut.* 12. to make shorter by trimming (hair, branches, etc.); pare. 13. to dilute, as alcohol. 14. to dissolve the fat globules of: as, lye *cuts* grease. 15. to make or do by or as by cutting; specif., *a*) to make (an opening, clearing, channel, etc.). *b*) to cut cloth so as to form (a garment). *c*) to perform: as, he *cut* a caper. *d*) in *sports*, to hit, drive, or throw (a ball) so that it spins or is deflected. 16. [Colloq.], to pretend not to see or know (a person). 17. [Colloq.], to stay away from (a school class, etc.) without being excused. 18. [Slang], to stop; discontinue. ***v.i.*** 1. to do the work of a sharp-edged instrument; pierce, sever, gash, etc. 2. to work as a cutter. 3. to take cutting: as, wood *cuts* easily. 4. to use an instrument that cuts. 5. to hurt as by sharp, piercing strokes: as, the wind *cut* through his coat. 6. in *sports*, to swing a bat, etc. (*at* a ball). *adj.* 1. that has been cut. 2. made or formed by cutting. 3. reduced; lessened. *n.* 1. a cutting or being cut. 2. a stroke or blow with a sharp-edged instrument, whip, etc. 3. an opening, wound, etc. made by a sharp-edged instrument. 4. the omission of a part. 5. a piece cut or cut off, as from a meat animal. 6. a reduction; decrease. 7. the shortest way across: usually **short cut.** 8. a passage or channel cut out. 9. the style in which a thing is cut; fashion: as, a stylish *cut.* 10. an act, remark, etc. that hurts one's feelings. 11. *a*) a block or plate engraved for printing. *b*) the impression from this. 12. [Colloq.], a snub. 13. [Colloq.], an unauthorized absence from a school class, etc. 14. [Slang], a share, as of profits or loot. **—a cut above,** [Colloq.], somewhat better than. **—cut across,** to take a shorter course by going straight across. **—cut a figure,** [Colloq.], to attract attention or make a (certain) impression. **—cut and dried,** 1. arranged beforehand. 2. lifeless; dull; boring. **—cut back,** 1. to make shorter as by cutting off the end: as, to *cut* back production. 2. to go back, as in telling a story. 3. to change direction suddenly, as a football player carrying the ball. **—cut dead,** [Colloq.], to snub completely. **—cut down (on),** to reduce; lessen; curtail. **—cut in,** 1. to move in suddenly. 2. to interrupt. 3. to interrupt two people dancing together in order to dance with one of them. **—cut it fine,** [Colloq.], to make exact distinctions. **—cut it out,** [Colloq.], to stop what one is doing. **—cut loose,** [Colloq.], to act without restraint. **—cut off,** 1. to sever. 2. to stop abruptly. 3. to shut off. 4. to interrupt. 5. to intercept. 6. to disinherit. **—cut out,** 1. to remove by cutting. 2. to remove; omit. 3. to eliminate and take the place of (a rival). 4. to make or form as by cutting. 5. [Colloq.], to discontinue; stop. **—cut out for,** suited for. **—cut short,** to stop abruptly before the end. **—cut up,** 1. to cut into pieces. 2. to inflict cuts on. 3. [Colloq.], to cause to be dejected. 4. [Slang], to clown, joke, etc. to attract attention.

**cu·ta·ne·ous** (kū-tā'ni-əs), *adj.* [< ML. < L. *cutis*, skin], of or on the skin; affecting the skin.

**cut·a·way** (kut'ə-wā'), *n.* a man's formal daytime coat with the front of the skirt cut so as to curve back to the tails: also **cutaway coat.**

CUTAWAY

**cute** (kūt), *adj.* [CUTER, CUTEST], [< *acute*], [Colloq.], 1. clever; shrewd. 2. pretty or attractive, especially in a delicate way. **—cute'ly,** *adv.* **—cute'ness,** *n.*

**cut glass,** glass, usually flint glass, shaped or ornamented by grinding and polishing. **—cut'-glass',** *adj.*

**cu·ti·cle** (kū'ti-k'l), *n.* [L. *cuticula*, skin, dim. < *cutis*, skin], 1. the outer layer of the skin; epidermis. 2. hardened skin, such as accumulates at the base and sides of a fingernail.

**cu·tin·ize** (kū'ti-nīz'), *v.i.* & *v.t.* [-IZED, -IZING], [< L. *cutis*, skin], to undergo or cause to undergo a process in which the outermost cells of a plant become much thickened and covered with a waxy substance (**cutin**), making them waterproof. **—cu'ti·ni·za'tion,** *n.*

**cu·tis** (kū'tis), *n.* [L., the skin], the dermis.

**cut·lass, cut·las** (kut'ləs), *n.* [< Fr. < It. < L. < *culter*, knife], a short, thick, curved sword with a single cutting edge, formerly used by sailors.

**cut·ler** (kut'lẽr), *n.* [< Anglo-Fr. < OFr. < LL. < L. < *culter*, knife], a person who makes, sells, or repairs knives and other cutting tools.

**cut·ler·y** (kut'lẽr-i), *n.* 1. the work or business of a cutler. 2. cutting instruments, often, specif., those used in preparing and eating food.

**cut·let** (kut'lit), *n.* [Fr. *côtelette*, dim. < *côte*, rib < L. *costa*, a rib], 1. a small slice of meat from the ribs or leg, for frying or broiling. 2. a small, flat croquette of chopped meat or fish.

**cut·off** (kut'ôf'), *n.* 1. a road or passage that is a short cut. 2. a stopping of steam, etc. from entering the cylinder of an engine. 3. a device for doing this, or the point where this is done.

**cut·out** (kut'out'), *n.* 1. a device for breaking or closing an electric circuit. 2. a device for letting the exhaust gases of an internal-combustion engine pass directly into the air instead of through a muffler. 3. a design to be cut out.

**cut·o·ver** (kut'ō'vẽr), *adj.* cleared of trees.

**cut·purse** (kut'pūrs'), *n.* 1. originally, a thief who cut purses from belts. 2. a pickpocket.

**cut-rate** (kut'rāt'), *adj.* 1. on sale at a lower price. 2. selling at a lower price.

**cut·ter** (kut'ẽr), *n.* 1. a device for cutting. 2. one whose work is cutting, as the sections of a garment. 3. a small, swift vessel; specif., *a*) a boat carried by large ships as a communications tender: also **ship's cutter.** *b*) an armed, single-masted sailing vessel, formerly used to pursue smugglers, etc.: also **revenue cutter.** *c*) an armed motor ship, used by the coast guard: also **coast-guard cutter.** *d*) a gaff-rigged racing yacht with a single mast: also **British cutter.** 4. a small, light sleigh.

**cut·throat** (kut'thrōt'), *n.* a murderer. *adj.* 1. murderous. 2. merciless; relentless.

**cut·ting** (kut'iŋ), *n.* 1. the act of one that cuts. 2. a piece cut off. 3. [Brit.], a newspaper clipping. 4. a shoot cut away from a plant for rooting or grafting. *adj.* 1. that cuts; sharp. 2. chilling or piercing. 3. sarcastic; harsh. **—cut'ting·ly,** *adv.*

**cut·tle·bone** (kut''l-bōn'), *n.* the internal shell of cuttlefish, used as a bird food and, when powdered, as a polishing agent: also **cut'tle.**

**cut·tle·fish** (kut''l-fish'), *n.* [*pl.* see FISH], [AS. *cudele*], a sea mollusk with ten sucker-bearing arms and a hard internal shell: when in danger, some cuttlefish eject an inky fluid: also **cuttle.**

CUTTLEFISH

**cut·up** (kut'up'), *n.* [Slang], one who clowns, plays practical jokes, etc. to attract attention.

**cut·wa·ter** (kut'wô'tẽr, -wot'ẽr), *n.* the fore part of a ship's prow.

**cut·worm** (kut'wūrm'), *n.* any of a number of caterpillars which attack young plants of cabbage, corn, etc., cutting them off at ground level.

**cwt.,** hundredweight.

**-cy** (si), [OFr. *-cie;* L. *-cia;* Gr. *-kia*], a suffix meaning: 1. *quality, condition, state,* or *fact of being,* as in *hesitancy.* 2. *position, rank,* or *office of,* as in *curacy.*

**cy·a·nate** (sī'ə-nāt'), *n.* a salt of cyanic acid.

**cy·an·ic** (sī-an'ik), *adj.* 1. of or containing cyanogen. 2. blue.

**cyanic acid,** a colorless, poisonous acid, HOCN.

**cy·a·nide** (sī'ə-nīd', -nid), *n.* a compound of cyanogen with some element or radical; esp., potassium cyanide, KCN, or sodium cyanide, NaCN, highly poisonous compounds used in electroplating and as a fluxing material: also **cy'a·nid** (-nid).

**cy·an·o·gen** (sī-an'ə-jən), *n.* [< Gr. *kyanos*, blue; + *-gen*], 1. a colorless, poisonous, inflammable gas, $C_2N_2$, smelling like peach blossoms. 2. the univalent radical CN, occurring in cyanides.

**cy·a·no·sis** (sī'ə-nō'sis), *n.* [< Gr. < *kyanos*, blue], a bluish skin color caused by lack of oxygen in the blood. **—cy'a·not'ic** (-not'ik), *adj.*

**Cyb·e·le** (sib''l-ē'), *n.* in *ancient Phrygian mythology*, the goddess of nature: identified with the Greek goddess Rhea.

**cy·ber·na·tion** (sī'bẽr-nā'shən), *n.* [*cyber*netics + *-ation*], the use of computers coupled with automatic machinery to perform complex operations, repetitive tasks, etc.

**cy·ber·net·ics** (sī'bẽr-net'iks), *n.pl.* [construed as sing.], [< Gr. *kybernētēs*, helmsman; + *-ics*], a science dealing with the comparative study of complex electronic calculating machines and the human nervous system in an attempt to explain the nature of the brain.

**cy·cad** (sī'kad), *n.* [< Gr. *kykas*, erroneous pl. of *koix*, palm], a large, tropical, palmlike plant with fernlike leaves growing in a cluster.

**Cyc·la·des** (sik'lə-dēz'), *n.pl.* a group of Greek islands in the Aegean: area, 1,023 sq. mi.

**cy·cla·mate** (sī'klə-māt', sik'lə-), *n.* [see CYCLO- & -ATE (sense 2)], a sodium or calcium salt used, esp. formerly, as an artificial sweetener.

**cyc·la·men** (sik'lə-mən, -men'), *n.* [*pl.* -MENS], [< L. < Gr. *kyklaminos*], a plant of the primrose family, having heart-shaped leaves and white, pink, or red flowers with reflexed petals.

**cy·cle** (sī'k'l), *n.* [< Fr. & LL. < Gr. *kyklos*, circle], 1. *a*) a period of time within which a round of regularly recurring events is completed. *b*) a complete set of such events. 2. a very long period of time; an age. 3. all the traditional poems, songs, etc. connected with a hero or an event. 4. a series of poems or songs on the same theme. 5. a bicycle, tricycle, or motorcycle. 6. in *electricity*, one complete period of the reversal of an alternating current. *v.i.* [CYCLED, CYCLING], 1. to occur in cycles; pass through a cycle. 2. to ride a cycle (*n.* 5).

**cy·clic** (sī'klik, sik'lik), *adj.* 1. of, or having the nature of, a cycle; moving or occurring in cycles. 2. in *chemistry*, arranged in a ring or closed-chain structure: said of atoms. Also **cy'cli·cal.** **—cy'cli·cal·ly,** *adv.*

**cy·clist** (sī′klist), *n.* one who rides a cycle.
**cy·clo-**, [< Gr. *kyklos*, circle], a combining form meaning *of a circle* or *wheel, circular:* also **cycl-**.
**cy·cloid** (sī′kloid), *adj.* [see CYCLE], circular: also **cy·cloi′dal.** —**cy·cloi′dal·ly,** *adv.*
**cy·clom·e·ter** (sī-klom′ə-tẽr), *n.* [*cyclo-* + *-meter*], an instrument that records the revolutions of a wheel for measuring distance traveled.
**cy·clone** (sī′klōn), *n.* [< Gr. < *kykloein*, to whirl < *kyklos*, a circle], 1. loosely, a violent, whirling windstorm; tornado or hurricane. 2. in *meteorology*, a storm with heavy rainfall and winds rotating about a moving center of low atmospheric pressure. —**cy·clon′ic** (-klon′ik), **cy·clon′i·cal,** *adj.*
**Cy·clo·pe·an** (sī′klə-pē′ən), *adj.* 1. of the Cyclopes. 2. [c-], huge; gigantic; enormous.
**cy·clo·pe·di·a, cy·clo·pae·di·a** (sī′klə-pē′di-ə), *n.* [see ENCYCLOPEDIA], an encyclopedia. —**cy′clo·pe′dic, cy′clo·pae′dic,** *adj.* —**cy′clo·pe′dist, cy′clo·pae′dist,** *n.*
**Cy·clops** (sī′klops), *n.* [*pl.* CYCLOPES (sī-klō′pēz)], [L. < Gr. < *kyklos*, a circle + *ōps*, eye], in *Gr. mythology*, one of a race of giants living in Sicily, who had a single eye, centered in the forehead.
**cy·clo·ra·ma** (sī′klə-ram′ə, -rä′mə), *n.* [*cyclo-* + Gr. *horama*, sight], 1. a series of large pictures, as of a landscape, put on the wall of a circular room so as to appear in natural perspective to a spectator. 2. a large, curved curtain or screen used as a background for stage settings. —**cy′clo·ram′ic,** *adj.*
**cy·clo·tron** (sī′klə-tron′), *n.* [*cyclo-* + elec*tron*], an apparatus for giving high energy to particles, usually protons and deuterons: it is used in atomic research.
**cyg·net** (sig′nit), *n.* [dim. < Fr. *cygne*, swan < LL. < Gr. *kyknos*, swan], a young swan.
**Cyg·nus** (sig′nəs), *n.* [L. < Gr. *kyknos*, swan], a northern constellation, the Swan, in the Milky Way.
**cyl.,** 1. cylinder. 2. cylindrical.
**cyl·in·der** (sil′in-dẽr), *n.* [< Fr. < L. < Gr. < *kylindein*, to roll], 1. in *geometry*, a solid figure described by the edge of a rectangle rotated around the parallel edge as axis: the ends of a cylinder are parallel and equal circles. 2. anything, hollow or solid, with the shape of a cylinder; specif., *a)* the turning part of a revolver, containing chambers for cartridges. *b)* a chamber in which force is exerted on the piston of a reciprocating engine. *c)* the barrel of a pump.

CYLINDER

**cy·lin·dri·cal** (si-lin′dri-k'l), *adj.* 1. having the shape of a cylinder. 2. of a cylinder. Also **cy·lin′dric.** —**cy·lin′dri·cal′i·ty** (-kal′ə-ti), *n.* —**cy·lin′dri·cal·ly,** *adv.*
**Cym.,** Cymric.
**cym·bal** (sim′b'l), *n.* [< OFr. & AS. < L. < Gr. < *kymbē*, hollow of a vessel], either of a pair of slightly concave plates of brass, used in orchestras or bands: when struck together they produce a sharp, ringing sound. —**cym′bal·ist,** *n.*
**cyme** (sīm), *n.* [< L. < Gr. *kyma*, swelling < *kyein*, to be pregnant], a cluster of flowers in which each main and secondary stem bears a single flower, as in phlox. —**cy·mose** (sī′mōs, sī-mōs′), *adj.*

CYMBALS

**Cym·ric** (kim′rik, sim′-), *adj.* [< W. *Cymru*, Wales], 1. of the Celtic people of Wales. 2. of their language. *n.* a group of Brythonic Celtic languages. Also **Kymric.**
**Cym·ry** (kim′ri, sim′-), *n.pl.* the Cymric Celts; the Welsh: also **Kymry.**
**cyn·ic** (sin′ik), *n.* [see CYNICAL], 1. [C-], a member of a sect of ancient Greek philosophers who held virtue to be the only good, and stressed independence from worldly needs and pleasures; they became critical of the rest of society. 2. a cynical person. *adj.* 1. [C-], of or like the Cynics or their doctrines. 2. cynical.
**cyn·i·cal** (sin′i-k'l), *adj.* [< L. < Gr. *kynikos*, canine < *kyōn*, dog], 1. inclined to question the sincerity and goodness of people's motives and actions. 2. morose, sarcastic, etc. —**cyn′i·cal·ly,** *adv.* —**cyn′i·cal·ness,** *n.*
**cyn·i·cism** (sin′ə-siz'm), *n.* 1. [C-], the philosophy of the Cynics. 2. the attitude or beliefs of a cynic. 3. a cynical expression or view.
**cy·no·sure** (sī′nə-shoor′, sin′ə-), *n.* [< Gr. *kynosoura*, dog's tail], 1. [C-], the constellation Ursa Minor. 2. [C-], the North Star. 3. anything that guides or directs. 4. any person or thing that is a center of attention or interest.
**Cyn·thi·a** (sin′thi-ə), *n.* 1. Artemis (or Diana), goddess of the moon. 2. the moon personified.
**cy·pher** (sī′fẽr), *n., v.t. & v.i.* cipher.
**cy·press** (sī′prəs), *n.* [< OFr. < L. *cypressus* < or akin to Gr. *kyparissos*], 1. an evergreen, cone-bearing tree of the pine family, native to North America, Europe, and Asia. 2. its hard wood. 3. any of a number of related trees.
**Cyp·ri·an** (sip′ri-ən), *adj.* of Cyprus, its people, or its language. *n.* a native or inhabitant of Cyprus. Also **Cyp′ri·ot** (-ot), **Cyp′ri·ote′** (-ōt′).
**cyp·ri·noid** (sip′ri-noid′, si-prī′noid), *adj.* [< Gr. *kyprinos*, carp; + *-oid*], of or like the fishes of the carp family, including the carps, goldfishes, dace, certain minnows, etc. *n.* a fish of this family. Also **cy·pri·nid** (si-prī′nid).
**Cy·prus** (sī′prəs), a country on an island in the E Mediterranean, a member of the British Commonwealth of Nations: area, 3,572 sq. mi.; pop., 562,000; capital, Nicosia.
**Cy·ril·lic** (si-ril′ik), *adj.* [attributed to St. Cyril, 9th-c. apostle to the Slavs], designating or of the alphabet used for Russian, Bulgarian, and some other Slavic languages.
**Cy·rus** (sī′rəs), *n.* Persian king; lived 600?–529 B.C.; founded the Persian empire: called *the Great.*
**cyst** (sist), *n.* [< Gr. *kystis*, sac, bladder], 1. any of certain saclike structures in plants or animals. 2. any saclike growth in the body, especially if filled with fluid or diseased matter. —**cyst′ic,** *adj.* —**cyst′oid,** *adj. & n.*
**-cyst,** [see CYST], a suffix meaning *sac, pouch, bladder*, as in *encyst.*
**cys·to-,** [see CYST], a combining form meaning *of* or *like a bladder* or *sac*: also **cyst-, cysti-.**
**cys·to·scope** (sis′tə-skōp′), *n.* [*cysto-* + *-scope*], an instrument for examining the interior of the urinary bladder. *v.t.* [-SCOPED, -SCOPING], to examine with a cystoscope. —**cys·tos′co·py** (-tos′kə-pi), *n.*
**-cyte** (sīt), [< Gr. *kytos*, a hollow], a combining form meaning *a cell*, as in *lymphocyte.*
**Cyth·er·e·a** (sith′ə-rē′ə), *n.* Aphrodite; Venus. —**Cyth′er·e′an,** *adj.*
**cy·to-,** [see -CYTE], a combining form meaning *of a cell* or *cells*: also **cyt-.**
**cy·tol·o·gy** (sī-tol′ə-ji), *n.* [*cyto-* + *-logy*], the branch of biology dealing with the structure, function, pathology, and life history of cells. —**cy′to·log′i·cal,** *adj.* —**cy·tol′o·gist,** *n.*
**cy·to·plasm** (sī′tə-plaz'm), *n.* [*cyto-* + *-plasm*], the protoplasm of a cell, exclusive of the nucleus: also **cy′to·plast′.** —**cy′to·plas′mic,** *adj.*
**C.Z.,** Canal Zone.
**czar** (zär), *n.* [< Russ. < OSlav. prob. via Goth. < L. *Caesar;* see CAESAR], 1. an emperor: title of any of the former emperors of Russia. 2. an autocrat; despot; absolute ruler. Also **tsar, tzar.** —**czar′dom,** *n.* —**czar′ism,** *n.* —**czar′ist,** *adj. & n.*
**czar·das** (chär′däsh), *n.* [Hung. *csárdás*], 1. a Hungarian dance with fast and slow movements. 2. the music for this dance.
**czar·e·vitch** (zär′ə-vich′), *n.* [< Russ.], 1. the eldest son of a Russian czar. 2. formerly, any son of a Russian czar. Also **tsarevitch, tzarevich.**
**cza·rev·na** (zä-rev′nə), *n.* [< Russ.], 1. a Russian czar's daughter. 2. the wife of a czarevitch. Also **tsarevna, tzarevna.**
**cza·ri·na** (zä-rē′nə), *n.* [< G. < Russ. *tsaritsa*], the wife of a czar; empress of Russia: also **cza·rit·za** (zä-rit′sə), **tsarina, tzarina.**
**Czech** (chek), *n.* 1. a Bohemian, Moravian, or Silesian Slav. 2. the West Slavic language of the Czechs: also called *Bohemian.* *adj.* of Czechoslovakia, its people, or their language: also **Czech′ic, Czech′ish.**
**Czech·o·slo·vak, Czech·o-Slo·vak** (chek′ə-slō′vak, -väk), *adj.* of Czechoslovakia, its people or language. *n.* 1. a Czech or Slovak living in Czechoslovakia. 2. the language spoken there.
**Czech·o·slo·va·ki·a, Czech·o-Slo·va·ki·a** (chek′ə-slō-vä′ki-ə, -vak′yə), *n.* a country in central Europe: area, 49,381 sq. mi.; pop., 13,649,000; capital, Prague. —**Czech′o·slo·vak′i·an, Czech′o-Slo·vak′i·an,** *adj. & n.*

# D

**D, d** (dē), *n.* [*pl.* D's, d's, Ds, ds], 1. the fourth letter of the English alphabet. 2. the sound of D or d. *adj.* fourth in a sequence or group.

**D** (dē), *n.* 1. a Roman numeral for 500. 2. in *chemistry, the symbol for* deuterium. 3. in *music, a*) the second tone in the scale of C major. *b*) the scale having D as the keynote. 4. in *physics, the symbol for* density. *adj.* shaped like D.

**D.,** 1. December. 2. Democrat(ic). 3. Dutch.

**d.,** 1. day(s). 2. dead. 3. degree. 4. delete. 5. [L.], *denarius*, penny; *denarii*, pence: as, 6*d*. 6. diameter. 7. died. 8. dollar. 9. dose.

**'d,** 1. abbreviated spelling of *had* or *would*, as in *I'd*, *they'd*, etc. 2. -ed, as in *foster'd*.

**D.A.,** District Attorney.

**dab** (dab), *v.t. & v.i.* [DABBED, DABBING], [ME. *dabben*, to strike], 1. to touch lightly and quickly. 2. to pat with something soft or moist. 3. to put on (paint, etc.) with light, quick strokes. *n.* 1. a light, quick blow; tap; pat. 2. a small, soft, or moist bit of something: as, a *dab* of rouge. —**dab'ber,** *n.*

**dab** (dab), *n.* [<ME. *dabben;* see DAB], 1. a small flounder. 2. any small, edible flatfish.

**dab·ble** (dab''l), *v.t.* [-BLED, -BLING], [< D. *dabben*, to strike], 1. to dip lightly in and out of a liquid. 2. to wet as by sprinkling. *v.i.* 1. to play in water, as with the hands. 2. to do something superficially (with *in* or *at*): as, he *dabbles* in art. —**dab'bler,** *n.*

**dab·chick** (dab'chik'), *n.* [*dab*, *v.* + *chick*], 1. the European little grebe. 2. the American pied-billed grebe.

**‡da ca·po** (dä kä'pô), [It.], in *music*, from the beginning: abbrev. **D.C.**

**dace** (dās), *n.* [*pl.* DACE, DACES; see PLURAL, II, D, 2], [< OFr. *dars* < ML. *darsus*], a small fresh-water fish of the carp family.

**Da·chau** (dä'khou), *n.* a Nazi concentration camp near Munich, Germany.

**dachs·hund** (däks'hoond', daks'hund', dash'-; G. däkhs'hoont'), *n.* [G. *dachs*, badger + *hund*, dog], a small dog of German breed, with a long body and short legs.

**da·cron** (dā'kron), *n.* a synthetic fiber, or a washable fabric made from this fiber that is resistant to wrinkling: a trade-mark (**Dacron**).

**dac·tyl** (dak'til, -t'l), *n.* < L. < Gr. *daktylos*, a finger], in *prosody*, a metrical foot of three syllables, the first accented and the others unaccented, in English verse (e.g., glō-ri-ous). —**dac·tyl'ic,** *adj.*

**-dac·ty·ly** (dak't'l-i), [< Gr. *daktylos*, a finger], a combining form meaning *a* (specified) *condition of the fingers, toes,* etc.: also **-dactylia.**

**dad** (dad), *n.* [< child's cry *dada*], [Colloq.], father: also **dad'dy** (dad'i), [*pl.* -DIES].

**Da·da** (dä'dä, -də), *n.* [Fr.; prob. < child's cry], a cult (1916–1922) in art and literature characterized by satiric nihilism and irrational, formless expression of supposedly subconscious matter: also **Da'da·ism.** —**Da'da·ist,** *adj. & n.*

**dad·dy-long·legs** (dad'i-lôŋ'legz'), *n.* [*pl.* DADDY-LONGLEGS], 1. [Brit.], the crane fly. 2. the harvestman, an arachnid with long legs.

**da·do** (dā'dō), *n.* [*pl.* -DOES], [< It. < L. *datum*, a die], 1. the part of a pedestal between the cap and the base. 2. the lower part of the wall of a room if decorated differently from the upper part.

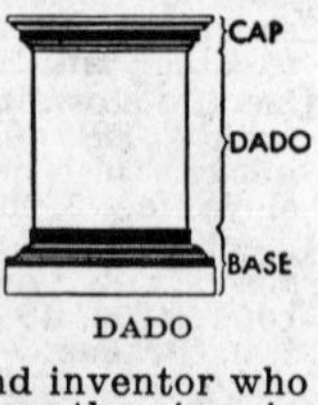

DADO

**Dae·da·li·an, Dae·da·le·an** (di-dā'li-ən, -dāl'yən), *adj.* 1. of Daedalus. 2. [d-], ingenious or intricate. Also sp. **Dedalian, Dedalean.**

**Daed·a·lus** (ded'ə-ləs, dē'də-), *n.* in *Gr. legend*, the skillful artist and inventor who built the labyrinth in Crete and was then imprisoned in it with his son Icarus: see **Icarus.**

**dae·mon** (dē'mən), *n.* [L. < Gr. *daimōn*], 1. in *Gr. mythology*, any of the secondary divinities ranking below the gods. 2. a guardian spirit. 3. a demon; devil. —**dae·mon·ic** (di-mon'ik), *adj.*

**daf·fa·down·dil·ly, daf·fy·down·dil·ly** (daf'ə-doun-dil'i), *n.* [*pl.* -LIES], [Dial.], a daffodil: also **daf'fo·dil'ly, daf'fa·dil'ly** [*pl.* -LIES].

**daf·fo·dil** (daf'ə-dil'), *n.* [< ML. < L. *asphodelus* < Gr. *asphodelos*], 1. a narcissus with long, narrow leaves and yellow flowers. 2. its flower. 3. yellow.

**daf·fy** (daf'i), *adj.* [-FIER, -FIEST], [? < obs. *daff*, a fool], [Colloq.], crazy; idiotic; silly.

**daft** (daft, däft), *adj.* [< AS. (*ge*)*dæfte*, mild, gentle], 1. silly; foolish. 2. insane. —**daft'ly,** *adv.* —**daft'ness,** *n.*

**dag·ger** (dag'ēr), *n.* [ME., as if < *daggen*, to slit], 1. a short weapon with a sharp point, used for stabbing. 2. in *printing*, a reference mark (†). *v.t.* 1. to stab with a dagger. 2. to mark with a dagger. —**look daggers at,** to look at with anger.

**dag·gle** (dag''l), *v.t. & v.i.* [-GLED, -GLING], [< dial. *dag*, to make muddy], to make or become dirty by trailing through mud.

**Da·gon** (dā'gon, -gən), *n.* [L.; Gr.; Heb. < *dāg*, a fish], the main god of the ancient Philistines, represented as half man and half fish.

**da·guerre·o·type** (də-ger'ə-tīp', -i-ə-tīp'), *n.* [after L. J. M. *Daguerre* (1789–1851), Fr. inventor], 1. a photograph made by an early method on a plate of chemically treated metal or glass. 2. the method itself. *v.t.* to photograph by this method. —**da·guerre'o·typ'er, da·guerre'o·typ'ist,** *n.* —**da·guerre'o·typ'y,** *n.*

**dahl·ia** (dal'yə, däl'-, dāl'-), *n.* [after A. *Dahl*, 18th-c. Swed. botanist], 1. a perennial plant of the composite family, with tuberous roots and large, showy flowers. 2. the flower.

**Da·ho·mey** (dä-hō'mā; Fr. då'ô'mā'), *n.* a country on the W coast of Africa, a member of the French community: area, 44,696 sq. mi.; pop., 1,713,000; capital, Porto Novo. —**Da·ho·man** (dä-hō'mən), *adj. & n.*

**Dail Eir·eann** (dôl âr'ən, doil, dīl), [Ir. *dāil*, assembly + *Eireann*, genit. of *Eire*, Ireland], the lower house of the legislature of Ireland.

**dai·ly** (dā'li), *adj.* relating to, done, happening, or published every day or every weekday. *n.* [*pl.* -LIES], a newspaper published every day or every weekday. *adv.* every day; day after day.

**daily dozen,** [Colloq.], gymnastic setting-up exercises (originally twelve) done daily.

**dain·ty** (dān'ti), *n.* [*pl.* -TIES], [< OFr. *deinté*, worth, delicacy < L. *dignitas*, worth, dignity], a delicacy. *adj.* [-TIER, -TIEST], 1. delicious and choice. 2. delicately pretty or lovely. 3. of delicate and refined taste. 4. fastidious; squeamish. —**dain'ti·ly,** *adv.* —**dain'ti·ness,** *n.*

**Dai·ren** (dī'ren'), *n.* a seaport in NE China, on the Yellow Sea: pop. (with near-by Port Arthur), 1,054,000. Chinese name, *Talien.*

**dair·y** (dâr'i), *n.* [*pl.* -IES], [ME. *deierie* < *deie*, dairymaid < AS. *dæge*, breadmaker], 1. a place where milk and cream are kept and made into butter, cheese, etc. 2. a store where milk and milk products are sold. 3. the business of producing or selling milk and milk products: also **dair'y·ing.** 4. a farm (**dairy farm**) in this business.

**dairy cattle,** cows raised mainly for milk.

**dair·y·maid** (dâr'i-mād'), *n.* a girl or woman who works in a dairy.

**dair·y·man** (dâr'i-mən), *n.* [*pl.* -MEN], 1. a man who works in or for a dairy. 2. a man who owns a dairy.

**da·is** (dā'is, dās), *n.* [*pl.* DAISES], [< OFr. < LL. *discus*, table < L. *discus*, platter, quoit], a platform raised above the floor at one end of a room, as in a banquet hall or classroom.

**dai·sy** (dā'zi), *n.* [*pl.* -SIES], [AS. *dæges eage*, lit., day's eye], 1. a plant of the composite family, bearing flowers with white or pink rays around a yellow disk: also **English daisy.** 2. a related tall chrysanthemum with large flowers that have long, white rays around a yellow disk. 3. [Slang], something outstanding or notable.

**Dak.,** Dakota.

**Da·kar** (då′kär′), *n.* capital and seaport of Senegal, in NW Africa: pop., 234,500.

**Da·ko·ta** (də-kō′tə), *n.* 1. a member of a group of Siouan tribes that lived in North and South Dakota. 2. their Siouan language. 3. a former U.S. Territory, now forming North Dakota and South Dakota (**the Dakotas**). *adj.* 1. of a Dakota. 2. of Dakota. 3. of the Dakotas. —**Da·ko′tan,** *adj.* & *n.*

**dal.,** decaliter.

**Da·lai La·ma** (dä-lī′ lä′mə), [Mong. *dalai*, ocean + *blama;* see LAMA], the high priest of the Lamaist religion in Tibet and Mongolia; Grand Lama.

**dale** (dāl), *n.* [AS. *dæl*], a small valley.

**Dal·las** (dal′əs), *n.* a city in NE Texas: pop., 680,000.

**dal·li·ance** (dal′i-əns, **dal′yəns**), *n.* the act of dallying; flirting, toying, trifling, etc.

**dal·ly** (dal′i), *v.i.* [-LIED, -LYING], [< OFr. *dalier*, to converse, trifle], 1. to play, especially in making love. 2. to flirt or toy: as, he *dallied* with the idea. 3. to loiter; waste time. *v.t.* to spend (time) in trifling (with *away*). —**dal′li·er,** *n.*

**Dal·ma·tia** (dal-mā′shə), *n.* a region of SW Yugoslavia.

**Dal·ma·tian** (dal-mā′shən), *adj.* of Dalmatia or its people. *n.* 1. a native or inhabitant of Dalmatia. 2. a large, lean, short-haired dog with a black-and-white coat: also called *coach dog.*

DALMATIAN (23 in. high)

**‡dal se·gno** (däl se′nyô), [It.], in *music*, from the sign: a direction to return and repeat from the sign 𝄋: abbrev. **D.S., d.s.**

**dam** (dam), *n.* [< MD. *damm*], 1. a barrier built to hold back flowing water. 2. the water thus kept back. 3. a thing like a dam. *v.t.* [DAMMED, DAMMING], 1. to put a dam in. 2. to keep back by means of a dam; hence, 3. to keep back or confine (usually with *in* or *up*).

**dam** (dam), *n.* [see DAME], 1. the female parent of any four-footed animal. 2. [Archaic], a mother.

**dam·age** (dam′ij), *n.* [OFr. < L. *damnum*, loss, injury], 1. injury; harm causing a loss. 2. the loss so caused. 3. *pl.* in *law*, money claimed by, or ordered paid to, a person to compensate for injury, loss, etc. that is another's fault. 4. *usually pl.* [Colloq.], cost or expense. *v.t.* [-AGED, -AGING], to do damage to. *v.i.* to incur damage. —**dam′age·a·ble,** *adj.* —**dam′ag·ing·ly,** *adv.*

**Dam·a·scene** (dam′ə-sēn′, dam′ə-sēn′), *adj.* [L. *Damascenus*, of Damascus], 1. of Damascus, its people, etc. 2. [d-], of damascening or damask. *n.* 1. a native or inhabitant of Damascus. 2. [d-], damascened work. *v.t.* [-SCENED, -SCENING], [d-], to decorate (metal) with wavy markings: also **dam′a·skeen′** (-skēn′).

**Da·mas·cus** (də-mas′kəs), *n.* the capital of Syria: it is one of the oldest cities in the world: pop., 455,000.

**dam·ask** (dam′əsk), *n.* [< It. < L. *Damascus*, the city], 1. a reversible fabric, usually of silk or linen, in figured weave. 2. a fine twilled table linen. 3. damascened steel. 4. the wavy markings of such steel. 5. deep pink or rose. *adj.* 1. of or from Damascus. 2. made of damask. 3. like damask. 4. deep-pink or rose. *v.t.* 1. to weave like damask cloth. 2. to damascene.

**damask rose,** a large, fragrant, deep-pink rose, used in the Orient for making attar of roses.

**damask steel,** steel decorated with wavy lines or inlaid work, originally made in Damascus and used for sword blades: also **Damascus steel.**

**dame** (dām), *n.* [OFr. < L. *domina*, lady, fem. of *dominus*, a lord], 1. a title formerly given to the mistress of a household. 2. a lady. 3. an elderly woman. 4. in Great Britain, *a*) the legal title of the wife or widow of a knight or baronet. *b*) [D-], a title awarded to a woman as the equivalent of a knight's title, *Sir.* 5. [Slang], a girl or woman.

**damn** (dam), *v.t.* [DAMNED, DAMNING], [< OFr. < L. *damnare*, to condemn < *damnum*, loss], 1. to condemn as bad, inferior, etc.: often used in the imperative as a curse. 2. to criticize adversely. 3. to ruin the chances of; make fail. 4. to swear at by saying "damn". 5. in *theology*, to condemn to eternal punishment, as in hell. *v.i.* to swear or curse; say "damn", etc. *n.* the saying of "damn" as a curse. *adj.* & *adv.* [Colloq.], damned: a clipped form, used as a strong intensive. *interj.* an expression of anger, annoyance, etc. Often euphemized as *darn, dog-gone*, etc. —**damn with faint praise,** to condemn by praising mildly. —**not care** (or **give**) **a damn,** [Colloq.], not care at all. —**damn′er,** *n.*

**dam·na·ble** (dam′nə-b′l), *adj.* 1. deserving damnation. 2. deserving to be sworn at; outrageous. —**dam′na·ble·ness,** *n.* —**dam′na·bly,** *adv.*

**dam·na·tion** (dam-nā′shən), *n.* 1. a damning or being damned. 2. condemnation to endless punishment, as in hell. 3. endless punishment. *interj.* an expression of anger, annoyance, etc. —**dam′na·to′ry** (-tôr′i, -tō′ri), *adj.*

**damned** (damd; *also, as in poetry*, dam′nid), *adj.* 1. condemned or deserving condemnation. 2. [Colloq.], cursed; outrageous: as, a *damned* shame. 3. in *theology*, doomed to endless punishment, as in hell. *adv.* [Colloq.], very: as, *damned* silly. —**the damned,** in *theology*, souls doomed to eternal punishment, as in hell.

**Dam·o·cles** (dam′ə-klēz′), *n.* in *Gr. legend*, a courtier of ancient Syracuse to whom the king, Dionysius, demonstrated the dangers of a ruler's life by seating him at a banquet just below a sword hanging by a hair. —**sword of Damocles,** any imminent danger.

**dam·oi·selle, dam·o·sel, dam·o·zel** (dam′ə-zel′), *n.* [Archaic], a damsel.

**Da·mon and Pyth·i·as** (dā′mən ən pith′i-əs), in *Rom. legend*, friends so devoted to each other that when Pythias, condemned to death, wanted time to arrange his affairs, Damon pledged his life that his friend would return: Pythias returned.

**damp** (damp), *n.* [MD., vapor], 1. moisture; wetness. 2. a harmful gas sometimes found in mines; firedamp; chokedamp. 3. a dejected or depressed state. *adj.* somewhat moist or wet. *v.t.* 1. to make damp; moisten. 2. to stifle; make choke. 3. to check or reduce (energy, action, etc.). —**damp′ish,** *adj.* —**damp′ly,** *adv.* —**damp′ness,** *n.*

**damp-dry** (damp′drī′), *v.t.* [-DRIED, -DRYING], to dry (laundry) so that some moisture is kept. *adj.* designating laundry so dried.

**damp·en** (dam′pən), *v.t.* 1. to make damp; moisten. 2. to depress; dishearten. 3. to deaden, reduce, or lessen. *v.i.* to become damp. —**damp′en·er,** *n.*

**damp·er** (dam′pẽr), *n.* 1. a person or thing that depresses or disheartens. 2. a movable plate or valve in the flue of a stove or furnace, for controlling the draft. 3. a device to check vibration in the strings of a piano, etc.

**dam·sel** (dam′z'l), *n.* [< OFr. *dameisele* < LL. < L. *domina;* see DAME], [Archaic], a girl; maiden.

**dam·son** (dam′z'n), *n.* [< OFr. < L. *Damascenus*, (plum) of Damascus], 1. a variety of small, purple plum. 2. the tree that it grows on.

**Dan** (dan), *n.* 1. in the *Bible*, *a*) the fifth son of Jacob. *b*) the tribe of Israel descended from him. 2. a town in N Palestine. —**from Dan to Beersheba,** from end to end (Beersheba was in S Palestine).

**Dan.,** 1. Daniel: also **Danl.** 2. Danish.

**Da·na·i·des, Da·na·ï·des** (də-nā′ə-dēz′), *n.pl.* [sing. DANAID, DANAID (dan′i-id)], in *Gr. legend*, the fifty daughters of Danaus: forty-nine murdered their husbands at their father's command, and were condemned in Hades to keep drawing water with a sieve.

**Dan·a·us, Dan·a·üs** (dan′i-əs), *n.* in *Gr. legend*, a king of Argos, a city in E Peloponnesus.

**dance** (dans, däns), *v.i.* [DANCED, DANCING], [< OFr. *danser* < OHG. *dansōn*, to draw out], 1. to move the body, especially the feet, in rhythm, ordinarily to music. 2. to move lightly, rapidly, or gaily about, as leaves in a wind. 3. to bob up and down. *v.t.* 1. to perform or take part in (a dance). 2. to cause to dance. 3. to dandle. *n.* 1. rhythmic movement of the feet or body, ordinarily to music. 2. a particular kind of dance, as the waltz or tango. 3. the art of dancing. 4. one round of a dance. 5. a party to which people come to dance. 6. a piece of music for dancing. 7. rapid, lively movement. —**dance attendance on,** to be always near so as to lavish attentions on. —**danc′er,** *n.* —**danc′ing,** *n.* —**danc′ing·ly,** *adv.*

**dan·de·li·on** (dan′di-lī′ən), *n.* [< Fr. *dent de lion* < L. *dens*, tooth + *de*, of, + *leo*, lion], a common weed with yellow flowers, and jagged, edible leaves.

**dan·der** (dan′dẽr), *n.* [? < Scot. *dunder*, resounding], [Colloq.], 1. anger. 2. temper. —**get one's dander up,** [Colloq.], to become angry.

**dan·di·fy** (dan′di-fī′), *v.t.* [-FIED, -FYING], to make look like a dandy; dress up. —**dan′di·fi·ca′tion** (-fi-kā′shən), *n.*

**dan·dle** (dan′d'l), *v.t.* [-DLED, -DLING], [< It. *dondolare*], 1. to dance (a child) up and down as on the knee. 2. to fondle; pet. —**dan′dler,** *n.*

**dan·druff** (dan′drəf), *n.* [folk etym. of earlier *dandro* + Eng. dial. *hurf*, scab], little scales of dead skin formed on the scalp.

**dan·dy** (dan′di), *n.* [*pl.* -DIES], [Scot. var. of *Andy* <*Andrew* (see MERRY-ANDREW)], 1. a man overly attentive to his clothes and appearance; fop. 2. [Slang], something very good; first-class thing. *adj.* 1. dressed like a fop. 2. [Slang], very good; first-class. —**dan′dy·ish,** *adj.* —**dan′dy·ism,** *n.*

**Dane** (dān), *n.* a native or inhabitant of Denmark.

**Dane·law, Dane·lagh** (dān′lô′), *n.* 1. the code of Scandinavian laws established in NE England by Norse invaders in the 9th and 10th centuries A.D. 2. the section of England under these laws.

**dan·ger** (dān′jēr), *n.* [< OFr. < LL. < L. < *dominus*, a master; ? infl. by LL. *damnum*, injury], 1. liability to injury, damage, or loss; peril. 2. a thing that may cause injury, pain, etc.

**dan·ger·ous** (dān′jēr-əs), *adj.* full of danger; unsafe; perilous. —**dan′ger·ous·ly,** *adv.* —**dan′ger·ous·ness,** *n.*

**dan·gle** (daŋ′g' ), *v.i.* [-GLED, -GLING], [< ON.], 1. to hang swinging loosely. 2. to follow (*after*); be a hanger-on. 3. in *grammar*, to lack clear connection with the proper substantive: as, a *dangling* participle. *v.t.* to cause to dangle. —**dan′gler,** *n.*

**Dan·iel** (dan′yəl), *n.* in the *Bible*, 1. a Hebrew prophet whose faith saved him in the lions' den. 2. the book of the Old Testament with his story.

**Dan·ish** (dān′ish), *adj.* of Denmark, the Danes, or their language. *n.* the language of the Danes.

**dank** (daŋk), *adj.* [? < ON.], disagreeably damp; moist and chilly. —**dank′ly,** *adv.* —**dank′ness,** *n.*

**dan·seuse** (dän-sooz′; Fr. dän′söz′), *n.* [*pl.* -SEUSES (-sooz′iz; Fr. -söz′)], [Fr.], a girl or woman dancer, especially a ballet dancer.

**Dan·te A·li·ghie·ri** (dän′te ä′lē-gyâr′ē; Eng. dan′ti), 1265–1321; Italian poet; wrote *The Divine Comedy*. —**Dan′te·an,** *adj.* & *n.* —**Dan·tesque′** (-tesk′), *adj.*

**Dan·ube** (dan′ūb), *n.* a river flowing from SW Germany eastward into the Black Sea: length, 1,725 mi. —**Dan·u′bi·an** (-ū′bi-ən), *adj.*

**Dan·zig** (dan′tsig, -sig; G. dän′tsikh), *n.* a seaport in Poland on the Baltic Sea: formerly an autonomous region (**Free City of Danzig**), 1920–1939: pop., 170,000.

**Daph·ne** (daf′ni), *n.* in *Gr. mythology*, a nymph who escaped from Apollo by becoming a laurel tree.

**dap·per** (dap′ēr), *adj.* [? < MD.], 1. small and active. 2. trim; neat; spruce. —**dap′per·ly,** *adv.* —**dap′per·ness,** *n.*

**dap·ple** (dap′'l), *adj.* [< ON. *depill*, a spot < *dapi*, a pool], spotted; mottled; variegated: also **dappled.** *n.* 1. a spotted condition. 2. an animal whose skin is spotted. *v.t.* [-PLED, -PLING], to cover with spots.

**dap·ple-gray** (dap′'l-grā′), *adj.* gray spotted with darker gray. *n.* a dapple-gray horse.

**D.A.R.,** Daughters of the American Revolution.

**Dar·by and Joan** (där′bi ən jōn), [< an old song (1753)], an old married couple who live in perfect harmony.

**Dar·da·nelles** (där′də-nelz′), *n.* the strait joining the Aegean and the Sea of Marmara: length, 40 mi.; width, 1–4 mi.: ancient name, *Hellespont.*

**dare** (dâr), *v.i.* [DARED or *archaic* DURST (dūrst), DARED, DARING; 3d pers. sing., pres. indic., DARE, DARES], [< AS. *dear*, 1st pers. sing. of *durran*], to have enough courage or boldness for some act; be fearless. *v.t.* 1. to have courage for; venture upon. 2. to oppose and defy. 3. to challenge (someone) to do something hard or dangerous. *n.* a challenge. —**dare say,** to think very likely; consider probable. —**dar′er,** *n.*

**dare·dev·il** (dâr′dev′'l), *adj.* reckless; foolhardy. *n.* a foolhardy or reckless person.

**Dar·i·en, Gulf of** (dâr′i-en′; Sp. dä′rē-en′), an inlet of the Caribbean, between Panama and Colombia.

**Darien, Isthmus of,** the Isthmus of Panama: the former name.

**dar·ing** (dâr′iŋ), *adj.* fearless; bold. *n.* bold courage. —**dar′ing·ly,** *adv.* —**dar′ing·ness,** *n.*

**Da·ri·us I** (də-rī′əs), 558?–486 B.C.; king of Persia (521–486 B.C.): called *the Great.*

**dark** (därk), *adj.* [< AS. *deorc*], 1. entirely or partly without light. 2. neither giving nor receiving light. 3. giving no performance: as, this theater is *dark* tonight. 4. almost black. 5. not light in color or complexion; brunet. 6. hidden. 7. not easily understood. 8. gloomy. 9. evil; sinister. 10. ignorant; unenlightened. *n.* 1. the state of being dark. 2. night; nightfall. 3. obscurity. 4. secrecy. 5. ignorance. —**in the dark,** uninformed; ignorant. —**keep dark,** to keep secret or hidden. —**dark′ish,** *adj.* —**dark′ish·ness,** *n.* —**dark′ly,** *adv.* —**dark′ness,** *n.*

**Dark Ages, dark ages,** [<*dark*, *adj.* 10], 1. the Middle Ages. 2. the earlier part of the Middle Ages, to about the end of the 10th century.

**Dark Continent,** Africa: so called because it was little known until the 19th century.

**dark·en** (där′kən), *v.i.* & *v.t.* to make or become dark or darker. —**not darken one's door** (or **doorway**), not come to one's home. —**dark′en·er,** *n.*

**dark horse,** [Colloq.], 1. an unexpected, almost unknown winner, as in a horse race. 2. in *politics*, one who gets or may get the nomination unexpectedly.

**dark lantern,** a lantern with a shutter that can hide the light.

**dark·ling** (därk′liŋ), *adv.* [*dark* + *-ling*], [Poetic], in the dark. *adj.* [Poetic], dusky; dim.

**dark·room** (därk′rōōm′, -room′), *n.* a room from which all actinic rays are excluded, so that photographs can be developed in it.

**dark·some** (därk′səm), *adj.* [Poetic], 1. dark. 2. dismal; gloomy. 3. obscure.

**dark·y** (där′ki), *n.* [*pl.* -IES], [Colloq.], a Negro: patronizing or contemptuous term: also sp. **darkey, darkie.**

**dar·ling** (där′liŋ), *n.* [AS. *deorling*, dim.; see DEAR], 1. a person much loved by another. 2. a favorite. *adj.* 1. very dear; beloved. 2. cherished.

**darn** (därn), *v.t.* & *v.i.* [< MFr. dial. *darner*, to mend], to mend by sewing a network of stitches across the gap. *n.* 1. a darning. 2. a darned place in fabric. —**darn′er,** *n.*

**darn** (därn), *v.t., n., adj., adv., interj.* [Colloq.], damn: a euphemism for the curse.

**dar·nel** (där′n'l), *n.* [< Fr. dial. *darnelle*], a poisonous weed resembling rye, often found in grainfields: also called *rye grass.*

**darn·ing** (därn′iŋ), *n.* 1. the act of one who darns. 2. things darned or to be darned.

**darning needle,** 1. a large needle for darning. 2. a dragonfly.

**Dar·row, Clarence Sew·ard** (sōō′ērd, sū′ērd dar′ō), 1857–1938; U.S. lawyer.

**dart** (därt), *n.* [< OFr. < Gmc. source], 1. a small, pointed weapon for throwing or shooting. 2. anything resembling this. 3. a sudden, quick movement. 4. an insect's stinger. 5. a short, tapered seam to make a garment fit more closely. *v.t.* & *v.i.* 1. to throw, shoot, etc. suddenly and fast. 2. to move suddenly and fast.

**dart·er** (där′tēr), *n.* a thing or animal that darts; specif., *a*) a tropical, fish-eating bird with a snakelike neck: also **snake′bird′**. *b*) any of several small, perchlike, fresh-water fishes.

**dar·tle** (där′t'l), *v.t.* & *v.i.* [-TLED, -TLING], to dart again and again; dart about.

**Dar·win, Charles Robert** (där′win), 1809–1882; English naturalist. —**Dar·win′i·an,** *adj.* & *n.*

**Darwinian theory,** Darwin's theory of evolution, which holds that all species of plants and animals developed from earlier forms by hereditary transmission of slight variations in successive generations, those forms surviving which are best adapted to the environment (*natural selection*): also called **Dar′win·ism.** —**Dar′win·ist,** *n.* & *adj.*

**dash** (dash), *v.t.* [ME. *daschen*], 1. to smash. 2. to strike violently against. 3. to throw or thrust (*away, down*, etc.). 4. to splash. 5. to mix with a little of another substance. 6. to destroy. 7. to frustrate; discourage. 8. to abash. 9. to do, write, etc. hastily (with *off*). *v.i.* 1. to strike violently (*against*). 2. to rush. *n.* 1. a smash. 2. a splash. 3. a bit of something. 4. a rush. 5. a short, swift run or race. 6. vigor; spirited quality or showy appearance. 7. a dashboard. 8. the mark (—), used in printing and writing to indicate a break in a sentence, a parenthetical element, or an omission. 9. in *telegraphy*, a long sound, as in the Morse code: opposed to *dot.* —**dash′er,** *n.*

**dash·board** (dash′bôrd′, -bōrd′), *n.* 1. a board or screen at the front of a carriage, boat, etc., to protect against splashing. 2. a panel with instruments and gauges on it, as in an automobile.

**dash·ing** (dash′iŋ), *adj.* 1. full of dash or spirit; lively. 2. showy. —**dash′ing·ly,** *adv.*

**dash·y** (dash′i), *adj.* [-IER, -IEST], 1. having dash; showy. 2. full of dashes. —**dash′i·ly,** *adv.*

**das·tard** (das′tẽrd), *n.* [akin to MD. *daasardt*, a fool, but prob. < ON. *dæstr* < *dæsa*, to groan; + *-ard*], a mean, skulking coward. *adj.* dastardly.
**das·tard·ly** (das′tẽrd-li), *adj.* mean and skulking; cowardly and brutal. —**das′tard·li·ness,** *n.*
**dat.,** dative.
**da·ta** (dā′tə, dat′ə, dä′tə), *n.pl.* [often construed as sing.], [see DATUM], things known or assumed; facts from which conclusions can be inferred.
**date** (dāt), *n.* [< OFr. < L. *data*, < *dare*, to give], 1. a statement on a writing, coin, etc. of when it was made. 2. the time at which a thing happens. 3. the time that anything lasts. 4. the day of the month. 5. [Colloq.], *a*) an appointment for a set time; specif., a social appointment with a person of the opposite sex. *b*) the person with whom one has such an appointment. *v.t.* [DATED, DATING], 1. to mark (a letter, etc.) with a date. 2. to find out or give the date of. 3. to reckon by dates. 4. [Colloq.], to have a social appointment with. *v.i.* 1. to be dated (usually with *from*). 2. to belong to, or have origin in, a definite period in the past (usually with *from*). —**out of date,** old-fashioned. —**to date,** until now; as yet. —**up to date,** modern; in accord with the latest ideas, facts, etc. —**dat′a·ble,** *adj.*
**date** (dāt), *n.* [< OFr. < L. < Gr. *daktylos*, a date, lit., a finger], 1. the sweet, fleshy fruit of a tall palm (**date palm**). 2. the tree itself.
**dat·ed** (dāt′id), *adj.* 1. marked with or showing a date. 2. out of date; old-fashioned.
**date·less** (dāt′lis), *adj.* 1. without a date. 2. without limit or end. 3. too old for its date to be fixed. 4. still good or interesting though old.
**date line,** 1. a line on which the date of writing or issue is given, as in a letter or newspaper. 2. an imaginary line north and south through the Pacific Ocean, largely along the 180th meridian: the line at which, by international agreement, each calendar day begins at midnight, so that when it is Sunday just west of the line, it is Saturday just east of it.
**da·tive** (dā′tiv), *adj.* [< L. *dativus*, of giving < *datus*, pp. of *dare*, to give], denoting or belonging to that case of a noun, pronoun, etc. which expresses the indirect object of a verb or approach toward something. *n.* 1. the dative case: in English, the dative notion is expressed by *to*, *for*, or word order (e.g., I gave the book *to Jack*, I did the task *for Jack*, I gave *Jack* the book). 2. a word or phrase in the dative. —**da·ti′val** (-tī′v'l), *adj.* —**da′tive·ly,** *adv.*
**da·tum** (dā′təm, dat′əm), *n.* [L., what is given; neut. of *datus;* see DATIVE], sing. of **data.**
**daub** (dôb), *v.t. & v.i.* [< OFr. < L. *dealbare*, to whitewash < *de-*, intens. + *albus*, white], 1. to cover or smear with sticky, soft stuff, such as plaster, grease, etc. 2. to paint badly and coarsely. *n.* 1. anything daubed on. 2. a daubing stroke or splash. 3. a poorly painted picture. —**daub′er,** *n.* —**daub′ing,** *n.*
**Dau·det, Al·phonse** (ål′fōns′ dō′de′; Eng. dō-dā′), 1840–1897; French novelist.
**daugh·ter** (dô′tẽr), *n.* [AS. *dohtor*], 1. a girl or woman in her relationship to either or both parents. 2. a female descendant. 3. a female thought of as if in relation to a parent: as, a *daughter* of France. 4. anything thought of as like a daughter in relation to its origin. —**daugh′ter·ly,** *adj.*
**daugh·ter-in-law** (dô′tẽr-'n-lô′), *n.* [*pl.* DAUGHTERS-IN-LAW], the wife of one's son.
**Dau·mier, Ho·no·ré** (ō′nô′rā′ dō′myā′), 1808–1879; French painter and caricaturist.
**daunt** (dônt, dänt), *v.t.* [< OFr. < L. < *domare*, to tame], 1. to make afraid; intimidate. 2. to dishearten.
**daunt·less** (dônt′lis, dänt′-), *adj.* that cannot be daunted or intimidated; brave. —**daunt′less·ly,** *adv.* —**daunt′less·ness,** *n.*
**dau·phin** (dô′fin; Fr. dō′fan′), *n.* [Fr., lit., dolphin (see DOLPHIN)], the eldest son of the king of France: a title used from 1349 to 1830.
**Dav·en·port** (dav′ən-pôrt′, -pōrt′), *n.* a city in E Iowa, on the Mississippi: pop., 89,000.
**dav·en·port** (dav′ən-pôrt′, -pōrt′), *n.* [< the name of the original manufacturer (19th c.)], a large sofa, sometimes convertible into a bed.
**Da·vid** (dā′vid), *n.* in the *Bible*, the second king of Israel, succeeded by his son Solomon.
**Da·vis, Jefferson** (dā′vis), 1808–1889; president of the Confederacy (1861–1865).
**dav·it** (dav′it), *n.* [< OFr. dim. of *David*], 1. either of a pair of uprights curving over the side of a ship for suspending or lowering a small boat. 2. a crane in a ship's bow, used to raise or lower the anchor.

DAVITS

**Da·vy,** Sir **Hum·phry** (hum′fri dā′vi), 1778–1829; English chemist.
**Da·vy Jones** (dā′vi jōnz′), the spirit of the sea: humorous name given by sailors.
**Davy Jones's locker,** the bottom of the sea; grave of those drowned at sea or buried there.
**Davy lamp,** [after Sir Humphry *Davy*], formerly, a miner's safety lamp in which the flame was enclosed by a screen of wire gauze.
**daw** (dô), *n.* [ME. *dawe*], a jackdaw.
**daw·dle** (dô′d'l), *v.i. & v.t.* [-DLED, -DLING], [var. of dial. *daddle*], to waste (time) in trifling; loiter (often with *away*). —**daw′dler,** *n.*
**dawn** (dôn), *v.i.* [< AS. < *dæg*, day], 1. to begin to be day; grow light. 2. to begin to appear, develop, etc. 3. to begin to be clear to the mind: as, the meaning *dawned* on me. *n.* 1. daybreak. 2. the beginning (*of* something).
**Daw·son** (dô′s'n), *n.* a city in Yukon Territory, Canada, on the Yukon River: pop., 850.
**day** (dā), *n.* [AS. *dæg*], 1. the period of light between sunrise and sunset. 2. daylight. 3. the time (24 hours) that it takes the earth to revolve once on its axis: the legal day is from midnight to midnight. 4. [often D-], a particular or special day: as, D-*Day*. 5. a period of time: as, the best writer of his *day*. 6. a period of power, glory, etc.: as, he's had his *day*. 7. hours of work; shift: as, an eight-hour *day*. 8. *pl.* time; era. 9. *pl.* life: as, he spent his *days* in study. 10. in *astronomy*, the time that it takes a celestial body to revolve once on its axis. —**call it a day,** [Colloq.], to stop working for the day. —**day after day,** every day. —**day by day,** each day. —**day in, day out,** every day. —**from day to day,** from one day to the next.
**day bed,** a sofa that can also be used as a bed.
**day·book** (dā′book′), *n.* 1. a diary. 2. in *bookkeeping*, a book used for keeping a record of the transactions of each day as they occur.
**day·break** (dā′brāk′), *n.* the time in the morning when light first appears; dawn.
**day coach,** a regular passenger car of a railroad train, as distinguished from a sleeping car, etc.
**day·dream** (dā′drēm′), *n.* 1. a pleasant, dreamy thought; reverie. 2. a pleasing but visionary idea. *v.i.* to have daydreams. —**day′dream′er,** *n.*
**day laborer,** an unskilled worker paid by the day.
**day letter,** a telegram with a minimum charge for fifty words or fewer, sent in the daytime: it is cheaper but slower than a regular telegram.
**day·light** (dā′līt′), *n.* 1. the light of day; sunlight. 2. dawn. 3. daytime. 4. understanding; solution (of a problem). 5. publicity.
**day·light-sav·ing time** (dā′līt′sāv′iŋ), time that is one hour later than standard time, generally used in the summer to give an hour more of daylight at the end of the working day: also **Daylight Saving Time.**
**day nursery,** a nursery for taking care of small children during the daytime.
**Day of Atonement,** Yom Kippur, a Jewish holiday: see **Jewish holidays.**
**day room,** in *military usage*, a recreation room for a company, troop, or battery.
**day school,** 1. a school that has classes only in the daytime. 2. a private school whose students live at home and attend classes daily.
**day·time** (dā′tīm′), *n.* the period of daylight.
**Day·ton** (dā′t'n), *n.* a city in SW Ohio, on the Miami River: pop., 262,000.
**daze** (dāz), *v.t.* [DAZED, DAZING], [< ON. *dasask*, to become weary < *dasi*, tired], 1. to stun or bewilder, as by a blow. 2. to dazzle. *n.* a dazed condition; bewilderment. —**daz′ed·ly,** *adv.*
**daz·zle** (daz′'l), *v.t.* [-ZLED, -ZLING], [freq. of *daze*], 1. to overpower, or dim, the vision of with very bright light or moving lights. 2. to surprise or overpower with brilliant qualities, display, etc. *v.i.* 1. to be overpowered by glare. 2. to arouse admiration by brilliant display. *n.* 1. a dazzling. 2. something that dazzles. —**daz′zler,** *n.* —**daz′zling·ly,** *adv.*

**db,** decibel.
**D.Bib.,** Douay Bible.
**D.C.,** District of Columbia.
**D.C., d.c.,** direct current.
**D.D.,** 1. demand draft: also **D/D.** 2. *Divinitatis Doctor,* [L.], Doctor of Divinity.
**dd., d/d,** delivered.
**D-Day** (dē′dā′), *n.* 1. the unspecified day on which a military operation is to take place. 2. June 6, 1944, the day Allied forces invaded W Europe in World War II.
**D.D.S.,** Doctor of Dental Surgery.
**DDT,** [*dichlorodiphenyltrichloroethane*], a powerful insecticide effective upon contact.
**de-,** [< Fr. *dé-* or L. *de* < L. *dis-;* see DIS-], a prefix meaning: 1. *away from, off,* as in *detrain.* 2. *down,* as in *decline.* 3. *wholly, entirely,* as in *derelict.* 4. *undo, reverse the action of,* as in *defrost, decode.*
**dea·con** (dē′k'n), *n.* [AS. < LL. < Gr. *diakonos,* servant], 1. a clergyman ranking just below a priest in the Roman Catholic and Anglican churches. 2. in certain other Christian churches, a layman appointed to help the minister, especially in secular matters, etc. —**dea′con·ry** [*pl.* -RIES], *n.*
**dea·con·ess** (dē′k'n-is), *n.* a woman appointed as an assistant in a church, as one who helps take care of the sick and poor of a parish.
**de·ac·ti·vate** (dē-ak′tə-vāt′), *v.t.* [-VATED, -VATING], in *military usage,* to place (a division, etc.) on a non-active status; disband.
**dead** (ded), *adj.* [AS.], 1. no longer living; having died. 2. without life. 3. deathlike. 4. lacking feeling, energy, warmth, etc. 5. motionless: as, *dead* waters. 6. no longer used or significant; obsolete: as, *dead* laws. 7. lacking interest, color, etc.; dull; flat. 8. barren; unprofitable: as, *dead* soil. 9. unerring; sure: as, a *dead* shot. 10. complete; absolute: as, a *dead* loss. 11. [Colloq.], very tired; exhausted. 12. in *electricity,* uncharged: as, a *dead* wire. 13. in *sports,* not in actual play: as, a *dead* ball. *n.* the time of most cold, most darkness, etc.: as, the *dead* of night. *adv.* 1. completely; absolutely. 2. directly. —**the dead,** those who have died. —**dead′ness,** *n.*
**dead-beat** (ded′bēt′), *adj.* [Colloq.], very tired.
**dead beat,** [Slang], 1. one who tries to evade paying for things. 2. a lazy, idle person.
**dead center,** in *mechanics,* that position of a crank and a connecting rod in which both are in the same straight line, so that no force is exerted: also **dead point.**
**dead·en** (ded′'n), *v.t.* 1. to lessen the vigor or intensity of; dull; muffle. 2. to make numb. 3. to make soundproof. *v.i.* to become as if dead; lose vigor, intensity, etc. —**dead′en·er,** *n.*
**dead end,** a street, alley, etc. closed at one end. —**dead′-end′,** *adj.*
**dead·eye** (ded′ī′), *n.* a round, flat block of wood with three holes in it for the lanyard, used on a ship to fasten the shrouds.
**dead·fall** (ded′fôl′), *n.* a trap arranged so that a heavy weight is dropped on the prey.
**dead·head** (ded′hed′), *n.* a person who rides on trains, goes to the theater, etc. using a free ticket. *v.t.* to treat as a deadhead. *v.i.* to go as a deadhead. *adv.* [Colloq.], without passengers.
**dead heat,** a race in which two or more contestants reach the finish line at the same time; tie.
**dead letter,** 1. a law or ordinance no longer enforced but not repealed. 2. an unclaimed letter, or one that cannot be delivered because of an incorrect address, etc.
**dead·line** (ded′līn′), *n.* 1. a boundary which it is forbidden to cross. 2. a time limit, as for a payment, news story, etc.
**dead·lock** (ded′lok′), *n.* a standstill resulting from the action of equal and opposed forces. *v.t. & v.i.* to bring or come to a deadlock.
**dead·ly** (ded′li), *adj.* [-LIER, -LIEST], 1. causing or liable to cause death; fatal. 2. until death: as, *deadly* combat. 3. as in death: as, *deadly* pale. 4. excessive. 5. [Colloq.], unbearable: as, a *deadly* party. 6. in *theology,* causing spiritual death: as, *deadly* sins. *adv.* 1. like death. 2. as if dead. 3. extremely. —**dead′li·ness,** *n.*
**deadly nightshade,** the belladonna.
**dead pan,** [Slang], an expressionless face. —**dead′-pan′,** *adj. & adv.*
**dead reckoning,** the finding of a ship's location by using compass readings and data recorded in the log (speed, course, etc.) rather than astronomical observations: used in fog, etc.
**Dead Sea,** an inland body of salt water between Israel and Jordan.
**dead weight,** 1. the weight of an inert person or thing. 2. the weight of a vehicle without a load.
**dead·wood** (ded′wood′), *n.* 1. dead wood on trees. 2. anything useless; burdensome person or thing.
**deaf** (def), *adj.* [AS.], 1. totally or partially unable to hear. 2. unwilling to hear or listen: as, *deaf* to her pleas. —**deaf′ly,** *adv.* —**deaf′ness,** *n.*
**deaf-and-dumb** (def′ən-dum′), *adj.* 1. deaf-mute. 2. of or for deaf-mutes. Now opprobrious.
**deaf·en** (def′'n), *v.t.* 1. to make deaf. 2. to overwhelm with noise. 3. to drown out (a sound) with a louder sound. 4. to make soundproof. —**deaf′en·ing,** *adj. & n.* —**deaf′en·ing·ly,** *adv.*
**deaf-mute** (def′mūt′, -mūt′), *n.* a person who is deaf, especially from birth, and therefore unable to speak: most deaf-mutes, having the necessary vocal organs, can be taught to speak. *adj.* unable to hear and speak.
**deal** (dēl), *v.t.* [DEALT, DEALING], [AS. *dælan*], 1. to portion out; distribute. 2. to give; administer, as a blow. 3. to distribute (playing cards) to the players. *v.i.* 1. to have to do (*with*): as, science *deals* with facts. 2. to act or conduct oneself (followed by *with*): as, *deal* fairly with others. 3. to take up; consider (followed by *with*): as, to *deal* with a problem. 4. to do business; trade (*with* or *in*): as, we *deal* in cutlery. *n.* 1. a dealing. 2. *a*) the distribution of playing cards. *b*) a player's turn to deal the cards. *c*) the playing of one deal of cards. 3. [Colloq.], a business transaction. 4. [Colloq.], an agreement, especially a secret one in politics. 5. [Colloq.], an arrangement, treatment, or plan: as, a new *deal.*—**deal′er,** *n.*
**deal** (dēl), *n.* [AS. *dæl,* a part], an indefinite amount. —**a good** (or **great**) **deal,** 1. a large amount. 2. very much: as, *a good deal* faster.
**deal** (dēl), *n.* [MD. *dele*], 1. a fir or pine board. 2. fir or pine wood. *adj.* made of deal.
**deal·ing** (dēl′iŋ), *n.* 1. distribution. 2. behavior; way of acting. 3. *usually pl.* transactions or relations, usually of business.
**dealt** (delt), pt. and pp. of **deal.**
**dean** (dēn), *n.* [< OFr. < LL. *decanus,* head of ten (monks, etc.) < L. *decem,* ten], 1. the presiding official of a cathedral or collegiate church. 2. a college or university official in charge of a school or faculty, or of the students. 3. the member of a group who has belonged to it the longest. —**dean′-ship′,** *n.*
**dean·er·y** (dēn′ēr-i), *n.* [*pl.* -IES], 1. the rank or authority of a dean. 2. the residence of a dean.
**dear** (dêr), *adj.* [AS. *deore*], 1. much loved; beloved. 2. highly thought of; esteemed: a polite form of address, as, *Dear* Sir. 3. *a*) high-priced; costly. *b*) charging high prices. 4. earnest: as, our *dearest* hope. *adv.* 1. with deep affection. 2. at a high cost. *n.* a loved person; darling. *interj.* an expression of surprise, pity, etc. —**dear′ly,** *adv.* —**dear′ness,** *n.*
**Dear·born** (dêr′bērn, dêr′bôrn′), *n.* a city in Michigan, near Detroit: pop., **112,000.**
**dearth** (dūrth), *n.* [ME. *derth* < *deere,* dear], 1. scarcity of food; famine. 2. scarcity; lack.
**dear·y, dear·ie** (dêr′i), *n.* [*pl.* -IES], [Colloq.], dear; darling.
**death** (deth), *n.* [AS.], 1. the act or fact of dying; permanent ending of life. 2. [D-], the personification of death, usually pictured as a skeleton holding a scythe. 3. the state of being dead. 4. any ending resembling dying: as, the *death* of fascism. 5. any experience thought of as like dying or being dead. 6. the cause of death. 7. murder or bloodshed. —**at death's door,** nearly dead. —**do to death,** to kill. —**put to death,** to kill; execute. —**to death,** very much: as, he worries me *to death.* —**death′-like′,** *adj.*
**death·bed** (deth′bed′), *n.* 1. the bed on which a person dies. 2. the last hours of a person's life. *adj.* said, done, or made in the last hours of life: as, a *deathbed* will.
**death·blow** (deth′blō′), *n.* 1. a blow that kills. 2. a thing destructive or fatal (*to* something).
**death cup,** a poisonous mushroom with a swollen, cuplike base.
**death duty,** [Brit.], an inheritance tax.
**death house,** a place where prisoners condemned to die are kept until their execution.
**death·less** (deth′lis), *adj.* that cannot die; immortal: as, *deathless* words. —**death′less·ly,** *adv.* —**death′less·ness,** *n.*
**death·ly** (deth′li), *adj.* 1. causing death; fatal. 2. like or characteristic of death. 3. [Poetic], of death. *adv.* 1. in a deathlike way. 2. extremely: as, *deathly* ill.
**death mask,** a cast of a dead person's face.

**death rate,** the number of deaths per year per thousand of population: sometimes other units of time or population are used.
**death's-head** (deths'hed'), *n.* a human skull or a representation of it, symbolizing death.
**death·trap** (deth'trap'), *n.* 1. any unsafe structure. 2. a very dangerous place, situation, etc.
**Death Valley,** a dry, hot region in E California: 276 ft. below sea level.
**death warrant,** 1. an official order to put a person to death. 2. anything that ends hope, joy, etc.
**death·watch** (deth'woch', -wôch'), *n.* 1. a vigil kept beside a dead or dying person. 2. a guard set over a person soon to be executed.
**deb.,** debenture.
**de·ba·cle** (dā-bä'k'l, di-bak''l), *n.* [< Fr. < *débâcler*, to break up], 1. a breaking up of ice in a river, etc. 2. a rush of debris-filled waters. 3. an overthrow; rout. 4. a sudden disaster.
**de·bar** (di-bär'), *v.t.* [-BARRED, -BARRING], [< Fr.; see DE- & BAR], 1. to exclude (*from* something). 2. to prevent or prohibit. —**de·bar'ment,** *n.*
**de·bark** (di-bärk'), *v.t.* & *v.i.* [< Fr.; see DE- & BARK (a ship)], to put or go ashore from a ship; disembark. —**de·bar·ka·tion** (dē'bär-kā'shən), *n.*
**de·base** (di-bās'), *v.t.* [-BASED, -BASING], [*de-* + *base* (low)], to make lower in value, quality, dignity, etc. —**de·base'ment,** *n.* —**de·bas'er,** *n.*
**de·bate** (di-bāt'), *v.i.* [-BATED, -BATING], [< OFr.; see DE- & BATTER (to beat)], 1. to consider. 2. to discuss opposing reasons; argue. 3. to take part in a debate (*n.* 2). *v.t.* 1. to dispute about, especially in a meeting or legislature. 2. to argue (a question) formally. 3. to consider reasons for and against. *n.* 1. discussion of opposing reasons; argument. 2. a formal contest of skill in reasoned argument, with two teams taking opposite sides of a specified question. —**de·bat'a·ble,** *adj.* —**de·bat'er,** *n.*
**de·bauch** (di-bôch'), *v.t.* [< Fr. < OFr. *desbaucher*, to draw away from work], to lead astray morally; corrupt. *v.i.* to indulge in debauchery; dissipate. *n.* 1. debauchery. 2. an orgy. —**de·bauch'ed·ly,** *adv.* —**de·bauch'er,** *n.* —**de·bauch'ment,** *n.*
**deb·au·chee** (deb'ô-chē', -shē'), *n.* one who debauches; dissipated or depraved person.
**de·bauch·er·y** (di-bôch'ēr-i), *n.* [*pl.* -IES], 1. extreme indulgence of one's appetites; dissipation. 2. *pl.* orgies. 3. a leading astray morally.
**de·ben·ture** (di-ben'chēr), *n.* [Fr. < L. *debentur*, there are owing < *debere*; see DEBT], 1. a voucher acknowledging a debt owed by the signer. 2. an interest-bearing bond issued, often without security, by a corporation.
**de·bil·i·tate** (di-bil'ə-tāt'), *v.t.* [-TATED, -TATING], [< L. pp. of *debilitare*, to weaken < *debilis*, weak], to make weak; enervate. —**de·bil'i·tat'ed,** *adj.* —**de·bil'i·ta'tion,** *n.* —**de·bil'i·ta'tive,** *adj.*
**de·bil·i·ty** (di-bil'ə-ti), *n.* [*pl.* -TIES], [< Fr. < L. < *debilis*, weak], weakness; feebleness.
**deb·it** (deb'it), *n.* [L. *debitum*, what is owing < *debere*, to owe], 1. an entry in an account of money owed. 2. the total of such entries. 3. the left-hand side of an account, where such entries are made. *adj.* of debt or debts. *v.t.* 1. to charge with a debt. 2. to enter as a debit.
**deb·o·nair, deb·o·naire** (deb'ə-nâr'), *adj.* [< OFr. *de bon aire*, lit., of good breed], 1. affable; genial; courteous. 2. gay; jaunty. Also **deb'on·naire'.** —**deb'o·nair'ly,** *adv.* —**deb'o·nair'ness,** *n.*
**de·bouch** (di-bōōsh'), *v.i.* [< Fr. < *dé-* (see DE-) + *bouche*, mouth < L. *bucca*, cheek], 1. in *military usage*, to come forth from a narrow or shut-in place into open country. 2. to come forth; emerge. —**de·bouch'ment,** *n.*
**de·brief** (dē'brēf'), *v.t.* [*de-* + *brief*, *v.*], to question and instruct (a pilot, emissary, etc.) following a flight or mission.
**de·bris, dé·bris** (də-brē', dā'brē; Brit. deb'rē), *n.* [Fr. < OFr. *desbrisier*, to break apart], 1. broken, scattered remains; rubbish; ruins. 2. a heap or heaps of rock fragments, as from a glacier.
**Debs, Eugene Victor** (debz), 1855–1926; American Socialist and labor leader.
**debt** (det), *n.* [< OFr. < L. *debitum*, neut. pp. of *debere*, to owe], 1. something owed by one person to another. 2. an obligation to pay or return something. 3. the condition of owing: as, to be in *debt*. 4. in *theology*, a sin.
**debt of honor,** a gambling or betting debt.
**debt·or** (det'ēr), *n.* one that owes a debt.
**de·bunk** (di-buŋk'), *v.t.* [*de-* + *bunk* (nonsense)], [Colloq.], to expose the false or exaggerated claims, pretensions, etc. of. —**de·bunk'er,** *n.*
**De·bus·sy, A·chille Claude** (á'shēl' klōd də-bü'sē'; Eng. də-bū'si), 1862–1918; French composer.
**de·but, dé·but** (di-bū', dā'bū), *n.* [Fr. < *débuter*, to lead off (at bowls, etc.) < (*jouer*) *de but*, (to play) for the mark], 1. a first appearance before the public, as of an actor. 2. the formal introduction of a girl to society.
**deb·u·tante, dé·bu·tante** (deb'yoo-tänt', deb'yə-tant'), *n.* [Fr.], a girl making a social debut.
**Dec.,** December.
**dec.,** 1. deceased. 2. decimeter. 3. declension.
**dec·a-,** [< Gr. *deka*, ten], a combining form meaning *ten*, as in *decagon*: also **dec-,** and in words referring to the metric system, **deka-.**
**dec·ade** (dek'ād), *n.* [< Fr. < L. < Gr. < *deka*, ten], 1. a group of ten. 2. a period of ten years.
**de·ca·dence** (di-kā'd'ns, dek'ə-dəns), *n.* [< Fr. < ML. < L. *de-*, from + ppr. of *cadere*, to fall], a falling away; process, condition, or period of decline, as in morals, art, literature, etc.; deterioration.
**de·ca·dent** (di-kā'd'nt, dek'ə-dənt), *adj.* in a state of decline; characterized by decadence. *n.* a decadent person, especially a decadent writer or artist. —**de·ca'dent·ly,** *adv.*
**dec·a·gon** (dek'ə-gon'), *n.* [see DECA- & -GON], a plane figure with ten sides and ten angles. —**de·cag·o·nal** (de-kag'ə-n'l), *adj.*
**dec·a·gram, dec·a·gramme** (dek'ə-gram'), *n.* [see DECA- & GRAM], a measure of weight, equal to 10 grams: abbrev. **dkg.**
**dec·a·he·dron** (dek'ə-hē'drən), *n.* [*pl.* -DRONS, -DRA (-drə)], [see DECA- & -HEDRON], a solid figure with ten plane surfaces. —**dec'a·he'dral,** *adj.*
**de·cal** (di-kal'), *n.* decalcomania.
**de·cal·ci·fy** (dē-kal'sə-fī'), *v.t.* [-FIED, -FYING], to remove calcium or lime from (bones, etc.). —**de·cal'ci·fi·ca'tion,** *n.* —**de·cal'ci·fi'er,** *n.*
**de·cal·co·ma·ni·a** (di-kal'kə-mā'ni-ə), *n.* [< Fr. < *décalquer*, to counterdraw + Gr. *mania*, madness], 1. the transferring of decorative pictures or designs from specially prepared paper to glass, wood, etc. 2. such a picture or design.
**dec·a·li·ter, dec·a·li·tre** (dek'ə-lē'tēr), *n.* [see DECA- & LITER], a measure of capacity, equal to 10 liters: abbrev. **dkl., dal.**
**Dec·a·logue, Dec·a·log** (dek'ə-lôg', -log'), *n.* [< Fr. < LL. < Gr. *dekalogos*; see DECA- & -LOGUE], [sometimes d-], the Ten Commandments.
**dec·a·me·ter, dec·a·me·tre** (dek'ə-mē'tēr), *n.* [see DECA- & METER], a measure of length, equal to 10 meters: abbrev. **dkm.**
**de·camp** (di-kamp'), *v.i.* [< Fr.; see DE- & CAMP], 1. to break or leave camp. 2. to go away suddenly and secretly. —**de·camp'ment,** *n.*
**de·cant** (di-kant'), *v.t.* [< Fr. < ML. < L. *de-*, from + *canthus*; see CANT (edge)], to pour off (a liquid) gently without stirring up the sediment. —**de·can·ta·tion** (dē'kan-tā'shən), *n.*
**de·cant·er** (di-kan'tēr), *n.* [*decant* + *-er*], a decorative glass bottle for serving wine, etc.
**de·cap·i·tate** (di-kap'ə-tāt'), *v.t.* [-TATED, -TATING], [< Fr. < ML. < L. *de-*, off + *caput*, the head], to cut off the head of; behead. —**de·cap'i·ta'tion,** *n.* —**de·cap'i·ta'tor** (-tēr), *n.*
**dec·a·pod** (dek'ə-pod'), *adj.* [*deca-* + *-pod*], ten-legged. *n.* 1. any crustacean with ten legs, as a lobster, shrimp, etc. 2. any cephalopod with ten arms, as a squid.
**de·car·bon·ize** (dē-kär'bə-nīz'), *v.t.* & *v.i.* to remove carbon (from): also **de·car'bu·rize'** (-byoo-rīz', -bə-rīz').
**dec·a·syl·la·ble** (dek'ə-sil'ə-b'l), *n.* a line of verse with ten syllables. —**dec'a·syl·lab'ic** (-si-lab'ik), *adj.*
**de·cath·lon** (di-kath'lon), *n.* [< *deca-* + Gr. *athlon*, a contest], an athletic contest consisting of ten events in track and field sports: the contestant receiving the highest total of points wins.
**De·ca·tur** (di-kā'tēr), *n.* a city in central Illinois: pop., 78,000.
**de·cay** (di-kā'), *v.i.* [< OFr. < L. < *de-*, down + *cadere*, to fall], 1. to lose strength, beauty, prosperity, etc. gradually; deteriorate. 2. to rot. *v.t.* to cause to decay. *n.* 1. a gradual decline; deterioration. 2. a rotting or rottenness. 3. the gradual disintegration of radioactive substances.
**Dec·can** (dek'ən), *n.* that part of the peninsula of India south of the Narbada River.

**de·cease** (di-sēs′), *n.* [< OFr. < L. *decessus*, pp. < *de-*, from + *cedere*, to go], death. *v.i.* [-CEASED, -CEASING], to die.
**de·ceased** (di-sēst′), *adj.* dead. —**the deceased,** the dead person or persons.
**de·ce·dent** (di-sē′d'nt), *n.* in *law*, the deceased.
**de·ceit** (di sēt′), *n.* 1. the act of deceiving or lying. 2. a lie; dishonest action or trick. 3. the quality of being deceitful.
**de·ceit·ful** (di-sēt′fəl), *adj.* 1. tending to deceive; apt to lie or cheat. 2. intended to deceive; deceptive; false. —**de·ceit′ful·ly,** *adv.* —**de·ceit′ful·ness,** *n.*
**de·ceive** (di-sēv′), *v.t.* [-CEIVED, -CEIVING], [< OFr. < L. *decipere*, to ensnare < *de-*, from + *capere*, to take], to make (a person) believe what is not true; mislead. *v.i.* to use deceit. —**de·ceiv′a·ble,** *adj.* —**de·ceiv′er,** *n.* —**de·ceiv′ing·ly,** *adv.*
**de·cel·er·ate** (dē-sel′ēr-āt′), *v.t.* & *v.i.* [-ATED, -ATING], [*de-* + *accelerate*], to slow down: opposed to *accelerate*. —**de·cel′er·a′tion,** *n.* —**de·cel′er·a′tor,** *n.*
**De·cem·ber** (di-sem′bēr), *n.* [< OFr. < L. < *decem*, ten: the early Romans reckoned from March], the twelfth and last month of the year, having 31 days.
**de·cem·vir** (di-sem′vēr), *n.* [*pl.* -VIRS, -VIRI(-ī′)], [< L. < *decem*, ten + *vir*, a man], a member of a council of ten magistrates in ancient Rome.
**de·cem·vi·rate** (di-sem′və-rit, -rāt′), *n.* the position or term of a decemvir.
**de·cen·cy** (dē′s'n-si), *n.* [*pl.* -CIES], 1. the quality or state of being decent; propriety; proper observance of modesty, good taste, etc. 2. *pl.* socially proper actions. 3. *pl.* things needed for a proper standard of living.
**de·cen·ni·al** (di-sen′i-əl), *adj.* [< LL. < L. *decem*, ten + *annus*, year; + *-al*], 1. of or lasting ten years. 2. occurring every ten years. *n.* a tenth anniversary. —**de·cen′ni·al·ly,** *adv.*
**de·cent** (dē′s'nt), *adj.* [< Fr. < L. ppr. of *decere*, to befit], 1. proper and fitting. 2. not immodest; not obscene. 3. conforming to approved social standards; respectable. 4. satisfactory; adequate: as, *decent* wages. 5. fair; kind; generous. 6. [Colloq.], adequately clothed for propriety. —**de′cent·ly,** *adv.* —**de′cent·ness,** *n.*
**de·cen·tral·ize** (dē-sen′trəl-īz′), *v.t.* [-IZED, -IZING], to break up the centralization of authority, as in a government, and distribute, as to local authorities. —**de·cen′tral·i·za′tion,** *n.*
**de·cep·tion** (di-sep′shən), *n.* 1. a deceiving or being deceived. 2. something deceiving, as an illusion, or meant to deceive, as a fraud.
**de·cep·tive** (di-sep′tiv), *adj.* deceiving or meant to deceive. —**de·cep′tive·ly,** *adv.* —**de·cep′tive·ness,** *n.*
**dec·i-,** [< Fr. < L. < *decem*, ten], a combining form meaning *one tenth of*, as in *decigram*.
**dec·i·bel** (des′ə-bel′), *n.* [*deci-* + *bel* (after A. G. *Bell*)], a unit for measuring the volume of a sound.
**de·cide** (di-sīd′), *v.t.* [-CIDED, -CIDING], [< Fr. < L. < *de-*, off + *caedere*, to cut], 1. to end (a contest, argument, etc.) by giving one side the victory. 2. to cause to reach a decision. *v.i.* 1. to pass judgment. 2. to reach a decision. —**de·cid′a·ble,** *adj.*
**de·cid·ed** (di-sīd′id), *adj.* [pp. of *decide*], 1. definite; unquestionable. 2. unhesitating; determined. —**de·cid′ed·ly,** *adv.* —**de·cid′ed·ness,** *n.*
**de·cid·u·ous** (di-sij′ōō-əs, -ū-əs), *adj.* [< L. < *de-*, off + *cadere*, to fall], 1. falling off at a certain season or stage of growth, as some leaves, antlers, etc. 2. shedding leaves annually: opposed to *evergreen*. —**de·cid′u·ous·ly,** *adv.* —**de·cid′u·ous·ness,** *n.*
**dec·i·gram, dec·i·gramme** (des′ə-gram′), *n.* [see DECI- & GRAM], a metric weight, equal to 1/10 gram: abbrev. **dg.**
**dec·i·li·ter, dec·i·li·tre** (des′ə-lē′tēr), *n.* [see DECI- & LITER], a metric measure of volume, equal to 1/10 liter: abbrev. **dl.**
**de·cil·lion** (di-sil′yən), *n.* [< L. *decem*, ten; + *million*], 1. in the U.S. and France, the number represented by 1 followed by 33 zeros. 2. in Great Britain and Germany, the number represented by 1 followed by 60 zeros. *adj.* amounting to one decillion in number.
**dec·i·mal** (des′ə-m'l), *adj.* [< OFr. < ML. < L. < *decem*, ten], relating to or based upon the number ten; progressing by tens. *n.* a decimal fraction. —**dec′i·mal·ly,** *adv.*
**decimal fraction,** a fraction with an unwritten denominator of ten or some power of ten, shown by a decimal point, as .5 = 5/10, .07 = 7/100.
**decimal point,** a period placed just to the left of a decimal fraction, as in 1.15, 0.9.
**dec·i·mate** (des′ə-māt′), *v.t.* [-MATED, -MATING], [< L. < *decem*, ten], 1. to select by lot and kill every tenth one of. 2. to destroy or kill a large part of. 3. to take or destroy a tenth part of. —**dec′i·ma′tion,** *n.* —**dec′i·ma′tor,** *n.*
**dec·i·me·ter, dec·i·me·tre** (des′ə-mē′tēr), *n.* [see DECI- & METER], a metric measure of length, equal to 1/10 meter: abbrev. **dec., decim., dm.**
**de·ci·pher** (di-sī′fēr), *v.t.* [*de-* + *cipher*], 1. to translate from secret writing or code; decode. 2. to make out the meaning of (ancient inscriptions, a scrawl, etc.). —**de·ci′pher·a·ble,** *adj.* —**de·ci′pher·ment,** *n.*
**de·ci·sion** (di-sizh′ən), *n.* 1. the act of deciding or settling a dispute or question. 2. the act of making up one's mind. 3. a judgment or conclusion reached or given. 4. determination; firmness of mind: as, a man of *decision*. 5. in *boxing*, a victory on points instead of by a knockout.
**de·ci·sive** (di-sī′siv), *adj.* 1. that settles a dispute, question, etc.; conclusive. 2. having the quality of decision; showing determination. —**de·ci′sive·ly,** *adv.* —**de·ci′sive·ness,** *n.*
**dec·i·stere** (des′ə-stêr′), *n.* [see DECI- & STERE], a metric measure of volume, 1/10 cubic meter.
**deck** (dek), *n.* [MD. *decke*, a covering], 1. a roof over a section of a ship's hold, serving as a floor. 2. any platform or floor like a ship's deck. 3. a pack of playing cards. *v.t.* 1. to cover with finery or ornaments; adorn; trim. 2. to furnish (a vessel) with a deck. —**clear the decks,** to get ready for action. —**hit the deck,** [Slang], 1. to get out of bed. 2. to get ready for action. —**on deck,** [Colloq.], ready; on hand.
**-deck·er** (dek′ēr), a combining form meaning *having* (a specified number of) *decks, layers*, etc.
**deck hand,** a sailor, usually one who works on deck.
**deck·le, deck·el** (dek′'l), *n.* [< G. dim. of *decke*, a cover], in *papermaking*, 1. a frame to guide the pulp into a desired width. 2. a deckle edge.
**deckle edge,** the untrimmed edge of paper made in a deckle. —**deck′le-edged′,** *adj.*
**de·claim** (di-klām′), *v.i.* & *v.t.* [< L. < *de-*, intens. + *clamare*, to cry, shout], to speak or recite loudly and rhetorically; specif., to give a recitation, set speech, etc. —**de·claim′er,** *n.*
**dec·la·ma·tion** (dek′lə-mā′shən), *n.* 1. a declaiming or being declaimed. 2. the giving of formal speeches or recitations. 3. a formal speech, passage of poetry, etc. for declaiming. —**de·clam·a·to·ry** (di-klam′ə-tôr′i, -tō′ri), *adj.*
**dec·la·ra·tion** (dek′lə-rā′shən), *n.* 1. a declaring or being declared; announcement. 2. a thing declared. 3. a formal statement; proclamation. 4. a statement of taxable goods. 5. in *bridge*, a bid; esp., the winning bid.
**Declaration of Independence,** a formal statement adopted July 4, 1776, by the Second Continental Congress, declaring the thirteen American colonies free and independent of Great Britain.
**de·clar·a·tive** (di-klar′ə-tiv), *adj.* making a statement or assertion: also **de·clar′a·to′ry** (-tôr′i, -tō′ri).
**de·clare** (di-klâr′), *v.t.* [-CLARED, -CLARING], [< OFr. < L. < *de-*, intens. + *clarus*, clear], 1. to make clearly known; announce openly or formally. 2. to show; reveal. 3. to say emphatically. 4. to make a statement of (goods) for taxation. 5. in *bridge*, to bid to play the hand in (a specific suit or no trump). *v.i.* 1. to make a declaration. 2. to state openly a choice, opinion, etc. —**declare oneself,** 1. to state strongly one's opinion. 2. to reveal one's true character, etc. —**I declare!** I am surprised, startled, etc. —**de·clar′er,** *n.*
**de·clas·si·fy** (dē-klas′ə-fī′), *v.t.* [-FIED, -FYING], to make (secret or restricted documents, codes, etc.) available to the public, as by executive order.
**de·clen·sion** (di-klen′shən), *n.* [prob. via ML. < L. pp. of *declinare*; see DECLINE], 1. a sloping; descent. 2. a falling off or away; decline; deterioration. 3. deviation, as from a standard. 4. [Rare], a polite refusal. 5. in *grammar*, *a*) a class of nouns, pronouns, or adjectives showing the same or a similar system of inflections. *b*) the inflection of such words. —**de·clen′sion·al,** *adj.*
**dec·li·na·tion** (dek′lə-nā′shən), *n.* 1. a bending or sloping downward. 2. an oblique variation from a given direction. 3. the angle made by a compass needle with a line pointing to true north. 4. a polite refusal. 5. [Archaic], decline; deterioration. 6. in *astronomy*, the angular distance of a heavenly body north or south from the celestial equator.
**de·cline** (di-klīn′), *v.i.* [-CLINED, -CLINING], [< OFr. < L. < *de-*, from + *clinare*, to bend], 1. to bend or slope downward or aside. 2. to deteriorate; decay. 3. to refuse something. *v.t.* 1. to cause to bend or slope downward or aside. 2. to refuse, especially politely. 3. in *grammar*, to give the inflected forms of (a noun, pronoun, or adjective). *n.* 1. a declin-

ing; deterioration; decay. 2. a failing (of health, etc.). 3. a period of decline. 4. the last part. 5. a downward slope. —**de·clin′a·ble,** *adj.* —**de·clin′a·to′ry** (-tôr′i, -tō′ri), *adj.* —**de·clin′er,** *n.*

**de·cliv·i·ty** (di-kliv′ə-ti), *n.* [*pl.* -TIES], [< L. < *de-*, down, from + *clivus*, a slope], a downward slope, as of a hill: opposed to *acclivity.* —**de·cliv′i·tous,** *adj.*

**de·coct** (di-kokt′), *v.t.* [< L. *decoctus*, pp. < *de-*, down + *coquere*, to cook], to extract the essence, flavor, etc. of by boiling. —**de·coc′tion,** *n.*

**de·code** (dē-kōd′), *v.t.* [-CODED, -CODING], to translate (something written in code) into comprehensible language. —**de·cod′er,** *n.*

**dé·col·le·té** (dā′kol-tā′, -ko-lə-tā′), *adj.* [Fr.; ult. < L. *de*, from + *collum*, the neck], 1. cut low so as to bare the neck and shoulders. 2. wearing a décolleté dress, etc.

**de·com·pose** (dē′kəm-pōz′), *v.t. & v.i.* [< Fr.], 1. to break up into basic components or parts. 2. to rot; decay. —**de′com·pos′a·ble,** *adj.* —**de′com·po·si′tion** (-kom-pə-zish′ən), *n.*

**de·com·press** (dē′kəm-pres′), *v.t.* to free from pressure. —**de′com·pres′sion,** *n.*

**decompression sickness,** a condition caused by the formation of air bubbles in the blood or body tissues as the result of a sudden lowering of pressure, resulting in collapse in severe cases: also called *caisson disease, bends.*

**de·con·gest·ant** (dē′kən-jes′tənt), *n.* a medication or treatment that relieves congestion, as in the nasal passages.

**de·con·tam·i·nate** (dē′kən-tam′ə-nāt′), *v.t.* [-NATED, -NATING], to rid of a harmful substance, as poison gas. —**de′con·tam′i·na′tion,** *n.*

**de·con·trol** (dē′kən-trōl′), *v.t.* [-TROLLED, -TROLLING], to free from controls. *n.* a decontrolling or being decontrolled.

**dé·cor** (dā-kôr′), *n.* [Fr. < L. < *decere*, to be suitable], 1. decoration. 2. the decorative scheme of a room, stage set, etc.

**dec·or·ate** (dek′ə-rāt′), *v.t.* [-ATED, -ATING], [< L. pp. of *decorare* < *decus*, an ornament], 1. to adorn; ornament. 2. to furnish a color scheme, drapes, etc. for. 3. to paint or wallpaper. 4. to give a medal or similar sign of honor to. *v.i.* to decorate a room, house, etc. —**dec′o·ra·tive** (-rə-tiv, -rā′tiv), *adj.* —**dec′o·ra·tive·ly,** *adv.* —**dec′o·ra′tor,** *n.*

**dec·o·ra·tion** (dek′ə-rā′shən), *n.* 1. a decorating. 2. anything used for decorating; ornament. 3. a medal, badge, or similar sign of honor.

**Decoration Day,** Memorial Day.

**dec·o·rous** (dek′ə-rəs, di-kôr′əs, -kō′rəs), *adj.* characterized by or showing decorum, good taste, etc. —**dec′o·rous·ly,** *adv.* —**dec′o·rous·ness,** *n.*

**de·co·rum** (di-kôr′əm, -kō′rəm), *n.* [*pl.* -RUMS, -RA (-ə, -rə)], [L.; see DÉCOR], 1. whatever is suitable or proper; propriety. 2. propriety and good taste in behavior, speech, dress, etc.

**de·cou·page, dé·cou·page** (dā′kōō-päzh′), *n.* [Fr.], the art of cutting out designs or illustrations from paper, foil, etc. and mounting them on a surface in a decorative arrangement.

**de·coy** (di-koi′; *also, for n.,* dē′koi), *n.* [< D. *de kooi*, the cage < L. *cavea*, cage], 1. a place into which wild ducks, etc. are lured for capture. 2. an artificial or trained bird or animal used to lure game to a place where it can be shot. 3. a thing or person used to lure into danger. *v.t. & v.i.* to lure or be lured into a trap, danger, etc. —**de·coy′er,** *n.*

**de·crease** (di-krēs′, dē′-; *for n., usually* dē′krēs), *v.i. & v.t.* [-CREASED, -CREASING], [< OFr. < L. < *de-*, from + *crescere*, to grow], to become or cause to become gradually less, smaller, etc.; diminish. *n.* 1. a decreasing; lessening. 2. amount of decreasing. —**on the decrease,** decreasing. —**de·creas′ing·ly,** *adv.*

**de·cree** (di-krē′), *n.* [< OFr. < L. *decretum* < *de-*, from + *cernere*, to see, judge], 1. an official order or decision, as of a government, etc. 2. anything settled and unchangeable: as, a *decree* of fate. *v.t.* [-CREED, -CREEING], to order, decide, or appoint by decree. *v.i.* to issue a decree.

**dec·re·ment** (dek′rə-mənt), *n.* 1. a decreasing or decrease; loss. 2. amount lost by decrease.

**de·crep·it** (di-krep′it), *adj.* [< Fr. < L. < *de-*, intens. + pp. of *crepare*, to creak], broken down or worn out by old age or long use. —**de·crep′it·ly,** *adv.*

**de·crep·i·tude** (di-krep′ə-tōōd′, -tūd′), *n.* a decrepit condition; feebleness, as from age.

**de·cre·scen·do** (dē′krə-shen′dō), *adj. & adv.* [It.], in *music*, with a gradual decrease in loudness: abbrev. **decresc.** or indicated by the sign >. *n.* [*pl.* -DOS], in *music*, 1. a gradual decrease in loudness. 2. a passage played decrescendo.

**de·cre·tal** (di-krē′t'l), *adj.* [< Fr. < LL. *decretalis*], of or containing a decree. *n.* 1. a decree. 2. in the *R. C. Church*, a decree by the Pope on a question of doctrine or ecclesiastical law.

**de·cry** (di-krī′), *v.t.* [-CRIED, -CRYING], [< Fr. < OFr. *descrier;* see DE- & CRY], 1. to denounce or condemn openly; censure. 2. to depreciate (money, etc.) officially. —**de·cri′al,** *n.* —**de·cri′er,** *n.*

**de·cum·bent** (di-kum′bənt), *adj.* [< L. *decumbens*, pp. < *de-*, down + *cumbere* < *cubare*, to recline], 1. lying down. 2. in *botany*, trailing on the ground and rising at the tip, as some stems.

**ded·i·cate** (ded′ə-kāt′), *v.t.* [-CATED, -CATING], [< L. < *de-*, intens. + *dicare*, to proclaim < *dicere*, to speak], 1. to set apart for a religious purpose. 2. to devote to some work, duty, etc. 3. to address (a book, etc.) to someone as a sign of honor, affection, etc. —**ded′i·ca′tor,** *n.*

**ded·i·ca·tion** (ded′ə-kā′shən), *n.* 1. a dedicating or being dedicated. 2. an inscription in a book, etc., dedicating it to someone. —**ded′i·ca′tive, ded′i·ca·to′ry** (-kə-tôr′i, -tō′ri), *adj.*

**de·duce** (di-dōōs′, -dūs′), *v.t.* [-DUCED, -DUCING], [< L. < *de-*, down + *ducere*, to lead], 1. to trace the course or derivation of. 2. to infer from a general principle by deductive reasoning. 3. to conclude by reasoning. —**de·duc′i·ble,** *adj.*

**de·duct** (di-dukt′), *v.t.* [< L. pp. of *deducere;* see DEDUCE], to take away or subtract (an amount or quantity). —**de·duct′i·ble,** *adj.*

**de·duc·tion** (di-duk′shən), *n.* 1. a deducting or being deducted; subtraction. 2. the amount deducted. 3. in *logic*, *a*) reasoning from the general to the specific or from a premise to a logical conclusion. *b*) a conclusion so deduced. Opposed to *induction* (in sense 3). —**de·duc′tive,** *adj.* —**de·duc′tive·ly,** *adv.*

**deed** (dēd), *n.* [ME. *dede*], 1. a thing done; act. 2. a feat of courage, skill, etc. 3. action; doing. 4. in *law*, a document under seal that states a transfer of property. *vt.* to transfer (property) by such a document. —**in deed,** in fact; really.

**deem** (dēm), *v.t. & v.i.* [AS. *deman*, to judge < *dom;* see DOOM], to think; believe; suppose.

**deep** (dēp), *adj.* [AS. *deop*], 1. extending far downward from the top, inward from the surface, or backward from the front. 2. placed far down or back. 3. coming from far down or back. 4. hard to understand; abstruse. 5. serious; extreme: as, *deep* disgrace. 6. wise. 7. tricky and sly. 8. dark and rich: said of colors. 9. absorbed by: as, *deep* in thought. 10. intense; profound. 11. of low pitch: said of sound. *n.* 1. a deep place. 2. the middle part; part that is darkest, etc.: as, the *deep* of night. *adv.* deeply; far down, far back, far on, etc. —**go off the deep end,** [Colloq.], to become angry or excited. —**the deep,** [Poetic], the sea or ocean. —**deep′ly,** *adv.* —**deep′ness,** *n.*

**deep·en** (dēp′'n), *v.t. & v.i.* to make or become deep or deeper.

**deep·freeze** (dēp′frēz′), *n.* a refrigerator for keeping perishable foods at a very low temperature for a long time: a trade-mark **(Deepfreeze).** *v.t.* [-FREEZED or -FROZE, -FREEZED or -FROZEN, -FREEZING], to put or keep in such a refrigerator.

**deep-fry** (dēp′frī′), *v.t.* [-FRIED, -FRYING], to fry by immersing in a deep pan of boiling fat.

**deep-root·ed** (dēp′rōōt′id, -root′-), *adj.* 1. having deep roots. 2. firmly established.

**deep-seat·ed** (dēp′sēt′id), *adj.* 1. buried far beneath the surface. 2. firmly established.

**deep-set** (dēp′set′), *adj.* 1. deeply set. 2. firmly established.

**deer** (dêr), *n.* [*pl.* DEER, *occas.* DEERS], [AS. *deor*, wild animal], any of a family of hoofed, cud-chewing animals, as the moose, reindeer, caribou, etc.: the males usually bear antlers that are shed annually.

**deer·hound** (dêr′hound′), *n.* a Scottish breed of large, shaggy-haired dog, used in hunting deer.

**deer·skin** (dêr′skin′), *n.* 1. the hide of a deer. 2. leather made from it. *adj.* made of deerskin.

**def.,** 1. defendant. 2. defense. 3. deferred. 4. defined. 5. definite. 6. definition.

**de·face** (di-fās′), *v.t.* [-FACED, -FACING], [OFr. *desfacier;* see DE- & FACE], to spoil the appearance of;

disfigure; mar. **—de·face′ment,** *n.* **—de·fac′er,** *n.*

‡**de fac·to** (dē fak′tō), [L.], in fact; actual: as, *de facto* government: cf. *de jure.*

**de·fal·cate** (di-fal′kāt, -fôl′-), *v.i.* [-CATED, -CATING], [< ML. pp. of *defalcare,* to cut off < L. *de-,* from + *falx,* sickle], to steal or misuse funds entrusted to one; embezzle. **—de·fal·ca·tion** (dē′fal-kā′shən, -fôl-), *n.* **—de·fal′ca·tor** (-tēr), *n.*

**de·fame** (di-fām′), *v.t.* [-FAMED, -FAMING], [< OFr. < L. < *dis-,* from + *fama;* see FAME], to attack the reputation of; slander or libel. **—def·a·ma·tion** (def′ə-mā′shən, dē′fə-), *n.* **—de·fam·a·to·ry** (di-fam′ə-tôr′i, -tō′ri), *adj.* **—de·fam′er,** *n.*

**de·fault** (di-fôlt′), *n.* [< OFr. < L. *de-,* away + *fallere,* to fail, deceive], 1. failure to do or appear as required: as, he lost the tennis match by *default.* 2. failure to pay money due. 3. failure to appear in court to defend or prosecute a case. *v.i.* 1. to fail to do or appear as required. 2. to fail to make payment when due. 3. to fail to appear in court. 4. to lose a contest by default. *v.t.* 1. to fail to do or pay (something) when required. 2. to lose (a contest) by default; forfeit. **—de·fault′er,** *n.*

**de·feat** (di-fēt′), *v.t.* [< OFr. < LL. < L. *dis-,* from + *facere,* to do], 1. to win victory over; overcome; beat. 2. to bring to nothing; frustrate. 3. to make null and void. *n.* a defeating or being defeated.

**de·feat·ist** (di-fēt′ist), *n.* one who too readily accepts defeat, and acts accordingly. *adj.* of or like a defeatist. **—de·feat′ism,** *n.*

**def·e·cate** (def′ə-kāt′), *v.t.* [-CATED, -CATING], [< L. pp. of *defaecare* < *de-,* from + *faex,* dregs], to remove impurities from; refine. *v.i.* 1. to become pure. 2. to excrete waste matter from the bowels. **—def′e·ca′tion,** *n.* **—def′e·ca′tor,** *n.*

**de·fect** (di-fekt′, dē′fekt), *n.* [< L. pp. of *deficere,* to fail < *de-,* from + *facere,* to do], 1. lack of something necessary for completeness; shortcoming. 2. an imperfection; fault; blemish. *v.i.* (di-fekt′), to forsake a party, cause, etc.; desert.

**de·fec·tion** (di-fek′shən), *n.* 1. failure. 2. abandonment of loyalty, duty, etc.; desertion.

**de·fec·tive** (di-fek′tiv), *adj.* 1. having a defect or defects; incomplete; faulty. 2. in *grammar,* lacking some of the usual grammatical forms. 3. subnormal in intelligence. *n.* 1. a person with some bodily or mental defect. 2. in *grammar,* a defective word. **—de·fec′tive·ly,** *adv.* **—de·fec′tive·ness,** *n.*

**de·fence** (di-fens′), *n.* defense: Brit. spelling.

**de·fend** (di-fend′), *v.t.* [< OFr. < L. *defendere* < *de-,* away + *fendere,* to strike], 1. to guard from attack; protect. 2. to support by speech or act. 3. to try to justify. 4. in *law, a*) to oppose (an action, etc.). *b*) to act for (an accused). *v.i.* to make a defense. **—de·fend′a·ble,** *adj.* **—de·fend′er,** *n.*

**de·fend·ant** (di-fen′dənt), *adj.* defending. *n.* in *law,* the person sued or accused: cf. *plaintiff.*

**de·fense** (di-fens′), *n.* [OFr. < L. pp. of *defendere*], 1. a defending against attack. 2. a being defended. 3. something that defends; means of defense. 4. justification or support by speech or writing. 5. self-protection, as by boxing. 6. the side that is defending in any contest. 7. *a*) the arguments of the defendant in contesting a case. *b*) the defendant and his counsel, collectively. **—de·fense′less,** *adj.* **—de·fense′less·ly,** *adv.* **—de·fense′less·ness,** *n.*

**defense mechanism** (or **reaction**), in *psychology,* an unconscious tendency to keep from oneself or others unpleasant feelings, memories, etc.

**de·fen·si·ble** (di-fen′sə-b'l), *adj.* that can be defended or justified. **—de·fen′si·bil′i·ty, de·fen′si·ble·ness,** *n.* **—de·fen′si·bly,** *adv.*

**de·fen·sive** (di-fen′siv), *adj.* 1. defending. 2. of or for defense. *n.* 1. [Obs.], something that defends. 2. attitude, position, or operation of defense. **—de·fen′sive·ly,** *adv.* **—de·fen′sive·ness,** *n.*

**de·fer** (di-fũr′), *v.t. & v.i.* [-FERRED, -FERRING], [OFr. *differer;* see DIFFER], 1. to put off; postpone; delay. 2. to postpone the induction of (a person) into the armed forces. **—de·fer′ment,** *n.*

**de·fer** (di-fũr′), *v.i.* [-FERRED, -FERRING], [< Fr. < L. < *de-,* down + *ferre,* to bear], to submit or yield in opinion or judgment. **—de·fer′rer,** *n.*

**def·er·ence** (def′ēr-əns), *n.* 1. a yielding in opinion, judgment, etc. 2. courteous regard or respect. **—in deference to,** because of regard for (a person, his wishes, etc.). **—def′er·ent,** *adj.*

**def·er·en·tial** (def′ēr-en′shəl), *adj.* showing deference; very respectful. **—def′er·en′tial·ly,** *adv.*

**de·fi·ance** (di-fī′əns), *n.* 1. a defying; open, bold resistance to authority or opposition. 2. a challenge. **—bid defiance to,** to defy. **—in defiance of,** in spite of. **—de·fi′ant,** *adj.* **—de·fi′ant·ly,** *adv.*

**de·fi·cien·cy** (di-fish′ən-si), *n.* 1. the quality or state of being deficient; absence of an essential; incompleteness. 2. [*pl.* -CIES], *a*) a shortage. *b*) the amount of shortage; deficit.

**de·fi·cient** (di-fish′ənt), *adj.* [< L. *deficiens,* ppr. of *deficere;* see DEFECT], 1. lacking in some essential; incomplete; defective. 2. inadequate in amount, quality, degree, etc. *n.* a deficient person or thing. **—de·fi′cient·ly,** *adv.*

**def·i·cit** (def′ə-sit), *n.* [L., it is lacking < *deficere,* to lack], the amount by which a sum of money is less than what is expected, due, etc.

**de·fi·er** (di-fī′ēr), *n.* a person who defies.

**de·file** (di-fīl′), *v.t.* [-FILED, -FILING], [< OFr. *defouler,* to tread underfoot; infl. by AS. *fylan,* make foul], 1. to make filthy; pollute. 2. to corrupt. 3. to profane; sully, as a person's name. 4. [Archaic], to violate the chastity of. **—de·file′ment,** *n.* **—de·fil′er,** *n.*

**de·file** (di-fīl′, dē′fīl), *v.i.* [-FILED, -FILING], [< Fr. < *dé-* (L. *de*), from + *file,* a file, line], to march in a line, in single file. *n.* 1. a narrow passage through which troops must defile. 2. any narrow valley or mountain pass.

**de·fine** (di-fīn′), *v.t.* [-FINED, -FINING], [< OFr. < L. *definire,* to limit < *de-,* from + *finis,* boundary], 1. to determine the boundaries of. 2. to determine the limits and nature of; describe exactly. 3. to state or explain the meaning or meanings of (a word, etc.). *v.i.* to construct a definition. **—de·fin′a·bil′i·ty,** *n.* **—de·fin′a·ble,** *adj.* **—de·fin′a·bly,** *adv.* **—de·fin′er,** *n.*

**def·i·nite** (def′ə-nit), *adj.* [< L. pp. of *definire;* see DEFINE], 1. having exact limits. 2. precise and clear in meaning; explicit. 3. certain; positive. 4. in *grammar,* limiting or specifying: as, *the* is the *definite* article. **—def′i·nite·ly,** *adv.* **—def′i·nite·ness,** *n.*

**def·i·ni·tion** (def′ə-nish′ən), *n.* 1. a defining or being defined. 2. an explanation of what a word or phrase means or has meant. 3. a putting or being in clear, sharp outline. 4. the power of a lens to show (an object) in clear, sharp outline. 5. in *radio & television,* the degree of accuracy with which sounds or images are reproduced.

**de·fin·i·tive** (di-fin′ə-tiv), *adj.* 1. decisive; conclusive; final. 2. most nearly complete and accurate. 3. serving to define; distinguishing. *n.* in *grammar,* a word that defines or limits a noun, as *this, that, any, some,* etc. **—de·fin′i·tive·ly,** *adv.* **—de·fin′i·tive·ness,** *n.*

**de·flate** (di-flāt′), *v.t. & v.i.* [-FLATED, -FLATING], [< L. *de-,* from + pp. of *flare,* to blow], 1. to collapse by letting out air or gas. 2. to lessen in amount, size, importance, etc., as currency. Opposed to *inflate.* **—de·fla′tor** (-tēr), *n.*

**de·fla·tion** (di-flā′shən), *n.* 1. a deflating or being deflated. 2. a lessening of the amount of money in circulation, causing a rise in its value and a fall in prices. **—de·fla′tion·ar′y,** *adj.*

**de·flect** (di-flekt′), *v.t. & v.i.* [< L. < *de-,* from + *flectere,* to bend], to bend or turn to one side; swerve. **—de·flec′tion** or Brit. **de·flex′ion,** *n.* **—de·flec′tive,** *adj.* **—de·flec′tor** (-tēr), *n.*

**de·flow·er** (di-flou′ēr), *v.t.* [see DE- & FLOWER], 1. to take away the virginity of (a woman). 2. to ravish; spoil. 3. to remove flowers from (a plant). **—def·lo·ra·tion** (def′lə-rā′shən), *n.*

**De·foe, Daniel** (di-fō′), 1660?–1731; English novelist and essayist: also sp. **De Foe.**

**de·fo·li·ant** (dē-fō′li-ənt), *n.* a chemical spray that strips growing plants of their leaves.

**de·fo·li·ate** (dē-fō′li-āt′), *v.t.* [-ATED, -ATING], [< LL. < L. *de-,* from + *folium,* a leaf], to strip (trees, etc.) of leaves.

**de·for·est** (dē-fôr′ist, -for′-), *v.t.* to clear (land) of forests or trees. **—de·for′est·a′tion,** *n.* **—de·for′est·er,** *n.*

**de·form** (di-fôrm′), *v.t.* [< Fr. < L. < *de-,* from + *forma,* form], 1. to mar the form or shape of. 2. to make ugly; disfigure. 3. in *physics,* to change the shape of by pressure or stress. *v.i.* to become deformed. **—de·form′a·bil′i·ty,** *n.* **—de·form′a·ble,** *adj.* **—de·for·ma·tion** (dē′fôr-mā′shən, def′ēr-), *n.* **—de·form′er,** *n.*

**de·formed** (di-fôrmd′), *adj.* 1. changed in form; misshapen. 2. ugly, hateful, etc. **—de·form′ed·ly,** *adv.*

**de·form·i·ty** (di-fôr′mə-ti), *n.* [*pl.* -TIES], 1. the condition of being deformed. 2. a deformed part, as of the body. 3. ugliness; depravity. 4. a deformed person or thing.

**de·fraud** (di-frôd′), *v.t.* [< OFr. < L.; cf. DE- & FRAUD], to take or hold back property, rights, etc. from by fraud; cheat. **—de·fraud′er,** *n.*

**de·fray** (di-frā′), *v.t.* [< Fr. < OFr. < *de-* (L. *de*), off + *frai,* expense], to pay (the cost or expenses).

—**de·fray′a·ble,** *adj.* —**de·fray′al, de·fray′ment,** *n.* —**de·fray′er,** *n.*
**de·frost** (dē-frôst′, -frost′), *v.t. & v.i.* to rid or become rid of frost or ice.
**de·fros·ter** (dē-frôs′tẽr, -fros′-), *n.* a device for defrosting, as on an automobile windshield.
**deft** (deft), *adj.* [see DAFT], skillful; dexterous. —**deft′ly,** *adv.* —**deft′ness,** *n.*
**de·funct** (di-fuŋkt′), *adj.* [< L. *defunctus*, pp. of *defungi*, to do, finish < *de-*, from, off + *fungi*, to perform], no longer living or existing; dead; extinct. —**de·funct′ness,** *n.*
**de·fy** (di-fī′; *also, for n.*, dē′fī), *v.t.* [-FIED, -FYING], [< OFr. < LL. < L. *dis-*, from + *fidus*, faithful], 1. to resist or oppose boldly or openly. 2. to resist completely; foil. 3. to dare (someone) to do or prove something. *n.* [*pl.* -FIES], [Slang], a defiance.
**De·gas, Hi·laire Ger·main Ed·gar** (ē′lâr′ zher′-man′ ed′gär′ də-gä′), 1834–1917; French painter.
**De Gaulle, Charles** (shärl′ də-gōl′; Eng. də-gôl′), 1890– ; French general; president (1959–69).
**de·gauss** (di-gous′), *v.t.* [*de-* + *gauss*], to neutralize the magnetic field surrounding (a ship) as a protection against magnetic mines.
**de·gen·er·a·cy** (di-jen′ẽr-ə-si), *n.* 1. a degenerate quality or condition. 2. a degenerating.
**de·gen·er·ate** (di-jen′ẽr-it), *adj.* [< L. pp. of *degenerare;* ult. < *de-*, from + *genus*, race], having sunk below a former or normal condition, etc.; deteriorated. *n.* a degenerate person, especially one who is subnormal mentally or morally. *v.i.* (-āt′), [-ATED, -ATING], 1. to lose former, normal, or higher qualities. 2. in *biology*, to change gradually to a lower type; deteriorate. —**de·gen′er·ate·ly,** *adv.* —**de·gen′er·ate·ness,** *n.* —**de·gen′er·a′tive,** *adj.*
**de·gen·er·a·tion** (di-jen′ẽr-ā′shən), *n.* 1. a degenerating. 2. a degenerate condition. 3. in *medicine*, biochemical change in tissues or organs.
**de·grade** (di-grād′), *v.t.* [-GRADED, -GRADING], [< OFr. < LL. *degradare* < L. *de-*, down + *gradus;* see GRADE], 1. to lower in rank or status; demote. 2. to lower or corrupt in quality, moral character, etc. 3. to bring into dishonor or contempt. 4. in *geology*, to lower (a surface) by erosion. *v.i.* to sink to a lower position or type; degenerate. —**deg·ra·da·tion** (deg′rə-dā′shən), *n.* —**de·grad′er,** *n.* —**de·grad′ing,** *adj.* —**de·grad′ing·ly,** *adv.*
**de·grad·ed** (di-grād′id), *adj.* disgraced; debased; depraved. —**de·grad′ed·ly,** *adv.* —**de·grad′ed·ness,** *n.*
**de·gree** (di-grē′), *n.* [< OFr. < LL. < *degradare;* see DEGRADE], 1. any of the successive steps or stages in a process. 2. a step in the direct line of descent. 3. social or official rank. 4. the relative condition, way, or respect. 5. intensity, extent, or amount: as, hungry to a slight *degree.* 6. in *algebra*, rank as determined by the sum of a term's exponents: as, $x^5$ is of the fifth *degree.* 7. in *education*, a rank given by a college or university to a student who has completed a required course of study, or to a distinguished person as an honor: as, an M.A. *degree.* 8. in *grammar*, a grade of comparison of adjectives and adverbs: as, the superlative *degree* of *good* is *best.* 9. in *law*, the seriousness of a crime: as, murder in the first *degree.* 10. in *mathematics*, *geography*, etc., a unit of measure for angles or arcs, 1/360 of the circumference of a circle. 11. in *music*, the interval between any two notes on an adjacent line and space. 12. in *physics*, a unit of measure for temperature: as, water boils at 212 *degrees* Fahrenheit (212° F.). —**by degrees,** step by step; gradually. —**to a degree,** 1. to a great extent. 2. somewhat.
**de·hisce** (di-his′), *v.i. & v.t.* [-HISCED, -HISCING], [< L. < *de-*, off, from + *hiscere*, to gape], to burst or split open, as a seed pod to discharge its contents. —**de·his′cence,** *n.* —**de·his′cent,** *adj.*
**de·horn** (dē-hôrn′), *v.t.* to remove the horns from.
**de·hu·man·ize** (dē-hū′mə-nīz′), *v.t.* [-IZED, -IZING], to deprive of human qualities; make inhuman. —**de·hu′man·i·za′tion,** *n.*
**de·hu·mid·i·fy** (dē′hū-mid′ə-fī′), *v.t.* [-FIED, -FYING], [*de-* + *humidify*], to remove moisture from (the air, etc.). —**de′hu·mid′i·fi·ca′tion,** *n.* —**de′hu·mid′i·fi′er,** *n.*
**de·hy·drate** (dē-hī′drāt), *v.t.* [< *de-* + Gr. *hydor*, water; + *-ate*], in *chemistry*, etc., to remove water from; dry. *v.i.* to lose water; become dry. —**de′hy·dra′tion,** *n.* —**de·hy′dra·tor** (-tẽr), *n.*
**de·ic·er** (dē-i′sẽr), *n.* a device for eliminating formations of ice, as on the wings of airplanes.
**de·i·fy** (dē′ə-fī′), *v.t.* [-FIED, -FYING], [< OFr. < LL. < L. *deus*, god + *facere*, to make], 1. to make a god of; rank among the gods. 2. to look upon as a god: worship. —**de·if′ic** (-if′ik), *adj.* —**de′i·fi·ca′tion** (-fi-kā′shən), *n.* —**de′i·fi′er,** *n.*
**deign** (dān), *v.i.* [< OFr. < L. *dignare* < *dignus*, worthy], to think befitting one's dignity (*to do* something); condescend. *v.t.* to condescend to give.
**de·ism** (dē′iz'm), *n.* [< Fr. < L. *deus*, god], the belief that God exists and created the world but thereafter assumed no control over it or the lives of people. —**de′ist,** *n.* —**de·is′tic, de·is′ti·cal,** *adj.* —**de·is′ti·cal·ly,** *adv.*
**de·i·ty** (dē′ə-ti), *n.* [*pl.* -TIES], [< OFr. < LL. < L. *deus*, god], 1. the state of being a god; divine nature. 2. a god. 3. a goddess. —**the Deity,** God.
**de·ject** (di-jekt′), *v.t.* [< L. pp. of *dejicere* < *de-*, down + *jacere*, to throw], to dishearten; depress.
**de·ject·ed** (di-jek′tid), *adj.* [pp. of *deject*], depressed; discouraged; disheartened; downcast. —**de·ject′ed·ly,** *adv.* —**de·ject′ed·ness,** *n.*
**de·jec·tion** (di-jek′shən), *n.* lowness of spirits; depression.
‡**dé·jeu·ner** (dā′zhë′nā′), *n.* [Fr.], 1. a breakfast, especially a late one. 2. a luncheon.
‡**de ju·re** (dē joor′i), [L.], by right; in accordance with law: distinguished from *de facto.*
**dek·a-,** deca-: also, before a vowel, **dek-.**
**Del.,** Delaware.
**del.,** 1. delete. 2. delegate.
**De·la·croix, Fer·di·nand Vic·tor Eu·gène** (fer′dē′-nän′ vēk′tôr′ ë′zhen′ də-là′krwä′), 1799–1863; French painter.
**Del·a·ware** (del′ə-wâr′), *n.* 1. an E State of the U.S.: area, 2,057 sq. mi.; pop., 446,000; capital, Dover: abbrev. **Del.** 2. a river flowing between Pennsylvania and New Jersey into the Atlantic. 3. any of a tribe of Algonquian Indians who lived in the Delaware River valley. —**Del′a·war′e·an,** *adj. & n.*
**de·lay** (di-lā′), *v.t.* [< OFr. < *de-*, from + *laier*, to leave], 1. to put off; postpone. 2. to make late; detain. *v.i.* to stop for a while; loiter. *n.* a delaying or being delayed. —**de·lay′er,** *n.*
**de·le** (dē′li), *v.t.* [DELED (-lid), DELEING (-li-iŋ)], [L., imperative sing. of *delere;* see DELETE], in *printing*, to delete (a letter, etc.): usually in the imperative as a direction to the printer. *n.* a mark (₰) showing that a letter, word, etc. is to be taken out.
**de·lec·ta·ble** (di-lek′tə-b'l), *adj.* [< L. < *delectare;* see DELIGHT], enjoyable; delightful. —**de·lec′ta·bil′i·ty, de·lec′ta·ble·ness,** *n.* —**de·lec′ta·bly,** *adv.*
**de·lec·ta·tion** (dē′lek-tā′shən), *n.* [OFr. < L. < *delectare;* see DELIGHT], delight; entertainment.
**del·e·gate** (del′ə-gāt′; *also, for n.*, -git), *n.* [< L. *delegatus*, pp. < *de-*, from + *legare*, to send], 1. a person authorized to act for others; representative. 2. a (non-voting) representative of a U.S. territory in the House of Representatives. 3. a member of a House of Delegates. *v.t.* [-GATED, -GATING], 1. to send or appoint as a delegate. 2. to entrust (authority, power, etc.) to a person acting as one's representative.
**del·e·ga·tion** (del′ə-gā′shən), *n.* 1. a delegating or being delegated. 2. a group of delegates.
**de·lete** (di-lēt′), *v.t. & v.i.* [-LETED, -LETING], [< L. pp. of *delere*, to destroy], to take out (a printed or written letter, word, etc.); cross out; dele. —**de·le′tion,** *n.*
**del·e·te·ri·ous** (del′ə-têr′i-əs), *adj.* [< ML. < Gr. < *dēleisthai*, to injure], harmful to health, well-being, etc.; injurious. —**del′e·te′ri·ous·ly,** *adv.* —**del′e·te′ri·ous·ness,** *n.*
**delft·ware** (delft′wâr′), *n.* 1. glazed pottery, usually blue, which originated in Delft, a city in W Holland. 2. brown earthenware with a white, decorated glaze. Also **delf** (delf), **delft.**
**Del·hi** (del′i), *n.* 1. a small territory of N India: area, 574 sq. mi.; pop., 2,659,000. 2. its capital: pop., 2,062,000: also called *Old Delhi;* formerly the capital of India: see **New Delhi.**
**de·lib·er·ate** (di-lib′ẽr-it; *for v.*, -āt′), *adj.* [< L. pp. of *deliberare* < *de-*, intens. + *librare*, to weigh < *libra*, a scales], 1. carefully thought out or formed; done on purpose. 2. careful in considering; not rash or hasty. 3. slow; unhurried. *v.i.* [-ATED, -ATING], 1. to consider carefully and fully. 2. to consider reasons for and against in order to make up one's mind. *v.t.* to consider carefully. —**de·lib′er·ate·ly,** *adv.* —**de·lib′er·ate·ness,** *n.* —**de·lib′er·a′tor** (-tẽr), *n.*
**de·lib·er·a·tion** (di-lib′ẽr-ā′shən), *n.* 1. a deliberat-

ing; considering carefully. 2. *often pl.* consideration and debate: as, the *deliberations* of statesmen. 3. carefulness; slowness.

**de·lib·er·a·tive** (di-lib′ẽr-ā′tiv), *adj.* 1. of or for deliberating: as, a *deliberative* assembly. 2. characterized by deliberation. —**de·lib′er·a′tive·ly,** *adv.* —**de·lib′er·a′tive·ness,** *n.*

**del·i·ca·cy** (del′i-kə-si), *n.* [*pl.* -CIES], 1. a delicate quality. 2. fineness; frailty; graceful slightness, softness, etc. 3. weakness of constitution or health. 4. a need for careful and deft handling. 5. fineness of feeling or appreciating; sensitiveness. 6. fineness of touch, skill, etc. 7. a fine regard for the feelings of others. 8. a sensitive distaste for what is considered improper or offensive. 9. a choice food or dainty.

**del·i·cate** (del′i-kit), *adj.* [L. *delicatus,* delightful < *delicere;* see DELIGHT], 1. pleasingly and finely flavored. 2. deliciously mild or soft: as, a *delicate* air. 3. beautifully fine in texture, workmanship, etc. 4. slight and subtle. 5. easily damaged, disordered, etc. 6. frail in health. 7. needing careful handling: as, a *delicate* situation. 8. finely sensitive: as, a *delicate* ear for music, a *delicate* gauge. 9. finely skilled. 10. considerate and tactful. 11. having a sensitive distaste for anything offensive or improper. —**del′i·cate·ly,** *adv.* —**del′i·cate·ness,** *n.*

**del·i·ca·tes·sen** (del′i-kə-tes′'n), *n.pl.* [< G. pl. < Fr. *délicatesse,* delicacy], 1. [often construed as sing.], prepared cooked meats, smoked fish, cheeses, salads, relishes, etc. 2. [construed as sing.], a shop where such foods are sold.

**de·li·cious** (di-lish′əs), *adj.* [< OFr. < L. < *deliciae,* delight < *delicere;* see DELIGHT], 1. very enjoyable; delightful. 2. very pleasing to taste or smell. *n.* [D-], a sweet, red winter apple. —**de·li′cious·ly,** *adv.* —**de·li′cious·ness,** *n.*

**de·light** (di-līt′), *v.t.* [< OFr. < L. < *delicere* < *de-,* from + *lacere,* to entice], to give great pleasure to. *v.i.* 1. to give great pleasure. 2. to be highly pleased. *n.* 1. great pleasure. 2. something giving great pleasure. —**de·light′ed,** *adj.* —**de·light′ed·ly,** *adv.* —**de·light′ed·ness,** *n.* —**de·light′er,** *n.*

**de·light·ful** (di-līt′fəl), *adj.* giving delight; very pleasing; charming. —**de·light′ful·ly,** *adv.* —**de·light′ful·ness,** *n.*

**De·li·lah** (di-lī′lə), *n.* 1. in the *Bible,* the mistress of Samson, who betrayed him to the Philistines: Judg. 16. 2. a false woman or harlot.

**de·lim·it** (di-lim′it), *v.t.* to set the limits or boundaries of. —**de·lim′i·ta′tion,** *n.*

**de·lin·e·ate** (di-lin′i-āt′), *v.t.* [-ATED, -ATING], [< L. < *de-,* from + *linea,* a line], 1. to trace the outline of. 2. to draw; depict. 3. to depict in words; describe. —**de·lin′e·a′tion,** *n.* —**de·lin′e·a′tive,** *adj.* —**de·lin′e·a′tor,** *n.*

‡**de·li·ne·a·vit** (di-lin′i-ā′vit), [L.], he (or she) drew (this): used with the artist's name on a painting, etc.: abbrev. **del., delt.**

**de·lin·quen·cy** (di-liŋ′kwən-si), *n.* [*pl.* -CIES], 1. failure or neglect to do what duty or law requires; guilt. 2. a fault; misdeed. 3. in *law,* the act or acts of a juvenile delinquent.

**de·lin·quent** (di-liŋ′kwənt), *adj.* [< L. *delinquens,* ppr. < *de-,* from + *linquere,* to leave], 1. failing to do what duty or law requires; guilty of a fault or misdeed. 2. overdue: as, *delinquent* taxes. *n.* a delinquent person; esp., a delinquent juvenile. —**de·lin′quent·ly,** *adv.*

**del·i·quesce** (del′ə-kwes′), *v.i.* [-QUESCED, -QUESCING], [< L. < *de-,* from + *liquere,* to be liquid], 1. to melt away. 2. to become liquid by absorbing moisture from the air. —**del′i·ques′cence,** *n.* —**del′i·ques′cent,** *adj.*

**de·lir·i·ous** (di-lir′i-əs), *adj.* 1. in a state of delirium. 2. of or caused by delirium. 3. in a state of wild excitement. —**de·lir′i·ous·ly,** *adv.* —**de·lir′i·ous·ness,** *n.*

**de·lir·i·um** (di-lir′i-əm), *n.* [*pl.* -UMS, -A (-ə)], [L. < *delirare,* to rave, lit., to make the furrow awry in plowing < *de-,* from + *lira,* a line], 1. a temporary state of extreme mental excitement, marked by confused speech and hallucinations: it sometimes occurs during fever, in some forms of insanity, etc. 2. an uncontrollably wild excitement.

**delirium tre·mens** (trē′mənz), [Mod. L., lit., trembling delirium], a violent delirium resulting from excessive drinking of alcoholic liquor: abbrev. **D.T.'s, d.t.**

**de·liv·er** (di-liv′ẽr), *v.t.* [< OFr. < LL. < L. *de-,* from + *liberare,* to free < *liber,* free], 1. to set free or save from evil, danger, etc. 2. to assist at the birth of (an offspring). 3. to express in words; utter: as, to *deliver* a speech. 4. to hand over; transfer (with *to*). 5. to distribute: as, *deliver* the mail. 6. to strike (a blow). 7. to throw (a ball, etc.). —**be delivered of,** to give birth to. —**deliver oneself of,** to express; utter. —**de·liv′er·a·ble,** *adj.* —**de·liv′er·er,** *n.*

**de·liv·er·ance** (di-liv′ẽr-əns), *n.* 1. a freeing or being freed. 2. an opinion, judgment, etc. formally or publicly expressed.

**de·liv·er·y** (di-liv′ẽr-i), *n.* [*pl.* -IES], 1. a handing over; transfer. 2. a distributing, as of mail. 3. a giving birth; childbirth. 4. any giving forth. 5. a striking (of a blow). 6. a throwing (of a ball). 7. the manner of speaking, throwing, etc. 8. something delivered.

**dell** (del), *n.* [AS. *dell*], a small, secluded valley, glen, or ravine, usually a wooded one.

**de·louse** (dē-lous′, -louz′) *v.t.* [-LOUSED, -LOUSING], to rid of lice.

**Del·phi** (del′fī), *n.* a city in ancient Greece: site of a celebrated oracle of Apollo. —**Del′phi·an** (-fi-ən), **Del′phic** (-fik), *adj.*

**del·phin·i·um** (del-fin′i-əm), *n.* [< Gr. *delphin,* dolphin: its nectary resembles a dolphin], a plant bearing spikes of spurred, irregular flowers, usually blue, on tall stalks; larkspur.

**del·ta** (del′tə), *n.* [< Gr.], 1. the fourth letter of the Greek alphabet (Δ, δ). 2. a deposit of sand and soil, usually triangular, formed at the mouth of some rivers.

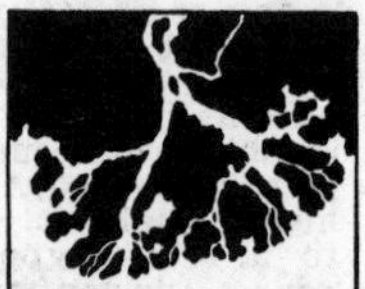

DELTA OF RIVER

**del·toid** (del′toid), *adj.* 1. shaped like a delta; triangular. 2. designating or of a large, triangular muscle of the shoulder. *n.* this muscle.

**de·lude** (di-lōōd′), *v.t.* [-LUDED, -LUDING], [< L. < *de-,* from + *ludere,* to play], to mislead; beguile; deceive. —**de·lud′er,** *n.*

**del·uge** (del′ūj), *n.* [OFr. < L. *diluvium* < *dis-,* off + *luere,* to wash], 1. a great flood. 2. a heavy rainfall. 3. an overwhelming, floodlike rush of anything *v.t.* [-LUGED, -LUGING], 1. to flood. 2. to overwhelm. —**the Deluge,** in the *Bible,* the great flood in Noah's time: Gen. 7.

**de·lu·sion** (di-lōō′zhən), *n.* 1. a deluding or being deluded. 2. a false belief or opinion. 3. in *psychiatry,* a false, persistent belief not substantiated by sensory evidence.

**de·lu·sive** (di-lōō′siv), *adj.* tending to delude; misleading: also **de·lu′so·ry** (-sə-ri). —**de·lu′sive·ly,** *adv.* —**de·lu′sive·ness,** *n.*

**de luxe** (di looks′, di luks′), [Fr., lit., of luxury], of especially good quality; elegant.

**delve** (delv), *v.i.* [DELVED, DELVING], [AS. *delfan*], 1. [Archaic or Brit. Dial.], to dig. 2. to make an investigation; search for facts: as, *delve* into books, etc. *v.t.* [Archaic or Brit. Dial.], to dig up (ground) with a spade. —**delv′er,** *n.*

**Dem.,** 1. Democrat. 2. Democratic.

**de·mag·net·ize** (dē-mag′nə-tīz′), *v.t.* [-IZED, -IZING], to deprive of magnetism. —**de·mag′net·i·za′tion,** *n.* —**de·mag′net·iz′er,** *n.*

**dem·a·gog·ic** (dem′ə-goj′ik, -gog′-), *adj.* of, like, or characteristic of a demagogue or demagogy: also **dem′a·gog′i·cal.** —**dem′a·gog′i·cal·ly,** *adv.*

**dem·a·gogue, dem·a·gog** (dem′ə-gôg′, -gog′), *n.* [< Gr. < *dēmos,* the people + *agōgos,* leader < *agein,* to lead], one who tries to stir up the people by appeals to emotion, prejudice, etc. in order to become a leader and accomplish selfish ends.

**dem·a·gog·y** (dem′ə-gō′ji, -gôg′i, -gog′i), *n.* the methods, actions, or principles of a demagogue: also **dem′a·gog′uer·y** (-gôg′ẽr-i, -gog′-).

**de·mand** (di-mand′, -mänd′), *v.t.* [< OFr. < L. < *de-,* from + *mandare,* to entrust < *manus,* a hand + *dare,* to give], 1. to ask for boldly or urgently. 2. to ask for as a right or with authority. 3. to ask to know or be informed. 4. to require; need: as, the work *demands* patience. *v.i.* to make a demand. *n.* 1. a demanding. 2. a thing demanded. 3. a strong request. 4. a requirement or claim. 5. an emphatic inquiry. 6. in *economics, a*) the desire for a commodity together with ability to pay for it. *b*) the amount people are ready to buy at a certain price. —**in demand,** demanded or sought. —**on demand,** when presented for payment. —**de·mand′a·ble,** *adj.* —**de·mand′er,** *n.*

**de·mar·cate** (di-mär′kāt, dē′mär-kāt′), *v.t.* [-CATED, -CATING], [< *demarcation*], 1. to mark the limits of. 2. to discriminate; separate.

**de·mar·ca·tion, de·mar·ka·tion** (dē′mär-kā′shən), *n.* [Fr. < Sp. < *de-* (L. *de*), from + *marcar,* to mark], 1. the act of setting and marking boundaries. 2. a limit or boundary line. 3. a separating.

‡**dé·marche** (dā'märsh'), *n.* [Fr.], 1. a line of action. 2. in *diplomacy*, a change of policy.
**de·mean** (di-mēn'), *v.t.* [*de-* + *mean* (low)], to degrade; humble: as, to *demean* oneself by cheating.
**de·mean** (di-mēn'), *v.t.* [see DEMEANOR], to behave, conduct, or comport (oneself).
**de·mean·or** (di-mēn'ẽr), *n.* [< OFr. < *de-* (L. *de*), from + *mener*, to lead < LL. < L. *minari*, to threaten], outward behavior; conduct; deportment: also Brit. **de·mean'our** (-ẽr).
**de·ment** (di-ment'), *v.t.* to cause dementia in.
**de·ment·ed** (di-men'tid), *adj.* mentally ill. —**de·ment'ed·ly,** *adv.* —**de·ment'ed·ness,** *n.*
**de·men·ti·a** (di-men'shə, -shi-ə), *n.* [< L. < *de-*, away + *mens, mentis*, the mind], loss or impairment of mental powers: cf. *amentia*.
**dementia prae·cox** (prē'koks), [L., lit., precocious dementia], a form of dementia, usually beginning in late adolescence, characterized by melancholia, withdrawal, hallucinations, etc.
**de·mer·it** (dē-mer'it), *n.* [< Fr.; ult. < L. *demerere*, to deserve well, with prefix *de-* mistaken as negative], 1. a fault; defect. 2. a mark recorded against a student, etc. for poor work or conduct.
**de·mesne** (di-mān', -mēn'), *n.* [OFr. *demaine;* see DOMAIN], 1. in *law*, possession (of real estate) as one's own. 2. a lord's mansion and the land around it. 3. a region; domain. 4. a realm (of activity): as, the *demesne* of science.
**De·me·ter** (di-mē'tẽr), *n.* in *Gr. mythology*, the goddess of agriculture and fruitfulness: identified by the Romans with Ceres.
**dem·i-,** [Fr. < L. < *dis-*, apart + *medius*, middle], a prefix meaning: 1. *half.* 2. *less than usual in size, power*, etc., as in *demigod*.
**dem·i·god** (dem'i-god'), *n.* 1. in *mythology*, a lesser god; minor deity. 2. a person regarded as partly divine. —**dem'i·god'dess,** *n.fem.*
**dem·i·john** (dem'i-jon'), *n.* [Fr. *dame-jeanne*], a large bottle of glass or earthenware, with a narrow neck and a wicker casing and handle.
**de·mil·i·ta·rize** (dē-mil'ə-tə-rīz'), *v.t.* [-RIZED, -RIZING], to free from military control or militarism. —**de·mil'i·ta·ri·za'tion,** *n.*
**dem·i·mon·daine** (dem'i-mon-dān'), *n.* [Fr.], a woman of the demimonde.
**dem·i·monde** (dem'i-mond', dem'i-mond') *n.* [Fr.; *demi-* + *monde* (< L. *mundus*), world], the class of women who have lost social standing because of sexual promiscuity.
**dem·i·qua·ver** (dem'i-kwā'vẽr), *n.* a semiquaver.
**de·mise** (di-mīz'), *n.* [< Fr. pp. of *démettre*, to dismiss < L. < *de-*, down + *mittere*, to send], 1. the transfer of an estate by will or lease. 2. the transfer of sovereignty by death or abdication. 3. death. *v.t.* [-MISED, -MISING], 1. to give or transfer (an estate) by will or lease. 2. to transfer (sovereignty) by death or abdication. *v.i.* to be passed on by bequest or inheritance. —**de·mis'a·ble,** *adj.*
**dem·i·sem·i·qua·ver** (dem'i-sem'i-kwā'vẽr), *n.* in *music*, a thirty-second note (♪).
**dem·i·tasse** (dem'i-tas', -täs'), *n.* [Fr.; *demi-* + *tasse*, cup], a small cup of or for after-dinner coffee.
**de·mo·bi·lize** (dē-mō'b'l-īz'), *v.t. & v.i.* [-LIZED, -LIZING], 1. to disband (troops). 2. to change over from war to peace. —**de·mo'bi·li·za'tion,** *n.*
**de·moc·ra·cy** (də-mok'rə-si), *n.* [*pl.* -CIES (-siz)], [< Fr. < ML. < Gr. < *dēmos*, the people + *kratein*, to rule], 1. government by the people, either directly or through elected representatives. 2. a country, state, etc. with such government. 3. majority rule. 4. the acceptance and practice of the principle of equality of rights, opportunity, and treatment. 5. [D-], the Democratic Party of the U.S., or the principles of this party.
**dem·o·crat** (dem'ə-krat'), *n.* 1. a person who believes in and upholds government by the people. 2. a person who believes in and practices the principle of equality of rights, opportunity, etc. 3. [D-], a member of the Democratic Party.
**dem·o·crat·ic** (dem'ə-krat'ik), *adj.* 1. of, belonging to, or upholding democracy or a democracy. 2. of or for all the people. 3. considering and treating others as one's equals. 4. [D-], of or belonging to the Democratic Party. Also **dem'o·crat'i·cal.** —**dem'o·crat'i·cal·ly,** *adv.*
**Democratic Party,** one of the two major political parties in the U.S., since about 1830.
**de·moc·ra·tize** (də-mok'rə-tīz'), *v.t. & v.i.* [-TIZED, -TIZING], to make or become democratic. —**de·moc'ra·ti·za'tion,** *n.*
‡**dé·mo·dé** (dā'mô'dā'), *adj.* [Fr.], out-of-date.
**de·mol·ish** (di-mol'ish), *v.t.* [< Fr. < L. *demoliri*, to destroy; *de-*, down + *moliri*, to build < *moles*, a mass], 1. to pull or tear down (a building, etc.); hence, 2. to destroy; ruin. —**de·mol'ish·er,** *n.* —**de·mol'ish·ment,** *n.*
**dem·o·li·tion** (dem'ə-lish'ən, dē'mə-), *n.* a demolishing or being demolished; destruction.
**demolition bomb,** a bomb designed for demolishing buildings, etc. by means of explosive force.
**de·mon** (dē'mən), *n.* [< Fr. < L. *daemon*], 1. a daemon. 2. a devil; evil spirit. 3. a person or thing regarded as evil, cruel, etc. 4. a person who has great energy or skill.
**de·mon·e·tize** (dē-mon'ə-tīz', -mun'-), *v.t.* [-TIZED, -TIZING], 1. to deprive (currency) of its standard value. 2. to stop using as money. —**de·mon'e·ti·za'tion,** *n.*
**de·mo·ni·ac** (di-mō'ni-ak'), *adj.* 1. possessed or influenced by a demon. 2. of a demon or demons. 3. devilish. 4. frenzied; frantic. Also **de·mo·ni·a·cal** (dē'mə-nī'ə-k'l). *n.* a person supposedly possessed by a demon. —**de'mo·ni'a·cal·ly,** *adv.*
**de·mon·ic** (dē-mon'ik), *adj.* 1. of or like a demon or demons. 2. having a guiding spirit.
**de·mon·ism** (dē'mən-iz'm), *n.* belief in the existence and powers of demons. —**de'mon·ist,** *n.*
**de·mon·o-,** a combining form meaning *demon:* also, before a vowel, **demon-.**
**de·mon·ol·a·try** (dē'mən-ol'ə-tri), *n.* [*demono-* + *-latry*], worship of demons. —**de'mon·ol'a·ter,** *n.*
**de·mon·ol·o·gy** (dē'mən-ol'ə-ji), *n.* [*demono-* + *-logy*], the study of demons or of beliefs about them. —**de'mon·ol'o·gist,** *n.*
**de·mon·stra·ble** (di-mon'strə-b'l, dem'ən-), *adj.* that can be demonstrated, or proved. —**de·mon'stra·bil'i·ty, de·mon'stra·ble·ness,** *n.* —**de·mon'stra·bly,** *adv.*
**dem·on·strate** (dem'ən-strāt'), *v.t.* [-STRATED, -STRATING], [< L. *demonstratus*, pp. < *de-*, from + *monstrare*, to show], 1. to show by reasoning; prove. 2. to explain by using examples, experiments, etc. 3. to show, or advertise by showing, the operation or working of. 4. to show (feelings) plainly. *v.i.* 1. to show feelings or ideas by public meetings, parades, etc. 2. to show military power or preparedness.
**dem·on·stra·tion** (dem'ən-strā'shən), *n.* 1. a making evident or proving. 2. an explanation by example, etc. 3. a practical showing of how something works or is done. 4. a display or outward show. 5. a public show of opinion, etc., as by a mass meeting. 6. a show of military force or preparedness. —**dem'on·stra'tion·al,** *adj.*
**de·mon·stra·tive** (di-mon'strə-tiv), *adj.* 1. showing clearly; illustrative. 2. giving evidence or proof (with *of*). 3. having to do with demonstration. 4. showing feelings openly and frankly. 5. in *grammar*, pointing out: as, *that* is a *demonstrative* pronoun. *n.* in *grammar*, a demonstrative pronoun or adjective. —**de·mon'stra·tive·ly,** *adv.* —**de·mon'stra·tive·ness,** *n.*
**dem·on·stra·tor** (dem'ən-strā'tẽr), *n.* [L.], a person or thing that demonstrates, as a person who takes part in a public demonstration.
**de·mor·al·ize** (di-môr'ə-līz', -mor'-), *v.t.* [-IZED, -IZING], 1. to corrupt the morals of. 2. to lower the morale of. 3. to throw into confusion. —**de·mor'al·i·za'tion,** *n.* —**de·mor'al·iz'er,** *n.*
**De·mos·the·nes** (di-mos'thə-nēz'), *n.* Greek orator and statesman; lived 385?–322 B.C.
**de·mote** (di-mōt'), *v.t.* [-MOTED, -MOTING], [*de-* + *-mote*, as in *promote*], to reduce to a lower grade; lower in rank. —**de·mo'tion,** *n.*
**de·mount** (dē-mount'), *v.t.* to remove from a mounting: as, *demount* the motor. —**de·mount'a·ble,** *adj.*
**de·mul·cent** (di-mul's'nt), *adj.* [< L. < *de-*, down + *mulcere*, to stroke], soothing. *n.* a medicine or ointment that soothes irritated surfaces.
**de·mur** (di-mũr'), *v.i.* [-MURRED, -MURRING], [< OFr. < L. < *de-*, from + *morari*, to delay < *mora*, a delay], 1. to hesitate; have scruples; object (with *at*). 2. in *law*, to enter a demurrer. *n.* 1. a demurring: also **de·mur'ral.** 2. an objection raised.
**de·mure** (di-myoor'), *adj.* [*de-* (prob. intens. < *demur*); + ME. *meur* < OFr.; prob. < L. *maturus*, mature], 1. sober; serious; sedate. 2. affectedly modest or sedate; coy. —**de·mure'ly,** *adv.* —**de·mure'ness,** *n.*
**de·mur·rage** (di-mũr'ij), *n.* 1. the delaying of a ship, freight car, etc., as by failure to load, unload,

or sail within the time allowed. 2. the compensation paid for this.

**de·mur·rer** (di-mũr′ẽr), *n.* [see DEMUR], 1. a plea for the dismissal of a lawsuit on the grounds that even if the statements of the opposition are true, they do not sustain the claim. 2. an objection. 3. a person who demurs.

**den** (den), *n.* [AS. *denn*], 1. the lair of a wild animal. 2. a retreat or headquarters, as of thieves. 3. a cozy room where one can be alone to read, work, etc. *v.i.* [DENNED, DENNING], to live or hide in a den.

**Den.,** Denmark.

**de·nar·i·us** (di-nâr′i-əs), *n.* [*pl.* -NARII(-Ī′)], [L. < *deni*, by tens < *decem*, ten], 1. an ancient Roman silver coin, the penny of the New Testament. 2. an ancient Roman gold coin.

**de·na·tion·al·ize** (dē-nash′ə-n'l-īz′), *v.t.* [-IZED, -IZING], to deprive of national rights, status, scope, etc. —**de·na′tion·al·i·za′tion,** *n.*

**de·nat·u·ral·ize** (dē-nach′ẽr-əl-īz′), *v.t.* [-IZED, -IZING], 1. to make unnatural. 2. to take citizenship away from. —**de·nat′u·ral·i·za′tion,** *n.*

**de·na·ture** (dē-nā′chẽr), *v.t.* [-TURED, -TURING], 1. to change the nature of. 2. to make unfit as food or drink without spoiling for other uses: as, *denatured* alcohol. —**de·na′tur·ant,** *n.* —**de·na′tur·a′tion,** *n.*

**de·na·zi·fy** (dē-nät′sə-fī′) *v.t.* [-FIED, -FYING], to rid of Nazi elements or influences.—**de·na′zi·fi·ca′tion,** *n.*

**den·drite** (den′drīt), *n.* [< Gr. < *dendron*, a tree], the branched part of a nerve cell that carries impulses toward the cell body: also **den′dron** (-drən). —**den·drit′ic** (-drit′ik), **den·drit′i·cal,** *adj.*

**den·dro-,** [< Gr. *dendron*], a combining form meaning *tree*: also **dendri-** or, before a vowel, **dendr-.**

**den·drol·o·gy** (den-drol′ə-ji), *n.* [*dendro-* + *-logy*], the scientific study of trees.

**-den·dron** (den′drən), [< Gr. *dendron*, tree], a combining form meaning *tree, treelike structure.*

**den·gue** (deŋ′gi, -gā), *n.* [W. Ind. Sp. < Swahili *dinga*, a cramp], an infectious tropical disease transmitted by mosquitoes and characterized by severe pains in the joints, fever, and rash.

**de·ni·al** (di-nī′əl), *n.* 1. a denying; saying "no" (to a request, etc.). 2. a contradiction: as, the *denial* of a statement. 3. a disowning; repudiation: as, the *denial* of one's family. 4. a refusal to believe or accept (a doctrine, etc.). 5. abstinence from desired things: also **self-denial.**

**de·nic·o·tin·ize** (dē-nik′ə-tin-īz′), *v.t.* [-IZED, -IZING], [< *de-* + *nicotine* + *-ize*], to remove nicotine from (tobacco).

**de·ni·er** (di-nī′ẽr), *n.* a person who denies.

**de·nier** (də-nêr′, den′yẽr), *n.* [Fr. < L.; see DENARIUS], a unit of weight for measuring the fineness of threads of silk, nylon, etc.

**den·i·grate** (den′ə-grāt′), *v.t.* [-GRATED, -GRATING], [< L. < *de-*, intens. + *nigrare*, to blacken < *niger*, black], to disparage the character or reputation of; defame. —**den′i·gra′tion,** *n.*

**den·im** (den′im), *n.* [< Fr. *serge de Nîmes*, serge of Nîmes, town in France], a coarse, twilled cotton cloth used for overalls, uniforms, etc.

**den·i·zen** (den′i-z'n), *n.* [< OFr. *denzein* < *denz*, within < LL. *de intus*, from within], 1. an inhabitant. 2. a naturalized animal, foreign word, etc.

**Den·mark** (den′märk), *n.* a country in N Europe, between the North and Baltic Seas: area, 16,576 sq. mi.; pop., 4,870,000; capital, Copenhagen.

**de·nom·in·ate** (di-nom′ə-nāt′; *for adj., usually* -nit), *v.t.* [-ATED, -ATING], [< L. *denominatus*, pp. < *de-*, intens. + *nominare*; see NOMINATE], to name; call. *adj.* having a specified name.

**de·nom·i·na·tion** (di-nom′ə-nā′shən), *n.* 1. the act of naming. 2. a name. 3. a class or kind having a specific name or value: as, coins of different *denominations*. 4. a religious sect.

**de·nom·i·na·tion·al** (di-nom′ə-nā′shən-'l), *adj.* of, or under the control of, some religious sect or sects. —**de·nom′i·na′tion·al·ly,** *adv.*

**de·nom·i·na·tion·al·ism** (di-nom′ə-nā′shən-'l-iz'm), *n.* 1. denominational principles. 2. division into denominations.

**de·nom·i·na·tive** (di-nom′ə-nā′tiv, -nə-tiv), *adj.* 1. denominating; naming. 2. in *grammar*, formed from a noun or adjective stem: as, *to eye* is a *denominative* verb. *n.* a denominative word.

**de·nom·i·na·tor** (di-nom′ə-nā′tẽr), *n.* 1. one that denominates. 2. in *mathematics*, the term below the line in a fraction, indicating the number of equal parts into which the whole is divided.

**de·no·ta·tion** (dē′nō-tā′shən), *n.* 1. a denoting. 2. the explicit meaning or reference of a word or term: cf. *connotation*. 3. an indication or sign.

**de·note** (di-nōt′), *v.t.* [-NOTED, -NOTING], [< Fr. < L. < *de-*, down + *notare*, to mark < *nota*, a mark], 1. to mark; indicate; make known by a sign. 2. to mean; signify explicitly; be a name of: cf. *connote*. —**de·not′a·ble,** *adj.* —**de·no·ta·tive** (di-nō′tə-tiv, dē′nō-tā′-), *adj.*

**de·noue·ment, dé·noue·ment** (dā-nōō′män; Fr. dā′nōō′män′), *n.* [Fr. < *dé-* (L. *dis-*), out + *nouer*, to tie < L. < *nodus*, a knot], 1. the outcome, solution, or unraveling of a plot in a drama, story, etc. 2. any final revelation or outcome.

**de·nounce** (di-nouns′), *v.t.* [-NOUNCED, -NOUNCING], [< OFr. < L. *denuntiare*; see DENUNCIATION], 1. to accuse publicly; inform against. 2. to condemn strongly as evil. 3. to give formal notice of the ending of (a treaty, armistice, etc.). —**de·nounce′ment,** *n.* —**de·nounc′er,** *n.*

‡**de no·vo** (dē nō′vō), [L.], anew; once more.

**dense** (dens), *adj.* [DENSER, DENSEST], [L. *densus*, compact], 1. packed tightly together. 2. thick; impenetrable. 3. stupid. 4. in *photography*, comparatively opaque: said of a negative. —**dense′ly,** *adv.* —**dense′ness,** *n.*

**den·si·ty** (den′sə-ti), *n.* [*pl.* -TIES], 1. the quality or condition of being dense or crowded. 2. quantity or number per unit, as of area: as, the *density* of population. 3. stupidity. 4. in *physics*, the ratio of the mass of an object to its volume: symbol, D (no period).

**dent** (dent), *n.* [ME., dial. var. of *dint*], a slight hollow made in a surface by a blow. *v.t.* to make a dent in. *v.i.* to become dented.

**den·tal** (den′t'l), *adj.* [< L. *dens*, *dentis*, a tooth], 1. of or for the teeth or dentistry. 2. in *phonetics*, formed by placing the tip of the tongue against or near the upper front teeth. *n.* in *phonetics*, a dental consonant, as *d*, *t*, *th*.

**den·tate** (den′tāt), *adj.* [< L. < *dens*, tooth], having teeth or toothlike projections; toothed or notched. —**den′tate·ly,** *adv.* —**den·ta′tion,** *n.*

**den·ti-,** [< L. *dens*, tooth], a combining form meaning: *tooth* or *teeth*: also **den′to-, dent-.**

**den·ti·frice** (den′tə-fris), *n.* [Fr. < L. < *dens*, tooth + *fricare*, to rub], any preparation for cleaning teeth, as a powder, paste, or liquid.

**den·tine** (den′tēn, -tin), *n.* [< L. *dens*, tooth], the hard, calcareous tissue forming the body of a tooth, under the enamel: also **den′tin** (-tin).

**den·tist** (den′tist), *n.* [< Fr. < L. *dens*, tooth], one whose profession is the care and repair of teeth and the replacement of missing teeth with artificial ones; doctor of dental surgery (**D.D.S.**).

**den·tist·ry** (den′tis-tri), *n.* the work or profession of a dentist.

**den·ti·tion** (den-tish′ən), *n.* [< L. < *dentire*, to cut teeth], 1. the teething process. 2. the number, sort, and arrangement of the teeth.

**den·ture** (den′chẽr), *n.* [Fr. < L. *dens*, a tooth], a set of teeth; esp., a set of artificial teeth.

**den·u·date** (den′yoo-dāt′, di-nū′dāt), *v.t.* [-DATED, -DATING], [< L. pp. of *denudare* < *de-*, off + *nudare*, to strip], to denude.

**de·nude** (di-nōōd′, -nūd′), *v.t.* [-NUDED, -NUDING], [see DENUDATE], 1. to make bare or naked; strip. 2. in *geology*, to lay bare by erosion. —**den·u·da·tion** (den′yoo-dā′shən, dē′nyoo-), *n.*

**de·nun·ci·ate** (di-nun′si-āt′, -shi-), *v.t.* & *v.i.* [-ATED, -ATING], to denounce. —**de·nun′ci·a′tor,** *n.* —**de·nun′ci·a·to′ry** (-ə-tôr′i, -tō′ri), *adj.*

**de·nun·ci·a·tion** (di-nun′si-ā′shən, -shi-ā′-), *n.* [< L. pp. of *denuntiare* < *de-*, intens. + *nuntiare*, to announce], a denouncing; specif., *a*) strong, public condemnation. *b*) a threat or warning. *c*) an accusation. *d*) a notice by a nation of its intention to end a treaty, etc.

**Den·ver** (den′vẽr), *n.* the capital of Colorado: pop., 494,000.

**de·ny** (di-nī′), *v.t.* [-NIED, -NYING], [< OFr. < L. < *de-*, intens. + *negare*, to refuse], 1. to declare (a statement) untrue; contradict. 2. to refuse to accept as true or right. 3. to refuse to recognize; repudiate. 4. to refuse access to. 5. to refuse to give. 6. to refuse a request of. *v.i.* to maintain a negative attitude. —**deny oneself,** to do without desired things.

**de·o·dar** (dē′ə-där′), *n.* [< Hind. < Sans. *devadāru*, divine tree], 1. a cedar tree, native to the Himalayas. 2. its wood.

**de·o·dor·ant** (dē-ō′dẽr-ənt), *adj.* that can destroy or counteract undesired odors. *n.* any deodorant substance or preparation.

**de·o·dor·ize** (dē-ō′dẽr-īz′), *v.t.* [-IZED, -IZING], to remove or counteract the odor of. —**de·o′dor·i·za′tion,** *n.* —**de·o′dor·iz′er,** *n.*

**de·ox·i·dize** (dē-ok′sə-dīz′), *v.t.* [-DIZED, -DIZING], to

remove oxygen, especially chemically combined oxygen, from. —**de·ox'i·diz'er,** *n.*
**dep.,** 1. department. 2. deposit. 3. deputy.
**de·part** (di-pärt'), *v.i.* [< OFr. < L. < *dis-*, apart + *partire*, to divide < *pars*, part], 1. to go away (*from*); leave. 2. to die. 3. to turn aside (*from* something): as, to *depart* from custom. *v.t.* [Archaic], to leave: now only in *depart this life.*
**de·part·ed** (di-pär'tid), *adj.* 1. gone away; past. 2. dead. —**the departed,** dead person or persons.
**de·part·ment** (di-pärt'mənt), *n.* [see DEPART], 1. a separate part or division: as, the police *department.* 2. a field of knowledge or activity. 3. a government administrative district in France. —**de·part·men·tal** (dē'pärt-men't'l), *adj.* —**de'part·men'tal·ly,** *adv.* —**de'part·men'tal·ism,** *n.*
**department store,** a retail store for the sale of many kinds of goods arranged in departments.
**de·par·ture** (di-pär'chēr), *n.* 1. a departing; leaving. 2. a starting out, as on a trip or new course of action. 3. a deviation or turning aside (*from* something). 4. [Archaic], death.
**de·pend** (di-pend'), *v.i.* [< OFr. < L. < *de-*, down + *pendere*, to hang], 1. to be influenced or determined by something else; be contingent (*on*). 2. to rely. 3. to rely for support or aid. 4. [Archaic], to hang down.
**de·pend·a·ble** (di-pen'də-b'l), *adj.* trustworthy; reliable. —**de·pend'a·bil'i·ty,** *n.* —**de·pend'a·bly,** *adv.*
**de·pend·ence** (di-pen'dəns), *n.* 1. the condition or fact of being dependent. 2. the state of being contingent upon. 3. subordination. 4. reliance (*on* someone else) for support or aid. 5. reliance; trust. Also sp. **de·pend'ance.**
**de·pend·en·cy** (di-pen'dən-si), *n.* [*pl.* -CIES], 1. dependence. 2. something dependent or subordinate. 3. a land or territory geographically distinct from the country governing it. Also sp. **de·pend'an·cy.**
**de·pend·ent** (di-pen'dənt), *adj.* 1. hanging down. 2. influenced, controlled, or determined by something else. 3. relying (*on* someone or something) for support or aid. 4. subordinate. *n.* 1. a thing that depends. 2. a person who relies on someone else for support, etc. Also sp. **de·pend'ant.**
**dependent clause,** a subordinate clause.
**de·pict** (di-pikt'), *v.t.* [< L. *depictus*, pp. < *de-*, intens. + *pingere*, to paint], 1. to represent by drawing, painting, etc. 2. to picture in words; describe. —**de·pict'er,** *n.* —**de·pic'tion,** *n.*
**dep·i·late** (dep'ə-lāt'), *v.t.* [-LATED, -LATING], [< L. *depilatus*, pp. < *de-*, from + *pilare*, to pull out the hair < *pilus*, hair], to remove hair from (a part of the body). —**dep'i·la'tor,** *n.*
**de·pil·a·to·ry** (di-pil'ə-tôr'i, -tō'ri), *adj.* serving to remove unwanted hair. *n.* [*pl.* -RIES], a depilatory substance or device.
**de·plane** (di-plān'), *v.i.* [-PLANED, -PLANING], to get out of an airplane after it lands.
**de·plete** (di-plēt'), *v.t.* [-PLETED, -PLETING], [< L. *depletus*, pp. < *de-*, from + *plere*, to fill], 1. to empty wholly or partly. 2. to exhaust. —**de·ple'tion,** *n.* —**de·ple'tive,** *adj.*
**de·plor·a·ble** (di-plôr'ə-b'l, -plō'rə-), *adj.* to be deplored; lamentable; regrettable; unfortunate. —**de·plor'a·bly,** *adv.*
**de·plore** (di-plôr', -plōr'), *v.t.* [-PLORED, -PLORING], [< Fr. < L. *de-*, intens. + *plorare*, to weep], to be regretful or sorry about; lament.
**de·ploy** (di-ploi'), *v.t. & v.i.* [< Fr. < OFr. *desployer*, to unroll < LL. < L. *dis-*, from + *plicare*, to fold], in *military science*, 1. to spread out so as to form a wider front. 2. to station (forces, equipment, etc.) in accordance with a plan. —**de·ploy'ment,** *n.*
**de·po·lar·ize** (dē-pō'lēr-īz'), *v.t.* [-IZED, -IZING], to destroy or counteract the polarization of. —**de·po'lar·i·za'tion,** *n.*
**de·pon·ent** (di-pō'nənt), *adj.* [< L. < *de-*, down + *ponere*, to set], in *Latin & Greek grammar*, denoting a verb with a passive voice form and an active meaning. *n.* 1. a deponent verb. 2. in *law*, a person who gives written testimony under oath.
**de·pop·u·late** (dē-pop'yoo-lāt'), *v.t.* [-LATED, -LATING], to reduce the population of, as by violence or pestilence. —**de·pop'u·la'tion,** *n.* —**de·pop'u·la'tor,** *n.*
**de·port** (di-pôrt', -pōrt'), *v.t.* [< OFr. < L. < *de-*, from + *portare*, to carry], 1. to behave or conduct (oneself) in a specified way. 2. to expel (someone) from a country; banish.
**de·por·ta·tion** (dē'pôr-tā'shən, -pōr-), *n.* expulsion, as of an undesirable alien, from a country.
**de·port·ment** (di-pôrt'mənt, -pōrt'-) *n.* the manner of conducting oneself; behavior.
**de·pose** (di-pōz'), *v.t.* [-POSED, -POSING], [< OFr. < *de-* (L. *de*), from + *poser*, to cease; confused with L. *deponere*, to set down], 1. to remove from office or a position of power; oust. 2. in *law*, to state under oath; testify. *v.i.* to bear witness. —**de·pos'a·ble,** *adj.* —**de·pos'al,** *n.*
**de·pos·it** (di-poz'it), *v.t.* [< L. pp. of *deponere*, to lay down], 1. to place or entrust, as for safekeeping: as, to *deposit* money in a bank. 2. to give as a pledge or partial payment: as, he *deposited* $500 on a house. 3. to put or set down. 4. to leave lying, as sediment. *n.* 1. the state of being placed for safekeeping (with *on*). 2. something so placed. 3. money put in a bank. 4. a pledge or part payment. 5. something left lying. 6. sand, clay, minerals, etc. deposited by natural forces.
**de·pos·i·tar·y** (di-poz'ə-ter'i), *n.* [*pl.* -IES], 1. a person, firm, etc. entrusted with something for safekeeping; trustee. 2. a depository.
**dep·o·si·tion** (dep'ə-zish'ən, dē'pə-), *n.* 1. a deposing or being deposed, as from office. 2. a testifying. 3. testimony, especially in the form of a sworn written statement. 4. a depositing or being deposited. 5. something deposited.
**de·pos·i·tor** (di-poz'i-tēr), *n.* one who deposits something, especially money in a bank.
**de·pos·i·to·ry** (di-poz'ə-tôr'i, -tō'ri), *n.* [*pl.* -RIES], 1. a place where things are put for safekeeping; storehouse. 2. a depositary; trustee.
**de·pot** (dē'pō; *Brit. or military* dep'ō), *n.* [< Fr. < OFr. *depost*, a deposit < L. *depositum;* see DEPOSIT], 1. a storehouse; warehouse. 2. a railroad station. 3. in *military usage*, *a*) a storage place for supplies. *b*) a station for assembling recruits or combat replacements. Abbrev. **dep.**
**de·prave** (di-prāv'), *v.t.* [-PRAVED, -PRAVING], [< OFr. < L. < *de-*, intens. + *pravus*, crooked], to make morally bad; corrupt. —**dep·ra·va·tion** (dep'rə-vā'shən), *n.* —**de·praved',** *adj.* —**de·prav'er,** *n.*
**de·prav·i·ty** (di-prav'ə-ti), *n.* 1. a depraved condition; corruption; perversion. 2. [*pl.* -TIES], a depraved act or practice.
**dep·re·cate** (dep'rə-kāt'), *v.t.* [-CATED, -CATING], [< L. pp. < *de-*, off + *precari*, to pray], to feel and express disapproval of. —**dep're·cat'ing·ly,** *adv.* —**dep're·ca'tion,** *n.* —**dep're·ca'tor,** *n.*
**dep·re·ca·to·ry** (dep'rə-kə-tôr'i, -tō'ri), *adj.* 1. deprecating. 2. apologetic. Also **dep're·ca'tive.** —**dep're·ca·to'ri·ly,** *adv.* —**dep're·ca·to'ri·ness,** *n.*
**de·pre·ci·ate** (di-prē'shi-āt'), *v.t. & v.i.*, [-ATED, -ATING], [< L. pp. < *de-*, from + *pretiare*, to value < *pretium*, price], 1. to lessen in value or price. 2. to belittle; disparage. —**de·pre'ci·a·ble,** *adj.* —**de·pre'ci·a'tor,** *n.* —**de·pre'ci·a'tive, de·pre'ci·a·to'ry,** *adj.*
**de·pre·ci·a·tion** (di-prē'shi-ā'shən), *n.* 1. a decrease in value of property through wear, deterioration, etc. 2. a decrease in the purchasing power of money. 3. a belittling; disparagement.
**dep·re·da·tion** (dep'ri-dā'shən), *n.* [< LL. pp. < L. *de-*, intens. + *praedari*, to rob < *praeda*, booty], a plundering or laying waste; robbery.
**de·press** (di-pres'), *v.t.* [< OFr. < L. *depressus*, pp. < *de-*, down + *premere*, to press], 1. to press down; lower. 2. to lower in spirits; make gloomy; sadden. 3. to decrease the activity of; weaken. 4. to lower in value, price, or amount. 5. in *music*, to lower the pitch of. —**de·press'ing,** *adj.* —**de·press'ing·ly,** *adv.* —**de·pres'sor** (-ēr), *n.*
**de·pres·sant** (di-pres'ənt), *adj.* lowering the rate of muscular or nervous activity. *n.* a depressant medicine, drug, etc.; sedative.
**de·pressed** (di-prest'), *adj.* 1. pressed down. 2. lowered in position, intensity, amount, etc. 3. flattened or hollowed, as if pressed down. 4. gloomy; dejected; sad. 5. in *botany*, flattened vertically, as if from downward pressure.
**de·pres·sion** (di-presh'ən), *n.* 1. a depressing or being depressed. 2. a depressed part or place; hollow or low place. 3. low spirits; dejection. 4. a decrease in force, activity, amount, etc. 5. a period marked by slackening of business activity, much unemployment, falling prices and wages, etc. —**de·pres'sive** (-pres'iv), *adj.* —**de·pres'sive·ly,** *adv.*
**dep·ri·va·tion** (dep'rə-vā'shən), *n.* a depriving or being deprived: also **de·priv·al** (di-prīv''l).
**de·prive** (di-prīv'), *v.t.* [-PRIVED, -PRIVING], [< OFr.

< L. *de-*, intens. + *privare*, to separate], 1. to take away from forcibly; dispossess. 2. to keep from having, using, or enjoying: as, *deprived* of one's rights. —**de·priv'a·ble,** *adj.*

**dept.,** 1. department. 2. deponent. 3. deputy.

**depth** (depth), *n.* [ME. < *dep*, deep + *-th*], 1. the distance from the top straight downward, or from front to back. 2. the quality of being deep; deepness. 3. intensity. 4. deepness of thought; profundity. 5. lowness (of tone). 6. the middle (of night or winter). 7. *usually pl.* the inmost part: as, the *depths* of a wood. 8. *usually pl.* the deep or deepest part (of the sea, earth, etc.). —**out of** (or **beyond) one's depth,** 1. in water too deep for one. 2. past one's ability or understanding.

**depth charge,** an explosive charge timed to explode under water at a certain depth: used especially against submarines: also **depth bomb.**

**dep·u·ta·tion** (dep'yoo-tā'shən), *n.* 1. a deputing or being deputed. 2. a person or persons appointed to represent others; delegation.

**de·pute** (di-pūt'), *v.t.* [-PUTED, -PUTING], [< L. < *de-*, from + *putare*, lit., to cleanse], 1. to give (authority, etc.) to someone else as deputy. 2. to appoint as one's substitute, agent, etc.

**dep·u·tize** (dep'yoo-tiz'), *v.t.* [-TIZED, -TIZING], to appoint as deputy. *v.i.* to act as deputy.

**dep·u·ty** (dep'yoo-ti), *n.* [*pl.* -TIES], [see DEPUTE], 1. a person appointed to act for, or in the place of, another or others. 2. a member of a legislature such as the Chamber of Deputies in France. *adj.* acting as deputy.

**De Quin·cey, Thomas** (di kwin'si), 1785–1859; English essayist.

**de·rail** (dē-rāl'), *v.t.* to cause (a train, etc.) to run off the rails. *v.i.* to run off the rails. —**de·rail'ment,** *n.*

**de·range** (di-rānj'), *v.t.* [-RANGED, -RANGING], [< Fr. < OFr. < *des-* (L. *dis-*), apart + *rengier;* see RANGE], 1. to upset the arrangement, order, or working of; disorder. 2. to make insane. —**de·ranged',** *adj.* —**de·range'ment,** *n.*

**Der·by** (dūr'bi; Brit. där'-), *n.* [*pl.* -BIES], 1. an annual race for three-year-old horses at Epsom Downs, begun by the Earl of Derby in 1780. 2. any similar horse race, especially the one (**Kentucky Derby**) run in Louisville, Kentucky. 3. [d-], a stiff felt hat with a round crown and curved brim.

DERBY

**der·e·lict** (der'ə-likt'), *adj.* [< L. *derelictus*, pp. < *de-*, intens. + *relinquere;* see RELINQUISH], 1. deserted by the owner; abandoned; forsaken. 2. neglectful of duty; negligent. *n.* 1. a property abandoned by the owner; esp., a ship deserted at sea. 2. a person or thing abandoned as worthless.

**der·e·lic·tion** (der'ə-lik'shən), *n.* 1. a forsaking or being forsaken. 2. a neglect of, or failure in, duty; being remiss.

**de·ride** (di-rīd'), *v.t.* [-RIDED, -RIDING], [< L. < *de-*, down + *ridere*, to laugh], to laugh at in contempt or scorn; ridicule. —**de·rid'er,** *n.* —**de·rid'ing·ly,** *adv.*

‡**de ri·gueur** (də rē'gēr'), [Fr.], required by etiquette; according to good form.

**de·ri·sion** (di-rizh'ən), *n.* 1. a deriding or being derided. 2. [Rare], a person or thing derided.

**de·ri·sive** (di-rī'siv), *adj.* showing derision; ridiculing; scoffing: also **de·ri'so·ry** (-sə-ri). —**de·ri'sive·ly,** *adv.* —**de·ri'sive·ness,** *n.*

**der·i·va·tion** (der'ə-vā'shən), *n.* 1. a deriving or being derived. 2. something derived; a derivative. 3. the source or origin of something. 4. the origin and development of a word; etymology. —**der'i·va'tion·al,** *adj.*

**de·riv·a·tive** (də-riv'ə-tiv), *adj.* derived; hence, not original. *n.* 1. something derived. 2. in *chemistry*, a substance derived from another by chemical change. 3. a word derived from another or others, as by the addition of affixes. —**de·riv'a·tive·ly,** *adv.* —**de·riv'a·tive·ness,** *n.*

**de·rive** (də-rīv'), *v.t.* [-RIVED, -RIVING], [< OFr. < L. *derivare*, to divert a stream < *de-*, from + *rivus*, a stream], 1. to get or receive (*from* a source). 2. to deduce or infer. 3. to trace from or to a source; show the derivation of. 4. in *chemistry*, to obtain (a compound) from another compound by replacing one element with another. *v.i.* to proceed (*from* a source); originate. —**de·riv'a·ble,** *adj.* —**de·riv'er,** *n.*

**-derm** (dūrm), [see DERMA], a suffix meaning *skin* or *covering*, as in *endoderm*.

**der·ma** (dūr'mə), *n.* [Mod. L. < Gr. *derma*, the skin], dermis. —**der'mal,** *adj.*

**der·ma·to-,** [< Gr. < *derma*, *dermatos*, skin], a combining form meaning *skin* or *hide*: also **dermo-, dermat-.**

**der·ma·tol·o·gy** (dūr'mə-tol'ə-ji), *n.* [*dermato-* + *-logy*], the branch of medicine dealing with the skin and its diseases. —**der'ma·to·log'i·cal** (-tə-loj'ə-kəl), *adj.* —**der'ma·tol'o·gist,** *n.*

**der·mis** (dūr'mis), *n.* [< Gr. *epidermis;* see EPIDERMIS], 1. the layer of skin just below the epidermis; derma. 2. the skin. —**der'mic,** *adj.*

**der·o·gate** (der'ə-gāt'), *v.i.* & *v.t.* [-GATED, -GATING], [< L. *derogatus*, pp. < *de-*, from + *rogare*, to ask], to take away (*from*) so as to lessen or impair; detract. —**der'o·ga'tion,** *n.*

**de·rog·a·to·ry** (di-rog'ə-tôr'i, -tō'ri), *adj.* 1. tending to lessen or impair; detracting. 2. disparaging; belittling. —**de·rog'a·to'ri·ly,** *adv.*

**der·rick** (der'ik), *n.* [after *Derrick*, 17th-c. London hangman: orig. applied to a gallows], 1. a large apparatus with tackle and beams, for lifting and moving heavy objects. 2. a tall, tapering framework, as over an oil well, to support drilling machinery, etc.

**der·ring-do** (der'iŋ-do͞o'), *n.* [ME. *durring don*, daring to do], daring action; reckless courage.

**der·rin·ger** (der'in-jēr), *n.* [< name of the inventor, Am. gunsmith, c. 1850], a small, short-barreled pistol of large caliber.

**der·vish** (dūr'vish), *n.* [< Turk. < Per. *darvīsh*, beggar], a member of any of various Moslem orders dedicated to poverty and chastity: some practice whirling, howling, etc. as religious acts.

**de·sal·i·na·tion** (dē-sal'ə-nā'shən), *n.* [*de-* + *saline* + *-ation*], the removal of salt, esp. from sea water to make it drinkable: also **de·sal'i·ni·za'tion.**

**desc.,** descendant.

**des·cant** (des'kant), *n.* [< OFr. < ML. < L. *dis-*, apart + *cantus*, song], 1. in *medieval music*, *a*) a counterpoint sung above the main melody. *b*) the art of composing part music. *c*) a piece of part music. 2. a comment; discourse. *v.i.* (des-kant', di-skant'), 1. to discourse. 2. to add a counterpoint to the main melody. 3. to sing.

**Des·cartes, Re·né** (rə-nā' dā-kärt'), 1596–1650; French philosopher and mathematician.

**de·scend** (di-send'), *v.i.* [< OFr. < L. < *de-*, down + *scandere*, to climb], 1. to move from a higher to a lower place; come or go down. 2. to pass from earlier to later time, from greater to less, from general to particular, etc. 3. to slope downward. 4. to come down (*from* a source): as, he is *descended* from pioneers. 5. to pass by inheritance or heredity. 6. to stoop (*to* some act). 7. to make a sudden visit or attack (*on* or *upon*). 8. in *astronomy*, to move toward the horizon. *v.t.* to move down, down along, or through. —**de·scend'er,** *n.*

**de·scend·ant** (di-sen'dənt), *adj.* [Rare], descending. *n.* a person who is an offspring of a certain ancestor, family, group, etc.

**de·scend·ent** (di-sen'dənt), *adj.* descending.

**de·scend·i·ble** (di-sen'də-b'l), *adj.* that may or does descend to an heir: also **de·scend'a·ble.**

**de·scent** (di-sent'), *n.* 1. a descending; coming or going down. 2. lineage; ancestry. 3. a generation (of a specified lineage). 4. a downward slope. 5. a way down. 6. a sudden attack or raid. 7. a decline; fall. 8. a stooping (to an act). 9. in *law*, transference (of property) to heirs.

**de·scribe** (di-skrīb'), *v.t.* [-SCRIBED, -SCRIBING], [< OFr. < L. < *de-*, from + *scribere*, to write], 1. to tell or write about. 2. to picture in words. 3. to trace the form or outline of. —**de·scrib'a·ble,** *adj.*

**de·scrip·tion** (di-skrip'shən), *n.* 1. the act, process, or technique of describing. 2. a statement or passage that describes. 3. sort, kind, or variety: as, books of every *description*. 4. the act of tracing or outlining.

**de·scrip·tive** (di-skrip'tiv), *adj.* describing; of or characterized by description. —**de·scrip'tive·ly,** *adv.* —**de·scrip'tive·ness,** *n.*

**de·scry** (di-skrī'), *v.t.* [-SCRIED, -SCRYING], [< OFr. *descrier*, to proclaim < *des-*, from + *crier;* see CRY], 1. to catch sight of (distant or obscure objects). 2. to look for and discover; detect.

**Des·de·mo·na** (dez'də-mō'nə), *n.* see **Othello.**

**des·e·crate** (des'i-krāt'), *v.t.* [-CRATED, -CRATING], [after *consecrate* < OFr. *dessacrer* < L. *dis-*, apart + *sacrare* < *sacer*, sacred], to violate the sacredness of; treat as not sacred; profane. —**des'e·crat'er, des'e·cra'tor,** *n.* —**des'e·cra'tion,** *n.*

**de·seg·re·gate** (dē-seg'ri-gāt'), *v.t.* & *v.i.* [-GATED, -GATING], to abolish racial segregation in (public schools, etc.). —**de·seg're·ga'tion,** *n.*

**de·sen·si·tize** (dē-sen′sə-tīz′), *v.t.* [-TIZED, -TIZING], to make insensitive or less sensitive. —**de·sen′si·ti·za′tion,** *n.* —**de·sen′si·tiz′er,** *n.*

**de·sert** (di-zũrt′), *v.t.* [< Fr. < LL. < L. *desertus*, pp. < *de-*, from + *serere*, to join], 1. to abandon; forsake. 2. to leave (one's post, etc.) without permission. *v.i.* to leave one's post, etc. without permission, specifically, in military usage, with no intent to return or, in war, to avoid hazardous duty. —**de·sert′er,** *n.*

**des·ert** (dez′ẽrt), *n.* [OFr. < L. < *desertus;* see DESERT, *v.*], 1. an uncultivated region without inhabitants; wilderness. 2. a dry, barren region, largely treeless and sandy. *adj.* 1. of a desert or deserts. 2. wild and uninhabited.

**de·sert** (di-zũrt′), *n.* [< OFr. < *deservir;* see DESERVE], 1. the fact of deserving reward or punishment. 2. *often pl.* deserved reward or punishment.

**de·ser·tion** (di-zũr′shən), *n.* 1. a deserting. 2. the fact or state of being deserted.

**de·serve** (di-zũrv′), *v.t.* [-SERVED, -SERVING], [< OFr. *deservir* < L. < *de-*, intens. + *servire*, to serve], to be worthy of; merit. *v.i.* to be worthy. —**de·serv′er,** *n.*

**de·serv·ed·ly** (di-zũr′vid-li), *adv.* in accordance with what is deserved; justly.

**de·serv·ing** (di-zũr′viŋ), *adj.* that deserves; worthy (*of* help, reward, etc.). —**de·serv′ing·ly,** *adv.* —**de·serv′ing·ness,** *n.*

**des·ha·bille** (dez′ə-bēl′), *n.* dishabille.

**des·ic·cant** (des′i-kənt), *adj.* drying. *n.* a substance, drug, etc. for drying something.

**des·ic·cate** (des′i-kāt′), *v.t.* [-CATED, -CATING], [< L. < *de-*, intens. + *siccare* < *siccus*, dry], 1. to dry completely. 2. to preserve (food) by drying. *v.i.* to become dry. —**des′ic·ca′tion,** *n.* —**des′ic·ca′tive,** *adj.* & *n.*

**de·sid·er·a·tum** (di-sid′ẽr-ā′təm), *n.* [*pl.* -TA (-tə)], [< L. pp. of *desiderare;* see DESIRE], something needed and wanted.

**de·sign** (di-zīn′), *v.t.* [< OFr. < L. < *de-*, out + *signare* < *signum*, a mark], 1. to plan; sketch a preliminary pattern or outline for. 2. to form in the mind; contrive. 3. to plan to do; intend. 4. to set apart for some purpose. *v.i.* to make original plans, patterns, etc. *n.* 1. a plan; scheme; project. 2. purpose; intention; aim. 3. *pl.* a secret or sinister scheme (often with *on* or *upon*). 4. a plan or sketch to work from; pattern. 5. the art of making designs. 6. the arrangement of parts, form, color, etc., especially so as to produce an artistic unit. 7. a finished artistic work. —**by design,** purposely.

**des·ig·nate** (dez′ig-nit; *also, and for v. always,* -nāt′), *adj.* [see DESIGN], named for office, etc.; appointed. *v.t.* [-NATED, -NATING], 1. to point out; indicate; specify. 2. to name; entitle. 3. to name for an office or duty; appoint. —**des′ig·na′tive,** *adj.* —**des′ig·na′tor,** *n.*

**des·ig·na·tion** (dez′ig-nā′shən), *n.* 1. a pointing out or marking out. 2. appointment to an office, post, etc. 3. a distinguishing name, title, etc.

**de·signed** (di-zīnd′), *adj.* done by design; purposed; intended. —**de·sign′ed·ly** (-zīn′id-li), *adv.*

**de·sign·er** (di-zīn′ẽr), *n.* 1. a person whose work is making designs. 2. a schemer; plotter.

**de·sign·ing** (di-zīn′iŋ), *adj.* 1. that designs; of or for making designs, etc. 2. planning. 3. scheming; artful. *n.* the art or work of making designs, etc. —**de·sign′ing·ly,** *adv.*

**de·sir·a·ble** (di-zīr′ə-b'l), *adj.* worth wanting or having; pleasing. —**de·sir′a·bil′i·ty, de·sir′a·ble·ness,** *n.* —**de·sir′a·bly,** *adv.*

**de·sire** (di-zīr′), *v.t.* [-SIRED, -SIRING], [< OFr. < L. *desiderare*], 1. to wish or long for; crave; covet. 2. to ask for; request. 3. to want sexually. *n.* 1. a wish or craving. 2. sexual appetite. 3. a request. 4. anything desired.

**de·sir·ous** (di-zīr′əs), *adj.* desiring; having desire (with *of*): as, he is *desirous* of winning.

**de·sist** (di-zist′), *v.i.* [< OFr. < L. < *de-*, from + *sistere*, to cause to stand < *stare*, to stand], to cease; stop; abstain. —**de·sist′ance** (-əns), *n.*

**desk** (desk), *n.* [< ML. < It. *desco* < L. *discus;* see DISK], 1. a frame or table, often with drawers, and with a flat or sloping top for writing, drawing, or reading. 2. a pulpit.

**Des Moines** (də-moin′, di-moinz′), the capital of Iowa: pop., 209,000.

**des·o·late** (des′ə-lit; *for v.*, -lāt′), *adj.* [< L. *desolatus*, pp. < *de-*, intens. + *solare*, to make lonely < *solus*, alone], 1. lonely; solitary. 2. uninhabited; deserted. 3. made uninhabitable; laid waste. 4. forlorn; wretched. *v.t.* [-LATED, -LATING], 1. to rid of inhabitants. 2. to lay waste; devastate. 3. to forsake; abandon. 4. to make forlorn, wretched, etc. —**des′o·late·ly,** *adv.* —**des′o·late·ness,** *n.* —**des′o·la′tor, des′o·lat′er,** *n.*

**des·o·la·tion** (des′ə-lā′shən), *n.* 1. a making desolate. 2. a desolate condition. 3. a desolate place. 4. lonely grief; misery. 5. loneliness.

**De So·to, Her·nan·do** (hẽr-nan′dō di sō′tō), 1500?–1542; Spanish explorer: also **de Soto.**

**de·spair** (di-spâr′), *v.i.* [< OFr. < L. < *de-*, without + *sperare*, to hope < *spes*, hope], to lose hope; be without hope (usually with *of*). *v.t.* [Archaic], to give up hope of. *n.* 1. loss of hope; state of having no hope. 2. a person or thing causing despair. —**de·spair′ing,** *adj.* —**de·spair′ing·ly,** *adv.*

**des·patch** (di-spach′), *v.t.* & *n.* dispatch. —**des·patch′er,** *n.*

**des·per·a·do** (des′pə-rā′dō, -rä′dō), *n.* [*pl.* -DOES, -DOS], [< OSp.; see DESPAIR], a dangerous, reckless criminal; bold outlaw.

**des·per·ate** (des′pẽr-it), *adj.* [< L. pp. of *desperare;* see DESPAIR], 1. rash or violent because of despair. 2. giving so little hope as to cause despair; extremely dangerous or serious. —**des′per·ate·ly,** *adv.* —**des′per·ate·ness,** *n.*

**des·per·a·tion** (des′pẽr-ā′shən), *n.* 1. the state of being desperate. 2. recklessness resulting from despair.

**des·pi·ca·ble** (des′pik-ə-b'l, di-spik′-), *adj.* that is or should be despised; contemptible. —**des′pi·ca·ble·ness,** *n.* —**des′pi·ca·bly,** *adv.*

**de·spise** (di-spīz′), *v.t.* [-SPISED, -SPISING], [< OFr. < L. *despicere* < *de*, down + *specere*, to look at], to look down on; be contemptuous or disdainful of; scorn. —**de·spis′er,** *n.*

**de·spite** (di-spīt′), *n.* [< OFr. < L. < *despicere;* see DESPISE], 1. a contemptuous act; insult; injury. 2. malice; spite. 3. [Archaic], contempt; scorn. *prep.* in spite of; notwithstanding. *v.t.* [-SPITED, -SPITING], [Archaic], to show contempt for. —**in despite of,** in spite of. —**de·spite′ful,** *adj.* —**de·spite′ful·ly,** *adv.*

**de·spoil** (di-spoil′), *v.t.* [< OFr. < L. < *de-*, intens. + *spoliare*, to strip], to deprive (*of* something) by force; rob; plunder. —**de·spoil′er,** *n.* —**de·spoil′ment, de·spo′li·a′tion** (-spō′li-ā′shən), *n.*

**de·spond** (di-spond′), *v.i.* [< L. < *de*, from + *spondere*, to promise], to lose courage, confidence, or hope; become disheartened. *n.* despondency: now only in *slough of despond.* —**de·spond′ing,** *adj.* —**de·spond′ing·ly,** *adv.*

**de·spond·en·cy** (di-spon′dən-si), *n.* loss of courage, confidence, or hope; dejection: also **de·spond′ence.** —**de·spond′ent,** *adj.*

**des·pot** (des′pət, -pot), *n.* [< OFr. < Gr. *despotēs*, a master], 1. an absolute ruler; king with unlimited power; autocrat. 2. a tyrant.

**des·pot·ic** (di-spot′ik), *adj.* of or like a despot; autocratic; tyrannical: also **des·pot′i·cal.** —**des·pot′i·cal·ly,** *adv.*

**des·pot·ism** (des′pət-iz'm), *n.* 1. rule by a despot; autocracy. 2. the methods of a despot; tyranny.

**des·sert** (di-zũrt′), *n.* [Fr. < *desservir*, to clear the table < *des-* (L. *de*), from + *servir* < L. *servire*, to serve], 1. a course, as of fruits, pie, or ice cream, served at the end of a meal. 2. [Brit.], uncooked fruit and nuts served after the sweet course.

**des·ti·na·tion** (des′tə-nā′shən), *n.* 1. [Rare], a destining or being destined. 2. the end or purpose for which something or someone is destined. 3. the place toward which someone or something is going or sent.

**des·tine** (des′tin), *v.t.* [-TINED, -TINING], [< OFr. < L. *destinare*, to secure < *de-*, intens. + *stare*, to stand], 1. to predetermine, as by fate: as, he was *destined* to lead them. 2. to set apart for a certain purpose; intend. —**destined for,** 1. bound for. 2. intended for.

**des·tin·y** (des′tə-ni), *n.* [*pl.* -IES], 1. the inevitable or necessary succession of events. 2. what will necessarily happen to one; (one's) fortune. 3. that which determines events.

**des·ti·tute** (des′tə-to͞ot′, -tūt′), *adj.* [< L. < *destituere*, to forsake < *de*, down + *statuere*, to set], 1. lacking (with *of*): as, *destitute* of brains. 2. lacking the necessities of life; living in complete poverty. —**des′ti·tu′tion,** *n.*

---

fat, āpe, bâre, cär; ten, ēven, hêre, ovẽr; is, bīte; lot, gō, hôrn, to͞ol, look; oil, out; up, ūse, fũr; get; joy; yet; chin; she; thin, *th*en; zh, leisure; ŋ, ring; ə for *a* in *ago*, *e* in *agent*, *i* in *sanity*, *o* in *comply*, *u* in *focus;* ′ in *able* (ā′b'l), Fr. bål; ë, Fr. coeur; ö, Fr. feu; Fr. mon; ô, Fr. coq; ü, Fr. duc; H, G. ich; kh, G. doch. ‡ foreign; < derived from.

**de·stroy** (di-stroi′), *v.t.* [< OFr. < L. < *de-*, down + *struere*, to build], 1. to tear down; demolish. 2. to spoil completely; ruin. 3. to put an end to. 4. to kill. 5. to neutralize the effect of. 6. to make useless. —**de·stroy′a·ble,** *adj.*

**de·stroy·er** (di-stroi′ẽr), *n.* 1. a person or thing that destroys. 2. a small, fast, heavily armed warship.

**de·struct** (di-strukt, dē′strukt′), *n.* the deliberate destruction of a malfunctioning missile, rocket, etc. after its launch.

**de·struct·i·ble** (di-struk′tə-b'l), *adj.* that can be destroyed. —**de·struct′i·bil′i·ty,** *n.*

**de·struc·tion** (di-struk′shən), *n.* 1. a destroying or being destroyed; ruin. 2. the cause or means of destroying.

**de·struc·tive** (di-struk′tiv), *adj.* 1. tending or likely to cause destruction. 2. destroying. 3. tearing down; negative: as, *destructive* criticism. —**de·struc′tive·ly,** *adv.* —**de·struc′tive·ness,** *n.*

**destructive distillation,** decomposition of coal, wood, etc. by heat in the absence of air, and the collection of the volatile products.

**des·ue·tude** (des′wi-tōōd′, -tūd′), *n.* [Fr. < L. < *de-*, from + *suescere*, to be accustomed], disuse: as, laws fallen into *desuetude*.

**de·sul·fur·ize** (dē-sul′fẽr-īz′), *v.t.* [-IZED, -IZING], to remove sulfur from: also **de·sul′fur.**

**des·ul·to·ry** (des′'l-tôr′i, -tō′ri), *adj.* [< L. < *desultor*, a jumper < *desilire* < *de-*, from + *salire*, to leap], 1. jumping from one thing to another; disconnected; not methodical. 2. random: as, a *desultory* thought. —**des′ul·to′ri·ly,** *adv.* —**des′ul·to′ri·ness,** *n.*

**de·tach** (di-tach′), *v.t.* [< Fr. < *dé-* (L. *dis-*), from + *-tacher* as in *attacher;* see ATTACH], 1. to unfasten and remove; separate; disconnect. 2. to send for a special task, as troops, ships, etc. —**de·tach′a·bil′i·ty,** *n.* —**de·tach′a·ble,** *adj.*

**de·tached** (di-tacht′), *adj.* 1. disconnected; separate. 2. aloof; disinterested; impartial.

**de·tach·ment** (di-tach′mənt), *n.* 1. a detaching; separation. 2. the sending of troops or ships on special service. 3. a unit of troops or ships so assigned: abbrev. **det.** 4. the state of being disinterested or impartial. 5. aloofness.

**de·tail** (di-tāl′; *also, for n.,* dē′tāl), *n.* [< Fr. < *dé-* (L. *de*), from + *tailler*, to cut], 1. a dealing with things item by item. 2. a minute account. 3. a small part; item. 4. a small secondary part of a picture, building, etc. 5. in *military usage, a)* one or more persons chosen for a special task. *b)* the special task. *v.t.* 1. to give the particulars of; tell minutely. 2. in *military usage*, to choose for a special task. —**in detail,** with particulars.

**de·tain** (di-tān′), *v.t.* [< OFr. < L. < *de-*, off + *tenere*, to hold], 1. to keep in custody; confine. 2. to keep; withhold. 3. to keep from going on; delay. —**de·tain′er,** *n.* —**de·tain′ment,** *n.*

**de·tect** (di-tekt′), *v.t.* [< L. *detectus*, pp. < *de-*, from + *tegere*, to cover], 1. to discover. 2. to discover the presence or existence of (anything hidden, not clear, etc.). 3. in *radio*, to rectify. —**de·tect′a·ble, de·tect′i·ble,** *adj.*

**de·tec·tion** (di-tek′shən), *n.* 1. a finding out or being found out. 2. in *radio*, the separating of a signal wave from its carrier wave in order to reproduce it as sound; rectification.

**de·tec·tive** (di-tek′tiv), *adj.* 1. of or for detection. 2. of detectives and their work. *n.* a person, often a policeman, whose work is investigating crimes, getting information, etc.

**de·tec·tor** (di-tek′tẽr), *n.* 1. a person or thing that detects. 2. in *radio*, a device, as a vacuum tube, for effecting detection; rectifier.

**dé·tente** (dā′tänt′), *n.* [Fr.], a lessening of tension or hostility, especially between nations.

**de·ten·tion** (di-ten′shən), *n.* 1. a detaining or being detained. 2. an enforced delay.

**de·ter** (di-tũr′), *v.t.* [-TERRED, -TERRING], [< L. < *de-*, from + *terrere*, to frighten], to keep (a person) from doing something through fear, anxiety, etc.; discourage. —**de·ter′ment,** *n.*

**de·terge** (di-tũrj′), *v.t.* [-TERGED, -TERGING], [< L. < *de-*, off + *tergere*, to wipe], to cleanse. —**de·ter′gen·cy, de·ter′gence,** *n.*

**de·ter·gent** (di-tũr′jənt), *adj.* cleansing. *n.* a cleansing substance, esp. one that is like soap, but is made synthetically and not from fats and lye.

**de·te·ri·o·rate** (di-tēr′i-ə-rāt′), *v.t.* & *v.i.* [-RATED, -RATING], [< LL. pp. of *deteriorare* < L. *deterior*, worse], to make or become worse; depreciate. —**de·te′ri·o·ra′tion,** *n.* —**de·te′ri·o·ra′tive,** *adj.*

**de·ter·mi·nant** (di-tũr′mə-nənt), *adj.* determining. *n.* a thing or factor that determines.

**de·ter·mi·nate** (di-tũr′mə-nit), *adj.* [see DETERMINE], 1. having exact limits; definite; fixed. 2 settled; conclusive. 3. resolute. 4. in *botany*, having a flower at the end of the primary axis and of each secondary axis. —**de·ter′mi·nate·ly,** *adv.*

**de·ter·mi·na·tion** (di-tũr′mə-nā′shən), *n.* 1. a determining or being determined. 2. a firm intention. 3. firmness of purpose.

**de·ter·mi·na·tive** (di-tũr′mə-nā′tiv, -nə-tiv), *adj.* determining. *n.* a thing that determines. —**de·ter′mi·na′tive·ly,** *adv.* —**de·ter′mi·na′tive·ness,** *n.*

**de·ter·mine** (di-tũr′min), *v.t.* [-MINED, -MINING], [< OFr. < L. < *de-*, from + *terminare*, to set bounds < *terminus*, an end], 1. to set limits to; define. 2. to settle conclusively or beforehand; resolve. 3. to reach a decision about; decide upon. 4. to be the deciding or regulating factor in. 5. to find out exactly; fix precisely. 6. to give a definite aim to; direct. *v.i.* 1. to decide. 2. in *law*, to come to an end. —**de·ter′mi·na·ble,** *adj.* —**de·ter′min·er,** *n.*

**de·ter·mined** (di-tũr′mind), *adj.* 1. having one's mind made up; resolved. 2. resolute; unwavering. —**de·ter′mined·ly,** *adv.* —**de·ter′mined·ness,** *n.*

**de·ter·min·ism** (di-tũr′min-iz'm), *n.* the doctrine that one's choice of action is not free but determined by a sequence of causes independent of his will. —**de·ter′min·ist,** *n.* & *adj.*

**de·ter·rent** (di-tũr′ənt, -ter′-), *adj.* deterring. *n.* a thing or factor that deters. —**de·ter′rence,** *n.*

**de·test** (di-test′), *v.t.* [< Fr. < L. *detestari*, to curse while calling the gods to witness < *de-*, down + *testis*, a witness], to dislike intensely; hate; abhor.

**de·test·a·ble** (di-tes′tə-b'l), *adj.* that is or should be detested; odious. —**de·test′a·bil′i·ty, de·test′a·ble·ness,** *n.* —**de·test′a·bly,** *adv.*

**de·tes·ta·tion** (dē′tes-tā′shən), *n.* 1. intense dislike; hatred. 2. a detested person or thing.

**de·throne** (dē-thrōn′), *v.t.* [-THRONED, -THRONING], to remove from a throne; depose. —**de·throne′ment,** *n.* —**de·thron′er,** *n.*

**det·o·nate** (det′ə-nāt′, dē′tō-), *v.i.* & *v.t.* [-NATED, -NATING], [< L. *detonatus*, pp. < *de-*, intens. + *tonare*, to sound], to explode noisily. —**det′o·na′tion,** *n.* —**det′o·na′tor,** *n.*

**de·tour** (dē′toor, di-toor′), *n.* [< Fr. < *détourner*, to evade; *dé-* (L. *de*), from + *tourner;* see TURN], 1. a roundabout way. 2. a route used when the regular route is closed to traffic. *v.i.* & *v.t.* to go or cause to go by way of a detour.

**de·tract** (di-trakt′), *v.t.* [< Fr. < L. < *detractus*, pp. < *de-*, from + *trahere*, to draw], 1. to take away. 2. [Rare], to belittle; disparage. *v.i.* to take something desirable (*from*). —**de·trac′tion,** *n.* —**de·trac′tive, de·trac′to·ry,** *adj.* —**de·trac′tor,** *n.*

**de·train** (dē-trān′), *v.i.* & *v.t.* to get off or cause to get off a railroad train. —**de·train′ment,** *n.*

**det·ri·ment** (det′rə-mənt), *n.* [< Fr. < L. *detrimentum*, loss < *de-*, off + *terere*, to rub], 1. damage; injury. 2. anything that causes damage or injury. —**det′ri·men′tal,** *adj.* —**det′ri·men′tal·ly,** *adv.*

**de·tri·tus** (di-trī′təs), *n.* [L., pp. of *deterere*, to wear away], fragments of rock, etc. produced by disintegration or wearing away; debris.

**De·troit** (di-troit′), *n.* a city in SE Michigan: pop., 1,670,000 (metropolitan area, 3,762,000).

‡**de trop** (də trō′), [Fr.], too much; superfluous.

**deuce** (dōōs, dūs), *n.* [Fr. *deux* < OFr. < L. acc. of *duo*, two], 1. a playing card with two spots. 2. the side of a die with two spots, or a throw of the dice totaling two. 3. in *tennis*, a tie score of 40 each (or five games each) after which one side must get two successive points (or games) to win.

**deuce** (dōōs, dūs), *n.* & *interj.* [orig. dicer's exclamation on making lowest score], bad luck, the devil, etc.: a mild curse.

**deu·ced** (dōō′sid, dōōst, dū′sid, dūst), *adj.* devilish; extreme: used in mild cursing. *adv.* devilishly; extremely. —**deu′ced·ly,** *adv.*

‡**De·us** (dē′əs, dā′oos), *n.* [L.], God: abbrev. **D.**

**Deut.,** Deuteronomy.

**deu·te·ri·um** (dōō-tēr′i-əm, dū-), *n.* [Mod. L.; see DEUTERO- & -IUM], the hydrogen isotope having an atomic weight of approximately 2; heavy hydrogen: symbol, D.

**deu·ter·o-,** [< Gr. *deuteros*, second], a combining form meaning *second* or *secondary:* also **deuto-, deuter-, deut-.**

**deu·ter·on** (dōō′tẽr-on′, dū′-), *n.* the nucleus of an atom of deuterium: also **deu′tron, deu′ton.**

**Deu·ter·on·o·my** (dōō′tẽr-on′ə-mi, dū′-), *n.* [< LL. < Gr. < *deuteros*, second + *nomos*, law], the fifth book of the Old Testament: abbrev. **Deut.**

‡**Deut·sches Reich** (doi′chəs rīH′), [G.], Germany: the former official name.

‡**Deutsch·land** (doich′länt), *n.* [G.], Germany.
**De Va·ler·a, Ea·mon** (ā′mən dev′ə-lâr′ə, də-və-lêr′ə), 1882– ; Irish statesman born in the U.S.
**de·val·u·ate** (dē-val′ū-āt′), *v.t.* [-ATED, -ATING], to lessen the value of. —**de·val′u·a′tion,** *n.*
**dev·as·tate** (dev′əs-tāt′), *v.t.* [-TATED, -TATING], [< L. pp. < *de-*, intens. + *vastare*, to make empty < *vastus*, empty], to lay waste; make desolate; ravage; destroy. —**dev′as·tat′ing·ly,** *adv.* —**dev′as·ta′tion,** *n.* —**dev′as·ta′tor** (-tēr), *n.*
**de·vel·op** (di-vel′əp), *v.t.* [< Fr. < *dé-* (L. *dis-*), apart + OFr. *voluper*, to wrap], 1. to cause to become gradually fuller, larger, better, etc. 2. to bring into activity, as an idea. 3. to expand, as a business. 4. in *music*, to elaborate (a theme). 5. in *photography*, *a*) to put (an exposed film, plate, or printing paper) in various chemical solutions in order to make the picture visible. *b*) to make (a picture) visible by doing this. 6. to show or work out by degrees; reveal; make known gradually. 7. to explain more clearly; enlarge upon. *v.i.* 1. to come into being or activity. 2. to become larger, fuller, better, etc.; grow; evolve. 3. to be disclosed. —**de·vel′op·a·ble,** *adj.*
**de·vel·op·er** (di-vel′əp-ēr), *n.* 1. a person or thing that develops. 2. in *photography*, a chemical used to develop film, plate, etc.
**de·vel·op·ment** (di-vel′əp-mənt), *n.* 1. a developing or being developed. 2. a stage in growth, advancement, etc. 3. an event or happening. 4. a thing that is developed. —**de·vel′op·men′tal,** *adj.* —**de·vel′op·men′tal·ly,** *adv.*
**de·vi·ant** (dē′vi-ənt), *adj.* [< LL. ppr. of *deviare*; see DEVIATE], deviating, especially from what is considered normal behavior. *n.* a deviant person.
**de·vi·ate** (dē′vi-āt′), *v.i.* [-ATED, -ATING], [< LL. pp. of *deviare* < L. *devius*; see DEVIOUS], to turn aside (*from* a course, direction, standard, etc.); diverge. *v.t.* to cause to deviate. *adj.* deviant. *n.* (-ət), a deviant; especially, one whose sexual behavior is deviant. —**de′vi·a′tion,** *n.* —**de′vi·a′tor,** *n.*
**de·vice** (di-vīs′), *n.* [ME. *devis*, intention; OFr. *devis*, fem. *devise*, division < *deviser*; see DEVISE], 1. a thing devised; plan. 2. an underhanded scheme; trick. 3. a mechanical contrivance; invention. 4. an ornamental figure or design. 5. a design, often with a motto, on a coat of arms; heraldic emblem. 6. any motto or emblem. —**leave to one's own devices,** to allow to do as one wishes.
**dev·il** (dev′'l), *n.* [AS. *deofol* < LL. < Gr. *diabolos*, lit., slanderer < *dia-*, across + *ballein*, to throw], 1. [sometimes D-], in *theology*, *a*) the chief evil spirit; Satan (with *the*): typically depicted as a man with horns, a tail, and cloven feet. *b*) any demon of hell. 2. something evil or bad. 3. a wicked or malevolent person. 4. one who is sprightly, mischievous, etc. 5. an unlucky, unhappy person. 6. a printer's apprentice. 7. any of various machines with teeth, as for tearing up rags. *v.t.* [-ILED or -ILLED, -ILING or -ILLING], 1. to prepare (food) with strong seasoning. 2. to annoy; torment; tease. —**between the devil and the deep (blue sea),** between equally unpleasant alternatives. —**give the devil his due,** to acknowledge the good qualities of a wicked or unpleasant person. —**go to the devil,** to fall into bad habits. —**play the devil with,** [Colloq.], to upset. —**the devil!** [Colloq.], an exclamation of anger, surprise, etc. —**the devil to pay,** trouble as a consequence.
**dev·iled** (dev′'ld), *adj.* prepared with strong seasoning: as, *deviled* ham: also sp. **devilled.**
**dev·il·fish** (dev′'l-fish′), *n.* [*pl.* see FISH], 1. the largest kind of ray, with pectoral fins that are hornlike when rolled up. 2. an octopus.

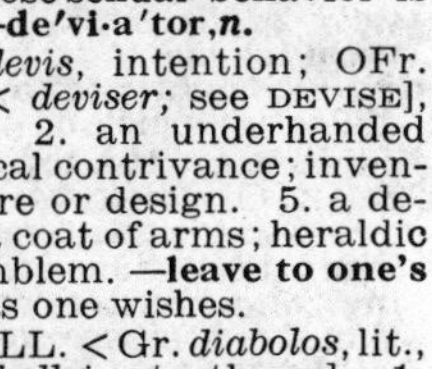

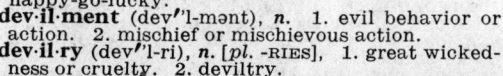

DEVILFISH
(20 ft. across)

**dev·il·ish** (dev′'l-ish, dev′lish), *adj.* 1. of, like, or characteristic of a devil; diabolical. 2. mischievous; energetic. 3. [Colloq.], extremely bad. *adv.* [Colloq.], extremely; very. —**dev′il·ish·ly,** *adv.* —**dev′il·ish·ness,** *n.*
**devil-may-care** (dev′'l-mā-kâr′), *adj.* reckless; careless; happy-go-lucky.
**dev·il·ment** (dev′'l-mənt), *n.* 1. evil behavior or action. 2. mischief or mischievous action.
**dev·il·ry** (dev′'l-ri), *n.* [*pl.* -RIES], 1. great wickedness or cruelty. 2. deviltry.
**devil's-food cake** (dev′'lz-fōōd′), reddish-brown chocolate cake made with sour milk.
**Devil's Island,** an island off the coast of French Guiana: site of a former French penal colony.
**dev·il·try** (dev′'l-tri), *n.* [*pl.* -TRIES], reckless mischief, fun, etc.
**de·vi·ous** (dē′vi-əs), *adj.* [< L. *devius* < *de-*, off, from + *via*, road], 1. roundabout; rambling. 2. going astray; not straightforward. —**de′vi·ous·ly,** *adv.* —**de′vi·ous·ness,** *n.*
**de·vise** (di-vīz′), *v.t.* & *v.i.* [-VISED, -VISING], [< OFr. *deviser*, to distribute, direct < LL. < L. < *dividere*, to divide], 1. to think out; contrive; plan; invent. 2. in *law*, to bequeath (real property) by will. *n.* in *law*, 1. a gift of real property by will. 2. a will, or clause in a will, granting such a gift. —**de·vis′a·ble,** *adj.* —**de·vis′al,** *n.* —**de·vis′er,** *n.*
**dev·i·see** (dev′i-zē′, di-vīz′ē′), *n.* in *law*, the person to whom real property has been bequeathed.
**de·vi·sor** (di-vī′zēr, -zôr), *n.* in *law*, a person who devises property; testator.
**de·vi·tal·ize** (dē-vī′t'l-īz′), *v.t.* [-IZED, -IZING], 1. to kill. 2. to lower the vitality of; weaken. —**de·vi′tal·i·za′tion,** *n.*
**de·void** (di-void′), *adj.* [< OFr. < *des-* (L. *dis-*), from + *vuidier*; see VOID], completely without; empty or destitute (*of*).
**de·voir** (də-vwär′, dev′wär), *n.* [Fr. < L. *debere*, to owe], 1. duty. 2. an act of due respect or courtesy: now used in the plural.
**de·volve** (di-volv′), *v.t.* & *v.i.* [-VOLVED, -VOLVING], [< L. < *de-*, down + *volvere*, to roll], to pass (*on*) to another: said of duties, rights, authority, etc. —**dev·o·lu·tion** (dev′ə-lōō′shən), **de·volve′ment,** *n.*
**De·vo·ni·an** (də-vō′ni-ən), *adj.* 1. of Devonshire. 2. in *geology*, designating or of the period after the Silurian in the Paleozoic Era: see **geology,** chart. *n.* 1. a native or inhabitant of Devonshire. 2. the Devonian Period.
**Dev·on·shire** (dev′ən-shir′), *n.* a county of SW England: pop., 824,000: also **Dev′on.**
**de·vote** (di-vōt′), *v.t.* [-VOTED, -VOTING], [< L. *devotus*, pp. < *de-*, from + *vovere*, to vow], 1. to dedicate; consecrate. 2. to apply (oneself or one's time, energy, etc.) to some purpose.
**de·vot·ed** (di-vōt′id), *adj.* 1. vowed; dedicated; consecrated. 2. very loyal; faithful. —**de·vot′ed·ly,** *adv.* —**de·vot′ed·ness,** *n.*
**dev·o·tee** (dev′ə-tē′), *n.* 1. a person warmly devoted to something or someone. 2. a religious zealot.
**de·vo·tion** (di-vō′shən), *n.* 1. a devoting or being devoted. 2. piety; devoutness. 3. religious worship. 4. *pl.* prayers. 5. loyalty; faithfulness; deep affection. —**de·vo′tion·al,** *adj.* —**de·vo′tion·al·ly,** *adv.*
**de·vour** (di-vour′), *v.t.* [< OFr. < L. < *de-*, intens. + *vorare*, to swallow whole], 1. to eat (up) hungrily or voraciously. 2. to consume; destroy. 3. to take in greedily with the eyes or ears: as, to *devour* novels. 4. to swallow up; engulf. —**de·vour′er,** *n.* —**de·vour′ing·ly,** *adv.*
**de·vout** (di-vout′), *adj.* [< OFr. < L. *devotus*; see DEVOTE], 1. very religious; pious. 2. showing reverence. 3. earnest; sincere; heartfelt. —**de·vout′ly,** *adv.* —**de·vout′ness,** *n.*
**dew** (dōō, dū), *n.* [AS. *deaw*], 1. the atmospheric moisture that condenses and appears during the night in little drops on cool surfaces. 2. anything refreshing, pure, etc., like dew. 3. any moisture in small drops: as, the *dew* of his brow. *v.t.* to wet, as with dew; make moist.
**dew·ber·ry** (dōō′ber′i, dū′-), *n.* [*pl.* -RIES], 1. any of various trailing blackberry plants. 2. the fruit of any of these plants.
**dew·claw** (dōō′klô′, dū′-), *n.* 1. a functionless digit on the foot of some animals, as on the inner side of a dog's hind leg. 2. the claw or hoof at the end of such a digit.
**dew·drop** (dōō′drop′, dū′-), *n.* a drop of dew.
**Dew·ey, George** (dōō′i, dū′i), 1837–1917; U.S. admiral in Spanish-American War.
**Dewey, John,** 1859–1952; U.S. educator.
**dew·lap** (dōō′lap′, dū′-), *n.* [< ME. < *dew*, prob. dew + *lappe*, a fold < AS. *lappa*], a loose fold of skin hanging from the throat of cattle and certain other animals. —**dew′lapped′** (-lapt′), *adj.*
**dew point,** the temperature at which dew starts to form or vapor to condense into liquid.
**dew·y** (dōō′i, dū′i), *adj.* [-IER, -IEST], 1. wet or damp with dew. 2. of dew. 3. [Poetic], dewlike; refreshing, etc. —**dew′i·ness,** *n.*

**dex·ter** (dek′stēr), *adj.* [L. *dexter*, right], of or on the right-hand side (in *heraldry*, the left of the viewer).
**dex·ter·i·ty** (dek-ster′ə-ti), *n.* 1. skill in using one's hands or body; adroitness. 2. skill in using one's mind; cleverness.
**dex·ter·ous** (dek′strəs, -stēr-əs), *adj.* 1. having or showing skill in using the hands or body. 2. having or showing mental skill. Also **dex′trous.** —**dex′ter·ous·ly,** *adv.* —**dex′ter·ous·ness,** *n.*
**dex·tral** (dek′strəl), *adj.* 1. on the right-hand side; right. 2. right-handed. —**dex·tral′i·ty,** *n.* —**dex′tral·ly,** *adv.*
**dex·trin** (dek′strin), *n.* a soluble, gummy substance obtained from starch and used as adhesive, sizing, etc.: also **dex′trine** (-strin, -strēn).
**dex·trorse** (dek′strôrs, dek-strôrs′), *adj.* [< L. < *dexter*, right + *vorsus*, pp. of *vortere*, to turn], in *botany*, twining upward to the right, as the stem of the hop.
**dex·trose** (dek′strōs), *n.* a sugar, $C_6H_{12}O_6$, found in plants and animals; glucose.
**dex·trous** (dek′strəs), *adj.* dexterous. —**dex′trous·ly,** *adv.* —**dex′trous·ness,** *n.*
**dey** (dā), *n.* [Fr. < Turk. *dāi*, maternal uncle], 1. the former title of the governor of Algiers. 2. formerly, a pasha or ruler in Tunis or Tripoli.
**dg.,** decigram; decigrams.
**dhole** (dōl), *n.* [*pl.* DHOLES (dōlz), DHOLE; see PLURAL, II, D, 1], [native name], a wild dog of India that hunts in packs.
**DHQ,** Division Headquarters.
**di** (dē), *n.* in *music*, the tone intermediate between do and re in solfeggio.
**di-,** [Gr. *di-* < *dis*, twice], a prefix meaning: 1. *twice, double, twofold.* 2. in *chemistry*, *having two* (atoms, molecules, radicals, etc.).
**di-,** dis- (*separation, deprivation*, etc.).
**Di,** in *chemistry*, didymium.
**di., dia.,** diameter.
**di·a-,** [< Gr.], a prefix meaning: 1. *through, across*, as in *diagonal.* 2. *apart, between*, as in *diagnose.* Also **di-.**
**di·a·be·tes** (dī′ə-bē′tis, -tēz), *n.* [L. < Gr. *diabētēs*, a siphon < *dia-*, through + *bainein*, to go], a disease characterized by an excessive discharge of urine. —**di·a·bet′ic** (-bet′ik, -bē′tik), *adj.*
**diabetes mel·li·tus** (mə-lī′təs), [< L. *mellitus* < *mel*, honey], a chronic form of diabetes characterized by excess sugar in the blood and urine, hunger, thirst, etc.: also *sugar diabetes.*
**di·a·bol·ic** (dī′ə-bol′ik), *adj.* [< Fr. < LL. < *diabolus;* see DEVIL], 1. of the Devil or devils. 2. very wicked or cruel; devilish. Also **di′a·bol′i·cal.** —**di′a·bol′i·cal·ly,** *adv.*
**di·ac·o·nal** (dī-ak′ə-n′l), *adj.* [< LL. < *diaconus;* see DEACON], of a deacon or deacons.
**di·ac·o·nate** (dī-ak′ə-nit, -nāt′), *n.* [LL. *diaconatus;* see DEACON], 1. the rank, office, or tenure of a deacon. 2. a group of deacons.
**di·a·crit·ic** (dī′ə-krit′ik), *adj.* [< Gr. *diakritikos* < *dia-*, across + *krinein*, to separate], diacritical. *n.* a diacritical mark.
**di·a·crit·i·cal** (dī′ə-krit′i-k′l), *adj.* used to distinguish. —**di′a·crit′i·cal·ly,** *adv.*
**diacritical mark,** a mark added to a letter to show pronunciation, etc. Examples: ä, ā, â, é.
**di·a·dem** (dī′ə-dem′), *n.* [< OFr. < L. < Gr. < *dia-*, through + *dein*, to bind], 1. a crown. 2. an ornamental cloth headband worn as a crown. 3. kingly power or authority. *v.t.* to crown.
**di·aer·e·sis** (dī-er′ə-sis), *n.* [*pl.* -SES (-sēz′)], dieresis. —**di·ae·ret·ic** (dī′ə-ret′ik), *adj.*
**di·ag·nose** (dī′əg-nōs′, -nōz′), *v.t. & v.i.* [-NOSED, -NOSING], to make a diagnosis (of).
**di·ag·no·sis** (dī′əg-nō′sis), *n.* [*pl.* -NOSES (-sēz)], [L. < Gr. < *dia-*, between + *gignōskein*, to know], 1. the act or process of deciding the nature of a disease by examination and observation. 2. a careful investigation of the facts to determine the nature of a thing. 3. the decision resulting from either of these. —**di′ag·nos′tic** (-nos′tik), *adj.* —**di′ag·nos′ti·cal·ly,** *adv.* —**di′ag·nos·ti′cian** (-tish′ən), *n.*
**di·ag·nos·ti·cate** (dī′əg-nos′ti-kāt′), *v.t. & v.i.* [-CATED, -CATING], to diagnose.
**di·ag·o·nal** (dī-ag′ə-n′l), *adj.* [< L. < Gr. < *dia-*, through + *gōnia*, an angle], 1. extending slantingly between opposite corners. 2. having the general direction of a diagonal; slanting; oblique. 3. having slanting markings, lines, etc. *n.* 1. a diagonal line or plane. 2. any diagonal course, row, or part. —**di·ag′o·nal·ly,** *adv.*

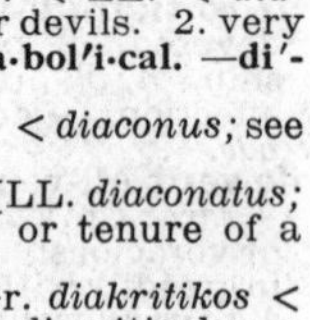

DIAGONAL (AB)

**di·a·gram** (dī′ə-gram′), *n.* [< Fr. < L. < Gr. *diagramma* < *dia-*, across + *graphein*, to write], 1. a geometrical figure, often used to illustrate a theorem. 2. a sketch, plan, graph, etc. that helps explain or illustrate something, as by outlining its parts. *v.t.* [-GRAMED or -GRAMMED, -GRAMING or -GRAMMING], to make a diagram of. —**di′a·gram·mat′ic** (-grə-mat′ik), **di′a·gram·mat′i·cal,** *adj.* —**di′a·gram·mat′i·cal·ly,** *adv.*
**di·al** (dī′əl, dīl), *n.* [< ML. *dialis*, daily < L. *dies*, day], 1. a sundial. 2. the face of a watch or clock. 3. the clocklike face of a gauge, meter, etc. for indicating, as by a moving pointer, the amount of something. 4. a knob or disk, as on a radio, for tuning in stations. 5. a rotating disk on a telephone, used in making connections automatically. *v.t. & v.i.* [-ALED or -ALLED, -ALING or -ALLING], 1. to show on or measure with a dial. 2. to tune in (a radio station, program, etc.). 3. to call by using a telephone dial. —**dial′er,** *n.*
**dial.,** 1. dialect. 2. dialectal. 3. dialectic(al).
**di·a·lect** (dī′ə-lekt′), *n.* [< Fr. < L. < Gr. *dialektos*, discourse < *dia-*, between + *legein*, to talk], 1. the sum total of local characteristics of speech as they differ from those of a real or imaginary standard speech. 2. loosely, any jargon, cant, or patois. 3. in *linguistics*, the form of a spoken language peculiar to a region, community, social group, or occupational group. 4. any language as part of a larger group of languages: as, English is a West Germanic *dialect.* *adj.* of or in dialect.
**di·a·lec·tal** (dī′ə-lek′t′l), *adj.* of or characteristic of a dialect. —**di′a·lec′tal·ly,** *adv.*
**di·a·lec·tic** (dī′ə-lek′tik), *n.* [< OFr. < L. < Gr. < *dialektikos;* see DIALECT], 1. the art or practice of examining ideas logically, often by question and answer, so as to determine their validity: also **dialectics.** 2. logical argumentation. 3. the method of logic used by Hegel and adapted by Marx to his materialist philosophy. *adj.* 1. of or using dialectic. 2. dialectal. Also **di′a·lec′ti·cal.** —**di′a·lec′ti·cal·ly,** *adv.*
**di·a·lec·ti·cian** (dī′ə-lek-tish′ən), *n.* an expert in dialectic; logician.
**di·a·logue, di·a·log** (dī′ə-lôg′, -log′), *n.* [Fr. < L. < Gr. *dialogos* < *dialegesthai;* see DIALECT], 1. a talking together; conversation. 2. open and frank discussion, as in seeking mutual understanding. 3. a written work in the form of a conversation. 4. the passages of talk in a play, story, etc. *v.i.* [-LOGUED (-lôgd′, -logd′), -LOGUING], to hold a conversation. *v.t.* to express in dialogue. —**di·al·o·gist** (dī-al′ə-jist), **di′a·logu′er,** *n.*
**di·al·y·sis** (dī-al′ə-sis), *n.* [*pl.* -SES (-sēz′)], [L. < Gr. < *dia-*, apart + *lyein*, to loose], in *chemistry*, the separation of crystalloids from colloids in solution by the faster diffusion of the former through a moist membrane. —**di′a·lyt′ic** (-ə-lit′ik), *adj.*
**diam.,** diameter.
**di·a·mag·net·ism** (dī′ə-mag′nə-tiz′m), *n.* the property that certain substances have of being repelled by both poles of a magnet. —**di′a·mag·net′ic** (-mag-net′ik), *adj. & n.* —**di′a·mag·net′i·cal·ly,** *adv.*
**di·am·e·ter** (dī-am′ə-tēr), *n.* [< OFr. < L. < Gr. < *dia-*, through + *metron*, a measure], 1. a straight line passing through the center of a circle, sphere, etc. from one side to the other. 2. the length of such a line; thickness.
**di·a·met·ri·cal** (dī′ə-met′ri-k′l), *adj.* 1. of or along a diameter. 2. directly opposite; contrary. Also **di′a·met′ric.** —**di′a·met′ri·cal·ly,** *adv.*
**di·a·mond** (dī′mənd, dī′ə-), *n.* [< OFr. < ML. *diamantis* < L. < Gr. *adamas*, adamant], 1. nearly pure carbon in crystalline form: it is the hardest mineral known, and has great brilliance. 2. a piece of this, used as a gem and in cutting tools, etc. 3. a figure shaped like this ◇; lozenge. 4. a red, lozenge-shaped mark on some playing cards. 5. *pl.* the suit of cards with this mark. 6. a card of this suit. 7. in *baseball*, *a*) the infield. *b*) the whole playing field. 8. in *printing*, a small size of type, 4½ point. *adj.* of, like, or set with a diamond. *v.t.* to adorn as with diamonds.
**diamond anniversary,** a sixtieth, or often seventy-fifth, anniversary: also **diamond jubilee.**
**di·a·mond·back** (dī′mənd-bak′, dī′ə-), *adj.* having diamond-shaped markings on the back: as, a *diamondback* rattlesnake. *n.* 1. a kind of moth. 2. an edible North American turtle found in salt marshes along the Atlantic and Gulf coasts: also **diamondback terrapin.**
**diamond wedding,** a sixtieth, or sometimes seventy-fifth, wedding anniversary.

**Di·an·a** (dī-an′ə), *n.* in *Rom. mythology*, the goddess of the moon, of hunting, and of virginity: identified with the Greek Artemis.

DIANA

**di·a·pa·son** (dī′ə-pā′z'n, -s'n), *n.* [L., contr. < Gr. < *dia*, through + *pasōn*, genit. pl. of *pas*, all (tones)], 1. the entire range of a musical instrument or voice. 2. either of two principal stops of an organ (**open diapason** and **stopped diapason**), covering the entire range: when either is used, any note played is sounded in two or more octaves.

**di·a·per** (dī′ə-pēr), *n.* [< OFr. < ML. *diasprus*, a precious cloth < Gr. *dia-*, through + *aspros*, white], 1. a white cotton or linen cloth woven in a pattern of repeated, small, diamond-shaped figures. 2. (*also* dī′pēr), a small cloth of cotton, etc. used as a baby's breechcloth. *adj.* 1. of diaper. 2. for diapers. *v.t.* 1. to pattern with diamond-shaped figures. 2. to put a diaper on (a baby).

**di·aph·a·nous** (dī-af′ə-nəs), *adj.* [< ML. < Gr. < *dia-*, through + *phainein*, to show], transparent or translucent, as gauzy cloth. —**di·aph′a·nous·ly,** *adv.* —**di·aph′a·nous·ness,** *n.*

**di·a·pho·re·sis** (dī′ə-fə-rē′sis), *n.* [LL. < Gr. < *dia-*, through + *phorein*, to bear], perspiration, especially when profuse and artificially induced. —**di′a·pho·ret′ic** (-ret′ik), *adj. & n.*

**di·a·phragm** (dī′ə-fram′), *n.* [< LL. < Gr. < *dia-*, through + *phragma*, a fence < *phrassein*, to enclose], 1. the partition of muscles and tendons between the chest cavity and the abdominal cavity; midriff. 2. any separating membrane or device. 3. a device to regulate the amount of light entering a camera lens, etc. 4. a vibrating disk that produces sound waves, as in an earphone. —**di′a·phrag·mat′ic** (-frag-mat′ik), *adj.* —**di′a·phrag·mat′i·cal·ly,** *adv.*

**di·a·rist** (dī′ə-rist), *n.* one who keeps a diary.

**di·ar·rhe·a, di·ar·rhoe·a** (dī′ə-rē′ə), *n.* [< LL. < Gr. < *dia-*, through + *rheein*, to flow], excessive frequency and looseness of bowel movements. —**di′ar·rhe′al, di′ar·rhoe′al, di′ar·rhe′ic, di′ar·rhoe′ic,** *adj.*

**di·a·ry** (dī′ə-ri), *n.* [*pl.* -RIES], [< L. *diarium* < *dies*, day], 1. a daily written record of the writer's own experiences, thoughts, etc. 2. a book for keeping such a record.

**Di·as·po·ra** (dī-as′pə-rə), *n.* [< Gr. < *dia-*, through + *speirein*, to sow], the dispersion of the Jews after the Babylonian exile.

**di·a·stase** (dī′ə-stās′), *n.* [Fr. < Gr. *diastasis*, separation < *dia-*, apart + *histanai*, to stand], an enzyme that changes starches into maltose and later into dextrose; amylase. —**di′a·stat′ic** (-stat′ik), *adj.*

**di·as·to·le** (dī-as′tə-lē′), *n.* [LL. < Gr. *diastolē*, expansion < *dia-*, apart + *stellein*, to put], 1. the usual rhythmic dilatation of the heart, especially of the ventricles, during which the chambers fill with blood. 2. in *Gr. & Latin prosody*, the lengthening of a short syllable. Opposed to *systole*. —**di·as·tol·ic** (dī′ə-stol′ik), *adj.*

**di·as·tro·phism** (dī-as′trə-fiz'm), *n.* [< Gr. *diastrophē*, distortion < *dia-*, aside + *strephein*, to turn; + *-ism*], 1. the process by which the earth's surface is reshaped through rock movements and displacements. 2. formations so made. —**di·a·stroph·ic** (dī′ə-strof′ik), *adj.*

**di·a·ther·mize** (dī′ə-thūr′mīz), *v.t.* [-MIZED, -MIZING], to treat by diathermy.

**di·a·ther·my** (dī′ə-thūr′mi), *n.* [< Gr. *dia-*, through + *thermē*, heat], medical treatment in which heat is produced in the tissues beneath the skin by a high-frequency electric current: also **di′a·ther′mi·a.** —**di′a·ther′mic** (-mik), **di′a·ther′ma·nous** (-mə-nəs), *adj.*

**di·a·tom** (dī′ə-təm, -tom′), *n.* [< Gr. < *dia-*, through + *temnein*, to cut], any of various microscopic one-celled algae whose walls contain silica. —**di′a·to·ma′ceous** (-tə-mā′shəs), *adj.*

**di·a·ton·ic** (dī′ə-ton′ik), *adj.* [< Fr. < LL. < Gr. *diatonikos*, stretched through (the notes) < *dia-*, through + *teinein*, to stretch], in *music*, designating, of, or using any standard major or minor scale of eight tones without the chromatic intervals. —**di′a·ton′i·cal·ly,** *adv.*

**di·a·tribe** (dī′ə-trīb′), *n.* [Fr. < L. < Gr. *diatribē*, a waste of time < *dia-*, through + *tribein*, to rub], a bitter, abusive denunciation.

**Dí·az, Ro·drí·go** (rô-thrē′gô dē′äth), see **Cid.**

**di·bas·ic** (dī-bās′ik), *adj.* denoting or of an acid with two hydrogen atoms which may be replaced by basic radicals or atoms to form a salt.

**dib·ble** (dib′'l), *n.* [Eng. dial. var. of *dabble*], a pointed tool used to make holes in the soil for seeds, bulbs, or young plants: also **dib′ber** (-bēr). *v.t.* [-BLED, -BLING], 1. to make a hole in (the soil) with a dibble. 2. to plant with a dibble. *v.i.* to use a dibble. —**dib′bler,** *n.*

DIBBLE

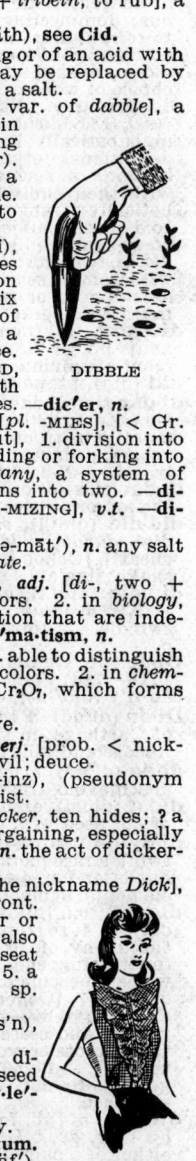

**dice** (dīs), *n.pl.* [sing. DIE (dī), DICE], [see DIE, *n.*], 1. small cubes of bone, plastic, etc. marked on each side with from one to six spots and used in games of chance. 2. [construed as sing.], a gambling game played with dice. 3. any small cubes. *v.i.* [DICED, DICING], to play or gamble with dice. *v.t.* to cut into small cubes. —**dic′er,** *n.*

**di·chot·o·my** (dī-kot′ə-mi), *n.* [*pl.* -MIES], [< Gr. < *dicha*, in two + *temnein*, to cut], 1. division into two parts. 2. in *biology*, a dividing or forking into parts; bifurcation. 3. in *botany*, a system of branching by repeated divisions into two. —**di·chot′o·mize′** (-mīz′), [-MIZED, -MIZING], *v.t.* —**di·chot′o·mous,** *adj.*

**di·chro·mate** (dī-krō′māt, dī′krə-māt′), *n.* any salt of dichromic acid: also *bichromate.*

**di·chro·mat·ic** (dī′krō-mat′ik), *adj.* [*di-*, two + *chromatic*], 1. having two colors. 2. in *biology*, having two varieties of coloration that are independent of sex or age. —**di·chro′ma·tism,** *n.*

**di·chro·mic** (dī-krō′mik), *adj.* 1. able to distinguish only two of the three primary colors. 2. in *chemistry*, designating an acid, $H_2Cr_2O_7$, which forms dichromates.

**dick** (dik), *n.* [Slang], a detective.

**dick·ens** (dik′'nz, -inz), *n. & interj.* [prob. < nickname for *Richard*], [Colloq.], devil; deuce.

**Dick·ens, Charles** (dik′'nz, -inz), (pseudonym *Boz*), 1812–1870; English novelist.

**dick·er** (dik′ēr), *v.i. & v.t.* [< *dicker*, ten hides; ? a unit of barter], to trade by bargaining, especially on a small scale; barter; haggle. *n.* the act of dickering.

**dick·ey** (dik′i), *n.* [*pl.* -EYS], [< the nickname *Dick*], 1. a man's detachable shirt front. 2. a woman's detachable collar or blouse front. 3. a small bird: also **dick′ey·bird′**. 4. the driver's seat in a carriage: also **dickey box.** 5. a back seat in a carriage. Also sp. **dicky** [*pl.* -IES].

DICKEY

**Dick·in·son, Emily** (dik′in-s'n), 1830–1886; U.S. poet.

**di·cot·y·le·don** (dī′kot-'l-ē′d'n, dī-kot′-), *n.* a plant with two seed leaves (cotyledons). —**di′cot·y·le′don·ous,** *adj.*

**dict.,** 1. dictator. 2. dictionary.

**dic·ta** (dik′tə), *n.* alt. pl. of **dictum.**

**dic·ta·graph** (dik′tə-graf′, -gräf′), *n.* a dictograph.

**dic·ta·phone** (dik′tə-fōn′), *n.* [< *dictate* + *-phone*], a machine for recording and reproducing words spoken into it, as for transcription by a typist: a trade-mark (**Dictaphone**).

**dic·tate** (dik′tāt; *also, for v.,* dik-tāt′), *v.t. & v.i.* [-TATED, -TATING], [< L. pp. of *dictare*, freq. of *dicere*, to speak], 1. to speak (something) aloud for someone else to write down. 2. to command expressly. 3. to impose or give (orders) with authority or arbitrarily. *n.* an authoritative order or command.

**dic·ta·tion** (dik-tā′shən), *n.* 1. the act of speaking (something) aloud for someone else to write down, as in shorthand. 2. the words so spoken or written down. 3. the giving of authoritative orders or commands. —**dic·ta′tion·al,** *adj.*

**dic·ta·tor** (dik′tā-tēr, dik-tā′-), *n.* 1. a ruler with absolute power and authority. 2. a person whose word must be obeyed. 3. a person who speaks aloud words for someone else to write down. **—dic·ta′tor·ship′**, *n.*

**dic·ta·to·ri·al** (dik′tə-tôr′i-əl, -tō′ri-), *adj.* of, like, or characteristic of a dictator; autocratic; imperious; domineering. **—dic′ta·to′ri·al·ly**, *adv.* **—dic′-ta·to′ri·al·ness**, *n.*

**dic·tion** (dik′shən), *n.* [Fr. < L. *dictio* < pp. of *dicere*, to say], 1. manner of expression in words; choice of words. 2. enunciation.

**dic·tion·ar·y** (dik′shən-er′i; *Brit.* -ẽr-i), *n.* [*pl.* -IES], [ML. *dictionarium;* see DICTION], 1. a book of alphabetically listed words in a language, with definitions, etymologies, pronunciations, etc.; lexicon. 2. such a book of words in one language with their equivalents in another. 3. any alphabetically arranged list of words or articles relating to a special subject.

**dic·to·graph** (dik′tə-graf′, -gräf′), *n.* [< L. pp. of *dicere*, to speak; + *-graph*], a telephonic instrument with a small, sensitive transmitter, used for secretly listening to or recording conversations: a trademark (**Dictograph**).

**dic·tum** (dik′təm), *n.* [*pl.* -TUMS, -TA (-tə)], [L., neut. pp. of *dicere*, to speak], 1. a formal statement of opinion; pronouncement. 2. a saying.

**did** (did), pt. of **do.**

**di·dac·tic** (dī-dak′tik), *adj.* [Gr. *didaktikos* < *didaskein*, to teach], 1. intended for instruction. 2. morally instructive. 3. too much inclined to teach others; pedantic. Also **di·dac′ti·cal. —di·dac′ti·cal·ly**, *adv.* **—di·dac′ti·cism** (-siz′m), *n.*

**di·dac·tics** (dī-dak′tiks), *n.pl.* [construed as sing.], the art or science of teaching; pedagogy.

**did·dle** (did′′l), *v.i. & v.t.* [-DLED, -DLING], [Eng. dial. *duddle, diddle*, to totter; akin to *diddle* (to cheat)], [Colloq.], to move back and forth jerkily; shake; jiggle.

**did·dle** (did′′l), *v.t. & v.i.* [-DLED, -DLING], [? ult. < AS. *dyderian*, to fool], [Colloq.], 1. to cheat; swindle. 2. to waste (time) in trifling. **—did′dler**, *n.*

**Di·de·rot, De·nis** (də-nē′ dē′drō′; Eng. dē′də-rō′), 1713–1784; French encyclopedist.

**did·n't** (did′′nt), did not.

**Di·do** (dī′dō), *n.* in *Rom. legend*, founder and queen of Carthage: in the *Aeneid*, she falls in love with Aeneas and kills herself when he leaves her.

**di·do** (dī′dō), *n.* [*pl.* -DOS, -DOES], [< ?], [Colloq.], a mischievous trick; prank.

**didst** (didst), archaic second pers. sing., past indic. of **do**: used with *thou.*

**di·dym·i·um** (dī-dim′i-əm, di-), *n.* [< Gr. *didymos*, twin], a rare metal, formerly considered an element but later found to be a mixture of two rare-earth elements: symbol D or Di.

**die** (dī), *v.i.* [DIED, DYING], [ME. *dien, deyen;* ON. *deyja*], 1. to stop living; become dead. 2. to suffer the agony of, or like that of, death. 3. to stop functioning; end. 4. to lose force or activity. 5. to wither; become extinct. 6. to pine away, as with desire. 7. [Colloq.], to wish very much: as, she's *dying* to tell. **—die away** (or **down**), to become weaker and cease gradually. **—die back**, to wither to the roots or woody part. **—die hard**, to resist to the last. **—die off**, to die one by one until all are gone. **—die out**, 1. to die away. 2. to go out of existence.

**die** (dī), *n.* [*pl.*, for 1, DICE (dīs); for 2, DIES (dīz)], [< OFr. *de* < L. pp of *dare*, to give, grant], 1. either of a pair of dice; small, marked cube used in games of chance. 2. any of various tools or devices for molding, stamping, cutting, or shaping. *v.t.* [DIED, DIEING], to mold, stamp, cut, or shape with a die. **—the die is cast**, the decision has been made and is irrevocable.

**die casting**, 1. the process of making a casting by forcing molten metal into a metallic mold, or die, under great pressure. 2. a casting made in this way. **—die caster.**

**di·e·cious** (dī-ē′shəs), *adj.* dioecious.

**die-hard, die·hard** (dī′härd′), *adj.* stubborn in resistance; unwilling to give in. *n.* a stubborn, resistant person; esp., an extreme conservative.

**di·e·lec·tric** (dī′ə-lek′trik), *n.* [< *dia-*, across + *electric*], a material, as rubber or glass, that does not conduct electricity; insulator. *adj.* nonconducting; insulating. **—di′e·lec′tri·cal·ly**, *adv.*

**di·er·e·sis** (dī-er′ə-sis), *n.* [*pl.* -SES (-sēz′)], [< LL. < Gr. *diairesis*, division < *dia-*, apart + *hairein*, to take], the mark (¨), placed over the second of two consecutive vowels to show that it is pronounced in a separate syllable: it is sometimes replaced by a hyphen (*coöperate, co-operate*): also sp. **diaeresis. —di·e·ret·ic** (dī′ə-ret′ik), *adj.*

**Die·sel** (dē′z'l, dē′s'l), *n.* [after R. *Diesel* (1858–1913), its G. inventor], a type of internal-combustion engine that burns crude oil: ignition is brought about by heat resulting from air compression: also **diesel, Diesel engine** (or **motor**).

**die·sink·er** (dī′siŋ′kẽr), *n.* a maker of dies for stamping or shaping.

**‡Di·es I·rae** (dī′ēz ī′rē, dē′ās êr′ī), [L., Day of Wrath], a medieval Latin hymn about Judgment Day, now often included in the Requiem Mass.

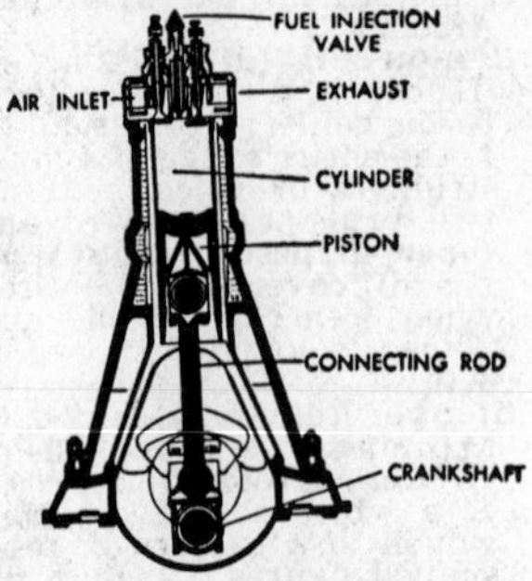

DIESEL ENGINE

**di·e·sis** (dī′ə-sis), *n.* [*pl.* -SES (-sēz′)], [L. < Gr. < *diienai*, to send through], a reference mark (‡) used in printing: also called *double dagger.*

**di·et** (dī′ət), *n.* [< OFr. < LL. < L. < Gr. *diaita*, manner of living], 1. what a person or animal usually eats and drinks; daily fare. 2. special, limited food and drink, chosen or prescribed for health or to gain or lose weight. *v.i. & v.t.* to adhere or cause to adhere to a diet, especially for losing weight. **—di′et·er**, *n.*

**di·et** (dī′ət), *n.* [< OFr. < ML. *dieta*, assembly, day's journey < L. *dies*, day], 1. a formal assembly. 2. in some countries, a national or, sometimes, local legislative assembly.

**di·e·tar·y** (dī′ə-ter′i), *n.* [*pl.* -IES], 1. a system of diet. 2. daily food allowance, as in a jail. *adj.* 1. of diet. 2. of a dietary.

**di·e·tet·ic** (dī′ə-tet′ik), *adj.* of diet (food): also **di′e·tet′i·cal. —di′e·tet′i·cal·ly**, *adv.*

**di·e·tet·ics** (dī′ə-tet′iks), *n.pl.* [construed as sing.], the study of the kinds and quantities of food needed for health.

**di·e·ti·tian, di·e·ti·cian** (dī′ə-tish′ən), *n.* an expert in dietetics; specialist in planning meals.

**dif-**, dis-: used before *f*, as in *differ.*

**dif., diff.**, 1. differ. 2. difference. 3. different.

**dif·fer** (dif′ẽr), *v.i.* [< OFr. < L. *differre* < *dis-*, apart + *ferre*, to carry], 1. to be unlike; be different (*from*). 2. to be of opposite or different opinions; disagree. 3. to quarrel (*with*).

**dif·fer·ence** (dif′ẽr-əns, dif′rəns), *n.* 1. condition or quality of being different. 2. the way in which people or things are different. 3. the state of holding a differing opinion; disagreement. 4. a dispute; quarrel. 5. in *mathematics*, the amount by which one quantity is greater or less than another. *v.t.* [-ENCED, -ENCING], to differentiate. **—make a difference**, 1. to have an effect. 2. to change the situation. **—what's the difference?** [Colloq.], what does it matter?

**dif·fer·ent** (dif′ẽr-ənt, dif′rənt), *adj.* 1. not alike; dissimilar (with *from*, or, colloquially, *than*, and, in British usage, *to*). 2. not the same; distinct; separate. 3. various. 4. unlike most others; unusual. **—dif′fer·ent·ly**, *adv.*

**dif·fer·en·ti·a** (dif′ẽr-en′shi-ə), *n.* [*pl.* -AE (-ē′)], in *logic*, a distinguishing characteristic.

**dif·fer·en·tial** (dif′ẽr-en′shəl), *adj.* 1. of, showing, or depending on a difference. 2. constituting a specific difference; distinguishing. 3. having different effects: as, a *differential* gear. 4. in *mathematics & mechanics*, involving differentials. *n.* 1. in *mathematics*, an infinitesimal difference between consecutive values of a variable quantity. 2. in *mechanics*, a differential gear. 3. in *railroading*, a difference in rates, as between different routes. **—dif′fer·en′tial·ly**, *adv.*

**differential calculus**, the branch of higher mathematics that deals with the relations of differentials to the constant on which they depend.

**differential gear**, a certain arrangement of gears connecting two axles in the same line: used in automobiles to allow one axle to turn faster than the other, as in turning curves.

**dif·fer·en·ti·ate** (dif′ẽr-en′shi-āt′), *v.t.* [-ATED, -ATING], 1. to constitute a difference in or between. 2. to make unlike. 3. to perceive or express the difference in; distinguish between. 4. in *mathematics*, to work out the differential of. *v.i.* 1. to become different or differentiated. 2. to perceive or express a difference. **—dif′fer·en′ti·a′tion**, *n.*

**dif·fi·cult** (dif′i-kəlt, -kult′), *adj.* 1. hard to do, make, understand, etc. 2. hard to satisfy, get along with, etc. —**dif′fi·cult·ly,** *adv.*

**dif·fi·cul·ty** (dif′i-kul′ti, -kəl-), *n.* [*pl.* -TIES], [< OFr. < L. *difficultas* < *dis-*, not + *facilis*, easy], 1. the condition or fact of being difficult. 2. something difficult; obstacle or objection. 3. trouble. 4. a disagreement or quarrel. —**be in difficulties,** to have financial troubles.

**dif·fi·dent** (dif′i-dənt), *adj.* [< L. *diffidens*, ppr. < *dis-*, not + *fidere*, to trust], lacking confidence in oneself; hesitant to assert oneself; shy. —**dif′fi·dence,** *n.* —**dif′fi·dent·ly,** *adv.*

**dif·fract** (di-frakt′), *v.t.* [< L. *diffractus*, pp. < *dis-*, apart + *frangere*, to break], 1. to break into parts. 2. to cause to undergo diffraction.

**dif·frac·tion** (di-frak′shən), *n.* 1. the breaking up of a ray of light into dark and light bands or into the colors of the spectrum, as when it is deflected at the edge of an opaque object. 2. a similar breaking up of other waves, as of sound or electricity. —**dif·frac′tive,** *adj.*

**dif·fuse** (di-fūs′; *for v.*, -fūz′), *adj.* [L. *diffusus*, pp. < *dis-*, apart + *fundere*, to pour], 1. spread out; not concentrated. 2. using more words than are needed. *v.t. & v.i.* [-FUSED, -FUSING], 1. to pour in every direction; spread widely; scatter. 2. in *physics*, to mix by diffusion, as gases, liquids, etc. —**dif·fuse′ly** (-fūs′-), *adv.* —**dif·fuse′ness,** *n.* —**dif·fus′er, dif·fus′or** (-fūz′ẽr), *n.* —**dif·fus′i·ble** (-fūz′-), *adj.*

**dif·fu·sion** (di-fū′zhən), *n.* 1. a diffusing or being diffused; spreading; dissemination. 2. wordiness. 3. the intermingling of the molecules of two or more substances. 4. a reflection, as of light, from an irregular surface.

**dif·fu·sive** (di-fū′siv), *adj.* 1. tending to diffuse. 2. characterized by diffusion. 3. diffuse. —**dif·fu′sive·ly,** *adv.* —**dif·fu′sive·ness,** *n.*

**dig** (dig), *v.t.* [DUG or *archaic & poetic* DIGGED, DIGGING], [< OFr. *diguer* < Gmc.], 1. to break and turn up or remove (ground) with a spade or other tool, or with hands, claws, etc. 2. to make (a hole, cellar, etc.) by digging. 3. to get out by digging: as, *dig* potatoes. 4. to find out, as by careful study; unearth (usually with *up* or *out*): as, to *dig* out the truth. 5. to nudge or prod. 6. [Slang], *a*) to understand. *b*) to observe. *v.i.* 1. to excavate. 2. to make a way by digging (*through, into, under*). 3. [Colloq.], to work or study hard. *n.* 1. the act of digging. 2. [Colloq.], a poke, nudge, etc.; hence, a sarcastic comment; taunt. —**dig in,** 1. to dig trenches for cover. 2. [Colloq.], to begin to work hard. —**dig into,** [Colloq.], to work hard at.

**di·gest** (dī′jest; *for v.*, di-jest′, dī-), *n.* [< L. pp. of *digerere*, to separate < *di-*, apart + *gerere*, to bear], a body of condensed, systematic information; summary or synopsis, as of legal material. *v.t.* 1. to arrange systematically, usually in condensed form; summarize. 2. to change (food) in the mouth, stomach, and intestines so that it can be absorbed by the body. 3. to aid the digestion of (food). 4. to think over and absorb. 5. to tolerate or accept. 6. in *chemistry*, to soften or dissolve with heat and moisture. *v.i.* 1. to be digested. 2. to digest food. —**di·gest′er,** *n.*

**di·gest·ant** (di-jes′tənt, dī-), *adj. & n.* digestive.

**di·gest·i·ble** (di-jes′tə-b'l, dī-), *adj.* that can be digested. —**di·gest′i·bil′i·ty,** *n.* —**di·gest′i·bly,** *adv.*

**di·ges·tion** (di-jes′chən, dī-), *n.* 1. a digesting or being digested: said of food. 2. the ability to digest food. 3. the absorption of ideas.

**di·ges·tive** (di-jes′tiv, dī-), *adj.* of or for digestion. *n.* any substance that aids digestion.

**dig·ger** (dig′ẽr), *n.* 1. a person or thing that digs. 2. a tool or machine for digging. 3. [D-], a member of any of several tribes of Indians in the western U.S. who dug up roots for food.

**dig·gings** (dig′iŋz), *n.pl.* 1. materials dug out. 2. [often construed as sing.], a place where digging or mining is carried on. 3. [Slang], the place where one lives.

**dight** (dīt), *v.t.* [DIGHT or DIGHTED, DIGHTING], [< AS. *dihtan*, to arrange < L. *dictare;* see DICTATE], [Archaic & Poetic], 1. to adorn. 2. to equip.

**dig·it** (dij′it), *n.* [L. *digitus*, a finger, toe], 1. a finger or toe. 2. any numeral from 0 to 9.

**dig·it·al** (dij′i-t'l), *adj.* 1. of or like a digit. 2. having digits. *n.* a key played with a finger, as on the piano. —**dig′it·al·ly,** *adv.*

**digital computer,** a computer using coded digits to solve problems by means of arithmetic.

**dig·i·ta·lis** (dij′i-tal′is, -tā′lis), *n.* [ML.; see DIGIT: from its thimblelike flowers], 1. the foxglove, a plant of the figwort family. 2. the dried leaves of the purple foxglove. 3. a medicine made from these leaves, used as a heart stimulant.

**dig·i·tate** (dij′i-tāt′), *adj.* [see DIGIT], 1. having separate fingers or toes. 2. fingerlike. 3. having fingerlike divisions, as some leaves. Also **dig′i·tat′ed.** —**dig′i·tate′ly,** *adv.*

**dig·ni·fied** (dig′nə-fīd′), *adj.* having and showing dignity or stateliness. —**dig′ni·fied′ly,** *adv.*

**dig·ni·fy** (dig′nə-fī′), *v.t.* [-FIED, -FYING], [< OFr. < ML. < L. *dignus*, worthy + *facere*, to make], to give dignity to; make worthy; honor; exalt.

**dig·ni·tar·y** (dig′nə-ter′i), *n.* [*pl.* -IES], [< L. *dignitas*, dignity; + *-ary*], a person holding a high, dignified position or office, as in a church.

**dig·ni·ty** (dig′nə-ti), *n.* [*pl.* -TIES], [< OFr. < L. < *dignus*, worthy], 1. worthiness; nobility. 2. high repute; honor. 3. the degree of worth, repute, or honor. 4. a high position, rank, or title. 5. loftiness of appearance or manner; stateliness. 6. calm self-possession and self-respect.

**di·graph** (dī′graf, -gräf), *n.* [*di-* + *-graph*], a combination of two letters to represent one sound, as *read*, *graphic*, etc. —**di·graph′ic,** *adj.*

**di·gress** (də-gres′, dī-), *v.i.* [< L. *digressus*, pp. < *dis-*, apart + *gradi*, to go, step], to depart temporarily from the main subject in talking or writing.

**di·gres·sion** (də-gresh′ən, dī-), *n.* a digressing; temporary departure from the main subject in talking or writing. —**di·gres′sion·al,** *adj.*

**di·gres·sive** (də-gres′iv, dī-), *adj.* digressing; given to digression. —**di·gres′sive·ly,** *adv.*

**di·he·dral** (dī-hē′drəl), *adj.* [< *di-* + Gr. *hedra*, a seat], 1. having two plane faces or sides: as, a *dihedral* angle. 2. having wings that form a dihedral angle with each other, as some airplanes. 3. in *solid geometry*, formed by two intersecting planes. *n.* a dihedral angle. —**di·he′dral·ly,** *adv.*

**dik-dik** (dik′dik′), *n.* [< the Ethiopian native name], a very small African antelope.

**dike** (dīk), *n.* [AS. *dic*], 1. a ditch or watercourse. 2. the bank of earth thrown up in digging a ditch. 3. a causeway or low dividing wall of earth or stone. 4. an embankment or dam made to prevent flooding by the sea or by a stream. 5. a protective barrier. 6. in *geology*, a hardened mass of igneous rock that has been forced into a fissure while in a melted state. *v.t.* [DIKED, DIKING], 1. to provide with a dike. 2. to drain by a ditch. Also sp. **dyke.** —**dik′er,** *n.*

**di·lan·tin** (di-lan′tin), *n.* [< *diphenylhydantoin* sodium], a drug used in the treatment of epileptic attacks: in full, **dilantin sodium**: a trade-mark (**Dilantin**).

**di·lap·i·date** (di-lap′ə-dāt′), *v.i. & v.t.* [-DATED, -DATING], [< L. *dilapidatus*, pp. < *dis-*, apart + *lapidare*, to throw stones at < *lapis*, a stone], to become or cause to become partially ruined and in need of repairs. —**di·lap′i·da′tion,** *n.*

**di·lap·i·dat·ed** (di-lap′ə-dāt′id), *adj.* falling to pieces; broken down; shabby and neglected.

**dil·a·ta·tion** (dil′ə-tā′shən, dī′lə-), *n.* dilation.

**di·late** (dī-lāt′, di-lāt′), *v.t.* [-ATED, -ATING], [L. *dilatare* < *dis-*, apart + *latus*, pp. of *ferre*, to bring], to make wider or larger; cause to expand or swell. *v.i.* 1. to become wider or larger; expand; swell. 2. to speak or write at length (*on* or *upon* a subject). —**di·lat′a·bil′i·ty,** *n.* —**di·lat′a·ble,** *adj.* —**di·la′tor, di·lat′er,** *n.*

**di·la·tion** (dī-lā′shən, di-), *n.* 1. a dilating or being dilated. 2. a dilated form or part.

**dil·a·to·ry** (dil′ə-tôr′i, -tō′ri), *adj.* [< LL. < L. < *dilatus;* see DILATE], 1. causing or tending to cause delay. 2. inclined to delay; slow; tardy. —**dil′a·to′ri·ly,** *adv.* —**dil′a·to′ri·ness,** *n.*

**di·lem·ma** (di-lem′ə), *n.* [LL. < Gr. < *di-*, two + *lēmma*, assumption], 1. an argument necessitating a choice between equally unfavorable alternatives. 2. any situation necessitating a choice between unpleasant alternatives; perplexing or awkward situation. —**on the horns of a dilemma,** faced with a choice between equally unfavorable alternatives.

**dil·et·tan·te** (dil′ə-tan′ti, -tänt′), *n.* [*pl.* -TES, -TI (-ti)], [It. < ppr. of *dilettare* < L. *delectare*, to delight], 1. a person who loves the fine arts. 2. a person who dabbles in art, literature, etc. in a superficial way; trifler. ***adj.*** of or characteristic of a dilettante. —**dil'et·tant'ish,** ***adj.*** —**dil'et·tant'ism, dil'et·tan'te·ism,** ***n.***

**dil·i·gence** (dil'ə-jəns), ***n.*** a being diligent; constant, careful effort; persevering hard work.

**dil·i·gence** (dil'ə-jəns; Fr. dē'lē'zhäns'), ***n.*** [Fr.], a public stagecoach formerly used in Europe.

**dil·i·gent** (dil'ə-jənt), ***adj.*** [OFr. < L. ppr. of *diligere,* to esteem highly < *dis-,* apart + *legere,* to choose], 1. persevering and careful in work; hardworking. 2. done with careful, steady effort; painstaking. —**dil'i·gent·ly,** ***adv.***

**dill** (dil), ***n.*** [AS. *dile*], 1. a plant of the carrot family, with aromatic seeds used to flavor pickles, etc. 2. the seeds of this plant.

**dill pickle,** a cucumber pickle flavored with dill.

**dil·ly·dal·ly** (dil'i-dal'i), ***v.i.*** [-LIED, -LYING], [redupl. form of dally], to waste time in hesitation; loiter or trifle.

**di·lute** (di-lōōt', dī-), ***v.t.*** [-LUTED, -LUTING], [< L. pp. of *diluere* < *dis-,* off + *luere,* to wash], 1. to thin down or weaken by mixing with water or other liquid. 2. to change or weaken (in brilliancy, force, etc.) by mixing with something else. ***adj.*** diluted. —**di·lute'ness,** ***n.***

**di·lu·tion** (di-lōō'shən, dī-), ***n.*** 1. a diluting or being diluted. 2. something diluted.

**di·lu·vi·al** (di-lōō'vi-əl), ***adj.*** [< LL. < L. *diluvium,* a deluge], of or caused by a flood, especially the Deluge: also **di·lu'vi·an.**

**dim** (dim), ***adj.*** [DIMMER, DIMMEST], [AS. *dimm*], 1. not bright; somewhat dark; dull. 2. not clear; indistinct. 3. not clearly seen, heard, or understood; vague. 4. not clearly seeing, hearing, or understanding. ***v.t. & v.i.*** [DIMMED, DIMMING], to make or grow dim. —**take a dim view of,** to view skeptically, etc. —**dim'ly,** ***adv.*** —**dim'ness,** ***n.***

**dim., dimin.,** 1. diminuendo. 2. diminutive.

**dime** (dīm), ***n.*** [< OFr. < L. *decimus,* a tenth < *decem,* ten], a silver coin of the U.S. and Canada equal to ten cents; tenth of a dollar. —**a dime a dozen,** [Colloq.], very common or cheap.

**dime novel,** a cheap, melodramatic novel without literary worth, originally costing a dime.

**di·men·sion** (də-men'shən), ***n.*** [Fr. < L. *dimensio* < *dis-,* off + *metiri,* to measure], 1. any measurable extent, as length, breadth, thickness, etc. 2. *pl.* measurement in length, breadth, and, often, height. 3. extent; size. 4. scope; importance. —**di·men'sion·al,** ***adj.*** —**di·men'sion·al·ly,** ***adv.***

**dime store,** a store where a wide variety of low-priced articles is sold.

**di·min·ish** (də-min'ish), ***v.t.*** [combination of ME. *diminuen* (ult. < L. *deminuere,* to make smaller) & Eng. *minish* (ult. < LL. *minutia,* smallness)], 1. to make smaller; reduce in size, degree, importance, etc. 2. in *music,* to reduce (a minor interval) by a semitone. ***v.i.*** to become smaller; lessen; dwindle. —**di·min'ish·a·ble,** ***adj.*** —**di·min'ish·ing·ly,** ***adv.***

**di·min·u·en·do** (də-min'ū-en'dō), ***adj. & adv.*** [It. < *diminuire,* to diminish], in *music,* with gradually diminishing volume; decrescendo: symbol, **>**. ***n.*** [*pl.* -DOS], 1. a gradual decrease in loudness. 2. a passage played diminuendo.

**dim·i·nu·tion** (dim'ə-nū'shən, -nōō'-), ***n.*** a diminishing or being diminished; lessening; decrease.

**di·min·u·tive** (də-min'yoo-tiv), ***adj.*** 1. very small; tiny. 2. expressing smallness or diminution: as, a *diminutive* suffix. ***n.*** 1. a very small person or thing. 2. a word formed from another by the addition of a suffix expressing smallness and, sometimes, endearment, as *ringlet, sonny, lambkin.* —**di·min'u·tive·ly,** ***adv.*** —**di·min'u·tive·ness,** ***n.***

**dim·i·ty** (dim'ə-ti), ***n.*** [*pl.* -TIES], [< It. < ML. < Gr. *dimitos,* double-threaded < *dis-,* two + *mitos,* a thread], a thin, strong, corded cotton cloth, often figured, used for curtains, dresses, etc.

**dim·mer** (dim'ẽr), ***n.*** 1. a person that dims. 2. a device for dimming an electric light, as in automobile headlights or theater stage lights.

**dim-out** (dim'out'), ***n.*** a dimming or reduction of the night lighting in a city, etc. to make it less easily visible, as to enemy aircraft.

**dim·ple** (dim'p'l), ***n.*** [ME. *dimpul*], 1. a small, natural hollow on the body, as on the cheek or chin. 2. any little hollow, as on water. ***v.t.*** [-PLED, -PLING], to make dimples in. ***v.i.*** to show or form dimples. —**dim'ply,** ***adv.***

**dim·wit** (dim'wit'), ***n.*** [Slang], a stupid person; simpleton. —**dim'wit'ted,** ***adj.***

**din** (din), ***n.*** [AS. *dyne*], a loud, continuous noise; confused clamor or uproar. ***v.t.*** [DINNED, DINNING], 1. to strike with din. 2. to repeat insistently or noisily: as, *din* the idea into his ears. ***v.i.*** to make a din.

**dine** (dīn), ***v.i.*** [DINED, DINING], [< OFr. *disner;* ult. < L. *dis-,* away + *jejunus,* fasting], to eat dinner. ***v.t.*** to give a dinner to; entertain at dinner. —**dine out,** to dine away from home.

**din·er** (dīn'ẽr), ***n.*** 1. a person eating dinner. 2. a railroad car equipped to serve meals. 3. a small restaurant built to look like such a car.

**din·ette** (dī-net'), ***n.*** an alcove or small, partitioned space used as a dining room.

**ding** (diŋ), ***v.i.*** [< ON. *dengja,* to hammer, merged with *din*], 1. to make the sound of a bell; ring. 2. [Colloq.], to speak repetitiously and tiresomely. ***v.t.*** [Colloq.], to impress by repetition. ***n.*** the sound of a bell, or a similar sound.

**ding-dong** (diŋ'dôŋ', -doŋ'), ***n.*** [echoic], 1. the sound of a bell struck repeatedly. 2. any similar sound. ***adj.*** [Colloq.], vigorously contested. ***adv.*** [Colloq.], with a will; vigorously.

**din·ghy** (diŋ'gi), ***n.*** [*pl.* -GHIES], [Hind. *dīngī*], 1. a rowboat, originally one used on the rivers of India. 2. any small boat used as a tender, etc. Also **din'gey** [*pl.* -GEYS], **din'gy** [*pl.* -GIES].

**din·go** (diŋ'gō), ***n.*** [*pl.* -GOES], [native name], the Australian wild dog.

**ding·us** (diŋ'əs), ***n.*** [S.Afr.D. < *ding,* thing], [Slang], any device; contrivance; gadget: humorous substitute for a name forgotten or not known.

**din·gy** (din'ji), ***adj.*** [-GIER, -GIEST], [via dial.; ? < *dung* + *-y*], 1. dirty-colored; not bright or clean; hence, 2. dismal; shabby. —**din'gi·ly,** ***adv.*** —**din'gi·ness,** ***n.***

**dining car,** a railroad car equipped to serve meals to passengers.

**dining room,** a room in which people eat their meals, especially dinner.

**din·key** (diŋ'ki), ***n.*** [*pl.* -KEYS], [see DINKY], [Colloq.], 1. a small locomotive for hauling cars, etc. in a railroad yard. 2. a small trolley car.

**din·ky** (diŋ'ki), ***adj.*** [-KIER, -KIEST], [Scot. & N. Eng. dial. *dink,* trim, neat; + *-y*], [Slang], small; of no consequence. ***n.*** a dinkey.

**din·ner** (din'ẽr), ***n.*** [< OFr. *disner* (Fr. *dîner*), inf. used as n.; see DINE], 1. the chief meal of the day, whether eaten in the evening or about noon. 2. a formal meal honoring some person or event.

**dinner jacket,** a tuxedo jacket.

**din·ner·ware** (din'ẽr-wâr'), ***n.*** plates, cups, saucers, etc., collectively, or a set of these.

**di·no·saur** (dī'nə-sôr'), ***n.*** [< Gr. *deinos,* terrible + *sauros,* lizard], any of a group of extinct reptiles of the Mesozoic Era. —**di'no·sau'ri·an,** ***adj. & n.***

DINOSAUR (Tyrannosaurus; 18 ft. high)

**dint** (dint), ***n.*** [AS. *dynt,* a blow, stroke], 1. force; exertion: as, by *dint* of great effort he got what he wanted. 2. a dent. ***v.t.*** to dent.

**di·oc·e·san** (dī-os'ə-s'n, dī'ə-sē's'n), ***adj.*** of a diocese. ***n.*** the bishop of a diocese.

**di·o·cese** (dī'ə-sēs', -sis), ***n.*** [< OFr. < LL. < L. < Gr. *dioikēsis,* administration < *dioikein,* to keep house < *dia-,* through + *oikos,* a house], the district under a bishop's jurisdiction; bishopric.

**di·oe·cious** (dī-ē'shəs), ***adj.*** [< *di-* + Gr. *oikos,* a house; + *-ous*], in *biology,* having the male reproductive organs in one individual and the female organs in another. —**di·oe'cious·ly,** ***adv.***

**Di·og·e·nes** (dī-oj'ə-nēz'), ***n.*** Greek Cynic philosopher; lived 412?–323 B.C.

**di·oi·cous** (dī-oi'kəs), ***adj.*** dioecious.

**Di·o·ny·sus, Di·o·ny·sos** (dī'ə-nī'səs), ***n.*** the Greek god of vegetation and wine: identified with the Roman god Bacchus. —**Di'o·ny'sian** (-nish'ən, -nis'i-ən), **Di'o·nys'i·ac** (-nis'i-ak), ***adj.***

**di·op·ter** (dī-op'tẽr), ***n.*** [< L. < Gr.; see DIOPTRICS], a unit of measure of the refractive power of a lens, equal to the power of a lens with a focal distance of one meter.

**di·op·trics** (dī-op'triks), ***n.pl.*** [construed as sing.], [< L. < Gr. < *dia-,* through + base of *opsis,* sight], the branch of optics dealing with the refraction of light through lenses. —**di·op'tric, di·op'tri·cal,** ***adj.*** —**di·op'tri·cal·ly,** ***adv.***

**di·o·ra·ma** (dī'ə-ram'ə, -rä'mə), ***n.*** [< Gr. *dia-,* through + *horama,* a sight], 1. a picture painted on transparent curtains and looked at through a small opening. 2. a miniature scene depicting three-dimensional figures in a naturalistic setting.

**di·ox·ide** (dī-ok′sīd), *n.* an oxide containing two atoms of oxygen per molecule: also **di·ox′id** (-sid).

**dip** (dip), *v.t.* [DIPPED or, *occas.*, DIPT, DIPPING], [AS. *dyppan*], 1. to put into liquid for a moment and then immediately take out. 2. to dye in this way. 3. to make (a candle) by putting a wick in melted tallow or wax. 4. to baptize by immersion. 5. to bathe (sheep) in disinfectant. 6. to take out as by scooping up with a container, the hand, etc. 7. to lower and immediately raise again: as, *dip* the flag in salute. *v.i.* 1. to plunge into water, etc. and quickly come out. 2. to sink down suddenly. 3. to seem to sink: as, the sun *dips* into the ocean. 4. to slope down. 5. to lower a container, the hand, etc. into water, etc., especially in order to take something out. 6. to read or study casually or at random (with *into*): as, *dip* into a book. 7. to drop suddenly before rising. *n.* 1. a dipping or being dipped. 2. a plunge into water or other liquid. 3. a liquid into which something is dipped, as for dyeing. 4. whatever is removed by dipping. 5. a candle made by dipping. 6. a downward slope or inclination. 7. the amount of this. 8. a slight hollow. 9. a short downward plunge, as of an airplane. 10. [Colloq.], liquid sauce. 11. [Slang], a pickpocket.

**diph·the·ri·a** (dif-thêr′i-ə, dip-), *n.* [< Fr. < Gr. *diphthera*, leather < *dephein*, to soften hides], an acute infectious disease characterized by high fever and the formation in the air passages of a membrane which interferes with breathing: it is caused by a bacillus. —**diph·the′ri·al,** *adj.*

**diph·the·rit·ic** (dif′thə-rit′ik, dip′-), *adj.* 1. of, characteristic of, or like diphtheria. 2. having diphtheria. Also **diph·ther′ic** (-ther′ik).

**diph·thong** (dif′thôŋ, dip′thoŋ), *n.* [< Fr. < LL. < Gr. < *di-*, two + *phthongos*, sound], a complex sound made by gliding continuously from the position for one vowel to that for another within the same syllable. Example: *ou* (ä + o͞o) in *house; oi* (ô + i) in *coil.* —**diph·thon′gal,** *adj.*

**diph·thong·ize** (dif′thôŋ-īz′, dip′thoŋ-), *v.t.* [-IZED, -IZING], to pronounce as a diphthong. *v.i.* to become a diphthong. —**diph′thong·i·za′tion,** *n.*

**di·plo·ma** (di-plō′mə), *n.* [L. < Gr. *diplōma*, letter folded double < *diploos*, double], 1. a certificate conferring honors, privileges, etc. 2. a certificate issued by a school, college, or university, indicating the completion of a prescribed course of study, or conferring a degree.

**di·plo·ma·cy** (di-plō′mə-si), *n.* [*pl.* -CIES], [< Fr.; see DIPLOMAT], 1. the conducting of relations between nations. 2. skill in doing this. 3. skill in dealing with people; tact.

**dip·lo·mat** (dip′lə-mat′), *n.* [< Fr.; ult. < L.; see DIPLOMA], 1. a representative of a government who conducts relations with another government in the interests of his own country. 2. a tactful person. Also **di·plo·ma·tist** (di-plō′mə-tist).

**dip·lo·mat·ic** (dip′lə-mat′ik), *adj.* 1. of or connected with diplomacy. 2. tactful and adroit in dealing with people. —**dip′lo·mat′i·cal·ly,** *adv.*

**diplomatic corps,** all the foreign envoys in residence at the capital of a nation.

**dip·per** (dip′ẽr), *n.* 1. one whose work is dipping something in liquid. 2. a thing for dipping, as a long-handled cup. 3. [D-], either of two groups of stars in the shape of a dipper: see **Big Dipper, Little Dipper.** 4. in *zoology*, any of several dipping or diving birds, as the grebe.

**dip·so·ma·ni·a** (dip′sə-mā′ni-ə), *n.* [< Gr. *dipsa*, thirst + *mania*, madness], an abnormal and insatiable craving for alcoholic drink. —**dip′so·ma′ni·ac** (-ak), *n.* —**dip′so·ma·ni′a·cal** (-mə-nī′ə-k′l), *adj.*

**dipt** (dipt), occasional pt. and pp. of **dip.**

**dip·ter·ous** (dip′tẽr-əs), *adj.* [Gr. *dipteros* < *di-*, two + *pteron*, a wing], 1. having two wings or two winglike appendages. 2. of the group of insects **(Diptera)**, including the housefly, mosquito, gnat, etc., having one pair of membranous wings.

**dip·tych** (dip′tik), *n.* [< LL. < Gr. < *di-*, twice + *ptyche*, a fold], 1. an ancient writing tablet made up of a hinged pair of wooden or ivory pieces. 2. a picture painted or carved on two hinged tablets.

**dir.,** director.

**dire** (dīr), *adj.* [DIRER, DIREST], [L. *dirus*], dreadful; terrible; horrible; disastrous. —**dire′ly,** *adv.* —**dire′ness,** *n.*

**di·rect** (də-rekt′, dī-), *adj.* [< OFr. < L. *directus*, pp. of *dirigere*, to lay straight < *dis-*, apart + *regere*, to rule], 1. straight; not deviating; not interrupted. 2. straightforward; not vague; frank. 3. immediate. 4. with nothing or no one between: as, *direct* contact. 5. in an unbroken line of descent; lineal. 6. exact; complete: as, the *direct* opposite. 7. by action of the people through popular vote instead of through representatives. *v.t.* 1. to manage the affairs of; guide; conduct. 2. to give authoritative instructions to; order; command. 3. to turn or point (a person or thing) toward a place or goal; aim; head. 4. to tell (a person) the way to a place. 5. to say (words, etc.) to a specific person or persons. 6. to write the address on (a letter, etc.). 7. to plan and supervise the actions and effects of (a play, motion picture, etc.). *v.i.* 1. to give directions. 2. to be a director. *adv.* directly. —**di·rect′ness,** *n.*

**direct current,** an electric current flowing in one direction: abbrev. **D.C., d.c.**

**direct discourse,** quotation of one's exact words.

**di·rec·tion** (də-rek′shən, dī-), *n.* 1. a directing; management; control. 2. the address on a letter or parcel. 3. *usually in pl.* instruction for doing, using, etc. 4. an order; command. 5. the point toward which a person or thing is moving or facing. 6. the line leading to a place: as, in the *direction* of Berlin. 7. a line of development, a way, etc.: as, work in that *direction*.

**di·rec·tion·al** (də-rek′shən-'l, dī-), *adj.* 1. of direction in space. 2. in *radio*, *a*) for telling the direction from which signals are coming. *b*) for sending radio waves on one directed beam.

**direction finder,** a device for finding out the direction from which radio waves or signals come.

**di·rec·tive** (də-rek′tiv, dī-), *adj.* 1. directing. 2. indicating direction. *n.* a general order issued by a central office, military unit, etc.

**di·rect·ly** (də-rekt′li, dī-), *adv.* 1. in a direct way or line; straight. 2. with nothing coming between: as, *directly* responsible. 3. exactly: as, *directly* opposite. 4. instantly; right away. *conj.* [Chiefly Brit.], as soon as.

**direct object,** the word or words denoting the thing or person that receives the action of a transitive verb, as *ball* in *he hit the ball.*

**di·rec·tor** (də-rek′tẽr, dī-), *n.* 1. one who directs, as the production of a play or motion picture. 2. a member of a board chosen to direct the affairs of a corporation or institution. —**di·rec′tor′i·al** (-tôr′i-əl, -tō′ri-), *adj.* —**di·rec′tor·ship′,** *n.* —**di·rec′tress,** *n.fem.*

**di·rec·to·rate** (də-rek′tə-rit, dī-), *n.* 1. the position of director. 2. a board of directors.

**di·rec·to·ry** (də-rek′tə-ri, dī-), *adj.* directing; advising. *n.* [*pl.* -RIES], 1. a book of directions. 2. a book listing the names and addresses of a specific group of persons. 3. a directorate.

**direct primary election,** a preliminary election at which candidates for public office are chosen by direct vote of the people instead of by delegates at a convention: also **primary (election).**

**direct tax,** a tax levied directly on the person by whom it is to be paid, as an income tax.

**dire·ful** (dīr′fəl), *adj.* dreadful; terrible. —**dire′ful·ly,** *adv.* —**dire′ful·ness,** *n.*

**dirge** (dũrj), *n.* [< L. *dirige* (imperative of *dirigere*, to direct), first word of the antiphon in the Latin burial service], 1. a funeral hymn. 2. a song, poem, etc. of grief or mourning; lament.

**dir·i·gi·ble** (dir′i-jə-b'l), *adj.* [< L. *dirigere* (see DIRECT); + *-ible*], that can be steered. *n.* a balloon that can be steered; esp., a long, cigar-shaped, motor-driven balloon with a cabin underneath. —**dir′i·gi·bil′i·ty** (-bil′ə-ti), *n.*

**dirk** (dũrk), *n.* [earlier *dork, durk*], a short, straight dagger. *v.t.* to stab with a dirk.

**dirn·dl** (dũrn′d'l), *n.* [G., dim. of *dirne*, girl], 1. a kind of dress with a full skirt, gathered waist, and closefitting bodice. 2. such a skirt without a bodice: also **dirndl skirt.**

**dirt** (dũrt), *n.* [ME. < *drit* < ON. *dritr*, excrement], 1. any unclean matter, as mud, trash, etc.; filth. 2. earth or garden soil. 3. dirtiness; uncleanness. 4. obscene writing or speaking. 5. malicious talk; gossip. 6. in *mining*, the gravel, soil, etc. from which gold is separated by washing or panning. —**do one dirt,** [Slang], to harm one.

**dirt-cheap** (dũrt′chēp′), *adj. & adv.* [Colloq.], as cheap as dirt; very cheap.

**dirt farmer,** [Colloq.], a farmer who does his own farming: distinguished from *gentleman-farmer*.
**dirt·y** (dũr′ti), *adj.* [-IER, -IEST], 1. soiled or soiling with dirt; unclean. 2. obscene; pornographic: as, *dirty* jokes. 3. contemptible; mean. 4. muddy or clouded: as, a *dirty* green. 5. rough: as, *dirty* weather. *v.t. & v.i.* [-IED, -YING], to make or become dirty; soil. **—dirt′i·ly,** *adv.* **—dirt′i·ness,** *n.*
**Dis** (dis), *n.* in *Rom. mythology*, the god of the lower world: identified with the Greek god Pluto.
**dis-,** [< OFr. or (usually) L.; OFr. *des-* < L. *dis-*; cf. DE-], a prefix denoting, in general, *separation, negation*, or *reversal:* 1. used to form verbs meaning: *a) away, apart*, as in *disperse; b) deprive of, expel from*, as in *disbar; c) cause to be the opposite of*, as in *disable; d) fail, cease, refuse to*, as in *dissatisfy, disappear; e) do the opposite of*, as in *disjoin*. 2. used to form adjectives meaning *not, the opposite of*, as in *dishonest*. 3. used to form nouns meaning *opposite of, lack of*, as in *disease, disunion*.
**dis-,** di- (twice, double).
**dis·a·bil·i·ty** (dis′ə-bil′ə-ti), *n.* [*pl.* -TIES], 1. a disabled condition. 2. that which disables, as illness, etc. 3. a legal disqualification.
**dis·a·ble** (dis-ā′b'l), *v.t.* [-BLED, -BLING], 1. to make unable or unfit; cripple; incapacitate. 2. to disqualify legally. **—dis·a′ble·ment,** *n.*
**dis·a·buse** (dis′ə-būz′), *v.t.* [-BUSED, -BUSING], [*dis-* + *abuse*], to rid of false ideas; undeceive.
**dis·ad·van·tage** (dis′əd-van′tij, -vän′-), *n.* 1. an unfavorable situation or circumstance; drawback; handicap. 2. loss; injury; detriment. *v.t.* [-TAGED, -TAGING], to act to the disadvantage of. **—at a disadvantage,** in an unfavorable situation.
**dis·ad·van·taged** (dis′əd-van′tijd), *adj.* deprived of a decent standard of living, education, etc. by poverty and a lack of opportunity.
**dis·ad·van·ta·geous** (dis-ad′vən-tā′jəs, dis′ad-), *adj.* causing disadvantage; unfavorable. **—dis·ad′van·ta′geous·ly,** *adv.* **—dis·ad′van·ta′geous·ness,** *n.*
**dis·af·fect** (dis′ə-fekt′), *v.t.* to make unfriendly, discontented, or disloyal, as toward the government. **—dis′af·fect′ed,** *adj.* **—dis′af·fec′tion,** *n.*
**dis·a·gree** (dis′ə-grē′), *v.i.* [-GREED, -GREEING], 1. to fail to agree; be different. 2. to differ in opinion. 3. to quarrel or dispute. 4. to be unsuitable or harmful (followed by *with*).
**dis·a·gree·a·ble** (dis′ə-grē′ə-b'l), *adj.* 1. not to one's taste; unpleasant; offensive. 2. hard to get along with; quarrelsome. **—dis′a·gree′a·ble·ness,** *n.* **—dis′a·gree′a·bly,** *adv.*
**dis·a·gree·ment** (dis′ə-grē′mənt), *n.* 1. a disagreeing. 2. difference; incongruity; discrepancy. 3. difference of opinion. 4. a quarrel or dispute.
**dis·al·low** (dis′ə-lou′), *v.t.* to refuse to allow; reject as invalid or illegal. **—dis′al·low′ance,** *n.*
**dis·ap·pear** (dis′ə-pêr′), *v.i.* 1. to cease to be seen; vanish. 2. to cease being; become lost or extinct. **—dis′ap·pear′ance,** *n.*
**dis·ap·point** (dis′ə-point′), *v.t.* 1. to fail to satisfy the hopes or expectations of. 2. to break one's promise to. 3. to prevent or undo the intended result of; balk; thwart.
**dis·ap·point·ed** (dis′ə-poin′tid), *adj.* made unhappy by the failure of one's expectations.
**dis·ap·point·ment** (dis′ə-point′mənt), *n.* 1. a disappointing. 2. the state or feeling of being disappointed. 3. a person or thing causing this.
**dis·ap·pro·ba·tion** (dis′ap-rə-bā′shən, dis-ap′-), *n.* disapproval; unfavorable opinion.
**dis·ap·prov·al** (dis′ə-prōōv′'l), *n.* 1. a disapproving; failure to approve. 2. unfavorable opinion; dislike.
**dis·ap·prove** (dis′ə-prōōv′), *v.t.* [-PROVED, -PROVING], 1. to have or express an unfavorable opinion of; condemn. 2. to refuse to approve; reject. *v.i.* to have or express an unfavorable opinion (*of*). **—dis′ap·prov′ing·ly,** *adv.*
**dis·arm** (dis-ärm′), *v.t.* 1. to take away weapons from. 2. to make harmless. 3. to overcome the hostility of. *v.i.* 1. to lay down arms. 2. to reduce or do away with armed forces and armaments.
**dis·ar·ma·ment** (dis-är′mə-mənt), *n.* 1. a disarming. 2. the reduction of armed forces and armaments, as to a limitation set by treaty.
**dis·arm·ing** (dis-ärm′iŋ), *adj.* removing suspicions, fears, or hostility.
**dis·ar·range** (dis′ə-rānj′), *v.t.* [-RANGED, -RANGING], to put out of order or arrangement; unsettle. **—dis′ar·range′ment,** *n.*
**dis·ar·ray** (dis′ə-rā), *v.t.* to throw into disorder or confusion; upset. *n.* 1. disorder; confusion. 2. disorder or insufficiency of clothing.
**dis·as·sem·ble** (dis′ə-sem′b'l), *v.t.* [-BLED, -BLING], to take apart. **—dis′as·sem′bly,** *n.*
**dis·as·so·ci·ate** (dis′ə-sō′shi-āt′), *v.t.* [-ATED, -ATING], to dissociate.
**dis·as·ter** (di-zas′tēr, -zäs′-), *n.* [< OFr. < It. < L. *dis-* + *astrum* < Gr. *astron*, a star; cf. ILL-STARRED], any happening that causes great harm or damage; sudden misfortune; calamity.
**dis·as·trous** (di-zas′trəs, -zäs′-), *adj.* of the nature of or causing a disaster; calamitous. **—dis·as′trous·ly,** *adv.*
**dis·a·vow** (dis′ə-vou′), *v.t.* to deny any knowledge or approval of, or responsibility for; disclaim; disown. **—dis′a·vow′al,** *n.* **—dis′a·vow′er,** *n.*
**dis·band** (dis-band′), *v.t.* 1. to break up (an association or organization). 2. to dismiss from military service. *v.i.* to cease to exist as an organization. **—dis·band′ment,** *n.*
**dis·bar** (dis-bär′), *v.t.* [-BARRED, -BARRING], to expel (a lawyer) from the bar; deprive of the right to practice law. **—dis·bar′ment,** *n.*
**dis·be·lief** (dis′bi-lēf′), *n.* refusal to believe; absence of belief.
**dis·be·lieve** (dis′bi-lēv′), *v.t.* [-LIEVED, -LIEVING], reject as untrue. *v.i.* to fail to believe (*in*). **—dis′be·liev′er,** *n.*
**dis·bur·den** (dis-būr′d'n), *v.t.* 1. to relieve of a burden or burdensome thing. 2. to get rid of (a burden). *v.i.* to rid oneself of a burden.
**dis·burse** (dis-būrs′), *v.t.* [-BURSED, -BURSING], [< OFr. *desbourser;* see DIS- & BOURSE], to pay out; expend. **—dis·burs′a·ble,** *adj.* **—dis·burse′ment,** *n.* **—dis·burs′er,** *n.*
**disc** (disk), *n.* a disk.
**disc.,** 1. discount. 2. discovered. 3. discoverer.
**dis·card** (dis-kärd′; *for n.*, dis′kärd), *v.t.* [< OFr.; see DIS- & CARD], 1. in *card games, a)* to throw away (undesired cards). *b)* to play (a card not a trump and not in the suit led). 2. to get rid of as no longer valuable or useful. *v.i.* in *card games*, to make a discard. *n.* 1. a discarding or being discarded. 2. something discarded. 3. in *card games*, the card or cards discarded. **—dis·card′er,** *n.*
**dis·cern** (di-zūrn′, -sūrn′), *v.t.* [< OFr. < L. < *dis-*, apart + *cernere*, to separate], 1. to recognize as separate or different. 2. to perceive or recognize; make out clearly. *v.i.* to perceive or recognize the difference. **—dis·cern′er,** *n.* **—dis·cern′i·ble,** *adj.* **—dis·cern′i·bly,** *adv.*
**dis·cern·ing** (di-zūrn′iŋ, -sūrn′-), *adj.* keenly perceptive; shrewd; astute. **—dis·cern′ing·ly,** *adv.*
**dis·cern·ment** (di-zūrn′mənt, -sūrn′-), *n.* 1. a discerning. 2. the power of discerning; keen perception or judgment; insight; acumen.
**dis·charge** (dis-chärj′; *also, for n.*, dis′chärj′), *v.t.* [-CHARGED, -CHARGING], [< OFr. < LL. < L. *dis-*, from + *carrus*, wagon], 1. to relieve of or release from something: as, *discharged* from the army. 2. *a)* to remove the cargo of (a ship). *b)* to unload (a cargo). 3. to fire (a gun) or shoot (a projectile). 4. to dismiss from service, as a servant. 5. to release (a prisoner) from jail, (a defendant) from suspicion, (a bankrupt) from obligations. 6. to throw off; emit: as, the sore *discharges* pus. 7. to pay (a debt) or perform (a duty). 8. in *electricity*, to remove stored energy from (a battery or condenser). 9. in *law*, to set aside, as a court order. *v.i.* 1. to get rid of a burden, load, etc. 2. to be released or thrown off. 3. to go off: said of a gun, etc. 4. to emit waste matter: said of a wound, etc. *n.* 1. a discharging or being discharged. 2. that which discharges, as a legal order for release from military service. 3. a seaman's record of service. 4. that which is discharged, as matter from a sore. 5. a flow of electricity across a gap, as in a spark. **—dis·charge′a·ble,** *adj.* **—dis·charg′er,** *n.*
**dis·ci·ple** (di-sī′p'l), *n.* [< OFr. or AS.; both < L.; orig., prob. < *dis-*, apart + *capere*, to hold], 1. a pupil or follower of any teacher or school. 2. an early follower of Jesus, especially an Apostle. **—dis·ci′ple·ship′,** *n.*
**dis·ci·pli·nar·i·an** (dis′ə-pli-nâr′i-ən), *adj.* disciplinary. *n.* 1. one who enforces discipline. 2. a believer in strict discipline.
**dis·ci·pli·nar·y** (dis′ə-pli-ner′i), *adj.* of or for discipline.
**dis·ci·pline** (dis′ə-plin), *n.* [see DISCIPLE], 1. training that develops self-control, character, or efficiency. 2. the result of such training; orderly conduct. 3. submission to authority and control. 4. a particular system of rules or methods, as for a monastic order. 5. treatment that corrects or punishes. *v.t.* [-PLINED, -PLINING], 1. to subject to discipline; train; control. 2. to punish. **—dis′ci·plin′a·ble,** *adj.* **—dis′ci·plin·er,** *n.*

**dis·claim** (dis-klām'), *v.t.* 1. to give up any claim to or connection with; disown. 2. to refuse to acknowledge; repudiate. **—dis·cla·ma·tion** (dis'-klə-mā'shən), *n.*
**dis·claim·er** (dis-klām'ẽr), *n.* a disclaiming; denial or renunciation, as of a claim or title.
**dis·close** (dis-klōz'), *v.t.* [-CLOSED, -CLOSING], 1. to uncover; bring into the open. 2. to reveal. **—dis-clos'er,** *n.*
**dis·clo·sure** (dis-klō'zhẽr), *n.* 1. a disclosing or being disclosed. 2. a thing disclosed.
**dis·cob·o·lus** (dis-kob'ə-ləs), *n.* [L. < Gr. < *diskos,* discus + *ballein,* to throw], a discus thrower.
**dis·coid** (dis'koid), *adj.* [< LL. < Gr. < *diskos,* a disk + *eidos,* form], shaped like a disk. *n.* anything shaped like a disk. **—dis·coi'dal,** *adj.*
**dis·col·or** (dis-kul'ẽr), *v.t. & v.i.* to change in color; stain; tarnish. **—dis·col'or·a'tion, dis·col'or·ment,** *n.*
**dis·col·our** (dis-kul'ẽr), *v.t. & v.i.* to discolor: Brit. spelling. **—dis·col'our·a'tion, dis·col'our·ment,** *n.*
**dis·com·fit** (dis-kum'fit), *v.t.* [< OFr. < LL. < L. *dis-* + *conficere;* see CONFECT], 1. originally, to defeat; overthrow. 2. to frustrate the plans or expectations of. 3. to embarrass; disconcert.
**dis·com·fi·ture** (dis-kum'fi-chẽr), *n.* 1. a discomfiting or being discomfited. 2. embarrassment.
**dis·com·fort** (dis-kum'fẽrt), *n.* 1. absence of comfort; uneasiness; inconvenience. 2. anything causing this. *v.t.* to cause discomfort to.
**dis·com·mode** (dis'kə-mōd'), *v.t.* [-MODED, -MODING], [< *dis-* + L. *commodare,* to make suitable], to put to trouble; inconvenience; disturb.
**dis·com·pose** (dis'kəm-pōz'), *v.t.* [-POSED, -POSING], 1. to disturb the calm of; ruffle; disconcert. 2. to disorder; disarrange. **—dis'com·pos'ed·ly,** *adv.* **—dis'com·pos'ing·ly,** *adv.*
**dis·com·po·sure** (dis'kəm-pō'zhẽr), *n.* lack of composure; discomfiture; embarrassment.
**dis·con·cert** (dis'kən-sũrt'), *v.t.* 1. to upset or frustrate (plans, etc.). 2. to upset the composure of; confuse. **—dis'con·cert'ed,** *adj.* **—dis'con·cert'ing·ly,** *adv.* **—dis'con·cer'tion,** *n.*
**dis·con·nect** (dis'kə-nekt'), *v.t.* to break or dissolve the connection between; separate; detach. **—dis'-con·nec'tion,** *n.*
**dis·con·nect·ed** (dis'kə-nek'tid), *adj.* 1. separated; detached. 2. broken up into unrelated parts; incoherent. **—dis'con·nect'ed·ly,** *adv.* **—dis'con·nect'-ed·ness,** *n.*
**dis·con·so·late** (dis-kon'sə-lit), *adj.* [< ML. < L.; see DIS- & CONSOLE, *v.*], 1. not to be comforted; inconsolable; hopeless. 2. causing dejection; cheerless. **—dis·con'so·late·ly,** *adv.* **—dis·con'so·late·ness, dis·con'so·la'tion** (-lā'shən), *n.*
**dis·con·tent** (dis'kən-tent'), *adj.* discontented. *n.* lack of contentment; dissatisfaction with one's situation: also **dis'con·tent'ment.** *v.t.* to make discontented.
**dis·con·tent·ed** (dis'kən-ten'tid), *adj.* not contented; dissatisfied; restless. **—dis'con·tent'ed·ly,** *adv.* **—dis'con·tent'ed·ness,** *n.*
**dis·con·tin·ue** (dis'kən-tin'ū), *v.t. & v.i.* [-UED, -UING], to stop; cease; give up; break off; specif., in *law,* to interrupt or terminate (a suit). **—dis'-con·tin'u·ance, dis'con·tin'u·a'tion,** *n.*
**dis·con·tin·u·ous** (dis'kən-tin'ū-əs), *adj.* not continuous; broken; intermittent. **—dis'con·ti·nu'i·ty** (-kon-tə-nōō'ə-ti, -nū'ə-ti), **dis'con·tin'u·ous·ness,** *n.* **—dis'con·tin'u·ous·ly,** *adv.*
**dis·cord** (dis'kôrd), *n.* [< OFr. < L. < *discors,* at variance < *dis-,* apart + *cor, cordis,* heart], 1. lack of concord; disagreement. 2. a harsh or confused noise, as the sound of battle. 3. in *music,* a lack of harmony in tones simultaneously sounded. *v.i.* (dis-kôrd'), to disagree; clash.
**dis·cord·ant** (dis-kôr'd'nt), *adj.* 1. not in accord; disagreeing; incongruous. 2. not in harmony; dissonant; jarring. **—dis·cord'ance, dis·cord'an·cy,** *n.* **—dis·cord'ant·ly,** *adv.*
**dis·co·thèque** (dis'kə-tek), *n.* [Fr. < *disque,* record + *bibliothèque,* library], a café or other public place for dancing to recorded popular music.
**dis·count** (dis'kount; *for v., also* dis-kount'), *n.* [< Fr. < OFr. < LL. < L. *dis-,* apart + *computare;* see COMPUTE], 1. a deduction from an original price or debt. 2. the interest deducted in advance by one who lends money on a bill, promissory note, etc. 3. the rate of interest charged for this: also **discount rate.** 4. a discounting. *v.t.* 1. to deduct; subtract. 2. to pay or receive the value of (a bill, promissory note, etc.), minus a deduction for interest. 3. to deduct from. 4. to take (a story, etc.) at less than face value, allowing for exaggeration, bias, etc. 5. to disbelieve or disregard entirely. 6. to lessen the effect of by anticipating. **—at a discount,** 1. below the regular price. 2. unwanted and easily obtained. 3. with allowance for exaggeration, bias, etc. **—dis'count·a·ble,** *adj.* **—dis'count·er,** *n.*
**dis·coun·te·nance** (dis-koun'tə-nəns), *v.t.* [-NANCED, -NANCING], 1. to put to shame; abash; disconcert. 2. to refuse approval or support to; discourage; frown on.
**dis·cour·age** (dis-kũr'ij), *v.t.* [-AGED, -AGING], [OFr. *descoragier*], 1. to deprive of courage; dishearten. 2. to advise or persuade (a person) to refrain. 3. to prevent or try to prevent by disapproving. **—dis-cour'age·ment,** *n.* **—dis·cour'ag·er,** *n.* **—dis·cour'-ag·ing,** *adj.* **—dis·cour'ag·ing·ly,** *adv.*
**dis·course** (dis'kôrs, -kōrs; *also, and for v. always,* dis-kôrs', -kōrs'), *n.* [< OFr. < LL. < L. pp. < *dis-,* from + *currere,* to run], 1. talk; conversation. 2. communication in general. 3. a formal treatment of a subject, in speech or writing. 4. [Archaic], ability to reason. *v.i.* [-COURSED, -COURSING], 1. to converse; talk. 2. to speak or write (*on* or *upon* a subject) formally. *v.t.* to utter. **—dis-cours'er,** *n.*
**dis·cour·te·ous** (dis-kũr'ti-əs), *adj.* not courteous; impolite; ill-mannered. **—dis·cour'te·ous·ly,** *adv.* **—dis·cour'te·ous·ness,** *n.*
**dis·cour·te·sy** (dis-kũr'tə-si), *n.* 1. lack of courtesy; impoliteness; rudeness. 2. [*pl.* -SIES], a rude or impolite act or remark.
**dis·cov·er** (dis-kuv'ẽr), *v.t.* [< OFr. < LL. *discooperire;* see DIS- & COVER], 1. to be the first to find, see, or learn about. 2. to find out; learn of the existence of. 3. [Archaic], to reveal; disclose. **—dis·cov'er·a·ble,** *adj.* **—dis·cov'er·er,** *n.*
**dis·cov·er·y** (dis-kuv'ẽr-i), *n.* [*pl.* -IES], 1. a discovering. 2. anything discovered.
**Discovery Day,** Columbus Day.
**dis·cred·it** (dis-kred'it), *v.t.* 1. to disbelieve. 2. to cast doubt on. 3. to damage the reputation of; disgrace. *n.* 1. loss of belief or trust; doubt. 2. damage to one's reputation; disgrace. 3. something that causes disgrace. **—dis·cred'it·a·ble,** *adj.* **—dis·cred'it·a·bly,** *adv.*
**dis·creet** (dis-krēt'), *adj.* [< OFr. < L. *descretus,* pp. of *discernere;* see DISCERN], careful about what one says or does; prudent. **—dis·creet'ly,** *adv.* **—dis-creet'ness,** *n.*
**dis·crep·an·cy** (dis-krep'ən-si), *n.* [< OFr. < L. ppr. < *dis-,* from + *crepare,* to rattle], 1. disagreement; contradiction; inconsistency. 2. [*pl.* -CIES], an instance of this. **—dis·crep'ant,** *adj.* **—dis·crep'ant·ly,** *adv.*
**dis·crete** (dis-krēt'), *adj.* [< L.; see DISCREET], 1. separate and distinct. 2. made up of distinct parts. **—dis·crete'ly,** *adv.* **—dis·crete'ness,** *n.*
**dis·cre·tion** (dis-kresh'ən), *n.* 1. the quality of being discrete; separation or distinction. 2. the freedom or power to make decisions and choices. 3. the quality of being discreet; caution; prudence. **—at one's discretion,** in accordance with one's judgment.
**dis·cre·tion·ar·y** (dis-kresh'ə-ner'i), *adj.* left to one's discretion: also **dis·cre'tion·al.**
**dis·crim·i·nate** (dis-krim'ə-nāt'), *v.t.* [-NATED, -NATING], [< L. pp. of *discriminare* < *discrimen,* division; *dis-,* apart + *crimen,* verdict], 1. to constitute a difference between; differentiate. 2. to recognize as being different; distinguish. *v.i.* 1. to see the difference (*between* things); distinguish. 2. to make distinctions in treatment; show partiality or prejudice. *adj.* (-nit), 1. distinct; distinguished. 2. involving discrimination; making distinctions. **—dis·crim'i·nate·ly,** *adv.* **—dis·crim'i·nat.ing,** *adj.* **—dis·crim'i·nat'ing·ly,** *adv.* **—dis·crim'i·na'tor** (-nā'-tẽr), *n.*
**dis·crim·i·na·tion** (dis-krim'ə-nā'shən), *n.* 1. the act of making or perceiving differences and distinctions. 2. the ability to do this. 3. a showing of favoritism in treatment. **—dis·crim'i·na'tive,** *adj.* **—dis·crim'i·na'tive·ly,** *adv.*
**dis·crim·i·na·to·ry** (dis-krim'ə-nə-tôr'i, -tō'ri), *adj.* showing discrimination or bias.
**dis·cur·sive** (dis-kũr'siv), *adj.* [see DISCOURSE], wandering from one topic to another; rambling; digressive. **—dis·cur'sive·ly,** *adv.* **—dis·cur'sive-ness,** *n.*

**dis·cus** (dis′kəs), *n.* [*pl.* -CUSES, -CI (dis′ī)], [L. < Gr. *diskos*], 1. a heavy disk of metal or stone, thrown in a contest of strength and skill. 2. such a contest: often **discus throw.**

DISCUS THROWER

**dis·cuss** (dis-kus′), *v.t.* [< L. *discussus*, pp. < *dis-*, apart + *quatere*, to shake], 1. to talk or write about; consider and argue the pros and cons of. 2. [Colloq.], to eat or drink with enjoyment. **—dis·cuss′er,** *n.*

**dis·cus·sion** (dis-kush′ən), *n.* talk or writing in which the pros and cons of a topic are considered. **—under discussion,** being discussed.

**dis·dain** (dis-dān′), *v.t.* [< OFr. < LL. < L. *dis-*, not + *dignari*, to deign < *dignus*, worthy], to regard as beneath one's dignity or status; treat with scorn. *n.* aloof contempt or scorn. **—dis·dain′ful,** *adj.* **—dis·dain′ful·ly,** *adv.*

**dis·ease** (di-zēz′), *n.* [OFr. *desaise*; see DIS- & EASE], 1. any departure from health; illness in general. 2. a particular destructive process in an organism; specific illness. 3. an evil or destructive tendency or state of affairs. *v.t.* [-EASED, -EASING], to cause disease in; infect; corrupt. **—dis·eased′,** *adj.*

**dis·em·bark** (dis′im-bärk′), *v.t.* to put ashore from a ship; unload. *v.i.* to go ashore from a ship; land. **—dis′em·bar·ka′tion,** *n.*

**dis·em·bar·rass** (dis′im-bar′əs), *v.t.* to rid or relieve of something embarrassing, entangling, perplexing, or burdensome.

**dis·em·bod·y** (dis′im-bod′i), *v.t.* [-BODIED, -BODYING], to free (a spirit, etc.) from bodily existence; make incorporeal. **—dis′em·bod′i·ment,** *n.*

**dis·em·bow·el** (dis′im-bou′əl, -boul′), *v.t.* [-ELED or -ELLED, -ELING or -ELLING], to take out the bowels of; eviscerate. **—dis′em·bow′el·ment,** *n.*

**dis·en·chant** (dis′in-chant′, -chänt′), *v.t.* to set free from an enchantment or illusion. **—dis′en·chant′er,** *n.* **—dis′en·chant′ment,** *n.*

**dis·en·cum·ber** (dis′in-cum′bẽr), *v.t.* to relieve of a burden; free from a hindrance.

**dis·en·fran·chise** (dis′in-fran′chīz), *v.t.* [-CHISED, -CHISING], to disfranchise. **—dis′en·fran′chise·ment** (-chiz-mənt), *n.*

**dis·en·gage** (dis′in-gāj′), *v.t.* [-GAGED, -GAGING], to release or loosen from something that engages, holds, entangles, etc.; detach; extricate. *v.i.* to release oneself; get loose. **—dis′en·gage′ment,** *n.*

**dis·en·tan·gle** (dis′in-taŋ′g′l), *v.t.* [-GLED, -GLING], 1. to free from something that entangles, confuses, etc.; extricate. 2. to straighten out (a tangle, confusion, etc.); untangle. *v.i.* to get free from a tangle. **—dis′en·tan′gle·ment,** *n.*

**dis·es·tab·lish** (dis′ə-stab′lish), *v.t.* 1. to deprive of the status of being established. 2. to deprive (a state church) of official connection with the government. **—dis′es·tab′lish·ment,** *n.*

**dis·es·teem** (dis′ə-stēm′), *v.t.* to hold in low esteem; dislike; slight. *n.* disfavor; dislike.

**dis·fa·vor** (dis-fā′vẽr), *n.* 1. an unfavorable opinion; dislike; disapproval. 2. the state of being disliked or disapproved of. *v.t.* to regard or treat unfavorably; slight.

**dis·fa·vour** (dis-fā′vẽr), *n.* & *v.t.* disfavor: Brit. spelling.

**dis·fig·ure** (dis-fig′yẽr), *v.t.* [-URED, -URING], to hurt the appearance or attractiveness of; deface; mar. **—dis·fig′ure·ment,** *n.* **—dis·fig′ur·er,** *n.*

**dis·fran·chise** (dis-fran′chīz), *v.t.* [-CHISED, -CHISING], 1. to deprive of the rights of citizenship, as of the right to vote. 2. to deprive of a privilege, right, or power. **—dis·fran′chise·ment** (-chiz-mənt), *n.*

**dis·gorge** (dis-gôrj′), *v.t.* & *v.i.* [-GORGED, -GORGING], [< OFr.; see DIS- & GORGE], 1. to vomit. 2. to give up (something wrongfully obtained). 3. to pour forth (its contents); empty (itself).

**dis·grace** (dis-grās′), *n.* [< Fr. < It. < *dis-* (L. *dis-*), not + *grazia*, favor < L. *gratia*; see GRACE], 1. a being in disfavor because of bad conduct, etc. 2. loss of respect; public dishonor; shame. 3. a person or thing that brings shame (*to* one). *v.t.* [-GRACED, -GRACING], to bring shame or dishonor upon; be a discredit to. **—dis·grac′er,** *n.*

**dis·grace·ful** (dis-grās′fəl), *adj.* causing or characterized by disgrace; shameful. **—dis·grace′ful·ly,** *adv.* **—dis·grace′ful·ness,** *n.*

**dis·grun·tle** (dis-grun′t′l), *v.t.* [-TLED, -TLING], [*dis-* + obs. freq. of *grunt*], to make peevishly discontented or disappointed. **—dis·grun′tle·ment,** *n.*

**dis·guise** (dis-gīz′), *v.t.* [-GUISED, -GUISING], [< OFr.; see DIS- & GUISE], 1. to make appear, sound, etc. different from usual so as to be unrecognizable. 2. to hide the real nature of: as, he *disguised* his fear. *n.* 1. any clothes, equipment, manner, etc. used for disguising. 2. the state of being disguised. 3. the act or practice of disguising. **—dis·guis′ed·ly,** *adv.* **—dis·guis′er,** *n.*

**dis·gust** (dis-gust′), *n.* [< MFr. < *des-* (see DIS-) + L. *gustus*, taste], a sickening distaste or dislike; deep aversion; repugnance. *v.t.* to cause to feel disgust; be sickening or repulsive to. **—dis·gust′ed,** *adj.* **—dis·gust′ed·ly,** *adv.*

**dis·gust·ing** (dis-gus′tiŋ), *adj.* sickening; repulsive; very disagreeable. **—dis·gust′ing·ly,** *adv.*

**dish** (dish), *n.* [AS. *disc* < L. *discus*; see DISK], 1. any container, generally shallow and concave, for holding food, as a plate, bowl, cup, etc. 2. a dishful. 3. a particular kind of food: as, one's favorite *dish*. 4. a dish-shaped object or concavity. *v.t.* 1. to serve (food) in a dish (with *up* or *out*). 2. to make concave. *v.i.* to be or become dish-shaped; cave in. **—dish it out,** [Slang], to administer punishment, reprimands, etc.

**dis·ha·bille** (dis′ə-bēl′), *n.* [< Fr. < *dés-* (see DIS-) + *habiller*, to dress], 1. the state of being dressed only partially or in night clothes. 2. clothing worn in this state. Also **deshabille.**

**dis·har·mo·ny** (dis-här′mə-ni), *n.* [*pl.* -NIES], absence of harmony; discord. **—dis′har·mo′ni·ous** (-mō′ni-əs), *adj.*

**dish·cloth** (dish′klôth′, -kloth′), *n.* a cloth for washing dishes; dishrag.

**dis·heart·en** (dis-här′t′n), *v.t.* to discourage; depress. **—dis·heart′en·ing·ly,** *adv.* **—dis·heart′en·ment,** *n.*

**di·shev·el** (di-shev′′l), *v.t.* [-ELED or -ELLED, -ELING or -ELLING], [< OFr. < *des-* (L. *dis-*), apart + *chevel* (< L. *capillus*), hair], 1. to cause (hair, clothing, etc.) to become disarranged and untidy; rumple. 2. to cause the hair or clothes of (a person) to become disarranged. **—di·shev′eled, di·shev′elled,** *adj.* **—di·shev′el·ment,** *n.*

**dish·ful** (dish′fool′), *n.* as much as a dish holds.

**dis·hon·est** (dis-on′ist), *adj.* not honest; not to be trusted. **—dis·hon′est·ly,** *adv.*

**dis·hon·es·ty** (dis-on′is-ti), *n.* 1. the quality of being dishonest. 2. [*pl.* -TIES], a dishonest act.

**dis·hon·or** (dis-on′ẽr), *n.* 1. loss of honor or respect; shame; disgrace. 2. a cause of dishonor; discredit. 3. a refusal or failure to pay a check, draft, etc. *v.t.* 1. to insult or disgrace. 2. to refuse or fail to pay (a check, draft, etc.).

**dis·hon·or·a·ble** (dis-on′ẽr-ə-b′l), *adj.* causing or deserving dishonor; shameful; disgraceful. **—dis·hon′or·a·ble·ness,** *n.* **—dis·hon′or·a·bly,** *adv.*

**dis·hon·our** (dis-on′ẽr), *n.* & *v.t.* dishonor: Brit. spelling.

**dish·pan** (dish′pan′), *n.* a pan in which dishes and cooking utensils are washed.

**dish·rag** (dish′rag′), *n.* a dishcloth.

**dis·il·lu·sion** (dis′i-lōō′zhən), *v.t.* to free from illusion; disenchant. *n.* a disillusioning or being disillusioned: also **disillusionment.**

**dis·in·cli·na·tion** (dis′in-klə-nā′shən, dis-in′-), *n.* a dislike (*for*) or unwillingness (*to*).

**dis·in·cline** (dis′in-klīn′), *v.t.* & *v.i.* to make or be unwilling.

**dis·in·fect** (dis′in-fekt′), *v.t.* to destroy the harmful bacteria, viruses, etc. in; sterilize. **—dis′in·fec′tion,** *n.* **—dis′in·fec′tor,** *n.*

**dis·in·fect·ant** (dis′in-fek′tənt), *adj.* disinfecting. *n.* any substance or device that disinfects.

**dis·in·gen·u·ous** (dis′in-jen′ū-əs), *adj.* not straightforward; not candid; insincere. **—dis′in·gen′u·ous·ly,** *adv.* **—dis′in·gen′u·ous·ness,** *n.*

**dis·in·her·it** (dis′in-her′it), *v.t.* to deprive of an inheritance. **—dis′in·her′i·tance,** *n.*

**dis·in·te·grate** (dis-in′tə-grāt′), *v.t.* & *v.i.* [-GRATED, -GRATING], to separate into parts or fragments; break up. **—dis·in′te·gra·ble** (-grə-b′l), *adj.* **—dis·in′te·gra′tion,** *n.* **—dis·in′te·gra′tor,** *n.*

**dis·in·ter** (dis′in-tũr′), *v.t.* [-TERRED, -TERRING], 1. to remove from a grave, tomb, etc.; dig up; exhume. 2. to bring to light. **—dis′in·ter′ment,** *n.*

**dis·in·ter·est·ed** (dis-in′tẽr-is-tid, -tris-tid), *adj.* 1. not influenced by selfish motives; impartial. 2. [Colloq.], uninterested. **—dis·in′ter·est·ed·ly,** *adv.* **—dis·in′ter·est·ed·ness,** *n.*

**dis·join** (dis-join′), *v.t.* to separate or detach. *v.i.* to become separated.

**dis·joint** (dis-joint′), *v.t.* 1. to put out of joint; dislocate. 2. to dismember. 3. to destroy the unity, connections, or orderliness of. *v.i.* to come apart at the joints. **—dis·joint′ed,** *adj.* **—dis·joint′ed·ly,** *adv.* **—dis·joint′ed·ness,** *n.*

**dis·junc·tion** (dis-juŋk′shən), *n.* a disjoining or being disjoined; separation.
**dis·junc·tive** (dis-juŋk′tiv), *adj.* 1. disjoining; separating or causing to separate. 2. in *grammar*, indicating a contrast or an alternative between ideas, clauses, etc.: as, *either . . . or, but,* and *although* are *disjunctive* conjunctions. 3. in *logic*, presenting alternatives: as, a *disjunctive* proposition. *n.* 1. in *grammar*, a disjunctive conjunction. 2. in *logic*, a disjunctive proposition. —**dis·junc′tive·ly,** *adv.*
**disk** (disk), *n.* [< L. *discus* < Gr. *diskos*, discus, dish, disk], 1. a thin, flat, circular thing of any material. 2. anything like this in shape: as, the moon's *disk*. 3. the disk-shaped center of certain composite flowers. 4. a phonograph record. 5. in *zoology*, a disk-shaped part or structure. 6. [Obs.], a discus. Also sp. **disc,** especially in sense 5. —**disk′like′,** *adj.*
**disk harrow,** a harrow with sharp, revolving disks, used to break up soil for sowing.
**disk jockey,** a person who conducts a radio program of recorded music, interspersed with chatter, jokes, commercials, etc.
**dis·like** (dis-lik′), *v.t.* to have a feeling of not liking; feel aversion to. *n.* a feeling of not liking; distaste; aversion. —**dis·lik′a·ble, dis·like′a·ble,** *adj.*
**dis·lo·cate** (dis′lō-kāt′, dis-lō′kāt), *v.t.* [-CATED, -CATING], 1. to put out of joint; disjoint. 2. to upset the order of; disarrange. —**dis′lo·ca′tion,** *n.*
**dis·lodge** (dis-loj′), *v.t. & v.i.* [-LODGED, -LODGING], to remove or go from a position or place of lodgment; drive out or depart. —**dis·lodg′ment,** *n.*
**dis·loy·al** (dis-loi′əl) *adj.* not loyal or faithful; perfidious. —**dis·loy′al·ly,** *adv.*
**dis·loy·al·ty** (dis-loi′əl-ti), *n.* 1. the quality of being disloyal. 2. [*pl.* -TIES], a disloyal act.
**dis·mal** (diz′m'l), *adj.* [< ME. *dismale*, evil days < OFr. < L. *dies mali*], 1. causing gloom or misery. 2. dark and gloomy; bleak; dreary; miserable. —**dis′mal·ly,** *adv.* —**dis′mal·ness,** *n.*
**dis·man·tle** (dis-man′t'l), *v.t.* [-TLED, -TLING], [< OFr. *desmanteller;* see DIS- & MANTLE], 1. to strip of covering. 2. to strip (a house, ship, etc.) of furniture, equipment, etc. 3. to take apart; raze. —**dis·man′tle·ment,** *n.* —**dis·man′tler,** *n.*
**dis·may** (dis-mā′), *v.t.* [< Anglo-Fr.; ? ult. < L. *ex-*, from + Gmc. base *mag*, power; see MAIN], to make afraid or discouraged at the prospect of trouble; fill with alarm; daunt. *n.* a loss of courage at the prospect of trouble; consternation.
**dis·mem·ber** (dis-mem′bẽr), *v.t.* [< OFr.; see DIS- & MEMBER], 1. to cut the limbs from; to tear limb from limb. 2. to cut or pull to pieces; separate into parts. —**dis·mem′ber·ment,** *n.*
**dis·miss** (dis-mis′), *v.t.* [< LL. < L. *dimissus*, pp. < *di-*, from + *mittere*, to send], 1. to send away; request or allow to go away. 2. to remove or discharge from an office, employment, etc. 3. to put aside mentally. 4. in *law*, to reject (a claim or action). —**dis·miss′al,** *n.* —**dis·miss′i·ble,** *adj.*
**dis·mount** (dis-mount′), *v.i.* to get off, as from a horse or bicycle. *v.t.* 1. to remove (a thing) from its mounting or setting. 2. to cause to get off. 3. to take (a machine) apart.
**dis·o·be·di·ence** (dis′ə-bē′di-əns), *n.* refusal to obey; failure to follow commands; insubordination. —**dis′o·be′di·ent,** *adj.* —**dis′o·be′di·ent·ly,** *adv.*
**dis·o·bey** (dis′ə-bā′), *v.t. & v.i.* to refuse to obey; fail to obey. —**dis′o·bey′er,** *n.*
**dis·o·blige** (dis′ə-blij′), *v.t.* [-BLIGED, -BLIGING], 1. to refuse to oblige, or do a favor for. 2. to slight; offend. 3. to inconvenience. —**dis′o·blig′ing,** *adj.* —**dis′o·blig′ing·ly,** *adv.*
**dis·or·der** (dis-ôr′dẽr), *n.* 1. a lack of order; confusion; jumble. 2. a breach of public peace; riot. 3. a disregard of system; irregularity. 4. an upset of normal function; disease. *v.t.* 1. to throw into disorder; disarrange; muddle. 2. to upset the normal functions or health of.
**dis·or·der·ly** (dis-ôr′dẽr-li), *adj.* 1. not orderly; untidy; unsystematic. 2. unruly; riotous. 3. in *law*, violating public peace, safety, or order. *adv.* in a disorderly manner. —**dis·or′der·li·ness,** *n.*
**dis·or·gan·ize** (dis-ôr′gə-nīz′), *v.t.* [-IZED, -IZING], to break up the order, arrangement, or system of; throw into confusion or disorder. —**dis·or′gan·i·za′tion,** *n.* —**dis·or′gan·i′zer,** *n.*
**dis·o·ri·ent** (dis-ôr′i-ent′, -ō′ri-), *v.t.* to cause to lose one's orientation; confuse: also **dis·o′ri·en·tate′** (-en-tāt′). —**dis·o′ri·en·ta′tion,** *n.*
**dis·own** (dis-ōn′), *v.t.* to refuse to acknowledge as one's own; repudiate; cast off.
**dis·par·age** (dis-par′ij), *v.t.* [-AGED, -AGING], [< OFr. *desparagier*, to marry one of inferior rank < *des-* (see DIS-) + *parage*, rank < *per;* see PEER, *n.*], 1. to lower in esteem; discredit. 2. to speak slightingly of; belittle. —**dis·par′age·ment,** *n.* —**dis·par′ag·er,** *n.* —**dis·par′ag·ing·ly,** *adv.*
**dis·pa·rate** (dis′pə-rit), *adj.* [< L. < *dis-*, apart, not + *parare*, to make equal < *par*, equal], distinct or different in kind; dissimilar. —**dis′pa·rate·ly,** *adv.* —**dis′pa·rate·ness,** *n.*
**dis·par·i·ty** (dis-par′ə-ti), *n.* [*pl.* -TIES], inequality or difference, as in rank, quality, etc.
**dis·pas·sion** (dis-pash′ən), *n.* freedom from passion, from emotion, or from bias.
**dis·pas·sion·ate** (dis-pash′ən-it), *adj.* free from emotion or bias; calm; unprejudiced; impartial. —**dis·pas′sion·ate·ly,** *adv.*
**dis·patch** (dis-pach′), *v.t.* [< Sp. & It.; ult. < L. *dis-* + LL. hyp. *pedicare*, to snare < L. < *pes*, a foot], 1. to send off or out on a specific errand or official business. 2. to kill. 3. to finish quickly or promptly. *n.* 1. a sending off or out. 2. a killing. 3. speed; haste; promptness. 4. a message; esp., an official message. 5. a news story sent to a paper, as by a syndicate or special reporter.
**dis·patch·er** (dis-pach′ẽr), *n.* one who dispatches; esp., one who sends out trains, buses, trucks, etc. according to schedule.
**dis·pel** (dis-pel′), *v.t.* [-PELLED, -PELLING], [< L. < *dis-*, away + *peller*, to drive], to scatter and drive away; disperse. —**dis·pel′ler,** *n.*
**dis·pen·sa·ble** (dis-pen′sə-b'l), *adj.* 1. that can be dispensed or dealt out. 2. that can be dispensed with; not needed. —**dis·pen′sa·bil′i·ty,** *n.* —**dis·pen′sa·ble·ness,** *n.*
**dis·pen·sa·ry** (dis-pen′sə-ri), *n.* [*pl.* -RIES], 1. a room, as in a hospital, where medicines are made up and given out. 2. a place where medical treatment is given free or for a small fee.
**dis·pen·sa·tion** (dis′pən-sā′shən, -pen-), *n.* 1. a dispensing; distribution. 2. anything distributed. 3. an administrative system; management. 4. a release from an obligation; special exemption. 5. in the *R.C. Church*, an official release from the provisions of a specific church law. 6. in *theology*, *a*) the ordering of events under divine authority. *b*) any religious system: as, the Moslem *dispensation*. —**dis′pen·sa′tion·al,** *adj.* —**dis′pen·sa′tor,** *n.*
**dis·pen·sa·to·ry** (dis-pen′sə-tôr′i, -tō′ri), *n.* [*pl.* -RIES], 1. a handbook on the preparation and use of medicines. 2. [Archaic], a dispensary. *adj.* granting privilege by dispensation.
**dis·pense** (dis-pens′), *v.t.* [-PENSED, -PENSING], [< OFr. < L. < *dis-*, out + *pendere*, to weigh], 1. to give out; deal out; distribute. 2. to prepare and give out (medicines, prescriptions, etc.). 3. to administer: as, he *dispensed* the law justly. 4. to exempt; excuse. —**dispense with,** 1. to get rid of. 2. to do without. —**dis·pens′er,** *n.*
**dis·perse** (dis-pũrs′), *v.t.* [-PERSED, -PERSING], [< Fr. < L. *dispersus*, pp. < *dis-*, out + *spargere*, to strew], 1. to break up and scatter in all directions; distribute widely. 2. to dispel (mist, etc.). 3. to break up (light) into its component colored rays. *v.i.* to move in different directions; scatter. —**dis·pers′ed·ly,** *adv.* —**dis·pers′er,** *n.* —**dis·pers′i·ble,** *adj.* —**dis·per′sive** (-pũr′siv), *adj.*
**dis·per·sion** (dis-pũr′shən, -zhən), *n.* 1. a dispersing or being dispersed. 2. the breaking up of light into its component colored rays, as by a prism.
**dis·pir·it** (di-spir′it), *v.t.* to depress; dishearten. —**dis·pir′it·ed,** *adj.* —**dis·pir′it·ed·ly,** *adv.*
**dis·place** (dis-plās′), *v.t.* [-PLACED, -PLACING], 1. to move from its customary place. 2. to remove from office; discharge. 3. to replace.
**dis·placed person** (dis-plāst′), a person left homeless in a foreign country by war.
**dis·place·ment** (dis-plās′mənt), *n.* 1. a displacing or being displaced. 2. the weight or volume of air, water, or other fluid displaced by a floating object, as a balloon or a ship.
**dis·play** (dis-plā′), *v.t.* [< OFr. < L. *dis-*, apart + *plicare*, to fold], 1. to unfold; spread out. 2. to show off; exhibit to advantage. 3. to disclose; reveal. *n.* 1. a displaying; exhibition. 2. anything displayed; exhibit. 3. ostentation; show. 4. in *printing*, the variation of type faces to attract attention. —**dis·play′er,** *n.*

**dis·please** (dis-plēz′), *v.t. & v.i.* [-PLEASED, -PLEASING], to fail to please; annoy; offend.

**dis·pleas·ure** (dis-plezh′ẽr), *n.* 1. the fact or feeling of being displeased; dissatisfaction. 2. [Archaic], trouble. 3. [Archaic], an injury.

**dis·port** (dis-pôrt′, -pōrt′), *v.i.* [< OFr. < *des-* (see DIS-) + *porter* < L. *portare*, to carry], to play; frolic. *v.t.* to amuse or divert (oneself).

**dis·pos·a·ble** (dis-pō′zə-b'l), *adj.* 1. that can be disposed of. 2. that can be disposed; not put to any particular use; subject to disposal.

**dis·pos·al** (dis-pō′z'l), *n.* 1. a disposing; arrangement in a particular order. 2. a dealing with matters; settling of affairs. 3. a giving away; transfer. 4. a getting rid of. 5. the power to dispose of. 6. a disposer (sense 2). —**at one's disposal,** available for use or service as one wishes.

**dis·pose** (dis-pōz′), *v.t.* [-POSED, -POSING], [< OFr.; see DIS- & POSE], 1. to place in a certain order; arrange. 2. to arrange (matters); settle (affairs). 3. to make use of. 4. to incline mentally. 5. to make susceptible or liable. *v.i.* to have the power of disposing. —**dispose of,** 1. to deal with; settle. 2. to give away or sell. 3. to get rid of; do away with.

**dis·pos·er** (dis-pō′zẽr), *n.* 1. one that disposes. 2. a device installed in the drain of a kitchen sink to grind up garbage.

**dis·po·si·tion** (dis′pə-zish′ən), *n.* 1. proper or orderly arrangement. 2. management of affairs. 3. a giving away (*of* something). 4. the power to dispose. 5. an inclination or tendency. 6. one's nature or temperament.

**dis·pos·sess** (dis′pə-zes′), *v.t.* to deprive of the possession of land, a house, etc.; oust. —**dis′pos·ses′sion,** *n.* —**dis′pos·ses′sor,** *n.*

**dis·praise** (dis-prāz′), *v.t.* [-PRAISED, -PRAISING], to speak of with disapproval; blame; disparage. *n.* a dispraising; reproach.

**dis·proof** (dis-proōf′), *n.* 1. a disproving; refutation. 2. evidence that disproves.

**dis·pro·por·tion** (dis′prə-pôr′shən, -pōr′-), *n.* a lack of proportion; lack of symmetry. *v.t.* to cause to be disproportionate. —**dis′pro·por′tion·al,** *adj.* —**dis′pro·por′tion·al·ly,** *adv.*

**dis·pro·por·tion·ate** (dis′prə-pôr′shən-it, -pōr′-), *adj.* not proportionate; not in proportion. —**dis′pro·por′tion·ate·ly,** *adv.*

**dis·prove** (dis-proōv′), *v.t.* [-PROVED, -PROVING], to prove to be false or in error; refute. —**dis·prov′a·ble,** *adj.* —**dis·prov′al,** *n.*

**dis·pu·ta·ble** (dis-pū′tə-b'l, dis′pyoo-), *adj.* that can be disputed; debatable. —**dis·pu′ta·bil′i·ty,** *n.* —**dis·pu′ta·bly,** *adv.*

**dis·pu·tant** (dis′pyoo-tənt, dis-pū′t'nt), *adj.* disputing. *n.* one who disputes, or debates.

**dis·pu·ta·tion** (dis′pyoo-tā′shən), *n.* 1. a disputing; dispute. 2. controversial discussion; debate.

**dis·pu·ta·tious** (dis′pyoo-tā′shəs), *adj.* inclined to dispute; fond of arguing: also **dis·pu·ta·tive** (dis-pū′tə-tiv). —**dis′pu·ta′tious·ly,** *adv.* —**dis′pu·ta′tious·ness,** *n.*

**dis·pute** (dis-pūt′), *v.i.* [-PUTED, -PUTING], [< OFr. < L. < *dis-*, apart + *putare*, to think], 1. to argue; debate. 2. to quarrel. *v.t.* 1. to argue or debate (a question). 2. to question the truth of; doubt. 3. to oppose in any way; resist. 4. to try to win (a game, prize, etc.). *n.* 1. a disputing; argument; debate. 2. a quarrel. —**beyond dispute,** 1. not open to dispute; settled. 2. indisputably. —**in dispute,** not settled. —**dis·put′er,** *n.*

**dis·qual·i·fi·ca·tion** (dis-kwôl′ə-fi-kā′shən, dis′-kwäl-), *n.* 1. a disqualifying or being disqualified. 2. anything that disqualifies.

**dis·qual·i·fy** (dis-kwôl′ə-fī′, -kwäl′-), *v.t.* [-FIED, -FYING], 1. to make unfit or unqualified; disable. 2. to make or declare ineligible, as to participate further in a sport, for breaking rules.

**dis·qui·et** (dis-kwī′ət), *v.t.* to make anxious or restless; disturb. *n.* restlessness; anxiety.

**dis·qui·e·tude** (dis-kwī′ə-toōd′, -tūd′), *n.* restlessness; uneasiness; anxiety.

**dis·qui·si·tion** (dis′kwə-zish′ən), *n.* [L. *disquisitio;* ult. < *dis-*, apart + *quaerere*, to seek], a formal discussion of some subject; a treatise.

**Dis·rae·li, Benjamin** (diz-rā′li), Earl of Beaconsfield, 1804–1881; English prime minister.

**dis·re·gard** (dis′ri-gärd′), *v.t.* 1. to pay little or no attention to. 2. to treat without due respect; slight. *n.* 1. lack of attention. 2. lack of due regard or respect. —**dis′re·gard′ful,** *adj.*

**dis·re·mem·ber** (dis′ri-mem′bẽr), *v.t.* [Dial. & Colloq.], to forget; be unable to remember.

**dis·re·pair** (dis′ri-pâr′), *n.* the condition of needing repairs; state of neglect; dilapidation.

**dis·rep·u·ta·ble** (dis-rep′yoo-tə-b'l), *adj.* 1. not reputable; discreditable. 2. not respectable. —**dis·rep′u·ta·bil′i·ty, dis·rep′u·ta·ble·ness,** *n.* —**dis·rep′u·ta·bly,** *adv.*

**dis·re·pute** (dis′ri-pūt′), *n.* lack or loss of repute; bad reputation; disgrace; disfavor.

**dis·re·spect** (dis′ri-spekt′), *n.* lack of respect; discourtesy; rudeness. *v.t.* to have or show lack of respect for. —**dis′re·spect′ful,** *adj.* —**dis′re·spect′ful·ly,** *adv.* —**dis′re·spect′ful·ness,** *n.*

**dis·robe** (dis-rōb′), *v.t. & v.i.* [-ROBED, -ROBING], to undress; strip. —**dis·robe′ment,** *n.* —**dis·rob′er,** *n.*

**dis·rupt** (dis-rupt′), *v.t. & v.i.* [< L. *disruptus*, pp. < *dis-*, apart + *rumpere*, to break], to break apart; split up; rend asunder. *adj.* disrupted. —**dis·rupt′er, dis·rup′tor** (-rup′tẽr), *n.* —**dis·rup′tion,** *n.* —**dis·rup′tive** (-tiv), *adj.*

**dis·sat·is·fac·tion** (dis′sat-is-fak′shən), *n.* the condition of being dissatisfied; discontent.

**dis·sat·is·fac·to·ry** (dis′sat-is-fak′tə-ri), *adj.* not satisfying; unsatisfactory.

**dis·sat·is·fy** (dis-sat′is-fī′), *v.t.* [-FIED, -FYING], to fail to satisfy; make discontented.

**dis·sect** (di-sekt′), *v.t.* [< L. *dissectus*, pp. < *dis-*, apart + *secare*, to cut], 1. to cut apart piece by piece; separate into parts, as a body for purposes of study. 2. to examine or analyze closely. —**dis·sec′tion,** *n.* —**dis·sec′tor** (-sek′tẽr), *n.*

**dis·sect·ed** (di-sek′tid), *adj.* 1. cut up into parts. 2. in *botany*, consisting of many lobes or segments, as some leaves. 3. in *physical geography*, cut up by valleys and ravines.

**dis·sem·ble** (di-sem′b'l), *v.t.* [-BLED, -BLING], [earlier *dissimule* < OFr. < L. *dissimulare;* re-formed after *resemble*], 1. to conceal, as one's true feelings, under a false appearance. 2. to resemble falsely; simulate. 3. to pretend not to observe; feign ignorance of. *v.i.* to conceal one's true feelings, motives, etc. by pretense; behave hypocritically. —**dis·sem′blance** (-bləns), *n.* —**dis·sem′bler,** *n.*

**dis·sem·i·nate** (di-sem′ə-nāt′), *v.t.* [-NATED, -NATING], [< L. < *dis-*, apart + *seminare*, to sow < *semen*, seed], to scatter far and wide; spread widely. —**dis·sem′i·na′tion,** *n.* —**dis·sem′i·na′tive** (-nā′tiv), *adj.* —**dis·sem′i·na′tor** (-nā′tẽr), *n.*

**dis·sen·sion** (di-sen′shən), *n.* 1. a dissenting in opinion; disagreement. 2. strife; quarreling.

**dis·sent** (di-sent′), *v.i.* [< L. < *dis-*, apart + *sentire*, to feel], 1. to disagree; think differently. 2. to refuse to accept the doctrines and forms of an established church. *n.* a dissenting; difference of opinion. —**dis·sent′er,** *n.*

**dis·sen·tient** (di-sen′shənt), *adj.* dissenting, especially from the majority opinion. *n.* a person who dissents; dissenter.

**dis·ser·ta·tion** (dis′ẽr-tā′shən), *n.* [< L. < *dissertare*, to discuss < *dis-*, apart + *serere*, to join], a formal and lengthy discussion in speech or writing; a discourse or treatise; a thesis.

**dis·serv·ice** (dis-sũr′vis), *n.* harm; injury.

**dis·sev·er** (di-sev′ẽr), *v.t.* 1. to sever; cut apart. 2. to divide into parts. *v.i.* to separate or part; disunite. —**dis·sev′er·ance,** *n.*

**dis·si·dence** (dis′ə-dəns), *n.* [< L. < *dissidens*, ppr. < *dis-*, apart + *sidere*, to sit], disagreement; dissent. —**dis′si·dent** (-dənt), *adj. & n.*

**dis·sim·i·lar** (di-sim′ə-lẽr, dis-sim′-), *adj.* not similar; not alike; different. —**dis·sim′i·lar′i·ty** (-lar′ə-ti), *n.* —**dis·sim′i·lar·ly,** *adv.*

**dis·sim·i·la·tion** (di-sim′ə-lā′shən, dis′sim-), *n.* 1. a making or becoming dissimilar. 2. in *linguistics*, the replacement or disappearance of a sound (usually *l*, *r*, or *n*) when it recurs within the same word. Example: Eng. mar*b*le < OFr. mar*b*re.

**dis·si·mil·i·tude** (dis′si-mil′ə-toōd′, -tūd′), *n.* dissimilarity; difference.

**dis·sim·u·late** (di-sim′yoo-lāt′), *v.t. & v.i.* [-LATED, -LATING], [< L.; see DIS- & SIMULATE], to hide (one's feelings, etc.) by pretense; dissemble. —**dis·sim′u·la′tion,** *n.* —**dis·sim′u·la′tor** (-lā′tẽr), *n.*

**dis·si·pate** (dis′ə-pāt′), *v.t.* [-PATED, -PATING], [< L. < *dis-*, apart + *sipare*, to throw], 1. to scatter; disperse. 2. to drive completely away; make disappear. 3. to waste; squander. *v.i.* 1. to be dispelled; vanish. 2. to indulge in pleasure to the point of harming oneself; be dissolute. —**dis′si·pat′er, dis′si·pa′tor** (-pā′tẽr), *n.*

**dis·si·pat·ed** (dis′ə-pāt′id), *adj.* 1. scattered. 2. squandered; wasted. 3. indulging in pleasure to excess; dissolute. 4. showing the harmful effects of dissipation.

**dis·si·pa·tion** (dis′ə-pā′shən), *n.* 1. a scattering or being scattered. 2. a squandering. 3. wasteful or frivolous diversion. 4. wasteful or excessive indulgence in pleasure; intemperance.

**dis·so·ci·ate** (di-sō′shi-āt′), *v.t.* [-ATED, -ATING], [< L. < *dis-*, apart + *sociare*, to join < *socius*, companion], 1. to break the ties between; sever association with; disunite. 2. in *chemistry*, to cause to undergo dissociation. *v.i.* 1. to stop associating. 2. in *chemistry*, to undergo dissociation. —**dissociate oneself from,** to deny or repudiate any connection with.

**dis·so·ci·a·tion** (di-sō′si-ā′shən, -shi-ā′-), *n.* 1. a dissociating or being dissociated. 2. in *chemistry*, the breaking up of a compound into simpler components. —**dis·so′ci·a′tive** (-shi-ā′tiv), *adj.*

**dis·sol·u·ble** (dis-sol′yoo-b'l), *adj.* that can be dissolved. —**dis·sol′u·bil′i·ty, dis·sol′u·ble·ness,** *n.*

**dis·so·lute** (dis′ə-lo͞ot′), *adj.* [< L. pp. of *dissolvere;* see DISSOLVE], dissipated and immoral; debauched. —**dis′so·lute′ly,** *adv.* —**dis′so·lute′ness,** *n.*

**dis·so·lu·tion** (dis′ə-lo͞o′shən), *n.* 1. a dissolving or being dissolved. 2. a breaking up or into parts; disintegration. 3. an ending; termination. 4. death. 5. the adjournment of a formal meeting. 6. the liquidation of a business. 7. in *law*, the annulment of a contract.

**dis·solve** (di-zolv′), *v.t. & v.i.* [-SOLVED, -SOLVING], [< L. < *dis-*, apart + *solvere*, to loosen], 1. to make or become liquid; melt. 2. to merge with a liquid; pass or make pass into solution. 3. to break up; decompose. 4. to end as by breaking up; terminate. 5. to disappear or make disappear. 6. in *motion pictures & television*, to fade or make fade into or out of view. *n.* a fade-in or fade-out. —**dissolved in tears,** weeping. —**dis·solv′a·ble,** *adj.* —**dis·solv′er,** *n.*

**dis·so·nance** (dis′ə-nəns), *n.* [Fr. < LL. < L. ppr. < *dis-*, apart + *sonare*, to sound], 1. an inharmonious combination of sounds; discord. 2. any lack of harmony or agreement; incongruity. 3. in *music*, a chord that sounds harsh and incomplete. Also **dis′so·nan·cy** [*pl.* -CIES].

**dis·so·nant** (dis′ə-nənt), *adj.* 1. characterized by or constituting a dissonance. 2. disagreeing or clashing; incongruous. —**dis′so·nant·ly,** *adv.*

**dis·suade** (di-swād′), *v.t.* [-SUADED, -SUADING], [< L. < *dis-*, away + *suadere*, to persuade], to turn (a person) aside (*from* a course, etc.) by persuasion or advice. —**dis·suad′er,** *n.* —**dis·sua′sion,** *n.* —**dis·sua′sive,** *adj.*

**dis·syl·la·ble** (di-sil′ə-b'l, dis′sil′-), *n.* [< Fr. < L. < Gr. < *di-*, two + *syllabē*, syllable], a word of two syllables, as *receive*: also **disyllable.** —**dis·syl·lab·ic** (dis′si-lab′ik, dis′i-), *adj.*

**dist.,** 1. distance. 2. distinguish. 3. district.

**dis·taff** (dis′taf, -täf), *n.* [< AS. < *dis-*, flax + *stæf*, a staff], 1. a staff on which flax, wool, etc. is wound for use in spinning. 2. a woman's work or concerns. 3. woman or women in general.

DISTAFF AND SPINDLE

**distaff side,** the maternal side of a family.

**dis·tal** (dis′t'l), *adj.* [*distant* + *-al*], in *anatomy*, farthest from the center or the point of attachment or origin. —**dis′tal·ly,** *adv.*

**dis·tance** (dis′təns), *n.* [< OFr. < L. < *distans*, ppr. < *dis-*, apart + *stare*, to stand], 1. the fact or condition of being separated in space or time; remoteness. 2. a space between two points. 3. an interval between two points in time. 4. the measure of a space or interval. 5. a remoteness in behavior; reserve. 6. a faraway place. 7. in *music*, an interval between two tones. *v.t.* [-TANCED, -TANCING], to do better or more than; outdistance; leave behind; excel. —**keep at a distance,** to treat aloofly.

**dis·tant** (dis′tənt), *adj.* 1. having a space between; separated. 2. widely separated; far apart in space or time. 3. away: as, ten miles *distant*. 4. far apart in relationship; remote: as, a *distant* cousin. 5. cool in manner; reserved. 6. from or at a distance. —**dis′tant·ly,** *adv.*

**dis·taste** (dis-tāst′), *n.* dislike; aversion.

**dis·taste·ful** (dis-tāst′fəl), *adj.* causing distaste; unpleasant; disagreeable. —**dis·taste′ful·ly,** *adv.* —**dis·taste′ful·ness,** *n.*

**dis·tem·per** (dis-tem′pẽr), *v.t.* [< OFr. < ML. *distemperare*, to mix up < L. *dis-*, apart + *temperare*, to mix in proportion], 1. to disturb; ruffle. 2. to upset the functions of; derange; disorder. *n.* 1. a mental or physical derangement or disorder; disease. 2. an infectious virus disease of young dogs. 3. civil disorder or turmoil.

**dis·tem·per** (dis-tem′pẽr), *v.t.* [< OFr. < ML. < L. *dis-*, intens. + *temperare*, to mix in proportion], 1. to mix (colors or pigments) with water and egg yolks. 2. to paint with such a mixture. *n.* 1. a method of painting using distempered pigment. 2. distempered paint. 3. painting done in or with distemper.

**dis·tend** (di-stend′), *v.t. & v.i.* [< L. < *dis-*, apart + *tendere*, to stretch], 1. to stretch out. 2. to expand; make or become swollen. —**dis·ten′si·ble,** *adj.* —**dis·ten′tion, dis·ten′sion,** *n.*

**dis·tich** (dis′tik), *n.* [< L. < Gr. < *di-*, two + *stichos*, a row], two successive lines of verse regarded as a unit; couplet.

**dis·till, dis·til** (di-stil′), *v.i.* [-TILLED, -TILLING], [< OFr. < L. < *de-*, down + *stillare*, to drop < *stilla*, a drop], 1. to fall in drops; drip. 2. to undergo distillation. *v.t.* 1. to let fall in drops. 2. to subject to distillation. 3. to purify by or as by distillation. —**dis·till′a·ble,** *adj.*

**dis·til·late** (dis′t'l-it, -āt′), *n.* a product of distillation; liquid obtained by distilling.

**dis·til·la·tion** (dis′t'l-ā′shən), *n.* 1. a distilling. 2. the process of heating a mixture to separate the more volatile from the less volatile parts, and condensing the resulting vapor to produce a more nearly pure substance. 3. a distillate. 4. the essence of anything. Also **dis·till′ment, dis·til′ment.**

**dis·till·er** (di-stil′ẽr), *n.* 1. a person or apparatus that distills. 2. a person, company, etc. in the business of distilling alcoholic liquors.

**dis·till·er·y** (di-stil′ẽr-i), *n.* [*pl.* -IES], a place where distilling is carried on.

**dis·tinct** (di-stiŋkt′), *adj.* [OFr. < L. pp. of *distinguere;* see DISTINGUISH], 1. not alike; different. 2. separate; individual. 3. clearly marked off; plain. 4. well-defined; unmistakable. —**dis·tinct′ly,** *adv.* —**dis·tinct′ness,** *n.*

**dis·tinc·tion** (di-stiŋk′shən), *n.* 1. the act of making or keeping distinct. 2. a particular quality or feature that differentiates. 3. fame; eminence: as, a singer of *distinction*. 4. the quality that makes one seem superior: as, he fought with *distinction*. 5. a mark or sign of honor.

**dis·tinc·tive** (di-stiŋk′tiv), *adj.* distinguishing from others; characteristic. —**dis·tinc′tive·ly,** *adv.* —**dis·tinc′tive·ness,** *n.*

**dis·tin·gué** (dis′taŋ-gā′, di-staŋ′gā), *adj.* [*fem.* -GUÉE (-gā′, -gā)], distinguished; having an air of distinction.

**dis·tin·guish** (di-stiŋ′gwish), *v.t.* [< L. *distinguere* + Eng. *-ish;* L. < *dis-*, apart + *stinguere*, orig., to prick], 1. to perceive or show the difference in; differentiate. 2. to characterize. 3. to recognize plainly by any of the senses. 4. to separate and classify. 5. to make famous or eminent. *v.i.* to make a distinction (*between* or *among*). —**dis·tin′guish·a·ble,** *adj.* —**dis·tin′guish·a·bly,** *adv.*

**dis·tin·guished** (di-stiŋ′gwisht), *adj.* 1. celebrated; famous. 2. having an air of distinction.

**dis·tort** (di-stôrt′), *v.t.* [< L. *distortus*, pp. < *dis-*, intens. + *torquere*, to twist], 1. to twist out of usual shape. 2. to misrepresent; pervert (facts, etc.). —**dis·tort′ed,** *adj.* —**dis·tort′ed·ly,** *adv.* —**dis·tort′ed·ness,** *n.* —**dis·tort′er,** *n.* —**dis·tor′tion,** *n.* —**dis·tor′tion·al,** *adj.*

**dis·tract** (di-strakt′), *v.t.* [< L. *distractus*, pp. < *dis-*, apart + *trahere*, to draw], 1. to draw (the mind, etc.) away in another direction; divert. 2. harass; confuse. 3. to derange; craze. —**dis·tract′ed,** *adj.* —**dis·tract′ed·ly,** *adv.* —**dis·tract′er,** *n.* —**dis·tract′i·ble,** *adj.* —**dis·tract′ing,** *adj.* —**dis·tract′ing·ly,** *adv.* —**dis·trac′tive** (-trak′tiv), *adj.* —**dis·trac′tive·ly,** *adv.*

**dis·trac·tion** (di-strak′shən), *n.* 1. a distracting or being distracted; confusion. 2. anything that distracts. 3. anything that gives freedom from worry, grief, etc.; diversion. 4. great mental agitation; madness.

**dis·train** (di-strān′), *v.t. & v.i.* [< OFr. < LL. < L. < *dis-*, apart + *stringere*, to stretch], in *law*, to seize and hold (property) as security or indemnity for a debt. —**dis·train′a·ble,** *adj.* —**dis·train′or** (-ẽr), **dis·train′er,** *n.* —**dis·traint′,** *n.*

**dis·trait** (di-strā′), *adj.* [Fr. < L.; see DISTRACT], absent-minded; inattentive.

**dis·traught** (di-strôt′), *adj.* [prob. var. of *distrait* or of *distract*, used as adj.], 1. distracted; harassed. 2. driven mad; crazed.

**dis·tress** (di-stres′), *v.t.* [< OFr. < L. pp. of *distringere*; see DISTRAIN], to cause sorrow, misery, or suffering to; pain; afflict. *n.* 1. the state of being distressed; pain; anxiety; grief. 2. anything that distresses; affliction. 3. a state of danger or trouble. 4. in *law*, *a*) distraint. *b*) the property distrained. **—dis·tress′ful,** *adj.* **—dis·tress′ful·ly,** *adv.* **—dis·tress′ing,** *adj.* **—dis·tress′ing·ly,** *adv.*

**dis·trib·ute** (di-strib′yoot), *v.t.* [-UTED, -UTING], [< L. *distributus*, pp. < *dis-*, apart + *tribuere*, to allot], 1. to divide and deal out in shares; allot. 2. to scatter or spread out, as over a surface. 3. to classify. 4. to put (things) in various distinct places. **—dis·trib′ut·a·ble,** *adj.*

**dis·tri·bu·tion** (dis′trə-bū′shən), *n.* 1. a distributing or being distributed. 2. the manner of being distributed. 3. anything distributed; share. 4. the system of distributing commodities to consumers. **—dis′tri·bu′tion·al,** *adj.*

**dis·trib·u·tive** (di-strib′yoo-tiv), *adj.* 1. distributing or tending to distribute. 2. relating to distribution. 3. referring to each member of a group regarded individually. *n.* a distributive word or expression, as *any* or *each*. **—dis·trib′u·tive·ly,** *adv.* **—dis·trib′u·tive·ness,** *n.*

**dis·trib·u·tor** (di-strib′yoo-tẽr), *n.* 1. a person or thing that distributes: also **distributer.** 2. an agent or business firm that distributes goods to consumers. 3. a device for distributing electric current to the spark plugs of a gasoline engine.

**dis·trict** (dis′trikt), *n.* [Fr. < ML. < L. pp. of *distringere;* see DISTRAIN], 1. a geographical or political division made for a specific purpose: as, a school *district*. 2. any region; part of a country, city, etc. *v.t.* to divide into districts.

**district attorney,** a lawyer elected or appointed in a specified district to serve as a prosecutor in criminal cases on behalf of the state.

**District of Columbia,** a federal district of the U.S., on the Potomac River: pop., 764,000: occupied by the city of Washington: abbrev. **D.C.**

**dis·trust** (dis-trust′), *n.* a lack of trust or of confidence; doubt; suspicion. *v.t.* to have no trust or confidence in; doubt; suspect. **—dis·trust′ful,** *adj.* **—dis·trust′ful·ly,** *adv.*

**dis·turb** (di-stũrb′), *v.t.* [< OFr. < L. < *dis-*, intens. + *turbare*, to disorder < *turba*, a mob], 1. to break up the quiet, stillness, or serenity of. 2. to make uneasy or anxious. 3. to break up the settled order of. 4. to break in on; interrupt. 5. to inconvenience. **—dis·turb′er,** *n.* **—dis·turb′ing·ly,** *adv.*

**dis·turb·ance** (di-stũr′bəns), *n.* 1. a disturbing or being disturbed. 2. anything that disturbs. 3. commotion; disorder.

**di·sul·fide, di·sul·phide** (dī-sul′fīd, di-sul′fid), *n.* a chemical compound of two sulfur atoms with a single radical or with a single atom of an element: also **di·sul′fid, di·sul′phid** (-fid).

**dis·un·ion** (dis-ūn′yən), *n.* 1. a breaking of a bond; separation. 2. absence of unity; discord.

**dis·u·nite** (dis′yoo-nīt′), *v.t.* [-NITED, -NITING], to destroy the unity of; make disagree; separate. *v.i.* to come apart. **—dis·un′i·ty** (-ūn′ə-ti), *n.*

**dis·use** (dis-ūz′; *for n.*, -ūs′), *v.t.* [-USED, -USING], to stop using. *n.* lack of use.

**ditch** (dich), *n.* [AS. *dic*], a long, narrow cut in the earth, usually for carrying water; channel for drainage or irrigation. *v.t.* 1. to make a ditch in. 2. throw into a ditch. 3. [Slang], to get rid of. *v.i.* to dig a ditch. **—ditch′er,** *n.*

**dith·er** (di*th*′ẽr), *n.* [var. of dial. *didder*, to tremble], a trembling or excited condition. *v.i.* to be in a dither.

**dith·y·ramb** (dith′ə-ram′, -ramb′), *n.* [< L. < Gr. *dithyrambos*], 1. in ancient Greece, a wild choric hymn in honor of Dionysus. 2. any wildly emotional song, speech, or writing. **—dith′y·ram′bic** (-ram′bik), *adj.* & *n.*

**dit·to** (dit′ō), *n.* [*pl.* -TOS], [It. < L. *dictum* < *dicere*, to say], 1. the same (as something said above or before): abbrev. **do.** 2. a duplicate. 3. a **ditto mark.** *adv.* as said above. *v.t.* [-TOED, -TOING], to repeat; copy.

**ditto mark,** a mark (″) used in lists or tables to show that the item above is to be repeated.

**dit·ty** (dit′i), *n.* [*pl.* -TIES], [< OFr. < L. < *dictare;* see DICTATE], a short, simple song.

**ditty bag** (or **box**), [< obs. *dutty*, coarse calico, orig. E.Ind.], a small bag (or box) used by sailors or soldiers for carrying sewing equipment, toilet articles, etc.

**di·u·ret·ic** (dī′yoo-ret′ik), *adj.* [< LL. < Gr. < *dia-*, through + *ourein*, to urinate], increasing the secretion and flow of urine. *n.* a diuretic drug.

**di·ur·nal** (dī-ũr′n'l), *adj.* [< L. < *diurnus* < *dies*, day], 1. daily; happening each day. 2. of the daytime: opposed to *nocturnal*. **—di·ur′nal·ly,** *adv.*

**div.,** 1. divide. 2. divided. 3. dividend. 4. division. 5. divisor. 6. divorced.

**di·va** (dē′və), *n.* [*pl.* -VAS; It. DIVE (-ve)], [It. < L., goddess], a prima donna.

**di·va·gate** (dī′və-gāt′), *v.i.* [-GATED, -GATING], [< L. < *dis-*, from + *vagari*, to wander], 1. to wander about. 2. to digress. **—di′va·ga′tion,** *n.*

**di·va·lent** (dī-vā′lənt, div′ə-), *adj.* 1. having a valence of two. 2. having two valences. Also, esp. for 2, **bivalent.**

**di·van** (dī′van, di-van′), *n.* [< Turk. < Per. *dīwān*], 1. a large, low couch or sofa, usually without arm rests or back. 2. a coffee room or smoking room.

**dive** (dīv), *v.i.* [DIVED or DOVE (dōv), DIVED, DIVING], [AS. *dyfan*], 1. to plunge head first into water. 2. to go suddenly under water: as, a submarine *dives*. 3. to plunge the hand or body suddenly into something. 4. to vanish from sight suddenly. 5. in *aviation*, to make a steep, sudden descent. *v.t.* 1. to plunge (a hand, head, etc.) into something. 2. to explore or penetrate as by diving. 3. to send (one's airplane) into a dive. *n.* 1. a diving into water. 2. any sudden plunge. 3. in *aviation*, a sharp descent. 4. [Colloq.], a cheap, disreputable saloon, gambling place, etc.

**dive bomber,** a kind of airplane that releases bombs while diving at the target. **—dive bombing.**

**div·er** (dīv′ẽr), *n.* one that dives; specif., *a*) one whose occupation is diving under water. *b*) any of various diving birds.

**di·verge** (də-vũrj′, dī-), *v.i.* [-VERGED, -VERGING], [< Mod. L. < L. *dis-*, apart + *vergere*, to incline], 1. to go or be in different directions from a common point or from each other; branch off. 2. to vary from a norm; differ; deviate.

**di·ver·gence** (də-vũr′jəns, dī-), *n.* 1. a diverging; branching off. 2. variation from a norm; difference; deviation. Also **di·ver′gen·cy** [*pl.* -CIES]. **—di·ver′gent,** *adj.* **—di·ver′gent·ly,** *adv.*

**di·vers** (dī′vẽrz), *adj.* [OFr. < L. *diversus*, pp. < *dis-*, apart + *vertere*, to turn], various or sundry.

**di·verse** (də-vũrs′, dī-, dī′vũrs), *adj.* [see DIVERS], 1. different; dissimilar. 2. varied; diversified. **—di·verse′ly,** *adv.* **—di·verse′ness,** *n.*

**di·ver·si·fy** (də-vũr′sə-fī′, dī-), *v.t.* [-FIED, -FYING], [see -FY], to make diverse; give variety to; vary. **—di·ver′si·fi·ca′tion,** *n.* **—di·ver′si·fied′,** *adj.* **—di·ver′si·fi′er,** *n.*

**di·ver·sion** (də-vũr′zhən, dī-vũr′shən), *n.* 1. a diverting; turning aside (*from*). 2. distraction of attention. 3. a pastime; amusement.

**di·ver·sion·ar·y** (də-vũr′zhən-er′i, dī-vũr′shən-), *adj.* serving to divert or distract: as, *diversionary* military tactics.

**di·ver·si·ty** (də-vũr′sə-ti, dī-), *n.* [*pl.* -TIES], 1. dissimilarity; difference. 2. variety.

**di·vert** (də-vũrt′, dī-), *v.t.* [< OFr. < L. *divertere;* see DIVERS], 1. to turn aside (*from* a course); deflect. 2. to amuse; entertain. **—di·vert′er,** *n.* **—di·vert′ing,** *adj.* **—di·vert′ing·ly,** *adv.* **—di·ver′tive** (-vũr′tiv), *adj.*

**‡di·ver·tisse·ment** (dē′ver′tēs′mäɴ′), *n.* [Fr.], 1. a diversion; amusement. 2. a short ballet or entr'acte

**di·vest** (də-vest′, dī-), *v.t.* [< earlier *devest* after ML. *divestire* < L. *dis-*, from + *vestire*, to dress], 1. to strip (*of* clothing, etc.). 2. to deprive or dispossess (*of* rank, rights, etc.).

**di·vide** (də-vīd′), *v.t.* [-VIDED, -VIDING], [< L. *dividere*], 1. to separate into parts; sever. 2. to separate into groups; classify. 3. to make or keep separate as by a partition. 4. to give out in shares; apportion. 5. to cause to disagree; alienate. 6. in *mathematics*, to separate into equal parts by a **divisor.** 7. to mark off the divisions of; graduate. *v.i.* 1. to be or become separate; part. 2. to disagree. 3. to separate into groups in voting on a question. 4. to share. *n.* a ridge that divides two drainage areas; watershed. **—di·vid′a·ble,** *adj.* **—di·vid′er,** *n.*

**di·vid·ed** (də-vid′id), *adj.* 1. separated into parts; parted. 2. in *botany*, segmented.

**div·i·dend** (div′ə-dend′), *n.* [< Fr. < L. *dividendum*, that which is to be divided], 1. the number or quantity to be divided. 2. *a*) a sum of money to be divided among stockholders, creditors, etc. *b*) a single share of this.

**di·vid·ers** (də-vīd′ẽrz), *n.pl.* an instrument for dividing lines, etc.; compasses.

**div·i·na·tion** (div′ə-nā′shən), *n.* [see DIVINE, *v.*], 1. the act or practice of trying to foretell the future or the unknown by occult means. 2. a prophecy; augury. 3. a successful or clever guess. —**di·vin·a·to·ry** (də-vin′ə-tôr′i, -tō′ri), *adj.*

**di·vine** (də-vin′), *adj.* [< OFr. < L. *divinus* < *divus*, a god], 1. of or like God or a god. 2. given or inspired by God; holy; sacred. 3. devoted to God; religious. 4. supremely great, good, etc. 5. [Colloq.], very pleasing, attractive, etc. *n.* 1. a clergyman. 2. a theologian. *v.t.* [-VINED, -VINING], 1. to prophesy. 2. to guess; conjecture. 3. to find out by intuition. *v.i.* to engage in divination. —**di·vine′ly,** *adv.* —**di·vine′ness,** *n.* —**di·vin′er,** *n.*

**Divine Comedy,** an elaborate narrative poem in Italian, written (1302–1321) by Dante Alighieri.

**diving bell,** a large, hollow, air-filled apparatus, in which divers can work under water.

**diving board,** a board projecting horizontally over a swimming pool, lake, etc., for diving.

**diving suit,** a heavy, waterproof garment worn by divers working under water: it has a detachable helmet into which air is pumped through a hose.

DIVING SUIT

**divining rod,** a forked stick allegedly useful in discovering underground water, minerals, etc.

**di·vin·i·ty** (də-vin′ə-ti), *n.* [*pl.* -TIES], 1. the quality or condition of being divine. 2. a god; deity. 3. a divine power or quality. 4. the study of religion; theology. —**the Divinity,** God.

**di·vis·i·ble** (də-viz′ə-b'l), *adj.* that can be divided, especially without leaving a remainder. —**di·vis′i·bil′i·ty,** *n.* —**di·vis′i·bly,** *adv.*

**di·vi·sion** (də-vizh′ən), *n.* 1. a dividing or being divided. 2. a difference of opinion; disagreement. 3. a sharing or distribution. 4. a separation into groups in voting. 5. anything that divides; partition; boundary. 6. a section, segment, group, etc. 7. the process of finding how many times a number (the *divisor*) is contained in another (the *dividend*): the answer is the *quotient*. 8. a section of an army corps, consisting generally of three regiments and auxiliary troops, under the command of a major general. —**di·vi′sion·al,** *adj.*

**division sign** (or **mark**), the symbol (÷), indicating that the preceding number is to be divided by the following number. Example: 8 ÷ 4 = 2.

**di·vi·sor** (də-vī′zẽr), *n.* [L.], in *mathematics*, the number or quantity by which the dividend is divided to produce the quotient.

**di·vorce** (də-vôrs′, -vōrs′), *n.* [OFr. < L. *divortium* < pp. of *divertere;* see DIVERS], 1. legal dissolution of a marriage. 2. complete separation; disunion: as, a *divorce* of church and state. *v.t.* [-VORCED, -VORCING], 1. to dissolve legally a marriage between. 2. to separate from (one's husband or wife) by divorce. 3. to separate; disunite. *v.i.* to get a divorce. —**di·vorce′ment,** *n.*

**di·vor·cée** (də-vôr′sā′, -vōr′sā′), *n.* [Fr.], a divorced woman. —**di·vor′cé′,** *n.masc.*

**di·vor·cee** (də-vôr′sē′, -vōr′sē′), *n.* a divorced person.

**div·ot** (div′ət), *n.* [Scot. dial.; ? < MLG. *dövicke*, a plug, or < ON.], in *golf*, a lump of turf dislodged in making a stroke.

**di·vulge** (də-vulj′), *v.t.* [-VULGED, -VULGING], [< L. < *dis-*, apart + *vulgare*, to make public < *vulgus*, the common people], to make known; make public; disclose; reveal. —**di·vul′gence** (-jəns), **di·vulge′ment,** *n.* —**di·vulg′er,** *n.*

**div·vy** (div′i), *v.t. & v.i.* [-VIED, -VYING], [< *divide*], [Slang], to share (often with *up*). *n.* [*pl.* -VIES], [Slang], a share; portion.

**Dix·ie** (dik′si), *n.* [? < *dixie* (< Fr. *dix*, ten) a ten-dollar bank note issued in Louisiana prior to the Civil War], 1. the Southern States of the U.S., collectively: also **Dixie Land.** 2. a popular Confederate song celebrating the South, composed (1859) by D. D. Emmett.

**Dix·ie·land** (dik′si-land′), *adj.* in, of, or like the style of jazz associated with New Orleans.

**diz·en** (diz′'n, dī′z'n), *v.t.* [MD. *disen*, to put flax on a distaff < LG. *dise*, bunch of flax], to dress up in finery; deck out; bedizen.

**diz·zy** (diz′i), *adj.* [-ZIER, -ZIEST], [AS. *dysig*, foolish], 1. feeling giddy or unsteady. 2. causing or likely to cause dizziness: as, *dizzy* heights. 3. confused; bewildered. 4. [Colloq.], silly. *v.t.* [-ZIED, -ZYING], to make dizzy. —**diz′zi·ly,** *adv.* —**diz′zi·ness,** *n.*

**dk.,** 1. dark. 2. deck. 3. dock.

**dkg.,** decagram; decagrams.

**dkl.,** decaliter.

**dkm.,** decameter.

**dl.,** deciliter; deciliters.

**dm.,** decimeter; decimeters.

**DNA,** [<*d*eoxyribo*n*ucleic *a*cid], a nucleic acid in a living cell, which contains the genetic code and transmits the hereditary pattern.

**Dne·pr** (nē′pẽr; Russ. dnye′p'r), *n.* a river in the western U.S.S.R., flowing into the Black Sea: length, 1,400 mi.: also sp. **Dnieper.**

**Dne·pro·pe·trovsk** (dnye′prô-pye-trôfsk′), *n.* a city in the Ukrainian S.S.R., on the Dnepr: pop., 658,000.

**Dnes·tr** (nēs′tẽr; Russ. dnye′st'r), *n.* a river in the southwestern U.S.S.R., flowing into the Black Sea: length, 800 mi.: also sp. **Dniester.**

**do** (do͞o), *v.t.* [DID, DONE, DOING], [AS. *don*], 1. to perform (an action, etc.); carry out: as, to *do* a deed. 2. to finish; bring to completion: as, dinner has been *done* for an hour. 3. to cause; bring about: as, it *does* no harm. 4. to exert (efforts, etc.): as, *do* your best. 5. to deal with as is required; attend to: as, *do* the ironing. 6. to work at; have as one's occupation. 7. to work out; solve: as, he *did* the problem. 8. to produce (a play, etc.): as, we *did* Hamlet. 9. to play the role of: as, I *did* Polonius. 10. to cover (distance): as, he *does* a mile in record time. 11. to give; render: as, *do* honor to the dead. 12. to suit; be convenient to: as, this will *do* me very well. 13. [Colloq.], to cheat; swindle: as, you've been *done.* 14. [Colloq.], to serve (a jail term). *v.i.* 1. to behave: as, he *does* well when praised. 2. to be active; work: as, *do*, don't talk. 3. to get along; fare: as, the patient is *doing* well. 4. to be adequate or suitable: as, the black dress will *do. Auxiliary uses* of *do*: 1. to give emphasis: as, please *do* stay. 2. to ask a question: as, *did* you write? 3. to emphasize negation: as, *don't* go. 4. to serve as a substitute verb: as, love me as I *do* (love) you. 5. to form inverted constructions after some adverbs: as, little *did* he realize. *n.* [Brit. Colloq.], 1. a hoax; swindle. 2. a party. —**do away with,** 1. to get rid of. 2. to destroy; kill. —**do by,** to act toward or for. —**do for,** [Colloq.], to ruin; destroy. —**do in,** [Slang], to kill. —**do over** [Colloq.], to redecorate. —**do to death,** [Archaic], to kill. —**do up,** [Colloq.], 1. to clean and prepare (laundry, etc.). 2. to wrap up; tie up. 3. to arrange (the hair) off the neck and shoulders. 4. to tire out; exhaust. —**do with,** to make use of. —**do without,** to get along without. —**have to do with,** to have relation with or to. —**make do,** to get along with what is available.

**do** (dō), *n.* [It.; used instead of earlier *ut;* see GAMUT], a syllable in solfeggio representing the first or last tone of the diatonic scale.

**do.,** ditto.

**D.O.,** Doctor of Osteopathy.

**do·a·ble** (do͞o′ə-b'l), *adj.* that can be done.

**dob·bin** (dob′in), *n.* [rhyme alteration < *Robin*], a horse, especially a plodding, patient horse.

**Do·ber·man pin·scher** (dō′bẽr-mən pin′shẽr), a terrier with smooth, dark hair and tan markings.

**doc** (dok), *n.* [Slang], doctor: often used as a general term of address like *Mac, Bud, Jack,* etc.

**doc.,** document.

**doc·ile** (dos′'l), *adj.* [Fr. < L. *docilis* < *docere*, to teach], 1. easy to teach; teachable. 2. easy to discipline; obedient; tractable. —**doc′ile·ly,** *adv.* —**do·cil·i·ty** (dō-sil′ə-ti, do-), *n.*

**dock** (dok), *n.* [< MD. < ML. *ductia*, channel < L. *ductio*, a leading away], 1. a large excavated basin equipped with floodgates, for receiving ships between voyages. 2. a landing pier; wharf. 3. the water between two docks. *v.t.* to pilot (a ship) to a dock. *v.i.* to come into a dock.

**dock** (dok), *n.* [< Fl. *dok*, cage], the place where the accused stands or sits in a courtroom.

**dock** (dok), *n.* [AS. *docce*], a coarse weed of the buckwheat family, with large leaves.

**dock** (dok), *n.* [< ON. *dockr*], 1. the solid part of an animal's tail. 2. an animal's bobbed tail. *v.t.* 1. to cut off the end of (a tail, etc.); bob. 2. to bob the tail of. 3. to deduct from (wages, etc.). 4. to deduct from the wages of. —**dock′er,** *n.*

**dock·age** (dok′ij), *n.* 1. docking accommodations. 2. the fee for this. 3. the docking of ships.

**dock·age** (dok′ij), *n.* a docking, or cutting off.

**dock·et** (dok′it), *n.* [merging of *cocket*, a seal & obs. *doggette*, register], 1. a summary of legal decisions. 2. a list of cases to be tried by a law court. 3. any list of things to be done; agenda. 4. a label listing the contents of a package, directions, etc. *v.t.* 1. to enter in a docket. 2. to put a docket on; label.
**dock·yard** (dok′yärd′), *n.* a place with docks, machinery, etc. for repairing or building ships.
**doc·tor** (dok′tēr), *n.* [< OFr. < L. *doctor*, teacher < pp. of *docere*, to teach], 1. a person on whom a university or college has conferred the doctorate: a Doctor of Medicine, Dentistry, Philosophy, etc. is properly addressed as *Doctor*: abbrev. **Dr.** (as a title), **D.** (as in *Ph. D.*, *D. Litt.*, etc.). 2. a physician or surgeon (M.D.). 3. a person licensed to practice any of the healing arts, as an osteopath, chiropractor, etc. 4. a witch doctor or medicine man. 5. [Archaic], a learned man. *v.t.* [Colloq.], 1. to try to heal; apply medicine to. 2. to repair; mend. 3. to tamper with. *v.i.* [Colloq.], 1. to practice medicine. 2. to be under a doctor's care. **—doc′tor·al,** *adj.* **—doc′tor·ship′,** *n.*
**doc·tor·ate** (dok′tēr-it), *n.* the degree or status of doctor conferred by a university
**doc·tri·naire** (dok′tri-nâr′), *n.* [Fr.], one who tries to apply theories regardless of practical problems which affect them; visionary. *adj.* impractical; visionary. **—doc′tri·nair′ism,** *n.*
**doc·trine** (dok′trin), *n.* [< L. *doctrina* < *doctor;* see DOCTOR], 1. something taught; teachings. 2. something taught as the principles of a religion, political party, etc.; tenet or tenets; dogma. **—doc′tri·nal,** *adj.* **—doc′tri·nal·ly,** *adv.*
**doc·u·ment** (dok′yoo-mənt; *for v.*, -ment′), *n.* [Fr < L. *documentum*, lesson, proof < *docere*, to teach], 1. anything printed, written, etc., relied upon to record or prove something. 2. any proof. *v.t.* 1. to provide, as a book, with documents or references. 2. to prove or support by reference to documents. **—doc′u·men′tal,** *adj.* **—doc′u·men·ta′tion,** *n.*
**doc·u·men·ta·ry** (dok′yoo-men′tə-ri), *adj.* 1. of, supported by, or serving as a document or documents. 2. recording news events or showing social conditions dramatically but without fictionalization. *n.* [*pl.* -RIES], a documentary motion picture, television program, etc.
**dod·der** (dod′ēr), *v.i.* [var. of dial. *dudder, dither*], 1. to shake or tremble as from old age. 2. to totter. **—dod′der·ing,** *adj.*
**do·dec·a-,** [< Gr. *dōdeka*, twelve], a prefix meaning *twelve*: also **dodec-.**
**do·dec·a·gon** (dō-dek′ə-gon′, -gən), *n.* [Gr.; see DODECA- & -GON], a plane figure with twelve angles and twelve sides.
**do·dec·a·he·dron** (dō′dek-ə-hē′drən), *n.* [*pl.* -DRONS, -DRA (-drə)], [< Gr.; see DODECA- & -HEDRON], a solid figure with twelve plane faces. **—do′dec·a·he′dral,** *adj.*
**Do·dec·a·nese (Islands)** (dō-dek′ə-nēs′, dō′dek-), a group of Greek islands in the Aegean.
**dodge** (doj), *v.i.* [DODGED, DODGING], [? < Scot. *dod*, to jog], 1. to move or twist quickly aside, as to avoid a blow. 2. to use tricks or evasions. *v.t.* 1. to avoid by moving quickly aside. 2. to evade by cunning, trickery, etc. *n.* 1. a dodging. 2. a trick used in cheating or evading.
**dodg·er** (doj′ēr), *n.* 1. one who dodges. 2. a tricky, dishonest person. 3. a bread or cake made of corn meal. 4. a small handbill.
**Dodg·son, Charles Lut·widge** (lut′wij doj′s′n), see **Carroll, Lewis.**
**do·do** (dō′dō), *n.* [*pl.* -DOS, -DOES], [Port. *doudo*, lit., foolish, stupid], a large bird, now extinct, that had rudimentary wings useless for flying: formerly found on Mauritius.

DODO (2 ft. high)

**Doe** (dō), a name (*John Doe*) used in legal papers, etc. to refer to any person whose name is unknown.
**doe** (dō), *n.* [*pl.* DOES, DOE; see PLURAL, II, D, 1], [AS. *da*], the female of the deer, or of the antelope, rabbit, or almost any other animal the male of which is called a buck.
**do·er** (do͞o′ēr), *n.* 1. a person who does something. 2. a person who gets things done.
**does** (duz), the 3d pers. sing., pres. indic., of **do.**
**doe·skin** (dō′skin′), *n.* 1. the skin of a female deer. 2. leather made from this. 3. a fine, soft, smooth woolen cloth.
**does·n't** (duz′′nt), does not.
**do·est** (do͞o′ist), archaic 2d pers. sing., pres. indic., of **do**: used with *thou*, and in auxiliary uses shortened to **dost.**
**do·eth** (do͞o′ith), archaic 3d pers. sing., pres. indic., of **do**: cf. **doth.**
**doff** (dof, dôf), *v.t.* [< *do* + *off*], 1. to take off (clothes, etc.). 2. to put aside; give up.
**dog** (dôg), *n.* [*pl.* DOGS, DOG; see PLURAL, II, D, 1], [AS. *docga*], 1. any of a large group of domesticated animals related to the fox, wolf, and jackal. 2. the male of any of these. 3. a low, contemptible fellow. 4. a prairie dog, dogfish, or other animal thought of as resembling a dog. 5. an andiron. 6. [Colloq.], a boy or man: as, a lucky *dog.* 7. *pl.* [Slang], feet. 8. [D-], either of the constellations Canis Major (**Great** or **Greater Dog**) or Canis Minor (**Little** or **Lesser Dog**). 9. in *mechanics*, a device for holding or grappling. *v.t.* [DOGGED, DOGGING], to follow or hunt like a dog. *adv.* very; completely: as, *dog*-tired. **—a dog's age,** [Colloq.], a long time. **—a dog's life,** a wretched existence. **—dog eat dog,** ruthless competition. **—dog in the manger,** one who keeps others from using something which he cannot or will not use. **—go to the dogs,** [Colloq.], to deteriorate; degenerate. **—put on the dog,** [Slang], to make a show of being very elegant, wealthy, etc.
**dog biscuit,** a hard biscuit containing ground bones, meat, etc., for feeding dogs.
**dog·cart** (dôg′kärt′), *n.* 1. a small, light cart drawn by dogs. 2. a small, light, open carriage having two seats arranged back to back.
**dog days,** the hot, humid days in July and August.
**doge** (dōj), *n.* [It. < L. *dux*, leader], the chief magistrate of either of the former republics of Venice and Genoa. **—doge′ship′,** *n.*
**dog-ear** (dôg′êr′), *n.* a turned-down corner of the leaf of a book. *v.t.* to turn down the corner of (a leaf or leaves in a book). Also **dog's-ear. —dog′-eared′, dog's′-eared′,** *adj.*
**dog·face** (dôg′fās′), *n.* [Slang], an enlisted man in the army, especially an infantryman.
**dogfight** (dôg′fīt′), *n.* a rough, violent fight, as between dogs; specif., combat between fighter planes or tanks at close quarters.
**dog·fish** (dôg′fish′), *n.* [*pl.* see FISH], 1. any of various small sharks. 2. any of several other fishes, as the mudfish.
**dog·ged** (dôg′id), *adj.* [see DOG], not giving in readily; persistent; stubborn. **—dog′ged·ly,** *adv.* **—dog′ged·ness,** *n.*
**dog·ger·el** (dôg′ēr-əl, dog′-), *n.* [prob. < It. *doga*, barrel stave], trivial, weakly constructed verse, usually of a comic sort; jingle. *adj.* designating or of such verse.
**dog·gish** (dôg′ish), *adj.* of or like a dog. **—dog′gish·ly,** *adv.* **—dog′gish·ness,** *n.*
**dog·gone** (dôg′gôn′), *interj.* damn! darn! *v.t.* [-GONED, -GONING], [Colloq.], to damn: as, I'll be *dog-goned* if I'll go.
**dog·grel** (dôg′rəl, dog′-), *n.* & *adj.* doggerel.
**dog·gy** (dôg′i), *n.* [*pl.* -GIES], a little dog: also sp. **doggie.** *adj.* [-GIER, -GIEST], 1. of or like a dog. 2. [Colloq.], stylish and showy.
**dog·house** (dôg′hous′), *n.* a dog's shelter; kennel. **—in the doghouse,** [Slang], in disfavor.
**do·gie, do·gy** (dō′gi), *n.* [*pl.* -GIES], [< ?], in the western U.S., a stray or motherless calf.
**dog·ma** (dôg′mə, dog′-), *n.* [*pl.* -MAS, -MATA (-mə-tə)], [L. < Gr. < *dokein*, to think], 1. a doctrine; tenet; belief. 2. doctrines or beliefs, collectively. 3. a positive, arrogant assertion of opinion. 4. in *theology*, a doctrine or body of doctrines formally and authoritatively affirmed.
**dog·mat·ic** (dôg-mat′ik, dog-), *adj.* 1. of or like dogma. 2. asserted without proof. 3. stating opinion in a positive, emphatic, or arrogant manner. Also **dog·mat′i·cal. —dog·mat′i·cal·ly,** *adv.* **—dog·mat′i·cal·ness,** *n.*
**dog·ma·tism** (dôg′mə-tiz′m, dog′-), *n.* dogmatic assertion of opinion, usually without reference to evidence. **—dog′ma·tist,** *n.*
**dog·ma·tize** (dôg′mə-tīz′, dog′-), *v.i.* [-TIZED, -TIZING], to speak or write in a dogmatic manner. *v.t.* to formulate or express as dogma. **—dog′ma·ti·za′tion,** *n.* **—dog′ma·tiz′er,** *n.*
**dog·rose,** a European wild rose with single, pink flowers and hooked thorns.
**dog sled** (or **sledge**), a sled (or sledge) drawn by dogs.
**Dog Star,** 1. Sirius. 2. Procyon.
**dog tag,** 1. an identification tag or license tag for a dog. 2. [Slang], a military identification tag worn about the neck.
**dog-tired** (dôg′tīrd′), *adj.* [Colloq.], very tired.

**dog·tooth** (dôg′to͞oth′), *n.* [*pl.* -TEETH], a canine tooth; eyetooth: also **dog tooth.**
**dogtooth violet,** 1. an American plant of the lily family, with either a yellow or a white flower: also called *adder's-tongue.* 2. a related similar European plant. Also **dog's-tooth violet.**
**dog·trot** (dôg′trot′), *n.* a slow, easy trot.
**dog·watch** (dôg′wôch′, -wäch′), *n.* in *nautical usage,* either of two duty periods, one from 4 to 6 P.M., the other from 6 to 8 P.M.
**dog·wood** (dôg′wood′), *n.* 1. a tree with pink or white flowers early in the spring and clusters of small red berries in the fall. 2. its hard wood.
**doi·ly** (doi′li), *n.* [*pl.* -LIES], [after a 17th-c. London draper], a small mat, as of linen or paper, used as a protection for table tops, etc.
**do·ings** (do͞o′iŋz), *n.pl.* 1. things done; deeds; activities. 2. behavior.
**dol.,** [*pl.* DOLS.], a dollar.
**dol·drums** (dol′drəmz), *n.pl.* [? < *dull*], 1. low spirits; dull, listless feeling. 2. equatorial ocean regions noted for dead calms and light, fluctuating winds.
**dole** (dōl), *n.* [< AS. *dal*], 1. a giving out of money or food in charity. 2. that which is thus given out. 3. anything given out sparingly. 4. a form of payment by a government to the unemployed. *v.t.* [DOLED, DOLING], to give sparingly or as a dole. **—on the dole,** receiving government relief funds.
**dole** (dōl), *n.* [see DOLEFUL], [Archaic], sorrow.
**dole·ful** (dōl′fəl), *adj.* [< OFr. < LL. < L. *dolere,* to suffer; + *-ful*], sad; sorrowful; dismal. **—dole′ful·ly,** *adv.* **—dole′ful·ness,** *n.*
**dol·i·cho·ce·phal·ic** (dol′i-kō′sə-fal′ik), *adj.* [< Gr. *dolichos,* long; + *-cephalic*], having a relatively long skull: opposed to *brachycephalic*: also **dol′i·cho·ceph′a·lous** (-sef′ə-ləs). **—dol′i·cho·ceph′a·ly,** *n.*
**doll** (dol), *n.* [orig., nickname for *Dorothy*], 1. a child's toy made to resemble a child or grown person. 2. a pretty but stupid woman. *v.t. & v.i.* [Slang], to dress stylishly or showily (with *up*).
**dol·lar** (dol′ẽr), *n.* [< LG. & Early Mod. D.; G. *thaler* contr. < *Joachimsthaler,* coin made at *Joachimstal,* Bohemia], 1. the monetary unit of the U.S., equal to 100 cents. 2. the standard monetary unit of Canada and some other British colonies. 3. a standard monetary unit of China: in full *People's Dollar.* 4. the Mexican peso. 5. any of several monetary units used only in trade, as the Levant dollar of Austria, etc. 6. a coin or paper bill of the value of a dollar.
**dollar diplomacy,** the use of the economic power of a government to promote in other countries the business interests of its corporations, etc.
**doll·y** (dol′i), *n.* [*pl.* -IES], 1. a doll: child's term. 2. a stick for stirring, as in washing ore. 3. any of several kinds of low, flat, wheeled frames for transporting heavy objects.
**dol·man** (dol′mən), *n.* [*pl.* -MANS], [< Fr. < Pol. < Turk. *dōlāmān,* long robe], a woman's coat or wrap with capelike arm pieces instead of sleeves.
**dol·men** (dol′men), *n.* [Fr.; prob. < Corn. *tolmen,* hole of stone], a prehistoric tomb or monument consisting of a large, flat stone laid across upright stones; cromlech.

DOLMEN

**dol·o·mite** (dol′ə-mīt′), *n.* [after the Fr. geologist *Dolomieu* (1750–1801)], rock consisting mainly of magnesium carbonate and calcium carbonate.
**Dol·o·mites** (dol′ə-mīts′), *n.pl.* that part of the Alps in NE Italy: also **Dolomite Alps.**
**do·lor** (dō′lẽr), *n.* [< OFr. < L. *dolor* < *dolere,* to suffer], [Poetic], sorrow; distress; grief.
**dol·or·ous** (dol′ẽr-əs, dō′lẽr-), *adj.* 1. sorrowful; sad; mournful. 2. painful. **—dol′or·ous·ly,** *adv.* **—dol′or·ous·ness,** *n.*
**do·lour** (dō′lẽr), *n.* dolor: Brit. spelling.
**dol·phin** (dol′fin), *n.* [< OFr. < L. < Gr. < *delphis*], 1. any of several mammals of the whale family, with a beaklike snout. 2. a buoy or spar used in mooring a boat.

DOLPHIN (about 8 ft.)

**dolt** (dōlt), *n.* [? < *dull*], a stupid, slow-witted person; blockhead. **—dolt′ish,** *adj.* **—dolt′ish·ly,** *adv.* **—dolt′ish·ness,** *n.*
**-dom** (dəm), [AS. < *dom,* state], a suffix meaning: 1. *the rank, position,* or *dominion of,* as in *kingdom.* 2. *the fact* or *state of being,* as in *martyrdom.* 3. *a total of all who are,* as in *officialdom.*
**dom.,** 1. domestic. 2. dominion.
**do·main** (dō-mān′), *n.* [< Fr. < L. < *dominus,* a lord, master], 1. territory under one government or ruler. 2. land belonging to one person; estate. 3. field or sphere of activity or influence.
**dome** (dōm), *n.* [< Fr. < It. or LL. < L. *domus,* house], 1. a roof formed by a series of rounded arches or vaults on a round or many-sided base; cupola. 2. any dome-shaped object. 3. [Slang], the head. *v.t.* [DOMED, DOMING], 1. to cover as with a dome. 2. to form into a dome. *v.i.* to swell out like a dome.
**do·mes·tic** (də-mes′tik), *adj.* [< OFr. < L. *domesticus* < *domus,* house], 1. of the home or family: as, *domestic* bliss. 2. of one's homeland: as, *domestic* trade. 3. made in the home country; native. 4. domesticated; tame: said of animals. 5. home-loving; enjoying household affairs. *n.* a domestic worker; maid, cook, butler, etc. **—do·mes′ti·cal·ly,** *adv.*
**do·mes·ti·cate** (də-mes′tə-kāt′), *v.t.* [-CATED, -CATING], 1. to accustom to home life; make domestic. 2. to cause (animals or plants) to be no longer wild; tame. 3. to civilize. *v.i.* to become domestic. **—do·mes′ti·ca′tion,** *n.*
**do·mes·tic·i·ty** (dō′mes-tis′ə-ti), *n.* [*pl.* -TIES], 1. home life; family life. 2. devotion to home and family life. 3. *pl.* household affairs.
**domestic science,** home economics.
**domestic worker,** one employed to do household work in another's home, as a maid, cook, etc.
**dom·i·cile** (dom′ə-sil, -sīl′), *n.* [Fr. < L. < *domus,* house], a customary dwelling place; home; residence. *v.t.* [-CILED, -CILING], to establish (oneself or another) in a domicile. *v.i.* [Rare], to dwell. **—dom′i·cil′i·ar′y (-sil′i-er′i),** *adj.*
**dom·i·cil·i·ate** (dom′ə-sil′i-āt′), *v.t. & v.i.* [-ATED, -ATING], to domicile. **—dom′i·cil′i·a′tion,** *n.*
**dom·i·nance** (dom′ə-nəns), *n.* a dominating; being dominant; control; authority: also **dom′i·nan·cy.**
**dom·i·nant** (dom′ə-nənt), *adj.* 1. dominating; ruling; prevailing. 2. in *genetics,* designating or of that one of any pair of opposite Mendelian characters which, when factors for both are present in the germ plasm, dominates over the other and appears in the organism: opposed to *recessive.* 3. in *music,* of or based upon the fifth tone of a diatonic scale. *n.* in *music,* the fifth note of a diatonic scale. **—dom′i·nant·ly,** *adv.*
**dom·i·nate** (dom′ə-nāt′), *v.t. & v.i.* [-NATED, -NATING], [< L. *dominus,* a master], 1. to rule or control by superior power. 2. to tower over; rise high above (the surroundings, etc.). **—dom′i·na′tive** (-tiv), *adj.* **—dom′i·na′tor (-nā′tẽr),** *n.*
**dom·i·na·tion** (dom′ə-nā′shən), *n.* a dominating or being dominated; rule; control.
**dom·i·neer** (dom′ə-nêr′), *v.i.* [< D. < Fr. < L.; see DOMINATE], to rule (*over*) in a harsh or an arrogant way; bully; tyrannize.
**dom·i·neer·ing** (dom′ə-nêr′iŋ), *adj.* overbearing; tyrannical. **—dom′i·neer′ing·ly,** *adv.*
**Dom·in·ic,** Saint (dom′ə-nik), (*Domingo de Guzmán*) 1170–1221; Spanish founder of the Dominican order.
**Do·min·i·can** (də-min′i-kən), *adj.* 1. of Saint Dominic or of the orders of friars and nuns founded by him. 2. of the Dominican Republic. *n.* 1. a member of one of the Dominican orders. 2. a native or inhabitant of the Dominican Republic.
**Dominican Republic,** a country in the E part of Hispaniola, in the West Indies: area, 18,711 sq. mi.; pop., 3,205,000; capital, Santo Domingo: formerly called *Santo Domingo*: abbrev. **Dom. Rep.**
**dom·i·nie** (dom′ə-ni), *n.* [< vocative case (*domine*) of L. *dominus,* a master], 1. in Scotland, a schoolmaster. 2. [Colloq.], a clergyman.
**do·min·ion** (də-min′yən), *n.* [Fr. (obs.) < ML. *dominio* < L. *dominus,* a lord], 1. rule or power to rule; sovereignty. 2. a governed territory or country. 3. [D-], a self-governing commonwealth of the British Empire: as, the *Dominion* of Canada.
**Dominion Day,** in Canada, July 1, a legal holiday, the anniversary of the proclamation in 1867 of the establishment of the Dominion of Canada.
**dom·i·no** (dom′ə-nō′), *n.* [*pl.* -NOES, -NOS], [Fr. & It. < L. *dominus,* a lord], 1. a loose cloak with wide sleeves, hood, and mask, worn at masquerades.

2. a small mask for the eyes; half mask. 3. one dressed in such a cloak or mask. 4. a small, oblong piece of wood, etc. marked with dots. 5. *pl.* [construed as sing.], a game played with such pieces.
**Don** (don; Russ. dôn), *n.* a river in the European U.S.S.R., flowing into the Sea of Azov.
**don** (don), *n.* [Sp. < L. *dominus*, a lord], 1. [D-], Sir; Mr.: a Spanish title of respect. 2. a Spanish nobleman or gentleman. 3. a distinguished man. 4. [Colloq.], a head, tutor, or fellow of any college of Oxford or Cambridge.
**don** (don), *v.t.* [DONNED, DONNING], [contr. of *do on*], to put on (a garment, etc.).
‡**Do·ña** (dô′nyä), *n.* [Sp. < L. *domina*, mistress], 1. Lady; Madam: a Spanish title of respect. 2. [d-], a Spanish lady.
**do·nate** (dō′nāt), *v.t.* [-NATED, -NATING], [< L. pp. of *donare* < *donus*, gift], to give or contribute, as to some cause. **—do′na·tor (-nā-tẽr), *n.***
**do·na·tion** (dō-nā′shən), *n.* 1. a donating; giving. 2. a gift or contribution.
**done** (dun), pp. of **do.** ***adj.*** 1. completed. 2. sufficiently cooked. **—done in,** [Colloq.], exhausted.
**do·nee** (dō-nē′), *n.* one who receives a donation.
**Do·nets** (do-nets′; Russ. dô-nyets′), *n.* a river in the European U.S.S.R., flowing into the Don.
**dong** (dôŋ, doŋ), *n.* [echoic], a sound of, or like that of, a large bell.
**don·jon** (dun′jən, don′-), *n.* [old sp. of *dungeon*], the heavily fortified inner tower of a castle.
**Don Ju·an** (don jo͞o′ən; Sp. dôn Hwän′), 1. in *Spanish legend*, a dissolute nobleman and seducer of women. 2. any man who seduces women; rake.
**don·key** (doŋ′ki, duŋ′-), *n.* [*pl.* -KEYS], [? nickname for *Duncan*], 1. a small domestic animal resembling the horse but with longer ears and a shorter mane; ass. 2. a stupid or stubborn person. 3. a small, portable steam engine; in full, **donkey engine.**
**Don·na** (don′ə; It. dôn′nä), *n.* [It. < L. *domina*, mistress], 1. Lady; Madam: an Italian title of respect. 2. [d-], an Italian lady.
**Donne, John** (dun), 1573–1631; English poet.
**don·nish** (don′ish), *adj.* of, characteristic of, or like a university don. **—don′nish·ly, *adv.***
**don·ny·brook** (don′i-brook′), *n.* [< a fair formerly held at *Donnybrook*, Ireland: scene of many fights], [Slang], a rough, rowdy fight or free-for-all.
**do·nor** (dō′nẽr), *n.* [< OFr. < L. *donator;* see DONATE], one who makes a donation, giver.
**Don Quix·ote** (don kwik′sət, don ki-hō′ti; Sp. dôn kē-Hô′te), 1. a satirical romance by Miguel de Cervantes, published in two parts (1605, 1615). 2. the chivalrous, unrealistic hero of this romance.
**don't** (dōnt), 1. do not. 2. does not: in this sense now generally considered substandard.
**do·nut** (dō′nut′), *n.* a doughnut.
**doo·dad** (do͞o′dad′), *n.* [fanciful extension of *do*], [Colloq.], 1. any small object whose name does not readily occur to one; gadget. 2. a bauble.
**doo·dle** (do͞o′d'l), *v.i.* [-DLED, -DLING], [G. *dudeln*, to play (the bagpipe), hence to trifle], to scribble aimlessly, especially when the attention is elsewhere. *n.* 1. a foolish person; simpleton. 2. a mark made in aimless scribbling. **—doo′dler, *n.* —doo′dling, *n.***
**doo·dle·bug** (do͞o′d'l-bug′), *n.* the larva of the ant lion.
**doo·hick·ey** (do͞o′hik′i), *n.* [fanciful extension of *do*], [Colloq.], any device or gadget: humorous substitute for a name not known.
**doom** (do͞om), *n.* [AS. *dom*], 1. a judgment; sentence. 2. destiny; fate. 3. tragic fate; ruin or death. *v.t.* 1. to pass judgment on; condemn. 2. to destine to a tragic fate. 3. to ordain as a penalty.
**dooms·day** (do͞omz′dā′), *n.* 1. Judgment Day; Last Judgment. 2. any day of judgment.
**door** (dôr, dōr), *n.* [AS. *duru*], 1. a movable structure for opening or closing the entrance to a building, room, closet, etc.: most doors turn on hinges, slide in grooves, or revolve on an axis. 2. the room or building to which a door belongs: as, two *doors* down the hall. 3. anything resembling a door. 4. any opening with a door in it; doorway. 5. any way to go in or out; access. **—lay at the door of,** to blame for. **—out of doors,** outdoors. **—show a person the door,** to command a person to leave.
**door·bell** (dôr′bel′, dōr′-), *n.* a bell that rings inside a building when someone pushes an outside button.
**door·jamb** (dôr′jam′, dōr′-), *n.* a vertical piece of wood, etc. forming the side of a doorway.
**door·keep·er** (dôr′kēp′ẽr, dōr′-), *n.* 1. a person guarding the entrance of a house, hotel, etc.; gatekeeper; porter. 2. a doorman.
**door·knob** (dôr′nob′, dōr′-), *n.* a small knob or lever on a door, for releasing the latch.
**door·man** (dôr′man′, dōr′mən), *n.* [*pl.* -MEN], 1. a man whose work is opening the street door of a public building for those who enter or leave, hailing taxicabs, etc. 2. a doorkeeper.
**door mat,** a mat to wipe the shoes on before entering a house, room, etc.
**door·nail** (dôr′nāl′, dōr′-), *n.* a large-headed nail used in studding some doors. **—dead as a doornail,** dead beyond a doubt.
**door·plate** (dôr′plāt′, dōr′-), *n.* a metal plate on an entrance door, having on it a number, name, etc.
**door·post** (dôr′pōst′, dōr′-), *n.* a doorjamb.
**door·sill** (dôr′sil′, dōr′-), *n.* a board, piece of metal, etc. placed beneath a door; threshold.
**door·step** (dôr′step′, dōr′-), *n.* a step that leads from an outer door to a path, lawn, etc.
**door·stop** (dôr′stop′, dōr′-), *n.* any device for controlling or stopping the closing of a door.
**door·way** (dôr′wā′, dōr′-), *n.* 1. an opening in a wall that can be closed by a door; portal. 2. a means of access: as, the *doorway* to China.
**door·yard** (dôr′yärd′, dōr′-), *n.* a yard onto which a door of a house opens.
**dope** (dōp), *n.* [D. *doop*, sauce < *doopen*, to dip], 1. any thick liquid or paste used as a lubricant, etc. 2. a varnish or filler used to protect a surface, as on the cloth covering of airplane wings. 3. [Slang], information; prediction. 4. [Slang], a drug or narcotic. 5. [Slang], a user of narcotics. 6. [Slang], a slow-witted, stupid person. *v.t.* [DOPED, DOPING], 1. to give dope to; hence, 2. to drug or stupefy. 3. [Slang], to make out or figure out; also, to predict (usually with *out*). **—dop′er, *n.***
**dope·y** (dō′pi), *adj.* [DOPIER, DOPIEST], [Slang], 1. in a drugged stupor. 2. lethargic or stupid.
**Do·ré, Paul Gus·tave** (pôl güs′tåv′ dô′rā′; Eng. dô-rā′), 1833–1883; French artist.
**Dor·ic** (dôr′ik, dor′-), *adj.* [< L. < Gr. *Dōrikos*, of *Dōris*, ancient region of Greece], designating or of the oldest architectural style of ancient Greece, characterized by simplicity of form: the **Doric order** is characterized by fluted, heavy columns with simple capitals.
**dorm** (dôrm), *n.* [Colloq.], a dormitory.
**dor·mant** (dôr′mənt), *adj.* [OFr., ppr. of *dormir* (< L. *dormire*), to sleep], 1. sleeping. 2. as if asleep; quiet; still. 3. inactive, as some animals or plants in winter. **—dor′man·cy (-mən-si), *n.***
**dor·mer** (dôr′mẽr), *n.* [< OFr. < L. *dormitorium;* see DORMITORY], 1. a window set upright in a sloping roof. 2. the roofed projection in which this window is set. Also **dormer window.**

DORMER

**dor·mi·to·ry** (dôr′mə-tôr′i, -tō′ri), *n.* [*pl.* -RIES], [L. *dormitorium* < *dormire*, to sleep], 1. a room with sleeping accommodations for a number of people. 2. a building with many rooms that provide sleeping and living accommodations for a number of people, as at a college.
**dor·mouse** (dôr′mous′), *n.* [*pl.* -MICE (-mīs′)], [prob. < Eng. dial. *dorm*, to doze < Fr. < L. *dormire*, to sleep; + *mouse*], a small, hibernating European rodent that resembles a squirrel.
**dor·sal** (dôr′s'l), *adj.* [< ML. < L. < *dorsum*, the back], of, on, or near the back. **—dor′sal·ly, *adv.***
**Dor·set·shire** (dôr′sit-shir′), *n.* a county on the S coast of England; also **Dor′set.**
**Dort·mund** (dôrt′moont; Eng. -mənd), *n.* a city in W Germany: pop., 507,000.
**do·ry** (dôr′i, dō′ri), *n.* [*pl.* -RIES], [Central Am. Ind. *dori*, a dugout], a small, flat-bottomed fishing boat with high sides.
**dos·age** (dōs′ij), *n.* 1. the giving of medicine in doses. 2. the amount in a single dose.
**dose** (dōs), *n.* [Fr. < ML. < Gr. *dosis*, gift < *didonai*, to give], 1. an amount of medicine to be taken at one time or at stated intervals. 2. amount of a remedy, punishment, etc. given at one time. *v.t.* [DOSED, DOSING], to give doses of medicine to. *v.i.* to take a dose of medicine. **—dos′er, *n.***
**do·sim·e·ter** (dō-sim′ə-tẽr), *n.* [see DOSE & -METER], a small device carried in the pocket, for measuring the radiation a person has absorbed.
**dos·si·er** (dos′i-ā′, -i-ẽr), *n.* [Fr.], a collection of documents about some person or matter.
**dost** (dust), [cf. DOEST], archaic 2d pers. sing., pres. indic., of **do**: used with *thou.*
**Dos·to·ev·ski, Fe·o·dor Mi·khai·lo·vich** (fyô′dôr mi-khī′lô-vich dôs′tô-yef′ski), 1821–1881; Russian novelist.

**dot** (dot), *n.* [AS. *dott,* head of boil], 1. a tiny spot, speck, or mark; any mark made with a pointed object; point. 2. a small, round spot. 3. the short sound of the Morse code, written as a dot: cf. *dash.* 4. in *music, a*) a mark after a note or rest, increasing its time value by one half. *b*) a staccato mark. *v.t.* [DOTTED, DOTTING], 1. to mark as with a dot or dots. 2. to cover as with dots: as, trees *dotted* the landscape. *v.i.* to make a dot or dots. **—dot one's *i*'s and cross one's *t*'s,** to be minutely correct. **—on the dot,** [Colloq.], at the exact time. **—dot′ter,** *n.*

**dot** (dot), *n.* [Fr. < L. *dos* < *dare,* to give], a woman's dowry at marriage. **—do·tal** (dō′t'l), *adj.*

**dot·age** (dōt′ij), *n.* [ME. < *doten,* to dote], 1. feeble and childish state due to old age; senility. 2. a doting; foolish or excessive affection.

**do·tard** (dō′tẽrd), *n.* [ME. < *doten,* to dote], a foolish and doddering old person.

**dote** (dōt), *v.i.* [DOTED, DOTING], [ME. *doten*], 1. to be foolish or weak-minded, especially because of old age. 2. to be excessively or foolishly fond (with *on* or *upon*). **—dot′er,** *n.* **—dot′ing,** *adj.* **—dot′ing·ly,** *adv.*

**doth** (duth), [cf. DOETH], archaic 3d pers. sing., pres. indic., of **do,** in auxiliary uses.

**dot·ter·el** (dot′ẽr-əl), *n.* [*pl.* -ELS, -EL; see PLURAL, II, D, 1], [< *dote,* because easy to catch], the European plover: also **dot′trel** (dot′rəl).

**dot·tle, dot·tel** (dot′'l), *n.* [< ?], tobacco left in the bowl of a pipe after it has been smoked.

**dot·ty** (dot′i), *adj.* [-TIER, -TIEST], 1. covered with dots; dotted. 2. [Colloq.], feeble; unsteady. 3. [Colloq.], feeble-minded or demented.

**Dou·ai, Dou·ay** (do͞o′ā′), *n.* a town in N France.

**Douay Bible,** an English version of the Bible translated from the Latin Vulgate edition for the use of Roman Catholics: the New Testament was published at Reims (1582), the Old Testament at Douai (1609–1610): also **Douay Version.**

**dou·ble** (dub′'l), *adj.* [OFr. < L. *duplus,* lit., twofold], 1. twofold; duplex. 2. having two layers; folded in two. 3. having two of one kind; repeated: as, a *double* consonant. 4. being of two kinds; dual: as, a *double* standard. 5. having two meanings; ambiguous. 6. twice as much, as many, as large, etc. 7. of extra size, value, strength, etc. 8. made for two: as, a *double* bed. 9. two-faced; deceiving. 10. having a tone an octave lower: as, a *double* bass. 11. in *botany,* having more than one set of petals. *adv.* 1. twofold. 2. twice. 3. two together; in pairs. *n.* 1. anything twice as much, as many, or as large as normal. 2. an exact duplication of something; counterpart. 3. a stand-in, as in motion pictures. 4. a fold; second ply. 5. a sharp shift of direction. 6. a trick; shift. 7. in *baseball,* a hit on which the batter reaches second base. 8. in *bridge, a*) the doubling of an opponent's bid. *b*) a hand that makes this possible. 9. *pl.* a game of tennis, handball, etc. with two players on each side. *v.t.* [-BLED, -BLING], 1. to make twice as much or many; as, *double* the recipe. 2. to fold. 3. to repeat or duplicate. 4. to be the double of. 5. in *bridge,* to increase the point value or penalty of (an opponent's bid). 6. in *nautical usage,* to sail around: as, they *doubled* Cape Horn. *v.i.* 1. to become double. 2. to turn sharply backward: as, the animal *doubled* on its tracks. 3. to serve as a double, serve two purposes, etc. 4. in *baseball,* to hit a double. **—double back,** 1. to fold back. 2. to turn back in the direction from which one came. **—double up,** 1. to fold completely; clench (one's fist). 2. to bend over, as in laughter or pain. 3. to share a room, etc. with someone. **—on the double,** [Colloq.], 1. in double time. 2. quickly. **—dou′ble·ness,** *n.* **—dou′bler,** *n.*

**dou·ble-bar·reled** (dub′'l-bar′'ld), *adj.* 1. having two barrels, as a kind of shotgun; hence, 2. having a double purpose or meaning.

**double bass,** the bass viol. **—dou′ble-bass′,** *adj.*

**double bassoon,** the contrabassoon.

**double bed,** a bed large enough for two people: the standard width is 54 inches.

**double boiler,** a utensil consisting of two pans, one of which fits into the other: food is cooked in the upper one by water boiling in the lower.

**dou·ble-breast·ed** (dub′'l-bres′tid), *adj.* overlapping across the breast and having two rows of buttons: as, a *double-breasted* coat.

**double chin,** a fold of flesh beneath the chin.

**dou·ble-cross** (dub′'l-krôs′), *v.t.* [Slang], to betray (a person) by doing the opposite of, or intentionally failing to do, what one has promised. **—dou′ble-cross′er,** *n.*

**double cross,** [Slang], double-crossing; treachery.

**double dagger,** a mark (‡) used in printing and writing to indicate a note or cross reference.

**double date,** [Colloq.], a social engagement in which two couples are together. **—dou′ble-date′** [-DATED, -DATING], *v.i.*

**dou·ble-deal·ing** (dub′'l-dēl′iŋ), *n.* the act of doing the opposite of what one pretends to do; duplicity. **—dou′ble-deal′er,** *n.*

**dou·ble-deck·er** (dub′'l-dek′ẽr), *n.* 1. any structure or vehicle with two levels. 2. [Colloq.], a sandwich with two layers of filling.

**dou·ble-edged** (dub′'l-ejd′), *adj.* 1. having two cutting edges. 2. applicable both ways, as an argument.

‡**dou·ble-en·ten·dre** (do͞o′bl′-än′tän′dr′), *n.* [Fr.; prob. altered < *double entente,* double meaning], a word or phrase with two meanings, especially when one of these is risqué or indecorous.

**double entry,** a system of bookkeeping in which every transaction is entered as both a debit and a credit.

**double exposure,** in *photography,* 1. the making of two exposures on the same film or plate. 2. a photograph made in this way.

**dou·ble-faced** (dub′'l-fāst′), *adj.* 1. having two faces or aspects. 2. hypocritical; insincere.

**double feature,** two full-length motion pictures on the same program.

**dou·ble-head·er** (dub′'l-hed′ẽr), *n.* two baseball games played in succession on the same day.

**double indemnity,** a clause in life insurance policies providing for the payment of twice the face value of the contract for accidental death.

**dou·ble-joint·ed** (dub′'l-join′tid), *adj.* having joints that permit limbs, fingers, etc. to bend at other than the usual angles.

**dou·ble-park** (dub′'l-pärk′), *v.t. & v.i.* to park (an automobile), usually unlawfully, alongside another parked next to a curb. **—dou′ble-park′ing,** *n.*

**double play,** in *baseball,* a play by which two players are put out.

**double pneumonia,** pneumonia of both lungs.

**dou·ble-quick** (dub′'l-kwik′), *adj.* very quick. *n.* a double-quick marching pace; double time. *v.i. & v.t.* to go or cause to go at this pace. *adv.* in this pace.

**dou·ble-reed** (dub′'l-rēd′), *adj.* designating or of a group of wood-wind instruments, as the oboe or bassoon, having two reeds separated by a narrow opening. *n.* a double-reed instrument.

**double standard,** the moral code imposing a more restrictive standard of behavior on women than on men, especially in matters of sex.

**dou·blet** (dub′lit), *n.* [OFr. dim. of *double,* orig., something folded], 1. a man's close-fitting jacket of the 14th to the 16th centuries. 2. either of a pair of similar things. 3. a pair; couple. 4. either of two words which derive ultimately from the same source but have changed in form (e.g., *card, chart*).

DOUBLET

**double take,** a delayed reaction to something unexpected, in which there is first unthinking acceptance and then a startled and obvious understanding of the true meaning: used as a piece of comic business in acting.

**double talk,** 1. ambiguous and deceptive talk. 2. meaningless syllables made to sound like talk.

**double time,** 1. a rate of payment twice as high as usual. 2. a marching cadence of 180 three-foot steps a minute: cf. **quick time.**

**dou·ble·tree** (dub′'l-trē′), *n.* [< *double,* after *singletree*], a crossbar on a wagon, plow, etc.

**dou·bloon** (du-blo͞on′), *n.* [< Fr. < Sp. < L. *duplus,* double], an obsolete Spanish gold coin.

**dou·bly** (dub′li), *adv.* 1. twice. 2. two at a time. 3. [Archaic], in a deceitful manner.

**doubt** (dout), *v.i.* [< OFr. < L. *dubitare*], to be unsettled in opinion or belief; be uncertain or undecided. *v.t.* 1. to be uncertain about; question. 2. to be inclined to disbelieve. 3. [Archaic], to be fearful of. *n.* 1. a wavering of opinion or belief. 2. a condition of uncertainty. 3. an unsettled point or matter; difficulty. **—beyond doubt,** certainly.

—**in doubt,** not certain. —**no doubt,** 1. certainly. 2. probably. —**without doubt,** certainly. —**doubt′a·ble,** *adj.* —**doubt′er,** *n.* —**doubt′ing·ly,** *adv.*

**doubt·ful** (dout′fəl), *adj.* 1. in doubt; not definite. 2. uncertain. 3. giving rise to doubt; of questionable reputation. 4. feeling doubt; undecided. —**doubt′ful·ly,** *adv.* —**doubt′ful·ness,** *n.*

**doubt·less** (dout′lis), *adj.* [Rare], feeling no doubt. *adv.* 1. without doubt; certainly. 2. probably. —**doubt′less·ly,** *adv.* —**doubt′less·ness,** *n.*

**douche** (dōōsh), *n.* [Fr. < It. *doccia,* water jet < LL. hyp. *ductia,* pipe < L. < *ducere,* to lead], 1. a jet of liquid applied externally or internally to some part of the body. 2. a bath or treatment of this kind. 3. a device for douching. *v.t.* & *v.i.* [DOUCHED, DOUCHING], to apply a douche (to).

**dough** (dō), *n.* [AS. *dag*], 1. a mixture of flour, liquid, and other ingredients, worked into a soft, thick mass for baking. 2. any pasty mass like this. 3. [Slang], money.

**dough·boy** (dō′boi′), *n.* [Colloq.], formerly, a U.S. infantryman.

**dough·nut** (dō′nut′), *n.* a small, usually ring-shaped cake, fried in deep fat.

**dough·ty** (dou′ti), *adj.* [-TIER, -TIEST], [< AS < *dugan,* to avail], [Archaic], valiant; brave; strong: now humorous. —**dough′ti·ly,** *adv.* —**dough′ti·ness,** *n.*

**dough·y** (dō′i), *adj.* [-IER, -IEST], of or like dough; soft, pasty, etc. —**dough′i·ness,** *n.*

**Doug·las, Stephen Arnold** (dug′ləs), 1813–1861; American political leader.

**Douglas fir** (or **spruce, pine, hemlock**), [after David *Douglas,* 19th-c. Scot. botanist], a tall evergreen tree of the pine family, found in the western part of North America.

**Doug·lass, Frederick** (dug′ləs), 1817?–1895; U.S. Negro leader, journalist, and statesman.

**dour** (dōōr, door, dour), *adj.* [< L. *durus,* hard], 1. [Scot.], stern; severe. 2. [Scot.], obstinate. 3. sullen; gloomy. —**dour′ly,** *adv.* —**dour′ness,** *n.*

**dou·ra, dou·rah** (door′ə), *n.* durra.

**douse** (dous), *v.t.* [DOUSED, DOUSING], [prob. < LG.], 1. to thrust suddenly into liquid. 2. to drench. 3. to pull down (sails), especially in haste. 4. [Colloq.], to pull off (shoes, etc.). 5. [Colloq.], to put out (a light or fire) quickly; extinguish. *v.i.* to be immersed or drenched. Also sp. **dowse.** —**dous′er,** *n.*

**dove** (duv), *n.* [< ON. *dūfa*], 1. a bird of the pigeon family, with a full-breasted body and short legs: a symbol of peace. 2. [D-], a symbol of the Holy Spirit. 3. a person regarded as gentle or innocent.

**dove** (dōv), alt. pt. of **dive.**

**dove·cote** (duv′kōt′, -kot′), *n.* [*dove* + *cote*], a small house or box with compartments for nesting pigeons: also **dove′cot′** (-kot′).

**Do·ver** (dō′vẽr), *n.* 1. the capital of Delaware: pop., 7,000. 2. a seaport in England, on the Strait of Dover: pop., 35,000.

**Dover, Strait** (or **Straits**) **of,** a strait between France and England.

**dove·tail** (duv′tāl′), *n.* 1. a thing shaped like a dove's tail; specif., a projecting, wedge-shaped part that fits into a corresponding indentation to form a joint. 2. a joint thus formed. *v.t.* 1. to join together by means of dovetails. 2. to piece together (facts, etc.). *v.i.* to fit together closely or logically.

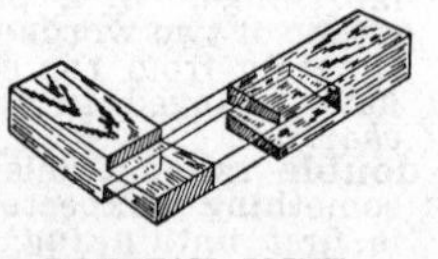

DOVETAIL JOINT

**dow·a·ger** (dou′ə-jẽr), *n.* [< OFr. < *douage,* dowry see DOWER], 1. a widow with a title or property derived from her dead husband. 2. [Colloq.], an elderly woman of wealth and dignity.

**dow·dy** (dou′di), *adj.* [-DIER, -DIEST], [< ME. *doude,* a slut], not neat or fashionable in dress; shabby. *n.* [*pl.* -DIES], a dowdy woman. —**dow′di·ly,** *adv.* —**dow′di·ness,** *n.*

**dow·el** (dou′əl), *n.* [ME. *duvel;* prob. < MLG. *dövel* via Fr.], a peg or pin of wood, metal, etc., usually fitted into corresponding holes in two pieces to fasten them together. *v.t.* [-ELED or -ELLED, -ELING or -ELLING], to fasten with dowels.

**dow·er** (dou′ẽr), *n.* [< OFr. < ML. *dotarium* < L. *dos;* see DOT (dower)], 1. that part of a husband's property which his widow inherits for life. 2. a dowry. 3. a natural talent, or endowment. *v.t.* 1. to give a dower to. 2. to endow (*with*).

DOWEL

**dow·er·y** (dou′ẽr-i), *n.* [*pl.* -IES], a dowry.

**down** (doun), *adv.* [AS. *adun,* from the hill < *a-,* off + *dun,* hill], 1. from a higher to a lower place. 2. in or on a lower position or level. 3. in a direction or place thought of as lower: as, *down*town. 4. from an earlier to a later period or person: as, *down* from the Middle Ages. 5. into a low condition, physically or emotionally. 6. in an inferior position; in check: as, they held him *down.* 7. to a lower amount or bulk: as, to come *down* in price. 8. to a heavier consistency: as, boil *down.* 9. in a serious manner: as, get *down* to work. 10. completely; to the full extent: as, loaded *down.* 11. in cash or when bought: as, $5 *down* and $80 on account. 12. in writing; on record: as, take *down* his name. *adj.* 1. directed toward a lower position. 2. in a lower place. 3. gone, brought, paid, etc. down. 4. dejected; discouraged. 5. prostrate; ill. 6. in *sports,* *a*) not in play: said of a football. *b*) trailing an opponent by a specified number of points, goals, etc. *prep.* down toward, along, through, into, or upon. *v.t.* to put, get, throw, or knock down. *v.i.* to go, come, or get down. *n.* 1. a descent. 2. a reverse; misfortune: as, one's ups and *downs.* 3. in *football,* *a*) one of four consecutive plays through which the team possessing the ball must either score or advance the ball ten yards or more to keep possession. *b*) the declaring of the ball as down, or the play just before this. —**down and out,** penniless, friendless, ill, etc. —**down on,** [Colloq.], hostile to; angry or annoyed with. —**down with!** do away with! overthrow!

**down** (doun), *n.* [< ON. *dūnn*], 1. soft, fine feathers. 2. soft, fine hair or hairy growth.

**down** (doun), *n.* [AS. *dun,* a hill], *usually in pl.* 1. an expanse of open, high, grassy land. 2. [confused with *dune*], a sandy mound formed by the wind.

**down·cast** (doun′kast′, -käst′), *adj.* 1. directed downward. 2. sad; very discouraged; dejected. *n.* 1. a casting down or pulling down. 2. in *mining,* a ventilating shaft.

**down-east** (doun′ēst′), *adj.* [Colloq.], of New England, especially Maine. —**down′-east′er,** *n.*

**Dow·ney** (doun′i), *n.* a city in SW California, near Los Angeles: pop., 83,000.

**down·fall** (doun′fôl′), *n.* 1. a sudden fall, as from prosperity or power. 2. a heavy fall of rain or snow. 3. a trap operated when the prey causes a weight to drop. —**down′fall′en,** *adj.*

**down·grade** (doun′grād′), *n.* a downward slope. *adv.* & *adj.* downhill; downward. *v.t.* [-GRADED, -GRADING], to demote to a less skilled job at lower pay. —**on the downgrade,** losing success, influence, health, etc.; declining; deteriorating.

**down·heart·ed** (doun′här′tid), *adj.* discouraged; dejected. —**down′heart′ed·ly,** *adv.*

**down·hill** (doun′hil′, doun′hil′), *adv.* toward the bottom of a hill; downward. *adj.* sloping or going downward; declining. —**go downhill,** to lose success, health, etc.; decline; deteriorate.

**Down·ing Street** (doun′iŋ), 1. a street in the West End of London, where some British government offices are located. 2. the British government.

**down·pour** (doun′pôr′, -pōr′), *n.* a heavy rain.

**down·right** (doun′rīt′, doun′rīt′), *adv.* 1. thoroughly; utterly. 2. [Rare], straight down. *adj.* 1. absolute; utter: as, a *downright* insult. 2. straightforward; frank: as, a *downright* fellow. 3. [Rare], going straight downward. —**down′right′ly,** *adv.* —**down′right′ness,** *n.*

**down·stairs** (doun′stârz′, doun′stârz′), *adv.* 1. down the stairs. 2. on or to a lower floor. *adj.* on a lower floor. *n.* a lower floor or floors.

**down·stream** (doun′strēm′, doun′strēm′), *adv.* & *adj.* in the direction of the current of a stream.

**down·town** (doun′toun′, doun′toun′), *adj.* 1. of or in the geographically lower part of a city. 2. of, in, or like the main business section of a city. *adv.* to, toward, or in the geographically lower part or main business section of a city. *n.* the main business section of a city.

**down·trod·den** (doun′trod′'n), *adj.* 1. trampled on or down. 2. oppressed. Also **down′trod′.**

**down·ward** (doun′wẽrd), *adv.* & *adj.* 1. toward a lower place, position, etc. 2. from an earlier to a later time. —**down′ward·ly,** *adv.*

**down·wards** (doun′wẽrdz), *adv.* downward.

**down·y** (doun′i), *adj.* [-IER, -IEST], 1. of or covered with soft, fine feathers or hair. 2. soft and fluffy, like down. —**down′i·ness,** *n.*

**dow·ry** (dou′ri), *n.* [*pl.* -RIES], [see DOWER], 1. the property that a woman brings to her husband at marriage. 2. a natural talent, gift, etc. 3. [Archaic], a widow's dower. 4. [Archaic], a gift by a man to his bride.

**dowse** (douz), ***v.i.*** [DOWSED, DOWSING], [? Corn.], to search for a source of water or minerals with a divining rod (**dowsing rod**).
**dowse** (dous), ***v.t.*** [DOWSED, DOWSING], to douse.
**dox·ol·o·gy** (doks-ol′ə-ji), ***n.*** [*pl.* -GIES], [< ML. < Gr. < *doxa*, praise + *logos* < *legein*, to speak], a hymn of praise to God; specif., *a*) the **greater doxology**, which begins "Glory to God in the highest." *b*) the **lesser doxology**, which begins "Glory to the Father." *c*) a hymn beginning "Praise God from whom all blessings flow."
**Doyle,** Sir **Arthur Co·nan** (kō′nən doil), 1859–1930; English writer of *Sherlock Holmes* stories.
**doz.,** dozen; dozens.
**doze** (dōz), ***v.i.*** [DOZED, DOZING], [orig., to stupefy < LG.], to sleep fitfully; nap. ***v.t.*** to spend (time) in dozing. ***n.*** a light sleep; nap. **—doze off,** to fall into a light sleep. **—doz′er,** ***n.***
**doz·en** (duz′'n), ***n.*** [*pl.* -ENS; *when preceded by a number*, -EN], [< OFr. < *douze*, twelve < L. < *duo*, two + *decem*, ten], a set of twelve: abbrev. **doz., dz. —doz′enth,** ***adj.***
**doz·y** (dōz′i), ***adj.*** [-IER, -IEST], sleepy; drowsy. **—doz′i·ly,** ***adv.*** **—doz′i·ness,** ***n.***
**DP, D.P.,** displaced person.
**dpt.,** 1. department. 2. deponent.
**Dr.,** Doctor.
**dr.,** 1. debtor. 2. dram; drams.
**drab** (drab), ***n.*** [< Fr. *drap*, cloth < LL. *drappus;* cf. DRAPE], a dull yellowish brown. ***adj.*** [DRABBER, DRABBEST], 1. dull yellowish-brown. 2. dull; monotonous. **—drab′ly,** ***adv.*** **—drab′ness,** ***n.***
**drab** (drab), ***n.*** [< Celt.; akin to Ir. *drabog*, slattern], 1. a slovenly woman; slut. 2. a prostitute. ***v.i.*** [DRABBED, DRABBING], to be a prostitute.
**drachm** (dram), ***n.*** 1. a drachma. 2. a dram.
**drach·ma** (drak′mə), ***n.*** [*pl.* -MAS, -MAE (-mē)], [L. < Gr. *drachmē* < *drachma*, handful < *drassesthai*, to grasp], 1. an ancient Greek silver coin. 2. a modern Greek monetary unit.
**draft** (draft, dräft), ***n.*** [ME. *draught*, *draht*, a stroke < AS. *dragan*, to draw], 1. a drawing, as of a vehicle or load. 2. the thing, quantity, or load pulled. 3. a drawing in of a fish net. 4. the amount of fish caught in a net. 5. a drinking. 6. the amount taken at one drink. 7. a drink. 8. a drawing into the lungs, as of air. 9. the air, etc. drawn in. 10. a drawing, as of beer, from a cask when ordered. 11. a rough sketch of a writing. 12. a plan or drawing of a work to be done. 13. a current of air, as in a room. 14. a device for regulating the current of air in a heating system. 15. a written order from one person, firm, etc., directing the payment of money to another; check. 16. a drain; heavy demand. 17. the taking of persons for compulsory military service. 18. those thus taken. 19. in *nautical usage*, the depth of water that a ship draws, or displaces. ***v.t.*** 1. to take, as for compulsory military service, by drawing from a group. 2. to draw off or away. 3. to make a preliminary sketch of or working plans for. ***adj.*** 1. used for pulling loads: as, *draft* animals. 2. drawn from a cask on order: as, *draft* beer. Also sp. **draught** in all senses, especially ***n.*** 3–10 and ***adj.*** 2. **—draft′er,** ***n.***
**draf·tee** (draf-tē′, dräf-), ***n.*** a person drafted, especially for service in the armed forces.
**drafts** (drafts, dräfts), ***n.pl.*** checkers: see **draughts.**
**drafts·man** (drafts′mən, dräfts′-), ***n.*** [*pl.* -MEN], 1. one who draws plans of structures or machinery. 2. one who draws up legal documents, speeches, etc. Also sp. **draughtsman. —drafts′man·ship′,** ***n.***
**draft·y** (draf′ti, dräf′-), ***adj.*** [-IER, -IEST], 1. in a draft (*n.* 13). 2. letting in, causing, or having a draft or drafts: as, a *drafty* house. Also sp. **draughty. —draft′i·ly,** ***adv.*** **—draft′i·ness,** ***n.***
**drag** (drag), ***v.t.*** [DRAGGED, DRAGGING], [< AS. *dragan* or ON. *draga;* see DRAW], 1. to pull or draw with effort, especially along the ground; haul. 2. to pull a grapnel, net, etc. over the bottom of (a river, etc.) in searching for something; dredge. 3. to draw a harrow over (land). 4. to draw (something) out over a period of time. ***v.i.*** 1. to be pulled along the ground; trail. 2. to lag behind. 3. to move or pass too slowly. 4. to search a river, etc., as with a grapnel or net. ***n.*** 1. something dragged along the ground; specif., *a*) a harrow for breaking ground. *b*) a heavy sledge (vehicle). *c*) a heavy coach with seats inside and on top. 2. a grapnel, dragnet, etc. 3. anything that hinders. 4. a dragging. 5. [Slang], influence. 6. [Slang], a puff of a cigarette, etc. 7. [Slang], a dull or boring person, situation, etc. **—drag on** (or **out**), to prolong or be prolonged tediously.
**drag·gle** (drag′'l), ***v.t. & v.i.*** [-GLED, -GLING], [freq. of *drag*], to make or become wet and dirty by dragging in mud or water.
**drag·net** (drag′net′), ***n.*** 1. a net dragged along the bottom of a river, lake, etc. for catching fish. 2. a net for catching small game. 3. an organized system or network for catching criminals, etc.
**drag·o·man** (drag′ə-mən), ***n.*** [*pl.* -MANS, -MEN], [Fr. < Late Gr. *dragoumanos* < OAr. < *targama*, to interpret], in the Near East, an interpreter.
**drag·on** (drag′ən), ***n.*** [OFr. < L. *draco* < Gr. *drakōn*], 1. a mythical monster, usually represented as a large reptile with wings and claws, breathing out fire. 2. a fierce person; esp., a strict chaperon.
**drag·on·fly** (drag′ən-flī′), ***n.*** [*pl.* -FLIES], a large, harmless insect with a long, slender body and four filmy wings: it feeds on flies, gnats, etc.
**dra·goon** (drə-gōōn′), ***n.*** [< Fr. *dragon;* see DRAGON], a heavily armed cavalryman. ***v.t.*** 1. to harass or persecute by dragoons. 2. to force by persecution.
**drag race,** a race between cars, as hot rods, to test their rates of acceleration from a complete stop, often held on a short, straight course.
**drain** (drān), ***v.t.*** [AS. *dreahnian* < base of *dryge*, dry], 1. to draw off (liquid, etc.) gradually. 2. to draw liquid from gradually: as, to *drain* an abscess. 3. to exhaust gradually; use up slowly: said of strength, etc. ***v.i.*** 1. to flow off gradually. 2. to become dry by the drawing or flowing off of liquid. 3. to discharge its waters: as, Central Europe *drains* into the Danube. ***n.*** 1. a channel, tube, or the like, carrying off water, sewage, pus, etc. 2. a draining or exhausting. 3. anything that drains or exhausts. **—drain′a·ble,** ***adj.*** **—drain′er,** ***n.***
**drain·age** (drān′ij), ***n.*** 1. the act, process, or method of draining. 2. a system of pipes, etc. for carrying off waste matter. 3. that which is drained off. 4. an area drained, as by a river.
**drainage basin,** the land drained by a river system.
**drain·pipe** (drān′pīp′), ***n.*** a large pipe used to carry off water, sewage, etc.
**drake** (drāk), ***n.*** [? < West Gmc.], a male duck.
**Drake,** Sir **Francis** (drāk), 1545?–1596; English admiral and navigator.
**dram** (dram), ***n.*** [< OFr. < L.; see DRACHMA], 1. in *apothecaries' weight*, a unit equal to 1/8 ounce. 2. in *avoirdupois weight*, a unit equal to 1/16 ounce. 3. a fluid dram. 4. a small drink of alcoholic liquor. 5. a small quantity of anything.
**dra·ma** (drä′mə, dram′ə), ***n.*** [LL. < Gr., a deed, drama < *dran*, to do], 1. a literary composition to be performed on the stage by actors; stage play. 2. the art or profession of writing, acting, or producing plays (often with *the*). 3. a series of events so interesting, vivid, etc. as to resemble those of a play. 4. the quality of being dramatic.
**Dram·a·mine** (dram′ə-mēn′), ***n.*** a drug to relieve seasickness, airsickness, etc.: a trade-mark.
**dra·mat·ic** (drə-mat′ik), ***adj.*** 1. of or connected with drama. 2. like a play; hence, 3. full of action; vivid, exciting, etc. **—dra·mat′i·cal·ly,** ***adv.***
**dra·mat·ics** (drə-mat′iks), ***n.pl.*** [construed as sing.], 1. the art of performing or producing plays. 2. plays presented by amateurs.
**dram·a·tis per·so·nae** (dram′ə-tis pẽr-sō′nē), [L.], the characters in a play. Abbrev. **dram. pers.**
**dram·a·tist** (dram′ə-tist), ***n.*** a person who writes plays; playwright.
**dram·a·tize** (dram′ə-tīz′), ***v.t.*** [-TIZED, -TIZING], 1. to make into a drama; adapt for performance on the stage, screen, etc. 2. to regard or show in a dramatic manner. ***v.i.*** to be capable of being dramatized. **—dram′a·ti·za′tion,** ***n.*** **—dram′a·tiz′er,** ***n.***
**dram·a·tur·gy** (dram′ə-tũr′ji), ***n.*** [< Fr. < Gr. < *drama* + *ergon*, work], the art of writing or producing plays. **—dram′a·tur′gic, dram′a·tur′gi·cal,** ***adj.*** **—dram′a·tur′gi·cal·ly,** ***adv.*** **—dram′a·tur′gist, dram′a·turge′** (-tũrj′), ***n.***
**drank** (draŋk), pt. and colloq. pp. of **drink.**
**drape** (drāp), ***v.t.*** [DRAPED, DRAPING], [< OFr. < *drap*, cloth < LL. *drappus*], 1. to cover, hang, or decorate as with cloth or clothes in loose folds. 2. to arrange (a garment, cloth, etc.) artistically in folds or hangings. ***v.i.*** to hang or fall in folds. ***n.*** *usually in pl.* cloth hanging in loose folds; curtain.
**drap·er** (drāp′ẽr), ***n.*** [Brit.], a dealer in cloth and dry goods.
**dra·per·y** (drā′pẽr-i), ***n.*** [*pl.* -IES], 1. cloth; fabric;

---

textile. 2. hangings or clothing arranged in loose folds. 3. an artistic arrangement of such hangings or clothing. 4. *pl.* curtains.

**dras·tic** (dras′tik), *adj.* [< Gr. *drastikos*, active < *dran*, to do], acting with force; having a violent effect; severe; harsh. —**dras′ti·cal·ly,** *adv.*

**draught** (draft, dräft), *n.*, *v.t.*, *adj.* draft.

**draughts** (drafts, dräfts), *n.pl.* [Brit.], the game of checkers: also sp. **drafts.**

**draughts·man** (drafts′mən, dräfts′-), *n.* [*pl.* -MEN], a draftsman. —**draughts′man·ship′,** *n.*

**draught·y** (draf′ti, dräf′-), *adj.* [-IER, -IEST], drafty. —**draught′i·ly,** *adv.* —**draught′i·ness,** *n.*

**drave** (drāv), archaic pt. of **drive.**

**Dra·vid·i·an** (drə-vid′i-ən), *n.* 1. any member of a group of intermixed races in S India and S Ceylon. 2. the family of non-Indo-European languages spoken by these races, including Tamil, Malayalam, Telugu, etc. *adj.* of the Dravidians or their languages: also **Dra·vid′ic.**

**draw** (drô), *v.t.* [DREW, DRAWN, DRAWING], [AS. *dragan*], 1. to make move toward one; pull; drag: as, a horse *draws* the cart. 2. to pull up, down, back, or in. 3. to need (a specified depth of water) to float in: said of a ship. 4. to attract; charm. 5. to breathe in; inhale. 6. to bring forth; elicit: as, his challenge *drew* no reply. 7. to cause to happen; bring on: as, the airplane *drew* the enemy's fire. 8. to pull out; extract, as a cork, sword, etc. 9. to take out (a liquid, etc.) by sucking, distilling, etc. 10. to bring up, as water from a well. 11. to disembowel. 12. to get from some source: as, he *draws* a good salary. 13. to withdraw (money) held in an account. 14. to write (a check or draft). 15. to bring (a game or contest) to a tie. 16. to deduce. 17. to stretch; make tense. 18. to distort. 19. to flatten or shape (metal) by die stamping, hammering, etc. 20. to make metal into (wire) by pulling it through holes. 21. to make (lines, pictures, etc.), as with a pencil or pen; sketch. *v.i.* 1. to draw something (in various senses of the *v.t.*). 2. to be drawn. 3. to come; move: as, he *drew* near. 4. to shrink; contract. 5. to allow a draft, as of smoke, to move through: as, the chimney *draws* well. *n.* 1. a drawing or being drawn (in various senses). 2. the result of drawing. 3. a thing drawn. 4. a tie; stalemate. 5. a thing that attracts. 6. the movable part of a drawbridge. 7. a land basin that water drains into. —**draw on,** to approach. —**draw out,** 1. to extend. 2. to get (a person) to talk. —**draw up,** 1. to arrange in order. 2. to compose (a document) in due form; draft. 3. to stop.

**draw·back** (drô′bak′), *n.* 1. money paid back from a charge previously made. 2. anything that prevents or lessens full satisfaction; shortcoming.

**draw·bridge** (drô′brij′), *n.* a bridge that can be raised, lowered, or drawn aside.

**draw·ee** (drô′ē′), *n.* the person on whom an order, bill of exchange, or draft is drawn.

**draw·er** (drô′ēr), *n.* 1. a person or thing that draws. 2. one who draws an order for the payment of money. 3. a draftsman. 4. (drôr), a sliding box in a table, chest, etc., which can be drawn out and then pushed back into place.

**draw·ers** (drôrz), *n.pl.* an undergarment for the lower part of the body, often covering the legs.

**draw·ing** (drô′iŋ), *n.* 1. the act of a person or thing that draws. 2. the art of representing something by lines drawn with a pencil, pen, etc. 3. a picture, design, etc. thus made. 4. a lottery.

**drawing card,** an entertainer, speaker, show, etc. that normally draws a large audience.

**drawing room,** [< *withdrawing room*: guests withdrew there after dinner], 1. a room where guests are received or entertained; parlor. 2. those assembled in such a room. 3. a private compartment on a railroad sleeping car.

**draw·knife** (drô′nīf′), *n.* [*pl.* -KNIVES (-nīvz′)], a knife with a handle at each end: the user draws it toward him in shaving a surface: also **drawing knife, draw′shave′** (-shāv′).

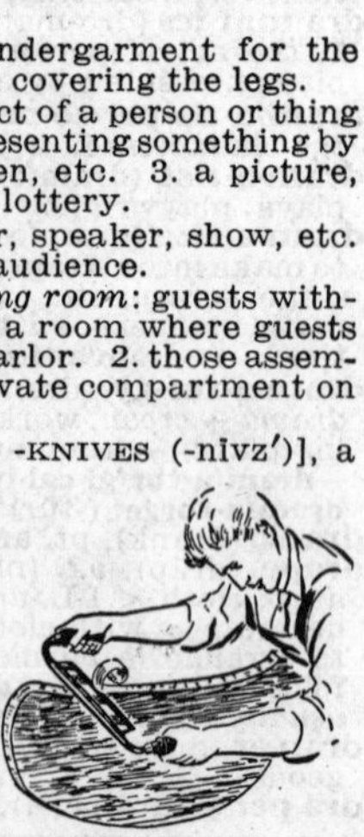

DRAWKNIFE

**drawl** (drôl), *v.t.* & *v.i.* [prob. < *draw*], to speak slowly, prolonging the syllables. *n.* speech characterized by slowness and prolongation of syllables. —**drawl′er,** *n.* —**drawl′ing·ly,** *adv.*

**drawn** (drôn), pp. of **draw.** *adj.* 1. pulled out of the sheath. 2. stalemated; even; tied: as, a *drawn* game. 3. disemboweled. 4. tense; haggard.

**drawn butter,** melted butter, sometimes thickened, used as a sauce.

**drawn work,** ornamental work done on textiles by pulling out threads and embroidering or hemstitching the edges.

**draw poker,** a form of poker in which each player is dealt five cards, and unwanted cards may be replaced from the deck before betting begins.

**dray** (drā), *n.* [AS. *dræge*, lit., something drawn < *dragan*, to draw], a low, sturdy cart with detachable sides, for carrying heavy loads. *v.t.* to carry or haul on a dray. *v.i.* to drive a dray.

**dray·age** (drā′ij), *n.* 1. the hauling of a load by dray. 2. the charge made for this.

**dray·man** (drā′mən), *n.* [*pl.* -MEN], a man who drives a dray.

**dread** (dred), *v.t.* & *v.i.* [AS. *on-drædan*], to anticipate with fear or distaste. *n.* 1. intense fear; apprehensive terror. 2. fear mixed with awe. *adj.* 1. dreaded or dreadful. 2. inspiring awe.

**dread·ful** (dred′fəl), *adj.* 1. inspiring dread; terrible or awesome. 2. [Colloq.], very bad, offensive, disagreeable, etc. —**dread′ful·ly,** *adv.* —**dread′ful·ness,** *n.*

**dread·nought, dread·naught** (dred′nôt′), *n.* a large, heavily armored battleship with big guns.

**dream** (drēm), *n.* [in form < AS. *dream*, joy, music; in sense < ON. *draum*, a dream], 1. a sequence of sensations, images, thoughts, etc. passing through a sleeping person's mind. 2. a fancy of the conscious mind; daydream; reverie. 3. the state in which such a daydream occurs. 4. a fond hope or aspiration. 5. anything so lovely, transitory, etc. as to seem dreamlike. *v.i.* [DREAMED or DREAMT (dremt), DREAMING], 1. to have dreams. 2. to have daydreams. 3. to have vague notions (*of*). *v.t.* 1. to dream of. 2. to spend in dreaming (with *away* or *out*). 3. to imagine as possible. —**dream up,** [Colloq.], to conceive of or devise. —**dream′er,** *n.* —**dream′ing·ly,** *adv.* —**dream′less,** *adj.* —**dream′like′,** *adj.*

**dream·y** (drēm′i), *adj.* [-IER, -IEST], 1. filled with dreams. 2. visionary; impractical: as, a *dreamy* idealist. 3. like something in a dream; shadowy; vague. 4. lulling; soothing: as, a *dreamy* melody. —**dream′i·ly,** *adv.* —**dream′i·ness,** *n.*

**drear** (drêr), *adj.* [< *dreary*], [Poetic], dreary.

**drear·y** (drêr′i), *adj.* [-IER, -IEST], [AS. *dreorig*, sad, orig., bloody, gory], 1. gloomy; cheerless; depressing; dismal; dull. 2. [Archaic], sad. —**drear′i·ly,** *adv.* —**drear′i·ness,** *n.*

**dredge** (drej), *n.* [< obs. D. *dregghe* or AS. *dragan*; see DRAW], 1. a net attached to a frame, dragged along the bottom of a river, bay, etc. to gather shellfish, etc. 2. an apparatus for scooping up mud, sand, etc., as in deepening or clearing channels, harbors, etc. *v.t.* [DREDGED, DREDGING], 1. to gather with a dredge. 2. to enlarge or clean out (a river channel, harbor, etc.) with a dredge. *v.i.* to use a dredge. —**dredg′er,** *n.*

**dredge** (drej), *v.t.* [DREDGED, DREDGING], [< ME. *dragge*, sweetmeat], 1. to sprinkle with flour or other powdery substance. 2. to sprinkle or sift (flour, etc.). —**dredg′er,** *n.*

**dregs** (dregz), *n.pl.* [< ON. *dregg*], 1. the particles of solid matter that go to the bottom in a liquid; lees. 2. the most worthless part: as, the *dregs* of society. —**dreg′gy** [-GIER, -GIEST], *adj.*

**Drei·ser, Theodore** (drī′sēr, -zēr), 1871–1945; American novelist.

**drench** (drench), *v.t.* [AS. *drencan*, caus. of *drincan*, to drink], 1. to make (a horse, cow, etc.) drink, especially medicine. 2. to wet all over; soak. *n.* 1. a large dose or draft, especially for a sick animal. 2. a drenching; soaking. 3. a solution for soaking. —**drench′er,** *n.*

**Dres·den** (drez′dən; G. drās′-), *n.* 1. a city in East Germany: pop., 468,000. 2. a fine porcelain or chinaware made near Dresden. *adj.* designating such porcelain or chinaware.

**dress** (dres), *v.t.* [DRESSED or DREST, DRESSING], [< OFr. *dresser*, to arrange < LL. < L. *directus*; see DIRECT], 1. to put clothes on; clothe. 2. to provide with clothing. 3. to decorate; trim; adorn. 4. to arrange a display in: as, he *dresses* store windows. 5. to arrange or do up (the hair). 6. to arrange (troops, etc.) in straight lines. 7. to apply medicines and bandages to (a wound, etc.). 8. to prepare; make ready for use: as, to *dress* a fowl. 9. to cultivate (fields or plants). 10. to smooth or finish (leather, stone, etc.). *v.i.* 1. to put on or wear clothes. 2. to dress in formal clothes. 3. to get into a straight line. *n.* 1. clothes; clothing; apparel. 2. the usual outer garment of women, generally of one piece with a skirt. 3. formal clothes. 4. external covering or appearance. *adj.* 1. of or for dresses: as, *dress* material. 2. worn on formal occasions: as, a *dress* suit. **—dress down,** [Colloq.], 1. to reprimand; scold. 2. to beat; thrash. **—dress up,** to dress in formal clothes, or in clothes more elegant, showy, etc. than usual.

**dress circle,** a section of seats in a theater or concert hall, usually behind and above the orchestra: so called because formal dress was formerly customary there.

**dress·er** (dres′ẽr), *n.* 1. one who dresses another person; valet, etc. 2. one who dresses store windows, leather, wounds, etc. 3. one who dresses elegantly or in a certain way: as, a fancy *dresser.*

**dress·er** (dres′ẽr), *n.* [< Fr. < OFr. *dresser;* see DRESS], 1. a table on which food is prepared for serving. 2. a cupboard for dishes and kitchen utensils. 3. a chest of drawers for clothes, with a mirror; bureau.

**dress·ing** (dres′iŋ), *n.* 1. the act of one that dresses. 2. something used to dress a person (as clothes) or a thing (as manure applied to soil, bandages applied to wounds, etc.). 3. a sauce for salads and other dishes. 4. a stuffing, as of bread, seasoning, etc., for roast fowl.

**dress·ing-down** (dres′iŋ-doun′), *n.* [Colloq.], 1. a reprimand; scolding. 2. a thrashing; beating.

**dressing gown,** a loose robe for wear when one is undressed or lounging.

**dressing room,** a room for getting dressed in, especially backstage in a theater.

**dressing table,** a low stand or table with a mirror, for use while putting on cosmetics, etc.

**dress·mak·er** (dres′māk′ẽr), *n.* one who makes women's dresses and the like. *adj.* designating or of a woman's suit, coat, etc. not cut on severe, mannish lines: cf. *tailored.* **—dress′mak′ing,** *n.*

**dress parade,** a military parade in dress uniform.

**dress rehearsal,** a final rehearsal, as of a play, performed in the way in which it is to take place.

**dress suit,** a man's formal suit for evening wear.

**dress·y** (dres′i), *adj.* [-IER, -IEST], [Colloq.], 1. wearing showy clothes. 2. stylish; elegant; smart. **—dress′i·ly,** *adv.* **—dress′i·ness,** *n.*

**drest** (drest), alt. pt. and pp. of **dress.**

**drew** (drōō), pt. of **draw.**

**Drey·fus, Alfred** (drā′fəs, drī′-; Fr. dre′füs′), 1859–1935; French army officer convicted of treason but later vindicated when shown to be the victim of anti-Semitism and conspiracy.

**drib** (drib), *v.i. & v.t.* [DRIBBED, DRIBBING], [< *drip*], [Obs.], to fall, or let fall, in or as in driblets. **—dribs and drabs,** [*drab* for *drap,* dial. form of *drop, n.*], [Colloq.], small amounts.

**drib·ble** (drib′'l), *v.i. & v.t.* [-BLED, -BLING], [freq. of *drip*], 1. to flow, or let flow, in drops or driblets; trickle. 2. to slaver; drool. 3. in certain games, to move (the ball) along by repeated bounces or by a series of short kicks. *n.* 1. a driblet; dribbling flow. 2. the act of dribbling a basketball, soccer ball, etc. 3. [Colloq.], a drizzling rain. **—drib′bler,** *n.*

**drib·let, drib·blet** (drib′lit), *n.* [*drib,* drip + *-let*], a small amount; bit.

**dried** (drid), pt. and pp. of **dry.**

**dri·er** (drī′ẽr), *n.* 1. a person or thing that dries. 2. an apparatus for drying by heating, blowing, etc. 3. a substance added to paint, varnish, etc. to make it dry fast. Also sp. **dryer.** *adj.* comparative of **dry.**

**dri·est** (drī′ist), *adj.* superlative of **dry.**

**drift** (drift), *n.* [<AS. *drifan,* to drive], 1. a driving. 2. a being driven along, as by a current of water. 3. the course on which something is directed. 4. the deviation of a ship or airplane from its path, caused by side currents or winds. 5. a tendency; trend. 6. meaning; intent. 7. something driven, as rain or snow before the wind. 8. a heap of snow, sand, etc., piled up by the wind. 9. in *geology,* rocks, gravel, etc. carried from one place and deposited in another by a river or glacier. 10. in *mining,* a horizontal passageway, as along the path of a vein. 11. in *physical geography,* a slow ocean current. *v.i.* 1. to be carried along as by a current. 2. to go along aimlessly. 3. to accumulate in heaps by force of wind or water. *v.t.* to cause to drift. **—drift′er,** *n.* **—drift′y** [-IER, -IEST], *adj.*

**drift·age** (drif′tij), *n.* 1. a drifting. 2. deviation caused by drifting. 3. that which has drifted.

**drift·wood** (drift′wood′), *n.* wood drifting in the water or washed ashore: often figurative.

**drill** (dril), *n.* [D. *dril* < *drillen,* to drill], 1. a tool or apparatus for boring holes in wood, metal, etc. 2. a snail that bores into the shells of oysters and kills them. 3. military or physical training, as in marching and the manual of arms. 4. the process or method of teaching by making those taught do an exercise repeatedly. *v.t.* 1. to bore a hole in as with a drill. 2. to train in military or physical exercises. 3. to teach by having do repeated exercises. *v.i.* 1. to bore a hole or holes. 2. to engage in military, physical, or mental exercises. **—drill′er,** *n.*

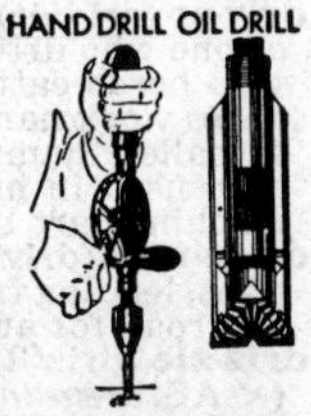

TYPES OF DRILL

**drill** (dril), *n.* [< ?], 1. a furrow in which seeds are planted. 2. a row of planted seeds. 3. a machine for making holes or furrows and dropping seeds into them. *v.t.* 1. to sow (seeds) in rows. 2. to plant (a field) in drills. **—drill′er,** *n.*

**drill** (dril), *n.* [< MHG. *dril(i)ch* < L. *trilix,* three-threaded], a coarse linen or cotton cloth, used for work clothes, etc.: also **drill′ing.**

**drill** (dril), *n.* [? < Fr. *drill,* a soldier], a baboon native to W Africa, like the mandrill.

**drill·mas·ter** (dril′mas′tẽr, -mäs′-), *n.* 1. an instructor in military drill. 2. a person who teaches by drilling.

**drill press,** a machine tool for drilling holes.

**dri·ly** (drī′li), *adv.* dryly.

**drink** (driŋk), *v.t.* [DRANK or *archaic* DRUNK, DRUNK or *colloq.* DRANK or *archaic* DRUNKEN, DRINKING], [AS. *drincan*], 1. to swallow (liquid). 2. to absorb (liquid). 3. to swallow the contents of. 4. to drink a toast to. *v.i.* 1. to swallow liquid. 2. to absorb anything as if in drinking. 3. to drink alcoholic liquor, especially to excess. *n.* 1. any liquid for drinking; beverage. 2. alcoholic liquor. 3. habitual or excessive use of alcoholic liquor. **—drink in,** to take in eagerly with the senses or the mind. **—drink to,** to drink a toast to. **—drink′a·ble,** *adj.* **—drink′er,** *n.*

**drip** (drip), *v.i. & v.t.* [DRIPPED or DRIPT, DRIPPING], [AS. *dryppan*], to fall, or let fall, in drops. *n.* 1. a falling in drops. 2. liquid falling in drops. 3. a projecting part of a sill, cornice, etc. that sheds rain water. 4. [Slang], a person regarded as unpleasant or insipid.

**drip-dry** (drip′drī′), *adj.* designating or of fabrics or garments that dry quickly when hung soaking wet and that require little or no ironing.

**drip·ping** (drip′iŋ), *adj.* thoroughly wet. *n.* 1. a falling of liquid drop by drop. 2. *usually pl.* anything that drips; esp., the fat and juices that drip from roasting meat.

**drive** (drīv), *v.t.* [DROVE, DRIVEN, DRIVING], [AS. *drifan*], 1. to force to go; push forward; impel. 2. to force into or from a state or act: as, he *drove* her insane. 3. to force to work, usually to excess. 4. to force as by a blow; hit (a ball) hard and swiftly. 5. to make penetrate. 6. to produce by penetrating: as, he *drove* an oil well. 7. to control the movement of (an automobile, wagon, etc.). 8. to transport as in an automobile. 9. to carry on with vigor; push (a bargain, etc.) through. *v.i.* 1. to advance violently; dash. 2. to drive a blow, ball, etc. 3. to be driven; operate: said of an automobile. 4. to go in a vehicle. 5. to operate a motor vehicle. *n.* 1. a driving. 2. a trip in a vehicle. 3. a road for automobiles, etc. 4. a rounding up of animals as for branding. 5. a hard, swift blow, hit, thrust, etc. 6. an organized movement to achieve some purpose; campaign. 7. energy; push: as, a person with *drive.* 8. that which is urgent or pressing: as, hunger is a basic *drive.* 9. a collection of logs floating down a river. 10. the propelling mechanism of a motor vehicle, machine, etc. 11. [Colloq.], a driveway. **—drive at,** 1. to aim at. 2. to mean; intend. **—let drive,** to hit or aim.

**drive-in** (drīv′in′), *adj.* designating or of a restaurant, movie theater, etc. designed to render its services to persons who drive up and remain in their cars. *n.* such a restaurant, etc.

**driv·el** (driv′'l), *v.i.* [-ELED or -ELLED, -ELING or -ELLING], [AS. *dreflian*], 1. to let saliva flow from one's mouth; slobber. 2. to speak in a silly or stupid manner. *v.t.* to say in a silly or stupid manner. *n.* 1. saliva running from the mouth. 2. silly, stupid talk. **—driv′el·er, driv′el·ler,** *n.*

**driv·en** (driv'’n), pp. of **drive.** ***adj.*** moved along and piled up by the wind: as, *driven* snow.
**driv·er** (drīv'ẽr), ***n.*** 1. a person who drives; specif., *a)* one who drives an automobile, horse, etc. *b)* one who herds cattle. *c)* one who makes his subordinates work hard. 2. a thing that drives; specif., *a)* a mallet, hammer, etc. *b)* a wooden-headed golf club used in hitting the ball from the tee. *c)* any machine part that communicates motion.
**drive·way** (drīv'wā'), ***n.*** 1. a path, as for automobiles, leading from a garage or house to the street. 2. a road for automobiles, etc.
**driz·zle** (driz''l), ***v.i.*** [-ZLED, -ZLING], [< ME. *dresen* (< AS. *dreosan*), to fall; + *-le*, freq. suffix], to rain in fine, mistlike drops. ***n.*** a rain of this kind. **—driz'zly,** ***adj.***
**droll** (drōl), ***adj.*** [< Fr. < D. *drol*, short, stout fellow], amusing in a quaint way; humorously odd. ***n.*** a droll person; jester. ***v.i.*** to joke; play the jester. **—drol'ly,** ***adv.***
**droll·er·y** (drōl'ẽr-i), ***n.*** [*pl.* -IES], 1. anything quaintly amusing; droll act, remark, etc. 2. the act of joking. 3. quaint humor.
**-drome** (drōm), [< Gr. *dromas*, running], a suffix meaning *running, racecourse*, as in *hippodrome*.
**drom·e·dar·y** (drom'ə-der'i), ***n.*** [*pl.* -IES], [< OFr. < LL. *dromedarius (camelus)*, running (camel) < L. < Gr. < *dramein*, to run], a camel trained for fast riding; esp., the one-humped Arabian camel.
**drone** (drōn), ***n.*** [AS. *dran*], 1. a male honeybee, which serves only in a reproductive capacity, has no sting, and does no work. 2. an idle person who lives by the work of others; loafer. ***v.i.*** [DRONED, DRONING], to live in idleness; loaf.
**drone** (drōn), ***v.i.*** [DRONED, DRONING], [< ME.; prob. < *drone* (bee)], 1. to make a continuous humming sound. 2. to talk in a monotonous voice. ***v.t.*** to utter in a monotonous tone. ***n.*** 1. a continuous humming sound. 2. a bagpipe. 3. its bass pipe.
**drool** (drōōl), ***v.i.*** [< *drivel*], 1. to let saliva flow from one's mouth; drivel. 2. to flow from the mouth, as saliva. 3. [Slang], to speak in a silly or stupid manner. ***v.t.*** 1. to let run from the mouth. 2. [Slang], to say in a silly or stupid manner. ***n.*** 1. saliva running from the mouth. 2. [Slang], silly, stupid talk.
**droop** (drōōp), ***v.i.*** [< ON. *drūpa* < base of *drop*, drip], 1. to sink, hang, or bend down. 2. to lose vitality or strength. 3. to become dejected. ***v.t.*** to let sink or hang down. ***n.*** a drooping.
**droop·y** (drōōp'i), ***adj.*** [-IER, -IEST], tending to droop. **—droop'i·ly,** ***adv.*** **—droop'i·ness,** ***n.***
**drop** (drop), ***n.*** [AS. *dropa*], 1. a small quantity of liquid that is somewhat spherical, as when falling. 2. a very small quantity of liquid. 3. *pl.* liquid medicine taken in drops. 4. a very small quantity of anything. 5. a thing like a drop in shape, size, etc. 6. a dropping; sudden fall, slump, descent, etc. 7. anything that drops or is used for dropping, as a drop curtain, a trap door, or a slot for depositing letters. 8. the distance between a higher and lower level. 9. in *football*, a drop kick. ***v.i.*** [DROPPED or, *occas.*, DROPT, DROPPING], 1. to fall in drops. 2. to fall; come down. 3. to sink to the ground exhausted, wounded, or dead. 4. to fall into a specified state: as, she *dropped* off to sleep. 5. to come to an end: as, let the matter *drop*. 6. to become lower or less, as prices, etc. 7. to move down with a current of water or air. 8. to be born: said of animals. ***v.t.*** 1. to let fall in drops. 2. to let fall; release hold of. 3. to give birth to: said of animals. 4. to utter (a hint, etc.) casually. 5. to send (a letter). 6. to cause to fall, as by wounding or killing. 7. to dismiss; have done with. 8. to lower. 9. to poach (an egg). 10. [Colloq.], to leave (a person or thing) at a specified place. 11. in *football*, *a)* to drop-kick (a ball). *b)* to make (a goal) in this way. **—at the drop of a hat,** immediately. **—drop behind,** to be outdistanced. **—drop in,** to pay a casual or unexpected visit. **—drop off,** 1. to go away or out of sight. 2. [Colloq.], to fall asleep. **—drop out,** to stop being a member or participant.
**drop curtain,** a theater curtain that can be lowered and raised.
**drop-forge** (drop'fôrj', -fōrj'), ***v.t.*** [-FORGED, -FORGING], to pound (heated metal) between dies with a drop hammer. **—drop'-forg'er,** ***n.*** **—drop forging.**
**drop hammer,** 1. a machine for pounding metal into shape, with a heavy weight that is raised and then dropped on the metal. 2. this weight. Also **drop press.**
**drop kick,** in *football*, a kick in which the ball is dropped to the ground and kicked just as it rebounds. **—drop'-kick',** ***v.t. & v.i.*** **—drop'-kick'er,** ***n.***
**drop·let** (drop'lit), ***n.*** a very small drop.
**drop·out** (drop'out'), ***n.*** a student who withdraws from school before graduating.
**drop·per** (drop'ẽr), ***n.*** 1. a person or thing that d ops. 2. a small glass tube with a rubber bulb at one end and a narrow opening at the other, for releasing liquid in drops.
**drop·si·cal** (drop'si-k'l), ***adj.*** 1. of or like dropsy. 2. having dropsy. **—drop'si·cal·ly,** ***adv.***
**drop·sy** (drop'si), ***n.*** [< OFr. < L. < Gr. *hydrōps*, dropsy < *hydōr*, water], an abnormal accumulation of serous fluid in cavities or tissues of the body. **—drop'sied,** ***adj.***
**dropt** (dropt), occas. pt. and pp. of **drop.**
**drosh·ky** (drosh'ki, drôsh'-), ***n.*** [*pl.* -KIES], [Russ. *drozhki*], a low, open, four-wheeled Russian carriage: also **dros·ky** (dros'ki), [*pl.* -KIES].
**dro·soph·i·la** (drō-sof'ə-lə, drə-), ***n.*** [*pl.* -LAE (-lē')], [Mod. L. < Gr. *drosos*, liquid + *philos*, loving], a small fly used in laboratory experiments in heredity: also called *fruit fly*.
**dross** (drôs, dros), ***n.*** [< AS. < *dreosan*, to fall], 1. a scum formed on the surface of molten metal. 2. waste matter; refuse; rubbish. **—dross'i·ness,** ***n.*** **—dross'y** [-IER, -IEST], ***adj.***
**drought** (drout), ***n.*** [AS. *drugoth*, dryness < base of *dryge;* see DRY], 1. dryness; lack of moisture, especially of rain. 2. prolonged dry weather. **—drought'y** [-IER, -IEST], ***adj.***
**drouth** (drouth), ***n.*** drought. **—drouth'y** [-IER, -IEST], ***adj.***
**drove** (drōv), ***n.*** [AS. *draf;* see DRIVE], 1. a number of cattle, sheep, etc. driven or moving along as a group; flock; herd. 2. a moving crowd of people. 3. a mason's broad-faced chisel **(drove chisel)** for smoothing stone. ***v.t. & v.i.*** [DROVED, DROVING], to finish (stone) with a drove chisel.
**drove** (drōv), pt. of **drive.**
**dro·ver** (drō'vẽr), ***n.*** 1. a person who takes a drove of animals to market. 2. a cattle dealer.
**drown** (droun), ***v.i.*** [< ON. *drukkna*], to die by suffocation in water or other liquid. ***v.t.*** 1. to kill by such suffocation. 2. to cover with water; flood; soak. 3. to deaden or muffle (sound, etc.): with *out.* 4. to get rid of: as, to *drown* one's sorrow in drink. **—drown'er,** ***n.***
**drowse** (drouz), ***v.i.*** [DROWSED, DROWSING], [< D. *droosen*], to be sleepy or almost asleep; doze. ***v.t.*** 1. to make sleepy. 2. to spend (time) in drowsing. ***n.*** the fact or state of drowsing; doze.
**drow·sy** (drou'zi), ***adj.*** [-SIER, -SIEST], 1. being or making sleepy or half asleep. 2. brought on by sleepiness. **—drow'si·ly,** ***adv.*** **—drow'si·ness,** ***n.***
**drub** (drub), ***v.t.*** [DRUBBED, DRUBBING], [Turk. < Ar. < *daraba*, to cudgel], 1. to beat with a stick; cudgel. 2. to defeat soundly in a fight, contest, etc. ***n.*** a blow with a club. **—drub'ber,** ***n.***
**drub·bing** (drub'iŋ), ***n.*** [see DRUB], a sound beating, thrashing, or defeat.
**drudge** (druj), ***n.*** [? < AS. *dreogan*, to suffer], a person who does hard, menial, or unpleasant work. ***v.i.*** [DRUDGED, DRUDGING], to do such work.
**drudg·er·y** (druj'ẽr-i), ***n.*** [*pl.* -IES], work that is hard, menial, or unpleasant.
**drug** (drug), ***n.*** [< OFr. *drogue*], 1. any substance used as or in a medicine. 2. a narcotic. ***v.t.*** [DRUGGED, DRUGGING], 1. to put a harmful drug in (a beverage, etc.). 2. to stupefy or poison as with a drug. 3. to administer something nauseating to. **—drug on the market,** a commodity for which there is little demand because of a plentiful supply.
**drug addict,** a habitual user of narcotics.
**drug·gist** (drug'ist), ***n.*** 1. a dealer in drugs, medical equipment, etc. 2. a person authorized to fill prescriptions; pharmacist.
**drug·store** (drug'stôr', -stōr'), ***n.*** a store where drugs and medical supplies are sold: most drugstores also sell cosmetics, tobacco, books, etc.
**dru·id, Dru·id** (drōō'id), ***n.*** [< Fr. < L. *druides*, *pl.* < Celt.], a member of a Celtic religious order in ancient Britain, Ireland, and France. **—dru·id'ic, dru·id'i·cal,** ***adj.*** **—dru'id·ism,** ***n.***
**drum** (drum), ***n.*** [< D. *trom* or MLG. *trumme*], 1. a percussion instrument consisting of a hollow cylinder with a membrane stretched tightly over the end or ends. 2. the sound produced by beating a drum, or any sound like this. 3. any drumlike cylindrical object. 4. a metal cylinder around which cable, etc. is wound in a machine. 5. a barrellike metal container for oil, etc. 6. in *anatomy*, *a)* the middle ear. *b)* the eardrum. ***v.i.*** [DRUMMED, DRUMMING], 1. to beat a drum. 2. to beat or tap continually, as with the fingers. ***v.t.*** 1. to play (a piece) on a drum. 2. to assemble by beating a drum. **—drum into,** to make known to by continued repetition. **—drum out of,** to expel from in disgrace. **—drum up,** 1. to

summon as by beating a drum. 2. to get (business, etc.) by soliciting.
**drum·beat** (drum'bēt'), *n.* a sound made by beating a drum.
**drum·head** (drum'hed'), *n.* 1. the membrane stretched over the open end or ends of a drum. 2. the eardrum. 3. the top of a capstan.
**drum·lin** (drum'lin), *n.* [< Ir. *druim* + *-lin*, dim. suffix], a long ridge formed by glacial drift.
**drum major,** a person who leads or precedes a marching band, often whirling a baton and prancing. —**drum ma'jor·ette',** *fem.*
**drum·mer** (drum'ẽr), *n.* 1. a drum player. 2. [cf. phr. *drum up*], [Colloq.], a traveling salesman.
**drum·stick** (drum'stik'), *n.* 1. a stick for beating a drum. 2. the lower half of the leg of a cooked fowl.
**drunk** (druŋk), pp. and archaic pt. of **drink.** *adj.* (usually used in the predicate) 1. overcome by alcoholic liquor; intoxicated. 2. overcome by any powerful emotion. *n.* [Slang], 1. a drunken person. 2. a drinking spree.
**drunk·ard** (druŋ'kẽrd), *n.* a person who often gets drunk; inebriate.
**drunk·en** (druŋ'kən), archaic pp. of **drink.** *adj.* (used before the noun) 1. intoxicated or habitually intoxicated. 2. caused by or in a drunken condition. —**drunk'en·ly,** *adv.* —**drunk'en·ness,** *n.*
**drupe** (dro͞op), *n.* [< L. < Gr. *dryppa*, overripe olive], any fruit with a soft, fleshy part around an inner stone that contains the seed, as an apricot, cherry, etc. —**dru·pa·ceous** (dro͞o-pā'shəs), *adj.*
**drupe·let** (dro͞op'lit), *n.* a small drupe: a loganberry or blackberry consists of many drupelets.
**dry** (drī), *adj.* [DRIER, DRIEST], [AS. *dryge*], 1. not under water: as, *dry* land. 2. having no moisture; not wet or moist. 3. not shedding tears. 4. lacking rain or water: as, a *dry* summer. 5. having lost moisture; arid. 6. needing water or drink; thirsty. 7. not yielding milk. 8. without butter, jam, etc.: as, *dry* toast. 9. solid: opposed to *liquid*. 10. not sweet: as, *dry* wine. 11. having no mucous or watery discharge: as, a *dry* cough. 12. without bleeding: as, a *dry* death. 13. prohibiting or opposed to the use or sale of alcoholic liquors: as, a *dry* county. 14. unemotional; plain: as, a *dry* remark. 15. boring; uninteresting: as, a *dry* lecture. *n.* [*pl.* DRYS], [Colloq.], one opposed to the use or sale of alcoholic liquors; prohibitionist. *v.t. & v.i.* [DRIED, DRYING], to make or become dry. —**dry up,** 1. to make or become thoroughly dry. 2. [Slang.], to stop talking. —**not dry behind the ears,** [Colloq.], immature; inexperienced.
**dry·ad, Dry·ad** (drī'əd, -ad), *n.* [*pl.* -ADS, -ADES (-ə-dēz')], [< L. < Gr. *dryas* < *drys*, an oak, tree], in *Gr. mythology*, any nymph living in a tree; wood nymph. —**dry·ad'ic** (-ad'ik), *adj.*
**dry battery,** 1. an electric battery made up of several connected dry cells. 2. a dry cell.
**dry cell,** a voltaic cell containing an absorbent so that its contents cannot spill.
**dry-clean** (drī'klēn', -klēn'), *v.t.* to clean (garments, etc.) with a solvent other than water, as naphtha or gasoline. —**dry cleaner.** —**dry cleaning.**
**Dry·den, John** (drī'd'n), 1631–1700; English poet, critic, and dramatist.
**dry-dock** (drī'dok'), *v.t. & v.i.* to place in or go into a dry dock.
**dry dock,** a dock from which the water can be emptied, used for building and repairing ships.
**dry·er** (drī'ẽr), *n.* a drier.
**dry-eyed** (drī'īd'), *adj.* shedding no tears.
**dry-farm** (drī'färm'), *v.i. & v.t.* to do dry farming on (land). —**dry farmer.**
**dry farming,** farming in an almost rainless region without irrigation: done by conserving the soil moisture and planting drought-resistant crops.
**dry goods,** cloth, cloth products, thread, etc.
**dry ice,** carbon dioxide highly compressed and in a solid state, used as a refrigerant.
**dry law,** a law prohibiting the manufacture and sale of alcoholic liquors.
**dry·ly** (drī'li), *adv.* in a dry manner; without emotion: also **dri'ly.**
**dry measure,** a system of measuring the volume of dry things, such as grain, vegetables, etc.; esp., the system in which 2 pints = 1 quart, 8 quarts = 1 peck, and 4 pecks = 1 bushel.
**dry·ness** (drī'nis), *n.* a dry quality or state.
**dry nurse,** a nurse who takes care of a baby without breast-feeding it: cf. *wet nurse.* —**dry'-nurse'** [-NURSED, -NURSING], *v.t.*
**dry point,** 1. a needle for engraving lines on a copper plate without using acid. 2. a print from such a plate. 3. this way of engraving.
**dry rot,** 1. a fungous decay causing seasoned timber to crumble to powder. 2. a similar fungous disease of plants, fruits, etc.
**dry run,** [Military Slang], 1. practice in firing small arms or guns without using live ammunition. 2. a rehearsal for any event.
**dry wash,** laundry washed and dried but not ironed.
**Ds,** in *chemistry*, dysprosium.
**d.s.,** daylight saving.
**D.S., d.s.,** *dal segno*, [It.], (repeat) from this sign.
**D.S., D.Sc.,** Doctor of Science.
**D.S.C.,** Distinguished Service Cross.
**D.S.T.,** Daylight Saving Time.
**d.t.,** 1. delirium tremens. 2. double time.
**D.T.'s, d.t.'s** (dē'tēz'), [Slang], delirium tremens.
**du·al** (do͞o'əl, dū'-), *adj.* [< L. < *duo*, two], 1. of two. 2. having or composed of two parts; double; twofold. *n.* in *linguistics*, dual number. —**du·al·i·ty** (do͞o-al'ə-ti, dū-), *n.* —**du'al·ly,** *adv.*
**du·al·ism** (do͞o'əl-iz'm, dū'-), *n.* 1. the state of being dual; duality. 2. any doctrine or theory that is based on a twofold distinction, as the theory that the world is ultimately composed of mind and matter. —**du'al·ist,** *n.* —**du'al·is'tic,** *adj.* —**du'al·is'ti·cal·ly,** *adv.*
**dual number,** in some languages, as Sanskrit, a grammatical number indicating *two*: distinguished from *singular* and *plural*.
**dub** (dub), *v.t.* [DUBBED, DUBBING], [< AS. *dubbian*, to strike], 1. to make (a man) a knight by tapping on the shoulder with a sword. 2. to confer a title, name, or nickname upon. 3. to make smooth, as by hammering, scraping, or rubbing. 4. [Slang], to bungle (a golf stroke, etc.). *n.* [Slang], a clumsy, unskillful player.
**dub** (dub), *v.t.* [DUBBED, DUBBING], [< *double*], to insert (dialogue, music, etc.) in the sound track of a motion picture: usually with *in*. *n.* dialogue, music, etc. so inserted.
**Du Bar·ry, Ma·rie** (må'rē' dü' bå'rē'; Eng. do͞o' bar'i, dū'), Comtesse, 1746?–1793; mistress of Louis XV of France.
**du·bi·e·ty** (do͞o-bī'ə-ti, dū-), *n.* [L. *dubietas*], 1. the quality of being dubious; uncertainty. 2. [*pl.* -TIES], a thing that is doubtful.
**du·bi·ous** (do͞o'bi-əs, dū'-), *adj.* [< L. < *dubius*, uncertain], 1. causing doubt; ambiguous. 2. feeling doubt; skeptical. 3. uncertain: as, *dubious* battle. 4. questionable: as, a *dubious* character. —**du'bi·ous·ly,** *adv.* —**du'bi·ous·ness,** *n.*
**Dub·lin** (dub'lin), *n.* the capital of Ireland: seaport on the Irish Sea: pop., 539,000.
**Du·Bois, William Edward Burghardt** (do͞o-bois'), 1868–1963; U.S. historian and Negro leader.
**du·bon·net** (do͞o'bə-nā'; Fr. dü'bô'ne'), *n.* [name of Fr. manufacturer], 1. a fortified French red wine: a trade-mark (**Dubonnet**). 2. a light maroon color. *adj.* of this color.
**Du·buque** (də-būk'), *n.* a city in E Iowa, on the Mississippi: pop., 57,000.
**du·cal** (do͞o'k'l, dū'-), *adj.* [LL. *ducalis*, of a leader], of a duke or dukedom. —**du'cal·ly,** *adv.*
**duc·at** (duk'ət), *n.* [< OFr. < It. < LL. *ducatus*; see DUCHY], 1. any of several former European coins of gold or silver. 2. [Slang], a ticket.
**‡du·ce** (do͞o'che), *n.* [It. < L. *dux*], chief; leader: title (*Il Duce*) taken by Benito Mussolini.
**duch·ess** (duch'is), *n.* 1. the wife or widow of a duke. 2. a woman who holds in her own right the sovereignty of a duchy.
**duch·y** (duch'i), *n.* [*pl.* -IES], [< OFr. < LL. *ducatus*, military command < L. *dux*, leader], the territory ruled by a duke or duchess; dukedom.
**duck** (duk), *n.* [< AS. *duce*, lit., diver < *duck, v.*], 1. [*pl.* DUCKS, DUCK; see PLURAL, II, D, 1], a swimming bird with a flat bill, short neck and legs, and webbed feet. 2. a female duck: opposed to *drake*. 3. the flesh of a duck as food. 4. [Colloq.], a darling; dear. 5. [Military Slang], an amphibious motor vehicle. —**like water off a duck's back,** with no effect.
**duck** (duk), *v.t. & v.i.* [ME. *duken, douken*], 1. to plunge or dip under water for a moment. 2. to lower, turn, or bend (the head, body, etc.) suddenly, as in avoiding a blow. 3. [Colloq.], to avoid (a task, person, etc.). *n.* a ducking.
**duck** (duk), *n.* [D. *doek*], 1. a cotton or linen cloth

like canvas but finer and lighter in weight. 2. *pl.* [Colloq.], trousers made of this cloth.

**duck·bill** (duk′bil′), *n.* a small, egg-laying water mammal with webbed feet, a tail like a beaver's, and a bill like a duck's: also called *platypus.*

DUCKBILL (1½ ft. long)

**duck·ling** (duk′liŋ), *n.* a young duck.

**duck·pins** (duk′pinz′), *n.pl.* 1. [construed as sing.], a game like bowling or tenpins, played with smaller pins and balls. 2. the pins used.

**duck·weed** (duk′wēd′), *n.* a small flowering plant that floats on fresh water like a green scum.

**duck·y** (duk′i), *adj.* [-IER, -IEST], [Slang], excellent, pleasing, delightful, etc.

**duct** (dukt), *n.* [< L. < *ducere*, to lead], 1. a tube or channel through which a gas, liquid, etc. moves. 2. a tube in the body for the passage of excretions or secretions: as, a bile *duct.* 3. a pipe enclosing wires. **—duct′less,** *adj.*

**duc·tile** (duk′t'l, -til), *adj.* [see DUCT], 1. that can be drawn or hammered thin without breaking: said of metals. 2. easily molded; pliant. 3. easily led; tractable. **—duc·til′i·ty** (-til′ə-ti), *n.*

**duct·less gland** (dukt′lis), a gland, as the thyroid, which has no excretory ducts and sends its secretions directly into the lymph or blood stream.

**dud** (dud), *n.* [ult. < D. *dood*, dead], [Slang], 1. a bomb or shell that fails to explode; hence, 2. a person or thing that fails.

**dude** (do͞od, dūd), *n.* [invented term, 1883], 1. a dandy; fop. 2. [Western Slang], a city fellow or tourist, especially an Easterner. **—dud′ish,** *adj.*

**dude ranch,** a ranch or farm operated as a resort for tourists, with horseback riding, etc.

**dudg·eon** (duj′ən), *n.* [prob. < Anglo-Fr. (*en*) *digeon*, (at) the dagger hilt], an angry or offended feeling; resentment. **—in high dudgeon,** very angry, offended, or resentful.

**duds** (dudz), *n.pl.* [prob. < ON. < *dutha*, to wrap up], [Slang], 1. clothes. 2. belongings.

**due** (do͞o, dū), *adj.* [< OFr. *deu*, pp. of *devoir*, to owe < L. *debere*], 1. owed or owing as a debt; payable. 2. suitable; proper: as, *due* respect. 3. as much as is required; enough: as, *due* care. 4. expected or scheduled to arrive or be ready: as, the train is *due* soon. ***adv.*** exactly; directly: as, *due* west. ***n.*** anything due. **—become (or fall) due,** to become payable as previously arranged. **—due to,** 1. caused by; owing to. 2. [Colloq.], because of: widely so used despite purists' objections.

**du·el** (do͞o′əl, dū′-), *n.* [Fr. < It. < ML. & OL. *duellum* (L. *bellum*), war < *duo*, two], 1. a formal, prearranged fight between two persons armed with deadly weapons. 2. any contest suggesting such a fight: as, a verbal *duel.* ***v.i. & v.t.*** [-ELED or -ELLED, -ELING or -ELLING], to fight a duel (with). **—du′el·ist, du′el·list, du′el·er, du′el·ler,** *n.*

**du·en·na** (do͞o-en′ə, dū-), *n.* [< Sp. < L. *domina*, mistress], 1. an elderly woman who has charge of the young unmarried women of a Spanish or Portuguese family. 2. a chaperon or governess.

**dues** (do͞oz, dūz), *n.pl.* [see DUE], 1. a fee or tax. 2. the sum of money paid, or to be paid, by a member to an organization.

**du·et** (do͞o-et′, dū-), *n.* [< It. < L. *duo*, two], 1. a musical composition for two voices or instruments. 2. the two performers of such a composition.

**duff** (duf), *n.* [dial. var. of *dough*], a thick flour pudding boiled in a cloth bag.

**duf·fel, duf·fle** (duf′'l), *n.* [D. < *Duffel*, town near Antwerp], 1. a coarse woolen cloth with a thick nap. 2. a camper's kit or equipment.

**duffel bag,** a large cloth bag for carrying clothing and personal belongings.

**duf·fer** (duf′ēr), *n.* [< thieves' slang *duff*, to fake], 1. [Obs.], a peddler of cheap jewelry. 2. [Slang], an awkward or stupid person.

**dug** (dug), pt. and pp. of **dig.**

**dug** (dug), *n.* [< same base as Dan. *dægge*, to suckle], a female animal's nipple or teat.

**du·gong** (do͞o′goŋ), *n.* [Malay *dūyung*], a large, whalelike, plant-eating mammal of tropical seas.

**dug·out** (dug′out′), *n.* 1. a boat or canoe hollowed out of a log. 2. a large hole dug in the ground or the side of a hill, used as a shelter against bombing in warfare. 3. in *baseball*, a covered shelter near the diamond for the players to sit in when not at bat or in the field.

**Duis·burg** (düs′boorkh), *n.* a city in Germany, on the Rhine: pop., 502,000.

**duke** (do͞ok, dūk), *n.* [< OFr. < L. *dux*, leader], 1. the ruler of an independent duchy. 2. a nobleman of the highest hereditary rank below that of a prince. 3. *pl.* [Slang], the fists. **—duke′dom,** *n.*

**dul·cet** (dul′sit), *adj.* [< OFr. < L. *dulcis*, sweet], soothing or pleasant to hear; melodious.

**dul·ci·mer** (dul′sə-mēr), *n.* [< OFr. < L. < *dulcis*, sweet + *melos* (< Gr. *melos*), a song], a musical instrument with metal strings, which are struck with two small hammers by the player.

DULCIMER

**dull** (dul), *adj.* [< AS. *dol*, stupid], 1. mentally slow; stupid. 2. lacking sensitivity; unfeeling. 3. physically slow; sluggish. 4. lacking spirit; depressed. 5. boring; tedious: as, a *dull* party. 6. not sharp; blunt: as, a *dull* blade. 7. not felt keenly or sharply: as, a *dull* headache. 8. not vivid: as, a *dull* color. 9. gloomy; cloudy: as, *dull* weather. ***v.t. & v.i.*** to make or become dull. **—dull′ish,** *adj.* **—dull′ness, dul′ness,** *n.* **—dul′ly,** *adv.*

**dull·ard** (dul′ērd), *n.* a stupid person.

**Dul·les, John Fos·ter** (fôs′tēr dul′əs), 1888–1959; United States secretary of state (1953–1959).

**dulse** (duls), *n.* [Ir. & Gael. *duileasg*], any of several edible seaweeds with large, red fronds.

**Du·luth** (də-lo͞oth′), *n.* a city in E Minnesota, on Lake Superior: pop., 107,000.

**du·ly** (do͞o′li, dū′-), *adv.* 1. in a due manner; as due; rightfully; properly. 2. when due; at the right time. 3. as required; sufficiently.

**Du·mas, A·lex·an·dre** (à′lek′sän′dr′ dü′mà′; Eng. do͞o-mä′, do͞o′mä), 1. 1802–1870; French novelist and dramatist. 2. 1824–1895; son of the above; French dramatist and novelist.

**dumb** (dum), *adj.* [AS.], 1. lacking the power of speech; mute. 2. unwilling to talk; silent. 3. not accompanied by speech. 4. temporarily speechless, as from fear. 5. [< G. *dumm*], [Colloq.], stupid; moronic. **—dumb′ly,** *adv.* **—dumb′ness,** *n.*

**dumb·bell** (dum′bel′), *n.* 1. a device consisting of two heavy weights joined by a short bar, used in exercises to develop the muscles of the arm, shoulder, and back. 2. [Slang], a stupid person.

**dumb show,** 1. formerly, a part of a play done in pantomime. 2. gestures without speech.

**dumb-wait·er** (dum′wāt′ēr), *n.* 1. a small serving stand placed near a dining table. 2. a small, often hand-operated elevator for sending food, trash, etc. from one floor to another.

**dum·dum (bullet)** (dum′dum), [< *Dumdum*, arsenal near Calcutta, India], a soft-nosed bullet that expands when it hits, inflicting a large wound.

**dum·found, dumb·found** (dum′found′), *v.t.* [< *dumb* + *confound*], to make speechless by surprising; amaze.

**dum·my** (dum′i), *n.* [*pl.* -MIES], 1. a figure made in human form, used for displaying clothing, practicing tackling in football, etc. 2. an imitation; sham. 3. a person secretly acting for another while apparently representing his own interests. 4. [Slang], a stupid person. 5. in *card games, a*) the declarer's partner, whose hand is exposed on the board and played by the declarer. *b*) the hand thus exposed. 6. the skeleton copy, as of a book, upon which the format is laid out. ***adj.*** 1. imitation; sham. 2. secretly acting as the tool of another. 3. in *card games*, played with a dummy.

**dump** (dump), *v.t.* [prob. < ON.], 1. to empty out or unload in a heap or mass. 2. to throw away as rubbish. 3. to throw (a large quantity of goods) on the market at low prices. ***v.i.*** 1. to fall in a heap or mass. 2. to unload rubbish. 3. to dump commodities. ***n.*** 1. a rubbish pile. 2. a place for dumping. 3. a temporary supply center, as of ammunition for an army. 4. [Slang], a place that is unpleasant, ugly, etc. **—dump′er,** *n.*

**dump** (dump), *n.* [? < D. *domp*, haze], [Archaic], a sad song. **—in the dumps,** in low spirits; depressed.

**dump·ling** (dump′liŋ), *n.* [< dial. *dump*, shapeless lump + *-ling*], 1. a small piece of dough, steamed or boiled and served with meat or soup. 2. a crust of dough filled with fruit and steamed or baked.

**dump truck,** a truck that is unloaded by tilting the truck bed backward with the tailgate open.

**dump·y** (dump′i), *adj.* [-IER, -IEST], short and thick; squat. **—dump′i·ly,** *adv.* **—dump′i·ness,** *n.*

**dump·y** (dump′i), *adj.* [-IER, -IEST], [see DUMP (sad song)], melancholy; depressed.

**dun** (dun), *adj.* [AS. *dunn*], dull grayish-brown. *n.* a dull grayish brown. *v.t.* [DUNNED, DUNNING], to give a dun color to.

**dun** (dun), *v.t. & v.i.* [DUNNED, DUNNING], [prob. dial. var. of *din*], to ask (a debtor) repeatedly for payment. *n.* 1. one who duns. 2. an insistent demand for payment of a debt.

**dunce** (duns), *n.* [< John *Duns* Scotus, 13th-c. Scottish scholar, whose followers were orig. called *Dunsmen, Duncemen*], 1. a dull, ignorant person. 2. a person who learns more slowly than others.

**dunce cap,** a cone-shaped hat which children slow at learning were formerly forced to wear in school.

**Dun·dee** (dun-dē′), *n.* a seaport in E Scotland: pop., 179,000.

**dun·der·head** (dun′dẽr-hed′), *n.* [< D. *donder*, thunder], a stupid person; dunce.

**dune** (do͞on, dūn), *n.* [Fr. < OD. *duna*], a rounded hill or ridge of sand heaped up by the wind.

**dung** (duŋ), *n.* [AS.], 1. animal excrement; manure. 2. filth. *v.t.* to spread or cover with dung, as in fertilizing. —**dung′y** [-IER, -IEST], *adj.*

**dun·ga·ree** (duŋ′gə-rē′), *n.* [Hind. *dungrī*], 1. a coarse cotton cloth used for tents, sails, etc. 2. *pl.* work trousers or overalls of this cloth.

**dun·geon** (dun′jən), *n.* [OFr. *donjon*], 1. a donjon. 2. a dark underground cell or prison. *v.t.* [Rare], to confine in a dungeon.

**dung·hill** (duŋ′hil′), *n.* 1. a heap of dung. 2. anything vile or filthy.

**dunk** (duŋk), *v.t. & v.i.* [G. *tunken*, to dip < OHG. *dunchôn*], to dip (bread, cake, etc.) into soup, coffee, etc. before eating it. —**dunk′er,** *n.*

**Dun·kirk** (dun′kẽrk), *n.* a town in N France: scene of evacuation of Allied troops (May, 1940): Fr. name, **Dun·kerque** (dön′kerk′).

**dun·lin** (dun′lin), *n.* [*pl.* -LINS, -LIN; see PLURAL, II, D, 1], [< *dun*, dark brown + *-ling*], a sandpiper which has a black stripe on its abdomen during the breeding season.

**dun·nage** (dun′ij), *n.* [? < MD. *dun* (< MLG. *dünne*), thin; + *-age*], 1. a loose packing of any bulky material put around cargo to protect it from damage. 2. personal baggage or belongings.

**du·o** (do͞o′ō, dū′ō), *n.* [*pl.* -OS, -I (-ē)], [It.], a duet (especially in sense 2).

**du·o-,** [< L. *duo*, two], a combining form meaning *two, double,* as in *duologue.*

**du·o·dec·i·mal** (do͞o′ə-des′ə-m'l, dū′-), *adj.* [< L. < *duo*, two + *decem*, ten + *-al*], 1. relating to twelve or twelfths. 2. consisting of or counting by twelves. *n.* 1. one twelfth. 2. *pl.* in *mathematics*, a system of numeration with twelve as its base.

**du·o·dec·i·mo** (do͞o′ə-des′ə-mō′, dū′-), *n.* [*pl.* -MOS], [< L. *in duodecimo*, (in) twelve], 1. the page size of a book made up of printer's sheets folded into twelve leaves, each leaf being about 5 by 7½ inches. 2. a book consisting of pages of this size: also called *twelvemo*, and written ***12mo*** or ***12°***. *adj.* consisting of pages of this size.

**du·o·de·num** (do͞o′ə-dē′nəm, dū′-), *n.* [*pl.* -NA (-nə)], [< L. *duodeni*, twelve each: so called because its length is about twelve fingers' breadth], the first section of the small intestine, below the stomach. —**du′o·de′nal,** *adj.*

**du·o·logue** (do͞o′ə-lôg′, dū′-ə-log′), *n.* [*duo-* + *monologue*], a conversation between two people.

**dup.,** duplicate.

**dupe** (do͞op, dūp), *n.* [Fr. < OFr. < L. *upupa*, hoopoe], a person easily tricked or fooled. *v.t.* [DUPED, DUPING], to deceive; cheat. —**dup′a·ble,** *adj.* —**dup′er,** *n.* —**dup′er·y** [*pl.* -IES], *n.*

**du·ple** (do͞o′p'l, dū′-), *adj.* [L. *duplus;* see DOUBLE], 1. double. 2. in *music*, containing an even number of beats to the measure.

**du·plex** (do͞o′pleks, dū′-), *adj.* [L. < *duo*, two + base akin to *plaga*, region (Gr. *plax*, area)], 1. double; twofold. 2. having two units operating in the same way or simultaneously. *n.* a duplex apartment or house. —**du·plex′i·ty,** *n.*

**duplex apartment,** an apartment with rooms on two floors and a private inner stairway.

**duplex house,** a house consisting of two separate family units.

**du·pli·cate** (do͞o′plə-kit, dū′-; *for v.*, -kāt′), *adj.* [< L. < *duplicare*, to double; see DUPLEX], 1. double. 2. having two similar parts. 3. corresponding exactly. 4. designating a game of bridge, etc. in which the hands dealt are played off again by other players. *n.* 1. an exact copy; replica; facsimile. 2. a counterpart or double. 3. a duplicate game of bridge, etc. *v.t.* [-CATED, -CATING], 1. to make double or twofold. 2. to make an exact copy of. 3. to make, do, or cause to happen again. —**in duplicate,** in two precisely similar forms. —**du′pli·ca′tion,** *n.* —**du′pli·ca′tive,** *adj.*

**du·pli·ca·tor** (do͞o′plə-kā′tẽr, dū′-), *n.* a machine for making exact copies of written or typewritten matter.

**du·plic·i·ty** (do͞o-plis′ə-ti, dū-), *n.* [*pl.* -TIES], [< Fr. < LL. *duplicitas;* see DUPLEX], hypocritical cunning or deception; double-dealing.

**du·ra·ble** (door′ə-b'l, dyoor′-), *adj.* [Fr. < L. < *durare*, to last < *durus*, hard], 1. lasting in spite of hard wear or frequent use. 2. continuing to exist; stable. —**du′ra·bil′i·ty, du′ra·ble·ness,** *n.* —**du′ra·bly,** *adv.*

**du·ral·u·min** (doo-ral′yoo-min′, dyoo-), *n.* [*durable* + *aluminum*], a strong, lightweight alloy of aluminum with copper, manganese, magnesium, and silicon: a trade-mark **(Duralumin).**

**du·ra ma·ter** (dyoor′ə mā′tẽr), [ML., lit., hard mother], the outermost and toughest of the three membranes covering the brain and spinal cord: also **dura.** —**du′ral,** *adj.*

**du·ra·men** (dyoo-rā′min), *n.* [< L.; see DURABLE], the hard wood at the center of the trunk of any tree that grows by annual rings; heartwood.

**dur·ance** (door′əns, dyoor′-), *n.* [OFr. < L. *durans*, ppr.; see DURABLE], imprisonment.

**du·ra·tion** (doo-rā′shən, dyoo-), *n.* [< LL. < L.; see DURABLE], 1. continuance in time. 2. the time that a thing continues or lasts.

**Dur·ban** (dũr′bən), *n.* a city on the coast of Natal, Union of South Africa: pop., 480,000.

**dur·bar** (dũr′bär), *n.* [< Hind. & Per. < *dar*, portal + *bār*, court], 1. in India, an official reception or audience held by a native prince, or by a British ruler or governor. 2. the place or hall where this is held.

**Dü·rer, Al·brecht** (äl′breHt dü′rẽr), 1471–1528; German painter and wood engraver.

**du·ress** (doo-res′, dyoo-, door′is, dyoor′-), *n.* [< OFr. < L. *duritia*, hardness < *durus*, hard], 1. imprisonment. 2. coercion or compulsion.

**Dur·ham** (dũr′əm), *n.* 1. one of a breed of shorthorned beef cattle, originally bred in Durham county, England. 2. a city in north central North Carolina: pop., 78,000.

**dur·ing** (door′iŋ, dyoor′-), *prep* [< ME. ppr. of *duren*, to last < OFr. < L.; see DURABLE], 1. throughout the entire time of. 2. at some point in the entire time of; in the course of.

**Du·roc-Jer·sey** (door′ok-jũr′zi, dyoor′-), *n.* any of a breed of large, red hog: also **Duroc.**

**dur·ra** (door′ə), *n.* [Ar. *dhurah*], a variety of grain-producing sorghum: also sp. **doura, dourah.**

**durst** (dũrst), archaic pt. of **dare.**

**du·rum (wheat)** (door′əm, dyoor′-), [L., neut. of *durus*, hard], a variety of hard wheat: flour made from it is used in macaroni, spaghetti, etc.

**Du·se, E·le·o·no·ra** (e′le-ô-nô′rä do͞o′ze), 1859–1924; Italian actress.

**dusk** (dusk), *adj.* [AS. *dosc, dox*, dark-colored], [Poetic], dark in color; dusky. *n.* 1. the dark part of twilight. 2. gloom; dusky quality. *v.t. & v.i.* to make or become dusky or shadowy.

**dusk·y** (dus′ki), *adj.* [-IER, -IEST], 1. somewhat dark in color. 2. lacking light; dim. 3. gloomy; melancholy. —**dusk′i·ly,** *adv.* —**dusk′i·ness,** *n.*

**Düs·sel·dorf** (düs′əl-dôrf′), *n.* a city in W Germany, on the Rhine: pop., 685,000.

**dust** (dust), *n.* [AS. *dust*], 1. powdery earth or any finely powdered matter. 2. a cloud of such matter; hence, 3. confusion; turmoil. 4. earth. 5. disintegrated mortal remains. 6. a humble or lowly condition. 7. anything worthless. 8. gold dust. 9. [Slang], money. *v.t.* 1. to sprinkle with dust, powder, etc. 2. to sprinkle (powder, etc.) on. 3. to make dusty. 4. to rid of dust, as by brushing. *v.i.* to remove dust, as from furniture. —**bite the dust,** to fall in battle; be defeated. —**shake the dust off one's feet,** to leave in anger or contempt. —**throw dust in (someone's) eyes,** to mislead (someone). —**dust′less,** *adj.*

**dust bowl,** those parts of the Great Plains of the U.S. where droughts and dust storms are common: also **Dust Bowl.**

**dust·er** (dus′tẽr), *n.* 1. a person or thing that dusts. 2. a brush or cloth for removing dust from furniture, etc. 3. a lightweight coat worn to protect the clothes from dust.

**dust jacket,** a removable paper covering folded around the binding of a book.
**dust·pan** (dust′pan′), *n.* a shovellike receptacle into which floor dust is swept.
**dust storm,** a windstorm that sweeps up clouds of dust when passing over an arid region.
**dust·y** (dus′ti), *adj.* [-IER, -IEST], 1. covered with or full of dust. 2. like dust; powdery. 3. of the color of dust. —**dust′i·ly,** *adv.* —**dust′i·ness,** *n.*
**Dutch** (duch), *adj.* 1. of the Netherlands, its people, language, or culture. 2. [Slang], German. *n.* 1. the language of the Netherlands. 2. [Slang], German. 3. [construed as pl.], the people of the Netherlands. 4. [construed as pl.], [Slang], the German people. —**beat the Dutch,** [Slang], to be very unusual. —**go Dutch,** [Colloq.], to have each pay his own expenses. —**in Dutch,** [Slang], in difficulties or disfavor.
**Dutch door,** a door with upper and lower halves that can be opened separately.
**Dutch East Indies,** the Netherlands Indies.
**Dutch Guiana,** Surinam, a Netherlands colony.
**Dutch Harbor,** the site of a U.S. naval station in the Aleutian Islands.
**Dutch·man** (duch′mən), *n.* [*pl.* -MEN], 1. a native or inhabitant of the Netherlands. 2. [Slang], a German.
**Dutch·man's-breech·es** (duch′mənz-brich′iz), *n. sing. & pl.* a spring wild flower with a formation shaped somewhat like wide breeches.
**Dutch oven,** 1. an iron kettle for baking, with a tight-fitting convex lid. 2. a metal container for roasting meats, etc., with an open side placed so that it is toward the fire.
**Dutch treat,** [Colloq.], any entertainment, etc. in which each participant pays his own expenses.
**Dutch uncle,** [Colloq.], a person who bluntly and sternly lectures or scolds someone else.
**Dutch West Indies,** see **Netherlands Antilles.**
**du·te·ous** (dōō′ti-əs, dū′-), *adj.* dutiful; obedient. —**du′te·ous·ly,** *adv.* —**du′te·ous·ness,** *n.*
**du·ti·a·ble** (dōō′ti-ə-b'l, dū′-), *adj.* necessitating payment of a duty or tax, as imported goods.
**du·ti·ful** (dōō′ti-fəl, dū′-), *adj.* 1. showing, or resulting from, a sense of duty. 2. performing one's duty; obedient. —**du′ti·ful·ly,** *adv.* —**du′ti·ful·ness,** *n.*
**du·ty** (dōō′ti, dū′-), *n.* [*pl.* -TIES], [< OFr. *duete,* what is due; see DUE & -TY], 1. conduct owed to one's parents, older people, etc.; respect. 2. any action necessary in one's occupation or position. 3. conduct resulting from a sense of justice, morality, etc. 4. a sense of obligation: as, *duty* calls. 5. a payment due to the government; esp., a tax imposed on imports, exports, etc. —**off duty,** temporarily relieved from one's work. —**on duty,** at one's assigned work.
**du·um·vir** (dōō-um′vẽr, dū-), *n.* [*pl.* -VIRS, -VIRI (-vi-rī′)], [L. < *duo,* two + *vir,* a man], either of a court of two judges in ancient Rome.
**du·um·vi·rate** (dōō-um′və-rit, dū-), *n.* 1. governmental position held jointly by two men. 2. two men jointly holding such position.
**du·ve·tyn, du·ve·tyne, du·ve·tine** (dōō′və-tēn′), *n.* [< Fr. *duvet,* eider down], a soft, velvety textile of wool mixed with some other fiber, as silk.
**D.V.,** *Deo volente,* [L.], God willing.
**Dvo·rák, An·ton** (än′tôn dvôr′zhäk, -zhak), 1841–1904; Czech composer.
**dwarf** (dwôrf), [AS. *dweorh*], *n.* 1. a person, animal, or plant that is much smaller than the usual one of its species. 2. in *folklore,* an ugly little being to whom magic powers are attributed. *v.t.* 1. to stunt the growth of. 2. to make smaller. 3. to make seem small in comparison. *v.i.* to become stunted or dwarfed. *adj.* undersized; stunted. —**dwarf′ish,** *adj.* —**dwarf′ish·ly,** *adv.* —**dwarf′ish·ness, dwarf′ness,** *n.*
**dwell** (dwel), *v.i.* [DWELT or DWELLED, DWELLING], [AS. *dwellan,* to deceive, hence hinder], to reside; make one's home. —**dwell on** (or **upon**), to linger over in thought or speech. —**dwell′er,** *n.*
**dwell·ing (place)** (dwel′iŋ), a place to live in; residence; house; abode.
**dwelt** (dwelt), alt. pt. and pp. of **dwell.**
**dwin·dle** (dwin′d'l), *v.i. & v.t.* [-DLED, -DLING], [dim. of ME. *dwinen* < AS. *dwinan,* to waste away], to make or become smaller or less; diminish; decrease; shrink.
**dwt.,** [*denarius weight*], pennyweight; pennyweights.
**DX, D.X.,** in *radio,* 1. distance. 2. distant.
**Dy,** in *chemistry,* dysprosium.
**Dy·ak** (dī′ak), *n.* [Malay *dayak,* savage], a member of one of the native tribes of Borneo.
**dye** (dī), *n.* [AS. *deah*], 1. color produced in something by saturating it with a coloring substance; tint; hue. 2. any such substance used to color fabric, hair, etc. *v.t.* [DYED, DYEING], 1. to color as with a dye. 2. to make (something) a specified color using a dye. *v.i.* to take on or give color in dyeing. —**of deepest dye,** of the worst sort.
**dyed-in-the-wool** (dīd′'n-*th*ə-wool′), *adj.* 1. having the yarn dyed before being woven; hence, 2. thoroughgoing; unchangeable.
**dye·ing** (dī′iŋ), *n.* the process or work of coloring fabrics with dyes.
**dy·er** (dī′ẽr), *n.* a person whose work or business is dyeing fabrics.
**dye·stuff** (dī′stuf′), *n.* any substance constituting or yielding a dye.
**dy·ing** (dī′iŋ), ppr. of **die.** *adj.* 1. at the point of death; about to die. 2. drawing to a close; about to end. 3. of or connected with death or dying. *n.* a ceasing to live or exist.
**dyke** (dīk), *n. & v.t.* [DYKED, DYKING], dike.
**dy·nam·ic** (dī-nam′ik), *adj.* [< Fr. < Gr. *dynamikos* < *dynamis,* power], 1. relating to energy or physical force in motion: opposed to *static.* 2. relating to dynamics. 3. energetic; vigorous; forceful. Also **dy·nam′i·cal.** —**dy·nam′i·cal·ly,** *adv.*
**dy·nam·ics** (dī-nam′iks), *n.pl.* [construed as sing. in senses 1 & 3], 1. the branch of physics that treats of the action of force on bodies in motion or at rest; kinetics, kinematics, and statics, collectively. 2. the various forces, physical or moral, operating in any field. 3. that aspect of musical expression which deals with degrees of loudness and softness in performance. Abbrev. **dyn.**
**dy·na·mite** (dī′nə-mīt′), *n.* [< Gr. *dynamis,* power; + *-ite*], a powerful explosive made by soaking nitroglycerin into some absorbent, such as sodium nitrate and wood pulp. *v.t.* [-MITED, -MITING], to blow up or destroy with dynamite. —**dy′na·mit′er,** *n.*
**dy·na·mo** (dī′nə-mō′), *n.* [*pl.* -MOS (-mōz′)], [< *dynamoelectric machine*], a device for converting mechanical energy into electrical energy by producing a relative periodic motion of a conductor and a surrounding magnetic field.

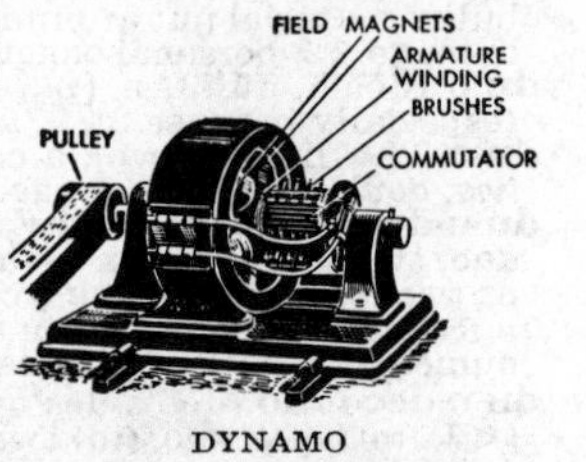

DYNAMO

**dy·na·mo-,** [< Gr. *dynamis,* power], a combining form meaning *power,* as in *dynamoelectric*: also **dynam-.**
**dy·na·mo·e·lec·tric** (dī′nə-mō-i-lek′trik), *adj.* having to do with the production of electrical energy from mechanical energy, or the reverse process: also **dy′na·mo·e·lec′tri·cal.**
**dy·na·mom·e·ter** (dī′nə-mom′ə-tẽr), *n.* an apparatus for measuring force or energy. —**dy′na·mo·met′ric** (-mō-met′rik), *adj.* —**dy′na·mom′e·try,** *n.*
**dy·na·mo·tor** (dī′nə-mō′tẽr), *n.* an electric generator combining dynamo and motor, for transforming the voltage of a current.
**dy·nast** (dī′nast, -nəst), *n.* [< L. < Gr. < *dynasthai,* to be strong], a ruler; esp., a hereditary ruler.
**dy·nas·ty** (dī′nəs-ti), *n.* [*pl.* -TIES], [see DYNAST], 1. a succession of rulers who are members of the same family. 2. the period during which a certain family reigns. —**dy·nas′tic** (-nas′tik), **dy·nas′ti·cal,** *adj.* —**dy·nas′ti·cal·ly,** *adv.*
**dy·na·tron** (dī′nə-tron′), *n.* [< Gr. *dynamis,* power + elec*tron*], a three-electrode vacuum tube in which the plate current decreases as the plate potential increases: often used as an oscillator.
**dyne** (dīn), *n.* [Fr. < Gr. *dynamis,* power], the amount of force that causes a mass of one gram to alter its speed by one centimeter per second for each second during which the force acts.
**dys-,** [Gr. *dys-*], a prefix meaning *bad, ill, difficult,* etc.
**dys·en·ter·y** (dis′'n-ter′i), *n.* [< OFr. < L. < Gr. < *dys-,* bad + *entera,* bowels], a painful intestinal disease characterized by inflammation and diarrhea with bloody, mucous feces. —**dys′en·ter′ic,** *adj.*
**dys·pep·sia** (dis-pep′shə, -si-ə), *n.* [L. < Gr. < *dys-,* bad + *peptos* < *peptein,* to digest], impaired digestion; indigestion.
**dys·pep·tic** (dis-pep′tik), *adj.* 1. of, causing, or having dyspepsia; hence, 2. gloomy; grouchy. Also **dys·pep′ti·cal.** *n.* a person who suffers from dyspepsia. —**dys·pep′ti·cal·ly,** *adv.*
**dysp·ne·a, dysp·noe·a** (disp-nē′ə), *n.* [< L. < Gr.

< *dys-*, hard + *pnein*, to breathe], difficult or painful breathing. —**dysp·ne′al, dysp·noe′al,** *adj.*
**dys·pro·si·um** (dis-prō′si-əm, -shi-), *n.* [< Gr. *dysprositos*, difficult of access], a chemical element of the rare-earth group: symbol, Dy; at. wt., 162.46; at. no., 66: it is the most magnetic of all known substances.
**dz.,** dozen; dozens.

# E

**E, e** (ē), *n.* [*pl.* E's, e's, Es, es], 1. the fifth letter of the English alphabet. 2. a sound of E or e. *adj.* fifth in a sequence or group.
**E** (ē), *n.* 1. in *chemistry, the symbol for* einsteinium. 2. in *music, a)* the third tone in the scale of C major. *b)* the scale having E as the keynote. *adj.* shaped like E.
**e-,** a prefix meaning *out, from,* etc.: see **ex-.**
**E.,** 1. Earl. 2. English.
**E, E., e, e.,** 1. east. 2. eastern.
**ea.,** each.
**each** (ēch), *adj. & pron.* [< AS. *ælc* < *a*, ever + *gelic*, alike], every one of two or more considered separately. *adv.* apiece: as, ten cents *each.* —**each other,** each the other: in formal usage restricted to two and distinguished from *one another.*
**ea·ger** (ē′gēr), *adj.* [< OFr. < L. *acer*, sharp, keen], keenly desiring; wanting very much; impatient or anxious. —**ea′ger·ly,** *adv.* —**ea′ger·ness,** *n.*
**ea·gle** (ē′g'l), *n.* [< OFr. < L. *aquila*], 1. a large, strong, flesh-eating bird of prey belonging to the falcon family, noted for its sharp vision and powerful wings. 2. a representation of the eagle as a symbol of a nation, etc.; esp., the national emblem of the U.S. 3. a former gold coin of the U.S., worth ten dollars. 4. in *golf*, a score of two below par on a hole.
**ea·gle-eyed** (ē′g'l-īd′), *adj.* having keen vision.
**ea·glet** (ē′glit), *n.* a young eagle.
**-e·an** (ē′ən), [< L. & Gr.], a suffix meaning *of, belonging to, like,* used to form adjectives and nouns, as *European*: also **-aean, -ian.**
**ear** (êr), *n.* [< AS. *eare*], 1. the part of the body that perceives sound; organ of hearing. 2. the visible, external part of the ear. 3. the sense of hearing. 4. the ability to recognize slight differences in sound or musical tones. 5. attention; heed, especially if favorable: as, they lent *ear* to his plea. 6. anything shaped or placed like an ear. —**be all ears,** to listen attentively or eagerly. —**fall on deaf ears,** to be ignored or unheeded. —**have** (or **keep**) **an ear to the ground,** to give careful attention to the trends of public opinion. —**play by ear,** to play (a musical instrument or piece) without the use of notation. —**turn a deaf ear,** to be unwilling to listen or heed. —**up to the ears,** very deeply involved.

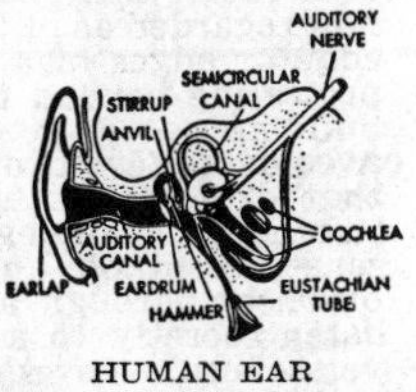

HUMAN EAR

**ear** (êr), *n.* [< AS. *ear*], the grain-bearing spike of a cereal plant: as, an *ear* of corn. *v.i.* to sprout ears; form ears.
**ear·ache** (êr′āk′), *n.* an ache or pain in the ear.
**ear·drum** (êr′drum′), *n.* 1. the tympanum. 2. the tympanic membrane; thin membrane that separates the middle ear from the external ear and vibrates when struck by sound waves.
**earl** (ũrl), *n.* [AS. *eorl*, warrior], a British nobleman ranking above a viscount and below a marquis. —**earl′dom, earl′ship′,** *n.*
**ear·lap** (êr′lap′), *n.* 1. the ear lobe. 2. the external ear.
**ear·ly** (ũr′li), *adv. & adj.* [-LIER, -LIEST], [< AS. < *ær*, before + *-lice* (see -LY)], 1. near the beginning of a given period of time or series of actions, events, or things. 2. before the expected or usual time. 3. in the far distant past. 4. in the near future; before long. —**ear′li·ness,** *n.*
**early bird,** [Colloq.], a person who arrives early or gets up early in the morning.
**Early Modern English,** English as spoken and written from about 1450 to about 1750.
**ear·mark** (êr′märk′), *n.* 1. an identification mark put on the ear of an animal to show ownership. 2. an identifying mark or feature; sign. *v.t.* 1. to mark the ears of (livestock) for identification. 2. to set a distinctive mark upon; identify. 3. to reserve for a special purpose: as, *earmark* these supplies for the army.
**ear·muffs** (êr′mufs′), *n.pl.* a pair of cloth or fur coverings for the ears, worn in cold weather.
**earn** (ũrn), *v.t.* [AS. *earnian*], 1. to receive (salary, wages, etc.) for one's labor or service. 2. to get as a result of merit or deserving. 3. to gain (interest, etc.) as profit. —**earn′er,** *n.*
**ear·nest** (ũr′nist), *adj.* [AS. *eornoste*], 1. serious and intense; zealous and sincere; not joking. 2. important; not petty. —**in earnest,** 1. serious; zealous. 2. with determination. —**ear′nest·ly,** *adv.* —**ear′nest·ness,** *n.*
**ear·nest** (ũr′nist), *n.* [< OFr. *erres* < L. *arrae*, pl. < Gr. *arrabōn* < Heb. *'ērābōn*], 1. money given as a part payment and pledge in binding a bargain: in full, **earnest money.** 2. something done as an indication of what is to come; token.
**earn·ings** (ũr′niŋz), *n.pl.* 1. wages or other recompense. 2. profits; interest; dividends.
**ear·phone** (êr′fōn′), *n.* a receiver as for telephone, usually part of a headset; headphone.
**ear·ring** (êr′riŋ′), *n.* a ring or other small ornament for the lobe of the ear.
**ear·shot** (êr′shot′), *n.* the distance within which a sound, especially that of the unaided human voice, can be heard: also **ear′reach′** (-rēch′).
**earth** (ũrth), *n.* [AS. *eorthe*], 1. the planet that we live on: it is the fifth largest planet of the solar system: diameter, 7,918 mi.: cf. **planet.** 2. this world, as distinguished from heaven and hell. 3. all the people on the earth. 4. land, as distinguished from sea or sky. 5. soil; ground. 6. [Poetic], *a)* the human body. *b)* worldly matters. 7. the hole of a burrowing animal. 8. in *chemistry*, any of the metallic oxides which are reduced with difficulty, as alumina. *v.t.* 1. to cover (*up*) with soil for protection, as seeds. 2. to chase (an animal) into a burrow. *v.i.* to hide in a burrow: said of a fox, etc. —**come back** (or **down**) **to earth,** to return to reality. —**down to earth,** practical; realistic. —**move heaven and earth,** to make every effort. —**run to earth,** to hunt down; to find by search.
**earth-bound, earth·bound** (ũrth′bound′), *adj.* confined to or by the earth and earthly things.
**earth·en** (ũr′thən), *adj.* 1. made of earth. 2. made of baked clay. 3. earthly.
**earth·en·ware** (ũr′thən-wâr′), *n.* 1. the coarser sort of containers, tableware, etc. made of baked clay. 2. baked clay. *adj.* made of earthenware.
**earth·ly** (ũrth′li), *adj.* 1. of the earth; specif., *a)* terrestrial. *b)* worldly. *c)* temporal. 2. conceivable; possible. —**earth′li·ness,** *n.*
**earth·nut** (ũrth′nut′), *n.* a root or tuber, or underground pod as of the peanut.
**earth·quake** (ũrth′kwāk′), *n.* a shaking of the crust of the earth, caused by underground volcanic forces or by shifting of rock.
**earth·ward** (ũrth′wẽrd), *adv. & adj.* toward the earth: also **earth′wards,** *adv.*
**earth·work** (ũrth′wũrk′), *n.* 1. a fortification made by piling up earth. 2. in *engineering*, the work of excavating and building embankments.
**earth·worm** (ũrth′wũrm′), *n.* a round, segmented worm that burrows in the soil.
**earth·y** (ũr′thi), *adj.* [-IER, -IEST], 1. of or like earth

or soil. 2. *a*) coarse; gross. *b*) simple and natural. **—earth′i·ness,** *n.*

**ear trumpet,** a trumpet-shaped tube formerly used as a hearing aid by the partially deaf.

**ear·wax** (êr′waks′), *n.* the yellowish, waxlike secretion in the canal of the outer ear; cerumen.

**ear·wig** (êr′wig′), *n.* [< AS. < *eare*, ear + *wicga*, beetle, worm], 1. any of a group of insects with thick, short forewings and a pincerlike part at the tail end. 2. any of various small centipedes.

**ease** (ēz), *n.* [< OFr. *aise* < LL. < L. *adjacens*, lying nearby; see ADJACENT], 1. freedom from pain or trouble; comfort. 2. freedom from constraint; poise; natural manner. 3. freedom from difficulty; facility; readiness. 4. freedom from poverty; affluence. ***v.t.*** [EASED, EASING], 1. to free from pain or trouble; comfort. 2. to lessen (pain, anxiety, etc.). 3. to facilitate. 4. to reduce the strain or pressure of; slacken (a rope, sail, etc.): often with *up* or *off*. 5. to move by careful shifting, etc.: as, they *eased* the piano into place. ***v.i.*** 1. to move or be moved by careful shifting, etc. 2. to lessen in tension, pain, etc. **—at ease,** 1. having no anxiety, pain, etc. 2. in *military usage*, in a relaxed position but maintaining attention and silence. **—take one's ease,** to make oneself comfortable. **—eas′er,** *n.* **—ease′ful,** *adj.*

**ea·sel** (ē′z'l), *n.* [< D. *ezel* (G. *esel*), ass], an upright frame or tripod to hold an artist's canvas, a picture on display, etc.

EASEL

**ease·ment** (ēz′mənt), *n.* 1. an easing or being eased. 2. a comfort, relief, or convenience. 3. in *law*, a right that one may have in another's land.

**eas·i·ly** (ē′z'l-i), *adv.* 1. in an easy manner. 2. without a doubt: as, it's *easily* the best. 3. very likely: as, it may *easily* rain today.

**eas·i·ness** (ēz′i-nis), *n.* 1. the quality or state of being easy. 2. careless indifference. 3. ease of manner; freedom from constraint; poise.

**east** (ēst), *n.* [AS. *east*], 1. the direction to the right of a person facing north; direction in which sunrise occurs (90° on the compass, opposite west). 2. a region or district in or toward this direction. 3. [E-], Asia and the nearby islands; the Orient. ***adj.*** 1. in, of, to, or toward the east. 2. from the east: as, an *east* wind. 3. [E-], designating the eastern part of a continent, country, etc. ***adv.*** in or toward the east. **—down East,** [Colloq.], (in, to, or toward) New England, especially Maine. **—the East,** the eastern part of the U.S.; specif., *a*) the part east of the Allegheny Mountains, from Maine through Maryland. *b*) the part east of the Mississippi and north of the Ohio.

**East., east.,** eastern.

**East Chicago,** a city in NW Indiana, near Chicago: pop., 58,000.

**East China Sea,** a sea off eastern China: also called *Eastern Sea.*

**East·er** (ēs′tēr), *n.* [< AS. < *Eastre*, dawn goddess], 1. an annual Christian festival celebrating the resurrection of Jesus, held on the first Sunday after the first full moon occurring on or after March 21. 2. this Sunday: often **Easter Sunday.**

**Easter egg,** a colored egg or an egg-shaped candy, etc., used as an Easter gift or ornament.

**Easter Island,** Chilean island in the South Pacific.

**east·er·ly** (ēs′tēr-li), *adj. & adv.* 1. toward the east. 2. from the east. **—east′er·li·ness,** *n.*

**east·ern** (ēs′tērn), *adj.* 1. in, of, or toward the east. 2. from the east. 3. [E-], of or characteristic of the East. **—east′ern·most′** (-mōst′), *adj.*

**Eastern Church,** 1. originally, the Christian Church in the Eastern Roman Empire, in E Europe, W Asia, and Egypt. 2. the Orthodox Eastern Church.

**east·ern·er** (ēs′tēr-nēr), *n.* 1. a native or inhabitant of the east. 2. [E-], a native or inhabitant of the E part of the U.S.

**Eastern Hemisphere,** that half of the earth which includes Europe, Africa, Asia, and Australia.

**Eastern (Roman) Empire,** the Byzantine Empire.

**Eastern Standard Time,** see **standard time.**

**East·er·tide** (ēs′tēr-tīd′), *n.* the period after Easter, extending in various churches to Ascension Day, Whitsunday, or Trinity Sunday.

**East Indies,** 1. the islands southeast of Asia; Malay Archipelago. 2. the Malay Archipelago, the Malay Peninsula, the Indochinese peninsula, and India. Also **East India. —East Indian.**

**east-north·east** (ēst′nôrth′ēst′; *nautical*, -nôr-ēst′), *n.* the direction halfway between due east and northeast (22° 30′ north of due east). ***adj. & adv.*** 1. in or toward this direction. 2. from this direction.

**East Orange,** a city in NE New Jersey, near Newark: pop., 77,000.

**East Prussia,** a former province of Prussia, Germany, on the Baltic Sea: now divided between the R.S.F.S.R. and Poland.

**east-south·east** (ēst′south′ēst′), *n.* the direction halfway between due east and southeast (22° 30′ south of due east). ***adj. & adv.*** 1. in or toward this direction. 2. from this direction.

**East St. Louis,** a city in W Illinois, on the Mississippi, opposite St. Louis: pop., 82,000.

**east·ward** (ēst′wērd), *adv. & adj.* toward the east: also **east′wards,** *adv.* ***n.*** an eastward direction, point, or region.

**east·ward·ly** (ēst′wērd-li), *adv. & adj.* 1. toward the east. 2. from the east: as, an *eastwardly* wind.

**eas·y** (ēz′i), *adj.* [-IER, -IEST], [< OFr. *aaisie* < *aise*; see EASE], 1. that can be done, got, etc. with ease; not difficult. 2. free from trouble, anxiety, pain, etc. 3. conducive to comfort or rest. 4. fond of comfort or ease. 5. free from constraint; not stiff or awkward. 6. not strict or severe. 7. compliant; tractable. 8. unhurried; moderate. 9. in *business*, in little demand: said of a commodity. ***adv.*** [Colloq.], easily. **—on easy street,** well-to-do. **—take it easy,** [Colloq.], 1. to refrain from anger, haste, etc. 2. to relax; rest.

**easy chair,** a stuffed or padded armchair.

**eas·y·go·ing, eas·y-go·ing** (ēz′i-gō′iŋ), *adj.* dealing with things in an easy, carefree manner.

**easy mark,** [Colloq.], a person easily duped.

**eat** (ēt), *v.t.* [ATE (āt; Brit. et) or *archaic & dial.* EAT (et, ēt), EATEN (ēt′'n) or *archaic* EAT (et, ēt), EATING], [AS. *etan*], 1. to chew and swallow (food). 2. to use up or destroy as by eating; consume or ravage (usually with *away* or *up*). 3. to penetrate and destroy, as acid does; corrode. 4. to make by or as by eating: as, acid *ate* holes in my suit. ***v.i.*** to eat food; have a meal or meals. **—eat into,** 1. to corrode. 2. to use up. **—eat one's words,** to retract something said earlier. **—eat up,** 1. to consume or use up thoroughly. 2. to engross deeply: as, *eaten up* with curiosity. **—eat′er,** *n.*

**eat·a·ble** (ēt′ə-b'l), *adj.* fit to be eaten; edible. ***n.*** *usually in pl.* a thing fit to be eaten; food.

**eat·en** (ēt′'n), pp. of **eat.**

**eats** (ēts), ***n.pl.*** [Colloq.], food; meals.

**eau de Co·logne** (ō′ də kə-lōn′), [Fr., lit., water of Cologne], cologne.

**eaves** (ēvz), ***n.pl.*** [*mod. sing.* EAVE (ēv)], [orig. sing. now regarded as pl.; AS. *efes*], the edge or edges of a roof, usually projecting beyond the sides of a building.

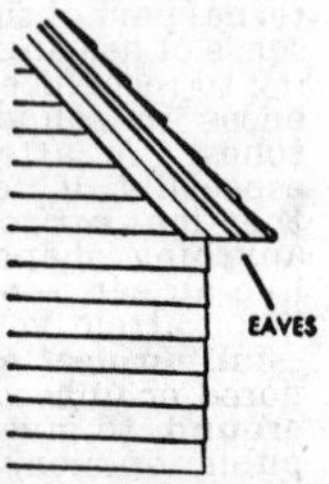


EAVES

**eaves·drop** (ēvz′drop′), *n.* water that drips from the eaves. ***v.i.*** [-DROPPED, -DROPPING], [orig. sense, to stand under eaves to overhear through a window], to listen secretly to a private conversation. **—eaves′drop′per,** *n.* **—eaves′drop′ping,** *n.*

**Eb,** in *chemistry*, erbium.

**ebb** (eb), *n.* [AS. *ebba*], 1. the flowing of the tide back toward the sea. 2. a weakening or lessening; decline: as, the *ebb* of one's hopes. ***v.i.*** 1. to flow back or out; recede, as the tide. 2. to weaken or lessen; decline.

**ebb tide,** the outgoing tide; falling tide.

**eb·on** (eb′ən), *adj. & n.* [< L. *ebenus* < Gr. *ebenos* < Egypt. *hebni*], [Poetic], ebony.

**eb·on·ite** (eb′ən-īt′), *n.* vulcanite.

**eb·on·ize** (eb′ən-īz′), *v.t.* [-IZED, -IZING], to make (wood, etc.) black; make look like ebony.

**eb·on·y** (eb′ən-i), *n.* [*pl.* -IES], [< L.; see EBON], 1. the hard, heavy, dark wood of certain tropical trees, used for furniture and decorative woodwork. 2. a tree that yields this wood. ***adj.*** 1. made of ebony. 2. like ebony; dark; black.

**e·bul·lient** (i-bul′yənt), *adj.* [< L. ppr. < *e-*, out + *bullire*, to boil], 1. bubbling; boiling. 2. overflowing with enthusiasm, etc.; exuberant. **—e·bul′lience, e·bul′lien·cy,** *n.* **—e·bul′lient·ly,** *adv.*

**e·bul·li·tion** (eb′ə-lish′ən), *n.* 1. a boiling or bubbling up. 2. a sudden outburst, as of emotion.

**ec-,** [Gr. *ek-*; see EX-], a prefix meaning *out of*, as in *ecstasy*: used before consonants: see **ex-.**

**ECA, E.C.A.,** Economic Co-operation Administration.

**é·car·té** (ā′kär-tā′) [Fr., pp. of *écarter*, to discard], a card game for two persons played with thirty-two cards (sevens up through aces).

**ec·cen·tric** (ik-sen′trik, ek-), *adj.* [< ML. < LL. < Gr. < *ek-*, out of + *kentron*, center], 1. not having the same center, as two circles: opposed to *concentric.* 2. not having the axis exactly in the center; off center. 3. not exactly circular in shape or motion. 4. out of the ordinary; deviating from the norm, as in conduct; odd; unconventional. *n.* 1. a disk set off center on a shaft converting the circular motion of the shaft into back-and-forth motion of a rod. 2. an odd or unconventional person. —**ec·cen′tri·cal·ly,** *adv.*

**ec·cen·tric·i·ty** (ek′sən-tris′ə-ti, -sen-), *n.* [*pl.* -TIES], 1. the state, quality, or amount of being eccentric. 2. deviation from what is ordinary or customary, as in conduct; oddity.

**eccl., eccles.,** ecclesiastical.

**Eccles., Eccl.,** Ecclesiastes.

**Ec·cle·si·as·tes** (i-klē′zi-as′tēz), *n.* [L. < Gr., lit., preacher], a book of the Old Testament.

**ec·cle·si·as·tic** (i-klē′zi-as′tik), *adj.* [< L. < Gr. *ekklēsia*, assembly of the people; ult. < *ek-*, out + *kalein*, to call], ecclesiastical. *n.* a clergyman.

**ec·cle·si·as·ti·cal** (i-klē′zi-as′ti-k'l), *adj.* of the church or the clergy. —**ec·cle′si·as′ti·cal·ly,** *adv.*

**Ec·cle·si·as·ti·cus** (i-klē′zi-as′ti-kəs), *n.* [L.], a book of proverbs in the Apocrypha: abbrev. **Ecclus.**

**ech·e·lon** (esh′ə-lon′), *n.* [< Fr. < OFr. *eschelle* < L. *scala*, ladder], 1. a steplike formation of units of troops, or of ships, aircraft, etc. 2. a subdivision of a military force, according to position or function. *v.t. & v.i.* to form or move in echelon.

**e·chid·na** (i-kid′nə), *n.* [L. < Gr. *echidna*, adder], a small, egg-laying, ant-eating Australian mammal with a spiny coat: also called *spiny anteater.*

**e·chi·no·derm** (i-kī′nə-dũrm′, ek′i-), *n.* [< Gr. *echinos*, sea urchin; + *-derm*], any of various small sea animals with a hard, spiny shell and radial body, as the starfish or sea urchin.

**ech·o** (ek′ō), *n.* [*pl.* -OES], [L. < Gr. < *ēchē*, a sound], 1. the repeating of a sound by reflection of sound waves from a surface. 2. a sound so produced. 3. any repeating or imitating of the words, acts, ideas, etc. of another; also, the person who repeats or imitates. 4. sympathetic response. 5. [E-], in *Greek mythology*, a nymph who pined away for Narcissus until only her voice remained. *v.i.* [-OED, -OING], to resound with an echo; reverberate. *v.t.* 1. *a)* to repeat (another's words, ideas, etc.). *b)* to repeat the words, etc. of (another person). 2. to reflect (sound) from a surface. —**ech′o·er,** *n.*

**echo chamber,** a room used in recording and broadcasting to increase resonance, etc.

**e·cho·ic** (e-kō′ik), *adj.* 1. having the nature of an echo. 2. imitative in sound; onomatopoeic, as a word formed in approximate imitation of some sound (e.g., *clash*). —**ech′o·ism,** *n.*

**é·clair** (ā-klâr′, i-), *n.* [Fr., lit., lightning], a small, oblong pastry shell filled with custard or whipped cream and covered with frosting.

**é·clat** (ā-klä′), *n.* [Fr. < *éclater*, to burst (out)], 1. brilliant success. 2. dazzling display; striking effect. 3. approval; acclaim. 4. fame.

**ec·lec·tic** (ik-lek′tik, ek-), *adj.* [< Gr. < *ek-*, out + *legein*, to pick], 1. selecting from various systems, doctrines, or sources. 2. composed of material gathered from various sources, systems, etc. *n.* one who uses eclectic methods. —**ec·lec′ti·cal·ly,** *adv.* —**ec·lec′ti·cism** (-siz'm), *n.*

**e·clipse** (i-klips′), *n.* [OFr. < L. < Gr. *ekleipsis* < *ek-*, out + *leipein*, to leave], 1. the partial or total darkening of the sun when the moon comes between it and the earth (**solar eclipse**), or of the moon when the earth's shadow is cast upon it (**lunar eclipse**). 2. any overshadowing or cutting off of light. 3. a temporary obscurity, as of fame, glory, etc. *v.t.* [ECLIPSED, ECLIPSING], 1. to cause an eclipse of; darken or obscure. 2. to overshadow; surpass.

**e·clip·tic** (i-klip′tik, ē-), *n.* 1. the sun's apparent annual path, or orbit, or that of the earth as seen from the sun; great circle of the celestial sphere. 2. the plane of the earth's orbit, cutting this circle. *adj.* of eclipses or the ecliptic: also **e·clip′ti·cal.**

**ec·logue** (ek′lôg, -log), *n.* [< Fr. < L. < Gr. < *eklegein*; see ECLECTIC], a short pastoral poem, usually a dialogue between two shepherds.

**e·col·o·gy** (ē-kol′ə-ji), *n.* [< Gr. *oikos*, house; + *-logy*], the branch of biology that deals with the relations between living organisms and their environment. —**ec·o·log·ic** (ek′ə-loj′ik, ē′kə-), **ec′o·log′i·cal,** *adj.* —**ec′o·log′i·cal·ly,** *adv.* —**e·col′o·gist,** *n.*

**econ.,** 1. economic. 2. economics. 3. economy.

**e·co·nom·ic** (ē′kə-nom′ik, ek′ə-), *adj.* 1. of the management of the income, expenditures, etc. of a community, government, etc. 2. of economics. 3. of the satisfaction of the material needs of people.

**e·co·nom·i·cal** (ē′kə-nom′i-k'l, ek′ə-), *adj.* 1. not wasting money, time, fuel, etc.; thrifty. 2. of economics; economic. —**e′co·nom′i·cal·ly,** *adv.*

**economic geography,** the branch of geography that deals with the relation of economic conditions to physical geography and natural resources.

**e·co·nom·ics** (ē′kə-nom′iks, ek′ə-), *n.pl.* [construed as sing.], the science that deals with the production, distribution, and consumption of wealth, and with the various related problems of labor, finance, taxation, etc.; political economy.

**e·con·o·mist** (i-kon′ə-mist), *n.* 1. an economical person. 2. a specialist in economics.

**e·con·o·mize** (i-kon′ə-mīz′), *v.i.* [-MIZED, -MIZING], to avoid waste or reduce expenses. *v.t.* to manage or use with thrift. —**e·con′o·miz′er,** *n.*

**e·con·o·my** (i-kon′ə-mi), *n.* [*pl.* -MIES], [< L. < Gr. < *oikonomos*, manager < *oikos*, house + *nomos*, managing < *nemein*, to distribute], 1. the management of the income, expenditures, etc. of a household, government, etc. 2. careful management of wealth, resources, etc.; thrift. 3. an instance of this. 4. an orderly arrangement of parts; organization or system. 5. a system of producing, distributing, and consuming wealth.

**e·co·sys·tem** (ē′kō-sis′təm), *n.* [<Gr. *oikos*, house; + *system*], a system made up of a community of animals, plants, and bacteria and the environment with which it is interrelated.

**ec·ru** (ek′rōō, ā′krōō), *adj. & n.* [< Fr. < OFr. *escru* < L. *ex*, out + *crudus*, raw], light tan; beige.

**ec·sta·sy** (ek′stə-si), *n.* [*pl.* -SIES], [< OFr. < LL. < Gr. *ekstasis*, distraction < *ek-*, out + *histanai*, to place], 1. a state of being overpowered with emotion, especially joy. 2. a feeling of overpowering joy; rapture. 3. a trance.

**ec·stat·ic** (ik-stat′ik, ek-), *adj.* 1. of or characterized by ecstasy. 2. causing, or caused by, ecstacy. —**ec·stat′i·cal·ly,** *adv.*

**ec·to-,** [< Gr. *ektos*, outside], a combining form meaning *outside, external*: also **ect-.**

**ec·to·derm** (ek′tə-dũrm′), *n.* [*ecto-* + *-derm*], the outer layer of cells of an embryo in its early stage. —**ec′to·der′mal, ec′to·der′mic,** *adj.*

**-ec·to·my** (ek′tə-mi), [< Gr. < *ek-*, out + *temnein*, to cut], a combining form meaning *a surgical excision of*, as in *appendectomy.*

**ec·to·plasm** (ek′tə-plaz'm), *n.* [*ecto-* + *-plasm*], 1. in *biology*, the outer layer of the cytoplasm of a cell. 2. in *spiritualism*, the luminous substance supposed to emanate from the medium's body during a trance. —**ec′to·plas′mic,** *adj.*

**Ec·ua·dor** (ek′wə-dôr′), *n.* a country in NW South America: area, 276,000 sq. mi.; pop., 5,890,000; capital, Quito. —**Ec′ua·do′re·an, Ec′ua·do′ri·an** (-dôr′i-ən, -dō′ri-ən), *adj. & n.*

**ec·u·men·i·cal** (ek′yoo-men′i-k'l), *adj.* [< LL. < Gr. < *oikoumenē* (*gē*), the inhabited (world) < *oikein*, to inhabit < *oikos*, a house], 1. general; universal; esp., of the Christian Church as a whole. 2. furthering religious unity, esp. among Christian churches. Also **ec′u·men′ic.** —**ec′u·men′i·cal·ly,** *adv.*

**ec·u·men·ism** (ek′yoo-mə-niz'm), *n.* 1. the ecumenical movement, esp. among Christian churches. 2. the principles or practice of promoting co-operation or better understanding among differing religious faiths.

**ec·ze·ma** (ek′sə-mə, eg′zi-, eg-zē′-), *n.* [< Gr. < *ek-*, out of + *zeein*, to boil], a skin disease characterized by inflammation, itching, and the formation of scales. —**ec·zem·a·tous** (eg-zem′ə-təs), *adj.*

**-ed** (id, əd, d, t), [AS.], 1. a suffix used: *a)* to form the past tense and past participle of weak verbs, as in *walked*: see **-t.** *b)* to form adjectives from nouns or verbs, as in *cultured*, or from other adjectives ending in *-ate*, as in *serrated.* 2. a suffix added to nouns, meaning: *having, characterized by*, as in *sugared.*

**ed.,** [*pl.*, for 2 & 3, EDS.], 1. edited. 2. edition. 3. editor.

**E·dam (cheese)** (ē′dəm, ē′dam), [< *Edam*, Holland, where orig. made], a mild, yellow cheese, made in a round mold, generally with a red coating.

**Ed·da** (ed′ə), *n.* [ON.], either of two early Icelandic works: *a)* the *Prose*, or *Younger, Edda* (c. 1230), a summary of Norse mythology. *b)* the *Poetic*, or *Elder, Edda* (c. 1200), a collection of old Norse poetry. —**Ed·da·ic** (i-dā′ik, e-), **Ed′dic,** *adj.*

**ed·dy** (ed′i), *n.* [*pl.* -DIES], [prob. < ON. *itha*], a current of air, water, etc. moving with a circular motion against the main current; little whirlpool or whirlwind. *v.i.* [-DIED, -DYING], to move as or in an eddy; whirl.

**Ed·dy, Mary Baker** (ed′i), 1821–1910; U.S. founder of Christian Science.

**e·del·weiss** (ā′d'l-vis′), *n.* [G.; *edel*, noble + *weiss*, white], a small Alpine plant having white, woolly leaves in star-shaped clusters with small, yellow flower heads at their center.

**e·de·ma** (i-dē′mə), *n.* [*pl.* -MATA (-mə-tə)], [< Gr. < *oidein*, to swell], an abnormal accumulation of fluid in tissues or cavities of the body, resulting in swelling; dropsy: also sp. **oedema.** —**e·de′ma·tous** (-təs), **e·de′ma·tose′** (-tōs′), *adj.*

**E·den** (ē′d'n), *n.* [LL. < Heb. *'edēn*, lit., delight], 1. in the *Bible*, the garden where Adam and Eve first lived; Paradise. 2. any delightful place.

**E·den, Sir Anthony** (ē′d'n), 1897– ; English statesman; prime minister (1955–1957).

**e·den·tate** (ē-den′tāt), *adj.* [< L. < *e-*, out + *dens*, tooth], 1. without teeth. 2. of the edentates. *n.* any of a group of mammals having only molars, or no teeth at all, as the sloths and anteaters.

**edge** (ej), *n.* [AS. *ecg*], 1. the sharp, cutting part of a blade. 2. the quality of being sharp or keen. 3. a projecting ledge, as of a cliff; brink. 4. the line or part where something begins or ends; border; margin. 5. [Colloq.], advantage: as, you have the *edge* on me. *v.t. & v.i.* [EDGED, EDGING], 1. to form an edge (on). 2. to make (one's way) sideways, as through a crowd. 3. to move gradually or cautiously. —**on edge,** 1. very tense or nervous; irritable. 2. eager; impatient. —**set one's teeth on edge,** 1. to give one a sensation of tingling discomfort, as a grating sound. 2. to irritate; provoke. —**take the edge off,** to dull the force or pleasure of. —**edged,** *adj.* —**edg′er,** *n.*

**edge·ways** (ej′wāz′), *adv.* with the edge foremost; on, by, or with the edge: also **edge′wise′** (-wīz′). —**get a word in edgeways,** to manage to say something in a conversation monopolized by others.

**edg·ing** (ej′iŋ), *n.* something forming an edge, as a fringe or border trimming.

**edg·y** (ej′i), *adj.* [-IER, -IEST], 1. having an edge or edges; sharp 2. irritable; on edge.

**ed·i·ble** (ed′ə-b'l), *adj.* [< LL. < *edere*, to eat], fit to be eaten. *n. usually pl.* anything fit to be eaten; food. —**ed′i·bil′i·ty, ed′i·ble·ness,** *n.*

**e·dict** (ē′dikt), *n.* [L. < *e-*, out + *dicere*, to speak], a public proclamation or order issued by authority; decree. —**e·dic′tal** (-təl), *adj.*

**ed·i·fi·ca·tion** (ed′ə-fi-kā′shən), *n.* an edifying or being edified; instruction; esp., moral or spiritual instruction or improvement.

**ed·i·fice** (ed′ə-fis), *n.* [< Fr. < L. *aedificium*, a building < *aedificare*; see EDIFY], a building, especially a large one of imposing appearance.

**ed·i·fy** (ed′ə-fī′), *v.t.* [-FIED, -FYING], [< OFr. < L. *aedificare*, to build < *aedes*, a house + *facere*, to make], 1. to instruct; esp., to instruct or improve morally or spiritually. 2. [Archaic], to build; establish. —**ed′i·fi′er,** *n.*

**e·dile** (ē′dīl), *n.* an aedile.

**Ed·in·burgh** (ed′'n-bũr′ō, -bũr′ə), *n.* the capital of Scotland, on the Firth of Forth: pop., 471,000.

**Ed·i·son, Thomas Alva** (ed′i-s'n), 1847–1931; U.S. inventor.

**ed·it** (ed′it), *v.t.* [< L. pp. of *edere* < *e-*, out + *dare*, to give], 1. to prepare (an author's works, a manuscript, etc.) for publication, as by selection, annotation, revision, etc. 2. to govern the policy of (a newspaper or periodical); decide what to print.

**edit.,** 1. edited. 2. edition. 3. editor.

**e·di·tion** (i-dish′ən), *n.* [< Fr. < L.; see EDIT], 1. the size, style, or form in which a book is published: as, a pocket *edition*. 2. *a*) the total number of copies of a book, newspaper, etc. published at about the same time. *b*) a single copy of such a printing.

**ed·i·tor** (ed′i-tẽr), *n.* [L.], 1. one who edits. 2. a writer of editorials. —**ed′i·tor·ship′,** *n.*

**ed·i·to·ri·al** (ed′ə-tôr′i-əl, -tō′ri-), *adj.* of, characteristic of, or written by an editor. *n.* a newspaper or magazine article explicitly stating opinions held by the editor or publisher. —**ed′i·to′ri·al·ly,** *adv.*

**ed·i·to·ri·al·ize** (ed′ə-tôr′i-əl-īz′, -tō′ri-), *v.t. & v.i.* [-IZED, -IZING], 1. to express editorial opinions about (something). 2. to put editorial opinions into (a newspaper article, etc.).

**editor in chief,** [*pl.* EDITORS IN CHIEF], the editor who heads the staff of a publication.

**Ed·mon·ton** (ed′mən-tən), *n.* the capital of Alberta, Canada: pop., 281,000.

**E·dom** (ē′dəm), *n.* an ancient kingdom near Judea. —**E′dom·ite′,** *n.* —**E′dom·it′ish** (-ī′tish), *adj.*

**ed·u·ca·ble** (ej′oo-kə-b'l), *adj.* that can be educated or trained. —**ed′u·ca·bil′i·ty,** *n.*

**ed·u·cate** (ej′oo-kāt′), *v.t.* [-CATED, -CATING], [< L. pp. of *educare*, to rear < *e-*, out + *ducere*, to lead], 1. to develop the knowledge, skill, or character of, especially by formal schooling; teach; instruct. 2. to pay for the schooling of (a person). —**ed′u·ca′tor** (-kā′tẽr), *n.*

**ed·u·ca·tion** (ej′oo-kā′shən), *n.* 1. the process of educating, especially by formal schooling; teaching; training. 2. knowledge, ability, etc. thus developed. 3. *a*) formal schooling. *b*) a kind or stage of this: as, a medical *education*. 4. systematic study of the methods and theories of teaching and learning.

**ed·u·ca·tion·al** (ej′oo-kā′shən-'l), *adj.* 1. relating to education. 2. educating; giving instruction or information. —**ed′u·ca′tion·al·ism,** *n.* —**ed′u·ca′tion·al·ist,** *n.* —**ed′u·ca′tion·al·ly,** *adv.*

**ed·u·ca·tion·ist** (ej′oo-kā′shən-ist), *n.* an educator, or authority on educational theory: often used with disparaging connotations.

**ed·u·ca·tive** (ej′oo-kā′tiv), *adj.* educating or tending to educate; instructive.

**e·duce** (i-dōōs′, ē-dūs′), *v.t.* [EDUCED, EDUCING], [< L. < *e-*, out + *ducere*, to lead], 1. to draw out; elicit; evolve. 2. to deduce; infer from data. —**e·duc′i·ble,** *adj.* —**e·duc·tion** (i-duk′shən, ē-), *n.*

**Ed·ward VII** (ed′wẽrd), 1841–1910; son of Queen Victoria; king of England (1901–1910).

**Ed·ward·i·an** (ed-wôr′di-ən), *adj.* designating or of the reign of any of the English kings named Edward; specif., of the time of Edward VII.

**Ed·wards, Jonathan** (ed′wẽrdz), 1703–1758; American theologian and preacher.

**Edward the Confessor,** 1002?–1066; king of England (1042–1066).

**-ee** (ē), [< Anglo-Fr. *-é*, masc. ending of pp. of verbs in *-er*], a noun-forming suffix, designating: 1. *the recipient of a specified action* or *benefit*, as in *appointee, mortgagee*. 2. *a person in a specified condition*, as in *refugee, employee*.

**E.E.,** 1. Early English. 2. Electrical Engineer.

**E.E.C.,** European Economic Community: see **Common Market.**

**eel** (ēl), *n.* [*pl.* EELS, EEL; see PLURAL, II, D, 1], [AS. *æl*], a fish with a long, slippery, snakelike body and no pelvic fins. —**eel′like′, eel′y,** *adj.*

**eel·grass** (ēl′gras′, -gräs′), *n.* an underwater plant of the North Atlantic coast, with long, narrow leaves.

**eel·pout** (ēl′pout′), *n.* [*pl.* -POUT, -POUTS; see PLURAL, II, D, 2], 1. a salt-water fish resembling the blenny. 2. the burbot.

**e'en** (ēn), *adv.* [Poetic], even. *n.* [Poetic or Dial.], even (evening).

**e'er** (âr), *adv.* [Poetic], ever.

**-eer** (êr), [Fr. *-ier*; L. *-arius*], a suffix used to form: 1. nouns meaning: *a*) *a person* or *thing that has to do with*, as *engineer*. *b*) *a person who writes, makes*, etc., as *profiteer*. 2. verbs meaning *to have to do with*, as *electioneer*.

**ee·rie** (êr′i, ē′ri), *adj.* [-RIER, -RIEST], [ME. *eri*; var. of *erg*, timid (AS. *earg*), or < *erg* + *-y*], 1. originally, timid or frightened; uneasy because of superstitious fear. 2. inspiring fear; weird; uncanny. —**ee′ri·ly,** *adv.* —**ee′ri·ness,** *n.*

**ee·ry** (êr′i, ē′ri), *adj.* [-RIER, -RIEST], eerie.

**ef-,** ex-: used before *f*, as in *efferent*.

**ef·face** (i-fās′, e-), *v.t.* [-FACED, -FACING], [Fr. *effacer* < L. *ex*, out + *facies*, form], 1. to rub out, as from a surface; erase; blot out: as, to *efface* a memory. 2. to make (oneself) inconspicuous. —**ef·face′a·ble,** *adj.* —**ef·face′ment,** *n.* —**ef·fac′er,** *n.*

**ef·fect** (ə-fekt′, i-), *n.* [< L. pp. of *efficere* < *ex-*, out + *facere*, to do], 1. anything brought about by a cause or agent; result. 2. the power to bring about results; efficacy. 3. influence or action: as, the drug had a cathartic *effect*. 4. purport; meaning; tenor: as, he spoke to this *effect*. 5. the impression produced, as by artistic design or manner of speaking, acting, etc. 6. the condition or fact of being operative or in force (with *in, into*, or *to*). 7. *pl.* belongings; property: as, one's personal *effects*. *v.t.* 1. to bring about; cause to happen; accomplish. 2. to make; produce. —**give effect to,** to put into practice. —**in effect,** 1. in result; actually. 2. in essence; virtually. 3. in practice; operative. —**of no effect,** producing no results. —**take effect,** to begin to act; become operative. —**to the effect,** with the purport or meaning. —**ef·fect′er,** *n.*

**ef·fec·tive** (ə-fek′tiv, i-), *adj.* 1. having an effect. 2. producing a desired result; efficient. 3. operative; in effect. 4. making a striking impression; impressive. 5. equipped and ready for combat, as a soldier or ship. *n. usually in pl.* a member of the armed forces equipped and ready for combat. —**ef·fec′tive·ly,** *adv.* —**ef·fec′tive·ness,** *n.*

**ef·fec·tu·al** (ə-fek′cho͞o-əl, i-), *adj.* 1. producing, or capable of producing, the desired effect. 2. having legal force; valid. —**ef·fec′tu·al′i·ty** (-al′ə-ti), *n.* —**ef·fec′tu·al·ly,** *adv.*

**ef·fec·tu·ate** (ə-fek′cho͞o-āt′, i-), *v.t.* [-ATED, -ATING], to bring about; cause to happen; effect; accomplish. —**ef·fec′tu·a′tion,** *n.*

**ef·fem·i·nate** (ə-fem′ə-nit, i-), *adj.* [< L. pp. < *ex-*, out + *femina*, a woman], having or showing qualities generally attributed to women, as weakness, delicacy, etc.; unmanly. —**ef·fem′i·na·cy** (-nə-si), [*pl.* -CIES], **ef·fem′i·nate·ness,** *n.* —**ef·fem′i·nate·ly,** *adv.*

**ef·fen·di** (i-fen′di), *n.* [*pl.* -DIS], [< Turk. < Mod. Gr. < Gr. *authentēs*, a master], Sir; Master: a Turkish title of respect.

**ef·fer·ent** (ef′ẽr-ənt), *adj.* [< L. ppr. < *ex-*, out + *ferre*, to bear], in *physiology*, carrying away: as, an *efferent* nerve carries impulses away from a nerve center: opposed to *afferent*. *n.* an efferent nerve, duct, or blood vessel.

**ef·fer·vesce** (ef′ẽr-ves′), *v.i.* [-VESCED, -VESCING], [< L. < *ex-*, out + *fervescere*, to begin to boil < *fervere*, to be hot], 1. to give off gas bubbles, as soda water; bubble; foam. 2. to be lively and high-spirited; be vivacious. —**ef′fer·ves′cence, ef′fer·ves′cen·cy,** *n.* —**ef′fer·ves′cent,** *adj.*

**ef·fete** (e-fēt′, i-), *adj.* [L. *effetus*, exhausted by bearing < *ex-*, out + *fetus*, that has brought forth], no longer able to produce; worn out; spent and sterile. —**ef·fete′ly,** *adv.* —**ef·fete′ness,** *n.*

**ef·fi·ca·cious** (ef′ə-kā′shəs), *adj.* [< L. < *efficere* (see EFFECT); + *-ous*], that produces the desired effect; effective: as, an *efficacious* drug. —**ef′fi·ca′cious·ly,** *adv.* —**ef′fi·ca′cious·ness,** *n.*

**ef·fi·ca·cy** (ef′i-kə-si), *n.* [*pl.* -CIES], power to produce intended results; effectiveness.

**ef·fi·cien·cy** (ə-fish′ən-si, i-), *n.* [*pl.* -CIES], 1. ability to produce the desired effect with a minimum of effort or waste; a being efficient. 2. the ratio of effective work to the energy expended in producing it: said of a machine, etc.

**efficiency expert,** one whose work is to find ways to increase efficiency, as of a business.

**ef·fi·cient** (ə-fish′ənt, i-), *adj.* [< L. ppr. of *efficere*; see EFFECT], 1. directly producing an effect or result; effective. 2. producing the desired effect or result with a minimum of effort, expense, or waste. —**ef·fi′cient·ly,** *adv.*

**ef·fi·gy** (ef′ə-ji), *n.* [*pl.* -GIES], [< Fr. < L. *effigies* < *ex-*, out + *fingere*, to form], a statue or other image; often, a crude representation of one who is hated or held in contempt. —**burn** (or **hang**) **in effigy,** to burn (or hang) an image of such a person.—**ef·fi·gi·al** (e-fij′i-əl), *adj.*

**ef·flo·resce** (ef′lô-res′, -lō-), *v.i.* [-RESCED, -RESCING], [< L. < *ex-*, out + *florescere*, to blossom < *flos*, a flower], 1. to blossom out; flower. 2. in *chemistry*, *a*) to change from a crystalline to a powdery state through loss of the water of crystallization. *b*) to develop a powdery crust by evaporation or chemical change.

**ef·flo·res·cence** (ef′lô-res′'ns, -lō-), *n.* 1. a flowering; blooming. 2. the time of flowering. 3. an eruption on the skin; rash. 4. in *chemistry*, act, process, or result of efflorescing. Also **ef′flo·res′cen·cy.** —**ef′flo·res′cent,** *adj.*

**ef·flu·ence** (ef′lo͞o-əns), *n.* [< L. *effluens*, ppr. < *ex-*, out + *fluere*, to flow], 1. a flowing out or forth; emanating. 2. a thing that flows out or forth; emanation. —**ef′flu·ent,** *adj.* & *n.*

**ef·flu·vi·um** (e-flo͞o′vi-əm, i-), *n.* [*pl.* -VIA (-ə), -VIUMS], [LL.; see EFFLUENCE], 1. a real or supposed outflow in the form of a vapor or stream of invisible particles; aura. 2. a disagreeable or noxious vapor or odor. —**ef·flu′vi·al,** *adj.*

**ef·fort** (ef′ẽrt), *n.* [Fr. < OFr. < *esforcier*, to make an effort < LL. < L. *ex-*, intens. + *fortis*, strong], 1. the using of energy to get something done; exertion of strength or mental power. 2. a try; attempt; endeavor. 3. a result of working or trying; achievement. —**ef′fort·less,** *adj.* —**ef′fort·less·ly,** *adv.* —**ef′fort·less·ness,** *n.*

**ef·fron·ter·y** (e-frun′tẽr-i, i-), *n.* [*pl.* -IES], [< Fr. < LL. < L. *effrons*, *effrontis*, shameless, barefaced < *ex-*, from + *frons*, forehead], impudence; unashamed boldness; audacity.

**ef·fulge** (e-fulj′, i-), *v.t.* & *v.i.* [-FULGED, -FULGING], [see EFFULGENT], to shine; radiate.

**ef·ful·gent** (e-ful′jənt, i-), *adj.* [< L. ppr. of *effulgere* < *ex-*, forth + *fulgere*, to shine], brightly shining; radiant. —**ef·ful′gence,** *n.* —**ef·ful′gent·ly,** *adv.*

**ef·fuse** (e-fūz′, i-; *for adj.*, e-fūs′, i-), *v.t.* & *v.i.* [-FUSED, -FUSING], [< L. pp. < *ex-*, out + *fundere*, to pour], 1. to pour out or forth. 2. to spread; diffuse. *adj.* 1. in botany, spread out loosely: said of a flower. 2. in *zoology*, with the lips divided by a gap: said of a shell.

**ef·fu·sion** (e-fū′zhən, i-), *n.* 1. a pouring forth. 2. unrestrained expression in speaking or writing.

**ef·fu·sive** (e-fū′siv, i-), *adj.* 1. pouring out or forth. 2. expressing excessive emotion in an unrestrained manner; overly demonstrative; gushing. —**ef·fu′sive·ly,** *adv.* —**ef·fu′sive·ness,** *n.*

**eft** (eft), *n.* [AS. *efeta*], a newt or small lizard.

**eft** (eft), *adv.* [AS. *eft*, orig. compar. of *aft*; cf. AFT], [Archaic], 1. again. 2. afterwards.

**eft·soon** (eft-so͞on′), *adv.* [< AS. < *eft*, again + *sona* (see SOON)], [Archaic], 1. immediately afterward. 2. often. 3. again. Also **eft·soons′** (-so͞onz′).

**e.g.,** *exempli gratia*, [L.], for example.

**e·gad** (i-gad′, ē-), *interj.* [prob. < *ah God*], a softened or euphemistic oath.

**egg** (eg), *n.* [ON.], 1. the oval body laid by a female bird, fish, or reptile, containing the germ of a new individual along with food for its development: it is enclosed in a shell or membrane. 2. a reproductive cell (**egg cell**) produced by the female; ovum. 3. a hen's egg, raw or cooked. 4. a thing resembling a hen's egg. 5. [Slang], a person: as, he's a good *egg*. *v.t.* 1. to mix or cover with the yolk or white of eggs, as in cooking. 2. [Colloq.], to throw eggs at. —**lay an egg,** [Slang], to fail completely: said of a joke, performance, etc.

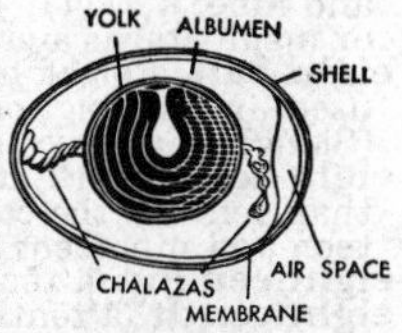

HEN'S EGG

**egg** (eg), *v.t.* [< ON. *eggja*, lit., to give edge to; cf. EDGE], to urge or incite (with *on*).

**egg·head** (eg′hed′), *n.* [Slang], an intellectual: a term of contempt as used by anti-intellectuals.

**egg·nog** (eg′nog′), *n.* [*egg*, *n.* + *nog*, strong beer or ale], a drink made of beaten eggs, milk, sugar, and nutmeg, usually with whisky, wine, etc.

**egg·plant** (eg′plant′, -plänt′), *n.* 1. a plant with a large, pear-shaped, usually purple-skinned fruit, eaten as a vegetable. 2. the fruit.

**egg·shell** (eg′shel′), *n.* the hard, brittle covering of a bird's egg. *adj.* 1. fragile and thin, like an eggshell. 2. yellowish-ivory.

**e·gis** (ē′jis), *n.* aegis.

**eg·lan·tine** (eg′lən-tin′, -tēn′), *n.* [< Fr. < OFr. *aiglent* < LL. < L. *aculeus*, a prickle, dim. of *acus*, a point], a sweet-smelling wild rose with pink flowers and a prickly stem; sweetbrier.

**e·go** (ē′gō, eg′ō), *n.* [*pl.* EGOS], [L., I], 1. the self; the individual as aware of himself. 2. [Colloq.], egotism; conceit. 3. in *psychoanalysis*, that part of the psyche which consciously controls the impulses of the id: cf. *superego*.

**e·go·cen·tric** (ē′gō-sen′trik, eg′ō-), *adj.* viewing everything in relation to oneself. *n.* an egocentric person. —**e′go·cen′tri·cal·ly,** *adv.* —**e′go·cen·tric′i·ty** (-sen-tris′ə-ti), *n.*

**e·go·ism** (ē′gō-iz'm, eg′ō-), *n.* 1. the tendency to consider only oneself and one's own interests; selfishness. 2. egotism; conceit. —**e′go·ist,** *n.* —**e′go·is′tic, e′go·is′ti·cal,** *adj.* —**e′go·is′ti·cal·ly,** *adv.*

**e·go·ma·ni·a** (ē′gō-mā′ni-ə, eg′ō-), *n.* abnormally excessive egotism. —**e′go·ma′ni·ac′** (-ak′), *n.*

**e·go·tism** (ē′gə-tiz'm, eg′ə-), *n.* 1. constant, excessive reference to oneself in speaking or writing. 2. self-conceit. 3. selfishness: see also **egoism**; *egotism* is generally considered the more opprobrious term. —**e′go·tist,** *n.* —**e′go·tis′tic, e′go·tis′ti·cal,** *adj.* —**e′go·tis′ti·cal·ly,** *adv.*

**e·gre·gious** (i-grē′jəs, -ji-əs), *adj.* [L. *egregius*, chosen from the herd, choice < *e-*, out + *grex*, a herd], 1. remarkably bad; flagrant. 2. [Archaic], outstanding. —**e·gre′gious·ly,** *adv.* —**e·gre′gious·ness,** *n.*

**e·gress** (ē′gres), *n.* [< L. pp. < *e-*, out + *gradi*, to step, go], 1. a going out; emergence. 2. the right to go out. 3. a way out; exit.

**e·gret** (ē′grit, eg′ret), *n.* [Fr. *aigrette* < Pr. < OHG. *haigiro*], 1. [*pl.* EGRETS, EGRET; see PLURAL, II, D, 1], any of various herons with long, white plumes. 2. such a plume: usually **aigrette.**

**E·gypt** (ē′jipt), *n.* a country in NE Africa, on the Mediterranean and Red seas: area, 386,000 sq. mi.; pop., 32,501,000; capital, Cairo: official name, *United Arab Republic.*

**Egypt., Eg.,** Egyptian.

**E·gyp·tian** (i-jip′shən, ē-), *adj.* 1. of Egypt, its people, etc. 2. [Obs.], gypsy. *n.* 1. a native or inhabitant of Egypt. 2. the Hamitic language of the ancient Egyptians. 3. [Obs.], a gypsy.

**E·gyp·tol·o·gy** (ē′jip-tol′ə-ji), *n.* the study of ancient Egyptian culture, language, etc. —**E·gyp·to·log·i·cal** (i-jip′tə-loj′i-k'l), *adj.* —**E′gyp·tol′o·gist,** *n.*

**eh** (ā, e), *interj.* a sound expressing: 1. surprise. 2. doubt or inquiry.

**Ehr·lich, Paul** (poul âr′liH; Eng. -lik), 1854–1915; German bacteriologist and physician.

**ei·der** (ī′dẽr), *n.* [ON. *æthr*], 1. [*pl.* -DERS, -DER; see PLURAL, II, D, 1], a large sea duck of the northern regions: often **eider duck.** 2. its down.

**eider down,** 1. the soft, fine breast feathers, or down, of the eider duck, used to stuff quilts, pillows, etc. 2. a bed quilt so stuffed.

**Eif·fel Tower** (ī′f'l), an iron tower in Paris, 984 ft. high, built for the Exposition of 1889.

**eight** (āt), *adj.* [AS. *eahta*], totaling one more than seven. *n.* 1. the cardinal number between seven and nine; 8; VIII. 2. anything having eight units or members, as a crew of eight oarsmen.

**eight ball,** a black ball with the number eight on it, used in playing pool. —**behind the eight ball,** [Slang], in a very unfavorable position.

**eight·een** (ā′tēn′), *adj.* [AS. *eahta-tyna*], eight more than ten. *n.* the cardinal number between seventeen and nineteen; 18; XVIII.

**eight·een·mo** (ā′tēn′mō′), *n. & adj.* octodecimo.

**eight·eenth** (ā′tēnth′), *adj.* 1. preceded by seventeen others in a series; 18th. 2. designating any of the eighteen equal parts of something. *n.* 1. the one following the seventeenth. 2. any of the eighteen equal parts of something; 1/18.

**eight·fold** (āt′fōld′), *adj.* [see -FOLD], 1. having eight parts. 2. having eight times as much or as many. *adv.* eight times as much or as many.

**eighth** (ātth, āth), *adj.* 1. preceded by seven others in a series; 8th. 2. designating any of the eight equal parts of something. *n.* 1. the one following the seventh. 2. any of the eight equal parts of something; ⅛. 3. in *music,* an octave.

**eighth note,** in *music,* a note (♪) having one eighth the duration of a whole note; a quaver.

**eight·i·eth** (ā′ti-ith), *adj.* 1. preceded by seventy-nine others in a series; 80th. 2. designating any of the eighty equal parts of something. *n.* 1. the one following the seventy-ninth. 2. any of the eighty equal parts of something; 1/80.

**eight·y** (ā′ti), *adj.* eight times ten. *n.* [*pl.* -IES], the cardinal number between seventy-nine and eighty-one; 80; LXXX. —**the eighties,** the years from eighty through eighty-nine (of a century or a person's age).

**Ein·stein, Albert** (īn′stīn′), 1879–1955; German-born physicist; became U.S. citizen in 1940; introduced theory of relativity. —**Ein·stein′i·an,** *adj.*

**ein·stein·i·um** (īn-stīn′i-əm), *n.* [after A. *Einstein*], a transuranic, radioactive chemical element: symbol, E; at. wt., 247 (?); at. no., 99.

**Eir·e** (âr′ə), *n.* Ireland (sense 2): Gaelic name.

**Ei·sen·how·er, Dwight David** (ī′z'n-hou′ẽr), 1890–1969; U.S. general; 34th president of the U.S. (1953–1961).

**ei·ther** (ē′thẽr, ī′-), *adj.* [AS. *æghwæther* < *a* (*æ*), always (see AY) + *gehwæther,* each of two (cf. WHETHER)], 1. one or the other (of two): as, use *either* hand. 2. each (of two): as, he had a tool in *either* hand. *pron.* one or the other (of two). *conj.* a correlative used with *or* to denote a choice of alternatives: as, *either* go or stay. *adv.* 1. any more than the other; also (after negative expressions): as, if she doesn't go, he won't *either.* 2. [Colloq.], an intensifier used in a statement of denial: e.g., "You took it." "I didn't *either!*"

**e·jac·u·late** (i-jak′yoo-lāt′, ē-), *v.t.* [-LATED, -LATING], [< L. pp. < *e-,* out + *jaculari,* to throw < *jaculum,* a dart < *jacere,* to throw], 1. to eject or discharge (fluids) suddenly. 2. to utter suddenly and vehemently; exclaim. —**e·jac′u·la′tion,** *n.* —**e·jac′u·la′tive,** *adj.* —**e·jac′u·la′tor** (-lā′tẽr), *n.* —**e·jac′u·la·to′ry** (-lə-tôr′i, -tō′ri), *adj.*

**e·ject** (i-jekt′, ē-), *v.t.* [< L. pp. of *ejicere* < *e-,* out + *jacere,* to throw], 1. to throw out; expel; discharge: as, to *eject* smoke. 2. to drive out; evict: as, his landlord *ejected* him. —**e·jec′tion, e·ject′ment,** *n.* —**e·jec′tive,** *adj.* —**e·jec′tor,** *n.*

**eke** (ēk), *v.t.* [EKED, EKING], [ME. *eken;* chiefly < *eke,* addition, partly < AS. *eacan*], [Archaic or Dial.], to make larger or longer; increase. —**eke out,** 1. to add something missing to; supplement: as, he *eked* out his income by writing. 2. to manage to make (a living) with difficulty.

**eke** (ēk), *adv. & conj.* [AS. *eac*], [Archaic], also.

**e·kis·tics** (i-kis′tiks), *n.pl.* [construed as sing.], [< Gr. *oikos,* house; + *-ics*], the science of city and area planning, dealing with individual and community needs, as transportation, education, entertainment, etc.

**el** (el), *n.* 1. an ell (sense 2). 2. [< *elevated*], [Colloq.], an elevated railway.

**e·lab·o·rate** (i-lab′ẽr-it; *for v.,* i-lab′ə-rāt′), *adj.* [< L. *elaboratus,* pp. < *e-,* out + *laborare* < *labor,* work], worked out carefully; developed in great detail; painstaking. *v.t.* [-RATED, -RATING], 1. to produce by effort or labor. 2. to work out carefully in great detail. *v.i.* to state something in detail; give additional information (with *on* or *upon*). —**e·lab′o·rate·ly,** *adv.* —**e·lab′o·rate·ness,** *n.* —**e·lab′o·ra′tion,** *n.* —**e·lab′o·ra′tive,** *adj.* —**e·lab′o·ra′tor** (-rā′tẽr), *n.*

**E·lam** (ē′ləm), *n.* an ancient kingdom in the region of modern SW Iran. —**E′lam·ite′,** *n. & adj.* —**E′lam·it′ic** (-it′ik), *adj.*

**‡é·lan** (ā′län′), *n.* [Fr. < *élancer,* to dart], ardor; enthusiasm; vigor; impetuosity.

**e·land** (ē′lənd), *n.* [*pl.* ELAND, ELANDS; see PLURAL, II, D, 2], [D., elk], a large, heavy African antelope with long, twisted horns.

**e·lapse** (i-laps′), *v.i.* [ELAPSED, ELAPSING], [< L. *elapsus,* pp. < *e-,* out + *labi,* to glide], to slip by; pass: as, a little time *elapsed.*

**e·las·mo·branch** (i-las′mə-braŋk′, -laz′-), *adj.* [< Gr. *elasmos,* beaten metal + L. *branchia,* gills], of a group of fishes having a cartilaginous skeleton and platelike scales and lacking air bladders. *n.* a fish of this group, as the shark or skate.

**e·las·tic** (i-las′tik), *adj.* [< Late Gr. *elastikos* < Gr. *elaunein,* to drive], 1. having the property of immediately returning to its original size, shape, or position after being stretched, squeezed, etc.; flexible; springy. 2. able to recover easily from dejection, fatigue, etc.; buoyant. 3. readily changed to suit circumstances; adaptable. *n.* 1. a loosely woven fabric made flexible by strands of rubber running through it. 2. a rubber band. —**e·las′ti·cal·ly,** *adv.* —**e·las·tic·i·ty** (i-las′tis′ə-ti, ē′las-), *n.*

**e·late** (i-lāt′, ē-), *v.t.* [ELATED, ELATING], [< L. *elatus,* pp. of *efferre* < *ex-,* out + *ferre,* to bear], to raise the spirits of; make proud, happy, etc. —**e·lat′ed,** *adj.* —**e·lat′ed·ly,** *adv.* —**e·lat′er,** *n.*

**e·la·tion** (i-lā′shən, ē-), *n.* a feeling of exultant joy, pride, or happiness; high spirits.

**El·ba** (el′bə), *n.* an Italian island between Corsica and Italy: site of Napoleon's first exile.

**El·be** (el′bə), *n.* a river in Bohemia and Germany, flowing into the North Sea.

**el·bow** (el′bō), *n.* [AS. *elnboga* < *eln,* forearm, hence ell + *boga,* a bow], 1. the joint between the upper and lower arm; esp., the outer part of the curve of a bent arm. 2. anything bent like an elbow. *v.t. & v.i.* to shove or jostle as with the elbows. —**out at the elbows,** shabby; poverty-stricken. —**rub elbows with,** to mingle with (famous people, etc.). —**up to the elbows,** deeply engaged (*in* work, etc.).

**elbow grease,** [Colloq.], vigorous physical effort.

**el·bow·room** (el′bō-rōōm′, -room′), *n.* room enough to move or work in; ample space.

**El·brus** (or **El·bruz), Mount** (el′broos, āl′brōōs), a volcanic mountain in the Caucasus, U.S.S.R.: height, 18,468 ft.

**El·burz Mountains** (el-bōōrz′), a mountain range in N Iran, along the Caspian.

**eld** (eld), *n.* [< AS. < base of *ald,* old], [Archaic], 1. old age. 2. ancient times; days of yore.

**eld·er** (el′dẽr), *adj.* [AS. *eldra,* compar. of *ald,* old], 1. older; born or brought forth earlier than another or others; senior. 2. superior in rank, position, validity, etc. 3. earlier; former. *n.* 1. an older person. 2. an aged person. 3. a forefather; ancestor. 4. an older person with some authority in a tribe or community. 5. any of certain church officials, as in the Presbyterian Church. —**eld′er·ship′,** *n.*

**el·der** (el′dẽr), *n.* [AS. *ellern*], a shrub or tree of the honeysuckle family, with white or pink flowers and red or blackish berries.

**el·der·ber·ry** (el′dẽr-ber′i, -bẽr-i), *n.* [*pl.* -RIES], 1. the elder plant. 2. the red or black berry, or drupe, of the elder, used for making wines.

**eld·er·ly** (el′dẽr-li), *adj.* somewhat old; approaching old age. —**eld′er·li·ness,** *n.*

**eld·est** (el′dist), *adj.* [AS., superl. of *ald*, old], oldest; esp., first-born or oldest surviving.

**El Do·ra·do** (el′ də-rä′dō), [*pl.* -DOS], [Sp., the gilded], 1. an imaginary country in South America, fabled to be rich in gold and jewels. 2. any fabulously rich place. Also sp. **Eldorado.**

**elec., elect.,** 1. electric. 2. electrical. 3. electricity.

**e·lect** (i-lekt′), *adj.* [L. *electus*, pp. of *eligere* < *e-*, out + *legere*, to choose], 1. chosen; given preference. 2. elected but not yet installed in office: as, mayor-*elect.* 3. in *theology*, chosen by God for salvation and eternal life. *n.* one who is elect. *v.t.* 1. to select (a person) for some office by voting. 2. to choose; select. *v.i.* to make a choice by vote. —**the elect,** 1. persons belonging to a specially privileged group. 2. in *theology*, those who are elect.

**e·lec·tion** (i-lek′shən), *n.* 1. a choosing or choice. 2. a choosing by vote. 3. in *theology*, the selection by God of certain people for salvation and eternal life.

**e·lec·tion·eer** (i-lek′shən-êr′), *v.i.* to canvass votes for a candidate, party, etc. in an election. —**e·lec′tion·eer′er,** *n.* —**e·lec′tion·eer′ing,** *n.*

**e·lec·tive** (i-lek′tiv), *adj.* 1. filled by election: as, an *elective* office. 2. chosen by election. 3. having the power to choose. 4. that may be chosen but is not required; optional. *n.* an optional course in a school or college curriculum. —**e·lec′tive·ly,** *adv.* —**e·lec′tive·ness,** *n.*

**e·lec·tor** (i-lek′tẽr, ə-), *n.* 1. one who elects; specif., a qualified voter. 2. a member of the electoral college. 3. [usually E-], any of the princes of the Holy Roman Empire who took part in the election of the emperor. —**e·lec′tor·al,** *adj.*

**electoral college,** an assembly elected by the voters to perform the formal duty of electing the president and the vice-president of the U.S.

**e·lec·tor·ate** (i-lek′tẽr-it), *n.* 1. all those qualified to vote in an election. 2. a district of voters. 3. the territory ruled by an elector of the Holy Roman Empire.

**E·lec·tra** (i-lek′trə), *n.* in *Gr. legend*, the daughter of Agamemnon and Clytemnestra: she persuaded her brother, Orestes, to kill their mother and their mother's lover, to avenge Agamemnon's murder.

**e·lec·tric** (i-lek′trik), *adj.* [Mod. L. *electricus* < L. < Gr. *ēlektron*, amber: from the effect of friction upon amber], 1. of or charged with electricity: as, an *electric* wire. 2. producing, or produced by, electricity: as, an *electric* generator. 3. operated by electricity: as, an *electric* iron. 4. electrifying; exciting; tense. *n.* a train, etc. operated by electricity.

**e·lec·tri·cal** (i-lek′tri-k'l), *adj.* 1. electric. 2. connected with the science or application of electricity: as, an *electrical* engineer. —**e·lec′tri·cal·ly,** *adv.*

**electrical transcription,** in *radio broadcasting*, 1. a large, long-playing phonograph record for recording programs. 2. the use of such records for broadcasting.

**electric chair,** a chair used in electrocuting those condemned to death.

**electric eel,** a South American eellike fish with special organs that can give electric shocks.

**electric eye,** a photoelectric cell: used for controlling mechanisms, as for opening doors.

**electric guitar,** a guitar whose tones are amplified through a loudspeaker by the use of an electrical pickup on its bridge.

**e·lec·tri·cian** (i-lek′trish′ən, ē′lek-), *n.* a person whose work is the construction, repair, or installation of electric apparatus.

**e·lec·tric·i·ty** (i-lek′tris′ə-ti, ē′lek-), *n.* 1. a form of energy generated by friction, induction, or chemical change, and having magnetic, chemical, and radiant effects: it is a property of the basic particles of all matter, consisting of protons (positive charges) and electrons (negative charges), which attract each other. 2. *a*) an electric current; stream of moving electrons. *b*) static electricity. 3. the branch of physics dealing with electricity. 4. electric current as a public utility for lighting, heating, etc.

**electric organ,** a musical instrument resembling an organ, but producing tones by means of vacuum tubes instead of pipes.

**e·lec·tri·fy** (i-lek′trə-fī′), *v.t.* [-FIED, -FYING], 1. to charge with electricity. 2. to give an electric shock to. 3. to excite; thrill; shock. 4. to equip for the use of electricity. —**e·lec′tri·fi·ca′tion,** *n.* —**e·lec′tri·fi′er,** *n.*

**e·lec·tro** (i-lek′trō), *n.* [*pl.* -TROS], 1. an electrotype. 2. an electroplate.

**e·lec·tro-,** a combining form meaning: 1. *electric*, as in *electromagnet.* 2. *electrically*, as in *electrocute.* 3. *electricity*, as in *electrostatics.*

**e·lec·tro·car·di·o·gram** (i-lek′trō-kär′di-ə-gram′), *n.* a tracing showing the changes in electric potential produced by contractions of the heart.

**e·lec·tro·car·di·o·graph** (i-lek′trō-kär′di-ə-graf′), *n.* an instrument for making electrocardiograms.

**e·lec·tro·chem·is·try** (i-lek′trō-kem′is-tri), *n.* the science dealing with the chemical effects of electrical action. —**e·lec′tro·chem′i·cal,** *adj.*

**e·lec·tro·cute** (i-lek′trə-kūt′), *v.t.* [-CUTED, -CUTING], [*electro-* + *execute*], to execute or kill by electricity. —**e·lec′tro·cu′tion,** *n.*

**e·lec·trode** (i-lek′trōd), *n.* [*electro-* + *-ode*], either of the two terminals of an electric source, such as a battery; anode or cathode.

**e·lec·tro·dy·nam·ics** (i-lek′trō-dī-nam′iks), *n.pl.* [construed as sing.], the branch of physics dealing with the phenomena of electric currents and associated magnetic forces. —**e·lec′tro·dy·nam′ic, e·lec′tro·dy·nam′i·cal,** *adj.*

**e·lec·tro·en·ceph·a·lo·gram** (i-lek′trō-en-sef′ə-lə-gram′), *n.* a tracing showing the changes in electric potential produced by the brain.

**e·lec·tro·en·ceph·a·lo·graph** (i-lek′trō-en-sef′ə-lə-graf′), *n.* an instrument for making electroencephalograms.

**e·lec·trol·y·sis** (i-lek′trol′ə-sis), *n.* [*electro-* + *-lysis*], 1. the decomposition into ions of a chemical compound in solution by the action of an electric current passing through the solution. 2. the removal of hair from the body by destroying the hair roots with an electrified needle.

**e·lec·tro·lyte** (i-lek′trə-līt′), *n.* [*electro-* + *-lyte*], any substance which in solution is dissociated into ions and thus made capable of conducting an electric current: when an electric current is passed through an electrolyte, a gas is generated or a solid deposited at the electrodes. —**e·lec′tro·lyt′ic** (-lit′ik), **e·lec′tro·lyt′i·cal,** *adj.* —**e·lec′tro·lyt′i·cal·ly,** *adv.*

**e·lec·tro·lyze** (i-lek′trə-līz′), *v.t.* [-LYZED, -LYZING], to subject to electrolysis. —**e·lec′tro·ly·za′tion,** *n.* —**e·lec′tro·lyz′er,** *n.*

**e·lec·tro·mag·net** (i-lek′trō-mag′nit), *n.* a soft iron core that temporarily becomes a magnet when an electric current flows through a coil surrounding it.

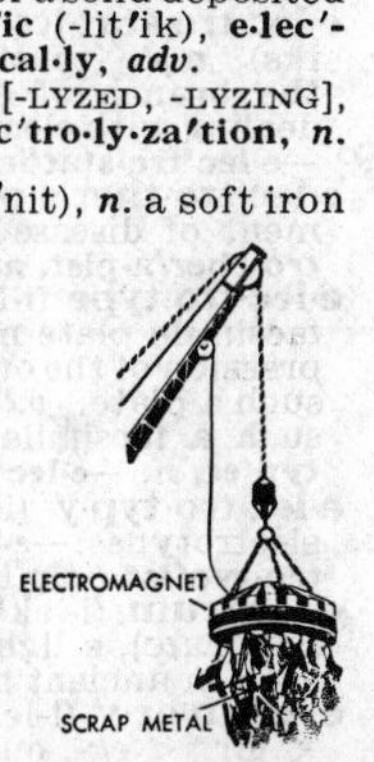

ELECTROMAGNET

**e·lec·tro·mag·net·ic** (i-lek′trō-mag-net′ik), *adj.* 1. of or produced by an electromagnet. 2. having to do with electromagnetism. Also **e·lec′tro·mag·net′i·cal.** —**e·lec′tro·mag·net′i·cal·ly,** *adv.*

**electromagnetic wave,** in *radio*, *television*, etc. a wave of electric energy radiated into space from an antenna.

**e·lec·tro·mag·net·ism** (i-lek′trō-mag′nə-tiz'm), *n.* 1. magnetism produced by an electric current. 2. the branch of physics that deals with the relations between electricity and magnetism.

**e·lec·trom·e·ter** (i-lek′trom′ə-tẽr, ē′lek-), *n.* [*electro-* + *-meter*], a device for detecting or measuring differences of potential by means of electrostatic forces. —**e·lec′tro·met′ric** (-trō-met′rik), **e·lec′tro·met′ri·cal,** *adj.* —**e·lec′trom′e·try** (-tri), *n.*

**e·lec·tro·mo·tive** (i-lek′trə-mō′tiv), *adj.* 1. producing an electric current through differences in potential. 2. relating to electromotive force.

**electromotive force,** the force that can alter the motion of electricity, measured in terms of the energy per unit charge imparted to electricity passing through the source of this force: abbrev. **E.M.F., e.m.f., EMF, emf, E, E., e.**

**e·lec·tro·mo·tor** (i-lek′trə-mō′tẽr), *n.* 1. any apparatus that produces an electric current, as a dynamo. 2. an electric motor.

**e·lec·tron** (i-lek′tron), *n.* [< Gr. *ēlektron*; see ELECTRIC], any of the nonnuclear, negatively charged particles that form a part of all atoms: the number of electrons circulating around a nucleus is equal to the number of positive charges on the nucleus.

**e·lec·tro·neg·a·tive** (i-lek'trō-neg'ə-tiv), *adj.* 1. having a negative electrical charge; tending to move to the positive electrode, or anode, in electrolysis; hence, 2. acid; not metallic. *n.* an electronegative substance.

**e·lec·tron·ic** (i-lek'tron'ik), *adj.* 1. of electrons. 2. operating, produced, or done by the action of electrons.

**e·lec·tron·ics** (i-lek'tron'iks), *n.pl.* [construed as sing.], the science that deals with electronic action in vacuums and gases, and with the use of vacuum tubes, photoelectric cells, etc.

**electron microscope,** an instrument for focusing rays of electrons, rather than light rays, to form an enlarged image of the object: it is much more powerful than any optical microscope.

**electron tube,** a type of vacuum tube whose functioning is largely dependent on the motion of electrons, as an X-ray tube: see also **vacuum tube.**

**e·lec·tron-volt** (i-lek'tron-vōlt'), *n.* a unit of energy equal to that attained by an electron falling unimpeded through a potential difference of one volt.

**e·lec·troph·o·rus** (i-lek'trof'ə-rəs, el'ek-), *n.* [*pl.* -RI (-rī')], [< *electro-* + Gr. *pherein*, to bear], an apparatus consisting of a resin disk, shellac, etc. and a metal plate, for generating static electricity by induction.

**e·lec·tro·plate** (i-lek'trə-plāt'), *v.t.* to deposit a coating of silver, nickel, etc. on by electrolysis. *n.* anything so plated. **—e·lec'tro·plat'er,** *n.* **—e·lec'tro·plat'ing,** *n.*

**e·lec·tro·pos·i·tive** (i-lek'trə-poz'ə-tiv), *adj.* 1. having a positive electrical charge; tending to move to the negative electrode, or cathode, in electrolysis; hence, 2. basic; not acid. *n.* an electropositive substance.

**e·lec·tro·scope** (i-lek'trə-skōp', ə-), *n.* [*electro-* + *-scope*], an instrument for detecting very small charges of electricity, and indicating whether they are positive or negative, as by the divergence of strips of gold leaf. **—e·lec'tro·scop'ic** (-skop'ik), *adj.*

ELECTROSCOPE

**e·lec·tro·stat·ics** (i-lek'trə-stat'iks), *n.pl.* [construed as sing.], the branch of electrodynamics dealing with electricity at rest, or static electricity. **—e·lec'tro·stat'ic,** *adj.*

**e·lec·tro·ther·a·py** (i-lek'trō-ther'ə-pi), *n.* the treatment of disease by means of electricity. **—e·lec'tro·ther'a·pist,** *n.*

**e·lec·tro·type** (i-lek'trə-tīp'), *n.* in *printing,* 1. a facsimile plate made by electroplating a wax impression of the original plate. 2. a print made from such a plate. *v.t. & v.i.* [-TYPED, -TYPING], to make such a facsimile plate or plates (of). **—e·lec'tro·typ'er,** *n.* **—e·lec'tro·typ'ing,** *n.*

**e·lec·tro·typ·y** (i-lek'trə-tīp'i), *n.* the making of electrotypes. **—e·lec'tro·typ'ic** (-tip'ik), *adj.* **—e·lec'tro·typ'ist** (-tīp'ist), *n.*

**e·lec·trum** (i-lek'trəm), *n.* [L. < Gr. *ēlektron*; see ELECTRIC], a light-yellow alloy of gold and silver, used in ancient times.

**e·lec·tu·ar·y** (i-lek'chōō-er'i), *n.* [*pl.* -IES], [< LL. < Gr. < *ek-*, out + *leichein*, to lick], a medicine mixed with honey or sirup to form a paste.

**el·ee·mos·y·nar·y** (el'ə-mos''n-er'i, el'i-ə-), *adj.* [< ML. < Gr. *eleēmosynē*, alms], 1. of or for charity; charitable. 2. supported by or dependent on charity. 3. given by charity; free.

**el·e·gance** (el'ə-gəns), *n.* 1. the quality of being elegant; tasteful luxury. 2. anything elegant. Also **el'e·gan·cy** [*pl.* -CIES].

**el·e·gant** (el'ə-gənt), *adj.* [< Fr. < L. *elegans* < *e-*, out + *legare*, to choose], 1. characterized by dignified richness and grace, as of manner, dress, design, etc.; tastefully luxurious. 2. characterized by a sense of propriety or refinement; fastidious in manners and tastes. 3. [Colloq.], excellent; fine. **—el'e·gant·ly,** *adv.*

**el·e·gi·ac** (el'ə-jī'ək, i-lē'ji-ak'), *adj.* 1. of or composed in dactylic hexameter couplets, the second line having only an accented syllable in the third and sixth feet, as in Greek and Latin elegies. 2. of, like, or fit for an elegy. 3. sad; mournful. Also **el'e·gi'a·cal.** *n.* 1. an elegiac couplet. 2. *pl.* a poem or poems in such couplets.

**el·e·gize** (el'ə-jīz'), *v.i.* [-GIZED, -GIZING], to write elegies. *v.t.* to lament as in an elegy.

**el·e·gy** (el'ə-ji), *n.* [*pl.* -GIES], [< Fr. < L. < Gr. *elegeia* < *elegos*, a lament], 1. a poem of lament and praise for the dead. 2. any poem in elegiac verse. 3. a poem written in a mournfully contemplative tone. **—el'e·gist,** *n.*

**elem.,** 1. element. 2. elementary. 3. elements.

**el·e·ment** (el'ə-mənt), *n.* [OFr. < L. *elementum*], 1. any of the four substances—earth, air, fire, water—formerly believed to constitute all physical matter. 2. the natural or fitting environment for a person or thing. 3. a component, feature, or principle of something; basic part. 4. in *chemistry*, any substance that cannot be separated into different substances except by nuclear disintegration: all matter is composed of such substances: see table, p. 243. 5. *pl.* in *ecclesiastical usage*, the bread and wine of the Eucharist. 6. the working part of an electrical appliance: as, the heating *element* of an iron. 7. in *military aviation*, the basic unit of an air force, consisting of one or more aircraft: it is a subdivision of a flight. **—the elements,** 1. the first or basic principles; rudiments. 2. wind, rain, etc.; forces of the atmosphere.

**el·e·men·tal** (el'ə-men't'l), *adj.* 1. of the four elements (earth, air, fire, and water). 2. of or like natural forces. 3. basic and powerful; primal: as, hunger is an *elemental* drive. 4. of first principles; elementary; basic. 5. being an essential part or parts. 6. in *chemistry*, of an element; not a compound. **—el'e·men'tal·ly,** *adv.*

**el·e·men·ta·ry** (el'ə-men'tēr-i, -tri), *adj.* 1. elemental. 2. of first principles or fundamentals; introductory. 3. consisting of one chemical element; not a compound. 4. of a chemical element or elements. **—el'e·men'ta·ri·ly,** *adv.* **—el'e·men'ta·ri·ness,** *n.*

**elementary school,** a school of the first eight grades (or six, in systems having a junior high school), where basic subjects are taught.

**el·e·phant** (el'ə-fənt), *n.* [*pl.* -PHANTS, -PHANT; see PLURAL, II, D, 1], [< OFr. < L. < Gr. *elephas*, elephant, ivory], a huge, thick-skinned mammal, the largest of extant four-footed animals, with a long, flexible snout (called a *trunk*) and two ivory tusks: the *African elephant* is larger and has much bigger ears than the *Indian elephant*.

**el·e·phan·ti·a·sis** (el'ə-fən-tī'ə-sis), *n.* a chronic disease of the skin characterized by the enlargement of the legs or other parts, and by the hardening of the skin: it is caused by small worms which obstruct the lymphatic glands.

**el·e·phan·tine** (el'ə-fan'tēn, -tin, -tīn), *adj.* 1. of an elephant or elephants. 2. like an elephant in size or gait; huge, heavy, slow, clumsy, etc.

**El·eu·sin·i·an** (el'yoo-sin'i-ən), *adj.* of Eleusis or the secret religious rites (**Eleusinian mysteries**) anciently celebrated there every spring in honor of Demeter and Persephone.

**E·leu·sis** (e-lōō'sis, el-ū'-), *n.* a city in ancient Greece, northwest of Athens.

**el·e·vate** (el'ə-vāt'), *v.t.* [-VATED, -VATING], [< L. pp. < *e-*, out + *levare*, to lift], 1. to raise; lift up. 2. to raise in rank or position. 3. to raise to a higher intellectual or moral level. 4. to raise the spirits of; elate; exhilarate.

**el·e·vat·ed** (el'ə-vāt'id), *adj.* 1. raised; lifted up; high. 2. dignified; noble; lofty. 3. high-spirited; elated. *n.* [Colloq.], a railway raised above street level: in full, **elevated railway.**

**el·e·va·tion** (el'ə-vā'shən), *n.* 1. an elevating or being elevated. 2. a high place or position. 3. height above the surface of the earth. 4. dignity; loftiness. 5. a flat scale drawing of the front, rear, or side of a building, etc. 6. in *astronomy*, altitude. 7. in *geography*, height above sea level.

**el·e·va·tor** (el'ə-vā'tēr), *n.* 1. one that raises or lifts up. 2. a machine for hoisting or lowering goods or people by means of a suspended cage; also, the cage itself: in Brit. usage, a *lift*. 3. a machine, usually consisting of buckets fastened to an endless belt, for hoisting grain, etc. 4. a warehouse for storing, hoisting, and discharging grain. 5. a movable airfoil like a horizontal rudder, for making an aircraft go up or down.

**e·lev·en** (i-lev''n), *adj.* [AS. *endleofan*, lit., one left over (ten)], totaling one more than ten. *n.* 1. the cardinal number between ten and twelve; 11; XI. 2. in *football & cricket*, a team.

**e·lev·enth** (i-lev''nth), *adj.* 1. preceded by ten others in a series; 11th. 2. designating any of the eleven equal parts of something. *n.* 1. the one following the tenth. 2. any of the eleven equal parts of something; 1/11. **—at the eleventh hour,** at the last possible time.

**elf** (elf), *n.* [*pl.* ELVES (elvz)], [AS. *ælf*], 1. in *folklore*, a small fairy, supposedly exercising magic powers and haunting woods and hills. 2. a mischievous child or small person. **—elf'ish,** *adj.* **—elf'ish·ly,** *adv.* **—elf'ish·ness,** *n.* **—elf'like',** *adj.*

**elf·in** (el'fin), *adj.* of, appropriate to, or like an elf; fairylike. *n.* an elf.

## CHEMICAL ELEMENTS

With International Atomic Weights. Carbon at 12 is the standard.

| | Symbol | Atomic Number | Atomic Weight |
|---|---|---|---|
| Actinium | Ac | 89 | 227(?) |
| Aluminum | Al | 13 | 26.97 |
| Americium | Am | 95 | 241(?) |
| Antimony | Sb | 51 | 121.76 |
| Argon | A | 18 | 39.944 |
| Arsenic | As | 33 | 74.91 |
| Astatine | At | 85 | 211(?) |
| Barium | Ba | 56 | 137.36 |
| Berkelium | Bk | 97 | 243(?) |
| Beryllium | Be | 4 | 9.02 |
| Bismuth | Bi | 83 | 209.00 |
| Boron | B | 5 | 10.82 |
| Bromine | Br | 35 | 79.916 |
| Cadmium | Cd | 48 | 112.41 |
| Calcium | Ca | 20 | 40.08 |
| Californium | Cf | 98 | 244(?) |
| Carbon | C | 6 | 12.01 |
| Cerium | Ce | 58 | 140.13 |
| Cesium | Cs | 55 | 132.91 |
| Chlorine | Cl | 17 | 35.457 |
| Chromium | Cr | 24 | 52.01 |
| Cobalt | Co | 27 | 58.94 |
| Columbium | *former name for* NIOBIUM | | |
| Copper | Cu | 29 | 63.54 |
| Curium | Cm | 96 | 242(?) |
| Dysprosium | Dy | 66 | 162.46 |
| Einsteinium | E | 99 | 247(?) |
| Erbium | Er | 68 | 167.2 |
| Europium | Eu | 63 | 152.0 |
| Fermium | Fm | 100 | 254(?) |
| Fluorine | F | 9 | 19.00 |
| Francium | Fr | 87 | 223(?) |
| Gadolinium | Gd | 64 | 156.9 |
| Gallium | Ga | 31 | 69.72 |
| Germanium | Ge | 32 | 72.60 |
| Gold | Au | 79 | 197.2 |
| Hafnium | Hf | 72 | 178.6 |
| Helium | He | 2 | 4.003 |
| Holmium | Ho | 67 | 164.94 |
| Hydrogen | H | 1 | 1.0080 |
| Indium | In | 49 | 114.76 |
| Iodine | I | 53 | 126.92 |
| Iridium | Ir | 77 | 193.1 |
| Iron | Fe | 26 | 55.85 |
| Krypton | Kr | 36 | 83.7 |
| Lanthanum | La | 57 | 138.92 |
| Lawrencium | Lw | 103 | 257(?) |
| Lead | Pb | 82 | 207.21 |
| Lithium | Li | 3 | 6.940 |
| Lutetium | Lu | 71 | 174.99 |
| Magnesium | Mg | 12 | 24.32 |
| Manganese | Mn | 25 | 54.93 |
| Mendelevium | Mv | 101 | 256(?) |
| Mercury | Hg | 80 | 200.61 |
| Molybdenum | Mo | 42 | 95.95 |
| Neodymium | Nd | 60 | 144.27 |
| Neon | Ne | 10 | 20.183 |
| Neptunium | Np | 93 | 239 |
| Nickel | Ni | 28 | 58.69 |
| Niobium | Nb | 41 | 92.91 |
| Niton | *alt. name for* RADON | | |
| Nitrogen | N | 7 | 14.008 |
| Nobelium | No | 102 | 255(?) |
| Osmium | Os | 76 | 190.2 |
| Oxygen | O | 8 | 16.00 |
| Palladium | Pd | 46 | 106.7 |
| Phosphorus | P | 15 | 30.98 |
| Platinum | Pt | 78 | 195.23 |
| Plutonium | Pu | 94 | 239 |
| Polonium | Po | 84 | 210.0 |
| Potassium | K | 19 | 39.096 |
| Praseodymium | Pr | 59 | 140.92 |
| Promethium | Pm | 61 | 147(?) |
| Protactinium | Pa | 91 | 231 |
| Radium | Ra | 88 | 226.05 |
| Radon | Rn | 86 | 222 |
| Rhenium | Re | 75 | 186.31 |
| Rhodium | Rh | 45 | 102.91 |
| Rubidium | Rb | 37 | 85.48 |
| Ruthenium | Ru | 44 | 101.7 |
| Samarium | Sm | 62 | 150.43 |
| Scandium | Sc | 21 | 45.10 |
| Selenium | Se | 34 | 78.96 |
| Silicon | Si | 14 | 28.06 |
| Silver | Ag | 47 | 107.880 |
| Sodium | Na | 11 | 22.997 |
| Strontium | Sr | 38 | 87.63 |
| Sulfur | S | 16 | 32.06 |
| Tantalum | Ta | 73 | 180.88 |
| Technetium | Tc | 43 | 99(?) |
| Tellurium | Te | 52 | 127.61 |
| Terbium | Tb | 65 | 159.2 |
| Thallium | Tl | 81 | 204.39 |
| Thorium | Th | 90 | 232.12 |
| Thulium | Tm | 69 | 169.4 |
| Tin | Sn | 50 | 118.70 |
| Titanium | Ti | 22 | 47.90 |
| Tungsten | W | 74 | 183.92 |
| Uranium | U | 92 | 238.07 |
| Vanadium | V | 23 | 50.95 |
| Wolfram | *alt. name for* TUNGSTEN | | |
| Xenon | Xe | 54 | 131.3 |
| Ytterbium | Yb | 70 | 173.04 |
| Yttrium | Y | 39 | 88.92 |
| Zinc | Zn | 30 | 65.38 |
| Zirconium | Zr | 40 | 91.22 |

**elf·lock** (elf′lok′), *n.* a tangled, matted lock of hair.

**El·gar,** Sir **Edward** (el′gẽr, -gär), 1857–1934; English composer.

**El Grec·o** (el grek′ō), (born *Kyriakos Theotokopoulos*), 1548?–1614?; painter and sculptor in Italy and Spain, born in Crete.

**E·li·a** (ē′li-ə, ēl′yə), see **Lamb, Charles.**

**e·lic·it** (i-lis′it), *v.t.* [< L. *elicitus*, pp. < *e-*, out + *lacere*, to entice], to draw forth; evoke: as, his irony *elicited* an angry reply. —**e·lic′i·ta′tion,** *n.* —**e·lic′i·tor,** *n.*

**e·lide** (i-lid′), *v.t.* [ELIDED, ELIDING], [< L. < *e-*, out + *laedere*, to strike], 1. to leave out; suppress. 2. to leave out or slur over (a vowel, syllable, etc.) in pronunciation. —**e·lid′i·ble,** *adj.*

**el·i·gi·bil·i·ty** (el′i-jə-bil′ə-ti), *n.* 1. the quality or state of being eligible. 2. [*pl.* -TIES], *usually in pl.* a quality that makes eligible.

**el·i·gi·ble** (el′i-jə-b'l), *adj.* [< Fr. < L. *eligere;* see ELECT], fit to be chosen; qualified. *n.* an eligible person. —**el′i·gi·bly,** *adv.*

**E·li·jah** (i-lī′jə), *n.* a prophet of Israel in the 9th century B.C.: I Kings 17–19, II Kings 2:1–11.

**e·lim·i·nate** (i-lim′ə-nāt′), *v.t.* [-NATED, -NATING], [< L. pp. of *eliminare* < *e-*, out + *limen*, threshold], 1. to take out; get rid of. 2. to leave out of consideration; reject; omit. 3. in *algebra*, to get rid of (an unknown quantity) by combining equations. 4. in *physiology*, to excrete. —**e·lim′i·na′tion,** *n.* —**e·lim′i·na′tive, e·lim′i·na·to′ry** (-nə-tôr′i, -tō′ri), *adj.* —**e·lim′i·na′tor,** *n.*

**El·i·ot, George** (el′i-ət), (pseudonym of *Mary Ann Evans*), 1819–1880; English novelist.

**Eliot, T.S.,** (*Thomas Stearns Eliot*), **1888–1965; U.S.** poet and essayist in England.

**E·li·sha** (i-lī′shə), *n.* in the *Bible*, a prophet of Israel, who succeeded Elijah: II Kings 2.

**e·li·sion** (i-lizh′ən), *n.* an eliding or being elided; specif., the omission or slurring over of a vowel, syllable, etc., as for euphony (e.g., "th' inevitable hour").

**e·lite, é·lite** (i-lēt′, ā-), *n.* [< Fr. < L. *eligere;* see ELECT], 1. [also construed as pl.], the choice or most carefully selected part of a group, as of a society. 2. a size of type for typewriters, equivalent to 10-point.

**e·lix·ir** (i-lik′sẽr), *n.* [< ML. < Ar. *al-iksīr;* prob. < Gr. *xērion*, powder for drying wounds < *xēros*, dry], 1. a hypothetical substance sought for by medieval alchemists to change base metals into gold or to prolong **life** indefinitely: also **philosopher's stone, elixir of life.** 2. [Rare], the quintessence. 3. a remedy for all ailments; cure-all. 4. a medicine made of drugs in alcoholic solution.

**Eliz.,** Elizabethan.

**E·liz·a·beth** (i-liz′ə-bəth), *n.* a city in NE New Jersey: pop., 108,000.

**Elizabeth I, 1533–1603;** daughter of Henry VIII; queen of England (1558–1603).

**Elizabeth II,** 1926–; daughter of George VI; queen of England (1952– ).

**E·liz·a·be·than** (i-liz′ə-bē′thən, -beth′ən), *adj.* of or characteristic of the time when Elizabeth I was queen of England. *n.* an English person, especially a writer, of the time of Queen Elizabeth I.

**Elizabethan sonnet,** see **Shakespearean sonnet.**

**elk** (elk), *n.* [*pl.* ELK, ELKS; see PLURAL, II, D, 2], [< AS. *elh, eolh*], 1. a large, mooselike deer of N Europe and Asia, with broad antlers. 2. the wapiti, a North American deer.

**ell** (el), *n.* 1. the letter L. 2. something shaped like an L; specif., an extension or wing at right angles to the main structure.

**ell** (el), *n.* [< AS. *eln*], a former measure of length, mainly for cloth (in England, 45 inches).

**el·lipse** (i-lips′), *n.* [*pl.* -LIPSES (-lip′siz)], [< L. < Gr. < *elleipein*, to fall short], in *geometry*, a closed curve, the path of a point that moves so that the sum of its distances from two fixed points (called *foci*) is constant.

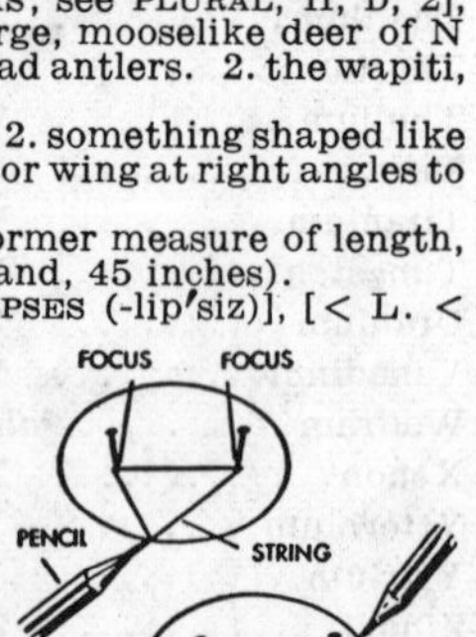

ELLIPSE

**el·lip·sis** (i-lip′sis), *n.* [*pl.* -SES (sēz)], [see ELLIPSE], 1. in *grammar*, the omission of a word or words necessary for complete construction but understood in the context. Example: "If (it is) possible, (you) come early." 2. in *writing & printing*, a mark (. . . or ***) indicating an omission of words or letters.

**el·lip·ti·cal** (i-lip′ti-k'l, ə-), *adj.* 1. of, or having the form of, an ellipse. 2. of or characterized by ellipsis; with a word or words omitted. Also **el·lip′tic.** —**el·lip′ti·cal·ly,** *adv.*

**El·lis, (Henry) Have·lock** (hav′lək el′is), 1859–1939; English scientist and writer.

**El·lis Island** (el′is), a small island in New York harbor: immigrants were formerly examined there before being allowed into the U.S.

**elm** (elm), *n.* [AS.], 1. a tall, hardy shade tree growing largely in the North Temperate Zone. 2. the hard, heavy wood of this tree.

**El·mi·ra** (el-mī′rə), *n.* a city in south central New York: pop., 47,000.

**el·o·cu·tion** (el′ə-kū′shən), *n.* [< L. < *eloqui;* see ELOQUENT], 1. style or manner of speaking or reading in public. 2. the art of public speaking or declaiming. —**el′o·cu′tion·ar′y** (-er′i), *adj.* —**el′o·cu′tion·ist,** *n.*

**E·lo·him** (e-lō′him), *n.* [Heb., pl.], God: Hebrew name used in parts of the Old Testament.

**e·lon·gate** (i-lôŋ′gāt), *v.t. & v.i.* [-GATED, -GATING], [< LL. pp. of *elongare*, to prolong < L. *e-*, out + *longus*, long], to lengthen; extend. *adj.* 1. lengthened; stretched. 2. long and narrow.

**e·lon·ga·tion** (i-lôŋ′gā′shən, ē′lôŋ-), *n.* 1. an elongating or being elongated. 2. something elongated.

**e·lope** (i-lōp′), *v.i.* [ELOPED, ELOPING], [< Anglo-Fr. *aloper;* prob. < ME. < AS. < *a-*, away + *hleapan*, to run], 1. to run away secretly, especially in order to get married. 2. to run away; escape. —**e·lope′ment,** *n.* —**e·lop′er,** *n.*

**el·o·quence** (el′ə-kwəns), *n.* 1. speech or writing that is vivid, forceful, fluent, etc. 2. *a*) the art or manner of such speech or writing. *b*) the power to persuade with speech or writing.

**el·o·quent** (el′ə-kwənt), *adj.* [< Fr. < L. pp. < *e-*, out + *loqui*, to speak], 1. having, or characterized by, eloquence. 2. vividly expressive. —**el′o·quent·ly,** *adv.*

**El Pas·o** (el pas′ō), **a city in the westernmost part of Texas, on the Rio Grande; pop., 277,000.**

**El Sal·va·dor** (el sal′və-dôr′), a country in W Central America: area, 8,259 sq. mi.; pop., 2,670,000; capital, San Salvador.

**else** (els), *adj.* [AS. *elles*, adv. genit. of n. base *el-*, other], 1. different; other: as, somebody *else*. 2. in addition; more: as, is there anything *else?* *adv.* 1. in a different time, place, or manner; otherwise: as, where *else* can I go? 2. if not: as, study, (or) *else* you will fail.

**else·where** (els′hwâr′), *adv.* in, at, or to some other place; somewhere else.

**e·lu·ci·date** (i-lōō′sə-dāt′), *v.t.* [-DATED, -DATING], [< LL. pp. of *elucidare* < L. *e-*, out + *lucidus*, light, clear], to make clear; explain. —**e·lu′ci·da′tion,** *n.* —**e·lu′ci·da′tor** (-tẽr), *n.*

**e·lude** (i-lōōd′), *v.t.* [ELUDED, ELUDING], [< L. < *e-*, out + *ludere*, to play], 1. to avoid or escape from by quickness, cunning, etc. 2. to escape detection by; evade; baffle. —**e·lud′er,** *n.* —**e·lu·sion** (i-lōō′zhən), *n.*

**E·lul** (e-lōōl′, el′ool), *n.* [Heb.], the twelfth month of the Jewish year: see **Jewish calendar.**

**e·lu·sive** (i-lōō′siv), *adj.* 1. tending to elude. 2. hard to grasp or retain mentally; baffling. Also **e·lu′so·ry** (-sẽr-i). —**e·lu′sive·ly,** *adv.* —**e·lu′sive·ness,** *n.*

**elves** (elvz), *n.* pl. of **elf.**

**elv·ish** (el′vish), *adj.* like an elf or elf's; elfish. —**elv′ish·ly,** *adv.*

**E·ly·si·um** (i-lizh′i-əm, i-liz′-), *n.* [L. < Gr.], 1. in *Gr. mythology*, the place where virtuous people went after death. 2. any place or condition of ideal bliss or complete happiness; paradise. —**E·ly′sian** (-lizh′ən, -lizh′i-ən), *adj.*

**em** (em), *n.* 1. the letter M, m. 2. in *printing*, formerly the letter M of any given font, now a square of any size of type, used as a unit of measure, as of column width.

**'em** (əm, 'm), *pron.* [Colloq.], them.

**em-,** en-: used before *p*, *b*, or *m*, as in *empower*.

**EM,** in the *U.S. Army*, enlisted man; enlisted men.

**e·ma·ci·ate** (i-mā′shi-āt′), *v.t.* [-ATED, -ATING], [< L. pp. of *emaciare;* ult. < *e-*, out + *macies*, leanness], to cause to become abnormally lean; cause to lose much flesh or weight. —**e·ma′ci·at′ed,** *adj.* —**e·ma′ci·a′tion** (-shi-ā′shən, -si-), *n.*

**em·a·nate** (em′ə-nāt′), *v.i.* [-NATED, -NATING], [< L. pp. < *e-*, out + *manare*, to flow], to come forth; issue, as from a source. *v.t.* [Rare], to send forth; emit. —**em′a·na′tive** (-tiv), *adj.*

**em·a·na·tion** (em′ə-nā′shən), *n.* 1. an emanating. 2. something that comes forth from a source. 3. in *chemistry*, a gas given off by some radioactive substance: abbrev. **Em.**

**e·man·ci·pate** (i-man′sə-pāt′), *v.t.* [-PATED, -PATING], [< L. pp. < *e-*, out + *mancipare*, to deliver up as property; ult. < *manus*, the hand + *capere*, to take], 1. to set free (a slave, etc.); release from bondage. 2. to free from restraint or influence. —**e·man′ci·pa′tion,** *n.* —**e·man′ci·pa′tor** (-tẽr), *n.* —**e·man′ci·pa·to′ry** (-pə-tôr′i, -tō′ri), **e·man′ci·pa′tive,** *adj.*

**e·mas·cu·late** (i-mas′kyoo-lāt′; *for adj.*, -lit), *v.t.* [-LATED, -LATING], [< L. pp. of *emasculare* < *e-*, out + *masculus*, male], 1. to remove the testicles of, so as to deprive of the power to reproduce; castrate. 2. to weaken; destroy the strength or vigor of. *adj.* deprived of virility, strength, or vigor. —**e·mas′cu·la′tion,** *n.* —**e·mas′cu·la′tor** (-tẽr), *n.* —**e·mas′cu·la·to′ry** (-lə-tôr′i, -tō′ri), *adj.*

**em·balm** (im-bäm′), *v.t.* [< OFr. *embaumer*; see EN- & BALM], 1. to keep (a dead body) from decaying by treating it with various chemicals. 2. to preserve in memory. 3. to perfume; make fragrant. —**em·balm′er,** *n.* —**em·balm′ment,** *n.*

**em·bank** (im-baŋk′), *v.t.* to protect, support, or enclose with a bank of earth, rubble, etc.

**em·bank·ment** (im-baŋk′mənt), *n.* 1. an embanking. 2. a bank (of earth, rubble, etc.) used to keep back water, hold up a roadway, etc.

**em·bar·go** (im-bär′gō), *n.* [*pl.* -GOES], [Sp. < L. *in*, in + *barra*, a bar], 1. a government order prohibiting the entry or departure of commercial ships at its ports. 2. any restriction imposed on commerce by law. 3. restriction; restraint; prohibition. *v.t.* to put an embargo upon.

**em·bark** (im-bärk′), *v.t.* [< Fr. < L. *in*, in + LL. *barca*, small boat], 1. to put aboard ship. 2. to take aboard: said of a ship. 3. to engage (a person) or invest (money, etc.) in an enterprise. *v.i.* 1. to go aboard a ship. 2. to begin a journey. 3. to engage in an enterprise. —**em·bar·ka·tion, em·bar·ca·tion** (em′bär-kā′shən), **em·bark′ment,** *n.*

**em·bar·rass** (im-bar′əs), *v.t.* [< Fr. < It. < *im-*, in + LL. *barra*, a bar], 1. to cause to feel self-conscious; disconcert. 2. to hinder; impede. 3. to cause to be in debt; cause financial difficulties to. 4. to complicate. —**em·bar′rass·ing,** *adj.* —**em·bar′rass·ing·ly,** *adv.* —**em·bar′rass·ment,** *n.*

**em·bas·sa·dor** (im-bas′ə-dẽr), *n.* ambassador.

**em·bas·sy** (em′bə-si), *n.* [*pl.* -SIES], [< OFr. < It. < Pr. < L. < Goth. *andbahts*, servant], 1. the position or functions of an ambassador. 2. the official residence or offices of an ambassador. 3. an ambassador and his staff. 4. a person or group sent on an official mission to a foreign government. 5. any important mission, errand, or message.

**em·bat·tle** (em-bat′'l), *v.t.* [-TLED, -TLING], to provide with battlements; build battlements on.

**em·bat·tle** (em-bat′'l), *v.t.* [-TLED, -TLING], [< OFr. < *en-*, in + *bataille*; see BATTLE], [Rare, except in pp.], to prepare or set in line for battle.

**em·bay** (em-bā′), *v.t.* to shut in; enclose or surround, as in a bay. —**em·bay′ment,** *n.*

**em·bed** (im-bed′), *v.t.* [-BEDDED, -BEDDING], to set or fix firmly in a surrounding mass: as, the knife was *embedded* in the wood.

**em·bel·lish** (im-bel′ish), *v.t.* [< OFr. *embellir* < *em-* (L. *in*) + *bel* < L. *bellus*, beautiful], 1. to decorate; ornament; adorn. 2. to improve (a story, etc.) by adding touches or details, often of a fictitious kind. —**em·bel′lish·er,** *n.* —**em·bel′lish·ment,** *n.*

**em·ber** (em′bẽr), *n.* [< AS. *æmerge*], 1. a glowing piece of coal, wood, peat, etc. from a fire. 2. *pl.* the smoldering remains of a fire.

**em·ber** (em′bẽr), *adj.* [< AS. < *ymbrene*, circuit], designating or of three days (**Ember days**) set aside in each season of the year for prayer and fasting: observed in the Roman Catholic and other churches.

**em·bez·zle** (im-bez′'l), *v.t.* [-ZLED, -ZLING], [< Anglo-Fr. < OFr. < *en-* (see EN-) + *besillier*, to destroy], to steal (money, etc. entrusted to one's care); take by fraud for one's own use. —**em·bez′zle·ment,** *n.* —**em·bez′zler,** *n.*

**em·bit·ter** (im-bit′ẽr), *v.t.* to make bitter or more bitter. —**em·bit′ter·ment,** *n.*

**em·bla·zon** (em-blā′z'n), *v.t.* [see BLAZON], 1. to decorate (*with* coats of arms, etc.). 2. to display brilliantly; decorate with bright colors. 3. to praise; celebrate. —**em·bla′zon·er,** *n.* —**em·bla′zon·ment,** *n.* —**em·bla′zon·ry** [*pl.* -RIES], *n.*

**em·blem** (em′bləm), *n.* [< OFr. < L. *emblema*, inlaid work < Gr. *emblēma*, insertion < *en-*, in + *ballein*, to throw], 1. a visible symbol of a thing, idea, etc.; object that stands for or suggests something else: as, the cross is an *emblem* of Christianity. 2. a sign, badge, or device.

**em·blem·at·ic** (em′blə-mat′ik), *adj.* of, containing, or serving as an emblem; symbolic: also **em′blem·at′i·cal.** —**em′blem·at′i·cal·ly,** *adv.*

**em·bod·i·ment** (im-bod′i-mənt), *n.* 1. an embodying or being embodied. 2. that in which some idea, quality, etc. is embodied: as, she is the *embodiment* of virtue. 3. anything embodied.

**em·bod·y** (im-bod′i), *v.t.* [-IED, -YING], 1. to give bodily form to; incarnate. 2. to give definite or visible form to. 3. to collect and include (material) in a book, system, etc. 4. to make (something) part of an organized whole; incorporate.

**em·bold·en** (im-bōl′d'n), *v.t.* to give courage to; cause to be bold or bolder.

**em·bo·lism** (em′bə-liz'm), *n.* in *medicine*, the obstruction of a blood vessel by an embolus.

**em·bo·lus** (em′bə-ləs), *n.* [*pl.* -LI (-lī′)], [L. < Gr. < *en-*, in + *ballein*, to throw], any foreign matter, as a blood clot or air bubble, carried in the blood stream. —**em·bol′ic** (-bol′ik), *adj.*

**‡em·bon·point** (äṅ′bōṅ′pwaṅ′), *n.* [Fr. < OFr., lit., in good condition], plumpness; stoutness.

**em·bos·om** (em-booz′əm, -bōō′zəm), *v.t.* 1. to embrace; cherish. 2. to enclose; surround; shelter.

**em·boss** (im-bôs′, -bos′), *v.t.* [< OFr.; see EN- & BOSS (raised ornament)], 1. to decorate with designs, etc. raised above the surface. 2. to raise in relief, as a design. —**em·boss′er,** *n.* —**em·boss′ment,** *n.*

**em·bou·chure** (om′boo-shoor′), *n.* [Fr. < *emboucher*, to put into the mouth < ML. < L. *in*, in + *bucca*, the cheek], 1. the mouth of a river. 2. in *music*, *a)* the mouthpiece of a wind instrument. *b)* the way of applying the lips and tongue to the mouthpiece of a wind instrument.

**em·bow·er** (em-bou′ẽr), *v.t.* to enclose or shelter in or as in a bower.

**em·brace** (im-brās′), *v.t.* [-BRACED, -BRACING], [< OFr. < LL. < L. *im-*, in + *brachium*, an arm], 1. to clasp in the arms lovingly or affectionately; hug. 2. to accept readily: as, to *embrace* an opportunity. 3. to take up; enter upon; adopt: as, to *embrace* a new profession. 4. to encircle; surround. 5. to include; contain. *v.i.* to clasp one another in the arms. *n.* an embracing; hug. —**em·brace′a·ble,** *adj.* —**em·brace′ment,** *n.* —**em·bra′cer,** *n.*

**em·bra·sure** (em-brā′zhẽr), *n.* [Fr. < *embraser*, to widen an opening], 1. an opening (for a door, window, etc.) with the sides slanted so that it is wider on the inside than on the outside. 2. an opening, as in a parapet, with the sides slanting outward to increase the angle of fire of a gun.

**em·bro·cate** (em′brō-kāt′), *v.t.* [-CATED, -CATING], [< ML. *embrocatus*, pp. < L. < Gr. < *en-*, in + *brechein*, to wet], in *medicine*, to moisten and rub with an oil, liniment, etc. —**em′bro·ca′tion,** *n.*

**em·broi·der** (im-broi′dẽr), *v.t.* [< OFr. < *en-* + *brosder*, to embroider], 1. to ornament (fabric) with a design in needlework. 2. to make (a design, etc.) on fabric with needlework. 3. to embellish (a story, etc.); exaggerate. *v.i.* to do embroidery. —**em·broi′der·er,** *n.*

**em·broi·der·y** (im-broi′dẽr-i), *n.* [*pl.* -IES], 1. the art or work of ornamenting fabric with needlework; embroidering. 2. embroidered work or fabric. 3. embellishment, as of a story.

**em·broil** (em-broil′), *v.t.* [< Fr.; see EN- & BROIL (to dispute)], 1. to confuse (affairs, etc.); mix up; entangle. 2. to cause (a person, government, etc.) to take part in a dispute; involve. —**em·broil′er,** *n.* —**em·broil′ment,** *n.*

**em·bry·o** (em′bri-ō′), *n.* [*pl.* -OS], [ML. < Gr. *embryon* < *en-*, in + *bryein*, to swell], 1. an animal in the earliest stages of its development in the uterus: the human organism in the first three months after conception is called an *embryo*, thereafter a *fetus*. 2. *a)* an early, undeveloped stage of something. *b)* anything in such a stage. 3. in *botany*, the rudimentary plant contained in the seed. *adj.* embryonic.

**em·bry·o-,** a combining form meaning *embryo*, *embryonic*, as in *embryology*.

**em·bry·ol·o·gy** (em′bri-ol′ə-ji), *n.* [*embryo-* + *-logy*], the branch of biology dealing with the formation and development of embryos: abbrev. **embryol.** —**em′bry·o·log′ic** (-ə-loj′ik), **em′bry·o·log′i·cal,** *adj.* —**em′bry·ol′o·gist,** *n.*

**em·bry·on·ic** (em'bri-on'ik), *adj.* 1. of or like an embryo. 2. undeveloped; rudimentary.

**em·cee** (em'sē'), *v.t. & v.i.* [-CEED, -CEEING], [< *M.C.*, Master of Ceremonies], [Slang], to act as master of ceremonies (for). *n.* [Slang], a master of ceremonies.

**e·meer** (ə-mêr'), *n.* an emir. —**e·meer'ate** (-it), *n.*

**e·mend** (i-mend'), *v.t.* [< L. < *e-*, out + *menda*, a fault], to correct or improve; specif., to make scholarly corrections in (a literary text, etc.). —**e·mend'a·ble,** *adj.* —**e·mend'er,** *n.*

**e·men·date** (ē'mən-dāt'), *v.t.* [-DATED, -DATING], to emend (a text). —**e·men·da·tion** (ē'men-dā'-shən, em'ən-), *n.* —**e'men·da'tor,** *n.* —**e·mend·a·to·ry** (i-men'də-tôr'i, -tō'ri), *adj.*

**em·er·ald** (em'ẽr-əld, em'rəld), *n.* [< OFr. *esmeralde* < LL. < L. < Gr. *(s)maragdos*], 1. a bright-green, transparent precious stone; green variety of beryl. 2. a similar variety of corundum: also called *Oriental emerald.* 3. bright green. *adj.* 1. bright-green. 2. made of or with an emerald or emeralds.

**Emerald Isle,** Ireland.

**e·merge** (i-mũrj'), *v.i.* [EMERGED, EMERGING], [< L. < *e-*, out + *mergere*, to dip], 1. to rise as from a fluid. 2. to come forth into view; become visible. —**e·mer'gence,** *n.* —**e·mer'gent,** *adj.*

**e·mer·gen·cy** (i-mũr'jən-si), *n.* [*pl.* -CIES], [orig. sense, an emerging], a sudden, generally unexpected occurrence or set of circumstances demanding immediate action. *adj.* for use in case of sudden necessity: as, an *emergency* exit.

**e·mer·i·tus** (i-mer'ə-təs), *adj.* [L. < *e-*, out + *mereri*, to serve], retired from active service, usually for age, but retaining one's rank or title: as, professor *emeritus.*

**e·mer·sion** (ē-mũr'shən, -zhən), *n.* an emerging.

**Em·er·son, Ralph Wal·do** (wôl'dō em'ẽr-s'n), 1803–1882; U.S. essayist, philosopher, and poet.

**em·er·y** (em'ẽr-i, em'ri), *n.* [*pl.* -IES], [< Fr. < OFr. < LL. < It. < Gr. *smyris*, emery], a dark, very hard, coarse variety of corundum used for grinding, polishing, etc.

**e·met·ic** (i-met'ik), *adj.* [< L. < Gr. *emetikos* < *emeein*, to vomit], causing vomiting. *n.* a medicine or other substance that causes vomiting.

**e·meu** (ē'mū), *n.* an emu.

**E.M.F., e.m.f., EMF, emf,** electromotive force.

**-e·mi·a** (ē'mi-ə), [Mod. L. < Gr. < *haima*, blood], a suffix meaning *a* (specified) *condition of the blood*, as in *leukemia*: also sp. **-aemia.**

**em·i·grant** (em'ə-grənt), *adj.* 1. emigrating. 2. of emigrants or emigration. *n.* one who emigrates.

**em·i·grate** (em'ə-grāt'), *v.i.* [-GRATED, -GRATING], [< L. *emigratus*, pp. < *e-*, out + *migrare*, to move], to leave one country or region to settle in another: opposed to *immigrate.* —**em'i·gra'tion,** *n.*

**‡é·mi·gré** (ā'mē'grā'; Eng. em'ə-grā'), *n.* [*pl.* -GRÉS (-grā'; Eng. -grāz')], [Fr.], 1. an emigrant. 2. a Royalist who fled from France during the French Revolution.

**em·i·nence** (em'ə-nəns), *n.* 1. an eminent or high place, thing, etc., as a hill. 2. superiority in rank, position, etc.; greatness. 3. [E-], in the *R.C. Church*, a title of honor given to a cardinal.

**em·i·nent** (em'ə-nənt), *adj.* [< L. ppr. of *eminere*, to project], 1. rising above others; high. 2. projecting; prominent. 3. standing high by comparison with others; exalted; distinguished. 4. outstanding; noteworthy. —**em'i·nent·ly,** *adv.*

**eminent domain,** in *law*, the right of a government to take private property for public use, just compensation being given to the owner.

**e·mir** (ə-mêr'), *n.* [Ar. *amīr*, commander], 1. an Arabian ruler, prince, or military commander. 2. a title given to Mohammed's descendants. 3. a Turkish honorary title. —**e·mir'ate** (-it), *n.*

**em·is·sar·y** (em'ə-ser'i), *n.* [*pl.* -IES], [< L. < pp. of *emittere;* see EMIT], a person or agent, especially a secret agent, sent on a specific mission. *adj.* of or serving as an emissary.

**e·mis·sion** (i-mish'ən), *n.* 1. an emitting; issuance. 2. something emitted; discharge. —**e·mis'sive** (-mis'-iv), *adj.*

**e·mit** (i-mit'), *v.t.* [EMITTED, EMITTING], [< L. < *e-*, out + *mittere*, to send], 1. to send out; give forth. 2. to utter (sounds, etc.). 3. to issue, as money; put into circulation. —**e·mit'ter,** *n.*

**Em·man·u·el** (i-man'ū-əl), *n.* Immanuel.

**EmnE., EMnE.,** Early Modern English.

**e·mol·li·ent** (i-mol'yənt), *adj.* [< L. ppr. < *e-*, out + *mollire*, to soften < *mollis*, soft], softening; soothing. *n.* a medicine that has a softening or soothing effect on surface tissues.

**e·mol·u·ment** (i-mol'yoo-mənt), *n.* [< L. < *e-*, out + *molere*, to grind], gain from employment or position; salary; wages; fees.

**e·mote** (i-mōt'), *v.i.* [EMOTED, EMOTING], [< *emotion*], [Colloq.], to conduct oneself in an emotional or theatrical manner.

**e·mo·tion** (i-mō'shən), *n.* [Fr.; prob. after *motion* < L. < *e-*, out + *movere*, to move], 1. strong, generalized feeling. 2. any specific feeling, as love, hate, fear, anger, etc. —**e·mo'tion·less,** *adj.* —**e·mo'tion·less·ly,** *adv.*

**e·mo·tion·al** (i-mō'shən-'l), *adj.* 1. of emotion or the emotions. 2. showing emotion. 3. easily aroused to emotion. 4. appealing to the emotions. —**e·mo'tion·al·ist,** *n.* —**e·mo'tion·al'i·ty** (-al'ə-ti), *n.* —**e·mo'tion·al·ly,** *adv.*

**e·mo·tion·al·ism** (i-mō'shən-'l-iz'm), *n.* 1. emotional character. 2. the tendency to be emotional. 3. display of emotion.

**e·mo·tion·al·ize** (i-mō'shən-'l-īz'), *v.t.* [-IZED, -IZING], to treat, present, or interpret in an emotional way; make emotional.

**e·mo·tive** (i-mō'tiv), *adj.* characterized by, expressing, or producing emotion. —**e·mo'tive·ly,** *adv.* —**e·mo'tive·ness,** *n.*

**Emp.,** 1. Emperor. 2. Empire. 3. Empress.

**em·pan·el** (im-pan''l), *v.t.* [-ELED or -ELLED, -ELING or -ELLING], 1. to enter the name or names of on a jury list. 2. to choose (a jury) from such a list. Also sp. **impanel.**

**em·pa·thy** (em'pə-thi), *n.* [< Gr. < *en-*, in + *pathos*, feeling], the projection of one's own personality into that of another or into an object; intellectual or emotional identification with another. —**em·path·ic** (em-path'ik), *adj.*

**em·per·or** (em'pẽr-ẽr), *n.* [< OFr. < L. *imperator* < *imperare*, to command < *in-*, in + *parare*, to set in order], a man who rules an empire. —**em'per·or·ship',** *n.*

**em·pha·sis** (em'fə-sis), *n.* [*pl.* -SES (-sēz')], [L. < Gr. < *en-*, in + *phasis*, appearance], 1. force of expression, feeling, action, etc. 2. special stress given to a syllable, word, phrase, etc. in speaking. 3. special attention given to something so as to make it stand out; importance.

**em·pha·size** (em'fə-sīz'), *v.t.* [-SIZED, -SIZING], to give emphasis, or special force, to; stress.

**em·phat·ic** (im-fat'ik), *adj.* 1. expressed, felt, or done with emphasis. 2. using emphasis in speaking, etc. 3. forcible; striking; definite. —**em·phat'i·cal·ly,** *adv.*

**em·pire** (em'pīr), *n.* [< OFr. < L. < *imperare;* see EMPEROR], 1. supreme rule; absolute power or authority. 2. government by an emperor or empress. 3. a group of states or territories under one sovereign power. 4. a state uniting many territories and peoples under one ruler. *adj.* [E-], of or characteristic of the first French Empire (1804–1815), under Napoleon: as, *Empire* furniture.

**em·pir·ic** (em-pir'ik), *n.* [< L. < Gr. < *empeiria*, experience < *en-*, in + *peira*, a trial], 1. a person who is ignorant of scientific principles and relies solely on practical experience. 2. a person who lacks regular training and proper qualifications; charlatan; quack. *adj.* empirical.

**em·pir·i·cal** (em-pir'i-k'l), *adj.* 1. relying or based on experiment and observation. 2. relying or based on practical experience without reference to scientific principles: as, an *empirical* remedy. —**em·pir'i·cal·ly,** *adv.*

**em·pir·i·cism** (em-pir'ə-siz'm), *n.* 1. experimental method; search for knowledge by observation and experiment. 2. *a*) a disregarding of scientific methods and relying solely on experience; hence, *b*) quackery. 3. in *philosophy*, the theory that sensory experience is the only source of knowledge. —**em·pir'i·cist,** *n.*

**em·place·ment** (im-plās'mənt), *n.* 1. a placing in position; assigning to a location. 2. the prepared position or platform from which a heavy gun is fired.

**em·ploy** (im-ploi'), *v.t.* [< Fr. < L. < *in-*, in + *plicare*, to fold], 1. to make use of; use. 2. to keep busy or occupied; devote. 3. to provide work and pay for. 4. to engage the services or labor of; hire. *n.* the state of being employed; paid service; employment. —**em·ploy'a·ble,** *adj.*

**em·ploy·ee, em·ploy·e** (im-ploi'ē, em'ploi-ē'), *n.* a person employed by another, or by a firm, etc., for wages or salary: also sp. **employé.**

**em·ploy·er** (im-ploi'ẽr), *n.* 1. a person, business firm, etc. that employs one or more persons for wages or salary. 2. a user.

**em·ploy·ment** (im-ploi'mənt), *n.* 1. an employing or being employed. 2. the thing at which one is employed; work; occupation; job.

**em·po·ri·um** (em-pôr'i-əm, -pō'ri-), *n.* [*pl.* -RIUMS. -RIA (-ə)], [L. <Gr . < *emporos*, traveler < *en-*, in +

*poros*, way], 1. a place of commerce; trading center. 2. a large store with a wide variety of things for sale.

**em·pow·er** (im-pou'ēr), *v.t.* 1. to give power or authority to; authorize. 2. to give ability to; enable. Also sp. **impower.** —**em·pow'er·ment,** *n.*

**em·press** (em'pris), *n.* 1. the wife of an emperor. 2. a woman ruler of an empire.

**emp·ty** (emp'ti), *adj.* [-TIER, -TIEST], [AS. *æmettig*, unoccupied < *æmetta*, leisure + *-tig* (see -TY)], 1. containing nothing; having nothing in it. 2. having no one in it; unoccupied: as, an *empty* house. 3. worthless; unsatisfying: as, *empty* pleasures. 4. meaningless; insincere; vain: as, *empty* promises. 5. [Colloq.], hungry. *v.t.* [-TIED, -TYING], 1. to make empty. 2. to pour out or remove (the contents) of something. *v.i.* 1. to become empty. 2. to pour out; discharge. *n.* [*pl.* -TIES], an empty freight car, truck, bottle, etc. —**empty of,** lacking; devoid of. —**emp'ti·ly,** *adv.* —**emp'ti·ness,** *n.*

**emp·ty-hand·ed** (emp'ti-han'did), *adj.* bringing or carrying away nothing.

**emp·ty-head·ed** (emp'ti-hed'id), *adj.* frivolous and stupid; silly. —**emp'ty-head'ed·ness,** *n.*

**em·pur·ple** (em-pũr'p'l), *v.t.* [-PLED, -PLING], to make purple.

**em·pyr·e·al** (em-pir'i-əl, em'pə-rē'əl, em'pi-), *adj.* [< LL. < Gr. *empyr(i)os*, fiery < *en-*, in + *pyr*, a fire], of the empyrean; heavenly; sublime.

**em·py·re·an** (em'pə-rē'ən, em'pi-), *n.* [see EMPYREAL], 1. the highest heaven: among the ancients, the sphere of pure light or fire. 2. the sky; the celestial vault; firmament. *adj.* empyreal.

**e·mu** (ē'mū), *n.* [prob. < Port. *ema*, a crane], a large, nonflying Australian bird, like the ostrich but smaller: also sp. **emeu.**

**em·u·late** (em'yoo-lāt'), *v.t.* [-LATED, -LATING], [< L. < *aemulus*, trying to equal], 1. to try to equal or surpass. 2. to rival successfully. —**em'u·la'tion,** *n.* —**em'u·la'tive,** *adj.* —**em'u·la'tor,** *n.*

**em·u·lous** (em'yoo-ləs), *adj.* 1. desirous of equaling or surpassing. 2. of or resulting from emulation. —**em'u·lous·ly,** *adv.* —**em'u·lous·ness,** *n.*

**e·mul·si·fy** (i-mul'sə-fī'), *v.t. & v.i.* [-FIED, -FYING], to form into an emulsion. —**e·mul'si·fi·ca'tion,** *n.* —**e·mul'si·fi'er,** *n.*

**e·mul·sion** (i-mul'shən), *n.* [< L. *emulsus*, pp. < *e-*, out + *mulgere*, to milk], a fluid, as milk, formed by the suspension of one liquid in another; specif., *a)* in *pharmacy*, a preparation of an oily substance held in suspension in a watery liquid. *b)* in *photography*, a suspension of a salt of silver in gelatin or collodion, used to coat plates and film. —**e·mul'sive,** *adj.*

**en** (en), *n.* 1. the letter N, n. 2. in *printing*, a space half the width of an em.

**en-,** [OFr. < L. *in-* < prep. *in*, in, into], a prefix meaning: 1. *to put into* or *on*, as in *enthrone; to cover with*, as in *enrobe.* 2. *to make, cause to be*, as in *endanger, enfeeble.* 3. *in* or *into*, as in *enclose. En-* often has the force of an intensifier as in *enliven.* Many words with *en-* are also spelled *in-* (e.g., *enquire, inquire*). See also **em-.**

**en-,** [Gr. *en-* < prep. *en*, in], a prefix meaning *in*, chiefly in Greek derivatives, as *endemic.*

**-en** (ən, 'n), [< AS. suffixes *-an*, *-en*, etc.], any of several suffixes: 1. meaning: *a) to become* or *cause to be*, as in *weaken. b) to come to have* or *cause to have*, as in *hearten.* 2. meaning *made of*, as in *woolen.* 3. used to form the past participle of strong verbs, as in *risen.* 4. used to form plurals, as in *children.* 5. used to form diminutives, as in *chicken.*

**en·a·ble** (in-ā'b'l), *v.t.* [-BLED, -BLING], to make able; provide with means, opportunity, or power (*to* do something). —**en·a'ble·ment,** *n.*

**en·act** (in-akt'), *v.t.* 1. to make (a bill, etc.) into a law; pass (a law); decree; ordain. 2. to do: usually in the passive. 3. to represent in or as in a play. —**en·ac'tive,** *adj.*

**en·act·ment** (in-akt'mənt), *n.* 1. an enacting or being enacted. 2. something enacted, as a law.

**en·am·el** (i-nam''l), *n.* [see the *v.*], 1. a glassy, colored, opaque substance fused to surfaces, as of metals, as an ornamental or protective coating. 2. any smooth, hard, glossy coating like enamel. 3. the hard, white, glossy coating of the crowns of teeth. 4. anything enameled; enameled ware. 5. paint or varnish that produces a smooth, hard, glossy surface when it dries. *v.t.* [-ELED or -ELLED, -ELING or -ELLING], [< Anglo-Fr. < *en-* (see EN-) + *amayl* < OFr. *esmail*, enamel], 1. to inlay or cover with enamel. 2. to decorate in various colors, as if with enamel. 3. to form an enamellike surface on. —**en·am'el·er, en·am'el·ler, en·am'el·ist, en·am'el·list,** *n.* —**en·am'el·work',** *n.*

**en·am·el·ware** (i-nam''l-wâr'), *n.* kitchen utensils, etc. made of enameled metal.

**en·am·or, en·am·our** (in-am'ēr), *v.t.* [< OFr. < *en-*, in + *amour* < L. *amor*, love], to fill wth love and desire; charm; captivate.

**en·am·ored, en·am·oured** (in-am'ērd), *adj.* charmed; captivated. —**enamored of,** in love with.

**en bloc** (en blok'; Fr. än' blôk'), [Fr., lit., in a block], in one lump; as a whole; all together.

**enc., encl.,** 1. enclosed. 2. enclosure.

**en·camp** (in-kamp'), *v.i.* to make, and stay in, a camp. *v.t.* to put in a camp. —**en·camp'ment,** *n.*

**en·case** (in-kās'), *v.t.* [-CASED, -CASING], 1. to cover completely; enclose. 2. to put into a case. Also sp. **incase.** —**en·case'ment,** *n.*

**en cas·se·role** (en kas'ə-rōl'; Fr. an'kas'rôl'), [Fr.], (baked and served) in a casserole.

**en·caus·tic** (en-kôs'tik), *adj.* [< L. < Gr. < *en-*, in + *kaiein*, to burn], done by a process of burning in: as, *encaustic* tile. *n.* a method of painting in which wax colors are fused with hot irons.

**-ence** (əns), [< Fr. & L.; Fr. *-ence;* L. *-entia*], a suffix meaning *act, fact, quality, state, result*, or *degree*, as in *conference, excellence.*

**‡en·ceinte** (än'sant'; Eng. en-sānt'), *adj.* [Fr.; ult. < L. *in-*, not + *cinctus*, pp. of *cingere*, to gird], pregnant.

**en·ceph·a·li·tis** (en'sef-ə-lī'tis, en-sef'-), *n.* [< *encephalo-* + *-itis*], inflammation of the brain. —**en'ceph·a·lit'ic** (-lit'ik), *adj.*

**en·ceph·a·lo-,** [< Gr. *enkephalos*, the brain], a combining form meaning *of the brain*: also **encephal-.**

**en·ceph·a·lon** (en-sef'ə-lon'), *n.* [*pl.* -LA (-lə)], [< Gr. < *en-*, in + *kephalē*, the head], in *anatomy*, the brain. —**en'ce·phal'ic** (-sə-fal'ik), *adj.*

**en·chain** (en-chān'), *v.t.* 1. to put in chains; fetter. 2. to captivate. —**en·chain'ment,** *n.*

**en·chant** (in-chant', -chänt'), *v.t.* [< OFr. < L. < *in-*, in + *cantare*, to sing], 1. to cast a spell over, as by magic; bewitch. 2. to charm greatly; delight. —**en·chant'er,** *n.* —**en·chant'ress,** *n.fem.*

**en·chant·ing** (in-chan'tiŋ, -chän'-), *adj.* 1. charming; delightful. 2. bewitching; fascinating. —**en·chant'ing·ly,** *adv.*

**en·chant·ment** (in-chant'mənt, -chänt'-), *n.* 1. an enchanting or being enchanted by magic. 2. a magic spell or charm. 3. something that charms or delights greatly. 4. great delight or pleasure.

**en·cir·cle** (in-sũr'k'l), *v.t.* [-CLED, -CLING], 1. to make a circle around; surround. 2. to move in a circle around. —**en·cir'cle·ment,** *n.*

**en·clave** (en'klāv), *n.* [< OFr. < LL. < L. *in*, in + *clavis*, a key or *clavus*, a nail], foreign territory surrounded by a specified country.

**en·close** (in-klōz'), *v.t.* [-CLOSED, -CLOSING], 1. to shut in all around; surround; fence in. 2. to put into a receptacle. 3. to insert in an envelope, etc. together with a letter. 4. to contain. Also sp. **inclose.**

**en·clo·sure** (in-klō'zhēr), *n.* 1. an enclosing or being enclosed. 2. something that encloses. 3. something enclosed. 4. an enclosed place. Also sp. **inclosure.**

**en·co·mi·ast** (en-kō'mi-ast'), *n.* a person who speaks or writes encomiums; eulogist. —**en·co'mi·as'tic, en·co'mi·as'ti·cal,** *adj.*

**en·co·mi·um** (en-kō'mi-əm), *n.* [*pl.* -UMS, -A (-ə)], [L. < Gr. *enkōmion*, song of praise < *en-*, in + *kōmos*, a revel], a formal expression of high praise; eulogy; panegyric.

**en·com·pass** (in-kum'pəs), *v.t.* 1. to shut in all around; surround; encircle. 2. to contain; include. —**en·com'pass·ment,** *n.*

**en·core** (äŋ'kôr, än-kōr'), *interj.* [Fr., yet, again], again; once more. *n.* (äŋ'kôr, än'kōr), 1. a demand by an audience, shown by applause, for further performance. 2. the performance or piece performed in answer to such a demand. *v.t.* (äŋ-kôr', än'kōr), [-CORED, -CORING], to demand a repetition of (a piece of music, etc.) or from (a performer) by applauding.

**en·coun·ter** (in-koun'tēr), *v.t.* [< OFr. < L. *in*, in + *contra*, against], 1. to meet unexpectedly. 2. to meet in conflict; engage in battle. 3. to face (difficulties, trouble, etc.). *v.i.* to meet accidentally or in opposition. *n.* 1. a meeting in conflict; fight. 2. an unexpected meeting.

**en·cour·age** (in-kũr′ij), *v.t.* [-AGED, -AGING], 1. to give courage, hope, or confidence to; hearten. 2. to help; give support to; be favorable to; foster. —**en·cour′ag·er,** *n.* —**en·cour′ag·ing,** *adj.* —**en·cour′ag·ing·ly,** *adv.*

**en·cour·age·ment** (in-kũr′ij-mənt), *n.* 1. an encouraging or being encouraged. 2. something that encourages.

**en·croach** (in-krōch′), *v.i.* [< OFr. *encrochier*, to seize upon < *en-*, in + *croc*, a hook], 1. to trespass or intrude (*on* or *upon* the rights, property, etc. of another). 2. to advance beyond the proper or customary limits. —**en·croach′er,** *n.* —**en·croach′ment,** *n.*

**en·crust** (in-krust′), *v.t. & v.i.* to incrust. —**en′crus·ta′tion,** *n.*

**en·cum·ber** (in-kum′bẽr), *v.t.* [< OFr.; see EN- & CUMBER], 1. to hold back the motion or action of, as with a burden; hinder; hamper. 2. to fill so as to obstruct; block up. 3. to burden; load or weigh down. Also sp. **incumber.**

**en·cum·brance** (in-kum′brəns), *n.* 1. something that encumbers; hindrance; burden. 2. [Rare], a dependent, especially a child. 3. a claim, as a mortgage, against property. Also sp. **incumbrance.**

**-en·cy** (ən-si), [L. *-entia*], a suffix equivalent to *-ence*, meaning *act, fact, quality, state*, etc., as in *dependency, emergency, efficiency.*

**ency., encyc., encycl.,** encyclopedia.

**en·cy·cli·cal** (en-sik′li-k'l, -sī′kli-), *adj.* [LL. *encyclicus* < Gr. < *en-*, in + *kyklos*, a circle], for general circulation. *n.* in the *R.C. Church*, a letter from the Pope to the clergy, having to do with church matters. Also **en·cy′clic.**

**en·cy·clo·pe·di·a, en·cy·clo·pae·di·a** (in-sī′klə-pē′di-ə), *n.* [Mod. L. < Gr. *enkyklopaideia*, < *enkyklios*, general + *paideia*, education], 1. a book or set of books giving information on all branches of knowledge, generally in articles alphabetically arranged. 2. a similar work giving information on one field of knowledge. —**en·cy′clo·pe′dic, en·cy′clo·pae′dic, en·cy′clo·pe′di·cal, en·cy′clo·pae′di·cal,** *adj.* —**en·cy′clo·pe′dist, en·cy′clo·pae′dist,** *n.*

**en·cyst** (en-sist′), *v.t. & v.i.* to enclose or become enclosed in a cyst, capsule, or sac. —**en·cyst′ment,** *n.*

**end** (end), *n.* [AS *ende*], 1. a boundary; a limit or limiting part. 2. the last part of anything; final point; finish; conclusion. 3. a ceasing to exist; death or destruction. 4. the part at or near either extremity of anything; tip. 5. an aim; purpose; intention. 6. an outcome; result; consequence. 7. a piece left over; fragment; remnant. 8. in *football*, a player at either end of the line of scrimmage. *v.t.* 1. to bring to an end; finish; stop. 2. to form the end of. 3. [Obs.], to kill. *v.i.* 1. to come to an end; terminate. 2. to die. *adj.* at the end; final: as, *end* product. —**at loose ends,** in an unsettled or confused condition. —**end up,** 1. in an upright position. 2. to finish. —**make an end of,** 1. to stop. 2. to do away with. —**make both ends meet,** 1. to keep one's expenses within one's income. 2. to manage merely to exist on one's income. —**no end,** [Colloq.], a great deal; very much or many. —**put an end to,** 1. to stop. 2. to do away with. —**end′er,** *n.*

**en·da·moe·ba, en·da·me·ba** (en′də-mē′bə), *n.* [*pl.* -BAS, -BAE (-bē)], [see ENDO- & AMOEBA], any of a large group of amoebas, some species of which are found as parasites in man and certain other animals, causing amoebic dysentery and other diseases.

**en·dan·ger** (in-dān′jẽr), *v.t.* to expose to danger, harm, or loss; imperil. —**en·dan′ger·ment,** *n.*

**en·dear** (in-dêr′), *v.t.* to make dear or beloved. —**en·dear′ing·ly,** *adv.*

**en·dear·ment** (in-dêr′mənt), *n.* 1. an endearing or being endeared; affection. 2. an expression of affection; caress. 3. something that endears.

**en·deav·or** (in-dev′ẽr), *v.i.* [< *en-* + OFr. *deveir*, duty < L. *debere*, to owe], to try hard; make an earnest attempt; strive. *v.t.* [Archaic], to try to achieve; attempt. *n.* an earnest effort to accomplish something. Brit. sp. **endeavour.**

**en·dem·ic** (en-dem′ik), *adj.* [< Gr. < *en-*, in + *dēmos*, the people; + *-ic*], prevalent in or restricted to a certain locality or group: also **en·dem′i·cal.** *n.* an endemic disease. —**en·dem′i·cal·ly,** *adv.*

‡**en dés·ha·bil·lé** (än′ dā′zȧ′bē′yā′), [Fr.], partly undressed or dressed in night clothes.

**end·ing** (en′diŋ), *n.* 1. the last part; finish. 2. death. 3. in *grammar*, the final letter or letters added to a word base to make a derivative or inflectional form: as, *-ed* is the *ending* in *wanted.*

**en·dive** (en′dīv, än′dēv), *n.* [Fr. < ML. < MGr. < L. *intibus* < Gr. *entybon*], 1. a kind of chicory with ragged, curly leaves used in salads: also called *escarole.* 2. another kind of chicory whose long leaves are blanched for use in salads.

**end·less** (end′lis), *adj.* 1. having no end; going on forever; eternal; infinite. 2. lasting too long: as, an *endless* speech. 3. with the ends joined to form a closed ring that can move continuously over wheels, etc.: as, an *endless* chain. —**end′less·ly,** *adv.* —**end′less·ness,** *n.*

**end·most** (end′mōst′), *adj.* at or nearest to the end; farthest; most remote; last.

**en·do-,** [< Gr. *endon*, within], a combining form meaning *within, inner*: also **end-.**

**en·do·blast** (en′də-blast′), *n.* the endoderm.

**en·do·carp** (en′də-kärp′), *n.* the inner layer of a ripened ovary or fruit, as the pit of a plum.

ENDOCARP OF PEACH

**en·do·crine** (en′də-krīn′, -krin), *adj.* [< *endo-* + Gr. *krinein*, to separate], 1. designating or of any gland (**endocrine gland**) producing one or more internal secretions that are carried by the blood or lymph to some part whose functions they regulate. 2. designating or of such a secretion. *n.* any such gland or its secretion, as the thyroid, adrenal, and pituitary glands. Also **en′do·crin′** (-krin′). —**en′do·cri′nal, en′do·crin′ic, en·doc′ri·nous,** *adj.*

**en·do·derm** (en′də-dũrm′), *n.* the inner layer of cells of the embryo, from which is formed the lining of the digestive tract and of other internal organs. —**en′do·der′mal, en′do·der′mic,** *adj.*

**en·dog·a·my** (en-dog′ə-mi), *n.* [*endo-* + *-gamy*], the custom of marrying only within one's own tribe or social group; inbreeding. —**en·dog′a·mous,** *adj.*

**en·dog·e·nous** (en-doj′ə-nəs), *adj.* 1. developing from within; originating internally. 2. in *biology*, growing or developing from or on the inside. —**en·dog′e·nous·ly,** *adv.* —**en·dog′e·ny,** *n.*

**en·do·plasm** (en′də-plaz′m), *n.* the inner part of the cytoplasm of a cell. —**en′do·plas′mic,** *adj.*

**en·dorse** (in-dôrs′), *v.t.* [-DORSED, -DORSING], [< OFr. < ML. < L. *in*, on + *dorsum*, the back], 1. to write on the back of (a document); specif., to sign one's name as payee or transferor on the back of (a check, etc.). 2. to give support to; sanction. Also sp. **indorse.** —**en·dors′a·ble,** *adj.* —**en·dor·see** (in-dôr′sē′, en′-), *n.* —**en·dorse′ment,** *n.* —**en·dors′er,** *n.*

**en·do·skel·e·ton** (en′də-skel′ə-t'n), *n.* the internal bony structure, or true skeleton, in vertebrates.

**en·do·sperm** (en′də-spũrm′), *n.* [*endo-* + *sperm*], the nourishment for the embryo, which surrounds the embryo in the seed of a plant.

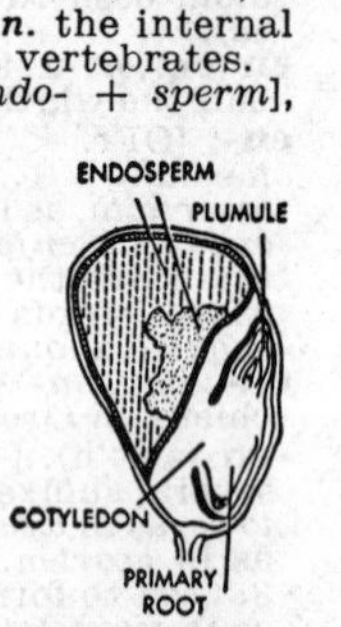

ENDOSPERM (of grain of corn)

**en·dow** (in-dou′), *v.t.* [< OFr. < *en-*, in + *douer* < L. *dotare*, to give], 1. to provide with some talent, quality, etc.: as, he is *endowed* with courage. 2. to give money or property for the support of (a college, hospital, etc.). 3. [Obs.], to provide with a dower. —**en·dow′er,** *n.*

**en·dow·ment** (in-dou′mənt), *n.* 1. an endowing. 2. that with which something is endowed; bequest. 3. a gift of nature; talent; ability.

**end product,** the final result of any series of changes, processes, or chemical reactions.

**end table,** a small table placed beside a chair, etc.

**en·due** (in-dōō′, -dū′), *v.t.* [-DUED, -DUING], [< OFr. < L. < *in-*, in + *ducere*, to lead], to provide (*with* something); specif., to endow (*with* qualities, talents, etc.): also sp. **indue.**

**en·dur·ance** (in-door′əns, -dyoor′-), *n.* 1. an enduring. 2. the ability to last, continue, or remain. 3. the ability to stand pain, distress, fatigue, etc.; fortitude. 4. duration.

**en·dure** (in-door′, -dyoor′), *v.t.* [-DURED, -DURING], [< OFr. < L. < *in-*, in + *durare*, to harden < *durus*, hard], 1. to stand (pain, fatigue, etc.); bear. 2. to put up with; tolerate. *v.i.* 1. to last; continue; remain. 2. to bear pain, etc. without flinching; hold out. Also **indure.** —**en·dur′a·ble,** *adj.* —**en·dur′a·bly,** *adv.*

**en·dur·ing** (in-door′iŋ, -dyoor′-), *adj.* 1. lasting; permanent. 2. long-suffering. —**en·dur′ing·ly,** *adv.* —**en·dur′ing·ness,** *n.*

**end·ways** (end′wāz′), *adv.* 1. on end; upright. 2.

with the end foremost. 3. lengthwise. 4. end to end. Also **end′wise′** (-wīz′).

**En·dym·i·on** (en-dim′i-ən), *n.* in *Gr. legend*, a beautiful young shepherd loved by Selene.

**-ene** (ēn), [after L. *-enus*, adj. suffix], a suffix used: 1. to form names for certain hydrocarbons, as in *benzene, acetylene*. 2. to form commercial names for some products.

**ENE, E.N.E., e.n.e.,** east-northeast.

**en·e·ma** (en′ə-mə), *n.* [LL.; Gr. < *en-*, in + *hienai*, to send], 1. a liquid injected into the rectum either as a purgative or a medicine. 2. the injection of such a liquid.

**en·e·my** (en′ə-mi), *n.* [*pl.* -MIES], [< OFr. < L. *inimicus* < *in-*, not + *amicus*, friend], 1. a person who hates another and wishes to injure him; also, one hostile to an idea, cause, etc.; foe. 2. *a*) a nation or force hostile to another. *b*) troops, ship, member, etc. of a hostile nation. 3. anything hostile or injurious. *adj.* of an enemy.

**en·er·get·ic** (en′ẽr-jet′ik), *adj.* having or showing energy; vigorous. —**en′er·get′i·cal·ly,** *adv.*

**en·er·gize** (en′ẽr-jīz′), *v.t.* [-GIZED, -GIZING], to give energy to; activate. *v.i.* to show energy; be active. —**en′er·giz′er,** *n.*

**en·er·gy** (en′ẽr-ji), *n.* [*pl.* -GIES], [< LL. < Gr. *energeia* < *en-*, in + *ergon*, work], 1. force of expression. 2. potential forces; capacity for action. 3. effective power. 4. in *physics*, the capacity for doing work and overcoming resistance.

**en·er·vate** (en′ẽr-vāt′), *v.t.* [-VATED, -VATING], [< L. < *enervis*, weak < *e-*, out + *nervus*, a nerve, sinew], to deprive of nerve, force, etc.; devitalize; debilitate. *adj.* (i-nũr′vit), enervated; weakened. —**en′er·va′tion,** *n.* —**en′er·va′tor,** *n.*

‡**en fa·mille** (än′fȧ′mē′y′), [Fr.], 1. with one's family; at home. 2. in an informal way.

‡**en·fant ter·ri·ble** (än′fän′ te′rē′bl′), [Fr.], 1. an unmanageable, mischievous child. 2. a person who causes trouble by making frank, bold remarks at the wrong times.

**en·fee·ble** (in-fē′b'l), *v.t.* [-BLED, -BLING], to make feeble; weaken. —**en·fee′ble·ment,** *n.* —**en·fee′bler,** *n.*

**en·fi·lade** (en′fə-lād′), *n.* [Fr. < *enfiler*, to thread < *en-* (L. *in*), in + *fil* (L. *filum*), a thread], 1. gunfire directed from either flank along the length of a line of troops. 2. a placement of troops that makes them vulnerable to such fire. *v.t.* [-LADED, -LADING], to direct such gunfire at (a column, etc.).

**en·fold** (in-fōld′), *v.t.* 1. to wrap in folds; wrap up. 2. to embrace. Also sp. **infold.** —**en·fold′er,** *n.* —**en·fold′ment,** *n.*

**en·force** (in-fôrs′, -fōrs′), *v.t.* [-FORCED, -FORCING], 1. to give force to; urge: as, he *enforced* his argument by examples. 2. to force; compel. 3. to impose by force: as, to *enforce* one's will. 4. to compel observance of (a law, etc.). —**en·force′a·ble,** *adj.* —**en·force′ment,** *n.* —**en·forc′er,** *n.*

**en·fran·chise** (en-fran′chīz), *v.t.* [-CHISED, -CHISING], 1. to free from slavery, bondage, etc. 2. to give a franchise to; admit to citizenship, especially to the right to vote. —**en·fran′chise·ment** (-chiz-mənt), *n.* —**en·fran′chis·er** (-chīz-), *n.*

**Eng.,** 1. England. 2. English.

**eng.,** 1. engineer(ing). 2. engraved. 3. engraving.

**en·gage** (in-gāj′), *v.t.* [-GAGED, -GAGING], [< Fr. & OFr. *engager;* see EN- & GAGE], 1. to bind (oneself) by a promise; pledge. 2. to bind by a promise of marriage; betroth. 3. to hire; employ. 4. to arrange for the use of; to reserve: as, he *engaged* a hotel room. 5. to involve, as in conversation. 6. to attract and hold (the attention, etc.). 7. to keep busy; occupy. 8. to enter into conflict with (the enemy). 9. to interlock with; to mesh together, as gears. *v.i.* 1. to pledge oneself; promise; undertake. 2. to involve oneself; be active: as, she *engaged* in dramatics. 3. to enter into conflict. 4. to interlock; mesh. —**en·gag′er,** *n.*

**en·gaged** (in-gājd′), *adj.* 1. pledged. 2. pledged in marriage; betrothed. 3. occupied; employed; busy. 4. involved in combat, as troops. 5. attached to or partly set into (a wall, etc.): as, *engaged* columns. 5. interlocked; meshed; in gear.

**en·gage·ment** (in-gāj′mənt), *n.* 1. an engaging or being engaged; specif., *a*) a betrothal. *b*) an appointment, obligation, or commitment. *c*) employment or period of employment. *d*) a conflict; battle. *e*) *usually pl.* in *business*, financial obligations. *f*) an interlocking; being in gear. 2. something that engages.

**en·gag·ing** (in-gāj′iŋ), *adj.* attractive; winning; charming. —**en·gag′ing·ly,** *adv.* —**en·gag′ing·ness,** *n.*

‡**en garde** (än′gärd′), [Fr.], in *fencing*, on guard: the opening position in which the fencer is prepared either to attack or defend.

**Eng·els, Frie·drich** (frē′driH eŋ′əls), 1820–1895; German socialist theoretician (with Karl Marx).

**en·gen·der** (in-jen′dẽr), *v.t.* [< OFr. < L. < *in-*, in + *generare*, to beget], to bring into being; cause; produce. —**en·gen′der·er,** *n.* —**en·gen′der·ment,** *n.*

**engin.,** 1. engineer. 2. engineering.

**en·gine** (en′jən), *n.* [< OFr. < L. *ingenium*, genius < *in-*, in + base of *gignere*, to produce], 1. any machine that uses energy to develop mechanical power; esp., a machine for starting motion in some other machine. 2. a railroad locomotive. 3. any instrument or machine; apparatus: as, *engines* of torture. 4. [Archaic], any means or device.

**en·gi·neer** (en′jə-nêr′), *n.* 1. one skilled in some branch of engineering: as, an electrical *engineer.* 2. the operator of an engine; esp., the driver of a railroad locomotive. 3. a member of that branch of the army which is concerned with the construction and demolition of bridges, roads, and fortifications, etc. *v.t.* 1. to plan, construct, or manage as an engineer. 2. to manage skillfully; guide artfully; as, to *engineer* a business merger.

**en·gi·neer·ing** (en′jə-nêr′iŋ), *n.* the planning, designing, construction, or management of machinery, roads, bridges, buildings, etc.

**Eng·land** (iŋ′glənd), *n.* a division of Great Britain, bounded by Wales and Scotland: area, 50,874 sq. mi.; pop., 41,148,000; capital, London.

**Eng·lish** (iŋ′glish), *adj.* [AS. *englisc*, lit., of the Angles], 1. of England, its people, their culture, etc. 2. of their language. *n.* 1. the people of England. 2. the language of the English, spoken also in the U.S. and most parts of the British Empire. 3. the English language of a specific period, place, group, etc.: see **Old English, Middle English, Modern English.** 4. [sometimes e-], in *billiards, bowling*, etc., a spinning motion given to a ball, as by striking it on one side. *v.t.* 1. to translate into English. 2. to Anglicize, as a foreign word.

**English Channel,** an arm of the Atlantic, between England and France: width, 20–100 mi.

**English horn,** a double-reed instrument of the wood-wind family, similar to the oboe but larger and a fifth lower in pitch.

ENGLISH HORN

**Eng·lish·man** (iŋ′glish-mən), *n.* [*pl.* -MEN], 1. a native or inhabitant of England. 2. a person of English ancestry, as in Canada, Australia, etc. —**Eng′lish·wom′an** [*pl.* -WOMEN], *n.fem.*

**English sonnet,** see **Shakespearean sonnet.**

**English sparrow,** the common street sparrow, a small, brownish-gray finch of European origin.

**English walnut,** 1. an Asiatic walnut now grown in Europe and North America. 2. its nut.

**en·gorge** (en-gôrj′), *v.t.* [-GORGED, -GORGING], 1. to gorge. 2. in *medicine*, to congest (a blood vessel, tissue, etc.) with blood or other fluid. *v.i.* to eat greedily. —**en·gorge′ment,** *n.*

**engr.,** 1. engineer. 2. engraved. 3. engraver.

**en·graft** (en-graft′, -gräft′), *v.t.* to insert (a shoot from one tree or plant) into another; graft. Also **ingraft.** —**en·graft′er,** *n.*

**en·grave** (in-grāv′), *v.t.* [-GRAVED, -GRAVING], [*en-* + *grave* (to carve)], 1. to cut or etch letters, designs, etc. in or on. 2. to make a deep or permanent impression on. 3. to cut or etch (a picture, letters, etc.) into a metal plate, wooden block, etc. for printing. 4. to print by means of such a plate, block, etc. —**en·grav′er,** *n.*

**en·grav·ing** (in-grāv′iŋ), *n.* 1. the act, process, or art of cutting or etching designs or letters on metal plates, wooden blocks, etc. for printing. 2. an engraved block, plate, design, etc. 3. any printed impression made from an engraved surface.

**en·gross** (in-grōs′), *v.t.* [< Anglo-Fr. *engrosser;* also < OFr. *engrossier*, to become thick < LL. < L. *in*, in + *grossus*, thick], 1. to write in large, distinct letters, as for a legal document. 2. to express formally or in legal form. 3. to take the entire

attention of; occupy wholly. —**en·gross′er,** *n.* —**en·gross′ing,** *adj.* —**en·gross′ment,** *n.*
**en·gulf** (in-gulf′), *v.t.* to swallow up; overwhelm: also sp. **ingulf.** —**en·gulf′ment,** *n.*
**en·hance** (in-hans′, -häns′), *v.t.* [-HANCED, -HANCING], [< Anglo-Fr.; prob. < OFr. *enhaucer;* ult. < L. *in,* in + *altus,* high], to make greater; heighten; intensify. —**en·hance′ment,** *n.* —**en·hanc′er,** *n.*
**e·nig·ma** (i-nig′mə), *n.* [*pl.* -MAS], [< L. < Gr. *ainigma* < *ainissesthai,* to speak in riddles < *ainos,* tale], 1. a perplexing statement; riddle. 2. a perplexing or baffling matter, person, etc. —**e·nig·mat·ic** (en′ig-mat′ik, ē′nig-), **e′nig·mat′i·cal,** *adj.* —**e′nig·mat′i·cal·ly,** *adv.*
**En·i·we·tok** (en′i-wē′tok, e-nē′we-tok′), *n.* an atoll in the NW Marshall Islands: site of U.S. hydrogen bomb tests in 1952 and 1954.
**en·join** (in-join′), *v.t.* [< OFr. < L. < *in-,* in + *jungere,* to join], 1. to command; order: as, to *enjoin* silence. 2. to prohibit, especially by legal injunction; forbid. —**en·join′er,** *n.*
**en·joy** (in-joi′), *v.t.* [< OFr. *enjoier,* to give joy to], 1. to have or experience with joy; get pleasure from; relish. 2. to have the use or benefit of. —**enjoy oneself,** to have a good time. —**en·joy′a·ble,** *adj.* —**en·joy′a·ble·ness,** *n.* —**en·joy′a·bly,** *adv.* —**en·joy′er,** *n.*
**en·joy·ment** (in-joi′mənt), *n.* 1. an enjoying. 2. something enjoyed. 3. pleasure; gratification; joy; happiness.
**en·kin·dle** (en-kin′d'l), *v.t.* [-DLED, -DLING], 1. to make blaze up; arouse (passions, etc.). 2. to light up. —**en·kin′dler,** *n.*
**en·lace** (in-lās′), *v.t.* [-LACED, -LACING], 1. to wind about as with a lace; encircle; enfold. 2. to entangle; interlace. —**en·lace′ment,** *n.*
**en·large** (in-lärj′), *v.t.* & *v.i.* [-LARGED, -LARGING], 1. to make or become larger; increase in size, volume, extent, etc.; expand. 2. in *photography,* to reproduce on a larger scale. —**enlarge on** (or **upon**), to discuss at greater length or in greater detail. —**en·large′ment,** *n.* —**en·larg′er,** *n.*
**en·light·en** (in-līt′'n), *v.t.* 1. to give the light of knowledge to; free from ignorance, prejudice, or superstition. 2. to inform; give clarification to (a person) as to meanings, intentions, etc. —**en·light′en·er,** *n.*
**en·light·en·ment** (in-līt′'n-mənt), *n.* an enlightening or being enlightened. —**the Enlightenment,** an 18th-century European philosophical and social movement characterized by rationalism.
**en·list** (in-list′), *v.t.* 1. to enroll in some branch of the armed forces. 2. to win the support of. 3. to get (the help, support, etc. of someone). *v.i.* 1. to join some branch of the armed forces (often with *in*). 2. to join or support a cause or movement (with *in*). —**en·list′er,** *n.*
**enlisted man,** any man in the armed forces who is not a commissioned or warrant officer.
**en·list·ment** (in-list′mənt), *n.* 1. an enlisting or being enlisted. 2. the period of time for which one enlists.
**en·liv·en** (in-līv′ən), *v.t.* to make active, interesting, or cheerful; liven up or brighten. —**en·liv′en·er,** *n.* —**en·liv′en·ment,** *n.*
**en masse** (en mas′; Fr. än′mås′), [Fr., lit., in mass], in a group; as a whole; all together.
**en·mesh** (en-mesh′), *v.t.* to entangle; catch in or as in the meshes of a net.
**en·mi·ty** (en′mə-ti), *n.* [*pl.* -TIES], [< OFr. *enemistie* < LL. < L.; see ENEMY], the attitude or feelings of an enemy or enemies; hostility.
**en·no·ble** (i-nō′b'l, en-nō′-), *v.t.* [-BLED, -BLING], 1. to raise to the rank of nobleman; make a member of the nobility. 2. to give nobility to; dignify. —**en·no′ble·ment,** *n.* —**en·no′bler,** *n.*
**en·nui** (än′wē; Fr. än′nwē′), *n.* [*pl.* -NUIS (-wēz; Fr. -nwē′)], [Fr.; see ANNOY], weariness and boredom resulting from inactivity or lack of interest.
**e·nor·mi·ty** (i-nôr′mə-ti), *n.* [*pl.* -TIES], [< Fr. < L. < *enormis,* irregular, immense < *e-,* out + *norma,* rule], 1. great wickedness. 2. a monstrous or outrageous act; very wicked crime.
**e·nor·mous** (i-nôr′məs), *adj.* [see ENORMITY], 1. very much exceeding the usual size, number, or degree; huge; vast. 2. [Archaic], outrageous; very wicked. —**e·nor′mous·ly,** *adv.* —**e·nor′mous·ness,** *n.*
**e·nough** (i-nuf′), *adj.* [AS. *genoh*], as much or as many as necessary or desired; sufficient. *n.* the amount or number needed or desired; sufficiency. *adv.* 1. as much or as often as necessary; sufficiently. 2. fully; quite: as, thankful *enough* to escape. 3. just adequately; tolerably: as, he played well *enough.* *interj.* no more!
**e·now** (i-nou′), *adj., n., adv.* [Archaic], enough.
**en·quire** (in-kwīr′), *v.t.* & *v.i.* [-QUIRED, -QUIRING], to inquire. —**en·quir′y** [*pl.* -IES], *n.*
**en·rage** (in-rāj′), *v.t.* [-RAGED, -RAGING], to put into a rage; infuriate. —**en·rage′ment,** *n.*
‡**en rap·port** (än′ rå′pôr′), [Fr.], in harmony; in sympathy; in accord.
**en·rapt** (in-rapt′), *adj.* enraptured; rapt.
**en·rap·ture** (in-rap′chẽr), *v.t.* [-TURED, -TURING], to fill with pleasure or delight; entrance.
**en·rich** (in-rich′), *v.t.* to make rich or richer; as, *a*) to give more wealth to. *b*) to give greater value or importance to: as, music *enriched* her life. *c*) to fertilize (soil). *d*) to decorate; adorn. *e*) to add vitamins, minerals, etc. to (bread, etc.) so as to increase the food value. —**en·riched′,** *adj.* —**en·rich′er,** *n.* —**en·rich′ment,** *n.*
**en·roll, en·rol** (in-rōl′), *v.t.* [-ROLLED, -ROLLING], 1. to record in a roll, or list. 2. to enlist. 3. to accept as a member. *v.i.* 1. to have one's name recorded on a list. 2. to enlist. 3. to become a member. —**en·roll′er,** *n.*
**en·roll·ment, en·rol·ment** (in-rōl′mənt), *n.* 1. an enrolling or being enrolled. 2. a list of those enrolled. 3. the number of those enrolled.
**en route** (än ro͞ot′), [Fr.], on or along the way.
**Ens.,** Ensign.
**en·sconce** (en-skons′), *v.t.* [-SCONCED, -SCONCING], [*en-* + *sconce* (fortification)], 1. to hide; conceal; shelter. 2. to place or settle snugly.
**en·sem·ble** (än-säm′b'l; Fr. än′sän′bl'), *n.* [Fr. < OFr. < LL. < *in-,* in + *simul,* at the same time], 1. all the parts considered as a whole; total effect. 2. a whole costume of matching parts. 3. in *music,* *a*) the performance together of all the instruments or voices of a group. *b*) a small group of musicians performing together. *c*) the instruments or voices constituting such a group.
**en·shrine** (in-shrīn′), *v.t.* [-SHRINED, -SHRINING], 1. to enclose in or as in a shrine. 2. to hold as sacred; cherish. —**en·shrine′ment,** *n.*
**en·shroud** (en-shroud′), *v.t.* to cover as if with a shroud; hide; veil; obscure.
**en·sign** (en′sīn), *n.* [< OFr. < L. < *insignis,* distinguished < *in-* + *signum,* a sign], 1. a badge, symbol, or token of office or authority. 2. a flag or banner. 3. in the *Brit. Army,* formerly, a commissioned officer who served as standard-bearer. 4. (en′s'n), in the *U.S. Navy,* a commissioned officer of the lowest rank, corresponding to a second lieutenant in the Army. —**en′sign·ship′** (-s'n-ship′), **en′sign·cy** (-s'n-si), *n.*
**en·si·lage** (en′s'l-ij), *n.* [Fr.], 1. the preserving of green fodder by storage in a silo. 2. green fodder so preserved; silage. *v.t.* [-LAGED, -LAGING], to ensile.
**en·sile** (en-sīl′, en′sīl), *v.t.* [-SILED, -SILING], to store (fodder) in a silo for preservation.
**en·slave** (in-slāv′), *v.t.* [-SLAVED, -SLAVING], 1. to put into slavery; make a slave of. 2. to dominate; subjugate. —**en·slave′ment,** *n.* —**en·slav′er,** *n.*
**en·snare** (en-snâr′), *v.t.* [-SNARED, -SNARING], to catch in or as in a snare; trap: also **insnare.** —**en·snare′ment,** *n.* —**en·snar′er,** *n.*
**en·sue** (en-so͞o′, -sū′), *v.i.* [-SUED, -SUING], [< OFr. pp. of *ensuivre* < LL. < L. < *in-* + *sequi,* to follow], 1. to come afterward; follow immediately. 2. to happen as a consequence; result.
**en·sure** (in-shoor′), *v.t.* & *v.i.* [-SURED, -SURING], to insure.
**-ent** (ənt), [< Fr. & L.; Fr. *-ent;* L. *-ent-,* stem ending of the ppr. of some verbs], a suffix used to form: 1. adjectives from verbs, as *insistent.* 2. nouns of agency from verbs, as *superintendent.*
**en·tab·la·ture** (en-tab′lə-chẽr), *n.* [MFr. < It. *intavolatura* < *in-,* in + *tavola* (< L. *tabula*), table], in *architecture,* a horizontal superstructure supported by columns and composed of architrave, frieze, and cornice.

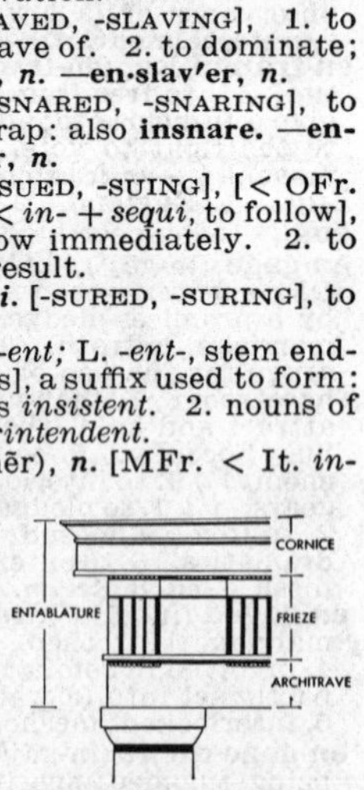

ENTABLATURE

**en·tail** (in-tāl′), *v.t.* [< ME. < *en-,* in + *taile,* an agreement < OFr. < *taillier,* to cut], 1. in *law,* to limit the inheritance of (property) to a specific line of heirs so that it can never be legally transferred. 2. to cause or require as a necessary consequence; necessitate. *n.* 1. an entailing or being entailed. 2. an entailed inheritance. 3. the order of descent for an entailed inheritance. —**en·tail′ment,** *n.*
**en·tan·gle** (in-tan′g'l), *v.t.* [-GLED, -GLING], 1. to involve in a tangle; ensnare. 2. to involve in

difficulty. 3. to confuse; perplex. 4. to cause to be tangled; complicate. —**en·tan′gle·ment,** *n.*

**en·tente** (än-tänt′), *n.* [Fr. < *entendre,* to understand], 1. an understanding or agreement, as between governments. 2. the parties to this.

**en·ter** (en′tẽr), *v.t.* [< OFr. < L. *intrare* < *intra,* within], 1. to come or go into or upon. 2. to force a way into; penetrate. 3. to put into; insert. 4. to write down in a record, list, etc. 5. to join; become a member of (a club, school, etc.). 6. to get (someone) admitted. 7. to begin; start upon. 8. to register (a ship or cargo) at a customhouse. 9. in *law,* to place (a record, evidence, etc.) before a court. *v.i.* 1. to come or go into some place. 2. to pierce; penetrate. —**enter into,** 1. to engage in; take part in. 2. to form a part or component of. 3. to deal with; discuss. —**enter on** (or **upon**), 1. to begin; start. 2. to begin to possess or enjoy. —**en′ter·er,** *n.*

**en·ter·ic** (en-ter′ik), *adj.* [< Gr. < *enteron,* intestine], intestinal.

**en·ter·o-** (en′tə-rō), [< Gr. *enteron,* intestine], a combining form meaning *intestine:* also **enter-.**

**en·ter·prise** (en′tẽr-prīz′), *n.* [< OFr. < *entre-* (< L. *inter*), in + *prendre* (< L. *prendere*), to take], 1. an undertaking; project. 2. a bold, hard, dangerous, or important undertaking. 3. willingness to venture on such undertakings; energy and initiative. 4. the carrying on of projects; participation in undertakings. —**en′ter·pris′er,** *n.*

**en·ter·pris·ing** (en′tẽr-prīz′iŋ), *adj.* showing enterprise; full of energy and initiative; venturesome. —**en′ter·pris′ing·ly,** *adv.*

**en·ter·tain** (en′tẽr-tān′), *v.t.* [< Fr. < OFr. *entre* (< L. *inter*), between + *tenir* (< L. *tenere*), to hold], 1. to amuse; interest; divert. 2. to give hospitality to; have as a guest. 3. to consider, as an idea. 4. to harbor in the mind. *v.i.* to have guests.

**en·ter·tain·er** (en′tẽr-tān′ẽr), *n.* a person who entertains; esp., one whose work is singing, dancing, etc., as at night clubs.

**en·ter·tain·ing** (en′tẽr-tān′iŋ), *adj.* interesting; diverting; amusing. —**en′ter·tain′ing·ly,** *adv.*

**en·ter·tain·ment** (en′tẽr-tān′mənt), *n.* 1. an entertaining or being entertained. 2. something that entertains; interesting, diverting, or amusing thing, as a show or performance.

**en·thrall, en·thral** (in-thrôl′), *v.t.* [-THRALLED, -THRALLING], 1. to make a slave of; enslave. 2. to fascinate; captivate; enchant. —**en·thrall′er,** *n.* —**en·thrall′ing,** *adj.* —**en·thrall′ing·ly,** *adv.* —**en·thrall′ment, en·thral′ment,** *n.*

**en·throne** (in-thrōn′), *v.t.* [-THRONED, -THRONING], 1. to place on a throne; make a king or bishop of. 2. to accord the highest place to; exalt. Also sp. **inthrone.** —**en·throne′ment,** *n.*

**en·thuse** (in-thōōz′, -thūz′), *v.t. & v.i.* [-THUSED, -THUSING], [< *enthusiasm*], [Colloq.], 1. to make or become enthusiastic. 2. to show or cause to show enthusiasm.

**en·thu·si·asm** (in-thōō′zi-az′m, -thū′-), *n.* [< Gr. < *enthous,* possessed by a god, inspired < *en-,* in + *theos,* god], 1. intense or eager interest; zeal; fervor. 2. something arousing this.

**en·thu·si·ast** (in-thōō′zi-ast, -thū′-), *n.* 1. one full of enthusiasm. 2. a religious zealot, etc.

**en·thu·si·as·tic** (in-thōō′zi-as′tik, -thū′-), *adj.* of, having, or showing enthusiasm; ardent. —**en·thu′si·as′ti·cal·ly,** *adv.*

**en·tice** (in-tīs′), *v.t.* [-TICED, -TICING], [< OFr. < LL. < L. *in,* in + *titio,* a burning brand], to attract by offering hope of reward or pleasure; tempt. —**en·tice′ment,** *n.* —**en·tic′er,** *n.* —**en·tic′ing·ly,** *adv.*

**en·tire** (in-tīr′), *adj.* [< OFr. < L. *integer,* untouched, whole], 1. not lacking any of the parts; whole; complete. 2. unbroken; intact. 3. being wholly of one piece. 4. not castrated. 5. in *botany,* having an unbroken margin, as some leaves. *n.* the whole; entirety. —**en·tire′ly,** *adv.* —**en·tire′ness,** *n.*

**en·tire·ty** (in-tīr′ti), *n.* [*pl.* -TIES], 1. the state or fact of being entire; wholeness; completeness. 2. an entire thing; whole. —**in its entirety,** as a whole.

**en·ti·tle** (in-tī′t'l), *v.t.* [-TLED, -TLING], 1. to give a title or name to. 2. to honor or dignify by a title. 3. to give a right, claim, or legal title to. Also sp. **intitle.**

**en·ti·ty** (en′tə-ti), *n.* [*pl.* -TIES], [< Fr. < ML. *entitas* < L. ppr. of *esse,* to be], 1. being; existence. 2. a thing that has real and individual existence in reality or in the mind.

**en·to-,** [< Gr. *entos,* within], a combining form meaning *within* or *inner:* also **ent-.**

**en·tomb** (in-tōōm′), *v.t.* to place in a tomb or grave; bury. Also sp. **intomb.** —**en·tomb′ment,** *n.*

**en·to·mo-,** [< Gr. *entomon,* insect], a combining form meaning *insect, insects,* as in *entomology.*

**en·to·mo·log·i·cal** (en′tə-mə-loj′i-k'l), *adj.* having to do with entomology: also **en′to·mo·log′ic.** —**en′to·mo·log′i·cal·ly,** *adv.*

**en·to·mol·o·gy** (en′tə-mol′ə-ji), *n.* [< Fr.; see ENTOMO- & -LOGY], the branch of zoology that deals with insects. —**en′to·mol′o·gist,** *n.*

**en·tou·rage** (än′too-räzh′), *n.* [Fr. < *entourer,* to surround], 1. environment. 2. a group of associates or attendants; retinue.

**en·tr'acte** (än-trakt′), *n.* [Fr. < *entre-,* between + *acte,* an act], 1. the interval between two acts of a play, opera, etc.; intermission. 2. music, a dance, etc. performed during this interval.

**en·trails** (en′trālz, -trəlz), *n.pl.* [< OFr. < LL. *intralia* < L. < *interaneus,* internal < *inter,* between], 1. the inner organs of men or animals; specif., the intestines; viscera; guts. 2. [Rare], the inner parts of a thing.

**en·train** (in-trān′), *v.t.* to put aboard a train. *v.i.* to go aboard a train. —**en·train′ment,** *n.*

**en·trance** (en′trəns), *n.* 1. the act or point of entering. 2. a place for entering; door, gate, etc. 3. permission or right to enter; admission.

**en·trance** (in-trans′, -träns′), *v.t.* [-TRANCED, -TRANCING], 1. to put into a trance. 2. to delight; charm; enrapture. —**en·trance′ment,** *n.* —**en·tranc′ing,** *adj.* —**en·tranc′ing·ly,** *adv.*

**en·trant** (en′trənt), *n.* a person who enters.

**en·trap** (in-trap′), *v.t.* [-TRAPPED, -TRAPPING], 1. to catch as in a trap. 2. to trick into difficulty; ensnare. —**en·trap′ment,** *n.* —**en·trap′per,** *n.*

**en·treat** (in-trēt′), *v.t. & v.i.* [< OFr. < *en-,* in + *traiter;* see TREAT], to ask earnestly; beg; beseech; implore: also sp. **intreat.** —**en·treat′ing·ly,** *adv.* —**en·treat′ment,** *n.*

**en·treat·y** (in-trēt′i), *n.* [*pl.* -IES], an earnest request; prayer.

**en·tree, en·trée** (än′trā; Fr. än′trā′), *n.* [< Fr. < *entrer;* see ENTER], 1. the right or freedom to enter. 2. the main course of a meal. 3. formerly, and still in some countries, a dish served before the roast or between the main courses.

**en·trench** (in-trench′), *v.t.* 1. to surround or fortify with a trench or trenches. 2. to establish securely. *v.i.* to encroach; infringe; trespass. Also sp. **intrench.** —**en·trench′ment,** *n.*

‡**en·tre nous** (än′tr′ nōō′), [Fr.], between ourselves; confidentially.

**en·tre·pre·neur** (än′trə-prə-nūr′), *n.* [Fr. < *entreprendre;* see ENTERPRISE], a person who organizes and manages a business undertaking, assuming the risk for the sake of the profit.

**en·tro·py** (en′trə-pi), *n.* [< Gr. *entropē,* a turning toward], 1. a measure of the energy unavailable for useful work in a system undergoing change. 2. the tendency of an energy system to run down.

**en·trust** (in-trust′), *v.t.* 1. to trust; charge with a trust or duty. 2. to assign the care of; turn over for safekeeping. Also sp. **intrust.**

**en·try** (en′tri), *n.* [*pl.* -TRIES], [< OFr.; see ENTER], 1. an entering; entrance. 2. a way or passage by which to enter; door, hall, etc. 3. the writing down of an item or note in a list, journal, etc. 4. a thing thus written down. 5. the registration of a ship or cargo at a customhouse. 6. one entered in a race, competition, etc. 7. in *law,* the taking possession of buildings, land, etc. by entering them.

**en·twine** (in-twīn′), *v.t. & v.i.* [-TWINED, -TWINING], to twine or twist together or around.

**e·nu·mer·ate** (i-nōō′mə-rāt′, -nū′-), *v.t.* [-ATED, -ATING], [< L. pp. < *e-,* out + *numerare,* to count < *numerus,* a number], 1. to count; count one by one. 2. to name one by one; specify, as in a list. —**e·nu′mer·a′tion,** *n.* —**e·nu′mer·a′tive,** *adj.* —**e·nu′mer·a′tor** (-tẽr), *n.*

**e·nun·ci·ate** (i-nun′si-āt′, -shi-āt′), *v.t.* [-ATED, -ATING], [< L. pp. < *e-,* out + *nuntiare,* to announce < *nuntius,* a messenger], 1. to state definitely. 2. to announce; proclaim. 3. to pronounce (words). *v.i.* to pronounce words; articulate. —**e·nun′ci·a·ble,** *adj.* —**e·nun′ci·a′tion,** *n.* —**e·nun′ci·a′tive,** *adj.* —**e·nun′ci·a′tor** (-ā′tẽr), *n.*

**en·u·re·sis** (en′yoo-rē′sis), *n.* [< Gr. *enourein,* to urinate], involuntary emission of urine.

**en·vel·op** (in-vel′əp), *v.t.* [< OFr.; see EN- & DEVELOP], 1. to wrap up; cover completely. 2. to surround. 3. to conceal; hide. *n.* an envelope. —**en·vel′op·er,** *n.* —**en·vel′op·ing·ly,** *adv.*

**en·ve·lope** (en′və-lōp′, än′-), *n.* [< Fr.; see ENVELOP], 1. a thing that envelops; wrapper; covering. 2. a folded paper container for letters, etc., usually with a gummed flap. 3. the bag that contains the gas in a dirigible or balloon.

**en·vel·op·ment** (in-vel′əp-mənt), *n.* 1. an enveloping or being enveloped. 2. something that envelops; wrapper; covering.

**en·ven·om** (en-ven′əm), *v.t.* 1. to put venom or poison in. 2. to fill with hate or bitterness.

**en·vi·a·ble** (en′vi-ə-b'l), *adj.* to be envied or desired. —**en′vi·a·ble·ness,** *n.* —**en′vi·a·bly,** *adv.*

**en·vi·ous** (en′vi-əs), *adj.* [< OFr. < L. < *invidia,* envy], feeling, showing, or resulting from envy. —**en′vi·ous·ly,** *adv.* —**en′vi·ous·ness,** *n.*

**en·vi·ron** (in-vī′rən), *v.t.* [< OFr. < *environ,* about; see ENVIRONS], to surround; encircle.

**en·vi·ron·ment** (in-vī′rən-mənt; -ērn-mənt), *n.* [*en-viron* + *-ment*], 1. a surrounding or being surrounded. 2. surroundings. 3. all the conditions, circumstances, and influences surrounding, and affecting the development of, an organism. —**en-vi′ron·men′tal** (-men′t'l), *adj.*

**en·vi·rons** (in-vī′rənz, en′və-), *n.pl.* [< OFr. < *en-,* in + *viron,* a circuit < *virer,* to turn], the districts surrounding a city; suburbs; vicinity.

**en·vis·age** (en-viz′ij), *v.t.* [-AGED, -AGING], [< Fr.; see EN- & VISAGE], 1. to face; confront. 2. to form an image of in the mind; visualize.

**en·vi·sion** (en-vizh′ən), *v.t.* to imagine (something not yet in existence). —**en·vi′sion·er,** *n.*

**en·voy** (en′voi), *n.* [< Fr. < *envoyer,* to send < OFr. < *en-* (< L. *in*), in + *voie* (< L. *via*), way], 1. a messenger; agent. 2. an agent sent by a government or ruler to transact diplomatic business: an envoy ranks just below an ambassador.

**en·voy** (en′voi), *n.* see **l'envoi.**

**en·vy** (en′vi), *n.* [*pl.* -VIES], [< OFr. < L. < *invidus* < *invidere,* to look askance at; *in-,* upon + *videre,* to look], 1. a feeling of discontent and ill will because of another's advantages, possessions, etc. 2. desire for something belonging to another. 3. an object of envious feeling. *v.t.* [-VIED, -VYING], to feel envy toward, at, or because of. —**en′vi·er** (-ēr), *n.* —**en′vy·ing·ly,** *adv.*

**en·wrap** (en-rap′), *v.t.* [-WRAPPED, -WRAPPING], to wrap; envelop: also **inwrap.**

**en·wreathe** (en-rēth′), *v.t.* [-WREATHED, -WREATHING], to encircle with or as with a wreath.

**en·zyme** (en′zīm, -zim), *n.* [< G. < LGr. *enzymos,* leavened < Gr. *en-,* in + *zymē,* leaven], an organic substance that is produced in plant and animal cells and causes changes in other substances by catalytic action: as, pepsin is an *enzyme* that helps in digestion: also **en′zym** (-zim). —**en·zy·mat·ic** (en′zī-mat′ik, -zi-), *adj.*

**e·o-,** [< Gr. *ēōs,* dawn], a prefix meaning *early, early part of a period,* as in *Eocene.*

**E·o·cene** (ē′ə-sēn′), *adj.* [*eo-* + Gr. *kainos,* new], designating or of the earliest epoch of the Tertiary Period in the Cenozoic Era: see **geology,** chart. *n.* the Eocene Epoch or its rocks.

**E·o·li·an** (ē-ō′li-ən), *adj.* Aeolian.

**e·o·lith·ic** (ē′ə-lith′ik), *adj.* [*eo-* + *-lithic*], designating or of that early stage of human culture in which crude stone tools were first used.

**e·on** (ē′ən, ē′on), *n.* [see AEON], an extremely long, indefinite period of time: also sp. **aeon.**

**E·os** (ē′os), *n.* in *Gr. mythology,* the goddess of dawn: identified with the Roman goddess Aurora.

**e·o·sin** (ē′ə-sin), *n.* [< Gr. *ēōs,* dawn; + *-in*], a rose-colored coal-tar dye and acid-base indicator: also **e′o·sine** (-sin, -sēn′). —**e′o·sin′ic,** *adj.*

**-e·ous** (i-əs), [L. *-eus;* + *-ous*], a suffix meaning *having the nature of, like,* used to form adjectives, as *beauteous.*

**ep·au·let, ep·au·lette** (ep′ə-let′), *n.* [< Fr. < OFr. < L. *spatula;* see SPATULA], a shoulder ornament, as on military uniforms.

**e·pee, é·pée** (e-pā′), *n.* [Fr. < OFr. < L. < Gr. *spathē,* blade], a sword, especially a thin, pointed sword without a cutting edge, used in fencing. —**e·pee′ist, é·pée′ist,** *n.*

**Eph.,** Ephesians.

**e·phah, e·pha** (ē′fə), *n.* [Heb. *'ēphāh*], an ancient Hebrew dry measure, equal to about 37 quarts.

**e·phed·rine** (e-fed′rin, ef′ə-drēn′), *n.* [< *Ephedra,* genus name of the plants < L.], an alkaloid, $C_{10}H_{15}NO$, derived from certain plants or made synthetically, used to relieve nasal congestion, as in asthma, hay fever, etc.: also **e·phed′rin** (-rin).

**e·phem·er·al** (ə-fem′ēr-əl), *adj.* [< Gr. < *epi-,* upon + *hēmera,* a day; + *-al*], 1. lasting only one day. 2. short-lived; transitory. *n.* an ephemeral thing. —**e·phem′er·al·ly,** *adv.* —**e·phem′er·al·ness,** *n.*

**e·phem·er·id** (ə-fem′ēr-id), *n.* [see EPHEMERAL], a delicate insect with gauzy wings, which lives for only a few hours or a few days; May fly: also **e·phem′er·a** (-ə), [*pl.* -ERAS, -ERAE (-ēr-ē′)], **e·phem′er·on′** (-on′), [*pl.* -ERA (-ēr-ə), -ERONS].

**Ephes.,** Ephesians.

**E·phe·sians** (i-fē′zhənz), *n.pl.* [construed as sing.], a book of the New Testament: an Epistle of the Apostle Paul to the Christians of Ephesus.

**Eph·e·sus** (ef′ə-səs), *n.* an ancient city in Asia Minor. —**E·phe′sian** (i-fē′zhən), *adj.* & *n.*

**eph·or** (ef′ôr, -ēr), *n.* [*pl.* -ORS, -ORI (-ə-rī′)], [< L. < Gr. < *epi-,* over + *horan,* to see], any of the five chief magistrates annually elected by the people of ancient Sparta.

**E·phra·im** (ē′fri-əm), *n.* in the *Bible,* 1. the younger son of Joseph. 2. the tribe of Israel descended from him. 3. the kingdom of Israel.

**ep·i-,** [< Gr. *epi,* at, on, upon, etc.], a prefix meaning *on, upon, over, on the outside, anterior, beside,* as in *epiglottis, epidemic, epistle:* also **ep-** (before a vowel) and **eph-** (in an aspirated word, as *ephemeral*).

**ep·ic** (ep′ik), *n.* [< L. < Gr. < *epos,* a word, tale, etc.], 1. a long narrative poem with a dignified style and certain formalities of structure, about the deeds of a traditional or historical hero or heroes, as the *Iliad* and *Odyssey.* 2. any long narrative poem regarded as having the style, structure, and importance of an epic. 3. a prose narrative, play, etc. regarded as having the qualities of an epic. 4. a series of events regarded as a proper subject for an epic. *adj.* of, or having the nature of, an epic; heroic; grand; majestic: also **ep′i·cal.** —**ep′i·cal·ly,** *adv.*

**ep·i·ca·lyx** (ep′ə-kā′liks, -kal′iks), *n.* [*pl.* -LYXES, -LYCES (-li-sēz′, -i-sēz′)], a ring of leaflets (called *bracts*) at the base of certain flowers, resembling an extra outer calyx.

**ep·i·can·thus** (ep′ə-kan′thəs), *n.* [< *epi-* + Gr. *kanthos,* corner of the eye], a small fold of skin sometimes covering the inner corner of the eye.

EPICANTHUS

**ep·i·car·di·um** (ep′ə-kär′di-əm), *n.* [*pl.* -DIA (-di-ə)], [< *epi-* + Gr. *kardia,* the heart], the innermost layer of the pericardium. —**ep′i·car′di·al,** *adj.*

**ep·i·carp** (ep′ə-kärp′), *n.* the outer layer of a ripened ovary or fruit, as the rind of an apple.

**ep·i·cene** (ep′ə-sēn′), *adj.* [< L. < Gr. < *epi-,* to + *koinos,* common], of, having characteristics of, or common to both sexes. *n.* an epicene person.

**ep·i·cen·ter** (ep′i-sen′tēr), *n.* 1. the area of the earth's surface directly above the place of origin, or focus, of an earthquake. 2. a focal point. Also sp. **epicentre.** —**ep′i·cen′tral,** *adj.*

**ep·i·cure** (ep′i-kyoor′), *n.* [< L. < Gr.; see EPICURUS], 1. a person who enjoys and has a discriminating taste for foods and liquors. 2. a person who is especially fond of luxury and sensuous pleasure. —**ep′i·cur·ism,** *n.*

**Ep·i·cu·re·an** (ep′i-kyoo-rē′ən), *adj.* 1. of Epicurus or his philosophy. 2. [e-], fond of luxury and sensuous pleasure, especially that of eating and drinking. 3. [e-], suited to or characteristic of an epicure. *n.* 1. a follower of Epicurus or his philosophy. 2. [e-], an epicure. —**Ep′i·cu·re′an·ism, ep′i·cu·re′an·ism,** *n.*

**Ep·i·cu·rus** (ep′i-kyoor′əs), *n.* Greek philosopher; 342?–270 B.C.; he held that the goal of man should be a life of pleasure regulated by morality, temperance, serenity, and cultural development.

**ep·i·cy·clic train** (ep′ə-sī′klik, -sik′lik), [< Fr. < LL. < Gr. < *epi-,* upon + *kyklos,* a circle], a system of cogwheels, etc., in which one wheel axis moves around the circumference of another.

**ep·i·dem·ic** (ep′ə-dem′ik), *adj.* [< Fr. < *épidémie* < LL. < Gr. < *epi-,* among + *dēmos,* people], prevalent and spreading rapidly among many people in a community at the same time, as a contagious disease: also **ep′i·dem′i·cal.** *n.* 1. an epidemic disease. 2. the rapid spreading of such a disease. 3. the rapid, widespread occurrence of a fad, belief, etc. —**ep′i·dem′i·cal·ly,** *adv.*

**ep·i·der·mis** (ep′ə-dũr′mis), *n.* [LL. < Gr. < *epi-,* upon + *derma,* the skin], 1. the outermost layer of the skin in vertebrates. 2. the outermost layer of cells covering seed plants and ferns. 3. the outer layer of the shells of many mollusks. 4. any of various other integuments. —**ep′i·der′mal, ep′i·der′mic,** *adj.*

**ep·i·der·moid** (ep′ə-dũr′moid), *adj.* like epidermis: also **ep′i·der·moi′dal.**

**ep·i·glot·tis** (ep'ə-glot'is), *n.* [< Gr. < *epi-*, upon + *glōtta, glōssa*, the tongue], the thin, triangular lid of cartilage that folds back to cover the opening of the windpipe during swallowing, thus preventing food, etc. from entering the lungs.

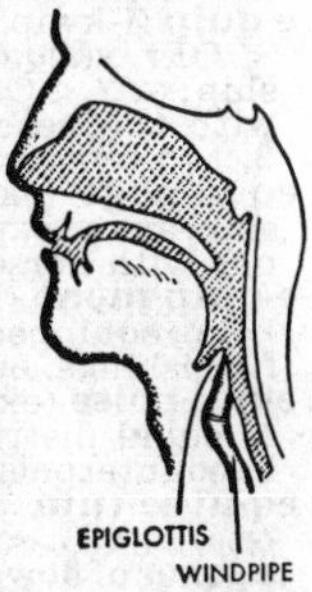

EPIGLOTTIS

**ep·i·gram** (ep'ə-gram'), *n.* [< L. < Gr. < *epi-*, upon + *graphein*, to write], 1. a short poem with a witty or satirical point. 2. any terse, witty, pointed statement, often antithetical. Example: "Crying is the refuge of plain women, but the ruin of pretty ones." 3. the use of epigrams. —**ep·i·gram·mat·ic** (ep'i-grə-mat'ik), **ep'i·gram·mat'i·cal**, *adj.* —**ep'i·gram·mat'i·cal·ly**, *adv.* —**ep'i·gram'ma·tist**, *n.*

**ep·i·gram·ma·tize** (ep'ə-gram'ə-tīz'), *v.t.* [-TIZED, -TIZING], to express (something) epigrammatically. *v.i.* to make epigrams.

**ep·i·graph** (ep'ə-graf', -gräf'), *n.* 1. an inscription on a building, monument, etc. 2. a motto or quotation, as at the beginning of a book.

**ep·i·graph·ic** (ep'ə-graf'ik), *adj.* of an epigraph or epigraphy: also **ep'i·graph'i·cal.**

**e·pig·ra·phy** (e-pig'rə-fi), *n.* 1. inscriptions collectively. 2. the study that deals with deciphering, interpreting, and classifying inscriptions. —**e·pig'ra·phist**, **e·pig'ra·pher**, *n.*

**ep·i·lep·sy** (ep'ə-lep'si), *n.* [< Fr. < L. < Gr. *epilēpsia* < *epi-*, upon + *lambanein*, to seize], a chronic disease of the nervous system, characterized by convulsions and, often, unconsciousness.

**ep·i·lep·tic** (ep'ə-lep'tik), *adj.* 1. of, or having the nature of, epilepsy. 2. having epilepsy. *n.* one who has epilepsy. —**ep'i·lep'ti·cal·ly**, *adv.*

**ep·i·logue, ep·i·log** (ep'ə-lôg', -log'), *n.* [< Fr. < L. < Gr. < *epi-*, upon + *legein*, to speak], 1. a closing section of a novel, play, etc., providing further comment. 2. a short speech or poem spoken to the audience by one of the actors at the end of a play. 3. the actor who speaks this.

**ep·i·neph·rine** (ep'ə-nef'rin, -rēn), *n.* [< *epi-* + Gr. *nephros*, kidney; + *-ine*], 1. the hormone produced by the adrenal glands. 2. a drug made from the adrenal glands of animals, or synthetically: see **adrenalin.** Also **ep'i·neph'rin** (-rin).

**E·piph·a·ny** (i-pif'ə-ni), *n.* [*pl.* -NIES], [< OFr. < LL. < Gr. < *epi-*, upon + *phainein*, to show], in most Christian churches, a festival (January 6) commemorating the revealing of Jesus as the Christ to the Gentiles in the persons of the Magi at Bethlehem: also called *Twelfth Night.*

**ep·i·phyte** (ep'ə-fīt'), *n.* [*epi-* + *-phyte*], a nonparasitic plant that grows on another plant but gets its nourishment from the air, as certain orchids, mosses, and lichens; air plant. —**ep'i·phyt'ic** (-fit'ik), **ep'i·phyt'i·cal**, *adj.* —**ep'i·phyt'i·cal·ly**, *adv.*

**Epis.**, Epistle.

**Epis., Episc.**, 1. Episcopal. 2. Episcopalian.

**e·pis·co·pa·cy** (i-pis'kə-pə-si), *n.* [*pl.* -CIES], [< LL. < *episcopus*, bishop < Gr. < *epi-*, over + *skopein*, to look], 1. church government by bishops. 2. the position, rank, or term of office of a bishop; episcopate. 3. bishops collectively.

**e·pis·co·pal** (i-pis'kə-p'l), *adj.* [< Fr. < LL.; see EPISCOPACY], 1. of or governed by bishops. 2. [E-], designating of or any of various churches governed by bishops, as the Protestant Episcopal or the Anglican Church. —**e·pis'co·pal·ly**, *adv.*

**E·pis·co·pa·li·an** (i-pis'kə-pā'li-ən, -pāl'yən), *adj.* Episcopal. *n.* a member of the Protestant Episcopal Church. —**E·pis'co·pa'li·an·ism**, *n.*

**e·pis·co·pate** (i-pis'kə-pit, -pāt'), *n.* 1. the position, rank, or term of office of a bishop. 2. a bishop's see. 3. bishops collectively.

**ep·i·sode** (ep'ə-sōd'), *n.* [< Gr. < *epeisodios*, coming in besides < *epi-*, besides + *eis-*, into + *hodos*, road], 1. any part of a novel, poem, musical composition, etc. that is complete in itself; incident. 2. any event or series of events complete in itself but forming part of a larger one. 3. any installment of a serialized story or drama.

**ep·i·sod·ic** (ep'ə-sod'ik), *adj.* 1. of the nature of an episode; incidental. 2. divided into episodes. Also **ep'i·sod'i·cal.** —**ep'i·sod'i·cal·ly**, *adv.*

**e·pis·te·mol·o·gy** (i-pis'tə-mol'ə-ji), *n.* [*pl.* -GIES], [< Gr. *epistēmē*, knowledge; + *-logy*], the study or theory of the origin, nature, methods, and limits of knowledge. —**e·pis'te·mo·log'i·cal** (-mə-loj'i-k'l), *adj.* —**e·pis'te·mol'o·gist**, *n.*

**e·pis·tle** (i-pis''l), *n.* [< OFr. < L. < Gr. *epistolē* < *epi-*, to + *stellein*, to send], 1. a letter; esp., a long, formal, instructive letter: now used humorously. 2. [E-], *a*) in the *New Testament*, any of the letters written by an Apostle. *b*) a selection from these Epistles, read as part of Mass, Communion, etc. in various churches.

**e·pis·to·lar·y** (i-pis'tə-ler'i), *adj.* [see EPISTLE], 1. of or suitable to letters or letter writing. 2. contained in or conducted by letters.

**ep·i·taph** (ep'ə-taf, -täf'), *n.* [< OFr. < L. *epitaphium*, eulogy < Gr. < *epi-*, upon + *taphos*, tomb], an inscription, as for a tomb, in memory of a dead person. —**ep'i·taph'ic**, *adj.* —**ep'i·taph'ist**, *n.*

**ep·i·the·li·um** (ep'ə-thē'li-əm), *n.* [*pl.* -LIUMS, -LIA (-li-ə)], [Mod. L. < Gr. *epi-*, upon + *thēlē*, nipple], cellular, membranelike tissue that covers surfaces, forms glands, and lines most cavities of the body. —**ep'i·the'li·al**, *adj.*

**ep·i·thet** (ep'ə-thet'), *n.* [< L. < Gr. < *epitheton* < *epi-*, on + *tithenai*, to put], a word or phrase expressing some quality considered characteristic of a person or thing. Examples: a *black-hearted* villain, Ivan *the Terrible.* —**ep'i·thet'ic, ep'i·thet'i·cal**, *adj.*

**e·pit·o·me** (i-pit'ə-mi), *n.* [*pl.* -MES (-miz)], [L. < Gr. < *epi-*, upon + *temnein*, to cut], 1. a short statement of the main points of a book, report, etc.; abstract; summary. 2. a part or thing that is representative of the characteristics of the whole.

**e·pit·o·mize** (i-pit'ə-mīz'), *v.t.* [-MIZED, -MIZING], to make or be an epitome of. —**e·pit'o·miz'er**, *n.*

**ep·i·zo·ot·ic** (ep'i-zō-ot'ik), *adj.* [< Fr. < Gr. *epi*, upon + *zōion*, animal], designating a disease temporarily prevalent among many animals. *n.* a disease of this kind: also **ep'i·zo'o·ty** (-ə-zō'ə-ti).

‡**e plu·ri·bus u·num** (ē ploor'ə-bəs ū'nəm), [L.], out of many, one: a motto of the U.S.

**ep·och** (ep'ək; *chiefly* Brit., ē'pok), *n.* [< LL. < Gr. *epochē*, a pause < *epi-*, upon + *echein*, to hold], 1. the beginning of a new and important period in the history of anything: as, radio marked an *epoch* in communication. 2. a period of time considered in terms of noteworthy events, developments, persons, etc.: as, an *epoch* of social revolution. 3. in *astronomy*, an arbitrary date for which are given the relative data determining the position of a heavenly body. 4. in *geology*, a subdivision of a geological period: as, the Eocene *Epoch.* —**ep'och·al**, *adj.*

**ep·ode** (ep'ōd), *n.* [< Fr. < L. < Gr. *epōidos*, aftersong < *epi-*, upon + *aeidein*, to sing], 1. a form of lyric poem in which a short line follows a longer one. 2. that part of a lyric ode which follows the strophe and antistrophe.

**ep·o·nym** (ep'ə-nim'), *n.* [< Gr. < *epi-*, upon + *onyma*, a name], 1. a real or mythical person from whose name the name of a nation, race, etc. is derived: as, William *Penn* is the *eponym* of *Penn*sylvania. 2. *a*) one whose name has become closely associated with some period, theory, etc. *b*) the name applied to the period, etc., as *Elizabethan.* —**ep·on·y·mous** (e-pon'ə-məs), *adj.*

**ep·ox·y** (ep-ok si), *adj.* [*ep-* + *oxy*gen], designating a compound in which an oxygen atom is joined to each of two other connected atoms; specifically, designating a resin used in glues, etc.

**ep·si·lon** (ep'sə-lon', -lən), *n.* [Gr.], the fifth letter of the Greek alphabet (**Ε, ε**).

**Ep·som** (ep'səm), *n.* a town in England, south of London: pop., 27,000: site of the race track (**Epsom Downs**) where the Derby is run.

**Epsom salts** (or **salt**), [< *Epsom*, England], a white, crystalline salt, magnesium sulfate, $MgSO_4 \cdot 7H_2O$, used as a cathartic.

**Ep·stein, Sir Jacob** (ep'stīn), 1880–1959; British sculptor, born in the U.S.

**eq.**, 1. equal. 2. equation. 3. equivalent.

**eq·ua·ble** (ek'wə-b'l, ē'kwə-), *adj.* [< L. < *aequare*, to make equal < *aequus*, equal], 1. not varying or fluctuating much; steady; uniform: as, an *equable* temperature. 2. even; serene: as, an *equable* temperament. —**eq'ua·bil'i·ty**, *n.* —**eq'ua·bly**, *adv.*

**e·qual** (ē'kwəl), *adj.* [< L. < *aequus*, plain, even], 1. of the same quantity, size, number, value, degree, etc. 2. having the same rights, ability, rank, etc. (with *to* or *with*). 3. evenly proportioned. 4. [Archaic], fair; just. *n.* any thing or person that is equal: as, men are *equals* under the law. *v.t.* [EQUALED OR EQUALLED, EQUALING OR EQUALLING],

fat, āpe, bâre, cär; ten, ēven, hêre, ovẽr; is, bīte; lot, gō, hôrn, tōōl, look; oil, out; up, ūse, fũr; get; joy; yet; chin; she; thin, *th*en; zh, leisure; ŋ, ring; ə for *a* in *ago*, *e* in *agent*, *i* in *sanity*, *o* in *comply*, *u* in *focus*; ' in *able* (ā'b'l); Fr. bål; ë, Fr. coeur; ö, Fr. feu; Fr. mon; ô, Fr. coq; ü, Fr. duc; H, G. ich; kh, G. doch. ‡ foreign; < derived from.

1. to be equal to; match. 2. to do or make something equal to: as, you can *equal* his record. —**equal to,** having the necessary ability, strength, etc. for.
**e·qual·i·tar·i·an** (i-kwäl′ə-târ′i-ən, -kwôl′-), *adj.* of or holding the belief that all men should have equal political and social rights. *n.* a person who holds this belief.
**e·qual·i·ty** (i-kwäl′ə-ti, i-kwôl′-), *n.* [*pl.* -TIES], state or instance of being equal; esp., the state of being equal in political, economic, and social rights.
**e·qual·ize** (ē′kwəl-īz′), *v.t.* [-IZED, -IZING], 1. to make equal. 2. to make uniform. —**e′qual·i·za′tion,** *n.* —**e′qual·iz′er,** *n.*
**e·qual·ly** (ē′kwəl-i), *adv.* in an equal manner; to an equal degree; uniformly; impartially.
**equal mark** (or **sign**), the arithmetical sign (=), indicating equality: as, 2 + 2 = 4.
**e·qua·nim·i·ty** (ē′kwə-nim′ə-ti, ek′wə-), *n.* [< L. < *aequus*, even + *animus*, the mind], calmness of mind; evenness of temper; composure.
**e·quate** (i-kwāt′), *v.t.* [EQUATED, EQUATING], [< L. pp. of *aequare*, to make equal < *aequus*, equal], 1. in *mathematics*, to state the equality of; put in the form of an equation. 2. to treat, regard, or express as equal or equivalent.
**e·qua·tion** (i-kwā′zhən, -shən), *n.* 1. an equating or being equated. 2. an expression of equality between two quantities as shown by the equal mark (=): as, x + 4x = 5x. 3. an expression in which symbols and formulas are used to represent a chemical reaction: as, $H_2SO_4 + 2NaCl = 2HCl + Na_2SO_4$.
**e·qua·tor** (i-kwā′tēr), *n.* [LL. *aequator* < L. *aequare*; see EQUABLE], 1. an imaginary circle around the earth, equally distant from both the North Pole and the South Pole: it divides the earth into the Northern Hemisphere and the Southern Hemisphere. 2. any circle that divides a sphere, etc. into two equal parts. 3. the imaginary circle formed by the intersection of the plane of the earth's equator with the celestial sphere: in full, **celestial equator.**
**e·qua·to·ri·al** (ē′kwə-tôr′i-əl, ek′wə-tō′ri-əl), *adj.* 1. of or near the earth's equator. 2. of an equator. 3. like or characteristic of conditions near the earth's equator. —**e′qua·to′ri·al·ly,** *adv.*
**Equatorial Guinea,** a country in central Africa, including a mainland section and two islands in the Atlantic: area, 10,832 sq. mi.; pop., 286,000.
**eq·uer·ry** (ek′wēr-i; *occas.* i-kwer′i), *n.* [*pl.* -RIES], [Fr. *écurie*, a stable < OFr.; associated in Eng. with L. *equus*, horse], 1. formerly, an officer in charge of the horses of a royal or noble household. 2. a personal attendant on some member of the king's family, as in England.
**e·ques·tri·an** (i-kwes′tri-ən), *adj.* [< L. *equester* < *eques*, horseman < *equus*, a horse], 1. of horses, horsemen, or horsemanship. 2. on horseback: as, an *equestrian* statue. *n.* a rider or circus performer on horseback. —**e·ques′tri·enne′** (-en′), *n.fem.*
**e·qui-,** [< L. *aequus*, equal], a combining form meaning *equal, equally*, as in *equidistant.*
**e·qui·an·gu·lar** (ē′kwi-aŋ′gyoo-lēr), *adj.* having all angles equal.
**e·qui·dis·tant** (ē′kwə-dis′tənt), *adj.* equally distant. —**e′qui·dis′tance,** *n.* —**e′qui·dis′tant·ly,** *adv.*
**e·qui·lat·er·al** (ē′kwə-lat′ēr-əl), *adj.* [< LL. < L. *aequus*, equal + *latus*, side], having all sides equal: as, an *equilateral* triangle. *n.* 1. a figure having equal sides. 2. a side exactly equal to another.
**e·quil·i·brant** (ē-kwil′ə-brənt), *n.* [< Fr. < L.; see EQUILIBRIUM], in *physics*, a force or combination of forces that can balance another.
**e·qui·li·brate** (ē′kwə-lī′brāt, i-kwil′ə-brāt′), *v.t.* & *v.i.* [-BRATED, -BRATING], to bring into or be in equilibrium; balance or counterbalance. —**e′qui·li·bra′tion,** *n.* —**e′qui·li′bra·tor** (-brā-tēr), *n.*
**e·qui·lib·ri·um** (ē′kwə-lib′ri-əm), *n.* [*pl.* -RIUMS, -RIA (-ri-ə)], [< L. < *aequus*, equal + *libra*, a balance], 1. a state of balance or equality between opposing forces. 2. a state of balance or adjustment of conflicting desires, interests, etc.
**e·quine** (ē′kwīn), *adj.* [< L. < *equus*, horse], of, like, or characteristic of a horse. *n.* a horse.
**e·qui·noc·tial** (ē′kwə-nok′shəl), *adj.* 1. relating to either of the equinoxes. 2. occurring at about the time of the equinox: as, an *equinoctial* storm. 3. equatorial. *n.* the celestial equator (see **equator**): also **equinoctial circle** (or **line**).
**e·qui·nox** (ē′kwə-noks′), *n.* [< Fr. < LL. < L. < *aequus*, equal + *nox*, night], 1. the time when the sun crosses the equator, making night and day of equal length in all parts of the earth: cf. **vernal equinox, autumnal equinox.** 2. either of the two points on the celestial equator where the sun crosses it on these dates: also **equinoctial point.**
**e·quip** (i-kwip′), *v.t.* [EQUIPPED, EQUIPPING], [< Fr. < OFr. *e(s)quiper*, embark; prob < AS. < *scip*, a ship; or ? < ON. *skipa*, make ready], 1. to furnish with the necessities for an undertaking; fit out. 2. to prepare intellectually; train. —**e·quip′per,** *n.*
**eq·ui·page** (ek′wə-pij), *n.* 1. the equipment of a ship, army, expedition, etc. 2. a carriage, especially one with horses and liveried servants.
**e·quip·ment** (i-kwip′mənt), *n.* 1. an equipping or being equipped. 2. whatever one is equipped with; furnishings, outfit, resources, etc.
**e·qui·poise** (ek′wə-poiz′, ē′kwə-), *n.* [*equi-* + *poise*], 1. equal distribution of weight; state of balance. 2. counterpoise; counterbalance.
**eq·ui·se·tum** (ek′wə-sē′təm), *n.* [*pl.* -TUMS, -TA (-tə)], [< L. < *equus*, horse + *saeta*, bristle], any of a genus of flowerless plants with hard, jointed stems, useful in preventing erosion; horsetail.
**eq·ui·ta·ble** (ek′wi-tə-b′l), *adj.* 1. characterized by equity; fair; just. 2. in *law*, *a*) having to do with equity, as distinguished from common or statute law. *b*) valid in equity. —**eq′ui·ta·ble·ness,** *n.* —**eq′ui·ta·bly,** *adv.*
**eq·ui·ty** (ek′wə-ti), *n.* [*pl.* -TIES], [< OFr. < L. *aequitas*, equality < *aequus*, equal], 1. fairness; impartiality; justice. 2. anything that is fair or equitable. 3. the value of property beyond the total amount owed on it. 4. in *law*, a system of rules and doctrines, as in the U.S., supplementing common and statute law and superseding such law when it proves inadequate for just settlement.
**equiv.,** equivalent.
**e·quiv·a·lence** (i-kwiv′ə-ləns), *n.* the condition of being equivalent; equality of quantity, value, meaning, etc.: also **e·quiv′a·len·cy** [*pl.* -CIES].
**e·quiv·a·lent** (i-kwiv′ə-lənt), *adj.* [Fr. < LL. < L. *aequus*, equal + *valere*, to be strong], 1. equal in quantity, value, force, meaning, etc. 2. in *chemistry*, having the same valence. 3. in *geometry*, equal in area or volume but not of the same shape. *n.* 1. an equivalent thing. 2. in *chemistry*, the quantity by weight (of a substance) that combines with one gram of hydrogen or eight grams of oxygen. —**e·quiv′a·lent·ly,** *adv.*
**e·quiv·o·cal** (i-kwiv′ə-k′l), *adj.* [< LL.; see EQUIVOCATE], 1. having two or more meanings; purposely vague or ambiguous: as, an *equivocal* reply. 2. uncertain; doubtful: as, an *equivocal* outcome. 3. suspicious; questionable: as, *equivocal* conduct. —**e·quiv′o·cal·ly,** *adv.* —**e·quiv′o·cal·ness,** *n.*
**e·quiv·o·cate** (i-kwiv′ə-kāt′), *v.i.* [-CATED, -CATING], [< LL. < *aequivocus*, of like sound < L. *aequus*, equal + *vox*, voice], to use equivocal terms in order to deceive or mislead; hedge. —**e·quiv′o·ca′tion,** *n.* —**e·quiv′o·ca′tor** (-kā′tēr), *n.*
**er** (*approx.* ə, u; ēr, ũr *is a sp. pronun.*), *interj.* a conventionalized expression of the sound often made by a speaker when hesitating briefly.
**Er,** in *chemistry*, erbium.
**-er** (ēr), a suffix of various origins: 1. [AS. *-ere*], *a*) meaning *a person having to do with*, as in *hatter*: also **-ier** or **-yer**, as in *hosier, lawyer. b*) meaning *a person living in*, as in *New Yorker. c*) in colloquial usage, meaning *a thing or action connected with*, as in *diner. d*) meaning *a person or thing that*, as in *sprayer, roller.* 2. [AS. *-ra*], added to many adjectives and adverbs to form the comparative degree, as in *greater.* 3. [Anglo-Fr. inf. suffix], in legal language, meaning *the action of —ing*, as in *demurrer, waiver.* 4. [AS. *-rian*, freq. suffix], meaning *repeatedly*, as in *flicker.*
**e·ra** (êr′ə), *n.* [LL. *aera*, era; earlier sense, "counters," < pl. of L. *aes*, brass], 1. a system of reckoning time by numbering the years from some given date: as, the Christian *Era.* 2. an event or date that marks the beginning of a new period in the history of something. 3. a period of time measured from some important occurrence or date. 4. a period of time considered in terms of noteworthy and characteristic events, men, etc.: as, an *era* of progress. 5. any of the five main divisions of geological time: as, the Paleozoic *Era*: see also **epoch, period, age.**
**e·ra·di·ate** (ē-rā′di-āt′), *v.i.* & *v.t.* [-ATED, -ATING], to radiate.
**e·rad·i·ca·ble** (i-rad′i-kə-b′l), *adj.* that can be eradicated.
**e·rad·i·cate** (i-rad′i-kāt′), *v.t.* [-CATED, -CATING], [< L. pp. of *eradicare*, to root out < *e-*, out + *radix*, a root], 1. to tear out by the roots; uproot. 2. to wipe out; destroy. —**e·rad′i·ca′tion,** *n.* —**e·rad′i·ca′tive,** *adj.* —**e·rad′i·ca′tor** (-kā′tēr), *n.*
**e·rase** (i-rās′), *v.t.* [ERASED, ERASING], [< L. *erasus*, pp. < *e-*, out + *radere*, to scrape], 1. to rub, scrape,

or wipe out, as writing; efface. 2. to remove all marks of; obliterate, as from the mind. 3. [Slang], to kill. —**e·ras′a·ble,** *adj.*

**e·ras·er** (i-rās′ẽr), *n.* a thing that erases; specif., a device made of rubber, for erasing marks made with ink or pencil, or a pad of felt or cloth, for removing chalk marks from a blackboard.

**E·ras·mus, Des·i·der·i·us** (des′i-dêr′i-əs i-raz′məs), (born *Gerhard Gerhards*), 1466?–1536; Dutch humanist and writer. —**E·ras′mi·an** (-mi-ən), *adj.* & *n.*

**e·ra·sure** (i-rā′shẽr, -zhẽr), *n.* 1. an erasing. 2. an erased word, mark, etc. 3. the place where some word, mark, etc. has been erased.

**Er·a·to** (er′ə-tō′), *n.* in *Gr. mythology*, the Muse of lyric poetry and love poetry.

**er·bi·um** (ũr′bi-əm), *n.* [Mod. L. < Ytt*erby*, Sweden], a metallic chemical element of the rare-earth group: symbol, Er; at. wt., 167.2; at. no., 68.

**ere** (âr), *prep.* [AS. *ær*], [Archaic or Poetic], before (in time). *conj.* [Archaic or Poetic], 1. before. 2. sooner than; rather than.

**Er·e·bus** (er′ə-bəs), *n.* in *Gr. mythology*, the dark place under the earth through which the dead passed before entering Hades.

**e·rect** (i-rekt′), *adj.* [L. *erectus*, pp. < *e-*, up + *regere*, to make straight], 1. upright; vertical. 2. bristling; stiff: said of hair, etc. *v.t.* 1. to raise or construct (a building, etc.). 2. to set up; cause to arise, as social barriers. 3. to set in an upright position; raise. 4. to assemble; put together. 5. [Archaic], to establish; found. 6. in *geometry*, to construct or draw (a perpendicular, figure, etc.) upon a base line. —**e·rect′er, e·rec′tor,** *n.* —**e·rec′tion,** *n.* —**e·rect′ly,** *adv.* —**e·rect′ness,** *n.*

**e·rec·tile** (i-rek′t'l, -til), *adj.* that can become erect: used especially of tissue that becomes swollen and hard when filled with blood. —**e·rec·til·i·ty** (i-rek′til′ə-ti, ē′rek-), *n.*

**ere·long** (âr′lôŋ′), *adv.* [Archaic or Poetic], before long; soon: also **ere long.**

**er·e·mite** (er′ə-mīt′), *n.* [< OFr. or LL.; see HERMIT], a hermit; religious recluse. —**er′e·mit′ic** (-mit′ik), **er′e·mit′i·cal,** *adj.*

**erg** (ũrg), *n.* [< Gr. *ergon*, work], in *physics*, the unit of work or energy in the C.G.S. (metric) system, being the work done by one dyne acting through a distance of one centimeter: abbrev. **e.**

‡**er·go** (ũr′gō), *conj.* & *adv.* [L.], therefore.

**er·gos·ter·ol** (ẽr-gos′tə-rōl′), *n.* [< *ergot* + *sterol*], an alcohol, $C_{28}H_{44}O$, formerly prepared from ergot but now chiefly from yeast: when exposed to ultraviolet rays it produces a vitamin ($D_1$) used to prevent or cure rickets.

**er·got** (ũr′gət), *n.* [Fr. < OFr. *argot*, a rooster's spur: from the shape of the growth], 1. a fungous growth on the grains of rye and other cereal plants. 2. the disease in which this occurs or the fungus causing it. 3. the dried fungus, used as a drug to stop bleeding and to contract muscles, as of the uterus during labor.

**er·i·ca·ceous** (er′ə-kā′shəs), *adj.* [< Mod. L. *Erica*, genus name (< L. *erice*, heath < Gr. *ereikē*)], of the heath family of plants and shrubs, including the rhododendrons, laurels, azaleas, etc.

**Er·ic·son, Leif** (lēf, lāv er′ik-s'n), fl. 1000 A.D.; son of Eric the Red· Norwegian discoverer of America.

**Er·ic the Red** (er′ik), fl. 10th century A.D.; Norwegian navigator; discovered Greenland.

**Er·ie** (êr′i), *n.* 1. [*pl.* ERIE, ERIES], a member of a tribe of Iroquoian Indians who lived in an area east and southeast of Lake Erie. 2. one of the Great Lakes, between Lake Huron and Lake Ontario: area, 9,940 sq. mi.; length, 240 mi.: usually **Lake Erie.** 3. a port on Lake Erie, in NW Pennsylvania: pop., 138,000.

**Erie Canal,** a former barge canal from Buffalo on Lake Erie to Albany on the Hudson, opened in 1825: see **New York State Barge Canal.**

**Er·in** (âr′in, êr′-), *n.* [Poetic], Ireland.

**E·rin·y·es** (i-rin′i-ēz′), *n.pl.* [*sing.* ERINYS (i-rin′is, i-rī′nis)], in *Gr. mythology*, the Furies.

**E·ris** (êr′is, er′-), *n.* in *Gr. mythology*, the goddess of strife and discord.

**Er·i·tre·a** (er′i-trē′ə), *n.* an autonomous unit of Ethiopia, in E Africa, on the Red Sea: former Italian colony: area, 48,000 sq. mi.; pop., 1,100,000. —**Er′i·tre′an,** *adj.* & *n.*

**Er·i·van** (er′i-vän′y′), *n.* the capital of the Armenian S.S.R.: pop., 509,000.

**erl·king** (ũrl′kiŋ′), *n.* [< G. *erlkönig* < Dan. *ellerkonge*, king of the elves], in *German & Scandinavian folklore*, a spirit who does mischief and evil, especially to children: probably a personification of the destructive forces of nature.

**er·mine** (ũr′min), *n.* [*pl.* -MINES, -MINE; see PLURAL, II, D, 1], [OFr.; prob. < MHG. < OHG. *harmo*, weasel], 1. a weasel of northern regions whose fur is brown in summer but white with a black-tipped tail in winter: also called *stoat.* 2. the soft, white fur of this animal. 3. the position, rank, or functions of a judge, whose state robe, in European countries, is trimmed with ermine as an emblem of honor and purity. —**er′mined,** *adj.*

ERMINE (15 in. long)

**erne, ern** (ũrn), *n.* [AS. *earn*], a kind of eagle that lives near the sea.

**e·rode** (i-rōd′), *v.t.* [ERODED, ERODING], [< Fr. < L. < *e-*, out, off + *rodere*, to gnaw], 1. to eat into; wear away; disintegrate: as, acid *erodes* metal. 2. to form by wearing away gradually: as, the stream *eroded* a gully. *v.i.* to become eroded. —**e·ro′dent** (i-rō′d'nt), *adj.*

**E·ros** (êr′os, er′-), *n.* in *Gr. mythology*, the god of love, son of Aphrodite: identified by the Romans with Cupid.

**e·rose** (i-rōs′), *adj.* [< L. pp.; see ERODE], 1. irregular, as if gnawed away. 2. in *botany*, having an irregularly notched edge, as some leaves.

**e·ro·sion** (i-rō′zhən), *n.* an eroding or being eroded: as, soil *erosion.* —**e·ro′sive,** *adj.*

**e·rot·ic** (i-rot′ik), *adj.* [< Gr. *erōtikos* < *erōs*, love], of or causing sexual feelings or desires; having to do with sexual love; amatory: also **e·rot′i·cal.** —**e·rot′i·cal·ly,** *adv.*

**e·rot·i·cism** (i-rot′ə-siz'm), *n.* 1. erotic quality or character. 2. sexual instincts and behavior. 3. preoccupation with sex.

**er·o·tism** (er′ə-tiz'm), *n.* eroticism (especially in sense 2).

**ERP, E.R.P.,** European Recovery Program.

**err** (ũr), *v.i.* [< OFr. < L. *errare*, to wander], 1. to be wrong or mistaken; fall into error. 2. to deviate from the established moral code; do wrong. —**err′ing,** *adj.* —**err′ing·ly,** *adv.*

**er·rand** (er′ənd), *n.* [AS. *ærende*], 1. a short trip to do a thing, often for someone else. 2. the thing to be done on such a trip; purpose or object for which one is sent.

**er·rant** (er′ənt), *adj.* [OFr. ppr. of *errer* < LL. < L. *iter*, a journey; cf. ERR], 1. roving in search of adventure; wandering: as, a knight-*errant.* 2. [OFr., ppr. of *errer* (see ERR)], erring; wrong; incorrect. —**er′rant·ly,** *adv.*

**er·rant·ry** (er′ənt-ri), *n.* the condition or behavior of a knight-errant; deeds of chivalry.

**er·rat·ic** (ə-rat′ik), *adj.* [< OFr. < L. pp. of *errare*, to wander], 1. having no fixed course; irregular; wandering. 2. eccentric; queer. *n.* an erratic person. —**er·rat′i·cal·ly,** *adv.*

**er·ra·tum** (i-rā′təm, e-rä′-), *n.* [*pl.* -TA (-tə)], [L., neut. pp. of *errare*, to wander], an error in printing or writing.

**er·ro·ne·ous** (ə-rō′ni-əs, e-), *adj.* containing or based on error; mistaken; wrong. —**er·ro′ne·ous·ly,** *adv.* —**er·ro′ne·ous·ness,** *n.*

**er·ror** (er′ẽr), *n.* [< OFr. < L. *errare*, to wander], 1. the state of believing what is untrue or incorrect. 2. a wrong belief; incorrect opinion. 3. something incorrect or wrong; inaccuracy; mistake. 4. transgression; wrongdoing. 5. in *baseball*, a misplay (by a fielder) of a chance that should have resulted in an out for the team at bat, or that permits a runner to advance.

**er·satz** (er-zäts′), *n.* & *adj.* [G.], substitute: the word usually suggests inferior quality.

**Erse** (ũrs), *adj.* & *n.* [Scot. var. of *Irish*], 1. formerly, Scottish Gaelic. 2. Irish Gaelic.

**erst** (ũrst), *adv.* [AS. *ærest*, superl. of *ær*, ere], [Archaic], formerly; long ago. *adj.* [Obs.], first.

**erst·while** (ũrst′hwīl′), *adv.* [Archaic], formerly; some time ago. *adj.* former.

**e·ruct** (i-rukt′), *v.t.* & *v.i.* [< L. *eructare* < *e-*, out + *ructare*, to belch], to belch.

**e·ruc·tate** (i-ruk′tāt), *v.t.* & *v.i.* [-TATED, -TATING], [see ERUCT], to belch. —**e·ruc·ta·tion** (i-ruk′tā′shən, ē′ruk-), *n.* —**e·ruc′ta·tive** (-tə-tiv), *adj.*

**er·u·dite** (er′yoo-dit′, er′oo-), *adj.* [< L. pp. of

*erudire*, to instruct < *e-*, out + *rudis*, rude], learned; scholarly. **—er′u·dite·ly,** *adv.* **—er′u·dite·ness,** *n.*

**er·u·di·tion** (er′yoo-dish′ən, er′oo-), *n.* learning acquired by reading and study; scholarship.

**e·rupt** (i-rupt′), *v.i.* [< L. *eruptus*, pp. < *e-*, out + *rumpere*, to break], 1. to burst forth or out, as lava from a volcano. 2. to throw forth lava, water, steam, etc.: as, geysers *erupt*. 3. to break out in a rash. *v.t.* to cause to burst forth; throw forth.

**e·rup·tion** (i-rup′shən), *n.* 1. a bursting forth or out. 2. a throwing forth of lava, water, steam, etc. 3. in *medicine*, *a*) a breaking out in a rash. *b*) a rash. **—e·rup′tive,** *adj.*

**-er·y** (ẽr-i), [< OFr. *-erie* < LL. *-aria*, or < OFr. *-ier* + *-ie* (L. *-ia*)], a suffix meaning: 1. *a place to*, as in *tannery*. 2. *a place for*, as in *nunnery*. 3. *the practice, act,* or *occupation of*, as in *surgery*. 4. *the product* or *goods of*, as in *pottery*. 5. *a collection of*, as in *jewelry*. 6. *the state* or *condition of*, as in *drudgery*. Also **-ry.**

**er·y·sip·e·las** (er′ə-sip′′l-əs, êr′ə-), *n.* [L. < Gr. < *erythros*, red + *pella*, skin], an acute infectious disease of the skin or mucous membranes caused by several kinds of streptococcus and characterized by local inflammation and fever.

**e·ryth·ro-,** [< Gr. *erythros*, red], a combining form meaning: 1. *red*, as in *erythrocyte*. 2. *erythrocyte*.

**e·ryth·ro·cyte** (i-rith′rō-sit′, e-), *n.* [*erythro-* + *-cyte*], a red blood corpuscle: it is a very small, circular disk and contains hemoglobin, which carries oxygen to the body tissues.

**-es** (iz, əz), [variously < AS. *-as*, *-s*, *-es*], a suffix used: 1. to form the plural of some nouns, as *fishes*: also **-s, -'s.** 2. to form the third person singular, present indicative, of verbs, as in (he) *kisses*: also **-s.** 3. formerly, to form the possessive case of nouns, as in *Wednesday* (*Woden's day*): now **'s.**

**E·sau** (ē′sô), *n.* in the *Bible*, the son of Isaac and Rebekah, who sold his birthright to his younger twin brother, Jacob: Gen. 25:21-34, 27.

**es·ca·drille** (es′kə-dril′; Fr. es′kȧ′drē′y′), *n.* [Fr., dim. of *escadre*, fleet], 1. a squadron of airplanes, usually six, as in the French armed forces. 2. a squadron of warships, usually eight.

**es·ca·lade** (es′kə-lād′), *n.* [Fr. < Sp. < L. *scala*, ladder], the act of climbing the walls of a fortified place by ladders. *v.t.* [-LADED, -LADING], to climb (a wall, etc.) or enter (a fortified place) by ladders.

**es·ca·late** (es′kə-lāt′), *v.i.* [-LATED, -LATING], [< *escalator*], 1. to rise as on an escalator. 2. to expand, as from a local conflict into a general nuclear war. **—es′ca·la′tion,** *n.*

**es·ca·la·tor** (es′kə-lā′tẽr), *n.* [see ESCALADE], a moving stairway consisting of treads linked in an endless belt: a former trade-mark.

ESCALATOR

**es·cal·op, es·cal·lop** (e-skol′əp, -skal′-), *n.* [< OFr.; see SCALLOP], scallop. *v.t.* to bake with crumbs or in a cream sauce.

**es·ca·pade** (es′kə-pād′, es′kə-pād′), *n.* [Fr.], 1. an escaping or breaking loose from restraint. 2. a reckless adventure or prank.

**es·cape** (ə-skāp′, e-), *v.i.* [-CAPED, -CAPING], [< OFr. < LL. < L. *ex-*, out of + *cappa*, cloak], 1. to get free; get away. 2. to avoid an illness, accident, pain, etc. 3. to flow, drain, or leak away: as, gas *escaping* from the stove. 4. to slip away; disappear. *v.t.* 1. to get away from; flee. 2. to avoid; manage to keep away from: as, he *escaped* punishment. 3. to come from involuntarily: as, a scream *escaped* his lips. 4. to slip away from; be missed or forgotten by: as, the date *escapes* me. *n.* 1. an escaping or state of having escaped. 2. a means of escape. 3. an outward flow or leakage. 4. a temporary mental release from reality. *adj.* 1. giving temporary mental release from reality. 2. giving a basis for evading a claim, responsibility, etc. **—es·cap′a·ble,** *adj.* **—es·cap′er,** *n.*

**es·cape·ment** (ə-skāp′mənt, e-), *n.* 1. [Rare], a means of escape. 2. the part in a clock or watch that controls the speed and regularity of the balance wheel or pendulum by the movement of a notched wheel (**escape wheel**), one tooth of which is permitted to escape from the detaining catch at a time. 3. the mechanism in typewriters that regulates the horizontal movement of the carriage.

ESCAPEMENT

**es·cap·ism** (ə-skāp′iz'm, e-), *n.* a tendency to escape from reality, the responsibilities of real life, etc., especially by unrealistic imaginative activity. **—es·cap′ist,** *adj. & n.*

**es·ca·role** (es′kə-rōl′), *n.* [Fr. < ML. < L. < *esca*, food], a kind of endive used in salads.

**es·carp·ment** (e-skärp′mənt), *n.* [< Fr.; see SCARP], 1. a steep slope or cliff. 2. ground formed into a steep slope as part of a fortification.

**-esce** (es), [< L. *-escere*], a suffix used to form verbs that designate an action just begun or still incomplete, as *acquiesce*.

**-es·cence** (es′'ns), a noun suffix corresponding to the adjective suffix *-escent*, as in *obsolescence*.

**-es·cent** (es′'nt), [< L. *-escens*, *-escentis*, ppr. ending], an adjective suffix meaning *starting to be, being,* or *becoming*, as in *obsolescent*.

**es·cheat** (es-chēt′), *n.* [< OFr. < pp. of *escheoir*, to fall to one's share < LL. < L. *es-*, out + *cadere*, to fall], in *law*, 1. the reverting of property to the lord of the manor or to the government when there are no legal heirs. 2. property so reverting. *v.t. & v.i.* to transfer or revert by escheat. **—es·cheat′a·ble,** *adj.*

**es·chew** (es-choo͞′, -chū′), *v.t.* [< Anglo-Fr. < OFr. < OHG. *sciuhan*, to fear], to keep away from (something harmful or bad); shun. **—es·chew′al,** *n.*

**es·cort** (es′kôrt), *n.* [< Fr. < It. < *scortare* < *scorgere*, to lead < LL. < L. *ex-*, out + *corrigere*, to correct], 1. one or more persons (or ships, airplanes, etc.) accompanying another or others to protect or show honor. 2. a man or boy accompanying a woman or girl in public. 3. accompaniment as an escort. *v.t.* (i-skôrt′), to go with as an escort.

**es·cri·toire** (es′kri-twär′, -twôr′), *n.* [< OFr. < LL. < pp. of L. *scribere*, to write], a writing desk or table: sometimes called *secretary*.

**es·crow** (es′krō, e-skrō′), *n.* [< OFr.; see SCROLL], in *law*, a written agreement, as a bond or deed, put in the care of a third party and not in effect until certain conditions are fulfilled. **—in escrow,** in *law*, put in the care of a third party until certain conditions are fulfilled.

**es·cu·do** (es-koo͞′dō), *n.* [*pl.* -DOS], [Sp. < L. *scutum*, a shield], 1. any of several obsolete coins of Spain, Portugal, and their former colonies. 2. the gold monetary unit of Portugal.

**es·cu·lent** (es′kyoo-lənt), *adj.* [< L. < *esca*, food], fit for food; edible. *n.* something fit for food, especially a vegetable.

**es·cutch·eon** (i-skuch′ən), *n.* [< ONorm.Fr. < LL. < L. *scutum*, shield], a shield or shield-shaped surface on which a coat of arms is displayed. **—a blot on one's escutcheon,** a stain on one's honor.

**Es·dras** (ez′drəs), *n.* 1. either of two books about Ezra in the Protestant Apocrypha. 2. in the *Douay Bible*, either of two books of the Old Testament (Ezra and Nehemiah). Abbrev. **Esd.**

**-ese** (ēz; *occas.* ēs), [< OFr. < L. *-ensis*], a suffix meaning: *a*) (*a native* or *inhabitant*) *of*, as in *Portuguese*. *b*) (*in*) *the language* or *dialect of*, as in *Chinese*. *c*) (*in*) *the style of*, as in *journalese*.

**ESE, E.S.E., e.s.e.,** east-southeast.

**Es·ki·mo** (es′kə-mō′), *n.* [? < Algonquian *eskimantik*, eater of raw flesh], 1. [*pl.* -MOS, -MO], a member of a race living in Greenland, the Arctic coasts of North America, the Labrador coast, Alaska, and the NE tip of Asia. 2. the language of the Eskimos. *adj.* of the Eskimos or their language. Also sp. **Esquimau.** **—Es′ki·mo′an,** *adj.*

**Eskimo dog,** a strong breed of dog with grayish, shaggy fur, used by the Eskimos to pull sleds.

**e·soph·a·gus** (i-sof′ə-gəs), *n.* [*pl.* -GI (-jī′)], [< L. < Gr. *oisophagos* < *oisein*, fut. inf. of *pherein*, to carry + *phagein*, to eat], the passage for food from the pharynx to the stomach; gullet: also sp. **oesophagus.**

**es·o·ter·ic** (es′ə-ter′ik), *adj.* [< Gr. < *esōteros*, inner < *esō*, within], 1. understood by only a chosen few; of or for only an inner group of disciples or initiates, as ideas, doctrines, etc. 2. confidential; private. **—es′o·ter′i·cal·ly,** *adv.*

**ESP, E.S.P.,** extrasensory perception.

**esp., espec.,** especially.

**es·pal·ier** (e-spal′yẽr), *n.* [Fr. < It. *spalliera*, support < *spalla* (< L. *spatula*), the shoulder], 1. a lattice or trellis on which trees and shrubs are trained to grow flat. 2. a plant, tree, etc. so trained. *v.t.* 1. to train as on an espalier. 2. to provide with an espalier.

ESPALIER

**Es·pa·ña** (es-pä′nyä), *n.* Spain: the Spanish name.

**es·pe·cial** (ə-spesh′əl), *adj.* special; particular; chief. **—es·pe′cial·ly,** *adv.*

**Es·pe·ran·to** (es'pə-rän'tō, -ran'-), *n.* [after pseudonym of Dr. L. L. Zamenhof (1859–1917), its inventor], an artificial language for international (chiefly European) use, based on word bases common to the main European languages.

**es·pi·al** (ə-spī'əl), *n.* 1. an espying or being espied; observation. 2. discovery.

**es·pi·o·nage** (es'pi-ə-nij, es'pi-ə-näzh'), *n.* [< Fr. < *espion*, a spy < It. *spione* < *spia*, a spy], 1. the act or practice of spying. 2. the use of spies, especially for military purposes.

**es·pla·nade** (es'plə-nād', -näd'), *n.* [Fr. < Sp. < It. < *spianare* (< L. *explanare*), to level], 1. a level, open space of ground; esp., a public walk or roadway, often along a shore; promenade. 2. a level, open space separating the citadel of a fortification from the town.

**es·pous·al** (i-spou'z'l), *n.* 1. *usually pl. a*) a betrothal ceremony. *b*) a wedding. 2. an espousing (of some cause, idea, etc.); advocacy.

**es·pouse** (i-spouz'), *v.t.* [-POUSED, -POUSING], [< OFr. < LL. *sponsare* < L. *sponsus*, pp. of *spondere*, to betroth], 1. to take as a spouse; marry. 2. to support, advocate, or adopt (some cause, idea, etc.). **—es·pous'er,** *n.*

**es·pres·so** (es-pres'ō), *n.* [*pl.* -sos], [It.], coffee made by forcing steam through ground coffee beans.

**‡es·prit** (es'prē'), *n.* [Fr.], 1. spirit. 2. lively intelligence or wit.

**‡es·prit de corps** (es'prē' də kôr'), [Fr.], group spirit; sense of pride, honor, etc. in common interests and activities.

**es·py** (ə-spī'), *v.t.* [-PIED, -PYING], [< OFr. *espier;* prob. < OHG. *spehōn*, to spy], to catch sight of; see; make out; spy; descry.

**Esq., Esqr.,** Esquire.

**-esque** (esk), [Fr.; It. *-esco*], a suffix meaning: 1. *in the manner* or *style of*, as in *Romanesque*. 2. *having the quality of, like*, as in *statuesque*.

**Es·qui·mau** (es'kə-mō'), *n.* [*pl.* -MAUX (-mō', -mōz')], *& adj.* Eskimo.

**es·quire** (ə-skwīr'; *occas. for n.* es'kwīr), *n.* [< OFr. < LL. *scutarius*, a shield-bearer < L. *scutum*, a shield], 1. formerly, a candidate for knighthood, acting as attendant for a knight. 2. in England, a member of the gentry ranking just below a knight. 3. [E-], a title of courtesy, usually abbrev. **Esq., Esqr.,** placed after a man's surname: as, John Davis, *Esq.* *v.t.* [-QUIRED, -QUIRING], 1. to raise to the rank of esquire. 2. to address as Esquire.

**ess** (es), *n.* [*pl.* ESSES (es'iz)], 1. the letter S, s. 2. something shaped like an S.

**-ess** (is, əs), [< OFr. < LL. *-issa* < Gr.], a suffix used to form feminine nouns, as in *lioness, actress*.

**es·say** (ə-sā', e-sā'), *v.t.* [< OFr. < LL. < L. *exagium*, a weighing < *ex-*, out of + *agere*, to drive], to try; attempt. *n.* 1. (e-sā', es'ā), an attempt; trial. 2. (es'ā, es'i), a short, personal literary composition dealing with a single subject. **—es·say'er,** *n.*

**es·say·ist** (es'ā-ist), *n.* one who writes essays.

**Es·sen** (es''n), *n.* a city in West Germany: pop., 728,000.

**es·sence** (es''ns), *n.* [Fr. < L. < ppr. of *esse*, to be], 1. an entity. 2. that which makes something what it is; fundamental nature (of something). 3. a substance that keeps, in concentrated form, the flavor, fragrance, etc. of the plant, drug, food, etc. from which it is extracted. 4. a solution of such a substance in alcohol. 5. a perfume. 6. in *philosophy*, true substance.

**es·sen·tial** (ə-sen'shəl), *adj.* 1. of or constituting the essence of something; basic; inherent. 2. absolute; pure: as, *essential* happiness. 3. necessary to make a thing what it is; indispensable: as, water is *essential* to life. *n.* something necessary, fundamental, or indispensable. **—es·sen'tial·ly,** *adv.* **—es·sen'tial·ness,** *n.*

**es·sen·ti·al·i·ty** (ə-sen'shi-al'ə-ti), *n.* [*pl.* -TIES], essential quality, fact, or thing.

**essential oil,** any volatile oil that gives distinctive odor, flavor, etc. as to a flower or fruit.

**Es·sex** (es'iks), *n.* a county in SE England: pop., 2,347,000.

**-est** (ist, əst, est), a suffix used to form: 1. the superlative degree of adjectives and adverbs, as in *greatest, soonest*. 2. the archaic 2d pers. sing., pres. indic., of verbs, as in *goest:* also **-st.**

**E.S.T., EST,** Eastern Standard Time.

**es·tab·lish** (ə-stab'lish), *v.t.* [< OFr. *establir* < L. < *stabilis*, stable], 1. to make stable; settle. 2. to order, ordain, or appoint (officials, laws, etc.) permanently. 3. to set up (a nation, business, etc.); found. 4. to set up in business, a profession, a position, etc. 5. to make a state institution of (a church). 6. to cause to be accepted or recognized, as a precedent. 7. to prove; demonstrate, as a case at law. **—es·tab'lish·er,** *n.*

**es·tab·lished church** (ə-stab'lisht), a church officially recognized by the government and supported as a national institution; specif., [E-C-], the Church of England.

**es·tab·lish·ment** (ə-stab'lish-mənt), *n.* 1. an establishing or being established. 2. a thing established, as a business, military organization, household, etc. **—the Establishment,** the ruling inner circle of any nation, institution, etc.

**es·tate** (ə-stāt') *n.* [< OFr. < L. *status*, a state, pp. of *stare*, to stand], 1. a condition or stage of life: as, to come to man's *estate*. 2. formerly, any of the three social classes having specific political powers: the clergy (**first estate**), the nobility (**second estate**), and the commons, or bourgeoisie (**third estate**). 3. one's property or possessions. 4. landed property; individually owned piece of land containing a residence. 5. in *law*, the degree, nature, and extent of ownership that a person has in land, etc. **—the fourth estate,** [cf. sense 2], journalism or journalists.

**es·teem** (ə-stēm'), *v.t.* [< Fr. < L. *aestimare*, to value, appraise], 1. to value highly; have a great regard for; prize. 2. to consider; regard. *n.* favorable opinion; high regard. **—es·teem'er,** *n.*

**es·ter** (es'tẽr), *n.* [G.; synthesis of *äther*, ether + *säure*, acid], an organic compound, comparable to an inorganic salt, formed by the reaction of an acid and an alcohol: the organic radical of the alcohol replaces the acid hydrogen of the acid.

**Es·ther** (es'tẽr), *n.* in the *Bible*, 1. the Jewish wife of a Persian king: she saved her people from slaughter. 2. the book of the Old Testament that tells her story. Abbrev. **Esth.**

**es·thete** (es'thēt), *n.* aesthete. **—es·thet'ic** (-thet'ik), *adj.* **—es·thet'i·cal·ly,** *adv.* **—es·thet'i·cism,** *n.*

**es·thet·ics** (es-thet'iks), *n.pl.* [construed as sing.], aesthetics.

**Es·tho·ni·a** (es-thō'ni-ə, -tō'-), *n.* Estonia. **—Es·tho'ni·an,** *adj. & n.*

**es·ti·ma·ble** (es'tə-mə-b'l), *adj.* 1. that can be estimated or evaluated. 2. worthy of esteem. **—es'ti·ma·ble·ness,** *n.* **—es'ti·ma·bly,** *adv.*

**es·ti·mate** (es'tə-māt'; *for n., usually* es'tə-mit), *v.t.* [-MATED, -MATING], [< L.; see ESTEEM], 1. to form an opinion about; gauge. 2. to determine roughly (the size, value, cost, etc.); calculate approximately. *v.i.* to make an estimate. *n.* 1. a rough calculation of size, value, etc.; esp., an approximate computation of the probable cost of a piece of work, made by a person undertaking to do the work. 2. an opinion or judgment. **—es'ti·ma'tive** (-tiv), *adj.* **—es'ti·ma'tor** (-mā'tẽr), *n.*

**es·ti·ma·tion** (es'tə-mā'shən), *n.* 1. an estimating. 2. an opinion or judgment. 3. esteem; regard; respect.

**Es·to·ni·a** (es-tō'ni-ə), *n.* a country in NE Europe annexed as the Estonian Soviet Socialist Republic: also **Esthonia. —Es·to'ni·an,** *adj. & n.*

**Estonian Soviet Socialist Republic,** a republic of the U.S.S.R., on the Baltic Sea: area, 18,050 sq. mi.; pop., 1,300,000; capital, Tallinn.

**es·top** (e-stop'), *v.t.* [-TOPPED, -TOPPING], [< Anglo-Fr. & OFr. < LL. < L. *stuppa*, oakum], 1. originally, to stop up; plug up. 2. to stop; obstruct; prevent; bar. **—es·top'page,** *n.*

**es·trange** (ə-strānj'), *v.t.* [-TRANGED, -TRANGING], [< OFr. < LL. < L. *extraneus*, foreign < *extra*, beyond], 1. to remove; keep apart or away. 2. to turn away; alienate. 3. to turn (a person) from an affectionate or friendly attitude to an indifferent, unfriendly, or hostile one; alienate the affections of. **—es·trange'ment,** *n.* **—es·trang'er,** *n.*

**es·tro·gen** (es'trə-jən), *n.* any of several estrus-producing compounds. **—es'tro·gen'ic,** *adj.*

**es·trus** (es'trəs, ēs'-), *n.* [< L. < Gr. *oistros*, frenzy] the sexual excitement, or heat, of female mammals or the period of this; also sp. **oestrus.**

**es·tu·ar·y** (es'chōō-er'i), *n.* [*pl.* -IES], [< L. < *aestus*, the tide], an inlet or arm of the sea; esp., the wide mouth of a river, where the tide meets the current. **—es'tu·ar'i·al,** *adj.*

**-et** (it, ət), [< OFr. *-et*, masc., *-ete* (Fr. *-ette*), fem.], a suffix added to nouns, meaning *little*, as in *islet*: it has lost its diminutive sense in most words, as in *bullet, hatchet, pocket,* etc.

**Et, et,** in *chemistry,* ethyl.

**e·ta** (ā′tə, ē′tə), *n.* the seventh letter of the Greek alphabet (Η, η).

**et al.,** [L.], 1. *et alibi.* 2. *et alii.*

‡**et a·li·bi** (et al′ə-bī′), [L.], and elsewhere.

‡**et a·li·i** (et ā′li-ī′), [L.], and others.

**etc.,** et cetera.

**et cet·er·a, et caet·er·a** (et set′ēr-ə, et set′rə), [L.], and others; and the like; and the rest; and so forth: abbrev. **etc., &c.**

**et·cet·er·as** (et-set′ēr-əz, -set′rəz), *n.pl.* additional things; odds and ends.

**etch** (ech), *v.t.* [< D. < G. < MHG. *etzen,* to cause to eat < *ezzen,* to eat], 1. to make (a drawing, design, etc.) on metal, glass, etc. by the action of an acid. 2. to engrave (a metal plate, etc.) in this way for use in printing. 3. to produce (drawings, designs, etc.) by this process. *v.i.* to make etchings. —**etch′er,** *n.*

**etch·ing** (ech′iŋ), *n.* 1. the art or process of producing drawings or designs on metal plates, etc. by the action of acid. 2. an etched plate, design, etc. 3. a print made from such a plate.

**e·ter·nal** (i-tũr′n'l), *adj.* [< OFr. < LL. *aeternalis* < L. < *aevum,* an age], 1. without beginning or end; everlasting. 2. timeless. 3. forever the same; unchangeable. 4. always going on or coming back; perpetual. 5. seeming never to stop; happening very often. —**the Eternal,** God. —**e·ter′nal·ly,** *adv.* —**e·ter′nal·ness,** *n.*

**Eternal City,** Rome.

**e·ter·nal·ize** (i-tũr′n'l-īz′), *v.t.* [-IZED, -IZING], to make eternal; eternize.

**e·ter·ni·ty** (i-tũr′nə-ti), *n.* [*pl.* -TIES], 1. the quality, state, or fact of being eternal; continuance without end. 2. infinite time; time without beginning or end. 3. a long period of time that seems endless. 4. the endless time after death.

**e·ter·nize** (i-tũr′nīz), *v.t.* [-NIZED, -NIZING], 1. to make eternal. 2. to make famous forever; immortalize. —**e·ter′ni·za′tion,** *n.*

**-eth,** see **-th** (suffix for ordinal numerals).

**-eth** (əth, ith), [AS. *-(a)th*], archaic ending of the 3d pers. sing., pres. indic., of verbs, as in *asketh, bringeth:* also **-th.**

**Eth.,** 1. Ethiopia. 2. Ethiopian. 3. Ethiopic.

**eth·ane** (eth′ān), *n.* [< *ether* + *-ane*], an odorless, colorless, gaseous hydrocarbon, $CH_3CH_3$: it is found in natural gas and illuminating gas.

**eth·ene** (eth′ēn), *n.* ethylene.

**e·ther** (ē′thēr), *n.* [< L. < Gr. *aithēr* < *aithein,* to kindle, burn], 1. the upper regions of space; clear sky. 2. [Rare], the air. 3. in *chemistry,* a volatile, colorless, highly inflammable liquid, $(C_2H_5)_2O$, with an aromatic odor: it is used as an anesthetic and a solvent for resins and fats: also **diethyl ether.** 4. in *physics,* an invisible substance that has been postulated as pervading space and serving as the medium for the transmission of light waves and other forms of radiant energy. Also sp. **aether** (in senses 1 and 2).

**e·the·re·al** (i-thêr′i-əl), *adj.* 1. of or like the ether, or upper regions of space. 2. very light; airy; delicate. 3. heavenly; not earthly. 4. in *chemistry,* of or like ether. Also sp. **aethereal** (in senses 1, 2, 3). —**e·the′re·al′i·ty** (-al′ə-ti), **e·the′re·al·ness,** *n.* —**e·the′re·al·ly,** *adv.*

**e·the·re·al·ize** (i-thêr′i-ə-līz′), *v.t.* [-IZED, -IZING], to make, or treat as being, ethereal. —**e·the′re·al·i·za′tion,** *n.*

**e·ther·ize** (ē′thə-rīz′), *v.t.* [-IZED, -IZING], 1. to change into ether. 2. to cause to inhale ether fumes so as to make unconscious. —**e′ther·i·za′tion,** *n.* —**e′ther·iz′er,** *n.*

**eth·ic** (eth′ik), *n.* ethics or a system of ethics. *adj.* ethical.

**eth·i·cal** (eth′i-k'l), *adj.* [< L. *ethicus* < Gr. < *ēthos,* character], 1. having to do with ethics or morality; of or conforming to moral standards. 2. conforming to professional standards of conduct. —**eth′i·cal·ly,** *adv.* —**eth′i·cal·ness,** *n.*

**eth·ics** (eth′iks), *n.pl.* [construed as sing. in 1 & 2], 1. the study of standards of conduct and moral judgment. 2. a treatise on this study. 3. the system or code of morals of a particular philosopher, religion, group, etc.

**E·thi·op** (ē′thi-op′), *n. & adj.* Ethiopian.

**E·thi·o·pi·a** (ē′thi-ō′pi-ə), *n.* 1. an ancient region in NE Africa, south of Egypt. 2. a country in E Africa: area, 395,000 sq. mi.; pop., c. 20,000,000; capital, Addis Ababa: also called *Abyssinia.*

**E·thi·o·pi·an** (ē′thi-ō′pi-ən), *adj.* of Ethiopia, its people, culture, etc. *n.* 1. a native or inhabitant of Ethiopia. 2. loosely, a Negro.

**E·thi·op·ic** (ē′thi-op′ik, -ō′pik), *adj.* 1. Ethiopian. 2. of the Semitic language of the Ethiopians. *n.* this language.

**eth·nic** (eth′nik), *adj.* [< Fr. < L. < Gr. < *ethnos,* nation, *ta ethnē,* the (gentile) nations], 1. of nations or groups neither Christian nor Jewish; heathen. 2. designating or of any of the basic divisions or groups of mankind, as distinguished by customs, characteristics, language, etc. Also **eth′ni·cal.** —**eth′ni·cal·ly,** *adv.*

**eth·no-,** [< Gr. *ethnos,* nation], a combining form meaning *race, peoples:* also **ethn-.**

**eth·nog·ra·phy** (eth-nog′rə-fi), *n.* [*ethno-* + *-graphy*], the branch of anthropology that deals descriptively with specific cultures, especially those of primitive peoples. —**eth·nog′ra·pher,** *n.* —**eth′no·graph′ic** (-nə-graf′ik), **eth′no·graph′i·cal,** *adj.* —**eth′no·graph′i·cal·ly,** *adv.*

**eth·nol·o·gy** (eth-nol′ə-ji), *n.* [*ethno-* + *-logy*], the branch of anthropology that deals with the comparative cultures of various peoples, including their distribution, classification, characteristics, etc. —**eth′no·log′ic** (-nə-loj′ik), **eth′no·log′i·cal,** *adj.* —**eth′no·log′i·cal·ly,** *adv.* —**eth·nol′o·gist,** *n.*

**eth·yl** (eth′əl), *n.* [< *ether* + *-yl*], 1. the monovalent hydrocarbon radical $CH_3CH_2$, which forms the base of common alcohol, ether, and many other compounds. 2. tetraethyl lead, $Pb(C_2H_5)_4$, a poisonous lead compound, added to gasoline as an antiknock: a trade-mark **(Ethyl).** *adj.* containing ethyl. —**e·thyl·ic** (i-thil′ik), *adj.*

**ethyl alcohol,** common alcohol: see **alcohol.**

**eth·yl·ene** (eth′ə-lēn′), *n.* [*ethyl* + *-ene*], a colorless, inflammable gas, $C_2H_4$, with a disagreeable odor: it is used as a fuel and anesthetic, and in hastening the ripening of fruits.

**e·ti·ol·o·gy** (ē′ti-ol′ə-ji), *n.* [*pl.* -GIES], [< LL. < Gr. < *aitia,* cause + *logia,* description], 1. the assignment of a cause: as, the *etiology* of a folkway. 2. the science of causes or origins. 3. science or theory of the causes of diseases. Also sp. **aetiology.** —**e′ti·o·log′i·cal** (-ə-loj′i-k'l), *adj.* —**e′ti·o·log′i·cal·ly,** *adv.* —**e′ti·ol′o·gist,** *n.*

**et·i·quette** (et′i-ket′, -kət), *n.* [Fr. *étiquette,* a ticket, label < OFr. < *estiquer,* to stick], the forms, manners, and ceremonies established by convention as acceptable or required in society, a profession, etc.

**Et·na** (et′nə), *n.* a volcanic mountain in E Sicily: also sp. **Aetna.**

**E·ton** (ē′t'n), *n.* a private preparatory school for boys near London, England: in full, **Eton College.** —**E·to·ni·an** (ē-tō′ni-ən), *adj. & n.*

**Eton collar,** 1. a broad, white linen collar worn with an Eton jacket. 2. a collar like this.

**Eton jacket** (or **coat**), 1. a boys' short, waist-length jacket with broad lapels, left open in front: worn by students at Eton. 2. a similar jacket, as worn by girls and women.

ETON COLLAR AND JACKET

**E·tru·ri·a** (i-troor′i-ə), *n.* an ancient country in the central part of W Italy.

**E·trur·i·an** (i-troor′i-ən), *adj. & n.* Etruscan.

**E·trus·can** (i-trus′kən), *adj.* of Etruria, its people, their language, or culture. *n.* 1. a native or inhabitant of Etruria. 2. the language of the Etruscans.

**et seq.,** [L. *et sequens*], 1. and the following. 2. [L. *et sequentes, et sequentia*], and those that follow: also **et seqq.**

**-ette** (et), [Fr., fem. of *-et*], a suffix meaning: 1. *little,* as in *dinette.* 2. *female,* as in *suffragette.* 3. *a substitute for,* as in *leatherette.*

**é·tude** (ā′tōōd, ā′tūd; Fr. ā-tüd′), *n.* [Fr.; see STUDY], 1. a study. 2. a musical composition for a solo instrument, designed to give practice in some special point of technique.

**ety., etym., etymol.,** 1. etymological. 2. etymology.

**et·y·mol·o·gy** (et′ə-mol′ə-ji), *n.* [*pl.* -GIES], [< Fr. < L. < Gr. < *etymon,* literal sense of a word (< *etymos,* true) + *logos,* word], 1. the origin and development of a word; the tracing of a word back as far as possible. 2. an account of this. 3. the branch of linguistics that deals with the origin and development of words. —**et′y·mo·log′i·cal** (-mə-loj′i-k'l), *adj.* —**et′y·mo·log′i·cal·ly,** *adv.* —**et′y·mol′o·gist,** *n.* —**et′y·mol′o·gize′** (-jīz′), [-GIZED, -GIZING], *v.t. & v.i.*

**Eu,** *in chemistry,* europium.

**eu-,** [Gr.], a prefix meaning *good, well,* as in *eulogy, eugenic:* opposed to *dys-, caco-.*

**Eu·boe·a** (yoo-bē′ə), *n.* Evvoia: the ancient name. —**Eu·boe′an,** *adj. & n.*

**eu·ca·lyp·tus** (ū′kə-lip′təs), *n.* [*pl.* -TUSES, -TI (-tī)], [< Gr. *eu-*, well + *kalyptos*, covered (from the covering of the buds) < *kalyptein*, to cover], any of a group of subtropical evergreen trees of the myrtle family, native to Australia, valued for their timber, gums, and oil: also **eu′ca·lypt′.**

**eucalyptus oil,** an essential oil derived from eucalyptus leaves: an antiseptic and disinfectant.

**Eu·cha·rist** (ū′kə-rist), *n.* [< OFr. < LL. < Gr. *eucharistia*, gratitude < *eu-*, well + *charis*, favor], in *Christian churches*, 1. Holy Communion; Lord's Supper. 2. the consecrated bread and wine used in this. —**Eu′cha·ris′tic, Eu′cha·ris′ti·cal,** *adj.*

**eu·chre** (ū′kẽr), *n.* [? < G. dial. (cf. G. *juchs*, joke, game)], 1. a card game for two, three, or four players, played with thirty-two cards. 2. a euchring or being euchred. *v.t.* [-CHRED, -CHRING], 1. to gain an advantage over (an opponent at euchre) by his failure to take three tricks. 2. [Colloq.], to outwit.

**Eu·clid** (ū′klid), *n.* 1. Greek mathematician; fl. c. 300 B.C. 2. his basic book on geometry. 3. a city in NE Ohio: suburb of Cleveland: pop., 63,000. —**Eu·clid′e·an, Eu·clid′i·an,** *adj.*

**eu·gen·ic** (yoo-jen′ik), *adj.* [< Gr.; see EU- & GENESIS], improving, or relating to the improvement of, the race; relating to the bearing of healthy offspring: also **eu·gen′i·cal.** —**eu·gen′i·cal·ly,** *adv.*

**eu·gen·i·cist** (yoo-jen′ə-sist), *n.* a specialist in or advocate of eugenics: also **eu′gen·ist.**

**eu·gen·ics** (yoo-jen′iks), *n.pl.* [construed as sing.], the science that deals with the improvement of races and breeds, especially the human race, through the control of hereditary factors.

**eu·lo·gist** (ū′lə-jist), *n.* one who eulogizes.

**eu·lo·gis·tic** (ū′lə-jis′tik), *adj.* of or expressing eulogy; praising highly; laudatory: also **eu′lo·gis′ti·cal.** —**eu′lo·gis′ti·cal·ly,** *adv.*

**eu·lo·gi·um** (yoo-lō′ji-əm), *n.* [*pl.* -GIUMS, -GIA (-ji-ə)], [ML.], eulogy.

**eu·lo·gize** (ū′lə-jīz′), *v.t.* [-GIZED, -GIZING], to compose a eulogy about; extol. —**eu′lo·giz′er,** *n.*

**eu·lo·gy** (ū′lə-ji), *n.* [*pl.* -GIES], [< ML. < Gr. < *eulegein*, to speak well of], 1. speech or writing in praise of a person, event, or thing; esp., a funeral oration. 2. high praise.

**Eu·men·i·des** (ū-men′ə-dēz′), *n.pl.* [L. < Gr. *Eumenidēs*, lit., the gracious ones: a propitiatory euphemism], in *Gr. mythology*, the Furies; Erinyes.

**eu·nuch** (ū′nək), *n.* [< L. < Gr. *eunouchos*, bed guardian < *eunē*, bed + *echein*, to keep], a castrated man; esp., one in charge of a harem or employed as a chamberlain in an Oriental palace.

**eu·pep·si·a** (yoo-pep′shə, -si-ə), *n.* [< Gr. < *eu-*, well + *peptein*, to digest], good digestion. —**eu·pep′tic,** *adj.* —**eu·pep′ti·cal·ly,** *adv.*

**eu·phe·mism** (ū′fə-miz′m), *n.* [< Gr. < *eu-*, good + *phēmē*, voice < *phanai*, to speak], 1. the use of a word or phrase that is less expressive or direct but considered less distasteful or offensive, than another. 2. a word or phrase so substituted (e.g., *remains* for *corpse*). —**eu′phe·mist,** *n.* —**eu′phe·mis′tic, eu′phe·mis′ti·cal,** *adj.* —**eu′phe·mis′ti·cal·ly,** *adv.*

**eu·phe·mize** (ū′fə-mīz′), *v.t. & v.i.* [-MIZED, -MIZING], to speak or write of (something) euphemistically. —**eu′phe·miz′er,** *n.*

**eu·phon·ic** (yoo-fon′ik), *adj.* 1. of euphony. 2. euphonious. Also **eu·phon′i·cal.** —**eu·phon′i·cal·ly,** *adv.* —**eu·phon′i·cal·ness,** *n.*

**eu·pho·ni·ous** (yoo-fō′ni-əs), *adj.* characterized by euphony; having a pleasant sound; harmonious. —**eu·pho′ni·ous·ly,** *adv.* —**eu·pho′ni·ous·ness,** *n.*

**eu·pho·ni·um** (yoo-fō′ni-əm), *n.* a brass-wind instrument resembling the tuba but having a slightly higher range and more mellow tone.

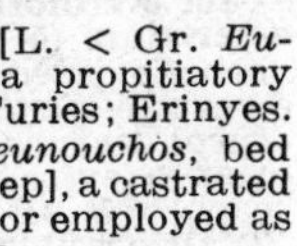

EUPHONIUM

**eu·pho·ny** (ū′fə-ni), *n.* [*pl.* -NIES], [< LL. < Gr. < *eu-*, well + *phōnē*, voice], 1. the quality of having a pleasing sound; pleasant combination of agreeable sounds, as in speech or music. 2. in *phonetics*, the tendency to make pronunciation easier, as by assimilation.

**eu·phor·bi·a** (yoo-fôr′bi-ə), *n.* [< L. < Gr. < *Euphorbos*, Gr. physician], any of a large group of cactuslike plants with a thick, milky juice, including the poinsettia, milkbush, etc.

**eu·pho·ri·a** (yoo-fôr′i-ə, -fō′ri-), *n.* [< Gr. < *eu-*, well + *pherein*, to bear], a feeling of well-being; esp., in *psychology*, an abnormal feeling of buoyant vigor and health. —**eu·phor′ic,** *adj.*

**Eu·phra·tes** (ū-frā′tēz), *n.* a river flowing through E Turkey, Syria, and Iraq, into the Persian Gulf: length, 1,700 mi.

**eu·phu·ism** (ū′fū-iz′m), *n.* [< *Euphues*, fictitious character in two prose romances by John Lyly, English writer (1554?–1606); < Gr. < *eu-*, well + *phyē*, growth], 1. an artificial, affected, high-flown style of speaking or writing of the late 16th century, characterized by alliteration, antithesis, farfetched figures of speech, etc. 2. any artificial, high-flown style of speech or writing. 3. an instance of this. —**eu′phu·ist,** *n.* —**eu′phu·is′tic, eu′phu·is′ti·cal,** *adj.* —**eu′phu·is′ti·cal·ly,** *adv.*

**Eur.,** 1. Europe. 2. European.

**Eur·a·sia** (yoo-rā′zhə, -shə), *n.* Europe and Asia, considered as a unit.

**Eur·a·sian** (yoo-rā′zhən, -shən), *adj.* 1. of Eurasia. 2. of mixed European and Asiatic descent. *n.* a person of mixed European and Asiatic descent.

**eu·re·ka** (yoo-rē′kə), *interj.* [< Gr., I have found (it)], an exclamation of triumphant achievement, equivalent to "I've got it!"

**eu·rhyth·mics** (yoo-rith′miks), *n.pl.* eurythmics. —**eu·rhyth′mic, eu·rhyth′mi·cal,** *adj.*

**Eu·rip·i·des** (yoo-rip′ə-dēz′), *n.* Greek tragic dramatist; lived 5th century B.C.

**Eu·ro·pa** (yoo-rō′pə), *n.* in *Gr. mythology*, a Phoenician princess loved by Zeus: taking on the form of a white bull, he carried her off to Crete.

**Eu·rope** (yoor′əp), *n.* the continent west of Asia: area, 3,872,000 sq. mi.; pop., c.560,000,000. —**Eu′ro·pe′an** (-ə-pē′ən), *adj. & n.*

**Eu·ro·pe·an·ize** (yoor′ə-pē′ən-īz′), *v.t.* [-IZED, -IZING], to make European in habits, dress, culture, etc. —**Eu′ro·pe′an·i·za′tion,** *n.*

**European plan,** a system of hotel operation in which guests are charged for rooms and service, and pay for meals separately if they wish them: distinguished from *American plan.*

**eu·ro·pi·um** (yoo-rō′pi-əm), *n.* [Mod. L. < *Europe*], a chemical element of the rare-earth group: symbol, Eu; at. wt., 152.0; at. no., 63.

**Eu·ryd·i·ce** (yoo-rid′ə-sē′), *n.* see **Orpheus**: also sp. **Euridice.**

**eu·ryth·mics** (yoo-rith′miks), *n.pl.* [construed as sing.], [< L. < Gr. < *eu-*, well + *rhythmos*, rhythm], the art of performing various bodily movements in rhythm, usually to musical accompaniment. —**eu·ryth′mic, eu·ryth′mi·cal,** *adj.*

**Eu·sta·chi·an tube** (yoo-stā′ki-ən, -shi-ən, -shən), [after Bartolommeo *Eustachio* (1520–1574), It. anatomist], a slender tube between the middle ear and the pharynx, which serves to equalize air pressure on both sides of the eardrum.

**Eu·ter·pe** (ū-tũr′pi), *n.* in *Gr. mythology*, the Muse of music and lyric poetry.

**eu·tha·na·si·a** (ū′thə-nā′zhə, -zhi-ə), *n.* [< Gr. < *eu-*, well + *thanatos*, death], 1. an easy and painless death. 2. act or practice of causing death painlessly to end suffering: advocated by some in cases of incurable diseases.

**eu·then·ics** (yoo-then′iks), *n.pl.* [construed as sing.], [< Gr. *euthēnein*, to flourish; + *-ics*], the science that deals with the improvement of races and breeds, especially the human race, through the control of environmental factors.

**Eux·ine Sea** (ūk′sin, -sīn), the Black Sea: the ancient name.

**e·vac·u·ant** (i-vak′ū-ənt), *adj. & n.* [see EVACUATE], cathartic or emetic.

**e·vac·u·ate** (i-vak′ū-āt′), *v.t.* [-ATED, -ATING], [< L. pp. < *e-*, out + *vacuare*, to make empty < *vacuus*, empty], 1. to make empty; remove the contents of. 2. to discharge (excrement, etc.); void. 3. to move or remove: as, to *evacuate* civilians from a battle area. 4. to give up military occupation of; withdraw from. *v.i.* to withdraw, as from a besieged town. —**e·vac′u·a′tion,** *n.* —**e·vac′u·a′tor** (-ā′tẽr), *n.* —**e·vac′u·ee′** (-ē′), *n.*

**e·vade** (i-vād′), *v.i.* [EVADED, EVADING], [< Fr. < L. < *e-*, out, from + *vadere*, to go], to avoid using evasion; be deceitful or clever in avoiding or escaping. *v.t.* 1. to avoid or escape from by deceit or cleverness; 2. to avoid doing or answering directly. —**e·vad′a·ble, e·vad′i·ble,** *adj.* —**e·vad′er,** *n.* —**e·vad′ing·ly,** *adv.*

**e·val·u·ate** (i-val′ū-āt′), *v.t.* [-ATED, -ATING], [< Fr. < *é-* (< L. *ex-*), out + *value;* see VALUE], to find the value or amount of; determine the worth of; appraise. —**e·val′u·a′tion,** *n.*

**ev·a·nesce** (ev′ə-nes′), *v.i.* [-NESCED, -NESCING], [< L. < *e-*, out + *vanescere*, to vanish < *vanus*, empty], to fade from sight, like mist or smoke; vanish.

**ev·a·nes·cent** (ev′ə-nes′'nt), *adj.* tending to fade from sight; vanishing; fleeting; ephemeral. —**ev′a·nes′cence,** *n.* —**ev′a·nes′cent·ly,** *adv.*

**e·van·gel** (i-van′jəl), *n.* [< OFr. < LL. < Gr. *euangelos*, bringing good news; *eu-*, well + *angelos*, messenger], 1. the gospel. 2. [E-], any of the four Gospels. 3. good news. 4. an evangelist.

**e·van·gel·i·cal** (ē′van-jel′i-k'l, ev′ən-), *adj.* 1. in, of, or according to the Gospels or the New Testament. 2. of those Protestant churches, as the Methodist and Baptist, that emphasize salvation by faith in the atonement of Jesus. 3. evangelistic. Also **e′van·gel′ic.** *n.* a member of an evangelical church. —**e′van·gel′i·cal·ism,** *n.* —**e′van·gel′i·cal·ly,** *adv.*

**e·van·gel·ism** (i-van′jə-liz'm), *n.* a preaching of, or zealous effort to spread, the gospel, as in revival meetings.

**e·van·gel·ist** (i-van′jə-list), *n.* 1. [E-], any of the four writers of the Gospels; Matthew, Mark, Luke, or John. 2. one who preaches the gospel; esp., a traveling preacher who conducts revival meetings. —**e·van′gel·is′tic,** *adj.* —**e·van′gel·is′ti·cal·ly,** *adv.*

**e·van·gel·ize** (i-van′jə-līz′), *v.t.* [-IZED, -IZING], 1. to preach the gospel to. 2. to convert to Christianity. —**e·van′gel·i·za′tion,** *n.* —**e·van′gel·iz′er,** *n.*

**Ev·ans·ton** (ev′ən-stən, -ənz-tən), *n.* a city in Illinois, near Chicago: pop., 79,000.

**Ev·ans·ville** (ev′ənz-vil′), *n.* a city in SW Indiana, on the Ohio River: pop., 142,000.

**e·vap·o·rate** (i-vap′ə-rāt′), *v.t.* [-RATED, -RATING], [< L. pp. < *e-*, out + *vaporare*, to emit vapor < *vapor*, steam], 1. to change (a liquid or solid) into vapor. 2. to remove moisture from (milk, vegetables, etc.), as by heating, so as to get a concentrated product. *v.i.* 1. to become vapor. 2. to give off vapor. 3. to disappear; vanish. —**e·vap′o·ra·bil′i·ty,** *n.* —**e·vap′o·ra·ble** (-ẽr-ə-b'l), *adj.* —**e·vap′o·ra′tion,** *n.* —**e·vap′o·ra′tive** (-tiv), *adj.* —**e·vap′o·ra′tor** (-tẽr), *n.*

**evaporated milk,** canned, unsweetened milk thickened by evaporation: cf. *condensed milk*.

**e·va·sion** (i-vā′zhən), *n.* 1. an evading; an avoiding of a duty, question, fact, etc. by deceit or cleverness. 2. a means of doing this; subterfuge.

**e·va·sive** (i-vā′siv), *adj.* 1. tending or seeking to evade; not straightforward or definite. 2. elusive. —**e·va′sive·ly,** *adv.* —**e·va′sive·ness,** *n.*

**Eve** (ēv), *n.* in the *Bible*, Adam's wife, the first woman: Gen. 3:20.

**eve** (ēv), *n.* [ME.; shortened < *even* (evening)], 1. [Poetic], evening. 2. the evening or day before a holiday: as, Christmas *Eve;* hence, 3. the period immediately before some event.

**e·ven** (ē′vən, -v'n), *adj.* [AS. *efne*], 1. flat; level; smooth: as, *even* country. 2. not varying; constant: as, an *even* tempo. 3. calm; tranquil: as, an *even* disposition. 4. in the same plane or line: as, *even* with the rim. 5. equally balanced. 6. owing and being owed nothing. 7. revenged for a wrong, insult, etc. 8. just; fair: as, an *even* exchange. 9. equal or identical in number, quantity, etc. 10. exactly divisible by two: said of numbers. 11. exact: as, an *even* mile. *adv.* 1. moreover; however improbable; indeed; fully: as, *even* a fool could do it. 2. exactly; just: as, it happened *even* as I expected. 3. just as; while: as, *even* as he spoke, I left. 4. comparatively; still; yet: as, he's *even* better. *v.t.* & *v.i.* to make, become, or be even; level off. —**break even,** [Slang], to finish as neither a winner nor loser. —**even if,** though; despite the fact that. —**e′ven·er,** *n.* —**e′ven·ly,** *adv.* —**e′ven·ness,** *n.*

**e·ven** (ē′vən), *n.* [< AS. *æfen*], [Poetic], evening.

**e·ven·fall** (ē′vən-fôl′), *n.* [Poetic], the fall of evening; twilight; dusk.

**e·ven·hand·ed** (ē′vən-han′did), *adj.* impartial; fair. —**e′ven·hand′ed·ly** *adv.* —**e′ven·hand′ed·ness,** *n.*

**eve·ning** (ēv′niŋ), *n.* [< AS. < *æfnian*, to grow toward evening < *æfen*], 1. the last part of the day and early part of night. 2. in some parts of the South, the period from noon through sunset. 3. the last period, as of life, a career, etc. *adj.* in, for, or of the evening.

**evening primrose,** a plant with spikes of night-blooming fragrant flowers of yellow or white.

**evening star,** a bright planet, usually Venus, seen in the western sky soon after sunset.

**e·ven·song** (ē′vən-sôŋ′), *n.* 1. in the *R.C. Church*, vespers. 2. in the *Church of England*, the service of evening prayer.

**e·vent** (i-vent′), *n.* [< OFr. < L. < *e-*, out + *venire*, to come], 1. a happening; occurrence, especially an important occurrence. 2. a result; consequence. 3. a particular contest or item in a program of sports. —**at all events,** in any case; anyhow: also **in any event.** —**in the event of,** in case of.

**e·ven-tem·pered** (ē′vən-tem′pẽrd), *adj.* not quickly angered or excited; placid; calm.

**e·vent·ful** (i-vent′fəl), *adj.* 1. full of outstanding events. 2. having an important outcome. —**e·vent′ful·ly,** *adv.* —**e·vent′ful·ness,** *n.*

**e·ven·tide** (ē′vən-tīd′), *n.* [Archaic], evening.

**e·ven·tu·al** (i-ven′cho͞o-əl), *adj.* 1. depending on events; contingent or possible. 2. happening at the end; final. —**e·ven′tu·al·ly,** *adv.*

**e·ven·tu·al·i·ty** (i-ven′cho͞o-al′ə-ti), *n.* [*pl.* -TIES], a possible event, outcome, or condition; contingency: as, ready for any *eventualities*.

**e·ven·tu·ate** (i-ven′cho͞o-āt′), *v.i.* [-ATED, -ATING], to happen in the end; result (often with *in*). —**e·ven′tu·a′tion,** *n.*

**ev·er** (ev′ẽr), *adv.* [AS. *æfre*], 1. always; at all times: as, *ever* the same. 2. repeatedly. 3. at any time: as, have you *ever* seen her? 4. at all; by any chance: as, if it *ever* starts, we can go. —**ever and anon,** [Archaic], once in a while. —**ever so,** [Colloq.], very. —**for ever and a day,** always.

**Ev·er·est, Mount** (ev′ẽr-ist, ev′rist), a peak of the Himalayas, between Tibet and Nepal: height, 29,002 ft.: highest known mountain in the world.

**ev·er·glade** (ev′ẽr-glād′), *n.* swampland. —**the Everglades,** a large tract of swampland in S Florida.

**ev·er·green** (ev′ẽr-grēn′), *adj.* having green leaves throughout the year, as most of the conifers: opposed to *deciduous*. *n.* 1. an evergreen plant or tree. 2. *pl.* the branches and twigs of evergreens, used for decoration.

**ev·er·last·ing** (ev′ẽr-las′tiŋ, -läs′-), *adj.* 1. lasting forever; eternal. 2. going on for a long time. 3. going on too long; seeming never to stop. *n.* 1. eternity. 2. any of various plants whose blossoms keep their color and shape when dried; immortelle. —**the Everlasting,** God. —**ev′er·last′ing·ly,** *adv.* —**ev′er·last′ing·ness,** *n.*

**ev·er·more** (ev′ẽr-môr′, -mōr′), *adv.* forever; always. —**for evermore,** always.

**e·ver·sion** (ē-vũr′shən, -zhən), *n.* an everting or being everted. —**e·ver′si·ble,** *adj.*

**e·vert** (ē-vũrt′), *v.t.* [< L. < *e-*, out + *vertere*, to turn], to turn outward or inside out.

**ev·er·y** (ev′ri, ev′ẽr-i), *adj.* [AS. *æfre ælc*, lit., ever each], 1. all, taken individually and separately. 2. all possible: as, he was given *every* chance. 3. each interval of (a specified number or time): as, a dose *every* three hours. —**every now and then,** once in a while. —**every other,** each alternate, as the first, third, fifth, etc. —**every so often,** [Colloq.], once in a while. —**every which way,** [Colloq.], in complete disorder.

**ev·er·y·bod·y** (ev′ri-bod′i, -bud′i), *pron.* every person; everyone.

**ev·er·y·day** (ev′ri-dā′), *adj.* 1. daily: as, one's *everyday* routine. 2. suitable for ordinary days: as, *everyday* shoes. 3. usual; common.

**ev·er·y·one** (ev′ri-wun′, -wən), *pron.* everybody.

**every one,** 1. everyone. 2. every person or thing.

**ev·er·y·thing** (ev′ri-thiŋ′), *pron.* 1. every thing; all. 2. all things pertinent. 3. the most important thing: as, money isn't *everything*.

**ev·er·y·where** (ev′ri-hwâr′), *adv.* in every place; in all places.

**e·vict** (i-vikt′), *v.t.* [< L. *evictus*, pp. < *e-*, from + *vincere*, to conquer], to put (a tenant) out by legal procedure, as for failure to pay rent. —**e·vic′tion,** *n.* —**e·vic′tor** (-tẽr), *n.*

**ev·i·dence** (ev′ə-dəns), *n.* 1. the condition of being evident. 2. something that makes another thing evident; indication; sign. 3. something that tends to prove. 4. in *law*, *a)* something presented before a court, as a statement of a witness, an object, etc., which bears on or establishes the point in question. *b)* one who presents testimony; witness: as, state's *evidence*. *v.t.* [-DENCED, -DENCING], 1. to make evident; indicate; show. 2. to bear witness to; attest. —**in evidence,** plainly visible or perceptible. —**turn state's evidence,** to give testimony against an accomplice.

**ev·i·dent** (ev′ə-dənt), *adj.* [< OFr. < L. *evidens*, clear < *e-*, from + *videre*, to see], easy to see or perceive; clear; obvious; plain. —**ev′i·dent·ly,** *adv.* —**ev′i·dent·ness,** *n.*

**ev·i·den·tial** (ev′ə-den′shəl), *adj.* of, serving as, or providing evidence.

**e·vil** (ē′v'l), *adj.* [AS. *yfel*], 1. morally bad or wrong; wicked; depraved. 2. harmful; injurious. 3. unlucky; disastrous. 4. resulting from conduct regarded as immoral: as, an *evil* reputation. *n.* 1. wickedness; depravity; sin. 2. anything that causes harm, pain, disaster, etc. **—the Evil One,** the Devil. **—e′vil·ly,** *adv.* **—e′vil·ness,** *n.*

**e·vil·do·er** (ē′v'l-do͞o′ẽr), *n.* one who does evil. **—e′vil-do′ing, e′vil·do′ing,** *n.*

**evil eye,** the supposed power of harming others by merely looking at them, superstitiously attributed to some people.

**e·vil-mind·ed** (ē′v'l-mīn′did), *adj.* having an evil mind or disposition; specif., *a)* malicious; wicked. *b)* obscene; lewd. **—e′vil-mind′ed·ness,** *n.*

**e·vince** (i-vins′), *v.t.* [EVINCED, EVINCING], [< L. < *e-*, out + *vincere*, to conquer], to show plainly; make manifest; esp., to show that one has (a quality, feeling, etc.). **—e·vin′ci·ble,** *adj.* **—e·vin′cive,** *adj.*

**e·vis·cer·ate** (i-vis′ə-rāt′), *v.t.* [-ATED, -ATING], [< L. pp. < *e-*, out + *viscera;* see VISCERA], 1. to remove the entrails from; disembowel. 2. to deprive of an essential part. **—e·vis′cer·a′tion,** *n.*

**ev·o·ca·ble** (ev′ə-kə-b'l), *adj.* that can be evoked.

**ev·o·ca·tion** (ev′ō-kā′shən), *n.* an evoking. **—e·voc·a·tive** (i-vok′ə-tiv, -vō′kə-), *adj.* **—ev′o·ca′tor** (-tẽr), *n.*

**e·voke** (i-vōk′), *v.t.* [EVOKED, EVOKING], [< Fr. < L. < *e-*, out + *vocare*, to call < *vox*, the voice], to call forth; summon; elicit, as a response, a mental image, etc. **—e·vok′er,** *n.*

**ev·o·lu·tion** (ev′ə-lo͞o′shən), *n.* [< L.; see EVOLVE], 1. an unfolding; process of development, formation, or growth. 2. a result of this; thing evolved. 3. a movement that is part of a series or pattern. 4. a setting free; giving off; emission. 5. in *biology*, *a)* the development of a species, organism, or organ from its original to its present state. *b)* the theory that all species of plants and animals developed from earlier forms by hereditary transmission of slight variations in successive generations: see also **natural selection.** 6. in *military & naval usage*, any of various maneuvers by which troops, ships, etc. change formation. **—ev′o·lu′tion·ar′y, ev′o·lu′tion·al,** *adj.* **—ev′o·lu′tion·al·ly,** *adv.*

**ev·o·lu·tion·ist** (ev′ə-lo͞o′shən-ist), *n.* one who believes in the theory of evolution. *adj.* 1. of the theory of evolution. 2. of evolutionists.

**e·volve** (i-volv′), *v.t.* [EVOLVED, EVOLVING], [< L. < *e-*, out + *volvere*, to roll], 1. to unfold; open out; develop gradually. 2. to set free or give off (gas, heat, etc.); emit. 3. to produce or change by evolution. *v.i.* 1. to develop gradually; become developed. 2. to unfold. **—e·volve′ment,** *n.* **—e·volv′er,** *n.*

**Ev·voi·a** (ev′ē-ə), *n.* a large Greek island in the Aegean: ancient name, *Euboea*.

**ewe** (ū; *dial.* yō), *n.* [AS. *eowu*], a female sheep.

**ew·er** (ū′ẽr), *n.* [< Anglo-Fr. < OFr. *ewere, aiguier*, < LL. < L. *aquarius*, for water < *aqua*, water], a large water pitcher with a wide mouth.

**ex** (eks), *prep.* [L.], in *business & finance*, without; exclusive of: as, *ex* dividend.

**ex-,** [< L. *ex* < Gr. *ex*, out, from], 1. a prefix meaning: *a) from, out*, as in *expel*. *b) beyond*, as in *excess*. *c) out of*, as in *expatriate*. *d) thoroughly*, as in *exterminate*. *e) upward*, as in *exalt*. It appears as *ef-* before *f; e-* before *b, d, g, h, l, m, n, r*, and *v;* and, often, *ec-* before *c* or *s*. 2. a prefix meaning *former, previously*, as in *ex-president, ex-convict*.

**ex-** (eks), exo-.

**Ex.,** Exodus.

**ex.,** 1. examined. 2. example. 3. except(ion).

**ex·ac·er·bate** (ig-zas′ẽr-bāt′, ik-sas′-), *v.t.* [-BATED, -BATING], [< L. pp.; ult. < ex-, intens. + *acerbus*, harsh, sour], 1. to make more intense or bitter; aggravate (disease, pain, etc.). 2. to exasperate; irritate. **—ex·ac′er·ba′tion,** *n.*

**ex·act** (ig-zakt′), *adj.* [< L. *exactus*, pp. of *exigere*, to measure < *ex-*, out + *agere*, to drive], 1. characterized by, requiring, or capable of accuracy of detail; methodical; correct. 2. leaving no room for error or doubt; precise. 3. strict; severe; rigorous. *v.t.* 1. to extort (with *from* or *of*). 2. to demand and get by authority or force (with *from* or *of*). 3. to require; make necessary. **—ex·act′a·ble,** *adj.* **—ex·act′er, ex·ac′tor** (-tẽr), *n.* **—ex·act′ness,** *n.*

**ex·act·ing** (ig-zak′tiŋ), *adj.* 1. making severe demands; tyrannical; not easily satisfied. 2. demanding great care, patience, effort, etc.; arduous. **—ex·act′ing·ly,** *adv.* **—ex·act′ing·ness,** *n.*

**ex·ac·tion** (ig-zak′shən), *n.* 1. an exacting. 2. an extortion. 3. something exacted, as a fee or tax.

**ex·act·i·tude** (ig-zak′tə-to͞od′, -tūd′), *n.* the quality of being exact; precision; accuracy.

**ex·act·ly** (ig-zakt′li), *adv.* in an exact manner; accurately; precisely: also used as an affirmative reply, equivalent to "I agree," "quite true."

**ex·ag·ger·ate** (ig-zaj′ə-rāt′), *v.t.* [-ATED, -ATING], [< L. pp. < *ex-*, out + *aggerare*, to heap up < *agger*, a heap], 1. to think, speak, or write of (something) as greater than it is; overstate. 2. to increase or enlarge to an abnormal degree. *v.i.* to give an exaggerated account. **—ex·ag′ger·at′ed·ly,** *adv.* **—ex·ag′ger·a′tion,** *n.* **—ex·ag′ger·a′tive** (-tiv), *adj.* **—ex·ag′ger·a′tor** (-tẽr), *n.*

**ex·alt** (ig-zôlt′), *v.t.* [< OFr. < L. *exaltare* < *ex-*, out, up + *altus*, high], 1. to lift up: obsolete in the physical sense. 2. to raise in status, dignity, power, wealth, etc. 3. to praise; glorify; extol. 4. to fill with joy, pride, fervor, etc.; elate. 5. to heighten or intensify the effect of (colors, etc.). **—ex·alt′ed·ly,** *adv.* **—ex·alt′er,** *n.*

**ex·al·ta·tion** (eg′zôl-tā′shən), *n.* 1. an exalting or being exalted. 2. elation; rapture.

**ex·am** (ig-zam′), *n.* [Colloq.], examination.

**exam.,** examination.

**ex·am·i·na·tion** (ig-zam′ə-nā′shən), *n.* 1. an examining or being examined; investigation; inquiry. 2. means or method of examining. 3. a set of questions asked or answers given in testing; test.

**ex·am·ine** (ig-zam′in), *v.t.* [-INED, -INING], [< OFr < L. < *examen*, tongue of a balance, examination] 1. to look at or into critically or methodically to find out the facts, physical condition, etc. of; investigate; inspect. 2. to test by questioning to find out the knowledge, skill, etc. of. **—ex·am′in·a·ble,** *adj.* **—ex·am′in·er,** *n.* **—ex·am′i·nee′,** *n.*

**ex·am·ple** (ig-zam′p'l, -zäm′-), *n.* [< OFr. < L. *exemplum* < *eximere*, to take out], 1. something selected to show the nature or character of the rest; sample. 2. a case that serves as a warning or caution. 3. a person or thing to be imitated; model. 4. a problem in mathematics, etc. that illustrates a principle or method. *v.t.* [-PLED, -PLING], [Obs. except in the passive], to exemplify. **—set an example,** to behave so as to be a pattern or model for others. **—without example,** having no precedent.

**ex·as·per·ate** (ig-zas′pə-rāt′), *v.t.* [-ATED, -ATING], [< L. pp. < *ex-*, out + *asperare*, to roughen < *asper*, rough], 1. to irritate or annoy very much; make angry; vex. 2. to intensify (a feeling, disease, etc.); aggravate. **—ex·as′per·at′er,** *n.* **—ex·as′per·at′ing·ly,** *adv.*

**ex·as·per·a·tion** (ig-zas′pə-rā′shən), *n.* an exasperating or being exasperated; great irritation or annoyance.

**Exc.,** Excellency.

**exc.,** 1. excellent. 2. except(ed). 3. exchange.

**Ex·cal·i·bur** (eks-kal′ə-bẽr), *n.* in *Arthurian legend*, King Arthur's sword.

**ex ca·the·dra** (eks kə-thē′drə, kath′i-), [L., lit. from the chair], with the authority of a rank or office: as, the Pope spoke *ex cathedra*.

**ex·ca·vate** (eks′kə-vāt′), *v.t.* [-VATED, -VATING], [< L. pp. < *ex-*, out + *cavare*, to make hollow < *cavus*, hollow], 1. to make a hole or cavity in, as by digging; hollow out. 2. to form by hollowing out, as a tunnel. 3. to uncover by digging; unearth. 4. to dig out; remove (earth, soil, etc.). **—ex′ca·va′tion,** *n.* **—ex′ca·va′tor,** *n.*

**ex·ceed** (ik-sēd′), *v.t.* [< OFr. < L. < *ex-*, out + *cedere*, to go], 1. to go or be beyond (a limit, measure, etc.). 2. to be more or greater than; surpass. *v.i.* to surpass others, as in a quality or quantity; be outstanding. **—ex·ceed′er,** *n.*

**ex·ceed·ing** (ik-sēd′iŋ), *adj.* surpassing; extraordinary; extreme. *adv.* [Archaic], extremely. **—ex·ceed′ing·ly,** *adv.*

**ex·cel** (ik-sel′), *v.i. & v.t.* [-CELLED, -CELLING], [< OFr. < L. < *ex-*, out of + *-cellere*, to rise], to be better or greater than (another or others).

**ex·cel·lence** (ek′s'l-əns), *n.* 1. the fact or condition of excelling; superiority. 2. something in which a person or thing excels; a particular virtue. 3. [E-], Excellency.

**ex·cel·len·cy** (ek′s'l-ən-si), *n.* [*pl.* -CIES], 1. [E-], a title of honor applied to various persons of high position, as an ambassador, bishop, etc. 2. [Archaic], excellence (in senses 1 & 2).

**ex·cel·lent** (ek′s'l-ənt), *adj.* unusually good of its

kind; of exceptional merit, virtue, etc. —**ex′cel·lent·ly,** *adv.*

**ex·cel·si·or** (ek-sel′si-ôr′; *for n.,* ik-sel′si-ẽr), *adj. & interj.* [L., compar. of *excelsus,* high < *excellere;* see EXCEL], higher; always upward. *n.* long, thin wood shavings used for packing or as stuffing in some upholstered furniture.

**ex·cept** (ik-sept′), *v.t.* [< Fr. < L. < *exceptus,* pp. < *ex-,* out + *capere,* to take], to leave out or take out; exclude; omit. *v.i.* to object; take exception. *prep.* leaving out; other than; but: as, everyone *except* John. *conj.* [Archaic], unless.

**ex·cept·ing** (ik-sep′tiŋ), *prep.* except; leaving out; but. *conj.* [Archaic], unless.

**ex·cep·tion** (ik-sep′shən), *n.* 1. an excepting or being excepted; exclusion. 2. a person or thing omitted or excluded; case to which a rule, principle, etc. does not apply. 3. a person or thing different from others of the same class. 4. an objection. —**take exception,** 1. to object. 2. to resent; feel offended. —**ex·cep′tion·less,** *adj.*

**ex·cep·tion·a·ble** (ik-sep′shən-ə-b′l), *adj.* liable to exception. —**ex·cep′tion·a·bly,** *adv.*

**ex·cep·tion·al** (ik-sep′shən-′l), *adj.* being an exception; unusual; extraordinary. —**ex·cep′tion·al·ly,** *adv.* —**ex·cep′tion·al·ness,** *n.*

**ex·cerpt** (ik-sũrpt′; *for n.,* ek′sẽrpt), *v.t.* [< L. pp. < *ex-,* out + *carpere,* to pick], to select or quote (passages from a book, etc.); make extracts from (a book, etc.); extract. *n.* a passage selected or quoted from a book, article, etc.; extract. —**ex·cerpt′i·ble,** *adj.* —**ex·cerp′tion,** *n.*

**ex·cess** (ik-ses′; *for adj., usually* ek′ses′), *n.* [< OFr. < L. pp. of *excedere;* see EXCEED], 1. action or conduct that goes beyond the usual, reasonable, or lawful limit. 2. intemperance; overindulgence. 3. an amount or quantity greater than is necessary, desirable, etc. 4. the amount or degree by which one thing is more than another; surplus. *adj.* more than usual; surplus. —**in excess of,** more than. —**to excess,** too much.

**ex·ces·sive** (ik-ses′iv), *adj.* characterized by excess; too much; immoderate. —**ex·ces′sive·ly,** *adv.* —**ex·ces′sive·ness,** *n.*

**ex·cess-prof·its tax** (ek′ses-prof′its), a tax on business profits that are greater than the average of profits over a certain period of years.

**exch.,** 1. exchange. 2. exchequer.

**ex·change** (iks-chānj′), *v.t.* [-CHANGED, -CHANGING], [< OFr. < LL. *excambiare;* see EX- & CHANGE], 1. *a*) to give or transfer (*for* another thing in return). *b*) to receive or give another thing for (something returned). 2. to interchange, as gifts. 3. to give up for a substitute or alternative: as, she *exchanged* honor for wealth. *v.i.* 1. to make an exchange; barter. 2. in *finance,* to pass in exchange. *n.* 1. a giving or taking of one thing for another; barter. 2. a reciprocal giving; interchange. 3. the substituting of one thing for another. 4. a thing given or received in exchange. 5. a place for exchanging; esp., a place where business is carried on by brokers, merchants, etc.: as, a stock *exchange.* 6. a central office, as one providing telephone communication in a community. 7. in *commerce & finance, a*) the payment of debts by negotiable drafts or bills of exchange. *b*) a bill of exchange. *c*) a fee paid for settling accounts or collecting a draft, bill of exchange, etc. *d*) an exchanging of a sum of money of one country for the equivalent in the money of another country. *e*) the rate of exchange; value of one currency in terms of the other. *adj.* 1. exchanged. 2. having to do with an exchange. —**ex·change′a·bil′i·ty,** *n.* —**ex·change′a·ble,** *adj.* —**ex·chang′er,** *n.*

**ex·cheq·uer** (iks-chek′ẽr, eks′chek-), *n.* [< OFr. < LL. *scaccarium,* chessboard: accounts of revenue were kept on a squared board], 1. [usually E-], the British state department in charge of the national revenue. 2. the funds in the national treasury. 3. a treasury. 4. money in one's possession; funds, finances.

**ex·cise** (ik-sīz′; *for n., also* ek′sīz), *n.* [prob. < MD. < OFr. < LL. < L. *ad-,* to + *census,* a tax], a tax on the manufacture, sale, or consumption of various commodities within a country, as liquor, tobacco, etc.: also **excise tax.** *v.t.* [-CISED, -CISING], to force payment of an excise from. —**ex·cis′a·ble,** *adj.*

**ex·cise** (ik-sīz′), *v.t.* [-CISED, -CISING], [< L. pp. of *excidere* < *ex-,* out + *caedere,* to cut], to cut out or away; remove, as a tumor. —**ex·cis′a·ble,** *adj.* —**ex·ci′sion** (-sizh′ən), *n.*

**ex·cise·man** (ik-sīz′mən), *n.* [*pl.* -MEN], in Great Britain, an official who collects excises.

**ex·cit·a·ble** (ik-sī′tə-b′l), *adj.* that can be excited; easily excited. —**ex·cit′a·bil′i·ty, ex·cit′a·ble·ness,** *n.* —**ex·cit′a·bly,** *adv.*

**ex·ci·ta·tion** (ek′sī-tā′shən, ek′si-), *n.* an exciting or being excited; excitement.

**ex·cite** (ik-sīt′), *v.t.* [-CITED, -CITING], [< OFr. < L. < *ex-,* out + pp. of *ciere,* to call], 1. to put into motion or activity; stir up; stimulate. 2. to arouse; provoke: as, she *excited* his jealousy. 3. to arouse the feelings or passions of: as, the news *excited* us. —**ex·cit′a·tive** (-tiv), **ex·cit′a·to′ry** (-tôr′i, -tō′ri), *adj.* —**ex·cit′ed,** *adj.* —**ex·cit′ed·ly,** *adv.* —**ex·cit′er,** *n.*

**ex·cite·ment** (ik-sīt′mənt), *n.* 1. an exciting or being excited; agitation. 2. that which excites.

**ex·cit·ing** (ik-sīt′iŋ), *adj.* causing excitement; stirring; thrilling. —**ex·cit′ing·ly,** *adv.*

**ex·claim** (iks-klām′), *v.i. & v.t.* [< Fr. < L. < *ex-,* out + *clamare,* to shout], to cry out; speak or say suddenly and vehemently, as in surprise, emotion, etc. —**ex·claim′er,** *n.*

**ex·cla·ma·tion** (eks′klə-mā′shən), *n.* 1. an exclaiming. 2. something exclaimed; interjection. —**ex·clam·a·to·ry** (iks-klam′ə-tôr′i, -tō′ri), *adj.*

**exclamation mark** (or **point**), a mark (!) used after a word or sentence in writing or printing to show surprise, strong emotion, etc.

**ex·clude** (iks-klo͞od′), *v.t.* [-CLUDED, -CLUDING], [< L. < *ex-,* out + *claudere,* to shut], 1. to refuse to admit, consider, etc.; shut out; reject; bar. 2. to put out; force out; expel. —**ex·clud′a·ble,** *adj.* —**ex·clud′er,** *n.*

**ex·clu·sion** (iks-klo͞o′zhən), *n.* 1. an excluding or being excluded. 2. a thing excluded. —**to the exclusion of,** so as to keep out, bar, etc.

**ex·clu·sive** (iks-klo͞o′siv), *adj.* 1. excluding all others; shutting out other considerations, happenings, etc.: as, *exclusive* terms. 2. having the tendency or power to exclude all others. 3. excluding all but what is specified. 4. not shared or divided; sole: as, an *exclusive* right. 5. excluding certain people or groups for social or economic reasons. 6. snobbish; undemocratic. —**exclusive of,** not including or allowing for. —**ex·clu′sive·ly,** *adv.* —**ex·clu′sive·ness,** *n.*

**ex·com·mu·ni·cate** (eks′kə-mū′nə-kāt′; *for adj. & n., also* -kit), *v.t.* [-CATED, -CATING], to cut off from communion with a church; exclude from membership in or the sacraments of a church by ecclesiastical authority. *adj.* excommunicated. *n.* an excommunicated person. —**ex′com·mu′ni·ca·ble,** *adj.* —**ex′com·mu′ni·ca′tion,** *n.* —**ex′com·mu′ni·ca′tive,** *adj.* —**ex′com·mu′ni·ca′tor** (-tẽr), *n.* —**ex′-com·mu′ni·ca·to′ry** (-tôr′i, -tō′ri), *adj.*

**ex·co·ri·ate** (ik-skôr′i-āt′, -skō′ri-), *v.t.* [-ATED, -ATING], [< L. pp. of *excoriare* < *ex-,* off + *corium,* the skin], 1. to strip, scratch, or peel off the skin of; abrade. 2. to denounce strongly. —**ex·co′ri·a′tion,** *n.* —**ex·co′ri·a′tor** (-tẽr), *n.*

**ex·cre·ment** (eks′krə-mənt), *n.* [< Fr. < L. < *excretus;* see EXCRETE], waste matter discharged from the bowels; feces. —**ex′cre·men′tal,** *adj.*

**ex·cres·cence** (iks-kres′′ns), *n.* [< L. < *ex-,* out + *crescere,* to grow], 1. a normal outgrowth, as fingernails, hair, etc. 2. an abnormal or disfiguring outgrowth, as a bunion. —**ex·cres′cent,** *adj.*

**ex·cres·cen·cy** (iks-kres′′n-si), *n.* 1. the condition of being excrescent. 2. [*pl.* -CIES], an excrescence.

**ex·cre·ta** (eks-krē′tə), *n.pl.* waste matter excreted from the body, as sweat, urine, or feces.

**ex·crete** (iks-krēt′), *v.t. & v.i.* [-CRETED, -CRETING], [< L. *excretus,* pp. < *ex-,* out of + *cernere,* to sift], to separate (waste matter) from the blood or tissue and eliminate from the body. —**ex·cre′tion,** *n.* —**ex·cre′tive,** *adj.*

**ex·cre·to·ry** (eks′kri-tôr′i, -tō′ri), *adj.* of or for excretion. *n.* an excretory organ.

**ex·cru·ci·ate** (iks-kro͞o′shi-āt′), *v.t.* [-ATED, -ATING], [< L. pp. < *ex-,* intens. + *cruciare,* to crucify < *crux,* a cross], 1. to torture; cause intense bodily pain to. 2. to subject to mental anguish; torment. —**ex·cru′ci·at′ing,** *adj.* —**ex·cru′ci·at′ing·ly,** *adv.* —**ex·cru′ci·a′tion,** *n.*

**ex·cul·pate** (eks′kəl-pāt′, ik-skul′pāt), *v.t.* [-PATED, -PATING], [< L. *ex,* out + pp. of *culpare,* to blame < *culpa,* fault], to free from blame; prove guiltless. —**ex·cul′pa·ble** (-pə-b′l), *adj.* —**ex′cul·pa′tion,** *n.* —**ex·cul′pa·to′ry** (-tôr′i, -tō′ri), *adj.*

**ex·cur·sion** (ik-skũr′zhən, -shən), *n.* [< L. *excursio* < *ex-,* out + *currere,* to run], 1. a short trip or journey, as for health or pleasure. 2. a round trip (on a train, bus, etc.) at special reduced rates. 3. a group taking such a trip. 4. a deviation or digression. 5. [Obs.], a military sortie; raid. *adj.* for an excursion. —**ex·cur′sion·ist,** *n.*

**ex·cur·sive** (ik-skũr′siv), *adj.* 1. having the character of an excursion. 2. rambling; desultory: as, *excursive* reading. 3. digressive; wandering. —**ex·cur′sive·ly,** *adv.* —**ex·cur′sive·ness,** *n.*

**ex·cuse** (ik-skūz′; *for n.,* -skūs′), *v.t.* [-CUSED, -CUSING], [< OFr. < L. *excusare* < *ex-*, from + *causa*, a charge], 1. to try to free (a person) of blame. 2. to try to minimize (a fault); apologize or give reasons for. 3. to disregard (an offense or fault); overlook: as, *excuse* my rudeness. 4. to release from an obligation, promise, etc. 5. to permit to leave. 6. to serve as explanation or justification for; justify; absolve. *n.* 1. a plea in defense of one's conduct; apology. 2. a release from obligation, duty, etc. 3. something that excuses; justifying factor. 4. a pretended reason; pretext; alibi. —**excuse oneself,** 1. to apologize. 2. to ask for permission to leave. —**ex·cus′a·ble,** *adj.* —**ex·cus′a·bly,** *adv.* —**ex·cus′er,** *n.*

**exec.,** 1. executive. 2. executor.

**ex·e·cra·ble** (ek′si-krə-b'l), *adj.* [L. *execrabilis*], abominable; detestable. —**ex′e·cra·bly,** *adv.*

**ex·e·crate** (ek′si-krāt′), *v.t.* [-CRATED, -CRATING], [< L. *execratus*, pp. < *ex-*, out + *sacrare*, to consecrate < *sacer*, sacred], 1. to call down evil upon; curse. 2. to loathe; detest; abhor. *v.i.* to curse. —**ex′e·cra′tion,** *n.* —**ex′e·cra′tive** (-tiv), *adj.* —**ex′e·cra′tor** (-tẽr), *n.* —**ex′e·cra·to′ry** (-krə-tôr′i), *adj.*

**ex·e·cute** (ek′si-kūt′), *v.t.* [-CUTED, -CUTING], [< OFr. < L. *executus*, pp. < *ex-*, out + *sequi*, to follow], 1. to carry out; do; perform; fulfill. 2. to carry into effect; administer (laws, etc.). 3. to put to death in accordance with a legally imposed sentence. 4. to create in accordance with an idea, plan, etc. 5. to perform (a piece of music, etc.). 6. in *law*, to make valid (a deed, contract, etc.), as by signing, sealing, and delivering. —**ex′e·cut′a·ble,** *adj.*

**ex·e·cu·tion** (ek′si-kū′shən), *n.* 1. an executing; a performing, administering, etc. 2. a putting to death in accordance with a legally imposed sentence. 3. *a*) the manner of doing or producing something. *b*) the manner of performing a piece of music, etc. 4. effective action, especially of a destructive nature: as, the bombs did heavy *execution.* 5. in *law*, a writ, issued by a court, giving authority to put a judgment into effect.

**ex·e·cu·tion·er** (ek′si-kū′shən-ẽr), *n.* one who carries out the death penalty imposed by a court.

**ex·ec·u·tive** (ig-zek′yoo-tiv), *adj.* 1. of or capable of carrying out duties, functions, etc.: as, *executive* ability. 2. empowered and required to administer (laws, government affairs, etc.). *n.* 1. a person, group, or branch of government empowered and required to administer the laws and affairs of a nation. 2. one whose function is to administer or manage affairs. —**ex·ec′u·tive·ly,** *adv.*

**Executive Mansion,** 1. the White House (in Washington, D.C.), official home of the President of the U.S. 2. the official home of the governor of a State.

**ex·ec·u·tor** (ek′si-kū′tẽr; *for 2,* ig-zek′yoo-), *n.* 1. a person who does something; performer of actions. 2. a person appointed to carry out the provisions of another's will. —**ex·ec′u·to′ri·al** (-tôr′i-əl, -tō′ri-), *adj.* —**ex·ec′u·trix** (-triks), [*pl.* -TRIXES, -TRICES (-zek′yoo-trī′sēz)], *n.fem.*

**ex·e·ge·sis** (ek′sə-jē′sis), *n.* [*pl.* -SES (-sēz)], [L. < Gr. < *ex-*, out + *hēgeisthai*, to guide], analysis or interpretation of a word, literary passage, etc., especially of the Bible. —**ex′e·get′ic** (-jet′ik), **ex′e·get′i·cal,** *adj.* —**ex′e·get′i·cal·ly,** *adv.*

**ex·em·plar** (ig-zem′plẽr, -plär), *n.* [< OFr. < LL. < L. *exemplum*, a pattern, copy], 1. a model; pattern; archetype. 2. a sample; specimen; example.

**ex·em·pla·ry** (ig-zem′plə-ri), *adj.* 1. serving as a model or example; worth imitating: as, *exemplary* behavior. 2. serving as a warning: as, *exemplary* punishment. 3. serving as a sample, etc.; typical. —**ex·em′pla·ri·ly,** *adv.* —**ex·em′pla·ri·ness,** *n.*

**exemplary damages,** in *law*, damages beyond the actual loss, imposed as a punishment.

**ex·em·pli·fy** (ig-zem′plə-fī′), *v.t.* [-FIED, -FYING], [< ML. < L. *exemplum*, an example + *facere*, to make], 1. to show by example; serve as an example of. 2. to make a certified copy of (a document, etc.) under seal. —**ex·em′pli·fi·ca′tion,** *n.*

‡**ex·em·pli gra·ti·a** (eg-zem′plī grā′shi-ə), [L.], for example; for instance: abbrev. **e.g.**

**ex·empt** (ig-zempt′), *v.t.* [< OFr. < L. *exemptus*, pp. < *ex-*, out + *emere*, to take], to free from a rule or obligation which others must observe; excuse; release. *adj.* freed from a rule, obligation, etc.; excused; released. *n.* an exempted person. —**exempt′i·ble,** *adj.* —**ex·emp′tion,** *n.*

**ex·er·cise** (ek′sẽr-sīz′), *n.* [< OFr. < L. < pp. of *exercere*, to drive out (farm animals to work) < *ex-*, out + *arcere*, to enclose], 1. active use or operation: as, the *exercise* of wit. 2. activity for training or developing the body or mind; esp., bodily exertion for the sake of health. 3. *usually in pl.* a series of movements to strengthen or develop some part of the body. 4. a problem or task to be worked out for developing some technical skill, as in mathematics. 5. *pl.* a program of speeches, etc., as at graduation. *v.t.* [-CISED, -CISING], 1. to use; employ: as, to *exercise* self-control. 2. to practice; train. 3. to put into action for the purpose of training or developing, as the body, mind, etc. 4. to take up the attention of; esp., to worry; perplex; trouble. 5. to perform (duties, etc.). 6. to exert or have (influence, control, etc.). *v.i.* to take exercise; do exercises. —**ex′er·cis′a·ble,** *adj.* —**ex′er·cis′er,** *n.*

**ex·ert** (ig-zũrt′), *v.t.* [< L. < *exerere*, to stretch out < *ex-*, out + *serere*, to join], exercise; put into action: as, *exert* your will. —**exert oneself,** to try or work hard. —**ex·er′tive,** *adj.*

**ex·er·tion** (ig-zũr′shən), *n.* 1. the act, fact, or process of exerting. 2. energetic activity; effort.

**ex·e·unt** (ek′si-ənt), [L.], they go off (the stage): a stage direction to actors.

**exeunt om·nes** (om′nēz), [L.], all (of the characters on stage) go off: a stage direction.

**ex·fo·li·ate** (eks-fō′li-āt′), *v.t. & v.i.* [-ATED, -ATING], [< LL. pp. of *exfoliare*, to strip of leaves < *ex-*, out + *folium*, a leaf], to cast or come off in flakes, scales, or layers, as skin, etc. —**ex·fo′li·a′tion,** *n.*

**ex·hale** (eks-hāl′, ig-zāl′), *v.i.* [-HALED, -HALING], [< Fr. < L. < *ex-*, out + *halare*, to breathe], 1. to breathe forth air. 2. to rise into the air as vapor; evaporate. *v.t.* 1. to breathe forth (air or smoke). 2. to give off (vapor, fumes, etc.). —**ex·ha·la·tion** (eks′hə-lā′shən, eg′zə-), *n.*

**ex·haust** (ig-zôst′), *v.t.* [< L. *exhaustus*, pp. < *ex-*, out + *haurire*, to draw], 1. to draw off or let out (air, gas, etc.), as from a container. 2. to use up; expend completely. 3. to empty completely; drain: as, they *exhausted* the well. 4. to drain of power, resources, etc. 5. to tire out; weaken. 6. to deal with or study completely and thoroughly: as, she has *exhausted* the subject. *v.i.* to be let out, as gas or steam from an engine. *n.* 1. a creating of an outflowing current of air by means of a partial vacuum. 2. the discharge of used steam, gas, etc. from the cylinders of an engine at the end of every working stroke of the pistons. 3. the pipe through which such steam, gas, etc. is released. 4. something discharged, as fumes from a gasoline engine. —**ex·haust′er,** *n.* —**ex·haust′i·bil′i·ty,** *n.* —**ex·haust′i·ble,** *adj.*

**ex·haus·tion** (ig-zôs′chən), *n.* 1. an exhausting. 2. the state of being exhausted; esp., *a*) great fatigue or weariness. *b*) complete consumption.

**ex·haus·tive** (ig-zôs′tiv), *adj.* exhausting or tending to exhaust; specif., leaving nothing out; complete; thorough. —**ex·haus′tive·ly,** *adv.* —**ex·haus′tive·ness,** *n.*

**ex·haust·less** (ig-zôst′lis), *adj.* that cannot be exhausted; inexhaustible. —**ex·haust′less·ly,** *adv.* —**ex·haust′less·ness,** *n.*

**ex·hib·it** (ig-zib′it), *v.t.* [< L. pp. of *exhibere* < *ex-*, out + *habere*, to hold, have], 1. to show; display. 2. to present to public view. 3. in *law*, to present (evidence, etc.) officially to a court. *v.i.* to put art objects, wares, etc. on public display. *n.* 1. a show; display. 2. an object or group of objects displayed publicly. 3. in *law*, an object produced as evidence in a court. —**ex·hib′i·tor** (-tẽr), **ex·hib′it·er,** *n.*

**ex·hi·bi·tion** (ek′sə-bish′ən), *n.* 1. an exhibiting or showing. 2. that which is shown. 3. a public show, as of art objects.

**ex·hi·bi·tion·ism** (ek′sə-bish′ən-iz′m), *n.* 1. a tendency to call attention to oneself or show off one's talents, skill, etc. 2. in *psychology*, a tendency to expose parts of the body that are conventionally concealed. —**ex′hi·bi′tion·ist,** *n.*

**ex·hil·a·rate** (ig-zil′ə-rāt′), *v.t.* [-RATED, -RATING], [< L. pp. of *exhilarare* < *ex-*, intens. + *hilaris*, glad], to make merry or lively; stimulate. —**ex·hil′a·rat′ing, ex·hil′a·ra·tive** (-tiv), *adj.* —**ex·hil′a·rat′ing·ly,** *adv.* —**ex·hil′a·ra′tion,** *n.*

**ex·hort** (ig-zôrt′), *v.t. & v.i.* [< L. < *ex-*, out + *hortari*, to urge], to urge earnestly by advice, warning, etc.; entreat. —**ex·hor·ta·tion** (eg'zôr-tā'shən, ek'sẽr-), *n.* —**ex·hor'ta·tive, ex·hor'ta·to'ry** (-tə-tôr'i, -tō'ri), *adj.* —**ex·hort'er,** *n.*

**ex·hume** (iks-hūm', ig-zūm'), *v.t.* [-HUMED, -HUMING], [< Fr. < ML. *exhumare* < L. *ex*, out + *humus*, the ground], 1. to dig out of the earth; disinter. 2. to reveal. —**ex·hu·ma·tion** (eks'hyoo-mā'shən), *n.*

**ex·i·gen·cy** (ek'sə-jən-si), *n.* [*pl.* -CIES], [see EXIGENT], 1. urgency. 2. a situation calling for immediate action or attention. 3. *pl.* pressing needs; demands; requirements: as, the *exigencies* of the situation. Also **ex'i·gence.**

**ex·i·gent** (ek'sə-jənt), *adj.* [< L. *exigens*, ppr. < *ex-*, out + *agere*, to drive], 1. calling for immediate action or attention; urgent. 2. requiring more than is reasonable; demanding; exacting.

**ex·ig·u·ous** (ig-zig'ū-əs, ik-sig'-), *adj.* [< L. < *exigere*, to weigh], scanty; little; small; meager. —**ex·i·gu·i·ty** (ek'sə-gū'ə-ti), *n.*

**ex·ile** (eg'zīl, ek'sīl), *n.* [< OFr. < L. *ex(s)ilium*, < *ex(s)ul*, an exile], 1. a prolonged, often enforced, living away from one's country, community, etc.; banishment, sometimes self-imposed. 2. a person in exile. *v.t.* (*also* ig-zīl'), [-ILED, -ILING], to force (a person) to leave his country, community, etc.; banish. —**ex·il·ic** (ig-zil'ik, ik-), *adj.*

**ex·ist** (ig-zist'), *v.i.* [< Fr. < L. < *ex-*, forth + *sistere* (< *stare*), to stand], 1. to be; have reality or actual being. 2. to occur; be present (*in*). 3. to continue being; live. —**ex·ist'ent,** *adj.*

**ex·ist·ence** (ig-zis'təns), *n.* 1. an existing; state or fact of being. 2. life; living; continuance of being. 3. occurrence. 4. a manner of existing. 5. a being; entity; thing that exists. —**ex'is·ten'tial** (-ten'shəl), *adj.*

**ex·is·ten·tial·ism** (eg'zis-ten'shəl-iz'm), *n.* a literary-philosophic cult popularized in France after World War II: it holds that man exists as an individual in a purposeless universe, and that he must oppose his hostile environment through exercise of his free will. —**ex'is·ten'tial·ist,** *n.*

**ex·it** (eg'zit, ek'sit), *n.* [< L. < *exitus*, pp. < *ex-*, out + *ire*, to go], 1. an actor's departure from the stage. 2. a going out; departure. 3. a way out. 4. [L., 3d pers. sing., pres. indic., of *exire*], he (or she) goes off (the stage): a stage direction.

‡**ex li·bris** (eks lī'bris, lē'-), [L.], 1. from the library of: an inscription on bookplates. 2. a bookplate. Abbrev. **ex lib.**

**ex·o-,** [< Gr. *exō*, without], a prefix meaning *outside, outer, outer part*: also **ex-.**

**ex·o·carp** (ek'sō-kärp'), *n.* [*exo-* + *-carp*], the outer layer of a ripened ovary or fruit; epicarp.

**Exod.,** Exodus.

**ex·o·dus** (ek'sə-dəs), *n.* [L. < Gr. < *ex-*, out + *hodos*, way], 1. a going out or forth; departure. 2. [E-], the departure of the Israelites from Egypt (with *the*). 3. [E-], the second book of the Old Testament, which describes this.

**ex of·fi·ci·o** (eks ə-fish'i-ō'), [L., lit., from office], by virtue of one's office, or position.

**ex·og·a·my** (eks-og'ə-mi), *n.* [*exo-* + *-gamy*], the custom of marrying only outside the tribe, clan, etc.; outbreeding. —**ex·og'a·mous** (-məs), **ex·o·gam·ic** (ek'sə-gam'ik), *adj.*

**ex·og·e·nous** (eks-oj'ə-nəs), *adj.* [*exo-* + *-genous*], 1. developing from without; originating externally. 2. in *biology*, growing or developing from or on the outside. —**ex·og'e·nous·ly,** *adv.*

**ex·on·er·ate** (ig-zon'ə-rāt'), *v.t.* [-ATED, -ATING], [< L. pp. < *ex-*, out + *onerare*, to load < *onus*, a burden], to free (a person) from a charge of guilt; declare or prove blameless. —**ex·on'er·a'tion,** *n.* —**ex·on'er·a'tive,** *adj.* —**ex·on'er·a'tor,** *n.*

**ex·oph·thal·mi·a** (ek'sof-thal'mi-ə), *n.* [< Gr. < *ex-*, out + *ophthalmos*, an eye], abnormal protrusion of the eyeball, caused by disease: also **ex'oph·thal'mos** (-mos), **ex'oph·thal'mus** (-məs). —**ex'oph·thal'mic,** *adj.*

**ex·or·bi·tant** (ig-zôr'bə-tənt), *adj.* [< L. ppr. of *exorbitare* < *ex-*, out + *orbita*, a track], going beyond what is reasonable, just, proper, usual, etc.; excessive; extravagant. —**ex·or'bi·tance, ex·or'bi·tan·cy** [*pl.* -CIES], *n.* —**ex·or'bi·tant·ly,** *adv.*

**ex·or·cise, ex·or·cize** (ek'sôr-sīz'), *v.t.* [-CISED or -CIZED, -CISING or -CIZING], [< OFr. < LL. < Gr. < *ex-*, out + *horkizein*, to make one swear < *horkos*, an oath], 1. to drive out (a supposed evil spirit) by ritual charms or incantation. 2. to free from such a spirit. —**ex'or·cis'er, ex'or·ciz'er,** *n.*

**ex·or·cism** (ek'sôr-siz'm), *n.* 1. an exorcising. 2. a verbal formula or ritual used in exorcising. —**ex'or·cist,** *n.*

**ex·or·di·um** (ig-zôr'di-əm, ik-sôr'-), *n.* [*pl.* -UMS, -A (-ə)], [L. < *ex-*, from + *ordiri*, to begin], 1. a beginning. 2. the opening part of a speech, treatise, etc. —**ex·or'di·al,** *adj.*

**ex·ot·ic** (ig-zot'ik), *adj.* [< L. < Gr. *exōtikos* < *exō*, outside], 1. foreign; imported. 2. strangely beautiful, enticing, etc. *n.* 1. a foreign or imported thing. 2. a plant that is not native. —**ex·ot'i·cal·ly,** *adv.* —**ex·ot'i·cism,** *n.*

**exp.,** 1. expenses. 2. export. 3. express.

**ex·pand** (ik-spand'), *v.t.* [< L. < *ex-*, out + *pandere*, to spread], 1. to spread out; open out; stretch out; unfold. 2. to increase in size, area, etc.; enlarge; dilate. 3. to enlarge upon (a topic, idea, etc.); develop in detail. *v.i.* to spread out, enlarge, swell, etc. —**ex·pand'er,** *n.*

**ex·panse** (ik-spans'), *n.* 1. a large, open area or unbroken surface; wide extent; great breadth. 2. expansion. 3. the amount of expansion.

**ex·pan·si·ble** (ik-span'sə-b'l), *adj.* that can be expanded. —**ex·pan'si·bil'i·ty,** *n.*

**ex·pan·sion** (ik-span'shən), *n.* 1. an expanding or being expanded; enlargement. 2. an expanded thing or part. 3. the extent or degree of expansion. 4. a development or full treatment, as of a topic.

**ex·pan·sive** (ik-span'siv), *adj.* 1. tending to expand; that can expand. 2. of, or working by means of, expansion. 3. broad; extensive; comprehensive. 4. sympathetic; demonstrative: as, an *expansive* person. —**ex·pan'sive·ly,** *adv.* —**ex·pan'sive·ness,** *n.*

**ex·pa·ti·ate** (ik-spā'shi-āt'), *v.i.* [-ATED, -ATING], [< L. pp. of *ex(s)patiari*, to wander < *ex-*, out + *spatium*, space], to speak or write at length (*on* or *upon*). —**ex·pa'ti·a'tion,** *n.* —**ex·pa'ti·a'tor,** *n.*

**ex·pa·tri·ate** (eks-pā'tri-āt'; *for adj. & n., also* -it), *v.t.* [-ATED, -ATING], [< L. *ex*, out of + *patria*, fatherland < *pater*, father], to exile or banish. *adj.* expatriated. *n.* an expatriated person. —**ex·pa'tri·a'tion,** *n.*

**ex·pect** (ik-spekt'), *v.t.* [< L. < *ex-*, out + *spectare*, to look], 1. to look forward to; look for as likely to occur or appear; anticipate. 2. to look for as due, proper, or necessary: as, you *expect* too much from the child. 3. [Colloq.], to suppose; presume; guess. —**be expecting,** [Colloq.], to be pregnant.

**ex·pect·an·cy** (ik-spek'tən-si), *n.* [*pl.* -CIES], 1. an expecting or being expected; expectation. 2. that which is expected, especially on a statistical basis: as, life *expectancy*. Also **ex·pect'ance.**

**ex·pect·ant** (ik-spek'tənt), *adj.* 1. expecting; specif., *a*) having or showing expectation. *b*) waiting, as for a position. *n.* a person who expects something. —**ex·pect'ant·ly,** *adv.*

**expectant mother,** a pregnant woman.

**ex·pec·ta·tion** (ek'spek-tā'shən), *n.* 1. a looking forward to; anticipation. 2. a looking for as due, proper, or necessary. 3. a thing looked forward to. 4. *also pl.* a reason or warrant for looking forward to something; prospect. —**in expectation,** in the state of being looked for.

**ex·pec·to·rant** (ik-spek'tə-rənt), *adj.* causing or stimulating expectoration. *n.* any expectorant medicine.

**ex·pec·to·rate** (ik-spek'tə-rāt'), *v.t. & v.i.* [-RATED, -RATING], [< L. pp. < *ex-*, out + *pectus*, breast], 1. to cough up and spit (phlegm, mucus, etc.). 2. to spit. —**ex·pec'to·ra'tion,** *n.*

**ex·pe·di·en·cy** (ik-spē'di-ən-si), *n.* [*pl.* -CIES], 1. the quality or state of being expedient; suitability for a given purpose. 2. the doing or consideration of what is selfish rather than what is right or just; self-interest. Also **ex·pe'di·ence.**

**ex·pe·di·ent** (ik-spē'di-ənt), *adj.* [< OFr. < L. ppr. of *expedire*; see EXPEDITE], 1. useful for effecting a desired result; suited to the circumstances; convenient. 2. based on what is of personal use or advantage rather than what is right or just; guided by self-interest. *n.* an expedient thing; means to an end. —**ex·pe'di·ent·ly,** *adv.*

**ex·pe·dite** (ek'spi-dīt'), *v.t.* [-DITED, -DITING], [< L. pp. of *expedire*, lit., to free one caught by the feet < *ex-*, out + *pes*, foot], 1. to speed up or make easy the progress or action of; facilitate. 2. to do quickly. 3. [Rare], to dispatch.

**ex·pe·dit·er** (ek'spi-dīt'ẽr), *n.* a person who expedites; esp., one employed, as in industry, to expedite urgent or involved projects.

**ex·pe·di·tion** (ek'spi-dish'ən), *n.* [Fr. < L.; see EXPEDITE], 1. a sending forth or embarking upon a voyage, march, etc., as for exploration or battle. 2. such a journey. 3. the people, ships, etc. participating. 4. efficient speed; dispatch.

**ex·pe·di·tion·ar·y** (ek'spi-dish'ən-er'i), *adj.* of or constituting an expedition.

**ex·pe·di·tious** (ek'spi-dish'əs), *adj.* efficient and speedy; prompt. —**ex'pe·di'tious·ly,** *adv.*

**ex·pel** (ik-spel′), *v.t.* [-PELLED, -PELLING], [< L. < *ex-*, out + *pellere*, to thrust], 1. to drive out by force; make leave; eject. 2. to dismiss or send away by authority: as, *expelled* from school. —**ex·pel′la·ble,** *adj.* —**ex·pel′ler,** *n.*

**ex·pend** (ik-spend′), *v.t.* [< L. *expendere*, to pay out < *ex-*, out + *pendere*, to weigh], to spend; consume by using; use up. —**ex·pend′er,** *n.*

**ex·pend·a·ble** (ik-spen′də-b'l), *adj.* 1. that can be expended. 2. in *military usage*, designating equipment (and hence, men) expected to be used up (or sacrificed) in service.

**ex·pend·i·ture** (ik-spen′di-chẽr), *n.* 1. an expending; using up of money, time, etc. 2. the amount of money, time, etc. expended.

**ex·pense** (ik-spens′), *n.* [< Anglo-Fr. < LL. *expensa* (*pecunia*), paid out (money) < L.; see EXPEND], 1. an expending of money. 2. *also in pl.* cost; fee; charge. 3. *pl.* *a*) charges met with in carrying out one's work, etc. *b*) money to pay for these charges. 4. a cause of spending. 5. loss; sacrifice. —**at the expense of,** 1. with the payment borne by. 2. with the loss of.

**ex·pen·sive** (ik-spen′siv), *adj.* necessitating or involving much expense; costly; high-priced. —**ex·pen′sive·ly,** *adv.* —**ex·pen′sive·ness,** *n.*

**ex·pe·ri·ence** (ik-spêr′i-əns), *n.* [< OFr. < L. < ppr. of *experiri*, to try < *ex-*, out + base of *peritus*, experienced], 1. an actual living through an event or events. 2. anything or everything observed or lived through. 3. effect on one of anything or everything that has happened to him. 4. *a*) activity that includes training and personal participation. *b*) the period of such activity. 5. knowledge, skill, or practice resulting from this. *v.t.* [-ENCED, -ENCING], to have experience of; undergo.

**ex·pe·ri·enced** (ik-spêr′i-ənst), *adj.* 1. having had much experience. 2. having learned from experience; made wise or competent by experience.

**ex·pe·ri·en·tial** (ik-spêr′i-en′shəl), *adj.* of or based on experience. —**ex·pe′ri·en′tial·ly,** *adv.*

**ex·per·i·ment** (ik-sper′ə-mənt), *n.* [< OFr. < L. *experimentum* < *experiri;* see EXPERIENCE], 1. any action or process undertaken to discover something not yet known or to demonstrate or test something known. 2. the conducting of such tests or trials. *v.i.* to make an experiment. —**ex·per′i·ment′er,** *n.*

**ex·per·i·men·tal** (ik-sper′ə-men′t'l, ek′sper-), *adj.* 1. of or based on experience rather than theory or authority. 2. based on, tested by, or having the nature of, experiment. 3. of or used for an experiment or experiments. —**ex·per′i·men′tal·ism,** *n.* —**ex·per′i·men′tal·ly,** *adv.*

**ex·per·i·men·ta·tion** (ik-sper′ə-men-tā′shən), *n.* an experimenting; using experiments.

**ex·pert** (ek′spẽrt; *also, for adj.,* ik-spũrt′), *adj.* [< OFr. < L. *expertus*, pp. of *experiri;* see EXPERIENCE], 1. very skillful; having much training and knowledge in some special field. 2. of or from an expert. *n.* one who is very skillful or highly trained and informed in some special field. —**ex·pert′ly,** *adv.* —**ex·pert′ness,** *n.*

**ex·pert·ise** (ek′spẽr-tēz′), *n.* [Fr.], the skill or knowledge of an expert.

**ex·pi·ate** (ek′spi-āt′), *v.t.* [-ATED, -ATING], [< L. pp. < *ex-*, out + *piare*, to appease < *pius*, devout], to make amends or reparation for (wrongdoing or guilt); atone for. —**ex′pi·a·ble** (-ə-b'l), *adj.* —**ex′pi·a′tion,** *n.* —**ex′pi·a′tor,** *n.*

**ex·pi·a·to·ry** (ek′spi-ə-tôr′i, -tō′ri), *adj.* expiating; intended or serving to expiate.

**ex·pi·ra·tion** (ek′spə-rā′shən), *n.* 1. a breathing out, as of air from the lungs. 2. something breathed out. 3. a breathing one's last; dying; hence, 4. a coming to an end; close. —**ex·pir·a·to·ry** (ik-spīr′ə-tôr′i, -tō′ri), *adj.*

**ex·pire** (ik-spīr′), *v.t.* [-PIRED, -PIRING], [< Fr. < L. < *ex-*, out + *spirare*, to breathe], to breathe out, as air. *v.i.* 1. to breathe out air from the lungs. 2. to breathe one's last breath; die. 3. to come to an end; terminate. —**ex·pir′er,** *n.*

**ex·plain** (iks-plān′), *v.t.* [< L. < *ex-*, out + *planare*, to make level < *planus*, level], 1. to make plain or understandable. 2. to give the meaning or interpretation of; expound. 3. to account for; state reasons for. *v.i.* to give an explanation. —**explain away,** to state reasons for so as to justify. —**explain oneself,** 1. to make clear what one means. 2. to give reasons explaining one's conduct. —**ex·plain′a·ble,** *adj.* —**ex·plain′er,** *n.*

**ex·pla·na·tion** (eks′plə-nā′shən), *n.* 1. an explaining. 2. something that explains. 3. the interpretation, meaning, etc. given in explaining.

**ex·plan·a·to·ry** (iks-plan′ə-tôr′i, -tō′ri), *adj.* explaining. —**ex·plan′a·to′ri·ly,** *adv.*

**ex·ple·tive** (eks′pli-tiv), *n.* [< LL. < L. *expletus*, pp. < *ex-*, out + *plere*, to fill], 1. an oath or exclamation. 2. a word, phrase, etc. used merely to fill out a sentence or metrical line. *adj.* used to fill out a sentence, line, etc.: also **ex′ple·to′ry** (-tôr′i, -tō′ri).

**ex·pli·ca·ble** (eks′pli-kə-b'l, iks-plik′ə-), *adj.* that can be explained. —**ex′pli·ca·ble·ness,** *n.*

**ex·pli·cate** (eks′pli-kāt′), *v.t.* [-CATED, -CATING], [< L. *explicatus*, pp. < *ex-*, out + *plicare*, to fold], to make clear or explicit (something obscure or implied); explain. —**ex′pli·ca′tion,** *n.*

**ex·plic·it** (iks-plis′it), *adj.* [< L. *explicitus*, pp.; see EXPLICATE], 1. clearly stated; distinctly expressed; definite. 2. saying what is meant, without reservation; outspoken. —**ex·plic′it·ly,** *adv.* —**ex·plic′it·ness,** *n.*

**ex·plode** (iks-plōd′), *v.t.* [-PLODED, -PLODING], [orig., to drive off the stage by clapping and hooting < L. < *ex-*, off + *plaudere*, to applaud], 1. to discredit; expose as false: as, that theory is *exploded*. 2. to make burst with a loud noise; detonate. *v.i.* 1. to burst noisily and violently. 2. to break forth noisily: as, he *exploded* with anger. —**ex·plod′er,** *n.*

**ex·ploit** (eks′ploit, iks-ploit′), *n.* [< OFr. < L. < *explicare;* see EXPLICATE], an act remarkable for brilliance or daring; bold deed. *v.t.* (iks-ploit′), 1. to make use of; utilize. 2. to make unethical use of for one's own advantage or profit. —**ex·ploit′a·ble,** *adj.* —**ex′ploi·ta′tion,** *n.* —**ex·ploit′a·tive,** *adj.* —**ex·ploit′er,** *n.*

**ex·plo·ra·tion** (eks′plô-rā′shən), *n.* an exploring; specif., a traveling for purposes of discovery in regions previously unknown or little known. —**ex·plor·a·to·ry** (iks-plôr′ə-tôr′i), **ex·plor′a·tive,** *adj.*

**ex·plore** (iks-plôr′, -plōr′), *v.t.* [-PLORED, -PLORING], [< L. *explorare*, to search out < *ex-*, out + *plorare*, to cry out], 1. to look into closely; investigate. 2. to travel in (a region previously unknown or little known) for discovery. 3. in *medicine*, to examine (an organ, etc.). *v.i.* to make explorations. —**ex·plor′er,** *n.*

**ex·plo·sion** (iks-plō′zhən), *n.* 1. an exploding; esp., a blowing up; detonation. 2. the noise made by exploding. 3. a noisy outburst.

**ex·plo·sive** (iks-plō′siv), *adj.* 1. of, causing, or having the nature of, an explosion. 2. tending to explode; esp., tending to burst forth noisily. 3. plosive. *n.* 1. a substance that can explode, as gunpowder. 2. a plosive. —**ex·plo′sive·ly,** *adv.* —**ex·plo′sive·ness,** *n.*

**ex·po·nent** (ik-spō′nənt), *adj.* [< L. ppr. of *exponere;* see EXPOUND], expounding; interpreting. *n.* 1. one who expounds, or interprets. 2. a person or thing that is an example or symbol (*of* something). 3. in *algebra*, a small figure or symbol placed at the upper right of another figure or symbol to show how many times the latter is to be multiplied by itself (e.g., $b^2 = b \times b$). —**ex·po·nen·tial** (ek′spō-nen′shəl), *adj.* —**ex′po·nen′tial·ly,** *adv.*

**ex·port** (ik-spôrt′, -spōrt′; *also, and for n. & adj. always,* ek′spôrt), *v.t.* [< L. < *ex-*, out + *portare*, to carry], to carry or send (goods, etc.) from one country to another, especially for purposes of sale. *n.* 1. an exporting. 2. something exported. Also **ex′por·ta′tion.** *adj.* of exporting or exports; for export. —**ex·port′a·ble,** *adj.* —**ex·port′er,** *n.*

**ex·pose** (ik-spōz′), *v.t.* [-POSED, -POSING], [< OFr.; prob. < L. pp. of *exponere* (see EXPOUND)], 1. *a*) to lay open (*to* danger, attack, ridicule, etc.); leave unprotected. *b*) to make accessible or subject (*to* an influence or action). 2. to allow to be seen; reveal; exhibit 3. *a*) to make (a crime, fraud, etc.) known; unmask. *b*) to make known the crimes, etc. of. 4. in *photography*, to subject (a sensitized film or plate) to the action of actinic rays.— **ex·pos′er,** *n.*

**ex·po·sé** (ek′spō-zā′), *n.* [Fr., pp. of *exposer*], a public disclosure of a scandal, crime, etc.

**ex·po·si·tion** (ek′spə-zish′ən), *n.* [< OFr. < L. < *exponere;* see EXPOUND], 1. a setting forth of facts, ideas, etc.; detailed explanation. 2. writing or speaking that sets forth or explains. 3. a large public exhibition or show.

**ex·pos·i·tor** (ik-spoz′ə-tẽr), *n.* a person, piece of writing, etc. that expounds or explains.

**ex·pos·i·to·ry** (ik-spoz′ə-tôr′i, -tō′ri), *adj.* of, containing, or having the nature of, exposition; explanatory: also **ex·pos′i·tive** (-tiv).

**ex post fac·to** (eks pōst fak′tō), [L., from the (thing) done afterward], done or made after something, but having retroactive effect.

**ex·pos·tu·late** (ik-spos′chə-lāt′), *v.i.* [-LATED, -LATING], [< L. pp. < *ex-*, intens. + *postulare*, to demand], to reason with a person earnestly, objecting to his actions or intentions; remonstrate (with). **—ex·pos′tu·la′tion,** *n.* **—ex·pos′tu·la′tor,** *n.* **—ex·pos′tu·la·to′ry** (-lə-tôr′i, -tō′ri), *adj.*

**ex·po·sure** (ik-spō′zhẽr), *n.* 1. an exposing or being exposed (in various senses). 2. a location, as of a house, in relation to the sun, winds, etc.: as, an eastern *exposure*. 3. *a*) a section of a film for taking one photograph. *b*) the time during which a film or plate is exposed.

**ex·pound** (ik-spound′), *v.t.* [< OFr. < L. < *ex-*, out + *ponere*, to put], 1. to set forth; state in detail. 2. to explain; interpret. **—ex·pound′er,** *n.*

**ex·press** (iks-pres′), *v.t.* [< OFr. < L. < *ex*, out + *pressare;* see PRESS], 1. to press out or squeeze out (juice, etc.). 2. to put into words; state. 3. to make known; reveal; show: as, his face *expressed* sorrow. 4. to show by a sign; symbolize; signify. 5. to send by express. *adj.* 1. expressed and not implied; explicit. 2. exact. 3. for a definite or special purpose. 4. fast, direct, and making few stops: as, an *express* train. 5. characterized by speed or velocity; specif., *a*) for fast driving: as, an *express* highway. *b*) having to do with express (transportation system). *adv.* by express. *n.* 1. a message delivered by a special messenger. 2. an express train, bus, truck, etc. 3. a method or service for transporting goods or sending money rapidly: express is usually more expensive and faster than freight. 4. the things sent by express. 5. any method or means of swift transmission. **—express oneself,** 1. to state one's thoughts. 2. to give expression to one's feelings, talents, imagination, etc. **—ex·press′er,** *n.* **—ex·press′i·ble,** *adj.*

**ex·press·age** (iks-pres′ij), *n.* 1. the carrying of packages, etc. by express. 2. the charge for this.

**ex·pres·sion** (iks-presh′ən), *n.* 1. a pressing out or squeezing out, as of juice. 2. a putting into words; stating. 3. a manner of expressing; esp., a meaningful and eloquent manner of speaking, singing, etc. 4. a particular word or phrase: as, an idiomatic *expression*. 5. a showing of feeling, character, etc.: as, laughter is often the *expression* of joy. 6. a look, intonation, etc. that conveys meaning or feeling: as, a quizzical *expression*. 7. a symbol or set of symbols expressing some algebraic fact. 8. a showing by a symbol, sign, etc. **—ex·pres′sion·less,** *adj.*

**ex·pres·sion·ism** (iks-presh′ən-iz′m), *n.* an early 20th-century movement in the arts, especially in drama, characterized by the use of symbols, stereotyped characters, stylization, etc. to give objective expression to inner experience. **—ex·pres′sion·ist,** *adj. & n.* **—ex·pres′sion·is′tic,** *adj.* **—ex·pres′sion·is′ti·cal·ly,** *adv.*

**ex·pres·sive** (iks-pres′iv), *adj.* 1. of or characterized by expression. 2. expressing; indicating: as, a song *expressive* of joy. 3. full of expression: as, an *expressive* nod. **—ex·pres′sive·ly,** *adv.* **—ex·pres′sive·ness,** *n.*

**ex·press·ly** (iks-pres′li), *adv.* 1. plainly; definitely; explicitly. 2. especially; on purpose.

**ex·press·man** (iks-pres′mən), *n.* [*pl.* -MEN], a person employed by an express company; esp., a driver of an express truck.

**ex·press·way** (iks-pres′wā′), *n.* a highway for high-speed traffic, usually of limited access.

**ex·pro·pri·ate** (eks-prō′pri-āt′), *v.t.* [-ATED, -ATING], [< ML. pp. of *expropriare* < L. *ex*, out + *proprius*, one's own], 1. to take (land, property, etc.) from its owner, especially for public use. 2. to deprive of ownership; dispossess. **—ex·pro′pri·a′tion,** *n.* **—ex·pro′pri·a′tor** (-tẽr), *n.*

**ex·pul·sion** (ik-spul′shən), *n.* 1. an expelling; forcing out. 2. the fact or state of being expelled. **—ex·pul′sive,** *adj.*

**ex·punge** (ik-spunj′), *v.t.* [-PUNGED, -PUNGING], [< L. < *ex-*, out + *pungere*, to prick], to blot, wipe, or strike out; erase. **—ex·pung′er,** *n.*

**ex·pur·gate** (ek′spẽr-gāt′), *v.t.* [-GATED, -GATING], [< L. pp. < *ex-*, out + *purgare*, to cleanse], to remove passages considered obscene or otherwise objectionable from (a book, etc.). **—ex′pur·ga′tion,** *n.* **—ex′pur·ga′tor** (-tẽr), *n.* **—ex·pur′ga·to′ry** (-gə-tôr′i, -tō′ri), *adj.*

**ex·qui·site** (eks′kwi-zit, ik-skwiz′it), *adj.* [< L. pp. of *exquirere*, to search out < *ex-*, out + *quaerere*, to ask], 1. carefully done or elaborately made. 2. very beautiful, especially in a delicate or carefully wrought way. 3. of highest quality; admirable. 4. highly sensitive; keenly discriminating: as, an *exquisite* ear for music. 5. intense; keen: as, *exquisite* pain. *n.* one who makes a great show of being refined and fastidious about his appearance, etc. **—ex′qui·site·ly,** *adv.* **—ex′qui·site·ness,** *n.*

**ext.,** 1. extension. 2. external(ly). 3. extinct. 4. extra. 5. extract.

**ex·tant** (ek′stənt, ik-stant′), *adj.* [< L. *ex(s)tans*, ppr. < *ex-*, out + *stare*, to stand], still existing.

**ex·tem·po·ra·ne·ous** (ik-stem′pə-rā′ni-əs), *adj.* [< LL. < L. *ex*, out + *tempus*, time], 1. made, done, or spoken with no preparation or with little advance thought; offhand: cf. **impromptu.** 2. speaking without preparation. 3. made for the occasion; improvised: as, an *extemporaneous* fireplace. **—ex·tem′po·ra′ne·ous·ly,** *adv.*

**ex·tem·po·rar·y** (ik-stem′pə-rer′i), *adj.* extemporaneous. **—ex·tem′po·rar′i·ly,** *adv.* **—ex·tem′po·rar′i·ness,** *n.*

**ex·tem·po·re** (ik-stem′pə-ri, -rē′), *adv. & adj.* [L. < *ex*, out of + *tempore*, abl. of *tempus*, time], without preparation; offhand; impromptu.

**ex·tem·po·rize** (ik-stem′pə-rīz′), *v.i. & v.t.* [-RIZED, -RIZING], to speak, perform, or compose extempore, or without preparation; improvise. **—ex·tem′po·ri·za′tion,** *n.* **—ex·tem′po·riz′er,** *n.*

**ex·tend** (ik-stend′), *v.t.* [< L. < *ex-*, out + *tendere*, to stretch], 1. to stretch out or draw out; to prolong; continue. 2. to enlarge in area, scope, influence, etc.; expand; spread. 3. to stretch forth; hold out. 4. to offer; accord; grant. 5. to straighten out, as an arm or leg: opposed to *flex*. *v.i.* to be extended. **—ex·tend′ed,** *adj.* **—ex·tend′ed·ly,** *adv.* **—ex·tend′ed·ness,** *n.* **—ex·tend′er,** *n.* **—ex·tend′i·ble,** *adj.*

**ex·ten·si·ble** (ik-sten′sə-b'l), *adj.* that can be extended. **—ex·ten′si·bil′i·ty, ex·ten′si·ble·ness,** *n.*

**ex·ten·sion** (ik-sten′shən), *n.* 1. an extending or being extended. 2. extent; range. 3. an extended part; continuation; addition: as, an *extension* to a factory. 4. a branch of a university away from the university proper. 5. an extra telephone on the same line as the main telephone. 6. in *physics*, that property of a body by which it occupies space. **—ex·ten′sion·al,** *adj.*

**ex·ten·sive** (ik-sten′siv), *adj.* 1. having great extent; covering a large area; vast. 2. having a wide scope, effect, influence, etc.; far-reaching. 3. of or characterized by extension. 4. in *agriculture*, using large areas of land. **—ex·ten′sive·ly,** *adv.* **—ex·ten′sive·ness,** *n.*

**ex·ten·sor** (ik-sten′sẽr), *n.* a muscle that extends or straightens some part of the body, especially an arm or leg: opposed to *flexor*.

**ex·tent** (ik-stent′), *n.* 1. the space, amount, or degree to which a thing extends; size; length; breadth. 2. scope; limits; comprehensiveness. 3. an extended space; vast area.

**ex·ten·u·ate** (ik-sten′ū-āt′), *v.t.* [-ATED, -ATING], [< L. pp. < *ex-*, out + *tenuare*, to make thin < *tenuis*, thin], 1. to diminish; weaken. 2. to lessen or seem to lessen the seriousness of (an offense, guilt, etc.) by giving excuses or serving as an excuse. **—ex·ten′u·a′tion,** *n.* **—ex·ten′u·a′tive,** *adj.* **—ex·ten′u·a′tor,** *n.*

**ex·te·ri·or** (ik-stêr′i-ẽr), *adj.* [L., compar. of *exterus*, on the outside; see EXTERNAL], 1. outer; outermost; on the outside. 2. acting or coming from without; as, *exterior* forces. 3. foreign; of foreign affairs. *n.* 1. an outside or outside surface. 2. an outward appearance: as, a misleading *exterior*. **—ex·te′ri·or·ly,** *adv.*

**exterior angle,** any of the four angles formed on the outside of two straight lines by a straight line cutting across them.

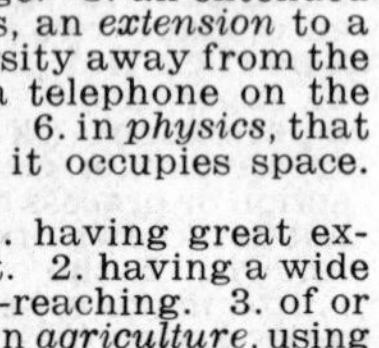

EXTERIOR ANGLES (CEL, LER, ADT, TDF)

**ex·ter·mi·nate** (ik-stũr′mə-nāt′), *v.t.* [-NATED, -NATING], [< L. pp. of *exterminare*, to drive out, destroy < *ex-*, out + *terminus*, a boundary], to destroy entirely; wipe out; annihilate. **—ex·ter′mi·na′tion,** *n.* **—ex·ter′mi·na′tive,** *adj.*

**ex·ter·mi·na·tor** (ik-stũr′mə-nā′tẽr), *n.* a person or thing that exterminates; esp., *a*) one whose work is exterminating rats, insects, and other vermin. *b*) any preparation for exterminating vermin.

**ex·ter·nal** (ik-stũr′n'l), *adj.* [< L. *externus* < *exter(us)*, on the outside, compar. form < *ex*, out of], 1. on the outside; outer; exterior. 2. on, or for use on, the outside of the body: as, a medicine for *external* use only. 3. outwardly visible; existing apart from the mind. 4. acting or coming from without. 5. for outward appearance or show;

superficial. 6. having to do with foreign countries and international affairs. *n.* 1. an outside or outward surface or part. 2. *pl.* outward appearance or behavior. —**ex′ter·nal′i·ty** (-nal′i-ti), [*pl.* -TIES], *n.* —**ex·ter′nal·ly,** *adv.*

**ex·ter·nal·ize** (ik-stũr′n'l-īz′), *v.t.* [-IZED, -IZING], to make or regard as external. —**ex·ter′nal·i·za′tion,** *n.*

**ex·tinct** (ik-stiŋkt′), *adj.* [< L. pp. of *ex(s)tinguere;* see EXTINGUISH], 1. having died down or gone out: as, an *extinct* fire. 2. no longer in existence.

**ex·tinc·tion** (ik-stiŋk′shən), *n.* 1. a putting out or being put out; extinguishing. 2. the fact or state of being or becoming extinct. 3. a destroying or being destroyed; annihilation.

**ex·tin·guish** (ik-stiŋ′gwish), *v.t.* [< L. *ex(s)tinguere;* prob. < *ex-,* intens. + *ting(u)ere,* to wet], 1. to put out (a fire, etc.); quench. 2. to put an end to; destroy. 3. to eclipse; obscure: as, her beauty *extinguished* all others. —**ex·tin′guish·a·ble,** *adj.* —**ex·tin′guish·er,** *n.* —**ex·tin′guish·ment,** *n.*

**ex·tir·pate** (ek′stēr-pāt′, ik-stũr′pāt), *v.t.* [-PATED, -PATING], [< L. pp. of *ex(s)tirpare* < *ex-,* out + *stirps,* root], 1. to pull up by the roots. 2. to destroy completely; abolish. —**ex′tir·pa′tion,** *n.* —**ex′tir·pa′tive,** *adj.* —**ex′tir·pa′tor** (-tẽr), *n.*

**ex·tol, ex·toll** (ik-stōl′, -stol′), *v.t.* [-TOLLED, -TOLLING], [< L. < *ex-,* up + *tollere,* to raise], to praise highly; laud. —**ex·tol′ler,** *n.* —**ex·tol′ment, ex·toll′ment,** *n.*

**ex·tort** (ik-stôrt′), *v.t.* [< L. *extortus,* pp. < *ex-,* out + *torquere,* to twist], to get (money, etc.) by violence, threats, misuse of authority, etc.; exact or wrest (*from*). —**ex·tort′er,** *n.* —**ex·tor′tive,** *adj.*

**ex·tor·tion** (ik-stôr′shən), *n.* 1. an extorting: sometimes applied to the exaction of too high a price. 2. something extorted. —**ex·tor′tion·ate, ex·tor′tion·ar′y,** *adj.*

**ex·tor·tion·er** (ik-stôr′shən-ẽr), *n.* a person guilty of extortion: also **ex·tor′tion·ist.**

**ex·tra** (eks′trə), *adj.* [contr. < *extraordinary;* also < L. < *extra, adv.,* more than, outside], more, larger, or better than what is normal, expected, necessary, etc.; additional. *n.* an extra person or thing; specif., *a*) *often in pl.* an additional charge. *b*) a special edition of a newspaper, covering news of unusual interest or importance. *c*) an extra worker. *d*) in *motion pictures,* an actor hired by the day to play a minor part. *adv.* more than usually; especially: as, *extra* good quality.

**ex·tra-,** [L. < *exter(us);* see EXTERNAL], a prefix meaning *outside, outside the scope of, beyond, besides.*

**ex·tract** (iks-trakt′; *for n.,* eks′trakt), *v.t.* [< L. *extractus,* pp. < *ex-,* out + *trahere,* to draw], 1. to draw out by effort; pull out: as, to *extract* teeth, to *extract* a promise. 2. to obtain by pressing, distilling, etc.: as, to *extract* juice from fruit. 3. to deduce; derive; manage to get. 4. to select or quote (a passage from a book, etc.). 5. in *mathematics,* to find out (the root of a quantity). *n.* something extracted; specif., *a*) a concentrated form of a food, flavoring, etc.: as, vanilla *extract. b*) a passage from a book, etc.; excerpt; quotation. —**ex·tract′a·ble, ex·tract′i·ble,** *adj.* —**ex·trac′tive** (-tiv), *adj.* —**ex·trac′tor** (-tẽr), *n.*

**ex·trac·tion** (iks-trak′shən), *n.* 1. an extracting or being extracted. 2. origin; lineage; descent. 3. a thing extracted; extract.

**ex·tra·cur·ric·u·lar** (eks′trə-kə-rik′yoo-lẽr), *adj.* not part of the regular curriculum: as, football is an *extracurricular* activity.

**ex·tra·dite** (eks′trə-dīt′), *v.t.* [-DITED, -DITING], [< *extradition*], 1. to turn over (an alleged criminal, fugitive, etc.) to the jurisdiction of another country, state, etc. 2. to obtain the extradition of. —**ex′tra·dit′a·ble,** *adj.*

**ex·tra·di·tion** (eks′trə-dish′ən), *n.* [Fr. < L. *ex,* out + *traditus,* pp. of *tradere,* to give up], the turning over of an alleged criminal, fugitive, etc. by one country, state, etc. to another.

**ex·tra·dos** (eks-trā′dos), *n.* [Fr. < L. *extra,* beyond + Fr. *dos* < L. *dorsum,* back], the outside curved surface of an arch.

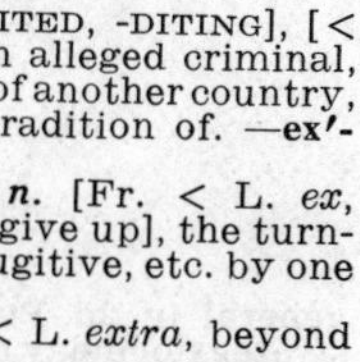

EXTRADOS

**ex·tra·le·gal** (eks′trə-lē′g'l), *adj.* outside of legal control or authority.

**ex·tra·ne·ous** (iks-trā′ni-əs), *adj.* [< L. *extraneus* < *extra;* see EXTRA- & STRANGE], 1. coming from outside; foreign: as, an *extraneous* substance. 2. not belonging to the matter under consideration; not pertinent. —**ex·tra′ne·ous·ly,** *adv.* —**ex·tra′ne·ous·ness,** *n.*

**ex·tra·or·di·nar·y** (iks-trôr′d'n-er′i), *adj.* [< L. < *extra ordinem,* out of the usual order], 1. not ordinary; out of the usual order. 2. going far beyond the ordinary degree, measure, limit, etc.; very unusual; remarkable. 3. (eks′trə-ôr′d'n-er′i), outside of the regular staff; sent on a special errand: as, an envoy *extraordinary.* —**ex·tra·or′di·nar′i·ly,** *adv.* —**ex·tra·or′di·nar′i·ness,** *n.*

**ex·trap·o·late** (eks-trap′ə-lāt′), *v.t. & v.i.* [-LATED, -LATING], [*extra* + inter*polate*], to estimate (a value, quantity, etc. beyond the known range) on the basis of certain known variables: as, future sales figures may be *extrapolated* from previous sales records. —**ex·trap′o·la′tion,** *n.*

**ex·tra·sen·so·ry** (eks′trə-sen′sə-ri), *adj.* apart from normal sense perception.

**ex·tra·ter·ri·to·ri·al** (eks′trə-ter′ə-tôr′i-əl, -tō′ri-), *adj.* outside the territorial limits or jurisdiction of the country, state, etc. —**ex′tra·ter′ri·to′ri·al′i·ty** (-al′ə-ti), *n.* —**ex′tra·ter′ri·to′ri·al·ly,** *adv.*

**ex·trav·a·gance** (iks-trav′ə-gəns), *n.* 1. a going beyond reasonable or moderate limits; unreasonable excess. 2. a spending of more than is reasonable or necessary; wastefulness. 3. an instance of excess in spending, behavior, etc. Also **ex·trav′a·gan·cy** [*pl.* -CIES].

**ex·trav·a·gant** (iks-trav′ə-gənt), *adj.* [Fr. < ML. < L. *extra,* beyond + *vagari,* to wander], 1. going beyond the limits of reason or moderation; excessive. 2. spending more than is reasonable or necessary; wasteful. —**ex·trav′a·gant·ly,** *adv.*

**ex·trav·a·gan·za** (iks-trav′ə-gan′zə), *n.* [< It. *estravaganza,* extravagance], a literary, musical, or dramatic composition characterized by loose structure and fantastic, often farcical content; now, any spectacular and elaborate theatrical production, as certain musical shows.

**ex·treme** (iks-trēm′), *adj.* [OFr. < L. *extremus,* superl. of *exterus,* outer], 1. at the end or outermost point; farthest away; utmost. 2. last; final. 3. in or to the greatest degree; very great: as, *extreme* poverty. 4. advanced; radical: as, *extreme* views. 5. very severe; drastic. *n.* 1. either of two things that are as different or far as possible from each other. 2. an extreme degree. 3. an extreme act, expedient, etc. 4. an extreme state: as, an *extreme* of distress. 5. in *mathematics,* the first or last term of a proportion or series. —**go to extremes,** to be immoderate in speech or action. —**in the extreme,** to the utmost degree. —**ex·treme′ly,** *adv.* —**ex·treme′ness,** *n.*

**extreme unction,** in the *R.C. Church,* the sacrament administered by a priest to a person who is dying or in danger of death through sickness.

**ex·trem·ist** (iks-trēm′ist), *n.* 1. a person who goes to extremes. 2. a person who holds extreme, or advanced, views, or advocates extreme measures. *adj.* of extremists or extreme views, actions, etc. —**ex·trem′ism,** *n.*

**ex·trem·i·ty** (iks-trem′ə-ti), *n.* [*pl.* -TIES], 1. the outermost or utmost point or part; end. 2. the greatest degree. 3. a state of extreme necessity, danger, etc. 4. the end of life; dying. 5. *usually in pl.* an extreme measure; severe or strong action. 6. *pl.* the hands and feet.

**ex·tri·cate** (eks′tri-kāt′), *v.t.* [-CATED, -CATING], [< L. pp. of *extricare* < *ex-,* out + *tricae,* trifles, vexations], to set free; disentangle (*from* a net, difficulty, embarrassment, etc.). —**ex′tri·ca·ble** (-kə-b'l), *adj.* —**ex′tri·ca·bil′i·ty,** *n.* —**ex′tri·ca·bly,** *adv.* —**ex′tri·ca′tion,** *n.*

**ex·trin·sic** (eks-trin′sik), *adj.* [< Fr. < L. *extrinsecus,* from without < *exter,* without + *secus,* besides], 1. not belonging to the real nature of a thing; not essential; not inherent. 2. being, coming, or acting from the outside; external. Opposed to *intrinsic.* —**ex·trin′si·cal·ly,** *adv.*

**ex·tro-,** extra- (when opposed to *intro-*).

**ex·tro·ver·sion** (eks′trō-vũr′zhən, -shən), *n.* [< *extro-* + L. *versus,* pp. of *vertere,* to turn], in *psychology,* an attitude in which a person directs his interest to phenomena outside himself rather than to his own experiences and feelings: opposed to *introversion.*

**ex·tro·vert** (eks′trō-vũrt′), *n.* in *psychology,* a person characterized by extroversion; person who is active and expressive: opposed to *introvert.*

**ex·trude** (iks-trōōd′), *v.t.* [-TRUDED, -TRUDING], [< L. < *ex-,* out + *trudere,* to thrust], to push or force out, as through a small opening. *v.i.* to stick out;

protrude; project. **—ex·tru′sion** (-trōō′zhən), *n.* **—ex·tru′sive,** *adj.*

**ex·u·ber·ance** (ig-zōō′bēr-əns, -zū′-), *n.* [< Fr. < LL. < L. < *ex-*, intens. + *uberare*, to bear abundantly < *uber*, udder], 1. the state or quality of being exuberant; great abundance. 2. an instance of this; esp., action or speech showing high spirits. Also **ex·u′ber·an·cy** [*pl.* -CIES].

**ex·u·ber·ant** (ig-zōō′bēr-ənt, -zū′-), *adj.* 1. growing profusely; luxuriant. 2. overflowing; superabundant; lavish; effusive: as, *exuberant* spirits. 3. overflowing with good health and spirits: said of a person. **—ex·u′ber·ant·ly,** *adv.*

**ex·ude** (ig-zōōd′, ik-sūd′), *v.i. & v.t.* [-UDED, -UDING], [< L. < *ex-*, out + *sudare*, to sweat < *sudor*, sweat], to pass out in drops, as through pores, an incision, etc.; ooze; discharge. **—ex·u·da·tion** (eks′yoo-dā′shən), *n.*

**ex·ult** (ig-zult′), *v.i.* [< Fr. < L. *ex(s)ultare*, to leap for joy < *ex-*, intens. + *saltare* (< *salire*), to leap], to rejoice greatly; be jubilant; glory.**—ex′ul·ta′tion,** *n.* **—ex·ult′ing·ly,** *adv.*

**ex·ult·ant** (ig-zul′t′nt), *adj.* exulting; triumphant; jubilant. **—ex·ult′ant·ly,** *adv.*

**ex·u·vi·ate** (ig-zōō′vi-āt′, ik-sū′-), *v.t. & v.i.* [-ATED, -ATING], [< L. < *exuere*, to strip off; + *-ate*], to cast off (a skin, shell, etc.); molt. **—ex·u′vi·a′tion,** *n.*

**-ey** (ē, i), -y (adjective-forming suffix): used especially after words ending in *y*.

**eye** (ī), *n.* [AS. *eage*], 1. organ of sight in man and animals. 2. the eyeball. 3. the iris: as, she has blue *eyes*. 4. the area around the eye: as, a black *eye*. 5. sight; vision. 6. a look; glance: as, cast your *eye* on this. 7. attention; observation. 8. the power of judging, estimating, etc. by eyesight: as, a good *eye* for distances. 9. *often in pl.* judgment; opinion: as, in the *eyes* of the law. 10. a thing like an eye in appearance or function: as, the *eye* of a needle. *v.t.* [EYED, EYING or EYEING], 1. to look at; observe; scrutinize. 2. to provide with eyes, or holes. **—an eye for an eye,** punishment or retaliation equivalent to the injury suffered. **—catch one's eye,** to attract one's attention. **—feast one's eyes on,** to look at with pleasure. **—have an eye for,** to have the ability to notice with discernment and appreciation. **—have an eye to,** to watch out for; attend to. **—in a pig's eye,** [Slang], never. **—in the public eye,** often brought to public attention. **—keep an eye on,** to look after; watch. **—keep one's eyes open,** to be watchful. **—lay** (or **set** or **clap**) **eyes on,** to see; look at. **—make eyes at,** to look at lovingly or flirtatiously. **—my eye!** [Slang], an exclamation of contradiction, astonishment, etc. **—open one's eyes,** to make one aware of the facts. **—run one's eye over,** to glance over. **—see eye to eye,** to be in full agreement. **—shut one's eyes to,** to be unwilling to see or think about. **—with an eye to,** paying attention to; considering.

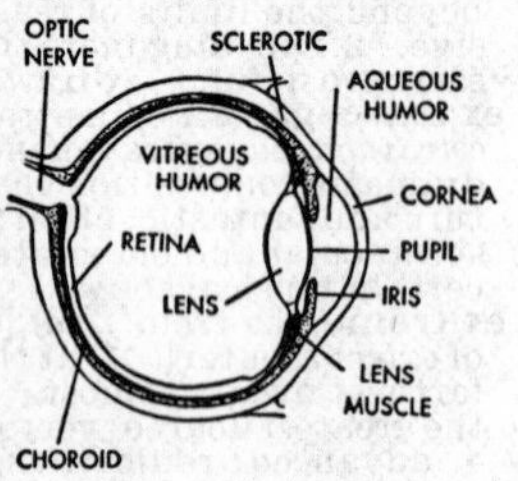

HUMAN EYE

**eye·ball** (ī′bôl′), *n.* the ball-shaped part of the eye, enclosed by the socket and eyelids.

**eye·brow** (ī′brou′), *n.* 1. the bony arch over each eye. 2. the arch of hair growing on this.

**eye·cup** (ī′kup′), *n.* a small cup used in applying medicine to the eyes or washing them.

**eyed** (īd), *adj.* having eyes: often used in compounds, as in *blue-eyed.*

**eye·ful** (ī′fool′), 1. a quantity of something in the eye. 2. [Slang], a person or thing that looks striking or unusual. **—get an eyeful,** [Colloq.], 1. to get a good look. 2. to see something very interesting.

**eye·glass** (ī′glas′, ī′gläs′), *n.* 1. a lens to help faulty vision; monocle. 2. *pl.* a pair of such lenses, usually in a frame: also called *glasses* or *spectacles*. 3. an eyepiece.

**eye·hole** (ī′hōl′), *n.* 1. the socket for the eyeball. 2. a peephole. 3. an opening for receiving a rope, cord, pin, etc.; eyelet.

**eye·lash** (ī′lash′), *n.* 1. any of the hairs on the edge of the eyelid. 2. a fringe of these hairs.

**eye·less** (ī′lis), *adj.* without eyes; blind.

**eye·let** (ī′lit), *n.* [< OFr. dim. < L. *oculus*, eye], 1. a small hole for receiving a rope, cord, hook, etc. 2. a metal ring or short tube for lining such a hole. 3. a small hole edged by stitching in embroidered work. 4. a peephole or loophole. *v.t.* to provide with eyelets.

**eye·lid** (ī′lid′), *n.* either of the two movable folds of flesh that cover and uncover the front of the eyeball.

**eye opener,** 1. something that causes the eyes to open in astonishment or realization. 2. [Slang], an alcoholic drink, especially one taken early in the day.

**eye·piece** (ī′pēs′), *n.* in a telescope, microscope, etc., the lens or lenses nearest the viewer's eye.

**eye shadow,** a cosmetic paste, usually green or blue, applied to the upper eyelids.

**eye·shot** (ī′shot′), *n.* range of vision.

**eye·sight** (ī′sīt′), *n.* 1. the power of seeing; sight; vision. 2. the range of vision.

**eye·sore** (ī′sôr′, ī′sōr′), *n.* a thing that is disagreeable to look at.

**eye·strain** (ī′strān′), *n.* a tired or strained condition of the eye muscles, caused by too much or incorrect use of the eyes, faulty vision, etc.

**eye·tooth** (ī′tōōth′), *n.* [*pl.* -TEETH (-tēth′)], a canine tooth of the upper jaw. **—cut one's eyeteeth,** to become experienced or sophisticated.

**eye·wash** (ī′wôsh′, ī′wäsh′), *n.* 1. a lotion for the eyes. 2. [Slang], *a)* nonsense. *b)* flattery. *c)* something done only to impress an observer.

**eye·wink** (ī′wiŋk′), *n.* 1. a wink, look, or glance; hence, 2. an instant.

**eye·wit·ness** (ī′wit′nis), *n.* 1. a person who sees or has seen a specific thing happen. 2. a person who testifies to what he has seen.

**ey·rie, ey·ry** (âr′i, ēr′i), *n.* [*pl.* -RIES], an aerie.

**E·zek·i·el** (i-zē′ki-əl, -kyəl), *n.* 1. a Hebrew prophet who lived in the 6th century B.C. 2. a book of the Old Testament containing his prophetic writings. Abbrev. **Ezek.**

**Ez·ra** (ez′rə), *n.* 1. a Hebrew scribe, prophet, and religious reformer of the 5th century B.C. 2. a book of the Old Testament telling of his life and teachings. Abbrev. **Ez., Ezr.**

# F

**F, f** (ef), *n.* [*pl.* F's, f's, Fs, fs], 1. the sixth letter of the English alphabet. 2. the sound of F or f. *adj.* sixth in a sequence or group.

**F** (ef), *n.* 1. in *chemistry, the symbol for* fluorine. 2. in *music, a)* the fourth tone in the scale of C major. *b)* the scale having F as the key note. *adj.* shaped like F.

**F/, f/, f:,** *f.*, F number.

**F.,** 1. Fahrenheit. 2. February. 3. Fellow. 4. France. 5. French. 6. Friday.

**F., f.,** 1. farad. 2. farthing. 3. fathom. 4. feminine. 5. fluid. 6. folio(s). 7. following. 8. franc. 9. in *music*, forte.

**fa** (fä), *n.* [It. < *famuli*; see GAMUT], in *music*, the fourth tone of the diatonic scale.

**Fa·bi·an** (fā′bi-ən), *adj.* [<L. < *Fabius*, Roman general in 2d Punic War], 1. using a cautious strategy of delay and avoidance of battle. 2. designating or of an English socialist organization (**Fabian Society**) advocating gradual reforms. *n.* a member of the Fabian Society. **—Fa′bi·an·ism,** *n.* **—Fa′bi·an·ist,** *n.*

**fa·ble** (fā′b'l), *n.* [< OFr. < L. *fabula*, a story < *fari*, to speak], 1. a fictitious story meant to teach a moral lesson: the characters are usually animals. 2. a myth or legend. 3. a story that is not true; falsehood. *v.i. & v.t.* [-BLED, -BLING], to write or tell (fables, fiction, falsehoods). **—fa′bled,** *adj.* **—fa′bler,** *n.*

**Fa·bre, Jean Hen·ri** (zhän än′rē′ fà′br′), 1823–1915; French entomologist.

**fab·ric** (fab′rik), *n.* [< Fr. < L. *fabrica*, a workshop

< *faber*, a workman], 1. anything made of parts put together; structure. 2. the style or plan of construction; texture. 3. any woven, knitted, or felted cloth.

**fab·ri·cate** (fab′ri-kāt′), *v.t.* [-CATED, -CATING], [see FABRIC], 1. to make; build; construct; manufacture. 2. to make by assembling parts. 3. to make up (a story, reason, falsehood, etc.); invent. —**fab′ri·ca′tion,** *n.* —**fab′ri·ca′tor,** *n.*

**fab·ri·koid** (fab′ri-koid′), *n.* [see FABRIC & -OID], a fabric made to resemble leather, used for upholstery, etc.: a trade-mark **(Fabrikoid).**

**fab·u·list** (fab′yoo-list), *n.* 1. a person who writes, tells, or invents fables. 2. a liar.

**fab·u·lous** (fab′yoo-ləs), *adj.* [< L. < *fabula;* see FABLE], 1. of or like a fable; imaginary; fictitious; legendary. 2. incredible; astounding. —**fab′u·lous·ly,** *adv.* —**fab′u·lous·ness,** *n.*

**fa·çade** (fə-säd′), *n.* [Fr. < It. < LL.; see FACE], the front or principal face of a building: often used figuratively of a deceptive outward aspect.

**face** (fās), *n.* [< OFr. < LL. *facia* < L. *facies*, the face], 1. the front of the head; countenance. 2. the expression of the countenance. 3. the surface of a thing; esp., *a)* the main surface or side. *b)* the front, upper, or outer surface. 4. the side or surface that is marked, finished, etc., as of a clock, fabric, etc. 5. the appearance; outward aspect. 6. [< Chin. idiom], dignity; self-respect: as, to lose *face*. 7. the value indicated on a note: usually **face value.** 8. the topography (of an area). 9. the functional side (of a tool, etc.). 10. [Colloq.], a grimace: as, he made a *face*. 11. [Colloq.], effrontery; audacity. 12. in *typography, a)* the printing part of a letter or plate. *b)* the design of type. *v.t.* [FACED, FACING], 1. to turn, or have the face turned, toward: as, the house *faces* the street. 2. to meet face to face. 3. to meet or confront, especially with boldness, courage, etc. 4. to cover with a new surface. 5. to put a smooth surface on (a stone, tool, etc.). 6. to turn (a card, etc.) with the face up. *v.i.* 1. to turn, or have the face turned, toward a specified thing or in a specified direction. 2. in *military science*, to pivot in a specified direction: as, right *face!* —**face to face,** 1. confronting one another. 2. in the presence of: followed by *with*. —**face up to,** 1. to confront and resist. 2. to realize and be ready to meet. —**in the face of,** 1. in the presence of. 2. in spite of. —**on the face of it,** apparently. —**pull (or wear) a long face,** to look sad, glum, disappointed, etc. —**face′a·ble,** *adj.* —**face′less,** *n.*

**face card,** any king, queen, or jack in a deck of cards.

**face lifting,** plastic surgery for removing wrinkles, sagging flesh, etc. from the face.

**face powder,** a cosmetic powder applied to the face to dull the shine, conceal blemishes, etc.

**fac·et** (fas′it), *n.* [Fr. *facette*, dim.; see FACE], 1. any of the small, polished plane surfaces of a cut gem; hence, 2. any of a number of sides or aspects, as of a personality. *v.t.* [-ETED, -ETING], to cut or make facets on.

**fa·ce·tious** (fə-sē′shəs), *adj.* [< Fr. < L. < *facetus*, witty], lightly joking; jocular, especially at an inappropriate time. —**fa·ce′tious·ly,** *adv.* —**fa·ce′tious·ness,** *n.*

**face value,** 1. the value printed or written on a bill, bond, etc. 2. the seeming value: as, I took his promise at *face value*.

**fa·cial** (fā′shəl), *adj.* of or for the face. *n.* [Colloq.], a cosmetic treatment for the skin of the face. —**fa′cial·ly,** *adv.*

**-fa·cient** (fā′shənt), [< L. ppr. of *facere*, to make], a suffix used to form adjectives, meaning *making* or *causing to become*, as in *liquefacient*.

**fac·ile** (fas′'l, -il), *adj.* [Fr. < L. *facilis* < *facere*, to make, do], 1. not hard to do; easy. 2. moving or working easily and quickly; fluent: as, a *facile* imagination. 3. easy to influence or persuade. —**fac′ile·ly,** *adv.* —**fac′ile·ness,** *n.*

**fa·cil·i·tate** (fə-sil′ə-tāt′), *v.t.* [-TATED, -TATING], [see FACILE], 1. to make easy or easier. 2. to lighten the work of; assist. —**fa·cil′i·ta′tion,** *n.*

**fa·cil·i·ty** (fə-sil′ə-ti), *n.* [*pl.* -TIES], [see FACILE], 1. ease; absence of difficulty. 2. a ready ability; skill; fluency. 3. a tendency to be easygoing, etc. 4. *pl.* the means by which something can be more easily done; conveniences.

**fac·ing** (fās′iŋ), *n.* 1. a lining or trimming sewn on the edge of a dress, coat, etc. 2. any material used for this. 3. a covering of contrasting material to decorate or protect a building.

**fac·sim·i·le** (fak-sim′ə-li), *n.* [< L. *fac*, imperative of *facere*, to make + *simile*, like], 1. an exact likeness, reproduction, or copy: abbrev. **fac.** 2. the transmission and reproduction of printed matter by a process involving the use of radio broadcast. *adj.* of, or having the nature of, a facsimile. *v.t.* [-LED, -LEING], to make a facsimile of. —**in facsimile,** as an exact likeness.

**fact** (fakt), *n.* [< L. *factum*, deed < *facere*, to do], 1. originally, a deed; act. 2. a thing that has actually happened or is true. 3. the state of things as they are; reality; truth. 4. something said to have occurred or supposed to be true. —**as a matter of fact,** in truth; really: also **in fact, in point of fact.**

**fac·tion** (fak′shən), *n.* [< Fr. < L. *factio*, a making < *facere*, to do, act], 1. a group of people in an organization who have common aims, usually dissident from the main body; clique. 2. dissension; partisan conflict within an organization or state. —**fac′tion·al,** *adj.* —**fac′tion·al·ism,** *n.*

**fac·tious** (fak′shəs), *adj.* 1. producing or tending to produce faction, or dissension. 2. of faction; produced or characterized by faction. —**fac′tious·ly,** *adv.* —**fac′tious·ness,** *n.*

**fac·ti·tious** (fak-tish′əs), *adj.* [< L. < *facere*, to do, act], not natural, genuine, or spontaneous; forced or artificial. —**fac·ti′tious·ly,** *adv.* —**fac·ti′tious·ness,** *n.*

**fac·tor** (fak′tēr), *n.* [< Fr. < OFr. < L. *factor* < *facere*, to do, make], 1. a person who carries on business transactions for another; commission merchant. 2. any of the circumstances, conditions, etc. that bring about a result. 3. in *mathematics*, any of two or more quantities which form a product when multiplied together. *v.t.* in *mathematics*, to resolve into factors: also **fac′tor·ize′** (-tə-rīz′), [-IZED, -IZING]. —**fac′tor·ship′,** *n.*

**fac·tor·age** (fak′tēr-ij), *n.* 1. the business of a factor. 2. a factor's commission.

**fac·to·ry** (fak′tə-ri, -tri), *n.* [*pl.* -RIES], [see FACTOR], a building or buildings in which things are manufactured; manufacturing plant.

**fac·to·tum** (fak-tō′təm), *n.* [ML. < L. < *fac*, imperative of *facere*, to do + *totum*, all], a person hired to do all sorts of work; handy man.

**fac·tu·al** (fak′chōō-əl), *adj.* of or containing facts; real; actual. —**fac′tu·al·ly,** *adv.*

**fac·ul·ty** (fak′'l-ti), *n.* [*pl.* -TIES], [< OFr. < L. *facultas* < *facilis;* see FACILE], 1. formerly, the ability to perform any action. 2. any natural or specialized power of a living organism: as, the *faculty* of hearing. 3. special aptitude or talent; knack. 4. any of the departments of learning in a university. 5. all the teachers of a school, college, or university. 6. all the members of any profession. 7. authorization. 8. in *psychology*, any of the powers formerly thought of as composing the mind, such as will, reason, etc.

**fad** (fad), *n.* [< Brit. Midland dial.] a custom, style, etc. that many people are interested in for a short time; passing fashion; craze. —**fad′dish,** *adj.* —**fad′dish·ness,** *n.* —**fad′dist,** *n.*

**fade** (fād), *v.i.* [FADED, FADING], [< OFr. *fader* < *fade*, pale], 1. to become less distinct; lose color or brilliance; dim. 2. to lose freshness or strength; wither; droop. 3. to disappear slowly; die out. *v.t.* to cause to fade. —**fade in** (or **out**), in *motion pictures, radio & television*, to appear (or disappear) gradually; become more (or less) distinct. —**fade′less,** *adj.*

**fade-in** (fād′in′), *n.* in *motion pictures, radio & television*, a fading in of a scene or sound.

**fade-out** (fād′out′), *n.* in *motion pictures, radio & television*, a fading out of a scene or sound.

**fae·ces** (fē′sēz), *n.pl.* feces. —**fae′cal** (-k'l), *adj.*

**fa·er·ie, fa·er·y** (fâr′i), *n.* [*pl.* -IES], [Archaic], 1. (fā′ēr-i), fairyland. 2. a fairy. *adj.* [Archaic], fairy. Also sp. **faërie, faëry.**

**fag** (fag), *v.i.* [FAGGED, FAGGING], [earlier form of *flag* (to droop)], 1. to work hard and become very tired. 2. to serve as a fag. *v.t.* to make tired by hard work. *n.* [Brit. Colloq.], 1. *a)* hard, tiring work; drudgery. *b)* fatigue. 2. in English schools, a boy who acts as servant for another in an upper grade.

**fag** (fag), *n.* [< *fag end*], [Slang], a cigarette.

**fag end,** 1. *a)* the last part or coarse end of a piece

of cloth. *b*) the frayed, untwisted end of a rope. 2. the last and worst part of anything.

**fag·ot, fag·got** (fag′ət), *n.* [< OFr.; ult. < Gr. *phakelos*, a bundle], 1. a bundle of sticks or twigs, especially for use as fuel. 2. in *metallurgy*, a bundle of iron or steel pieces to be worked into bars. *v.t.* 1. to make into a fagot or fagots. 2. in *sewing*, to decorate with fagoting.

**fag·ot·ing, fag·got·ing** (fag′ət-iŋ), *n.* 1. a decorative stitch made by pulling horizontal threads out of the fabric and tying the cross threads together in bunches. 2. openwork decoration in which the thread is drawn in crisscross stitches across the open seam.

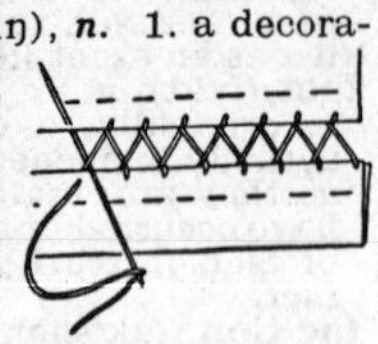
FAGOTING

**Fahr·en·heit** (far′ən-hīt′, fär′-), *adj.* [< G. D. *Fahrenheit* (1686–1736), G. physicist who devised the scale], designating or of a thermometer on which the boiling point of pure water is 212° and the freezing point 32°. *n.* this thermometer or its scale. Abbrev. **F., Fah., Fahr.**

**fail** (fāl), *v.i.* [< OFr. < L. *fallere*, to deceive], 1. to be lacking or insufficient; fall short. 2. to lose power or strength; weaken; die away. 3. to be deficient or negligent in an obligation, duty, or expectation. 4. to be unsuccessful in obtaining a desired end. 5. to become bankrupt. 6. in *education*, to get a grade of failure. *v.t.* 1. to be useless or not helpful to; disappoint. 2. to leave; abandon. 3. to neglect or omit: as, to *fail* to go. 4. in *education*, *a*) to give a grade of failure to. *b*) to get a grade of failure in. *n.* failure: now only in **without fail,** without failing (to occur, do, etc.). **—fail of,** to fail to achieve.

**fail·ing** (fāl′iŋ), *n.* 1. a failure. 2. a weakness; slight fault or defect. *prep.* without; in the lack of. *adj.* that fails. **—fail′ing·ly,** *adv.*

**faille** (fāl, fīl; Fr. fá′y′), *n.* [Fr.], a ribbed, soft fabric of silk or rayon, for dresses, etc.

**fail·ure** (fāl′yẽr), *n.* [see FAIL], 1. the state or fact of being lacking or insufficient. 2. a losing of power or strength. 3. neglect or omission. 4. a not succeeding in doing or becoming. 5. a person or thing that does not succeed. 6. a becoming bankrupt. 7. in *education*, *a*) a failing to pass. *b*) a grade or mark indicating this.

**fain** (fān), *adj.* [AS. *fæg(e)n*, glad], [Archaic & Poetic], 1. glad; ready. 2. reluctantly willing. 3. eager. *adv.* with eagerness.

**faint** (fānt), *adj.* [< OFr. pp. of *feindre;* see FEIGN], 1. without strength; weak; feeble. 2. without courage or vigor; timid. 3. done without strength or enthusiasm. 4. feeling weak and dizzy, as if about to swoon. 5. dim; indistinct. *n.* a condition of temporary loss of consciousness. *v.i.* to fall into a faint; swoon. **—faint′ish,** *adj.* **—faint′ly,** *adv.* **—faint′ness,** *n.*

**faint·heart·ed** (fānt′här′tid), *adj.* lacking courage; cowardly; timid. **—faint′heart′ed·ly,** *adv.* **—faint′heart′ed·ness,** *n.*

**fair** (fâr), *adj.* [AS. *fæger*, beautiful], 1. attractive; beautiful: as, *fair* women. 2. unblemished; clean: as, a *fair* reputation. 3. light in color; blond: as, *fair* hair. 4. clear and sunny; unclouded: as, *fair* weather. 5. without obstacles; clear and open: as, a *fair* road. 6. just and honest; impartial: as, a *fair* judge. 7. according to the rules: as, a *fair* defeat. 8. likely; promising. 9. pleasant and courteous. 10. lawfully hunted: as, *fair* game. 11. of moderately good size. 12. neither very bad nor very good; average: as, in *fair* condition. *n.* [Archaic], 1. beauty. 2. a pretty woman. *adv.* 1. in a fair manner: as, play *fair*. 2. straight; squarely: as, struck *fair* in the face. **—bid fair,** to appear likely. **—fair and square,** [Colloq.], with justice and honesty. **—fair to middling,** [Colloq.], moderately good; passable. **—fair′ish,** *adj.* **—fair′ness,** *n.*

**fair** (fâr), *n.* [< OFr. < LL. < L. *feriae, pl.*, holidays], 1. originally, a gathering of people at regular intervals for barter and sale of goods. 2. a carnival where there is entertainment and things are sold, often for charity; bazaar. 3. an exhibition varying in scope (**county fair, state fair, world's fair**) and often competitive, of farm, household, and manufactured products, with various amusement facilities and educational displays.

**fair ball,** in *baseball*, a batted ball that first strikes the ground inside the foul line and does not pass the foul line before first or third base.

**fair employment practices,** the employment of persons without prejudicial regard to race, religion, sex, etc.

**fair·ground** (fâr′ground′), *n.* an open space where fairs are held: also **fair′grounds′.**

**fair-haired** (fâr′hârd′), *adj.* 1. having blond hair. 2. [Colloq.], favorite: as, the teacher's *fair-haired* boy.

**fair·ish** (fâr′ish), *adj.* moderately good, well, etc.

**fair·ly** (fâr′li), *adv.* 1. justly; equitably. 2. moderately; somewhat. 3. clearly; distinctly. 4. completely or really: as, his voice *fairly* rang.

**fair-mind·ed** (fâr′mīn′did), *adj.* just; impartial; unprejudiced. **—fair′-mind′ed·ly,** *adv.* **—fair′-mind′ed·ness,** *n.*

**fair play,** an abiding by the rules or by decency and honor in sports, business, etc.

**fair sex,** women.

**fair-spo·ken** (fâr′spō′kən), *adj.* speaking or spoken politely; courteous.

**fair-trade** (fâr′trād′), *adj.* designating or of an agreement whereby a distributor of a product undertakes to charge no less than the minimum price set by the manufacturer. *v.t. & v.i.* [-TRADED, -TRADING], to sell under a fair-trade agreement.

**fair·way** (fâr′wā′), *n.* 1. a navigable channel in a river, harbor, etc. 2. the mowed part of a golf course between the tees and the putting greens.

**fair-weath·er** (fâr′weth′ẽr), *adj.* 1. suitable only for fair weather. 2. dependable only in easy circumstances: as, *fair-weather* friends.

**fair·y** (fâr′i), *n.* [*pl.* -IES], [< OFr. *faerie;* see FAY], 1. a tiny, graceful imaginary being in human form, supposed to have magic powers. 2. [Slang], a male homosexual: contemptuous term. *adj.* 1. of fairies. 2. fairylike; graceful; delicate.

**fair·y·land** (fâr′i-land′), *n.* 1. the imaginary land where the fairies live; hence, 2. a lovely and enchanting place.

**fairy tale,** 1. a story about fairies, magic deeds, etc. 2. an unbelievable or untrue story.

‡**fait ac·com·pli** (fe′tá′kōn′plē′), [Fr., lit., an accomplished fact], a thing already done, so that opposition or argument is useless.

**faith** (fāth), *n.* [< OFr. < L. *fides* < *fidere*, to trust], 1. unquestioning belief. 2. unquestioning belief in God, religion, etc 3. a particular religion. 4. anything believed. 5. complete trust or confidence. 6. loyalty. *interj.* indeed. **—bad faith,** insincerity; duplicity. **—good faith,** sincerity; honesty. **—in faith,** indeed; really.

**faith·ful** (fāth′fəl), *adj.* 1. keeping faith; loyal. 2. reliable; dependable. 3. accurate; exact. 4. [Rare], full of faith. **—the faithful,** 1. the true believers. 2. the loyal adherents. **—faith′ful·ly,** *adv.* **—faith′ful·ness,** *n.*

**faith·less** (fāth′lis), *adj.* 1. not keeping faith; not worthy of trust; dishonest. 2. unreliable; undependable. 3. [Rare], without faith. **—faith′less·ly,** *adv.* **—faith′less·ness,** *n.*

**fake** (fāk), *v.t. & v.i.* [FAKED, FAKING], [? < G. *fegen*, to clean, sweep], [Colloq.], to make (something) seem real, satisfactory, etc. by deception. *n.* [Colloq.], anything or anyone not genuine; fraud. *adj.* [Colloq.], fraudulent; sham; false. **—fak′er,** *n.*

**fa·keer** (fə-kêr′), *n.* a fakir.

**fa·kir** (fə-kêr′, fā′kẽr), *n.* [Ar. *faqīr*, lit., poor], 1. a member of a Moslem holy sect who lives by begging. 2. any Hindu ascetic.

**Fa·lange** (fā′lanj; Sp. fä-läŋ′hā), *n.* [Sp., lit., phalanx], a fascist organization established in Spain in 1934: it became the only official political party under Franco's regime. **—Fa·lang·ism** (fə-lan′jiz′m), *n.* **—Fa·lang′ist,** *n.*

**fal·cate** (fal′kāt), *adj.* [< L. < *falx*, a sickle], shaped like a sickle; curved or hooked.

**fal·chion** (fôl′chən, -shən), *n.* [< OFr. < L. *falx*, a sickle], 1. a medieval sword with a short, broad, slightly curved blade. 2. [Poetic], any sword.

**fal·con** (fôl′k′n, fô′k′n), *n.* [< OFr. < LL. *falco;* prob. < L. *falx*, a sickle], 1. any hawk trained to hunt and kill small game. 2. a hawk with long, pointed wings and a short, curved, notched beak.

**fal·con·ry** (fôl′k′n-ri, fô′k′n-), *n.* 1. the art of training falcons to hunt game. 2. the sport of hunting with falcons. **—fal′con·er,** *n.*

**fal·de·ral** (fal′də-ral′), *n.* [nonsense syllables], 1. a trifle. 2. mere nonsense. 3. a refrain in some old songs. Also **fal′de·rol′** (-rol′), **fol′de·rol′** (fol′-).

**Falk·land Islands** (fôk′lənd), a group of British islands, east of the S tip of South America.

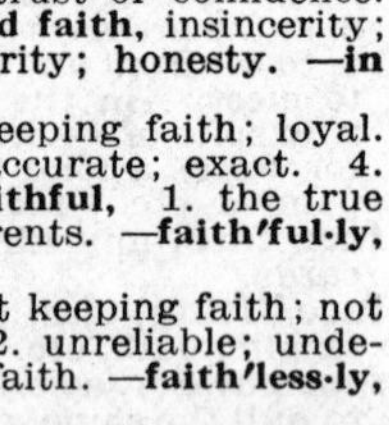
FALCON
(17 in. long)

**fall** (fôl), *v.i.* [FELL, FALLEN, FALLING], [AS. *feallan*], 1. to come down by the force of gravity, as when detached, pushed, dropped, etc: as, apples *fall* from the tree. 2. to come down suddenly from a standing or sitting position; tumble: as, the child *fell*. 3. to be wounded or killed in battle. 4. to collapse: as, the building *fell*. 5. to hang down: as, the coat *falls* well from the shoulders. 6. to strike; hit: as, to *fall* wide of the mark. 7. to take a downward direction: as, her glance *fell*. 8. to become lower in amount, degree, etc.; lessen: as, prices are *falling*. 9. to lose power: as, the government *fell*. 10. to lose status, reputation, dignity, etc. 11. to do wrong; sin. 12. to be captured or conquered: as, Berlin *fell* to the Allies. 13. to pass into a particular mental or physical state: as, the child *fell* ill. 14. to take on a dejected look: as, his face *fell*. 15. to become lower in pitch or volume: as, her voice *fell*. 16. to take place; occur: as, the meeting *fell* on a Friday. 17. to come by chance: as, the prize *fell* to us. 18. to come as a right or inheritance: as, the estate *falls* to the son. 19. to come at a specified place: as, the accent *falls* on the third syllable. 20. to be directed: as, his eye *fell* on me. 21. to be divided (*into*): as, these poems *fall* into two classes. *n.* 1. a dropping; descending. 2. a coming down suddenly from a standing or sitting position. 3. a hanging down. 4. a downward direction or slope. 5. a becoming less; reduction in value, price, etc. 6. a capture; overthrow; ruin. 7. a loss of status, reputation, virtue, etc. 8. something that has fallen: as, a *fall* of leaves. 9. autumn. 10. the amount of what has fallen: as, a six-inch *fall* of snow. 11. the distance that something falls. 12. *usually pl.* water falling over a cliff, etc.; cascade. 13. *a*) in *wrestling*, the throwing of an opponent so that both shoulders touch the floor. *b*) a division of a wrestling match. *adj.* of, for, or in the autumn. **—fall away,** 1. to take away friendship, support, etc.; desert. 2. to become less in size, strength, etc.; specif., to grow thin and weak. **—fall back,** to withdraw; retreat; recede. **—fall back on** (or **upon**), to turn, or return, to for help. **—fall flat,** to fail to have the desired effect. **—fall for,** [Slang], 1. to fall in love with. 2. to be tricked by. **—fall in,** 1. to agree. 2. to line up in proper formation. **—fall off,** 1. to drop. 2. to become smaller, less, worse, etc. **—fall on** (or **upon**), 1. to attack. 2. to be the duty of. **—fall out,** 1. to quarrel. 2. to happen; result. 3. to leave one's place in line. **—fall through,** to fail; come to nothing. **—fall to,** 1. to begin; start. 2. to start attacking. **—fall under,** 1. to come under (an influence, etc.). 2. to be classified as. **—the Fall (of Man),** in *Christian theology*, Adam's sin of yielding to temptation in eating the forbidden fruit.

**fal·la·cious** (fə-lā'shəs), *adj.* [see FALLACY], 1. faulty in logic; erroneous. 2. misleading; deceptive. **—fal·la'cious·ly,** *adv.* **—fal·la'cious·ness,** *n.*

**fal·la·cy** (fal'ə-si), *n.* [*pl.* -CIES], [< OFr. < L. *fallacia* < *fallere*, to deceive], 1. aptness to mislead: as, the *fallacy* of the senses. 2. a false or mistaken idea, opinion, etc.; error. 3. false reasoning; illogical or misleading argument.

**fall·en** (fôl''n), *adj.* 1. having come down; dropped. 2. prostrate; on the ground. 3. degraded. 4. captured; overthrown. 5. ruined. 6. dead.

**fall guy,** [Slang], a person left to face the consequences, as of a scheme that has miscarried.

**fal·li·ble** (fal'ə-b'l), *adj.* [< ML. < L. *fallere*, to deceive], 1. liable to be mistaken or deceived. 2. liable to be erroneous or inaccurate. **—fal'li·bil'i·ty, fal'li·ble·ness,** *n.* **—fal'li·bly,** *adv.*

**falling sickness,** [Rare], epilepsy.

**falling star,** a meteor.

**Fal·lo·pi·an tube** (fə-lō'pi-ən), [after Gabriel *Fallopio*, It. anatomist (1523–1562)], either of two slender tubes that carry ova from the ovaries to the uterus: also called *oviduct*.

**fall·out** (fôl'out'), *n.* the descent to earth of radioactive particles following a nuclear explosion.

**fal·low** (fal'ō), *n.* [< AS. *fealh*], 1. land plowed but not seeded for one or more seasons, to kill weeds, enrich the soil, etc. 2. the plowing of land to be left idle in this way. *adj.* 1. left uncultivated or unplanted. 2. untrained; inactive, as the mind. *v.t.* to leave (land) unplanted after plowing.

**fal·low** (fal'ō), *adj.* [< AS. *fealo*], pale-yellow; brownish-yellow.

**fallow deer,** a small European deer having a yellowish coat spotted with white in summer.

**Fall River,** a seaport in SE Massachusetts: pop., 100,000.

**false** (fôls), *adj.* [FALSER, FALSEST], [< OFr. < L. *falsus*, pp. of *fallere*, to deceive], 1. not true; in error; incorrect; wrong. 2. untruthful; lying; dishonest. 3. disloyal; unfaithful. 4. deceiving; misleading: as, a *false* scent. 5. not real; artificial; counterfeit. 6. not properly so named: as, *false* jasmine. 7. temporary, inessential, or added on for protection, disguise, etc.: as, a *false* drawer, a *false* bottom. 8. in *music*, pitched incorrectly. *adv.* in a false manner. **—play (a person) false,** to deceive or betray (a person). **—false'ly,** *adv.* **—false'ness,** *n.*

**false·heart·ed** (fôls'här'tid), *adj.* disloyal; deceitful; treacherous. **—false'heart'ed·ly,** *adv.* **—false'heart'ed·ness,** *n.*

**false·hood** (fôls'hood), *n.* 1. lack of accuracy or truth; falsity. 2. the telling of lies; lying. 3. a false statement; lie. 4. a false belief, theory, idea, etc.

**false imprisonment,** unlawful imprisonment.

**false ribs,** the five lower ribs on each side of the body: so called because they are not directly attached to the breastbone.

**false step,** 1. a misstep; stumble. 2. a blunder.

**fal·set·to** (fôl-set'ō), *n.* [*pl.* -TOS], [It. dim. < L.; see FALSE], 1. an artificial way of singing in which the voice is placed in a register much higher than that of the natural voice. 2. the voice so used. 3. a person singing in falsetto. *adj.* of or singing in falsetto. *adv.* in falsetto.

**fal·si·fy** (fôl'sə-fī'), *v.t.* [-FIED, -FYING,] [< Fr. < ML. < L.; see FALSE & -FY], 1. to make false; specif., *a*) to misrepresent; give an untrue account of. *b*) to alter (a record, etc.) fraudulently. 2. to prove to be untrue. *v.i.* to tell falsehoods; lie. **—fal'si·fi·ca'tion,** *n.* **—fal'si·fi'er,** *n.*

**fal·si·ty** (fôl'sə-ti), *n.* [*pl.* -TIES], 1. the condition or quality of being false; specif., *a*) incorrectness. *b*) dishonesty. *c*) deceitfulness. *d*) disloyalty. 2. something false; esp., a lie.

**Fal·staff, Sir John** (fôl'staf, -stäf), a character in Shakespeare's plays, a fat, blustering, witty knight. **—Fal·staff'i·an,** *adj.*

**fal·ter** (fôl'tēr), *v.i.* [ME. *faltren*, prob. < ON.], 1. to move uncertainly or unsteadily; stumble. 2. to stumble in speech; stammer. 3. to act hesitantly; show uncertainty; waver. *v.t.* to say hesitantly or timidly. *n.* 1. a faltering. 2. a faltering sound. **—fal'ter·er,** *n.* **—fal'ter·ing·ly,** *adv.*

**fame** (fām), *n.* [< OFr. < L. *fama*, fame; from same base as *fari*, to speak], 1. [Archaic], public report; rumor. 2. reputation, especially for good. 3. the state of being well known or much talked about; renown. *v.t.* [FAMED, FAMING], [Archaic], 1. to tell about widely. 2. to make famous.

**famed** (fāmd), *adj.* 1. reported; popularly believed. 2. widely known; celebrated; renowned.

**fa·mil·ial** (fə-mil'yəl), *adj.* of, involving, or common to a family.

**fa·mil·iar** (fə-mil'yēr), *adj.* [< OFr. < L. < *familia*; see FAMILY], 1. friendly; intimate; close. 2. too friendly; unduly intimate or bold. 3. closely acquainted (*with*). 4. well-known; ordinary: as, a *familiar* sight. *n.* 1. a close friend. 2. formerly, a spirit believed to act as an intimate servant. **—fa·mil'iar·ly,** *adv.*

**fa·mil·i·ar·i·ty** (fə-mil'i-ar'ə-ti, -mil'yar'-), *n.* [*pl.* -TIES], 1. intimacy. 2. free and intimate behavior; absence of formality. 3. undue intimacy. 4. close acquaintance (*with* something).

**fa·mil·iar·ize** (fə-mil'yə-rīz'), *v.t.* [-IZED, -IZING], 1. to make commonly known. 2. to make (another or oneself) accustomed or fully acquainted. **—fa·mil'iar·i·za'tion,** *n.*

**fam·i·ly** (fam'ə-li, fam'li), *n.* [*pl.* -LIES], [L. *familia*, household < *famulus*, servant], 1. all the people living in the same house. 2. *a*) parents and their children as a group. *b*) the children of the same parents. 3. a group of people related by blood or marriage; relatives. 4. all those descended from a common ancestor; tribe or clan. 5. *a*) descent; lineage. *b*) good or noble lineage. 6. a group of things having a common source or similar features: as, a *family* of languages. 7. in *biology*, a subdivision in the classification of plants or animals, above a genus and below an order.

**family name,** a surname.

**family tree,** the ancestors and descendants in a

given family, often as shown in a branching chart indicating relationship.

**fam·ine** (fam′in), *n.* [< OFr. < LL. < L. *fames*, hunger], 1. *a*) an acute and general shortage of food. *b*) the time of this. 2. starvation; great hunger. 3. an acute and general lack of anything.

**fam·ish** (fam′ish), *v.t. & v.i.* [< OFr. < L. *ad*, to + *fames*, hunger], 1. to be or make very hungry. 2. to kill or die with hunger; starve.

**fa·mous** (fā′məs), *adj.* [< OFr. < L. < *fama*, fame], 1. having fame, or celebrity; renowned. 2. [Colloq.], excellent; first-rate. —**fa′mous·ly,** *adv.* —**fa′mous·ness,** *n.*

**fan** (fan), *n.* [AS. *fann* < L. *vannus*, basket for winnowing grain], 1. originally, a device for separating grain from chaff. 2. any device used to set up a current of air for ventilating or cooling; specif., *a*) any flat surface moved by hand. *b*) a folding device of paper, cloth, etc. that opens as a sector of a circle. *c*) a motor-driven device with revolving blades. 3. anything in the shape of a fan (sense 2, b). *v.t.* [FANNED, FANNING], 1. to move or agitate (air) as with a fan. 2. to direct a current of air toward with or as with a fan; blow on. 3. to stir up; excite. 4. to blow away with a fan. 5. to spread out into the shape of a fan (sense 2, b). 6. to separate (grain) from chaff. 7. [Slang], in *baseball*, to strike (a batter) out. *v.i.* 1. to scatter or spread (*out*) like a fan. 2. [Slang], in *baseball*, to strike out. —**fan′like′,** *adj.* —**fan′ner,** *n.*

**fan** (fan), *n.* [prob. < *fanatic*], [Colloq.], a person enthusiastic about a specified sport, pastime, or performer; devotee: as, a football *fan*.

**fa·nat·ic** (fə-nat′ik), *adj.* fanatical. *n.* a fanatical person.

**fa·nat·i·cal** (fə-nat′i-k'l), *adj.* [< L. < *fanum*, a temple], unreasonably enthusiastic; overly zealous. —**fa·nat′i·cal·ly,** *adv.* —**fa·nat′i·cism,** *n.*

**fan·cied** (fan′sid), *adj.* imaginary; imagined.

**fan·ci·er** (fan′si-ẽr), *n.* a person with a special interest in and knowledge of something, especially plant or animal breeding: as, a dog *fancier*.

**fan·ci·ful** (fan′si-fəl), *adj.* 1. full of fancy; imaginative. 2. created in the fancy; imaginary; not real. 3. quaint; odd: as, *fanciful* costumes. —**fan′ci·ful·ly,** *adv.* —**fan′ci·ful·ness,** *n.*

**fan·cy** (fan′si), *n.* [*pl.* -CIES], [contr. < *fantasy*], 1. *a*) originally, imagination in general. *b*) light, whimsical, or capricious imagination. 2. a mental image. 3. an arbitrary idea; notion; caprice; whim. 4. an inclination or fondness, often temporary. 5. critical taste in art, dress, etc. *adj.* [-CIER, -CIEST], 1. whimsical; capricious; fanciful. 2. higher than real value; extravagant: as, a *fancy* price. 3. made or added to please the fancy; ornamental: as, a *fancy* necktie. 4. of superior skill: as, *fancy* diving. 5. of superior quality. 6. for expensive tastes: as, *fancy* groceries. 7. bred for some special feature or excellence of type: said of animals. *v.t.* [-CIED, -CYING], 1. to imagine. 2. to be fond of. 3. to believe without conviction; suppose. —**fancy (that)!** can you imagine (that)! —**fan′ci·less,** *adj.*

**fan·cy-free** (fan′si-frē′), *adj.* 1. free to fall in love; not married or engaged. 2. carefree.

**fan·cy·work** (fan′si-wũrk′), *n.* embroidery, crocheting, and other ornamental needlework.

**fan·dan·go** (fan-daŋ′gō), *n.* [*pl.* -GOS], [Sp.], 1. a lively Spanish dance in rhythm varying from slow to quick 3/4 time. 2. music for this.

**fane** (fān), *n.* [L. *fanum*], [Archaic & Poetic], a temple or church.

**fan·fare** (fan′fâr′), *n.* [< Fr. < *fanfaron*, braggart], 1. a loud blast or flourish of trumpets. 2. noisy or showy display.

**fang** (faŋ), *n.* [AS. < base of *fon*, to seize], 1. *a*) one of the long, pointed teeth with which meat-eating animals seize and tear their prey. *b*) one of the long, hollow or grooved teeth through which poisonous snakes inject their venom. 2. the pointed part of something. —**fanged,** *adj.* —**fang′less,** *adj.* —**fang′like′,** *adj.*

FANGS

FANGS
(of bushmaster)

**fan·light** (fan′līt′), *n.* a semicircular window, often with sash bars in a fanlike arrangement, over a door or larger window.

**fan mail,** letters of praise or adulation sent to a prominent actor, author, etc. by admirers.

**fan·tail** (fan′tāl′), *n.* 1. a part, tail, or end spread out like an opened fan. 2. a variety of domestic pigeon or goldfish with such a tail.

**fan-tan** (fan′tan′), *n.* [< Chin. *fan*, number of times + *t'an*, apportion], 1. a Chinese gambling game. 2. a card game in which the players discard their cards in proper sequence, the winner being the one who first gets rid of all his cards.

**fan·ta·si·a** (fan-tā′zi-ə, -zhə, fan′tə-zē′ə), *n.* [It.; see FANTASY], 1. a musical composition of no fixed form. 2. a medley of familiar tunes.

**fan·tas·tic** (fan-tas′tik), *adj.* [< OFr. < ML. < LL. < Gr. *phantastikos*, able to present to the mind < *phainein*, to show], 1. imaginary; unreal: as, *fantastic* reasons. 2. grotesque; odd; quaint: as, a *fantastic* hat. 3. extravagant; capricious; eccentric: as, *fantastic* whims. Also **fan·tas′ti·cal.** *n.* a person who is fantastic in behavior, dress, etc.; eccentric. —**fan·tas′ti·cal·ly,** *adv.* —**fan·tas′ti·cal·ness, fan·tas′ti·cal′i·ty** (-kal′ə-ti), *n.*

**fan·ta·sy** (fan′tə-si, -zi), *n.* [*pl.* -SIES], [< OFr. < LL. < Gr. *phantasia*, appearance < *phainein*, to show], 1. imagination or fancy. 2. *a*) an unreal mental image; illusion. *b*) a daydream. 3. a whim; caprice. 4. an imaginative poem, play, etc. 5. in *music*, a fantasia. Also sp. **phantasy.**

**far** (fär), *adj.* [FARTHER, FARTHEST], [AS. *feor(r)*], 1. distant in space or time; not near: as, a *far* land, the *far* future. 2. extending a long way: as, a *far* journey. 3. more distant: as, the *far* side of the stage. 4. very different in quality or nature. 5. advanced, as in years. *adv.* 1. very distant in space, time, or degree. 2. to or from a distance in time or position. 3. very much: as, *far* better. *n.* a distant place: as, from *far*. —**as far as,** to the distance or degree that. —**by far,** considerably. —**far and away,** very much; beyond doubt. —**far and near (or wide),** everywhere. —**far be it from me,** I would not presume or wish. —**go far,** 1. to cover much extent; last long. 2. to have a strong tendency. 3. to accomplish much. —**in so far as,** to the extent that. —**so far,** 1. to that extent. 2. up to this or now. —**so far as,** to the extent or point that. —**so far, so good,** up to this point everything is all right. —**far′ness,** *n.*

**far·ad** (far′əd, -ad), *n.* [after M. *Faraday*], a unit of electrical capacity, equal to the amount that permits the storing of one coulomb of charge for each volt of potential difference: symbol, **F.**

**Far·a·day, Michael** (far′ə-dā′), 1791–1867; English chemist and physicist.

**far·a·way** (fär′ə-wā′), *adj.* 1. distant in time or place. 2. dreamy: as, a *faraway* look.

**farce** (färs), *n.* [Fr. < L. *farcire*, to stuff: early farces were used to fill in the interludes of a play], 1. an exaggerated comedy based on broadly humorous situations. 2. broad humor of the kind found in such plays. 3. something absurd or ridiculous. *v.t.* [FARCED, FARCING], to fill out with or as with stuffing or seasoning: as, to *farce* a play with old jokes.

**far·ci·cal** (fär′si-k'l), *adj.* of, or having the nature of, a farce; absurd; ridiculous: also **far′cial** (-shəl). —**far′ci·cal′i·ty** (-kal′ə-ti), [*pl.* -TIES], **far′ci·cal·ness,** *n.* —**far′ci·cal·ly,** *adv.*

**far cry,** a great distance or extent; long way.

**far·del** (fär′d'l), *n.* [OFr.], [Archaic], a burden.

**fare** (fâr), *v.i.* [FARED, FARING], [< AS. *faran*, to go, wander], 1. [Poetic], to travel; go. 2. to happen; result: as, how did it *fare* with him? 3. to be in a specified condition; get on: as, he *fared* well in business. 4. to eat or be given food. *n.* 1. the charge for transportation. 2. a passenger in a train, bus, etc. 3. food; diet. —**far′er,** *n.*

**Far East,** E Asia, including China, Japan, etc.

**fare·well** (fâr′wel′), *interj.* [*fare* (imperative) + *well*], good-by. *n.* (fâr′wel′), 1. parting words; good wishes at parting. 2. a departure. *adj.* (fâr′wel′), parting; last: as, a *farewell* gesture.

**far·fetched** (fär′fecht′), *adj.* not naturally resulting or introduced; strained; forced.

**far-flung** (fär′fluŋ′), *adj.* extending for a great distance.

**fa·ri·na** (fə-rē′nə), *n.* [L., < *far*, kind of grain], flour or meal made from cereal grains, potatoes, nuts, etc., eaten as a cooked cereal.

**far·i·na·ceous** (far′ə-nā′shəs), *adj.* [see FARINA], 1. consisting of or made from flour or meal. 2. mealy. 3. starchy.

**far·kle·ber·ry** (fär′k'l-ber′i), *n.* [*pl.* -RIES], [< ?], a shrub or small tree of the southern U.S., with black, inedible berries.

**farm** (färm), *n.* [< Fr. < ML. *firma*, fixed payment < *firmare*, to fix < *firmus*, steadfast], 1. the letting out, for a fixed amount, of the privilege to collect and keep taxes. 2. a piece of land (with house, barns, etc.) on which crops or animals are raised: originally, such land let out to tenants. 3. something similar to this: as, a tract of water for raising fish is a fish *farm*. 4. in *baseball*, a minor-league team owned by a major-league team. *v.t.* 1. to cultivate (land). 2. to collect the taxes, etc. of (a business) for a fixed fee. 3. to rent (a business, land, etc.) for a fixed payment. 4. to send (work) from the main shop to workers on the outside (with *out*). 5. to let out the labor of (a convict, etc.) for a fixed amount. 6. in *baseball*, to assign to a farm (with *out*). ***v.i.*** to work on or operate a farm; be a farmer.

**farm·er** (fär′mẽr), ***n.*** 1. a person who earns his living by farming; esp., one who manages or operates a farm. 2. a person who contracts to collect taxes or revenues by paying a fixed sum to the government for the right to do so.

**farm hand,** a man employed on a farm.

**farm·house** (färm′hous′), ***n.*** a house on a farm; esp., the main dwelling house on a farm.

**farm·ing** (fär′miŋ), ***adj.*** of or for agriculture. ***n.*** 1. the business of operating a farm; agriculture. 2. the letting out to farm of taxes, etc.

**farm·stead** (färm′sted′), ***n.*** the land and buildings of a farm.

**farm·yard** (färm′yärd′), ***n.*** the yard surrounding or enclosed by the farm buildings.

**far·o** (fâr′ō), ***n.*** [? < *pharaoh*], a gambling game in which players bet on the cards to be turned up from the top of the dealer's pack.

**far-off** (fär′ôf′), ***adj.*** distant; remote.

**far·ra·go** (fə-rā′gō, -rä′-), ***n.*** [*pl.* -GOES], [L., mixed fodder, mixture < *far*, kind of grain], a confused mixture; jumble; hodgepodge.

**Far·ra·gut, David Glasgow** (far′ə-gət), 1801–1870; American admiral.

**far-reach·ing** (fär′rēch′iŋ), ***adj.*** having a wide range, extent, influence, or effect.

**far·ri·er** (far′i-ẽr), ***n.*** [< OFr. < L. < *ferrum*, iron], 1. a blacksmith. 2. [Obs.], a veterinary who treats horses. —**far′ri·er·y** [*pl.* -IES], ***n.***

**far·row** (far′ō), ***n.*** [AS. *fearh*, young pig], a litter of pigs. ***v.t. & v.i.*** to give birth to (a litter of pigs).

**far·see·ing** (fär′sē′iŋ), ***adj.*** 1. capable of seeing far. 2. planning ahead; provident.

**far·sight·ed** (fär′sīt′id), ***adj.*** 1. farseeing. 2. seeing distant objects more clearly than near ones. —**far′sight′ed·ly,** ***adv.*** —**far′sight′ed·ness,** ***n.***

**far·ther** (fär′thẽr), ***adj.*** [compar. of *far*], [ME. *ferther*, var. of *further*, substituted for *ferrer*, compar.], 1. more distant. 2. additional; more. ***adv.*** 1. at or to a greater distance or more remote point. 2. to a greater degree. 3. in addition. Cf. **further** for differences in usage.

**far·ther·most** (fär′thẽr-mōst′, -məst), ***adj.*** most distant; most remote; farthest.

**far·thest** (fär′thist), ***adj.*** [superl. of *far*], [ME. *ferthest;* see FARTHER], 1. most distant. 2. longest. ***adv.*** 1. at or to the greatest distance or most remote point. 2. to the greatest degree.

**far·thing** (fär′thiŋ), ***n.*** [AS. *feorthing*, dim. of *feortha*, fourth], a small British coin, equal to half of a halfpenny: abbrev. **F., f.**

**far·thin·gale** (fär′thiŋ-gāl′), ***n.*** [OFr. *verdugalle* < Sp. < *verdugo*, tree shoot, rod < *verde* (< L. *viridis*), green], a hoop skirt worn by women in the 16th and 17th centuries.

**fas·ces** (fas′ēz), ***n.pl.*** [L., pl. of *fascis*, a bundle], a bundle of rods bound about an ax, carried before ancient Roman magistrates as a symbol of authority: later the symbol of Italian fascism.

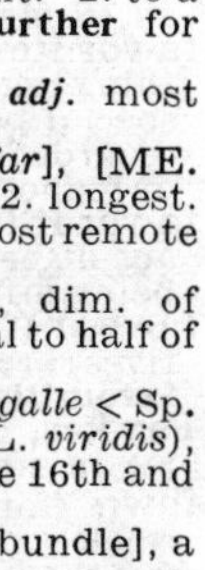
FASCES

**fas·ci·a** (fash′i-ə), ***n.*** [*pl.* -CIAE (-i-ē′)], [L., a band], 1. a band; fillet. 2. in *anatomy*, a thin layer of connective tissue. —**fas′ci·al,** ***adj.***

**fas·ci·cle** (fas′i-k'l), ***n.*** [< L. dim. of *fascis*, a bundle], 1. a small bundle or cluster, as of flowers, leaves, stems, etc. 2. an installment of a book published in parts. —**fas′ci·cled,** ***adj.***

**fas·cic·u·late** (fə-sik′yoo-lit, -lāt′), ***adj.*** formed of, or growing in, fascicles. Also **fas·cic′u·lat′ed, fas·cic′u·lar** (-lẽr).

**fas·ci·nate** (fas′'n-āt′), ***v.t.*** [-NATED, -NATING], [< L. pp. of *fascinare*, to bewitch < *fascinum*, witchcraft], 1. originally, to bewitch. 2. to hold motionless, as by inspiring terror. 3. to attract by delightful qualities; charm. —**fas′ci·nat′ing,** ***adj.*** —**fas′ci·nat′ing·ly,** ***adv.***

**fas·ci·na·tion** (fas′'n-ā′shən), ***n.*** 1. a fascinating or being fascinated. 2. charm; allure.

**fas·ci·na·tor** (fas′'n-ā′tẽr), ***n.*** 1. one who fascinates. 2. a woman's scarf of lace, net, or crocheted wool.

**fas·cism** (fash′iz'm), ***n.*** [It. *fascismo* < L. *fascis;* see FASCES], 1. [F-], the doctrines, methods, or movement of the Fascisti. 2. a system of government characterized by dictatorship, belligerent nationalism and racism, glorification of war, etc.: first instituted in Italy in 1922. 3. fascist behavior.

**fas·cist** (fash′ist), ***n.*** 1. [F-], *a*) a member of the Fascisti. *b*) a member of some similar party; Nazi, Falangist, etc. 2. an adherent of fascism. ***adj.*** 1. [F-], of Fascists or Fascism. 2. of, believing in, or practicing fascism: also **fa·scis′tic** (fə-shis′tik). —**fa·scis′ti·cal·ly,** ***adv.***

**Fa·scis·ti** (fä-shē′stē), ***n.pl.*** [*sing.* -TA (-tä)], [It. < L. *fasces;* see FASCES], an Italian political organization, founded in 1919, which set up an antidemocratic dictatorship (1922–1943) under Mussolini.

**fash·ion** (fash′ən), ***n.*** [< OFr. *façon* < L. pp. of *facere*, to make], 1. the make, form, or shape of a thing. 2. kind; sort. 3. way; manner. 4. the current style of dress, conduct, etc. 5. something fashionable. 6. fashionable society. ***v.t.*** 1. to make; form; shape. 2. to contrive. 3. to adapt (with *to*). —**after** (or **in**) **a fashion,** to some extent. —**fash′ion·er,** ***n.***

**fash·ion·a·ble** (fash′ən-ə-b'l), ***adj.*** 1. in fashion; stylish. 2. of, characteristic of, or used by people who follow fashion. ***n.*** a fashionable person. —**fash′ion·a·ble·ness,** ***n.*** —**fash′ion·a·bly,** ***adv.***

**fashion plate,** 1. a picture showing a current style in dress. 2. a fashionably dressed person.

**fast** (fast, fäst), ***adj.*** [AS. *fæst*], 1. firm; firmly fastened. 2. loyal; devoted. 3. complete; sound. 4. unfading: said of colors. 5. swift; quick; speedy. 6. permitting swift movement: as, a *fast* highway. 7. lasting a short time. 8. ahead of time: as, a *fast* clock. 9. having loose morals; promiscuous. 10. in *photography*, having a high shutter speed. ***adv.*** 1. firmly; fixedly. 2. thoroughly; soundly: as, *fast* asleep. 3. rapidly; swiftly. 4. in a reckless, dissipated way; wildly. 5. [Obs. or Poetic], close; near: as, *fast* by the river. —**play fast and loose,** to behave with duplicity or insincerity.

**fast** (fast, fäst), ***v.i.*** [AS. *fæstan*], 1. to abstain from all or certain foods, as in observing a holy day. 2. to eat very little. ***n.*** 1. a fasting. 2. a day or period of fasting. —**break one's fast,** to eat food for the first time after fasting.

**fast day,** a holy day, etc. observed by fasting.

**fas·ten** (fas′'n, fäs′'n), ***v.t.*** [AS. *fæstnian* < *fæst*, fast, *adj.*], 1. to attach; connect. 2. to make secure, as by locking, buttoning, etc. 3. to hold or direct (the attention, etc.) steadily (*on*). 4. to cause to be attributed; impute: as, he *fastened* the crime on his friend. ***v.i.*** 1. to become attached or connected. 2. to take hold; cling. —**fas′ten·er,** ***n.***

**fas·ten·ing** (fas′'n-iŋ, fäs′-), ***n.*** anything used to fasten; bolt, clasp, hook, lock, etc.

**fas·tid·i·ous** (fas-tid′i-əs), ***adj.*** [< L. < *fastidium*, a loathing < *fastus*, disdain], 1. not easy to please; very critical. 2. daintily refined; oversensitive; squeamish. —**fas·tid′i·ous·ly,** ***adv.*** —**fas·tid′i·ous·ness,** ***n.***

**fast·ness** (fast′nis, fäst′-), ***n.*** 1. the quality or condition of being fast. 2. a stronghold.

**fat** (fat), ***adj.*** [FATTER, FATTEST], [AS. *fætt*, contracted pp. of *fættian*, to fatten], 1. containing or full of fat; oily; greasy. 2. *a*) fleshy; plump. *b*) too plump; obese. 3. thick; broad. 4. fertile; productive: as, *fat* land. 5. profitable; lucrative: as, a *fat* job. 6. prosperous. 7. plentiful; ample. 8. stupid; dull. ***n.*** 1. *a*) an oily, yellow or white substance formed in animal tissue. *b*) a similar substance in vegetable matter. 2. fleshiness; corpulence. 3. the richest part of anything. 4. in *chemistry*, a class of glyceryl esters of fatty acids, insoluble in water. ***v.t. & v.i.*** [FATTED, FATTING], to make or become fat. —**a fat chance,** [Slang], very little or no chance. —**chew the fat,** [Slang], to talk together; chat. —**the fat of the land,** the best obtainable; great luxury. —**fat′ly,** ***adv.*** —**fat′ness,** ***n.***

**fa·tal** (fā′t'l), ***adj.*** [OFr. < L. *fatalis* < *fatum*, fate], 1. fateful; decisive: as, the *fatal* day arrived. 2. resulting in death. 3. destructive; ruinous. —**fa′tal·ly,** ***adv.*** —**fa′tal·ness,** ***n.***

**fa·tal·ism** (fā′t'l-iz'm), ***n.*** 1. the belief that all events are determined by fate and are therefore inevitable. 2. the acceptance of every event as inevitable. —**fa′tal·ist,** ***n.*** —**fa′tal·is′tic,** ***adj.*** —**fa′tal·is′ti·cal·ly,** ***adv.***

**fa·tal·i·ty** (fə-tal′ə-ti, fā-), ***n.*** [*pl.* -TIES], 1. the agency of fate or necessity; subjection to fate. 2. an inevitable liability to disaster. 3. a fatal quality; deadliness: as, the *fatality* of disease. 4. an event resulting in death; death.

**fate** (fāt), ***n.*** [< L. *fatum*, oracle; neut. pp. of *fari*, to speak], 1. the power supposed to determine the outcome of events; destiny. 2. something supposedly determined by this power. 3. a person's lot or fortune: as, it was his *fate* to be a bachelor. 4. final outcome. 5. death; destruction. ***v.t.*** [FATED, FATING], [Obs. except in passive], to destine. —**the Fates,** in *Gr. & Rom. mythology*, the three goddesses who control human destiny and life; Clotho, Lachesis, and Atropos.

**fat·ed** (fāt′id), ***adj.*** 1. destined. 2. doomed.

**fate·ful** (fāt′fəl), ***adj.*** 1. prophetic. 2. having important consequences; decisive. 3. controlled as if by fate. 4. bringing death or destruction. —**fate′ful·ly,** ***adv.*** —**fate′ful·ness,** ***n.***

**fat·head** (fat′hed′), ***n.*** a stupid person. —**fat′head′ed,** ***adj.***

**fa·ther** (fä′*th*ẽr), ***n.*** [AS. *fæder*], 1. a male parent. 2. a guardian or protector. 3. [F-], God. 4. a forefather; ancestor. 5. an originator; founder; inventor. 6. *pl.* the leaders of a city, assembly, etc. 7. [often F-], any of the important early Christian religious writers: also **Church Father.** 8. in the *R.C. Church, a)* a priest. *b)* his title. ***v.t.*** 1. to be the father of; beget. 2. to act as a father to; protect. 3. to originate; found; invent. —**fa′ther·hood′,** ***n.*** —**fa′ther·less,** ***adj.*** —**fa′ther·like′,** ***adj.***

**father confessor,** 1. a priest who hears confessions. 2. one in whom people habitually confide.

**fa·ther-in-law** (fä′*th*ẽr-′n-lô′), ***n.*** [*pl.* FATHERS-IN-LAW], the father of one's wife or husband.

**fa·ther·land** (fä′*th*ẽr-land′), ***n.*** 1. one's native land. 2. the land of one's ancestors.

**fa·ther·ly** (fä′*th*ẽr-li), ***adj.*** of or like a father; kindly; protective. ***adv.*** [Archaic], in a fatherly manner. —**fa′ther·li·ness,** ***n.***

**fath·om** (fa*th*′əm), ***n.*** [AS. *fæthm*, the two arms outstretched (to measure, etc.)], a nautical unit of depth or length, equal to 6 feet: abbrev. **f., fthm., fm.** ***v.t.*** 1. to measure the depth of; sound. 2. to understand thoroughly. —**fath′om·a·ble,** ***adj.*** —**fath′om·er,** ***n.*** —**fath′om·less,** ***adj.***

**fa·tigue** (fə-tēg′), ***n.*** [Fr. < L. *fatigare*, to weary], 1. physical or mental exhaustion; weariness. 2. fatigue duty. 3. *pl.* fatigue clothes. 4. a weakening in metal caused by strain. ***v.t.*** [-TIGUED, -TIGUING], 1. to tire out; weary. 2. to weaken by continued use. —**fat·i·ga·ble** (fat′i-gə-b'l), ***adj.***

**fatigue clothes,** clothing of denim or twill worn in doing fatigue duty.

**fatigue duty,** any labor, other than drill or instruction, assigned to soldiers in training.

**Fat·i·ma** (fat′i-mə, fä′ti-; *now often* fə-tē′-), ***n.*** the daughter of Mohammed; 606–632 A.D.

**fat·ling** (fat′liŋ), ***n.*** a calf, lamb, kid, or young pig fattened before being slaughtered.

**fat·ten** (fat′'n), ***v.t. & v.i.*** to make or become fat (in various senses). —**fat′ten·er,** ***n.***

**fat·tish** (fat′ish), ***adj.*** somewhat fat.

**fat·ty** (fat′i), ***adj.*** [-TIER, -TIEST], 1. of or containing fat. 2. resembling fat; greasy; oily. *n* [Colloq.]- a fat person. —**fat′ti·ly,** ***adv.*** —**fat′ti·ness,** ***n.***

**fatty acid,** any of a series of organic acids having the general formula $C_nN_{2n}O_2$.

**fa·tu·i·ty** (fə-tū′ə-ti, -tōō′-), ***n.*** [*pl.* -TIES], 1. complacent stupidity; folly. 2. something fatuous.

**fat·u·ous** (fach′ōō-əs), ***adj.*** [L. *fatuus*, foolish], 1. complacently stupid; foolish. 2. [Rare], unreal; illusory. —**fat′u·ous·ly,** ***adv.*** —**fat′u·ous·ness,** ***n.***

**fau·ces** (fô′sēz), ***n.pl.*** [L., throat], the passage leading from the back of the mouth into the pharynx. —**fau′cal** (-kəl), **fau′cial** (-shəl), ***adj.***

**fau·cet** (fô′sit), ***n.*** [< Fr.; prob. < OFr. *faulser*, to breach, falsify < L. *falsus*, false], a device with a valve for regulating the flow of a liquid from a pipe, etc.; cock; tap.

**Faulk·ner, William** (fôk′nẽr), 1897–1962; U.S. novelist.

**fault** (fôlt), ***n.*** [< OFr. *faute* < pp. of L. *fallere*, to deceive], 1. something that mars; flaw; defect. 2. *a)* a misdeed; offense. *b)* an error; mistake. 3. responsibility for something wrong; blame: as, it's my *fault* that he's late. 4. in *geology*, a break in rock strata or veins that causes dislocation along the line of fracture. 5. in *tennis, squash*, etc., an improper serve. ***v.t. & v.i.*** in *geology*, to develop, or cause to have, a fault. —**at fault,** in the wrong; deserving blame. —**find fault,** to seek and point out faults; complain. —**find fault with,** to criticize. —**to a fault,** too much; excessively.

FAULT

**fault·find·ing** (fôlt′fīn′diŋ), ***n. & adj.*** finding fault; criticizing. —**fault′find′er,** ***n.***

**fault·less** (fôlt′lis), ***adj.*** without blemish, imperfection, or error; perfect. —**fault′less·ly,** ***adv.*** —**fault′less·ness,** ***n.***

**fault·y** (fôl′ti), ***adj.*** [-IER, -IEST], 1. having a fault or faults; imperfect. 2. [Obs.], deserving blame. —**fault′i·ly,** ***adv.*** —**fault′i·ness,** ***n.***

**faun** (fôn), ***n.*** [L. *Faunus*, a Roman nature god], any of a class of minor Roman rural deities, represented as having the body of a man, but the horns, ears, tail, and hind legs of a goat.

FAUN

**fau·na** (fô′nə), ***n.*** [*pl.* -NAS, -NAE (-nē)], [< LL. *Fauna*, Roman goddess], the animals of a specified region or time: as, the *fauna* of North America.

**Faust** (foust), ***n.*** the hero of a medieval legend (and in literature) who sells his soul to the devil in exchange for knowledge and power.

**faux pas** (fō′pä′), [*pl.* FAUX PAS (-päz′; Fr. -pä′)], [Fr., lit., false step], a social blunder; error in etiquette.

**fa·vor** (fā′vẽr), ***n.*** [< OFr. < L. < *favere*, to favor], 1. friendly regard; approval. 2. *a)* kind indulgence. *b)* too kind indulgence; unfair partiality. 3. a kind or obliging act. 4. a small gift, souvenir, or token. ***v.t.*** 1. to regard with favor; approve; like. 2. to be partial to; prefer unfairly. 3. to support; advocate. 4. to make easier; help: as, the rain *favored* his escape. 5. to do a kindness for. 6. to look like; resemble: as, he *favors* his mother. 7. to use gently; spare: as, to *favor* an injured hand. —**find favor,** to be pleasing to. —**in favor of,** 1. approving; supporting. 2. to the advantage of. 3. payable to, as a check. —**in one's favor,** to one's advantage or credit. —**fa′vor·er,** ***n.***

**fa·vor·a·ble** (fā′vẽr-ə-b'l), ***adj.*** favoring; specif., *a)* approving. *b)* helpful; advantageous. —**fa′vor·a·ble·ness,** ***n.*** —**fa′vor·a·bly,** ***adv.***

**fa·vored** (fā′vẽrd), ***adj.*** 1. treated with favor; specially privileged. 2. having (specified) features: as, *ill-favored.*

**fa·vor·ite** (fā′vẽr-it, fāv′rit), ***n.*** 1. a person or thing regarded with special liking. 2. one granted special privileges, as by a king. 3. a contestant regarded as most likely to win. ***adj.*** held in special or highest regard; preferred.

**fa·vor·it·ism** (fā′vẽr-it-iz'm, fāv′rit-), ***n.*** 1. the act of being unfairly partial. 2. the condition of being a favorite.

**fa·vour** (fā′vẽr), ***n. & v.t.*** favor: British sp.: derivatives are similarly spelled (**favoured, favourite, favouritism,** etc.).

**Fawkes, Guy** (fôks), 1570–1606; English conspirator in a plot to blow up Parliament.

**fawn** (fôn), ***v.i.*** [AS. *fagnian*, var. of *fægnian*, to rejoice < *fægen*, fain], 1. to show affection by licking the hand, wagging the tail, etc.: said of a dog. 2. to act servilely; cringe and flatter. —**fawn′er,** ***n.*** —**fawn′ing·ly,** ***adv.***

**fawn** (fôn), ***n.*** [< OFr. *faon* < L. *fetus*, fetus], 1. a young deer less than one year old. 2. a pale, yellowish brown. ***adj.*** of this color.

**fay** (fā), ***n.*** [< OFr. < LL. < *fatum*, fate], a fairy.

**faze** (fāz), ***v.t.*** [FAZED, FAZING], [< AS. *fes(i)an*, to drive], [Colloq.], to disturb; disconcert.

**FBI, F.B.I.,** Federal Bureau of Investigation.

**fcap., fcp.,** foolscap.

**FCC, F.C.C.,** Federal Communications Commission.

**F clef,** the bass clef.

**Fe,** *ferrum*, [L.], in *chemistry*, iron.

**fe·al·ty** (fē′əl-ti), ***n.*** [*pl.* -TIES], [< OFr. *feaulte* < L. *fidelitas;* see FIDELITY], 1. the loyalty owed by a vassal to his feudal lord. 2. [Archaic or Poetic], loyalty; fidelity.

**fear** (fēr), ***n.*** [AS. *fær*, danger], 1. anxiety and agitation caused by the presence of danger, evil, pain, etc.; dread; fright. 2. awe; reverence. 3. a feeling of uneasiness; anxiety; concern. 4. a cause for fear; danger. ***v.t.*** 1. to be afraid of; dread. 2. to feel reverence or awe for. 3. to expect with misgiving: as, I *fear* he'll be late. ***v.i.*** 1. to feel fear. 2. to be uneasy or anxious. —**for fear of,** in order to avoid or prevent. —**fear′er,** ***n.*** —**fear′less,** ***adj.*** —**fear′less·ly,** ***adv.*** —**fear′less·ness,** ***n.***

**fear·ful** (fēr′fəl), ***adj.*** 1. causing fear; dreadful. 2. feeling fear; afraid. 3. showing fear: as, a *fearful* look. 4. [Colloq.], very bad, great, etc.: as, a *fearful* liar. —**fear′ful·ly,** *adv.* —**fear′ful·ness,** *n.*

**fear·some** (fêr′səm), *adj.* 1. causing fear; frightful. 2. frightened; timid. —**fear′some·ly,** *adv.* —**fear′some·ness,** *n.*

**fea·si·ble** (fē′zə-b'l), *adj.* [< OFr. *faisible* < *faire*, to make, do < L. *facere*], 1. capable of being done or carried out; practicable; possible. 2. likely; reasonable; probable. 3. capable of being used effectively; suitable. —**fea′si·bil′i·ty** [*pl.* -TIES], **fea′si·ble·ness,** *n.* —**fea′si·bly,** *adv.*

**feast** (fēst), *n.* [< OFr. < L. *festa*, pl. of *festum* < *festus*, festal], 1. a festival; esp., a religious festival. 2. a rich and elaborate meal; banquet. 3. anything that gives pleasure by its abundance or richness. *v.i.* to have a feast. *v.t.* 1. to entertain with a feast. 2. to please; delight: as, he *feasted* his eyes on her. —**feast′er,** *n.*

**feat** (fēt), *n.* [< OFr. < L. *factum*, a deed, pp. of *facere*, to do], an act or accomplishment showing unusual daring, skill, etc.; remarkable deed.

**feath·er** (feth′ẽr), *n.* [AS. *fether*], 1. any of the outgrowths covering the body of a bird and making up a large part of the wing surface. 2. anything like a feather in appearance, lightness, etc. 3. *pl.* *a)* plumage. *b)* attire. 4. class; kind: as, birds of a *feather*. 5. the act of feathering an oar. *v.t.* 1. to provide or adorn as with feathers. 2. to join by inserting a wedge-shaped part into a groove. 3. to turn the edge of (an oar or propeller blade) toward the line of movement: as, rowers *feather* their oars between strokes. *v.i.* 1. to grow feathers. 2. to move, grow, or look like feathers. 3. to feather an oar or propeller. —**feather in one's cap,** an achievement worthy of pride. —**feather one's nest,** to provide for one's comfort or security. —**in fine** (or **high** or **good**) **feather,** in good humor, spirits, etc. —**feath′ered,** *adj.* —**feath′er·less,** *adj.* —**feath′er·like′,** *adj.*

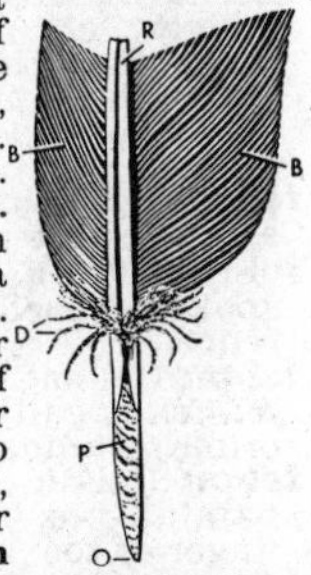

FEATHER
B, barbs (with barbules); D, down; R, shaft; O, opening at end of shaft; P, pith

**feather bed,** a large, heavy quilt thickly filled with feathers or down, used as a mattress.

**feath·er·brain** (feth′ẽr-brān′), *n.* a foolish, silly, frivolous person. —**feath′er·brained′,** *adj.*

**feath·er·edge** (feth′ẽr-ej′), *n.* a very thin edge, easily broken or curled. —**feath′er·edged′,** *adj.*

**feath·er·stitch** (feth′ẽr-stich′), *n.* an embroidery stitch forming a zigzag line. *v.t.* & *v.i.* to embroider with such stitches.

**feath·er·weight** (feth′ẽr-wāt′), *n.* 1. a person or thing of light weight or small size. 2. a boxer or wrestler who weighs between 119 and 126 pounds. *adj.* 1. of featherweights. 2. light or trivial.

**feath·er·y** (feth′ẽr-i), *adj.* 1. covered with or as with feathers. 2. resembling feathers; soft, light, etc. —**feath′er·i·ness,** *n.*

**fea·ture** (fē′chẽr), *n.* [< OFr. < L. *factura*, a making < *facere*, to make], 1. originally, the make, form, or appearance of a person or thing. 2. *a)* *pl.* the form or cast of the face. *b)* any of the parts of the face, as the eyes, nose, mouth, etc. 3. a distinct or outstanding part or quality of something. 4. a prominently displayed attraction or item in a program, sale, etc. 5. a special story, article, etc. in a newspaper or magazine. 6. a full-length motion picture. *v.t.* [-TURED, -TURING], 1. to portray; represent. 2. to make a feature or specialty of. 3. to sketch or show the features of. 4. to be a feature of. 5. [Slang], to conceive of. —**fea′ture·less,** *adj.*

**fea·tured** (fē′chẽrd), *adj.* 1. having (a specified kind of) facial features: as, *broad-featured*. 2. formed; shaped. 3. given special prominence.

**feaze** (fēz, fāz), *v.t.* [FEAZED, FEAZING], to faze.

**Feb.,** February.

**feb·ri-,** [< L. *febris*], a combining form meaning *fever*, as in *febrifuge*.

**feb·ri·fuge** (feb′ri-fūj′), *n.* [< Fr.; see FEBRI- & -FUGE], any substance for reducing or removing fever. *adj.* reducing or removing fever. —**fe·brif·u·gal** (fi-brif′yoo-gəl, feb′rə-fū′-), *adj.*

**fe·brile** (fē′brəl, feb′rəl), *adj.* [< Fr. < L. *febris*, fever], 1. of or characterized by fever; feverish. 2. caused by fever.

**Feb·ru·ar·y** (feb′roo-er′i; *now often* feb′yoo-), *n.* [L. *Februarius* < *februa*, Roman festival of purification held Feb. 15], the second month of the year, having 28 days (or 29 days in leap years).

**fe·cal** (fē′kəl), *adj.* of feces: also sp. **faecal.**

**fe·ces** (fē′sēz), *n.pl.* [< L. *faeces*, dregs], 1. waste matter expelled from the bowels; excrement. 2. dregs; sediment. Also sp. **faeces.**

**feck·less** (fek′lis), *adj.* [Scot. < *effect* + *-less*], 1. weak; ineffective. 2. thoughtless; careless. —**feck′less·ly,** *adv.* —**feck′less·ness,** *n.*

**fe·cund** (fē′kənd, fek′ənd), *adj.* [< Fr. < L. *fecundus*, fruitful], fruitful; fertile; productive. —**fe·cun·di·ty** (fi-kun′də-ti), *n.*

**fe·cun·date** (fē′kən-dāt′, fek′ən-), *v.t.* [-DATED, -DATING], [< L. pp.; ult. < *fecundus*, fruitful], 1. to make fruitful, fertile, or productive. 2. to impregnate; pollinate. —**fe′cun·da′tion,** *n.*

**fed** (fed), pt. and pp. of **feed.** —**fed up,** [Slang], having had enough to become disgusted, bored, etc.

**Fed.,** 1. Federal. 2. Federation.

**fed·er·al** (fed′ẽr-əl, fed′rəl), *adj.* [< Fr. < L. *foedus*, a league], 1. of or formed by a compact; specif., designating or of a union of states, groups, etc. in which each member subordinates its power to a central authority in common affairs. 2. designating or of a central government of this sort. 3. [usually F-], designating or of the central government of the United States. 4. [F-], of or supporting the Federalist Party or its principles. 5. [F-], of or supporting the central government of the U.S. in the Civil War. *n.* 1. [F-], a Federalist. 2. [F-], a supporter or soldier of the Federal government in the Civil War. —**fed′er·al·ly,** *adv.*

**Federal Bureau of Investigation,** a branch of the U.S. Department of Justice whose duty is to investigate and bring to trial violators of Federal criminal laws: abbrev. **FBI, F.B.I.**

**fed·er·al·ism** (fed′ẽr-əl-iz'm, fed′rəl-), *n.* 1. the federal principle of government or organization. 2. [F-], the principles of the Federalist Party.

**fed·er·al·ist** (fed′ẽr-əl-ist, fed′rəl-), *n.* 1. one who believes in or supports federalism. 2. [F-], a member or supporter of the Federalist Party. *adj.* 1. of or supporting federalism. 3. [F-], of or supporting the Federalist Party or its principles. —**fed′er·al·is′tic,** *adj.*

**Federalist** (or **Federal**) **Party,** a political party in the U.S. (1789–1816) which advocated the adoption of the Constitution and the establishment of a strong, centralized government.

**fed·er·al·ize** (fed′ẽr-əl-īz′, fed′rəl-), *v.t.* [-IZED, -IZING], 1. to unite (states, etc.) in a federal union. 2. to put under the authority of a federal government. —**fed′er·al·i·za′tion,** *n.*

**fed·er·ate** (fed′ẽr-it; *for v.*, -āt′), *adj.* [< L. *foederatus*, pp. < *foedus*; see FEDERAL], united by common agreement under a central government or authority. *v.t.* & *v.i.* [-ATED, -ATING], to unite in a federation.

**fed·er·a·tion** (fed′ə-rā′shən), *n.* 1 a uniting by compact; union of states, groups, etc. by agreement of each member to subordinate its power to that of the central authority in common affairs. 2. a federated organization; league. —**fed′er·a′tive,** *adj.* —**fed′er·a′tive·ly,** *adv.*

**fe·do·ra** (fi-dôr′ə), *n.* [Fr. < *Fédora* (1882), play by V. Sardou, Fr. dramatist], a soft felt hat with the crown creased lengthwise and a curved brim.

**fee** (fē), *n.* [< Anglo-Fr. *fee, fie*; ult. < Gmc.; sense influences < ML. *feudum*, prob. lit., cattle-wealth], 1. originally, a fief; feud. 2. a payment asked or given for professional services, licenses, tuition, etc.; charge. 3. a present of money; tip. 4. in *law*, an inheritance in land: an estate can be held with unrestricted rights of disposition (**fee simple**) or with restrictions as to a specified class of heirs (**fee tail**). *v.t.* to give a fee to. —**hold in fee,** to own.

**fee·ble** (fē′b'l), *adj.* [-BLER, -BLEST], [< OFr. < L. *flebilis*, to be wept over < *flere*, to weep], weak; not strong; specif., *a)* infirm: as, a *feeble* old man. *b)* without force or effectiveness: as, a *feeble* light. *c)* easily broken; frail: as, a *feeble* barrier. —**fee′ble·ness,** *n.* —**fee′blish,** *adj.* —**fee′bly,** *adv.*

**fee·ble-mind·ed** (fē′b'l-mīn′did), *adj.* mentally weak; subnormal in intelligence. —**fee′ble-mind′ed·ly,** *adv.* —**fee′ble-mind′ed·ness,** *n.*

**feed** (fēd), *v.t.* [FED, FEEDING], [< AS. *fedan* < *fod*, food], 1. to give food to; provide food for. 2. to provide as food: as, to *feed* oats to horses. 3. to provide something necessary for the growth or existence of; nourish: as, the news *fed* his anger. 4. to provide (material to be used up): as, *feed* coal to the stove. 5. to provide with material: as, *feed* the stove. 6. to provide satisfaction for; gratify: as, to *feed* one's vanity. *v.i.* to eat: said chiefly of animals. *n.* 1. food given to animals; fodder. 2. the amount of fodder given at one time. 3. material supplied to a machine. 4. the part of a machine supplying this material. 5. the supplying of this material. 6. [Colloq.], a meal. **—feed on** (or **upon**), to be nourished or gratified by. **—off one's feed,** [Slang], lacking appetite; sickish. **—feed'er,** *n.*

**feed·back** (fēd'bak'), *n.* 1. in *electronics*, the transfer of part of the output back to the input, either as an unwanted effect or to reduce distortion, etc. 2. a process in which the factors that produce a result are themselves modified, corrected, etc. by that result.

**feel** (fēl), *v.t.* [FELT, FEELING], [AS. *felan*], 1. to touch; to examine by touching or handling. 2. to be aware of through physical sensation: as, he *felt* tears on his cheeks. 3. to be influenced or moved by. 4. to be aware of: as, I *feel* his sincerity. 5. to think; believe; consider. *v.i.* 1. to have physical sensation. 2. to appear to be to the senses, especially to the sense of touch: as, the water *feels* warm. 3. to search by touching; grope. 4. to be aware of being: as, I *feel* sad. 5. to be moved to sympathy, pity, etc. *n.* 1. the act of feeling. 2. the sense of touch. 3. the nature of a thing perceived through touch. 4. an emotional sensation. **—feel (a person) out,** to try cautiously to find out the opinions of (a person). **—feel like,** [Colloq.], to have a desire for. **—feel up to,** [Colloq.], to feel capable of.

**feel·er** (fēl'ẽr), *n.* 1. a person or thing that feels. 2. a specialized organ of touch in an animal or insect, as an antenna. 3. a remark, question, etc. made to find out another's attitude.

**feel·ing** (fēl'iŋ), *adj.* sensitive and sympathetic. *n.* 1. that sense by which sensations of contact, pressure, temperature, and pain are transmitted through the skin; sense of touch. 2. the ability to experience physical sensation. 3. an awareness; consciousness: as, a *feeling* of pain. 4. an emotion. 5. *pl.* sensitivities; susceptibilities: as, her *feelings* are easily hurt. 6. a kindly attitude; sympathy; pity. 7. *a*) an opinion or sentiment. *b*) a premonition: as, a *feeling* of impending doom. 8. air; atmosphere: as, a *feeling* of excitement in the room. 9. the emotional quality in a work of art. **—feel'ing·ly,** *adv.*

**feet (fēt),** *n.* pl. of **foot**: abbrev. **ft., f., F. —carry** (or **sweep**) **off one's feet,** 1. to fill with enthusiasm. 2. to impress deeply. **—on one's feet,** firmly established. **—sit at the feet of,** to be an admiring disciple or pupil of. **—stand on one's own feet,** to be independent.

**feign** (fān), *v.t.* [< OFr. *feindre* < L. *fingere*, to shape], 1. to make up (a story, excuse, etc.); fabricate. 2. to imagine. 3. to make a false show of; pretend. *v.i.* to pretend; dissemble. **—feigned,** *adj.* **—feign'er,** *n.* **—feign'ing·ly,** *adv.*

**feint** (fānt), *n.* [< Fr. pp. of *feindre;* see FEIGN], 1. a false show; pretense. 2. a pretended attack intended to take the opponent off his guard, as in boxing or fencing. *v.i.* to deliver such an attack.

**feld·spar** (feld'spär', fel'spär'), *n.* [< G. < *feld*, field + *spat(h)*, spar], any of several crystalline minerals made up mainly of aluminum silicates, usually glassy and moderately hard: also **felspar.** **—feld·spath'ic** (-spath'ik), **feld·spath'ose,** *adj.*

**fe·lic·i·tate** (fə-lis'ə-tāt'), *v.t.* [-TATED, -TATING], [< L. pp. of *felicitare* < *felix*, happy], to congratulate; wish happiness to. **—fe·lic'i·ta'tion,** *n.*

**fe·lic·i·tous** (fə-lis'ə-təs), *adj.* [< *felicity* + *-ous*], 1. used or expressed in a way suitable to the occasion; appropriate. 2. having the knack of appropriate and pleasing expression. **—fe·lic'i·tous·ly,** *adv.* **—fe·lic'i·tous·ness,** *n.*

**fe·lic·i·ty** (fə-lis'ə-ti), *n.* [*pl.* -TIES], [< OFr. < L. < *felix*, happy], 1. happiness; bliss. 2. anything producing happiness. 3. a quality of appropriate and pleasing expression in writing, speaking, etc. 4. an apt expression or thought.

**fe·line** (fē'līn), *adj.* [< L. < *felis*, cat], 1. of a cat or the cat family. 2. catlike; sly; stealthy. *n.* any animal of the cat family, including the cat, lion, panther, tiger, etc. **—fe'line·ly,** *adv.* **—fe'line·ness, fe·lin·i·ty** (fi-lin'ə-ti), *n.*

**fell** (fel), pt. of **fall.**

**fell** (fel), *v.t.* [AS. *fellan*], 1. to make fall; knock down. 2. to cut down (a tree). 3. to turn over (the rough edge of a seam) and sew down flat. *n.* 1. the trees cut down in one season. 2. a felled seam. **—fell'a·ble,** *adj.* **—fell'er,** *n.*

**fell** (fel), *adj.* [< OFr. < LL. hyp. *fello;* see FELON], 1. fierce; terrible; cruel. 2. [Archaic or Poetic], causing death; deadly: as, a *fell* plague. **—fell'ness,** *n.* **—fel'ly,** *adv.*

**fell** (fel), *n.* [AS. *fel*], an animal's hide or skin.

**fell** (fel), *n.* [< Anglo-N.], [Brit.], a moor; down.

**fel·lah** (fel'ə), *n.* [*pl.* -LAHS; Ar. -LAHEEN, -LAHIN (fel'ə-hēn')], [< Ar. < *falāḥa*, to plow], a peasant or laborer in Egypt or some other countries where Arabic is spoken.

**fel·loe** (fel'ō), *n.* a felly (rim).

**fel·low** (fel'ō, fel'ə), *n.* [< AS. *feolaga* < ON. *félagi*, partner], 1. a companion; associate. 2. one of the same class or rank; equal. 3. either of a pair of similar things; mate. 4. one holding a fellowship in a university or college. 5. a member of a learned society. 6. [Brit.], a member of a governing body of a college. 7. [Colloq.], *a*) a man or boy. *b*) a person; one: as, a *fellow* must eat. 8. [Colloq], a suitor; beau. *adj.* having the same ideas, position, work, etc.; associated: as, *fellow* workers.

**fel·low·ship** (fel'ō-ship'), *n.* 1. companionship; friendly association. 2. a mutual sharing, as of activity, etc. 3. a group of people with the same interests. 4. *a*) an endowment, or a sum paid from it, for the support of a graduate student in a university or college. *b*) the rank or position of such a fellow.

**fellow traveler,** a nonmember who supports or approves the cause of a party.

**fel·ly** (fel'i), *n.* [*pl.* -LIES], [AS. *felg*], 1. the rim of a spoked wheel. 2. a segment of such a rim. Also **felloe.**

**fel·on** (fel'ən), *n.* [< OFr. < LL. hyp. *fello;* ? < L. *fel, fellis*, gall], in *law*, a person guilty of a major crime; criminal. *adj.* wicked; base; criminal.

**fel·on** (fel'ən), *n.* [prob. < same base as prec.], a painful, pus-producing infection at the end of a finger or toe, near the nail.

**fe·lo·ni·ous** (fə-lō'ni-əs), *adj.* 1. wicked; base; criminal. 2. of, like, or constituting a felony. **—fe·lo'ni·ous·ly,** *adv.* **—fe·lo'ni·ous·ness,** *n.*

**fel·o·ny** (fel'ə-ni), *n.* [*pl.* -NIES], [< OFr. < LL.; see FELON], a major crime, as murder, arson, rape, etc., for which statute provides a greater punishment than for a misdemeanor.

**fel·spar** (fel'spär'), *n.* feldspar.

**felt** (felt), *n.* [AS.] 1. a fabric of wool, often mixed with fur or hair, worked together by pressure, heat, chemical action, etc: also **felt'ing.** 2. anything made of felt. *adj.* made of felt. *v.t.* 1. to make into felt. 2. to cover with felt.

**felt** (felt), pt. and pp. of **feel.**

**fe·luc·ca** (fə-luk'ə, fe-), *n.* [< It. & Sp.; ? < Ar. *fulk*, a ship], a small, narrow ship propelled by oars or lateen sails or both, used along the Mediterranean coasts.

**fem.,** feminine.

**fe·male** (fē'māl), *adj.* [< OFr. < L. dim. of *femina*, a woman], 1. designating or of the sex that produces ova and bears offspring. 2. of, like, or suitable to members of this sex; feminine. 3. of women or girls. 4. in *botany*, having a pistil and no stamens. 5. in *mechanics*, designating or having a hollow part shaped to receive a corresponding inserted part: said of a gauge, plug, etc. *n.* a female person, animal, or plant. **—fe'male·ness,** *n.*

**fem·i·nine** (fem'ə-nin), *adj.* [< L. < *femina*, woman], 1. of women or girls. 2. having qualities regarded as characteristic of women and girls, as gentleness, delicacy, etc. 3. suitable to or characteristic of a woman. 4. effeminate: said of men. 5. in *grammar*, designating or of the gender of words referring to females or things originally regarded as female. *n.* in *grammar*, 1. the feminine gender. 2. a word or form in this gender. **—fem'i·nine·ly,** *adv.* **—fem'i·nin'i·ty, fem'i·nine·ness,** *n.*

**feminine rhyme,** a rhyme of two or, sometimes, three syllables of which only the first is stressed (e.g., haziness, laziness).

**fem·i·nism** (fem'ə-niz'm), *n.* 1. the theory that women should have political, economic, and social rights equal to those of men, or the movement to win these. 2. [Rare], feminine qualities. **—fem'i·nist,** *n. & adj.* **—fem'i·nis'tic,** *adj.*

**fem·i·nize** (fem'ə-nīz'), *v.t. & v.i.* [-NIZED, -NIZING], to make or become feminine or effeminate. **—fem'i·ni·za'tion,** *n.*

‡**femme** (fàm), *n.* [Fr.], a woman or wife.

**fe·mur** (fē'mẽr), *n.* [*pl.* -MURS, -MORA (fem'ẽr-ə)], [L., thigh], the thighbone. **—fem'o·ral** (fem'ẽr-əl), *adj.*

**fen** (fen), *n.* [AS. *fen, fenn*], low, flat, marshy land; swamp; bog. **—fen'ny,** *adj.*

**fe·na·gle** (fi-nā′g'l), *v.i.* & *v.t.* [-GLED, -GLING], to finagle. —**fe·na′gler,** *n.*
**fence** (fens), *n.* [ME., abbrev. of *defence*], 1. a barrier of posts, wire, rails, etc., used as a boundary or means of protection or confinement. 2. the art of self-defense with foil, saber, etc.; fencing. 3. expertness in conversation or debate. 4. one who buys and sells stolen goods, or his shop. *v.t.* [FENCED, FENCING], 1. to enclose as with a fence. 2. [Archaic], to ward off; protect. *v.i.* 1. to practice the art of fencing. 2. to avoid giving a direct reply; evade. 3. to buy or sell stolen goods. —**on the fence,** not having chosen to join one side or the other. —**fence′less,** *adj.* —**fence′less·ness,** *n.* —**fence′-like′,** *adj.* —**fenc′er,** *n.*
**fenc·ing** (fen′siŋ), *n.* 1. the art of fighting with a foil or other sword. 2. debating. 3. material for making fences. 4. a system of fences.
**fend** (fend), *v.t.* [< *defend*], [Archaic], to defend. *v.i.* to resist; parry. —**fend for oneself,** to manage by oneself. —**fend off,** to ward off; repel.
**fend·er** (fen′dẽr), *n.* anything that fends off or protects something else; specif., *a*) any of the metal frames over the wheels of an automobile or other vehicle; mudguard. *b*) a device on the front of a streetcar or locomotive to catch or push aside anything on the track; cowcatcher. *c*) a screen or guard placed in front of a fireplace.
**Fe·ni·an** (fē′ni-ən, fēn′yən), *n.* [< *Fiann*(*a*), the old militia of Ireland], a member of a secret Irish revolutionary group (**Fenian Brotherhood**) formed in New York about 1858 to free Ireland from English rule. *adj.* of the Fenians. —**Fe′ni·an·ism,** *n.*
**fen·nel** (fen′'l), *n.* [< AS. < L. *feniculum*, dim. of *fenum*, hay], a tall herb of the carrot family, with yellow flowers: its aromatic seeds are used as a seasoning and in medicine.
**feoff** (fef, fēf), *v.t.* [< Anglo-Fr. < OFr. < *fieu*, fief], to give or sell a fief to. *n.* a fief. —**feoff′ment,** *n.* —**feof′for, feoff′er,** *n.*
**FEPC,** Fair Employment Practices Committee.
**-fer** (fẽr), [see -FEROUS], a suffix meaning *one that bears* or *produces*, as in *conifer*.
**fe·ral** (fêr′əl), *adj.* [< L. < *ferus*, wild; + *-al*], 1. untamed; uncultivated; wild. 2. savage; brutal.
**fer·de·lance** (fâr′də-läns′), *n.* [Fr., iron tip of a lance], a large, poisonous snake related to the rattlesnake, found in tropical American countries.
**fer·ment** (fũr′mənt; *for v.*, fẽr-ment′), *n.* [Fr. < L. *fermentum* < *fervere*, to boil], 1. a substance causing fermentation in other substances, as yeast, bacteria, etc. 2. fermentation. 3. a state of excitement; agitation. *v.t.* 1. to cause fermentation in. 2. to excite; agitate. *v.i.* 1. to be in the process of fermentation. 2. to be excited or agitated; seethe. —**fer·ment′a·ble,** *adj.* —**fer·ment′er,** *n.*
**fer·men·ta·tion** (fũr′mən-tā′shən, -men-), *n.* 1. the breakdown of complex molecules in organic compounds, caused by the influence of a ferment: as bacteria curdle milk by *fermentation*. 2. excitement; agitation. —**fer·ment′a·tive (-men′tə-tiv),** *adj.*
**Fer·mi, En·ri·co** (en-rē′kô fâr′mē), 1901–1954; Italian nuclear physicist in U.S.
**fer·mi·um** (fâr′mi-əm), *n.* [after E. *Fermi*], a transuranic, radioactive chemical element: symbol, Fm; at. wt., 254 (?); at. no., 100.
**fern** (fũrn), *n.* [AS. *fearn*], any of a large group of shrubby, nonflowering plants having roots, stems, and fronds, and reproducing by spores instead of by seeds. —**fern′like′,** *adj.* —**fern′y,** *adj.*
**fern·er·y** (fũr′nẽr-i), *n.* [*pl.* -IES], a place where ferns are grown; collection of growing ferns.
**fe·ro·cious** (fi-rō′shəs), *adj.* [< L. *ferox* < *ferus*, fierce; + *-ous*], 1. fierce; savage; violently cruel. 2. [Colloq.], very great: as, a *ferocious* appetite. —**fe·ro′cious·ly,** *adv.* —**fe·ro′cious·ness,** *n.*
**fe·roc·i·ty** (fi-ros′ə-ti), *n.* [*pl.* -TIES], the quality or condition of being ferocious; fierceness; savagery.
**-fer·ous** (fẽr-əs), [L. *-fer* < *ferre*, to bear; + *-ous*], a suffix meaning *bearing, yielding,* as in *coniferous*.
**fer·ret** (fer′it), *n.* [< OFr. < LL. *furo* < L. *fur*, thief], a kind of weasel, easily tamed and used for hunting rabbits, rats, etc. *v.t.* 1. to force out of hiding with a ferret. 2. to look for carefully; search out. *v.i.* 1. to hunt with ferrets. 2. to search. —**fer′ret·er,** *n.* —**fer′ret·y,** *adj.*
**fer·ri-** (fer′i, -ī), a combining form meaning *containing ferric iron*: see **ferro-.**
**fer·ric** (fer′ik), *adj.* [< L. *ferrum*, iron; + *-ic*], 1. of, containing, or derived from iron. 2. in *chemistry*, designating or of iron with a valence higher than two, or compounds containing such iron.
**Fer·ris wheel** (fer′is), [after George W. G. *Ferris* (1859–1896), U.S. engineer who invented it], a large, upright wheel revolving on a fixed axle and having seats hanging from the frame: used in amusement parks, etc.

FERRIS WHEEL

**fer·ro-,** [< L. *ferrum*, iron], a combining form meaning: 1. *iron, connection with iron*. 2. *iron and*, as in *ferromanganese*. 3. in *chemistry, containing ferrous iron*.
**fer·ro·con·crete** (fer′ō-kon′krēt, -kon-krēt′), *n.* concrete having an iron or steel framework embedded in it: also called *reinforced concrete*.
**fer·ro·mag·net·ic** (fer′ō-mag-net′ik), *adj.* highly magnetic, as iron, nickel, etc. —**fer′ro·mag′net·ism** (-nə-tiz'm), *n.*
**fer·ro·man·ga·nese** (fer′ō-maŋ′gə-nēs′, -nēz′), *n.* an alloy of iron and manganese, used for making hard steel.
**fer·rous** (fer′əs), *adj.* [< L. *ferrum*, iron; + *-ous*], 1. of, containing, or derived from iron. 2. in *chemistry*, designating or of bivalent iron or compounds containing it.
**fer·ru·gi·nous** (fə-rōō′ji-nəs), *adj.* [< L. < *ferrugo*, iron rust < *ferrum*, iron], 1. of, containing, or having the nature of, iron. 2. having the color of iron rust; reddish-brown.
**fer·rule** (fer′əl, -ool), *n.* [< OFr. < LL. < L. *viriola*, dim. of *viriae*, bracelets], a metal ring or cap put around the end of a stick, tool, cane, etc. to give added strength. *v.t.* [-RULED, -RULING], to furnish with a ferrule.
**fer·ry** (fer′i), *v.t.* [-RIED, -RYING], [AS. *ferian*, to carry, caus. of *faran*, to go], 1. to take across a river, etc. in a boat. 2. to cross (a river, etc.), as on a ferry. 3. to deliver (airplanes) by flying to the destination. *v.i.* to cross a river, etc. in a ferryboat. *n.* [*pl.* -RIES], 1. a transportation system for carrying people, goods, etc. across a river, etc. 2. a ferryboat. 3. the place where a ferryboat crosses. 4. the delivery of airplanes from one point to another by flying them. —**fer′ry·man** [*pl.* -MEN], *n.*
**fer·ry·boat** (fer′i-bōt′), *n.* a boat for transporting people or goods across a river, etc.
**fer·tile** (fũr′t'l), *adj.* [< OFr. < L. *fertilis* < *ferre*, to bear], 1. producing abundantly; rich in resources or invention; fruitful. 2. able to produce young, seeds, fruit, etc. 3. capable of development into a new individual; fertilized. —**fer′tile·ly,** *adv.* —**fer′tile·ness,** *n.*
**fer·til·i·ty** (fẽr-til′ə-ti), *n.* [*pl.* -TIES], the quality or state of being fertile; productivity.
**fer·ti·lize** (fũr′t'l-īz′), *v.t.* [-LIZED, -LIZING], 1. to make fertile; make fruitful or productive. 2. to spread fertilizer on. 3. to make (the female reproductive cell or female individual) fruitful by introducing the male germ cell; impregnate. —**fer′ti·liz′a·ble,** *adv.* —**fer′ti·li·za′tion,** *n.*
**fer·ti·liz·er** (fũr′t'l-īz′ẽr), *n.* one that fertilizes; specif., manure, chemicals, etc. put in soil to improve the quality or quantity of plant growth.
**fer·ule** (fer′əl, -ōōl), *n.* [L. *ferula*, rod], a flat stick or ruler used for punishing children. *v.t.* [-ULED, -ULING], to strike with a ferule.
**fer·vent** (fũr′vənt), *adj.* [< L. ppr. of *fervere*, to glow, boil], 1. hot; burning; glowing. 2. having or showing great warmth of feeling; intensely earnest. —**fer′ven·cy, fer′vent·ness,** *n.* —**fer′vent·ly,** *adv.*
**fer·vid** (fũr′vid), *adj.* [< L. < *fervere*, to boil, glow], 1. hot; burning; glowing. 2. impassioned; fervent. —**fer′vid·ly,** *adv.* —**fer′vid·ness,** *n.*
**fer·vor** (fũr′vẽr), *n.* [< OFr. < L.; see FERVENT], 1. intense heat. 2. great warmth of emotion; intense feeling; ardor; zeal. Also, Brit. sp., **fervour.**
**fes·cue** (fes′kū), *n.* [< OFr. < L. *festuca*, a straw], a tough meadow grass, used for pasture.
**fess, fesse** (fes), *n.* [< OFr. < L. *fascia*, a band], in *heraldry*, a horizontal band forming the middle third of an escutcheon.
**-fest** (fest), [< G. *fest*, a feast], a combining form used in forming colloquial and slang words, meaning *an occasion of much*, as in *songfest*.
**fes·tal** (fes′t'l), *adj.* [OFr. < L. *festum*, feast], of, or having the character of, a feast or festival; gay; joyous. —**fes′tal·ly,** *adv.*

**fes·ter** (fes′tẽr), *n.* [< OFr. < L. *fistula*, ulcer], a small sore producing pus; pustule. *v.i.* 1. to form pus; ulcerate. 2. to grow embittered; rankle. 3. to decay. *v.t.* 1. to cause the formation of pus in. 2. to make rankle; embitter.

**fes·ti·val** (fes′tə-v'l), *n.* [< OFr. < LL. < L. *festivus;* see FESTIVE], 1. a time or day of feasting or celebration. 2. a celebration, entertainment, or series of performances of a certain kind: as, the Bach *festival*. 3. merrymaking; festivity. *adj.* of, for, or fit for a festival.

**fes·tive** (fes′tiv), *adj.* [< L. *festivus* < *festum*, feast], of or for a feast or festival; merry; gay; joyous. —**fes′tive·ly,** *adv.* —**fes′tive·ness,** *n.*

**fes·tiv·i·ty** (fes-tiv′ə-ti), *n.* [*pl.* -TIES], 1. gaiety; merrymaking. 2. *a*) a festival. *b*) *pl.* festive proceedings.

**fes·toon** (fes-to͞on′), *n.* [< Fr. < It. *festone* < *festa*, feast], 1. a garland of flowers, leaves, etc. hanging in a loop or curve. 2. any molding or decoration like this. *v.t.* to adorn with, form into, or join by festoons. —**fes·toon′er·y,** *n.*

**fe·tal** (fē′t'l), *adj.* of or characteristic of a fetus: also sp. **foetal.**

**fetch** (fech), *v.t.* [AS. *feccan*], 1. to go after and come back with; bring; get. 2. to cause to come; produce. 3. to draw (a breath); heave (a sigh, groan, etc.). 4. [Dial.], to come to; reach. 5. to bring as a price; sell for. 6. [Colloq.], to attract; charm. 7. [Colloq.], to deliver or deal, as a blow. *v.i.* 1. to go after things and bring them back. 2. in *nautical usage*, to take or hold a course. *n.* 1. a fetching. 2. a trick; dodge. —**fetch up,** to reach; stop. —**fetch′er,** *n.*

**fetch·ing** (fech′iŋ), *adj.* [Colloq.], attractive; charming; captivating. —**fetch′ing·ly,** *adv.*

**fete, fête** (fāt), *n.* [Fr. < OFr.; see FEAST], a festival; entertainment; esp., one held outdoors. *v.t.* [FETED or FETED, FETING or FETING], to celebrate or honor with festivities; entertain.

**fet·id** (fet′id, fē′tid), *adj.* [< L. *f(o)etidus* < *f(o)etere*, to stink], having a bad smell; stinking. —**fet′id·ly,** *adv.* —**fet′id·ness,** *n.*

**fe·tish, fe·tich** (fē′tish, fet′ish), *n.* [< Fr. < Port. *feitiço*, a charm < L. *facticius*, artificial < *facere*, to make], 1. any object believed by primitive peoples to have magic power. 2. anything held in unreasoning devotion. 3. in *psychiatry*, any nonsexual object that excites erotic feelings. —**fe′tish·like′, fe′tich·like′,** *n.*

**fe·tish·ism, fe·tich·ism** (fē′tish-iz'm, fet′ish-), *n.* 1. worship of or belief in fetishes. 2. in *psychiatry*, an abnormal condition in which erotic feelings are excited by a nonsexual object, as a foot, glove, etc. —**fe′tish·ist, fe′tich·ist,** *n.* —**fe′ti·shis′tic, fe′ti·chis′tic,** *adj.*

**fet·lock** (fet′lok′), *n.* [ME. *fitlok;* prob. < MLG. or MD.], 1. a tuft of hair on the back of a horse's leg just above the hoof. 2. the joint or projection bearing this tuft.

**fet·ter** (fet′ẽr), *n.* [AS. *feter* < base of *fot*, foot], 1. *usually pl.* a shackle or chain for the feet. 2. anything that holds in check; restraint. *v.t.* 1. to bind with fetters; shackle; chain. 2. to hold in check; restrain; confine.

**fet·tle** (fet′'l), *v.t.* [-TLED, -TLING], [ME. *fetlen;* prob. < AS. *fetel*, belt, with idea of "to gird up"], [Dial.], to arrange. *n.* condition; state; trim: as, the speaker was in fine *fettle*.

**fe·tus** (fē′təs), *n.* [*pl.* -TUSES], [L., a bringing forth], the unborn young of an animal while still in the uterus or egg, especially in its later stages: cf. **embryo.** Also sp. **foetus.**

**feud** (fūd), *n.* [< OFr.; prob. ult. < OHG. *fehida*, enmity], a bitter, deadly quarrel; esp., a quarrel between clans or families, through several generations. *v.i.* to carry on a feud. —**feu′dal,** *adj.*

**feud** (fūd), *n.* [ML. *feudum* < Gmc.], land held under feudalism; a fief: also **fee, feoff.**

**feu·dal** (fū′d'l), *adj.* 1. of or having to do with a feud, or fief. 2. of or having to do with feudalism: abbrev. **feud.** —**feu′dal·ly,** *adv.*

**feu·dal·ism** (fū′d'l-iz'm), *n.* the economic, political, and social organization of medieval Europe, in which land, worked by serfs attached to it, was held by vassals in exchange for military and other services given to overlords. —**feu′dal·ist,** *n.* —**feu′dal·is′tic,** *adj.*

**feudal system,** feudalism.

**feu·da·to·ry** (fū′də-tôr′i, -tō′ri), *n.* [*pl.* -RIES], 1. a feudal vassal. 2. a feudal estate; fief. *adj.* 1. of the feudal relationship between vassal and lord. 2. owing feudal allegiance (*to*).

**feud·ist** (fū′dist), *n.* a participant in a feud.

**fe·ver** (fē′vẽr), *n.* [< AS. < L. *febris*, fever], 1. a state of abnormally increased body temperature. 2. any disease characterized by fever and, usually, a quickened pulse, delirium, etc. 3. a restless, emotional excitement. *v.t.* to cause fever in. —**fe′vered,** *adj.* —**fe′ver·less,** *adj.*

**fe·ver·few** (fē′vẽr-fū′), *n.* [< AS.; ult. < L. *febris*, fever + *fugare*, to drive away], a plant of the aster family, with small, white flowers.

**fe·ver·ish** (fē′vẽr-ish), *adj.* 1. having fever, especially slight fever. 2. of, or having the nature of, fever. 3. causing fever. 4. infested by fever. 5. excited; agitated. Also **fe′ver·ous.** —**fe′ver·ish·ly,** *adv.* —**fe′ver·ish·ness,** *n.*

**fe·ver·root** (fē′vẽr-ro͞ot′, -root′), *n.* [from use in medicine], a coarse herb of the honeysuckle family, with small, purplish flowers.

**fever sore** (or **blister**), a cold sore: see **herpes.**

**few** (fū), *adj.* [AS. *feawe*, *pl.*], not many; of small number. *pron.* & *n.* not many; a small number. —**quite a few,** [Colloq.], a good many. —**some few,** a few. —**the few,** the minority.

**fez** (fez), *n.* [*pl.* FEZZES], [Fr. < Turk. < *Fez*, city in Morocco], a tapering felt cap, usually red with a black tassel, formerly worn by Turkish men.

**ff.,** 1. folios. 2. following (pages). 3. in *music*, fortissimo.

**FHA, F.H.A.,** Federal Housing Administration.

**fi·an·cé** (fē′än-sā′, fē-än′sā), *n.* [Fr., pp. of *fiancer* < *fiance*, a promise], the man to whom a woman is engaged to be married.

**fi·an·cée** (fē′än-sā′, fē-än′sā), *n.* [Fr., fem. pp; see FIANCÉ], the woman to whom a man is engaged to be married.

**fi·as·co** (fi-as′kō), *n.* [*pl.* -COES, -COS], [It., lit., a flask], a complete failure; action that comes to a ridiculous end.

**fi·at** (fī′ət, fī′at), *n.* [L., let it be done], 1. an order issued by legal authority; decree. 2. a sanction; authorization.

**fiat money,** paper currency made legal tender by law or fiat, although not backed by gold or silver and not necessarily redeemable in coin.

**fib** (fib), *n.* [? ult. < *fable*], a lie about something unimportant. *v.i.* [FIBBED, FIBBING], to tell such a lie or lies. —**fib′ber,** *n.*

**fi·ber, fi·bre** (fī′bẽr), *n.* [< Fr. < L. *fibra*], 1. a slender, threadlike structure that combines with others to form animal or vegetable tissue. 2. any substance that can be separated into threadlike structures for weaving, etc. 3. a threadlike root. 4. the texture of something. 5. character; nature. —**fi′ber·less, fi′bre·less,** *adj.* —**fi′ber·like′, fi′bre·like′,** *adj.*

**fi·ber·board, fi·bre·board** (fī′bẽr-bôrd′, -bōrd′), *n.* a boardlike material made from pressed fibers, used in building.

**fi·ber·glas** (fī′bẽr-glas′, -gläs′), *n.* finespun filaments of glass made into textiles or used as insulation material: a trade-mark (**Fiberglas**).

**fi·bril** (fī′brəl), *n.* 1. a small fiber. 2. a hairlike subdivision of a root. —**fi′bril·lar,** *adj.*

**fi·brin** (fī′brin), *n.* 1. an elastic, threadlike, insoluble protein formed in the clotting of blood. 2. gluten: also called *plant* (or *vegetable*) *fibrin.* —**fi′brin·ous,** *adj.*

**fi·bro-,** [< L. *fibra*, fiber], a combining form meaning *of fibrous matter* or *structure*: also **fibr-.**

**fi·broid** (fī′broid), *adj.* like, composed of, or forming fibrous tissue. *n.* a fibrous tumor.

**fi·brous** (fī′brəs), *adj.* 1. containing or composed of fibers. 2. like fiber.

**fib·u·la** (fib′yoo-lə), *n.* [*pl.* -LAE (-lē′), -LAS], [L., a clasp], 1. the long, thin outer bone of the human leg below the knee. 2. a similar bone in the hind leg of animals. —**fib′u·lar,** *adj.*

**-fic** (fik), [< Fr. *-fique* < L. *-ficus* < *facere*, to make], an adjectival suffix meaning *making, creating,* as in *terrific.*

**-fi·ca·tion** (fi-kā′shən), [< Fr. & L.; ult. < *facere*, to make], a suffix meaning *a making, creating, causing,* as in *glorification.*

**fich·u** (fish′o͞o), *n.* [Fr.], a three-cornered lace or muslin cape worn over the shoulders by women.

**fick·le** (fik′'l), *adj.* [AS. *ficol*], changeable or unstable in affection, interest, etc.; capricious; inconstant. —**fick′le·ness,** *n.*

**fic·tion** (fik′shən), *n.* [Fr. < L. *fictio* < *fingere*, to form, mold], 1. a making up of imaginary happenings; feigning. 2. anything made up or imagined, as a statement, story, etc. 3. *a*) any literary work portraying imaginary characters and events. *b*) such works collectively; esp., novels and stories. 4. in *law*, something accepted as fact for convenience, although not necessarily true. —**fic′tion·al,** *adj.* —**fic′tion·al·ly,** *adv.*

**fic·ti·tious** (fik-tish′əs), *adj.* 1. of or like fiction, imaginary; not real. 2. false; assumed for deception: as, a *fictitious* name. —**fic·ti′tious·ly,** *adv.* —**fic·ti′tious·ness,** *n.*

**fid** (fid), *n.* [? < L. *findere*, to cleave, via Fr. or It.], 1. a hard, tapering pin for separating the strands of a rope in splicing. 2. a bar or pin for supporting something. 3. in *nautical usage*, a square bar for supporting a topmast.

**-fid** (fid), [< L. < *findere*, to cleave], a combining form meaning *cleft, split*, as in *palmatifid*.

**fid·dle** (fid′'l), *n.* [AS. *fithele* < ML. < L. *vitula*], [Colloq.], 1. a violin. 2. any instrument of the viol class. *v.t.* [-DLED, -DLING], 1. [Colloq.], to play (a tune) on the violin. 2. to waste (time). *v.i.* 1. [Colloq.], to play on a violin. 2. to fidget. —**fit as a fiddle,** in excellent health. —**play second fiddle,** to act in a subordinate position. —**fid′dler,** *n.*

**fiddler crab,** a small, burrowing crab of the Atlantic coast.

**fid·dle·stick** (fid′'l-stik′), *n.* 1. [Colloq.], a violin bow. 2. a trifle; mere nothing.

FIDDLER CRAB (1 in. across)

**fid·dle·sticks** (fid′'l-stiks′), *interj.* nonsense!

**fi·del·i·ty** (fi-del′ə-ti, fə-), *n.* [*pl.* -TIES], [< L. < *fides*, faith], 1. faithful devotion to duty, obligations, or vows; loyalty. 2. accuracy of reproduction.

**fidg·et** (fij′it), *n.* [< ME. *fiken* < ON. *fīkja*], 1. the state of being restless, nervous, or uneasy. 2. a person in this state. *v.i.* to make restless or nervous movements. *v.t.* to cause to fidget. —**the fidgets,** a restless or nervous state. —**fidg′et·i·ness,** *n.* —**fidg′et·y,** *adj.*

**fi·du·ci·ar·y** (fi-dōō′shi-er′i, -dū′-), *adj.* [< L. < *fiducia*, trust], 1. designating or of one who holds something in trust for another: as, a *fiduciary* guardian for a child. 2. held in trust: as, *fiduciary* property. 3. valuable only because of public confidence: said of certain paper money. *n.* [*pl.* -IES], a trustee.

**fie** (fī), *interj.* shame!: now often humorous.

**fief** (fēf), *n.* [Fr.; see FEE], in feudalism, *a)* heritable land held from a lord in return for service. *b)* the right to hold such land. Also **feoff.**

**field** (fēld), *n.* [AS. *feld*], 1. *often pl.* a wide stretch of open land; plain. 2. a piece of cleared land for raising crops or pasturing livestock. 3. a piece of land for some particular purpose: as, a football *field*. 4. an area of land producing some natural resource: as, a gold *field*. 5. any wide, unbroken space: as, a *field* of ice. 6. *a)* a battlefield. *b)* a battle. 7. an area of military operations. 8. a realm of knowledge or of special work: as, the *field* of television. 9. an area of observation, as in a microscope. 10. the background, as on a flag or coin. 11. *a)* an area where athletic events are held. *b)* the part of such an area, usually inside a closed racing track, where contests in jumping, shot-put, pole vault, etc. are held. *c)* all the entrants in a contest. 12. in *physics*, a space within which magnetic or electrical lines of force are active. *adj.* 1. of, in, or for a field. 2. living or growing in fields. 3. of or held on the field (sense 11, b): distinguished from *track*. *v.t.* in *baseball*, etc., 1. to stop or catch and return (a ball) in play. 2. to put (a player) into a field position. *v.i.* in *baseball*, etc., to play in a field position. —**play the field,** to take a broad area of operations. —**take the field,** to begin activity in a game, military operation, etc.

**field artillery,** 1. movable artillery capable of accompanying an army into battle. 2. [F- A-], the branch of the army that uses such artillery.

**field day,** 1. a day of military exercises and display, or of athletic events. 2. a day of pleasantly exciting or successful events.

**field·er** (fēl′dẽr), *n.* in *baseball & cricket*, a player in the field.

**field glass, field glasses,** a small, portable, binocular telescope.

**field goal,** 1. in *basketball*, a basket toss made from play, scoring two points. 2. in *football*, a goal kicked from the field, scoring three points.

**field gun,** a mobile artillery piece for use in the field: also called **field′piece′.**

**field hand,** a hired farm laborer.

**Fiel·ding, Henry** (fēl′diŋ), 1707–1754; English novelist.

**field magnet,** the magnet used to create and maintain the magnetic field, as in a motor.

**field marshal,** in some European armies, an officer ranking just below the commander in chief.

**field officer,** a colonel, lieutenant colonel, or major in the army.

**field·work** (fēld′wūrk′), *n.* any temporary defensive fortification made by troops in the field.

**field work,** the work of collecting scientific data in the field. —**field′work′er,** *n.*

**fiend** (fēnd), *n.* [AS. *feond*], 1. an evil spirit; devil. 2. an inhumanly wicked person. 3. [Colloq.], *a)* an addict: as, a dope *fiend*. *b)* one who is excellent at some activity: as, a *fiend* at tennis. —**the Fiend,** the Devil; —**fiend′like′,** *adj.*

**fiend·ish** (fēn′dish), *adj.* like or characteristic of a fiend; inhumanly wicked or cruel; devilish. —**fiend′ish·ly,** *adv.* —**fiend′ish·ness,** *n.*

**fierce** (fêrs), *adj.* [FIERCER, FIERCEST], [< OFr. < L. *ferus*, wild], 1. of a violently cruel nature; savage: as, a *fierce* dog. 2. violent; uncontrolled: as, a *fierce* storm. 3. intensely eager; ardent: as, *fierce* labor. 4. [Slang], very distasteful, disagreeable, etc. —**fierce′ly,** *adv.* —**fierce′ness,** *n.*

**fi·er·y** (fī′ri, fī′ẽr-i), *adj.* [-IER, -IEST], 1. containing or consisting of fire. 2. like fire; glaring, hot, etc. 3. characterized by strong emotion; ardent. 4. easily stirred up; excitable: as, a *fiery* nature. 5. inflamed: said of a sore. —**fi′er·i·ly,** *adv.* —**fi′er·i·ness,** *n.*

**fi·es·ta** (fi-es′tə; Sp. fyes′tä), *n.* [Sp. < ML. *festa*; see FEAST], 1. a religious festival; saint's day. 2. any gala celebration; holiday.

**fife** (fīf), *n.* [prob. < G. < MHG. < OHG. < ML. hyp. *pipa*, a pipe], a small, shrill-toned musical instrument resembling a flute. *v.t. & v.i.* [FIFED, FIFING], to play on a fife. —**fif′er,** *n.*

**fif·teen** (fif′tēn′), *adj.* [< AS. *fiftene*], five more than ten. *n.* the cardinal number between fourteen and sixteen; 15; XV.

**fif·teenth** (fif′tēnth′), *adj.* 1. preceded by fourteen others in a series; 15th. 2. designating any of the fifteen equal parts of something. *n.* 1. the one following the fourteenth. 2. any of the fifteen equal parts of something; 1/15.

**fifth** (fifth), *adj.* [< AS. < *fif*, five], 1. preceded by four others in a series; 5th. 2. designating any of the five equal parts of something. *n.* 1. the one following the fourth. 2. any of the five equal parts of something; 1/5. 3. a fifth of a gallon. 4. in *music*, *a)* an interval of five degrees in a diatonic scale. *b)* a tone five degrees above or below a given tone. *c)* the combination of two notes separated by this interval. —**fifth′ly,** *adv.*

**fifth column,** [orig. (1939) applied to Franco sympathizers inside Madrid, then besieged by four of his columns on the outside], a group of people who secretly aid and support the enemy from within their own country. —**fifth columnist.**

**fifth wheel,** any superfluous person or thing.

**fif·ti·eth** (fif′ti-ith), *adj.* 1. preceded by forty-nine others in a series; 50th. 2. designating any of the fifty equal parts of something. *n.* 1. the one following the forty-ninth. 2. any of fifty equal parts of something; 1/50.

**fif·ty** (fif′ti), *adj.* [< AS. *fiftig*], five times ten. *n.* [*pl.* -TIES], the cardinal number between forty-nine and fifty-one; 50; L. —**the fifties,** the years from fifty through fifty-nine (of a century or a person's age).

**fif·ty-fif·ty** (fif′ti-fif′ti), *adj.* [Colloq.], equal; even. *adv.* [Colloq.], equally.

**fig** (fig), *n.* [< OFr. < LL. < L. *ficus*], 1. a small, pear-shaped fruit with sweet, seed-filled flesh: usually dried for eating. 2. the tree bearing this fruit. 3. a trifle: as, not worth a *fig*.

**fig.,** 1. figurative(ly). 2. figure(s).

**fig·eat·er** (fig′ēt′ẽr), *n.* a large beetle that eats ripe fruit; the June bug of the southern U.S.

**fight** (fīt), *v.i.* [FOUGHT, FIGHTING], [AS. *feohtan*], 1. to take part in a physical struggle or battle. 2. to struggle against opposition; contend. *v.t.* 1. to oppose physically or in battle, as with fists, weapons, etc. 2. to struggle against; contend with as by argument. 3. to engage in or carry on (a war, conflict, etc.). 4. to gain by struggle: as, he *fought* his way to the top. 5. to cause to fight; manage, as a boxer. *n.* 1. a physical struggle; combat. 2. any struggle, contest, or quarrel. 3. power or readiness to fight. —**fight it out,** to fight until one side is defeated. —**fight off,** to fight to keep away. —**fight′a·ble,** *adj.*

**fight·er** (fīt′ẽr), *n.* 1. one that fights or is inclined to fight. 2. a prizefighter; pugilist. 3. a small, light, highly maneuverable airplane for aerial combat: often **fighter plane.**

**fig·ment** (fig′mənt), *n.* [< L. *figmentum* < *fingere*, to make, devise], something imagined or made up in the mind; fictitious story.

**fig·u·ra·tion** (fig′yoo-rā′shən), *n.* 1. a forming; shaping. 2. form; appearance. 3. an ornamenting with or representing by figures or symbols.

**fig·ur·a·tive** (fig′yoor-ə-tiv), *adj.* 1. representing by means of a figure or symbol. 2. not in its usual, literal, or exact sense or reference; metaphorical. 3. containing or using figures of speech. —**fig′ur·a·tive·ly,** *adv.* —**fig′ur·a·tive·ness,** *n.*

**fig·ure** (fig′yoor), *n.* [< OFr. < L. *figura* < *fingere*, to form], 1. the outline or shape of something; form. 2. the human form. 3. a person seen or thought of in a specified way: as, a minor historical *figure*. 4. a likeness of a person or thing. 5. an illustration; diagram; picture. 6. an artistic design in fabrics, etc.; pattern. 7. the symbol for a number: as, the *figure* 5. 8. *pl.* arithmetic. 9. a sum of money. 10. in *dancing*, a series of steps and movements. 11. in *geometry*, a surface or space bounded on all sides by lines or planes. 12. in *music*, a series of consecutive tones or chords forming a distinct group. 13. in *rhetoric*, a figure of speech. *v.t.* [-URED, -URING], 1. to represent in definite form. 2. to represent mentally; imagine. 3. to ornament with a design. 4. to compute with figures. 5. [Colloq.], to believe; predict. 6. in *rhetoric*, to represent by a figure of speech. *v.i.* 1. to appear prominently; be conspicuous. 2. to do arithmetic. 3. [Colloq.], to consider; calculate. —**figure on,** 1. to count on; rely on. 2. to consider as part of a project. —**figure out,** 1. to solve; compute. 2. to reason out. —**figure up,** to add; total. —**fig′ur·er,** *n.*

**fig·ured** (fig′yoord), *adj.* 1. shaped; formed. 2. having a design or pattern.

**fig·ure·head** (fig′yoor-hed′), *n.* 1. a carved figure on the bow of a ship. 2. a person put in a position of leadership because of his name, rank, etc. but having no real power or authority.

**figure of speech,** an expression using words in an unusual or nonliteral sense to give beauty or vividness of style; metaphor, simile, etc.

**figure skating,** ice skating in which the performer traces various elaborate figures on the ice.

**fig·u·rine** (fig′yoo-rēn′), *n.* [Fr. < It. *figurina*], a small sculptured or molded figure.

**fig·wort** (fig′wūrt′), *n.* any of a group of tall, coarse, strong-smelling plants with small flowers, including the snapdragon, foxglove, etc.

**Fi·ji** (fē′jē), *n.* 1. the Fiji Islands. 2. a British colony including the Fiji Islands. —**Fi′ji·an,** *adj. & n.*

**Fiji Islands,** a group of British islands in the South Pacific, east of the New Hebrides.

**fil·a·gree** (fil′ə-grē′), *n., adj., & v.t.* [-GREED, -GREEING], filigree.

**fil·a·ment** (fil′ə-mənt), *n.* [Fr. < LL. < L. *filum*, a thread], 1. a very slender thread or threadlike part; specif., the fine metal wire in a light bulb or vacuum tube, which is made incandescent by an electric current. 2. in *botany*, the stalk of a stamen bearing the anther. —**fil′a·men′ta·ry** (-men′tēr-i), **fil′a·men′tous,** *adj.*

**fi·la·ri·a** (fi-lâr′i-ə), *n.* [*pl.* -RIAE (-ē′)], [Mod. L. < L. *filum*, a thread], any of several kinds of threadlike parasitic worms that live in the blood and tissues of vertebrate animals. —**fi·lar′i·al, fi·lar′i·an,** *adj.*

**fil·bert** (fil′bērt), *n.* [< St. *Philibert*, whose feast came in the nutting season], the cultivated hazelnut or the tree it grows on.

**filch** (filch), *v.t.* [< slang *filch*, a hooked staff; orig., "to steal with a filch"], to steal (something small or petty); pilfer. —**filch′er,** *n.*

**file** (fil), *n.* [Fr. < OFr. *fil*, a file, row < LL. < L. *filum*, a thread], 1. folder, cabinet, etc., for keeping papers in order. 2. an orderly arrangement of papers, reference cards, etc. 3. a line of persons or things situated one behind another. *v.t.* [FILED, FILING], 1. to put (papers, etc.) in order for future reference. 2. to put (a legal document) on public record. *v.i.* to move or march in a line. —**on file,** kept in order for reference. —**fil′er,** *n.*

**file** (fil), *n.* [AS. *feol*], a steel tool with a rough, ridged surface for smoothing or grinding away something. *v.t.* [FILED, FILING], to smooth or grind away, as with a file. —**fil′er,** *n.*

**file·fish** (fil′fish′), *n.* [*pl.* see FISH], a fish having hard, rough spines instead of scales.

**fi·let** (fi-lā′, fil′ā, fil′it), *n.* [see FILLET], 1. a net or lace with a simple pattern on a square mesh background. 2. a fillet (*n.* 3).

**fi·let mi·gnon** (fi-lā′ min-yōn′, fil′ā min′yon; Fr. fē′le′mē′nyōn′), [Fr.], a round cut of lean beefsteak broiled, often with mushrooms and bacon.

**fil·i·al** (fil′i-əl, fil′yəl), *adj.* [< LL. < L. *filius*, son, *filia*, daughter], 1. of, suitable to, or due from a son or daughter: as, *filial* devotion. 2. in *genetics*, designating or of any generation following the parental. —**fil′i·al·ly,** *adv.*

**fil·i·bus·ter** (fil′ə-bus′tēr), *n.* [< Sp. < Fr. < D. *vrijbuiter*, freebooter], 1. an adventurer who engages in unauthorized warfare against another country; freebooter. 2. a member of a legislative body who obstructs the passage of a bill by making long speeches, introducing irrelevant issues, etc. 3. such deliberate obstruction of a bill. *v.i.* 1. to engage in unauthorized warfare as a freebooter. 2. to obstruct the passage of a bill by making long speeches, etc. *v.t.* to obstruct the passage of (a bill) by such methods. —**fil′i·bus′ter·er,** *n.*

**fil·i·gree** (fil′ə-grē′), *n.* [< earlier *filigrain* < Fr. & It. < L. *filum*, a thread + *granum*, grain], 1. lacelike ornamental work of intertwined wire of gold, silver, etc. 2. any delicate work or figure like this. *adj.* like, made of, or made into filigree. *v.t.* [-GREED, -GREEING], to ornament with filigree.

**fil·ing** (fil′iŋ), *n.* *usually in pl.* a small piece of metal, etc. scraped off with a file.

**Fil·i·pine** (fil′ə-pēn′), *adj.* Philippine.

**Fil·i·pi·no** (fil′ə-pē′nō), *n.* [*pl.* -NOS], [Sp.], a native of the Philippines. *adj.* Philippine.

**fill** (fil), *v.t.* [AS. *fyllan* < base of *full*, *adj.*], 1. to put as much as possible into (a container or space); make full. 2. to take up the whole of; occupy: as, the crowd *filled* the room. 3. to occupy (an office, position, etc.). 4. to put a person into (an office, position, etc.). 5. to supply the things called for in (an order, prescription, etc.). 6. to close or plug (holes, cracks, etc.). 7. to satisfy the hunger of. 8. to be plentiful in. 9. to put into a container as if to fill it. *v.i.* to become full. *n.* 1. all that is needed to make full. 2. all that is needed to satisfy. 3 anything that fills. —**fill in,** 1. to fill with some substance. 2. to make complete by supplying something. 3. to supply for completion. 4. to be a substitute. —**fill one in on,** [Colloq.], to provide one with additional details of. —**fill out,** 1. to make or become rounder, shapelier, etc. 2. to complete (a document, etc.) by inserting information. —**fill up,** to make or become completely full.

**fill·a·gree** (fil′ə-grē′), *n., adj., & v.t.* [-GREED, -GREEING], filigree.

‡**fille** (fē′y′), *n.* [Fr.], 1. a daughter. 2. a girl.

**fill·er** (fil′ēr), *n.* a person or thing that fills; specif., *a*) matter added to increase bulk, solidity, etc. *b*) a preparation used to fill in cracks, etc. *c*) the tobacco rolled in the leaf of a cigar.

**fil·let** (fil′it), *n.* [< OFr. dim. of *fil*; see FILE (a line)], 1. a narrow headband for ornament or to hold the hair in place. 2. a thin strip or band. 3. (fil′ā, fil′it), a boneless, lean piece of fish or meat: also sp. **filet.** *v.t.* 1. to bind or decorate with a band, molding, etc. 2. (fil′ā, fi-lā′, fil′it), to bone and slice (meat or fish).

**fill·ing** (fil′iŋ), *n.* 1. a thing used to fill something else; esp., the gold, amalgam, etc. inserted by a dentist into a prepared cavity in a tooth. 2. the woof in a woven fabric; weft.

**filling station,** a service station.

**fil·lip** (fil′əp), *n.* [echoic extension of *flip*], 1. the snap made by a finger held down by the thumb and then suddenly released. 2. a light tap given in this way. 3. anything that stirs up or arouses; stimulus. *v.t.* 1. to toss with a fillip. 2. to stir up; stimulate. *v.i.* to make a fillip.

**Fill·more, Mill·ard** (mil′ērd fil′môr, -mōr), 1800–1874; 13th president of the U.S. (1850–1853).

**fil·ly** (fil′i), *n.* [*pl.* -LIES], [ON. *fylja*], 1. a young mare. 2. [Colloq.], a vivacious girl.

**film** (film), *n.* [AS. *filmen*], 1. a fine, thin skin or coating. 2. a flexible cellulose material covered with a substance sensitive to light and used in taking photographs. 3. a haze or blur, as over the eyes. 4. a motion picture. 5. a fine thread. *v.t.* 1. to cover as with a film. 2. to take a photograph of. 3. to make a motion picture of. *v.i.* 1. to be or become covered with a film. 2. to be photographed for motion pictures.

**film·strip** (film′strip′), *n.* a length of film containing still photographs, often of illustrations, diagrams, etc., arranged in sequence for projection separately: used in teaching.

**film·y** (fil′mi), *adj.* [-IER, -IEST], 1. of or like a film; hazy, gauzy, etc. 2. covered as with a film. —**film′i·ly,** *adv.* —**film′i·ness,** *n.*

‡**fils** (fēs), *n.* [Fr.], a son or a youth.

**fil·ter** (fil′tẽr), *n.* [< Fr. < LL. *filtrum*, felt (used for filters)], 1. a device for straining out solid particles, impurities, etc. from a fluid. 2. any porous substance so used, as sand, charcoal, etc. 3. *a*) a device that passes electric currents of only certain frequencies. *b*) a device for absorbing certain light rays: as, a *filter* for a camera lens. *v.t.* 1. to pass (fluids) through a filter. 2. to remove or separate (solid particles, etc.) from a fluid with a filter. 3. to act as a filter for (electric currents or light rays). *v.i.* 1. to be filtered. 2. to pass slowly: as, the news *filtered* through town. —**fil′ter·er,** *n.*

**fil·ter·a·ble** (fil′tẽr-ə-b'l), *adj.* 1. that can be filtered. 2. that goes through a filter. —**fil′ter·a·bil′i·ty, fil′ter·a·ble·ness,** *n.*

**filter paper,** a porous paper for straining liquids.

**filth** (filth), *n.* [AS. *fylthe* < *ful*, foul], 1. foul dirt; disgusting matter. 2. moral corruption or something causing it; indecency; obscenity.

**filth·y** (fil′thi), *adj.* [-IER, -IEST], 1. full of filth; revoltingly dirty; foul. 2. indecent; obscene; lewd. —**filth′i·ly,** *adv.* —**filth′i·ness,** *n.*

**fil·tra·ble** (fil′trə-b'l), *adj.* filterable. —**fil′tra·bil′i·ty, fil′tra·ble·ness,** *n.*

**filtrable virus,** any virus of ultramicroscopic size, capable of passing through filters that bacteria cannot pass through.

**fil·trate** (fil′trāt; *also, for n.*, -trit), *v.t.* [-TRATED, -TRATING], to strain; filter. *n.* a liquid that has been filtered. —**fil·tra′tion,** *n.*

**fin** (fin), *n.* [AS. *finn*], 1. any of several winglike, membranous organs on the body of a fish, dolphin, etc., used in swimming and balancing. 2. anything like a fin in shape or use, as on an aircraft or boat. 3. [Slang], a five-dollar bill. *v.t.* [FINNED, FINNING], to cut the fins from. *v.i.* 1. to move the fins, especially in a violent way. —**fin′less,** *adj.* —**fin′like′,** *adj.*

**fin.,** 1. finance. 2. financial.

**fi·na·gle** (fi-nā′g'l), *v.i.* [-GLED, -GLING], [prob. < *Feinagel*, G. whist expert], 1. in *card games*, to renege; revoke. 2. to use trickery; be crafty; cheat. *v.t.* 1. to cheat. 2. to get or manage by trickery or craftiness. —**fi·na′gler,** *n.*

**fi·nal** (fī′n'l), *adj.* [OFr. < L. *finalis* < *finis*, end], 1. of or coming at the end; last; concluding. 2. deciding; conclusive: as, a *final* decree. 3. of purpose or result: as, a *final* cause. *n.* 1. anything final. 2. *pl.* the last of a series of contests. 3. [Colloq.], a final examination. —**fi′nal·ly,** *adv.*

**fi·na·le** (fi-nä′li; It. fē-nä′le), *n.* [It.], 1. the concluding part of a musical composition or an entertainment. 2. the conclusion; end.

**fi·nal·ist** (fī′n'l-ist), *n.* a contestant who participates in the final, deciding contest of a series.

**fi·nal·i·ty** (fī-nal′ə-ti), *n.* 1. the quality or condition of being final, settled, or complete. 2. [*pl.* -TIES], anything final or conclusive.

**fi·nal·ize** (fī′n'l-īz′), *v.t.* [-IZED, -IZING], [U.S. neologism], to make final.

**fi·nance** (fə-nans′, fī′nans), *n.* [< OFr. < *finer*, to end, settle accounts < *fin* (< L. *finis*), an end], 1. *pl.* the money resources, income, etc. of a nation, organization, or person. 2. the science of managing money matters. *v.t.* [-NANCED, -NANCING], 1. to supply money for. 2. to manage the money of.

**fi·nan·cial** (fə-nan′shəl, fī-), *adj.* of finance, finances, or financiers. —**fi·nan′cial·ly,** *adv.*

**fin·an·cier** (fin′ən-sêr′, fī′nən-), *n.* [Fr.], 1. a person skilled in finance. 2. one who engages in financial operations on a large scale.

**fin·back** (fin′bak′), *n.* a large whalebone whale with a dorsal fin; rorqual: also **finback whale.**

**finch** (finch), *n.* [AS. *finc*], any of a large group of small, short-beaked songbirds, including the bunting, canary, cardinal, and sparrow.

**find** (fīnd), *v.t.* [FOUND, FINDING], [AS. *findan*], 1. to happen on by chance; come upon. 2. to get by searching. 3. to get sight or knowledge of; perceive; learn. 4. *a*) to recover (something lost). *b*) to recover the use of. 5. to consider; think. 6. to reach; attain: as, the blow *found* his chin. 7. to decide: as, the jury *found* him innocent. 8. to supply; furnish. *v.i.* to reach a decision: as, the jury *found* for the accused. *n.* 1. a finding. 2. something found. —**find oneself,** to learn what one's real talents are and begin to apply them. —**find out,** 1. to discover; learn. 2. to learn the true character or identity of.

**find·er** (fīn′dẽr), *n.* 1. a person or thing that finds. 2. a camera device that shows what will appear in the photograph. 3. a small, low-powered telescope attached to a larger one, used to locate objects for closer view with the larger one.

‡**fin de siè·cle** (fan′də-sye′kl′), [Fr., end of the century], of or like the last years of the 19th century.

**find·ing** (fīn′diŋ), *n.* 1. discovery. 2. something found or discovered. 3. the conclusion reached after examination of facts, as by a judge or jury.

**fine** (fīn), *adj.* [FINER, FINEST], [OFr. *fin* < LL. < L. *finitus*, pp. of *finire*; see FINISH], 1. originally, perfected. 2. superior in quality, character, ability, etc.; excellent. 3. with no impurities; refined. 4. containing a specified proportion of pure metal: said of gold or silver. 5. clear and bright, as the weather. 6. not heavy, gross, or coarse: as, *fine* sand. 7. very thin: as, *fine* thread. 8. sharp; keen: as, a knife with a *fine* edge. 9. discriminating; subtle: as, *fine* distinctions. 10. good-looking; handsome: as, a *fine* baby. 11. too elegant; showy: as, *fine* writing. *adv.* [Colloq.], very well. *v.t. & v.i.* [FINED, FINING], to make or become fine or finer. —**fine′ly,** *adv.* —**fine′ness,** *n.*

**fine** (fīn), *n.* [< OFr. < L. *finis*; see FINISH], a sum of money paid as punishment for an offense. *v.t.* [FINED, FINING], to require the payment of a fine from. —**in fine,** 1. in conclusion. 2. in brief.

**fine arts,** the graphic arts, as drawing, painting, sculpture, ceramics, and architecture; also, often, literature, music, dramatic art, and dancing.

**fine-drawn** (fīn′drôn′), *adj.* 1. drawn out until very fine, as wire. 2. extremely subtle: said of reasoning, arguments, etc.

**fine-grained** (fīn′grānd′), *adj.* having a fine, smooth grain, as some wood, leather, etc.

**fin·er·y** (fīn′ẽr-i), *n.* [*pl.* -IES], showy, gay, elaborate decoration, clothes, jewelry, etc.

**fine·spun** (fīn′spun′), *adj.* 1. spun or drawn out to extreme fineness. 2. extremely subtle.

**fi·nesse** (fi-nes′), *n.* [Fr. < *fin*; see FINE, *adj.*], 1. skill; adroitness and delicacy of performance. 2. the ability to handle delicate situations diplomatically. 3. cunning; artfulness; craft. 4. in *bridge*, *whist*, etc., an attempt to take a trick with a lower card while holding a higher card not in sequence with this. *v.t.* [-NESSED, -NESSING], 1. to change by finesse. 2. in *bridge*, *whist*, etc., to make a finesse with (a card). *v.i.* to use or make a finesse.

**fine-toothed comb** (fīn′tōōtht′), a comb with fine, closely set teeth. —**go over with a fine-toothed comb,** to examine very thoroughly.

**fin·ger** (fiŋ′gẽr), *n.* [AS.], 1. any of the five parts at the end of the hand; esp., any of these other than the thumb. 2. the part of a glove covering a finger. 3. anything like a finger in shape or use. 4. a unit of measurement based on the breadth of a finger (about ¾ inch) or the length of a finger (about 4½ inches). *v.t.* 1. to touch with the fingers; handle. 2. to play (an instrument) by using the fingers on strings, keys, etc. *v.i.* to be fingered, as a violin. —**have a finger in the pie,** to participate. —**put one's finger on,** to indicate or ascertain exactly. —**twist around one's little finger,** to be able to manage with ease. —**fin′ger·er,** *n.* —**fin′ger·less,** *adj.*

**finger bowl,** a small bowl to hold water for rinsing the fingers at table after a meal.

**fin·gered** (fiŋ′gẽrd), *adj.* having (specified) fingers: in compounds, as, *light-fingered.*

**fin·ger·ing** (fiŋ′gẽr-iŋ), *n.* 1. a touching with the fingers. 2. in *music*, *a*) technique of using the fingers on the strings, keys, etc. to produce tones. *b*) directions on a score for using the fingers.

**fin·ger·ling** (fiŋ′gẽr-liŋ), *n.* 1. any small object. 2. a small fish about the size of a finger.

**fin·ger·nail** (fiŋ′gẽr-nāl′), *n.* the horny substance on the upper part of the end joint of a finger.

**fin·ger·print** (fiŋ′gẽr-print′), *n.* an impression of the lines and whorls on the inner surface of the last joint of a finger, used to identify a person. *v.t.* to take the fingerprints of.

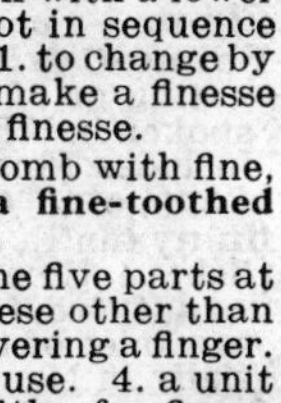

FINGERPRINT

**finger tip,** the tip of a finger. —**have at one's finger tips,** 1. to have available for instant use. 2. to be completely familiar with. —**to one's** (or **the**) **finger tips,** entirely; altogether.

**fin·i·al** (fin′i-əl, fī′ni-), *n.* [< *finis* + *-ial*], an ornament at the top of a spire, lamp, etc.

**fin·i·cal** (fin′i-k'l), *adj.* [< *fine*, *adj.*], too particular; fussy; fastidious. —**fin′i·cal′i·ty** (-kal′ə-ti), **fin′i·cal·ness,** *n.* —**fin′i·cal·ly,** *adv.*

**fin·ick·y** (fin'i-ki), *adj.* finical: also **fin'ick·ing.**
**fi·nis** (fi'nis; *now often* fin'is), *n.* [*pl.* -NISES], [L.], the end, as of a book; conclusion.
**fin·ish** (fin'ish), *v.t.* [< OFr. < L. *finire* < *finis*, an end], 1. to come to the end of; end. 2. to complete; accomplish. 3. to use up; consume entirely. 4. to perfect; polish. 5. to give a desired surface to, as by polishing, brushing, etc. 6. [Colloq.], to overthrow completely; kill. 7. [Colloq.], to reduce to worthlessness. *v.i.* to come to an end. *n.* 1. the last part; end. 2. anything used to finish something else. 3. completeness; perfection. 4. the manner or method of completion. 5. the way in which a surface is finished. 6. polish in manners, speech, etc. —**finish off,** 1. to end or complete. 2. to kill or destroy. —**finish up,** 1. to end or complete. 2. to consume all of. —**finish with,** 1. to end or complete. 2. to end relations with. —**fin'ished,** *adj.* —**fin'ish·er,** *n.* —**fin'ish·ing,** *adj.* & *n.*
**finishing school,** a private school that trains girls for life in society.
**fi·nite** (fi'nit), *adj.* [< L. *finitus*, pp. of *finire;* see FINISH], 1. having definable limits; not infinite. 2. in *grammar*, having limits of person, number, and tense: said of a verb that can be used to form a predicate. *n.* anything that is finite. —**fi'nite·ly,** *adv.* —**fi'nite·ness,** *n.*
**fink** (fiŋk), *n.* [? < name of notorious Am. strikebreaker], [Slang], an informer or strikebreaker.
**Fin·land** (fin'lənd), *n.* a country in N Europe: area, 119,113 sq. mi.; pop., 4,464,000; capital, Helsinki: Finnish name, **Suomi** (soo-ô'mi).
**Finland, Gulf of,** an arm of the Baltic Sea, south of Finland.
**Finn** (fin), *n.* a native or inhabitant of Finland.
**Finn., Fin.,** Finnish.
**fin·nan had·die** (fin'ən had'i), [prob. < *Findhorn haddock*, after *Findhorn*, Scotland], smoked haddock: also **finnan haddock.**
**Finn·ish** (fin'ish), *adj.* 1. of Finland. 2. of the Finns, their language, or culture. *n.* the language of the Finns.
**Fin·no-,** a combining form meaning *Finn, Finnish*
**Fin·no-U·gric** (fin'ō-ōō'grik, -ū'grik), *adj.* designating or of a subfamily of the Uralic languages spoken in NE Europe, W Siberia, and Hungary: it includes Finnish, Estonian, Hungarian (Magyar), Lapp, etc. *n.* this subfamily of languages.
**fin·ny** (fin'i), *adj.* 1. having fins. 2. like a fin. 3. of fish. 4. [Poetic], full of fish.
**fiord** (fyôrd, fyōrd), *n.* [Norw. < ON. *fjǫrthr*], a narrow inlet of the sea bordered by steep cliffs, especially in Norway: also sp. **fjord.**
**fip·ple** (fip''l), *n.* [cf. ON. *flipi*, horse's lip], a plug forming the mouthpiece of certain wind instruments, as the recorder.
**fir** (fũr), *n.* [AS. *fyrh*], 1. a cone-bearing evergreen tree somewhat like a pine. 2. its wood.
**fire** (fir), *n.* [AS. *fyr*], 1. the flame, heat, and light of combustion. 2. something burning, as fuel in a furnace. 3. a destructive burning: as, a forest *fire*. 4. any preparation that will burn in a brilliant display: as, red *fire*. 5. anything like a fire in heat, brilliance, etc.: as, the *fire* of lightning. 6. torture by fire. 7. great trouble; tribulation. 8. fever or inflammation. 9. strong feeling; excitement; ardor. 10. vivid imagination. 11. a discharge of firearms or artillery. 12. anything like this in speed and continuity: as, a *fire* of criticism. *v.t.* [FIRED, FIRING], 1. to make burn; ignite. 2. to supply with fuel: as, he *fired* the furnace. 3. to bake in a kiln, as bricks, pottery, etc. 4. to dry by heat. 5. to make bright; illuminate, as if by fire. 6. to excite; stimulate; inflame. 7. to shoot; discharge (a gun, bullet, etc.). 8. [Colloq.], to direct with force; hurl: as, *fire* questions. 9. [Colloq.], to dismiss from a position; discharge. *v.i.* 1. to start burning; flame; glow with heat. 2. to tend a fire. 3. to become excited or aroused. 4. to shoot a firearm. 5. to discharge a projectile. —**between two fires,** shot at, criticized, etc. from both sides. —**catch fire,** to ignite. —**fire up,** to start a fire, as in a stove. —**go through fire and water,** to undergo great difficulties or dangers. —**hang fire,** 1. to delay in firing: said of a gun. 2. to delay or be delayed. —**lay a fire,** to place fuel ready for starting a fire. —**miss fire,** 1. to fail to fire, as a gun. 2. to fail in an attempt. —**on fire,** 1. burning. 2. greatly excited. —**open fire,** 1. to begin to shoot. 2. to begin; start. —**play with fire,** to do something risky. —**set fire to,** to make burn; ignite. —**set the world on fire,** to become very successful, famous, etc. —**take fire,** 1. to begin to burn. 2. to become excited. —**under fire,** 1. under attack by the enemy. 2. under attack; criticized. —**fir'er,** *n.*
**fire·arm** (fir'ärm'), *n.* any weapon from which a shot is fired by explosive force; esp., such a weapon small enough to be carried, as a rifle.
**fire boat,** a boat equipped with fire-fighting equipment, used along water fronts.
**fire·box** (fir'boks'), *n.* the place for the fire in a locomotive engine, furnace, stove, etc.
**fire·brand** (fir'brand'), *n.* 1. a piece of burning wood. 2. a person who stirs up strife, etc.
**fire·break** (fir'brāk'), *n.* a strip of land cleared to stop the spread of fire, as in a forest.
**fire·brick** (fir'brik'), *n.* a brick made to withstand great heat, used to line furnaces, etc.
**fire·bug** (fir'bug'), *n.* [Colloq.], a person who deliberately sets fire to buildings, etc.
**fire clay,** a clay that can resist intense heat, used for firebricks, furnace linings, etc.
**fire·crack·er** (fir'krak'ẽr), *n.* a roll of paper that contains an explosive and an attached fuse, set off as a noisemaker at celebrations, etc.
**fire·damp** (fir'damp'), *n.* a gas, largely methane, formed in coal mines, which is explosive when mixed with a certain proportion of air.
**fire·dog** (fir'dôg', -dog'), *n.* an andiron.
**fire-eat·er** (fir'ēt'ẽr), *n.* 1. an entertainer who pretends to eat fire. 2. a belligerent person.
**fire engine,** 1. a machine for spraying water, chemicals, etc. to extinguish fires. 2. a motor truck for carrying firemen and equipment to a fire.
**fire escape,** any device, as a ladder, stairway, etc., for escape from a burning building.
**fire extinguisher,** a device containing chemicals for spraying on a fire to extinguish it.
**fire·fly** (fir'fli'), *n.* [*pl.* -FLIES], a winged beetle whose abdomen glows with a phosphorescent light; lightning bug: the larvae and wingless females are called *glowworms*.
**fire insurance,** insurance against loss or damage resulting from fire.
**fire·light** (fir'lit'), *n.* the light from an open fire.
**fire·man** (fir'mən), *n.* [*pl.* -MEN], 1. a man whose work is fighting fires. 2. a man who tends a fire in a furnace, locomotive engine, etc.
**fire·place** (fir'plās'), *n.* a place for a fire; esp., an open place built in a wall, at a chimney base.
**fire·plug** (fir'plug'), *n.* a street hydrant to which a hose can be attached for fighting fires.
**fire·pow·er** (fir'pou'ẽr), *n.* in *military usage*, 1. the effectiveness of a weapon in terms of the accuracy and volume of its fire. 2. the capacity of a given unit to deliver fire.
**fire·proof** (fir'proof'), *adj.* almost impossible to destroy by fire. *v.t.* to make fireproof.
**fire sale,** a sale of goods damaged in a fire.
**fire·side** (fir'sid'), *n.* 1. the space around a fireplace; hearth; hence, 2. home. 3. home life. *adj.* of or at the hearth or home.
**fire station,** place where fire engines are kept: also **fire house.**
**fire·trap** (fir'trap'), *n.* a building unsafe in case of fire, as because it lacks adequate exits.
**fire·wa·ter** (fir'wô'tẽr, -wä'-), *n.* [prob. transl. of Am. Ind. term], alcoholic liquor: now humorous.
**fire·weed** (fir'wēd'), *n.* any of various weeds that grow readily on cleared or burned-over land.
**fire·wood** (fir'wood'), *n.* wood used as fuel.
**fire·works** (fir'wũrks'), *n.pl.* 1. devices, as firecrackers, rockets, etc., used, as in celebrations, to produce loud noises or brilliant lighting effects. 2. a display of or as of fireworks.
**firing line,** 1. the line from which gunfire is directed against the enemy. 2. the front position in any kind of activity.
**fir·kin** (fũr'kin), *n.* [< D. < *vierde*, a fourth + *-kin*, -kin], 1. a small wooden tub for butter, lard, etc. 2. a measure of capacity equal to ¼ barrel.
**firm** (fũrm), *adj.* [< OFr. < L. *firmus*], 1. not yielding easily under pressure; solid; hard. 2. not moved or shaken easily; fixed. 3. not fluctuating; steady: as, a *firm* market. 4. resolute; constant: as, a *firm* faith. 5. showing determination; positive: as, a firm command. 6. formally concluded; final; definite: as, a *firm* contract. *v.t.* & *v.i.* to make or become firm. —**firm'ly,** *adv.* —**firm'ness,** *n.*
**firm** (fũrm), *n.* [It. *firma*, signature < L. < *firmus*, firm], a business company or partnership.
**fir·ma·ment** (fũr'mə-mənt), *n.* [< L. < *firmare*, to strengthen < *firmus*, firm], the sky, viewed poetically as a solid arch or vault.
**first** (fũrst), *adj.* [AS. *fyrst*], 1. before any others; 1st: used as the ordinal of *one*. 2. happening or acting before all others; earliest. 3. foremost in rank, quality, importance, etc. 4. in *music*, of highest pitch; playing or singing the part highest in pitch. *adv.* 1. before any other person or thing; at

the beginning. 2. for the first time. 3. sooner; preferably. *n.* 1. any person, thing, class, place, etc. that is first. 2. the first day of the month. 3. the beginning; start. 4. *pl.* the best quality of merchandise: as, these sheets are *firsts.* 5. the winning place, as in a race. 6. in *music,* the highest or leading voice or instrument in an ensemble.

**first aid,** emergency treatment for injury or sudden illness, before regular medical treatment is available. **—first′-aid′,** *adj.*

**first base,** in *baseball,* the base on the pitcher's left, first from home plate: see **base, baseball.**

**first-born** (fũrst′bôrn′), *adj.* born first in a family; oldest. *n.* the first-born child.

**first-class** (fũrst′klas′, -kläs′), *adj.* 1. of the highest class, rank, quality, etc. 2. designating or of the best accommodations, as on a ship. 3. designating or of a class of mail consisting of sealed matter and carrying the highest regular postage rates. *adv.* 1. with the best accommodations. 2. as or by first-class mail.

**first finger,** the forefinger.

**first·hand** (fũrst′hand′), *adj. & adv.* from the original producer or source; direct.

**first lady,** the wife of the president of the U.S.

**first lieutenant,** an army officer ranking just above a second lieutenant.

**first·ling** (fũrst′liŋ), *n.* 1. the first of a kind. 2. the first fruit, produce, etc. 3. the first-born of an animal.

**first·ly** (fũrst′li), *adv.* in the first place; first.

**first mate,** a ship's officer next in rank below the captain: also **first officer.**

**first mortgage,** a mortgage having priority over all others as a lien on property.

**first papers,** the documents by which an alien makes preliminary application for U.S. citizenship.

**first person,** that form of a pronoun or verb which refers to the speaker, as in *I* (or *we*) *do.*

**first-rate** (fũrst′rāt′), *adj.* 1. of the highest class, rank, quality, etc. 2. [Colloq.], very good; excellent. *adv.* [Colloq.], very well.

**first sergeant,** in the *U.S. Army,* the occupational title of the master sergeant serving as assistant to the commander of a company, battery, etc.

**first water,** the best quality and purest luster: said of gems, but often used figuratively.

**firth** (fũrth), *n.* [< ON. *fjörthr*], a narrow arm of the sea; estuary, especially in Scotland.

**fis·cal** (fis′k'l), *adj.* [Fr. < LL. < L. *fiscus,* money bag], 1. relating to the public treasury or revenues. 2. financial. **—fis′cal·ly,** *adv.*

**fiscal year,** the twelve-month period between settlements of financial accounts: in the U.S. the government fiscal year legally ends June 30.

**fish** (fish), *n.* [*pl.* FISH; in referring to different species, FISHES; see PLURAL, II, D, 2], [AS. *fisc*], 1. any of a large group of cold-blooded animals living in water and having backbones, gills for breathing, fins, and, usually, scales. 2. loosely, any animal living in water only, as a crab, oyster, etc. 3. the flesh of a fish used as food. 4. [Colloq.], a person thought of as like a fish, as in being easily lured. 5. [F-], *pl.* in *astronomy,* the constellation Pisces. *v.i.* 1. to catch or try to catch fish. 2. to try to get something indirectly or by cunning. *v.t.* 1. to fish in (a stream, lake, etc.). 2. to get by fishing. 3. to grope for, find, and bring to view: as, he *fished* a coin out of his pocket. *adj.* 1. of fish or fishing. 2. selling fish. **—drink like a fish,** to drink heavily. **—like a fish out of water,** out of one's element; not adapted. **—neither fish, flesh, nor fowl,** —not anything definite or recognizable. **—other fish to fry,** other, more important things to attend to. **—fish′a·ble,** *adj.* **—fish′less,** *adj.* **—fish′like′,** *adj.*

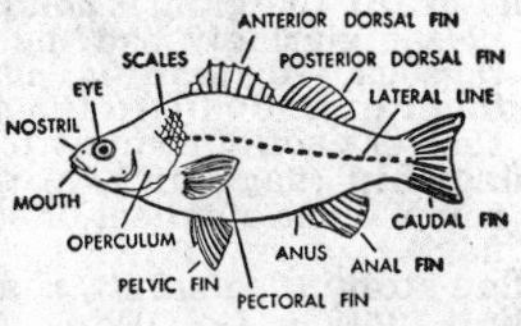

FISH

**fish and chips,** [Chiefly Brit.], small fillets of fish and strips of potato French fried.

**fish·er** (fish′ẽr), *n.* 1. a fisherman. 2. [*pl.* -ERS, -ER; see PLURAL, II, D, 1], a fish-eating animal of the marten family, larger than a weasel.

**fish·er·man** (fish′ẽr-mən), *n.* [*pl.* -MEN], 1. a person who fishes for sport or for a living. 2. a ship used in fishing.

**fish·er·y** (fish′ẽr-i), *n.* [*pl.* -IES], 1. the business of catching fish. 2. a place where fish are caught. 3. a legal right to catch fish in certain waters or at certain times. 4. a place where fish are bred.

**fish hawk,** the osprey, a large, fish-eating hawk.

**fish·hook** (fish′hook′), *n.* a hook, usually barbed, for catching fish.

**fish·ing** (fish′iŋ), *n.* 1. the catching of fish for sport or for a living. 2. a place to fish.

**fishing rod,** a slender pole with an attached line, hook, and, sometimes, a reel, used in fishing.

**fish joint,** a joint, as of two railroad rails, held together by fishplates along the sides.

**fish·mon·ger** (fish′muŋ′gẽr), *n.* a dealer in fish.

**fish·plate** (fish′plāt′), *n.* [prob. < Fr. *fiche,* means of fixing], either of a pair of steel plates bolting two railroad rails together lengthwise.

**fish story,** [Colloq.], an exaggerated story.

**fish·wife** (fish′wīf′), *n.* [*pl.* -WIVES], 1. a woman who sells fish. 2. a coarse, scolding woman.

**fish·y** (fish′i), *adj.* [-IER, -IEST], 1. of or full of fish. 2. like a fish in odor, taste, etc. 3. dull; without expression; lusterless: as, a *fishy* stare. 4. [Colloq.], questionable; suspicious. **—fish′i·ly,** *adv.* **—fish′i·ness,** *n.*

**fis·sile** (fis′'l, fis′il), *adj.* [< L. < *fissus,* pp. of *findere,* to split], that can be split; easily cleft. **—fis·sil′i·ty,** *n.*

**fis·sion** (fish′ən), *n.* [< L. < *fissus;* see FISSILE], 1. a splitting apart; division into parts; cleavage: see also *nuclear fission.* 2. in *biology,* a form of asexual reproduction in which the parent organism divides into two or more parts, each becoming an independent individual.

**fis·sion·a·ble** (fish′ən-ə-b'l), *adj.* that can undergo fission; specif., designating a substance, as uranium, whose nuclei can undergo fission.

**fis·sure** (fish′ẽr), *n.* [Fr. < L. < *fissus;* see FISSILE], 1. a cleft or crack. 2. a dividing or breaking into parts. *v.t. & v.i.* [-SURED, -SURING], to crack or split apart.

**fist** (fist), *n.* [AS. *fyst*], 1. a hand with the fingers closed tightly into the palm. 2. [Colloq.], *a)* a hand. *b)* the grasp. *c)* handwriting. 3. in *printing,* the sign (☞), used to point out something. *v.t.* to hit with the fist.

**fist·ic** (fis′tik), *adj.* [Colloq.], having to do with boxing; fought with the fists; pugilistic.

**fis·ti·cuffs** (fis′ti-kufs′), *n.pl.* 1. a fight with the fists. 2. blows with the fists; punches. 3. the science of boxing. **—fis′ti·cuff′er,** *n.*

**fis·tu·la** (fis′choo-lə), *n.* [*pl.* -LAS, -LAE (-lē′)], [L.], 1. a pipe or tube. 2. an abnormal hollow passage from an abscess, cavity, or hollow organ to the skin or to another abscess, cavity, or organ. **—fis′tu·lous, fis′tu·lar,** *adj.*

**fit** (fit), *v.t.* [FITTED, FITTING], [< the *adj.*], 1. to be suitable or adapted to. 2. to be the proper size, shape, etc. for. 3. to make, adjust, or alter so as to fit. 4. to make suitable or qualified. 5. to equip; outfit. *v.i.* 1. to be suitable or proper. 2. to be as specified in size, shape, etc.: as, his coat *fits* well. *adj.* [FITTER, FITTEST], [ME. *fyt;* prob. ult. < L. *factus* (see FACT)], 1. adapted, qualified, or suited to some purpose, function, etc. 2. proper; right. 3. prepared; ready. 4. in good physical condition; healthy. *n.* 1. a fitting or being fitted. 2. the manner of fitting: as, a tight *fit.* 3. anything that fits. **—fit out (or up),** to equip; outfit, as a ship. **—fit′ly,** *adv.* **—fit′ness,** *n.* **—fit′ter,** *n.*

**fit** (fit), *n.* [AS. *fitt,* conflict], 1. any sudden, uncontrollable attack: as, a *fit* of coughing. 2. a sharp, brief display of feeling: as, a *fit* of anger. 3. a temporary burst of activity: as, he works by *fits.* 4. in *medicine,* a convulsion with loss of consciousness. **—by fits and starts,** in an irregular way. **—have (or throw) a fit,** [Colloq.], to become very angry or upset.

**fitch·ew** (fich′ōō), *n.* [< OFr. < MD. *fisse, vitsche* < OHG. *wiessa*], 1. the European polecat. 2. its fur. Also **fitch, fitchet.**

**fit·ful** (fit′fəl), *adj.* characterized by intermittent bursts of activity; spasmodic; irregular. **—fit′ful·ly,** *adv.* **—fit′ful·ness,** *n.*

**fit·ting** (fit′iŋ), *adj.* suitable; proper; appropriate. *n.* 1. an adjustment or trying on of clothes, etc. for fit. 2. something used in an adjustment: as, a pipe *fitting.* 3. *pl.* fixtures, furnishings, etc., as of a house or office. **—fit′ting·ly,** *adv.* **—fit′ting·ness,** *n.*

**Fiu·me** (fū′me), *n.* [It.] a seaport in NW Yugoslavia; in Italy 1924–1947: pop., 75,000: cf. **Rieka.**

**five** (fīv), *adj.* [AS. *fif, fife*], totaling one more than four. *n.* 1. the cardinal number between four and six; 5; V. 2. anything having five units or members, as a basketball team.

**five-and-ten-cent store** (fīv′′n-ten′sent′), a dime store: also **five-and-ten, five-and-dime,** *n.*

**five·fold** (fīv′fōld′), *adj.* [see -FOLD], 1. having five parts. 2. having five times as much or as many. *adv.* five times as much or as many.

**Five Nations,** a confederation of Iroquoian Indians, consisting originally of the Mohawks, Oneidas, Onondagas, Cayugas, and Senecas, and later including the Tuscaroras.

**fiv·er** (fīv′ẽr), *n.* [Slang], a five-dollar bill.

**fix** (fiks), *v.t.* [FIXED or FIXT, FIXING], [< ML. < *fixus*, pp. of *figere*, to fasten], 1. to make firm; fasten firmly. 2. to set firmly in the mind. 3. to direct steadily, as one's eyes. 4. to make rigid. 5. to make permanent or lasting. 6. to establish; set: as, he *fixed* the rent at $40. 7. to find out definitely; determine. 8. to set in order; adjust. 9. to repair; mend. 10. to prepare (food or meals). 11. [Colloq.], to influence the result or action of (a horse race, jury, etc.) by bribery, trickery, etc. 12. [Colloq.], to punish; revenge oneself on. 13. in *chemistry, a)* to make solid or nonvolatile. *b)* to combine (free nitrogen) in the form of useful compounds, as nitrates, ammonia, etc. 14. in *photography*, to make (a film, slide, etc.) permanent by washing in a chemical solution. *v.i.* 1. to become fixed. 2. [Colloq. or Dial.], to prepare or intend: as, I'm *fixing* to go hunting. *n.* 1. [Colloq.], a difficult or awkward situation; predicament. 2. in *aviation, navigation*, etc., a position determined from the bearings of two or more known points. 3. [Slang], a situation that is fixed (sense 11). **—fix on** (or **upon**), to choose; settle on. **—fix up,** [Colloq.], 1. to repair; mend. 2. to set in order. **—fix′a·ble,** *adj.* **—fix′er,** *n.*

**fix·a·tion** (fik-sā′shən), *n.* 1. a fixing or being fixed, as in chemistry, photography, etc. 2. in *psychology*, a morbid preoccupation; obsession.

**fix·a·tive** (fik′sə-tiv), *adj.* that can or tends to make permanent, prevent fading, etc. *n.* a fixative substance, as a mordant.

**fixed** (fikst), *adj.* 1. firm; not movable. 2. established; set. 3. steady; resolute. 4. obsessive: as, a *fixed* idea. 5. in *chemistry, a)* nonvolatile: as, *fixed* oils. *b)* incorporated into a stable compound from its free state, as atmospheric nitrogen. **—fix·ed·ly** (fik′sid-li), *adv.* **—fix′ed·ness,** *n.*

**fixed star,** a star that appears to keep the same position in relation to other stars.

**fix·ings** (fik′siŋz), *n.pl.* [Colloq.], furnishings; accessories; trimmings.

**fix·i·ty** (fik′sə-ti), *n.* 1. the quality or state of being fixed; steadiness; stability; permanence. 2. [*pl.* -TIES], anything fixed.

**fixt** (fikst), poetic pt. and pp. of **fix.**

**fix·ture** (fiks′chẽr), *n.* [< obs. *fixure* (< L. *fixura*), after *mixture*], 1. anything firmly in place. 2. *usually in pl.* any of the firmly attached fittings of a house, store, etc. 3. [Colloq.], a person long-established in a place or a job.

**fiz** (fiz), *n.* & *v.t.* [FIZZED, FIZZING], fizz.

**fizz** (fiz), *n.* [echoic], 1. a hissing, sputtering sound. 2. a drink, as champagne, soda water, etc. that hisses and bubbles. *v.i.* [FIZZED, FIZZING], to make a hissing or bubbling sound. **—fizz′er,** *n.* **—fiz′zy** [-ZIER, -ZIEST], *adj.*

**fiz·zle** (fiz′′l), *v.i.* [-ZLED, -ZLING], [echoic], 1. to fizz. 2. [Colloq.], to fail, especially after a successful beginning. *n.* 1. a hissing or sputtering sound. 2. [Colloq.], a failure.

**fjord** (fyôrd, fyōrd), *n.* a fiord.

**Fl,** in *chemistry*, fluorine.

**Fl.,** 1. Flanders. 2. Flemish.

**fl.,** 1. florin(s). 2. *floruit*, [L.], (he or she) flourished. 3. fluid.

**Fla.,** Florida.

**flab·ber·gast** (flab′ẽr-gast′), *v.t.* [prob. < *flabby* + *aghast*], [Colloq.], to amaze; dumfound.

**flab·by** (flab′i), *adj.* [-BIER, -BIEST], [var. of *flappy* < *flap*], 1. lacking firmness; limp and soft. 2. lacking force; weak. **—flab′bi·ly,** *adv.* **—flab′bi·ness,** *n.*

**flac·cid** (flak′sid), *adj.* [< Fr. < L. < *flaccus*, flabby], 1. soft and limp; flabby: as, *flaccid* muscles. 2. weak; feeble. **—flac·cid′i·ty, flac′cid·ness,** *n.* **—flac′cid·ly,** *adv.*

**‡fla·con** (flȧ′kōn′), *n.* [Fr.; see FLAGON], a small bottle with a stopper, for holding perfume, etc.

**flag** (flag), *n.* [prob. < *flag*, *v.i.* in sense "to flutter"], 1. a piece of cloth with colors, patterns, or devices, used as a symbol of a nation, state, organization, etc. or as a signal; banner; standard. 2. *pl. a)* the quills on the second joint of a bird's wing. *b)* the long feathers on the leg of a hawk, owl, etc. 3. the bushy tail of certain dogs, as setters. *v.t.* [FLAGGED, FLAGGING], 1. to decorate or mark with flags. 2. to signal with or as with a flag: as, to *flag* a train. 3. to send (a message) by signaling. **—flag down,** to flag (a train, etc.) as a signal to stop. **—strike the** (or **one's**) **flag,** 1. to lower the flag. 2. to surrender.

**flag** (flag), *n.* [ON. *flaga*; cf. FLAKE], any hard, flat stone used for paving; flagstone. *v.t.* [FLAGGED, FLAGGING], to pave with flagstones. **—flag′ger,** *n.*

**flag** (flag), *n.* [< ME.; prob. < *flag*, *v.i.* in sense "to flutter"], an iris or a sweet flag, with sword-shaped leaves and blue, yellow, or white flowers.

**flag** (flag), *v.i.* [FLAGGED, FLAGGING], [prob. var. of ME. *flacken*, to flutter], 1. to become limp; droop. 2. to lose strength; grow weak or tired.

**Flag Day,** June 14, anniversary of the day in 1777 when the U.S. flag was adopted.

**flag·el·lant** (flaj′ə-lənt, flə-jel′ənt), *n.* a person who whips; esp., one who whips himself or has himself whipped as a religious discipline or in abnormal eroticism. *adj.* engaging in flagellation.

**flag·el·late** (flaj′ə-lāt′), *v.t.* [-LATED, -LATING], [< L. < *flagellum*, a whip], to whip; flog. *adj.* having flagella or shaped like a flagellum: also **flag′el·lat′ed.** **—flag′el·la′tion,** *n.* **—flag′el·la′tor,** *n.*

**fla·gel·lum** (flə-jel′əm), *n.* [*pl.* -LA (-ə), -LUMS], [L., a whip], 1. a whip. 2. in *biology*, a whiplike part serving as an organ of locomotion in bacteria and certain cells. 3. in *botany*, a shoot or runner.

**flag·eo·let** (flaj′ə-let′), *n.* [Fr., dim. of OFr. *flageol*, a flute < LL. < L. *flare*, to blow], a small wind instrument of the fipple flute family, similar to a recorder.

FLAGEOLET

**flag·ging** (flag′iŋ), *adj.* losing strength; drooping; growing weak. **—flag′ging·ly,** *adv.*

**flag·ging** (flag′iŋ), *n.* [< *flag* (flagstone)], 1. a pavement made of flagstones. 2. flagstones.

**fla·gi·tious** (flə-jish′əs), *adj.* [L. < *flagitium*, shameful act < *flagitare*, to demand], shamefully wicked; vile and scandalous; heinous. **—fla·gi′tious·ly,** *adv.* **—fla·gi′tious·ness,** *n.*

**flag officer,** a naval officer in command of a fleet or squadron and hence entitled to display a flag indicating his rank or command.

**flag·on** (flag′ən), *n.* [< OFr. *flascon*; see FLASK], 1. a container for liquids, usually with a handle, spout, and lid. 2. the contents of a flagon.

**flag·pole** (flag′pōl′), *n.* a pole on which a flag is flown: also **flag′staff′** (-staf′, -stäf′).

**fla·gran·cy** (flā′grən-si), *n.* the quality or state of being flagrant: also **fla′grance** (-grəns).

**fla·grant** (flā′grənt), *adj.* [< L. ppr. of *flagrare*, to blaze], glaringly bad; notorious; scandalous; outrageous. **—fla′grant·ly,** *adv.*

**‡fla·gran·te de·lic·to** (flə-gran′tē di-lik′tō), [L.], in the very act of committing the crime.

**flag·ship** (flag′ship′), *n.* the ship that carries the commander of a fleet or squadron and displays his flag.

**flag·stone** (flag′stōn′), *n.* a large, flat paving stone.

**flail** (flāl), *n.* [< OFr. < L. *flagellum*, a whip], an implement used to thresh grain by hand. *v.t.* 1. to thresh with a flail. 2. to beat; thrash.

FLAIL

**flair** (flâr), *n.* [< OFr. < *flairer* (ult. < L. *fragrare*), to emit an odor], 1. a keen natural discernment. 2. an aptitude; knack.

**flak** (flak), *n.* [< G. *Fl*ieger*a*bwehr*k*anone, antiaircraft gun], antiaircraft fire.

**flake** (flāk), *n.* [< ON. *flaki*], 1. a small, thin mass: as, a *flake* of snow. 2. a thin piece split, cut, or peeled from anything; chip. *v.t.* & *v.i.* [FLAKED, FLAKING], 1. to form into flakes. 2. to chip or peel off in flakes. 3. to make or become spotted with flakes. **—flak′er,** *n.*

**flak·y** (flāk′i), *adj.* [-IER, -IEST], 1. containing or made up of flakes. 2. breaking easily into flakes. **—flak′i·ly,** *adv.* **—flak′i·ness,** *n.*

**flam·beau** (flam′bō), *n.* [*pl.* -BEAUX (-bōz), -BEAUS], [< Fr. < OFr. < L. *flammula*, dim. of *flamma*, a flame], a lighted torch.

**flam·boy·ant** (flam-boi′ənt), *adj.* [< Fr.; see FLAMBEAU], 1. characterized by flamelike tracery of windows and florid decoration, as 16th century French Gothic architecture. 2. flamelike or brilliant. 3. ornate; too showy; flowery. —**flam·boy′ance, flam·boy′an·cy,** *n.* —**flam·boy′ant·ly,** *adv.*

**flame** (flām), *n.* [< OFr. < L. *flamma* < *flagrare,* to burn], 1. the burning gas of a fire, seen as a shimmering light; blaze. 2. a tongue of light rising from a fire. 3. the state of burning with a blaze of light. 4. a thing like a flame in heat, etc. 5. an intense emotion. 6. [Slang], a sweetheart. *v.i.* [FLAMED, FLAMING], 1. to blaze; burst into flame. 2. to act or be like a flame. 3. to grow red or hot. 4. to become very excited. *v.t.* [Poetic], to inflame. —**flame up** (or **out**), to burst out as in flames.

**flame·out** (flām′out′), *n.* the stopping of combustion in a jet engine, esp. as a result of some abnormal flight condition.

**flame thrower** a weapon for shooting a stream of flaming liquid, as oil, at enemy troops and positions.

**flam·ing** (flām′iŋ), *adj.* 1. burning with flames. 2. like a flame in brilliance or heat. 3. ardent; passionate. 4. startling. —**flam′ing·ly,** *adv.*

**fla·min·go** (flə-miŋ′gō), *n.* [*pl.* -GOS, -GOES], [Port. < Sp. *flamenco;* associated with *flama,* flame], a tropical wading bird with long legs, a long neck, and bright feathers colored pink to red.

**flam·ma·ble** (flam′ə-b'l), *adj.* easily set on fire; inflammable. —**flam′ma·bil′i·ty,** *n.*

**Flan·ders** (flan′dẽrz), *n.* a region in NW Europe, in Belgium and N France.

**flange** (flanj), *n.* [prob. < OFr. *flangir,* to turn], a projecting rim or collar on a wheel, etc., to hold it in place, give it strength, or attach it to something else. *v.t.* [FLANGED, FLANGING], to put a flange on.

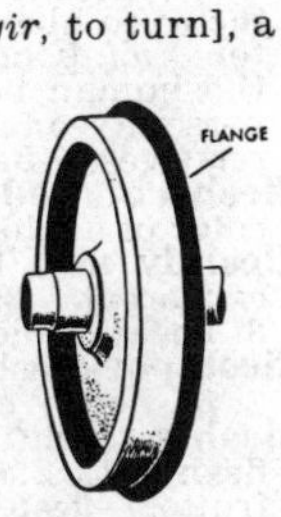

FLANGE

**flank** (flaŋk), *n.* [< OFr. *flanc*], 1. the fleshy side of a person or animal between the ribs and the hip. 2. a cut of beef from this part. 3. the side of anything. 4. the right or left side of a military formation or force. *adj.* of or on the flank. *v.t.* 1. to be at the side of. 2. to attack, or pass around, the side of (enemy troops). *v.i.* to be in a flanking position (with *on* or *upon*).

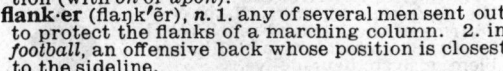

**flank·er** (flaŋk′ẽr), *n.* 1. any of several men sent out to protect the flanks of a marching column. 2. in *football,* an offensive back whose position is closest to the sideline.

**flan·nel** (flan′'l), *n.* [prob. < W. *gwlanen* < *gwlan,* wool], 1. a lightweight, loosely woven woolen cloth. 2. *pl.* clothes made of this cloth. 3. flannelette. 4. [Colloq.], *pl.* heavy woolen underwear. *v.t.* [-NELED or -NELLED, -NELING or -NELLING], to wrap in flannel. —**flan′nel·ly,** *adj.*

**flan·nel·ette, flan·nel·et** (flan′'l-et′), *n.* a soft cotton cloth resembling flannel.

**flap** (flap), *n.* [ME. *flap(pe)*], 1. anything flat and broad that hangs loose and is attached at one end: as, the *flap* of a pocket. 2. the movement of such a part: as, the *flap* of an awning. 3. the sound made by such a movement. 4. a slap. 5. a hinged section on an airplane wing, used in landing and taking off. *v.t.* [FLAPPED, FLAPPING], 1. to strike with something flat and broad; slap. 2. to move back and forth or up and down: as, the bird *flapped* its wings. *v.i.* 1. to move with a slapping motion; flutter. 2. to fly by flapping the wings.

**flap·jack** (flap′jak′), *n.* a large pancake.

**flap·per** (flap′ẽr), *n.* 1. one that flaps. 2. [Colloq.], in the 1920's, a young girl rather bold in behavior.

**flare** (flâr), *v.i.* [FLARED, FLARING], [? < D. *vlederen,* to flutter], 1. to blaze up brightly and unsteadily. 2. to curve or spread outward, as a bell, a ship's sides, etc. *v.t.* to make flare. *n.* 1. a bright, brief, unsteady blaze of light. 2. a brief, dazzling light used as a signal. 3. a sudden, brief outburst, as of emotion or sound. 4. a curving outward, as of a skirt. 5. a part that curves or spreads outward. —**flare up** (or **out**), 1. to burst into flame. 2. to become suddenly angry, violent, etc.

**flare-up** (flâr′up′), *n.* a sudden outburst of flame or of emotion, violence, etc.

**flar·ing** (flâr′iŋ), *adj.* 1. blazing brightly for a little while. 2. gaudy. 3. curving or spreading outward.

**flash** (flash), *v.i.* [ME. *flaschen,* to splash; prob. echoic], 1. to send out a sudden, brief blaze or light. 2. to sparkle; gleam. 3. to come or pass swiftly and suddenly. *v.t.* 1. to cause to flash. 2. to send (news, etc.) swiftly or suddenly. 3. [Colloq.], to show briefly or ostentatiously: as, he *flashed* a roll of money. *n.* 1. a sudden, brief light. 2. a brief time; moment. 3. a sudden, brief display: as, a *flash* of wit. 4. a brief item of news sent by telegraph, radio, etc. 5. a gaudy display. 6. anything that flashes. *adj.* flashy. —**flash in the pan** [orig. of priming in pan of a flintlock], 1. a sudden, apparently brilliant effort that fails. 2. one who fails after such an effort. —**flash′er,** *n.*

**flash-back** (flash′bak′), *n.* 1. an interruption in the continuity of a story, play, etc. by the narration of some earlier episode. 2. such an episode.

**flash·bulb** (flash′bulb′), *n.* an electric light bulb giving a brief, dazzling light, for taking photographs.

**flash burn,** a severe burn caused by exposure to a flash or sudden release of intense radiant heat, especially the heat of a nuclear explosion.

**flash·cube** (flash′kūb′), *n.* a small rotating cube containing a flashbulb in each of four sides, designed for taking photographs rapidly.

**flash flood,** a sudden flood, as after heavy rain.

**flash·ing** (flash′iŋ), *n.* sheets of metal, etc. used to weatherproof joints or edges, as of a roof.

**flash·light** (flash′līt′), *n.* 1. a portable electric light, usually operated by a small battery. 2. the light of a flashbulb.

**flash·y** (flash′i), *adj.* [-IER, -IEST], 1. flashing; dazzling or bright for a little while. 2. gaudy; showy. —**flash′i·ly,** *adv.* —**flash′i·ness,** *n.*

**flask** (flask, fläsk), *n.* [< Fr. < OFr. < ML. *flasca,* wine bottle], 1. any of various bottles used in chemical laboratories, etc. 2. a small, flattened pocket container for liquor, etc.

**flat** (flat), *adj.* [FLATTER, FLATTEST], [< ON. *flatr*], 1. having a smooth, level surface. 2. lying extended or spread out. 3. broad, even, and thin. 4. absolute; positive: as, a *flat* denial. 5. not fluctuating: as, a *flat* rate. 6. without much business activity: as, a *flat* market. 7. having little or no sparkle or taste: as, a *flat* drink. 8. of little interest; dull. 9. not clear or full; blurred: as, a *flat* sound. 10. emptied of air: as, a *flat* tire. 11. in *art, a)* designating figures lacking relief or perspective. *b)* uniform in tint. *c)* without gloss. 12. in *grammar,* not having an inflectional ending: *fast* in *drive fast* is a *flat* adverb. 13. in *music, a)* below the true pitch. *b)* lower in pitch by a half note: as, *D-flat.* 14. in *phonetics,* sounded with the tongue in a relatively level position (e.g., *a* in *can*). *adv.* 1. in a flat manner. 2. in a flat position. 3. exactly; precisely: as, ten seconds *flat.* 4. in *music,* below the true pitch. *n.* 1. a flat surface or part: as, the *flat* of the hand. 2. an expanse of level land. 3. a low-lying marsh. 4. a shallow; shoal. 5. a piece of theatrical scenery on a flat frame. 6. a deflated tire. 7. *a)* a note or tone one half step below another. *b)* the symbol (♭) for such a note. *v.t. & v.i.* [FLATTED, FLATTING], to flatten. —**fall flat,** to arouse no response. —**flat′ly,** *adv.* —**flat′ness,** *n.* —**flat′tish,** *adj.*

**flat** (flat), *n.* [altered < Scot. dial. *flet* (AS. *flet*) a floor, story], an apartment or suite of rooms on one floor of a building.

**flat·boat** (flat′bōt′), *n.* a flat-bottomed boat for carrying freight in shallow waters or on rivers.

**flat·car** (flat′kär′), *n.* a railroad car without sides or a roof, for carrying certain freight.

**flat·fish** (flat′fish′), *n.* [*pl.* see FISH], a fish with a flat body and both eyes on the uppermost side, as the flounder, halibut, etc.

**flat·foot** (flat′foot′), *n.* 1. a condition in which the instep arch of the foot has been flattened. 2. [Slang], a policeman.

**flat-foot·ed** (flat′foot′id), *adj.* 1. having feet with flattened instep arches. 2. [Colloq.], firm and uncompromising. —**catch flat-footed,** [Colloq.], to take by surprise. —**flat′-foot′ed·ly,** *adv.* —**flat′-foot′ed·ness,** *n.*

**flat·i·ron** (flat′ī′ẽrn), *n.* an iron (sense 2, b).

**flat silver,** silver knives, forks, spoons, etc.

**flat·ten** (flat′'n), *v.t. & v.i.* to make or become flat or flatter. —**flat′ten·er,** *n.*

**flat·ter** (flat′ẽr), *v.t.* [prob. < OFr. *flater,* to smooth], 1. to praise too much or insincerely. 2. to try to please, or get the favor of, as by praise. 3. to make seem more attractive than is so: as, my picture *flatters* me. 4. to make feel pleased or honored. *v.i.* to use flattery. —**flatter oneself,** to be pleased to think (*that*). —**flat′ter·er,** *n.* —**flat′ter·ing·ly,** *adv.*

**flat·ter·y** (flat′ẽr-i), *n.* [*pl.* -IES], 1. a flattering. 2. excessive or insincere praise.

**flat·top, flat-top** (flat′top′), *n.* [Slang], an aircraft carrier.

**flat·u·lent** (flach′ə-lənt, -yoo-), *adj.* [Fr.; ult. < L. < *flare*, to blow], 1. of, having, or producing gas in the stomach or intestines. 2. windy or empty in speech; vain; pompous. —**flat′u·lence, flat′u·len·cy,** *n.* —**flat′u·lent·ly,** *adv.*

**flat·ware** (flat′wâr′), *n.* flat table utensils, as knives, forks, and spoons, or plates, etc.

**flat·worm** (flat′wũrm′), *n.* any of a large group of worms with a flattened, unsegmented body, as the tapeworm: many flatworms are parasitic.

**Flau·bert, Gus·tave** (güs′tȧv′ flō′bâr′), 1821–1880; French novelist.

**flaunt** (flônt), *v.i.* [ult. source prob. ON.], 1. to make a gaudy or impudent display: as, brazen women *flaunt* through the town. 2. to flutter or wave freely. *v.t.* to show off proudly or impudently. *n.* a flaunting. —**flaunt′er,** *n.* —**flaunt′ing·ly,** *adv.* —**flaunt′y** [-IER, -IEST], *adj.*

**flau·tist** (flô′tist), *n.* [It. *flautista*], flutist.

**fla·vin** (flā′vin, flav′in), *n.* [< L. *flavus*, yellow], 1. a complex ketone, $C_{10}H_6N_4O_2$. 2. a yellow compound found in certain plant and animal products or prepared synthetically. Also **fla′vine** (flā′vēn, flav′in).

**fla·vor** (flā′vẽr), *n.* [< OFr. *flaor;* prob. < L. *flare*, to blow + *foetor*, foul smell], 1. an odor; smell; aroma. 2. that quality of a substance which gives it a characteristic taste. 3. flavoring. 4. characteristic quality: as, the *flavor* of adventure. *v.t.* to give flavor to. —**fla′vor·er,** *n.* —**fla′vor·less,** *adj.* —**fla′vor·ous,** *adj.*

**fla·vor·ing** (flā′vẽr-iŋ), *n.* an essence, extract, etc. added to a food or drink to give it a certain taste: also **fla′vour·ing.**

**fla·vour** (flā′vẽr), *n. & v.t.* flavor: British sp. —**fla′vour·er,** *n.* —**fla′vour·less,** *adj.* —**fla′vour·ous,** *adj.*

**flaw** (flô), *n.* [prob. < ON. *fla*, break in a cliff], 1. a crack, as in a gem; broken or faulty place; blemish. 2. a defect; fault; error. *v.t. & v.i.* to make or become faulty. —**flaw′less,** *adj.* —**flaw′less·ly,** *adv.* —**flaw′less·ness,** *n.*

**flaw** (flô), *n.* [prob. < ON. *flaga*, sudden onset], a sudden, brief rush of wind; squall.

**flax** (flaks), *n.* [AS. *fleax*], 1. a slender, erect plant with delicate blue flowers and narrow leaves: its seed (**flaxseed**) is used to make linseed oil, and the fibers of the stem are spun into linen thread. 2. the threadlike fibers of this plant, ready for spinning. —**flax′y** [-IER, -IEST], *adj.*

**flax·en** (flak′s′n), *adj.* 1. of or made of flax. 2. like flax in color; pale-yellow.

**flay** (flā), *v.t.* [AS. *flean*], 1. to strip off the skin or hide of. 2. to criticize or scold mercilessly. 3. to rob; plunder; pillage. —**flay′er,** *n.*

**flea** (flē), *n.* [AS. *fleah*], a small, wingless, jumping insect that is parasitic and blood-sucking.

FLEA (⅛ in. long)

**flea·bane** (flē′bān′), *n.* a plant of the composite family that supposedly drives away fleas.

**flea-bit·ten** (flē′bit′′n), *adj.* 1. bitten by fleas. 2. infested with fleas. 3. wretched; decrepit.

**fleck** (flek), *n.* [ON. *flekkr*], 1. a spot or small patch, as of color; speck. 2. a particle; flake. *v.t.* to spot; speckle. —**flecked,** *adj.*

**flec·tion** (flek′shən), *n.* [< L. pp. of *flectere*, to bend], 1. a bending; flexing. 2. a bent part or bend. Also sp. **flex′ion.** —**flec′tion·al,** *adj.*

**fled** (fled), pt. and pp. of **flee.**

**fledge** (flej), *v.i.* [FLEDGED, FLEDGING], [AS. (*un*)*flycge*, (un)fledged], to grow the feathers necessary for flying. *v.t.* 1. to rear (a young bird) until it is able to fly. 2. to supply or cover (an arrow, etc.) with feathers.

**fledg·ling, fledge·ling** (flej′liŋ), *n.* 1. a young bird just fledged. 2. a young, inexperienced person.

**flee** (flē), *v.i.* [FLED, FLEEING], [AS. *fleon*], 1. to run away or escape from danger, pursuit, etc. 2. to pass away quickly; vanish. 3. to go swiftly. *v.t.* to run away from; avoid. —**fle′er,** *n.*

**fleece** (flēs), *n.* [AS. *fleos*], 1. the wool covering a sheep or similar animal. 2. the amount of wool cut from a sheep in one shearing. 3. a covering like a sheep's. 4. a soft, warm, napped fabric. *v.t.* [FLEECED, FLEECING], 1. to shear the fleece from. 2. to take money, property, etc. from by fraud; cheat; swindle. —**fleec′er,** *n.*

**fleec·y** (flēs′i), *adj.* [-IER, -IEST], 1. made of or covered with fleece. 2. like fleece; soft and light. —**fleec′i·ly,** *adv.* —**fleec′i·ness,** *n.*

**fleer** (flêr), *v.i. & v.t.* [prob. < ON.], to laugh derisively (at); sneer. *n.* a derisive grimace, laugh, or remark; gibe. —**fleer′ing·ly,** *adv.*

**fleet** (flēt), *n.* [AS. *fleot* < *fleotan*, to float], 1. *a*) a number of warships under one command. *b*) the entire navy of a country. 2. any group of ships, trucks, airplanes, etc. under one control.

**fleet** (flēt), *v.i.* [AS. *fleotan*, to float], to move swiftly; fly. *adj.* 1. swift; rapid. 2. [Poetic], evanescent. —**fleet′ly,** *adv.* —**fleet′ness,** *n.*

**fleet·ing** (flēt′iŋ), *adj.* passing swiftly; transitory. —**fleet′ing·ly,** *adv.* —**fleet′ing·ness,** *n.*

**Flem.,** Flemish.

**Flem·ing** (flem′iŋ), *n.* 1. a native of Flanders. 2. a Belgian who speaks Flemish.

**Flem·ish** (flem′ish), *adj.* of Flanders, the Flemings, or their language. *n.* the Low German language of the Flemings. Abbrev. **Fl., Flem.** —**the Flemish,** the people of Flanders.

**flesh** (flesh), *n.* [AS. *flæsc*], 1. the soft substance of the body (of a person or animal); esp., the muscular tissue. 2. the pulpy or edible part of fruits and vegetables. 3. meat; esp., meat other than fish or fowl. 4. the human body, as distinguished from the soul. 5. the nature of the human body; esp., the sensual nature. 6. all human beings; mankind. 7. all living beings. 8. the usual color of a white person's skin; yellowish pink. *v.t.* 1. to feed (animals) with flesh so as to incite them to kill. 2. to incite to bloodshed, etc. by a foretaste. 3. to fatten. *v.i.* [Colloq.], to grow fat. —**flesh and blood,** the human body. —**in the flesh,** 1. alive. 2. in person. —**one's (own) flesh and blood,** one's close relatives. —**flesh′less,** *adj.*

**flesh-col·ored** (flesh′kul′ẽrd), *adj.* having the usual color of a white person's skin; yellowish-pink.

**flesh·ly** (flesh′li), *adj.* [-LIER, -LIEST], 1. of the body; corporeal. 2. fond of bodily pleasures; sensual. 3. fleshy. —**flesh′li·ness,** *n.*

**flesh·pot** (flesh′pot′), *n.* 1. a pot for cooking meat. 2. *pl.* bodily comforts; luxury.

**flesh·y** (flesh′i), *adj.* [-IER, -IEST], 1. having much flesh; fat. 2. of or like flesh. 3. pulpy: said of some fruits. —**flesh′i·ness,** *n.*

**fleur-de-lis** (flũr′də-lē′, -lēs′), *n.* [*pl.* FLEURS-DE-LIS (-lēz′)], [Fr., flower of the lily], 1. the iris (plant or flower). 2. the coat of arms of the former French royal family. 3. in *heraldry*, a lilylike emblem: also sp. **fleur-de-lys.**

FLEUR-DE-LIS

**flew** (flōō), pt. of **fly.**

**flex** (fleks), *v.t. & v.i.* [< L. pp. of *flectere*, to bend], 1. to bend, as an arm. 2. to contract, as a muscle.

**flex·i·ble** (flek′sə-b′l), *adj.* [< L.; see FLEX], 1. able to bend without breaking; not stiff; pliant. 2. easily persuaded or influenced. 3. adjustable to change; easily adaptable. —**flex′i·bil′i·ty, flex′i·ble·ness,** *n.* —**flex′i·bly,** *adv.*

**flex·or** (flek′sẽr, -sôr), *n.* any muscle that bends a limb or other part of the body.

**flex·u·ous** (flek′shōō-əs), *adj.* 1. full of bends or curves; winding. 2. wavering. —**flex′u·os′i·ty** (-os′ə-ti), [*pl.* -TIES], *n.*

**flex·ure** (flek′shẽr), *n.* 1. a bending, curving, or flexing. 2. a bend; curve. —**flex′ur·al,** *adj.*

**flib·ber·ti·gib·bet** (flib′ẽr-ti-jib′it), *n.* [? echoic of nonsense chatter], 1. a person, especially a woman, who chatters constantly. 2. an irresponsible, flighty person.

**flick** (flik), *n.* [prob. echoic], 1. a light, quick stroke, as with a whip; snap. 2. a light, snapping sound. 3. a fleck; streak; dash. *v.t.* 1. to strike, throw, etc. with a light, quick, snapping stroke. 2. to make such a stroke with (a whip, etc.). *v.i.* to move quickly and jerkily; flutter.

**flick·er** (flik′ẽr), *v.i.* [AS. *flicorian*], 1. to move with a quick, light, wavering motion. 2. to burn or shine unsteadily, as a candle in the wind. *v.t.* to cause to flicker. *n.* 1. a flickering. 2. a dart of flame or light. 3. a brief, passing feeling: as, a *flicker* of fear. —**flick′er·ing·ly,** *adv.*

**flick·er** (flik′ẽr), *n.* [echoic of its cry], a North American woodpecker with wings colored golden on the underside.

**flied** (flīd), pt. and pp. of **fly** (only in reference to baseball); see **fly,** *v.i.*).

**fli·er** (flī′ẽr), *n.* 1. a thing that flies. 2. an aviator. 3. a bus, train, etc. with a fast schedule. 4. [Slang], a reckless gamble. Also sp. **flyer.**

**flight** (flīt), *n.* [AS. *flyht*], 1. the act, manner, or power of flying. 2. the distance flown at one time by an airplane, bird, etc. 3. a group of things flying through the air together. 4. *a*) a formation of military airplanes in flight. *b*) a basic unit of an air force, consisting of a small number of planes of the same type. 5. an airplane scheduled to fly a certain trip. 6. a trip by airplane. 7. an outburst or soaring above the ordinary: as, a *flight* of fancy. 8. a set of stairs, especially between landings. 9. in *archery*, a special arrow for distance shooting: also **flight arrow.**

**flight** (flīt), *n.* [< AS. < *fleon*, to flee], a fleeing, as from danger. —**put to flight,** to force to flee.

**flight·less** (flīt′lis), *adj.* not able to fly.

**flight·y** (flīt′i), *adj.* [-IER, -IEST], 1. given to sudden whims or flights of fancy; unsettled; frivolous. 2. mentally unbalanced. —**flight′i·ly,** *adv.* —**flight′i·ness,** *n.*

**flim·sy** (flim′zi), *adj.* [-SIER, -SIEST], [prob. < W. *llymsi*, flimsy], 1. thin and easily broken or damaged; frail. 2. trivial; ineffectual: as, a *flimsy* excuse. *n.* 1. thin paper used by newspaper reporters. 2. copy written on this. —**flim′si·ly,** *adv.* —**flim′si·ness,** *n.*

**flinch** (flinch), *v.i.* [< OFr. *flenchir*], to draw back, as from a blow or from anything difficult, dangerous, or painful. *n.* a flinching. —**flinch′er,** *n.* —**flinch′ing·ly,** *adv.*

**flin·der** (flin′dẽr), *n.* [ME. *flender;* prob. < Anglo-N.], a little piece; splinter; fragment: chiefly in the phrase **break (or fly) into flinders.**

**fling** (fliŋ), *v.t.* [FLUNG, FLINGING], [ME. *flingen*, to rush; prob. < ON.], 1. to throw, especially with force; hurl. 2. to put abruptly or violently: as, the crowd was *flung* into confusion. 3. to throw down; overthrow. 4. to move (one's arms, legs, etc.) suddenly or impulsively. 5. to move into with spirit: as, he *flung* himself into the task. 6. to give out; emit. *v.i.* to move suddenly and violently; dash: as, she *flung* out of the room. *n.* 1. a flinging. 2. a taunting remark; sneer. 3. a brief time of wild actions and unrestrained pleasures. 4. a spirited dance: as, the Highland *fling.* 5. [Colloq.], a trial effort. —**fling′er,** *n.*

**Flint** (flint), *n.* a city in E Michigan: pop., 197,000.

**flint** (flint), *n.* [AS.], 1. a very hard, grayish or brown quartz, which produces sparks when struck against steel. 2. a piece of this stone, used to start a fire, for primitive tools, etc. 3. anything extremely hard or firm.

**flint glass,** a hard, bright glass containing lead, used for lenses, crystal, etc.

**flint·lock** (flint′lok′), *n.* 1. a gunlock in which the powder is exploded by a spark produced by the striking of a flint against a metal plate. 2. an old-fashioned gun with such a lock.

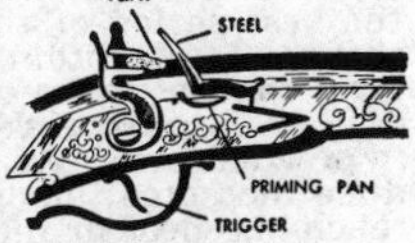

FLINTLOCK

**flint·y** (flin′ti), *adj.* [-IER, -IEST], 1. made of or containing flint. 2. like flint; extremely hard and firm. —**flint′i·ly,** *adv.* —**flint′i·ness,** *n.*

**flip** (flip), *v.t.* [FLIPPED, FLIPPING], [echoic], 1. to toss or move with a quick jerk; flick. 2. to toss (a coin, etc.) by snapping the thumb against the finger, as in betting on which side will land uppermost. *v.i.* 1. to make a quick, light stroke; snap. 2. to move jerkily. *n.* a flipping; snap, tap, or jerk.

**flip** (flip), *n.* [prob. < *flip*, to toss], a hot, sweetened drink of beer, cider, etc. with spices and, sometimes, milk and eggs.

**flip** (flip), *adj.* [FLIPPER, FLIPPEST], [Colloq.], flippant; saucy; pert; impertinent.

**flip·pan·cy** (flip′ən-si), *n.* 1. a flippant quality or state. 2. [*pl.* -CIES], a flippant act or remark.

**flip·pant** (flip′ənt), *adj.* [Early Mod. Eng., nimble; prob. < *flip*, *v.*], frivolous and disrespectful; saucy. —**flip′pant·ly,** *adv.* —**flip′pant·ness,** *n.*

**flip·per** (flip′ẽr), *n.* [< *flip*, *v.*], 1. a broad, flat limb adapted for swimming, as in seals, turtles, etc. 2. [Slang], the hand.

**flirt** (flũrt), *v.t.* [? echoic, but infl. by OFr. *fleureter*, to touch lightly], to throw or move quickly and jerkily: as, the bird *flirted* its tail. *v.i.* 1. to move jerkily. 2. to make love without serious intentions; play at love. 3. to trifle; play: as, to *flirt* with an idea. *n.* 1. a quick, jerky movement. 2. a quick, jerky toss. 3. one who plays at love. —**flirt′er,** *n.* —**flirt′ing·ly,** *adv.* —**flirt′y** [-IER, -IEST], *adj.*

**flir·ta·tion** (flũr-tā′shən), *n.* 1. a playing at love without serious intentions. 2. a superficial, rather playful love affair. —**flir·ta′tious,** *adj.* —**flir·ta′tious·ly,** *adv.* —**flir·ta′tious·ness,** *n.*

**flit** (flit), *v.i.* [FLITTED, FLITTING], [< ON. *flytja*], 1. to pass lightly and rapidly, as through the mind. 2. to fly lightly and rapidly; flutter. *n.* a flitting. —**flit′ter,** *n.* —**flit′ting·ly,** *adv.*

**flitch** (flich), *n.* [AS. *flicce*], the cured and salted side of a hog; side of bacon. *v.t.* to cut so as to form flitches.

**flit·ter** (flit′ẽr), *v.i.* & *v.t.* [freq. of *flit*], [Dial.], to move rapidly and lightly; flutter.

**fliv·ver** (fliv′ẽr), *n.* [arbitrary coinage], [Slang], a small, cheap automobile, airplane, etc.

**float** (flōt), *n.* [AS. *flota* < *fleotan*, to float], 1. anything that stays, or causes something else to stay, on the surface of a liquid; specif., *a)* a cork on a fishing line. *b)* a floating ball that regulates water level, as in a tank. *c)* a raft. 2. a low, flat, decorated vehicle for carrying exhibits in a parade. *v.i.* 1. to stay on the surface of a liquid. 2. to drift gently on water, in air, etc. 3. to move about vaguely and without purpose: as, idle thoughts *floated* through his mind. *v.t.* 1. *a)* to cause to float. *b)* to bring to the surface and cause to float. 2. to flood. 3. to put into circulation; start: as, they *floated* a bond issue. —**float′a·ble,** *adj.*

**float·a·tion** (flō-tā′shən), *n.* flotation.

**float·er** (flōt′ẽr), *n.* 1. a person or thing that floats. 2. a person who illegally votes at several polling places. 3. [Colloq.], a person who changes his place of residence or work frequently.

**float·ing** (flōt′iŋ), *adj.* 1. that floats. 2. not remaining in one place. 3. in *finance*, *a)* designating an unfunded, short-time debt. *b)* not permanently invested: as, *floating* capital. 4. in *medicine*, displaced, especially downward, from the normal position: as, a *floating* kidney. —**float′ing·ly,** *adv.*

**floating ribs,** the eleventh and twelfth pairs of ribs, which are not attached to the breastbone or to other ribs.

**floc·cu·late** (flok′yoo-lāt′), *v.t.* & *v.i.* [-LATED, -LATING], to collect, as soils, clouds, etc., into small, flocculent lumps or masses.

**floc·cu·lent** (flok′yoo-lənt), *adj.* [< L. *floccus*, flock of wool], 1. woolly; fluffy. 2. containing or consisting of small woolly masses. —**floc′cu·lence,** *n.* —**floc′cu·lent·ly,** *adv.*

**flock** (flok), *n.* [AS. *flocc*, a troop], 1. a group of certain animals, as goats, sheep, or birds, living, feeding, etc. together. 2. a large number of people or things. 3. the members of a church. *v.i.* to assemble or travel in a flock or crowd.

**flock** (flok), *n.* [< OFr. < L. *floccus*], 1. a small tuft of wool. 2. wool or cotton waste used to stuff upholstered furniture, mattresses, etc.

**floe** (flō), *n.* [ON. *flo*, a layer], 1. a large field or sheet of floating ice. 2. a piece of this broken off and floating free.

**flog** (flog, flôg), *v.t.* [FLOGGED, FLOGGING], [? cant abbrev. of L. *flagellare*, to whip], to beat with a strap, stick, whip, etc. —**flog′ger,** *n.*

**flood** (flud), *n.* [AS. *flod*], 1. an overflowing of water on land usually dry; deluge. 2. *a)* the flowing of the tide toward the shore: opposed to *ebb.* *b)* the rising tide: also **flood tide.** 3. a great flow or outpouring: as, a *flood* of words. 4. [Poetic], a large body of water; ocean, sea, etc. *v.t.* 1. to cover or fill with a flood; overflow. 2. to cover, fill, or overwhelm like a flood: as, music *flooded* the room. 3. to put much water on or in. *v.i.* 1. to rise in a flood. 2. to gush out like a flood. —**the Flood,** in the *Bible*, the great flood in Noah's time: Gen. 7. —**flood′a·ble,** *adj.* —**flood′er,** *n.*

**flood control,** the protection of land from floods by the construction of river embankments, soil conservation, reforestation, etc.

**flood·gate** (flud′gāt′), *n.* 1. a gate in a stream or canal, to control the flow of water. 2. anything like this in controlling an outburst.

**flood·light** (flud′līt′), *n.* 1. a lamp that casts a broad beam of bright light. 2. such a beam of light. *v.t.* [-LIGHTED or -LIT, -LIGHTING], to illuminate by a floodlight.

**floor** (flôr, flōr), *n.* [AS. *flor*], 1. the inside bottom surface of a room. 2. the corresponding surface of anything: as, the ocean *floor.* 3. a level or story in a building. 4. the part of a legislative chamber, stock exchange, etc. occupied by the members and not including the gallery or platform. 5. the right to speak in an assembly: as, the chairman gave him the *floor.* 6. a minimum price level for any commodity. *v.t.* 1. to cover or furnish with a floor. 2.

to knock down. 3. [Colloq.], *a*) to defeat. *b*) to puzzle; confuse. —**floor′less,** *adj.*
**floor·ing** (flôr′iŋ, flōr′-), *n.* 1. a floor or floors. 2. material for making a floor.
**floor leader,** a member of a legislature who is chosen by fellow members of his political party to direct their actions on the floor.
**floor plan,** an architectural scale drawing showing the size and arrangement of rooms, halls, etc. on one floor of a house or other building.
**floor show,** an entertainment, as singing, dancing, etc., presented in a restaurant or night club.
**floor·walk·er** (flôr′wôk′ẽr, flōr′-), *n.* a person employed by a department store to direct customers, supervise sales, etc.: now often **floor manager.**
**floo·zy, floo·zie** (flōō′zi), *n.* [*pl.* -ZIES], [Slang], a loose, disreputable woman: also sp. **floosy.**
**flop** (flop), *v.t.* [FLOPPED, FLOPPING], [var. of *flap*], to flap or throw noisily and clumsily. *v.i.* 1. to move or flap around loosely or clumsily. 2. to fall or drop in this way: as, to *flop* into a chair. 3. to make a sudden change. 4. [Colloq.], to fail. 5. [Slang], to sleep. *n.* 1. a flopping. 2. the sound of flopping. 3. [Colloq.], a failure. *adv.* with a flop. —**flop′per,** *n.*
**flop·house** (flop′hous′), *n.* a cheap hotel.
**flop·py** (flop′i), *adj.* [-PIER, -PIEST], [Colloq.], flopping or inclined to flop. —**flop′pi·ly,** *adv.* —**flop′pi·ness,** *n.*
**Flo·ra** (flôr′ə, flō′rə), *n.* [L. < *flos*, a flower], 1. in *Rom. mythology*, the goddess of flowers. 2. [f-], [*pl.* -RAS, -RAE (-ē, -rē)], the plants of a specified region or time.
**flo·ral** (flôr′əl, flō′rəl), *adj.* of, made of, or like flowers. —**flo′ral·ly,** *adv.*
**Flor·ence** (flôr′əns, flor′-), *n.* a city in Tuscany, Italy: pop., 391,000: Italian name, **Fi·ren·ze** (fē-ren′dze). —**Flor′en·tine′** (-tēn′), *adj. & n.*
**flo·res·cence** (flô-res′′ns, flō-), *n.* [< L. *florescens*, ppr. < *florere*, to bloom < *flos*, a flower], 1. a blooming. 2. the condition or period of blooming. —**flo·res′cent,** *adj.*
**flo·ret** (flôr′it, flō′rit), *n.* [< OFr. dim. of *flor* < L. *flos*, a flower], 1. a small flower. 2. any of the small flowers making up the head of a composite flower, as the daisy or aster.
**flo·ri·cul·ture** (flôr′i-kul′chẽr, flō′ri-), *n.* the cultivation of flowers. —**flo′ri·cul′tur·al,** *adj.* —**flo′ri·cul′tur·ist,** *n.*
**flor·id** (flôr′id, flor′-), *adj.* [< L. *floridus* < *flos*, a flower], 1. rosy; ruddy: said of the complexion. 2. highly decorated; gaudy; showy: as, a *florid* passage in music. —**flo·rid·i·ty** (flô-rid′ə-ti, flō-), **flor′id·ness,** *n.* —**flor′id·ly,** *adv.*
**Flor·i·da** (flôr′i-də, flor′-), *n.* a State on a peninsula in the southeastern U.S.: area, 58,560 sq. mi.; pop., 4,952,000; capital, Tallahassee: abbrev. **Fla., Flor.** —**Flo·rid′i·an** (flô-rid′i-ən, flō-), **Flor′i·dan,** *adj. & n.*
**flor·in** (flôr′in, flor′-), *n.* [< OFr. < It. < L. *flos*, flower: the figure of a lily was stamped on the original coins], 1. originally, a gold coin of medieval Florence, issued in 1252. 2. an English silver coin equal to two shillings. 3. any of various European silver or gold coins.
**flo·rist** (flôr′ist, flō′rist, flor′-), *n.* [< L. *flos*, a flower], one who cultivates or sells flowers.
**-flo·rous** (flə-rəs), [< L. < *flos*, a flower], a suffix meaning *having many* or *a* (specified) *number of flowers*, as in *multiflorous*.
**floss** (flôs, flos), *n.* [prob. < Fr. < L. *floccus;* see FLOCK (a tuft)], 1. the rough silk covering a silkworm's cocoon. 2. the short, downy waste fibers of silk. 3. floss silk. 4. a soft, silky substance like floss, as in corn tassels.
**floss silk,** soft, untwisted silk fibers, used in embroidery and cheap silk fabrics.
**floss·y** (flôs′i, flos′i), *adj.* [-IER, -IEST], 1. of or like floss; downy; light; fluffy. 2. [Slang], showy and frilly.
**flo·ta·tion** (flō-tā′shən), *n.* 1. a floating or launching. 2. the act of financing a business by selling an entire issue of bonds, securities, etc. Also sp. **floatation.**
**flo·til·la** (flō-til′ə), *n.* [Sp., dim. of *flota*, a fleet], 1. a small fleet. 2. a fleet of boats or small ships.
**flot·sam** (flot′səm), *n.* [< OFr. *flotaison* < AS. *flotian*, to float], the wreckage of a ship or its cargo found floating on the sea. —**flotsam and jetsam,** 1. the wreckage of a ship or its cargo found floating on the sea or washed ashore. 2. miscellaneous trifles or worthless things. 3. transient, unemployed people.
**flounce** (flouns), *v.i.* [FLOUNCED, FLOUNCING], [prob. < Scand.], 1. to move with quick, flinging motions of the body, as in anger. 2. to jerk; twist or turn abruptly. *n.* a flouncing.
**flounce** (flouns), *n.* [earlier *frounce* < OFr. < *froncir*, to wrinkle], a wide, gathered piece of cloth sewed on by its upper edge to a skirt, sleeve, etc. *v.t.* [FLOUNCED, FLOUNCING], to trim with a flounce or flounces.
**floun·der** (floun′dẽr), *v.i.* [prob. var. of *founder*], 1. to struggle awkwardly, as in deep mud or snow. 2. to speak or act in an awkward, confused manner. *n.* a floundering. —**floun′der·ing·ly,** *adv.*
**floun·der** (floun′dẽr), *n.* [*pl.* -DERS, -DER; see PLURAL, II, D, 1], [< Anglo-Fr. < OFr. *flondre;* prob. < Scand.], any of various flatfishes caught for food, as the halibut or the plaice.
**flour** (flour), *n.* [var. of *flower;* after Fr. *fleur de farine*, lit., flower (i.e., best) of meal], 1. a fine, powdery substance produced by grinding and sifting grain. 2. any finely powdered substance. *v.t.* 1. to put flour in or on. 2. to make into flour. —**flour′less,** *adj.* —**flour′y,** *adj.*
**flour·ish** (flũr′ish), *v.i.* [< OFr. *florir;* ult. < L. < *flos*, a flower], 1. to grow vigorously; succeed; prosper. 2. to be at the peak of development, activity, etc. 3. to make showy, wavy motions, as of the arms. 4. to write in an ornamental style. 5. to perform a fanfare, as of trumpets. *v.t.* to brandish (a sword, arm, etc.). *n.* 1. anything done in a showy way. 2. a brandishing. 3. a decorative line or lines in writing. 4. an ornate musical passage; fanfare. —**flour′ish·er,** *n.* —**flour′ish·ing,** *adj.* —**flour′ish·ing·ly,** *adv.*
**flout** (flout), *v.t.* [? < ME. *flouten*, to play the flute], to mock; show scorn or contempt for. *v.i.* to jeer; scoff. *n.* a scornful or contemptuous act or remark. —**flout′er,** *n.* —**flout′ing·ly,** *adv.*
**flow** (flō), *v.i.* [AS. *flowan*], 1. to move as a liquid does. 2. to move like a stream: as, *flowing* crowds. 3. to move gently and smoothly; glide. 4. to pour out. 5. to be derived; proceed. 6. to fall in waves; hang loose: as, *flowing* hair. 7. to come in; rise, as the tide. 8. to be overflowing or plentiful. *v.t.* to overflow; flood. *n.* 1. the act or manner of flowing. 2. the rate of flow. 3. anything that flows. 4. the rising of the tide.
**flow·er** (flou′ẽr, flour), *n.* [< OFr. < L. *flos*, a flower], 1. the part of a plant with the reproductive organs; blossom; bloom. 2. a plant cultivated for its blossoms. 3. the best or finest part or example. 4. the best period of a person or thing. 5. something decorative; esp., a figure of speech. 6. *pl.* in *chemistry*, a substance in powder form. *v.i.* 1. to produce blossoms; bloom. 2. to reach the best or most vigorous stage. *v.t.* to decorate as with flowers. —**in flower,** in a state of flowering. —**flow′er·less,** *adj.*

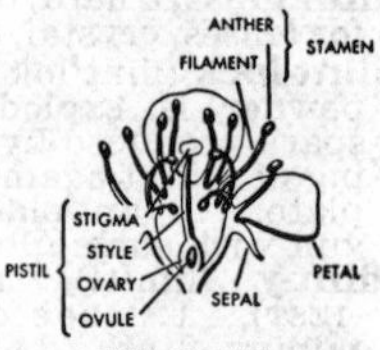


DIAGRAM OF FLOWER

**flow·ered** (flou′ẽrd), *adj.* 1. bearing or containing flowers. 2. decorated with flowers.
**flow·er·et** (flou′ẽr-it, flou′rit), *n.* 1. a small flower. 2. a floret.
**flow·er·ing** (flou′ẽr-iŋ, flou′riŋ), *adj.* 1. having flowers; in bloom. 2. having conspicuous flowers.
**flow·er·pot** (flou′ẽr-pot′, flour′pot′), *n.* a container to hold earth for a plant to grow in.
**flow·er·y** (flou′ẽr-i, flou′ri), *adj.* [-IER, -IEST], 1. covered or decorated with flowers. 2. full of figurative and ornate expressions and fine words. —**flow′er·i·ly,** *adv.* —**flow′er·i·ness,** *n.*
**flown** (flōn), pp. of **fly.**
**flu** (flōō), *n.* [Colloq.], influenza.
**fluc·tu·ate** (fluk′chōō-āt′), *v.i.* [-ATED, -ATING], [< L. pp. of *fluctuare* < *fluctus*, a wave], 1. to move back and forth or up and down; rise and fall, as waves. 2. to be continually changing or varying in an irregular way. *v.t.* to cause to fluctuate. —**fluc′tu·ant,** *adj.* —**fluc′tu·a′tion,** *n.*
**flue** (flōō), *n.* [? < dial. *flew*, flaring, or OFr. *flue*, a flowing], 1. a tube or shaft for the passage of smoke, hot air, etc., as in a chimney. 2. a flue pipe in an organ. 3. the passage for air in such a flue pipe.
**flu·ent** (flōō′ənt), *adj.* [< L. ppr. of *fluere*, to flow], 1. flowing smoothly and easily. 2. able to write or speak easily, smoothly, and expressively. —**flu′en·cy, flu′ent·ness,** *n.* —**flu′ent·ly,** *adv.*
**flue pipe,** an organ pipe in which the tone is produced by a current of air striking the lip of the mouth, or opening, in the pipe.
**fluff** (fluf), *n.* [? a merging of rare *flue*, a soft mass & *puff*], 1. soft, light down. 2. a loose soft mass

as of fur. 3. in the *theater, radio,* etc., an error in reading lines. ***v.t.*** 1. to shake or pat until loose and fluffy. 2. to make an error in reading (a word, one's lines, etc.), as an actor. ***v.i.*** to become fluffy. **—fluff′er,** ***n.***

**fluf·fy** (fluf′i), ***adj.*** [-FIER, -FIEST], 1. like fluff; soft and light; feathery. 2. covered with fluff. **—fluff′i·ly,** ***adv.*** **—fluff′i·ness,** ***n.***

**flu·id** (flo͞o′id), ***adj.*** [< Fr. < L. *fluidus* < *fluere,* to flow], 1. that can flow as a liquid or gas does. 2. of fluids. 3. that can change rapidly or easily; not settled. ***n.*** any substance that can flow; liquid or gas. **—flu·id′ic,** ***adj.*** **—flu·id′i·ty, flu′id·ness,** ***n.*** **—flu′id·ly,** ***adv.***

**fluid dram** (or **drachm**), a liquid measure equal to 1/8 fluid ounce.

**fluid ounce,** a liquid measure equal to 1/16 pint, or 29.6 cc: abbrev. **fl. oz.:** also **flu′id·ounce′,** ***n.***

**fluke** (flo͝ok), ***n.*** [AS. *floc*], 1. a flatfish; esp., a flounder. 2. any of a number of flat, parasitic worms, living especially in sheep's livers.

**fluke** (flo͝ok), ***n.*** [prob. < prec. *fluke*], 1. either of the pointed blades on an anchor, which catch in the ground. 2. a barb of an arrow, harpoon, etc. 3. either of the lobes of a whale's tail.

**fluke** (flo͝ok), ***n.*** [? < slang *fluke,* a dupe < *fluke,* flatfish (which is easily caught)], [Slang], 1. an accidentally good stroke in billiards or pool. 2. a stroke of luck. ***v.i.*** [FLUKED, FLUKING], [Slang], to make a fluke. ***v.t.*** [Slang], to get by a fluke.

**fluk·y, fluk·ey** (flo͝ok′i), ***adj.*** [-IER, -IEST], [see prec.], [Slang], resulting from chance.

**flume** (flo͞om), ***n.*** [< OFr. < L. *flumen,* river < *fluere,* to flow], 1. an inclined chute or trough for carrying water to furnish power, transport logs, etc. 2. a narrow gorge with a stream running through it. ***v.t.*** [FLUMED, FLUMING], to send (logs, etc.) down a flume.

**flum·mer·y** (flum′ẽr-i), ***n.*** [*pl.* -IES], [W. *llymru*], 1. any soft food; esp., thick, boiled oatmeal or flour. 2. meaningless flattery or silly talk.

**flung** (fluŋ), pt. and pp. of **fling.**

**flunk** (fluŋk), ***v.t.*** [? < *funk* (orig., Oxford Univ. slang)], [Colloq.], 1. to fail in (schoolwork). 2. to give a mark of *failure* to. 3. to cause to fail. ***v.i.*** [Colloq.], 1. to fail, as in schoolwork. 2. to give up; retreat. ***n.*** [Colloq.], 1. a failure. 2. a mark of *failure.* **—flunk out,** [Colloq.], to send or be sent away from school because of failure.

**flunk·y** (fluŋ′ki), ***n.*** [*pl.* -IES], [orig. Scot.; ? < Fr. *flanquer,* to flank], 1. a liveried manservant, as a footman: term of contempt. 2. a flattering, servile person; toady. Also **flunk′ey** [*pl.* -EYS]. **—flunk′y·ism, flunk′ey·ism,** ***n.***

**flu·o-,** a combining form meaning: 1. *fluorine.* 2. *fluorescent.*

**flu·o·resce** (flo͞o′ə-res′), ***v.i.*** [-RESCED, -RESCING], to produce, show, or undergo fluorescence.

**flu·o·res·cence** (flo͞o′ə-res′'ns), ***n.*** [< *fluor* spar (fluorite)], 1. the property of some substances, as fluorite, of producing light when acted upon by radiant energy, such as ultraviolet rays or X rays. 2. the production of such light. 3. light so produced. **—flu′o·res′cent,** ***adj.***

**fluorescent lamp,** a glass tube coated on the inside with a fluorescent substance that gives off light (**fluorescent light**) when acted upon by a stream of electrons from the cathode.

**flu·o·ri·date** (flo͞o′ə-ri-dāt′), ***v.t.*** [-DATED, -DATING], to add fluorides to (a water supply) in order, as is claimed, to reduce the incidence of tooth decay. **—flu′o·ri·da′tion,** ***n.***

**flu·o·ride** (flo͞o′ə-rīd′, -rid), ***n.*** a compound of fluorine and one or more elements or radicals: also **flu′o·rid** (-rid).

**flu·o·rine** (flo͞o′ə-rēn′, -rin), ***n.*** [< *fluorite* (in which it occurs)], a very active chemical element of the halogen family, a corrosive, greenish-yellow gas: symbol, F, Fl; at. wt., 19.00; at. no., 9: also **flu′o·rin** (-rin). **—flu·or′ic** (-ôr′ik, -or′-), ***adj.***

**flu·o·rite** (flo͞o′ə-rīt′), ***n.*** [L. *fluor,* flux; + *-ite*], calcium fluoride, $CaF_2$, a transparent, crystalline mineral of various colors: it is used as a flux, etc.: also **fluor, fluor spar.**

**flu·o·ro-,** a combining form meaning: 1. *fluorine.* 2. *fluorescence.* Also **fluor-.**

**flu·o·ro·scope** (floor′ə-skōp′, flo͞o′ə-rə-), ***n.*** [*fluoro-* + *-scope*], a machine for examining internal structures by viewing the shadows cast on a fluorescent screen by objects through which X rays are directed. **—flu′or·os′co·py** (-os′kə-pi), ***n.***

**flur·ry** (flũr′i), ***n.*** [*pl.* -RIES], [prob. echoic], 1. a sudden gust of wind. 2. a gust of rain or snow. 3. a sudden confusion, commotion, or agitation. ***v.t.*** [-RIED, -RYING], to confuse; agitate.

**flush** (flush), ***v.i.*** [blend of *flash, v.* & ME. *flusschen,* to fly up suddenly], 1. to flow suddenly and rapidly: as, the blood *flushed* in his face. 2. to become red in the face; blush. 3. to glow. 4. to become cleaned or emptied with a sudden flow of water, etc. 5. to start up from cover: said of birds. ***v.t.*** 1. to clean or empty out with a sudden flow of water, etc. 2. to make blush or glow. 3. to excite; exhilarate. 4. to drive (birds) from cover. 5. to make level or even. ***n.*** 1. a rapid flow, as of water. 2. a sudden, vigorous growth: as, the first *flush* of youth. 3. sudden excitement or exhilaration. 4. a blush; glow. 5. a sudden feeling of heat, as in a fever. ***adj.*** 1. well supplied, as with money. 2. abundant; plentiful. 3. lavish; profuse. 4. full of vigor. 5. having a ruddy color; glowing. 6. making an even line or surface: as, a door *flush* with the wall. 7. direct; full: as, a blow *flush* in the face. ***adv.*** 1. so as to be level. 2. directly; squarely. **—flush′er,** ***n.***

**flush** (flush), ***n.*** [Fr. *flux;* see FLUX], in *card games,* a hand of cards all in the same suit.

**flus·ter** (flus′tẽr), ***v.t. & v.i.*** [prob. < ON.], to make or be confused and excited. ***n.*** the state of being flustered. **—flus·tra′tion, flus′ter·a′tion,** ***n.***

**flute** (flo͞ot), ***n.*** [< OFr. < Pr. *flaüt;* prob. < *flauja* (ult. < L. *flare,* to blow) + *laüt,* lute], 1. a high-pitched wind instrument consisting of a long, slender tube with finger holes and keys, played by blowing across a hole near the upper end. 2. a groove in cloth, in the shaft of a column, etc. ***v.t. & v.i.*** [FLUTED, FLUTING], 1. to sing, speak, etc. in a flutelike tone. 2. to play on the flute. 3. to make long, rounded grooves in (a column, etc.). **—flut′ed,** ***adj.*** **—flute′like′,** ***adj.***

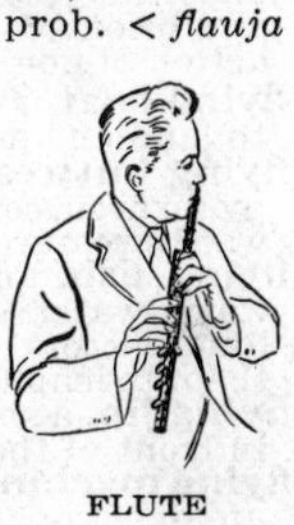

FLUTE

**flut·ing** (flo͞ot′iŋ), ***n.*** 1. decoration with flutes, as in a column. 2. the act of playing the flute.

**flut·ist** (flo͞ot′ist), ***n.*** a person who plays the flute: also **flautist.**

**flut·ter** (flut′ẽr), ***v.i.*** [AS. *flotorian,* freq. < base of *fleotan,* to float], 1. to flap the wings rapidly, without flying. 2. to wave rapidly and irregularly: as, the flag *flutters* in the wind. 3. to move with quick vibrations, flaps, etc. 4. to tremble; quiver. 5. to move restlessly. ***v.t.*** 1. to cause to move in quick, irregular motions. 2. to excite; confuse. ***n.*** 1. a fluttering movement. 2. a state of excitement or confusion. **—flut′ter·er,** ***n.*** **—flut′ter·ing·ly,** ***adv.*** **—flut′ter·y,** ***adj.***

**flut·y** (flo͞ot′i), ***adj.*** [-IER, -IEST], flutelike in tone; soft, clear, and high-pitched. **—flut′i·ly,** ***adv.*** **—flut′i·ness,** ***n.***

**flu·vi·al** (flo͞o′vi-əl), ***adj.*** [OFr. < L. < *fluere,* to flow], of, found in, or produced by a river.

**flux** (fluks), ***n.*** [OFr. < L. *fluxus* < *fluere,* to flow], 1. a flowing or flow. 2. a coming in of the tide. 3. a continual change. 4. any abnormal discharge of fluid matter from the body. 5. a substance used to help metals to fuse together, as in soldering. 6. in *physics,* the rate of flow of energy, fluids, etc. over a surface. ***v.t.*** 1. to fuse (metals) by melting. 2. in *medicine,* to purge.

**flux·ion** (fluk′shən), ***n.*** 1. a flowing. 2. continuous change. 3. a discharge. **—flux′ion·al, flux′ion·ar′y,** ***adj.*** **—flux′ion·al·ly,** ***adv.***

**fly** (flī), ***v.i.*** [FLEW, FLOWN, FLYING], [AS. *fleogan*], 1. to move through the air by using wings, as a bird. 2. to travel through the air in an aircraft. 3. to operate an aircraft. 4. to wave or float in the air, as a flag or kite. 5. to move swiftly. 6. to appear to pass swiftly: as, time *flies.* 7. to be used up swiftly: said of money, etc. 8. to flee. 9. [FLIED, FLYING], in *baseball,* to hit a fly. ***v.t.*** 1. to cause to float in the air: as, *fly* a kite. 2. to operate (an aircraft). 3. to go over in an aircraft: as, he *flew* the Pacific. 4. to carry in an aircraft. 5. to flee from; avoid. ***n.*** [*pl.* FLIES], 1. a flap of cloth that conceals buttons, etc. in a garment. 2. a flap serving as the door of a tent. 3. the width of an extended flag. 4. a flyleaf. 5. [Brit.], a hackney carriage. 6. in *baseball,* a ball batted high in the air within the foul lines. 7. *pl.* in the *theater,* the space behind and above the proscenium arch. —**fly in the face of,** to be openly opposed to. —**fly into,** to have a violent outburst of. —**fly off,** to hurry off. —**fly out,** in *baseball*, to be put out by hitting a fly that is caught before it touches the ground. —**let fly (at),** 1. to shoot or throw (at). 2. to direct a verbal attack (at). —**on the fly,** 1. while in flight. 2. [Slang], while in a hurry.

**fly** (flī), *n.* [*pl.* FLIES], [AS. *fleoge*], 1. *a*) a housefly. *b*) any of a large group of insects with two transparent wings, as the housefly, gnat, mosquito, and May fly. 2. a flylike device of feathers, colored silk, etc. used as fishing bait.

**fly** (flī), *adj.* [FLIER, FLIEST], [orig., thieves' slang], [Slang], 1. agile. 2. alert and knowing.

**fly·blown** (flī'blōn'), *adj.* 1. full of flies' eggs or larvae; hence, 2. spoiled; tainted.

**fly-by-night** (flī'bī-nīt'), *adj.* financially unsound. *n.* a debtor who evades his debts.

**fly·catch·er** (flī'kach'ēr), *n.* 1. any of a group of small birds, including the kingbird, pewee, and phoebe, that catch insects in flight. 2. any plant that catches and ingests insects.

**fly·er** (flī'ēr), *n.* a flier.

**fly-fish** (flī'fish'), *v.i.* to fish with flies, especially artificial flies, as bait. —**fly'-fish'er,** *n.* —**fly'-fish'ing,** *n.*

**fly·ing** (flī'iŋ), *adj.* 1. that flies or can fly. 2. moving swiftly; fast. 3. streaming in the air. 4. hasty and brief. 5. of or for aircraft or aviators. *n.* the action of one that flies.

**flying boat,** an airplane with a hull that permits it to land on and take off from water.

**flying buttress,** a buttress connected with a wall by an arch, serving to resist outward pressure.

FLYING BUTTRESS

**flying fish,** any of a number of warm-water sea fishes with winglike pectoral fins that enable them to leap through the air.

**flying jib,** a small, triangular sail in front of the jib.

**flying machine,** an aircraft; esp., an airplane.

**flying saucer,** any of various unidentified objects frequently reported since 1947 to have been seen flying at great heights and high speeds, and variously regarded as light phenomena, hallucinations, secret military missiles, etc.

**fly·leaf** (flī'lēf'), *n.* [*pl.* -LEAVES (-lēvz')], a blank leaf at the beginning or end of a book, etc.

**fly·pa·per** (flī'pā'pēr), *n.* a sticky or poisonous paper set out to kill flies: also **fly paper.**

**fly·speck** (flī'spek'), *n.* 1. a speck of excrement left by a fly; hence, 2. any speck or tiny spot. *v.t.* to make flyspecks on.

**fly·trap** (flī'trap'), *n.* a plant that catches insects.

**fly·weight** (flī'wāt'), *n.* a boxer who weighs 112 pounds or less. *adj.* of flyweights.

**fly·wheel** (flī'hwēl'), *n.* a heavy wheel for regulating the speed and uniformity of motion of the machine to which it is attached.

**FM,** frequency modulation.

**Fm,** in *chemistry*, fermium.

**F number,** in *photography*, the ratio of a lens diameter to its focal distance: the lower the F number, the shorter the exposure required.

**foal** (fōl), *n.* [AS. *fola*], a young horse, mule, etc. colt or filly. *v.t.* & *v.i.* to give birth to (a foal).

**foam** (fōm), *n.* [AS. *fam*], 1. the whitish mass of bubbles formed on liquids by violent shaking, fermentation, etc. 2. something like foam, as frothy saliva. *v.i.* to form or gather foam; froth. *v.t.* to cause to foam. —**foam at the mouth,** to rage. —**foam'ing·ly,** *adv.* —**foam'less,** *adj.* —**foam'like',** *adj.*

**foam rubber,** rubber prepared in a firm spongy mass, used in upholstered seats, mattresses, etc.

**foam·y** (fōm'i), *adj.* [-IER, -IEST], 1. foaming or covered with foam. 2. consisting of foam. 3. like foam. —**foam'i·ly,** *adv.* —**foam'i·ness,** *n.*

**fob** (fob), *n.* [prob. < dial. G. *fuppe*, a pocket], 1. a small pocket in the front of a man's trousers; watch pocket. 2. a short ribbon or chain attached to a watch and hanging out of such a pocket. 3. any ornament worn at the end of such a ribbon or chain.

**fob** (fob), *v.t.* [FOBBED, FOBBING], [< ME. *fobbe*, cheater], to get rid of (something worthless) by deceit or trickery (with *off*).

**F.O.B., f.o.b.,** free on board.

**fo·cal** (fō'k'l), *adj.* of or placed at a focus. —**fo'cal·ly,** *adv.*

**focal distance,** the distance from the optical center of a lens to the point where the light rays converge: also **focal length.**

**fo·cal·ize** (fō'k'l-īz'), *v.t.* & *v.i.* [-IZED, -IZING], to adjust or come to a focus. —**fo'cal·i·za'tion,** *n.*

**fo'c's'le** (fōk's'l), *n.* forecastle: phonetic sp.

**fo·cus** (fō'kəs), *n.* [*pl.* -CUSES, -CI (-sī)], [L., hearth], 1. the point where rays of light, heat, etc. or waves of sound come together, or from which they spread or seem to spread; specif., the point where rays of light reflected by a mirror or refracted by a lens meet. 2. focal distance. 3. an adjustment of this distance to make a clear image: as, move the lens into *focus*. 4. any center of activity, attention, etc. 5. a part of the body where an infection is most active. 6. in *mathematics* *a*) either of two fixed points that determine an ellipse: cf. **ellipse.** *b*) any analagous point for a hyperbola or parabola. *v.t.* [-CUSED or -CUSSED, -CUSING or -CUSSING], 1. to bring into focus. 2. to adjust the focal distance of (the eye, a lens, etc.) so as to produce a clear image. 3. to concentrate: as, to *focus* one's attention. *v.i.* to meet at a focus. —**in focus,** clear; distinct. —**out of focus,** indistinct; blurred. —**fo'cus·er,** *n.*

**fod·der** (fod'ēr), *n.* [AS. *fodor* < base of *foda*, food], coarse food for cattle, horses, etc., as hay and straw. *v.t.* to feed with fodder.

**foe** (fō), *n.* [AS. *fah*, hostile, (*ge*)*fah*, enemy], an enemy; opponent.

**foe·man** (fō'mən), *n.* [*pl.* -MEN], [Archaic], a foe.

**foe·tus** (fē'təs), *n.* a fetus. —**foe'tal,** *adj.*

**fog** (fôg, fog), *n.* [back-formation < *foggy*], 1. a large mass of water vapor condensed to fine particles, just above the earth's surface. 2. a similar mass of smoke, dust, etc. obscuring the atmosphere. 3. a state of mental confusion. 4. a blur on a photograph or film. *v.i.* [FOGGED, FOGGING], 1. to become covered by fog. 2. to be or become blurred or dimmed. *v.t.* 1. to surround or cover with fog. 2. to blur; dim. 3. to confuse; bewilder. 4. in *photography*, to make blurred.

**fog bank,** a dense mass of fog.

**fog·gy** (fôg'i, fog'i), *adj.* [-GIER, -GIEST], [orig., covered with *fog* (long, rank grass)], 1. full of fog; misty. 2. dim; blurred. 3. confused; perplexed. —**fog'gi·ly,** *adv.* —**fog'gi·ness,** *n.*

**fog·horn** (fôg'hôrn', fog'-), *n.* a horn blown to give warning to ships in a fog.

**fo·gy** (fō'gi), *n.* [*pl.* -GIES], [? < *foggy*, *adj.* in obs. sense "flabby, fat"], a person who is old-fashioned in ideas and actions: also **fo'gey** [*pl.* -GEYS]. —**fo'gy·ish, fo'gey·ish,** *adj.*

**foi·ble** (foi'b'l), *n.* [obs. form of Fr. *faible*, feeble], a small weakness in character; frailty.

**foil** (foil), *v.t.* [< OFr. *f(o)uler*, to trample], to baffle; thwart; frustrate. *n.* 1. a long, thin fencing sword with a button on the point to prevent injury. 2. the art of fencing with foils.

**foil** (foil), *n.* [< OFr. < L. < *folium*, a leaf], 1. a leaflike, rounded design in windows, etc., as in Gothic architecture. 2. a very thin sheet of metal: as, gold *foil*. 3. a thin leaf of polished metal placed under a gem to give it brilliance. 4. a person or thing that sets off or enhances another by contrast. *v.t.* 1. to cover or back with foil. 2. [Rare], to serve as a contrast to. 3. to decorate (windows, etc.) with foils.

**foist** (foist), *v.t.* [prob. < dial. D. *vuisten*, to hide in the hand < *vuist*, a fist], 1. to put in slyly or stealthily. 2. to impose by fraud; palm off.

**fol.,** 1. folio. 2. following.

**fold** (fōld), *v.t.* [AS. *faldan*], 1. to double (material) up on itself. 2. to draw together and intertwine: as, *fold* your arms. 3. to draw close to the body: as, wings *folded*. 4. to clasp in the arms; embrace. 5. to wrap up; envelop. *v.i.* 1. to be or become folded 2. [Slang], to fail, as a play, business, etc. *n.* 1. a folding. 2. a folded part or layer. 3. a mark made by folding. 4. a hollow or crease produced by folded parts. 5. in *geology*, a rock layer folded by pressure. —**fold up,** 1. to make or become more compact by folding. 2. [Slang], to fail.

**fold** (fōld), *n.* [AS. *falod*], 1. a pen in which to keep sheep. 2. a flock of sheep. 3. *a*) the members of a church. *b*) a church. *v.t.* to keep or confine (sheep) in a pen.

**-fold** (fōld), [AS. *-feald*], a suffix meaning: 1. *having* (a specified number of) *parts*. 2. (a specified number of) *times as many* or *as much*, as in *tenfold*.

**fold·er** (fōl'dēr), *n.* 1. a person or thing that folds. 2. a sheet of heavy paper folded as a holder for papers. 3. a booklet of folded, unstitched sheets.

**fol·de·rol** (fol'də-rol'), *n.* falderal.

**fo·li·a·ceous** (fō'li-ā'shəs), *adj.* [< L. < *folium*, a leaf], 1. of or like the leaf of a plant. 2. having leaves. 3. consisting of thin layers.

**fo·li·age** (fō′li-ij), *n.* [< OFr. < L. *folia,* leaves], 1. leaves, as of a plant or tree; leafage. 2. a decoration consisting of a representation of leaves, branches, flowers, etc. **—fo′li·aged,** *adj.*

**fo·li·ate** (fō′li-āt′; *for adj., usually* -it), *v.t.* [-ATED, -ATING], [< L. pp. of *foliare* < *folium,* a leaf], to divide into thin layers. *v.i.* 1. to separate into layers. 2. to send out leaves. *adj.* having or covered with leaves: also **fo′li·at′ed.**

**fo·li·a·tion** (fō′li-ā′shən), *n.* 1. a growing of or developing into a leaf or leaves. 2. the state of being in leaf. 3. the act of beating metal into layers. 4. the consecutive numbering of leaves of a book. 5. a leaflike decoration. 6. in *botany,* the way leaves are arranged in the bud.

**fo·lic acid** (fō′lik), [< L. *folium,* a leaf; + *-ic*], a nitrogenous acid found in green leaves, etc., believed to be one of the vitamin B complex.

**fo·li·o** (fō′li-ō′, fōl′yō), *n.* [*pl.* -OS], [L. abl. of *folium,* a leaf], 1. a large sheet of paper folded once, so that it forms two leaves, or four pages, of a book, etc. 2. a book (the largest regular size), usually more than 11 inches in height, made of sheets so folded. 3. a leaf of a book, etc. numbered on only one side. 4. the number of a page in a book, etc. *adj.* having sheets folded once; of the size of a folio. *v.t.* [-OED, -OING], to number the pages of (a book, etc.). **—in folio,** in the form of a folio.

**folk** (fōk), *n.* [*pl.* FOLK, FOLKS], [AS. *folc*], 1. a people; nation; ethnic group. 2. *pl.* people; persons: as, *folks* don't agree. *adj.* of the common people. **—(one's) folks,** [Colloq.], (one's) family.

**folk dance,** 1. a traditional dance of the common people of a country. 2. music for this.

**folk etymology,** the change that occurs in the form of a word over a period of prolonged usage so as to give it an apparent connection with some other word, as *cole slaw* becomes *cold slaw*: also **popular etymology. —folk′-et′y·mol′o·gize′** [-GIZED, GIZING], *v.t. & v.i.*

**folk·lore** (fōk′lôr′, -lōr′), *n.* the traditional beliefs, legends, sayings, etc. of a people. **—folk′lor′ist,** *n.* **—folk′lor·is′tic,** *adj.*

**folk music,** music made and handed down among the common people.

**folk song,** 1. a song made and handed down among the common people. 2. a song composed in imitation of such a song.

**folk·sy** (fōk′si), *adj.* [Colloq.], 1. of or like the common people. 2. sociable.

**folk tale,** a story, often with legendary or mythical elements, made and handed down among the common people: also **folk story.**

**folk·way** (fōk′wā′), *n.* any way of thinking, feeling, behaving, etc. common to members of the same social group.

**fol·li·cle** (fol′i-k'l), *n.* [< L. *folliculus,* dim. of *follis,* bellows], 1. in *anatomy,* any small sac, cavity, or gland for excretion or secretion: as, a hair *follicle.* 2. in *botany,* a dry, one-celled seed capsule, opening along one side, as a milkweed pod. **—fol·lic·u·lar** (fə-lik′yoo-lẽr), *adj.*

**fol·low** (fol′ō), *v.t.* [AS. *folgian*], 1. to come or go after. 2. to accompany; attend. 3. to chase; pursue. 4. to go along: as, *follow* the road. 5. to come after in time, in a series, etc. 6. to take the place of in rank, position, etc. 7. to take up; engage in, as a trade. 8. to result from. 9. to take as a model; imitate. 10. to accept the authority of; obey. 11. to watch or listen to closely. 12. to understand the continuity or logic of: as, do you *follow* me? *v.i.* 1. to come, go, or happen after something else in place, sequence, or time. 2. to attend. 3. to result. *n.* the act of following. **—follow out,** to carry out fully. **—follow through,** to continue and complete a stroke or action. **—follow up,** 1. to follow closely and persistently. 2. to carry out fully. 3. to add to the effectiveness of by doing something more. **—fol′low·a·ble,** *adj.*

**fol·low·er** (fol′ō-ẽr), *n.* one that follows; specif., *a)* a person who follows another's beliefs or teachings; disciple. *b)* a servant or attendant.

**fol·low·ing** (fol′ō-iŋ), *adj.* that follows; next after. *n.* a group of followers or attendants. **—the following,** 1. the one or ones to be mentioned immediately. 2. what follows.

**fol·low-through** (fol′ō-thrōō′), *n.* 1. the act or manner of continuing the swing of a club, racket, etc. after striking the ball, as in tennis, golf, etc. 2. this final part of a swing.

**fol·low-up** (fol′ō-up′), *adj.* designating or of anything that follows as a repetition or addition. *n.* 1. a follow-up thing or event. 2. the use of follow-up letters, visits, etc. 3. a following up.

**fol·ly** (fol′i), *n.* [*pl.* -LIES], [< OFr. < *fol;* see FOOL], 1. a lack of sense or rational conduct; a being foolish. 2. any foolish action or belief. 3. any foolish but expensive undertaking.

**fo·ment** (fō-ment′), *v.t.* [< Fr. < L. *fomentare* < *fovere,* to keep warm], 1. to treat with warm water, medicated lotions, etc. 2. to stir up; arouse; incite: as, to *foment* rebellion. **—fo′men·ta′tion,** *n.* **—fo·ment′er,** *n.*

**fond** (fond), *adj.* [< ME. *fonned,* pp. of *fonnen,* to be foolish], 1. [Now Rare], foolishly naive or hopeful. 2. foolishly tender; too loving; doting. 3. affectionate; loving; tender: as, *fond* caresses. 4. greatly cherished. **—fond of,** having a liking for. **—fond′ly,** *adv.* **—fond′ness,** *n.*

**fon·dant** (fon′dənt), *n.* [Fr., ppr. of *fondre,* to melt], a soft, creamy candy made of sugar, used especially as a filling for other candies.

**fon·dle** (fon′d'l), *v.t.* [-DLED, -DLING], [freq. of obs. *fond, v.*], to caress; pet. **—fon′dler,** *n.*

**fon·due** (fon′dōō, fon-dōō′), *n.* [Fr., fem. pp. of *fondre,* to melt], a dish made of cheese, eggs, etc.

**font** (font), *n.* [AS. < L. *fons,* spring], 1. a bowl to hold the water used in baptismal services. 2. a basin for holy water. 3. [Poetic], a fountain or spring. 4. a source; origin.

**font** (font), *n.* [< Fr. *fonte* < *fondre;* see FOUND (to cast)], in *printing,* a complete assortment of type in one size and style: also *fount.*

**Fon·taine·bleau** (fōn′ten′blō′; Eng. fon′tin-blō′), *n.* a town near Paris: site of an old royal palace.

**Foo·chow** (fōō′chou′; Chin. -jō′), *n.* a seaport in SE China: pop., 390,000: also called *Minhow.*

**food** (fōōd), *n.* [AS. *foda*], 1. any substance taken into and assimilated by a plant or animal to keep it alive and enable it to grow; nourishment. 2. solid substances of this sort: opposed to *drink.* 3. a specified kind of food. 4. anything that nourishes or stimulates: as, *food* for thought.

**food·stuff** (fōōd′stuf′), *n.* any material made into or used as food.

**fool** (fōōl), *n.* [< OFr. *fol* < LL. < L. *follis,* windbag], 1. a silly person; simpleton. 2. a man formerly kept by a nobleman or king to entertain as a clown; jester. 3. a victim of a trick; dupe. *v.i.* 1. to act like a fool; be silly. 2. to joke; be playful. *v.t.* to trick; deceive; dupe. **—be no** (or **nobody's**) **fool,** to be shrewd and capable. **—fool around,** [Colloq.], to trifle. **—fool away,** [Colloq.], to squander. **—fool with,** [Colloq.], to trifle or meddle with. **—play the fool,** to clown. **—fool′ing,** *n.*

**fool·er·y** (fōōl′ẽr-i), *n.* [*pl.* -IES], foolish activity.

**fool·har·dy** (fōōl′här′di), *adj.* [-DIER, -DIEST], foolishly daring; rash. **—fool′har′di·ly,** *adv.* **—fool′har′di·ness,** *n.*

**fool·ish** (fōōl′ish), *adj.* 1. without good sense; silly; unwise. 2. absurd. 3. [Archaic], worthless. **—fool′ish·ly,** *adv.* **—fool′ish·ness,** *n.*

**fool·proof** (fōōl′prōōf′), *adj.* so harmless, simple, or indestructible as not to be mishandled, injured, misunderstood, etc. even by a fool.

**fools·cap** (fōōlz′kap′), *n.* 1. [from former watermark], a size of writing paper varying from 12 by 15 inches to 13½ by 17 inches. 2. a fool's cap.

**fool's cap,** a jester's cap with bells.

**fool's gold,** iron pyrites or copper pyrites, like gold in color.

**foot** (foot), *n.* [*pl.* FEET], [AS. *fot*], 1. the end part of the leg, on which a person or animal stands or moves. 2. the base or bottom: as, the *foot* of a page. 3. the last of a series. 4. the end, as of a bed, toward which the feet are directed. 5. the part of a stocking, etc. covering the foot. 6. a measure of length, equal to 12 inches (the approximate length of the human foot): symbol, ′ (e.g., 10′). 7. foot soldiers; infantry. 8. a group of syllables serving as a unit of meter in verse, as a dactyl or trochee. *v.i.* 1. to dance. 2. to walk. *v.t.* 1. to walk, dance, or run over or through. 2. to make the foot of (a stocking, etc.). 3. to add (a column of figures) and set down a total. 4. [Colloq.], to pay (costs, etc.). **—foot it,** [Colloq.], to dance, walk, or run. **—on foot,** 1. standing. 2. walking or running. 3. in process. **—put one's best foot forward,** [Colloq.], to do the best that one can. **—put one's foot down,** [Colloq.], to be firm. **—put one's foot in it** (or **in one's mouth**), [Colloq.], to make an embarrassing

blunder. —**under foot,** 1. on the floor, etc. 2. in the way. —**foot′less,** *adj.*
**-foot** (foot), a combining form meaning (a specified number of) *feet long, deep,* etc., as in *six-foot.*
**foot·age** (foot′ij), *n.* length expressed in feet.
**foot-and-mouth disease** (foot″n-mouth′), an acute, contagious disease of cattle, deer, etc., characterized by fever and blisters in the mouth and around the hoofs: it can be transmitted to man.
**foot·ball** (foot′bôl′), *n.* 1. any of several field games played with an inflated leather ball by two teams, the object being to get the ball across the opponents' goal: in *American football,* the players may kick, throw, or run with the ball, and may run ahead of it for interference, forward passes, etc.: cf. **soccer, Rugby.** 2. the elliptical or (for soccer) round ball used in playing these games.
**foot·board** (foot′bôrd′, -bōrd′), *n.* 1. a board or small platform for supporting the feet. 2. a vertical piece across the foot of a bed.
**foot·bridge** (foot′brij′), *n.* a narrow bridge for use by pedestrians only.
**foot-can·dle** (foot′kan′d'l), *n.* a unit for measuring illumination: it is equal to the amount of direct light thrown by one standard candle on a surface one foot away.
**foot·ed** (foot′id), *adj.* having (a specified number or kind of) feet: as, *four-footed.*
**-foot·er** (foot′ẽr), a combining form meaning *a person* or *thing* (a specified number of) *feet tall* or *high,* as in *six-footer.*
**foot·fall** (foot′fôl′), *n.* 1. a footstep. 2. the sound of a footstep or footsteps.
**foot·hill** (foot′hil′), *n.* a low hill at or near the foot of a mountain or mountain range.
**foot·hold** (foot′hōld′), *n.* 1. a place to put the feet, as in climbing. 2. a secure position.
**foot·ing** (foot′iŋ), *n.* 1. a moving on the feet; walking, dancing, etc. 2. a secure placing of the feet. 3. a secure place to put the feet; foothold. 4. a secure position or basis. 5. a basis for relationship: as, to be on a friendly *footing.* 6. *a*) the adding of a column of figures. *b*) the sum obtained.
**foot·lights** (foot′līts′), *n.pl.* 1. a row of lights along the front of a stage floor. 2. the theater; acting as a profession.
**foot-loose** (foot′lōōs′), *adj.* free to go wherever one likes or do as one likes.
**foot·man** (foot′mən), *n.* [*pl.* -MEN], a manservant who waits on table, opens the door, etc.
**foot·note** (foot′nōt′), *n.* a note of comment or reference at the bottom of a page. *v.t.* [-NOTED, -NOTING], to add such a note or notes to.
**foot·pad** (foot′pad′), *n.* [see PAD (path)], a highway robber or holdup man who travels on foot.
**foot·path** (foot′path′, -päth′), *n.* a narrow path for use by pedestrians only.
**foot-pound** (foot′pound′), *n.* a unit of energy, equal to the amount of energy required to raise a weight of one pound a distance of one foot.
**foot·print** (foot′print′), *n.* a mark left by a foot.
**foot·rest** (foot′rest′), *n.* a support to rest the feet.
**foot soldier,** a soldier who moves and fights largely on foot; infantryman.
**foot·sore** (foot′sôr′, -sōr′), *adj.* having sore or tender feet, as from much walking.
**foot·step** (foot′step′), *n.* 1. the distance covered in a step. 2. the sound of a step; footfall. 3. a footprint. 4. a step by which to go up or down. —**follow in (someone's) footsteps,** to repeat or imitate (someone's) actions.
**foot·stool** (foot′stōōl′), *n.* a low stool for supporting the feet of a seated person.
**foot·wear** (foot′wâr′), *n.* anything to wear on the feet; shoes, boots, slippers, etc.
**foot·work** (foot′wûrk′), *n.* the manner of using the feet, as in boxing, dancing, tennis, etc.
**foo·zle** (fōō′z'l), *v.t. & v.i.* [-ZLED, -ZLING], [? < G. *fuseln,* to bungle], to make or do (something) awkwardly; bungle (a stroke in golf, etc.). *n.* an awkward, unskillful act or stroke.
**fop** (fop), *n.* [ME. *foppe,* a fool; prob. < MD. or MLG.], a vain, affected man who pays too much attention to his clothes, appearance, etc.; dandy. —**fop′per·y** [*pl.* -IES], *n.* —**fop′pish,** *adj.* —**fop′pish·ly,** *adv.* —**fop′pish·ness,** *n.*
**for** (fôr; *unstressed* fẽr), *prep.* [< AS. weakened form of *fore,* before], 1. in place of: as, we used blankets *for* coats. 2. in the interest of: as, his agent acted *for* him. 3. in defense of; in favor of. 4. in honor of: as, the banquet was given *for* him. 5. with the aim or purpose of: as, a gun *for* protection. 6. with the purpose of going to: as, she left *for* Rome. 7. in order to be, become, get, have, keep, etc.: as, walk *for* exercise. 8. in search of: as, look *for* his dog. 9. meant to be received by a specified person or thing, or to be used in a specified way: as, flowers *for* a girl. 10. suitable to: as, a room *for* sleeping. 11. with a feeling toward: as, an ear *for* music. 12. as affecting (a person or thing) in a specified way: as, that is bad *for* you. 13. as being: as, we left him *for* dead. 14. considering the nature of: as, it is cool *for* July. 15. because of: as, he cried *for* pain. 16. in spite of: as, she is stupid *for* all her learning. 17. in proportion to: as, a good day *for* every ten bad ones. 18. to the amount of: as, a bill *for* $50. 19. at the price of: as, he sold it *for* $10. 20. throughout; through: as, the movie lasts *for* an hour. 21. at (a specified time): as, a date *for* two o'clock. *conj.* because; seeing that: as, he will win, *for* he is prepared. —**for** (one) **to,** that (one) will, should, must, etc.: as, an order *for* the grocer *to* fill. —**O! for,** I wish that I had.
**for-,** [AS. *for-,* replacing *fer-*], a prefix used chiefly with verbs, meaning *away, apart, off,* as in *forbid, forget, forgo*: the original senses are now largely obscured.
**for·age** (fôr′ij, for′-), *n.* [< OFr. < Frank. *fodr,* food], 1. food for domestic animals; fodder. 2. a search for food or provisions. *v.i.* [-AGED, -AGING], 1. to search for food or provisions. 2. to search for what one needs or wants (with *for* or *about*). *v.t.* 1. *a*) to get or take food or provisions from. *b*) to plunder. 2. to provide with forage; feed. 3. to get by foraging. —**for′ag·er,** *n.*
**fo·ra·men** (fō-rā′mən), *n.* [*pl.* -MENS, -MINA (fō-ram′i-nə)], [L. < *forare,* to bore], a small opening; esp., a small, natural opening in a bone.
**for·a·min·i·fer** (fôr′ə-min′ə-fẽr), *n.* [*pl.* -FERA (fə-ram′ə-nif′ẽr-ə)], [< L. (see FORAMEN); + *-fer*], any of several small, one-celled sea animals with hard shells full of tiny holes through which slender filaments project. —**fo·ram′i·nif′er·al,** *adj.*
**for·as·much** (fôr′əz-much′), *conj.* inasmuch (*as*).
**for·ay** (fôr′ā, for′ā), *v.t. & v.i.* [< OFr. < *forrer,* to forage], to raid for spoils; plunder. *n.* a raid, as for spoils. —**for′ay·er,** *n.*
**for·bade, for·bad** (fẽr-bad′, fôr-), pt. of **forbid.**
**for·bear** (fôr-bâr′), *v.t.* [-BORE or *archaic* -BARE, -BORNE, -BEARING], [< AS.; see FOR- & BEAR (to carry)], to refrain from; avoid (doing, saying, etc.). *v.i.* 1. to refrain or abstain. 2. to control oneself. —**for·bear′er,** *n.* —**for·bear′ing·ly,** *adv.*
**for·bear** (fôr′bâr′), *n.* a forebear; ancestor.
**for·bear·ance** (fôr-bâr′əns), *n.* 1. the act of forbearing. 2. self-control; patient restraint.
**for·bid** (fẽr-bid′, fôr-), *v.t.* [-BADE or -BAD, -BIDDEN or *archaic* -BID, -BIDDING], [< AS.; see FOR- & BID, *v.*], 1. to rule against; prohibit. 2. to command to stay away from. 3. to make impossible; prevent. —**for·bid′dance,** *n.* —**for·bid′der,** *n.*
**for·bid·ding** (fẽr-bid′iŋ, fôr-), *adj.* looking dangerous or disagreeable; frightening; repellent. —**for·bid′ding·ly,** *adv.* —**for·bid′ding·ness,** *n.*
**for·bore** (fôr-bôr′, -bōr′), pt. of **forbear.**
**for·borne** (fôr-bôrn′, -bōrn′), pp. of **forbear.**
**force** (fôrs, fōrs), *n.* [OFr. < LL. < L. *fortis,* strong], 1. strength; energy; power. 2. impetus: as, the *force* of a blow. 3. physical power or coercion exerted against a person or thing. 4. the power to control, persuade, etc.; effectiveness. 5. military, naval, or air power. 6. any group of soldiers, sailors, etc. 7. any group of people organized for some activity: as, a sales *force.* 8. in *law,* binding power; validity. 9. in *physics,* the cause of motion, or of change or stoppage of motion, of a body. *v.t.* [FORCED, FORCING], 1. to make do something by force; compel. 2. to rape. 3. *a*) to break open, into, or through by force. *b*) to overpower or capture in this way. 4. to take by force; wrest; extort. 5. to drive as by force; impel. 6. to impose as by force (with *on* or *upon*). 7. to effect or produce as by force: as, she *forced* a smile. 8. to strain: as, she *forced* her voice. 9. to cause (plants, fruit, etc.) to develop faster by artificial means. 10. in *baseball,* to cause (a base runner) to be put out at an advanced base by occupying the base behind him. 11. in *card games, a*) to play so as to cause (an opponent) to play a particular card. *b*) to cause (a particular card) to be played. —**in force,** 1. in full strength. 2. in effect; valid. —**force′a·ble,** *adj.* —**force′less,** *adj.* —**forc′er,** *n.*
**forced** (fôrst, fōrst), *adj.* 1. done or brought about by force; compulsory: as, *forced* labor. 2. produced by unusual effort; not natural; strained: as, a *forced* smile. —**forc·ed·ly** (fôr′sid-li), *adv.*
**force·ful** (fôrs′fəl, fōrs′-), *adj.* full of force; powerful; strong; vigorous; effective. —**force′ful·ly,** *adv.* —**force′ful·ness,** *n.*
**force·meat** (fôrs′mēt′, fōrs′-), *n.* [< *farce meat* < Fr.

*farcir*, to stuff], meat chopped up and seasoned, usually for stuffing.

**for·ceps** (fôr′səps, -seps), ***n.*** [*pl.* -CEPS, rarely -CEPSES], [L., orig., smith's tongs < *formus*, hot + *capere*, to take], small tongs or pincers for grasping, compressing, and pulling, used especially by surgeons and dentists.

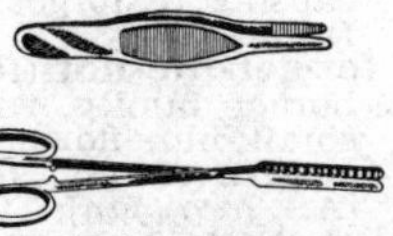

FORCEPS

**force pump,** a pump with a valveless plunger for forcing a liquid through a pipe under pressure.

**for·ci·ble** (fôr′sə-b'l, fōr′-), ***adj.*** 1. done or effected by force. 2. having force; forceful. **—for′ci·ble·ness,** ***n.*** **—for′ci·bly,** ***adv.***

**ford** (fôrd, fōrd), ***n.*** [AS.], a shallow place in a stream, river, etc. that can be crossed by walking, on horseback, etc. ***v.t.*** to cross at a ford. **—ford′a·ble,** ***adj.*** **—ford′less,** ***adj.***

**Ford, Henry** (fôrd, fōrd), 1863–1947; U.S. automobile manufacturer.

**for·done** (fôr-dun′), ***adj.*** [AS. *fordon*], [Archaic], completely exhausted: also sp. **foredone.**

**fore** (fôr, fōr), ***adv.*** [AS.], at, in, or toward the front part, or bow, of a ship: opposed to *aft.* ***adj.*** situated at or toward the front. ***n.*** the front thing or part. ***interj.*** in *golf*, a shout warning those ahead that one is about to drive the ball. **—to the fore,** 1. to the front; into view. 2. at hand.

**'fore** (fôr), ***prep.*** [Poetic], before.

**fore-** (fôr, fōr), [< AS. *fore*], a prefix meaning: 1. *before in time, place, order,* or *rank,* as in *forecast.* 2. *the front part of,* as in *forearm.*

**fore-and-aft** (fôr′'n-aft′, fōr′'n-äft′), ***adj.*** in *nautical usage*, from the bow to the stern; set lengthwise, as a rig.

**fore and aft,** in *nautical usage*, 1. from the bow to the stern; lengthwise. 2. at, in, or toward both the bow and the stern.

**fore·arm** (fôr′ärm′, fōr′-), ***n.*** the part of the arm between the elbow and the wrist.

**fore·arm** (fôr-ärm′, fōr-), ***v.t.*** to arm in advance; prepare beforehand for any difficulty.

**fore·bear** (fôr′bâr′, fōr′-), ***n.*** [< *fore* + *be* + *-er*], an ancestor: also sp. **forbear.**

**fore·bode** (fôr-bōd′, fōr-), ***v.t.*** & ***v.i.*** [< AS.], 1. to foretell; predict; portend: usually of something bad or harmful. 2. to have a presentiment of (something bad or harmful). **—fore·bod′er,** ***n.*** **—fore·bod′ing,** ***n.***

**fore·brain** (fôr′brān′, fōr′-), ***n.*** the front part of the brain.

**fore·cast** (fôr-kast′, fōr′käst′), ***v.t.*** [-CAST or -CASTED, -CASTING], 1. to plan in advance; foresee. 2. to estimate in advance; prophesy. 3. to serve as a prediction of. ***n.*** (fôr′kast′, fōr′käst′), 1. [Rare], foresight. 2. a prediction or prophecy. **—fore′cast′er,** ***n.***

**fore·cas·tle** (fōk's'l, fôr′kas′'l, fōr′käs′'l), ***n.*** 1. the upper deck of a ship in front of the foremast. 2. the front part of a merchant ship, where the sailors' quarters are located. Also **fo'c's'le.**

**fore·close** (fôr-klōz′, fōr-), ***v.t.*** [-CLOSED, -CLOSING], [< OFr. pp. of *forclore*, to exclude < *fors*, outside + *clore*, to close], 1. to shut out; exclude; bar. 2. to take away the right to redeem (a mortgage, etc.). ***v.i.*** to foreclose a mortgage, etc. **—fore·clos′a·ble,** ***adj.***

**fore·clo·sure** (fôr-klō′zhẽr, fōr-), ***n.*** the foreclosing of a mortgage, etc.

**fore·done** (fôr-dun′, fōr-), ***adj.*** [Archaic], fordone.

**fore·doom** (fôr-do͞om′, fōr-), ***v.t.*** to doom in advance; condemn beforehand.

**fore·fa·ther** (fôr′fä′*th*ẽr, fōr′-), ***n.*** an ancestor.

**fore·fin·ger** (fôr′fiŋ′gẽr, fōr′-), ***n.*** the finger nearest the thumb; index finger; first finger.

**fore·foot** (fôr′foot′), ***n.*** [*pl.* -FEET], 1. either of the front feet of an animal with four or more feet. 2. the meeting point of the keel and the stem of a ship.

**fore·front** (fôr′frunt′, fōr′-), ***n.*** 1. the extreme front. 2. the position of most activity, importance, etc.

**fore·gath·er** (fôr-gath′ẽr, fōr-), ***v.i.*** to forgather.

**fore·go** (fôr-gō′, fōr-), ***v.t.*** & ***v.i.*** [-WENT, -GONE, -GOING], 1. [AS. *foregan*], to go before in place or time; precede. 2. to forgo. **—fore·go′er,** ***n.***

**fore·go·ing** (fôr′gō′iŋ, fōr′gō′-), ***adj.*** preceding; previously said, written, etc.

**fore·gone** (fôr-gôn′, fōr′gon), ***adj.*** 1. that has gone before; previous. 2. *a*) previously determined. *b*) inevitable: said of a conclusion.

**fore·ground** (fôr′ground′, fōr′-), ***n.*** 1. the part of a scene, picture, etc. nearest the viewer. 2. the most noticeable or conspicuous place.

**fore·hand** (fôr′hand′, fōr′-), ***adj.*** 1. foremost; front. 2. designating or of a stroke, as in tennis, made with the palm of the hand turned forward. ***n.*** 1. the position in front or above; advantage. 2. a forehand stroke, as in tennis.

**fore·hand·ed** (fôr′han′did, fōr′-), ***adj.*** 1. making provision for the future; thrifty; prudent. 2. done beforehand. **—fore′hand′ed·ness,** ***n.***

**fore·head** (fôr′id, for′əd, fôr′hed′), ***n.*** 1. the part of the face between the eyebrows and the hairline. 2. the front part of anything.

**for·eign** (fôr′in, for′ən), ***adj.*** [< OFr. *forain* < LL. < L. *foras*, out of doors], 1. situated outside one's own country, locality, etc. 2. of, from, or characteristic of another country: as, a *foreign* language. 3. as if coming from another person or thing; not characteristic: as, lying is *foreign* to his nature. 4. not organically connected, as substances found in parts of the body where they do not naturally occur. **—for′eign·ness,** ***n.***

**foreign affairs,** matters concerning a country in its relations with other countries.

**for·eign-born** (fôr′in-bôrn′, for′ən-), ***adj.*** born in some other country; not native.

**for·eign·er** (fôr′in-ẽr, for′ən-), ***n.*** a person born in another country; alien.

**foreign office,** in some countries, the department of government in charge of foreign affairs.

**fore·know** (fôr-nō′, fōr-), ***v.t.*** [-KNEW, -KNOWN, -KNOWING], to know beforehand. **—fore′knowl′edge** (-nol′ij), ***n.***

**fore·land** (fôr′lənd, fōr′-), ***n.*** a headland; cape.

**fore·leg** (fôr′leg′, fōr′-), ***n.*** either of the front legs of an animal with four or more legs.

**fore·lock** (fôr′lok′, fōr′-), ***n.*** a lock of hair growing just above the forehead.

**fore·man** (fôr′mən, fōr′-), ***n.*** [*pl.* -MEN], [orig., foremost man], 1. the chairman of a jury. 2. a man in charge of a department or group of workers, as in a factory. **—fore′man·ship′,** ***n.*** **—fore′wom′an** [*pl.* -WOMEN], ***n.fem.***

**fore·mast** (fôr′mast′, fōr′mäst′), ***n.*** the mast nearest the bow of a ship.

**fore·most** (fôr′mōst′, fōr′məst), ***adj.*** [< AS. superl. of *forma*, superl. of *fore*, fore], 1. first in place or time. 2. first in rank or importance. ***adv.*** first.

**fore·named** (fôr′nāmd′, fōr′-), ***adj.*** named before; previously mentioned.

**fore·noon** (fôr′no͞on′, fōr-no͞on′), ***n.*** the time from sunrise to noon. ***adj.*** of or in the forenoon.

**fo·ren·sic** (fə-ren′sik), ***adj.*** [< L. *forensis*, public < *forum*, market place], of, characteristic of, or suitable for a law court or public debate. **—fo·ren′si·cal·ly,** ***adv.***

**fore·or·dain** (fôr′ôr-dān′, fōr′-), ***v.t.*** to ordain beforehand; predestine. **—fore′or·di·na′tion** (-d'n-ā′shən), **fore′or·dain′ment,** ***n.***

**fore·paw** (fôr′pô′, fōr′-), ***n.*** a front paw.

**fore·quar·ter** (fôr′kwôr′tẽr, fōr′-), ***n.*** the front half of a side of beef, pork, mutton, etc.

**fore·run** (fôr-run′, fōr-), ***v.t.*** [-RAN, -RUN, -RUNNING], [Rare], 1. to run before; precede. 2. to be a sign of (a thing to follow). 3. to forestall.

**fore·run·ner** (fôr-run′ẽr, fōr′run′-), ***n.*** 1. a messenger sent before or going before; herald. 2. a sign that tells or warns of something to follow. 3. *a*) a predecessor. *b*) an ancestor.

**fore·sail** (fôr′sāl′, fôr′s'l, fō′s'l), ***n.*** 1. the main, square sail on the foremast of a square-rigged ship. 2. the main triangular sail on the mast of a fore-and-aft-rigged ship.

**fore·see** (fôr-sē′, fōr-), ***v.t.*** [-SAW, -SEEN, -SEEING], to see or know beforehand. **—fore·see′a·ble,** ***adj.*** **—fore·se′er** (-sē′ẽr), ***n.***

**fore·shad·ow** (fôr-shad′ō, fōr-), ***v.t.*** to indicate or suggest beforehand; presage. **—fore·shad′ow·er,** ***n.***

**fore·sheet** (fôr′shēt′, fōr′-), ***n.*** 1. one of the ropes used to trim a foresail. 2. *pl.* the space in the bows of an open boat.

**fore·shore** (fôr′shôr′, fōr′shōr′), ***n.*** the part of a shore between high-water and low-water marks.

**fore·short·en** (fôr-shôr′t'n, fōr-), ***v.t.*** in *drawing, painting,* etc., to represent some lines of (an object) as shorter than they actually are in order to give the illusion of proper relative size.

**fore·show** (fôr-shō′, fōr-), *v.t.* [-SHOWED, -SHOWN or -SHOWED, -SHOWING], to show or indicate beforehand; foretell.
**fore·sight** (fôr′sīt′, fōr′-), *n.* 1. *a*) a foreseeing. *b*) the power to foresee. 2. a looking forward. 3. prudent regard or provision for the future. —**fore′sight′ed,** *adj.* —**fore′sight′ed·ness,** *n.*
**fore·skin** (fôr′skin′, fōr′-), *n.* the fold of skin that covers the end of the penis; prepuce.
**for·est** (fôr′ist, for′-), *n.* [OFr. < ML. (*silva*) *forestis,* (wood) unenclosed < L. *foris,* out of doors], 1. a large tract of land covered with trees; woodland. 2. such trees. *adj.* of or in a forest. *v.t.* to plant with trees; make into a forest. —**for′est·ed,** *adj.* —**for′est·less,** *adj.* —**for′est·like′,** *adj.*
**fore·stall** (fôr-stôl′, fōr-), *v.t.* [< AS. *foresteall,* ambush], 1. to prevent by doing something beforehand. 2. to act in advance of; anticipate. —**fore·stall′er,** *n.* —**fore·stall′ment, fore·stal′ment,** *n.*
**for·est·a·tion** (fôr′is-tā′shən, for′-), *n.* the planting or care of forests.
**fore·stay** (fôr′stā′, fōr′-), *n.* a rope or cable reaching from the head of a ship's foremast to the bowsprit, for supporting the foremast.
**for·est·er** (fôr′is-tēr, for′-), *n.* 1. one trained in forestry or charged with the care of a forest. 2. a person or animal that lives in a forest.
**for·est·ry** (fôr′is-tri, for′-), *n.* 1. [Rare], forest land. 2. the science of planting and taking care of forests. 3. systematic forest management for the production of timber, for conservation, etc.
**fore·taste** (fôr′tāst′, fōr′-), *n.* a preliminary taste; anticipation. *v.t.* [-TASTED, -TASTING], (fôr-tāst′, fōr-), [Rare], to taste beforehand.
**fore·tell** (fôr-tel′, fōr-), *v.t.* [-TOLD, -TELLING], to tell, announce, or indicate beforehand; prophesy; predict. —**fore·tell′er,** *n.*
**fore·thought** (fôr′thôt′, fōr′-), *n.* 1. a thinking or planning beforehand. 2. foresight; prudence.
**fore·to·ken** (fôr′tō′kən, fōr′-), *n.* a prophetic sign; omen. *v.t.* (fôr-tō′kən, fōr-), to be a prophetic sign or omen of; foreshadow.
**fore·top** (fôr′top′, fōr′-; *also* -təp), *n.* the platform at the top of a ship's foremast.
**fore-top·gal·lant** (fôr′top-gal′ənt, fōr′tə-gal′-), *adj.* designating or of the mast, sail, etc. just above the fore-topmast.
**fore-top·mast** (fôr-top′mast′, fōr-top′mäst′; *also* -məst), *n.* the mast extending above the foremast.
**fore-top·sail** (fôr-top′sāl′, fōr-top′s'l), *n.* a sail set on the fore-topmast, above the foresail.
**for·ev·er** (fēr-ev′ēr, fôr-), *adv.* 1. for eternity; for always; endlessly. 2. always; at all times. Also **for·ev′er·more′** (-môr′, -mōr′).
**fore·warn** (fôr-wôrn′, fōr-), *v.t.* to warn beforehand. —**fore·warn′er,** *n.*
**fore·word** (fôr′wūrd′, fōr′-), *n.* an introductory remark, preface, or prefatory note.
**for·feit** (fôr′fit), *n.* [< OFr. < *forfaire,* to transgress; ult. < L. *foris,* beyond + *facere,* to do], 1. something that one has to give up because of some crime, fault, or neglect; fine; penalty. 2. the act or process of paying a forfeit. *adj.* lost or taken away as a forfeit. *v.t.* to lose or be deprived of as a forfeit. —**for′feit·a·ble,** *adj.* —**for′feit·er,** *n.*
**for·fei·ture** (fôr′fi-chēr), *n.* 1. a forfeiting. 2. anything forfeited; penalty or fine.
**for·gat** (fôr-gat′), archaic pt. of **forget.**
**for·gath·er** (fôr-gath′ēr), *v.i.* 1. to come together; assemble. 2. to meet by chance. 3. to associate or be friendly (*with*). Also **foregather.**
**for·gave** (fēr-gāv′, fôr-), pt. of **forgive.**
**forge** (fôrj, fōrj), *n.* [< OFr. < L. *fabrica,* workshop < *faber,* workman], 1. a furnace for heating metal to be wrought. 2. a place where metal is heated and wrought into shape; smithy. 3. a place where wrought iron is made, as from iron ore. *v.t.* [FORGED, FORGING], 1. to shape (metal) by heating and hammering. 2. to form; shape; produce. 3. to imitate for purposes of deception or fraud; counterfeit (a check, etc.). *v.i.* 1. to work at a forge. 2. to commit forgery. —**forge′a·ble,** *adj.* —**forg′er,** *n.*
**forge** (fôrj, fōrj), *v.t. & v.i.* [FORGED, FORGING], [prob. alt. < *force*], to move forward consistently but slowly, as if against difficulties.
**for·ger·y** (fôr′jēr-i, fōr′-), *n.* [*pl.* -IES], 1. the act or legal offense of forging documents, signatures, etc. to deceive. 2. anything forged.
**for·get** (fēr-get′, fôr-), *v.t.* [-GOT or *archaic* FORGAT, -GOTTEN or -GOT, -GETTING], [AS. *forgietan*], 1. to lose (facts, etc.) from the mind; be unable to remember. 2. to overlook or neglect, either unintentionally or intentionally. *v.i.* to forget things. —**forget oneself,** 1. to think only of others. 2. to behave in an improper or unseemly manner. —**for·get′ter,** *n.*
**for·get·ful** (fēr-get′fəl, fôr-), *adj.* 1. apt to forget; having a poor memory. 2. negligent. 3. [Poetic], causing to forget. —**for·get′ful·ly,** *adv.* —**for·get′ful·ness,** *n.*
**for·get-me-not** (fēr-get′mi-not′), *n.* a plant of the borage family, with hairy leaves and clusters of small, blue flowers.
**for·give** (fēr-giv′, fôr-), *v.t.* [-GAVE, -GIVEN, -GIVING], [AS. *forgiefan*], 1. to give up resentment against or the desire to punish; pardon. 2. to overlook (an offense). 3. to cancel (a debt). *v.i.* to show forgiveness. —**for·giv′a·ble,** *adj.* —**for·giv′er,** *n.*
**for·give·ness** (fēr-giv′nis, fôr-), *n.* 1. a forgiving; pardon. 2. inclination to forgive.
**for·giv·ing** (fēr-giv′iŋ, fôr-), *adj.* that forgives; inclined to forgive. —**for·giv′ing·ly,** *adv.* —**for·giv′ing·ness,** *n.*
**for·go** (fôr-gō′), *v.t.* [-WENT, -GONE, -GOING], [AS. *forgan*], to do without; abstain from; give up. Also **forego.** —**for·go′er,** *n.*
**for·got** (fēr-got′, fôr-), pt. and alt. pp. of **forget.**
**for·got·ten** (fēr-got′'n, fôr-), pp. of **forget.**
**fork** (fôrk), *n.* [AS. *forca* < L. *furca,* hayfork], 1. an instrument consisting of a handle and two or more pointed prongs at one end, used for spearing or picking up something. 2. something like a fork in shape. 3. a division into branches; bifurcation. 4. the point where a river, road, etc. is divided into two or more branches. 5. one of these branches. *v.i.* to divide into branches, as a river or road. *v.t.* 1. to make into the shape of a fork. 2. to pick up, spear, or pitch with a fork. —**fork over** (or **out, up**), [Colloq.], to pay out; hand over.
**forked** (fôrkt; *poetic,* fôr′kid), *adj.* 1. having a fork or forks. 2. zigzag: as, *forked* lightning. —**fork·ed·ly** (fôr′kid-li), *adv.* —**fork′ed·ness,** *n.*
**for·lorn** (fēr-lôrn′, fôr-), *adj.* [< AS. pp. of *forleosan,* to lose utterly], 1. left behind; deserted; forsaken. 2. wretched; miserable. 3. without hope; desperate. 4. bereft (*of*). —**for·lorn′ly,** *adv.* —**for·lorn′ness,** *n.*
**form** (fôrm), *n.* [< OFr. < L. *forma*], 1. the shape or outline of anything; structure, excluding color, texture, and density. 2. the body or figure of a person or animal. 3. anything used to give shape to something else; mold. 4. the combination of qualities making something what it is; intrinsic character. 5. orderly arrangement; style: distinguished from *content.* 6. a way of doing something: as, one's golf *form.* 7. a customary way of acting or behaving; ceremony; formality. 8. a fixed order of words; formula. 9. a printed document with blank spaces to be filled in. 10. a particular kind or type; species or variety. 11. a condition of mind or body: as, the boxer was in good *form.* 12. a long, wooden bench, as formerly in a schoolroom. 13. a grade or class in school. 14. in *grammar,* any of the different appearances of a word in changes of inflection, spelling, etc.: as, *am* is a *form* of *be.* 15. in *printing,* the type, plates, etc. locked in a frame for printing. *v.t.* 1. to shape; fashion; make: as, a school *formed* after Oxford. 2. to train; instruct. 3. to develop (habits). 4. to think of; conceive. 5. to organize into: as, the boys *formed* lines. 6. to make up; constitute. *v.i.* 1. to be formed. 2. to come into being; take form. 3. to take a specific form. —**good** (or **bad**) **form,** conduct in (or not in) accord with social custom.
**-form** (fôrm), [< L. *-formis*], a suffix meaning: 1. *having the form of,* as in *cuneiform.* 2. *having* (a specified number of) *forms,* as in *uniform.*
**for·mal** (fôr′m'l), *adj.* [L. *formalis*], 1. of external form; apparent. 2. of the internal form; essential. 3. according to fixed customs, rules, etc. 4. done for outward appearance only; stiff; ceremonious. 5. *a*) designed for wear at ceremonies, etc.: as, *formal* dress. *b*) requiring such clothes: as, a *formal* dinner. 6. done or made in orderly, regular fashion; methodical. 7. rigidly symmetrical: as, a *formal* garden. 8. done or made according to the forms that make explicit, definite, etc.: as, a *formal* contract. 9. designating or of that level of language usage characterized by expanded vocabulary, syntactical constructions, complex sentences, etc.: distinguished from *colloquial.* *n.* [Colloq.], 1. a dance requiring formal clothes. 2. a woman's long, evening dress. —**for′mal·ly,** *adv.* —**for′mal·ness,** *n.*
**form·al·de·hyde** (fôr-mal′də-hīd′), *n.* [< *formic* + *aldehyde*], a colorless, pungent gas, HCHO, used in solution as a disinfectant and preservative.
**for·mal·ism** (fôr′m'l-iz'm), *n.* strict attention to outward forms and customs, as in art or religion. —**for′mal·ist,** *n.* —**for′mal·is′tic,** *adj.*

**for·mal·i·ty** (fôr-mal′ə-ti), *n.* [*pl.* -TIES], 1. a being formal; specif., *a*) an observing of prescribed customs, rules, ceremonies, etc.; propriety. *b*) strict or excessive attention to order, regularity, or convention; stiffness. 2. a formal or conventional act or requirement; ceremony or form.

**for·mal·ize** (fôr′m'l-īz′), *v.t.* [-IZED, -IZING], 1. to give definite form to; shape. 2. to make formal. **—for′mal·i·za′tion,** *n.* **—for′mal·iz′er,** *n.*

**for·mat** (fôr′mat), *n.* [Fr. < L. (*liber*) *formatus*, (a book) formed], 1. the shape, size, and general make-up of a book, magazine, etc. 2. general arrangement, as of a television program.

**for·ma·tion** (fôr-mā′shən), *n.* 1. a forming or being formed. 2. a thing formed. 3. the way in which something is formed or arranged; structure; order. 4. in *geology*, a series of strata of the same sort of rock or mineral. 5. in *military usage*, the arrangement of troops, ships, etc.

**form·a·tive** (fôr′mə-tiv), *adj.* 1. helping to shape, develop, or mold: as, a *formative* influence. 2. of formation or development: as, one's *formative* years. 3. in *grammar*, serving to form words. *n.* 1. an element, as a prefix or suffix, used with other elements to form words. 2. a word thus formed. **—form′a·tive·ly,** *adv.* **—form′a·tive·ness,** *n.*

**for·mer** (fôr′mēr), *adj.* [ME. *formere*, compar., back-formation < *formest*, foremost], 1. previous; earlier; past. 2. first-mentioned of two: opposed to *latter*: often a noun (with *the*).

**form·er** (fôr′mēr), *n.* a person or thing that forms.

**for·mer·ly** (fôr′mēr-li), *adv.* at or in a former time; in the past; some time ago.

**for·mic** (fôr′mik), *adj.* [< L. *formica*, an ant], 1. of ants. 2. designating or of a colorless acid, HCOOH, found in ants, spiders, nettles, etc.

**for·mi·da·ble** (fôr′mi-də-b'l), *adj.* [Fr. < L. < *formidare*, to dread], 1. causing dread, fear, or awe. 2. hard to handle or overcome. **—for′mi·da·ble·ness, for′mi·da·bil′i·ty,** *n.* **—for′mi·da·bly,** *adv.*

**form·less** (fôrm′lis), *adj.* having no definite or regular form or plan; shapeless; amorphous. **—form′less·ly,** *adv.* **—form′less·ness,** *n.*

**form letter,** one of a number of duplicated letters, with the inside address, etc. filled in separately.

**For·mo·sa** (fôr-mō′sə), *n.* Taiwan, an island province off SE China: see **Taiwan.**

**for·mu·la** (fôr′myoo-lə), *n.* [*pl.* -LAS, -LAE (-lē′)], [L., dim. of *forma*, form], 1. a fixed form of words, especially one that is used only as a conventional expression: as, "Very truly yours" is a *formula*. 2. any conventional rule or method for doing something, especially when used, applied, or repeated without thought. 3. an exact statement of religious faith or doctrine. 4. a prescription for a medicine, a baby's food, etc. 5. a set of algebraic symbols expressing a mathematical fact, rule, etc. 6. in *chemistry*, an expression of the composition, as of a compound, by a combination of symbols and figures (e.g., $C_6H_6$, benzene).

**for·mu·lar·ize** (fôr′myoo-lə-rīz′), *v.t.* [-IZED, -IZING] to express in a formula; formulate.

**for·mu·lar·y** (fôr′myoo-ler′i), *n.* [*pl.* -IES], 1. a collection of formulas or prescribed forms, as of prayers. 2. a formula. 3. in *pharmacy*, a list of medicines with their formulas. *adj.* of formulas.

**for·mu·late** (fôr′myoo-lāt′), *v.t.* [-LATED, -LATING], 1. to express in or reduce to a formula. 2. to express in a definite or systematic way. **—for′mu·la′tion,** *n.* **—for′mu·la′tor,** *n.*

**for·mu·lize** (fôr′myoo-līz′), *v.t.* [-LIZED, -LIZING], to formulate. **—for′mu·liz′er,** *n.*

**for·myl** (fôr′mil), *n.* [< *formic* + *-yl*], the radical, HCO, of formic acid.

**for·ni·cate** (fôr′ni-kāt′), *v.i.* [-CATED, -CATING], [< LL. pp. of *fornicari* < L. *fornix*, a brothel], to commit fornication. **—for′ni·ca′tor,** *n.*

**for·ni·ca·tion** (fôr′ni-kā′shən), *n.* voluntary sexual intercourse between unmarried persons.

**for·sake** (fēr-sāk′, fôr-), *v.t.* [-SOOK (-sook′), -SAKEN, -SAKING], [< AS. < *for-* + *sacan*, to strive], 1. to give up; renounce (a habit, idea, etc.). 2. to leave; abandon; desert.

**for·sak·en** (fēr-sāk′ən, fôr-), *adj.* abandoned; desolate; forlorn. **—for·sak′en·ly,** *adv.*

**for·sooth** (fēr-sōōth′, fôr-), *adv.* [AS. *forsoth*], [Archaic], in truth; no doubt; indeed.

**for·spent** (fôr-spent′), *adj.* [< AS.; see FOR- & SPEND], [Archaic], exhausted with toil; fatigued.

**for·swear** (fôr-swâr′), *v.t.* [-SWORE, -SWORN, -SWEARING], 1. to swear or promise earnestly to give up. 2. to deny earnestly or on oath. *v.i.* to swear falsely; commit perjury. **—forswear oneself,** to perjure oneself. **—for·swear′er,** *n.*

**for·syth·i·a** (fēr-sith′i-ə, fôr-sī′thi-ə), *n.* [Mod. L., after William *Forsyth* (1737–1804), Eng. botanist], a shrub with yellow bell-shaped flowers, which appear in early spring before the leaves.

**fort** (fôrt, fōrt), *n.* [Fr. < L. *fortis*, strong], a fortified place or building for military defense.

**forte** (fôrt), *n.* [< Fr.; see FORT], that which one does particularly well; one's strong point.

**for·te** (fôr′ti, -tā), *adj.* & *adv.* [It. < L. *fortis*, strong], in *music*, loud: a direction to the performer: abbrev. **f., F.** *n.* a forte note or passage.

**Forth** (fôrth, fōrth), *n.* a river in E Scotland.

**forth** (fôrth, fōrth), *adv.* [AS.], 1. forward; onward. 2. out; into view, as from hiding. **—and so forth,** and so on: equivalent to *etc.*

**Forth, Firth of** (fôrth, fōrth), the long estuary of the Forth River, E Scotland.

**forth·com·ing** (fôrth′kum′iŋ, fōrth′-), *adj.* 1. approaching; about to appear. 2. ready when needed: as, the promised money was not *forthcoming*. *n.* an appearing or approaching.

**forth·right** (fôrth′rīt′, fōrth′-), *adj.* straightforward; direct; frank. *adv.* 1. straight ahead. 2. at once. **—forth′right′ly,** *adv.* **—forth′right′ness,** *n.*

**forth·with** (fôrth′with′, fōrth′*with*′), *adv.* without delay; at once.

**for·ti·eth** (fôr′ti-ith), *adj.* 1. preceded by thirty-nine others in a series; 40th. 2. designating any of the forty equal parts of something. *n.* 1. the one following the thirty-ninth. 2. any of the forty equal parts of something; 1/40.

**for·ti·fi·ca·tion** (fôr′tə-fi-kā′shən), *n.* 1. the act or science of fortifying. 2. a fort or defensive earthwork, etc. 3. a fortified place.

**for·ti·fy** (fôr′tə-fī′), *v.t.* [-FIED, -FYING], [< Fr. < LL. < L. *fortis*, strong + *facere*, to make], 1. to strengthen physically or structurally. 2. to strengthen against attack, as by building forts, walls, etc. 3. to support; corroborate, as an argument. 4. to strengthen (liquor, etc.) by adding alcohol. 5. to add vitamins, minerals, etc. to (bread, etc.) so as to increase the food value. *v.i.* to build military defenses. **—for′ti·fi′a·ble,** *adj.* **—for′ti·fi′er,** *n.*

**for·tis·si·mo** (fôr-tis′ə-mō′), *adj.* & *adv.* [It. superl. of *forte*, strong], in *music*, very loud: a direction to the performer: abbrev. **ff.**

**for·ti·tude** (fôr′tə-tōōd′, -tūd′), *n.* [Fr. < L. < *fortis*, strong], firm courage; patient endurance of trouble, pain, etc. **—for′ti·tu′di·nous,** *adj.*

**Fort Lau·der·dale** (lô′dēr-dāl′), a city on the SE coast of Florida: pop., 84,000.

**fort·night** (fôrt′nīt, -nit), *n.* [< AS.; lit., fourteen nights], [Chiefly Brit.], two weeks.

**fort·night·ly** (fôrt′nīt-li), *adv.* once in every fortnight; at two-week intervals. *adj.* happening or appearing at two-week intervals. *n.* [*pl.* -LIES], a periodical issued at two-week intervals.

**for·tress** (fôr′tris), *n.* [< OFr. < ML. < L. *fortis*, strong], a fortified place; fort; stronghold. *v.t.* to protect by a fortress.

**for·tu·i·tous** (fôr-tōō′ə-təs, -tū′-), *adj.* [< L. < *fors*, luck], happening by chance; accidental. **—for·tu′i·tous·ly,** *adv.* **—for·tu′i·tous·ness,** *n.*

**for·tu·i·ty** (fôr-tōō′ə-ti, -tū′-), *n.* [*pl.* -TIES], [< Fr. < L.; see FORTUITOUS], chance; accident.

**for·tu·nate** (fôr′chə-nit), *adj.* [< L. *fortunatus*, pp. < *fortuna*; see FORTUNE], 1. having good luck; lucky. 2. bringing, or coming by, good luck; favorable. **—for′tu·nate·ly,** *adv.* **—for′tu·nate·ness,** *n.*

**for·tune** (fôr′chən), *n.* [OFr. < L. *fortuna* < *fors*, luck], 1. the supposed power that brings good or bad to people; luck; chance; fate: often personified. 2. what happens to one; one's lot, especially future lot, good or bad. 3. good luck; success. 4. wealth; riches. *v.t.* [-TUNED, -TUNING], [Rare], to provide with wealth. *v.i.* [Archaic], to happen. **—for′tune·less,** *adj.*

**fortune hunter,** one who tries to become rich, especially by marrying a rich person.

**for·tune·tell·er** (fôr′chən-tel′ēr), *n.* a person who professes to foretell events in other people's lives. **—for′tune·tell′ing,** *n.* & *adj.*

**Fort Wayne** (wān), a city in NE Indiana: pop., 162,000.

**Fort Worth** (wūrth), a city in N Texas: pop., 356,000.

**for·ty** (fôr′ti), *adj.* [AS. *feowertig*], four times ten. *n.* [*pl.* -TIES], the cardinal number between thirty-

nine and forty-one; 40; XL. **—the forties,** the years from forty through forty-nine (of a century or a person's age).
**for·ty-nin·er, For·ty-Nin·er** (fôr'ti-nīn'ẽr), *n.* a participant in the California gold rush of 1849.
**forty winks,** [Colloq.], a short sleep; nap.
**fo·rum** (fôr'əm, fō'rəm), *n.* [*pl.* -RUMS, -RA (-ə, -rə)], [L.], 1. the public square or market place of an ancient Roman city, where legal and political business was conducted. 2. a law court; tribunal. 3. an assembly for the discussion of public matters. **—the Forum,** the forum of ancient Rome.
**for·ward** (fôr'wẽrd), *adj.* [AS. *foreweard*], 1. at, toward, or of the front. 2. advanced; specif., *a*) early. *b*) mentally advanced. *c*) advanced socially or politically. 3. onward; advancing. 4. prompt; ready; eager: as, he was *forward* in helping. 5. bold; presumptuous. 6. of or for the future: as, *forward* buying. *adv.* 1. toward the front; ahead; onward. 2. toward the future: as, look *forward*. *n.* in *basketball, hockey*, etc., any of the players in a front position. *v.t.* 1. to promote. 2. to send; transmit: as, *forward* her mail to New York. **—for'ward·er,** *n.* **—for'ward·ly,** *adv.* **—for'ward·ness,** *n.*
**forward pass,** in *football*, a pass from behind the line of scrimmage toward the opponents' goal.
**for·wards** (fôr'wẽrdz), *adv.* forward.
**for·went** (fôr-went'), pt. of **forgo.**
**fos·sa** (fos'ə), *n.* [*pl.* -SAE (-ē)], [L., a ditch], in *anatomy*, a cavity, pit, or small hollow.
**fosse, foss** (fôs, fos), *n.* [< OFr. < L. *fossa*, ditch], a ditch or moat, especially in fortifications.
**fos·sil** (fos''l, fô's'l), *n.* [< Fr. < L. *fossilis*, dug up < pp. of *fodere*, to dig up], 1. any hardened remains or traces of plant or animal life of some previous geological age, preserved in the earth's crust. 2. [Colloq.], a person who has outmoded, fixed ideas. *adj.* 1. of, like, or forming a fossil. 2. antiquated, as ideas. **—fos'sil·like',** *adj.*
**fos·sil·if·er·ous** (fos''l-if'ẽr-əs), *adj.* containing fossils.
**fos·sil·ize** (fos''l-īz'), *v.t.* [-IZED, -IZING], 1. to change into a fossil; petrify. 2. to make out of date, rigid, or incapable of change. *v.i.* to become fossilized. **—fos'sil·i·za'tion,** *n.*
**fos·ter** (fôs'tẽr, fos'-), *v.t.* [AS. *fostrian*, to nourish; ult. < *foda*, food], 1. to bring up; rear. 2. to help to develop; promote: as, hunger *fosters* disease. 3. to cherish: as, she *fostered* hopes of success. *adj.* having the standing of a specified member of a family but not by birth: as, a *foster* brother. **—fos'ter·er,** *n.*
**Fos·ter, Stephen Collins** (fôs'tẽr, fos'-), 1826–1864; U.S. composer of songs.
**fought** (fôt), pt. and pp. of **fight.**
**foul** (foul), *adj.* [AS. *ful*], 1. stinking; loathsome: as, a *foul* odor. 2. extremely dirty; disgustingly filthy. 3. full of dirt or foreign objects: as, a *foul* pipe. 4. rotten: said of food. 5. indecent; profane: as, *foul* language. 6. wicked; abominable. 7. stormy; unfavorable: as, *foul* weather. 8. tangled; jammed: as, a *foul* rope. 9. not according to the rules of a game; unfair. 10. dishonest. 11. [Colloq.], unpleasant, disagreeable, etc. 12. in *baseball*, of foul balls or foul lines. *n.* anything foul; specif., *a*) a collision of boats, contestants, etc. *b*) an infraction of rules, as of a game. *c*) in *baseball*, a foul ball. *v.t.* 1. to make foul; dirty; soil. 2. to dishonor; disgrace. 3. to obstruct; fill up: as, grease *fouls* sink drains. 4. to cover (a ship's bottom) with impeding growths. 5. to entangle; catch: as, a rope *fouled* in the shrouds. 6. to collide with. 7. to make a foul against, as in a game. 8. in *baseball*, to bat (the ball) so that it falls outside the foul lines. *v.i.* 1. to be or become fouled (in various senses). 2. to break the rules of a game. 3. in *baseball*, to hit a foul ball. **—foul out,** to be put out by a fielder's catch of a foul ball. **—foul up,** [Colloq.], to entangle or bungle. **—go** (or **fall** or **run**) **foul of,** 1. to collide with and become tangled in. 2. to get into trouble with. **—foul'ly,** *adv.* **—foul'ness,** *n.*
**fou·lard** (fōō-lärd'), *n.* [Fr.], 1. a lightweight material of silk, rayon, or silk and cotton. 2. a necktie, scarf, etc. of this material.
**foul ball,** in *baseball*, a batted ball that falls outside the foul lines: opposed to *fair ball*.
**foul line,** in *baseball*, 1. either of the lines extending from home plate through the outside corners of first base or third base and onward along the outfield. 2. in *tennis, bowling*, etc., any of various lines bounding the playing area, beyond which the ball must not be hit, the player must not go, etc.
**foul play,** 1. unfair play. 2. treacherous action or violence, as in assault, murder, etc.
**found** (found), *v.t.* [< OFr. < L. < *fundus*, bottom], 1. to set for support; base: as, a statement *founded* on facts. 2. to begin construction of; establish: as, a city *founded* in 1815. *v.i.* [Rare], to be based.
**found** (found), *v.t.* [< Fr. < L. *fundere*, to pour], 1. to melt and pour (metal) into a mold. 2. to make by founding metal; cast.
**found** (found), pt. and pp. of **find.**
**foun·da·tion** (foun-dā'shən), *n.* 1. a founding or being founded; establishment. 2. the establishment of an institution with provision for its upkeep. 3. a fund or endowment to maintain a hospital, school, etc. 4. an institution maintained by an endowment. 5. basis. 6. the supporting part of a wall, house, etc.; base.
**foundation garment,** a corset or girdle.
**foun·der** (foun'dẽr), *v.i.* [< OFr. < L. *fundus*, bottom], 1. to stumble, fall, or go lame. 2. to fill with water and sink: said of a ship. 3. to break down; collapse; fail. *v.t.* to cause to founder.
**found·er** (foun'dẽr), *n.* a person who founds, or establishes.
**found·er** (foun'dẽr), *n.* a person who founds metals.
**found·ling** (found'liŋ), *n.* a child found after it has been abandoned by its parents.
**found·ry** (foun'dri), *n.* [*pl.* -RIES], 1. the act or work of founding metals; casting. 2. metal castings. 3. a place where metal is cast.
**fount** (fount), *n.* [< Fr. < L. *fons*, a fountain], 1. a fountain; spring. 2. a source.
**fount** (fount), *n.* in *printing*, a font: Brit. form.
**foun·tain** (foun't'n), *n.* [< OFr. < LL. *fontana* < L. < *fons*, fountain], 1. a natural spring of water. 2. the source or origin of anything. 3. *a*) an artificial spring, jet, or flow of water. *b*) the basin, pipes, etc. where this flows. *c*) a water cooler or other device for supplying drinking water. 4. a container or reservoir, as for ink, oil, etc. **—foun'tain·less,** *adj.*
**foun·tain·head** (foun't'n-hed', -tin-), *n.* 1. a spring that is the source of a stream. 2. the original or main source of anything.
**fountain pen,** a pen which is fed writing fluid from a supply in the reservoir.
**four** (fôr, fōr), *adj.* [< AS. *feower*], totaling one more than three. *n.* 1. the cardinal number between three and five; 4; IV. 2. something that has four of anything as its outstanding characteristic. **—on all fours,** 1. on all four feet. 2. on hands and knees (or feet).
**four-flush** (fôr'flush', fōr'-), *v.i.* 1. in *poker*, to pretend that one's hand has five cards of the same suit when it has only four (**four flush**); hence, 2. [Slang], to bluff.
**four-flush·er** (fôr'flush'ẽr, fōr'-), *n.* 1. a poker player who four-flushes. 2. [Slang], one who bluffs.
**four·fold** (fôr'fōld', fōr'-), *adj.* 1. having four parts. 2. having four times as much or as many. *adv.* four times as much or as many.
**four-foot·ed** (fôr'foot'id, fōr'-), *adj.* having four feet; quadruped.
**four hundred,** the social set regarded as wealthiest and most exclusive (with *the*).
**four-in-hand** (fôr'in-hand', fōr'-), *n.* 1. a team of four horses. 2. a coach drawn by such a team. 3. a necktie tied in a slipknot with the ends left hanging. *adj.* designating or of a four-in-hand.
**four·pence** (fôr'pəns, fōr'-), *n.* 1. the sum of four pence; four British pennies. 2. a former British silver coin of this value.
**four·pen·ny** (fôr'pen'i, fōr'pən-i), *adj.* costing or valued at fourpence. *n.* [*pl.* -NIES], fourpence.
**four-post·er** (fôr'pōs'tẽr, fōr'-), *n.* a large bedstead with tall corner posts that sometimes support a canopy or curtains.
**four·score** (fôr'skôr', fōr'skōr'), *adj.* & *n.* [Archaic or Poetic], four times twenty; eighty.
**four·some** (fôr'səm, fōr'-), *n.* 1. a group of four people. 2. in *golf*, *a*) a game involving four players, usually two to a team. *b*) these players.
**four·square** (fôr'skwâr', fōr'-), *adj.* 1. square. 2. unyielding; firm. 3. frank; forthright. *adv.* in a square form or manner. *n.* a square. **—four'-square'ly,** *adv.* **—four'square'ness,** *n.*
**four·teen** (fôr'tēn', fōr'-), *adj.* [AS. *feowertyne*], four more than ten. *n.* the cardinal number between thirteen and fifteen; 14; XIV.
**four·teenth** (fôr'tēnth', fōr'-), *adj.* 1. preceded by thirteen others in a series; 14th. 2. designating any of the fourteen equal parts of something. *n.* 1. the one following the thirteenth. 2. any of the fourteen equal parts of something; 1/14.
**fourth** (fôrth, fōrth), *adj.* [AS. *feortha*], 1. preceded by three others in a series; 4th. 2. designating any

of the four equal parts of something. *n.* 1. the one following the third. 2. any of the four equal parts of something; $^1/_4$. 3. in *music*, *a*) the tone four degrees above a given tone in a diatonic scale. *b*) the interval between, or a combination of, these tones. **—fourth′ly,** *adv.*

**fourth dimension,** a dimension in addition to those of length, width, and depth: in the theory of relativity, time is regarded as this dimension.

**Fourth of July,** Independence Day.

**fowl** (foul), *n.* [*pl.* FOWLS, FOWL; see PLURAL, II, D, 1], [< AS. *fugol*], 1. any bird: used in combination, as, wild *fowl*. 2. any of the larger domestic birds used as food, as the chicken, duck, turkey, etc. 3. the flesh of any of these birds used for food. *v.i.* to hunt wild birds for food or sport. **—fowl′er,** *n.* **—fowl′ing,** *adj.* & *n.*

**fowling piece,** a shotgun for shooting wild birds.

**fox** (foks), *n.* [*pl.* FOXES, FOX; see PLURAL, II, D, 1], [AS.], 1. a small, wild, flesh-eating animal of the dog family, with a bushy tail: thought of as sly and crafty. 2. its fur, commonly reddish brown. 3. a sly, crafty person. *v.t.* 1. to stain (book leaves, prints, etc.) with reddish-brown discolorations. 2. to trick by slyness or craftiness. *v.i.* to become stained, as book leaves.

FOX ($3^1/_2$ ft. long including tail)

**fox·glove** (foks′gluv′), *n.* a plant of the figwort family, with thimblelike flowers: cf. **digitalis.**

**fox·hole** (foks′hōl′), *n.* a hole dug in the ground as a temporary protection for one or two soldiers against enemy gunfire or tanks.

**fox·hound** (foks′hound′), *n.* a strong, swift hound with a keen scent, bred to hunt foxes.

**fox·tail** (foks′tāl′), *n.* 1. the tail of a fox. 2. a tall grass with spikes of brushlike flowers.

**fox terrier,** a small, active terrier with a smooth or wire-haired coat, formerly trained to drive foxes out of hiding.

**fox trot,** 1. a slow, mixed gait of a horse in which it trots with the forelegs and paces with the hind legs. 2. a ballroom dance in 4/4 time with a variety of steps, both fast and slow. 3. the music for such a dance. **—fox′-trot′,** *v.i.*

WIRE-HAIRED FOX TERRIER (15 in. high at shoulder)

**fox·y** (fok′si), *adj.* [-IER, -IEST], 1. foxlike; crafty; sly. 2. covered with brownish or yellowish stains. **—fox′i·ly,** *adv.* **—fox′i·ness,** *n.*

**foy·er** (foi′ẽr, foi′ā; Fr. fwȧ′yā′), *n.* [Fr. < LL. < L. *focus*, hearth], an entrance hall or lobby, as in a theater or hotel.

**fp., F.P., f.p.,** foot-pound; foot-pounds.

**f.p., fp, fp.,** freezing point.

**Fr,** in *chemistry*, francium.

**Fr.,** 1. Father. 2. France. 3. French. 4. Friday.

**fr.,** 1. fragment. 2. franc; francs. 3. from.

**Fra** (frä), *n.* [It., abbrev. of *frate* < L. *frater*], brother: title given to a friar or monk.

**fra·cas** (frā′kəs), *n.* [Fr. < It. < *fracassare*, to smash], a noisy dispute or fight; brawl.

**frac·tion** (frak′shən), *n.* [Fr. < L. < pp. of *frangere*, to break], 1. a small part, amount, etc.; fragment. 2. in *mathematics*, *a*) a quantity less than a whole number expressed as a decimal (.4) or with a numerator and denominator ($^1/_2$). *b*) any quantity expressed by a numerator and denominator, as $^{13}/_4$. **—frac′tion·al,** *adj.* **—frac′tion·al·ly,** *adv.*

**frac·tious** (frak′shəs), *adj.* [? < obs. *fraction*, brawling, after *factious*], 1. unruly; rebellious; refractory. 2. peevish; irritable; cross. **—frac′tious·ly,** *adv.* **—frac′tious·ness,** *n.*

**frac·ture** (frak′chẽr), *n.* [Fr. < L. *fractura* < *frangere*, to break], 1. a breaking or being broken. 2. a break; crack; split. 3. a break in a bone or, occasionally, a tear in a cartilage. 4. the texture of the surface of a mineral broken across the line of cleavage. *v.t.* & *v.i.* [-TURED, -TURING], to break; crack; split. **—frac′tur·al,** *adj.*

**frae** (frā), *prep.* [Scot.], from. *adv.* [Scot.], fro.

**frag·ile** (fraj′əl), *adj.* [< L. *fragilis* < *frangere*, to break], easily broken, damaged, or destroyed; brittle; frail; delicate. **—frag′ile·ly,** *adv.* **—fra·gil·i·ty** (frə-jil′ə-ti), **frag′ile·ness,** *n.*

**frag·ment** (frag′mənt), *n.* [Fr. < L. < *frangere*, to break], 1. a part broken away; broken piece. 2. a detached or incomplete part: as, *fragments* of music, a novel, etc. **—frag·men′tal** (-men′t'l), *adj.*

**frag·men·tar·y** (frag′mən-ter′i), *adj.* consisting of fragments; not complete; disconnected. **—frag′men·tar′i·ly,** *adv.* **—frag′men·tar′i·ness,** *n.*

**frag·men·ta·tion** (frag′mən-tā′shən), *n.* a breaking into fragments.

**fra·grance** (frā′grəns), *n.* a fragrant smell; pleasant odor: also **fra′gran·cy** [*pl.* -CIES].

**fra·grant** (frā′grənt), *adj.* [Fr. < L. ppr. of *fragrare*, to emit a smell], having a pleasant odor; sweet-smelling. **—fra′grant·ly,** *adv.*

**frail** (frāl), *adj.* [< OFr. < L. *fragilis*; see FRAGILE], 1. easily broken, damaged, or destroyed; fragile; delicate. 2. slender and delicate; weak. 3. easily tempted; morally weak. *n.* [Slang], a woman or girl. **—frail′ly,** *adv.* **—frail′ness,** *n.*

**frail·ty** (frāl′ti), *n.* 1. the quality or condition of being frail; weakness; esp., moral weakness. 2. [*pl.* -TIES], any fault or failing arising from such weakness.

**frame** (frām), *v.t.* [FRAMED, FRAMING], [< AS. *framian*, to be helpful & < ON. *frama*, to further], 1. to shape or form according to a pattern; design: as, they *framed* a constitution. 2. to put together the parts of; construct. 3. to compose; put into words; devise. 4. to adjust; fit: as, the tax is *framed* to benefit a few. 5. to enclose in a border, as a mirror or picture. 6. [Slang], to falsify evidence, testimony, etc. beforehand, so as to make (a person) appear guilty. *n.* 1. anything made of parts fitted together according to a design; framework, as of a house. 2. the human skeleton; body structure in general; build. 3. the structural case or border into which a window, door, etc. is set. 4. an ornamental border, as of a picture or mirror. 5. the way that anything is constructed or put together; form. 6. mood; temper. 7. an established order or system, especially of government. 8. [Colloq.], in *baseball*, an inning. 9. in *bowling*, etc., any of the divisions of a game. 10. in *motion pictures*, each of the small exposures composing a strip of film. 11. in *pool*, the triangular form in which the balls are set up at the beginning of a game. **—frame′less,** *adj.* **—fram′er,** *n.*

**frame house,** a house with a wooden framework, usually covered with boards.

**frame of mind,** mental or emotional state; mood.

**frame-up** (frām′up′), *n.* [Colloq.], 1. a falsifying of evidence, testimony, etc. to make an innocent person seem guilty. 2. a secret, deceitful arrangement or scheme made beforehand.

**frame·work** (frām′wũrk′), *n.* 1. a structure to hold together or to support something built or stretched over or around it: as, the *framework* of a house. 2. a basic structure, arrangement, or system.

**franc** (fraŋk), *n.* [Fr. < L. *Francorum rex* (king of the French), former device on the coin], 1. the monetary unit and a coin of France. 2. the similar monetary unit of Belgium and of Switzerland.

**France** (frans, fräns), *n.* a country in W Europe: area, 212,737 sq. mi.; pop., 45,355,000; capital, Paris: abbrev. **Fr., F.**

**France, A·na·tole** (an′ə-tōl′ frans, fräns), (pseudonym of *Jacques Anatole François Thibault*), 1844–1924; French writer.

**fran·chise** (fran′chīz), *n.* [< OFr. < *franc*, free], 1. *a*) any special right or privilege granted by a government, as to operate a public utility, etc. *b*) the jurisdiction over which this extends. 2. the right to vote; suffrage. **—fran′chised,** *adj.*

**Fran·cis·can** (fran-sis′kən), *adj.* 1. of Saint Francis of Assisi. 2. designating or of the monastic order founded by him in 1209. *n.* any member of this order.

**Fran·cis of As·si·si, Saint** (**fran′sis, frän′-, ə-sē′zi**), 1182–1226; Italian founder of the Franciscan order.

**fran·ci·um** (fran′si-əm), *n.* [< *France*], a metallic chemical element of the alkali group: symbol, Fr; at. wt., 223 (?); at. no., 87.

**Franck, Cé·sar Au·guste** (sā′zȧr′ ō′güst′ fränk), 1822–1890; French composer born in Belgium.

**Fran·co, Fran·cis·co** (frän-thēs′kô fräŋ′kô; Eng. fraŋ′kō), 1892– ; Spanish general; dictator of Spain (1939– ).

**Fran·co-,** a combining form meaning: 1. *Frankish.* 2. *of France, of the French.* 3. *France and*, as in *Franco-German.*

**Fran·co·phile** (fraŋ′kə-fīl′), *n.* [*Franco-* + *-phile*], a person who admires or is extremely fond of France, its people, customs, etc. *adj.* of Francophiles. Also **Fran'co·phil** (-fil).

**Fran·co·phobe** (fraŋ'kə-fōb'), *n.* [*Franco-* + *-phobe*], a person who hates or fears France, its people, customs, etc. *adj.* of Francophobes. —**Fran'co·pho'bi·a** (-fō'bi-ə), *n.*

**fran·gi·ble** (fran'jə-b'l), *adj.* [< OFr. < L. *frangere*, to break], breakable; fragile. —**fran'gi·bil'i·ty, fran'gi·ble·ness,** *n.*

**fran·gi·pan·i** (fran'ji-pan'i, -pä'ni), *n.* [? < proper name], 1. any of several tropical American shrubs with large, fragrant flowers; esp., the red jasmine. 2. a perfume obtained from this flower. Also **fran'gi·pane'** (-jə-pān').

**Frank** (fraŋk), *n.* [< AS.; see FRANK, *adj.*], 1. a member of the Germanic tribes that established the Frankish Empire, which, at its height (9th century A.D.), extended over what is now France, Germany, and Italy. 2. any western European: term used by Moslems and Greeks.

**frank** (fraŋk), *adj.* [< OFr. *franc*, free < ML. < *Francus* (< OHG. *Franco*), a Frank], 1. free in expressing what one thinks or feels; outspoken; candid. 2. free from disguise or guile; clearly evident. *v.t.* 1. to send (mail) free of postage. 2. to mark (mail) so that it can be sent free. *n.* 1. the right to send mail free. 2. a mark or signature authorizing mail to be sent free. 3. any letter, etc. sent free. —**frank'a·ble,** *adj.* —**frank'er,** *n.* —**frank'ly,** *adv.* —**frank'ness,** *n.*

**Frank.,** Frankish.

**Frank·en·stein** (fraŋk'ən-stīn'), *n.* 1. the title character in a novel (1818) by Mary Shelley: he is a young medical student who creates a monster that destroys him. 2. popularly, the monster; hence, anything that becomes dangerous to its creator.

**Frank·fort** (fraŋk'fērt), *n.* the capital of Kentucky, in the north central part of the State: pop., 18,000.

**Frank·furt am Main** (fräŋk'foort äm mīn'), a city in W Germany, on the Main River: pop., 648,000.

**Frankfurt an der O·der** (än dēr ō'dēr), a city in E Germany, on the Oder River: pop., 52,000.

**frank·furt·er, frank·fort·er** (fraŋk'fēr-tēr), *n.* [G. < *Frankfurt*, Germany], a smoked sausage of beef or beef and pork, usually enclosed in a membranous casing; wiener: also **frankfurt** (or **frankfort**) **sausage, frank.**

**frank·in·cense** (fraŋk'in-sens'), *n.* [< OFr.; see FRANK & INCENSE], a gum resin from various Asiatic and East African trees, burned as incense.

**Frank·ish** (fraŋk'ish), *adj.* of the Franks, their language, or culture. *n.* the West Germanic language of the Franks.

**frank·lin** (fraŋk'lin), *n.* [< Anglo-Fr. < ML. < *francus*; see FRANK, *adj.*], in England in the 14th and 15th centuries, a landowner of free but not noble birth, ranking just below the gentry.

**Frank·lin, Benjamin** (fraŋk'lin), 1706–1790; American statesman, scientist, and writer.

**fran·tic** (fran'tik), *adj.* [< OFr. < L. < Gr. *phrenitikos* < *phrenitis*; see FRENZY], greatly excited by anger, grief, pain, etc.; frenzied. —**fran'ti·cal·ly, fran'tic·ly,** *adv.* —**fran'tic·ness,** *n.*

**frap·pé** (fra-pā'; Fr. frȧ'pā'), *adj.* [Fr., pp. of *frapper*, to strike], partly frozen; iced; cooled. *n.* 1. a dessert made of partly frozen beverages, fruit juices, etc. 2. a drink made of some beverage poured into a glassful of shaved ice.

**frat** (frat), *n.* [Slang], a fraternity, as at a college.

**fra·ter·nal** (frə-tũr'n'l), *adj.* [< ML. < L. *fraternus* < *frater*, a brother], 1. of or characteristic of brothers; brotherly. 2. of or like a fraternal order. 3. designating either of a pair of twins (**fraternal twins**) developed from separately fertilized ova. —**fra·ter'nal·ism,** *n.* —**fra·ter'nal·ly,** *adv.*

**fraternal order** (or **society, association**), a society, often secret, organized for fellowship or for work toward a common goal.

**fra·ter·ni·ty** (frə-tũr'nə-ti), *n.* [*pl.* -TIES], 1. fraternal relationship or spirit; brotherliness. 2. a group of men joined together by common interests, for fellowship, etc., as a Greek-letter college organization. 3. a group of people with the same beliefs, interests, work, etc.: as, the writing *fraternity*.

**frat·er·nize** (frat'ēr-nīz'), *v.i.* & *v.t.* [-NIZED, -NIZING], to associate in a brotherly manner. —**frat'er·ni·za'tion,** *n.* —**frat'er·niz'er,** *n.*

**frat·ri·cide** (frat'rə-sīd', frā'trə-), *n.* [Fr. < LL. *fratricidium* < L. < *frater*, brother + *caedere*, to kill], 1. the act of killing one's own brother or sister. 2. a person who kills his own brother or sister. —**frat'ri·cid'al,** *adj.*

‡**Frau** (frou), *n.* [*pl.* FRAUEN (frou'ən); Eng. FRAUS], [G.], a married woman; wife: used in Germany as a title corresponding to *Mrs.*

**fraud** (frôd), *n.* [< OFr. < L. *fraus*], 1. deceit; trickery; cheating. 2. an intentional deception or dishonesty; trick. 3. [Colloq.], a person who deceives or is not what he pretends to be.

**fraud·u·lent** (frô'jə-lənt), *adj.* 1. acting with fraud; deceitful. 2. based on or characterized by fraud. 3. done or obtained by fraud. —**fraud'u·lence, fraud'u·len·cy,** *n.* —**fraud'u·lent·ly,** *adv.*

**fraught** (frôt), *adj.* [< MD. < *vracht*, a load], filled, charged, or loaded (*with*): as, the situation is *fraught* with danger.

‡**Fräu·lein** (froi'līn), *n.* [*pl.* FRAULEIN; Eng. -LEINS], [G.], an unmarried woman: used in Germany as a title corresponding to *Miss*.

**fray** (frā), *n.* [< *affray*], 1. a noisy quarrel; brawl. 2. a fight; conflict.

**fray** (frā), *v.t.* & *v.i.* [< Fr. < OFr. < L. *fricare*, to rub], to make or become worn or ragged by rubbing.

**fraz·zle** (fraz''l), *v.t.* & *v.i.* [-ZLED, -ZLING], [Brit. dial. & U.S., prob. < LG.], [Colloq.], 1. to wear to tatters; fray. 2. to tire completely; weary. *n.* [Colloq.], the state of being frazzled.

**freak** (frēk), *n.* [? via dial. < AS. *frician*, to dance], 1. a sudden fancy; odd notion; whim. 2. a whimsical nature; capriciousness. 3. any abnormal animal, person, or plant; monstrosity. *adj.* oddly different from what is normal; queer. —**freak'ish,** *adj.* —**freak'ish·ly,** *adv.* —**freak'ish·ness,** *n.* —**freak'y** [-IER, -IEST], *adj.*

**freck·le** (frek''l), *n.* [< ON.], a small, yellowish-brown spot on the skin, especially on parts exposed to the sun. *v.t.* [-LED, -LING], to cause freckles to appear on. *v.i.* to become spotted with freckles. —**freck'led,** *adj.* —**freck'ly,** *adj.*

**Frederick the Great,** (*Frederick II*), 1712–1786; king of Prussia (1740–1786).

**Fred·er·ic·ton** (fred'ēr-ik-tən, fred'rik-), *n.* the capital of New Brunswick, Canada: pop., 18,000.

**free** (frē), *adj.* [FREER, FREEST], [AS. *freo*], 1. *a*) not under the control or power of another; able to act or think without arbitrary restriction; having liberty; independent. *b*) characterized by or resulting from liberty. 2. having, or existing under, a government that does not impose arbitrary restrictions on the right to speak, assemble, petition, vote, etc. 3. able to move in any direction; not held; loose. 4. not held or confined by a court, the police, etc. 5. not burdened by obligations, debts, discomforts, etc.; unhindered: as, *free* from pain. 6. not confined to the usual rules or conventions: as, *free* verse. 7. not literal; not exact: as, a *free* translation. 8. not busy or engaged: as, I'm *free* this morning. 9. not constrained or stilted: as, a *free* gait. 10. *a*) generous; lavish: as, a *free* spender. *b*) profuse; abundant. 11. frank; straightforward. 12. too frank or familiar in speech, action, etc.; forward. 13. without cost or payment: as, a *free* ticket. 14. exempt from certain impositions, as taxes or duties. 15. clear of obstructions; open: as, a *free* road ahead. 16. open to all: as, a *free* port. 17. not fastened: as, the *free* end of a rope. 18. not united; not combined: as, *free* oxygen. *adv.* 1. without cost or payment. 2. in a free manner. *v.t.* [FREED, FREEING], to make free; specif., *a*) to release from bondage or arbitrary power, obligation, etc. *b*) to clear of obstruction, etc.; disengage. —**free and easy,** unceremonious; informal. —**free from** (or **of**), 1. lacking; without. 2. beyond. —**make free with,** to use freely. —**set free,** to release; liberate. —**with a free hand,** with generosity; lavishly. —**free'ly,** *adv.* —**free'ness,** *n.*

**free·board** (frē'bôrd', -bōrd'), *n.* the part of a ship's side between the deck or gunwale and the water line.

**free·boot·er** (frē'bōōt'ēr), *n.* [< D. < *vrij*, free + *buit*, plunder], a pirate; buccaneer.

**free·born** (frē'bôrn'), *adj.* 1. born free, not in slavery. 2. of or fit for a free person.

**free city,** a city that is an autonomous state.

**freed·man** (frēd'mən), *n.* [*pl.* -MEN], a man legally freed from slavery or bondage.

**free·dom** (frē'dəm), *n.* 1. the state or quality of being free. 2. exemption or liberation from the control of some other person or some arbitrary power; liberty. 3. exemption from arbitrary restrictions on a specified civil right; political liberty: as, *freedom* of speech. 4. exemption or immunity from a specified obligation, discomfort, etc.: as, *freedom* from want. 5. a being able to act, move, use, etc. without hindrance. 6. ease of movement or performance; facility. 7. a being free from the usual rules, conventions, etc. 8. frankness; straightforwardness. 9. an excessive frankness or familiarity.

**freed·wom·an** (frēd′woom′ən), *n.* [*pl.* -WOMEN], a woman legally freed from slavery or bondage.
**free enterprise,** the economic doctrine of permitting private industry to operate with a minimum of control by the government.
**free fall,** the unchecked fall of a body through the air, as that of a parachutist before he opens the parachute.
**free-for-all** (frē′fẽr-ôl′), *n.* a disorganized, general fight; brawl. *adj.* open to anyone.
**free-form** (frē′fôrm′), *adj.* 1. having an irregular, nonrectangular, or curvilinear form or outline. 2. not conventional in idea, artistic form, etc.
**free·hand** (frē′hand′), *adj.* drawn by hand without the use of instruments, measurements, etc.
**free·hand·ed** (frē′han′did), *adj.* generous; liberal.
**free·hold** (frē′hōld′), *n.* 1. the holding of a piece of land, an office, etc. for life or with the right to pass it on by inheritance. 2. land, etc. held in this way. *adj.* of or held by freehold. —**free′hold′er,** *n.*
**free lance,** 1. a medieval soldier who sold his services to any state or army. 2. one who acts according to his principles and is not influenced by any group. 3. a writer, actor, etc. not under contract, who sells his services to individual buyers. —**free-lance** (frē′lans′, -läns′), *adj.* & *v.i.*
**free·load·er** (frē′lōd′ẽr), *n.* [Slang], a person who seizes every chance to get free food, lodging, etc.
**free·man** (frē′mən), *n.* [*pl.* -MEN], 1. a person not in slavery or bondage. 2. a citizen; person who has all civil and political rights.
**Free·ma·son** (frē′mā′s'n, frē′mā′-), *n.* a member of an international secret society having as its principles brotherliness, charity, and mutual aid: also **Free and Accepted Mason, Mason.**
**Free·ma·son·ry** (frē′mā s'n-ri, frē′mā′-), *n.* 1. the principles, rituals, etc. of Freemasons. 2. [f-], a natural sympathy and understanding among persons with similar interests.
**free on board,** delivered (by the seller) aboard the train, ship, etc. at the point of shipment, without additional charge to the buyer.
**free·si·a** (frē′zhi-ə, -zhə, -si-ə), *n.* [after E. M. *Fries* (1794–1878), Swed. botanist], a South African plant of the iris family, with fragrant flowers.
**free silver,** the free coinage of silver, especially at a fixed ratio to the gold coined in the same period.
**free-soil** (frē′soil′), *adj.* opposed to the extension of slavery into U.S. Territories before the Civil War.
**free-spo·ken** (frē′spō′kən), *adj.* speaking frankly and freely; outspoken. —**free′-spo′ken·ly,** *adv.*
**free·stone** (frē′stōn′), *n.* 1. a stone, especially sandstone or limestone, that can be cut easily without splitting. 2. a peach, plum, etc. in which the stone, or pit, does not cling to the pulp of the ripened fruit. *adj.* having such a pit.
**free·think·er** (frē′thiŋk′ẽr), *n.* a person who forms his opinions about religion independently of tradition, authority, or established belief. —**free′think′ing,** *n.* & *adj.* —**free thought.**
**free trade,** trade conducted without restrictions, protective tariffs, customs duties, etc.
**free verse,** poetry not adhering to regular metrical, rhyming, or stanzaic forms.
**free·way** (frē′wā′), *n.* a multiple-lane highway designed to move traffic along quickly and smoothly, as by the use of interchanges.
**free·will** (frē′wil′), *adj.* voluntary; spontaneous.
**free will,** the human will regarded as free from restraints, compulsions, etc.; freedom of choice.
**freeze** (frēz), *v.i.* [FROZE, FROZEN, FREEZING], [AS. *freosan*], 1. to be formed into ice; be hardened by cold. 2. to become covered or clogged with ice. 3. to be or become very cold. 4. to become fixed or attached by freezing. 5. to die or be damaged by exposure to cold. 6. to become motionless or stiff. 7. to be chilled or stunned by a strong, sudden emotion. 8. to become formal or unfriendly. 9. in *mechanics,* to stick or become tight as a result of expansion of parts from overheating. *v.t.* 1. to cause to form into ice. 2. to cover or clog with ice. 3. to make very cold. 4. to preserve (food) by rapid refrigeration. 5. to make fixed or attached by freezing. 6. to kill or damage by exposure to cold. 7. to make or keep motionless or stiff. 8. to discourage as by cool behavior. 9. to make formal or unfriendly. 10. [Colloq.], to fix (prices, wages, an employee, etc.) at a given level or place by authoritative regulation. *n.* 1. a freezing or being frozen. 2. a period of cold, freezing weather. —**freeze (on) to,** [Colloq.], to hold fast to. —**freeze out,** [Colloq.], to force out by a cold manner, competition, etc. —**freeze over,** to become covered with ice.
**freeze-dry** (frēz′drī′), *v.t.* [-DRIED, -DRYING], to subject (food, vaccines, etc.) to quick-freezing followed by drying under high vacuum.
**freez·er** (frēz′ẽr), *n.* 1. a machine for making ice cream and sherbet. 2. a refrigerator for freezing foods and storing frozen foods.
**freezing point,** the temperature at which a liquid freezes: for water, it is 32° F. or 0° C.
**freight** (frāt), *n.* [< MD. *vraht,* a load], 1. a method or service for transporting goods by water, land, or air. 2. the cost for such transportation. 3. the goods transported; cargo. 4. a freight train. 5. any load or burden. *v.t.* 1. to load with freight. 2. to load; burden. 3. to transport as by freight.
**freight·age** (frāt′ij), *n.* 1. the charge for transporting goods. 2. freight; cargo. 3. the transportation of goods.
**freight car,** a railroad car for transporting freight.
**freight·er** (frāt′ẽr), *n.* a ship for carrying freight.
**freight train,** a railroad train of freight cars.
**Fré·mont, John Charles** (frē′mont), 1813–1890; U.S. politician, general, and explorer.
**French** (french), *adj.* of France, its people, their language, or culture. *n.* the Romance language of the French. —**the French,** the people of France. —**French′man** [*pl.* -MEN], *n.* —**French′wom′an** [*pl.* -WOMEN], *n.fem.*
**French chalk,** a very soft chalk used for marking lines on cloth or removing grease spots.
**French Community,** a political union comprising France and its overseas departments and territories, and six other fully independent member states, Senegal, Gabon, Congo, Central African Republic, Chad, and Malagasy Republic.
**French cuff,** a shirt-sleeve cuff turned back on itself and fastened with a link.
**French doors,** two adjoining doors with glass panes from top to bottom, hinged at opposite sides of a doorway and opening in the middle.
**French dressing,** a salad dressing made of vinegar, oil, and various seasonings.
**French fried,** fried in very hot, deep fat until crisp: French fried potatoes (colloquially **French fries**) are first cut lengthwise into strips.
**French Guiana,** a French overseas department in N South America.
**French horn,** a brass-wind instrument with a long, coiled tube ending in a wide, flaring bell.

FRENCH HORN

**French·i·fy** (fren′chə-fī′), *v.t.* & *v.i.* [-FIED, -FYING], to make or become French or like the French in customs, ideas, manners, etc.
**French Indochina,** Indochina (sense 2): the former name.
**French leave,** an unauthorized or unceremonious departure; act of leaving secretly or in haste.
**French Revolution,** the revolution of the people against the monarchy in France: it began in 1789, resulted in the establishment of a republic, and ended in 1799 with the Consulate.
**French Somaliland,** a French overseas territory in E Africa, on the Gulf of Aden.
**French toast,** sliced bread dipped in a batter of egg and milk and then fried.
**French windows,** a pair of long casement windows hinged at opposite sides of a window frame so that they open in the middle.
**fre·net·ic** (frə-net′ik), *adj.* [see PHRENETIC], frantic; frenzied. *n.* a frantic person. —**fre·net′i·cal·ly,** *adv.*
**fren·zy** (fren′zi), *n.* [*pl.* -ZIES], [< OFr. < LL. < L. *phrenesis;* ult. < Gr. *phrenitis,* madness < *phrēn,* mind], wild excitement; brief delirium that is almost insanity. *v.t.* [-ZIED, -ZYING], to make frantic; drive mad. —**fren′zied,** *adj.*
**freq.,** 1. frequent. 2. frequentative.
**fre·quen·cy** (frē′kwən-si), *n.* [*pl.* -CIES], 1. frequent occurrence. 2. the number of times any action or occurrence is repeated in a given period. 3. in *physics, a*) the number of vibrations or cycles per unit of time. *b*) the number of cycles per second of an alternating electric current. 4. in *statistics,* the ratio of the number of individuals occurring in a specific class to the total number of individuals under survey. Also **fre′quence.**
**frequency modulation,** 1. the changing of the frequency of the transmitting radio wave in accordance with the sound being broadcast. 2.

broadcasting that uses this, characterized by freedom from static. Abbrev. **FM, F.M.** Distinguished from *amplitude modulation.*

**fre·quent** (frē′kwənt; *for v.*, fri-kwent′), *adj.* [Fr. < L. *frequens*, crowded], 1. occurring often; happening repeatedly at brief intervals. 2. constant; habitual. *v.t.* to go to constantly; be at or in habitually. —**fre′quen·ta′tion,** *n.* —**fre·quent′er,** *n.* —**fre′quent·ly,** *adv.*

**fre·quen·ta·tive** (fri-kwen′tə-tiv), *adj.* in *grammar*, expressing frequent and repeated action. *n.* in *grammar*, a frequentative verb: *prickle* is a frequentative of *prick.*

‡**frère** (frâr), *n.* [Fr.], 1. a brother. 2. a friar.

**fres·co** (fres′kō), *n.* [*pl.* -COES, -COS], [It., fresh < OHG. *frisc*], 1. the art of painting with water colors on wet plaster. 2. a painting or design so made. *v.t.* to paint in fresco. —**in fresco,** with water colors on wet plaster. —**fres′co·er,** *n.*

**fresh** (fresh), *adj.* [AS. *fersc;* infl. by OFr. *freis, fresche* < same Gmc. base], 1. recently made, obtained, or grown: as, *fresh* coffee. 2. not salted, preserved, etc. 3. not spoiled or stale. 4. not tired; vigorous; lively. 5. not worn, faded, etc.; bright; clean. 6. youthful or healthy in appearance. 7. new; recent; not known before. 8. additional; further: as, a *fresh* start. 9. inexperienced; untutored. 10. cool and refreshing: as, a *fresh* spring day. 11. brisk; strong: said of the wind. 12. not salt: said of water. 13. giving milk because having borne a calf: said of a cow. —**fresh out of,** [Slang], having just sold or used up. —**fresh′ly,** *adv.* —**fresh′ness,** *n.*

**fresh** (fresh), *adj.* [< G. *frech*, bold], [Slang], saucy; impertinent; impudent.

**fresh·en** (fresh′ən), *v.t.* to make fresh. *v.i.* to become fresh. —**fresh′en·er,** *n.*

**fresh·et** (fresh′it), *n.* 1. a rush of fresh water flowing into the sea. 2. a flooding of a stream because of melting snow or heavy rain.

**fresh·man** (fresh′mən), *n.* [*pl.* -MEN], 1. a beginner. 2. a first-year student in a high school or college. *adj.* of or for first-year students.

**fresh-wa·ter** (fresh′wô′tẽr, -wät′ẽr), *adj.* 1. of or living in water that is not salty. 2. sailing only on inland waters, not on the sea; hence, 3. unskilled. 4. inland, provincial, etc.

**Fres·no** (frez′nō), *n.* a city in central California: pop., 134,000.

**fret** (fret), *v.t.* [FRETTED, FRETTING], [AS. *fretan*, to eat up], 1. to wear away by gnawing, rubbing, rusting, etc. 2. to make by wearing away. 3. to make rough; disturb. 4. to irritate; vex; worry. *v.i.* 1. to gnaw (*into, on,* or *upon*). 2. to become corroded, worn, etc. 3. to become rough or disturbed. 4. to be irritated, vexed, etc.; worry. *n.* 1. a wearing away. 2. a worn place. 3. irritation; worry. —**fret′ter,** *n.*

**fret** (fret), *n.* [? < OFr. *frete*, interlaced work & AS. *frætwa*, ornament], an ornamental pattern of straight bars joining one another at right angles to form a regular design. *v.t.* [FRETTED, FRETTING], to ornament with fretwork.

**fret** (fret), *n.* [Fr., a band], any of the lateral ridges on the finger board of a banjo, guitar, etc. to regulate the fingering. *v.t.* [FRETTED, FRETTING], to furnish with frets. —**fret′ted,** *adj.*

**fret·ful** (fret′fəl), *adj.* tending to fret; peevish. —**fret′ful·ly,** *adv.* —**fret′ful·ness,** *n.*

**fret·work** (fret′wũrk′), *n.* work ornamented with frets; decorative carving or openwork.

**Freud, Sigmund** (froid), 1856-1939; Austrian psychiatrist; founder of psychoanalysis.

**Freud·i·an** (froi′di-ən), *adj.* of or according to Freud or his theories and practice. *n.* one who believes in Freud's theories or uses his methods. See **psychoanalysis.** —**Freud′i·an·ism,** *n.*

**Fri.,** Friday.

**fri·a·ble** (frī′ə-b′l), *adj.* [< Fr. < L. *friabilis* < *friare*, to rub], easily crumbled into powder. —**fri′a·bil′i·ty, fri′a·ble·ness,** *n.*

**fri·ar** (frī′ẽr), *n.* [< OFr. *frere* < L. *frater*, brother], in the *R.C. Church*, a member of any of several religious orders, especially those living as mendicant traveling ministers.

**fri·ar·y** (frī′ẽr-i), *n.* [*pl.* -IES], 1. a monastery where friars live. 2. a brotherhood of friars.

**fric·as·see** (frik′ə-sē′), *n.* [< Fr. < *fricasser*, to cut up and fry], meat cut into pieces, stewed or fried, and served in a sauce of its own gravy. *v.t.* [-SEED, -SEEING], to prepare as a fricassee.

**fric·a·tive** (frik′ə-tiv), *adj.* [< L. pp. of *fricare*, to rub; + *-ive*], formed and pronounced by forcing the breath through a narrow opening between the teeth, lips, etc.: said of certain consonants, as *f, s, v,* and *z.* *n.* a fricative consonant.

**fric·tion** (frik′shən), *n.* [Fr. < L. pp. of *fricare*, to rub], 1. a rubbing, especially of one object against another. 2. conflict because of differences of opinion, temperament, etc. 3. the resistance to motion of surfaces that touch. —**fric′tion·al,** *adj.* —**fric′tion·al·ly,** *adv.* —**fric′tion·less,** *adj.*

**Fri·day** (frī′di), *n.* [AS. *frigedæg*, lit., day of the goddess *Frig*, wife of Woden], 1. the sixth day of the week. 2. the devoted servant of Robinson Crusoe. 3. a faithful follower or helper: usually **man** (or **girl**) **Friday.**

**fried** (frīd), pt. and pp. of **fry.** *adj.* 1. cooked by frying. 2. [Slang], drunk; intoxicated.

**fried·cake** (frīd′kāk′), *n.* a small cake fried in deep fat; doughnut or cruller.

**friend** (frend), *n.* [AS. *freond*], 1. a person whom one knows well and is fond of; close acquaintance. 2. a person on the same side in a struggle; ally: opposed to *foe.* 3. a supporter or sympathizer: as, a *friend* of labor. 4. [F-], a member of the Society of Friends; Quaker. —**be** (or **make**) **friends with,** to be (or become) a friend of. —**friend′less,** *adj.* —**friend′less·ness,** *n.*

**friend·ly** (frend′li), *adj.* [-LIER, -LIEST], 1. like, characteristic of, or suitable for a friend or friendship; kindly. 2. not hostile; amicable. 3. supporting; helping; favorable. 4. desiring friendship. *adv.* in a friendly manner; amicably. —**friend′li·ly,** *adv.* —**friend′li·ness,** *n.*

**friend·ship** (frend′ship), *n.* 1. the state of being friends. 2. friendly feeling or attitude.

**fri·er** (frī′ẽr), *n.* a fryer.

**Frie·sian** (frē′zhən), *adj.* & *n.* Frisian.

**Fries·land** (frēz′lənd, -land′), *n.* a province of the N Netherlands, on the North Sea.

**frieze** (frēz), *n.* [< Fr. < ML. *frisium* < Frank.], 1. a decoration forming an ornamental band around a room, mantel, etc. 2. a horizontal band, usually decorated with sculpture, between the architrave and cornice of a building.

**frieze** (frēz), *n.* [Fr. & MD. *frise*], a heavy wool cloth with a shaggy, uncut nap on one side.

**frig·ate** (frig′it), *n.* [< Fr. < It. *fregata*], a fast, medium-sized sailing warship of the 18th and early 19th centuries.

**frigate bird,** a strong-winged tropical sea bird that robs other birds of their prey.

**fright** (frīt), *n.* [AS. *fyrhto, fryhto*], 1. sudden fear or terror; alarm. 2. [Colloq.], an ugly, ridiculous, or startling person or thing. *v.t.* [Rare & Poetic], to frighten; terrify.

**fright·en** (frīt′'n), *v.t.* 1. to cause to feel fright; make suddenly afraid; scare. 2. to make go (*away* or *into* a specified condition) or to force (*out* or *off*) by frightening. *v.i.* to become suddenly afraid. —**fright′ened,** *adj.* —**fright′en·er,** *n.* —**fright′en·ing·ly,** *adv.*

**fright·ful** (frīt′fəl), *adj.* 1. causing fright; alarming. 2. shocking; disgusting. 3. [Colloq.], *a)* unpleasant; annoying. *b)* great: as, a *frightful* bore. —**fright′ful·ly,** *adv.* —**fright′ful·ness,** *n.*

**frig·id** (frij′id), *adj.* [< L. < *frigus*, coldness], 1. extremely cold. 2. without warmth of feeling or manner; stiff and formal. 3. habitually unaroused sexually: said of women. —**fri·gid′i·ty, frig′id·ness,** *n.* —**frig′id·ly,** *adv.*

**Frigid Zone,** the Arctic (or Antarctic) Zone.

**fri·jol, fri·jole** (frē′hōl), *n.* [*pl.* -JOLES (-hōlz; Sp. frē-hō′les)], [Sp. *fríjol, fréjol*], any bean cultivated for food, especially in Mexico and the Southwest.

**frill** (fril), *n.* [? < OFr. *fresel*, dim. of *fraise*, a ruff], 1. a fringe of hair or feathers around the neck of a bird or animal. 2. [Colloq.], any unnecessary ornament; thing added only for show. 3. a ruffle. *v.t.* to decorate with a ruffle. —**frill′er,** *n.* —**frill′y** [-IER, -IEST], *adj.*

**fringe** (frinj), *n.* [< OFr. < L. *fimbria*], 1. a border or trimming of cords or threads, hanging loose or tied in bunches at the top. 2. an outer edge; border; margin. *v.t.* [FRINGED, FRINGING], 1. to decorate with or as with fringe. 2. to be a fringe for; line: as, trees *fringed* the lawn. —**fringe′less,** *adj.* —**fringe′like′,** *adj.* —**frin′gy,** *adj.*

**frip·per·y** (frip′ẽr-i), *n.* [*pl.* -IES], [< Fr. < OFr. < *frepe*, a rag], 1. cheap, gaudy clothes; tawdry finery. 2. showy display in dress, manners, speech, etc.; affectation of elegance.

**Fris·co** (fris′kō), *n.* [Colloq.], San Francisco.

**fri·sé** (fri-zā′), *n.* [Fr. < *friser*, to curl], a type of upholstery fabric with a thick pile of loops, some of which are sometimes cut to form a design.

**Fri·sian** (frizh′ən, -i-ən), *adj.* of Friesland, the Frisian Islands, their people, or their language. *n.* 1. a native or inhabitant of Friesland or the Frisian Islands. 2. the Low German language of the Frisians. Abbrev. **Fris.**

**Frisian Islands,** a chain of islands in the North Sea off the coast of the Netherlands and Germany.

**frisk** (frisk), *adj.* [OFr. *frisque;* prob. < OHG. *frisc*], [Obs.], frisky. *n.* a frolic; gambol. *v.t.* 1. to move in a playful, lively manner. 2. [Slang], to search (a person) for weapons, stolen articles, etc. by passing the hands quickly over his clothing. 3. [Slang], to steal something from (a person) thus. *v.i.* to frolic; gambol. —**frisk'er,** *n.*

**frisk·y** (fris'ki), *adj.* [-IER, -IEST], lively; frolicsome. —**frisk'i·ly,** *adv.* —**frisk'i·ness,** *n.*

**frith** (frith), *n.* [var. of *firth*], a firth.

**frit·il·lar·y** (frit'ə-ler'i), *n.* [*pl.* -IES], [< L. *fritillus,* dice box: from markings on the petals or wings], 1. a plant of the lily family, with spotted, bell-shaped flowers. 2. any of a large group of butterflies having spotted wings.

**frit·ter** (frit'ẽr), *n.* [< OFr. < L. *fractura;* see FRACTURE], [Rare], a small piece; shred. *v.t.* 1. [Rare], to break, cut, or tear into small pieces. 2. to waste (money, time, etc.) bit by bit on petty things. —**frit'ter·er,** *n.*

**frit·ter** (frit'ẽr), *n.* [< Fr. *friture* < LL. *frigere,* to fry], a small cake of fried batter, usually containing corn, fruit, or other filling.

**fri·vol·i·ty** (fri-vol'ə-ti), *n.* 1. a frivolous quality. 2. [*pl.* -TIES], a frivolous act or thing.

**friv·o·lous** (friv'ə-ləs), *adj.* [L. *frivolus*], 1. trifling; trivial; paltry. 2. not properly serious or sensible; silly and light-minded; giddy. —**friv'o·lous·ly,** *adv.* —**friv'o·lous·ness,** *n.*

**friz, frizz** (friz), *v.t. & v.i.* [FRIZZED, FRIZZING], [Fr. *friser*], 1. to form into small, tight curls: said of hair. 2. to form into small tufts, as the nap of cloth. *n.* something frizzed, as hair.

**friz·zle** (friz''l), *v.t. & v.i.* [-ZLED, -ZLING], [prob. < *fry*], 1. to make or cause to make a sputtering, hissing noise, as in frying; sizzle. 2. to make or become crisp by broiling or frying.

**friz·zle** (friz''l), *v.t. & v.i.* [-ZLED, -ZLING], [prob. < *friz* + *-le,* freq. suffix], to friz (sense 1). *n.* a small, tight curl. —**friz'zler,** *n.*

**friz·zly** (friz'li), *adj.* full of or covered with small, tight curls.

**friz·zy** (friz'i), *adj.* frizzly. —**friz'zi·ly,** *adv.* —**friz'zi·ness,** *n.*

**fro** (frō), *adv.* [< ON. *frā*], backward; back: now only in *to and fro. prep.* [Scot.], from. —**to and fro,** forward and backward; back and forth.

**frock** (frok), *n.* [< OFr. < ML. < OHG. *hroc,* a cloak], 1. *a*) a robe worn by friars, monks, etc. *b*) the office of a priest, etc. 2. any of various other garments; specif., *a*) a smock. *b*) a dress; gown. *c*) a frock coat. *v.t.* to clothe in a frock. —**frock'less,** *adj.*

**frock coat,** a man's double-breasted dress coat with a full skirt reaching to the knees, worn chiefly in the 19th century.

**frog** (frôg, frog), *n.* [AS. *frogga*], 1. *a*) a small, four-legged, leaping animal with webbed feet and no tail: it can live either in water or on land. *b*) an animal like this, as a tree frog. 2. a horny pad in the sole of a horse's foot. 3. a corded or braided loop used as a fastener or decoration on clothing. 4. a device on railroad tracks for keeping cars on the proper rails at intersections or switches. —**frog in the throat,** hoarseness due to throat irritation.

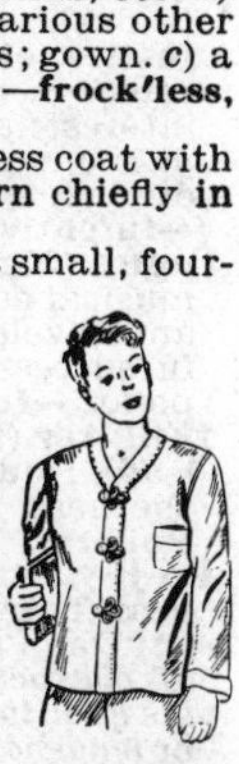
FROGS ON JACKET

**frog·gy** (frôg'i, frog'i), *adj.* [-GIER, -GIEST], 1. of or like a frog. 2. full of frogs.

**Frois·sart, Jean** (zhän frwȧ'sȧr'; Eng. froi'särt), 1333?–1400?; French historian and poet.

**frol·ic** (frol'ik), *adj.* [< D. < MD. *vrō,* merry], full of fun and pranks; gay; merry. *n.* 1. a gay trick. 2. a gay party or game. 3. merriment; fun. *v.i.* [-ICKED, -ICKING], to make merry; have fun; play. —**frol'ick·er,** *n.*

**frol·ic·some** (frol'ik-səm), *adj.* full of gaiety or high spirits; playful; merry: also **frol'ick·y.**

**from** (frum, from; *unstressed* frəm), *prep.* [AS. *from, fram*], 1. beginning at: as, he walked *from* the door. 2. starting with: as, I stayed *from* three to six. 3. out of: as, he took a comb *from* his pocket. 4. with (a person or thing) as the maker, speaker, source, etc.: as, facts learned *from* reading. 5. at a place not near to: as, keep away *from* me. 6. out of the whole of or alliance with: as, take two *from* four. 7. out of the possibility or use of: as, he kept me *from* going. 8. out of the possession or control of: as, released *from* jail. 9. as not being like: as, I don't know him *from* Adam. 10. by reason of; because of: as, he trembled *from* fear.

**frond** (frond), *n.* [L. *frons,* leafy branch], 1. the leaflike, spore-bearing organ of a fern. 2. the leaflike shoot of a lichen, seaweed, etc. 3. [Poetic], a leaf, especially of a palm. —**frond'ed,** *adj.*

**front** (frunt), *n.* [< OFr. < L. *frons,* forehead], 1. outward attitude, behavior, or countenance: as, he puts on a bold *front.* 2. the part of something that faces forward; most important side. 3. first part; beginning. 4. the place or position directly before a person or thing. 5. the first available bellhop, as in a hotel. 6. the land bordering a lake, ocean, street, etc. 7. the advanced area of contact between opposing sides in warfare. 8. a broad movement in which different groups are united for the achievement of common political or social aims. 9. one who serves as a public representative of a business, group, etc., as because of his prestige. 10. a person or group whose work or reputation serves to obscure its real objectives. 11. a stiff shirt bosom, worn with formal clothes. 12. [Colloq.], an appearance, usually pretended, of social standing, wealth, etc. 13. a face of a building; esp., the face with the principal entrance. 14. in *meteorology,* the boundary between two masses of air that are different, as in density. *adj.* 1. at, to, in, on, or of the front. 2. in *phonetics,* articulated with the front of the tongue, as *i* (in *bid*) and *e* (in *met*). *v.t.* 1. to face; be opposite to. 2. to be before in place. 3. to meet; confront. 4. to defy; oppose. *v.i.* 1. to face in a certain direction. 2. to be a front (sense 9): with *for.* —**in front of,** before.

**front·age** (frun'tij), *n.* 1. the front part of a building. 2. the direction toward which this faces. 3. the land between the front edge of a building and the street. 4. *a*) the front boundary line of a lot. *b*) the length of this line. 5. land bordering a street, river, etc.

**fron·tal** (frun't'l), *adj.* 1. of, in, on, or at the front. 2. of or for the forehead. *n.* the bone of the forehead. —**fron'tal·ly,** *adv.*

**fron·tier** (frun-têr', fron'têr), *n.* [< OFr. < *front;* see FRONT], 1. that part of a country which borders on another country. 2. that part of a settled country which lies next to an unexplored region. 3. any new or incompletely investigated field of learning, etc.: as, the *frontiers* of medicine. *adj.* of, on, or near the frontier.

**fron·tiers·man** (frun-têrz'mən), *n.* [*pl.* -MEN], a man who lives on the frontier.

**fron·tis·piece** (frun'tis-pēs', fron'-), *n.* [OFr. < ML. *frontispicium,* front view < L. *frons,* front + *specere,* to look], 1. an illustration facing the first page or title page of a book or division of a book. 2. in *architecture, a*) the main façade. *b*) a small pediment over a door, window, etc.

**front·let** (frunt'lit), *n.* [< OFr.; ult. < L. *frons,* front], a band or fillet worn on the forehead.

**front-page** (frunt'pāj'), *adj.* fit to be printed on the front page of a newspaper; important.

**frost** (frôst, frost), *n.* [AS. < *freosan* (see FREEZE)], 1. a freezing or being frozen. 2. temperature below the freezing point of water. 3. frozen dew or vapor; hoarfrost. 4. coolness of action, feeling, etc. 5. [Slang], a failure. *v.t.* 1. to cover with frost. 2. to damage or kill by freezing. 3. to cover with frosting. —**frost'less,** *adj.* —**frost'like',** *adj.*

**Frost, Robert Lee** (frôst, frost), 1874–1963; U.S. poet.

**frost·bite** (frôst'bīt', frost'-), *v.t.* [-BIT, -BITTEN, -BITING], to injure the tissues of (a part of the body) by exposure to intense cold. *n.* injury caused by such exposure. —**frost'bit'ten,** *adj.*

**frost·ing** (frôs'tiŋ, fros'-), *n.* 1. a mixture of sugar, butter, eggs, etc., for covering a cake; icing. 2. a dull, frostlike finish on glass, metal, etc.

**frost·y** (frôs'ti, fros'-), *adj.* [-IER, -IEST], 1. cold enough to produce frost; freezing. 2. covered as with frost. 3. cold in manner or feeling; unfriendly. 4. having gray hair. 5. *a*) old. *b*) of or like old age. —**frost'i·ly,** *adv.* —**frost'i·ness,** *n.*

**froth** (frôth, froth), *n.* [ON. *frotha*], 1. foam. 2. foaming saliva, as in disease or great excitement. 3. any light, trifling, or worthless thing. *v.t.* 1. to cause to foam. 2. to cover with foam. 3. to spill forth as foam. *v.i.* to foam.

**froth·y** (frôth'i, froth'i), *adj.* [-IER, -IEST], 1. foamy. 2. light; trifling; worthless. —**froth'i·ly,** *adv.*

**frou·frou** (frōō'frōō'), *n.* [Fr.; echoic], 1. a rustling or swishing, as of a skirt. 2. [Colloq.], excessive or affected elegance, fanciness, etc.

**frou·zy, frou·sy** (frou'zi), *adj.* frowzy.

**fro·ward** (frō'ẽrd, -wẽrd), *adj.* [< *fro* + *-ward*], not easily controlled; stubbornly willful; contrary. **—fro'ward·ly,** *adv.* **—fro'ward·ness,** *n.*

**frown** (froun), *v.i.* [< OFr. *frognier;* prob. < Gmc.], 1. to contract the brows, as in sternness, displeasure, or concentration. 2. to look with disapproval (*on* or *upon*). *v.t.* to express (disapproval, etc.) by contracting the brows. *n.* 1. a contracting of the brows in sternness, thought, etc. 2. any expression of displeasure or disapproval. **—frown'er,** *n.* **—frown'ing·ly,** *adv.*

**frow·zy** (frou'zi), *adj.* [-ZIER, -ZIEST], [prob. akin to or < Brit. dial. *frowsty,* musty], 1. [Rare], bad-smelling; musty. 2. dirty and untidy; slovenly; unkempt. Also sp. **frowsy. —frow'zi·ly, frow'si·ly,** *adv.* **—frow'zi·ness, frow'si·ness,** *n.*

**froze** (frōz), pt. of **freeze.**

**fro·zen** (frō'z'n), pp. of **freeze.** *adj.* 1. turned into or covered with ice. 2. damaged or killed by freezing. 3. having heavy frosts and extreme cold: as, the *frozen* polar wastes. 4. as if turned into ice: as, *frozen* with terror. 5. without warmth or affection. 6. prohibited in sale or exchange; not marketable as because of legal restrictions. **—fro'zen·ly,** *adv.* **—fro'zen·ness,** *n.*

**frozen custard,** a food like ice cream, but with less butterfat content and of a looser consistency.

**frs.,** francs.

**frt.,** freight.

**fruc·ti·fy** (fruk'tə-fī'), *v.i.* [-FIED, -FYING], [< OFr. < L. *fructificare;* see FRUIT & -FY], to bear fruit; become fruitful. *v.t.* to cause to bear fruit; fertilize. **—fruc'ti·fi·ca'tion,** *n.*

**fruc·tose** (fruk'tōs, frook'-), *n.* [< L. *fructus,* fruit; + *-ose*], a crystalline sugar, $C_6H_{12}O_6$, found in sweet fruits and in honey: also called *fruit sugar, levulose.*

**fru·gal** (frōō'g'l), *adj.* [L. *frugalis* < *frugi,* fit for food < *frux,* fruits], 1. not wasteful; thrifty; economical. 2. *a*) not costly; inexpensive. *b*) sparingly provided: as, a *frugal* meal. **—fru'gal·ly,** *adv.* **—fru·gal'i·ty** (-gal'ə-ti), [*pl.* -TIES], **fru'gal·ness,** *n.*

**fruit** (frōōt), *n.* [see PLURAL, II, D, 3], [OFr. < L. *fructus* < pp. of *frui,* to enjoy], 1. *usually in pl.* any plant product, as grain, flax, vegetables, etc. 2. the edible part of a plant or tree, consisting of the seeds and pulpy surrounding tissues: often distinguished from *vegetable.* 3. the result or product of any action: as, prosperity is the *fruit* of planning. 4. [Archaic], offspring. 5. in *botany,* the mature ovary of a plant or tree, including the seed and its envelope, as an apple, pea pod, etc. *v.i.* to produce or bear fruit. *v.t.* to cause to bear fruit. **—fruit'like',** *adj.*

**fruit·age** (frōōt'ij), *n.* 1. the bearing of fruit. 2. a crop of fruit. 3. a result; product.

**fruit·cake** (frōōt'kāk'), *n.* a rich cake containing nuts, preserved fruit, citron, spices, etc.

**fruit·er** (frōōt'ẽr), *n.* 1. a tree that bears fruit. 2. a ship for transporting fruit.

**fruit·er·er** (frōōt'ẽr-ẽr), *n.* [Chiefly Brit.], a person who deals in fruit.

**fruit fly,** 1. a small fly whose larvae feed on fruits and vegetables. 2. the drosophila.

**fruit·ful** (frōōt'fəl), *adj.* 1. bearing much fruit. 2. producing much; productive; fertile. 3. producing results; profitable: as, a *fruitful* scheme. **—fruit'ful·ly,** *adv.* **—fruit'ful·ness,** *n.*

**fru·i·tion** (frōō-ish'ən), *n.* [OFr. < L. < pp. of *fruire,* to use, enjoy], 1. a pleasure obtained from using or possessing something. 2. the bearing of fruit. 3. a coming to fulfillment; realization.

**fruit·less** (frōōt'lis), *adj.* 1. without results; unsuccessful; vain. 2. bearing no fruit; sterile. **—fruit'less·ly,** *adv.* **—fruit'less·ness,** *n.*

**fruit sugar,** fructose: also called *levulose.*

**fruit·y** (frōōt'i), *adj.* [-IER, -IEST], 1. like fruit in taste or smell. 2. [Colloq.], rich in interest; spicy; juicy. **—fruit'i·ness,** *n.*

**frump** (frump), *n.* [< D. *frompelen* < *rompelen,* to rumple], a dowdy, sometimes ill-tempered, woman.

**frump·ish** (frump'ish), *adj.* dowdy, and sometimes ill-tempered. **—frump'ish·ly,** *adv.* **—frump'ish·ness,** *n.*

**frump·y** (frump'i), *adj.* [-IER, -IEST], frumpish. **—frump'i·ly,** *adv.* **—frump'i·ness,** *n.*

**frus·trate** (frus'trāt), *v.t.* [-TRATED, -TRATING], [< L. pp. of *frustrare* < *frustra,* in vain], 1. to cause to have no effect; nullify: as, he *frustrated* our plans. 2. to keep from an objective; baffle; foil: as, he *frustrated* his enemies. 3. in *psychology,* to prevent from gratifying certain impulses and desires. **—frus'trat·er,** *n.* **—frus·tra'tion,** *n.*

**frus·tum** (frus'təm), *n.* [*pl.* -TUMS, -TA (-tə)], [L, a piece, bit], the solid figure formed when the top of a cone or pyramid is cut off by a plane parallel to the base.

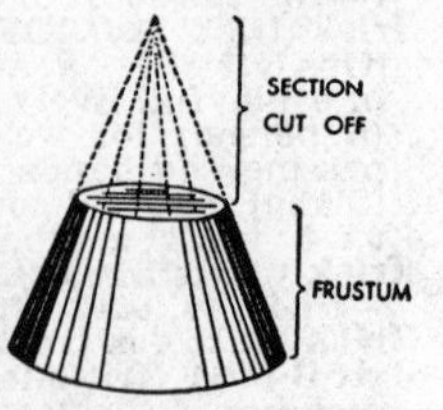


FRUSTUM

**fry** (frī), *v.t. & v.i.* [FRIED, FRYING], [< OFr. < L. *frigere,* to fry], to cook or be cooked in hot fat or oil over direct heat. *n.* [*pl.* FRIES], 1. a dish of fried food, especially meat. 2. a social gathering, usually outdoors, at which food is fried and eaten: as, a fish *fry.*

**fry** (frī), *n.* [*pl.* FRY], [a merging of ON. *frio,* seed, with Anglo-Fr. *frei,* spawn], 1. young fish. 2. small adult fish, especially when in large groups. 3. young; offspring; children. **—small fry,** 1. children. 2. unimportant people or things.

**fry·er** (frī'ẽr), *n.* 1. a person or thing that fries. 2. food to be cooked by frying; esp., a young, tender chicken. Also sp. **frier.**

**ft.,** 1. foot; feet. 2. fort. 3. fortification.

**FTC, F.T.C.,** Federal Trade Commission.

**fth., fthm.,** fathom.

**fub** (fub), *v.t.* [FUBBED, FUBBING], to fob (trick).

**fuch·si·a** (fū'shə, -shi-ə), *n.* [after L. *Fuchs,* 16th-c. G. botanist], 1. a shrubby plant of the evening primrose family, with pink, red, or purple flowers. 2. purplish red. *adj.* purplish-red.

**fud·dle** (fud''l), *v.t.* [-DLED, -DLING], [? < D. or LG. via thieves' slang], to muddle, confuse, or stupefy as with alcoholic liquor. *n.* a fuddled condition.

**fud·dy-dud·dy** (fud'i-dud'i), *n.* [*pl.* -DIES], [? < *fuddle*], [Slang], 1. a fussy, critical person. 2. an old-fashioned person.

**fudge** (fuj), *n.* [? < an echoic interj.], 1. empty talk; nonsense. 2. a soft candy made of butter, milk, sugar, flavoring, etc. *interj.* nonsense! *v.t.* [FUDGED, FUDGING], to make or put together dishonestly or carelessly; fake.

**fu·el** (fū''l), *n.* [< OFr. *fouaille;* ult. < L. *focus,* fireplace], 1. coal, oil, gas, wood, etc., burned to supply heat or power. 2. anything that maintains or intensifies strong feeling. *v.t.* [-ELED or -ELLED, -ELING or -ELLING], to supply with fuel. *v.i.* to get fuel. **—fu'el·er, fu'el·ler,** *n.*

**-fuge** (fūj), [Fr. < L. *fugere,* to flee], a suffix meaning *something that drives away,* as in *febrifuge.*

**fu·gi·tive** (fū'jə-tiv), *adj.* [< OFr. < L. pp. of *fugere,* to flee], 1. fleeing or having fled, as from danger, justice, etc. 2. passing quickly; fleeting; evanescent. 3. having to do with matters of temporary interest: as, *fugitive* essays. 4. roaming; shifting. *n.* 1. one who flees or has fled from danger, justice, etc. 2. a thing that is fleeting or hard to grasp. **—fu'gi·tive·ly,** *adv.* **—fu'gi·tive·ness,** *n.*

**fugue** (fūg), *n.* [Fr. < It. < L. < *fugere,* to flee], a musical composition in which a theme is taken up and developed by the various instruments or voices in succession, according to the laws of counterpoint. **—fugue'like',** *adj.* **—fu·guist** (fū'gist), *n.*

‡**Füh·rer** (fü'rẽr; Eng. fyoor'ẽr), *n.* [G. < *führen,* to lead], leader: the title assumed by Adolf Hitler as the head of Nazi Germany (1933–1945): also sp. **Fuehrer.**

**Fu·ji·ya·ma** (fōō'jē-yä'mä), *n.* a volcanic mountain near Tokyo, Japan: also **Fu'ji.**

**-ful** (fəl, f'l), [< *full, adj.*], a suffix meaning: 1. *full of, characterized by, having,* as in *joyful.* 2. *having the qualities of,* as in *masterful.* 3. *having the ability* or *tendency to,* as in *helpful.* 4. *the quantity that will fill,* as in *handful.*

**ful·crum** (ful'krəm), *n.* [*pl.* -CRUMS, -CRA (-krə)], [L. < *fulcire,* to prop], 1. the support or point of support on which a lever turns in raising or moving something. 2. a means of exerting influence, pressure, etc.

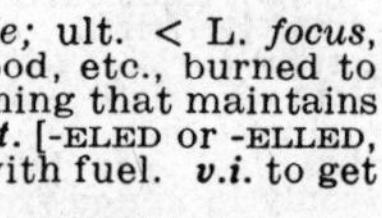


FULCRUM OF A LEVER

**ful·fill, ful·fil** (fool-fil'), *v.t.* [-FILLED, -FILLING], [AS. *full-fyllan*], 1. to carry out (something promised, predicted, etc.); cause to be or happen. 2. to do (something required); obey. 3. to answer (a purpose); satisfy (a condition). 4. to bring to an end; complete. **—fulfill oneself,** to realize completely one's ambitions, potentialities, etc. **—ful·fill'er,** *n.* **—ful·fill'ment, ful·fil'ment,** *n.*

**ful·gent** (ful'jənt), *adj.* [< L. ppr. of *fulgere,* to flash], [Poetic], very bright; glittering; radiant. **—ful'gent·ly,** *adv.*

**full** (fool), *adj.* [AS.], 1. having in it all there is space for; filled: as, a *full* pail. 2. having eaten all that one wants. 3. occupying all of a given space: as, a *full* load. 4. well supplied or provided with: as, woods *full* of game. 5. filling the required number, measure, etc.; complete: as, a *full* dozen. 6. having reached the greatest development, size, etc.: as, a *full* moon. 7. entirely visible: as, a *full* view. 8. having clearness, volume, and depth: as, a *full* tone. 9. plump; round; chubby: as, a *full* face. 10. with loose, wide folds; with plenty of material: as, a *full* skirt. *n.* the greatest amount, extent, number, etc. *adv.* 1. completely; to the greatest degree: as, a *full*-grown boy. 2. directly; exactly: as, struck *full* in the face. *v.t.* & *v.i.* to have, or make with, loose folds; gather, as a skirt. —**full many,** [Archaic & Poetic], very many. —**full of,** 1. filled by or with. 2. having had all that one wants of. 3. occupied or engrossed with. —**full well,** very well. —**in full,** 1. to, for, or with the full amount, value, etc. 2. not abbreviated, as a name.

**full** (fool), *v.t.* & *v.i.* [< OFr. < LL. < L. *fullo*, cloth fuller], to clean, shrink, and thicken (cloth) using moisture, heat, and pressure.

**full·back** (fool′bak′), *n.* in *football*, one of the backs, originally the one farthest behind the scrimmage line.

**full-blood·ed** (fool′blud′id), *adj.* 1. vigorous; lusty. 2. of unmixed breed or race; thoroughbred.

**full-blown** (fool′blōn′), *adj.* 1. in full bloom: said of flowers. 2. fully developed; matured.

**full-bod·ied** (fool′bod′id), *adj.* having a rich flavor and much strength: as, a *full-bodied* wine.

**full dress,** formal clothes worn on important occasions; esp., formal evening clothes. —**full′-dress′,** *adj.*

**full·er** (fool′ẽr), *n.* one whose work is to full cloth.

**full·er's earth** (fool′ẽrz), a highly absorbent, claylike substance used to remove grease from woolen cloth in fulling, to purify oil, etc.

**full-fash·ioned** (fool′fash′′nd), *adj.* knitted to conform to the shape of the foot and leg.

**full-fledged** (fool′flejd′), *adj.* completely developed or trained; of full rank or status.

**full-grown** (fool′grōn′), *adj.* fully grown.

**full house,** a poker hand containing three cards of one denomination and a pair of another.

**full moon,** the moon seen as a circle when its whole disk reflects the sun's light.

**full·ness, ful·ness** (fool′nis), *n.* the quality or state of being full.

**full·y** (fool′i), *adv.* 1. to the full; completely; entirely. 2. exactly. 3. abundantly; amply. 4. at least: as, there were *fully* 200 people there.

**ful·mi·nate** (ful′mə-nāt′), *v.i.* [-NATED, -NATING], [< L. pp. of *fulminare* < *fulmen*, lightning], 1. [Rare], to thunder and lighten. 2. to explode with violence; detonate. 3. to shout forth denunciations, decrees, etc. *v.t.* 1. to cause to explode. 2. to shout forth (decrees, etc.). *n.* any highly explosive compound. —**ful′mi·na′tion,** *n.* —**ful′mi·na′tor,** *n.* —**ful′mi·na·to′ry** (-nə-tôr′i, -tō′ri), *adj.*

**ful·some** (fool′səm, ful′-), *adj.* [see FULL, *adj.* & -SOME; but infl. by *foul*], disgusting or offensive, especially because of excess or insincerity: as, *fulsome* flattery. —**ful′some·ly,** *adv.* —**ful′some·ness,** *n.*

**Ful·ton, Robert** (fool′t'n), 1765–1815; U.S. inventor: designed first successful American steamboat.

**fum·ble** (fum′b'l), *v.i.* & *v.t.* [-BLED, -BLING], [? < ON. *famla*, to grope], 1. to grope clumsily. 2. to handle (a thing) clumsily; bungle. 3. in *football*, etc., to fail to catch, hold, or handle (the ball) properly. *n.* 1. a clumsy groping or handling. 2. a failing to catch, hold, or handle the ball properly. —**fum′bler,** *n.* —**fum′bling·ly,** *adv.*

**fume** (fūm), *n.* [< OFr. < L. *fumus*], 1. a gas, smoke, or vapor, especially if offensive or suffocating. 2. anything imaginary or without substance. 3. [Rare], an outburst of anger, etc. *v.i.* [FUMED, FUMING], 1. to give off fumes. 2. to rise up or pass off in fumes. 3. to show, or give way to, anger, annoyance, etc. *v.t.* to expose to fumes. —**fume′-less,** *adj.* —**fum′er,** *n.* —**fum′ing·ly,** *adv.*

**fu·mi·gate** (fū′mə-gāt′), *v.t.* [-GATED, -GATING], [< L. *fumigatus*, pp. < *fumus*, smoke + *agere*, to make], to expose to the action of fumes, especially in order to disinfect or kill the vermin in. —**fu′mi·ga′tion,** *n.* —**fu′mi·ga′tor,** *n.*

**fum·y** (fūm′i), *adj.* [-IER, -IEST], full of, or producing, fumes. —**fum′i·ly,** *adv.* —**fum′i·ness,** *n.*

**fun** (fun), *n.* [< obs. *v. fon*, to act foolishly], 1. lively, gay play or playfulness; merriment; amusement; sport; joking. 2. a source of amusement. *v.i.* [FUNNED, FUNNING], [Colloq.], to make fun; play or joke. —**for** (or **in**) **fun,** playfully or jokingly. —**like fun,** [Slang], by no means; not at all. —**make fun of,** to ridicule; mock laughingly.

**func·tion** (fuŋk′shən), *n.* [< OFr. < L. *functio* < pp. of *fungi*, to perform], 1. the normal or characteristic action of anything; esp., any of the specialized actions of an organ or part of an animal or plant. 2. a special duty or performance required of a person or thing in the course of work. 3. a formal ceremony or social occasion. 4. a thing that depends on and varies with something else. 5. in *mathematics*, a variable quantity whose value depends on and varies with that of another quantity or quantities. *v.i.* to act in a required manner; work; be used. —**func′tion·less,** *adj.*

**func·tion·al** (fuŋk′shən-'l), *adj.* 1. of a function or functions. 2. performing a function. 3. in *medicine*, affecting a function of some organ without apparent structural or organic changes: as, a *functional* disease. —**func′tion·al·ly,** *adv.*

**func·tion·ar·y** (fuŋk′shən-er′i), *n.* [*pl.* -IES], one who performs a certain function; official.

**fund** (fund), *n.* [L. *fundus*, bottom, land], 1. a supply that can be drawn upon; stock; store: as, a *fund* of good humor. 2. *a)* a sum of money set aside for some particular purpose. *b)* *pl.* ready money. 3. *pl.* [Brit.], a permanent government debt on which interest is paid; public securities (with *the*). *v.t.* 1. to provide money for the payment of interest on (a debt). 2. to put or convert into a long-term debt that bears interest.

**fun·da·ment** (fun′də-mənt), *n.* [< OFr. < L. < *fundus*, the bottom], 1. the buttocks. 2. the anus.

**fun·da·men·tal** (fun′də-men′t'l), *adj.* [< ML. *fundamentalis* < L.; see FUNDAMENT], 1. of or forming a foundation or basis; basic; essential. 2. in *music*, designating or of the lowest, or root, tone of a chord. *n.* 1. a principle, law, etc. serving as a basis; essential part. 2. in *music*, the lowest, or root, tone of a chord. 3. in *physics*, the component having the lowest frequency in a complex vibration. —**fun′da·men·tal′i·ty** (-tal′ə-ti), *n.* —**fun′da·men′tal·ly,** *adv.*

**fun·da·men·tal·ism** (fun′də-men′t'l-iz'm), *n.* [sometimes F-], 1. orthodox religious beliefs based on a literal interpretation of the Bible and regarded as fundamental to Christian faith. 2. among some American Protestants, the movement based on this belief. —**fun′da·men′tal·ist,** *adj.* & *n.*

**Fun·dy, Bay of** (fun′di), an arm of the Atlantic, between New Brunswick and Nova Scotia.

**fu·ner·al** (fū′nẽr-əl), *adj.* [OFr. < ML. *funeralis* < L. *funus*, a funeral], of, like, or suitable for burial or cremation ceremonies. *n.* 1. the ceremonies connected with burial or cremation of the dead. 2. the procession accompanying the body to the place of burial or cremation.

**fu·ne·re·al** (fū-nêr′i-əl), *adj.* suitable for a funeral; sad and solemn; gloomy; dismal. —**fu·ne′re·al·ly,** *adv.*

**fun·gi·cide** (fun′jə-sīd′), *n.* [< *fungus* + *-cide*], any substance that kills fungi. —**fun′gi·cid′al,** *adj.*

**fun·goid** (fuŋ′goid), *adj.* like or characteristic of a fungus. *n.* a fungus.

**fun·gous** (fuŋ′gəs), *adj.* of, like, or caused by a fungus or fungi.

**fun·gus** (fuŋ′gəs), *n.* [*pl.* -GI (fun′jī), -GUSES], [L.; altered < Gr. *sp(h)ongos*, a sponge], 1. any of a group of plants, including mildews, molds, mushrooms, rusts, etc., that have no leaves, flowers, or green color and reproduce by means of spores. 2. something that grows rapidly like a fungus. 3. in *medicine*, a spongy, diseased growth on the body. *adj.* fungous. —**fun′gal,** *adj.* & *n.* —**fun′gus-like′,** *adj.*

**fu·nic·u·lar** (fū-nik′yoo-lẽr), *adj.* [< L. *funiculus*, dim. of *funis*, a rope; + *-ar*], of, worked by, or hanging from a rope or cable. *n.* a mountain railway on which the cars are pulled up and lowered by cables: in full, **funicular railway.**

**funk** (fuŋk), *n.* [? < Fl. *fonck*, dismay], [Colloq.], 1. a cowering through fear; panic. 2. a cowering person. *v.i.* [Colloq.], to be in a funk. *v.t.* [Colloq.], 1. to be afraid of. 2. to shrink from in fear. 3. to frighten.

**fun·nel** (fun′'l), *n.* [< Pr. < L. *(in)fundibulum* < *in-*, in + *fundere*, to pour], 1. a slender tube with a wide, cone-shaped mouth, for pouring liquids and powders into containers with small openings. 2. a thing shaped like a funnel. 3. a cylindrical chimney or smokestack, as of a steamship. 4. a flue. *v.i.* & *v.t.* [-NELED or -NELLED, -NELING or -NELLING], to move or pour through, or as if through, a funnel.

**fun·ny** (fun′i), *adj.* [-NIER, -NIEST], 1. causing laughter; laughable; amusing; humorous. 2. [Colloq.], out of the ordinary; strange; queer. *n.* [*pl.* -NIES], *usually in pl.* [Colloq.], a comic strip. —**fun′ni·ly**, *adv.* —**fun′ni·ness**, *n.*

**funny bone**, [? < pun on *humerus* (*humorous*)], a place on the elbow where the ulnar nerve passes close to the surface: a sharp impact at this place causes a sudden, painful tingling in the arm: also called *crazy bone*.

**fur** (fũr), *n.* [< OFr. *forre*, a sheath < Gmc. *fodr*], 1. the soft, thick hair covering the bodies of certain animals. 2. a skin bearing such hair, processed for use as material. 3. any garment made of such skins. 4. any fuzzy coating, as diseased matter on the tongue. *adj.* of fur. *v.t.* [FURRED, FURRING], 1. to line, cover, or trim with fur. 2. to coat with a deposit. 3. in *architecture*, to put furring on. *v.i.* to become coated with a deposit. —**make the fur fly**, to cause dissension or fighting.

**fur·be·low** (fũr′bə-lō′), *n.* [var. of Fr. *falbala*], 1. a flounce or ruffle. 2. *usually pl.* showy trimming. *v.t.* to decorate with furbelows.

**fur·bish** (fũr′bish) *v.t.* [< OFr. *forbir* < OHG. *furban*, to clean], 1. to brighten by rubbing or scouring; polish; burnish. 2. to put into usable condition again; renovate. —**fur′bish·er**, *n.*

**fur·cate** (fũr′kāt; *also, for adj.*, -kit), *adj.* [< ML. < L. *furca*, a fork], forked. *v.i.* [-CATED, -CATING], to branch; fork. —**fur·ca′tion**, *n.*

**Fu·ries** (fyoor′iz), *n.pl.* in *Gr. & Rom. mythology*, the three female spirits who punished the doers of unavenged crimes: also *Erinyes*, *Eumenides*.

**fu·ri·ous** (fyoor′i-əs), *adj.* [< OFr. < L. < *furia*, fury], 1. full of fury or intense feeling; violent. 2. violently overpowering: as, a *furious* attack. —**fu′ri·ous·ly**, *adv.* —**fu′ri·ous·ness**, *n.*

**furl** (fũrl), *v.t.* [prob. < Fr. *ferler* < OFr. *fermlier* < L. *firmum*, firm + *ligare*, to lay], to roll up tightly and make secure, as a flag to a staff. *v.i.* to become curled or rolled up. *n.* 1. a roll or coil of something furled. 2. a furling or being furled. —**furl′er**, *n.*

**fur·long** (fũr′lôŋ), *n.* [AS. *furlang* < *furh*, a furrow + *lang*, long], a measure of distance equal to 1/8 of a mile, or 220 yards: abbrev. **fur.**

**fur·lough** (fũr′lō), *n.* [< D. *verlof*], a leave of absence; esp., in *military usage*, a leave granted to enlisted personnel. *v.t.* to grant a furlough to.

**fur·nace** (fũr′nis), *n.* [< OFr. < L. *fornax* < *fornus*, oven], 1. an enclosed structure in which heat is produced for heating a building, reducing ores and metals, etc. 2. any extremely hot place.

**fur·nish** (fũr′nish), *v.t.* [< OFr. < *furnir* < Frank. < Gmc.], 1. to equip with whatever is necessary; esp., to put furniture into (a room, apartment, etc.). 2. to supply; provide. —**fur′nish·er**, *n.*

**fur·nish·ings** (fũr′nish-iŋz), *n.pl.* 1. the furniture and fixtures for a room, apartment, etc. 2. articles of dress; things to wear.

**fur·ni·ture** (fũr′ni-chẽr), *n.* [Fr. *fourniture*; see FURNISH], 1. the movable things in a room, etc. which equip it for living, as chairs, beds, etc. 2. the necessary equipment of a ship, trade, etc.

**fu·ror** (fyoor′ôr), *n.* [< Fr. *fureur* & L. *furor*], 1. fury; rage; frenzy. 2. a great, widespread outburst of admiration or enthusiasm; craze; rage.

**furred** (fũrd), *adj.* 1. made, trimmed, or lined with fur. 2. having fur. 3. wearing fur.

**fur·ri·er** (fũr′i-ẽr, fũr′yẽr), *n.* 1. a dealer in furs. 2. one who processes furs or makes and repairs fur garments. —**fur′ri·er·y** [*pl.* -IES], *n.*

**fur·ring** (fũr′iŋ), *n.* 1. the act of trimming, lining, etc. with fur. 2. fur so used. 3. a coating of diseased matter, as on the tongue. 4. the formation of such a coating. 5. in *architecture*, *a*) the leveling of a floor, wall, etc. with thin strips of wood or metal before adding boards or plaster. *b*) the strips so used.

**fur·row** (fũr′ō), *n.* [AS. *furh*], 1. a narrow groove made in the ground by a plow. 2. anything like this, as a wrinkle on the face. *v.t.* to make furrows in. *v.i.* 1. to make furrows. 2. to become wrinkled. —**for′row·er**, *n.* —**fur′row·like′**, *adj.*

**fur·ry** (fũr′i), *adj.* [-RIER, -RIEST], 1. of or made of fur. 2. covered with or wearing fur. 3. like fur, as in texture. —**fur′ri·ness**, *n.*

**fur·ther** (fũr′*th*ẽr), *adj.* [AS. *furthra*], 1. more distant; farther. 2. additional; more. *adv.* [AS. *furthor*], 1. at or to a greater distance in space or time. 2. to a greater degree or extent. 3. in addition; moreover. *Further* is now generally interchangeable with *farther* in senses 1 & 2 of the *adv.* and 1 of the *adj.*, though preference is often given to *farther* in reference to space and to *further* in reference to time, degree, or addition. *v.t.* to promote; give aid to. —**fur′ther·er**, *n.*

**fur·ther·ance** (fũr′*th*ẽr-əns), *n.* 1. a furthering, or helping forward; promotion. 2. an aid.

**fur·ther·more** (fũr′*th*ẽr-môr′, -mōr′), *adv.* besides; moreover; in addition.

**fur·ther·most** (fũr′*th*ẽr-mōst′), *adj.* furthest.

**fur·thest** (fũr′*th*ist), *adj.* [ME., formed as superl. on analogy of *further*], most distant; farthest. *adv.* 1. at or to the greatest distance in space or time. 2. to the greatest degree or extent.

**fur·tive** (fũr′tiv), *adj.* [< Fr. < L. *furtivus*, stolen < *fur*, thief], done or acting in a stealthy manner; stealthy; sly; shifty. —**fur′tive·ly**, *adv.* —**fur′tive·ness**, *n.*

**fu·ry** (fyoor′i), *n.* [*pl.* -RIES], [< OFr. < L. *furia* < *furere*, to rage], 1. *a*) violent anger; wild rage. *b*) a fit of this. 2. violence; vehemence; fierceness. 3. a violent, uncontrollable person. 4. [F-], one of the Furies. —**like fury**, [Colloq.], 1. with violence. 2. swiftly.

**furze** (fũrz), *n.* [AS. *fyrs*], a prickly evergreen shrub with dark-green spines and yellow flowers, common in Europe, especially on wastelands: also called *gorse*, *whin*. —**furz′y**, *adj.*

**fuse** (fūz), *v.t.* & *v.i.* [FUSED, FUSING], [< L. *fusus*, pp. of *fundere*, to shed], 1. to make or become liquid by great heat; melt. 2. to unite as if by melting together; blend. Also sp. **fuze.**

**fuse** (fūz), *n.* [< It. < L. *fusus*, hollow spindle], 1. a tube or wick filled with combustible material for setting off an explosive charge. 3. in *electricity*, a strip of easily melted metal placed in a circuit as a safeguard: when the current becomes too strong, the metal melts, thus breaking the circuit. Also sp. **fuze.**

**fu·see** (fū-zē′), *n.* [< Fr. *fusée*, spindleful < ML. < L. *fusus*; see FUSE, *n.*], 1. a friction match with a large head, that burns in a wind. 2. a colored flare used as a railroad signal. Also sp. **fuzee.**

**fu·se·lage** (fū′z'l-ij, fū′zə-läzh′), *n.* [Fr.; prob. < OFr. *fusel*, dim. of L. *fusus*, a spindle], the body of an airplane, exclusive of the wings and tail.

**fu·sel oil** (fū′z'l, fū′s'l), [G. *fusel*, inferior liquor], an oily, acrid, poisonous liquid occurring in insufficiently distilled alcoholic products: also **fusel.**

**fu·si·ble** (fū′zə-b'l), *adj.* that can be fused. —**fu′si·bil′i·ty**, **fu′si·ble·ness**, *n.* —**fu′si·bly**, *adv.*

**fu·si·form** (fū′zə-fôrm′), *adj.* [< L. *fusus*, a spindle; + *-form*], shaped like a spindle.

**fu·sil** (fū′z'l), *n.* [Fr., orig., steel for striking sparks < LL. < L. *focus*, hearth], an old-fashioned light flintlock musket.

**fu·sil·ier, fu·sil·eer** (fū′z'l-êr′), *n.* [Obs.], a soldier armed with a fusil: the term *Fusiliers* is still applied to certain British regiments.

**fu·sil·lade** (fū′z'l-ād′), *n.* [Fr. < *fusiller*, to shoot; see FUSIL, *n.*], 1. a simultaneous discharge of many firearms. 2. something like this: as, a *fusillade* of questions. *v.t.* [-LADED, -LADING], to shoot down or attack with a fusillade.

**fu·sion** (fū′zhən), *n.* 1. a fusing; melting or melting together: see also *nuclear fusion*. 2. a blending; coalition: as, a *fusion* of political parties. 3. anything made by fusing.

**fu·sion·ism** (fū′zhən-iz'm), *n.* the theory or practice of bringing about a coalition of political parties, factions, etc. —**fu′sion·ist**, *n.* & *adj.*

**fuss** (fus), *n.* [prob. echoic], 1. a nervous, excited activity or state; unnecessary bother or worry. 2. a fussy person. *v.i.* to bustle about or worry over trifles. *v.t.* [Colloq.], to bother; make nervous. —**fuss′er**, *n.*

**fuss·y** (fus′i), *adj.* [-IER, -IEST], 1. habitually fussing; bustling about or worrying over trifles. 2. showing or needing careful attention. 3. full of details, especially if unnecessary or showy. —**fuss′i·ly**, *adv.* —**fuss′i·ness**, *n.*

**fus·tian** (fus′chən), *n.* [< OFr. < ML. < L. *fustis*, wooden stick], 1. orig., a coarse cloth of cotton and linen. 2. now, cotton corduroy or velveteen. 3. pompous, pretentious talk or writing; bombast. *adj.* of or characterized by fustian.

**fust·y** (fus′ti), *adj.* [-IER, -IEST], [< dial. *fust*, moldiness < OFr., cask < L. *fustis*, wooden stick], 1. musty; moldy; smelling stale or stuffy. 2. old-fashioned. —**fust′i·ly**, *adv.* —**fust′i·ness**, *n.*

**fut.**, future.

**fu·tile** (fū′t'l), *adj.* [Fr. < L. *futilis*, lit., that easily pours out, hence worthless < *fundere*, to pour], 1. useless; ineffectual; vain. 2. trifling; unimportant. —**fu′tile·ly**, *adv.* —**fu·til′i·ty** (-til′ə-ti), [*pl.* -TIES], **fu′tile·ness**, *n.*

**fut·tock** (fut′ək), *n.* [? < *foot* + *hook*], any of the curved timbers forming the ribs of a wooden ship.

**fu·ture** (fū′chẽr), *adj.* [< OFr. < L. *futurus*, used as fut. part. of *esse*, to be], 1. that is to be or come. 2. indicating time to come: as, the *future* tense of a verb. *n.* 1. the time that is to come. 2. what will happen; what is going to be. 3. the prospective condition of a person or thing: as, he has a great *future* in politics. 4. *pl.* commodities bought or sold by speculators, theoretically to be delivered in time to come. 5. in *grammar, a)* the future tense. *b)* a verb form in this tense. **—fu′ture·less,** *adj.*

**fu·tur·ism** (fū′chẽr-iz'm), *n.* a movement in art, literature, music, etc., during World War I, which opposed traditional form, balance, etc. and stressed the dynamic movement and violence of the machine age. **—fu′tur·ist,** *n. & adj.*

**fu·tu·ri·ty** (fū-toor′ə-ti, -tyoor′-), *n.* [*pl.* -TIES], 1. the future. 2. a future condition or event. 3. the quality of being future.

**fuze** (fūz), *n.* a fuse.

**fuze** (fūz), *v.t. & v.i.* [FUZED, FUZING], to fuse.

**fu·zee** (fū-zē′), *n.* a fusee.

**fuzz** (fuz), *n.* [? echoic, but cf. D. *voos*, spongy], very loose, light particles of down, wool, etc.; fine hairs or fibers: as, the *fuzz* on a peach. *v.i. & v.t.* to cover or become covered with fuzz. **—the fuzz,** [Slang], a policeman or the police.

**fuzz·y** (fuz′i), *adj.* [-IER, -IEST], 1. of, like, or covered with fuzz. 2. not clear; blurred. **—fuzz′i·ly,** *adv.* **—fuzz′i·ness,** *n.*

**-fy** (fī), [< OFr. *-fier* < L. *-ficare* < *facere*, to make, do], a suffix meaning: 1. *to make, cause to be,* as in *liquefy.* 2. *to cause to have, imbue with,* as in *glorify.* 3. *to become,* as in *putrefy.*

# G

**G, g** (jē), *n.* [*pl.* G's, g's, Gs, gs], 1. the seventh letter of the English alphabet. 2. a sound of G or g. *adj.* seventh in a sequence or group.

**G** (jē), *n.* 1. [Slang], one thousand dollars. 2. in *music, a)* the fifth tone in the scale of C major. *b)* the scale having G as the keynote. *adj.* shaped like G.

**G.,** German.

**G., g.,** 1. gauge. 2. gold. 3. gram. 4. gulf. 5. in *electricity*, conductance.

**Ga,** in *chemistry*, gallium.

**Ga.,** Georgia.

**gab** (gab), *v.i.* [GABBED, GABBING], [prob. < ON. *gabba*, to mock], [Colloq.], to talk much or idly; chatter. *n.* [Colloq.], chatter; talkativeness. **—gift of (the) gab,** [Colloq.], the ability to speak fluently; eloquence. **—gab′ber,** *n.*

**gab·ar·dine** (gab′ẽr-dēn′, gab′ẽr-dēn′), *n.* [see GABERDINE], 1. a twilled cloth of wool, cotton, etc., with a fine, diagonal weave, used for suits, coats, etc. 2. a gaberdine.

**gab·ble** (gab′'l), *v.i.* [-BLED, -BLING], [freq. of *gab*], 1. to talk rapidly and incoherently; jabber. 2. to utter rapid sounds, as a goose. *v.t.* to utter rapidly and incoherently. *n.* rapid, incoherent or meaningless utterance. **—gab′bler,** *n.*

**gab·by** (gab′i), *adj.* [-BIER, -BIEST], [Colloq.], talkative.

**gab·er·dine** (gab′ẽr-dēn′, gab′ẽr-dēn′), *n.* [< OFr. *galvardine* < MHG. *walvart*, pilgrimage], 1. a loose coat of coarse cloth worn in the Middle Ages, especially by Jews. 2. gabardine.

**ga·bi·on** (gā′bi-ən), *n.* [Fr. < It. < *gabbia*, cage < L. *cavea*, cave], 1. a cylinder of wicker filled with earth or stones, formerly used in building fortifications. 2. a similar cylinder of metal, used in building dams, foundations, etc.

**ga·ble** (gā′b'l), *n.* [< OFr.; prob. < ON. *gafl*], 1. the triangular wall enclosed by the sloping ends of a ridged roof. 2. the end wall of a building, the upper part of which is a gable. 3. a triangular decorative feature, as over a door or window. *v.t.* [-BLED, -BLING], to put a gable or gables on. *v.i.* to be in the form of a gable. **—ga′bled,** *adj.*

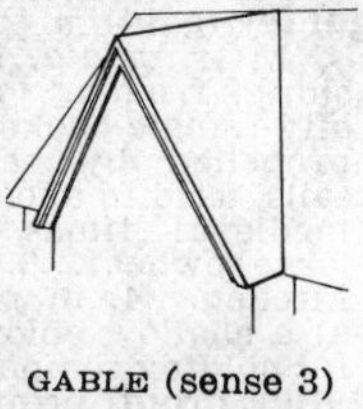

GABLE (sense 3)

**gable roof,** a ridged roof forming a gable at one end or both ends.

**Ga·bon** (gȧ′bōn′) *n.* a country on the W coast of Africa, a member of the French Community: area, 102,300 sq. mi.; pop., 480,000; capital, Libreville.

**Ga·bri·el** (gā′bri-əl), *n.* in the *Bible*, the angel of the Annunciation and the herald of good news.

**ga·by** (gā′bi), *n.* [*pl.* -BIES], [? < *gape*, after *baby*], [Colloq.], a foolish person; simpleton.

**Gad, gad** (gad), *interj.* a mild oath or expression of surprise, disgust, etc.: a euphemism for *God.*

**gad** (gad), *v.i.* [GADDED, GADDING], [? a back-formation < AS. *gædeling*, companion], to roam about aimlessly or restlessly; go about seeking excitement. *n.* [Colloq.], a gadding. **—gad′der,** *n.*

**gad** (gad), *n.* [ON. *gaddr*], a goad. *v.t.* [GADDED, GADDING], to goad.

**gad·a·bout** (gad′ə-bout′), *n.* [Colloq.], a person who gads about, looking for fun, excitement, etc. *adj.* fond of gadding.

**gad·fly** (gad′flī′), *n.* [*pl.* -FLIES], [*gad* (goad) + *fly*], 1. a large fly that stings cattle, etc.; horsefly. 2. one who annoys or irritates others.

**gadg·et** (gaj′it), *n.* [? ult. < *gauge*], 1. any small mechanical contrivance. 2. any small object.

**gad·o·lin·i·um** (gad′ə-lin′i-əm), *n.* [after J. *Gadolin*, 18th-c. Finn. chemist], a chemical element of the rare-earth group: symbol, Gd; at. wt., 156.9; at. no., 64.

**Gads·den** (gadz′dən), *n.* a city in NE Alabama: pop., 58,000.

**gad·wall** (gad′wôl), *n.* [*pl.* -WALLS, -WALL; see PLURAL, II, D, 1], a grayish-brown wild duck of the northern fresh-water regions of America.

**Gae·a** (jē′ə), *n.* [Gr. *Gaia* < *gē*, earth], in *Gr. mythology*, the earth personified as a goddess.

**Gael** (gāl), *n.* [contr. < Gael. *Gaidheal*], a Celt of Scotland, Ireland, or the Isle of Man; esp., a Celt of the Scottish Highlands.

**Gael.,** Gaelic.

**Gael·ic** (gāl′ik), *adj.* 1. of the Gaels. 2. of the Goidelic subfamily of languages; esp., of Scottish Gaelic. *n.* 1. the Goidelic subfamily of languages. 2. one of these languages, especially that of the Scottish Highlands (*Scottish Gaelic*).

**gaff** (gaf), *n.* [MFr. *gaffe*, prob. < Celt.], 1. a large, strong hook on a pole, or a barbed spear, for landing large fish. 2. a sharp metal spur fastened to the leg of a gamecock. 3. a spar or pole supporting a fore-and-aft sail. *v.t.* to strike or land (a fish) with a gaff. **—stand the gaff,** [Slang], to bear up well under difficulties, punishment, etc.

**gaf·fer** (gaf′ẽr), *n.* [altered < *godfather*], an old man: often used contemptuously or humorously.

**gag** (gag), *v.t.* [GAGGED, GAGGING], [echoic], 1. to cause to retch or choke. 2. to cover or stuff the mouth of, so as to keep from talking, crying out, etc. 3. to keep (a person) from expressing himself freely, as by intimidation. 4. to prevent or limit speech in (a legislative body). *v.i.* to retch or choke. *n.* 1. something put into or over the mouth to prevent talking, etc. 2. any restraint of free speech. 3. [Slang], *a)* a joke or comic remark. *b)* a practical joke or bit of comic stage business. **—gag′ger,** *n.*

**gage** (gāj), *n.* [< OFr. *g(u)age* < Gmc.], 1. something pledged to insure that an obligation will be fulfilled; security. 2. a pledge to appear and fight, as a glove thrown down by a challenger. 3. a challenge. *v.t.* [GAGED, GAGING], [Archaic], to offer as or bind by a pledge.

**gage** (gāj), *n. & v.t.* [GAGED, GAGING], gauge.

**gag man,** a man who devises jokes, bits of comic business, etc., as for professional comedians.

**gai·e·ty** (gā′ə-ti), *n.* [*pl.* -TIES], 1. the state or quality of being gay; cheerfulness. 2. merrymak-

ing; lively entertainment. 3. finery; showy display: as, *gaiety* of plumage. Also sp. **gayety.**
**gai·ly** (gā'li), *adv.* in a gay manner; specif., *a*) happily; merrily. *b*) brightly; with bright display. Also sp. **gayly.**
**gain** (gān), *n.* [< OFr. < *gaaignier;* ult. < OHG. *weide,* pasture], 1. an increase; addition; specif., *a*) *often in pl.* an increase in wealth, earnings, etc.; profit. *b*) an increase in advantage; improvement. 2. the act of getting something; acquisition. *v.t.* 1. to get by labor; earn. 2. to get by effort or merit; win. 3. to get as an addition, profit, or advantage. 4. to get to; reach. *v.i.* to make progress; improve or advance, as in health. **—gain on,** 1. to draw nearer to (an opponent in a race). 2. to make more progress than (a competitor). **—gain over,** to win over to one's side. **—gain'a·ble,** *adj.* **—gain'less,** *adj.*
**gain·er** (gān'ẽr), *n.* 1. a person or thing that gains. 2. a fancy dive in which the diver faces forward and does a backward somersault in the air.
**gain·ful** (gān'fəl), *adj.* producing gain; profitable. **—gain'ful·ly,** *adv.* **—gain'ful·ness,** *n.*
**gain·ly** (gān'li), *adj.* [< ON. *gegn,* straight, favorable], shapely and graceful. **—gain'li·ness,** *n.*
**gain·say** (gān'sā'), *v.t.* [-SAID, -SAYING], [*gain-* < AS. *gegn,* against], 1. to deny. 2. to contradict. 3. to speak or act against; oppose. *n.* (gān'sā'), a gainsaying. **—gain'say'er,** *n.*
**Gains·bor·ough, Thomas** (gānz'bũr'ō, -bẽr-ə), 1727–1788; English painter.
**'gainst, gainst** (genst, gānst), *prep.* [Poetic], against.
**gait** (gāt), *n.* [< ON. *gata,* path], 1. manner of walking or running. 2. any of the various foot movements of a horse, as a trot, canter, etc. *v.t.* to train (a horse) to certain gaits. **—gait'ed,** *adj.*
**gai·ter** (gā'tẽr), *n.* [Fr. *guêtre*], 1. a cloth or leather covering for the instep and ankle, and, sometimes, the calf of the leg; spat or legging. 2. formerly, a kind of high-topped shoe.
**gal** (gal), *n.* [Slang], a girl.
**Gal.,** Galatians.
**gal.,** gallon; gallons.
**ga·la** (gā'lə, gal'ə, gä'lə), *n.* [< Fr. & It. < OFr. *gale,* enjoyment], a festive occasion; festival; celebration. *adj.* festive; suitable for a festive occasion.**—in gala,** in festive dress.
**ga·lac·tic** (gə-lak'tik), *adj.* [< Gr. *galaktikos,* milky < *gala,* milk], 1. of or obtained from milk. 2. in *astronomy,* of the Milky Way, or Galaxy.
**Gal·a·had** (gal'ə-had'), *n.* in *Arthurian legend,* a knight who was successful in the quest for the Holy Grail because of his purity and nobility.
**gal·an·tine** (gal'ən-tēn'), *n.* [< OFr. < ML. < L. pp. of *gelare,* to congeal], a mold of boned, seasoned, boiled white meat, as chicken or veal, chilled and served cold in its own jelly.
**Ga·lá·pa·gos Islands** (gə-lä'pə-gōs'), a group of islands in the Pacific, on the equator: a possession of Ecuador.
**Gal·a·te·a** (gal'ə-tē'ə), *n.* see **Pygmalion.**
**Ga·la·tia** (gə-lā'shə), *n.* an ancient kingdom, and later a Roman province, in central Asia Minor. **—Ga·la'tian,** *adj. & n.*
**Ga·la·tians** (gə-lā'shənz), *n.* the Epistle to the Galatians, a book of the New Testament written by the Apostle Paul.
**gal·ax·y** (gal'ək-si), *n.* [< Fr. < L. *galaxias* < Gr. < *gala,* milk], 1. [often G-], the Milky Way. 2. [*pl.* -IES], any similar but smaller group of stars. 3. an assembly of brilliant or illustrious people.
**gale** (gāl), *n.* [prob. < Anglo-N. hyp. *gaul,* wind], 1. a strong wind, especially one having a velocity between 32 and 63 miles an hour. 2. an outburst: as, a *gale* of laughter.
**Ga·len** (gā'lən), *n.* (*Claudius Galen*), Greek physician and writer of the 2nd century A.D.
**ga·le·na** (gə-lē'nə), *n.* [L., lead ore], native lead sulfide, PbS, a lead-gray mineral with metallic luster: it is the principal ore of lead: also **ga·le'nite** (-nīt).
**Ga·len·ic, ga·len·ic** (gə-len'ik), *adj.* of Galen or his methods: also **Ga·len'i·cal, ga·len'i·cal.**
**Ga·li·cia** (gə-lish'ə), *n.* 1. a former province of NW Spain. 2. a region in south central Europe, partly in Poland and the U.S.S.R. **—Ga·li'cian,** *adj. & n.*
**Gal·i·le·an** (gal'ə-lē'ən), *adj.* of Galilee or its people. *n.* 1. a native or inhabitant of Galilee. 2. a Christian. **—the Galilean,** Jesus.
**Gal·i·le·an** (gal'ə-lē'ən), *adj.* of Galileo.
**Gal·i·lee** (gal'ə-lē'), *n.* an ancient division of N Palestine.
**Galilee, Sea of,** a small lake in NE Palestine.
**Gal·i·le·o** (gal'ə-lē'ō), *n.* (*Galileo Galilei*), Italian astronomer and physicist; 1564–1642.

**gal·i·ot** (gal'i-ət), *n.* [< OFr. < ML. *galea;* see GALLEY], 1. a small, swift galley with sails and oars. 2. a light, Dutch merchant ship with a single mast and leeboards. Also sp. **galliot.**
**gall** (gôl), *n.* [AS. *galla*], 1. a bitter, greenish fluid secreted by the liver and stored in the gall bladder; bile. 2. the gall bladder. 3. something bitter or distasteful. 4. bitter feeling. 5. [Colloq.], impudence; effrontery.
**gall** (gôl), *n.* [AS. *gealla;* ? < L. *galla,* gallnut, but prob. connected with OFr. *galle,* a sore], 1. a sore on the skin caused by chafing; esp., such a sore on a horse. 2. *a*) irritation; annoyance. *b*) a cause of this. *v.t.* 1. to make (the skin) sore by chafing. 2. to irritate; annoy; vex. *v.i.* to become sore from chafing.
**gall** (gôl), *n.* [< OFr. < L. *galla,* gallnut], a tumor on plant tissue caused by irritation due to fungi, insects, or bacteria: galls formed on oak trees have a high tannic acid content.
**gal·lant** (gal'ənt), *adj.* [< OFr. < *gale;* see GALA], 1. fine; showy: as, *gallant* attire. 2. stately; imposing; grand. 3. brave and noble; daring. 4. (gə-lant', gal'ənt), polite and attentive to women. *n.* (gal'ənt, gə-lant'), 1. a brave, noble man. 2. a man attentive and polite to women. 3. a lover. *v.t.* (gə-lant'), to pay court to (a woman). *v.i.* to behave like a gallant. **—gal'lant·ly,** *adv.* **—gal'lant·ness,** *n.*
**gal·lant·ry** (gal'ən-tri), *n.* [*pl.* -RIES], 1. nobility of behavior or spirit; heroic courage. 2. the behavior of a gallant. 3. *usually in pl.* an act or speech characteristic of a gallant. 4. amorous intrigue. 5. [Archaic], gay or showy appearance.
**gall bladder,** a membranous sac attached to the liver, in which excess gall or bile is stored.
**gal·le·ass** (gal'i-as', -əs), *n.* [< Fr. < OFr. < It. < ML. *galea;* see GALLEY], a large, three-masted vessel having sails and oars and carrying heavy guns: used in the 16th and 17th centuries.
**gal·le·on** (gal'i-ən), *n.* [Fr. *galion* or Sp. *galeón;* both < ML. *galea;* see GALLEY], a large, heavy Spanish warship and trader of the 15th and 16th centuries, with three or four decks at the stern.

GALLEON

**gal·ler·y** (gal'ẽr-i), *n.* [*pl.* -IES], [< Fr. < ML. *galeria*], 1. a covered walk or porch open at one side; portico. 2. a long, narrow platform, or balcony, on the outside of a building. 3. a similar platform around the stern of an early sailing ship. 4. a platform or projecting upper floor in a church, theater, etc.; esp., the highest of a series of such platforms in a theater, with the cheapest seats. 5. the people occupying these seats. 6. any group of spectators. 7. a long, narrow corridor or room. 8. a place or establishment for art exhibitions. 9. a collection of paintings, statues, etc. 10. a place or establishment for taking photographs, shooting at targets, etc. 11. an underground passage, as one used in mining. *v.t.* [-IED, -YING], to furnish with a gallery. *v.i.* to make a gallery (sense 11). **—play to the gallery,** to try to win the approval of the public.
**gal·ley** (gal'i), *n.* [*pl.* -LEYS], [< OFr. < ML. *galea,* < MGr. *galaia,* kind of ship], 1. a long, low, usually single-decked ship propelled by oars and sails, used in ancient and medieval times. 2. a large rowboat. 3. a ship's kitchen. 4. in *printing,* *a*) a shallow oblong tray for holding composed type. *b*) a galley proof.

GALLEY

**galley proof,** printer's proof taken from type in a galley to permit correction of errors before the type is made up in pages.
**galley slave,** 1. a slave or convict sentenced or compelled to pull an oar on a galley. 2. a drudge.
**gall·fly** (gôl'flī'), *n.* [*pl.* -FLIES], an insect whose eggs cause galls on plant stems.
**Gal·lic** (gal'ik), *adj.* 1. of ancient Gaul or its people. 2. French.
**gal·lic** (gal'ik), *adj.* [< Fr. < L. *galla,* gallnut], designating or of an acid, $(OH)_3C_6H_2 \cdot COOH$, prepared from nutgalls, tannin, etc. and used in the manufacture of inks, dyes, etc.
**Gal·li·cism, gal·li·cism** (gal'ə-siz'm), *n.* French idiom or expression, used in another language.
**Gal·li·cize** (gal'ə-sīz'), *v.t. & v.i.* [-CIZED, -CIZING], to

make or become French or like the French in thought, language, etc.

**gal·li·gas·kins** (gal'i-gas'kinz), *n.pl.* [altered < Fr. *garguesque* < OFr. < It. < *Grechesca*, Grecian], loosely fitting breeches: now a humorous usage.

**gal·li·na·cean** (gal'ə-nā'shən), *adj.* gallinaceous. *n.* any gallinaceous bird.

**gal·li·na·ceous** (gal'ə-nā'shəs), *adj.* [< L. < *gallina*, hen < *gallus*, a cock], of or belonging to a large group of birds that nest on the ground, including poultry, pheasants, etc.

**gall·ing** (gôl'iŋ), *adj.* that galls; chafing; vexing.

**gal·li·nule** (gal'ə-nūl', -nōōl'), *n.* [< L. dim. of *gallina;* see GALLINACEOUS], any of several wading birds of the rail family.

**Gal·lip·o·li** (gə-lip'ə-li), *n.* a peninsula in European Turkey, along the Dardanelles north shore.

**gal·li·pot** (gal'ə-pot'), *n.* [prob. < *galley* + *pot*], a small pot or jar of glazed earthenware, especially one used by druggists as a container for medicine.

**gal·li·um** (gal'i-əm), *n.* [< L. *Gallia*, Gaul; also a pun on L. *gallus*, a cock, transl. of *Lecoq* (de Boisbaudran), its 19th-c. Fr. discoverer], a soft, bluish-white, metallic chemical element with a low melting point (85.5° F.), used as a substitute for mercury: symbol, Ga; at. wt., 69.72; at. no., 31.

**gal·li·vant** (gal'ə-vant', gal'ə-vant'), *v.i.* [arbitrary elaboration of *gallant*], 1. to play the gallant or beau. 2. to go about in search of amusement; gad about. —**gal'li·vant'er,** *n.*

**gall·nut** (gôl'nut'), *n.* a nutlike gall, as on oaks.

**Gal·lo-** (gal'ō), [L. < *Gallus*, a Gaul], a combining form meaning: 1. *French.* 2. *French and.*

**gal·lon** (gal'ən), *n.* [< ONorm. Fr. < OFr. *jalon* < base of LL. *galleta*, a jug], 1. a liquid measure, equal to 4 quarts (231 cubic inches): the British imperial gallon equals 277.42 cubic inches. 2. a dry measure, equal to 1/8 bushel. 3. any container with a capacity of one gallon.

**gal·loon** (gə-lōōn'), *n.* [< Fr. < *galonner*, to braid], a braid of cotton, silk, worsted, or metal thread used for trimming or binding.

**gal·lop** (gal'əp), *n.* [< OFr. < *galoper*, to gallop < Frank.], 1. the fastest gait of a horse, etc., consisting of a succession of leaping strides with all the feet off the ground at one time. 2. a ride on a galloping animal. 3. [Colloq.], any fast pace or speedy action. *v.i.* 1. to go at a gallop. 2. to move or act very fast; hurry. *v.t.* to cause to gallop. —**gal'lop·er,** *n.*

**gal·lows** (gal'ōz), *n.* [*pl.* -LOWSES, -LOWS], [AS. *galga*], 1. an upright frame with a crossbeam, for hanging condemned persons. 2. any structure like this. 3. the punishment of hanging.

**gallows bird,** [Colloq.], a person who deserves to be hanged.

**gallows humor,** morbid or cynical humor.

**gall·stone** (gôl'stōn'), *n.* a small, solid mass sometimes formed in the gall bladder or bile duct.

**gal·lus·es** (gal'əs-iz), *n.pl.* [< *gallus*, dial. var. of *gallows*], [Colloq.], suspenders; braces.

**gal·op** (gal'əp), *n.* [Fr.; see GALLOP], 1. a lively dance in 2/4 time. 2. music for this. *v.i.* to dance a galop.

**ga·lore** (gə-lôr'), *adv.* [Ir. *go leōr*, enough], in abundance; plentifully: as, she has hats *galore.*

**ga·losh, ga·loshe** (gə-losh'), *n.* [OFr. *galoche*], *usually in pl.* any protective overshoe; esp., a high overshoe of rubber and waterproof fabric.

**gals.,** gallons.

**Gals·wor·thy, John** (gôlz'wũr'*th*i, galz'-), 1867–1933; English novelist and dramatist.

**Gal·ton,** Sir **Francis** (gôl't'n), 1822–1911; English anthropologist; pioneer in eugenics.

**Gal·va·ni, Lu·i·gi** (lōō-ē'jē gäl-vä'nē), 1737–1798; Italian physiologist and physicist.

**gal·van·ic** (gal-van'ik), *adj.* 1. of, caused by, or producing an electric current, especially from a battery. 2. stimulating or stimulated as if by electric shock; startling. —**gal·van'i·cal·ly,** *adv.*

**gal·va·nism** (gal'və-niz'm), *n.* [< Fr. < It.: after L. *Galvani*], 1. electricity produced by chemical action. 2. the branch of physics that deals with this. 3. the use of electricity in therapy.

**gal·va·nize** (gal'və-nīz'), *v.t.* [-NIZED, -NIZING], 1. to apply an electric current to. 2. to stimulate as if by electric shock; startle; excite. 3. to plate (metal) with zinc. —**gal'va·ni·za'tion,** *n.* —**gal'va·niz'er,** *n.*

**galvanized iron,** iron coated with zinc as a protection against rust.

**gal·va·no-,** a combining form meaning *galvanic, galvanism.*

**gal·va·nom·e·ter** (gal'və-nom'ə-tẽr), *n.* [*galvano-* + *-meter*], an instrument for detecting, and determining the intensity and direction of, an electric current. —**gal'va·no·met'ric** (-nō-met'rik), *adj.* —**gal'va·nom'e·try,** *n.*

**gal·va·no·scope** (gal-van'ə-skōp', gal'və-nō-), *n.* an instrument for detecting very weak electric currents and indicating their direction. —**gal'va·no·scop'ic** (-skop'ik), *adj.*

**Gal·ves·ton** (gal'vis-t'n), *n.* a seaport in SE Texas: pop., 66,000.

**gam** (gam), *n.* [< dial. Fr. *gambe;* ult. < Gr. *kampē*, a joint], [Slang], a leg; esp., a woman's leg.

**Gam·a, Vas·co da** (vas'kō də gam'ə; Port. dä gä'mä), 1469?–1524; Portuguese navigator.

**Gam·bi·a** (gam'bi-ə), *n.* a country on the coast of W Africa: a member of the British Commonwealth of Nations: area, 4,000 sq. mi.; pop., 316,000; capital, Bathurst.

**gam·bit** (gam'bit), *n.* [Fr. < OFr. < Sp. *gambeta*, a tripping < *gamba*, a leg; see GAM], 1. in *chess*, an opening in which a pawn or other piece is sacrificed to get an advantage in position; hence, 2. a maneuver or action intended to gain an advantage.

**gam·ble** (gam'b'l), *v.i.* [-BLED, -BLING], [AS. *gamenian*, to play, game], 1. to play games of chance for money, etc. 2. to take a risk in order to gain some advantage. *v.t.* 1. to squander or lose in gambling (with *away*). 2. to bet; wager. *n.* an act or undertaking involving risk of a loss. —**gam'bler,** *n.* —**gam'bling,** *n.*

**gam·boge** (gam-bōj', -bōōzh'), *n.* [Mod. L. *gambogium* < *Cambodia*], a gum resin extracted from certain Asiatic trees, used as a yellow pigment and as a cathartic.

**gam·bol** (gam'bəl), *n.* [< Fr. < It. *gambata*, a kick < *gamba*, a leg; see GAMBIT], a jumping and skipping about in play; frolic. *v.i.* [-BOLED or -BOLLED, -BOLING or -BOLLING], to jump and skip about in play; frolic.

**gam·brel** (gam'brəl), *n.* [< OFr.; prob. < It. *gamba*, a leg; see GAM], 1. the hock of a horse or similar animal. 2. a gambrel roof.

**gambrel roof,** a roof with two slopes on each side, the lower steeper than the upper, which form the ridge.

GAMBREL ROOF

**game** (gām), *n.* [AS. *gamen*], 1. any form of play; amusement; sport; frolic. 2. *a*) any specific amusement or sport involving competition under specific rules: as, football and chess are *games. b*) a single contest in such a competition. 3. *a*) the number of points required for winning. *b*) a winning; victory. 4. a set of equipment for a specific game: as, toys and *games* are sold here. 5. a way or quality of playing: as, that halfback plays a good *game.* 6. any test of skill, endurance, etc. 7. a scheme; plan: as, he saw through my *game.* 8. wild birds, fish, or animals hunted for sport or food. 9. the flesh of such creatures used as food. 10. [Colloq.], any object of pursuit. 11. [Slang], a business or vocation, especially a risky one: as, the stock-market *game. v.i.* [GAMED, GAMING], to play cards, etc. for stakes; gamble. *v.t.* to squander in gambling (with *away*). *adj.* 1. designating or of wild birds, fish, etc. hunted for sport or food. 2. [Colloq.], *a*) plucky; courageous. *b*) having enough spirit; ready: as, he's *game* for anything. —**big game,** large wild animals, as lions, elephants, etc., hunted for sport. —**make game of,** to make fun of; ridicule. —**play the game,** [Colloq.], to act according to the rules; behave as fairness or custom requires. —**the game is up,** failure is certain. —**game'ly,** *adv.* —**game'ness,** *n.*

**game** (gām), *adj.* [? < Fr. dial. *gambi*, limping], [Colloq.], lame: as, a *game* leg. —**game'ness,** *n.*

**game·cock** (gām'kok'), *n.* a specially bred rooster trained for cockfighting.

**game·keep·er** (gām'kēp'ẽr), *n.* a game warden, especially on a private estate.

**game·some** (gām'səm), *adj.* playful; frolicsome; merry. —**game'some·ly,** *adv.* —**game'some·ness,** *n.*

**game·ster** (gām'stẽr), *n.* a gambler.

**gam·ete** (gam'ēt, gə-mēt'), *n.* [< Gr. *gametē*, a wife, ult. < *gamos*, marriage], a reproductive cell that can unite with another similar one to form the cell that develops into a new individual. —**ga·met·ic** (gə-met'ik), *adj.*

**ga·me·to-,** a combining form meaning *gamete.*

**ga·me·to·phyte** (gə-mē'tə-fīt'), *n.* [*gameto-* +

-*phyte*], the gamete-bearing phase of certain plants: cf. *sporophyte*.
**game warden,** an official in charge of enforcing the game laws in a certain area.
**gam·in** (gam'in), *n.* [Fr.], a homeless or neglected child left to roam the streets; street urchin.
**gam·ing** (gām'iŋ), *n.* the playing of games of chance for stakes; gambling.
**gam·ma** (gam'ə), *n.* [Gr.], the third letter of the Greek alphabet (Γ, γ): often used to mark the third of a series.
**gamma glob·u·lin** (glob'yoo-lin), that fraction of blood serum which contains most antibodies: used in experimental inoculation against poliomyelitis.
**gamma rays,** one of the three kinds of rays emitted by radioactive substances: they are similar to X rays, but shorter in wave length.
**gam·mer** (gam'ẽr), *n.* [altered < *godmother*], an old woman: often used contemptuously or humorously.
**gam·mon** (gam'ən), *n.* [< ONorm.Fr. < *gambe*, a leg < ML. < Gr. *kampē*, a joint], 1. the bottom end of a side of bacon. 2. a ham, smoked or cured.
**gam·mon** (gam'ən), *n.* [ME. *gammen*, game], in *backgammon*, a victory in which the winner gets rid of all his men before his opponent gets rid of any. *v.t.* to defeat by scoring a gammon.
**gam·mon** (gam'ən), *n. & interj.* [prob. jocular use of *gammon* (bacon)], [Colloq.], nonsense; humbug. *v.t. & v.i.* [Colloq.], to talk humbug (to).
**gam·o-,** [< Gr. *gamos*, marriage], a combining form meaning: 1. *sexually united*. 2. *joined*, as in *gamosepalous*.
**gam·o·pet·al·ous** (gam'ə-pet''l-əs), *adj.* [*gamo-* + *petalous*], having the petals united so as to form a tubelike corolla.
**gam·o·sep·al·ous** (gam'ə-sep''l-əs), *adj.* [*gamo-* + -*sepalous*], having the sepals united.
**-ga·mous** (gə-məs), [< Gr. *gamos*, marriage], a combining form meaning *marrying*, *uniting sexually*, as in *heterogamous*, *polygamous*.
**gam·ut** (gam'ət), *n.* [ML. *gamma ut; gamma*, the lowest note of the medieval scale < Gr. *gamma* (the letter) + *ut* < L. *ut*, that, in a medieval song whose phrases began on successive ascending major tones: *Ut* queant laxis *Re*sonare fibris, *Mi*ra gestorum *Fa*muli tuorum, *Sol*ve polluti *La*bii reatum, *S*ancte *I*ohannes], 1. in *music*, *a*) the entire series of recognized notes in modern music. *b*) any complete musical scale, especially the major scale. 2. the entire range or extent of anything: as, she ran the *gamut* of emotions.
**gam·y** (gām'i), *adj.* [-IER, -IEST], 1. having a strong, tangy flavor like that of cooked game. 2. slightly tainted in smell or taste. 3. plucky; high-spirited. **—gam'i·ly,** *adv.* **—gam'i·ness,** *n.*
**-ga·my** (gə-mi), [< Gr.; see -GAMOUS], a combining form meaning *marriage*, *sexual union*, as in *polygamy*.
**gan·der** (gan'dẽr), *n.* [AS. *gan(d)ra*], 1. a male goose. 2. a stupid or silly fellow. 3. [Slang], a look: chiefly in the phrase *take a gander*.
**Gan·dhi, Mo·han·das Ka·ram·chand** (mō'hən-däs' kə-rəm-chund' gän'dē; Eng. gan'di), 1869–1948; Indian nationalist leader: called *Mahatma Gandhi*.
**gang** (gaŋ), *n.* [AS. *gang*, a going], 1. a group of people associated together in some way; specif., *a*) a group of workers directed by a foreman. *b*) an organized group of criminals. 2. a set of tools or machines designed to work together. *v.i.* to form a gang. *v.t.* [Colloq.], to attack as a gang. **—gang up on,** [Slang], to oppose as a group.
**gang** (gaŋ), *v.i.* [AS. *gangan*], [Scot.], to go; walk.
**Gan·ges** (gan'jēz), *n.* a river in N India, flowing from the Himalayas into the Bay of Bengal.
**gan·gling** (gaŋ'gliŋ), *adj.* [? ppr. of hyp. *gangle*, freq. of *gang*, to go], thin, tall, and awkward; of loose, lanky build: also **gan'gly.**
**gan·gli·on** (gaŋ'gli-ən), *n.* [*pl.* -GLIA (-ə), -GLIONS] [LL. < Gr. *ganglion*, tumor], 1. a mass of nerve cells serving as a center from which nerve impulses are transmitted. 2. a center of force, energy, etc. **—gan'gli·on'ic (-on'ik)** *adj.*
**gang·plank** (gaŋ'plaŋk'), *n.* a narrow, movable platform by which to board or leave a ship.
**gan·grene** (gaŋ'grēn), *n.* [OFr. < L. < Gr. *gaggraina* < *grainein*, to gnaw], decay of tissue in a part of the body when the blood supply is obstructed by injury, disease, etc. *v.t.* [-GRENED, -GRENING], to cause gangrene in. *v.i.* to decay. **—gan'gre·nous** (-gri-nəs), *adj.*
**gang·ster** (gaŋ'stẽr), *n.* 1. a member of a gang of criminals. 2. any criminal or tough.
**gang·way** (gaŋ'wā'), *n.* [AS. *gangweg*], a passageway; specif., *a*) an opening in a ship's side for freight or for passengers. *b*) a gangplank. *interj.* make room! clear the way!
**gan·net** (gan'it), *n.* [*pl.* -NETS, -NET; see PLURAL, II, D, 1], [AS. *ganot*], a large, web-footed water bird related to the heron and somewhat like a pelican.
**gan·oid** (gan'oid), *adj.* [< Fr. < Gr. *ganos*, brightness; + -*oid*], of a group of fishes that are covered by rows of hard, enameled scales, including the sturgeons and gars. *n.* a ganoid fish.
**gant·let** (gônt'lit, gant'-), *n.* [< Sw. *gatlopp*, a run down a lane < *gata*, lane + *lopp*, a run], 1. a former military punishment in which the offender ran between two rows of men who struck him with clubs, etc. as he passed. 2. a series of troubles or difficulties. Also sp. **gauntlet. —run the gantlet,** 1. to be punished by means of the gantlet. 2. to act while under attack, as by gossip, etc.
**gant·let** (gônt'lit, gant'-), *n.* a glove: see **gauntlet.**
**gan·try** (gan'tri), *n.* [*pl.* -TRIES], [< OFr. < L. *canterius*, rafter], 1. a frame for holding barrels horizontally. 2. a framework supported at each end so that it spans a distance, as for displaying railroad signals. 3. a wheeled framework with a crane, platforms, etc., for readying a rocket to be launched. Also **gauntry.**
**Gan·y·mede** (gan'ə-mēd'), *n.* in *Gr. mythology*, a beautiful youth who was cupbearer to the gods.
**gaol** (jāl), *n.* a jail: British sp. **—gaol'er,** *n.*
**gap** (gap), *n.* [ON. *gap* < *gapa*, to gape], 1. a hole or opening made by breaking or parting; breach. 2. a mountain pass or ravine. 3. a blank space; hiatus. 4. a difference between ideas, natures, etc. *v.t.* [GAPPED, GAPPING], to breach.
**gape** (gāp), *v.i.* [GAPED, GAPING], [< ON. *gapa*], 1. to open the mouth wide, as in yawning. 2. to stare with the mouth open, as in wonder. 3. to open wide, as a chasm. *n.* 1. an open-mouthed stare. 2. a yawn. 3. a wide opening. 4. in *zoology*, the measure of the widest possible opening of a mouth. **—the gapes,** 1. a disease of poultry and birds, characterized by gaping. 2. a fit of yawning. **—gap'er,** *n.* **—gap'ing·ly,** *adv.*
**gar** (gär), *n.* [*pl.* GAR, GARS; see PLURAL, II, D, 2], [AS. *gar*, a spear], any of a group of ganoid fishes with elongated bodies and long beaklike snouts.
**G.A.R.,** Grand Army of the Republic.
**ga·rage** (gə-räzh', -räj'; Brit. gar'ij), *n.* [Fr. < *garer*, to protect], 1. a shelter for automobiles. 2. a business establishment where automobiles are stored, repaired, etc. *v.t.* [-RAGED, -RAGING], to put or keep in a garage.
**Gar·and rifle** (gar'ənd, gə-rand'), [after John C. *Garand* (1888– ), Am. who invented it], a semi-automatic, rapid-firing, .30-caliber rifle.
**garb** (gärb), *n.* [< OFr. < It. *garbo*, elegance < OHG. < *garawen*, to dress < Gmc.], 1. clothing; manner or style of dress. 2. external form, covering, or appearance. *v.t.* to clothe; attire.
**gar·bage** (gär'bij), *n.* [ME., entrails of fowls], 1. waste parts of food, as from a market or kitchen; animal or vegetable matter that is thrown away. 2. any worthless or offensive matter.
**gar·ble** (gär'b'l), *v.t.* [-BLED, -BLING], [< OFr. < It. < Ar. *gharbala* < LL. *cribellare*, to sift < dim. of *cribrum*, a sieve], 1. to select, suppress, or otherwise distort parts of (a story, etc.) in telling, in order to mislead or misrepresent. 2. to confuse or mix up (a story, etc.) innocently. **—gar'bler,** *n.*
**‡gar·çon** (gȧr'sōn'), *n.* [*pl.* -CONS (-sōn')], [Fr.], 1. a boy or young man. 2. a waiter or servant.
**gar·den** (gär'd'n), *n.* [< ONorm.Fr. < Frank. *gardo*], 1. a piece of ground, usually close to a house, for the growing of fruits, flowers, or vegetables. 2. an area of fertile, richly cultivated land. 3. *often pl.* a parklike place for public enjoyment, often having special displays of animal or plant life. *v.i.* to make, work in, or take care of a garden, lawn, etc. *adj.* 1. of, for, or grown in a garden. 2. commonplace. **—gar'den·er,** *n.*
**Garden Grove,** a city in SW California, near Los Angeles: pop., 84,000.
**gar·de·ni·a** (gär-dēn'yə, -dē'ni-ə), *n.* [after Alexander *Garden* (1730–1791), Am. botanist], 1. a white or yellowish flower with fragrant, waxy petals. 2. the shrub on which it grows.
**Gar·field, James Abram** (gär'fēld), 1831–1881; 20th president of the U.S. (1881); assassinated.
**gar·fish** (gär'fish'), *n.* [*pl.* see FISH], a gar.
**Gar·gan·tu·a** (gär-gan'choo-ə), *n.* a giant king with prodigious appetites in *Gargantua and Pantagruel*, a satire by Rabelais. **—Gar·gan'tu·an,** *adj.*
**gargle** (gär'g'l), *v.i. & v.t.* [-GLED, -GLING], [< Fr. < *gargouille*, gargoyle < L. *gurgulio*, throat], to rinse (the throat) with a liquid kept in motion in the throat by the expulsion of air from the lungs. *n.* a liquid used for gargling.

**gar·goyle** (gär′goil), *n.* [OFr. *gargouille;* see GARGLE], a waterspout, usually carved in the form of a fantastic creature, projecting from the gutter of a building. —**gar′goyled,** *adj.*

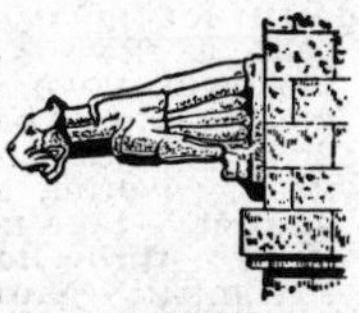
GARGOYLE

**Gar·i·bal·di, Giu·sep·pe** (jo͞o-zep′pe gä′rē-bäl′dē; Eng. gar′ə-bôl′di), 1807–1882; Italian patriot.

**gar·ish** (gâr′ish), *adj.* [prob. < ME. *gauren,* to stare], too bright or gaudy; showy; glaring. —**gar′ish·ly,** *adv.* —**gar′ish·ness,** *n.*

**gar·land** (gär′lənd), *n.* [< OFr. *garlande*], 1. a wreath of flowers, leaves, etc. 2. an anthology of poems, songs, etc. *v.t.* to form into or decorate with a garland or garlands.

**gar·lic** (gär′lik), *n.* [AS. *garleac; gar,* a spear + *leac,* a leek], 1. a bulbous plant of the lily family. 2. its strong-smelling bulb, made up of small sections called cloves, used as seasoning in meats, salads, etc. —**gar′lick·y,** *adj.*

**gar·ment** (gär′mənt), *n.* [< OFr. *garnement* < *garnir;* see GARNISH], 1. any article of clothing. 2. a covering. *v.t.* to clothe.

**gar·ner** (gär′nẽr), *n.* [< OFr. < L. *granarium* < *granum,* grain], 1. a granary. 2. a store of anything. *v.t.* to gather up and store.

**gar·net** (gär′nit), *n.* [< OFr. < ML. *granatus* < L. *granum,* a grain], 1. a hard, glasslike silicate mineral of various colors: the most precious variety, used as a gem, is of a deep, transparent red. 2. deep red. —**gar′net·like′,** *adj.*

**gar·nish** (gär′nish), *v.t.* [< OFr. *g(u)arnir,* to protect; prob. < MHG. *warnen,* to prepare], 1. to decorate; adorn; trim. 2. to decorate (food) with something that adds color or flavor. 3. in *law,* to bring garnishment proceedings against. *n.* 1. a decoration; ornament. 2. something used to garnish food, as parsley. —**gar′nish·er,** *n.*

**gar·nish·ee** (gär′ni-shē′), *n.* in *law,* a person served with a garnishment (sense 2*b*), *v.t.* [-EED, -EEING], in *law, a)* to attach (a debtor's property, wages, etc.) by the authority of a court, so that it can be used to pay the debt. *b)* to order (a person) not to dispose of the defendant's money or property in his possession pending settlement of the lawsuit.

**gar·nish·ment** (gär′nish-mənt), *n.* 1. a decoration; embellishment. 2. in *law, a)* a summons to a person other than the litigants to appear in a lawsuit. *b)* a notice ordering a person not to dispose of a defendant's property or money in his possession pending settlement of the lawsuit.

**gar·ni·ture** (gär′ni-chẽr), *n.* garnish; trimming.

**ga·rotte** (gə-rot′), *n.* & *v.t.* [-ROTTED, -ROTTING], garrote.

**gar pike,** a North American fresh-water fish of the gar family.

**gar·ret** (gar′it), *n.* [< OFr. *garite,* watchtower < *garir,* to watch < Gmc.], the space or rooms just below the sloping roof of a house; attic.

**Gar·rick, David** (gar′ik), 1717–1779; English actor.

**gar·ri·son** (gar′i-s'n), *n.* [< OFr. < *garir* (see GARRET)], 1. troops stationed in a fort. 2. a fortified place with troops, guns, etc. *v.t.* 1. to station troops in (a fortified place) for its defense. 2. to station (troops) in a garrison.

**Gar·ri·son, William Lloyd** (gar′i-s'n), 1805–1879; U.S. editor and abolitionist.

**gar·rote** (gə-rot′, -rōt′), *n.* [Sp., orig., a stick used to wind a cord < Celt.], 1. a Spanish method of execution by strangling with an iron collar. 2. the iron collar so used. 3. any device used in strangling a person. 4. a disabling by strangling, especially in an attack for robbery. *v.t.* [-ROTED or -ROTTED, -ROTING or -ROTTING], 1. to execute or attack with a garrote or by strangling. 2. to strangle and rob. —**gar·rot′er, gar·rot′ter, ga·rot′ter,** *n.*

**gar·rotte** (gə-rot′), *n.* & *v.t.* [-ROTTED, -ROTTING], garrote.

**gar·ru·lous** (gar′oo-ləs, -yoo-), *adj.* [< L. < *garrire,* to chatter], talking much, often about unimportant things; loquacious. —**gar′ru·lous·ly,** *adv.* —**gar·ru·li·ty** (gə-ro͞o′lə-ti), **gar′ru·lous·ness,** *n.*

**gar·ter** (gär′tẽr), *n.* [ONorm.Fr. *gartier* < OFr. *garet,* the back of the knee < Celt.], 1. an elastic band or strap for holding a stocking in position. 2. [G-], *a)* the badge of the Order of the Garter, the highest order of British knighthood. *b)* the order itself. *v.t.* to fasten with a garter.

**garter belt,** a belt, usually of elastic fabric, with garters suspended from it, worn by women.

**garter snake,** any of various small, harmless, striped snakes, common in North America.

**Gar·y** (gâr′i), *n.* a city in NW Indiana, on Lake Michigan: pop., 178,000.

**gas** (gas), *n.* [coined by the Belgian chemist, Van Helmont (1577–1644), after Gr. *chaos,* chaos], 1. the fluid form of a substance in which it can expand indefinitely; form neither liquid nor solid; vapor. 2. any mixture of inflammable gases used for lighting or heating. 3. any gas used as an anesthetic. 4. any substance dispersed through the atmosphere, as in war, to act as a poison or irritant. 5. [Colloq.], gasoline. 6. [Slang], idle or boastful talk. 7. in *mining,* a mixture of firedamp with air that explodes if ignited. *v.t.* [GASSED, GASSING], 1. to supply with gas. 2. to subject to the action of gas. 3. to attack, injure, or kill by gas, as in war. *v.i.* 1. to give off gas. 2. [Slang], to talk in an idle or boastful way. *adj.* of or using gas.

**Gas·con** (gas′kən), *adj.* 1. of Gascony or its people, noted for boastfulness. 2. [g-], boastful. *n.* 1. a native of Gascony. 2. [g-], a boaster.

**gas·con·ade** (gas′kə-nād′), *n.* [see GASCON & -ADE], boastful talk; brag. *v.i.* [-ADED, -ADING], to boast or bluster.

**Gas·co·ny** (gas′kə-ni), *n.* a former province of SW France: French name, **Gas·cogne** (gȧs′kôn′y′).

**gas engine,** an internal-combustion engine.

**gas·e·ous** (gas′i-əs, gas′yəs), *adj.* of, like, or in the form of, gas. —**gas′e·ous·ness,** *n.*

**gas fitter,** a person whose work is installing and repairing gas pipes and fixtures.

**gas furnace,** 1. a furnace that distills gas from coal, etc. 2. a furnace that burns gas as fuel.

**gash** (gash), *v.t.* [< OFr. *garser*], to make a long, deep cut in; slash. *n.* a long, deep cut.

**gas·i·fy** (gas′ə-fī′), *v.t.* & *v.i.* [-FIED, -FYING], to change into gas. —**gas′i·fi′a·ble,** *adj.* —**gas′i·fi·ca′tion,** *n.* —**gas′i·fi′er,** *n.*

**gas jet,** 1. a flame of illuminating gas. 2. a nozzle at the end of a gas lamp or burner.

**gas·ket** (gas′kit), *n.* [prob. < It. *gaschetta,* a rope end], 1. a piece or ring of rubber, metal, etc. placed around a piston or joint to make it leakproof. 2. in *nautical usage,* a rope or cord by which a furled sail is tied to the yard.

**gas·light** (gas′līt′), *n.* 1. the light produced by burning illuminating gas. 2. a gas jet or burner. *adj.* of or characteristic of the period of gaslight illumination: as, *gaslight* melodrama.

**gas mantle,** a tube of fabric fastened over a gas burner to give off light when heated.

**gas mask,** a filtering device for the face to protect against breathing in poisonous gases.

**gas·o·line, gas·o·lene** (gas′'l-ēn′, gas′'l-ēn′), *n.* [< *gas* + L. *oleum,* oil; + *-ine, -ene*], a volatile, highly inflammable, colorless liquid produced by the distillation of petroleum and used chiefly as a fuel in internal-combustion engines.

**gas·om·e·ter** (gas-om′ə-tẽr), *n.* 1. a container for holding and measuring gas. 2. a gas reservoir.

**gasp** (gasp), *v.i.* [< ON. *geispa,* to yawn], to catch the breath suddenly or with effort, as in surprise or in choking. *v.t.* to say with gasps. *n.* a gasping; catching of the breath with difficulty.

**gas station,** a place for the sale of gasoline, oil, services, etc. for motor vehicles.

**gas·sy** (gas′i), *adj.* [-SIER, -SIEST], 1. full of or containing gas. 2. like gas. 3. [Colloq.], full of pretentious or boastful talk. —**gas′si·ness,** *n.*

**gas·tric** (gas′trik), *adj.* [< *gastro-* + *-ic*], of, in, or near the stomach.

**gastric juice,** the acid digestive fluid produced by glands in the mucous membrane lining the stomach: it contains enzymes and hydrochloric acid.

**gastric ulcer,** an ulcer of the stomach lining.

**gas·tri·tis** (gas-trī′tis), *n.* [< *gastro-* + *-itis*], inflammation of the stomach, especially of the stomach lining. —**gas·trit′ic** (-trit′ik), *adj.*

**gas·tro-,** [< Gr. *gastēr,* the stomach], a combining form meaning *the stomach (and)*: also **gastr-.**

**gas·tro·in·tes·ti·nal** (gas′trō-in-tes′ti-n'l), *adj.* of the stomach and the intestines.

**gas·tro·nome** (gas′trə-nōm′), *n.* a person who enjoys and has a discriminating taste for foods: also **gas·tron′o·mer** (-tron′ə-mẽr), **gas·tron′o·mist.**

**gas·tron·o·my** (gas-tron′ə-mi), *n.* [< Fr. < Gr. < *gastēr,* the stomach + *nomos,* law], the art of good eating. —**gas·tro·nom·ic** (gas′trə-nom′ik), **gas′tro·nom′i·cal,** *adj.* —**gas′tro·nom′i·cal·ly,** *adv.*

**gas·tro·pod** (gas′trə-pod′), *n.* [*gastro-* + *-pod*], any of a large group of mollusks having single spiral shells, as the snail, nautilus, etc., or no shells, as certain slugs: gastropods move by means of a broad, muscular, ventral disk. *adj.* of or like a gastropod.

**gas·tru·la** (gas′troo-lə), *n.* [*pl.* -LAE (-lē′), -LAS (-ləz)], [Mod. L., dim. < Gr. *gastēr*, the stomach], an embryo in the early stage of development, consisting of a sac with two layers, the ectoderm and endoderm. —**gas′tru·lar,** *adj.*

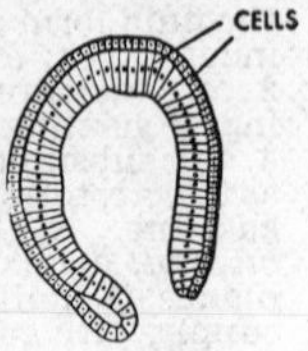

GASTRULA

**gat** (gat), archaic pt. of **get.**

**gat** (gat), *n.* [< *Gat*ling gun], [Slang], a pistol.

**gate** (gāt), *n.* [< AS. *geat*], 1. a movable structure controlling entrance or exit through an opening in a fence or wall. 2. an opening for passage through a fence or wall, with or without such a structure; gateway. 3. any means of entrance: as, the *gate* to one's heart. 4. a movable barrier, as at a railroad crossing. 5. a structure controlling the flow of water, as in a pipe, canal, etc. 6. *a)* the total amount of admission money paid by spectators to a performance or exhibition. *b)* the total number of such spectators. —**give the gate,** [Slang], to get rid of; dismiss. —**gate′like′,** *adj.* —**gate′man** [*pl.* -MEN], *n.*

**gate-leg table** (gāt′leg′), a table with drop leaves supported by gatelike legs that swing back to let the leaves drop: also **gate-legged table.**

**gate·way** (gāt′wā′), *n.* 1. an entrance in a wall, fence, etc. fitted with a gate. 2. a means of going in or out; means of getting at something.

**gath·er** (gath′ēr), *v.t.* [AS. *gad(e)rian*], 1. to bring together in one place or group. 2. to get gradually from various places, sources, etc.; accumulate. 3. to pick or collect by picking, as a harvest. 4. to infer; conclude. 5. to prepare (oneself, one's energies) to meet a situation. 6. to gain or acquire gradually: as, to *gather* speed. 7. to draw (cloth) into fixed folds or pleats. 8. to wrinkle (one's brow). *v.i.* 1. to come together; assemble. 2. to form pus; come to a head, as a boil. 3. to increase. 4. to become wrinkled: said of the brow. *n.* a pleat. —**gath′er·a·ble,** *adj.* —**gath′er·er,** *n.*

**gath·er·ing** (gath′ēr-iŋ), *n.* 1. the act of one that gathers. 2. what is gathered; specif., *a)* a meeting; assemblage; crowd; party. *b)* a collection for charity. 3. a festering; boil; abscess.

**Gat·ling gun** (gat′liŋ), [after R. J. *Gatling* (1818–1903), U.S. inventor], an obsolete kind of machine gun consisting of a rotating cluster of barrels arranged parallel with and around an axis.

**gauche** (gōsh), *adj.* [Fr. < MFr. *gauchir*, to become warped; ult. < Frank.], awkward; tactless; lacking social grace. —**gauche′ly,** *adv.* —**gauche′ness,** *n.*

**gau·che·rie** (gō′shə-rē′), *n.* quality, fact, or instance of being awkward or tactless.

**Gau·cho** (gou′chō), *n.* [*pl.* -CHOS], [Sp.], a cowboy of mixed Indian and Spanish ancestry, living on the South American pampas.

**gaud** (gôd), *n.* [prob. < OFr. *gaudir*, to make merry < L. *gaudere*], a cheap, showy ornament; trinket.

**gaud·y** (gôd′i), *adj.* [-IER, -IEST], bright and showy, but in bad taste; cheaply brilliant and ornate. —**gaud′i·ly,** *adv.* —**gaud′i·ness,** *n.*

**gauge** (gāj), *n.* [< the *v.*], 1. a measure; standard measure or scale of measurement. 2. dimensions; capacity; extent. 3. any device for measuring something: as, a pressure *gauge*, wire *gauge*, etc. 4. any means of estimating. 5. the distance between the two rails of a railway (**standard gauge** is 56½ inches) or between parallel wheels on a vehicle. 6. the size of the bore of a shotgun as determined by the number per pound of spherical projectiles fitting the bore. *v.t.* [GAUGED, GAUGING], [ONorm.Fr. *gauger*], 1. to measure accurately by means of a gauge. 2. to measure the size, amount, or capacity of. 3. to estimate; judge. 4. to make conform with a standard. Also sp. **gage.** —**gauge′a·ble,** *adj.*

**gaug·er** (gāj′ēr), *n.* 1. a person or thing that gauges; esp., an official who measures the contents of casks of liquor, etc. to be taxed. 2. a collector of excise taxes. Also sp. **gager.**

**Gau·guin, Paul** (pôl gō′gan′), 1848–1903; French painter; in Tahiti after 1890.

**Gaul** (gôl), *n.* 1. an ancient division of the Roman Empire, consisting of France and Belgium, northern Italy, and parts of the Netherlands, Germany, and Switzerland. 2. any of the Celtic-speaking people of ancient Gaul. 3. a Frenchman.

**Gaul·ish** (gôl′ish), *adj.* of Gaul or the Gauls. *n.* the Celtic language spoken in ancient Gaul.

**gaunt** (gônt, gänt), *adj.* [ME. *gawnte;* infl. by ON. *gandr*, thin pole], 1. thin and bony; hollow-eyed and haggard, as from great hunger or age. 2. looking grim, forbidding, or desolate. —**gaunt′ly,** *adv.* —**gaunt′ness,** *n.*

**gaunt·let** (gônt′lit, gänt′-), *n.* [< OFr. dim. of *gant*, a glove < Frank. *want*, a mitten], 1. a medieval glove, usually of leather covered with metal plates, worn to protect the hand in combat. 2. a long glove with a flaring cuff, or the cuff itself, covering the lower part of the arm. Also **gantlet.** —**take up the gauntlet,** to accept a challenge. —**throw down the gauntlet,** to challenge, as to combat. —**gaunt′let·ed,** *adj.*

**gaunt·let** (gônt′lit, gänt′-), *n.* a gantlet (form of punishment).

**gauss** (gous), *n.* [after K. *Gauss* (1777–1855), G. physicist], in *electricity*, a unit used in measuring magnetic induction or magnetic intensity.

**Gau·ta·ma** (gou′tə-mə, gô′-), *n.* see **Buddha.**

**gauze** (gôz), *n.* [Fr. *gaze;* ? < *Gaza*, a city in Palestine], 1. any very thin, transparent, loosely woven material, as of cotton, silk, or wire. 2. a thin mist. *adj.* made of or resembling gauze.

**gauz·y** (gôz′i), *adj.* [-IER, -IEST], thin, light, and transparent, like gauze. —**gauz′i·ly,** *adv.* —**gauz′i·ness,** *n.*

**gave** (gāv), pt. of **give.**

**gav·el** (gav′′l), *n.* [? akin to MD. *gaffele*, a fork], a small mallet rapped on the table by a presiding officer in calling for attention or silence.

**ga·vi·al** (gā′vi-əl), *n.* [Fr. < Hind. *ghariyāl*], a large crocodile of India, with a long muzzle.

**ga·votte, ga·vot** (gə-vot′), *n.* [Fr. < Pr. *gavoto*, dance of the *Gavots*, an Alpine people], 1. a 17th-century dance like the minuet, but livelier. 2. the music for this, in **4/4** time.

**Ga·wain** (gä′win), *n.* in *Arthurian legend*, a knight of the Round Table, nephew of King Arthur.

**gawk** (gôk), *n.* [prob. dial. var. of *gowk*, stupid person], a clumsy, stupid fellow; simpleton. *v.i.* [Colloq.], to stare in a stupid way.

**gawk·y** (gôk′i), *adj.* [-IER, -IEST], clumsy; ungainly. *n.* a gawk. —**gawk′i·ly,** *adv.* —**gawk′i·ness,** *n.*

**gay** (gā), *adj.* [< OFr. *gai*], 1. joyous and lively; merry. 2. bright; brilliant: as, *gay* colors. 3. given to social pleasures: as, a *gay* life. 4. wanton; licentious: as, a *gay* dog. —**gay′ness,** *n.*

**gay·e·ty** (gā′ə-ti), *n.* [*pl.* -TIES], gaiety.

**gay·ly** (gā′li), *adv.* gaily.

**gaze** (gāz), *v.i.* [GAZED, GAZING], [prob. < ON.], to look intently and steadily; stare. *n.* a steady look. —**gaz′er,** *n.*

**ga·zelle** (gə-zel′), *n.* [*pl.* -ZELLES, -ZELLE; see PLURAL, II, D, 1], [Fr.; Ar. *ghazāl*], any of various small, swift, graceful antelopes of Africa, the Near East, and Asia, with spirally twisted horns and large, lustrous eyes.

**ga·zette** (gə-zet′), *n.* [Fr. < It. *gazzetta* < dial. *gazeta*, a small coin (price of the paper)], 1. a newspaper. 2. in England, any of various official government publications, containing announcements and bulletins. *v.t.* [-ZETTED, -ZETTING], to announce or list in a gazette.

**gaz·et·teer** (gaz′ə-têr′), *n.* 1. *a)* a person who writes for a gazette. *b)* an official appointed to publish a gazette. 2. a dictionary or index of geographical names.

**G.B.,** Great Britain.

**G clef,** the treble clef.

**Gd,** in *chemistry*, gadolinium.

**G.D.,** 1. Grand Duchess. 2. Grand Duke.

**Gdy·nia** (g′dēn′yä), *n.* a seaport in Poland, on the Bay of Danzig: pop., 111,000.

**Ge** (jē, gē), *n.* Gaea.

**Ge,** in *chemistry*, germanium.

**gear** (gêr), *n.* [< ON. *gervi*, preparation], 1. clothing and personal equipment. 2. apparatus or equipment for some particular task, as a workman's tools, a harness, a ship's rigging, etc. 3. in *mechanics*, *a)* a system of toothed wheels meshed together so that the motion of one is passed on to the others. *b)* a gearwheel. *c)* proper working order: as, out of *gear*. *d)* a specific adjustment: in motor-vehicle transmissions, *high gear* provides greatest speed and *low gear* greatest power. *e)* a part of a mechanism performing a specific function: as a steering *gear*. *v.t.* 1. to furnish with gear; equip. 2. *a)* to connect by gears. *b)* to furnish with gears. *c)* to put into gear. *v.i.* to be in, or come into, proper adjustment or working order. —**in** (or **out of**) **gear,** 1. (not) connected to the motor; (not) in adjustment for use. 2. (not) in order. —**shift gears,** in a multiple gear system, to change from one gear arrangement to another. —**geared,** *adj.* —**gear′less,** *adj.*

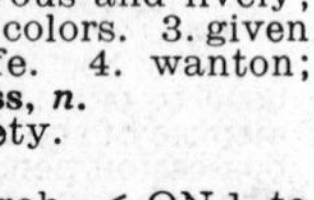
GEARS

**gear·ing** (gêr′iŋ), *n.* 1. the arrangement of gears in a machine. 2. in *mechanics*, a system of gears or other parts for transmitting motion.
**gear·shift** (gêr′shift′), *n.* a device for connecting or disconnecting any of a number of sets of transmission gears to a motor, etc.
**gear·wheel** (gêr′hwēl′), *n.* a toothed wheel designed to mesh with another or others: also **gear wheel.**
**geck·o** (gek′ō), *n.* [*pl.* -OS, -OES], [Malay *gekoq*, echoic of its cry], a soft-skinned, insect-eating lizard with suction pads on its feet.
**gee** (jē), *interj.* & *n.* [cf. *haw* (command)], a word of command to a horse, ox, etc., meaning "turn to the right!" *v.t.* & *v.i.* [GEED, GEEING], to turn to the right. Also sp. **jee.** Opposed to *haw*.
**gee** (jē), *interj.* [euphemistic contraction of *Jesus*], [Slang], an exclamation of surprise, etc.
**geese** (gēs), *n.* pl. of **goose.**
**gee·zer** (gē′zēr), *n.* [< dial. *guiser*, a mummer < *guise*], [Slang], an eccentric old man.
**Ge·hen·na** (gi-hen′ə), *n.* [< Heb. *gēhinnōm*, the valley of Hinnom, near Jerusalem, where fires were kept burning for refuse], 1. a place of torment and burning. 2. in the *New Testament*, hell.
**Gei·ger counter** (gī′gēr), [after Hans *Geiger* (1882–1945), G. physicist], a gas-filled instrument with a needlelike electrode, for detecting and counting ionizing particles (**Geigers**), as from radioactive ores: the **Geiger-Müller** (-mü′lēr) **counter** is similar but has an electrical amplifying system.
**gei·sha** (gā′shə), *n.* [*pl.* -SHA, -SHAS], [Japan.], a Japanese professional singing and dancing girl.
**gel** (jel), *n.* [< *gelatin*], a jellylike substance formed by a colloidal solution in its solid phase. *v.i.* [GELLED, GELLING], to form a gel.
**gel·a·tin, gel·a·tine** (jel′ə-t'n), *n.* [< Fr. < It. < *gelata*, a jelly < pp. of L. *gelare*, to freeze], 1. *a*) the tasteless, odorless, brittle substance extracted by boiling bones, hoofs, etc. *b*) a similar vegetable substance: gelatin dissolves in hot water, forming a jellylike substance when cool, and is used in various foods, photographic film, etc. 2. a jelly made with gelatin.
**ge·lat·i·nize** (ji-lat′'n-īz′), *v.t.* [-NIZED, -NIZING], 1. to change into gelatin or gelatinous matter. 2. in *photography*, to coat with gelatin. *v.i.* to be changed into gelatin or gelatinous matter.
**ge·lat·i·nous** (ji-lat′'n-əs), *adj.* 1. of or containing gelatin. 2. like gelatin or jelly; viscous. —**ge·lat′i·nous·ly,** *adv.* —**ge·lat′i·nous·ness,** *n.*
**geld** (geld), *v.t.* [GELDED or GELT, GELDING], [< ON. *gelda* < *geldr*, barren], 1. to remove the testicles of (a horse, etc.); castrate. 2. to devitalize.
**geld·ing** (gel′diŋ), *n.* a gelded animal, especially a horse.
**gel·id** (jel′id), *adj.* [< L. *gelidus* < *gelu*, frost], frozen; frosty; extremely cold. —**ge·lid′i·ty** (jə-lid′ə-ti), **gel′id·ness,** *n.* —**gel′id·ly,** *adv.*
**gem** (jem), *n.* [< OFr. < L. *gemma*, a bud, gem], 1. a precious stone, cut and polished for use as a jewel. 2. anything prized for its beauty and value. 3. a kind of muffin. *v.t.* [GEMMED, GEMMING], to adorn or set with or as with gems.
**gem·i·nate** (jem′ə-nāt′), *adj.* [< L. pp. of *geminare*, to double < *geminus*, twin], growing or combined in pairs; coupled. *v.t.* & *v.i.* [-NATED, -NATING], to double; arrange or be arranged in pairs. —**gem′i·nate·ly,** *adv.* —**gem′i·na′tion,** *n.*
**Gem·i·ni** (jem′ə-nī′), *n.pl.* [L., twins], 1. a northern constellation containing the stars Castor and Pollux, represented as twins sitting together. 2. the third sign of the zodiac (♊ or □ or ♊), entered by the sun about May 21.
**gem·ma** (jem′ə), *n.* [*pl.* -MAE (-ē)], [L.], in *biology*, 1. a bud. 2. a budlike outgrowth which becomes detached and develops into a new organism.
**gem·mate** (jem′āt), *adj.* [< L. *gemmatus*, pp. < *gemma*, a bud], having or reproducing by gemmae. *v.i.* [-MATED, -MATING], to have, or reproduce by, gemmae; bud. —**gem·ma′tion,** *n.*
**gem·mule** (jem′ūl), *n.* in *biology*, a small gemma.
**gems·bok** (gemz′bok′), *n.* [*pl.* -BOK, -BOKS; see PLURAL, II, D, 2], [D. < G. *gemse*, chamois + *bock*, a buck], a large, South African antelope with long, straight horns.
**-gen** (jen, jən), [< Fr. < Gr. < base of *gignesthai*, to be born], a suffix meaning: 1. *something that produces*, as in *oxygen*. 2. *something produced* (in a specified way), as in *endogen*.
**Gen.,** 1. General. 2. Genesis.
**gen.,** 1. gender. 2. general. 3. genitive.
**gen·darme** (zhän′därm), *n.* [*pl.* -DARMES (-därmz)], [Fr., ult. < L. *gens*, a people + *de*, of + *arma*, arms], 1. in France, Belgium, etc., an armed policeman; hence, 2. any policeman.
**gen·dar·me·rie** (zhän′där-mēr-i), *n.* [Fr.], gendarmes collectively; the police: also **gen′darm·er·y.**
**gen·der** (jen′dēr), *n.* [< OFr. < L. *genus*, descent, origin], 1. in *grammar*, *a*) the classification by which nouns and pronouns (and often their modifiers) are grouped and inflected as masculine, feminine, or neuter. *b*) any one of such groupings. 2. [Colloq.], sex.
**gene** (jēn), *n.* [see -GEN], in *genetics*, any of the elements in the chromosome by which hereditary characters are transmitted and determined.
**ge·ne·al·o·gist** (jē′ni-al′ə-jist, jen′i-äl′-), *n.* a person who studies genealogies or traces them.
**ge·ne·al·o·gy** (jē′ni-al′ə-ji, jen′i-äl′-), *n.* [*pl.* -GIES], [< OFr. < LL. < Gr. < *genea*, race + *logos*, a discourse < *legein*, to speak], 1. a recorded history of the ancestry or descent of a person or family. 2. the study of family descent. 3. descent from an ancestor; pedigree; lineage. —**ge′ne·a·log′i·cal** (-ə-loj′i-k'l), **ge′ne·a·log′ic,** *adj.* —**ge′ne·a·log′i·cal·ly,** *adv.*
**gen·er·a** (jen′ēr-ə), *n.* pl. of **genus.**
**gen·er·al** (jen′ēr-əl, jen′rəl), *adj.* [< OFr. < L. *generalis* < *genus*, kind, class], 1. of, for, or from the whole or all; not particular or specialized: as, a *general* anesthetic. 2. of, for, or applying to a whole genus, kind, class, order, or race: as, *man* is a *general* term for all human beings. 3. existing or occurring extensively; widespread: as, *general* unrest in the country. 4. most common; usual: as, the *general* pronunciation of a word. 5. concerned with the main or over-all features; lacking in details; hence, 6. vague; not precise: as, he spoke in *general* terms. 7. highest in rank: as, the attorney *general*. *n.* 1. the main or over-all fact, idea, etc. 2. the head of a religious order. 3. *a*) an army officer ranking just above a lieutenant general: also **full general.** *b*) any general officer. —**in general,** 1. in the main; usually. 2. without specific details. —**gen′er·al·ness,** *n.*
**General American,** the English language as spoken by most people in the U.S., exclusive of much of New England and most of the South.
**General Assembly,** 1. the legislative assembly of some States. 2. the UN legislative assembly.
**gen·er·al·cy** (jen′ēr-əl-si, jen′rəl-si), *n.* [*pl.* -CIES], the rank or authority of a general.
**general election,** an election to choose between candidates nominated in a primary election.
**gen·er·al·is·si·mo** (jen′ēr-əl-is′ə-mō, jen rəl-), *n.* [*pl.* -MOS], [It.; see GENERAL], 1. in certain countries, the commander in chief of all the armed forces. 2. the commanding officer of several armies in the field.
**gen·er·al·i·ty** (jen′ə-ral′ə-ti), *n.* [*pl.* -TIES], 1. the condition or quality of being general. 2. a general, or nonspecific, statement, expression, etc. 3. the bulk; main body; majority.
**gen·er·al·i·za·tion** (jen′ēr-əl-i-zā′shən, jen′rəl-ī-), *n.* 1. the act or process of generalizing. 2. an idea, statement, etc. resulting from this.
**gen·er·al·ize** (jen′ēr-əl-īz′, jen′rəl-), *v.t.* [-IZED, -IZING], to make general; esp., *a*) to state in terms of a general law. *b*) to infer from particular instances. *c*) to draw or infer general principles, etc. from. *d*) to emphasize the general character rather than specific details of; make vague. *e*) to cause to be widely known or used. *v.i.* 1. to formulate general principles from particulars. 2. to talk in generalities; make vague statements. —**gen′er·al·iz′er,** *n.*
**gen·er·al·ly** (jen′ēr-əl-i, jen′rəl-i), *adv.* 1. widely; popularly; extensively. 2. in most instances; usually. 3. in a general way; not specifically.
**general officer,** any army officer above a colonel in rank.
**General of the Army,** the highest rank in the U.S. Army, having the insigne of five stars.
**gen·er·al·ship** (jen′ēr-əl-ship′, jen′rəl-), *n.* 1. *a*) the rank, commission, tenure of office, or authority of a general. *b*) the military skill of a general. 2. skillfulness of directing; leadership.
**general staff,** a group of high-ranking army officers who plan military operations.
**gen·er·ate** (jen′ə-rāt′), *v.t.* [-ATED, -ATING], [< L. pp. of *generare* < *genus*, race, kind], 1. to produce (offspring); beget. 2. to bring into being; produce. 3. in *mathematics*, to trace out or form (a line, plane, figure, or solid) by the motion of a point, line, or plane.

**gen·er·a·tion** (jen'ə-rā'shən), *n.* 1. the act or process of producing offspring. 2. a bringing into being; production, as of electricity. 3. a single stage in the succession of descent: as, father and son are two *generations*. 4. the average time (about thirty years) between the birth of successive generations. 5. all the people born at about the same time. 6. in *mathematics*, the formation of a line, plane, figure, or solid by the motion of a point, line, or plane.

**gen·er·a·tive** (jen'ə-rā'tiv, jen'ẽr-ə-), *adj.* of, or having the power of, generation or production. —**gen'er·a'tive·ly,** *adv.* —**gen'er·a'tive·ness,** *n.*

**gen·er·a·tor** (jen'ə-rā'tẽr), *n.* a person or thing that generates; esp., *a*) a machine for producing gas or steam. *b*) a machine for changing mechanical energy into electrical energy; dynamo.

**gen·er·a·trix** (jen'ə-rā'triks), *n.* [*pl.* -TRICES (-ẽr-ə-trī'sēz)], in *mathematics*, a generating point, line, or plane: see **generate,** sense 3.

**ge·ner·ic** (jə-ner'ik), *adj.* [< L. *genus*, race, kind; + *-ic*], 1. of, applied to, or referring to a kind, class, or group; inclusive or general: opposed to *specific*. 2. in *biology*, of or characteristic of a genus. —**ge·ner'i·cal·ly,** *adv.*

**gen·er·os·i·ty** (jen'ə-ros'ə-ti), *n.* 1. the quality of being generous; specif., *a*) nobility of mind; magnanimity. *b*) willingness to give or share; unselfishness. 2. [*pl.* -TIES], a generous act.

**gen·er·ous** (gen'ẽr-əs), *adj.* [< OFr. < L. *generosus*, of noble birth, excellent < *genus*, race, kind], 1. noble-minded; gracious; magnanimous. 2. willing to give or share; unselfish; liberal. 3. large; ample: as, a *generous* portion. 4. fertile: said of land. 5. full-flavored and strong: said of wine. —**gen'er·ous·ly,** *adv.* —**gen'er·ous·ness,** *n.*

**gen·e·sis** (jen'ə-sis), *n.* [*pl.* -SES (-sēz')], [L. < Gr.], 1. [G-], the first book of the Old Testament, giving an account of the creation of the universe. 2. a beginning; origin; creation.

**-gen·e·sis,** a combining form, meaning *origination, creation, evolution* (of something specified).

**gen·et** (jen'it), *n.* a jennet.

**ge·net·ic** (jə-net'ik), *adj.* [< *genesis*], 1. of the genesis, or origin, of something. 2. of genetics. —**ge·net'i·cal·ly,** *adv.*

**ge·net·ics** (jə-net'iks), *n.pl.* [construed as sing.], [< *genetic*], the branch of biology that deals with heredity and variation in similar or related animals and plants. —**ge·net'i·cist** (-ə-sist), *n.*

**Ge·ne·va** (jə-nē'və), *n.* 1. a city in Switzerland, on Lake Geneva: pop., 144,000. 2. a lake between SW Switzerland and France: also called *Lake Leman*. —**Ge·ne'van, Gen·e·vese** (jen'ə-vēz'), [*pl.* -VESE], *n.* & *adj.*

**Geneva Convention,** an international agreement signed at Geneva in 1864, establishing a code for the care and protection in wartime of the sick, wounded, and prisoners of war.

**Gen·ghis Khan** (jeŋ'giz kän'), 1167–1227; Mongol conqueror of central Asia: also sp. **Jenghiz Khan.**

**gen·ial** (jēn'yəl; *occas.* jē'ni-əl), *adj.* [L. *genialis*, of (one's) genius, or guardian deity], 1. good for life and growth; warm and mild: as, a *genial* climate. 2. cheerful, friendly, and sympathetic; amiable. —**ge·ni·al·i·ty** (jē'ni-al'ə-ti, jēn-yal'-), **gen'ial·ness,** *n.* —**gen'ial·ly,** *adv.*

**-gen·ic** (jen'ik), a combining form used to form adjectives corresponding to nouns ending in *-gen* or *-geny*, as in *phylogenic*.

**ge·nie** (jē'ni), *n.* [< Fr. *génie*], a jinni; spirit.

**gen·i·tal** (jen'ə-t'l), *adj.* [< OFr. < L. *genitalis* < pp. of *genere, gignere*, to beget], of reproduction or the sexual organs.

**gen·i·tals** (jen'ə-t'lz), *n.pl.* [< *genital*], the reproductive organs; esp., the external sex organs: also **gen'i·ta'li·a** (-ə-tāl'yə).

**gen·i·tive** (jen'ə-tiv), *adj.* of or in the genitive case. *n.* 1. the genitive case. 2. a word or construction in the genitive case. —**gen'i·ti'val** (-tī'v'l), *adj.* —**gen'i·ti'val·ly,** *adv.*

**genitive case,** [after L. *casus genitivus*, lit., case of birth or origin; mistransl. < Gr. *genikē*, generic (case) < Gr. *genos*, genus], 1. a case in Latin grammar shown by inflection of nouns, pronouns, and adjectives, chiefly expressing possession, origin, source, etc. 2. loosely, any similar case, as the possessive case in English.

**gen·i·to·u·ri·nar·y, gen·i·to-u·ri·nar·y** (jen'i-tō-yoor'ə-ner'i), *adj.* designating or of the genital and urinary organs together.

**gen·ius** (jēn'yəs, jē'ni-əs), *n.* [*pl.* for 3, 4, 5, 6 GENIUSES, for 1 & 2 GENII (jē'ni-ī')], [L., guardian deity < base of *genere*, to produce], 1. *a*) [often G-], the guardian spirit of a person, place, etc. *b*) either of two spirits, one good and one evil, supposed to influence one's destiny. *c*) a person considered as having strong influence over another. 2. a jinni; spirit. 3. particular character or spirit of a nation, place, age, etc. 4. natural ability; strong inclination (with *to* or *for*). 5. great mental capacity and inventive ability. 6. a person having such capacity or ability.

**Gen·o·a** (jen'ō-ə, ji-nō'ə), *n.* a seaport in NW Italy: pop., 683,000: Italian name, **Ge·no·va** (je'nô-vä'). —**Gen'o·ese'** (-ēz'), *adj.* & *n.* [*pl.* -ESE].

**gen·o·cide** (jen'ə-sīd'), *n.* [< Gr. *genos*, race, kind; + *-cide*], the systematic killing or extermination of a whole people or nation. —**gen'o·cid'al,** *adj.*

**-ge·nous** (jə-nəs), [*-gen* + *-ous*], a suffix meaning: 1. *producing, generating*, as in *nitrogenous*. 2. *produced by, generated in*, as in *endogenous*.

**gen·re** (zhän'rə; Fr. zhän'r'), *n.* [Fr. < L. *genus*; see GENUS], 1. a kind; sort; type: said of works of literature, art, etc. 2. genre painting.

**genre painting,** painting in which subjects from everyday life are treated realistically.

**gens** (jenz), *n.* [*pl.* GENTES (jen'tēz)], [L. < *gignere*, to beget], 1. in ancient Rome, a clan united by descent through the male line from a common ancestor. 2. any tribe or clan.

**gent** (jent), *n.* [Slang], a gentleman; man.

**gen·teel** (jen-tēl'), *adj.* [< Fr. *gentil;* akin to *gentle*], 1. formerly, gentlemanly or ladylike; well-bred. 2. affectedly or pretentiously well-bred, polite, etc. —**gen·teel'ly,** *adv.* —**gen·teel'ness,** *n.*

**gen·tian** (jen'shən), *n.* [< OFr. < L. *gentiana* < *Gentius*, Illyrian king who discovered its properties], 1. any of a group of plants with blue, white, red, or yellow flowers. 2. the bitter root of the yellow gentian.

**gen·tile** (jen'tīl), *n.* [< Fr. *gentil* & L. *gentilis*, of the same gens, or clan], 1. any person not a Jew. 2. formerly, among Christians, a heathen; pagan. 3. among Mormons, any person not a Mormon. *adj.* 1. not Jewish. 2. heathen; pagan. 3. not Mormon. Also [G-] for *n.* & *adj.* 1 & 3.

**gen·til·i·ty** (jen-til'ə-ti), *n.* [*pl.* -TIES], [< OFr. < L. < *gentilis;* see GENTLE], 1. originally, gentle birth; position of a person of the upper classes. 2. politeness; refinement; respectability.

**gen·tle** (jen't'l), *adj.* [-TLER, -TLEST], [< OFr. < L. *gentilis*, of the same gens, or clan; see GENS], 1. of the upper classes; of good birth. 2. having qualities considered appropriate to those of good birth; refined; polite. 3. [Archaic], noble; chivalrous: as, a *gentle* knight. 4. generous; kind. 5. easily handled; tame: as, a *gentle* dog. 6. kindly; patient: as, a *gentle* disposition. 7. mild; moderate: as, a *gentle* tap. 8. gradual: as, a *gentle* slope. *n. usually in pl.* [Archaic], one born into a family of social standing. *v.t.* [-TLED, -TLING], [Rare], 1. to make gentle. 2. to tame or train (a horse). —**the gentle sex,** women. —**gen'tle·ness,** *n.* —**gen'tly,** *adv.*

**gen·tle·folk** (jen't'l-fōk'), *n.pl.* people of good birth and social standing: also **gentlefolks.**

**gen·tle·man** (jen't'l-mən), *n.* [*pl.* -MEN], 1. a man of good birth and social standing. 2. a well-bred, courteous man. 3. a man in attendance on a person of rank. 4. *often in pl.* any man: polite term.

**gen·tle·man-farm·er** (jen't'l-mən-fär'mẽr), *n.* [*pl.* -MEN-FARMERS], a wealthy man who owns and manages a farm, but usually does not work on it.

**gen·tle·man·ly** (jen't'l-mən-li), *adj.* of, characteristic of, or fit for a gentleman; well-mannered: also **gen'tle·man·like'.** —**gen'tle·man·li·ness,** *n.*

**gentleman's** (or **gentlemen's**) **agreement,** an unwritten agreement secured only by the parties' pledge of honor and not legally binding.

**gentleman's gentleman,** [*pl.* -MEN'S GENTLEMEN], a valet.

**gen·tle·wom·an** (jen't'l-woom'ən), *n.* [*pl.* -WOMEN], 1. a woman of good birth and social standing; lady. 2. a well-bred, courteous woman. 3. formerly, a woman in attendance on a lady of rank. —**gen'tle·wom'an·ly,** *adv.* —**gen'tle·wom'an·li·ness,** *n.*

**gen·try** (jen'tri), *n.* [< OFr. *genterise* < *gentil;* see GENTEEL], 1. people of good birth and social standing; esp., in Great Britain, the class of people ranking just below the nobility. 2. people of a particular class or group.

**gen·u·flect** (jen'yoo-flekt'), *v.i.* [< ML. < L. *genu*, the knee + *flectere*, to bend], to bend the knee, as in reverence or worship. —**gen'u·flec'tion, gen'u·flex'ion,** *n.* —**gen'u·flec'tor,** *n.*

**gen·u·ine** (jen'ū-in), *adj.* [< L. *genuinus* < base of *gignere*, to be born], 1. of the original stock; purebred. 2. really being what it is said to be; true; authentic. 3. sincere; without hypocrisy. —**gen'u·ine·ly,** *adv.* —**gen'u·ine·ness,** *n.*

**ge·nus** (jē'nəs), *n.* [*pl.* GENERA (jen'ẽr-ə), sometimes GENUSES], [L., birth, race, kind], 1. a class;

kind; sort. 2. in *logic*, class of things made up of subordinate classes, or species. 3. in *biology*, a classification of plants or animals with common distinguishing characteristics: a genus is the main subdivision of a family and includes one or more species; the genus name is capitalized, the species name is not (e.g., *Homo sapiens*, the scientific name for man).

**-gen·y** (jə-ni), [< Gr.; see -GEN], a suffix meaning *manner of origin* or *development*, as in *phylogeny*.

**ge·o-,** [< Gr. < *gaia*, *gē*, the earth], a combining form meaning *earth*, *of the earth*.

**ge·o·cen·tric** (jē'ō-sen'trik), *adj.* [*geo-* + *centric*], 1. measured or viewed as from the earth's center. 2. having or regarding the earth as a center. Also **ge'o·cen'tri·cal.** —**ge'o·cen'tri·cal·ly,** *adv.*

**ge·od·e·sy** (jē-od'ə-si), *n.* [< Fr. < Mod. L. < Gr. < *gē*, the earth + *daiein*, to divide], the branch of mathematics concerned with measuring, or determining the shape of, the earth or a large part of its surface, or with locating exactly points on its surface. —**ge·o·des·ic** (jē'ə-des'ik, -dē'sik), **ge'o·des'i·cal,** *adj.* —**ge·od'e·sist,** *n.*

**ge·o·det·ic** (jē'ə-det'ik), *adj.* of or determined by geodesy: also **ge'o·det'i·cal.** —**ge'o·det'i·cal·ly,** *adv.*

**ge·o·det·ics** (jē'ə-det'iks), *n.pl.* [construed as sing.], geodesy.

**geog.,** 1. geographic(al). 2. geography.

**ge·o·graph·i·cal** (jē'ə-graf'i-k'l), *adj.* of or according to geography: also **ge'o·graph'ic.** —**ge'o·graph'i·cal·ly,** *adv.*

**ge·og·ra·phy** (jē-og'rə-fi, -ôg'-), *n.* [*pl.* -PHIES], [< L. < Gr. < *gē*, the earth + *graphein*, to write], 1. the science dealing with the surface of the earth, its division into continents and countries, and the climate, plants, animals, natural resources, people, and industries of the various divisions. 2. the physical features of a region or place. 3. a book about geography. —**ge·og'ra·pher,** *n.*

**geol.,** 1. geologic(al). 2. geologist. 3. geology.

**ge·o·log·i·cal** (jē'ə-loj'i-k'l), *adj.* of or according to geology: also **ge'o·log'ic.** —**ge'o·log'i·cal·ly,** *adv.*

**ge·ol·o·gy** (jē-ol'ə-ji), *n.* [*pl.* -GIES], [*geo-* + *-logy*], 1. the science dealing with the structure of the earth's crust and the development of its various layers: it includes the study of rock types and fossil forms. 2. the structure of the earth's crust in a given region or place. 3. a book about geology. **See chart, p. 314.** —**ge·ol'o·gist,** *n.*

**geom.,** 1. geometric(al). 2. geometry.

**ge·o·met·ric** (jē'ə-met'rik), *adj.* 1. of or according to geometry. 2. characterized by straight lines, triangles, circles, etc., as a pattern. Also **ge'o·met'ri·cal.** —**ge'o·met'ri·cal·ly,** *adv.*

**geometric(al) progression,** a sequence of terms in which the ratio of each term to the preceding one is the same throughout (e.g., 1, 2, 4, 8, etc.).

**ge·om·e·trid** (jē-om'ə-trid), *n.* [< L. < Gr. < *gē*, the earth + *metron*, measure], any of a group of small moths whose larvae (**measuring worms**) move by looping their bodies.

**ge·om·e·try** (jē-om'ə-tri), *n.* [*pl.* -TRIES], [< OFr. < L. < Gr. < *gē*, earth + *metrein*, to measure], 1. the branch of mathematics that deals with points, lines, planes, and solids, and examines their properties, measurement, and mutual relations in space. 2. a book about geometry. —**ge·om'e·tri'cian** (-trish'ən), **ge·om'e·ter,** *n.*

**ge·o·phys·ics** (jē'ō-fiz'iks), *n.pl.* [construed as sing.], the science that deals with weather, winds, tides, etc. and their effect on the earth. —**ge'o·phys'i·cal,** *adj.* —**ge'o·phys'i·cist,** *n.*

**ge·o·pol·i·tics** (jē'ō-pol'ə-tiks), *n.pl.* [construed as sing.], [< G. *geopolitik*], the study of the relation of a nation's policies to geography, especially as developed in Nazi Germany. —**ge'o·po·lit'i·cal** (-pə-lit'ə-kəl), **ge'o·pol'i·tic,** *adj.* —**ge'o·po·lit'i·cal·ly,** *adv.* —**ge'o·pol'i·ti'cian** (-tish'ən), *n.*

**George III** (jôrj), 1738–1820; king of England (1760–1820).

**George V,** 1865–1936; king of England (1910–1936).

**George VI,** 1895–1952; king of England (1936–1952).

**George, Saint,** ?–303? A.D.; patron saint of England.

**George, Henry,** 1839–1897; U.S. political economist; advocate of single tax.

**geor·gette** (jôr-jet'), *n.* [after *Georgette* de la Plante, Parisian modiste], a thin, transparent, slightly crinkled cloth of silk, etc., used for women's dresses, etc.: also **georgette crepe.**

**Geor·gia** (jôr'jə), *n.* 1. a Southern State of the U.S.: area, 58,876 sq. mi.; pop., 3,943,000; capital, Atlanta. 2. Georgian S.S.R.

**Geor·gi·an** (jôr'jən, -ji-ən), *adj.* 1. of the reigns of George I, II, III, and IV of England (1714–1830). 2. of the Georgian S.S.R., its people, language, or culture. 3. of the State of Georgia. *n.* 1. a native or inhabitant of the Georgian S.S.R. 2. a native or inhabitant of the State of Georgia. 3. the language of the Transcaucasian Georgians: see **Caucasian.**

**Georgian Soviet Socialist Republic,** a republic of the U.S.S.R., in the Transcaucasus, on the Black Sea: area, 26,875 sq. mi.; pop., 4,049,000; capital, Tiflis.

**ge·o·stat·ics** (jē'ō-stat'iks), *n.pl.* [construed as sing.], [< *geo-* + *static*], the branch of physics dealing with the mechanics of the equilibrium of forces in rigid bodies.

**ge·ot·ro·pism** (jē-ot'rə-piz'm), *n.* [*geo-* + *-tropism*], movement or growth of a living organism in response to the force of gravity, either toward the center of the earth (**positive geotropism**) or away from the center of the earth (**negative geotropism**). —**ge·o·trop·ic** (jē'ō-trop'ik), *adj.* —**ge'o·trop'i·cal·ly,** *adv.*

**Ger.,** 1. German. 2. Germany.

**ger.,** gerund.

**ge·ra·ni·um** (ji-rā'ni-əm), *n.* [L. < Gr. < *geranos*, a crane], 1. a plant with strong-smelling flowers of pink or purple and leaves with many lobes. 2. any of a group of plants related to these; pelargonium.

**ger·fal·con** (jũr'fôl'k'n, -fô'-), *n.* a gyrfalcon.

**ger·i·at·rics** (jer'i-at'riks), *n.pl.* [construed as sing.], [< Gr. *gēras*, old age; + *-iatrics*], the branch of medicine that deals with the diseases and hygiene of old age.

**germ** (jũrm), *n.* [< Fr. < L. *germen*, sprout], 1. the rudimentary form from which a new organism is developed; seed, bud, etc. 2. any microscopic organism, especially one of the bacteria, that can cause disease. 3. that from which something can develop: as, the *germ* of an idea. —**germ'less,** *adj.*

**Ger·man** (jũr'mən), *adj.* [L. *Germanus*; prob. < Celt.], of or like Germany, its people, language, or culture. *n.* 1. a native or inhabitant of Germany. 2. the Germanic language of the Germans, technically called *New High German.*

**ger·man** (jũr'mən), *adj.* [< OFr. < L. *germanus*; see GERM], closely related; specif., *a*) having the same parents (**brother-german** or **sister-german**). *b*) being a first cousin (**cousin-german**).

**ger·man** (jũr'mən), *n.* [short for *German cotillion*], 1. a cotillion (sense 1). 2. a party at which the german is danced.

**ger·man·der** (jẽr-man'dẽr), *n.* [< OFr. < ML.; ult. < Gr. *chamai*, on the ground + *drys*, tree], 1. a shrubby plant of the mint family, with showy flowers and mintlike leaves. 2. a kind of speedwell.

**ger·mane** (jẽr-mān'), *adj.* [var. of *german* (closely related)], 1. closely related; relevant; pertinent; to the point. 2. akin; german.

**Ger·man·ic** (jẽr-man'ik), *adj.* 1. of Germany or the Germans; German. 2. designating or of the original language of the German peoples or the languages descended from it; Teutonic. *n.* 1. the original language of the German peoples: usually **Primitive Germanic** or **Primitive Teutonic.** 2. a branch of the Indo-European family of languages, comprising this language and the languages descended from it, including Norwegian, Icelandic, Swedish, Danish (**North Germanic**); German, Dutch, Frisian, and English (**West Germanic**); and the extinct language Gothic (**East Germanic**).

**ger·ma·ni·um** (gẽr-mā ni-əm), *n.* [< L. *Germania*, Germany], a rare, grayish-white, metallic chemical element of the carbon family: symbol, Ge; at. wt., 72.60; at. no., 32.

**Ger·man·ize** (jũr'mə-nīz'), *v.t.* & *v.i.* [-IZED, -IZING], to make or become German in character, thought, language, etc. —**Ger'man·i·za'tion,** *n.*

**German measles,** an acute, contagious disease resembling measles but less severe.

**Ger·ma·no-** (jũr'mə-nō, jẽr-man'ō), a combining form meaning *German*, *of Germany*, *of the Germans.*

**German shepherd dog,** a breed of dog somewhat like a wolf in form and size, used in sheepherding, police work, etc.: also **(German) police dog.**

**German silver,** a white alloy of zinc, nickel, and copper: also called *nickel silver.*

**Ger·ma·ny** (jũr'mə-ni), *n.* a country in north central Europe, on the North and Baltic seas: area, 136,462 sq. mi.; pop., 72,951,000: in 1949, Germany was constituted as two states, (**the Federal Re-**

# Geological Time Chart

| ERAS | PERIODS (OF TIME) or SYSTEMS (OF ROCK) | EPOCHS (OF TIME) or SERIES (OF ROCK) | APPROXIMATE TIME IN YEARS SINCE BEGINNING OF EACH | PHYSICAL & BIOLOGICAL FEATURES |
|---|---|---|---|---|
| CENOZOIC | QUATERNARY | RECENT | 50,000 | Development of modern man. |
| | | PLEISTOCENE | 1,000,000 | Ice sheets over Europe and North America; appearance of early man. |
| | TERTIARY | PLIOCENE | 12,000,000 | Development of modern plants and animals; formation of mountains in western America. |
| | | MIOCENE | 30,000,000 | Highest development of larger mammals; formation of mountains, including the Alps, Andes, and Himalayas. |
| | | OLIGOCENE | 40,000,000 | Development of higher mammals. |
| | | EOCENE (& PALEOCENE) | 60,000,000 | Rise to dominance of mammals; appearance of ancestral horse and primates. |
| MESOZOIC | CRETACEOUS | | 120,000,000 | Extinction of dinosaurs; development of early mammals and flowering plants; chalk deposits. |
| | JURASSIC | | 155,000,000 | Appearance of flying reptiles and birds; dominance of dinosaurs; appearance of primitive mammals; many coniferous trees. |
| | TRIASSIC | | 190,000,000 | Appearance of dinosaurs; dominance of reptiles; appearance of primitive cycads. |
| PALEOZOIC | PERMIAN | | 215,000,000 | Development of reptiles; decline of huge Carboniferous plants. |
| | CARBONIFEROUS PENNSYLVANIAN MISSISSIPPIAN | | 300,000,000 | Age of coal; formation of coal beds from luxuriant plant life in warm, swampy forests; great, fernlike trees; appearance of primitive conifers; abundance of insect life; first reptiles; development of amphibians. |
| | DEVONIAN | | 350,000,000 | Age of the fish; appearance of primitive amphibians; development of primitive plant life on dry continents. |
| | SILURIAN | | 390,000,000 | Appearance of scorpions, the first animals to live on land; extensive coral reefs. |
| | ORDOVICIAN | | 480,000,000 | Floods and recessions of shallow seas; deposits of limestone, lead, and zinc ores; abundance of marine invertebrate life; a few primitive, fishlike vertebrates. |
| | CAMBRIAN | | 550,000,000 | Shallow seas over much of the land; formation of sedimentary rocks; development of marine invertebrate life (brachiopods, snails, trilobites, etc.). |
| PRE-CAMBRIAN: PROTEROZOIC | | | 1,200,000,000 | Formation of mountains; deposits of iron ore; abundance of lime-secreting algae; first sponges. |
| PRE-CAMBRIAN: ARCHEOZOIC | | | 2,000,000,000 | Great volcanic activity; formation of igneous rocks; some microscopic algae; probably some protozoa. |

public of) **West Germany** and the **East German Democratic Republic (East Germany).**

**germ cell,** a cell from which a new organism can develop; egg or sperm cell.

**ger·mi·cide** (jũr′mə-sīd′), *n.* [< *germ* + *-cide*], anything used to destroy germs. —**ger′mi·cid′al,** *adj.*

**ger·mi·nal** (jũr′mə-n'l), *adj.* 1. of, like, or characteristic of germs or germ cells. 2. in the first stage of growth or development.

**ger·mi·nant** (jũr′mə-nənt), *adj.* germinating.

**ger·mi·nate** (jũr′mə-nāt′), *v.i.* & *v.t.* [-NATED, -NATING], [< L. *germinatus*, pp. < *germen*, a sprout], to start developing or growing; sprout or cause to sprout, as from a seed. —**ger′mi·na′tion,** *n.* —**ger′mi·na′tive** (-tiv), *adj.* —**ger′mi·na′tor** (-tẽr), *n.*

**germ plasm** (or **plasma**), the substance in germ cells by which hereditary characteristics are believed to be transmitted.

**ger·on·tol·o·gy** (jer′ən-tol′ə-ji), *n.* [< Gr. *gerōn*, old man; + *-logy*], the scientific study of the process of aging and of the problems of aged people.

**-ger·ous** (jẽr-əs), [< L. < *gerere*, to bear], a suffix meaning *producing* or *bearing.*

**ger·ry·man·der** (ger′i-man′dẽr, jer′-), *v.t.* [< E. *Gerry*, governor of Mass. when the method was employed (1812) + *salamander*, from the shape of the redistricted Essex County], 1. to divide (a voting area) in such a way as to give an unfair advantage to one political party. 2. to manipulate unfairly. *v.i.* to engage in gerrymandering. *n.* a redistricting of voting districts to the advantage of one party. —**ger′ry·man′der·er,** *n.*

**ger·und** (jer′ənd), *n.* [< L. < *gerere*, to do or carry out], in *grammar*, a verbal noun ending in *-ing*: it has all the uses of the noun but retains certain characteristics of the verb, such as the ability to take an object or an adverbial modifier (e.g., *doing* in "Doing a job well is commendable."). —**ge·run·di·al** (jə-run′di-əl), *adj.*

**ge·run·dive** (jə-run′div), *n.* 1. a Latin verbal adjective with a typical gerund stem form, used as a future passive participle expressing duty, necessity, etc. 2. a similar form in any language.

**gest, geste** (jest), *n.* [< OFr. < L. *gesta*, deeds < *gerere*, to do], 1. an adventure; exploit. 2. a romantic story of adventure, especially in verse.

**Ge·stalt psychology** (gə-shtält′), [< G., form, configuration], a school of psychology, developed in Germany, which affirms that the response of an organism to a situation is a complete and unanalyzable whole rather than a sum of the responses to specific elements in the situation.

**Ge·sta·po** (gə-stä′pō; G. -shtä′-), *n.* [< G. *Geheime Staatspolizei*, secret state police], in Nazi Germany, the state police, organized to operate against political opposition.

**ges·tate** (jes′tāt), *v.t.* [-TATED, -TATING], [< L. *gestatus*, pp.; ult. < *gerere*, to bear], to carry in the uterus during pregnancy. —**ges·ta′tion,** *n.*

**ges·tic·u·late** (jes-tik′yoo-lāt′), *v.i.* [-LATED, -LATING], [< L. *gesticulatus*, pp.; ult. < pp. of *gerere*, to bear], 1. to use gestures to help express one's meaning, as in speaking. 2. to make or use many energetic gestures. *v.t.* to express by gesticulating. —**ges·tic′u·la′tive,** *adj.* —**ges·tic′u·la′tor,** *n.*

**ges·tic·u·la·tion** (jes-tik′yoo-lā′shən), *n.* 1. a gesticulating. 2. a gesture. —**ges·tic′u·la·to′ry** (-lə-tôr′i, -tō′ri), *adj.*

**ges·ture** (jes′chẽr), *n.* [< ML. < L. *gestus*, pp. of *gerere*, to bear], 1. movement of the body, or of part of the body, to express or emphasize ideas, emotions, etc. 2. any action, statement, etc. intended to convey a state of mind or intention, sometimes one made only for effect. *v.i.* [-TURED, -TURING], to make or use gestures. —**ges′tur·er,** *n.*

**get** (get), *v.t.* [GOT (got), or *archaic & dial.* GAT, GOT or GOTTEN, GETTING], [< ON. *geta*], 1. to come into the state of having (anything); receive; gain; obtain; acquire. 2. *a*) to reach; arrive at: as, we *got* home early. *b*) to be in communication with: as, I *got* Paris on the radio. 3. to go and bring: as, *get* your books. 4. to catch; capture; gain hold of. 5. to learn; commit to memory. 6. to persuade (a person) to do something: as, *get* him to leave. 7. to cause to act in a certain way: as, can you *get* the door to shut? 8. to cause to be: as, he *got* his hands dirty. 9. to be sentenced to: as, he *got* ten years. 10. to prepare: as, I'll *get* breakfast. 11. to give birth to; beget: usually said of animals. 12. [Colloq.], to be obliged to; feel a necessity to (with *have* or *has*): as, he's *got* to pass. 13. [Colloq.], to own; possess (with *have* or *has*): as, he's *got* red hair. 14. [Colloq.], to be or become the master of; esp., *a*) to overpower: as, narcotics will *get* him. *b*) to puzzle; baffle: as, this problem *gets* me. *c*) to take into custody, wound, or kill. *d*) in *baseball*, to put (an opponent) out. 15. [Colloq.], to strike; hit: as, the blow *got* him in the eye. 16. [Colloq.], to catch the meaning or import of; understand. 17. [Slang], to cause an emotional response in; irritate, please, thrill, etc.: as, that singer *gets* me. 18. [Slang], to notice: as, *get* the look on his face. *v.i.* 1. to come or arrive (with *from*, *to*, etc.): as, when do we *get* to New York? 2. to come to be (doing something); come to be (in a situation, condition, etc.): as, he *got* caught in the rain. *Get* is used as an auxiliary for emphasis in passive constructions: as, we *got* beaten. *n.* 1. the young of an animal; offspring. 2. a begetting. —**get across,** [Colloq.], 1. to explain convincingly. 2. to succeed, as in making oneself understood. —**get along,** 1. to proceed. 2. to leave. 3. to succeed or be fairly successful. 4. to agree. —**get around,** 1. to move from place to place. 2. to go to many social events, places, etc. 3. to circulate, as news. 4. to circumvent. 5. to influence or gain favor with by cajoling, flattering, etc. —**get away,** 1. to go away; leave. 2. to escape. 3. to start. —**get away with,** [Slang], to succeed in doing or taking without being discovered or punished. —**get back,** 1. to return. 2. to recover. 3. [Slang], to get revenge (usually with *at*). —**get by,** 1. to pass. 2. [Colloq.], to succeed without being discovered or punished. 3. [Colloq.], to survive; manage. —**get down to,** to begin to consider or act on. —**get in,** 1. to enter; join in. 2. to arrive. 3. to put in. —**get off,** 1. to come off, down, or out of. 2. to leave; go away. 3. to take off. 4. to escape. 5. to help to escape punishment. 6. to start, as in a race. 7. to utter (a joke, retort, etc.). —**get on,** 1. to go on or into. 2. to put on. 3. to proceed. 4. to grow older. 5. to succeed. 6. to agree. —**get out,** 1. to go out. 2. to go away. 3. to take out. 4. to become no longer a secret. 5. to issue; publish. —**get over,** 1. to recover from. 2. to forget or overlook. —**get there,** [Colloq.], to succeed. —**get through,** 1. to finish. 2. to manage to survive. —**get to,** [Colloq.], 1. to succeed in. 2. to succeed in reaching. 3. to influence, as by bribery: also **get at.** —**get together,** 1. to bring or come together; assemble. 2. [Colloq.], to reach an agreement. —**get up,** 1. to rise (from a chair, from sleep, etc.). 2. to contrive; organize. 3. to dress elaborately. 4. to advance; make progress. —**get′ta·ble, get′a·ble,** *adj.* —**get′ter,** *n.*

**get·a·way** (get′ə-wā′), *n.* 1. the act of starting, as in a race. 2. the act of escaping.

**Geth·sem·a·ne** (geth-sem′ə-ni), *n.* in the *Bible*, a garden outside of Jerusalem, scene of the agony, betrayal, and arrest of Jesus: Matt. 26:36.

**get-to·geth·er** (get′tə-geth′ẽr), *n.* an informal social gathering or meeting.

**Get·tys·burg** (get′iz-bũrg′), *n.* a town in S Pennsylvania: site of a crucial battle (July 1–3, 1863) of the Civil War.

**get-up** (get′up′), *n.* [Colloq.], 1. general arrangement or composition of a thing. 2. costume; outfit; dress. 3. driving ambition.

**gew·gaw** (gū′gô), *n.* [ME. *giuegoue*, *gugaw*, etc.], something showy but worthless or useless; trinket. *adj.* showy but worthless.

**gey·ser** (gī′zẽr, -sẽr), *n.* [< Ice. *Geysir*, name of a hot spring in Iceland < ON. *gōysa*, to gush], a spring from which columns of boiling water and steam gush into the air at intervals.

**Gha·na** (gä′nə), *n.* a country on the W coast of Africa: a member of the British Commonwealth of Nations: area, 91,843 sq. mi.; pop., 8,143,000; capital, Accra.

**ghast·ly** (gast′li, gäst′-), *adj.* [-LIER, -LIEST], [AS. *gastlic*, lit., ghostly], 1. horrible; frightful. 2. ghostlike; pale. 3. [Colloq.], very unpleasant. *adv.* in a ghastly manner. —**ghast′li·ness,** *n.*

**ghat, ghaut** (gôt), *n.* [Hind. *ghāṭ*], in India, 1. a mountain pass. 2. a flight of steps leading down to a river landing for ritual bathers.

**ghee** (gē), *n.* [Hind. *ghī*], in India, a type of liquid butter made especially from buffalo milk.

**Ghent** (gent), *n.* a city in NW Belgium: pop., 161,000: Flemish sp. **Gent.**

**gher·kin** (gũr′kin), *n.* [< D. dim. of *agurk* < Czech < Late Gr. *angourion*], 1. a variety of cucumber bearing small, prickly fruit, used for pickles. 2. any small, immature cucumber when pickled.

**ghet·to** (get′ō), *n.* [*pl.* -TOS], [It.], 1. in certain

European cities, a section to which Jews are, or were, restricted. 2. any section of a city in which many members of some ethnic or racial group live, or to which they are restricted.

**ghost** (gōst), *n.* [AS. *gast*], 1. originally, the spirit or soul: now only in **give up the ghost,** to die. 2. the supposed disembodied spirit of a dead person, conceived of as appearing to the living as a pale, shadowy apparition. 3. a faint semblance; slight trace: as, not a *ghost* of a chance. 4. [Colloq.], a ghost writer. 5. in *optics & television,* an unwanted secondary image or bright spot. *v.i.* [Colloq.], to work as a ghost writer. *v.t.* [Colloq.], to be the ghost writer of. **—ghost′like′,** *adj.*

**ghost·ly** (gōst′li), *adj.* [-LIER, -LIEST], 1. of, like, or characteristic of a ghost. 2. of the soul or religion; spiritual. **—ghost′li·ness,** *n.*

**ghost writer,** one who writes speeches, articles, etc. for another who professes to be the author. **—ghost′write′** [-WROTE, -WRITTEN, -WRITING], *v.t. & v.i.*

**ghoul** (go͞ol), *n.* [Ar. *ghūl*, demon < *ghāla*, to seize], 1. in *Oriental folklore,* an evil spirit that robs graves and feeds on the dead. 2. a robber of graves. 3. one who performs horrible acts or enjoys loathsome things. **—ghoul′ish,** *adj.* **—ghoul′ish·ly,** *adv.* **—ghoul′ish·ness,** *n.*

**GHQ, G.H.Q.,** General Headquarters.

**gi.,** gill; gills.

**GI, G.I.** (jē′ī′), *adj.* 1. in *military usage,* government issue: designating clothing, equipment, etc. issued to military personnel. 2. [Colloq.], *a*) of or characteristic of the U.S. armed forces: as, a *GI* haircut. *b*) inclined to a strict observance of military regulations and customs: as, our captain is very *GI.* *n.* [Colloq.], any member of the U.S. armed forces; esp., an enlisted soldier.

**g.i., G.I.,** gastrointestinal.

**gi·ant** (jī′ənt), *n.* [< ONorm.Fr. < LL. < L. *gigas* < Gr. *gigas*], 1. any imaginary being of human form but of superhuman size and strength. 2. a person or thing of great size, strength, intellect, etc. *adj.* of great size, strength, etc. **—gi′ant·ess,** *n.fem.*

**gi·ant·ism** (jī′ən-tiz′m), *n.* gigantism.

**giant panda,** a panda (sense 2).

**giaour** (jour), *n.* [< Turk. < Per. *gaur;* prob. < Ar. *kāfir,* infidel], a non-Moslem: term applied by Moslems to unbelievers, especially Christians.

**gib·ber** (jib′ẽr, gib′-), *v.i. & v.t.* [echoic], to speak or utter rapidly and incoherently; chatter. *n.* unintelligible chatter; gibberish.

**gib·ber·ish** (jib′ẽr-ish, gib′-), *n.* rapid and incoherent talk; unintelligible chatter; jargon.

**gib·bet** (jib′it), *n.* [< OFr. *gibet* < Frank. *gibb* forked stick], 1. a gallows. 2. a structure like a gallows, from which bodies of executed criminals were hung and exposed to public scorn. *v.t.* 1. to execute by hanging. 2. to hang on a gibbet. 3. to expose to public scorn.

**gib·bon** (gib′ən), *n.* [Fr.], a small, slender, long-armed ape of India, southern China, and the East Indies.

GIBBON (3 ft. high)

**Gib·bon, Edward** (gib′ən), 1737–1794; English historian.

**gib·bose** (gib′ōs, gi-bōs′), *adj.* gibbous.

**gib·bos·i·ty** (gi-bos′ə-ti), *n.* 1. the state or quality of being gibbous. 2. [*pl.* -TIES], a rounded swelling or protuberance.

**gib·bous** (gib′əs), *adj.* [< L. *gibbus,* a hump], 1. rounded and bulging. 2. designating the moon in a phase between half-moon and full moon. 3. humpbacked. **—gib′bous·ly,** *adv.* **—gib′bous·ness,** *n.*

**gibe** (jīb), *v.i. & v.t.* [GIBED, GIBING], [? < OFr. *giber,* to handle roughly], to jeer; taunt; sneer or scoff (at). *n.* a jeer; taunt; scoff. Also sp. **jibe. —gib′er,** *n.*

**gib·let** (jib′lit), *n.* [< OFr. *gibelet,* stew made of game], *usually in pl.* any of the edible internal parts of a fowl, as the gizzard.

**Gi·bral·tar** (ji-brôl′tẽr), *n.* 1. a British colony and fortress on the Rock of Gibraltar: area, 2¼ sq. mi.; pop., 24,000. 2. any strong fortress.

**Gibraltar, Rock of,** a large rock forming a peninsula in S Spain, at the Strait of Gibraltar.

**Gibraltar, Strait of,** the strait between Spain and Africa, joining the Atlantic and the Mediterranean.

**gid·dy** (gid′i), *adj.* [-DIER, -DIEST], [< AS. *gydig,* insane < base of AS. *god,* a god (i.e., "possessed by a god")], 1. having a whirling, dazed sensation; dizzy. 2. causing such a sensation. 3. turning around very rapidly; whirling. 4. *a*) inconstant; fickle. *b*) frivolous; flighty. *v.t. & v.i.* [-DIED, -DYING], to make or become giddy. **—gid′di·ly,** *adv.* **—gid′di·ness,** *n.*

**Gide, An·dré** (än′drā′ zhēd′), 1869–1951; French novelist and critic.

**Gid·e·on** (gid′i-ən), *n.* in the *Bible,* a hero of Israel who led his people in the defeat of the Midianites: Judg. 6:11 ff.

**Gideon Society,** an organization for placing Bibles in hotel rooms, etc., founded in 1899 by a group of commercial travelers.

**gie** (gē, gi), *v.t. & v.i.* [GIED or GAE (gā), GIEN, GIEING], [Scot. & Brit. Dial.], to give.

**gift** (gift), *n.* [AS. < *giefan,* to give; infl. by ON. *gipt,* gift], 1. something given or bestowed; present. 2. the act, power, or right of giving. 3. a natural ability; talent: as, a *gift* for art.

**gift·ed** (gif′tid), *adj.* having a natural ability or aptitude; talented. **—gift′ed·ness,** *n.*

**gig** (gig), *n.* [prob. < ON.], 1. a light, two-wheeled, open carriage drawn by one horse. 2. a long, light ship's boat with oars and sail. *v.i.* [GIGGED, GIGGING], to travel in a gig.

**gi·gan·tic** (jī-gan′tik), *adj.* [see GIANT], 1. of, like, or fit for a giant. 2. huge; enormous; immense. **—gi·gan′ti·cal·ly,** *adv.* **—gi·gan′tic·ness,** *n.*

**gi·gan·tism** (jī′gan-tiz′m, jī-gan′-), *n.* [see GIANT], abnormal growth of the body, caused by a disorder of the pituitary gland: also **giantism.**

**gig·gle** (gig′′l), *v.i.* [-GLED, -GLING], [? < MD. or LG.], to laugh with uncontrollable, rapid, high-pitched sounds, suggestive of foolishness, nervousness, etc.; titter. *n.* such a laugh. **—gig′gler,** *n.* **—gig′gling·ly,** *adv.* **—gig′gly** [-GLIER, -GLIEST], *adj.*

**gig·o·lo** (jig′ə-lō′), *n.* [*pl.* -LOS], [Fr.], 1. a man who is paid to be a woman's dancing partner or escort. 2. a man supported by a prostitute.

**gig·ot** (jig′ət), *n.* [Fr.; OFr., dim. < OHG. *giga,* a fiddle], 1. a leg of mutton, lamb, veal, etc. 2. a leg-of-mutton sleeve: also **gigot sleeve.**

**Gi·la monster** (hē′lə), [< the *Gila* River, Arizona], a stout, poisonous lizard covered with beadlike scales in alternating rings of black and orange: found in desert regions of the Southwest: also called **Gila.**

**Gil·bert,** Sir **William Schwen(c)k** (shweŋk gil′bẽrt), 1836–1911; English librettist of comic operas; collaborated with Sir Arthur Sullivan. **—Gil·ber′ti·an** (-ti-ən), *adj.*

**Gilbert and Ellice Islands,** a British colony consisting of several groups of equatorial islands in the SW Pacific.

**gild** (gild), *v.t.* [GILDED or GILT, GILDING], [AS. *gyldan* < base of AS. *gold*], 1. *a*) to overlay with a thin layer of gold. *b*) to coat with a gold color. 2. to make appear bright and attractive. 3. to make (something) seem more attractive or more valuable than it is. **—gild′ed,** *adj.* **—gild′er,** *n.* **—gild′ing,** *n.*

**gild** (gild), *n.* a guild. **—gilds′man** [*pl.* -MEN], *n.*

**Gil·e·ad** (gil′i-əd), *n.* a region in ancient Palestine, east of the Jordan: Gen. 37:25.

**gill** (gil), *n.* [prob. < Anglo-N.], 1. the organ for breathing of most animals that live in water, as fish, lobsters, etc. 2. *often pl.* *a*) the wattle of a fowl. *b*) the jowl of a person. 3. *pl.* the thin, leaflike, radiating plates on the undersurface of a mushroom. **—gill′-like′,** *adj.*

**gill** (jil), *n.* [< OFr. < L. *gillo,* cooling vessel], a liquid measure, equal to ¼ pint: abbrev. **gi.**

**gil·lie, gil·ly** (gil′i), *n.* [*pl.* -LIES], [Scot. < Gael. *gille,* boy, page], 1. in the Scottish Highlands, a sportsman's attendant. 2. a servant.

**gil·ly·flow·er, gil·li·flow·er** (jil′i-flou′ẽr), *n.* [OFr. *gilofre* < LL. < Gr. < *karyon,* nut + *phyllon,* leaf], any of several plants with clove-scented flowers, including the clove pink.

**gilt** (gilt), alt. pt. and pp. of **gild.** *adj.* gilded. *n.* a thin layer of gold, or a substance like gold, covering a surface.

**gilt-edged** (gilt′ejd′), *adj.* 1. having the edge gilded. 2. of the highest quality or value: said of bonds, securities, etc. Also **gilt′-edge′.**

**gim·bals** (jim′b'lz, gim′-), *n.pl.* [< OFr. *gemelle,* twin < L. dim. of *geminus*], a device consisting of a pair of rings pivoted on axes at right angles to each other so that one is free to swing within the other: a ship's compass will keep a horizontal position when suspended in gimbals.

**gim·crack** (jim′krak′), *adj.* [< ?], showy but cheap and useless. *n.* a showy, useless thing; knickknack.

**gim·let** (gim′lit), *n.* [< OFr. < MD. *wimpel;* see WIMBLE], a small boring tool with a handle at right angles to a shaft with a spiral, pointed cutting edge.

GIMLET

**gim·let-eyed** (gim′lit-īd′), *adj.* sharp-eyed.

**gim·mick** (gim′ik), *n.* [? < G. *gemach*, a convenience], [Slang], 1. a secret means of controlling a prize wheel, etc. 2. any deceptive device. 3. [Slang], an attention-getting device or feature for promoting the success of a product, campaign, etc.

**gimp** (gimp), *n.* [Fr. *guimpe*, wimple < OFr. < OHG. *wimpal*], a ribbonlike silk, worsted, or cotton braided fabric, sometimes stiffened with wire, used to trim garments, furniture, etc.

**gin** (jin), *n.* [< D. *genever* < OFr. < L. *juniperus*, juniper], 1. a strong alcoholic liquor distilled from grain and usually flavored with juniper berries. 2. alcoholic liquor generally.

**gin** (jin), *n.* [ME., abbrev. of *engin;* see ENGINE], 1. a snare or trap, as for game. 2. a machine for separating cotton from the seeds. *v.t.* [GINNED, GINNING], 1. to catch in a trap. 2. to remove seeds from (cotton) with a gin. —**gin′ner,** *n.*

**gin** (gin), *v.t. & v.i.* [GAN, GINNING], [ME. *ginnen* (< AS. *beginnan*, to begin & *onginnan*, to attempt)], [Archaic & Poetic], to begin.

**gin** (jin), *n.* gin rummy. *v.i.* [GINNED, GINNING], to win in gin by matching all one's cards first.

**gin·ger** (jin′jẽr), *n.* [< AS. & < OFr.; both < LL. *zingiber* < Gr. < Sans.], 1. a tropical herb grown for its rootstalks, used for flavoring and in medicine. 2. the rootstalk, or the spice made from this. 3. [Colloq.], vigor; spirit. —**gin′ger·y,** *adj.*

**ginger ale,** an effervescent, nonalcoholic drink flavored with ginger.

**ginger beer,** a ginger-flavored drink similar to ginger ale, popular in England.

**gin·ger·bread** (jin′jẽr-bred′), *n.* 1. a cake flavored with ginger and molasses. 2. cheap, showy ornamentation. *adj.* tawdry; gaudy.

**gin·ger·ly** (jin′jẽr-li), *adv.* carefully; timidly. *adj.* careful; timid. —**gin′ger·li·ness,** *n.*

**gin·ger·snap** (jin′jẽr-snap′), *n.* a crisp, spicy cooky flavored with ginger and molasses.

**ging·ham** (giŋ′əm), *n.* [D. *gingang* < Malay *giŋgaŋ*, striped], a cotton cloth, usually woven in stripes, checks, or plaids. *adj.* made of gingham.

**gin·gi·vi·tis** (jin′jə-vī′tis), *n.* [< L. *gingiva*, the gum; + *-itis*], inflammation of the gums.

**gink** (giŋk), *n.* [? < dial. *gink*, a trick], [Slang], a person, especially one regarded as odd, etc.

**gink·go** (giŋ′kō, jiŋ′-), *n.* [*pl.* -GOES], [Japan. *ginko*, < Chin.], a large tree with fan-shaped leaves and edible yellow fruit, native to N China and Japan: also **ging·ko** (giŋ′kō), [*pl.* -KOES].

**gin rummy,** a variety of the card game rummy, for two or more players.

**gin·seng** (jin′seŋ), *n.* [Chin. *jen shen*], 1. an herb with a thick, forked, aromatic root: some species are found in China and North America. 2. the root of this plant, used medicinally.

**Giot·to (di Bon·do·ne)** (jôt′tô dē bôn-dô′ne; Eng. jot′ō), 1276?–1337?; Florentine painter.

**gip** (jip), *n., v.t. & v.i.* gyp.

**gip·sy** (jip′si), *n.* [*pl.* -SIES], *adj., v.i.* [-SIED, -SYING], gypsy.

**gipsy moth,** a gypsy moth.

**gi·raffe** (jə-raf′, -räf′), *n.* [*pl.* -RAFFES, -RAFFE; see PLURAL, II, D, 1], [Fr.; via Sp., Port., or It. < Ar. *zarāfah*], a large cud-chewing animal of Africa, with a very long neck and legs: it is the tallest of existing animals.

**gird** (gũrd), *v.t.* [GIRT or GIRDED, GIRDING], [AS. *gyrdan*], 1. to encircle or fasten with a belt or band. 2. to encircle; enclose. 3. to equip; clothe; invest. 4. to prepare (oneself) for action.

**gird** (gũrd), *n., v.i. & v.t.* [? < AS. *gierd*, a rod; infl. by prec. *gird*], gibe; taunt; sneer.

**gird·er** (gũr′dẽr), *n.* [*gird* (encircle) + *-er*], a large beam of timber or steel, for supporting the joists of a floor, a framework, etc.

**gir·dle** (gũr′d'l), *n.* [AS. *gyrdel*], 1. a belt or sash for the waist. 2. anything that surrounds or encircles. 3. a light, corsetlike garment, for supporting the waist and hips. 4. the rim of a cut gem. 5. a ring around the trunk of a tree, made by removing bark. *v.t.* [-DLED, -DLING], 1. to surround or bind as with a girdle. 2. to encircle. 3. to cut a ring of bark from (a tree), usually killing it. —**gir′dle·like′,** *adj.* —**gir′dler,** *n.*

**girl** (gũrl), *n.* [ME. *girle, gurle, gerle*, youngster] 1. a female child. 2. a young, unmarried woman. 3. a female servant. 4. [Colloq.], a woman of any age. 5. [Colloq.], a sweetheart. —**girl′ish,** *adj.* —**girl′ish·ly,** *adv.* —**girl′ish·ness,** *n.*

**girl·hood** (gũrl′hood), *n.* 1. the state or time of being a girl. 2. girls collectively.

**girl scout,** a member of the Girl Scouts.

**Girl Scouts,** a U.S. organization founded in 1912 (as **Girl Guides**) to provide character-building activities for girls.

**girt** (gũrt), pt. and pp. of **gird** (encircle).

**girt** (gũrt), *v.t.* [< *gird* (encircle)], 1. to gird; girdle. 2. to fasten with a girdle, belt, etc.

**girth** (gũrth), *n.* [< base of ON. *gyrtha*, to encircle], 1. a band put around the belly of a horse, donkey, etc. to hold a saddle or pack. 2. the circumference, as of a tree trunk or person's waist. 3. a girdle. *v.t.* 1. to encircle. 2. to fasten or bind with a girth. *v.i.* to measure in girth.

**gist** (jist), *n.* [< OFr. *giste*, point at issue < *gesir* (< L. *jacere*), to lie], the essence or main point, as of an article or argument.

**git·tern** (git′ẽrn), *n.* [< OFr. *guiterne* < L. *cithara* < Gr. *kithara*, guitar], an obsolete, wire-strung musical instrument somewhat resembling a guitar.

**give** (giv), *v.t.* [GAVE, GIVEN, GIVING], [AS. *giefan;* infl. by ON. *gefa*], 1. to hand over without cost or exchange; present as a gift. 2. to hand or pass over; deliver: as, he *gave* the porter his bag, her father *gave* Ruth in marriage. 3. to hand over in exchange for money, etc.; pay. 4. to cause to have; impart: as, this oil *gives* a wave to hair. 5. to confer (a title, position, etc.). 6. to grant; allow: as, God *give* us peace. 7. to produce; supply: as, cows *give* milk. 8. to part with for some cause: as, he *gave* his life for his men. 9. to yield; concede: as, I'll *give* you that point. 10. to offer; proffer: as, may I *give* advice? 11. to make (gestures, etc.): as, to *give* a shrug. 12. to utter (words, etc.); state: as, *give* a reply. 13. to perform: as, they *gave* a concert. 14. to inflict (punishment, etc.): as, they *gave* him a whipping. *v.i.* 1. to make gifts. 2. to bend, sink, move, etc. from force or pressure. *n.* a bending, moving, etc. under pressure, often with resilience. —**give and take,** to exchange on an even basis. —**give away,** 1. to make a gift of. 2. to give (the bride) to the bridegroom. 3. [Colloq.], to reveal; expose. —**give back,** to return. —**give forth** (or **off**), to send forth; emit. —**give in,** 1. to hand in. 2. to yield. —**give it to,** [Colloq.], to beat or scold. —**give out,** 1. to emit. 2. to make public. 3. to distribute. 4. to become worn out, spent, etc. —**give to understand** (or **know,** etc.), to cause to understand (or know, etc.). —**give up,** 1. to hand over; relinquish. 2. to stop; cease. 3. to admit failure and stop trying. 4. to lose hope for. 5. to devote wholly. —**give upon,** to open upon; afford a view of: a Gallicism. —**giv′er,** *n.*

**give-and-take** (giv′ən-tāk′), *n.* 1. an exchange on equal terms. 2. an exchange of talk, banter, etc.

**give·a·way** (giv′ə-wā′), *n.* [Colloq.], an unintentional revelation or betrayal. *adj.* [Colloq.], in *radio & television*, designating a type of program in which prizes are given to contestants.

**giv·en** (giv′'n), pp. of **give.** *adj.* 1. bestowed; presented. 2. accustomed, as from habit or inclination: as, he is *given* to drink. 3. stated; specified. 4. in *logic & mathematics*, assumed; granted. 5. in *law*, issued; executed.

**given name,** the first name of a person, as distinguished from the family name.

**giz·zard** (giz′ẽrd), *n.* [< OFr. *giser* < L. *gigeria*, cooked entrails of poultry], 1. the second stomach of a bird: it has thick muscular walls and a tough lining for grinding food. 2. [Colloq.], the stomach: humorous usage.

**Gk.,** Greek.

**Gl,** in *chemistry*, glucinum.

**gla·brous** (glā′brəs), *adj.* [< L. *glaber*, bald], without hair, down, or fuzz; smooth; bald.

**‡gla·cé** (glȧ′sā′; Eng. gla-sā′), *adj.* [Fr., pp. of *glacer*, to freeze < L. *glacies*, ice], 1. having a smooth, glossy surface. 2. covered with icing or sugar, as fruits; candied. 3. frozen; iced. *v.t.* [-CÉED, -CÉING], to glaze.

**gla·cial** (glā′shəl), *adj.* [< L. < *glacies*, ice], 1. of ice or glaciers. 2. of or produced by a glacial epoch. 3. cold and hard; icy. 4. having an icelike appearance. —**gla′cial·ly,** *adv.*

fat, āpe, bâre, cär; ten, ēven, hêre, ovẽr; is, bīte; lot, gō, hôrn, tōōl, look; oil, out; up, ūse, fũr; get; joy; yet; chin; she; thin, *th*en; zh, leisure; ŋ, ring; ə for *a* in *ago*, *e* in *agent*, *i* in *sanity*, *o* in *comply*, *u* in *focus;* ′ in *able* (ā′b'l); Fr. bál; ë, Fr. coeur; ö, Fr. feu; Fr. mo*n*; ô, Fr. coq; ü, Fr. duc; H, G. ich; kh, G. doch. ‡ foreign; < derived from.

**glacial epoch,** any geological period when much of the earth was covered with glaciers.
**gla·ci·ate** (glā′shi-āt′), *v.t.* [-ATED, -ATING], 1. *a*) to cover over with ice or a glacier. *b*) to freeze. 2. to expose to or change by glacial action. —**gla′ci·a′tion,** *n.*
**gla·cier** (glā′shẽr), *n.* [Fr. < LL. < L. *glacies*, ice], a large mass of ice and snow that forms in areas where the rate of snowfall exceeds the melting rate: it moves slowly down a mountain or valley until it melts or breaks away. —**gla′ciered,** *adj.*
**gla·cis** (glā′sis, glas′is), *n.* [Fr. < OFr. *glacier*, to slip < *glace*, ice], 1. a gradual slope. 2. an embankment sloping gradually up to a fortification so as to expose attackers to defending gunfire.
**glad** (glad), *adj.* [GLADDER, GLADDEST], [AS. *glæd*], 1. happy; pleased. 2. causing pleasure or joy; making happy. 3. pleased; willing: as, I'm *glad* to do it. 4. bright; beautiful; gay. *v.t. & v.i.* [GLADDED, GLADDING], [Archaic], to gladden. —**glad′ly** *adv.* —**glad′ness,** *n.*
**glad** (glad), *n.* [Slang], a gladiolus.
**glad·den** (glad′'n), *v.t. & v.i.* to make or become glad. —**glad′den·er,** *n.*
**glade** (glād), *n.* [prob. akin to *glad*], 1. an open space in a wood or forest. 2. an everglade.
**glad hand,** [Slang], cordial welcome.
**glad·i·a·tor** (glad′i-ā′tẽr), *n.* [L. < *gladius*, sword], 1. in ancient Rome, a man who fought with a sword, etc. in an arena as a public show: gladiators were slaves, captives, or paid performers. 2. any person involved in a controversy or fight. —**glad′i·a·to′ri·al** (-ə-tôr′i-əl, -tō′ri-), *adj.*
**glad·i·o·lus** (glad′i-ō′ləs, glə-dī′ə-), *n.* [*pl.* -LUSES, -LI (-lī, -li′)], [L. < *gladius*, sword], a plant of the iris family, with swordlike leaves and tall spikes of funnel-shaped flowers in various colors: also **glad′i·o′la.**
**glad rags,** [Slang], fine or dressy clothes.
**glad·some** (glad′səm), *adj.* 1. giving joy; cheering; pleasing; delightful. 2. joyful; cheerful. —**glad′some·ly,** *adv.* —**glad′some·ness,** *n.*
**Glad·stone, William Ew·art** (ū′ẽrt glad′stōn′, -stən), 1809–1898; British statesman.
**Gladstone bag,** [after William E. *Gladstone*], a traveling bag hinged so that it can open flat into two compartments of equal size: also **Gladstone.**
**glair** (glâr), *n.* [< OFr. < LL. < L. *clarus*, clear], 1. raw white of egg, used in sizing or glossing. 2. a size or glaze made from this. 3. any sticky matter resembling white of egg. —**glair′y,** *adj.*
**glaive, glave** (glāv), *n.* [< OFr. < L. *gladius*, sword], [Archaic], a sword; esp., a broadsword.
**glam·or·ous, glam·our·ous** (glam′ẽr-əs), *adj.* full of glamour; fascinating; alluring. —**glam′or·ous·ly, glam′our·ous·ly,** *adv.*
**glam·our, glam·or** (glam′ẽr), *n.* [Scot. var. of *grammar* in sense of *gramarye*, magic], 1. originally, magic spell or charm; hence, 2. seemingly mysterious and elusive fascination or allure, as of some person, scene, etc.; bewitching charm.
**glance** (glans, gläns), *v.i.* [GLANCED, GLANCING], [< OFr. *glacier*, to slip], 1. to strike obliquely and go off at an angle. 2. to make an indirect or passing reference. 3. to flash; gleam. 4. to look suddenly and briefly. *v.t.* to cause to strike (a surface) at an angle and be deflected. *n.* 1. a glancing off. 2. a flash or gleam. 3. a quick glimpse.
**gland** (gland), *n.* [< Fr. < OFr. < L. *glandula*, dim. of *glans*, acorn], any organ that separates certain elements from the blood and secretes them in the form of a substance for the body to use, as adrenalin, or throw off, as urine.
**glan·ders** (glan′dẽrz), *n.pl.* [construed as sing.], [OFr. *glandres*, lit., glands], a contagious disease of horses, mules, etc. characterized by fever, swelling of glands beneath the jaw, nasal inflammation, etc. —**glan′der·ous, glan′dered,** *adj.*
**glan·du·lar** (glan′joo-lẽr), *adj.* of, like, or having a gland or glands: also **glan′du·lous.**
**glan·dule** (glan′jo͞ol), *n.* [Fr.], a small gland.
**glare** (glâr), *v.i.* [GLARED, GLARING], [ME. *glaren;* prob. < OD. or OLG.], 1. to shine with a strong, steady, dazzling light. 2. to be too bright and showy. 3. to stare fiercely or angrily. *v.t.* to express with a glare. *n.* 1. a strong, steady, dazzling light or reflection. 2. a fierce or angry stare. 3. a too bright or showy display.
**glare** (glâr), *n.* [prob. < *glare*, brightness], a smooth, bright, glassy surface, as of ice. *adj.* smooth, bright, and glassy.
**glar·ing** (glâr′iŋ), *adj.* 1. dazzlingly bright. 2. too bright and showy. 3. staring in a fierce, angry manner. 4. flagrant: as, a *glaring* mistake. —**glar′ing·ly,** *adv.* —**glar′ing·ness,** *n.*
**glar·y** (glâr′i), *adj.* [-IER, -IEST], glaring.

**Glas·gow** (glas′gō, gläs′kō), *n.* a city in west central Scotland: pop., 1,085,000. —**Glas·we′gi·an** (-wē′jən, -ji-ən), *adj. & n.*
**glass** (glas, gläs), *n.* [AS. *glæs*], 1. a hard, brittle substance, usually transparent, made by fusing silicates with soda or potash, lime, and, sometimes, metallic oxides. 2. glassware. 3. *a*) an article made of glass, as a drinking container, mirror, telescope, barometer, etc. *b*) *pl.* eyeglasses. *c*) *pl.* binoculars. 4. the quantity contained in a drinking glass. *v.t.* 1. to enclose in glass. 2. to mirror; reflect. 3. to equip with glass; glaze. *adj.* of or made of glass.
**glass blowing,** the art or process of shaping molten glass by blowing air into a mass of it at the end of a tube. —**glass blower.**
**glass·ful** (glas′fool′, gläs′-), *n.* [*pl.* -FULS], the amount that will fill a glass.
**glass·house** (glas′hous′, gläs′-), *n.* a greenhouse.
**glass snake,** a legless lizard found in the South: so called because its tail breaks off easily.
**glass·ware** (glas′wâr′, gläs′-), *n.* articles made of glass.
**glass·wort** (glas′wũrt′, gläs′-), *n.* a European plant of the goosefoot family, with fleshy stems, growing in salt-water marshes.
**glass·y** (glas′i, gläs′i), *adj.* [-IER, -IEST], 1. like glass in appearance or quality; smooth; transparent. 2. expressionless or lifeless: as, a *glassy* stare. —**glass′i·ly,** *adv.* —**glass′i·ness,** *n.*
**glau·co·ma** (glô-kō′mə), *n.* [L. < Gr. < *glaukos;* see GLAUCOUS], a disease of the eye, with hardening of the eyeball: it leads to a gradual loss of sight. —**glau·co′ma·tous** (-kō′mə-təs, -kom′ə-), *adj.*
**glau·cous** (glô′kəs), *adj.* [< L. < Gr. *glaukos*, orig., gleaming], 1. green with a grayish-blue cast. 2. in *botany*, covered with a whitish bloom that can be rubbed off, as grapes, plums, etc.
**glaze** (glāz), *v.t.* [GLAZED, GLAZING], [ME. *glasen* < *glas*, glass], 1. to furnish (windows, etc.) with glass. 2. to give a hard, smooth, glossy finish to; specif., *a*) to overlay (pottery, etc.) with a substance which gives a glassy finish when fused. *b*) to cover (food) with a coating of sugar sirup, etc. *v.i.* to become glassy, glossy, or filmy. *n.* 1. a glassy coating, as on pottery. 2. any substance used to produce this. 3. a film or coating. —**glaz′er,** *n.* —**glaz′i·ness,** *n.* —**glaz′y** [-IER, -IEST], *adj.*
**gla·zier** (glā′zhẽr), *n.* 1. one whose work is cutting glass and setting it in windows, etc. 2. one whose work is glazing pottery. —**gla′zier·y,** *n.*
**glaz·ing** (glā′ziŋ), *n.* 1. the work of a glazier. 2. glass set or to be set in frames. 3. matter applied as glaze. 4. the applying of a glaze.
**gleam** (glēm), *n.* [AS. *glæm*], 1. a flash or beam of light. 2. a faint light. 3. a reflected brightness, as from a polished surface. 4. a brief, faint manifestation, as of hope, etc. *v.i.* 1. to shine with a gleam. 2. to be manifested briefly; appear suddenly. —**gleam′y** [-IER, -IEST], *adj.*
**glean** (glēn), *v.t. & v.i.* [< OFr. < LL. *glennare* < Celt.], 1. to collect (grain left by reapers). 2. to collect the remaining grain from (a field). 3. to collect (facts, etc.) gradually. —**glean′er,** *n.*
**glean·ings** (glēn′iŋz), *n.pl.* that which is gleaned.
**glebe** (glēb), *n.* [< Fr. < L. *gleba*, clod], 1. church land used by the holder of a benefice during his tenure. 2. [Poetic], soil; land; earth; field.
**glee** (glē), *n.* [AS. *gleo*], 1. gaiety; mirth; joy; merriment. 2. a part song for three or more voices, usually unaccompanied.
**glee club,** a group formed to sing part songs.
**glee·ful** (glē′fəl), *adj.* full of glee; joyful; merry. —**glee′ful·ly,** *adv.* —**glee′ful·ness,** *n.*
**glee·man** (glē′mən), *n.* [*pl.* -MEN], [Archaic], a wandering minstrel.
**glee·some** (glē′səm), *adj.* gleeful. —**glee′some·ly,** *adv.* —**glee′some·ness,** *n.*
**glen** (glen), *n.* [< Scot. Gael. *glenn* (now *gleann*)], a narrow, secluded valley.
**Glen·dale** (glen′dāl), *n.* a city in California, near Los Angeles: pop., 119,000.
**Glen·gar·ry** (glen-gar′i), *n.* [*pl.* -RIES], [< *Glengarry*, valley in Scotland], [sometimes g-], a Scottish cap for men, creased lengthwise across the top and often having short ribbons at the back: also **Glengarry bonnet** (or **cap**).

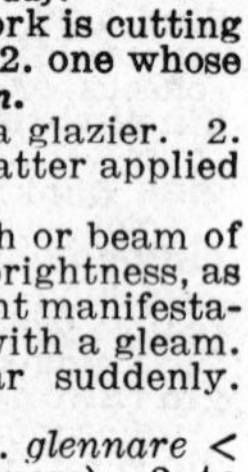
GLENGARRY

**glib** (glib), *adj.* [GLIBBER, GLIBBEST], [orig., slippery; cf. D. *glibberig*, slippery], 1. done in a smooth, offhand fashion. 2. *a*) speaking or spoken in a smooth, easy manner; fluent. *b*) speaking or spoken in a manner too smooth and easy to be convincing. —**glib′ly,** *adv.* —**glib′ness,** *n.*

**glide** (glīd), *v.i.* [GLIDED, GLIDING], [AS. *glidan*], 1. to flow or move smoothly and easily. 2. to pass gradually and unnoticed, as time. 3. to descend slowly in an airplane without using an engine. 4. in *music & phonetics*, to make a glide. *v.t.* to cause to glide. *n.* 1. a smooth, easy flow. 2. a slow descent in an airplane without using an engine. 3. in *music*, a slur. 4. in *phonetics*, the sound made when the speech organs are passing from the position for one sound to that for another. —**glid′ing·ly,** *adv.*

**glid·er** (glīd′ẽr), *n.* 1. a person or thing that glides. 2. an engineless airplane flown by being manipulated into air currents that keep it aloft. 3. a porch seat suspended in an upright frame so that it can swing back and forth.

GLIDER (sense 2)

**glim·mer** (glim′ẽr), *v.i.* [< base of AS. *glæm* (see GLEAM) & *gleomu*, splendor], 1. to give a faint, flickering light. 2. to appear or be seen faintly or dimly. *n.* 1. a faint, flickering light. 2. a faint manifestation; dim perception; glimpse; inkling. —**glim′mer·ing,** *n.* —**glim′mer·ing·ly,** *adv.*

**glimpse** (glimps), *v.t.* [GLIMPSED, GLIMPSING], [< base of *glimmer*], to catch a brief, quick view of, as in passing. *v.i.* to look quickly; glance. *n.* 1. a flash. 2. a faint, fleeting appearance; slight trace; inkling. 3. a brief, quick view.

**glint** (glint), *v.i.* [prob. < ON.], 1. to gleam; flash. 2. to move quickly; dart. *n.* a gleam.

**glis·sade** (gli-säd′, -sād′), *n.* [Fr. < *glisser*, to slide], 1. an intentional slide by a mountain climber down a steep slope covered with snow. 2. in *ballet dancing*, a gliding step to the side. *v.i.* [-SADED, -SADING], to make a glissade; slide.

**glis·san·do** (gli-sän′dō), *n.* [*pl.* -DI (-di)], [formed as if It. ppr., equivalent to Fr. *glissant*, ppr. of *glisser*, to slide], in *music*, a gliding effect achieved by sounding a series of adjacent tones in rapid succession. *adj.* performed with such an effect.

**glis·ten** (glis′'n), *v.i. & n.* [AS. *glisnian*], shine; sparkle; gleam; glitter. —**glis′ten·ing·ly,** *adv.*

**glis·ter** (glis′tẽr), *v.i. & n.* [prob. < LG. source], [Archaic], glitter; sparkle; gleam.

**glit·ter** (glit′ẽr), *v.i.* [prob. < ON. *glitra*], 1. to shine with a sparkling light. 2. to be showy, colorful, and attractive. *n.* 1. a bright, sparkling light. 2. showiness; brilliance. —**glit′ter·ing, glit′ter·y,** *adj.* —**glit′ter·ing·ly,** *adv.*

**gloam·ing** (glōm′iŋ), *n.* [AS. *glomung* < *glom*, twilight], evening dusk; twilight.

**gloat** (glōt), *v.i.* [prob. < ON. *glotta*, to grin scornfully], to gaze or meditate with malicious pleasure. —**gloat′er,** *n.* —**gloat′ing·ly,** *adv.*

**glob·al** (glō′b'l), *adj.* 1. globe-shaped. 2. world-wide: as, *global* warfare. —**glob′al·ly,** *adv.*

**globe** (glōb), *n.* [Fr. < L. *globus*, a ball], 1. any round, ball-shaped thing; sphere; specif., *a*) the earth; world. *b*) a spherical model of the earth. 2. anything shaped somewhat like a globe, as an electric light bulb. *v.t. & v.i.* [GLOBED, GLOBING], to form or gather into a globe. —**glo′bate,** *adj.*

**globe·fish** (glōb′fish′), *n.* [*pl.* see FISH], a tropical fish that can puff itself into a globular form.

**globe-trot·ter** (glōb′trot′ẽr), *n.* one who travels widely about the world, especially for pleasure or sightseeing. —**globe′-trot′ting,** *adj. & n.*

**glo·bose** (glō′bōs), *adj.* [L. *globosus*], globular; spherical or almost spherical. —**glo′bose·ly,** *adv.* —**glo·bos·i·ty** (glō-bos′ə-ti), *n.*

**glob·u·lar** (glob′yoo-lẽr), *adj.* 1. shaped like a globe or ball; spherical. 2. made up of globules. —**glob′u·lar′i·ty,** *n.* —**glob′u·lar·ly,** *adv.*

**glob·ule** (glob′yool), *n.* [Fr. < L. *globulus*, dim. of *globus*, a ball], a tiny ball; very small drop.

**glock·en·spiel** (glok′ən-spēl′), *n.* [G. < *glocke*, a bell + *spiel*, play], in *music*, a percussion instrument with flat metal bars, formerly bells or tubes, set in a frame and chromatically tuned: it is played with one or two small hammers.

**glom·er·ate** (glom′ẽr-it), *adj.* [< L. *glomeratus*, pp. < *glomus*, a ball], formed into a rounded mass; clustered. —**glom′er·a′tion,** *n.*

**gloom** (glōōm), *v.i.* [prob. < AS. *glom*, twilight], 1. to be or look morose, displeased, or dejected. 2. to be or become dark, dim, or dismal. *v.t.* to make dark, dim, or dismal. *n.* 1. darkness; dimness; obscurity. 2. a dark or dim place. 3. melancholy; sadness; dejection.

**gloom·y** (glōōm′i), *adj.* [-IER, -IEST], 1. overspread with or enveloped in darkness or dimness. 2. melancholy; sad. 3. causing gloom; dismal; depressing. —**gloom′i·ly,** *adv.* —**gloom′i·ness,** *n.*

**Glo·ri·a** (glôr′i-ə, glō′ri-), [L., glory], *n.* 1. [also g-], *a*) glory; praise: a word of worship. *b*) any of several Latin hymns beginning with this word, as *Gloria in Excelsis Deo* (glory be to God on high), or *Gloria Patri* (glory be to the Father). *c*) the music for any of these. 2. [g-], a halo (sense 2).

**glo·ri·fy** (glôr′ə-fī′, glō′rə-), *v.t.* [-FIED, -FYING], [< OFr. < L. *gloria*, glory + *facere*, to make], 1. to make glorious; give glory to. 2. to exalt in worship. 3. to honor; extol. 4. to make, or make seem, better, larger, or more beautiful. —**glor′i·fi′a·ble,** *adj.* —**glo′ri·fi·ca′tion,** *n.* —**glor′i·fi′er,** *n.*

**glo·ri·ous** (glôr′i-əs, glō′ri-), *adj.* 1. full of glory; illustrious. 2. giving glory. 3. receiving or deserving glory. 4. splendid; magnificent. 5. [Colloq.], very delightful or enjoyable. —**glo′ri·ous·ly,** *adv.* —**glo′ri·ous·ness,** *n.*

**glo·ry** (glôr′i, glō′ri), *n.* [*pl.* -RIES], [< OFr. < L. *gloria*], 1. great honor and admiration; fame; renown. 2. anything bringing this. 3. worship; adoration. 4. the condition of highest achievement, prosperity, etc. 5. the highest degree of pleasure, pride, etc. 6. splendor; magnificence. 7. heaven or the bliss of heaven. 8. a halo (sense 2). *v.i.* [-RIED, -RYING], to be very proud; exult (with *in*). —**gone to glory,** dead.

**gloss** (glôs), *n.* [? < ON. *glossi*, a blaze], 1. the luster of a smooth, polished surface; sheen. 2. a deceiving outward appearance; superficial show, as in manners or speech. *v.t.* 1. to give a polished, shiny surface to. 2. to make (an error, fault, etc.) appear right or trivial (often with *over*). *v.i.* to become shiny. —**gloss′er,** *n.*

**gloss** (glôs), *n.* [< OFr. < L. < Gr. *glōssa*, the tongue], 1. a translation inserted between the lines of a text. 2. a note of comment or explanation, as in a footnote. 3. a glossary. *v.t.* 1. to furnish (a text) with notes of comment or explanation. 2. to interpret falsely. *v.i.* to annotate. —**gloss′er,** *n.*

**glos·sa·ry** (glos′ẽr-i, glôs′-), *n.* [*pl.* -RIES], [< L. < Gr. *glōssa*, the tongue], a list of foreign, difficult, or technical terms with explanations or translations, as for a particular author, subject, book, etc. —**glos·sar·i·al** (glo-sâr′i-əl), *adj.* —**glos·sar′i·al·ly,** *adv.* —**glos′sar·ist,** *n.*

**gloss·y** (glôs′i), *adj.* [-IER, -IEST], 1. having a smooth, shiny, polished surface. 2. specious. —**gloss′i·ly,** *adv.* —**gloss′i·ness,** *n.*

**-glot** (glot), [< Gr. < *glotta*; see GLOTTIS], a combining form meaning *knowledge* or *use of* (a specified number of) *languages*, as in *polyglot*.

**glot·tal** (glot′'l), *adj.* of or articulated at the glottis: as, English *h* is produced by a gradual *glottal* narrowing.

**glot·tis** (glot′is), *n.* [< Gr. < *glōtta*, var. of *glōssa*, the tongue], the opening between the vocal cords in the larynx.

**Glouces·ter·shire** (glos′tẽr-shir′, glôs′-), *n.* a county of SW England: also **Glouces′ter.**

**glove** (gluv), *n.* [AS. *glof*], 1. a covering for the hand, with a separate sheath for each finger and the thumb. 2. in *sports*, *a*) a baseball player's mitt. *b*) a boxing glove. *v.t.* [GLOVED, GLOVING], 1. to supply with gloves. 2. to cover as with a glove. 3. to be a glove for. —**be hand in glove with,** to be closely associated with. —**handle with (kid) gloves,** to deal with gently and tactfully. —**glove′-like′,** *adj.*

**glov·er** (gluv′ẽr), *n.* a maker or seller of gloves.

**glow** (glō), *v.i.* [AS. *glowan*], 1. to give off a bright light as a result of great heat; be red-hot or white-hot. 2. to give out a steady, even light without heat. 3. to be or feel hot. 4. to radiate health. 5. to be elated or enlivened by emotion. 6. to be bright with color. *n.* 1. light given off as a result of great heat. 2. steady, even light without flame or heat. 3. brightness of color, as of the skin, the dawn, etc. 4. a sensation of warmth and well-being. 5. intensity of emotion; ardor, etc. —**glow′ing,** *adj.* —**glow′ing·ly,** *adv.*

**glow·er** (glou′ẽr), *v.i.* [prob. < ON.], to stare with sullen anger; scowl. *n.* a sullen, angry stare; scowl. —**glow′er·ing·ly,** *adv.*

**glow·worm** (glō′wũrm′), *n.* a wingless insect or insect larva that gives off a phosphorescent light; esp., the larva or wingless female of the firefly.

**glox·in·i·a** (glok-sin′i-ə), *n.* [after B. P. *Gloxin*, 18th-c. G. botanist], a cultivated tropical plant with bell-shaped flowers of various colors.

**gloze** (glōz), ***v.t.*** [GLOZED, GLOZING], [< OFr. < *glose;* see GLOSS (explanation)], to explain away; gloss (over). ***v.i.*** [Obs.], to flatter.

**glu·ci·num** (glōō-sī'nəm), ***n.*** [< Fr. *glucine* < Gr. *glykys*, sweet], beryllium: symbol, Gl: the former name: also **glu·cin'i·um** (-sin'i-əm).

**glu·cose** (glōō'kōs), ***n.*** [< Gr. *glykys*, sweet; + *-ose*], a crystalline sugar, $C_6H_{12}O_6$, occurring naturally in fruits and honey: also called *dextrose*, *grape sugar*: the commercial form is prepared as a sweet sirup by the hydrolysis of starch in the presence of dilute acids.

**glue** (glōō), ***n.*** [< OFr. *glu*, birdlime < LL. *glus*, glue], 1. a gelatin made by boiling animal skins, bones, hoofs, etc. to a jelly: when heated in water, it forms a sticky, viscous liquid used to stick things together. 2. any substance used to stick things together. ***v.t.*** [GLUED, GLUING], to stick together as with glue. —**glu'er, *n.***

**glue·y** (glōō'i), ***adj.*** [GLUIER, GLUIEST], 1. like glue; sticky. 2. covered with or full of glue. —**glue'y·ness, *n.***

**glum** (glum), ***adj.*** [GLUMMER, GLUMMEST], [< ME. var. of *gloum(b)en*, to look morose], gloomy; sullen; morose. —**glum'ly, *adv.*** —**glum'ness, *n.***

**glume** (glōōm), ***n.*** [L. *gluma*, husk < base of *glubere*, to cast off the shell], the husk or chafflike bract of grains or grasses.

**glut** (glut), ***v.i.*** [GLUTTED, GLUTTING], [< OFr. *glotir*, to swallow < L. *glutire*], to overindulge. ***v.t.*** 1. to feed, fill, etc. to excess; surfeit. 2. to flood (the market) with certain goods so that the supply is greater than the demand. ***n.*** 1. a glutting or being glutted. 2. a supply of certain goods that is greater than the demand.

**glu·ten** (glōō't'n), ***n.*** [L., glue], a gray, sticky, nutritious substance found in wheat flour. —**glu'te·nous, *adj.***

**glu·te·us** (glōō-tē'əs), ***n.*** [*pl.* -I(-ī)], [Gr. *gloutos*, rump], any of the three muscles that form each of the buttocks. —**glu·te'al, *adj.***

**glu·ti·nous** (glōō'ti-nəs), ***adj.*** [< L. < *gluten*, glue], gluey; sticky. —**glu'ti·nous·ly, *adv.*** —**glu'ti·nous·ness, glu'ti·nos'i·ty** (-tə-nos'ə-ti), ***n.***

**glut·ton** (glut''n), ***n.*** [< OFr. < L. *gluto* < *glutire*, to devour], 1. one who eats too much. 2. a person with a great capacity for something. 3. a furry, northern animal related to the marten and weasel: the American variety is called *wolverine*.

**glut·ton·ous** (glut''n-əs), ***adj.*** inclined to eat greedily or too much. —**glut'ton·ous·ly, *adv.*** —**glut'ton·ous·ness, *n.***

**glut·ton·y** (glut''n-i), ***n.*** [*pl.* -IES], the habit or act of eating too much.

**glyc·er·in** (glis'ēr-in), ***n.*** [< Fr. < Gr. *glykeros*, sweet], an odorless, colorless, sirupy liquid, $C_3H_5(OH)_3$, prepared by the hydrolysis of fats and oils: used as a solvent, skin lotion, etc., and in explosives: also **glyc'er·ine** (-in, -ēn').

**glyc·er·ol** (glis'ēr-ōl', -ol'), ***n.*** glycerin: the name in chemistry.

**glyc·er·yl** (glis'ēr-il'), ***n.*** [*glycerin* + *-yl*], the trivalent radical of glycerin, $C_3H_5$.

**gly·co-,** [< Gr. < *glykeros*, sweet], a combining form meaning *glycerin, glycerol, glycogen.*

**gly·co·gen** (glī'kə-jən), ***n.*** [*glyco-* + *-gen*], an insoluble, starchlike substance, $(C_6H_{10}O_5)_x$, produced in animal tissues, especially in the liver and muscles, and changed into a simple sugar as the body needs it. —**gly'co·gen'ic** (-jen'ik), ***adj.***

**gly·col** (glī'kōl, -kol), ***n.*** [< *glycerin* + *-ol*], 1. a colorless, sirupy liquid, $C_2H_4(OH)_2$, prepared by heating any of certain ethylene compounds with an alkali carbonate and used as an antifreeze: more accurately, **ethylene glycol.** 2. any of a group of alcohols of which this compound is the type. —**gly·col·ic** (glī-kol'ik), ***adj.***

**gm.,** gram; grams.

**G-man** (jē'man'), ***n.*** [*pl.* G-MEN], [Government *man*], [Colloq.], an agent of the Federal Bureau of Investigation.

**Gmc.,** Germanic.

**gnarl** (närl), ***n.*** [back-formation < *gnarled*], a knot on the trunk or branch of a tree. ***v.t.*** to twist; contort; make knotted. ***v.i.*** to form gnarls.

**gnarled** (närld), ***adj.*** [< ME. *knarre*, a knot], knotty, as a tree trunk; contorted; twisted; rugged: also **gnarl'y** [-IER, -IEST].

**gnash** (nash), ***v.t.*** [ME. *gnasten;* prob. < ON.], 1. to grind or strike (the teeth) together. 2. to bite by grinding the teeth. ***v.i.*** to grind the teeth together in anger or pain.

**gnat** (nat), ***n.*** [AS. *gnæt*], 1. any of a number of small, two-winged insects that bite or sting. 2. [Brit.], a mosquito. —**gnat'like', *adj.***

**gnaw** (nô), ***v.t.*** [GNAWED, GNAWED or GNAWN, GNAWING], [AS. *gnagen*], 1. to bite and wear away bit by bit. 2. to make by gnawing. 3. to consume; waste away; corrode. 4. to torment, as by constant pain, fear, etc. ***v.i.*** 1. to bite repeatedly (*on, at*, etc.). 2. to produce an effect of continual biting, consuming, etc. —**gnaw'er, *n.*** —**gnaw'ing, *n.* & *adj.*** —**gnaw'ing·ly, *adv.***

**gneiss** (nīs), ***n.*** [< G. < OHG. *gneisto*, a spark], a coarse-grained, granitelike rock formed of layers of feldspar, quartz, mica, etc. —**gneiss'ic, *adj.***

**gnome** (nōm), ***n.*** [Fr.; ult. < Gr. *gnōmē*, thought], in *folklore*, a dwarf supposed to dwell in the earth and guard its treasures. —**gnom'ish, *adj.***

**gno·mic** (nō'mik, nom'ik), ***adj.*** [< Gr. *gnōmikos* < *gnōmē*, thought], wise and pithy; full of aphorisms: also **gno'mi·cal.** —**gno'mi·cal·ly, *adv.***

**gno·mon** (nō'mon), ***n.*** [< Gr. < base of *gignōskein*, to know], a column, pin on a sundial, etc. that casts a shadow indicating the time of day.

**-gnomy,** [Gr. *-gnōmia* < *gnōmē*, thought], a combining form meaning *art* or *science of judging* or *determining*, as in *physiognomy.*

**-gnosis,** [see GNOSTIC], a combining form meaning *knowledge, recognition*, as in *diagnosis.*

**gnos·tic** (nos'tik), ***adj.*** [< Gr. *gnōstikos* < *gnōsis*, knowledge], 1. of or having knowledge. 2. [G-], of the Gnostics or Gnosticism: also **Gnos'ti·cal. *n.*** [G-], a believer in Gnosticism.

**-gnostic,** [see GNOSTIC], a combining form meaning *of knowledge, of recognition*, as in *diagnostic.*

**Gnos·ti·cism** (nos'tə-siz'm), ***n.*** a system of mystical religious and philosophical doctrines, combining Christianity with Greek and Oriental philosophies, propagated by early Christian sects.

**gnu** (nōō, nū), ***n.*** [*pl.* GNUS, GNU; see PLURAL, II, D, 1], [< the native (Hottentot) name], a large African antelope with an oxlike head and horns and a horselike mane and tail: also called *wildebeest.*

GNU (4½ ft. high)

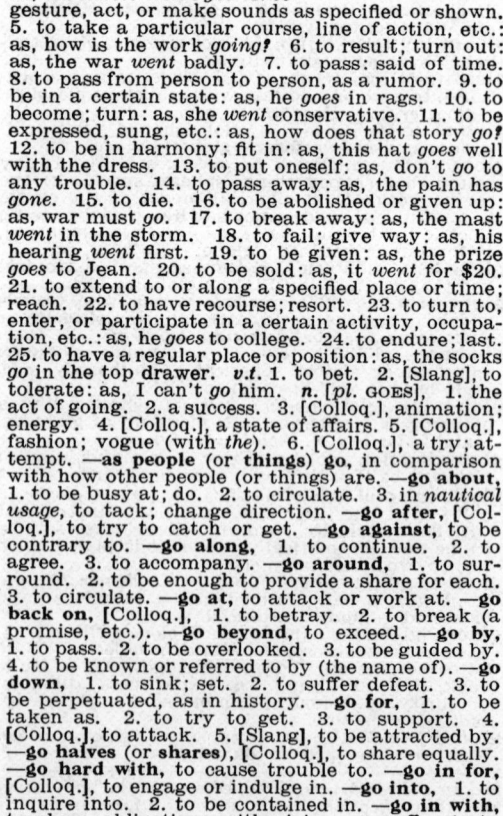

**go** (gō), ***v.i.*** [WENT, GONE, GOING], [AS. *gan*], 1. to move along; travel; proceed: as, *go* fast, *go* to the city. 2. to move off; leave; depart. 3. to move; work; operate: as, the motor won't *go*. 4. to gesture, act, or make sounds as specified or shown. 5. to take a particular course, line of action, etc.: as, how is the work *going?* 6. to result; turn out: as, the war *went* badly. 7. to pass: said of time. 8. to pass from person to person, as a rumor. 9. to be in a certain state: as, he *goes* in rags. 10. to become; turn: as, she *went* conservative. 11. to be expressed, sung, etc.: as, how does that story *go?* 12. to be in harmony; fit in: as, this hat *goes* well with the dress. 13. to put oneself: as, don't *go* to any trouble. 14. to pass away: as, the pain has *gone*. 15. to die. 16. to be abolished or given up: as, war must *go*. 17. to break away: as, the mast *went* in the storm. 18. to fail; give way: as, his hearing *went* first. 19. to be given: as, the prize *goes* to Jean. 20. to be sold: as, it *went* for $20. 21. to extend to or along a specified place or time; reach. 22. to have recourse; resort. 23. to turn to, enter, or participate in a certain activity, occupation, etc.: as, he *goes* to college. 24. to endure; last. 25. to have a regular place or position: as, the socks *go* in the top drawer. ***v.t.*** 1. to bet. 2. [Slang], to tolerate: as, I can't *go* him. ***n.*** [*pl.* GOES], 1. the act of going. 2. a success. 3. [Colloq.], animation; energy. 4. [Colloq.], a state of affairs. 5. [Colloq.], fashion; vogue (with *the*). 6. [Colloq.], a try; attempt. —**as people** (or **things**) **go,** in comparison with how other people (or things) are. —**go about,** 1. to be busy at; do. 2. to circulate. 3. in *nautical usage*, to tack; change direction. —**go after,** [Colloq.], to try to catch or get. —**go against,** to be contrary to. —**go along,** 1. to continue. 2. to agree. 3. to accompany. —**go around,** 1. to surround. 2. to be enough to provide a share for each. 3. to circulate. —**go at,** to attack or work at. —**go back on,** [Colloq.], 1. to betray. 2. to break (a promise, etc.). —**go beyond,** to exceed. —**go by,** 1. to pass. 2. to be overlooked. 3. to be guided by. 4. to be known or referred to by (the name of). —**go down,** 1. to sink; set. 2. to suffer defeat. 3. to be perpetuated, as in history. —**go for,** 1. to be taken as. 2. to try to get. 3. to support. 4. [Colloq.], to attack. 5. [Slang], to be attracted by. —**go halves** (or **shares**), [Colloq.], to share equally. —**go hard with,** to cause trouble to. —**go in for,** [Colloq.], to engage or indulge in. —**go into,** 1. to inquire into. 2. to be contained in. —**go in with,** to share obligations with; join. —**go off,** 1. to depart. 2. to explode. 3. to happen. **—go on,** 1. to continue. 2. to behave. 3. to happen. **—go out,** 1. to be extinguished, become outdated, etc. 2. to attend social affairs, the theater, etc. 3. to sympathize. 4. to go on strike. **—go over,** 1. to examine thoroughly. 2. to do again. 3. to review. 4. [Colloq.], to be successful. **—go through,** 1. to perform thoroughly. 2. to endure; experience. 3. to search. 4. to get acceptance. **—go through with,** to complete. **—go together,** 1. to harmonize. 2. [Colloq.], to be sweethearts. **—go under,** 1. to sink. 2. to be defeated, ruined, etc. **—go up,** 1. to ascend. 2. to increase. **—go with,** 1. to accompany. 2. to harmonize. 3. [Colloq.], to be a sweetheart of. **—go without,** to do without. **—let go,** 1. to let escape. 2. to release one's hold. 3. to give up; abandon. **—let oneself go,** to be unrestrained in emotion, action, etc. **—no go,** [Colloq.], not possible; no use. **—on the go,** [Colloq.], in constant motion or action. **—to go,** [Slang], to be taken out: said of food in a restaurant.

**Go·a** (gō′ə), *n.* a Portuguese colony on the SW coast of India.

**goad** (gōd), *n.* [AS. *gad*], 1. a sharp-pointed stick used in driving oxen. 2. any driving impulse; spur. *v.t.* to drive as with a goad; urge on. **—goad′like′,** *adj.*

**go-a·head** (gō′ə-hed′), *adj.* 1. moving forward. 2. [Colloq.], enterprising; pushing. *n.* permission or an order to proceed: usually with *the.*

**goal** (gōl), *n.* [ME. *gol,* boundary], 1. the place at which a race, trip, etc. is ended. 2. an end that one strives to attain; aim. 3. in certain games, *a*) the line, net, etc. over or into which the ball or puck must go to score. *b*) a scoring in this way. *c*) the score made. *d*) a goalkeeper.

**goal·ie** (gōl′i), *n.* [Colloq.], a goalkeeper.

**goal·keep·er** (gōl′kēp′ẽr), *n.* in certain games, a player stationed at a goal to prevent the ball or puck from reaching it: also **goal tender.**

**goat** (gōt), *n.* [*pl.* GOATS, GOAT; see PLURAL, II, D, 1], [AS. *gat*], 1. a cud-chewing mammal related to the sheep: it has hollow horns that curve backward and straight hair. 2. a lecherous man. 3. [Slang], a scapegoat. 4. [G-], the constellation Capricorn. **—get one's goat,** [Slang], to annoy, anger, or irritate one. **—goat′ish,** *adj.* **—goat′ish·ly,** *adv.* **—goat′ish·ness,** *n.* **—goat′like′,** *adj.*

**goat·ee** (gō-tē′), *n.* a pointed beard on a man's chin.

**goat·herd** (gōt′hũrd′), *n.* one who herds goats.

**goat·skin** (gōt′skin′), *n.* 1. the skin of a goat. 2. leather made from this. 3. a container for wine, water, etc. made of this leather.

**goat·suck·er** (gōt′suk′ẽr), *n.* a large-mouthed, nocturnal bird that feeds on insects: American species include the whippoorwill and nighthawks.

**gob** (gob), *n.* [< OFr. *gobe;* see GOBBET], [Colloq.], a lump, chunk, or mass.

**gob** (gob), *n.* [< ?], [Slang], a sailor in the U.S. Navy.

**gob·bet** (gob′it), *n.* [OFr. *gobet,* mouthful < *gobe,* mouth], 1. a lump; chunk; mass. 2. a mouthful.

**gob·ble** (gob′'l), *n.* [echoic; var. of *gabble*], the characteristic throaty sound made by a male turkey. *v.i.* [-BLED, -BLING], to make this sound.

**gob·ble** (gob′'l), *v.t. & v.i.* [-BLED, -BLING], [prob. < OFr. *gober,* to swallow < *gobe,* mouth], 1. to eat quickly and greedily. 2. [Slang], to seize eagerly. **—gob′bler,** *n.*

**gob·ble·dy·gook** (gob′'l-di-gook′), *n.* [Slang], pompous and wordy talk or writing, as of officialdom.

**gob·bler** (gob′lẽr), *n.* a male turkey.

**Gob·e·lin** (gob′ə-lin, gō′bə-), *adj.* designating or like a kind of tapestry or upholstery made at the Gobelin works in Paris. *n.* Gobelin tapestry.

**go-be·tween** (gō′bi-twēn′), *n.* one who passes back and forth between others with messages, suggestions, etc.; intermediary.

**Go·bi** (gō′bi), *n.* a large desert in Asia, chiefly in Mongolia.

**gob·let** (gob′lit), *n.* [OFr. *gobelet;* ult. < LL. *cuppa,* cup], 1. originally, a cup without handles. 2. now, a drinking glass with a base and stem.

**gob·lin** (gob′lin), *n.* [< OFr. < ML. *gobelinus;* ? ult. < Gr. *kobalos,* rogue], in *folklore,* an evil or mischievous spirit, conceived of as ugly or misshapen.

**go·by** (gō′bi), *n.* [*pl.* -BIES, -BY; see PLURAL, II, D, 1], [L. *gobio,* gudgeon < Gr. *kōbios*], any of a group of small, spiny-finned fishes: the ventral fins are modified to form a suction disk.

**go-by** (gō′bī′), *n.* [Colloq.], a passing by; esp., an intentional disregard or slight. **—give** (or **get**) **the go-by,** to slight (or be slighted).

**go·cart** (gō′kärt′), *n.* 1. a child's low carriage that can be drawn or pushed by hand. 2. a type of light carriage.

**god** (god), *n.* [AS.], 1. any of various beings conceived of as supernatural, immortal, and having special powers over people and nature; esp., a male deity. 2. an image that is worshiped; idol. 3. a person or thing deified or excessively honored and admired. 4. [G-], (*also* gôd), in *monotheistic religions,* the creator and ruler of the universe, eternal, all powerful, and all-knowing; Supreme Being; Almighty.

**god·child** (god′child′), *n.* [*pl.* -CHILDREN], the person for whom a godparent is sponsor.

**god·daugh·ter** (god′dô′tẽr), *n.* a female godchild.

**god·dess** (god′is), *n.* 1. a female god. 2. a woman of very great charm or beauty.

**god·fa·ther** (god′fä′*th*ẽr), *n.* a male godparent.

**God-fear·ing** (god′fêr′iŋ), *adj.* [also g-], 1. fearing God. 2. devout; pious.

**God·for·sak·en** (god′fẽr-sā′kən), *adj.* [also g-], 1 depraved; wicked. 2. [Colloq.], desolate; forlorn.

**God-giv·en** (god′giv′ən), *adj.* [also g-], 1. given by God. 2. very welcome; opportune.

**god·head** (god′hed), *n.* 1. godhood. 2. [G-], God.

**god·hood** (god′hood), *n.* the state or quality of being a god; divinity.

**Go·di·va** (gə-dī′və), *n.* in *English legend,* the 11th-century patroness of Coventry who rode naked through the streets on a white horse on condition that her husband abolish a heavy tax.

**god·less** (god′lis), *adj.* 1. denying the existence of God or a god; irreligious. 2. impious; wicked. **—god′less·ly,** *adv.* **—god′less·ness,** *n.*

**god·like** (god′līk′), *adj.* like or suitable to God or a god; divine. **—god′like′ness,** *n.*

**god·ly** (god′li), *adj.* [-LIER, -LIEST], devoted to God; pious; devout; religious. **—god′li·ness,** *n.*

**god·moth·er** (god′mu*th*′ẽr), *n.* a female godparent.

**go·down** (gō-doun′), *n.* [altered < Malay *godon,* warehouse], in the Far East, a warehouse.

**god·par·ent** (god′pâr′ənt), *n.* a person who sponsors a newborn child and assumes responsibility for its faith; godmother or godfather.

**God's acre,** a burial ground; cemetery.

**god·send** (god′send′), *n.* anything unexpected and needed or desired that comes at the opportune moment, as if sent by God.

**god·ship** (god′ship), *n.* the character or status of a god; deity; divinity.

**god·son** (god′sun′), *n.* a male godchild.

**God·speed** (god′spēd′), *n.* [contr. of *God speed you*], success; good fortune: a wish for the welfare of a person starting on a journey.

**God·win Aus·ten, Mount** (god′win ôs′tin), the second highest mountain in the world, in N Kashmir, India: height, 28,250 ft.: also called *K2.*

**god·wit** (god′wit), *n.* [? echoic], a long-billed wading bird of the snipe family.

**Goe·the, Jo·hann Wolf·gang von** (yō′hän vôlf′gäŋ fôn gö′tə; *sometimes Anglicized to* gā′ti, gũr′tə), 1749–1832; German poet and dramatist.

**go-get·ter** (gō′get′ẽr), *n.* [Slang], an active, aggressive person who usually gets what he wants.

**gog·gle** (gog′'l), *v.i.* [-GLED, -GLING], [ME. *gogelen*], 1. *a*) to stare with bulging eyes. *b*) to roll the eyes. 2. to bulge or roll: said of the eyes, as when staring. *v.t.* to roll (the eyes). *n.* 1. a bulging or rolling of the eyes. 2. *pl.* large spectacles, often fitted with side guards, to protect the eyes against dust, wind, etc. *adj.* bulging or rolling: said of the eyes. **—gog′gle-eyed′ (-īd′),** *adj.*

**Gogh, Vincent van** (vän′ gokh′; Eng. van gō′, gôk′), 1853–1890; Dutch painter.

**Go·gol, Ni·ko·lai Va·sil·ie·vich** (ni-kô-lī′ vä-sil-yā′vich gô′gôl; Eng. gō′gəl), 1809–1852; Russian novelist and dramatist.

**Goi·del·ic** (goi-del′ik, goi′*th*əl-), *adj.* [< Ir. *Gaedheal* < OIr. *Góidel*], 1. of the Gaels. 2. designating or of their languages. *n.* the subfamily of the Celtic languages that includes Erse (Irish Gaelic), Scottish Gaelic, and Manx.

**go·ing** (gō′iŋ), *n.* 1. a departure. 2. the condition of the ground or land with reference to the ease with which it can be traveled. 3. [Colloq.], circumstances affecting progress. *adj.* 1. moving; running; working. 2. conducting its regular business: as, a *going* concern. **—be going to,** to be intending to; will or shall. **—get going,** [Colloq.], to start; begin. **—going on,** [Colloq.], nearing or nearly (a specified age or time). **—goings on,** [Colloq.], behavior or actions.

**goi·ter, goi·tre** (goi′tẽr), *n.* [< Fr. < LL. < L. *guttur*, throat], 1. a diseased condition and enlargement of the thyroid gland, seen as a swelling in the front of the neck. 2. the enlargement or swelling. —**goi′trous,** *adj.*
**gold** (gōld), *n.* [AS.], 1. a heavy, yellow, metallic chemical element with a high degree of ductility and malleability: it is a precious metal and is used in coins, jewelry, alloys, etc.: symbol, Au; at. wt., 197.2; at. no., 79. 2. gold coin; hence, 3. money; wealth. 4. the bright yellow color of gold. 5. a thing having the value, brilliance, etc. of gold: as, his voice is pure *gold. adj.* 1. of, made of, or like gold. 2. having the color of gold.
**gold·brick** (gōld′brik′), *v.i.* [Military Slang], to try to avoid work; shirk; loaf. *n.* a gold brick. —**gold′-brick′er,** *n.*
**gold brick,** 1. [Colloq.], anything worthless passed off as genuine or valuable. 2. [Military Slang], one who tries to avoid work; shirker.
**Gold Coast,** a former British territory in W Africa: merged with British Togoland to form Ghana.
**gold digger,** [Slang], a woman who tries to get money and gifts from her men friends.
**gold dust,** gold in very small bits or as a powder.
**gold·en** (gōl′d′n), *adj.* 1. made of, containing, or yielding gold. 2. having the color and luster of gold; bright-yellow. 3. very valuable or precious; excellent. 4. prosperous and joyful; flourishing. —**gold′en·ly,** *adv.* —**gold′en·ness,** *n.*
**gold·en·eye** (gōl′d′n-ī′), *n.* [*pl.* -EYES, -EYE; see PLURAL, II, D, 1], a wild duck noted for its expert diving and speed in flying.
**Golden Fleece,** in *Gr. legend,* the fleece of gold guarded by a dragon until captured by Jason.
**Golden Gate,** the strait leading into San Francisco Bay from the Pacific.
**golden glow,** a tall, hardy North American plant with doubled, yellow, globular flowers.
**golden mean,** the safe, prudent way between extremes; happy medium; moderation.
**gold·en·rod** (gōl′d′n-rod′), *n.* a North American plant of the composite family, typically with long, branching stalks bearing clusters of small, yellow flowers through the late summer and fall.
**golden rule,** the precept that one should behave toward others as he would want them to behave toward him: see Matt. 7:12, Luke 6:31.
**golden wedding,** a 50th wedding anniversary.
**gold-filled** (gōld′fild′), *adj.* made of a base metal overlaid with gold.
**gold·finch** (gōld′finch′), *n.* [AS. *goldfinc*], 1. a European songbird with yellow-streaked wings. 2. a small American songbird the male of which has a yellow body with black markings.
**gold·fish** (gōld′fish′), *n.* [*pl.* see FISH], a small, typically golden-yellow or orange-colored fish, often kept in ponds or fish bowls.
**gold leaf,** gold beaten into very thin sheets, used for gilding. —**gold′-leaf′,** *adj.*
**gold plate,** tableware made of gold.
**gold rush,** a rush of people to territory where gold has recently been discovered.
**gold·smith** (gōld′smith′), *n.* a skilled worker who makes articles of gold.
**Gold·smith, Oliver** (gōld′smith′), 1728–1774; British poet, playwright, and novelist.
**gold standard,** a monetary standard in which the basic currency unit is made equal to and redeemable by a specified quantity of gold.
**golf** (gôlf, golf), *n.* [? < D. *kolf*, a club, or Scot. *gowf*, to strike], an outdoor game played on a large tract of land (**golf course or golf links**) with a small, hard rubber ball and a set of clubs, the object being to drive the ball into a series of small holes (usually 9 or 18) with the fewest possible strokes. *v.i.* to play golf. —**golf′er,** *n.*
**golf club,** 1. any of the various clubs with wooden or metal heads and long, slender handles, used in golf. 2. an organization operating a golf course, clubhouse, etc.

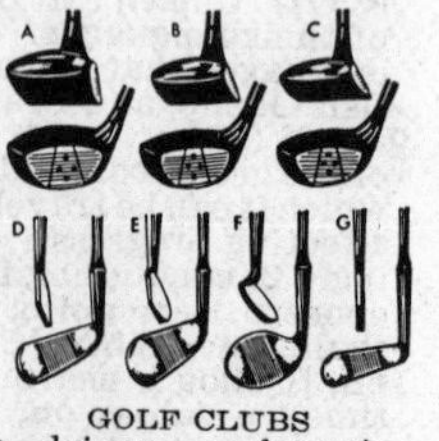

GOLF CLUBS
A, driver; B, brassie; C, spoon; D, midiron; E, mashie; F, niblick; G, putter

**Gol·go·tha** (gol′gə-thə), *n.* 1. the place where Jesus was crucified; Calvary. 2. [g-], a burial place.
**Go·li·ath** (gə-lī′əth), *n.* in the *Bible,* the Philistine giant killed by David with a sling.
**gol·ly** (gol′i), *interj.* an exclamation of surprise, etc.: a euphemism for *God.*
**go·losh, go·loshe** (gə-losh′), *n.* a galosh.
**Go·mor·rah, Go·mor·rha** (gə-môr′ə, -mor′ə), *n.* in the *Bible,* a city destroyed together with a neighboring city, Sodom, by fire from heaven because of the sinfulness of the people: Gen. 19:24.
**Gom·pers, Samuel** (gom′pẽrz), 1850–1924; American labor leader born in England.
**-gon** (gon, gən), [< Gr. < *gōnia*, an angle], a combining form meaning *a figure having* (a specified number of) *angles,* as in *pentagon.*
**gon·ad** (gon′ad, gō′nad), *n.* [ Gr. *gonē*, a seed], a gland that produces reproductive cells; ovary or testis. —**gon′ad·al, go·na·di·al** (gō-nā′di-əl), **go·nad·ic** (gō-nad′ik), *adj.*
**gon·do·la** (gon′də-lə), *n.* [It. (Venetian)], 1. a long, narrow canalboat with a high, pointed prow and stern, used on the canals of Venice. 2. a flat-bottomed river barge. 3. a gondola car. 4. a cabin suspended under a dirigible or balloon.

GONDOLA

**gondola car,** a railroad freight car with low sides and no top.
**gon·do·lier** (gon′də-lêr′), *n.* a man who rows or poles a gondola.
**gone** (gôn, gon), pp. of **go.** *adj.* 1. moved away; departed. 2. ruined. 3. lost. 4. dying; dead. 5. faint; weak. 6. used up; consumed. 7. ago; past. —**far gone,** much advanced; deeply involved. —**gone on,** [Colloq.], in love with.
**gon·er** (gôn′ẽr, gon′-), *n.* [Colloq.], a person or thing that seems certain to die soon, be ruined, etc.; person or thing beyond help.
**gon·fa·lon** (gon′fə-lən), *n.* [Fr. < It. < OFr. < OHG. < *gund*, a battle + *fano*, banner], a flag or ensign hanging from a crosspiece instead of an upright staff and usually ending in streamers.
**gong** (gôŋ, goŋ), *n.* [Malay *gun;* echoic], 1. a slightly convex metallic disk that gives a loud, resonant tone when struck. 2. a saucer-shaped bell with a similar tone. —**gong′like′,** *adj.*
**-go·ni·um** (gō′ni-əm), [< Gr. *gonos*, seed], a combining form meaning *a cell* or *structure in which reproductive cells are formed.*
**gon·or·rhe·a, gon·or·rhoe·a** (gon′ə-rē′ə), *n.* [< LL. < Gr. < *gonos*, a seed, semen + *rheein*, to flow], a venereal disease characterized by inflammation of the mucous membrane of the genito-urinary tract and a discharge of mucus and pus. —**gon′or·rhe′al, gon′or·rhoe′al,** *adj.*
**-go·ny,** [< L. < Gr. < base of *gignesthai*, to be born], a combining form meaning *something generated, produced, descended,* etc., as in *cosmogony.*
**goo** (gōō), *n.* [Slang], 1. anything sticky, as glue. 2. anything sticky and sweet.
**goo·ber** (gōō′bẽr), *n.* [of Afr. origin; said to be < Congo *nguba*], a peanut.
**good** (good), *adj.* [BETTER, BEST], [AS. *god*], 1. *a*) having the proper qualities; as one should be: as, a *good* mayor. *b*) suitable to a purpose; efficient: as, chamois is *good* for polishing. *c*) producing favorable results; beneficial: as, milk is *good* for children. 2. fresh; unspoiled: as, *good* eggs. 3. valid; genuine; real: as, *good* money. 4. healthy; sound: as, *good* eyesight. 5. honorable; worthy: as, one's *good* name. 6. enjoyable, happy, etc.: as, life is *good* here. 7. dependable; reliable: as, *good* advice. 8. thorough: as, a *good* job of cleaning up. 9. adequate; satisfying: as, a *good* meal. 10. morally sound or excellent; specif., *a*) virtuous. *b*) kind, benevolent, etc. *c*) well-behaved; dutiful. *d*) proper; becoming: as, *good* manners. 11. able; skilled: as, a *good* swimmer. 12. considerable: as, a *good* many. *n.* something good; specif., *a*) worth; virtue; merit: as, there is much *good* in him. *b*) benefit; advantage: as, for the *good* of all. *c*) something desirable or desired. See also **goods.** *interj.* an exclamation of satisfaction, pleasure, etc. *adv.* well, fully, etc.: variously regarded as substandard, dialectal, or colloquial. —**as good as,** virtually; nearly. —**for good (and all),** for the last time; permanently. —**good for,** 1. able to survive, endure, work, etc. for (a period of time). 2. worth. 3. able to pay. —**make good,** 1. to repay or replace. 2. to fulfill. 3. to succeed in doing; be successful. 4. to prove. —**no good,** useless; worthless. —**to the good,** as a profit, benefit, or advantage.
**Good Book,** the Bible (usually with *the*).
**good-by, good-bye** (good′bī′), *interj.* & *n.* [*pl.* -BYS, -BYES], [contr. of *God be with ye*], farewell: also **goodby, goodbye.**
**good day,** a salutation of greeting or farewell.
**good-for-noth·ing** (good′fẽr-nuth′iŋ), *adj.* useless or worthless. *n.* a useless or worthless person.

**Good Friday,** Friday before Easter Sunday, observed to commemorate the crucifixion of Jesus.
**good-heart·ed** (good′här′tid), *adj.* kind, generous, etc. **—good′-heart′ed·ly,** *adv.* **—good′-heart′ed·ness,** *n.*
**Good Hope, Cape of,** a cape at the S tip of Africa.
**good humor,** a cheerful, agreeable, pleasant mood. **—good′-hu′mored,** *adj.* **—good′-hu′mored·ly,** *adv.*
**good·ish** (good′ish), *adj.* 1. fairly good; rather good. 2. fairly large.
**good looks,** attractive personal appearance; handsomeness. **—good′-look′ing,** *adj.*
**good·ly** (good′li), *adj.* [-LIER, -LIEST], 1. handsome. 2. of good quality; pleasing. 3. ample; rather large. **—good′li·ness,** *n.*
**good·man** (good′mən), *n.* [*pl.* -MEN], [Obs.], 1. a husband or master of a household. 2. a title equivalent to *Mr.*, for a man ranking below a gentleman.
**good morning,** a salutation of greeting or farewell in the morning.
**good nature,** a pleasant or kindly disposition; amiability; geniality. **—good′-na′tured,** *adj.* **—good′-na′tured·ly,** *adv.* **—good′-na′tured·ness,** *n.*
**good·ness** (good′nis), *n.* 1. the state or quality of being good; specif., *a*) virtue; excellence. *b*) kindness; generosity. 2. best part or quality of a thing. *interj.* an exclamation of surprise.
**good night,** a salutation of farewell at night.
**goods** (goodz), *n.pl.* 1. movable personal property. 2. merchandise; wares. 3. fabric; cloth. 4. [Brit.], freight. **—deliver the goods,** to do or produce the thing required, promised, etc. **—get** (or **have**) **the goods on,** [Slang], to discover (or know) something incriminating about.
**good Samaritan,** anyone who pities or helps others unselfishly: Luke 10:30–37.
**Good Shepherd,** Jesus: John 10:11.
**good-sized** (good′sīzd′), *adj.* ample; fairly big.
**good-tem·pered** (good′tem′pērd), *adj.* not easily angered or annoyed. **—good′-tem′pered·ly,** *adv.*
**good turn,** a good deed; friendly, helpful act.
**good·wife** (good′wīf′), *n.* [*pl.* -WIVES], [Obs.], 1. a mistress of a household. 2. a title equivalent to *Mrs.*, for a woman ranking below a lady.
**good·will** (good′wil′), *n.* good will.
**good will,** 1. a friendly or kindly attitude. 2. cheerful consent; readiness. 3. the value of a business in patronage, reputation, etc., over and beyond its tangible assets. **—good′-will′,** *adj.*
**good·y** (good′i), *n.* [*pl.* -IES], [Colloq.], 1. *usually in pl.* something considered very good to eat, as a candy. 2. a sanctimonious person. *adj.* [Colloq.], weakly or cantingly pious. *interj.* [Colloq.], a child's exclamation of delight. Often **goody-goody** (for *n.* 2, *adj.*, *& interj.*).
**good·y** (good′i), *n.* [*pl.* -IES], [< *goodwife*], an old woman or housewife of lowly social status.
**Good·year, Charles** (good′yêr′), 1800–1860; U.S. inventor of process for vulcanizing rubber.
**goof** (gōōf), *n.* [Slang], a stupid or silly person. *v.i.* [Slang], to err or fail clumsily.
**goof·y** (gōōf′i), *adj.* [-IER, -IEST], [Slang], like or characteristic of a goof; stupid and silly. **—goof′i·ly,** *adv.* **—goof′i·ness,** *n.*
**goon** (gōōn), *n.* [after a comic-strip character of E. C. Segar], [Slang], 1. a person who is awkward, stupid, etc. 2. a ruffian or thug, especially one used in breaking a strike.
**goose** (gōōs), *n.* [AS. *gos*], 1. [*pl.* GEESE, rarely GOOSE; see PLURAL, II, D, 1], a long-necked, web-footed, wild or domestic bird that is like a duck but larger; esp., the female of this bird. 2. the flesh of a goose, used for food. 3. a silly person. 4. [*pl.* GOOSES], a tailor's pressing iron with a gooseneck handle. 5. [*pl.* GOOSES], [Slang], a sudden, playful prod in the backside. *v.t.* [GOOSED, GOOSING], [Slang], 1. to prod suddenly and playfully in the backside so as to startle. 2. to feed gasoline to (an engine) in irregular spurts. **—cook one's goose,** [Colloq.], to spoil one's chances, hopes, etc. **—goose′-like′,** *adj.*
**goose·ber·ry** (gōōs′ber′i, gōōz′bēr-i), *n.* [*pl.* -RIES], 1. a small, sour berry used in making preserves, pies, etc.: it resembles a currant but is larger. 2. the prickly shrub on which it grows.
**goose flesh,** a roughened condition of the skin in which its papillae are erected, caused by cold, shock, etc.: also **goose pimples** (or **skin**).
**goose·foot** (gōōs′foot′), *n.* [*pl.* -FOOTS], any of a group of plants, including spinach, beets, etc., with large, coarse leaves.
**goose·neck** (gōōs′nek′), *n.* any of various mechanical devices shaped like a goose's neck, as a flexible rod for supporting a desk lamp, etc.
**goose step,** a marching step in which the legs are raised high and kept unbent: a German infantry parade step. **—goose′-step′** [-STEPPED, -STEPPING], *v.i.*
**G.O.P.,** Grand Old Party (the Republican Party).
**go·pher** (gō′fēr), *n.* [Fr. *gaufre*, honeycomb: from its burrowing], 1. a burrowing rodent, about the size of a large rat, with wide cheek pouches: also **pocket gopher.** 2. a striped ground squirrel of the prairies, related to the chipmunk.
**Gor·di·an knot** (gôr′di-ən), in *Gr. legend*, a knot tied by King Gordius of Phrygia, to be undone only by the future master of Asia: Alexander the Great, failing to untie it, cut the knot with his sword. **—cut the Gordian knot,** to find a quick, efficient solution for a perplexing problem.
**gore** (gôr, gōr), *n.* [AS. *gor*, dung, filth], blood shed from a wound; esp., clotted blood.
**gore** (gôr, gōr), *v.t.* [GORED, GORING], [? < ME. *gore*, a spear], to pierce as with a horn or tusk.
**gore** (gôr, gōr), *n.* [AS. *gara*, corner < base of *gar*, a spear], a tapering piece of cloth made or inserted in a garment, sail, etc. to give it further width. *v.t.* [GORED, GORING], to make or insert a gore or gores in. **—gored,** *adj.*
**gorge** (gôrj), *n.* [< OFr. < LL. < L. *gurges*, whirlpool], 1. the throat; gullet. 2. what has been swallowed. 3. a deep, narrow pass between steep heights. 4. a mass that blocks up a passage: as, an ice *gorge*. *v.i.* [GORGED, GORGING], to eat gluttonously. *v.t.* 1. to fill the gorge of; glut. 2. to swallow greedily. **—make one's gorge rise,** to make one nauseated, angry, etc. **—gorg′er,** *n.*
**gor·geous** (gôr′jəs), *adj.* [< OFr. *gorgias*, beautiful], 1. brilliantly colored; magnificent. 2. [Slang], beautiful; wonderful; delightful. **—gor′geous·ly,** *adv.* **—gor′geous·ness,** *n.*
**gor·get** (gôr′jit), *n.* [< OFr. < *gorge*, throat], a piece of armor to protect the throat: see **armor,** illus.
**Gor·gon** (gôr′gən), *n.* 1. in *Gr. mythology*, any of three sisters with snakes for hair, so horrible that the beholder was turned to stone: cf. *Medusa*. 2. [g-], any ugly, terrifying, or repulsive woman. **—Gor·go′ni·an** (-gō′ni-ən), *adj.*
**Gor·gon·zo·la** (gôr′gən-zō′lə), *n.* [< *Gorgonzola*, town in Italy], a white Italian pressed cheese like Roquefort in appearance and flavor.
**go·ril·la** (gə-ril′ə), *n.* [< an ancient W. African name], 1. the largest and most powerful of the manlike apes, native to the jungles of equatorial Africa. 2. [Slang], *a*) a person regarded as like a gorilla in appearance, strength, etc. *b*) a gangster; thug. **—go·ril′la-like′,** *adj.*

GORILLA
(5 ft. high)

**Gor·ki, Gor·ky** (gôr′ki), *n.* a city in the central R.S.F.S.R., on the Volga: pop., 1,000,000: formerly called *Nizhni Novgorod*.
**Gor·ki, Max·im** (mák-sēm′ gôr′ki), (pseudonym of *Aleksei Maksimovich Pyeshkov*), 1868–1936: Russian novelist, playwright, etc.: also sp. **Gorky.**
**gor·mand** (gôr′mənd), *n.* a gourmand.
**gor·mand·ize** (gôr′mən-dīz′), *v.i.* [-IZED, -IZING], [< Fr. *gourmandise*, gluttony], to eat like a glutton; gorge. **—gor′mand·iz′er,** *n.*
**gorse** (gôrs), *n.* [AS. *gorst*], furze. **—gors′y,** *adj.*
**gor·y** (gôr′i, gō′ri), *adj.* [-IER, -IEST], 1. covered with gore; bloody. 2. with much bloodshed or slaughter. **—gor′i·ly,** *adv.* **—gor′i·ness,** *n.*
**gosh** (gosh), *interj.* an exclamation of surprise, etc.: a euphemism for *God*.
**gos·hawk** (gos′hôk′, gôs′-), *n.* [< AS.; see GOOSE & HAWK], a large, swift hawk with short wings.
**Go·shen** (gō′shən), *n.* 1. in the *Bible*, the fertile land assigned to the Israelites in Egypt: Gen. 45:10. 2. a land of plenty.
**gos·ling** (goz′liŋ), *n.* [< ON.], a young goose.
**gos·pel** (gos′p'l), *n.* [AS. *gōdspel*, lit., good news], 1. the teachings of Jesus and the Apostles. 2. the history of the life and teachings of Jesus. 3. [G-], any of the first four books of the New Testament, ascribed to Matthew, Mark, Luke, and John. 4. [G-], an excerpt from any of these books read in a religious service. 5. a belief or body of beliefs pro-

claimed or accepted as absolutely true. 6. any doctrine or rule of conduct widely maintained.

**gos·sa·mer** (gos'ə-mēr), *n.* [ME. *gosesomer*, lit., goose summer: the period in fall when goose is in season], 1. a filmy cobweb floating in the air. 2. a very thin, soft, filmy cloth. 3. *a*) a lightweight waterproof cloth. *b*) a coat of this cloth. *adj.* light, thin, and filmy: also **gos'sa·mer·y.**

**gos·sip** (gos'əp), *n.* [< AS. *godsibbe*, godparent; see GOD & SIB], 1. [Obs. or Dial.], *a*) a godparent. *b*) a close friend. 2. one who chatters idly or repeats rumors about others. 3. such talk or rumors. *v.i.* [-SIPED, -SIPING], to indulge in idle talk or rumors about others. **—gos'sip·er,** *n.* **—gos'sip·y,** *adj.*

**gos·soon** (go-sōōn'), *n.* [altered < Fr. *garçon*, boy], [Irish], 1. a boy. 2. a servant boy.

**got** (got), pt. and alt. pp. of **get.**

**Gö·te·borg** (yö'tə-bôr'y'; Eng. jā'tə-bôrg'), *n.* a seaport in SW Sweden: pop., 354,000: also **Goth·en·burg** (got'ən-būrg', goth'-).

**Goth** (goth, gôth), *n.* [< LL. < Gr. *Gothoi*, pl.], 1. any member of a Germanic people that invaded and conquered most of the Roman Empire in the 3d, 4th, and 5th centuries A.D. 2. an uncivilized person.

**Goth·am** (goth'əm, gō'thəm), *n.* 1. (Brit. got'əm), an English village near Nottingham whose inhabitants were, according to legend, very foolish. 2. New York City. **—Goth'am·ite'** (-īt'), *n.*

**Goth·ic** (goth'ik), *adj.* 1. of the Goths or their language. 2. designating or of a style of architecture developed in W Europe between the 12th and 16th centuries, characterized by flying buttresses, pointed arches, etc. 3. [sometimes g-], *a*) medieval. *b*) not classical. *c*) barbarous; uncivilized. *n.* 1. the East Germanic language of the Goths. 2. Gothic architecture. 3. in *printing*, [often g-], a type characterized by straight lines of even width, and lacking serifs. Abbrev. **Goth., goth. —Goth'i·cal·ly,** *adv.*

**Goth·i·cize** (goth'ə-sīz'), *v.t.* [-CIZED, -CIZING], to make Gothic.

**got·ten** (got''n), alt. pp. of **get.**

**‡gouache** (gwash), *n.* [Fr. < It. *guazzo*, water color < L. < *aqua*, water], 1. a way of painting with opaque water colors mixed with gum. 2. such a pigment or a picture so painted.

**gouge** (gouj), *n.* [Fr. < LL. *gu(l)bia*], 1. a chisel with a curved, hollowed blade, for cutting grooves or holes in wood. 2. [Colloq.], *a*) the act of making a groove or hole as with a gouge. *b*) the groove or hole. 3. [Colloq.], a trick to rob; swindle. *v.t.* [GOUGED, GOUGING], 1. to make grooves or holes in as with a gouge. 2. to scoop out. 3. [Colloq.], to defraud; swindle. **—goug'er,** *n.*

**gou·lash** (gōō'läsh, -lash), *n.* [< G. < Hung. *gulyás*, shepherd, hence shepherds' food], a stew made of beef or veal and vegetables, seasoned with paprika: also **Hungarian goulash.**

**Gou·nod, Charles Fran·cois** (shärl frän'swà' gōō'nō'; Eng. gōō'nō), 1818-1893; Fr. composer.

**gourd** (gôrd, gōrd, goord), *n.* [< OFr. < L. *cucurbita*], 1. any trailing or climbing plant of a family that includes the squash, melon, pumpkin, etc. 2. the bulb-shaped fruit **(bottle gourd)** of one species of this family. 3. any plant producing such a fruit. 4. the dried, hollowed-out shell of such a fruit, used as a drinking cup, dipper, etc. **—gourd'like',** *adj.*

GOURDS

**gour·mand** (goor'mənd), *n.* [Fr.], a person who has a great liking for fine foods: also **gormand.**

**gour·met** (goor'mā), *n.* [Fr. < OFr. *gourmet*, wine taster], a person who likes and is a judge of fine foods and drinks; epicure.

**gout** (gout), *n.* [< OFr. < L. *gutta*, a drop], 1. a disease characterized by deposits of uric acid salts around the joints, with swelling and severe pain, especially in the big toe. 2. a drop; clot.

**‡goût** (gōō), *n.* [Fr. < L. *gustus*], taste.

**gout·y** (gout'i), *adj.* [-IER, -IEST], 1. having, or tending to have, gout. 2. of or like gout. 3. resulting from or causing gout. 4. swollen with gout. **—gout'i·ly,** *adv.* **—gout'i·ness,** *n.*

**gov., Gov.,** 1. government. 2. governor.

**gov·ern** (guv'ērn), *v.t.* [< OFr. < L. *gubernare* < Gr. *kybernan*, to steer], 1. to exercise authority over; direct; control; rule; manage. 2. to influence the action or conduct of; guide. 3. to restrain; curb: as, *govern* your temper. 4. to determine; be a rule or law for: as, the bylaws *governing* procedure. 5. in *grammar*, *a*) to require (a word) to be in a particular case or mood. *b*) to require (a particular case or mood). *v.i.* 1. to rule. 2. to be a determinant. **—gov'ern·a·ble,** *adj.*

**gov·ern·ance** (guv'ēr-nəns), *n.* control or rule.

**gov·ern·ess** (guv'ēr-nis), *n.* a woman employed in a private home to train and teach the children.

**gov·ern·ment** (guv'ēr-mənt, guv'ērn-), *n.* 1. the exercise of authority over an organization, state, district, etc.; control; rule; management. *b*) the right, function, or power of governing. 2. *a*) a system of ruling, controlling, etc. *b*) an established system of political administration by which a state, district, etc. is governed. 3. all the people who direct the affairs of a state, organization, etc.; administration. 4. a governed territory. 5. in *grammar*, the influence of one word over the case or mood of another. **—gov'ern·men'tal,** *adj.* **—gov'ern·men'tal·ly,** *adv.*

**gov·er·nor** (guv'ēr-nēr, guv'ə-), *n.* 1. one who governs; esp., *a*) one appointed to govern a dependency, province, etc. *b*) the elected head of any State of the U.S. *c*) a person, often one of a group, who directs or manages an organization or institution. 2. a mechanical device for automatically controlling the speed of an engine by regulating the intake of fuel, steam, etc. 3. [Chiefly Brit. Colloq.], a person having authority; esp., one's father or employer. **—gov'er·nor·ship',** *n.*

**governor general,** [*pl.* -NORS GENERAL, -NOR GENERALS], a governor who has deputy governors under him, as in the British dominions: also **gov'er·nor-gen'er·al. —gov'er·nor-gen'er·al·ship',** *n.*

**govt., Govt.,** government.

**gow·an** (gou'ən), *n.* [< Obs. *gollan*, yellow flower], [Scot.], the English daisy.

**gown** (goun), *n.* [< OFr. < ML. *gunna*], 1. a woman's dress. 2. a dressing gown. 3. a nightgown. 4. a long, flowing robe worn by certain officials, clergymen, etc., and by graduates receiving degrees. *v.t.* to clothe in a gown.

**gowns·man** (gounz'mən), *n.* [*pl.* -MEN], a person wearing a gown as an indication of his profession or office, as a lawyer, judge, etc.

**Go·ya, Fran·cis·co Jo·sé de** (frän-thēs'kô hô-se' de gô'yä; Eng. goi'ə), 1746–1828; Spanish painter.

**Gr.,** 1. Grecian. 2. Greece. 3. Greek.

**gr.,** 1. grain(s). 2. gram(s). 3. great. 4. gross.

**grab** (grab), *v.t.* [GRABBED, GRABBING], [prob. < MD., MLG. *grabben*], 1. to seize or snatch suddenly. 2. to get possession of by unscrupulous methods. *n.* 1. a grabbing. 2. something grabbed. 3. any mechanical device for clutching or holding something to be hoisted. **—grab'ber,** *n.*

**grab bag,** any of a number of closed bags of merchandise to be bought unseen at a fixed price.

**grace** (grās), *n.* [< OFr. < L. *gratia*, pleasing quality < *gratus*, pleasing], 1. beauty or charm of form, movement, or expression. 2. an attractive quality, feature, manner, etc. 3. a sense of what is right and proper; decency. 4. disposition to grant something freely; favor; good will. 5. mercy; clemency. 6. a delay granted beyond the date set for the performance or payment of an obligation. 7. favor shown by granting such a delay. 8. a short prayer in which blessing is asked, or thanks are given, for a meal. 9. [G-], a title of respect in speaking to or of an archbishop, duke, or duchess. 10. in *music*, one or more grace notes. 11. in *theology*, *a*) the unmerited love and favor of God toward man. *b*) divine influence acting in man. *c*) the condition of a person thus influenced. *v.t.* [GRACED, GRACING], 1. to honor; dignify. 2. to give or add grace to; adorn. 3. in *music*, to add grace notes to. **—fall from grace,** to sin. **—in the good** (or **bad**) **graces of,** in favor (or disfavor) with. **—with bad grace,** sullenly or reluctantly. **—with good grace,** graciously or willingly.

**grace·ful** (grās'fəl), *adj.* having grace, or beauty of form, movement, or expression. **—grace'ful·ly,** *adv.* **—grace'ful·ness,** *n.*

**grace·less** (grās'lis), *adj.* 1. lacking any sense of what is right. 2. without grace; awkward. **—grace'less·ly,** *adv.* **—grace'less·ness,** *n.*

**grace note,** in *music*, a note not necessary to the melody, added only for ornamentation.

**Grac·es** (grās'iz), *n.pl.* in *Gr. mythology*, three sister goddesses who controlled pleasure, charm, elegance, and beauty in human life and in nature.

**gra·cious** (grā'shəs), *adj.* 1. having or showing kindness, courtesy, charm, etc. 2. merciful; compassionate. 3. indulgent or polite to supposed inferiors. *interj.* an expression of surprise. **—gra'cious·ly,** *adv.* **—gra'cious·ness,** *n.*

**grack·le** (grak''l), *n.* [L. *graculus*, jackdaw], any of

various blackbirds somewhat smaller than a crow; esp., the American purple grackle.
**grad** (grad), *n.* [Colloq.], a graduate.
**grad.,** 1. graduate. 2. graduated.
**gra·da·tion** (grā-dā′shən), *n.* [Fr. < L. *gradatio* < *gradus;* see GRADE], 1. a forming or arranging in grades, stages, or steps. 2. a gradual change by steps or stages. 3. a gradual shading of one tone or color into another. 4. a step, stage, or degree in a graded series. **—gra·da′tion·al,** *adj.* **—gra·da′tion·al·ly,** *adv.*
**grade** (grād), *n.* [Fr.; L. *gradus*, a step < *gradi*, to step], 1. any of the stages in a systematic progression. 2. *a*) a degree in a scale of quality, rank, etc. *b*) a group of people of the same rank, merit, etc. 3. the degree of rise or descent of a slope, as of a highway, railroad, etc. 4. a sloping part. 5. one of the divisions by years in a school curriculum. 6. a mark or rating on an examination, school work, etc. *v.t.* [GRADED, GRADING], 1. to classify by distinct steps or stages; sort. 2. to give a grade (sense 6) to. 3. to make (ground) level or slope (ground) evenly for a roadway, etc. *v.i.* 1. to be of a certain grade. 2. to change gradually. **—make the grade,** 1. to get to the top of a steep incline. 2. to overcome obstacles; succeed. **—the grades,** elementary school. **—up to grade,** with standard quality.
**-grade,** [< L. *gradi*, to walk], a combining form meaning *walking* or *moving*, as in *plantigrade*.
**grade crossing,** a place where two railroads or a railroad and roadway intersect on the same level.
**grad·er** (grād′ẽr), *n.* 1. a person or thing that grades. 2. a pupil in a specified grade at school.
**grade school,** elementary school.
**gra·di·ent** (grā′di-ənt, -dyənt), *adj.* [< L. ppr. of *gradi*, to step], 1. in *zoology*, moving by taking steps; walking. 2. ascending or descending with a uniform slope. *n.* 1. a slope, as of a road or railroad. 2. the degree of slope. 3. in *physics*, the rate of change of temperature, pressure, etc.
**grad·u·al** (graj′o͞o-əl), *adj.* [< ML. < L. *gradus;* see GRADE], taking place by almost imperceptible steps or degrees; little by little. *n.* 1. a response sung after the Epistle. 2. a book containing choral responses of the Mass. **—grad′u·al·ly,** *adv.* **—grad′u·al·ness,** *n.*
**grad·u·ate** (graj′o͞o-it; *for v. and occas. for n. & adj.,* -āt′), *n.* [< ML. *graduatus*, pp. < L. *gradus;* see GRADE], 1. one who has completed a course of study at a school or college and has received a degree or diploma. 2. a flask, tube, etc. marked with a progressive series of degrees for measuring liquids or solids. *v.t.* [-ATED, -ATING], 1. to give a degree or diploma to upon completion of a course of study. 2. to mark with degrees for measuring. 3. to classify into grades according to size, quality, etc. *v.i.* 1. to receive a degree or diploma upon completion of a course of study. 2. to change by degrees. *adj.* 1. being a graduate of a school, college, etc. 2. of or for graduates. **—grad′u·a′tor,** *n.*
**grad·u·a·tion** (graj′o͞o-ā′shən), *n.* 1. a graduating or being graduated from a school or college. 2. the ceremony connected with this; commencement. 3. a marking with a series of degrees for measuring. 4. one or all of the degrees marked. 5. classification into grades according to amount, size, etc.
**Grae·cism** (grē′siz'm), *n.* Grecism.
**Grae·cize** (grē′sīz), *v.t. & v.i.* [-CIZED, -CIZING], to Grecize.
**Grae·co-** (grē′kō), Greco-.
**graft** (graft, gräft), *n.* [< ME. & OFr. *graffe* < L. < Gr. *grapheion*, stylus < *graphein*, to write], 1. a shoot or bud of one plant or tree inserted into the stem or trunk of another, where it grows permanently. 2. the act or process of inserting such a bud or shoot. 3. the place on a plant or tree where it has been inserted. 4. a tree or plant with such an insertion. 5. *a*) a taking advantage of one's position to gain money, property, etc. dishonestly, as in politics. *b*) anything so gained. 6. in *surgery*, a piece of skin, bone, or other living tissue transplanted from one body or area to another, where it grows permanently. *v.t.* 1. to insert (a graft). 2. to produce (a fruit, flower, etc.) by means of a graft. 3. to obtain (money, etc.) by graft. 4. in *surgery*, to transplant (a graft). *v.i.* 1. to be grafted. 2. to make a graft on a plant. 3. to obtain money, etc. by graft. **—graft′age, graft′ing** *n.* **—graft′er,** *n.*
**gra·ham** (grā′əm), *adj.* [< S. *Graham* (1794–1851), Am. physician], designating or made of unsifted, whole-wheat flour: as, *graham* crackers.

**Grail** (grāl), *n.* [< OFr. *graal* < ML. *gradalis*, cup; ? < dim. of L. *crater*, a bowl], in *medieval legend*, the Holy Grail, the cup or platter used by Jesus at the Last Supper and the receptacle of drops of blood from Jesus' body at the Crucifixion.
**grain** (grān), *n.* [< OFr. < L. *granum*], 1. a small, hard seed or seedlike fruit, especially that of any cereal plant, as wheat, rice, corn, etc. 2. *a*) cereal seeds in general. *b*) any plant or plants producing cereal seeds. 3. a tiny, solid particle, as of salt or sand. 4. a tiny bit; slightest amount: as, a *grain* of sense. 5. the smallest unit in the system of weights used in the U.S. and Great Britain: one pound avoirdupois equals 7,000 grains; one pound troy equals 5,760 grains. 6. *a*) the arrangement of fibers, layers, or particles of wood, leather, stone, etc. *b*) the markings or texture due to a particular arrangement. 7. that side of a piece of leather from which the hair has been removed. 8. disposition; nature. *v.t.* 1. to form into grains; crystallize. 2. to paint or otherwise finish (a surface) in imitation of the grain of wood, marble, etc. 3. to put a finish on the grain surface of (leather). *v.i.* to form grains. **—against the** (or **one's**) **grain,** contrary to one's feelings, nature, etc. **—grained,** *adj.* **—grain′er,** *n.*
**grain alcohol,** ethyl alcohol, especially when made from grain.
**grain elevator,** a tall building for storing grain.
**grain·y** (grān′i), *adj.* [-IER, -IEST], 1. having a well-defined grain, as a wood surface. 2. full of grain (cereal). 3. granular. **—grain′i·ness,** *n.*
**gram** (gram), *n.* [< Fr. < LL. < Gr. *gramma*, a small weight, letter < *graphein*, to write], the basic unit of weight in the metric system, equal to about 1/28 of an ounce: also sp. **gramme.**
**-gram** (gram), [< Gr.; see GRAM], a combining form meaning: 1. *something written* or *drawn*, as in *telegram*. 2. *a*) (a specified number of) *grams*, as in *kilogram*. *b*) (a specified fraction of) *a gram*, as in *centigram*.
**gram.,** 1. grammar. 2. grammatical.
**gram·mar** (gram′ẽr), *n.* [< OFr. < L. < Gr. *grammatikē* (*technē*), (art) of grammar, learning; ult. < *graphein*, to write], 1. that part of the study of language which deals with the forms of words (*morphology*) and with their arrangement in sentences (*syntax*). 2. the system of word structures and arrangements of a given language at a given time. 3. a system of rules for speaking and writing a given language. 4. *a*) a book containing such rules. *b*) a book or treatise on grammar (senses 1 & 2). 5. one's manner of speaking or writing as judged by conventional grammatical rules. 6. the elementary principles of a field of knowledge. Abbrev. **gram., gr.**
**gram·mar·i·an** (grə-mâr′i-ən), *n.* a specialist or expert in grammar.
**grammar school,** 1. an elementary school, especially in the level between the fifth and eighth grades. 2. in England, a secondary school.
**gram·mat·i·cal** (grə-mat′i-k'l), *adj.* 1. of grammar. 2. conforming to the rules of grammar. **—gram·mat′i·cal·ly,** *adv.* **—gram·mat′i·cal·ness,** *n.*
**gram-mo·lec·u·lar weight** (gram′mə-lek′yoo-lẽr), a gram molecule.
**gram molecule,** in *chemistry*, the quantity of a substance having a weight in grams numerically equal to its molecular weight: also **mole, mol** (mōl).
**gram·o·phone** (gram′ə-fōn′), *n.* [< Gr. *gramma*, something written; + *-phone*], a phonograph: a trade-mark (**Gramophone**).
**gram·pus** (gram′pəs), *n.* [*pl.* -PUSES], [< OFr. *graspeis* < L. *crassus*, fat + *pisces*, fish], 1. a small, black, fierce variety of toothed whale, related to the dolphins; killer whale. 2. any of several animals related to this.
**Gra·na·da** (grə-nä′də; Sp. grä-nä′*th*ä), *n.* a city in S Spain: pop., 154,000.
**gran·a·ry** (gran′ẽr-i, grā′nẽr-i), *n.* [*pl.* -RIES], [< L. < *granum*, grain], 1. a building for storing grain. 2. a region that produces much grain.
**grand** (grand), *adj.* [OFr. < L. *grandis*, large], 1. higher in rank or status than others with the same title: as, a *grand* duke. 2. great; most important; main: as, the *grand* ballroom. 3. imposing because of size, beauty, and extent: as, *grand* scenery. 4. handsome and luxurious: as, a *grand* banquet. 5. distinguished; illustrious. 6. self-important; haughty. 7. complete; over-all: as, the *grand* total. 8. [Colloq.], admirable; delightful; very satisfactory. *n.* 1. a grand piano. 2. [Slang], a thousand dollars. **—grand′ly,** *adv.* **—grand′ness,** *n.*

**grand-**, a combining form meaning, in general, *of the generation older* (or *younger*) *than*, as in *grandfather, grandson.*
**gran·dam** (gran′dam, -dəm), *n.* [Anglo-Fr.; see GRAND- & DAME], [Archaic], 1. a grandmother. 2. an old woman. Also sp. **gran′dame** (-dām, -dəm).
**Grand Army of the Republic,** an association (1866–1949) of veterans who served with the Union during the Civil War: abbrev. **G.A.R.**
**grand·aunt** (grand′ant′, -änt′), *n.* a great-aunt.
**Grand Bank,** a shoal SE of Newfoundland: noted fishing grounds: also **Grand Banks.**
**Grand Canyon,** the deep gorge of the Colorado River, in N Arizona.
**grand·child** (gran′child′, grand′-), *n.* [*pl.* -CHILDREN], a child of one's son or daughter.
**Grand Cou·lee** (kōō′li), a dam on the Columbia River, in central Washington: height, 550 ft.
**grand·dad, grand-dad** (gran′dad′), *n.* [Colloq.], grandfather: also **grandad.**
**grand·daugh·ter** (gran′dô′tẽr, grand′-), *n.* a daughter of one's son or daughter.
**grand duchess,** 1. the wife or widow of a grand duke. 2. a lady whose rank is equivalent to that of a grand duke. 3. in czarist Russia, a princess of the royal family.
**grand duchy,** the territory ruled by a grand duke or a grand duchess.
**grand duke,** 1. in certain European countries, a member of the nobility ranking just below a king and ruling a grand duchy. 2. in czarist Russia, a prince of the royal family.
**gran·dee** (gran-dē′), *n.* [Sp. & Port. *grande;* see GRAND], 1. in Spain or Portugal, a nobleman of the highest rank. 2. a person of high rank.
**gran·deur** (gran′jẽr, -joor), *n.* [Fr. < *grand;* see GRAND], 1. greatness of position; eminence. 2. splendor; magnificence. 3. nobility; dignity.
**grand·fa·ther** (gran′fä′thẽr, grand′-), *n.* 1. the father of one's father or mother. 2. a forefather.
**grand·fa·ther·ly** (gran′fä′thẽr-li, grand′-), *adj.* 1. of a grandfather. 2. having the conventional characteristics of a grandfather; kindly; indulgent.
**gran·dil·o·quent** (gran-dil′ə-kwənt), *adj.* [< L. < *grandis*, grand + *loqui*, to speak], using high-flown, pompous, bombastic language. —**gran·dil′o·quence,** *n.* —**gran·dil′o·quent·ly,** *adv.*
**gran·di·ose** (gran′di-ōs′), *adj.* [Fr. < It. < L. *grandis*, great], 1. having grandeur; imposing; impressive. 2. pompous and showy. —**gran′di·ose′ly,** *adv.* —**gran′di·os′i·ty** (-os′ə-ti), *n.*
**grand jury,** a jury that investigates accusations against persons charged with crime and indicts them for trial if there is sufficient evidence.
**Grand Lama,** the Dalai Lama.
**grand·ma** (gran′mä, gram′mä, gram′ə, grand′mä), *n.* [Colloq.], grandmother.
**grand·moth·er** (gran′muth′ẽr, grand′-), *n.* 1. the mother of one's father or mother. 2. a female ancestor; ancestress.
**grand·moth·er·ly** (gran′muth′ẽr-li, grand′-), *adj.* 1. of a grandmother. 2. having the conventional characteristics of a grandmother; kindly; indulgent.
**grand·neph·ew** (gran′nef′ū, grand′nev′ū), *n.* a great-nephew.
**grand·niece** (gran′nēs′, grand′-), *n.* a great-niece.
**Grand Old Party,** the Republican Party.
**grand opera,** opera, generally on a serious theme, in which the whole text is set to music.
**grand·pa** (gran′pä, gram′pä, gram′pə, grand′pä), *n.* [Colloq.], grandfather.
**grand·par·ent** (gran′pâr′ənt, grand′-), *n.* a grandfather or grandmother.
**grand piano,** a large piano with strings set horizontally in a harp-shaped case.
**Grand Rapids,** a city in SW Michigan: pop., 176,000.
**grand·sire** (gran′sīr′, grand′-), *n.* [Archaic], 1. a grandfather. 2. a male ancestor. 3. an old man.
**grand slam,** in *bridge*, the winning of all the tricks in a deal.
**grand·son** (gran′sun′, grand′-), *n.* a son of one's son or daughter.
**grand·stand** (gran′stand′, grand′-), *n.* the main seating structure for spectators at a sporting event, etc. *v.i.* [Colloq.], to make grandstand plays.
**grandstand play,** [Colloq.], an unnecessarily showy play, as in baseball, to get applause.
**grand tour,** a tour of continental Europe.
**grand·un·cle** (grand′uŋ′k'l), *n.* a great-uncle.
**grange** (grānj), *n.* [< Anglo-Fr. < OFr. < ML. *granica* < L. *granum*, grain], 1. a farm with its dwelling house, barns, etc. 2. [G-], the Patrons of Husbandry, an association of farmers organized in the U.S. in 1867 for mutual welfare and advancement. 3. any local lodge of this association.
**grang·er** (grān′jẽr), *n.* 1. a member of a grange. 2. [G-], a member of the Grange. 3. a farmer.
**gran·ite** (gran′it), *n.* [< It. *granito*, grained, pp. of *granire* < L. *granum*, grain], a very hard, igneous rock consisting chiefly of crystalline quartz, feldspar, and mica. —**gran′ite·like′,** *adj.* —**gra·nit·ic** (grə-nit′ik, gra-), *adj.*
**gran·ite·ware** (gran′it-wâr′), *n.* a variety of ironware coated with a hard, grained enamel.
**gra·niv·o·rous** (grə-niv′ẽr-əs), *adj.* [< L. *granum*, grain; + *-vorous*], feeding on grain and seeds.
**gran·ny, gran·nie** (gran′i), *n.* [*pl.* -NIES], [Colloq.], 1. a grandmother. 2. an old woman. 3. any fussy, exacting person. 4. a granny knot.
**granny knot,** a knot like a square knot but with the ends crossed the wrong way, forming an awkward, insecure knot: also **granny's knot.**
**grant** (grant, gränt), *v.t.* [< OFr. < *craanter*, to promise, yield < LL. < L. ppr. of *credere*, to believe], 1. to give (what is requested), as permission, etc.; assent to. 2. *a*) to give formally or according to legal procedure. *b*) to transfer (property) by a deed. 3. to admit as true without proof; concede. *n.* 1. a granting. 2. something granted, as property, right, money, etc. —**take for granted,** to consider or treat as a fact. —**grant′a·ble,** *adj.* —**grant′er,** *n.*
**Grant, Ulysses Simp·son** (simp′sən grant), 1822–1885; 18th president of the U.S. (1869–1877); commander of Union forces in the Civil War.
**gran·tee** (gran′tē′, grän′-), *n.* in *law*, a person to whom a grant is made.
**grant·or** (gran′tẽr, grän′tôr′), *n.* in *law*, a person who makes a grant.
**gran·u·lar** (gran′yoo-lẽr), *adj.* 1. containing or consisting of grains or granules, as the inner surface of eyelids made rough by disease (**granular eyelids**). 2. like grains or granules. —**gran′u·lar′i·ty** (-lar′ə-ti), *n.* —**gran′u·lar·ly,** *adv.*
**gran·u·late** (gran′yoo-lāt′), *v.t.* & *v.i.* [-LATED, -LATING], 1. to form into grains or granules. 2. to make or become rough on the surface by the development of granules. —**gran′u·lat′ed,** *adj.* —**gran′u·la′tor** (-tẽr), **gran′u·lat′er,** *n.* —**gran′u·la′tion,** *n.* —**gran′u·la′tive,** *adj.*
**gran·ule** (gran′yool), *n.* [< LL. *granulum*, dim. of L. *granum*, a grain], 1. a small grain. 2. a small, grainlike particle or spot.
**grape** (grāp), *n.* [< OFr. dial. *crape*, bunch of grapes < Frank. *krappo*, hook; prob. via OFr. *graper*, to gather with a hook], 1. a small, round, smooth-skinned, juicy fruit, growing in clusters on a woody vine: grapes are used to make wine. 2. a grapevine. 3. a dark purplish red. 4. grapeshot. —**grape′like′,** *adj.*
**grape·fruit** (grāp′frōōt′), *n.* a large, round, edible citrus fruit with a pale-yellow rind, juicy pulp, and a somewhat sour taste.
**grape·shot** (grāp′shot′), *n.* a cluster of small iron balls formerly fired as a cannon charge.
**grape·stone** (grāp′stōn′), *n.* a seed of the grape.
**grape sugar,** a simple sugar occurring in plants and fruits, especially in ripe grapes; dextrose.
**grape·vine** (grāp′vin′), *n.* 1. a woody vine bearing grapes. 2. a secret means of spreading information: also **grapevine telegraph.** 3. a rumor.
**graph** (graf, gräf), *n.* [short for *graphic formula*], 1. a diagram representing the successive changes in the value of a variable quantity or quantities. 2. in *mathematics*, a curve or surface showing the locus of a function on a series of co-ordinates set at right angles to each other. *v.t.* to represent by a graph.

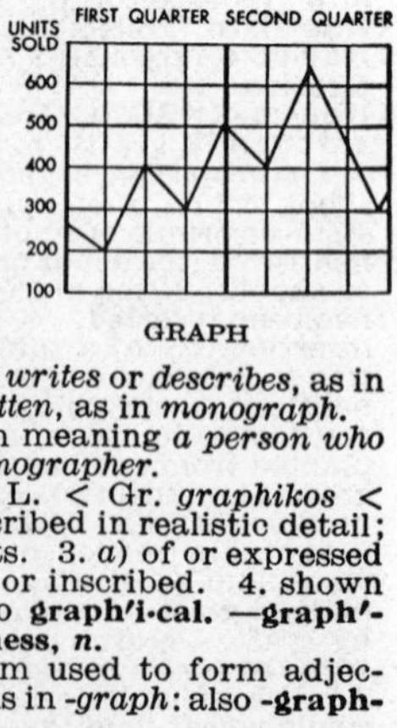

GRAPH

**-graph** (graf, gräf), [Gr. *-graphos* < *graphein*, to write], a combining form meaning: 1. *something that writes* or *describes*, as in *telegraph*. 2. *something written*, as in *monograph.*
**-grapher,** a combining form meaning *a person who writes*, as in *telegrapher, stenographer.*
**graph·ic** (graf′ik), *adj.* [< L. < Gr. *graphikos* < *graphein*, to write], 1. described in realistic detail; vivid. 2. of the graphic arts. 3. *a*) of or expressed in handwriting. *b*) written or inscribed. 4. shown by a graph or graphs. Also **graph′i·cal.** —**graph′i·cal·ly,** *adv.* —**graph′i·cal·ness,** *n.*
**-graph·ic,** a combining form used to form adjectives corresponding to nouns in *-graph*: also **-graphical.**
**graphic arts,** any form of visual artistic representation; esp., painting, drawing, etching, etc.
**graph·ite** (graf′it), *n.* [G. *graphit* < Gr. *graphein*, to write], a soft, black, lustrous form of carbon used

for lead in pencils, for lubricants, electrodes, etc. —**gra·phit·ic** (grə-fit′ik), *adj.*

**graph·ol·o·gy** (gra-fol′ə-ji), *n.* [< Gr. *graphein*, to write; + *-logy*], the study of handwriting, especially as it is supposed to indicate character, aptitudes, etc. —**graph·ol′o·gist,** *n.*

**-graphy,** [< L. < Gr. < *graphein*, to write], a combining form meaning: 1. *a process* or *manner of writing*, or *graphically representing*, as in *lithography*. 2. *a descriptive science*, as in *geography*.

**grap·nel** (grap′n'l), *n.* [< OFr. *grapin*; Pr. < *grapa* (< Frank. *krappo*), a hook], 1. a small anchor with several flukes, or claws. 2. a grappling iron.

**grap·ple** (grap′'l), *n.* [OFr. *grappil*], 1. a grappling iron or grapnel (sense 2). 2. a seizing; grip or hold, as in wrestling. 3. a close fight in which the fighters grip one another. *v.t.* [-PLED, -PLING], to grip and hold; seize. *v.i.* 1. to use a grappling iron. 2. to come to grips, as in wrestling; seize one another. —**grap′pler,** *n.*

GRAPNEL

**grappling iron** (or **hook**), a device consisting of an iron bar with claws or hooks at one end for grasping and holding things; grapnel.

**grap·y** (grāp′i), *adj.* [-IER, -IEST], of or like grapes.

**grasp** (grasp, gräsp), *v.t.* [ME. *graspen*; ? akin to AS. *grapian* (see GROPE)], 1. to take hold of firmly as with the hand; grip. 2. to take hold of eagerly; seize. 3. to understand; comprehend. *n.* 1. a grasping; grip or clasp of the hand. 2. control; possession. 3. the power to hold or seize. 4. comprehension. —**grasp at,** 1. to try to seize. 2. to take eagerly. —**grasp′a·ble,** *adj.* —**grasp′er,** *n.*

**grasp·ing** (gras′piŋ, gräs′-), *adj.* 1. that grasps. 2. greedy; eager for gain; avaricious. —**grasp′ing·ly,** *adv.* —**grasp′ing·ness,** *n.*

**grass** (gras, gräs), *n.* [AS. *gærs, græs*], 1. any of various green plants with bladelike leaves that are eaten by grazing animals. 2. any of a group of plants with long, narrow leaves, jointed stems, and seedlike fruit, as wheat, rye, oats, sugar cane, etc. 3. ground covered with grass; pasture land or lawn. 4. [Slang], marijuana. *v.t.* 1. to pasture or graze (cattle). 2. to grow grass over. 3. to lay (textiles, etc.) on the grass for bleaching. —**go to grass,** 1. to graze. 2. to decay; go to ruin.

**grass·hop·per** (gras′hop′ẽr, gräs′-), *n.* 1. any of a group of leaping insects with two pairs of membranous wings and powerful hind legs adapted for jumping. 2. [Military Slang], a light airplane for scouting and observation.

**grass·land** (gras′land′, gräs′-), *n.* land with grass growing on it, used for grazing; pasture land.

**grass-roots** (gras′rōōts′, gräs′-), *adj.* [Colloq.], originating among or carried on by the common people: as, a *grass-roots* political movement.

**grass widow,** a woman divorced or otherwise separated from her husband. —**grass widower.**

**grass·y** (gras′i, gräs′i), *adj.* [-IER, -IEST], 1. of or consisting of grass. 2. covered with grass. 3. like grass. —**grass′i·ly,** *adv.* —**grass′i·ness,** *n.*

**grate** (grāt), *v.t.* [GRATED, GRATING], [< OFr. *grater* < Gmc.], 1. to grind into particles by scraping. 2. to rub against (an object) with a harsh, scraping sound. 3. to grind (the teeth) together with a rasping sound. 4. to irritate; annoy; fret. *v.i.* 1. to grind or rub with a rasping sound. 2. to make a rasping sound. 3. to have an irritating effect: as, a *grating* voice. —**grat′er,** *n.*

**grate** (grāt), *n.* [< ML. < L. *cratis*, a hurdle], 1. a framework of parallel bars set in a window, etc. 2. a frame of metal bars for holding fuel in a fireplace, etc. 3. a fireplace. *v.t.* [GRATED, GRATING], to provide with a grate or grates.

**grate·ful** (grāt′fəl), *adj.* [obs. *grate* (< L. *gratus*), pleasing; + *-ful*], 1. feeling or expressing gratitude; thankful. 2. causing gratitude; welcome. —**grate′ful·ly,** *adv.* —**grate′ful·ness,** *n.*

**grat·i·fy** (grat′ə-fī′), *v.t.* [-FIED, -FYING], [< Fr. < L. < *gratus*, pleasing + *facere*, to make], 1. to give pleasure or satisfaction to. 2. to indulge; humor. —**grat′i·fi·ca′tion,** *n.* —**grat′i·fi′er,** *n.* —**grat′i·fy′ing·ly,** *adv.*

**grat·ing** (grāt′iŋ), *n.* a framework of parallel or latticed bars set in a window, door, etc.; grate.

**grat·ing** (grāt′iŋ), *adj.* 1. sounding harsh and rasping. 2. irritating. —**grat′ing·ly,** *adv.*

**gra·tis** (grā′tis, grat′is), *adv. & adj.* [L. < *gratia*, a favor], without charge or payment; free.

**grat·i·tude** (grat′ə-tōōd′, -tūd′), *n.* [Fr. < LL. < L. *gratus*, thankful], a feeling of thankful appreciation for favors received; thankfulness.

**gra·tu·i·tous** (grə-tōō′ə-təs, -tū′-), *adj.* [< L. < *gratus*, pleasing], 1. given or received without charge; granted without obligation; free. 2. without cause or justification; uncalled-for. —**gra·tu′i·tous·ly,** *adv.* —**gra·tu′i·tous·ness,** *n.*

**gra·tu·i·ty** (grə-tōō′ə-ti, -tū′-), *n.* [*pl.* -TIES], [see GRATUITOUS], a gift of money, etc., especially one given for a service rendered; tip.

**gra·va·men** (grə-vā′men), *n.* [*pl.* -MENS, -VAMINA (-vam′in-ə)], [LL. < L. < *gravis*, heavy], 1. a grievance. 2. in *law*, the gist of an accusation.

**grave** (grāv), *adj.* [< L. *gravis*, heavy], 1. important; weighty. 2. threatening; ominous: as, a *grave* illness. 3. solemn; sedate. 4. somber; dull. 5. in *music*, low in pitch: cf. *acute*. 6. in *phonetics*, having a grave accent. *n.* the grave accent. —**grave′ly,** *adv.* —**grave′ness,** *n.*

**grave** (grāv), *n.* [AS. *græf* < *grafan*, to dig], 1. a hole in the ground in which to bury a dead body. 2. a burial mound or monument. 3. any place for receiving something dead. 4. death. *v.t.* [GRAVED, GRAVEN or GRAVED, GRAVING], 1. to carve out; sculpture. 2. to engrave; incise. 3. to impress or fix sharply and clearly. —**grav′er,** *n.*

‡**gra·ve** (grä′ve), *adj. & adv.* [It.], in *music*, slow and with solemnity.

**grave accent,** a mark (\`) used to show: 1. in French, the quality of an open e (è), as in *chère*. 2. full pronunciation of a syllable normally elided, as in *lovèd*. 3. falling pitch, as in Chinese.

**grave·clothes** (grāv′klōz′, -klōthz′), *n.pl.* the clothes in which a dead body is buried.

**grave·dig·ger** (grāv′dig′ẽr), *n.* a person whose work is digging graves.

**grav·el** (grav′'l), *n.* [< OFr. dim. of *grave*, coarse sand, beach], 1. a loose mixture of pebbles and rock fragments coarser than sand. 2. in *medicine*, a deposit of small concretions in the kidneys and bladder. *v.t.* [-ELED or -ELLED, -ELING or -ELLING], 1. to cover (a walk, etc.) with gravel. 2. to perplex. 3. [Colloq.], to annoy. —**grav′el·ly,** *adj.*

**grav·en** (grāv′'n), alt. pp. of **grave** (to engrave). *adj.* 1. engraved; carved; sculptured. 2. sharply impressed; permanently fixed.

**graven image,** an idol.

**grave·stone** (grāv′stōn′), *n.* a memorial stone placed at a grave; tombstone.

**grave·yard** (grāv′yärd′), *n.* a burial ground; cemetery.

**grav·i·tate** (grav′ə-tāt′), *v.i.* [-TATED, -TATING], 1. to move or tend to move in accordance with the force of gravity. 2. to sink or fall; tend to settle at a bottom level. 3. to be attracted or tend to move (*toward*). —**grav′i·ta′tive,** *adj.*

**grav·i·ta·tion** (grav′ə-tā′shən), *n.* 1. the act, process, or fact of gravitating. 2. in *physics*, *a*) the force by which every mass or particle of matter attracts and is attracted by every other mass or particle of matter. *b*) tendency of these masses or particles toward each other. —**grav′i·ta′tion·al,** *adj.* —**grav′i·ta′tion·al·ly,** *adv.*

**grav·i·ty** (grav′ə-ti), *n.* [*pl.* -TIES], [< L. < *gravis*, heavy], 1. the state or condition of being grave; esp., *a*) solemnity; sedateness; earnestness. *b*) danger or menace. *c*) seriousness. 2. weight; heaviness, as in specific *gravity*. 3. lowness of musical pitch. 4. in *physics*, gravitation; esp., the force that tends to draw all bodies in the earth's sphere toward the center of the earth.

**gra·vure** (grə-vyoor′, grā′vyoor), *n.* [Fr.], 1. photogravure. 2. a plate or print prepared by photogravure.

**gra·vy** (grā′vi), *n.* [*pl.* -VIES], [? < a misreading of OFr. *grané* < *grain*, cooking ingredients], 1. the juice given off by meat in cooking. 2. a sauce made with this juice and flour, seasoning, etc. 3. [Slang], easily obtained profit.

**gravy boat,** a dish for serving gravy.

**gray** (grā), *adj.* [< AS. *græg*], 1. of the color gray; hence, 2. *a*) darkish; dull. *b*) dreary; dismal. 3. having hair that is gray. 4. old. *n.* 1. a color made by mixing black and white pigments. 2. a gray animal or thing. 3. a person dressed in a gray uniform. *v.t. & v.i.* to make or become gray. Also sp. **grey.** —**gray′ly,** *adv.* —**gray′ness,** *n.*

**Gray, Thomas** (grā), 1716–1771; English poet.

**gray·beard** (grā′bẽrd′), *n.* an old man: also sp. **greybeard.**

**gray·hound** (grā′hound′), *n.* a greyhound.

**gray·ish** (grā′ish), *adj.* somewhat gray: also sp. **greyish.**
**gray·lag** (grā′lag′), *n.* [said to be *gray* + *lag*: so called from its color and its late migration], the European wild gray goose: also sp. **greylag.**
**gray·ling** (grā′liŋ), *n.* [*pl.* -LING, -LINGS; see PLURAL, II, D, 2], 1. a fresh-water game fish of the trout family. 2. any of several varieties of gray or brown butterflies.
**gray market,** a place or system for selling scarce goods secretly at above prevailing prices. —**gray mar·ket·eer** (mär′kə-têr′).
**gray matter,** 1. grayish nerve tissue of the brain and spinal cord, consisting of nerve cells and some nerve fibers. 2. [Colloq.], intelligence.
**graze** (grāz), *v.t.* [GRAZED, GRAZING], [AS. *grasian* < *græs*, grass], 1. to feed (livestock) on growing grass, etc. 2. to put livestock to feed on (a pasture, etc.). 3. to feed on (growing grass, etc.). 4. to tend (feeding livestock) in a pasture. *v.i.* to feed on growing grass or herbage. —**graz′er,** *n.*
**graze** (grāz), *v.t.* [GRAZED, GRAZING], [prob. < prec. *v.*], 1. to touch or rub lightly in passing. 2. to scrape or scratch in passing: as, the shot *grazed* him. *v.i.* to scrape, touch, or rub lightly against something in passing. *n.* 1. a grazing. 2. a slight scratch or scrape caused by grazing. —**graz′ing·ly,** *adv.*
**gra·zier** (grā′zhẽr), *n.* [Chiefly Brit.], a person who grazes beef cattle for sale.
**graz·ing** (grāz′iŋ), *n.* pasturage for livestock.
**Gr. Brit., Gr. Br.,** Great Britain.
**grease** (grēs), *n.* [< OFr. < LL. < L. *crassus*, fat], 1. the soft fat of game animals. 2. melted animal fat. 3. any thick, oily substance or lubricant. *v.t.* (grēs, grēz), [GREASED, GREASING], 1. to smear or lubricate with grease. 2. to bribe or tip: often **grease the hand** (or **palm**). —**greas′er,** *n.*
**grease paint,** a mixture of grease and coloring matter used by actors in making up for the stage.
**grease·wood** (grēs′wood′), *n.* a shrubby, stiff, prickly plant growing in alkaline soils in the western U.S.: also **grease′bush′** (-boosh′).
**greas·y** (grēs′i, grēz′i), *adj.* [-IER, -IEST], 1. smeared or soiled with grease. 2. containing grease; full of grease. 3. like grease; oily; slippery. —**greas′i·ly,** *adv.* —**greas′i·ness,** *n.*
**great** (grāt), *adj.* [AS. *great*], 1. of much more than ordinary size, extent, volume, etc.: as, the *Great* Lakes, a *great* company. 2. much above the ordinary or average in some quality or degree; esp., *a*) existing in a high degree; intense: as, *great* pain. *b*) very much of a: as, a *great* reader. *c*) eminent; important; superior: as, a *great* playwright. *d*) very impressive or imposing: as, *great* ceremony. *e*) having or showing nobility of mind, purpose, etc.: as, a *great* man. 3. of most importance; main; chief: as, the *Great* War. 4. designating a relationship one generation removed: as, *great-grandmother*. 5. [Colloq.], clever; skillful: as, he is *great* at golf. 6. [Colloq.], excellent; splendid; fine. 7. [Archaic], pregnant. *adv.* [Colloq.], very well. *n.* the whole or gross. —**the great,** those who are great. —**great′ly,** *adv.* —**great′ness,** *n.*
**great-aunt** (grāt′ant′, grāt′änt′), *n.* a sister of any of one's grandparents; grandaunt.
**Great Barrier Reef,** a coral reef off the NE coast of Queensland, Australia.
**Great Bear,** the constellation Ursa Major.
**Great Britain,** England, Wales, and Scotland: a division of the United Kingdom and the British Commonwealth of Nations: area, 89,041 sq. mi.; pop., 50,622,000; capital, London.
**great calorie,** see **calorie** (sense 2).
**great circle,** any circle described on the surface of the earth or other sphere so that its plane passes through the center of the sphere.
**great·coat** (grāt′kōt′), *n.* a heavy overcoat.
**great Dane,** any of a breed of large, powerful dog with short, smooth hair: also **Great Dane.**
**Great Divide,** a principal mountain watershed; specif., the Rocky Mountains.
**Greater Antilles,** a group of islands in the West Indies, including the islands of Cuba, Jamaica, Hispaniola, and Puerto Rico.
**great-grand·child** (grāt′gran′child′, -grand′-), *n.* a child of any of one's grandchildren (**great-granddaughter** or **great-grandson**).
**great-grand·par·ent** (grāt′gran′pâr′ənt, -grand′-), *n.* a parent of any of one's grandparents (**great-grandfather** or **great-grandmother**).
**great-great-** (grāt′grāt′), a combining form used with nouns of relationship to indicate *two degrees of removal*, as in *great-great-grandparent*.
**great gross,** twelve gross.
**great·heart·ed** (grāt′här′tid), *adj.* 1. brave; fearless; courageous. 2. generous; unselfish. —**great′heart′ed·ly,** *adv.* —**great′heart′ed·ness,** *n.*
**Great Lakes,** a chain of fresh-water lakes in Canada and the U.S.; Lakes Superior, Michigan, Huron, Erie, and Ontario.
**Great Mogul,** 1. the title of the ruler of the empire founded by the Mongols in India in the 16th century. 2. [g- m-], a person of importance.
**great-neph·ew** (grāt′nef′ū, -nev′ū), *n.* a grandson of one's brother or sister; grandnephew.
**great-niece** (grāt′nēs′), *n.* a granddaughter of one's brother or sister; grandniece.
**Great Plains,** the large area of low valleys and plains east of the Rockies in the U.S. and Canada.
**Great Salt Lake,** a shallow salt lake in N Utah.
**great seal,** the chief seal of a nation, state, etc., with which official documents are stamped.
**Great Slave Lake,** a lake in S Northwest Territories, Canada.
**Great Smoky Mountains,** a mountain range of the Appalachians, between Tennessee and North Carolina: also **Smoky Mountains, (Great) Smokies.**
**great-un·cle** (grāt′uŋ′k'l), *n.* a brother of any of one's grandparents; granduncle.
**Great White Way,** [from its bright lights], the theater district in New York City along Broadway.
**greaves** (grēvz), *n.pl.* [< OFr. *greve*, shin], armor for the legs from the ankle to the knee.
**grebe** (grēb), *n.* [*pl.* GREBES, GREBE; see PLURAL, II, D, 1], [Fr. *grèbe*], a diving and swimming bird of the loon family, with partially webbed feet and legs set far back on the body.
**Gre·cian** (grē′shən), *adj.* Greek. *n.* 1. a Greek. 2. a scholar of Greek.
**Gre·cism** (grē′siz'm), *n.* 1. an idiom of the Greek language. 2. the spirit of Greek culture.
**Gre·cize** (grē′sīz), *v.t.* [-CIZED, -CIZING], to make Greek; give a Greek form to. *v.i.* to imitate the Greeks in language, manner, etc.
**Gre·co-,** a combining form meaning: 1. *Greek, Greeks.* 2. *Greek and.*
**Gre·co-Ro·man** (grē′kō-rō′mən), *adj.* of or influenced by both Greece and Rome.
**Greece** (grēs), *n.* a country in the S Balkan Peninsula, on the Mediterranean: area, 51,246 sq. mi.; pop., 8,300,000; capital, Athens.
**greed** (grēd), *n.* [back-formation < *greedy*], excessive desire for acquiring or having; avarice.
**greed·y** (grēd′i), *adj.* [-IER, -IEST], [AS. *grædig*], 1. wanting excessively to have or acquire; desiring more than one needs or deserves; avaricious. 2. wanting to eat and drink too much; gluttonous. —**greed′i·ly,** *adv.* —**greed′i·ness,** *n.*
**Greek** (grēk), *n.* 1. a native or inhabitant of ancient or modern Greece. 2. the Hellenic language of Greece, ancient or modern. *adj.* of ancient or modern Greece, its people, language, or culture. —**be Greek to one,** to be incomprehensible to one.
**Greek fire,** an incendiary material used in ancient warfare, said to have burned in water.
**Greek Orthodox Church,** 1. the established church of Greece, an autonomous part of the Orthodox Eastern Church. 2. the Orthodox Eastern Church: popularly so called. Also **Greek Church.**
**Gree·ley, Horace** (grē′li), 1811–1872; U.S. journalist and politician.
**green** (grēn), *adj.* [AS. *grene*], 1. of the color that is characteristic of growing grass. 2. overspread with green foliage: as, a *green* field. 3. keeping the green grass of summer; snowless: as, a *green* December. 4. sickly or bilious, as from illness, fear, etc. 5. unripe; not mature. 6. inexperienced; not trained. 7. easily imposed on or deceived; naive. 8. not dried, seasoned, or cured. 9. fresh; new. 10. [Colloq.], jealous. *n.* 1. the color of growing grass; color between blue and yellow in the spectrum. 2. any green pigment or dye. 3. anything colored green, as clothing. 4. *pl.* green leaves, branches, etc., used for ornamentation. 5. *pl.* green leafy vegetables, as spinach, etc. 6. an area of smooth turf set aside for special purposes: as, a village *green*. 7. in *golf*, a putting green. *v.t. & v.i.* to make or become green. —**the Green,** Ireland's national color. —**green′ish,** *adj.* —**green′ness,** *n.*
**green·back** (grēn′bak′), *n.* any piece of U.S. paper money printed in green ink on the back.
**Green Bay,** a city in NE Wisconsin: pop., 63,000.
**green·bri·er** (grēn′brī′ẽr), *n.* a woody, climbing vine of the lily family, with spiny stems.
**green corn,** unripe ears of sweet corn, used for cooking and eating.
**green·er·y** (grēn′ẽr-i), *n.* [*pl.* -IES], 1. green vegetation; verdure. 2. a greenhouse.
**green-eyed** (grēn′īd′), *adj.* 1. having green eyes. 2. jealous.

**green·gage** (grēn'gāj'), *n.* [after Sir William *Gage,* who introduced it into England, c. 1725], a large plum with golden-green skin and flesh.
**green·gro·cer** (grēn'grō'sẽr), *n.* [Brit.], a retail dealer in fresh vegetables and fruit. —**green'gro'-cer·y** [*pl.* -IES], *n.*
**green·horn** (grēn'hôrn'), *n.* [prob. orig. with reference to a young animal with immature horns], an inexperienced person; beginner; novice.
**green·house** (grēn'hous'), *n.* a building with the roof and sides of glass, artificially heated for growing plants; hothouse.
**green·ing** (grēn'iŋ), *n.* any of various apples having a greenish-yellow skin when ripe.
**Green·land** (grēn'lənd), *n.* a Danish island northeast of North America: it is the world's largest island: area, 840,000 sq. mi.; pop., 30,000.
**green light,** the green phase of a traffic light, a direction to go ahead. —**to give** (or **get**) **the green light,** [Colloq.], to give (or get) authorization to proceed with some undertaking.
**Green Mountains,** a mountain range extending the length of Vermont.
**green onion,** an immature onion with a long stalk and green leaves, eaten raw; scallion.
**green pepper,** the green, immature fruit of the sweet red pepper, eaten as a vegetable.
**green·room** (grēn'ro͞om', -room'), *n.* a waiting room in some theaters, for use by actors and actresses when they are off-stage.
**Greens·bor·o** (grēnz'bũr'ō), *n.* a city in north central North Carolina: pop., 120,000.
**green·sward** (grēn'swôrd'), *n.* green grass or turf.
**green tea,** tea prepared from leaves not fermented before drying.
**Green·ville** (grēn'vil), *n.* a city in NW South Carolina: pop., 66,000.
**Green·wich** (grin'ij, gren'ich), *n.* a borough of London, on the Prime Meridian: pop., 91,000.
**Greenwich time,** mean solar time of the meridian at Greenwich, England, used as the basis for standard time throughout most of the world.
**Green·wich Village** (gren'ich), a section of New York City, a center for artists, authors, etc.
**green·wood** (grēn'wood'), *n.* a forest in leaf.
**greet** (grēt), *v.t.* [AS. *gretan*], 1. to address with expressions of friendliness, respect, etc., as in meeting or by letter; hail; welcome. 2. to meet, receive, or acknowledge (a person, event, etc.) in a specified way: as, he was *greeted* by a rifle shot. 3. to come or appear to; meet: as, the aroma of coffee *greeted* us. —**greet'er,** *n.*
**greet·ing** (grēt'iŋ), *n.* 1. the act or words of a person who greets; salutation; welcome. 2. *often pl.* a message of regards from someone absent.
**gre·gar·i·ous** (gri-gâr'i-əs), *adj.* [< L. *gregarius* < *grex,* a flock, herd], 1. living in herds or flocks. 2. fond of the company of others; sociable. 3. having to do with a herd, flock, or crowd. 4. in *botany,* growing in clusters. —**gre·gar'i·ous·ly,** *adv.* —**gre·gar'i·ous·ness,** *n.*
**Gre·go·ri·an** (gri-gôr'i-ən, -gō'ri-), *adj.* of or introduced by Pope Gregory I or Pope Gregory XIII.
**Gregorian calendar,** a corrected form of the Julian calendar, introduced by Pope Gregory XIII in 1582 and now used in most countries of the world.
**Gregorian chant,** the ritual plain song of the Roman Catholic Church, introduced by Pope Gregory I: it is unaccompanied and without meter.
**Greg·o·ry I** (greg'ẽr-i), Saint, 540?–604 A.D.; Pope (590–604 A.D.): called *the Great.*
**Gregory XIII,** Saint, 1502–1585; Pope (1572–1585).
**grem·lin** (grem'lin), *n.* [Eng. dial. < Fr. dial. *grimelin,* a brat, dim. < *grimaud,* a dunce], an imaginary impish creature humorously blamed for the faulty operation of airplanes or the upsetting of any procedure.
**gre·nade** (gri-nād'), *n.* [< Fr. & Sp.; ult. < L. *granatus,* having seeds < *granum,* a seed], 1. a small bomb detonated by a fuse and thrown by hand (**hand grenade**) or fired from a rifle (**rifle grenade**). 2. a glass container to be thrown so that it will break and disperse the chemicals inside: used for putting out fires, etc.
**gren·a·dier** (gren'ə-dêr'), *n.* [Fr. < *grenade*], 1. originally, an infantry soldier employed to carry and throw grenades. 2. a member of a special regiment or corps, as the British Grenadier Guards.
**gren·a·dine** (gren'ə-dēn', gren'ə-dēn'), *n.* [Fr., dim. of *grenade,* pomegranate], a sirup made from pomegranate juice, used for flavoring cocktails.
**gren·a·dine** (gren'ə-dēn', gren'ə-dēn'), *n.* [Fr.], a thin, loosely woven cloth of cotton, wool, silk, etc. used for blouses, dresses, etc.
**Gret·na Green** (gret'nə), 1. a village in S Scotland where, formerly, many eloping English couples went to be married. 2. any similar village.
**grew** (gro͞o), pt. of **grow.**
**grew·some** (gro͞o'səm), *adj.* gruesome. —**grew'-some·ly,** *adv.* —**grew'some·ness,** *n.*
**grey** (grā), *adj., n., v.t. & v.i.* gray: British sp. —**grey'ly,** *adv.* —**grey'ness,** *n.*
**grey·hound** (grā'hound'), *n.* [AS. *grighund*], any of a breed of tall, slender, swift hound with a narrow, pointed head: also (rarely) sp. **grayhound.**
**grid** (grid), *n.* [< *gridiron*], 1. a framework of parallel bars; gridiron; grating. 2. a lead plate in a storage battery. 3. an electrode of wire mesh in an electron tube to control the flow of electrons through the tube. *adj.* [Slang], of football.
**grid circuit,** the part of an electric circuit between the grid and the cathode of an electron tube.
**grid condenser,** a condenser in series with the grid circuit of an electron tube.
**grid·der** (grid'ẽr), *n.* [< *grid, adj. & gridiron*], [Slang], a football player.
**grid·dle** (grid''l), *n.* [< Anglo-Fr. *gridil* < OFr. < L. < *craticula,* gridiron < *cratis,* wickerwork], a heavy, flat, metal plate or pan for cooking pancakes, etc. *v.t.* [-DLED, -DLING], to cook on a griddle.
**grid·dle·cake** (grid''l-kāk'), *n.* a thin, flat batter cake cooked on a griddle; pancake.
**grid·i·ron** (grid'ī'ẽrn), *n.* [ME. *gridirne,* folk etym. on *irne* (see IRON) < *gridire,* var. of *gredil;* see GRIDDLE], 1. a framework of metal bars or wires for broiling meat or fish; grill. 2. anything suggesting a gridiron in design. 3. a football field.
**grid leak,** a high resistance in parallel with a grid condenser to prevent an excess of negative charge on the grid.
**grief** (grēf), *n.* [< OFr. < *grever;* see GRIEVE], 1. intense emotional suffering caused by loss, disaster, etc.; acute sorrow; deep sadness. 2. a cause or the subject of such suffering. —**come to grief,** to meet with difficulty or failure.
**grief-strick·en** (grēf'strik'ən), *adj.* stricken with grief; keenly distressed; sorrowful.
**Grieg, Ed·vard** (ed'värt grig; Eng. grēg), 1843–1907; Norwegian composer.
**griev·ance** (grēv'əns), *n.* 1. a circumstance thought to be unjust and ground for complaint or resentment. 2. complaint or resentment, or a ground for this, against a wrong, real or imagined.
**grieve** (grēv), *v.t.* [GRIEVED, GRIEVING], [OFr. *grever* < L. *gravare,* to burden < *gravis,* heavy], to cause to feel grief; afflict with deep sorrow; make sad. *v.i.* to feel deep sorrow; be sad; lament. —**griev'er,** *n.* —**griev'ing·ly,** *adv.*
**griev·ous** (grēv'əs), *adj.* 1. causing grief. 2. showing or full of grief. 3. causing physical suffering; severe. 4. deplorable; atrocious. —**griev'ous·ly,** *adv.* —**griev'ous·ness,** *n.*
**grif·fin** (grif'in), *n.* [< OFr. < OHG. or It.; both < L. *gryphus* < Gr. < *grypos,* curved], a mythical animal, part eagle and part lion: also **grif'fon** (-ən), **gryph'on.**

GRIFFIN

**Grif·fith, David Wark** (wôrk grif'ith), 1875–1948; U.S. motion-picture producer.
**grift·er** (grif'tẽr), *n.* [prob. altered < *grafter*], [Slang], a person who runs a gambling device at a carnival, resort, etc.; confidence man.
**grig** (grig), *n.* [prob. < ON.], 1. a lively person. 2. [Obs. or Dial.], a small eel. 3. [Obs. or Dial.], *a*) a grasshopper. *b*) a cricket.
**grill** (gril), *n.* [Fr. *gril;* akin to *griddle*], 1. a gridiron. 2. grilled food. 3. a grillroom. *v.t.* 1. to broil. 2. to torture by applying heat. 3. to question or cross-examine relentlessly. *v.i.* to be subjected to grilling. —**grilled,** *adj.* —**grill'er,** *n.*
**grille** (gril), *n.* [Fr. < OFr.; see GRIDDLE], an open grating of wrought iron, wood, etc., forming a screen to a door, window, or the like: sometimes sp. **grill.** —**grilled,** *adj.*
**grill·room** (gril'ro͞om', -room'), *n.* a restaurant that makes a specialty of grilled foods.
**grilse** (grils), *n.* [*pl.* GRILSE, GRILSES; see PLURAL, II, D, 2], a young salmon on its first return from the sea to fresh water.
**grim** (grim), *adj.* [GRIMMER, GRIMMEST], [AS. *grimm*], 1. fierce; cruel; savage. 2. hard and unyielding; relentless; stern. 3. appearing stern,

threatening, forbidding, etc. 4. hideous; ghastly. **—grim′ly,** ***adv.*** **—grim′ness,** ***n.***
**gri·mace** (gri-mās′), ***n.*** [Fr.; prob. < OHG. < base of *grim*], a distortion of the face; a wry or ugly smile or expression of pain, contempt, etc. ***v.i.*** [-MACED, MACING], to make grimaces. **—gri·mac′er,** ***n.***
**gri·mal·kin** (gri-mal′kin, -môl′-), ***n.*** [? < *gray* + *malkin*, dim. of *Matilda*, etc.; ? < Fr. *grimaud*, dunce], 1. a cat; esp., an old female cat. 2. a malicious old woman.
**grime** (grīm), ***n.*** [< D. or LG.], sooty dirt rubbed into a surface, as of the skin. ***v.t.*** [GRIMED, GRIMING], to make very dirty or grimy.
**Grimm, Ja·kob** (yä′kôp grim), 1785–1863; German philologist and collector of fairy tales.
**Grimm, Wil·helm** (vil′helm), 1786–1859; brother and collaborator of *Jakob.*
**grim·y** (grīm′i), ***adj.*** [-IER, -IEST], covered with grime; very dirty. **—grim′i·ly,** ***adv.*** **—grim′i·ness,** ***n.***
**grin** (grin), ***v.i.*** [GRINNED, GRINNING], [AS. *grennian*], 1. to smile broadly. 2. to draw back the lips and show the teeth in pain, scorn, etc. ***v.t.*** to express by means of a broad smile: as, he *grinned* his approval. ***n.*** 1. the act of grinning. 2. a facial expression resulting from grinning. **—grin′ner,** ***n.*** **—grin′ning·ly,** ***adv.***
**grind** (grīnd), ***v.t.*** [GROUND, GRINDING], [AS. *grindan*], 1. to crush into bits or fine particles between two hard surfaces; pulverize. 2. to afflict with cruelty, hardship, etc.; oppress. 3. to sharpen, shape, or smooth by friction. 4. to press down or rub together harshly or gratingly: as, he *ground* his teeth. 5. to operate by turning the crank of: as, *grind* a coffee mill. 6. to produce as by grinding. ***v.i.*** 1. to perform the act of grinding something. 2. to grate. 3. [Colloq.], to work or study hard and steadily. ***n.*** 1. the act of grinding. 2. a long, difficult task or study. 3. [Colloq.], a student who studies very hard. **—grind′ing·ly,** ***adv.***
**grind·er** (grīn′dẽr), ***n.*** 1. a person or thing that grinds; specif., *a*) a tool sharpener. *b*) a machine for crushing a substance. *c*) a molar tooth.
**grind·stone** (grīnd′stōn′), ***n.*** a revolving stone disk for sharpening tools or shaping and polishing things. **—keep (or have or put) one's nose to the grindstone,** to work hard and steadily.
**grin·go** (griŋ′gō), ***n.*** [*pl.* -GOS], [Mex. Sp.; Sp., gibberish], in Latin America, a foreigner, especially an American or Englishman: hostile term.
**grip** (grip), ***n.*** [AS. *gripe* < *gripan*, to seize], 1. a secure grasp; firm hold, as with the hand, teeth, etc. 2. any special manner of clasping hands: as, Freemasons have a secret *grip.* 3. the power of grasping firmly. 4. mental grasp. 5. firm control; mastery. 6. a mechanical contrivance for clutching or grasping. 7. the part by which something is grasped; handle. 8. a small traveling bag; valise. 9. a sudden, intense pain. 10. in *sports*, the manner of holding a bat, golf club, etc. ***v.t.*** [GRIPPED or GRIPT, GRIPPING], 1. to take firmly and hold fast with the hand, teeth, etc. 2. to give a grip (sense 2) to. 3. to fasten or join firmly (*to*). 4. to get and hold the attention of. 5. to control (the attention, emotions, etc.). ***v.i.*** to get a grip. **—come to grips,** to struggle; try to cope (*with*). **—grip′per,** ***n.*** **—grip′ping·ly,** ***adv.***
**gripe** (grīp), ***v.t.*** [GRIPED, GRIPING], [AS. *gripan*, to seize], 1. to grasp; clutch. 2. to distress; afflict. 3. to cause sudden, sharp pain in the bowels of. 4. [Slang], to annoy; irritate. ***v.i.*** 1. to feel sharp pains in the bowels. 2. [Slang], to complain. ***n.*** 1. a griping; clutching. 2. control; mastery. 3. distress; affliction. 4. *pl.* sudden, sharp pains in the bowels. 5. [Slang], a complaint. **—grip′er,** ***n.*** **—grip′y** [-IER, -IEST], ***adj.***
**grippe** (grip), ***n.*** [Fr. < Russ. *chripu*, huskiness], influenza: also sp. **grip.**
**grip·py** (grip′i), ***adj.*** [-PIER, -PIEST], [Colloq.], having the grippe.
**grip·sack** (grip′sak′), ***n.*** a valise.
**gript** (gript), alt. pt. and pp. of **grip.**
**Gri·sel·da** (gri-zel′də, -sel′-), ***n.*** in *medieval romance*, a heroine famous for her patience.
**gri·sette** (gri-zet′), ***n.*** [orig., gray woolen cloth used for dresses of French working girls < Fr. *gris*, gray], a French working girl or shop girl.
**gris·ly** (griz′li), ***adj.*** [-LIER, -LIEST], [AS. *grislic*], terrifying; ghastly. **—gris′li·ness,** ***n.***
**grist** (grist), ***n.*** [AS.], grain that is to be or has been ground; esp., a batch of such grain. **—grist to one's mill,** anything one can use profitably.
**gris·tle** (gris′'l), ***n.*** [AS.], cartilage.
**gris·tly** (gris′li), ***adj.*** [-TLIER, -TLIEST], 1. of or containing gristle. 2. having the nature of gristle. Also sp. **gris′ly. —gris′tli·ness,** ***n.***
**grist·mill** (grist′mil′), ***n.*** a mill for grinding grain, especially for individual customers.
**grit** (grit), ***n.*** [AS. *greot*], 1. rough, hard particles of sand, stone, etc. 2. a hard, coarse sandstone. 3. obstinate courage; pluck. ***v.t.*** [GRITTED, GRITTING], to grind (the teeth) in anger or determination. ***v.i.*** to make a grating or grinding sound.
**grits** (grits), ***n.pl.*** [AS. *grytt(e)*], grain hulled and coarsely ground; esp., coarse hominy.
**grit·ty** (grit′i), ***adj.*** [-TIER, -TIEST], 1. of, like, or containing grit; sandy. 2. brave; plucky. **—grit′ti·ly,** ***adv.*** **—grit′ti·ness,** ***n.***
**griz·zle** (griz′'l), ***n.*** [< OFr. < *gris* (< OHG. *gris*), gray], 1. gray hair. 2. gray. ***v.t. & v.i.*** [-ZLED, -ZLING], to make or become gray. ***adj.*** gray.
**griz·zled** (griz′'ld), ***adj.*** 1. gray or streaked with gray. 2. having gray hair.
**griz·zly** (griz′li), ***adj.*** [-ZLIER, -ZLIEST], grayish; grizzled. ***n.*** [*pl.* -ZLIES], a grizzly bear.
**grizzly bear,** a large, ferocious, yellow-brown bear, found in western North America.
**groan** (grōn), ***v.i.*** [AS. *granian*], 1. to utter a deep sound expressing pain, distress, or disapproval. 2. to make a sound like this: as, the wind *groans.* 3. to suffer deeply from cruelty, etc. 4. to be loaded or weighed down. ***v.t.*** to utter with a groan or groans. ***n.*** a sound made in groaning. **—groan′er,** ***n.*** **—groan′ing·ly,** ***adv.***
**groat** (grōt), ***n.*** [< MD. *groot* or MLG. *grote*, thick], 1. an obsolete English silver coin worth fourpence. 2. a trifling sum.
**groats** (grōts), ***n.pl.*** [< AS. *grotan*, pl. ], hulled, or hulled and coarsely cracked, grain.
**gro·cer** (grō′sẽr), ***n.*** [< OFr. < ML. *grossarius*, wholesale dealer < *grossus*, great], a storekeeper who sells food and various household supplies.
**gro·cer·y** (grō′sẽr-i), ***n.*** [*pl.* -IES], 1. the business or store of a grocer. 2. *pl.* the food and supplies sold by a grocer.
**grog** (grog), ***n.*** [after Old *Grog* (< his *grogram* cloak), nickname of E. Vernon (1684–1757), Brit. admiral], 1. an alcoholic liquor, originally rum, diluted with water. 2. any alcoholic liquor.
**grog·ger·y** (grog′ẽr-i), ***n.*** [*pl.* -IES], a saloon.
**grog·gy** (grog′i), ***adj.*** [-GIER, -GIEST], [< *grog*], [Colloq.], 1. drunk; intoxicated. 2. shaky or dizzy. **—grog′gi·ly,** ***adv.*** **—grog′gi·ness,** ***n.***
**grog·ram** (grog′rəm), ***n.*** [< OFr. < *gros*, coarse + *grain*, grain], a coarse fabric made of silk, or of silk, worsted, and mohair.
**grog·shop** (grog′shop′), ***n.*** [*grog* + *shop*], a place where alcoholic drinks are sold; saloon.
**groin** (groin), ***n.*** [? < AS. *grynde*, abyss], 1. the depressed part or the fold where the abdomen joins either thigh. 2. in *architecture*, the sharp, curved edge at the junction of two intersecting vaults. ***v.t.*** to build with a groin.

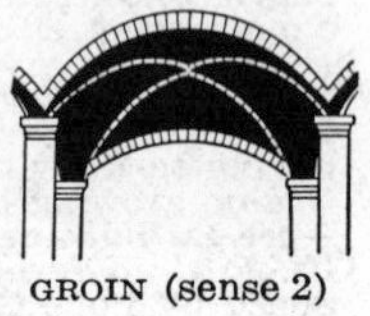

GROIN (sense 2)

**grom·met** (grom′it), ***n.*** [Fr. *gourmette*, a curb], 1. a ring of rope or metal used to fasten the edge of a sail to its stay, hold an oar in place, etc. 2. a metal eyelet.
**groom** (grōōm, groom), ***n.*** [ME. *grome*, boy; akin to OFr. *gromet*, servant], 1. a man or boy whose work is tending horses. 2. any of various officials of the British Royal household. 3. a bridegroom. 4. [Archaic], a manservant. ***v.t.*** 1. to tend (horses); feed and curry. 2. to make neat, tidy, and smart. 3. to train (a person) for a particular purpose: as, he was *groomed* for political office. **—groom′er,** ***n.***
**grooms·man** (grōōmz′mən, groomz′-), ***n.*** [*pl.* -MEN], a man who attends a bridegroom at the wedding.
**groove** (grōōv), ***n.*** [< ON. *grof*, a pit], 1. a long, narrow furrow cut in a surface with a tool. 2. any channel like this; rut. 3. a habitual way of doing things; settled routine. ***v.t.*** [GROOVED, GROOVING], to make a groove or grooves in. **—in the groove,** [Slang], performing or performed with smooth, effortless skill, as musicians or music. **—groove′less,** ***adj.*** **—groov′er,** ***n.***
**grope** (grōp), ***v.i.*** [GROPED, GROPING], [< AS. *grapian* < base of *grap*, a grasp], to feel or search about blindly, or uncertainly. ***v.t.*** to seek or find by groping; feel (one's way). ***n.*** a groping. **—grop′er,** ***n.*** **—grop′ing·ly,** ***adv.***
**gros·beak** (grōs′bēk′), ***n.*** [< Fr.; see GROSS & BEAK], any of various birds of the finch family, with a thick, strong, conical bill.
**gros·grain** (grō′grān′), ***adj.*** [Fr.; see GROGRAM], having heavy, crosswise cords: as, *grosgrain* silk. ***n.*** 1. grosgrain silk. 2. ribbon made of this.
**gross** (grōs), ***adj.*** [< OFr. < LL. *grossus*, thick], 1. too fat; overfed; burly. 2. flagrant; very wrong.

3. dense; thick. 4. coarse; not delicate. 5. vulgar; obscene: as, *gross* language. 6. total; entire; with no deductions: as, one's *gross* income: opposed to *net*. ***n.*** 1. [*pl.* GROSSES], the mass or bulk; whole amount. 2. [*pl.* GROSS], twelve dozen. ***v.t. & v.i.*** [Colloq.], to make (a specified total amount) before expenses are deducted. **—in the gross,** 1. in bulk; as a whole. 2. wholesale. **—gross'ly,** ***adv.*** **—gross'ness,** ***n.***

**gross ton,** a unit of weight, 2,240 pounds.

**gross weight,** the total weight of a commodity, including the weight of the wrapper or container.

**gro·tesque** (grō-tesk'), ***adj.*** [< Fr. < It. < *grotta*, a grotto: from designs found in grottoes], 1. in or of a style of painting, sculpture, etc. in which forms of persons and animals are intermingled with foliage, etc. in a fantastic design. 2. characterized by distortions or incongruities in appearance, shape, etc.; bizarre. 3. ludicrously eccentric; absurd. ***n.*** 1. a grotesque painting, sculpture, etc. 2. grotesque quality, character, etc. 3. a grotesque figure or design. **—gro·tesque'ly,** ***adv.*** **—gro·tesque'ness,** ***n.***

**grot·to** (grot'ō), ***n.*** [*pl.* -TOES, -TOS], [< It. < LL. *grupta* < L. *crypta*, crypt], 1. a cave. 2. a cavelike summerhouse, shrine, etc.

**grouch** (grouch), ***v.i.*** [< OFr. *grouchier*], [Colloq.], to grumble or sulk. ***n.*** [Colloq.], 1. a person who grouches. 2. a grumbling or sulky mood.

**grouch·y** (grouch'i), ***adj.*** [-IER, -IEST], [Colloq.], grumbling; sulky. **—grouch'i·ly,** ***adv.*** **—grouch'i·ness,** ***n.***

**ground** (ground), ***n.*** [AS. *grund*, bottom], 1. *a*) originally, the lowest part or bottom of anything. *b*) the bottom of the sea. 2. the solid surface of the earth. 3. the soil of the earth; earth; land. 4. *often pl.* a particular piece of land: as, a hunting *ground*, the *grounds* of an estate. 5. any area or distance: as, *ground* covered in work, discussion, a race, etc. 6. basis; foundation; groundwork. 7. *usually pl.* the logical basis of a conclusion, action, etc.; valid reason or cause: as, *grounds* for a divorce. 8. the background, as in a painting, colored pattern, etc. 9. *pl.* particles that settle to the bottom of a liquid; dregs: as, coffee *grounds*. 10. in *electricity*, the connection of an electrical conductor with the ground. ***adj.*** 1. of, on, or near the ground. 2. growing or living in or on the ground. ***v.t.*** 1. to set on, or cause to touch, the ground. 2. to cause to run aground. 3. to found on a firm basis; establish. 4. to base (a claim, argument, etc.) on something specified. 5. to instruct (a person) in the elements or first principles of. 6. to provide with a background. 7. in *aviation*, to cause to remain on the ground; keep from flying. 8. in *electricity*, to connect (a conductor) with the ground. ***v.i.*** 1. to strike or fall to the ground. 2. to strike the bottom or run ashore: said of a ship. 3. in *baseball*, to be put out on a grounder (usually with *out*). **—break ground,** 1. to dig; excavate. 2. to plow. 3. to start any undertaking. **—cover ground,** 1. to traverse a certain distance. 2. to travel. 3. to get a certain amount of work done. **—cut the ground from under one's feet,** to deprive one of effective defense or argument. **—from the ground up,** completely; thoroughly. **—gain ground,** 1. to move forward. 2. to make progress. 3. to gain in strength, popularity, etc. **—give ground,** to withdraw under attack; yield. **—hold** (or **stand**) **one's ground,** to keep one's position against opposition. **—lose ground,** 1. to fall behind. 2. to lose in strength, popularity, etc. **—on the ground of,** because of. **—run into the ground,** [Colloq.], to do too long or too often; overdo. **—shift one's ground,** to change one's argument or defense.

**ground** (ground), pt. and pp. of **grind.**

**ground crew,** a group of people in charge of the maintenance and repair of aircraft.

**ground·er** (groun'dẽr), ***n.*** in *baseball*, etc., a batted ball that rolls or bounces along the ground.

**ground floor,** that floor of a building which is on or near the ground level; first floor. **—in on the ground floor,** [Colloq.], 1. in at the beginning of an enterprise. 2. in a position of advantage.

**ground glass,** glass whose surface has been ground so that it is translucent and not transparent.

**ground hog,** a woodchuck: also **ground'hog',** ***n.***

**ground-hog** (or **groundhog**) **day** (ground'hôg', -hog'), February 2, when, in legend, if the ground hog sees his shadow, he returns to his hole for another six weeks of winter weather.

**ground·less** (ground'lis), ***adj.*** without reason or cause. **—ground'less·ly,** ***adv.*** **—ground'less·ness,** ***n.***

**ground·ling** (ground'liŋ), ***n.*** 1. *a*) a fish that lives close to the bottom of the water. *b*) an animal that lives on or in the ground. *c*) a plant that grows close to the ground. 2. [orig. of spectators in a theater pit], a person lacking critical ability or taste.

**ground·nut** (ground'nut'), ***n.*** 1. any of various plants with edible tubers or tuberlike parts, as the peanut. 2. the tuber or tuberlike part.

**ground pine,** any of several kinds of club moss, an evergreen with creeping or underground stems and erect, treelike branches.

**ground plan,** 1. a plan of the ground floor or of any floor of a building. 2. a first or basic plan.

**ground·sel** (ground's'l, groun's'l), ***n.*** [< AS.; ? < *gund*, pus + *swelgan*, to swallow: from use in poultices], any of a large group of plants with yellow, rayed flowers, as the golden ragwort.

**ground·sel** (ground's'l, groun's'l), ***n.*** [see SILL], the bottom horizontal timber in a framework.

**ground·sill** (ground'sil), ***n.*** a groundsel (timber).

**ground squirrel,** any of various small, burrowing animals of the squirrel family; esp., the chipmunk or the gopher.

**ground swell,** a violent swelling or rolling of the ocean, caused by a distant storm or earthquake.

**ground water,** water found underground in porous rock strata and soils, as in a spring.

**ground wire,** a wire acting as a conductor from an electric circuit, radio, etc. to the ground.

**ground·work** (ground'wũrk'), ***n.*** foundation; basis.

**group** (grōōp), ***n.*** [< Fr. < It. *gruppo*], 1. a number of persons or things gathered together and forming a unit; cluster; band. 2. a collection of objects or figures forming a design. 3. a number of persons or things classified together because of common characteristics, interests, etc. 4. in *biology*, a large number of plants or animals related to each other because of certain similarities. 5. in *chemistry*, a radical. 6. in the *U.S. Air Force*, a unit consisting of four squadrons of the same kind of aircraft. ***v.t. & v.i.*** to assemble or form into a group or groups.

**group·er** (grōōp'ẽr), ***n.*** [*pl.* -ERS, -ER; see PLURAL, II, D, 1], [Port. *garoupa*], a large, tropical food fish related to the sea bass.

**grouse** (grous), ***n.*** [*pl.* GROUSE], [? < ME. *grewe*, a crane], any of a group of game birds with a round, plump body, feathered legs, and mottled feathers, as the ruffed grouse, sage hen, etc.

**grouse** (grous), ***v.i.*** [GROUSED, GROUSING], [? < OFr. *groucier*], [Slang], to complain; grumble. ***n.*** [Slang], 1. a complaint. 2. a person who habitually complains. **—grous'er,** ***n.***

**grove** (grōv), ***n.*** [AS. *graf*], a small wood; group of trees standing together without undergrowth.

**grov·el** (gruv''l, grov''l), ***v.i.*** [-ELED or -ELLED, -ELING or -ELLING], [back-formation < *grovelling*, *adv.*, down on one's face], 1. to lie prone or crawl in a prostrate position, especially abjectly. 2. to behave humbly or abjectly. 3. to take pleasure in base or contemptible things. **—grov'el·er, grov'el·ler,** ***n.*** **—grov'el·ing·ly, grov'el·ling·ly,** ***adv.***

**grow** (grō), ***v.i.*** [GREW, GROWN, GROWING], [< AS. *growan*], 1. to come into being or be produced naturally; sprout. 2. to exist as living vegetation; thrive: as, it *grows* in sandy soil. 3. to increase in size and develop toward maturity. 4. to increase in size, quantity, or degree. 5. to become; turn: as, he *grew* weary. 6. to become attached or united by growth. ***v.t.*** 1. to cause to grow; raise; cultivate. 2. to cover with a growth. 3. to allow to grow: as, he *grew* a beard. 4. to develop. **—grow on,** to have a gradually increasing effect on. **—grow out of,** to issue or develop from. **—grow up,** to reach maturity; become adult. **—grow'er,** ***n.***

**growl** (groul), ***v.i.*** [prob. echoic], 1. to make a rumbling, throaty, menacing sound, as a dog does. 2. to complain in an angry or surly manner. ***v.t.*** to express by growling. ***n.*** 1. a rumbling, throaty, menacing sound made by an angry dog. 2. a sound like this. **—growl'er,** ***n.*** **—growl'ing·ly,** ***adv.***

**grown** (grōn), pp. of **grow.** ***adj.*** 1. having completed its growth; mature. 2. covered with a growth.

**grown-up** (grōn'up'), ***adj.*** of, for, or characteristic of an adult. ***n.*** an adult: also **grown'up'.**

**growth** (grōth), ***n.*** 1. a growing or developing. 2. *a*) increase in size, weight, etc. *b*) the amount of this. 3. something that grows or has grown: as, a *growth* of grass. 4. an abnormal mass of tissue, as a tumor, in or on the body.

**grub** (grub), ***v.i.*** [GRUBBED, GRUBBING], [ME. *grubben*], 1. to dig in the ground. 2. to work hard; drudge. ***v.t.*** 1. to clear (ground) of roots by digging

them up. 2. to uproot. *n.* 1. the short, fat, wormlike larva of an insect, especially of a beetle. 2. a person who works hard at some menial work; drudge. 3. [Slang], food. —**grub'ber,** *n.*
**grub·by** (grub'i), *adj.* [-BIER, -BIEST], 1. infested with grubs. 2. dirty; messy; untidy. —**grub'bi·ly,** *adv.* —**grub'bi·ness,** *n.*
**grub·stake** (grub'stāk'), *n.* [*grub* (food) + *stake*], [Colloq.], 1. money or supplies advanced to a prospector in return for a share in his findings. 2. money advanced for any enterprise. *v.t.* [Colloq.], to provide with a grubstake. —**grub'stak'er,** *n.*
**grudge** (gruj), *v.t.* [GRUDGED, GRUDGING], [< Late ME. var. of *grucchen*, to grouch], 1. to envy (a person) because of his possession or enjoyment of (something). 2. to give or allow with reluctance. *n.* a strong feeling of resentment or malice held against someone; ill will. —**grudg'ing·ly,** *adv.*
**gru·el** (grōō'əl), *n.* [< OFr. < ML. dim. of *grutum*, meal], thin, easily digested broth made by cooking meal in water or milk. *v.t.* [-ELED or -ELLED, -ELING or -ELLING], to subject to intense strain; exhaust, as by severe punishment, etc.
**gru·el·ing, gru·el·ling** (grōō'əl-iŋ, grōōl'iŋ), *adj.* tormenting; exhausting. *n.* an experience that has a grueling effect.
**grue·some** (grōō'səm), *adj.* [< obs. *grue*, to shudder + *-some*], causing fear and loathing; horrifying and revolting: also sp. **grewsome.** —**grue'some·ly,** *adv.* —**grue'some·ness,** *n.*
**gruff** (gruf), *adj.* [D. *grof*], 1. rough or surly in manner or speech; rude. 2. harsh and throaty; hoarse. —**gruff'ly,** *adv.* —**gruff'ness,** *n.*
**gruff·y** (gruf'i), *adj.* [-IER, -IEST], gruff.
**grum·ble** (grum'b'l), *v.i.* [-BLED, -BLING], [prob. < D. *grommelen*], 1. to make low, unintelligible sounds in the throat. 2. to mutter in discontent; complain in a surly manner. 3. to rumble. *v.t.* to express by grumbling. *n.* 1. a grumbling, as in complaint. 2. a rumble. —**grum'bler,** *n.* —**grum'bling·ly,** *adv.* —**grum'bly** [-BLIER, -BLIEST], *adj.*
**grump·y** (grum'pi), *adj.* [-IER, -IEST], [prob. < *grumble*], peevish; bad-tempered; surly: also **grump'ish.** —**grump'i·ly,** *adv.* —**grump'i·ness,** *n.*
**Grun·dy·ism** (grun'di-iz'm), *n.* [< Mrs. *Grundy*, a fictitious personification of this in an 18th-c. play], prudish and narrow-minded conventionality.
**grunt** (grunt), *v.i.* [AS. *grunnettan*, freq. of *grunian*, to grunt], 1. to make a deep, gruff sound in the throat: said of a hog. 2. to make a sound like this, as in annoyance. *v.t.* to express by grunting. *n.* 1. the deep, gruff, throaty sound made by a hog. 2. a sound like this. 3. a salt-water fish that grunts when removed from water. —**grunt'er,** *n.* —**grunt'ing·ly,** *adv.*
**Gru·yère (cheese)** (grē-yer', grōō-), [< *Gruyère*, Switzerland], a light-yellow Swiss cheese, rich in butterfat, or an American cheese like this.
**gr. wt.,** gross weight.
**gryph·on** (grif'ən), *n.* a griffin.
**GS,** German silver.
**G.S., g.s.,** 1. general secretary. 2. general staff.
**G.S.A.,** Girl Scouts of America.
**G string,** 1. a loincloth. 2. a similar cloth with ornamentation, worn by strip-tease dancers. 3. a string tuned to G, as on a violin.
**gt.,** 1. great. 2. *gutta*, [L.], [*pl.* GTT.], in *pharmacy*, a drop.
**Gt. Brit., Gt. Br.,** Great Britain.
**G.T.C., g.t.c.,** good till canceled (or countermanded).
**g.u., g.-u.,** genitourinary.
**Gua·da·la·ja·ra** (gwä'dä-lä-hä'rä), *n.* a city in W Mexico: pop., 590,000.
**Gua·dal·ca·nal** (gwä'd'l-kə-nal'), *n.* one of the Solomon Islands, in the South Pacific.
**Gua·de·loupe** (gô'd'l-ōōp'; Fr. gwȧd'lōōp'), *n.* a French overseas department consisting of two islands of the Leeward group in the West Indies.
**Guam** (gwäm), *n.* one of the Marianas Islands, in the W Pacific: it is a U.S. territory.
**gua·no** (gwä'nō), *n.* [*pl.* -NOS], [Sp. < Quechua *huanu*, dung], 1. the manure of sea birds, found especially on islands off the coast of Peru: it is used as a fertilizer. 2. any manure, artificial or natural, resembling this.
**guar.,** guaranteed.
**Gua·ra·ni** (gwä'rä-nē'), *n.* 1. [*pl.* -NIS, -NI], a member of a tribe of South American Indians who lived east of the Paraguay River. 2. their language.
**guar·an·tee** (gar'ən-tē'), *n.* [prob. < *guaranty*], 1. a guaranty (senses 1 & 3). 2. *a*) a pledge that something will be replaced if it is not as represented. *b*) a positive assurance that something will be done in the manner specified. 3. a guarantor. 4. one who receives a guaranty. *v.t.* [-TEED, -TEEING], 1. to give a guarantee or guaranty for. 2. to promise; affirm: as, I *guaranteed* that I'd be there.
**guar·an·tor** (gar'ən-tēr, -tôr'), *n.* a person who makes or gives a guaranty or guarantee.
**guar·an·ty** (gar'ən-ti), *n.* [*pl.* -TIES], [< OFr. < *guarant*, a warrant < OHG. < *weren*, to protect; cf. WARRANT], 1. a pledge by which a person promises to pay another's debt or fulfill another's obligation in the event of default. 2. an agreement that secures the existence or maintenance of something. 3. something given or held as security. *v.t.* [-TIED, -TYING], to guarantee.
**guard** (gärd), *v.t.* [< OFr. *guarder* < Gmc.; see WARD], 1. to watch over and protect; defend; shield. 2. *a*) to keep from escape or trouble. *b*) to supervise or control; check. *v.i.* 1. to keep watch; take precautions (with *against*). 2. to act as a guard. *n.* 1. the act or duty of guarding; defense; protection. 2. caution; safeguard. 3. a posture of defense, as in fencing, boxing, etc. 4. any device that protects against injury or loss. 5. a person or group that guards; specif., *a*) a sentinel or sentry. *b*) a railway brakeman or gateman. *c*) a person who guards prisoners. *d*) *pl.* a special unit of troops connected with the household of the British sovereign. 6. in *basketball*, either of the two players whose special duties are defensive. 7. in *football*, either of the two players at the left and right of the center. —**mount guard,** to go on sentry duty. —**on (one's) guard,** vigilant. —**stand guard,** to do sentry duty. —**guard'er,** *n.*
**guard·ed** (gär'did), *adj.* 1. kept safe; watched over and protected; defended. 2. held in check; supervised. 3. cautious; careful; restrained. —**guard'ed·ly,** *adv.* —**guard'ed·ness,** *n.*
**guard·house** (gärd'hous'), *n.* in *military usage*, 1. a building used by the members of a guard when they are not walking a post. 2. a building used as a jail for temporary confinement.
**guard·i·an** (gär'di-ən), *n.* 1. a person who guards or cares for another person, property, etc.; custodian. 2. a person legally placed in charge of the affairs of a minor or of someone incapable of taking care of his own affairs. *adj.* protecting. —**guard'i·an·ship',** *n.*
**guard·room** (gärd'rōōm', -room'), *n.* a room having the same uses as a guardhouse.
**guards·man** (gärdz'mən), *n.* [*pl.* -MEN], 1. a guard. 2. a member of the National Guard or of any military body called a guard.
**Gua·te·ma·la** (gwä'te-mä'lə), *n.* 1. a country in Central America, south and east of Mexico: area, 45,042 sq. mi.; pop., 3,759,000. 2. its capital: pop., 374,000. —**Gua'te·ma'lan,** *adj.* & *n.*
**gua·va** (gwä'və), *n.* [Sp. *guayaba* < native name in Brazil], 1. a tropical American tree or shrub bearing a yellowish, pear-shaped, edible fruit. 2. the fruit, used for jelly, preserves, etc.
**Guay·a·quil** (gwī'ä-kēl'), *n.* a seaport in Ecuador: pop., 296,000.
**gua·yu·le** (gwä-ū'lā), *n.* [Sp. < Nahuatl < *quauitl*, plant + *olli*, gum], 1. a small shrub of N Mexico and Texas, cultivated for the rubber obtained from its sap. 2. this rubber: also **guayule rubber.**
**gu·ber·na·to·ri·al** (gōō'bēr-nə-tôr'i-əl, gū'-, -tō'ri-əl), *adj.* [L. *gubernator*, governor < *gubernare*, to steer], of a governor or his office.
**gudg·eon** (guj'ən), *n.* [< OFr. < L. *gobio* < Gr. *kōbios*], 1. a small, European fresh-water fish of the carp family, easily caught, and used for bait. 2. a minnow. 3. a person easily cheated or tricked; dupe; gull. *v.t.* to cheat; trick; dupe.
**Guelph, Guelf** (gwelf), *n.* 1. a member of a German royal family from which the present line of British sovereigns is descended. 2. any member of a political party in medieval Italy that supported the Pope. —**Guelph'ic, Guelf'ic,** *adj.*
**guer·don** (gũr'd'n), *n.* [< OFr. < ML. *widerdonum* < OHG. *widar*, again + L. *donum*, gift], [Poetic], a reward; recompense. *v.t.* [Poetic], to reward. —**guer'don·er,** *n.*
**Guern·sey** (gũrn'zi), *n.* 1. a British island in the English Channel. 2. [*pl.* -SEYS], any of a breed of dairy cattle, originally from this island: usually fawn-colored with white markings.
**guer·ril·la, gue·ril·la** (gə-ril'ə), *n.* [Sp. dim. of *guerra*, war < OHG.], a member of a small defensive force of irregular soldiers, usually volunteers, making surprise raids behind the lines of an invading enemy army. *adj.* of or by guerrillas.
**guess** (ges), *v.t.* & *v.i.* [prob. < ON.], 1. to form a judgment or estimate of (something) without actual knowledge; conjecture; surmise. 2. to judge correctly by doing this. 3. to think or suppose: as, I *guess* you can do it. *n.* 1. a guessing. 2. something

guessed; conjecture; surmise. —**guess′er**, *n.*

**guess·work** (ges′wũrk′), *n.* 1. a guessing. 2. a view, work, etc. based on guessing.

**guest** (gest), *n.* [AS. *giest*], 1. a person entertained at the home of another; visitor. 2. one paying for his lodgings, meals, etc., as at a hotel. 3. one receiving the hospitality of a club, etc. of which he is not a member. *adj.* 1. for guests. 2. performing by invitation: as, a *guest* artist.

**guff** (guf), *n.* [echoic], [Slang], foolish talk.

**guf·faw** (gə-fô′), *n.* [echoic], a loud, coarse burst of laughter. *v.i.* to laugh in this way.

**Gui·a·na** (gi-an′ə, -ä′nə), *n.* a region in N South America, including Guyana, French Guiana, and Surinam (Dutch Guiana).

**guid·ance** (gīd′′ns), *n.* 1. a guiding; direction; leadership. 2. something that guides.

**guide** (gīd), *v.t.* [GUIDED, GUIDING], [< OFr. *guider*, var. of *guier* < Gmc.], 1. to point out the way for; conduct; lead. 2. to direct the course of (a vehicle, hand, etc.) by physical action. 3. to manage; regulate. *v.i.* to act as a guide. *n.* one that guides; specif., *a*) a person whose work is conducting strangers through a region, building, etc. *b*) a part that controls the motion of other parts of a machine. *c*) a guidebook. *d*) a book giving instruction in the elements of some subject. —**guid′a·ble**, *adj.* —**guid′er**, *n.*

**guide·book** (gīd′book′), *n.* a book containing directions and information for tourists.

**guided missile,** a military missile whose course is controlled by radio signals, radar devices, etc.

**guide·post** (gīd′pōst′), *n.* a post, as at a roadside, with a sign and directions for travelers.

**gui·don** (gī′d'n), *n.* [Fr. < It. *guidone*], 1. formerly, a small flag or pennant carried by the guide of mounted cavalry. 2. in the *U.S. Army*, *a*) the identification flag of a unit. *b*) a soldier carrying this; also **guidon bearer.**

**guild** (gild), *n.* [< AS. *gyld* and *gegyld* and ON. *gildi*; all < base seen in AS. *gieldan*, to pay], 1. in medieval times, a union of men in the same craft or trade to uphold standards and protect the members. 2. any association for mutual aid and the promotion of common interests. Also sp. **gild.**

**guil·der** (gil′dẽr), *n.* [< D. *gulden*, florin, lit., golden], 1. a former gold or silver coin of the Netherlands, Germany, or Austria. 2. the unit of currency and a silver coin in the Netherlands. Also **gulden.**

**guild·hall** (gild′hôl′), *n.* 1. a hall where a guild meets. 2. a town hall.

**guilds·man** (gildz′mən), *n.* [*pl.* -MEN], a member of a guild.

**guile** (gīl), *n.* [OFr. *guile* < Gmc.], crafty, deceitful talk or conduct; cunning. —**guile′less**, *adj.* —**guile′less·ly**, *adv.* —**guile′less·ness**, *n.*

**guile·ful** (gīl′fəl), *adj.* full of guile; deceitful; tricky. —**guile′ful·ly**, *adv.* —**guile′ful·ness**, *n.*

**guil·le·mot** (gil′i-mot′), *n.* [Fr., dim. of *Guillaume*, William], any of various narrow-billed arctic diving birds of the auk family.

**guil·lo·tine** (gil′ə-tēn′), *n.* [Fr., after J. I. *Guillotin* (1738–1814), who advocated its use], an instrument for beheading, consisting of a heavy blade dropped between two grooved uprights. *v.t.* (gil′ə-tēn′), [-TINED, -TINING], to behead with a guillotine. —**guil′lo·tin′er**, *n.*

GUILLOTINE

**guilt** (gilt), *n.* [AS. *gylt*, a sin], 1. the act or state of having done a wrong or committed an offense. 2. conduct that involves guilt; crime or sin.

**guilt·less** (gilt′lis), *adj.* 1. not guilty; innocent. 2. having no knowledge or experience (with *of*). —**guilt′less·ly**, *adv.*

**guilt·y** (gil′ti), *adj.* [-IER, -IEST], 1. having guilt; deserving blame or punishment. 2. having one's guilt proved; legally judged an offender. 3. showing or conscious of guilt: as, a *guilty* look. 4. of or involving guilt: as, a *guilty* conscience. —**guilt′i·ly**, *adv.* —**guilt′i·ness**, *n.*

**guimpe** (gimp, gamp), *n.* [Fr.], a short-sleeved blouse worn under a pinafore or jumper.

**Guin·ea** (gin′i), *n.* 1. a country in W Africa, on the Atlantic: a former French colony: area, 94,925 sq. mi.; pop., 3,702,000; capital, Conakry. 2. a region along the W coast of Africa, including Guinea, Portuguese Guinea, and Spanish Guinea.

**guin·ea** (gin′i), *n.* 1. [first coined of gold from Guinea], a former English gold coin, last minted in 1813, equal to 21 shillings; hence, 2. the sum of 21 English shillings. 3. a guinea fowl.

**guinea fowl,** a domestic fowl with a rounded body and dark feathers finely spotted with white.

**guinea hen,** 1. a guinea fowl. 2. a female guinea fowl.

**guinea pig,** [prob. from being brought to England (from S. America) by ships in the Guinea slave trade], 1. a small, fat rodent, with short ears and a short tail, used in biological experiments. 2. any person or thing used in an experiment.

**Guin·e·vere** (gwin′ə-vêr′), *n.* in *Arthurian legend*, the wife of King Arthur and mistress of Sir Lancelot: also **Guin′e·ver** (-vẽr).

**guise** (gīz), *n.* [OFr. < OHG. *wisa*, manner], 1. manner of dress; garb. 2. outward aspect; semblance. 3. a false appearance; pretense: as, under the *guise* of friendship. *v.t.* [GUISED, GUISING], [Brit. Dial.], to disguise.

**gui·tar** (gi-tär′), *n.* [< Fr. < Sp. *guitarra* < Gr. *kithara*, lyre], a musical instrument of the lute family, usually with six strings which are plucked with the fingers or a plectrum. —**gui·tar′ist**, *n.*

GUITAR

**gulch** (gulch), *n.* [prob. < dial. *gulch*, to swallow greedily], a steep-walled valley cut by a swift stream; deep, narrow ravine.

**gul·den** (gool′dən), *n.* [*pl.* -DENS, -DEN], [D. & G., a florin, lit., golden], a guilder.

**gules** (gūlz), *n.* [< OFr. *gueules*, red-dyed ermine; ult. < L. *gula*, throat], in *heraldry*, red.

**gulf** (gulf), *n.* [< Fr. < It. *golfo*; ult. < Gr. *kolpos*, bosom], 1. a large area of ocean partially enclosed by land, larger than a bay. 2. a wide, deep chasm or abyss. 3. a wide or impassable gap or separation. *v.t.* to engulf.

**Gulf Stream,** a warm ocean current flowing from the Gulf of Mexico northward into the Atlantic toward Europe.

**gull** (gul), *n.* [*pl.* GULLS, GULL; see PLURAL, II, D, 1], [ME. < Celt.], a sea bird with large wings, webbed feet, and feathers of gray and white.

**gull** (gul), *n.* [prob. < obs. *gull*, to swallow], a person easily tricked; dupe. *v.t.* to cheat; trick.

**Gul·lah** (gul′ə), *n.* [< *Gola* or *Gora*, names of African tribes], 1. any of a group of Negroes living on the South Carolina and Georgia coast or near-by islands. 2. their English dialect.

**gul·let** (gul′it), *n.* [OFr. *goulet* (< L. *gula*), throat], 1. the tube leading from the mouth to the stomach; esophagus. 2. the throat or neck.

**gul·li·ble** (gul′ə-b'l), *adj.* easily cheated or tricked; credulous: also sp. **gull′a·ble.** —**gul′li·bil′i·ty**, *n.* —**gul′li·bly**, *adv.*

**gul·ly** (gul′i), *n.* [*pl.* -LIES], [< Fr. < OFr. *goulet*; see GULLET], a channel worn by water; narrow ravine. *v.t.* [-LIED, -LYING], to make a gully in.

**gulp** (gulp), *v.t.* [prob. < MD. or MFl.], 1. to swallow hastily, greedily, or in large amounts. 2. to choke back as if swallowing. *v.i.* to catch the breath as after swallowing. *n.* 1. a gulping. 2. a swallow. 3. the amount swallowed at one time. —**gulp′er**, *n.* —**gulp′ing·ly**, *adv.*

**gum** (gum), *n.* [< OFr. < L. *gummi* < Gr. *kommi*], 1. a sticky substance given off by certain trees and plants, which dries into a brittle mass soluble in water. 2. any similar plant secretion, as resin. 3. any plant gum processed for use in industry, art, etc. 4. an adhesive, as on the back of a postage stamp; glue; mucilage. 5. *a*) any gum tree or its wood. *b*) rubber. 6. *pl.* rubber overshoes. 7. chewing gum. *v.t.* [GUMMED, GUMMING], to coat, unite, or stiffen with gum. *v.i.* 1. to secrete or form gum. 2. to become sticky or clogged. —**gum up**, [Slang], to cause to go awry. —**gum′like′**, *adj.*

**gum** (gum), *n.* [AS. *goma*], *often pl.* the firm flesh surrounding the base of the teeth.

**gum ammoniac,** ammoniac, a natural gum resin.

**gum arabic,** a gum from certain acacia trees, used in medicine, in candy, etc.

**gum·bo** (gum′bō), *n.* [*pl.* -BOS], [prob. of Negro origin], 1. the okra plant or its edible, sticky pods. 2. a soup thickened with unripe okra pods. 3. a fine, silty soil of the Western prairies, which becomes

sticky and nonporous when wet: also **gumbo soil.**
**gum·boil** (gum'boil'), *n.* an abscess on the gums.
**gum·drop** (gum'drop'), *n.* a small, firm, jellylike piece of candy, made of sweetened gum arabic or gelatin, usually colored and flavored.
**gum·my** (gum'i), *adj.* [-MIER, -MIEST], 1. having the nature of gum; sticky. 2. covered with or containing gum. 3. yielding gum. **—gum'mi·ness,** *n.*
**gump·tion** (gump'shən), *n.* [< Scot. dial.], [Colloq.], 1. common sense. 2. courage and initiative; enterprise: the current sense.
**gum resin,** a mixture of gum and resin, given off by certain trees and plants.
**gum·shoe** (gum'shōō'), *n.* 1. *a)* a rubber overshoe. *b)* *pl.* sneakers. 2. [Slang], a detective. *v.i.* [-SHOED, -SHOEING], [Slang], to go about quietly.
**gum tree,** any of various trees that yield gum, as the sour gum, sweet gum, eucalyptus, etc.
**gun** (gun), *n.* [prob. < *Gunna,* dim. of *Gunhilda,* fem. name given to a ballista in 1330], 1. a weapon consisting of a metal tube from which a projectile is discharged, by the explosion of gunpowder: technically restricted to a heavy weapon, as a cannon, etc., but also applied to rifles, pistols, etc. 2. any similar device not discharged by an explosive: as, an air *gun.* 3. a discharge of a gun in signaling or saluting. 4. anything like a gun in shape or use. *v.i.* [GUNNED, GUNNING], to shoot or hunt with a gun. *v.t.* 1. [Colloq.], to shoot (a person). 2. [Slang], to advance the throttle of (an engine) so as to increase the speed. **—give it the gun,** [Slang], to cause something to start or gain speed. **—gun for,** 1. to hunt for with a gun. 2. [Slang], to seek. **—stick to one's guns,** to hold one's position under attack.
**gun·boat** (gun'bōt'), *n.* a small armed ship of shallow draft, used to patrol rivers, etc.
**gun·cot·ton** (gun'kot''n), *n.* an explosive made of cotton treated with nitric and sulfuric acids.
**gun·fire** (gun'fīr'), *n.* firing of a gun or guns.
**gun·lock** (gun'lok'), *n.* in some guns, the mechanism by which the charge is set off.
**gun·man** (gun'mən), *n.* [*pl.* -MEN], a gangster, bandit, or thug armed with a gun.
**gun metal,** 1. a kind of bronze formerly used for making cannon. 2. any of several metals or alloys treated to resemble this. 3. dark gray, the color of tarnished gun metal. **—gun'-met'al,** *adj.*
**gun moll,** [Slang], the mistress or female accomplice of a gunman.
**gun·nel** (gun''l), *n.* [< ?], a small North Atlantic fish of the blenny family.
**gun·nel** (gun''l), *n.* a gunwale.
**gun·ner** (gun'ēr), *n.* 1. a soldier, sailor, etc. who helps fire artillery. 2. a naval warrant officer in charge of a ship's guns. 3. a hunter with a gun.
**gun·ner·y** (gun'ēr-i), *n.* 1. heavy guns. 2. the science of making and using heavy guns and projectiles. 3. the firing of heavy guns.
**gun·ny** (gun'i), *n.* [*pl.* -NIES], [< Hind. < Sans. *gonī,* a sack], 1. a coarse, heavy fabric of jute or hemp, used for sacks and bags. 2. a sack or bag made of this: also **gunny sack** (or **bag**).
**gun·play** (gun'plā'), *n.* an exchange of gunshots.
**gun·pow·der** (gun'pou'dēr), *n.* an explosive powder used as a charge in cartridges, shells, etc., for blasting, and in firecrackers.
**gun·run·ning** (gun'run'iŋ), *n.* the smuggling of guns and ammunition. **—gun'run'ner,** *n.*
**gun·shot** (gun'shot'), *n.* 1. *a)* shot fired from a gun. *b)* [Rare], the shooting of a gun. 2. the range of a gun. *adj.* caused by a shot from a gun.
**gun·smith** (gun'smith'), *n.* a person who makes or repairs small guns.
**gun·stock** (gun'stok'), *n.* the wooden handle or butt to which the barrel of a gun is attached.
**Gun·ther** (goon'tēr), *n.* in the *Nibelungenlied,* a king of Burgundy, husband of Brunhild.
**gun·wale** (gun''l), *n.* [first applied to bulwarks supporting a ship's guns], the upper edge of the side of a ship or boat: also sp. **gunnel.**
**gup·py** (gup'i), *n.* [*pl.* -PIES], [after R. J. L. *Guppy,* of Trinidad], a tiny, brilliantly colored fresh-water fish of the West Indies, Venezuela, etc.
**gur·gle** (gūr'g'l), *v.i.* [-GLED, -GLING], [prob. < Gmc.; ult. < L. *gurgulio,* gullet], 1. to flow with a bubbling or rippling sound. 2. to make such a sound. *v.t.* to utter with a gurgling sound. *n.* 1. a gurgling. 2. a gurgling sound. **—gur'gler,** *n.*
**gur·nard** (gūr'nērd), *n.* [*pl.* -NARDS, -NARD; see PLURAL II D, 1], [< OFr. < *grogner,* to grunt], a spiny-finned sea fish with a bone-plated head and winglike pectoral fins which have feelers.
**gu·ru** (goor'ōō, goo-rōō'), *n.* [Hindi < Sans. *guru-h,* venerable], in Hinduism, one's personal spiritual adviser or teacher.
**gush** (gush), *v.i.* [prob. < ON. *gusa* < base of *giosa,* to pour], 1. to flow out suddenly and plentifully. 2. to have a sudden, heavy flow of blood, tears, etc. 3. [Colloq.], to express exaggerated enthusiasm or feeling. *v.t.* to cause to flow out suddenly and plentifully. *n.* 1. a sudden, heavy flow. 2. [Colloq.], gushing talk or writing. **—gush'ing·ly,** *adv.*
**gush·er** (gush'ēr), *n.* 1. a person who gushes. 2. an oil well from which oil spouts without pumping.
**gush·y** (gush'i), *adj.* [-IER, -IEST], [Colloq.], given to or characterized by gush (*n.* 2); effusive. **—gush'i·ly,** *adv.* **—gush'i·ness,** *n.*
**gus·set** (gus'it), *n.* [< OFr. dim. of *gousse,* a husk], 1. a triangular piece inserted in a garment, glove, etc. to make it stronger or roomier. 2. a triangular metal brace for reinforcing a corner or angle. *v.t.* to furnish with a gusset.
**gust** (gust), *n.* [< ON. < *gjosa,* to gush], 1. a sudden, strong rush of air or wind. 2. a sudden outburst of rain, laughter, rage, etc.
**gus·ta·to·ry** (gus'tə-tôr'i, -tō'ri), *adj.* of tasting or the sense of taste: also **gus'ta·tive.**
**gus·to** (gus'tō), *n.* [*pl.* -TOS], [It. & Sp. < L. *gustus,* taste], 1. taste; liking. 2. keen enjoyment; zest; relish. 3. artistic style.
**gust·y** (gus'ti), *adj.* [-IER, -IEST], characterized by gusts; windy or blustery. **—gust'i·ly,** *adv.* **—gust'i·ness,** *n.*
**gut** (gut), *n.* [AS. *guttas,* pl. < base of *geotan,* to pour], 1. *pl.* the bowels; entrails: regarded as an indelicate usage. 2. all or part of the alimentary canal; intestine. 3. tough cord made from animal intestines, used for violin strings, surgical sutures, etc. 4. a narrow passage or gully. 5. *pl.* [Slang], *a)* pluck; courage. *b)* impudence; effrontery. *c)* force; power. *v.t.* [GUTTED, GUTTING], 1. to remove the intestines from; eviscerate. 2. to destroy the interior of, as by fire. *adj.* [Slang], urgent and basic: as, the *gut* issues of a campaign. **—gut'ter,** *n.*
**Gu·ten·berg, Jo·hann** (yō'hän gōō't'n-bērg), 1398?–1468; German printer: reputedly the first European to print with movable type.
**gut·less** (gut'lis), *adj.* [Slang], lacking courage.
**guts·y** (gut'si), *adj.* [-IER, -IEST], [Slang], full of guts; daring, courageous, forceful, etc.
**gut·ta-per·cha** (gut'ə-pūr'chə), *n.* [Malay *gĕtah,* gum + *pĕrca,* tree from which it is obtained], a rubberlike substance formed by the milky juice of certain trees of Malaysia, used in electric insulation, dentistry, golf balls, etc.
**gut·ter** (gut'ēr), *n.* [< OFr. < L. *gutta,* a drop], 1. a trough along or under the eaves of a roof, to carry off rain water. 2. a narrow channel along the side of a road or street, to carry off surface water. 3. any channel or groove. *v.t.* to furnish with gutters. *v.i.* 1. to flow in a stream. 2. to melt rapidly so that the wax runs off in channels: said of a candle.
**gut·ter·snipe** (gut'ēr-snīp'), *n.* [Colloq.], a poor, neglected child who spends most of his time in the streets: contemptuous term.
**gut·tur·al** (gut'ēr-'l), *adj.* [< L. *guttur,* throat], 1. of the throat. 2. loosely, produced in the throat; rasping: said of sounds. 3. formed with the back of the tongue close to or against the soft palate, as the *k* in *keen.* *n.* a sound produced in this way. **—gut'tur·al·ly,** *adv.* **—gut'tur·al·ness,** *n.*
**guy** (gī), *n.* [< OFr. < *guier,* to guide], a rope, chain, etc. used to steady or guide something. *v.t.* [GUYED, GUYING], to guide or steady with a guy.
**guy** (gī), *n.* [after *Guy* Fawkes], 1. an odd or eccentric person. 2. [Slang], a boy or man; fellow. *v.t.* [GUYED, GUYING], [Colloq.], to make fun of; ridicule.
**Guy·a·na** (gī-an'ə, -än'ə), *n.* a country in NE South America: a member of the British Commonwealth of Nations: area, 83,000 sq. mi.; pop., 742,000.
**guz·zle** (guz''l), *v.i.* & *v.t.* [-ZLED, -ZLING], [? < OFr. < *gosier,* throat], to drink greedily or immoderately. **—guz'zler,** *n.*
**gybe** (jīb), *v.i.* & *v.t.* [GYBED, GYBING], *n.* in *nautical usage,* jibe.
**gym** (jim), *n.* [Colloq.], gymnasium.
**gym·na·si·um** (jim-nā'zi-əm), *n.* [*pl.* -SIUMS, -SIA (-zi-ə)], [L. < Gr. *gymnasion;* ult. < *gymnos,* naked], 1. a room or building equipped for physical training and athletic sports. 2. [G-], (G. güm-nä'-zi-oom'), in Germany and some other European countries, a secondary school for students preparing to enter a university.
**gym·nast** (jim'nast), *n.* an expert in gymnastics.
**gym·nas·tic** (jim-nas'tik), *adj.* [< L. < Gr.; see GYMNASIUM], of physical exercises or athletics: also **gym·nas'ti·cal.** **—gym·nas'ti·cal·ly,** *adv.*
**gym·nas·tics** (jim-nas'tiks), *n.pl.* exercises to develop and train the muscles.
**gym·no-,** [< Gr. *gymnos,* naked], a combining form meaning *naked, stripped, bare:* also **gymn-.**

**gym·no·sperm** (jim′nə-spũrm′), *n.* [< *gymno-* + Gr. *sperma*, a seed], any of a large class of plants producing seeds not enclosed in a seed case or ovary, as certain evergreens. —**gym′no·sper′mous,** *adj.*
**gyn·e·co-,** [< Gr. < *gynē*, a woman], a combining form meaning *woman, female*: words beginning with *gyneco-* may also be spelled **gynaeco-.**
**gyn·e·col·o·gy** (jī′ni-kol′ə-ji, jin′i-, gī′ni-), *n.* [*gyneco-* + *-logy*], the branch of medicine dealing with the study and treatment of women's diseases. —**gyn′e·co·log′ic** (-kə-loj′ik), **gyn′e·co·log′i·cal,** *adj.* —**gyn′e·col′o·gist,** *n.*
**gy·noe·ci·um** (ji-nē′si-əm, ji-nē′-), *n.* [*pl.* -CIA (-si-ə)], [Mod.L. < Gr. *gynē*, a woman + *oikos*, house], the female organ or organs of a flower; pistil or pistils: also sp. **gynaeceum, gynecium.**
**gyn·o·phore** (jī′nə-fôr′, jin′ə-), *n.* [< Gr. *gynē*, woman; + *-phore*], a stalk bearing the gynoecium.
**-gyn·ous** (jin-əs), [< Mod.L. < Gr. < *gynē*, a woman], a combining form meaning: 1. *woman, female*, as in *polygynous*. 2. *having female organs* or *pistils*, as in *androgynous*.
**-gyn·y** (jin-i), a combining form used in nouns corresponding to adjectives ending in *-gynous*.
**gyp** (jip), *n.* [prob. < *gypsy*], [Slang], 1. a swindle; cheat. 2. a swindler. *v.t. & v.i.* [GYPPED, GYPPING], [Slang], to swindle; cheat. —**gyp′per,** *n.*
**gyp·soph·i·la** (jip-sof′ə-lə), *n.* [see GYPSUM & -PHIL], any of a group of plants bearing clusters of small white or pink flowers with a delicate fragrance, as babies'-breath.
**gyp·sum** (jip′səm), *n.* [L. < Gr. *gypsos*], a hydrated sulfate of calcium, $CaSO_4·2H_2O$, occurring naturally in sedimentary rocks and used for making plaster of Paris, in treating soil, etc.
**gyp·sy** (jip′si), *n.* [*pl.* -SIES], [< *Egipcien*, Egyptian: because formerly thought to have come from Egypt], 1. [often G-], a member of a wandering Caucasian people with dark skin and black hair, believed to have originated in India: known throughout the world as musicians, fortune tellers, etc. 2. [G-], their Indo-European, Indic language. 3. one whose appearance or habits are like those of a gypsy. *adj.* of or like a gypsy or gypsies. *v.i.* [-SIED, -SYING], to wander or live like a gypsy. Also sp. **gipsy.** —**gyp′sy·like′,** *adj.*
**gypsy moth,** a European moth, brownish or white, common in the eastern U.S.: its larvae feed on leaves, damaging trees and plants: also **gipsy moth.**
**gy·rate** (jī′rāt, ji-rāt′), *v.i.* [-RATED, -RATING], [< L. pp. of *gyrare*, to turn; ult. < Gr. *gyros*, a circle], to move in a circular or spiral path; revolve; whirl. *adj.* (jī′rāt), coiled; spiral; circular. —**gy·ra′tion,** *n.* —**gy·ra′tor,** *n.* —**gy·ra·to·ry** (jī′rə-tôr′i, -tō′ri), *adj.*
**gyre** (jīr), *n.* [< L. < Gr. *gyros*, a circle], 1. a circular or spiral motion; whirl. 2. a circular or spiral form. *v.i. & v.t.* [GYRED, GYRING], [Rare], to whirl.
**gyr·fal·con** (jũr′fôl′k'n, -fô′k'n), *n.* [< OFr. < Gmc. *ger*, spear + *falco*, falcon], a large, fierce falcon of the arctic regions: also sp. **gerfalcon.**
**gy·ro** (jī′rō), *n.* [Colloq.], 1. an autogiro. 2. a gyroscope. 3. a gyrocompass.
**gy·ro-,** [< Gr. *gyros*, a circle], a combining form meaning: 1. *whirling around, gyrating*, as in *gyroscope*. 2. *gyroscope*, as in *gyrocompass*.
**gy·ro·com·pass** (jī′rō-kum′pəs), *n.* a compass consisting of a motor-operated gyroscope whose rotating axis points to the geographic north pole instead of the magnetic pole.
**gy·ro·pi·lot** (jī′rō-pī′lət), *n.* [*gyro-* + *pilot*], a gyroscopic instrument that automatically keeps an airplane flying evenly at the same height and on a set course: also called *automatic pilot*.
**gy·ro·scope** (jī′rə-skōp′), *n.* [*gyro-* + *-scope*], a wheel mounted in a ring so that its axis is free to turn in any direction: when the wheel is spun rapidly, it will keep its original plane of rotation no matter which way the ring is turned. —**gy·ro·scop·ic** (jī′rə-skop′ik), *adj.* —**gy′ro·scop′i·cal·ly,** *adv.*

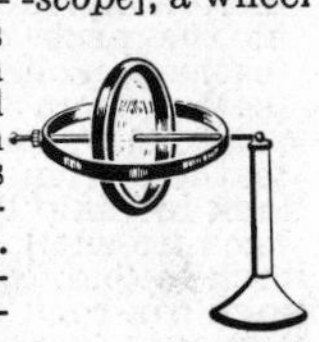
GYROSCOPE

**gy·ro·sta·bi·liz·er** (jī′rō-stā′bə-līz′ẽr), *n.* a device consisting of a gyroscope spinning in a vertical plane, used to stabilize the rocking of a ship or airplane.
**gyve** (jīv), *n. & v.t.* [GYVED, GYVING], [< Anglo-Fr. *guives*, pl.], [Archaic], fetter; shackle.

# H

**H, h** (āch), *n.* [*pl.* H's, h's, Hs, hs], 1. the eighth letter of the English alphabet. 2. the sound of H or h. *adj.* eighth in a sequence or group.
**H** (āch), *n.* 1. in *chemistry, the symbol for* hydrogen. 2. in *physics, the symbol for* henry. *adj.* shaped like H.
**H., h.,** 1. harbor. 2. hard(ness). 3. height. 4. high. 5. in *baseball*, hits. 6. hour(s).
**ha** (hä), *interj.* [echoic], an exclamation variously expressing wonder, surprise, anger, etc. *n.* the sound of this exclamation or of a laugh.
**ha.,** hectare; hectares.
**Haa·kon VII** (hô′koon), 1872–1957; king of Norway (1905–1957).
**Haar·lem** (här′ləm), *n.* a city in NW Netherlands: pop., 165,000.
**Ha·bak·kuk** (hə-bak′ək, hab′ə-kuk′), *n.* in the *Bible*, 1. a Hebrew prophet of about 450 B.C. 2. a book of the Old Testament containing his prophecies: abbrev. **Hab.**
**Ha·ba·na** (ä-bä′nä), *n.* Havana: the Spanish name.
‡**ha·be·as cor·pus** (hā′bi-əs kôr′pəs), [L., (that) you have the body], in *law*, a writ requiring that a prisoner be brought before a court to decide the legality of his detention or imprisonment.
**hab·er·dash·er** (hab′ẽr-dash′ẽr), *n.* [prob. < Anglo-Fr. *hapertas*, kind of cloth], 1. one who sells men's furnishings, such as hats, shirts, gloves, etc. 2. [Chiefly Brit.], a dealer in various small articles, such as lace, thread, etc.
**hab·er·dash·er·y** (hab′ẽr-dash′ẽr-i), *n.* [*pl.* -IES], 1. things sold by a haberdasher. 2. a haberdasher's shop.
**hab·er·geon** (hab′ẽr-jən), *n.* [OFr. *haubergeon*, dim. of *hauberc*, hauberk], 1. a short, high-necked jacket of mail. 2. a hauberk.
**ha·bil·i·ment** (hə-bil′ə-mənt), *n.* [< Fr. < *habiller*, to clothe], 1. a garment. 2. *pl.* clothing; dress.
**ha·bil·i·tate** (hə-bil′ə-tāt′), *v.t.* [-TATED, -TATING], [< ML. < *habilitare*, to qualify], to clothe; equip; dress; outfit. —**ha·bil′i·ta′tion,** *n.*
**hab·it** (hab′it), *n.* [OFr. < L. *habitus*, pp. of *habere*, to have], 1. costume; dress. 2. a distinctive religious costume. 3. a costume for certain occasions: as, a riding *habit*. 4. characteristic condition of mind or body; disposition. 5. a thing done often and, hence, easily; practice; custom. 6. a usual way of doing. 7. in *biology*, characteristic growth of an animal or plant. *v.t.* to dress.
**hab·it·a·ble** (hab′i-tə-b'l), *adj.* fit to be lived in. —**hab′it·a·bil′i·ty, hab′it·a·ble·ness,** *n.* —**hab′it·a·bly,** *adv.*
**hab·it·ant** (hab′i-tənt), *n.* [Fr. < L. pp. of *habitare;* see HABIT], an inhabitant; resident.
**hab·i·tat** (hab′ə-tat′), *n.* [L., it inhabits], 1. native environment. 2. the place where a person or thing is ordinarily found.
**hab·i·ta·tion** (hab′ə-tā′shən), *n.* 1. an inhabiting. 2. a place in which to live; dwelling; home.
**ha·bit·u·al** (hə-bich′o͞o-əl), *adj.* 1. done or caused by habit; customary. 2. being or doing a certain thing by habit; steady: as, a *habitual* smoker. 3. usual; frequent; much seen, done, or used. —**ha·bit′u·al·ly,** *adv.* —**ha·bit′u·al·ness,** *n.*
**ha·bit·u·ate** (hə-bich′o͞o-āt′), *v.t.* [-ATED, -ATING], [< LL. < L. *habitus;* see HABIT], 1. to make used (*to*); accustom; familiarize. 2. [Colloq.], to frequent. —**ha·bit′u·a′tion,** *n.*

**hab·i·tude** (hab'ə-tōōd', -tūd'), *n.* 1. habitual condition of mind or body; disposition. 2. custom.
**ha·bit·u·é** (hə-bich'ōō-ā'), *n.* [Fr.], one who frequents a certain club, restaurant, etc.
**ha·cien·da** (hä'si-en'də), *n.* [Sp. < L. *facienda*, things to be done < *facere*, to do], in Spanish America, a large estate, ranch, or country home.
**hack** (hak), *v.t.* [AS. *haccian*], 1. to chop or cut roughly or irregularly. 2. to break up (land) with a hoe, etc. *v.i.* 1. to make rough or irregular cuts. 2. to give harsh, dry coughs. *n.* 1. a tool for hacking; ax, hoe, etc. 2. a slash, gash, or notch. 3. a harsh, dry cough. **—hack'er,** *n.*
**hack** (hak), *n.* [< *hackney*], 1. a horse for hire. 2. a saddle-horse. 3. an old, worn-out horse. 4. a person hired to do routine writing. 5. a carriage or coach for hire. 6. a taxicab. *v.t.* 1. to employ as a hack. 2. to hire out (a horse, etc.). 3. to wear out by constant use. *v.i.* 1. to ride a horse for pleasure or exercise. 2. [Colloq.], to drive a taxicab. *adj.* 1. employed as a hack: as, a *hack* writer. 2. done by a hack. 3. trite.
**hack·a·more** (hak'ə-môr', -mōr'), *n.* [? < Sp. *jaquima*, halter], in the Western U.S., a rope or rawhide halter, used in breaking horses.
**hack·ber·ry** (hak'ber'i, -bẽr-i), *n.* [*pl.* -RIES], [< Scand.], 1. an American tree of the elm family, with a small, cherrylike fruit. 2. its fruit. 3. its wood.
**hack·le** (hak''l), *n.* [ME. *hakell*, var. of *hechele* (see HATCHEL)], 1. *a*) any of the long, slender feathers at the neck of a rooster, pigeon, etc. *b*) such feathers, collectively. 2. in *fishing*, a tuft of feathers from a rooster's neck, used as the legs of an artificial fly (**hackle fly**). *v.t.* [-LED, -LING], to put feathers from a rooster's neck on (a fishing fly).
**hack·le** (hak''l), *v.t. & v.i.* [-LED, -LING], [freq. of *hack* (to cut)], to hack; cut roughly; mangle.
**hack·le** (hak''l), *n. & v.t.* [-LED, -LING], hatchel.
**hack·ma·tack** (hak'mə-tak'), *n.* [Am. Ind. (Algonquian)], 1. the tamarack. 2. the juniper. 3. the wood of either of these trees.
**hack·ney** (hak'ni), *n.* [*pl.* -NEYS], [< *Hackney*, England], 1. a horse for ordinary driving or riding. 2. a carriage for hire. 3. a drudge. *adj.* 1. hired out. 2. stale; trite; commonplace. *v.t.* 1. to hire out. 2. to make trite by overuse.
**hack·neyed** (hak'nid), *adj.* made trite and commonplace by overuse.
**hack·saw** (hak'sô'), *n.* a hack saw.
**hack saw,** a saw for cutting metal, consisting of a narrow, fine-toothed blade held in a frame.

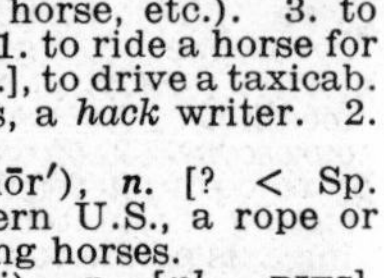

HACK SAW

**had** (had; *unstressed* həd, əd), pt. and pp. of **have**: also used to indicate preference or necessity, with adverbs, adjectives, and phrases of comparison, such as *rather, better, as well* (e.g., I *had* better leave).
**had·dock** (had'ək), *n.* [*pl.* -DOCK, -DOCKS; see PLURAL, II, D, 2], [prob. < OFr. *hadot*], a small, edible fish of the Atlantic, related to the cod.
**Ha·des** (hā'dēz), *n.* 1. in *Gr. mythology*, *a*) the home of the dead, beneath the earth. *b*) Pluto. 2. in the *New Testament*, the state or resting place of the dead. 3. [often h-], [Colloq.], hell.
**hadj** (haj), *n.* [Ar. *hajj*], a pilgrimage; specif., the journey to Mecca that every Moslem is expected to take at least once.
**hadj·i** (haj'ē), *n.* a Moslem who has made his hadj.
**had·n't** (had''nt), had not.
**Ha·dri·an** (hā'dri-ən), *n.* Roman emperor (117–138 A.D.); lived 76–138 A.D.
**hadst** (hadst), archaic second pers. sing., past indic., of **have**: used with *thou*.
**hae** (hā, ha), *v.t.* [Scot.], to have.
**Haeck·el, Ernst Hein·rich** (ernst hīn'riH hek'əl), 1834–1919; German biologist and writer.
**haem-, haema-, haemat-, hae·ma·to-, haemo-,** see **hemo-, hemato-.**
**haem·a·tite** (hem'ə-tīt', hē'mə-), *n.* hematite.
**hae·mo·glo·bin** (hē'mə-glō'bin, hem'ə-), *n.* hemoglobin.
**hae·mo·phil·i·a** (hē'mə-fil'i-ə, hem'ə-fil'yə), *n.* hemophilia. **—hae'mo·phil'i·ac** (-ak, -yak), *n.*
**haf·ni·um** (haf'ni-əm), *n.* [< L. *Hafnia*, ancient name of Copenhagen], a metallic chemical element found with zirconium and somewhat resembling it: symbol, Hf; at. wt., 178.6; at. no., 72.
**haft** (haft, häft), *n.* [AS. *hæft*], a handle or hilt of a knife, sword, etc. *v.t.* to fit with a haft.
**hag** (hag), *n.* [< AS. *hægtes*, a witch], 1. a witch. 2. an ugly, repulsive old woman, especially an evil and malevolent one. **—hag'gish,** *adj.*
**Ha·gar** (hā'gẽr), *n.* in the *Bible*, a concubine of Abraham and slave of his wife, Sarah: Gen. 16.
**hag·ber·ry** (hag'ber'i, -bẽr-i), *n.* [*pl.* -RIES], the hackberry.
**hag·fish** (hag'fish'), *n.* [*pl.* see FISH], [< *hag*], a small, eellike salt-water fish with a round, sucking mouth and horny teeth, with which it bores into other fish and devours them.
**Hag·ga·da, Hag·ga·dah** (hə-gä'də), *n.* [*pl.* -DOTH (-dōth)], [Heb. *haggadah* < *higgid*, to tell], 1. [often h-], in the *Talmud*, an anecdote that explains some point of law. 2. the part of the Talmud devoted to such narratives. 3. the narrative of the Exodus read at the start of Passover. **—hag·gad·ic** (hə-gad'ik, -gäd'-), **hag·gad'i·cal,** *adj.*
**Hag·ga·i** (hag'i-ī', hag'ī), *n.* in the *Bible*, 1. a Hebrew prophet of c. 500 B.C. 2. a book of the Old Testament attributed to him: abbrev. **Hag.**
**hag·gard** (hag'ẽrd), *adj.* [< MFr. *hagard*, untamed (hawk); prob. < MHG. *hag*, a hedge], having a wild, wasted, worn look, as from grief or illness; gaunt. **—hag'gard·ly,** *adv.* **—hag'gard·ness,** *n.*
**hag·gis** (hag'is), *n.* [ME. *hagas*, kind of pudding], a Scottish dish made of the lungs, heart, etc. of a sheep or calf, mixed with suet, seasoning, and oatmeal and boiled in the animal's stomach.
**hag·gle** (hag''l), *v.t.* [-GLED, -GLING], [freq. of Scot. *hag*, to chop, cut], to hack; mangle. *v.i.* to argue about terms, price, etc.; wrangle. *n.* a haggling. **—hag'gler,** *n.*
**hag·i·ol·o·gy** (hag'i-ol'ə-ji, hā'ji-), *n.* [*pl.* -GIES], [< Gr. *hagios*, holy; + *-logy*], 1. literature about saints' lives and legends, sacred writings, etc. 2. a list of saints. **—hag'i·o·log'ic** (-ə-loj'ik), **hag'i·o·log'i·cal,** *adj.* **—hag'i·ol'o·gist,** *n.*
**hag·rid·den** (hag'rid''n), *adj.* obsessed or harassed as by fears or nightmares.
**Hague, The** (hāg), the political capital of the Netherlands: pop., 584,000.
**hah** (hä), *interj. & n.* ha.
**Hai·fa** (hī'fə), *n.* a seaport in N Palestine, in the state of Israel: pop., 190,000.
**hail** (hāl), *v.t.* [< ON. < *heill*, whole, sound], 1. to shout to in greeting, welcome, etc. 2. to salute as: as, they *hailed* him their leader. 3. to shout to or after: as, I *hailed* a taxi. *v.i.* in *nautical usage*, to call out or signal to a ship. *n.* 1. a hailing; greeting. 2. the distance that a shout will carry: as, within *hail*. *interj.* an exclamation of tribute, greeting, etc. **—hail fellow well met,** very friendly to everyone, especially in a superficial way: also **hail fellow, hail-fellow. —hail from,** to come from (one's birthplace, etc.). **—hail'er,** *n.*
**hail** (hāl), *n.* [AS. *hægel*], 1. small, rounded pieces of ice that sometimes fall during thunderstorms; hailstones. 2. a falling, showering, etc. of or like hail: as, a *hail* of explosives. *v.i.* to pour down hail: as, it is *hailing*. *v.t.* to shower, hurl, etc. violently like hail (with *on* or *upon*): as, he *hailed* curses upon us.
**Hai·le Se·las·sie** (hī'li sə-las'i, sə-lä'si), 1891– ; emperor of Ethiopia (1930– ).
**hail·stone** (hāl'stōn'), *n.* a piece of hail.
**hail·storm** (hāl'stôrm'), *n.* a storm with hail.
**hair** (hâr), *n.* [AS. *hær*], 1. any of the fine, threadlike outgrowths from the skin of an animal or human being. 2. a growth of these; esp., the growth covering the human head or the skin of most mammals. 3. an extremely small space, degree, etc. 4. a threadlike growth on a plant. *adj.* 1. made of or with hair. 2. for the care of the hair: as, *hair* tonic. **—get in one's hair,** [Slang], to annoy one. **—let one's hair down,** [Slang], to be very informal, relaxed, etc. **—make one's hair stand on end,** to horrify one. **—split hairs,** to quibble; cavil. **—to a hair,** exactly; perfectly. **—hair'less,** *adj.* **—hair'less·ness,** *n.* **—hair'like',** *adj.*
**hair·breadth** (hâr'bredth'), *n.* a very short distance; extremely small space. *adj.* very narrow; close. Also **hairs'breadth', hair's'-breadth'.**
**hair·cloth** (hâr'klôth'), *n.* cloth woven from horsehair or camel's hair: used mainly for covering furniture.
**hair·cut** (hâr'kut'), *n.* 1. a cutting of the hair of the head. 2. the style in which the hair is cut. **—hair'cut'ter,** *n.*
**hair-do** (hâr'dōō'), *n.* the style in which (a woman's) hair is arranged; coiffure.
**hair·dress·er** (hâr'dres'ẽr), *n.* a person whose work is dressing (women's) hair.
**hair·dress·ing** (hâr'dres'iŋ), *n.* the business or work of a hairdresser. *adj.* of or for the dressing of hair.
**hair·line** (hâr'līn'), *n.* 1. a very thin line or stripe. 2. the lower line of the hair on the head.
**hair·pin** (hâr'pin'), *n.* a small, usually U-shaped,

piece of wire, shell, etc., for keeping the hair in place. *adj.* U-shaped: as, a *hairpin* turn.
**hair-raising** (hâr′rāz′iŋ), *adj.* [Colloq.], causing the hair to stand on end; horrifying.
**hair shirt,** a shirt or girdle of haircloth, worn for self-punishment, as by religious ascetics.
**hair·split·ting** (hâr′split′iŋ), *adj.* & *n.* making petty distinctions; quibbling. —**hair′split′ter,** *n.*
**hair·spring** (hâr′spriŋ′), *n.* a very slender, hairlike coil that controls the regular movement of the balance wheel in a watch or clock.
**hair trigger,** a trigger so delicately adjusted that slight pressure on it discharges the firearm.
**hair·y** (hâr′i), *adj.* [-IER, -IEST], 1. covered with hair. 2. of or like hair. —**hair′i·ness,** *n.*
**Hai·ti** (hā′ti), *n.* 1. a republic on the island of Hispaniola, West Indies: area, 10,714 sq. mi.; pop., 3,505,000; capital, Port-au-Prince. 2. Hispaniola: the former name. Also sp. **Hayti.** —**Hai·ti·an** (hā′ti-ən, hā′shən), *adj.* & *n.*
**haj·i, haj·ji** (haj′ē), *n.* a hadji.
**hake** (hāk), *n.* [*pl.* HAKE, HAKES; see PLURAL, II, D, 2], [prob. < ON. *haki*, a hook (so called from shape of the jaw)], any of various edible sea fishes related to the cod.
**ha·keem** (hä-kēm′), *n.* [Ar. *hakīm*, wise, learned], in Moslem regions, a physician: also sp. **hakim.**
**ha·kim** (hä′kim), *n.* [Ar. *hākim*, governor], 1. in Moslem regions, a ruler or judge. 2. (hä-kēm′), a hakeem; physician.
**hal·berd** (hal′bērd), *n.* [< Fr. < It. < MHG. *helmbarte*], a combination spear and battle-ax used in the 15th and 16th centuries: also **halbert** (-bērt).

HALBERD

**hal·berd·ier** (hal′bēr-dêr′), *n.* a soldier, guard, etc. armed with a halberd.
**hal·cy·on** (hal′si-ən), *n.* [< L. < Gr. *alkyōn*, kingfisher], in *ancient legend*, a bird, believed to have been the kingfisher, supposed to have a calming influence on the sea at the time of the winter solstice. *adj.* tranquil; happy: as, *halcyon* days.
**hale** (hāl), *adj.* [HALER, HALEST], [AS. *hal*], sound in body; vigorous and healthy. —**hale′ness,** *n.*
**hale** (hāl), *v.t.* [HALED, HALING], [< OFr. *haler;* prob. < Gmc.], 1. to pull forcibly; drag. 2. to force (one) to go: as, he was *haled* into court.
**Hale, Nathan,** 1755–1776; American Revolutionary soldier, hanged by the British as a spy.
**half** (haf, häf), *n.* [*pl.* HALVES], [AS. *healf*], 1. either of the two equal, or almost equal, parts of something. 2. either of the two equal periods of certain games, between which the players rest. *adj.* 1. being either of the two equal parts. 2. being about fifty per cent of the whole. 3. incomplete; partial. *adv.* 1. to an extent approximately or exactly fifty per cent of the whole. 2. [Colloq.], to some extent: as, I was *half* convinced. —**by half,** considerably; very much. —**in half,** into halves. —**not half bad,** not really bad but rather good. —**not the half of,** only a small part of. —**one's better half,** [Slang], one's spouse.
**half-and-half** (haf′′nd-haf′, häf′′n-häf′), *n.* something that is half one thing and half another; esp., *a*) a mixture of equal parts of milk and cream. *b*) a mixture of equal parts of porter and ale, beer and stout, etc. *adj.* 1. combining two things equally. 2. partly one thing and partly the other. *adv.* in two equal parts.
**half·back** (haf′bak′, häf′-), *n.* in *football*, 1. either of two players whose position is behind the line of scrimmage together with the fullback and the quarterback. 2. this position.
**half-baked** (haf′bākt′, häf′-), *adj.* 1. only partly baked. 2. not completely thought out. 3. having or showing little intelligence and experience.
**half-blood** (haf′blud′, häf′-), *n.* 1. a person related to another through one parent only. 2. a half-breed. —**half′blood′ed,** *adj.*
**half blood,** 1. kinship through one parent only: as, sisters of the *half blood.* 2. a half-blood.
**half-breed** (haf′brēd′, häf′-), *n.* one whose parents are of different races.
**half brother,** a brother related through one parent only.
**half-caste** (haf′kast′, häf′käst′), *n.* 1. a half-breed. 2. an offspring of one European parent and one Asiatic parent. *adj.* of a half-caste.
**half cock,** the halfway position of the hammer of a firearm, when the trigger is locked. —**go off at half cock,** 1. to go off too soon: said of a firearm. 2. to speak or act thoughtlessly or too hastily. Also **go off half cocked.**
**half crown,** a British silver coin equal to two shillings and sixpence (2½ shillings).
**half dollar,** a silver coin of the U.S. and Canada, worth 50 cents.
**half gainer,** a back dive made from the stance for a front dive.
**half·heart·ed** (haf′här′tid, häf′-), *adj.* with little enthusiasm, determination, interest, etc. —**half′-heart′ed·ly,** *adv.* —**half′heart′ed·ness,** *n.*
**half hitch,** a knot made by passing the end of the rope around the rope and then through the loop thus made: it is the simplest kind of hitch.
**half-hour** (haf′our′, häf′-), *n.* 1. half of an hour; thirty minutes. 2. the point thirty minutes after any given hour. *adj.* 1. lasting for thirty minutes. 2. occurring every thirty minutes. —**half′-hour′ly,** *adj.* & *adv.*
**half life,** in *nuclear physics*, the period required for the disintegration of half of the atoms in a sample of a radioactive substance.
**half-mast** (half′mast′, häf′mäst′), *n.* the position of a flag lowered about halfway down its staff, as in public mourning. *adv.* about halfway on the staff. *v.t.* to hang (a flag) at half-mast.
**half-moon** (haf′mōōn′, häf′mōōn′), *n.* 1. the moon when only half its disk is clearly seen. 2. anything shaped like a half-moon or crescent. *adj.* shaped like a half-moon.
**half nelson** (nel′s′n), in *wrestling*, a hold in which one arm is placed under the opponent's arm from behind with the hand pressed against the back of his neck.
**half note,** in *music*, a note (𝅗𝅥) having one half the duration of a whole note: also called **minim.**
**half·pen·ny** (hā′pən-i, hāp′ni), *n.* [*pl.* -PENCE (hā′pəns), -PENNIES (hā′pən-iz, hāp′niz)], a British bronze coin equal to half a penny. *adj.* 1. worth a halfpenny. 2. worth very little; trifling.
**half pint,** 1. a liquid or dry measure equal to ¼ quart. 2. [Slang], a small person.
**half sister,** a sister related through one parent only.
**half-sole** (haf′sōl′, häf′-), *v.t.* [-SOLED, -SOLING], to repair (shoes or boots) by attaching new half soles.
**half sole,** a sole (of a shoe or boot) from the arch to the toe.
**half step,** 1. in *military usage*, a short marching step of fifteen inches (in double time, eighteen inches). 2. in *music*, the difference in pitch between two adjacent keys on the piano; half tone.
**half-tim·bered** (haf′tim′bērd, häf′-), *adj.* in *architecture*, made of a wooden framework having the spaces filled with plaster, brick, etc.
**half-tone** (haf′tōn′, häf′-), *n.* a half tone. *adj.* designating, of, or producing half tones.
**half tone,** 1. in *art*, a tone or shading between light and dark. 2. in *music*, a half step. 3. in *photoengraving*, *a*) a technique of shading by dots produced by photographing the object from behind a fine screen. *b*) a photoengraving so made.
**half-track** (haf′trak′, häf′-), *n.* an army truck, armored vehicle, etc. with caterpillar treads instead of rear wheels.
**half·way** (haf′wā′, häf′-), *adj.* 1. equally distant between two points, states, etc. 2. incomplete; partial. *adv.* 1. half the distance; to the midway point. 2. incompletely; partially. —**meet halfway,** to be willing to compromise with.
**half-wit** (haf′wit′, häf′-), *n.* 1. a person who is feeble-minded, moronic, etc. 2. a stupid, silly person; fool; dolt. —**half′-wit′ted,** *adj.*
**hal·i·but** (hal′ə-bət, häl′-), *n.* [*pl.* -BUT, -BUTS; see PLURAL, II, D, 2], [ME. *hali*, holy + *butt*, a flounder: because eaten on holidays], a large, edible flatfish found in northern seas: it sometimes weighs hundreds of pounds: also **holibut.**
**hal·ide** (hal′īd, -id, hā′līd, -lid), *n.* [*halo*gen + *-ide*], in *chemistry*, a compound of a halogen with another element or radical: also **hal·id** (hal′id, hā′lid). *adj.* of or like a halide.
**hal·i·dom** (hal′i-dəm), *n.* [< AS.; see HOLY & -DOM], [Archaic], 1. holiness. 2. a holy place; sanctuary. 3. a sacred relic. Also **hal′i·dome′** (-dōm′).
**Hal·i·fax** (hal′ə-faks′), *n.* the capital of Nova Scotia, Canada: pop., 93,000.
**hal·ite** (hal′īt, hā′līt), *n.* [< Gr. *hals*, salt; + *-ite*], native sodium chloride; rock salt.
**hal·i·to·sis** (hal′ə-tō′sis), *n.* [< L. *halitus*, breath; + *-osis*], bad-smelling breath.
**hall** (hôl), *n.* [< AS. *heall* < base of *helan*, to cover],

1. the dwelling of a baron, squire, etc. 2. [sometimes H-], a building containing public offices or the headquarters of an organization. 3. a large public or semipublic room for gatherings, entertainments, etc. 4. [sometimes H-], *a*) a college dormitory, classroom building, etc. *b*) any of the minor colleges of an English university. 5. a passageway or room between the entrance and the interior of a building. 6. a passageway or corridor onto which rooms open.

**Hal·le** (häl′ə; Eng. hal′i), ***n.*** a city in E Germany: pop., 276,000.

**hal·le·lu·jah, hal·le·lu·iah** (hal′ə-lo͞o′yə), ***interj.*** [< Heb. < *hallelū*, praise + *yāh*, Jehovah], praise (ye) the Lord! ***n.*** an exclamation, hymn, or song of praise to God. Also **alleluia.**

**Hal·ley's comet** (hal′iz), a comet, last seen in 1910, whose periodic reappearance was predicted by Edmund Halley (1656–1742), Eng. astronomer.

**hal·liard** (hal′yẽrd), ***n.*** a halyard.

**hall·mark** (hôl′märk′), ***n.*** 1. the official mark stamped on gold and silver articles at Goldsmiths' Hall in London as a guarantee of genuineness. 2. any mark or symbol of genuineness or high quality. Also **hall mark.** ***v.t.*** to put a hallmark on.

**hal·loo** (hə-lo͞o′), ***v.i. & v.t.*** [-LOOED, -LOOING], 1. to call out in order to attract the attention of (a person). 2. to urge on (hounds) by shouting. 3. to shout; yell. ***interj. & n.*** a shout or call.

**hal·low** (hal′ō), ***v.t.*** [AS. *halgian* < *halig*, holy], 1. to make holy or sacred; consecrate. 2. to regard as holy; honor as sacred.

**hal·lowed** (hal′ōd; *in poetry or liturgy, often* hal′ō-id), ***adj.*** 1. made holy or sacred. 2. honored as sacred. —**hal′lowed·ness,** ***n.***

**Hal·low·een, Hal·low·e'en** (hal′ō-ēn′, häl′ə-wēn′), ***n.*** [contr. < *all hallow even*], the evening of October 31, followed by All Saints' Day.

**Hal·low·mas** (hal′ō-məs, -mas′), ***n.*** [contr. < *all hallow mass*], All Saints' Day: the former name.

**hal·lu·ci·nate** (hə-lo͞o′sə-nāt′), ***v.t.*** [-NATED, -NATING], [< L. pp. of *hallucinari*, to wander mentally], to cause to have hallucinations.

**hal·lu·ci·na·tion** (hə-lo͞o′sə-nā′shən), ***n.*** 1. the apparent perception of sights, sounds, etc. that are not actually present. 2. the imaginary thing apparently seen, heard, etc. —**hal·lu′ci·na·to′ry** (-nə-tôr′i, -tō′ri), ***adj.***

**hal·lu·ci·no·gen** (hə-lo͞o′sə-nə-jen, hal′yoo-sin′ə-jən), ***n.*** a drug or other substance that produces hallucinations.

**hall·way** (hôl′wā′), ***n.*** 1. a passageway or room between the entrance and the interior of a building. 2. a passageway; corridor.

**ha·lo** (hā′lō), ***n.*** [*pl.* -LOS, -LOES], [< L. < Gr. *halōs*, threshing floor on which oxen trod in a circular path < *halein*, to grind], 1. a ring of light that seems to encircle the sun, moon, etc. 2. a symbolic ring or disk of light shown around the head of a saint, etc. 3. the glory attributed to a person or thing famed or idealized in legend or history. ***v.t.*** [-LOED, -LOING], to encircle with a halo.

**hal·o·gen** (hal′ə-jən), ***n.*** [< Gr. *hals*, salt; + *-gen*], any of five nonmetallic chemical elements: fluorine, chlorine, bromine, astatine, and iodine.

**hal·oid** (hal′oid, hā′loid), ***adj.*** [< Gr. *hals*, salt; + *-oid*], of or like a halide. ***n.*** a halide.

**Hals, Frans** (fräns häls; Eng. hals), 1580?–1666; Dutch painter.

**halt** (hôlt), ***n.*** [< Fr. < G. < *halten*, to hold], a temporary stop, as in marching; pause. ***v.i. & v.t.*** to stop; cease or cause to cease. —**call a halt,** to order a stop. —**come to a halt,** to stop.

**halt** (hôlt), ***v.i.*** [< AS. < *healt, adj.*], 1. to walk with a crippled gait; limp. 2. to be uncertain; hesitate: as, he *halts* in his speech. 3. to have defects in flow, as of rhythm or logic. ***adj.*** [Archaic], halting; lame. ***n.*** [Archaic], a halting; lameness. —**the halt,** those who are lame. —**halt′ing·ly,** ***adv.***

**hal·ter** (hôl′tẽr), ***n.*** [AS. *hælftre*], 1. a rope, strap, etc. for tying or leading an animal. 2. a rope for hanging a person; noose. 3. execution by hanging. 4. a woman's garment for covering the breast, held up by a loop around the neck. ***v.t.*** to put a halter on (an animal); tie with a halter.

**hal·vah** (häl-vä′), ***n.*** [Turk. *helwa;* Ar. *halwa*], a Turkish confection made of ground sesame seeds and nuts mixed with honey, etc.

**halve** (hav, häv), ***v.t.*** [HALVED, HALVING], 1. to divide into two equal parts. 2. to share equally (*with* someone). 3. to reduce to half. 4. in *golf*, to play (a hole, match, etc.) in the same number of strokes as one's opponent.

**halves** (havz, hävz), ***n.*** pl. of **half.** —**by halves,** 1. halfway; incompletely. 2. halfheartedly. —**go halves,** to share expenses, etc. equally.

**hal·yard** (hal′yẽrd), ***n.*** [earlier *halier* < ME. *halien* (see HALE, *v.*)], a rope or tackle for raising or lowering a flag, sail, etc.: also sp. **halliard.**

**Ham** (ham), ***n.*** in the *Bible*, Noah's second son.

**ham** (ham), ***n.*** [AS. *hamm*], 1. the part of the leg behind the knee. 2. *a*) the back of the thigh. *b*) the thigh and buttock together. 3. the hock or hind leg of a four-legged animal. 4. the upper part of a hog's hind leg, salted, smoked, etc. 5. [Slang], an incompetent actor, especially one who overacts. 6. [Slang], an amateur radio operator.

**ham·a·dry·ad** (ham′ə-drī′əd, -ad), ***n.*** [< L. < Gr. < *hama*, together with + *drys*, a tree], in *Gr. mythology*, a dryad; wood nymph whose life was bound up with that of the tree in which she lived.

**Ha·man** (hā′mən), ***n.*** in the *Bible*, a Persian official who sought the destruction of the Jews but was hanged from his own gallows: Esth. 7.

**Ham·burg** (ham′bẽrg; G. häm′boorkh), ***n.*** a city in NW Germany: pop., 1,854,000.

**ham·burg** (ham′bẽrg), ***n.*** (a) hamburger.

**ham·burg·er** (ham′bũr′gẽr), ***n.*** [earlier *Hamburg steak*, after *Hamburg*, Germany], 1. ground beef. 2. a fried or broiled patty of such meat, often eaten as a sandwich in a round bun.

**Hamburg** (or **hamburger**) **steak,** hamburger.

**hame** (hām), ***n.*** [< AS. *hama*, a cover, skin], either of the two rigid pieces along the sides of a horse's collar, to which the traces are attached.

**Ham·il·ton** (ham′il-t'n), ***n.*** 1. a city in Ontario, Canada, west of Toronto: pop., 274,000. 2. a city in SW Ohio: pop., 72,000. 3. the capital of Bermuda: pop., 3,200.

**Hamilton, Alexander,** 1757–1804; U.S. statesman; first secretary of the treasury (1789–1795).

**Ham·ite** (ham′īt), ***n.*** 1. a person regarded as descended from Ham. 2. a member of any of several dark-skinned peoples of N and E Africa.

**Ham·it·ic** (ham-it′ik, hə-mit′-), ***adj.*** 1. of Ham or the Hamites. 2. designating or of a group of African languages related to the Semitic languages and including ancient Egyptian, the modern Berber dialects, and Cushitic.

**Ham·let** (ham′lit), ***n.*** 1. a famous tragedy by Shakespeare (c. 1602). 2. the hero of this play.

**ham·let** (ham′lit), ***n.*** [< OFr. dim. of *hamel* < LG. *hām*, home], a very small village.

**Ham·mar·skjöld, Dag Hjal·mar** (dåg yål′mår håm′år-shüld′), 1905–1961; Swedish statesman; secretary-general of the United Nations (1953–1961).

**ham·mer** (ham′ẽr), ***n.*** [AS. *hamor*], 1. a tool for pounding, usually consisting of a metal head and a handle. 2. a thing like this in shape or use; specif., *a*) the mechanism that strikes the firing pin or cap in a firearm. *b*) any of the felted mallets that strike against the strings of a piano. 3. the malleus, one of the bones of the middle ear: see **ear,** illus. 4. an auctioneer's gavel. ***v.t.*** 1. to strike repeatedly as with a hammer. 2. to make or fasten with a hammer. 3. to drive, force, or shape as with hammer blows. ***v.i.*** to strike repeated blows as with a hammer. —**hammer (away) at,** 1. to work energetically at. 2. to keep emphasizing. —**hammer out,** 1. to shape or flatten by hammering. 2. to take out by hammering. 3. to develop by careful thought or repeated effort. —**ham′mer·er,** ***n.*** —**ham′mer·less,** ***adj.*** —**ham′mer·like′,** ***adj.***

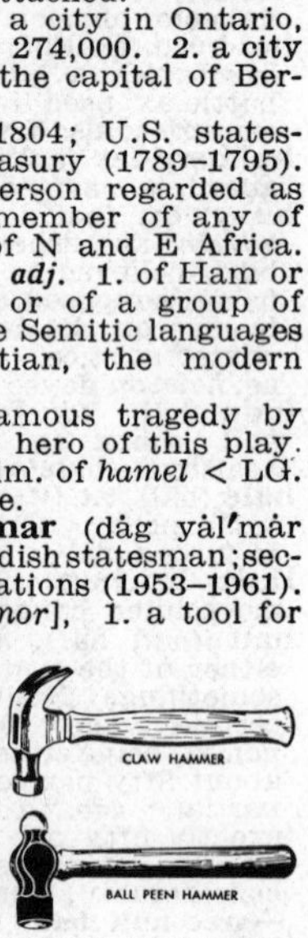

TYPES OF HAMMER

**ham·mer·head** (ham′ẽr-hed′), ***n.*** a savage shark that has a mallet-shaped head.

**hammer lock,** in *wrestling*, a hold in which the opponent's arm is twisted behind his back.

**ham·mock** (ham′ək), ***n.*** [Sp. *hamaca;* of W. Ind. origin], a length of netting, canvas, etc. swung from ropes at both ends and used as a bed or couch. —**ham′mock·like′,** ***adj.***

**Ham·mond** (ham′ənd), ***n.*** a city in Indiana, near Chicago: pop., 112,000.

**ham·my** (ham′i), ***adj.*** [-MIER, -MIEST], [Slang], like or characteristic of a ham (actor).

**ham·per** (ham′pẽr), ***v.t.*** [ME. *hampren*], to hinder; impede; encumber.

**ham·per** (ham′pẽr), ***n.*** [< OFr. < *hanap*, a cup < Gmc.], a large basket, usually with a cover.

**Hamp·ton** (hamp′tən), ***n.*** a city in SE Virginia, on Hampton Roads: pop., 89,000.

**Hampton Roads,** a channel of Chesapeake Bay, SE Virginia.

**ham·ster** (ham′stẽr), ***n.*** [G.], a ratlike animal of Europe and Asia, with large cheek pouches: one variety is used in scientific experiments.

**ham·string** (ham′striŋ′), ***n.*** 1. one of the tendons

at the back of the human knee. 2. the great tendon at the back of the hock in a four-legged animal. *v.t.* [-STRUNG, -STRINGING], 1. to disable by cutting a hamstring. 2. to cripple; disable.

**Han·cock, John** (han′kok), 1737–1793; U.S. statesman; first signer of the Declaration of Independence.

**hand** (hand), *n.* [AS.], 1. the part of the human arm below the wrist, used for grasping. 2. the corresponding part in apes, etc. 3. a side, direction, or position indicated by a hand: as, at one's right *hand.* 4. possession: as, the papers are in my *hands.* 5. control; power: as, he rules with an iron *hand.* 6. an active part; share: as, take a *hand* in this work. 7. *a*) a handshake as a pledge. *b*) a promise to marry. 8. skill; ability: as, a master's *hand.* 9. handwriting. 10. a signature. 11. a clapping of hands; applause: as, they gave the singer a *hand.* 12. assistance; help: as, lend me a *hand.* 13. one whose chief work is with his hands, as a sailor, farm laborer, etc. 14. one regarded as having some special skill: as, he's quite a *hand* at the piano. 15. source; origin: as, I got the news at first *hand.* 16. anything like a hand, as the pointer on a clock. 17. the breadth of a hand, about 4 inches. 18. in *card games, a*) the cards held by a player at one time. *b*) a player. *c*) a round of play. *adj.* of, for, or controlled by the hand. *v.t.* 1. to give as with the hand; transfer. 2. to help or conduct with the hand: as, *hand* the lady to her car. **—at hand,** 1. near; close by. 2. ready. **—(at) second hand,** 1. not from the original source. 2. previously used. **—at the hand** (or **hands**) **of,** through the action of. **—by hand,** not by machines but with the hands. **—change hands,** to pass to another's ownership. **—from hand to mouth,** with nothing saved for the future. **—hand down,** 1. to bequeath. 2. to announce (a verdict, etc.). **—hand in,** to give; submit. **—hand in hand,** 1. holding one another's hand. 2. together. **—hand it to,** [Slang], to give deserved credit to. **—hand on,** to pass along; transmit. **—hand out,** to distribute. **—hand over,** to give up; deliver. **—hand over fist,** [Colloq.], easily and in large amounts. **—hands down,** easily; without effort. **—hands off!** don't touch! don't interfere! **—hand to hand,** at close quarters: said of fighting. **—have one's hands full,** to be extremely busy. **—in hand,** 1. in order or control. 2. in possession. 3. in process. **—lay hands on,** 1. to attack physically. 2. to seize; take. 3. to touch with the hands in blessing, etc. **—off one's hands,** no longer in one's care. **—on every hand,** on all sides. **—on hand,** 1. near. 2. available. 3. present. **—on one's hands,** in one's care. **—on the one hand,** from one point of view. **—on the other hand,** from the opposed point of view. **—out of hand,** 1. out of control. 2. immediately. 3. over and done with. **—show one's hand,** to disclose one's intentions. **—take in hand,** 1. to take control of. 2. to handle; treat. 3. to try; attempt. **—to hand,** 1. near; accessible. 2. in one's possession. **—turn** (or **put**) **one's hand to,** to undertake; work at. **—upper hand,** the advantage. **—wash one's hands of,** to refuse to go on with or take responsibility for. **—with a high hand,** with arrogance. **—with clean hands,** without guilt.

**hand-,** a combining form meaning *of, with, by, or for a hand or hands,* as in *handclasp, handmade.*

**hand·bag** (hand′bag′), *n.* 1. a small container for money, toilet articles, keys, etc., carried by women; purse. 2. a small satchel.

**hand·ball** (hand′bôl′), *n.* 1. a game in which players bat a small ball against a wall or walls with the hand. 2. the small rubber ball.

**hand·bar·row** (hand′bar′ō), *n.* 1. a rack or frame carried by a pair of handles attached at each end. 2. a wheelbarrow.

**hand·bill** (hand′bil′), *n.* a small printed notice, advertisement, etc. to be passed out by hand.

**hand·book** (hand′book′), *n.* 1. a compact reference book; manual. 2. a guidebook.

**hand·breadth** (hand′bredth′), *n.* the breadth of the human palm, used as a unit of measurement: now usually about 4 inches.

**hand·cart** (hand′kärt′), *n.* a small cart, often with only two wheels, pulled or pushed by hand.

**hand·clasp** (hand′klasp′, -kläsp′), *n.* a clasping of hands in greeting, farewell, promise, etc.

**hand·cuff** (hand′kuf′), *n. usually in pl.* either of a pair of connected rings that can be locked about the wrists, as in fastening a prisoner to a policeman. *v.t.* to put handcuffs on; manacle.

**hand·ed** (han′did), *adj.* 1. having (a specified number or kind of) hands: usually in hyphenated compounds, as, *left-handed.* 2. involving (a specified number of) players: as, *three-handed* bridge.

**Han·del, George Frederick** (han′d'l; G. hen′dəl), 1685–1759; English composer, born in Germany.

**hand·ful** (hand′fool′), *n.* [*pl.* -FULS], 1. as much or as many as the hand will hold. 2. a relatively small number or amount. 3. [Colloq.], someone or something hard to control.

**hand·gun** (hand′gun′), *n.* any firearm that is held and fired with one hand, as a pistol.

**hand·i·cap** (han′di-kap′), *n.* [< *hand in cap,* former kind of lottery], 1. a race or other competition in which difficulties are imposed on the superior contestants, or advantages given to the inferior, to equalize their chances of winning. 2. such a difficulty or advantage. 3. something that hampers one; disadvantage. *v.t.* [-CAPPED, -CAPPING], 1. to give a handicap to. 2. to cause to be at a disadvantage; hinder. **—hand′i·cap′per,** *n.*

**hand·i·craft** (han′di-kraft′, -kräft′), *n.* [AS. *handcræft;* infl. by *handiwork*], 1. expertness with the hands; manual skill. 2. an occupation or art calling for skillful use of the hands, as weaving.

**hand·i·work** (han′di-wûrk′), *n.* [AS. *handgeweorc*], 1. handwork. 2. work done by a person himself. 3. the result of one's actions.

**hand·ker·chief** (haŋ′kẽr-chif, -chēf′), *n.* [*pl.* -CHIEFS (-chivz, -chēfs′)], 1. a small, square piece of cloth for wiping the nose, eyes, or face, or worn for ornament. 2. a larger piece of cloth worn around the neck or the head; kerchief.

**han·dle** (han′d'l), *n.* [AS. < *hand,* hand], 1. that part of a utensil, tool, etc. which is to be held, turned, etc. with the hand. 2. a thing like a handle. 3. occasion; pretext. *v.t.* [-DLED, -DLING], 1. to touch, lift, etc. with the hand or hands. 2. to operate or use with the hands. 3. to manage; control. 4. to deal with: as, I *handle* many requests. 5. to trade in; deal in. 6. to behave toward; treat. *v.i.* to respond to control: as, the car *handles* well. **—fly off the handle,** [Colloq.], to become violently angry or excited. **—han′dled,** *adj.* **—han′dle·less,** *adj.*

**handle bar,** *often in pl.* 1. a curved metal bar with handles on the ends, for steering a bicycle, etc. 2. [Colloq.], a long mustache like this.

**hand·ler** (han′dlẽr), *n.* 1. a person or thing that handles. 2. a boxer's trainer or second.

**hand·made** (hand′mād′), *adj.* made by hand, not by machine.

**hand·maid** (hand′mād′), *n.* a woman or girl servant or attendant: also **hand′maid′en.**

**hand-me-down** (hand′mi-doun′), *adj.* [Colloq.], 1. ready-made. 2. used; secondhand. *n.* [Colloq.], a hand-me-down garment.

**hand·off** (hand′ôf′), *n.* in *football,* an offensive maneuver in which a back hands the ball directly to another back.

**hand organ,** a barrel organ.

**hand·out** (hand′out′), *n.* a gift of food, clothing, etc., as to a beggar or tramp.

**hand-picked** (hand′pikt′), *adj.* 1. picked by hand: said of fruit or vegetables; hence, 2. chosen with care, or for a special purpose.

**hand·rail** (hand′rāl′), *n.* a rail serving as a guard or hand support, as along a stairway.

**hand·saw** (hand′sô′), *n.* a saw used with one hand.

**hand's-breadth** (handz′bredth′), *n.* handbreadth.

**hand·sel** (hand′s'l, han′s'l), *n.* [< ON. *handsal*(*i*), confirmation of bargain by giving one's hand], a present for good luck, as on New Year's or on launching a new business. *v.t.* [-SELED or -SELLED, -SELING or -SELLING], to give a handsel to.

**hand·set** (hand′set′), *n.* a telephone mouthpiece and receiver mounted together on a handle.

**hand·shake** (hand′shāk′), *n.* a gripping of each other's hand in greeting, promise, etc.

**hand·some** (han′səm), *adj.* [orig., easily handled < ME.; see HAND & -SOME], 1. *a*) moderately large. *b*) considerable: as, a *handsome* sum. 2. proper; gracious. 3. good-looking; of pleasing appearance, especially in a manly or dignified way. **—hand′some·ly,** *adv.* **—hand′some·ness,** *n.*

**hand·spike** (hand′spīk′), *n.* [< Early Mod. D. < *hand,* hand + *spaeke,* rod, pole], a heavy bar used as a lever, especially on ships.

**hand·spring** (hand′spriŋ′), *n.* a gymnastic feat in which the performer turns over in mid-air with one or both hands touching the ground.

**hand-to-hand** (hand′tə-hand′), *adj.* in close contact; at close quarters: said of fighting.

**hand-to-mouth** (hand′tə-mouth′), *adj.* with nothing saved for the future.
**hand·work** (hand′wũrk′), *n.* work done or made by hand, not by machine.
**hand·writ·ing** (hand′rit′iŋ), *n.* 1. writing done by hand, with pen, pencil, etc. 2. a style or way of forming letters and words in writing.
**hand·y** (han′di), *adj.* [-IER, -IEST], 1. close at hand; easily reached; easily used. 2. easily managed. 3. clever with the hands; deft. —**hand′i·ly,** *adv.* —**hand′i·ness,** *n.*
**handy man,** a man who does odd jobs.
**hang** (haŋ), *v.t.* [HUNG, HANGING; for *v.t.* 3. & *v.i.* 3, HANGED is preferred pt. & pp.], [AS. *hangian*], 1. to attach to something above with no support from below; suspend. 2. to attach so as to permit free motion: as, a door is *hung* on its hinges. 3. to put to death by suspending from a rope about the neck. 4. to fasten (pictures, etc.) to a wall. 5. to ornament or cover: as, she *hung* the walls with pictures. 6. to paste (wallpaper) to walls. 7. to deadlock (a jury), as by withholding one's vote. *v.i.* 1. to be suspended. 2. to swing, as on a hinge. 3. to die by hanging. 4. to droop; bend. 5. to hesitate; be undecided. 6. to exhibit one's pictures in a museum, etc. *n.* 1. the way that a thing hangs. 2. the way that a thing is done or used. 3. significance; general idea. 4. [Colloq.], a bit: as, I don't care a *hang.* —**hang around** (or **about**), 1. to cluster around. 2. [Colloq.], to loiter around. —**hang back,** to be reluctant to advance. —**hang fire,** to be unsettled or undecided. —**hang on,** 1. to keep hold. 2. to persevere. 3. to depend on. 4. to listen attentively to. —**hang out,** 1. to lean out. 2. [Slang], *a*) to reside. *b*) to frequent. —**hang over,** to project, hover, or loom over. —**hang together,** to stick together. —**hang up,** 1. to put on a hanger, hook, etc. 2. to end a telephone conversation by replacing the receiver. —**hang′a·ble,** *adj.*
**hang·ar** (haŋ′ẽr, -gär), *n.* [Fr., a shed], a shed or other shelter, especially one for aircraft.
**Hang·chow** (haŋ′chou′; Chin. häŋ′jō′), *n.* a seaport in E China: pop., 784,000.
**hang·dog** (haŋ′dôg′), *n.* a low, skulking person; sneak. *adj.* low, sneaking, or abject.
**hang·er** (haŋ′ẽr), *n.* 1. a person who hangs things: as, a paper *hanger.* 2. a thing that hangs. 3. a thing on which objects, as garments, are hung.
**hang·er-on** (haŋ′ẽr-on′), *n.* [*pl.* HANGERS-ON], a follower or dependent; specif., *a*) one who attaches himself to another, to some group, etc. although not wanted. *b*) a sycophant; parasite.
**hang·ing** (haŋ′iŋ), *adj.* 1. suspended. 2. leaning over. 3. located on a steep slope or slant. 4. downcast. 5. deserving the death penalty. *n.* 1. a suspending or being suspended. 2. a putting to death by hanging. 3. *usually in pl.* something hung on a wall, etc., as drapery, etc.
**hang·man** (haŋ′mən), *n.* [*pl.* -MEN], an executioner who hangs condemned persons.
**hang·nail** (haŋ′nāl′), *n.* [alt. < *agnail* (AS. *angnægl*), a sore around the nail], a bit of torn skin hanging at the side or base of a fingernail.
**hang-out** (haŋ′out′), *n.* [Slang], a place frequented by some person or group.
**hang·o·ver** (haŋ′ō′vẽr), *n.* 1. something remaining from a previous time or state; a survival. 2. headache, nausea, etc. occurring as an aftereffect of drinking much alcoholic liquor.
**hang-up** (haŋ′up′), *n.* [Slang], a problem or difficulty, esp. of an emotional nature.
**hank** (haŋk), *n.* [prob. < Anglo-N.], 1. a loop or coil of something flexible. 2. a standard length of coiled thread or yarn; skein.
**hank·er** (haŋ′kẽr), *v.i.* [prob. < D. or LG.], to crave or long (followed by *after, for,* or an infinitive). —**hank′er·er,** *n.* —**hank′er·ing,** *n.*
**hank·y-pank·y** (haŋ′ki-paŋ′ki), *n.* [redupl. & dim. formation < *hand*], [Colloq.], trickery; jugglery; deception. *adj.* [Colloq.], deceptive.
**Han·ni·bal** (han′ə-b'l), *n.* Carthaginian general; 247 B.C.–183 B.C.; crossed Alps to invade Italy.
**Ha·noi** (hä′noi′), *n.* the capital of North Vietnam: pop., 644,000.
**Han·o·ver** (han′ō-vẽr), *n.* 1. a city in northern West Germany: pop., 553,000. 2. a ruling family of England (1714–1901). —**Han·o·ve·ri·an** (han′ō-vêr′i-ən), *adj.* & *n.*
**hanse** (hans), *n.* [OFr.; MHG. < OHG. *hansa,* band of men], 1. a medieval guild of merchants. 2. [H-], a medieval league of free towns in N Germany and adjoining countries, for economic advancement and protection: also **Hanseatic League.**
**Han·se·at·ic** (han′si-at′ik), *adj.* of the Hanse.
**han·sel** (han′s'l), *n.* a handsel.
**han·som** (han′səm), *n.* [after J.A. *Hansom* (1803–1882), Eng. inventor], a two-wheeled covered carriage for two passengers, pulled by one horse: the driver's seat is above and behind the cab: also **hansom cab.**

HANSOM

**Ha·nuk·kah, Ha·nuk·ka** (hä′noo-kä′; Heb. khä′noo-kô), *n.* a Jewish festival commemorating the rededication of the Temple by the Maccabees in 165 B.C.: also **Chanukah**: see **Jewish holidays.**
**hap** (hap), *n.* [< ON. *happ*], [Archaic], chance; luck. *v.i.* [HAPPED, HAPPING], [Archaic], to happen.
**hap·haz·ard** (hap′haz′ẽrd; *for adj. & adv.* hap′haz′-), *n.* mere chance; accident. *adj.* not planned; random. *adv.* casually; by chance. —**hap′haz′ard·ly,** *adv.* —**hap′haz′ard·ness,** *n.*
**hap·less** (hap′lis), *adj.* unfortunate; unlucky. —**hap′less·ly,** *adv.* —**hap′less·ness,** *n.*
**hap·ly** (hap′li), *adv.* [Archaic], by chance.
**hap·pen** (hap′'n), *v.i.* [ME. *happenen;* see HAP & -EN], 1. to take place; occur. 2. to be or occur by chance. 3. to have the luck or occasion; chance: as, she *happened* to see it. 4. [Colloq.], to come by chance (*along, by, in,* etc.). —**happen on** (or **upon**), to meet or find by chance. —**happen to,** to be done to; befall.
**hap·pen·ing** (hap′'n-iŋ), *n.* something that happens; occurrence; incident; event.
**hap·pen·stance** (hap′'n-stans′), *n.* [*happen* + circum*stance*], [Colloq.], chance occurrence.
**hap·py** (hap′i), *adj.* [-PIER, -PIEST], [ME. *happi* < *hap*], 1. favored by circumstances; lucky; fortunate. 2. having, showing, or causing a feeling of pleasure, joy, etc.; glad. 3. suitable and clever; apt; felicitous: as, a *happy* suggestion. —**hap′pi·ly,** *adv.* —**hap′pi·ness,** *n.*
**hap·py-go-luck·y** (hap′i-gō-luk′i), *adj.* easygoing; trusting to luck. *adv.* haphazardly; by chance.
**Haps·burg** (haps′bẽrg), *n.* the ruling family of Austria (1276–1918), of Spain (1516–1700), and of the Holy Roman Empire (1438–1806): also sp. **Habsburg.**
**ha·ra-ki·ri** (hä′rä-kêr′i, har′ə-), *n.* [Japan. *hara,* belly + *kiri,* cutting], ritual suicide by disembowelment: it was practiced by high-ranking Japanese to avoid facing disgrace: also **hara-kari** (-kar′i), **hari-kari.**
**ha·rangue** (hə-raŋ′), *n.* [Fr. < ML. *harenga* < Frank. < *hari,* army + *hringa,* a ring, assembly], a long, blustering, or pompous speech; tirade. *v.i.* [-RANGUED, -RANGUING], to give a harangue. *v.t.* to address in a harangue. —**ha·rangu′er,** *n.*
**har·ass** (har′əs, hə-ras′), *v.t.* [< Fr. *harasser* < OFr. *harer,* to set a dog on], 1. to trouble, worry, or torment, as with cares, debts, etc. 2. in *military usage,* to trouble (the enemy) by constant raids or attacks; harry. —**har′ass·er,** *n.* —**har′ass·ing·ly,** *adv.* —**har′ass·ment,** *n.*
**Har·bin** (här′bin′, -bēn′), *n.* a city in central Manchuria: pop., 1,800,000.
**har·bin·ger** (här′bin-jẽr), *n.* [OFr. *herbergeor,* one who provides a lodging < *herberge,* a shelter < OHG.], a person or thing that comes before to announce or indicate what follows; forerunner. *v.t.* to serve as harbinger of; announce; foretell.
**har·bor** (här′bẽr), *n.* [< AS. < *here,* army + *beorg,* a shelter], 1. a place of refuge, safety, etc.; shelter. 2. a protected inlet of a sea, lake, etc., for anchoring ships; port. *v.t.* 1. to serve as a place of protection to; shelter; house. 2. to hold in the mind; cherish: as, he *harbors* no resentment. *v.i.* to take shelter, as in a harbor. —**har′bor·er,** *n.* —**har′bor·less,** *adj.*
**har·bor·age** (här′bẽr-ij), *n.* 1. a shelter for ships; port. 2. *a*) shelter. *b*) lodgings.
**harbor master,** the official in charge of enforcing the regulations governing the use of a harbor.
**har·bour** (här′bẽr), *n., v.t. & v.i.* harbor: Brit. sp. —**har′bour·er,** *n.* —**har′bour·less,** *adj.*
**har·bour·age** (här′bẽr-ij), *n.* harborage: Brit. sp.
**hard** (härd), *adj.* [AS. *heard*], 1. not easily pierced or crushed; firm to the touch; solid and compact: opposed to *soft.* 2. having firm muscles; vigorous and robust. 3. powerful; violent: as, a *hard* blow. 4. demanding great effort or labor; difficult; specif., *a*) difficult to do: as, *hard* work. *b*) difficult to understand or explain: as, a *hard* question. *c*) firmly fastened or tied: as, a *hard* knot. 5. not easily moved; unfeeling: as, a *hard* heart. 6. practical and shrewd: as, a *hard* customer. 7. causing pain or discomfort; specif., *a*) difficult to endure: as, a *hard* life. *b*) harsh; severe; stern: as, a *hard* master. 8. having in solution mineral salts that interfere with the lathering of soap: said of water. 9.

energetic and persistent: as, a *hard* worker. 10. containing much alcohol: said of alcoholic liquors. 11. high in gluten content: as, *hard* wheat. 12. in *phonetics*, popularly, designating *c* and *g* when they are explosive rather than fricative or affricative, as in *cake* and *gun*. ***adv.*** 1. energetically and persistently: as, work *hard*. 2. with vigor, strength, or violence: as, hit *hard*. 3. with difficulty: as, *hard*-earned. 4. firmly; tightly: as, hold on *hard*. 5. close; near: as, we live *hard* by. 6. so as to be or make firm or solid: as, it will freeze *hard*. 7. in *nautical usage*, with vigor and to the fullest extent: as, *Hard* alee! —**be hard on,** 1. to treat severely. 2. to be difficult or unpleasant for. —**hard and fast,** invariable; strict. —**hard of hearing,** partially deaf. —**hard put to it,** having considerable difficulty. —**hard up,** [Colloq.], in great need of something, especially money. —**hard′ness,** ***n.***

**hard-bit·ten** (härd′bit″'n), ***adj.*** stubborn; tough; enduring; dogged.

**hard-boiled** (härd′boild′), ***adj.*** 1. boiled in water until both the white and yolk solidify: said of eggs. 2. [Colloq.], not affected by sentiment, appeal, etc.; callous.

**hard-bound** (härd′bound′), ***adj.*** designating any book bound in a relatively stiff cover: also **hard′-cov′er** (-kuv′ẽr).

**hard cash,** 1. metal coins. 2. ready money; cash.

**hard cider,** fermented apple juice; alcoholic cider.

**hard coal,** anthracite coal.

**hard·en** (här′d'n), ***v.t. & v.i.*** to make or become hard (in various senses). —**hard′en·er,** ***n.***

**hard·fist·ed** (härd′fis′tid), ***adj.*** selfish; stingy; niggardly. —**hard′fist′ed·ness,** ***n.***

**hard·head·ed** (härd′hed′id), ***adj.*** 1. shrewd and unsentimental; practical. 2. stubborn. —**hard′head′ed·ly,** ***adv.*** —**hard′head′ed·ness,** ***n.***

**hard·heart·ed** (härd′här′tid), ***adj.*** unfeeling; pitiless. —**hard′heart′ed·ly,** ***adv.*** —**hard′heart′ed·ness,** ***n.***

**har·di·hood** (här′di-hood′), ***n.*** 1. resolute boldness; daring. 2. impudence; insolence.

**Har·ding, Warren Ga·ma·li·el** (gə-mā′li-əl här′diŋ), 1865–1923; 29th president of the U.S. (1921–1923).

**hard·ly** (härd′li), ***adv.*** 1. with effort or difficulty. 2. severely; harshly. 3. only just; barely; scarcely: often used ironically to mean "not at all." 4. improbably; not likely.

**hard palate,** the bony part of the roof of the mouth, behind the upper teeth.

**hard·pan** (härd′pan′), ***n.*** 1. a layer of hard subsoil difficult to work. 2. the hard, underlying part of anything; firm, solid foundation.

**hard sauce,** a sweet creamy mixture of butter, sugar, and flavoring, served on puddings, etc.

**hard-shell** (härd′shel′), ***adj.*** 1. having a hard shell. 2. [Colloq.], strict; uncompromising; strait-laced.

**hard·ship** (härd′ship), ***n.*** 1. hard circumstances of life. 2. a thing hard to bear.

**hard·tack** (härd′tak′), ***n.*** unleavened bread made in very hard, large wafers: it is traditionally a part of army and navy rations.

**hard·ware** (härd′wâr′), ***n.*** articles made of metal, as tools, nails, fittings, utensils, etc.

**hard·wood** (härd′wood′), ***n.*** 1. any tough, heavy timber with a compact texture. 2. in *forestry*, wood other than that from a conifer; deciduous timber. 3. a tree yielding hardwood.

**har·dy** (här′di), ***adj.*** [-DIER, -DIEST], [< OFr. pp. of *hardir*, to make bold < OHG. *hartjan*, to make hard], 1. bold and resolute; courageous. 2. too bold; rash. 3. able to withstand fatigue, privation, etc. 4. in *gardening*, able to survive the winter without special care: said of plants. —**har′di·ly,** ***adv.*** —**har′di·ness,** ***n.***

**Har·dy, Thomas** (här′di), 1840–1928; English poet and novelist.

**hare** (hâr), ***n.*** [*pl.* HARES, HARE; see PLURAL, II, D, 1], [AS. *hara*], 1. a swift animal of the rodent family, with long ears, soft fur, a cleft upper lip, a short tail, and long, powerful hind legs. 2. the common American rabbit.

**hare·bell** (hâr′bel′), ***n.*** a slender plant with clusters of blue, bell-shaped flowers; bluebell.

**hare·brained** (hâr′brānd′), ***adj.*** having no more intelligence than a hare; reckless, flighty, giddy, rash, etc.

**hare·lip** (hâr′lip′), ***n.*** 1. a congenital deformity consisting of a harelike cleft of the lip. 2. a lip with such a deformity. —**hare′lipped′,** ***adj.***

**ha·rem** (hâr′əm), ***n.*** [< Ar. *harīm*, lit., prohibited (place)], 1. that part of a Moslem's house in which the women live. 2. the wives, concubines, women servants, etc. in a harem. Also **ha·reem** (hä-rēm′).

**har·i·cot** (har′i-kō′), ***n.*** [Fr. < *harigoter*, to cut to pieces], 1. a highly seasoned stew of lamb or mutton. 2. [? < Nahuatl *ayecotli* or < name of stew (because used in it)], *a)* the kidney bean. *b)* its pod or seed.

**ha·ri-ka·ri** (hä′ri-kä′ri, har′ə-kar′i), ***n.*** hara-kiri.

**hark** (härk), ***v.i.*** [? < AS. *heorcnian*, to hearken], to listen carefully: usually in the imperative. —**hark back,** to go back; revert.

**hark·en** (här′k'n), ***v.i. & v.t.*** to hearken. —**hark′en·er,** ***n.***

**Har·lem** (här′ləm), ***n.*** a section of New York City with a large Negro population.

**Har·le·quin** (här′lə-kwin, -kin), ***n.*** [< Fr. < It. *arlecchino* < OFr. *hierlekin*, demon], 1. a comic character in pantomime, who wears a mask and gay, spangled tights of many colors, and sometimes carries a wooden sword. 2. [h-], a clown; buffoon. ***adj.*** [h-], 1. comic; ludicrous. 2. of many colors; colorful.

HARLEQUIN

**har·lot** (här′lət), ***n.*** [OFr., rogue], a prostitute.

**har·lot·ry** (här′lət-ri), ***n.*** prostitution.

**harm** (härm), ***n.*** [AS. *hearm*], 1. hurt; injury; damage. 2. moral wrong; evil. ***v.t.*** to do harm to; hurt; injure; damage. —**harm′er,** ***n.***

**harm·ful** (härm′fəl), ***adj.*** causing harm; hurtful. —**harm′ful·ly,** ***adv.*** —**harm′ful·ness,** ***n.***

**harm·less** (härm′lis), ***adj.*** causing no harm; inoffensive. —**harm′less·ly,** ***adv.*** —**harm′less·ness,** ***n.***

**har·mon·ic** (här-mon′ik), ***adj.*** 1. harmonious in feeling or effect; agreeing. 2. in *music*, *a)* of or in harmony. *b)* designating a tone whose rate of vibration is a precise multiple of that of a given fundamental tone. ***n.*** an overtone, especially one produced by lightly stopping a vibrating string at some specified point. —**har·mon′i·cal·ly,** ***adv.***

**har·mon·i·ca** (här-mon′i-kə), ***n.*** [L.; see HARMONY], a small wind instrument with a series of graduated metal reeds that vibrate and produce tones when air is blown or sucked across them: also called *mouth organ*.

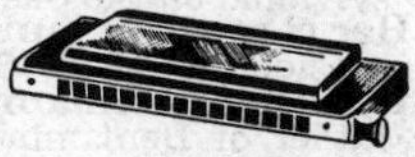

HARMONICA

**har·mon·ics** (här-mon′iks), ***n.pl.*** [construed as sing.], the science of musical sounds.

**har·mo·ni·ous** (här-mō′ni-əs), ***adj.*** [see HARMONY], 1. having parts combined in a proportionate, orderly, or pleasing arrangement. 2. having conforming feelings, ideas, interests, etc. 3. in *music*, having tones combined to give a pleasing effect. —**har·mo′ni·ous·ly,** ***adv.*** —**har·mo′ni·ous·ness,** ***n.***

**har·mo·nist** (här′mə-nist), ***n.*** a musician or composer; esp., an expert in harmony.

**har·mo·ni·um** (här-mō′ni-əm), ***n.*** [see HARMONY], a small keyboard organ in which the tones are produced by forcing air through metal reeds by means of a bellows operated by pedals.

**har·mo·nize** (här′mə-nīz′), ***v.i.*** [-NIZED, -NIZING], to be, sing, or play in harmony; agree. ***v.t.*** 1. to make harmonious; bring into agreement. 2. to add chords to (a melody) so as to form a harmony. —**har′mon·i·za′tion,** ***n.*** —**har′mo·niz′er,** ***n.***

**har·mo·ny** (här′mə-ni), ***n.*** [*pl.* -NIES], [< Fr. < L. < Gr. *harmonia*; ult. < *harmozein*, to fit together], 1. a combination of parts into a proportionate or orderly whole. 2. agreement in feeling, action, ideas, etc.; a being peaceable or friendly. 3. pleasing agreement of color, size, shape, etc. 4. agreeable sounds; music. 5. in *music*, *a)* the pleasing combination of two or more tones in a chord. *b)* structure in terms of the arrangement, progression, etc. of chords. *c)* the study of this structure.

**har·ness** (här′nis), ***n.*** [< OFr. *harneis*, armor], 1. originally, armor for a man or horse. 2. the leather straps and metal pieces by which a horse, mule, etc. is fastened to a vehicle, plow, or load. 3. any trappings or gear similar to this. ***v.t.*** 1. to put harness on. 2. to bring into a condition for producing power: as, they *harnessed* the power of the water. —**in harness,** in or at one's routine work. —**har′ness·er,** ***n.*** —**har′ness·like′,** ***adj.***

**Harold II,** 1022?–1066; last Saxon king of England (1066); killed in the Norman invasion.

**harp** (härp), *n.* [AS. *hearpe*], 1. a musical instrument with strings stretched across an open, triangular frame, played by being plucked with the fingers. 2. a harp-shaped object or implement. *v.i.* 1. to play a harp. 2. to persist in talking or writing tediously or continuously (*on* or *upon* something). *v.t.* [Rare], to give voice to; express. **—harp′er,** *n.* **—harp′like′,** *adj.*

HARP

**harp·ist** (här′pist), *n.* a harp player.

**har·poon** (här-po͞on′), *n.* [Fr. *harpon* < *harpe*, a claw; < Gmc.], a barbed spear with a line attached to it, used for spearing whales or other large sea animals. *v.t.* to strike or kill with a harpoon. **—har·poon′er,** *n.*

**harp·si·chord** (härp′si-kôrd′), *n.* [< obs. Fr. < *harpe* (see HARP) + *chorde* (see CORD)], a stringed musical instrument with a keyboard, forerunner of the piano: the strings are plucked by points rather than struck by hammers, as in the piano.

**Har·py** (här′pi), *n.* [*pl.* -PIES], [< OFr. < L. < Gr. < *harpazein*, to seize], 1. in *Gr. mythology*, any of several hideous, winged monsters with the head of a woman and the body of a bird, who carried off the souls of the dead. 2. [h-], a relentless or greedy person.

HARPY

**har·que·bus** (här′kwi-bəs), *n.* an arquebus, an early type of firearm. **—har′que·bus·ier′** (-êr′), *n.*

**har·ri·dan** (har′i-dən), *n.* [< OFr. *haridelle*, worn-out horse], a haggard, disreputable, shrewish old woman.

**har·ri·er** (har′i-ẽr), *n.* [< *hare* + *-ier*], 1. an English breed of dog, used for hunting hares and rabbits. 2. a cross-country runner.

**har·ri·er** (har′i-ẽr), *n.* 1. one who harries. 2. a hawk that preys on insects and small animals.

**Har·ris, Joel Chand·ler** (chand′lẽr har′is), 1848–1908; U.S. writer.

**Har·ris·burg** (har′is-bũrg′), *n.* the capital of Pennsylvania, on the Susquehanna: pop., 80,000.

**Har·ri·son, Benjamin** (har′ə-s′n), 1833–1901; 23d president of the U.S. (1889–1893).

**Harrison, William Henry,** 1773–1841; grandfather of Benjamin; ninth president of the U.S. (1841).

**har·row** (har′ō), *n.* [prob. < ON.], a heavy frame with spikes or sharp-edged disks, used for leveling and breaking up plowed ground, covering seeds, etc. *v.t.* 1. to draw a harrow over (land). 2. to hurt; wound. 3. to torment; distress; vex. *v.i.* to take harrowing: as, this ground *harrows* well. **—har′row·er,** *n.* **—har′row·ing,** *adj.* **—har′row·ing·ly,** *adv.*

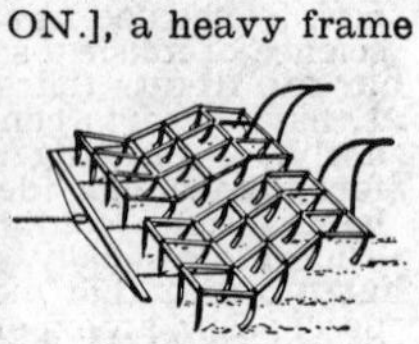
HARROW

**har·ry** (har′i), *v.t.* [-RIED, -RYING], [< AS. *hergian* < base of *here*, army], 1. to raid and destroy or rob; plunder. 2. to torment; worry.

**harsh** (härsh), *adj.* [prob. < ON.], 1. unpleasantly sharp or rough to the eye, ear, taste, or touch; grating, glaring, bitter, coarse, etc. 2. unpleasantly crude or abrupt. 3. rough, crude, or forbidding in appearance. 4. stern; severe; cruel. **—harsh′ly,** *adv.* **—harsh′ness,** *n.*

**hart** (härt), *n.* [*pl.* HARTS, HART; see PLURAL, II, D, 1], [AS. *heor(o)t*], a male deer, especially a red deer after its fifth year; stag.

**Harte, Bret** (bret härt), (*Francis Brett Harte*), 1836–1902; U.S. writer.

**har·te·beest** (här′tə-bēst′, härt′bēst′), *n.* [*pl.* -BEESTS, -BEEST; see PLURAL, II, D, 1], [S.Afr.D.; *harte*, hart + *beest*, beast], a large, swift South African antelope having long horns curved backward at the tips: also **hart′beest′.**

**Hart·ford** (härt′fẽrd), *n.* the capital of Connecticut, in the central part: pop., 162,000.

**harts·horn** (härts′hôrn′), *n.* 1. ammonia in water solution. 2. ammonium carbonate, used in smelling salts; sal volatile: so called because formerly obtained from deer's antlers.

**har·um-scar·um** (hâr′əm-skâr′əm), *adj.* [prob. < *hare* + *scare* + *'em*], reckless; rash; wild; irresponsible. *adv.* in a harum-scarum manner. *n.* a harum-scarum person or action.

**har·us·pex** (hə-rus′peks, har′əs-peks′), *n.* [*pl.* -PICES (hə-rus′pi-sēz′)], [L.], a soothsayer in ancient Rome, who professed to foretell the future by interpreting the entrails of sacrificial animals. **—ha·rus·pi·cal** (hə-rus′pi-k'l), *adj.*

**har·vest** (här′vist), *n.* [AS. *hærfest*], 1. the time of the year when grain, fruit, vegetables, etc. are reaped and gathered in. 2. a season's yield of grain, fruit, etc.; crop. 3. the gathering in of a crop. 4. the outcome of any effort. *v.t. & v.i.* 1. to gather in (a crop, etc.). 2. to gather the crop from (a field). **—har′vest·ing,** *n.*

**har·vest·er** (här′vis-tẽr), *n.* 1. a person who gathers in a crop of grain, fruit, etc.; reaper. 2. a harvesting machine.

**har·vest·man** (här′vist-mən), *n.* [*pl.* -MEN (-mən)], 1. a man who harvests. 2. a daddy-longlegs.

**harvest moon,** the full moon at or about the time of the autumnal equinox, September 22 or 23.

**Har·vey, William** (här′vi), 1578–1657; English physician; discovered circulation of the blood.

**has** (haz; *unstressed* həz, əz), the 3d pers. sing., pres. indic., of **have.**

**has-been** (haz′bin′), *n.* [Colloq.], a person or thing whose popularity or effectiveness is past.

**ha·sen·pfef·fer** (hä′s'n-fef′ẽr), *n.* [G. < *hase*, rabbit + *pfeffer*, pepper], a German dish of marinated rabbit, seasoned and braised.

**hash** (hash), *v.t.* [< Fr. < *hache*, a hatchet], 1. to chop (meat and vegetables) into small pieces for cooking. 2. [Colloq.], to make a mess of; bungle. *n.* 1. a chopped mixture of cooked meat and vegetables, usually baked or browned. 2. a mixture. 3. a hodgepodge; muddle. **—settle one's hash,** [Colloq.], to overcome or subdue one.

**hash house,** [Slang], a cheap restaurant.

**hash·ish** (hash′ēsh, -ish), *n.* [Ar. *hashīsh*, dried hemp], a drug made from the leaves and stalks of Indian hemp, used in the Orient for its intoxicating and narcotic effects: also **hash′eesh** (-ēsh).

**has·n't** (haz′'nt), has not.

**hasp** (hasp, häsp), *n.* [AS. *hæpse*], a hinged metal fastening for a door, window, lid, etc.; esp., a metal piece fitted over a staple or into a hole and fastened by a bolt or padlock. *v.t.* to fasten or lock as with a hasp.

HASP

**has·sle, has·sel** (has′'l), *n.* [? < dial. *hassle*, to breathe noisily], [Slang], a heated discussion; a squabble.

**has·sock** (has′ək), *n.* [AS. *hassuc* (clump of) coarse grass], 1. a thick clump of grass. 2. a firmly stuffed cushion used as a footstool or seat.

**hast** (hast; *unstressed* həst), archaic 2d pers. sing., pres. indic., of **have**: used with *thou.*

**has·tate** (has′tāt), *adj.* [< L. < *hasta*, a spear], shaped like a spearhead, as certain leaves.

**haste** (hāst), *n.* [OFr. *haste* < Gmc.], 1. quickness of motion; hurrying. 2. careless hurrying: as, *haste* makes waste. 3. necessity for hurrying; urgency. *v.t. & v.i.* [Rare], to hasten. **—in haste,** 1. in a hurry. 2. in too great a hurry. **—make haste,** to hasten; hurry.

**has·ten** (hās′'n), *v.t.* to make hurry; speed up. *v.i.* to move swiftly; be quick. **—has′ten·er,** *n.*

**hast·y** (hās′ti), *adj.* [-IER, -IEST], 1. done or made with haste; hurried. 2. done or made too quickly and with too little thought. 3. short-tempered or impetuous. 4. showing irritation or impatience. **—hast′i·ly,** *adv.* **—hast′i·ness,** *n.*

**hasty pudding,** 1. mush made of corn meal. 2. [Brit.], mush made of flour or oatmeal.

**hat** (hat), *n.* [AS. *hætt*], a head covering, usually with a brim and a crown. *v.t.* [HATTED, HATTING], to cover or provide with a hat. **—pass the hat,** to take up a collection. **—take one's hat off to,** to salute; compliment. **—talk through one's hat,** [Colloq.], to talk nonsense. **—under one's hat,** [Colloq.], secret. **—hat′less,** *adj.*

**hat·band** (hat′band′), *n.* a band of cloth around the crown of a hat, just above the brim.

**hatch** (hatch), *v.t.* [ME. *hacchen*], 1. to bring forth (young) from an egg or eggs by applying warmth. 2. to bring forth young from (an egg or eggs). 3. *a*) to bring (a plan, idea, etc.) into existence. *b*) to plot. *v.i.* 1. to bring forth young: said of eggs. 2. to come forth from the egg. *n.* 1. the process of hatching. 2. the brood hatched. **—hatch′er,** *n.*

**hatch** (hach), *n.* [AS. *hæc*, grating], 1. the lower half of a door, gate, etc. with two separately movable halves. 2. *a*) an opening in a ship's deck through which cargo can be lowered. *b*) a similar opening in the floor or roof of a building. 3. a lid for such an opening.

**hatch** (hach), *v.t.* [< OFr. < *hache*, an ax], to mark or engrave with fine, crossed or parallel lines.

**hatch·el** (hach′əl), *n.* [ME. *hecchel*], a comblike instrument for cleaning and dressing flax, hemp.

etc. *v.t.* [-ELED or -ELLED, -ELING or -ELLING], to clean and dress (flax, hemp, etc.) with a hatchel. **—hatch′el·er, hatch′el·ler,** *n.*

**hatch·er·y** (hach′ẽr-i), *n.* [*pl.* -IES], a place for hatching eggs, as of fish or poultry.

**hatch·et** (hach′it), *n.* [< OFr. dim. of *hache*, an ax], 1. a small ax with a short handle, for use with one hand. 2. a tomahawk. **—bury the hatchet,** to stop fighting; make peace. **—dig** (or **take**) **up the hatchet,** to start fighting.

**hatch·ing** (hach′iŋ), *n.* [see HATCH (to engrave)], 1. the drawing or engraving of fine, parallel or crossed lines to show shading. 2. such lines.

**hatch·ment** (hach′mənt), *n.* [alt. < *achievement*], in *heraldry*, a square tablet or panel bearing the coat of arms of a man who has recently died.

**hatch·way** (hach′wā′), *n.* an opening for cargo in a ship's deck, or a similar opening in the floor or roof of a building; hatch.

**hate** (hāt), *v.t.* [HATED, HATING], [AS. *hatian*], 1. to have strong dislike or ill will for; despise. 2. to dislike; wish to avoid: as, he *hates* to work. *v.i.* to feel hatred. *n.* 1. a strong feeling of dislike or ill will. 2. a person or thing hated. **—hate′a·ble, hat′a·ble,** *adj.* **—hat′er,** *n.*

**hate·ful** (hāt′f'l), *adj.* 1. [Rare], feeling or showing hate; malevolent. 2. deserving hate; odious. **—hate′ful·ly,** *adv.* **—hate′ful·ness,** *n.*

**hath** (hath), archaic 3d pers. sing., pres. indic., of **have.**

**hat·rack** (hat′rak′), *n.* a rack, set of hooks, etc. to hold hats.

**ha·tred** (hā′trid), *n.* [ME.; *hate* + AS. *ræden*, state], strong dislike or ill will; hate.

**hat·ter** (hat′ẽr), *n.* one who makes or sells hats.

**hau·ber·geon** (hô′bẽr-jən), *n.* a habergeon.

**hau·berk** (hô′bẽrk), *n.* [< OFr. < OHG. *halsberc*, gorget < *hals*, the neck + *bergan*, to protect], a medieval coat of armor, usually of chain mail.

**haugh·ty** (hô′ti), *adj.* [-TIER, -TIEST], [< OFr. *haut*, high < L. *altus* (with *h-* after OHG. *hoh*, high)], 1. having or showing great pride in oneself and disdain or contempt for others. 2. [Archaic], lofty; noble. **—haugh′ti·ly,** *adv.* **—haugh′ti·ness,** *n.*

**haul** (hôl), *v.t.* [< OFr. *haler*, to draw < OFrank. *halōn*, to fetch], 1. to move by pulling or drawing; drag. 2. to transport by wagon, truck, etc.: as, he *hauls* coal. 3. in *nautical usage*, to change the course of (a ship). *v.i.* 1. to pull; tug. 2. to shift direction: said of the wind. 3. to change one's opinion or course of action. 4. in *nautical usage*, to change the course of a ship. *n.* 1. the act of hauling; pull; tug. 2. the amount gained, caught, etc. at one time; catch: as, a good *haul* of fish. 3. the distance or route over which something is transported: as, a long *haul*. 4. the load transported. **—haul off,** [Colloq.], to draw the arm back before hitting. **—haul on** (or **to, onto**) **the wind,** to haul in sails in order to sail closer to the wind. **—haul up,** to sail nearer the direction of the wind. **—haul′er,** *n.*

**haul·age** (hôl′ij), *n.* 1. the act or process of hauling. 2. the force used in hauling something. 3. the charge made for hauling.

**haunch** (hônch, hänch), *n.* [< OFr. *hanche* < Gmc.], 1. the part of the body including the hip, buttock, and thickest part of the thigh; hindquarter. 2. an animal's loin and leg together.

**haunt** (hônt, hänt), *v.t.* [< OFr. *hanter*, to frequent], 1. to visit (a place) often or continually. 2. to annoy (a person) by constant visiting, following, etc. 3. to recur frequently to: as, memories *haunted* her. 4. to fill the atmosphere of; pervade: as, gay memories *haunt* the house. *n.* 1. a place often visited: as, a saloon that was the *haunt* of criminals. 2. (*also* hant), [Dial.], a ghost. **—haunt′er,** *n.*

**haunt·ed** (hôn′tid, hän′-), *adj.* supposedly frequented by ghosts: as, a *haunted* house.

**haunt·ing** (hôn′tiŋ, hän′-), *adj.* recurring often to the mind; not easily forgotten: as, a *haunting* melody. **—haunt′ing·ly,** *adv.*

**haut·boy** (hō′boi, ō′-), *n.* [< Fr. < *haut*, high (pitch) + *bois*, wood], an oboe.

**hau·teur** (hō-tũr′; Fr. ō′tẽr′), *n.* [Fr. < *haut*, high, proud], haughtiness; disdainful pride.

‡**haut monde** (ō′mōnd′), [Fr.], high society.

**Ha·van·a** (hə-van′ə), *n.* 1. the capital of Cuba: pop., 785,000: Spanish name, *Habana*. 2. a cigar made in Cuba or of Cuban tobacco.

**have** (hav; *unstressed* həv, əv), *v.t.* [HAD, HAVING], [AS. *habban*], 1. to hold; own; possess: as, he *has* money. 2. to possess as a part, feature, etc.: as, the week *has* seven days. 3. to experience; undergo: as, *have* a good time. 4. to grasp or hold mentally; know: as, I *have* an idea. 5. to believe or declare: as, so gossip *has* it. 6. to get; take; acquire: as, *have* a drink. 7. to beget (offspring). 8. to perform; engage in: as, we *had* an argument. 9. to cause to; cause to be: as, *have* this done at once. 10. to be in a certain relation to: as, we *had* empty seats beside us. 11. to permit; tolerate: as, I won't *have* this noise! 12. [Colloq.], to hold in a position of disadvantage: as, I *had* my opponent now. *Have* is used as an auxiliary to form phrases expressing completed action, as in the perfect tenses (e.g., I *had* left), and with infinitives to express obligation or necessity (e.g., we *have* to go). *Have got* often replaces *have*. *Have* is conjugated in the present indicative (I) *have*, (he, she, it) *has*, (we, you, they) *have;* in the past indicative (I, he, she, it, we, you, they) *had*. Archaic forms are (thou) *hast, hadst*, (he, she, it) *hath*. *n.* [Colloq.], a person or nation with relatively much wealth or rich resources. **—have at,** to attack; strike. **—have done,** to stop; finish. **—have it in for,** [Colloq.], to bear a grudge against. **—have it out,** to settle a conflict by fighting or discussion. **—have on,** to be wearing. **—have to do with,** 1. to be related to or connected with. 2. to deal with.

**ha·ven** (hā′v'n), *n.* [AS. *hæfen*], 1. a port; harbor. 2. any place of shelter and safety; refuge. *v.t.* to provide a haven for. **—ha′ven·less,** *adj.*

**have-not** (hav′not′), *n.* [Colloq.], a person or nation relatively unwealthy or poor in resources.

**have·n't** (hav′'nt), have not.

**hav·er·sack** (hav′ẽr-sak′), *n.* [< Fr. < G. *habersack*, lit., sack of oats], a canvas bag for provisions, worn on the back by soldiers and hikers.

**hav·oc** (hav′ək), *n.* [< OFr. *havot*, plunder; of Gmc. origin], great destruction and devastation. *v.t.* [-OCKED, -OCKING], [Archaic], to lay waste; devastate. **—cry havoc,** formerly, to give (an army) the signal for pillage. **—play havoc with,** to cause great harm to; destroy; ruin.

**Ha·vre** (hä′vẽr, häv′rə), *n.* a seaport in NW France: pop., 140,000: French name, *Le Havre*.

**haw** (hô), *n.* [AS. *haga*], 1. the berry of the hawthorn. 2. the hawthorn.

**haw** (hô), *interj.* & *n.* [? < echoic *geehaw*, meaning "a horse's neigh"], a word of command to a horse, ox, etc., meaning "turn to the left!" *v.t.* & *v.i.* to turn to the left. Opposed to *gee*.

**haw** (hô), *v.i.* [echoic], to hesitate in speaking: usually in *hem and haw*. *interj.* & *n.* a conventionalized expression of the sound often made by a speaker when hesitating briefly.

**Ha·wai·i** (hə-wä′ē, -wä′yə), *n.* 1. a State of the U.S., consisting of a group of islands in the North Pacific: a Territory, 1900–1959: area, 6,415 sq. mi.; pop., 633,000; capital, Honolulu. 2. the largest of the Hawaiian Islands.

**Ha·wai·ian** (hə-wä′yən), *adj.* of Hawaii, its people, language, etc. *n.* 1. a native or inhabitant of Hawaii; specif., a Polynesian. 2. the Polynesian language of the Hawaiians: abbrev. **Haw.**

**Hawaiian Islands,** the islands comprising the State of Hawaii.

**hawk** (hôk), *n.* [AS. *hafoc*], any bird of prey of a family characterized by short, rounded wings, a long tail, and a hooked beak and claws; hawks include the falcons, buzzards, harriers, and kites, but not vultures and eagles. *v.i.* to hunt birds with the help of hawks. *v.t.* to prey on as a hawk does. **—hawk′er,** *n.* **—hawk′ing,** *n.* **—hawk′like′,** *adj.*

**hawk** (hôk), *v.t.* & *v.i.* [< *hawker* (peddler)], 1. to advertise or peddle (goods) in the streets by shouting. 2. to spread (rumors, etc.).

**hawk** (hôk), *v.i.* [echoic], to clear the throat audibly. *v.t.* to bring up (phlegm) by coughing. *n.* an audible clearing of the throat.

**hawk·er** (hôk′ẽr), *n.* [prob. < MLG. *hoker*] a street peddler; huckster.

**hawk-eyed** (hôk′īd′), *adj.* keen-sighted as a hawk.

**hawk moth,** a moth with a thick, tapering body, slender wings, and a long feeding tube used for sucking the nectar of flowers.

**hawks·bill, hawk's-bill** (hôks′bil′), *n.* a small turtle found in tropical seas, having a hawklike beak and a horny shell from which tortoise shell is obtained: also **hawk′bill′, hawksbill turtle.**

**hawk·weed** (hôk′wēd′), *n.* a weedy plant of the composite family, with red, yellow, or orange flowers.

**hawse** (hôz), *n.* [prob. < ON. *hals*, the neck], 1. that part of the bow of a ship containing the hawse;

holes. 2. a hawsehole. 3. the space between the bow of a ship and the anchors.

**hawse·hole** (hôz′hōl′), *n.* any of the holes in a ship's bow through which a hawser is passed.

**haw·ser** (hô′zẽr), *n.* [OFr. *haulser* < LL. < L. *altus*, high], a large rope or small cable by which a ship is anchored, towed, etc.

**haw·thorn** (hô′thôrn′), *n.* [< AS. < *haga*, hedge + *thorn*], a spiny shrub or small tree of the rose family, with fragrant flowers of white, pink, or red, and red berries (called *haws*).

**Haw·thorne, Nathaniel** (hô′thôrn′), 1804–1864; U.S. novelist and writer of short stories.

**hay** (hā), *n.* [AS. *hieg*], grass, clover, etc. cut and dried for use as fodder. *v.i.* to mow grass, clover, etc., and spread it out to dry. **—hit the hay,** [Slang], to go to bed. **—make hay while the sun shines,** to make the most of an opportunity.

**hay·cock** (hā′kok′), *n.* a small heap of hay drying in a field.

**Hay·dn, Franz Jo·seph** (fränts yō′zef hī′d'n), 1732–1809; Austrian composer.

**Hayes, Ruth·er·ford Bir·chard** (ruth′ẽr-fẽrd bũr′chẽrd hāz), 1822–1893; 19th president of the U.S. (1877–1881).

**hay fever,** an acute inflammation of the eyes and upper respiratory tract: it is an allergic reaction, caused by the pollen of some grasses and trees.

**hay·field** (hā′fēld′), *n.* a field of grass, clover, etc. to be made into hay.

**hay·loft** (hā′lôft′), *n.* a loft, or upper story, in a barn or stable, for storing hay; haymow.

**hay·mak·er** (hā′māk′ẽr), *n.* 1. a person who tosses cut hay and spreads it out to dry. 2. [Slang], a powerful blow with the fist.

**hay·mow** (hā′mou′), *n.* 1. hay stored in a barn. 2. a hayloft.

**hay·seed** (hā′sēd′), *n.* 1. grass seed shaken from mown hay. 2. [Slang], a person with the awkwardness and simplicity regarded as characteristic of rural people: somewhat contemptuous term.

**hay·stack** (hā′stak′), *n.* a large heap of hay piled up outdoors: also **hay′rick′** (-rik′).

**Hay·ti** (hā′ti), *n.* Haiti. **—Hay′ti·an** (-ti-ən, -shən), *adj. & n.*

**Hay·ward** (hā′wẽrd), *n.* a city in W California: suburb of Oakland: pop., 73,000.

**hay·wire** (hā′wīr′), *n.* wire for tying up bales of hay, straw, etc. *adj.* [Slang], 1. out of order; confused; wrong. 2. crazy.

**haz·ard** (haz′ẽrd), *n.* [OFr., game of dice; ? < Ar. *al-zār*, the die], 1. an early game of chance played with dice. 2. chance. 3. risk; peril; danger. 4. any obstacle on a golf course. *v.t.* to chance; risk; venture. **—at all hazards,** in spite of everything. **—haz′ard·a·ble,** *adj.* **—haz′ard·er,** *n.* **—haz′ard·less,** *adj.*

**haz·ard·ous** (haz′ẽr-dəs), *adj.* risky; dangerous. **—haz′ard·ous·ly,** *adv.* **—haz′ard·ous·ness,** *n.*

**haze** (hāz), *n.* [prob. < LG. dial.], 1. a thin vapor of fog, smoke, dust, etc. in the air. 2. slight confusion or vagueness of mind.

**haze** (hāz), *v.t.* [HAZED, HAZING], [OFr. *haser*, to irritate], to initiate or discipline (fellow students) by means of horseplay, practical jokes, etc., often in the nature of humiliating or painful ordeals. **—haz′er,** *n.* **—haz′ing,** *n.*

**ha·zel** (hā′z'l), *n.* [AS. *hæsel*], 1. a tree or shrub of the birch family, with edible nuts. 2. a reddish brown. *adj.* 1. of the hazel. 2. light reddish-brown. **—ha′zel·ly,** *adv.*

**ha·zel·nut** (hā′z'l-nut′), *n.* the small, edible, roundish nut of the hazel; filbert.

**Haz·litt, William** (haz′lit), 1778–1830; English essayist and critic.

**ha·zy** (hā′zi), *adj.* [-ZIER, -ZIEST], 1. characterized by haze; somewhat foggy or smoky. 2. somewhat vague, obscure, or indefinite: as, *hazy* thinking. **—ha′zi·ly,** *adv.* **—ha′zi·ness,** *n.*

**Hb,** *the symbol for* hemoglobin.

**H-bomb** (āch′bom′), *n.* hydrogen bomb.

**hd.,** head.

**hdqrs.,** headquarters.

**he** (hē; *unstressed* hi, ē, i), *pron.* [for *pl.* see THEY], [AS.], 1. the man, boy, or male animal previously mentioned. 2. the one; anyone: as, *he* who laughs last laughs best. *He* is the nominative case form, *him* the objective, *his* the possessive, and *himself* the intensive and reflexive, of the masculine third personal pronoun. *n.* a man, boy, or male animal: as, our dog is a *he*.

**He,** in *chemistry*, helium.

**head** (hed), *n.* [AS. *heafod*], 1. the top part of the body in man, the apes, etc., or the front part in most other animals: in higher animals it is a bony structure containing the brain, and including the eyes, ears, nose, and mouth. 2. the head as the seat of reason, memory, and imagination; mind; intelligence: as, use your *head*. 3. a person: as, dinner at five dollars a *head*. 4. [*pl.* HEAD], the head as a unit of counting: as, ten *head* of cattle. 5. the main side of a coin, usually showing a head. 6. the highest or uppermost part or thing; top; specif., *a*) the top of a page, column, etc. *b*) a topic of a section, chapter, etc. *c*) a headline. *d*) froth floating on newly poured effervescent beverages. *e*) the end of a cask or drum. 7. the foremost part of a thing; front; specif., *a*) the front part of a ship; bow. *b*) the front position, as of a column of marching men. *c*) either end of something. 8. the projecting part of something; specif., *a*) the part designed for holding, striking, etc.: as, the *head* of a nail. *b*) a headland. *c*) a projecting place, as in a boil, where pus is about to break through. *d*) the part of a tape recorder that imposes or plays back the magnetic arrangements on the tape. 9. the membrane stretched across the end of a drum, tambourine, etc. 10. the source of a river or stream. 11. a source of water kept at some height to supply a mill, etc. 12. pressure: as, a *head* of steam. 13. a position of leadership. 14. a foremost person; leader, ruler, etc. 15. a headmaster. 16. a crisis or culmination: as, things may soon come to a *head*. 17. strength; momentum: as, the campaign is gathering *head*. 18. [Nautical Slang], a toilet. 19. [Slang], a drug addict: often in combination. 20. in *botany*, *a*) a flat or rounded cluster of little flowers. *b*) a large, compact bud: as, a *head* of cabbage. 21. in *music*, the rounded part of a note, at the end of the stem. *adj.* 1. most important; principal; first. 2. to be found at the top or front. 3. striking against the front: as, *head* currents. *v.t.* 1. to be chief of; command. 2. to lead; precede. 3. to supply with a head. 4. [Rare], to behead. 5. to trim the higher part from (a tree or plant); poll. 6. to cause to go in a specified direction. *v.i.* 1. to grow or come to a head. 2. to set out; go: as, they *headed* eastward. **—by a head,** by a small margin. **—come to a head,** 1. to be about to suppurate, as a boil. 2. to culminate. **—give one his head,** to let one do as he likes. **—go to one's head,** 1. to confuse or intoxicate one. 2. to make one vain. **—hang (or hide) one's head,** to lower one's head or conceal one's face as in shame. **—head and shoulders above,** definitely superior to. **—head off,** to get ahead of and intercept. **—head over heels,** 1. deeply; completely. 2. hurriedly; recklessly. **—heads up!** [Colloq.], look out! be careful! **—keep (or lose) one's head,** to keep (or lose) one's poise, self-control, etc. **—lay (or put) heads together,** to consult or scheme together. **—make head,** to go forward; advance. **—not make head or tail of,** not to understand. **—on (or upon) one's head,** as one's responsibility or misfortune. **—out of (or off) one's head,** [Colloq.], 1. crazy. 2. raving. **—over one's head,** 1. too difficult for one to understand. 2. to a higher authority. **—take it into one's head,** to conceive the notion, plan, etc. **—turn one's head,** 1. to make one dizzy. 2. to make one vain.

**-head,** -hood, as in *godhead*.

**head·ache** (hed′āk′), *n.* 1. a continuous pain in the head. 2. [Colloq.], a cause of worry or trouble.

**head·board** (hed′bôrd′, -bōrd′), *n.* a board or frame that forms the head of a bed, etc.

**head·cheese** (hed′chēz′), *n.* a loaf of jellied and seasoned meat from the head and feet of hogs.

**head·dress** (hed′dres′), *n.* 1. a covering or decoration for the head. 2. the style in which hair is worn or arranged; coiffure.

**head·ed** (hed′id), *adj.* 1. formed into a head, as cabbage. 2. having a heading. 3. having a head or heads: usually in hyphenated compounds, as, clear-*headed*, two-*headed*.

**head·er** (hed′ẽr), *n.* 1. a person or device that puts heads on pins, nails, rivets, etc. 2. a machine that takes off the heads of grain and loads them into a truck. 3. [Colloq.], a headlong fall or dive. 4. in *masonry*, a brick or stone laid across the thickness of a wall with one end toward the face of the wall.

**head·first** (hed′fũrst′), *adv.* 1. with the head in front; headlong. 2. recklessly; rashly. Also **head·fore·most** (hed′fôr′mōst′, -fōr′məst).

**head·gear** (hed′gêr′), *n.* 1. a covering for the head. 2. the harness for the head of a horse, mule, etc.

**head-hunt·er** (hed′hun′tẽr), *n.* a member of any of certain primitive tribes who remove the heads of slain enemies and preserve them as trophies. **—head′-hunt′ing,** *n. & adj.*

**head·ing** (hed′iŋ), *n.* 1. something forming or used to form the head, top, edge, or front. 2. an inscription at the top of a chapter, page, etc., giving the title, topic, etc.

**head·land** (hed′lənd), *n.* a cape; promontory.

**head·less** (hed′lis), *adj.* 1. without a head. 2. without a leader. 3. stupid; foolish.
**head·light** (hed′līt), *n.* 1. a light with a reflector and lens, at the front of a vehicle. 2. a white light at the masthead of a ship.
**head·line** (hed′līn′), *n.* 1. a line at the top of a page, giving the running title, page number, etc. 2. printed lines at the top of a newspaper article, giving the topic. *v.t.* [-LINED, -LINING], 1. to provide with a headline. 2. to give (a performer or performance) featured billing.
**head·lin·er** (hed′līn′ẽr), *n.* a featured entertainer.
**head·long** (hed′lôŋ′), *adv.* [folk-etymologized form < ME. *hedelinge*(*s*)], 1. with the head first; headforemost. 2. with uncontrolled speed and force. 3. recklessly; rashly. *adj.* 1. having the head first. 2. moving with uncontrolled speed and force. 3. reckless; rash.
**head·man** (hed′mən, -man′), *n.* [*pl.* -MEN], a leader; chief; foreman.
**head·mas·ter** (hed′mas′tẽr, -mäs′-), *n.* in certain schools, the principal: also **head master.**
**head·mis·tress** (hed′mis′tris), *n.* in certain schools, a woman principal: also **head mistress.**
**head·most** (hed′mōst′), *adj.* foremost; in the lead.
**head-on** (hed′on′), *adj.* & *adv.* with the head or front foremost: as, a *head-on* collision.
**head·phone** (hed′fōn′), *n.* 1. a telephone or radio receiver held to the ear by a band over the head. 2. *usually pl.* a pair of such receivers.
**head·piece** (hed′pēs′), *n.* 1. a helmet, cap, or other covering for the head. 2. a headphone. 3. the head; mind; intellect.
**head·quar·ters** (hed′kwôr′tẽrz), *n.pl.* [sometimes construed as sing.], 1. the main office, or center of operations, of one in command, as in an army or police force. 2. the main office in any organization.
**head·set** (hed′set′), *n.* a headphone.
**head·ship** (hed′ship′), *n.* the position or authority of a chief or leader; leadership; command.
**heads·man** (hedz′mən), *n.* [*pl.* -MEN], a person who executes by beheading.
**head·stall** (hed′stôl′), *n.* the part of a bridle or halter that fits over a horse's head.
**head start,** a start ahead of other contestants or competitors, taken or given as an advantage.
**head·stock** (hed′stok′), *n.* the part of a lathe supporting the spindle or chuck.
**head·stone** (hed′stōn′), *n.* 1. cornerstone. 2. a stone marker placed at the head of a grave.
**head·stream** (hed′strēm′), *n.* a stream forming the source of another and larger stream.
**head·strong** (hed′strôŋ′), *adj.* 1. determined not to follow orders, advice, etc. but to do as one pleases; self-willed. 2. showing such determination: as, *headstrong* desire. —**head′strong′ness,** *n.*
**head·wait·er** (hed′wāt′ẽr), *n.* a supervisor of waiters in a restaurant, night club, etc.
**head·wa·ters** (hed′wô′tẽrz, -wät′ẽrz), *n.pl.* the small streams that are the sources of a river.
**head·way** (hed′wā′), *n.* 1. forward motion. 2. progress in work, etc. 3. clearance overhead. 4. the difference in time or miles between two trains, ships, etc. traveling the same route.
**head wind,** a wind blowing in the direction directly opposite the course of a ship or aircraft.
**head·work** (hed′wũrk′), *n.* mental effort; thinking.
**head·y** (hed′i), *adj.* [-IER, -IEST], 1. impetuous; rash; reckless. 2. tending to affect the head; intoxicating. —**head′i·ly,** *adv.* —**head′i·ness,** *n.*
**heal** (hēl), *v.t.* [AS. *hælan* < *hal,* sound, healthy], 1. to make well or healthy again. 2. to cure (a disease) or mend (a wound, sore, etc.). 3. to free from grief, troubles, evil, etc. 4. to remedy (grief, troubles, etc.). *v.i.* 1. to become well or healthy again; be cured. 2. to become scarred or closed: said of a wound. —**heal′er,** *n.* —**heal′ing,** *adj.* & *n.*
**health** (helth), *n.* [AS. *hælth* < *hal,* sound, healthy + *-th*], 1. physical and mental well-being; freedom from disease, etc. 2. condition of body or mind: as, bad *health.* 3. a wish for a person's health and happiness, expressed as in a toast.
**health·ful** (helth′fəl), *adj.* 1. helping to produce or maintain health; wholesome. 2. [Rare], healthy. —**health′ful·ly,** *adv.* —**health′ful·ness,** *n.*
**health·y** (hel′thi), *adj.* [-IER, -IEST], 1. having good health. 2. showing or resulting from good health: as, a *healthy* appetite. 3. healthful. —**health′i·ly,** *adv.* —**health′i·ness,** *n.*
**heap** (hēp), *n.* [< AS. *heap,* a troop, band], 1. many things lying together in a pile; mass. 2. [Colloq.], a large amount; great deal. *v.t.* 1. to make a heap of. 2. to give in large amounts: as, he *heaped* gifts upon me. 3. to fill (a plate, etc.) full or to overflowing. *v.i.* to accumulate or rise in a heap, or pile. —**heap′er,** *n.*
**hear** (hêr), *v.t.* [HEARD (hũrd), HEARING], [AS. *hieran, heran*], 1. to become aware of (sounds) by the ear. 2. to listen to and consider: as, *hear* this piece of news. 3. to listen to formally: as, he will *hear* your lessons now. 4. to conduct a hearing of (a law case, etc.); try. 5. to consent to; grant: as, he *heard* my entreaty. 6. to permit to speak: as, I cannot *hear* you now. 7. to be informed of; learn. *v.i.* 1. to be able to hear sounds. 2. to listen. 3. to learn. —**hear from,** to get a letter, telegram, etc. from. —**hear! hear!** well said! bravo! —**not hear of,** not assent to or permit. —**hear′er,** *n.*
**hear·ing** (hêr′iŋ), *n.* 1. the act or process of perceiving sounds. 2. the sense by which sounds are perceived. 3. opportunity to speak, sing, etc.; audience. 4. an investigation or trial before a judge, etc. 5. the distance that a sound will carry: as, he is within *hearing.*
**heark·en** (här′k'n), *v.i.* [< AS. *heorcnean* < *hieran;* see HEAR], to give careful attention; listen carefully. *v.t.* [Archaic], to hear; heed. Also sp. **harken.** —**heark′en·er,** *n.*
**hear·say** (hêr′sā′), *n.* common talk or report; gossip. *adj.* based on hearsay.
**hearse** (hũrs), *n.* [< OFr. < L. *hirpex,* a harrow], 1. a vehicle for carrying a dead body to a grave. 2. [Archaic], a bier.
**heart** (härt), *n.* [AS. *heorte*], 1. the hollow, muscular organ that circulates the blood by alternate dilation and contraction. 2. any place or part centrally located like the heart: as, *hearts* of celery, the *heart* of the city. 3. the central, vital, or main part; essence; core. 4. the human heart considered as the center of emotions, personal attributes, etc.; specif., *a*) inmost thoughts and feelings: as, I know in my *heart. b*) one's emotional nature; disposition: as, a kind *heart. c*) any of various humane feelings; love, sympathy, etc. *d*) mood; feeling: as, I have a heavy *heart. e*) spirit or courage: as, take *heart.* 5. a person loved or admired in some way: as, he is a valiant *heart.* 6. *a*) a conventionalized design of a heart, shaped like this (♥). *b*) anything in this shape. 7. any of a suit of playing cards marked with such symbols in red. 8. *pl.* this suit of cards. 9. *pl.* a card game in which the object is to avoid getting hearts in the tricks taken. —**after one's own heart,** that suits or pleases one perfectly. —**at heart,** in one's innermost nature; basically. —**break one's heart,** to overwhelm one with grief or disappointment. —**by heart,** by memorizing or from memory. —**change of heart,** a change of mind, affections, etc. —**eat one's heart out,** to be overcome with grief, remorse, or longing. —**have one's heart in one's mouth** (or **boots**), to be full of fear or nervous anticipation. —**have one's heart in the right place,** to be well-meaning. —**heart and soul,** with all one's effort, love, enthusiasm, etc. —**lose one's heart to,** to fall in love with. —**set one's heart on,** to have a fixed desire for. —**take heart,** to have more courage or confidence. —**take to heart,** 1. to consider seriously. 2. to be troubled by. —**to one's heart's content,** as much as one desires. —**wear one's heart on one's sleeve,** to behave so that one's feelings are plainly evident. —**with all one's heart,** with complete sincerity, devotion, etc.

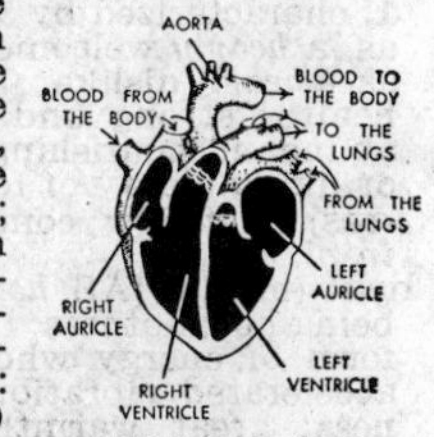

HUMAN HEART

**heart·ache** (härt′āk′), *n.* sorrow; grief.
**heart·beat** (härt′bēt′), *n.* one pulsation, or full contraction and dilation, of the heart: also **heart throb.**
**heart·break** (härt′brāk′), *n.* overwhelming sorrow, grief, or disappointment. —**heart′break′er,** *n.* —**heart′break′ing,** *adj.* —**heart′break′ing·ly,** *adv.*
**heart·bro·ken** (härt′brō′k'n), *adj.* overwhelmed with sorrow, grief, or disappointment. —**heart′bro′ken·ly,** *adv.* —**heart′bro′ken·ness,** *n.*
**heart·burn** (härt′bũrn′), *n.* 1. a burning, acid sensation in the esophagus and stomach. 2. jealousy; discontent; envy: also **heart′burn′ing.**
**heart·ed** (här′tid), *adj.* having (a specified kind of) heart: used in compounds, as *downhearted.*
**heart·en** (här′t'n), *v.t.* to cheer up; encourage.

**heart·felt** (härt′felt′), *adj.* with or expressive of deep feeling; sincere; genuine.
**hearth** (härth), [AS. *heorth*], 1. the stone or brick floor of a fireplace. 2. *a*) the fireside. *b*) the home. 3. the lowest part of a blast furnace, on which the molten metal and slag are deposited.
**hearth·stone** (härth′stōn′), *n.* 1. the stone forming a hearth; hence, 2. fireside; home.
**heart·i·ly** (här′t'l-i), *adv.* 1. in a sincere, cordial way. 2. with enthusiasm or vigor. 3. with zestful appetite. 4. completely; fully; very.
**heart·i·ness** (här′ti-nis), *n.* a being hearty.
**heart·less** (härt′lis), *adj.* 1. lacking in spirit, courage, or enthusiasm. 2. unkind; unfeeling. —**heart′less·ly,** *adv.* —**heart′less·ness,** *n.*
**heart-rend·ing** (härt′ren′diŋ), *adj.* causing much grief or mental anguish. —**heart′-rend′ing·ly,** *adv.*
**hearts·ease, heart's-ease** (härts′ēz′), *n.* 1. peace of mind. 2. the wild pansy.
**heart·sick** (härt′sik′), *adj.* sick at heart; extremely unhappy; despondent. —**heart′sick′ness,** *n.*
**heart·sore** (härt′sôr′, -sōr′), *adj.* feeling or showing grief. —**heart′sore′ness,** *n.*
**heart-strick·en** (härt′strik′'n), *adj.* deeply affected by grief, sorrow, dismay, etc.: also **heart′-struck′.**
**heart·string** (härt′striŋ′), *n. usually pl.* deepest feelings or affections.
**heart-to-heart** (härt′tə-härt′), *adj.* intimate and candid; frank.
**heart·wood** (härt′wood′), *n.* the hard wood at the core of a tree trunk; duramen.
**heart·y** (här′ti), *adj.* [-IER, -IEST], [see HEART & -Y], 1. characterized by warmth and sincerity; cordial: as, a *hearty* welcome. 2. strongly felt; vigorous: as, a *hearty* dislike. 3. in or resulting from excellent health; strong and healthy. 4. satisfying and abundant; nourishing: as, a *hearty* meal. 5. needing or liking plenty of food: as, a *hearty* eater. *n.* [*pl.* -IES], 1. fellow; comrade: sailor's term. 2. *usually in pl.* a sailor.
**heat** (hēt), *n.* [AS. *hætu;* see HOT], 1. the quality of being hot; hotness: in physics, heat is considered a form of energy whose effect is produced by the accelerated vibration of molecules. 2. much hotness; great warmth. 3. degree of hotness or warmth. 4. the perception of hotness or warmth. 5. hot weather or climate. 6. the warming of a room, house, etc., as by a furnace. 7. appearance as an indication of hotness: as, blue *heat* in metals. 8. *a*) intensity of feeling; excitement, ardor, anger, etc. *b*) the period or condition of such feeling: as, in the *heat* of battle. 9. a single effort, bout, or trial; esp., a preliminary round of a race, etc. 10. *a*) sexual excitement. *b*) the period of this in animals. 11. in *metallurgy*, a single heating, as of metal, in a furnace or forge. 12. [Slang], *a*) intense activity. *b*) coercion, as by torture. *v.t. & v.i.* 1. to make or become warm or hot. 2. to make or become excited. —**heat′less,** *adj.*
**heat·ed·ly** (hēt′id-li), *adv.* with anger, vehemence, or excitement.
**heat·er** (hēt′ēr), *n.* an apparatus for giving heat or warmth; stove, furnace, radiator, etc.
**heat exhaustion,** a form of heatstroke characterized by low body temperature and collapse: also **heat prostration.**
**heath** (hēth), *n.* [AS. *hæth*], 1. a tract of open wasteland, especially in the British Isles, covered with heather, low shrubs, etc. 2. any of various shrubs and plants growing on heaths; esp., heather. —**one's native heath,** the place of one's birth or childhood. —**heath′like′,** *adj.* —**heath′y,** *adj.*
**heath·bird** (hēth′būrd′), *n.* the black grouse.
**hea·then** (hē′thən), *n.* [*pl.* -THENS, -THEN], [AS. *hæthen*], 1. originally, a member of any people not worshiping the God of Israel. 2. anyone not a Jew, Christian, or Moslem. 3. a person regarded as uncivilized, irreligious, etc. *adj.* 1. of heathen tribes or culture. 2. pagan; hence, 3. irreligious. —**hea′then·dom,** *n.* —**hea′then·ish,** *adj.* —**hea′then·ish·ly,** *adv.* —**hea′then·ish·ness,** *n.* —**hea′then·ism,** *n.*
**hea·then·ize** (hē′thən-īz′), *v.t. & v.i.* [-IZED, -IZING], to make or become heathen.
**heath·er** (heth′ēr), *n.* [ME. *haddyr*, altered after *heath*], a low-growing plant of the heath family, especially common in the British Isles, with stalks of small, bell-shaped, purplish-pink flowers. *adj.* like heather in color or appearance. —**heath′er·y,** *adj.*
**heat lightning,** lightning without thunder, seen near the horizon, especially on summer evenings.
**heat·stroke** (hēt′strōk′), *n.* any of several conditions resulting from exposure to excessive heat.
**heat wave,** 1. unusually hot weather, resulting from a slowly moving air mass of relatively high temperature. 2. a period of such weather.
**heaume** (hōm), *n.* [Fr.; OFr. *helme;* see HELMET], a heavy helmet worn in the Middle Ages.
**heave** (hēv), *v.t.* [HEAVED or HOVE, HEAVING], [< AS. *hebban*], 1. to raise or lift, especially with effort. 2. to lift in this way and throw. 3. to make rise or swell, as one's chest. 4. to make (a sigh, etc.) with great effort. 5. in *nautical usage*, *a*) to raise, haul, etc. by pulling with a rope or cable. *b*) to move (a ship) in a specified manner or direction. *v.i.* 1. to swell up; bulge out. 2. to rise and fall rhythmically: as, his chest *heaved* with sobs. 3. *a*) to retch or vomit. *b*) to pant; breathe hard; gasp. 4. in *nautical usage*, *a*) to tug or haul (*on* or *at* a cable, rope, etc.). *b*) to proceed; move: as, the ship *heaves* into sight. *n.* the act or effort of heaving. —**heave ho!** pull hard! —**heave to,** 1. in *nautical usage*, to stop forward movement. 2. to stop. —**heav′er,** *n.*
**heav·en** (hev′'n), *n.* [AS. *heofon*], 1. *usually pl.* the space surrounding the earth; firmament. 2. [H-], God; Providence. 3. any place of great beauty and pleasure. 4. a state of great happiness. 5. in *theology*, the place where God and his angels are and where the blessed go after death. —**move heaven and earth,** to do all that can be done.
**heav·en·ly** (hev′'n-li), *adj.* 1. of the visible heavens: as, the sun is a *heavenly* body. 2. causing or characterized by great happiness, beauty, etc. 3. in *theology*, of or living in heaven; holy; divine. —**heav′en·li·ness,** *n.*
**heav·en·ward** (hev′'n-wērd), *adv. & adj.* toward heaven: also **heav′en·wards,** *adv.*
**heaves** (hēvz), *n.pl.* [construed as sing.], a respiratory disease of horses, marked by forced breathing, coughing, and heaving of the flanks.
**Heav·i·side layer** (hev′i-sīd′), the Kennelly-Heaviside layer.
**heav·y** (hev′i), *adj.* [-IER, -IEST], [AS. *hefig* < base of *habban*, to have & *hebban*, to heave], 1. hard to lift or move because of its weight; weighty. 2. of concentrated weight for its size. 3. above the usual or defined weight, as certain goods. 4. larger, greater, or more intense than usual; specif., *a*) striking with great force: as, a *heavy* blow. *b*) of more than usual quantity: as, a *heavy* vote. *c*) violent; rough: as, a *heavy* sea. *d*) loud and deep: as, *heavy* thunder. *e*) thick; coarse: as, *heavy* features. *f*) to an unusual extent: as, a *heavy* drinker. *g*) prolonged and intense: as, *heavy* applause. 5. serious; grave: as, a *heavy* responsibility. 6. hard to endure: as, *heavy* sorrow. 7. hard to do, work, or manage; difficult: as, *heavy* work, *heavy* soil. 8. causing grief or sorrow: as, *heavy* news. 9. sorrowful; depressed: as, a *heavy* heart. 10. burdened with sleep or fatigue: as, *heavy* eyelids. 11. hard to digest: as, a *heavy* meal. 12. not leavened properly; doughy: as, a *heavy* cake. 13. clinging; penetrating: as, a *heavy* odor. 14. cloudy; gloomy: as, a *heavy* sky. 15. tedious; dull. 16. clumsy; awkward: as, a *heavy* walk. 17. steeply inclined: as, a *heavy* grade. 18. in *military usage*, heavily armed. *adv.* in a heavy manner; heavily. *n.* [*pl.* -IES], 1. something heavy. 2. in the *theater*, *a*) a tragic or villainous role. *b*) an actor who plays such roles. —**hang heavy,** to pass tediously; drag. —**heavy with child,** pregnant. —**heav′i·ly,** *adv.* —**heav′i·ness,** *n.*
**heav·y-du·ty** (hev′i-do͞o′ti, -dū′ti), *adj.* that can resist great strain, weather, wear, etc.
**heav·y-hand·ed** (hev′i-han′did), *adj.* 1. clumsy; tactless. 2. cruel; tyrannical. —**heav′y-hand′ed·ly,** *adv.* —**heav′y-hand′ed·ness,** *n.*
**heav·y-heart·ed** (hev′i-här′tid), *adj.* sad; unhappy; depressed. —**heav′y-heart′ed·ness,** *n.*
**heavy hydrogen,** deuterium: cf. *heavy water.*
**heavy spar,** native barium sulfate; barite.
**heavy water,** a compound like water, composed of oxygen and deuterium, the isotope of hydrogen of atomic weight 2; deuterium oxide, $D_2O$.
**heav·y·weight** (hev′i-wāt′), *n.* 1. a person or animal weighing much more than average. 2. a boxer or wrestler who weighs 176 pounds or more. 3. [Slang], a very intelligent or important person. *adj.* of heavyweights.
**Heb., Hebr.,** 1. Hebrew. 2. Hebrews.
**heb·dom·a·dal** (heb-dom′ə-d'l), *adj.* [< L. < Gr. < *hebdomas*, seven (days) < *hepta*, seven], weekly. —**heb·dom′a·dal·ly,** *adv.*
**He·be** (hē′bi), *n.* in *Gr. mythology*, the goddess of youth: she was the gods' cupbearer until succeeded by Ganymede.
**He·bra·ic** (hi-brā′ik), *adj.* of or characteristic of the Hebrews, their language, or culture; Hebrew. —**He·bra′i·cal·ly,** *adv.*
**He·bra·ism** (hē′bri-iz'm), *n.* 1. a Hebrew idiom,

custom, etc. 2. Hebrew character, thought, or ethical system. 3. Judaism. —**He′bra·ist,** *n.* —**He′bra·is′tic, He′bra·is′ti·cal,** *adj.*

**He·brew** (hē′brōō), *n.* 1. any member of a group of northern Semitic peoples; specif., an Israelite: in modern usage interchangeable with *Jew.* 2. *a*) the ancient Semitic language of the Israelites, in which most of the Old Testament was written. *b*) its modern form, the official language of Israel. *adj.* 1. of Hebrew or the Hebrews. 2. Jewish.

**Hebrew calendar,** the Jewish calendar.

**He·brews** (hē′brōōz), *n.pl.* [construed as sing.], in the *Bible,* the Epistle to the Hebrews, a book of the New Testament.

**Heb·ri·des** (heb′rə-dēz′), *n.pl.* Scottish island group off NW Scotland. —**Heb′ri·de′an** (-dē′ən), *adj. & n.*

**Hec·a·te** (hek′ə-ti; *occas.* hek′it), *n.* in *Gr. mythology,* a goddess of the moon, earth, and underground realm of the dead, later regarded as the goddess of sorcery: also sp. **Hekate.**

**hec·a·tomb** (hek′ə-tōm′, -tōōm′), *n.* [< L. < Gr. < *hekaton,* a hundred + *bous,* ox], 1. in ancient Greece, the mass slaughter of 100 cattle as an offering to the gods. 2. any large-scale slaughter.

**heck** (hek), *interj. & n.* [Slang], hell: a euphemism.

**heck·le** (hek′'l), *v.t.* [-LED, -LING], [ME. *hekelin* < *hechele,* a hatchel], 1. to hatchel. 2. to annoy or badger (a speaker) by interrupting with questions or taunts. *n.* a hatchel. —**heck′ler,** *n.*

**hec·tare** (hek′târ), *n.* [Fr.; see HECTO- & ARE, *n.*], a metric measure of surface, equal to 10,000 square meters (100 ares or 2.471 acres).

**hec·tic** (hek′tik), *adj.* [< Fr. < LL. < Gr. *hektikos,* habitual], 1. of or characteristic of a wasting disease, as tuberculosis; consumptive. 2. designating the fever accompanying this. 3. feverish; flushed. 4. [Colloq.], characterized by haste, agitation, etc. *n.* 1. hectic fever. 2. the flush of a person with hectic fever. —**hec′ti·cal·ly,** *adv.*

**hec·to-** [Fr. < Gr. *hekaton,* a hundred], a combining form meaning *a hundred:* also **hect-.**

**hec·to·graph** (hek′tə-graf′, -gräf′), *n.* a duplicating device by which written or typed matter is transferred to a sheet of gelatin, from which many copies can be taken. *v.t.* to duplicate by means of a hectograph. —**hec′to·graph′ic,** *adj.*

**Hec·tor** (hek′tẽr), *n.* in Homer's *Iliad,* a Trojan hero killed by Achilles: he was Priam's son.

**hec·tor** (hek′tẽr), *n.* [< prec.] a swaggering bully. *v.t. & v.i.* 1. to bully. 2. to tease.

**Hec·u·ba** (hek′yoo-bə), *n.* in Homer's *Iliad,* the wife of Priam and mother of Hector, Troilus, Cassandra, and Paris.

**he'd** (hēd), 1. he had. 2. he would.

**hedge** (hej), *n.* [AS. *hecg*], 1. a row of closely planted shrubs, bushes, etc. forming a boundary or fence. 2. any fence or barrier. 3. a hedging. *v.t.* [HEDGED, HEDGING], 1. to place a hedge around or along. 2. to hinder or guard as with a barrier (usually with *in*). 3. to try to avoid loss in (a bet, risk, etc.) by making counterbalancing bets, etc. *v.i.* 1. to hide or protect oneself, as if behind a hedge. 2. to refuse to commit oneself; avoid direct answers. 3. to try to avoid loss by making counterbalancing bets, etc. —**hedg′er,** *n.*

**hedge·hog** (hej′hôg′, -hog′), *n.* 1. a small, insect-eating mammal of Europe, with sharp spines on the back, which bristle and form a hedgelike defense when the animal curls up. 2. the American porcupine.

HEDGEHOG
(10 in. long)

**hedge·hop** (hej′hop′), *v.i.* [-HOPPED, -HOPPING], [Slang], in *aviation,* to fly very close to the ground. —**hedge′hop′per,** *n.* —**hedge′hop′ping,** *n.*

**hedge·row** (hej′rō′), *n.* a row of shrubs, bushes, etc., forming a hedge.

**He·djaz** (he-jäz′, hē-jaz′), *n.* Hejaz.

**he·don·ism** (hē′d'n-iz'm), *n.* [< Gr. *hēdonē,* pleasure], the doctrine that pleasure is the principal good and should be the aim of action. —**he′don·ist,** *n.* —**he′do·nis′tic,** *adj.* —**he′do·nis′ti·cal·ly,** *adv.*

**-he·dral** (hē′drəl), a combining form for adjectives corresponding to nouns ending in *-hedron.*

**-he·dron** (hē′drən), [< Gr. < *hedra,* a side, face], a combining form meaning *a geometric figure* or *crystal with a* (specified) *number of surfaces.*

**heed** (hēd), *v.t. & v.i.* [AS. *hedan*], to pay close attention (to); take careful notice (of). *n.* close attention; careful notice. —**heed′er,** *n.*

**heed·ful** (hēd′fəl), *adj.* careful; attentive. —**heed′ful·ly,** *adv.* —**heed′ful·ness,** *n.*

**heed·less** (hēd′lis), *adj.* careless; inattentive. —**heed′less·ly,** *adv.* —**heed′less·ness,** *n.*

**hee·haw** (hē′hô′), *n. & v.i.* [echoic], bray.

**heel** (hēl), *n.* [AS. *hela*], 1. the back part of the human foot, under the ankle. 2. the corresponding part of the hind foot of an animal. 3. that part of a stocking, etc. which covers the heel. 4. the built-up part of a shoe, supporting the heel. 5. anything like the heel in location, shape, or function, as the end of a loaf of bread. 6. [Slang], a contemptible person. *v.t.* 1. to furnish with a heel. 2. to follow closely; chase. 3. [Slang], to furnish with money, etc. *v.i.* to go along at the heels of someone. —**at heel,** just behind. —**cool one's heels,** [Colloq.], to be kept waiting for some time. —**down at the heel** (or **heels**), 1. with the heels of one's shoes in need of repair. 2. shabby; run-down. —**kick up one's heels,** to have fun. —**on** (or **upon**) **the heels of,** close behind. —**out at the heels,** 1. having holes in the heels of one's shoes or socks. 2. shabby; run-down. —**show one's** (or **a clean pair of**) **heels,** to run away. —**take to one's heels,** to run away. —**to heel,** 1. just behind. 2. under control. —**heel′less,** *adj.*

**heel** (hēl), *v.i.* [AS. *hieldan*], to lean to a side; list: said especially of a ship. *v.t.* to make (a ship) list. *n.* the act of heeling.

**heeled** (hēld), *adj.* [Slang], 1. having money. 2. armed as with a pistol.

**heel·er** (hēl′ẽr), *n.* 1. one who puts heels on shoes or boots. 2. [Colloq.], a servile supporter of a politician; hanger-on: as, a ward *heeler.*

**heel·tap** (hēl′tap′), *n.* 1. a layer of leather, etc. serving as a lift in the heel of a shoe. 2. a bit of liquor left in a glass after drinking.

**heft** (heft), *n.* [< base of *heave*], [Colloq.], 1. weight; heaviness. 2. importance; influence. 3. the larger part or bulk of something. *v.t.* [Colloq.], 1. to lift or heave. 2. to try to determine the weight of by lifting. *v.i.* [Colloq.], to weigh.

**heft·y** (hef′ti), *adj.* [-IER, -IEST], [Colloq.], 1. weighty; heavy. 2. large and powerful. —**heft′i·ly,** *adv.* —**heft′i·ness,** *n.*

**He·gel, Ge·org Wil·helm Frie·drich** (gā-ôrkh′ vil′helm frē′driH hā′gəl), 1770–1831; German philosopher. —**He·ge·li·an** (hā-gā′li-ən, hi-jēl′yən), *adj. & n.* —**He·ge′li·an·ism,** *n.*

**he·gem·o·ny** (hi-jem′ə-ni, hej′i-mō′-), *n.* [*pl.* -NIES], [< Gr. < *hēgemōn,* leader], leadership or dominance, especially that of one nation in a league. —**heg·e·mon·ic** (hej′ə-mon′ik, hē′jə-), *adj.*

**he·gi·ra** (hi-jī′rə, hej′i-), *n.* [ML. < Ar. *hijrah,* lit., flight], 1. [often H-], the forced journey of Mohammed from Mecca to Medina in 622 A.D.: the Moslem era dates from this event. 2. any journey for safety; flight. Also sp. **hejira.**

**Hei·del·berg** (hī′d'l-bẽrg), *n.* a city in SW Germany: site of university founded in 1386.

**heif·er** (hef′ẽr), *n.* [AS. *heahfore*], a young cow that has not borne a calf.

**heigh** (hā, hī), *interj.* an exclamation to attract notice, show pleasure, express surprise, etc.

**heigh-ho** (hī′hō′, hā′hō′), *interj.* an exclamation of mild surprise, boredom, sorrow, etc.

**height** (hīt), *n.* [AS. *hiehthu* < *heah,* high], 1. the topmost point of anything. 2. the highest limit; greatest degree; extreme; climax: as, the *height* of lunacy. 3. the distance from the bottom to the top. 4. elevation or distance above a given level, as the earth or sea; altitude. 5. a relatively great distance above a given level or from bottom to top. 6. *often pl.* an eminence; hill.

**height·en** (hīt′'n), *v.t. & v.i.* 1. to bring or come to a higher position. 2. to make or become larger, greater, etc.; increase. —**height′en·er,** *n.*

**‡heil** (hīl), *interj.* [G.], hail! *v.t.* to say "heil" to.

**Hei·ne, Hein·rich** (hīn′riH hī′nə), 1797–1856: German poet and prose writer.

**hei·nous** (hā′nəs), *adj.* [< OFr. < *haine,* hatred; < Gmc.], hateful; odious; very wicked; outrageous. —**hei′nous·ly,** *adv.* —**hei′nous·ness,** *n.*

**heir** (âr), *n.* [< OFr. < L. *heres*], 1. one who inherits or is entitled to inherit another's property or title upon the other's death. 2. one who seems to get some trait from a predecessor or to carry on in his tradition. *v.t.* to inherit. —**heir′dom, heir′ship′,** *n.* —**heir′less,** *adj.*

**heir apparent,** [*pl.* HEIRS APPARENT], the heir whose right to a certain property or title cannot be denied if he outlives the ancestor.

**heir·ess** (âr′is), *n.* a woman or girl who is an heir, especially of great wealth.
**heir·loom** (âr′lōōm′), *n.* [*heir* + *loom* (tool)], 1. a piece of personal property that goes to an heir. 2. any valuable or interesting possession handed down from generation to generation.
**heir presumptive,** [*pl.* HEIRS PRESUMPTIVE], an heir whose right to a certain property or title will be lost if someone more closely related is born before the ancestor dies.
**He·jaz** (he-jäz′, hē-jaz′), *n.* a former country in W Arabia: now a province of Saudi Arabia.
**he·ji·ra** (hi-jī′rə, hej′i-), *n.* a hegira.
**Hek·a·te** (hek′ə-ti; *occas.* hek′it), *n.* Hecate.
**hek·to-,** hecto-: also **hekt-.**
**held** (held), pt. and pp. of **hold.**
**Hel·e·na** (hel′i-nə), *n.* the capital of Montana: pop., 20,000.
**Helen of Troy,** in *Gr. legend*, the beautiful wife of Menelaus, king of Sparta: the Trojan War was started by her elopement with Paris to Troy.
**hel·i·cal** (hel′i-k′l), *adj.* of, or having the form of, a helix; spiral. —**hel′i·cal·ly,** *adv.*
**hel·i·ces** (hel′i-sēz′), *n.* alt. pl. of **helix.**
**hel·i·coid** (hel′i-koid′), *adj.* [< Gr. < *helix*, a spiral + *eidos*, form], shaped like a spiral; coiled: also **hel′i·coi′dal.** *n.* in *geometry*, a surface generated by a straight line moving so that it passes through a fixed helix at all points, as a propeller screw.
**Hel·i·con** (hel′i-kon′, -kən), *n.* 1. a mountain in S Greece, regarded by the ancient Greeks as the home of the Muses. 2. [h-], a brass-wind instrument, similar to a bass tuba.
**hel·i·cop·ter** (hel′i-kop′tẽr, hē′li-), *n.* [< Fr. < Gr. *helix*, a spiral + *pteron*, wing], a kind of aircraft lifted and moved by a large propeller mounted horizontally above the fuselage.
**he·li·o-,** [< Gr. *hēlios*, the sun], a combining form meaning *the sun, radiant*: also **heli-.**
**he·li·o·cen·tric** (hē′li-ō-sen′trik), *adj.* [*helio-* + *centric*], 1. calculated from, or viewed as from, the center of the sun. 2. having or taking the sun as the center. Also **he′li·o·cen′tri·cal.**
**he·li·o·graph** (hē′li-ə-graf′, -gräf′), *n.* [*helio-* + *-graph*], a device for sending a message (**heliogram**) or signaling by flashing the sun's rays from a mirror. *v.t. & v.i.* to signal or communicate by heliograph. —**he·li·og·ra·pher** (hē′li-og′rə-fẽr), *n.* —**he′li·o·graph′ic,** *adj.* —**he′li·og′ra·phy,** *n.*
**He·li·os** (hē′li-os′), *n.* in *Gr. mythology*, the sun god: see also **Apollo, Hyperion.**
**he·li·o·scope** (hē′li-ə-skōp′), *n.* [*helio-* + *-scope*], a telescopic device for looking at the sun without hurting the eye.
**he·li·o·ther·a·py** (hē′li-ō-ther′ə-pi), *n.* the treatment of disease by exposure to sunlight.
**he·li·o·trope** (hē′li-ə-trōp′, hēl′yə-), *n.* [< Fr. < L. < Gr. < *hēlios*, the sun + *trepein*, to turn], 1. formerly, a sunflower. 2. a plant of the borage family, with fragrant clusters of small, reddish-purple or white flowers. 3. reddish purple. 4. bloodstone. *adj.* reddish-purple.
**he·li·ot·ro·pism** (hē′li-ot′rə-piz′m), *n.* the tendency of certain plants or other organisms to turn toward or from light, especially sunlight. —**he′li·o·trop′ic** (-ə-trop′ik), *adj.*
**hel·i·port** (hel′ə-pôrt′), *n.* [*heli*copter + air*port*], a flat place where helicopters land and take off.
**he·li·um** (hē′li-əm), *n.* [< Gr. *hēlios*, the sun], one of the chemical elements, a very light, inert, colorless gas, used, in preference to the lighter hydrogen, for inflating balloons, etc. because it is not inflammable: symbol, He; at. wt., 4.003; at. no., 2.
**he·lix** (hē′liks), *n.* [*pl.* -LIXES, -LICES (hel′i-sēz′)], [L.; Gr., a spiral < *helissein*, to turn round], 1. any spiral, either lying in a single plane or, especially, moving around a cone, cylinder, etc., as the thread of a screw. 2. the folded rim of cartilage around the outer ear. 3. in *architecture*, an ornamental spiral.
**hell** (hel), *n.* [AS. *hel* < base of *helan*, to hide], 1. in the *Bible*, the place where the spirits of the dead are. 2. *a*) in *Christianity*, the place to which sinners and unbelievers go after death for torment. *b*) the people in hell. *c*) the powers of evil or darkness. 3. any place or condition of evil, misery, cruelty, etc. *interj.* an exclamation of irritation, anger, emphasis, etc.: regarded as a profanity. —**be hell on,** [Slang], 1. to be very difficult or painful for. 2. to be very strict with. 3. to be very damaging to. —**catch** (or **get**) **hell,** [Slang], to receive a severe scolding, punishment, etc. —**play hell with,** [Slang], to cause much damage or trouble to. —**raise hell,** [Slang], to cause trouble, uproar, etc.
**he'll** (hēl, hil), 1. he will. 2. he shall.
**Hel·las** (hel′əs), *n.* [Now Poetic], Greece.
**hell·bend·er** (hel′ben′dẽr), *n.* a large, edible salamander, found especially in the Ohio Valley.
**hell·bent** (hel′bent′), *adj.* [Slang], firmly or recklessly resolved to have or do (with *on* or *for*).
**hell·cat** (hel′kat′), *n.* 1. a witch. 2. an evil, spiteful, bad-tempered woman.
**hell-div·er** (hel′dīv′ẽr), *n.* any of several diving birds, as the dabchick.
**hel·le·bore** (hel′ə-bôr′, -bōr′), *n.* [< OFr. < L. < Gr. *helleboros*], 1. any of a group of winter-blooming plants of the crowfoot family, with flowers shaped like buttercups but of various colors. 2. any of a group of plants belonging to the lily family. 3. the poisonous powdered roots of certain species of either of these, used in medicine, as an insecticide, etc.
**Hel·lene** (hel′ēn), *n.* [*pl.* -LENES], [< Gr.], a Greek.
**Hel·len·ic** (he-len′ik, -lē′nik), *adj.* 1. of the Hellenes; Greek. 2. of the history, language, or culture of the ancient Greeks from 776 B.C. to the era of Alexander the Great: cf. *Hellenistic. n.* the language of ancient Greece.
**Hel·len·ism** (hel′ən-iz′m), *n.* 1. a Greek phrase, idiom, or custom. 2. the character, thought, culture, or ethics of ancient Greece. 3. adoption of the Greek language, customs, etc. —**Hel′len·ist,** *n.*
**Hel·len·is·tic** (hel′ə-nis′tik), *adj.* 1. of or characteristic of Hellenism. 2. of Greek history, art, etc. after the death of Alexander the Great (323 B.C.): cf. *Hellenic.* Also **Hel′len·is′ti·cal.**
**Hel·len·ize** (hel′ə-nīz′), *v.t.* [-IZED, -IZING], to make Greek in character, form, etc. *v.i.* to adopt the Greek language, customs, ideals, etc. —**Hel′len·i·za′tion,** *n.* —**Hel′len·iz′er,** *n.*
**Hel·les·pont** (hel′əs-pont′), *n.* the Dardanelles: the ancient name.
**hell-fire, hell·fire** (hel′fīr′), *n.* the fire, hence punishment, of hell.
**hel·lion** (hel′yən), *n.* [Colloq.], a person fond of deviltry; mischievous troublemaker.
**hell·ish** (hel′ish), *adj.* 1. of or from hell. 2. appropriate to hell; devilish; fiendish. 3. [Colloq.], very unpleasant; detestable. —**hell′ish·ly,** *adv.* —**hell′ish·ness,** *n.*
**hel·lo** (he-lō′, hə-, hel′ō, hul′ō), *interj.* 1. an exclamation of greeting or of response, as in telephoning. 2. an exclamation to attract attention. 3. an exclamation of surprise. *n.* [*pl.* -LOS], a saying or shouting of "hello." *v.i.* [-LOED, -LOING], to shout or say "hello." *v.t.* to say "hello" to.
**helm** (helm), *n. & v.t.* [AS.], [Archaic], helmet.
**helm** (helm), *n.* [AS. *halma*], 1. *a*) the wheel or tiller by which a ship is steered. *b*) the complete steering gear. 2. the control or leadership of an organization, enterprise, etc. *v.t.* to guide; control; steer. —**helm′less,** *adj.*
**hel·met** (hel′mit), *n.* [OFr., dim. of *helme*, helmet; < Gmc.], 1. a protective head covering usually made of or with metal and variously designed for use in combat, certain sports, diving, etc. 2. something like such a headpiece in appearance or function. *v.t.* to equip with a helmet. —**hel′met·ed,** *adj.* —**hel′met·less,** *adj.*
**hel·minth** (hel′minth), *n.* [Gr. *helmins*], a worm or wormlike parasite, especially of the intestine: tapeworms and roundworms are helminths.
**helms·man** (helmz′mən), *n.* [*pl.* -MEN], the man at the helm; man who steers a ship.
**Hé·lo·ïse** (ā′lô′ēz′), *n.* mistress and, later, wife of Pierre Abélard; 1101?–1164?: see **Abélard.**
**Hel·ot** (hel′ət, hē′lət), *n.* [< L. < Gr. *Heilōtes*, serfs; prob. < *helein*, to seize], 1. a member of the lowest class of serfs in ancient Sparta. 2. [h-], a serf or slave. —**hel′ot·ism,** *n.* —**hel′ot·ry,** *n.*
**help** (help), *v.t.* [HELPED or *archaic* HOLP, HELPED or *archaic* HOLPEN or *obs.* HOLP, HELPING], [AS. *helpan*], 1. to make it easier for (a person) to do something; aid; assist; specif., *a*) to give (one in need) relief, money, etc. *b*) to share the labor of: as, *help* us lift this. *c*) to aid in getting (*up, down, to, into, out of*, etc.). 2. to make it easier for (something) to exist, happen, etc.; promote: as, ignorance *helps* war. 3. to remedy; relieve: as, this will *help* your cough. 4. to prevent: as, I can't *help* his cheating. 5. to keep from; avoid: as, I can't *help* liking him. 6. to serve or wait on: said of waiters, clerks, etc. *v.i.* 1. to give assistance; be useful or beneficial. 2. to act as a waiter at table. *n.* 1. a helping; aid; assistance. 2. relief; remedy. 3. a person or thing that helps; helper. 4. *a*) a hired helper, as a servant, farm hand, etc. *b*) hired helpers; employees. 5. a serving of food; helping. —**cannot help but,** be compelled or obliged to. —**help oneself to,** 1. to serve oneself, as with food. 2. to take without asking or being given. —**help out,** to help in getting or doing something. —**so**

**help me God,** as God is my witness: used in oaths. —**help′a·ble,** *adj.* —**help′er,** *n.*
**help·ful** (help′fəl), *adj.* giving help; useful. —**help′ful·ly,** *adv.* —**help′ful·ness,** *n.*
**help·ing** (hel′piŋ), *n.* 1. a giving of aid; assisting. 2. a portion of food served to one person.
**help·less** (help′lis), *adj.* 1. without power to help oneself; weak. 2. without help or protection. 3. incompetent; inefficient. —**help′less·ly,** *adv.* —**help′less·ness,** *n.*
**help·mate** (help′māt′), *n.* [< *helpmeet*], a companion and helper, as a wife or husband.
**help·meet** (help′mēt′), *n.* [misreading of "an *help meet* for him" (Gen. 2:18)], a helpmate.
**Hel·sin·ki** (hel′siŋ-ki), *n.* the capital of Finland, a seaport in the S part: pop., 445,000.
**hel·ter-skel·ter** (hel′tēr-skel′tēr), *adv.* in haste and confusion; in a disorderly, hurried manner. *adj.* hurried and confused; disorderly. *n.* anything helter-skelter.
**helve** (helv), *n.* [AS. *hielfe*], the handle of a tool, especially of an ax or hatchet. *v.t.* [HELVED, HELVING], to put a helve on.
**Hel·ve·tia** (hel-vē′shə), *n.* Switzerland: the Latin name. —**Hel·ve′tian,** *adj.* & *n.*
**hem** (hem), *n.* [AS. *hem(m)*], 1. the border on a garment or piece of cloth, usually made by folding the edge and sewing it down. 2. any border, edge, or margin. *v.t.* [HEMMED, HEMMING], 1. to fold back the edge of and sew down. 2. *a*) to encircle; surround. *b*) to confine or restrain: with *in, around,* or *about.* —**hem′mer,** *n.*
**hem** (hem), *interj.* & *n.* a conventionalized expression of the sound made in clearing the throat to attract attention or show doubt. *v.i.* [HEMMED, HEMMING], to make this sound. —**hem and haw,** to pause or hesitate in speaking.
**he-man** (hē′man′), *n.* [*pl.* HE-MEN], [Slang], a strong, virile man.
**hem·a·tite** (hem′ə-tīt′, hē′mə-), *n.* [< L. < Gr. *haimatitēs,* bloodlike < *haima,* blood], native ferric oxide, $Fe_2O_3$, an important iron ore, brownish red when pulverized. —**hem′a·tit′ic** (-tit′ik), *adj.*
**hem·a·to-,** [< Gr. *haima,* blood], a combining form meaning *blood*: also **hemat-, haemato-.**
**hem·a·tol·o·gy** (hem′ə-tol′ə-ji, hē′mə-), *n.* the study of blood and its diseases. —**hem′a·tol′o·gist,** *n.*
**he·ma·to·ma** (hē′mə-tō′mə, hem′ə-), *n.* [*pl.* -MATA (-mə-tə), -MAS], [see HEMATO- & -OMA], a local swelling or tumor filled with effused blood.
**hem·i-,** [Gr. *hēmi-*], a prefix meaning *half,* as in *hemisphere.*
**hem·i·dem·i·sem·i·qua·ver** (hem′i-dem′i-sem′i-kwā′vēr), *n.* in *music,* a sixty-fourth note (♪).
**Hem·ing·way, Ernest** (hem′iŋ-wā′), 1899–1961; U.S. novelist and short-story writer.
**he·mip·ter·ous** (hi-mip′tēr-əs), *adj.* [*hemi-* + *-pterous*], belonging to a group of insects, including bedbugs, water bugs, lice, etc., with piercing and sucking mouth parts: also **he·mip′ter·al.**
**hem·i·sphere** (hem′ə-sfêr′), *n.* [< Fr. < L. < Gr.; cf. HEMI- & SPHERE], 1. half of a sphere or globe. 2. *a*) any of the halves of the earth; the Northern, Southern, Eastern, or Western Hemisphere. *b*) a model or map of any of these halves. —**hem′i·spher′i·cal** (-sfer′i-k′l), **hem′i·spher′ic,** *adj.* —**hem′i·spher′i·cal·ly,** *adv.*
**hem·i·stich** (hem′i-stik′), *n.* [< L. < Gr. < *hēmi-,* half + *stichos,* a line], 1. half a line of verse, especially as divided by the caesura. 2. a metrically short line of verse. —**he·mis·ti·chal** (hi-mis′ti-k′l, hem′ə-stik′əl), *adj.*
**hem·lock** (hem′lok), *n.* [AS. *hymlic*], 1. a poisonous weed of the carrot family, with small, white flowers and finely divided leaves: also **poison hemlock.** 2. poison made from this weed. 3. an evergreen tree of the pine family, with horizontal, drooping branches and short, flat needles: the bark is used in tanning. 4. the wood of this tree.
**he·mo-,** [< Gr. < *haima,* blood], a combining form meaning *blood*: also **hem-, hema-**: words beginning with *hemo-* may also be spelled **haemo-.**
**he·mo·glo·bin** (hē′mə-glō′bin, hem′ə-), *n.* [< *hem(at)o* + *globule* + *-in*], the red coloring matter of the red blood corpuscles: it carries oxygen from the lungs to the tissues, and carbon dioxide from the tissues to the lungs.
**he·mol·y·sis** (hi-mol′i-sis), *n.* [*hemo-* + *-lysis*], the destruction of the red corpuscles with liberation of hemoglobin into the surrounding fluid. —**he·mo·lyt·ic** (hē′mə-lit′ik, hem′ə-), *adj.*
**he·mo·phil·i·a** (hē′mə-fil′i-ə, hem′ə-fil′yə), *n.* [Mod. L.; see HEMO-, -PHILE, & -IA], a hereditary condition in which the blood fails to clot quickly enough, causing prolonged, uncontrollable bleeding from even the smallest cut. —**he′mo·phil′i·ac** (-ak), **he′mo·phile′** (-fīl′, -fil), *n.*
**hem·or·rhage** (hem′ēr-ij), *n.* [< Fr. < L. < Gr. < *haima,* blood + *rhēgnynai,* to break], the escape of blood from its vessels; bleeding; esp., heavy bleeding. *v.i.* [-RHAGED, -RHAGING], to suffer a hemorrhage. —**hem·or·rhag·ic** (hem′ə-raj′ik), *adj.*
**hem·or·rhoid** (hem′ə-roid′), *n.* [< Fr. < L. < Gr. < *haima,* blood + *rhein,* to flow], *usually in pl.* a painful swelling or tumor of a vein in the region of the anus: also called, in the plural, *piles.* —**hem′or·rhoi′dal** (-roi′d′l), *adj.*
**he·mo·stat** (hē′mə-stat′, hem′ə-), *n.* [< *hemo-* + Gr. *stasis,* a standing], anything used to stop bleeding; specif., a clamplike device used in surgery.
**hemp** (hemp), *n.* [AS. *henep*], 1. a tall Asiatic plant of the nettle family, having tough fiber. 2. the fiber, used to make rope, sailcloth, etc. 3. a drug, especially hashish, made from the flowers and leaves of this plant. —**hemp′en,** *adj.*
**hem·stitch** (hem′stich′), *n.* 1. an ornamental stitch, used especially at a hem, made by pulling out several parallel threads and tying the cross threads into small bunches. 2. decorative needlework done with this stitch. *v.t.* to put hemstitches on. —**hem′stitch′er,** *n.* —**hem′stitch′ing,** *n.*

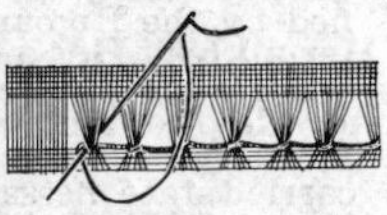
HEMSTITCH

**hen** (hen), *n.* [< AS. *henn,* fem. of *hana,* rooster], 1. the female of the chicken, or domestic fowl. 2. the female of various other birds.
**hen·bane** (hen′bān′), *n.* a coarse, hairy, foul-smelling plant of the nightshade family, poisonous to animals, especially fowls.
**hence** (hens), *adv.* [ME. *hennes* < *henne* (< AS. *heonan,* from here) + *-(e)s,* adv. genit. suffix], 1. from this place; away: as, go *hence.* 2. from this time; after now: as, a year *hence.* 3. from this life: as, departed *hence.* 4. from this origin or source. 5. as a result; therefore. *interj.* go away! —**hence with!** away with!
**hence·forth** (hens′fôrth′, hens′fōrth′), *adv.* from this time on: also **hence′for′ward** (-fôr′wērd).
**hench·man** (hench′mən), *n.* [*pl.* -MEN], [AS. *hengest,* male horse + *-man;* orig. sense prob. "groom"], a trusted helper or follower.
**hen·e·quen, hen·e·quin** (hen′ə-kin), *n.* [< Sp. < native Yucatan name], 1. fiber obtained from a Central American plant; sisal hemp: used for making rope, cloth, etc. 2. this plant, a kind of agave.
**hen·house** (hen′hous′), *n.* a shelter for poultry.
**hen·na** (hen′ə), *n.* [Ar. *hinnā′*], 1. an ornamental tropical shrub of Asia. 2. a dye extracted from the leaves of this plant, often used to tint the hair auburn. 3. reddish brown. *adj.* reddish-brown. *v.t.* [-NAED, -NAING], to tint with henna.
**hen·ner·y** (hen′ēr-i), *n.* [*pl.* -IES], a place where poultry is kept or raised.
**hen·peck** (hen′pek′), *v.t.* to domineer over (one's husband). —**hen′pecked′,** *adj.*
**hen·ry** (hen′ri), *n.* [*pl.* -RIES, -RYS], [after J. *Henry* (1797–1878), Am. physicist], in *electricity,* the unit by which inductance is measured: equal to the inductance of a circuit in which the variation of a current at the rate of one ampere per second induces an electromotive force of one volt.
**Henry IV,** 1553–1610; first Bourbon king of France (1589–1610): called *Henry of Navarre.*
**Henry VIII,** 1491–1547; king of England (1509–1547); established the Church of England.
**Henry, O.,** (pseudonym of *William Sydney Porter*), 1862–1910; U.S. short-story writer.
**Henry, Patrick,** 1736–1799; U.S. statesman and orator.
**hep** (hep), *adj.* [Slang], informed; conversant.
**he·pat·ic** (hi-pat′ik), *adj.* [< L. < Gr. < *hēpar,* the liver], 1. of or affecting the liver. 2. like the liver in color or shape. *n.* a medicine affecting the liver.
**he·pat·i·ca** (hi-pat′i-kə), *n.* [Mod. L.; see HEPATIC: it has liver-shaped leaves], a small plant of the crowfoot family, with small, spring flowers of white, pink, blue, or purple.
**hep·a·ti·tis** (hep′ə-tī′tis), *n.* [Mod. L. < L. *hepar,* liver; + -ITIS], inflammation of the liver.
**hep·cat** (hep′kat′), *n.* [*hep* + *cat,* slang for "swing dancer"], [Slang], a jazz expert or enthusiast.

**He·phaes·tus** (hi-fes′təs), *n.* the Greek god of fire and forge, identified with the Roman Vulcan.
**Hep·ple·white** (hep′'l-hwīt′), *adj.* designating or of a style of furniture, with graceful curves, designed by George Hepplewhite (?–1786), English cabinet-maker. *n.* furniture in this style.
**hep·ta-,** [< Gr. *hepta*], a combining form meaning *seven*: also **hept-.**
**hep·ta·gon** (hep′tə-gon′), *n.* [< Gr. < *hepta*, seven + *gōnia*, a corner, angle], a plane figure with seven angles and seven sides. —**hep·tag·o·nal** (hep-tag′ə-n'l), *adj.*
**hep·tam·e·ter** (hep-tam′ə-tẽr), *n.* [*hepta-* + *-meter*], a line of verse with seven metrical feet. *adj.* containing seven metrical feet.
**hep·tarch·y** (hep′tär-ki), *n.* [*pl.* -IES], 1. government by seven rulers. 2. [sometimes H-], a group of seven allied kingdoms.
**her** (hũr), *pron.* [AS. *hire*], the objective case of **she**: also used colloquially as a predicate complement with a linking verb (e.g., that's *her*). *possessive pronominal adj.* of, belonging to, or done by her: as, *her* father, *her* poem.
**her.,** heraldry.
**He·ra** (hêr′ə), *n.* in *Gr. mythology*, the wife of Zeus, queen of the gods, and goddess of marriage: identified by the Romans with Juno.
**Her·a·kles, Her·a·cles** (her′ə-klēz′), *n.* Hercules. —**Her′a·kle′an, Her′a·cle′an,** *adj.*
**her·ald** (her′əld), *n.* [< OFr. *heralt* < Gmc.], 1. formerly, an official who made proclamations, carried state messages, took charge of tournaments, etc. 2. in England, an official in charge of genealogies, heraldic arms, etc. 3. a person who announces significant news; messenger. 4. a person or thing that presages what is to follow; forerunner; harbinger. *v.t.* to announce; foretell; usher in.
**he·ral·dic** (he-ral′dik), *adj.* of heraldry or heralds. —**he·ral′di·cal·ly,** *adv.*
**her·ald·ry** (her′əld-ri), *n.* [*pl.* -RIES], 1. the art or science having to do with coats of arms, genealogies, etc. 2. a coat of arms or heraldic device. 3. heraldic ceremony or pomp.
**herb** (ũrb, hũrb), *n.* [< OFr. < L. *herba*], 1. any seed plant whose stem withers away annually, as distinguished from a tree or shrub whose woody stem lives from year to year. 2. any such plant used as a medicine, seasoning, etc., as mint, thyme, basil, and sage. 3. grass; herbage. —**herb′less,** *adj.* —**herb′like′,** *adj.* —**herb′y** [-IER, -IEST], *adj.*
**her·ba·ceous** (hẽr-bā′shəs), *adj.* 1. of or like an herb or herbs. 2. like a green leaf in texture, color, shape, etc. —**her·ba′ceous·ly,** *adv.*
**herb·age** (ũr′bij, hũr′-), *n.* 1. herbs collectively, especially those used as pasturage; grass. 2. the green foliage and juicy stems of herbs.
**herb·al** (hũr′b'l, ũr′-), *adj.* of herbs. *n.* formerly, a book about herbs or plants.
**herb·al·ist** (hũr′b'l-ist, ũr′-), *n.* 1. formerly, a botanist. 2. one who collects or deals in herbs.
**her·bar·i·um** (hẽr-bâr′i-əm), *n.* [*pl.* -IUMS, -IA (-i-ə)], [LL. < L. *herba*, herb], 1. a collection of dried plants used for botanical study. 2. a room, building, etc. for keeping such a collection.
**Her·bert, Victor** (hũr′bẽrt), 1859–1924; U.S. composer and conductor, born in Ireland.
**her·bi·cide** (hũr′bə-sīd′), *n.* [< L. *herba*, herb; + *-cide*], any substance used to destroy plants, especially weeds. —**her′bi·cid′al,** *adj.*
**her·bi·vore** (hũr′bi-vôr′, -vōr′), *n.* a herbivorous animal: opposed to *carnivore*.
**her·biv·o·rous** (hẽr-biv′ẽr-əs), *adj.* [< L. *herba*, herb + *vorare*, to devour], feeding chiefly on grass or other plants: opposed to *carnivorous*.
**Her·cu·le·an** (hẽr-kū′li-ən, hũr′kyoo-lē′-), *adj.* 1. of Hercules. 2. [usually h-], having the great size and strength of Hercules. 3. [usually h-], calling for great strength, size, or courage; very difficult to do: as, a *herculean* task.
**Her·cu·les** (hũr′kyoo-lēz′), *n.* 1. in *Gr. & Rom. mythology*, a hero renowned for feats of strength, particularly the twelve labors imposed on him by Hera. 2. [h-], any very large, strong man. 3. a northern constellation.
**herd** (hũrd), *n.* [AS. *heord*], 1. a number of cattle or other large animals feeding, living, or being driven together. 2. the common people; public; crowd: contemptuous term. *v.t. & v.i.* to form into a herd, group, crowd, etc. —**herd′er,** *n.*
**herd** (hũrd), *n.* [AS. *h(i)erde*], a herdsman: now only in combination, as in *cowherd, shepherd. v.t.* to tend or drive as a herdsman.
**herds·man** (hũrdz′mən), *n.* [*pl.* -MEN], a person who tends or drives a herd.
**here** (hêr), *adv.* [AS. *her*], 1. at or in this place: often used as an intensive, as, John *here* is a good player. 2. toward, to, or into this place: as, come *here*. 3. at this point in action, speech, etc.; now. 4. on earth. Opposed to *there*. *interj.* an exclamation used to call attention, answer a roll call, etc. *n.* 1. this place (where the speaker or writer is). 2. this life or time. —**here and there,** 1. at irregular intervals. 2. hither and thither. —**here goes!** an exclamation of decision on starting some act requiring courage, etc. —**neither here nor there,** beside the point; irrelevant.
**here·a·bout** (hêr′ə-bout′), *adv.* in this general vicinity; about or near here: also **here′a·bouts′.**
**here·af·ter** (hêr-af′tẽr, -äf′-), *adv.* 1. from now on; in the future. 2. following this, as in a writing. 3. in the state or life after death. *n.* 1. the future. 2. the state or life after death.
**here·at** (hêr-at′), *adv.* 1. at this time; when this occurred. 2. at this; for this reason.
**here·by** (hêr-bī′), *adv.* by this means.
**he·red·i·ta·ble** (hə-red′i-tə-b'l), *adj.* that can be inherited; heritable. —**he·red′i·ta·bil′i·ty,** *n.* —**he·red′i·ta·bly,** *adv.*
**he·red·i·tar·y** (hə-red′ə-ter′i), *adj.* [< L. < *hereditas*; see HEREDITY], 1. *a*) of, or passed down by, inheritance from an ancestor; *b*) having title, etc. by inheritance. 2. of or passed down by heredity. 3. being such because of emotional attitudes, etc. passed down from predecessors. —**he·red′i·tar′i·ly,** *adv.* —**he·red′i·tar′i·ness,** *n.*
**he·red·i·ty** (hə-red′ə-ti), *n.* [*pl.* -TIES], [< Fr. < L. *hereditas*, heirship < *heres*, heir], 1. the transmission from parent to offspring of certain characteristics; tendency of offspring to resemble parents or ancestors: see **genetics.** 2. the characteristics transmitted in this way.
**Her·e·ford** (hũr′fẽrd, her′ə-fẽrd), *n.* any of a breed of beef cattle having a white face and a red body with white markings. *adj.* of this breed.
**here·in** (hêr-in′), *adv.* 1. in here. 2. in this writing, container, etc. 3. in this matter, detail, etc.
**here·in·af·ter** (hêr′in-af′tẽr, -äf′-), *adv.* in the following part (of this document, speech, etc.).
**here·in·be·fore** (hêr′in-bi-fôr′, -fōr′), *adv.* in the preceding part (of this document, speech, etc.).
**here·in·to** (hêr-in′tōō), *adv.* 1. into this place. 2. into this matter, condition, etc.
**here·of** (hêr-uv′, -ov′), *adv.* 1. of this. 2. concerning this. 3. [Archaic], from this; hence.
**here·on** (hêr-on′), *adv.* hereupon.
**here's** (hêrz), here is.
**here's to!** here's a toast to! I wish joy, etc. to!
**her·e·sy** (her′ə-si), *n.* [*pl.* -SIES], [< OFr. < L. < Gr. *hairesis*, a selection, sect < *hairein*, to take], 1. a religious belief opposed to the orthodox doctrines of a church; esp., such a belief denounced by the church as likely to cause schism. 2. any opinion opposed to established views or doctrines.
**her·e·tic** (her′ə-tik), *n.* [< Fr. < LL. < Gr. *hairetikos*, able to choose < *hairein*, to take], one who professes any heresy; esp., a church member who holds beliefs opposed to the official church doctrines. *adj.* heretical.
**he·ret·i·cal** (hə-ret′i-k'l), *adj.* 1. of heresy or heretics. 2. characterized by, or having the nature of, heresy. —**he·ret′i·cal·ly,** *adv.*
**here·to** (hêr-tōō′), *adv.* to this.
**here·to·fore** (hêr′too-fôr′, -tə-fōr′), *adv.* up to now; until the present; before this.
**here·un·to** (hêr′un-tōō′), *adv.* hereto.
**here·up·on** (hêr′ə-pon′), *adv.* 1. immediately following this. 2. concerning this subject, etc.
**here·with** (hêr-with′, -wiŧh′), *adv.* 1. along with this. 2. by this method or means.
**her·it·a·ble** (her′i-tə-b'l), *adj.* 1. that can be inherited. 2. that can inherit. —**her′it·a·bil′i·ty,** *n.*
**her·it·age** (her′ə-tij), *n.* [OFr. < LL. < L. *hereditas*; see HEREDITY], 1. property that is or can be inherited. 2. *a*) something handed down from one's ancestors or the past, as a culture, tradition, etc. *b*) birthright.
**her·maph·ro·dite** (hẽr-maf′rə-dīt′), *n.* [< L. < Gr. < *Hermaphroditos*, son of Hermes and Aphrodite, united in a single body with a nymph], 1. a person or animal with the sexual organs of both the male and the female. 2. a plant having stamens and pistils in the same flower. 3. a hermaphrodite brig. *adj.* of or like a hermaphrodite: also **her·maph′ro·dit′ic** (-dit′ik), **her·maph′ro·dit′i·cal.** —**her·maph′ro·dit′i·cal·ly,** *adv.*
**hermaphrodite brig,** a ship with a square-rigged foremast and a fore-and-aft-rigged mainmast.
**Her·mes** (hũr′mēz), *n.* in *Gr. mythology*, a god who served as messenger of the other gods, identified by the Romans with Mercury and pictured with winged shoes and hat, carrying a caduceus.
**her·met·ic** (hẽr-met′ik), *adj.* [< ML. < L. < Gr.

*Hermēs* (reputed founder of alchemy)], airtight: also **her·met'i·cal.** —**her·met'i·cal·ly,** *adv.*
**her·mit** (hũr'mit), *n.* [< OFr. < LL. < Gr. *erēmitēs* < *erēmos*, solitary], a person who lives by himself in a secluded spot, often from religious motives; recluse. —**her·mit'ic, her·mit'i·cal,** *adj.* —**her·mit'i·cal·ly,** *adv.* —**her'mit·like',** *adj.*
**her·mit·age** (hũr'mə-tij), *n.* 1. the place where a hermit lives. 2. a place where a person can live away from other people; secluded retreat.
**hermit crab,** any of various soft-bodied crabs that live in the empty shells of certain mollusks, as snails, etc.
**her·ni·a** (hũr'ni-ə), *n.* [*pl.* -AS, -AE (-ē')], [L.], the protrusion of all or part of an organ, especially a part of the intestine, through a tear in the wall of the surrounding structure; rupture. —**her'ni·al,** *adj.*
**He·ro** (hêr'ō), *n.* in *Gr. legend*, a priestess of Aphrodite: her lover, Leander, swam the Hellespont every night to be with her; when he drowned one night, Hero threw herself into the sea.
**he·ro** (hêr'ō), *n.* [*pl.* -ROES], [< L. < Gr. *hērōs*], 1. in *mythology & legend*, a man of great strength and courage, favored by the gods and in part descended from them. 2. any man admired for his courage, nobility, or exploits. 3. any person regarded as an ideal or model. 4. the central, usually sympathetic, male character, in a novel, play, poem, etc. 5. a central figure who played an admirable role in any important event or period.
**Her·od** (her'əd), *n.* king of Judea (37–4 B.C.); lived 73?–4 B.C.: called *Herod the Great*.
**Herod An·ti·pas** (an'ti-pas'), ? B.C.–40? A.D.; son of Herod; ruler of Galilee (4 B.C.–39 A.D.).
**He·rod·o·tus** (hi-rod'ə-təs), *n.* Greek historian; 5th century B.C.: called the *Father of History*.
**he·ro·ic** (hi-rō'ik), *adj.* 1. like or characteristic of a hero or his deeds: as, *heroic* conduct. 2. of, about, or characterized by heroes and their deeds; epic: as, a *heroic* poem, etc. 3. exalted; eloquent: as, *heroic* words. 4. exceptionally daring and risky: as, *heroic* measures. 5. in *art*, somewhat larger than life-size: as, a *heroic* statue. Also **he·ro'i·cal.** *n.* 1. *a*) a heroic poem. *b*) *pl.* heroic verse. 2. *pl* extravagant or melodramatic talk or action, meant to seem heroic. —**he·ro'i·cal·ly,** *adv.*
**heroic couplet,** a pair of rhymed lines in iambic pentameter.
**heroic verse,** the verse form in which epic poetry is traditionally written, as iambic pentameter.
**her·o·in** (her'ō-in, hêr'-), *n.* [G.], a very powerful, habit-forming narcotic, a derivative of morphine: a trade-mark (**Heroin).**
**her·o·ine** (her'ō-in), *n.* a girl or woman hero in life or literature.
**her·o·ism** (her'ō-iz'm), *n.* the qualities and actions of a hero or heroine; bravery, nobility, etc.
**her·on** (her'ən), *n.* [*pl.* -ONS, -ON; see PLURAL, II, D, 1], [< OFr. *hairon* < Frank.], any of a group of wading birds with a long neck, long legs, and a long, tapered bill.
**her·on·ry** (her'ən-ri), *n.* [*pl.* -RIES], a place where many herons gather to breed.
**hero worship,** exaggerated admiration for heroes.
**her·pes** (hũr'pēz), *n.* [L. < Gr. < *herpein*, to creep], a virus disease of the skin, characterized by the eruption of small blisters on the skin or mucous membranes. —**her·pet·ic** (hẽr-pet'ik), *adj.*
‡**herpes zos·ter** (zos'tẽr), [Gr. *zōstēr*, a girdle], shingles (the disease).
**her·pe·tol·o·gy** (hũr'pi-tol'ə-ji), *n.* [< Gr. *herpeton*, reptile; + *-logy*], the branch of zoology having to do with the study of reptiles. —**her·pe·to·log·i·cal** (hũr'pi-tə-loj'i-k'l), *adj.* —**her'pe·tol'o·gist,** *n.*
‡**Herr** (her), *n.* [*pl.* HERREN (-ən)], in Germany, a man; gentleman: also used as a title corresponding to *Mr.* or *Sir.*
**Her·rick, Robert** (her'ik), 1591–1674; Eng. poet.
**her·ring** (her'iŋ), *n.* [*pl.* -RINGS, -RING; see PLURAL, II, D, 1], [AS. *hæring*], any of an abundant group of small food fishes of the N Atlantic.
**her·ring·bone** (her'iŋ-bōn'), *n.* 1. the spine of a herring with the ribs extending from opposite sides in rows of parallel, slanting lines. 2. anything made in this pattern. *adj.* having the pattern of a herringbone: as, a *herringbone* stitch. *v.i. & v.t.* [-BONED, -BONING], to use a herringbone stitch or pattern (on).
**hers** (hũrz), *pron.* that or those belonging to her: often after *of*, as, a friend of *hers*, that book is *hers*, *hers* are better.
**her·self** (hẽr-self'), *pron.* a form of the 3d pers. sing., feminine pronoun, used: *a*) as an intensive: as, she went *herself*. *b*) as a reflexive: as, she hurt *herself*. *c*) as a quasi-noun meaning "her real or true self" (e.g., she's not *herself* today).
**hertz** (hũrts), *n.* [*pl.* HERTZ, HERTZES], [see next entry], the international unit of frequency, equal to one cycle per second.
**Hertz·i·an waves** (hert'si-ən, hũrt'-), [after H.R. *Hertz* (1857–1894), G. physicist], [sometimes h-], radio waves or other electromagnetic radiation resulting from oscillations of electricity in a conductor.
**Her·ze·go·vi·na** (her'tsi-gō-vē'nə), *n.* a former province of Austria-Hungary, now in Yugoslavia.
**he's** (hēz), 1. he is. 2. he has.
**Hesh·van** (hesh'vən), *n.* Cheshvan.
**hes·i·tan·cy** (hez'ə-tən-si), *n.* [*pl.* -CIES], hesitation; indecision; doubt: also **hes'i·tance.**
**hes·i·tant** (hez'ə-tənt), *adj.* hesitating; undecided; doubtful. —**hes'i·tant·ly,** *adv.*
**hes·i·tate** (hez'ə-tāt'), *v.i.* [-TATED, -TATING], [< L. < *haerere*, to stick], 1. to stop in indecision; pause or delay in acting or deciding. 2. to pause; stop momentarily. 3. to be reluctant: as, I *hesitate* to ask. 4. to pause continually in speaking. —**hes'i·tat'er, hes'i·ta'tor,** *n.* —**hes'i·tat'ing·ly,** *adv.*
**hes·i·ta·tion** (hez'ə-tā'shən), *n.* a hesitating; specif., *a*) indecision. *b*) a pausing. *c*) reluctance. *d*) a stammering. —**hes'i·ta'tive,** *adj.*
**Hes·per·i·des** (hes-per'ə-dēz'), *n.pl.* in *Gr. mythology*, 1. the nymphs who guarded the golden apples given as a wedding present by Gaea to Hera. 2. the garden where these apples grew.
**Hes·per·us** (hes'pẽr-əs), *n.* [L.], the evening star, especially Venus: also **Hes'per.**
**Hesse** (hes, hes'i), *n.* 1. a former duchy of W central Germany. 2. later, a district of W Germany.
**Hes·sian** (hesh'ən), *adj.* of Hesse or its people. *n.* 1. a native or inhabitant of Hesse. 2. any of the Hessian mercenaries who fought for the British in the Revolutionary War.
**Hessian fly,** a small, two-winged fly whose larvae destroy wheat crops.
**hest** (hest), *n.* [< AS. *hæs*, command < *hatan*, to call], [Archaic], behest; order.
**he·tae·ra** (hi-têr'ə), *n.* [*pl.* -RAE (-ē)], [< Gr. < *hetairos*, companion], in ancient Greece, a courtesan, usually an educated slave: also **he·tai·ra** (hi-tī'rə).
**het·er·o-,** [< Gr. < *heteros*, the other (of two)], a combining form meaning *other, another, different*: opposed to *homo-*: also **heter-.**
**het·er·o·cy·clic** (het'ẽr-ə-sī'klik, -sik'lik), *adj.* designating or of a cyclic molecular arrangement of atoms of carbon and other elements.
**het·er·o·dox** (het'ẽr-ə-doks'), *adj.* [< Gr. < *hetero-*, other + *doxa*, opinion], departing from or opposed to the usual beliefs or established doctrines, especially in religion; unorthodox.
·**het·er·o·dox·y** (het'ẽr-ə-dok'si), *n.* [*pl.* -IES], 1. the quality or fact of being heterodox. 2. a heterodox belief or doctrine.
**het·er·o·dyne** (het'ẽr-ə-din'), *adj.* having to do with the combination of radio oscillations of somewhat different frequencies coupled in such a way as to produce beats of intermediate frequency. *v.t.* [-DYNED, -DYNING], to combine (a series of waves) with a series of a different frequency.
**het·er·o·ge·ne·ous** (het'ẽr-ə-jē'ni-əs), *adj.* [< ML. < Gr. < *hetero-*, other + *genos*, a kind], 1. differing or opposite in structure, quality, etc.; dissimilar. 2. composed of unrelated or unlike elements or parts; miscellaneous. —**het'er·o·ge·ne'i·ty** (-ō-jə-nē'ə-ti), [*pl.* -TIES], *n.* —**het'er·o·ge'ne·ous·ly,** *adv.*
**het·er·o·nym** (het'ẽr-ə-nim'), *n.* [< Gr. < *hetero-*, other + *onyma*, name], a word with the same spelling as another but with a different meaning and pronunciation (e.g., *tear*, a drop from the eye, *tear*, to rip). —**het'er·on'y·mous** (-on'ə-məs), *adj.*
**het·er·o·sex·u·al** (het'ẽr-ō-sek'shōō-əl), *adj.* 1. of or having sexual desire for those of the opposite sex. 2. in *biology*, of different sexes. *n.* a heterosexual individual. Opposed to *homosexual.* —**het'er·o·sex'u·al'i·ty** (-al'ə-ti), *n.*
**het·man** (het'mən), *n.* [*pl.* -MANS], [Pol. < G. < *haupt*, head + *mann*, man], a Cossack chief.
**het up** (het), [*het*, dial. pt. & pp. of *heat*], [Slang], excited.
**HEW,** (Dept. of) Health, Education, and Welfare.
**hew** (hū), *v.t.* [HEWED, HEWED or HEWN, HEWING], [AS. *heawan*], 1. to chop or cut with an ax, knife, etc. 2. to make or shape as by cutting or chopping

with an ax, etc. 3. to chop down (a tree) with an ax. *v.i.* to make cutting or chopping blows with an ax, knife, etc. —**hew'er,** *n.*

**hewn** (hūn), *adj.* cut or formed by hewing.

**hex** (heks), *n.* [< G. *hexe*, a witch < OHG.], 1. [Dial.], a witch or sorcerer. 2. [Colloq.], something supposed to bring bad luck; jinx. *v.t.* [Colloq.], to bewitch; cause bad luck to.

**hex·a-,** [< Gr. *hex*, six], a combining form meaning *six*: also **hex-.**

**hex·a·gon** (hek'sə-gon'), *n.* [< L. < Gr. < *hex*, six + *gōnia*, a corner, angle], a plane figure with six angles and six sides. —**hex·ag'o·nal** (-sag'ə-n'l), *adj.* —**hex·ag'o·nal·ly,** *adv.*

**hex·a·gram** (hek'sə-gram'), *n.* [*hexa-* + *-gram*], a six-pointed star formed by extending all sides of a regular hexagon to points of intersection.

**hex·a·he·dron** (hek'sə-hē'drən), *n.* [*pl.* -DRONS, -DRA (-drə)], a solid figure with six plane surfaces. —**hex'a·he'dral,** *adj.*

**hex·am·e·ter** (hek-sam'ə-tēr), *n.* [< L. < Gr.; see HEXA- & METER (rhythm)], 1. a line of verse containing six metrical feet. 2. verse consisting of hexameters. *adj.* having six metrical feet. —**hex'-a·met'ric** (-sə-met'rik), **hex'a·met'ri·cal,** *adj.*

**hex·a·pod** (hek'sə-pod'), *n.* [*hexa-* + *-pod*], an invertebrate animal with six feet; esp., any of the true insects. *adj.* having six feet. —**hex·ap·o·dous** (hek-sap'ə-dəs), *adj.*

**hey** (hā), *interj.* [ME. *hei;* echoic formation], an exclamation used to attract attention, express surprise, etc., or in asking a question.

**hey·day** (hā'dā'), *n.* the time of greatest health, vigor, beauty, prosperity, etc.; prime.

**Hez·e·ki·ah** (hez'ə-kī'ə), *n.* in the *Bible*, a king of Judah: II Kings 18–20.

**Hf,** in *chemistry*, hafnium.

**hf.,** half.

**H.F.,** high-frequency.

**Hg,** *hydrargyrum*, [L.], in *chemistry*, mercury.

**HG., H.G.,** High German.

**hg.,** hectogram; hectograms.

**hgt.,** height.

**H.H.,** 1. His (or Her) Highness. 2. His Holiness.

**hhd.,** hogshead.

**hi** (hī), *interj.* [contr. < *hiya*, contr. < *how are you?*], an exclamation of greeting.

**Hi·a·le·ah** (hī'ə-lē'ə), *n.* a city in SE Florida, near Miami: pop., 67,000.

**hi·a·tus** (hī-ā'təs), *n.* [*pl.* -TUSES, -TUS], [L., pp. of *hiare*, to gape], 1. a break or gap where a part is missing or lost; blank space; lacuna. 2. a slight pause in pronunciation between two successive vowels in adjacent words or syllables, as between the successive *e*'s in *re-enter*.

**Hi·a·wa·tha** (hī'ə-wô'thə, hē'ə-wä'-), *n.* 1. a Mohawk Indian chief who was responsible for the confederation of the Five Nations (the Iroquois League). 2. the Indian hero of *The Song of Hiawatha*, a long narrative poem (1855) by Longfellow.

**hi·ber·nal** (hī-būr'nəl), *adj.* [< L. < *hibernus*, wintry], of winter; wintry.

**hi·ber·nate** (hī'bēr-nāt'), *v.i.* [-NATED, -NATING], [< L. pp. of *hibernare* < *hibernus*, wintry], 1. to spend the winter. 2. to spend the winter in a dormant state. —**hi'ber·na'tion,** *n.*

**Hi·ber·ni·a** (hī-būr'ni-ə), *n.* [L.], [Poetic], Ireland. —**Hi·ber'ni·an,** *adj. & n.*

**hi·bis·cus** (hī-bis'kəs, hi-), *n.* [L.; Gr. *hibiskos*, marsh mallow], a plant, shrub, or small tree of the mallow family, with large, colorful flowers.

**hic·cup, hic·cough** (hik'əp), *n.* [? < Walloon Fr. *hikett; hiccough* is a late sp. after *cough*], 1. a sudden, involuntary contraction of the diaphragm that closes the glottis at the moment of breathing in. 2. the sharp, quick sound made by this. *v.i.* to make a hiccup. *v.t.* to utter with a hiccup.

**‡hic ja·cet** (hik jā'sit), [L.], 1. here lies: inscribed on tombstones. 2. an epitaph.

**hick** (hik), *n.* [altered < *Richard*], [Colloq.], a country person, regarded as unsophisticated, simple, etc.; hayseed: somewhat contemptuous term. *adj.* [Colloq.], of or like a hick.

**hick·o·ry** (hik'ēr-i), *n.* [*pl.* -RIES], [< Am. Ind. *powcohicora*], 1. an American tree of the walnut family, with smooth-shelled, edible nuts. 2. its hard, tough wood. 3. its nut: also **hickory nut.**

**hi·dal·go** (hi-dal'gō), *n.* [*pl.* -GOS], [Sp., contr. of *hijo de algo*, son of something], in Spain, a nobleman of secondary rank, below a grandee.

**hid·den** (hid''n), alt. pp. of **hide** (conceal). *adj.* concealed; obscure; secret.

**hide** (hīd), *v.t.* [HID (hid), HIDDEN or HID, HIDING], [AS. *hydan*], 1. to put or keep out of sight; secrete; conceal. 2. to keep secret. 3. to obstruct the view of. 4. to turn away, as one's face, head, etc. *v.i.* 1. to be concealed. 2. to conceal oneself. —**hid'er,** *n.*

**hide** (hīd), *n.* [AS. *hyd*], 1. an animal skin or pelt, either raw or tanned. 2. the human skin: now humorous or contemptuous. *v.t.* [HIDED, HIDING], 1. to take the hide off; skin. 2. [Colloq.], to thrash; flog. —**neither hide nor hair,** nothing whatsoever.

**hide-and-seek** (hīd'ən-sēk'), *n.* a children's game in which some players hide and others then try to find them: also **hide-and-go-seek.**

**hide·bound** (hīd'bound'), *adj.* 1. having the hide tight over the body structure: said of animals. 2. obstinately conservative and narrow-minded.

**hid·e·ous** (hid'i-əs), *adj.* [< OFr. < *hi(s)de*, fright], horrible; very ugly; revolting; dreadful. —**hid'-e·ous·ly,** *adv.* —**hid'e·ous·ness,** *n.*

**hide-out** (hīd'out'), *n.* [Colloq.], a hiding place for gangsters or the like.

**hid·ing** (hīd'iŋ), *n.* 1. *a)* the act of one that hides. *b)* the condition of being hidden: usually in the phrase *in hiding*. 2. a place to hide.

**hid·ing** (hīd'iŋ), *n.* [Colloq.], a severe beating.

**hie** (hī), *v.i. & v.t.* [HIED, HIEING or HYING], [AS. *higian*], to speed; hasten: often reflexive.

**hi·er·arch·y** (hī'ēr-är'ki), *n.* [*pl.* -IES], [< OFr. < LL. < Gr. < *hieros*, sacred + *archos*, ruler < *archein*, to rule], 1. a system of church government by priests or other clergy in graded ranks. 2. the group of officials in such a system. 3. a group of persons or things arranged in order of rank, grade, class, etc. —**hi'er·ar'chi·cal, hi'er·ar'chic,** *adj.* —**hi'er·ar'chi·cal·ly,** *adv.*

**hi·er·at·ic** (hī'ə-rat'ik), *adj.* [< L. < Gr. *hieratikos* < *hieros*, sacred], 1. of or used by priests; priestly; sacerdotal. 2. designating or of the abridged form of cursive hieroglyphic writing once used by Egyptian priests. Also **hi'er·at'i·cal.** —**hi'er·at'i·cal·ly,** *adv.*

**hi·er·o·glyph** (hī'ēr-ə-glif', hī'rə-), *n.* a hieroglyphic.

**hi·er·o·glyph·ic** (hī'ēr-ə-glif'ik, hī'rə-), *adj.* [< Fr. < LL. < Gr. < *hieros*, sacred + *glyphein*, to carve], 1. of, like, or written in hieroglyphics. 2. symbolical; emblematic. 3. hard to read or understand. Also **hi'er·o·glyph'i·cal.** *n.* 1. a picture or symbol representing a word, syllable, or sound, used by the ancient Egyptians and others. 2. *usually pl.* a method of writing using hieroglyphics; picture writing. 3. a symbol, sign, etc. hard to understand. 4. *pl.* writing hard to decipher. —**hi'er·o·glyph'i·cal·ly,** *adv.*

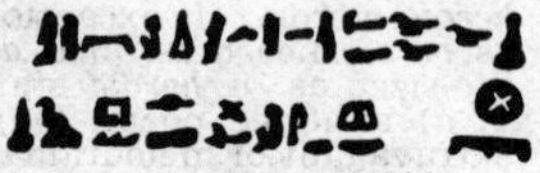

HIEROGLYPHICS

**hi-fi** (hī'fī'), *adj.* of or having high fidelity of sound reproduction.

**hig·gle** (hig''l), *v.i.* [-GLED, -GLING], [prob. weakened form of *haggle*], to argue about terms, price, etc.; haggle; chaffer. —**hig'gler,** *n.*

**hig·gle·dy-pig·gle·dy** (hig''l-di-pig''l-di), *adv.* [redupl., prob. after *pig*], in disorder; in jumbled confusion. *adj.* disorderly; jumbled; confused.

**high** (hī), *adj.* [AS. *heah*], 1. lofty; tall; of more than normal height: not used of persons. 2. extending upward a (specified) distance. 3. situated far above the ground or other level. 4. reaching to or done from a height: as, a *high* jump, a *high* dive. 5. above others in rank, position, quality, character, etc.; superior. 6. main; principal; chief: as, a *high* priest. 7. grave; very serious: as, *high* treason. 8. complex; profound: usually in the comparative, as, *higher* mathematics. 9. greater in size, amount, degree, power, etc. than usual: as, *high* stakes. 10. expensive; costly. 11. luxurious and extravagant: as, *high* living. 12. haughty; overbearing. 13. advanced to its acme or fullness: as, *high* noon. 14. raised or acute in pitch; sharp; shrill. 15. slightly tainted; strong-smelling: as, this meat is *high*. 16. extreme or inflexible in matters of ceremony, doctrine, etc. 17. hilarious; elated; excited: as, *high* spirits. 18. [Slang], *a)* drunk; intoxicated. *b)* under the influence of a drug. 19. in *geography*, designating a latitude far from the equator. 20. in *machinery*, of or adjusted at the highest transmission ratio: said of gears. 21. in *phonetics*, produced with part of the tongue raised toward the roof of the mouth: said of a vowel. *adv.* 1. in a high manner. 2. in or to a high level, degree, rank, etc. *n.* 1. a high level, degree, etc. 2. an area of high barometric pressure. 3. an arrangement of gears giving the greatest speed. —**fly high,** to have high hopes or ambitions. —**high and dry,** stranded. —**high and low,** everywhere. —**high and mighty,** [Colloq.], arrogant; haughty. —**on high,** 1. high above. 2. in heaven.

**high·ball** (hī'bôl'), *n.* 1. liquor, usually whisky or

brandy, mixed with soda water, ginger ale, etc. and served with ice in a tall glass: also **high ball.** 2. a railroad signal meaning "go ahead." ***v.i.*** [Slang], to proceed at great speed.

**high·born** (hī′bôrn′), ***adj.*** of noble birth.

**high·boy** (hī′boi′), ***n.*** [*high* + *boy*], a high chest of drawers mounted on legs.

**high·bred** (hī′bred′), ***adj.*** 1. of superior stock or breed. 2. showing good breeding; well-mannered.

HIGHBOY

**high-brow, high·brow** (hī′brou′), ***n.*** [Slang], one having or pretending to have highly cultivated tastes; intellectual. ***adj.*** [Slang], of or fit for such a person. Usually a term of derision.

**High Church,** that party of the Anglican Church which emphasizes the importance of the priesthood, rituals, and sacraments. **—High′-Church′,** ***adj.*** **—High′-Church′man** [*pl.* -MEN], ***n.***

**high comedy,** comedy reflecting the life of the upper social classes, characterized by witty, often sophisticated, dialogue; comedy of manners.

**high·er-up** (hī′ẽr-up′), ***n.*** [Colloq.], a person of higher rank or position.

**high·fa·lu·tin, high·fa·lu·ting** (hī′fə-lōō′t'n), ***adj.*** [Colloq.], high-flown; pompous; pretentious.

**high fidelity,** in radio, sound recording, etc., nearly exact reproduction of a wide range of sound waves, as from 50 to 15,000 cycles per second.

**high·fli·er, high·fly·er** (hī′flī′ẽr), ***n.*** 1. a person or thing that flies high. 2. one who acts or talks in an extravagant manner.

**high-flown** (hī′flōn′), ***adj.*** 1. extravagantly ambitious. 2. trying to be eloquent; bombastic.

**high-fre·quen·cy** (hī′frē′kwən-si), ***adj.*** designating or of an alternating electric current or oscillation with a relatively high frequency, now usually more than 20,000 cycles per second.

**High German,** 1. the Germanic dialects spoken in the high regions of central and southern Germany: distinguished from *Low German.* 2. the official and literary form of the German language, technically called *New High German*: see also **Old High German, Middle High German.**

**high-grade** (hī′grād′), ***adj.*** excellent.

**high·hand·ed** (hī′han′did), ***adj.*** overbearing; arbitrary; arrogant. **—high′hand′ed·ly,** ***adv.*** **—high′-hand′ed·ness,** ***n.***

**high-hat** (hī′hat′), ***adj.*** [Slang], 1. elegant; stylish. 2. snobbish. ***n.*** [Slang], a snob. ***v.t.*** [-HATTED, -HATTING], [Slang], to treat snobbishly; snub.

**high·jack** (hī′jak′), ***v.t.*** [Colloq.], to hijack.

**high jump,** an athletic contest in which the contestants jump for height over a horizontal bar.

**high·land** (hī′lənd), ***n.*** region higher than adjacent land and containing many hills or mountains. ***adj.*** of, in, or from such a region. **—the Highlands,** the elevated mountainous region in N and W Scotland. **—high′land·er, High′land·er,** ***n.***

**Highland fling,** a lively dance of the Highlands.

**high life,** the way of life of fashionable society.

**high·light** (hī′līt′), ***v.t.*** 1. to give a high light or high lights to. 2. to give prominence to.

**high light,** 1. *a*) a part on which light is brightest. *b*) a part of a painting, etc. on which light is represented as brightest. *c*) the representation or effect of such light in a painting, etc. 2. the most important or interesting part, scene, etc.: also **high spot.**

**high·ly** (hī′li), ***adv.*** 1. extremely. 2. favorably. 3. at a high price. 4. in a high office or rank.

**High Mass,** in the *R. C. Church,* a Mass with full ceremonials and music, usually with a deacon and a subdeacon assisting the celebrant.

**high-mind·ed** (hī′mīn′did), ***adj.*** having or showing high ideals, principles, and feelings. **—high′-mind′ed·ly,** ***adv.*** **—high′-mind′ed·ness,** ***n.***

**high·ness** (hī′nis), ***n.*** 1. the quality or state of being high; height. 2. [H-], a title used in speaking to or of a member of a royal family.

**high-pitched** (hī′picht′), ***adj.*** 1. high in pitch; shrill. 2. lofty; exalted. 3. steep in slope.

**High Point,** a city in central North Carolina: pop., 62,000.

**high-powered** (hī′pou′ẽrd), ***adj.*** very powerful.

**high-pres·sure** (hī′presh′ẽr), ***adj.*** 1. having, using, or withstanding relatively high pressure. 2. using energetic or strongly persuasive methods or arguments. ***v.t.*** [-SURED, -SURING], [Colloq.], to urge with such methods or arguments.

**high priest,** 1. a chief priest. 2. the chief priest of the ancient Jewish priesthood.

**high-proof** (hī′prōōf′), ***adj.*** high in alcohol content.

**high-rise** (hī′rīz′), ***adj.*** designating or of a tall apartment house, office building, etc. of many stories. ***n.*** a high-rise building.

**high·road** (hī′rōd′), ***n.*** 1. a main road; highway. 2. an easy or direct way.

**high school,** a school offering academic or vocational subjects, attended by students who have completed elementary school or, in many systems, junior high school.

**high seas,** ocean waters not under the jurisdiction of any country.

**high-sound·ing** (hī′soun′diŋ), ***adj.*** sounding pretentious or imposing.

**high-spir·it·ed** (hī′spir′it-id), ***adj.*** 1. having or showing a courageous or noble spirit. 2. spirited; lively. **—high′-spir′it·ed·ly,** ***adv.***

**high-strung** (hī′struŋ′), ***adj.*** highly sensitive; nervous and tense; excitable.

**hight** (hīt), ***adj.*** [< AS. < *hatan,* to call], [Archaic], named; called: as, a maiden *hight* Elaine.

**high-ten·sion** (hī′ten′shən), ***adj.*** having or carrying a high voltage.

**high-test** (hī′test′), ***adj.*** 1. passing severe tests; meeting difficult requirements. 2. having a low boiling point: said of gasoline.

**high tide,** 1. the highest level to which the tide rises. 2. the time when the tide is at this level. 3. any culminating point or time.

**high time,** 1. time beyond the proper time but before it is too late. 2. [Slang], a gay time.

**high-toned** (hī′tōnd′), ***adj.*** 1. high in tone; high-pitched. 2. characterized by dignity, lofty quality, etc. 3. [Colloq.], stylish; fashionable.

**high treason,** treason against the ruler or government.

**high water,** 1. high tide. 2. the highest level reached by a body of water.

**high-wa·ter mark** (hī′wô′tẽr, hī′wät′ẽr), 1. the highest level reached by a body of water. 2. the mark left after high water has receded. 3. a culminating point; highest point.

**high·way** (hī′wā′), ***n.*** 1. a public road. 2. a main road; thoroughfare. 3. a direct way to some objective.

**high·way·man** (hī′wā′mən), ***n.*** [*pl.* -MEN], a man who robs travelers on a highway.

**hi·jack** (hī′jak′), ***v.t.*** [prob. *hi* (for *high*) + *jack, v.*], [Colloq.], 1. to steal (goods in transit, especially bootlegged liquor) by force. 2. to steal such goods from (a person) by force. 3. to force the pilot of (an aircraft) to fly to a nonscheduled landing point. Also sp. **highjack.** **—hi′jack′er,** ***n.***

**hike** (hīk), ***v.i.*** [HIKED, HIKING], [< dial. *heik*], to take a long, vigorous walk; tramp or march. ***v.t.*** [Colloq.], 1. to pull up; hoist. 2. to raise (prices, etc.). ***n.*** a hiking; march. **—hik′er,** ***n.***

**hi·lar·i·ous** (hi-lâr′i-əs, hī-), ***adj.*** [< L. < Gr. *hilaros,* cheerful], very gay; boisterously merry. **—hi·lar′i·ous·ly,** ***adv.*** **—hi·lar′i·ous·ness,** ***n.***

**hi·lar·i·ty** (hi-lar′ə-ti, hī-), ***n.*** the state or quality of being hilarious; noisy merriment.

**hill** (hil), ***n.*** [< AS. *hyll*], 1. a natural raised part of the earth's surface, often rounded, smaller than a mountain. 2. a small pile, heap, or mound: as, an ant*hill.* 3. a small mound of soil heaped over and around plant roots: as, a *hill* of corn. 4. the plant or plants rooted in such a mound. ***v.t.*** 1. to shape into or like a hill. 2. to cover with a hill (sense 3). **—hill′er,** ***n.***

**hill·bill·y** (hil′bil′i), ***n.*** [*pl.* -IES], [< nickname *Billy*], [Colloq.], a person who lives in or comes from the mountains or backwoods, especially of the South: somewhat contemptuous term. ***adj.*** [Colloq.], of or characteristic of hillbillies.

**hill·ock** (hil′ək), ***n.*** a small hill; mound.

**hill of beans,** [< *hill, n.* 3], [Colloq.], a trifle.

**hill·side** (hil′sīd′), ***n.*** the side or slope of a hill.

**hill·top** (hil′top′), ***n.*** the top of a hill.

**hill·y** (hil′i), ***adj.*** [-IER, -IEST], 1. full of hills. 2. like a hill; steep. **—hill′i·ness,** ***n.***

**hilt** (hilt), ***n.*** [AS.], the handle of a sword, dagger, tool, etc. ***v.t.*** to put a hilt on. **—(up) to the hilt,** thoroughly; entirely. **—hilt′ed,** ***adj.***

**hi·lum** (hī′ləm), ***n.*** [*pl.* -LA (-lə)], [L., little thing], in *botany,* a scar on a seed, marking the place where it was attached to the seed vessel.

**him** (him), ***pron.*** [AS.], the objective case of **he:** also used colloquially as a predicate complement with a linking verb (e.g., that's *him*).

**Hi·ma·la·yas** (hi-mäl′yəz, him′ə-lā′əz), *n.pl.* a mountain system between India and Tibet, the highest known: also **Himalaya Mountains.** —**Hi·ma′la·yan,** *adj.*

**him·self** (him-self′), *pron.* a form of the 3d pers. sing., masculine pronoun, used: *a*) as an intensive: as, he went *himself.* *b*) as a reflexive: as, he hurt *himself.* *c*) as a quasi-noun meaning "his real or true self" (e.g., he is not *himself* today).

**hind** (hīnd), *adj.* [HINDER, HINDMOST or HINDERMOST], [prob. < *hinder,* adj.], back; rear; posterior.

**hind** (hīnd), *n.* [*pl.* HINDS, HIND; see PLURAL, II, D, 1], [AS.], the female of the red deer, in and after its third year.

**hind** (hīnd), *n.* [AS. *hina, higna*], 1. in northern England and Scotland, a skilled farm worker or servant. 2. a peasant; rustic.

**Hind.,** 1. Hindu. 2. Hindustan. 3. Hindustani.

**hind·brain** (hīnd′brān′), *n.* the hindmost part of the brain.

**hin·der** (hin′dẽr), *v.t.* [AS. *hindrian*], 1. to keep back; obstruct; prevent; stop. 2. to make difficult for; thwart; frustrate. —**hin′der·er,** *n.*

**hind·er** (hīn′dẽr), *adj.* [AS. *hinder, adv.;* now felt as compar. of *hind*], hind; rear; posterior.

**Hin·di** (hin′di), *adj.* [see HINDU], of or associated with northern India. *n.* the group of Indo-European, Indic languages spoken there.

**hind·most** (hīnd′mōst′), *adj.* farthest back; last.

**Hin·doo** (hin′dōō), *adj.* & *n.* [*pl.* -DOOS], Hindu.

**hind·quar·ter** (hīnd′kwôr′tẽr), *n.* the hind leg and loin of a carcass of veal, beef, lamb, etc.

**hin·drance** (hin′drəns), *n.* 1. a hindering. 2. any person or thing that hinders; obstacle.

**hind·sight** (hīnd′sīt′), *n.* an understanding, after the event, of what should have been done.

**Hin·du** (hin′dōō), *n.* [< Per. < *Hind,* India], 1. any of the peoples of India that speak languages derived from the Indic branch of Indo-European. 2. a follower of Hinduism. *adj.* 1. of the Hindus, their language, culture, etc. 2. of Hinduism.

**Hin·du·ism** (hin′dōō-iz'm), *n.* the religion and social system of the Hindus.

**Hin·du·stan** (hin′doo-stan′, -stän′), *n.* 1. the northern part of India. 2. the Indian peninsula north of the Deccan. 3. popularly, India.

**Hin·du·sta·ni** (hin′doo-stan′i, -stä′ni), *n.* the most important of the Western Hindi group of languages, used as a trade language throughout India. *adj.* 1. of Hindustan or its people. 2. of Hindustani.

**hinge** (hinj), *n.* [< ME. *hengen,* to hang], 1. a joint on which a door, gate, lid, etc. swings. 2. a natural joint, as of the bivalve shell of a clam or oyster. 3. anything on which matters turn or depend. *v.t.* [HINGED, HINGING], to equip with or attach by a hinge. *v.i.* 1. to hang or swing as on a hinge. 2. to depend. —**hinged,** *adj.*

**hin·ny** (hin′i), *n.* [*pl.* -NIES], [L. *hinnus* < Gr. *ginnos*], the offspring of a male horse and a female donkey: distinguished from *mule.*

**hint** (hint), *n.* [< AS. *henten,* to seize], a slight indication; faint suggestion; indirect allusion. *v.t.* to give a hint of; intimate. *v.i.* to make a hint or hints. —**hint at,** to suggest indirectly. —**take a hint,** to perceive and act on a hint. —**hint′er,** *n.*

**hin·ter·land** (hin′tẽr-land′), *n.* [G.; *hinter,* back + *land,* land], 1. the land or district behind that bordering on a coast or river. 2. an area far from big cities and towns; back country.

**hip** (hip), *n.* [AS. *hype*], 1. the part of the body surrounding and including the joint formed by each thigh bone and the pelvis. 2. the angle formed by the meeting of two sloping sides of a roof. *v.t.* [HIPPED, HIPPING], to make (a roof) with such an angle. —**on** (or **upon**) **the hip,** at a disadvantage.

**hip** (hip), *n.* [AS. *heop*], the small, fleshy, ripened fruit of a rosebush.

**hip** (hip), *adj.* [? < *hep*], [Slang], informed, aware, sophisticated, etc.

**hip·bone** (hip′bōn′), *n.* 1. the innominate bone. 2. the ilium. 3. the neck of the femur.

**hipped** (hipt), *adj.* 1. having hips (of a specified sort): as, broad-*hipped.* 2. in *architecture,* having a hip or hips: as, a *hipped* roof.

**hipped** (hipt), *adj.* [< *hypochondria*], [Colloq.], 1. in low spirits; depressed. 2. obsessed (with *on*).

**hip·pie** (hip′i), *n.* [Slang], a young person who, in his alienation from conventional society, has turned to mysticism, psychedelic drugs, communal living, experimental arts, etc.

**hip·po** (hip′ō), *n.* [*pl.* -POS], [Colloq.], a hippopotamus.

**Hip·poc·ra·tes** (hi-pok′rə-tēz′), *n.* Greek physician; 460?–377? B.C.: called the *Father of Medicine.* —**Hip·po·crat·ic** (hip′ə-krat′ik), *adj.*

**Hippocratic oath,** the oath, attributed to Hippocrates, generally taken by medical graduates: it sets forth an ethical code for the profession.

**Hip·po·crene** (hip′ə-krēn′, hip′ə-krē′ni), *n.* in *Gr. mythology,* a fountain on Mt. Helicon, sacred to the Muses, and supposed to inspire poets.

**hip·po·drome** (hip′ə-drōm′), *n.* [< Fr. < L. < Gr. < *hippos,* a horse + *dromos,* a course], 1. in ancient Greece and Rome, an oval course for horse races and chariot races, surrounded by tiers of seats. 2. an arena or building for a circus, etc.

**hip·po·pot·a·mus** (hip′ə-pot′ə-məs), *n.* [*pl.* -MUSES, -MI (-mī′), -MUS; see PLURAL, II, D, 1], [L. < Gr. < *hippos,* a horse + *potamos,* river], a large, plant-eating mammal of the hog family, with a heavy, thick-skinned, almost hairless body: it lives chiefly in or near rivers in Africa.

**hip roof,** a roof with sloping ends and sides.

**hip·ster** (hip′stẽr), *n.* [Slang], 1. a hip person, esp., a devotee of modern jazz. 2. a beatnik, specif. one who professes total indifference to the value of any human activity.

**hir·cine** (hũr′sīn, -sin), *adj.* [< L. < *hircus,* goat], of or like a goat, especially in smell.

**hire** (hīr), *n.* [AS. *hyr*], 1. the amount paid for the services of a person or the use of a thing. 2. a hiring. *v.t.* [HIRED, HIRING], 1. to pay for the services of (a person) or the use of (a thing); employ. 2. to give the use of (a thing) in return for payment. —**for hire,** available for work or use in return for payment: also **on hire.** —**hire out,** to give one's work in return for payment. —**hir′a·ble, hire′a·ble,** *adj.* —**hir′er,** *n.*

**hire·ling** (hīr′liŋ), *n.* [see HIRE & -LING], a person who will follow anyone's orders for pay; mercenary. *adj.* of or like a hireling; mercenary.

**Hi·ro·hi·to** (hêr′ō-hē′tō), *n.* emperor of Japan (1926– ); born 1901.

**Hi·ro·shi·ma** (hêr′ō-shē′mä), *n.* a city on the SW coast of Honshu, Japan: pop., 259,000: on August 6, 1945, it was largely destroyed by an American atomic bomb, the first ever used in warfare.

**hir·sute** (hũr′sōōt, hẽr-sūt′), *adj.* [L. *hirsutus*], hairy; shaggy; bristly. —**hir′sute·ness,** *n.*

**his** (hiz), *pron.* [AS.], that or those belonging to him: often after *of,* as, a friend of *his,* that book is *his, his* are better. *possessive pronominal adj.* of, belonging to, or done by him: as, *his* father, *his* poem.

**His·pa·ni·a** (his-pā′ni-ə, -pä′nyə), *n.* [Poetic], Spain: the Latin name. —**His·pan′ic** (-pan′ik), *adj.*

**His·pan·io·la** (his′pən-yō′lə), *n.* an island in the West Indies, between Cuba and Puerto Rico: area, 28,242 sq. mi.: divided between Haiti and the Dominican Republic: formerly called **Haiti.**

**hiss** (his), *v.i.* [echoic], 1. to make a sound like that of a prolonged *s,* as of a goose, snake, escaping steam, etc. 2. to show hatred or disapproval by hissing. *v.t.* 1. to say or indicate by hissing. 2. to condemn, force, or drive by hissing. *n.* a sound like a prolonged *s.* —**hiss′er,** *n.*

**hist** (st, hist), *interj.* be quiet! listen!

**hist.,** 1. historian. 2. historical. 3. history.

**his·ta·mine** (his′tə-mēn′, -min), *n.* [see HISTO- & AMINE], an amine, $C_5H_9N_3$, discharged by the tissues in allergic reactions: it dilates blood vessels, stimulates gastric secretion, etc. —**his·ta·min·ic** (his′tə-min′ik), *adj.*

**his·to-,** [< Gr. *histos,* a loom, web], a combining form meaning *tissue,* as in *histology*: also **hist-.**

**his·tol·o·gy** (his-tol′ə-ji), *n.* [*histo-* + *-logy*], the branch of biology concerned with the microscopic study of the structure of tissues. —**his·to·log·i·cal** (his′tə-loj′i-k'l), *adj.* —**his·tol′o·gist,** *n.*

**his·to·ri·an** (his-tôr′i-ən, -tō′ri-), *n.* 1. a writer of history; chronicler. 2. an authority on or specialist in history.

**his·tor·ic** (his-tôr′ik, -tor′-), *adj.* historical; esp., famous in history.

**his·tor·i·cal** (his-tôr′i-k'l, -tor′-), *adj.* 1. of or concerned with history as a science: as, the *historical* method. 2. providing evidence for a fact of history: as, a *historical* document. 3. based on people or events of the past: as, a *historical* novel. 4. established by history; not legendary or fictional; factual. 5. famous in history: now usually *historic.* —**his·tor′i·cal·ly,** *adv.* —**his·tor′i·cal·ness,** *n.*

**historical present,** the present tense used in telling about past events: also **historic present.**

**his·to·ri·og·ra·pher** (his-tôr′i-og′rə-fẽr, -tō′ri-), *n.* [< LL. < Gr. < *historia,* history + *graphein,* to write], a historian; esp., one appointed to write the history of some institution, country, etc. —**his·to′ri·og′ra·phy,** *n.*

**his·to·ry** (his′tə-ri, his′tri), *n.* [*pl.* -RIES], [< L. < Gr. *historia* < *histōr,* learned], 1. an account of what has happened; narrative. 2. *a*) what has happened in the life of a people, country, etc. *b*) a systematic account of this. 3. all recorded events of the past. 4. the branch of knowledge that deals systematically with the recording, analyzing, and co-ordinating of past events. 5. a known or recorded past: as, this coat has a *history*. **—make history,** to be or do something important enough to be recorded.

**his·tri·on·ic** (his'tri-on'ik), *adj.* [< LL. < L. *histrio*, actor], 1. of, or having the nature of, acting or actors. 2. overacted or overacting; theatrical; artificial. **—his'tri·on'i·cal·ly,** *adv.*

**his·tri·on·ics** (his'tri-on'iks), *n.pl.* 1. [construed as sing.], theatricals; dramatics. 2. an artificial or affected manner; theatricality.

**hit** (hit), *v.t.* [HIT, HITTING], [AS. *hittan* < ON. *hitta*, to meet with], 1. to come against, usually with force; strike: as, the car *hit* the tree. 2. to give a blow to; strike. 3. to strike by throwing or shooting a missile: as, he fired and *hit* the deer. 4. to cause (something) to bump or strike, as in falling, moving, etc. 5. to affect strongly; distress: as, they were hard *hit* by the famine. 6. to come upon by accident or after search: as, he *hit* the right answer. 7. to appeal to; suit: as, the hat *hit* her fancy. 8. [Slang], to arrive at or in: as, to *hit* town. 9. in *baseball*, to get (a specified base hit). *v.i.* 1. to give a blow or blows; strike. 2. to knock, bump, or strike. 3. to come by accident or after search: as, we *hit* upon the clue. 4. to ignite the combustible mixture in its cylinders: said of an internal-combustion engine. 5. in *baseball*, to get a base hit. *n.* 1. a blow that strikes its mark. 2. a collision. 3. an effectively witty or sarcastic remark. 4. a stroke of good fortune. 5. a successful and popular song, book, play, etc. 6. in *baseball*, a base hit. **—hit it off,** to get along well together; be congenial. **—hit or miss,** in a haphazard or aimless way. **—hit'ter,** *n.*

**hit-and-run** (hit''n-run'), *adj.* hitting and then escaping: also **hit'-skip'.**

**hitch** (hich), *v.i.* [prob. < OFr. *hocier*, to move jerkily], 1. to move jerkily; limp; hobble. 2. to become fastened or caught. *v.t.* 1. to move, pull, or shift with jerks. 2. to fasten with a hook, knot, etc. 3. [Slang], to get (a ride) in hitchhiking. *n.* 1. a short, sudden movement or pull; tug; jerk. 2. a hobble; limp. 3. a hindrance; obstacle. 4. a catching or fastening; catch. 5. [Military Slang], a period of enlistment. 6. in *nautical usage*, a kind of knot that can be easily undone. **—without a hitch,** smoothly and successfully. **—hitch'er,** *n.*

**hitch·hike** (hich'hīk'), *v.i.* [-HIKED, -HIKING], to travel by asking for rides from motorists along the way. **—hitch'hik'er,** *n.*

**hith·er** (hith'ẽr), *adv.* [AS. *hider*], to this place; here. *adj.* on or toward this side; nearer.

**hith·er·most** (hith'ẽr-mōst'), *adj.* nearest.

**hith·er·to** (hith'ẽr-to͞o'), *adv.* until this time.

**hith·er·ward** (hith'ẽr-wẽrd), *adv.* [Rare], toward this place; hither: also **hith'er·wards.**

**Hit·ler, A·dolf** (ä'dôlf hit'lẽr), 1889–1945; leader of the Nazis and chancellor of Germany (1933–1945).

**Hit·ler·ism** (hit'lẽr-iz'm), *n.* the fascist program, ideas, and methods of Hitler and the Nazis. **—Hit'ler·ite,** *n. & adj.*

**Hit·tite** (hit'īt), *n.* 1. any of an ancient people of Asia Minor and Syria (c. 2000–700 B.C.). 2. the language of the Hittites. *adj.* of the Hittites, their language, or culture.

**hive** (hīv), *n.* [AS. *hyf*], 1. a box or other shelter for a colony of domestic bees; beehive. 2. a colony of bees living in a hive. 3. a crowd of busy, bustling people. 4. a place of great bustle and activity. *v.t.* [HIVED, HIVING], 1. to gather (bees) into a hive. 2. to store up (honey) in a hive. *v.i.* 1. to enter a hive. 2. to live together as in a hive. **—hive'less,** *adj.* **—hive'like',** *adj.*

**hives** (hīvz), *n.* [orig. Scot. dial.], an allergic skin condition characterized by itching and the formation of smooth patches, usually red.

**H.M.,** 1. Her Majesty. 2. His Majesty.

**H.M.S.,** 1. His (or Her) Majesty's Service. 2. His (or Her) Majesty's Ship.

**ho** (hō), *interj.* an exclamation of pleasure, surprise, etc., or to attract attention.

**Ho,** in *chemistry*, holmium.

**hoar** (hôr, hōr), *adj.* [AS. *har*], 1. white or grayish-white. 2. hoary. *n.* 1. hoariness. 2. hoarfrost.

**hoard** (hôrd, hōrd), *n.* [AS. *hord*], a supply stored up and hidden or kept in reserve. *v.i.* to store away money, goods, etc. *v.t.* to accumulate and store away. **—hoard'er,** *n.* **—hoard'ing,** *n.*

**hoard·ing** (hôr'diŋ, hōr'-), *n.* [< OFr. < Frank. *hurda*, a pen, fold], [Brit.], 1. a temporary wooden fence around a site of building construction or repair. 2. a billboard.

**hoar·frost** (hôr'frôst', hōr'frost'), *n.* white, frozen dew on the ground, leaves, etc.; rime.

**hoar·hound** (hôr'hound', hōr'-), *n.* horehound.

**hoarse** (hôrs, hōrs), *adj.* [HOARSER, HOARSEST], [AS. *has*], 1. harsh and grating in sound; sounding rough and husky. 2. having a rough, husky voice. **—hoarse'ly,** *adv.* **—hoarse'ness,** *n.*

**hoar·y** (hôr'i, hō'ri), *adj.* [-IER, -IEST], 1. white, gray, or grayish-white. 2. having white or gray hair because very old. 3. very old; ancient. **—hoar'i·ness,** *n.*

**hoax** (hōks), *n.* [< *hocus*], a trick or fraud, especially one meant as a practical joke. *v.t.* to deceive with a hoax. **—hoax'er,** *n.*

**hob** (hob), *n.* [? var. of *hub*], 1. a projecting ledge at the back or side of a fireplace, for keeping a kettle, pan, etc. warm. 2. a peg used as a target in quoits, etc.

**hob** (hob), *n.* [old form of *Rob*, for *Robin* Goodfellow, elf of English folklore], an elf; goblin. **—play** (or **raise**) **hob,** to cause mischief.

**Ho·bart** (hō'bẽrt, -bärt), *n.* seaport and capital of Tasmania: pop., 93,000.

**Hobbes, Thomas** (hobz), 1588–1679; English social philosopher and writer. **—Hob'bism,** *n.*

**hob·ble** (hob''l), *v.i.* [-BLED, -BLING], [ME. *hobelen;* prob. < base of *hop* + freq. *-le*], 1. to go unsteadily, haltingly, etc. 2. to walk lamely; limp. *v.t.* 1. to cause to limp. 2. to hamper the movement of (a horse, etc.) by tying two legs together. 3. to hinder. *n.* 1. a halting walk; limp. 2. a rope, strap, etc. used to hobble a horse. **—hob'bler,** *n.* **—hob'bling,** *adj.* **—hob'bling·ly,** *adv.*

**hob·ble·de·hoy** (hob''l-di-hoi'), *n.* [prob. based on Eng. dial. *hob*, a rustic], 1. a youth between boyhood and manhood. 2. a gawky youth or boy.

**hob·by** (hob'i), *n.* [*pl.* -BIES], [< dim. of *Hob*, old familiar form of *Robin, Robert:* formerly applied to horses], 1. [Rare], a hobbyhorse. 2. something that a person likes to do or study in his spare time; favorite pastime or avocation.

**hob·by·horse** (hob'i-hôrs'), *n.* 1. a child's toy consisting of a stick with a horse's head. 2. a rocking horse.

**hob·gob·lin** (hob'gob'lin), *n.* [< *Hob* (see HOB, an elf) + *goblin*], 1. an elf; goblin. 2. a bogy; bugbear.

**hob·nail** (hob'nāl'), *n.* [*hob* (a peg) + *nail*], a short nail with a broad head, put on the soles of heavy shoes to prevent wear or slipping. *v.t.* to put hobnails on. **—hob'nailed',** *adj.*

**hob·nob** (hob'nob'), *v.i.* [-NOBBED, -NOBBING], [< ME. *habben*, to have + *nabben*, not to have, esp. with reference to alternation in drinking], 1. to drink together. 2. to be on close terms (*with*); associate in a familiar way.

**ho·bo** (hō'bō), *n.* [*pl.* -BOS, -BOES], 1. a migratory worker. 2. a vagrant; tramp. Sometimes shortened to **bo.**

**Ho·bo·ken** (hō'bō-kən), *n.* a city in NE New Jersey, on the Hudson River: pop., 51,000.

**Hob·son's choice** (hob's'nz), [after T. *Hobson*, Eng. liveryman, who let horses in strict order according to their position near the door], a choice of taking what is offered or nothing at all.

**hock** (hok), *n.* [AS. *hoh*, the heel], the joint bending backward in the hind leg of a horse, ox, etc., corresponding to the human ankle. *v.t.* to disable by cutting the tendons of the hock.

**hock** (hok), *n.* [< *Hochheimer* < *Hochheim*, Germany], [Chiefly Brit.], a white Rhine wine.

**hock** (hok), *v.t. & n.* [? < *hock*, obs. card game < D. *hok*, prison, debt], [Slang], pawn.

**hock·ey** (hok'i), *n.* [prob. < OFr. *hoquet*, bent stick], 1. a team game played on ice, in which the players, using curved sticks (**hockey sticks**) and wearing skates, try to drive a rubber disk (*puck*) into their opponents' goal: also **ice hockey.** 2. a similar game played on a field with a small ball instead of a puck: also **field hockey.**

**hock·shop** (hok'shop'), *n.* [Slang], a pawnshop.

**ho·cus** (hō'kəs), *v.t.* [-CUSED or -CUSSED, -CUSING or -CUSSING], [abbrev. of *hocus-pocus*], 1. to play a trick on; dupe; hoax. 2. to drug. 3. to put drugs in (a drink).

**ho·cus-po·cus** (hō'kəs-pō'kəs), *n.* [imitation L.], 1. meaningless words used as a formula by conjurers. 2. sleight of hand; legerdemain. 3. trickery;

deception. ***v.t. & v.i.*** [-CUSED or -CUSSED, -CUSING or -CUSSING], [Colloq.], to trick; dupe.

**hod** (hod), *n.* [< OFr. < MD. *hodde*], 1. a long-handled wooden trough used for carrying bricks, mortar, etc. on the shoulder. 2. a coal scuttle.

**hodge·podge** (hoj′poj′), *n.* [< earlier *hotchpot(ch)* < OFr. < Walloon *hosepot*, kind of stew < OD. *hutspot*], any jumbled mixture; mess; medley.

**Hodg·kin's disease** (hoj′kinz), [after Dr. T. *Hodgkin* (1798–1866), by whom first described], a disease characterized by progressive enlargement of the lymph nodes.

**hoe** (hō), *n.* [< OFr. *houe* < OHG. < *houwan*, to hew], a tool with a thin blade set across the end of a long handle, used for weeding, loosening soil, etc. ***v.t. & v.i.*** [HOED, HOEING], to dig, cultivate, weed, etc. with a hoe. —**ho′er,** *n.*

**hoe·cake** (hō′kāk′), *n.* a thin bread made of corn meal, originally baked on a hoe at the fire.

**hog** (hôg, hog), *n.* [*pl.* HOGS, HOG; see PLURAL, II, D, 1], [AS. *hogg*], 1. a pig; esp., a full-grown pig raised for its meat. 2. [Colloq.], a selfish, greedy, or filthy person. ***v.t.*** [HOGGED, HOGGING], [Slang], to take all of or an unfair share of. —**go the whole hog,** [Slang], to go all the way.

**Ho·garth, William** (hō′gärth), 1697–1764; English painter and engraver.

**hog·back** (hôg′bak′, hog′-), *n.* a ridge with a sharp crest and abruptly sloping sides.

**hog·gish** (hôg′ish, hog′-), *adj.* like a hog; very selfish, greedy, gluttonous, coarse, or filthy. —**hog′gish·ly,** *adv.* —**hog′gish·ness,** *n.*

**hog·nose snake** (hôg′nōz′, hog′-), a small, harmless North American snake with a flat snout.

**hogs·head** (hôgz′hed′, hogz′-), *n.* [ME. *hogsheved*, lit., hog's head], 1. a large barrel or cask, especially one holding from 100 to 140 gallons. 2. a liquid measure, especially one equal to 63 gallons (52½ imperial gallons).

**hog·tie** (hôg′tī′, hog′-), ***v.t.*** [-TIED, -TYING or TIEING], 1. to tie the four feet or the hands and feet of. 2. [Colloq.], to make incapable of effective action, as if by tying up.

**hog·wash** (hôg′wôsh′, hog′wäsh′), *n.* 1. refuse fed to hogs; swill. 2. empty talk, writing, etc.

**Hoh·en·zol·lern** (hō′ən-tsôl′ẽrn; Eng. hō′ən-zol′ẽrn), *n.* the ruling family of Prussia and Germany (1701–1918).

**hoicks** (hoiks), *interj.* [earlier *hoika;* cf. YOICKS], a hunter's call to the hounds: also **hoick.** ***v.t. & v.i.*** to urge as with this call.

**hoi·den** (hoi′d'n), ***n., adj., v.i.*** hoyden.

**hoi·den·ish** (hoi′d'n-ish), *adj.* hoydenish.

‡**hoi pol·loi** (hoi′ pə-loi′), [Gr., the many], the common people; the masses: usually patronizing.

**hoist** (hoist), *v.t.* [var. of earlier *hoise* < D. < LG. *hissen*], to raise aloft; lift, especially by means of a pulley, crane, etc. *n.* 1. a hoisting. 2. an apparatus for raising heavy things; elevator or tackle. 3. in *nautical usage*, the perpendicular height of a sail or flag. —**hoist′er,** *n.*

**hoi·ty-toi·ty** (hoi′ti-toi′ti), *adj.* [redupl. of obs. *hoit*, to indulge in noisy mirth], 1. giddy; flighty. 2. haughty; arrogant. 3. fussy; huffy. *n.* hoity-toity behavior. *interj.* an exclamation of surprise and somewhat derisive disapproval.

**ho·key-po·key** (hō′ki-pō′ki), *n.* hocus-pocus.

**Hok·kai·do** (hôk′kī-dô′), *n.* one of the islands forming Japan.

**ho·kum** (hō′kəm), *n.* [< *hocus*], [Slang], 1. mawkishly sentimental elements in a play, story, etc., used to gain an immediate emotional response. 2. nonsense; humbug; bunk.

**Hol·bein, Hans** (häns hōl′bīn), 1. 1465?–1524; German painter: called *the Elder*. 2. 1497?–1543; his son; German painter: called *the Younger*.

**hold** (hōld), *v.t.* [HELD, HOLDING; *archaic* pp. HOLDEN], [AS. *haldan*], 1. to take and keep with the hands, arms, or other means; grasp; clutch. 2. to keep from going away; not let escape: as, *hold* the prisoner. 3. to keep in a certain position or condition: as, *hold* your head up. 4. to restrain or control; specif., *a)* to keep from falling; support. *b)* to keep from acting; keep back: as, *hold* your tongue. *c)* to get and keep control of. 5. to be in possession of; own; occupy: as, he *holds* the office of mayor. 6. to guard; defend: as, *hold* the fort. 7. to have or conduct together; carry on (a meeting, etc.). 8. to contain: as, this bottle *holds* a quart. 9. to have or keep in the mind. 10. to regard; consider: as, I *hold* the story to be true. 11. in *law*, *a)* to decide; decree. *b)* to possess by legal title: as, to *hold* a mortgage. *v.i.* 1. to go on being firm, loyal, etc.: as, *hold* to your resolution. 2. to remain unbroken or unyielding: as, the rope *held*. 3. to have right or title (usually with *from* or *of*). 4. to be true or valid: as, this rule *holds* for most cases. 5. to keep up; continue: as, the wind *held* steady. *n.* 1. a grasping or seizing; grip. 2. a thing to hold or hold on by. 3. a thing for holding something else. 4. a controlling force; strong influence: as, she has a *hold* over him. 5. a prison. 6. [Archaic], a stronghold. 7. in *music*, a symbol for a pause. 8. in *wrestling*, a way of holding an opponent. —**catch hold of,** to seize; grasp. —**get hold of,** 1. to seize; grasp. 2. to acquire. —**hold back,** 1. to restrain. 2. to refrain. 3. to retain. —**hold down,** 1. to restrain. 2. [Colloq.], to have and keep (a job). —**hold forth,** 1. to preach; lecture. 2. to offer. —**hold in,** 1. to keep in or back. 2. to control oneself. —**hold off,** 1. to keep at a distance. 2. to keep from attacking or doing something. —**hold on,** 1. to retain one's hold. 2. to persist. 3. [Colloq.], stop! wait! —**hold one's own,** to keep up. —**hold out,** 1. to last; endure. 2. to stand firm. 3. to offer. 4. [Slang], to refuse to give (what is to be given). —**hold over,** 1. to postpone. 2. to stay for an additional period or term. —**hold up,** 1. to prop up. 2. to show. 3. to last; endure. 4. to stop; delay. 5. to stop forcibly and rob. —**hold with,** 1. to agree with. 2. to side with. —**lay** (or **take**) **hold of,** 1. to take; seize; grasp. 2. to get control of.

**hold** (hōld), *n.* [altered < *hole* or < MD. *hol*], the interior of a ship below decks, especially below the lower deck, in which the cargo is carried.

**hold·back** (hōld′bak′), *n.* 1. a check; restraint; hindrance. 2. a strap or iron attached to the shaft of a wagon, etc. and to the harness, to enable a horse to stop or back the vehicle.

**hold·er** (hōl′dẽr), *n.* 1. a person or thing that holds. 2. a person who holds, and is legally entitled to payment of, a bill, note, or check.

**hold·fast** (hōld′fast′, -fäst′), *n.* a device that holds something in place; hook, nail, etc.

**hold·ing** (hōld′iŋ), *n.* 1. land, especially a farm, rented from another. 2. *usually pl.* property owned, especially stocks and bonds.

**holding company,** a corporation organized to hold bonds or stocks of other corporations, which it usually controls.

**hold·out** (hōld′out′), *n.* [Colloq.], in *baseball*, etc., a player who delays signing his contract because he wants better terms.

**hold·o·ver** (hōld′ō′vẽr), *n.* [Colloq.], a person or thing staying on from a previous period, as from one term of office to another.

**hold·up** (hōld′up′), *n.* 1. a stoppage; delay. 2. the act of stopping forcibly and robbing.

**hole** (hōl), *n.* [AS. *hol*], 1. a hollow place; cavity: as, a *hole* in the ground, a swimming *hole*. 2. an animal's burrow or lair; den. 3. a small, dingy, squalid place. 4. a prison cell. 5. *a)* an opening in or through anything; gap. *b)* a tear or rent, as in a garment. 6. a flaw; fault; defect: as, *holes* in an argument. 7. [Colloq.], an embarrassing situation; predicament. 8. in *golf*, *a)* a small, round, hollow place into which the ball is to be hit. *b)* the tee, fairway, greens, etc. leading to this. *v.t.* [HOLED, HOLING], 1. to make holes in. 2. to put or drive into a hole. —**hole in one,** in *golf*, the act of getting the ball into a hole with one drive from the tee. —**hole out,** in *golf*, to hit the ball into a hole. —**hole up,** to hibernate, as in a hole. —**in the hole,** [Colloq.], financially embarrassed or behind. —**pick holes in,** to find fault with. —**hole′less,** *adj.* —**hole′y,** *adj.*

**hol·i·but** (hol′ə-bət), *n.* [*pl.* -BUT, -BUTS; see PLURAL, II, D, 2], a halibut.

**hol·i·day** (hol′ə-dā′), *n.* 1. a religious festival; holy day: usually **holyday.** 2. a day of freedom from labor; day for leisure and recreation. 3. *often pl.* [Chiefly Brit.], a vacation. 4. a day set aside, as by law, in celebration of some event. *adj.* of or suited to a holiday; joyous; gay.

**ho·li·ly** (hō′lə-li), *adv.* in a holy manner.

**ho·li·ness** (hō′li-nis), *n.* 1. a being holy. 2. [H-], a title of the Pope: used with *his* or *your*.

**Hol·land** (hol′ənd), *n.* the Netherlands. —**Hol′land·er,** *n.*

**hol·land** (hol′ənd), *n.* [< *Holland*, where first made], a linen or cotton cloth used for children's clothing, upholstery, etc.

**hol·lan·daise sauce** (hol′ən-dāz′), [Fr., of Holland], a creamy sauce, as for vegetables, made of butter, egg yolks, vinegar, lemon juice, etc.

**Hol·lands** (hol′əndz), *n.* gin made in Holland: also **Holland gin,** originally **Hollands geneva.**

**hol·ler** (hol′ẽr), ***v.i. & v.t., n.*** [var. of *hollo*], shout; yell: often considered substandard.

**hol·lo** (hol′ō, hə-lō′), ***interj. & n.*** [*pl.* -LOS], 1. a shout or call, as to attract one's attention, or to urge on hounds in hunting. 2. a shout of greeting or surprise. *v.i. & v.t.* [-LOED, -LOING], 1. to shout so as to attract the attention of (a person). 2. to urge on (hounds) by shouting "hollo." 3. to shout in greeting or surprise. Also **hallo, halloa, hullo.** See **hello.**

**hol·low** (hol'ō), *adj.* [AS. *holh*], 1. having a cavity within it; not solid. 2. shaped like a cup or bowl; concave. 3. deeply set; sunken: as, *hollow* cheeks. 4. empty, worthless, or insincere: as, *hollow* praise. 5. hungry. 6. deep-toned and muffled, as though resounding from something hollow. *adv.* in a hollow manner. *n.* 1. a hollow place; cavity; hole. 2. a valley. *v.t. & v.i.* to make or become hollow. —**beat all hollow,** [Colloq.], to beat fully. —**hollow out,** to make by hollowing. —**hol'low·ly,** *adv.* —**hol'low·ness,** *n.*

**hol·ly** (hol'i), *n.* [*pl.* -LIES], [AS. *holegn*], 1. a small evergreen tree or shrub with glossy, sharp-pointed leaves and bright-red berries. 2. the leaves and berries, used as Christmas ornaments.

**hol·ly·hock** (hol'i-hok'), *n.* [ME. < *holi*, holy + *hoc*, mallow], 1. a tall, hardy plant of the mallow family, with a hairy stem and large, showy flowers of various colors. 2. its flower.

**Hol·ly·wood** (hol'i-wood'), *n.* a section of Los Angeles, California, regarded as the center of the American motion-picture industry.

**holm** (hōm), *n.* a holm oak.

**Holmes, Oliver Wendell** (hōmz), 1. 1809–1894; U.S. writer and physician. 2. 1841–1935; his son; associate justice, U.S. Supreme Court (1902–1932).

**Holmes, Sher·lock** (shūr'lok), a fictitious British detective in stories by A. Conan Doyle.

**hol·mi·um** (hōl'mi-əm), *n.* [< *Holmia*, Latinized form of *Stockholm*], a metallic chemical element of the rare-earth group: symbol, Ho; at. wt., 164.94; at. no., 67. —**hol'mic** (-mik), *adj.*

**holm oak,** [AS. *holegn*, holly], 1. a south European evergreen oak with leaves like those of the holly. 2. its wood.

**hol·o·caust** (hol'ə-kôst'), *n.* [< Fr. < LL. < Gr. < *holos*, whole + *kaustos*, burnt < *kaiein*, to burn], 1. a burnt offering to be burned entirely. 2. complete destruction of people or animals by fire. 3. great or widespread destruction. —**hol'o·caus'tic, hol'o·caus'tal,** *adj.*

**hol·o·graph** (hol'ə-graf', -gräf'), *adj.* [< Fr. < LL. < Gr. < *holos*, whole + *graphein*, to write], written entirely in the handwriting of the person under whose name it appears. *n.* a holograph document, letter, will, etc. —**hol'o·graph'ic,** *adj.*

**holp** (hōlp), archaic pt. and obs. pp. of **help.**

**hol·pen** (hōl'p'n), archaic pp. of **help.**

**Hol·stein** (hōl'stin, -stēn), *n.* [after Schleswig-*Holstein*, where originally bred], any of a breed of large, black-and-white, dairy cattle: also **Hol'stein-Frie'sian** (-frē'zhən).

**hol·ster** (hōl'stēr), *n.* [< D.; ult. < ON. *hulstr*, sheath], a leather pistol case, usually attached to a belt or a saddle.

**ho·ly** (hō'li), *adj.* [-LIER, -LIEST], [AS. *halig* < base of *hal*, sound, whole], [often H-], 1. dedicated to religious use; consecrated; sacred. 2. spiritually pure; sinless. 3. deserving reverence or worship. 4. associated with Jesus and his life. 5. [Slang], very much of a: a generalized intensive, as, a *holy* terror. *n.* something holy; a sanctuary.

**Holy City,** 1. a city regarded as sacred by the believers of some religion: as, Jerusalem, Mecca, and Rome are *Holy Cities.* 2. Heaven.

**Holy Communion,** any of various church rites in which bread and wine are consecrated and received as (symbols of) the body and blood of Jesus; sacrament of the Eucharist.

**ho·ly·day** (hō'li-dā'), *n.* a religious festival: also **holy day.**

**Holy Father,** a title of the Pope: also **Most Holy Father.**

**Holy Ghost,** the third person of the Trinity; spirit of God: also called *Holy Spirit.*

**Holy Grail,** see **Grail.**

**Holy Land,** Palestine.

**holy of holies,** 1. the innermost part of the Jewish tabernacle and Temple, where the ark of the covenant was kept. 2. any most sacred place.

**Hol·yoke** (hōl'yōk), *n.* a city in central Massachusetts: pop., 54,000.

**holy orders,** 1. the sacrament or rite of ordination. 2. the rank of an ordained Christian minister or priest. 3. three higher ranks of Christian ministers or priests; specif., *a*) in the *R. C. Church,* priests, deacons, and subdeacons. *b*) in the *Anglican Church,* bishops, priests, and deacons.

**Holy Roman Empire,** the central European empire established in 962 A.D. (or, according to some, in 800 A.D.) and ending in 1806, regarded as a political unity over which the Pope had spiritual control.

**Holy Scripture,** the Bible.

**Holy See,** the position, authority, or court of the Pope; Apostolic See.

**Holy Spirit,** the Holy Ghost.

**ho·ly·stone** (hō'li-stōn'), *n.* a flat piece of sandstone for scouring a ship's decks. *v.t.* [-STONED, -STONING], to scour with a holystone.

**Holy Synod,** the administrative council of any Orthodox church.

**Holy Week,** the week before Easter.

**Holy Writ,** the Bible.

**hom·age** (hom'ij, om'-), *n.* [< OFr. < ML. *hominaticum* < L. *homo*, a man], 1. originally, *a*) a public avowal of allegiance by a vassal to his lord. *b*) anything given or done to show the relationship between lord and vassal. 2. anything given or done to show the reverence, honor, etc. in which a person is held: as, the town paid *homage* to the hero.

**hom·bre** (ôm'brā, om'bri), *n.* [*pl.* -BRES], [Sp. < L. *homo*, man], [Slang], a man; fellow.

**Hom·burg** (hom'bērg), *n.* [< *Homburg*, Prussia], a man's felt hat with a crown dented from front to back and a stiffened, slightly upturned brim.

**home** (hōm), *n.* [AS. *ham*], 1. the place where a person (or family) lives; one's dwelling place. 2. the city, state, or country where one was born or reared. 3. a place where one likes to be; restful or congenial place. 4. one's final resting place; the grave. 5. the members of a family; household or the life around it. 6. an institution for orphans, the infirm, aged, etc. 7. the natural environment, or habitat, of an animal, plant, etc. 8. the place of origin, development, etc.: as, Paris is the *home* of fashion. 9. in many games, the base or goal; esp., the home plate in baseball. *adj.* 1. of one's home or country; domestic. 2. of or at the center of operations: as, a *home* office. 3. to the point; effective. *adv.* 1. at, to, or in the direction of home. 2. to the point aimed at: as, he drove the nail *home.* 3. to the center or heart of a matter; closely. *v.i.* [HOMED, HOMING], 1. to go to one's home. 2. to have a home. *v.t.* to send to or provide with a home. —**at home,** 1. in one's own house, city, or country. 2. as if in one's own home; comfortable; at ease. 3. willing to receive visitors. —**bring home to,** to impress upon or make clear to. —**see a person home,** to escort a person to his home. —**home'like',** *adj.*

**home-bred** (hōm'bred'), *adj.* 1. bred at home; domestic; native. 2. not sophisticated; crude.

**home-brew** (hōm'brōō'), *n.* alcoholic liquor, especially beer, made at home.

**home-com·ing** (hōm'kum'iŋ), *n.* in many colleges, an annual celebration for returning alumni.

**home economics,** the science and art of homemaking, including nutrition, clothing, budgeting, etc.

**home·land** (hōm'land'), *n.* the country in which one was born or makes one's home.

**home·less** (hōm'lis), *adj.* without a home. —**home'less·ly,** *adv.* —**home'less·ness,** *n.*

**home·ly** (hōm'li), *adj.* [-LIER, -LIEST], 1. suitable for home or home life; simple; plain; everyday: as, *homely* virtues. 2. crude; unpolished. 3. not good-looking; plain; ugly. —**home'li·ness,** *n.*

**home·made** (hōm'mād'), *adj.* 1. made, or as if made, at home. 2. plain; simple; crude.

**home·mak·er** (hōm'māk'ēr), *n.* a woman who manages a home; housewife. —**home'mak'ing,** *n.*

**ho·me·o-,** [Gr. *homoio-* < *homos*, same], a combining form meaning *like, similar*: also **home-**: words beginning with *homeo-* may also be sp. **homoeo-.**

**ho·me·op·a·thy** (hō'mi-op'ə-thi, hom'i-), *n.* [*homeo-* + *-pathy*], a system of medical treatment based on the theory that certain diseases can be cured with small doses of drugs which in a healthy person and in large doses would produce symptoms like those of the disease: opposed to *allopathy.* —**ho'me·o·path'** (-ə-path'), **ho'me·op'a·thist,** *n.* —**ho'me·o·path'ic,** *adj.* —**ho'me·o·path'i·cal·ly,** *adv.*

**home plate,** in *baseball,* the slab that the batter stands beside, across which the pitcher must throw the ball for a strike: it is the last of the four bases that a runner must touch in succession to score a run.

**Ho·mer** (hō′mẽr), *n.* Greek epic poet; c. 8th century B.C.; according to legend, the author of the *Iliad* and the *Odyssey*.

**hom·er** (hōm′ẽr), *n.* [Colloq.], a home run.

**Ho·mer·ic** (hō-mer′ik), *adj.* of, like, or characteristic of the legendary Homer, his style, his poems, or the Greek civilization that they describe: also **Ho-mer′i·cal.**

**Homeric laughter,** loud, unrestrained laughter.

**home rule,** the administration of the affairs of a country, colony, city, etc. by the citizens who live in it; local self-government; autonomy.

**home run,** in *baseball*, a safe hit that permits the batter to touch all the bases and score a run.

**home·sick** (hōm′sik′), *adj.* longing for home. —**home′sick′ness,** *n.*

**home·spun** (hōm′spun′), *n.* 1. cloth made of yarn spun at home. 2. coarse, loosely woven cloth like this. *adj.* 1. spun at home. 2. made of homespun. 3. plain; homely: as, *homespun* virtues.

**home·stead** (hōm′sted′), *n.* 1. a place where a family makes its home, including the land, house, and outbuildings. 2. a 160-acre tract of public land granted by the U.S. government to a settler to be developed as a farm. *v.i.* to become a settler on a homestead. —**home′stead′er,** *n.*

**homestead law,** 1. a law exempting a homestead (sense 1) from seizure or forced sale to meet general debts. 2. a U.S. law granting homesteads (sense 2).

**home·stretch** (hōm′strech′), *n.* 1. the part of a race track between the last turn and the finish line. 2. the final part of any undertaking.

**home·ward** (hōm′wẽrd), *adv. & adj.* toward home.

**home·wards** (hōm′wẽrdz), *adv.* homeward.

**home·work** (hōm′wũrk′), *n.* 1. work done at home. 2. schoolwork to be done outside the classroom.

**home·y** (hōm′i), *adj.* [HOMIER, HOMIEST], [Colloq.], having qualities usually associated with home; comfortable, friendly, cozy, etc.

**hom·i·cide** (hom′ə-sīd′), *n.* [< OFr. < LL. < L. < *homo*, a man + *caedere*, to cut, kill], 1. any killing of one human being by another: *justifiable homicide* is homicide committed in the performance of duty, in self-defense, etc. 2. a person who kills another. —**hom′i·cid′al,** *adj.* —**hom′i·cid′al·ly,** *adv.*

**hom·i·let·ics** (hom′ə-let′iks), *n.pl.* [construed as sing.], [< Gr. < *homilein*, to converse < *homilos*; see HOMILY], the art of writing and preaching sermons. —**hom′i·let′ic, hom′i·let′i·cal,** *adj.* —**hom′i-let′i·cal·ly,** *adv.*

**hom·i·ly** (hom′′l-i), *n.* [*pl.* -LIES], [< OFr. < LL. *homilia* < Gr. < *homilos*, assembly < *homos*, the same + *ile*, a crowd], 1. a sermon, especially one about something in the Bible. 2. a solemn moral talk or writing. —**hom′i·list,** *n.*

**homing pigeon,** a pigeon trained to find its way home from distant places, and hence used to carry messages; carrier pigeon.

**hom·i·ny** (hom′ə-ni), *n.* [Am. Ind. (Algonquian) *rockahominie*, parched corn], dry corn hulled and coarsely ground: it is boiled for food.

**ho·mo** (hō′mō), *n.* [*pl.* HOMINES (hom′ə-nēz′)], [L.], 1. man. 2. [H-], the genus of primates including modern man.

**ho·mo-,** [< Gr. < *homos*, the same], a combining form meaning *same, equal, like:* also **hom-.**

**ho·moe·o-,** homeo-.

**ho·mo·ge·ne·ous** (hō′mə-jē′ni-əs, hom′ə-), *adj.* [< ML. < Gr. < *homos*, the same + *genos*, a race, kind], 1. the same in structure, quality, etc.; similar or identical. 2. composed of similar or identical parts; uniform. —**ho′mo·ge·ne′i·ty** (-jə-nē′ə-ti), **ho′mo·ge′ne·ous·ness,** *n.* —**ho′mo·ge′-ne·ous·ly,** *adv.*

**ho·mo·gen·ize** (hə-moj′ə-nīz′), *v.t.* [-IZED, -IZING], 1. to make homogeneous. 2. to make more uniform throughout.

**homogenized milk,** milk in which the fat particles are so finely divided and emulsified that the cream does not separate on standing.

**hom·o·graph** (hom′ə-graf′, hō′mə-gräf′), *n.* [< Gr. < *homos*, the same + *graphein*, to write], a word with the same spelling as another but with a different meaning and origin (e.g., *bow*, a tie, *bow*, to bend). —**hom′o·graph′ic,** *adj.*

**ho·mol·o·gize** (hō-mol′ə-jīz′), *v.t.* [-GIZED, -GIZING], 1. to make homologous. 2. to demonstrate homology in. *v.i.* to be homologous.

**ho·mol·o·gous** (hō-mol′ə-gəs), *adj.* [< Gr. < *homos*, the same + *legein*, to speak], 1. matching in structure, position, character, etc. 2. in *biology*, corresponding in structure and deriving from a common origin: as, the wing of a bat and the foreleg of a mouse are *homologous.*

**ho·mol·o·gy** (hō-mol′ə-ji), *n.* [*pl.* -GIES], 1. the quality or state of being homologous. 2. a homologous correspondence or relationship.

**ho·mol·o·sine projection** (hə-mol′ə-sin, -sīn′), [< Gr. *homalos*, even; + *sine*], a map of the earth's surface with land areas shown in their proper relative size and form, with a minimum of distortion.

HOMOLOSINE PROJECTION

**ho·mo·mor·phy** (hō′mə-môr′fi, hom′ə-), *n.* [< *homo-* + Gr. *morphē*, form], in *biology*, external resemblance without actual relationship in structure or origin. —**ho′mo·mor′phic, ho′mo·mor′phous,** *adj.*

**hom·o·nym** (hom′ə-nim′, hō′mə-), *n.* [< Fr. < L. < Gr. < *homos*, the same + *onyma*, *onoma*, name], a word with the same pronunciation as another but with a different meaning, origin, and, usually, spelling (e.g., *bore* and *boar*). —**ho·mon·y·mous** (hō-mon′ə-məs), **hom′o·nym′ic,** *adj.*

**hom·o·phone** (hom′ə-fōn′), *n.* [< Gr. < *homos*, same + *phōnē*, sound], 1. any of two or more letters having a sound in common, as *c* and *s*. 2. a homonym.

**ho·moph·o·ny** (hō-mof′ə-ni), *n.* [*pl.* -NIES], 1. music in which a single voice carries the melody. 2. in *phonetics*, the quality of homophones. —**hom·o·phon·ic** (hom′ə-fon′ik), **ho·moph′o·nous,** *adj.*

**ho·mop·ter·ous** (hō-mop′tẽr-əs), *adj.* [*homo-* + *-pterous*], belonging to a group of insects with sucking mouth parts and wings of uniform thickness throughout, as aphids, cicadas, etc.

**Ho·mo sa·pi·ens** (hō′mō sā′pi-enz′), [L.; see HOMO & SAPIENT], man; human being: the only living species of the genus *Homo.*

**ho·mo·sex·u·al** (hō′mə-sek′shōō-əl), *adj.* of or having sexual desire for those of the same sex. *n.* a homosexual person. —**ho′mo·sex′u·al′i·ty,** *n.*

**ho·mun·cu·lus** (hō-muŋ′kyoo-ləs), *n.* [*pl.* -LI (-lī′)], [L., dim. of *homo*, man], a little man; dwarf.

**hom·y** (hōm′i), *adj.* [-IER, -IEST], [Colloq.], homey.

**Hon., hon.,** 1. honorable. 2. honorary.

**Hon·du·ras** (hon-door′əs, -dyoor′əs), *n.* a country in Central America, on the Caribbean and the Pacific: area, 59,160 sq. mi.; pop., 1,950,000; capital, Tegucigalpa. —**Hon·du′ran,** *adj. & n.*

**hone** (hōn), *n.* [< AS. *han*, a stone], a whetstone used to sharpen cutting tools, especially razors. *v.t.* [HONED, HONING], to sharpen on a hone.

**hon·est** (on′ist), *adj.* [< OFr. < L. *honestus* < *honor*, honor], 1. that will not lie, cheat, or steal; trustworthy; truthful: as, an *honest* man. 2. *a*) showing fairness and sincerity: as, an *honest* effort. *b*) gained by fair methods: as, an *honest* living. 3. being what it seems; genuine: as, *honest* wool. 4. frank and open: as, an *honest* face. 5. [Archaic], chaste. —**hon′est·ly,** *adv.*

**hon·es·ty** (on′is-ti), *n.* the state or quality of being honest; specif., *a*) a being truthful, trustworthy, or upright. *b*) sincerity; straightforwardness. *c*) [Archaic], chastity.

**hon·ey** (hun′i), *n.* [*pl.* -EYS], [AS. *hunig*], 1. a thick, sweet, sirupy substance that bees make as food from the nectar of flowers. 2. anything like honey in quality; sweetness. 3. sweet one; darling. *adj.* 1. of or like honey. 2. sweet; dear. *v.t.* [-EYED or -IED, -EYING], 1. to make sweet with or as with honey. 2. to speak sweetly or lovingly to. 3. to flatter. *v.i.* to speak sweetly or lovingly.

**hon·ey·bee** (hun′i-bē′), *n.* a bee that makes honey.

**hon·ey·comb** (hun′i-kōm′), *n.* 1. the structure of six-sided wax cells made by bees to hold their honey, eggs, etc. 2. anything like this. *v.t.* 1. to fill with holes like a honeycomb. 2. to permeate or undermine: as, *honeycombed* with intrigue. *v.i.* to become full of holes like a honeycomb. *adj.* of or like a honeycomb. —**hon′ey·combed′,** *adj.*

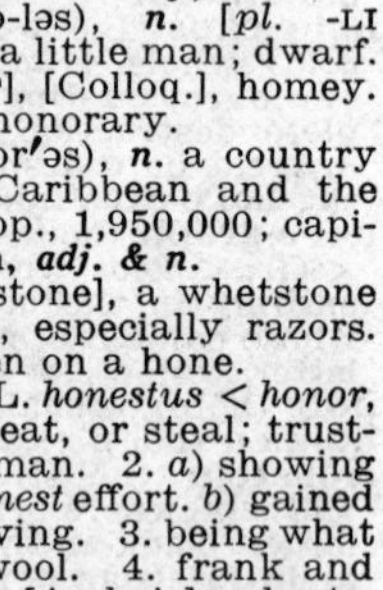

HONEYCOMB

**hon·ey·dew** (hun′i-dōō′, -dū′), *n.* 1. a sweet fluid exuded from the leaves of some plants in summer. 2. a sweet substance secreted by some juice-sucking plant insects. 3. a honeydew melon.

**honeydew melon,** a variety of muskmelon with a smooth, whitish rind and sweet, green flesh.

**hon·eyed** (hun id), alt. pt. and pp. of honey. *adj.* 1. sweetened, covered, or filled with honey. 2. sweet as honey; flattering: as, *honeyed* words.

**honey locust,** a North American tree of the pea

family, with strong, spiny branches, featherlike foliage, and glossy, flat pods.
**hon·ey·moon** (hun'i-mōōn'), *n.* 1. formerly, the first month of marriage. 2. the holiday or vacation spent together by a newly married couple. *v.i.* to have or spend a honeymoon. —**hon'ey·moon'er,** *n.*
**hon·ey·suck·le** (hun'i-suk''l), *n.* 1. any of a group of climbing, twining vines with small, fragrant flowers of red, yellow, or white. 2. any of several similar plants.
**Hong Kong** (hoŋ' koŋ', hôŋ' kôŋ'), a British crown colony in SE China: also **Hongkong.**
**hon·ied** (hun'id), alt. pt. and pp. of **honey.** *adj.* honeyed.
**honk** (hôŋk, hoŋk), *n.* [echoic], 1. the call of a wild goose. 2. any similar sound, as of an automobile horn. *v.i. & v.t.* to make or cause to make such a sound. —**honk'er,** *n.*
**hon·ky-tonk** (hôŋ'ki-tôŋk', hoŋ'ki-toŋk'), *n.* [prob. echoic], [Slang], a cheap, disreputable saloon, cabaret, etc.; dive.
**Hon·o·lu·lu** (hon'ə-lōō'lōō), *n.* the capital of the State of Hawaii, on Oahu: pop., 294,000.
**hon·or** (on'ēr), *n.* [< OFr. < L. *honor, honos*], 1. high regard or great respect given or received; esp., *a*) glory; fame; renown. *b*) credit; good reputation. 2. a keen sense of right and wrong; adherence to principles considered right: as, to behave with *honor.* 3. chastity; purity. 4. high rank or position; distinction: as, the *honor* of being president. 5. [H-], a title given to certain officials, as judges (with *his, her,* or *your*). 6. something done or given as a token of respect; specif., *a*) a social courtesy: as, do me the *honor* of visiting us. *b*) *pl.* public ceremonies of respect: as, funeral *honors.* *c*) *pl.* special distinction given to students who receive unusually high marks. 7. a source or cause of respect and fame. 8. in *bridge,* etc., any of the four or five highest cards of the trump suit; in a no-trump hand, any of the four aces. 9. in *golf,* the privilege of driving first from the tee. *v.t.* 1. to respect greatly; regard highly. 2. to show great respect or high regard for. 3. to worship. 4. to confer an honor on; exalt. 5. to accept and pay when due: as, to *honor* a check. —**do honor to,** 1. to show great respect for. 2. to bring honor to. —**do the honors,** to act as host or hostess. —**on** (or **upon**) **one's honor,** staking one's good name on one's truthfulness or reliability. —**hon'or·er,** *n.*
**hon·or·a·ble** (on'ēr-ə-b'l), *adj.* 1. worthy of being honored; specif., *a*) of, or having a position of, high rank or worth: used as a title of courtesy. *b*) noble; illustrious. *c*) of good reputation; respectable. 2. having or showing a sense of right and wrong; upright. 3. bringing honor to the owner or doer: as, *honorable* mention. 4. doing honor; worthy of respect: as, an *honorable* discharge. —**hon'or·a·ble·ness,** *n.* —**hon'or·a·bly,** *adv.*
**hon·o·rar·i·um** (on'ə-râr'i-əm), *n.* [*pl.* -IUMS, -IA (-i-ə)], [< LL. < *honorarius,* honorary], a payment to a professional man for services on which no fee is set.
**hon·or·ar·y** (on'ə-rer'i), *adj.* [L. *honorarius,* of or conferring honor], 1. done or given as an honor: as, an *honorary* degree. 2. designating an office held as an honor only, without service or pay. 3. holding such an office.
**hon·or·if·ic** (on'ə-rif'ik), *adj.* [< L. < *honor* + *facere,* to make], conferring honor: showing respect. *n.* a complimentary form or phrase, as in Japanese, for describing or addressing a person or thing. —**hon'or·if'i·cal,** *adj.* —**hon'or·if'i·cal·ly,** *adv.*
**honor system,** in various schools and colleges, a system whereby students are trusted to do their work, take tests, etc. without supervision.
**hon·our** (on'ēr), *n. & v.t.* honor: British spelling. —**hon'our·a·ble,** *adj.* —**hon'our·a·ble·ness,** *n.* —**hon'our·a·bly,** *adv.* —**hon'our·er,** *n.*
**Hon·shu** (hon'shōō'), *n.* the largest of the islands forming Japan: chief city, Tokyo.
**hooch** (hōōch), *n.* [< Alaskan Ind. *hoochinoo,* crude alcoholic liquor], [Slang], alcoholic liquor; esp., liquor made or obtained surreptitiously.
**hood** (hood), *n.* [AS. *hod*], 1. a covering for the head and neck, worn separately or as part of a robe or cloak. 2. anything like a hood in shape or use; specif., *a*) the metal cover over the engine of an automobile. *b*) in *falconry,* a covering for a falcon's head, used when the falcon is not chasing game. *v.t.* to cover as with a hood. —**hood'ed,** *adj.* —**hood'less,** *adj.* —**hood'like',** *adj.*
**-hood,** [< AS. *had,* order, condition, rank], a suffix meaning: 1. *state, quality, condition,* as in *childhood.* 2. *the whole group of* (a specified class, profession, etc.), as in *priesthood.*
**Hood, Mount,** a volcanic mountain of the Cascade Range, in N Oregon: height, 11,245 ft.
**Hood, Robin,** see **Robin Hood.**
**hood·lum** (hōōd'ləm), *n.* [said to be < *huddle 'em,* as used by gangs], [Colloq.], a rowdy or ruffian; hooligan. —**hood'lum·ism,** *n.*
**hoo·doo** (hōō'dōō), *n.* [*pl.* -DOOS], [var. of *voodoo*], 1. voodoo. 2. [Colloq.], a person or thing that causes bad luck. 3. [Colloq.], bad luck. *v.t.* [Colloq.], to bring bad luck to.
**hood·wink** (hood'wiŋk'), *v.t.* [*hood* + *wink*], 1. to blindfold. 2. to play a deceiving trick on; deceive.
**hoo·ey** (hōō'i), *interj. & n.* [echoic], [Slang], nonsense; bunk.
**hoof** (hoof, hōōf), *n.* [*pl.* HOOFS, rarely HOOVES], [AS. *hof*], the horny covering on the feet of cattle, deer, etc., or the entire foot. *v.t. & v.i.* 1. [Colloq.], to walk; tramp. 2. [Slang], to dance. —**on the hoof,** not butchered; alive. —**hoofed,** *adj.* —**hoof'less,** *adj.* —**hoof'like',** *adj.*
**hoof·beat** (hoof'bēt', hōōf'-), *n.* the sound made by the hoof of an animal when it walks, etc.
**hoof·er** (hoof'ēr, hōōf'-), *n.* [Slang], a professional dancer, especially a tap dancer.
**hook** (hook), *n.* [AS. *hoc*], 1. a curved or bent piece of metal, wood, etc. used to catch, hold, or pull something; specif., *a*) a curved piece of wire with a barbed end, for catching fish. *b*) a curved piece used to hang things on, etc.: as, a coat *hook.* 2. a curved metal implement for cutting grain, etc.; sickle. 3. something shaped like a hook, as a curving cape or headland. 4. a trap; snare. 5. in *baseball,* a curve. 6. in *boxing,* a short blow delivered with the arm bent at the elbow. 7. in *golf,* a stroke in which the ball curves to the left. 8. in *music,* one of the lines at the end of a stem. *v.t.* 1. to fasten as with a hook. 2. to take hold of or catch as with a hook. 3. to catch or deceive by a trick. 4. to steal; snatch. 5. to shape into a hook. 6. in *baseball,* to throw (a ball) so that it curves. 7. in *boxing,* to hit with a hook. 8. in *golf,* to drive (a ball) so that it curves to the left. *v.i.* 1. to curve as a hook does. 2. to be fastened with a hook or hooks. 3. to be caught by a hook. —**by hook or by crook,** by any means, honest or dishonest. —**hook it,** [Slang], to run away. —**hook up,** to arrange and connect the parts of (a radio, etc.). —**on one's own hook,** [Colloq.], by oneself.
**hook·ah, hook·a** (hook'ə), *n.* [Ar. *huqqah*], an Oriental pipe with a long, flexible tube by means of which the smoke is drawn through water so as to be cooled.

HOOKAH

**hooked** (hookt, hook'id), *adj.* 1. curved like a hook. 2. having a hook or hooks. 3. made with a hook: as, a *hooked* rug. —**hook'ed·ness,** *n.*
**hooked rug,** a rug made by drawing strips of cloth or yarn back and forth through canvas or burlap.
**hook·up** (hook'up'), *n.* 1. the arrangement and connection of parts, circuits, etc., as in (a) radio. 2. [Colloq.], a connection or alliance.
**hook·worm** (hook'wũrm'), *n.* a small, parasitic roundworm with hooks around the mouth, infesting the small intestine and causing a disorder (**hookworm disease**) characterized by anemia, fever, weakness, and abdominal pain.
**hook·y** (hook'i), *n.* see **play hooky.**
**hoo·li·gan** (hōō'li-gən), *n.* [< *Hooligan,* name of an Irish family in London], a ruffian; hoodlum. —**hoo'li·gan·ism,** *n.*
**hoop** (hōōp, hoop), *n.* [AS. *hop*], 1. a circular band or ring for holding together the staves of a barrel, cask, etc. 2. anything like a hoop; specif., *a*) *usually in pl.* a ring for spreading out a woman's skirt. *b*) a finger ring. 3. in *croquet,* any of the arches through which the balls are hit. *v.t.* to bind or fasten with a hoop or hoops. —**hooped,** *adj.* —**hoop'like',** *adj.*
**hoop·er** (hōōp'ēr, hoop'-), *n.* a person whose work is putting hoops on barrels, casks, etc.
**hoop·la** (hōōp'lä), *n.* [Colloq.], great excitement.
**hoo·poe** (hōō'pōō), *n.* [< Fr. *huppe* < L. *upupa;* prob. echoic], a brightly colored European bird with a long, curved bill and an erectile crest.

**hoop skirt,** a woman's skirt worn over a framework of hoops to make it spread out.
**hoo·ray** (hoo-rā′, hə-, hōō-), *interj., n., v.i. & v.t.* hurrah.
**hoose·gow, hoos·gow** (hōōs′gou), *n.* [prob. < Sp. *juzgado,* a court, sentenced], [Slang], a jail.
**Hoo·sier** (hōō′zhẽr), *n.* [prob. < dial. *hoosier,* mountaineer, used of Kentucky settlers of S Indiana], a native or inhabitant of Indiana: a nickname.
**hoot** (hōōt), *v.i.* [? < ON.; orig. echoic], 1. to utter its characteristic hollow sound: said of an owl. 2. to utter a sound like this. 3. to shout, especially in scorn or disapproval. *v.t.* 1. to express (scorn, disapproval, etc.) by hooting. 2. to express scorn or disapproval of by hooting. 3. to chase away by hooting: as, they *hooted* him out of the room. *n.* 1. the sound that an owl makes. 2. any sound like this. 3. a loud shout of scorn or disapproval. 4. the least bit; whit: as, not worth a *hoot.* —**hoot′er,** *n.*

HOOP SKIRT

**hoot·en·an·ny** (hōōt′'n-an′i), *n.* [*pl.* -NIES], [Slang], a meeting of folk singers, as for public entertainment.
**Hoo·ver, Herbert Clark** (hōō′vẽr), 1874–1964; 31st president of the U.S. (1929–1933).
**Hoover, J. Edgar,** (*John Edgar Hoover*), 1895– ; Am. criminal investigator; director of the FBI (1924– ).
**Hoover Dam,** a dam on the Colorado River, between Nevada and Arizona: formerly called *Boulder Dam.*
**hooves** (hōōvz, hoovz), *n.* rare pl. of **hoof.**
**hop** (hop), *v.i.* [HOPPED, HOPPING], [AS. *hoppian*], 1. to make a short leap or leaps on one foot. 2. to move by leaping or springing on both (or all) feet at once, as a bird, frog, etc. 3. [Colloq.], to dance. 4. [Slang], to go. *v.t.* 1. to jump over: as, *hop* the hedge. 2. to jump onto: as, *hop* a train. 3. [Colloq.], to fly over in an airplane. *n.* 1. a hopping. 2. [Colloq.], a dance. 3. [Colloq.], a flight in an airplane.
**hop** (hop), *n.* [< MD. *hoppe*], 1. a climbing vine with cone-shaped female flowers. 2. *pl.* the dried ripe cones, used for flavoring beer, ale, etc. *v.t.* [HOPPED, HOPPING], to flavor with hops.
**hope** (hōp), *n.* [AS. *hopa*], 1. a feeling that what is wanted will happen. 2. the object of this. 3. a person or thing from which something may be hoped. 4. [Archaic], trust; reliance. *v.t.* [HOPED, HOPING], 1. to want and expect. 2. to want very much. *v.i.* 1. to have hope (*for*). 2. [Archaic], to trust or rely. —**hope against hope,** to go on hoping though it seems baseless. —**hop′er,** *n.*
**hope chest,** a chest in which a young woman collects linen, clothing, etc. in anticipation of getting married.
**hope·ful** (hōp′fəl), *adj.* 1. feeling or showing hope. 2. inspiring or giving hope. *n.* a young person who seems likely to succeed. —**hope′ful·ness,** *n.*
**hope·ful·ly** (hōp′fəl-i), *adv.* 1. in a hopeful manner. 2. it is to be hoped that: as, *hopefully* we will win: regarded by some as a loose usage.
**hope·less** (hōp′lis), *adj.* 1. without hope. 2. arousing no hope: as, a *hopeless* situation. —**hope′less·ly,** *adv.* —**hope′less·ness,** *n.*
**Ho·pi** (hō′pi), *n.* 1. a member of a Pueblo tribe of Indians in NE Arizona. 2. their language.
**hop·lite** (hop′līt), *n.* [< Gr. < *hoplon,* a tool], a heavily armed foot soldier of ancient Greece.
**hopped up,** [Slang], stimulated as by a drug.
**hop·per** (hop′ẽr), *n.* 1. a person or thing that hops. 2. any hopping insect. 3. a container for material that is passed or fed into something else: as, the *hopper* of an automatic coal stoker.
**hop·scotch** (hop′skoch′), *n.* [*hop* (to jump) + *scotch,* a line], a children's game in which each player hops from one compartment to another of a figure drawn on the ground.
**Hor·ace** (hôr′is, hor′-), *n.* (*Quintus Horatius Flaccus*), Roman poet; 65–8 B.C. —**Ho·ra·ti·an** (hə-rā′shən, hō-rā′shi-ən), *adj.*
**horde** (hôrd, hōrd), *n.* [< Fr. < G. < Pol. *horda* < Turk. *ordū,* a camp], 1. a nomadic tribe or clan of Mongols. 2. a crowd; pack; swarm. *v.i.* [HORDED, HORDING], to form a horde.
**hore·hound** (hôr′hound′, hōr′-), *n.* [AS. < *har,* white + *hune,* horehound], 1. a bitter plant of the mint family, with white, downy leaves. 2. a bitter juice extracted from its leaves. 3. cough medicine or candy made with this juice. Also sp. **hoarhound.**
**ho·ri·zon** (hə-rī′z'n), *n.* [< OFr. < L. < Gr. *horizōn* (*kyklos*), the bounding (circle) < *horos,* boundary], 1. the line where the sky seems to meet the earth (**visible** or **apparent horizon**). 2. the limit of one's experience, interest, knowledge, etc.
**hor·i·zon·tal** (hôr′ə-zon′t'l, hor′-), *adj.* 1. parallel to the plane of the horizon: opposed to *vertical.* 2. placed or acting chiefly in a horizontal direction. 3. flat and even; level. *n.* a horizontal line, plane, etc. —**hor′i·zon·tal′i·ty,** *n.* —**hor′i·zon′tal·ly,** *adv.*
**horizontal union,** a labor union whose members all work at the same trade but not necessarily in the same industry; craft union.
**hor·mone** (hôr′mōn), *n.* [< Gr. < *hormē,* impulse], 1. a chemical substance formed in some organ of the body, as the ovary, adrenal glands, etc., and carried to another organ or tissue, where it has a specific effect. 2. a similar substance in plants. —**hor·mo′nal, hor·mon′ic** (-mon′ik), *adj.*
**horn** (hôrn), *n.* [AS.], 1. *a*) a hard, bonelike, permanent projection that grows on the head of a cow, sheep, goat, etc. *b*) the antler of a deer, shed annually. 2. anything that protrudes from the head of an animal, as the tentacle of a snail, etc. 3. the substance that horns are made of. 4. *a*) a container made by hollowing out a horn: as, a drinking *horn.* *b*) a drink contained in a horn. 5. a cornucopia. 6. anything shaped like a horn; specif., *a*) a peninsula or cape. *b*) the end of a crescent. *c*) the beak of an anvil. *d*) the pommel of a saddle. 7. *a*) an instrument made of horn and sounded by blowing. *b*) any brass-wind instrument; specif., the French horn. 8. a horn-shaped loud-speaker. 9. a device sounded to give a warning: as, a fog*horn.* *v.t.* 1. to furnish with horns. 2. to butt with the horns; gore. *adj.* made of horn. —**blow one's own horn,** [Colloq.], to boast. —**horn in,** [Slang], to intrude or meddle. —**pull** (or **draw** or **haul**) **in one's horns,** 1. to restrain one's impulses, efforts, etc. 2. to withdraw; recant. —**horned,** *adj.* —**horn′less,** *adj.* —**horn′like′,** *adj.*
**Horn, Cape,** the southernmost point of South America, on Horn Island, Tierra del Fuego.
**horn·bill** (hôrn′bil′), *n.* any of a family of large tropical birds with a huge, curved bill, often with a bony protuberance on it.
**horn·blende** (hôrn′blend′), *n.* [G.], a common black, blackish-green, or dark-brown mineral, a variety of amphibole found in igneous rocks.
**horn·book** (hôrn′book′), *n.* 1. a sheet of parchment with the alphabet, numbers, etc. on it, mounted on a small board with a handle and protected by a thin, clear plate of horn: formerly used as a child's primer. 2. an elementary treatise.
**horned pout,** a catfish or other bullhead: also **horn pout, horn′pout′,** *n.*
**horned toad,** a small, scaly, insect-eating lizard with a short tail and hornlike spines.
**horned viper,** a poisonous African snake with a hornlike spine above each eye.
**hor·net** (hôr′nit), *n.* [AS. *hyrnet*], a large wasp whose sting is very painful.
**horn of plenty,** a cornucopia.
**horn·pipe** (hôrn′pīp′), *n.* 1. an obsolete wind instrument with a bell and mouthpiece made of horn. 2. a lively dance formerly popular with sailors. 3. music for this.
**horn·swog·gle** (hôrn′swog′'l), *v.t.* [-GLED, -GLING], [fanciful coinage], [Slang], to swindle; humbug.
**horn·y** (hôr′ni), *adj.* [-IER, -IEST], 1. made of horn or a hornlike substance. 2. having horns or hornlike growths. 3. hard like horn; callous and tough. —**horn′i·ness,** *n.*
**ho·ro·loge** (hôr′ə-lōj′, hor′ə-loj′), *n.* [< OFr. < L. < Gr. < *hōra,* hour + *legein,* to tell], a timepiece; clock, watch, hourglass, sundial, etc.
**ho·rol·o·gist** (hō-rol′ə-jist, hō-), *n.* an expert in horology; a maker of or dealer in timepieces: also **ho·rol′o·ger** (-jẽr).
**ho·rol·o·gy** (hō-rol′ə-ji, hō-), *n.* [< Gr. *hōra,* hour; + *-logy*], the science or art of measuring time or making timepieces. —**hor·o·log·ic** (hôr′ə-loj′ik, hor′-), **hor′o·log′i·cal,** *adj.*
**hor·o·scope** (hôr′ə-skōp′, hor′-), *n.* [Fr. < L. < Gr. < *hōra,* hour + *skopein,* to view], in *astrology,* 1. the position of the planets and stars with relation to one another at a given time, as at a person's birth, regarded as determining his destiny. 2. a chart of the zodiacal signs and the positions of the planets, etc., by which astrologers profess to tell a person's future. —**cast a horoscope,** to calculate the supposed influence of the stars and planets on a person's life. —**hor′o·scop′er,** *n.* —**ho·ros·co·py** (hō-ros′kə-pi, hō-), *n.*
**hor·ren·dous** (hō-ren′dəs, ho-), *adj.* [< L. < ppr. of *horrere,* to bristle], horrible; frightful; fearful; dreadful. —**hor·ren′dous·ly,** *adv.*
**hor·ri·ble** (hôr′i-b'l, hor′-), *adj.* [< OFr. < L. < *horrere*, to bristle], 1. causing a feeling of horror;

terrible; dreadful; frightful. 2. [Colloq.], very bad, ugly, shocking, unpleasant, etc. —**hor′ri·ble·ness,** *n.* —**hor′ri·bly,** *adv.*

**hor·rid** (hôr′id, hor′-), *adj.* 1. causing a feeling of horror; terrible; detestable. 2. [Colloq.], very bad, ugly, unpleasant, etc. —**hor′rid·ly,** *adv.* —**hor′rid·ness,** *n.*

**hor·ri·fy** (hôr′ə-fī′, hor′-), *v.t.* [-FIED, -FYING], 1. to cause to feel horror. 2. [Colloq.], to shock greatly. —**hor′ri·fi·ca′tion,** *n.*

**hor·ror** (hôr′ẽr, hor′-), *n.* [< OFr. < L. *horror* < *horrere*, to bristle, be afraid], 1. the strong feeling caused by something frightful or shocking; terror and repugnance. 2. strong dislike or aversion. 3. the quality of causing horror. 4. something that causes horror. 5. [Colloq.], something very bad, disagreeable, etc.

‡**hors de com·bat** (ôr′ də kōn′bä′), [Fr., out of combat], put out of action; disabled.

**hors d'oeu·vre** (ôr′dũrv′, ôr′duv′; Fr. ôr′dö′vr′), [*pl.* D'OEUVRES (-dũrvz′, -duvz′; Fr. -dö′vr′)], [Fr., lit., outside of work], *usually in pl.* an appetizer, as olives, anchovies, etc., served usually at the beginning of a meal.

**horse** (hôrs), *n.* [*pl.* HORSES, HORSE; see PLURAL, II, D, 1], [AS. *hors*], 1. a large, strong animal with four legs, solid hoofs, and flowing mane and tail, long ago domesticated for drawing loads, carrying riders, etc. 2. the full-grown male of the horse. 3. a frame on legs to support something: as, a saw*horse*. 4. a padded block on legs, used in gymnastics for jumping or vaulting. 5. mounted troops; cavalry. *v.t.* [HORSED, HORSING], 1. to supply with a horse or horses; put on horseback. 2. [Slang], to subject (a person) to horseplay; make fun of. *v.i.* to mount or go on horseback. *adj.* 1. of a horse or horses. 2. mounted on horses. 3. large, strong, or coarse of its kind: as, *horse*radish. —**be on one's high horse,** [Colloq.], to behave in an arrogant or haughty manner. —**hold one's horses,** [Slang], to curb one's impatience. —**horse around,** [Slang], to engage in horseplay. —**horse of another** (or **different**) **color,** an entirely different matter. —**to horse!** mount your horse!

**horse·back** (hôrs′bak′), *n.* the back of a horse. *adv.* on horseback.

**horse·car** (hôrs′kär′), *n.* 1. a streetcar drawn by horses. 2. a car for transporting horses.

**horse chestnut,** 1. a tree with large palmate leaves, clusters of white flowers, and glossy brown nuts. 2. its nut. 3. any of various related shrubs or trees.

**horse·flesh** (hôrs′flesh′), *n.* 1. the flesh of the horse, especially as food. 2. horses collectively.

**horse·fly** (hôrs′flī′), *n.* [*pl.* -FLIES], any of various large flies the female of which sucks the blood of horses, cattle, etc.; gadfly.

**horse·hair** (hôrs′hâr′), *n.* 1. hair from the mane or tail of a horse. 2. the stiff fabric made from this hair; haircloth. *adj.* 1. of horsehair. 2. covered or stuffed with horsehair.

**horse·hide** (hôrs′hīd′), *n.* 1. the hide of a horse. 2. leather made from this.

**horse latitudes,** either of two belts of calms, light winds, and high barometric pressure, situated at about 30° N. and 30° S. latitude.

**horse·laugh** (hôrs′laf′, -läf′), *n.* a loud, boisterous laugh, usually derisive; guffaw.

**horse·less** (hôrs′lis), *adj.* 1. without a horse. 2. self-propelled: as, a *horseless* carriage.

**horse·man** (hôrs′mən), *n.* [*pl.* -MEN], 1. a man who rides on horseback. 2. a man skilled in the riding or care of horses. —**horse′man·ship′,** *n.*

**horse pistol,** a large pistol formerly carried by men on horseback.

**horse·play** (hôrs′plā′), *n.* rough, boisterous play.

**horse·pow·er** (hôrs′pou′ẽr), *n.* a unit for measuring the power of motors or engines, equal to a rate of 33,000 foot-pounds per minute.

**horse·rad·ish** (hôrs′rad′ish), *n.* 1. a plant of the mustard family, grown for its pungent, white root. 2. a relish made by grating this root.

**horse sense,** [Colloq.], plain common sense.

**horse·shoe** (hôr′shōō′, hôrs′-), *n.* 1. a flat, U-shaped, protective metal plate nailed to a horse's hoof. 2. anything shaped like this. 3. *pl.* a game in which the players toss horseshoes in an attempt to encircle a stake or come as close to it as possible. *v.t.* [-SHOED, -SHOEING], to fit with a horseshoe or horseshoes. —**horse′sho′er,** *n.*

**horseshoe crab,** a horseshoe-shaped sea animal with a long, spinelike tail; king crab.

**horse·tail** (hôrs′tāl′), *n.* 1. a horse's tail. 2. a rushlike, flowerless plant with hollow, jointed stems and scalelike leaves.

**horse·whip** (hôrs′hwip′), *n.* a whip for driving or managing horses. *v.t.* [-WHIPPED or -WHIPT, -WHIPPING], to lash with a horsewhip.

**horse·wom·an** (hôrs′woom′ən), *n.* [*pl.* -WOMEN], 1. a woman who rides on horseback. 2. a woman skilled in the riding or care of horses.

**hors·y** (hôr′si), *adj.* [-IER, -IEST], 1. of, like, or suggesting a horse. 2. of, like, or characteristic of people who are fond of horses, fox hunting, or horse racing. —**hors′i·ly,** *adv.* —**hors′i·ness,** *n.*

**hort.,** 1. horticultural. 2. horticulture.

**hor·ta·to·ry** (hôr′tə-tôr′i, -tō′ri), *adj.* [< L. < pp. of *hortari*, freq. of *horiri*, to urge], 1. encouraging or urging to good deeds. 2. exhorting; giving advice. Also **hor′ta·tive.** —**hor′ta·tive·ly,** *adv.*

**hor·ti·cul·ture** (hôr′ti-kul′chẽr), *n.* [< L. *hortus*, a garden + *cultura*, culture], the art or science of growing flowers, fruit, and vegetables. —**hor′ti·cul′tur·al,** *adj.* —**hor′ti·cul′tur·ist,** *n.*

**Hos.,** Hosea.

**ho·san·na** (hō-zan′ə), *n.* & *interj.* [LL. < Gr. *hōsanna* < Heb. *hōshī'āh nnā*, lit., save, we pray], an exclamation or shout of praise to God.

**hose** (hōz), *n.* [*pl.* HOSE, *archaic* HOSEN (hō′z'n)], [AS. *hosa*], 1. formerly, a man's tight-fitting outer garment covering the hips, legs, and feet. 2. *pl.* *a*) stockings. *b*) socks. 3. [*pl.* HOSE, HOSES], a flexible pipe or tube, used to convey fluids, especially water from a hydrant. *v.t.* [HOSED, HOSING], 1. to water with a hose. 2. [Slang], to beat with a hose.

**Ho·se·a** (hō-zē′ə, -zā′ə), *n.* 1. a Hebrew prophet who lived in the 8th century B.C. 2. a book of the Old Testament containing his writings.

**ho·sier** (hō′zhẽr), *n.* a person who makes or sells hosiery or similar knitted or woven goods.

**ho·sier·y** (hō′zhẽr-i), *n.* 1. hose; stockings and socks. 2. the business of a hosier.

**hos·pice** (hos′pis), *n.* [Fr. < L. < *hospes*, host, guest], a shelter for travelers, especially that belonging to the monks of St. Bernard in the Alps.

**hos·pi·ta·ble** (hos′pi-tə-b'l, hos-pit′ə-), *adj.* [MFr. < L. < *hospes*, host, guest], 1. entertaining guests in a friendly, generous manner. 2. characterized by generosity and friendliness to guests: as, a *hospitable* act. 3. receptive or open, as to new ideas. —**hos′pi·ta·ble·ness,** *n.* —**hos′pi·ta·bly,** *adv.*

**hos·pi·tal** (hos′pi-t'l), *n.* [< OFr. < ML. *hospitale*, inn < L. < *hospes*, host, guest], an institution where the ill or injured may receive medical or surgical treatment, nursing, lodging, etc.

**hos·pi·tal·i·ty** (hos′pi-tal′ə-ti), *n.* [*pl.* -TIES], the act, practice, or quality of being hospitable.

**hospitalization insurance,** insurance providing hospitalization for the subscriber and, usually, members of his immediate family.

**hos·pi·tal·ize** (hos′pi-t'l-īz′), *v.t.* [-IZED, -IZING], to send or admit to, or put in, a hospital. —**hos′pi·tal·i·za′tion,** *n.*

**Host, host** (hōst), *n.* [< OFr. < L. *hostia*, sacrifice], the bread of the Eucharist.

**host** (hōst), *n.* [< OFr. < L. *hospes*, host, guest], 1. a man who entertains guests in his own home or at his own expense. 2. a man who keeps an inn or hotel. 3. any organism on or in which another (called a *parasite*) lives.

**host** (hōst), *n.* [< OFr. < ML. < L. *hostis*, enemy], 1. an army. 2. a multitude; great number.

**hos·tage** (hos′tij), *n.* [< OFr.; prob. merging of *hostage*, lodging & *ostage*, hostage; both ult. < L.], 1. a person kept or given as a pledge for the fulfillment of certain agreements. 2. the state of such a person. —**hos′tage·ship′,** *n.*

**hos·tel** (hos′t'l), *n.* [see HOSPITAL], a lodging place; inn; esp., a supervised shelter (**youth hostel**) used by young people on hikes, etc.

**hos·tel·ry** (hos′t'l-ri), *n.* [*pl.* -RIES], a lodging place; inn; hotel. —**hos′tel·er,** *n.*

**host·ess** (hōs′tis), *n.* 1. a woman who entertains guests in her own home; often, the host's wife. 2. *a*) a woman employed in a restaurant to supervise the waitresses, seating, etc. *b*) a woman who serves as a paid partner at a public dance hall.

**hostess gown,** a long, dresslike negligee worn for lounging and entertaining at home.

**hos·tile** (hos′t'l; Brit. -tīl), *adj.* [< L. < *hostis*, enemy], 1. of or characteristic of an enemy. 2. unfriendly; antagonistic. —**hos′tile·ly,** *adv.*

**hos·til·i·ty** (hos-til′ə-ti), *n.* [*pl.* -TIES], [see HOSTILE], 1. a feeling of enmity, ill will, unfriendliness, etc.

2. *a*) expression of enmity and ill will; active opposition. *b*) *pl.* warfare.
**hos·tler** (hos′lẽr, os′-), *n.* [contr. of *hosteler*], one who takes care of horses at an inn, stable, etc.
**hot** (hot), *adj.* [HOTTER, HOTTEST], [AS. *hat*], 1. *a*) having much heat or warmth; having a temperature higher than that of the human body. *b*) having a relatively or abnormally high temperature. 2. producing a burning sensation: as, *hot* pepper. 3. full of or characterized by any intense feeling or activity; specif., *a*) impetuous; excitable: as, a *hot* temper. *b*) violent; angry: as, a *hot* battle. *c*) full of enthusiasm; eagerly intent. *d*) lustful. *e*) very controversial. 4. following closely: as, *hot* pursuit. 5. as if heated by friction; specif., *a*) in constant use: as, the news kept the wires *hot*. *b*) electrically charged: as, a *hot* wire. *c*) [Colloq.], radioactive. 6. [Slang], that has not yet lost heat, freshness, etc.; specif., *a*) recent; new: as, *hot* news. *b*) clear; strong, as a scent in hunting. *c*) recent and seemingly valid: as, a *hot* tip. *d*) recently stolen or smuggled; illegally obtained. 7. [Slang], excellent; good. 8. in *jazz music*, designating or of music or playing characterized by exciting rhythmic and tonal effects and imaginative improvisation. *adv.* in a hot manner. **—get hot,** [Slang], to act, perform, etc. with great spirit or enthusiasm. **—make it hot for,** [Colloq.], to make things uncomfortable for. **—hot′ly,** *adv.* **—hot′ness,** *n.*
**hot air,** [Slang], empty or pretentious talk.
**hot·bed** (hot′bed′), *n.* 1. a bed of earth covered with glass and heated by manure, for forcing plants. 2. any place that fosters rapid growth.
**hot-blood·ed** (hot′blud′id), *adj.* easily excited; excitable, ardent, passionate, reckless, etc.
**hot·box** (hot′boks′), *n.* an overheated bearing on an axle or shaft.
**hot cake,** a griddlecake. **—sell like hot cakes,** [Colloq.], to be sold rapidly and in large quantities.
**hot cross bun,** a bun marked with a cross, eaten especially during Lent.
**hot dog,** [Colloq.], 1. a frankfurter or wiener. 2. a frankfurter or wiener served in a soft roll.
**ho·tel** (hō-tel′), *n.* [< Fr. < OFr. *hostel;* see HOSPITAL], an establishment or building providing a number of bedrooms, baths, etc., and usually food, for the accommodation of travelers, etc.
**hot·foot** (hot′foot′), *adv.* [Colloq.], in great haste. *v.i.* [Colloq.], to hurry; hasten.
**hot·head** (hot′hed′), *n.* a hotheaded person.
**hot·head·ed** (hot′hed′id), *adj.* 1. quick-tempered; easily made angry. 2. hasty; impetuous. **—hot′-head′ed·ly,** *adv.* **—hot′head′ed·ness,** *n.*
**hot·house** (hot′hous′), *n.* a greenhouse.
**hot line,** a telephone or telegraph line for immediate communication between heads of state in an emergency or crisis.
**hot plate,** a small gas or electric stove for cooking.
**hot rod,** [Slang], an automobile, usually a jalopy, whose motor has been supercharged.
**hot-tem·pered** (hot′tem′pẽrd), *adj.* having a fiery temper; easily made angry.
**Hot·ten·tot** (hot′′n-tot′), *n.* 1. a member of a Negroid race living in South Africa. 2. their language. *adj.* of the Hottentots or their language.
**hot water,** [Colloq.], trouble: preceded by *in.*
**Hou·din·i, Harry** (hōō-dē′ni), (born *Ehrich Weiss*), 1874–1926; U.S. stage magician.
**hough** (hok; Scot. hokh), *n.* hock (joint).
**hound** (hound), *n.* [AS. *hund*, a dog], 1. any of several breeds of hunting dog characterized by long, drooping ears and short hair. 2. any dog. 3. a contemptible person. *v.t.* 1. to hunt or chase with or as with hounds; pursue: as, creditors *hound* him. 2. to urge on; incite to pursuit. **—follow the** (or **ride to) hounds,** to hunt (a fox, etc.) on horseback with hounds. **—hound′ed,** *adj.*
**hour** (our), *n.* [< OFr. < L. < Gr. *hōra*, hour, time], 1. a division of time, one of the twenty-four equal parts of a day; sixty minutes. 2. a point or period of time; specif., *a*) a fixed point or period of time for a particular activity, etc.: as, the dinner *hour*. *b*) the period of time in a classroom: as, the *hour* lasts fifty minutes. *c*) *pl.* a special period for work, etc.: as, his office *hours* are 2–5. *d*) *pl.* the usual times for getting up and going to bed: as, he keeps late *hours*. 3. the time of day as indicated by a timepiece: as, the *hour* is 2:30. 4. a measure of distance set by the time it takes to travel it. 5. the 24th part of a great circle, as of the earth; 15° of longitude. 6. *pl.* in *ecclesiastical usage*, *a*) the seven times of the day set aside for prayers. *b*) these prayers. **—after hours,** after the regular hours for business, school, etc. **—hour after hour,** every hour. **—hour by hour,** each hour. **—the small** (or **wee) hours,** the hours just after midnight.
**hour·glass** (our′glas′, -gläs′), *n.* an instrument for measuring time by the trickling of sand, mercury, etc. from one glass bulb to another below it: the shift of contents takes one hour.

HOURGLASS

**hou·ri** (hoo′ri, hou′-), *n.* [*pl.* -RIS], [Fr. < Per. *hūri* < Ar.; ult. < *hawira*, to be dark-eyed], a nymph of the Moslem Paradise, thought of as always young and beautiful.
**hour·ly** (our′li), *adj.* 1. done or happening every hour. 2. done or happening in the course of an hour: as, the *hourly* output. 3. done or happening very often; frequent. *adv.* 1. once an hour. 2. hour by hour; at any hour. 3. often; frequently.
**house** (hous; *for v.*, houz), *n.* [*pl.* HOUSES (houz′iz)], [AS. *hus*], 1. a building for human beings to live in; specif., *a*) the building or part of a building occupied by one family. *b*) a building where a group of people live as a unit: as, a fraternity *house*. 2. the people who live in a house; family; household. 3. a family as including kin, ancestors, and descendants, especially a royal family: as, the *House* of Tudor. 4. something regarded as a house, in providing shelter, etc.; specif., *a*) the habitation of an animal, as the shell of a mollusk. *b*) a building where things are kept or stored. 5. *a*) a theater. *b*) the audience in a theater. 6. *a*) a place of business. *b*) a business firm. 7. *a*) the building or rooms where a legislative assembly meets. *b*) a legislative assembly: as, the *House* of Representatives. 8. in *astrology*, one of the twelve parts into which the heavens are divided. *v.t.* [HOUSED, HOUSING], 1. to provide a house or lodgings for. 2. to store in a house. 3. to cover, shelter, etc. as if by putting in a house. *v.i.* 1. to take shelter. 2. to reside; live. **—bring down the house,** [Colloq.], to receive enthusiastic applause from the audience. **—keep house,** to take care of the affairs of a home. **—on the house,** given free, at the expense of the establishment. **—set** (or **put) one's house in order,** to put one's affairs in order. **—house′less,** *adj.*
**house·boat** (hous′bōt′), *n.* a large, flat-bottomed boat used as a dwelling place.
**house·break·ing** (hous′brāk′iŋ), *n.* the act of breaking into another's house to commit theft or some other felony. **—house′break′er,** *n.*
**house·bro·ken** (hous′brō′k′n), *adj.* trained to live in a house (i.e., to void in the proper place): said of a dog, cat, etc.: also **house′broke′.**
**house·coat** (hous′kōt′), *n.* a woman's long, loose garment for informal wear about the house.
**house·dress** (hous′dres′), *n.* an inexpensive dress, as of printed cotton, worn for household chores.
**house·fly** (hous′flī′), *n.* [*pl.* -FLIES], a two-winged fly found in and around houses: it feeds on garbage, manure, and food.
**house·ful** (hous′fool′), *n.* as many as a house will accommodate.
**house·hold** (hous′hōld′), *n.* 1. all the persons who live in one house; family, or family and servants. 2. the home and its affairs. 3. [H-], a royal household. *adj.* of a household; domestic.
**household arts,** home economics.
**house·hold·er** (hous′hōl′dẽr), *n.* 1. one who owns or maintains a house. 2. the head of a household.
**household word,** a very familiar word or saying.
**house·keep·er** (hous′kēp′ẽr), *n.* 1. a woman who runs a home, does the housework, etc. 2. a woman hired to run a home, etc. **—house′keep′ing,** *n.*
**house·maid** (hous′mād′), *n.* a girl or woman servant who does housework.
**housemaid's knee,** an inflammation of the saclike cavity covering the kneecap.
**house·moth·er** (hous′mu*th*′ẽr), *n.* a woman who has charge of a dormitory, sorority house, etc. as chaperon and, often, housekeeper.
**House of Burgesses,** the lower branch of the colonial legislature of Virginia or Maryland.
**house of cards,** any flimsy structure, plan, etc.
**House of Commons,** the lower branch of the legislature of Great Britain or Canada.
**house of correction,** a place of short-term confinement for persons convicted of minor offenses and regarded as capable of being reformed.
**House of Delegates,** the lower branch of the legislature of Maryland, Virginia, or West Virginia.
**House of Lords,** the upper branch of the legislature of Great Britain, made up of the nobility and high-ranking clergy.
**House of Representatives,** the lower branch of the legislature of: *a*) the United States. *b*) any State of the U.S. *c*) Australia. *d*) New Zealand.
**house organ,** a periodical published by a business firm for its employees.

**house party,** the entertainment of guests overnight or over a period of a few days in a home.
**house physician,** a resident physician of a hospital, hotel, etc.: also **house doctor.**
**house·top** (hous′top′), *n.* the top of a house; roof. **—from the housetops,** publicly and widely.
**house·warm·ing** (hous′wôr′miŋ), *n.* a party given by or for someone moving into a new home.
**house·wife** (hous′wīf′; *for 2, usually* huz′if), *n.* [*pl.* -WIVES (*for 2,* -ivz)], 1. a woman in charge of her own household. 2. a small sewing kit. **—house′wife′li·ness,** *n.* **—house′wife′ly,** *adj. & adv.*
**house·wif·er·y** (hous′wīf′ẽr-i, -wīf′ri), *n.* the work of a housewife; housekeeping.
**house·work** (hous′wũrk′), *n.* the work involved in housekeeping; cleaning, cooking, etc.
**hous·ing** (houz′iŋ), *n.* 1. the act of providing shelter or lodging. 2. shelter or lodging, as in houses, apartments, etc. 3. houses collectively. 4. a shelter; covering. 5. in *mechanics,* a frame, box, etc. for containing some part.
**hous·ing** (houz′iŋ), *n.* [< OFr. *huche, houce*], an ornamental blanket or covering for a horse.
**Hous·man, A. E.** (hous′mən), (*Alfred Edward Housman*), 1859–1936; English poet.
**Hous·ton** (hūs′tən), *n.* a city in SE Texas: pop., 938,000: a port on a ship canal.
**Hous·ton, Samuel** (hūs′tən), 1793–1863; U.S. statesman and general; president of the Republic of Texas (1836–1838; 1841–1844).
**hove** (hōv), alt. pt. and pp. of **heave.**
**hov·el** (huv′'l, hov′'l), *n.* [? < OFr. < Frank. *huba,* a hood], 1. a low, open shed for sheltering animals, storing equipment, etc. 2. any small, miserable dwelling; hut. *v.t.* [-ELED or -ELLED, -ELING or -ELLING], to shelter in a hovel.
**hov·er** (huv′ẽr, hov′-), *v.i.* [< ME. freq. of *hoven,* to stay], 1. to stay suspended or flutter in the air near one place. 2. to linger or wait close by. 3. to be in an uncertain condition; waver (*between*). *n.* a hovering. **—hov′er·er,** *n.* **—hov′er·ing·ly,** *adv.*
**how** (hou), *adv.* [AS. *hu*], 1. in what manner or way; by what means. 2. in what state or condition. 3. for what reason; why. 4. by what name. 5. with what meaning; to what effect. 6. to what extent, degree, amount, etc. 7. at what price. 8. [Colloq.], what?: usually a request to repeat something said. *How* is also used in exclamations and as an intensive. *n.* the way of doing; manner; method. **—how now?** what is the meaning of this? **—how so?** how is it so? why?
**how·be·it** (hou-bē′it), *adv.* [Archaic], however it may be; nevertheless.
**how·dah** (hou′də), *n.* [< Hind. < Ar. *haudaj*], a canopied seat for riding on the back of an elephant or camel: also sp. **houdah.**

HOWDAH

**how·dy** (hou′di), *interj.* [contr. < *how do you* (*do*)?], [Colloq.], an expression of greeting.
**Howe, Elias** (hou), 1819–1867; U.S. inventor of the sewing machine.
**how·e'er** (hou-er′), *adv. & conj.* however.
**How·ells, William Dean** (dēn hou′əlz), 1837–1920; U.S. novelist and editor.
**how·ev·er** (hou-ev′ẽr), *adv.* 1. no matter how; by whatever means. 2. to whatever degree or extent. *conj.* nevertheless; yet; but.
**how·itz·er** (hou′it-sẽr), *n.* [< G. < Czech *haufnice,* orig., a sling], a short cannon, firing shells in a relatively high trajectory.
**howl** (houl), *v.i.* [ME. *houlen;* prob. echoic], 1. to utter the long, wailing cry of wolves, dogs, etc. 2. to utter a similar cry of pain, anger, etc. 3. to make a sound like this: as, the wind *howls.* 4. to shout or laugh in scorn, mirth, etc. *v.t.* 1. to utter with a howl. 2. to drive or effect by howling. *n.* 1. the long, wailing cry of a wolf, dog, etc. 2. any similar cry or sound. **—howl down,** to drown out with shouts of scorn, etc.
**howl·er** (houl′ẽr), *n.* 1. a person or thing that howls. 2. [Colloq.], a stupid, ridiculous blunder.
**howl·ing** (houl′iŋ), *adj.* 1. that howls. 2. filled with howls; mournful. 3. [Slang], great: as, a *howling* success. **—howl′ing·ly,** *adv.*
**how·so·ev·er** (hou′sō-ev′ẽr), *adv.* 1. to whatever degree or extent. 2. by whatever means.
**hoy·den** (hoi′d'n), *n.* [? < D. *heiden,* heathen], a bold, boisterous girl; tomboy. *adj.* bold and boisterous; tomboyish. *v.i.* to behave like a hoyden. Also sp. **hoiden. —hoy′den·ish,** *adj.* **—hoy′den·ish·ly,** *adv.* **—hoy′den·ish·ness,** *n.*
**Hoyle** (hoil), *n.* a book of rules and instructions for card games, originally compiled by Edmond Hoyle (1672–1769). **—according to Hoyle,** according to the rules and regulations; in a fair way.
**H.P., HP, h.p., hp,** horsepower.
**H.Q., Hq.,** Headquarters.
**hr.,** [*pl.* HRS.], hour; hours.
**H.R.,** House of Representatives.
**H.R.H.,** His (or Her) Royal Highness.
**Hsin·king** (shin′kiŋ′; Chin. -jiŋ′), *n.* Changchun.
**ht.,** 1. heat. 2. [*pl.* HTS.], height.
**hub** (hub), *n.* [prob. var. of *hob* (a peg)], 1. the center part of a wheel. 2. a center of interest, importance, or activity. **—the Hub,** Boston.
**hub·bub** (hub′ub), *n.* [said to be < Ir. cry], a confused sound of many voices; uproar; tumult.
**hub·by** (hub′i), *n.* [*pl.* -BIES], [Colloq.], a husband: familiar diminutive.
**huck·a·back** (huk′ə-bak′), *n.* [< ?], a coarse linen or cotton cloth with a rough surface, used for toweling: also [Colloq.], **huck.**
**huck·le·ber·ry** (huk′'l-ber′i), *n.* [*pl.* -RIES], [? < AS. *wyrtil,* small shrub + *berie,* a berry], 1. a shrub having dark-blue berries resembling blueberries. 2. the fruit of this shrub.
**huck·ster** (huk′stẽr), *n.* [< or akin to MD. *hokester;* prob. < *hoek,* a corner], 1. a peddler, especially of fruits, vegetables, etc. 2. a mean, haggling tradesman. 3. [Colloq.], an advertising man. Also **huck′ster·er.** *v.t.* 1. to peddle; sell. 2. to bargain in or haggle over.
**HUD,** (Dept. of) Housing and Urban Development.
**hud·dle** (hud′'l), *v.i.* [-DLED, -DLING], [? var. of ME. *hoderen,* to cover up], 1. to crowd close together: as, animals *huddle* together from fear. 2. to draw oneself up tightly. 3. in *football,* to gather in a huddle. *v.t.* 1. to crowd close together. 2. to hunch or draw (oneself) up. 3. to do, put, or make hastily and carelessly. 4. to push in a hurried manner. *n.* 1. a confused crowd or heap. 2. confusion; jumble. 3. in *football,* a grouping of a team behind the line of scrimmage to receive signals before a play. 4. [Slang], a secret discussion. **—go into a huddle,** [Slang], to have a secret discussion. **—hud′dler,** *n.*
**Hud·son** (hud′s'n), *n.* a river in E New York, with its mouth at New York City.
**Hudson, Henry,** ?–1611; English navigator; discovered the river and bay named for him.
**Hudson Bay,** a part of the Atlantic extending into central Canada.
**Hudson seal,** muskrat fur treated to resemble seal.
**hue** (hū), *n.* [AS. *heow*], 1. color. 2. a particular variety of a color; shade; tint. **—hued,** *adj.*
**hue** (hū), *n.* [< OFr. *hu,* hunting cry], a shouting; outcry: now only in *hue and cry.* **—hue and cry,** 1. originally, a loud shout or cry by those pursuing a felon. 2. any loud outcry or clamor.
**huff** (huf), *v.t.* [prob. echoic], to make angry; offend. *v.i.* 1. to blow; puff. 2. to become angry. *n.* a burst of anger or resentment.
**huff·y** (huf′i), *adj.* [-IER, -IEST], [see HUFF], 1. easily offended; touchy. 2. angered or offended. **—huff′i·ly,** *adv.* **—huff′i·ness,** *n.*
**hug** (hug), *v.t.* [HUGGED, HUGGING], [prob. < ON. *hugga,* to comfort], 1. to put the arms around and hold closely and fondly. 2. to squeeze tightly with the forelegs or arms. 3. to cling to (a belief, opinion, etc.). 4. to keep close to: as, the bus *hugged* the curb. *v.i.* to embrace one another closely. *n.* 1. a close, fond embrace. 2. a tight hold with the arms, as in wrestling. 3. a bear's squeeze.
**huge** (hūj), *adj.* [OFr. *ahuge*], very large; immense; enormous. **—huge′ly,** *adv.* **—huge′ness,** *n.*
**hug·ger-mug·ger** (hug′ẽr-mug′ẽr), *n.* [prob. based on ME. *mokeren,* to conceal], a confusion; muddle; jumble. *adj.* confused; muddled. *adv.* in a confused or jumbled manner.
**Hughes, Charles Evans** (hūz), 1862–1948; U.S. chief justice (1930–1941).
**Hu·go, Victor Marie** (hū′gō), 1802–1885; French poet, novelist, and dramatist.
**Hu·gue·not** (hū′gə-not′), *n.* [Fr. < G. *eidgenosse,* confederate], any French Protestant of the 16th or 17th century.
**huh** (hu), *interj.* an exclamation used to express contempt, surprise, etc., or to ask a question.

**hu·la-hu·la** (hōō'lə-hōō'lə), *n.* [Haw.], a native Hawaiian dance performed by women: also **hula.**
**hulk** (hulk), *n.* [AS. *hulc*], 1. a big, unwieldy ship. 2. the body of a ship, especially if old and dismantled. 3. formerly, an old, dismantled ship or one specially built, for use as a prison. 4. a big, clumsy person or thing. *v.i.* to rise bulkily (usually with *up*).
**hulk·ing** (hul'kiŋ), *adj.* bulky and clumsy.
**hulk·y** (hul'ki), *adj.* [-IER, -IEST], hulking.
**Hull** (hul), *n.* a seaport in Yorkshire, England: pop., 299,000: officially *Kingston-upon-Hull.*
**hull** (hul), *n.* [AS. *hulu*], 1. the outer covering of a seed or fruit, as the husk of grain, shell of nuts, etc. 2. the calyx of some fruits, as the strawberry. 3. any outer covering. *v.t.* to take the hull or hulls off. **—hull'er,** *n.*
**hull** (hul), *n.* [special use of prec. *hull*], 1. the frame or body of a ship, excluding the spars, sails, and rigging. 2. the frame or main body of a flying boat or amphibian. *v.t.* to put a shell, torpedo, etc. through the hull of a ship.
**hul·la·ba·loo** (hul'ə-bə-lōō', hul'ə-bə-lōō'), *n.* [echoic; based on *hullo*], clamor; uproar.
**hul·lo** (hə-lō'), *interj., n., v.t. & v.i.* 1. hollo. 2. hello.
**hum** (hum), *v.i.* [HUMMED, HUMMING], [echoic], 1. to make the low, murmuring sound of a bee, a revolving electric fan, etc. 2. to sing with closed lips, not saying the words. 3. to give forth a confused, droning sound: as, the room *hummed* with voices. 4. [Colloq.], to be full of activity. *v.t.* 1. to sing (a tune, etc.) with the lips closed. 2. to produce an effect on by humming: as, to *hum* a child to sleep. *n.* 1. a humming. 2. a continuous, murmuring sound. **—hum'mer,** *n.*
**hum** (həm), *interj.* a conventionalized expression of a sound made in clearing the throat to attract attention, show doubt, etc. or of a sound made with closed lips to express contempt, pleasure, etc. *v.i.* [HUMMED, HUMMING], to make either of these sounds.
**hu·man** (hū'mən), *adj.* [< OFr. < L. *humanus*], 1. of or characteristic of a person or people. 2. having the form or nature of a person; consisting of people. 3. having or showing the qualities characteristic of people. *n.* a person: usually **human being. —hu'man·ness,** *n.*
**hu·mane** (hyoo-mān'), *adj.* [earlier var. of *human*], 1. kind, tender, merciful, considerate, etc. 2. civilizing; refining; humanizing: as, *humane* learning. **—hu·mane'ly,** *adv.* **—hu·mane'ness,** *n.*
**hu·man·ism** (hū'mən-iz'm), *n.* 1. the quality of being human; human nature. 2. any system or way of thought or action concerned with the interests and ideals of people. 3. the study of the humanities. 4. [H-], the intellectual and cultural movement that stemmed from the study of Greek and Latin classics during the Middle Ages and was one of the factors giving rise to the Renaissance. **—hu'man·ist,** *adj. & n.* **—hu'man·is'tic,** *adj.* **—hu'man·is'ti·cal·ly,** *adv.*
**hu·man·i·tar·i·an** (hyoo-man'ə-târ'i-ən), *n.* a person devoted to promoting the welfare of humanity; philanthropist. *adj.* helping humanity; philanthropic. **—hu·man'i·tar'i·an·ism,** *n.*
**hu·man·i·ty** (hyoo-man'ə-ti), *n.* [*pl.* -TIES], 1. the fact or quality of being human; human nature. 2. the human race; mankind; people. 3. the fact or quality of being humane; kindness, mercy, sympathy, etc. **—the humanities,** 1. languages and literature, especially the classical Greek and Latin. 2. the branches of learning concerned with human thought and relations; esp., literature and philosophy, and, often, the fine arts, history, etc.
**hu·man·ize** (hū'mə-nīz'), *v.t.* [-IZED, -IZING], 1. to make human. 2. to make humane; civilize; refine. *v.i.* to become human or humane. **—hu'man·i·za'tion,** *n.* **—hu'man·iz'er,** *n.*
**hu·man·kind** (hū'mən-kīnd'), *n.* the human race; mankind; people.
**hu·man·ly** (hū'mən-li), *adv.* 1. in a human manner. 2. by human means. 3. according to the experience or knowledge of human beings.
**hum·ble** (hum'b'l, um'-), *adj.* [-BLER, -BLEST], [OFr. < L. *humilis*, low; akin to *humus*, earth], 1. having or showing a consciousness of one's defects or shortcomings; not proud; modest. 2. low in condition or rank; lowly; unimportant; unpretentious. *v.t.* [-BLED, -BLING], 1. to lower in condition or rank; abase. 2. to make modest or humble in mind. **—hum'ble·ness,** *n.* **—hum'bler,** *n.* **—hum'bling·ly,** *adv.* **—hum'bly,** *adv.*
**hum·ble·bee** (hum'b'l-bē'), *n.* [< ME. < *hum(b)len*, to keep on humming + *bee*], a bumblebee.
**humble pie,** [< *umbles*, entrails of a deer < OFr. *nombles* < L. < *lumbus*, loin], formerly, a pie made of the inner parts of a deer, served to the servants after a hunt. **—eat humble pie,** to undergo humiliation, as by admitting one's error.
**hum·bug** (hum'bug'), *n.* [< ?], 1. *a)* fraud; sham; hoax. *b)* misleading or empty talk. 2. a dishonest person; impostor. 3. a spirit of trickery, deception, etc.: also **hum'bug'ger·y.** *v.t.* [-BUGGED, -BUGGING], to dupe; cheat. **—hum'bug'ger,** *n.*
**hum·ding·er** (hum'diŋ'ẽr), *n.* [Slang], a person or thing considered excellent of its kind.
**hum·drum** (hum'drum'), *adj.* [echoic], having no variety; dull; monotonous. *n.* 1. a humdrum person. 2. humdrum talk, routine, etc.
**Hume, David** (hūm), 1711–1776; Scottish philosopher and historian.
**hu·mer·us** (hū'mẽr-əs), *n.* [*pl.* -MERI (-mẽr-ī')], [L. *humerus, umerus*, the upper arm], the bone of the upper arm or forelimb, extending from the shoulder to the elbow. **—hu'mer·al,** *adj.*
**hu·mid** (hū'mid), *adj.* [< Fr. < L. *umidus* < *umere*, to be moist], damp; moist; specif., containing much water vapor. **—hu'mid·ly,** *adv.* **—hu'mid·ness,** *n.*
**hu·mid·i·fy** (hyoo-mid'ə-fī'), *v.t.* [-FIED, -FYING], to make humid; moisten; dampen. **—hu·mid'i·fi·ca'tion,** *n.* **—hu·mid'i·fi'er,** *n.*
**hu·mid·i·ty** (hyoo-mid'ə-ti), *n.* 1. moistness; dampness. 2. the amount of moisture in the air. **—relative humidity,** the amount of moisture in the air as compared with the greatest amount that the air could contain at the same temperature, expressed as a percentage.
**hu·mi·dor** (hū'mi-dôr'), *n.* a jar, case, etc. with a device for keeping tobacco, etc. moist.
**hu·mil·i·ate** (hyoo-mil'i-āt'), *v.t.* [-ATED, -ATING], [< LL. *humiliatus*, pp. < L. *humilis*, humble], to lower the pride or dignity of; mortify. **—hu·mil'i·at'er,** *n.* **—hu·mil'i·at'ing,** *adj.* **—hu·mil'i·at'ing·ly,** *adv.* **—hu·mil'i·a'tion,** *n.*
**hu·mil·i·ty** (hyoo-mil'ə-ti), *n.* [*pl.* -TIES], [< OFr. < L. < *humilis*, lowly], 1. the state or quality of being humble. 2. *pl.* acts of self-abasement.
**hum·ming·bird** (hum'iŋ-būrd'), *n.* any of a group of very small, brightly colored birds with a long, slender bill and narrow wings that vibrate rapidly and make a humming sound in flight.
**hum·mock** (hum'ək), *n.* [earlier also *hammock*], 1. a low, rounded hill; knoll; hillock. 2. a ridge or bump in an ice field. **—hum'mock·y,** *adj.*
**hu·mor** (hū'mẽr, ū'mẽr), *n.* [OFr. < L. *humor, umor*, moisture, fluid], 1. formerly, any of the four fluids **(cardinal humors)** considered responsible for one's health and disposition; blood, phlegm, choler (yellow bile), or melancholy (black bile); hence, 2. *a)* a person's temperament. *b)* a mood; state of mind. 3. whim; fancy; caprice. 4. comicality. 5. *a)* the ability to appreciate or express what is funny, amusing, or ludicrous. *b)* the expression of this in speech, writing, or action. *v.t.* 1. to comply with the mood or whim of (another); indulge. 2. to adapt oneself to. **—out of humor,** cross; out of sorts. **—hu'mor·less,** *adj.*
**hu·mor·esque** (hū'mə-resk'), *n.* a light, fanciful, or humorous musical composition; caprice.
**hu·mor·ist** (hū'mẽr-ist, ū'-), *n.* 1. a person with a well-developed sense of humor. 2. a professional writer or teller of amusing stories, jokes, etc.
**hu·mor·ous** (hū'mẽr-əs, ū'-), *adj.* 1. having or expressing humor; funny; amusing; comical. 2. [Archaic], capricious. **—hu'mor·ous·ly,** *adv.* **—hu'mor·ous·ness,** *n.*
**hu·mour** (hū'mẽr, ū'-), *n. & v.t.* humor: British sp.: derivatives are similarly spelled **(humourist, humourous,** etc.).
**hump** (hump), *n.* [cf. LG. *humpe*], 1. a rounded, protruding lump, as the fleshy mass on the back of a camel: in man, a hump is caused by a deformity of the spine. 2. a hummock; mound. *v.t.* 1. to arch; hunch: as, the cat *humped* its back. 2. [Slang], to exert (oneself). **—humped,** *adj.*
**hump·back** (hump'bak'), *n.* 1. a humped, deformed back. 2. a person having a humped back; hunchback. 3. a large whale with a dorsal fin resembling a humpback. **—hump'backed',** *adj.*
**humph** (humf; *conventionalized pronun.*), *interj. & n.* a grunting sound expressing doubt, surprise, disdain, disgust, etc.
**Hum·phrey, Hubert Horatio** (hum'fri), 1911– ; vice-president of the U.S. (1965–1969).
**Hump·ty Dump·ty** (hump'ti dump'ti), the personified egg of a well-known nursery rhyme.
**hump·y** (hump'i), *adj.* [-IER, -IEST], 1. having humps. 2. like a hump. **—hump'i·ness,** *n.*
**hu·mus** (hū'məs), *n.* [L., earth], the brown or black organic part of the soil, resulting from the partial decay of leaves and other vegetable matter.
**Hun** (hun), *n.* 1 a member of a savage Asiatic

people who invaded eastern and central Europe in the 4th and 5th centuries A.D. 2. [h-], any savage or destructive person; vandal. —**Hun′nish,** *adj.*
**hunch** (hunch), *v.t.* [< *hunchback*], to form into a hump: as, don't *hunch* your back so. *v.i.* to move forward jerkily; push; shove. *n.* 1. a hump. 2. a chunk; hunk. 3. [Colloq.], a feeling that something is going to happen; premonition.
**hunch·back** (hunch′bak′), *n.* 1. a humped back. 2. a person having a humped back. —**hunch′-backed′,** *adj.*
**hun·dred** (hun′drid, -dẽrd), *n.* [AS.], 1. the cardinal number next above ninety-nine; ten times ten; 100; C. 2. a division of an English county. *adj.* ten times ten.
**hun·dred·fold** (hun′drid-fōld′), *adj.* having or being a hundred times as much or as many. *adv.* a hundred times as much or as many.
**hun·dredth** (hun′dridth), *adj.* 1. preceded by ninety-nine others in a series; 100th. 2. designating any of the hundred equal parts of something. *n.* 1. the one following the ninety-ninth. 2. any of the hundred equal parts of something; 1/100.
**hun·dred·weight** (hun′drid-wāt′), *n.* a unit of weight, equal to 100 pounds in the United States and 112 pounds in England.
**hung** (huŋ), pt. and pp. of **hang**: see **hang.**
**Hung.,** 1. Hungarian. 2. Hungary.
**Hun·gar·i·an** (huŋ-gâr′i-ən), *adj.* of Hungary, its people, their language, or culture. *n.* 1. a native or inhabitant of Hungary; esp., a Magyar. 2. the Finno-Ugric language of the Magyars.
**Hun·ga·ry** (huŋ′gẽr-i), *n.* a country in central Europe: area, 35,912 sq. mi.; pop., 9,977,000; capital, Budapest.
**hun·ger** (huŋ′gẽr), *n.* [AS. *hungor*], 1. the discomfort, pain, or weakness caused by a need for food. 2. a need or appetite for food. 3. any strong desire; craving. *v.i.* 1. to be hungry. 2. to crave; long. *v.t.* to starve; famish. —**hun′ger·ing·ly,** *adv.*
**hunger strike,** a refusal, as of a prisoner, to eat until the authorities grant certain demands.
**hun·gry** (huŋ′gri), *adj.* [-GRIER, -GRIEST], 1. feeling or showing hunger; specif., *a*) wanting or needing food. *b*) craving; eager: as, a *hungry* glance. 2. [Rare], producing hunger. 3. not fertile; barren: said of soil. —**hun′gri·ly,** *adv.* —**hun′gri·ness,** *n.*
**hunk** (huŋk), *n.* [prob. < Fl. *hunke*], [Colloq.], a large piece, lump, or slice of bread, meat, etc.
**hunk·y-do·ry** (huŋ′ki-dôr′i, -dō′ri), *adj.* [Slang], as it should be; fine; satisfying.
**hunt** (hunt), *v.t.* [AS. *huntian*], 1. to chase (game) for food or sport. 2. to search carefully for; try to find. 3. *a*) to chase; drive. *b*) to hound; harry. 4. *a*) to go through (an area) in pursuit of game. *b*) to search (a place) carefully. 5. to use (dogs or horses) in chasing game. *v.i.* 1. to go out after game. 2. to search; seek. *n.* 1. a hunting. 2. a group of people who hunt together. 3. a district covered in hunting. 4. a search.
**hunt·er** (hun′tẽr), *n.* 1. a person who hunts. 2. a horse or dog trained for hunting.
**hunt·ing** (hun′tiŋ), *n.* the act of a person or animal that hunts. *adj.* of or for hunting.
**hunting ground,** a region used for hunting.
**hunting horn,** a horn for signaling during a hunt.
**Hunt·ing·ton** (hun′tiŋ-tən), *n.* a city in W West Virginia, on the Ohio: pop., 84,000.
**hunt·ress** (hun′tris), *n.* a woman who hunts.
**hunts·man** (hunts′mən), *n.* [*pl.* -MEN], [Chiefly Brit.], 1. a hunter. 2. the manager of a hunt.
**Hunts·ville** (hunts′vil), *n.* a city in N Alabama: pop., 72,000.
**Hu·pa** (hōō′pə), *n.* 1. any member of a tribe of North American Indians of NW California. 2. their Athapascan language.
**hur·dle** (hũr′d'l), *n.* [AS. *hyrdel*], 1. a portable frame of interlaced twigs, etc., used for temporary enclosures. 2. a kind of frame on which prisoners in England were drawn through the streets to execution. 3. a movable, framelike barrier for horses or runners to jump over in a race. 4. an obstacle; difficulty to be overcome. *v.t.* [-DLED, -DLING], 1. to fence off with hurdles. 2. to jump over (a hurdle), as in a race. 3. to overcome (an obstacle). —**the hurdles,** a race in which the contestants must jump over a series of hurdles. —**hur′dler,** *n.*

HURDLE

**hur·dy-gur·dy** (hũr′di-gũr′di), *n.* [*pl.* -DIES], [prob. echoic], 1. a boxed, lutelike instrument played by turning a crank: used by street musicians. 2. a barrel organ.

HURDY-GURDY

**hurl** (hũrl), *v.t.* [ME. *hurlen;* prob. < ON.] 1. to throw with force or violence. 2. to cast down; overthrow. 3. to utter vehemently. *v.i.* 1. to throw something. 2. [Archaic], to rush. 3. [Slang], in *baseball,* to pitch. *n.* a violent throw. —**hurl′er,** *n.*
**hurl·y-burl·y** (hũr′li-bũr′li), *n.* [*pl.* -IES], a turmoil; uproar. *adj.* disorderly and confused.
**Hu·ron** (hyoor′ən), *n.* 1. a member of a confederation of Iroquoian Indian tribes that lived between Georgian Bay and Lake Ontario. 2. the second largest of the Great Lakes, between Michigan and Ontario, Canada: usually **Lake Huron.** *adj.* of the Hurons.
**hur·rah** (hoo-rô′, hə-rä′), *interj. & n.* [echoic], a shout of joy, approval, etc. *v.i. & v.t.* to cheer; to shout "hurrah" (for).
**hur·ray** (hoo-rā′, hə-), *interj., n., v.t. & v.i.* hurrah.
**hur·ri·cane** (hũr′i-kān′), *n.* [< Sp. < W. Ind. *huracan*], 1. a violent cyclone, usually tropical, with winds moving from 73 to 100 miles an hour, usually accompanied by rain, thunder, and lightning. 2. a violent outburst.
**hurricane deck,** the top deck of a passenger ship plying inland waters.
**hur·ried** (hũr′id), *adj.* 1. forced to do, act, etc. in a hurry. 2. done, carried on, etc. in a hurry; hasty. —**hur′ried·ly,** *adv.* —**hur′ried·ness,** *n.*
**hur·ry** (hũr′i), *v.t.* [-RIED, -RYING], [prob. akin to *hurl*], 1. to move, send, or carry with haste. 2. to cause to occur or be done more rapidly or too rapidly. 3. to urge or cause to act soon or too soon. *v.i.* to move or act with haste. *n.* [*pl.* -RIES], 1. rush; haste; urgency. 2. eagerness to do, act, go, etc. quickly. —**hur′ry·ing·ly,** *adv.*
**hur·ry-scur·ry, hur·ry-skur·ry** (hũr′i-skũr′i), *n.* a disorderly confusion. *v.i.* to hurry and scurry about. *adj.* hurried and confused. *adv.* in a hurried, confused manner.
**hurt** (hũrt), *v.t.* [HURT, HURTING], [OFr. *hurter,* to push, hit; prob. < Frank.], 1. to cause pain or injury to; wound. 2. to harm or damage in some way. 3. to offend. *v.i.* 1. to cause injury, damage, or pain. 2. to give or have the sensation of pain; be sore: as, my leg *hurts. n.* 1. a pain or injury. 2. harm; damage. 3. something that wounds the feelings. —**hurt′er,** *n.* —**hurt′less,** *adj.*
**hurt·ful** (hũrt′fəl), *adj.* causing hurt; damaging; injurious. —**hurt′ful·ly,** *adv.* —**hurt′ful·ness,** *n.*
**hur·tle** (hũr′t'l), *v.i.* [-TLED, -TLING], [ME. *hurtlen*], 1. to come with a crash; clash; collide (with *against* or *together*). 2. to make a crashing sound as when colliding; clatter. 3. to move violently and swiftly. *v.t.* to throw, shoot, or cast with violence; hurl.
**hus·band** (huz′bənd), *n.* [AS. *husbonda* < ON. < *hūs,* house + *-bondi,* freeholder], a married man: the correlative of *wife. v.t.* 1. to marry (a woman). 2. to manage economically; conserve.
**hus·band·man** (huz′bənd-mən), *n.* [*pl.* -MEN], [Archaic or Poetic], a farmer.
**hus·band·ry** (huz′bənd-ri), *n.* 1. originally, management of domestic affairs, resources, etc. 2. careful, thrifty management. 3. farming.
**hush** (hush), *v.t.* [< ME. < *huscht,* quiet], 1. to make quiet or silent. 2. to soothe; lull. *v.i.* to be or become quiet or silent. *n.* quiet; silence. *interj.* an exclamation calling for silence. —**hush up,** 1. to keep quiet. 2. to keep secret; suppress.
**hush·a·by** (hush′ə-bī′), *interj.* [see HUSH & LULLABY], an exclamation used to hush infants.
**hush money,** money paid to a person to keep him from telling something.
**hush puppy,** in the southern U.S., a small, fried ball of corn-meal dough.
**husk** (husk), *n.* [prob. < MD. *huuskijn,* dim. of *huus,* a house], 1. the dry outer covering of various fruits or seeds, as of an ear of corn. 2. the dry, rough, or useless outside covering of anything. *v.t.* to remove the husk from. —**husk′er,** *n.*
**husk·ing (bee)** (hus′kiŋ), a cornhusking.
**Hus·ky** (hus′ki), *n.* [*pl.* -KIES], [? < *Eskimo*], 1. an Eskimo. 2. [sometimes h-] an Eskimo dog.
**husk·y** (hus′ki), *adj.* [-IER, -IEST], 1. *a*) full of or

consisting of husks. *b*) like a husk. 2. dry in the throat; hoarse and rough. **—husk′i·ly,** ***adv.*** **—husk′i·ness,** ***n.***

**hus·ky** (hus′ki), ***adj.*** [-KIER, -KIEST], big and strong; robust; burly. ***n.*** [*pl.* -KIES], a husky person. **—hus′ki·ly,** ***adv.*** **—hus′ki·ness,** ***n.***

**Huss, John** (hus), (*Jan Hus*), 1369?–1415; Bohemian religious reformer and martyr. **—Huss′ite** (-īt), ***n. & adj.***

**hus·sar** (hoo-zär′), ***n.*** [< Hung. < Serb. *husar, gusar* < MGr. < LL. *cursarius;* see CORSAIR], a member of any European regiment of light-armed cavalry, usually with brilliant dress uniforms.

**hus·sy** (huz′i, hus′i), ***n.*** [*pl.* -SIES], [contr. < ME. *huswife,* housewife], 1. a woman, especially one of low morals. 2. a saucy, pert girl; minx.

**hust·ings** (hus′tiŋz), ***n.pl.*** [usually construed as sing.], [AS. < ON. < *hūs,* a house + *thing,* assembly], 1. the proceedings at an election. 2. any place where political campaign speeches are made.

**hus·tle** (hus′'l), ***v.t.*** [-TLED, -TLING], [D. *husselen,* to shake up], 1. to push about; jostle in a rude, rough manner. 2. to force in a rough, hurried manner: as, he *hustled* them into the patrol wagon. 3. [Colloq.], to hurry (a person, a job, etc.). ***v.i.*** 1. to move hurriedly. 2. [Colloq.], to work or act rapidly or energetically. ***n.*** 1. a hustling; rough pushing or shoving. 2. [Colloq.], energetic action; drive. **—hus′tler,** ***n.***

**hut** (hut), ***n.*** [< Fr. < OHG. *hutta*], a small, shedlike house; hovel; roughly made little cabin. ***v.i.*** [HUTTED, HUTTING], to live in a hut. **—hut′like′,** ***adj.***

**hutch** (huch), ***n.*** [OFr. *huche,* bin < LL. *hutica,* a chest], 1. a bin, chest, or box for storage. 2. pen or coop for animals or poultry. 3. a hut. ***v.t.*** to store or put in or as in a hutch.

**Hux·ley, Thomas Henry** (huks′li), 1825–1895; English biologist and writer.

**huz·za** (hə-zä′, hoo-), ***interj. & n.*** [*pl.* -ZAS], a shout of joy, approval, etc. ***v.i. & v.t.*** [-ZAED, -ZAING], to cheer. Now replaced by *hurrah.*

**H.V., h.v.,** high voltage.

**Hwang Ho, Hwang·ho** (hwäŋ′ hō′), a river in China, flowing into the Yellow Sea: length, 2,700 mi.: also called *Yellow River.*

**hy·a·cinth** (hī′ə-sinth′), ***n.*** [< Fr. < L. < Gr. *hyakinthos*], 1. a gem; specif., *a*) among the ancients, a blue gem. *b*) a reddish-orange gem; jacinth. 2. a plant of the lily family, with spikes of fragrant, bell-shaped flowers. 3. bluish purple. **—hy′a·cin′thine** (-thin, -thīn), ***adj.***

**hy·ae·na** (hī-ē′nə), ***n.*** a hyena.

**hy·a·line** (hī′ə-lin, -līn′), ***adj.*** [< L. < Gr. < *hyalos,* glass], transparent as glass; glassy: also **hy′a·loid′** (-loid′). ***n.*** anything transparent or glassy.

**hy·brid** (hī′brid), ***n.*** [L. *hybrida,* offspring of tame sow and wild boar], 1. the offspring of two animals or plants of different species, etc. 2. anything of mixed origin. 3. in *linguistics,* a word made up of elements from different languages. ***adj.*** of, or having the nature of, a hybrid. **—hy′brid·ism, hy·brid′i·ty,** ***n.***

**hy·brid·ize** (hī′bri-dīz′), ***v.t.*** [-IZED, -IZING], to produce or cause to produce hybrids; interbreed; cross. **—hy′brid·i·za′tion,** ***n.***

**Hyde Park** (hīd), 1. a park in London. 2. a village in S New York: the estate and burial place of Franklin D. Roosevelt is near by.

**Hy·der·a·bad** (hī′dēr-ə-bad′, hī′drə-bäd′), ***n.*** 1. a state of south central India. 2. its capital: pop., 1,086,000.

**hydr-,** hydro-.

**Hy·dra** (hī′drə), ***n.*** [*pl.* -DRAS, -DRAE (-drē)], [< OFr. *ydre* < L. < Gr. *hydra,* water serpent], 1. in *Gr. mythology,* the nine-headed serpent slain by Hercules: each head grew back double when cut off. 2. [h-], any persistent or ever-increasing evil. 3. [h-], a very small fresh-water polyp, with a tubelike body and a mouth surrounded by tentacles.

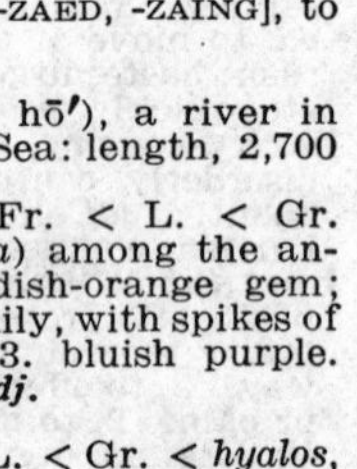

HYDRA

**hy·dran·ge·a** (hī-drān′jə, -dran′ji-ə), ***n.*** [< *hydr-* + Gr. *angeion,* vessel], a shrub of the saxifrage family, with opposite leaves and large, showy clusters of white, blue, or pink flowers.

**hy·drant** (hī′drənt), ***n.*** [< Gr. *hydōr,* water], a large discharge pipe with a valve for drawing water from a water main; fireplug.

**hy·drar·gy·rum** (hī-drär′ji-rəm), ***n.*** [< L. < Gr. *hydrargyros* < *hydōr,* water + *argyros,* silver], mercury: symbol, Hg. **—hy′drar·gyr′ic,** ***adj.***

**hy·drate** (hī′drāt), ***n.*** [*hydr-* + *-ate*], a compound formed by the chemical combination of water and some other substance: as, plaster of Paris, $2CaSO_4 \cdot H_2O$, is a *hydrate.* ***v.t. & v.i.*** [-DRATED, -DRATING], 1. to become or cause to become a hydrate. 2. to combine with water. **—hy′drat·ed,** ***adj.*** **—hy·dra′tion,** ***n.*** **—hy′dra·tor,** ***n.***

**hy·drau·lic** (hī-drô′lik), ***adj.*** [< Fr. < L. < Gr. *hydraulikos;* ult. < *hydōr,* water + *aulos,* tube], 1. of hydraulics. 2. operated by the movement and force of liquid: as, a *hydraulic* brake. 3. setting or hardening under water: as, *hydraulic* mortar. **—hy·drau′li·cal·ly,** ***adv.***

**hy·drau·lics** (hī-drô′liks), ***n.pl.*** [construed as sing.], the branch of physics having to do with the mechanical properties of liquids, as water, and their application in engineering.

**hy·dric** (hī′drik), ***adj.*** [*hydr-* + *-ic*], of or containing hydrogen.

**hy·dride** (hī′drīd, -drid), ***n.*** [*hydr-* + *-ide*], a compound of hydrogen with either another element or a radical: also **hy′drid** (-drid).

**hy·dro-,** [< Gr. *hydōr,* water], a combining form meaning: 1. *water,* as in *hydrometer.* 2. *the presence of hydrogen,* as in *hydrocyanic.* Also **hydr-.**

**hy·dro·car·bon** (hī′drə-kär′bən), ***n.*** any compound containing only hydrogen and carbon: benzene and methane are hydrocarbons.

**hy·dro·ceph·a·lus** (hī′drə-sef′ə-ləs), ***n.*** [< Gr. < *hydōr,* water + *kephalē,* head], a condition characterized by an abnormal amount of fluid in the cranium, causing enlargement of the head: also **hy′dro·ceph′a·ly.** **—hy′dro·ceph′a·loid, hy′dro·ceph′a·lous,** ***adj.***

**hy·dro·chlo·ric** (hī′drə-klôr′ik, -klō′rik), ***adj.*** [*hydro-* + *chloric*], designating or of an acid, HCl, produced by the combination of hydrogen and chlorine, and existing as a colorless gas or as a colorless solution of this gas in water.

**hy·dro·cy·an·ic** (hī′drō-sī-an′ik), ***adj.*** [*hydro-* + *cyanic*], designating or of a weak, highly poisonous acid, HCN (also called *prussic acid*), a colorless liquid with the odor of bitter almonds.

**hy·dro·dy·nam·ics** (hī′drō-dī-nam′iks), ***n.pl.*** [construed as sing.], the branch of physics having to do with the motion and action of water and other liquids. **—hy′dro·dy·nam′ic,** ***adj.***

**hy·dro·e·lec·tric** (hī′drō-i-lek′trik), ***adj.*** producing, or relating to the production of, electricity by water power. **—hy′dro·e·lec′tric′i·ty** (-tris′ə-ti), ***n.***

**hy·dro·flu·or·ic** (hī′drō-flōō-ôr′ik, -or′ik), ***adj.*** [*hydro-* + *fluoric*], designating or of an acid, HF, existing as a colorless, fuming, corrosive liquid: it is used in etching glass.

**hy·dro·gen** (hī′drə-jən), ***n.*** [< Fr.; see HYDRO- & -GEN], an inflammable, colorless, odorless, gaseous chemical element, the lightest of all known substances: symbol, H; at. wt., 1.0080; at. no., 1. **—hy·drog·en·ous** (hī-droj′ə-nəs), ***adj.***

**hy·dro·gen·ate** (hī′drə-jə-nāt′), ***v.t.*** [-ATED, -ATING], to combine or treat with hydrogen, as in making a solid fat of oil. **—hy′dro·gen·a′tion,** ***n.***

**hydrogen bomb,** an extremely destructive, thermonuclear atom bomb, in which the atoms of heavy hydrogen are fused into helium by explosion of a nuclear-fission unit in the bomb: the first hydrogen bomb was exploded in 1952 by the U.S.: also **H-bomb, fusion bomb.**

**hydrogen ion,** the positively charged ion in all acids: symbol, $H^+$.

**hy·dro·gen·ize** (hī′drə-jə-nīz′), ***v.t.*** [-IZED, -IZING], to hydrogenate.

**hydrogen peroxide,** an unstable liquid, $H_2O_2$, often used, diluted, as a bleach or disinfectant.

**hydrogen sulfide,** a gaseous compound, $H_2S$, with the characteristic odor of rotten eggs.

**hy·drog·ra·phy** (hī-drog′rə-fi), ***n.*** [< Fr.; see HYDRO- & -GRAPHY], the study, description, and mapping of oceans, lakes, and rivers. **—hy·drog′ra·pher,** ***n.*** **—hy·dro·graph·ic** (hī′drə-graf′ik), **hy′dro·graph′i·cal,** ***adj.***

**hy·droid** (hī′droid), ***adj.*** [< *hydra* + *-oid*], 1. like a hydra or polyp. 2. of or related to the group of hydrozoans of which the hydra is the typical member. ***n.*** any member of this group; esp., a polyp.

**hy·drol·y·sis** (hī-drol′ə-sis), ***n.*** [*pl.* -SES (-sēz′)], [*hydro-* + *-lysis*], a chemical reaction in which a compound reacts with the ions of water ($H^+$ and $OH^-$) to produce a weak acid, a weak base, or both. **—hy·dro·lyt·ic** (hī′drə-lit′ik), ***adj.***

**hy·dro·lyte** (hī′drə-līt′), ***n.*** any substance undergoing hydrolysis.

**hy·dro·lyze** (hī′drə-līz′), ***v.t. & v.i.*** [-LYZED, -LYZING], to undergo or cause to undergo hydrolysis. **—hy′dro·ly·za′tion,** ***n.***

**hy·drom·e·ter** (hī-drom′ə-tẽr), *n.* [*hydro-* + *-meter*], an instrument consisting of a graduated, weighted tube, used for determining the specific gravity of liquids. —**hy·dro·met·ric** (hī′drə-met′rik), **hy′dro·met′ri·cal,** *adj.* —**hy·drom′e·try,** *n.*

**hy·drop·a·thy** (hī-drop′ə-thi), *n.* [*hydro-* + *-pathy*], a system of treating all diseases by the external or internal use of water. —**hy·dro·path·ic** (hī′drə-path′ik), **hy′dro·path′i·cal,** *adj.* —**hy·drop′a·thist′,** *n.*

**hy·dro·pho·bi·a** (hī′drə-fō′bi-ə), *n.* [see HYDRO- & -PHOBIA], 1. an abnormal fear of water. 2. [from the symptomatic inability to swallow liquids], rabies (especially in man). —**hy′dro·pho′bic,** *adj.*

**hy·dro·phyte** (hī′drə-fīt′), *n.* [*hydro-* + *-phyte*], any plant growing only in water or very wet earth.

**hy·dro·plane** (hī′drə-plān′), *n.* [*hydro-* + *plane*], 1. a small, light motorboat with a flat bottom that can skim along the water at high speeds. 2. a seaplane. 3. an attachment for an airplane that enables it to glide along on the water. ***v.i.*** to drive or ride in a hydroplane.

**hy·dro·pon·ics** (hī′drə-pon′iks), *n.pl.* [construed as sing.], [< *hydro-* + Gr. *ponos*, labor; + *-ics*], the science of growing plants in mineral solutions instead of in soil. —**hy′dro·pon′ic,** *adj.*

**hy·dro·sphere** (hī′drə-sfêr′), *n.* [*hydro-* + *-sphere*], 1. all the water on the surface of the earth. 2. the moisture in the earth's atmosphere.

**hy·dro·stat** (hī′drə-stat′), *n.* [*hydro-* + *-stat*], 1. an electrical device for regulating the level of water in a reservoir, etc. 2. an apparatus for preventing the explosion of a steam boiler.

**hy·dro·stat·ics** (hī′drə-stat′iks), *n.pl.* [construed as sing.], the branch of physics having to do with the pressure and equilibrium of water and other liquids. —**hy′dro·stat′ic, hy′dro·stat′i·cal,** *adj.* —**hy′dro·stat′i·cal·ly,** *adv.*

**hy·dro·sul·fide** (hī′drə-sul′fīd), *n.* a compound containing the HS radical and some other radical or element: also called *bisulfide.*

**hy·dro·ther·a·peu·tics** (hī′drə-ther′ə-pū′tiks), *n.pl.* [construed as sing.], hydrotherapy. —**hy′dro·ther′a·peu′tic,** *adj.*

**hy·dro·ther·a·py** (hī′drə-ther′ə-pi), *n.* [*hydro-* + *therapy*], the treatment of disease by the internal or external use of water.

**hy·drot·ro·pism** (hī-drot′rə-piz′m), *n.* [*hydro-* + *-tropism*], the tendency of a plant to grow or turn in the direction of moisture. —**hy·dro·trop·ic** (hī′drə-trop′ik), *adj.*

**hy·drous** (hī′drəs), *adj.* [*hydr-* + *-ous*], 1. containing water; watery. 2. containing water in chemical combination.

**hy·drox·ide** (hī-drok′sīd, -sid), *n.* [*hydr-* + *oxide*], a compound consisting of an element or radical combined with the hydroxyl radical (OH).

**hy·drox·yl** (hī-drok′sil), *n.* the monovalent radical OH, present in all hydroxides.

**hy·dro·zo·an** (hī′drə-zō′ən), *adj.* [< *hydra* + Gr. *zōion*, an animal], of a class of water animals having a saclike body and a mouth that opens directly into the body cavity. *n.* any animal of this class, including hydras, polyps, etc.

**hy·e·na** (hī-ē′nə), *n.* [< L. < Gr. *hyaina* < *hys*, a hog], a wolflike, flesh-eating animal of Africa and Asia, with a characteristic shrill cry: hyenas feed on carrion and are considered cowardly: also sp. **hyaena.**

**Hy·ge·ia** (hī-jē′ə), *n.* the ancient Greek goddess of health.

**hy·giene** (hī′jēn, -ji-ēn′), *n.* [< Fr. < Gr. *hygieinē* < *hygiēs*, healthy], the science of health and its maintenance; system of principles for the preservation of health and prevention of disease: also **hy′gi·en′ics** (-ji-en′iks, -jē′niks), *n.pl.* [construed as sing.].

**hy·gi·en·ic** (hī′ji-en′ik, hī-jē′nik), *adj.* 1. of hygiene or health. 2. promoting health; sanitary. Also **hy′gi·en′i·cal.** —**hy′gi·en′i·cal·ly,** *adv.*

**hy·gi·en·ist** (hī′ji-ən-ist), *n.* an expert in hygiene: also **hy·ge·ist, hy·gie·ist** (hī′ji-ist).

**hy·gro-,** [< Gr. *hygros*, wet], a combining form meaning *wet, moisture:* also **hygr-.**

**hy·grom·e·ter** (hī-grom′ə-tẽr), *n.* [*hygro-* + *-meter*], an instrument for measuring humidity.

**hy·grom·e·try** (hī-grom′ə-tri), *n.* [*hygro-* + *-metry*], the branch of physics having to do with measuring the amount of moisture in the air. —**hy·gro·met·ric** (hī′grə-met′rik), *adj.*

**hy·gro·scope** (hī′grə-skōp′), *n.* [*hygro-* + *-scope*], an instrument for recording changes in the amount of moisture in the air.

**hy·gro·scop·ic** (hī′grə-skop′ik), *adj.* 1. of or measurable by a hygroscope. 2. absorbing moisture from the air. —**hy′gro·scop′i·cal·ly,** *adv.*

**hy·ing** (hī′iŋ), alt. ppr. of **hie.**

**hy·la** (hī′lə), *n.* [< Gr. *hylē*, wood], a tree toad.

**Hy·men** (hī′mən), *n.* 1. the ancient Greek god of marriage. 2. [h-], *a*) marriage. *b*) a wedding song.

**hy·men** (hī′mən), *n.* [Gr. *hymēn*, skin], the thin mucous membrane that usually covers part of the opening of the vagina in a virgin.

**hy·me·ne·al** (hī′mə-nē′əl), *adj.* [see HYMEN], of a wedding or marriage: also **hy′me·ne′an.** *n.* a wedding song or poem.

**hy·me·nop·ter·on** (hī′mə-nop′tẽr-on), *n.* [*pl.* -TERA (-tẽr-ə)], a hymenopterous insect.

**hy·me·nop·ter·ous** (hī′mə-nop′tẽr-əs), *adj.* [< Gr. < *hymēn*, membrane + *pteron*, a wing], belonging to a large group of insects, including wasps, bees, ants, etc., which have a sucking mouth and four membranous wings.

**hymn** (him), *n.* [< AS. & OFr. < LL. < Gr. *hymnos*], 1. a song in praise or honor of God, a god, or gods. 2. any song of praise. ***v.t. & v.i.*** to praise in a hymn. —**hym·nist** (him′nist), *n.*

**hym·nal** (him′nəl), *n.* a collection of hymns: also **hymn′book′.** *adj.* of or using hymns.

**hym·nol·o·gy** (him-nol′ə-ji), *n.* [< Gr.; see HYMN & -LOGY], 1. the study of hymns, their use, history, etc. 2. hymns collectively. 3. the composition of hymns. —**hym·no·log·ic** (him′nə-loj′ik), **hym′no·log′i·cal,** *adj.* —**hym·nol′o·gist,** *n.*

**hy·oid** (hī′oid), *adj.* [< Fr. < Gr. *hyoeidēs*, shaped like the letter Υ (upsilon) < name of this letter + *eidos*, form], designating or of a U-shaped bone at the base of the tongue. *n.* a hyoid bone.

**hyp.,** 1. hypodermic. 2. hypotenuse. 3. hypothesis.

**hy·per-,** [Gr. < *hyper*, over, above], a prefix meaning: *over, above, more than the normal, excessive,* as in *hypercritical:* opposed to *hypo-.*

**hy·per·a·cid·i·ty** (hī′pẽr-ə-sid′ə-ti), *n.* excessive acidity, especially of the gastric juice. —**hy′per·ac′id** (-as′id), *adj.*

**hy·per·bo·la** (hī-pũr′bə-lə), *n.* [*pl.* -LAS], [Mod.L. < Gr. *hyperbolē* < *hyper-*, over + *ballein*, to throw], a curve formed by the section of a cone cut by a plane that makes a greater angle with the base than the side of the cone makes.

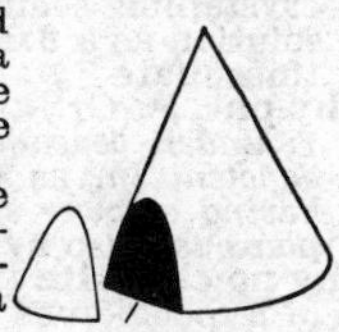

HYPERBOLA

**hy·per·bo·le** (hī-pũr′bə-li), *n.* [see HYPERBOLA], exaggeration for effect, not meant to be taken literally. Example: He's as big as a house.

**hy·per·bol·ic** (hī′pẽr-bol′ik), *adj.* 1. of, having the nature of, or using hyperbole; exaggerated or exaggerating. 2. of, or having the form of, a hyperbola. —**hy′per·bol′i·cal·ly,** *adv.*

**hy·per·bo·lize** (hī-pũr′bə-līz′), ***v.t. & v.i.*** [-LIZED, -LIZING], to express with hyperbole.

**hy·per·bo·re·an** (hī′pẽr-bôr′i-ən, -bō′ri-), *adj.* [< L. < Gr. *hyperboreos*, beyond the north wind], 1. of the far north. 2. very cold. *n.* [H-], in *Gr. legend*, an inhabitant of a region of sunshine and eternal spring beyond the north wind.

**hy·per·crit·i·cal** (hī′pẽr-krit′i-k'l), *adj.* too critical. —**hy′per·crit′i·cal·ly,** *adv.*

**Hy·pe·ri·on** (hī-pêr′i-ən), *n.* in *Gr. mythology*, 1. a Titan, father of the sun god Helios. 2. Helios, in later mythology identified with Apollo.

**hy·per·me·tro·pi·a** (hī′pẽr-mi-trō′pi-ə), *n.* [Mod. L. < Gr. *hypermetros*, excessive + *ōps*, eye], farsightedness; abnormal vision in which distant objects are seen more clearly than near ones: also **hy′per·o′pi·a** (-ō′pi-ə). —**hy′per·me·trop′ic** (-trop′ik), **hy′per·op′ic** (-op′ik), *adj.*

**hy·per·sen·si·tive** (hī′pẽr-sen′sə-tiv), *adj.* abnormally or excessively sensitive. —**hy′per·sen′si·tive·ness, hy′per·sen′si·tiv′i·ty,** *n.*

**hy·per·son·ic** (hī′pẽr-son′ik), *adj.* [*hyper-*, over + L. *sonus*, sound], designating, of, or moving at a speed greater than five times the speed of sound (in air), or over 3,700 miles per hour.

**hy·per·ten·sion** (hī′pẽr-ten′shən), *n.* 1. abnormally high blood pressure. 2. the condition caused by this. —**hy′per·ten′sive,** *adj. & n.*

**hy·per·thy·roid·ism** (hī′pẽr-thī′roid-iz′m), *n.* 1. excessive activity of the thyroid gland. 2. the condition caused by this, characterized by a rapid pulse, sleeplessness, etc. —**hy′per·thy′roid,** *adj. & n.*

**hy·per·tro·phy** (hī-pūr′trə-fi), *n.* [*hyper-* + *-trophy*], an abnormal increase in the size of an organ or tissue. *v.i. & v.t.* [-PHIED, -PHYING], to increase abnormally in size. **—hy·per·troph·ic** (hī′pẽr-trof′ik), *adj.*

**hy·pha** (hī′fə), *n.* [*pl.* -PHAE (-fē)], [< Gr. *hyphē*, a web], any of the threadlike parts making up the mycelium of a fungus.

**hy·phen** (hī′f′n), *n.* [LL. < Gr. < *hypo-*, under + *hen*, neut. acc. of *heis*, one], a mark (-) used between the parts of a compound word or the syllables of a divided word, as at the end of a line. *v.t.* to hyphenate.

**hy·phen·ate** (hī′f′n-āt′), *v.t.* [-ATED, -ATING], 1. to connect by a hyphen. 2. to write or print with a hyphen. *adj.* hyphenated. **—hy′phen·a′tion,** *n.*

**hyp·no-,** [< Gr. *hypnos*, sleep], a combining form meaning *sleep*: also **hypn-.**

**hyp·noid** (hip′noid), *adj.* resembling hypnosis: also **hyp·noi′dal.**

**hyp·nol·o·gy** (hip-nol′ə-ji), *n.* [*hypno-* + *-logy*], the science dealing with sleep and hypnotism.

**hyp·no·sis** (hip-nō′sis), *n.* [*pl.* -SES (-sēz)], [< Gr. *hypnos*, sleep; + *-osis*], a sleeplike condition psychically induced, usually by another person, in which the subject loses consciousness but responds, with certain limitations, to the suggestions of the hypnotist.

**hyp·not·ic** (hip-not′ik), *adj.* [< Fr. or L. < Gr. *hypnōtikos*, tending to sleep < *hypnos*, sleep], 1. causing sleep; soporific. 2. of, like, or inducing hypnosis. 3. easily hypnotized. *n.* 1. any drug causing sleep. 2. a hypnotized person or one easily hypnotized. **—hyp·not′i·cal·ly,** *adv.*

**hyp·no·tism** (hip′nə-tiz′m), *n.* 1. the act or practice of inducing hypnosis. 2. the science of hypnosis. **—hyp′no·tist,** *n.*

**hyp·no·tize** (hip′nə-tīz′), *v.t.* [-TIZED, -TIZING], 1. to induce hypnosis in. 2. [Colloq.], to entrance, as by eloquent speech. **—hyp′no·tiz′a·ble,** *adj.* **—hyp′no·ti·za′tion,** *n.* **—hyp′no·tiz′er,** *n.*

**hy·po** (hī′pō), *n.* [*pl.* -POS], 1. [Colloq.], a hypodermic. 2. [Slang], a hypochondriac.

**hy·po** (hī′pō), *n.* [contr. < *hyposulfite*], a colorless, crystalline sodium salt, $Na_2S_2O_3 \cdot 5H_2O$, used in solution as a fixing agent in photography; sodium thiosulfate.

**hy·po-,** [< Gr. < *hypo*, less than], a prefix meaning: 1. *under, beneath*, as in *hypodermic*. 2. *less than, deficient in*, as in *hypothyroid*. 3. in *chemistry, having a lower state of oxidation*, as in *hypophosphorous*. Also **hyp-.** Opposed to *hyper-*.

**hy·po·chlo·rite** (hī′pə-klôr′īt, -klō′rīt), *n.* any salt of hypochlorous acid.

**hy·po·chlo·rous** (hī′pə-klôr′əs, -klō′rəs), *adj.* [*hypo-* + *chlorous*], designating or of an unstable acid, $HClO$, known only in solution and used as a bleach and oxidizer.

**hy·po·chon·dri·a** (hī′pə-kon′dri-ə, hip′ə-), *n.* [LL., *pl.*, abdomen (supposed seat of this condition) < Gr. < *hypo-*, under + *chondros*, cartilage], abnormal anxiety over one's health, often with imaginary illnesses and severe melancholy: also **hy′po·chon·dri′a·sis** (-dri′ə-sis).

**hy·po·chon·dri·ac** (hī′pə-kon′dri-ak′, hip′ə-), *adj.* 1. designating or of the region of the hypochondrium. 2. of or having hypochondria. Also **hy′po·chon·dri′a·cal** (-kən-dri′ə-k'l). *n.* one who has hypochondria. **—hy′po·chon·dri′a·cal·ly,** *adv.*

**hy·po·chon·dri·um** (hī′pə-kon′dri-əm, hip′ə-), *n.* [*pl.* -DRIA (-dri-ə)], [see HYPOCHONDRIA], either side of the abdomen just below the lowest rib.

**hy·po·cot·yl** (hī′pə-kot′'l, hip′ə-), *n.* the part of the axis, or stem, below the cotyledons in the embryo of a plant. **—hy′po·cot′y·lous,** *adj.*

**hy·poc·ri·sy** (hi-pok′rə-si), *n.* [*pl.* -SIES], [< OFr. < L. < Gr. *hypokrisis*, a reply, acting a part; ult. < *hypo-*, under + *krinesthai*, to dispute], a pretending to be what one is not, or to feel what one does not feel; esp., a pretense of virtue, etc.

**hyp·o·crite** (hip′ə-krit), *n.* [< OFr. < L. *hypocrita*, an actor; see HYPOCRISY], a person who pretends to be better than he really is, or pious, virtuous, etc. without really being so. **—hyp′o·crit′i·cal,** *adj.* **—hyp′o·crit′i·cal·ly,** *adv.*

**hy·po·der·mic** (hī′pə-dūr′mik), *adj.* [see HYPO- & -DERM], 1. of the parts under the skin. 2. injected under the skin. *n.* 1. a hypodermic injection. 2. a hypodermic syringe or needle. **—hy′po·der′mi·cal·ly,** *adv.*

**hypodermic injection,** the injection of a medicine or drug under the skin.

**hypodermic syringe,** a glass syringe attached to a hollow needle **(hypodermic needle)**, used for giving hypodermic injections.

HYPODERMIC SYRINGE

**hy·po·der·mis** (hī′pə-dūr′mis), *n.* [see HYPO- & DERMIS], a layer of cells that lies beneath, and secretes, the cuticle of annelids, arthropods, etc.

**hy·po·gas·tri·um** (hī′pə-gas′tri-əm), *n.* [*pl.* -TRIA (-tri-ə)], [Mod. L. < Gr. < *hypo-*, under + *gastēr*, the belly], the lower, middle part of the abdomen. **—hy′po·gas′tric,** *adj.*

**hy·po·phos·phate** (hī′pə-fos′fāt), *n.* a salt of hypophosphoric acid.

**hy·po·phos·phite** (hī′pə-fos′fīt), *n.* a salt of hypophosphorous acid.

**hy·po·phos·phor·ic** (hī′pō-fos-fôr′ik, -for′ik), *adj.* designating or of an acid, $H_4P_2O_6$, obtained when phosphorus is slowly oxidized in moist air.

**hy·po·phos·pho·rous** (hī′pə-fos′fẽr-əs), *adj.* designating or of a monobasic acid of phosphorus, $H_3PO_2$: it is a strong reducing agent.

**hy·po·sul·fite** (hī′pə-sul′fīt), *n.* 1. a salt of hyposulfurous acid. 2. popularly but incorrectly, sodium thiosulfate, $Na_2S_2O_3$: see **hypo.**

**hy·po·sul·fu·rous** (hī′pō-sul-fyoor′əs, -sul′fẽr-əs), *adj.* designating or of a dibasic acid, $H_2S_2O_4$, used as a bleaching and reducing agent.

**hy·pot·e·nuse** (hī-pot′'n-ōōs′, hi-pot′'n-ūs′), *n.* [< L. < Gr. *hypoteinousa*, lit., subtending < *hypo-*, under + *teinein*, to stretch], the side of a right-angled triangle opposite the right angle: also **hy·poth′e·nuse′** (-poth′-).

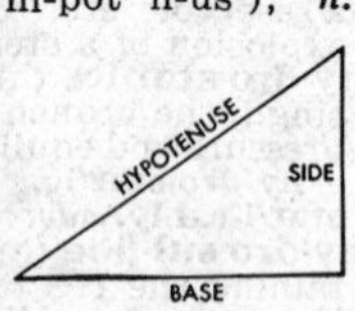


HYPOTENUSE

**hy·poth·e·cate** (hī-poth′ə-kāt′, hi-), *v.t.* [-CATED, -CATING], [< ML. < L. < Gr. < *hypotithenai*, to pledge], to pledge (property) to another as security; mortgage. **—hy·poth′e·ca′tion,** *n.* **—hy·poth′e·ca′tor,** *n.*

**hy·poth·e·sis** (hī-poth′ə-sis, hi-), *n.* [*pl.* -SES (-sēz′)], [Mod. L. < Gr. < *hypo-*, under + *tithenai*, to place], an unproved theory, proposition, etc. tentatively accepted to explain certain facts or **(working hypothesis)** to provide a basis for further investigation, argument, study, etc.

**hy·poth·e·size** (hī-poth′ə-sīz′, hi-), *v.i.* [-SIZED, -SIZING], to make a hypothesis. *v.t.* to assume; suppose. **—hy·poth′e·siz′er,** *n.*

**hy·po·thet·i·cal** (hī′pə-thet′i-k'l), *adj.* 1. based on or involving a hypothesis; assumed; supposed. 2. given to the use of hypotheses: as, a *hypothetical* mind. 3. in *logic*, conditional: as, a *hypothetical* proposition. Also **hy′po·thet′ic.** **—hy′po·thet′i·cal·ly,** *adv.*

**hy·po·thy·roid·ism** (hī′pō-thī′roid-iz′m), *n.* 1. deficient activity of the thyroid gland. 2. the condition caused by this, characterized by sluggishness, goiter, etc. **—hy′po·thy′roid,** *adj. & n.*

**hy·son** (hī′s'n), *n.* [Chin. *hsi-tchun*, lit., blooming spring], a variety of Chinese green tea.

**hys·sop** (his′əp), *n.* [< OFr. < L. < Gr. *hyssōpos* < Heb. *ēzōb*, aromatic plant], 1. a fragrant, blue-flowered plant of the mint family, used in medicine as a tonic, stimulant, etc. 2. in the *Bible*, a plant whose twigs were used in ancient Jewish religious rites: Psalms 51:7.

**hys·ter·ec·to·my** (his′tẽr-ek′tə-mi), *n.* [*pl.* -MIES], [< Gr. *hystera*, uterus; + *-ectomy*], surgical removal of all or part of the uterus.

**hys·te·ri·a** (his-têr′i-ə, -ter′-), *n.* [< *hysterical*], 1. a psychiatric condition characterized by excitability, sensory and motor disturbances, and the simulation of organic disorders. 2. any outbreak of wild, uncontrolled excitement, such as fits of laughing and crying.

**hys·ter·ic** (his-ter′ik), *adj.* hysterical. *n.* 1. *usually pl.* [occas. construed as sing.], a hysterical fit. 2. a person subject to hysteria.

**hys·ter·i·cal** (his-ter′i-k'l), *adj.* [< L. < Gr. < *hystera*, uterus: hysteria in women was attributed to disturbances of the uterus], 1. of, like, or characteristic of hysteria. 2. having or subject to hysteria. **—hys·ter′i·cal·ly,** *adv.*

**hys·ter·ot·o·my** (his′tə-rot′ə-mi), *n.* [*pl.* -MIES], [< Gr. *hystera*, uterus; + *-tomy*], 1. a Caesarean operation. 2. an incision of the uterus.

**Hz, hz,** hertz.

# I

**I, i** (ī), *n.* [*pl.* I's, i's, Is, is], 1. the ninth letter of the English alphabet. 2. a sound of I or i. *adj.* ninth in a sequence or group.
**I** (ī), *n.* 1. a Roman numeral for 1. 2. in *chemistry, the symbol for* iodine. *adj.* shaped like I.
**I** (ī), *pron.* [for *pl.* see WE], [AS. *ic*], the person speaking or writing: *I* is the nominative case form, *me* the objective, *my* and *mine* the possessive, and *myself* the intensive and reflexive, of the first person singular pronoun. *n.* [*pl.* I's], 1. this pronoun thought of as a word. 2. the ego.
**I., i.,** 1. island; islands. 2. isle; isles.
**Ia.,** Iowa.
**-i·a** (i-ə, yə), [L. & Gr.], a noun-forming suffix used variously, as in names of certain diseases.
**I·a·go** (i-ä'gō), *n.* the villain in Shakespeare's *Othello.*
**-i·al** (yəl, i-əl), [L. *-ialis, -iale*], an adjective-forming suffix, as in *artificial.*
**i·amb** (ī'amb), *n.* [< Fr. < L. < Gr. *iambos*], a metrical foot of two syllables, the first unaccented and the other accented, as in English verse, or the first short and the other long, as in Greek and Latin verse. Example: "Tŏ bé,|ŏr nót|tŏ bé."
**i·am·bic** (ī-am'bik), *adj.* of or made up of iambs. *n.* 1. an iamb. 2. an iambic verse.
**i·am·bus** (ī-am'bəs), *n.* [*pl.* -BUSES, -BI (-bī)], [L.], an iamb.
**-i·an** (i-ən, yən), -an, as in *Grecian, reptilian.*
**-i·an·a** (i-an'ə), -ana.
**-i·a·sis** (ī'ə-sis), [< Gr. *-iasis*], a combining form meaning *process* or *condition.*
**-i·at·rics** (i-at'riks), [< Gr. < *iatros,* physician], a combining form meaning *treatment of disease,* as in *pediatrics.*
**-i·a·try** (ī'ə-tri), [< Gr. *iatreia,* healing], a combining form meaning *medical treatment,* as in *psychiatry.*
**I·be·ri·a** (ī-bêr'i-ə), *n.* the Spanish-Portuguese peninsula: Latin name. —**I·be'ri·an,** *adj.* & *n.*
**i·bex** (ī'beks), *n.* [*pl.* IBEXES, IBICES (ib'ə-sēz', ī'bə-), IBEX; see PLURAL, II, D, 1], [L.], any of certain wild goats of Europe, Asia, or Africa: the male has large, backward-curved horns.
**‡i·bi·dem** (i-bī'dem), *adv.* [L.], in the same place: used in referring again to the book, chapter, etc. cited just before: abbrev. **ibid., ib.**
**-i·bil·i·ty** (ə-bil'ə-ti), [*pl.* -TIES], [< L. *-ibilitas*], a suffix used to form nouns from adjectives ending in *-ible,* as in *sensibility.*
**i·bis** (ī'bis), *n.* [*pl.* IBISES, IBIS; see PLURAL, II, D, 1], [L. < Gr. *ibis*], a large wading bird related to the herons, with long legs and a long, curved bill, as the **sacred ibis** of the Nile, held sacred by the ancient Egyptians.

IBIS (3 ft. high)

**-i·ble** (i-b'l), [L. *-ibilis*], -able, as in *legible:* see **-able.**
**Ib·sen, Hen·rik** (hen'rik ib's'n), 1828–1906; Norwegian dramatist and poet.
**-ic** (ik), [< Fr. *-ique* or L. *-icus* or Gr. *-ikos*], a suffix meaning: *a*) *of, having to do with,* as in *volcanic. b*) *like, having the nature of,* as in *angelic. c*) *produced by, caused by,* as in *photographic. d*) *made up of, containing,* as in *alcoholic. e*) in *chemistry, of a higher valence than the compound ending in -ous,* as in *nitric.*
**-i·cal** (i-k'l), a suffix corresponding to *-ic,* used to form adjectives from nouns ending in *-ic,* as in *physical,* or from other adjectives ending in *-ic,* as in *poetical:* such adjectives sometimes have meanings differentiated from the corresponding *-ic* forms (e.g., *historical, economical*).
**Ic·a·rus** (ik'ə-rəs, ī'kə-), *n.* in *Gr. legend,* the son of Daedalus: escaping from Crete by flying with wings made by Daedalus, Icarus flew so high that the sun's heat melted the wax by which his wings were fastened, and he fell to his death in the sea. —**I·car·i·an** (i-kâr'i-ən, ī-), *adj.*
**ICBM,** intercontinental ballistic missile.
**I.C.C., ICC,** Interstate Commerce Commission.
**ice** (īs), *n.* [AS. *is*], 1. water frozen solid by cold. 2. a piece, layer, or sheet of this. 3. anything like frozen water in appearance. 4. a frozen dessert, usually of water, fruit juice, egg white, and sugar. 5. icing. 6. [Slang], diamonds. *v.t.* [ICED, ICING], 1. to change into ice; freeze. 2. to cover with ice. 3. to cool by putting ice on, in, or around. 4. to cover with icing. *v.i.* to freeze (often with *up* or *over*). —**break the ice,** 1. to make a start by getting over initial difficulties. 2. to make a start toward getting better acquainted. —**cut no ice,** [Colloq.], to have no effect. —**on thin ice,** [Colloq.], in a risky situation. —**ice'less,** *adj.* —**ic'er,** *n.*
**-ice** (is), [< OFr. *-ice* < L. *-itius*], a suffix meaning *the condition* or *quality of,* as in *justice.*
**Ice.,** 1. Iceland. 2. Icelandic.
**ice age,** the glacial epoch.
**ice bag,** an ice pack (sense 2).
**ice·berg** (īs'būrg'), *n.* [prob. < D. *ijsberg,* lit., ice mountain], a great mass of ice broken off from a glacier and floating in the sea.
**ice·boat** (īs'bōt'), *n.* 1. a light, boatlike frame, often triangular, equipped with runners and propelled over ice by a sail. 2. an icebreaker.
**ice·bound** (īs'bound'), *adj.* 1. held fast by ice, as a boat. 2. blocked up by ice, as a coast.
**ice·box** (īs'boks'), *n.* a refrigerator, especially one in which ice is used for cooling foods, etc.
**ice·break·er** (īs'brāk'ēr), *n.* a sturdy boat for breaking a channel through ice.
**ice·cap** (īs'kap'), *n.* a large, permanent ice sheet with a raised center, as on a mountain top.
**ice cream,** [orig., *iced cream*], a food consisting of cream or milk, and sometimes eggs, sweetened, flavored, and frozen. —**ice'-cream',** *adj.* & *n.*
**iced** (īst), *adj.* 1. having ice on, in, or around it; cooled by ice. 2. covered with icing.
**ice field** (or **floe**), a large sheet of floating sea ice.
**ice-free** (īs'frē'), *adj.* 1. without ice. 2. never frozen: as, an *ice-free* harbor.
**ice hockey,** see **hockey.**
**ice·house** (īs'hous'), *n.* 1. a building where ice is stored. 2. a place where artificial ice is made.
**Ice·land** (īs'lənd), *n.* a country on an island in the North Atlantic, between Norway and Greenland: area, 39,709 sq. mi.; pop., 192,000; capital, Reykjavik. —**Ice'land'er** (-lan'dẽr, -lən-dẽr), *n.*
**Ice·lan·dic** (īs-lan'dik), *adj.* of Iceland, its people, their language, or culture. *n.* the North Germanic language of the Icelanders.
**ice·man** (īs'man', -mən), *n.* [*pl.* -MEN], a person who sells or delivers ice.
**ice pack,** 1. a large, floating expanse of ice masses frozen together. 2. a bag holding ice, applied to a part of the body to reduce swelling, ease pain, etc.
**ice pick,** a pointed metal tool used to break up pieces of ice.
**ice sheet,** a thick layer of ice covering an extensive area for a long period, as in the ice age.
**ich·neu·mon** (ik-nū'mən, ik-nōō'-), *n.* [L. < Gr. *ichneumōn,* lit., tracker < *ichnos,* a track], 1. an Egyptian species of mongoose. 2. the ichneumon fly.
**ichneumon fly,** a wasplike but stingless insect having wormlike larvae that live as parasites in or on the larvae of other insects.
**i·chor** (ī'kôr, ī'kẽr), *n.* [Gr. *ichōr*], 1. in *Gr. mythology,* the fluid flowing instead of blood in the veins of the gods. 2. a watery discharge from a wound or ulcer. —**i·chor·ous** (ī'kẽr-əs), *adj.*
**ich·thy·o-,** [< Gr. < *ichthys,* a fish], a combining form meaning *fish* or *like a fish:* also **ichthy-.**

**ich·thy·ol·o·gy** (ik'thi-ol'ə-ji), *n.* [*ichthyo-* + *-logy*], 1. the branch of zoology dealing with fishes. 2. [*pl.* -GIES], a treatise on fishes. —**ich'thy·o·log'i·cal** (-thi-ə-loj'i-k'l), **ich'thy·o·log'ic,** *adj.* —**ich'thy·ol'o·gist,** *n.*

**ich·thy·o·saur** (ik'thi-ə-sôr'), *n.* [< *ichthyo-* + Gr. *sauros*, lizard], a prehistoric marine reptile, now extinct, which had a fishlike body, four paddle-shaped flippers, and a dolphinlike head: also **ich'thy·o·sau'rus** [*pl.* -RI (-rī)].

**-i·cian** (ish'ən), [< Fr.; see -IC & -IAN], a suffix meaning *a person engaged in, practicing,* or *specializing in,* as in *magician.*

**i·ci·cle** (ī'si-k'l), *n.* [< AS. < *is*, ice + *gicel*, piece of ice], a hanging piece of ice, formed by the freezing of dripping water. —**i'ci·cled,** *adj.*

**ic·ing** (is'iŋ), *n.* a mixture of sugar, water or other liquid, flavoring, and, sometimes, whites of eggs, etc. for covering a cake; frosting.

**i·con** (ī'kon), *n.* [*pl.* ICONS, ICONES (ī'kə-nēz')], [L. < Gr. *eikōn*, an image], 1. an image or picture. 2. in the *Orthodox Eastern Church*, a sacred image or picture of Jesus, Mary, a saint, etc. Also sp. **ikon, eikon.** —**i·con'ic, i·con'i·cal,** *adj.*

**i·con·o-,** [< Gr. *eikōn*, an image], a combining form meaning *image, figure*: also **icon-.**

**i·con·o·clast** (ī-kon'ə-klast'), *n.* [< ML. < MGr. < Gr. *eikōn*, an image + *klaein*, to break], 1. one who advocates the destruction of church images. 2. one who attacks or ridicules traditional or venerated institutions or ideas. —**i·con'o·clasm,** *n.* —**i·con'o·clas'tic,** *adj.* —**i·con'o·clas'ti·cal·ly,** *adv.*

**i·con·o·scope** (ī-kon'ə-skōp'), *n.* [*icono-* + *-scope*], an electronic device in a television transmitter, consisting of a vacuum tube enclosing a photosensitive plate on which the image is projected and an electronic scanning device: a trade-mark (**Iconoscope**).

**-ics,** [see -IC], a suffix used to form plural nouns meaning: 1. (a specified) *art* or *science*, as in *physics*: such nouns are construed as singular. 2. (specified) *activities, practice, system, properties,* as in *statistics*: such nouns are usually construed as plural.

**ic·tus** (ik'təs), *n.* [*pl.* -TUSES, -TUS], [< L. < *icere*, to hit], 1. rhythmical or metrical stress, or accent. 2. in *medicine*, a stroke or sudden attack.

**i·cy** (ī'si), *adj.* [ICIER, ICIEST], 1. having much ice; full of or covered with ice. 2. of ice. 3. like ice; slippery or very cold. 4. cold in manner; unfriendly. —**i'ci·ly,** *adv.* —**i'ci·ness,** *n.*

**id** (id), *n.* [L., it], in *psychoanalysis*, that part of the psyche which is the source of instinctive energy, dominated by the pleasure principle and impulsive wishing: cf. *ego, superego.*

**-id,** [ult. < L. or Gr.], a suffix of various meanings: *a*) used to form nouns meaning *a thing belonging to* or *connected with*, as in *Aeneid, arachnid.* *b*) in chemistry, *-ide.*

**I'd** (īd), 1. I had. 2. I would. 3. I should.

**id.,** *idem*, [L.], the same.

**Ida., Id.,** Idaho.

**-i·dae** (i-dē'), [< Mod. L.], a suffix used in forming the scientific names of zoological families, as *Canidae* (the dog family).

**I·da·ho** (ī'də-hō'), *n.* a Northwestern State of the U.S.: area, 83,557 sq. mi.; pop., 667,000; capital, Boise. —**I'da·ho'an,** *adj.* & *n.*

**-ide** (īd, id), [< ox*ide*], a suffix added to part of the name of one of the elements in a binary compound, as in sodium *chloride*, hydrogen *sulfide.*

**i·de·a** (ī-dē'ə), *n.* [L. < Gr. *idea*, appearance of a thing], 1. a thought; mental conception or image; notion. 2. an opinion or belief. 3. a plan; scheme; intention. 4. a hazy perception; vague impression; inkling. 5. in *philosophy*, according to Plato, a model or archetype of which all real things are but imperfect imitations. —**i·de'a·less,** *adj.*

**i·de·al** (ī-dē'əl, ī-dēl'), *adj.* [< Fr. < LL. < L. *idea*, an idea], 1. existing as an idea, model, or archetype. 2. thought of as perfect; exactly as one would desire. 3. of, or having the nature of, an idea. 4. existing only in the mind as an image or concept; imaginary: distinguished from *real, material.* 5. in *philosophy*, of idealism. *n.* 1. a conception of something in its most excellent form. 2. a perfect model or standard. —**i·de'al·ness,** *n.*

**i·de·al·ism** (ī-dē'əl-iz'm), *n.* 1. behavior or thought based on a conception of things as one thinks they should be. 2. such an idealization of persons or things in art or literature. 3. a striving to achieve one's ideals. 4. in *philosophy*, any theory which holds that the objects of perception are actually ideas of the perceiving mind and that it is impossible to know whether reality exists apart from the mind.

**i·de·al·ist** (ī-dē'əl-ist), *n.* 1. a person whose behavior or thought is based on ideals: often used contemptuously to mean an impractical visionary. 2. an adherent or practitioner of idealism in art, literature, or philosophy. *adj.* idealistic.

**i·de·al·is·tic** (ī'dē-ə-lis'tik, ī-dē'-), *adj.* 1. of or characteristic of an idealist. 2. of, characterized by, or based on idealism. Also **i'de·al·is'ti·cal.** —**i'de·al·is'ti·cal·ly,** *adv.*

**i·de·al·ize** (ī-dē'ə-līz'), *v.t.* [-IZED, -IZING], to make ideal; regard or show as perfect or more nearly perfect than is true. *v.i.* to represent things in the manner of an idealist. —**i·de'al·i·za'tion,** *n.* —**i·de'al·iz'er,** *n.*

**i·de·al·ly** (ī-dē'əl-i), *adv.* 1. in an ideal manner; perfectly. 2. in theory; in idea.

**i·de·ate** (ī-dē'āt), *v.t.* & *v.i.* [-ATED, -ATING], to form an idea or ideas (of). —**i'de·a'tion,** *n.* —**i'de·a'tion·al,** *adj.*

**‡i·dée fixe** (ē'dā'fēks'), [Fr.], a fixed idea; obsession.

**‡i·dem** (ī'dem), *pron.* & *adj.* [L.], the same; the same as that previously mentioned.

**i·den·ti·cal** (ī-den'ti-k'l), *adj.* [< ML. < L. *identidem*, repeatedly < *idem*, the same; + *-al*], 1. the very same. 2. exactly alike. Also **i·den'tic.** —**i·den'ti·cal·ly,** *adv.* —**i·den'ti·cal·ness,** *n.*

**identical twins,** a pair of twins of the same sex, developed from a single fertilized ovum.

**i·den·ti·fi·ca·tion** (ī-den'tə-fi-kā'shən), *n.* 1. an identifying or being identified. 2. anything by which a person or thing can be identified. 3. in *psychiatry*, an emotional tie with a person unconsciously causing one to think, feel, or act as he imagines the person does.

**i·den·ti·fy** (ī-den'tə-fī'), *v.t.* [-FIED, -FYING], 1. to make identical; treat as the same. 2. to show to be a certain person or thing; show to be the same as described or claimed. 3. to join or associate closely (*with*). 4. in *psychiatry*, to make identification with someone else: used reflexively. —**i·den'ti·fi'a·ble,** *adj.* —**i·den'ti·fi'er,** *n.*

**i·den·ti·ty** (ī-den'tə-ti), *n.* [*pl.* -TIES], [< Fr. < ML.; see IDENTICAL], 1. the condition or fact of being the same; sameness. 2. *a*) the condition or fact of being some specific person or thing; individuality. *b*) the condition of being the same as something or someone described or claimed.

**id·e·o-,** [< Fr. *ideo-* or < Gr. *idea*], a combining form meaning *idea*, as in *ideology.*

**id·e·o·gram** (id'i-ə-gram', ī'di-), *n.* [*ideo-* + *-gram*], 1. a graphic symbol representing an object or idea without expressing the sounds that form its name. 2. a symbol representing an idea rather than a word (e.g., 5, +, =).

**id·e·o·graph** (id'i-ə-graf', ī'di-ə-gräf'), *n.* an ideogram. —**id'e·o·graph'ic, id'e·o·graph'i·cal,** *adj.* —**id'e·o·graph'i·cal·ly,** *adv.*

**id·e·o·log·i·cal** (ī'di-ə-loj'i-k'l, id'i-), *adj.* of or concerned with ideology: also **id'e·o·log'ic.** —**id'e·o·log'i·cal·ly,** *adv.*

**id·e·ol·o·gy** (ī'di-ol'ə-ji, id'i-), *n.* [*pl.* -GIES], [see IDEO- & -LOGY], 1. the study of ideas, their nature and source. 2. thinking of an idealistic, abstract, or impractical nature. 3. the doctrines, opinions, or way of thinking of an individual, class, etc. —**id'e·ol'o·gist,** *n.*

**ides** (īdz), *n.pl.* [Fr. < L. *idus*], in the ancient Roman calendar, the 15th day of March, May, July, or October, or the 13th of the other months.

**‡id est** (id est), [L.], that is to say: abbrev. **i.e.**

**id·i·o·cy** (id'i-ə-si), *n.* [*pl.* -CIES], 1. the state of being an idiot. 2. great foolishness or stupidity.

**id·i·om** (id'i-əm), *n.* [< Fr. & LL. < Gr. < *idios*, one's own], 1. the language or dialect of a people, region, etc. 2. the usual way in which words of a language are joined together to express thought. 3. an accepted phrase or expression having a meaning different from the literal. 4. the style of expression characteristic of an individual. 5. a characteristic style, as in art or music.

**id·i·o·mat·ic** (id'i-ə-mat'ik), *adj.* 1. characteristic of a particular language. 2. using or having many idioms. 3. of or like an idiom or idioms. Also **id'i·o·mat'i·cal.** —**id'i·o·mat'i·cal·ly,** *adv.*

**id·i·o·syn·cra·sy** (id'i-ə-siŋ'krə-si, -sin'-), *n.* [*pl.* -SIES], [< Gr. < *idio-*, one's own + *synkrasis*, mixture < *syn-*, together + *kerannynai*, to mix], 1. the temperament peculiar to a person or group. 2. any personal peculiarity, mannerism, etc. —**id'i·o·syn·crat'ic** (-ō-sin-krat'ik), *adj.* —**id'i·o·syn·crat'i·cal·ly,** *adv.*

**id·i·ot** (id'i-ət), *n.* [OFr. < L. < Gr. *idiōtēs*, ignorant person < *idios*, one's own], 1. a mentally deficient person with an intelligence quotient of less than 25: *idiot* is the lowest classification of mental deficiency: cf. **imbecile, moron.** 2. loosely, a very foolish or stupid person.

**id·i·ot·ic** (id'i-ot'ik), *adj.* of, having the nature of, or characteristic of an idiot; very foolish or stupid. —**id'i·ot'i·cal·ly,** *adv.*

**i·dle** (ī'd'l), *adj.* [IDLER, IDLEST], [AS. *idel*, empty], 1. worthless; useless. 2. baseless; unfounded: as, *idle* rumors. 3. *a*) unemployed; not busy: as, *idle* men. *b*) inactive; not used: as, *idle* machines. 4. not inclined to work; lazy. *v.i.* [IDLED, IDLING], 1. to move slowly or aimlessly; loaf. 2. to be unemployed or inactive. 3. to operate slowly without transmitting power: said of machinery. *v.t.* 1. to waste; squander: as, he *idled* away his youth. 2. to cause (a motor, etc.) to idle. —**i'dle·ness,** *n.* —**i'dler,** *n.* —**i'dly,** *adv.*

**i·dol** (ī'd'l), *n.* [< OFr. < L. < Gr. *eidōlon*, an image < *eidos*, form], 1. an image of a god, used as an object of worship: sometimes applied to any heathen deity. 2. any object of ardent or excessive devotion or admiration. 3. [Obs.], an effigy. 4. in *logic*, a fallacy.

**i·dol·a·ter** (ī-dol'ə-tẽr), *n.* [< OFr. < LL. < Gr. < *eidōlon*, an image + *latris*, servant], 1. one who worships an idol or idols. 2. a devoted admirer; adorer. —**i·dol'a·tress** (-tris), *n.fem.*

**i·dol·a·trous** (ī-dol'ə-trəs), *adj.* 1. of, or having the nature of, idolatry. 2. worshiping idols. 3. having excessive admiration or devotion. —**i·dol'a·trous·ly,** *adv.* —**i·dol'a·trous·ness,** *n.*

**i·dol·a·try** (ī-dol'ə-tri), *n.* [*pl.* -TRIES], 1. worship of idols. 2. excessive devotion to or reverence for some person or thing.

**i·dol·ize** (ī'd'l-īz'), *v.t.* [-IZED, -IZING], 1. to make an idol of. 2. to love or admire excessively. *v.i.* to worship idols. —**i'dol·i·za'tion,** *n.* —**i'dol·iz'er,** *n.*

**i·dyl, i·dyll** (ī'd'l), *n.* [< L. < Gr. dim. of *eidos*, a form, image], 1. a short poem or prose work describing a simple, pleasant scene of rural or pastoral life. 2. a scene or incident suitable for such a work. —**i'dyl·ist, i'dyll·ist,** *n.*

**i·dyl·lic** (ī-dil'ik), *adj.* 1. of or like an idyl. 2. pleasing and simple. —**i·dyl'li·cal·ly,** *adv.*

**-ie** (i), [earlier form of *-y*], a suffix meaning *small, little,* as in *lassie:* often used to express affection.

**IE.,** Indo-European.

**i.e.,** *id est*, [L.], that is.

**-ier** (êr, i-ẽr), [< OFr. < L. *-arius*], a suffix meaning *a person concerned with* (a specified action or thing), as in *bombardier, collier.*

**if** (if), *conj.* [AS. *gif*], 1. on condition that; in case that: as, *if* I come, I'll see him. 2. although; granting that: as, *if* it was wrong, it was at least meant well. 3. whether: as, I don't know *if* I can go. *n.* 1. the word *if;* hence, 2. a supposition; condition. —**as if,** as the situation would be if; as though.

**ig·loo** (ig'lo͞o), *n.* [*pl.* -LOOS], [Esk. *igdlu*, snow house], an Eskimo hut, dome-shaped and usually built of blocks of packed snow: also sp. **iglu.**

IGLOO

**Ig·na·tius (of) Loy·o·la,** Saint (ig-nā'shəs loi-ō'lə), (*Iñigo de Oñez y Loyola*), 1491–1556; Spanish founder of the Jesuit Order.

**ig·ne·ous** (ig'ni-əs), *adj.* [< L. < *ignis*, a fire], 1. of, like, or containing fire. 2. produced by the action of fire; specif., formed by volcanic action or great heat: as, *igneous* rock.

‡**ig·nis fat·u·us** (ig'nis fach'o͞o-əs), [*pl.* IGNES FATUI (ig'nēz fach'o͞o-ī')], [ML. < L. *ignis*, a fire + *fatuus*, foolish], 1. a light seen at night moving over swamps or marshy places, believed to be caused by the combustion of marsh gas: popularly called *will-o'-the-wisp, jack-o'-lantern.* 2. a deceptive hope, goal, etc.; delusion.

**ig·nite** (ig-nīt'), *v.t.* [-NITED, -NITING], [< L. pp. of *ignire* < *ignis*, a fire], 1. to set fire to. 2. to heat to a great degree; make glow with heat. 3. to excite: as, his speech *ignited* the crowd. *v.i.* to catch on fire. —**ig·nit'a·ble, ig·nit'i·ble,** *adj.* —**ig·nit'a·bil'i·ty, ig·nit'i·bil'i·ty,** *n.* —**ig·nit'er, ig·ni'tor** (-ẽr), *n.*

**ig·ni·tion** (ig-nish'ən), *n.* 1. a setting on fire or catching fire. 2. the means by which a thing is ignited. 3. in an internal-combustion engine, *a*) the igniting of the explosive mixture in the cylinder. *b*) the electrical system for doing this.

**ig·no·ble** (ig-nō'b'l), *adj.* [Fr. < L. < *in-*, not + (*g*)*nobilis*, known], 1. [Rare], of low origin or humble condition. 2. not noble in character or quality; dishonorable; base. —**ig'no·bil'i·ty, ig·no'ble·ness,** *n.* —**ig·no'bly,** *adv.*

**ig·no·min·i·ous** (ig'nə-min'i-əs), *adj.* 1. marked by or bringing on ignominy; disgraceful. 2. contemptible; despicable. 3. degrading; humiliating. —**ig'no·min'i·ous·ly,** *adv.* —**ig'no·min'i·ous·ness,** *n.*

**ig·no·min·y** (ig'nə-min'i), *n.* [*pl.* -IES], [< Fr. < L. *ignominia* < *in-*, without + *nomen*, name], 1. loss of one's reputation; shame and dishonor. 2. disgraceful or shameful quality or action.

**ig·no·ra·mus** (ig'nə-rā'məs, -ram'əs), *n.* [*pl.* -MUSES], [< L. 1st pers. pl., pres. indic., of *ignorare*, to ignore], an ignorant person.

**ig·no·rance** (ig'nẽr-əns), *n.* the condition or quality of being ignorant; lack of knowledge.

**ig·no·rant** (ig'nẽr-ənt), *adj.* [< OFr. < L. ppr. of *ignorare;* see IGNORE], 1. lacking knowledge, education, or experience. 2. caused by or showing lack of knowledge, education, etc. 3. uninformed (*in*) or unaware (*of*). —**ig'no·rant·ly,** *adv.*

**ig·nore** (ig-nôr', -nōr'), *v.t.* [-NORED, -NORING], [< Fr. < L. *ignorare* < *in-*, not + base of *gnarus*, knowing], to disregard deliberately; pay no attention to; refuse to consider. —**ig·nor'er,** *n.*

**Ig·o·rot** (ig'ə-rōt', ē'gə-), *n.* [*pl.* -ROT, -ROTS], 1. a member of a Malayan people living in Luzon, in the Philippines. 2. their Indonesian language. Also **Ig'or·ro'te** (-rō'tā), [*pl.* -ROTE, -ROTES].

**i·gua·na** (i-gwä'nə), *n.* [Sp. < Haitian name], a large tropical American lizard usually living in trees.

**IHS,** a contraction misread from the Greek word IH(ΣΟΥ)Σ, Jesus, used as a symbol or monogram.

**i·kon** (ī'kon), *n.* an icon.

**Il,** in *chemistry*, illinium.

**il-,** 1. in- (not). 2. in- (in). Used before *l.*

‡**Il Du·ce** (ēl do͞o'che), see **duce.**

**-ile** (il), [< Fr. *-il, -ile* or L. *-ilis*], a suffix meaning *of, having to do with, like, suitable for,* as in *docile, missile*: also **-il,** as in *civil.*

**il·e·um** (il'i-əm), *n.* [L. *ilium, ileum*, pl. *ilia*, the flank, groin], the lowest part of the small intestine. —**il'e·ac'** (-ak'), *adj.*

**i·lex** (ī'leks), *n.* [*pl.* ILEXES], [L.], 1. the holm oak. 2. any tree or shrub of the holly family.

**Il·i·ad** (il'i-əd), *n.* [< L. < Gr. < *Ilios*, Troy], a long Greek epic poem, ascribed to Homer, about the siege of Troy by the Greeks in the Trojan War.

**-il·i·ty** (-il'ə-ti), [< Fr. < L. *-ilitas*], a suffix used to form nouns from adjectives ending in *-ile, -il, -able, -ible,* as in *imbecility, ability.*

**il·i·um** (il'i-əm), *n.* [*pl.* ILIA (il'i-ə)], [see ILEUM], the uppermost of the three sections of the hipbone. —**il'i·ac'** (-ak'), *adj.*

**Il·i·um** (il'i-əm), *n.* [see ILIAD], ancient Troy.

**ilk** (ilk), *adj.* [Scot. dial. < AS. *ilca*, same], [Obs.], same; like. *pron.* [Obs.], the same. *n.* [Colloq.], a family; kind; sort. —**of that ilk,** 1. in Scotland, of the same name. 2. of the same sort.

**ill** (il), *adj.* [WORSE, WORST], [< ON. *illr*], 1. *a*) morally bad or wrong; evil: as, *ill* repute. *b*) harsh; not kind: as, *ill* will. *c*) unfavorable; unfortunate: as, an *ill* omen. 2. not healthy; not well; sick. 3. imperfect; improper: as, *ill* breeding. *n.* anything causing harm, trouble, pain, etc.; an evil or disease. *adv.* [WORSE, WORST], 1. in an ill manner; specif., *a*) badly; wrongly; imperfectly. *b*) harshly; unkindly. 2. with difficulty; scarcely: as, he can *ill* afford to refuse. —**ill at ease,** uncomfortable.

**I'll** (il), 1. I shall. 2. I will.

**Ill.,** Illinois.

**ill.,** 1. illustrated. 2. illustration.

**ill-ad·vised** (il'əd-vīzd'), *adj.* showing or resulting from improper consideration or unsound advice; unwise. —**ill'ad·vis'ed·ly** (-vīz'id-li), *adv.*

**ill-be·ing** (il'bē'iŋ), *n.* an unhealthy, unhappy, or evil condition: opposed to *well-being.*

**ill-bred** (il'bred'), *adj.* badly brought up; lacking good manners; rude; impolite.

**ill breeding,** bad manners; rudeness.

**ill-con·sid·ered** (il'kən-sid'ẽrd), *adj.* not properly considered; not suitable; not wise.

**ill-dis·posed** (il'dis-pōzd'), *adj.* 1. having a bad disposition. 2. unfriendly (*toward*).

**il·le·gal** (i-lē'gəl), *adj.* prohibited by law; against the law; not sanctioned. —**il·le·gal·i·ty** (il'ē-gal'ə-ti), [*pl.* -TIES], **il·le'gal·ness,** *n.* —**il·le'gal·ly,** *adv.*

**il·leg·i·ble** (i-lej'ə-b'l), *adj.* not legible; difficult or impossible to read because badly written or printed. —**il'leg·i·bil'i·ty, il·leg'i·ble·ness,** *n.* —**il·leg'i·bly,** *adv.*

**il·le·git·i·mate** (il'i-jit'ə-mit), *adj.* 1. born of parents not married to each other. 2. incorrectly deduced. 3. contrary to law or rules; unlawful.

—**il'le·git'i·ma·cy** (-mə-si), [*pl.* -CIES], *n.* —**il'le·git'i·mate·ly,** *adv.* —**il'le·git'i·mate·ness,** *n.*
**ill-fat·ed** (il'fāt'id), *adj.* 1. certain to have an evil fate or unlucky end. 2. unlucky.
**ill-fa·vored** (il'fā'vērd), *adj.* 1. of unpleasant or evil appearance; ugly. 2. unpleasant; offensive. Also **ill'-fa'voured.** —**ill'-fa'vored·ly,** *adv.* —**ill'-fa'vored·ness,** *n.*
**ill-found·ed** (il'foun'did), *adj.* not supported by facts or sound reasons.
**ill-got·ten** (il'got''n), *adj.* obtained by evil, unlawful, or dishonest means: as, *ill-gotten* gains.
**ill-hu·mor** (il'hū'mēr), *n.* a disagreeable or sullen mood: also **ill humor.** —**ill'-hu'mored,** *adj.* —**ill'-hu'mored·ly,** *adv.* —**ill'-hu'mored·ness,** *n.*
**ill-hu·mour** (il'hū'mēr), *n.* ill-humor: British sp. —**ill'-hu'moured,** *adj.* —**ill'-hu'moured·ly,** *adv.* —**ill'-hu'moured·ness,** *n.*
**il·lib·er·al** (i-lib'ēr-əl), *adj.* 1. lacking a liberal education or training; without culture. 2. intolerant; narrow-minded. 3. miserly; stingy. —**il·lib'er·al'i·ty, il·lib'er·al·ness,** *n.* —**il·lib'er·al·ly,** *adv.*
**il·lic·it** (i-lis'it), *adj.* [< Fr. < L.; see IN- (not) & LICIT], not allowed by law, custom, etc.; unlawful. —**il·lic'it·ly,** *adv.* —**il·lic'it·ness,** *n.*
**il·lim·it·a·ble** (i-lim'i-tə-b'l), *adj.* without limit or boundary; immeasurable; endless. —**il·lim'it·a·bil'i·ty, il·lim'it·a·ble·ness,** *n.* —**il·lim'it·a·bly,** *adv.*
**il·lin·i·um** (i-lin'i-əm), *n.* [Mod. L., after the University of *Illinois*], a former name for chemical element 61: see **promethium.**
**Il·li·nois** (il'ə-noi', -noiz'), *n.* 1. [*pl.* -NOIS], a member of a confederation of Algonquian Indian tribes that lived in Illinois. 2. a Middle Western State of the U.S.: area, 56,400 sq. mi.; pop., 10,081,000; capital, Springfield. —**Il'li·nois'an** (-noi'ən, -noiz'ən), *adj.* & *n.*
**il·lit·er·a·cy** (i-lit'ēr-ə-si), *n.* 1. the state of being illiterate. 2. [*pl.* -CIES], a mistake (in writing or speaking) resulting from ignorance.
**il·lit·er·ate** (i-lit'ēr-it), *adj.* 1. ignorant; uneducated; esp., unable to read or write. 2. having or showing limited knowledge, experience, or culture. *n.* an illiterate person. —**il·lit'er·ate·ly,** *adv.* —**il·lit'er·ate·ness,** *n.*
**ill-man·nered** (il'man'ērd), *adj.* having bad manners; rude; impolite. —**ill'-man'nered·ly,** *adv.* —**ill'-man'nered·ness,** *n.*
**ill nature,** an unpleasant, disagreeable disposition; peevishness; sullenness. —**ill-na·tured** (il'nā'chērd), *adj.* —**ill'-na'tured·ly,** *adv.* —**ill'-na'tured·ness,** *n.*
**ill·ness** (il'nis), *n.* an unhealthy condition of the body or mind; sickness; disease.
**il·log·i·cal** (i-loj'i-k'l), *adj.* not logical or reasonable. —**il·log'i·cal'i·ty, il·log'i·cal·ness,** *n.* —**il·log'i·cal·ly,** *adv.*
**ill-spent** (il'spent'), *adj.* misspent; wasted.
**ill-starred** (il'stärd'), *adj.* as if born or conceived under an evil star; unlucky.
**ill-suit·ed** (il's o͞ot'id, -sūt'-), *adj.* not well-suited; not appropriate.
**ill-tem·pered** (il'tem'pērd), *adj.* having or showing a bad temper; quarrelsome; cross. —**ill'-tem'pered·ly,** *adv.* —**ill'-tem'pered·ness,** *n.*
**ill-timed** (il'tīmd'), *adj.* unsuitable at the time; inappropriate: as, an *ill-timed* remark.
**ill-treat** (il'trēt'), *v.t.* to treat unkindly, cruelly, or unfairly; abuse. —**ill'-treat'ment,** *n.*
**il·lu·mi·nant** (i-lo͞o'mə-nənt), *adj.* giving light; illuminating. *n.* something that gives light.
**il·lu·mi·nate** (i-lo͞o'mə-nāt'), *v.t.* [-NATED, -NATING], [< L. *illuminatus*, pp. < *in-*, in + *luminare*, to light < *lumen*, a light], 1. to give light to; light up. 2. *a*) to make clear; explain. *b*) to inform; enlighten. 3. to make famous. 4. to decorate with lights. 5. to decorate (an initial letter, a page border, etc.) with designs or tracings of gold, silver, or bright colors, as in old manuscripts. *v.i.* to light up. —**il·lu'mi·nat'ing·ly,** *adv.* —**il·lu'mi·na'tive,** *adj.* —**il·lu'mi·na'tor,** *n.*
**il·lu·mi·na·tion** (i-lo͞o'mə-nā'shən), *n.* 1. an illuminating; specif., *a*) a lighting up. *b*) explanation. *c*) enlightenment. *d*) decoration with lights. *e*) decoration, as of manuscripts, with designs, colors, etc. 2. light; intensity of light per unit area.
**il·lu·mine** (i-lo͞o'min), *v.t.* & *v.i.* [-MINED, -MINING], to illuminate or be illuminated; light up. —**il·lu'mi·na·ble,** *adj.*
**illus., illust.,** 1. illustrated. 2. illustration.
**ill-us·age** (il'ūs'ij, -ūz'-), *n.* unfair, unkind, or cruel treatment; abuse: also **ill usage.**
**ill-use** (il'ūz'; *for n.*, -ūs'), *v.t.* to treat unfairly, unkindly, or cruelly. *n.* ill-usage.
**il·lu·sion** (i-lo͞o'zhən), *n.* [< L. < pp. of *illudere*, to mock], 1. a false idea or conception. 2. an unreal or misleading appearance or image. 3. a false perception or conception of what one sees, where one is, etc. —**il·lu'sion·al,** *adj.*
**il·lu·sion·ist** (i-lo͞o'zhən-ist), *n.* an entertainer who produces illusions.
**il·lu·sive** (i-lo͞o'siv), *adj.* producing, based on, or having the nature of, illusion; deceptive; unreal. —**il·lu'sive·ly,** *adv.* —**il·lu'sive·ness,** *n.*
**il·lu·so·ry** (i-lo͞o'sēr-i), *adj.* illusive; deceptive. —**il·lu'so·ri·ly,** *adv.* —**il·lu'so·ri·ness,** *n.*
**il·lus·trate** (il'əs-trāt', i-lus'trāt), *v.t.* [-TRATED, -TRATING], [< L. *illustratus*, pp. < *in-*, in + *lustrare*, to illuminate], 1. *a*) to explain; make clear. *b*) to make clear or easily understood by examples, comparisons, etc. 2. *a*) to furnish (books, etc.) with explanatory or decorative drawings, pictures, etc. *b*) to explain or decorate: said of pictures, etc. —**il'lus·tra'tor,** *n.*
**il·lus·tra·tion** (il'əs-trā'shən), *n.* 1. an illustrating or being illustrated. 2. an example, analogy, etc. used to help explain. 3. a picture, diagram, etc. used to decorate or explain something.
**il·lus·tra·tive** (i-lus'trə-tiv, il'əs-trā'-), *adj.* illustrating or tending to illustrate; serving as an example. —**il·lus'tra·tive·ly,** *adv.*
**il·lus·tri·ous** (i-lus'tri-əs), *adj.* [< L. *illustris*, bright], distinguished; famous; celebrated.—**il·lus'tri·ous·ly,** *adv.* —**il·lus'tri·ous·ness,** *n.*
**ill will,** hostility; hate; dislike. —**ill'-willed',** *adj.*
**il·ly** (il'li), *adv.* badly; ill: now generally regarded as substandard or dialectal.
**Il·lyr·i·a** (i-lêr'i-ə), *n.* an ancient country on the east coast of the Adriatic. —**Il·lyr'i·an,** *adj.* & *n.*
**I'm** (īm), I am.
**im-,** 1. in- (not). 2. in- (in). Used before *b*, *m*, and *p*.
**im·age** (im'ij), *n.* [OFr. < L. *imago* < *imitari*, to imitate], 1. a representation of a person or thing, drawn, painted, etc.; especially, a statue. 2. the visual impression of something produced by a lens, mirror, etc. 3. a copy; counterpart; likeness. 4. a mental picture of something; idea; impression. 5. a type; embodiment: as, he is the *image* of laziness. 6. a figure of speech, especially a metaphor or simile. 7. the total impression created by a person, company, etc. as a result of practices, policies, etc. *v.t.* [-AGED, -AGING], 1. to make a representation of; portray. 2. to reflect; mirror. 3. to picture in the mind; imagine. 4. to typify. 5. to describe graphically or vividly.
**im·age·ry** (im'ij-ri, -ij-ēr-i), *n.* [*pl.* -RIES], 1. images generally; esp., statues. 2. mental images, as produced by memory or imagination. 3. descriptions and figures of speech.
**im·ag·i·na·ble** (i-maj'i-nə-b'l), *adj.* that can be imagined. —**im·ag'i·na·bly,** *adv.*
**im·ag·i·nar·y** (i-maj'i-ner'i), *adj.* existing only in the imagination; unreal. —**im·ag'i·nar'i·ly,** *adv.*
**im·ag·i·na·tion** (i-maj'i-nā'shən), *n.* 1. *a*) the act or power of forming mental images of what is not actually present. *b*) the act or power of creating mental images of what has never been actually experienced, or of creating new images or ideas by combining previous experiences. 2. anything imagined; creation of the mind. 3. a foolish notion. —**im·ag'i·na'tion·al,** *adj.*
**im·ag·i·na·tive** (i-maj'i-nā'tiv, -nə-tiv), *adj.* 1. having, using, or showing imagination; able to imagine or fond of imagining. 2. of or resulting from imagination. —**im·ag'i·na'tive·ly,** *adv.* —**im·ag'i·na'tive·ness,** *n.*
**im·ag·ine** (i-maj'in), *v.t.* & *v.i.* [-INED, -INING], [< OFr. < L. *imaginari* < *imago*, an image], 1. to make a mental image (of); conceive in the mind. 2. to suppose; guess; think.
**im·ag·ism** (im'əj-iz'm), *n.* a movement in modern poetry (c. 1912–1924) using precise, concrete images and extensive free verse.
**im·ag·ist** (im'əj-ist), *n.* any of the poets who practiced imagism. *adj.* of imagism or the imagists: also **im·ag·is·tic** (im'ə-jis'tik).
**i·ma·go** (i-mā'gō), *n.* [*pl.* -GOS, -GINES (i-maj'ə-nēz')], [L., an image, likeness], 1. the final, adult, reproductive stage in the development of an insect. 2. an insect in this stage.
**im·be·cile** (im'bə-s'l), *adj.* [< Fr. < L. *imbecilis*, feeble], 1. of or showing feeble intellect. 2. very foolish or stupid. *n.* 1. a mentally deficient person with an intelligence quotient ranging from 25 to 50: *imbecile* is the second-lowest classification of mental deficiency, above *idiot* and below *moron*. 2. loosely, a very foolish or stupid person. —**im'be·cil'ic,** *adj.*
**im·be·cil·i·ty** (im'bə-sil'ə-ti), *n.* [*pl.* -TIES], 1. the state of being imbecile. 2. great foolishness or stupidity. 3. an imbecile act or remark.
**im·bed** (im-bed'), *v.t.* [-BEDDED, -BEDDING], to embed.

**im·bibe** (im-bīb′), *v.t.* [-BIBED, -BIBING], [< OFr. < L. < *in-*, in + *bibere*, to drink], 1. to drink or drink in. 2. to absorb (moisture). 3. to absorb into the mind. *v.i.* to drink. —**im·bib′er,** *n.*
**im·bri·cate** (im′bri-kāt′; *also, for adj.*, -kit), *adj.* [< L. pp. of *imbricare*, to cover with tiles < *imbrex*, gutter tile < *imber*, rain], 1. overlapping evenly, as tiles, fish scales, etc. 2. ornamented as with overlapping scales. Also **im′bri·cat′ed.** *v.t.* [-CATED, -CATING], to place in overlapping order. *v.i.* to overlap. —**im′bri·cate·ly,** *adv.* —**im′bri·ca′tion,** *n.*
**im·bro·glio** (im-brōl′yō), *n.* [*pl.* -GLIOS], [It. < *broglio*, confusion], 1. an involved and confusing situation. 2. a confused misunderstanding or disagreement; entanglement.
**im·brue** (im-brōō′), *v.t.* [-BRUED, -BRUING], [< OFr.; ult. < L. *imbibere;* see IMBIBE], to wet or stain, especially with blood. —**im·brue′ment,** *n.*
**im·bue** (im-bū′), *v.t.* [-BUED, -BUING], [< L. *imbuere*], 1. to fill with moisture; saturate. 2. to fill with color; dye. 3. to fill (the mind, etc.); inspire (*with* feelings, etc.). —**im·bue′ment,** *n.*
**imit.,** 1. imitation. 2. imitative.
**im·i·ta·ble** (im′i-tə-b'l), *adj.* that can be imitated. —**im′i·ta·bil′i·ty,** *n.*
**im·i·tate** (im′ə-tāt′), *v.t.* [-TATED, -TATING], [< L. pp. of *imitari*, to imitate], 1. to try to be the same as; follow the example of. 2. to mimic. 3. to reproduce in form, color, etc.; copy. 4. to be like in appearance; resemble. —**im′i·ta′tor** (-ēr), *n*
**im·i·ta·tion** (im′ə-tā′shən), *n.* 1. an imitating. 2. the result or product of imitating; copy. *adj.* made to resemble something else, usually something superior or genuine: as, *imitation* leather. —**im′i·ta′tion·al,** *adj.*
**im·i·ta·tive** (im′ə-tā′tiv), *adj.* 1. formed from a model. 2. given to imitating others. 3. not genuine; imitation. 4. approximating in sound the thing signified; echoic. —**im′i·ta′tive·ly,** *adv.* —**im′i·ta′tive·ness,** *n.*
**im·mac·u·late** (i-mak′yoo-lit), *adj.* [< L. < *in-*, not + *maculatus*, pp. < *macula*, a spot], 1. perfectly clean; without a spot or stain. 2. without a flaw or error. 3. pure: innocent; sinless. —**im·mac′u·late·ly,** *adv.* —**im·mac′u·late·ness,** *n.*
**Immaculate Conception,** in the *R. C. Church*, the doctrine that the Virgin Mary was from the moment of conception free from original sin.
**im·ma·nence** (im′ə-nəns), *n.* the fact or condition of being immanent: also **im′ma·nen·cy.**
**im·ma·nent** (im′ə-nənt), *adj.* [< LL. < *in-*, in + *manere*, to remain], living, remaining, or operating within; inherent. —**im′ma·nent·ly,** *adv.*
**Im·man·u·el** (i-man′ū-əl), *n.* a name given by Isaiah to the Messiah of his prophecy (Is. 7:14), often applied to Jesus (Matt. 1:23).
**im·ma·te·ri·al** (im′ə-têr′i-əl), *adj.* 1. not consisting of matter; spiritual. 2. that does not matter; unimportant. —**im′ma·te′ri·al·ly,** *adv.* —**im′ma·te′ri·al·ness,** *n.*
**im·ma·ture** (im′ə-tyoor′, -toor′, -choor′), *adj.* 1. not mature; not completely developed; not ripe. 2. not finished or perfected. —**im′ma·ture′ly,** *adv.* —**im′ma·tu′ri·ty, im′ma·ture′ness,** *n.*
**im·meas·ur·a·ble** (i-mezh′ēr-ə-b'l), *adj.* that cannot be measured; boundless; vast; immense. —**im·meas′ur·a·bil′i·ty, im·meas′ur·a·ble·ness,** *n.* —**im·meas′ur·a·bly,** *adv.*
**im·me·di·a·cy** (i-mē′di-ə-si), *n.* the quality or state of being immediate.
**im·me·di·ate** (i-mē′di-it), *adj.* [< ML.; see IN- (not) & MEDIATE], with nothing coming between; specif., *a*) not separated in space; in direct contact; nearest. *b*) not separated in time; happening at once; instant; of the present. *c*) next in order, succession, etc.; directly related: as, one's *immediate* family. *d*) directly affecting; direct: as, an *immediate* cause. —**im·me′di·ate·ness,** *n.*
**im·me·di·ate·ly** (i-mē′di-it-li), *adv.* in an immediate manner; specif., *a*) without intervening agency or cause; directly. *b*) without delay; instantly. *conj.* [Chiefly Brit.], as soon as: as, return *immediately* you are done.
**im·me·mo·ri·al** (im′ə-môr′i-əl, -mō′ri-), *adj.* extending back beyond the reach of memory or record; very old. —**im′me·mo′ri·al·ly,** *adv.*
**im·mense** (i-mens′), *adj.* [Fr. < L. < *in-*, not + *mensus*, pp. of *metiri*, to measure], 1. very large; vast; enormous. 2. [Slang], very good; excellent. —**im·mense′ly,** *adv.* —**im·mense′ness,** *n.*
**im·men·si·ty** (i-men′sə-ti), *n.* [*pl.* -TIES], 1. vastness; great size or limitless extent. 2. infinite space or being; infinity.
**im·merge** (i-mũrj′), *v.t.* [-MERGED, -MERGING], [see IMMERSE], to immerse. *v.i.* to plunge or disappear, as in liquid.
**im·merse** (i-mũrs′), *v.t.* [-MERSED, -MERSING], [< L. pp. of *immergere*, to plunge], 1. to plunge or dip into or as if into a liquid. 2. to baptize by dipping under water. 3. to absorb or involve deeply; engross: as, *immersed* in thought. —**im·mer′sion,** *n.*
**im·mi·grant** (im′ə-grənt), *n.* a person who immigrates. *adj.* immigrating.
**im·mi·grate** (im′ə-grāt′), *v.i.* [-GRATED, -GRATING], [< L. pp. of *immigrare;* see IN- (in) & MIGRATE], to come into a new country or region in order to settle there: opposed to *emigrate.*
**im·mi·gra·tion** (im′ə-grā′shən), *n.* 1. an immigrating. 2. the immigrants during a specified period.
**im·mi·nence** (im′ə-nəns), *n.* 1. a being imminent. 2. something imminent; impending evil, danger, etc. Also **im′mi·nen·cy** [*pl.* -CIES].
**im·mi·nent** (im′ə-nənt), *adj.* [< L. *imminens*, ppr. < *in-*, on + *minere*, to project], likely to happen without delay; impending. —**im′mi·nent·ly,** *adv.*
**im·mis·ci·ble** (i-mis′ə-b'l), *adj.* [*im-* (not) + *miscible*], that cannot be mixed or blended. —**im·mis′ci·bil′i·ty,** *n.* —**im·mis′ci·bly,** *adv.*
**im·mo·bile** (i-mō′b'l, -bēl), *adj.* 1. firmly set or placed; stable. 2. motionless. —**im′mo·bil′i·ty,** *n.*
**im·mo·bi·lize** (i-mō′b'l-īz′), *v.t.* [-LIZED, -LIZING], 1. to make immobile. 2. to prevent the movement of (a limb or joint) with splints or a cast. —**im·mo′bi·li·za′tion,** *n.*
**im·mod·er·ate** (i-mod′ēr-it), *adj.* not moderate; without restraint; excessive. —**im·mod′er·ate·ly,** *adv.* —**im·mod′er·ate·ness, im·mod′er·a′tion,** *n.*
**im·mod·est** (i-mod′ist), *adj.* not modest; specif., *a*) indecent; improper. *b*) bold; impudent. —**im·mod′est·ly,** *adv.* —**im·mod′es·ty,** *n.*
**im·mo·late** (im′ə-lāt′), *v.t.* [-LATED, -LATING], [< L. pp. of *immolare*, to sprinkle with sacrificial meal < *in-*, on + *mola*, meal], to sacrifice; esp., to kill as a sacrifice. —**im′mo·la′tion,** *n.* —**im′mo·la′tor** (-lā′tēr), *n.*
**im·mor·al** (i-môr′əl, i-mor′-), *adj.* not in conformity with accepted principles of right and wrong behavior; not moral; esp., unchaste; lewd; obscene. —**im·mor′al·ly,** *adv.*
**im·mo·ral·i·ty** (im′ə-ral′ə-ti), *n.* 1. the state or quality of being immoral. 2. immoral behavior. 3. [*pl.* -TIES], an immoral act or practice; vice.
**im·mor·tal** (i-môr′t'l), *adj.* 1. not mortal; living forever. 2. of immortal beings or immortality; heavenly. 3. lasting as long as this world; enduring. 4. having lasting fame. *n.* an immortal being; specif., *a*) *pl.* the gods of ancient Greece or Rome. *b*) a person having lasting fame. —**im·mor′tal·ly,** *adv.*
**im·mor·tal·i·ty** (im′ôr-tal′ə-ti), *n.* the quality or state of being immortal; specif., *a*) endless existence. *b*) lasting fame.
**im·mor·tal·ize** (i-môr′t'l-īz′), *v.t.* [-IZED, -IZING], to make immortal in existence or fame. —**im·mor′tal·i·za′tion,** *n.* —**im·mor′tal·iz′er,** *n.*
**im·mor·telle** (im′ôr-tel′), *n.* [Fr. fem. of *immortel*, undying], an everlasting (the plant).
**im·mov·a·ble** (i-mōōv′ə-b'l), *adj.* 1. that cannot be moved; firmly fixed. 2. motionless; stationary. 3. unyielding; steadfast. 4. unemotional; unfeeling. *n.pl.* in *law*, immovable possessions or property, as land, buildings, etc. —**im·mov′a·bil′i·ty, im·mov′a·ble·ness,** *n.* —**im·mov′a·bly,** *adv.*
**im·mune** (i-mūn′), *adj.* [OFr. < L. < *in-*, without + *munus*, duty], having immunity; exempt from or protected against something disagreeable or harmful; esp., protected against a disease, as by inoculation.
**immune body,** an antibody.
**im·mu·ni·ty** (i-mū′nə-ti), *n.* [*pl.* -TIES], 1. exemption from taxes, military service, etc. 2. resistance to a specified disease or toxic substance.
**im·mu·nize** (im′yoo-nīz′), *v.t.* [-NIZED, -NIZING], to make immune; give immunity to, as by inoculation. —**im′mu·ni·za′tion,** *n.*
**im·mu·nol·o·gy** (im′yoo-nol′ə-ji), *n.* the branch of medicine dealing with immunity to disease. —**im·mu·no·log·ic** (i-mū′nə-loj′ik), **im·mu′no·log′i·cal,** *adj.* —**im′mu·nol′o·gist,** *n.*
**im·mure** (i-myoor′), *v.t.* [-MURED, -MURING], [< OFr. < ML. < L. *im-*, in + *murus*, a wall], to shut up as within walls; confine. —**im·mure′ment,** *n.*

**im·mu·ta·ble** (i-mū′tə-b'l), *adj.* never changing or varying; unchangeable. **—im·mu′ta·bil′i·ty, im·mut′a·ble·ness,** *n.* **—im·mut′a·bly,** *adv.*

**imp** (imp), *n.* [< AS. < LL. *impotus*, a shoot < Gr. < *em-*, in + *phyein*, to produce], 1. a devil's offspring; young demon. 2. a mischievous child.

**imp.,** 1. imperative. 2. imperfect. 3. imperial. 4. import. 5. imprimatur. 6. imprint.

**im·pact** (im-pakt′; *for n.,* im′pakt), *v.t.* [< L. pp. of *impingere*, to press firmly together], to force tightly together; wedge. *n.* 1. a striking together; collision. 2. the force of a collision; shock. **—im·pac′tion,** *n.*

**im·pact·ed** (im-pak′tid), *adj.* firmly lodged in the jaw: said of a tooth unable to erupt because of its abnormal position.

**im·pair** (im-pâr′), *v.t.* [< OFr.; ult. < L. *in-*, intens. + *pejor*, worse], to make worse, less, etc.; damage; deteriorate. **—im·pair′er,** *n.* **—im·pair′ment,** *n.*

**im·pale** (im-pāl′), *v.t.* [-PALED, -PALING], [< Fr. < L. < *in-*, on + *palus*, a pole], 1. *a*) to pierce through with, or fix on, something pointed. *b*) to punish or torture by fixing on a stake. 2. to make helpless, as if fixed on a stake: as, her glance *impaled* him. **—im·pale′ment,** *n.* **—im·pal′er,** *n.*

**im·pal·pa·ble** (im-pal′pə-b'l), *adj.* 1. not perceptible to the touch. 2. too slight or subtle to be grasped easily by the mind. **—im′pal·pa·bil′i·ty,** *n.* **—im·pal′pa·bly,** *adv.*

**im·pan·el** (im-pan′'l), *v.t.* [-ELED or -ELLED, -ELING or -ELLING], to empanel.

**im·part** (im-pärt′), *v.t.* [< OFr. < L. *impartire;* see IN- (in) & PART], 1. to give a share or portion of; give. 2. to make known; reveal. **—im′par·ta′tion,** *n.* **—im·part′er,** *n.* **—im·part′i·ble,** *adj.*

**im·par·tial** (im-pär′shəl), *adj.* favoring no one side or party more than another; fair; just. **—im·par′tial·ly,** *adv.* **—im·par′tial·ness,** *n.*

**im·par·ti·al·i·ty** (im′pär-shi-al′ə-ti), *n.* freedom from favoritism, bias, or prejudice; fairness.

**im·pass·a·ble** (im-pas′ə-b'l), *adj.* that cannot be passed, crossed, or traveled over: as, an *impassable* highway. **—im·pas′sa·bil′i·ty, im·pas′sa·ble·ness,** *n.* **—im·pas′sa·bly,** *adv.*

**im·passe** (im′pas, im-pas′), *n.* [Fr.], 1. a passage open only at one end; blind alley. 2. a situation from which there is no escape; deadlock.

**im·pas·si·ble** (im-pas′ə-b'l), *adj.* [< OFr. < LL. < L. *im-*, not + *passibilis* < *pati*, to suffer], 1. that cannot feel pain. 2. that cannot be injured. 3. that cannot be moved or aroused emotionally; unfeeling. **—im·pas′si·bil′i·ty, im·pas′si·ble·ness,** *n.* **—im·pas′si·bly,** *adv.*

**im·pas·sion** (im-pash′ən), *v.t.* to fill with passion; arouse emotionally.

**im·pas·sioned** (im-pash′ənd), *adj.* filled with passion; passionate; fiery; ardent. **—im·pas′sioned·ly,** *adv.* **—im·pas′sioned·ness,** *n.*

**im·pas·sive** (im-pas′iv), *adj.* 1. not feeling pain; insensible. 2. not feeling or showing emotion; calm; serene. **—im·pas′sive·ly,** *adv.* **—im·pas′sive·ness, im·pas·siv·i·ty** (im′pa-siv′ə-ti), *n.*

**im·pa·tience** (im-pā′shəns), *n.* lack of patience; specif., *a*) annoyance because of delay, bother, etc. *b*) restless eagerness to do something, etc.

**im·pa·ti·ens** (im-pā′shi-ənz), *n.* [L.; see IMPATIENT], a flower of the balsam family, with spurred flowers and pods that burst and scatter their seeds when ripe: also called *touch-me-not.*

**im·pa·tient** (im-pā′shənt), *adj.* feeling or showing a lack of patience; specif., *a*) annoyed because of delay, opposition, etc. *b*) restlessly eager to do something, go somewhere, etc. **—im·pa′tient·ly,** *adv.* **—im·pa′tient·ness,** *n.*

**im·peach** (im-pēch′), *v.t.* [< OFr. < LL. *impedicare*, to entangle < L. *in-*, in + *pedica*, a fetter < *pes*, foot], 1. to challenge or discredit (a person's honor, etc.). 2. to challenge the practices or honesty of; esp., to bring (a public official) before the proper tribunal on a charge of wrongdoing. **—im·peach′a·bil′i·ty,** *n.* **—im·peach′a·ble,** *adj.* **—im·peach′ment,** *n.*

**im·pec·ca·ble** (im-pek′ə-b'l), *adj.* [< LL. < L. *in-*, not + *peccare*, to sin], 1. not liable to sin or wrongdoing. 2. without defect or error; flawless. *n.* an impeccable person. **—im·pec′ca·bil′i·ty,** *n.* **—im·pec′ca·bly,** *adv.*

**im·pe·cu·ni·ous** (im′pi-kū′ni-əs), *adj.* [< Fr. < L. *in-*, not + *pecunia*, money], having no money; poor. **—im′pe·cu′ni·os′i·ty** (-os′ə-ti), *n.* **—im′pe·cu′ni·ous·ly,** *adv.* **—im′pe·cu′ni·ous·ness,** *n.*

**im·ped·ance** (im-pēd′'ns), *n.* [< *impede* + *-ance*], the apparent resistance in an alternating electrical current, corresponding to the true resistance in a direct current.

**im·pede** (im-pēd′), *v.t.* [-PEDED, -PEDING], [< L. *impedire* < *in-*, in + *pes*, foot], to bar or hinder the progress of; obstruct; retard. **—im·ped′er,** *n.* **—im·ped′ing·ly,** *adv.*

**im·ped·i·ment** (im-ped′ə-mənt), *n.* 1. an impeding or being impeded. 2. anything that impedes; specif., a speech defect; stutter, lisp, etc. **—im·ped′i·men′tal, im·ped′i·men′ta·ry** (-tə-ri), *adj.*

**im·ped·i·men·ta** (im-ped′ə-men′tə, im′ped-), *n.pl.* [L.], things impeding progress, as on a trip; specif., *a*) baggage. *b*) the supplies or baggage carried along with an army.

**im·pel** (im-pel′), *v.t.* [-PELLED, -PELLING], [< L. < *in-*, on + *pellere*, to drive], 1. to push, drive, or move forward; propel. 2. to force, compel, or urge. **—im·pel′lent,** *adj. & n.* **—im·pel′ler,** *n.*

**im·pend** (im-pend′), *v.i.* [< L. < *in-*, in + *pendere*, to hang], 1. to hang or be suspended (*over*). 2. to be about to happen; be imminent: as, an *impending* disaster. **—im·pend′ence, im·pen′den·cy,** *n.*

**im·pend·ing** (im-pen′diŋ), *adj.* 1. overhanging. 2. about to happen; imminent or threatening.

**im·pen·e·tra·ble** (im-pen′i-trə-b'l), *adj.* 1. that cannot be penetrated or pierced; impervious. 2. that cannot be solved or understood; unfathomable. 3. unreceptive to ideas, influences, etc. **—im·pen′e·tra·bil′i·ty, im·pen′e·tra·ble·ness,** *n.* **—im·pen′e·tra·bly,** *adv.*

**im·pen·i·tent** (im-pen′i-tənt), *adj.* without regret, shame, or remorse; not penitent. *n.* an impenitent person. **—im·pen′i·tence, im·pen′i·ten·cy,** *n.* **—im·pen′i·tent·ly,** *adv.*

**im·per·a·tive** (im-per′ə-tiv), *adj.* [< LL. < L. *imperare*, to order], 1. indicating authority or command: as, an *imperative* gesture. 2. absolutely necessary; urgent. 3. in *grammar*, designating or of the mood of a verb that expresses a command, strong request, etc. *n.* 1. a command; order. 2. in *grammar*, *a*) the imperative mood. *b*) a verb in this mood. **—im·per′a·tive·ly,** *adv.* **—im·per′a·tive·ness,** *n.*

**im·pe·ra·tor** (im′pə-rā′tēr, -tôr), *n.* [L. < pp. of *imperare*, to command], in ancient Rome, a title of honor for generals and, later, emperors. **—im·per·a·to·ri·al** (im-pêr′ə-tôr′i-əl, -tō′ri-əl), *adj.* **—im·per′a·to′ri·al·ly,** *adv.*

**im·per·cep·ti·ble** (im′pēr-sep′tə-b'l), *adj.* not easily perceived by the senses or the mind; very slight, gradual, subtle, etc. **—im′per·cep′ti·bil′i·ty, im′per·cep′ti·ble·ness,** *n.* **—im′per·cep′ti·bly,** *adv.* **—im′per·cep′tive,** *adj.*

**imperf.,** 1. imperfect. 2. imperforate.

**im·per·fect** (im-pūr′fikt), *adj.* 1. not finished or complete; lacking in something. 2. not perfect; having a defect or error. 3. in certain languages, designating or of the tense of a verb that indicates a past action or state as incomplete or continuous: in English, "was writing" is a form corresponding to the imperfect tense. 4. in *music*, diminished. *n.* in *grammar*, 1. the imperfect tense. 2. a verb of this tense. **—im·per′fect·ly,** *adv.* **—im·per′fect·ness,** *n.*

**im·per·fec·tion** (im′pēr-fek′shən), *n.* 1. a being imperfect. 2. a shortcoming; defect; fault.

**im·per·fo·rate** (im-pūr′fēr-it), *adj.* 1. having no holes or openings. 2. having a straight edge without perforations: said of a postage stamp. Also **im·per′fo·rat′ed** (-fə-rā′tid). *n.* an imperforate stamp. **—im·per′fo·ra′tion,** *n.*

**im·pe·ri·al** (im-pêr′i-əl), *adj.* [< OFr. < L. < *imperium*, empire], 1. of an empire. 2. of a country having control over other countries or colonies. 3. of, or having the rank of, an emperor or empress. 4. having supreme authority. 5. majestic; magnificent. 6. of great size or superior quality. 7. according to the standard of weights and measures fixed by British law. *n.* 1. a size of writing paper measuring 23 by 31 inches. 2. a pointed tuft of beard on the lower lip and chin. **—im·pe′ri·al·ly,** *adv.* **—im·pe′ri·al·ness,** *n.*

**imperial gallon,** the British gallon, equal to 277.42 cu. in. or about 1$^1/_5$ U.S. gallons.

**im·pe·ri·al·ism** (im-pêr′i-əl-iz'm), *n.* 1. imperial state, authority, or government. 2. the policy and practice of forming and maintaining an empire, characterized by the subjugation and control of territories, the establishment of colonies, etc. **—im·pe′ri·al·ist,** *n. & adj.* **—im·pe′ri·al·is′tic,** *adj.* **—im·pe′ri·al·is′ti·cal·ly,** *adv.*

**Imperial Valley,** an irrigated agricultural region in SE California, reclaimed from the desert.

**im·per·il** (im-per′əl), *v.t.* [-ILED or -ILLED, -ILING or -ILLING], to put in peril; endanger.

**im·pe·ri·ous** (im-pêr′i-əs), *adj.* [< L. < *imperium*, command], 1. overbearing; arrogant; domineering. 2. urgent; imperative. **—im·pe′ri·ous·ly,** *adv.* **—im·pe′ri·ous·ness,** *n.*

**im·per·ish·a·ble** (im-per′ish-ə-b'l), *adj.* not perishable; that will not decay; immortal. —**im·per′ish·a·bil′i·ty, im·per′ish·a·ble·ness,** *n.* —**im·per′ish·a·bly,** *adv.*

**im·per·ma·nent** (im-pūr′mə-nənt), *adj.* not permanent; not lasting; temporary. —**im·per′ma·nence, im·per′ma·nen·cy,** *n.* —**im·per′ma·nent·ly,** *adv.*

**im·per·me·a·ble** (im-pūr′mi-ə-b'l), *adj.* not permeable; not permitting passage, especially of fluids. —**im·per′me·a·bil′i·ty, im·per′me·a·ble·ness,** *n.* —**im·per′me·a·bly,** *adv.*

**im·per·son·al** (im-pūr′s'n-əl), *adj.* 1. not personal; specif., *a*) without reference to any particular person: as, an *impersonal* attitude. *b*) not existing as a person: as, time is an *impersonal* force. 2. in *grammar,* designating or of a verb occurring only in the third person singular, with *it* as the subject (e.g., "it's raining"). *n.* an impersonal verb. —**im·per′son·al·ly,** *adv.*

**im·per·son·al·i·ty** (im′pēr-sə-nal′ə-ti, im-pūr′-), *n.* 1. the condition or quality of being impersonal. 2. [*pl.* -TIES], an impersonal thing.

**im·per·son·ate** (im-pūr′sə-nāt′), *v.t.* [-NATED, -NATING], 1. to represent in the form of a person; personify: as, he *impersonates* pride. 2. to act the part of: as, he *impersonated* Caesar in the play. 3. to mimic the appearance, behavior, etc. of (a person). *adj.* embodied in a person; personified. —**im′per·son·a′tion,** *n* —**im·per′son·a·tor,** *n.*

**im·per·ti·nence** (im-pūr′t'n-əns), *n.* 1. the quality or fact of being impertinent; specif., *a*) irrelevance. *b*) unsuitability; inappropriateness. *c*) insolence; impudence. 2. an impertinent act, remark, etc. Also **im·per′ti·nen·cy** [*pl.* -CIES].

**im·per·ti·nent** (im-pūr′t'n-ənt), *adj.* 1. not pertinent; irrelevant. 2. not suitable; inappropriate. 3. saucy; impudent; insolent. —**im·per′ti·nent·ly,** *adv.*

**im·per·turb·a·ble** (im′pēr-tūr′bə-b'l), *adj.* that cannot be perturbed, disconcerted, or excited; impassive. —**im′per·turb′a·bil′i·ty, im′per·turb′a·ble·ness,** *n.* —**im′per·turb′a·bly,** *adv.*

**im·per·vi·ous** (im-pūr′vi-əs), *adj.* 1. not pervious; incapable of being penetrated, as by moisture. 2. not affected or influenced by (with *to*). —**im·per′vi·ous·ly,** *adv.* —**im·per′vi·ous·ness,** *n.*

**im·pe·ti·go** (im′pi-tī′gō), *n.* [L. < *in-*, in + *petere,* to assault], a skin disease with eruption of pustules; esp., a contagious disease of this kind.

**im·pet·u·os·i·ty** (im′pech-ōō-os′ə-ti, im-pech′-), *n.* 1. the quality of being impetuous. 2. [*pl.* -TIES], an impetuous action or feeling.

**im·pet·u·ous** (im-pech′ōō-əs), *adj.* [< Fr. < L. *impetuosus;* see IMPETUS], 1. moving with great force or violence; rushing. 2. acting with sudden energy and little thought; impulsive. —**im·pet′u·ous·ly,** *adv.* —**im·pet′u·ous·ness,** *n.*

**im·pe·tus** (im′pə-təs), *n.* [*pl.* -TUSES], [< L. < *in-*, in + *petere,* to seek], 1. the force with which a body moves against resistance, resulting from its mass and velocity. 2. anything that stimulates activity; incentive.

**im·pi·e·ty** (im-pī′ə-ti), *n.* 1. a lack of piety; specif., *a*) lack of reverence for God. *b*) disrespect. 2. [*pl.* -TIES], an impious act.

**im·pinge** (im-pinj′), *v.i.* [-PINGED, -PINGING], [L. *impingere* < *in-*, in + *pangere,* to strike], 1. to strike, hit, etc. (*on, upon,* or *against*). 2. to make inroads or encroach (*on* or *upon*). —**im·pinge′ment,** *n.* —**im·ping′er,** *n.*

**im·pi·ous** (im′pi-əs), *adj.* not pious; specif., lacking reverence for God. —**im′pi·ous·ly,** *adv.* —**im′pi·ous·ness,** *n.*

**imp·ish** (imp′ish), *adj.* of or like an imp; mischievous. —**imp′ish·ly,** *adv.* —**imp′ish·ness,** *n.*

**im·pla·ca·ble** (im-plā′kə-b'l, -plak′ə-), *adj.* not placable; not to be appeased or pacified; relentless. —**im′pla·ca·bil′i·ty, im·pla′ca·ble·ness,** *n.* —**im·pla′ca·bly,** *adv.*

**im·plant** (im-plant′, -plänt′), *v.t.* 1. to plant firmly or deeply; embed. 2. to fix firmly in the mind; instill. —**im′plan·ta′tion,** *n.* —**im·plant′er,** *n.*

**im·plau·si·ble** (im-plô′zə-b'l), *adj.* not plausible. —**im·plau′si·bly,** *adv.*

**im·ple·ment** (im′plə-mənt; *for v.,* -ment′), *n.* [< LL. *implementum,* a filling up < L. < *in-*, in + *plere,* to fill], something used or needed in a given activity; tool, instrument, etc. *v.t.* 1. to fulfill; accomplish. 2. to give practical effect to. 3. to provide with implements. —**im′ple·men′tal,** *adj.* —**im′ple·men·ta′tion,** *n.*

**im·pli·cate** (im′pli-kāt′), *v.t.* [-CATED, -CATING], [< L. pp. of *implicare,* to enfold < *in-*, in + *plicare,* to fold], 1. to twist together; entangle. 2. to imply. 3. to show to be a party to a crime, fault, etc.; involve. —**im′pli·ca′tive, im′pli·ca·to′ry** (-kə-tôr′i, -tō′ri), *adj.*

**im·pli·ca·tion** (im′pli-kā′shən), *n.* 1. an implicating or being implicated. 2. an implying or being implied. 3. something implied, from which an inference may be drawn.

**im·plic·it** (im-plis′it), *adj.* [< Fr. < L. pp. of *implicare,* to involve], 1. suggested or to be understood though not plainly expressed; implied: cf. *explicit.* 2. necessarily or naturally involved though not plainly apparent or expressed; inherent. 3. without reservation or doubt; absolute. —**im·plic′it·ly,** *adv.* —**im·plic′it·ness,** *n.*

**im·plied** (im-plīd′), *adj.* involved, suggested, or understood without being openly expressed.

**im·plore** (im-plôr′, -plōr′), *v.t.* [-PLORED, -PLORING], [< L. < *in-*, intens. + *plorare,* to cry out], 1. to ask earnestly for; beseech. 2. to beg (a person) to do something; entreat. —**im′plo·ra′tion,** *n.* —**im·plor′er,** *n.* —**im·plor′ing·ly,** *adv.*

**im·ply** (im-plī′), *v.t.* [-PLIED, -PLYING], [< OFr. < L. *implicare,* to involve], 1. to have as a necessary part, condition, or effect: as, drama *implies* conflict. 2. to indicate without saying openly; suggest; intimate: as, his attitude *implied* boredom.

**im·po·lite** (im′pə-līt′), *adj.* not polite; ill-mannered; discourteous; rude. —**im′po·lite′ly,** *adv.* —**im′po·lite′ness,** *n.*

**im·pol·i·tic** (im-pol′ə-tik), *adj.* not politic; unwise; injudicious; inexpedient. —**im·pol′i·tic·ly,** *adv.* —**im·pol′i·tic·ness,** *n.*

**im·pon·der·a·ble** (im-pon′dēr-ə-b'l), *adj.* not ponderable; that cannot be weighed or measured. *n.* anything imponderable. —**im·pon′der·a·bil′i·ty, im·pon′der·a·ble·ness,** *n.* —**im·pon′der·a·bly,** *adv.*

**im·port** (im-pôrt′, im′pôrt; *for n.,* im′pôrt, -pōrt), *v.t.* [< L. < *in-*, in + *portare,* to bring], 1. *a*) to bring in from the outside. *b*) to bring (goods) into one country from another in commerce. 2. to mean; signify: as, this action *imports* trouble. *v.i.* to be of importance; matter. *n.* 1. the act or business of importing (goods). 2. something imported. 3. meaning; signification. 4. importance. —**im·port′a·ble,** *adj.* —**im·port′a·bil′i·ty,** *n.*

**im·por·tance** (im-pôr′t'ns), *n.* the state or quality of being important; significance; consequence.

**im·por·tant** (im-pôr′t'nt), *adj.* [Fr. < ML. ppr. of *importare;* see IMPORT], 1. meaning a great deal; having much significance or consequence. 2. having, or acting as if having, power, authority, high position, etc. —**im·por′tant·ly,** *adv.*

**im·por·ta·tion** (im′pôr-tā′shən, -pōr-), *n.* 1. an importing, as of goods. 2. something imported.

**im·port·er** (im-pôr′tēr, -pōr′-), *n.* a person or firm in the business of importing goods.

**im·por·tu·nate** (im-pôr′chə-nit), *adj.* urgent or annoyingly persistent in asking or demanding. —**im·por′tu·nate·ly,** *adv.* —**im·por′tu·nate·ness,** *n.*

**im·por·tune** (im′pôr-tōōn′, -tūn′, im-pôr′choon), *v.t.* [-TUNED, -TUNING], [< Fr. < ML. < L. *importunus,* troublesome], to trouble with requests or demands; urge persistently or repeatedly. *v.i.* to be importunate. —**im′por·tune′ly,** *adv.* —**im′por·tun′er,** *n.*

**im·por·tu·ni·ty** (im′pôr-tōō′nə-ti, -tū′-), *n.* [*pl.* -TIES], an importuning or being importunate; persistence in requesting or demanding.

**im·pose** (im-pōz′), *v.t.* [-POSED, -POSING], [< Fr.; see IN- (in) & POSE], 1. to place (a burden, tax, etc. *on* or *upon*). 2. to force (oneself) on another or others. 3. to pass off by deception; foist. 4. to arrange (pages of type) in a frame for printing. —**impose on** (or **upon**), 1. to take advantage of. 2. to get the better of by deceiving. —**im·pos′a·ble,** *adj.* —**im·pos′er,** *n.*

**im·pos·ing** (im-pōz′iŋ), *adj.* making a strong impression because of great size, strength, dignity, etc. —**im·pos′ing·ly,** *adv.* —**im·pos′ing·ness,** *n.*

**im·po·si·tion** (im′pə-zish′ən), *n.* 1. an imposing or imposing on; specif., a taking advantage of friendship, etc. 2. something imposed; specif., *a*) a tax, fine, etc. *b*) an unjust burden, requirement, etc. *c*) a deception; fraud.

**im·pos·si·bil·i·ty** (im-pos′ə-bil′ə-ti), *n.* 1. the fact or quality of being impossible. 2. [*pl.* -TIES], something impossible.

**im·pos·si·ble** (im-pos′ə-b'l), *adj.* 1. not capable of being, being done, or happening. 2. [Colloq.], not capable of being endured, used, etc., because disagreeable or unsuitable: as, an *impossible* person. **—im·pos′si·ble·ness,** *n.* **—im·pos′si·bly,** *adv.*

**im·post** (im′pōst), *n.* [OFr. < LL. *impositus* < L. *in-*, in + pp. of *ponere*, to place], a tax; esp., a duty on imported goods. *v.t.* to classify (imported goods) in order to assess the proper taxes.

**im·post** (im′pōst), *n.* [ult. < L.; see prec. entry], the top part of a pillar supporting an arch.

**im·pos·tor** (im-pos′tẽr), *n.* [see IMPOSE], a cheat or fraud; esp., one who deceives by pretending to be someone or something that he is not.

**im·pos·ture** (im-pos′chẽr), *n.* the act or practice of an impostor; fraud; deception.

**im·po·tence** (im′pə-təns), *n.* the quality or condition of being impotent: also **im′po·ten·cy.**

**im·po·tent** (im′pə-tənt), *adj.* [see IN- (not) & POTENT], 1. lacking physical strength. 2. ineffective, powerless, or helpless. 3. unable to engage in sexual intercourse: said of males. **—im′po·tent·ly,** *adv.* **—im′po·tent·ness,** *n.*

**im·pound** (im-pound′), *v.t.* 1. to shut up (an animal) in a pound. 2. to take into legal custody. 3. to gather and enclose (water) for irrigation, etc. **—im·pound′er,** *n.*

**im·pov·er·ish** (im-pov′ẽr-ish), *v.t.* [< OFr. < L. *in*, in + *pauper*, poor], 1. to make poor. 2. to deprive of strength, resources, etc. **—im·pov′er·ish·er,** *n.* **—im·pov′er·ish·ment,** *n.*

**im·pow·er** (im-pou′ẽr), *v.t.* to empower.

**im·prac·ti·ca·ble** (im-prak′ti-kə-b'l), *adj.* 1. not capable of being carried out in practice: as, an *impracticable* plan. 2. not capable of being used. 3. difficult to manage or deal with: as, an *impracticable* person. **—im′prac·ti·ca·bil′i·ty, im·prac′ti·ca·ble·ness,** *n.* **—im·prac′ti·ca·bly,** *adv.*

**im·prac·ti·cal** (im-prak′ti-k'l), *adj.* not practical. **—im′prac·ti·cal′i·ty** [*pl.* -TIES], *n.*

**im·pre·cate** (im′pri-kāt′), *v.t.* [-CATED, -CATING], [< L. *imprecatus*, pp. < *in-*, on + *precari*, to pray < *prex*, prayer], 1. to pray for (evil, misfortune, etc.); invoke (a curse). 2. [Rare], to curse. **—im′pre·ca′tion,** *n.* **—im′pre·ca′tor,** *n.* **—im′pre·ca·to′ry** (-kə-tôr′i, -tō′ri), *adj.*

**im·preg·na·ble** (im-preg′nə-b'l), *adj.* [< OFr.; see IN- (not) & PREGNABLE], 1. not capable of being captured or entered by force. 2. unshakable; unyielding; firm. **—im′preg·na·bil′i·ty, im·preg′na·ble·ness,** *n.* **—im·preg′na·bly,** *adj.*

**im·preg·nate** (im-preg′nāt), *v.t.* [-NATED, -NATING], [< LL. < L. *in-*, in + *praegnans*, pregnant], 1. to fertilize. 2. to make pregnant. 3. to fill or saturate. 4. to imbue (*with* ideas, feelings, etc.). *adj.* (-nit), impregnated. **—im·preg′na·ble,** *adj.* **—im′preg·na′tion,** *n.* **—im·preg′na·tor** (-nā-tẽr), *n.*

**im·pre·sa·ri·o** (im′pri-sä′ri-ō′), *n.* [*pl.* -OS], [It. < *impresa*, enterprise], the organizer, manager, or director of an opera, concert series, etc.

**im·pre·scrip·ti·ble** (im′pri-skrip′tə-b'l), *adj.* that cannot rightfully be taken away or revoked; inviolable: as, *imprescriptible* rights. **—im′pre·scrip′ti·bil′i·ty,** *n.* **—im′pre·scrip′ti·bly,** *adv.*

**im·press** (im-pres′), *v.t.* [*im-* (in) + *press* (to force into service)], 1. to force (men) to serve in an army or a navy. 2. to levy or seize for public use. 3. to introduce and make use of (a fact, etc.). **—im·press′ment,** *n.*

**im·press** (im-pres′; *for n.*, im′pres), *v.t.* [< OFr. < L.; see IN- (in) & PRESS (to squeeze)], 1. to use pressure on so as to leave a mark. 2. to mark by using pressure; stamp; imprint. 3. to affect strongly the mind or emotions of. 4. to fix in the memory. *n.* 1. an impressing. 2. any mark, imprint, etc.; stamp. 3. an effect produced on the mind or feelings by some strong influence. **—im·press′er,** *n.* **—im·press′i·bil′i·ty,** *n.* **—im·press′i·ble,** *adj.*

**im·pres·sion** (im-presh′ən), *n.* 1. an impressing. 2. *a*) a mark, imprint, etc. made by physical pressure. *b*) an effect produced on the mind or senses: as, his talk made little *impression* on us. *c*) the effect produced by an effort or activity: as, cleaning made no *impression* on the dirt. 3. a vague notion: as, I have the *impression* that he was there. 4. in *printing*, *a*) a printed copy. *b*) all the copies printed as a single edition.

**im·pres·sion·a·ble** (im-presh′ən-ə-b'l), *adj.* easily affected by impressions; capable of being influenced; sensitive. **—im·pres′sion·a·bil′i·ty, im·pres′sion·a·ble·ness,** *n.*

**im·pres·sion·ism** (im-presh′ən-iz'm), *n.* a theory and school of art, whose chief aim is to reproduce only the immediate, over-all impression, without much attention to detail: the term has been extended to literature and to music which seeks to suggest impressions and atmosphere. **—im·pres′sion·ist,** *adj.* & *n.* **—im·pres′sion·is′tic,** *adj.*

**im·pres·sive** (im-pres′iv), *adj.* impressing or tending to impress the mind or emotions. **—im·pres′sive·ly,** *adv.* **—im·pres′sive·ness,** *n.*

**im·pri·ma·tur** (im′pri-mā′tẽr), *n.* [Mod. L., let it be printed], 1. license to publish or print a book, article, etc.; esp., sanction given by the Roman Catholic Church. 2. sanction or approval.

**im·print** (im-print′; *for n.*, im′print), *v.t.* [< OFr. < LL. < L. *im-*, in + *premere*, to press], 1. to mark by pressing or stamping; impress. 2. to press: as, to *imprint* a kiss on the cheek. 3. to fix in the memory. *n.* 1. a mark made by imprinting. 2. a characteristic effect or result. 3. a publisher's note, as on the title page of a book, giving his name, the time and place of publication, etc. **—im·print′er,** *n.*

**im·pris·on** (im-priz′'n), *v.t.* 1. to put or keep in prison; jail. 2. to restrict, limit, or confine in any way. **—im·pris′on·ment,** *n.*

**im·prob·a·ble** (im-prob′ə-b'l), *adj.* not probable; unlikely to happen or be true. **—im′prob·a·bil′i·ty, im·prob′a·ble·ness,** *n.* **—im·prob′a·bly,** *adv.*

**im·promp·tu** (im-promp′tōō, -tū), *adj.* & *adv.* [Fr. < L. *in promptu*, in readiness], without preparation or advance thought; offhand. *n.* an impromptu speech, performance, etc.

**im·prop·er** (im-prop′ẽr), *adj.* 1. not suitable or appropriate; unfit. 2. not in accordance with the truth, fact, etc.; incorrect. 3. contrary to good taste or decency. **—im·prop′er·ly,** *adv.* **—im·prop′er·ness,** *n.*

**improper fraction,** a fraction in which the denominator is less than the numerator (e.g., 5/3).

**im·pro·pri·e·ty** (im′prə-prī′ə-ti), *n.* [*pl.* -TIES], 1. the quality of being improper. 2. improper action or behavior. 3. an improper use of a word or phrase (e.g., "borrow" for "lend").

**im·prove** (im-prōōv′), *v.t.* [-PROVED, -PROVING], [< Anglo-Fr. < *en-*, in + *prou*, gain < L. *prodesse*, to profit], 1. to use (time, etc.) profitably. 2. to make better. 3. to make (land) more valuable by cultivation, etc. *v.i.* to become better. **—improve on** (or **upon**), to do or make better than. **—im·prov′a·bil′i·ty, im·prov′a·ble·ness,** *n.* **—im·prov′a·ble,** *adj.* **—im·prov′a·bly,** *adv.*

**im·prove·ment** (im-prōōv′mənt), *n.* 1. an improving or being improved; esp., *a*) betterment. *b*) an increase in value. *c*) profitable use. 2. *a*) an addition or change that improves something or adds to its value. *b*) a person or thing representing a higher degree of excellence.

**im·prov·i·dent** (im-prov′ə-dənt), *adj.* not providing for the future; lacking foresight or thrift. **—im·prov′i·dence,** *n.* **—im·prov′i·dent·ly,** *adv.*

**im·pro·vise** (im′prə-vīz, im′prə-vīz′), *v.t.* & *v.i.* [-VISED, -VISING], [< Fr. It. *improvvisare* < L. < *in-*, not + pp. of *providere*, to foresee], 1. to compose and simultaneously utter, sing, or play, without any preparation; extemporize. 2. to make, provide, or do with whatever is at hand. **—im·pro·vi·sa·tion** (im-prov′ə-zā′shən, im′prə-vi-), *n.* **—im·pro′vi·sa′tion·al,** *adj.* **—im′pro·vis′er,** *n.*

**im·pru·dent** (im-prōō′d'nt), *adj.* not prudent; without thought of the consequences; rash; indiscreet. **—im·pru′dence,** *n.* **—im·pru′dent·ly,** *adv.*

**im·pu·dence** (im′pyoo-dəns), *n.* 1. the quality of being impudent. 2. impudent speech or behavior: also **im′pu·den·cy** [*pl.* -CIES].

**im·pu·dent** (im′pyoo-dənt), *adj.* [< Fr. < L. < *in-*, not + ppr. of *pudere*, to feel shame], 1. originally, immodest; shameless. 2. shamelessly bold; disrespectful; insolent. **—im′pu·dent·ly,** *adv.*

**im·pugn** (im-pūn′), *v.t.* [< OFr. < L. < *in-*, against + *pugnare*, to fight], to attack by argument or criticism; oppose or challenge as false. **—im·pugn′a·ble,** *adj.* **—im·pug·na·tion** (im′pəg-nā′shən), **im·pugn′ment,** *n.* **—im·pugn′er,** *n.*

**im·pulse** (im′puls), *n.* [< L. < *impellere;* see IMPEL], 1. *a*) an impelling, or driving forward with sudden force. *b*) an impelling force; push; impetus. *c*) the motion or effect caused by such a force. 2. *a*) incitement to action arising from a state of mind or an external stimulus. *b*) a sudden inclination to act, without conscious thought. 3. in *physiology*, a stimulus transmitted in a muscle or nerve, which causes or inhibits activity in the body.

**im·pul·sion** (im-pul′shən), *n.* 1. an impelling or being impelled. 2. an impelling force; impetus.

**im·pul·sive** (im-pul′siv), *adj.* 1. impelling; driving forward. 2. *a*) given to acting on impulse: as, an *impulsive* person. *b*) produced by or resulting from impulse: as, an *impulsive* remark. **—im·pul′sive·ly,** *adv.* **—im·pul′sive·ness,** *n.*

**im·pu·ni·ty** (im-pū′nə-ti), *n.* [< Fr. < L. < *impunis* < *in-*, without + *poena*, punishment], freedom from punishment, penalty, harm, or loss.

**im·pure** (im-pyoor′), *adj.* not pure; specif., *a*) unclean; dirty. *b*) unclean according to religious ritual. *c*) immoral; obscene. *d*) mixed with foreign matter; adulterated. *e*) mixed; having more than one color, style, etc. *f*) not idiomatic or grammatical. —**im·pure′ly,** *adv.* —**im·pure′ness,** *n.*

**im·pu·ri·ty** (im-pyoor′ə-ti), *n.* 1. a being impure. 2. [*pl.* -TIES], an impure thing or element.

**im·pu·ta·tion** (im′pyoo-tā′shən), *n.* 1. an imputing or being imputed. 2. a fault or crime imputed. —**im·put·a·tive** (im-pūt′ə-tiv), *adj.* —**im·put′a·tive·ly,** *adv.* —**im·put′a·tive·ness,** *n.*

**im·pute** (im-pūt′), *v.t.* [-PUTED, -PUTING], [< OFr. < L. < *in-*, to + *putare*, to charge], to attribute (something, especially a crime or fault) to another; charge with; ascribe. —**im·put′a·bil′i·ty,** *n.* —**im·put′a·ble,** *adj.* —**im·put′er,** *n.*

**in** (in), *prep.* [AS.], 1. contained or enclosed by; inside: as, *in* the room. 2. wearing: as, the lady *in* red. 3. during the course of: as, done *in* a day. 4. at or near the end of: as, meet me *in* an hour. 5. perceptible to (a specified sense): as, he is *in* sight. 6. amidst; surrounded by: as, *in* a storm. 7. affected by; having: as, *in* trouble. 8. occupied by or employed at: as, *in* a search for truth, a man *in* business. 9. with regard to; as concerns: as, weak *in* faith, *in* my opinion. 10. with; by; using: as, he spoke *in* French. 11. made of: as, it was done *in* wood. 12. because of; for: as, he cried *in* pain. 13. by way of: as, do this *in* recompense. 14. belonging to: as, it is not *in* his nature. 15. into: as, come *in* the house. *In* expresses inclusion with relation to space, place, time, state, circumstances, manner, quality, a class, etc. *adv.* 1. from a point outside to one inside: as, he went *in*. 2. so as to be contained by a certain space, condition, or position: as, labor's vote put him *in*. 3. so as to be agreeing with: as, he fell *in* with our plans. 4. so as to form a part of: as, mix cream *in* the sauce. *adj.* 1. that is in power: as, the *in* group. 2. inner; inside. 3. coming or going inside; inward: as, the *in* door. *n.* 1. *usually in pl.* a person or thing that is in power or having its turn. 2. [Colloq.], special access, influence, favor, etc. *v.t.* [INNED, INNING], to enclose. —**have it in for,** [Colloq.], to hold a grudge against. —**in for,** certain to have or get (usually an unpleasant experience). —**ins and outs,** all the parts, details, and intricacies. —**in that,** because; since. —**in with,** associated with in partnership, friendship, etc.

**in-,** [< the Eng. or L. prep. *in*], a prefix used: 1. to mean *in, into, within, on, toward*, as in *infer, induct.* 2. as an intensifier in some words of Latin origin, as in *instigate.* Assimilated in words of Latin origin to *il-* before *l*, *ir-* before *r*, and *im-* before *m, p,* and *b*.

**in-,** [L. *in-*], a prefix meaning *no, not, without, non-*, as in *inhumane:* assimilated to *il-* before *l*, *ir-* before *r*, and *im-* before *m, p,* and *b*.

**-in** (in), in *chemistry*, -ine.

**In,** in *chemistry*, indium.

**in.,** [*pl.* IN., INS.], inch; inches.

**in·a·bil·i·ty** (in′ə-bil′ə-ti), *n.* a being unable; lack of ability, capacity, means, or power.,

**‡in ab·sen·ti·a** (in ab-sen′shi-ə, in əb-sen′shə), [L.], in absence; although not present.

**in·ac·ces·si·ble** (in′ək-ses′ə-b'l), *adj.* not accessible; specif., *a*) impossible to reach or enter. *b*) that cannot be seen, talked to, etc. *c*) not obtainable. —**in′ac·ces′si·bil′i·ty, in′ac·ces′si·ble·ness,** *n.* —**in′ac·ces′si·bly,** *adv.*

**in·ac·cu·ra·cy** (in-ak′yoo-rə-si), *n.* 1. lack of accuracy. 2. [*pl.* -CIES], error; mistake.

**in·ac·cu·rate** (in-ak′yoo-rit), *adj.* not accurate; not correct; not exact; in error. —**in·ac′cu·rate·ly,** *adv.* —**in·ac′cu·rate·ness,** *n.*

**in·ac·tion** (in-ak′shən), *n.* absence of action or motion; inertness or idleness.

**in·ac·ti·vate** (in-ak′tə-vāt′), *v.t.* [-VATED, -VATING], 1. to make inactive. 2. to cause (a military unit, etc.) to go out of existence; dissolve. —**in·ac′ti·va′tion** (-vā′shən), *n.*

**in·ac·tive** (in-ak′tiv), *adj.* 1. not active or moving; inert. 2. not industrious; idle. —**in·ac′tive·ly,** *adv.* —**in′ac·tiv′i·ty, in·ac′tive·ness,** *n.*

**in·ad·e·quate** (in-ad′i-kwit), *adj.* not adequate; insufficient. —**in·ad′e·qua·cy** (-kwə-si), [*pl.* -CIES], **in·ad′e·quate·ness,** *n.* —**in·ad′e·quate·ly,** *adv.*

**in·ad·mis·si·ble** (in′əd-mis′ə-b'l), *adj.* not admissible; not to be admitted, allowed, etc. —**in′ad·mis′si·bil′i·ty,** *n.* —**in′ad·mis′si·bly,** *adv.*

**in·ad·vert·ence** (in′əd-vūr′t'ns), *n.* 1. a being inadvertent. 2. an instance of this; oversight; mistake. Also **in′ad·ver′ten·cy** [*pl.* -CIES].

**in·ad·vert·ent** (in′əd-vūr′t'nt), *adj.* 1. not attentive or observant; negligent. 2. due to oversight. —**in′ad·vert′ent·ly,** *adv.*

**in·ad·vis·a·ble** (in′əd-viz′ə-b'l), *adj.* not advisable; not wise or prudent. —**in′ad·vis′a·bil′i·ty, in′ad·vis′a·ble·ness,** *n.* —**in′ad·vis′a·bly,** *adv.*

**in·al·ien·a·ble** (in-āl′yən-ə-b'l), *adj.* that cannot be taken away or transferred. —**in·al′ien·a·bil′i·ty,** *n.* —**in·al′ien·a·bly,** *adv.*

**in·am·o·ra·ta** (in-am′ə-rä′tə), *n.* [< It. < *innamorare*, to fall in love], a woman loved; one's sweetheart or mistress.

**in·ane** (in-ān′), *adj.* [L. *inanis*], 1. empty. 2. lacking sense; silly; foolish. —**in·ane′ly,** *adv.*

**in·an·i·mate** (in-an′ə-mit), *adj.* 1. not animate. 2. not animated; dull. —**in·an′i·mate·ly,** *adv.* —**in·an′i·mate·ness,** *n.*

**in·a·ni·tion** (in′ə-nish′ən), *n.* [< OFr. < LL. < L. pp. of *inanire*, to empty; see INANE], 1. emptiness. 2. exhaustion from lack of food.

**in·an·i·ty** (in-an′ə-ti), *n.* 1. a being inane; specif., *a*) emptiness. *b*) silliness. 2. [*pl.* -TIES], something inane; silly act, remark, etc.

**in·ap·pli·ca·ble** (in-ap′li-kə-b'l), *adj.* not applicable; not suitable; inappropriate. —**in′ap·pli·ca·bil′i·ty, in·ap′pli·ca·ble·ness,** *n.* —**in·ap′pli·ca·bly,** *adv.*

**in·ap·po·site** (in-ap′ə-zit), *adj.* not apposite; inappropriate. —**in·ap′po·site·ly,** *adv.*

**in·ap·pre·ci·a·ble** (in′ə-prē′shi-ə-b'l, -shə-b'l), *adj.* too small to be observed or have any value; negligible. —**in′ap·pre′ci·a·bly,** *adv.*

**in·ap·pro·pri·ate** (in′ə-prō′pri-it), *adj.* not appropriate; not suitable or proper. —**in′ap·pro′pri·ate·ly,** *adv.* —**in′ap·pro′pri·ate·ness,** *n.*

**in·apt** (in-apt′), *adj.* 1. not apt; inappropriate. 2. lacking skill or aptitude; awkward. —**in·apt′ly,** *adv.* —**in·apt′ness,** *n.*

**in·apt·i·tude** (in-ap′tə-tōōd′, -tūd′), *n.* lack of aptitude; specif., *a*) lack of suitability. *b*) lack of skill.

**in·ar·tic·u·late** (in′är-tik′yoo-lit), *adj.* 1. produced without the articulation of normal speech: as, an *inarticulate* cry. 2. *a*) unable to speak; mute. *b*) unable to speak clearly or expressively. 3. in *zoology*, without joints, hinges, etc. —**in′ar·tic′u·late·ly,** *adv.* —**in′ar·tic′u·late·ness,** *n.*

**in·ar·tis·tic** (in′är-tis′tik), *adj.* not artistic; lacking artistic taste. —**in′ar·tis′ti·cal·ly,** *adv.*

**in·as·much** (in′əz-much′), *conj.* because; since; seeing that (followed by *as*).

**in·at·ten·tion** (in′ə-ten′shən), *n.* failure to give attention or pay heed; negligence.

**in·at·ten·tive** (in′ə-ten′tiv), *adj.* not attentive; heedless; negligent. —**in′at·ten′tive·ly,** *adv.* —**in′at·ten′tive·ness,** *n.*

**in·au·di·ble** (in-ô′də-b'l), *adj.* not audible; that cannot be heard. —**in′au·di·bil′i·ty,** *n.* —**in·aud′i·bly,** *adv.*

**in·au·gu·ral** (in-ô′gyoo-rəl), *adj.* [Fr.], of an inauguration. *n.* a speech made at an inauguration.

**in·au·gu·rate** (in-ô′gyoo-rāt′), *v.t.* [-RATED, -RATING], [< L. pp. of *inaugurare*, to practice augury], 1. to induct into office with a formal ceremony. 2. to make a formal beginning of. 3. to celebrate formally the first public use of: as, to *inaugurate* a new bridge. —**in·au′gu·ra′tion,** *n.* —**in·au′gu·ra′tor** (-rā′tēr), *n.*

**in·aus·pi·cious** (in′ôs-pish′əs), *adj.* not auspicious; unfavorable; unlucky. —**in′aus·pi′cious·ly,** *adv.* —**in′aus·pi′cious·ness,** *n.*

**in·board** (in′bôrd′, -bōrd′), *adv.* & *adj.* inside the hull or bulwarks of a ship or boat. *n.* a marine motor mounted inboard.

**in·born** (in′bôrn′), *adj.* present in the organism at birth; innate; natural.

**in·bound** (in′bound′), *adj.* inward bound.

**in·bred** (in′bred′; *for* 2, *often* in′bred′), *adj.* 1. inborn; natural. 2. resulting from inbreeding.

**in·breed** (in′brēd′, in′brēd′), *v.t.* [-BRED, -BREEDING], 1. to form or develop within. 2. to breed by continual mating of individuals of the same or closely related stocks. —**in′breed′ing,** *n.*

**inc.,** 1. inclosure. 2. including. 3. inclusive. 4. incorporated: also **Inc.** 5. increase.

**In·ca** (iŋ′kə), *n.* any member of a group of Indian tribes that dominated ancient Peru until the Spanish conquest: the Incas had a highly developed civilization. —**In′can,** *adj.* & *n.*

**in·cal·cu·la·ble** (in-kal′kyoo-lə-b'l), *adj.* 1. that cannot be calculated; too great or too many to be counted. 2. too uncertain to be counted on; unpredictable. —**in′cal·cu·la·bil′i·ty** [*pl.* -TIES], **in·cal′cu·la·ble·ness,** *n.* —**in·cal′cu·la·bly,** *adv.*

**in·can·desce** (in'kən-des'), *v.i. & v.t.* [-DESCED, -DESCING], to become or make incandescent.

**in·can·des·cent** (in'kən-des''nt), *adj.* [< L.; see IN- (in) & CANDESCENT], 1. glowing with intense heat; red-hot or, especially, white-hot. 2. very bright; shining brilliantly. **—in'can·des'cence, in'can·des'cen·cy,** *n.* **—in'can·des'cent·ly,** *adv.*

**incandescent lamp,** a lamp in which the light is produced by a filament contained in a vacuum and heated to incandescence by an electric current.

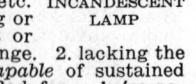

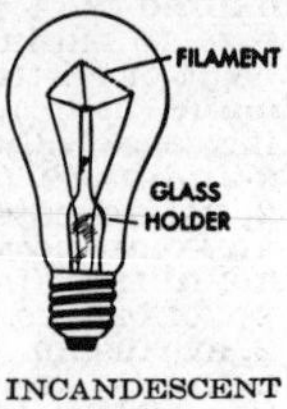

INCANDESCENT LAMP

**in·can·ta·tion** (in'kan-tā'shən), *n.* [< LL. < L. < *in-*, in + *cantare*, to chant], 1. the chanting of special words or a formula in magic spells or rites. 2. the words or formula so chanted.

**in·ca·pa·ble** (in-kā'pə-b'l), *adj.* not capable; lacking the necessary ability, competence, qualifications, etc. **—incapable of,** 1. not allowing or admitting; not able to accept or experience: as, *incapable* of change. 2. lacking the ability or fitness for: as, *incapable* of sustained thought. 3. not legally qualified for. **—in'ca·pa·bil'i·ty, in·ca'pa·ble·ness,** *n.* **—in·ca'pa·bly,** *adv.*

**in·ca·pac·i·tate** (in'kə-pas'ə-tāt'), *v.t.* [-TATED, -TATING], 1. to make unable or unfit; esp., to make incapable of normal activity; disable. 2. in *law*, to disqualify. **—in'ca·pac'i·ta'tion,** *n.*

**in·ca·pac·i·ty** (in'kə-pas'ə-ti), *n.* [*pl.* -TIES], 1. lack of capacity, power, or fitness; disability. 2. legal ineligibility.

**in·car·cer·ate** (in-kär'sə-rāt'), *v.t.* [-ATED, -ATING], [< ML. pp. of *incarcerare* < L. *in*, in + *carcer*, prison], 1. to imprison; jail. 2. to confine. **—in·car'cer·a'tion,** *n.* **—in·car'cer·a'tor** (-rā'tēr), *n.*

**in·car·na·dine** (in-kär'nə-dīn', -din), *adj.* [< Fr. < It. *incarnatino* < LL; see INCARNATE], 1. flesh-colored; pink. 2. red; esp., blood-red. *n.* the color of either flesh or blood. *v.t.* [-DINED, -DINING], to make incarnadine.

**in·car·nate** (in-kär'nit; *also, and for v. always,* -nāt), *adj.* [< LL. *incarnatus* < L. *in-*, in + *caro*, flesh], endowed with a human body; personified: as, he is evil *incarnate*. *v.t.* [-NATED, -NATING], 1. to give bodily form to; embody. 2. to give concrete form to. 3. to be the type or embodiment of.

**in·car·na·tion** (in'kär-nā'shən), *n.* 1. endowment with a human body. 2. [I-], the taking on of human form and nature by Jesus as the Son of God. 3. any person or animal serving as the embodiment of a god or spirit. 4. any person or thing serving as the embodiment of a quality or concept.

**in·case** (in-kās'), *v.t.* [-CASED, -CASING], to encase. **—in·case'ment,** *n.*

**in·cau·tion** (in-kô'shən), *n.* lack of caution.

**in·cau·tious** (in-kô'shəs), *adj.* not cautious; not careful or prudent; reckless; rash. **—in·cau'tious·ly,** *adv.* **—in·cau'tious·ness,** *n.*

**in·cen·di·ar·y** (in-sen'di-er'i), *adj.* [< L. < *incendium*, a fire < *incendere;* see INCENSE (to anger)], 1. having to do with the willful destruction of property by fire. 2. designed to cause fires, as certain bombs. 3. willfully stirring up strife, riot, etc. *n.* [*pl.* -IES], 1. one who willfully destroys property by fire. 2. one who willfully stirs up strife, riot, etc. 3. an incendiary bomb, substance, etc. **—in·cen'di·a·rism** (-ə-riz'm), *n.*

**in·cense** (in'sens), *n.* [< OFr. < LL. < L. pp. of *incendere;* see INCENSE (to anger)], 1. any substance burned to produce a pleasant odor. 2. the smoke or fragrance from such a substance. 3. any pleasant odor. 4. pleasing attention, praise, or admiration. *v.t.* [-CENSED, -CENSING], 1. to make fragrant as with incense. 2. to burn or offer incense to. *v.i.* to burn incense. **—in'cense·like',** *adj.*

**in·cense** (in-sens'), *v.t.* [-CENSED, -CENSING], [< OFr. < L. pp. of *incendere*, to set on fire < *in-*, in + *candere*, to glow], to make very angry; fill with wrath; enrage. **—in·cense'ment,** *n.*

**in·cen·tive** (in-sen'tiv), *adj.* [< L. *incentivus* < *in-*, on + *canere*, to sing], stimulating to action; encouraging; motivating. *n.* a stimulus; encouragement; motive.

**in·cep·tion** (in-sep'shən), *n.* [< L. < pp. of *incipere;* see INCIPIENT], a beginning; start; commencement.

**in·cep·tive** (in-sep'tiv), *adj.* [< OFr. < L. pp. of *incipere;* see INCIPIENT], 1. beginning; introductory. 2. in *grammar*, expressing the beginning of an action. *n.* an inceptive verb. **—in·cep'tive·ly,** *adv.*

**in·cer·ti·tude** (in-sũr'tə-tōōd', -tūd'), *n.* [Fr. < ML. < L. *incertus*, uncertain], an uncertain state of mind; doubt.

**in·ces·sant** (in-ses''nt), *adj.* [Fr. < LL. < L. *in-*, not + ppr. of *cessare*, to cease], never ceasing; continuing or repeated without interruption; constant. **—in·ces'san·cy,** *n.* **—in·ces'sant·ly,** *adv.*

**in·cest** (in'sest), *n.* [< L. < *in-*, not + *castus*, chaste], sexual intercourse between persons too closely related to marry legally.

**in·ces·tu·ous** (in-ses'chōō-əs), *adj.* 1. guilty of incest. 2. involving incest. **—in·ces'tu·ous·ly,** *adv.* **—in·ces'tu·ous·ness,** *n.*

**inch** (inch), *n.* [AS. *ynce* < L. *uncia*, twelfth part], 1. a measure of length, equal to 1/12 foot: symbol," (e.g., 10"). 2. a fall (of rain, snow, etc.) that would cover a surface to the depth of one inch. 3. a very small amount, degree, or distance. *v.t. & v.i.* to move by degrees; move very slowly. **—by inches,** gradually; slowly: also **inch by inch. —every inch,** in all respects; thoroughly. **—within an inch of,** not far from; very near. **—within an inch of one's life,** almost to one's death.

**inch·meal** (inch'mēl'), *adv.* [*inch* + *meal*], gradually; inch by inch: also **by inchmeal.**

**in·cho·ate** (in-kō'it, in'kō-āt'), *adj.* [< L. pp. of *inchoare, incohare*, to begin], just begun; in the early stages; rudimentary. **—in·cho'ate·ly,** *adv.* **—in·cho'ate·ness,** *n.*

**in·cho·a·tive** (in-kō'ə-tiv, in'kō-ā'-), *adj.* in *grammar*, inceptive; expressing the beginning of an action. *n.* an inceptive verb.

**inch·worm** (inch'wũrm'), *n.* a measuring worm.

**in·ci·dence** (in'si-dəns), *n.* 1. the act, fact, or manner of falling upon or influencing. 2. the degree or range of occurrence or effect; extent of influence. See also **angle of incidence.**

**in·ci·dent** (in'si-dənt), *adj.* [Fr. < L. *incidens*, ppr. < *in-*, on + *cadere*, to fall], 1. likely to happen in connection with; attendant on: as, the cares *incident* to leadership. 2. falling upon or affecting: as, *incident* rays. *n.* 1. something that happens; event; occurrence. 2. a minor event or episode, especially one in a novel, play, etc.

**in·ci·den·tal** (in'si-den't'l), *adj.* 1. happening or likely to happen in connection with something more important; casual. 2. secondary or minor. *n.* 1. something incidental. 2. *pl.* miscellaneous items.

**in·ci·den·tal·ly** (in'si-den't'l-i), *adv.* 1. in an incidental manner; accidentally. 2. by the way.

**in·cin·er·ate** (in-sin'ə-rāt'), *v.t. & v.i.* [-ATED, -ATING], [< ML. pp. of *incinerare* < L. *in*, to + *cinis*, ashes], to burn to ashes; burn up; cremate. **—in·cin'er·a'tion,** *n.*

**in·cin·er·a·tor** (in-sin'ə-rā'tēr), *n.* one that incinerates; specif., a furnace for burning trash.

**in·cip·i·ent** (in-sip'i-ənt), *adj.* [< L. ppr. of *incipere*, to begin < *in-*, on + *capere*, to take], just beginning to exist or to come into notice: as, an *incipient* tumor. **—in·cip'i·ence, in·cip'i·en·cy,** *n.* **—in·cip'i·ent·ly,** *adv.*

**in·cise** (in-sīz'), *v.t.* [-CISED, -CISING], [< Fr. < L. *incisus*, pp. < *in-*, into + *caedere*, to cut], 1. to cut into with a sharp tool. 2. to engrave; carve. **—in·cised',** *adj.*

**in·ci·sion** (in-sizh'ən), *n.* 1. an incising. 2. a result of incising; cut. 3. incisive quality. 4. in *surgery*, a cut made into a tissue or organ.

**in·ci·sive** (in-sī'siv), *adj.* 1. cutting into. 2. sharp; keen; piercing; acute: as, an *incisive* mind. **—in·ci'sive·ly,** *adv.* **—in·ci'sive·ness,** *n.*

**in·ci·sor** (in-sī'zēr), *n.* any of the front cutting teeth between the canines in either jaw.

**in·ci·ta·tion** (in'sī-tā'shən, in'si-), *n.* an inciting.

**in·cite** (in-sīt'), *v.t.* [-CITED, -CITING], [< Fr. < L. < *in-*, in, on + *citare*, to urge], to urge to action; stimulate; rouse. **—in·cite'ment,** *n.* **—in·cit'er,** *n.* **—in·cit'ing·ly,** *adv.*

**in·ci·vil·i·ty** (in'si-vil'ə-ti), *n.* [*pl.* -TIES], 1. a lack of civility or politeness; rudeness. 2. a rude or discourteous act.

**incl.,** 1. inclosure. 2. including. 3. inclusive.

**in·clem·ent** (in-klem'ənt), *adj.* [< L.; see IN (not) & CLEMENT], 1. rough; severe; stormy. 2. lacking mercy or leniency; harsh. **—in·clem'en·cy** [*pl.* -CIES], *n.* **—in·clem'ent·ly,** *adv.*

**in·cli·na·tion** (in'klə-nā'shən), *n.* 1. an inclining, bending, or sloping. 2. bend; slope. 3. the extent or degree of incline from the horizontal or vertical. 4. the angle made by two lines or planes. 5. *a*) a particular bent of mind; tendency. *b*) a liking or preference. **—in'cli·na'tion·al,** *adj.*

**in·cline** (in-klīn'), *v.i.* [-CLINED, -CLINING], [< OFr. < L. < *in-*, on + *clinare*, to lean], 1. to lean; slope; slant. 2. to bow the body or head. 3. to have a tendency. 4. to have a preference or liking. *v.t.* 1. to cause to lean, slope, etc. 2. to make willing; influence. *n.* (in'klīn, in-klīn'), an inclined plane or surface; slope; grade. **—incline one's ear,** to listen willingly. **—in·cli'na·ble,** *adj.* **—in·clined',** *adj.* **—in·clin'er,** *n.*

**inclined plane,** any plane surface set at an angle against a horizontal surface; sloping plane.

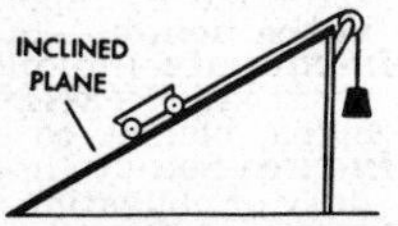

INCLINED PLANE

**in·cli·nom·e·ter** (in'kli-nom'ə-tẽr), *n.* [< *incline* + *-meter*], an instrument for indicating an airplane's angle of inclination from the horizontal.

**in·close** (in-klōz'), *v.t.* [-CLOSED, -CLOSING], to enclose.

**in·clo·sure** (in-klō'zhẽr), *n.* enclosure.

**in·clude** (in-klōōd'), *v.t.* [-CLUDED, -CLUDING], [< L. < *in-*, in + *claudere*, to close], 1. to enclose; shut up or in. 2. to have as part of a whole; contain; comprise. 3. to take into account; put in a total, category, etc. —**in·clud'a·ble, in·clud'i·ble,** *adj.*

**in·clu·sion** (in-klōō'zhən), *n.* 1. an including or being included. 2. something included.

**in·clu·sive** (in-klōō'siv), *adj.* 1. including or tending to include; esp., taking everything into account. 2. including the terms, limits, or extremes mentioned: as, the first to the tenth *inclusive.* —**inclusive of,** including. —**in·clu'sive·ly,** *adv.* —**in·clu'sive·ness,** *n.*

**in·cog** (in-kog'), *adj., adv., n.* [Colloq.], incognito.

**in·cog·ni·to** (in-kog'ni-tō', in'kəg-nē'tō), *adv.* & *adj.* [It. < L. < *in-*, not + *cognitus*, pp., known], with true identity unrevealed or disguised; under an assumed name, rank, etc. *n.* [*pl.* -TOS], 1. a person who is incognito. 2. *a*) the state of being incognito. *b*) the disguise assumed.

**in·co·her·ence** (in'kō-hêr'əns), *n.* 1. a being incoherent. 2. incoherent speech, thought, etc. Also **in'co·her'en·cy** [*pl.* -CIES].

**in·co·her·ent** (in'kō-hêr'ənt), *adj.* not coherent; specif., *a*) lacking cohesion; not sticking together. *b*) not logically connected; disjointed. *c*) characterized by incoherent speech, thought, etc. —**in'co·her'ent·ly,** *adv.*

**in·com·bus·ti·ble** (in'kəm-bus'tə-b'l), *adj.* not combustible; that cannot be burned. *n.* an incombustible substance. —**in'com·bus'ti·bil'i·ty, in'com·bus'ti·ble·ness,** *n.* —**in'com·bus'ti·bly,** *adv.*

**in·come** (in'kum), *n.* the money or other gain periodically received by an individual, corporation, etc., for labor or services, or from property, investments, etc.

**income tax,** a tax on income or on that part of income which exceeds a certain amount.

**in·com·ing** (in'kum'iŋ), *adj.* coming in or about to come in. *n.* 1. a coming in. 2. what comes in.

**in·com·men·su·ra·ble** (in'kə-men'shoor-ə-b'l, -sẽr-ə-b'l), *adj.* 1. not commensurable; that cannot be measured or compared by the same standard or measure. 2. not worthy of comparison. 3. having no common divisor. *n.* an incommensurable thing, quantity, etc. —**in'com·men'su·ra·bil'i·ty, in'com·men'su·ra·ble·ness,** *n.* —**in'com·men'su·ra·bly,** *adv.*

**in·com·men·su·rate** (in'kə-men'shoor-it, -sẽr-it), *adj.* not commensurate; specif., *a*) not equal in measure or size. *b*) not proportionate; not adequate. *c*) incommensurable (sense 1). —**in'com·men'su·rate·ly,** *adv.* —**in'com·men'su·rate·ness,** *n.*

**in·com·mode** (in'kə-mōd'), *v.t.* [-MODED, -MODING], [< Fr. < L. < *in-*, not + *commodus*, convenient], to inconvenience; put out; bother.

**in·com·mo·di·ous** (in'kə-mō'di-əs), *adj.* 1. causing inconvenience; uncomfortable. 2. inconveniently small, narrow, etc. —**in'com·mo'di·ous·ly,** *adv.* —**in'com·mo'di·ous·ness,** *n.*

**in·com·mu·ni·ca·ble** (in'kə-mū'ni-kə-b'l), *adj.* that cannot be communicated or told. —**in'com·mu'ni·ca·bil'i·ty, in'com·mu'ni·ca·ble·ness,** *n.* —**in'com·mu'ni·ca·bly,** *adv.*

**in·com·mu·ni·ca·do** (in'kə-mū'ni-kä'dō), *adj.* [Sp.], unable or not allowed to communicate: as, the prisoners were held *incommunicado.*

**in·com·pa·ra·ble** (in-kom'pẽr-ə-b'l, -prə-b'l), *adj.* that cannot be compared; specif., *a*) having no basis of comparison; incommensurable. *b*) beyond comparison; unequalled; matchless: as, *incomparable* skill. —**in·com'pa·ra·bil'i·ty, in·com'pa·ra·ble·ness,** *n.* —**in·com'pa·ra·bly,** *adv.*

**in·com·pat·i·ble** (in'kəm-pat'ə-b'l), *adj.* not compatible; specif., *a*) unable to live together harmoniously. *b*) not suitable for being used together. *n.* *usually in pl.* an incompatible person or thing. —**in'com·pat'i·bil'i·ty** [*pl.* -TIES], **in'com·pat'i·ble·ness,** *n.* —**in'com·pat'i·bly,** *adv.*

**in·com·pe·tent** (in-kom'pə-tənt), *adj.* 1. without adequate ability, knowledge, fitness, etc. 2. not legally qualified. *n.* an incompetent person; esp., one who is mentally deficient. —**in·com'pe·tence, in·com'pe·ten·cy,** *n.* —**in·com'pe·tent·ly,** *adv.*

**in·com·plete** (in'kəm-plēt'), *adj.* 1. lacking a part or parts. 2. unfinished; not concluded. 3. not perfect; not thorough. —**in'com·plete'ly,** *adv.* —**in'com·plete'ness, in'com·ple'tion,** *n.*

**in·com·pre·hen·si·ble** (in'kom-pri-hen'sə-b'l), *adj.* 1. not comprehensible; that cannot be understood. 2. [Archaic], illimitable. —**in'com·pre·hen'si·bil'i·ty, in'com·pre·hen'si·ble·ness,** *n.* —**in'com·pre·hen'si·bly,** *adv.*

**in·com·press·i·ble** (in'kəm-pres'ə-b'l), *adj.* that cannot be compressed. —**in'com·press'i·bil'i·ty,** *n.*

**in·con·ceiv·a·ble** (in'kən-sēv'ə-b'l), *adj.* that cannot be conceived; that cannot be thought of, imagined, etc. —**in'con·ceiv'a·bil'i·ty, in'con·ceiv'a·ble·ness,** *n.* —**in'con·ceiv'a·bly,** *adv.*

**in·con·clu·sive** (in'kən-klōō'siv), *adj.* not conclusive; not decisive; ineffective. —**in'con·clu'sive·ly,** *adv.* —**in'con·clu'sive·ness,** *n.*

**in·con·gru·i·ty** (in'kən-grōō'ə-ti), *n.* 1. a being incongruous; specif., *a*) lack of harmony or agreement. *b*) lack of fitness or appropriateness. 2. [*pl.* -TIES], something incongruous.

**in·con·gru·ous** (in-koŋ'grōō-əs), *adj.* not congruous; not congruent; specif., *a*) lacking harmony or agreement. *b*) having inharmonious parts, elements, etc. *c*) unsuitable; inappropriate. —**in·con'gru·ous·ly,** *adv.* —**in·con'gru·ous·ness,** *n.*

**in·con·se·quent** (in-kon'si-kwent', -kwənt), *adj.* not consequent; specif., *a*) not following as a result. *b*) not following as a logical inference; irrelevant. *c*) not proceeding in logical sequence. —**in·con'se·quence,** *n.* —**in·con'se·quent·ly,** *adv.*

**in·con·se·quen·tial** (in'kon-si-kwen'shəl), *adj.* 1. inconsequent; illogical. 2. of no consequence; unimportant. *n.* something inconsequential. —**in·con'se·quen'ti·al'i·ty** (-shi-al'ə-ti), *n.* —**in'con·se·quen'tial·ly,** *adv.*

**in·con·sid·er·a·ble** (in'kən-sid'ẽr-ə-b'l), *adj.* not worth consideration; trivial; small. —**in'con·sid'er·a·ble·ness,** *n.* —**in'con·sid'er·a·bly,** *adv.*

**in·con·sid·er·ate** (in'kən-sid'ẽr-it), *adj.* 1. insufficiently considered. 2. without thought or consideration for others; thoughtless. —**in'con·sid'er·ate·ly,** *adv.* —**in'con·sid'er·ate·ness, in'con·sid'er·a'tion,** *n.*

**in·con·sist·en·cy** (in'kən-sis'tən-si), *n.* 1. the quality or state of being inconsistent. 2. [*pl.* -CIES], an inconsistent act, remark, etc.

**in·con·sist·ent** (in'kən-sis'tənt), *adj.* not consistent; specif., *a*) lacking agreement in kind, nature, form, etc.; not in harmony or accord. *b*) not uniform; self-contradictory: as, an *inconsistent* narrative. *c*) not holding to the same principles or practice; changeable: as, *inconsistent* behavior. —**in'con·sist'ent·ly,** *adv.*

**in·con·sol·a·ble** (in'kən-sōl'ə-b'l), *adj.* that cannot be consoled. —**in'con·sol'a·bil'i·ty, in'con·sol'a·ble·ness,** *n.* —**in'con·sol'a·bly,** *adv.*

**in·con·so·nant** (in-kon'sə-nənt), *adj.* not consonant; not in harmony or agreement. —**in·con'so·nance,** *n.* —**in·con'so·nant·ly,** *adv.*

**in·con·spic·u·ous** (in'kən-spik'ū-əs), *adj.* not conspicuous; attracting little attention. —**in'con·spic'u·ous·ly,** *adv.* —**in'con·spic'u·ous·ness,** *n.*

**in·con·stant** (in-kon'stənt), *adj.* not constant; changeable; specif., *a*) not remaining firm in mind or purpose. *b*) fickle. *c*) irregular. —**in·con'stan·cy,** *n.* —**in·con'stant·ly,** *adv.*

**in·con·test·a·ble** (in'kən-tes'tə-b'l), *adj.* not to be contested; unquestionable. —**in'con·test'a·bil'i·ty, in'con·test'a·ble·ness,** *n.* —**in'con·test'a·bly,** *adv.*

**in·con·ti·nent** (in-kon'tə-nənt), *adj.* [< OFr. < L.; see IN- (not) & CONTINENT], 1. without self-restraint, especially in regard to sexual activity. 2. incapable of containing, holding, etc. —**in·con'ti·nence,** *n.* —**in·con'ti·nent·ly,** *adv.*

**in·con·tro·vert·i·ble** (in'kon-trə-vũr'tə-b'l), *adj.* not to be controverted; not disputable; undeniable. —**in'con·tro·vert'i·bil'i·ty, in'con·tro·vert'i·ble·ness,** *n.* —**in'con·tro·vert'i·bly,** *adv.*

**in·con·ven·ience** (in'kən-vēn'yəns), *n.* 1. a being inconvenient; lack of comfort, ease, etc. 2. anything inconvenient. *v.t.* [-IENCED, -IENCING], to cause inconvenience to; trouble; bother.

**in·con·ven·ient** (in'kən-vēn'yənt), *adj.* not convenient; not favorable to one's comfort; causing trouble, bother, etc. —**in'con·ven'ient·ly,** *adv.*

**in·con·vert·i·ble** (in'kən-vũr'tə-b'l), *adj.* that cannot be converted; that cannot be changed or ex-

changed. **—in′con·vert′i·bil′i·ty, in′con·vert′i·ble·ness,** *n.* **—in′con·vert′i·bly,** *adv.*
**in·cor·po·rate** (in-kôr′pẽr-it; *for v.*, -pə-rāt′), *adj.* [< LL.; see IN- (in) & CORPORATE], 1. combined into one body or unit. 2. incorporated. *v.t.* [-RATED, -RATING], 1. to combine with something already formed; embody. 2. to bring together into a single whole; merge. 3. to admit into association as a member. 4. to form into a corporation. 5. to give material form to. *v.i.* to unite into one group or substance; form a corporation. **—in·cor′po·ra′tive,** *adj.* **—in·cor′po·ra′tor,** *n.*
**in·cor·po·rat·ed** (in-kôr′pə-rāt′id), *adj.* 1. combined; united. 2. organized as a legal corporation.
**in·cor·po·ra·tion** (in-kôr′pə-rā′shən), *n.* 1. an incorporating or being incorporated. 2. a corporation.
**in·cor·po·re·al** (in′kôr-pôr′i-əl, -pō′ri-), *adj.* 1. without material body or substance. 2. of spirits or angels. **—in′cor·po′re·al·ly,** *adv.*
**in·cor·rect** (in′kə-rekt′), *adj.* not correct; specif., *a*) improper. *b*) untrue; inaccurate; wrong; faulty. **—in′cor·rect′ly,** *adv.* **—in′cor·rect′ness,** *n.*
**in·cor·ri·gi·ble** (in-kôr′i-jə-b′l, -kor′-), *adj.* not corrigible; that cannot be corrected, improved, or reformed, especially because firmly set, as a habit, or set in bad habits, as a child. *n.* an incorrigible person. **—in·cor′ri·gi·bil′i·ty, in·cor′ri·gi·ble·ness,** *n.* **—in·cor′ri·gi·bly,** *adv.*
**in·cor·rupt** (in′kə-rupt′), *adj.* not corrupt; sound, uncontaminated, pure, upright, honest, etc.
**in·cor·rupt·i·ble** (in′kə-rup′tə-b′l), *adj.* that cannot be corrupted; specif., *a*) that cannot be bribed. *b*) not liable to decay or destruction. **—in′cor·rupt′i·bil′i·ty, in′cor·rupt′i·ble·ness,** *n.* **—in′cor·rupt′i·bly,** *adv.*
**incr.,** 1. increase. 2. increased. 3. increasing.
**in·crease** (in-krēs′; *for n.*, in′krēs), *v.i.* [-CREASED, -CREASING], [< OFr. < L. < *in-*, in + *crescere*, to grow], 1. to become greater in size, amount, etc.; grow. 2. to become greater in numbers by producing offspring: multiply. *v.t.* to cause to become greater in size, amount, etc. *n.* 1. an increasing or becoming increased; multiplication, as of offspring. 2. the result or amount of an increasing. **—on the increase,** increasing. **—in·creas′a·ble,** *adj.* **—in·creas′er,** *n.*
**in·creas·ing·ly** (in-krēs′iŋ-li), *adv.* more and more; to an ever-increasing degree.
**in·cred·i·ble** (in-kred′ə-b′l), *adj.* not credible; unbelievable; seeming too unusual or improbable to be possible. **—in·cred′i·bil′i·ty, in·cred′i·ble·ness,** *n.* **—in·cred′i·bly,** *adv.*
**in·cre·du·li·ty** (in′krə-dōō′lə-ti, -dū′-), *n.* unwillingness or inability to believe; doubt.
**in·cred·u·lous** (in-krej′oo-ləs), *adj.* 1. not credulous; unwilling or unable to believe; doubting. 2. showing doubt or disbelief. **—in·cred′u·lous·ly,** *adv.* **—in·cred′u·lous·ness,** *n.*
**in·cre·ment** (in′krə-mənt, iŋ′-), *n.* [< L. *incrementum* < *increscere;* see INCREASE], 1. a becoming greater or larger; increase; gain. 2. amount of increase. **—in′cre·men′tal,** *adj.*
**in·crim·i·nate** (in-krim′ə-nāt′), *v.t.* [-NATED, -NATING], [< ML.; see IN- (in) & CRIMINATE], 1. to charge with a crime; accuse. 2. to involve in, or make appear guilty of, a crime or fault. **—in·crim′i·na′tion,** *n.* **—in·crim′i·na′tor,** *n.* **—in·crim′i·na·to′ry** (-nə-tôr′i, -tō′ri), *adj.*
**in·crust** (in-krust′), *v.t.* to cover as with a crust, or hard outer layer. *v.i.* to form, or form into, a crust. Also **encrust. —in′crus·ta′tion,** *n.*
**in·cu·bate** (in′kyoo-bāt′, iŋ′-), *v.t.* [-BATED, -BATING], [< L. *incubatus*, pp. < *in-*, on + *cubare*, to lie], 1. to sit on and hatch (eggs). 2. to keep (eggs, embryos, etc.) in a favorable environment for hatching or developing. *v.i.* to go through the process of incubation.
**in·cu·ba·tion** (in′kyoo-bā′shən, iŋ′-), *n.* 1. an incubating or being incubated. 2. the phase in the development of a disease between the infection and the first appearance of symptoms. **—in′cu·ba′tion·al,** *adj.* **—in′cu·ba′tive,** *adj.*
**in·cu·ba·tor** (in′kyoo-bā′tẽr, iŋ′-), *n.* a person or thing that incubates; specif., *a*) an artificially heated container for hatching eggs. *b*) a similar apparatus in which premature babies are kept for a period. *c*) an apparatus for developing bacterial cultures.
**in·cu·bus** (in′kyoo-bəs, iŋ′-), *n.* [*pl.* -BUSES, -BI (-bī′)], [LL., nightmare (in ML., a demon) < L.; see INCUBATE], 1. a spirit or demon thought in medieval times to lie with sleeping women. 2. a nightmare. 3. anything oppressive; burden.
**in·cul·cate** (in-kul′kāt, in′kul-kāt′), *v.t.* [-CATED, -CATING], [< L. *inculcatus*, pp. < *in-*, in + *calcare*, to trample underfoot < *calx*, heel], to impress upon the mind by repetition or insistent urging. **—in′cul·ca′tion,** *n.* **—in·cul′ca·tor,** *n.*
**in·cul·pate** (in-kul′pāt, in′kul-pāt′), *v.t.* [-PATED, -PATING], [< ML. *inculpatus*, pp. < L. *in*, on + *culpa*, blame], to incriminate. **—in′cul·pa′tion,** *n.*
**in·cum·ben·cy** (in-kum′bən-si), *n.* [*pl.* -CIES], 1. a duty or obligation. 2. *a*) the holding and administering of a position. *b*) term of office.
**in·cum·bent** (in-kum′bənt), *adj.* [< L. *incumbens*, ppr. < *in-*, on + *cubare*, to lie down], lying, resting, or pressing with its weight on something else. *n.* the holder of a benefice or office. **—incumbent on (or upon),** resting upon as a duty or obligation. **—in·cum′bent·ly,** *adv.*
**in·cum·ber** (in-kum′bẽr), *v.t.* to encumber.
**in·cum·brance** (in-kum′brəns), *n.* encumbrance.
**in·cu·nab·u·la** (in′kyoo-nab′yoo-lə), *n.pl.* [*sing.* -LUM (-ləm)], [< L. < *in-*, in + *cunabula*, neut. pl., a cradle], 1. the very first stages of anything; beginnings. 2. early printed books; esp., books printed before 1500. **—in′cu·nab′u·lar,** *adj.*
**in·cur** (in-kūr′), *v.t.* [-CURRED, -CURRING], [< L. < *in-*, in + *currere*, to run], to come into or meet with (something undesirable), especially through one's own actions; bring upon oneself.
**in·cur·a·ble** (in-kyoor′ə-b′l), *adj.* not curable; that cannot be remedied or corrected. *n.* a person having an incurable disease. **—in·cur′a·bil′i·ty, in·cur′a·ble·ness,** *n.* **—in·cur′a·bly,** *adv.*
**in·cu·ri·ous** (in-kyoor′i-əs), *adj.* not curious; uninterested; indifferent. **—in·cu·ri·os·i·ty** (in′kyoor-i-os′ə-ti), **in·cu′ri·ous·ness,** *n.* **—in·cu′ri·ous·ly,** *adv.*
**in·cur·sion** (in-kūr′zhən, -shən), *n.* [< L. *incursio;* see INCUR], an unfriendly entry; invasion; raid. **—in·cur′sive** (-siv), *adj.*
**in·curve** (in-kūrv′), *v.t. & v.i.* to curve inward. *n.* (in′kūrv′), 1. an incurving. 2. in *baseball*, a pitched ball that curves toward the batter. Also, *for n.*, **in-curve.**
**in·cus** (iŋ′kəs), *n.* [*pl.* INCUDES (in-kū′dēz)], [L., anvil], the central one of the three small bones in the middle ear: also called *anvil.*
**Ind.,** 1. India. 2. Indian. 3. Indiana. 4. Indies.
**ind.,** 1. independent. 2. index. 3. industrial.
**in·debt·ed** (in-det′id), *adj.* 1. in debt. 2. obliged; owing gratitude.
**in·debt·ed·ness** (in-det′id-nis), *n.* 1. a being indebted. 2. the amount owed; all one's debts.
**in·de·cen·cy** (in-dē′s′n-si), *n.* 1. a being indecent. 2. [*pl.* -CIES], an indecent act or remark.
**in·de·cent** (in-dē′s′nt), *adj.* not decent; specif., *a*) not proper and fitting; improper. *b*) morally offensive; obscene. **—in·de′cent·ly,** *adv.*
**in·de·ci·pher·a·ble** (in′di-sī′fẽr-ə-b′l), *adj.* that cannot be deciphered; illegible. **—in′de·ci′pher·a·bil′i·ty,** *n.*
**in·de·ci·sion** (in′di-sizh′ən), *n.* inability to decide or a tendency to change the mind frequently.
**in·de·ci·sive** (in′di-sī′siv), *adj.* 1. not decisive. 2. showing indecision; hesitating or vacillating. **—in′de·ci′sive·ly,** *adv.* **—in′de·ci′sive·ness,** *n.*
**in·de·clin·a·ble** (in′di-klīn′ə-b′l), *adj.* not declinable; having no case inflections. **—in′de·clin′a·bly,** *adv.*
**in·dec·o·rous** (in-dek′ə-rəs, in′di-kôr′əs, -kō′rəs), *adj.* lacking decorum, good taste, etc. **—in·dec′o·rous·ly,** *adv.* **—in·dec′o·rous·ness,** *n.*
**in·de·co·rum** (in′di-kôr′əm, -kō′rəm), *n.* 1. lack of decorum. 2. an indecorous act, remark, etc.
**in·deed** (in-dēd′), *adv.* [see IN, *prep.* & DEED], certainly; truly; admittedly. *interj.* an exclamation of surprise, doubt, sarcasm, etc.
**indef.,** indefinite.
**in·de·fat·i·ga·ble** (in′di-fat′i-gə-b′l), *adj.* [< MFr. < L. < *in-*, not + *defatigare*, to tire out], that cannot be tired out; tireless; untiring. **—in′de·fat′i·ga·bil′i·ty, in′de·fat′i·ga·ble·ness,** *n.* **—in′de·fat′i·ga·bly,** *adv.*
**in·de·fea·si·ble** (in′di-fē′zə-b′l), *adj.* that cannot be undone or made void. **—in′de·fea′si·bil′i·ty,** *n.* **—in′de·fea′si·bly,** *adv.*
**in·de·fen·si·ble** (in′di-fen′sə-b′l), *adj.* 1. that cannot be defended. 2. that cannot be justified. **—in′de·fen′si·bil′i·ty, in′de·fen′si·ble·ness,** *n.* **—in′de·fen′si·bly,** *adv.*
**in·de·fin·a·ble** (in′di-fīn′ə-b′l), *adj.* that cannot be defined. **—in′de·fin′a·ble·ness,** *n.* **—in′de·fin′a·bly,** *adv.*
**in·def·i·nite** (in-def′ə-nit), *adj.* not definite; specif., *a*) having no exact limits. *b*) not precise in meaning; vague. *c*) not clear in outline; blurred. *d*) not certain; unsure. *e*) in *grammar*, not limiting or specifying: as, *a* and *an* are *indefinite* articles. **—in·def′i·nite·ly,** *adv.* **—in·def′i·nite·ness,** *n.*
**in·de·his·cent** (in′di-his′′nt), *adj.* not dehiscent; not

opening at maturity to discharge its seeds. —**in'de·his'cence,** *n.*

**in·del·i·ble** (in-del'ə-b'l), *adj.* [< L.; ult. < *in-*, not + *delere*, to destroy], 1. that cannot be erased, washed out, etc.; permanent. 2. leaving an indelible mark: as, *indelible* ink. —**in'del·i·bil'i·ty,** *n.* —**in·del'i·bly,** *adv.*

**in·del·i·ca·cy** (in-del'i-kə-si), *n.* 1. a being indelicate. 2. [*pl.* -CIES], something indelicate.

**in·del·i·cate** (in-del'i-kit), *adj.* not delicate; coarse; esp., lacking propriety or modesty. —**in·del'i·cate·ly,** *adv.* —**in·del'i·cate·ness,** *n.*

**in·dem·ni·fy** (in-dem'nə-fī'), *v.t.* [-FIED, -FYING], [< L. *indemnis*, unhurt < *in-*, not + *damnum*, hurt; + *-fy*], 1. to protect against loss, damage, etc.; insure. 2. *a*) to repay for loss or damage; reimburse. *b*) to make good (a loss). —**in·dem'ni·fi·ca'tion,** *n.* —**in·dem'ni·fi'er,** *n.*

**in·dem·ni·ty** (in-dem'nə-ti), *n.* [*pl.* -TIES], 1. protection or insurance against loss, damage, etc. 2. legal exemption from penalties incurred by one's actions. 3. repayment for loss, damage, etc.

**in·dent** (in-dent'; *for n., usually* in'dent), *v.t.* [< OFr. < ML. < L. *in*, in + *dens*, tooth], 1. *a*) to cut toothlike points into (an edge or border); notch. b) to make jagged in outline. 2. to indenture. 3. to space (the beginning of a paragraph, etc.) in from the regular margin. *v.i.* 1. to form or be marked by notches, points, or a jagged border. 2. to enter into an indenture, or contract. 3. to space in from the margin. *n.* 1. a notch or cut in an edge. 2. an indenture. 3. an indented line, paragraph, etc. —**in·dent'er,** *n.*

**in·dent** (in-dent'; *for n.*, in'dent), *v.t.* [*in-* (in) + *dent*], 1. to make a dent in. 2. to apply (a mark, etc.) with pressure; stamp in. *n.* a dent.

**in·den·ta·tion** (in'den-tā'shən), *n.* 1. an indenting or being indented. 2. a notch or cut. 3. a dent. 4. an indention; space in from the margin.

**in·den·tion** (in-den'shən), *n.* 1. a spacing in from the margin. 2. an empty or blank space left by this. 3. *a*) a dent. *b*) the making of a dent.

**in·den·ture** (in-den'chẽr), *n.* 1. indentation. 2. a written contract or agreement. 3. *usually pl.* a contract binding one person to work for another, as an apprentice to a master. *v.t.* [-TURED, -TURING], 1. to bind by indenture. 2. to indent.

**In·de·pend·ence** (in'di-pen'dəns), *n.* a city in W Missouri: pop., 62,000: see **Santa Fe Trail.**

**in·de·pend·ence** (in'di-pen'dəns), *n.* 1. a being independent; freedom from the control of another. 2. an income sufficient for a livelihood.

**Independence Day,** the Fourth of July, the anniversary of the adoption of the Declaration of Independence on July 4, 1776.

**in·de·pend·en·cy** (in'di-pen'dən-si), *n.* [*pl.* -CIES], 1. independence. 2. an independent state.

**in·de·pend·ent** (in'di-pen'dənt), *adj.* 1. free from the influence or control of others; specif., *a*) free from the rule of another; self-governing. *b*) free from persuasion or bias; self-determined, self-reliant, etc. *c*) not connected with any political party: as, an *independent* voter. *d*) not connected with others; separate: as, an *independent* grocer. 2. *a*) not depending on another for financial support. *b*) designating, of, or having an income large enough to enable one to live without working. 3. [I-], of or having to do with the Independents. *n.* one who is independent in thinking, action, etc.; specif. [often I-], a person not an adherent of any political party. —**independent of,** apart from; regardless of. —**in'de·pend'ent·ly,** *adv.*

**independent clause,** in *grammar*, a main clause.

**in·de·scrib·a·ble** (in'di-skrīb'ə-b'l), *adj.* that cannot be described; beyond the power of description. —**in'de·scrib'a·bil'i·ty,** **in'de·scrib'a·ble·ness,** *n.* —**in'de·scrib'a·bly,** *adv.*

**in·de·struct·i·ble** (in'di-struk'tə-b'l), *adj.* that cannot be destroyed. —**in'de·struct'i·bil'i·ty, in'de·struct'i·ble·ness,** *n.* —**in'de·struct'i·bly,** *adv.*

**in·de·ter·mi·na·ble** (in'di-tũr'mi-nə-b'l), *adj.* not determinable; specif., *a*) that cannot be decided. *b*) that cannot be ascertained. —**in'de·ter'mi·na·ble·ness,** *n.* —**in'de·ter'mi·na·bly,** *adv.*

**in·de·ter·mi·nate** (in'di-tũr'mə-nit), *adj.* not determinate; specif., *a*) having inexact limits; indefinite; vague. *b*) unsettled; inconclusive. —**in'de·ter'mi·nate·ly,** *adv.* —**in'de·ter'mi·nate·ness,** *n.*

**in·de·ter·mi·na·tion** (in'di-tũr'mə-nā'shən), *n.* 1. a being indeterminate. 2. lack of determination.

**in·dex** (in'deks), *n.* [*pl.* -DEXES, -DICES (-də-sēz')], [L. < *indicare;* see INDICATE], 1. the forefinger: also **index finger.** 2. a pointer, as the needle on a dial. 3. an indication or sign: as, performance is an *index* of ability. 4. *a*) an alphabetical list of names, subjects, etc. together with page numbers, usually placed at the end of a publication. *b*) a catalogue: as, a library *index*. 5. the relation or proportion of one amount or dimension to another. 6. [I-], in the *R.C. Church*, a list of books forbidden to be read. 7. in *mathematics*, an exponent. 8. in *printing*, a sign (☞) calling special attention to certain information. *v.t.* 1. *a*) to make an index of or for. *b*) to include in an index. 2. to indicate. —**in'dex·er,** *n.*

**In·di·a** (in'di-ə), *n.* 1. a large peninsula of S Asia, between the Bay of Bengal and the Arabian Sea: it was partitioned in 1947 into the states of India (see sense 2), Pakistan, and several smaller unaffiliated states. 2. a republic in the British Commonwealth of Nations in central and southern India: area, 1,260,000 sq. mi.; pop., 357,000,000; capital, New Delhi.

**India ink,** 1. a black pigment of lampblack mixed with a gelatinous substance, used in writing, painting, etc. 2. a liquid ink made from this.

**In·di·a·man** (in'di-ə-mən), *n.* [*pl.* -MEN], formerly, a merchant ship traveling regularly between England and India.

**In·di·an** (in'di-ən), *adj.* 1. of India or the East Indies, their people, or culture. 2. of the American aboriginal races (**American Indians**) or their culture. 3. of a type used or made by Indians. *n.* 1. a native of India or the East Indies. 2. a member of any of the aboriginal races of North America, South America, or the West Indies. 3. any of the languages spoken by the American Indians.

**In·di·an·a** (in'di-an'ə), *n.* a Middle Western State of the U.S.: area, 36,291 sq. mi.; pop., 4,662,000; capital, Indianapolis: abbrev. **Ind.** —**In'di·an'i·an,** *adj. & n.*

**In·di·an·ap·o·lis** (in'di-ən-ap''l-is), *n.* the capital of Indiana, in the central part of the State: pop., 476,000.

**Indian club,** a wooden or metallic club shaped like a tenpin, swung in the hand for exercise.

**Indian corn,** 1. a kind of grain that grows in kernels on large ears. 2. its ears. 3. its seeds, or kernels. Also called *maize* or *corn*.

**Indian file,** single file.

**Indian giver,** [Colloq.], a person who gives something and then asks for it back.

**Indian meal,** corn meal.

**Indian Ocean,** an ocean south of Asia, between Africa and Australia.

**Indian pipe,** a leafless wild herb with one waxy, pipe-shaped flower on each stem.

**Indian pudding,** a pudding containing chiefly corn meal, milk, and molasses.

**Indian summer,** a period of mild, warm, hazy weather following the first frosts of late autumn.

**Indian tobacco,** a hardy weed with spikes of light-blue flowers, growing in the northwestern U.S.

**India paper,** 1. a thin, absorbent paper used in taking prints from engraved plates. 2. a thin, tough, opaque printing paper used for Bibles, etc.

**India rubber, india rubber,** natural rubber; esp., crude rubber obtained from latex. —**In'di·a-rub'ber,** *adj.*

**In·dic** (in'dik), *adj.* 1. of India. 2. designating or of a branch of the Indo-European languages, including many of the languages of India.

**indic.,** indicative.

**in·di·cate** (in'də-kāt'), *v.t.* [-CATED, -CATING], [< L. < *in-*, in + *dicare*, to declare], 1. to direct attention to; point out. 2. to be or give a sign of; signify: as, thunder *indicates* a storm. 3. to show the need for; make necessary. 4. to show or point out as a cause, treatment, or outcome: said of a disease. 5. to express briefly or generally.

**in·di·ca·tion** (in'də-kā'shən), *n.* 1. an indicating. 2. something that indicates. 3. the amount or degree registered by an indicator.

**in·dic·a·tive** (in-dik'ə-tiv), *adj.* 1. giving an indication or intimation; signifying. 2. designating or of that mood of a verb used to express an act, state, or occurrence as actual, or to ask a question of fact. *n.* 1. the indicative mood. 2. a verb in this mood. —**in·dic'a·tive·ly,** *adv.*

**in·di·ca·tor** (in'də-kā'tẽr), *n.* 1. a person or thing that indicates; specif., any device, as a gauge, dial, pointer, etc., that measures something. 2. any substance used to indicate by change of color the acidity or alkalinity of a solution, the beginning or end of a chemical reaction, etc. —**in·di·ca·to·ry** (in′di-kə-tôr′i, -tō′ri), *adj.*

**in·di·ces** (in′də-sēz′), *n.* alt. pl. of **index.**

**in·dict** (in-dīt′), *v.t.* [< Anglo-Fr. & OFr. *enditer,* to inform; ult. < L. *in,* against + *dictare;* see DICTATE], to charge with the commission of a crime; esp., to make formal accusation against on the basis of positive legal evidence. —**in·dict′a·ble,** *adj.* —**in·dict′er, in·dict′or,** *n.*

**in·dict·ment** (in-dīt′mənt), *n.* 1. an indicting or being indicted. 2. a charge; specif., a formal accusation charging someone with a crime, presented by a grand jury to the court.

**In·dies** (in′dēz), *n.pl.* 1. the East Indies. 2. the East Indies, India, and Indochina. 3. the West Indies.

**in·dif·fer·ence** (in-dif′ēr-əns, -dif′rəns), *n.* a being indifferent; specif., *a*) lack of concern or interest. *b*) lack of importance or meaning.

**in·dif·fer·ent** (in-dif′ēr-ənt, -dif′rənt), *adj.* 1. having or showing no preference; neutral. 2. having or showing no interest, concern, etc.; uninterested. 3. of no importance. 4. not particularly good or bad, large or small, etc.; fair. 5. not particularly good. 6. inactive; neutral in quality, as a chemical or magnet. —**in·dif′fer·ent·ly,** *adv.*

**in·di·gence** (in′di-jəns), *n.* poverty.

**in·dig·e·nous** (in-dij′ə-nəs), *adj.* [< LL. < L. *indigena* < OL. *indu,* in + L. *gignere,* to be born], 1. born, growing, or produced naturally in a region or country; native. 2. innate; inherent. —**in·dig′e·nous·ly,** *adv.* —**in·dig′e·nous·ness,** *n.*

**in·di·gent** (in′di-jənt), *adj.* [Fr. < L. ppr. of *indigere,* to be in need < OL. *indu,* in + *egere,* to need], poor; needy. —**in′di·gent·ly,** *adv.*

**in·di·gest·i·ble** (in′də-jes′tə-b′l), *adj.* not digestible; not easily digested. —**in′di·gest′i·bil′i·ty, in′di·gest′i·ble·ness,** *n.* —**in′di·gest′i·bly,** *adv.*

**in·di·ges·tion** (in′də-jes′chən), *n.* inability to digest, or difficulty in digesting, food.

**in·dig·nant** (in-dig′nənt), *adj.* [< L. *indignans,* ppr.; ult. < *in-,* not + *dignus,* worthy], feeling or expressing anger or scorn, especially at unjust or mean action. —**in·dig′nant·ly,** *adv.*

**in·dig·na·tion** (in′dig-nā′shən), *n.* anger or scorn resulting from injustice or meanness.

**in·dig·ni·ty** (in-dig′nə-ti), *n.* [*pl.* -TIES], something that humiliates, insults, or injures the dignity or self-respect; an affront.

**in·di·go** (in′di-gō′), *n.* [*pl.* -GOS, -GOES], [< Sp. < L. *indicum* < Gr. < *Indikos,* Indian], 1. a blue dye obtained from certain plants or made synthetically. 2. a plant of the pea family that yields indigo. 3. a deep violet-blue: also **indigo blue.** *adj.* of this color: also **in′di·go′-blue′.**

**indigo bunting** (or **bird**), a small finch native to the eastern U.S.: the male is indigo-blue, the female brown.

**in·di·rect** (in′də-rekt′), *adj.* not direct; specif., *a*) not straight; roundabout. *b*) not straight to the point or object: as, an *indirect* reply. *c*) not straightforward; dishonest: as, *indirect* dealing. *d*) not immediate; secondary: as, an *indirect* result. —**in′di·rect′ly,** *adv.* —**in′di·rect′ness,** *n.*

**indirect discourse,** statement of what a person said, without quoting his exact words (e.g., *she said that she could not go*).

**in·di·rec·tion** (in′də-rek′shən), *n.* 1. roundabout act, procedure, or means. 2. deceit; dishonesty.

**indirect lighting,** lighting reflected, as from a ceiling, or diffused so as to avoid glare.

**indirect object,** in *grammar,* the person or thing indirectly affected by the action of the verb, i.e., the one to which something is given or for which something is done (e.g., *us* in *give us time*).

**indirect tax,** a tax on manufactured goods, imports, etc. that is paid indirectly by the consumer because it is added to the price.

**in·dis·cern·i·ble** (in′di-zũr′nə-b′l, -sũr′-), *adj.* that cannot be discerned; imperceptible. —**in′dis·cern′i·ble·ness,** *n.* —**in′dis·cern′i·bly,** *adv.*

**in·dis·creet** (in′dis-krēt′), *adj.* not discreet; lacking prudence; unwise. —**in′dis·creet′ly,** *adv.* —**in′dis·creet′ness,** *n.*

**in·dis·cre·tion** (in′dis-kresh′ən), *n.* 1. lack of discretion. 2. an indiscreet act or remark.

**in·dis·crim·i·nate** (in′dis-krim′ə-nit), *adj.* 1. confused; random. 2. not discriminating; making no distinctions. —**in′dis·crim′i·nate·ly,** *adv.* —**in′dis·crim′i·nate·ness, in′dis·crim′i·na′tion,** *n.*

**in·dis·pen·sa·ble** (in′dis-pen′sə-b′l), *adj.* not dispensable; absolutely necessary. *n.* an indispensable person or thing. —**in′dis·pen′sa·bil′i·ty, in′dis·pen′sa·ble·ness,** *n.* —**in′dis·pen′sa·bly,** *adv.*

**in·dis·pose** (in′dis-pōz′), *v.t.* 1. to make unfit or unable. 2. to dispose against; make unwilling or disinclined. 3. to make slightly ill.

**in·dis·posed** (in′dis-pōzd′), *adj.* 1. slightly ill. 2. unwilling; disinclined.

**in·dis·po·si·tion** (in′dis-pə-zish′ən), *n.* the condition of being indisposed; specif., *a*) slight illness. *b*) unwillingness; disinclination.

**in·dis·pu·ta·ble** (in′dis-pū′tə-b′l, in-dis′pyoo-), *adj.* that cannot be disputed or doubted; unquestionable. —**in′dis·pu′ta·bil′i·ty, in′dis·pu′ta·ble·ness,** *n.* —**in′dis·pu′ta·bly,** *adv.*

**in·dis·sol·u·ble** (in′di-sol′yoo-b′l), *adj.* that cannot be dissolved, decomposed, or destroyed; firm; lasting. —**in′dis·sol′u·bil′i·ty, in′dis·sol′u·ble·ness,** *n.* —**in′dis·sol′u·bly,** *adv.*

**in·dis·tinct** (in′di-stiŋkt′), *adj.* not distinct; specif., *a*) not seen or heard clearly; obscure. *b*) not separate or separable; not plainly defined. —**in′dis·tinct′ly,** *adv.* —**in′dis·tinct′ness,** *n.*

**in·dis·tin·guish·a·ble** (in′di-stiŋ′gwish-ə-b′l), *adj.* that cannot be distinguished; imperceptible. —**in′dis·tin′guish·a·ble·ness,** *n.* —**in′dis·tin′guish·a·bly,** *adv.*

**in·dite** (in-dīt′), *v.t.* [-DITED, -DITING], [see INDICT], to put in writing; compose and write. —**in·dite′ment,** *n.* —**in·dit′er,** *n.*

**in·di·um** (in′di-əm), *n.* [Mod. L. < L. *indicum,* indigo: from its spectrum], a rare metallic chemical element, soft, ductile, and silver-white: symbol, In; at. wt., 114.76; at. no., 49.

**in·di·vid·u·al** (in′də-vij′o͞o-əl), *adj.* [< ML. < L. *individuus,* not divisible], 1. existing as a separate thing or being; single; particular. 2. of, for, or by a single person or thing. 3. of or characteristic of a single person or thing. 4. of a peculiar or striking character: as, an *individual* style. *n.* 1. a single thing or being. 2. a person.

**in·di·vid·u·al·ism** (in′də-vij′o͞o-əl-iz′m), *n.* 1. the leading of one's life in one's own way without regard for others. 2. individuality. 3. the doctrine that individual freedom in economic enterprise should not be restricted. 4. the doctrine that the state exists for the individual and not the individual for the state. 5. egoism.

**in·di·vid·u·al·ist** (in′də-vij′o͞o-əl-ist), *n.* a person who practices or believes in individualism. —**in′di·vid′u·al·is′tic,** *adj.*

**in·di·vid·u·al·i·ty** (in′də-vij′o͞o-al′ə-ti), *n.* [*pl.* -TIES], 1. the sum of the characteristics that set one person or thing apart from others; individual character. 2. the condition of existing as an individual. 3. an individual.

**in·di·vid·u·al·ize** (in′də-vij′o͞o-ə-līz′), *v.t.* [-IZED, -IZING], 1. to make individual; mark as different from other persons or things. 2. to consider individually; particularize. —**in′di·vid′u·al·i·za′tion,** *n.* —**in′di·vid′u·al·iz′er,** *n.*

**in·di·vid·u·al·ly** (in′də-vij′o͞o-əl-i), *adv.* 1. as individuals; one at a time. 2. showing individual characteristics; distinctively.

**in·di·vis·i·ble** (in′də-viz′ə-b′l), *adj.* 1. that cannot be divided. 2. in *mathematics,* that cannot be divided without leaving a remainder. *n.* anything indivisible. —**in′di·vis′i·bil′i·ty, in′di·vis′i·ble·ness,** *n.* —**in′di·vis′i·bly,** *adv.*

**In·do·chi·na, In·do-Chi·na** (in′dō-chī′nə), *n.* 1. the peninsula in SE Asia, including Malaya, Thailand, Burma, North Vietnam, South Vietnam, Laos, and Cambodia. 2. a former region in this peninsula including Vietnam, Laos, and Cambodia.

**In·do·chi·nese, In·do-Chi·nese** (in′dō-chī-nēz′), *adj.* 1. of Indochina, its Mongoloid people, or their culture. 2. Sino-Tibetan: now seldom used.

**in·doc·tri·nate** (in-dok′tri-nāt′), *v.t.* [-NATED, -NATING], [< ML. *in-,* in + pp. of *doctrinare,* to instruct], 1. to instruct in doctrines, principles, theories, or beliefs. 2. to instruct; teach. —**in·doc′tri·na′tion,** *n.* —**in·doc′tri·na′tor,** *n.*

**In·do-Eu·ro·pe·an** (in′dō-yoor′ə-pē′ən), *adj.* designating or of a family of languages that includes most of those spoken in Europe and many of those spoken in SW Asia and India. *n.* this family of languages: its branches include Indic, Hellenic, Italic, Germanic, and Slavic.

**In·do-Ger·man·ic** (in′dō-jẽr-man′ik), *adj.* & *n.* Indo-European.

**In·do-I·ra·ni·an** (in′dō-ī-rā′ni-ən), *adj.* designating or of the Indic and Iranian branches of the Indo-European family of languages as spoken or formerly spoken in India, Afghanistan, Iran, etc.

**in·do·lent** (in′də-lənt), *adj.* [Fr. < LL. < L. *in-,* not + *dolens,* ppr. of *dolere,* to feel pain], disliking or avoiding work; idle; lazy. —**in′do·lence,** *n.* —**in′do·lent·ly,** *adv.*

**in·dom·i·ta·ble** (in-dom′i-tə-b′l), *adj.* [< LL. < L. < *in-,* not + *domitus* < *domere,* to tame], not easily

discouraged or defeated; unyielding. —**in·dom′i·ta·ble·ness,** *n.* —**in·dom′i·ta·bly,** *adv.*
**In·do·ne·si·a** (in′dō-nē′zhə, -shə), *n.* 1. the Malay Archipelago; East Indies. 2. a republic in the Malay Archipelago, consisting of Java, Sumatra, Celebes, Borneo, and other islands: area, 735,268 sq. mi.; pop., 92,600,000; capital, Jakarta: formerly the Netherlands Indies.
**In·do·ne·sian** (in′dō-nē′zhən, -shən), *adj.* 1. of Indonesia, its people, etc. 2. designating or of a large group of Austronesian languages spoken in Indonesia, the Philippines, Java, etc. *n.* 1. a member of a light-brown, non-Malay race of Indonesia, the Philippines, Java, etc. 2. an inhabitant of Indonesia. 3. the Indonesian languages.
**in·door** (in′dôr′, -dōr′), *adj.* 1. of the inside of a house or building. 2. living, belonging, etc. in a house or building.
**indoor baseball,** softball.
**in·doors** (in′dôrz′, -dōrz′), *adv.* in or into a house or building.
**in·dorse** (in-dôrs′), *v.t.* [-DORSED, -DORSING], to endorse. —**in·dors′a·ble,** *adj.* —**in·dor′see′,** *n.* —**in·dorse′ment,** *n.* —**in·dors′er,** *n.*
**In·dra** (in′drə), *n.* [Sans.], the chief god of the early Hindu religion.
**in·du·bi·ta·ble** (in-do͞o′bi-tə-b'l, in-dū′-), *adj.* that cannot be doubted; unquestionable. —**in·du′bi·ta·ble·ness,** *n.* —**in·du′bi·ta·bly,** *adv.*
**in·duce** (in-do͞os′, -dūs′), *v.t.* [-DUCED, -DUCING], [< L. < *in-*, in + *ducere*, to lead], 1. to lead on to some action, condition, etc.; persuade. 2. to bring on: as, indigestion is *induced* by overeating. 3. to draw (a general rule or conclusion) from particular facts. 4. in *physics*, to bring about (an electric or magnetic effect) in a body by exposing it to the influence of a field of force. —**in·duc′er,** *n.* —**in·duc′i·ble,** *adj.*
**in·duce·ment** (in-do͞os′mənt, in-dūs′-), *n.* 1. an inducing or being induced. 2. anything that induces; motive; incentive.
**in·duct** (in-dukt′), *v.t.* [< L. pp. of *inducere;* see INDUCE], 1. to bring in; introduce. 2. to place formally in an official position. 3. *a*) to initiate into a society. *b*) to bring formally into the armed forces.
**in·duct·ance** (in-duk′təns), *n.* 1. the property of an electric circuit by which a varying current in it induces voltages in the same circuit or in a near-by circuit. 2. a circuit, condenser, etc. having inductance.
**in·duct·ee** (in-duk′tē′), *n.* a person inducted or being inducted.
**in·duc·tile** (in-duk′t'l), *adj.* not ductile, malleable, or pliant. —**in′duc·til′i·ty,** *n.*
**in·duc·tion** (in-duk′shən), *n.* 1. an inducting or being inducted; installation. 2. *a*) reasoning from particular facts to a general conclusion. *b*) the conclusion so reached. 3. in *physics*, the act or process by which an electric or magnetic effect is produced in an electrical conductor or magnetizable body when it is exposed to the influence or variation of a field of force.
**induction coil,** a coiled apparatus made up of two coupled circuits: interruptions in the direct current in one circuit produce an alternating current of high potential in the other.
**in·duc·tive** (in-duk′tiv), *adj.* 1. inducing; persuasive. 2. of or using logical induction: as, *inductive* reasoning. 3. produced by induction. 4. of inductance or electrical or magnetic induction. —**in·duc′tive·ly,** *adv.* —**in·duc′tive·ness,** *n.*
**in·duc·tiv·i·ty** (in′duk-tiv′ə-ti), *n.* 1. inductance (sense 1). 2. [*pl.* -TIES], specific inductive capacity.
**in·duc·tor** (in-duk′tẽr), *n.* a person or thing that inducts; specif., a part of an electrical apparatus acting, or acted upon, by induction.
**in·due** (in-do͞o′, -dū′), *v.t.* [-DUED, -DUING], to endue.
**in·dulge** (in-dulj′), *v.t.* [-DULGED, -DULGING], [< L. *indulgere*, to be kind to], 1. to satisfy (a desire). 2. to gratify the wishes of; humor. *v.i.* to give way to one's desires; indulge oneself (*in* something). —**in·dulg′er,** *n.* —**in·dulg′ing·ly,** *adv.*
**in·dul·gence** (in-dul′jəns), *n.* 1. an indulging or being indulgent. 2. what is indulged in. 3. a giving way to one's own desires. 4. a favor or privilege. 5. in the *R.C. Church*, a remission of temporal or purgatorial punishment still due for a sin after the guilt has been forgiven.
**in·dul·gent** (in-dul′jənt), *adj.* indulging or inclined to indulge; kind or lenient, often to excess. —**in·dul′gent·ly,** *adv.*
**in·du·rate** (in′doo-rāt′, in′dyoo-), *v.t. & v.i.* [-RATED, -RATING], [< L.; ult. < *in-*, in + *durus*, hard], 1. to harden. 2. to make or become callous or unfeeling. *adj.* 1. hardened. 2. callous or unfeeling. —**in′du·ra′tion,** *n.* —**in′du·ra′tive,** *adj.*
**In·dus** (in′dəs), *n.* a river in NW India, flowing into the Arabian Sea: length, 2,000 mi.
**in·dus·tri·al** (in-dus′tri-əl), *adj.* 1. having the nature of or characterized by industries. 2. of, connected with, or resulting from industries. 3. working in industries. 4. of or concerned with people working in industries. 5. for use by industries: said of products. *n.* a person working in an industry. —**in·dus′tri·al·ly,** *adv.*
**industrial arts,** the technical arts used in industry, especially as a subject for study in schools.
**in·dus·tri·al·ism** (in-dus′tri-əl-iz'm), *n.* social and economic organization characterized by large industries, machine production, concentration of workers in cities, etc.
**in·dus·tri·al·ist** (in-dus′tri-əl-ist), *n.* one who owns or manages an industrial enterprise.
**in·dus·tri·al·ize** (in-dus′tri-əl-īz′), *v.t.* [-IZED, -IZING], 1. to develop industrialism in. 2. to organize as an industry. —**in·dus′tri·al·i·za′tion,** *n.*
**industrial relations,** relations between employers and employees.
**industrial union,** a labor union to which all the workers in a given industry can belong, no matter what their occupation or trade: cf. *craft union:* also called *vertical union.*
**in·dus·tri·ous** (in-dus′tri-əs), *adj.* characterized by earnest, steady effort; hard-working. —**in·dus′tri·ous·ly,** *adv.* —**in·dus′tri·ous·ness,** *n.*
**in·dus·try** (in′dəs-tri), *n.* [*pl.* -TRIES], [< Fr. < L. *industria* < *industrius*, active], 1. earnest, steady effort; diligence in work. 2. systematic work. 3. any branch of trade, production, or manufacture, or all of these collectively. 4. the owners and managers of industry.
**in·dwell** (in′dwel′), *v.i. & v.t.* [-DWELT, -DWELLING], to dwell (in); reside within. —**in′dwell′er,** *n.*
**-ine** (īn, in, ēn), [< Fr. < L. *-inus*], a suffix meaning *of, having the nature of, like,* as in *divine, marine, crystalline.*
**-ine** (in, īn, ēn), [< L. < Gr. *-inē*], a suffix used to form feminine nouns, as in *heroine.*
**-ine** (in), [Fr. < L. *-ina*], a suffix used to form certain abstract nouns, as in *medicine, doctrine.*
**-ine** (ēn, in, īn), [arbitrary use of L. *-inus*], a suffix used to form the chemical names of *a*) *halogens,* as in *iodine. b*) *alkaloids or nitrogen bases,* as in *morphine:* also **-in.**
**in·e·bri·ate** (in-ē′bri-āt′; *for adj. & n., usually* -it), *v.t.* [-ATED, -ATING], [< L.; ult. < *in-*, intens. + *ebrius*, drunk], 1. to make drunk; intoxicate. 2. to excite; exhilarate. *adj.* drunk; intoxicated. *n.* a drunken person, especially a habitual drunkard. —**in·e′bri·at′ed,** *adj.* —**in·e′bri·a′tion,** *n.*
**in·e·bri·e·ty** (in′i-brī′ə-ti), *n.* drunkenness.
**in·ed·i·ble** (in-ed′ə-b'l), *adj.* not edible; not fit to be eaten. —**in′ed·i·bil′i·ty,** *n.*
**in·ef·fa·ble** (in-ef′ə-b'l), *adj.* [< L. < *in-*, not + *effabilis*, utterable < *ex-*, out + *fari*, to speak], 1. too overwhelming to be expressed in words; inexpressible. 2. too sacred to be spoken. —**in′ef·fa·bil′i·ty, in·ef′fa·ble·ness,** *n.* —**in·ef′fa·bly,** *adv.*
**in·ef·face·a·ble** (in′i-fās′ə-b'l), *adj.* that cannot be effaced; impossible to wipe out. —**in′ef·face′a·bil′i·ty,** *n.* —**in′ef·face′a·bly,** *adv.*
**in·ef·fec·tive** (in′ə-fek′tiv), *adj.* 1. not effective; not producing the desired effect. 2. not capable of performing satisfactorily; incompetent. —**in′ef·fec′tive·ly,** *adv.* —**in′ef·fec′tive·ness,** *n.*
**in·ef·fec·tu·al** (in′ə-fek′cho͞o-əl), *adj.* not effectual; not producing or not able to produce the desired effect. —**in′ef·fec′tu·al′i·ty, in′ef·fec′tu·al·ness,** *n.* —**in′ef·fec′tu·al·ly,** *adv.*
**in·ef·fi·ca·cious** (in′ef-i-kā′shəs), *adj.* not efficacious; unable to produce the desired effect: said of medicines, etc. —**in′ef·fi·ca′cious·ly,** *adv.* —**in′ef·fi·ca′cious·ness,** *n.*
**in·ef·fi·ca·cy** (in-ef′i-kə-si), *n.* lack of efficacy; inability to produce the desired effect.
**in·ef·fi·cient** (in′ə-fish′ənt), *adj.* not efficient; specif., *a*) not producing the desired effect with a minimum use of energy, time, etc. *b*) lacking the necessary ability; incapable. —**in′ef·fi′cien·cy,** *n.* —**in′ef·fi′cient·ly,** *adv.*
**in·e·las·tic** (in′i-las′tik), *adj.* not elastic; inflexible, rigid, unyielding, unadaptable, etc. —**in′e·las·tic′i·ty** (-tis′ə-ti), *n.*

**in·el·e·gance** (in-el′ə-gəns), *n.* 1. lack of elegance; quality of being inelegant. 2. something inelegant. Also **in·el′e·gan·cy** [*pl.* -CIES].

**in·el·e·gant** (in-el′ə-gənt), *adj.* not elegant; lacking refinement, good taste, grace, etc.; coarse; crude. —**in·el′e·gant·ly,** *adv.*

**in·el·i·gi·ble** (in-el′i-jə-b'l), *adj.* not eligible; not qualified, as for office. *n.* a person who is ineligible. —**in·el′i·gi·bil′i·ty,** *n.* —**in·el′i·gi·bly,** *adv.*

**in·e·luc·ta·ble** (in′i-luk′tə-b'l), *adj.* [< L. < *in-*, not + *eluctabilis*, resistible < *eluctari*, to struggle], not to be avoided or escaped; inevitable. —**in′e·luc′ta·bil′i·ty,** *n.* —**in′e·luc′ta·bly,** *adv.*

**in·ept** (in-ept′), *adj.* [< Fr. < L. < *in-*, not + *aptus*, fit], 1. unsuitable; unfit. 2. foolish; absurd. 3. awkward; clumsy —**in·ept′ly,** *adv.* —**in·ept′ness,** *n.*

**in·ept·i·tude** (in-ep′tə-to͞od′, -tūd′), *n.* 1. a being inept. 2. an inept act, remark, etc.

**in·e·qual·i·ty** (in′i-kwäl′ə-ti, -kwôl′-), *n.* [*pl.* -TIES], 1. a being unequal; lack of equality. 2. an instance of this; specif., *a*) variation in size, amount, quality, etc. *b*) unevenness in surface. *c*) lack of proper proportion; unequal distribution. 3. in *mathematics*, *a*) the relation between two unequal quantities. *b*) an expression of this.

**in·eq·ui·ta·ble** (in-ek′wi-tə-b'l), *adj.* not equitable; unfair; unjust. —**in·eq′ui·ta·bly,** *adv.*

**in·eq·ui·ty** (in-ek′wi-ti), *n.* [*pl.* -TIES], (a) lack of equity or justice; unfairness.

**in·e·rad·i·ca·ble** (in′i-rad′i-kə-b'l), *adj.* that cannot be eradicated, or rooted out. —**in′e·rad′i·ca·ble·ness,** *n.* —**in′e·rad′i·ca·bly,** *adv.*

**in·ert** (in-ũrt′), *adj.* [< L. < *in-*, not + *ars*, skill], 1. without power to move or to resist an opposing force. 2. inactive; dull; slow. 3. with few or no active properties, as some ingredients of a medicine. —**in·ert′ly,** *adv.* —**in·ert′ness,** *n.*

**in·er·tia** (in-ũr′shə), *n.* [see INERT], 1. in *physics*, the tendency of matter to remain at rest (or to keep moving in the same direction) unless affected by some outside force. 2. a tendency to remain in a fixed condition without change. —**in·er′tial,** *adj.*

**in·es·cap·a·ble** (in′ə-skāp′ə-b'l), *adj.* that cannot be escaped; unavoidable; inevitable.

**in·es·ti·ma·ble** (in-es′ti-mə-b'l), *adj.* too great or valuable to be properly measured or estimated. —**in·es′ti·ma·bly,** *adv.*

**in·ev·i·ta·ble** (in-ev′i-tə-b'l), *adj.* [< L. *in-*, not + *evitabilis*, avoidable], that cannot be avoided; certain to happen. —**in′ev·i·ta·bil′i·ty, in·ev′i·ta·ble·ness,** *n.* —**in·ev′i·ta·bly,** *adv.*

**in·ex·act** (in′ig-zakt′), *adj.* not exact; not accurate. —**in′ex·act′ly,** *adv.* —**in′ex·act′ness,** *n.*

**in·ex·cus·a·ble** (in′ik-skūz′ə-b'l), *adj.* that cannot or should not be excused; unjustifiable. —**in′ex·cus′a·bil′i·ty,** *n.* —**in′ex·cus′a·bly,** *adv.*

**in·ex·haust·i·ble** (in′ig-zôs′tə-b'l), *adj.* that cannot be exhausted; specif., *a*) that cannot be used up or emptied. *b*) tireless. —**in′ex·haust′i·bil′i·ty,** *n.* —**in′ex·haust′i·bly,** *adv.*

**in·ex·o·ra·ble** (in-ek′sẽr-ə-b'l), *adj.* [< L. < *in-*, not + *exorare*, to move by entreaty], that cannot be influenced by persuasion or entreaty; unrelenting. —**in·ex′o·ra·bil′i·ty, in·ex′o·ra·ble·ness,** *n.* —**in·ex′o·ra·bly,** *adv.*

**in·ex·pe·di·ent** (in′ik-spē′di-ənt), *adj.* not expedient; not suitable or practicable; unwise. —**in′ex·pe′di·en·cy** [*pl.* -CIES], **in′ex·pe′di·ence,** *n.* —**in′ex·pe′di·ent·ly,** *adv.*

**in·ex·pen·sive** (in′ik-spen′siv), *adj.* not expensive; costing relatively little; cheap. —**in′ex·pen′sive·ly,** *adv.* —**in′ex·pen′sive·ness,** *n.*

**in·ex·pe·ri·ence** (in′ik-spêr′i-əns), *n.* lack of experience or of the knowledge or skill resulting from experience. —**in′ex·pe′ri·enced,** *adj.*

**in·ex·pert** (in′ik-spũrt′, in-ek′spẽrt), *adj.* not expert; unskillful; amateurish. —**in′ex·pert′ly,** *adv.* —**in′ex·pert′ness,** *n.*

**in·ex·pi·a·ble** (in-ek′spi-ə-b'l), *adj.* that cannot be expiated or atoned for: as, an *inexpiable* sin. —**in·ex′pi·a·ble·ness,** *n.* —**in·ex′pi·a·bly,** *adv.*

**in·ex·pli·ca·ble** (in-eks′pli-kə-b'l, in′ik-splik′ə-), *adj.* not explicable; that cannot be explained or understood. —**in·ex′pli·ca·bil′i·ty, in·ex′pli·ca·ble·ness,** *n.* —**in·ex′pli·ca·bly,** *adv.*

**in·ex·press·i·ble** (in′iks-pres′ə-b'l), *adj.* that cannot be expressed; indescribable or unutterable. —**in′ex·press′i·bil′i·ty, in′ex·press′i·ble·ness,** *n.* —**in′ex·press′i·bly,** *adv.*

**in·ex·pres·sive** (in′iks-pres′iv), *adj.* not expressive; lacking meaning or expression. —**in′ex·pres′sive·ly,** *adv.* —**in′ex·pres′sive·ness,** *n.*

**in·ex·ten·si·ble** (in′ik-sten′sə-b'l), *adj.* not extensible. —**in′ex·ten′si·bil′i·ty,** *n.*

‡**in ex·ten·so** (in ik-sten′sō), [L.], at full length.

**in·ex·tin·guish·a·ble** (in′ik-stiŋ′gwish-ə-b'l), *adj.* not extinguishable; that cannot be put out or suppressed. —**in′ex·tin′guish·a·bly,** *adv.*

‡**in ex·tre·mis** (in iks-trē′mis), [L., in extremity], at the point of death.

**in·ex·tri·ca·ble** (in-eks′tri-kə-b'l), *adj.* 1. that one cannot extricate himself from. 2. that cannot be disentangled or untied. 3. insolvable. —**in·ex′tri·ca·bil′i·ty, in·ex′tri·ca·ble·ness,** *n.* —**in·ex′tri·ca·bly,** *adv.*

**inf.,** 1. infantry: also **Inf.** 2. infinitive. 3. information. 4. *infra*, [L.], below.

**in·fal·li·ble** (in-fal′ə-b'l), *adj.* [< ML.; see IN- (not) & FALLIBLE], 1. incapable of error; never wrong. 2. not liable to fail, go wrong, etc.; reliable. 3. in the *R.C. Church*, incapable of error in setting forth doctrine on faith and morals. *n.* an infallible person or thing. —**in·fal′li·bil′i·ty, in·fal′li·ble·ness,** *n.* —**in·fal′li·bly,** *adv.*

**in·fa·mous** (in′fə-məs), *adj.* 1. having a very bad reputation; notorious; in disgrace or dishonor. 2. causing or deserving a bad reputation; scandalous. —**in′fa·mous·ly,** *adv.* —**in′fa·mous·ness,** *n.*

**in·fa·my** (in′fə-mi), *n.* [*pl.* -MIES], [< Fr. < L.; see IN- (not) & FAMOUS], 1. very bad reputation; disgrace; dishonor. 2. the quality of being infamous; great wickedness. 3. an infamous act.

**in·fan·cy** (in′fən-si), *n.* [*pl.* -CIES], 1. the state or period of being an infant; babyhood. 2. the beginning or earliest stage of anything. 3. in *law*, the state of being a minor; period before the age of legal majority, usually twenty-one.

**in·fant** (in′fənt), *n.* [< OFr. < L. < *in-*, not + *fans*, ppr. of *fari*, to speak], 1. a very young child; baby. 2. in *law*, a minor. *adj.* 1. of or for infants or infancy. 2. in a very early stage.

**in·fan·ta** (in-fan′tə), *n.* [Sp. & Port., fem. of *infante*, child], 1. any daughter of a king of Spain or Portugal. 2. the wife of an infante.

**in·fan·te** (in-fan′tā), *n.* [Sp. & Port.; see INFANT], any son of a king of Spain or Portugal, except the heir to the throne.

**in·fan·ti·cide** (in-fan′tə-sīd′), *n.* [Fr. < LL. < L. *infans*, infant + *caedere*, to kill], 1. the murder of a baby. 2. a person guilty of this. —**in·fan′ti·cid′al,** *adj.*

**in·fan·tile** (in′fən-tīl′, -til), *adj.* 1. of infants or infancy. 2. like or characteristic of an infant; babyish. 3. in the earliest stage of development.

**infantile paralysis,** poliomyelitis.

**in·fan·ti·lism** (in-fan′tə-liz'm), *n.* an abnormal state in which infantile, or childish, characteristics persist into adult life.

**in·fan·tine** (in′fən-tīn′, -tin), *adj.* infantile.

**in·fan·try** (in′fən-tri), *n.* [*pl.* -TRIES], [< Fr. < Sp. < Sp. & Port. *infante*, child, knight's page, foot soldier], foot soldiers collectively; esp., that branch of an army consisting of soldiers trained and equipped to fight on foot.

**in·fan·try·man** (in′fən-tri-mən), *n.* [*pl.* -MEN], a soldier in the infantry.

**in·fat·u·ate** (in-fach′o͞o-āt′), *v.t.* [-ATED, -ATING], [< L. pp. of *infatuare* < *in-*, intens. + *fatuus*, foolish], 1. to make foolish. 2. to inspire with unreasoning passion or attraction. *adj.* infatuated. *n.* one who is infatuated. —**in·fat′u·a′tion,** *n.*

**in·fat·u·at·ed** (in-fach′o͞o-āt′id), *adj.* 1. foolish. 2. completely carried away by unreasoning passion or attraction. —**in·fat′u·at′ed·ly,** *adv.*

**in·fect** (in-fekt′), *v.t.* [< OFr. < L. pp. of *inficere*, to stain < *in-*, in + *facere*, to make], 1. to contaminate with a disease-producing organism. 2. to cause to become diseased by bringing into contact with such an organism. 3. to imbue with one's feelings or beliefs, especially in a way considered harmful. —**in·fec′tor,** *n.*

**in·fec·tion** (in-fek′shən), *n.* 1. an infecting; specif., *a*) a causing to become diseased. *b*) an affecting with one's feelings or beliefs. 2. a being infected. 3. something resulting from an infecting; specif., a disease resulting from the presence of certain microorganisms or matter in the body. 4. anything that infects.

**in·fec·tious** (in-fek′shəs), *adj.* 1. likely to cause infection. 2. designating a disease caused by the presence in the body of certain microorganisms: it may or may not be contagious. 3. tending to spread to others: as, an *infectious* laugh. —**in·fec′tious·ly,** *adv.* —**in·fec′tious·ness,** *n.*

**in·fec·tive** (in-fek′tiv), *adj.* likely to cause infection. —**in·fec′tive·ness, in′fec·tiv′i·ty,** *n.*

**in·fe·lic·i·tous** (in′fə-lis′ə-təs), *adj.* not felicitous; specif., *a*) unhappy; unfortunate. *b*) inappropriate; unsuitable. —**in′fe·lic′i·tous·ly,** *adv.*

**in·fe·lic·i·ty** (in′fə-lis′ə-ti), *n.* 1. a being infelicitous. 2. [*pl.* -TIES], something infelicitous; inappropriate remark, action, etc.

**in·fer** (in-fũr′), *v.t.* [-FERRED, -FERRING], [< L. < *in-*, in + *ferre*, to bring], 1. to conclude by reasoning from something known or assumed. 2. to lead to as a conclusion; imply: generally regarded as a loose usage. *v.i.* to draw inferences. —**in·fer′a·ble, in·fer′ri·ble,** *adj.* —**in·fer′rer,** *n.*

**in·fer·ence** (in′fēr-əns), *n.* 1. an inferring. 2. something inferred; logical conclusion.

**in·fer·en·tial** (in′fə-ren′shəl), *adj.* of or based on inference. —**in′fer·en′tial·ly,** *adv.*

**in·fe·ri·or** (in-fêr′i-ēr, -fêr′yēr), *adj.* [< L., compar. of *inferus*, low], 1. lower in space; placed lower down. 2. lower in order, status, rank, etc. 3. lower in quality or value than (with *to*). 4. poor in quality; below average; mediocre. *n.* an inferior person or thing. —**in·fe′ri·or·ly,** *adv.*

**in·fe·ri·or·i·ty** (in-fêr′i-ôr′ə-ti, in′fêr-i-or′-), *n.* the quality or condition of being inferior.

**inferiority complex,** in *psychology*, a neurotic condition resulting from various feelings of inferiority or inadequacy, often manifested in excessive aggressiveness.

**in·fer·nal** (in-fũr′n'l), *adj.* [< OFr. < LL. *infernalis;* ult. < L. *inferus*, below], 1. *a*) of the ancient mythological world of the dead. *b*) of hell. 2. hellish; fiendish. 3. [Colloq.], hateful; outrageous. —**in′fer·nal′i·ty,** *n.* —**in·fer′nal·ly,** *adv.*

**infernal machine,** any hidden device designed to explode and cause injury or destruction.

**in·fer·no** (in-fũr′nō), *n.* [*pl.* -NOS], [It. < L.; see INFERNAL], 1. hell. 2. any place suggesting hell.

**in·fer·tile** (in-fũr′t'l), *adj.* not fertile; barren; sterile. —**in·fer·til·i·ty** (in′fēr-til′ə-ti), *n.*

**in·fest** (in-fest′), *v.t.* [< Fr. < L. < *infestus*, hostile], to overrun or swarm about in large numbers, usually so as to be harmful or bothersome. —**in′fes·ta′tion,** *n.* —**in·fest′er,** *n.*

**in·fi·del** (in′fə-d'l), *adj.* [< Fr. < L. < *in-*, not + *fidelis*, faithful], 1. *a*) not believing in religion. *b*) not believing in a certain, especially the prevailing, religion. 2. of infidels or infidelity. *n.* 1. one who does not believe in a certain, especially the prevailing, religion. 2. one who does not believe in any religion.

**in·fi·del·i·ty** (in′fə-del′ə-ti), *n.* [*pl.* -TIES], 1. lack of belief in all religion or in any one religion. 2. lack of faith, trust, or loyalty. 3. unfaithfulness of a husband or wife; adultery. 4. an unfaithful or disloyal act.

**in·field** (in′fēld′), *n.* 1. the square area enclosed by the four base lines on a baseball field. 2. the infielders collectively.

**in·field·er** (in′fēl′dēr), *n.* in *baseball*, a player whose position is in the infield; shortstop, first baseman, second baseman, or third baseman.

**in·fil·trate** (in-fil′trāt, in′fil-trāt′), *v.t. & v.i.* [-TRATED, -TRATING], 1. to filter, or cause (a fluid) to filter, through something. 2. to pass through, as in filtering; specif., in *military usage*, to pass through weak places in (the enemy's lines). *n.* something that infiltrates. —**in′fil·tra′tion,** *n.* —**in·fil′tra·tive,** *adj.*

**infin.,** infinitive.

**in·fi·nite** (in′fə-nit), *adj.* [< L.; see IN- (not) & FINITE], 1. lacking limits or bounds; endless; immeasurable. 2. very great; vast; immense. *n.* something infinite, as time. —**the Infinite (Being),** God. —**in′fi·nite·ly,** *adv.* —**in′fi·nite·ness,** *n.*

**in·fin·i·tes·i·mal** (in′fin-ə-tes′ə-m'l), *adj.* [< L. *infinitus*, infinite, after *centesimus*, hundredth], too small to be measured; minute. *n.* an infinitesimal quantity. —**in′fin·i·tes′i·mal·ly,** *adv.*

**in·fin·i·tive** (in-fin′ə-tiv), *adj.* [< LL. < L. *infinitus;* see INFINITE], in *grammar*, 1. of or connected with an infinitive. 2. not defined or limited. *n.* a form of a verb, expressing existence or action without reference to person, number, or tense: usually following *to* (as, *to go*) or another verb form (as, *let* him *go*). —**in·fin′i·tive·ly,** *adv.*

**in·fin·i·tude** (in-fin′ə-tōōd′, -tūd′), *n.* 1. a being infinite. 2. an infinite quantity or extent.

**in·fin·i·ty** (in-fin′ə-ti), *n.* [*pl.* -TIES], [< OFr. < L. *infinitas*], 1. the quality of being infinite. 2. endless or unlimited space, time, distance, etc. 3. an indefinitely large number or amount. —**to infinity,** without limit or end.

**in·firm** (in-fũrm′), *adj.* 1. not firm or strong physically; weak; feeble. 2. not firm in mind or purpose; unstable. 3. not secure or valid. —**in·firm′ly,** *adv.* —**in·firm′ness,** *n.*

**in·fir·ma·ry** (in-fũr′mə-ri), *n.* [*pl.* -RIES], a place for the care of the sick, injured, or infirm; hospital; esp., the building or room in a school, etc. that serves as a hospital.

**in·fir·mi·ty** (in-fũr′mə-ti), *n.* 1. a being infirm; feebleness; weakness. 2. [*pl.* -TIES], *a*) a physical weakness or defect. *b*) a moral weakness.

**in·fix** (in-fiks′; *for n.,* in′fiks′), *v.t.* 1. to fix or set firmly in or on. 2. to instill; teach. 3. to place (an infix) within the body of a word. *n.* in *linguistics*, an element consisting of one or more syllables placed within the body of a word to modify its meaning.

**in·flame** (in-flām′), *v.t.* [-FLAMED, -FLAMING], [< OFr. < L.; see IN- (in) & FLAME], 1. to set on fire. 2. to arouse passion, desire, or violence in. 3. to increase the intensity of (passion, desire, etc.). 4. in *medicine*, to cause inflammation in. *v.i.* 1. to become roused, excited, etc. 2. in *medicine*, to undergo inflammation. —**in·flam′er,** *n.* —**in·flam′ing·ly,** *adv*

**in·flam·ma·ble** (in-flam′ə-b'l), *adj.* 1. easily set on fire; combustible. 2. easily excited. *n.* anything inflammable. —**in·flam′ma·bil′i·ty, in·flam′ma·ble·ness,** *n.* —**in·flam′ma·bly,** *adv.*

**in·flam·ma·tion** (in′flə-mā′shən), *n.* 1. an inflaming or being inflamed. 2. in *medicine*, a diseased condition of some part of the body, characterized by redness, pain, heat, and swelling.

**in·flam·ma·to·ry** (in-flam′ə-tôr′i, -tō′ri), *adj.* 1. rousing or likely to rouse excitement, anger, violence, etc. 2. in *medicine*, of, caused by, or characterized by inflammation.

**in·flate** (in-flāt′), *v.t.* [-FLATED, -FLATING], [< L. *inflatus*, pp. < *in-*, in + *flare*, to blow], 1. to blow full or swell out with air or gas. 2. to raise in spirits; make proud. 3. to increase, as prices, beyond normal proportions. 4. to increase the amount of (currency in circulation). *v.i.* to become inflated. —**in·flat′a·ble,** *adj.* —**in·flat′er, in·fla′tor,** *n.*

**in·fla·tion** (in-flā′shən), *n.* 1. an inflating or being inflated. 2. an increase in the amount of currency in circulation or a marked expansion of credit, resulting in a fall in the value of the currency and a sharp rise in prices.

**in·fla·tion·ar·y** (in-flā′shən-er′i), *adj.* of, causing, or characterized by inflation.

**in·fla·tion·ist** (in-flā′shən-ist), *n.* a person who favors inflation.

**in·flect** (in-flekt′), *v.t.* [< L. < *in-*, in + *flectere*, to bend], 1. to turn, bend, or curve. 2. to vary the tone or pitch of (the voice). 3. to change the form of (a word) by inflection, as in conjugating or declining. —**in·flec′tive,** *adj.*

**in·flec·tion** (in-flek′shən), *n.* 1. a turn, bend, or curve. 2. a change in the tone or pitch of the voice. 3. *a*) the change of form by which some words indicate certain grammatical relationships, as number, case, gender, tense, etc. *b*) an inflected form. *c*) an inflectional element. Also sp. **in·flex′ion.**

**in·flec·tion·al** (in-flek′shən-'l), *adj.* of, having, or showing grammatical inflection: also sp. **in·flex′ion·al.**

**in·flex·i·ble** (in-flek′sə-b'l), *adj.* 1. not flexible; specif., *a*) that cannot be bent or curved; rigid. *b*) firm in mind or purpose; stubborn. 2. that cannot be changed; unalterable. —**in·flex′i·bil′i·ty, in·flex′i·ble·ness,** *n.* —**in·flex′i·bly,** *adv.*

**in·flict** (in-flikt′), *v.t.* [< L. *inflictus*, pp. < *in-*, against + *figere*, to strike], 1. to cause (pain, wounds, etc.) as by striking. 2. to impose (a punishment, chore, etc.). —**in·flict′er, in·flic′tor,** *n.* —**in·flic′tive,** *adj.*

**in·flic·tion** (in-flik′shən), *n.* 1. an inflicting. 2. something inflicted, as pain or punishment.

**in·flo·res·cence** (in′flō-res′'ns, in′flō-), *n.* [< Mod. L. < LL.; see IN- (in) & FLORESCENCE], in *botany*, 1. a flowering. 2. the arrangement of flowers on a stem or axis. 3. a single flower cluster. 4. flowers collectively. —**in′flo·res′cent,** *adj.*

**in·flow** (in′flō′), *n.* 1. a flowing in or into. 2. anything that flows in.

**in·flu·ence** (in′flōō-əns), *n.* [< OFr. < ML. < L. *influens*, ppr. < *in-*, in + *fluere*, to flow], 1. *a*) the power of persons or things to affect others. *b*) the effect of such power. 2. the power of a person or group to produce effects without the use of force or authority, based on wealth, position, ability, etc. 3. one that has influence. *v.t.* [-ENCED, -ENCING], to have influence on; affect the nature or behavior of. —**in′flu·enc·er,** *n.*

**in·flu·en·tial** (in′flōō-en′shəl), *adj.* 1. having or

exerting influence. 2. having great influence; powerful. **—in′flu·en′tial·ly,** *adv.*

**in·flu·en·za** (in′flo͞o-en′zə), *n.* [It., lit., an influence: formerly attributed to astrological influences], an acute, contagious, infectious disease, caused by a virus and characterized by inflammation of the respiratory tract, fever, muscular pain, and, often, intestinal disorders. **—in′flu·en′zal,** *adj.*

**in·flux** (in′fluks′), *n.* [Fr. < LL. *influxus,* pp. of *influere;* see INFLUENCE], 1. a flowing in or continual coming in; inflow. 2. the point where a river joins another body of water.

**in·fold** (in-fōld′), *v.t.* 1. to wrap in folds; wrap up. 2. to embrace. Also sp. **enfold.** **—in·fold′er,** *n.*

**in·form** (in-fôrm′), *v.t.* [< OFr. < L.; see IN- (in) & FORM], 1. *a*) to give form or character to. *b*) to animate. 2. to give knowledge of something to; tell. *v.i.* to give information, especially in blaming or accusing another. **—in·form′ing·ly,** *adv.*

**in·for·mal** (in-fôr′m'l), *adj.* not formal; specif., *a*) not according to fixed customs, rules, etc. *b*) casual, easy, or relaxed. *c*) not requiring formal dress. *d*) colloquial. **—in·for′mal·ly,** *adv.*

**in·for·mal·i·ty** (in′fôr-mal′ə-ti), *n.* 1. a being informal. 2. [*pl.* -TIES], an informal act.

**in·form·ant** (in-fôr′mənt), *n.* a person who gives information.

**in·for·ma·tion** (in′fẽr-mā′shən), *n.* 1. an informing or being informed; transmission of knowledge. 2. news; word; tidings. 3. knowledge acquired in any manner; facts; data; learning. 4. a person or agency answering questions as a service to others. 5. in *law,* an accusation of criminal offense by a public officer. **—in′for·ma′tion·al,** *adj.*

**in·form·a·tive** (in-fôr′mə-tiv), *adj.* giving information; instructive. **—in·form′a·tive·ly,** *adv.*

**in·form·er** (in-fôr′mẽr), *n.* one who informs; esp., one who accuses or implicates others, as for gain.

**in·fra-,** [< L. *infra,* below], a prefix meaning *below, beneath,* as in *infrared.*

**in·frac·tion** (in-frak′shən), *n.* [< L.; see IN- (in) & FRACTION], a violation of a law, pact, etc.

**in·fran·gi·ble** (in-fran′jə-b'l), *adj.* 1. that cannot be broken or separated. 2. that cannot be violated or infringed. **—in·fran′gi·bil′i·ty, in·fran′gi·ble·ness,** *n.* **—in·fran′gi·bly,** *adv.*

**in·fra·red** (in′frə-red′), *adj.* designating or of those invisible rays just beyond the red of the visible spectrum: their waves are longer than those of the spectrum colors and have a penetrating heating effect.

**in·fra·struc·ture** (in′frə-struk′chẽr), *n.* the basic installations and facilities on which the continuance and growth of a community, state, etc. depend.

**in·fre·quent** (in-frē′kwənt), *adj.* not frequent; happening seldom; rare. **—in·fre′quen·cy, in·fre′quence,** *n.* **—in·fre′quent·ly,** *adv.*

**in·fringe** (in-frinj′), *v.t.* [-FRINGED, -FRINGING], [< L. < *in-,* in + *frangere,* to break], to break (a law or agreement); violate. **—infringe on** (or **upon**), to break in on; encroach on (the rights, etc. of others). **—in·fringe′ment,** *n.* **—in·fring′er,** *n.*

**in·fu·ri·ate** (in-fyoor′i-it; *for v.,* -i-āt′), *adj.* [< ML. < L. *in-,* in + *furia,* rage], furious; very angry. *v.t.* [-ATED, -ATING], to make very angry; enrage. **—in·fu′ri·ate·ly,** *adv.* **—in·fu′ri·a′tion,** *n.*

**in·fuse** (in-fūz′), *v.t.* [-FUSED, -FUSING], [< L. *infusus,* pp. < *in-,* in + *fundere,* to pour], 1. to pour (a liquid) into or upon. 2. to instill or impart (qualities, etc.). 3. to fill; pervade; inspire. 4. to steep or soak, as tea in hot water, to extract certain qualities. **—in·fus′er,** *n.*

**in·fu·si·ble** (in-fū′zə-b'l), *adj.* that cannot be fused or melted. **—in·fu′si·bil′i·ty, in·fu′si·ble·ness,** *n.*

**in·fu·sion** (in-fū′zhən), *n.* 1. an infusing. 2. something infused. 3. the liquid extract that results when a substance is infused in water.

**in·fu·so·ri·an** (in′fyoo-sôr′i-ən, -sō′ri-ən), *n.* [from their occurrence in infusions], one of a class (*Infusoria*) of very small one-celled animals, characterized by cilia which permit free movement.

**-ing,** a suffix of various origins: 1. [AS.], used primarily to form nouns, meaning *related to, made of, descended from,* as in *farthing:* also used to form diminutives. 2. [< AS. *-ende*], used to form the present participle, as in *hearing.* 3. [AS. *-ung*], added to verbs or nouns, to form verbal nouns meaning: *a*) *the act* or *an instance of,* as in *talking.* *b*) *something produced by the action of,* as in *painting.* *c*) *something that does the action of,* as in a *covering* for her head. *d*) *material used for,* as in *carpeting.*

**in·gen·ious** (in-jēn′yəs), *adj.* [< Fr. < L. < *ingenium,* inclination < *in-,* in + *gignere,* to produce], 1. clever, resourceful, and inventive. 2. cleverly or originally made or done. **—in·gen′ious·ly,** *adv.* **—in·gen′ious·ness,** *n.*

**in·gé·nue** (an′zhi-no͞o′; Fr. an′zhā′nü′), *n.* [*pl.* -NUES (-no͞oz′; Fr. -nü′)], [< Fr. < L. *ingenuus,* ingenuous], 1. an innocent, inexperienced young woman. 2. in the *theater, a*) the role of such a character. *b*) an actress playing such a role.

**in·ge·nu·i·ty** (in′jə-no͞o′ə-ti, -nū′ə-ti), *n.* [< L. < *ingenuus,* ingenuous: associated with *ingenious*], a being ingenious; cleverness, originality, etc.

**in·gen·u·ous** (in-jen′ū-əs), *adj.* [< L. < *in-,* in + *gignere,* to produce], 1. frank; open; straightforward. 2. simple; artless; innocent; naive. **—in·gen′u·ous·ly,** *adv.* **—in·gen′u·ous·ness,** *n.*

**in·gest** (in-jest′), *v.t.* [< L. *ingestus,* pp. < *in-,* into + *gerere,* to carry], to take (food, drugs, etc.) into the body for digestion. **—in·ges′tion,** *n.* **—in·ges′tive,** *adj.*

**in·gle** (iŋ′g'l), *n.* [Scot. < Gael. *aingeal,* fire], 1. a fire or blaze. 2. a fireplace.

**in·gle·nook** (iŋ′g'l-nook′), *n.* [Chiefly Brit.], a corner by a fireplace: also **ingle nook.**

**In·gle·wood** (iŋ′g'l-wood′), *n.* a city in SW California: pop., 63,000.

**in·glo·ri·ous** (in-glôr′i-əs, in-glō′ri-), *adj.* 1. not giving or deserving glory; shameful; disgraceful. 2. without glory; not famous. **—in·glo′ri·ous·ly,** *adv.* **—in·glo′ri·ous·ness,** *n.*

**in·go·ing** (in′gō′iŋ), *adj.* going in; entering.

**in·got** (iŋ′gət), *n.* [ME. < *in,* in + *goten,* pp. of *geten,* to pour], a mass of metal cast into a bar or other convenient shape.

**in·graft** (in-graft′, -gräft′), *v.t.* to engraft. **—in·graft′er,** *n.*

**in·grained** (in-grānd′), *adj.* 1. worked into the grain; deeply imbued; firmly established. 2. inveterate; thoroughgoing: as, an *ingrained* liar.

**in·grate** (in′grāt), *n.* [< OFr. < L. < *in-,* not + *gratus,* grateful], an ungrateful person.

**in·gra·ti·ate** (in-grā′shi-āt′), *v.t.* [-ATED, -ATING], [< L. < *in,* in + *gratia,* favor], to bring (oneself) into another's favor or good graces. **—in·gra′ti·at′ing·ly,** *adv.* **—in·gra′ti·a′tion,** *n.*

**in·grat·i·tude** (in-grat′ə-to͞od′, -tūd′), *n.* lack of gratitude; ungratefulness.

**in·gre·di·ent** (in-grē′di-ənt), *n.* [< Fr. < L. ppr. of *ingredi;* see INGRESS], 1. any of the things that a mixture is made of: as, the *ingredients* of ice cream. 2. a component part of anything.

**in·gress** (in′gres), *n.* [< L. pp. of *ingredi,* to enter in < *in-,* into + *gradi,* to go], 1. the act of entering. 2. the right to enter. 3. an entrance. **—in·gres′sion** (-gresh′ən), *n.* **—in·gres′sive,** *adj.*

**in·grow·ing** (in′grō′iŋ), *adj.* growing within, inward, or into; esp., growing into the flesh.

**in·grown** (in′grōn′), *adj.* grown within, inward, or into; esp., grown into the flesh, as a toenail.

**in·gui·nal** (iŋ′gwi-n'l), *adj.* [< L. < *inguen,* the groin], of or near the groin.

**in·gulf** (in-gulf′), *v.t.* to engulf.

**in·hab·it** (in-hab′it), *v.t.* [< OFr. < L. < *in-,* in + *habitare,* to dwell], to live in; occupy (a region, house, etc.). **—in·hab′it·a·bil′i·ty,** *n.* **—in·hab′it·a·ble,** *adj.* **—in·hab′i·ta′tion,** *n.*

**in·hab·it·ant** (in-hab′i-tənt), *n.* a person or animal that inhabits some specified region, house, etc.: also **in·hab′it·er.**

**in·hal·ant** (in-hāl′ənt), *adj.* used in inhalation. *n.* 1. a medicine to be inhaled. 2. an inhaler (sense 2).

**in·hale** (in-hāl′), *v.t.* & *v.i.* [-HALED, -HALING], [< L. < *in-,* in + *halare,* to breathe], to breathe in; draw (air, tobacco smoke, etc.) into the lungs. **—in·ha·la·tion** (in′hə-lā′shən), *n.*

**in·hal·er** (in-hāl′ẽr), *n.* 1. one who inhales. 2. a device for inhaling medicinal vapors.

**in·har·mon·ic** (in′här-mon′ik), *adj.* not harmonic: discordant: also **in′har·mon′i·cal.**

**in·har·mo·ni·ous** (in′här-mō′ni-əs), *adj.* not harmonious; discordant, in conflict, etc. **—in′har·mo′ni·ous·ly,** *adv.* **—in′har·mo′ni·ous·ness,** *n.*

**in·here** (in-hêr′), *v.i.* [-HERED, -HERING], [< L. < *in-,* in + *haerere,* to stick], to be inherent; exist (*in*) as a quality, characteristic, or right.

**in·her·ent** (in-hêr′ənt, -her′-), *adj.* [see INHERE], existing in someone or something as a natural and inseparable quality or right; inborn. **—in·her′ence, in·her′en·cy** [*pl.* -CIES], *n.* **-in·her′ent·ly,** *adv.*

**in·her·it** (in-her′it), *v.t.* [< OFr. < LL.; ult. < L. *in,* in + *heres* heir], 1. to receive (property) as an heir from a predecessor. 2. to have (certain characteristics) by heredity. *v.i.* to receive an inheritance. **—in·her′i·tor,** *n.*

**in·her·it·a·ble** (in-her′i-tə-b'l), *adj.* 1. capable of inheriting; having the rights of an heir. 2. that can be inherited. **—in·her′it·a·bil′i·ty, in·her′it·a·ble·ness,** *n.* **—in·her′it·a·bly,** *adv.*

**in·her·it·ance** (in-her′i-təns), *n.* 1. the action of inheriting. 2. something inherited or to be

inherited; legacy; bequest. 3. right to inherit. 4. any characteristic passed on by heredity.
**inheritance tax,** a tax on inherited property.
**in·hib·it** (in-hib′it), *v.t.* [< L. pp. of *inhibere*, to curb < *in-*, in + *habere*, to hold], 1. to prohibit; forbid. 2. to restrain or suppress, as by a mental or psychological process. —**in·hib′it·a·ble,** *adj.* —**in·hib′i·tor, in·hib′it·er,** *n.*
**in·hi·bi·tion** (in′hi-bish′ən, in′i-), *n.* 1. an inhibiting or being inhibited. 2. a mental or psychological process that restrains an action, emotion, or thought. —**in·hib·i·to·ry** (in-hib′ə-tôr′i, -tō′ri), **in·hib′i·tive,** *adj.*
**in·hos·pi·ta·ble** (in-hos′pi-tə-b'l, in′hos-pit′ə-), *adj.* 1. not hospitable. 2. not offering protection or refuge; barren; forbidding. —**in·hos′pi·ta·ble·ness,** *n.* —**in·hos′pi·ta·bly,** *adv.*
**in·hos·pi·tal·i·ty** (in′hos-pə-tal′ə-ti, in-hos′-), *n.* lack of hospitality; inhospitable treatment.
**in·hu·man** (in-hū′mən), *adj.* not human; not having normal human characteristics; esp., cruel, brutal, etc. —**in·hu′man·ly,** *adv.* —**in·hu′man·ness,** *n.*
**in·hu·mane** (in′hyoo-mān′), *adj.* not humane; unmoved by the suffering of others; unfeeling, unkind, etc. —**in′hu·mane′ly,** *adv.*
**in·hu·man·i·ty** (in′hyoo-man′ə-ti), *n.* 1. a being inhuman. 2. [*pl.* -TIES], an inhuman act or remark.
**in·im·i·cal** (in-im′i-k'l), *adj.* [< LL. < L. < *in-*, not + *amicus*, friend], 1. hostile; unfriendly. 2. in opposition; adverse. —**in·im′i·cal·ly,** *adv.*
**in·im·i·ta·ble** (in-im′i-tə-b'l), *adj.* that cannot be imitated or matched; too good to be equaled or copied. —**in·im′i·ta·bil′i·ty,** *n.* —**in·im′i·ta·bly,** *adv.*
**in·iq·ui·tous** (in-ik′wə-təs), *adj.* showing iniquity; wicked; unjust. —**in·iq′ui·tous·ly,** *adv.* —**in·iq′ui·tous·ness,** *n.*
**in·iq·ui·ty** (in-ik′wə-ti), *n.* [< OFr. < L. < *iniquus*, unequal < *in-*, not + *aequus*, equal], 1. lack of righteousness or justice; wickedness; sin. 2. [*pl.* -TIES], a wicked or unjust act.
**in·i·tial** (i-nish′əl), *adj.* [< Fr. or < L. *initialis* < *in-*, in + *ire*, to go], having to do with or occurring at the beginning; first. *n.* a letter beginning a word; specif., the first letter of a name. *v.t.* [-TIALED or -TIALLED, -TIALING or -TIALLING], to mark or sign with (one's) initials.
**in·i·tial·ly** (i-nish′əl-i), *adv.* at the beginning.
**Initial Teaching Alphabet,** an alphabet of 44 characters, each representing one sound, devised by Sir James Pitman (1901– ) of England, for teaching beginners to read English: abbrev. **i/t/a, I.T.A.**
**in·i·ti·ate** (i-nish′i-āt′; *for adj. & n., usually* -it), *v.t.* [-ATED, -ATING], [< L. pp. of *initiare;* see INITIAL], 1. to bring into practice or use. 2. to teach the fundamentals of some subject to. 3. to admit as a member into a fraternity, club, etc., as through use of secret ceremony or rites. *adj.* initiated. *n.* one who has recently been, or is about to be, initiated. —**in·i′ti·a′tor,** *n.*
**in·i·ti·a·tion** (i-nish′i-ā′shən), *n.* 1. an initiating or being initiated. 2. the ceremonies or rites by which one is initiated into a fraternity, etc.
**in·i·ti·a·tive** (i-nish′i-ə-tiv, -i-ā′tiv), *adj.* of, or having the nature of, initiation; introductory. *n.* 1. the action of taking the first step or move. 2. the characteristic of originating new ideas or methods. 3. the right of a legislature to introduce new legislation. 4. *a*) the right of a group of citizens to introduce a matter for legislation directly to the voters. *b*) the procedure by which this is done.
**in·i·ti·a·to·ry** (i-nish′i-ə-tôr′i, -tō′ri), *adj.* 1. beginning; introductory. 2. of or used in an initiation.
**in·ject** (in-jekt′), *v.t.* [< L. pp. < *in-*, in + *jacere*, to throw], 1. to force or drive (a fluid) into some passage or cavity or into some part of the body by means of a syringe, etc. 2. to fill (a cavity, etc.) by injection. 3. to introduce (a remark, etc.). —**in·jec′tion,** *n.* —**in·jec′tor,** *n.*
**in·ju·di·cious** (in′jōō-dish′əs), *adj.* not judicious; showing poor judgment; not prudent. —**in′ju·di′cious·ly,** *adv.* —**in′ju·di′cious·ness,** *n.*
**in·junc·tion** (in-juŋk′shən), *n.* [< LL.; see IN- (in) & JUNCTION], 1. an enjoining; command. 2. an order. 3. a legal order from a court prohibiting a person or group from carrying out a given action, or ordering a given action to be done.
**in·jure** (in′jẽr), *v.t.* [-JURED, -JURING], [see INJURY], 1. to do physical harm to; hurt. 2. to wrong or offend deeply; be unjust to. —**in′jur·er,** *n.*
**in·ju·ri·ous** (in-joor′i-əs), *adj.* 1. injuring or likely to injure; harmful. 2. offensive; abusive. —**in·ju′ri·ous·ly,** *adv.* —**in·ju′ri·ous·ness,** *n.*
**in·ju·ry** (in′jẽr-i), *n.* [*pl.* -RIES], [< Anglo-Fr. < OFr. < L. *injuria;* ult. < *in-*, not + *jus, juris*, right], 1. physical harm to a person, etc. 2. unjust treatment; offense; wrong. 3. an injurious act.
**in·jus·tice** (in-jus′tis), *n.* 1. the quality of being unjust or unfair. 2. an unjust act; injury.
**ink** (iŋk), *n.* [OFr. *enque* < LL. < Gr. *enkauston*, red ink < *enkaiein*, to burn in], 1. a colored liquid used for writing, etc. 2. a sticky, colored paste used in printing. 3. a dark, liquid secretion squirted out by cuttlefish, etc. for protection. *v.t.* 1. to cover with ink. 2. to mark or color with ink. —**ink′er,** *n.* —**ink′like′,** *adj.*
**ink·horn** (iŋk′hôrn′), *n.* a small container made of horn, etc., formerly used to hold ink.
**ink·ling** (iŋk′liŋ), *n.* 1. a hint; suggestion. 2. a vague idea or notion.
**ink·stand** (iŋk′stand′), *n.* 1. a small stand holding an inkwell, pens, etc. 2. an inkwell.
**ink·well** (iŋk′wel′), *n.* a container for holding ink, usually set in a desk, inkstand, etc.
**ink·y** (iŋ′ki), *adj.* [-IER, -IEST], 1. like ink in color; dark; black. 2. colored, marked, or covered with ink. —**ink′i·ness,** *n.*
**in·laid** (in′lād′, in-lād′), *adj.* [pp. of *inlay*], 1. set in a surface so as to form a decoration. 2. decorated with material set in the surface.
**in·land** (in′lənd; *for n. & adv., also* -land′), *adj.* 1. of, located in, or confined to the interior of a country or region; away from the coast or border. 2. carried on within the borders of a country; domestic. *n.* the interior of a country or region. *adv.* into or toward the interior.
**in-law** (in′lô′), *n.* [contr. < *mother-in-law*, etc.], [Colloq.], a relative by marriage.
**in·lay** (in-lā′; *also, and for n., always,* in′lā′), *v.t.* [-LAID, -LAYING], 1. to set (pieces of wood, gold, etc.) in a surface so as to form a decoration. 2. to decorate with pieces of wood, gold, etc. set in the surface. *n.* [*pl.* -LAYS], 1. inlaid decoration or material. 2. a filling of metal, porcelain, etc. for a tooth, made from a mold and cemented into the cavity. —**in′lay′er,** *n.*
**in·let** (in′let), *n.* 1. *a*) a narrow strip of water extending into a body of land from a river, lake, ocean, etc. *b*) a narrow strip of water between islands. 2. an entrance, as to a culvert.
‡**in lo·co pa·ren·tis** (in lō′kō pə-ren′tis), [L.], in the place of a parent.
**in·ly** (in′li), *adv.* [Poetic], 1. inwardly; within. 2. deeply; intimately.
**in·mate** (in′māt′), *n.* [*in-* (in) + *mate*], 1. a person living with others in the same building. 2. a person confined with others in an institution, asylum, etc. 3. an inhabitant.
‡**in me·di·as res** (in mē′di-əs rēz), [L.], into the midst of things; in the middle of the action.
**in me·mo·ri·am** (in′ mə-môr′i-əm, -mō′ri-), [L.], in memory (of).
**in·most** (in′mōst′, -məst), *adj.* 1. located farthest within; innermost. 2. most intimate or secret: as, *inmost* thoughts.
**inn** (in), *n.* [AS., a lodging < *inn(e)*, *adv.*, within], 1. an establishment providing food and lodging for travelers; hotel. 2. a restaurant or tavern. Now usually only in the names of such places.
**in·nards** (in′ẽrdz), *n.pl.* [< *inwards*], [Dial.], the internal organs of the body; viscera.
**in·nate** (in′āt, i-nāt′), *adj.* [< L. *innatus*, pp. < *in-*, in + *nasci*, to be born], natural; inborn; not acquired. —**in·nate′ly,** *adv.* —**in·nate′ness,** *n.*
**in·ner** (in′ẽr), *adj.* 1. located farther within; interior. 2. of the mind or spirit. 3. more intimate or secret: as, the *inner* emotions. *n.* the inside. —**in′ner·ly,** *adv.* —**in′ner·ness,** *n.*
**inner man,** humorously, one's stomach or palate.
**Inner Mongolia,** an autonomous region of China, in the north central part.
**in·ner·most** (in′ẽr-mōst′, -məst), *adj.* inmost; farthest in.
**in·ning** (in′iŋ), *n.* [< AS. *innung*, a getting in], 1. in *baseball* and (*often pl.*) *cricket*, *a*) the period of play in which a team has a turn at bat. *b*) a numbered round of play in which both teams have a turn at bat. 2. *often pl.* the time a person or political party is in power.
**inn·keep·er** (in′kēp′ẽr), *n.* the owner of an inn.
**in·no·cence** (in′ə-s'ns), *n.* a being innocent; specif., *a*) freedom from sin, evil, or guilt. *b*) guilelessness; simplicity. *c*) harmlessness. Also **in′no·cen·cy.**
**in·no·cent** (in′ə-s'nt), *adj.* [< OFr. < L. < *in-*, not + ppr. of *nocere*, to do wrong to], 1. free from sin,

evil, or guilt; specif., *a)* doing or thinking nothing morally wrong; pure. *b)* not guilty of a specific crime or offense. *c)* free from evil or harmful effect or cause. 2. *a)* knowing no evil. *b)* without guile or cunning; artless; simple. *n.* a person knowing no evil or sin, as a child. **—in′no·cent·ly,** *adv.*

**in·noc·u·ous** (i-nok′ū-əs), *adj.* [< L. < *in-*, not + *nocuus*, harmful < *nocere*, to harm], that cannot injure or harm; harmless. **—in·noc′u·ous·ly,** *adv.* **—in·noc′u·ous·ness,** *n.*

**in·nom·i·nate bone** (i-nom′ə-nit), [see IN- (not) & NOMINATE], either of the two large, flat bones that, together with the sacrum, make up the pelvis; hipbone.

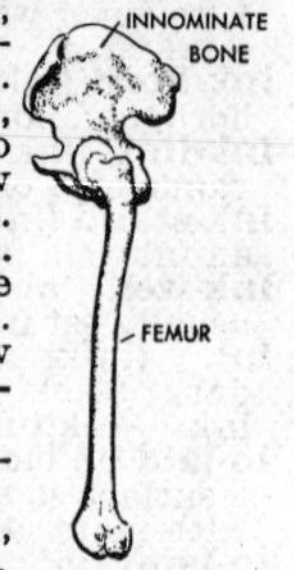

INNOMINATE BONE

**in·no·vate** (in′ə-vāt′), *v.i.* [-VATED, -VATING], [< L. < *in-*, in + *novare*, to alter < *novus*, new], to introduce new methods, devices, etc.; make changes. **—in′no·va′tive,** *adj.* **—in′no·va′tor,** *n.*

**in·no·va·tion** (in′ə-vā′shən), *n.* 1. the act or process of innovating. 2. something newly introduced; new method, custom, device, etc. **—in′no·va′tion·al,** *adj.*

**in·nox·ious** (i-nok′shəs), *adj.* not noxious; harmless.

**in·nu·en·do** (in′ū-en′dō), *n.* [*pl.* -DOES], [L., by nodding (or hinting) to < *in-*, in + *-nuere*, to nod], an indirect remark, reference, etc. usually implying something derogatory; insinuation.

**in·nu·mer·a·ble** (i-nōō′mẽr-ə-b'l, in-nū′-), *adj.* too numerous to be counted; countless. **—in·nu′mer·a·ble·ness,** *n.* **—in·nu′mer·a·bly,** *adv.*

**in·oc·u·late** (in-ok′yoo-lāt′), *v.t.* [-LATED, -LATING], [< L. pp. of *inoculare*, to engraft a bud < *in-*, in + *oculus*, an eye, bud], 1. *a)* to inject a serum, vaccine, etc. into, especially in order to make immune by causing a mild form of the disease. *b)* to inject (a disease virus, etc.) into a person or animal. 2. to implant bacteria, etc. into (soil, etc.). 3. to introduce ideas, etc. into the mind of; imbue. **—in·oc′u·la·ble,** *adj.* **—in·oc′u·la′tion,** *n.* **—in·oc′u·la′tive,** *adj.* **—in·oc′u·la′tor,** *n.*

**in·of·fen·sive** (in′ə-fen′siv), *adj.* not offensive; unobjectionable; causing no harm or annoyance. **—in′of·fen′sive·ly,** *adv.* **—in′of·fen′sive·ness,** *n.*

**in·op·er·a·ble** (in-op′ẽr-ə-b'l), *adj.* not operable; specif., *a)* not practicable. *b)* in surgery, not suitable to be operated on.

**in·op·er·a·tive** (in-op′ə-rā′tiv, -ẽr-ə-tiv), *adj.* not operative; without effect. **—in·op′er·a′tive·ness,** *n.*

**in·op·por·tune** (in-op′ẽr-tōōn′, in′op-ẽr-tūn′), *adj.* not opportune; coming or happening at a poor time; not appropriate. **—in·op′por·tune′ly,** *adv.* **—in·op′por·tune′ness,** *n.*

**in·or·di·nate** (in-ôr′d'n-it), *adj.* [< L.; see IN- (not) & ORDINATE], 1. disordered; not regulated. 2. without restraint or moderation; excessive. **—in·or′di·na·cy** (-d'n-ə-si), [*pl.* -CIES], **in·or′di·nate·ness,** *n.* **—in·or′di·nate·ly,** *adv.*

**in·or·gan·ic** (in′ôr-gan′ik), *adj.* not organic; specif., *a)* designating or composed of matter that is not animal or vegetable; not living. *b)* not like an organism in structure. *c)* designating or of any chemical compound not organic. *d)* designating or of the branch of chemistry dealing with these compounds. **—in′or·gan′i·cal·ly,** *adv.*

**in per·pe·tu·um** (in pẽr-pet′ū-əm), [L.], forever.

**in·put** (in′poot′), *n.* what is put in, as money, material, etc. into a project, power into a machine, information into a computer, etc.

**in·quest** (in′kwest), *n.* [< OFr. < LL. pp. of hyp. *inquaerere;* see INQUIRE], 1. a judicial inquiry, especially when held before a jury, as a coroner's investigation of a death. 2. a jury holding such an investigation. 3. the verdict of such an inquiry.

**in·qui·et** (in-kwī′ət), *adj.* not quiet; uneasy; disturbed. **—in·qui′e·tude′** (-ə-tōōd′, -tūd′), *n.*

**in·quire** (in-kwīr′), *v.i.* [-QUIRED, -QUIRING], [< OFr. < LL. hyp. *inquaerere* < L. *inquirere* < *in*, into + *quaerere*, to seek], 1. to ask a question or questions. 2. to carry out an examination or investigation (often with *into*). *v.t.* to ask about in order to learn: as, I'll *inquire* the way. Also sp. **enquire. —inquire after,** to pay respects by asking about the health of. **—inquire for,** to ask to see (someone). **—in·quir′er,** *n.* **—in·quir′ing·ly,** *adv.*

**in·quir·y** (in-kwīr′i, in′kwə-ri), *n.* [*pl.* -IES], 1. the act of inquiring. 2. an investigation or examination. 3. a question. Also **enquiry.**

**in·qui·si·tion** (in′kwə-zish′ən), *n.* 1. an inquiring; investigation. 2. in *law*, an inquest. 3. [I-], in the *R. C. Church*, *a)* a search for and punishment of heretics. *b)* the general tribunal established to discover and suppress heresy and heretics. *c)* the activities of this tribunal. 4. any strict or arbitrary suppression of nonconformity. **—in′qui·si′tion·al,** *adj.*

**in·quis·i·tive** (in-kwiz′ə-tiv), *adj.* 1. inclined to ask many questions or seek information. 2. unnecessarily curious; meddlesome; prying. *n.* an inquisitive person. **—in·quis′i·tive·ly,** *adv.* **—in·quis′i·tive·ness,** *n.*

**in·quis·i·tor** (in-kwiz′ə-tẽr), *n.* 1. an official whose work is making an inquisition; investigator. 2. [I-], an official of the Inquisition.

**in·quis·i·to·ri·al** (in-kwiz′ə-tôr′i-əl, -tō′ri-), *adj.* 1. of, or having the nature of, an inquisitor or an inquisition. 2. inquisitive. **—in·quis′i·to′ri·al·ly,** *adv.* **—in·quis′i·to′ri·al·ness,** *n.*

**‡in re** (in rē′), [L.], in the matter (of); concerning.

**‡I.N.R.I.,** *Iesus Nazarenus, Rex Iudaeorum*, [L.], Jesus of Nazareth, King of the Jews.

**in·road** (in′rōd′), *n.* 1. a sudden invasion or raid. 2. *usually in pl.* any injurious encroachment.

**in·rush** (in′rush′), *n.* a rushing in; inflow; influx. **—in′rush′ing,** *adj.* & *n.*

**INS, I.N.S.,** International News Service: see **UPI.**

**ins.,** 1. inches. 2. insulated. 3. insurance.

**in·sane** (in-sān′), *adj.* 1. not sane; mentally ill or deranged; mad; crazy. 2. of or for insane people: as, an *insane* asylum. 3. very foolish; senseless. **—the insane,** insane people. **—in·sane′ly,** *adv.* **—in·sane′ness,** *n.*

**in·san·i·tar·y** (in-san′ə-ter′i), *adj.* not sanitary; unhealthful. **—in·san′i·tar′i·ness,** *n.*

**in·san·i·ty** (in-san′ə-ti), *n.* [*pl.* -TIES], 1. the state of being insane; mental illness or derangement: a term used formally in law but not in psychiatry. 2. great folly; extreme senselessness.

**in·sa·ti·a·ble** (in-sā′shə-b'l, -shi-ə-b'l), *adj.* constantly wanting more; that cannot be satisfied; very greedy. **—in·sa′ti·a·bil′i·ty, in·sa′ti·a·ble·ness,** *n.* **—in·sa′ti·a·bly,** *adv.*

**in·sa·ti·ate** (in-sā′shi-it), *adj.* insatiable. **—in·sa′ti·ate·ly,** *adv.* **—in·sa′ti·ate·ness,** *n.*

**in·scribe** (in-skrīb′), *v.t.* [-SCRIBED, -SCRIBING], [< L.; see IN- (in) & SCRIBE], 1. to mark or engrave (words, symbols, etc.) on some surface. 2. to mark or engrave (a surface) with words, symbols, etc. 3. to add the name of (a person) to a list; enroll. 4. to dedicate (a book, song, etc.) informally to a person. 5. to fix or impress deeply in the mind, memory, etc. 6. in *geometry*, to draw (a figure) inside another figure so that their boundaries touch at as many points as possible. **—in·scrib′a·ble,** *adj.* **—in·scrib′er,** *n.*

**in·scrip·tion** (in-skrip′shən), *n.* 1. an inscribing. 2. something inscribed or engraved, as on a coin or monument. 3. an informal dedication, as in a book. **—in·scrip′tive, in·scrip′tion·al,** *adj.*

**in·scru·ta·ble** (in-skrōō′tə-b'l), *adj.* [< LL. < L. *in-*, not + *scrutari*, to examine], that cannot be learned or understood; completely obscure or mysterious; enigmatic. **—in·scru′ta·bil′i·ty, in·scru′ta·ble·ness,** *n.* **—in·scru′ta·bly,** *adv.*

**in·sect** (in′sekt), *n.* [< L. *insectum*, neut. of pp. of *insecare*, to cut into: from the segmented bodies], 1. any of a large group of small invertebrate animals, including beetles, bees, flies, wasps, etc., having, in the adult state, a head, thorax, and abdomen, three pairs of legs, and, usually, two pairs of membranous wings. 2. popularly, any small animal with a segmented body and several pairs of legs, as spiders, centipedes, etc.

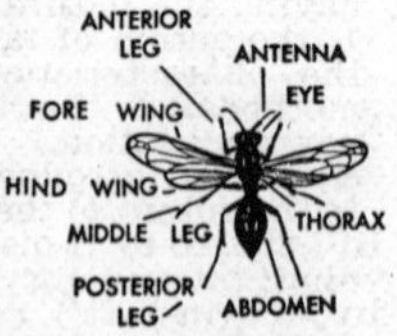

INSECT (Chinese wasp)

**in·sec·ti·cide** (in-sek′tə-sīd′), *n.* [< L. *insectum*, insect; + *-cide*], any substance used to kill insects. **—in·sec′ti·cid′al,** *adj.*

**in·sec·tiv·o·rous** (in′sek-tiv′ẽr-əs), *adj.* [< L. *insectum*, insect; + *-vorous*], 1. feeding chiefly on insects. 2. of an order of insect-eating mammals, including moles, shrews, and hedgehogs. **—in·sec′ti·vore′** (-tə-vôr′, -vōr′), *n.*

**in·se·cure** (in′si-kyoor′), *adj.* not secure; specif., *a)* not safe; unprotected. *b)* feeling more anxiety than seems warranted. *c)* not firm or dependable. **—in′se·cure′ly,** *adv.* **—in′se·cure′ness,** *n.*

**in·se·cu·ri·ty** (in′si-kyoor′ə-ti), *n.* 1. a being insecure. 2. [*pl.* -TIES], something insecure.

**in·sem·i·nate** (in-sem′ə-nāt′), *v.t.* [-NATED, -NATING], [< L. pp. < *in-*, in + *seminare*, to sow < *semen*, seed], to sow seeds in; esp., to impregnate with semen. **—in·sem′i·na′tion,** *n.*

**in·sen·sate** (in-sen′sāt, -sit), *adj.* 1. lacking sensation; inanimate. 2. without sense or reason;

stupid. 3. without regard or feeling; cold. —**in·sen′sate·ly,** *adv.* —**in·sen′sate·ness,** *n.*

**in·sen·si·ble** (in-sen′sə-b'l), *adj.* 1. lacking sensation; unable to perceive with the senses. 2. having lost sensation; unconscious. 3. not recognizing or realizing; unaware; indifferent: as, *insensible* to insult. 4. so small or slight as to be virtually imperceptible. —**in·sen′si·bil′i·ty, in·sen′si·ble·ness,** *n.* —**in·sen′si·bly,** *adv.*

**in·sen·si·tive** (in-sen′sə-tiv), *adj.* not sensitive; not feeling or perceiving; insensate. —**in·sen′si·tive·ness, in·sen′si·tiv′i·ty,** *n.*

**in·sen·ti·ent** (in-sen′shi-ənt, -shənt), *adj.* not sentient; without life, consciousness, or perception. —**in·sen′ti·ence,** *n.*

**in·sep·a·ra·ble** (in-sep′ēr-ə-b'l), *adj.* that cannot be separated or parted. *n.pl.* inseparable persons or things. —**in′sep·a·ra·bil′i·ty, in·sep′a·ra·ble·ness,** *n.* —**in·sep′a·ra·bly,** *adv.*

**in·sert** (in-sūrt′; *for n.,* in′sērt), *v.t.* [< L. *insertus,* pp. < *in-,* into + *serere,* to join], to put or fit (something) into something else; set in. *n.* anything inserted or for insertion; esp., an extra leaf or section inserted in a newspaper, etc. —**in·sert′er,** *n.*

**in·ser·tion** (in-sūr′shən), *n.* 1. an inserting or being inserted. 2. something inserted; specif., *a*) a piece of lace or embroidery that can be set into a piece of cloth for ornamentation. *b*) an advertisement in a newspaper.

**in·set** (in-set′; *for n.,* in′set′), *v.t.* [-SET, -SETTING], to set in; to insert. *n.* something set in or inserted.

**in·shore** (in′shôr′, in′shōr′), *adv. & adj.* 1. in toward the shore. 2. near the shore. —**inshore of,** nearer than (something else) to the shore.

**in·side** (in′sīd′; *for prep., usually* in′sīd′), *n.* 1. the part within; inner side, surface, or part. 2. *pl.* [Colloq.], the internal organs of the body; viscera. *adj.* 1. on or in the inside; internal. 2. working or used indoors. 3. known only to insiders; secret or private: as, the *inside* story. *adv.* 1. on or in the inside; within. 2. indoors. *prep.* inside of; in; within. —**inside of,** [Colloq.], within the space of. —**inside out,** with the inside where the outside should be; reversed.

**in·sid·er** (in′sīd′ēr), *n.* 1. a person inside a given place or group. 2. a person having or likely to have secret or confidential information.

**in·sid·i·ous** (in-sid′i-əs), *adj.* [< Fr. < L. < *insidiae,* an ambush < *in-,* in + *sedere,* to sit], 1. characterized by treachery or slyness; crafty. 2. more dangerous than seems evident: as, an *insidious* disease. —**in·sid′i·ous·ly,** *adv.* —**in·sid′i·ous·ness,** *n.*

**in·sight** (in′sīt′), *n.* 1. the ability to see and understand clearly the inner nature of things; intuition. 2. a clear understanding of the inner nature of some specific thing.

**in·sig·ni·a** (in-sig′ni-ə), *n.pl.* [*sing.* -NE (-nē); occas. -NIA], [< L. pl. of *insigne;* ult. < *in-,* in + *signum,* a mark], badges, emblems, or other distinguishing marks, as of rank, membership, etc.

**in·sig·nif·i·cant** (in′sig-nif′ə-kənt), *adj.* 1. meaningless. 2. unimportant; trivial. 3. small; unimposing. —**in′sig·nif′i·cance, in′sig·nif′i·can·cy,** *n.* —**in′sig·nif′i·cant·ly,** *adv.*

**in·sin·cere** (in′sin-sêr′), *adj.* not sincere; deceptive or hypocritical. —**in′sin·cere′ly,** *adv.*

**in·sin·cer·i·ty** (in′sin-ser′ə-ti), *n.* 1. a being insincere. 2. [*pl.* -TIES], an insincere remark, etc.

**in·sin·u·ate** (in-sin′ū-āt′), *v.t.* [-ATED, -ATING], [< L. pp. of *insinuare* < *in-,* in + *sinus,* curved surface], 1. to get in or introduce slowly, indirectly, etc. 2. to suggest (something) indirectly; hint. —**in·sin′u·at′ing·ly,** *adv.* —**in·sin′u·a′tive,** *adj.* —**in·sin′u·a′tor,** *n.*

**in·sin·u·a·tion** (in-sin′ū-ā′shən), *n.* 1. an insinuating. 2. something insinuated; specif., *a*) a sly hint. *b*) an act or remark intended to win favor.

**in·sip·id** (in-sip′id), *adj.* [< Fr. < LL. < L. *in-,* not + *sapidus,* savory < *sapere,* to taste], 1. without flavor; tasteless. 2. not exciting; dull; lifeless. —**in·sip′id·ly,** *adv.* —**in·sip′id·ness,** *n.*

**in·si·pid·i·ty** (in′si-pid′ə-ti), *n.* 1. a being insipid. 2. [*pl.* -TIES], something insipid.

**in·sist** (in-sist′), *v.i.* [< Fr. < L. < *in-,* in + *sistere,* to stand], to take and maintain a stand; make a firm demand (often with *on* or *upon*). *v.t.* to demand strongly. —**in·sist′er,** *n.*

**in·sist·ent** (in-sis′tənt), *adj.* 1. insisting or demanding; persistent in demands or assertions. 2. compelling attention: as, an *insistent* rhythm. —**in·sist′ence, in·sist′en·cy** [*pl.* -CIES], *n.*

**‡in si·tu** (in sī′tū), [L.], in its original position.

**in·snare** (in-snâr′), *v.t.* [-SNARED, -SNARING], to ensnare.

**in·so·bri·e·ty** (in′sə-brī′ə-ti, in′sō-), *n.* lack of sobriety; intemperance, as in drinking.

**in·so·far** (in′sō-fär′, in′sə-), *adv.* to the degree that (with *as*): often **in so far.**

**in·sole** (in′sōl′), *n.* 1. the inside sole of a shoe. 2. an extra, removable inside sole for comfort, etc.

**in·so·lent** (in′sə-lənt), *adj.* [< OFr. < L. < *in-,* not + ppr. of *solere,* to be accustomed], disrespectful of custom or authority; impertinent; impudent. —**in′so·lence,** *n.* —**in′so·lent·ly,** *adv.*

**in·sol·u·ble** (in-sol′yoo-b'l), *adj.* 1. that cannot be solved; unsolvable. 2. that cannot be dissolved; not soluble. —**in′sol·u·bil′i·ty, in·sol′u·ble·ness,** *n.* —**in·sol′u·bly,** *adv.*

**in·solv·a·ble** (in-sol′və-b'l), *adj.* not solvable.

**in·sol·vent** (in-sol′vənt), *adj.* 1. not solvent; unable to pay debts; bankrupt. 2. not enough to pay all debts. 3. of insolvents. *n.* an insolvent person. —**in·sol′ven·cy** [*pl.* -CIES], *n.*

**in·som·ni·a** (in-som′ni-ə), *n.* [< L. < *in-,* without + *somnus,* sleep], abnormal inability to sleep. —**in·som′ni·ac′,** *n.* —**in·som′ni·ous,** *adj.*

**in·so·much** (in′sō-much′), *adv.* 1. to such a degree or extent; so (usually with *as* or *that*). 2. inasmuch (with *as*).

**in·sou·ci·ant** (in-sōō′si-ənt), *adj.* [Fr.], calm and unbothered; carefree; indifferent. —**in·sou′ci·ance,** *n.* —**in·sou′ci·ant·ly,** *adv.*

**in·spect** (in-spekt′), *v.t.* [< L. pp. < *in-,* at + *specere,* to look], 1. to look at carefully; examine critically. 2. to review officially, as troops.

**in·spec·tion** (in-spek′shən), *n.* 1. careful investigation. 2. official examination, as of troops.

**in·spec·tor** (in-spek′tēr), *n.* 1. one who inspects; official examiner. 2. an officer on a police force, ranking next below a superintendent. —**in·spec′to·ral, in′spec·to′ri·al** (-tôr′i-əl, -tō′ri-), *adj.* —**in·spec′tor·ship′,** *n.*

**in·spi·ra·tion** (in′spə-rā′shən), *n.* 1. a breathing in; inhaling. 2. an inspiring or being inspired mentally or emotionally. 3. any stimulus to creative thought or action. 4. an inspired idea, action, etc. 5. a prompting of something written or said; suggestion. 6. in *theology,* a divine influence upon human beings. —**in′spi·ra′tion·al,** *adj.* —**in′spi·ra′tion·al·ly,** *adv.*

**in·spire** (in-spīr′), *v.t.* [-SPIRED, -SPIRING], [< OFr. < L. < *in-,* in + *spirare,* to breathe], 1. to draw (air) into the lungs; inhale. 2. to influence, stimulate, or impel, as to some creative or effective effort. 3. to guide or motivate by divine influence. 4. to arouse (a thought or feeling): as, kindness *inspires* love. 5. to affect with a specified feeling: as, it *inspired* us with fear. 6. to cause to be written or said. *v.i.* 1. to inhale. 2. to give inspiration. —**in·spir′a·ble,** *adj.* —**in·spir′er,** *n.* —**in·spir′ing·ly,** *adv.*

**in·spir·it** (in-spir′it), *v.t.* to put spirit or life into; cheer; hearten. —**in·spir′it·ing·ly,** *adv.*

**in·spis·sate** (in-spis′āt), *v.t. & v.i.* [-SATED, -SATING], [< LL.; ult. < L. *in-,* in + *spissus,* thick], to thicken by evaporation, etc.; condense. —**in′spis·sa′tion,** *n.* —**in′spis·sa′tor,** *n.*

**Inst.,** 1. Institute. 2. Institution.

**inst.,** instant (the present month).

**in·sta·bil·i·ty** (in′stə-bil′ə-ti), *n.* [*pl.* -TIES], 1. lack of firmness. 2. lack of determination.

**in·sta·ble** (in-stā′b'l), *adj.* unstable.

**in·stall** (in-stôl′), *v.t.* [< Fr. < ML. < *in-,* in + *stallum* < OHG. *stal,* a place], 1. to place (a person) in an office, rank, etc., with formality. 2. to establish in a place or condition: as, we *installed* ourselves in the seats. 3. to fix in position for use: as, to *install* light fixtures. —**in·stal·la·tion** (in′stə-lā′shən), *n.* —**in·stall′er,** *n.*

**in·stall·ment, in·stal·ment** (in-stôl′mənt), *n.* [< earlier *estall,* to arrange payments for < OFr. < OHG. *stal;* see INSTALL], 1. any of the parts of a debt or other sum of money to be paid at regular times over a specified period. 2. any of several parts, as of a magazine novel, appearing at intervals.

**in·stall·ment, in·stal·ment** (in-stôl′mənt), *n.* an installing or being installed; installation.

**installment plan,** a system by which debts, as for purchased articles, are paid in installments.

**in·stance** (in′stəns), *n.* [OFr. < L. *instantia,* a being present < *instans;* see INSTANT], 1. a request; suggestion; instigation: as, he resigned at the *instance* of the council. 2. an example; case; illustration. 3. a step in processing; occasion: as, in the

fat, āpe, bâre, cär; ten, ēven, hêre, ovẽr; is, bīte; lot, gō, hôrn, tōōl, look; oil, out; up, ūse, fũr; get; joy; yet; chin; she; thin, *th*en; zh, leisure; ŋ, ring; ə for *a* in *ago, e* in *agent, i* in *sanity, o* in *comply, u* in *focus;* ′ in *able* (ā′b'l); Fr. bȧl; ë, Fr. coeur; ö, Fr. feu; Fr. mon; ô, Fr. coq; ü, Fr. duc; H, G. ich; kh, G. doch. ‡ foreign; < derived from.

first *instance.* ***v.t.*** [-STANCED, -STANCING], 1. to exemplify. 2. to give as an example; cite. —**for instance,** as an example.

**in·stant** (in′stənt), ***adj.*** [OFr. < L. *instans,* ppr. < *in-,* upon + *stare,* to stand], 1. urgent; pressing. 2. of the current month: as, your letter of the 13th *instant.* 3. soon to happen; imminent. 4. without delay; immediate. 5. designating coffee, tea, etc. in readily soluble form, prepared by adding water or other liquid. ***adv.*** [Poetic], at once. ***n.*** 1. a moment. 2. a particular moment. —**on the instant,** immediately. —**the instant,** as soon as.

**in·stan·ta·ne·ous** (in′stən-tā′ni-əs), ***adj.*** 1. done, made, or happening in an instant. 2. done or made without delay; immediate. —**in′stan·ta′ne·ous·ly,** ***adv.*** —**in′stan·ta′ne·ous·ness,** ***n.***

**in·stan·ter** (in-stan′tēr), ***adv.*** [L., pressingly], immediately.

**in·stant·ly** (in′stənt-li), ***adv.*** 1. in an instant; without delay; immediately. 2. [Archaic], urgently. ***conj.*** as soon as; the instant that.

**in·state** (in-stāt′), ***v.t.*** [-STATED, -STATING], to put in a particular status, position, or rank; install. —**in·state′ment,** ***n.***

**in·stead** (in-sted′), ***adv.*** [*in* + *stead*], in place of the person or thing mentioned: as, since we had no sugar, we used honey *instead.* —**instead of,** in place of.

**in·step** (in′step′), ***n.*** 1. the upper surface of the arch of the foot, between the ankle and the toes. 2. the part of a shoe or stocking covering this.

**in·sti·gate** (in′stə-gāt′), ***v.t.*** [-GATED, -GATING], [< L. pp. < *in-,* on + *-stigare,* to prick], 1. to urge on or incite to some action. 2. to cause by inciting; foment, as a rebellion. —**in′sti·ga′tion,** ***n.*** —**in′sti·ga′tive,** ***adj.*** —**in′sti·ga′tor,** ***n.***

**in·still, in·stil** (in-stil′), ***v.t.*** [-STILLED, -STILLING], [< Fr. < L. < *in-,* in + *stilla,* a drop], 1. to put in drop by drop. 2. to put (a notion, principle, feeling, etc.) *in* or *into* gradually. —**in·stil·la·tion** (in′sti-lā′shən), ***n.*** —**in·still′er,** ***n.*** —**in·still′ment, in·stil′ment,** ***n.***

**in·stinct** (in′stiŋkt; *for adj.,* in-stiŋkt′), ***n.*** [< L. *instinctus,* pp. of *instinguere,* to impel], 1. (an) inborn tendency to behave in a way characteristic of a species: natural, unacquired response to stimuli: as, suckling is an *instinct* in mammals. 2. a natural or acquired tendency or talent; knack; gift: as, an *instinct* for doing the right thing. ***adj.*** filled or charged (*with*): as, a speech *instinct* with emotion.

**in·stinc·tive** (in-stiŋk′tiv), ***adj.*** 1. of, or having the nature of, instinct. 2. prompted or done by instinct. —**in·stinc′tive·ly,** ***adv.***

**in·stinc·tu·al** (in-stiŋk′chōō-əl), ***adj.*** of instinct.

**in·sti·tute** (in′stə-tōōt′, -tūt′), ***v.t.*** [-TUTED, -TUTING], [< L. pp. of *instituere* < *in-,* in + *statuere,* to set up], 1. to set up; establish; found. 2. to start; initiate: as, to *institute* an investigation. 3. to install in an office, position, etc. ***n.*** something instituted; specif., *a*) an established principle, law, or custom. *b*) an organization for the promotion or teaching of art, science, etc. *c*) the building in which this is housed. —**in′sti·tut′er, in′sti·tu′tor,** ***n.***

**in·sti·tu·tion** (in′stə-tōō′shən, -tū′-), ***n.*** 1. an instituting or being instituted; establishment. 2. an established law, custom, practice, etc. 3. an organization having a social, educational, or religious purpose, as a school, church, reformatory, etc. 4. the building housing such an organization. 5. [Colloq.], a familiar person or thing.

**in·sti·tu·tion·al** (in′stə-tōō′shən-'l, -tū′-), ***adj.*** 1. of, or having the nature of, an institution. 2. in *advertising,* intended primarily to gain prestige rather than to increase immediate sales. —**in′sti·tu′tion·al·ly,** ***adv.***

**in·sti·tu·tion·al·ize** (in′stə-tōō′shən-'l-iz′, -tū′-), ***v.t.*** [-IZED, -IZING], 1. to make into an institution. 2. to make institutional. 3. [Colloq.], to put (a person) into an institution.

**in·struct** (in-strukt′), ***v.t.*** [< L. pp. of *instruere,* to erect < *in-,* in + *struere,* to pile up], 1. to communicate knowledge to; teach. 2. to inform: as, a judge *instructs* the jury. 3. to give directions or orders to.

**in·struc·tion** (in-struk′shən), ***n.*** 1. an instructing; education. 2. knowledge, information, etc. given or taught; lesson. 3. *pl.* directions; orders. —**in·struc′tion·al,** ***adj.***

**in·struc·tive** (in-struk′tiv), ***adj.*** instructing; giving knowledge. —**in·struc′tive·ly,** ***adv.*** —**in·struc′tive·ness,** ***n.***

**in·struc·tor** (in-struk′tēr), ***n.*** 1. a teacher. 2. a college teacher ranking below an assistant professor. —**in·struc′tor·ship′,** ***n.*** —**in·struc′tress,** ***n.fem.***

**in·stru·ment** (in′stroo-mənt), ***n.*** [< OFr. < L. *instrumentum* < *instruere;* see INSTRUCT], 1. *a*) a thing by means of which something is done; means. *b*) a person used by another to bring something about. 2. a tool or implement. 3. any of various devices producing musical sound. 4. in *law,* a formal document, as a deed, contract, etc.

**in·stru·men·tal** (in′stroo-men′t'l), ***adj.*** 1. serving as a means; helpful. 2. of or performed with an instrument or tool. 3. of, performed on, or written for a musical instrument or instruments. —**in′stru·men′tal·ly,** ***adv.***

**in·stru·men·tal·ist** (in′stroo-men′t'l-ist), ***n.*** one who performs on a musical instrument.

**in·stru·men·tal·i·ty** (in′stroo-men-tal′ə-ti), ***n.*** [*pl.* -TIES], a being instrumental; means; agency.

**in·stru·men·ta·tion** (in′stroo-men-tā′shən), ***n.*** 1. the arrangement of music for instruments. 2. the use of, or work with, scientific instruments.

**instrument panel** (or **board**), a panel or board with instruments, gauges, etc. mounted on it, as in an automobile or airplane.

**in·sub·or·di·nate** (in′sə-bôr′d'n-it), ***adj.*** not submitting to authority; disobedient. ***n.*** an insubordinate person. —**in′sub·or′di·nate·ly,** ***adv.*** —**in′sub·or′di·na′tion** (-d'n-ā′shən), ***n.***

**in·sub·stan·tial** (in′səb-stan′shəl), ***adj.*** not substantial; specif., *a*) unreal; imaginary. *b*) not solid or firm; flimsy. —**in′sub·stan′ti·al′i·ty** (-al′ə-ti), ***n.***

**in·suf·fer·a·ble** (in-suf′ēr-ə-b'l), ***adj.*** not sufferable; intolerable; unbearable. —**in·suf′fer·a·ble·ness,** ***n.*** —**in·suf′fer·a·bly,** ***adv.***

**in·suf·fi·cien·cy** (in′sə-fish′ən-si), ***n.*** lack of sufficiency; deficiency; inadequacy.

**in·suf·fi·cient** (in′sə-fish′ənt), ***adj.*** not sufficient; inadequate. —**in′suf·fi′cient·ly,** ***adv.***

**in·su·lar** (in′sə-lēr, in′syoo-), ***adj.*** [< L. < *insula,* island], 1. of, or having the form of, an island. 2. living or situated on an island. 3. like an island. 4. of, like, or characteristic of islanders; hence, 5. narrow-minded; prejudiced. —**in′su·lar·ism, in·su·lar·i·ty** (in′sə-lar′ə-ti, in′syoo-), ***n.*** —**in′su·lar·ly,** ***adv.***

**in·su·late** (in′sə-lāt′, in′syoo-), ***v.t.*** [-LATED, -LATING], [< L. *insulatus,* made like an island < *insula,* island], 1. to set apart; detach from the rest; isolate. 2. to separate or cover with a nonconducting material in order to prevent the leakage of electricity, heat, or sound.

**in·su·la·tion** (in′sə-lā′shən, in′syoo-), ***n.*** 1. an insulating or being insulated. 2. any material used to insulate.

**in·su·la·tor** (in′sə-lā′tēr, in′syoo-), ***n.*** anything that insulates; esp., a device of glass, porcelain, etc. for insulating electric wires.

**in·su·lin** (in′sə-lin, in′syoo-), ***n.*** [< L. *insula,* island: referring to islands of special tissue in the pancreas], 1. a secretion of the pancreas which helps the body use sugar and other carbohydrates. 2. an extract from the pancreas of sheep or oxen, used hypodermically in the treatment of diabetes: a trademark (**Insulin**).

**in·sult** (in′sult; *for v.,* in-sult′), ***n.*** [Fr. < LL. < L. pp. < *in-,* on + *salire,* to leap], an act, remark, etc. meant to hurt the feelings or self-respect of another; indignity. ***v.t.*** to subject to an insult; treat with insolence; affront. —**in·sult′er,** ***n.*** —**in·sult′ing,** ***adj.*** —**in·sult′ing·ly,** ***adv.***

**in·su·per·a·ble** (in-sōō′pēr-ə-b'l, in-sū′-), ***adj.*** not superable; that cannot be overcome or passed over; insurmountable. —**in·su′per·a·bil′i·ty, in·su′per·a·ble·ness,** ***n.*** —**in·su′per·a·bly,** ***adv.***

**in·sup·port·a·ble** (in′sə-pôr′tə-b'l, -pōr′-), ***adj.*** not supportable; intolerable; unbearable. —**in′sup·port′a·ble·ness,** ***n.*** —**in′sup·port′a·bly,** ***adv.***

**in·sur·a·ble** (in-shoor′ə-b'l), ***adj.*** that can be insured. —**in·sur′a·bil′i·ty,** ***n.***

**in·sur·ance** (in-shoor′əns), ***n.*** 1. an insuring or being insured against loss by fire, accident, death, etc. 2. a contract (**insurance policy**) whereby the insurer guarantees the insured that a certain sum will be paid for a specified loss. 3. the fixed payment made by the insured; premium. 4. the amount for which life, property, etc. is insured. 5. the business of insuring against loss.

**in·sure** (in-shoor′), ***v.t.*** [-SURED, -SURING], [< OFr.; see IN- (in) & SURE], 1. to make sure; guarantee: as, to *insure* maximum efficiency. 2. to get as a certainty; secure: as, your degree will *insure* you a job. 3. to make safe; protect: as, care *insures* one against error. 4. to assure against loss; contract to be paid or to pay money in the case of loss of (life, property, etc.). ***v.i.*** to give or take out insurance. Also sp. **ensure.**

**in·sured** (in-shoord′), ***n.*** a person whose life, property, etc. is insured against loss.

**in·sur·er** (in-shoor′ēr), ***n.*** a person or company that insures others against loss or damage.

**in·sur·gence** (in-sũr′jəns), *n.* a rising in revolt; insurrection: also **in·sur′gen·cy.**

**in·sur·gent** (in-sũr′jənt), *adj.* [< L. *insurgens*, ppr. < *in-*, upon + *surgere*, to rise], rising up against political or governmental authority; rebellious. *n.* an insurgent person.

**in·sur·mount·a·ble** (in′sẽr-moun′tə-b'l), *adj.* not surmountable; that cannot be overcome. **—in′-sur·mount′a·bil′i·ty,** *n.* **—in′sur·mount′a·bly,** *adv.*

**in·sur·rec·tion** (in′sə-rek′shən), *n.* [< LL. < pp. of L. *insurgere*, to rise up], a rising up against established authority; rebellion; revolt. **—in′sur·rec′-tion·al,** *adj.* **—in′sur·rec′tion·ar′y** [*pl.* -IES], *n.* & *adj.* **—in′sur·rec′tion·ist,** *n.*

**in·sus·cep·ti·ble** (in′sə-sep′tə-b'l), *adj.* not susceptible; not easily affected or influenced. **—in′sus-cep′ti·bil′i·ty,** *n.* **—in′sus·cep′ti·bly,** *adv.*

**int.,** 1. interest. 2. interior. 3. internal. 4. international. 5. intransitive.

**in·tact** (in-takt′), *adj.* [< L. < *in-*, not + *tactus*, pp. of *tangere*, to touch], untouched or uninjured; kept or left whole. **—in·tact′ness,** *n.*

**in·tagl·io** (in-tal′yō, -täl′-), *n.* [*pl.* -IOS], [It. < *in-*, in + *tagliare*, to cut], 1. a design or figure carved or engraved below the surface. 2. a gem ornamented in this way. 3. the art of making such designs or figures. *v.t.* 1. to engrave a design on. 2. to cut (a design) in a surface.

**in·take** (in′tāk′), *n.* 1. a taking in. 2. the amount or thing taken in. 3. the place in a pipe, channel, etc. where a fluid is taken in.

**in·tan·gi·ble** (in-tan′jə-b'l), *adj.* not tangible; specif., *a*) that cannot be touched; incorporeal. *b*) that cannot be easily defined or grasped. *n.* something intangible. **—in·tan′gi·bil′i·ty, in·tan′gi·ble-ness,** *n.* **—in·tan′gi·bly,** *adv.*

**in·te·ger** (in′tə-jẽr), *n.* [L., untouched, whole], 1. anything complete in itself; whole. 2. a whole number (e.g., 5, 10, 748, etc.): cf. *fraction.*

**in·te·gral** (in′tə-grəl), *adj.* [see INTEGER], 1. necessary for completeness; essential. 2. whole or complete. 3. in *mathematics*, of or having to do with integers; not fractional. *n.* a whole. **—in′te·gral′i·ty** (-gral′ə-ti), *n.* **—in′te·gral·ly,** *adv.*

**integral calculus,** the branch of calculus dealing with the process (*integration*) of finding the quantity or function of which a given quantity or function is the differential.

**in·te·grate** (in′tə-grāt′), *v.t.* [-GRATED, -GRATING], [< L. pp. of *integrare* < *integer*, whole], 1. to make whole or complete. 2. to bring (parts) together into a whole; unify. 3. to indicate the sum or total of. 4. to remove legal and social barriers imposing segregation upon (racial groups). *v.i.* to unite or become whole. **—in′te·gra′tion,** *n.* **—in′te·gra′tor,** *n.*

**in·teg·ri·ty** (in-teg′rə-ti), *n.* [see INTEGER], 1. a being complete; wholeness. 2. unimpaired condition; soundness. 3. uprightness, honesty, and sincerity.

**in·teg·u·ment** (in-teg′yoo-mənt), *n.* [< L. < *in-*, upon + *tegere*, to cover], an outer covering, as of the body or of a plant; skin, shell, hide, etc.

**in·tel·lect** (in′tə-lekt′), *n.* [< L. < *intellegere*, to understand < *inter-*, between + *legere*, to choose], 1. the ability to reason or understand. 2. great mental ability; high intelligence. 3. *a*) a mind or intelligence. *b*) a person of (high) intelligence.

**in·tel·lec·tu·al** (in′tə-lek′choo-əl), *adj.* 1. of or done by the intellect. 2. appealing to the intellect. 3. requiring or using intelligence. 4. having or showing high intelligence. *n.* 1. a person with intellectual interests. 2. a person who does intellectual work. **—in′tel·lec′tu·al′i·ty, in′tel·lec′tu·al-ness,** *n.* **—in′tel·lec′tu·al·ly,** *adv.*

**in·tel·lec·tu·al·ism** (in′tə-lek′choo-əl-iz'm), *n.* a being intellectual; devotion to intellectual matters. **—in′tel·lec′tu·al·ist,** *n.* **—in′tel·lec′tu·al·is′tic,** *adj.*

**in·tel·li·gence** (in-tel′ə-jəns), *n.* [< OFr. < L. *intelligentia* < *intelligere;* see INTELLECT], 1. *a*) the ability to learn or understand from experience; mental ability. *b*) the ability to respond successfully to a new situation. 2. news; information. 3. the gathering of secret information, as for military purposes. 4. the persons or agency employed at this. 5. an intelligent being.

**intelligence quotient,** a number indicating a person's level of intelligence: it is the mental age multiplied by 100 and divided by the chronological age: abbrev. **IQ, I.Q.**

**intelligence test,** a series of problems intended to test the intelligence of an individual.

**in·tel·li·gent** (in-tel′ə-jənt), *adj.* 1. having or using intelligence. 2. having or showing a high intelligence; quick to learn. 3. having knowledge, understanding, or awareness (*of* something). **—in-tel′li·gent·ly,** *adv.*

**in·tel·li·gent·si·a** (in-tel′ə-jent′si-ə, -gent′-), *n.* [< Russ. < It. < L.; see INTELLIGENCE], the people regarded as, or regarding themselves as, the educated class; intellectuals collectively.

**in·tel·li·gi·ble** (in-tel′i-jə-b'l), *adj.* [< L. < *intelligere;* see INTELLECT], that can be understood; clear; comprehensible. **—in·tel′li·gi·bil′i·ty, in·tel′li·gi·ble-ness,** *n.* **—in·tel′li·gi·bly,** *adv.*

**in·tem·per·ance** (in-tem′pẽr-əns), *n.* 1. a lack of temperance or restraint; excess. 2. excessive drinking of alcoholic liquor.

**in·tem·per·ate** (in-tem′pẽr-it), *adj.* 1. not temperate; specif., *a*) not moderate; excessive. *b*) severe or violent: as, an *intemperate* wind. 2. drinking too much alcoholic liquor. **—in·tem′per·ate·ly,** *adv.* **—in·tem′per·ate·ness,** *n.*

**in·tend** (in-tend′), *v.t.* [< OFr. < L. *intendere*, to aim at < *in-*, at + *tendere*, to stretch], 1. to have in mind as a purpose; plan; purpose. 2. to mean (something) to be or be used for; design; destine. 3. to mean; signify. *v.i.* to have a purpose or intention. **—in·tend′er,** *n.*

**in·tend·an·cy** (in-ten′dən-si), *n.* [*pl.* -CIES], 1. the position or duties of an intendant. 2. intendants collectively.

**in·tend·ant** (in-ten′dənt), *n.* [Fr. < L. ppr. of *intendere;* see INTEND], a director, manager of a public business, superintendent, etc.

**in·tend·ed** (in-ten′did), *adj.* 1. meant; planned; purposed. 2. prospective; future. *n.* [Colloq.], one's prospective wife or husband.

**intens.,** 1. intensified. 2. intensifier. 3. intensive.

**in·tense** (in-tens′), *adj.* [< L. pp. of *intendere;* see INTEND], 1. occurring or existing in a high degree; very strong: as, an *intense* light. 2. strained to the utmost; earnest: as, *intense* thought. 3. having or showing strong emotion, great seriousness, etc. 4. characterized by much action, emotion, etc. **—in·tense′ness,** *n.*

**in·tense·ly** (in-tens′li), *adv.* 1. in an intense manner. 2. in a high degree; extremely.

**in·ten·si·fy** (in-ten′sə-fī′), *v.t.* & *v.i.* [-FIED, -FYING], to make or become intense or more intense; increase; strengthen. **—in·ten′si·fi·ca′tion,** *n.* **—in-ten′si·fi′er,** *n.*

**in·ten·si·ty** (in-ten′sə-ti), *n.* [*pl.* -TIES], 1. a being intense; specif., *a*) extreme degree of anything. *b*) great energy or vehemence, as of emotion. 2. in *physics*, the amount of force or energy of heat, light, sound, etc. per unit area, volume, etc.

**in·ten·sive** (in-ten′siv), *adj.* 1. increasing in degree or amount. 2. of or characterized by intensity; thorough; exhaustive. 3. in *agriculture*, designating a system of farming which aims at the increase of crop yield per unit area. 4. in *grammar*, giving force or emphasis: as, *oneself* is frequently *intensive.* *n.* 1. anything that intensifies. 2. in *grammar*, an intensive word, prefix, etc. **—in·ten′sive·ly,** *adv.* **—in·ten′sive·ness,** *n.*

**in·tent** (in-tent′), *adj.* [< L. pp. of *intendere;* see INTEND], 1. firmly directed; earnest. 2. *a*) having the attention firmly fixed; engrossed. *b*) strongly resolved: as, *intent* on going. *n.* 1. an intending. 2. something intended; specif., *a*) a purpose; intention. *b*) [Obs.], meaning; import. **—to all intents and purposes,** in almost every respect; practically. **—in·tent′ly,** *adv.* **—in·tent′ness,** *n.*

**in·ten·tion** (in-ten′shən), *n.* 1. an intending; determination to do a specified thing or act in a specified way. 2. *a*) anything intended; ultimate purpose. *b*) *pl.* purpose in regard to marriage.

**in·ten·tion·al** (in-ten′shən-'l), *adj.* done purposely; intended. **—in·ten′tion·al·ly,** *adv.*

**in·ter** (in-tũr′), *v.t.* [-TERRED, -TERRING], [< OFr. < LL. < L. *in*, in + *terra*, earth], to put (a dead body) into the ground or a tomb; bury.

**in·ter-,** [L. < *inter, prep.*], a combining form meaning: 1. *between, among*, as in *intercede.* 2. *with* or *on each other* (or *one another*), *together, mutual, reciprocal, mutually*, as in *interact.*

**in·ter·act** (in′tẽr-akt′), *v.i.* to act on each other. **—in′ter·ac′tion,** *n.* **—in′ter·ac′tive,** *adj.*

**‡in·ter a·li·a** (in′tẽr ā′li-ə), [L.], among other things.

**in·ter·breed** (in′tẽr-brēd′), *v.t.* [-BRED, -BREEDING], to cross different varieties of (animals or plants) in breeding. *v.i.* to breed in this way.

**in·ter·ca·lar·y** (in-tũr′kə-ler′i), *adj.* [< L.; see INTERCALATE], added to the calendar: said of a day, month, etc. added as in leap year to make the calendar correspond to the solar year.

**in·ter·ca·late** (in-tũr′kə-lāt′), *v.t.* [-LATED, -LATING], [< L. pp. < *inter-*, between + *calare*, to call], 1. to add (a day, month, etc.) to the calendar. 2. to interpolate. —**in·ter′ca·la′tion,** *n.*

**in·ter·cede** (in′tẽr-sēd′), *v.i.* [-CEDED, -CEDING], [< L. < *inter-*, between + *cedere*, to go], 1. to plead or make a request in behalf of another or others. 2. to intervene for the purpose of producing agreement; mediate. —**in′ter·ced′er,** *n.*

**in·ter·cel·lu·lar** (in′tẽr-sel′yoo-lẽr), *adj.* located between or among cells.

**in·ter·cept** (in′tẽr-sept′), *v.t.* [< L. pp. < *inter-*, between + *capere*, to take], 1. to seize, stop, or interrupt on the way: as, to *intercept* a message. 2. to stop or prevent: as, to *intercept* the escape of a thief. 3. to cut off communication with, sight of, etc. 4. in *mathematics*, to mark off between two points, lines, or planes. —**in′ter·cep′tion,** *n.* —**in′ter·cep′tive,** *adj.*

**in·ter·cep·tor** (in′tẽr-sep′tẽr), *n.* a person or thing that intercepts; esp., a fast-climbing military airplane used in fighting off enemy attacks: also **in′ter·cept′er.**

**in·ter·ces·sion** (in′tẽr-sesh′ən), *n.* an interceding; mediation, pleading, or prayer in behalf of another or others. —**in′ter·ces′sion·al,** *adj.* —**in′ter·ces′so·ry** (-ses′ẽr-i), *adj.*

**in·ter·ces·sor** (in′tẽr-ses′ẽr, in′tẽr-ses′-), *n.* a person who intercedes.

**in·ter·change** (in′tẽr-chānj′; *for n.*, in′tẽr-chānj′), *v.t.* [-CHANGED, -CHANGING], 1. to give and take mutually; exchange: as, to *interchange* presents. 2. to put (each of two things) in the other's place. 3. to alternate: as, to *interchange* work with play. *v.i.* to make an interchange. *n.* 1. a mutual giving in exchange. 2. alternation. 3. any of the places on a freeway where traffic can enter or depart, as by means of a cloverleaf. —**in′ter·chang′er,** *n.*

**in·ter·change·a·ble** (in′tẽr-chān′jə-b'l), *adj.* that can be interchanged, especially in position or use. —**in′ter·change′a·bil′i·ty, in′ter·change′a·ble·ness,** *n.* —**in′ter·change′a·bly,** *adv.*

**in·ter·col·le·gi·ate** (in′tẽr-kə-lē′jit, -ji-it), *adj.* between or among colleges and universities.

**in·ter·com** (in′tẽr-kom′), *n.* [Slang], an intercommunication system, as between the pilot and the bombardier in an airplane.

**in·ter·com·mu·ni·cate** (in′tẽr-kə-mū′ni-kāt′), *v.t.* & *v.i.* [-CATED, -CATING], to communicate with or to each other or one another. —**in′ter·com·mu′ni·ca′tion,** *n.* —**in′ter·com·mu′ni·ca′tive,** *adj.*

**in·ter·con·nect** (in′tẽr-kə-nekt′), *v.t.* & *v.i.* to connect with each other. —**in′ter·con·nec′tion,** *n.*

**in·ter·cos·tal** (in′tẽr-kos′t'l), *adj.* [*inter-* + *costal*], between the ribs. —**in′ter·cos′tal·ly,** *adv.*

**in·ter·course** (in′tẽr-kôrs′, -kōrs′), *n.* [< OFr. < L.; see INTER- & COURSE], 1. communication or dealings between or among people, countries, etc.; interchange of products, services, ideas, etc. 2. the sexual joining of two individuals; copulation: usually **sexual intercourse.**

**in·ter·de·nom·i·na·tion·al** (in′tẽr-di-nom′ə-nā′shən-'l), *adj.* between, among, shared by, or involving different religious denominations.

**in·ter·de·pend·ence** (in′tẽr-di-pen′dəns), *n.* dependence on each other; mutual dependence: also **in′ter·de·pend′en·cy.** —**in′ter·de·pend′ent,** *adj.* —**in′ter·de·pend′ent·ly,** *adv.*

**in·ter·dict** (in′tẽr-dikt′; *for n.*, in′tẽr-dikt′), *v.t.* [< ME. *entrediten*, remodeled after L. *interdictus*, pp. < *inter-*, between + *dicere*, to say], 1. to prohibit (an action); forbid with authority. 2. to restrain from doing or using something. 3. in the *R. C. Church*, to exclude (a person, parish, etc.) from certain offices or privileges. *n.* an official prohibition or restraint; specif., in the *R. C. Church*, an interdicting of a person, parish, etc. —**in′ter·dic′tion,** *n.* —**in′ter·dic′tor,** *n.* —**in′ter·dic′to·ry, in′ter·dic′tive,** *adj.*

**in·ter·est** (in′tẽr-ist, in′trist; *also, for v.*, in′tə-rest′), *n.* [< ML. *interesse*, compensation < L. < *inter-*, between + *esse*, to be; modified by L. *interest*, it concerns], 1. a right or claim to something. 2. a share in something. 3. anything in which one participates or has a share. 4. *often pl.* profit; welfare; benefit. 5. a group of people having a common concern in some industry, occupation, cause, etc.: as, the steel *interest.* 6. social or political influence. 7. *a)* a feeling of intentness, concern, or curiosity about something. *b)* the power of causing this feeling. *c)* something causing this feeling. 8. importance; consequence: as, a matter of little *interest.* 9. *a)* money paid for the use of money. *b)* the rate of such payment, expressed as a percentage per unit of time. 10. an increase over what is owed: as, he repaid her kindness with *interest.* *v.t.* 1. to involve the interest of. 2. to cause to have an interest, or share, in. 3. to excite the attention or curiosity of. —**in the interest** (or **interests**) **of,** for the sake of; in order to promote.

**in·ter·est·ed** (in′tẽr-is-tid, in′tris-, in′tə-res′-), *adj.* 1. having an interest or share. 2. influenced by personal interest; prejudiced. 3. feeling or showing interest, or curiosity. —**in′ter·est·ed·ly,** *adv.* —**in′ter·est·ed·ness,** *n.*

**in·ter·est·ing** (in′tẽr-is-tiŋ, in′tris-, in′tə-res′-), *adj.* exciting interest, curiosity, or attention. —**in′ter·est·ing·ly,** *adv.* —**in′ter·est·ing·ness,** *n.*

**in·ter·fere** (in′tẽr-fêr′), *v.i.* [-FERED, -FERING], [< OFr. < L. *inter*, between + *ferire*, to strike], 1. to strike against each other; clash; collide. 2. *a)* to come between for some purpose; intervene. *b)* to meddle. 3. in *football*, to effect an interference. 4. in *physics*, to affect each other by interference: said of vibrating waves. —**interfere with,** to hinder; prevent. —**in′ter·fer′er,** *n.* —**in′ter·fer′ing·ly,** *adv.*

**in·ter·fer·ence** (in′tẽr-fêr′əns), *n.* 1. an interfering. 2. in *football*, the obstruction of opposing tacklers to clear the way for the ball carrier. 3. in *physics*, the mutual action of two waves of vibration, as of sound, light, etc., in reinforcing or neutralizing each other. 4. in *radio*, static, unwanted signals, etc., producing a confusion of sounds.

**in·ter·fold** (in′tẽr-fōld′), *v.t.* & *v.i.* to fold together or inside each other.

**in·ter·fuse** (in′tẽr-fūz′), *v.t.* [-FUSED, -FUSING], 1. to combine by mixing or fusing together. 2. to spread itself through; pervade. *v.i.* to fuse; blend. —**in′ter·fu′sion,** *n.*

**in·ter·im** (in′tẽr-im), *n.* [L. < *inter*, between], the period of time between; meantime. *adj.* temporary; provisional: as, an *interim* government.

**in·te·ri·or** (in-têr′i-ẽr), *adj.* [OFr. < L., compar. of *inter*, between], 1. situated within; inner. 2. away from the coast, border, etc.; inland. 3. of the domestic affairs of a country. 4. private. *n.* 1. the interior part of anything; specif., *a)* the inside of a room or building. *b)* the inland part of a country or region. *c)* the inner nature of a person or thing. 2. the domestic affairs of a country: as, the Department of the *Interior.* —**in·te′ri·or′i·ty** (-ôr′ə-ti, -or′-), *n.* —**in·te′ri·or·ly,** *adv.*

**interior decoration,** the decorating and furnishing of the interior of a room, house, etc.

**interj.,** interjection.

**in·ter·ject** (in′tẽr-jekt′), *v.t.* [< L. pp. of *interjicere* < *inter-*, between + *jacere*, to throw], to throw in between; insert; interpose. *v.i.* [Obs.], to come between. —**in′ter·jec′tor** (-jek′tẽr), *n.*

**in·ter·jec·tion** (in′tẽr-jek′shən), *n.* 1. an interjecting. 2. something interjected; exclamation. 3. in *grammar*, an exclamation thrown in without grammatical connection (e.g., ah! pshaw!). —**in′ter·jec′tion·al,** *adj.* —**in′ter·jec′tion·al·ly,** *adv.*

**in·ter·lace** (in′tẽr-lās′), *v.t.* & *v.i.* [-LACED, -LACING], [< OFr.; see INTER- & LACE], 1. to unite by passing over and under each other; weave together; intertwine. 2. to connect intricately. —**in′ter·lace′ment,** *n.*

**in·ter·lard** (in′tẽr-lärd′), *v.t.* [< Fr.; see INTER- & LARD], 1. to intersperse; diversify: as, he *interlarded* his lecture with quotations. 2. to be intermixed in. —**in′ter·lard′ment,** *n.*

**in·ter·lay** (in′tẽr-lā′), *v.t.* [-LAID, -LAYING], 1. to lay or put between or among. 2. ornament with something laid or put between.

**in·ter·leaf** (in′tẽr-lēf′), *n.* [*pl.* -LEAVES], a leaf, usually blank, bound between the other leaves of a book, for notes, etc.

**in·ter·leave** (in′tẽr-lēv′), *v.t.* [-LEAVED, -LEAVING], to put an interleaf or interleaves in.

**in·ter·line** (in′tẽr-lin′), *v.t.* [-LINED, -LINING], to write or print (something) between the lines of (a text, document, etc.).

**in·ter·line** (in′tẽr-līn′), *v.t.* [-LINED, -LINING], to put an inner lining between the outer material and the ordinary lining of (a garment).

**in·ter·lin·e·ar** (in′tẽr-lin′i-ẽr), *adj.* 1. written or printed between the lines. 2. having the same text in different languages printed in alternate lines. Also **in′ter·lin′e·al.**

**in·ter·lin·ing** (in′tẽr-līn′iŋ), *n.* 1. an inner lining between the outer material and the ordinary lining of a garment. 2. any fabric so used.

**in·ter·link** (in′tẽr-liŋk′), *v.t.* to link together.

**in·ter·lock** (in′tẽr-lok′), *v.t.* & *v.i.* to lock together; join with one another. —**in′ter·lock′er,** *n.*

**interlocking directorates,** boards of directors having some members in common, so that the corporations concerned are more or less under the same control.

**in·ter·loc·u·tor** (in'tēr-lok'yoo-tēr), *n.* [< L. pp. < *inter*, between and *loqui*, to talk], 1. a person taking part in a conversation. 2. an entertainer in a minstrel show who acts as master of ceremonies.

**in·ter·loc·u·to·ry** (in'tēr-lok'yoo-tôr'i, -tō'ri), *adj.* 1. of, having the nature of, or occurring in dialogue; conversational. 2. in *law*, not final.

**in·ter·lop·er** (in'tēr-lōp'ēr), *n.* [prob. < D. *enterlooper* < Fr. *entre*, between + D. *loopen*, to run], a person who meddles in others' affairs.

**in·ter·lude** (in'tēr-lōōd'), *n.* [< OFr. < ML. < L. *inter*, between + *ludus*, play], 1. a type of short humorous play formerly presented between the parts of miracle plays or moralities, etc. 2. any performance between the acts of a play. 3. music played between the parts of a song, play, etc. 4. anything that fills time between two events.

**in·ter·mar·ry** (in'tēr-mar'i), *v.i.* [-RIED, -RYING], 1. to become connected by marriage: said of different families, clans, tribes, races, etc. 2. to marry: said of closely related persons. —**in'ter·mar'riage,** *n.*

**in·ter·med·dle** (in'tēr-med''l), *v.i.* [-DLED, -DLING], to meddle in the affairs of others.

**in·ter·me·di·ar·y** (in'tēr-mē'di-er'i), *adj.* 1. acting between two persons; acting as mediator. 2. intermediate. *n.* [*pl.* -IES], a go-between; mediator.

**in·ter·me·di·ate** (in'tēr-mē'di-it), *adj.* [< ML. < L. < *inter-*, between + *medius*, middle], being or happening between; in the middle. *n.* 1. anything intermediate. 2. an intermediary. *v.i.* (-āt'), [-ATED, -ATING], to act as intermediary; mediate. —**in'ter·me'di·ate·ly,** *adv.* —**in'ter·me'di·ate·ness,** *n.*

**in·ter·ment** (in-tūr'mənt), *n.* [see INTER], burial.

**in·ter·mez·zo** (in'tēr-met'sō, -med'zō), *n.* [*pl.* -ZOS, -ZI (-si, -zi)], [It.], 1. a short, light dramatic or musical entertainment between the acts of a play or opera. 2. in *music*, *a)* a short movement connecting the main parts of a composition. *b)* any of certain short works similar to this.

**in·ter·mi·na·ble** (in-tūr'mi-nə-b'l), *adj.* not terminating; lasting, or seeming to last, forever; endless. —**in·ter'mi·na·bly,** *adv.*

**in·ter·min·gle** (in'tēr-miŋ'g'l), *v.t. & v.i.* [-GLED, -GLING], to mix together; mingle; blend.

**in·ter·mis·sion** (in'tēr-mish'ən), *n.* 1. an intermitting or being intermitted; interruption. 2. an interval of time between periods of activity: as, *intermissions* between acts of a play.

**in·ter·mit** (in'tēr-mit'), *v.t. & v.i.* [-MITTED, -MITTING], [< L. < *inter-*, between + *mittere*, to send], to stop for a time; cease at intervals. —**in'ter·mit'ter,** *n.* —**in'ter·mit'ting·ly,** *adv.*

**in·ter·mit·tent** (in'tēr-mit''nt), *adj.* stopping and starting again at intervals; pausing from time to time; periodic. —**in'ter·mit'tence, in'ter·mit'ten·cy,** *n.* —**in'ter·mit'tent·ly,** *adv.*

**in·ter·mix** (in'tēr-miks'), *v.t. & v.i.* to mix together; blend. —**in'ter·mix'ture,** *n.*

**in·tern** (in'tērn), *n.* [< Fr. < L. *internus*, internal], a doctor serving as an assistant resident in a hospital, generally just after graduation from medical school: also sp. **interne.** *v.i.* to serve as an intern. —**in'tern·ship,** *n.*

**in·tern** (in-tūrn'), *v.t.* to detain and confine within a country or a definite area: as, to *intern* aliens in time of war. —**in·tern'ment,** *n.*

**in·ter·nal** (in-tūr'n'l), *adj.* [< ML. < L. *internus*], 1. of or on the inside; inward; inner. 2. of or belonging to the inner nature of a thing; intrinsic: as, *internal* evidence. 3. of or belonging to the inner nature of man; subjective. 4. domestic: as, *internal* revenue. 5. to be taken inside the body: as, *internal* remedies. *n.* 1. *pl.* the internal organs of the body. 2. inner or essential quality or attribute. —**in·ter·nal·i·ty** (in'tēr-nal'ə-ti), *n.* —**in·ter'nal·ly,** *adv.*

**in·ter·nal-com·bus·tion engine** (in-tūr'n'l-kəm-bus'chən), an engine, as in an automobile, in which the power is produced by the explosion of a fuel-and-air mixture within the cylinders.

**in·ter·nal·ize** (in-tūr'n'l-īz'), *v.t.* [-IZED, -IZING], to make internal; specif., to make (others' attitudes, norms, etc.) a part of one's own patterns of thinking. —**in·ter'nal·i·za'tion,** *n.*

**internal medicine,** the branch of medicine that deals with the diagnosis and nonsurgical treatment of diseases of the internal organs and systems.

**internal revenue,** governmental income from taxes on income, profits, luxuries, etc.

**in·ter·na·tion·al** (in'tēr-nash'ən-'l), *adj.* 1. between or among nations: as, an *international* treaty. 2. concerned with the relations between nations: as, an *international* court. *n.* [I-], any of several international socialist organizations. —**in'ter·na'tion·al'i·ty,** *n.* —**in'ter·na'tion·al·ly,** *adv.*

**international date line,** the date line (sense 2).

**in·ter·na·tion·al·ism** (in'tēr-nash'ən-'l-iz'm), *n.* the principle of international co-operation for the common good. —**in'ter·na'tion·al·ist,** *n.*

**in·ter·na·tion·al·ize** (in'tēr-nash'ən-'l-īz'), *v.t.* [-IZED, -IZING], to make international; bring under international control. —**in'ter·na'tion·al·i·za'tion,** *n.*

**International Phonetic Alphabet,** a phonetic alphabet used by most phoneticians and linguists: it has the same symbol for the same sound irrespective of the language.

**in·terne** (in'tērn), *n.* an intern.

**in·ter·ne·cine** (in'tēr-nē'sin, -sīn), *adj.* [< L. < *inter-*, between + *necare*, to kill], deadly or destructive, especially to both sides.

**in·tern·ee** (in'tēr-nē'), *n.* a person interned as a prisoner of war or enemy alien.

**in·ter·nist** (in-tūr'nist), *n.* a doctor who specializes in internal medicine.

**in·ter·pel·late** (in'tēr-pel'āt, in-tūr'pi-lāt'), *v.t.* [-LATED, -LATING], [< L. *interpellatus*, interrupted < *inter-*, between + *pellere*, to drive], to ask (a person) formally for an explanation of his action or policy: a form of political challenge to governmental ministers, etc. —**in'ter·pel'lant,** *adj. & n.* —**in'ter·pel·la'tion,** *n.*

**in·ter·pen·e·trate** (in'tēr-pen'ə-trāt'), *v.t.* [-TRATED, -TRATING], to penetrate thoroughly; permeate. *v.i.* to penetrate each other. —**in'ter·pen'e·tra'tion,** *n.* —**in'ter·pen'e·tra'tive,** *adj.*

**in·ter·phone** (in'tēr-fōn'), *n.* a telephone system for communication between the members of the crew of an airplane, tank, etc.

**in·ter·plan·e·tar·y** (in'tēr-plan'ə-ter'i), *adj.* 1. between planets. 2. within the solar system but outside the atmosphere of any planet or the sun.

**in·ter·play** (in'tēr-plā'), *n.* action, effect, or influence on each other; interaction.

**In·ter·pol** (in'tēr-pōl'), *n.* [*inter*national *pol*ice], an international police organization.

**in·ter·po·late** (in-tūr'pə-lāt'), *v.t.* [-LATED, -LATING], [< L. pp. < *inter-*, between + *polire*, to polish], 1. to change (a book, text, etc.) by putting in new words, subject matter, etc. 2. to insert between or among others. 3. in *mathematics*, to supply (intermediate terms) in a series of terms. *v.i.* to make interpolations. —**in·ter'po·la'tion,** *n.* —**in·ter'po·la'tive,** *adj.* —**in·ter'po·la'tor,** *n.*

**in·ter·pose** (in'tēr-pōz'), *v.t.* [-POSED, -POSING], 1. to place between; insert. 2. to introduce by way of intervention. 3. to put in as an interruption. *v.i.* 1. to be or come between. 2. to intervene. 3. to interrupt. —**in'ter·pos'er,** *n.* —**in'ter·pos'ing·ly,** *adv.* —**in'ter·po·si'tion** (-pə-zish'ən), **in'ter·pos'al,** *n.*

**in·ter·pret** (in-tūr'prit), *v.t.* [< Fr. < L. *interpretari* < *interpres*, negotiator], 1. to explain the meaning of; clarify or translate. 2. to have one's own understanding of; construe: as, he *interpreted* the silence as contempt. 3. to bring out the meaning of, especially to give one's own conception of, as in performing a play. *v.i.* to act as an interpreter; translate. —**in·ter'pret·a·bil'i·ty,** *n.* —**in·ter'pret·a·ble,** *adj.* —**in·ter'pre·ta'tive, in·ter'pre·tive,** *adj.*

**in·ter·pre·ta·tion** (in-tūr'pri-tā'shən), *n.* 1. an interpreting. 2. the result of this; explanation; translation. 3. the expression of a person's conception of a work of art, subject, etc. through acting, writing, etc. —**in·ter'pre·ta'tion·al,** *adj.*

**in·ter·pret·er** (in-tūr'pri-tēr), *n.* a person who interprets; specif., a person whose work is translating a foreign language orally.

**in·ter·ra·cial** (in'tēr-rā'shəl), *adj.* between, among, or for persons of different races.

**in·ter·reg·num** (in'tēr-reg'nəm), *n.* [*pl.* -NUMS, -NA (-nə)], [L. < *inter-*, between + *regnum*, rule], 1. an interval between two successive reigns, when the country has no sovereign. 2. any period without the usual ruler, governor, etc. 3. any break in a series or in a continuity; interval. —**in'ter·reg'nal,** *adj.*

**in·ter·re·lat·ed** (in'tēr-ri-lā'tid), *adj.* having a close connection with each other or one another; mutually related. —**in'ter·re·la'tion,** *n.* —**in'ter·re·la'tion·ship,** *n.*

**in·ter·ro·gate** (in-ter'ə-gāt'), *v.t.* [-GATED, -GATING],

[< L. pp. < *inter-*, between + *rogare*, to ask], to examine by formal questioning: as, he *interrogated* the witness. *v.i.* to ask questions. —**in·ter′ro·gat′·ing·ly,** *adv.* —**in·ter′ro·ga′tor,** *n.*

**in·ter·ro·ga·tion** (in-ter′ə-gā′shən), *n.* 1. an interrogating; a questioning or examination. 2. a question. —**in·ter′ro·ga′tion·al,** *adj.*

**interrogation mark** (or **point**), a mark of punctuation (?) indicating that the sentence preceding it is a direct question, or showing doubt, uncertainty, etc.: also called *question mark*.

**in·ter·rog·a·tive** (in′tə-rog′ə-tiv), *adj.* asking, or having the form of, a question. *n.* an interrogative word, element, etc. (e.g., what? where?). —**in′·ter·rog′a·tive·ly,** *adv.*

**in·ter·rog·a·to·ry** (in′tə-rog′ə-tôr′i, -tō′ri), *adj.* expressing a question. *n.* [*pl.* -RIES], an interrogating. —**in′ter·rog′a·to′ri·ly,** *adv.*

**in·ter·rupt** (in′tə-rupt′), *v.t.* [< L. *interruptus*, pp. < *inter-*, between + *rumpere*, to break], 1. to break into (a discussion, etc.), or break in upon (a person) while he is speaking, singing, etc. 2. to make a break in the continuity of; obstruct. *v.i.* to break in upon an action, talk, etc. —**in′ter·rupt′er,** *n.* —**in′ter·rup′tive,** *adj.*

**in·ter·rup·tion** (in′tə-rup′shən), *n.* 1. an interrupting or being interrupted. 2. anything that interrupts. 3. an intermission.

**in·ter·scho·las·tic** (in′tẽr-skə-las′tik), *adj.* between or among schools: as, *interscholastic* sports.

**in·ter·sect** (in′tẽr-sekt′), *v.t.* [< L. *intersectus*, pp. < *inter-*, between + *secare*, to cut], to dividei nto two parts by passing through or across. *v.i.* to cross each other.

**in·ter·sec·tion** (in′tẽr-sek′shən), *n.* 1. an intersecting. 2. a place of intersecting; specif., *a*) the point or line where two lines or surfaces meet or cross. *b*) the place where two streets cross.

**in·ter·sperse** (in′tẽr-spũrs′), *v.t.* [-SPERSED, -SPERSING], [< L. *interspersus*, pp. < *inter-*, among + *spargere*, to scatter], 1. to scatter among other things; put here and there. 2. to decorate or diversify with things scattered here and there. —**in′ter·sper′sion** (-spũr′zhən, -shən), *n.*

**in·ter·state** (in′tẽr-stāt′), *adj.* between states of a federal government: as, *interstate* commerce.

**in·ter·stel·lar** (in′tẽr-stel′ẽr), *adj.* [*inter-* + *stellar*], between or among the stars.

**in·ter·stice** (in-tũr′stis), *n.* [*pl.* -STICES], [Fr. < L. < *inter-*, between + *sistere*, to set < *stare*, to stand], a small space between things or parts of things; crevice; crack. —**in·ter·sti·tial** (in′tẽr-stish′əl), *adj.* —**in′ter·sti′tial·ly,** *adv.*

**in·ter·twine** (in′tẽr-twīn′), *v.t.* & *v.i.* [-TWINED, -TWINING], to twine together; intertwist. —**in′·ter·twine′ment,** *n.* —**in′ter·twin′ing·ly,** *adv.*

**in·ter·twist** (in′tẽr-twist′), *v.t.* & *v.i.* to twist together; intertwine. —**in′ter·twist′ing·ly,** *adv.*

**in·ter·ur·ban** (in′tẽr-ũr′bən), *adj.* [*inter-* + *urban*], between cities or towns. *n.* an interurban railway, train, etc.

**in·ter·val** (in′tẽr-v′l), *n.* [< OFr. < L. < *inter-*, between + *vallum*, wall], 1. a space between two things; distance. 2. a period of time between two events. 3. the extent of difference between two qualities, conditions, etc. 4. in *music*, the difference in pitch between two tones. —**at intervals,** 1. now and then. 2. here and there.

**in·ter·vene** (in′tẽr-vēn′), *v.i.* [-VENED, -VENING], [< L. < *inter-*, between + *venire*, to come], 1. to come or be between. 2. to occur between two events, etc. 3. to come or be in between as something irrelevant. 4. to come in to modify, settle, or hinder some action, dispute, etc. —**in′ter·ven′er,** *n.* —**in′ter·ven′ient** (-yənt), *adj.* & *n.*

**in·ter·ven·tion** (in′tẽr-ven′shən), *n.* 1. an intervening. 2. any interference in the affairs of others; esp., interference of one state in the affairs of another. —**in′ter·ven′tion·ist,** *n.* & *adj.*

**in·ter·view** (in′tẽr-vū′), *n.* [< Fr.; see INTER- & VIEW], 1. a meeting of people face to face to confer about something. 2. a meeting between a reporter and a person whose activities, views, etc. are to be the subject of a published article. 3. an article giving such information. *v.t.* to have an interview with. —**in′ter·view′er,** *n.*

**in·ter·weave** (in′tẽr-wēv′), *v.t.* & *v.i.* [-WOVE or *rarely* -WEAVED, -WOVEN or -WOVE, -WEAVING], 1. to weave together; intertwine. 2. to connect closely; intermingle. —**in′ter·wo′ven** (-wō′vən), *adj.*

**in·tes·tate** (in-tes′tāt, -tit), *adj.* [< OFr. < L. < *in-*, not + *testatus*, pp. of *testari*, to make a will], 1. having made no will. 2. not disposed of by a will. *n.* a person who has died intestate. —**in·tes′ta·cy** (-tə-si), *n.*

**in·tes·ti·nal** (in-tes′ti-n′l), *adj.* of or in the intestines. —**in·tes′ti·nal·ly,** *adv.*

**in·tes·tine** (in-tes′tin), *adj.* [< L. *intestinus* < *intus*, within < *in*, in], internal; esp., within a country or community; domestic. *n.* *usually pl.* the lower part of the alimentary canal, extending from the stomach to the anus and consisting of a convoluted upper part (**small intestine**) and a lower part of greater diameter (**large intestine**); bowel(s).

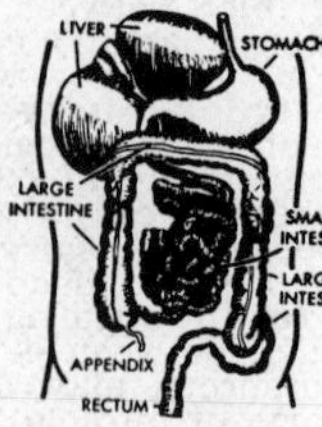

INTESTINES

**in·thrall, in·thral** (in-thrôl′), *v.t.* [-THRALLED, -THRALLING], to enthrall. —**in·thrall′ment, in·thral′ment,** *n.*

**in·throne** (in-thrōn′), *v.t.* [-THRONED, -THRONING], to enthrone. —**in·throne′ment,** *n.*

**in·ti·ma·cy** (in′tə-mə-si), *n.* [*pl.* -CIES], 1. a being intimate; familiarity. 2. an intimate act; esp., illicit sexual intercourse: a euphemism.

**in·ti·mate** (in′tə-mit), *adj.* [< Fr. < L. *intimus*, superl. of *intus*, within], 1. inmost; intrinsic: as, the *intimate* structure of matter. 2. most private or personal: as, one's *intimate* feelings. 3. closely associated; very familiar: as, an *intimate* friend. 4. *a*) resulting from careful study. *b*) very close: as, an *intimate* acquaintance with the facts. 5. having illicit sexual relations: a euphemism. *n.* an intimate friend or companion. —**in′ti·mate·ly,** *adv.* —**in′ti·mate·ness,** *n.*

**in·ti·mate** (in′tə-māt′), *v.t.* [-MATED, -MATING], [< L. pp. of *intimare*, to announce < *intimus*: see prec. entry], 1. to make known formally; announce. 2. to hint or imply. —**in′ti·mat′er,** *n.*

**in·ti·ma·tion** (in′tə-mā′shən), *n.* 1. an intimating. 2. a formal announcement or notice. 3. a hint.

**in·tim·i·date** (in-tim′ə-dāt′), *v.t.* [-DATED, -DATING], [< ML. pp. of *intimidare* < L. *in-*, in + *timidus*, afraid], 1. to make timid; make afraid. 2. to force or deter as with threats; cow. —**in·tim′i·da′·tion,** *n.* —**in·tim′i·da′tor,** *n.*

**in·ti·tle** (in-tī′t′l), *v.t.* [-TLED, -TLING], to entitle.

**in·to** (in′to͞o, -too, -tə), *prep.* [AS.], 1. to the inside of; toward and within: as, *into* a house. 2. advancing to the midst of (a period of time): as, they talked *into* the night. 3. to the form, substance, etc. of: as, divided *into* parts.

**in·tol·er·a·ble** (in-tol′ẽr-ə-b′l), *adj.* not tolerable; unbearable; too severe, painful, etc. to be endured. —**in·tol′er·a·bil′i·ty, in·tol′er·a·ble·ness,** *n.* —**in·tol′er·a·bly,** *adv.*

**in·tol·er·ance** (in-tol′ẽr-əns), *n.* 1. lack of tolerance, especially in matters of religion; bigotry. 2. inability to endure.

**in·tol·er·ant** (in-tol′ẽr-ənt), *adj.* not tolerant; unwilling to tolerate others' opinions, religious beliefs, etc.; illiberal. *n.* an intolerant person. —**intolerant of,** not able or willing to tolerate. —**in·tol′er·ant·ly,** *adv.*

**in·tomb** (in-to͞om′), *v.t.* to entomb.

**in·to·na·tion** (in′tō-nā′shən), *n.* 1. an intoning. 2. the manner of uttering tones with regard to rise and fall in pitch. 3. the manner of applying final pitch to a spoken sentence or phrase.

**in·tone** (in-tōn′), *v.t.* [-TONED, -TONING], [< ML; see IN- (in) & TONE], 1. to utter or recite in a singing tone or in prolonged monotones; chant. 2. to give a particular intonation to. *v.i.* to speak or recite in a singing tone or in prolonged monotones; chant. —**in·ton′er,** *n.*

‡**in to·to** (in tō′tō), [L.], as a whole; entirely.

**in·tox·i·cant** (in-tok′sə-kənt), *n.* something that intoxicates; specif., *a*) a drug that intoxicates. *b*) alcoholic liquor. *adj.* intoxicating.

**in·tox·i·cate** (in-tok′sə-kāt′), *v.t.* [-CATED, -CATING], [< ML. pp. < L. *in-*, in + *toxicum*, poison], 1. to make drunk. 2. to excite greatly; elate to a frenzy. —**in·tox′i·cat′ing·ly,** *adv.* —**in·tox′i·ca′tive,** *adj.* —**in·tox′i·ca′tor,** *n.*

**in·tox·i·ca·tion** (in-tok′sə-kā′shən), *n.* 1. a making or becoming drunk. 2. in *medicine*, a poisoning or becoming poisoned. 3. great excitement.

**intr.,** intransitive.

**in·tra-,** [L. < *intra*, within], a combining form meaning *within*, *inside of*, as in *intramural*.

**in·trac·ta·ble** (in-trak′tə-b′l), *adj.* not tractable; specif., *a*) hard to manage; unruly; stubborn. *b*) hard to work, cure, etc. —**in·trac′ta·bil′i·ty, in·trac′ta·ble·ness,** *n.* —**in·trac′ta·bly,** *adv.*

**in·tra·dos** (in-trā′dos), *n.* [Fr. < L. *intra*, within + Fr. *dos* < L. *dorsum*, the back], the inside curve or surface of an arch or vault.

**in·tra·mu·ral** (in′trə-myoor′əl), *adj.* [*intra-* +

*mural*], within the walls or limits of a city, college, etc.: as, *intramural* athletics.
**in·tra·mus·cu·lar** (in'trə-mus'kyoo-lẽr), ***adj.*** located or injected within the muscle.
**intrans.,** intransitive.
**in·tran·si·gent** (in-tran'si-jənt), ***adj.*** [< Fr. < Sp. < L. *in-*, not + pp. of *transigere*, to settle], refusing to compromise, be reconciled, etc.; uncompromising. ***n.*** one who is intransigent, especially in politics. **—in·tran'si·gence, in·tran'si·gen·cy, *n.* —in·tran'si·gent·ly, *adv.***
**in·tran·si·tive** (in-tran'sə-tiv), ***adj.*** not transitive; not used with an object to complete its meaning: said of certain verbs. ***n.*** an intransitive verb. **—in·tran'si·tive·ly, *adv.***
**in·tra·state** (in'trə-stāt'), ***adj.*** within a state; esp., within a State of the United States.
**in·tra·ve·nous** (in'trə-vē'nəs), ***adj.*** [*intra-* + *venous*], in, into, or within a vein or veins: as, an *intravenous* injection.
**in·treat** (in-trēt'), ***v.t. & v.i.*** to entreat.
**in·trench** (in-trench'), ***v.t. & v.i.*** to entrench. **—in·trench'er, *n.* —in·trench'ment, *n.***
**in·trep·id** (in-trep'id), ***adj.*** [< L. < *in-*, not + *trepidus*, alarmed], unafraid; bold; fearless; very brave. **—in'tre·pid'i·ty, *n.* —in·trep'id·ly, *adv.***
**Int. Rev.,** internal revenue.
**in·tri·ca·cy** (in'tri-kə-si), ***n.*** 1. an intricate quality or state; complexity. 2. [*pl.* -CIES], something intricate; involved matter, etc.
**in·tri·cate** (in'tri-kit), ***adj.*** [< L. pp. of *intricare*, to entangle < *in-*, in + *tricae*, vexations], hard to follow or understand because entangled, complicated, perplexing, etc.: as, an *intricate* path, *intricate* directions. **—in'tri·cate·ly, *adv.* —in'tri·cate·ness, *n.***
**in·trigue** (in-trēg'; *for n., also* in'trēg), ***v.i.*** [-TRIGUED, -TRIGUING], [< Fr. < It. < L. *intricare;* see INTRICATE], 1. to carry on a secret love affair. 2. to plot or scheme secretly or underhandedly. ***v.t.*** 1. to get by secret or underhanded plotting. 2. to excite the interest or curiosity of: as, the puzzle *intrigued* her. ***n.*** 1. secret or underhanded plotting. 2. a secret or underhanded plot or scheme. 3. a secret love affair. **—in·tri'guer, *n.* —in·tri'guing·ly, *adv.***
**in·trin·sic** (in-trin'sik), ***adj.*** [< Fr. < ML. < L. *intrinsecus*, inwardly < *intra-*, within + *secus*, otherwise], belonging to the real nature of a thing; essential; inherent: opposed to *extrinsic*. Also **in·trin'si·cal. —in·trin'si·cal·ly, *adv.***
**introd., intro.,** 1. introduction. 2. introductory.
**in·tro·duce** (in'trə-dōōs', -dūs'), ***v.t.*** [-DUCED, -DUCING], [< L. < *intro-*, in + *ducere*, to lead], 1. to conduct in. 2. to bring formally into society. 3. to put in; insert: as, to *introduce* a drain into a wound. 4. to add as a new feature: as, *introduce* some humor into the play. 5. to bring into use, knowledge, or fashion: as, the war *introduced* new words. 6. *a*) to make acquainted with; present to: as, *introduce* me to her. *b*) to give knowledge or experience of: as, they *introduced* him to music. 7. to bring forward: as, *introduce* a bill into Congress. 8. to start; begin: as, he *introduced* his speech with a joke. **—in'tro·duc'er, *n.* —in'tro·duc'i·ble, *adj.***
**in·tro·duc·tion** (in'trə-duk'shən), ***n.*** 1. an introducing or being introduced. 2. anything brought into use, knowledge, or fashion. 3. anything that introduces; specif., *a*) the preliminary section of a book, speech, etc.; preface; foreword. *b*) a preliminary guide or text. 4. the formal presentation of one person to another, to society, etc.
**in·tro·duc·tive** (in'trə-duk'tiv), ***adj.*** introductory. **—in'tro·duc'tive·ly, *adv.***
**in·tro·duc·to·ry** (in'trə-duk'tẽr-i), ***adj.*** used as an introduction; serving to introduce; preliminary. **—in'tro·duc'to·ri·ly, *adv.***
**in·tro·it** (in-trō'it), ***n.*** [< Fr. < L. < *intro-*, within + *ire*, to go], 1. in the *Anglican Church*, a psalm or hymn at the opening of the Communion service. 2. [I-], in the *R. C. Church*, the first variable part of the Mass, consisting of a psalm verse and an antiphon followed by the *Gloria Patri.*
**in·tro·spec·tion** (in'trə-spek'shən), ***n.*** [< L. *introspectus*, pp. < *intro-*, within + *specere*, to look], a looking into one's own mind, feelings, etc. **—in'tro·spec'tive, *adj.* —in'tro·spec'tive·ly, *adv.***
**in·tro·ver·sion** (in'trə-vũr'zhən, -shən), ***n.*** [see INTROVERT], a tendency to direct one's interest upon oneself rather than upon external objects or events. **—in'tro·ver'sive, *adj.***
**in·tro·vert** (in'trə-vũrt'; *for n. & adj.*, in'trə-vũrt'), ***v.t.*** [< L. *intro*, within + *vertere*, to turn], 1. to direct (one's interest, mind, etc.) upon oneself. 2. to bend (something) inward. ***v.i.*** to become introverted. ***n.*** a person characterized by introversion: opposed to *extrovert*. ***adj.*** of or characterized by introversion.
**in·trude** (in-trōōd'), ***v.t.*** [-TRUDED, -TRUDING], [< L. < *in-*, in + *trudere*, to thrust], 1. to force (oneself) upon others without being asked or welcomed. 2. in *geology*, to force (melted rock) into another stratum. ***v.i.*** to intrude oneself. **—in·trud'er, *n.* —in·trud'ing·ly, *adv.***
**in·tru·sion** (in-trōō'zhən), ***n.*** 1. an intruding. 2. intrusive rock.
**in·tru·sive** (in-trōō'siv), ***adj.*** 1. intruding. 2. in *geology*, formed by intruding. **—in·tru'sive·ly, *adv.* —in·tru'sive·ness, *n.***
**in·trust** (in-trust'), ***v.t.*** to entrust.
**in·tu·i·tion** (in'tōō-ish'ən, -tū-), ***n.*** [< ML. < L. *intuitus*, pp. < *in-*, in + *tueri*, to look at], 1. the immediate knowing or learning of something without the conscious use of reasoning. 2. something known or learned in this way. **—in'tu·i'tion·al, *adj.* —in'tu·i'tion·al·ly, *adv.***
**in·tu·i·tive** (in-tōō'i-tiv, -tū'-), ***adj.*** 1. knowing, learning, or characterized by intuition. 2. perceived by intuition: as, an *intuitive* truth. **—in·tu'i·tive·ly, *adv.* —in·tu'i·tive·ness, *n.***
**in·un·date** (in'ən-dāt', in-un'-), ***v.t.*** [-DATED, -DATING], [< L. pp. < *in-*, in + *undare*, to flood < *unda*, a wave], to cover as with a flood; deluge; overflow or overwhelm. **—in·un'dant** (-dənt), ***adj.* —in'un·da'tion, *n.* —in'un·da'tor, *n.***
**in·ure** (in-yoor'), ***v.t.*** [-URED, -URING], [*in-*, in + obs. *ure*, work < OFr. *eure* < L. *opera*, work], to cause to become used to (something difficult, painful, etc.); habituate. ***v.i.*** to come into use or take effect. **—in·ure'ment, *n.***
**inv.,** 1. invented. 2. inventor. 3. invoice.
**‡in va·cu·o** (in vak'ū-ō'), [L.], in a vacuum.
**in·vade** (in-vād'), ***v.t.*** [-VADED, -VADING], [< L. < *in-*, in + *vadere*, to go], 1. to enter forcibly, as to conquer. 2. to crowd into; throng: as, we *invaded* the kitchen. 3. to intrude upon; violate: as, he *invaded* my privacy. 4. to spread through with harmful effects: as, disease *invades* tissue. ***v.i.*** to make an invasion. **—in·vad'er, *n.***
**in·va·lid** (in'və-lid), ***adj.*** [Fr. < L. < *in-*, not + *validus*, strong], 1. not well; weak and sickly. 2. of or for invalids: as, an *invalid* home. ***n.*** a weak, sickly person; esp., one who is chronically ill or disabled. ***v.t.*** 1. to disable or weaken. 2. to dismiss (a soldier, sailor, etc.) from active service because of injury or illness. ***v.i.*** to become an invalid. **—in'va·lid·ism, *n.***
**in·val·id** (in-val'id), ***adj.*** not valid; having no force; null or void. **—in·va·lid·i·ty** (in'və-lid'ə-ti), ***n.* —in·val'id·ly, *adv.***
**in·val·i·date** (in-val'ə-dāt'), ***v.t.*** [-DATED, -DATING], to make invalid; deprive of legal force. **—in·val'i·da'tion, *n.* —in·val'i·da'tor, *n.***
**in·val·u·a·ble** (in-val'ū-ə-b'l), ***adj.*** too valuable to be measured; priceless; precious. **—in·val'u·a·ble·ness, *n.* —in·val'u·a·bly, *adv.***
**in·var·i·a·ble** (in-vâr'i-ə-b'l), ***adj.*** not variable; unchanging; constant; uniform. **—in·var'i·a·bil'i·ty, in·var'i·a·ble·ness, *n.* —in·var'i·a·bly, *adv.***
**in·va·sion** (in-vā'zhən), ***n.*** an invading; specif., *a*) an entering or being entered by an attacking army. *b*) an intrusion or infringement. *c*) the onset (*of* a disease). **—in·va'sive, *adj.***
**in·vec·tive** (in-vek'tiv), ***adj.*** [< Late OFr. < L. < pp. of *invehere;* see INVEIGH], inveighing; vituperative. ***n.*** 1. a violent verbal attack; denunciation; vituperation. 2. *often in pl.* an abusive word.
**in·veigh** (in-vā'), ***v.i.*** [< L. *invehere*, to scold < *in-*, in + *vehere*, to carry], to make a violent verbal attack; utter invective; rail (usually with *against*). **—in·veigh'er, *n.***
**in·vei·gle** (in-vē'g'l, -vā'-), ***v.t.*** [-GLED, -GLING], [prob. < Fr. *aveugler*, to blind < LL. < L. *ab*, from + *oculus*, an eye], to lead on with deception; entice or trick into doing something, etc. **—in·vei'gle·ment, *n.* —in·vei'gler, *n.***
**in·vent** (in-vent'), ***v.t.*** [< OFr. < L. *inventus*, pp. < *in-*, on + *venire*, to come], 1. to think up; devise in the mind: as, *invent* an alibi. 2. to think out or produce (a new device, etc.); devise for the first time: as, Edison *invented* the phonograph. **—in·vent'i·ble, *adj.***
**in·ven·tion** (in-ven'shən), ***n.*** 1. an inventing or

being invented. 2. the power of inventing; ingenuity. 3. something invented; specif., *a*) something thought up; falsehood. *b*) a new device or contrivance. —**in·ven′tion·al,** *adj.*

**in·ven·tive** (in-ven′tiv), *adj.* 1. of invention. 2. skilled in inventing. 3. indicating an ability to invent. —**in·ven′tive·ly,** *adv.* —**in·ven′tive·ness,** *n.*

**in·ven·tor, in·vent·er** (in-ven′tẽr), *n.* one who invents; esp., one who devises a new contrivance or system.

**in·ven·to·ry** (in′vən-tôr′i, -tō′ri), *n.* [*pl.* -RIES], [< ML. < L. < *inventus;* see INVENT], 1. an itemized list of goods, property, etc., as of a business, often prepared annually. 2. the store of goods, etc. for such listing; stock. *v.t.* [-RIED, -RYING], 1. to make an inventory of. 2. to place on an inventory. —**in′ven·to′ri·al,** *adj.* —**in′ven·to′ri·al·ly,** *adv.*

**In·ver·ness** (in′vẽr-nes′), *n.* [often i-], 1. a kind of overcoat with a long, removable, sleeveless cape. 2. the cape: also **Inverness cape.**

**in·verse** (in-vũrs′; *also, for adj.,* in′vũrs′), *adj.* inverted; reversed in order or relation; directly opposite. *n.* any inverse thing; direct opposite: as, love is the *inverse* of hate. *v.t.* [-VERSED, -VERSING], to invert. —**in·verse′ly,** *adv.*

**in·ver·sion** (in-vũr′zhən, -shən), *n.* 1. an inverting or being inverted. 2. something inverted; reversal. 3. in *grammar & rhetoric,* a reversal of the normal order of words in a sentence. 4. in *meteorology,* an increase with altitude in the temperature of the air, preventing the normal rising of surface air. 5. in *music,* the reversal of the position of the tones in an interval, chord, etc., as by raising the lower tone by an octave. —**in·ver′sive,** *adj.*

**in·vert** (in-vũrt′), *v.t.* [< L. < *in-,* to + *vertere,* to turn], 1. to turn upside down. 2. to change to the direct opposite; reverse the order, position, direction, etc. of. 3. to subject to inversion. *n.* (in′-vũrt′), an inverted person or thing. —**in·vert′er,** *n.* —**in·vert′i·ble,** *adj.*

**in·ver·te·brate** (in-vũr′tə-brit, -brāt′), *adj.* 1. not vertebrate; having no backbone, or spinal column. 2. of invertebrates. *n.* any animal without a backbone: the classification includes all animals except fishes, amphibians, reptiles, birds, and mammals.

**in·vest** (in-vest′), *v.t.* [< L. < *in-,* in + *vestis,* clothing], 1. [Rare], to clothe; array. 2. *a*) to cover or surround as with a garment: as, fog *invests* the city. *b*) to endue. 3. to install in office with ceremony. 4. to furnish with power, privilege, or authority. 5. to put (money) into business, stocks, bonds, etc., for the purpose of obtaining a profit; hence, 6. to spend or pay (time, money, etc.) with the expectation of some satisfaction. 7. in *military usage,* to besiege (a town, port, etc.). *v.i.* to invest money. —**in·ves′tor,** *n.*

**in·ves·ti·gate** (in-ves′tə-gāt′), *v.t.* [-GATED, -GATING], [< L. pp. < *in-,* in + *vestigare,* to track], to search or inquire into; examine in detail. *v.i.* to make an investigation. —**in·ves′ti·ga·ble** (-ti-gə-b'l), *adj.* —**in·ves′ti·ga′tive, in·ves′ti·ga·to′ry** (-gə-tôr′i, -tō′-ri), *adj.* —**in·ves′ti·ga′tor,** *n.*

**in·ves·ti·ga·tion** (in-ves′tə-gā′shən), *n.* an investigating; careful search; systematic inquiry.

**in·ves·ti·ture** (in-ves′tə-chẽr), *n.* 1. a formal investing with an office, power, authority, etc. 2. anything that clothes or covers; vesture.

**in·vest·ment** (in-vest′mənt), *n.* 1. an investing or being invested. 2. clothing; covering. 3. an investiture. 4. *a*) the investing of money. *b*) the amount of money invested. *c*) anything in which money is or may be invested.

**in·vet·er·ate** (in-vet′ẽr-it), *adj.* [< L. pp. of *inveterare,* to age < *in-,* in + *vetus,* old], 1. firmly established over a long period; deep-rooted. 2. settled in a habit, practice, prejudice, etc.; habitual. —**in·vet′er·a·cy,** *n.* —**in·vet′er·ate·ly,** *adv.*

**in·vid·i·ous** (in-vid′i-əs), *adj.* [< L. < *invidia,* envy], 1. *a*) such as to excite ill will or envy; giving offense. *b*) giving offense by discriminating unfairly: as, *invidious* comparisons. —**in·vid′i·ous·ly,** *adv.* —**in·vid′i·ous·ness,** *n.*

**in·vig·or·ate** (in-vig′ə-rāt′), *v.t.* [-ATED, -ATING], [see VIGOR], to give vigor to; fill with energy; strengthen; enliven. —**in·vig′or·at′ing·ly,** *adv.* —**in·vig′or·a′tion,** *n.* —**in·vig′or·a′tive,** *adj.* —**in·vig′or·a′tive·ly,** *adv.* —**in·vig′or·a′tor,** *n.*

**in·vin·ci·ble** (in-vin′sə-b'l), *adj.* [< Late OFr. < L; see IN- (not) & VINCIBLE], that cannot be overcome; unconquerable. —**in·vin′ci·bil′i·ty, in·vin′ci·ble·ness,** *n.* —**in·vin′ci·bly,** *adv.*

**in·vi·o·la·ble** (in-vī′ə-lə-b'l), *adj.* 1. not to be violated; not to be profaned or injured; sacred: as, an *inviolable* promise. 2. that cannot be violated; indestructible. —**in·vi′o·la·bil′i·ty, in·vi′o·la·ble·ness,** *n.* —**in·vi′o·la·bly,** *adv.*

**in·vi·o·late** (in-vī′ə-lit, -lāt′), *adj.* not violated; kept sacred or unbroken. —**in·vi′o·la·cy** (-lə-si), **in·vi′o·late·ness,** *n.* —**in·vi′o·late·ly,** *adv.*

**in·vis·i·ble** (in-viz′ə-b'l), *adj.* 1. not visible; that cannot be seen. 2. out of sight. 3. imperceptible. 4. kept hidden: as, *invisible* assets. *n.* an invisible thing or being. —**the Invisible,** 1. God. 2. the unseen world. —**in·vis′i·bil′i·ty, in·vis′i·ble·ness,** *n.* —**in·vis′i·bly,** *adv.*

**in·vi·ta·tion** (in′və-tā′shən), *n.* 1. an inviting to come somewhere or do something. 2. the message or note used in inviting. —**in′vi·ta′tion·al,** *adj.*

**in·vite** (in-vīt′), *v.t.* [-VITED, -VITING], [< Fr. < L. *invitare*], 1. to ask (a person) courteously to come somewhere or do something. 2. to make a request for: as, the speaker *invited* questions. 3. to give occasion for: as, such conduct *invites* scandal. 4. to tempt; entice. *n.* (in′vīt), [Slang], an invitation. —**in·vit′er,** *n.*

**in·vit·ing** (in-vīt′iŋ), *adj.* tempting; enticing. —**in·vit′ing·ly,** *adv.* —**in·vit′ing·ness,** *n.*

**in·vo·ca·tion** (in′və-kā′shən), *n.* 1. an invoking of God, the Muses, etc. for blessing, help, etc. 2. a formal prayer used in invoking, as at the beginning of a church service. 3. *a*) a conjuring of evil spirits. *b*) an incantation. —**in·voc·a·to·ry** (in-vok′-ə-tôr′i, -tō′ri), *adj.*

**in·voice** (in′vois), *n.* [< Fr. *envois,* pl. of *envoi,* a sending; see ENVOY], 1. an itemized list of goods shipped to a buyer, stating quantities, prices, shipping charges, etc. 2. a shipment of invoiced goods. *v.t.* [-VOICED, -VOICING], to make an invoice of; enter in an invoice.

**in·voke** (in-vōk′), *v.t.* [-VOKED, -VOKING], [< Fr. < L. < *in-,* on + *vocare,* to call], 1. to call on (God, the Muses, etc.) for blessing, help, etc. 2. to summon (evil spirits) by incantation; conjure. 3. to ask solemnly for; implore. —**in·vok′er,** *n.*

**in·vo·lu·cre** (in′və-lōō′kẽr), *n.* [Fr. < L. *involucrum,* wrapper < *involvere;* see INVOLVE], in *botany,* a ring of bracts at the base of a flower cluster or fruit. —**in′vo·lu′cral,** *adj.*

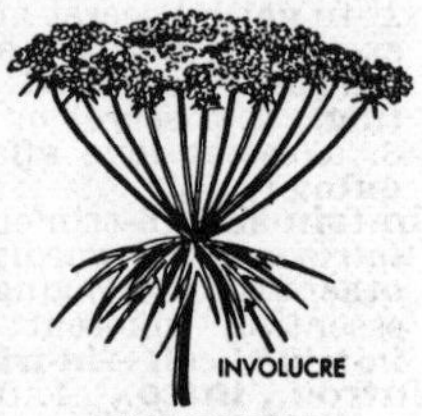

INVOLUCRE

**in·vol·un·tar·y** (in-vol′ən-ter′i), *adj.* not voluntary; specif., *a*) not done of one's own free will. *b*) unintentional; accidental. *c*) not consciously controlled: as, digestion is *involuntary.* —**in·vol′un·tar′i·ly,** *adv.* —**in·vol′un·tar′i·ness,** *n.*

**in·vo·lute** (in′və-lōōt′), *adj.* [L. *involutus,* pp. of *involvere;* see INVOLVE], 1. intricate; involved. 2. rolled up or curled in a spiral; having the whorls wound closely: as, *involute* shells. 3. in *botany,* rolled inward at the edges: as, *involute* leaves. *n.* [Rare], anything involved. —**in′vo·lut′ed,** *adj.* —**in′vo·lut′ed·ly,** *adv.*

**in·vo·lu·tion** (in′və-lōō′shən), *n.* 1. an involving or being involved; entanglement. 2. something involved; complication; intricacy. —**in′vo·lu′tion·al, in′vo·lu′tion·ar′y,** *adj.*

**in·volve** (in-volv′), *v.t.* [-VOLVED, -VOLVING], [< OFr. < L. < *in-,* in + *volvere,* to roll], 1. to wrap; enfold; envelop: as, fog *involved* the shore. 2. to wind spirally; coil up. 3. to make intricate; complicate. 4. to entangle in difficulty, danger, etc.; implicate. 5. to roll up within itself; include: as, the epidemic *involved* thousands. 6. to bring into connection; require: as, saving money *involves* thrift. 7. to occupy the attention of: as, he was *involved* in solving a problem. —**in·volve′ment,** *n.* —**in·volv′er,** *n.*

**in·vul·ner·a·ble** (in-vul′nẽr-ə-b'l), *adj.* 1. that cannot be wounded or injured. 2. proof against attack. —**in·vul′ner·a·bil′i·ty, in·vul′ner·a·ble·ness,** *n.* —**in·vul′ner·a·bly,** *adv.*

**in·ward** (in′wẽrd), *adj.* [AS. *inweard;* see IN- (in) & -WARD], 1. situated within; internal: as, the *inward* organs of the body. 2. mental or spiritual. 3. directed toward the inside: as, the *inward* pull of a centrifuge. 4. inland: as, *inward* Asia. *n.* 1. the inside. 2. *pl.* the entrails. *adv.* 1. toward the inside or center. 2. into the mind or soul. Also **in′wards,** *adv.*

**in·ward·ly** (in′wẽrd-li), *adv.* 1. in or on the inside; internally. 2. in the mind or spirit. 3. toward the inside or center.

**in·ward·ness** (in′wẽrd-nis), *n.* 1. the inner nature or meaning. 2. spirituality. 3. sincerity.

**in·weave** (in-wēv′), *v.t.* [-WOVE or *rarely* -WEAVED, -WOVEN or -WOVE, -WEAVING], to weave in.

**in·wrap** (in-rap′), *v.t.* [-WRAPPED, -WRAPPING], to enwrap.

**in·wreathe** (in-rēth′), *v.t.* [-WREATHED, -WREATHING], to enwreathe.
**in·wrought** (in′rôt′, in-rôt′), *adj.* 1. inwoven; interwoven. 2. having a decoration worked in. 3. closely blended with other things.
**I·o** (ī′ō), *n.* in *Gr. mythology*, a maiden loved by Zeus and changed into a heifer by Hera.
**Io,** in *chemistry*, ionium.
**i·o·dide** (ī′ə-dīd′, -did), *n.* a compound of iodine with another element or with a radical: also **i′o·did** (-did).
**i·o·dine** (ī′ə-dīn′, -din; *in chemistry, often* -dēn′), *n.* [Fr. *iode* < Gr. *iōdēs*, violetlike (< *ion*, a violet + *eidos*, form)], 1. a nonmetallic chemical element of the halogen family, consisting of grayish-black crystals that volatilize into a violet-colored vapor: used as an antiseptic, in photography, etc.: symbol, I; at. wt., 126.92; at. no., 53. 2. [Colloq.], tincture of iodine, used as an antiseptic. Also **i′o·din** (-din).
**i·o·dize** (ī′ə-dīz′), *v.t.* [-DIZED, -DIZING], to treat (a wound, photographic plate, etc.) with iodine or an iodide.
**iodized salt,** common table salt with a little sodium iodide or potassium iodide added.
**i·o·do·form** (ī-ō′də-fôrm′, ī-od′ə-), *n.* [< Mod. L. *iodum*, iodine; + *formyl*], a yellowish, crystalline compound of iodine, $CHI_3$, used as an antiseptic in surgical dressings.
**i·on** (ī′ən, ī′on), *n.* [Gr. *ion*, ppr. of *ienai*, to go], an electrically charged atom or group of atoms, the electrical charge of which results when a neutral atom or group of atoms loses or gains one or more electrons: such loss (resulting in a *cation*), or gain (resulting in an *anion*), occurs during electrolysis, by the action on matter of radiant energy, etc. —**i·on·ic** (ī-on′ik), *adj.*
**-ion,** [< Fr. < L. *-io*, *-ionis*], a noun-forming suffix meaning *the act or state of*, or *the result of*, as in *fusion, translation, correction*.
**I·o·ni·a** (ī-ō′ni-ə), *n.* an ancient district on the W coast of Asia Minor, colonized by the Greeks in the 11th century B.C. —**I·o′ni·an,** *adj.* & *n.*
**Ionian Sea,** that part of the Mediterranean between S Italy and Greece.
**I·on·ic** (ī-on′ik), *adj.* 1. of Ionia or its people; Ionian. 2. designating or of a Greek style of architecture characterized by ornamental scrolls on the capitals.

IONIC CAPITAL

**i·o·ni·um** (ī-ō′ni-əm), *n.* [*ion* + uran*ium*], a radioactive isotope of thorium, resulting from the disintegration of uranium.
**i·on·ize** (ī′ə-nīz′), *v.t.* & *v.i.* [-IZED, -IZING], to change or be changed into ions; dissociate into ions, as a salt dissolved in water, or become electrically charged, as a gas under radiation. —**i′on·i·za′tion,** *n.* —**i′on·iz′er,** *n.*
**i·on·o·sphere** (ī-on′ə-sfêr′, ī-ō′nə-), *n.* the outer part of the earth's atmosphere, consisting of changing layers of heavily ionized molecules.
**i·o·ta** (ī-ō′tə), *n.* 1. the ninth letter of the Greek alphabet (Ι, ι). 2. a very small quantity; jot.
**IOU, I.O.U.** (ī′ō′ū′), 1. I owe you. 2. a signed note bearing these letters, acknowledging a debt.
**-i·ous** (i-əs, yəs, əs), [see -OUS], a suffix used to form adjectives of nouns ending in *-ion*, as in *rebellious*, or to form analogous adjectives meaning *having, characterized by*, as in *furious*.
**I·o·wa** (ī′ə-wə; *locally, also* -wā′), *n.* a Middle Western State of the U.S.: area, 56,280 sq. mi.; pop., 2,758,000; capital, Des Moines: abbrev. **Ia.** —**I′o·wan,** *adj.* & *n.*
**IPA,** International Phonetic Alphabet.
**ip·e·cac** (ip′i-kak′), *n.* [contr. < *ipecacuanha*], 1. a tropical South American creeping plant of the madder family. 2. the dried roots of this plant. 3. a preparation from the dried roots, used in stomach disorders, as an emetic, etc.
**ip·e·cac·u·an·ha** (ip′i-kak′ū-an′ə), *n.* [Port. < Tupi *ipe-kaa-guéne*, small emetic plant], ipecac.
**Iph·i·ge·ni·a** (if′ə-ji-nī′ə), *n.* in *Gr. mythology*, a daughter of Agamemnon, offered by him as a sacrifice to Artemis and saved by the goddess.
‡**ip·se dix·it** (ip′si dik′sit), [L., he himself has said (it)], a dogmatic statement.
‡**ip·so fac·to** (ip′sō fak′tō), [L.], by the fact (or act) itself; by that very fact.
**IQ, I.Q.,** intelligence quotient.
**ir-,** 1. in- (not). 2. in- (in). Used before *r*.
**Ir,** in *chemistry*, iridium.
**Ir.,** 1. Ireland. 2. Irish.
**I·ran** (ē-rän′, ī-ran′), *n.* a country in SW Asia: area, 628,000 sq. mi.; pop., 19,395,000; capital, Teheran: formerly called *Persia*.
**I·ra·ni·an** (ī-rā′ni-ən), *adj.* of Iran, its people, their language, or culture. *n.* 1. one of the people of Iran; Persian. 2. a branch of the Indo-European family of languages, including Persian and Kurdish. Abbrev. **Iran.**
**I·raq** (ē-räk′, i-rak′), *n.* a country in SW Asia, on the Persian Gulf: area, 116,600 sq. mi.; pop., 6,538,000; capital, Bagdad: formerly called *Mesopotamia*: also sp. **Irak.**
**I·ra·qi** (ē-rä′ki), *n.* 1. a native of Iraq. 2. the Arabic dialect of the Iraqis. *adj.* of Iraq, its people, their language, or culture.
**i·ras·ci·ble** (i-ras′ə-b'l, ī-), *adj.* [< Late OFr. < LL. < L. *irasci*; see IRATE], easily angered; quick-tempered; irritable. —**i·ras′ci·bil′i·ty, i·ras′ci·ble·ness,** *n.* —**i·ras′ci·bly,** *adv.*
**i·rate** (ī′rāt, ī-rāt′), *adj.* [L. *iratus* < *irasci*, to be angry < *ira*, anger], angry; wrathful; incensed. —**i′rate·ly,** *adv.* —**i′rate·ness,** *n.*
**IRBM,** intermediate range ballistic missile.
**ire** (īr), *n.* [< OFr. < L. *ira*], anger; wrath. —**ire′ful,** *adj.* —**ire′ful·ly,** *adv.* —**ire′ful·ness,** *n.*
**Ire.,** Ireland.
**Ire·land** (īr′lənd), *n.* 1. one of the British Isles, comprising Ireland (sense 2) and Northern Ireland: area, 31,839 sq. mi. 2. an independent country comprising the southern provinces of this island and three counties of Ulster province: area, 26,601 sq. mi.; pop., 2,898,000; capital, Dublin: former name, *Eire*. See also **Northern Ireland.**
**ir·i·des·cent** (ir′ə-des′'nt), *adj.* [< L. *iris* (< Gr. *iris*), rainbow], having or showing an interplay of rainbowlike colors. —**ir′i·des′cence,** *n.* —**ir′i·des′cent·ly,** *adv.*
**i·rid·i·um** (i-rid′i-əm, ī-rid′-), *n.* [< L. *iris* (< Gr. *iris*), rainbow], a white, heavy, brittle, metallic chemical element found in platinum ores: alloys of iridium are used for pen points and bearings of watches: symbol, Ir; at. wt., 193.1; at. no., 77.
**I·ris** (ī′ris), *n.* in *Gr. mythology*, the goddess of the rainbow and a messenger of the gods.
**i·ris** (ī′ris), *n.* [*pl.* IRISES, IRIDES (ī′rə-dēz′)], [L. (< Gr. *iris*), rainbow], 1. a rainbow. 2. the round, pigmented membrane surrounding the pupil of the eye: see **eye,** illus. 3. *a*) a plant with sword-shaped leaves and a showy flower composed of three petals and three drooping sepals. *b*) this flower: also called *flag*.
**I·rish** (ī′rish), *adj.* of Ireland, its people, their language, etc. *n.* 1. the Celtic language spoken by some of the Irish; Erse. 2. the English dialect of Ireland. —**the Irish,** the Irish people. —**I′rish·man** [*pl.* -MEN], *n.* —**I′rish·wom′an** [*pl.* -WOMEN], *n.fem.*
**Irish Free State,** Ireland (sense 2): especially so called from 1922 to 1937.
**Irish potato,** the common white potato.
**Irish Sea,** the part of the Atlantic between Ireland and England.
**Irish setter,** any of a breed of setter with a coat of long, silky, reddish-brown hair.
**Irish stew,** meat, potatoes, carrots, and onions, cooked with a small amount of water.
**Irish terrier,** any of a breed of small, lean dog with a wiry, reddish-brown coat.
**Irish wolfhound,** any of a breed of very large, heavy, powerful dog with a hard, rough coat.

IRISH TERRIER (18 in. high)

**irk** (ũrk), *v.t.* [ME. *irken*, to be weary of], to make tired; disgust; annoy; trouble; vex; bore.
**irk·some** (ũrk′səm), *adj.* tiresome; troublesome; tedious. —**irk′some·ly,** *adv.* —**irk′some·ness,** *n.*
**Ir·kutsk** (êr-kootsk′), *n.* a city in the S Asiatic U.S.S.R., near Lake Baikal: pop., 365,000.
**i·ron** (ī′ērn), *n.* [see PLURAL, II, D, 3], [AS. *iren, isern, isen*; ? < Celt.], 1. a metallic chemical element, white, malleable, and ductile, the most common and most useful of all the metals: symbol, Fe; at. wt., 55.85; at. no., 26. 2. *a*) any tool, device, etc. made of iron. *b*) such a device with a flat undersurface, used, when heated, for pressing clothes or cloth. 3. *pl.* iron shackles or chains. 4. firm strength; power. 5. a golf club with a metal head. 6. a medicine containing iron. *adj.* 1. of or consisting of iron. 2. like iron; strong; firm: as, an *iron*

will. 3. cruel; merciless. *v.t.* 1. to furnish or cover with iron. 2. to put (a prisoner) in irons. 3. to press (clothes or cloth) with a hot iron. *v.i.* to iron clothes or cloth. **—have irons in the fire,** to be engaged in activities, etc. **—iron out,** to smooth out; eliminate. **—strike while the iron is hot,** to act at an opportune time. **—i′ron·like′,** *adj.*

**Iron Age,** a period of civilization (c. 1000 B.C.–100 A.D.), characterized by the introduction and development of iron tools and weapons.

**i·ron·bound** (ī′ẽrn-bound′), *adj.* 1. bound with iron. 2. hard; rigid; unyielding; inflexible. 3. edged with rocks or cliffs, as a coast.

**i·ron·clad** (ī′ẽrn-klad′), *adj.* 1. covered or protected with iron. 2. difficult to change or break: as, an *ironclad* lease. *n.* a warship armored with thick iron plates: 19th-century term.

**iron curtain,** 1. secrecy and censorship regarded as forming a barrier around the Soviet Union. 2. any barrier like this.

**iron hand,** firm, rigorous, severe control. **—i′ron-hand′ed,** *adj.*

**i·ron·i·cal** (ī-ron′i-k'l), *adj.* [< L. < Gr. < *eirōneia* (see IRONY)], 1. meaning the contrary of what is expressed. 2. using or tending to use irony. 3. directly opposite to what might be expected. Also **i·ron′ic.** **—i·ron′i·cal·ly,** *adv.* **—i·ron′i·cal·ness,** *n.*

**ironing board,** a cloth-covered board on which clothes are ironed.

**iron lung,** a large metal respirator, used for maintaining artificial respiration.

**i·ron·mon·ger** (ī′ẽrn-muŋ′gẽr), *n.* [Brit.], a dealer in articles made of iron and other metals; hardware dealer. **—i′ron·mon′ger·y,** *n.*

**iron pyrites,** a gold-colored ore of iron; pyrite.

**i·ron·side** (ī′ẽrn-sīd′), *n.* 1. a courageous, resolute man. 2. [I-], *a)* Oliver Cromwell: also **Ironsides.** *b)* [I-], *pl.* the regiment he led in the English Civil War. 3. *pl.* [construed as sing.], an ironclad.

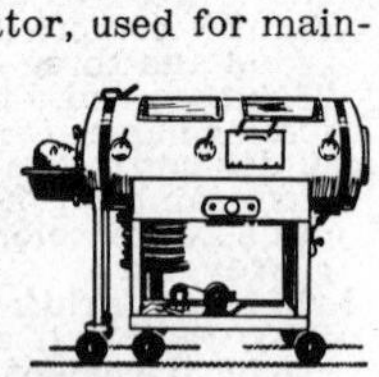

IRON LUNG

**i·ron·ware** (ī′ẽrn-wâr′), *n.* things made of iron; hardware.

**i·ron·weed** (ī′ẽrn-wēd′), *n.* a plant of the aster family, with clusters of tubular flowers.

**i·ron·wood** (ī′ẽrn-wood′), *n.* 1. any of various trees with extremely hard wood. 2. the wood.

**i·ron·work** (ī′ẽrn-wũrk′), *n.* 1. articles or parts made of iron. 2. work in iron. **—i′ron·work′er,** *n.*

**i·ron·works** (ī′ẽrn-wũrks′), *n.pl.* [also construed as sing.], a place where iron is smelted or heavy iron goods are made.

**i·ro·ny** (ī′rə-ni), *n.* [*pl.* -NIES], [< Fr. < L. < Gr. *eirōneia* < *eirōn,* dissembler in speech], 1. expression in which the intended meaning of the words is the direct opposite of their usual sense: as, in *irony* she called the stupid plan "very clever." 2. a set of circumstances or a result that is the opposite of what might be expected: as, the *irony* of having the fireboat burn and sink.

**Ir·o·quoi·an** (ir′ə-kwoi′ən), *adj.* of an important linguistic family of North American Indians, including tribes of the Five Nations, and the Cherokees, Hurons, etc. *n.* 1. a member of an Iroquoian tribe. 2. the Iroquoian languages collectively.

**Ir·o·quois** (ir′ə-kwoi′, -kwoiz′), *n.* [*pl.* -QUOIS], a member of a confederation of Iroquoian Indian tribes that lived in W and N New York: see **Five Nations.** *adj.* of the Iroquois or their tribes.

**ir·ra·di·ate** (i-rā′di-āt′), *v.t.* [-ATED, -ATING], [< L. pp. of *irradiare;* see IN- (in) & RADIATE], 1. to shine upon; light up; make bright. 2. to enlighten. 3. to radiate; diffuse. 4. to treat by exposing to X-rays, ultraviolet rays, etc. *v.i.* to emit rays; shine. *adj.* (-it), irradiated. **—ir·ra′di·ance,** *n.* **—ir·ra′di·ant,** *adj.* **—ir·ra′di·a′tion,** *n.* **—ir·ra′di·a′tive,** *adj.* **—ir·ra′di·a′tor,** *n.*

**ir·ra·tion·al** (i-rash′ən-'l), *adj.* 1. not rational; lacking the power to reason. 2. senseless; unreasonable; absurd. 3. in *mathematics,* not capable of being expressed as an integer or as a quotient of an integer. **—ir·ra′tion·al′i·ty, ir·ra′tion·al·ness,** *n.* **—ir·ra′tion·al·ly,** *adv.*

**Ir·ra·wad·dy** (ir′ə-wä′di, -wô′-), *n.* a river in E Asia, flowing through Burma into the Bay of Bengal.

**ir·re·claim·a·ble** (ir′i-klām′ə-b'l), *adj.* that cannot be reclaimed. **—ir′re·claim′a·bil′i·ty, ir′re·claim′a·ble·ness,** *n.* **—ir′re·claim′a·bly,** *adv.*

**ir·rec·on·cil·a·ble** (i-rek′ən-sīl′ə-b'l, ir′rek-ən-sīl′-), *adj.* that cannot be reconciled; that cannot be brought into agreement; incompatible. *n.* one who is irreconcilable and refuses to compromise. **—ir·rec′on·cil′a·bil′i·ty, ir·rec′on·cil′a·ble·ness,** *n.* **—ir·rec′on·cil′a·bly,** *adv.*

**ir·re·cov·er·a·ble** (ir′i-kuv′ẽr-ə-b'l), *adj.* that cannot be recovered, regained, rectified, or remedied; irretrievable. **—ir′re·cov′er·a·ble·ness,** *n.* **—ir′re·cov′er·a·bly,** *adv.*

**ir·re·deem·a·ble** (ir′i-dēm′ə-b'l), *adj.* 1. that cannot be redeemed, or bought back. 2. that cannot be converted into coin, as certain kinds of paper money. 3. that cannot be changed or reformed. **—ir′re·deem′a·bly,** *adv.*

**Ir·re·den·tist** (ir′i-den′tist), *n.* [< It. < (*Italia*) *irredenta,* unredeemed (Italy)], any member of an Italian political party, organized in 1878, seeking to recover for Italy adjacent regions inhabited largely by Italians and under foreign control. **—Ir′re·den′tism,** *n.*

**ir·re·duc·i·ble** (ir′i-dōōs′ə-b'l, -dūs′-), *adj.* that cannot be reduced. **—ir′re·duc′i·bil′i·ty, ir′re·duc′i·ble·ness,** *n.* **—ir′re·duc′i·bly,** *adv.*

**ir·ref·ra·ga·ble** (i-ref′rə-gə-b'l), *adj.* [< LL. < L. *in-,* not + *refragari,* to oppose], that cannot be refuted; indisputable. **—ir·ref′ra·ga·bil′i·ty,** *n.* **—ir·ref′ra·ga·bly,** *adv.*

**ir·ref·u·ta·ble** (i-ref′yoo-tə-b'l, ir′ri-fū′-), *adj.* that cannot be refuted; indisputable. **—ir·ref′u·ta·bil′i·ty,** *n.* **—ir·ref′u·ta·bly,** *adv.*

**irreg.,** 1. irregular. 2. irregularly.

**ir·re·gard·less** (ir′i-gärd′lis), *adj.* & *adv.* regardless: a substandard or humorous redundancy.

**ir·reg·u·lar** (i-reg′yoo-lẽr), *adj.* 1. not regular; not conforming to established rule, method, usage, standard, etc.; out of the ordinary. 2. lawless, immoral, or disorderly. 3. not straight or even; not symmetrical; not uniform in shape, design, etc. 4. uneven in occurrence. 5. in *grammar,* not inflected in the normal manner: as, *go* is an *irregular* verb. 6. in *military usage,* not belonging to the regularly established army. *n.* a person or thing that is irregular. **—ir·reg′u·lar·ly,** *adv.*

**ir·reg·u·lar·i·ty** (i-reg′yoo-lar′ə-ti), *n.* 1. lack of regularity. 2. [*pl.* -TIES], something irregular.

**ir·rel·e·vant** (i-rel′ə-vənt), *adj.* not relevant; not pertinent; not to the point. **—ir·rel′e·vance, ir·rel′e·van·cy,** *n.* **—ir·rel′e·vant·ly,** *adv.*

**ir·re·li·gion** (ir′i-lij′ən), *n.* a being irreligious; lack of religion. **—ir′re·li′gion·ist,** *n.*

**ir·re·li·gious** (ir′i-lij′əs), *adj.* 1. not religious; indifferent or hostile to religion. 2. profane; impious. **—ir′re·li′gious·ly,** *adv.* **—ir′re·li′gious·ness,** *n.*

**ir·re·me·di·a·ble** (ir′i-mē′di-ə-b'l), *adj.* that cannot be remedied; incurable. **—ir′re·me′di·a·ble·ness,** *n.* **—ir′re·me′di·a·bly,** *adv.*

**ir·re·mis·si·ble** (ir′i-mis′ə-b'l), *adj.* not remissible; that cannot be excused or pardoned.

**ir·re·mov·a·ble** (ir′i-mōōv′ə-b'l), *adj.* that cannot be removed. **—ir′re·mov′a·bil′i·ty,** *n.* **—ir′re·mov′a·bly,** *adv.*

**ir·rep·a·ra·ble** (i-rep′ẽr-ə-b'l), *adj.* not reparable; that cannot be repaired, mended, remedied, etc. **—ir·rep′a·ra·bil′i·ty, ir·rep′a·ra·ble·ness,** *n.* **—ir·rep′a·ra·bly,** *adv.*

**ir·re·place·a·ble** (ir′i-plās′ə-b'l), *adj.* that cannot be replaced.

**ir·re·press·i·ble** (ir′i-pres′ə-b'l), *adj.* that cannot be repressed or restrained. **—ir′re·press′i·bil′i·ty, ir′re·press′i·ble·ness,** *n.* **—ir′re·press′i·bly,** *adv.*

**ir·re·proach·a·ble** (ir′i-prōch′ə-b'l), *adj.* blameless; faultless. **—ir′re·proach′a·bil′i·ty, ir′re·proach′a·ble·ness,** *n.* **—ir′re·proach′a·bly,** *adv.*

**ir·re·sist·i·ble** (ir′i-zis′tə-b'l), *adj.* that cannot be resisted; too strong, fascinating, etc. to be withstood. **—ir′re·sist′i·bil′i·ty, ir′re·sist′i·ble·ness,** *n.* **—ir′re·sist′i·bly,** *adv.*

**ir·res·o·lute** (i-rez′ə-lōōt′), *adj.* not resolute; wavering in decision or purpose; indecisive. **—ir·res′o·lute·ly,** *adv.* **—ir·res′o·lu′tion, ir·res′o·lute·ness,** *n.*

**ir·re·spec·tive** (ir′i-spek′tiv), *adj.* [Rare], regardless of persons or consequences. **—irrespective of,** regardless of. **—ir′re·spec′tive·ly,** *adv.*

**ir·re·spon·si·ble** (ir′i-spon′sə-b'l), *adj.* 1. not responsible; not accountable for actions. 2. lacking a sense of responsibility. *n.* an irresponsible person. **—ir′re·spon′si·bil′i·ty, ir′re·spon′si·ble·ness,** *n.* **—ir′re·spon′si·bly,** *adv.*

**ir·re·spon·sive** (ir′i-spon′siv), *adj.* not responsive.

**ir·re·triev·a·ble** (ir′i-trēv′ə-b'l), *adj.* that cannot be retrieved, recovered, restored, or recalled. **—ir′re·triev′a·bil′i·ty, ir′re·triev′a·ble·ness,** *n.* **—ir′re·triev′a·bly,** *adv.*

**ir·rev·er·ence** (i-rev′ẽr-əns), *n.* 1. lack of reverence. 2. an act or statement showing this.

**ir·rev·er·ent** (i-rev′ẽr-ənt), *adj.* not reverent; showing disrespect. **—ir·rev′er·ent·ly,** *adv.*

**ir·re·vers·i·ble** (ir′i-vũr′sə-b'l), *adj.* that cannot be reversed; esp., that cannot be repealed or annulled.

**—ir're·vers'i·bil'i·ty, ir're·vers'i·ble·ness,** *n.* **—ir're·vers'i·bly,** *adv.*
**ir·rev·o·ca·ble** (i-rev'ə-kə-b'l), *adj.* that cannot be revoked or undone. **—ir·rev'o·ca·bil'i·ty, ir·rev'o·ca·ble·ness,** *n.* **—ir·rev'o·ca·bly,** *adv.*
**ir·ri·ga·ble** (ir'i-gə-b'l), *adj.* that can be irrigated.
**ir·ri·gate** (ir'ə-gāt'), *v.t.* [-GATED, -GATING], [< L. pp. < *in-*, in + *rigare*, to water], 1. to supply (land) with water as by means of artificial ditches. 2. in *medicine*, to wash out (a cavity or canal) with water or other fluid. **—ir'ri·ga'tion,** *n.* **—ir'ri·ga'tion·al,** *adj.* **—ir'ri·ga'tor,** *n.*
**ir·ri·ta·bil·i·ty** (ir'ə-tə-bil'ə-ti), *n.* [*pl.* -TIES], 1. a being irritable, or easily provoked. 2. in *medicine*, excessive responsiveness of an organ or part to mild stimulation. 3. in *physiology*, the property of living matter to react when stimulated.
**ir·ri·ta·ble** (ir'ə-tə-b'l), *adj.* 1. easily irritated or provoked; impatient. 2. in *medicine*, excessively sensitive to a stimulus. 3. in *physiology*, able to respond when stimulated. **—ir'ri·ta·ble·ness,** *n.* **—ir'ri·ta·bly,** *adv.*
**ir·ri·tant** (ir'ə-tənt), *adj.* causing irritation. *n.* something causing irritation. **—ir'ri·tan·cy,** *n.*
**ir·ri·tate** (ir'ə-tāt'), *v.t.* [-TATED, -TATING], [< L. pp. of *irritare*, to excite], 1. to provoke to impatience or anger; annoy. 2. to make inflamed or sore. 3. in *physiology*, to excite (an organ, muscle, etc.) to a characteristic action by a stimulus. **—ir'ri·tat'ing, ir'ri·ta'tive,** *adj.* **—ir'ri·tat'ing·ly,** *adv.* **—ir'ri·ta'tor,** *n.*
**ir·ri·ta·tion** (ir'ə-tā'shən), *n.* 1. an irritating or being irritated. 2. something that irritates. 3. in *medicine*, an excessive response to stimulation in an organ or part.
**ir·rup·tion** (i-rup'shən), *n.* [< L. pp. < *in-*, in + *rumpere*, to break], 1. a bursting or breaking in. 2. a swift, violent invasion. **—ir·rup'tive,** *adj.*
**Ir·ving, Washington** (ũr'viŋ), 1783–1859; U.S. writer.
**Ir·ving·ton** (ũr'viŋ-tən), *n.* a city in NE New Jersey: pop., 59,000.
**is** (iz), [AS.], the 3d pers. sing., pres. indic., of **be.** **—as is,** as it now is; without change.
**is.,** 1. island. 2. isle.
**Isa., Is.,** Isaiah.
**I·saac** (ī'zək), *n.* in the *Bible*, one of the patriarchs, son of Abraham and Sarah, and father of Jacob and Esau: Gen. 21:3.
**Is·a·bel·la I** (iz'ə-bel'ə), 1451–1504; queen of Castile (1474–1504) and (from 1479) León; gave help to Columbus.
**is·a·cous·tic** (īs'ə-kōōs'tik), *adj.* [*iso-* + *acoustic*], of or having to do with equal intensity of sound.
**i·sa·go·ge** (ī'sə-gō'ji), *n.* [L.; < Gr. ult. < *eis-*, into + *agein*, to lead], an introduction, as to a branch of study. **—i'sa·gog'ic** (-goj'ik), *adj.*
**I·sa·iah** (ī-zā'ə, ī-zī'ə), *n.* 1. a Hebrew prophet of the 8th century B.C. 2. a book of the Old Testament with his teachings. Also **I·sai'as** (-əs).
**Is·car·i·ot** (is-kar'i-ət), *n.* 1. in the *Bible*, the surname of the disciple Judas, who betrayed Jesus: Luke 22:3; hence, 2. a traitor.
**is·che·mi·a, is·chae·mi·a** (is-kē'mi-ə), *n.* [Mod.L. < Gr. *ischein*, to hold + *haima*, blood], a temporary lack of blood in an organ or tissue; local anemia. **—is·che'mic** (-kē'mik, -kem'ik), *adj.*
**is·chi·um** (is'ki-əm), *n.* [*pl.* -CHIA (-ki-ə)], [< L. < Gr. *ischion*, hip], the lowermost of the three sections of the hipbone. **—is'chi·al,** *adj.*
**-ise** (īz), -ize.
**I·seult** (i-sōōlt'), *n.* [Fr.], Isolde.
**-ish** (ish), 1. [AS. *-isc*], a suffix meaning: *a*) *of* or *belonging to* (a specified people), as in *Spanish*. *b*) *like* or *characteristic of*, as in *devilish*. *c*) *tending to*, *verging on*, as in *bookish*, *knavish*. *d*) *somewhat*, *rather*, as in *tallish*. *e*) [Colloq.], *approximately*, *about*, as in *thirtyish*. 2. [< OFr.], a suffix used in verbs of French origin, as in *finish*.
**Ish·ma·el** (ish'mi-əl), *n.* 1. in the *Bible*, the son of Abraham and Hagar: at Sarah's insistence, he and his mother were made outcasts: Gen. 16:12; hence, 2. an outcast.
**Ish·ma·el·ite** (ish'mi-əl-īt'), *n.* 1. a descendant of Ishmael. 2. an outcast. **—Ish'ma·el·it'ish,** *adj.*
**Ish·tar** (ish'tär), *n.* the Babylonian and Assyrian goddess of love and fertility.
**i·sin·glass** (ī'ziŋ-glas', ī'z'n-gläs'), *n.* [prob. < MD. < *huizen*, sturgeon + *blas*, bladder], 1. a form of gelatin prepared from fish bladders, used as a clarifying agent and adhesive. 2. mica, especially in thin sheets.
**I·sis** (ī'sis), *n.* the Egyptian goddess of fertility, sister and wife of Osiris.
**isl.,** [*pl.* ISLS.], 1. island. 2. isle.

ISIS

**Is·lam** (is'ləm, is-läm', iz'ləm), *n.* [Ar. *islām*, lit., submission (to God's will)], 1. the Moslem religion, a monotheistic religion whose supreme deity is called Allah and whose chief prophet and founder was Mohammed. 2. Moslems collectively. 3. all the lands in which the Moslem religion predominates. **—Is'lam·ism,** *n.* **—Is'lam·ite',** *n.*
**Is·lam·ic** (is-lam'ik, -läm'-, iz-lam'-), *adj.* of Islam: also **Is·lam·it·ic** (is'lə-mit'ik, iz'-).
**Is·lam·ize** (is'ləm-īz, iz'-), *v.i.* & *v.t.* [-IZED, -IZING], to make or become Islamic. **—Is'lam·i·za'tion,** *n.*
**is·land** (ī'lənd), *n.* [< ME. *iland* (respelled after unrelated *isle*) < AS. *igland*, lit., island land & *ealand*, lit., water land], 1. a land mass not as large as a continent, surrounded by water. 2. anything like an island in position or isolation. 3. in *anatomy*, a cluster of cells differing from surrounding tissue in formation, etc. *v.t.* to make into or like an island; isolate.
**is·land·er** (ī'lən-dẽr), *n.* a native or inhabitant of an island.
**isle** (īl), *n.* [< OFr. < LL. < L. *insula*], an island, especially a small island. *v.t.* [ISLED, ISLING], to island. *v.i.* to live on an isle.
**is·let** (ī'lit), *n.* a very small island.
**ism** (iz'm), *n.* any doctrine, theory, system, etc. whose name ends in *-ism*: usually disparaging.
**-ism** (iz'm), [< L. < Gr. *-ismos*], a suffix meaning: 1. *the act, practice*, or *result of*, as in *terrorism*. 2 *the condition of being*, as in *barbarism*. 3. *conduct* or *qualities characteristic of*, as in *patriotism*. 4. *the doctrine* or *theory of*, as in *socialism*. 5. *devotion to*, as in *nationalism*. 6. *an instance, example*, or *peculiarity of*, as in *witticism*. 7. *an abnormal condition caused by*, as in *alcoholism*.
**is·n't** (iz''nt), is not.
**i·so-,** [< Gr. *isos*, equal], a combining form meaning *equal, similar, alike, identical*: also **is-.**
**i·so·bar** (ī'sə-bär'), *n.* [< *iso-* + Gr. *baros*, weight], 1. a line on a map connecting points on the earth's surface having equal barometric pressure. 2. any of two or more forms of an atom having the same atomic weight but different atomic numbers: cf. *isotope*. **—i'so·bar'ic** (-bar'ik), *adj.*

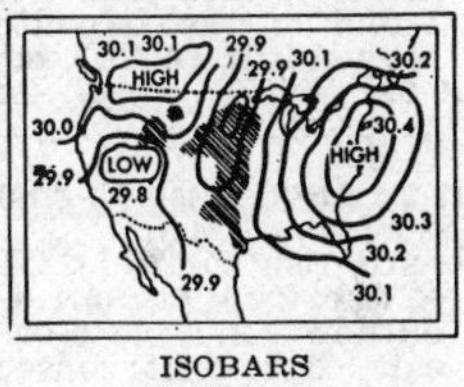


ISOBARS

**i·soch·ro·nal** (ī-sok'rə-n'l), *adj.* [< Mod. L. < Gr. < *isos*, equal + *chronos*, time], 1. equal in length of time. 2. occurring at equal intervals of time: also **i·soch'ro·nous.** **—i·soch'ro·nism,** *n.*
**i·so·cline** (ī'sə-klīn'), *n.* [< *iso-* + Gr. *kleinein*, to slope], a fold of rock in which the strata have the same angle of dip on each side. **—i'so·cli'nal, i'so·clin'ic** (-klin'ik), *adj.*
**i·so·gon·ic** (ī'sə-gon'ik), *adj.* [*iso-* + *-gon* + *-ic*], 1. of or having equal angles. 2. connecting or showing points on the earth's surface having the same magnetic declination. *n.* an isogonic line.
**i·so·late** (ī'sə-lāt', is'ə-), *v.t.* [-LATED, -LATING], [back-formation < *isolated* < It. < *isola* (< L. *insula*), island], 1. to set apart from others; place alone. 2. in *chemistry*, to separate (an element or compound) in pure form from another compound or mixture. 3. in *medicine*, to place (a patient with a contagious disease) apart from others to prevent the spread of infection. **—i'so·la·ble,** *adj.* **—i'so·la'tion,** *n.* **—i'so·la'tor,** *n.*
**i·so·la·tion·ist** (ī'sə-lā'shən-ist, is'ə-), *n.* one who advocates isolation; esp., one who wants his country to take no part in international leagues, etc. *adj.* of isolationists. **—i'so·la'tion·ism,** *n.*
**I·solde** (i-sōld', i-sōl'də), *n.* see **Tristram.**
**i·so·mer** (ī'sə-mẽr), *n.* [< Gr. < *isos*, equal + *meros*, a part], any of two or more chemical compounds having the same elements in the same proportion by weight but differing in properties because of differences in the structure of their molecules.
**i·som·er·ism** (ī-som'ẽr-iz'm), *n.* the state or relation of isomers. **—i·so·mer·ic** (ī'sə-mer'ik), *adj.*
**i·som·er·ous** (ī-som'ẽr-əs), *adj.* [*iso-* + *-merous*], in

*botany,* having the same number of parts in each whorl.

**i·so·met·ric** (ī'sə-met'rik), ***adj.*** [< Gr. < *isos,* equal + *metron,* measure]. 1. of or having equality of measure: also **i'so·met'ri·cal.** 2. designating or of isometrics. ***n. pl.*** exercise in which one set of muscles is briefly tensed in opposition to another set of muscles or to an immovable object.

**i·so·mor·phic** (ī'sə-môr'fik), ***adj.*** [*iso-* + *-morphic*], having similar or identical structure or form, but of different species or races. —**i'so·mor'phism,** ***n.***

**i·sos·ce·les** (ī-sos'ə-lēz'), ***adj.*** [L. < Gr. *isoskelēs* < *isos,* equal + *skelos,* a leg], designating a triangle with two equal sides.

**i·so·therm** (ī'sə-thūrm'), ***n.*** [< *iso-* + Gr. *thermē,* heat], a line on a map connecting points on the earth's surface having the same mean temperature or the same temperature at a given time.

**i·so·ther·mal** (ī'sə-thūr'm'l), ***adj.*** 1. of or indicating equality of temperature. 2. of isotherms. ***n.*** an isotherm. —**i'so·ther'mal·ly,** ***adv.***

**i·so·ton·ic** (ī'sə-ton'ik), ***adj.*** [< Gr. < *isos,* equal + *tonos,* a stretching], 1. having equal tension. 2. designating or of a salt solution, as for medical use, having the same osmotic pressure as blood.

**i·so·tope** (ī'sə-tōp'), ***n.*** [< *iso-* + Gr. *topos,* place], any of two or more forms of an element having the same or very closely related properties and the same atomic number but different atomic weights: as, uranium *isotopes* U 235, U 238, U 239: cf. *isobar.* —**i'so·top'ic** (-top'ik), ***adj.***

**i·so·trop·ic** (ī'sə-trop'ik, -trō'pik), ***adj.*** [*iso-* + *-tropic*], having physical properties, as conductivity, elasticity, etc., that are the same regardless of the direction of measurement: also **i·sot·ro·pous** (ī-sot'rə-pəs).

**Is·ra·el** (iz'ri-əl), ***n.*** 1. in the *Bible,* Jacob: Gen. 32:28. 2. the Jewish people, as descendants of Jacob. 3. the kingdom in the northern part of ancient Palestine. 4. a republic comprising parts of Palestine, established in 1948 as a Jewish state: area, 7,993 sq. mi.; pop., 2,428,000; capital, Jerusalem.

**Is·ra·el·i** (iz-rā'li), ***adj.*** of Israel (sense 4) or its people. ***n.*** a native or inhabitant of Israel (sense 4).

**Is·ra·el·ite** (iz'ri-əl-īt'), ***n.*** any of the people of Israel or their descendants; Jew; Hebrew. ***adj.*** of Israel or the Israelites; Jewish. —**Is'ra·el·it'ish, Is'ra·el·it'ic** (-it'ik), ***adj.***

**is·sei** (ēs'sā'), ***n.*** [*pl.* -SEI, -SEIS], [Japan., lit., first generation], [also I-], a Japanese emigrant to the U.S.

**is·su·ance** (ish'ōō-əns), ***n.*** an issuing; issue. —**is'su·ant,** ***adj.***

**is·sue** (ish'ōō), ***n.*** [< OFr. pp. of *(e)isser,* to go out < L. *exire* < *ex-,* out + *ire,* to go], 1. an outgoing; outflow. 2. a place or means of going out; outlet; exit. 3. a result; consequence. 4. offspring; a child or children. 5. profits, as from property; proceeds. 6. a point or matter under dispute. 7. a sending or giving out. 8. the entire amount put forth and circulated at one time: as, the May *issue* of a magazine, an *issue* of bonds. 9. in *medicine,* a discharge of blood, pus, etc. ***v.i.*** [-SUED, -SUING], 1. to go, pass, or flow out; emerge. 2. to be descended; be born. 3. to result, as from a cause. 4. to end (*in*); result, as in an effect. 5. to come as revenue. 6. to be published; be put forth and circulated. ***v.t.*** 1. to let out; discharge. 2. to give or deal out: as, to *issue* supplies. 3. to publish; put forth publicly or officially, as periodicals, bonds, an edict, etc. —**at issue,** in dispute; to be decided. —**join issue,** to meet in conflict, argument, etc. —**take issue,** to disagree. —**is'su·a·ble,** ***adj.*** —**is'su·er,** ***n.***

**-ist** (ist), [< Fr. < L. < Gr. *-istēs*], a suffix meaning: 1. *one who does* or *practices,* as in *moralist, satirist.* 2. *one skilled in* or *occupied with,* as in *chemist, violinist.* 3. *an adherent of,* as in *anarchist, hedonist.*

**Is·tan·bul** (is'tan-bōōl', -tän-; Turk. is-täm'bool), ***n.*** a city in European Turkey, on the Bosporus: pop., 1,467,000: formerly *Constantinople.*

**isth·mi·an** (is'mi-ən), ***adj.*** 1. of an isthmus. 2. [I-], of the Isthmus of Panama. 3. [I-], of the Isthmus of Corinth. ***n.*** a native or inhabitant of an isthmus.

**isth·mus** (is'məs; *rarely* isth'-), ***n.*** [*pl.* -MUSES, -MI (-mī)], [L. < Gr. *isthmos,* a neck], a narrow strip of land having water on either side and connecting two larger bodies of land.

**-is·tic** (is'tik), [< Fr. < L. < Gr. *-istikos,* or < Eng. *-ist* + *-ic*], a suffix forming adjectives corresponding to nouns ending in *-ism* and *-ist,* as in *artistic.*

**is·tle** (ist'li), ***n.*** [Mex.], the fiber of certain tropical American plants, used for baskets, etc.

**it** (it), ***pron.*** [for *pl.* see THEY], [AS. *hit*], the animal or thing under discussion. *It* is used as: *a*) the subject of an impersonal verb: as, *it* is snowing. *b*) the grammatical subject of a clause of which the actual subject follows: as, *it* is well that he can go. *c*) an object of indefinite sense: as, to lord *it* over someone. *d*) the antecedent to a relative pronoun from which it is separated by a predicate: as, *it* is your car that I want. *e*) a reference to something indefinite but understood: as, *it*'s all right, I didn't hurt myself. *f*) [Colloq.], an emphatic predicate pronoun referring to that person, thing, situation, etc. which is ultimate or final: as, zero hour is here; this is *it.* ***n.*** in the game of "tag," etc., the player who must do some specific thing.

**It., Ital.,** 1. Italian. 2. Italic. 3. Italy.

**i/t/a, I.T.A.,** Initial Teaching Alphabet.

**ital.,** italic; italics. Also **it.**

**I·tal·ia** (ē-täl'yä), ***n.*** Italy: the Italian name.

**I·tal·ian** (i-tal'yən), ***adj.*** of Italy, its people, their language, etc. ***n.*** 1. a native or inhabitant of Italy. 2. the Romance language of the Italians.

**I·tal·ic** (i-tal'ik), ***adj.*** 1. of ancient Italy, its people, etc. 2. designating or of the subfamily of the Indo-European languages that includes Latin and the languages descended from Latin. ***n.*** the Italic languages collectively.

**i·tal·ic** (i-tal'ik), ***adj.*** [< its first use in an *Italian* edition of Virgil], designating a type in which the letters slant upward to the right, used to give emphasis to words, etc.: *this is italic type.* ***n.*** italic type or print: also **italics,** *pl.* (sometimes construed as sing.).

**i·tal·i·cize** (i-tal'ə-sīz'), ***v.t.*** [-CIZED, -CIZING], 1. to print in italics. 2. to underscore (copy) to indicate that it is to be printed in italics.

**It·a·ly** (it''l-i), ***n.*** a country in S Europe, including the islands of Sicily and Sardinia: area, 119,768 sq. mi.; pop., 51,945,000; capital, Rome.

**itch** (ich), ***v.i.*** [AS. *giccan*], 1. to feel an irritating sensation on the skin, with the desire to scratch. 2. to have a restless desire. ***n.*** 1. an itching of the skin. 2. a contagious skin disease caused by a parasitic mite and accompanied by itching (with *the*). 3. a restless desire; hankering: as, an *itch* to travel. —**itch'y** [-IER, -IEST], ***adj.*** —**itch'i·ness,** ***n.***

**-ite** (īt), [< Fr. < L. < Gr. *-itēs*], a suffix meaning: 1. *a native* or *inhabitant of,* as in *Brooklynite.* 2. *an adherent of,* as in *laborite.* 3. *a commercially manufactured product,* as in *dynamite.* 4. *a fossil,* as in *trilobite.* 5. *a salt* or *ester of an acid whose name ends in -ous,* as in *nitrite.* 6. *a* (specified) *mineral* or *rock,* as in *anthracite.*

**i·tem** (ī'təm), ***adv.*** [L.], also: used before each article in a series being enumerated. ***n.*** 1. an article; unit; separate thing. 2. a bit of news or information. ***v.t.*** to itemize.

**i·tem·ize** (ī'təm-īz'), ***v.t.*** [-IZED, -IZING], to specify the items of; set down by items: as, *itemize* my bill. —**i'tem·i·za'tion,** ***n.*** —**i'tem·iz'er,** ***n.***

**it·er·ate** (it'ə-rāt'), ***v.t.*** [-ATED, -ATING], [< L. pp. of *iterare* < *iterum,* again], to utter or do again; repeat. —**it'er·a'tion,** ***n.***

**it·er·a·tive** (it'ə-rā'tiv, it'ēr-ə-), ***adj.*** repetitious.

**Ith·a·ca** (ith'ə-kə), ***n.*** an island off the west coast of Greece: legendary home of Odysseus.

**i·tin·er·an·cy** (ī-tin'ēr-ən-si, i-), ***n.*** 1. an itinerating or being itinerant. 2. official work requiring constant travel from place to place or frequent change of residence. Also **i·tin'er·a·cy.**

**i·tin·er·ant** (ī-tin'ēr-ənt, i-), ***adj.*** [< LL. ppr. of *itinerari,* to travel < L. *iter,* a walk], traveling from place to place or on a circuit. ***n.*** one who travels from place to place. —**i·tin'er·ant·ly,** ***adv.***

**i·tin·er·ar·y** (ī-tin'ə-rer'i, i-), ***adj.*** of traveling, journeys, roads, etc. ***n.*** [*pl.* -IES], 1. a route. 2. a record of a journey. 3. a guidebook. 4. a plan or outline of a journey or route.

**i·tin·er·ate** (ī-tin'ə-rāt', i-), ***v.i.*** [-ATED, -ATING], [< LL. pp.; see ITINERANT], to travel from place to place or on a circuit. —**i·tin'er·a'tion,** ***n.***

**-i·tion** (ish'ən), [< Fr. *-ition* or L. *-itio, -itionis*], a noun-forming suffix corresponding to *-ation,* as in *nutrition.*

**-i·tious** (ish'əs), [L. *-icius, -itius*], a suffix meaning *of, having the nature of, characterized by,* used to form adjectives corresponding to nouns ending in *-ition,* as in *nutritious.*

**-i·tis** (ī'tis), [Gr. *-itis*] a suffix meaning *inflammatory disease* or *inflammation of* (a specified part or organ), as in *neuritis.*

**it'll** (it''l), 1. it will. 2. it shall.

**its** (its), ***pron.*** that or those belonging to it. ***possessive pronominal adj.*** of, belonging to, or done by it.

**it's** (its), 1. it is. 2. it has.

**it·self** (it-self'), ***pron.*** a form of the 3d pers. sing., neuter pronoun, used: *a*) as an intensive: as, the

picture frame *itself* is a work of art. *b*) as a reflexive: as, the dog scratched *itself.*
**-i·ty** (ə-ti, i-ti), [< Fr. *-ité* or L. *-itas*], a suffix meaning *state* or *quality*, as in *chastity.*
**i.v.,** 1. initial velocity. 2. intravenous.
**I·van III** (ī′vən; Russ. i-vän′), 1440–1505; grand duke of Muscovy (1462–1505): called *the Great.*
**Ivan IV,** 1530–1584; grandson of Ivan III; grand duke of Muscovy (1533–1584); first czar of Russia (1547–1584): called *the Terrible.*
**I've** (iv), I have.
**-ive** (iv), [< Fr. *-if*, fem. *-ive* or L. *-ivus*], a suffix meaning: 1. *of, relating to, having the nature of,* as in *substantive.* 2. *tending to,* as in *creative.*
**i·vied** (ī′vid), *adj.* covered or overgrown with ivy.
**i·vo·ry** (ī′vẽr-i), *n.* [*pl.* -RIES], [< OFr. < L. *ebur*], 1. the hard, white substance forming the tusks of elephants, walruses, etc. 2. any substance like ivory. 3. the color of ivory; creamy white. 4. a tusk of an elephant. 5. *pl.* things made of or suggesting ivory; specif., [Slang], *a*) piano keys. *b*) teeth. *c*) dice. *adj.* 1. of or like ivory. 2. creamy-white. **—i′vo·ry·like′,** *adj.*
**Ivory Coast,** a country on the W coast of Africa, a member of the French Community: area, 124,500 sq. mi.; pop., 3,103,000; capital, Abidjan.
**ivory nut,** the seed of a certain tropical palm tree (**ivory palm**), resembling ivory when dried.
**ivory tower,** figuratively, a place of mental withdrawal from reality and action.
**i·vy** (ī′vi), *n.* [*pl.* IVIES], [AS. *ifig*], 1. a variety of climbing vine with a woody stem and evergreen leaves: also **English ivy.** 2. any of various similar climbing plants: as, poison *ivy.*
**I.W.W.,** Industrial Workers of the World.
**Ix·i·on** (ik-sī′ən), *n.* in *Gr. legend,* a Thessalian king, who was bound to a constantly revolving wheel in Tartarus for seeking the love of Hera.
**ix·tle** (iks′tli, is′tli), *n.* istle.
**I·yar** (ē′yär), *n.* [Heb.], the eighth month of the Jewish year: see **Jewish calendar.**
**-i·za·tion** (ə-zā′shən, ī-), a compound suffix forming nouns from verbs ending in *-ize*, as in *realization.*
**-ize** (īz), [< Fr. < LL. < Gr. *-izein*], a suffix meaning: 1. *to cause to be* or *become, make,* as in *sterilize.* 2. *to become, become like,* as in *crystallize.* 3. *to subject to, combine with,* as in *oxidize.* 4. *to engage in, concern oneself with,* as in *theorize.* Sometimes sp. **-ise.**
**Iz·mir** (iz′mir), *n.* Smyrna: the Turkish name.
**iz·zard** (iz′ẽrd), *n.* [< OFr. *ezed* < Pr. < Gr. *zēta*], [Archaic or Dial.], the letter Z.

# J

**J, j** (jā), *n.* [*pl.* J's, j's, Js, js], 1. the tenth letter of the English alphabet. 2. the sound of J or j. *adj.* tenth in a sequence or group.
**J,** in *physics,* joule.
**J.,** 1. Judge. 2. Justice.
**Ja.,** January.
**J.A.,** Judge Advocate.
**jab** (jab), *v.t. & v.i.* [JABBED, JABBING], [< ME. *jobben,* to peck], 1. to poke or thrust, as with a sharp instrument. 2. to punch with short, straight blows. *n.* a quick thrust or blow.
**jab·ber** (jab′ẽr), *v.i. & v.t.* [prob. echoic], to speak or say quickly, incoherently, or nonsensically; chatter. *n.* fast, incoherent, nonsensical talk. **—jab′ber·er,** *n.* **—jab′ber·ing·ly,** *adv.*
**ja·bot** (zha′bō′; Fr. zhà′bō′), *n.* [*pl.* -BOTS (-bōz′; Fr. -bō′)], [Fr., bird's crop], 1. a trimming or frill, usually of lace, attached to the neck of a woman's blouse or bodice. 2. formerly, a similar ruffle on a man's shirt front.
**ja·cinth** (jā′sinth, jas′inth), *n.* [< OFr. < L. *hyacinthus;* see HYACINTH], a reddish-orange precious stone, a variety of zircon; hyacinth.
**jack** (jak), *n.* [*pl.* for 5, 6, JACKS, JACK; see PLURAL, II, D, 1], [< OFr. < LL. *Jacobus* < Gr. < Heb. *ya'aqob,* Jacob], 1. [often J-], a man or boy; fellow. 2. [often J-], a sailor. 3. *a*) a device for turning a roast. *b*) a bootjack. 4. any of various machines used to lift or hoist something heavy a short distance: as, a hydraulic *jack,* automobile *jack,* etc. 5. a male donkey. 6. a jack rabbit. 7. [Slang], money. 8. a playing card with a page boy's picture on it; knave. 9. a jackstone. 10. a small flag flown on a ship's bow as a signal or to show nationality. 11. in *electricity,* a plug-in receptacle used to make electric contact. *v.t.* to raise by means of a jack. *adj.* male: of some animals. **—every man jack,** everyone. **—jack up,** 1. to raise by means of a jack. 2. [Colloq.], to raise (prices, salaries, etc.). 3. [Colloq.], to encourage to duty.

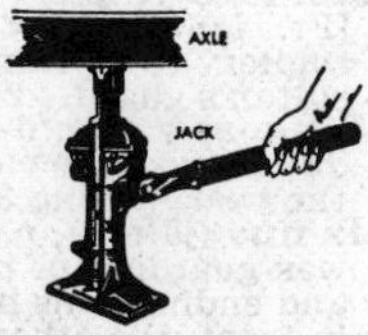

JACK

**jack-,** [see JACK], a combining form meaning: 1 *male,* as in *jackass, jackdaw.* 2. *large* or *strong,* as in *jackknife.* 3. *boy, fellow:* used in hyphenated compounds, as *jack-in-the-box.*
**jack·al** (jak′ôl, -əl), *n.* [*pl.* -ALS, -AL; see PLURAL, II, D, 1], [< Turk. < Per. *shagāl* < Sans.], 1. a yellowish-gray, meat-eating wild dog of Asia and N Africa, smaller than the wolf. 2. one who does low or dishonest work for another.
**jack·a·napes** (jak′ə-nāps′), *n.* [< nickname of a 15th-c. Duke of Suffolk], 1. formerly, a monkey. 2. a conceited, insolent fellow.
**jack·ass** (jak′as′), *n.* [*jack-* + *ass*], 1. a male donkey. 2. a stupid or foolish person; nitwit.
**jack·boot** (jak′bōōt′), *n.* [*jack-* + *boot*], a heavy, sturdy boot reaching above the knee: also **jack boot.**
**jack·daw** (jak′dô′), *n.* [*jack-* + *daw*], a European black bird like the crow, but smaller.
**jack·et** (jak′it), *n.* [< OFr. dim. of *jaque* < Sp. *jaco,* coat; prob. < Ar. *shakk*], 1. a short coat. 2. an outer covering, as the removable paper cover of a book, the insulating casing on a boiler, the skin of a potato, etc. *v.t.* 1. to put a jacket, or coat, on. 2. to cover with a wrapper, etc. **—jack′et·ed,** *adj.* **—jack′et·less,** *adj.*
**Jack Frost,** frost or cold weather personified.
**jack-in-the-box** (jak′in-*th*ə-boks′), *n.* [*pl.* -BOXES], [see JACK-], a toy consisting of a box from which a little figure on a spring jumps up when the lid is lifted: also **jack′-in-a-box′.**
**jack-in-the-pul·pit** (jak′in-*th*ə-pool′pit), *n.* [*pl.* -PITS], [see JACK-], an American plant of the lily family, with a flower spike partly arched over by a hoodlike covering.
**Jack Ketch,** [Brit.], an official hangman.
**jack·knife** (jak′nīf′), *n.* [*pl.* -KNIVES], [*jack-* + *knife*], 1. a large pocketknife. 2. a dive in which the diver keeps his legs straight and touches his feet with his hands just before plunging into the water. *v.i.* to bend at the middle, as in a dive.
**jack-of-all-trades** (jak′əv-ôl′trādz′), *n.* [*pl.* JACKS-], [see JACK-], [often J-], a person who can do many kinds of work acceptably; handy man.
**jack-o'-lan·tern** (jak′ə-lan′tẽrn), *n.* [*pl.* -TERNS], [see JACK-], 1. an ignis fatuus. 2. a hollow pumpkin cut to look like a face and used as a lantern.
**jack·pot** (jak′pot′), *n.* [*jack,* the playing card + *pot*], 1. cumulative stakes in a poker game, played for only when some player has a pair of jacks or better to open. 2. any cumulative stakes, as in a slot machine. Also **jack pot. —hit the jackpot,** [Slang], 1. to win the jackpot. 2. to attain the highest success.
**jack rabbit,** a large hare of W North America, with long ears and strong hind legs.
**jacks** (jaks), *n.pl.* [construed as sing.], the game of jackstones.
**jack·screw** (jak′skrōō′), *n.* [*jack-* + *screw*], a machine for raising heavy things a short distance, operated by turning a screw.
**Jack·son** (jak′s'n), *n.* 1. the capital of Mississippi,

in the central part: pop., 144,000. 2. a city in S Michigan: pop., 51,000.

**Jack·son, Andrew** (jak′s'n), 1767–1845; the seventh president of the U.S. (1829–1837).

**Jackson, Thomas Jonathan,** 1824–1863; Confederate general in the Civil War: called *Stonewall Jackson.*

**Jack·son·ville** (jak′s'n-vil′), *n.* a city of NE Florida: pop., 201,000.

**jack·stone** (jak′stōn′), *n.* [for dial. *checkstone* < *check*, pebble], 1. *pl.* [construed as sing.], a children's game of tossing, catching, or picking up pebbles or small metal pieces: often **jacks.** 2. a pebble or small metal piece used in this game.

**jack·straw** (jak′strô′), *n.* [*jack-* + *straw*], 1. a narrow strip of wood, bone, etc. used in a game played by tossing a number of these into a jumbled heap and trying to remove them one at a time without moving any of the others. 2. *pl.* [construed as sing.], this game.

**Ja·cob** (jā′kəb), *n.* in the *Bible*, a son of Isaac and father of the founders of the twelve tribes of Israel: also called *Israel*: Gen. 25–50.

**Jac·o·be·an** (jak′ə-bē′ən), *adj.* [< *Jacobus*, Latinized form of *James*], 1. of James I of England. 2. of the period in England when he was king (1603–1625). *n.* a poet, diplomat, etc. of this period.

**Jac·o·bin** (jak′ə-bin), *n.* [< the Church of St. *Jacques* in Paris, the society's meeting place], 1. any member of a society of revolutionary democrats in France during the Revolution of 1789. 2. a political radical. *adj.* of the Jacobins or their policies: also **Jac′o·bin′ic, Jac′o·bin′i·cal. —Jac′o·bin·ism,** *n.*

**Jac·o·bite** (jak′ə-bīt′), *n.* [cf. JACOBEAN], a supporter of James II of England after his abdication, or of his descendants' claims to the throne. **—Jac′o·bit′ic** (-bit′ik), **Jac′o·bit′i·cal,** *adj.*

**Jacob's ladder,** 1. in the *Bible*, the ladder to heaven that Jacob saw in a dream: Gen. 28:12. 2. a ladder made of rope, wire, etc., used on ships.

**Jac·quard** (jə-kärd′), *n.* [after the French inventor, J. M. *Jacquard* (1752–1834)], the figured weave (also **Jacquard weave**) produced by a loom (**Jacquard loom**) having an endless belt of cards with holes in them arranged to produce the desired pattern.

**jade** (jād), *n.* [Fr. < Sp. < *piedra de ijada*, stone of the side: from the notion that it cured pains in the side], 1. a hard ornamental stone, usually green. 2. the green color of this stone. *adj.* 1. made of jade. 2. green like jade.

**jade** (jād), *n.* [? < ON. *jalda*, a mare], 1. a horse, especially a worn-out, worthless one. 2. a loose or disreputable woman. 3. any woman: a playful usage. *v.t. & v.i.* [JADED, JADING], to make or become tired, weary, or worn out. **—jad′ish,** *adj.*

**jad·ed** (jād′id), *adj.* 1. tired; worn-out; wearied. 2. satiated. **—jad′ed·ly,** *adv.* **—jad′ed·ness,** *n.*

**jae·ger** (yā′gẽr, jā′-), *n.* [< G. *jäger*, huntsman], a robber bird of the gull family, which forces other weaker birds to yield their prey: also sp. **jäger.**

**Jaf·fa** (jaf′ə, yä′fä), *n.* a seaport in Israel, part of Tel Aviv since 1950.

**jag** (jag), *n.* [ME. *jagge*], 1. a notch or pointed tear, as in cloth. 2. a sharp, toothlike projection. *v.t.* [JAGGED, JAGGING], 1. to cut jags in; notch. 2. to cut or tear unevenly.

**jag** (jag), *n.* [Slang], 1. an intoxicated condition due to alcohol or drugs. 2. a drunken spree.

**jag·ged** (jag′id), *adj.* having sharp projecting points or notches; raggedly cut or torn. **—jag′ged·ly,** *adv.* **—jag′ged·ness,** *n.*

**jag·uar** (jag′wär, jag′ū-är′), *n.* [*pl.* -UARS, -UAR; see PLURAL, II, D, 1], [Port. < Tupi], a wild animal, like a large leopard, yellowish with black spots, found in Central and South America.

**Jah·veh, Jah·ve** (yä′ve), *n.* Jehovah.

**Jah·weh** (yä′we), *n.* Jehovah.

**jai-a·lai** (hī′ə-lī′), *n.* [Sp. < Basque *jai*, celebration + *alai*, merry], a Latin-American game like handball, played with a basketlike racket fastened to the arm.

**jail** (jāl), *n.* [< OFr. *gaole* < LL. *caveola*, dim. of L. *cavea*, a cage], a prison for confining those convicted of minor offenses or awaiting trial. *v.t.* to put or keep in jail.

**jail·bird** (jāl′būrd′), *n.* [Colloq.], 1. a jailed person; prisoner. 2. a person often put in jail.

**jail·er, jail·or** (jāl′ẽr), *n.* a person in charge of a jail or of prisoners.

**Ja·kar·ta** (jä-kär′tä), *n.* the capital of Indonesia, on the NW coast of Java: pop., c. 3,000,000: former, Dutch name, *Batavia.*

**jake** (jāk), *adj.* [Slang], just right; satisfactory.

**jal·ap** (jal′əp), *n.* [Fr. < Sp. < *Jalapa*, city in Mexico], 1. the dried root of a Mexican plant, used as a purgative. 2. the plant.

**ja·lop·y** (jə-lop′i), *n.* [*pl.* -IES], [prob. < Fr. *chaloupe*, lit., a skiff], [Slang], an old, ramshackle automobile or airplane: also sp. **jallopy.**

**jal·ou·sie** (jal′oo-sē′, zhal′oo-zē′), *n.* [Fr. < OFr. *jalousie*, jealousy; see JEALOUS], a window, shade, door, etc. of wooden, metal, or glass slats arranged as in a Venetian blind.

**jam** (jam), *v.t.* [JAMMED, JAMMING], [< ?], 1. to squeeze into or through a confined space. 2. to bruise; crush. 3. to push; crowd. 4. to fill or block (a passageway, etc.) by crowding into it. 5. to wedge so that it cannot move. 6. in *radio*, to make (signals) unintelligible by sending out others on the same wave length. *v.i.* 1. *a)* to become wedged or stuck fast. *b)* to become unworkable through such jamming of parts. 2. to push against one another in a confined space. 3. [Slang], in *jazz*, to improvise. *n.* 1. a jamming or being jammed: as, a traffic *jam.* 2. [Colloq.], a difficult situation.

**jam** (jam), *n.* [as if from *jam, v.*], a food made by boiling fruit with sugar to a thick mixture.

**Ja·mai·ca** (jə-mā′kə), *n.* a country on an island of the West Indies, in the British Commonwealth of Nations: area, 4,411 sq. mi.; pop., 1,651,000; capital, Kingston. **—Ja·mai′can,** *adj. & n.*

**jamb, jambe** (jam), *n.* [< Fr. < OFr. *jambe* (< LL. *gamba*), a leg], a side post of a doorway, window frame, fireplace, etc.

**jam·bo·ree** (jam′bə-rē′), *n.* [coined word; prob. < *jam, v.*], 1. [Colloq.], a noisy revel. 2. a large, especially international, assembly of boy scouts.

**James** (jāmz), *n.* 1. in the *Bible*, *a)* either of two Christian apostles. *b)* one of the books of the New Testament. 2. a river of Virginia flowing eastward into Chesapeake Bay.

**James I,** 1566–1625; king of England (1603–1625).

**James II,** 1633–1701; son of *Charles I;* king of England (1685–1688); deposed.

**James, Henry** (jāmz), 1843–1916; brother of *William;* U.S. novelist and essayist in England.

**James, Jesse,** 1847–1882; U.S. outlaw.

**James, William,** 1842–1910; U.S. psychologist and philosopher.

**James·town** (jāmz′toun′), *n.* a colonial settlement (1607) at the mouth of the James River, Virginia.

**Jam·mu and Kashmir** (jum′ōō), see **Kashmir.**

**jam session,** [Slang], an informal gathering of jazz musicians to play improvisations.

**Jan.,** January.

**jan·gle** (jaŋ′g'l), *v.i.* [-GLED, -GLING], [< OFr. *jangler*], 1. to make a harsh, inharmonious sound, as a bell out of tune. 2. to quarrel; bicker. *v.t.* 1. to utter in a harsh, inharmonious manner. 2. to cause to make a harsh sound. *n.* 1. a harsh sound. 2. bickering; quarrel. **—jan′gler,** *n.*

**Jan·is·sar·y** (jan′ə-ser′i), *n.* a Janizary.

**jan·i·tor** (jan′i-tẽr), *n.* [L., doorkeeper < *janua*, door], 1. a doorman. 2. one who takes care of a building, apartment house, etc. **—jan′i·to′ri·al** (-tôr′i-əl, -tō′ri-), *adj.* **—jan′i·tress,** *n.fem.*

**Jan·i·zar·y, jan·i·zar·y** (jan′ə-zer′i), *n.* [*pl.* -IES], [Fr. *janissaire* < Turk. < *yeñi*, new + *cheri*, soldiery], 1. formerly, a soldier in the Turkish sultan's guard. 2. any Turkish soldier.

**Jan·u·ar·y** (jan′ū-er′i), *n.* [*pl.* -IES], [L. (*mensis*) *Januarius*, (the month of) Janus], the first month of the year, having 31 days: abbrev. **Jan.**

**Ja·nus** (jā′nəs), *n.* in *Rom. mythology*, the god who was guardian of portals and patron of beginnings and endings: his head is shown with two faces, one in front, the other at the back.

**Jap** (jap), *n. & adj.* Japanese: a shortened form often expressing contempt, hostility, etc.

**Jap.,** 1. Japan. 2. Japanese.

**Ja·pan** (jə-pan′), *n.* an island country east of Asia, including Hokkaido, Honshu, Shikoku, Kyushu, and smaller islands: area, 142,727 sq. mi.; pop., 93,407,000; capital, Tokyo: Japanese name, *Nippon.*

**ja·pan** (jə-pan′), *n.* [< *Japan*], 1. a hard lacquer or varnish giving a glossy finish. 2. a liquid mixture used as a paint drier. 3. objects decorated and lacquered in the Japanese style. *v.t.* [-PANNED, -PANNING], to varnish with japan.

**Jap·a·nese** (jap′ə-nēz′), *adj.* of Japan, its people, language, culture, etc. *n.* 1. [*pl.* -NESE], a native of Japan. 2. the language of Japan.

**Japanese beetle,** a green-and-brown beetle, originally from Japan, which eats leaves, fruits, and grasses, and is damaging to crops.

**jape** (jāp), *v.t.* [JAPED, JAPING], [ME. *japen*], 1. to joke; jest. 2. to play tricks. *v.t.* to play tricks on; fool. *n.* 1. a joke; jest. 2. a trick. **—jap′er,** *n.* **—jap′er·y** (-ẽr-i), [*pl.* -IES], *n.*

**Ja·pheth** (jā′fith), *n.* in the *Bible*, the youngest of Noah's three sons: Gen. 5:32.
**ja·pon·i·ca** (jə-pon′i-kə), *n.* [Mod. L. (< Fr. *Japon*, Japan) adj., mistakenly used as n.], the camellia or any of several other unrelated plants.
**jar** (jär), *v.i.* [JARRED, JARRING], [ME. *jarren* < OFr. < Gmc. echoic base], 1. to make a harsh sound; grate. 2. to have a harsh, irritating effect (*on* one). 3. to vibrate from a sudden impact. 4. to clash; quarrel. *v.t.* 1. to make vibrate by sudden impact. 2. to cause to give a harsh, grating sound. 3. to jolt or shock. *n.* 1. a harsh, grating sound. 2. a vibration due to a sudden impact. 3. a jolt or shock. 4. a clash; petty quarrel.
**jar** (jär), *n.* [< Fr. *jarre* < Sp. < Ar. *jarrah*, earthen water container], 1. a container made of glass, stone, or earthenware, with a large opening and no spout. 2. as much as a jar will hold.
**jar·di·niere** (jär′d'n-êr′; Fr. zhȧr′dē′nyâr′), *n.* [Fr. < *jardin*, a garden], an ornamental bowl, pot, or stand for flowers or plants.
**jar·gon** (jär′gən, -gon), *n.* [OFr., a chattering], 1. incoherent speech; gibberish. 2. a language or dialect that is incomprehensible, outlandish, etc. to one. 3. a mixed or hybrid language or dialect, as pidgin English. 4. the specialized vocabulary and idioms of those in the same work, way of life, etc., as of journalists, gangsters, etc.: see **slang.** *v.i.* to talk jargon.
**jar·gon·ize** (jär′gən-īz′), *v.i. & v.t.* [-IZED, -IZING], to talk, write, or express in jargon.
**Jas.**, James.
**jas·mine, jas·min** (jas′min, jaz′-), *n.* [< Fr. < Ar. < Per. *yāsamīn*], 1. a tropical and subtropical shrub of the olive family, with fragrant flowers of yellow, red, or white: also called *jessamine*. 2. any of several other similar plants with fragrant flowers.
**Ja·son** (jā′s'n), *n.* in *Gr. legend*, a prince who led the Argonauts and got the Golden Fleece.
**jas·per** (jas′pēr), *n.* [< OFr. < L. < Gr. *iaspis*], 1. an opaque variety of colored quartz, usually reddish, yellow, or brown. 2. in the *Bible*, probably a green ornamental stone.
**jaun·dice** (jôn′dis, jän′-), *n.* [< OFr. *jaunisse;* ult. < L. *galbinus*, greenish yellow < *galbus*, yellow], 1. a diseased condition in which the eyeballs, skin, and urine become abnormally yellow, caused by the presence of bile pigments in the blood. 2. a soured state of mind, caused by jealousy, envy, etc., in which judgment is distorted. *v.t.* [-DICED, -DICING], 1. to cause to have jaundice. 2. to make soured or prejudiced through jealousy, envy, etc.
**jaunt** (jônt, jänt), *v.i.* [as if < OFr. *jante*, inner rim of a wheel], to take a short trip for pleasure. *n.* a short trip for pleasure; excursion.
**jaun·ty** (jôn′ti, jän′-), *adj.* [-TIER, -TIEST], [< Fr. *gentil*, genteel], 1. stylish; chic. 2. easy and careless; gay and swaggering; sprightly. **—jaun′ti·ly,** *adv.* **—jaun′ti·ness,** *n.*
**Jav.**, Javanese.
**Ja·va** (jä′və, jav′ə), *n.* 1. a large island of Indonesia, between the Malay peninsula and Australia: area, 48,842 sq. mi.; pop., with Madura, 63,060,000. 2. a coffee grown in Java and the islands near it. 3. [often j-], [Slang], any coffee.
**Java man,** a type of primitive man known from fossil remains found in Java in 1891: also called *Pithecanthropus (erectus)*.
**Jav·a·nese** (jav′ə-nēz′), *adj.* of Java, its people, their language, etc. *n.* 1. [*pl.* -NESE], a native of Java. 2. the Malay language of Java.
**jave·lin** (jav′lin, -ə-lin), *n.* [< Fr. *javeline;* ult. < Celt.], 1. a light spear for throwing. 2. a pointed wooden shaft, about 8½ feet long, thrown for distance in a contest.
**jaw** (jô), *n.* [< OFr. *joue*, cheek < L. *gabata*, dish], 1. either of the two bony parts that hold the teeth and frame the mouth. 2. either of two parts that open and close to grasp or crush something, as in a monkey wrench or vise. 3. *pl.* the entrance of (a canyon, valley, etc.). 4. [Slang], talk; esp., abusive talk. *v.i.* [Slang], to talk. *v.t.* [Slang], to scold or reprove.
**jaw·bone** (jô′bōn′), *n.* 1. a bone of a jaw. 2. either of the two bones of the lower jaw.
**jaw·break·er** (jô′brāk′ēr), *n.* [Slang], 1. a word that is hard to pronounce. 2. a hard candy ball.
**jay** (jā), *n.* [< OFr. *gai* < LL. *gaius*, a jay], 1. any of several birds of the crow family. 2. a bluejay. 3. [Slang], a stupid, foolish person.
**Jay, John** (jā), 1745–1829; first chief justice of the U.S. (1789–1795).
**Jay·hawk·er** (jā′hôk′ēr), *n.* [Colloq.], a native or inhabitant of Kansas.
**jay·walk** (jā′wôk′), *v.i.* [*jay*, stupid person + *walk*], [Colloq.], to walk in or across a street without regard to traffic rules and signals. **—jay′walk′er,** *n.* **—jay′walk′ing,** *n.*
**jazz** (jaz), *n.* [< Creole patois *jass*, sexual term applied to the Congo dances (New Orleans)], 1. a kind of music characterized by syncopation, heavily accented 4/4 time, melodic variations, and unusual tonal effects on the saxophone, clarinet, trumpet, trombone, etc. 2. loosely, any popular dance music. 3. [Slang], lively spirit. *adj.* of, in, or like jazz. *v.t.* to play or arrange as jazz. **—jazz up,** [Slang], to enliven. **—jazz′i·ly,** *adv.* **—jazz′i·ness,** *n.* **—jazz′y** [-IER, -IEST], *adj.*
**J.C.D.,** *Juris Civilis Doctor*, [L.], Doctor of Civil Law.
**jct.,** junction.
**J.D.,** *Jurum Doctor*, [L.], Doctor of Laws.
**Je.,** June.
**jeal·ous** (jel′əs), *adj.* [< OFr. *gelos* < LL. *zelosus;* see ZEAL], 1. watchful or solicitous in guarding or keeping: as, he is *jealous* of his rights. 2. resentfully suspicious, as of a rival: as, her husband was *jealous* of the other man. 3. resulting from such a feeling: as, a *jealous* rage. 4. demanding exclusive loyalty: as, a *jealous* God. 5. resentfully envious. **—jeal′ous·ly,** *adv.* **—jeal′ous·ness,** *n.*
**jeal·ous·y** (jel′əs-i), *n.* [*pl.* -IES], a jealous quality, state of mind, or feeling.
**jean** (jēn, jān), *n.* [< OFr. *Janne* < LL. < L. *Genua*, Genoa], 1. a durable, twilled cotton cloth, used for work clothes. 2. *pl.* trousers or overalls of this material.
**Jeans,** Sir **James Hop·wood** (hop′wood′ jēnz), 1877–1946; English mathematician, astronomer, physicist, and writer.
**jee** (jē), *interj., n., v.t. & v.i.* gee.
**jeep** (jēp), *n.* [< Eugene the *Jeep*, an animal in a comic strip by E.C. Segar; ? suggested by *G.P.*, *G*eneral *P*urpose Car], 1. a small, rugged, military automobile with a ¼-ton capacity and a four-wheel drive. 2. a similar vehicle for civilian use.
**jeer** (jêr), *v.i. & v.t.* [? < *cheer*], to make fun of (a person or thing) in a rude, sarcastic manner; mock; scoff (at). *n.* a jeering remark; derisive comment. **—jeer′er,** *n.* **—jeer′ing·ly,** *adv.*
**Jef·fer·son, Thomas** (jef′ēr-s'n), 1743–1826; American Revolutionary leader; drew up the Declaration of Independence; third president of the U.S. (1801–1809). **—Jef′fer·son′i·an** (-sō′ni-ən), *adj. & n.*
**Jefferson City,** the capital of Missouri, on the Missouri River: pop., 28,000.
**Je·hol** (jə-hol′, re-hō′), *n.* a former province of NE China.
**Je·hosh·a·phat** (ji-hosh′ə-fat′, -hos′-), *n.* in the *Bible*, a king of Judah noted for his righteousness: II Chron. 17 ff.
**Je·ho·vah** (ji-hō′və), *n.* [transliteration of Heb. sacred name for God], God; (the) Lord.
**Jehovah's Witnesses,** a Christian sect founded by Charles T. Russell (1852–1916): its members refuse to accept the authority of any government in matters of religious conscience.
**Je·hu** (jē′hū), *n.* [< *Jehu* in the Bible: II Kings 9:20], a fast, reckless driver: humorous term.
**je·june** (ji-jōōn′), *adj.* [L. *jejunus*, empty], 1. not nourishing. 2. not satisfying or interesting; dull. **—je·june′ly,** *adv.* **—je·june′ness,** *n.*
**je·ju·nec·to·my** (ji′jōō-nek′tə-mi), *n.* [*jejunum* + *-ectomy*], the surgical removal of all or part of the jejunum.
**je·ju·num** (ji-jōō′nəm), *n.* [< L.; see JEJUNE], the middle part of the small intestine, between the duodenum and the ileum.
**jell** (jel), *v.i. & v.t.* [< *jelly*], [Colloq.], 1. to become or make into jelly. 2. to take or give definite form; crystallize. *n.* [Colloq.], jelly.
**jel·lied** (jel′id), *adj.* 1. changed into jelly. 2. served in or with jelly. 3. coated with jelly.
**jel·li·fy** (jel′ə-fī′), *v.t. & v.i.* [-FIED, -FYING], to change into jelly. **—jel′li·fi·ca′tion,** *n.*
**jel·ly** (jel′i), *n.* [*pl.* -LIES], [< OFr. pp. of *geler* (< L. *gelare*), to freeze], 1. a soft, partially transparent, gelatinous food resulting from the cooling of fruit juice boiled with sugar, or of meat juice cooked down. 2. any substance like this. *v.t.* [-LIED, -LYING], 1. to make into jelly. 2. to put jelly on. *v.i.* to become jelly. **—jel′ly·like′,** *adj.*
**jel·ly·bean** (jel′i-bēn′), *n.* a small gelatinous candy shaped like a bean.

**jel·ly·fish** (jel′i-fish′), *n.* [*pl.* see FISH], 1. a sea animal with a body largely of jelly-like substance shaped like an umbrella; medusa: it has long, hanging tentacles with stinging hairs on them. 2. [Colloq.], a weak-willed person.

JELLYFISH (16 in. long)

**jel·ly·roll** (jel′i-rōl′), *n.* a thin sheet of sponge cake spread with jelly and rolled to form layers.

‡**je ne sais quoi** (zhə nə sā′ kwȧ′), [Fr.], 1. I know not what. 2. a thing hard to describe.

**Jenghiz Khan,** see **Genghis Khan.**

**Jen·ner, Edward** (jen′ẽr), 1749–1823; English physician; introduced vaccination.

**jen·net** (jen′it), *n.* [< OFr. < Sp. *jinete,* horseman; prob. < Ar. *Zenāta,* a tribe of Barbary], any of a breed of small Spanish horses.

**jen·ny** (jen′i), *n.* [*pl.* -NIES], [< *Jenny,* a feminine name], 1. a spinning jenny. 2. the female of some animals: as, a *jenny* wren.

**jeop·ard·ize** (jep′ẽr-dīz′), *v.t.* [-IZED, -IZING], to put in jeopardy; endanger: also **jeop′ard** (-ẽrd).

**jeop·ard·y** (jep′ẽr-di), *n.* [*pl.* -IES], [< OFr. *jeu parti,* lit., a game with even chances; ult. < L. *jocus,* a game + *partire,* to divide], 1. risk; danger; peril. 2. in *criminal law,* the situation of a person on trial.

**Jer.,** Jeremiah.

**jer·bo·a** (jẽr-bō′ə), *n.* [Mod. L. < Ar. *yarbū*], a small, leaping rodent of N Africa and Asia, with long hind legs and a long tail.

**jer·e·mi·ad** (jer′ə-mī′əd), *n.* a lamentation or tale of woe: in allusion to the *Lamentations of Jeremiah* in the Bible.

**Jer·e·mi·ah** (jer′ə-mī′ə), *n.* in the *Bible,* 1. a Hebrew prophet of the 6th and 7th centuries B.C. 2. a book of the Old Testament containing his prophecies. Also **Jer′e·mi′as.**

**Jer·i·cho** (jer′ə-kō′), *n.* a city in W Jordan: site of an ancient city whose walls were miraculously destroyed when trumpets were sounded: Josh. 6.

**jerk** (jũrk), *v.t.* [< ?], 1. to pull at, twist, push, or throw with a sudden, sharp movement. 2. to utter sharply and abruptly (with *out*). *v.i.* 1. to move with a jerk or in jerks. 2. to twitch. *n.* 1. a sharp, abrupt pull, twist, push, etc. 2. a sudden muscular contraction caused by a reflex action. 3. [Slang], a person regarded as stupid, dull, etc.

**jerk** (jũrk), *v.t.* [< Sp. *charqui,* dried meat < Peruv. *ccharqui*], to preserve (meat) by slicing it into strips and drying these in the sun or over a fire. *n.* jerked meat, especially beef.

**jer·kin** (jũr′kin), *n.* [cf. OFr. *jergot,* doublet], 1. a short, closefitting coat or jacket, often sleeveless, of the 16th and 17th centuries. 2. a woman's short, sleeveless vest.

**jerk·wa·ter** (jũrk′wô′tẽr, -wät′ẽr), *n.* [*jerk* (to pull) + *water*], a train on an early branch railroad; hence, *adj.* [Colloq.], small, unimportant, etc.: as, a *jerkwater* town.

**jerk·y** (jũr′ki), *adj.* [-IER, -IEST], characterized by jerks; making sudden starts and stops; spasmodic. —**jerk′i·ly,** *adv.* —**jerk′i·ness,** *n.*

**Jer·ome,** Saint (jə-rōm′; Brit. jer′əm), (*Eusebius Hieronymus*), 340?–420 A.D.; monk and church scholar; author of the Vulgate.

**jer·ry-built** (jer′i-bilt′), *adj.* [prob. < name *Jerry,* reinforced by nautical term *jury*], built poorly, of cheap, inferior materials; flimsy.

**Jer·sey** (jũr′zi), *n.* 1. one of the Channel Islands off the French coast. 2. [*pl.* -SEYS], any of a breed of small, reddish-brown dairy cattle originating there. 3. [j-], *a)* a soft, elastic, knitted cloth. *b)* [*pl.* -SEYS], a closefitting, knitted upper garment.

**Jersey City,** a seaport of NE New Jersey, across the Hudson from New York City: pop., 276,000.

**Je·ru·sa·lem** (jə-rōō′sə-ləm), *n.* a city divided between Israel and Jordan: pop., 231,000: the Israeli part is the capital of Israel, pop., 156,000: a holy city for Jews, Christians, and Moslems.

**Jerusalem artichoke,** [altered < It. *girasole,* sunflower], 1. a kind of sunflower with edible potato-like tubers. 2. a tuber of this plant.

**Jes·per·sen, Jens Ot·to Har·ry** (yens ot′ō hä′ri yes′pẽr-s′n), 1860–1943; Danish linguist.

**jess** (jes), *n.* [OFr. *ge(t)s,* pl. < L. *jactus,* a casting], a strap for fastening around a falcon's leg. *v.t.* to fasten a jess on.

**jes·sa·mine** (jes′ə-min), *n.* jasmine.

**jest** (jest), *n.* [OFr. *geste,* an exploit < L. pp. of *gerere,* to perform], 1. a mocking remark; jibe; taunt. 2. a joke. 3. joking; fun; ridicule. 4. something to be laughed at or joked about. *v.i.* 1. to jeer; mock; banter. 2. to be playful in speech and actions; joke. —**jest′ing·ly,** *adv.*

**jest·er** (jes′tẽr), *n.* one who jests; esp., a professional fool employed by a ruler in the Middle Ages to amuse him with antics, jokes, etc.

**Je·su** (jē′zū, -zōō, -sū, -sōō), *n.* [Poetic], Jesus.

**Jes·u·it** (jezh′ōō-it, jez′ū-), *n.* a member of the Society of Jesus, a Roman Catholic religious order founded by Ignatius Loyola in 1534. *adj.* 1. of the Jesuits. 2. [j-], jesuitic.

**Jes·u·it·ic** (jezh′ōō-it′ik, jez′ū-), *adj.* 1. of or like the Jesuits, or their doctrines, practices, etc. 2. [j-], crafty; cunning; casuistic: hostile term, as used by anti-Jesuits. Also **Jes′u·it′i·cal.** —**Jes′u·it′i·cal·ly,** *adv.*

**Je·sus** (jē′zəs), [L. *Iesus* < Gr. *Iēsous* < Heb. *yēshūʻa,* contr. of *yehōshuʻa,* help of Jehovah], *n.* the founder of the Christian religion: often **Jesus Christ, Jesus of Nazareth.**

**jet** (jet), *v.t.* & *v.i.* [JETTED, JETTING], [< Fr. *jeter* < LL. < L. *jactare* (< *jacere*), to throw], to spout, gush, or shoot out in a stream. *n.* 1. a stream of liquid or gas suddenly emitted, as from a spout; gush. 2. a spout or nozzle for emitting a jet. 3. a jet-propelled airplane: also **jet (air)plane.** *adj.* 1. jet-propelled. 2. used for jet propulsion.

**jet** (jet), *n.* [< OFr. < L.; Gr. *gagatēs,* jet < *Gagas,* town in Asia Minor], 1. a hard, black mineral like coal: used in jewelry when polished. 2. a lustrous black. *adj.* 1. made of jet. 2. black, like jet.

**jet-black** (jet′blak′), *adj.* very black, like jet.

**jet-pro·pelled** (jet′prə-peld′), *adj.* driven by jet propulsion.

**jet propulsion,** a method of propelling airplanes, boats, bombs, etc. by causing gases to be emitted under pressure through a vent at the rear.

JET-PROPELLED PLANE

**jet·sam** (jet′səm), *n.* [OFr. *jetaison;* see JETTISON], 1. that part of the cargo thrown overboard to lighten a ship in danger: cf. *flotsam.* 2. such cargo washed ashore. 3. discarded things.

**jet stream,** 1. a stream of strong wind moving in the upper troposphere around either of the earth's poles, usually from west to east. 2. a stream of exhaust, as from a rocket.

**jet·ti·son** (jet′ə-s′n, -z′n), *n.* [OFr. *getaison* < L. < *jactare,* to throw], 1. a throwing overboard of goods to lighten a ship, airplane, etc. in an emergency. 2. jetsam. *v.t.* 1. to throw (goods) overboard. 2. to discard (something).

**jet·ty** (jet′i), *n.* [*pl.* -TIES], [< OFr. *jetee;* orig. pp. of *jeter;* see JET, *v.*], 1. a kind of wall built out into the water to restrain currents, protect a harbor, etc. 2. a landing pier.

‡**jeu d'es·prit** (zhö′des′prē′), [Fr., lit., play of intellect], a witticism; clever turn of phrase.

**Jew** (jōō), *n.* [< OFr. < L. *Judaeus* < Gr. < Heb. *yehūdī,* citizen of Judah], 1. a person descended, or regarded as descended, from the ancient Hebrews. 2. a person whose religion is Judaism.

**jew·el** (jōō′əl), *n.* [< OFr. *jouel;* ult. < L. *jocus,* a joke], 1. a valuable ornament, often set with gems. 2. a precious stone; gem. 3. any person or thing very dear to one. 4. a small gem or gemlike object used as one of the bearings in a watch. *v.t.* [-ELED or -ELLED, -ELING or -ELLING], to set with jewels.

**jew·el·er, jew·el·ler** (jōō′əl-ẽr), *n.* one who makes, deals in, or repairs jewelry, watches, etc.

**jew·el·ry** (jōō′əl-ri), *n.* jewels collectively: also, Brit., **jew′el·ler·y.**

**jew·el·weed** (jōō′əl-wēd′), *n.* any of various plants bearing yellow or orange-yellow flowers and seed pods that curl at the touch when ripe.

**Jew·ess** (jōō′is), *n.* a Jewish woman or girl: often a patronizing or contemptuous term.

**jew·fish** (jōō′fish′), *n.* [*pl.* see FISH], 1. the giant black sea bass. 2. any of several species of large fish found in warm seas.

**Jew·ish** (jōō′ish), *adj.* of, belonging to, or characteristic of the Jews. *n.* popularly, Yiddish.

**Jewish calendar,** a calendar used by the Jews in calculating holidays, etc., based on the lunar month and reckoned from 3761 B.C., the traditional date of the Creation. The months of the year, which begins in late September or early October, are: 1. *Tishri* (30 days), 2. *Cheshvan* (29 or 30 days), 3. *Kislev* (29 or 30 days), 4. *Tebet* (29 days), 5. *Shebat* (30 days), 6. *Adar* (29 or 30 days), 7. *Nisan* (30 days), 8. *Iyar* (29 days), 9. *Sivan* (30 days), 10. *Tammuz* (29 days), 11. *Ab* (30 days), and 12. *Elul* (29 days). About once every three years an extra month, *Veadar* (29 days), falls between *Adar* and *Nisan*.

**Jewish holidays,** the holidays of Judaism, including: ***Rosh Hashana,*** New Year (*Tishri* 1, 2); ***Yom Kippur,*** Day of Atonement (*Tishri* 10); ***Sukkoth,*** Feast of Tabernacles (*Tishri* 15–22); ***Simchath Torah,*** Rejoicing in the Law (*Tishri* 23); ***Hanukkah,*** Feast of the Dedication (*Kislev* 25–*Tebet* 2); ***Purim,*** Feast of Lots (*Adar* 14); ***Pesach,*** the Passover (*Nisan* 15–22); ***Lag b'Omer,*** 33d day from the 2d of Passover (*Iyar* 18); ***Shabuoth,*** Pentecost (*Sivan* 6, 7); ***Tishah b'Ab,*** day of fasting (*Ab* 9), in commemoration of the destruction of the Temple.

**Jewish National Autonomous Region,** an autonomous region of the R.S.F.S.R., in far E Siberia, set aside for Jewish colonization: area, 14,204 sq. mi.; pop., 150,000: also called *Birobijan*.

**Jew·ry** (jo͞o′ri), *n.* [*pl.* -RIES], 1. a district inhabited by Jews; ghetto. 2. the Jewish people; Jews collectively. 3. [Obs.], Judea.

**jew's-harp, jews'-harp** (jo͞oz′härp′), *n.* a small musical instrument made of metal, held between the teeth and played by plucking a projecting bent piece with the fingers.

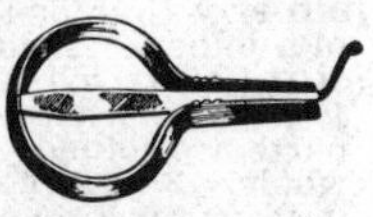
JEW'S-HARP

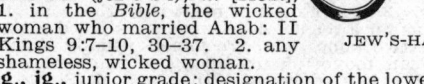

**Jez·e·bel** (jez′ə-b'l), *n.* [Heb.], 1. in the *Bible*, the wicked woman who married Ahab: II Kings 9:7–10, 30–37. 2. any shameless, wicked woman.

**j.g., jg.,** junior grade: designation of the lower rank of lieutenant in the U.S. Navy.

**jib** (jib), *n.* [prob. < *gibbet*], the projecting arm of a crane; boom of a derrick.

**jib** (jib), *v.i. & v.t.* [JIBBED, JIBBING], in *nautical usage*, to jibe; shift: also sp. **jibb.** *n.* a triangular sail projecting ahead of the foremast. **—cut of one's jib,** [Colloq.], one's appearance or way of dressing.

**jib** (jib), *v.i.* [JIBBED, JIBBING], [prob. < OFr. *regibber*, to kick back < *giber*, to shake < *gibet;* see GIBBET], 1. to refuse to go forward; balk. 2. to move backward or sideways instead of going on. *n.* an animal that jibs, as a horse.

**jib boom,** a spar fixed to and extending beyond the bowsprit of a ship: the jib is attached to it.

**jibe** (jīb), *v.i.* [JIBED, JIBING], [< D. *gijpen*], 1. to shift from one side of a ship to the other, as a fore-and-aft sail when the course is changed in a following wind. 2. to change the course of a ship so that the sails jibe. 3. [Colloq.], to be in harmony, agreement, etc. *v.t.* in *nautical usage*, to cause to jibe. *n.* 1. a shift of sail or boom from one side of a ship to another. 2. a change of course brought about by jibing. Also, in nautical senses, sp. **gibe, gybe.**

**jibe** (jīb), *v.i. & v.t.* [JIBED, JIBING], [var. of *gibe*], to jeer; taunt; scoff (at). *n.* a jeer; taunt. Also sp. **gibe. —jib′er,** *n.*

**Jid·da** (jid′ə), *n.* a city in Arabia, on the Red Sea, near Mecca: pop., 40,000: also **Jedda.**

**jif·fy** (jif′i), *n.* [*pl.* -FIES], [Colloq.], a very short time; instant: as, done in a *jiffy:* also **jiff.**

**jig** (jig), *n.* [merging of OFr. *gigue* (< OHG.) with ON. base of Dan. *gig*, spinning top], 1. a fast, gay, springy dance, usually in triple time. 2. the music for such a dance. 3. a fishhook having a spoonlike part that twirls in trolling. 4. any of several mechanical devices operating with a jerky motion, as a sieve for separating ores, a drill, etc. 5. a device used to guide a tool, as a drill. *v.i. & v.t.* [JIGGED, JIGGING], 1. to dance (a jig). 2. to move jerkily up and down or to and fro. **—the jig is up,** [Slang], all chances for success are gone: said of enterprises involving risk.

**jig·ger** (jig′ẽr), *n.* [altered < *chigoe*], 1. a small tropical flea. 2. a mite larva or tick that burrows into the skin. See **chigoe, chigger.**

**jig·ger** (jig′ẽr), *n.* 1. one who jigs. 2. a small glass used to measure liquor, containing usually 1½ ounces. 3. the quantity of liquor in a jigger. 4. any device or contraption whose name does not occur to one; gadget. 5. in *fishing*, a jig. 6. in *mechanics*, any of several devices with a jerky motion in operation. 7. in *nautical usage*, *a*) a small tackle. *b*) a small sail. *c*) a jigger mast.

**jigger mast,** a mast in the stern of a ship.

**jig·gle** (jig′'l), *v.t. & v.i.* [-GLED, -GLING], [freq. of *jig, v.*], to move in quick, slight jerks; rock lightly. *n.* a jiggling.

**jig·saw** (jig′sô′), *n.* a saw consisting of a narrow blade set in a frame and operated with a vertical reciprocating motion for cutting along wavy or irregular lines, as in scroll work: also **jig saw.**

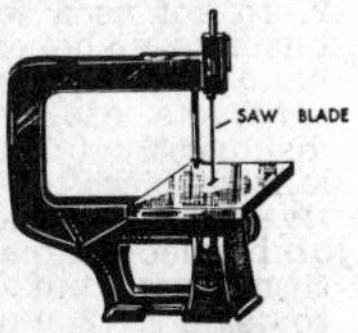

JIGSAW

**jigsaw puzzle,** a toy consisting of irregularly cut pieces of pasteboard, wood, etc. which when correctly fitted together form a picture, etc.

**Jill** (jil), *n.* [often j-], 1. a girl or young woman. 2. a sweetheart.

**jilt** (jilt), *n.* [? dim. of *Jill*, sweetheart], a woman who rejects (a lover or suitor) after encouraging him. *v.t.* to reject or cast off (a previously accepted lover or sweetheart).

**Jim Crow** (jim′ krō′), [name of an early Negro minstrel song], [Colloq.], discrimination against or segregation of Negroes. **—Jim Crow′ism.**

**jim-crow** (jim′krō′), *adj.* [also J-C-], [Colloq.], discriminating against or segregating Negroes: as, *jim-crow* laws. *n.* [also J-C-], [Colloq.], Jim Crow. *v.t.* [Colloq.], to subject to jim-crow practices.

**jim·my** (jim′i), *n.* [*pl.* -MIES], [< dim. of *James*], a short crowbar, used by burglars to pry open windows, etc. *v.t.* [-MIED, -MYING], to pry open with or as with a jimmy.

**jim·son weed, Jim·son weed** (jim′s'n), [< *Jamestown*, Virginia], a poisonous plant of the nightshade family, with bad-smelling leaves, and white or purplish, trumpet-shaped flowers.

**jin·gle** (jiŋ′g'l), *v.i.* [-GLED, -GLING], [ME. *ginglen;* echoic], 1. to make light, ringing sounds, as of bits of metal striking together; tinkle. 2. to have obvious, easy rhythm, simple rhymes, etc., as some poetry and music. *v.t.* to cause to jingle. *n.* 1. a jingling sound. 2. a verse that jingles. **—jin′gling·ly,** *adv.* **—jin′gly,** *adj.*

**jin·go** (jiŋ′gō), *n.* [*pl.* -GOES], [< phr. *by jingo* in a patriotic Brit. music-hall song (1878)], one who favors an aggressive, warlike foreign policy; chauvinist. *adj.* of jingoes. **—jin′go·ism,** *n.* **—jin′go·ist,** *n.* **—jin′go·is′tic,** *adj.*

**jinn** (jin), *n.* 1. plural of **jinni.** 2. [*pl.* JINNS], popularly, a jinni.

**jin·ni** (ji-nē′), *n.* [*pl.* JINN], [< Ar.], in *Moslem legend*, a supernatural being that can take human or animal form and influence human affairs: also **jinnee, jinn, genie.**

**jin·rik·i·sha** (jin-rik′shə, -shô), *n.* [< Japan. < *jin*, a man + *riki*, power + *sha*, carriage], a small, two-wheeled oriental carriage with a hood, pulled by one or two men: also sp. **jinricksha, jinriksha, jinrickshaw.**

**jinx** (jiŋks), *n.* [? < L. *iynx*, Gr. *iynx*, the wryneck, bird used in casting spells], [Slang], a person or thing supposed to cause bad luck. *v.t.* [JINXED, JINXING], [Slang], to cause bad luck to.

**jit·ney** (jit′ni), *n.* [*pl.* -NEYS], [c. 1903; ? < Fr. *jeton*, a token], [Slang], 1. a five-cent coin; nickel. 2. a bus or car that carries passengers for a small fare, originally five cents.

**jit·ter** (jit′ẽr), *v.i.* [? echoic], [Slang], 1. to be nervous; fidget. 2. to jitterbug. **—the jitters,** [Slang], a nervous feeling; fidgets.

**jit·ter·bug** (jit′ẽr-bug′), *n.* [*jitter* + *bug*], [Slang], a person who dances in a fast, acrobatic manner to jazz music. *v.i.* [-BUGGED, -BUGGING], [Slang], to dance in the manner of a jitterbug.

**jit·ter·y** (jit′ẽr-i), *adj.* [Slang], having the jitters.

**jiu·jit·su, jiu·jut·su** (jo͞o-jit′so͞o), *n.* jujitsu.

**jive** (jīv), *n.* [? coinage, after *jibe*], [Slang], 1. the jargon of jazz musicians and devotees. 2. loosely, jazz. *v.i.* to play jazz.

**Jl.,** July.

**jo** (jō), *n.* [*pl.* JOES], [Scot.], a sweetheart: also sp. **joe.**

**Jo.,** Joel.

**Joan of Arc,** Saint (jōn əv ärk), (Fr. *Jeanne d'Arc*), 1412–1431; French heroine; defeated the English at Orléans (1429); burned as a witch; canonized in 1920: called the *Maid of Orleans*.

**Job** (jōb), *n.* in the *Bible*, 1. a man who endured much suffering but did not lose his faith in God. 2. a book of the Old Testament telling of him.

**job** (job), *n.* [ME. *gobbe*, a lump, portion < Celt. *gob*, the mouth], 1. a piece of work; esp., a definite piece of work, done by agreement for pay. 2. task; chore; duty. 3. the thing or material being worked on. 4. a dishonest piece of official business. 5. a position of employment; work. 6. [Colloq.], any happening, affair, etc. *adj.* hired or done by the job. *v.i.* [JOBBED, JOBBING], 1. to do odd jobs. 2. to act as a jobber or broker. 3. to do public business dishonestly for private gain. *v.t.* 1. to handle (goods) as middleman. 2. to sublet (work, contracts, etc.). 3. to transact (public business) dishonestly for private gain. **—odd jobs,** miscellaneous pieces of work. **—on the job,** [Slang], attentive to one's task or duty. **—job′less,** *adj.*

**job·ber** (job′ẽr), *n.* 1. one who buys goods in quantity from manufacturers or importers and sells them to dealers. 2. a person who works by the job; also, one who does piecework.

**job·ber·y** (job′ẽr-i), *n.* the carrying on of public business dishonestly for private gain.

**job lot,** goods, often of various sorts, brought together for sale as one quantity.

**Jo·cas·ta** (jō-kas′tə), *n.* in *Gr. legend,* the woman who unwittingly married her own son, Oedipus.

**jock·ey** (jok′i), *n.* [*pl.* -EYS], [< Scot. dim. of *Jack*], a person whose job is to ride a horse in a race. *v.t. & v.i.* [-EYED, -EYING], 1. to ride (a horse) in a race. 2. to cheat; swindle. 3. to maneuver for position or advantage.

**jo·cose** (jō-kōs′), *adj.* [< L. < *jocus,* a joke], humorous; joking. **—jo·cose′ly,** *adv.* **—jo·cose′ness, jo·cos′i·ty** (-kos′ə-ti), [*pl.* -TIES], *n.*

**joc·u·lar** (jok′yoo-lẽr), *adj.* [< L. < *jocus,* a joke], joking; humorous. **—joc′u·lar′i·ty** (-lar′ə-ti), [*pl.* -TIES], *n.* **—joc′u·lar·ly,** *adv.*

**joc·und** (jok′ənd, jō′kənd), *adj.* [< OFr. < LL. < L. *jucundus,* pleasant < *juvare,* to help], cheerful; genial; gay. **—jo·cun·di·ty** (jō-kun′də-ti), [*pl.* -TIES], *n.* **—joc′und·ly,** *adv.*

**jodh·purs** (jod′pẽrz, jōd′-), *n.pl.* [after *Jodhpur,* state in India], riding breeches made loose and full above the knees and closefitting below.

**Jo·el** (jō′əl), *n.* in the *Bible,* 1. an ancient Hebrew prophet, probably of the 5th century B.C. 2. the book of his preachings, in the Old Testament.

**joe-pye weed** (jō′pī′), [? < Ind. name], a tall plant of the composite family, with clusters of pink or purplish flowers.

**jog** (jog), *v.t.* [JOGGED, JOGGING], [ME. *joggen*], 1. to give a little shake or jerk to. 2. to nudge. 3. to shake up or revive (a person's memory). *v.i.* to move along at a slow, steady, jolting pace or trot (often with *on* or *along*). *n.* 1. a little shake or nudge. 2. a slow, steady, jolting motion: also **jog trot.** **—jog′ger,** *n.*

**jog** (jog), *n.* [var. of *jag*], a projecting or notched part, especially one at right angles, in a surface or line. *v.i.* to form or make a jog.

**jog·gle** (jog′'l), *v.t. & v.i.* [-GLED, -GLING], [freq. of *jog*], to shake or jolt slightly. *n.* a slight jolt.

**jog·gle** (jog′'l), *n.* [? < *jog,* projection], 1. a joint made by putting a notch in one surface and a projection in the other to fit into it. 2. a notch or projection for such a joint. *v.t.* [-GLED, -GLING], to join by joggles.

**Jo·han·nes·burg** (jō-han′is-bũrg′, yō-hän′-), *n.* a city in the Transvaal, Union of South Africa: pop., 1,111,000; gold-mining center.

**John** (jon), *n.* 1. in the *Bible, a*) a Christian apostle, to whom are credited the Gospel of St. John, the three Epistles of John, and Revelation: called *the Evangelist* and *the Divine. b*) the fourth book of the New Testament. *c*) John the Baptist. 2. 1167?–1216; king of England (1199–1216); forced to sign the Magna Charta (1215).

**john** (jon), *n.* [Slang], a toilet.

**John XXIII,** 1881–1963; Pope (1958–1963).

**John Barleycorn,** [see BARLEYCORN], a personification of corn liquor, malt liquor, etc.

**John Bull,** England, or an Englishman, personified.

**John Doe** (dō), a fictitious name used in legal papers, etc. for that of an unknown person.

**John Han·cock** (han′kok), [Colloq.], a person's signature.

**john·ny·cake** (jon′i-kāk′), *n.* [altered < *Shawnee-cake,* kind of bread made by Shawnee Indians], a kind of corn bread baked on a griddle.

**John·ny-jump-up** (jon′i-jump′up′), *n.* 1. any early spring violet. 2. the wild pansy.

**John·son, Andrew** (jon′s'n), 1808–1875; 17th president of the U.S. (1865–1869).

**Johnson, Lyn·don Baines** (lin′dən bānz), 1908– ; 36th president of the U.S. (1963–1969).

**Johnson, Samuel,** 1709–1784; English writer, critic, and lexicographer; known as *Dr. Johnson.*

**John·so·ni·an** (jon-sō′ni-ən), *adj.* 1. of or like Samuel Johnson or his writings. 2. heavy, pompous, erudite, etc. in style. *n.* an admirer of or specialist in Johnson and his work.

**Johns·town** (jonz′toun′), *n.* a city in SW Pennsylvania: pop., 54,000: site of a flood, 1889.

**John the Baptist,** in the *Bible,* the forerunner and baptizer of Jesus: Matt. 3.

**Jo·hore** (jə-hôr′), *n.* a state of the Federation of Malaya: area, 7,330 sq. mi.; pop., 1,065,000.

**‡joie de vi·vre** (zhwȧ′də-vē′vr′), [Fr.], joy of living; zestful enjoyment of life.

**join** (join), *v.t.* [< OFr. *joindre* < L. *jungere*], 1. to bring together; connect; fasten; combine. 2. to make into one; unite: as, *join* forces, *joined* in wedlock. 3. to become a part or member of (a club, etc.). 4. to go to and combine with: as, the path *joins* the highway. 5. to enter into the company of; accompany: as, *join* us soon. 6. to go and take one's proper place in (a military or naval unit). 7. [Colloq.], to adjoin. *v.i.* 1. to come together; meet. 2. to enter into association. 3. to participate (*in* a conversation, singing, etc.). *n.* 1. a joining or being joined. 2. a place of joining, as a seam in a coat. **—join battle,** to start fighting.

**join·er** (join′ẽr), *n.* 1. a person or thing that joins. 2. a carpenter who finishes interior woodwork, as doors, molding, stairs, etc. 3. [Colloq.], a person given to joining various organizations.

**join·er·y** (join′ẽr-i), *n.* 1. the work, trade, or skill of a joiner. 2. the things made by a joiner.

**joint** (joint), *n.* [< OFr. < L. pp. of *jungere,* to join], 1. a place where, or way in which, two things or parts are joined. 2. one of the parts of a jointed whole. 3. a large cut of meat with the bone still in it, as for a roast. 4. in *anatomy,* a place or part where two bones, etc. are joined, usually so that they can move. 5. in *botany,* a point where a branch or leaf grows out of the stem. 6. [Slang], *a*) a saloon, cheap restaurant, etc. *b*) any house, building, etc. *adj.* 1. common to two or more as to ownership or action: as, a *joint* declaration, a *joint* savings account. 2. sharing with someone else: as, a *joint* owner. *v.t.* 1. to fasten together by a joint or joints. 2. to furnish with a joint or joints. 3. to cut (meat) into joints. **—out of joint,** 1. not in place at the joint; dislocated. 2. disordered. **—joint′er,** *n.* **—joint′less,** *adj.*

**joint·ly** (joint′li), *adv.* in common; together.

**joint return,** a single income tax return filed by a married couple, combining their incomes.

**joint-stock company** (joint′stok′), a business firm owned by the stockholders in shares which each may sell without the consent of the others.

**join·ture** (join′chẽr), *n.* [< OFr. < L. < *jungere,* to join], in *law,* 1. an arrangement by which a husband settles property on his wife for her use after his death. 2. the property thus settled.

**joist** (joist), *n.* [< OFr. *giste,* a bed; ult. < L. *jacere,* to lie], any of the parallel timbers that hold up the planks of a floor or the laths of a ceiling. *v.t.* to provide with joists.

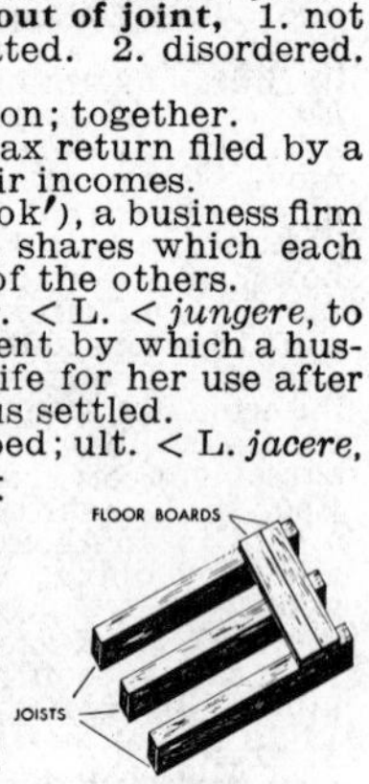

JOISTS

**joke** (jōk), *n.* [L. *jocus*], 1. anything said or done to arouse laughter; funny remark or anecdote; amusing trick. 2. something not meant to be taken seriously. 3. a person or thing to be laughed at. *v.i.* [JOKED, JOKING], to make jokes; to say or do something as a joke; jest. *v.t.* to make fun of. **—no joke,** a serious matter. **—jok′ing·ly,** *adv.*

**jok·er** (jōk′ẽr), *n.* 1. one who jokes. 2. a hidden provision put into a law, legal document, etc. to make it different from what it seems to be. 3. any hidden, unsuspected difficulty. 4. an extra playing card used in some games.

**Jo·li·et** (jō′li-et′, jō′li-et′, jol′i-et′), *n.* a city in NE Illinois: pop., 67,000.

**jol·li·fy** (jol′ə-fī′), *v.t. & v.i.* [-FIED, -FYING], [Colloq.], to make or be jolly or merry. **—jol′li·fi·ca′tion,** *n.*

**jol·li·ty** (jol′ə-ti), *n.* 1. a being jolly; gaiety. 2. [*pl.* -TIES], [Brit.], a jolly occasion.

**jol·ly** (jol′i), *adj.* [-LIER, -LIEST], [< OFr. *joli,* joyful; prob. < Gmc.], 1. full of high spirits and good humor; merry; gay. 2. [Colloq.], enjoyable; pleasant. *adv.* [Brit. Colloq.], very; altogether. *v.t. & v.i.* [-LIED, -LYING], [Colloq.], 1. to try to make (a person) feel good or agreeable by coaxing, flattering, etc. (often with *along*). 2. to make fun of (someone). **—jol′li·ly,** *adv.* **—jol′li·ness,** *n.*

**jol·ly-boat** (jol′i-bōt′), *n.* [prob. < D. *jol,* yawl], a ship's small boat: also **jolly boat, jolly.**

**Jol·ly Rog·er** (jol′i roj′ẽr), a black flag with white skull and crossbones, emblem of piracy.

**jolt** (jōlt), *v.t.* [earlier *jot, v.,* infl. by *jowl*], to shake up, as a vehicle running on a rough road. *v.i.* to move along in a bumpy, jerky manner. *n.* 1. a sudden jerk, bump, etc., as from a blow. 2. a shock or surprise. **—jolt′er,** *n.* **—jolt′y,** *adj.*

**Jo·nah** (jō′nə), *n.* 1. in the *Bible,* a Hebrew prophet:

thrown overboard in a storm, he was swallowed by a big fish, but later was cast up unharmed. 2. a book of the Old Testament telling Jonah's story. 3. any person said to bring bad luck by his presence. Also **Jo′nas** (-nəs).

**Jon·a·than** (jon′ə-thən), *n.* 1. in the *Bible*, Saul's oldest son, a close friend of David: I Sam. 18–20. 2. a late fall variety of apple.

**Jones, John Paul** (jōnz), (born *John Paul*), 1747–1792; American naval officer in the Revolutionary War, born in Scotland.

**jon·gleur** (joŋ′glẽr; Fr. zhōn′glẽr′), *n.* [Fr. < OFr.; see JUGGLE], a wandering minstrel of the Middle Ages in France and England.

**jon·quil** (joŋ′kwil, jon′-), *n.* [< Fr. < Sp. *junquillo*, dim. < L. *juncus*, a rush], 1. a variety of narcissus with yellow or white flowers and long, slender leaves. 2. its flower.

**Jon·son, Ben** (ben jon′s'n), 1573?–1637; English dramatist and poet.

**Jor·dan** (jôr′d'n), *n.* 1. a river in the Near East, flowing into the Dead Sea. 2. an Arab kingdom in SW Asia, east of Israel: area, 37,000 sq. mi.; pop., c. 1,600,000; capital, Amman: former name *Trans-Jordan.*

**Jordan almond,** [prob. < OFr. *jardin*, garden], a variety of large Spanish almond used in candies.

**Jo·seph** (jō′zəf), *n.* in the *Bible*, 1. one of Jacob's sons, who was sold into slavery in Egypt by his jealous brothers but became a high official there: Gen. 37, 39-41. 2. the husband of Mary, mother of Jesus: Matt. 1:18-25.

**Joseph of Ar·i·ma·the·a** (ar′i-mə-thē′ə), in the *Bible*, a wealthy disciple who provided a tomb for Jesus' body: Matt. 27:57–60.

**josh** (josh), *v.t. & v.i.* [said to merge *joke* and *bosh*], [Slang], to ridicule in a good-humored way; tease jokingly; banter. **—josh′er,** *n.*

**Josh·u·a** (josh′oo-ə), *n.* in the *Bible*, 1. Moses' successor, and leader of the Israelites into the Promised Land. 2. a book of the Old Testament telling about him.

**joss** (jos), *n.* [Pid. Eng.; var. of Port. *deos* < L. *deus*, a god], a figure of a Chinese god.

**joss house,** a Chinese temple.

**joss stick,** a thin stick of dried fragrant wood dust, burned by the Chinese as incense.

**jos·tle** (jos′'l), *v.t. & v.i.* [-TLED, -TLING], [earlier *justle*, freq.; see JOUST], to bump or push, as in a crowd; elbow or shove roughly. *n.* a jostling. **—jos′tle·ment,** *n.* **—jos′tler,** *n.*

**jot** (jot), *n.* [< L. < Gr. *iōta*, *i*, the smallest letter], a very small amount: as, I don't care a *jot* for him. *v.t.* [JOTTED, JOTTING], to make a brief note of (usually with *down*). **—jot′ter,** *n.*

**Jo·tunn, Jo·tun** (yô′toon, yō′-), *n.* in *Norse mythology*, a giant: also **Jö·tunn** (yö′-).

**Jo·tunn·heim, Jo·tun·heim** (yô′toon-hām′, yō′-), *n.* in *Norse mythology*, the home of the giants: also **Jötunnheim** (yö′-).

**joule** (joul, jōōl), *n.* [after J.P. *Joule* (1818–1889), Eng. physicist], in *physics*, a unit of work or energy equal to 10,000,000 ergs.

**jounce** (jouns), *v.t. & v.i.* [JOUNCED, JOUNCING], [prob. < *jaunt*], to jolt or bounce. *n.* a jolt.

**jour·nal** (jũr′n'l), *n.* [OFr. < L. *diurnalis*, daily < *dies*, day], 1. a daily record of happenings. 2. a diary. 3. a record of the transactions of a legislature, club, etc. 4. a ship's logbook. 5. a newspaper, magazine, etc. 6. in *bookkeeping*, a book of original entry for recording every transaction with an indication of its proper account. 7. in *mechanics*, the part of a rotatory axle or shaft that turns in a bearing.

**journal box,** in *mechanics*, a bearing for a journal.

**jour·nal·ese** (jũr′n'l-ēz′, -ēs′), *n.* a style of writing characteristic of many newspapers; facile style, with hackneyed expressions.

**jour·nal·ism** (jũr′n'l-iz'm), *n.* 1. the work of gathering news for, writing for, editing, or publishing a newspaper or other journal. 2. newspapers and magazines collectively.

**jour·nal·ist** (jũr′n'l-ist), *n.* one whose occupation is journalism; reporter, editor, etc. **—jour′nal·is′tic,** *adj.* **—jour′nal·is′ti·cal·ly,** *adv.*

**jour·ney** (jũr′ni), *n.* [*pl.* -NEYS], [< OFr. *journee* < LL. < L. *diurnus*, daily < *dies*, day], a traveling from one place to another; trip. *v.i.* [-NEYED, -NEYING], to go on a trip; travel.

**jour·ney·man** (jũr′ni-mən), *n.* [*pl.* -MEN], [archaic *journey*, day's work + *man*], 1. formerly, a worker who had served his apprenticeship and thus qualified himself to work at his trade. 2. now, a worker who has learned his trade.

**joust** (just, joust, jōōst), *n.* [< OFr. < *j(o)uster* < LL. *juxtare*, to approach < L. *juxta*, close to], 1. a combat with lances, between two knights on horseback. 2. *pl.* a tournament. *v.i.* to engage in a joust. **—joust′er,** *n.*

**Jove** (jōv), *n.* [Poetic], Jupiter (the god or planet). **—by Jove!** an exclamation expressing astonishment, emphasis, etc.

**jo·vi·al** (jō′vi-əl), *adj.* [Fr. < LL. *Jovialis*, of Jupiter: from astrological notion of planet's influence], full of hearty, playful good humor; genial and gay. **—jo′vi·al′i·ty** (-al′ə-ti), [*pl.* -TIES], **jo′vi·al·ness,** *n.* **—jo′vi·al·ly,** *adv.*

**jowl** (joul, jōl), *n.* [AS. *ceafl*, jaw], 1. a jaw, especially the lower jaw with the chin. 2. the cheek.

**jowl** (joul, jōl), *n.* [AS. *ceole*, throat], a fleshy, hanging part under the lower jaw.

**joy** (joi), *n.* [< OFr. *joie* < LL. < L. *gaudium*, joy], 1. a very glad feeling; happiness; delight. 2. anything causing this feeling. 3. the expression of this feeling. *v.i.* to be full of joy; rejoice. *v.t.* to make joyful; gladden.

**Joyce, James** (jois), 1882–1941; Irish author.

**joy·ful** (joi′fəl), *adj.* 1. full of joy. 2. feeling, expressing, or causing joy; glad; happy. **—joy′ful·ly,** *adv.* **—joy′ful·ness,** *n.*

**joy·less** (joi′lis), *adj.* without joy; unhappy; sad. **—joy′less·ly,** *adv.* **—joy′less·ness,** *n.*

**joy·ous** (joi′əs), *adj.* joyful; happy; gay; glad. **—joy′ous·ly,** *adv.* **—joy′ous·ness,** *n.*

**joy-ride** (joi′rīd′), *v.i.* [-RODE, -RIDDEN, -RIDING], [Colloq.], to take a joy ride.

**joy ride,** [Colloq.], an automobile ride merely for pleasure, often with reckless speed, rowdyism, etc.

**J.P.,** Justice of the Peace.

**Jr., jr.,** junior.

**Ju.,** June.

**Jua·rez, Be·ni·to Pa·blo** (be-nē′tô pä′blô hwä′res), 1806–1872; president of Mexico (1857–1863; 1863–1867).

**ju·bi·lant** (jōō′b'l-ənt), *adj.* [L. *jubilans*, ppr.; see JUBILATE], joyful and triumphant; rejoicing; elated. **—ju′bi·lance,** *n.* **—ju′bi·lant·ly,** *adv.*

**ju·bi·late** (jōō′b'l-āt′), *v.i.* [-LATED, -LATING], [< L. pp. of *jubilare*, to shout for joy < *jubilum*, wild shout], to rejoice, as in triumph; exult.

**ju·bi·la·tion** (jōō′b'l-ā′shən), *n.* 1. a jubilating; rejoicing. 2. a happy celebration, as of victory.

**ju·bi·lee** (jōō′b'l-ē′), *n.* [< OFr. < LL. < Gr. < Heb. *yōbēl*, a ram's horn (trumpet); infl. by L. *jubilum*, wild shout], 1. in *Jewish history*, a celebration held every fifty years in which all bondmen were freed, mortgaged lands restored to the owners, etc.: Lev. 25:8–17. 2. a 50th or 25th anniversary. 3. a time or occasion of rejoicing. 4. jubilation; rejoicing. 5. in the *R.C. Church*, a year during which plenary indulgence is granted on certain conditions, as for a pilgrimage to Rome.

**Jud.,** 1. Judges. 2. Judith.

**Ju·dah** (jōō′də), *n.* in the *Bible*, 1. one of Jacob's sons. 2. the tribe descended from him. 3. the kingdom in the S part of ancient Palestine formed by the tribes of Judah and Benjamin.

**Ju·da·ic** (jōō-dā′ik), *adj.* of the Jews or Judaism; Jewish: also **Ju·da′i·cal.**

**Ju·da·ism** (jōō′di-iz'm), *n.* 1. the Jewish religion. 2. observance of Jewish customs, rules, etc.

**Ju·das** (jōō′dəs), *n.* 1. Judas Iscariot, the disciple who betrayed Jesus for pay. 2. a betrayer; informer. **—Ju′das·like′,** *adj.*

**Judas tree,** a shrub or tree of the pea family, with clusters of rose-pink or purplish flowers.

**Jude** (jōōd), *n.* in the *Bible*, 1. a Christian apostle and saint: also called *Judas* (not Iscariot). 2. a book of the New Testament, the Epistle of Jude.

**Ju·de·a, Ju·dae·a** (jōō-dē′ə), *n.* a part of S Palestine that was under Roman rule.

**Ju·de·an, Ju·dae·an** (jōō-dē′ən), *adj.* 1. of Judea or its people. 2. Jewish. *n.* 1. a native of Judea. 2. a Jew.

**Judg.,** Judges.

**judge** (juj), *n.* [< OFr. < L. *judex* < *jus*, law + *dicere*, to say], 1. a public official with authority to hear and decide cases in a court of law. 2. a person designated to determine the winner, settle a controversy, etc. 3. a person qualified to decide on the relative worth of anything: as, a good *judge* of music. 4. any of the governing leaders of the ancient Israelites before the time of the kings. *v.t. & v.i.* [JUDGED, JUDGING], 1. to hear and pass judgment (on) in a court of law. 2. to determine the winner of (a contest) or settle (a controversy). 3. to form an opinion about. 4. to criticize or censure. 5. to think or suppose. 6. in *Jewish history*, to govern. **—judg′er,** ***n.*** **—judge′like′,** ***n.*** **—judge′ship,** ***n.***

**judge advocate,** [*pl.* JUDGE ADVOCATES], a military legal officer; esp., an officer designated to act as prosecutor at a court-martial.

**Judg·es** (juj′iz), ***n.pl.*** [construed as sing.], a book of the Old Testament telling the history of the Jews from the death of Joshua to the birth of Samuel.

**judg·ment** (juj′mənt), ***n.*** 1. a judging; deciding. 2. a legal decision; order or sentence given by a judge or law court. 3. a debt resulting from a court order. 4. an opinion or estimate. 5. criticism or censure. 6. the ability to come to an opinion; power of comparing and deciding. 7. [J-], in *theology*, the Last Judgment. Also sp. **judgement.**

**judgment day, Judgment Day,** in *theology*, the day of God's final judgment of all people.

**ju·di·ca·to·ry** (jōō′di-kə-tôr′i, -tō′ri), ***adj.*** [< LL. < L. pp. of *judicare*, to judge < *judex;* see JUDGE], judging; having to do with administering justice. ***n.*** [*pl.* -RIES], 1. a court of law; tribunal. 2. law courts collectively.

**ju·di·ca·ture** (jōō′di-kə-chẽr), ***n.*** 1. the administering of justice. 2. the position, functions, or legal power of a judge. 3. the extent of legal power of a judge or court of law. 4. a court of law. 5. judges or courts of law collectively.

**ju·di·cial** (jōō-dish′əl), ***adj.*** [L. *judicialis* < *judex;* see JUDGE], 1. of judges, law courts, or their functions. 2. allowed, enforced, or set by order of a judge or law court. 3. like or befitting a judge. 4. fair; unbiased. **—ju·di′cial·ly,** ***adv.***

**ju·di·ci·ar·y** (jōō-dish′i-er′i, -ẽr-i), ***adj.*** of judges, law courts, or their functions. ***n.*** [*pl.* -IES], 1. the part of government that administers justice; system of law courts. 2. judges collectively.

**ju·di·cious** (jōō-dish′əs), ***adj.*** [< Fr. < L. *judicium*, judgment < *judex;* see JUDGE], having, applying, or showing sound judgment; wise and careful. **—ju·di′cious·ly,** ***adv.*** **—ju·di′cious·ness,** ***n.***

**Ju·dith** (jōō′dith), ***n.*** 1. a book of the Apocrypha and the Douay Bible. 2. the Jewish woman told about in this book, who saved her people by killing an Assyrian general.

**ju·do** (jōō′dō), ***n.*** jujitsu.

**jug** (jug), ***n.*** [a pet form of *Judith* or *Joan*], 1. a container for liquids, with a small opening and a handle. 2. [Slang], a jail. ***v.t.*** [JUGGED, JUGGING], 1. to put into a jug. 2. [Slang], to jail.

**ju·gate** (jōō′git, -gāt), ***adj.*** [< L. pp. of *jugare*, to yoke < *jugum*, a yoke], 1. in *biology*, paired. 2. in *botany*, having paired leaflets.

**Jug·ger·naut** (jug′ẽr-nôt′), ***n.*** [< Hind. < Sans. < *jagat*, world + *nātha*, lord], 1. an incarnation of the Hindu god Vishnu: it was once erroneously believed that his worshipers threw themselves to be crushed under the wheels of a car bearing his idol. 2. [often j-], anything that exacts blind devotion or terrible sacrifice.

**jug·gle** (jug′'l), ***v.t.*** [-GLED, -GLING], [< OFr. *jogler* < L. *joculari*, to joke < *jocus*, a joke], 1. to perform skillful tricks of sleight of hand with (balls, knives, etc.). 2. to practice trickery on so as to deceive or cheat: as, he *juggled* the figures to show a profit. ***v.i.*** to toss up a number of balls, knives, etc. and keep them continuously in the air. ***n.*** 1. an act of juggling. 2. a clever trick or deception. **—jug′gler,** ***n.***

**jug·gler·y** (jug′lẽr-i), ***n.*** [*pl.* -IES], 1. the art or act of juggling. 2. trickery; deception.

**Ju·go·slav, Ju·go-Slav** (ū′gō-släv′, -slav′), ***n.*** **&** ***adj.*** Yugoslav. **—Ju′go·slav′ic,** ***adj.***

**Ju·go·sla·vi·a, Ju·go-Sla·vi·a** (ū′gō-slä′vi-ə), ***n.*** Yugoslavia. **—Ju′go·sla′vi·an,** ***adj.*** **&** ***n.***

**jug·u·lar** (jug′yoo-lẽr, jōō′gyoo-), ***adj.*** [< Mod. L. < L. *jugulum*, collarbone < *jugum*, a yoke], 1. of the neck or throat. 2. of a jugular vein. ***n.*** either of two large veins in the neck carrying blood back from the head to the heart: in full, **jugular vein.**

**juice** (jōōs), ***n.*** [< OFr. < L. *jus*, soup], 1. the liquid part of a plant, fruit, or vegetable. 2. a liquid in or from animal tissue: as, gastric *juice*. 3. [Slang], electricity. 4. [Slang], gasoline, oil, or any other liquid that supplies power. ***v.t.*** [JUICED, JUICING], [Colloq.], to extract juice from. **—juice′less,** ***adj.*** **—juic′er,** ***n.***

**juic·y** (jōō′si), ***adj.*** [-IER, -IEST], 1. full of juice; containing much juice. 2. full of interest; lively; spicy. **—juic′i·ly,** ***adv.*** **—juic′i·ness,** ***n.***

**ju·jit·su, ju·jut·su** (jōō-jit′sōō), ***n.*** [< Japan. < *jū*, soft, pliant + *jutsu*, art], a Japanese system of wrestling in which the strength and weight of an opponent are used against him: also **jiujitsu, jiujutsu, judo.**

**ju·jube** (jōō′jōōb), ***n.*** [Fr. < ML. < L. *zizyphum* < Gr. < Per. *zīzafūn*], 1. the edible, datelike fruit of a tree or shrub of the buckthorn family. 2. this tree or shrub. 3. a lozenge of gelatinous candy flavored with or like this fruit.

**juke box** (jook), [< Negro Gullah *jook-house*, roadhouse], [Colloq.], an electric phonograph operated by dropping a coin in a slot and pushing a button to choose the record.

**Jul.,** July.

**ju·lep** (jōō′lip), ***n.*** [Fr. < Ar. < Per. < *gul*, rose + *āb*, water], an iced drink of whisky or brandy flavored with sugar and fresh mint: also **mint julep.**

**Jul·ian** (jōōl′yən), ***adj.*** of Julius Caesar.

**Julian calendar,** the calendar introduced by Julius Caesar in 46 B.C., in which the ordinary year had 365 days and every fourth year (leap year) had 366 days: replaced by the Gregorian calendar.

**ju·li·enne** (jōō′li-en′; Fr. zhü′lyen′), ***n.*** [Fr.; after *Julien*, a French caterer], a clear soup containing vegetables cut into thin strips. ***adj.*** in *cooking*, cut into strips: said of vegetables.

**Ju·li·et** (jōōl′yət, jōō′li-ət, jōō′li-et′), ***n.*** the heroine of Shakespeare's tragedy *Romeo and Juliet.*

**Julius Caesar,** see **Caesar, Julius.**

**Ju·ly** (jōō-lī′), ***n.*** [*pl.* -LIES], [< Anglo-Fr. < L. (*mensis*) *Julius*, (the month of) Julius (Caesar)], the seventh month of the year, having 31 days: abbrev. **Jul., Jl., Jy.**

**jum·ble** (jum′b'l), ***v.t.*** **&** ***v.i.*** [-BLED, -BLING], [merging of *jump* with *tumble*, *stumble*, etc.], to mix or be mixed in a confused, disorderly heap. ***n.*** a confused mixture or heap.

**jum·bo** (jum′bō), ***n.*** [*pl.* -BOS], [after *Jumbo*, the elephant exhibited by P. T. Barnum], a large, clumsy person, animal, or thing. ***adj.*** very large.

**jump** (jump), ***v.i.*** [? It. loan word (16th c.)], 1. to move oneself suddenly from the ground, etc. by using the leg muscles; leap; spring. 2. to jerk; bob; bounce. 3. to start in sudden surprise. 4. to move abruptly as from one topic to another. 5. to rise suddenly, as prices. 6. in *checkers*, to move a piece over an opponent's piece, thus capturing it. ***v.t.*** 1. to leap over. 2. to cause to leap: as, he *jumped* his horse over the fence. 3. to spring aboard or leap from (a train, etc.). 4. to cause (prices, etc.) to rise. 5. [Slang], to attack suddenly. 6. [Slang], to leave suddenly; flee: as, he *jumped* town. 7. in *contract bridge*, to make an unnecessarily high bid in (a partner's suit). 8. in *checkers*, to capture (an opponent's piece). ***n.*** 1. a jumping; leap. 2. a distance jumped. 3. a thing to be jumped over. 4. a sudden transition. 5. a sudden rise, as in prices. 6. a sudden, nervous start or jerk; twitch. 7. *pl.* [Slang], chorea; also, delirium tremens (usually with *the*). 8. in *athletics*, a contest in jumping: as, the high *jump*. 9. in *checkers*, a move by which an opponent's piece is captured. **—get** (or **have**) **the jump on,** [Slang], to get (or have) an advantage over. **—jump a claim,** to seize land claimed by someone else. **—jump at,** to accept hastily and eagerly. **—jump bail,** to forfeit one's bail by running away. **—jump off,** [Military Slang], to start an attack. **—jump on,** [Slang], to scold; censure. **—jump the gun,** [Slang], to begin something before the proper time. **—jump the track,** to go suddenly off the rails. **—on the jump,** [Colloq.], very busy. **—jump′er,** ***n.***

**jump·er** (jum′pẽr), ***n.*** [< dial. *jump*, short coat; prob. < Fr. *juppe* < Sp. < Ar. *jubbah*, loose outer garment], 1. a loose jacket or blouse, worn to protect clothing. 2. a sleeveless dress for wearing over a blouse or sweater. 3. *pl.* rompers.

JUMPER

**jumping bean,** the seed of a Mexican plant, which is made to jump and roll about by the movements of a moth larva inside it.

**jumping jack,** a child's toy consisting of a jointed figure made to jump about by pulling a string.

**jump·y** (jum′pi), ***adj.*** [-IER, -IEST], 1. moving in jumps, jerks, etc. 2. easily made nervous; apprehensive. **—jump′i·ly,** ***adv.*** **—jump′i·ness,** ***n.***

**Jun.,** 1. June. 2. Junior.

**Junc., junc.,** junction.

**jun·co** (juŋ′kō), ***n.*** [*pl.* -COS], [prob. < Sp. < L. *juncus*, a rush], an American finch found from the Arctic to Central America; snowbird.

**junc·tion** (juŋk′shən), ***n.*** [< L. < *jungere*, to join], 1. a joining or being joined. 2. a place or point of joining or crossing, as of highways or railroads.

**junc·ture** (juŋk′chẽr), *n.* [see JUNCTION], 1. a joining or being joined. 2. a point or line of joining or connection; joint. 3. a point of time. 4. a crisis. 5. a state of affairs.

**June** (jo͞on), *n.* [< Fr. < L. (*mensis*) *Junius*, (the month of) Junius (a Roman family)], the sixth month of the year, having 30 days: abbrev. **Je., Ju., Jun.**

**Ju·neau** (jo͞o′nō), *n.* the capital of Alaska, on the SE coast: pop., 7,000.

**June bug** (or **beetle**), 1. a large, brownish beetle of the cockchafer group, found in the northern U.S.: it appears in early June. 2. the figeater.

**Jung, Carl Gus·tav** (kärl goos′täf yooŋ), 1875–1961; Swiss psychologist.

**Jung·frau** (yooŋ′frou′), *n.* a mountain in the Swiss Alps.

**jun·gle** (juŋ′g'l), *n.* [< Hind. < Sans. *jangala*, wasteland], 1. land covered with dense growth of trees, vines, etc., as in the tropics, usually inhabited by predatory animals. 2. any thick, tangled growth. 3. [Slang], a hoboes' camp. —**jun′gly** [-GLIER, -GLIEST], *adj.*

**jun·ior** (jo͞on′yẽr), *adj.* [L. compar. of *juvenis*, young], 1. the younger: written *Jr.* after the name of a son who bears the same name as his father. 2. of more recent position or lower status: as, a *junior* partner. 3. of later date. 4. made up of younger members. 5. relating to a third-year student or class in a high school or college. *n.* 1. a younger person. 2. a person of lower standing or rank. 3. a member of a third-year class in a high school or college. —**one's junior**, a person younger than oneself.

**junior college,** a school offering only the first one or two years of the standard college course.

**junior high school,** a school intermediate between elementary school and senior high school: it usually has the 7th, 8th, and 9th grades.

**Junior League,** any of the branches of a national society whose members are young women of the upper social class organized to engage in volunteer welfare work. —**Junior Leaguer.**

**ju·ni·per** (jo͞o′nə-pẽr), *n.* [L. *juniperus*], a small evergreen shrub or tree of the pine family, with scalelike foliage and berrylike cones.

**junk** (juŋk), *n.* [? < Port. *junco* (< L. *juncus*), a reed, rush], 1. old rope used for making oakum, mats, etc. 2. old metal, paper, rags, etc. 3. a piece or chunk. 4. [Colloq.], useless stuff; rubbish. *v.t.* [Colloq.], to throw away as worthless; discard.

**junk** (juŋk), *n.* [Sp. & Port. *junco* < Malay *dgong*], a Chinese flat-bottomed ship.

JUNK

**Jun·ker, jun·ker** (yooŋ′-kẽr), *n.* [G.], a German of the privileged land-owning class; Prussian aristocrat. *adj.* of or like the Junkers.

**jun·ket** (juŋ′kit), *n.* [< It. *giuncata*, cream cheese (in baskets) < L. *juncus*, a rush], 1. curds with cream. 2. milk sweetened, flavored, and thickened into curd. 3. a feast or picnic. 4. an excursion for pleasure. 5. an excursion by an official, paid for out of public funds. *v.i.* to go on a junket. *v.t.* to entertain, as on a junket. —**jun′ket·er,** *n.*

**junk·man** (juŋk′man′), *n.* [*pl.* -MEN], a dealer in old metal, glass, paper, rags, etc.

**Ju·no** (jo͞o′nō), *n.* [L.], 1. in *Rom. mythology*, the goddess of marriage, Jupiter's wife and queen of the gods: identified with the Greek Hera. 2. [*pl.* -NOS], a stately, regal woman.

**jun·ta** (jun′tə), *n.* [Sp. < L. pp. of *jungere*, to join], 1. a Spanish or Latin-American legislative or administrative body. 2. a junto.

**jun·to** (jun′tō), *n.* [*pl.* -TOS], [altered form of *junta*], a group of political intriguers; cabal.

**Ju·pi·ter** (jo͞o′pə-tẽr), *n.* [L.], 1. the chief Roman god: identified with the Greek Zeus. 2. the largest planet in the solar system: diameter, 87,000 mi.

**Ju·ra Mountains** (joor′ə), a mountain range between Switzerland and France.

**Ju·ras·sic** (joo-ras′ik), *adj.* designating or of the second period of the Mesozoic Era, immediately following the Triassic: see **geology,** chart. *n.* the Jurassic Period.

**ju·rid·i·cal** (joo-rid′i-k'l), *adj.* [< L. < *jus*, law + *dicere*, to declare], of judicial proceedings, or of law: also **ju·rid′ic.** —**ju·rid′i·cal·ly,** *adv.*

**ju·ris·dic·tion** (joor′is-dik′shən), *n.* [< L. < *jus*, *juris*, law + *dictio* < *dicere*, to declare], 1. the administering of justice; authority to hear and decide cases. 2. authority or power in general. 3. the range of authority. —**ju′ris·dic′tion·al,** *adj.* —**ju′ris·dic′tion·al·ly,** *adv.*

**ju·ris·pru·dence** (joor′is-pro͞o′d'ns), *n.* [< L. < *jus*, law + *prudentia*, a foreseeing], 1. the science or philosophy of law. 2. a system of laws. 3. a branch of law. —**ju′ris·pru·den′tial** (-pro͞o-den′shəl), *adj.*

**ju·rist** (joor′ist), *n.* [< Fr. < ML. < L. *jus*, law], an expert in law; writer on law.

**ju·ris·tic** (joo-ris′tik), *adj.* of jurists or jurisprudence; having to do with law; legal: also **ju·ris′ti·cal.** —**ju·ris′ti·cal·ly,** *adv.*

**ju·ror** (joor′ẽr), *n.* a member of a jury; juryman.

**ju·ry** (joor′i), *n.* [*pl.* -RIES], [< OFr. < ML. < L. *jurare*, to swear < *jus*, law], 1. a group of people sworn to hear evidence in a law case, and to give a decision in accordance with their findings. 2. a committee selected to decide the winners in a contest.

**ju·ry** (joor′i), *adj.* [? < OFr. *ajurie*, relief < L. *adjutare*, to help], for temporary use on a ship: as, a *jury* mast.

**ju·ry·man** (joor′i-mən), *n.* [*pl.* -MEN], a juror.

‡**jus** (zhü), *n.* [Fr.], juice; gravy: as, *au jus*, with gravy.

**just** (just), *adj.* [< OFr. < L. *justus*, lawful < *jus*, law], 1. right or fair: as, a *just* decision. 2. righteous; upright: as, a *just* man. 3. deserved; merited: as, a *just* rebuke. 4. lawful. 5. right; proper. 6. well-founded: as, a *just* suspicion. 7. correct; true. 8. accurate; exact. *adv.* 1. exactly; precisely: as, *just* one o'clock. 2. almost exactly. 3. only: as, *just* a simple soul. 4. barely: as, he *just* missed the train. 5. a very short time ago: as, she has *just* left the room. 6. [Colloq.], quite; really: as, it's *just* beautiful. —**just now,** a moment ago. —**just the same,** [Colloq.], nevertheless. —**just′ness,** *n.*

**just** (just), *n.* & *v.i.* joust.

**jus·tice** (jus′tis), *n.* 1. a being righteous. 2. fairness. 3. a being correct. 4. sound reason; rightfulness. 5. reward or penalty as deserved. 6. the use of authority to uphold what is right, just, or lawful. 7. the administration of law. 8. a judge. 9. a justice of the peace. —**bring to justice,** to cause (a wrongdoer) to be tried in court and duly punished. —**do justice to,** 1. to treat fitly or fairly. 2. to treat with due appreciation. —**do oneself justice,** to do something in a manner worthy of one's abilities. —**jus′tice·ship′,** *n.*

**justice of the peace,** a local magistrate, authorized to decide minor cases, commit persons to trial in a higher court, perform marriages, etc.

**jus·ti·fi·a·ble** (jus′tə-fī′ə-b'l), *adj.* that can be justified or defended as correct. —**jus′ti·fi′a·bil′i·ty, jus′ti·fi′a·ble·ness,** *n.* —**jus′ti·fi′a·bly,** *adv.*

**jus·ti·fi·ca·tion** (jus′tə-fi-kā′shən), *n.* 1. a justifying or being justified. 2. a fact that justifies or vindicates. —**jus′ti·fi·ca′tive,** *adj.*

**justification by faith,** in *Christian theology*, the act by which a sinner is freed through faith from the penalty of his sin.

**jus·ti·fy** (jus′tə-fī′), *v.t.* [-FIED, -FYING], [< OFr. < LL. < L. *justus*, just + *facere*, to make], 1. to show to be just, right, or reasonable. 2. to free from blame or guilt; absolve. 3. to supply good grounds for; warrant. 4. to space (type) so that the lines will be of the correct length. *v.i.* in *law*, to show an adequate reason for something done. —**jus′ti·fi′er,** *n.*

**Jus·tin·i·an I** (jus-tin′i-ən), 483–565 A.D.; Byzantine emperor (527–565 A.D.); had Roman law codified (**Justinian Code**): called *the Great*.

**jus·tle** (jus′'l), *n.*, *v.t.* & *v.i.* [-TLED, -TLING], jostle.

**just·ly** (just′li), *adv.* 1. in a just manner. 2. rightly. 3. deservedly.

**jut** (jut), *v.i.* [JUTTED, JUTTING], [var. of *jet*, *v.*], to stick out; project. *n.* a part that juts.

**Jute** (jo͞ot), *n.* a member of any of several early Germanic tribes in Jutland: Jutes settled in SE England in the 5th century A.D. —**Jut′ish,** *adj.*

**jute** (jo͞ot), *n.* [< E.Ind. *jhuto* < Sans. < *juṭa*, matted hair], 1. a strong fiber used for making burlap, sacks, rope, etc. 2. either of two East Indian plants having this fiber. *adj.* of jute.

**Jut·land** (jut′lənd), *n.* the peninsula of N Europe which forms the mainland of Denmark.

**Ju·ve·nal** (jo͞o′və-n'l), *n.* (*Decimus Junius Juvenalis*), Roman satirical poet; lived 60?–140? A.D.

**ju·ven·ile** (jo͞o′və-n'l, -nīl′), *adj.* [< L. < *juvenis*, young], 1. young; youthful; immature. 2. of,

characteristic of, or suitable for children or young persons. *n.* 1. a young person; child. 2. an actor who takes youthful roles. 3. a book for children. —**ju′ven·ile·ly,** *adv.* —**ju′ven·ile·ness, ju′ve·nil′i·ty** [*pl.* -TIES], *n.*
**juvenile court,** a law court for cases involving children under a fixed age.
**jux·ta·pose** (juks′tə-pōz′), *v.t.* [-POSED, -POSING], [< L. *juxta*, beside; + *pose*, *v.*], to put side by side; place close together.
**jux·ta·po·si·tion** (juks′tə-pə-zish′ən), *n.* a putting or being side by side or close together.
**Jy.,** July.
**Jyl·land** (yül′län), *n.* Jutland: the Danish name.

# K

**K, k** (kā), *n.* [*pl.* K's, k's, Ks, ks], 1. the eleventh letter of the English alphabet. 2. the sound of K or k. *adj.* eleventh in a sequence or group.
**K** (kā), *n.* 1. in *assaying, the symbol for* carat. 2. *kalium*, [Mod. L.], in *chemistry, the symbol for* potassium. *adj.* shaped like K.
**K., k.,** 1. karat (carat). 2. kilogram. 3. king. 4. knight. 5. in *nautical usage*, knot.
**Kaa·ba** (kä′bə, -ə-bə), *n.* the sacred Moslem shrine at Mecca, toward which believers turn when praying: it is a small structure in the great mosque, containing a black stone supposedly given to Abraham by the angel Gabriel: also sp. **Caaba.**
**kab·a·la, kab·ba·la** (kab′ə-lə, kə-bä′-), *n.* cabala.
**Ka·bul** (kä′bool), *n.* the capital of Afghanistan: pop., 300,000.
**ka·di** (kä′di, kā′di), *n.* a cadi.
**Kaf·fir** (kaf′ẽr), *n.* [< Ar. < *kafara*, to be agnostic], 1. a South African Bantu. 2. the language of the Kaffirs. Also **Ka·fir** (käf′ẽr, kaf′-).
**kaf·fir** (kaf′ẽr), *n.* any of a group of grain sorghums grown in dry regions for grain and fodder: also **kaffir corn, ka·fir** (kä′fẽr, kaf′ẽr).
**Kaf·ka, Franz** (fränts käf′kä), 1883–1924; Austrian writer.
**kaf·tan** (kaf′tən, käf′tän′), *n.* a caftan.
**kai·ak** (kī′ak), *n.* a kayak.
**kai·ser** (kī′zẽr), *n.* [< AS. < ON. or G. < L. *Caesar*], emperor: the title [K-] of *a*) the rulers of the Holy Roman Empire, 962–1806. *b*) the rulers of Austria, 1804–1918. *c*) the rulers of Germany, 1871–1918. —**kai′ser·ship′, Kai′ser·ship′,** *n.*
**Kal·a·ma·zoo** (kal′ə-mə-zōō′), *n.* a city in SW Michigan: pop., 82,000.
**Ka·lat** (kə-lät′), *n.* a former state in western India and Pakistan: now a division of West Pakistan.
**kale, kail** (kāl), *n.* [Scot. var. of *cole*], 1. a hardy, nonheading cabbage with loose, spreading, curled leaves. 2. [Slang], money.
**ka·lei·do·scope** (kə-lī′də-skōp′), *n.* [< Gr. *kalos*, beautiful + *eidos*, form; + *-scope*], 1. a small tube containing loose bits of colored glass reflected by mirrors so that various symmetrical patterns appear as the instrument is rotated. 2. anything that constantly changes.
**ka·lei·do·scop·ic** (kə-lī′də-skop′ik), *adj.* 1. of a kaleidoscope. 2. constantly changing, as in pattern. —**ka·lei′do·scop′i·cal·ly,** *adv.*
**kal·ends** (kal′əndz), *n.pl.* calends.
**Ka·le·va·la** (kä′li-vä′lä), *n.* a Finnish epic poem in unrhymed trochaic verse.
**Ka·li·nin, Mi·kha·il I·va·no·vich** (mē′khä-ēl′ i-vän′ô-vich kä-lē′nin), 1875–1946; president of the Soviet Union (1923–1946).
**Ka·lin·in·grad** (kä-lē′nin-grät′), *n.* a city in the western U.S.S.R.: pop., 202,000: former name *Königsberg.*
**ka·liph, ka·lif** (kā′lif, kal′if), *n.* a caliph.
**kal·mi·a** (kal′mi-ə), *n.* [after P. *Kalm* (1715–1779), Swed. botanist], any of a group of North American evergreen shrubs of the heath family, with flower clusters of white, rose, or purple.
**Kal·muck** (kal′muk), *n.* 1. a member of a group of Mongol peoples living chiefly in the NE Caucasus and NW China. 2. their Altaic, western Mongolic language. Also **Kal′myk** (-mik).
**kal·so·mine** (kal′sə-mīn′, -min), *n.* & *v.t.* calcimine.
**Kam·chat·ka** (kam-chat′kə; Russ. käm-chät′kä), *n.* a peninsula in NE Siberia, between the Sea of Okhotsk and the Bering Sea.
**Kan., Kans.,** Kansas.
**Kan·a·ka** (kə-nak′ə, kan′ə-kə), *n.* [Haw., man], 1. a Hawaiian. 2. a native of the South Sea Islands.
**kan·ga·roo** (kaŋ′gə-rōō′), *n.* [*pl.* -ROOS, -ROO; see PLURAL, II, D, 1], [prob. < native name], a leaping, plant-eating mammal native to Australia and neighboring islands, with short forelegs, strong large hind legs, and a long, thick tail: the female has a pouch in front, in which she carries her young.
**kangaroo court,** [Colloq.], a mock court illegally passing and executing judgment, as among frontiersmen, hoboes, or prison inmates.
**kangaroo rat,** a small mouselike rodent living in desert regions of the U.S. and Mexico.
**Kan·sas** (kan′zəs), *n.* 1. a Middle Western State of the U.S.: area, 82,276 sq. mi.; pop., 2,179,000; capital, Topeka: abbrev. **Kan., Kans.** 2. a river flowing from NE Kansas into the Missouri. —**Kan′san,** *adj.* & *n.*
**Kansas City,** 1. a city in W Missouri, on the Missouri River: pop., 476,000. 2. an adjoining city in Kansas, on the Missouri and Kansas rivers: pop., 122,000.
**Kant, Im·ma·nu·el** (i-mä′nōō-el känt; Eng. kant), 1724–1804; German philosopher. —**Kant′i·an,** *adj.* & *n.*
**ka·o·lin, ka·o·line** (kā′ə-lin), *n.* [Fr. < Chin. name of hill where it was found], a fine white clay used in making porcelain, in medicine, etc.
**ka·pok** (kā′pok), *n.* [Malay *kapoq*], the silky fibers around the seeds of the tropical silk-cotton tree (**kapok tree**), used for stuffing pillows, mattresses, etc: also called *Java cotton.*
**kap·pa** (kap′ə), *n.* [Gr.], the tenth letter of the Greek alphabet (K, κ).
**ka·put** (kä-po͝ot′), *adj.* [G.], [Colloq.], lost, ruined, destroyed, defeated, etc.
**Ka·ra·chi** (kə-rä′chi), *n.* a city in West Pakistan, on the Arabian Sea: pop., 2,153,000.
**kar·a·kul** (kar′ə-kəl), *n.* [< *Kara Kul*, lake in Uzbek], 1. a sheep of central Asia. 2. the loosely curled, usually black fur from the fleece of its newborn lambs. Also sp. **caracul, karakule.**
**kar·at** (kar′ət), *n.* a carat.
**ka·ra·te** (kä-rä′tē), *n.* [Japan., lit., open hand], a Japanese system of self-defense in which blows are struck with the side of the open hand.
**Ka·re·li·a** (kə-rē′li-ə, -rēl′yə), *n.* an autonomous republic of the R.S.F.S.R., east of Finland. —**Ka·re′li·an,** *adj.* & *n.*
**Ka·re·lo-Fin·nish Soviet Socialist Republic** (kə-rē′lō-fin′ish), a former republic of the U.S.S.R., east of Finland, composed of Karelia and territory ceded by Finland in 1940: now part of the R.S.F.S.R.
**Kar·nak** (kär′nak), *n.* a village on the Nile, Egypt: site of ancient Thebes.
**kar·y·o-,** [< Gr. *karyon*, a nut, kernel], a combining form meaning: 1. *nut, kernel.* 2. in *biology, the nucleus of a cell.* Also sp. **caryo-.**
**kar·y·o·tin** (kar′i-ō′tin), *n.* [*karyo-* + chroma*tin*], in *biology*, chromatin: also sp. **caryotin.**
**Kas·bah** (käz′bä), *n.* the native quarter of Algiers: also sp. **Casbah.**
**ka·sher** (kä′shẽr), *adj.* & *n.* kosher. *v.t.* to make or declare kosher: also **kosher.**
**Kash·mir** (kash-mêr′), *n.* a state of N India, control of which is disputed by Pakistan: in full, **Jammu and Kashmir.** —**Kash·mir′i·an,** *adj.* & *n.*
**kat·a-,** cata-: also **kat-.**
**kath·ode** (kath′ōd), *n.* a cathode.
**kat·i·on** (kat′ī′ən), *n.* a cation.
**Kat·man·du** (kät′män-dōō′), *n.* the capital of Nepal: pop., 195,000.
**Kat·te·gat** (kat′i-gat′), *n.* an arm of the North Sea, between Sweden and Denmark.
**ka·ty·did** (kā′ti-did′), *n.* a large, green, tree insect resembling the grasshopper: so called from the shrill sound made by the males.
**Kau·nas** (kou′näs), *n.* a city in the Lithuanian S.S.R.: pop., 214,000.
**kau·ri, kau·ry** (kou′ri), *n.* [Maori], 1. a tall pine tree of New Zealand. 2. its wood. 3. a resin (**kauri**

**resin, kauri gum**) from this tree, used in varnish.

**kay·ak** (kī′ak), *n.* [Esk.], an Eskimo canoe made of skins completely covering a wooden frame except for an opening for the paddler: also sp. **kaiak, kyak.**

KAYAK

**kay·o** (kā′ō′), *v.t.* [-OED, -OING], [< *k*nock out], [Slang], in *boxing*, to knock out. *n.* [Slang], in *boxing*, a knockout. Often written **K.O., KO, k.o.**

**Ka·zak Soviet Socialist Republic** (kȧ-zäk′), a republic of the U.S.S.R., in W Asia: area, 1,059,700 sq. mi.; capital, Alma-Ata: also **Ka′zak·stan′** (-stän′).

**Ka·zan** (kä-zän′), *n.* a city in the R.S.F.S.R., on the Volga: pop., 804,000.

**ka·zoo** (kə-zōō′), *n.* [echoic], a toy musical instrument consisting of a small tube containing a piece of paper that vibrates and produces a buzzing sound when one hums into the tube.

**kc.,** kilocycle; kilocycles.

**K.C.,** 1. King's Counsel. 2. Knights of Columbus.

**ke·a** (kā′ä, kē′ə), *n.* [Maori], a large, green, mountain parrot of New Zealand, which kills sheep to eat their fat.

**Keats, John** (kēts), 1795–1821; English poet.

**ke·bab** (kə-bäb′), *n.* [Ar. *kabāb*], [*often pl.*], a dish consisting of small pieces of marinated meat stuck on a skewer, often with vegetables, and broiled or roasted.

**kedge** (kej), *n.* [prob. < *cadge*, var. of *catch*], a light anchor, used especially in warping a ship: also **kedge anchor.** *v.t.* & *v.i.* [KEDGED, KEDGING], to warp or pull (a ship) along by means of a rope fastened to an anchor dropped at some distance.

**keel** (kēl), *n.* [< ON. *kjölr*], 1. the chief timber or steel piece extending along the entire length of the bottom of a boat or ship. 2. [Poetic], a ship. 3. anything like a ship's keel, as the beams, girders, etc. at the bottom of a rigid or semirigid airship. *v.t.* 1. to furnish with a keel. 2. to turn (a ship) over on its side. *v.i.* to turn up the keel. **—keel over,** [Colloq.], 1. to turn over; turn upside down. 2. to fall over suddenly. **—on an even keel,** in an upright, level position.

**keel·haul** (kēl′hôl′), *v.t.* to haul (a person) under the keel of a ship as a punishment.

**keel·son** (kel′s'n, kēl′-), *n.* [prob. < Sw. < *köl*, a keel + *svin*, swine], a beam or set of timbers or metal plates fastened along a ship's keel to add structural strength: also **kelson.**

**keen** (kēn), *adj.* [AS. *cene*, wise], 1. having a sharp edge or point: as, a *keen* knife. 2. sharp; cutting; piercing: as, a *keen* wind. 3. very sensitive or perceptive; acute: as, *keen* eyes. 4. sharp-witted; shrewd. 5. eager; enthusiastic. 6. strong; vivid; pungent. 7. [Slang], good; excellent. **—keen′ly,** *adv.* **—keen′ness,** *n.*

**keen** (kēn), *n.* [< Ir. < *caoinim*, I wail], [Irish], a wailing for the dead; dirge. *v.t.* & *v.i.* [Irish], to lament or wail for (the dead). **—keen′er,** *n.*

**keep** (kēp), *v.t.* [KEPT, KEEPING], [AS. *cepan*, to behold], 1. to observe with due ceremony; celebrate: as, *keep* the Sabbath. 2. to fulfill (a promise, etc.). 3. to protect; guard; defend. 4. to watch over; tend. 5. to raise (livestock). 6. to maintain in good condition; preserve. 7. to provide for; support. 8. to supply with food or lodging for pay: as, she *keeps* boarders. 9. to have in one's service: as, they *keep* servants. 10. to make regular entries in, detailing transactions, happenings, etc.: as, to *keep* books, a diary, etc. 11. to carry on; conduct; manage. 12. to cause to stay in a specified condition, position, etc.: as, *keep* your engine running. 13. to hold for future use or for a long time. 14. to have usually in stock for sale. 15. to have or hold and not let go; specif., *a*) to detain. *b*) to hold back; restrain. *c*) to withhold. *d*) to conceal. *e*) to stay in, on, or at (a path, course, or place). *v.i.* 1. to stay in a specified condition, position, etc. 2. to continue; go on; persevere. 3. to hold oneself back; refrain: as, he can't *keep* from talking. 4. to stay fresh; not spoil; last. 5. [Colloq.], to continue in session: as, will school *keep* all day? *n.* 1. care, charge, or custody. 2. *a*) the donjon of a castle. *b*) a fort; castle. 3. food and shelter; support; livelihood. **—for keeps,** [Colloq.], 1. with the winner keeping what he wins. 2. permanently. **—keep in with,** [Colloq.], to remain on good terms with. **—keep to oneself,** 1. to avoid the company of others. 2. to refrain from telling. **—keep up,** 1. to maintain in good condition. 2. to continue. 3. to maintain the pace. 4. to remain informed about.

**keep·er** (kēp′ẽr), *n.* a person or thing that keeps; specif., *a*) a guard, as of prisoners, animals, etc. *b*) a guardian or protector. *c*) a custodian.

**keep·ing** (kēp′iŋ), *n.* 1. observance (of a rule, holiday, etc.). 2. care; charge. 3. maintenance or means of maintenance; keep. 4. reservation for future use; preservation. 5. agreement; conformity: as, in *keeping* with his character.

**keep·sake** (kēp′sāk′), *n.* something kept, or to be kept, in memory of the giver; memento.

**keg** (keg), *n.* [< ON. (*vin*)*kaggr*, (wine) barrel], 1. a small barrel, usually one of less than ten gallons. 2. a unit of weight for nails, equal to 100 pounds.

**keg·ler** (keg′lẽr), *n.* [G. < *kegel*, (nine)pin], [Colloq.], a person who bowls; bowler.

**Kel·ler, Helen Adams** (kel′ẽr), 1880–1968; U.S. writer and lecturer; blind and deaf from infancy, she learned to speak and read.

**kelp** (kelp), *n.* [ME. *culp*(*e*)], 1. any of various large, coarse, brown seaweeds. 2. ashes of seaweed, from which iodine is obtained.

**kel·pie, kel·py** (kel′pi), *n.* [*pl.* -PIES], [Scot.], in *Gaelic folklore*, a water spirit, supposed to take the form of a horse and drown people or warn them that they will be drowned.

**kel·son** (kel′s'n), *n.* a keelson.

**Kelt** (kelt), *n.* a Celt. **—Kel′tic,** *adj.* & *n.*

**kel·ter** (kel′tẽr), *n.* [Colloq.], kilter.

**Ke·mal A·ta·turk, Mus·ta·fa** (moos-tä-fä′ ke-mäl′ ä-tä-türk′), (*Mustafa Kemal*), 1881–1938; president of Turkey (1923–1938).

**Kempis, Thomas à,** see **Thomas à Kempis.**

**ken** (ken), *v.t.* [KENNED, KENNING], [AS. *cennan*, lit., to cause to know], [Scot.], to know. *v.i.* [Scot.], to know (*of* or *about*). *n.* 1. [Rare], range of vision. 2. range of knowledge.

**Ken·ne·dy, Cape** (ken′ə-di), a cape on the E coast of Florida: U.S. launching site for rockets, spacecraft, etc.: former name, *Cape Canaveral.*

**Kennedy, John Fitzgerald,** 1917–1963; 35th president of the U.S. (1961–1963); assassinated.

**ken·nel** (ken′'l), *n.* [< OFr. < LL. *canile* < L. *canis*, a dog], 1. a doghouse. 2. *often pl.* a place where dogs are bred or kept. 3. a pack of dogs. *v.t.* [-NELED or -NELLED, -NELING or -NELLING], to place or keep in a kennel. *v.i.* to live in a kennel.

**Ken·nel·ly-Heav·i·side layer** (ken′'l-i-hev′i-sīd′), [after A.E. *Kennelly* (1861–1939), Am. electrical engineer & Oliver *Heaviside* (1850–1925), Eng. physicist], a highly ionized layer of the upper atmosphere, believed to reflect radio waves so that they travel parallel to the earth's surface.

**ke·no** (kē′nō), *n.* [prob. < Fr. *quine*, five winners], a gambling game resembling lotto.

**Ke·no·sha** (ki-nō′shə), *n.* a city in SE Wisconsin, on Lake Michigan: pop., 68,000.

**Kent** (kent), *n.* 1. a former Anglo-Saxon kingdom. 2. a county of SE England.

**Kent·ish** (ken′tish), *adj.* of Kent or its people. *n.* the dialect of Kent, especially in its Anglo-Saxon and Middle English stages of development.

**Ken·tuck·y** (kən-tuk′i, ken-), *n.* an East Central State of the U.S.: area, 40,395 sq. mi.; pop., 3,038,000; capital, Frankfort: abbrev. **Ky., Ken.** **—Ken·tuck′i·an,** *adj.* & *n.*

**Ken·ya** (ken′yə, kēn′-), *n.* a country in east central Africa, on the Indian Ocean: a member of the British Commonwealth of Nations: area, 224,960 sq. mi.; pop., 10,506,000; capital, Nairobi.

**kep·i** (kep′i), *n.* [Fr. *képi*; G. dial. *käppi* < *kappe*, a cap], a cap with a flat, round top and stiff visor, worn by French soldiers.

**Kep·ler, Jo·han·nes** (yō-hä′nəs kep′lẽr), 1571–1630; German astronomer and mathematician.

**kept** (kept), pt. and pp. of **keep.**

**ke·ram·ic** (ki-ram′ik), *adj.* ceramic.

**ker·a·tin** (ker′ə-tin), *n.* [< Gr. *keras*, horn], an albuminous substance forming the principal matter of hair, nails, horn, etc.

**kerb** (kũrb), *n.* curb (of a pavement): Brit. sp.

**ker·chief** (kũr′chif), *n.* [OFr. *covrechef* < *covrir*, to cover + *chef*, the head], 1. a piece of cloth worn over the head or around the neck. 2. a handkerchief. **—ker′chiefed, ker′chieft** (-chift), *adj.*

**kerf** (kũrf, kärf), *n.* [AS. *cyrf* < *ceorfan*, to cut, carve], 1. a cut or notch made by an ax, saw, etc. 2. a strip or piece cut off.

**ker·mes** (kũr′mēz), *n.* [< Fr. < Ar. *qirmiz*, insect],

1. the dried bodies of certain Mediterranean insects. 2. a red dye made from these bodies.

**ker·mis, ker·mess** (kũr′mis), *n.* [< D. < *kirk*, a church + *mis*, Mass], 1. an annual outdoor fair or carnival, held in the Netherlands, Belgium, etc. 2. in the U.S., an indoor fair or entertainment, usually for charity. Also sp. **kirmess.**

**kern** (kũrn), *n.* [< Fr. *carne*, a hinge < OFr. < L. *cardo*], that part of the face of a letter of type which projects beyond the body.

**ker·nel** (kũr′n'l), *n.* [AS. *cyrnel*, dim. of *corn*, seed], 1. a grain or seed, as of corn, wheat, etc. 2. the inner, softer part of a nut, fruit stone, etc. 3. the central, most important part of something; gist. *v.t.* [-NELED or -NELLED, -NELING or -NELLING], to enclose as a kernel.

**ker·o·sene** (ker′ə-sēn′, ker′ə-sēn′), *n.* [< Gr. *kēros*, wax], a thin oil distilled from petroleum, coal, etc., used in lamps, stoves, etc.; coal oil: in chemistry and industry now usually spelled **kerosine.**

**ker·sey** (kũr′zi), *n.* [*pl.* -SEYS], [< *Kersey*, village in England], a coarse woolen cloth, usually ribbed and with a cotton warp.

**kes·trel** (kes′trəl), *n.* [OFr. *cresserelle;* origin echoic], a small European falcon that can hover in the air against the wind; windhover.

**ketch** (kech), *n.* [? var. of *cache*, catch], a fore-and-aft rigged sailing vessel with a mainmast toward the bow and a mizzenmast, forward of the rudder post, toward the stern: cf. *yawl.*

**ketch·up** (kech′əp), *n.* [Malay *kēchap*, taste < Chin. *ke-tsiap*], a sauce for meat, fish, etc.; esp., a thick sauce (**tomato ketchup**) of tomatoes flavored with onion, salt, etc.: also **catsup, catchup.**

**ke·tone** (kē′tōn), *n.* [G. *keton*, var. of Fr. *acétone;* see ACETONE], an organic chemical compound containing the divalent radical CO in combination with two hydrocarbon radicals.

**ket·tle** (ket′'l), *n.* [AS. *cetel* < L. dim. of *catinus*, bowl], 1. a metal container for boiling liquids, etc. 2. a teakettle. 3. a kettledrum. —**kettle of fish,** a difficult or embarrassing situation.

**ket·tle·drum** (ket′'l-drum′), *n.* a drum consisting of a hollow hemisphere of copper or brass and a parchment top that can be tightened or loosened to change the pitch; timpano.

KETTLEDRUM

**key** (kē), *n.* [*pl.* KEYS], [AS. *cæge*], 1. an instrument, usually of metal, for moving the bolt of a lock and thus locking or unlocking something. 2. any device resembling or suggesting this in form or use; specif., *a*) a device to turn a bolt, etc.: as, a skate *key.* *b*) a pin, bolt, wedge, cotter, etc. put into a hole or space to hold parts together. *c*) any of the levers, or the disks, etc. connected to them, pressed down in operating a piano, clarinet, typewriter, etc. *d*) a device for opening or closing an electric circuit. 3. a place so located as to give control of a region; strategic gateway. 4. a thing that explains or solves, as a book of answers, a code to secret writing, the legend of a map, etc. 5. a controlling or essential person or thing. 6. tone of voice; pitch. 7. style of thought or expression: as, in a cheerful *key.* 8. in *music*, a system of related notes or tones based on and named after a certain note (*keynote*) and forming a given scale. *adj.* controlling; important: as, a *key* position in the office. *v.t.* [KEYED, KEYING], 1. to fasten or lock with a key. 2. to furnish with a key. 3. to regulate the tone or pitch of. 4. to bring into harmony, as in style of expression. —**key up,** to make nervous or excited.

**key** (kē), *n.* [*pl.* KEYS], [Sp. *cayo*, small island], a reef or low island.

**Key, Francis Scott** (kē), 1780–1843; U.S. lawyer; wrote "The Star-Spangled Banner."

**key·board** (kē′bôrd′, -bōrd′), *n.* the row or rows of keys of a piano, typewriter, linotype, etc.

**keyed** (kēd), *adj.* 1. having keys, as some musical instruments. 2. fastened or reinforced with a key. 3. set or pitched in a specified key.

**key·hole** (kē′hōl′), *n.* an opening (in a lock) into which a key is inserted.

**key·note** (kē′nōt′), *n.* 1. the lowest, basic note or tone of a musical scale, or key; tonic. 2. the basic idea or ruling principle, as of a speech, policy, etc. *v.t.* [-NOTED, -NOTING], to give the keynote of.

**keynote speech,** a speech, as at a political convention, that sets forth the main line of policy.

**key ring,** a metal ring for holding keys.

**key signature,** in *music*, an indication of the key, as by sharps or flats placed after the clef at the beginning of the staff.

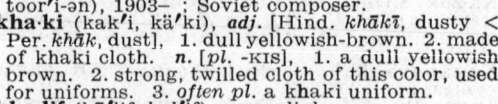

**key·stone** (kē′stōn′), *n.* 1. the central, topmost stone or piece of an arch, which holds the others in place. 2. that one of a number of associated parts or things that supports or holds together the others; main part or principle.

KEYSTONE

**Key West,** the westernmost island in the Florida Keys.

**kg.,** 1. keg; kegs. 2. kilogram; kilograms.

**Kha·cha·tur·i·an, A·ram** (a-räm′ khä′chä-too-ryän′; Eng. kach′ə-toor′i-ən), 1903– ; Soviet composer.

**kha·ki** (kak′i, kä′ki), *adj.* [Hind. *khākī*, dusty < Per. *khāk*, dust], 1. dull yellowish-brown. 2. made of khaki cloth. *n.* [*pl.* -KIS], 1. a dull yellowish brown. 2. strong, twilled cloth of this color, used for uniforms. 3. *often pl.* a khaki uniform.

**kha·lif** (kā′lif, kal′if), *n.* a caliph.

**khan** (kän, kan), *n.* [Turki *khān*, lord < Tatar], 1. a title given to the rulers of Turkish, Tatar, and Mongol tribes who dominated Asia in the Middle Ages. 2. a title of various dignitaries in Pakistan, Iran, Afghanistan, etc. —**khan′ate** (-āt), *n.*

**khan** (kän, kan), *n.* [Ar. *khān*], in Turkey and other Eastern countries, an inn or caravansary.

**Khar·kov** (khär′kôf; Eng. kär′kôf, -kov), *n.* a city in the Ukrainian S.S.R.: pop., 1,048,000.

**Khar·toum, Khar·tum** (kär-tōōm′), *n.* the capital of the Sudan, on the Nile: pop., 135,000.

**khe·dive** (kə-dēv′), *n.* [< Fr. < Turk. *khidīv* < Per. *khidīw*, prince], the title of the Turkish viceroys of Egypt, from 1867 to 1914.

**Khrush·chev, Ni·ki·ta Ser·gey·e·vich** (ni-kē′tä syer-gā′ye-vich khrōōs′chyôf; Eng. krōōs′chev), 1894– ; premier of the U.S.S.R. (1958–1964).

**Khu·fu** (kōō′fōō), *n.* Cheops.

**Khy·ber Pass** (kī′bẽr), a mountain pass between Pakistan and Afghanistan: also sp. **Khaibar.**

**kibe** (kīb), *n.* [prob. < W. *cibi*], a chapped or ulcerated chilblain, especially on the heel.

**kib·itz** (kib′its), *v.i.* [Colloq.], to act as a kibitzer.

**kib·itz·er** (kib′it-sẽr), *n.* [Yid. < colloq. G. *kiebitzen* < *kiebitz*, meddlesome onlooker], [Colloq.], 1. an onlooker at a card game, especially one who volunteers advice. 2. a giver of unwanted advice.

**ki·bosh** (kī′bosh, ki-bosh′), *n.* [prob. < Yid.], [Slang], nonsense: now usually in *put the kibosh on*, to put an end to; squelch; veto.

**kick** (kik), *v.i.* [? < ON. *kika*, to bend at the knee], 1. to strike out with the foot or feet. 2. to spring back suddenly, as a gun when fired; recoil. 3. [Colloq.], to complain; grumble. *v.t.* 1. to strike suddenly as with the foot. 2. to drive (a ball, etc.) by striking with the foot. 3. to force (one's way, etc.) by kicking. 4. to score (a goal or point in football) by kicking. *n.* 1. *a*) a blow with the foot. *b*) the act of kicking. 2. a sudden recoil, as of a gun when fired. 3. [Colloq.], a complaint; protest. 4. [Colloq.], *a*) a stimulating effect, as of alcoholic liquor. *b*) pleasurable excitement; thrill. 5. in *football, a*) a kicking of the ball. *b*) the kicked ball. —**kick around (or about),** [Colloq.], 1. to treat roughly. 2. to move from place to place. 3. to consider or discuss. —**kick back,** 1. [Colloq.], to recoil suddenly and unexpectedly. 2. [Slang], *a*) to give back (stolen goods). *b*) to give back (part of money received as pay, etc.). —**kick in,** [Slang], 1. to pay (one's share); contribute. 2. to die. —**kick off,** 1. to put a football into play with a kickoff. 2. [Slang], to die. —**kick out,** [Colloq.], to get rid of; eject. —**kick up,** [Slang], to make or cause (trouble, etc.). —**kick′er,** *n.*

**kick·back** (kik′bak′), *n.* [Slang], 1. a giving back of stolen goods. 2. *a*) a giving back of part of money received as payment, commission, etc. *b*) the money so returned.

**kick·off** (kik′ôf′), *n.* in *football*, a place kick that puts the ball into play.

**kick·shaw** (kik′shô′), *n.* [< Fr. *quelque chose*, something], 1. a fancy food or dish; delicacy. 2. a trinket; trifle; gewgaw. Also **kick′shaws′.**

**kick·up** (kik′up′), *n.* [Colloq.], a fuss; row.

**kid** (kid), *n.* [prob. < Anglo-N.], 1. a young goat. 2. its flesh, used as food. 3. leather from the skin of young goats, used for gloves, shoes, etc. 4. [Colloq.], a child or young person. *adj.* 1. made of kidskin. 2. [Colloq.], younger: as, my *kid* sister. *v.t. & v.i.* [KIDDED, KIDDING], [Slang], 1. to deceive; hoax. 2. to tease playfully; banter. —**kid′der,** *n.*

**Kidd, Captain** (kid), (*William Kidd*), 1645?–1701; Scottish privateer and pirate; hanged.

**kid·dy, kid·die** (kid′i), *n.* [*pl.* -DIES], [dim. of *kid* (child)], [Colloq.], a child.

**kid gloves,** soft, smooth gloves made of kidskin.

**—handle with kid gloves,** [Colloq.], to treat with care, tact, etc.

**kid·nap** (kid′nap), *v.t.* [-NAPED or -NAPPED, -NAPING or -NAPPING], [*kid*, child + dial. var. of *nab*, to snatch], 1. to steal (a child). 2. to seize and hold (a person) against his will, by force or fraud, as for ransom. **—kid′nap′er, kid′nap′per,** *n.*

**kid·ney** (kid′ni), *n.* [*pl.* -NEYS], [< ME. < *kiden-*, ? genit. pl. of *kid* (young goat) + *ei, ey*, an egg], 1. either of a pair of glandular organs in vertebrates, which separate water and waste products from the blood and excrete them as urine through the bladder. 2. an animal's kidneys, used as food. 3. *a*) disposition; nature. *b*) class; kind.

**kidney bean,** 1. a bean shaped like a kidney. 2. the scarlet runner, a tropical American bean.

**kidney stone,** a hard, mineral deposit formed in the kidney from phosphates, urates, etc.

**kid·skin** (kid′skin′), *n.* leather from the skin of young goats, used for gloves, shoes, etc.

**Kiel** (kēl), *n.* a seaport in N Germany, on the Kiel Canal: pop., 254,000.

**Kiel Canal,** a ship canal in Germany, connecting the North Sea with the Baltic.

**Ki·ev** (kē′yef; Eng. kē′ev), *n.* the capital of the Ukrainian S.S.R., on the Dnepr: pop., 846,000.

**kil.,** kilometer; kilometers.

**Ki·lau·e·a** (kē′lou-ā′ə), *n.* the active crater of Mauna Loa, on the island of Hawaii.

**Kil·i·man·ja·ro, Mount** (kil′i-män-jä′rō), a mountain in N Tanganyika Territory, the highest in Africa: height, 19,321 ft.

**kill** (kil), *v.t.* [ME. *killen*; prob. < AS. *cwellan*], 1. to cause the death of; slay. 2. *a*) to destroy the vital or active qualities of. *b*) to destroy; put an end to. 3. to defeat or veto (legislation). 4. to spend (time) on trivial matters. 5. to stop (an engine, etc.). 6. to prevent publication of: as, the editor *killed* the story. 7. to destroy by contrast: said of colors, etc. 8. [Colloq.], to overcome, as with laughter or embarrassment. *v.i.* 1. to destroy life. 2. to be killed: as, these plants *kill* easily. *n.* 1. the act of killing. 2. an animal or animals killed. **—in at the kill,** present at the end of some action or undertaking.

**kill** (kil), *n.* [< D. < MD. *kille*], a stream; channel; creek: used especially in place names.

**Kil·lar·ney** (ki-lär′ni), *n.* a town in SW Ireland.

**Killarney, Lakes of,** three lakes near Killarney.

**kill·dee** (kil′dē′), *n.* [*pl.* -DEES, -DEE; see PLURAL, II, D, 1], a killdeer.

**kill·deer** (kil′dêr′), *n.* [*pl.* -DEERS, -DEER; see PLURAL, II, D, 1], [echoic of its cry], a small, North American wading bird of the plover family.

**kill·er** (kil′ẽr), *n.* 1. a person, animal, or thing that kills. 2. a killer whale.

**killer whale,** a fierce dolphin that hunts in packs and preys on large fish, seals, and whales.

**kill·ing** (kil′iŋ), *adj.* 1. causing death; deadly. 2. exhausting; fatiguing. 3. [Colloq.], very comical. *n.* 1. slaughter; murder. 2. [Colloq.], a sudden great profit. **—kill′ing·ly,** *adv.*

**kill-joy** (kil′joi′), *n.* a person who destroys or lessens other people's enjoyment.

**kiln** (kil, kiln), *n.* [AS. *cyl(e)ne* < L. *culina*, cookstove], a furnace or oven for drying, burning, or baking something, as bricks, lime, etc. *v.t.* to dry, burn, or bake in a kiln.

**kiln-dry** (kil′drī′, kiln′-), *v.t.* to dry in a kiln.

**ki·lo** (kē′lō, kil′ō), *n.* [*pl.* -LOS], [Fr.], 1. a kilogram. 2. a kilometer.

**kil·o-,** [Fr. < Gr. *chilioi*, thousand], a combining form used in the metric system, meaning *one thousand*, as in *kilogram, kilowatt*.

**kil·o·cal·o·rie** (kil′ə-kal′ẽr-i), *n.* 1,000 calories; a great calorie.

**kil·o·cy·cle** (kil′ə-sī′k′l), *n.* 1. 1,000 cycles. 2. 1,000 cycles per second: used in radio to express the frequency of electromagnetic waves.

**kil·o·gram, kil·o·gramme** (kil′ə-gram′), *n.* a unit of weight and mass, equal to 1,000 grams (2.2046 pounds).

**kil·o·gram-me·ter, kil·o·gram-me·tre** (kil′ə-gram-mē′tẽr), *n.* a unit of energy or work, being the amount needed to raise one kilogram one meter: it is equal to 7.2334 foot-pounds.

**kil·o·li·ter, kil·o·li·tre** (kil′ə-lē′tẽr), *n.* a unit of capacity, equal to 1,000 liters, or one cubic meter (264.18 gallons, or 1.308 cubic yards).

**kil·o·me·ter, kil·o·me·tre** (kil′ə-mē′tẽr, ki-lom′ə-), *n.* a unit of length or distance, equal to 1,000 meters (3,280.8 feet, or about ⅝ mile). **—kil·o·met·ric** (kil′ə-met′rik), *adj.*

**kil·o·watt** (kil′ə-wot′, -wôt′), *n.* a unit of electrical power, equal to 1,000 watts.

**kil·o·watt-hour** (kil′ə-wot′our′, -wôt′-), *n.* a unit of electrical energy or work, equal to that done by one kilowatt acting for one hour.

**kilt** (kilt), *v.t.* [ME. *kilte*; prob. < ON.], 1. [Scot.], to tuck or fasten (*up*). 2. to pleat. *n.* a short, pleated skirt reaching to the knees, worn by men of the Scottish Highlands.

KILT

**kil·ter** (kil′tẽr), *n.* [Colloq.], good condition; proper order: also **kelter**: now always preceded by *in* or *out of*.

**Kim·ber·ley** (kim′bẽr-li), *n.* a city in the central part of the Union of South Africa: pop., 62,000: large diamond mines are located near by.

**ki·mo·no** (kə-mō′nə), *n.* [*pl.* -NOS], [Japan.], 1. a loose outer garment with a sash, worn, especially formerly, by both men and women in Japan. 2. a woman's loose dressing gown like this.

**kin** (kin), *n.* [AS. *cynn*], 1. relatives; family; kindred. 2. family relationship; connection by birth or, sometimes, by marriage. *adj.* related, as by blood; kindred. **—near of kin,** closely related. **—of kin,** related. **—kin′less,** *adj.*

**-kin** (kin), [prob. < MD. *-ken, -kijn*, dim. suffix], a noun suffix meaning *little*, as in *lambkin*.

**kind** (kīnd), *n.* [AS. *(ge)cynd*], 1. [Archaic], manner; way. 2. a natural group or division; race: as, the rodent *kind*. 3. sort; variety; class. *adj.* 1. sympathetic, friendly, gentle, benevolent, generous, etc. 2. cordial: as, *kind* regards. **—in kind,** 1. in goods or produce instead of money. 2. with something like that received. **—kind of,** [Colloq.], somewhat; rather. **—of a kind,** 1. of the same kind; alike. 2. of poor quality; mediocre.

**kin·der·gar·ten** (kin′dẽr-gär′t'n), *n.* [G.; *kinder*, children + *garten*, garden], a school or class for young children, usually four to six years old, that develops basic skills and social behavior by games, toys, simple handicraft, etc.

**kin·der·gart·ner, kin·der·gar·ten·er** (kin′dẽr-gärt′nẽr), *n.* 1. a kindergarten teacher. 2. a child who attends kindergarten.

**kind·heart·ed** (kīnd′här′tid), *adj.* having or resulting from a kind heart; sympathetic; kindly. **—kind′heart′ed·ly,** *adv.* **—kind′heart′ed·ness,** *n.*

**kin·dle** (kin′d'l), *v.t.* [-DLED, -DLING], [freq. of ON. *kynda*], 1. to set on fire; ignite. 2. to excite (interest, feelings, etc.). 3. to make bright. *v.i.* 1. to catch fire; start burning. 2. to become aroused or excited. 3. to become bright: as, her eyes *kindled* with joy. **—kin′dler,** *n.*

**kin·dling** (kin′dliŋ), *n.* bits of wood or other easily lighted material for starting a fire.

**kind·ly** (kīnd′li), *adj.* [-LIER, -LIEST], 1. kind; gracious; benign. 2. agreeable; pleasant: as, a *kindly* climate. *adv.* 1. in a kind, gracious manner. 2. agreeably; favorably. **—take kindly to,** to be naturally attracted to. **—kind′li·ness,** *n.*

**kind·ness** (kīnd′nis), *n.* 1. the state, quality, or habit of being kind. 2. kind act or treatment.

**kin·dred** (kin′drid), *n.* [< AS. *cynn*, kin + *-ræden*, condition], 1. relationship by birth or, sometimes, by marriage; kinship. 2. relatives or family; kin. 3. resemblance in qualities; likeness. *adj.* 1. related by birth or common origin. 2. similar: as, *kindred* spirits.

**kine** (kīn), *n.pl.* [< AS. *cy*, pl. of *cu*, cow + *-(e)n*], [Archaic or Dial.], cows; cattle.

**kin·e·mat·ics** (kin′ə-mat′iks), *n.pl.* [construed as sing.], [< Gr. *kinēma*, motion < *kinein*, to move], the branch of mechanics that deals with motion in the abstract, without reference to the force or mass. **—kin′e·mat′ic, kin′e·mat′i·cal,** *adj.*

**kin·e·mat·o·graph** (kin′ə-mat′ə-graf′, -gräf′), *n., v.t. & v.i.* a cinematograph.

**kin·e·scope** (kin′ə-skōp′), *n.* [< Gr. *kinein*, to move; + *-scope*], a form of cathode-ray receiving tube used in television: it has a luminescent screen at one end, on which the images are reproduced: a trade-mark (**Kinescope**).

**kin·es·the·si·a** (kin′is-thē′zhə, -zhi-ə), *n.* [< Gr. *kinein*, to move + *aisthēsis*, perception], the sensation of position, movement, etc. of parts of the body, perceived through nerve end organs in muscles, tendons, and joints: also sp. **kinaesthesia.** **—kin′es·thet′ic** (-thet′ik), *adj.*

**ki·net·ic** (ki-net′ik, kī-), *adj.* [Gr. *kinētikos* < *kinein*, to move], of or resulting from motion.
**ki·net·ics** (ki-net′iks, kī-), *n.pl.* [construed as sing.], the science dealing with the motion of masses in relation to the forces acting on them.
**kin·folk** (kin′fōk′), *n.pl.* [Dial.], kinsfolk.
**king** (kiŋ), *n.* [AS. *cyning*], 1. a male ruler or sovereign of a state, either limited or absolute. 2. a man who is supreme in some field: as, an oil *king*. 3. something supreme in its class. 4. in *card games*, a playing card with a picture of a king on it. 5. in *checkers*, a piece that has moved across the board to the opponent's base. 6. in *chess*, the chief piece. *adj.* chief (in size, importance, etc.).
**King, William Lyon Mac·ken·zie** (mə-ken′zi kiŋ), 1874–1950; prime minister of Canada (1921–June, 1926; September, 1926–1930; 1935–1948).
**king·bird** (kiŋ′bŭrd′), *n.* any of several American birds called tyrant flycatchers.
**king·bolt** (kiŋ′bōlt′), *n.* a vertical bolt connecting the front axle of a wagon, etc., or the truck of a railroad car, with the body; kingpin.
**king crab,** a horseshoe crab.
**king·dom** (kiŋ′dəm), *n.* [AS. *cynedom*], 1. a government or country headed by a king or queen; monarchy. 2. a realm; domain: as, the *kingdom* of poetry. 3. one of the three great divisions into which all natural objects have been classified (the animal, vegetable, and mineral kingdoms).
**king·fish** (kiŋ′fish′), *n.* 1. [*pl.* see FISH], any of several large food fishes found along the Atlantic or Pacific coast. 2. [Colloq.], the acknowledged head of some group, place, etc.
**king·fish·er** (kiŋ′fish′ẽr), *n.* a bright-colored, short-tailed bird with a large head and strong beak: many kingfishers eat fish.
**King James Version,** the Authorized Version of the Bible, a revised English translation published in 1611 with the authorization of King James I.
**King Lear** (lêr), 1. a famous tragedy by Shakespeare (1606?). 2. the main character of this play, a legendary British king.
**king·let** (kiŋ′lit), *n.* a petty, unimportant king, as of a small country.
**king·ly** (kiŋ′li), *adj.* [-LIER, -LIEST], of, like, or fit for a king; royal; regal; noble. *adv.* [Archaic], in the manner of a king. **—king′li·ness,** *n.*
**king·pin** (kiŋ′pin′), *n.* 1. a kingbolt. 2. the pin at the apex in bowling, tenpins, etc. 3. [Colloq.], the main or essential person or thing.
**king post,** in *carpentry*, a vertical supporting post between the apex of a triangular truss and the base, or tie beam.

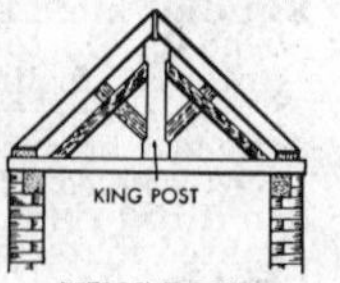

KING POST

**Kings** (kiŋz), *n.pl.* 1. the two books (*I Kings, II Kings*) in the Old Testament which give the history of the reigns of the Jewish kings after David. 2. four books in the Douay Bible which include I & II Samuel and I & II Kings.
**king's** (or **queen's**) **English, the,** standard (especially British) English.
**king's evil,** scrofula: so called from the old notion that a king's touch could cure it.
**king·ship** (kiŋ′ship), *n.* 1. the position, rank, dignity, or dominion of a king. 2. the rule of a king. 3. majesty: a title (with *his*).
**king-size** (kiŋ′sīz′), *adj.* [Colloq.], of greater than normal size: as, *king-size* cigarettes: also **king′-sized′.**
**king snake,** a large, harmless snake found in the southern U.S.: it eats mice, rats, and lizards.
**king's ransom,** a large sum of money.
**Kings·ton** (kiŋz′tən, kiŋ′stən), *n.* seaport and capital of Jamaica: pop., 109,000.
**kink** (kiŋk), *n.* [prob. < D. or Sw.], 1. a short twist, curl, or bend in a thread, rope, hair, etc. 2. a painful cramp in the neck, back, etc.; crick. 3. *a*) a mental twist; queer notion; whim. *b*) a quirk; peculiarity. *v.i. & v.t.* to form or cause to form a kink or kinks.
**kin·ka·jou** (kiŋ′kə-jo͞o′), *n.* [< native Brazilian (Tupi) name], a flesh-eating mammal of Central and South America, somewhat like a raccoon, with yellowish-brown fur and a long prehensile tail.
**kink·y** (kiŋ′ki), *adj.* [-IER, -IEST], full of kinks; tightly curled: as, *kinky* hair. **—kink′i·ly,** *adv.* **—kink′i·ness,** *n.*
**kins·folk** (kinz′fōk′), *n.pl.* relatives; family; kin; kindred.
**kin·ship** (kin′ship), *n.* 1. family relationship. 2. relationship; close connection.
**kins·man** (kinz′mən), *n.* [*pl.* -MEN], a relative; esp., a male relative.
**kins·wom·an** (kinz′woom′ən), *n.* [*pl.* -WOMEN], a female relative.

**ki·osk** (ki-osk′; *also, for 2,* kī′osk), *n.* [< Fr. < Turk. < Per. *kūshk*, palace], 1. in Turkey and Persia, an open summerhouse or pavilion. 2. a somewhat similar small structure open at one or more sides, used as a newsstand, bandstand, etc.
**kip** (kip), *n.* [prob. < D.], the untanned hide of a calf, lamb, or other young or small animal.
**Kip·ling, Rud·yard** (rud′yẽrd kip′liŋ), 1865–1936; British poet, short-story writer, and novelist.
**kip·per** (kip′ẽr), *v.t.* [? < *n.*], to cure (herring, salmon, etc.) by cleaning, salting, and drying or smoking. *n.* [AS. *cypera*], 1. a male salmon or sea trout during or shortly after the spawning season. 2. a kippered herring, salmon, etc.
**Kir·ghiz** (kir-gēz′), *n.* 1. [*pl.* -GHIZ, -GHIZES], a member of a Mongolian people living in west central Asia. 2. their Turko-Tatar language.
**Kirghiz Soviet Socialist Republic,** a republic of the U.S.S.R., in south central Asia: area, 75,950 sq. mi.; pop., 1,533,000; capital, Frunze.
**kirk** (kŭrk; Scot. kirk), *n.* [Scot. & North Eng.], a church. **—the Kirk,** the (Presbyterian) Church of Scotland.
**kir·mess** (kŭr′mis), *n.* a kermis.
**kir·tle** (kŭr′t'l), *n.* [AS. *cyrtel;* prob. < L. *curtus*, short], [Archaic], 1. a man's tunic or coat. 2. a woman's dress or skirt. **—kir′tled,** *adj.*
**Kis·lev, Kis·lew** (kis′lef), *n.* [Heb.], the third month of the Jewish year: see **Jewish calendar.**
**kis·met** (kiz′met, kis′-), *n.* [< Turk. < Ar. < *qasama*, to divide], fate; destiny: also **kis′mat** (-mət).
**kiss** (kis), *v.t. & v.i.* [AS. *cyssan*], 1. to touch or caress with the lips as an act of affection, desire, greeting, etc. 2. to touch lightly or gently. *n.* 1. an act of kissing. 2. a light, gentle touch, as of billiard balls in motion. 3. *a*) any of various candies. *b*) a baked confection of egg white and powdered sugar. **—kiss′a·ble,** *adj.*
**kiss·er** (kis′ẽr), *n.* 1. a person who kisses. 2. [Slang], *a*) the mouth or lips. *b*) the face.
**kit** (kit), *n.* [prob. < MD. *kitte*], 1. a small wooden tub or bucket, as for holding fish. 2. *a*) a soldier's equipment, exclusive of arms; pack. *b*) personal equipment, especially as packed for travel. *c*) a set of tools. *d*) equipment for some particular activity, sport, etc. 3. a box, bag, etc. for carrying such tools or equipment. 4. [Colloq.], a set; lot; collection. **—the whole kit and caboodle,** [Colloq.], the whole lot.
**kitch·en** (kich′ən), *n.* [AS. *cycene;* ult. < L. *coquina* < *coquere*, to cook], 1. a room or place for the preparation and cooking of food. 2. the cooking department; cuisine.
**kitch·en·ette, kitch·en·et** (kich′ən-et′), *n.* a small, compact kitchen.
**kitchen police,** 1. soldiers detailed to assist the cooks in an army kitchen. 2. this duty.
**kitch·en·ware** (kich′ən-wâr′), *n.* kitchen utensils.
**kite** (kīt), *n.* [AS. *cyta*], 1. a bird of the hawk family, with long, pointed wings. 2. a light wooden frame covered with paper or cloth, to be flown in the wind at the end of a string. 3. *pl.* the highest sails of a ship. 4. in *business*, a worthless commercial paper, as a bad check, used to raise money or maintain credit temporarily. *v.i.* [KITED, KITING], 1. [Colloq.], to fly like a kite; soar or glide. 2. in *business*, to get money or credit by using bad checks, etc. *v.t.* in *business*, to issue (a bad check, etc.) as a kite.
**kith** (kith), *n.* [< AS. *cyth;* prob. < base of *cuth*, known], [Archaic], friends, acquaintances, etc.: now only in *kith and kin*. **—kith and kin,** friends, acquaintances, and relatives.
**kit·ten** (kit′'n), *n.* [< OFr. var. of *chaton*, dim. of *chat*, cat], a young cat.
**kit·ten·ish** (kit′'n-ish), *adj.* like a kitten; playful; frisky; often, playfully coy. **—kit′ten·ish·ly,** *adv.* **—kit′ten·ish·ness,** *n.*
**kit·ti·wake** (kit′i-wāk′), *n.* [*pl.* -WAKES, -WAKE; see PLURAL, II, D, 1], [echoic of its cry], any of several sea gulls of the Arctic and North Atlantic.
**kit·ty** (kit′i), *n.* [*pl.* -TIES], 1. a kitten. 2. a pet name for a cat of any age.
**kit·ty** (kit′i), *n.* [*pl.* -TIES], [as if < *kit* (tub) + *-y*], 1. the stakes in a poker game. 2. money pooled by card players, etc. for some particular purpose, as to pay for the cards.
**kit·ty-cor·nered** (kit′i-kôr′nẽrd), *adj. & adv.* cater-cornered: also **kitty-corner.**
**Kitty Hawk,** a place in NE North Carolina where the first successful airplane flight in the U.S. was made by Orville and Wilbur Wright in 1903.
**Kiu·shu** (kū′sho͞o′), *n.* Kyushu.
**Ki·wa·nis** (kə-wä′nis, kə-wô′-), *n.* [< Am. Ind. *keewanis*, to make (oneself) known], an international group of clubs of business and professional men,

organized for civic service, etc. —**Ki·wa′ni·an,** *adj. & n.*
**ki·wi** (kē′wi), *n.* [*pl.* -WIS], [Maori: echoic of its cry], the apteryx.
**K.K.K., KKK,** Ku Klux Klan.
**kl.,** kiloliter; kiloliters.
**Klan** (klan), *n.* the Ku Klux Klan. —**Klans′man** [*pl.* -MEN], *n.*
**klep·to·ma·ni·a** (klep′tə-mā′ni-ə), *n.* [< Gr. *kleptēs,* thief; + *mania*], an abnormal, persistent impulse to steal. —**klep′to·ma′ni·ac′** (-ak′), *n.*
**klieg light** (klēg), [after the *Kliegl* brothers, its inventors], a very bright, hot arc light used to light motion-picture sets: also sp. **kleig.**
**Klon·dike** (klon′dīk), *n.* a region in E Alaska and W Yukon Territory, Canada, celebrated for its gold fields.
**km.,** 1. kilometer; kilometers. 2. kingdom.
**kn.,** 1. krona; kronor. 2. krone; kronen; kroner.
**knack** (nak), *n.* [ME. *knak,* sharp blow; prob. echoic], 1. *a*) a trick; device. *b*) a clever way of doing something. 2. ability to do something easily; dexterity. 3. [Rare], a knickknack.
**knap·sack** (nap′sak′), *n.* [< D. *knapzak* < *knappen,* to eat + *zak,* a sack], a leather or canvas bag for carrying equipment or supplies on the back: used by soldiers, hikers, etc.
**knave** (nāv), *n.* [AS. *cnafa,* boy], 1. [Archaic], *a*) a male servant. *b*) a man of humble birth or status. 2. a dishonest, deceitful person; rogue. 3. a playing card bearing a page's picture; jack.
**knav·er·y** (nāv′ẽr-i), *n.* [*pl.* -IES], 1. behavior or act characteristic of a knave; rascality; dishonesty. 2. [Obs.], mischievous quality.
**knav·ish** (nāv′ish), *adj.* like or characteristic of a knave; esp., dishonest; tricky. —**knav′ish·ly,** *adv.* —**knav′ish·ness,** *n.*
**knead** (nēd), *v.t.* [AS. *cnedan*], 1. to work into a plastic mass by pressing and squeezing, usually with the hands: said of dough, clay, etc. 2. to massage with kneading motions. 3. to make by kneading. —**knead′er,** *n.*
**knee** (nē), *n.* [AS. *cneow*], 1. the joint between the thigh and the lower part of the human leg. 2. a joint corresponding to this, as in the forelimb of an animal. 3. anything like a knee, especially a bent knee. 4. the part of a stocking, trouser leg, etc. covering the knee. *v.t.* [KNEED, KNEEING], to hit or touch with the knee. —**bring to one's knees,** to force to submit.
**knee·cap** (nē′kap′), *n.* the patella, a movable bone at the front of the human knee; kneepan.
**knee-deep** (nē′dēp′), *adj.* 1. so deep as to reach to the knees, as water. 2. sunk to the knees.
**knee·hole** (nē′hōl′), *n.* a space for the knees in a desk, etc. *adj.* having such a space.
**kneel** (nēl), *v.i.* [KNELT or KNEELED, KNEELING], [AS. *cneowlian* < *cneow,* knee], to bend or rest on one's knee or knees. —**kneel′er,** *n.*
**knee·pad** (nē′pad′), *n.* a protective pad worn around the knee, as by basketball players.
**knee·pan** (nē′pan′), *n.* the kneecap; patella.
**knell** (nel), *v.i.* [AS. *cnyllan*], 1. to ring in a slow, solemn way; toll. 2. to sound ominously or mournfully. *v.t.* to call or announce by or as by a knell. *n.* 1. the sound of a bell rung slowly, as at a funeral. 2. an omen of death, extinction, failure, etc. 3. a mournful sound.
**knelt** (nelt), alt. pt. and pp. of **kneel.**
**knew** (nōō, nū), pt. of **know.**
**Knick·er·bock·er** (nik′ẽr-bok′ẽr), *n.* [< Diedrich *Knickerbocker,* fictitious D. author of Washington Irving's *History of New York*], 1. a descendant of the early Dutch settlers of New York. 2. any New Yorker. 3. [k-], *pl.* short, loose trousers gathered at or just below the knees; knickers.
**knick·ers** (nik′ẽrz), *n.pl.* 1. knickerbockers. 2. a woman's bloomerlike undergarment.
**knick·knack** (nik′nak′), *n.* [redupl. of *knack*], a small ornamental article; gimcrack; trinket: also sp. **nicknack.**
**knife** (nīf), *n.* [*pl.* KNIVES (nīvz)], [AS. *cnif*], 1. a cutting instrument with one or more sharp-edged blades set in a handle. 2. a cutting blade, as in a machine. *v.t.* [KNIFED, KNIFING], 1. to cut or stab with a knife. 2. [Colloq.], to injure or defeat by treachery. —**under the knife,** [Colloq.], undergoing surgery. —**knife′like′,** *adj.*
**knight** (nīt), *n.* [AS. *cniht,* boy], 1. in the Middle Ages, *a*) a military attendant of the king or other feudal superior, typically holding land in fief. *b*) later, a man of high birth who after serving as page and squire was formally raised to honorable military rank and pledged to chivalrous conduct. 2. in Great Britain, a man who for some achievement is given honorary nonhereditary rank next below a baronet, entitling him to use *Sir* before his given name. 3. a member of any society that officially calls its members *knights.* 4. [Poetic], a lady's devoted champion or attendant. 5. in *chess,* a piece shaped like a horse's head. *v.t.* to make (a man) a knight. —**knight′like′,** *adj.*
**knight-er·rant** (nīt′er′ənt), *n.* [*pl.* KNIGHTS-ERRANT], 1. a medieval knight wandering in search of adventure. 2. a chivalrous or quixotic person.
**knight-er·rant·ry** (nīt′er′ən-tri), *n.* [*pl.* KNIGHT-ERRANTRIES], the behavior, character, or action of a knight-errant.
**knight·hood** (nīt′hood), *n.* 1. the rank or status of a knight. 2. the vocation of a knight. 3. knightliness. 4. knights collectively.
**knight·ly** (nīt′li), *adj.* 1. of, characteristic of, or like a knight; chivalrous, brave, etc. 2. consisting of knights. *adv.* [Archaic], in a knightly manner. —**knight′li·ness,** *n.*
**Knights of Columbus,** an international fraternal society of Roman Catholic men.
**Knight Templar,** [*pl.* KNIGHTS TEMPLARS for 1, KNIGHTS TEMPLAR for 2], 1. a member of a military and religious order established among the Crusaders in 1118 to protect pilgrims. 2. a member of a certain order of Masons.
**knit** (nit), *v.t.* [KNITTED or KNIT, KNITTING], [AS. *cnyttan* < base of *cnotta,* a knot], 1. to make (cloth or a garment) by looping together yarn or thread by means of special needles. 2. to form into cloth in this way instead of by weaving. 3. to fasten together closely and firmly; unite. 4. to draw (the brows) together. *v.i.* 1. to make cloth or a garment by looping together yarn or thread. 2. to grow together, as a broken bone. 3. to become drawn together in wrinkles: as, his brows *knit* in thought. —**knit′ter,** *n.*
**knit·ting** (nit′iŋ), *n.* 1. the action of a person or thing that knits. 2. knitted work.
**knitting needle,** an eyeless, long needle used in pairs, etc. in knitting by hand.
**knives** (nīvz), *n.* pl. of **knife.**
**knob** (nob), *n.* [prob. < MLG. *knobbe,* a knot, bud, etc.], 1. a rounded lump or protuberance. 2. a handle, usually round, of a door, drawer, etc. 3. a rounded hill or mountain. —**knobbed,** *adj.*
**knob·by** (nob′i), *adj.* [-BIER, -BIEST], 1. covered with knobs. 2. like a knob. —**knob′bi·ness,** *n.*
**knock** (nok), *v.i.* [< AS. *cnocian*], 1. to strike a blow, as with the fist; esp., to rap on a door. 2. to bump; collide. 3. to make a thumping or rattling noise: said of an engine, etc. 4. [Colloq.], to find fault; criticize adversely. *v.t.* 1. to hit; strike. 2. to hit so as to cause to fall (with *down* or *off*). 3. to make by hitting or striking: as, he *knocked* a hole in the screen. 4. [Colloq.], to find fault with; criticize. *n.* 1. a knocking. 2. a hit; rap, as on a door. 3. a thumping or rattling noise in an engine, etc. 4. [Colloq.], an adverse criticism. —**knock about** (or **around**), [Colloq.], to wander about; roam. —**knock down,** 1. to take apart. 2. to indicate the sale of (an article) at an auction. —**knock off,** 1. [Colloq.], to stop working. 2. [Colloq.], to deduct. 3. [Colloq.], to do. 4. [Slang], to kill, overcome, etc. —**knock out,** 1. in *boxing,* to score a knockout over. 2. to make unconscious or exhausted. —**knock together,** to make or compose hastily or crudely.
**knock·a·bout** (nok′ə-bout′), *n.* a small, one-masted yacht with a mainsail, a jib, and a centerboard, but no bowsprit. *adj.* 1. rough; noisy; boisterous. 2. made or suitable for rough use.
**knock·down** (nok′doun′), *adj.* 1. that knocks down; overwhelming. 2. made so as to be easily taken apart: as, a *knockdown* table. *n.* 1. a knocking down; felling. 2. a blow that fells one.
**knock·er** (nok′ẽr), *n.* one that knocks; esp., a small ring, knob, etc. on a door, for use in knocking.
**knock-knee** (nok′nē′), *n.* a condition in which the legs bend inward so that the knees touch each other in walking. —**knock′-kneed′,** *adj.*
**knock·out** (nok′out′), *adj.* that knocks out: said of a blow, etc. *n.* 1. a knocking out or being knocked out. 2. a blow that causes a boxer to fall and fail to resume the fight before a count of ten. 3. [Slang], a person or thing that is very attractive or striking.

**knockout drops,** [Slang], a drug put into a drink to cause the drinker to become unconscious.

**knoll** (nōl), *n.* [AS. *cnoll*], a little rounded hill or hilltop; hillock; mound.

**Knos·sos** (nos′əs), *n.* the chief city of ancient Crete: also **Cnossus.**

**knot** (not), *n.* [AS. *cnotta*], 1. a lump or knob in a thread, cord, etc., as formed by a tangle drawn tight. 2. a fastening made by intertwining or tying together pieces of string, rope, etc. 3. an ornamental bow of ribbon or twist of braid. 4. a small group or cluster. 5. something that ties closely or intricately; esp., the bond of marriage. 6. a problem; difficulty. 7. a knotlike part, as in a tense muscle; specif., *a*) a hard lump on a tree where a branch grows out. *b*) a cross section of such a lump, appearing cross-grained in a board. *c*) a joint on a plant stem where leaves grow out. 8. in *nautical usage*, a unit of speed of one nautical mile (6,076.10 feet) an hour: as, a speed of 10 *knots*. *v.t.* [KNOTTED, KNOTTING], 1. to tie or intertwine in or with a knot. 2. to tie closely or intricately; entangle. *v.i.* 1. to form a knot or knots; become entangled. 2. to make fringe by tying knots. **—knot′ted,** *adj.* **—knot′ter,** *n.*

**knot·grass** (not′gras′, -gräs′), *n.* a common weed with jointed or knotty stems: also **knot′weed′** (-wēd′).

**knot·hole** (not′hōl′), *n.* a hole in a board, etc. where a knot has fallen out.

**knot·ty** (not′i), *adj.* [-TIER, -TIEST], 1. full of knots: as, a *knotty* board. 2. hard to solve; puzzling: as, a *knotty* problem. **—knot′ti·ness,** *n.*

**knout** (nout), *n.* [Russ. *knut*], a leather whip formerly used in Russia to flog criminals. *v.t.* to flog with a knout.

**know** (nō), *v.t.* [KNEW, KNOWN, KNOWING], AS. (*ge*)*cnawan*], 1. to be well informed about: as, we *know* the facts. 2. to be aware of; have perceived or learned: as he *knew* that we were home. 3. to have securely in the memory: as, the actor *knows* his lines. 4. to be acquainted or familiar with. 5. to have understanding of or skill in as a result of study or experience: as, she *knows* music. 6. to recognize as distinct; distinguish: as, to *know* right from wrong. 7. in *Biblical & legal usage*, to have sexual intercourse with. *v.i.* 1. to have knowledge. 2. to be sure, informed, or aware. **—in the know,** [Colloq.], having confidential information. **—know′a·ble,** *adj.* **—know′a·ble·ness,** *n.* **—know′er,** *n.*

**know-how** (nō′hou′), *n.* [Colloq.], knowledge of how to do something; technical skill.

**know·ing** (nō′iŋ), *adj.* 1. having knowledge or information. 2. shrewd; worldly-wise. 3. implying shrewd understanding or secret knowledge: as, a *knowing* look. 4. deliberate. **—know′ing·ly,** *adv.* **—know′ing·ness,** *n.*

**knowl·edge** (nol′ij), *n.* 1. the act, fact, or state of knowing. 2. acquaintance with facts; range of information, awareness, or understanding. 3. what is known; learning; enlightenment. 4. the body of facts accumulated by mankind. **—to (the best of) one's knowledge,** as far as one knows; within the range of one's information.

**knowl·edge·a·ble** (nol′ij-ə-b'l), *adj.* [Colloq.], having or showing knowledge or intelligence.

**known** (nōn), pp. of **know.**

**know-noth·ing** (nō′nuth′iŋ), *n.* 1. an ignoramus. 2. [K- N-], a member of a U.S. secret political party (1853–1856) that sought to exclude from governmental office all but native-born Americans: so called because members professed ignorance of the party's activities.

**Knox, John** (noks), 1505–1572; Scottish Protestant preacher and religious reformer.

**Knox·ville** (noks′vil), *n.* a city in E Tennessee, on the Tennessee River: pop., 112,000.

**knuck·le** (nuk′'l), *n.* [ME. *knokyl;* prob. < LG.], 1. a joint of the finger; esp., any of the joints connecting the fingers to the rest of the hand. 2. the knee or hock joint of a pig or other animal, used as food. 3. *pl.* brass knuckles. *v.i.* [-LED, -LING], to rest the knuckles on the ground in shooting a marble. *v.t.* to strike or press with the knuckles. **—knuckle down,** 1. to work hard or earnestly. 2. to yield; give in: also **knuckle under.**

**knurl** (nūrl), *n.* [as if dim. of earlier *knur*, a knot], 1. a knot, knob, nodule, etc. 2. a ridge or any of a series of small ridges on a metal surface, as on the edge of a coin or nut. *v.t.* to make knurls on the edge of. **—knurled,** *adj.*

**knurl·y** (nūr′li), *adj.* [-IER, -IEST], full of knurls, as wood; gnarled.

**KO** (kā′ō′), *v.t.* [KO'D, KO'ING], [Slang], in *boxing*, to knock out. *n.* [*pl.* KO'S], [Slang], in *boxing*, a knockout. Also **kayo, K.O., k.o.**

**ko·a·la** (kō-ä′lə), *n.* [< the native name], an Australian tree-dwelling animal with thick, gray fur, which carries its young in a pouch.

KOALA
(24 in. long)

**Ko·be** (kô′be′; Eng. kō′bi), *n.* a city on the S coast of Honshu, Japan: pop., 1,217,000.

**Kö·ben·havn** (kö′p'n-houn′), *n.* Copenhagen: the Danish name.

**Ko·dak** (kō′dak), *n.* [arbitrary formation], a small, portable camera for taking photographs on a roll of film: a trade-mark.

**ko·di·ak bear** (kō′di-ak′), a large, brown bear found on Kodiak Island.

**Ko·di·ak Island** (kō′di-ak′), an island off the SW coast of Alaska.

**Koh-i-noor, Koh-i-nur, Koh·i·noor** (kō′i-noor′), *n.* [< Per.], a famous large Indian diamond, now one of the British crown jewels.

**kohl·ra·bi** (kōl′rä′bi, kōl′rä′-), *n.* [*pl.* -BIES], [G. < It. pl. of *cavolo rapa*, cole rape; cf. COLE (kale) & RAPE (herb)], a kind of cabbage with an edible stem that looks like a turnip.

KOHLRABI

**ko·la** (kō′lə), *n.* [< W. Afr. name], 1. the kola nut. 2. the tree that it grows on. 3. an extract or stimulant made from kola nuts. Also sp. **cola.**

**kola nut,** the brown, bitter nut of either of two tropical trees: it contains some caffeine.

**ko·lin·sky** (kə-lin′ski, kō-), *n.* [< Russ. < *Kola*, Russian district], 1. any of several minks of Asia. 2. the golden-brown fur of such a mink.

**Köln** (köln), *n.* Cologne (the city): German name.

**Kö·nigs·berg** (kö′niHs-berkh′; Eng. kā′nigz-būrg′), *n.* Kaliningrad: the former name.

**koo·doo** (kōō′dōō), *n.* a kudu.

**kook** (kōōk), *n.* [? < *cuckoo*], [Slang], a person regarded as silly, eccentric, crazy, etc. **—kook′ie, kook′y** [-IER, -IEST], *adj.*

**‡kop** (kop), *n.* [S. Afr. D. < D. *kop*, a head], in South Africa, a hill or mountain.

**ko·peck, ko·pek** (kō′pek), *n.* [Russ. *kopeika*], a small Russian coin of bronze or copper, equal to 1/100 ruble: also sp. **copeck.**

**Ko·ran** (kô-rän′, kō′ran), *n.* [Ar. *qur'ān*, lit., book, reading < *qara'a*, to read], the sacred book of the Moslems: its contents are reported revelations made to Mohammed by Allah.

**Ko·re·a** (kô-rē′ə, kō-), *n.* a country in eastern Asia, west of Japan: area, 85,228 sq. mi.; pop., 41,578,000: since 1948 divided into two republics: capitals, Seoul (South), Pyongyang (North).

**Ko·re·an** (kô-rē′ən, kō-), *adj.* of Korea, its people, etc. *n.* 1. a native of Korea. 2. the language of the Koreans.

**ko·ru·na** (kô-rōō′nä), *n.* [*pl.* -RUNY (-rōō′ni), -RUN (-rōōn′)], [Czech < L. *corona*, crown], the monetary unit and a coin of Czechoslovakia.

**Kos·ci·us·ko, Thaddeus** (kos′i-us′kō; Pol. kôsh-chōōsh′kô), 1746–1817; Polish hero and general; served in the American Revolutionary army.

**ko·sher** (kō′shēr), *adj.* [Heb. *kāshēr*, fit, proper], 1. in *Judaism*, *a*) clean or fit to eat according to the dietary laws: Lev. 11. *b*) dealing in such food. 2. [Slang], fit; proper. *n.* kosher food. *v.t.* (kosh′ēr), to make kosher. Also **kasher.**

**Kos·suth, Louis** (kos′ōōth; Hung. kô′shoot), 1802–1894; Hungarian patriot and statesman.

**kow·tow** (kou′tou′, kō′-), *n.* [Chin. *k'o-t'ou*, lit., knock head], the act of kneeling and touching the ground with the forehead to show great deference, submissive respect, homage, etc. *v.i.* to show great deference, etc. (*to* a person). Also **ko′tow′** (kō′-).

**KP, K.P.,** kitchen police.

**Kr,** in *chemistry*, krypton.

**kr.,** 1. krona; kronor. 2. krone; kronen; kroner.

**kraal** (kräl), *n.* [S. Afr. D.; prob. < Port. *curral*, pen for cattle], 1. a village of South African natives, enclosed by a stockade. 2. a fenced enclosure for cattle or sheep in South Africa.

**krait** (krīt), *n.* [Hind. *karait*], a very poisonous snake of India.

**Kra·ków** (krä′kō, krak′ou; Pol. krä′koof), *n.* Cracow, a city in Poland: the Polish name.

**Kras·no·dar** (kräs′nô-där′), *n.* a city in SW Soviet Russia: pop., 395,000.

**K ration,** a compactly boxed U.S. Army field ration.

**Kreis·ler, Fritz** (frits krīs′lēr), 1875–1962; Austrian violinist and composer in America.

**krem·lin** (krem′lin), *n.* [Fr. < Russ. *kreml′*], in Russia, the citadel of a city. —**the Kremlin,** 1. the citadel of Moscow, formerly housing many of the government offices of the Soviet Union. 2. the government of the Soviet Union.

**kreut·zer, kreu·zer** (kroit′sẽr), *n.* [G. *kreuzer*], a former copper coin of Germany and Austria.

**krim·mer** (krim′ẽr), *n.* [G. < *Krim*, Crimea], a grayish, tightly curled fur made from the pelts of Crimean lambs: also sp. **crimmer.**

**kris** (krēs), *n.* a creese, a Malay dagger.

**Krish·na** (krish′nə), *n.* an important Hindu god, an incarnation of Vishnu.

**Kriss Krin·gle** (kris kriŋ′g'l), [< G. < *Christ*, Christ + dim. of *kind*, child], Santa Claus.

**kro·na** (krō′nə; Sw. kroo′nə), *n.* [*pl.* -NOR (-nôr)], [Sw. < L. *corona*, crown], the monetary unit and a silver coin of Sweden.

**kro·ne** (krō′nə), *n.* [*pl.* -NEN (-nən)], [G. < L. *corona*, crown], 1. a former German gold coin, worth ten marks. 2. the former monetary unit or a silver coin of Austria.

**kro·ne** (krō′ne), *n.* [*pl.* -NER (-nẽr)], [Dan. < L. *corona*, crown], the monetary unit and a silver coin of Denmark or Norway.

**Kron·stadt** (krôn-shtät′), *n.* a Soviet fortified port on an island near Leningrad.

**Kru·ger, Paul** (kroo′gẽr), (*Stephanus Johannes Paulus Kruger*), 1825–1904; Dutch South African statesman: called *Oom Paul.*

**krul·ler** (krul′ẽr), *n.* a cruller.

**kryp·ton** (krip′ton), *n.* [< Gr. neut. of *kryptos*, hidden < *kryptein*, to hide], a rare chemical element, an inert gas present in very small quantities in air: symbol, Kr; at. wt., 83.7; at. no., 36.

**Kt,** in *chess*, knight.

**kt.,** carat.

**Kua·la Lum·pur** (kwä′lə loom-poor′), the capital of the Federation of Malaya: pop., 316,000.

**Ku·blai Khan** (koo′bli kän′), 1216?–1294; Mongol emperor (1259–1294); founder of the Mongol dynasty in China.

**ku·chen** (koo′khən), *n.* [G., cake], a kind of German coffeecake, made of yeast dough and often frosted or filled with raisins, nuts, etc.

**ku·dos** (kū′dos), *n.* [Gr. *kydos*, glory], [Colloq.], credit for an achievement; glory; fame.

**ku·du** (koo′doo), *n.* [*pl.* -DUS, -DU; see PLURAL, II, D, 1], [*Hottentot*], a large, grayish-brown African antelope: also sp **koodoo.**

**Ku-Klux, Ku·klux** (kū′kluks′, koo′-), *n.* [< Gr. *kyklos*, a circle], 1. the Ku Klux Klan. 2. a member of the Ku Klux Klan.

**Ku Klux Klan** (kū′kluks′klan′, koo′) [for *Ku-Klux Clan*], 1. a secret society of white men founded in the South after the Civil War to re-establish and maintain white supremacy. 2. a U.S. secret society organized in 1915: it is anti-Negro, anti-Semitic, anti-Catholic, etc., and uses terrorist methods. —**Ku Klux Klan′ner.**

**ku·lak** (koo-läk′), *n.* [Russ., lit., fist < Estonian], a well-to-do farmer in Russia who profited from the labor of poorer peasants: the kulaks as a class opposed Soviet policies, especially the collectivization of the land.

**ku·miss** (koo′mis), *n.* [G. < Russ. < Tatar *kumiz*], mare's or camel's milk fermented (or distilled) and used as a drink by Tatar nomads of Asia. Also sp. **koumis, koumiss, koumyss.**

**küm·mel** (kim′'l; G. küm′əl), *n.* [G. < OHG. *kumil* < L. *cuminum;* see CUMIN], a liqueur flavored with caraway seeds, anise, cumin, etc.

**kum·quat** (kum′kwot), *n.* [< Chin. *chin-chü*, golden orange], 1. a small, orange-colored, oval fruit, with a sour pulp and a sweet rind, used in preserves. 2. the tree that it grows on. Also sp. **cumquat.**

**Kuo·min·tang** (kwō′min-taŋ′; Chin. gwō′min′-däŋ′), *n.* [Chin.], nationalist political party of China, organized chiefly by Sun Yat-sen in 1911 and afterward led by Chiang Kai-shek.

**Kurd** (kūrd, koord), *n.* [Turk. & Ar.], any of a nomadic Moslem people living chiefly in Kurdistan. —**Kurd′ish,** *adj. & n.*

**Kur·di·stan** (kūr′di-stan′, koor′di-stän′), *n.* a region in SE Turkey, N Iraq, and NW Iran inhabited chiefly by Kurds.

**Ku·re** (koo′re), *n.* a city on the SW coast of Honshu, Japan: pop., 210,000.

**Ku·rile Islands** (koo′ril, koo-rēl′), one of the chains of islands between Japan and Kamchatka: ceded to the U.S.S.R. in 1945.

**Kush·it·ic** (kush-it′ik), *adj. & n.* Cushitic.

**Ku·wait** (koo-wit′), *n.* an independent Arab sheikdom in E Arabia, on the Persian Gulf.

**kw.,** kilowatt.

**kwh., K.W.H., kw-h, kw-hr,** kilowatt-hour.

**Ky.,** Kentucky.

**ky·ak** (kī′ak), *n.* a kayak.

**Kym·ric** (kim′rik), *adj. & n.* Cymric; Welsh.

**Kym·ry, Kym·ri** (kim′ri), *n.* [*pl.* -RY or -RI, -RIES], Cymry; the Welsh.

**Kyo·to, Kio·to** (kyô′tô′), *n.* a city in S Honshu, Japan: pop., 1,285,000.

**Kyu·shu** (kū′shoo′), *n.* one of the islands forming Japan: chief city, Nagasaki: also sp. **Kiushu.**

# L

**L, l** (el), *n.* [*pl.* L's, l's, Ls, ls], 1. the twelfth letter of the English alphabet. 2. the sound of L or l. *adj.* twelfth in a sequence or group.

**L** (el), *n.* 1. an object shaped like L. 2. an extension at right angles to, and forming an L with, the main structure. 3. a Roman numeral for 50. *adj.* shaped like L.

**L., l.,** 1. lake. 2. latitude. 3. law. 4. leaf. 5. league. 6. left. 7. length. 8. liberal. 9. [L.], *libra(e)*, pound(s). 10. [*pl.* LL.], line. 11. link. 12. lira; lire. 13. liter(s). 14. low.

**L.,** Latin.

**la** (lä, lô), *interj.* [Dial. or Archaic], oh! look!: an exclamation of surprise.

**la** (lä), *n.* [see GAMUT], in *music*, a syllable representing the sixth tone of the diatonic scale.

**La,** in *chemistry*, lanthanum.

**La.,** Louisiana.

**L.A.,** [Colloq.], Los Angeles.

**lab** (lab), *n.* [Colloq.], a laboratory.

**Lab.,** 1. Laborite. 2. Labrador.

**la·bel** (lā′b'l), *n.* [OFr. < OHG. *lappa*, a rag], 1. a card, strip of paper, etc. marked and attached to an object to indicate its nature, contents, ownership, destination, etc. 2. a descriptive word or phrase applied to a person, group, etc. as a convenient generalized classification. *v.t.* [-BELED or -BELLED, -BELING or -BELLING], 1. to attach a label to. 2. to classify as; call; name; describe. —**la′bel·er, la′bel·ler,** *n.*

**la·bi·a** (lā′bi-ə), *n.* pl. of **labium.**

**la·bi·al** (lā′bi-əl), *adj.* [< ML. < L. *labium*, a lip], 1. of the labia, or lips. 2. in *phonetics*, formed mainly with the lips, as *b, m,* and *p.* *n.* a labial sound. —**la′bi·al·ly,** *adv.*

**la·bi·ate** (lā′bi-āt′, -it), *adj.* [< L. *labium*, a lip], 1. formed or functioning like a lip. 2. having a lip or lips. 3. in *botany*, having the calyx or corolla so divided that one part overlaps the other like a lip.

**la·bile** (lā′b'l, -bil), *adj.* [< L. < *labi*, to slip], unstable, as certain chemical compounds.

**la·bi·o·den·tal** (lā′bi-ō-den′t'l), *adj.* [< L. *labium*, a lip; + *dental*], in *phonetics*, formed with the lower lip against the upper teeth: said of *f* and *v.* *n.* a labiodental sound.

**la·bi·um** (lā′bi-əm), *n.* [*pl.* -BIA (-bi-ə)], [L., a lip], in *anatomy, botany*, etc., a lip or liplike organ; specif., *pl.* the outer folds of skin (**labia majora**) or the inner folds of mucous membrane (**labia minora**) of the vulva.

**la·bor** (lā′bẽr), *n.* [< OFr. < L. *labor*], 1. physica. or mental exertion; work; toil. 2. a specific taskl

3. *a*) all wage-earning workers: distinguished from *capital* or *management*. *b*) all manual workers whose work is characterized largely by physical exertion: distinguished from *white-collar* or *professional workers*. 4. the work accomplished by workers collectively. 5. in *medicine*, the process of childbirth. ***v.i.*** 1. to work; toil. 2. to work hard. 3. *a*) to move slowly and with difficulty: as, the car *labored* up the hill. *b*) to pitch and roll heavily: as, the ship *labored* in the rough sea. 4. to be in childbirth. ***v.t.*** to develop in too great detail: as, do not *labor* the point. **—labor under,** to be subjected to or suffer from: as, to *labor under* a delusion. **—la'bor·ing·ly, *adv.***

**lab·o·ra·to·ry** (lab'rə-tôr'i, -ēr-ə-tō'ri), ***n.*** [*pl.* -RIES], [< ML. < L.; see LABOR], 1. a room or building for scientific experimentation or research. 2. a place for preparing chemicals, drugs, etc. ***adj.*** of or performed in, or as in, a laboratory. **—lab'o·ra·to'ri·al, *adj.***

**Labor Day,** the first Monday in September, set aside in the U.S. as a legal holiday in honor of labor.

**la·bored** (lā'bērd), ***adj.*** made or done with great effort; strained; not natural: Brit. sp., **laboured.**

**la·bor·er** (lā'bēr-ēr), ***n.*** one who labors; esp., a wage-earning worker whose work is characterized largely by physical exertion: Brit. sp., **labourer.**

**la·bo·ri·ous** (lə-bôr'i-əs, -bō'ri-), ***adj.*** 1. involving or calling for much hard work; difficult. 2. industrious; hard-working. **—la·bo'ri·ous·ly, *adv.* —la·bo'ri·ous·ness, *n.***

**la·bor·ite** (lā'bēr-īt'), ***n.*** 1. a member or supporter of a labor party. 2. [L-], a member or supporter of the British Labor Party: Brit. sp., **Labourite.**

**labor party,** 1. a political party organized to protect and further the rights of workers. 2. [L- P-], such a party in Great Britain: Brit. sp., **Labour Party.**

**la·bor-sav·ing** (lā'bēr-sāv'iŋ), ***adj.*** lessening the work required: as, *labor-saving* devices.

**labor union,** an association of workers to promote and protect the welfare, interests, and rights of its members.

**la·bour** (lā'bēr), ***n., v.t. & v.i.*** labor: Brit. sp.

**Lab·ra·dor** (lab'rə-dôr'), ***n.*** 1. a peninsula in NE North America, between the Atlantic and Hudson Bay. 2. the eastern part of this peninsula, a part of Newfoundland.

**la·bur·num** (lə-būr'nəm), ***n.*** [L.] a small tree or shrub of the pea family, with drooping clusters of yellow flowers.

**lab·y·rinth** (lab'ə-rinth'), ***n.*** [< L. < Gr. *labyrinthos*], 1. an intricate structure containing winding passages hard to follow without losing one's way; maze. 2. [L-], in *Gr. legend*, such a structure built for King Minos, to house the Minotaur. 3. a complicated, perplexing arrangement, condition, etc. 4. in *anatomy*, the inner ear.

LABYRINTH

**lab·y·rin·thine** (lab'ə-rin'thin), ***adj.*** of, constituting, or like a labyrinth; intricate: also **lab'y·rin'thi·an** (-thi-ən), **lab'y·rin'thic** (-thik).

**lac** (lak), ***n.*** [< Hind. < Sans. *lākshā*], a resinous substance formed on certain trees in S Asia by a variety of scale insect: when melted, strained, and rehardened, it forms shellac.

**lac** (lak), ***n.*** [< Hind. < Sans. *lākshā*, a mark], in India, 1. the sum of 100,000 (rupees, etc.). 2. any indefinitely large number. Also sp. **lakh.**

**lace** (lās), ***n.*** [OFr. *laz* < L. *laqueus*, a noose], 1. a string, ribbon, etc. used to draw together and fasten the parts of a shoe, corset, etc. 2. braid of gold or silver, as for trimming uniforms. 3. a fine netting or openwork fabric of linen, silk, etc., woven in ornamental designs. ***v.t.*** [LACED, LACING], 1. to draw the ends of (a garment, shoe, etc.) together and fasten by means of a lace. 2. to compress the waist of by lacing a corset, etc. 3. to weave together; intertwine. 4. to decorate with lace. 5. to streak, as with color. 6. to thrash; whip. 7. to add a dash of alcoholic liquor to (a beverage). ***v.i.*** to be fastened with a lace: as, these shoes *lace*. **—lace into,** [Colloq.], 1. to assail. 2. to berate.

**lac·er·ate** (las'ə-rāt'), ***v.t.*** [-ATED, -ATING], [< L. pp. of *lacerare* < *lacer*, mangled], 1. to tear jaggedly; mangle. 2. to hurt (one's feelings, etc.). ***adj.*** (-ēr-it), 1. torn; mangled. 2. in *botany*, having jagged edges, as a leaf.

**lac·er·a·tion** (las'ə-rā'shən), ***n.*** 1. a lacerating. 2. the result of lacerating; jagged tear or wound.

**lace·wing** (lās'wiŋ'), ***n.*** any of a large group of insects with four delicate, gauzy wings.

**lace·work** (lās'wūrk'), ***n.*** 1. lace. 2. any openwork decoration like lace.

**lach·es** (lach'iz), ***n.*** [OFr. *laschesse* < LL. < L. < *laxus*, lax], in *law*, failure to do the required thing at the proper time.

**Lach·e·sis** (lak'ə-sis), ***n.*** [L. < Gr. < *lanchanein*, to happen], in *Gr. & Rom. mythology*, that one of the three Fates who determines the span of life.

**lach·ry·mal** (lak'rə-m'l), ***adj.*** [< ML. < L. *lacrima*, a tear], of, for, or producing tears. ***n. pl.*** the lachrymal glands, which produce tears. Also sp. **lacrimal.**

**lach·ry·ma·to·ry** (lak'rə-mə-tôr'i, -tō'ri), ***n.*** [*pl.* -RIES], a small vase found in ancient Roman tombs, popularly supposed to have been used to catch the tears of mourners. ***adj.*** of or producing tears.

**lach·ry·mose** (lak'rə-mōs'), ***adj.*** [< L. < *lacrima*, a tear], 1. mournful; shedding tears. 2. causing to shed tears; sad. **—lach'ry·mose·ly, *adv.***

**lac·ing** (lās'iŋ), ***n.*** 1. the act of a person who laces. 2. a thrashing; whipping. 3. a cord or lace, as a shoelace. 4. gold or silver braid used to trim a uniform, etc.

**lack** (lak), ***n.*** [prob. < MLG., MD. *lak*], 1. the fact or condition of not having enough; shortage; deficiency. 2. the fact or condition of not having any; complete absence. 3. the thing that is lacking or needed. ***v.i.*** 1. to be wanting or missing. 2. *a*) to be short (with *of* or *in*). *b*) to be in need. ***v.t.*** 1. to be deficient in or entirely without. 2. to want; need. **—supply the lack,** to provide with whatever is needed.

**lack·a·dai·si·cal** (lak'ə-dā'zi-k'l), ***adj.*** [< *alackaday*], showing lack of interest or spirit; listless; languid. **—lack'a·dai'si·cal·ly, *adv.* —lack'a·dai'si·cal·ness, *n.***

**lack·ey** (lak'i), ***n.*** [*pl.* -EYS], [< Fr. < Sp. *lacayo*], 1. a male servant of low rank; footman. 2. a servile follower; toady. ***v.t. & v.i.*** [-EYED, -EYING], to serve as a lackey.

**lack·lus·ter, lack·lus·tre** (lak'lus'tēr), ***adj.*** lacking brightness; dull: as, *lackluster* eyes. ***n.*** [Rare], absence of brightness; dullness.

**La·co·ni·a** (lə-kō'ni-ə), ***n.*** an ancient country in the SE Peloponnesus: capital, Sparta. **—La·co'ni·an, *adj. & n.***

**la·con·ic** (lə-kon'ik), ***adj.*** [< L. < Gr. < *Lakōn*, a Laconian, Spartan], expressing much in few words; concise: also **la·con'i·cal. —la·con'i·cal·ly, *adv.***

**lac·quer** (lak'ēr), ***n.*** [Fr. & Port. *lacre* < *laca*, gum lac], 1. a clear varnish consisting of shellac or gum resins dissolved in alcohol: *lacquer enamels* are formed by adding pigment. 2. a resinous varnish obtained from certain trees in China and Japan, used to give a hard, highly polished finish to wood. 3. a wooden article coated with this lacquer. ***v.t.*** to coat with lacquer.

**lac·quey** (lak'i), ***n.*** [*pl.* -QUEYS], ***v.t. & v.i.*** [-QUEYED, -QUEYING], [Obs.], lackey.

**lac·ri·mal** (lak'rə-m'l), ***adj. & n.*** lachrymal.

**lac·ri·ma·to·ry** (lak'rə-mə-tôr'i, -tō'ri), ***adj. & n.*** [*pl.* -RIES], lachrymatory.

**lac·ri·mose** (lak'rə-mōs'), ***adj.*** lachrymose.

**la·crosse** (lə-krôs', -kros'), ***n.*** [Fr. < *la*, the + *crosse*, a crutch], a ball game in which two teams of ten men each, using long-handled, webbed rackets, try to advance the ball across the field into the opponents' goal.

LACROSSE

**lac·tate** (lak'tāt), ***v.i.*** [-TATED, -TATING], [< L. pp. of *lactare* < *lac*, milk], to secrete milk. ***n.*** any salt or ester of lactic acid.

**lac·ta·tion** (lak-tā'shən), ***n.*** 1. the secretion of milk by a mammary gland. 2. the period during which milk is secreted. 3. the suckling of young.

**lac·te·al** (lak'ti-əl), ***adj.*** [< L. *lacteus* < *lac*, milk], 1. of or like milk; milky. 2. containing or carrying chyle, the milky fluid that is a product of digestion. ***n.*** any of the lymphatic vessels that carry chyle from the small intestine to the blood.

**lac·tic** (lak'tik), ***adj.*** [*lact(o)-* + *-ic*], 1. of or obtained from milk. 2. designating or of a clear, sirupy acid, $C_3H_6O_3$, formed by the fermentation of lactose when milk sours.

**lac·to-,** [< L. *lac*, milk], a combining form meaning: 1. *milk*. 2. *lactic* or *lactate*. Also **lact-.**

**lac·to·fla·vin** (lak'tō-flā'vin), ***n.*** [*lacto-* + *flavin*], riboflavin; vitamin $B_2$.

**lac·tom·e·ter** (lak-tom'ə-tēr), ***n.*** [*lacto-* + *-meter*], an instrument for testing the richness of milk.

**lac·tose** (lak′tōs), *n.* [*lact*(*o*)- + -*ose*], a white, crystalline sugar, $C_{12}H_{22}O_{11}$, found in milk and used in infant foods, etc.: also called *milk sugar, sugar of milk.*
**la·cu·na** (lə-kū′nə), *n.* [*pl.* -NAS, -NAE (-nē)], [L., a ditch < *lacus*, pond], 1. a space where something has been omitted or has come out; gap; hiatus. 2. in *anatomy*, any of the very small cavities in bone that are filled with bone cells. —**la·cu′nar** (-nēr), **la·cu′nal** (-n'l), *adj.*
**lac·y** (lās′i), *adj.* [-IER, -IEST], 1. of lace. 2. like lace; having a delicate open pattern. —**lac′i·ly,** *adv.* —**lac′i·ness,** *n.*
**lad** (lad), *n.* [ME. *ladde*], 1. a boy; young man. 2. a man of any age: familiar term.
**lad·der** (lad′ēr), *n.* [AS. *hlæd*(*d*)*er*], 1. a framework of two parallel sidepieces connected by narrow crosspieces, on which a person steps in climbing up or down. 2. anything by means of which a person climbs: as, the *ladder* of success.
**lad·die** (lad′i), *n.* [Chiefly Scot.], a lad.
**lade** (lād), *v.t.* & *v.i.* [LADED, LADEN or LADED, LADING], [AS. *hladan*], 1. to load. 2. to dip (water, etc.) with a ladle; bail; ladle.
**lad·en** (lād′'n), alt. pp. of **lade.** *adj.* 1. loaded. 2. burdened; afflicted.
**lad·ing** (lād′iŋ), *n.* 1. a loading. 2. a load; cargo; freight.
**la·dle** (lā′d'l), *n.* [AS. *hlædel* < *hladan*, to draw water], a long-handled, cuplike spoon for dipping out liquids. *v.t.* [-DLED, -DLING], 1. to dip out, as with a ladle. 2. to carry in a ladle. —**la′dle·ful′,** *n.* —**la′dler,** *n.*
**La·do·ga, Lake** (lä′dô-gȧ), a lake in NW U.S.S.R., near Leningrad: area, 7,000 sq. mi.
**La·drone Islands** (lə-drōn′), the Marianas Islands, in the Pacific: the former name.
**la·dy** (lā′di), *n.* [*pl.* -DIES], [AS. *hlæfdige* < *hlaf*, loaf + base of *dæge*, kneader], 1. a woman with the rights, rule, or authority of a lord. 2. a woman of good breeding or some social position: corresponding to *gentleman.* 3. any woman. 4. a woman loved by a man; sweetheart. 5. a wife. 6. [L-], the Virgin Mary (usually with *Our*). 7. [L-], in the British Empire, the title given to women of certain ranks. *adj.* 1. female: as, a *lady* barber. 2. of or suitable for a lady or ladies.
**la·dy·bug** (lā′di-bug′), *n.* a small, roundish beetle with a spotted back, that feeds on insect pests and their eggs: also **ladybird, lady beetle.**
**Lady Day,** the church festival on March 25 commemorating the Annunciation; Annunciation Day.
**la·dy·fin·ger** (lā′di-fiŋ′gēr), *n.* a cooky made of spongecake dough and shaped somewhat like a finger: also **lady's-finger.**
**lady in waiting,** a woman attending, or waiting upon, a queen or princess.
**la·dy-kill·er** (lā′di-kil′ēr), *n.* [Slang], a man to whom women are supposed to be irresistibly attracted.
**la·dy·like** (lā′di-lik′), *adj.* like or suitable for a lady; refined; well-bred. —**la′dy·like′ness,** *n.*
**la·dy·love** (lā′di-luv′), *n.* a sweetheart.
**la·dy·ship** (lā′di-ship′), *n.* 1. the rank or position of a lady. 2. [often L-], the form used in speaking to or of a woman having the title of *Lady*: always preceded by *your* or *her.*
**la·dy's-slip·per** (lā′diz-slip′ēr), *n.* a wild orchid whose flowers somewhat resemble a slipper: also **lady-slipper.**
**La·fa·yette,** Marquis **de** (də lä′fi-yet′, laf′i-), 1757–1834; French statesman and general; served in the American Revolutionary army.
**La Fol·lette, Robert Marion** (lə fol′it), 1855–1925; U.S. statesman and political leader.
**La Fon·taine, Jean de** (zhän də lȧ′fōn′ten′; Eng. lə fon-tān′), 1621–1695; French poet and writer of fables.
**lag** (lag), *v.i.* [LAGGED, LAGGING], [prob. < *lack, v.t.*], 1. to fall behind; move slowly; loiter. 2. in *marbles*, to toss one's marble toward a line on the ground (**lag line**) in order to decide the order of play. *n.* 1. a falling behind or being retarded in motion, development, etc. 2. the amount of such falling behind. —**lag′ger,** *n.*
**lag bolt,** a bolt with a square head.
**Lag b'O·mer** (läg′ bō′mēr), see **Jewish holidays.**
**la·ger beer** (lä′gēr, lô′-), [G. *lager bier*, lit., storehouse beer], a beer, originally made in Germany, which is aged for several months after it has been brewed: also **lager.**
**lag·gard** (lag′ērd), *n.* [< *lag* (to loiter) + -*ard*], a slow person, especially one who is always falling behind. *adj.* backward; slow; hanging back.
**la·gniappe, la·gnappe** (lan-yap′, lan′yap), *n.* [Creole < Fr. *la*, the + Sp. *ñapa*, lagniappe < Peruv. *yapa*], [Dial.], a small present given to a customer with a purchase.
**la·goon** (lə-gōōn′), *n.* [< Fr. *lagune* & It. *laguna;* both < L. *lacuna*, a pond], 1. a shallow lake or pond, especially one connected with a larger body of water. 2. the water enclosed by a circular coral reef. 3. shallow salt water separated from the sea by sand dunes. Also sp. **lagune.**
**La·gos** (lä′gōs, lā′gos), *n.* the capital of Nigeria: pop., 350,000.
**La·hore** (lə-hôr′, lä-hōr′), *n.* the capital of West Pakistan: pop., 849,000.
**la·ic** (lā′ik), *adj.* [< LL. *laicus* < Gr. < *laos*, the people], of the laity; secular; lay: also **la′i·cal.** *n.* a layman. —**la′i·cal·ly,** *adv.*
**laid** (lād), pt. and pp. of **lay.** —**laid up,** 1. *a*) stored away. *b*) dismantled and out of use, as a ship. 2. so ill or injured as to be confined or disabled.
**laid paper,** paper having evenly spaced parallel lines watermarked in it.
**lain** (lān), pp. of **lie** (to recline).
**lair** (lâr), *n.* [AS. *leger*], a bed or resting place, especially of a wild animal; den.
**laird** (lârd), *n.* [Scot. form of *lord*], in Scotland, a landowner, especially a wealthy one.
**lais·sez faire, lais·ser faire** (les′ā fâr′), [Fr., let (people) do (as they please)], noninterference; esp., the policy of letting the owners of industry and business operate without governmental regulation or control. —**lais′sez-faire′, lais′ser-faire′,** *adj.*
**la·i·ty** (lā′ə-ti), *n.* [*pl.* -TIES], [< *lay, adj.*], 1. all the people not included among the clergy; laymen collectively. 2. all the people not belonging to any given profession.
**lake** (lāk), *n.* [merging of AS. *lacu*, a stream, with OFr. *lac* < L. *lacus*, pond], 1. a large inland body of water, usually fresh water. 2. a pool of oil or other liquid. 3. a place where a river widens out.
**lake** (lāk), *n.* [see LAC (resin)], 1. a dark-red pigment prepared from cochineal. 2. its color. 3. an insoluble coloring compound precipitated from a solution of a dye by adding a metallic salt.
**Lake Charles,** a city in SW Louisiana: pop., 63,000.
**Lake District** (or **Country**), a section of mountain and lake country in NW England: home of Wordsworth, Coleridge, and Southey (the **Lake poets**).
**lake dwelling,** a dwelling built on wooden piles rising above the surface of a lake, especially in prehistoric times. —**lake dweller.**
**lake trout,** any of several varieties of trout and salmon found in lakes, especially of the northern U.S. and Canada.
**Lake·wood** (lāk′wood′), *n.* 1. a city in NE Ohio, on Lake Erie: suburb of Cleveland: pop., 66,000. 2. a city in SW California, near Los Angeles: pop., 67,000.
**lakh** (lak), *n.* a lac (one hundred thousand).
**lam** (lam), *v.t.* [LAMMED, LAMMING], [? < ON. *lemja*], [Slang], to beat; thrash; flog.
**lam** (lam), *n.* [? < prec. *lam*], [Slang], headlong flight, usually to escape arrest or punishment. *v.i.* [LAMMED, LAMMING], [Slang], to flee; escape. —**on the lam,** [Slang], in headlong flight. —**take it on the lam,** [Slang], to escape.
**Lam.,** Lamentations.
**la·ma** (lä′mə), *n.* [Tibetan *blama*], a Buddhist priest or monk in Tibet and Mongolia.
**La·ma·ism** (lä′mə-iz'm), *n.* the religious system of the lamas, a form of Buddhism characterized by elaborate ritual and a strong hierarchy. —**La′ma·ist,** *adj.* & *n.* —**La′ma·is′tic,** *adj.*
**La·marck,** Chevalier **de** (də lȧ′mȧrk′; Eng. lə-märk′), (*Jean Baptiste Pierre Antoine de Monet*), 1744–1829; French naturalist who advanced the evolutionary theory that acquired characteristics can be inherited. —**La·marck′i·an,** *adj.* & *n.* —**La·marck′ism,** *n.*
**la·ma·ser·y** (lä′mə-ser′i), *n.* [*pl.* -IES], [< Fr.], a monastery of lamas.
**lamb** (lam), *n.* [AS.] 1. a young sheep. 2. its flesh used as food. 3. lambskin. 4. a gentle or innocent person, particularly a child. 5. a person easily tricked or outwitted. *v.i.* to give birth: said of a ewe. —**like a lamb,** 1. gently; mildly; timidly. 2. innocent and easily tricked. —**the Lamb,** Jesus. —**lamb′like′,** *adj.*
**Lamb, Charles** (lam), 1775–1834; English essayist, poet, and critic; pen name, *Elia.*
**lam·bast** (lam-bast′), *v.t.* [Dial.], to lambaste.

**lam·baste** (lam-bāst′), *v.t.* [-BASTED, -BASTING], [*lam* (to beat) + *baste*], [Slang], 1. to beat soundly; thrash. 2. to scold severely.

**lamb·da** (lam′də), *n.* the eleventh letter of the Greek alphabet (Λ, λ).

**lam·bent** (lam′bənt), *adj.* [< L. ppr. of *lambere*, to lick], 1. playing lightly over a surface; flickering: said of a flame, etc. 2. giving off a soft radiance. 3. light and graceful: said of wit, humor, etc. —**lam′ben·cy,** *n.* —**lam′bent·ly,** *adv.*

**lamb·kin** (lam′kin), *n.* 1. a little lamb. 2. a child or young person: a term of affection.

**Lamb of God,** Jesus: John 1:29, 36.

**lam·bre·quin** (lam′bēr-kin, -brə-), *n.* [Fr. < D. < *lamper*, a veil + *-kin*, -kin], a drapery hanging from a shelf or covering the upper part of a window or doorway.

**lamb·skin** (lam′skin′), *n.* 1. the skin of a lamb, especially with the fleece left on it. 2. leather or parchment made from the skin of a lamb.

**lame** (lām), *adj.* [AS. *lama*], 1. crippled; esp., unable to walk well because of an injured or disabled leg or foot. 2. stiff and painful: as, a *lame* back. 3. poor; halting; ineffectual: as, a *lame* excuse. *v.t.* & *v.i.* [LAMED, LAMING], to make or become lame. —**lame′ly,** *adv.* —**lame′ness,** *n.*

**la·mé** (la-mā′), *n.* [Fr., laminated < *lame*, metal plate], a cloth made of or with metal threads, especially of gold or silver.

**lame duck,** 1. a disabled, inefficient, or helpless person or thing. 2. an elected official whose term extends beyond the time of the election at which he was not re-elected.

**la·mel·la** (lə-mel′ə), *n.* [*pl.* -LAE (-ē), -LAS], [L., dim. of *lamina*, thin plate], 1. a thin plate, scale, or layer, as of bone or animal tissue. 2. a platelike part or organ. —**la·mel·lar** (-ēr, lam′ə-lēr), **lam·el·late** (lam′ə-lāt′, lə-mel′āt), *adj.*

**la·mel·li·branch** (lə-mel′i-braŋk′), *n.* [see LAMELLA & BRANCHIA], any of a group of mollusks, including the clams, oysters, etc., in bivalve shells.

**la·ment** (lə-ment′), *v.i.* [< Fr. < L. < *lamentum*, a wailing], to feel or express deep sorrow; mourn; grieve. *v.t.* 1. to mourn or grieve for. 2. to regret deeply. *n.* 1. a lamentation; wail. 2. a literary or musical composition, as an elegy or dirge, mourning some loss or calamity. —**la·ment′er,** *n.* —**la·ment′ing,** *adj.* —**la·ment′ing·ly,** *adv.*

**lam·en·ta·ble** (lam′ən-tə-b'l), *adj.* to be lamented; deplorable. —**lam′en·ta·bly,** *adv.*

**lam·en·ta·tion** (lam′ən-tā′shən), *n.* a lamenting.

**Lamentations,** a book of the Old Testament attributed to Jeremiah.

**lam·i·na** (lam′ə-nə), *n.* [*pl.* -NAE (-nē′), -NAS], [L.], 1. a thin flake, scale, or layer, as of metal, etc. 2. the flat, expanded part of a leaf. —**lam′i·nal, lam′i·nar,** *adj.*

**lam·i·nate** (lam′ə-nāt′; *for adj., usually* -nit), *v.t.* [-NATED, -NATING], 1. to form or press into a thin sheet or layer. 2. to separate into thin sheets or layers. 3. to cover with thin layers. 4. to make by building up in layers, as plywood. *v.i.* to split into thin layers. *adj.* laminated. —**lam′i·na′tion,** *n.*

**lam·i·nat·ed** (lam′ə-nāt′id), *adj.* composed of thin layers, as of wood or plastic, that have been bonded or pressed together.

**lamp** (lamp), *n.* [< OFr. < L. < Gr. < *lampein*, to shine], 1. a container with a wick for burning oil, alcohol, etc. to produce light or heat. 2. any device for producing light or therapeutic rays, as a gas jet, electric light, etc. 3. a holder, base, etc. for such a device.

**lamp·black** (lamp′blak′), *n.* fine soot produced by the incomplete combustion of tars, oils, and other forms of carbon: used as a pigment.

**lam·per eel** (lam′pēr), a lamprey.

**lam·poon** (lam-po͞on′), *n.* [< Fr. < *lampons*, let us drink (refrain in a drinking song)], a piece of strongly satirical writing, usually attacking or ridiculing someone. *v.t.* to attack or ridicule in a lampoon. —**lam·poon′er, lam·poon′ist,** *n.* —**lam·poon′er·y,** *n.*

**lamp·post** (lamp′pōst′), *n.* a post supporting a street lamp.

**lam·prey** (lam′pri), *n.* [*pl.* -PREYS], [< OFr. < ML. *lampreda*], an eellike water animal with a funnel-shaped, jawless, sucking mouth.

**Lan·ca·shire** (laŋ′kə-shir′), *n.* a county on the NW coast of England.

**Lan·cas·ter** (laŋ′kə-stēr), *n.* the ruling family of England (1399–1461). —**Lan·cas′tri·an** (-kas′tri-ən), *adj.* & *n.*

**Lan·cas·ter** (lan′kas′tēr), *n.* a city in SE Pennsylvania: pop., 64,000.

**lance** (lans, läns), *n.* [OFr. < L. *lancea*], 1. a thrusting weapon consisting of a long wooden shaft with a sharp metal head. 2. a lancer. 3. any sharp instrument like a lance, as a fish spear. 4. a lancet. *v.t.* [LANCED, LANCING], 1. to attack or pierce with a lance. 2. to cut open with a lancet.

**lance corporal,** 1. in the *Brit. army*, a private acting as a corporal, without the extra pay. 2. in the *U.S. Marine Corps*, an enlisted man ranking below a corporal and above a private first class.

**lance·let** (lans′lit, läns′-), *n.* [*lance* + *-let*], a small, fishlike sea animal, closely related to the vertebrates: also called *amphioxus*.

**Lan·ce·lot** (lan′sə-lot′, län′sə-lət), *n.* in *Arthurian legend*, the most celebrated of the Knights of the Round Table: he was Guinevere's lover.

**lan·ce·o·late** (lan′si-ə-lit, -lāt′), *adj.* [< LL. < *lanceola*, little lance], narrow and tapering like the head of a lance, as certain leaves.

**lan·cer** (lan′sēr, län′-), *n.* a soldier, especially a cavalry soldier, armed with a lance.

**lance sergeant,** in the *Brit. army*, a corporal acting as a sergeant, without the extra pay.

**lan·cet** (lan′sit, län′-), *n.* [< OFr. dim. of *lance*], 1. a small, pointed surgical knife, usually two-edged. 2. a lancet arch or window.

**lancet arch,** a narrow, sharply pointed arch.

**lancet window,** a narrow, sharply pointed window without tracery, set in a lancet arch.

**lance·wood** (lans′wood′, läns′-), *n.* 1. a tough, elastic wood used for fishing rods, etc. 2. a tropical American tree yielding this wood.

**Lan·chow** (län′chō′), *n.* a city in north central China: pop., 699,000.

**land** (land), *n.* [AS.], 1. the solid part of the earth's surface. 2. *a*) a country, region, etc. *b*) a country's people; nation. 3. ground or soil: as, rich *land*, high *land*. 4. ground considered as property; estate: as, to invest in *land*. 5. rural regions. 6. in *economics*, natural resources. *v.t.* 1. to put or set on shore from a ship. 2. to bring into; cause to enter a particular place: as, their fight *landed* them in jail. 3. to set (an aircraft) down on land or water. 4. to catch: as, to *land* a fish. 5. [Colloq.], to get or win: as, he *landed* a job. 6. [Colloq.], to deliver (a blow). *v.i.* 1. to leave a ship and go on shore. 2. to come to a port or to shore: said of a ship. 3. to arrive at a specified place. 4. to alight or come to rest, as after a flight, jump, or fall. —**make land,** to see or reach the shore.

**lan·dau** (lan′dô, -dou), *n.* [< *Landau*, German town where made], a four-wheeled carriage with the top in two sections, either of which can be lowered independently.

**land bank,** a bank that finances transactions in real estate.

**land·ed** (lan′did), *adj.* 1. owning land: as, *landed* gentry. 2. consisting of land or real estate: as, a *landed* estate.

**land·fall** (land′fôl′), *n.* 1. a sighting of land from a ship at sea. 2. the land sighted. 3. a landing by ship or airplane.

**land·fill** (land′fil′), *n.* the disposal of garbage or rubbish under a layer of ground.

**land grant,** a grant of public land by the government for a State college, railroad, etc.

**land·grave** (land′grāv′), *n.* [< G. < *land*, land + *graf*, a count], 1. in medieval Germany, a count having jurisdiction over a specified territory. 2. later, the title of certain German princes.

**land·hold·er** (land′hōl′dēr), *n.* an owner or occupant of land. —**land′hold′ing,** *adj.* & *n.*

**land·ing** (lan′diŋ), *n.* 1. the act of coming to shore or putting ashore. 2. the place where a ship is unloaded or loaded. 3. a platform at the end of a flight of stairs. 4. the act of alighting, as after a flight, jump, or fall.

**landing field,** a field with a smooth surface to enable airplanes to land and take off easily.

**landing gear,** the undercarriage of an aircraft, including wheels, pontoons, etc.

**landing net,** a baglike net attached to a long handle, for taking a hooked fish from the water.

**land·la·dy** (land′lā′di), *n.* [*pl.* -DIES], 1. a woman who leases land, houses, etc. to others. 2. a woman who keeps a rooming house, inn, etc.

**land·less** (land′lis), *adj.* not owning land.

**land·locked** (land′lokt′), *adj.* 1. entirely or almost entirely surrounded by land, as a bay. 2. cut off from the sea and confined to fresh water: as, the *landlocked* salmon.

**land·lord** (land′lôrd′), *n.* 1. a man who leases land, houses, etc. to others. 2. a man who keeps a rooming house, inn, etc.

**land·lub·ber** (land′lub′ēr), *n.* one who has had little experience at sea, and is therefore awkward aboard a ship: a sailor's term of contempt.

**land·mark** (land′märk′), *n.* 1. any fixed object

used to mark the boundary of a piece of land. 2. any prominent feature of the landscape, as a tree, marking a particular locality. 3. an event considered as a high point of a period.
**land mine,** an explosive charge hidden under the surface of the ground and discharged by the pressure of troops or vehicles upon it.
**land office,** a government office that handles and records the sales and transfers of public lands. —**land'-of'fice business,** [Colloq.], a booming business.
**Land of Promise,** 1. in the *Bible*, Canaan, promised by God to Abraham and his descendants: Gen. 15:18, 17:8; hence, 2. [l- p-], a place where one expects to improve his lot.
**land·own·er** (land'ōn'ẽr), *n.* one who owns land. —**land'own'er·ship',** *n.* —**land'own'ing,** *adj.* & *n.*
**land·scape** (land'skāp'), *n.* [< D. < *land*, land + *-schap*, -ship], 1. a picture representing natural, inland scenery. 2. an expanse of natural scenery seen in one view. *v.t.* [-SCAPED, -SCAPING], to change the natural features of (a plot of ground) so as to make it more attractive, as by adding lawns, bushes, etc. —**land'scap'er,** *n.*
**landscape architecture,** the art of changing the natural scenery of a place to produce the most desirable effect. —**landscape architect.**
**landscape gardening,** the art or work of arranging lawns, bushes, etc. on a plot of ground to make it more attractive. —**landscape gardener.**
**land·scap·ist** (land'skāp'ist), *n.* a painter of landscapes.
**land·slide** (land'slīd'), *n.* 1. the sliding of a mass of rocks or earth down a hillside or slope. 2. the mass sliding down. 3. an overwhelming majority of votes for one candidate or party in an election. 4. any overwhelming victory.
**land·slip** (land'slip'), *n.* [Chiefly Brit.], a landslide (senses 1 & 2).
**lands·man** (landz'mən), *n.* [*pl.* -MEN], 1. a person who lives on land: distinguished from *seaman*. 2. a new, inexperienced sailor.
**land·ward** (land'wẽrd), *adv.* toward the land: also **land'wards.** *adj.* situated or facing toward the land.
**lane** (lān), *n.* [AS. *lanu*], 1. a narrow way between hedges, walls, etc.; narrow country road or city street. 2. any narrow way, as an opening in a crowd of people, a path for each contestant in a race, etc. 3. a path or course designated, for reasons of safety, for ships, aircraft, automobiles, etc.
**lang.,** language.
**Lang·ley, Samuel Pier·pont** (pêr'pont laŋ'li), 1834–1906; U.S. astronomer and inventor.
**lang·syne** (laŋ'sin'; -zīn'), *adv.* [Scot.; *lang*, long + *syne*, since], [Scot.], long ago. *n.* [Scot.], the long ago; bygone days. Also **lang syne.**
**lan·guage** (laŋ'gwij), *n.* [< OFr. < *langue*, tongue < L. *lingua*], 1. *a*) human speech. *b*) the ability to communicate by human speech. *c*) the vocal sounds used in speech, or the written symbols for them. 2. any means of communicating, as gestures, animal sounds, etc. 3. all the words and ways of combining them common to a particular nation, tribe, etc.: as, the English *language*. 4. *a*) form or style of expression: as, the *language* of poetry. *b*) the particular words and phrases of a profession, group, etc.: as, the *language* of the army. 5. the study of language or languages; linguistics.
**lan·guid** (laŋ'gwid), *adj.* [< Fr. < L. < *languere*, to be faint], 1. without vigor or vitality; drooping; weak. 2. without interest or spirit; listless; indifferent. 3. sluggish; dull; slow. —**lan'guid·ly,** *adv.* —**lan'guid·ness,** *n.*
**lan·guish** (laŋ'gwish), *v.i.* [< OFr. < L. < *languere*], 1. to lose vigor or vitality; become weak; droop. 2. to live under distressing conditions: as, to *languish* in poverty. 3. to become slack or dull: as, his interest *languished*. 4. to suffer with longing; pine. 5. to put on a sentimental or wistful air. —**lan'guish·er,** *n.* —**lan'guish·ment,** *n.*
**lan·guish·ing** (laŋ'gwish-iŋ), *adj.* 1. becoming weak; drooping. 2. lingering. 3. pining; longing. 4. tender; sentimental; wistfully amorous. —**lan'guish·ing·ly,** *adv.*
**lan·guor** (laŋ'gẽr), *n.* [< OFr. < L. < *languere*, to be weary], 1. a lack of vigor or vitality; weakness. 2. a lack of interest or spirit; listlessness. 3. tenderness of mood or feeling. 4. a lack of activity; sluggishness; dullness. —**lan'guor·ous,** *adj.* —**lan'guor·ous·ly,** *adv.*
**lan·gur** (luŋ-goor'), *n.* [< Hind. < Sans.], a monkey of SE Asia, with a very long tail and a chin tuft.
**lan·iard** (lan'yẽrd), *n.* a lanyard.
**lank** (laŋk), *adj.* [AS. *hlanc*], 1. long and slender; lean. 2. straight and flat; not curly: said of hair. —**lank'ly,** *adv.* —**lank'ness,** *n.*
**lank·y** (laŋ'ki), *adj.* [-IER, -IEST], awkwardly tall and lean or long and slender. —**lank'i·ly,** *adv.* —**lank'i·ness,** *n.*
**lan·o·lin** (lan'ə-lin), *n.* [< L. *lana*, wool + *oleum*, oil; + *-in*], a fatty substance obtained from wool and used in ointments, cosmetics, etc.
**lan·o·line** (lan'ə-lin, -lēn'), *n.* lanolin.
**Lan·sing** (lan'siŋ), *n.* the capital of Michigan: pop., 108,000.
**lan·tern** (lan'tẽrn), *n.* [< Fr. < L. *lanterna* < Gr. *lamptēr* < *lampein*, to shine], 1. a transparent case for holding a light and protecting it from wind and weather. 2. the room containing the lamp at the top of a lighthouse. 3. an open structure on the roof, in a tower, etc. to admit light and air. 4. a magic lantern.
**lantern jaw,** 1. a projecting lower jaw. 2. *pl.* long, thin jaws that hollow the cheeks. —**lan'tern-jawed'** (-jôd'), *adj.*
**lantern slide,** a photographic slide for projection, as, originally, by a magic lantern.

KEROSENE LANTERN

**lan·tha·num** (lan'thə-nəm), *n.* [< Gr. *lanthanein*, to be concealed], a silvery, lustrous metallic chemical element of the rare-earth group: symbol, La; at. wt., 138.92; at. no., 57.
**lan·yard** (lan'yẽrd), *n.* [< Fr. < OFr. < *lasne*, noose; altered after *yard* (spar)], 1. a short rope used on board ship for holding or fastening something. 2. a cord used by sailors to hang a knife around their necks. 3. a cord used in firing certain types of cannon. Also sp. **laniard.**
**La·oc·o·ön** (lā-ok'ə-won'), *n.* in *Gr. legend*, a Trojan priest who was destroyed by two sea serpents after he had warned against the wooden horse.
**La·os** (lä'ōs), *n.* a kingdom on the Indochinese peninsula: area, 91,500 sq. mi.; pop., 1,760,000; capital, Vientiane.
**Lao-tse** (lou'dzu'), *n.* Chinese philosopher; 604–531 B.C.; founder of Taoism: also sp. **Lao-tzu.**
**lap** (lap), *n.* [AS. *læppa*], 1. the loose lower part of a garment, which may be folded over. 2. *a*) the front part from the waist to the knees of a person in a sitting position. *b*) the part of the clothing covering this. 3. that in which one is cared for, sheltered, etc.: as, in the *lap* of luxury. 4. *a*) an overlapping part. *b*) such overlapping. *c*) amount or place of this. 5. one complete circuit of a race track. 6. a lapping. *v.t.* [LAPPED, LAPPING], 1. to fold (*over* or *on*). 2. to wrap; enfold. 3. to hold as in the lap; envelop. 4. to place partly upon something else: as, *lap* one board over the other. 5. to lie partly upon: as, one board *laps* the other. 6. to get a lap ahead of (an opponent) in a race. *v.i.* 1. to lie partly upon something or upon one another; overlap. 2. to project or extend beyond something in space or time (with *over*). —**lap'per,** *n.*
**lap** (lap), *v.i.* & *v.t.* [LAPPED, LAPPING], [AS. *lapian*], 1. to drink (a liquid) by dipping it up with the tongue as a dog does. 2. to move or strike gently with a light splash: said of waves, etc. *n.* 1. a lapping. 2. the sound of lapping. —**lap up,** 1. to take up (liquid) by lapping. 2. [Colloq.], to take in eagerly. —**lap'per,** *n.*
**La Paz** (lä päs'), the actual seat of government of Bolivia, in the W part (the nominal capital is Sucre): pop., 339,000.
**lap dog,** a pet dog small enough to hold in the lap.
**la·pel** (lə-pel'), *n.* [dim. of *lap* (a fold)], the front part of a coat folded back and forming a continuation of the collar.
**lap·ful** (lap'fool'), *n.* as much as a lap can hold.
**lap·i·dar·y** (lap'ə-der'i), *n.* [*pl.* -IES], [< L. *lapidarius* < *lapis*, a stone], a workman who cuts, polishes, and engraves precious stones. *adj.* of the art of cutting and engraving precious stones.
**lap·in** (lap'in; Fr. là'pan'), *n.* [Fr., rabbit], rabbit fur, generally dyed in imitation of other skins.
**lap·is laz·u·li** (lap'is laz'yoo-lī'), [< L. *lapis*, a stone + ML. genit. of *lazulus*, azure], an azure-blue, opaque, semiprecious stone.

LAPELS

**Lap·land** (lap′land′), *n.* a region in N Norway, Sweden, Finland, and the U.S.S.R., inhabited by the Lapps. —**Lap′land′er,** *n.*

**La Pla·ta** (lä plä′tä), a seaport in E Argentina: pop., 410,000: called *Eva Perón* (1952–1955).

**Lapp** (lap), *n.* 1. a member of a Mongoloid people living in Lapland. 2. their Finno-Ugric language.

**lap·pet** (lap′it), *n.* [dim. of *lap* (a fold)], 1. a small, loose fold of a garment. 2. any fleshy or membranous part hanging loosely or in a fold, as an ear lobe.

**lap robe,** a heavy blanket, etc. laid over the lap for warmth, as when watching outdoor sports.

**lapse** (laps), *n.* [< L. *lapsus,* a fall, pp. of *labi,* to slip], 1. a small error; fault. 2. a falling away from a moral standard; moral slip. 3. a falling or slipping into a lower condition. 4. a passing away, as of time. 5. in *law,* the termination of a right or privilege through disuse or failure to meet stated obligations. *v.i.* [LAPSED, LAPSING], 1. to slip or fall into a specified state: as, he *lapsed* into silence. 2. to slip or deviate from virtue. 3. to pass away; elapse. 4. to become forfeit or void because of failure to pay the premium at the stipulated time: said of an insurance policy. —**laps′a·ble, laps′i·ble,** *adj.* —**laps′er,** *n.*

‡**lap·sus lin·guae** (lap′səs liŋ′gwē), [L.], a slip of the tongue.

**lap·wing** (lap′wiŋ′), *n.* [< AS. < *hleapan,* to leap + *wince* (prob. < *wincan,* to totter)], an Old World crested plover noted for its irregular, wavering flight and its shrill cry.

**lar·board** (lär′bẽrd, -bôrd′, -bōrd′), *n.* [< AS. *hladan,* to lade + *bord,* side], the left-hand side of a ship when facing the bow; port. *adj. & adv.* on or toward this side. Now largely replaced by *port.*

**lar·ce·ner** (lär′sə-nẽr), *n.* a person guilty of larceny: also **lar′ce·nist.**

**lar·ce·ny** (lär′sə-ni), *n.* [*pl.* -NIES], [< OFr. < L. < *latrocinari,* to rob < *latro,* robber], in *law,* the unlawful taking away of another's property with the intention of depriving him of it; theft: sometimes differentiated as *grand larceny* (more than a stated amount) and *petty,* or *petit, larceny* (less than this amount). —**lar′ce·nous,** *adj.*

**larch** (lärch), *n.* [< G. < L. *larix*], 1. a tree of the pine family, found throughout the Northern Hemisphere, bearing cones and needlelike leaves that are shed annually. 2. the tough wood of this tree.

**lard** (lärd), *n.* [< OFr. < L. *lardum*], the fat of hogs, melted down and clarified. *v.t.* 1. to smear with lard or other fat; grease. 2. to stuff (meat or poultry) with bits of bacon or fat pork before cooking. 3. to enrich; garnish: as, his speech was *larded* with oaths.

**lard·er** (lär′dẽr), *n.* [< OFr. *lardier* < ML. < L. *lardum,* lard], 1. a place where the food supplies of a household are kept; pantry. 2. the food supplies.

**Lard·ner, Ring** (riŋ lärd′nẽr), (*Ringgold Wilmer Lardner*), 1885–1933; U.S. writer.

**lard·y** (lär′di), *adj.* [-IER, -IEST], 1. containing or covered with lard. 2. like lard.

**La·re·do** (lə-rā′dō), *n.* a city in S Texas, on the Rio Grande: pop., 61,000.

**la·res** (lâr′ēz, lā′rēz), *n.pl.* [*sing.* LAR (lär)], [L.], in ancient Rome, guardian spirits.

**lares and penates,** 1. the household gods of the ancient Romans. 2. the treasured belongings of a family or household.

**large** (lärj), *adj.* [LARGER, LARGEST], [OFr. < L. *largus*], 1. big; great; specif., *a*) taking up much space; bulky. *b*) enclosing much space; spacious: as, a *large* office. *c*) of great extent or amount: as, a *large* sum. 2. bigger than others of its kind. 3. operating on a big scale: as, a *large* manufacturer. *adv.* in a large way: as, do not write so *large.* *n.* liberty: now only in the following phrase. —**at large,** 1. free; not imprisoned. 2. fully; in complete detail. 3. in general; taken altogether. 4. representing an entire State or district rather than only a subdivision: as, a congressman *at large.*

**large·ly** (lärj′li), *adv.* 1. much; in great amounts. 2. for the most part; mainly.

**large-scale** (lärj′skāl′), *adj.* 1. drawn to a large scale. 2. of wide scope; extensive: as, *large-scale* business operations.

**lar·gess, lar·gesse** (lär′jis, -jes), *n.* [OFr. < LL. < L. *largus,* large], 1. generous giving. 2. a gift or gifts generously given.

**lar·ghet·to** (lär-get′ō), *adj. & adv.* [It., dim. of *largo*], in *music,* rather slow, but faster than largo. *n.* [*pl.* -TOS], a larghetto movement or passage.

**larg·ish** (lär′jish), *adj.* rather large.

**lar·go** (lär′gō), *adj. & adv.* [It., large, slow < L. *largus,* large], in *music,* slow and stately. *n.* [*pl.* -GOS], a largo movement or passage.

**lar·i·at** (lar′i-ət), *n.* [Sp. *la reata,* the rope], 1. a rope used for tethering grazing horses, etc. 2. a lasso. *v.t.* to tie or catch with a lariat.

**lark** (lärk), *n.* [AS. *lāwerce*], 1. any of a large group of songbirds found throughout the world; esp., the English skylark. 2. any of a number of similar birds, as the meadow lark.

**lark** (lärk), *v.i.* [ME. *laike* < ON.], [Colloq.], to play or frolic. *v.t.* [Colloq.], to tease. *n.* a frolic or spree.

**lark·spur** (lärk′spũr′), *n.* a plant with green, feathery leaves and spurred flowers of blue or, occasionally, white or pink; delphinium.

**lar·rup** (lar′əp), *v.t.* [-RUPED, -RUPING], [akin to or < D. *larpen*], [Colloq.], to whip; flog; beat.

**lar·va** (lär′və), *n.* [*pl.* -VAE (-vē)], [L., ghost], 1. an insect in the earliest stage after hatching, before it is changed into a pupa; caterpillar, maggot, or grub. 2. the early form of any animal that changes structurally when it becomes an adult, as the tadpole. —**lar′val,** *adj.*

**la·ryn·ge·al** (lə-rin′ji-əl), *adj.* 1. of, in, or near the larynx. 2. used for treating the larynx.

**lar·yn·gi·tis** (lar′in-jī′tis), *n.* [*laryng(o)-* + *-itis*], inflammation of the larynx, often with a temporary loss of voice. —**lar′yn·git′ic** (-jit′ik), *adj.*

**la·ryn·go-,** [< Gr.], a combining form meaning: 1. the *larynx.* 2. *laryngeal and.* Also **laryng-.**

**la·ryn·go·scope** (lə-riŋ′gə-skōp′), *n.* [*laryngo-* + *-scope*], an instrument for examining the larynx. —**la·ryn·gos·co·py** (lar′iŋ-gos′kə-pi), *n.*

**lar·ynx** (lar′iŋks), *n.* [*pl.* -YNGES (lə-rin′jēz), -YNXES], [< Gr. *larynx*], 1. the structure of muscle and cartilage at the upper end of the human trachea, containing the vocal cords, and serving as the organ of voice: see **pharynx,** illus. 2. a similar structure in other animals.

**la·sa·gna** (lə-zän′yə), *n.* [It. < L. *lasanum* (< Gr. *lasanon*), a pot], broad macaroni, often baked in a dish with ground meat, cheeses, etc.

**La Salle,** Sieur **Ro·bert Ca·ve·lier de** (rô′bâr′ kȧ′və-lyā′ də lȧ′sȧl′; Eng. lə sal′), 1643–1687; French explorer in America.

**las·car** (las′kẽr), *n.* [< Hind. < Per. *lashkar* (< Ar. *al-'askar*), army], an East Indian sailor.

**las·civ·i·ous** (lə-siv′i-əs), *adj.* [< ML. < L. < *lascivus,* wanton], 1. characterized by or expressing lust or lewdness; wanton. 2. tending to excite lust. —**las·civ′i·ous·ly,** *adv.* —**las·civ′i·ous·ness,** *n.*

**la·ser** (lā′zẽr), *n.* [*l*ight *a*mplification by *s*timulated *e*mission of *r*adiation], a device that amplifies light waves and concentrates them in a narrow, very intense beam: also called *optical maser.*

**lash** (lash), *n.* [prob. merging of MLG. *lasch,* flap, with OFr. *laz* (see LACE)], 1. a whip, especially the flexible striking part. 2. a stroke as with a whip; switch. 3. a sharp remark, rebuke, etc. 4. an eyelash. *v.t.* 1. to strike or drive as with a lash; flog. 2. to switch energetically or angrily: as, the cat *lashed* her tail. 3. to strike with great force: as, the waves *lashed* the cliffs. 4. to attack violently in words; censure, rebuke, etc. *v.i.* 1. to move quickly or violently; switch. 2. to make strokes as with a whip (often with *at*). —**lash out,** 1. to strike out violently. 2. to speak angrily.

**lash** (lash), *v.t.* [< OFr. *lachier;* see LACE], to fasten or tie with a rope, etc.

**lash·ing** (lash′iŋ), *n.* 1. a whipping. 2. a strong rebuke: as, a tongue *lashing.*

**lash·ing** (lash′iŋ), *n.* 1. the act of lashing with a rope, etc. 2. a rope, etc. so used.

**lass** (las), *n.* [ME. *lasse;* ? < N.], 1. a young woman; girl. 2. a sweetheart.

**las·sie** (las′i), *n.* [dim. of *lass*], [Scot.], 1. a young girl. 2. a sweetheart.

**las·si·tude** (las′ə-tōōd′, -tūd′), *n.* [Fr. < L. < *lassus,* faint], a state or feeling of being tired or weak; weariness; languor.

**las·so** (las′ō), *n.* [*pl.* -SOS, -SOES], [Sp. *lazo* < L. *laqueus,* noose], a long rope with a sliding noose at one end, used in catching cattle, etc. *v.t.* [-SOED, -SOING], to catch with a lasso. —**las′so·er,** *n.*

**last** (last, läst), [alt. superl. of *late*], *adj.* [AS. *latost,* superl. of *læt;* see LATE], 1. being or coming after all others in place or time; furthest from the first; final. 2. only remaining: as, my *last* dime. 3. most recent: as, *last* month. 4. least likely: as, she was the *last* person one would suspect. 5. utmost; greatest: as, of the *last* importance. 6. lowest in rank, as a prize. 7. newest: as, the *last* thing in topcoats. 8. conclusive: as, the *last* word. *adv.* 1. after all others; at the end. 2. at the most recent time or occasion. 3. finally. *n.* 1. someone or something which comes last: as, this is the *last* of the apples. 2. end: as, he was a cynic to the *last.* —**at last,** finally. —**breathe one's last,** to die. —**see the last of,** to see for the last time.

**last** (last, läst), *v.i.* [AS. *læstan*], 1. to remain in existence or operation; continue; endure. 2. to remain in good condition. 3. to be enough (*for*); continue unconsumed. —**last′er,** *n.*

**last** (last, läst), *n.* [AS. *læst* < *last*, footstep], a form shaped like a foot, used by shoemakers in building or repairing shoes. *v.t.* to form with a last. —**stick to one's last,** to attend to one's own business. —**last′er,** *n.*

**las·tex** (las′teks), *n.* [coined word], a fine, round rubber thread wound with cotton, silk, etc. and woven into cloth: a trade-mark (**Lastex**).

**last·ing** (las′tiŋ, läs′-), *adj.* that lasts a long time; durable; permanent: as, a *lasting* peace. *n.* endurance; durability; permanence. —**last′ing·ly,** *adv.* —**last′ing·ness,** *n.*

**Last Judgment,** in *theology*, the final judgment of mankind at the end of the world.

**last·ly** (last′li, läst′-), *adv.* in conclusion; finally.

**last offices,** final rites for a dead person.

**last straw,** [< the last straw that broke the camel's back in the fable], the last of a sequence of troubles that results in a breakdown, etc.

**Last Supper,** the last supper eaten by Jesus with his disciples before the Crucifixion.

**last word,** 1. the final word or speech, regarded as settling the argument. 2. something regarded as incapable of improvement. 3. [Colloq.], the very latest style, model, etc.

**Las Ve·gas** (läs vā′gəs), a city in SE Nevada: pop., 64,000: a gambling center.

**Lat.,** Latin.

**lat.,** latitude.

**La·ta·ki·a** (lat′ə-kē′ə), *n.* [< *Latakia*, a seaport in Syria], a fine grade of Turkish tobacco.

**latch** (lach), *n.* [< AS. *læccan*], 1. a fastening for a door or gate consisting of a bar that falls into a notch on the doorjamb: sometimes used of a spring lock. 2. a fastening for a window, etc. *v.t. & v.i.* to fasten with a latch. —**latch on to,** [slang], to get or obtain. —**on the latch,** fastened by the latch but not bolted.

**latch·key** (lach′kē′), *n.* a key for drawing back or unfastening the latch of a door.

**latch·string** (lach′striŋ′), *n.* a cord fastened to a latch so that it can be raised from the outside.

**late** (lāt), *adj.* [LATER or LATTER, LATEST or LAST], [AS. *læt*], 1. happening, coming, etc. after the usual or expected time; tardy. 2. *a*) happening, continuing, etc. far on in the day, night, year, etc.: as, a *late* dinner. *b*) far advanced in a period, development, etc.: as, the *late* Middle Ages. 3. recent: as, *late* years. 4. *a*) recently dead. *b*) recently gone out of office. *adv.* [LATER, LATEST or LAST], 1. after the usual or expected time. 2. at or until an advanced time of the day, night, year, etc. 3. toward the end of a period, development, etc. 4. recently. —**of late,** lately; recently. —**late′ness,** *n.*

**la·teen** (la-tēn′), *adj.* [< Fr. (*voile*) *latine*, Latin (sail)], 1. designating or of a triangular sail attached to a long yard suspended from a short mast: used chiefly on Mediterranean vessels. 2. having such a sail. *n.* a vessel having such a sail.

LATEEN SAIL

**Late Greek,** the Greek language of the period after classical Greek, seen chiefly in writings from c. 200 A.D. to c. 600 A.D.: abbrev. **Late Gr.**

**Late Latin,** the Latin language of the period after classical Latin, seen chiefly in writings from c. 200 A.D. to c. 600 A.D.: abbrev. **LL.**

**late·ly** (lāt′li), *adv.* recently; a short while ago.

**la·tent** (lā′t'nt), *adj.* [< L. ppr. of *latere*, to lurk], lying hidden and undeveloped within a person or thing; concealed, dormant, etc. —**la′ten·cy,** *n.* —**la′tent·ly,** *adv.*

**lat·er** (lāt′ẽr), alt. compar. of **late.** —**later on,** subsequently.

**lat·er·al** (lat′ẽr-əl), *adj.* [< L. < *latus*, a side], 1. of, at, from, or toward the side; sideways: as, *lateral* movement. 2. tracing descent from a brother or sister of a person. *n.* 1. any lateral part, growth, etc. 2. in *football*, a lateral pass. —**lat′er·al·ly,** *adv.*

**lateral pass,** in *football*, a short pass more or less parallel to the goal line.

**Lat·er·an** (lat′ẽr-ən), *n.* [< name of a Roman family whose palace once occupied the site], 1. the church of St. John Lateran, the cathedral church of the Pope as bishop of Rome. 2. the palace adjoining this church. *adj.* of this church or palace; specif., of certain Catholic general councils held there.

**la·tes·cent** (lə-tes′'nt), *adj.* [< L. *latescens*, ppr. < *latere*, to lurk], becoming latent, or hidden. —**la·tes′cence,** *n.* —**la·tes′cent·ly,** *adv.*

**lat·est** (lāt′ist), alt. superl. of **late.** —**at the latest,** no later than (the time specified). —**the latest,** the most recent thing, newest development, etc.

**la·tex** (lā′teks), *n.* [-TEXES, -TICES (lat′ə-sēz′)], [L., a fluid], a milky liquid in certain plants and trees, as the rubber tree, milkweed, etc.: it is the basis of various products, notably rubber.

**lath** (lath, läth), *n.* [*pl.* LATHS (la*th*z, läths)], [AS. *lætt*], 1. any of the thin, narrow strips of wood used in building lattices or, in frameworks of walls, etc., as a groundwork for plastering, tiling, etc. 2. wire cloth or perforated sheet metal designed for similar uses. 3. lathing. *v.t.* to cover with laths. —**lath′er,** *n.*

**lathe** (lā*th*), *n.* [prob. < MD. *lade*], a machine for shaping an article of wood, metal, etc. by holding and turning it rapidly against the edge of a cutting tool. *v.t.* [LATHED, LATHING], to shape on a lathe.

**lath·er** (la*th*′ẽr), *n.* [AS. *leathor*, washing soda or soap], 1. the foam formed by soap and water. 2. foamy sweat, as on a race horse. *v.t.* 1. to cover with lather. 2. [Colloq.], to flog soundly. *v.i.* to form or become covered with lather. —**lath′er·er,** *n.* —**lath′er·y,** *adj.*

**lath·ing** (lath′iŋ, läth′-), *n.* 1. laths collectively. 2. the putting up of laths on walls, etc. Also **lath′work′** (-wũrk′).

**Lat·in** (lat′'n), *adj.* 1. of ancient Latium or its people. 2. of ancient Rome or its people. 3. of or in the language of ancient Latium and ancient Rome. 4. designating or of the languages derived from Latin, the peoples who speak them, their countries, etc. *n.* 1. a native or inhabitant of ancient Latium or ancient Rome. 2. the Italic language of ancient Latium and ancient Rome. 3. a person, as a Spaniard or an Italian, whose language is derived from Latin. —**La·tin′ic** (-tin′ik), *adj.*

**Latin America,** all of the Western Hemisphere south of the U.S. where Spanish, Portuguese, and French are spoken. —**Lat′in-A·mer′i·can,** *adj.* —**Latin American.**

**Lat·in·ate** (lat′'n-āt′), *adj.* of or from Latin.

**Latin Church,** that part of the Catholic Church which adheres to the Latin Rite; Roman Catholic Church.

**Lat·in·ism** (lat′'n-iz'm), *n.* a Latin idiom or expression, used in another language.

**Lat·in·ist** (lat′'n-ist), *n.* a scholar in Latin.

**Lat·in·ize** (lat′'n-īz′), *v.t.* [-IZED, -IZING], 1. to translate into Latin. 2. to give Latin form or characteristics to. *v.i.* to use Latin expressions, forms, etc. —**Lat′in·i·za′tion,** *n.*

**Latin Quarter,** a section of Paris, south of the Seine, where many artists and students live.

**Latin Rite,** 1. the Latin liturgies used in the Latin Church. 2. the Latin Church.

**lat·ish** (lāt′ish), *adj. & adv.* somewhat late.

**lat·i·tude** (lat′ə-tōōd′, -tūd′), *n.* [OFr. < L. < *latus*, wide], 1. extent; scope; range of applicability. 2. freedom from narrow restrictions. 3. a region with reference to its distance north or south of the equator: as, in this *latitude* it rarely snows. 4. in *geography*, angular distance, measured in degrees, north or south from the equator. —**lat′i·tu′di·nal,** *adj.* —**lat′i·tu′di·nal·ly,** *adv.*

**lat·i·tu·di·nar·i·an** (lat′ə-tōō′d'n-âr′i-ən, -tū′-), *adj.* liberal in one's views; permitting free thought, especially in religious matters. *n.* one who is very liberal in his views and, in religion, cares little about particular creeds and forms. —**lat′i·tu′di·nar′i·an·ism,** *n.*

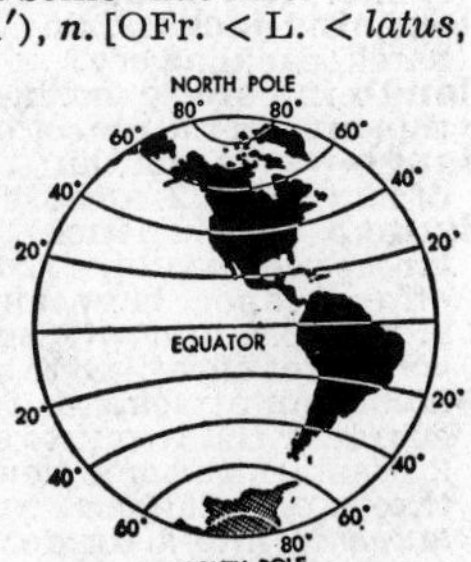

PARALLELS SHOWING LATITUDE

**La·ti·um** (lā′shi-əm), *n.* an ancient country in central Italy, southeast of Rome.

**la·trine** (lə-trēn′), *n.* [Fr. < L. < *lavare*, to wash], a toilet, or privy, for the use of a large number of people, as in an army camp.

**-la·try** (lə-tri), [< Gr. < *latreia*, service], a com-

bining form meaning *worship of* or *excessive devotion to*, as in *idolatry*.
**lat·ter** (lat'ẽr), *adj.* [alt. compar. of *late*], 1. *a*) later; more recent. *b*) nearer the end or close: as, in the *latter* part of the year. 2. last mentioned of two: opposed to *former:* often a noun (with *the*).
**lat·ter-day** (lat'ẽr-dā'), *adj.* modern.
**Lat·ter-day Saint** (lat'ẽr-dā'), a Mormon.
**lat·ter·ly** (lat'ẽr-li), *adv.* lately; recently.
**lat·tice** (lat'is), *n.* [OFr. *lattis* < MHG. *latte*, a lath], 1. an openwork structure of crossed strips of wood, metal, etc., used as a screen, support, etc. 2. a window, door, etc. screened by such a structure. *v.t.* [-TICED, -TICING], 1. to arrange like a lattice. 2. to furnish with a lattice.
**lat·tice·work** (lat'is-wũrk'), *n.* 1. a lattice. 2. lattices collectively. Also **lat'tic·ing.**
**Lat·vi·a** (lat'vi-ə), *n.* a country in NE Europe annexed as the Latvian Soviet Socialist Republic in August, 1940. —**Lat'vi·an,** *adj. & n.*
**Latvian Soviet Socialist Republic,** a republic of the U.S.S.R., on the Baltic Sea: area, 24,700 sq. mi.; pop., 1,951,000; capital, Riga.
**laud** (lôd), *n.* [< OFr. < L. *laus*], 1. praise. 2. any song or hymn of praise. 3. *pl. a*) [often L-], a morning church service that includes psalms of praise to God. *b*) [L-], in the *R. C. Church*, the service of dawn which constitutes the second (or together with matins, the first) of the canonical hours. *v.t.* to praise; extol. —**laud'er,** *n.*
**laud·a·ble** (lôd'ə-b'l), *adj.* worthy of being lauded; praiseworthy; commendable. —**laud'a·bil'i·ty, laud'a·ble·ness,** *n.* —**laud'a·bly,** *adv.*
**laud·a·num** (lôd''n-əm), *n.* [altered use of ML. var. of L. *ladanum*, mastic], 1. formerly, any of various opium preparations. 2. a tincture of opium.
**lau·da·tion** (lô-dā'shən), *n.* a lauding or being lauded; praise; commendation.
**laud·a·to·ry** (lôd'ə-tôr'i, -tō'ri), *adj.* expressing praise; commendatory: also **laud'a·tive.**
**laugh** (laf, läf), *v.i.* [AS. *hleahhan*], 1. to make the vocal sounds and facial movements that express mirth, amusement, ridicule, etc. 2. to feel or suggest joyousness. *v.t.* 1. to express with laughter. 2. to bring, drive, or influence by means of laughter: as, *laugh* your gloom away. *n.* 1. the act or sound of laughing. 2. a cause of or for laughter. —**have the last laugh,** to win after apparent defeat and discomfiture. —**laugh at,** 1. to be amused by. 2. to make fun of. —**laugh off,** to scorn, avoid, or reject by laughter or ridicule. —**laugh out of** (or **on**) **the other** (or **wrong**) **side of the mouth,** to change from joy to sorrow, from amusement to annoyance, etc. —**no laughing matter,** a serious thing. —**laugh'er,** *n.*
**laugh·a·ble** (laf'ə-b'l, läf'-), *adj.* of such a nature as to cause laughter; amusing or ridiculous. —**laugh'a·ble·ness,** *n.* —**laugh'a·bly,** *adv.*
**laugh·ing** (laf'iŋ, läf'-), *adj.* 1. that laughs: as, a *laughing* face. 2. causing laughter: as, a *laughing* matter. —**laugh'ing·ly,** *adv.*
**laughing gas,** nitrous oxide, $N_2O$, used as an anesthetic, especially in dentistry: it often causes exhilaration or laughter.
**laughing jackass,** an Australian kingfisher with a harsh, cackling cry.
**laugh·ing·stock** (laf'iŋ-stok', läf'-), *n.* a person or thing made the object of ridicule.
**laugh·ter** (laf'tẽr, läf'-), *n.* 1. the action or sound of laughing. 2. a cause of laughter.
**launch** (lônch, länch), *v.t.* [< OFr. *lanc(h)ier* < *lance;* see LANCE], 1. to hurl, discharge, or send off (a weapon, blow, airplane, verbal attack, etc.). 2. to cause (a newly built vessel) to slide into the water; set afloat. 3. to set in operation; start: as, to *launch* an attack. 4. to start (a person) on some course. *v.i.* 1. to put to sea (often with *out* or *forth*). 2. to start on some new course, career, etc. 3. to throw oneself (*into*) with vigor; plunge: as, she *launched* into a tirade. *n.* the sliding of a vessel from the land into the water. —**launch out,** to begin something new. —**launch'er,** *n.*
**launch** (lônch, länch), *n.* [Sp. or Port. *lancha;* prob. < Malay < *lancār*, speedy], 1. the largest boat carried by a warship. 2. a large, open motorboat.
**launching pad** (or **platform**), the platform from which a rocket, guided missile, etc. is launched.
**laun·der** (lôn'dẽr, län'-), *v.t.* [< OFr. < LL. < L. *lavare*, to wash], to wash or wash and iron (clothes, etc.). *v.i.* 1. to withstand washing; be washable: as, this fabric *launders* well. 2. to do laundry. —**laun'der·er,** *n.*
**laun·dress** (lôn'dris, län'-), *n.* a woman whose work is washing clothes, ironing, etc.
**laun·dry** (lôn'dri, län'-), *n.* [*pl.* -DRIES], 1. a laundering. 2. a place where laundering is done. 3. clothes, etc. laundered or to be laundered.
**laun·dry·man** (lôn'dri-mən, län'-), *n.* [*pl.* -MEN], a man who works for a laundry, especially collecting and delivering clothes, etc. for laundering.
**laun·dry·wom·an** (lôn'dri-woom'ən, län'-), *n.* [*pl.* -WOMEN], a laundress.
**lau·re·ate** (lô'ri-it), *adj.* [< L. < *laurus*, laurel], 1. crowned with a laurel wreath as a mark of honor or distinction. 2. worthy of honor; distinguished. *n.* 1. a person crowned with laurel. 2. a poet laureate. —**lau're·ate·ship',** *n.*
**lau·rel** (lô'rəl, lär'əl), *n.* [< OFr. < L. *laurus*], 1. an evergreen tree or shrub, native to S Europe, with large, glossy, aromatic leaves: also called *bay tree.* 2. the foliage of this tree, especially as woven into wreaths: used by the ancient Greeks to crown victors in contests. 3. *pl. a*) fame; honor. *b*) victory. 4. any of a family of trees and shrubs including the bay, cinnamon, etc. 5. a tree or shrub resembling the true laurel, as the azalea, rhododendron, etc. *v.t.* [-RELED or -RELLED, -RELING or -RELLING], 1. to crown with laurel. 2. to honor. —**look to one's laurels,** to beware of having one's achievements surpassed. —**rest on one's laurels,** to be satisfied with what one has already achieved. —**lau'reled, lau'relled,** *adj.*
**Laurentian Mountains** (lô-ren'shi-ən, lä-ren'shən), a mountain range in Canada, between Hudson Bay and the St. Lawrence River.
**Lau·sanne** (lō-zan'), *n.* a city in W Switzerland, near Lake Geneva: pop., 107,000.
‡**laus De·o** (lôs dē'ō), [L.], praise (be) to God.
**la·va** (lä'və, lav'ə), *n.* [It. < *lavare* < L. *lavare*, to wash], 1. melted rock issuing from a volcano. 2. such rock when solidified by cooling.
**lav·a·liere, lav·a·lier** (lav'ə-lêr'), *n.* [Fr. *lavallière*, kind of tie], an ornament hanging from a chain, worn around the neck.
**la·val·lière** (lav'ə-lêr'; Fr. là'và'lyâr'), *n.* [Fr.], a lavaliere.
**lav·a·to·ry** (lav'ə-tôr'i, -tō'ri), *n.* [*pl.* -RIES], [LL. *lavatorium* < L. *lavare*, to wash], 1. a bowl or basin for washing the face and hands. 2. a room equipped with such a basin or basins: now often a euphemism for *toilet.*
**lave** (lāv), *v.t. & v.i.* [LAVED, LAVING], [< OFr. < L. *lavare*], [Poetic], 1. to wash; bathe. 2. to flow along or against.
**lav·en·der** (lav'ən-dẽr), *n.* [< Anglo-Fr. < ML. *lavendula*], 1. a fragrant European plant of the mint family, having spikes of pale-purplish flowers and yielding an aromatic oil (**oil of lavender**). 2. the dried flowers, leaves, and stalks of this plant, used to perfume clothes, linens, etc. 3. a pale purple. *adj.* pale-purple. *v.t.* to perfume with lavender.
**la·ver** (lā'vẽr), *n.* [< OFr.; ult. < L. *lavare*, to wash], [Archaic], a large basin to wash in.
**lav·ish** (lav'ish), *adj.* [< OFr. *lavasse*, torrent of rain < Pr.; ult. < L. *lavare*, to wash], 1. very generous or liberal in giving or spending; prodigal. 2. more than enough; very abundant: as, *lavish* praise. *v.t.* to give or spend liberally. —**lav'ish·er,** *n.* —**lav'ish·ly,** *adv.* —**lav'ish·ness,** *n.*
**law** (lô), *n.* [Late AS. *lagu* < Anglo-N.], 1. all the rules of conduct established and enforced by the authority, legislation, or custom of a given community or other group. 2. any one of such rules. 3. the condition existing when obedience to such rules is general: as, to establish *law* and order. 4. the branch of knowledge dealing with such rules; jurisprudence. 5. the system of courts in which such rules are referred to in securing justice: as, to resort to *law.* 6. all such rules dealing with a particular activity: as, business *law.* 7. in England, common law. 8. the profession of lawyers, judges, etc. 9. knowledge of the law (sense 1): as, his *law* is sound. 10. *a*) a sequence of events in nature or in human activities occurring with unvarying uniformity under the same conditions: often **law of nature.** *b*) the stating of such a sequence. 11. any rule or principle expected to be observed: as, the *laws* of health. 12. in *ecclesiastical usage*, a divine commandment. 13. in *mathematics*, a general principle to which all applicable cases must conform: as, the *laws* of exponents. —**go to law,** to take a dispute to a law court for settlement. —**lay down the law,** 1. to give orders in an authoritative manner. 2. to give a scolding (*to*). —**read law,** to study to become a lawyer. —**the Law,** 1. the Mosaic code, or the part of the Old Testament containing it. 2. the Old Testament. 3. [l-], [Colloq.], a policeman, or the police.
**law-a·bid·ing** (lô'ə-bīd'iŋ), *adj.* obeying the law; abiding by the law.
**law·break·er** (lô'brāk'ẽr), *n.* one who violates the law. —**law'break'ing,** *n. & adj.*

**law court,** a court for the administration of justice under the law; judicial tribunal.

**law·ful** (lô′f'l), *adj.* 1. in conformity with the law; permitted by law: as, a *lawful* act. 2. recognized by law; just: as, *lawful* debts. —**law′ful·ly,** *adv.*

**law·giv·er** (lô′giv′ẽr), *n.* one who draws up or enacts a code of laws for a nation or people; lawmaker; legislator. —**law′giv′ing,** *n. & adj.*

**law·less** (lô′lis), *adj.* 1. without law; not regulated by the authority of law: as, a *lawless* city. 2. not in conformity with law; illegal: as, *lawless* practices. 3. not obeying the law; unruly. —**law′less·ly,** *adv.* —**law′less·ness,** *n.*

**law·mak·er** (lô′māk′ẽr), *n.* one who makes or helps to make laws; esp., a legislator. —**law′mak′ing,** *adj. & n.*

**lawn** (lôn), *n.* [< OFr. < Bret. *lann,* country], land covered with grass kept closely mown, especially around a house. —**lawn′y,** *adj.*

**lawn** (lôn), *n.* [< *Laon,* city in France, where made], a fine, sheer cloth of linen or cotton, used for blouses, curtains, etc. —**lawn′y,** *adj.*

**lawn mower,** a hand-propelled or power-driven machine for cutting the grass of a lawn, typically with rotating steel blades.

**lawn tennis,** see **tennis.**

**Law of Moses,** the first five books of the Old Testament; Pentateuch; Torah.

**Law·rence** (lôr′əns, lär′-), *n.* a city in NE Massachusetts: pop., 71,000.

**Law·rence, D. H.** (lôr′əns, lär′-), (*David Herbert Lawrence*), 1885–1930; English novelist and poet.

**Lawrence, T. E.,** (name changed, 1927, to *Thomas Edward Shaw*), 1888–1935; British adventurer and writer: called *Lawrence of Arabia.*

**law·ren·ci·um** (lô-ren′si-əm, lä-), *n.* [after E. O. *Lawrence* (1901–1958), Am. physicist], a radioactive chemical element produced by bombarding californium with boron nuclei: symbol, Lw; at. wt. 257(?); at. no., 103.

**law·suit** (lô′so͞ot′, -sūt′), *n.* a suit at law; case presented before a civil court for decision.

**Law·ton** (lô′t'n), *n.* a city in SW Oklahoma: pop., 62,000.

**law·yer** (lô′yẽr), *n.* a person whose profession is advising others in matters of law or representing them in lawsuits.

**lax** (laks), *adj.* [L. *laxus*], 1. loose; slack; not rigid or tight. 2. not strict or exact; careless: as, *lax* morals. —**lax′ly,** *adv.* —**lax′ness,** *n.*

**lax·a·tive** (lak′sə-tiv), *adj.* [< Late OFr. < L. *laxativus*], tending to make lax; specif., making the bowels loose and relieving constipation. *n.* any laxative medicine.

**lax·i·ty** (lak′sə-ti), *n.* lax quality or condition.

**lay** (lā), *v.t.* [LAID, LAYING], [AS. *lecgan* < pt. base of AS. *licgan,* to lie], 1. to cause to fall with force; knock down: as, one punch *laid* him low. 2. to place or put (*on* or *in*) so as to be in a recumbent position: as, *lay* the book on the table. 3. *a*) to put down in the correct position for a specific purpose, as bricks, carpeting, etc. *b*) to situate in a particular place: as, the scene is *laid* in France. 4. to place; put; set: as, he *lays* great emphasis on accuracy. 5. to produce (an egg or eggs), as a hen. 6. to put to rest; allay, suppress, etc.: as, his doubts were *laid.* 7. to smooth down: as, she *laid* the nap of the cloth. 8. to bet (a specified sum, etc.). 9. to impose (a tax, penalty, etc.). 10. to work out; devise: as, to *lay* plans. 11. to set (a table) with silverware, plates, etc. 12. to present or assert: as, he *laid* claim to the mill. 13. to attribute; charge; impute: as, the murder was *laid* to Jones. *v.i.* 1. to lay an egg or eggs. 2. to bet; wager. 3. to lie; recline: substandard usage. 4. to apply oneself with energy: as, *lay* to your oars. *n.* the way or position in which something is situated: as, the *lay* of the land. —**lay aside,** to set aside for future use; save: also **lay by.** —**lay away,** 1. to save; lay aside. 2. to bury (usually in the passive). —**lay down,** 1. to sacrifice (one's life). 2. to declare. 3. to bet; wager 4. to store away, as wine. —**lay for,** [Colloq.], to be waiting to attack. —**lay in,** to get and store away. —**lay into,** [Slang], 1. to hit repeatedly; beat. 2. to scold. —**lay it on,** [Colloq.], 1. to exaggerate. 2. to flatter effusively. —**lay off,** 1. to put aside. 2. to discharge (employees), especially temporarily. 3. to mark off the boundaries of. 4. [Slang], to cease. —**lay on,** 1. to spread on. 2. to attack with force. —**lay oneself open,** to expose oneself to attack, blame, etc. —**lay open,** 1. to cut open. 2. to expose. —**lay out,** 1. to spend. 2. to arrange according to a plan. 3. to spread out (clothes, equipment, etc.). 4. to make (a dead body) ready for burial. —**lay over,** to stop a while in a place before continuing a journey. —**lay to,** 1. to attribute to. 2. to apply oneself with vigor. —**lay up,** 1. to store for future use. 2. to disable; confine to a sick bed. 3. to put (a ship) in dock.

**lay** (lā), pt. of **lie** (to recline).

**lay** (lā), *adj.* [< OFr. < L. *laicus* < Gr. < *laos,* the people], 1. of the laity, or ordinary people, as distinguished from the clergy. 2. not belonging to or connected with a given profession.

**lay** (lā), *n.* [< OFr. *lai*], 1. a short poem, especially a narrative poem for singing. 2. [Archaic or Poetic], a song or melody.

**lay·er** (lā′ẽr), *n.* 1. a person or thing that lays. 2. a single thickness, coat, fold, or stratum. 3. a shoot (of a living plant) bent down and partly covered with earth so that it may take root. *v.t. & v.i.* to grow (plants) by layering.

**layer cake,** a cake of two or more layers placed one on the other, with icing, etc. in between.

**lay·ette** (lā-et′), *n.* [Fr., dim. of *laie,* drawer < Fl. < MD. *lade,* a chest], a complete outfit for a newborn baby, including clothes, bedding, etc.

**lay figure,** [earlier *layman* < D. < MD. < *led,* limb + *man,* man], 1. an artist's jointed model of the human form, on which drapery is arranged. 2. a mere puppet; figurehead.

**lay·man** (lā′mən), *n.* [*pl.* -MEN], 1. a member of the laity; person not a clergyman. 2. a person not belonging to or skilled in a given profession.

**lay·off** (lā′ôf′), *n.* 1. a putting out of work or being put out of work, especially temporarily. 2. the period of such unemployment.

**lay of the land,** 1. the way the land is situated. 2. the existing state of affairs. Also **lie of the land.**

**lay·out** (lā′out′), *n.* 1. the act of laying something out. 2. the manner in which anything is laid out; arrangement; specif., the plan or make-up of a newspaper, advertisement, etc. 3. the thing laid out. 4. an outfit or set.

**lay·o·ver** (lā′ō′vẽr), *n.* a stopping for a while in some place during a journey.

**la·zar** (lā′zẽr, laz′ẽr), *n.* [< OFr. < ML. < L. < Gr. *Lazaros,* Lazarus (the beggar)], [Rare], an impoverished, diseased beggar, especially a leper.

**laz·a·ret, laz·a·rette** (laz′ə-ret′), *n.* a lazaretto.

**laz·a·ret·to** (laz′ə-ret′ō), *n.* [*pl.* -TOS], [It. < (Santa Madonna di) *Nazaret,* Venetian church used as a plague hospital; after *lazzaro,* lazar], 1. a public hospital for poor people having contagious diseases, especially for lepers. 2. a building or ship used as a quarantine station. 3. in certain ships, a space between decks, used for storing provisions.

**Laz·a·rus** (laz′ə-rəs), *n.* in the *Bible, a*) the brother of Mary and Martha, raised from the dead by Jesus: John 11. *b*) the diseased beggar in Jesus' parable: Luke 16:19-31.

**laze** (lāz), *v.i.* [LAZED, LAZING], to be lazy or idle. *v.t.* to spend (time, etc.) in idleness.

**la·zy** (lā′zi), *adj.* [-ZIER, -ZIEST], [prob. < MLG. or MD.], 1. not eager or willing to work or exert oneself; slothful. 2. slow and heavy; sluggish: as, a *lazy* motion. —**la′zi·ly,** *adv.* —**la′zi·ness,** *n.*

**la·zy·bones** (lā′zi-bōnz′), *n.* [Colloq.], a lazy person.

**lb.,** [L.], 1. *libra,* pound. 2. *librae,* pounds: also **lbs.**

**L/C, l/c,** letter of credit.

**l.c.,** 1. *loco citato,* [L.], in the place cited. 2. in *typography,* lower case.

**LD, L.D.,** Low Dutch.

**lea** (lē), *n.* [AS. *leah*], [Chiefly Poetic], a meadow, grassy field, or pasture; grassland.

**leach** (lēch), *v.t.* [prob. < AS. *leccan,* to water], 1. to cause (a liquid) to filter down through some material. 2. to wash (wood ashes, etc.) with a filtering liquid. 3. to extract (a soluble substance) from some material: as, lye is *leached* from wood ashes. *v.i.* 1. to lose soluble matter through a filtering liquid. 2. to dissolve and be washed away. *n.* 1. a leaching. 2. a sievelike container used in leaching. —**leach′er,** *n.*

**lead** (lēd), *v.t.* [LED, LEADING], [AS. *lædan*], 1. to direct the course of by going before or along with; conduct; guide. 2. to guide by physical contact, pulling a rope, etc.: as, he *led* the horse. 3. to show the way to: as, the lights *led* me here. 4. to guide the course of (water, steam, rope, etc.). 5. to direct by influence; prompt: as, she *led* us to victory. 6. to be the head or leader of (an expedition, orchestra, etc.). 7. to be at the head of: as, she *leads* the class. 8. to live; spend: as, he *leads* a fast life.

9. to begin or open. 10. in *card games*, to begin the play with (a specified card or suit). ***v.i.*** 1. to show the way by going before or along; guide. 2. to submit to being led. 3. to tend in a certain direction; go (with *to, from*, etc.). 4. to bring as a result (with *to*): as, one thing *led* to another. 5. to be first, chief, or head. 6. to begin. 7. in *boxing*, to strike a first blow. 8. in *card games*, to play the first card. ***n.*** 1. leadership; example: as, follow his *lead*. 2. first or front place; precedence. 3. the extent of distance ahead: as, we now hold a safe *lead*. 4. anything that leads, as a clue. 5. in *boxing*, a blow used in leading. 6. in *card games*, the right of playing first or the card or suit played. 7. in *electricity*, a wire carrying current from one point to another in a circuit. 8. in the *theater*, *a*) a leading role. *b*) an actor or actress playing such a role. 9. in *journalism*, the opening paragraph of a news story. 10. in *mining*, a stratum of ore in an old river bed. ***adj.*** acting as leader: as, the *lead* horse. **—lead off,** to begin. **—lead on,** 1. to conduct further. 2. to lure. **—lead out,** to begin. **—lead up to,** to prepare the way for.

**lead** (led), ***n.*** [AS.], 1. a heavy, soft, malleable, bluish-gray metallic chemical element used for piping and in numerous alloys: symbol, Pb: at. wt., 207.21; at. no., 82. 2. anything made of this metal; specif., *a*) a weight for sounding depths at sea, etc. *b*) in *printing*, a thin strip of type metal inserted to increase the space between lines of type. 3. bullets. 4. a thin stick of graphite, used in pencils. ***adj.*** made of or containing lead. ***v.t.*** 1. to cover, line, or weight with lead. 2. in *printing*, to increase the space between (lines of type) by inserting leads. ***v.i.*** to become covered with lead.

**lead·en** (led'n), ***adj.*** 1. made of lead. 2. having the heaviness of lead; hard to move. 3. sluggish; dull. 4. depressed; gloomy. 5. of a dull gray. **—lead'en·ly,** ***adv.*** **—lead'en·ness,** ***n.***

**lead·er** (lēd'ēr), ***n.*** 1. a person or thing that leads; guiding head. 2. a horse harnessed before all others or in the foremost span. 3. a pipe for carrying water, etc. 4. a featured, low-priced article of trade. 5. in *fishing*, a short piece of catgut, etc. attaching the hook, lure, etc. to the fishline. 6. in *journalism*, one of the main editorials or articles: also **leading article.** 7. in *music*, *a*) a conductor, as of a dance band. *b*) the main performer, as in a vocal section. 8. *pl.* in *printing*, dots, dashes, etc. in a line, used to direct the eye across the page. **—lead'er·less,** ***adj.*** **—lead'er·ship',** ***n.***

**lead-in** (lēd'in'), ***n.*** the wire leading from the aerial to a radio or television receiver or transmitter. **—lead'-in',** ***adj.***

**lead·ing** (led'iŋ), ***n.*** 1. a covering or being covered with lead. 2. strips or sheets of lead.

**lead·ing** (lēd'iŋ), ***n.*** direction; guidance. ***adj.*** 1. that leads; guiding. 2. principal; chief. 3. playing the lead in a play, motion picture, etc.

**leading light,** [Slang], one of the most important members of a club, community, etc.

**leading question,** a question put in such a way as to suggest the answer sought.

**lead-off** (lēd'ôf'), ***n.*** the first play, turn, etc., as in certain games and sports. **—lead'-off',** ***adj.***

**lead pencil** (led), a pencil consisting of a stick of graphite encased in wood, etc.

**lead poisoning,** an acute or chronic poisoning caused by the absorption of lead into the body.

**lead tetraethyl,** tetraethyl lead: see **ethyl.**

**leaf** (lēf), ***n.*** [*pl.* LEAVES (lēvz)], [AS. *leaf*], 1. any of the flat, thin, expanded organs, usually green, growing from the stem of a plant. 2. popularly, *a*) the blade of a leaf. *b*) a petal: as, a tulip *leaf*. 3. leaves collectively: as, choice tobacco *leaf*. 4. a sheet of paper with a page on each side. 5. *a*) a thin sheet of metal. *b*) such sheets collectively: as, gold *leaf*. 6. *a*) a hinged section of a table top. *b*) a board inserted into a table top to increase its surface. 7. a flat, hinged or movable part of a folding door, shutter, etc. ***v.i.*** to bear leaves (often with *out*). ***v.t.*** to turn the pages of (a book, etc.): often with *through*. **—in leaf,** with foliage. **—take a leaf from one's book,** to follow one's example. **—turn over a new leaf,** to make a new start. **—leaf'less,** ***adj.*** **—leaf'like',** ***adj.***

**leaf·age** (lēf'ij), ***n.*** leaves collectively; foliage.

**leaf lard,** lard made from the heavily flaked or layered fat (**leaf fat**) around the kidneys of a pig.

**leaf·let** (lēf'lit), ***n.*** 1. one of the divisions of a compound leaf. 2. a small or young leaf. 3. a separate sheet of printed matter, often folded but not stitched: as, propaganda *leaflets*.

**leaf·stalk** (lēf'stôk'), ***n.*** a petiole.

**leaf·y** (lēf'i), ***adj.*** [-IER, -IEST], 1. of, consisting of, or like a leaf or leaves. 2. having many leaves. 3. having broad leaves, as lettuce, spinach, etc. **—leaf'i·ness,** ***n.***

**league** (lēg), ***n.*** [< OFr. < It. < *legare* (< L. *ligare*), to bind], 1. a covenant made by nations, groups, or individuals for promoting common interests, etc. 2. an association or alliance formed by such a covenant. ***v.t. & v.i.*** [LEAGUED, LEAGUING], to form into a league. **—in league,** associated for a common purpose; allied. **—the League,** the League of Nations. **—lea'guer,** ***n.***

**league** (lēg), ***n.*** [< OFr. < LL. *leuga*, Gallic mile < Celt.], a measure of distance varying in different times and countries: in English-speaking countries it is usually about 3 miles.

**League of Nations,** an association of nations (1920–1946) to promote international co-operation and peace.

**Le·ah** (lē'ə), ***n.*** in the *Bible*, the elder of the two wives of Jacob: Gen. 29:13-30.

**leak** (lēk), ***v.i.*** [< ON. *leka*, to drip], 1. to let a fluid substance out or in accidentally: as, the ship *leaks*. 2. to enter or escape in this way, as a fluid (often with *in* or *out*). 3. to become known little by little: as, the truth *leaked* out. ***v.t.*** to allow to leak. ***n.*** 1. an accidental crack, hole, etc. that lets something out or in. 2. any means of escape for something that ought not to be let out, lost, etc. 3. leakage. 4. *a*) a loss of electrical charge through faulty insulation. *b*) the point where this occurs.

**leak·age** (lēk'ij), ***n.*** 1. a leaking in or out; leak. 2. something that leaks in or out. 3. the amount that leaks in or out.

**leak·y** (lēk'i), ***adj.*** [-IER, -IEST], having a leak or leaks. **—leak'i·ness,** ***n.***

**leal** (lēl), ***adj.*** [< OFr. *leal* < L. *legalis*], [Archaic or Scot.], loyal; true. **—leal'ly,** ***adv.***

**lean** (lēn), ***v.i.*** [LEANED or LEANT (lent), LEANING], [AS. *hlinian*], 1. to bend or deviate from an upright position; stand slanting; incline. 2. to bend the body so as to rest part of one's weight upon something: as, he *leaned* on the desk. 3. to rely; depend for advice, etc. (with *upon* or *on*). 4. to tend; favor slightly: as, to *lean* toward pacifism. ***v.t.*** to cause to stand slanting or to rest against something. ***n.*** a bend or deviation from the upright; incline; slant. **—lean over backward,** [Colloq.], to counterbalance a tendency, prejudice, etc. by an extreme effort in the opposite direction. **—lean'er,** ***n.***

**lean** (lēn), ***adj.*** [AS. *hlæne*], 1. with little flesh or fat; thin; spare: opposed to *fat*. 2. containing little or no fat: said of meat. 3. lacking in richness, gain, etc.; meager. ***n.*** meat containing little or no fat. **—lean'ly,** ***adv.*** **—lean'ness,** ***n.***

**Le·an·der** (li-an'dẽr), ***n.*** see **Hero.**

**lean·ing** (lēn'iŋ), ***n.*** 1. the act of a person or thing that leans. 2. tendency; inclination.

**lean-to** (lēn'tōō'), ***n.*** [*pl.* -TOS], 1. a shed with a sloping roof resting against trees, etc. 2. a structure, as the wing of a building, whose sloping roof abuts a wall or building.

**leap** (lēp), ***v.i.*** [LEAPED or LEAPT (lept, lēpt), LEAPING], [AS. *hleapan*], 1. to jump; spring. 2. to move suddenly or swiftly, as if by jumping; bound. ***v.t.*** 1. to pass over by a jump. 2. to cause to leap: as, to *leap* a horse over a fence. ***n.*** 1. a jump; spring; bound. 2. the distance covered in a jump. 3. a place that is, or is to be, leaped over or from. **—leap in the dark,** a risky act whose consequences cannot be foreseen. **—leap'er,** ***n.***

**leap·frog** (lēp'frôg', -frog'), ***n.*** a game in which each of the players takes a turn jumping over the bent backs of the other players.

**leap year,** a year of 366 days, occurring every fourth year: the additional day is given to February: a leap year is a year whose number is exactly divisible by four, or, in the case of century years, by 400.

**Lear** (lêr), ***n.*** King Lear.

**Lear, Edward** (lêr), 1812–1888; English humorist.

**learn** (lũrn), ***v.t.*** [LEARNED (lũrnd) or LEARNT (lũrnt), LEARNING], [AS. *leornian*], 1. to get knowledge of (a subject) or skill in (an art, trade, etc.) by study, experience, etc. 2. to come to know: as, I *learned* that he's here. 3. to come to know how: as, to *learn* to swim. 4. to memorize. 5. to acquire as a habit or attitude. 6. [Dial.], to teach. ***v.i.*** 1. to gain knowledge or skill. 2. to be informed; hear (*of*). **—learn'er,** ***n.***

**learn·ed** (lũr'nid), ***adj.*** 1. having or showing much learning; erudite. 2. characterized by or requiring study. **—learn'ed·ly,** ***adv.*** **—learn'ed·ness,** ***n.***

**learn·ing** (lũr'niŋ), ***n.*** 1. the acquiring of knowledge or skill. 2. acquired knowledge or skill.

**lease** (lēs), ***n.*** [< OFr. < L. *laxare*, to loosen < *laxus*, loose], 1. a contract by which a landlord gives to a tenant the use of lands, buildings, etc.

for a specified time and for fixed payments. 2. the period of time for which such a contract is in force. *v.t.* [LEASED, LEASING], 1. to give by a lease; let. 2. to get by a lease. —**leas′a·ble,** *adj.* —**leas′er,** *n.*

**leash** (lēsh), *n.* [< OFr. < L. *laxa*, fem. of *laxus*, loose], a cord, strap, etc. by which a dog or the like is held in check. *v.t.* to check or hold as by a leash. —**hold in leash,** to control. —**strain at the leash,** to be impatient to have freedom.

**least** (lēst), *adj.* [alt. superl. of *little*], [AS. *læst*, superl. of *læssa*, less], smallest in size, degree, importance, etc. *adv.* in the smallest degree. *n.* the smallest in size, amount, importance, etc. —**at (the) least,** 1. with no less. 2. at any rate. —**not in the least,** not at all.

**least·wise** (lēst′wīz′), *adv.* [Colloq.], at least; at any rate: also **least′ways′** (-wāz′).

**leath·er** (le*th*′ẽr), *n.* [AS. *lether-*], 1. animal skin prepared for use by removing the hair and tanning. 2. any of various articles made of this. *adj.* of or made of leather. *v.t.* 1. to cover or furnish with leather. 2. [Colloq.], to whip as with a leather strap.

**leath·ern** (le*th*′ẽrn), *adj.* 1. made of leather. 2. like leather.

**leath·er·neck** (le*th*′ẽr-nek′), *n.* [Slang], a U.S. marine.

**leath·er·y** (le*th*′ẽr-i), *adj.* like leather; tough and flexible. —**leath′er·i·ness,** *n.*

**leave** (lēv), *v.t.* [LEFT, LEAVING], [AS. *læfan*, lit., to let remain], 1. to allow to remain: as, *leave* some cake for me. 2. to make, place, etc., and cause to remain behind one: as, the dog *left* tracks on the rug. 3. to have remaining after one: as, the deceased *leaves* a widow. 4. to bequeath. 5. to let remain in a certain condition: as, *leave* the door open. 6. to go away from. 7. to abandon; forsake. 8. to stop living in, working for, or belonging to. 9. [Slang], to let: as, *leave* us go now. *v.i.* to go away or set out. —**leave off,** 1. to stop; cease. 2. to stop doing or using. —**leave one alone,** not to bother one. —**leave out,** 1. to omit. 2. to fail to consider; neglect. —**leav′er,** *n.*

**leave** (lēv), *n.* [AS. *leaf*], 1. permission. 2. permission to be absent from duty. 3. the period for which this is granted. —**by your leave,** with your permission. —**on leave,** absent from duty with permission. —**take leave of,** to say good-by to. —**take one's leave,** to depart.

**leave** (lēv), *v.i.* [LEAVED, LEAVING], [see LEAF], to put forth, or bear, leaves; leaf.

**leaved** (lēvd), *adj.* 1. in leaf. 2. having (a specified number or kind of) leaves: as, *oval-leaved*.

**leav·en** (lev′′n), *n.* [< OFr. < L. *levamen*, alleviation < *levare*, to raise], 1. *a*) a substance, such as yeast, used to produce fermentation, especially in dough. *b*) a small piece of fermenting dough put aside for this use. 2. any influence working on something to bring about a gradual change. *v.t.* 1. to produce fermentation in as by means of yeast; make (dough) rise. 2. to spread through, causing a gradual change.

**leav·en·ing** (lev′′n-iŋ), *n.* 1. a causing to ferment by leaven. 2. a thing that leavens.

**Leav·en·worth** (lev′′n-wũrth′), *n.* 1. a city in NE Kansas: pop., 22,000. 2. a Federal prison there.

**leave of absence,** a leave (*n.* sense 2).

**leaves** (lēvz), *n.* pl. of **leaf.**

**leave-tak·ing** (lēv′tāk′iŋ), *n.* the act of taking leave, or saying good-by.

**leav·ing** (lēv′iŋ), *n.* 1. *usually in pl.* a thing left; leftover; remnant. 2. *pl.* refuse; offal.

**Leb·a·non** (leb′ə-nən), *n.* a country in W Asia, on the Mediterranean: capital, Beirut; area, 3,400 sq. mi.; pop., 1,760,000. —**Leb′a·nese′** (-nēz′), *adj.* & *n.* [*pl.* -NESE].

‡**Le·bens·raum** (lā′bəns-roum′), *n.* [G.], living space; territory for political and economic expansion: term of German imperialism.

**lech·er** (lech′ẽr), *n.* [OFr. *leicheor*, debauchee, glutton < OHG. *leccōn*, to lick], a lewd, grossly sensual man.

**lech·er·ous** (lech′ẽr-əs), *adj.* lustful; lewd. —**lech′er·ous·ly,** *adv.* —**lech′er·ous·ness,** *n.*

**lech·er·y** (lech′ẽr-i), *n.* gross sensuality; lewdness.

**lec·i·thin** (les′ə-thin), *n.* [< Gr. *lekithos*, yolk of an egg], a nitrogenous, fatty substance found in animal tissue, egg yolk, and some vegetables: used in medicine, foods, etc.

**Le Cor·bu·sier** (lə kôr′bü′zyā′), (*Charles Edouard Jeanneret*), 1887–1965; Swiss architect in France.

**lec·tern** (lek′tẽrn), *n.* [< OFr. < LL. *lectrum* < L. pp. of *legere*, to read], 1. a reading desk in a church; esp., such a desk from which a part of the Scriptures is read during service. 2. a small stand for holding the notes, speech, etc., as of a lecturer.

**lec·ture** (lek′chẽr), *n.* [< L. *lectura* < pp. of *legere*, to read], 1. an informative talk given before an audience, class, etc., and usually prepared beforehand. 2. a lengthy scolding. *v.i.* [-TURED, -TURING], to give a lecture. *v.t.* 1. to give a lecture to. 2. to scold at length. —**lec′tur·er,** *n.* —**lec′ture·ship′,** *n.*

**led** (led), pt. and pp. of **lead** (to guide).

**Le·da** (lē′də), *n.* in *Gr. mythology*, the mother of Clytemnestra and (by Zeus, who visited her in the form of a swan) of Helen of Troy and Castor and Pollux.

**ledge** (lej), *n.* [ME. *legge*], 1. a shelf or shelflike projection. 2. a projecting ridge of rocks. 3. in *mining*, a vein.

**ledg·er** (lej′ẽr), *n.* [prob. < ME. *leggen*, to lay, or *liggen*, to lie], in *bookkeeping*, the book of final entry, in which a record of debits, credits, and all money transactions is kept.

**ledger line,** in *music*, a short line written above or below the staff, for notes beyond the range of the staff: also **leger line.**

**ledg·y** (lej′i), *adj.* [-IER, -IEST], having ledges.

**lee** (lē), *n.* [AS. *hleo*, shelter], 1. shelter; protection. 2. a sheltered place, especially one on the side away from the wind. 3. in *nautical usage*, the side or part away from the wind. *adj.* 1. of or on the side sheltered from the wind. 2. of or in the direction toward which the wind is blowing: opposed to *weather*.

**Lee, Henry** (lē), 1756–1818; American general in the Revolutionary War: called *Light-Horse Harry*.

**Lee, Robert Edward,** 1807–1870; son of *Henry;* commander in chief of the Confederate army.

**leech** (lēch), *n.* [AS. *læce*], 1. formerly, a physician. 2. any of a number of bloodsucking worms living in water or wet earth and used, especially in former times, to bleed patients. 3. a person who clings to another to get some gain out of him. *v.t.* to bleed with leeches.

LEECH (2–4 in. long)

**leech** (lēch), *n.* [ME. *lich*], the free or outside edge of a sail.

**Leeds** (lēdz), *n.* a city in Yorkshire, England: pop., 514,000.

**leek** (lēk), *n.* [AS. *leac*], a vegetable related to the onion but of milder flavor, with a cylindrical bulb and long, broad, succulent leaves.

**leer** (lêr), *n.* [AS. *hleor*], a sly, sidelong look showing ill will, lustfulness, etc. *v.i.* to look with a leer. —**leer′ing·ly,** *adv.*

**leer·y** (lêr′i), *adj.* [Colloq.], wary; suspicious.

**lees** (lēz), *n.pl.* [< OFr. *lie* < ML. *lia*], dregs; grounds; sediment, as of wine.

**lee·ward** (lē′wẽrd; *in nautical usage,* lo͞o′ẽrd), *adj.* in the direction toward which the wind blows; of the lee side: opposed to *windward*. *n.* the lee part or side. *adv.* toward the lee.

**Lee·ward Islands** (lē′wẽrd), 1. the northern group of islands in the Lesser Antilles, in the West Indies. 2. a British colony made up of some of these islands.

**lee·way** (lē′wā′), *n.* 1. the leeward drift of a ship or aircraft from its course. 2. [Colloq.], *a*) margin of time, money, etc. *b*) room for freedom of action.

**left** (left), *adj.* [ME. var. of *lift*], 1. *a*) of or designating that side of one's body which is toward the west when one faces north, usually the side of the less-used hand. *b*) of or designating the corresponding side of anything. *c*) closer to the left side of a person directly facing the thing mentioned. 2. of the political left; liberal or radical. *n.* 1. all or part of the left side. 2. in *boxing*, *a*) the left hand. *b*) a blow delivered with the left hand. 3. [often L-], in *politics*, a liberal or radical position, party, etc. (often with *the*): from the location of their seats in some European legislatures. *adv.* on or toward the left hand or side.

**left** (left), pt. and pp. of **leave** (to go away).

**left-hand** (left′hand′), *adj.* 1. on or directed toward the left. 2. of, for, or with the left hand.

**left-hand·ed** (left′han′did), *adj.* 1. using the left hand more skillfully than the right. 2. done with the left hand. 3. clumsy; awkward. 4. insincere; dubious: as, a *left-handed* compliment. 5. made for use with the left hand. 6. turning from right to left. ***adv.*** with the left hand: as, he writes *left-handed.* **—left′-hand′ed·ly,** ***adv.*** **—left′-hand′ed·ness,** ***n.***

**left·ist** (lef′tist), ***n.*** in *politics,* a person who is liberal or radical; member of the left. ***adj.*** in *politics,* liberal or radical.

**left·o·ver** (left′ō′vẽr), ***n.*** something left over, as from a meal. ***adj.*** remaining unused, etc.

**left wing,** in *politics,* the more liberal or radical section of a party, group, etc. **—left′-wing′,** ***adj.*** **—left′-wing′er,** ***n.***

**left·y** (lef′ti), ***n.*** [*pl.* -IES], [Slang], a left-handed person: often used as a nickname.

**leg** (leg), ***n.*** [ON. *leggr*], 1. one of the parts of the body by means of which men and animals stand and walk. 2. the part of a garment covering the leg. 3. anything resembling a leg in shape or use, as one of the supports of a piece of furniture. 4. the run made by a sailing vessel on one tack. 5. one of the stages of a journey, etc. 6. in *mathematics,* any of the sides of a triangle other than its base or hypotenuse. ***v.i.*** [LEGGED, LEGGING], [Colloq.], to walk or run (usually with *it*): as, we had to *leg* it back. **—have not a leg to stand on,** [Colloq.], to have absolutely no defense, excuse, etc. **—on one's last legs,** [Colloq.], not far from death, failure, etc. **—pull one's leg,** [Colloq.], to make fun of or fool one. **—shake a leg,** [Slang], to hurry. **—stretch one's legs,** to walk, especially after sitting a long time. **—leg′less,** ***adj.***

**leg.,** 1. legal. 2. legislative. 3. legislature.

**leg·a·cy** (leg′ə-si), ***n.*** [*pl.* -CIES], [< OFr. *legacie* < ML. < L. *legatus;* see LEGATE], 1. money or property left to someone by a will. 2. anything handed down from, or as from, an ancestor.

**le·gal** (lē′g'l), ***adj.*** [< Fr. < L. *legalis* < *lex,* law], 1. of, based on, or authorized by law. 2. permitted by law: as, a *legal* act. 3. that can be enforced in a court of law: cf. *equitable.* 4. of or applicable to lawyers: as, *legal* ethics. 5. in terms of the law: as, a *legal* offense. **—le′gal·ly,** ***adv.***

**le·gal·ism** (lē′g'l-iz'm), ***n.*** strict, often too strict and literal, adherence to law. **—le′gal·ist,** ***n.*** **—le′gal·is′tic,** ***adj.***

**le·gal·i·ty** (li-gal′ə-ti), ***n.*** [*pl.* -TIES], quality, condition, or instance of being legal or lawful.

**le·gal·ize** (lē′g'l-īz′), ***v.t.*** [-IZED, -IZING], to make legal or lawful. **—le′gal·i·za′tion,** ***n.***

**legal tender,** money which the law requires a creditor to accept in payment of a debt.

**leg·ate** (leg′it), ***n.*** [< OFr. < L. pp. of *legare,* to send as ambassador < *lex,* law], an envoy or ambassador, especially one officially representing the Pope. **—leg′ate·ship′,** ***n.***

**leg·a·tee** (leg′ə-tē′), ***n.*** one to whom a legacy is bequeathed.

**le·ga·tion** (li-gā′shən), ***n.*** 1. a legate and his staff, representing their government in a foreign country and ranking just below an embassy. 2. the building housing such a legation.

**le·ga·to** (li-gä′tō), ***adj. & adv.*** [It., pp. of *legare* < L. *ligare,* to tie], in *music,* in a smooth, even style, with no noticeable interruption between the notes.

**leg·end** (lej′ənd), ***n.*** [< OFr. < ML. *legenda,* things read < L. < *legere,* to read], 1. a story of some wonderful event, handed down for generations and popularly believed to have a historical basis: cf. *myth.* 2. all such stories belonging to a particular group of people. 3. an inscription on a coin, medal, etc. 4. a title, key, etc. accompanying an illustration or map.

**leg·end·ar·y** (lej′ən-der′i), ***adj.*** of, based on, or presented in a legend or legends; traditional.

**leg·end·ry** (lej′ən-dri), ***n.*** legends collectively.

**leg·er·de·main** (lej′ẽr-di-mān′), ***n.*** [Fr. *léger de main,* lit., light of hand], 1. sleight of hand; tricks of a stage magician. 2. trickery; deceit. **—leg′er·de·main′ist,** ***n.***

**leg·ged** (leg′id, legd), ***adj.*** having (a specified number or kind of) legs: as, *long-legged.*

**leg·ging** (leg′iŋ), ***n.*** *usually in pl.* a covering of canvas, leather, etc. for protecting the leg below the knee.

**leg·gy** (leg′i), ***adj.*** [-IER, -IEST], having long, or long and awkward, legs; as, a *leggy* colt.

**Leg·horn** (leg′hôrn′; *for* 2 & 3, *usually* leg′ẽrn), ***n.*** 1. a seaport in W Italy: pop., 146,000. 2. [sometimes l-], any of a breed of small chicken. 3. [l-], *a*) a plaiting made of an Italian wheat straw. *b*) a wide-brimmed hat of this straw.

**leg·i·ble** (lej′ə-b'l), ***adj.*** [< LL. *legibilis* < *legere,* to read], 1. that can be read or deciphered. 2. that can be read easily. **—leg′i·bil′i·ty, leg′i·ble·ness,** ***n.*** **—leg′i·bly,** ***adv.***

**le·gion** (lē′jən), ***n.*** [< OFr. < L. *legio* < *legere,* to select], 1. in ancient Rome, a military division varying at times from 3,000 to 6,000 foot soldiers, with additional cavalrymen. 2. a large group of soldiers; army. 3. a large number; multitude.

**le·gion·ar·y** (lē′jən-er′i), ***adj.*** of or constituting a legion. ***n.*** [*pl.* -IES], a member of a legion.

**le·gion·naire** (lē′jən-âr′), ***n.*** [< Fr.], a member of a legion.

**leg·is·late** (lej′is-lāt′), ***v.i.*** [-LATED, -LATING], [< *legislator*], to make or pass a law or laws. ***v.t.*** to cause to become, go, etc. by making laws: as, we cannot *legislate* evil out of existence.

**leg·is·la·tion** (lej′is-lā′shən), ***n.*** 1. the making of a law or laws. 2. the law or laws made.

**leg·is·la·tive** (lej′is-lā′tiv), ***adj.*** 1. of legislation. 2. having the power to make laws: as, a *legislative* assembly. 3. enforced by legislation. ***n.*** a legislature. **—leg′is·la′tive·ly,** ***adv.***

**leg·is·la·tor** (lej′is-lā′tẽr), ***n.*** [L. *legis lator; legis,* genit. of *lex,* law + *lator,* proposer], a member of a legislative assembly; lawmaker.

**leg·is·la·ture** (lej′is-lā′chẽr), ***n.*** a body of persons given the responsibility and power to make laws for a country or state.

**le·git** (li-jit′), ***n.*** [Slang], the legitimate theater, drama, etc. ***adj.*** [Slang], legitimate.

**le·git·i·ma·cy** (li-jit′ə-mə-si), ***n.*** a being legitimate: also **le·git′i·mate·ness.**

**le·git·i·mate** (li-jit′ə-mit; *for v.,* -māt′), ***adj.*** [< ML. pp. of *legitimare,* to make lawful; ult. < L. *lex,* law], 1. born of parents legally married to each other. 2. lawful; allowed: as, a *legitimate* claim. 3. ruling by the rights of heredity: as, a *legitimate* king. 4. reasonable; logically correct: as, a *legitimate* inference. 5. in the *theater,* designating or of stage plays, as distinguished from motion pictures, vaudeville, etc. ***v.t.*** [-MATED, -MATING], 1. to make or declare legitimate. 2. to justify or authorize. **—le·git′i·mate·ly,** ***adv.*** **—le·git′i·ma′tion,** ***n.***

**le·git·i·ma·tize** (li-jit′ə-mə-tīz′), ***v.t.*** [-TIZED, -TIZING], to legitimate. **—le·git′i·ma·ti·za′tion,** ***n.***

**le·git·i·mist** (li-jit′ə-mist), ***n.*** a supporter of legitimate authority or, especially, of claims to monarchy based on the rights of heredity. **—le·git′i·mism,** ***n.*** **—le·git′i·mis′tic,** ***adj.***

**le·git·i·mize** (li-jit′ə-mīz′), ***v.t.*** [-MIZED, -MIZING], to legitimate. **—le·git′i·mi·za′tion,** ***n.***

**leg-of-mut·ton** (leg′ə-mut′'n, leg′əv-), ***adj.*** shaped like a leg of mutton; much larger at one end than the other, as a sleeve, sail, etc.

**leg·ume** (leg′ūm, li-gūm′), ***n.*** [< Fr. < L. *legumen* < *legere,* to gather], 1. any plant of the pea family, characterized by true pods enclosing seeds: legumes are able to store up nitrates. 2. the edible fruit of any plant of the pea family; pod or its seed.

**le·gu·mi·nous** (li-gū′mi-nəs), ***adj.*** 1. of, having the nature of, or bearing legumes. 2. of the group of plants to which peas and beans belong.

**leg work,** [Colloq.], research or investigation, as by a reporter (**leg man**), that serves as the basis for a news story, article, etc.

**Le Ha·vre** (lə å′vr′; Eng. lə hä′vẽr), Havre, a seaport in France: the French name.

**le·i** (lā, lā′i), ***n.*** [*pl.* -IS], [Haw.], in Hawaii, a garland or wreath of flowers and leaves.

**Leib·nitz,** Baron **Gott·fried Wil·helm von** (gôt′frēt vil′helm fôn līp′nits), 1646–1716; German philosopher and mathematician.

**Leices·ter** (les′tẽr), ***n.*** a city in central England: pop., 286,000.

**Leicester,** Earl of, (*Robert Dudley*), 1532?–1588; English courtier; favorite of Queen Elizabeth I.

**Lei·den** (lī′d'n), ***n.*** a university city in the W Netherlands: pop., 92,000: also sp. **Leyden.**

**Leip·zig** (līp′sig, -sik; G. -tsikh), ***n.*** a city in East Germany: pop., 608,000.

**lei·sure** (lē′zhẽr, lezh′ẽr), ***n.*** [< OFr. < L. *licere,* to be permitted], free, unoccupied time during which one may indulge in rest, recreation, etc. ***adj.*** 1. free and unoccupied; spare: as, *leisure* time. 2. having much leisure: as, the *leisure* class. **—at leisure,** 1. having free time. 2. with no hurry. 3. not occupied or engaged. **—at one's leisure,** when it is convenient for one.

**lei·sured** (lē′zhẽrd, lezh′ẽrd), ***adj.*** 1. having leisure. 2. without haste; leisurely.

**lei·sure·ly** (lē′zhẽr-li, lezh′ẽr-), ***adj.*** without haste; deliberate; slow. ***adv.*** in an unhurried manner. **—lei′sure·li·ness,** ***n.***

**leit·mo·tiv, leit·mo·tif** (līt′mō-tēf′), ***n.*** [< G. < *leiten,* to lead + *motiv,* motif], a short musical phrase representing and recurring with a given character, situation, etc. in an opera.

**lem·an** (lem′ən, lē′mən), ***n.*** [ME. *lemman* < *lef,* dear + *man*], [Archaic], a sweetheart or lover (man or woman); esp., a mistress.

**Le·man, Lake** (lē′mən), Lake Geneva.

**Lem·berg** (lem′berkh; Eng. -bẽrg), *n.* Lvov, a city in U.S.S.R.: the German name.

**lem·ming** (lem′iŋ), *n.* [*pl.* -MINGS, -MING; see PLURAL, II, D, 1], [Norw.], a small arctic rodent resembling the mouse but having a short tail and fur-covered feet.

**lem·on** (lem′ən), *n.* [< OFr. < Sp. < Ar. *laimūn* < Per. *līmūn*], 1. a small, edible citrus fruit with a pale-yellow rind and a juicy, sour pulp. 2. the small, spiny, semitropical tree that it grows on. 3. [Slang], something or someone undesirable or inadequate. *adj.* 1. pale-yellow. 2. made with or from lemons.

**lem·on·ade** (lem′ən-ād′), *n.* a drink made of lemon juice, sugar, and water.

**le·mur** (lē′mẽr), *n.* [< L. *lemures*, ghosts], a mammal related to the monkey, with large eyes and soft, woolly fur, found mainly in Madagascar.

**lend** (lend), *v.t.* [LENT, LENDING], [AS. *lænan* < *læn*, a loan], 1. to let another use or have (a thing) temporarily. 2. to let out (money) at interest. 3. to give; impart: as, to *lend* an air of mystery. *v.i.* to make a loan or loans. **—lend itself** (or **oneself**) **to,** to be useful for or open to. **—lend′er,** *n.*

**lending library,** a library from which books can be borrowed, usually for a fee.

**lend-lease** (lend′lēs′), *n.* in World War II, material aid in the form of munitions, tools, food, etc., granted to foreign countries whose defense was deemed vital to the defense of the U.S.

**length** (leŋkth, leŋth), *n.* [< AS. < base of *lang*, long], 1. the measure of how long a thing is from end to end; the greatest dimension of anything. 2. extent in space or time. 3. a long stretch or extent. 4. the fact or state of being long. 5. a piece of a certain length: as, a *length* of pipe. 6. a unit of measure consisting of the length of an object or animal in a race: as, the boat won by two *lengths*. **—at full length,** completely extended. **—at length,** 1. finally. 2. in full. **—go to any length,** to do whatever is necessary. **—keep at arm's length,** to act coldly toward.

**length·en** (leŋk′th'n, leŋ′-), *v.t. & v.i.* to make or become longer.

**length·wise** (leŋkth′wīz′, leŋth′-), *adv. & adj.* in the direction of the length: also **length′ways′** (-wāz′).

**length·y** (leŋk′thi, leŋ′-), *adj.* [-IER, -IEST], 1. long; esp., too long. 2. [Colloq.], tall: said of a person. **—length′i·ly,** *adv.* **—length′i·ness,** *n.*

**le·ni·en·cy** (lē′ni-ən-si, lēn′yən-), *n.* 1. the quality or condition of being lenient. 2. [*pl.* -CIES], a lenient act. Also **le′ni·ence.**

**le·ni·ent** (lē′ni-ənt, lēn′yənt), *adj.* [< L. ppr. of *lenire*, to soften < *lenis*, soft], not harsh or severe; mild; merciful; gentle. **—le′ni·ent·ly,** *adv.*

**Len·in, V. I.** (len′in), (born *Vladimir Ilich Ulianov*), 1870–1924; Russian revolutionary and Communist leader; premier of U.S.S.R. (1918–1924): also **Nikolai Lenin.**

**Len·in·grad** (len′in-grad′, -gräd′), *n.* a seaport in NW U.S.S.R.: pop., 3,665,000: formerly called *Petrograd, St. Petersburg.*

**Len·in·ism** (len′in-iz'm), *n.* the communist theories and policies of Lenin, including his theory of the dictatorship of the proletariat. **—Len′in·ist, Len′in·ite′,** *adj. & n.*

**len·i·tive** (len′ə-tiv), *adj.* [< ML. < L. pp. of *lenire*, to soften], softening, soothing, lessening pain, etc. *n.* a lenitive medicine, etc.

**len·i·ty** (len′ə-ti), *n.* [< OFr. < L. < *lenis*, mild], 1. a being lenient; gentleness; mercifulness. 2. [*pl.* -TIES], a lenient act.

**lens** (lenz), *n.* [L., lentil: a biconvex lens is shaped like the seed], 1. a piece of glass, or other transparent substance, with two curved surfaces, or one plane and one curved, bringing together or spreading rays of light passing through it: lenses are used in optical instruments to form an image. 2. a combination of two or more lenses. 3. a transparent, biconvex body of the eye: it focuses upon the retina light rays entering the pupil.

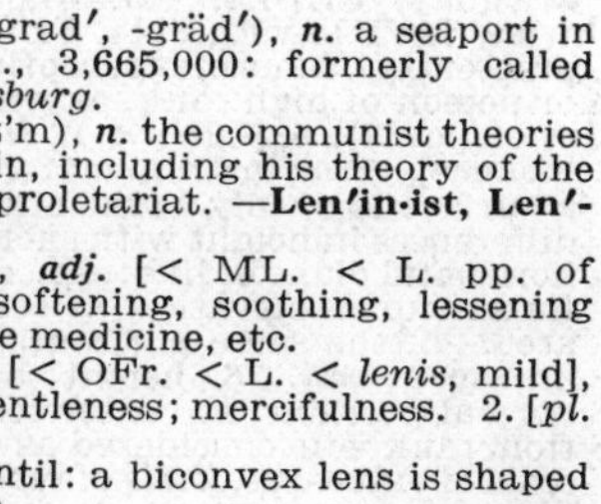

LENS

**Lent** (lent), *n.* [AS. *lengten*, the spring < *lang*, long: from the lengthening spring days], the period of forty weekdays from Ash Wednesday to Easter, observed in Christian churches by fasting and penitence.

**lent** (lent), pt. and pp. of **lend.**

**-lent,** [L. *-lentus*, -ful], a suffix meaning *full of, characterized by*, as in *virulent, fraudulent.*

**Lent·en, lent·en** (len′tən), *adj.* of, connected with, or suitable for Lent.

**len·til** (len′t'l, -til), *n.* [< Fr. < L. *lenticula*, dim. of *lens*, lentil], 1. a plant of the pea family, with small, edible seeds shaped like double-convex lenses. 2. the seed of this plant.

**len·to** (len′tō), *adv. & adj.* [It. < L. *lentus*, slow], in *music*, slow.

**l'en·voi, l'en·voy** (len′voi, len-voi′; Fr. län′vwȧ′), *n.* [Fr. < *le*, the + *envoi*, a sending], a concluding stanza added to a ballade and some other verse forms: also **envoy.**

**Le·o** (lē′ō), *n.* [L., lion], 1. a northern constellation supposedly outlining a lion. 2. the fifth sign of the zodiac (♌), entered by the sun about July 22.

**Leo XIII,** 1810–1903; Pope (1878–1903).

**Le·ón** (le-ôn′), *n.* a former province of NW Spain.

**Le·o·nid** (lē′ə-nid), *n.* [*pl.* -NIDS, -NIDES (li-on′ə-dēz′)], any of a shower of meteors visible yearly about November 15, appearing to radiate from the constellation Leo.

**le·o·nine** (lē′ə-nīn′), *adj.* [< OFr. < L. < *leo*, lion], of, characteristic of, or like a lion.

**leop·ard** (lep′ẽrd), *n.* [*pl.* -ARDS, -ARD; see PLURAL, II, D, 1], [< OFr. < LL. < Gr. *leopardos* < *leōn*, lion + *pardos*, panther], 1. a large, ferocious animal of the cat family, with a black-spotted tawny coat, found in Africa and Asia. 2. the jaguar, or American leopard. **—leop′ard·ess,** *n.fem.*

**lep·er** (lep′ẽr), *n.* [< OFr. < L. < Gr. *lepra* < *lepros*, scaly], a person having leprosy.

**lep·i·dop·ter·ous** (lep′ə-dop′tẽr-əs), *adj.* [< Gr. *lepis*, a scale + *pteron*, a wing], of a large group of insects, including the butterflies and moths, characterized by two pairs of broad, membranous wings covered with very fine scales: also **lep′i·dop′ter·al.** **—lep′i·dop′ter·an,** *adj. & n.*

**lep·re·chaun** (lep′rə-kôn′; Ir. lep′rə-khôn′), *n.* [Ir. *lupracān* < OIr. < *lu*, little + dim. of *corp* (< L. *corpus*), body], in *Irish folklore*, a fairy in the form of a little old man who can reveal hidden treasure to anyone who catches him.

**lep·ro·sy** (lep′rə-si), *n.* [< OFr. < LL.; see LEPER], a chronic infectious disease of the skin, tissues, or nerves, characterized by ulcers, white scaly scabs, deformities, and wasting of body parts.

**lep·rous** (lep′rəs), *adj.* [< OFr. < LL. *leprosus* < L. *lepra* < Gr.; see LEPER], 1. of or like leprosy. 2. having leprosy. **—lep′rous·ly,** *adv.*

**-lep·sy** (lep′si), [< Gr. *-lēpsia*], a combining form meaning *a fit, attack*, as in *catalepsy:* also **-lep′si·a.**

**Les·bi·an** (lez′bi-ən), *adj.* [in allusion to Sappho and her followers, in Lesbos], homosexual: said only of women. *n.* a homosexual woman.

**Les·bi·an·ism** (lez′bi-ən-iz'm), *n.* homosexuality between women.

**Les·bos** (lez′bəs, -bos), *n.* Mytilene, an island in the Aegean: the ancient name.

**lese maj·es·ty** (lēz′ maj′is-ti), [< Fr. < L. fem. of *laesus*, pp. of *laedere*, to hurt + *majestas*, majesty], a crime against the sovereign; treason: also **leze majesty.**

**le·sion** (lē′zhən), *n.* [< Fr. < L. pp. of *laedere*, to harm], 1. an injury; hurt. 2. an injury, etc. of an organ or tissue of the body resulting in impairment or loss of function.

**Le·sot·ho** (le-sut′hō, -sō′thō), *n.* a country in SE Africa, surrounded by South Africa: area, 11,716 sq. mi.; pop., 975,000.

**less** (les), *adj.* [alt. compar. of *little*], [AS. *læs(sa)*], not so much, so great, so many, etc.; smaller; fewer. *adv.* [compar. of *little*], not so much; to a smaller extent. *n.* a smaller amount. *prep.* minus: as, total income *less* earned income. **—no less a person than,** a person of no lower importance, rank, etc. than.

**-less** (lis), [AS. *-leas* < *leas*, free], a suffix meaning: 1. *without, lacking*, as in *valueless*. 2. *not* ——*ing*, as in *tireless*. 3. *not capable of being*——*ed*, as in *dauntless.*

**les·see** (les-ē′), *n.* [< OFr. pp. of *lesser*, to lease], one to whom a lease is given; tenant.

**less·en** (les′'n), *v.t.* 1. to make less; decrease. 2. to belittle; depreciate. *v.i.* to become less.

**less·er** (les′ẽr), *adj.* [alt. compar. of *little*], [*less* + *-er*], smaller, less, or less important.

**Lesser Antilles,** a group of islands in the West

Indies, southeast of Puerto Rico, including the Leeward Islands and the Windward Islands.
**Lesser Bear,** Ursa Minor.
**les·son** (les′'n), *n.* [< OFr. *leçon* < L. < pp. of *legere*, to read], 1. something to be learned; specif., *a*) an exercise that a student is to prepare or learn. *b*) something that needs to be learned for one's safety, etc. *c*) *pl.* course of instruction: as, music *lessons*. 2. a selection from the Bible, read as part of a church service. 3. a lecture; rebuke. *v.t.* 1. to give a lesson or lessons to. 2. to rebuke; reprove.
**les·sor** (les′ôr, les-ôr′), *n.* [Anglo-Fr. < *lesser*, to lease], one who gives a lease; landlord.
**lest** (lest), *conj.* [< AS. < *thy læs the*, lit., by the less that], 1. for fear that; in case: as, we spoke low *lest* we be overheard. 2. that: after expressions denoting fear, as, I was afraid *lest* he should fall.
**let** (let), *v.t.* [LET or *obs.* LETTED, LETTING], [AS. *lætan*, to leave behind], 1. to leave; abandon: now only in *let alone, let be.* 2. *a*) to rent; hire out. *b*) to assign (a contract). 3. to allow or cause to escape: as, *let* blood. 4. to allow to pass, come, or go. 5. to allow; permit: as, *let* me think. 6. to cause: usually with *know* or *hear*, as, *let* me hear from you. 7. to suppose; assume. When used in commands or suggestions, *let* serves as an auxiliary: as, *let* us go. *v.i.* to be rented or leased: as, this place *lets* for $53 a month. **—let alone,** 1. to refrain from disturbing, touching, etc. 2. not to mention; much less: as, he can't walk, *let alone* run. **—let be,** to have nothing to do with. **—let down,** 1. to lower. 2. to slow up. 3. to disappoint. **—let in,** to allow to come, pass, etc.; admit. **—let off,** 1. to give forth, as steam. 2. to deal leniently with. **—let on,** [Colloq.], 1. to pretend. 2. to indicate one's awareness of some fact. **—let out,** 1. to release. 2. to rent out. 3. to reveal (a secret, etc.). 4. to make a garment larger by reducing (the hem, etc.). 5. [Colloq.], to dismiss or be dismissed, as school. **—let up,** 1. to relax. 2. to cease.
**let** (let), *v.t.* [LETTED or LET, LETTING], [AS. *lettan*, lit., to make late], [Archaic], to hinder; obstruct. *n.* 1. an obstacle; hindrance: usually in *without let or hindrance*. 2. in *tennis*, etc., an interference with the course of the ball in some specific way, making it necessary to play the point over again.
**-let,** [< Fr. *-el* (< L. *-ellus*) + *-et*, both dim. suffixes], a suffix, generally meaning *small*, as in *ringlet:* used in some words (e.g., *anklet, armlet*) to mean *small object worn as a band on.*
**let·down** (let′doun′), *n.* 1. a slowing up or slackening, as after great excitement, effort, etc. 2. [Colloq.], a disappointment or disillusionment.
**le·thal** (lē′thəl), *adj.* [< L. *let(h)alis* < *let(h)um*, death], 1. causing death; fatal; deadly. 2. of or suggestive of death. **—le′thal·ly,** *adv.*
**le·thar·gic** (li-thär′jik), *adj.* 1. of or producing lethargy. 2. abnormally drowsy; dull; sluggish. Also **le·thar′gi·cal.** **—le·thar′gi·cal·ly,** *adv.*
**leth·ar·gize** (leth′ēr-jīz′), *v.t.* [-GIZED, -GIZING], to make lethargic.
**leth·ar·gy** (leth′ēr-ji), *n.* [*pl.* -GIES], [< OFr. < LL. < Gr. *lēthargos*, forgetful < *lēthē;* see LETHE], 1. *a*) an abnormal drowsiness; great lack of energy. *b*) a prolonged and unnatural sleep. 2. total indifference; apathy.
**Le·the** (lē′thi), *n.* [L. < Gr. *lēthē*, oblivion], 1. in *Gr. & Rom. mythology*, the river of forgetfulness, in Hades, whose water produced loss of memory in those who drank of it. 2. oblivion; forgetfulness. **—Le·the·an** (lē-thē′ən), *adj.*
**let's** (lets), let us.
**Lett** (let), *n.* 1. a member of a people living in Latvia and adjacent Baltic regions. 2. Lettish.
**let·ter** (let′ēr), *n.* [< OFr. < L. *littera*], 1. any of the characters of the alphabet, theoretically representing a speech sound. 2. a written or printed message, usually sent by mail. 3. an official document giving certain authorities or privileges. 4. literal meaning; exact wording. 5. the first letter of the name of a school or college, awarded and worn for superior activity in sports, etc. *v.t.* 1. to mark with letters: as, to *letter* a poster. 2. to set down in hand-printed letters. *v.i.* to make hand-printed letters. **—letters,** 1. literature generally. 2. learning; knowledge, especially of literature. 3. the profession of a writer. **—to the letter,** just as written or directed; exactly. **—let′ter·er,** *n.*
**let·tered** (let′ērd), *adj.* 1. able to read and write; literate. 2. very well educated. 3. inscribed with letters.
**let·ter·head** (let′ēr-hed′), *n.* 1. the name, address, etc. of a person or firm printed as a heading on letter paper. 2. a sheet of letter paper with such a heading.
**let·ter·ing** (let′ēr-iŋ), *n.* 1. the act of making letters or of inscribing in or with letters, as by hand-printing. 2. letters so made or inscribed.
**letter of credit,** a letter from a bank asking that the holder of the letter be allowed to draw specified sums of money from other banks or agencies.
**let·ter-per·fect** (let′ēr-pũr′fikt), *adj.* 1. correct in every respect. 2. knowing one's lines, part, or lesson perfectly: said of an actor, etc.
**let·ter·press** (let′ēr-pres′), *n.* printed words; esp., reading matter, as distinguished from illustrations.
**letter press,** a device for making copies of letters.
**letters** (or **letter**) **of marque,** a governmental document authorizing an individual to arm a ship and capture the merchant ships of an enemy nation: also **letters** (or **letter**) **of marque and reprisal.**
**letters pat·ent** (pat′'nt), a document issued by a government to a person, authorizing him to perform some act or to enjoy some privilege.
**Let·tish** (let′ish), *adj.* of the Letts or their language. *n.* the Baltic language of the Letts. Abbrev. **Lett.**
**let·tuce** (let′is), *n.* [< OFr. < L. *lactuca* < *lac*, milk: from its milky juice], 1. a plant of the composite family, with crisp, green leaves; esp., *head lettuce* (in cabbagelike form) or *leaf lettuce* (with spread leaves). 2. the leaves, much used for salads. 3. [Slang], paper money.
**let·up** (let′up′), *n.* [Colloq.], 1. a slackening; lessening. 2. a stop; pause; cessation.
**le·u** (le′oo), *n.* [*pl.* LEI (lā)], [Romanian < L. *leo*, lion], the monetary unit and a silver coin of Romania: also **ley.**
**leu·ce·mi·a, leu·cae·mi·a** (lōō-sē′mi-ə), *n.* leukemia.
**leu·co-** [< Gr. *leukos*, white], a combining form meaning *white* or *colorless*, as in *leucocyte:* also **leuc-**: now often spelled **leuk-** or **leuko-.**
**leu·co·cyte** (lōō′kə-sīt′), *n.* [*leuco-* + *-cyte*], any of the small, colorless cells in the blood, lymph, and tissues, which destroy organisms that cause disease; white blood corpuscle.
**leu·ke·mi·a, leu·kae·mi·a** (lōō-kē′mi-ə), *n.* [see LEUCO- & -EMIA], a disease of the blood-forming tissues, characterized by an abnormal and persistent increase in the number of leucocytes.
**Lev.,** Leviticus.
**Le·vant** (lə-vant′), *n.* [Fr. *levant* (ult. < L. *levare*, to raise), rising (of the sun)], 1. the regions on the E Mediterranean and the Aegean, from Greece to Egypt. 2. [l-], Levant morocco. **—Le·van·tine** (-van′tin, lev′ən-tīn′), *adj. & n.*
**Levant morocco,** a fine morocco leather with a large, irregular grain, used in bookbinding.
**le·va·tor** (lə-vā′tēr), *n.* [*pl.* -TORES (lev′ə-tôr′ēz, -tō′rēz)], [Mod. L. < pp. of *levare*, to raise], a muscle that raises a limb or other part of the body.
**lev·ee** (lev′i), *n.* [< Fr. pp. of *lever* (< L. *levare*), to raise], 1. an embankment built alongside a river to prevent high water from flooding bordering land. 2. a quay. *v.t.* [-EED, -EEING], to build a levee along.
**lev·ee** (lev′i, lə-vē′), *n.* [< Fr. < *se lever*, to rise; see prec. entry], a morning reception held by a sovereign or person of high rank, as when arising.
**lev·el** (lev′'l), *n.* [OFr. < L. *libella*, dim. of *libra*, a balance], 1. an instrument for determining whether a surface is evenly horizontal. 2. a measuring of differences in height with such an instrument. 3. a horizontal plane or line; esp., such a plane as a basis for measuring elevation: as, sea *level.* 4. a horizontal area. 5. the same horizontal plane: as, the seats are on a *level.* 6. height; altitude. 7. usual or normal position: as, water seeks its *level.* 8. position, rank, etc. considered as one of the planes in a scale of values: as, *levels* of reading. *adj.* 1. perfectly flat and even. 2. not sloping. 3. even in height (*with*). 4. not heaping: as, a *level* teaspoonful. 5. *a*) equal in importance, rank, degree, etc. *b*) equally advanced in development. *c*) uniform in tone, color, pitch, volume, etc. 6. well balanced; equable. *adv.* on a level line. *v.t.* [-ELED or -ELLED, -ELING or -ELLING], 1. to make level, even, flat, equal (as in rank), etc. 2. to knock to the ground; demolish. 3. to raise and aim (a gun, etc.). *v.i.* 1. to aim a gun or other weapon (with *at*). 2. to bring people or things to an equal rank, condition, etc. (usually with *down* or *up*). 3. [Slang], to be frank and honest (*with* someone). **—find one's** (or **its**) **level,** to reach one's proper or natural place. **—level off,** 1. to give a flat, horizontal surface to. 2. in *aviation*, to come, or bring, to a horizontal position just before landing. **—one's level best,** [Colloq.], the best one can do. **—on the level,** [Slang], honest(ly) and fair(ly).**—lev′el·er, lev′el·ler,** *n.* **—lev′el·ly,** *adv.* **—lev′el·ness,** *n.*
**lev·el-head·ed** (lev′'l-hed′id), *adj.* having or showing an even temper and sound judgment.

**lev·er** (lev′ẽr, lē′vẽr), *n.* [< OFr. *leveour* < *lever* < L. *levare*, to raise], 1. a bar used as a pry. 2. in *mechanics*, a device consisting of a bar turning about a fixed point, the fulcrum, using power or force applied at a second point to lift or sustain a weight at a third point. *v.t.* to move, lift, etc. with a lever. *v.i.* to use a lever. —**lev′er-like′**, *adj.*

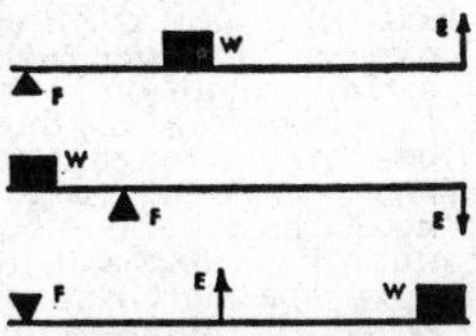

TYPES OF LEVER
E, energy; F, fulcrum; W, weight

**lev·er·age** (lev′ẽr-ij, lē′vẽr-), *n.* 1. the action of a lever. 2. the mechanical power resulting from this. 3. increased means of effecting an aim.

**lev·er·et** (lev′ẽr-it), *n.* [< OFr. dim. of *levre* (< L. *lepus*), hare], a hare during its first year.

**Le·vi** (lē′vī), *n.* in the *Bible*, the third son of Jacob and Leah: Gen. 29:34: see also **Levite**.

**le·vi·a·than** (lə-vī′ə-thən), *n.* [LL. < Heb. *liwyāthān*], 1. in the *Bible*, a sea monster, variously thought of as a reptile or a whale. 2. anything huge of its kind.

**lev·i·er** (lev′i-ẽr), *n.* one who levies taxes, etc.

**le·vis** (lē′vīz), *n.pl.* [after *Levi* Strauss, the Am. maker], overalls; esp., bibless overalls, reinforced at the seams, etc. with small copper rivets: a trademark (**Levi's**).

**lev·i·tate** (lev′ə-tāt′), *v.t.* [-TATED, -TATING], [< L. *levis*, light; by analogy with *gravitate*], [Rare], to cause to rise and float in the air. *v.i.* to rise and float in the air. —**lev′i·ta′tor**, *n.*

**lev·i·ta·tion** (lev′ə-tā′shən), *n.* 1. a levitating or being levitated. 2. the illusion of raising and keeping a heavy body in the air with little or no physical support.

**Le·vite** (lē′vīt), *n.* in the *Bible*, any member of the tribe of Levi, chosen to assist the Jewish priests.

**Le·vit·i·cal** (lə-vit′i-k'l), *adj.* 1. of the Levites. 2. of Leviticus or its laws.

**Le·vit·i·cus** (lə-vit′i-kəs), *n.* the third book of the Old Testament, containing the laws relating to priests and Levites.

**lev·i·ty** (lev′ə-ti), *n.* [*pl.* -TIES], [< OFr. < L. *levitas* < *levis*, light], 1. [Rare], buoyancy. 2. lightness of disposition, conduct, etc.; esp., improper gaiety; frivolity. 3. fickleness.

**lev·u·lose** (lev′yoo-lōs′), *n.* fructose.

**lev·y** (lev′i), *n.* [*pl.* -IES], [< Late OFr. fem. pp. of *lever*, to raise; see LEVER], 1. an imposing and collecting of a tax, fine, etc. 2. the amount collected. 3. the compulsory enlistment of personnel for military service. 4. a group so enlisted. *v.t.* [-IED, -YING], 1. to impose (a tax, fine, etc.). 2. to enlist or collect (troops) for military service. 3. to wage (war). *v.i.* 1. to make a levy. 2. in *law*, to seize property in order to satisfy a judgment (often with *on*).

**lewd** (lo͞od), *adj.* [AS. *lǣwede*, lay, unlearned], indecent; lustful; unchaste; lascivious. —**lewd′ly**, *adv.* —**lewd′ness**, *n.*

**Lew·is, John Llewellyn** (lo͞o′is), 1880–1969; U.S. labor leader.

**Lewis, Mer·i·weth·er** (mer′i-weth′ẽr), 1774–1809; U.S. explorer, with William Clark (1770–1838).

**Lewis, Sinclair**, 1885–1951; U.S. novelist.

**lew·is·ite** (lo͞o′is-īt′), *n.* [after W. L. *Lewis* (1878–1943), U.S. chemist], an arsenical compound, ClCH—CHAsCl$_2$, used as a blistering poison gas.

‡**lex** (leks), *n.* [*pl.* LEGES (lē′jēz)], [L.], law.

**lex·i·cog·ra·pher** (lek′sə-kog′rə-fẽr), *n.* [< Late Gr. < Gr. *lexikon*, lexicon + *graphein*, to write], a person who writes or compiles a dictionary.

**lex·i·cog·ra·phy** (lek′sə-kog′rə-fi), *n.* [see prec. entry], the act, art, or work of writing or compiling a dictionary. —**lex′i·co·graph′ic** (-si-kə-graf′ik), **lex′i·co·graph′i·cal**, *adj.* —**lex′i·co·graph′i·cal·ly**, *adv.*

**lex·i·con** (lek′si-kən), *n.* [Gr. *lexikon* < *lexis*, a word], 1. a dictionary, especially of an ancient language. 2. a special vocabulary, as of an author.

**Lex·ing·ton** (lek′siŋ-tən), *n.* 1. a town in E Massachusetts: pop., 28,000: site of the first battle (April 19, 1775) of the American Revolution. 2. a city in north central Kentucky: pop., 63,000.

**Ley·den** (lī′d'n), *n.* Leiden.

**Leyden jar** (or **vial**), [< *Leiden*, Netherlands], a glass jar coated outside and inside with tin foil and having a metallic rod connecting with the inner lining and passing through the lid: it acts as a condenser for static electricity.

**Ley·te** (lā′tā, lā′ti), *n.* one of the Philippine Islands, in the central part.

**LG., L.G.,** Low German: also **L.Ger.**

**LGr.,** Late Greek.

**l.h.,** in *music*, left hand.

**Lha·sa** (lä′sə), *n.* the capital of Tibet: pop., 50,000.

**Li,** in *chemistry*, lithium.

**L. I.,** Long Island.

**li·a·bil·i·ty** (lī′ə-bil′ə-ti), *n.* [*pl.* -TIES], 1. the state of being liable. 2. anything for which a person is liable. 3. *usually in pl.* a debt: as, accounts payable, surplus, losses, and capital stock are corporation *liabilities*: opposed to *asset*. 4. something that works to one's disadvantage.

**li·a·ble** (lī′ə-b'l), *adj.* [< Fr. < L. *ligare*, to bind], 1. legally bound, as to make good a loss; responsible. 2. likely to have, suffer from, etc.; subject to: as, he is *liable* to heart attacks. 3. *a*) disagreeably likely. *b*) [Colloq.], likely: as, I am *liable* to be there. —**li′a·ble·ness**, *n.*

**li·ai·son** (lē′ā-zōn′, -ə-zon′, lī′ə-z'n, li-ā′z'n), *n.* [Fr. < L. < *ligare*, to bind], 1. a connecting of the parts of a whole, intended to bring about proper co-ordination of activities; esp., intercommunication between units of a military force. 2. an illicit love affair. 3. in spoken French, the linking of words by pronouncing the final consonant of one word as if it were the initial consonant of a following word, as in the phrase *chez elle* (pronounced shā′zel′).

**li·a·na** (li-ä′nə, -an′ə), *n.* [< Norm. Fr. *liane*], any luxuriantly growing, woody, tropical vine that roots in the ground and climbs, as around tree trunks: also **li·ane** (li-än′).

**li·ar** (lī′ẽr), *n.* a person who tells lies.

**lib.,** 1. *liber*, [L.], book. 2. librarian. 3. library.

**li·ba·tion** (lī-bā′shən), *n.* [< L. *libatio* < *libare*, to pour out], 1. the ritual of pouring out wine or oil in honor of a god. 2. the liquid poured out. 3. an alcoholic drink: used humorously.

**li·bel** (lī′b'l), *n.* [OFr. < L. *libellus*, dim. of *liber*, a book], 1. any written or printed statement, or any sign, picture, etc., tending to injure a person's reputation unjustly. 2. the act or crime of publishing such a thing. 3. anything that gives an unflattering or damaging picture of the subject with which it is dealing. *v.t.* [-BELED or -BELLED, -BELING or -BELLING], 1. to publish or make a libel against. 2. to give an unflattering or damaging picture of. —**li′bel·er, li′bel·ler**, *n.*

**li·bel·ous, li·bel·lous** (lī′b'l-əs), *adj.* 1. involving a libel. 2. given to writing and publishing libels; defamatory. —**li′bel·ous·ly, li′bel·lous·ly**, *adv.*

**lib·er·al** (lib′ẽr-əl, lib′rəl), *adj.* [OFr. < L. *liberalis* < *liber*, free], 1. originally, suitable for a freeman; not restricted: now only in *liberal arts, education*, etc. 2. giving freely; generous. 3. ample; abundant: as, a *liberal* reward. 4. not restricted to the literal meaning: as, a *liberal* interpretation of the law. 5. broad-minded. 6. favoring reform or progress, as in religion, education, etc.; specif., [also L-], favoring political reforms; not conservative: as, the *Liberal* Party in England. *n.* 1. a person favoring liberalism. 2. [L-], a member of a liberal political party, especially that of England. —**lib′er·al·ly**, *adv.* —**lib′er·al·ness**, *n.*

**liberal arts,** [arts open to study only by freemen (L. *liberi*) in ancient Rome], the subjects of an academic college course, including literature, philosophy, languages, history, etc., as distinguished from professional or technical subjects.

**liberal education,** an education mainly in the liberal arts.

**lib·er·al·ism** (lib′ẽr-əl-iz'm, lib′rəl-), *n.* 1. the quality or state of being liberal, as in politics or religion. 2. liberal principles and ideals. —**lib′er·al·ist**, *adj. & n.* —**lib′er·al·is′tic**, *adj.*

**lib·er·al·i·ty** (lib′ə-ral′ə-ti), *n.* [*pl.* -TIES], 1. the quality or state of being liberal; esp., generosity. 2. a gift. 3. broad-mindedness.

**lib·er·al·ize** (lib′ẽr-ə-līz, lib′rə-) *v.t. & v.i.* [-IZED, -IZING], to make or become liberal. —**lib′er·al·i·za′tion**, *n.* —**lib′er·al·iz′er**, *n.*

**lib·er·ate** (lib′ə-rāt′), *v.t.* [-ATED, -ATING], [< L. pp. of *liberare*, to free < *liber*, free], 1. to release from slavery, enemy occupation, etc. 2. to free from chemical combination. —**lib′er·a′tion**, *n.* —**lib′er·a′tor**, *n.*

**Li·ber·i·a** (lī-bêr′i-ə), *n.* a country on the W coast of Africa, founded in 1847 by freed American Negro slaves: area, 43,000 sq. mi.; pop., c. 1,200,000; capital, Monrovia. —**Li·ber'i·an,** *adj. & n.*

**lib·er·tine** (lib'ēr-tēn', -tin), *n.* [< L. < *libertus*, freedman < *liber*, free], a man who leads an unrestrained, immoral life; rake. *adj.* morally unrestrained; licentious. —**lib'er·tin·ism,** *n.*

**lib·er·ty** (lib'ēr-ti), *n.* [*pl.* -TIES], [< OFr. < L. *libertas* < *liber*, free], 1. freedom from slavery, captivity, or any other form of arbitrary control. 2. the sum of rights possessed in common by the people of a community, state, etc.: see also **civil liberties.** 3. a particular right, franchise, freedom, etc.: as, he has the *liberty* of coming with us. 4. *usually pl.* unnecessary or excessive freedom or familiarity. 5. the limits within which a certain amount of freedom may be exercised: as, he has the *liberty* of the third floor. 6. leave given to a sailor to go ashore for 48 hours or less. 7. in *philosophy*, freedom to choose. —**at liberty,** 1. not confined; free. 2. permitted; allowed. 3. not busy or in use. —**take liberties,** to be too free or familiar in action or speech.

**Liberty Bell,** the bell of Independence Hall in Philadelphia, rung on July 4, 1776, to proclaim the independence of the U.S.

**Liberty Ship,** a U.S. merchant ship carrying about 10,000 gross tons, built in large numbers during World War II.

**li·bid·i·nous** (li-bid''n-əs), *adj.* [see LIBIDO], full of or characterized by lust; lascivious. —**li·bid'i·nous·ly,** *adv.* —**li·bid'i·nous·ness,** *n.*

**li·bi·do** (li-bī'dō, -bē'-), *n.* [L., desire, wantonness < *libet*, it pleases], 1. the sexual urge or instinct. 2. in *psychoanalysis*, psychic energy generally; driving force behind all human action. —**li·bid'i·nal** (-bid''n-əl), *adj.*

**Li·bra** (lī'brə), *n.* [L., a balance], 1. a southern constellation supposedly resembling a pair of scales in shape. 2. the seventh sign of the zodiac (♎), entered by the sun about September 23.

**li·bra** (lī'brə), *n.* [*pl.* -BRAE (-brē)], [L.], pound.

**li·brar·i·an** (lī-brâr'i-ən), *n.* 1. a person in charge of a library. 2. a person trained in library science and working in a library.

**li·brar·y** (lī'brer'i, -brə-ri), *n.* [*pl.* -IES], [< OFr. < *libraire*, copyist < L. < *liber*, a book], 1. a room or building where a collection of books, etc. is kept for reading or reference. 2. *a*) a public or private institution in charge of the care and circulation of such a collection. *b*) a commercial establishment that rents books. 3. a collection of books.

**li·bret·tist** (li-bret'ist), *n.* a writer of librettos.

**li·bret·to** (li-bret'ō), *n.* [*pl.* -TOS, -TI (-i)], [It., dim. of *libro*, a book < L. *liber*, a book], 1. the words, or text, of an opera, oratorio, etc. 2. a book containing these words.

**Lib·y·a** (lib'i-ə), *n.* 1. northern Africa west of Egypt: the ancient Greek and Roman name. 2. a country in N Africa, on the Mediterranean: area, 679,358 sq. mi.; pop., 1,869,000; capital, Tripoli: Italian name, *Libia.* —**Lib'y·an,** *adj. & n.*

**lice** (līs), *n.* pl. of **louse.**

**li·cense, li·cence** (lī's'ns), *n.* [< OFr. < L. *licentia* < ppr. of *licere*, to be permitted], 1. formal or legal permission to do something specified: as, *license* to marry, hunt, etc. 2. a document indicating that such permission has been granted. 3. *a*) freedom to deviate from strict conduct, rule, or practice: as, poetic *license.* *b*) an instance of this. 4. excessive, undisciplined freedom, constituting an abuse of liberty. *v.t.* [-CENSED or -CENCED, -CENSING or -CENCING], to give license or a license to or for; permit formally. —**li'cense·a·ble, li'cence·a·ble,** *adj.*

**li·cen·see, li·cen·cee** (lī's'n-sē'), *n.* a person to whom a license is granted.

**li·cen·ser, li·cen·cer** (lī's'n-sēr), *n.* a person with authority to grant licenses: also, in *law*, **li'cen·sor** (-sēr).

**li·cen·ti·ate** (lī-sen'shi-it, -āt'), *n.* 1. a person licensed to practice a specified profession. 2. in certain European universities, an academic degree between that of bachelor and that of doctor. —**li·cen'ti·ate·ship',** *n.*

**li·cen·tious** (lī-sen'shəs), *adj.* [< Fr. < L. < *licentia*; see LICENSE], 1. [Rare], disregarding accepted rules and standards. 2. morally unrestrained; lascivious; libertine. —**li·cen'tious·ly,** *adv.* —**li·cen'tious·ness,** *n.*

‡**li·cet** (lī'set), [L.], it is allowed; it is legal.

**li·chee** (lē'chē'), *n.* a litchi.

**li·chen** (lī'kən), *n.* [L. < Gr. < *leichein*, to lick], any of a group of mosslike plants consisting of algae and fungi growing in close association in patches on rocks and tree trunks. —**li'chen·ous,** *adj.*

**licht** (likht), *adj., n., v.i. & v.t.* [Scot.], light.

**lic·it** (lis'it), *adj.* [< Fr. < L. *licitus*, pp. of *licere*, to be permitted], permitted; lawful.

**lick** (lik), *v.t.* [AS. *liccian*], 1. to pass the tongue over: as, dogs *lick* their wounds. 2. to bring into a certain condition by passing the tongue over: as, the child *licked* his fingers clean. 3. to pass lightly over like a tongue: as, the flames are *licking* the logs. 4. [Colloq.], *a*) to whip; thrash. *b*) to vanquish. *n.* 1. the act of licking with the tongue. 2. a small quantity. 3. a salt lick. 4. [Colloq.], *a*) a sharp blow. *b*) a short, rapid burst of activity. *c*) a spurt of speed. 5. [Slang], a phrase of jazz music, especially an interpolated ornamentation. 6. *often in pl.* [Slang], chance; turn: as, I'll get my *licks* in later. —**lick into shape,** [Colloq.], to bring into proper condition. —**lick up,** to consume by or as by licking. —**lick'er,** *n.*

**lick·er·ish** (lik'ēr-ish), *adj.* [< Anglo-Fr. form of OFr. *lecheros*], 1. lecherous; lustful; lewd. 2. greedy or eager, especially to eat or taste. Also sp. **liquorish.** —**lick'er·ish·ness,** *n.*

**lick·e·ty-split** (lik'ə-ti-split'), *adv.* [prob. echoism based on *lick*, *n.* 4*c*], [Slang], at great speed.

**lick·spit·tle** (lik'spit''l), *n.* a servile flatterer; toady: also **lick'spit'.**

**lic·o·rice** (lik'ēr-is, lik'rish, -ēr-ish), *n.* [< OFr. < LL. *liquiritia* < L. < Gr. *glycyrrhiza* < *glykys*, sweet + *rhiza*, root], 1. a European plant of the pea family. 2. its dried root or the black flavoring extract made from this. 3. candy flavored with or as with this extract. Also sp. **liquorice.**

**lic·tor** (lik'tēr), *n.* [L.], a minor Roman official who carried the fasces and went before the chief magistrates to clear the way.

**lid** (lid), *n.* [AS. *hlid*], 1. a movable cover, as for a box, pot, etc. 2. an eyelid. 3. [Slang], a cap, hat, etc. —**lid'ded,** *adj.* —**lid'less,** *adj.*

**lie** (lī), *v.i.* [LAY, LAIN, LYING], [AS. *licgan*], 1. to be or put oneself in a reclining position along a relatively horizontal surface. 2. to rest on a support in a more or less horizontal position: said of inanimate things. 3. to be or remain in a specified condition: as, his motives *lie* hidden. 4. to be situated: as, Canada *lies* to the north. 5. to extend: as, the road *lies* straight across the prairie. 6. to be; exist: as, the remedy *lies* within yourself. 7. to be buried or entombed. 8. [Archaic], to stay overnight or for a short while; lodge. *n.* 1. the way in which something is situated or arranged; lay. 2. an animal's lair. —**lie down on the job,** [Colloq.], to put forth less than one's best efforts. —**lie in,** to be in confinement for childbirth. —**lie over,** to stay and wait until some future time. —**lie to,** in *nautical usage*, to lie stationary with the head to the wind: said of a ship. —**li'er,** *n.*

**lie** (lī), *v.i.* [LIED, LYING], [AS. *leogan*], 1. to make a statement or statements that one knows to be false, especially with intent to deceive. 2. to give a false impression. *v.t.* to bring, put, accomplish, etc. by lying: as, he *lied* himself into office. *n.* 1. a thing said or done in lying; falsehood. 2. anything that gives or is meant to give a false impression. —**give the lie to,** 1. to charge with telling a lie. 2. to prove to be false.

**Lie, Tryg·ve Halv·dan** (trig'və hälv'dän lē), 1896–1968; Norwegian statesman; secretary-general of the United Nations (1946–1953).

**Liech·ten·stein** (lēH'tən-shtīn'), *n.* a country in Europe, between Switzerland and Austria: area, 62 sq. mi.; pop., 21,000.

**lied** (lēd; G. lēt), *n.* [*pl.* LIEDER (lē'dēr)], [G.], a German lyric or song.

**Lie·der·kranz** (lē'dēr-kränts'), *n.* [G., choral society, lit., garland of songs], a soft cheese having a strong odor and flavor: a trade-mark.

**lief** (lēf), *adj.* [AS. *leof*], [Obs.], 1. dear; beloved. 2. willing. *adv.* [Rare], willingly; gladly: only in *would* (or *had*) *as lief*, etc.

**Li·ège** (li-āzh'), *n.* a city in E Belgium, on the Meuse River: pop., 157,000.

**liege** (lēj), *adj.* [< OFr.; prob. < OHG. *ledig*, free, but infl. by L. *ligare*, to bind], 1. in *feudal law*, *a*) entitled to the service and allegiance of his vassals: as, a *liege* lord. *b*) bound to give service and allegiance to the lord: as, *liege* subjects. 2. loyal; faithful. *n.* in *feudal law*, 1. a lord or sovereign. 2. a subject or vassal.

**li·en** (lēn, lē'ən), *n.* [Fr. < L. *ligamen*, a band < *ligare*, to bind], in *law*, a claim on the property of another as security against the payment of a debt.

**lieu** (lōō), *n.* [OFr. < L. *locus*, place], stead; place. —**in lieu of,** instead of; in place of.

**lieu·ten·an·cy** (lōō-ten'ən-si), *n.* [*pl.* -CIES], the rank, commission, or authority of a lieutenant.

**lieu·ten·ant** (lōō-ten'ənt; Brit., *esp. army*, lef-ten'-), *n.* [Late OFr. < *lieu*, place + *tenant*, holding

< L. *tenere*, to hold], 1. one who acts for a superior, as during the latter's absence. 2. a military officer normally commanding a platoon: for relative rank see **first lieutenant, second lieutenant.** 3. a naval officer ranking just above a lieutenant junior grade. Abbrev. **Lieut., Lt.**

**lieutenant colonel,** a military officer ranking just above a major: abbrev. **Lieut. Col., Lt. Col.**

**lieutenant commander,** a naval officer ranking just above a lieutenant: abbrev. **Lieut. Comdr., Lt. Comdr., Lt.-Comm.**

**lieutenant general,** a military officer ranking just above a major general: abbrev. **Lieut. Gen., Lt. Gen.**

**lieutenant governor,** 1. an elected official of a State who ranks below and substitutes for the governor in case of the latter's absence or death. 2. in certain countries, an official substituting for the governor general of a province or district. Abbrev. **Lt. Gov., Lieut. Gov.**

**lieutenant junior grade,** a naval officer ranking just above an ensign: abbrev. **Lt. (j.g.), Lieut. (j.g.).**

**life** (līf), *n.* [*pl.* LIVES], [AS. *lif*], 1. that property of plants and animals (ending at death and distinguishing them from inorganic matter) which makes it possible for them to take in food, get energy from it, grow, etc. 2. the state of possessing this property: as, brought back to *life.* 3. a living being, especially a human being: as, the cyclone took many *lives.* 4. living things collectively: as, plant *life.* 5. the time a person or thing is alive, or a specific portion of such time: as, a long *life,* his early *life.* 6. one's manner of living: as, a *life* of poverty. 7. the people and activities of a given time, or in a given setting or class: as, military *life,* low *life.* 8. human existence and activity: as, to learn from *life.* 9. *a)* all that is experienced by an individual during his existence. *b)* an account of this. 10. the existence of the soul: as, the eternal *life.* 11. something essential to the continued existence of something else: as, freedom of speech is the *life* of democracy. 12. the source of vigor or liveliness: as, the *life* of the party. 13. vigor; liveliness. 14. the period of flourishing, usefulness, functioning, etc.: as, fads have a short *life.* 15. representation in art from living models: as, a class in *life.* **—as large** (or **big**) **as life,** life-size. **—for dear life,** with a desperate intensity. **—for life,** 1. for the duration of one's life. 2. to save one's life. **—from life,** from a living model. **—see life,** to have a wide variety of experiences. **—take life,** to kill. **—take one's own life,** to commit suicide. **—to the life,** like the living original; exactly. **—true to life,** true to reality.

**life belt,** a life preserver in the form of a belt.

**life·blood** (līf′blud′), *n.* 1. the blood necessary to life. 2. the vital part or animating influence of anything.

**life·boat** (līf′bōt′), *n.* 1. a strong, especially buoyant boat kept in readiness on the shore for use in rescuing people in danger of drowning. 2. one of the small boats carried by a ship for use in case the ship has to be abandoned.

**life buoy,** a life preserver.

**life expectancy,** the average number of years that an individual of a given age may expect to live.

**life-giv·ing** (līf′giv′iŋ), *adj.* 1. that gives or can give life. 2. refreshing. **—life′-giv′er,** *n.*

**life·guard** (līf′gärd′), *n.* an expert swimmer employed at bathing beaches, pools, etc. to prevent drownings.

**life insurance** (or **assurance**), insurance in which a stipulated sum is paid to the beneficiary or beneficiaries at the death of the insured, or to the insured when he reaches a specified age.

**life·less** (līf′lis), *adj.* 1. without life; specif., *a)* inanimate. *b)* dead. 2. dull; listless. **—life′less·ly,** *adv.* **—life′less·ness,** *n.*

**life·like** (līf′līk′), *adj.* 1. resembling actual life. 2. closely resembling a real person or thing: as, a *lifelike* portrait. **—life′like′ness,** *n.*

**life line,** 1. a rope shot to a ship in distress near the shore, connecting it with the shore. 2. the rope by means of which a diver is raised and lowered. 3. a commercial route or transport line of great importance.

**life·long** (līf′lôŋ′), *adj.* lasting, or remaining as such, for all one's life: as, a *lifelong* reformer.

**life net,** a strong net used by firemen, etc. to catch people jumping, as from a burning building.

**life of Riley,** [Slang], a life of ease and pleasure.

**life preserver,** a device for saving a person from drowning by keeping his body afloat: it is usually a ring or sleeveless jacket of canvas-covered cork.

LIFE PRESERVER

**lif·er** (līf′ẽr), *n.* [Slang], a person sentenced to imprisonment for life.

**life·sav·er** (līf′sāv′ẽr), *n.* 1. a lifeguard. 2. [Colloq.], a person or thing that is essential to one's work, welfare, etc. **—life′sav′ing,** *adj.* & *n.*

**life-size** (līf′sīz′), *adj.* as big as the person or thing represented, as a picture, etc.

**life·time** (līf′tīm′), *n.* the time during which the life of an individual lasts. *adj.* lasting for such a period: as, a *lifetime* job.

**life·work** (līf′wūrk′), *n.* the work or task to which a person devotes his life; chief work in life.

**lift** (lift), *v.t.* [< ON. *lypta* < base of AS. *lyft,* air], 1. to bring up to a higher position; raise. 2. to pick up and set: as, to *lift* a baby down from its high chair. 3. to hold up. 4. to raise in rank, condition, spirits, etc.; elevate; exalt. 5. to cancel (a mortgage) by paying it off. 6. to perform plastic surgery on (the face) to remove wrinkles, sagging, etc. 7. [Colloq.], to plagiarize: as, he *lifted* a passage from Milton. 8. [Slang], to steal. *v.i.* 1. to exert strength in raising or trying to raise something. 2. to rise and vanish: as, the gloom *lifted.* 3. to become raised; go up. *n.* 1. a lifting, raising, or rising. 2. the amount lifted. 3. the distance through which something is lifted. 4. lifting force, power, or influence. 5. elevation of spirits or mood. 6. elevated position or carriage: as, the proud *lift* of her head. 7. a ride in the direction one is going. 8. help of any kind. 9. a rise in the ground. 10. the means by which something is lifted; specif., *a)* any layer of leather in the heel of a shoe. *b)* [Brit.], an elevator. **—lift a cry** (or **one's voice**), to call, cry, or speak out loudly. **—lift′a·ble,** *adj.* **—lift′er,** *n.*

**lift-off** (lift′ôf′), *n.* 1. the vertical thrust of a spacecraft, missile, etc. at launching. 2. the moment at which this occurs.

**lig·a·ment** (lig′ə-mənt), *n.* [< L. < *ligare,* to bind], 1. a bond or tie. 2. in *anatomy,* a band of tough tissue connecting bones or holding organs in place.

**li·gate** (lī′gāt), *v.t.* [-GATED, -GATING], to tie with a ligature, as a bleeding artery. **—li·ga′tion,** *n.*

**lig·a·ture** (lig′ə-chẽr), *n.* [Late OFr. < LL. *ligatura* < pp. of L. *ligare,* to bind], 1. a tying or binding together. 2. a thing used for this; tie, bond, bandage, etc. 3. in *music, a)* a curved line indicating a slur. *b)* the notes slurred. 4. in *surgery,* a thread or wire used to tie up an artery, etc. 5. in *printing,* a character containing two or more letters united, as *æ, fi, fl.* *v.t.* [-TURED, -TURING], to tie or bind together with a ligature.

**light** (līt), *n.* [AS. *leoht*], 1. *a)* that which makes it possible to see; form of radiant energy that acts upon the retina of the eye, optic nerve, etc., making sight possible: the speed of light is 186,000 miles per second. *b)* a similar form of radiant energy not acting on the normal retina, as ultraviolet and infrared radiation. 2. the sensation that light stimulates in the organs of sight. 3. brightness; illumination, often of a specified kind. 4. the source of light, as a lamp, the sun, etc. 5. the light from the sun; daylight or dawn. 6. a thing by means of which something can be started burning: as, a *light* for a cigar. 7. the means by which light is let in; window. 8. *a)* knowledge; enlightenment. *b)* spiritual enlightenment or inspiration. 9. public knowledge or view. 10. the way in which something is seen; aspect: as, presented in an unfavorable *light.* 11. facial expression: as, a *light* of recognition in his eyes. 12. an outstanding figure: as, he was a shining *light* in school. *adj.* 1. having light; bright. 2. pale in color; whitish; fair. *adv.* palely: as, a *light* blue color. *v.t.* [LIGHTED or LIT, LIGHTING], 1. to set on fire; ignite: as, let's *light* a bonfire. 2. to cause to give off light: as, she *lit* the lamp. 3. to furnish with light: as, lamps *light* the streets. 4. to brighten; animate. 5. to show the way to by giving light. *v.i.* 1. to catch fire. 2. to be lighted; brighten (usually with *up*). **—according to one's lights,** as one's opinions, abilities, etc. may direct. **—bring to light,** to reveal; disclose. **—come to light,** to be revealed or disclosed. **—in the light of,** considering. **—see the light (of day),** 1. to come into exist-

ence. 2. to come to public view. 3. to understand. —**shed** (or **throw**) **light on,** to explain; clarify.
**light** (līt), *adj.* [AS. *leoht*], 1. having little weight; not heavy. 2. having little weight for its size. 3. below the usual or defined weight: as, a *light* coin. 4. less than usual or normal in amount, extent, force, etc.; specif., *a*) striking with little force: as, a *light* blow. *b*) of less than the usual quantity or density: as, a *light* rain. *c*) not coarse, massive, etc.; graceful: as, *light* architecture. *d*) soft, muted, or muffled: as, a *light* sound. *e*) not prolonged or intense: as, *light* applause. 5. of little importance; not serious: as, *light* conversation. 6. easy to bear; not burdensome: as, a *light* tax. 7. easy to do; not difficult: as, *light* work. 8. gay; happy; buoyant: as, *light* spirits. 9. flighty; frivolous; fickle. 10. loose in morals; wanton. 11. dizzy; giddy. 12. of an amusing or nonserious nature: as, *light* reading. 13. containing little alcohol: as, *light* wine. 14. *a*) not as full as usual: as, a *light* meal. *b*) easy to digest. 15. well leavened; soft and spongy: as, a *light* cake. 16. loose in consistency; porous: as, *light* sand. 17. moving with ease and nimbleness: as, she is *light* on her feet. 18. unstressed or slightly stressed: said of syllables. 19. having light weapons, armor, etc.: as, a *light* tank. 20. in *meteorology*, designating a breeze less than 8 miles per hour. ***adv.*** lightly. ***v.i.*** [LIGHTED or LIT, LIGHTING], 1. [Rare], to dismount; alight. 2. to come to rest after traveling through the air: as, a fly *lighted* on the cake. 3. to come by chance (*on* or *upon*). 4. to strike suddenly, as a blow. —**light in the head,** 1. dizzy. 2. simple; foolish. —**light into,** [Slang], 1. to attack. 2. to scold. —**light out,** [Slang], to depart suddenly. —**make light of,** to treat as unimportant.
**light-armed** (līt'ärmd'), *adj.* bearing light weapons.
**light·en** (līt''n), *v.t.* to make light; illuminate. ***v.i.*** 1. to become light; grow brighter. 2. to shine brightly; flash. 3. to give off flashes of lightning. —**light'en·er,** *n.*
**light·en** (līt''n), *v.t.* 1. *a*) to make lighter in weight. *b*) to reduce the load of. 2. to make less severe, harsh, etc. 3. to make more cheerful. ***v.i.*** to become lighter, as in weight. —**light'en·er,** *n.*
**light·er** (līt'ēr), *n.* a person or thing that lights something or starts it burning.
**light·er** (līt'ēr), *n.* [< D. < *licht*, light], a large, open barge used chiefly in loading or unloading larger ships lying offshore. ***v.t. & v.i.*** to transport (goods) in a lighter.
**light·er·age** (līt'ēr-ij), *n.* 1. the loading or unloading of a ship, or transportation of goods, by means of a lighter. 2. the charge for this.
**light·face** (līt'fās'), *n.* in *printing*, type having thin, light lines. ***adj.*** having thin, light lines.
**light-fin·gered** (līt'fiŋ'gērd), *adj.* skillful at stealing, especially by picking pockets.
**light-foot·ed** (līt'foot'id), *adj.* stepping lightly and gracefully: also [Poetic], **light'-foot'.** —**light'-foot'ed·ly,** *adv.* —**light'-foot'ed·ness,** *n.*
**light-hand·ed** (līt'han'did), *adj.* 1. having a light, delicate touch. 2. having little to carry.
**light·head·ed** (līt'hed'id), *adj.* 1. delirious. 2. giddy; dizzy. 3. flighty; frivolous. —**light'head'ed·ly,** *adv.* —**light'head'ed·ness,** *n.*
**light·heart·ed** (līt'här'tid), *adj.* free from care; gay. —**light'heart'ed·ly,** *adv.* —**light'heart'ed·ness,** *n.*
**light heavyweight,** a boxer or wrestler who weighs between 161 and 175 pounds.
**light·house** (līt'hous'), *n.* a tower with a very bright light at the top, by which ships are guided and warned at night.
**light·ing** (līt'iŋ), *n.* 1. a giving light or being lighted; illumination or ignition. 2. the distribution of light and shade in a painting. 3. the art or manner of arranging stage lights.
**light·ly** (līt'li), *adv.* 1. with little weight or pressure. 2. gently. 3. to a small degree or amount: as, to spend *lightly*. 4. nimbly; deftly. 5. cheerfully; merrily. 6. with indifference or neglect. 7. with little or no reason. 8. wantonly.
**light-mind·ed** (līt'mīn'did), *adj.* flighty; thoughtless; frivolous. —**light'-mind'ed·ly,** *adv.* —**light'-mind'ed·ness,** *n.*
**light·ness** (līt'nis), *n.* 1. the quality or intensity of lighting; brightness. 2. paleness; whitishness.
**light·ness** (līt'nis), *n.* 1. the state of being light, not heavy. 2. mildness, nimbleness, delicacy, cheerfulness, lack of seriousness, etc.
**light·ning** (līt'niŋ), *n.* [< *lighten*, to illuminate], 1. a flash of light in the sky caused by the discharge of atmospheric electricity from one cloud to another or from a cloud to the earth. 2. such a discharge of electricity.
**lightning bug** (or **beetle**), a firefly.
**lightning rod,** a pointed metal rod placed high on a building, etc. and grounded at the lower end to divert lightning from the structure.
**light opera,** light operetta.
**lights** (līts), *n.pl.* [from their light weight], the lungs of animals, used as food.
**light·ship** (līt'ship'), *n.* a ship moored in a place dangerous to navigation and bearing a bright light to warn pilots away from the spot.
**light·some** (līt'səm), *adj.* 1. nimble, graceful, or lively. 2. cheerful; gay. 3. frivolous. —**light'some·ly,** *adv.* —**light'some·ness,** *n.*
**light·weight** (līt'wāt'), *n.* 1. one below normal weight. 2. [Colloq.], a person of little mentality or importance. 3. a boxer or wrestler who weighs between 127 and 135 pounds. ***adj.*** light in weight.
**light-year** (līt'yêr'), *n.* a unit of astronomical distance, the distance that light travels in one year, approximately 6,000,000,000,000 miles.
**lig·ne·ous** (lig'ni-əs), *adj.* [< L. *ligneus* < *lignum*, wood], of, or having the nature of, wood; woody.
**lig·ni-** (lig'ni), [< L. lignum, wood], a combining form meaning *wood*: also **ligno-** or **lign-.**
**lig·nite** (lig'nīt), *n.* [< Fr.; see LIGNI- & -ITE], a soft, brownish-black coal in which the texture of the original wood can still be seen. —**lig·nit·ic** (-nit'ik), *adj.*
**lig·num vi·tae** (lig'nəm vī'tē), [L., wood of life], 1. a tropical American tree with very hard, heavy, greenish-brown wood. 2. the wood of this tree.
**lik·a·ble, like·a·ble** (līk'ə-b'l), *adj.* having qualities that inspire liking; attractive, genial, etc. —**lik'a·ble·ness, like'a·ble·ness,** *n.*
**like** (līk), *adj.* [AS. *gelic*], 1. having almost or exactly the same characteristics; similar; equal: as, a cup of sugar and a *like* amount of flour. 2. [Dial.], likely: as, not many are *like* to fall. ***adv.*** 1. in the manner of one that is: as, he works *like* mad. 2. [Colloq.], likely: as, *like* as not, we will go. ***prep.*** 1. similar to; resembling: as, she is *like* a bird. 2. similarly to: as, she sings *like* a bird. 3. characteristic of: as, it was not *like* him to cry. 4. in the mood for; desirous of: as, I feel *like* sleeping. 5. indicative of: as, it looks *like* a clear day tomorrow. *Like* was originally an adjective in senses 1, 3, 4, 5, and an adverb in sense 2, and is still considered so by some grammarians. ***conj.*** [Colloq.], 1. as: as, it was just *like* you said. 2. as if: as, it looks *like* he is signaling. ***n.*** a person or thing regarded as the equal or counterpart of another or of the person or thing being discussed: as, I have never seen the *like* of it. ***v.t.*** [LIKED, LIKING], [Obs.], to liken. ***v.i.*** [Dial.], to come near (*to* doing something). —**and the like,** and others of the same kind. —**like anything** (or **blazes, crazy, the devil, mad,** etc.), [Colloq. or Slang], with furious energy, speed, etc. —**nothing like,** not at all like. —**something like,** almost like; about. —**the like** (or **likes**) **of,** [Colloq.], any person or thing like.
**like** (līk), *v.i.* [LIKED, LIKING], [AS. *lician*], to be so inclined; choose: as, you may leave whenever you *like*. ***v.t.*** 1. to be pleased with; have a preference for; enjoy. 2. to wish: as, I should *like* to go. ***n. pl.*** preferences, tastes, or affections: as, one's *likes* and dislikes. —**lik'er,** *n.*
**-like** (līk), [see LIKE, *adj.*], a suffix used to form adjectives meaning *like, characteristic of, suitable for*, as in *ball-like, homelike, owllike*.
**like·li·hood** (līk'li-hood'), *n.* (a) probability.
**like·ly** (līk'li), *adj.* [-LIER, -LIEST], [< AS. *geliclic* or cognate ON. *likligr*], 1. credible; probable: as, a *likely* account. 2. reasonably to be expected: as, the fog is *likely* to lift soon. 3. suitable: as, a *likely* place to hunt. 4. promising: as, a *likely* lad. ***adv.*** probably: as, he will very *likely* go.
**like-mind·ed** (līk'mīn'did), *adj.* having the same ideas, tastes, etc.; agreeing mentally.
**lik·en** (līk''n), *v.t.* to represent as like or similar; compare.
**like·ness** (līk'nis), *n.* 1. the state or quality of being like; similarity. 2. (the same) form; shape: as, Zeus took on the *likeness* of a bull. 3. something that is like; copy; portrait; picture.
**like·wise** (līk'wīz'), *adv.* [short for *in like wise*], 1. in the same manner. 2. also; too; moreover.
**lik·ing** (līk'iŋ), *n.* 1. fondness; affection. 2. preference; taste; pleasure: as, not to my *liking*.
**li·lac** (lī'lək), *n.* [OFr. < Sp. < Ar. < Per. *nīlak*, bluish < *nīl*, indigo], 1. a shrub with large clusters of tiny, fragrant flowers ranging in color from white to lavender. 2. the flower cluster of this plant. 3. a pale-purple color. ***adj.*** of a pale-purple color.
**lil·i·a·ceous** (lil'i-ā'shəs), *adj.* 1. of or characteristic of lilies. 2. of the lily family.
**Lille** (lēl), *n.* a city in N France: pop., 189,000.

**Lil·li·put** (lil′ə-put′, -pət), *n.* in Swift's *Gulliver's Travels*, a land inhabited by tiny people.

**Lil·li·pu·tian** (lil′ə-pū′shən), *adj.* 1. of Lilliput or its people. 2. tiny; dwarfed. *n.* 1. an inhabitant of Lilliput. 2. a very small person.

**lilt** (lilt), *v.t. & v.i.* [ME. *lilten*], to sing, speak, or play with a light, graceful rhythm. *n.* 1. a gay song or tune with a swingy rhythm. 2. a light, swingy, and graceful rhythm or movement.

**lil·y** (lil′i), *n.* [*pl.* -IES], [AS. *lilie* < L. *lilium* < Gr. *leirion*, lily], 1. any of a large group of plants grown from a bulb and having typically trumpet-shaped flowers, white or colored. 2. the flower or the bulb of any of these. 3. any of several plants related or similar to the true lily: as, the water *lily*. 4. the fleur-de-lis, as in the royal arms of France. *adj.* like a lily, as in whiteness, delicacy, purity, etc. —**lil′y·like′**, *adj.*

**lil·y-liv·ered** (lil′i-liv′ẽrd), *adj.* cowardly.

**lily of the valley,** [*pl.* LILIES OF THE VALLEY], a low plant with a single, one-sided spike of fragrant, small, white, bell-shaped flowers.

**Li·ma** (lē′mə), *n.* 1. capital of Peru: pop., 1,186,000. 2. (lī′-), a city in NW Ohio: pop., 51,000.

**Li·ma bean** (lī′mə), [after *Lima*, Peru], 1. a bean plant with creamy flowers and broad pods. 2. the broad, flat, edible bean of this plant.

**limb** (lim), *n.* [AS. *lim*], 1. an arm, leg, or wing. 2. a large branch of a tree. 3. a part that projects like an arm or leg. 4. a person or thing regarded as a part or agent. *v.t.* to dismember. —**out on a limb,** [Colloq.], in a precarious position or situation. —**limb′less,** *adj.*

**limb** (lim), *n.* [< Fr.; L. *limbus*, edge], a border or edge; specif., in *astronomy*, the outer edge of a heavenly body.

**limbed** (limd), *adj.* having (a specified number or kind of) limbs: as, crooked-*limbed*.

**lim·ber** (lim′bẽr), *adj.* [prob. < *limb* (arm or leg)], 1. easily bent; flexible. 2. able to bend the body easily; lithe. *v.t.* to make limber. *v.i.* to make oneself limber: as, the dancers were *limbering* up. —**lim′ber·ly,** *adv.* —**lim′ber·ness,** *n.*

**lim·ber** (lim′bẽr), *n.* [prob. < Fr. *limonière* < *limon*, a shaft], the two-wheeled, detachable front part of a gun carriage. *v.t. & v.i.* to attach the limber to (a gun carriage).

**lim·bo** (lim′bō), *n.* [< L. (*in*) *limbo*, (in or on) the border], 1. [often L-], in some Christian theologies, a region bordering upon hell, the abode after death of unbaptized children and righteous people who lived before Jesus. 2. a place or condition of neglect or oblivion for unwanted things or persons.

**Lim·burg·er (cheese)** (lim′bẽr-gẽr), [< *Limb(o)urg*, a province of Belgium], a soft, white brick cheese with a strong odor: also **Limburg cheese.**

**lime** (līm), *n.* [AS. *lim*], 1. [Rare], birdlime. 2. a white substance, calcium oxide, CaO, obtained by the action of heat on limestone, shells, etc. and used in making mortar and cement and in neutralizing acid soil: also called *quicklime, burnt lime, caustic lime*. *v.t.* [LIMED, LIMING], 1. to cement. 2. to smear with birdlime. 3. to catch with birdlime. 4. to treat with lime.

**lime** (līm), *n.* [Fr. < Sp. < Ar. *līmah* < Per. *līmūn*, lemon], 1. a small, lemon-shaped, greenish-yellow fruit with a juicy, sour pulp. 2. the small, semitropical tree that it grows on. *adj.* 1. made with or of limes. 2. having a flavor like that of limes.

**lime** (līm), *n.* [< earlier *line* < ME. *lind;* see LINDEN], the linden tree.

**lime·ade** (līm′ād′), *n.* a drink of lime juice, sugar, and water.

**lime·kiln** (līm′kil′, -kiln′), *n.* a furnace in which limestone, shells, etc. are burned to make lime.

**lime·light** (līm′līt′), *n.* 1. a brilliant light created by the oxidation of lime and formerly used in theaters to throw an intense beam of light upon a particular actor, part of the stage, etc. 2. a prominent position before the public.

**Lim·er·ick** (lim′ẽr-ik), *n.* 1. a county of SW Ireland. 2. [l-], [prob. < Ir. refrain containing the name], a rhymed, nonsense poem of five anapestic lines.

**lime·stone** (līm′stōn′), *n.* rock consisting mainly of calcium carbonate, from which building stones, lime, etc. are made: cf. **marble.**

**lime·wa·ter** (līm′wô′tẽr, -wät′ẽr), *n.* a solution of lime in water, used to neutralize acids.

**lim·ey** (līm′i), *n.* [*lime* juice was formerly served to British sailors to prevent scurvy], [Slang], 1. an English soldier or sailor. 2. any Englishman. A patronizing or contemptuous term.

**lim·it** (lim′it), *n.* [< OFr. < L. *limes*], 1. the point, line, or edge where something ends or must end; boundary. 2. *pl.* bounds. 3. the greatest amount allowed: as, a catch of ten trout is the *limit*, a ten-cent *limit* on raising a bet in poker. *v.t.* to set a limit to or for; restrict; curb. —**the limit,** [Colloq.], any person or thing regarded as quite unbearable, remarkable, etc. —**lim′it·a·ble,** *adj.* —**lim′it·er,** *n.*

**lim·i·ta·tion** (lim′ə-tā′shən), *n.* 1. a limiting or being limited. 2. qualification; restriction. 3. in *law*, a period of time, fixed by statute, during which legal action can be brought, as for the settlement of a claim. —**lim′i·ta′tive,** *adj.*

**lim·it·ed** (lim′it-id), *adj.* 1. confined within bounds; restricted. 2. making a restricted number of stops, and often charging extra fare: said of a train, bus, etc. 3. exercising governmental powers under constitutional restrictions: as, a *limited* monarch. *n.* a limited train, bus, etc. —**lim′it·ed·ly,** *adv.* —**lim′it·ed·ness,** *n.*

**lim·it·ing** (lim′it-iŋ), *adj.* designating any of a class of adjectives that limit or restrict the words modified (e.g., *several, these, four,* etc.).

**lim·it·less** (lim′it-lis), *adj.* without limits; unbounded; infinite; vast.

**limn** (lim), *v.t.* [LIMNED, LIMNING (-iŋ, -niŋ)], [< OFr. *enluminer*, < L. *illuminare*, to make light], 1. to paint or draw. 2. to portray in words; describe. —**limn′er** (-ẽr, -nẽr), *n.*

**Li·moges** (lē′mōzh′), *n.* 1. a city in W France. 2. fine porcelain made there: also **Limoges ware.**

**lim·ou·sine** (lim′ə-zēn′, lim′ə-zēn′), *n.* [Fr., lit., a hood], 1. an automobile with a closed compartment seating three or more passengers: the top extends forward over the driver's open seat. 2. any large, luxurious sedan.

**limp** (limp), *v.i.* [< specialized sense of AS. *limpan*, to befall], 1. to walk with or as with a lame leg. 2. to move jerkily, laboriously, etc. *n.* a halt or lameness in walking. —**limp′er,** *n.*

**limp** (limp), *adj.* [< base of *limp*, *v.*], 1. lacking stiffness; wilted; flexible. 2. lacking firmness or vigor. —**limp′ly,** *adv.* —**limp′ness,** *n.*

**limp·et** (lim′pit), *n.* [< AS. < LL. *lempreda*], a shellfish which clings to rocks and timbers by means of a thick, fleshy foot.

**lim·pid** (lim′pid), *adj.* [< Fr. < L. *limpidus*], perfectly clear; transparent. —**lim·pid′i·ty, lim′pid·ness,** *n.* —**lim′pid·ly,** *adv.*

**lim·y** (līm′i), *adj.* [-IER, -IEST], 1. covered with, consisting of, or like birdlime; sticky. 2. of, like, or containing lime.

**lin·age** (līn′ij), *n.* 1. alignment. 2. the number of written or printed lines on a page. 3. payment based on the number of lines produced by a writer. Also sp. **lineage.**

**linch·pin** (linch′pin′), *n.* [ME. *lynspin*], a pin that goes through the end of an axle outside the wheel to keep the wheel from coming off.

**Lin·coln** (liŋ′kən), *n.* the capital of Nebraska: pop., 129,000.

**Lincoln, Abraham,** 1809–1865; 16th president of the U.S. (1861–1865); assassinated.

**Lind, Jenny** (lind), 1820–1887; Swedish soprano.

**Lind·bergh, Charles Augustus** (lind′bẽrg), 1902–; U.S. aviator.

**lin·den** (lin′dən), *n.* [AS., *adj.* (*lind* + *-en*)], a tree with heart-shaped leaves and fragrant, yellowish flowers; the basswood.

**line** (līn), *n.* [merging of AS. *line*, a cord, with OFr. *ligne* (both < L. *linea*, lit., linen thread < *linum*, flax)], 1. *a*) a cord, rope, wire, or string. *b*) a fine, strong cord with a hook, used in fishing. *c*) a cord, steel tape, etc. used in measuring or leveling. 2. *a*) a wire or wires connecting stations in a telephone or telegraph system. *b*) any connection made in such a system. *c*) the whole system. 3. any wire, pipe, etc., or system of these, conducting fluid, electricity, etc. 4. a very thin threadlike mark; specif., *a*) a long, thin mark made by a pencil, pen, chalk, knife, etc. *b*) a thin crease in the palm or on the face. 5. a border or boundary: as, the State *line*. 6. a limit; demarcation. 7. outline; contour. 8. *pl.* circumstances of life; one's fate. 9. *usually pl.* a plan of making or doing. 10. a row or series of persons or like things; specif., a row of written or printed characters across a page or column. 11. *a*) alignment; straight row or line. *b*) agreement; conformity. In the phrases *in* (or *out of*) *line, bring* (or *come*) *into line*. 12. a connected series of persons or things following each other in time or place: as, a *line* of Democratic presidents. 13. lineage. 14. *a*) a transportation system consisting of regular trips by buses, ships, etc. between two or more points. *b*) a company operating such a system. *c*) one branch of such a system: as, the main *line* of a railroad. *d*) a single track of a railroad. 15. the course or direction anything moving takes: as, the *line* of fire. 16. a course of conduct, action, explanation, etc. 17. a person's trade or occupation, or the things he deals in: as, his *line* is leather goods. 18. a stock of goods of a particular quality, quantity, variety, etc. 19. the field of one's special knowledge or interest: as, debating was right in his *line*. 20. a short letter, note, or card: as, drop me a *line*. 21. a verse of poetry. 22. *pl.* all the speeches of any one character in a play. 23. in *football*, the players arranged in a row even with the ball at the start of each play, or those directly opposite them. 24. in *geography & astronomy*, an imaginary circle or arc used for convenience of division: as, the date *line*, the equinoctial *line*. 25. in *mathematics*, *a*) the path of a moving point. *b*) such a path when considered perfectly straight. 26. in *military usage*, *a*) a formation of ships, troops, etc. abreast of each other. *b*) the area or position in closest contact with the enemy during combat. *c*) the troops in this area. *d*) combat troops, as distinguished from *staff*, etc. 27. in *music*, any of the long parallel marks forming the staff. ***v.t.*** [LINED, LINING], 1. to mark with lines. 2. to trace with or as with lines; outline. 3. to bring into alignment (often with *up*). 4. to form a line along. 5. to place objects along the edge of. ***v.i.*** to form a line (usually with *up*). —**all along the line,** 1. everywhere. 2. at every turn of events. —**draw the** (or **a**) **line,** to set a limit. —**get a line on,** [Colloq.], to find out about. —**hold the line,** to stand firm. —**line out,** in *baseball*, to be put out by hitting a liner straight to a fielder. —**line up,** to bring into or take a specified position. —**on a line,** in the same plane; level. —**read between the lines,** to discover a hidden meaning or purpose in something written, said, or done.

**line** (līn), ***v.t.*** [LINED, LINING], [< AS. *lin* < L. *linum*, flax], 1. to put a layer or lining on the inside of. 2. to fill with money: chiefly in *line one's pockets*. 3. to be used as a lining in.

**lin·e·age** (lin′i-ij), ***n.*** [< OFr. *lignage* < *ligne;* see LINE, *n.*], 1. direct descent from an ancestor; hence, 2. ancestry; family.

**line·age** (līn′ij), ***n.*** linage.

**lin·e·al** (lin′i-əl), ***adj.*** 1. in the direct line of descent from an ancestor. 2. hereditary. 3. of or composed of a line or lines; linear. —**lin′e·al·ly,** ***adv.***

**lin·e·a·ment** (lin′i-ə-mənt), ***n.*** [< L. *lineamentum* < *linea*, a line], *usually in pl.* 1. any of the features of the face, especially with regard to its outline. 2. a distinctive feature.

**lin·e·ar** (lin′i-ēr), ***adj.*** 1. of a line or lines. 2. in a line. 3. made of or using lines. 4. narrow and long, as a willow leaf. —**lin′e·ar·ly,** ***adv.***

**linear measure,** 1. measurement of length. 2. a system of measuring length; esp., the system in which 12 inches = 1 foot, 3 feet = 1 yard, etc.

**line·man** (līn′mən), ***n.*** [*pl.* -MEN], 1. a man who carries a surveying line, tape, etc. 2. a man whose work is setting up and repairing telephone or electric wires, or the like. 3. in *football*, a player in the line; center, tackle, guard, or end.

**lin·en** (lin′ən), ***n.*** [see PLURAL, II, D, 3], [AS. < *lin*, flax], 1. thread or cloth made of flax. 2. articles made of linen, or of cotton, etc., as tablecloths, sheets, shirts, etc. ***adj.*** made of linen.

**line of fire,** 1. the course of a bullet, shell, etc. 2. a position open to attack of any kind.

**line of force,** a line in a field of electrical or magnetic force that shows the direction taken by the force at any point.

**lin·er** (līn′ēr), ***n.*** 1. a person or thing that traces lines. 2. a steamship, airplane, etc. in regular service for a specific line. 3. a cosmetic applied in a fine line, as along the eyelid. 4. in *baseball*, a batted ball that travels parallel with and not high above the ground: also **line drive.**

**lin·er** (līn′ēr), ***n.*** 1. a person who makes or attaches linings. 2. a lining. 3. the jacket of a long-playing phonograph record.

**lines·man** (līnz′mən), ***n.*** [*pl.* -MEN], 1. a lineman. 2. in *football*, an official who measures and records the gains or losses in ground. 3. in *tennis*, an official who watches one or more lines on the court and reports faults in service or in play.

**line-up, line·up** (līn′up′), ***n.*** an arrangement of persons or things in or as in a line; specif., *a*) a group of suspected criminals lined up by the police for identification. *b*) in *football, baseball*, etc., the list of a team's players arranged according to position, order at bat, etc.

**ling** (liŋ), ***n.*** [*pl.* LING, LINGS; see PLURAL, II, D, 2], [prob. < MLG. or MD], an edible fish of the cod family, found in the North Atlantic.

**ling** (liŋ), ***n.*** [ON. *lyng*], heather.

**-ling** (liŋ), [AS.], a suffix added to nouns, meaning: 1. *small*, as in *duckling*. 2. *unimportant* or *contemptible*, as in *princeling, hireling*.

**-ling** (liŋ), [AS.], [Archaic or Dial.], a suffix meaning *extent* or *condition*, as in *darkling*.

**lin·ger** (liŋ′gēr), ***v.i.*** [< North ME. freq. of *lengen*, to delay < base of *long*], 1. to continue to stay, as through reluctance to leave. 2. to continue to live or exist although very close to death. 3. to be unnecessarily slow in doing something; loiter. —**lin′ger·er,** ***n.*** —**lin′ger·ing·ly,** ***adv.***

**lin·ge·rie** (län′zhə-rā′, -rē′; lan′-), ***n.*** [Fr.], women's underwear of linen, silk, rayon, etc.

**lin·go** (liŋ′gō), ***n.*** [*pl.* -GOES], [Pr. < L. *lingua*, tongue], language; esp., a dialect, jargon, or special vocabulary that one is not familiar with: a humorous or disparaging term.

**lin·gua fran·ca** (liŋ′gwə fraŋ′kə), [It., lit., Frankish language], 1. a hybrid language of Italian, Spanish, French, Greek, Arabic, and Turkish elements, spoken in certain Mediterranean ports. 2. any hybrid language used for communication between different peoples, as pidgin English.

**lin·gual** (liŋ′gwəl), ***adj.*** [< ML. < L. *lingua*, the tongue], 1. of the tongue. 2. pronounced by using the tongue. ***n.*** in *phonetics*, a sound, or a letter representing it, pronounced by using the tongue especially, as *l* and *t*. —**lin′gual·ly,** ***adv.***

**lin·guist** (liŋ′gwist), ***n.*** [< L. *lingua*, the tongue], 1. a person who can speak, read, and write several languages. 2. a specialist in linguistics.

**lin·guis·tic** (liŋ-gwis′tik), ***adj.*** of language or linguistics: also **lin·guis′ti·cal.** —**lin·guis′ti·cal·ly,** ***adv.***

**lin·guis·tics** (liŋ-gwis′tiks), ***n.pl.*** [construed as sing.], 1. the science of language, including phonology, morphology, syntax, and semantics: often **general linguistics.** 2. the study of the structure, development, etc. of a particular language.

**lin·i·ment** (lin′ə-mənt), ***n.*** [< LL. < L. *linere*, to smear], a medicated liquid to be rubbed on the skin for soothing sore or inflamed areas.

**lin·ing** (līn′iŋ), ***n.*** [see LINE (to cover on the inside)], the material covering an inner surface.

**link** (liŋk), ***n.*** [< Anglo-N.], 1. any of the series of rings or loops making up a chain. 2. *a*) a section of something resembling a chain: as, a *link* of sausage. *b*) an element in a series of circumstances: as, a weak *link* in the evidence. 3. anything serving to connect or tie: as, a *link* with the past. 4. one length in a surveyor's chain, equal to 7.92 inches. ***v.t.*** to join together with a link or links. ***v.i.*** to connect. —**linked,** ***adj.***

**link** (liŋk), ***n.*** [? < prec., as being made in links], a torch made of tow and pitch.

**link·age** (liŋk′ij), ***n.*** 1. a linking or being linked. 2. a series or system of links.

**linking verb,** a verb that functions chiefly as a connection between a subject and a predicate complement (e.g., *be, appear, seem*, etc.).

**links** (liŋks), ***n.pl.*** [AS. *hlinc*, a slope], a golf course.

**Lin·nae·us, Car·o·lus** (kar′ə-ləs li-nē′əs), (born *Karl von Linné*), 1707–1778; Swedish botanist. —**Lin·nae′an, Lin·ne′an,** ***adj.***

**lin·net** (lin′it), ***n.*** [OFr. *linette* < *lin* (< L. *linum*), flax: the bird feeds on flaxseed], a small finch found in Europe, Asia, and Africa.

**li·no·le·um** (li-nō′li-əm), ***n.*** [< L. *linum*, flax + *oleum*, oil], a hard, washable floor covering made of a mixture of ground cork and oxidized linseed oil spread over a burlap or canvas backing.

**lin·o·type** (līn′ə-tīp′), ***n.*** [< *line of type*], a keyboard-operated typesetting machine that casts an entire line of type in one bar: a trade-mark (**Linotype**). ***v.t. & v.i.*** [-TYPED, -TYPING], to set (matter) with this machine. —**lin′o·typ′er,** ***n.***

**lin·seed** (lin′sēd′), ***n.*** [AS. *linsæd*], flaxseed.

**linseed oil,** a yellowish oil extracted from flaxseed, used in oil paints, etc.

**lin·sey** (lin′zi), ***n.*** [*pl.* -SEYS], linsey-woolsey.

**lin·sey-wool·sey** (lin′zi-wool′zi), ***n.*** [*pl.* -WOOLSEYS], [ME. < *lin*, flax + *wool*], a coarse cloth made of linen and wool or cotton and wool.

**lint** (lint), ***n.*** [< L. *linteum*, linen cloth < *linum*, flax], 1. scraped and softened linen formerly used as a dressing for wounds. 2. fine bits of thread, ravelings, or fluff from cloth or yarn. —**lint′y** [-IER, -IEST], ***adj.***

**lin·tel** (lin′t'l), ***n.*** [OFr. < LL. < L. *limes*, border], the horizontal crosspiece over a door or window, carrying the weight of the structure above it.

**lint·ers** (lin′tẽrz), *n.pl.* the short fibers clinging to cotton seeds after ginning, used in making cotton batting.
**lin·y** (lin′i), *adj.* [-IER, -IEST], 1. like a line; thin. 2. marked with lines. Also **line′y.**
**li·on** (lī′ən), *n.* [*pl.* LIONS, LION; see PLURAL, II, D, 1], [OFr. < L. *leo* < Gr. *leōn*], 1. a large, powerful mammal of the cat family, found in Africa and SW Asia, with a tawny coat, a tufted tail, and, in the adult male, a shaggy mane. 2. a person of great courage or strength. 3. a celebrity. 4. [L-], the constellation Leo.
**li·on·ess** (lī′ən-is), *n.* a female lion.
**li·on·heart** (lī′ən-härt′), *n.* 1. a lionhearted person. 2. [L-], Richard I of England.
**li·on·heart·ed** (lī′ən-här′tid), *adj.* very brave.
**li·on·ize** (lī′ən-īz′), *v.t.* [-IZED, -IZING], to treat as a celebrity. **—li′on·i·za′tion,** *n.*
**lion's share,** the largest or best portion.
**lip** (lip), *n.* [AS. *lippa*], 1. either of the two fleshy folds forming the edges of the mouth. 2. anything like a lip; specif., *a*) the projecting rim of a pitcher, cup, etc. *b*) the mouthpiece of a wind instrument. *c*) in *anatomy*, a labium. *d*) in *botany*, any liplike structure. 3. [Slang], insolent talk. *v.t.* [LIPPED, LIPPING], to touch with the lips; specif., *a*) to kiss. *b*) to place the lips in the proper position for playing (a wind instrument). *adj.* merely spoken or superficial; not sincere: as, *lip* service. **—bite one's lips,** to keep back one's anger, annoyance, etc. **—hang on the lips of,** to listen to with close attention or great admiration. **—keep a stiff upper lip,** [Colloq.], to avoid becoming frightened or discouraged.
**lip·o-** (lip′ō, -ə), [< Gr. *lipos*, fat], a combining form meaning *of* or *like fat, fatty*: also **lip-.**
**lip·oid** (lip′oid, lī′poid), *adj.* [*lip*(*o*)- + *-oid*], in biochemistry, resembling fat.
**lipped** (lipt), *adj.* having a lip or lips: often in compounds: as, *tight-lipped.*
**lip-read** (lip′rēd′), *v.t. & v.i.* [-READ, -READING], to recognize (a speaker's words) by lip reading.
**lip reading,** the art of recognizing a speaker's words by watching the movement of his lips: it is often taught to the deaf. **—lip reader.**
**lip·stick** (lip′stik′), *n.* a small stick of rouge for coloring the lips.
**liq.,** 1. liquid. 2. liquor.
**liq·ue·fac·tion** (lik′wə-fak′shən), *n.* a liquefying or being liquefied.
**liq·ue·fy** (lik′wə-fī′), *v.t. & v.i.* [-FIED, -FYING], [< Fr. < L. < *liquere*, to be liquid + *facere*, to make], to change into a liquid. **—liq′ue·fi′a·ble,** *adj.* **—liq′ue·fi′er,** *n.*
**li·ques·cent** (li-kwes′'nt), *adj.* [L. *liquescens*, ppr. < *liquere*, to be liquid], becoming liquid; melting. **—li·ques′cence, li·ques′cen·cy,** *n.*
**li·queur** (li-kūr′), *n.* [Fr.], any of certain sweet, sirupy alcoholic liquors, variously flavored.
**liq·uid** (lik′wid), *adj.* [< OFr. < L. *liquidus* < *liquere*, to be liquid], 1. readily flowing; fluid. 2. clear; transparent: as, the *liquid* air. 3. flowing smoothly and musically: as, *liquid* verse. 4. readily convertible into cash. 5. flowing and vowellike, as the consonants *l* and *r*. *n.* a substance that, unlike a solid, flows readily but, unlike a gas, does not tend to expand indefinitely. **—li·quid′i·ty, liq′uid·ness,** *n.* **—liq′uid·ly,** *adv.*
**liquid air,** air brought to a liquid state by being subjected to great pressure and then cooled by its own expansion.
**liq·ui·date** (lik′wi-dāt′), *v.t.* [-DATED, -DATING], [< ML. pp. of *liquidare* < L. *liquidus*, liquid], 1. to settle the amount of (indebtedness, damages, etc.). 2. to clear up the affairs of (a bankrupt business, etc.); settle the accounts of, by apportioning assets and debts. 3. to pay (a debt). 4. to convert into cash. 5. to dispose of; get rid of, as by killing. *v.i.* to liquidate one's debts. **—liq′ui·da′tion,** *n.* **—liq′ui·da′tor,** *n.*
**liquid measure,** 1. the measurement of liquids. 2. a system of measuring liquids; esp., the system in which 2 pints = 1 quart, 4 quarts = 1 gallon, etc.
**liq·uor** (lik′ẽr), *n.* [< OFr. *licor* < L. *liquor*], 1. any liquid or juice. 2. an alcoholic drink, especially one made by distilling, as whisky or rum. *v.t. & v.i.* [Slang], to drink or supply with alcoholic liquor, especially in large quantities (usually with *up*).
**liq·uo·rice** (lik′ẽr-is, lik′rish, -ẽr-ish), *n.* licorice.
**liq·uor·ish** (lik′ẽr-ish), *adj.* lickerish.
**li·ra** (lêr′ə), *n.* [*pl.* LIRE (-ā), -RAS], [It. < L. *libra*, pound], 1. the monetary unit and a silver coin of Italy. 2. the monetary unit and a gold coin of Turkey.
**Lis·bon** (liz′bən), *n.* the capital of Portugal: pop., 790,000: Portuguese name, **Lis·bo·a** (lēzh-bô′ä).
**lisle** (līl), *n.* [< *Lisle*, earlier sp. of *Lille*, France], 1. a fine, hard, extra-strong cotton thread: in full, **lisle thread.** 2. a fabric, stockings, etc. woven of this. *adj.* made of lisle.
**lisp** (lisp), *v.i.* [< AS. < *wlisp*, a lisping], 1. to substitute the sounds (th) and (*th*) for the sounds of *s* and *z*. 2. to speak imperfectly or like a child. *v.t.* to utter with a lisp. *n.* 1. the act or habit of lisping. 2. the sound of lisping. **—lisp′er,** *n.* **—lisp′ing·ly,** *adv.*
**lis·some, lis·som** (lis′əm), *adj.* [altered < *lithesome*], 1. supple; limber; flexible. 2. nimble; agile. **—lis′some·ly, lis′som·ly,** *adv.* **—lis′some·ness, lis′som·ness,** *n.*
**list** (list), *n.* [< AS. *liste* & Anglo-Fr. *liste*], 1. a narrow strip of cloth; esp., the selvage. 2. a stripe of color. 3. a strip or ridge. 4. a boundary. 5. a series of names, words, numbers, etc. set forth in order; catalogue; roll. *v.t.* 1. to edge with a strip or strips of cloth. 2. to arrange in stripes or bands. 3. *a*) to set forth (a series of names, words, etc.) in order. *b*) to enter in a list, directory, etc. **—list′ing,** *n.*
**list** (list), *v.i.* [AS. *lystan* < base of *lust*, desire], [Archaic], 1. to be pleasing (*to* someone). 2. to wish; like; choose.
**list** (list), *v.t. & v.i.* [< prec. word in basic sense "to incline"], to tilt to one side, as a ship. *n.* a tilting or inclining to one side.
**list** (list), *v.t. & v.i.* [AS. *hlystan* < base of *hlyst*, hearing], [Archaic], to listen (to).
**lis·ten** (lis′'n), *v.i.* [AS. *hlysnan;* see prec. entry], 1. to make a conscious effort to hear; attend closely, so as to hear. 2. to give heed; take advice. *n.* a listening. **—listen in,** to be a listener to a telephone conversation of others, a radio program, etc. **—lis′ten·er,** *n.*
**list·er** (lis′tẽr), *n.* [*list* (a strip) + *-er*], a plow with a double moldboard, which heaps the earth on both sides of the furrow.
**Lis·ter, Joseph** (lis′tẽr), 1827–1912; English surgeon; introduced antiseptic surgery.
**list·less** (list′lis), *adj.* [*list* (var. of *lust*) + *less*], feeling or showing only indifference to what is going on about one, as a result of illness, weariness, dejection, etc.; spiritless; languid. **—list′less·ly,** *adv.* **—list′less·ness,** *n.*
**list price,** price shown in a list or catalogue: dealers usually receive a discount from it.
**lists** (lists), *n.pl.* [ME. *listes*, specialized use of *liste*, strip, border], 1. the high fence enclosing an area in which knights held tournaments. 2. this area itself or a tournament held there. 3. any arena or place of combat. **—enter the lists,** to enter a contest or struggle.
**Liszt, Franz** (fränts list), 1811–1886; Hungarian pianist and composer.
**lit** (lit), alt. pt. and pp. of **light** (to illuminate) and of **light** (to alight).
**lit.,** 1. liter; liters. 2. literal. 3. literally. 4. literary. 5. literature.
**lit·a·ny** (lit′'n-i), *n.* [*pl.* -NIES], [< OFr. < LL. < Gr. *litaneia*], a form of prayer in which the clergy and the congregation take part alternately, with recitation and response.
**li·tchi** (lē′chē′), *n.* [Chin. *li-chih*], 1. a Chinese evergreen tree. 2. the fresh or dried fruit of this tree, with a single seed, a sweet, edible pulp, and a rough, papery shell. Also sp. **lichee.**
**litchi nut,** the dried fruit of the litchi tree.
**-lite** (līt), [Fr., for *-lithe;* see -LITH], a combining form meaning *stone*, used in the names of minerals and rocks, as in *chrysolite*: also **-lyte.**
**li·ter** (lē′tẽr), *n.* [Fr. *litre* < ML. < Gr. *litra*, a pound], the basic unit of capacity in the metric system, equal to 1 cubic decimeter (1.0567 liquid quarts or .908 dry quart): also sp. **litre.**
**lit·er·a·cy** (lit′ẽr-ə-si), *n.* the state or quality of being literate; ability to read and write.
**lit·er·al** (lit′ẽr-əl), *adj.* [OFr. < LL. *lit*(*t*)*eralis* < L. *lit*(*t*)*era*, a letter], 1. following the exact words of the original: as, a *literal* translation. 2. based on the actual words in their ordinary meaning; in a basic or strict sense: as, the *literal* meaning of a passage, word, etc. 3. habitually interpreting statements or words according to their actual denotation; matter-of-fact: as, a *literal* mind. 4. real; not going beyond the actual facts: as, the

*literal* truth. 5. [Colloq.], virtual: used as an intensive. —**lit′er·al′i·ty** [*pl.* -TIES], *n.* —**lit′er·al·ly,** *adv.* —**lit′er·al·ness,** *n.*

**lit·er·al·ism** (lit′ẽr-əl-iz′m), *n.* 1. the tendency to take words, statements, etc. in their literal sense. 2. in *art,* thoroughgoing realism. —**lit′er·al·ist,** *n.* —**lit′er·al·is′tic,** *adj.*

**lit·er·ar·y** (lit′ə-rer′i), *adj.* 1. of or dealing with literature. 2. appropriate to literature: as, a *literary* style. 3. *a*) skilled in learning and literature. *b*) making literature a profession. —**lit′er·ar′i·ly,** *adv.* —**lit′er·ar′i·ness,** *n.*

**lit·er·ate** (lit′ẽr-it), *adj.* [< L. < *lit(t)era,* a letter], 1. educated; esp., able to read and write. 2. having or showing extensive culture. 3. of or skilled in literature. *n.* a literate person.

**lit·e·ra·ti** (lit′ə-rä′tī, -rä′ti), *n.pl.* [L.], men of letters; scholarly or literary people.

‡**lit·e·ra·tim** (lit′ə-rā′tim), *adv.* [L. < *lit(t)era,* a letter], letter for letter; literally.

**lit·er·a·ture** (lit′ẽr-ə-chẽr, lit′rə-choor′), *n.* [< OFr.; L. *lit(t)eratura* < *lit(t)era,* a letter], 1. the profession of an author. 2. *a*) all the writings of a particular time, country, etc., especially those of an imaginative or critical character valued for excellence of form and expression: as, French *literature.* *b*) all the writings dealing with a particular subject. 3. [Colloq.], printed matter of any kind.

**-lith** (lith), [Fr. *-lithe* < Gr. *lithos,* stone], a combining form meaning *stone,* as in *monolith.*

**Lith.,** 1. Lithuania. 2. Lithuanian.

**lith., litho., lithog.,** 1. lithograph. 2. lithography.

**lith·arge** (lith′ärj, li-thärj′), *n.* [< OFr. < L. < Gr. *lithargyros* < *lithos,* a stone + *argyros,* silver], a yellowish-red oxide of lead, PbO, used in the manufacture of glass, enamel, paints, etc.

**lithe** (līth), *adj.* [AS. *lithe,* soft, mild], bending easily; flexible; supple; limber. —**lithe′ly,** *adv.* —**lithe′ness,** *n.*

**lithe·some** (līth′səm), *adj.* lithe; lissome.

**lith·i·a** (lith′i-ə), *n.* [< Gr. *lithos,* stone], lithium oxide, $Li_2O$, a white, crystalline compound.

**-lith·ic** (lith′ik), a combining form meaning *of a* (specified) *stage in the use of stone,* as in *neolithic.*

**lith·i·um** (lith′i-əm), *n.* [< Gr. *lithos,* a stone], a soft, silver-white, metallic chemical element, the lightest known metal: symbol, Li; at. wt., 6.940; at. no., 3.

**lith·o-** [< Gr. *lithos,* a stone], a combining form meaning *stone, rock:* also **lith-.**

**lith·o·graph** (lith′ə-graf′, -gräf′), *n.* a print made by lithography. *v.i.* to make prints by this process. *v.t.* to reproduce (a picture, writing, etc.) by this process. —**li·thog·ra·pher** (li-thog′rə-fẽr), *n.*

**li·thog·ra·phy** (li-thog′rə-fi), *n.* [*litho-* + *-graphy*], the art or process of printing from a flat stone or metal plate: the design is put on the surface with a greasy material, and then water and printing ink are successively applied; the greasy parts, which repel water, absorb the ink, but the wet parts do not. —**lith·o·graph·ic** (lith′ə-graf′ik), **lith′o·graph′i·cal,** *adj.* —**lith′o·graph′i·cal·ly,** *adv.*

**lith·o·sphere** (lith′ə-sfêr′), *n.* [*litho-* + *sphere*], the solid part of the earth; earth's crust.

**li·thot·o·my** (li-thot′ə-mi), *n.* [*pl.* -MIES], [see LITHO- & -TOMY], the surgical removal of a stone from the bladder. —**lith·o·tom·ic** (lith′ə-tom′ik), **lith′o·tom′i·cal,** *adj.*

**Lith·u·a·ni·a** (lith′oo-wā′ni-ə, -ū-ān′yə), *n.* a country in NE Europe annexed as the Lithuanian Soviet Socialist Republic. —**Lith′u·a′ni·an,** *adj. & n.*

**Lithuanian Soviet Socialist Republic,** a republic of the U.S.S.R., on the Baltic Sea: area, 25,500 sq. mi.; pop., 2,948,000; capital, Vilna.

**lit·i·ga·ble** (lit′i-gə-b'l), *adj.* that can be litigated, or contested in law.

**lit·i·gant** (lit′ə-gənt), *adj.* engaged in or inclined to litigation. *n.* a party to a lawsuit.

**lit·i·gate** (lit′ə-gāt′), *v.t.* [-GATED, -GATING], [< L. pp. of *litigare* < *lis,* dispute + *agere,* to do], to contest in a lawsuit. *v.i.* to carry on a lawsuit. —**lit′i·ga′tor** (-tẽr), *n.*

**lit·i·ga·tion** (lit′ə-gā′shən), *n.* 1. a litigating; carrying on of a lawsuit. 2. a lawsuit.

**li·ti·gious** (li-tij′əs), *adj.* 1. given to carrying on litigations. 2. disputable at law. 3. of lawsuits. —**li·ti′gious·ly,** *adv.* —**li·ti′gious·ness,** *n.*

**lit·mus** (lit′məs), *n.* [< Anglo-Fr. < ON. *litmose,* lichen used in dyeing < *litr,* color + *mosi,* moss], a purple coloring matter obtained from various lichens: it turns blue in bases and red in acids.

**litmus paper,** absorbent paper treated with litmus and used as an acid-base indicator.

**li·tre** (lē′tẽr), *n.* a liter.

**Litt.D.,** *Lit(t)erarum Doctor,* [L.], Doctor of Letters; Doctor of Literature: also **Lit.D.**

**lit·ter** (lit′ẽr), *n.* [< OFr. *litiere* < ML. < L. *lectus,* a couch], 1. a framework having long horizontal shafts near the bottom and enclosing a couch on which a person can be carried. 2. a stretcher for carrying the sick or wounded. 3. straw, hay, etc. used as bedding for animals, as a covering for plants, etc. 4. the young borne at one time by a dog, cat, etc. 5. things lying about in disorder. 6. untidiness; disorder. *v.t.* 1. to bring forth (a number of young) at one time: said of certain animals. 2. to make untidy (often with *up*). 3. to scatter about in a careless manner: as, he *littered* peanuts over the floor. *v.i.* to bear a litter of young.

**lit·té·ra·teur, lit·te·ra·teur** (lit′ẽr-ə-tũr′), *n.* [Fr.], a literary man; man of letters.

**lit·ter·bug** (lit′ẽr-bug′), *n.* a person who litters a public place with refuse, or trash.

**lit·tle** (lit′'l), *adj.* [LITTLER or LESS or LESSER, LITTLEST or LEAST], [AS. *lytel*], 1. small in size; not big, large, or great. 2. small in amount, number, or degree. 3. short in duration or distance; brief. 4. small in importance or power: as, the rights of the *little* man. 5. small in force, intensity, etc.; weak. 6. trivial; trifling. 7. lacking in breadth of vision; narrow-minded: as, a *little* mind. 8. young: of children or animals. *Little* is sometimes used to express endearment, as in bless your *little* heart. *adv.* [LESS, LEAST], 1. in a small degree; only slightly; not much. 2. not in the least: as, he *little* suspects his fate. *n.* 1. a small amount, degree, etc.: as, *little* will be done. 2. a short time or distance. —**little by little,** by slow degrees or small amounts; gradually. —**make little of,** to treat as not very important. —**not a little,** very much; very. —**think little of,** 1. to consider as not very important or valuable. 2. to have no hesitancy about. —**lit′tle·ness,** *n.*

**Little Bear,** Ursa Minor.

**Little Dipper,** a dipper-shaped group of stars in the constellation Ursa Minor (the Little Bear).

**Little Rock,** the capital of Arkansas, on the Arkansas River: pop., 108,000.

**little theater,** 1. a theater of a small community, college, etc., usually noncommercial and amateur, that produces experimental or low-cost drama. 2. drama produced by such theaters.

**lit·to·ral** (lit′ə-rəl), *adj.* [Fr. < L. *littoralis* < *littus,* seashore], of, on, or along the shore. *n.* the region along the shore.

**li·tur·gi·cal** (li-tũr′ji-k'l), *adj.* of or connected with liturgies or public worship: also **li·tur′gic.** —**li·tur′gi·cal·ly,** *adv.*

**lit·ur·gy** (lit′ẽr-ji), *n.* [*pl.* -GIES], [< Fr. < ML. < Gr. *leitourgia;* ult. < *leos,* people + *ergon,* work], 1. prescribed forms or ritual for public worship in any of various Christian churches. 2. the Eucharistic service.

**Lit·vi·nov, Max·im** (måk-sēm′ lit-vē′nôf), 1876–1951; Soviet Russian statesman.

**liv·a·ble** (liv′ə-b'l), *adj.* 1. fit or pleasant to live in, as a house. 2. that can be lived through; endurable. 3. agreeable to live with. Also sp. **liveable.** —**liv′a·ble·ness, live′a·ble·ness,** *n.*

**live** (liv), *v.i.* [LIVED, LIVING], [AS. *liflan, libban*], 1. to be alive; have life. 2. *a*) to remain alive. *b*) to endure. 3. *a*) to pass life in a specified manner: as, they *lived* wretchedly. *b*) to conduct one's life: as, to *live* by a strict moral code. 4. to enjoy a full and varied life. 5. to maintain life: as, she *lives* on twenty dollars a week. 6. to feed; subsist: as, bats *live* on insects and fruit. 7. to make one's dwelling; reside. *v.t.* 1. to carry out in one's life: as, he *lives* his faith. 2. to spend; pass: as, she *lived* a useful life. —**live down,** to live in such a way as to wipe out the shame of (some fault, misdeed, etc.). —**live high** (or **well**), to live in luxury. —**live up to,** to act in accordance with (ideals, promises, etc.).

**live** (līv), *adj.* [short for *alive*], 1. having life; not dead. 2. of the living state or living beings. 3. energetic; wide-awake: as, a *live* executive. 4. of immediate or present interest: as, a *live* issue. 5. still burning or glowing: as, a *live* spark. 6. unexploded: as, a *live* shell. 7. unused; unexpended: as, *live* steam. 8. bright; vivid: as, a *live* color. 9. carrying electrical current: as, a *live* wire. 10. stirring or swarming with living beings. 11. involving a performance in person, rather than a filmed or recorded one: as, a *live* concert. 12. in *mechanics,* imparting motion or power.

**-lived** (līvd; *occas.* livd), [< *life* + *-ed*], a combining form meaning *having* (a specified kind or duration of) *life,* as in *short-lived.*

**live·li·hood** (līv′li-hood′), *n.* [AS. *liflad* < *lif,* life + *-lad,* course], means of supporting life; subsistence.

**live·long** (liv′lôŋ′), *adj.* [ME. *lefe longe,* lit., lief long (cf. LIEF), phr. in which *lief* is merely intens.], long or tediously long in passing; whole; entire: as, the *livelong* day.

**live·ly** (līv′li), *adj.* [-LIER, -LIEST], [AS. *liflic*], 1. full of life; active; vigorous. 2. full of spirit; exciting; animated: as, a *lively* debate. 3. gay; cheerful. 4. moving quickly and lightly, as a dance. 5. vivid; keen: as, *lively* colors. 6. bounding back with great resilience: as, a *lively* ball. *adv.* in a lively manner. —**live′li·ly** (-lə-li), *adv.* —**live′li·ness,** *n.*

**liv·en** (līv′ən), *v.t.* & *v.i.* to make or become lively or gay; cheer (*up*). —**liv′en·er,** *n.*

**live oak,** 1. an evergreen oak of the southeastern U.S. 2. its hard wood, used in shipbuilding and other construction.

**liv·er** (liv′ẽr), *n.* [AS. *lifer*], 1. the largest glandular organ in vertebrate animals: it secretes bile and has an important function in metabolism. 2. the flesh of this organ in cattle, fowl, etc., used as food. 3. the liver thought of as the seat of emotion or desire.

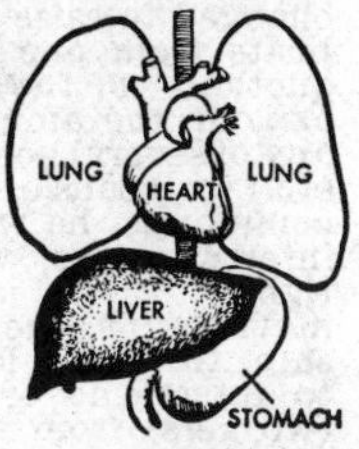

LIVER

**liv·er** (liv′ẽr), *n.* a person who lives (in a specified way or place): as, a plain *liver.*

**liv·er-col·ored** (liv′ẽr-kul′ẽrd), *adj.* reddish-brown to purplish-brown.

**liv·er·ied** (liv′ẽr-id), *adj.* wearing a livery.

**liv·er·ish** (liv′ẽr-ish), *adj.* [Colloq.], 1. bilious. 2. peevish; cross. —**liv′er·ish·ness,** *n.*

**Liv·er·pool** (liv′ẽr-pōōl′), *n.* a seaport in NW England: pop., 790,000.

**liv·er·wort** (liv′ẽr-wũrt′), *n.* 1. any of a group of green, red, purple, or yellow-brown plants resembling the mosses. 2. a hepatica.

**liv·er·wurst** (liv′ẽr-wũrst′), *n.* [*liver* + G. *wurst*, sausage], a sausage containing ground liver.

**liv·er·y** (liv′ẽr-i), *n.* [*pl.* -IES], [< OFr. *livree*, gift of clothes to a servant < *livrer*, to deliver < L. *liberare*, to free], 1. an identifying uniform such as is worn by servants or those in some particular group, trade, etc. 2. the people wearing such uniforms. 3. characteristic dress or appearance. 4. *a*) the keeping and feeding of horses for a fixed charge. *b*) the keeping of horses or vehicles, or both, for hire. *c*) a stable providing these services: also **livery stable.**

**liv·er·y·man** (liv′ẽr-i-mən), *n.* [*pl.* -MEN], a person who owns or works in a livery stable.

**lives** (līvz), *n.* pl. of **life.**

**live·stock** (līv′stok′), *n.* domestic animals kept for use on a farm or raised for sale and profit.

**live wire,** 1. a wire carrying an electric current. 2. [Colloq.], an alert and energetic person.

**liv·id** (liv′id), *adj.* [< Fr. < L. *lividus*], 1. discolored by a bruise; black-and-blue: said of the flesh. 2. grayish-blue; lead-colored: as, *livid* with rage. —**liv′id·ly,** *adv.* —**liv′id·ness, li·vid′i·ty,** *n.*

**liv·ing** (liv′iŋ), *adj.* 1. alive; having life. 2. in active operation or use: as, a *living* institution. 3. of persons alive: as, within *living* memory. 4. still spoken as a native tongue: said of a language. 5. true; lifelike: as, the *living* image. 6. *a*) of life or the sustaining of life: as, *living* conditions. *b*) enough to maintain a reasonable standard of existence: as, a *living* wage. *n.* 1. the state of being alive. 2. the means of sustaining life; livelihood. 3. the manner of existence: as, the standard of *living.* 4. in England, a church benefice. —**the living,** those that are still alive. —**liv′ing·ly,** *adv.* —**liv′ing·ness,** *n.*

**living death,** a life of unrelieved misery.

**living room,** a room (in a home) furnished with sofas, chairs, etc., used as for conversation, reading, or entertaining guests, etc.

**Liv·ing·stone, David** (liv′iŋ-stən), 1813–1873; Scottish missionary and explorer in Africa.

**living wage,** a wage sufficient to maintain a person and his dependents in reasonable comfort.

**Liv·y** (liv′i), *n.* (*Titus Livius*), Roman historian; 59 B.C.–17 A.D.

**liz·ard** (liz′ẽrd), *n.* [< OFr. *lesard* < L. *lacertus*], 1. any of a large group of reptiles with long slender bodies and tails, a scaly skin, and four legs (sometimes vestigial), as the gecko, chameleon, and iguana. 2. loosely, any of various similar animals, as the salamanders.

**'ll,** contraction of **will** or **shall**: as, *I'll* go.

**LL., L.L.,** 1. Late Latin. 2. Low Latin.

**ll.,** lines.

**lla·ma** (lä′mə), *n.* [*pl.* -MAS, -MA; see PLURAL, II, D, 1], [Sp. < Peruv. native name], a South American animal related to the camel but smaller and without humps: it is used as a beast of burden and as a source of wool, meat, and milk.

LLAMA (3 ft. high at shoulder)

**lla·no** (lä′nō; Sp. lyä′nô), *n.* [*pl.* -NOS], [Sp. < L. *planus*, plain], any of the level, grassy plains of Spanish America.

**LL.B.,** *Legum Baccalaureus,* [L.], Bachelor of Laws.

**LL.D.,** *Legum Doctor,* [L.], Doctor of Laws.

**Lloyd George, David** (loid jôrj), 1863–1945; British statesman; prime minister (1916–1922).

**lo** (lō), *interj.* [AS. *la*], look! see!

**loach** (lōch), *n.* [< OFr. *loche* < Celt.], a small European fresh-water fish of the carp family.

**load** (lōd), *n.* [AS. *lad*, a course; infl. in sense by *lade*], 1. something carried or to be carried at one time; burden. 2. a measure of weight or quantity, varying with the type of conveyance: as, a *load* of wood. 3. something carried with difficulty; specif., *a*) a heavy burden or weight. *b*) a great mental burden: as, that's a *load* off my mind. 4. the weight borne up by a structure. 5. a single charge, as of powder and bullets, for a firearm. 6. *often in pl.* [Colloq.], a great amount or quantity: as, she has *loads* of friends. 7. in *electricity*, the amount of current supplied by a source of electric power. 8. in *mechanics*, the external resistance offered to an engine by the machine that it is operating. *v.t.* 1. to put something to be carried into or upon; fill with a load: as, to *load* a truck. 2. to put into or upon a carrier: as, to *load* coal. 3. to burden; oppress. 4. to supply in large quantities: as, they *loaded* him with honors. 5. to put a charge of ammunition into (a firearm, etc.). 6. to put film into (a camera). 7. to add weight to unevenly: as, he *loaded* the dice. *v.i.* 1. to put a charge of ammunition into a firearm. 2. to supply or take a load. —**get a load of,** [Slang], 1. to listen to or hear. 2. to look at or see. —**have a load on,** [Slang], to be intoxicated. —**load′ed,** *adj.* —**load′er,** *n.*

**load·star** (lōd′stär′), *n.* a lodestar.

**load·stone** (lōd′stōn′), *n.* [*load, lode* + *stone*], 1. a strongly magnetic variety of the mineral magnetite. 2. something that attracts as with magnetic force. Also sp. **lodestone.**

**loaf** (lōf), *n.* [*pl.* LOAVES (lōvz)], [AS. *hlaf*], 1. a portion of bread baked in one piece. 2. a fairly large cake baked in one piece: also **loaf cake.** 3. any mass of food shaped somewhat like a loaf of bread and baked: as, a salmon *loaf.* 4. a mass of sugar shaped like a cone.

**loaf** (lōf), *v.i.* [< *loafer*], 1. to loiter or lounge about doing nothing. 2. to work in a lazy way: as, he *loafs* on the job. *v.t.* to spend (time) idly (often with *away*). *n.* the act of loafing.

**loaf·er** (lōf′ẽr), *n.* [prob. < Hudson Valley D.; cf. D. *landlooper*, a vagabond], 1. one who loafs; idler. 2. a moccasinlike sport shoe.

**loam** (lōm), *n.* [AS. *lam*], 1. a rich soil composed of clay, sand, and some organic matter. 2. popularly, any rich, dark soil. *v.t.* to fill or cover with loam. —**loam′y** [-IER, -IEST], *adj.*

**loan** (lōn), *n.* [< ON. *lān*], 1. the act of lending. 2. something lent; esp., a sum of money lent, often at interest. *v.t.* & *v.i.* to lend. —**loan′er,** *n.*

**loan shark,** [Colloq.], a person who lends money at exorbitant or illegal rates of interest.

**loan word,** [after G. *lehnwort*], a word of one language adopted into another and naturalized. English example: *depot* (< French).

**loath** (lōth), *adj.* [AS. *lath*, hostile], unwilling; reluctant: as, they were *loath* to depart: sometimes sp. **loth.** —**nothing loath,** willing(ly).

**loathe** (lōth), *v.t.* [LOATHED, LOATHING], [AS. *lathian*, to be hateful], to feel intense dislike or disgust for; abhor; detest. —**loath′er,** *n.*

**loath·ing** (lōth′iŋ), *n.* intense dislike, disgust, or hatred; abhorrence. —**loath′ing·ly,** *adv.*

**loath·ly** (lōth′li), *adv.* [Rare], unwillingly.

**loath·ly** (lōth′li), *adj.* [Rare], loathsome.

**loath·some** (lōth′səm), *adj.* causing loathing; disgusting. —**loath′some·ly,** *adv.* —**loath′some·ness,** *n.*

**loaves** (lōvz), *n.* pl. of **loaf.**

**lob** (lob), *n.* [ME. *lobbe, lob-*, lit., "heavy, thick"], in *tennis*, a stroke in which the ball is sent high into the air, dropping into the back of the opponent's court. ***v.t.*** [LOBBED, LOBBING], to send (a ball) in a lob. ***v.i.*** 1. to move heavily and clumsily. 2. to lob a ball. —**lob'ber, *n.***

**lo·bar** (lō'bẽr), ***adj.*** of a lobe or lobes.

**lo·bate** (lō'bāt), ***adj.*** having or formed into a lobe or lobes: also **lo'bat·ed.** —**lo'bate·ly, *adv.***

**lo·ba·tion** (lō-bā'shən), ***n.*** 1. lobate formation; a being lobed. 2. a lobe.

**lob·by** (lob'i), ***n.*** [*pl.* -BIES], [ML. *lobium, lobia*], 1. a hall; waiting room or vestibule, as of a hotel, theater, capitol, etc. 2. a group of political lobbyists representing the same special interest. ***v.i.*** [-BIED, -BYING], to act as a lobbyist. ***v.t.*** to get or try to get legislators to vote for (a measure) by lobbying. —**lob'by·ism, *n.***

**lob·by·ist** (lob'i-ist), ***n.*** a person who tries to get legislators to introduce or vote for measures favorable to the special interest he represents.

**lobe** (lōb), ***n.*** [Fr. < LL. < Gr. *lobos*], a rounded projecting part; specif., *a*) the fleshy lower end of the human ear. *b*) any of the main divisions of an organ: as, a *lobe* of the brain, lung, or liver. *c*) any of the rounded divisions of the leaves of certain trees. —**lobed, *adj.***

**lo·be·li·a** (lō-bē'li-ə, -bēl'yə), ***n.*** [after Matthias de *Lobel* (1538–1616), Fl. botanist], any of a large group of plants with long clusters of blue, red, or white flowers.

**lob·lol·ly** (lob'lol'i), ***n.*** [*pl.* -LIES], [prob. < *lob*, in basic sense "heavy, thick" + dial. *lolly*, broth: the tree grows in swamps], 1. a thick-barked pine of the southern U.S. 2. its coarse wood. Also **loblolly pine.**

**lo·bo** (lō'bō), ***n.*** [*pl.* -BOS], [Sp. < L. *lupus*], the large, gray timber wolf of the western U.S.

**lob·ster** (lob'stẽr), ***n.*** [*pl.* -STERS, -STER; see PLURAL, II, D, 1], [AS. *lopustre;* altered < L. *locusta*, locust, lobster, after AS. *loppe*, spider], 1. an edible sea crustacean with compound eyes, long antennae, and five pairs of legs, the first pair of which are modified into large pincers. 2. the flesh of this animal used as food.

**lob·ule** (lob'ūl), ***n.*** 1. a small lobe. 2. a subdivision of a lobe. —**lob'u·lar** (-yoo-lẽr), ***adj.***

**lo·cal** (lō'k'l), ***adj.*** [Fr. < LL. *localis* < L. *locus*, a place], 1. relating to place. 2. of, characteristic of, or confined to a particular place: as, items of *local* interest. 3. narrow; confined: as, *local* outlook. 4. of or for a particular part of the body. 5. making all stops along its run: as, a *local* train. ***n.*** 1. a local train, bus, etc. 2. a newspaper item having interest only to the residents of a particular community. 3. a chapter or branch, as of a labor union. —**lo'cal·ly, *adv.***

**local color,** customs and other features characteristic of a certain region or time, introduced into a novel, play, etc. to supply realism.

**lo·cale** (lō-kal', -käl'), ***n.*** [Fr. *local*], a place; locality, especially with reference to events, etc. associated with it.

**lo·cal·ism** (lō'k'l-iz'm), ***n.*** 1. a local custom. 2. a word, meaning, expression, pronunciation, etc. peculiar to one locality. 3. provincialism.

**lo·cal·i·ty** (lō-kal'ə-ti), ***n.*** [*pl.* -TIES], 1. position with regard to surrounding objects, landmarks, etc. 2. a place; district.

**lo·cal·ize** (lō'k'l-īz'), ***v.t.*** [-IZED, -IZING], to make local; limit, confine, or trace to a particular place, area, or locality. —**lo'cal·iz'a·ble, *adj.*** —**lo'cal·i·za'tion, *n.***

**local option,** the right of determining by a vote of the residents whether something, especially the sale of intoxicating liquors, shall be permitted in their locality.

**lo·cate** (lō'kāt, lō-kāt'), ***v.t.*** [-CATED, -CATING], [< L. pp. of *locare* < *locus*, a place], 1. to designate the site of, as a mining claim. 2. to establish in a certain place: as, the office is *located* downtown. 3. to discover the position of after a search: as, he *located* the seat of the trouble. 4. to show the position of: as, *locate* Guam on this map. 5. to assign to a particular place, etc. ***v.i.*** [Colloq.], to settle: as, he *located* in Cleveland. —**lo'ca·tor, *n.***

**lo·ca·tion** (lō-kā'shən), ***n.*** 1. a locating or being located. 2. position; place; situation. 3. an area marked off for a specific purpose. 4. an outdoor set, away from the studio, where scenes for a motion picture are photographed.

**loc·a·tive** (lok'ə-tiv), ***adj.*** [< pp. of L. *locare;* see LOCATE], in *grammar*, expressing place at which or in which. ***n.*** 1. the locative case (in Latin, Greek, etc.). 2. a word in this case.

**loc. cit.,** *loco citato*, [L.], in the place cited.

**loch** (lok, lokh), ***n.*** [Gael. & OIr.], [Scot.], 1. a lake. 2. an arm of the sea, especially when narrow and nearly surrounded by land.

**lo·ci** (lō'sī), ***n.*** pl. of **locus.**

**lock** (lok), ***n.*** [AS. *loc*, a bolt, enclosure], 1. a mechanical device for fastening a door, strongbox, etc. by means of a key or combination. 2. anything that fastens something else and prevents it from operating. 3. a locking together; jam. 4. an enclosed part of a canal, waterway, etc. equipped with gates so that the level of the water can be changed to raise or lower boats from one level to another. 5. the mechanism of a firearm used to explode the ammunition charge. 6. in *wrestling*, any of several holds. ***v.t.*** 1. to fasten (a door, trunk, etc.) by means of a lock. 2. to shut (*up, in,* or *out*); confine: as, he was *locked* in jail. 3. to fit; link; intertwine: as, we *locked* arms. 4. to embrace tightly. 5. to jam together so as to make immovable: as, the gears are *locked*. 6. to move (a ship) through a lock. ***v.i.*** 1. to become locked. 2. to intertwine or interlock. —**lock out,** to keep (workers) from a place of employment in an attempt to make them accept the employer's terms. —**lock, stock, and barrel,** [Colloq.], completely.

LOCK IN CANAL

**lock** (lok), ***n.*** [AS. *loc*], 1. a curl of hair; ringlet. 2. *pl.* [Poetic], the hair of the head. 3. a tuft of wool, cotton, etc.

**Locke, John** (lok), 1632–1704; English philosopher.

**lock·er** (lok'ẽr), ***n.*** 1. a person or thing that locks. 2. a chest, closet, drawer, etc. which can be locked, especially one for individual use.

**locker room,** a room equipped with lockers.

**lock·et** (lok'it), ***n.*** [< OFr. *locquet*, dim. of *loc*, a lock < Frank.], a small, hinged case of gold, silver, etc., for holding a picture, lock of hair, etc.: it is usually worn on a necklace.

**lock·jaw** (lok'jô'), ***n.*** a form of the disease tetanus, in which the jaws become firmly closed because of spasmodic muscular contraction.

**lock·out** (lok'out'), ***n.*** the refusal by an employer to allow his employees to come in to work unless they agree to his terms.

**lock·smith** (lok'smith'), ***n.*** a person whose work is making or repairing locks and keys.

**lock step,** a method of marching in very close file.

**lock·up** (lok'up'), ***n.*** a jail.

**lo·co** (lō'kō), ***n.*** [Sp., insane], 1. the locoweed. 2. loco disease. ***v.t.*** [-COED, -COING], to poison with locoweed. ***adj.*** [Slang], crazy; demented.

**lo·co-,** [< L. *locus*, a place], a combining form meaning *from place to place*, as in *locomotion*.

**‡lo·co ci·ta·to** (lō'kō sī-tā'tō), [L.], in the place cited or quoted.

**loco disease,** a nervous disease of horses, cattle, and sheep, caused by locoweed poisoning.

**lo·co·mo·tion** (lō'kə-mō'shən), ***n.*** [*loco-* + *motion*], motion, or the power of moving, from one place to another: as, walking is a form of *locomotion*.

**lo·co·mo·tive** (lō'kə-mō'tiv), ***adj.*** 1. of locomotion. 2. moving or capable of moving from one place to another. 3. of engines that move under their own power: as, *locomotive* design. ***n.*** an engine that can move about by its own power; esp., an electric, steam, or Diesel engine on wheels, designed to push or pull a railroad train.

**lo·co·mo·tor** (lō'kə-mō'tẽr), ***n.*** a person or thing with power of locomotion. ***adj.*** of locomotion.

**locomotor ataxia,** a disease of the nervous system, usually caused by syphilis: it is characterized by loss of reflexes and of muscular co-ordination.

**lo·co·weed** (lō'kō-wēd'), ***n.*** any of certain plants of the pea family, found in the western U.S.: it causes loco disease in cattle, etc. that eat it.

**lo·cus** (lō'kəs), ***n.*** [*pl.* -CI (-sī)], [L.], 1. a place. 2. in *mathematics*, a line, plane, etc. every point of which satisfies a given condition.

**lo·cust** (lō'kəst), ***n.*** [< OFr. < L. *locusta*], 1. any of various large, winged insects related to the grasshoppers and crickets: certain locusts travel in large swarms destroying vegetation. 2. a cicada. 3. a tree of the pulse family, common in the eastern U.S.: it has a compound leaf and clusters of fragrant white flowers: also called *black locust.* 4. the yellowish, very hard wood of this tree. 5. the honey locust.

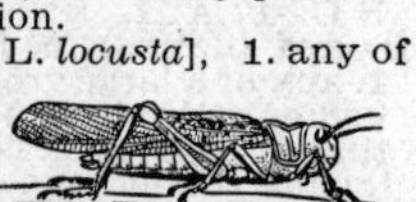

LOCUST (3 in. long)

**lo·cu·tion** (lō-kū'shən), ***n.*** [< L. *locutio* < pp. of *loqui*, to speak], 1. a word, phrase, or expression. 2. a particular style of speech.

**lode** (lōd), *n.* [var. of *load* (AS. *lad*, course)], in *mining*, 1. a vein containing metallic ore and filling a fissure in rock. 2. any deposit of ore separated from the adjoining rock.

**lode·star** (lōd′stär′), *n.* [see LODE], 1. a star by which one directs his course; esp., the North Star. 2. a guiding ideal; model for imitation. Also sp. **loadstar.**

**lode·stone** (lōd′stōn′), *n.* a loadstone.

**lodge** (loj), *n.* [< OFr. *loge*, arbor < OHG. *louba*, upper story, hut, etc.], 1. a small house for special or seasonal use: as, a caretaker's *lodge*, hunting *lodge*. 2. *a*) the place where members of a local chapter of a secret fraternal society hold their meetings. *b*) the local chapter itself. 3. the den of certain animals, as the beaver. 4. *a*) the hut or tent of an American Indian. *b*) those who live in it. *v.t.* [LODGED, LODGING], 1. to house, especially temporarily. 2. to rent rooms to. 3. to deposit for safekeeping. 4. to place or land by shooting, thrusting, etc. (with *in*). 5. to bring (a complaint, etc.) before legal authorities. 6. to confer (powers) upon (with *in*). *v.i.* 1. to live in a certain place for a time. 2. to live (*with* another or *in* his home) as a paying guest. 3. to come to rest and remain firmly fixed (*in*): as, the bullet *lodged* in her spine.

**lodg·er** (loj′ēr), *n.* a person or thing that lodges; esp., one who rents a room in another's home.

**lodg·ing** (loj′iŋ), *n.* 1. a place to live in, especially temporarily. 2. *pl.* a room or rooms rented in a private home.

**lodging house,** a rooming house.

**lodg·ment** (loj′mənt), *n.* 1. a lodging or being lodged. 2. a lodging place. 3. an accumulation of deposited material. Also sp. **lodgement.**

**Lódz** (lodz; Pol. looj), *n.* a city in W Poland: pop., 615,000.

**lo·ess** (lō′is, lös), *n.* [G. *löss* < *lösen*, to loosen], a fine-grained, yellowish-brown, extremely fertile loam deposited by the wind.

**loft** (lôft, loft), *n.* [AS. *loft* < ON. *loft*, upper room, air, sky], 1. *a*) an attic or atticlike space just below the roof of a house, barn, etc. *b*) an upper story of a warehouse or factory. 2. a gallery: as, the choir *loft* in a church. 3. in *golf*, *a*) the slope given to the face of a club to aid in driving the ball upward. *b*) a stroke that knocks the ball in a high curve. *v.t.* 1. to store in a loft. 2. to provide with a loft. 3. in *golf*, to strike (a ball) in such a way as to knock it in a high curve. *v.i.* in *golf*, to loft a ball.

**loft·y** (lôf′ti, lof′-), *adj.* [-IER, -IEST], 1. very high: as, a *lofty* peak in the Alps. 2. elevated; noble; grand. 3. haughty; overproud; arrogant. **—loft′i·ly,** *adv.* **—loft′i·ness,** *n.*

**log** (lôg, log), *n.* [ME. *logge;* prob. < MScand.], 1. a section of the trunk of a felled tree. 2. a device (orig. a quadrant of wood) for measuring the speed of a ship: see also **log chip.** 3. a daily record of a ship's speed, progress, etc. and of the events in its voyage; logbook. 4. *a*) a record of the operating history of an aircraft or of its engines. *b*) a record of a pilot's flying time, experience, etc. 5. any record of progress or operations. *adj.* made of a log or logs. *v.t.* [LOGGED, LOGGING], 1. to saw (trees) into logs. 2. to cut down the trees of (a region). 3. to enter in a ship's log. 4. to sail (a specified distance) as indicated by a log. *v.i.* to cut down trees and transport the logs to a sawmill.

**log,** logarithm.

**Lo·gan** (lō′gən), *n.* a mountain in the Yukon, in NW Canada: height, 19,850 ft.

**lo·gan·ber·ry** (lō′gən-ber′i), *n.* [*pl.* -RIES], [after J. H. *Logan*, who developed it], 1. a hybrid bramble developed from the blackberry and the red raspberry. 2. its purplish-red fruit.

**log·a·rithm** (lôg′ə-rith′m, log′-), *n.* [< Gr. *logos*, a ratio + *arithmos*, number], in *mathematics*, the exponent of the power to which a fixed number (the *base*) must be raised in order to produce a given number (the *antilogarithm*): logarithms are normally computed to the base of 10 and are used for shortening mathematical calculations. **—log′a·rith′mic, log′a·rith′mi·cal,** *adj.* **—log′a·rith′mi·cal·ly,** *adv.*

**log·book** (lôg′book′, log′-), *n.* a log (senses 3 & 4).

**log chip,** a flat piece of wood attached to a line (**log line**) and reel (**log reel**) and thrown into the water to measure a ship's rate of speed.

**loge** (lōzh), *n.* [Fr.; see LODGE], any of a series of compartments in a theater, etc.; box.

**log·ger** (lôg′ēr, log′-), *n.* 1. a person whose work is logging. 2. a machine for loading logs.

**log·ger·head** (lôg′ēr-hed′, log′-), *n.* [< *log* + *head*], 1. a stupid fellow. 2. a tropical sea turtle with a large head: also **loggerhead turtle. —at loggerheads,** in disagreement; in a quarrel.

**log·gia** (loj′i-ə, lô′jə; It. lôd′jä), *n.* [*pl.* -GIAS, It. -GIE (-je)], [It.; see LODGE], an arcaded or roofed gallery projecting from the side of a building, often one overlooking an open court.

LOGGIA

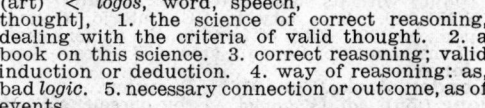

**log·ging** (lôg′iŋ, log′-), *n.* the occupation of cutting down trees, cutting them into logs, and transporting them to the sawmill.

**log·ic** (loj′ik), *n.* [< OFr. < L. < Gr. *logikē* (*technē*), logical (art) < *logos*, word, speech, thought], 1. the science of correct reasoning, dealing with the criteria of valid thought. 2. a book on this science. 3. correct reasoning; valid induction or deduction. 4. way of reasoning: as, bad *logic*. 5. necessary connection or outcome, as of events.

**log·i·cal** (loj′i-k'l), *adj.* 1. of or used in the science of logic. 2. according to the principles of logic, or correct reasoning. 3. necessary or expected because of what has gone before. 4. using correct reasoning. **—log′i·cal′i·ty** (-kal′ə-ti), **log′i·cal·ness,** *n.* **—log′i·cal·ly,** *adv.*

**-log·i·cal** (loj′i-k'l), a suffix used to form adjectives corresponding to nouns ending in *-logy*, as in *biological*: also **-logic.**

**lo·gi·cian** (lō-jish′ən), *n.* an expert in logic.

**lo·gis·tics** (lə-jis′tiks), *n.pl.* [construed as sing.], [< Fr. < *loger*, to quarter], the branch of military science having to do with moving, supplying, and quartering troops. **—lo·gis′tic, lo·gis′ti·cal,** *adj.*

**log·roll** (lôg′rōl′, log′-), *v.i.* to take part in logrolling. *v.t.* to get passage of (a bill) by logrolling. **—log′roll′er,** *n.*

**log·roll·ing** (lôg′rōl′iŋ, log′-), *n.* 1. the act of rolling logs away, as in a community land-clearing. 2. mutual aid, specifically among politicians, as by reciprocal voting for each other's bills. 3. the sport of birling.

**-logue** (lôg, log), [Fr. < L. < Gr. < *logos;* see LOGIC], a combining form meaning *a* (specified kind of) *speaking* or *writing*, as in *monologue*: also **-log.**

**log·wood** (lôg′wood′, log′-), *n.* [so called from being imported in logs], 1. the hard, brownish-red wood of a Central American and West Indian tree, used in dyeing. 2. this tree.

**lo·gy** (lō′gi), *adj.* [-GIER, -GIEST], [? < D. *log*, heavy, dull], [Colloq.], dull or sluggish, as from overeating.

**-lo·gy** (lə-ji), [ult. < Gr. < *logos;* see LOGIC], a combining form meaning 1. *a* (specified kind of) *speaking*, as in *eulogy*. 2. *science, doctrine, theory of*, as in *geology*.

**Lo·hen·grin** (lō′ən-grin′), *n.* in *German legend*, a knight of the Holy Grail: title character of an opera (1850) by Richard Wagner.

**loin** (loin), *n.* [< OFr. *loigne* < ML. < L. *lumbus*], 1. *usually in pl.* the lower part of the back on either side of the backbone between the hipbones and the ribs. 2. the front part of the hindquarters of beef, lamb, veal, etc. with the flank removed. 3. *pl.* the hips and the lower abdomen regarded as the region of strength, procreative power, or unseemly nakedness. **—gird up one's loins,** to get ready to do something difficult.

**loin·cloth** (loin′klôth′, -kloth′), *n.* a cloth worn about the loins, as by some tropical tribes.

**Loire** (lwär), *n.* a river in S France, flowing into the Bay of Biscay.

**loi·ter** (loi′tēr), *v.i.* [< MD. *loteren*], 1. to spend time idly (often with *about*); linger. 2. to move slowly and indolently, as with frequent pauses. *v.t.* to spend (time) idly. **—loi′ter·er,** *n.* **—loi′ter·ing·ly,** *adv.*

**Lo·ki** (lō′ki), *n.* in Norse mythology, the god who constantly created discord and mischief.

**loll** (lol), *v.i.* [< MD. *lollen*], 1. to lean or lounge about in a lazy manner. 2. to hang in a relaxed manner; droop. *v.t.* to let hang loosely, as the tongue. *n.* the act of lolling. **—loll′er,** *n.*

**lol·la·pa·loo·za, lol·la·pa·loo·sa** (lol′ə-pə-lōō′zə), *n.* [< ?], [Slang], something very striking or excellent: also **lollypalooza, lollypaloosa.**

**Lol·lard** (lol′ẽrd), *n.* [< MD. *lollaerd*, a mutterer (of prayers)], a member of a group of political and religious reformers of 14th- and 15th-century England, followers of John Wycliffe.
**lol·li·pop, lol·ly·pop** (lol′i-pop′), *n.* [prob. < dial. *lolly*, the tongue + *pop*], a piece of hard candy on the end of a small stick.
**Lom·bard** (lom′bẽrd, lum′-, lom′bärd′), *n.* 1. a native or inhabitant of Lombardy. 2. one of a Germanic tribe that settled in the Po Valley. ***adj.*** of Lombardy or the Lombards. **—Lom·bar′dic,** ***adj.***
**Lom·bar·dy** (lom′bẽr-di, lum′-), *n.* a region of N Italy: pop., 6,566,000.
**Lo·mond, Loch** (lō′mənd), a lake in W Scotland.
**Lon·don** (lun′dən), *n.* 1. an administrative county of SE England, including the City of London and 28 metropolitan boroughs: it is the capital of the United Kingdom and the British Empire. 2. this county with its suburbs (**Greater London**): pop., 8,251,000. 3. a city in SE Ontario, Canada: pop., 99,000. **—City of London,** the ancient center of the county of London: area, 677 acres. **—Lon′don·er,** ***n.***
**London, Jack,** 1876–1916; U.S. author.
**lone** (lōn), ***adj.*** [< *alone*], 1. by oneself; solitary. 2. lonesome. 3. unmarried or widowed: a humorous usage. 4. *a*) isolated. *b*) unfrequented.
**lone·ly** (lōn′li), ***adj.*** [-LIER, -LIEST], [*lone* + *-ly*], 1. alone; solitary. 2. *a*) isolated. *b*) unfrequented. 3. unhappy at being alone; longing for friends, etc. **—lone′li·ly,** ***adv.*** **—lone′li·ness,** ***n.***
**lone·some** (lōn′səm), ***adj.*** 1. having or causing a lonely feeling. 2. unfrequented; desolate. **—lone′some·ly,** ***adv.*** **—lone′some·ness,** ***n.***
**long** (lôŋ), ***adj.*** [AS. *long, lang*], 1. measuring much from end to end in space or time. 2. of a specified extent in length: as, six feet *long*. 3. of greater than usual or standard length, quantity, etc.: as, a *long* ton, a *long* list. 4. overextended in length; hence, 5. tedious; slow. 6. extending to what is distant in space or time; far-reaching: as, a *long* view of the matter. 7. large; big: as, *long* odds, a *long* chance. 8. well supplied: as, he was *long* on excuses. 9. holding a large supply of a commodity or stock in anticipation of a scarcity and rise in price. 10. requiring a relatively long time to pronounce: said of vowels, consonants, or syllables. ***adv.*** 1. for a long time. 2. for the duration of: as, all day *long*. 3. at a much earlier or a much later time than the time indicated: as, it happened *long* ago. ***n.*** a long vowel, consonant, or syllable. **—as** (or **so**) **long as,** 1. during the time that. 2. seeing that; since. 3. provided that. **—before long,** soon. **—the long and the short of,** the whole story in a few words. **—long′ish,** ***adj.***
**long** (lôŋ), ***v.i.*** [AS. *langian*], to feel a strong yearning; wish earnestly: as, we *long* to go home.
**long.,** longitude.
**Long Beach,** a city in SW California, on the Pacific: pop., 344,000.
**long·boat** (lôŋ′bōt′), *n.* the largest boat carried on a merchant sailing ship.
**long·bow** (lôŋ′bō′), *n.* a bow drawn by hand and shooting a long, feathered arrow: cf. *crossbow*.
**long·cloth** (lôŋ′klôth′, -kloth′), *n.* a soft cotton fabric of fine quality.
**long-dis·tance** (lôŋ′dis′təns), ***adj.*** to or from a distant place: as, *long-distance* telephone calls.
**long distance,** a telephone exchange or operator that puts through long-distance calls.
**long division,** the process of dividing one number by another and putting the steps down in full.
**long-drawn** (lôŋ′drôn′), ***adj.*** prolonged.
**lon·gev·i·ty** (lon-jev′ə-ti), *n.* [< L. < *longus*, long + *aevum*, age], long life; great span of life.
**long-faced** (lôŋ′fāst′), ***adj.*** glum; disconsolate.
**Long·fel·low, Henry Wads·worth** (wädz′wẽrth lôŋ′fel′ō), 1807–1882; U.S. poet.
**long green,** [Slang], paper money.
**long·hair** (lôŋ′hâr′), ***adj.*** [Colloq.], designating or of intellectuals or intellectual tastes; specif., preferring classical music rather than jazz or popular tunes. ***n.*** [Colloq.], an intellectual.
**long·hand** (lôŋ′hand′), *n.* ordinary handwriting: distinguished from *shorthand*.
**long-head·ed, long·head·ed** (lôŋ′hed′id), ***adj.*** 1. having a relatively long skull; dolichocephalic. 2. having much foresight; shrewd; sensible; clever. **—long′-head′ed·ness, long′head′ed·ness,** ***n.***
**long·horn** (lôŋ′hôrn′), *n.* any of a breed of long-horned cattle of the Southwest: also **Texas long-horn.**
**long·ing** (lôŋ′iŋ), *n.* earnest desire; yearning. ***adj.*** feeling or showing a yearning. **—long′ing·ly,** ***adv.***
**Long Island,** an island in New York State, between Long Island Sound and the Atlantic: area, 1,411 sq. mi.; pop., 6,404,000.
**Long Island Sound,** the arm of the Atlantic between Connecticut and Long Island.
**lon·gi·tude** (lon′jə-tōōd′, -tūd′), *n.* [< L. *longitudo* < *longus*, long], 1. length: now humorous. 2. angular distance east or west on the earth's surface, measured by the angle (expressed in degrees up to 180° in either direction) which the meridian passing through a particular place makes with a standard or prime meridian, usually the one passing through Greenwich, England.

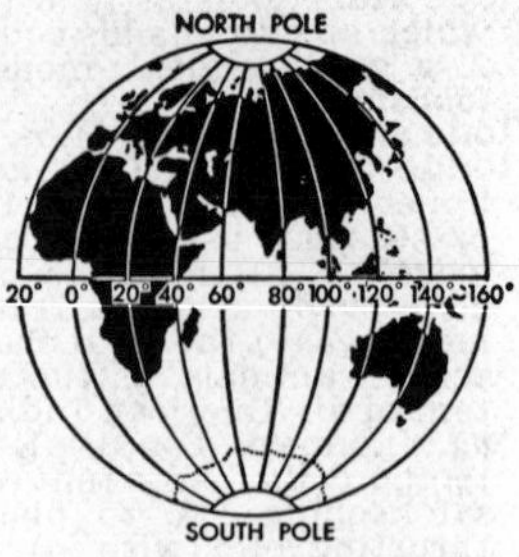

MERIDIANS SHOWING LONGITUDE

**lon·gi·tu·di·nal** (lon′jə-tōō′di-n'l, -tū′-), ***adj.*** 1. of or in length. 2. running or placed lengthwise. 3. of longitude. **—lon′gi·tu′di·nal·ly,** ***adv.***
**long-lived** (lôŋ′līvd′; *occas.* -livd′), ***adj.*** having or tending to have a long life span or existence.
**long-range** (lôŋ′rānj′), ***adj.*** taking the future into consideration: as, *long-range* plans.
**long·shore·man** (lôŋ′shôr′mən, -shōr′-), *n.* [*pl.* -MEN], [< *alongshore* + *man*], a person who works on a water front loading and unloading ships.
**long shot,** [Colloq.], in betting, a choice that is little favored and, hence, carries great odds. **—not by a long shot,** [Colloq.], absolutely not.
**long-sight·ed** (lôŋ′sīt′id), ***adj.*** farsighted. **—long′-sight′ed·ness,** ***n.***
**long-stand·ing** (lôŋ′stan′diŋ), ***adj.*** having continued for a long time.
**long-suf·fer·ing** (lôŋ′suf′ẽr-iŋ), ***adj.*** bearing injuries, trouble, etc. patiently for a long time. ***n.*** long and patient endurance of trials.
**long suit,** 1. the fullest suit in a card player's hand. 2. something at which one excels.
**long ton,** a unit of weight, equal to 2,240 pounds.
**long·ways** (lôŋ′wāz′), ***adv.*** lengthwise.
**long-wind·ed** (lôŋ′win′did), ***adj.*** 1. not easily winded by exertion. 2. speaking or writing at great length. 3. tiresomely long. **—long′-wind′ed·ly,** ***adv.*** **—long′-wind′ed·ness,** ***n.***
**long·wise** (lôŋ′wīz′), ***adv.*** lengthwise.
**loo** (lōō), *n.* [< Fr. *lanturelu*], a card game played for a pool made up of stakes and forfeits.
**look** (look), ***v.i.*** [AS. *locian*], 1. to see. 2. *a*) to direct one's eyes in order to see. *b*) to direct one's attention mentally upon something. 3. to search. 4. to appear; seem. 5. to be facing in a specified direction. 6. to expect (followed by an infinitive). ***v.t.*** 1. to direct one's eyes on: as, *look* him in the face. 2. to express by one's looks: as, he *looked* his despair. 3. to appear as having attained (some age): as, she *looks* her years. ***n.*** 1. the act of looking; glance. 2. appearance; aspect. 3. *pl.* [Colloq.], *a*) appearance: as, I don't like the *looks* of things. *b*) personal appearance, especially of a pleasing nature. ***interj.*** 1. see! 2. pay attention! **—look after,** to take care of. **—look alive!** [Colloq.], be alert! **—look down on** (or **upon**), to regard with contempt; despise. **—look for,** 1. to search for. 2. to expect. **—look forward to,** to anticipate. **—look in** (**on**), to pay a brief visit (to). **—look into,** to investigate. **—look on,** 1. to be an observer or spectator. 2. to consider; regard. **—look oneself,** to seem in normal health, spirits, etc. **—look out,** to be on the watch; be careful. **—look over,** to examine; inspect. **—look to,** 1. to take care of. 2. to rely upon. 3. to expect. **—look up,** 1. to search for in a book of reference, etc. 2. [Colloq.], to pay a visit to. 3. [Colloq.], to improve. **—look up to,** to admire. **—look′er,** ***n.***
**look·er-on** (look′ẽr-on′), *n.* [*pl.* LOOKERS-ON], an observer or spectator.
**looking glass,** a (glass) mirror.
**look·out** (look′out′), *n.* 1. a careful watching for someone or something. 2. *a*) a place for keeping watch. *b*) in *nautical usage*, a crow's-nest. 3. a person detailed to watch. 4. outlook. 5. [Colloq.], concern; worry: as, that's not my *lookout*.
**loom** (lōōm), *n.* [AS. (*ge*)*loma*, tool, utensil], a machine for weaving thread or yarn into cloth.
**loom** (lōōm), ***v.i.*** [prob. < LG. or Scand.], to appear, take shape, or come in sight indistinctly, especially in a large or threatening form: as, the peak *loomed* up before us, disaster *loomed* ahead.
**loon** (lōōn), *n.* [earlier *loom* < ON. *lomr*], a fish-

eating, diving bird somewhat like a duck but with a pointed bill and a weird cry.

**loon** (lōōn), *n.* [Scot.; ? < D. *loen*, stupid fellow], 1. a clumsy, stupid person; dolt. 2. [Archaic], a rogue; scamp.

**loon·y** (lōōn'i), *adj.* [-IER, -IEST], [< *lunatic*], [Slang], crazy; demented. *n.* [*pl.* -IES], [Slang], a loony person.

**loop** (lōōp), *n.* [< Anglo-N. forms corresponding to ON. *hlaup*, a leap, *hlaupa*, to run], 1. the more or less circular figure formed by a line, thread, wire, etc. that crosses itself. 2. anything having or forming this figure, as a written *l*. 3. a sharp bend, as in a mountain road. 4. a ring-shaped fastening or ornament, as a staple, eyelet, etc. 5. a plastic contraceptive device inserted into the uterus (usually with *the*). 6. in *aeronautics*, a movement in which an airplane describes a closed curve or circle in the vertical plane. *v.t.* 1. to make a loop or loops in or of. 2. to wrap around one or more times: as, *loop* the wire around that post. 3. to fasten with a loop or loops. *v.i.* 1. to form into a loop or loops. 2. in *aeronautics*, to perform a loop or loops. **—loop the loop,** to make a vertical loop in the air, as in an airplane or roller coaster. **—loop'er,** *n.*

**loop·hole** (lōōp'hōl'), *n.* [prob. < MD. *lupen*, to peer; + *hole*], 1. a hole or narrow slit in the wall of a fort, etc. for looking or shooting through. 2. a means of evading something unpleasant.

**loose** (lōōs), *adj.* [< Anglo-N.; cf. ON. *lauss*], 1. not confined or restrained; free. 2. not put up in a container: as, *loose* salt. 3. readily available: as, *loose* cash. 4. not firmly fastened down or in: as, this table leg is *loose*. 5. not tight: as, *loose* clothing. 6. not compact or compactly constructed: as, a *loose* frame. 7. not restrained: as, *loose* talk. 8. not precise; inexact: as, a *loose* translation. 9. sexually immoral; lewd. 10. moving freely or excessively: as, *loose* bowels. *adv.* loosely; in a loose manner. *v.t.* [LOOSED, LOOSING], 1. to make loose; specif., *a*) to set free; unbind. *b*) to make less tight. *c*) to make less compact. *d*) to free from restraint; relax. 2. to let fly; release: as, he *loosed* the arrow. *v.i.* to loose something or become loose. **—cast loose,** to untie or unfasten. **—cut loose,** 1. to break or cut from a connecting tie. 2. to become free. 3. [Colloq.], to have fun in a free, unrestrained manner. **—let loose (with),** to set free; release. **—on the loose,** 1. not confined or bound; free. 2. [Colloq.], having fun in a free, unrestrained manner. **—set** (or **turn**) **loose,** to make free; release. **—loose'ly,** *adv.* **—loose'ness,** *n.*

**loose-joint·ed** (lōōs'join'tid), *adj.* 1. having loose joints. 2. limber; moving freely.

**loose-leaf** (lōōs'lēf'), *adj.* having leaves or sheets which can easily be removed or inserted.

**loos·en** (lōōs''n), *v.t. & v.i.* to make or become loose or looser. **—loos'en·er,** *n.*

**loose·strife** (lōōs'strīf'), *n.* [transl. of L. *lysimachia* < Gr. < *lyein*, to loose + *machē*, battle], 1. a plant of the primrose family with leafy stems and loose spikes of white, rose, or yellow flowers. 2. a variety of this plant with whorls of yellow flowers. 3. any of a number of related plants with whorled leaves and spikes of purple flowers.

**loot** (lōōt), *n.* [Hind. *lūt* < Sans. *luṇṭ*, to rob], goods stolen or taken by force; plunder; spoils. *v.t. & v.i.* to plunder. **—loot'er,** *n.*

**lop** (lop), *v.t.* [LOPPED, LOPPING], [ME. *loppen*], 1. to trim (a tree, etc.) by cutting off branches or twigs. 2. to remove by or as by cutting off. *n.* something lopped off. **—lop'per,** *n.*

**lop** (lop), *v.i.* [LOPPED, LOPPING], [< same base as *lob*], to hang down loosely. *v.t.* to let hang down loosely. *adj.* hanging down loosely.

**lope** (lōp), *v.i.* [LOPED, LOPING], [< ON. *hlaupa*, to leap], to move with a long, swinging stride, as in galloping. *v.t.* to cause to lope. *n.* a long, swinging stride. **—lop'er,** *n.*

**lop-eared** (lop'ērd'), *adj.* having drooping ears.

**lop·sid·ed** (lop'sīd'id), *adj.* noticeably heavier, bigger, or lower on one side. **—lop'sid'ed·ly,** *adv.* **—lop'sid'ed·ness,** *n.*

**lo·qua·cious** (lō-kwā'shəs), *adj.* [< L. *loquax* < *loqui*, to speak], very talkative; fond of talking. **—lo·qua'cious·ly,** *adv.*

**lo·quac·i·ty** (lō-kwas'ə-ti), *n.* talkativeness, especially when excessive.

**Lo·rain** (lô-rān'), *n.* a city in N Ohio, on Lake Erie: pop., 69,000.

**Lor·an, lor·an** (lôr'an, lō'ran), *n.* [< *Long Range Navigation*], a system by which a ship or aircraft can determine its position by radar and radio signals sent from known stations.

**lord** (lôrd), *n.* [AS. *hlaford* < *hlaf*, loaf + *weard*, keeper], 1. a person having great power and authority; ruler; master. 2. the head of a feudal estate. 3. [L-], *a*) God. *b*) Jesus Christ. 4. in Great Britain, *a*) a nobleman holding the rank of baron, viscount, earl, or marquis; member of the House of Lords. *b*) a man who by courtesy or because of his office is given the title of Lord. 5. [L-], *pl.* the House of Lords in the British Parliament (usually with *the*). 6. [L-], in Great Britain, the title of a lord, variously used. *v.i.* to act like a lord; rule. *v.t.* to make a lord of. **—lord it (over),** to act in an overbearing manner (toward).

**lord·ly** (lôrd'li), *adj.* [-LIER, -LIEST], of, like, characteristic of, or suitable to a lord; specif., *a*) noble; magnificent. *b*) haughty. *adv.* in the manner of a lord. **—lord'li·ness,** *n.*

**lor·do·sis** (lôr-dō'sis), *n.* [< Gr. < *lordos*, bent backward], forward curvature of the spine, producing a hollow in the back.

**Lord's day,** Sunday.

**lord·ship** (lôrd'ship), *n.* 1. the rank or authority of a lord. 2. rule; dominion. 3. a title used in speaking of or to a lord: with *his* or *your*.

**Lord's Prayer,** the prayer beginning *Our Father*, which Jesus taught his disciples: Matt. 6:9-13.

**lords spiritual,** the archbishops and bishops who are members of the British House of Lords.

**Lord's Supper,** 1. the Last Supper. 2. Holy Communion; Eucharist.

**lords temporal,** those members of the British House of Lords who are not clergy.

**lore** (lôr, lōr), *n.* [AS. *lar*], knowledge; learning; specif., all the knowledge concerning a particular subject, especially that of a traditional nature.

**Lor·e·lei** (lôr'ə-lī'), *n.* [G.], in *German legend*, a siren whose singing on a rock in the Rhine lured sailors to shipwreck on the reefs.

**lor·gnette** (lôr-nyet'), *n.* [Fr. < *lorgner*, to spy, peep < OFr. *lorgne*, squinting], a pair of eyeglasses, or an opera glass, attached to a handle.

**lorn** (lôrn), *adj.* [ME.; pp. of *losen*, to lose], 1. [Obs.], lost; ruined. 2. [Archaic], forsaken, forlorn, bereft, or desolate.

**Lor·raine** (lô-rān', lō-; Fr. lô'ren'), *n.* a former province of NE France.

**lor·ry** (lôr'i, lor'i), *n.* [*pl.* -RIES], [prob. < dial. *lurry, lorry*, to tug], 1. a low, flat wagon without sides. 2. [Brit.], a motor truck.

**lo·ry** (lō'ri, lôr'i), *n.* [*pl.* -RIES], [Malay *lūrī*], a small, brightly colored parrot, native to Australia and near-by islands.

**Los Al·a·mos** (lôs al'ə-mōs'), a town in north-central New Mexico, established as the site of an atomic-bomb laboratory: pop., 13,000.

**Los An·gel·es** (lôs an'j'l-əs, aŋ'gəl-əs, los an'jə-lēz'), a city on the SW coast of California: pop., 2,479,000; with suburbs, 6,743,000.

**lose** (lōōz), *v.t.* [LOST, LOSING], [< AS. *losian*, to be lost & *leosan*, to lose], 1. to bring to ruin or destruction. 2. to become unable to find; mislay: as, he *lost* his keys. 3. to have taken from one by accident, death, removal, etc.; be deprived of. 4. to fail to keep (a state of mind or body, one's position, etc.): as, to *lose* one's temper. 5. *a*) to fail to see, hear, or understand: as, she did not *lose* a word of his lecture. *b*) to fail to keep in sight, mind, etc. 6. to fail to have, get, etc.; miss: as, he *lost* his chance. 7. to fail to win: as, we *lost* the game. 8. to cause the loss of: as, it *lost* him his job. 9. to wander from and not be able to find (one's way, etc.). 10. to waste; squander: as, don't *lose* any time. 11. to outdistance in a race. 12. to engross or preoccupy: as, *lost* in reverie. *v.i.* 1. to suffer loss. 2. to be defeated in a contest, etc. **—lose oneself,** 1. to go astray; become bewildered. 2. to become absorbed. **—los'a·ble,** *adj.* **—los'er,** *n.*

**los·ing** (lōōz'iŋ), *n. pl.* losses by gambling. *adj.* 1. that loses: as, the *losing* team. 2. resulting in loss: as, a *losing* proposition.

**loss** (lôs), *n.* [AS. *los*, ruin], 1. a losing or being lost. 2. the damage, disadvantage, etc. caused by losing something. 3. the person, thing, or amount lost. 4. in *insurance*, death, damage, etc. that is the basis for a valid claim for indemnity. 5. in *military usage*, *a*) the losing of soldiers in battle by death, injury, or capture. *b*) *pl.* soldiers thus lost. **—at a loss (to),** puzzled or uncertain (how to).

**loss leader,** any article that a store sells cheaply or below cost in order to attract customers.

**lost** (lôst), pt. and pp. of **lose.** *adj.* 1. ruined; destroyed. 2. not to be found; missing. 3. no longer held, possessed, seen, heard, etc. 4. not gained or won. 5. having wandered from the way. 6. bewildered; perplexed. 7. wasted; squandered. —**lost in,** engrossed in. —**lost on,** without effect on. —**lost to,** 1. no longer in the possession of. 2. no longer available to. 3. insensible to.

**Lot** (lot), *n.* in the *Bible,* Abraham's nephew, who, warned by angels, fled from Sodom: his wife, who glanced back to behold its destruction, was turned into a pillar of salt: Gen. 19:1-26.

**lot** (lot), *n.* [AS. *hlot*], 1. any of a number of counters, etc. drawn from at random to decide a matter by chance. 2. the use of such a method: as, ten men were chosen by *lot.* 3. the decision arrived at by this means. 4. what one receives as the result of such a decision; share; hence, 5. one's portion in life; fortune: as, his unhappy *lot.* 6. a plot of ground. 7. a number of persons or things regarded as a group. 8. *often pl.* [Colloq.], a great number or amount: as, a *lot* (or *lots*) of ducks. 9. [Colloq.], sort (of person): as, he's a bad *lot.* 10. a motion-picture studio. *adv.* very much: as, a *lot* happier. *v.t.* [LOTTED, LOTTING], 1. to divide into lots. 2. [Rare], to allot. *v.i.* to draw or cast lots. —**cast** (or **throw**) **in one's lot with,** to share the fortunes of. —**draw** (or **cast**) **lots,** to decide an issue by using lots. —**the lot,** [Colloq.], the whole of a quantity or number.

**loth** (lōth), *adj.* loath.

**Lo·thar·i·o** (lō-thâr′i-ō′), *n.* [*pl.* -OS], [after the young rake in a play by Nicholas Rowe (1674–1718)], a gay seducer of women; rake; libertine.

**lo·tion** (lō′shən), *n.* [< L. pp. of *lavare,* to wash], a liquid preparation used, as on the skin, for washing, soothing, healing, etc.

**lot·ter·y** (lot′ẽr-i), *n.* [*pl.* -IES], [It. *lotteria* < *lotto,* lot < Fr. *lot*], a game of chance in which subscribers buy numbered chances on prizes, the winning numbers being chosen by lot.

**lot·to** (lot′ō), *n.* [It.; see LOTTERY], a game of chance played with cards having squares numbered in rows: counters are placed on those numbers corresponding to numbered disks drawn by lot.

**lo·tus, lo·tos** (lō′təs), *n.* [< L. < Gr. *lōtos*], 1. in *Gr. legend,* a plant whose fruit was supposed to induce a dreamy languor and forgetfulness. 2. any of several tropical water lilies; esp., the blue African lotus, a similar species from India, or the white lotus of Egypt. 3. a plant of the pea family, with yellow, purple, or white flowers.

**lo·tus-eat·er** (lō′təs-ēt′ẽr), *n.* 1. in *Gr. legend,* one of a people who ate the fruit of the lotus and became indolent and forgetful. 2. anyone thought of as living a life of indolence and ease, forgetful of reality and duty.

**loud** (loud), *adj.* [AS. *hlud*], 1. of great intensity; strongly audible: said of sound. 2. sounding with great intensity: as, a *loud* bell. 3. noisy. 4. clamorous; emphatic: as, *loud* denials. 5. [Colloq.], showy; flashy: as, a *loud* pattern. 6. [Colloq.], unrefined; vulgar. *adv.* in a loud manner. —**loud′ly,** *adv.* —**loud′ness,** *n.*

**loud·ish** (loud′ish), *adj.* somewhat loud.

**loud·mouthed** (loud′mouthd′, -moutht′), *adj.* talking in a loud, irritating voice; blatant.

**loud-speak·er** (loud′spēk′ẽr), *n.* in *radio,* etc., a device for converting electrical energy to sound and for amplifying this sound.

**lou·is** (lo͞o′i), *n.* [*pl.* LOUIS (-iz)], a louis d'or.

**Lou·is XIV** (lo͞o′i), 1638–1715; king of France (1643–1715): called *the Great.*

**Louis XV,** 1710–1774; king of France (1715–1774).

**Louis XVI,** 1754–1793; king of France (1774–1792); guillotined.

**lou·is d'or** (lo͞o′i dôr′), [Fr., gold louis], 1. an old French gold coin of varying value. 2. a later French gold coin worth 20 francs.

**Louise, Lake** (loo-wēz′), a small lake in Alberta, Canada.

**Lou·i·si·an·a** (lo͞o′i-zi-an′ə, loo-wē′zi-an′ə), *n.* a Southern State of the U.S., on the Gulf of Mexico: area, 48,523 sq. mi.; pop., 3,257,000; capital, Baton Rouge: abbrev. **La.** —**Lou′i·si·an′i·an, Lou′i·si·an′an,** *adj. & n.*

**Lou·is ville** (lo͞o′i-vil′), *n.* a city in N Kentucky, on the Ohio: pop., 391,000.

**lounge** (lounj), *v.i.* [LOUNGED, LOUNGING], [? < Scot. dial. *lungis,* laggard], 1. to stand, move, sit, etc. in a relaxed or lazy way. 2. to spend time in idleness. *v.t.* to spend (time) by lounging. *n.* 1. an act or time of lounging. 2. a room equipped with comfortable furniture for lounging. 3. a couch or sofa. —**loung′er,** *n.*

**lour** (lour), *v.i. & n.* lower (scowl).

**Lourdes** (loord; Fr. lo͞ord), *n.* a town in SW France: pop., 14,000: site of a famous shrine.

**louse** (lous; *for v.,* louz), *n.* [*pl.* LICE], [AS. *lus*], 1. a small, wingless parasitic insect that infests the hair or skin of man and other warm-blooded animals. 2. any similar insect, arachnid, etc. parasitic on plants or animals. 3. [*pl.* LOUSES], [Slang], a person regarded as mean, contemptible, etc. *v.t.* [LOUSED, LOUSING], [Rare], to delouse. —**louse up** (lous), [Slang], to botch; bungle.

**lous·y** (lou′zi), *adj.* [-IER, -IEST], 1. infested with lice. 2. [Slang], dirty or disgusting. 3. [Slang], poor; inferior: a generalized epithet of disapproval. 4. [Slang], well supplied (*with*). —**lous′i·ly,** *adv.* —**lous′i·ness,** *n.*

**lout** (lout), *n.* [prob. < ME. *lowt,* a rag], a clumsy, stupid fellow; boor. —**lout′ish,** *adj.* —**lout′ish·ly,** *adv.* —**lout′ish·ness,** *n.*

**lou·ver** (lo͞o′vẽr), *n.* [OFr. *lover*], 1. *a*) an opening in a turret, etc. furnished with louver boards. *b*) a louver board. 2. any ventilating slit.

**louver board,** any of a series of sloping slats set in a window or other opening to provide air and light but to shed rain: also **louver boarding.**

LOUVER BOARDS

**Lou·vre** (lo͞o′vrə, lo͞ov), *n.* an ancient royal palace in Paris, now an art museum.

**lov·a·ble, love·a·ble** (luv′ə-b'l), *adj.* inspiring love; worthy of love; endearing. —**lov′a·bil′i·ty, love′a·bil′i·ty, lov′a·ble·ness, love′a·ble·ness,** *n.* —**lov′a·bly, love′a·bly,** *adv.*

**love** (luv), *n.* [AS. *lufu*], 1. strong affection for or attachment to someone. 2. a strong liking for or interest in something: as, her *love* of acting. 3. a strong, usually passionate, affection for a person of the opposite sex. 4. the person who is the object of such an affection; sweetheart. 5. [L-], *a*) Cupid. *b*) [Rare], Venus. 6. in *tennis,* a score of zero. *v.t.* [LOVED, LOVING], 1. to feel love for. 2. to show love for by fondling, kissing, etc. 3. to take great pleasure in: as, she *loves* good music. *v.i.* to feel the emotion of love. —**fall in love,** to begin to love. —**for the love of,** for the sake of. —**in love,** feeling love. —**make love,** to woo or embrace, kiss, etc.

**love apple,** the tomato: former name.

**love·bird** (luv′bũrd′), *n.* a small bird of the parrot family often kept as a cage bird: the mates appear to be greatly attached to each other.

**love knot,** a knot of ribbon, etc. that serves as a token between lovers.

**love·less** (luv′lis), *adj.* without love; specif., *a*) feeling no love. *b*) unloved. —**love′less·ly,** *adv.* —**love′less·ness,** *n.*

**love-lies-bleed·ing** (luv′līz′blēd′iŋ), *n.* a variety of amaranth with spikes of small, red flowers.

**love·lorn** (luv′lôrn′), *adj.* deserted by one's sweetheart; pining from love. —**love′lorn′ness,** *n.*

**love·ly** (luv′li), *adj.* [-LIER, -LIEST], having qualities that inspire love, admiration, etc.; specif., *a*) beautiful. *b*) morally or spiritually attractive. *c*) [Colloq.], highly enjoyable: as, a *lovely* party. —**love′li·ly,** *adv.* —**love′li·ness,** *n.*

**love potion,** a magic drink supposedly arousing love for a certain person in the drinker.

**lov·er** (luv′ẽr), *n.* one who loves; specif., *a*) a sweetheart. *b*) *pl.* a man and a woman in love with each other. *c*) a paramour. *d*) one who greatly enjoys some (specified) thing: as, a *lover* of good music. —**lov′er·ly,** *adj. & adv.*

**love seat,** a small sofa seating two persons.

**love·sick** (luv′sik′), *adj.* 1. so much in love as to be incapable of normal behavior. 2. expressive of such a condition. —**love′sick′ness,** *n.*

**lov·ing** (luv′iŋ), *adj.* feeling or expressing love. —**lov′ing·ly,** *adv.* —**lov′ing·ness,** *n.*

**loving cup,** a large drinking cup with two handles, formerly passed among guests at banquets: now often given as a prize in sports, etc.

**lov·ing-kind·ness** (luv′iŋ-kīnd′nis), *n.* kindness resulting from or expressing love.

**low** (lō), *adj.* [AS. *lah*], 1. not high or tall. 2. depressed below the surrounding surface: as, water stood in the *low* places. 3. of little depth; shallow: as, the river is *low.* 4. of little quantity, degree, value, etc.: as, a *low* cost. 5. of less than normal height, depth, degree, etc. 6. near the horizon: as, the sun was *low.* 7. near the equator: as, a *low* latitude. 8. exposing the neck and shoulders: as, a dress with a *low* neckline. 9. prostrate or dead: as, he was laid *low.* 10. deep: as, a *low* bow. 11. lacking energy; weak. 12. depressed in spirits; melancholy. 13. not of high rank; humble. 14. vulgar; coarse; undignified. 15. poor; unfavorable:

as, she has a *low* opinion of him. 16. not advanced in evolution, development, etc.: as, a *low* form of plant life. 17. relatively recent: as, a manuscript of *low* date. 18. *a*) not well supplied with: as, *low* on ammunition. *b*) [Colloq.], short of ready cash. 19. not loud: said of a sound. 20. designating or producing tones made by relatively slow vibrations; deep in pitch. 21. designating the gear ratio producing the lowest speed and the greatest power. 22. in *phonetics*, pronounced with the tongue depressed in the mouth: said of certain vowels. ***adv.*** 1. in, to, or toward a low position, direction, etc.: as, hit them *low*. 2. in a low manner. 3. quietly; softly. 4. with a deep pitch. 5. in a humble position. 6. cheaply. 7. so as to be near the horizon or near the equator. ***n.*** something low; specif., *a*) that gear of a motor vehicle, etc. producing the lowest speed and the greatest power. *b*) [Colloq.], a low level of accomplishment. *c*) in *meteorology*, a low-pressure area. —**lay low,** 1. to cause to fall by hitting. 2. to overcome or kill. —**lie low,** to keep oneself hidden. —**low′ness,** ***n.***

**low** (lō), ***v.i.*** [AS. *hlowan*], to make the characteristic sound of a cow; moo. ***v.t.*** to express by lowing. ***n.*** the characteristic sound of a cow.

**low-born** (lō′bôrn′), ***adj.*** of humble origin.

**low·boy** (lō′boi′), ***n.*** a chest of drawers mounted on short legs to about the height of a table.

**low·bred** (lō′bred′), ***adj.*** ill-mannered; vulgar.

**low-brow, low·brow,** (lō′brou′), ***n.*** [Slang], a person lacking or considered to lack intellectual tastes. ***adj.*** [Slang], of or for a low-brow. Usually a term of contempt or of false humility.

**Low Church,** that party of the Anglican Church which attaches little importance to rituals, sacraments, etc., and holds to an evangelical doctrine: cf. *High Church*. —**Low′-Church′,** ***adj.***

**low comedy,** comedy that gets its effect mainly from action and situation, as burlesque, farce, etc.

**Low Countries,** the Netherlands, Belgium, and Luxemburg. —**low′-coun′try,** ***adj.***

**low-down** (lō′doun′), ***n.*** [Slang], the pertinent facts (with *the*). ***adj.*** (lō′doun′), [Colloq.], mean; contemptible; despicable.

**Low·ell** (lō′əl), ***n.*** a city in NE Massachusetts: pop., 92,000.

**Lowell, James Russell,** 1819–1891; U.S. poet, essayist, editor, and diplomat.

**low·er** (lō′ẽr), ***adj.*** [compar. of *low*], 1. below or farther down in place, physical condition, rank, etc. 2. [L-], in *geology*, less recent; earlier: used of a division of a period. ***v.t.*** 1. to let or put down: as, *lower* the window. 2. to reduce in height, amount, etc.: as, he will *lower* his prices. 3. to weaken or lessen: as, a cold *lowered* his resistance. 4. to cause to be less respected. 5. to reduce (a sound) in volume or in pitch. ***v.i.*** to become lower; sink; fall.

**low·er** (lou′ẽr), ***v.i.*** [ME. *l(o)uren*], 1. to scowl or frown. 2. to appear black and threatening. ***n.*** a frowning or threatening look. Also **lour.**

**Lower California,** a peninsula in Mexico, between the Pacific and the Gulf of California.

**low·er-case** (lō′ẽr-kās′), ***adj.*** designating, of, or in small (not capital) letters. ***v.t.*** [-CASED, -CASING], to set in, or change to, small letters.

**lower case,** small-letter type used in printing as distinguished from capital letters (*upper case*).

**low·er·class·man** (lō′ẽr-klas′mən), ***n.*** [*pl.* -MEN], a freshman or sophomore in a school or college.

**Lower House,** [sometimes l- h-], the larger and more representative branch of a legislature having two branches, as the U.S. House of Representatives.

**low·er·ing** (lou′ẽr-iŋ, lour′iŋ), ***adj.*** 1. scowling; frowning darkly. 2. dark, as if about to rain or snow. Also **louring.** —**low′er·ing·ly,** ***adj.***

**low·er·most** (lō′ẽr-mōst′), ***adj.*** lowest.

**lower world,** 1. the supposed abode of the dead; hell; Hades. 2. the earth.

**low-fre·quen·cy** (lō′frē′kwən-si), ***adj.*** in *electricity*, designating or of an alternating current or oscillation with a relatively low frequency.

**Low German,** 1. the German dialects spoken in the northern lowlands of Germany, the Netherlands, etc. 2. the branch of Germanic languages which includes English, Frisian, Dutch, Flemish, Old Saxon, etc.: distinguished from *High German*.

**low-grade** (lō′grād′), ***adj.*** of inferior quality.

**low·land** (lō′lənd), ***n.*** land that is below the level of the surrounding land. ***adj.*** of or from such a region. —**the Lowlands,** lowlands of S and E Scotland. —**low′land·er, Low′land·er,** ***n.***

**Low Latin,** the Latin language from 200–300 A.D. to the time when Latin disappeared as a distinct vernacular language.

**low·ly** (lō′li), ***adj.*** [-LIER, -LIEST], 1. of or suited to a low position or rank. 2. humble; meek. 3. low. ***adv.*** 1. humbly; meekly. 2. in a low manner, position, etc. —**low′li·ness,** ***n.***

**Low Mass,** a Mass without music and with less ceremonialism than High Mass, conducted by one priest with, usually, only one altar boy.

**low-mind·ed** (lō′mīn′did), ***adj.*** having or showing a coarse, vulgar mind. —**low′-mind′ed·ly,** ***adv.***

**low-pitched** (lō′picht′), ***adj.*** having a low tone or low range of tone: as, a *low-pitched* voice.

**low-pres·sure** (lō′presh′ẽr), ***adj.*** having or using relatively low pressure.

**low-spir·it·ed** (lō′spir′i-tid), ***adj.*** in low spirits; sad; melancholy. —**low′-spir′it·ed·ly,** ***adv.***

**low tide,** 1. the lowest level reached by the ebbing tide. 2. the time when this point is reached. 3. the lowest point reached by something.

**low water,** 1. water at its lowest level. 2. low tide.

**low-wa·ter mark** (lō′wô′tẽr, -wät′ẽr), 1. a mark showing low water. 2. the lowest point reached.

**lox** (loks), ***n.*** [via Yid. < G. *lachs*, salmon], a variety of salty smoked salmon.

**loy·al** (loi′əl), ***adj.*** [Fr. < OFr. < L. *legalis;* see LEGAL], 1. faithful to one's country. 2. faithful to those persons, ideals, etc. that one stands under an obligation to defend or support. 3. relating to or indicating loyalty. —**loy′al·ly,** ***adj.***

**loy·al·ist** (loi′əl-ist), ***n.*** 1. one who supports the established government of his country during times of revolt. 2. [often L-], in the American Revolution, a colonist who was loyal to the British government. 3. [L-], in the Spanish Civil War (1936–1939), one who remained loyal to the Republic. —**loy′al·ism, Loy′al·ism,** ***n.***

**loy·al·ty** (loi′əl-ti), ***n.*** [*pl.* -TIES], quality, state, or instance of being loyal; faithful adherence, etc.

**Loyola,** Saint **Ignatius of,** see **Ignatius of Loyola.**

**loz·enge** (loz′inj), ***n.*** [OFr. *losenge;* prob. < Pr. *lausa*, slab], 1. a plane figure with four equal sides and two obtuse angles; diamond. 2. a cough drop, candy, etc., originally in this shape.

**LP,** ***adj.*** [*L*ong *P*laying], designating or of a phonograph record marked with microgrooves. ***n.*** an LP record: a trade-mark.

**LSD,** [*l*y*s*ergic acid *d*iethylamide], a chemical compound extracted from ergot alkaloids, used in the study of schizophrenia and other mental disorders and as a psychedelic drug.

**L.S.D., £.s.d., l.s.d.,** *librae, solidi, denarii,* [L.], pounds, shillings, pence.

**Lt.,** Lieutenant.

**Ltd., ltd.,** limited.

**Lu,** in *chemistry*, lutetium.

**lu·au** (lōō-ou′, lōō′ou′), ***n.*** [Haw.], a Hawaiian feast, usually with entertainment.

**lub·ber** (lub′ẽr), ***n.*** [< ME. < *lobbe* (see LOB)], 1. a big, slow, clumsy person. 2. an inexperienced, clumsy sailor. ***adj.*** big and clumsy. —**lub′ber·li·ness,** ***n.*** —**lub′ber·ly,** ***adj. & adv.***

**Lub·bock** (lub′ək), ***n.*** a city in NW Texas: pop., 129,000.

**Lü·beck** (lōō′bek; G. lü′bek), ***n.*** a city in NW Germany: pop., 237,000.

**lu·bri·cant** (lōō′bri-kənt), ***adj.*** reducing friction by providing a smooth film as a covering over parts that move against each other. ***n.*** a substance for reducing friction in this way, as oil.

**lu·bri·cate** (lōō′bri-kāt′), ***v.t.*** [-CATED, -CATING], [< L. pp. < *lubricus*, smooth], 1. to make slippery or smooth. 2. to apply a lubricant to (machinery, etc.) in order to reduce friction. ***v.i.*** to serve as a lubricant. —**lu′bri·ca′tion,** ***n.*** —**lu′bri·ca′tor,** ***n.***

**lu·bric·i·ty** (lōō-bris′ə-ti), ***n.*** [*pl.* -TIES], [< Fr. < LL. *lubricitas*], 1. slipperiness; smoothness. 2. trickiness. 3. lewdness.

**lu·cent** (lōō′s'nt), ***adj.*** [< L. ppr. of *lucere*, to shine], 1. giving off light; shining. 2. translucent. —**lu′cen·cy,** ***n.*** —**lu′cent·ly,** ***adv.***

**lu·cerne, lu·cern** (lōō-sũrn′), ***n.*** [< Fr. < OFr. < L. *lucerna*, a lamp < *lucere*, to shine], alfalfa: the common name in Australia and New Zealand.

**Lucerne, Lake of** (lōō-sũrn′), a lake in central Switzerland.

**lu·cid** (lōō′sid), ***adj.*** [< L. < *lucere*, to shine], 1. [Poetic], bright; shining. 2. transparent. 3. sane. 4. clear; readily understood: as, a *lucid* talk. —**lu·cid′i·ty, lu′cid·ness,** ***n.*** —**lu′cid·ly,** ***adv.***

**Lu·ci·fer** (lo͞o′sə-fẽr), *n.* [L. < *lux*, light + *ferre*, to bear], 1. [Poetic], the planet Venus when it is the morning star. 2. Satan, the leader of the revolt of the angels before his fall. 3. [l-], a match ignited by friction.

**lu·cite** (lo͞o′sīt), *n.* [< L. *lux*, light], a crystal-clear synthetic resin, plastic under heat: a trade-mark (**Lucite**).

**luck** (luk), *n.* [prob. < D. (*ge*)*luk* < OD.], 1. the seemingly chance happening of events which affect one; fortune; fate. 2. good fortune; success, etc. —**down on one's luck,** in misfortune; unlucky. —**in luck,** lucky. —**out of luck,** unlucky. —**try one's luck,** to try to do something without being sure of the outcome. —**worse luck,** unfortunately.

**luck·less** (luk′lis), *adj.* having no good luck; unlucky. —**luck′less·ly,** *adv.* —**luck′less·ness,** *n.*

**Luck·now** (luk′nou), *n.* the capital of Uttar Pradesh, India: pop., 497,000.

**luck·y** (luk′i), *adj.* [-IER, -IEST], 1. having good luck; fortunate. 2. resulting fortunately: as, a *lucky* change. 3. believed to bring good luck. —**luck′i·ly,** *adv.* —**luck′i·ness,** *n.*

**lu·cra·tive** (lo͞o′krə-tiv), *adj.* [< L. pp. of *lucrari*, to gain < *lucrum*, riches], producing wealth or profit; profitable. —**lu′cra·tive·ly,** *adv.* —**lu′cra·tive·ness,** *n.*

**lu·cre** (lo͞o′kẽr), *n.* [OFr. < L. *lucrum*], riches; money: chiefly in a derogatory sense.

**Lu·cre·tius** (lo͞o-krē′shəs), *n.* (*Titus Lucretius Carus*), Roman poet and philosopher; 96?–55 B.C.

**lu·cu·brate** (lo͞o′kyoo-brāt′), *v.i.* [-BRATED, -BRATING], [< L. pp. of *lucubrare*, to work by candlelight < *lux*, light], 1. to work, study, or write laboriously, especially late at night. 2. to write in a scholarly manner.

**lu·cu·bra·tion** (lo͞o′kyoo-brā′shən), *n.* 1. a lucubrating. 2. a learned or carefully elaborated production. 3. *often in pl.* any literary composition: humorous usage suggesting pedantry.

**lu·di·crous** (lo͞o′di-krəs), *adj.* [< L. < *ludus*, a game], causing laughter because absurd or ridiculous. —**lu′di·crous·ly,** *adv.* —**lu′di·crous·ness,** *n.*

**luff** (luf), *n.* [ME. *lof*, *loof*, a leeboard; prob. < OD.], 1. a sailing close to the wind. 2. the forward edge of a fore-and-aft sail. *v.i.* to turn the bow of a ship toward the wind.

‡**Luft·waf·fe** (lo͝oft′vä′fə), *n.* [G., lit., air weapon], the Nazi air force in World War II.

**lug** (lug), *v.t.* [LUGGED, LUGGING], [prob. < ON.; cf. Sw. *lugga*, to pull by the hair], to carry or drag (something heavy) with effort. *n.* 1. an earlike projection by which a thing is held or supported. 2. [Slang], a stupid fellow.

**lug** (lug), *n.* a lugsail.

**lug** (lug), *n.* [< *lug*, *v.*], a lugworm.

**lug·gage** (lug′ij), *n.* [< *lug*, *v.*], suitcases, valises, trunks, etc.; baggage.

**lug·ger** (lug′ẽr), *n.* a small vessel equipped with a lugsail or lugsails.

**lug·sail** (lug′s'l, -sāl′), *n.* [prob. < *lug*, *v.*], a four-cornered sail attached to an upper yard which hangs obliquely on the mast.

LUGSAIL

**lu·gu·bri·ous** (loo-go͞o′bri-əs, -gū′-), *adj.* [L. *lugubris* < *lugere*, to mourn], dismal; mournful: usually implying ridiculously excessive grief. —**lu·gu′bri·ous·ly,** *adv.* —**lu·gu′bri·ous·ness,** *n.*

**lug·worm** (lug′wũrm′), *n.* [*lug*, lugworm + *worm*], a bristly, segmented worm that burrows in muddy sand along the shore and is used for bait.

**Luke** (lo͝ok), *n.* in the *Bible*, 1. one of the four Evangelists, a physician and the reputed author of the third book of the New Testament. 2. the third book of the New Testament.

**luke·warm** (lo͞ok′wôrm′), *adj.* [< ME. *leuke*, tepid; + *warm*], 1. barely warm; tepid: said of liquids. 2. lacking warmth of feeling or enthusiasm. —**luke′warm′ly,** *adv.* —**luke′warm′ness,** *n.*

**lull** (lul), *v.t.* [ME. *lullen*], 1. to calm by gentle sound or motion or both: chiefly in *lull to sleep*. 2. to bring (a person) into a specified condition by soothing and reassuring him. 3. to mitigate; allay. *v.i.* to become calm. *n.* a short period of quiet or of comparative calm.

**lull·a·by** (lul′ə-bī′), *n.* [*pl.* -BIES], a song for lulling a baby to sleep. *v.t.* [-BIED, -BYING], to lull as with a lullaby.

**lum·ba·go** (lum-bā′gō), *n.* [LL. < L. *lumbus*, loin], backache, especially in the lower back.

**lum·bar** (lum′bẽr), *adj.* [< L. *lumbus*, loin], of or near the loins. *n.* a lumbar nerve, artery, vertebra, etc.

**lum·ber** (lum′bẽr), *n.* [< *Lombard*: orig., pawnshop, hence pawned (or stored) articles], 1. discarded household articles, furniture, etc. stored away or taking up room. 2. timber sawed into beams, boards, etc. of convenient sizes. *v.t.* 1. to clutter with useless articles or rubbish. 2. to cut down (trees). *v.i.* to cut down timber and saw it into lumber. —**lum′ber·er,** *n.* —**lum′ber·ing,** *n.*

**lum·ber** (lum′bẽr), *v.i.* [< ON.], 1. to move heavily and noisily. 2. to rumble. *n.* a rumbling sound. —**lum′ber·ing,** *adj.* —**lum′ber·ing·ly,** *adv.*

**lum·ber·jack** (lum′bẽr-jak′), *n.* [*lumber* + *jack* (man, boy, etc.)], a man whose work is cutting down timber and preparing it for the sawmill.

**lum·ber·man** (lum′bẽr-mən), *n.* [*pl.* -MEN], 1. a lumberjack. 2. one who deals in lumber or timber.

**lum·ber·yard** (lum′bẽr-yärd′), *n.* a place where lumber is kept for sale.

**lu·men** (lo͞o′mən), *n.* [*pl.* -MINA (-mi-nə), -MENS], [L., light], a unit of measure for the flow of light, equal to the amount of flow from a uniform point source of one candle power.

**lu·mi·nar·y** (lo͞o′mə-ner′i), *n.* [*pl.* -IES], [< OFr. < ML. < L. *luminare* < *lumen*, light], 1. a body that gives off light, such as the sun or moon. 2. a famous intellectual.

**lu·mi·nesce** (lo͞o′mə-nes′), *v.i.* [-NESCED, -NESCING], [a back-formation], to exhibit luminescence.

**lu·mi·nes·cence** (lo͞o′mə-nes′'ns), *n.* [< L. *lumen*, a light; + *-escence*], any giving off of light caused by the absorption of radiant or corpuscular energy and not by incandescence; any cold light. —**lu′mi·nes′cent,** *adj.*

**lu·mi·nif·er·ous** (lo͞o′mə-nif′ẽr-əs), *adj.* [< L. *lumen*, a light; + *-ferous*], giving off or transmitting light.

**lu·mi·nous** (lo͞o′mə-nəs), *adj.* [L. *luminosus* < *lumen*, a light], 1. giving off light; bright. 2. flooded with light. 3. clear; readily understood. —**lu′mi·nos′i·ty** (-nos′ə-ti), [*pl.* -TIES], **lu′mi·nous·ness,** *n.* —**lu′mi·nous·ly,** *adv.*

**lum·mox** (lum′əks), *n.* [? < pers. name *Lomax*], [Colloq.], a clumsy or stupid person.

**lump** (lump), *n.* [ME. *lumpe*], 1. an indefinitely shaped mass of something. 2. a swelling. 3. aggregate; collection. 4. a dull, clodlike person. *adj.* forming or formed into a lump or lumps: as, *lump* sugar. *v.t.* 1. to put together in a lump or lumps. 2. to treat or deal with in a mass, or collectively. 3. to make lumps in. *v.i.* to become lumpy. —**in the lump,** all together.

**lump** (lump), *v.t.* [Early Mod. Eng., to look sour], [Colloq.], to put up with (something disagreeable): as, if you don't like it, *lump* it.

**lump·ish** (lump′ish), *adj.* 1. like a lump; heavy. 2. dull; stupid. —**lump′ish·ly,** *adv.* —**lump′ish·ness,** *n.*

**lump sum,** a gross sum paid at one time.

**lump·y** (lump′i), *adj.* [-IER, -IEST], 1. full of lumps: as, *lumpy* pudding. 2. covered with lumps. 3. rough: said of water. 4. like a lump; heavy; clumsy. —**lump′i·ly,** *adv.* —**lump′i·ness,** *n.*

**Lu·na** (lo͞o′nə), *n.* [L.], 1. in *Rom. mythology*, the goddess of the moon. 2. the moon personified.

**lu·na·cy** (lo͞o′nə-si), *n.* [*pl.* -CIES], [*lunatic* + *-cy*], 1. insanity. 2. utter foolishness.

**Luna moth,** a large North American moth with crescent-marked, pastel-green wings, the hind pair of which end in elongated tails.

**lu·nar** (lo͞o′nẽr), *adj.* [< L. < *luna*, the moon], 1. of the moon. 2. like the moon; specif., *a*) pale; pallid. *b*) crescent-shaped. 3. measured by the moon's revolutions: as, a *lunar* month.

**lunar month,** the interval from one new moon to the next, equal to about 29½ days.

**lunar year,** a period of 12 lunar months.

**lu·nate** (lo͞o′nāt), *adj.* [< L. < *luna*, the moon], crescent-shaped: also **lu′nat·ed** (-nā-tid).

**lu·na·tic** (lo͞o′nə-tik), *adj.* [< OFr. < LL. *lunaticus* < L. *luna*, the moon], 1. insane. 2. of lunacy. 3. of or for insane persons. 4. utterly foolish. Also **lu·nat′i·cal** (-nat′i-k'l). *n.* an insane person. —**lu·nat′i·cal·ly,** *adv.*

**lunatic asylum,** a hospital for the mentally ill: term no longer in good usage.

**lunatic fringe,** the minority considered fanatical in any political, social, or other movement.

**lunch** (lunch), *n.* [earlier, a piece; ? < Sp. *lonja*, slice of ham], any light meal; esp., the midday meal between breakfast and dinner. *v.i.* to eat lunch. *v.t.* to provide lunch for. —**lunch′er,** *n.*

**lunch·eon** (lun′chən), *n.* [< *lunch*], a lunch; esp., a formal lunch.

**lunch·eon·ette** (lun′chən-et′), *n.* a small restaurant where light lunches can be had.

**lunch·room** (lunch′ro͞om′, -ro͝om′), *n.* a restaurant where lunches are served.

**lung** (luŋ), *n.* [AS. *lungen*], either of the two sponge-like respiratory organs in the thorax of vertebrates, that oxygenate the blood and remove carbon dioxide from it. **—at the top of one's lungs,** in one's loudest voice.

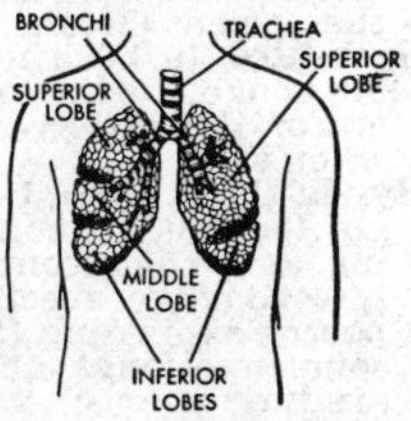

LUNGS

**lunge** (lunj), *n.* [< Fr. < *allonger*, to lengthen < *a-* (< L. *ad*), to + *long* (< L. *longus*), long], 1. a sudden thrust as with a sword. 2. a sudden plunge forward. *v.i. & v.t.* [LUNGED, LUNGING], to move, or cause to move, with a lunge. **—lung'er,** *n.*

**lung·fish** (luŋ'fish'), *n.* [*pl.* see FISH], any of a group of fishes having lungs as well as gills.

**lung·wort** (luŋ'wŭrt'), *n.* [AS. *lungenwyrt*], a plant of the borage family with spotted leaves and clusters of blue or purple flowers.

**Lu·per·ca·li·a** (lo͞o'pēr-kā'li-ə), *n.pl.* an ancient Roman fertility festival, held on February 15: also **Lu'per·cal'** (-kal'). **—Lu'per·ca'li·an,** *adj.*

**lu·pine** (lo͞o'pin), *adj.* [< L. < *lupus*, a wolf], 1. of or related to the wolf. 2. wolflike; fierce.

**lu·pine** (lo͞o'pin), *n.* [< L. < *lupus*, a wolf], 1. a plant of the pea family, with long spikes of rose, yellow, or blue flowers and pods containing white, beanlike seeds. 2. this seed, used in some parts of Europe as food.

**lu·pus** (lo͞o'pəs), *n.* [L., a wolf], a chronic, tuberculous skin disease.

**lurch** (lũrch), *v.i.* [earlier *lee-larch*, a falling to leeward; ult. < Fr. *lâcher*, to let go], to roll, pitch, or sway suddenly to one side. *n.* a lurching movement.

**lurch** (lũrch), *n.* [Fr. *lourche*, name of a game; prob. < OFr. *lourche*, duped], in *cribbage*, the condition of a loser who fails to score a specified number of points. **—leave in the lurch,** to leave in a difficult situation.

**lurch** (lũrch), *v.i.* [var. of *lurk*], [Obs.], to lurk. *v.t.* [Archaic], to cheat; trick; rob.

**lure** (loor), *n.* [< OFr. *leurre;* prob. < Gmc.], 1. a feathered device on the end of a long cord, used in falconry to recall the hawk. 2. anything that tempts or entices: as, the *lure* of the stage. 3. a bait used in fishing. *v.t.* [LURED, LURING], to attract; tempt; entice. **—lur'er,** *n.*

**lu·rid** (loor'id), *adj.* [L. *luridus*], 1. [Rare], deathly pale. 2. glowing through a haze, as flames enveloped by smoke. 3. *a*) startling; sensational. *b*) characterized by violence or crime: as, a *lurid* tale. **—lu'rid·ly,** *adv.* **—lu'rid·ness,** *n.*

**lurk** (lũrk), *v.i.* [ME. *lurken;* ? freq. of *louren* (see LOWER, to scowl)], 1. to stay hidden, ready to attack, etc. 2. to be concealed. 3. to move furtively. **—lurk'er,** *n.* **—lurk'ing·ly,** *adv.*

**lus·cious** (lush'əs), *adj.* [ME. *lucius;* ? var. of *delicious*], 1. highly gratifying to taste or smell; delicious. 2. delighting any of the senses. 3. sickeningly sweet; cloying. **—lus'cious·ly,** *adv.* **—lus'cious·ness,** *n.*

**lush** (lush), *adj.* [< OFr. *lasche*, lax], 1. tender and full of juice. 2. of or characterized by luxuriant growth: as, *lush* vegetation, *lush* fields. **—lush'ly,** *adv.* **—lush'ness,** *n.*

**lush** (lush), *n.* [? < *Lushington*, former actors' club in London], [Slang], 1. alcoholic liquor. 2. a drunkard. *v.i. & v.t.* [Slang], to drink (liquor).

**lust** (lust), *n.* [AS., pleasure, appetite], 1. bodily appetite; esp., excessive sexual desire. 2. overmastering desire: as, a *lust* for power. *v.i.* to feel an intense desire, especially sexual desire.

**lus·ter** (lus'tẽr), *n.* [< Fr. < It. < L. *lustrare*, to illumine], 1. gloss; sheen. 2. brightness; radiance. 3. brilliant beauty or fame; glory. 4. a glossy dress fabric of cotton and wool. 5. the reflecting quality and brilliance of the surface of a mineral. 6. the metallic, sometimes iridescent, appearance of glazed pottery. *v.t.* to give a lustrous finish to. *v.i.* to be or become lustrous.

**lus·ter·ware** (lus'tẽr-wâr'), *n.* highly glazed earthenware decorated by the application of metallic oxides to the glaze: also sp. **lustreware.**

**lust·ful** (lust'fəl), *adj.* full of or characterized by lust. **—lust'ful·ly,** *adv.* **—lust'ful·ness,** *n.*

**lus·trate** (lus'trāte), *v.t.* [-TRATED, -TRATING], [< L. pp. of *lustrare;* see LUSTRUM], to purify by means of certain ceremonies. **—lus·tra'tion,** *n.* **—lus'tra·tive** (-trə-tiv), *adj.*

**lus·tre** (lus'tẽr), *n., v.t. & v.i.* [-TRED (-tẽrd), -TRING], luster.

**lus·trous** (lus'trəs), *adj.* having luster; shining; bright. **—lus'trous·ly,** *adv.* **—lus'trous·ness,** *n.*

**lus·trum** (lus'trəm), *n.* [*pl.* -TRUMS, -TRA (-trə)], [L., orig., prob. illumination], 1. in ancient Rome, a purification of all the people by means of ceremonies held every five years. 2. a five-year period.

**lust·y** (lus'ti), *adj.* [-IER, -IEST], [ME. *lusti*, joyful, merry, etc.], full of youthful vigor; robust; strong. **—lust'i·ly,** *adv.* **—lust'i·ness,** *n.*

**lu·ta·nist, lu·te·nist** (lo͞ot''n-ist), *n.* a player on or composer for the lute.

**lute** (lo͞ot), *n.* [< OFr. < Sp. < Ar. *al'ūd*, lit., the wood], an old stringed instrument like the guitar, with a rounded body, and six to thirteen strings stretched along the fretted neck, which is often bent in a sharp angle.

LUTE

**lute** (lo͞ot), *n.* [< OFr. < L. *lutum*, mud < *luere*, to wash], a clayey cement used as a sealing agent for the joints of pipes, etc. *v.t.* [LUTED, LUTING], to seal with lute.

**lu·te·ti·um** (lo͞o-tē'shi-əm), *n.* [L. *Lutetia*, city in Gaul (now Paris)], a metallic chemical element of the rare-earth group: symbol, Lu; at. wt., 174.99; at. no., 71: formerly sp. **lutecium.**

**Lu·ther, Martin** (lo͞o'thẽr), 1483–1546; leader of the German Reformation.

**Lu·ther·an** (lo͞o'thẽr-ən), *adj.* 1. of Martin Luther. 2. of the Protestant denomination founded by Luther, or of its doctrines, etc. *n.* a member of the Lutheran Church. **—Lu'ther·an·ism,** *n.*

**lut·ist** (lo͞ot'ist), *n.* a lute player.

**Lux·em·burg** (luk'səm-bũrg'), *n.* 1. a grand duchy in W Europe, bounded by Belgium, Germany, and France: area, 999 sq. mi.; pop., 325,000. 2. its capital: pop., 70,000. Abbrev. **Lux.**

**Lux·or** (luk'sôr, look'-), *n.* a town in Egypt on the Nile, near the ruins of ancient Thebes.

**lux·u·ri·ance** (lug-zhoor'i-əns, luk-shoor'-), *n.* the quality or condition of being luxuriant: also **lux·u'ri·an·cy.**

**lux·u·ri·ant** (lug-zhoor'i-ənt, luk-shoor'-), *adj.* [< L. ppr. of *luxuriare;* see LUXURIATE], 1. growing with vigor and in abundance; lush; teeming. 2. characterized by rich ornamentation, etc., often to excess. **—lux·u'ri·ant·ly,** *adv.*

**lux·u·ri·ate** (lug-zhoor'i-āt', luk-shoor'-), *v.i.* [-ATED, -ATING], [< L. pp. of *luxuriare*, to be too fruitful < *luxuria*, luxury], 1. to grow with vigor and in abundance. 2. to live in great luxury. 3. to revel (with *in*). **—lux·u'ri·a'tion,** *n.*

**lux·u·ri·ous** (lug-zhoor'i-əs, luk-shoor'-), *adj.* 1. fond of or indulging in luxury. 2. constituting luxury; splendid, rich, comfortable, etc. **—lux·u'ri·ous·ly,** *adv.* **—lux·u'ri·ous·ness,** *n.*

**lux·u·ry** (luk'shə-ri; *occas.* lug'zhə-), *n.* [*pl.* -RIES], [< OFr. < L. *luxuria* < *luxus*, luxury], 1. the enjoyment of the best and most costly things that offer the greatest comfort and satisfaction. 2. anything contributing to such enjoyment, especially when considered unnecessary to life and health.

**Lu·zon** (lo͞o-zon'), *n.* the main island of the Philippine Islands: area, 40,420 sq. mi.; pop., 8,090,000.

**Lvov** (lvôf), *n.* a city in the W Ukrainian S.S.R.: German name, *Lemberg;* Polish name, *Lwów.*

**Lw,** in *chemistry*, lawrencium.

**Lwów** (lvo͞of), *n.* Lvov: the Polish name.

**-ly** (li), [AS. *-lic*], an adjective-forming suffix meaning: 1. *like, characteristic of, suitable to*, as in *manly.* 2. *happening* (*once*) *every* (specified period of time), as in *monthly.*

**-ly** (li), [AS. *-lice* < *-lic*], an adverb-forming suffix meaning: 1. *in* (a specified) *manner, to* (a specified) *extent* or *direction, in* or *at* (a specified) *time* or *place*, as in *harshly, outwardly, hourly.* 2. *in the* (specified) *order of sequence*, as in *secondly, thirdly.*

**‡ly·cée** (lē'sā'), *n.* [Fr.], in France, a public, college-preparatory secondary school.

**ly·ce·um** (li-sē'əm, li'si-), *n.* [L.; Gr. *Lykeion*, the Lyceum: from the temple of *Apollōn Lykeios* near it], 1. [L-], the grove at Athens where Aristotle taught. 2. a lecture hall. 3. an organization providing public lectures, concerts, etc.

**lydd·ite** (lid'īt), *n.* [< *Lydd*, in Kent, England], a powerful explosive containing picric acid.

**Lyd·i·a** (lid'i-ə), *n.* an ancient country in W Asia Minor. **—Lyd'i·an,** *adj. & n.*

**lye** (lī), *n.* [AS. *leag*], 1. originally, a strong, alkaline solution obtained by leaching wood ashes. 2. any strongly alkaline substance. Lye is used in cleaning and in making soap.
**ly·ing** (lī′iŋ), ppr. of **lie** (to tell lies). *adj.* false; not truthful. *n.* the telling of a lie.
**ly·ing** (lī′iŋ), ppr. of **lie** (to recline).
**ly·ing-in** (lī′iŋ-in′), *n.* confinement in childbirth. *adj.* of or for childbirth: as, a *lying-in* hospital.
**lymph** (limf), *n.* [L. *lympha* < Gr. *nymphē*; see NYMPH], a clear, yellowish, alkaline fluid found in the lymphatic vessels of the body: it resembles blood plasma but contains colorless corpuscles.
**lym·phat·ic** (lim-fat′ik), *adj.* 1. of, containing, or conveying lymph. 2. sluggish; without energy. *n.* a lymphatic vessel.
**lymph gland,** any of the glandlike structures lying in groups in the lymphatic vessels and producing lymphocytes: also **lymphatic gland, lymph node.**
**lym·pho-,** a combining form meaning *of lymph* or *the lymphatics*: also **lymph-.**
**lym·pho·cyte** (lim′fə-sīt′), *n.* [*lympho-* + *-cyte*], a variety of colorless corpuscle found in lymph.
**lymph·oid** (lim′foid), *adj.* of or like lymph or the tissue of the lymph glands.
**lynch** (linch), *v.t.* [< *lynch* law], to kill (an accused person) by mob action and without lawful trial, usually in defiance of local authority. **—lynch′er,** *n.* **—lynch′ing,** *n.*
**lynch law,** [after Capt. William *Lynch* (1742–1820), member of a vigilance committee in Pittsylvania, Virginia, in 1780], the practice of killing by lynching.
**Lynn** (lin), *n.* a city in NE Massachusetts, on Massachusetts Bay: pop., 94,000.
**lynx** (liŋks), *n.* [*pl.* LYNXES, LYNX; see PLURAL, II, D, 1], [L. < Gr. *lynx*], any of a group of wildcats found throughout the Northern Hemisphere and characterized by long legs, a short tail, long, tufted ears, and keen vision.
**lynx-eyed** (liŋks′īd′), *adj.* having very keen sight.
**Lyon** (lyōn), *n.* a city in SE France, on the Rhone River: pop., 471,000.
**ly·on·naise** (lī′ə-nāz′), *adj.* [Fr., fem. of *Lyonnais*, of Lyon], prepared with finely sliced, fried onions: as, *lyonnaise* potatoes.
**Ly·ons** (lī′ənz), *n.* Lyon: the English name.
**Ly·ra** (lī′rə), *n.* a northern constellation supposedly outlining a lyre.
**ly·rate** (lī′rāt), *adj.* shaped like a lyre.
**lyre** (līr), *n.* [< L.; Gr. *lyra*], a small stringed instrument of the harp family, used by the ancient Greeks.

LYRE

**lyre·bird** (līr′bũrd′), *n.* an Australian songbird: the long tail feathers of the male resemble a lyre when spread.
**lyr·ic** (lir′ik), *adj.* [< Fr. or L. < Gr. *lyrikos*], 1. suitable for singing, as to the accompaniment of a lyre; songlike; specif., designating poetry expressing the poet's personal emotion: sonnets, odes, etc. are lyric poems. 2. of or writing lyric poetry. 3. of or having a relatively high voice with a light, flexible quality: as, a *lyric* tenor. *n.* 1. a lyric poem. 2. *usually pl.* the words of a song.
**lyr·i·cal** (lir′i-k'l), *adj.* 1. lyric. 2. expressing feelings of enthusiasm, etc. in strong, emotional language. **—lyr′i·cal·ly,** *adv.* **—lyr′i·cal·ness,** *n.*
**lyr·i·cism** (lir′i-siz'm), *n.* lyric quality, style, expression, etc.
**lyr·i·cist** (lir′i-sist), *n.* a writer of lyrics, especially lyrics for popular songs.
**Ly·san·der** (lī-san′dẽr), *n.* Spartan admiral and general; ?–395 B.C.
**ly·sin** (lī′sin), *n.* [see LYSIS], any antibody dissolving bacteria, blood corpuscles, etc.
**ly·sis** (lī′sis), *n.* [< Gr. *lysis*, a loosening < *lyein*, to loose], the gradual and successful ending of a disease.
**-ly·sis** (lə-sis), [see LYSIS], a combining form meaning *a loosing, dissolution, dissolving, destruction*, as in *catalysis, paralysis.*
**ly·sol** (lī′sol, -sôl), *n.* [< Gr. *lysis* (see LYSIS); + *-ol*], a brown liquid mixture of soap and cresol, used as an antiseptic and disinfectant: a trade-mark **(Lysol).**
**-lyte** (līt), [< Gr. *lytos*; see LYSIS], a combining form meaning *a substance subjected to a process of decomposition*, as in *hydrolyte.*
**-lyt·ic** (lit′ik), 1. a suffix used to form adjectives corresponding to nouns ending in *-lysis*, as in *catalytic.* 2. in *biochemistry*, a suffix meaning *undergoing hydrolysis by enzymes.*
**-lyze** (līz), a combining form used to form verbs corresponding to nouns ending in *-lysis*, as in *paralyze*: also sp. **-lyse.**

# M

**M, m** (em), *n.* [*pl.* M's, m's, Ms, ms], 1. the thirteenth letter of the English alphabet. 2. the sound of M or m. *adj.* thirteenth in a sequence or group.
**M** (em), *n.* 1. an object shaped like M. 2. a Roman numeral for 1,000. *adj.* shaped like M.
**M.,** 1. Manitoba. 2. Medieval. 3. Monday. 4. [*pl.* MM.], Monsieur.
**M., m.,** 1. majesty. 2. male. 3. married. 4. masculine. 5. meridian. 6. *meridies*, [L.], noon, as in *A.M., P.M.* 7. meter(s). 8. middle. 9. mile(s). 10. mill. 11. minim. 12. minute(s). 13. month. 14. in *mechanics*, mass.
**ma** (mä; *dial.* mô), *n.* [Colloq.], mamma; mother.
**Ma,** in *chemistry*, masurium.
**M.A.,** *Magister Artium*, [L.], Master of Arts: also A.M.
**ma'am** (mam, mäm; *unstressed* məm, 'm), *n.* [Colloq.], madam: used in direct address.
**ma·ca·bre** (mə-kä′brə, -bẽr), *adj.* [Fr.; OFr. (*danse*) *Macabré*, (dance) of death], gruesome; grim and horrible: also sp. **ma·ca′ber** (-bẽr).
**mac·ad·am** (mə-kad′əm), *n.* [after John L. *MacAdam* (1756–1836), Scot. engineer], 1. small broken stones, used in making roads: see **macadamize.** 2. a road made with layers of such stones.
**mac·ad·am·ize** (mə-kad′əm-īz′), *v.t.* [-IZED, -IZING], 1. to make or repair (a road) by rolling successive layers of macadam on a dry earth roadbed, often with tar or asphalt.
**Ma·ca·o** (mə-kou′, -kä′ō), *n.* 1. an island at the mouth of the Pearl River, China. 2. a Portuguese colony comprising this and two near-by islands.
**ma·caque** (mə-käk′), *n.* [Fr. < Port. *macaco* < African native name], any of a group of short-tailed monkeys of Asia, Africa, and the East Indies.
**mac·a·ro·ni** (mak′ə-rō′ni), *n.* [*pl.* -NIS, -NIES], [It. *maccaroni*, pl. < LGr. *makaria*, broth of barley], 1. long, thin, hollow tubes, collectively, made of dried flour paste, to be cooked for food. 2. an 18th-century English dandy. Also sp. **maccaroni.**
**mac·a·roon** (mak′ə-rōōn′), *n.* [< Fr. < It.; see MACARONI], a small, sweet cooky made chiefly of egg white, crushed almonds or coconut, and sugar.
**Ma·cau·lay, Thomas Bab·ing·ton** (bab′iŋ-tən mə-kô′li), first Baron Macaulay, 1800–1859; English historian, essayist, and statesman.
**ma·caw** (mə-kô′), *n.* [Port. *macao*; prob. < Braz. native name], a large, bright-colored, harsh-voiced parrot of Central and South America.
**Mac·beth** (mək-beth′, mak-), *n.* 1. a tragedy by Shakespeare (1606?). 2. its main character.
**Mac·ca·bae·us, Judas** (mak′ə-bē′əs), 2d century B.C.; leader of the successful Jewish revolt against the Syrians.
**Mac·ca·bees** (mak′ə-bēz′), *n.pl.* 1. a family of Jewish patriots who headed a successful revolt against Syria (175–164 B.C.). 2. two books of the Old Testament Apocrypha that tell of this revolt: abbrev. **Macc., Mac. —Mac′ca·be′an,** *adj.*
**Mac·Dow·ell, Edward Alexander** (mək-dou′əl), 1861–1908; U.S. composer and pianist.
**mace** (mās), *n.* [< OFr.], 1. a heavy, spiked, armor-breaking club, used in the Middle Ages. 2. a staff used as a symbol of authority by certain officials. 3. a person who carries a mace.
**mace** (mās), *n.* [OFr. *macis* < L. < Gr. *maker*, bark

from India], a spice, usually ground, made from the dried outer covering of the nutmeg.

**Mac·e·do·ni·a** (mas'ə-dō'ni-ə), *n.* 1. an ancient kingdom north of Greece: also **Mac'e·don'** (-don'). 2. now, a region comprising parts of Greece, Bulgaria, and Yugoslavia. —**Mac'e·do'ni·an,** *adj. & n.*

**mac·er·ate** (mas'ə-rāt'), *v.t.* [-ATED, -ATING], [< L. pp. of *macerare,* to soften], 1. to soften or separate the parts of by soaking in liquid for some time. 2. to cause to waste away or grow thin. 3. to torment. *v.i.* to waste away; grow thin. —**mac'er·at'er, mac'er·a'tor,** *n.* —**mac'er·a'tion,** *n.*

**mach.,** 1. machine. 2. machinery. 3. machinist.

**ma·che·te** (mä-chā'tā, mə-shet', -shet'i), *n.* [Sp. < L. < *marcus,* hammer], a large, heavy-bladed knife used, as in Central and South America, for cutting sugar cane, etc., or as a weapon.

MACHETE

**Mach·i·a·vel·li, Nic·co·lò** (nik'ə-lō' mak'i-ə-vel'i, mak'yə-), 1469–1527; Florentine statesman and writer on government.

**Mach·i·a·vel·li·an, Mach·i·a·vel·i·an** (mak'i-ə-vel'i-ən, mak'yə-vel'yən), *adj.* of or like Machiavelli or the political principles of craftiness and duplicity advocated by him. *n.* a follower of such principles. —**Mach'i·a·vel'lism, Mach'i·a·vel'li·an·ism, Mach'i·a·vel'i·an·ism,** *n.*

**ma·chi·co·late** (mə-chik'ə-lāt'), *v.t.* [-LATED, -LATING], [< ML. pp. of *machicolare* < MFr. < Pr. *machacol,* balcony], to put machicolations in.

**ma·chic·o·la·tion** (mə-chik'ə-lā'shən), *n.* an opening, as in the floor of a gallery or parapet, through which hot liquids, rocks, etc. could be dropped by the defenders of a medieval fortress.

**mach·i·nate** (mak'ə-nāt'), *v.i. & v.t.* [-NATED, -NATING], [< L. pp. of *machinari,* to plot < *machina;* see MACHINE], to devise, plan, or plot artfully, especially to do evil. —**mach'i·na'tor,** *n.*

**mach·i·na·tion** (mak'ə-nā'shən), *n.* 1. [Rare], a machinating. 2. *usually in pl.* an artful or secret plot or scheme, especially an evil one.

**ma·chine** (mə-shēn'), *n.* [Fr. < L. *machina* < Gr. < *mēchos,* a contrivance], 1. a mechanical vehicle; specif., an automobile. 2. a structure consisting of a framework and various fixed and moving parts, for doing some kind of work; mechanism: as, a sewing *machine.* 3. a person or organization regarded as acting like a machine, without thought or will. 4. the members of a political party who control policy and confer patronage. 5. in *mechanics,* a device, as the lever or screw, that transmits, or changes the application of, energy. *adj.* 1. of a machine or machines. 2. made or done by machinery. *v.t.* [-CHINED, -CHINING], to make, shape, etc. by machinery.

**machine gun,** an automatic gun, usually with a cooling apparatus, firing a rapid stream of bullets fed into it by a belt, clip, etc. —**ma·chine'-gun'** [-GUNNED, -GUNNING], *v.t.*

**ma·chin·er·y** (mə-shēn'ēr-i, -shēn'ri), *n.* [*pl.* -IES], 1. machines collectively. 2. the working parts of a machine. 3. any means by which something is kept in action or a desired result is obtained.

**machine shop,** a factory for making or repairing machines or machine parts.

**machine tool,** a power-driven tool, as an electric lathe or drill. —**ma·chine'-tool',** *v.t. & adj.*

**ma·chin·ist** (mə-shēn'ist), *n.* 1. one who makes or repairs machinery. 2. a worker skilled in using machine tools or one who operates a machine.

**‡ma·chis·mo** (mä-chēz'mô), *n.* [Sp. < *macho* (see MACHO) + *-ismo,* -ism], masculinity, characterized by virility, courage, etc.

**Mach (number)** (mäk), [after Ernst *Mach* (1838–1916), Austrian physicist], in *aerodynamics,* a number representing the ratio of the air speed of an object to the speed of sound in the same region of the atmosphere.

**‡ma·cho** (mä'chô), *n.* [*pl.* -CHOS (-chôs)], [Sp. < Port. < L. *masculus,* masculine], a strong, virile man. *adj.* masculine, courageous, etc.

**-ma·chy** (mə-ki), [< Gr. *machē,* a battle], a combining form meaning *struggle, contest of.*

**Mac·ken·zie** (mə-ken'zi), *n.* a river in NW Canada.

**mack·er·el** (mak'ēr-əl), *n.* [*pl.* -EL, -ELS; see PLURAL, II, D, 2], [< OFr. < ML. *macarellus*], an edible fish of the North Atlantic, with a greenish, blue-striped back and a silvery belly.

**mackerel sky,** a sky covered with rows of small, fleecy, white clouds, suggesting the streaks on a mackerel's back.

**Mack·i·nac, Strait of** (mak'ə-nô'), the strait connecting Lake Huron and Lake Michigan.

**Mackinac Island,** a small island in the Strait of Mackinac.

**Mack·i·naw coat** (mak'ə-nô'), [< *Mackinac* Island], a short, double-breasted coat of heavy woolen cloth, often plaid: also **mackinaw.**

**mack·in·tosh, mac·in·tosh** (mak'in-tosh'), *n.* [after Charles *Macintosh* (1766–1843), the Scot. inventor], 1. a waterproof outer coat; raincoat. 2. the fabric used for such a coat.

**Ma·con** (mā'kən, -kon), *n.* a city in central Georgia: pop., 70,000.

**mac·ro-,** [< Gr. *makros,* long], a combining form meaning *long* (*in extent* or *duration*), *large, enlarged* or *elongated:* also **macr-.**

**mac·ro·bi·ot·ics** (mak'rō-bī-ot'iks), *n.pl.* [construed as sing.] [<*macro-* + Gr. *bios,* life], the art of prolonging life, as by a special diet.—**mac'ro·bi·ot'ic,** *adj.*

**mac·ro·ceph·a·ly** (mak'rə-sef'ə-li), *n.* [*macro-* + *cephal-* + *-y*], a condition in which the head or cranial capacity is abnormally large. —**mac'ro·ceph'a·lous, mac'ro·ce·phal'ic** (-sə-fal'ik), *adj.*

**mac·ro·cosm** (mak'rə-koz'm), *n.* [< Fr.; see MACRO- & COSMOS], the universe.

**ma·cron** (mā'krən, mak'ron), *n.* [< Gr. neut. of *makros,* long], a short, straight mark (¯) placed horizontally over a vowel to indicate that it is long or is to be pronounced in a certain way.

**mac·u·la** (mak'yoo-lə), *n.* [*pl.* -LAE (-lē')], [L.], 1. a stain, blotch, etc. 2. a sunspot. —**mac'u·lar,** *adj.*

**mad** (mad), *adj.* [MADDER, MADDEST], [< AS. pp. of (*ge*)*mædan,* to drive mad], 1. mentally ill; insane; crazy. 2. frenzied; frantic: as, *mad* with fear. 3. foolish and rash; unwise. 4. foolishly enthusiastic; infatuated: as, she's *mad* about him. 5. wildly gay; hilarious. 6. having rabies: as, a *mad* dog. 7. [Colloq.], angry; furious (often with *at*). —**have a mad on,** [Colloq.], to be angry. —**like mad,** with furious energy, speed, etc. —**mad as a hatter** (or **March hare**), completely crazy.

**Mad·a·gas·car** (mad'ə-gas'kēr), *n.* an island off the SE coast of Africa: coextensive with the republic of Malagasy. —**Mad'a·gas'can,** *adj. & n.*

**mad·am** (mad'əm), *n.* [*pl.* -AMS; *for 1, usually* MESDAMES (mā-däm')], [< Fr., orig. *ma dame,* my lady], 1. a woman; lady: a polite title used in speaking to or of a woman: often **ma'am.** 2. a woman in charge of a brothel. Abbrev. **Mdm., Mad., Madm.**

**mad·ame** (mad'əm; Fr. mȧ'dȧm'), *n.* [*pl.* MESDAMES (mā-däm')], [Fr.; see MADAM], a married woman: French title equivalent to *Mrs.:* abbrev. **Mme., Mdme.**

**mad·cap** (mad'kap'), *n.* [*mad* + *cap,* fig. for head], a reckless, impulsive person, especially a girl. *adj.* reckless and impulsive.

**mad·den** (mad''n), *v.t. & v.i.* to make or become mad; make or become insane, angry, or wildly excited. —**mad'den·ing,** *adj.* —**mad'den·ing·ly,** *adv.*

**mad·der** (mad'ēr), *n.* [AS. *mædere*], 1. any of various plants; esp., a vine with small, yellow flowers and berries. 2. *a*) the red root of this plant. *b*) a red dye made from this. 3. crimson.

**mad·ding** (mad'iŋ), *adj.* [Rare], raving; frenzied.

**made** (mād), pt. and pp. of **make.** *adj.* 1. constructed; formed. 2. produced artificially: as, *made* ground. 3. invented: as, a *made* word. 4. specially prepared: as, a *made* dish. 5. sure of success.

**Ma·deir·a** (mə-dêr'ə; Port. mȧ-de'rə), *n.* 1. a group of five Portuguese islands, off the coast of Morocco. 2. the chief island of this group. 3. [also m-], a white wine made on this island.

**ma·de·moi·selle** (mad'ə-mə-zel'; *popularly, often* mam'zel'; Fr. mȧd'mwȧ'zel'), *n.* [*pl.* MESDEMOISELLES (mād'-)], [Fr.; *ma,* my + *demoiselle,* young lady], an unmarried woman or girl: French title equivalent to *Miss:* abbrev. **Mlle., Mdlle.**

**made-to-or·der** (mād'tə-ôr'dēr), *adj.* made to conform to the customer's specifications; custom-made.

**made-up** (mād'up'), *adj.* 1. put together; arranged: as, a *made-up* page of type. 2. invented; false: as, a *made-up* story. 3. with cosmetics applied.

**mad·house** (mad'hous'), *n.* 1. an insane asylum. 2. any place of turmoil, noises, and confusion.

**Mad·i·son** (mad'i-s'n), *n.* the capital of Wisconsin: pop., 127,000.

**Madison, James,** 1751–1836; fourth president of the U.S. (1809–1817).

**mad·ly** (mad'li), *adv.* 1. insanely. 2. wildly; furiously. 3. foolishly.

**mad·man** (mad′man′, -mən), *n.* [*pl.* -MEN], a demented person; lunatic; maniac. —**mad′wom′an** [*pl.* -WOMEN], *n.fem.*
**mad·ness** (mad′nis), *n.* 1. insanity; lunacy. 2. great anger; fury. 3. great folly.
**Ma·doe·ra** (mä-do͞o′rä), *n.* Madura: Dutch spelling.
**Ma·don·na** (mə-don′ə), *n.* [It. < *ma*, my + *donna*, lady], 1. Mary, mother of Jesus. 2. a picture or statue of Mary.
**Ma·dras** (mə-dras′, -dräs′), *n.* a seaport in SE India: pop., 1,729,000.
**ma·dras** (mad′rəs, mə-dras′, -dräs′), *n.* [< *Madras*, India], a fine, firm cotton cloth, usually striped, used for shirts, dresses, etc.
‡**ma·dre** (mä′dre), *n.* [Sp.], mother.
**mad·re·pore** (mad′ri-pôr′, -pōr′), *n.* [< Fr. < It. < *madre*, mother + *poro*, a pore (or Gr. *pōros*, soft stone)], any of a group of corals which form coral reefs and islands in tropical seas.
**Ma·drid** (mə-drid′; Sp. mä-*th*rē′), *n.* the capital of Spain, in the central part: pop., 2,559,000.
**mad·ri·gal** (mad′ri-g'l), *n.* [< It. < LL.; ult. < *matricalis*, of the womb], 1. a short poem, as of love, which can be set to music. 2. a contrapuntal part song, without accompaniment, popular in the 15th to 17th centuries. 3. loosely, any song.
**Ma·du·ra** (mä-do͞o′rä), *n.* an island of Indonesia, NE of Java: Dutch spelling, **Madoera.**
**Mae·ce·nas** (mi-sē′nəs), *n.* 1. (*Gaius Cilnius Maecenas*), Roman patron of literature, friend of Horace and Virgil; 70?–8 B.C. 2. any generous patron, especially of literature or art.
**mael·strom** (māl′strəm), *n.* [Early Mod. D. < *malen*, to grind + *stroom*, a stream], 1. [M-], a dangerous whirlpool off the west coast of Norway. 2. any large or violent whirlpool. 3. a turbulent or agitated state of mind, emotions, affairs, etc.
**mae·nad** (mē′nad), *n.* [*pl.* -NADS, -NADES (men′ə-dēz′)], [< L. < Gr. < *mainesthai*, to rave], 1. in *Gr. & Rom. mythology*, a nymph who attended Dionysus; bacchante. 2. a frenzied woman. Also sp. **menad.** —**mae·nad·ic** (mi-nad′ik), *adj.*
‡**ma·es·to·so** (mä′es-tô′sô), *adj. & adv.* [It.], in *music*, with majesty or dignity.
**ma·es·tro** (mīs′trō, mä-es′-), *n.* [*pl.* -TROS, -TRI (-tri)], [It. < L. *magister*, a master], a master in any art; esp., a great composer, conductor, or teacher of music.
**Mae·ter·linck,** Count **Maurice** (mā′tēr-liŋk′, met′ēr-), 1862–1949; Belgian dramatist and poet.
**ma·fi·a, maf·fi·a** (mä′fi-ä′), *n.* [It. *maffia*], 1. in Sicily, popular hostility to law. 2. [M-], an alleged secret society of criminals in the U.S. and other countries, engaging in blackmail, illicit trade in narcotics, etc.
**mag.,** 1. magazine. 2. magnetic. 3. magnitude.
**mag·a·zine** (mag′ə-zēn′, mag′ə-zēn′), *n.* [< Fr. < OFr. < It. < Ar. < *makhzan*, a granary < *khazana*, to store up], 1. a warehouse or military supply depot. 2. a space in which explosives are stored, as in a fort or warship. 3. a supply chamber, as the space in a rifle from which the cartridges are fed, the space in a camera from which the film is fed, etc. 4. things kept in a magazine, as munitions or supplies. 5. a publication that appears at regular intervals and contains stories, articles, etc. and, usually, advertisements.
**Mag·da·lene** (mag′də-lēn′), *n.* 1. (*also* mag′də-lē′ni), Mary Magdalene (preceded by *the*). 2. [m-], a reformed and repentant prostitute.
**Mag·de·burg** (mag′də-bûrg′; G. mäg′də-boorkh′), *n.* a city in East Germany: pop., 266,000.
**mage** (māj), *n.* [Fr. < L. *magus;* see MAGI], [Archaic], a magician; wizard.
**Ma·gel·lan, Ferdinand** (mə-jel′ən), 1480?–1521; Portuguese navigator.
**Magellan, Strait of,** a narrow strait between the South American mainland and Tierra del Fuego.
**ma·gen·ta** (mə-jen′tə), *n.* [< *Magenta*, town in Italy], 1. a purplish-red aniline dye. 2. purplish red. *adj.* purplish-red.
**mag·got** (mag′ət), *n.* [ME. *magotte*], 1. a wormlike insect larva, as the legless larva of the housefly. 2. an odd notion; whim. —**mag′got·y,** *adj.*
**Ma·gi** (mā′ji), *n.pl.* [*sing.* -GUS (-gəs)], [L., pl. of *magus* < Gr. < OPer. *magu*], 1. the priestly caste in ancient Media and Persia. 2. in the *Bible*, the wise men from the East who came bearing gifts to the infant Jesus: Matt. 2:1-13.
**mag·ic** (maj′ik), *n.* [< OFr. < LL. < L. < Gr. < *magikos*, of the Magi], 1. the pretended art of producing effects by charms, spells, and rituals; sorcery. 2. any mysterious, seemingly inexplicable, power or influence: as, the *magic* of love. 3. the art of producing illusions by sleight of hand, etc. *adj.* 1. of, produced by, or using magic. 2. producing extraordinary results, as if by magic. —**mag′i·cal,** *adj.* —**mag′i·cal·ly,** *adv.*
**ma·gi·cian** (mə-jish′ən), *n.* [OFr. *magicien*], an expert in magic; specif., *a*) a sorcerer; wizard. *b*) a performer skilled in magic (sense 3).
**magic lantern,** an instrument with an arrangement of lenses and a light for projecting on a screen a magnified image of a picture on a slide.
**mag·is·te·ri·al** (maj′is-têr′i-əl), *adj.* [< ML. < LL. < L. *magister*, a master], 1. of or suitable for a magistrate or master. 2. authoritative. 3. domineering; pompous; arrogant. —**mag′is·te′ri·al·ly,** *adv.* —**mag′is·te′ri·al·ness,** *n.*
**mag·is·tra·cy** (maj′is-trə-si), *n.* [*pl.* -CIES], 1. the position, office, or jurisdiction of a magistrate. 2. magistrates collectively.
**mag·is·trate** (maj′is-trāt′, -trit), *n.* [< L. < *magister*, a master], 1. a civil officer empowered to administer and enforce the law: the President of the U.S. is sometimes called the *first* (or *chief*) *magistrate.* 2. a minor official with limited judicial powers, as a justice of the peace.
**mag·ma** (mag′mə), *n.* [*pl.* -MAS, -MATA (-mə-tə)], [L. < Gr. < *massein*, to knead], molten rock deep in the earth, from which igneous rock is formed.
**Mag·na Char·ta** (or **Car·ta**) (mag′nə kär′tə), [ML., great charter], 1. the charter that King John was forced by the English barons to grant at Runnymede, June 15, 1215: it guaranteed certain civil and political liberties to the English people. 2. any constitution guaranteeing such liberties.
‡**mag·na cum lau·de** (mag′nə kum lô′di, mäg′nä koom lou′di), [L.], with great praise: phrase used to signify graduation with high honors from a college.
**mag·na·nim·i·ty** (mag′nə-nim′ə-ti), *n.* 1. a magnanimous quality or state. 2. [*pl.* -TIES], a magnanimous act.
**mag·nan·i·mous** (mag-nan′ə-məs), *adj.* [< L. < *magnus*, great + *animus*, soul], generous in overlooking injury or insult; rising above pettiness or meanness; noble. —**mag·nan′i·mous·ly,** *adv.*
**mag·nate** (mag′nāt), *n.* [< LL. < L. *magnus*, great], a very influential person, especially in business.
**mag·ne·sia** (mag-nē′shə, -zhə), *n.* [< ML. < Gr. *Magnēsia lithos*, stone of Magnesia (district in Thessaly)], magnesium oxide, MgO, a white, tasteless powder, used as a mild laxative and as an insulating substance.
**mag·ne·si·um** (mag-nē′shi-əm, -zhi-), *n.* [< *magnesia*], a light, silver-white, malleable metallic chemical element: it burns with a hot, white light, and is used in photographic flash bulbs, etc.: symbol, Mg; at. wt., 24.32; at. no., 12.
**mag·net** (mag′nit), *n.* [< OFr. < L. *magnes* < Gr. *Magnētis lithos*, stone of Magnesia; see MAGNESIA], 1. any piece of iron, steel, or loadstone that has the property of attracting iron or steel, etc. 2. a person or thing that attracts.
**mag·net·ic** (mag-net′ik), *adj.* 1. having the properties of a magnet. 2. of, producing, or caused by magnetism. 3. of the earth's magnetism. 4. that can be magnetized. 5. powerfully attractive: as, a *magnetic* personality. —**mag·net′i·cal·ly,** *adv.*
**magnetic field,** the space around a magnet in which the magnetic force exerted is appreciable.
**magnetic force,** the force with which a magnet attracts (or repels) a piece of iron or steel.
**magnetic mine,** a naval mine exploded when the metal hull of a ship passing near it deflects a magnetic needle, thus detonating the charge.
**magnetic needle,** a slender bar of magnetized steel which, when swinging freely on a pivot, points toward the Magnetic Poles.
**magnetic north,** the direction toward which a magnetic needle points, usually not true north.
**magnetic pickup,** a phonograph pickup in which the movements of the needle produce variations in electrical output to the amplifier through an arrangement of a magnet and coils.
**magnetic pole,** 1. either pole of a magnet. 2. [M-P-], either point on the earth's surface toward which a magnetic needle points: these points do not precisely coincide with the geographical poles.
**magnetic tape,** a thin plastic ribbon coated with ferromagnetic iron oxide particles, used as a medium for storing electrical signals in the recording of sound, computer data, etc.
**mag·net·ism** (mag′nə-tiz'm), *n.* 1. the property, quality, or condition of being magnetic. 2. the force to which this is due. 3. the branch of physics dealing with magnetic phenomena. 4. personal charm.
**mag·net·ite** (mag′nə-tīt′), *n.* a black iron oxide, $Fe_3O_4$, an iron ore: called *loadstone* when magnetic.
**mag·net·ize** (mag′nə-tīz′), *v.t.* [-IZED, -IZING], 1. to

give magnetic properties to (steel, iron, etc.). 2. to attract or charm (a person). *v.i.* to become magnetic. —**mag′net·iz′a·ble,** *adj.* —**mag′net·i·za′tion,** *n.* —**mag′net·iz′er,** *n.*

**mag·ne·to** (mag-nē′tō), *n.* [*pl.* -TOS], a small generator in which one or more permanent magnets produce the magnetic field; esp., a device connected with an internal-combustion engine to generate the current providing a spark for the ignition: in full, **magnetoelectric machine.**

**mag·ne·to-,** a combining form meaning: 1. *magnetism, magnetic force.* 2. *magnetoelectric.*

**mag·ne·to·e·lec·tric** (mag-nē′tō-i-lek′trik, -net′ō-), *adj.* of or characterized by electricity produced by magnets: also **mag·ne′to·e·lec′tri·cal.**

**mag·ne·tom·e·ter** (mag′nə-tom′ə-tẽr), *n.* an instrument for measuring magnetic forces.

**mag·ni-,** [< L. *magnus,* great], a combining form meaning *great, big, large,* as in *magnificent.*

**mag·nif·ic** (mag-nif′ik), *adj.* [Archaic], 1. magnificent. 2. pompous. Also **mag·nif′i·cal.**

**Mag·nif·i·cat** (mag-nif′i-kat′), *n.* [L.], 1. the hymn of the Virgin Mary in Luke 1:46-55. 2. any musical setting for this.

**mag·ni·fi·ca·tion** (mag′nə-fi-kā′shən), *n.* 1. a magnifying or being magnified. 2. the power of magnifying. 3. a magnified image or representation.

**mag·nif·i·cence** (mag-nif′ə-s′ns), *n.* [OFr. < L. < *magnificus,* noble < *magnus,* great + *facere,* to do], richness and splendor, as of furnishings, color, dress, etc.; imposing beauty; grandeur.

**mag·nif·i·cent** (mag-nif′ə-s′nt), *adj.* [OFr. < LL. *magnificens;* see MAGNIFICENCE], 1. splendid; stately; grand; rich or sumptuous, as in construction, decoration, etc. 2. exalted: said of ideas, etc. —**mag·nif′i·cent·ly,** *adv.*

**mag·nif·i·co** (mag-nif′ə-kō′), *n.* [*pl.* -COES], [It. < L. *magnificus;* see MAGNIFICENCE], a person of high rank or great importance.

**mag·ni·fy** (mag′nə-fī′), *v.t.* [-FIED, -FYING], [< OFr. < L. *magnificare;* see MAGNIFICENCE], 1. [Rare], to enlarge. 2. to exaggerate: as, she *magnified* her sufferings. 3. to increase the apparent size of (an object), as by means of a lens. 4. [Archaic], to praise; extol. *v.i.* to have the power of increasing the apparent size of an object. —**mag′ni·fi′er,** *n.*

**magnifying glass,** a lens that increases the apparent size of an object seen through it.

**mag·nil·o·quent** (mag-nil′ə-kwənt), *adj.* [< L. *magnus,* great + ppr. of *loqui,* to speak], 1. pompous or grandiose in talking or writing. 2. boastful; bombastic. —**mag·nil′o·quence** (-kwəns), *n.* —**mag·nil′o·quent·ly,** *adv.*

**Mag·ni·to·gorsk** (mäg′ni-tô-gôrsk′), *n.* a city in W Siberia, U.S.S.R.: pop., 200,000.

**mag·ni·tude** (mag′nə-tōōd′, -tūd′), *n.* [< L. < *magnus,* great], 1. greatness; specif., *a*) of size. *b*) of extent. *c*) of influence. 2. *a*) size. *b*) importance. 3. in *astronomy,* the degree of brightness of a fixed star: the brightest stars are of the first magnitude. —**of the first magnitude,** of the greatest importance.

**mag·no·li·a** (mag-nō′li-ə, -nōl′yə), *n.* [< Pierre *Magnol* (1638–1715), Fr. botanist], 1. any of a group of trees or shrubs with large, fragrant flowers of white, pink, or purple. 2. the flower.

**mag·num** (mag′nəm), *n.* [L., neut. sing. of *magnus,* great], 1. a bottle holding two quarts, used for wine or liquor. 2. the amount that it holds.

‡**mag·num o·pus** (mag′nəm ō′pəs), [L.], 1. a great work of art or literature; masterpiece. 2. a person's greatest work or undertaking.

**mag·pie** (mag′pī′), *n.* [< *Mag,* dim. of *Margaret* + *pie,* magpie], 1. a noisy bird of the crow family, related to the jays, with black-and-white coloring and a long tail. 2. one who chatters.

**mag·uey** (mag′wā), *n.* [Sp.], a fleshy-leaved or fiber-yielding plant of the SW United States, Mexico, and Central America; agave; century plant.

**Mag·yar** (mag′yär; Hung. môd′-), *n.* [Hung.], 1. a member of the people constituting the main ethnic group in Hungary. 2. their language; Hungarian. *adj.* of the Magyars, their language, etc.

**Ma·ha·bha·ra·ta** (mə-hä′bä′rə-tə), *n.* [Sans.], one of the two great epics of India, written in Sanskrit about 200 B.C.

**ma·ha·ra·jah, ma·ha·ra·ja** (mä′hə-rä′jə; Hind. mə-hä′-), *n.* [< Sans. < *maha,* great + *rājā,* king], in India, a sovereign prince, especially the prince of any of the chief native states.

**ma·ha·ra·ni, ma·ha·ra·nee** (mä′hə-rä′nē; Hind. mə-hä′-), *n.* [< Hind. < *maha,* great + *rānī,* queen], in India, the wife of a maharajah.

**ma·hat·ma** (mə-hat′mə, -hät′-), *n.* [< Sans. < *maha,* great + *ātman,* soul], in *theosophy & esoteric Buddhism,* one of a class of wise and holy persons supposed to have unusual powers.

**Ma·hi·can** (mə-hē′kən), *n.* 1. a confederacy of Algonquian Indians that lived chiefly in the upper Hudson Valley. 2. a member of this confederacy. 3. Mohegan. *adj.* of this confederacy. Also **Mohican.**

**mah-jongg, mah·jong** (mä′jôŋ′, -joŋ′, -zhoŋ′), *n.* [< Chin. *ma-ch'iao,* lit., house sparrow (a figure on one of the tiles)], a game of Chinese origin, played with 136 or more small tiles.

**Mah·ler, Gus·tav** (goos′täf mä′lẽr), 1860–1911; Bohemian conductor and composer.

**ma·hog·a·ny** (mə-hog′ə-ni, -hôg′-), *n.* [*pl.* -NIES], [obs. Sp. *mahogani* < the native W. Ind. name], 1. *a*) the reddish-brown hard wood of a tropical American tree, much used for furniture. *b*) the tree. 2. reddish brown. *adj.* 1. made of mahogany. 2. reddish-brown.

**Ma·hom·et** (mə-hom′it), *n.* Mohammed. —**Ma·hom′et·an,** *adj. & n.* —**Ma·hom′et·an·ism,** *n.*

**ma·hout** (mə-hout′), *n.* [< Hind. < Sans. *mahāmātra,* lit., great in measure], in India and the East Indies, an elephant driver or elephant keeper.

**maid** (mād), *n.* [< *maiden*], 1. *a*) a girl or young unmarried woman. *b*) a virgin. 2. an unmarried woman. 3. a girl or woman servant.

**maid·en** (mād′'n), *n.* [AS. *mægden*], 1. a girl or young unmarried woman. 2. a virgin. *adj.* 1. of, characteristic of, or suitable for a maiden. 2. *a*) unmarried. *b*) virgin. 3. untried; unused; new; fresh. 4. first or earliest: as, a *maiden* voyage.

**maid·en·hair** (mād′'n-hâr′), *n.* any of a group of ferns with delicate fronds and slender stalks: also **maidenhair fern.**

**maid·en·head** (mād′'n-hed′), *n.* 1. [Archaic], maidenhood; virginity. 2. the hymen.

**maid·en·hood** (mād′'n-hood′), *n.* the state or time of being a maiden.

**maid·en·ly** (mād′'n-li), *adj.* 1. of a maiden. 2. like or suitable for a maiden; modest, gentle, etc. *adv.* in a maidenly manner. —**maid′en·li·ness,** *n.*

**maiden name,** the surname that a woman had when not yet married.

**maid of honor,** 1. an unmarried woman acting as chief attendant to the bride at a wedding. 2. an unmarried woman, usually of noble birth, attending a queen or princess.

**maid·ser·vant** (mād′sũr′vənt), *n.* a girl or woman servant.

**mail** (māl), *n.* [OFr. *male;* OHG. *malha,* wallet], 1. letters, packages, etc. transported and delivered by the post office. 2. a boat, train, etc. that transports these. 3. the postal system. *adj.* of mail. *v.t.* to send by mail; put into a mailbox. —**mail′a·ble,** *adj.* —**mail′er,** *n.*

**mail** (māl), *n.* [OFr. *maile* < L. *macula,* a mesh of a net], 1. a flexible body armor made of small metal rings, scales, or loops of chain. 2. any defensive armor. 3. the hard protective covering of some animals, as turtles. *v.t.* to cover or protect as with mail. —**mailed,** *adj.*

**mail·box** (māl′boks′), *n.* 1. a box into which mail is put when delivered, as at one's home. 2. a box, as on a street, into which mail is put for collection. Also **mail box.**

**mail·man** (māl′man′, -mən), *n.* [*pl.* -MEN], a man who carries or delivers mail; postman.

**mail order,** an order for goods to be sent by mail. —**mail′-or′der,** *adj.*

**mail-order house,** a business establishment that takes mail orders and sends goods by mail.

**maim** (mām), *v.t.* [OFr. *mahaigner*], to deprive of the use of some necessary part of the body; cripple; mutilate; disable.

**Mai·mon·i·des** (mī-mon′ə-dēz′), *n.* 1135–1204; Spanish rabbi, theologian, and philosopher.

**Main** (mīn; Eng. mān), *n.* a river in West Germany, flowing westward into the Rhine.

**main** (mān), *n.* [AS. *mægen*], 1. physical strength; force: now only in **with might and main,** with all one's strength. 2. the principal part or point: chiefly in **in the main,** mostly; chiefly. 3. a principal pipe or line in a distributing system for water, gas, etc. 4. a railroad trunk line. 5. [Poetic], the high sea; ocean. 6. [Archaic], the mainland. 7. [Obs.], any broad expanse. *adj.* 1. originally, strong; powerful. 2. chief in size, importance, etc.;

principal. 3. designating a broad expanse of land, sea, or space. —**by main force** (or **strength**), by sheer force (or strength).
**main** (mān), *n.* [prob. < *main, adj.*], in *cockfighting*, a match between two birds.
**main clause,** in a complex sentence, a clause that can function syntactically as a complete sentence by itself; independent clause.
**main drag,** [Slang], the main street of a city.
**Maine** (mān), *n.* a New England State of the U.S.: area, 33,215 sq. mi.; pop., 969,000; capital, Augusta: abbrev. **Me.**
**main·land** (mān′land′, -lənd), *n.* the principal land mass of a continent, as distinguished from near-by small islands, etc.
**main·ly** (mān′li), *adv.* chiefly; principally.
**main·mast** (mān′məst, -mast′, -mäst′), *n.* the principal mast of a vessel.
**main·sail** (mān′s'l, -sāl′), *n.* 1. in a square-rigged vessel, the sail set from the main yard: also **main course.** 2. in a fore-and-aft-rigged vessel, the large sail set from the mainmast.
**main·sheet** (mān′shēt′), *n.* the line controlling the angle at which a mainsail is set.
**main·spring** (mān′spriŋ′), *n.* 1. the principal, or driving, spring in a clock, watch, etc. 2. the chief motive, incentive, etc.
**main·stay** (mān′stā′), *n.* 1. the supporting line extending forward from the mainmast. 2. a chief support: as, her son is her *mainstay.*
**main stem,** [Slang], the main street of a city.
**Main Street,** 1. the principal street of a small town. 2. the typical inhabitants of a small town.
**main·tain** (mān-tān′), *v.t.* [OFr. *maintenir* < L. *manu tenere,* to hold in the hand], 1. to keep or keep up; carry on. 2. *a*) to keep in continuance: as, food *maintains* life. *b*) to keep in a certain condition, as of repair: as, the state *maintains* the roads. 3. to hold against attack; defend. 4. to declare to be true: as, he *maintains* his contentions. 5. to support by aid, influence, etc. 6. to provide the means of existence for: as, to *maintain* a family. —**main·tain′a·ble,** *adj.* —**main·tain′er,** *n.*
**main·te·nance** (mān′tə-nəns), *n.* 1. a maintaining or being maintained. 2. means of support or sustenance; livelihood.
**main·top** (mān′top′), *n.* a platform at the head of the lower section of the mainmast.
**main·top·mast** (mān′top′məst), *n.* the section of the mainmast above the maintop.
**main·top·sail** (mān′top′s'l, -sāl), *n.* the sail above the mainsail on the mainmast.
**main yard,** the lower yard on the mainmast.
‡**maî·tre d'hô·tel** (me′tr′ dō′tel′), [Fr., lit., master of the house], 1. a butler or steward. 2. a hotel manager. 3. a headwaiter. 4. (with) a sauce of melted butter, chopped parsley, and lemon juice or vinegar.
**maize** (māz), *n.* [Sp. *maíz* < W. Ind. *mahiz*], 1. *a*) a kind of grain that grows in kernels on large ears. *b*) its ears. *c*) its seeds or kernels. Also called *Indian corn* or *corn.* 2. its color (when ripe); yellow. *adj.* yellow.
**Maj.,** Major.
**ma·jes·tic** (mə-jes′tik), *adj.* grand; dignified; noble: also **ma·jes′ti·cal.** —**ma·jes′ti·cal·ly,** *adv.*
**maj·es·ty** (maj′is-ti), *n.* [*pl.* -TIES], [< OFr. < L. *majestas;* ult. < base of *magnus,* great], 1. the dignity or power of a sovereign. 2. [M-], a title used in speaking to or of a sovereign, with *His, Her,* or *Your.* 3. grandeur; dignity.
**ma·jol·i·ca** (mə-jol′i-kə, -yol′-), *n.* [It. *maiolica;* prob. < *Majorca*], a kind of Italian pottery, enameled, glazed, and richly decorated.
**ma·jor** (mā′jēr), *adj.* [L., compar. of *magnus,* great], 1. *a*) greater in size, amount, or extent. *b*) greater in importance or rank. 2. of full legal age. 3. constituting the majority. 4. in *education,* designating a field of study in which a student specializes. 5. in *music, a*) designating an interval higher than the minor by a half tone. *b*) designating a tone distant from another by a major interval. *c*) designating or based on a mode characterized by major intervals. *v.i.* in *education,* to specialize (*in* a field of study): as, to *major* in physics. *n.* 1. a superior in some class or group. 2. a military officer ranking just above a captain. 3. in *education,* a major field of study. 4. in *law,* a person of legal age. 5. in *music,* a major interval, key, etc.
**Ma·jor·ca** (mə-jôr′kə), *n.* the largest of the Balearic Islands: Spanish name, *Mallorca.*
**ma·jor-do·mo** (mā′jēr-dō′mō), *n.* [*pl.* -MOS], [< Sp. or It. < ML. < L. *major,* greater + genit. of *domus,* house], 1. a man in charge of a great or royal household. 2. a steward or butler: humorous usage.
**major general,** [*pl.* MAJOR GENERALS], a military officer ranking just above a brigadier general.
**ma·jor·i·ty** (mə-jôr′ə-ti, -jor′-), *n.* [*pl.* -TIES], [< Fr. < L. *major;* see MAJOR], 1. the greater part or larger number; more than half. 2. the excess of the larger number of votes cast for one candidate, bill, etc. over all the rest of the votes. 3. the group or party with the majority of votes. 4. the full legal age, at which one is no longer a minor. 5. the military rank or position of a major.
**major leagues,** the two main leagues of professional baseball clubs in the U.S. —**ma′jor-league′,** *adj.* —**ma′jor-lea′guer,** *n.*
**major scale,** one of the two standard diatonic musical scales, consisting of eight tones with half steps after the third and seventh tones.
**major suit,** in *bridge,* spades or hearts.
**make** (māk), *v.t.* [MADE, MAKING], [AS. *macian*], 1. to bring into being; specif., *a*) to form by shaping or putting parts together; build, create, devise, etc. *b*) to cause; bring about: as, it *made* a change. 2. to cause to be, become, or seem: as, we *made* him president: sometimes used reflexively, as, *make* yourself comfortable. 3. to prepare for use: as, *make* the beds. 4. to amount to: as, four quarts *make* a gallon. 5. to have, or prove to have, the qualities of: as, he will *make* a good doctor. 6. to set up; establish: as, to *make* a rule. 7. *a*) to acquire, as by one's behavior: as, to *make* friends. *b*) to get by earning, etc.: as, to *make* money. 8. to cause the success of: as, this venture *made* him. 9. to understand: as, what do you *make* of that? 10. to estimate to be: as, I *make* the distance about 500 miles. 11. to execute, do, accomplish, etc.: as, to *make* a quick turn, a speech, etc. 12. to cause or force to: as, *make* him behave. 13. to arrive at; reach: as, the ship *made* port. 14. to go; travel; traverse: as, they *made* the distance in five hours. 15. [Colloq.], to succeed in getting a position on, etc.: as, he *made* the team. 16. [Slang], to succeed in becoming the lover of. 17. in *electricity,* to close (a circuit). *v.i.* 1. to start (to do something): as, she *made* to go. 2. *a*) to go; proceed: as, he *made* for the door. *b*) to tend, extend, or point (*to, toward,* etc.). 3. to behave in a specified manner: as, *make* merry. 4. to cause something to be in a specified condition: as, *make* ready. *n.* 1. the act or process of making. 2. the amount made; output. 3. the way in which something is made; style; build. 4. type, sort, or brand. 5. character; nature: as, a man of this *make.* 6. in *electricity,* the closing of a circuit. —**make after,** to chase or follow. —**make away with,** 1. to steal. 2. to get rid of. 3. to kill. —**make believe,** to pretend. —**make for,** 1. to head for. 2. to attack. 3. to help effect. —**make like,** [Slang], to imitate. —**make off with,** to steal. —**make out,** 1. to see with some difficulty. 2. to understand. 3. to write out. 4. to fill out (a blank form, etc.). 5. to (try to) show or prove to be. 6. to succeed; get along. —**make over,** 1. to change; renovate. 2. to transfer the ownership of. —**make up,** 1. to put together; compose. 2. to form; constitute. 3. to invent. 4. to complete by providing what is lacking. 5. to compensate (*for*). 6. to become friendly again after a quarrel. 7. to put on cosmetics, etc., as for a role in a play. 8. to decide (one's mind). 9. to select and arrange type, illustrations, etc. for (a book, page, etc.). —**make up to,** to flatter, or try to be agreeable to. —**on the make,** 1. [Colloq.], trying to succeed financially, socially, etc. 2. [Slang], trying to get a lover.
**make-be·lieve** (māk′bə-lēv′), *n.* 1. pretense; feigning. 2. a pretender. *adj.* pretended; feigned.
**mak·er** (māk′ēr), *n.* 1. a person or thing that makes. 2. [M-], God. 3. in *law,* the signer of a promissory note.
**make·shift** (māk′shift′), *n.* a thing that will do as a substitute or temporary expedient. *adj.* that will do for a while as a substitute.
**make-up** (māk′up′), *n.* 1. the way in which something is put together; composition. 2. nature; disposition. 3. *a*) the way in which an actor is costumed, painted, etc. for a role. *b*) the costumes, cosmetics, etc. used. 4. cosmetics generally. 5. the arrangement of type, illustrations, etc. in a book, magazine, etc. *adj.* of or for making up.
**mak·ing** (māk′iŋ), *n.* 1. the act of one that makes or the process of being made. 2. the cause of success or advancement: as, this experience will be the *making* of him. 3. *a*) something made. *b*) the quantity made at one time. 4. *often pl.* the material or potential qualities (*of*): as, he has the *making(s)* of a good doctor.
**mal-,** [Fr. < L. *male,* badly < *malus,* bad], a prefix meaning *bad* or *badly, wrong, ill,* as in *maladjustment*: also **male-.**

**Mal.,** 1. Malachi. 2. Malay. 3. Malayan.
**Mal·a·bar** (mal'ə-bär'), *n.* a coastal region in SW India: also **Malabar Coast.**
**Ma·lac·ca** (mə-lak'ə), *n.* a state of Malaya.
**Malacca, Strait of,** the strait between the Malay Peninsula and Sumatra.
**Malacca cane,** a lightweight, rattan walking stick.
**Mal·a·chi** (mal'ə-kī'), *n.* 1. a Hebrew prophet of the 5th century B.C. 2. a book of the Old Testament attributed to him.
**mal·a·chite** (mal'ə-kīt'), *n.* [Fr. < OFr. < L. < Gr. *malachē,* mallow: from its color], native basic copper carbonate, $CuCO_3 \cdot Cu(OH)_2$, a green mineral used for table tops, vases, etc.
**mal·ad·just·ed** (mal'ə-jus'tid), *adj.* poorly adjusted, esp. to the environment. **—mal'ad·just'ment,** *n.*
**mal·ad·min·is·ter** (mal'əd-min'ə-stēr), *v.t.* to administer badly. **—mal'ad·min'is·tra'tion,** *n.*
**mal·a·droit** (mal'ə-droit'), *adj.* [Fr.; see MAL- & ADROIT], awkward; clumsy; bungling. **—mal'a·droit'ly,** *adv.* **—mal'a·droit'ness,** *n.*
**mal·a·dy** (mal'ə-di), *n.* [*pl.* -DIES], [< OFr. *malade,* sick < L. *male habitus,* badly kept < *male,* badly + pp. of *habere,* to hold], an ailment; disease; illness.
**Má·la·ga** (mä'lä-gä'; Eng. mal'ə-gə), *n.* a seaport in S Spain: pop., 301,000.
**Mal·a·ga** (mal'ə-gə), *n.* 1. a large, white, oval grape. 2. a white wine, originally from Málaga.
**Mal·a·gas·y** (mal'ə-gas'i), *n.* 1. [*pl.* -GASY, -GASIES], a native of Madagascar. 2. the Indonesian language of the Malagasy. 3. a country coextensive with the island of Madagascar: a member of the French Community: area, 230,000 sq. mi.; pop., 5,803,000; capital, Tananarive. *adj.* of the Malagasy or their language.
**ma·laise** (ma-lāz'), *n.* [Fr. < *mal,* bad + *aise,* ease], a vague feeling of physical discomfort.
**ma·la·mute** (mä'lə-mūt'), *n.* [< native name], a large, strong Alaskan dog with a thick coat: also sp. **malemute, malemiut.**
**mal·a·pert** (mal'ə-pūrt'), *adj.* [< OFr. < *mal,* badly + *appert,* deft], [Archaic], saucy; impudent.
**Mal·a·prop, Mrs.** (mal'ə-prop'), a character in Sheridan's play *The Rivals,* who makes ridiculous misuse of words, especially through confusion caused by likeness in sound. **—mal'a·prop·ism,** *n.*
**mal·ap·ro·pos** (mal'ap-rə-pō'), *adj.* [Fr.; see MAL- & APROPOS], at an improper time or place. *adv.* in an inopportune or inappropriate manner.
**ma·lar·i·a** (mə-lâr'i-ə), *n.* [It., contr. of *mala aria,* bad air], 1. unwholesome or poisonous air; miasma. 2. an infectious disease, generally recurrent, caused by protozoa transmitted by the bite of an infected anopheles mosquito: characterized by intermittent chills and fever. **—ma·lar'i·al, ma·lar'i·ous,** *adj.*
**ma·lar·key, ma·lar·ky** (mə-lär'ki), *n.* [? < Irish pers. name], [Slang], nonsense; buncombe.
**mal·a·thi·on** (mal'ə-thī'ən), *n.* an organic phosphate, $C_{10}H_{19}O_6PS_2$, used as an insecticide.
**Mal·a·wi** (mäl'ə-wē'), *n.* a country in SE Africa: a member of the British Commonwealth of Nations: area, 46,066 sq. mi.; pop., 2,980,000; capital, Zomba: formerly, *Nyasaland.*
**Ma·lay** (mā'lā, mə-lā'), *n.* 1. a member of a large group of brown-skinned peoples living in the Malay Peninsula, the Malay Archipelago, and near-by islands. 2. their Indonesian language. *adj.* of the Malays, their language, etc. Also **Ma·lay'an.**
**Ma·lay·a** (mə-lā'ə), *n.* 1. a state of the Federation of Malaysia, consisting of eleven native states on the Malay Peninsula: in full, **Federation of Malaya.** 2. the Malay Peninsula.
**Mal·a·ya·lam** (mal'ə-yä'ləm), *n.* a Dravidian language spoken on the Malabar Coast.
**Malay Archipelago,** a chain of islands between the Malay Peninsula and Australia.
**Malay Peninsula,** a peninsula in SE Asia, including the Federation of Malaya and part of Thailand.
**Ma·lay·sia** (mə-lā'zhə, -shə), *n.* 1. a country consisting of Malaya (sense 1) and two states on Borneo: a member of the British Commonwealth of Nations: area, 128,429 sq. mi.; pop., 8,510,000; capital, Kuala Lumpur: in full, **Federation of Malaysia.** 2. the Malay Archipelago. **—Ma·lay'sian,** *adj.* & *n.*
**mal·con·tent** (mal'kən-tent'), *adj.* [Fr.; see MAL- & CONTENT], dissatisfied; rebellious. *n.* a dissatisfied or rebellious person.
‡**mal de mer** (mål' də mâr'), [Fr.], seasickness.
**Mal·dive Islands** (mal'dīv), an independent sultanate on a group of islands, southwest of India: area, 115 sq. mi.; pop., 93,000.
**male** (māl), *adj.* [< OFr. < L. *masculus,* dim. of *mas,* a male], 1. designating or of the sex that fertilizes the ovum and begets offspring. 2. of, like, or suitable for members of this sex; masculine. 3. consisting of men or boys. 4. in *botany,* designating or of fertilizing bodies, organs, etc.: as, *male* gametes. 5. in *mechanics,* designating or having a part shaped to fit into a corresponding hollow part. *n.* a male person, animal, or plant.
**mal·e·dic·tion** (mal'ə-dik'shən), *n.* [OFr. < L. *maledictio* < pp. < *male,* evil + *dicere,* to speak], 1. a calling down of evil on someone; curse. 2. a speaking of evil; slander. **—mal'e·dic'to·ry,** *adj.*
**mal·e·fac·tion** (mal'ə-fak'shən), *n.* wrongdoing; evil action; crime.
**mal·e·fac·tor** (mal'ə-fak'tēr), *n.* [L. < pp. of *malefacere* < *male,* evil + *facere,* to do], an evildoer; criminal. **—mal'e·fac'tress,** *n.fem.*
**ma·lef·i·cent** (mə-lef'ə-s'nt), *adj.* [see MALEFACTOR], harmful; hurtful; evil. **—ma·lef'i·cence,** *n.*
**ma·lev·o·lent** (mə-lev'ə-lənt), *adj.* [< OFr. < L. < *male,* evil + ppr. of *velle,* to wish], wishing evil or harm to others; spiteful; malicious. **—ma·lev'o·lence,** *n.* **—ma·lev'o·lent·ly,** *adv.*
**mal·fea·sance** (mal-fē'z'ns), *n.* [obs. Fr. *malfaisance* < *mal,* evil + ppr. of *faire,* to do], wrongdoing or misconduct, especially in handling public affairs. **—mal·fea'sant,** *adj.* & *n.*
**mal·for·ma·tion** (mal'fôr-mā'shən), *n.* faulty, irregular, or abnormal formation of a body or part.
**mal·formed** (mal-fôrmd'), *adj.* faultily or abnormally formed; misshapen.
**mal·func·tion** (mal-fuŋk'shən), *v.i.* [*mal-* + *function*], to fail to function as it should. *n.* the act or an instance of malfunctioning.
**Mal·gache** (mål'gåsh'), *n.* the country of Malagasy: the French name.
**Ma·li** (mä'li), *n.* a country in W Africa, south of Algeria: area, 590,966 sq. mi.; pop., 4,305,000; capital, Bamako.
**mal·ic acid** (mal'ik, mā'lik), [< Fr. < L. < Gr. *mēlon,* apple], a colorless acid, $C_4H_6O_5$, occurring in apples and other fruits.
**mal·ice** (mal'is), *n.* [OFr. < L. < *malus,* bad], 1. active ill will; desire to harm others; spite. 2. in *law,* evil intent. **—malice aforethought,** a deliberate intention and plan to do something unlawful.
**ma·li·cious** (mə-lish'əs), *adj.* having, showing, or caused by malice; spiteful. **—ma·li'cious·ly,** *adv.*
**ma·lign** (mə-līn'), *v.t.* [< OFr. < L. < *malignus,* wicked < *male,* ill + base of *genus,* born], to speak evil of; slander. *adj.* 1. malevolent; malicious. 2. evil; sinister. 3. very harmful; malignant. **—ma·lign'er,** *n.* **—ma·lign'ly,** *adv.*
**ma·lig·nant** (mə-lig'nənt), *adj.* [< L. ppr. < *malignus;* see MALIGN], 1. having an evil influence; malign. 2. wishing evil; very malevolent. 3. very harmful. 4. virulent; causing or likely to cause death: as, a cancer is a *malignant* tumor. **—ma·lig'nan·cy, ma·lig'nance,** *n.* **—ma·lig'nant·ly,** *adv.*
**ma·lig·ni·ty** (mə-lig'nə-ti), *n.* 1. ill will or desire to harm others; great malice. 2. the quality of being very harmful or dangerous. 3. [*pl.* -TIES], a malignant act, event, or feeling.
**ma·lines, ma·line** (mə-lēn'), *n.* [Fr. < *Malines,* Belgian city], a thin, somewhat stiff, silk net.
**ma·lin·ger** (mə-liŋ'gēr), *v.i.* [< Fr. *malingre,* sickly], to pretend to be ill in order to escape duty or work. **—ma·lin'ger·er,** *n.*
**mall** (môl; *occas.* mal), *n.* [var. of *maul,* mallet], a shaded walk or public promenade.
**mall** (môl), *n.* & *v.t.* maul.
**mal·lard** (mal'ērd), *n.* [*pl.* -LARDS, -LARD; see PLURAL, II, D, 1], [OFr. *mal(l)art*], the common wild duck from which the domestic duck is descended; esp., the male, or drake, which has a green head and a band of white around the neck.
**mal·le·a·ble** (mal'i-ə-b'l), *adj.* [< OFr. < L. *malleare,* to hammer < *malleus,* a hammer], 1. that can be hammered, pounded, or pressed into various shapes without breaking. 2. pliable; adaptable. **—mal'le·a·bil'i·ty, mal'le·a·ble·ness,** *n.*
**mal·let** (mal'it), *n.* [< Fr. dim. of *mail;* see MAUL], 1. a kind of hammer, usually with a wooden head and short handle, as for driving a chisel. 2. *a)* a long-handled hammer used in playing croquet. *b)* a similar instrument used in playing polo.
**mal·le·us** (mal'i-əs), *n.* [*pl.* -LEI (-i-ī')], [L., a hammer], the outermost of the three small bones of the middle ear, shaped somewhat like a hammer.
**Mal·lor·ca** (mäl-yôr'kä), *n.* Majorca: Spanish name.
**mal·low** (mal'ō), *n.* [AS. *mealuwe* < L. *malva*],

1. any of a family of plants, including the hollyhock, cotton, marsh mallow, and okra, typically with large, showy flowers. 2. any of a genus of plants in this family; esp., the wild mallow, with purplish, pink, or white flowers.

**malm·sey** (mäm′zi), *n.* [< ML. < Gr. *Monembasia*, Greek town], 1. a strong, full-flavored, sweet white wine. 2. the grape from which this is made.

**mal·nu·tri·tion** (mal′nōō-trish′ən, mal′nū-), *n.* faulty or inadequate nutrition; undernourishment.

**mal·o·dor·ous** (mal-ō′dẽr-əs), *adj.* having a bad odor; stinking. —**mal·o′dor,** *n.* —**mal·o′dor·ous·ly,** *adv.* —**mal·o′dor·ous·ness,** *n.*

**Mal·o·ry, Sir Thomas** (mal′ə-ri), fl. 1470; English writer and translator: compiler of Arthurian tales translated from French.

**mal·prac·tice** (mal-prak′tis), *n.* 1. injurious or unprofessional treatment of a patient by a physician or surgeon. 2. misconduct or improper practice in any professional or official position. —**mal·prac·ti·tion·er** (mal′prak-tish′ən-ẽr), *n.*

**malt** (môlt), *n.* [AS. *mealt*], 1. barley or other grain softened by soaking and then kiln-dried: used in brewing and distilling certain alcoholic liquors. 2. such liquor; beer, ale, etc. *adj.* made with malt. *v.t.* 1. to change (barley, etc.) into malt. 2. to prepare (milk, etc.) with malt or malt extract. *v.i.* 1. to be changed into malt. 2. to change barley, etc. into malt. —**malt′y,** *adj.*

**Mal·ta** (môl′tə), *n.* 1. a country on a group of islands in the Mediterranean, south of Sicily: a member of the British Commonwealth of Nations: area, 122 sq. mi.; pop., 328,000; capital, Valletta. 2. the chief island of this group.

**malted milk,** a drink made by mixing a powdered preparation of dried milk and malted cereals with milk and, usually, ice cream and flavoring.

**Mal·tese** (môl′tēz′), *adj.* of Malta, its inhabitants, etc. *n.* 1. [*pl.* -TESE], a native or inhabitant of Malta. 2. the language spoken in Malta.

**Maltese cat,** a variety of domestic cat with bluish-gray fur.

**Maltese cross,** a cross whose arms look like arrowheads pointing inward.

**malt extract,** a sticky, sugary substance obtained from malt soaked in water.

**Mal·thus, Thomas Robert** (mal′thəs), 1766–1834; English clergyman and economist; known for his theory that population increase is a major cause of poverty and war. —**Mal·thu′sian** (-thōō′zhən, -thū′zi-ən), *adj. & n.*

**malt liquor,** beer, ale, or other fermented liquor made with malt or barley.

**malt·ose** (môl′tōs), *n.* a white, crystalline sugar, $C_{12}H_{22}O_{11}$, obtained by the action of the diastase of malt on starch: also called *malt sugar.*

**mal·treat** (mal-trēt′), *v.t.* [< Fr.; see MAL- & TREAT], to treat roughly, unkindly, or brutally; abuse. —**mal·treat′ment,** *n.*

**malt·ster** (môlt′stẽr), *n.* one who makes malt.

**mam·bo** (mäm′bō), *n.* [Sp. Am.], a rhythmic ballroom dance to music of Cuban Negro origin in 4/4 time with a heavy accent on the second and fourth beats. *v.i.* to dance the mambo.

**Mam·e·luke** (mam′ə-lōōk′, -lūk′), *n.* [< Fr. < Ar. *mamlūk*, slave < *malaka*, to possess], 1. a member of a military force, originally of slaves, that seized and held power in Egypt from c. 1250 until 1811. 2. [m-], in Moslem countries, a slave.

**mam·ma** (mä′mə; *occas.* mə-mä′), *n.* [like L. *mamma*, mother, Sans. *mā*, Gr. *mammē* < baby talk], mother: a child's word: also **mama, ma,** etc.

**mam·ma** (mam′ə), *n.* [*pl.* -MAE (-ē)], [AS. < L., breast], a gland for secreting milk, present in the female of all mammals; mammary gland.

**mam·mal** (mam′əl), *n.* [< LL. genit. pl. < L. *mamma*, breast], any of a group of vertebrates (*Mammalia*) the females of which have milk-secreting glands for feeding their offspring. —**mam·ma·li·an** (ma-mā′li-ən), *adj. & n.*

**mam·ma·ry** (mam′ə-ri), *adj.* designating or of the milk-secreting glands; of the mammae.

**mam·mon** (mam′ən), *n.* [< LL. < Gr. < Aram. *māmōnā*, riches], 1. [usually M-], the false god of riches and avarice. 2. riches regarded as an object of worship and greedy pursuit. —**mam′mon·ism,** *n.*

**mam·moth** (mam′əth), *n.* [Russ. *mammot'*], a huge, extinct elephant with a hairy skin and long tusks curving upward. *adj.* very big; huge.

**mam·my** (mam′i), *n.* [*pl.* -MIES], [dial. var. of *mamma* (mother)], 1. mamma; mother: a child's word. 2. especially in the South, a Negro woman who takes care of white children.

**man** (man), *n.* [*pl.* MEN], [AS. *mann*], 1. a human being; person. 2. the human race; mankind: without *the* or *a*. 3. an adult male human being. 4. *a*) an adult male servant, follower, etc. *b*) a male employee. *c*) [Archaic], a vassal. 5. a husband. 6. a person with qualities conventionally regarded as manly. 7. one of the pieces used in chess, checkers, etc. *v.t.* [MANNED, MANNING], 1. to furnish with men for work, defense, etc.: as, to *man* a ship. 2. to take assigned places in, on, or at: as, *man* the guns! 3. to strengthen; brace: as, he *manned* himself for the ordeal. *interj.* [Slang], an exclamation of pleasure, surprise, etc. *adj.* male. —**as a** (or **one**) **man,** in unison; unanimously. —**be one's own man,** 1. to be free and independent. 2. to be in full control of oneself. —**man and boy,** from boyhood. —**to a man,** with no exception; every one.

**-man** (mən, man), a combining form meaning *man* or *person;* specif., *a*) *a member of a* (specified) *nation*, as in *Frenchman*. *b*) *a person doing a* (specified) *kind of work*, as in *laundryman*. *c*) *a person operating a* (specified) *device*, as in *motorman*.

**Man.,** 1. Manila (paper). 2. Manitoba.

**Man, Isle of,** one of the British Isles, between Northern Ireland and England.

**man about town,** a man who spends much time in fashionable restaurants, clubs, bars, etc.

**man·a·cle** (man′ə-k'l), *n.* [< OFr. < L. *manicula*, dim. of *manus*, hand], *usually in pl.* 1. a handcuff; fetter or shackle for the hand. 2. any restraint. *v.t.* [-CLED, -CLING], 1. to put handcuffs on; fetter. 2. to restrain; hamper.

**man·age** (man′ij), *v.t.* [-AGED, -AGING], [It. *maneggiare* < LL. < L. *manus*, hand], 1. originally, to train (a horse) in his paces. 2. *a*) to handle (a weapon, etc.). *b*) to control or guide (a vehicle, boat, etc.). 3. to have charge of; direct; conduct: as, he *manages* a hotel. 4. [Rare], to handle or use (money, supplies, etc.) carefully. 5. to get (a person) to do what one wishes, especially by tact, flattery, etc. 6. to contrive; succeed in accomplishing. *v.i.* 1. to carry on business. 2. to contrive to get along.

**man·age·a·ble** (man′ij-ə-b'l), *adj.* that can be managed; controllable. —**man′age·a·bil′i·ty, man′age·a·ble·ness,** *n.* —**man′age·a·bly,** *adv.*

**man·aged currency** (man′ijd), currency whose buying power is arbitrarily stabilized to control price fluctuations.

**man·age·ment** (man′ij-mənt), *n.* 1. a managing or being managed; control, direction, etc. 2. skillful managing or executive ability. 3. the persons managing a business, institution, etc.

**man·ag·er** (man′ij-ẽr), *n.* a person who manages; esp., one who manages a business, institution, etc.

**man·a·ge·ri·al** (man′ə-jêr′i-əl), *adj.* of a manager or management. —**man′a·ge′ri·al·ly,** *adv.*

**Ma·na·gua** (mä-nä′gwä), *n.* 1. a lake in W Nicaragua. 2. the capital of Nicaragua, on this lake: pop., 275,000.

‡**ma·ña·na** (mä-nyä′nä), *n.* [Sp.], tomorrow. *adv.* 1. tomorrow. 2. at an indefinite future time.

**Ma·nas·seh** (mə-nas′ə), *n.* in the *Bible*, 1. the elder son of Joseph. 2. the tribe of Israel descended from him.

**man-at-arms** (man′ət-ärmz′), *n.* [*pl.* MEN-AT-ARMS], 1. a soldier. 2. a heavily armed cavalryman in a medieval army.

**man·a·tee** (man′ə-tē′), *n.* [Sp. *manatí* < native (Carib) name], a large, plant-eating aquatic mammal living in shallow tropical waters, having flippers and a broad, flat tail; sea cow.

MANATEE
(about 13 ft. long)

**Man·ches·ter** (man′ches′tẽr, -chis-), *n.* 1. a city in Lancashire, England: pop., 655,000. 2. a city in S New Hampshire: pop., 88,000.

**Man·chu, Man·choo** (man-chōō′, man′chōō), *n.* 1. a member of a Mongolian people of Manchuria: the Manchus conquered China in 1644 and ruled until 1912. 2. the language of the Manchus. *adj.* of Manchuria, the Manchus, their language, etc.

**Man·chu·kuo, Man·chou·kuo** (man′chōō-kwō′, man-chōō′kwō), *n.* a former state in E Asia, including Manchuria, under Japanese control (1932–1945).

**Man·chu·ri·a** (man-choor′i-ə), *n.* a region in NE China, on the Yellow Sea: area, c. 364,000 sq. mi. —**Man·chu′ri·an,** *adj. & n.*

**-man·cy** (man′si), [< OFr. or LL. < Gr. *manteia*, divination], a combining form meaning *divination*, as in *necromancy*.

**Man·da·lay** (man′də-lā′, man′də-lā′), *n.* a city in Burma, on the Irrawaddy River: pop., 213,000.

**man·da·mus** (man-dā′məs), *n.* [L., we command],

in *law*, a writ requiring that a specified thing be done, issued by a higher court to a lower court, or to a person, city, etc.

**man·da·rin** (man′də-rin), *n.* [< Port. < Malay *mantrī*, minister of state < Hind. < Sans. < *mantra*, counsel], 1. a high official of China under the Empire. 2. [M-], the main and official dialect of Chinese. 3. a small, sweet orange with a loose rind; tangerine.

**man·da·tar·y** (man′də-ter′i), *n.* [*pl.* -IES], a country to which, or, rarely, a person to whom, a mandate has been given: also **mandatory.**

**man·date** (man′dāt; *also, for n.*, -dit), *n.* [< L. neut. pp. of *mandare*, to command < *manus*, a hand + pp. of *dare*, to give], 1. an authoritative order or command. 2. *a*) formerly, a commission from the League of Nations to a country to administer some region, colony, etc. *b*) the area so administered. 3. the wishes of constituents expressed to a representative, etc., and regarded as an order. 4. in *law*, an order from a higher court or official to a lower one. *v.t.* [-DATED, -DATING], to assign (a region, etc.) as a mandate. **—man·da′tor,** *n.*

**man·da·to·ry** (man′də-tôr′i, -tō′ri), *adj.* 1. of, like, or containing a mandate. 2. authoritatively commanded; obligatory. 3. having received a mandate over some territory. *n.* a mandatary.

**man·di·ble** (man′də-b′l), *n.* [OFr. < LL. < *mandibulum* < L. *mandere*, to chew], 1. the jaw; esp., the lower jaw. 2. either part of a bird's beak. 3. either of the pair of outermost, biting jaws of an insect or other arthropod. Also **man·dib′u·la** (-dib′yoo-lə). **—man·dib′u·lar,** *adj.*

**man·do·lin** (man′d'l-in′, man′də-lin′), *n.* [< Fr. < It. dim. of *mandola* < LL. < Gr. *pandoura*, kind of lute], a musical instrument with from eight to twelve metal strings, usually paired, and a deep, rounded sound box: it is played with a plectrum.

**man·drag·o·ra** (man-drag′ə-rə), *n.* mandrake.

**man·drake** (man′drāk), *n.* [by folk etym. < AS. *mandragora* < LL. < L. < Gr. *mandragoras*], 1. a poisonous plant of the nightshade family, with a short stem and a thick root. 2. the root, used in medicine as a narcotic. 3. the May apple.

MANDOLIN

**man·drel, man·dril** (man′drəl), *n.* [prob. < Fr. *mandrin*], 1. a spindle or bar inserted into something to hold it while it is being machined. 2. a metal bar used as a core around which metal, glass, etc. is cast, molded, or shaped.

**man·drill** (man′dril), *n.* [*man* + *drill* (baboon)], a large, fierce, strong baboon of W Africa.

**mane** (mān), *n.* [AS. *manu*], the long hair growing from the top or sides of the neck of certain animals, as the horse, lion, etc. **—maned,** *adj.*

**man-eat·er** (man′ēt′ẽr), *n.* 1. a cannibal. 2. an animal that eats, or is thought to eat, human flesh, as a tiger, shark, etc.

**ma·nège, ma·nege** (ma-nezh′, mə-nāzh′), *n.* [Fr. < It. *maneggio;* see MANAGE], 1. the art of riding and training horses; horsemanship. 2. the paces of a trained horse. 3. a riding academy.

**ma·nes, Ma·nes** (mā′nēz), *n.pl.* [L.], in *ancient Rom. religion*, the souls of the dead, especially of dead ancestors, regarded as gods.

**ma·neu·ver** (mə-nōō′vẽr, -nū′-), *n.* [Fr. *manœuvre* < LL. < L. *manu operare*, to work by hand], 1. a planned and controlled movement of troops, warships, etc. 2. *pl.* large-scale practice movements of troops, warships, etc. 3. a stratagem; scheme. *v.i.* & *v.t.* 1. to perform or cause to perform maneuvers. 2. to manage or plan skillfully; scheme. 3. to move, get, put, make, etc. by some stratagem or scheme. Also sp. **manoeuvre. —ma·neu′ver·a·bil′i·ty,** *n.* **—ma·neu′ver·a·ble,** *adj.*

**man** (or **girl**) **Friday,** a loyal and devoted follower or servant: see **Friday.**

**man·ful** (man′fəl), *adj.* manly; brave, resolute, etc. **—man′ful·ly,** *adv.* **—man′ful·ness,** *n.*

**man·ga·nese** (maŋ′gə-nēs′, maŋ′gə-nēz′), *n.* [< Fr. < It.; by metathesis < ML. *magnesia;* see MAGNESIA], a grayish-white metallic chemical element, usually hard and brittle, which rusts like iron but is not magnetic: used in various alloys: symbol, Mn; at. wt., 54.93; at. no., 25.

**mange** (mānj), *n.* [< OFr. *mangeue*, an itch; ult. < L. *manducare;* see MANGER], a skin disease of domestic animals, and occasionally of man, especially one causing a loss of hair.

**man·gel-wur·zel** (maŋ′g'l-wũr′z'l, -wũrt′s'l), *n.* [G. < *mangold*, beet + *wurzel*, a root], a variety of large beet, used as food for cattle, especially in Europe: also **mangel.**

**man·ger** (mān′jẽr), *n.* [OFr. *mangeoire* < LL. < pp. of L. *manducare*, to eat < *mandere*, to chew], a box or trough to hold hay, etc. for horses or cattle to eat.

**man·gle** (maŋ′g'l), *v.t.* [-GLED, -GLING], [Anglo-Fr. *mangler* < OFr. *mehaigner*, to maim], 1. to mutilate by repeatedly and roughly cutting, hacking, etc. 2. to spoil; botch; mar. **—man′gler,** *n.*

**man·gle** (maŋ′g'l), *n.* [D. *mangel* < MD. < It. < LL. < Gr. *manganon*, war machine], a machine for pressing and smoothing cloth, especially sheets and other flat pieces, between rollers. *v.t.* [-GLED, -GLING], to press in a mangle. **—man′gler,** *n.*

**man·go** (maŋ′gō), *n.* [*pl.* -GOES, -GOS], [Port. *manga* < Malay < Tamil *mān-kāy*], 1. a yellow-red, somewhat acid tropical fruit with a thick rind and juicy pulp. 2. the tree that it grows on.

**man·grove** (man′grōv), *n.* [< Port. *mangue* or Sp. *mangle* < the W.Ind. name; infl. by Eng. *grove*], a tropical tree with branches that spread and send down roots, thus forming more trunks.

**man·gy** (mān′ji), *adj.* [-GIER, -GIEST], 1. having or caused by the mange. 2. shabby and filthy; squalid. 3. mean and low. **—man′gi·ly,** *adv.* **—man′gi·ness,** *n.*

**man·han·dle** (man′han′d'l), *v.t.* [-DLED, -DLING], 1. [Rare], to move or do by human strength only, without mechanical aids. 2. to handle roughly.

**Man·hat·tan** (man-hat′ən), *n.* 1. an island between the Hudson and East rivers, forming part of New York City: also **Manhattan Island.** 2. a borough of New York City consisting of this island: pop., 1,698,000. 3. a cocktail made of whisky and vermouth, usually with a dash of bitters.

**Manhattan District,** a division of the U.S. Army Corps of Engineers (1942–1946), which produced the atomic bomb.

**man·hole** (man′hōl′), *n.* a hole through which a man can get into a sewer, pipe, conduit, etc. for repair work or inspection.

**man·hood** (man′hood), *n.* 1. the state or time of being a man. 2. manly qualities; virility, courage, resolution, etc. 3. men collectively.

**man-hour** (man′our′), *n.* a unit of work, equal to that done by one man in one hour.

**man·hunt** (man′hunt′), *n.* a hunt for a man, especially for a fugitive: also **man hunt.**

**ma·ni·a** (mā′ni-ə), *n.* [L. < Gr. *mania* < *mainesthai*, to rage], 1. wild or violent insanity; specif., the manic phase of manic-depressive psychosis, characterized generally by abnormal excitability, flight of ideas, etc. 2. an excessive, persistent enthusiasm; obsession; craze.

**-ma·ni·a** (mā′ni-ə), [see MANIA], a combining form meaning: 1. *a* (specified) *type of mental disorder*, as in *kleptomania*. 2. *an excessive, persistent enthusiasm* or *craze for*, as in *bibliomania*.

**ma·ni·ac** (mā′ni-ak′), *adj.* wildly insane; raving. *n.* a violently insane person; lunatic. **—ma·ni·a·cal** (mə-nī′ə-k'l), *adj.* **—ma·ni′a·cal·ly,** *adv.*

**man·ic** (man′ik, mā′nik), *adj.* 1. having or characterized by mania. 2. of or like mania.

**man·ic-de·pres·sive** (man′ik-di-pres′iv, mā′nik-), *adj.* designating, of, or having a psychosis characterized by alternating periods of mania and melancholia. *n.* a person who has this psychosis.

**man·i·cure** (man′ə-kyoor′), *n.* [Fr. < L. *manus*, a hand + *cura*, care], the care of the hands; esp., trimming, polishing, etc. of the fingernails. *v.t.* & *v.i.* [-CURED, -CURING], to take care of (the hands and fingernails). **—man′i·cur′ist,** *n.*

**man·i·fest** (man′ə-fest′), *adj.* [< OFr. < L. *manifestus*, lit., struck by the hand, palpable], apparent to the senses, especially to sight, or to the mind; evident; obvious. *v.t.* 1. to make clear or evident; reveal. 2. to prove; be evidence of. *v.i.* to appear to the senses. *n.* an itemized list of a ship's cargo, to be shown to customs officials. **—man′i·fest′ly,** *adv.* **—man′i·fest′ness,** *n.*

**man·i·fes·ta·tion** (man′ə-fes-tā′shən), *n.* 1. a manifesting or being manifested. 2. something that manifests: as, his silence was a *manifestation* of fear. 3. a public demonstration.

**man·i·fes·to** (man′ə-fes′tō), *n.* [*pl.* -TOES], [It. < L.

---

fat, āpe, bâre, cär; ten, ēven, hêre, ovẽr; is, bīte; lot, gō, hôrn, tōōl, look; oil, out; up, ūse, fũr; get; joy; yet; chin; she; thin, *th*en; zh, leisure; ŋ, ring; ə for *a* in *ago*, *e* in *agent*, *i* in *sanity*, *o* in *comply*, *u* in *focus;* ′ in *able* (ā′b'l); Fr. bål; ë, Fr. coeur; ö, Fr. feu; Fr. mo*n*; ô, Fr. coq; ü, Fr. duc; H, G. ich; kh, G. doch. ‡ foreign; < derived from.

*manifestus;* see MANIFEST], a public declaration of motives and intentions by a government or by an important person or group.

**man·i·fold** (man'ə-fōld'), *adj.* [AS. *manigfeald;* see MANY & -FOLD], 1. having many and various forms, parts, etc.: as, *manifold* wisdom. 2. of many sorts; multifarious: as, *manifold* duties. 3. being such in many and various ways: as, a *manifold* villain. 4. operating several units or parts of one kind. *n.* 1. any of many copies made by manifolding. 2. a pipe with at least one inlet and two or more outlets, as for conducting cylinder exhaust from an automobile engine. *v.t.* 1. to multiply. 2. to make several copies of: as, to *manifold* a letter with carbon paper. —**man'i·fold'ly,** *adv.* —**man'i·fold'ness,** *n.*

MANIFOLD PIPE

**man·i·kin** (man'ə-kin), *n.* [D. *manneken* < *man,* man + dim. suffix *-ken*], 1. a little man; dwarf. 2. a mannequin. Also sp. **manakin, mannikin.**

**Ma·nil·a** (mə-nil'ə), *n.* 1. the principal city and former capital of the Philippine Islands, on Luzon: pop., 1,200,000: see **Quezon City.** 2. [often m-], *a)* Manila hemp. *b)* Manila paper.

**Manila hemp,** a strong fiber from the leafstalk of a Philippine tree related to the banana: it is used for making rope, paper, etc.

**Manila paper,** a strong, brownish wrapping paper, originally made of Manila hemp.

**man in the street,** the average man.

**man·i·oc** (man'i-ok', mā'ni-), *n.* [Fr. < Braz. (Tupi) *mandioca*], cassava.

**ma·nip·u·late** (mə-nip'yoo-lāt'), *v.t.* [-LATED, -LATING], [< Fr.; ult. < L. *manipulus,* handful < *manus,* a hand + base of *plere,* to fill], 1. to work or operate skillfully with or as with the hands. 2. to manage artfully or by shrewd use of influence, especially in an unfair way: as, the politician *manipulated* the voting. 3. to change or falsify (figures, accounts, etc.) for one's own purposes. —**ma·nip'u·lat'a·ble,** *adj.* —**ma·nip'u·la'tion,** *n.* —**ma·nip'u·la'tor,** *n.*

**ma·nip·u·lat·ive** (mə-nip'yoo-lā'tiv), *adj.* of or done by manipulation: also **ma·nip'u·la·to'ry** (-lə-tôr'i, -tō'ri).

**man·i·to** (man'ə-tō'), *n.* [Am. Ind. *manitto,* he is a god], in *Algonquian Indian religion,* a spirit understood as a nature spirit of both good and evil influence: also **man'i·tou', man'i·tu'** (-too').

**Man·i·to·ba** (man'ə-tō'bə), *n.* 1. a province of S Canada: pop., 777,000; capital, Winnipeg. 2. a lake in S Manitoba. —**Man'i·to'ban,** *adj.* & *n.*

**man·kind** (man'kīnd'; *also, and for* 2 *always,* man'-kīnd'), *n.* 1. all human beings; the human race. 2. all human males; the male sex.

**man·like** (man'līk'), *adj.* 1. like or characteristic of a man or men. 2. fit for a man; masculine.

**man·ly** (man'li), *adj.* [-LIER, -LIEST], 1. having the qualities regarded as suitable for a man; manlike; virile; brave, strong, honorable, etc. 2. fit for a man; masculine: as, *manly* sports. *adv.* in a manly way. —**man'li·ness,** *n.*

**Mann, Horace** (man), 1796–1859; American educator.

**Mann, Tho·mas** (tō'mäs män), 1875–1955; German novelist in U.S., etc.

**man·na** (man'ə), *n.* [AS. < LL. < Gr. < Aram. *mannā* < Heb. *mān*], 1. in the *Bible,* food miraculously provided for the Israelites in the wilderness: Ex. 16:14-36. 2. any needed sustenance that seems miraculously supplied. 3. a sweet, gummy juice from certain European ash trees, used as a laxative.

**man·ne·quin** (man'ə-kin), *n.* [Fr. < D.; see MANIKIN], 1. a model of the human body, used by tailors, artists, etc. 2. a woman whose work is modeling clothes in stores, etc.

**man·ner** (man'ẽr), *n.* [< OFr. < LL. < L. *manuarius,* of the hand < *manus,* a hand], 1. a way or method of doing something; mode of procedure. 2. a way of acting; personal behavior: as, his *manner* showed anger. 3. a usual way of acting; habit: as, their *manner* of living. 4. *pl. a)* ways of social life: as, a comedy of *manners. b)* ways of social behavior; deportment: as, good *manners,* bad *manners. c)* polite ways of social behavior: as, the child has no *manners.* 5. distinctive style in art, music, literature, etc. 6. kind; sort: as, what *manner* of man is he? —**by all manner of means,** of course; surely. —**by no manner of means,** in no way; definitely not. —**in a manner of speaking,** in a certain sense or way. —**to the manner born,** accustomed from birth to the way or usage spoken of. —**man'ner·less,** *adj.*

**man·nered** (man'ẽrd), *adj.* 1. having manners of a specified sort: as, ill-*mannered.* 2. affected: as, a *mannered* literary style.

**man·ner·ism** (man'ẽr-iz'm), *n.* 1. excessive use of some distinctive manner in art, literature, speech, or behavior. 2. a peculiarity of manner in behavior, speech, etc. —**man'ner·ist,** *n.*

**man·ner·ly** (man'ẽr-li), *adj.* showing good manners; polite. *adv.* politely. —**man'ner·li·ness,** *n.*

**man·ni·kin** (man'ə-kin), *n.* a manikin.

**man·nish** (man'ish), *adj.* characteristic of, like, or imitating a man; masculine. —**man'nish·ly,** *adv.* —**man'nish·ness,** *n.*

**ma·noeu·vre** (mə-nōō'vẽr, -nū'-), *n., v.i.* & *v.t.* [-VRED, -VRING], maneuver.

**man of god,** 1. a holy man; saint, hermit, etc. 2. a minister, priest, rabbi, etc.

**man of letters,** a writer or scholar, editor, etc. whose work is in the field of literature.

**man of the world,** a man familiar with and tolerant of various sorts of people and their ways.

**man-of-war** (man'əv-wôr', -ə-wôr'), *n.* [*pl.* MEN-OF-WAR], an armed naval vessel; warship.

**man-of-war bird** (or **hawk**), a frigate bird.

**ma·nom·e·ter** (mə-nom'ə-tẽr), *n.* [< Fr. < Gr. *manos,* rare + Fr. *-mètre,* -meter], 1. an instrument for measuring the pressure of gases. 2. an instrument for measuring blood pressure. —**man·o·met·ric** (man'ə-met'rik), **man'o·met'ri·cal,** *adj.*

**man on horseback,** a military man whose popular influence threatens the current regime.

**man·or** (man'ẽr), *n.* [< OFr. < *manoir,* to dwell < L. *manere,* to remain], 1. in England, a landed estate, originally of a feudal lord and subject to the jurisdiction of his court. 2. in colonial America, a district granted by the king as a manor and leased to tenants at a set rental. —**ma·no·ri·al** (mə-nôr'i-əl, -nō'ri-), *adj.*

**manor house,** the house of the lord of a manor.

**man·pow·er** (man'pou'ẽr), *n.* 1. power furnished by human physical strength. 2. the collective strength or availability for work of the people in a given area, nation, etc. Also **man power.**

**man·sard** (man'särd), *n.* [after F. *Mansard,* 17th-c. Fr. architect], a roof with two slopes on each of the four sides, the lower steeper than the upper: also **mansard roof.**

MANSARD ROOF

**manse** (mans), *n.* [< ML. < pp. of L. *manere,* to dwell], a parsonage; residence of a minister.

**man·ser·vant** (man'sũr'vənt), *n.* [*pl.* MENSERVANTS], a male servant: also **man servant.**

**man·sion** (man'shən), *n.* [OFr. < L. *mansio,* a dwelling < pp. of *manere,* to dwell], a large, imposing house; stately residence.

**man·slaugh·ter** (man'slô'tẽr), *n.* the killing of a human being by another; esp., such killing when unlawful but without malice.

**man·tel** (man't'l), *n.* [see MANTLE], 1. the facing of stone, marble, etc. about a fireplace, including a projecting shelf. 2. this shelf.

**man·tel·et** (man't'l-et', mant'lit), *n.* [OFr., dim. of *mantel;* see MANTLE], 1. a short mantle or cape. 2. a protective shelter or screen; esp., a bulletproof shield, as about a gun to protect the gun crew. Also (for 2) **mantlet.**

**man·tel·piece** (man't'l-pēs'), *n.* a mantel (sense 2).

**man·til·la** (man-til'ə), *n.* [Sp. < LL. < *mantellum,* a cloak], a woman's veil or scarf worn over the hair and shoulders, as in Spain, Mexico, etc.

**man·tis** (man'tis), *n.* [*pl.* -TISES, -TES (-tēz)], [< Gr. *mantis,* prophet, seer], an insect that holds its forelegs folded as if praying, and feeds on other insects: often **praying mantis.**

**man·tle** (man't'l), *n.* [< AS. & OFr. < L. *mantel(l)um*], 1. a loose, sleeveless cloak or cape. 2. anything that cloaks, envelops, or conceals. 3. a small, meshwork hood which when placed over a flame becomes white-hot and gives off light. 4. in *zoology,* the membranous fold of the body wall of a mollusk, etc., containing glands that secrete a shell-forming fluid. *v.t.* [-TLED, -TLING], 1. to cover with a mantle. 2. to cover; envelop; conceal. *v.i.* 1. to be or become covered, as a surface with scum. 2. to form a covering. 3. to blush or flush: as, her cheeks *mantled* at the praise.

**man·tu·a** (man'chōō-ə, -tōō-ə), *n.* [altered < Fr. *manteau,* a mantle], a mantle or loose gown or cloak formerly worn by women.

**man·u·al** (man'ū-əl), *adj.* [< OFr. < L. < *manus,* a hand], of a hand or the hands; made, done, or worked by the hands. *n.* 1. a handy book for use as a guide, reference, etc.; handbook. 2. a hand-operated keyboard on an organ. 3. prescribed drill in the handling of a weapon, especially a rifle: also **manual of arms.** —**man′u·al·ly,** *adv.*

**manual training,** training in woodwork, metal-working, and similar arts and crafts.

**man·u·fac·ture** (man′yoo-fak′chẽr), *n.* [Fr. < ML. < L. < *manus*, a hand + *factura*, a making < *facere*, to make], 1. the making of goods by hand or, especially, by machinery, often on a large scale and with division of labor. 2. anything so made. 3. the making of something in a merely mechanical way. *v.t.* [-TURED, -TURING], 1. to make by hand or, especially, by machinery. 2. to work (wool, steel, etc.) into usable form. 3. to produce (art, literature, etc.) mechanically. 4. to make up (excuses, etc.); invent.

**man·u·fac·tur·er** (man′yoo-fak′chẽr-ẽr), *n.* a person in the business of manufacturing; esp., a factory owner.

**man·u·mis·sion** (man′yoo-mish′ən), *n.* a freeing or being freed from slavery; liberation.

**man·u·mit** (man′yoo-mit′), *v.t.* [-MITTED, -MITTING], [< L. < *manus*, a hand + *mittere*, to send], to free from slavery; liberate (a slave, serf, etc.).

**ma·nure** (mə-nyoor′, -noor′), *v.t.* [-NURED, -NURING], [< Anglo-Fr. < OFr. *manouvrer*, to work with the hands, cultivate], to put manure on or into. *n.* animal excrement or other substance used to fertilize soil. —**ma·nur′er,** *n.*

**man·u·script** (man′yoo-skript′), *adj.* [< L. < *manus*, a hand + pp. of *scribere*, to write], written by hand or with a typewriter. *n.* a written or typewritten document, book, or paper; esp., an author's copy of his work, as submitted to a publisher.

**Manx** (maŋks), *adj.* of the Isle of Man, its people, etc. *n.* the Gaelic language spoken on the Isle of Man. —**the Manx,** the people of the Isle of Man.

**manx cat, Manx cat,** a variety of domestic cat with a rudimentary tail.

**Manx·man** (maŋks′mən), *n.* [*pl.* -MEN], a native or inhabitant of the Isle of Man.

**man·y** (men′i), *adj.* [MORE, MOST], [AS. *manig*], 1. consisting of some large, indefinite number; numerous. 2. relatively numerous (preceded by *as*, *too*, etc.). *n.* a large number (of persons or things). *pron.* many persons or things. —**a good many,** [construed as pl.], a relatively large number. —**a great many,** [construed as pl.], an extremely large number. —**be one too many for,** to defeat; overwhelm. —**the many,** 1. the majority of people. 2. the people; the masses.

**man·y-sid·ed** (men′i-sīd′id), *adj.* 1. having many sides or faces. 2. having many possibilities, qualities, etc.: as, a *many-sided* woman.

**man·za·ni·ta** (man′zə-nē′tə), *n.* [Sp., dim. of *manzana*, apple], any of several evergreen shrubs or small trees of the western U.S.

**Mao·ism** (mou′iz′m), *n.* the communist theories and policies of Mao Tse-tung.

**Ma·o·ri** (mä′ō-ri, mou′ri), *n.* 1. [*pl.* -RIS], one of a brown-skinned people native to New Zealand, of Polynesian origin. 2. their Polynesian language. *adj.* of the Maoris, their language, etc.

**Mao Tse-tung** (mou′ dzu′dooŋ′), 1893– ; Chinese communist leader.

**map** (map), *n.* [< OFr. < ML. *mappa (mundi)*, map (of the world) < L. *mappa*, napkin], 1. a representation, usually flat, of all or part of the earth's surface, ordinarily showing countries, bodies of water, cities, etc. 2. a similar representation of the sky, showing the stars, planets, etc. 3. any map-like representation. 4. [Slang], the face. *v.t.* [MAPPED, MAPPING], 1. to make a map of; represent on a map. 2. to work out in detail; plan: as, he *mapped* out his idea. 3. to survey for the purpose of making a map. —**off the map,** out of existence. —**put on the map,** [Colloq.], to make well known. —**map′per,** *n.*

**ma·ple** (mā′p'l), *n.* [AS. *mapel (treow)*, maple (tree)], 1. any of a large group of trees with dry, two-winged fruits and opposite leaves, grown for wood, sap, or shade. 2. the hard, light-colored wood of such a tree. 3. the flavor of maple sirup or of maple sugar. *adj.* 1. of or made of maple. 2. flavored with maple.

**maple sirup,** sirup made by boiling down the sap of a certain variety of maple.

**maple sugar,** sugar made from maple sirup.

**ma·quis** (mä-kē′), *n.* [Fr. < It. *macchia*, a thicket], 1. a zone of shrubby, evergreen plants in the Mediterranean area, used as a hiding place by guerrilla fighters, etc. 2. [often M-], [*pl.* -QUIS (-kē′)], a member of the French military underground against the Nazis in World War II.

**mar** (mär), *v.t.* [MARRED, MARRING], [AS. *merran*, to hinder], to injure so as to make imperfect, etc.; spoil; impair. *n.* something that mars; blemish.

**Mar.,** March.

**mar·a·bou** (mar′ə-bōō′), *n.* [Fr. < Port. < Ar. *murābiṭ*, hermit], 1. a large stork, especially one of a kind found in Africa. 2. the adjutant, a bird of India. 3. soft wing and tail feathers of the marabou, used in millinery. Also **mar′a·bout′** (-bōōt′).

**ma·ra·ca** (mə-rä′kə; Port. mä-rä′kä), *n.* [Port. *maracá* < the Braz. native name], a percussion instrument consisting of a dried gourd or gourd-shaped rattle with loose pebbles in it.

**mar·a·schi·no** (mar′ə-skē′nō), *n.* [It. < *marasca*, kind of cherry < *amaro*, bitter], a strong, sweet liqueur or cordial made from the fermented juice of a kind of black wild cherry.

**maraschino cherries,** cherries in a sirup flavored with maraschino.

**Mar·a·thon** (mar′ə-thon′), *n.* a plain on the E coast of Attica: site of a battle (490 B.C.), in which the Athenians defeated the Persians.

**mar·a·thon** (mar′ə-thon′, -thən), *n.* 1. a foot race of 26 miles, 385 yards: so called in allusion to the Greek runner who went from Marathon to Athens with news of the Athenian victory. 2. any long-distance or endurance contest.

**ma·raud** (mə-rôd′), *v.i.* [< Fr. < *maraud*, vagabond < OFr. *marault*], to rove in search of plunder; make raids. *v.t.* to raid; plunder. *n.* a raid; foray. —**ma·raud′er,** *n.* —**ma·raud′ing,** *adj.* & *n.*

**mar·ble** (mär′b'l), *n.* [OFr. < L. < Gr. *marmaros*, white glistening stone], 1. a hard, metamorphic limestone, white or colored and sometimes streaked or mottled, which can take a high polish. 2. a piece or slab of this stone, used as a monument, etc. 3. anything like marble in hardness, coldness, etc. 4. a little ball of stone, glass, or clay, used in games. 5. *pl.* *a)* [construed as sing.], a children's game in which a marble is propelled with the thumb at other marbles in a marked circle. *b)* a group of sculptures in marble. *adj.* 1. made of marble. 2. like marble; hard, cold, smooth, etc. *v.t.* [-BLED, -BLING], to make (paper, book edges, etc.) look mottled like marble. —**mar′ble-like′,** **mar′bly** [-BLIER, -BLIEST], *adj.*

**marble cake,** a cake made of light and dark batter mixed to give a marblelike appearance.

**mar·ble·ize** (mär′b'l-īz′), *v.t.* [-IZED, -IZING], to make, color, or streak in imitation of marble.

**Marc An·to·ny** (märk an′tə-ni), see **Antonius, Marcus.**

**mar·ca·site** (mär′kə-sīt′), *n.* [< Fr. < ML. < Ar. *marqashīṭā*], 1. formerly, crystallized iron pyrites, used in the 18th century for ornaments. 2. iron disulfide, a mineral resembling iron pyrites.

**mar·cel** (mär-sel′), *n.* [after M. *Marcel*, 19th-c. Fr. hairdresser], a series of even waves or tiers put in the hair: also **marcel wave.** *v.t.* [-CELLED, -CELLING], to put such waves in (hair).

**March** (märch), *n.* [< OFr. < L. *Martius (mensis)*, (month) of Mars], the third month of the year, having 31 days: abbrev. **Mar.**

**march** (märch), *v.i.* [Fr. *marcher*, orig., to trample < L. *marcus*, a hammer], 1. to walk with regular, steady steps, as in a military formation. 2. to walk in a grave, stately way. 3. to advance or progress steadily. *v.t.* to cause to march or go. *n.* 1. a marching. 2. a steady advance; progress: as, the *march* of events. 3. a regular, steady step or pace. 4. the distance covered in marching: as, a day's *march*. 5. a long, tiring walk. 6. a piece of music for marching. —**on the march,** marching. —**steal a march on,** to get an advantage over secretly. —**march′er,** *n.*

**march** (märch), *n.* [OFr. *marche* < Gmc. base of *mark*], a border or frontier, as of a country.

**‡Mär·chen** (mâr′Hən), *n.* [*pl.* MÄRCHEN], [G.], a story; tale; esp., a fairy tale or folk tale.

**March hare,** a hare in breeding time, proverbially regarded as an example of madness.

**mar·chion·ess** (mär′shən-is, mär′shə-nes′), *n.* [< ML. fem. of *marchio*, prefect of the marches, or borderlands], 1. the wife or widow of a marquis. 2. a lady whose own rank equals that of a marquis.

**march·pane** (märch′pān′), *n.* [< It. *marzapane* < ML. < Ar. *mauthaban*, coin; G. *marzipan* is < the It.], a confection of ground almonds, sugar, and egg white made into a paste: also **marzipan.**

**Mar·co·ni, Gu·gliel·mo** (gōō-lyel′mō mär-kō′ni),

fat, āpe, bâre, cär; ten, ēven, hêre, ovẽr; is, bīte; lot, gō, hôrn, tōōl, look; oil, out; up, ūse, fũr; get; joy; yet; chin; she; thin, *th*en; zh, leisure; ŋ, ring; ə for *a* in *ago*, *e* in *agent*, *i* in *sanity*, *o* in *comply*, *u* in *focus*; ′ in *able* (ā′b'l); Fr. bȧl; ë, Fr. coeur; ö, Fr. feu; Fr. mon; ô, Fr. coq; ü, Fr. duc; H, G. ich; kh, G. doch. ‡ foreign; < derived from.

Marquis, 1874–1937; Italian physicist: developed wireless telegraphy.
**mar·co·ni·gram** (mär-kō'ni-gram'), *n.* a radiogram.
**Marco Polo,** see **Polo, Marco.**
**Mar·cus Au·re·li·us** (mär'kəs ô-rē'li-əs), (*Marcus Aurelius Antoninus*), 121–180 A.D.; Stoic philosopher; emperor of Rome (161–180 A.D.).
**Mar·di gras** (mär'di grä'), [Fr., lit., fat Tuesday], Shrove Tuesday, the last day before Lent: a day of carnival in New Orleans, Paris, etc.
**mare** (mâr), *n.* [AS. *mere*, fem. of *mearh*, horse], a female horse, mule, donkey, etc.
**mare's-nest** (mârz'nest'), *n.* something supposed to be a wonderful discovery but turning out to be a hoax: earlier called *horse-nest.*
**mare's-tail** (mârz'tāl'), *n.* long, narrow formations of cirrus cloud, shaped somewhat like a horse's tail.
**mar·ga·rine** (mär'jə-rin, -rēn'; *occas.* -gə-rēn'), *n.* [Fr.], a blend of refined, edible, usually vegetable oil, churned with cultured skim milk: it is used like butter: also **mar'ga·rin** (-jə-rin), **oleomargarine.**
**marge** (märj), *n.* [Fr. < L. *margo*, margin], [Archaic or Poetic], a border; edge; margin.
**mar·gin** (mär'jin), *n.* [L. *margo*], 1. a border; edge: as, the *margin* of a pond. 2. the blank border of a printed or written page. 3. a limit. 4. an amount of money, supplies, etc. beyond what is needed. 5. provision for increase, error, etc. 6. in *business*, *a*) the difference between the cost and the selling price of a commodity. *b*) money or collateral deposited with a broker to insure him against loss on contracts which he undertakes for a buyer or seller of stocks, etc. *v.t.* 1. to provide with a margin. 2. in *business*, to deposit a margin upon.
**mar·gin·al** (mär'ji-n'l), *adj.* 1. written or printed in the margin. 2. of a margin. 3. at, on, or close to the margin. —**mar'gin·al·ly,** *adv.*
**mar·gin·ate** (mär'jə-nāt'; *for adj., also* -nit), *v.t.* [-ATED, -ATING], to provide with a margin. *adj.* having a distinct margin: also **mar'gin·at'ed.** —**mar'gin·a'tion,** *n.*
**mar·grave** (mär'grāv), *n.* [< MD. < MHG. < *mark*, a border + *graf*, a count], 1. originally, a military governor of a border province in Germany. 2. the title of certain princes of Germany.
**mar·gra·vine** (mär'grə-vēn'), *n.* a margrave's wife.
**mar·gue·rite** (mär'gə-rēt'), *n.* [Fr., a pearl], 1. a daisy with a yellow center and white petals. 2. a chrysanthemum with a single flower.
**Mar·i·an** (mâr'i-ən), *adj.* of the Virgin Mary. *n.* a worshiper or devotee of the Virgin Mary.
**Ma·ri·a·nas Islands** (mä'rē-ä'näs), a chain of islands in the Pacific, east of the Philippines: (except Guam) formerly a Japanese mandate, now under U.S. trusteeship: formerly called *Ladrone Islands.*
**Ma·rie An·toi·nette** (mə-rē' an'twə-net', an'tə-), 1755–1793; wife of Louis XVI; queen of France (1774–1792); guillotined.
**mar·i·gold** (mar'i-gōld'), *n.* [? < Virgin *Mary* + *gold*], 1. a plant of the composite family, with red, yellow, or orange flowers. 2. the flower.
**ma·ri·jua·na, ma·ri·hua·na** (mâr'i-wä'nə, mä'ri-hwä'nə), *n.* [Am. Sp.; ? < native word], 1. the hemp plant. 2. its narcotic dried leaves and flowers, smoked in cigarettes by addicts.
**ma·rim·ba** (mə-rim'bə), *n.* [< Afr. (Bantu) pl. of *limba*, kind of musical instrument], a kind of xylophone, usually with resonators beneath the wooden bars.

MARIMBA

**ma·ri·na** (mə-rē'nə), *n.* [It. & Sp., seacoast < L. *marinus;* see MARINE], a small harbor with dockage, supplies, and services for small pleasure craft.
**mar·i·nade** (mar'ə-nād'), *n.* [Fr. < Sp. < *marinar*, to pickle; ult. < L. *marinus;* see MARINE], 1. vinegar or wine, usually spiced, in which meats and fish are pickled. 2. meat or fish so pickled. *v.t.* (mar'ə-nād'), [-NADED, -NADING], to marinate.
**mar·i·nate** (mar'ə-nāt'), *v.t.* [-NATED, -NATING], [< *marinade* + *-ate*], 1. to soak (meat or fish) in marinade; steep in brine. 2. to steep in oil and vinegar. —**mar'i·na'tion,** *n.*
**ma·rine** (mə-rēn'), *adj.* [< Late OFr. < L. *marinus* < *mare*, the sea], 1. of, found in, or formed by the sea or ocean. 2. *a*) of navigation on, or shipping by, the sea; maritime; nautical. *b*) naval. 3. used, or to be used, at sea: as, a *marine* engine. 4. trained for service at sea, etc. *n.* 1. one of a class of troops trained for service at sea, etc.; specif., [often M-], a member of the Marine Corps. 2. naval or merchant ships collectively: as, the merchant *marine.* 3. in some countries, the department of government in charge of naval affairs. 4. a picture of a ship or sea scene.
**Marine Corps,** a branch of the U.S. armed forces trained for land, sea, and aerial combat.
**mar·i·ner** (mar'ə-nēr), *n.* [< Anglo-Fr. < ML. *marinarius* < L.; see MARINE], a sailor; seaman.
**mar·i·o·nette** (mar'i-ə-net'), *n.* [Fr., dim. of *Marion* < *Marie*, Mary], a little jointed doll moved by strings or wires, often on a miniature stage.
**Mar·i·po·sa lily** (or **tulip**) (mar'ə-pō'sə, -zə), [Sp. *mariposa*, butterfly], 1. a plant of the lily family, found in the western U.S. and Mexico, with tuliplike flowers. 2. the flower.
**mar·i·tal** (mar'ə-t'l), *adj.* [< L. < *maritus*, a husband], 1. of a husband. 2. of marriage; matrimonial; connubial. —**mar'i·tal·ly,** *adv.*
**mar·i·time** (mar'ə-tīm'), *adj.* [Fr. < L. *maritimus* < *mare*, the sea], 1. on, near, or living near the sea: as, a *maritime* people. 2. of the sea in relation to navigation, shipping, etc.: as, *maritime* law. 3. characteristic of sailors.
**Maritime Provinces,** the Canadian provinces of Nova Scotia, New Brunswick, and Prince Edward Island: also called **the Maritimes.**
**mar·jo·ram** (mär'jēr-əm), *n.* [< OFr. < ML. *majorana;* prob. ult. < L. *amaracus* < Gr. *amarakos*], any of various plants of the mint family; esp., a fragrant plant (*sweet marjoram*) used in cooking.
**Mark** (märk), *n.* in the *Bible*, 1. one of the four Evangelists (*John Mark*), the reputed author of the second book of the New Testament. 2. this book, telling the story of Jesus' life.
**mark** (märk), *n.* [AS. *mearc*, orig., boundary], 1. a line, spot, stain, scratch, mar, etc. on a surface. 2. a sign, symbol, or indication; specif., *a*) a printed or written symbol: as, punctuation *marks.* *b*) a brand, label, etc. put on an article to show the owner, maker, etc. *c*) a sign of some quality, character, etc.: as, courtesy is the *mark* of a gentleman. *d*) a grade; rating: as, a *mark* of B in history. *e*) a cross, etc. made by a person unable to write his signature. 3. a standard of quality, propriety, etc.: as, this novel isn't up to the *mark.* 4. importance; distinction: as, a man of *mark.* 5. impression; influence: as, he left his *mark* on history. 6. a visible object of known position, serving as a guide. 7. a line, dot, etc. used to indicate position, as on a graduated scale. 8. an object aimed at; target; end; goal. 9. an observing; heed. 10. in *sports*, the starting line of a race. *v.t.* 1. to put or make a mark or marks on. 2. to identify as by a mark. 3. to draw, write, etc. 4. to indicate by a mark or marks. 5. to show plainly; manifest: as, her smile *marked* her happiness. 6. to set off; characterize. 7. to pay attention to; heed: as, *mark* my words. 8. to give a grade to; rate. 9. to put price tags on. 10. to keep (score, etc.); record. *v.i.* 1. to make a mark or marks. 2. to observe; take note. 3. in *games*, to keep score. —**hit the mark,** 1. to achieve one's aim. 2. to be right. —**make one's mark,** to achieve fame. —**mark down,** 1. to write down; record. 2. to mark for sale at a reduced price. —**mark off** (or **out**), to mark the limits of. —**mark time,** 1. to keep time while at a halt by lifting the feet as if marching. 2. to suspend progress for a time. —**mark up,** 1. to cover with marks. 2. to mark for sale at an increased price. —**miss the mark,** 1. to fail in achieving one's aim. 2. to be wrong. —**wide of** (or **beside**) **the mark,** irrelevant. —**mark'er,** *n.*
**mark** (märk), *n.* [AS. *marc;* prob. < LL. *marca*], formerly, a silver coin and the monetary unit of Germany: it was superseded in 1924 by the reichsmark: now, in full, *Deutschemark* (in West Germany), *Ostmark* (in East Germany).
**Mark An·to·ny** (an'tə-ni), see **Antonius, Marcus.**
**mark·down** (märk'doun'), *n.* 1. a marking for sale at a reduced price. 2. the amount of reduction.
**marked** (märkt), *adj.* 1. having a mark or marks: as, *marked* cards. 2. noticeable; obvious: as, a *marked* change in behavior. 3. singled out as an object of suspicion, etc.: as, a *marked* man. —**mark'ed·ly** (mär'kid-li), *adv.* —**mark'ed·ness,** *n.*
**mar·ket** (mär'kit), *n.* [Late AS. < ONorm. Fr. < L. *mercatus*, trade < pp. of *mercari*, to trade < *merx*, merchandise], 1. *a*) a gathering of people for buying and selling things. *b*) the people gathered. 2. an open space or a building where goods are shown for sale: also **market place.** 3. a shop for the sale of provisions: as, a meat *market.* 4. a region in which goods can be bought and sold: as, the Latin-American *market.* 5. *a*) trade in goods, stocks, etc.: as, an active *market.* *b*) trade in a specified commodity: as, the wheat *market.* *c*) the people associated in such trade. 6. demand for

(goods or services): as, a good *market* for tea in England. *v.t.* 1. to send or take to market. 2. to offer for sale. 3. to sell. *v.i.* 1. to buy or sell. 2. to buy provisions. **—be in the market for,** to be seeking to buy. **—be on the market,** to be offered for sale. **—buyer's market,** a state of trade favorable to the buyer (relatively heavy supply and low prices). **—put on the market,** to offer for sale. **—seller's market,** a state of trade favorable to the seller (relatively heavy demand and high prices). **—mar'ket·a·bil'i·ty,** *n.* **—mar'ket·a·ble,** *adj.* **—mar'ket·er,** *n.*

**market price,** the prevailing price.

**market value,** the price that a commodity can be expected to bring in a given market.

**mark·ing** (mär'kiŋ), *n.* 1. the act of making a mark or marks. 2. a mark or marks. 3. the characteristic arrangement of marks, as on fur or feathers.

**mark·ka** (märk'kä), *n.* [*pl.* -KAA(-kä)], [Finn.; see MARK (money)], the monetary unit and a nickeled bronze coin of Finland.

**marks·man** (märks'mən), *n.* [*pl.* -MEN], a person who shoots, especially one who shoots well. **—marks'man·ship',** *n.*

**mark·up** (märk'up'), *n.* 1. a marking for sale at an increased price. 2. the amount of increase.

**marl** (märl), *n.* [< OFr. < LL. dim. of L. *marga,* marl; ? < Celt.], a crumbly soil, mainly clay, sand, and calcium carbonate, used as a fertilizer and in making cement or bricks. *v.t.* to fertilize with marl. **—marl'y** [-IER, -IEST], *adj.*

**Marl·bor·ough** (märl'bẽr-ō; Brit. môl'bẽr-ə, -brə), Duke of, (*John Churchill*), 1650–1722; English general.

**mar·lin** (mär'lin), *n.* [< *marlinespike*], a large, slender deep-sea fish related to the sailfish.

**mar·line** (mär'lin), *n.* [D. *marlijn* < *marren,* to tie + *lijn,* a line], a small cord of two loose strands for winding around the ends of ropes to prevent fraying: also **mar'ling** (-liŋ).

**mar·line·spike, mar·lin·spike** (mär'lin-spīk'), *n.* a tapered, pointed iron instrument for separating the strands of a rope in splicing: also **mar'ling·spike** (-liŋ-).

**Mar·lowe, Christopher** (mär'lō), 1564–1593; English dramatist and poet.

**mar·ma·lade** (mär'mə-lād'), *n.* [< OFr. < Port. < *marmeol,* quince < L. *melimelum* < Gr. < *meli,* honey + *mēlon,* apple], a jamlike preserve made of oranges or some other fruits and sugar.

**Mar·ma·ra, Sea of** (mär'mə-rə), a sea between Asiatic and European Turkey, connected with the Black Sea by the Bosporus and with the Mediterranean by the Dardanelles: also **Sea of Mar·mo·ra** (mär'mə-rə, mär-môr'ə, -mō'rə).

**mar·mo·set** (mär'mə-zet'), *n.* [< OFr. *marmouset,* grotesque figure], a very small monkey of South and Central America, with thick, soft fur.

**mar·mot** (mär'mət), *n.* [< Fr. < earlier *marmottaine;* prob. < L. *mus montanus,* mountain mouse], any of a group of small, thick-bodied, gnawing or burrowing rodents with coarse fur and a short, bushy tail, as the ground hog or woodchuck.

**Marne** (märn), *n.* a river in NE France, flowing into the Seine at Paris.

**ma·roon** (mə-rōōn'), *n.* & *adj.* [Fr. *marron,* chestnut < It. *marrone*], dark brownish red.

**ma·roon** (mə-rōōn'), *n.* [< Fr. < Sp. *cimarrón,* wild], in the West Indies and Dutch Guiana, *a*) originally, an escaped Negro slave. *b*) a descendant of such slaves. *v.t.* 1. to put (a person) ashore in some desolate place and leave him there. 2. to leave abandoned, helpless, etc.

**mar·plot** (mär'plot'), *n.* one who mars or spoils a plan by officious interference.

**marque** (märk), *n.* [Fr. < Pr. < *marcar,* to seize as a pledge < *marc,* token of pledge], reprisal: obsolete except in **letters of marque.**

**mar·quee** (mär-kē'), *n.* [< Fr. *marquise,* misunderstood as pl.: orig. a shelter for a marquise], 1. a large tent, especially for some outdoor entertainment. 2. a rooflike structure projecting over the entrance to a theater, store, hotel, etc.

**Mar·que·sas Islands** (mär-kā'səs), a group of French islands in the South Pacific. **—Mar·que'san,** *adj.* & *n.*

**mar·quess** (mär'kwis), *n.* a marquis.

**mar·que·try, mar·que·te·rie** (mär'kə-tri), *n.* [< Fr. < *marque,* a mark], decorative inlaid work of wood, ivory, etc., as in furniture or flooring.

**mar·quis** (mär'kwis; Fr. mȧr'kē'), *n.* [< OFr. < ML. *marchensis,* prefect of a frontier town < *marca,* border], in some European countries, a nobleman ranking above an earl or count and below a duke. **—mar'quis·ate** (-kwiz-it), *n.*

**mar·quise** (mär-kēz'), *n.* 1. the wife or widow of a marquis. 2. a lady whose rank in her own right equals that of a marquis.

**mar·qui·sette** (mär'ki-zet', -kwi-zet'), *n.* [dim. of Fr. *marquise,* awning], a thin, lightweight fabric of cotton, silk, rayon, etc. with square, open meshes, used for curtains, dresses, etc.

**Mar·ra·kech, Mar·ra·kesh** (mä-rä'kesh), *n.* one of the traditional capitals of the sultanate of Morocco: pop., 245,000: also called *Morocco.*

**mar·riage** (mar'ij), *n.* [OFr. < *marier;* see MARRY], 1. the state of being married; relation between husband and wife; wedlock. 2. the act or rite of marrying; wedding. 3. any intimate union.

**mar·riage·a·ble** (mar'ij-ə-b'l), *adj.* 1. old enough to get married. 2. suitable for marriage. **—mar'riage·a·bil'i·ty, mar'riage·a·ble·ness,** *n.*

**marriage portion,** a dowry.

**mar·ried** (mar'id), *adj.* 1. living together as husband and wife. 2. having a husband or wife. 3. of marriage or married people. 4. closely or intimately joined.

**mar·row** (mar'ō), *n.* [AS. *mearg*], 1. the soft, vascular, fatty tissue that fills the cavities of most bones. 2. the innermost, essential, or choicest part. **—mar'row·y** (-ə-wi), *adj.*

**mar·row·bone** (mar'ō-bōn'), *n.* 1. a bone containing marrow: also **marrow bone.** 2. *pl.* the knees.

**mar·row·fat** (mar'ō-fat'), *n.* a variety of large, rich pea: also **marrowfat pea, marrow pea.**

**mar·ry** (mar'i), *v.t.* [-RIED, -RYING], [< OFr. *marier* < L. < *maritus,* a husband], 1. to join as husband and wife. 2. to join (a man) to a woman as her husband, or (a woman) to a man as his wife. 3. to take as husband or wife. 4. to give in marriage (often with *off*). 5. to join closely. *v.i.* 1. to get married. 2. to enter into a close relationship. **—mar'ri·er,** *n.*

**mar·ry** (mar'i), *interj.* [euphemistic respelling of (the Virgin) *Mary*], [Archaic or Dial.], an exclamation of surprise, anger, etc.

**Mars** (märz), *n.* 1. the Roman god of war: identified with the Greek Ares. 2. war. 3. a planet of the solar system: diameter, c. 4,230 mi.

**Mar·sa·la** (mär-sä'lä), *n.* [< *Marsala,* a Sicilian seaport], a light, sweet white wine.

**Mar·seil·laise** (mär'sə-lāz'; Fr. mȧr'se'yez'), *n.* [Fr., lit., of Marseilles], the national anthem of France, composed in 1792 during the French Revolution.

**Mar·seille** (mȧr'se'y'; *for 2,* mär-sāl'), *n.* 1. Marseilles. 2. [m-], marseilles.

**Mar·seilles** (mär-sālz'), *n.* 1. a seaport in SE France, on the Mediterranean: pop., 636,000. 2. [m-], a thick, strong, figured or striped cotton, used for bedspreads, etc.

**marsh** (märsh), *n.* [AS. *mersc*], a tract of low, wet, soft land; swamp; bog.

**mar·shal** (mär'shəl), *n.* [< OFr. *mareschal* < OHG. < *marah,* horse + *scalh,* servant], 1. a high official of a medieval royal household. 2. a military commander; specif., *a*) a field marshal. *b*) in various foreign armies, a general officer of the highest rank. 3. an official in charge of ceremonies, processions, etc. 4. in the U.S., an officer of various kinds; specif., *a*) a Federal officer appointed to a judicial district to perform functions like those of a sheriff. *b*) the head of the police or fire department in some cities. *v.t.* [-SHALED or -SHALLED, -SHALING or -SHALLING], 1. to arrange (troops, things, ideas, etc.) in order; array: as, he *marshaled* his thoughts. 2. *a*) to direct as a marshal; manage. *b*) to lead or guide ceremoniously. **—mar'shal·cy** (-si), **mar'shal·ship',** *n.*

**Mar·shall, George Cat·lett** (kat'lit mär'shəl), 1880–1959; American general and statesman.

**Marshall, John,** 1755–1835; chief justice, U.S. Supreme Court (1801–1835).

**Marshall Islands,** a group of atolls in the North Pacific, east of the Caroline Islands: formerly a Japanese mandate, now under U.S. trusteeship.

**marsh gas,** methane.

**marsh hawk,** a large hawk that lives in marshes.

**marsh·mal·low** (märsh'mal'ō), *n.* 1. originally, a confection made from the root of the marsh mallow. 2. a soft, spongy candy made of sugar, starch, corn sirup, and gelatin.

**marsh mallow,** a plant of the mallow family, with large, pink flowers, growing in marshes.

**marsh marigold,** a swamp plant of the crowfoot family, with bright-yellow flowers; cowslip.
**marsh·y** (mär′shi), *adj.* [-IER, -IEST], 1. of or containing a marsh or marshes. 2. like a marsh; swampy. 3. growing in marshes. —**marsh′i·ness,** *n.*
**mar·su·pi·al** (mär-so͞o′pi-əl, -sū′-), *adj.* 1. of or like a marsupium. 2. of a group of lower mammals that lack a placenta and carry the prematurely born young in a marsupium. *n.* an animal of this kind, as a kangaroo, opossum, etc.
**mar·su·pi·um** (mär-so͞o′pi-əm, -sū′-), *n.* [*pl.* -PIA (-ə)], [L. < Gr. dim. of *marsypos*, a pouch], a fold of skin on the abdomen of a female marsupial, forming an external pouch in which the prematurely born young are carried.
**mart** (märt), *n.* [D. *markt*], a market.
**Mar·tel, Charles** (mär-tel′), 689?–741 A.D.; ruler of the Franks (715–741 A.D.).
**mar·ten** (mär′t'n), *n.* [*pl.* -TENS, -TEN; see PLURAL, II, D, 1], [< OFr. < *martre*], 1. a small flesh-eating mammal like a weasel but larger, with soft, thick fur. 2. the fur: also called *sable.*
**Mar·tha** (mär′thə), *n.* in the *Bible*, a friend of Jesus rebuked by him for doing housework while he talked with her sister, Mary: Luke 10:40.
**Mar·tial** (mär′shəl), *n.* (*Marcus Valerius Martialis*), Roman epigrammatist; 1st century A.D.
**mar·tial** (mär′shəl), *adj.* [Fr. < L. *martialis*, of Mars], 1. of or suitable for war: as, *martial* songs. 2. warlike; bold. 3. of the army or navy; military: as, court *martial.* —**mar′tial·ly,** *adv.*
**martial law,** temporary rule by the military authorities over the civilians, as in time of war.
**Mar·tian** (mär′shən), *adj.* of Mars (god or planet). *n.* a hypothetical inhabitant of Mars.
**mar·tin** (mär′t'n), *n.* [Fr.], any of various birds of the swallow family, as the *purple martin, sand martin, house martin,* etc.
**mar·ti·net** (mär′t'n-et′, mär′t'n-et′), *n.* [after *Martinet*, 17th-c. Fr. general], a very strict disciplinarian.
**mar·tin·gale** (mär′t'n-gāl′), *n.* [Fr. < Pr. *marte(n)galo*], 1. the strap of a horse's harness passing from the noseband to the girth between the forelegs, to keep the horse from rearing or throwing back its head. 2. a lower stay for the jib boom of a sailing vessel. Also **mar′tin·gal′** (-gal′).
**mar·ti·ni** (mär-tē′ni), *n.* [*pl.* -NIS], [< *Martini* and Rossi, firm that makes vermouth], [also M-], a cocktail made of gin and dry vermouth.
**Mar·ti·nique** (mär′t'n-ēk′), *n.* a French island of the Windward group, in the West Indies.
**Mar·tin·mas** (mär′t'n-məs), *n.* Saint Martin's Day, a church festival held on November 11.
**mar·tyr** (mär′tẽr), *n.* [AS. < LL. < Gr. *martyr*, a witness], 1. one who chooses to suffer or die rather than give up his faith or his principles. 2. one who suffers great pain or misery for a long time. *v.t.* 1. to kill or torture for adherence to a belief. 2. to persecute. —**mar′tyr·dom,** *n.*
**mar·tyr·ize** (mär′tẽr-īz′), *v.t.* [-IZED, -IZING], to make a martyr of. *v.i.* to be or become a martyr. —**mar′tyr·i·za′tion,** *n.*
**mar·vel** (mär′v'l), *n.* [< OFr. *merveille* < L. neut. pl. of *mirabilis*, wonderful < *mirari*, to admire], a wonderful or astonishing thing; miracle. *v.i.* [-VELED or -VELLED, -VELING or -VELLING], to become full of wonder; be astonished. *v.t.* to wonder at or about (followed by a clause).
**mar·vel·ous, mar·vel·lous** (mär′v'l-əs), *adj.* 1. causing wonder; astonishing, extraordinary, etc. 2. so extraordinary as to be improbable, incredible, etc. 3. [Colloq.], fine; splendid. —**mar′vel·ous·ly, mar′vel·lous·ly,** *adv.* —**mar′vel·ous·ness, mar′vel·lous·ness,** *n.*
**Marx, Karl** (märks), 1818–1883; German socialist leader and writer on political economy.
**Marx·ism** (märk′siz'm), *n.* the system of thought developed by Karl Marx, his co-worker Friedrich Engels, and their followers, serving as a basis for socialism and communism: also **Marx′i·an·ism.** —**Marx′ist, Marx′i·an,** *adj. & n*
**Mar·y** (mâr′i), *n.* [*pl.* -YS, -IES], in the *Bible*, 1. the mother of Jesus: Matt. 1:18-25. 2. the sister of Martha: Luke 10:38-42. 3. Mary Magdalene.
**Mary I,** (*Mary Tudor*), 1516–1558; queen of England (1553–1558) and wife of Philip II of Spain: called *Bloody Mary.*
**Mary II,** 1662–1694; queen of England (1689–1694), ruling jointly with her husband, William III.
**Mar·y·land** (mer′i-lənd), *n.* an Eastern State of the U.S.: area, 10,577 sq. mi.; pop., 3,101,000; capital, Annapolis: abbrev. **Md.**
**Mary Magdalene,** in the *Bible*, a woman out of whom Jesus cast seven devils: Luke 8:2: identified with the repentant woman in Luke 7:37 ff.
**Mary, Queen of Scots,** (*Mary Stuart*), 1542–1587; queen of Scotland (1542–1567); beheaded.
**mar·zi·pan** (mär′zi-pan′), *n.* marchpane.
**Ma·sa·ryk, To·más Gar·rigue** (tô′mäsh gə-rēg′ má′sá-rik), 1850–1937; first president of Czechoslovakia (1918–1935).
**masc., mas.,** masculine.
**mas·ca·ra** (mas-kar′ə), *n.* [< Sp. < Ar. *maskharah*, buffoon], a cosmetic for coloring the eyelashes. *v.t.* [-RAED, -RAING], to put mascara on.
**mas·cot** (mas′kot, -kət), *n.* [< Fr. < Pr. dim. of *masco*, sorcerer], any person, animal, or thing supposed to bring good luck by being present.
**mas·cu·line** (mas′kyoo-lin), *adj.* [< OFr. < L. < *masculus*, male < *mas*, male], 1. male; of men or boys. 2 having qualities regarded as characteristic of men and boys, as strength, vigor, etc. 3. suitable for a man. 4. mannish: said of women. 5. in *grammar*, designating or of the gender of words referring to males or things originally regarded as male. *n.* 1. the masculine gender. 2. a word or form in this gender. —**mas′cu·line·ly,** *adv.* —**mas′cu·lin′i·ty,** *n.*
**masculine rhyme,** a rhyme of only a single stressed syllable (e.g., *enjoy, destroy*).
**mas·cu·lin·ize** (mas′kyoo-lə-nīz′), *v.t.* [-IZED, -IZING], to make masculine; esp., to produce male characteristics in (a female).
**Mase·field, John** (mās′fēld′, māz′-), 1878–1967; English poet and dramatist.
**ma·ser** (mā′zẽr), *n.* [*m*icrowave *a*mplification by *s*timulated *e*mission of *r*adiation], an electronic device that amplifies microwaves, infrared rays, etc. and emits them in a very intense beam.
**mash** (mash), *n.* [AS. *masc-*, in *mascwyrt*, infused malt], 1. crushed malt or meal soaked in hot water for making wort, used in brewing beer. 2. a mixture of bran, meal, etc. in warm water, for feeding horses, etc. 3. any soft mixture or mass. *v.t.* 1. to mix (crushed malt, etc.) in hot water for making wort. 2. to change into a soft mass by beating, crushing, etc.
**mash·er** (mash′ẽr), *n.* 1. a person or thing that mashes. 2. [Slang], a man who annoys women by attempting familiarities.
**mash·ie, mash·y** (mash′i), *n.* [*pl.* -IES], [? < Fr. *massue*, a club], an iron-headed golf club of medium loft: now usually called *number 5 iron.*
**mask** (mask, mäsk), *n.* [< Fr. *masque* < It. *maschera* < Ar. *maskharah*, buffoon], 1. a covering to conceal or disguise all or part of the face. 2. anything that conceals or disguises: as, a *mask* of snow on the ground. 3. a masquerade: often sp. **masque.** 4. a person wearing a mask. 5. *a*) a sculptured or molded likeness of the face. *b*) a grotesque or comic representation of a face, worn to amuse or frighten. 6. a protective covering for the face: as, a gas mask. 7. a masque (sense 2). *v.t.* 1. to cover (the face) with a mask. 2. to conceal, disguise, or protect by covering. *v.i.* to put on a mask; wear a disguise. —**masked,** *adj.*
**masking tape,** an adhesive tape for covering and protecting margins, etc., as during painting.
**mas·och·ism** (mas′ə-kiz'm, maz′-), *n.* [after L. von Sacher-*Masoch* (1835–1895), Austrian writer], 1. the getting of abnormal sexual pleasure from being dominated or pained. 2. the getting of pleasure from being hurt or humiliated. —**mas′och·ist,** *n.* —**mas′och·is′tic,** *adj.* —**mas′och·is′ti·cal·ly,** *adv.*
**ma·son** (mā′s'n), *n.* [< OFr. < ML. *matio*], 1. a person whose work is building with stone, brick, etc. 2. [M-], a Freemason.
**Ma·son-Dix·on line** (mā′s'n-dik′s'n), the boundary between Pennsylvania and Maryland, surveyed by C. Mason and J. Dixon from 1763 to 1767: regarded as the line of demarcation between the North and the South: also **Mason and Dixon's line.**
**Ma·son·ic, ma·son·ic** (mə-son′ik), *adj.* of Freemasons or Freemasonry.
**ma·son·ite** (mā′s'n-īt′), *n.* [after W. H. *Mason* (1877–1947?), Am. engineer], a kind of fiberboard made from pressed wood fibers, used as building material, etc.: a trade-mark (**Masonite**).
**ma·son·ry** (mā′s'n-ri), *n.* [*pl.* -RIES], 1. the trade or art of a mason. 2. something built by a mason or masons; brickwork or stonework. 3. [usually M-], Freemasonry.
**masque** (mask, mäsk), *n.* [see MASK], 1. a masquerade; masked ball. 2. a former kind of dramatic entertainment, based on a mythical or allegorical theme, with lavish costumes, scenery, music, etc. Also sp. **mask.** —**mas′quer,** *n.*
**mas·quer·ade** (mas′kə-rād′, mäs′-), *n.* [< Fr. < Sp. *mascarada* or It. *mascherata;* see MASK], 1. a ball or party at which masks and fancy costumes are worn. 2. a costume for such an event. 3. *a*) a disguise. *b*) a living or acting under false pretenses.

*v.i.* [-ADED, -ADING], 1. to take part in a masquerade. 2. to live or act under false pretenses. *v.t.* to cover with a disguise. —**mas′quer·ad′er,** *n.*

**Mass, mass** (mas, mäs), *n.* [AS. *mæsse* < LL. < L. pp. of *mittere*, to dismiss < the words *ite, missa est* (go, you are dismissed)], 1. the service of the Eucharist in the Roman Catholic Church and some other churches, consisting of a series of prayers and ceremonies. 2. a musical setting for certain parts of this service.

**mass** (mas), *n.* [OFr. *masse* < L. < Gr. *maza*, barley cake], 1. a quantity of matter forming a body of indefinite shape and size; lump. 2. a large quantity or number: as, a *mass* of bruises. 3. bulk; size. 4. the main part; majority. 5. in *physics*, the quantity of matter in a body as measured in its relation to inertia. *adj.* 1. of a large number of things: as, *mass* production. 2. of, like, or for the masses: as, *mass* education. *v.t.* & *v.i.* to gather or assemble into a mass. —**in the mass,** collectively. —**the masses,** the common people; the working people.

**Mas·sa·chu·setts** (mas′ə-chōō′sits), *n.* a New England State of the U.S.: area, 8,257 sq. mi.; pop., 5,149,000; capital, Boston: abbrev. **Mass.**

**mas·sa·cre** (mas′ə-kẽr), *n.* [Fr. < OFr. *maçacre*, shambles], the indiscriminate, merciless killing of human beings or animals; wholesale slaughter. *v.t.* [-CRED, -CRING], to kill (many people or animals) indiscriminately and mercilessly; slaughter wholesale. —**mas′sa·crer** (-kẽr-ẽr, -krẽr), *n.*

**mas·sage** (mə-säzh′), *n.* [Fr. < *masser* < Port. *amassar*, to knead; ult. < L. *massa*, a lump], a rubbing, kneading, etc. of part of the body, as to stimulate circulation and make muscles or joints supple. *v.t.* [-SAGED, -SAGING], to give a massage to. —**mas·sag′er, mas·sag′ist,** *n.*

**mas·sé** (ma-sā′), *n.* [Fr. < *masse*, billiard cue], a stroke in billiards made by hitting the cue ball with the cue held vertically so as to make the ball move in a curve: also **massé shot.**

**mas·seur** (ma-sũr′; Fr. må′sër′), *n.* [Fr.], a man whose work is massaging. —**mas·seuse′** (-sooz′; Fr. -söz′), *n.fem.*

**mas·sive** (mas′iv), *adj.* 1. forming or consisting of a large mass; large and heavy; big and solid; bulky. 2. large and imposing or impressive. —**mas′sive·ly,** *adv.* —**mas′sive·ness,** *n.*

**mass meeting,** a large public meeting to hear speakers, discuss public affairs, demonstrate public approval or disapproval, etc.

**mass number,** the sum of the numbers of protons and neutrons in the nucleus of an atom.

**mass production,** quantity production of goods, especially by machinery and division of labor.

**mass·y** (mas′i), *adj.* [-IER, -IEST], [Archaic or Poetic], massive. —**mass′i·ness,** *n.*

**mast** (mast, mäst), *n.* [AS. *mæst*], 1. a tall spar rising vertically from the keel or deck of a vessel and used to support the sails, yards, etc. 2. any vertical pole, as in a crane. *v.t.* to put masts on. —**before the mast,** as a common sailor.

**mast** (mast, mäst), *n.* [AS. *mæst*], beechnuts, acorns, etc., especially as food for hogs.

**mas·ta·ba, mas·ta·bah** (mas′tə-bə), *n.* [< Ar.], an oblong structure built over the opening of a mummy chamber or burial pit in ancient Egypt.

**mas·ter** (mas′tẽr, mäs′-), *n.* [< AS. *mægester* & OFr. *maistre;* both < L. *magister* < base of L. *magnus*, great], 1. a man who rules others or has control, authority, or power over something; specif., *a*) a man who is head of a household or institution. *b*) an employer. *c*) an owner of an animal or slave. *d*) the captain of a merchant ship. *e*) a victor. *f*) [Chiefly Brit.], a male schoolteacher. *g*) a person whose teachings in religion, philosophy, etc. one follows. *h*) [M-], Jesus Christ (with *our, the*, etc.). 2. a person very skilled in some work, profession, etc.; expert; specif., *a*) a skilled workman qualified to follow his trade independently. *b*) an artist regarded as great. 3. a work by such an artist. 4. [M-], a title variously applied to *a*) any man or youth: now superseded by *Mister*, usually written *Mr. b*) a boy regarded as too young to be addressed as *Mr. c*) a man who heads some institution, group, etc. *d*) in Scotland, the heir apparent of a viscount or baron. *e*) a person holding a certain degree from a college or university, denoting completion of a prescribed course of graduate study: as, *Master* of Arts. 5. in *law*, any of several court officers appointed to assist the judge. *adj.* 1. being master. 2. of a master. 3. chief; main; controlling; specif., designating a mechanism or contrivance that controls others or sets a standard: as, a *master* switch. *v.t.* 1. to be or become master of; control, conquer, etc. 2. to become an expert in (an art, science, etc.). —**mas′ter·less,** *adj.*

**master builder,** 1. a person skilled in building; esp., an architect. 2. a building contractor.

**mas·ter·ful** (mas′tẽr-fəl, mäs′-), *adj.* 1. acting the part of a master; domineering. 2. having or showing the ability of a master; expert; skillful. —**mas′ter·ful·ly,** *adv.* —**mas′ter·ful·ness,** *n.*

**master key,** a key for opening a set of locks.

**mas·ter·ly** (mas′tẽr-li, mäs′-), *adj.* showing the ability or skill of a master; expert. *adv.* in a masterly manner. —**mas′ter·li·ness,** *n.*

**master mechanic,** a skilled mechanic, especially one serving as foreman: abbrev. **M.M.**

**mas·ter·mind** (mas′tẽr-mīnd′, mäs′-), *n.* a person of great intelligence, especially one with the ability to plan or direct a group project. *v.t.* to be the mastermind of (a project, etc.).

**Master of Arts** (or **Science,** etc.), 1. a degree given by a college or university to a person who has completed a prescribed course of graduate study in the humanities (or in science, etc.). 2. a person who has this degree.

**master of ceremonies,** 1. a person who supervises a ceremony. 2. a person who presides over an entertainment, introducing the participants, filling in the intervals with jokes, etc.

**mas·ter·piece** (mas′tẽr-pēs′, mäs′-), *n.* 1. a thing made or done with masterly skill. 2. the greatest work of a person or group. Also **mas′ter·work′.**

**Mas·ters, Edgar Lee** (mas′tẽrz, mäs′-), 1869–1950; American poet and novelist.

**master sergeant,** in the *U.S. armed forces*, a noncommissioned officer of the highest rank.

**mas·ter·ship** (mas′tẽr-ship′, mäs′-), *n.* 1. the state of being a master; rule; control. 2. the position, duties, or term of office of a master, especially a schoolmaster. 3. masterly ability.

**master stroke,** a masterly move, achievement, etc.

**mas·ter·y** (mas′tẽr-i, mäs′-), *n.* [*pl.* -IES], 1. mastership. 2. ascendancy or victory; the upper hand. 3. expert skill or knowledge: as, his *mastery* of chess. Also **mas′ter·dom.**

**mast·head** (mast′hed′, mäst′-), *n.* 1. the top part of a ship's mast. 2. that part of a newspaper or magazine stating its address, publishers, editors, etc. *v.t.* to display at the masthead.

**mas·tic** (mas′tik), *n.* [OFr. < LL. < L. < Gr. *mastichē*], 1. a yellowish resin obtained from a Mediterranean evergreen tree, used as an astringent and in making varnish, chewing gum, etc. 2. the tree: often **mastic tree.**

**mas·ti·cate** (mas′tə-kāt′), *v.t.* [-CATED, -CATING], [< LL. pp. of *masticare* < Gr. *mastichan*, to gnash < *mastax*, a mouth], 1. to chew up. 2. to grind, cut, or knead (rubber, etc.) to a pulp. —**mas′ti·ca′tion,** *n.* —**mas′ti·ca′tor,** *n.*

**mas·ti·ca·to·ry** (mas′ti-kə-tôr′i, -tō′ri), *adj.* of or for mastication; specif., adapted for chewing. *n.* [*pl.* -RIES], any substance chewed to increase saliva flow.

**mas·tiff** (mas′tif, mäs′-), *n.* [< OFr. *mastin* < LL. < L. *mansuetus*, tame], a large, powerful, smooth-coated dog with powerful jaws and drooping ears.

MASTIFF (30 in. high at shoulder)

**mas·to-,** [< Gr. *mastos*, the breast], a combining form meaning *of* or *like a breast:* also **mast-.**

**mas·to·don** (mas′tə-don′), *n.* [< Gr. *mastos*, a breast + *odous*, a tooth: from the nipplelike processes on its molars], a large, extinct animal resembling the elephant but larger.

**mas·toid** (mas′toid), *adj.* [< Gr. < *mastos*, a breast + *eidos*, form], 1. shaped like a breast. 2. designating, of, or near a projection of the temporal bone behind the ear. *n.* 1. the mastoid projection. 2. [Colloq.], mastoiditis.

**mas·toid·i·tis** (mas′toid-ī′tis), *n.* inflammation of the mastoid.

**mas·tur·bate** (mas′tẽr-bāt′), *v.i.* [-BATED, -BATING], to engage in masturbation. —**mas′tur·ba′tor,** *n.*

**mas·tur·ba·tion** (mas′tẽr-bā′shən), *n.* [< L. < pp. of *masturbari*], genital self-excitation, usually by manipulation.

**ma·su·ri·um** (mə-soor′i-əm, -syoor′-), *n.* [< *Masu-*

*ria*, a region in NE Poland], a name formerly given to chemical element 43: cf. **technetium.**
**mat** (mat), *n.* [< AS. < LL. *matta*], 1. a flat, coarse fabric of woven or plaited hemp, straw, etc. 2. a piece of this, or any similar article, put near a door, etc. to wipe the shoes on; door mat. 3. a flat piece of cloth, woven straw, etc. put under a vase, dish, etc. 4. a thickly padded floor covering, as in a gymnasium for wrestling, etc. 5. anything growing or interwoven in a thick tangle: as, a *mat* of hair. *v.t.* [MATTED, MATTING], 1. to cover as with a mat or mats. 2. to interweave. *v.i.* to be interwoven.
**mat** (mat), *adj.* [Fr. < OFr. *mat*, overcome < Ar. *māt*, he is dead], not glossy or shiny; dull. *n.* 1. a dull surface or finish. 2. a border, as of white cardboard, put around a picture, usually between the picture and the frame. 3. in *printing*, a matrix. *v.t.* [MATTED, MATTING], to produce a dull surface or finish on.
**mat·a·dor** (mat′ə-dôr′), *n.* [Sp. < *matar*, to kill < *mate*, checkmate], the bullfighter who kills the bull with a sword after performing a series of formalized actions with a cape to anger and tire the animal.
**match** (mach), *n.* [< OFr. *mesche;* prob. < L. *myxa*, wick of a candle < Gr.], 1. originally, a wick or cord prepared to burn at a uniform rate, used for firing guns or explosives. 2. a slender piece of wood, cardboard, etc. tipped with a composition that catches fire by friction, sometimes only on a specially prepared surface.
**match** (mach), *n.* [AS. *gemæcca*, mate], 1. any person or thing equal or similar to another in some way; specif., *a*) a person, group, or thing able to cope with another as an equal. *b*) a counterpart or facsimile. 2. two or more persons or things that go together in appearance, size, etc. 3. a contest or game; competition. 4. a marriage or mating. 5. a person regarded as a suitable mate. *v.t.* 1. to join in marriage; mate. 2. to compete with successfully. 3. to put in opposition (*with*); pit (*against*). 4. to be equal, similar, or suitable to. 5. to make, show, or get a competitor, counterpart, or equivalent to: as, *match* this cloth. 6. to suit or fit (one thing) to another. 7. to fit (things) together. 8. to compare. 9. *a*) to flip or reveal (coins) to decide something contested, the winner being determined by the combination of faces thus exposed. *b*) to match coins with (another person). *v.i.* 1. to get married; mate. 2. to be equal, similar, suitable, etc. in some way. **—match′a·ble,** *adj.* **—match′er,** *n.*
**match·box** (mach′boks′), *n.* a small box for holding matches.
**match·less** (mach′lis), *adj.* having no equal; peerless. **—match′less·ly,** *adv.* **—match′less·ness,** *n.*
**match·lock** (mach′lok′), *n.* 1. an old type of gunlock in which the charge was ignited by a slow match (of cord). 2. a musket with such a gunlock.
**match·mak·er** (mach′māk′ẽr), *n.* one who makes matches (for burning). **—match′mak′ing,** *adj. & n.*
**match·mak·er** (mach′māk′ẽr), *n.* 1. one who arranges or seeks to arrange marriages for others. 2. one who arranges wrestling matches, prize fights, etc. **—match′mak′ing,** *adj. & n.*
**match play,** in *golf*, a form of play in which the score is calculated by counting holes won rather than strokes taken: cf. *medal play.*
**mate** (māt), *n.* [prob. < MLG. *mate*, a companion < *gemate* < *ge-*, together + *mat*, meat], 1. a companion or fellow worker. 2. one of a matched pair. 3. *a*) a husband or wife. *b*) the male or female of paired animals. 4. in *nautical usage*, *a*) an officer of a merchant ship, ranking below the captain. *b*) an assistant. 5. in the *U.S. Navy*, any of various petty officers: as, a carpenter's *mate*. *v.t. & v.i.* [MATED, MATING], 1. to join as a pair. 2. to couple in marriage or sexual union.
**mate** (māt), *n., interj., v.t.* [MATED, MATING], checkmate.
**ma·té, ma·te** (mä′tā, mat′ā), *n.* [Sp. < Peruv. *mati*, calabash (used for steeping the brew)], 1. a kind of tea made from the dried leaves of a certain South American plant. 2. the plant or its leaves.
**ma·ter** (mā′tẽr, mä′-), *n.* [L.], [Chiefly Brit. Colloq.], mother: often preceded by *the.*
**ma·te·ri·al** (mə-têr′i-əl), *adj.* [< LL. < L. *materia*, matter], 1. of matter; relating to or consisting of what occupies space; physical: as, a *material* object. 2. *a*) of the body or bodily needs, etc.: as, *material* pleasures. *b*) of or fond of comfort, wealth, etc. rather than spiritual values: as, *material* success. 3. important, essential, etc. (*to* the matter under discussion). *n.* 1. what a thing is, or may be, made of; elements or parts. 2. ideas, notes, etc. that may be worked up; data. 3. cloth or other fabric. 4. *pl.* tools, articles, etc. for a specified use: as, writing *materials.*
**ma·te·ri·al·ism** (mə-têr′i-əl-iz′m), *n.* 1. in *philosophy*, the doctrine that everything in the world, including thought, will, and feeling, can be explained only in terms of matter. 2. the tendency to be more concerned with material than with spiritual values. **—ma·te′ri·al·ist,** *adj. & n.* **—ma·te′ri·al·is′tic,** *adj.* **—ma·te′ri·al·is′ti·cal·ly,** *adv.*
**ma·te·ri·al·ize** (mə-têr′i-ə-liz′), *v.t.* [-IZED, -IZING], 1. to represent in material form. 2. to make (a spirit, etc.) appear in bodily form. *v.i.* 1. to become fact; be realized: as, this project never *materialized.* 2. to take on, or appear in, bodily form: said of spirits, etc. **—ma·te′ri·al·i·za′tion,** *n.* **—ma·te′ri·al·iz′er,** *n.*
**ma·te·ri·al·ly** (mə-têr′i-əl-i), *adv.* 1. with regard to the matter, content, etc. and not the form. 2. physically. 3. to a great extent; substantially.
**ma·te·ri·a med·i·ca** (mə-têr′i-ə med′i-kə), [ML. < L. *materia*, matter + fem. of *medicus*, medical], 1. the drugs and other remedial substances used in medicine. 2. the branch of medical science that deals with such substances.
**ma·te·ri·el, ma·té·ri·el** (mə-têr′i-el′), *n.* [Fr.; see MATERIAL], the necessary materials and tools; specif., weapons, supplies, etc. of armed forces.
**ma·ter·nal** (mə-tũr′n′l), *adj.* [< Fr. < L. < *mater*, a mother], 1. of or like a mother; motherly. 2. derived or inherited from a mother. 3. on the mother's side of the family: as, a *maternal* uncle. **—ma·ter′nal·ly,** *adv.*
**ma·ter·ni·ty** (mə-tũr′nə-ti), *n.* [*pl.* -TIES], 1. the state of being a mother; motherhood. 2. the qualities of a mother; motherliness. *adj.* for pregnant women: as, a *maternity* dress.
**maternity hospital,** a hospital for women giving birth and for the care of newborn babies.
**math** (math), *n.* [Colloq.], mathematics.
**math·e·mat·i·cal** (math′ə-mat′i-k′l), *adj.* 1. of, like, or concerned with mathematics. 2. rigorously precise, accurate, etc. **—math′e·mat′i·cal·ly,** *adv.*
**math·e·ma·ti·cian** (math′ə-mə-tish′ən), *n.* an expert or specialist in mathematics.
**math·e·mat·ics** (math′ə-mat′iks), *n.pl.* [construed as sing.], [< L. < Gr. *mathēmatikos;* ult. < *manthanein*, to learn], the group of sciences (arithmetic, geometry, algebra, calculus, etc.) dealing with quantities, magnitudes, and forms, and their relationships, attributes, etc., by the use of numbers and symbols.
**mat·in** (mat′in), *n.* [< OFr. < L. *matutinus*, of the morning < *Matuta*, goddess of dawn], 1. *pl.* [sometimes M-], *a*) in the *R.C.Church*, the first of the seven canonical hours. *b*) in the *Anglican Church*, the service of public morning prayer: Brit. sp. often **mattins.** 2. [Poetic], a morning song. *adj.* 1. of matins. 2. of morning. **—mat′in·al,** *adj.*
**mat·i·nee, mat·i·née** (mat′′n-ā′, mat′′n-ā′), *n.* [< Fr. < *matin*, morning], a daytime reception, etc.; esp., an afternoon performance of a play.
**mat·ing** (māt′iŋ), *n.* a pairing or matching. *adj.* of or for mating: as, the *mating* season.
**Ma·tisse, Hen·ri** (än′rē′ mȧ′tēs′), 1869–1954; French painter.
**ma·tri-,** [< L. *mater*, a mother], a combining form meaning *mother*, as in *matriarch.*
**ma·tri·arch** (mā′tri-ärk′), *n.* [*matri-* + patri*arch*], 1. a woman who rules her family or tribe. 2. a woman of great age and dignity. **—ma′tri·ar′chal, ma′tri·ar′chic,** *adj.*
**ma·tri·arch·y** (mā′tri-är′ki), *n.* [*pl.* -IES], a form of social organization in which descent is traced through the mother as head of the family.
**ma·tri·cide** (mā′trə-sid′, mat′rə-), *n.* [< L. < *mater*, mother + *caedere*, to kill], 1. the murder of a woman by her child. 2. a person who kills his own mother. **—ma′tri·cid′al,** *adj.*
**ma·tric·u·late** (mə-trik′yoo-lāt′; *for n.*, -lit), *v.t. & v.i.* [-LATED, -LATING], [< ML. *matriculatus*, pp. < LL. dim. of *matrix;* see MATRIX], to enroll, especially as a student in a college or university. *n.* a person so enrolled. **—ma·tric′u·lant, ma·tric′u·la′tor,** *n.* **—ma·tric′u·la′tion,** *n.*
**mat·ri·mo·ny** (mat′rə-mō′ni), *n.* [*pl.* -NIES], [< OFr. < L. *matrimonium* < *mater*, a mother], 1. the act or rite of marriage. 2. the state of being husband and wife. 3. married life. **—mat′ri·mo′ni·al,** *adj.* **—mat′ri·mo′ni·al·ly,** *adv.*
**ma·trix** (mā′triks, mat′riks), *n.* [*pl.* -TRICES (mā′trə-sēz′, mat′rə-), -TRIXES], [LL., womb < L. stem of *mater*, a mother], 1. originally, the womb; uterus. 2. that within which something originates, takes form, etc.; specif., *a*) a die or mold for casting or shaping. *b*) a metal plate, usually of copper, for molding the face of a type. *c*) an impression, as of

papier-mâché, from which a printing plate can be made: also **mat.**

**ma·tron** (mā′trən), *n.* [< OFr. < L. *matrona* < *mater*, a mother], 1. a wife or widow, especially one who has had children. 2. a woman manager of the domestic arrangements of a hospital, prison, or other institution. **—ma′tron·al,** *adj.* **—ma′tron·ly,** *adj. & adv.* **—ma′tron·li·ness,** *n.*

**matron of honor,** a married woman acting as chief attendant to the bride at a wedding.

**Matt.,** Matthew.

**mat·ted** (mat′id), *adj.* 1. closely tangled in a dense mass. 2. covered with a mat or mats.

**mat·ter** (mat′ẽr), *n.* [< OFr. *mat(i)ere* < L. *materia*, material], 1. what a thing is made of; constituent material. 2. whatever occupies space and is perceptible to the senses in some way: in modern physics, matter and energy are regarded as mutually convertible equivalents. 3. any specified sort of substance: as, coloring *matter.* 4. material or content of thought or expression, as distinguished from style or form. 5. an amount or quantity: as, a *matter* of a few days. 6. *a*) a thing or affair: as, business *matters. b*) cause or occasion: as, no laughing *matter.* 7. importance; significance: as, it's of no *matter.* 8. trouble; difficulty (with *the*): as, what's the *matter?* 9. mail: as, second-class *matter.* 10. pus. 11. in *printing, a*) copy. *b*) type set up. *v.i.* 1. to be of importance; signify. 2. to form and discharge pus; suppurate. **—as a matter of fact,** in fact; really. **—for that matter,** as far as that is concerned: also **for the matter of that. —no matter,** 1. it is of no importance. 2. regardless of: as, *no matter* what you say.

**Mat·ter·horn** (mat′ẽr-hôrn′), *n.* a mountain of the Alps, between Switzerland and Italy.

**mat·ter-of-course** (mat′ẽr-əv-kôrs′, -kōrs′), *adj.* 1. to be expected; routine. 2. taking things as a matter of course.

**matter of course,** a thing to be expected as a natural or logical occurrence.

**mat·ter-of-fact** (mat′ẽr-əv-fakt′), *adj.* sticking to facts; literal, unimaginative, practical, etc.

**matter of opinion,** a debatable question.

**Mat·thew** (math′ū), *n.* in the *Bible,* 1. one of the twelve apostles, reputed author of the first book of the New Testament. 2. this book, telling the story of Jesus' life.

**mat·ting** (mat′iŋ), *n.* a mat, or border.

**mat·ting** (mat′iŋ), *n.* 1. a fabric of fiber, as straw or hemp, for mats, floor covering, etc. 2. mats collectively. 3. the making of mats.

**mat·tins** (mat′inz), *n.pl.* matins: Anglican sp.

**mat·tock** (mat′ək), *n.* [AS. *mattuc*], a tool like a pickax but with at least one flat blade, for loosening the soil, digging up roots, etc.

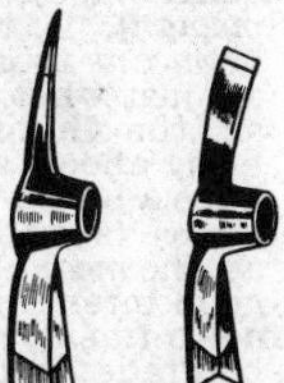

TYPES OF MATTOCK

**mat·tress** (mat′ris), *n.* [< OFr. < It. *materasso* < Ar. *maṭrah*, cushion], a casing of strong cloth filled with cotton, hair, foam rubber, etc. and used on or as a bed: some mattresses **(innerspring mattresses)** are made with wire springs inside.

**mat·u·rate** (mach′oo-rāt′, mat′yoo-), *v.i.* [-RATED, -RATING], [< L. pp. of *maturare;* see MATURE], 1. to suppurate; discharge pus. 2. to ripen; mature. **—mat′u·ra′tion,** *n.*

**ma·ture** (mə-tyoor′, -toor′, -choor′), *adj.* [< L. *maturus*, ripe], 1. full-grown, as plants or animals; ripe, as fruit. 2. fully developed, perfected, etc.: as, a *mature* scheme. 3. of a state of full development: as, of *mature* age. 4. due: said of a note, bond, etc. *v.t.* [-TURED, -TURING], 1. to bring to full growth; cause to ripen. 2. to develop fully. *v.i.* 1. to become fully grown; ripen. 2. to become due: said of a note, etc. **—ma·ture′ly,** *adv.* **—ma·ture′ness,** *n.*

**ma·tu·ri·ty** (mə-tyoor′ə-ti, -toor′-, -choor′-), *n.* 1. a being full-grown or ripe. 2. a being fully developed, complete, or ready. 3. *a*) a becoming due. *b*) the time at which a note, etc. becomes due. 4. [*pl.* -TIES], a mature act, trait, etc.

**ma·tu·ti·nal** (mə-tū′ti-n'l, -tōō′-), *adj.* [< L. < *matutinus;* see MATIN], of or in the morning; early. **—ma·tu′ti·nal·ly,** *adv.*

**matz·os** (mät′sōs, -səs), *n.pl.* matzoth.

**matz·oth** (mät′sōth, -sōs), *n.pl.* [*sing.* MATZO (-sô, -sə)], [< Heb., pl. of *matstsāh*, unleavened], flat, thin pieces of unleavened bread, eaten by Jews during the Passover.

**maud·lin** (môd′lin), *adj.* [< ME. *Maudeleyne*, (Mary) Magdalene (often represented as weeping)], 1. foolishly and tearfully or weakly sentimental. 2. tearfully sentimental from too much drink.

**Maugham, William Som·er·set** (sum′ẽr-set′ môm), 1874–1965; English writer and dramatist.

**mau·gre, mau·ger** (mô′gẽr), *prep.* [< OFr. *maugré*, lit., with displeasure < *mal*, ill + *gré*, pleasure], [Archaic], in spite of; notwithstanding.

**Mau·i** (mou′ē), *n.* one of the Hawaiian Islands.

**maul** (môl), *n.* [< OFr. < L. *malleus*, a hammer], 1. a very heavy hammer or mallet for driving stakes, etc. 2. [Archaic], a mace. *v.t.* 1. to bruise or lacerate. 2. to handle roughly or clumsily. Also sp. **mall. —maul′er,** *n.*

**Mau Mau** (mou′mou′), [*pl.* MAU MAU, MAU MAUS], a member of a secret society of natives in Kenya, Africa, organized to oppose white rule.

**Mau·na Lo·a** (mou′nä lō′ä), an active volcano on the island of Hawaii.

**maun·der** (môn′dẽr), *v.i.* [prob. freq. of obs. *maund*, to beg], 1. to move or act in a vague, aimless way. 2. to talk in an incoherent, rambling way. **—maun′der·er,** *n.*

**Maun·dy Thursday** (môn′di), [OFr. *mandé* < L. *mandatum*, a command: used in a prayer on that day], the Thursday before Easter.

**Mau·pas·sant, Guy de** (gē′ də mō′på′sän′; Eng. mō′pə-sänt′), 1850–1893; French writer.

**Mau·ri·ta·ni·a** (môr′ə-tā′ni-ə), *n.* a country in W Africa, on the Atlantic: a member of the French Community: area, c. 450,000 sq. mi.; pop., 1,100,000; capital, Nouakchott.

**Mau·ri·ti·us** (mô-rish′i-əs, mô-rish′əs), *n.* a country on an island in the Indian Ocean, east of Madagascar: a member of the British Commonwealth of Nations: area, 720 sq. mi.; pop., 774,000.

**mau·so·le·um** (mô′sə-lē′əm), *n.* [*pl.* -LEUMS, -LEA (-lē′ə)], 1. [M-], the tomb of Mausolus, king of an ancient land in Asia Minor, at Halicarnassus. 2. a large, imposing tomb. **—mau′so·le′an,** *adj.*

**mauve** (mōv), *n.* [Fr., mallow < L. *malva*, mallow], any of several shades of delicate purple. *adj.* of such a color.

**mav·er·ick** (mav′ẽr-ik), *n.* [after S. *Maverick*, 19th-c. Texas rancher who did not brand his cattle], 1. an unbranded animal, especially a lost calf, formerly the property of the first one who branded it. 2. [Colloq.], a person who acts independently of any political party, faction, etc.

**ma·vis** (mā′vis), *n.* [OFr. *mauvis*], the European song thrush.

**ma·vour·neen, ma·vour·nin** (mə-voor′nēn, -vôr′-), *n.* [Ir. *mo muirnīn*], my darling.

**maw** (mô), *n.* [AS. *maga*], 1. originally, the stomach. 2. the craw or crop of a bird. 3. the throat, gullet, jaws, etc. (of some voracious animals).

**mawk·ish** (môk′ish), *adj.* [lit., maggoty < ON. *mathkr*, maggot], 1. nauseating; sickening. 2. sentimental in a weak, sickly way. **—mawk′ish·ly,** *adv.* **—mawk′ish·ness,** *n.*

**max.,** maximum.

**max·il·la** (mak-sil′ə), *n.* [*pl.* -LAE (-ē)], [L.], 1. in vertebrates, a jaw or jawbone, especially the upper one. 2. in insects, crabs, etc., either of a pair of jaws just behind the mandibles.

**max·il·lar·y** (mak′sə-ler′i, mak-sil′ə-ri), *adj.* designating, of, or near the jaw or jawbone. *n.* [*pl.* -IES], a maxilla.

**max·im** (mak′sim), *n.* [< Late OFr. < L. *maxima* (*propositio*), the greatest (premise); see MAXIMUM], a concise rule of conduct; precept; adage.

**max·i·ma** (mak′sə-mə), *n.* alt. pl. of **maximum.**

**max·i·mal** (mak′sə-m'l), *adj.* highest or greatest possible; of or constituting a maximum. **—max′i·mal·ly,** *adv.*

**Max·i·mil·ian** (mak′sə-mil′yən), *n.* (*Ferdinand Maximilian Joseph*), 1832–1867; archduke of Austria; emperor of Mexico (1864–1867); executed.

**max·i·mize** (mak′sə-mīz′), *v.t.* [-MIZED, -MIZING], to increase to the maximum.

**max·i·mum** (mak′sə-məm), *n.* [*pl.* -MUMS, -MA (-mə)], [L., neut. of *maximus*, superl. of *magnus*, great], 1. the greatest quantity, number, etc. possible or permissible. 2. the highest degree or point reached or recorded. *adj.* 1. greatest or highest possible, permissible, or reached. 2. of, marking, or setting a maximum.

**May** (mā), *n.* [OFr. < L. *Maius*], 1. the fifth month of the year, having 31 days: abbrev. **My.** 2. the springtime of life; youth.

**may** (mā), *v.* [pt. MIGHT; *archaic* 2d pers. sing. MAYEST or MAYST], [ME. *mai*], an auxiliary preceding an infinitive (without *to*) and expressing: 1. originally, ability or power: now generally replaced by *can.* 2. possibility or likelihood: as, it *may* rain. 3. permission: as, you *may* go: see also **can.** 4. contingency, as in clauses of purpose, result, or concession: as, tell us so that we *may* be forewarned. 5. wish, hope, or prayer: as, *may* he go!

**Ma·ya** (mä′yə), *n.* 1. a member of a race of Indians of SE Mexico and Central America, who had a highly developed civilization. 2. their language. *adj.* of the Mayas or Maya. —**Ma′yan,** *adj. & n.*

**May apple,** 1. a North American plant with shield-shaped leaves and a single large, white flower. 2. its edible, yellow, lemon-shaped fruit.

**may·be** (mā′bi, -bē), *adv.* [ME. (for *it may be*)], perhaps; possibly.

**May Day,** May 1: as a traditional spring festival, often celebrated by dancing, crowning a May queen, etc.; as an international labor holiday, observed in many countries by parades, demonstrations, etc.

**May·fair** (mā′fâr′), *n.* a fashionable residential district of the West End, London.

**May·flow·er** (mā′flou′ẽr), *n.* 1. a plant that flowers in early spring; esp., *a*) in the U.S., the trailing arbutus, etc. *b*) in England, the hawthorn, marsh marigold, etc. 2. the ship on which the Pilgrims came to America (1620).

**May fly,** a slender insect with large forewings and small hind wings: it has a very short life in the adult stage.

**may·hap** (mā′hap′, mā′hap′), *adv.* [< *it may hap*(*pen*)], [Archaic], perhaps; maybe; perchance.

**may·hem** (mā′hem, -əm), *n.* [see MAIM], in *law*, the offense of maiming a person; act of intentionally injuring a person so as to deprive him of some part or function that he needs to defend himself.

**May·ing** (mā′iŋ), *n.* the celebration of May Day, as by gathering flowers, dancing, etc.

**may·n't** (mā′′nt, mānt), may not.

**may·on·naise** (mā′ə-nāz′, mā′ə-nāz′), *n.* [Fr.; ? < *Mahón*, Minorca], a creamy salad dressing made by beating together egg yolks, olive oil, lemon juice or vinegar, and seasoning.

**may·or** (mā′ẽr, mâr), *n.* [< OFr. *maire* < L. *major*, greater], the chief administrative official of a municipality. —**may′or·ship,** *n.*

**may·or·al·ty** (mā′ẽr-əl-ti, mâr′-), *n.* [*pl.* -TIES], the office or term of office of a mayor.

**May·pole** (mā′pōl′), *n.* a high pole wreathed with flowers, streamers, etc., around which merry-makers dance on May Day.

**May queen,** a girl chosen to be queen of the merry-makers on May Day.

**mayst** (māst), archaic 2d pers. sing. of **may**: used with *thou*: also **may·est** (mā′ist).

**May·tide** (mā′tīd′), *n.* the month of May: also **May′time′.**

**may tree,** [Brit.], the hawthorn.

**Ma·za·rin, Jules** (zhül mȧ′zȧ′ran′; Eng. maz′ə-rin), Cardinal, 1602–1661; French statesman, born in Italy.

**maze** (māz), *n.* [< AS. < *amazian*, to amaze & pp. *amasod*, puzzled], 1. a confusing, intricate network of winding pathways; labyrinth. 2. a state of confusion or bewilderment. —**ma′zy** [-ZIER, -ZIEST], *adj.* —**ma′zi·ly,** *adv.* —**ma′zi·ness,** *n.*

**ma·zur·ka, ma·zour·ka** (mə-zũr′kə, -zoor′-), *n.* [Pol. *mazurka*, woman from Mazovia, in Poland], 1. a lively Polish dance like the polka. 2. music for this, generally in 3/4 or 3/8 time.

**Maz·zi·ni, Giu·sep·pe** (jōō-zep′pe mät-tsē′nē), 1805–1872; Italian patriot and revolutionist.

**M.B.S., MBS,** Mutual Broadcasting System.

**M.C.,** 1. Master of Ceremonies. 2. Member of Congress.

**Mc·Car·thy·ism** (mə-kär′thi-iz′m), *n.* [after J. *McCarthy*, U.S. senator (1946–57)], the use of indiscriminate, often unfounded, accusations, inquisitorial investigative methods, sensationalism, etc., ostensibly in the suppression of communism.

**Mc·Cor·mick, Cyrus Hall** (mə-kôr′mik), 1809–1884; U.S. inventor of the reaping machine.

**Mc·Coy, the (real)** (mə-koi′), [Slang], the genuine person or thing, not a substitute.

**Mc·Guf·fey, William Holmes** (mə-guf′i), 1800–1873; U.S. educator; editor of *McGuffey's Readers.*

**Mc·In·tosh** (mak′in-tosh′), *n.* [after J. *McIntosh*, of Ontario, who first cultivated it (1796)], a late-maturing variety of red apple: also **McIntosh Red.**

**Mc·Kin·ley, William** (mə-kin′li), 1843–1901; 25th president of the U.S. (1897–1901); assassinated.

**McKinley, Mount,** a mountain in south central Alaska: highest peak in North America (20,300 ft.).

**MD.,** Middle Dutch.

**Md.,** Maryland.

**M.D.,** *Medicinae Doctor*, [L.], Doctor of Medicine.

**M-day** (em′dā′), *n.* the day on which active mobilization for war is ordered.

**Mdlle.,** [*pl.* MDLLES.], Mademoiselle.

**Mdm.,** [*pl.* MDMS.], Madam.

**Mdme.,** [*pl.* MDMES.], Madame.

**mdse.,** merchandise.

**me** (mē; *unstressed* mi), *pron.* [AS.], the objective case of **I**: also used colloquially as a predicate complement (e.g., that's *me*).

**ME.,** Middle English.

**Me.,** Maine.

**M.E.,** 1. Mechanical Engineer. 2. Methodist Episcopal. 3. Middle English. 4. Mining Engineer.

**mead** (mēd), *n.* [AS. *meodu*], an alcoholic liquor made of fermented honey, water, malt, etc.

**mead** (mēd), *n.* [< AS. *mæd*], [Poetic], a meadow.

**Mead, Lake** (mēd), a lake in the Colorado River, formed by Hoover Dam.

**mead·ow** (med′ō), *n.* [< AS. *mædwe*, oblique case of *mæd*], 1. a piece of grassland, especially one whose grass is grown for hay. 2. low, level grassland near a stream, etc. —**mead′ow·y,** *adj.*

**meadow lark,** [*pl.* MEADOW LARKS, MEADOW LARK; see PLURAL, II, D, 1], any of various North American songbirds with a yellow breast.

**mea·ger, mea·gre** (mē′gẽr), *adj.* [< OFr. < L. *macer*, lean], 1. thin; lean; emaciated. 2. poor; inadequate; not rich or fertile. —**mea′ger·ly, mea′gre·ly,** *adv.* —**mea′ger·ness, mea′gre·ness,** *n.*

**meal** (mēl), *n.* [AS. *mæl*], 1. any of the times for eating; breakfast, lunch, dinner, etc. 2. the food served or eaten at one time.

**meal** (mēl), *n.* [AS. *melu*], 1. any edible grain, coarsely ground and unbolted: as, corn *meal.* 2. any substance similarly ground or powdered.

**meal·ies** (mēl′iz), *n.pl.* [*sing.* -IE, -Y], [< S.Afr.D. < Port. *milho*, millet], in South Africa, 1. maize; corn. 2. *sing.* an ear of maize.

**meal ticket,** 1. a ticket entitling one to meals at a particular restaurant. 2. [Slang], a person, job, etc. depended on for one's livelihood.

**meal·time** (mēl′tīme′), *n.* the usual time for serving or eating a meal.

**meal·y** (mēl′i), *adj.* [-IER, -IEST], 1. like meal; powdery, dry, etc. 2. of or containing meal. 3. covered with meal. 4. pale; floury in color. 5. mealy-mouthed. —**meal′i·ness,** *n.*

**meal·y-mouthed** (mēl′i-mouthd′, -moutht′), *adj.* not willing to state the facts in simple, direct words; euphemistic and insincere.

**mean** (mēn), *v.t.* [MEANT (ment), MEANING], [AS. *mænan*], 1. to have in mind; intend; purpose: as, he *means* to go. 2. to intend to express or imply: as, just what do you *mean?* 3. to signify; denote: as, the German word "ja" *means* "yes." 4. to bring about: as, money *means* happiness. *v.i.* 1. to have a purpose in mind: chiefly in *mean well.* 2. to have a (specified) degree of importance, effect, etc.: as, she *means* little to him. —**mean well by,** to have good intentions toward.

**mean** (mēn), *adj.* [AS. (*ge*)*mæne*], 1. low in quality or grade; poor. 2. low in social status or rank. 3. of slight value, importance, etc. 4. poor in appearance; shabby: as, a *mean* appearance. 5. ignoble; base; petty. 6. stingy; miserly. 7. bad-tempered; unmanageable: said of a horse, etc. 8. [Colloq.], *a*) contemptibly selfish, bad-tempered, etc. *b*) humiliated. *c*) in poor health; ill. 9. [Slang], difficult: as, he throws a *mean* curve. —**mean′ly,** *adv.* —**mean′ness,** *n.*

**mean** (mēn), *adj.* [< OFr. < L. *medianus* < *medius*, middle], 1. halfway between extremes; intermediate as to quantity, quality, etc. 2. average; middling. *n.* 1. what is between extremes; intermediate state, quality, etc. 2. moderation. 3. in *mathematics*, *a*) a quantity with a value intermediate between the values of other quantities; esp., the average (**arithmetical mean**) obtained by dividing the sum of two or more quantities by the number of these quantities. *b*) the second or third term of a four-term proportion. See also **means.**

**me·an·der** (mi-an′dẽr), *n.* [< L. < Gr. *maiandros* < the name of a winding river in Asia Minor], 1. *often in pl.* a winding course, as of a stream. 2. an aimless wandering. *v.i.* 1. to take a winding course: said of a stream. 2. to wander aimlessly or idly. —**me·an′der·er,** *n.*

**mean·ing** (mēn′iŋ), *n.* 1. what is meant; what is intended to be, or in fact is, signified, indicated, etc.; import; sense; significance: as, the *meaning* of a word, a look full of *meaning.* 2. [Archaic], intention. *adj.* 1. that has meaning; significant.

2. intending. —**mean′ing·ful,** *adj.* —**mean′ing·ful·ly,** *adv.* —**mean′ing·ly,** *adv.*

**mean·ing·less** (mēn′iŋ-lis), *adj.* having no meaning; without significance. —**mean′ing·less·ly,** *adv.* —**mean′ing·less·ness,** *n.*

**means** (mēnz), *n.pl.* [< *mean, n.*], 1. [construed as sing. or pl.], that by which something is done or obtained; agency: as, a *means* to an end. 2. resources; property: as, a man of *means.* —**by all means,** 1. without fail. 2. certainly. —**by any means,** in any way possible; somehow. —**by means of,** by using; with the aid of. —**by no (manner of) means,** in no way; certainly not. —**means to an end,** a method of getting what one wants.

**mean (solar) time,** time having exactly equal divisions.

**meant** (ment), pt. and pp. of **mean.**

**mean·time** (mēn′tīm′), *adv.* 1. in or during the intervening time. 2. at the same time. *n.* the intervening time. Also **mean′while′.**

**mea·sles** (mē′z'lz), *n.pl.* [construed as sing.], [ME. *maseles;* infl. by ME. *mesel* (< OFr.), leper < L. *misellus,* wretch], 1. an acute, infectious, communicable virus disease, occurring most frequently in childhood, characterized by a skin eruption, high fever, nasal catarrh, etc. 2. any of various similar but milder diseases; esp., German measles.

**mea·sly** (mēz′li), *adj.* [-SLIER, -SLIEST], 1. infected with measles. 2. [Colloq.], contemptibly slight, worthless, or skimpy.

**meas·ur·a·ble** (mezh′ēr-ə-b'l), *adj.* that can be measured. —**meas′ur·a·bil′i·ty, meas′ur·a·ble·ness,** *n.* —**meas′ur·a·bly,** *adv.*

**meas·ure** (mezh′ēr), *n.* [< OFr. *mesure* < L. *mensura* < pp. of *metiri,* to measure], 1. the extent, dimensions, capacity, etc. of anything, especially as determined by a standard. 2. a determining of extent, dimensions, etc.; measurement. 3. *a*) unit of measurement, as an inch, yard, or bushel. *b*) any standard of valuation; criterion. 4. a system of measurement: as, dry *measure.* 5. an instrument or container for measuring: as, a quart *measure.* 6. a definite quantity measured out. 7. *a*) an extent or degree not to be exceeded. *b*) a reasonable limit: as, grieved beyond *measure.* 8. (certain) proportion, quantity, or degree: as, in large *measure.* 9. a course of action; step: as, reform *measures.* 10. a statute; law. 11. *a*) rhythm in verse; meter. *b*) a metrical unit; foot of verse. 12. a dance or dance movement. 13. *pl.* in *geology,* related beds, as of coal. 14. in *music, a*) the notes or rests, or both, contained between two bars on the staff. *b*) musical time. *v.t.* [-URED, -URING], 1. to find out or estimate the extent, dimensions, etc. of, especially by a standard. 2. to set apart or mark off by measuring (often with *off* or *out*). 3. to estimate by comparison: as, he *measured* his foe. 4. to bring into comparison or rivalry (*against*). 5. to be a measure of: as, a clock *measures* time. 6. to adjust by a standard: as, *measure* your speech by your listeners' reactions. 7. to traverse as if measuring. *v.i.* 1. to get or take measurements. 2. to be of specified measurements. 3. to allow of measurement. —**beyond measure,** exceedingly; extremely. —**in a measure,** to some extent; somewhat. —**made to measure,** custom-made: said of clothes. —**measure up to,** to meet (expectations, a standard, etc.). —**take one's measure,** to estimate one's ability, character, etc. —**meas′ur·er,** *n.*

**meas·ured** (mezh′ērd), *adj.* 1. determined by a standard. 2. regular or uniform. 3. *a*) rhythmical. *b*) metrical. 4. calculated, deliberate, etc., as speech. —**meas′ured·ly,** *adv.* —**meas′ured·ness,** *n.*

**meas·ure·less** (mezh′ēr-lis), *adj.* too large to be measurable; vast; immense; unlimited. —**meas′ure·less·ly,** *adv.* —**meas′ure·less·ness,** *n.*

**meas·ure·ment** (mezh′ēr-mənt), *n.* 1. a measuring or being measured. 2. extent or quantity determined by measuring. 3. a system of measuring.

**measuring worm,** the caterpillar larva of any geometrid moth.

**meat** (mēt), *n.* [AS. *mete*], 1. food: now dialectal except in *meat and drink.* 2. the flesh of animals, usually of mammals, used as food, as distinguished from fish and fowl. 3. the edible part: as, the *meat* of a nut. 4. the substance or essence: as, the *meat* of a story. 5. a meal: now only in *at meat, before meat,* etc. 6. [Slang], something that one especially enjoys or is skillful at: as, golf's my *meat.* —**meat′less,** *adj.*

**me·a·tus** (mi-ā′təs), *n.* [*pl.* -TUSES, -TUS], [L., a passage, pp. of *meare,* to pass], a natural passage or duct in the body, or its opening.

**meat·y** (mēt′i), *adj.* [-IER, -IEST], 1. of, or having the flavor of, meat. 2. like meat. 3. full of meat. 4. full of substance; thought-provoking; pithy. —**meat′i·ness,** *n.*

**Mec·ca** (mek′ə), *n.* 1. one of the capitals of Saudi Arabia: pop., c. 200,000: birthplace of Mohammed and hence a holy city of Islam, to which Moslems make pilgrimages. 2. [often m-], *a*) any place that one yearns to go to. *b*) anything that one greatly desires. —**Mec′can,** *adj. & n.*

**mech.,** 1. mechanical. 2. mechanics. 3. mechanism.

**me·chan·ic** (mə-kan′ik), *adj.* [< L. < Gr. < *mēchanē,* a machine], [Archaic], 1. of manual labor or skill. 2. mechanical. *n.* a worker skilled in using tools or making, operating, and repairing machines.

**me·chan·i·cal** (mə-kan′i-k'l), *adj.* 1. having to do with machinery or tools. 2. produced or operated by machinery. 3. of, or in accordance with, the science of mechanics. 4. machinelike; automatic, as if from force of habit: as, her acting is *mechanical.* —**me·chan′i·cal·ly,** *adv.*

**mechanical drawing,** a drawing made with the use of T squares, scales, compasses, etc.

**mech·a·ni·cian** (mek′ə-nish′ən), *n.* a person skilled in the design, operation, care, etc. of machinery.

**me·chan·ics** (mə-kan′iks), *n.pl.* [construed as sing.], 1. the branch of physics that deals with motion and the action of forces on bodies: see also **kinetics, kinematics, dynamics, statics.** 2. knowledge of machinery. 3. the mechanical aspect; technical part: as, the *mechanics* of writing.

**mech·a·nism** (mek′ə-niz'm), *n.* [< Gr. *mēchanē,* a machine], 1. the working parts of a machine; works: as, the *mechanism* of a clock. 2. *a*) a system whose parts work together as in a machine: as, the *mechanism* of the universe. *b*) any physical or mental process by which some result is produced: as, his boasting is a defense *mechanism.* 3. the mechanical aspect; technical part. 4. the theory that all phenomena can ultimately be explained in terms of physics and chemistry. —**mech′a·nist,** *n.* —**mech′a·nis′tic,** *adj.* —**mech′a·nis′ti·cal·ly,** *adv.*

**mech·a·nize** (mek′ə-nīz′), *v.t.* [-NIZED, -NIZING], 1. to make mechanical. 2. to do or operate by machinery, not by hand. 3. to bring about the use of machinery in (an industry, etc.). 4. to equip (an army, etc.) with motor vehicles, tanks, etc. —**mech′a·ni·za′tion,** *n.*

**mech·an·o·ther·a·py** (mek′ə-nō-ther′ə-pi), *n.* [< Gr. *mēchanē,* a machine; + *therapy*], the treatment of disease by mechanical means, such as massage. —**mech′an·o·ther′a·pist,** *n.*

**med.,** 1. medical. 2. medicine. 3. medieval.

**M.Ed.,** Master of Education.

**med·al** (med′'l), *n.* [< Fr. < It. *medaglia* < LL. < L. *metallum,* metal], a small, flat piece of metal with a design or inscription on it, made to commemorate some event, or awarded for some distinguished action, merit, etc. *v.t.* [-ALED or -ALLED, -ALING or -ALLING], to honor with a medal.

**med·al·ist, med·al·list** (med′'l-ist), *n.* 1. a person who designs or makes medals. 2. a person who has been awarded a medal. 3. in *golf,* the winner at medal play.

**me·dal·lion** (mə-dal′yən), *n.* [< Fr. < It.; see MEDAL], 1. a large medal. 2. a circular design, portrait, etc. shaped like a medal.

**medal play,** in *golf,* a form of competitive play in which the score is calculated by counting the total number of strokes taken to play the designated number of holes: cf. *match play.*

**med·dle** (med′'l), *v.i.* [-DLED, -DLING], [< OFr. *medler* (< L. *miscere*), to mix], to concern oneself with other people's affairs without being asked or needed; interfere (*in* or *with*). —**med′dler,** *n.*

**med·dle·some** (med′'l-səm), *adj.* meddling or inclined to meddle. —**med′dle·some·ness,** *n.*

**Mede** (mēd), *n.* a native or inhabitant of Media.

**Me·de·a** (mi-dē′ə), *n.* in *Gr. legend,* a sorceress who helped Jason get the Golden Fleece.

**Med·ford** (med′fērd), *n.* a city in E Massachusetts, near Boston: pop., 66,000.

**Me·di·a** (mē′di-ə), *n.* an ancient country in what is now NW Iran. —**Me′di·an,** *adj. & n.*

**me·di·a** (mē′di-ə), *n.* alt. pl. of **medium.**

**me·di·ae·val** (mē′di-ē′v'l, med′i-), *adj.* medieval.

fat, āpe, bâre, cär; ten, ēven, hêre, ovẽr; is, bīte; lot, gō, hôrn, tōōl, look; oil, out; up, ūse, fũr; get; joy; yet; chin; she; thin, *th*en; zh, leisure; ŋ, ring; ə for *a* in *ago, e* in *agent, i* in *sanity, o* in *comply, u* in *focus;* ′ in *able* (ā′b'l); Fr. bål; ë, Fr. coeur; ö, Fr. feu; Fr. mo*n*; ô, Fr. coq; ü, Fr. duc; H, G. ich; kh, G. doch. ‡ foreign; < derived from.

—**me'di·ae'val·ism,** *n.* —**me'di·ae'val·ist,** *n.* —**me'di·ae'val·ly,** *adv.*
**me·di·al** (mē'di-əl), *adj.* [< LL. < L. *medius,* middle], 1. of or in the middle; median. 2. average; mean. —**me'di·al·ly,** *adv.*
**me·di·an** (mē'di-ən), *adj.* [< L. < *medius,* middle], 1. middle; intermediate. 2. in *statistics, a)* designating the middle number in a series (e.g., 7 in the series 1, 4, 7, 16, 43). *b)* designating the number midway between the two middle numbers in a series containing an even number of items (e.g., 10 in the series 4, 8, 12, 46). *n.* a median number, point, or line. —**me'di·an·ly,** *adv.*
**me·di·ate** (mē'di-āt'; *for adj.,* -it), *v.i.* [-ATED, -ATING], [< LL. *mediatus,* pp. < L. *medius,* middle], 1. to be in an intermediate position. 2. to be an intermediary between persons or sides. *v.t.* 1. to settle by mediation. 2. to be the medium for bringing about (a result). *adj.* 1. intermediate. 2. dependent on, acting by, or connected through some intervening agency. —**me'di·a·cy,** *n.* —**me'di·ate·ly,** *adv.* —**me'di·a'tive,** *adj.*
**me·di·a·tion** (mē'di-ā'shən), *n.* a mediating; intercession for settling differences between persons, nations, etc. —**me'di·a'tor,** *n.*
**me·di·a·to·ry** (mē'di-ə-tôr'i, -tō'ri), *adj.* of, or having the nature of, a mediator or mediation.
**med·ic** (med'ik), *n.* [< L. < Gr. *mēdikē* (*poa*), (grass) of Media], any of various cloverlike plants; esp., alfalfa.
**med·ic** (med'ik), *n.* [Colloq.], 1. a physician or surgeon. 2. a medical student or intern. 3. a member of a military medical corps.
**med·i·ca·ble** (med'i-kə-b'l), *adj.* that can be cured, healed, or relieved by medical treatment.
**med·i·cal** (med'i-k'l), *adj.* [< Fr. < LL. < L. *medicus,* physician], of or connected with the practice or study of medicine. —**med'i·cal·ly,** *adv.*
**me·dic·a·ment** (mə-dik'ə-mənt, med'i-kə-), *n.* a medicine; substance for curing, healing, etc.
**Med·i·care** (med'i-kâr'), *n.* a system of government insurance for providing medical and hospital care for the aged from Federal social security funds.
**med·i·cate** (med'i-kāt'), *v.t.* [-CATED, -CATING], [< L. pp. of *medicari,* to heal], 1. to treat with medicine. 2. to apply or add a medicinal substance to. —**med'i·ca'tion,** *n.* —**med'i·ca'tive,** *adj.*
**Med·i·ci** (med'ə-chē'), *n.* name of a rich, powerful family of Florence, Italy, in the 14th to 16th centuries. —**Med·i·ce·an** (med'ə-sē'ən, -chē'ən), *adj.*
**Medici, Catherine de',** 1519–1589; queen of Henry II of France (1547–1559).
**Medici, Lo·ren·zo de'** (lô-ren'tsô de), 1449–1492; prince of Florence, statesman, scholar, and patron of the arts: called *Lorenzo the Magnificent.*
**me·dic·i·nal** (mə-dis''n-'l), *adj.* of, or having the properties of, medicine; curing, healing, or relieving. —**me·dic'i·nal·ly,** *adv.*
**med·i·cine** (med'ə-s'n), *n.* [< OFr. < L. < *medicus,* physician], 1. the science and art of diagnosing, treating, and preventing disease. 2. the branch of this science that makes use of drugs, diet, etc., especially as distinguished from surgery. 3. any substance, as a drug, used in treating disease, healing, relieving pain, etc. 4. among North American Indians, *a)* any object, rite, etc. supposed to have supernatural powers as a remedy, preventive, etc. *b)* magical power or rite. *v.t.* [-CINED, -CINING], to give medicine to. —**take one's medicine,** to endure punishment, etc.
**medicine ball,** a large, heavy, leather-covered ball, tossed from one person to another for exercise.
**medicine man,** among North American Indians, etc., a man supposed to have supernatural powers of curing disease and controlling spirits.
**med·i·co** (med'i-kō'), *n.* [*pl.* -COS], [It.], [Colloq.], 1. a doctor. 2. a medical student.
**me·di·e·val** (mē'di-ē'v'l, med'i-), *adj.* [< L. *medius,* middle + *aevum,* age], of, like, characteristic of, or suggestive of the Middle Ages: also sp. **mediaeval.** —**me'di·e'val·ly,** *adv.*
**Medieval Greek,** the Greek language as it was used in the Middle Ages, from about 700 A.D. to about 1500: also called *Middle Greek.*
**me·di·e·val·ism** (mē'di-ē'v'l-iz'm, med'i-), *n.* 1. the spirit, beliefs, customs, etc. of the Middle Ages. 2. devotion to or acceptance of these. 3. a medieval belief, custom, etc.
**me·di·e·val·ist** (mē'di-ē'v'l-ist, med'i-), *n.* 1. a specialist in medieval history, literature, art, etc. 2. one devoted to medieval customs, beliefs, etc.
**Medieval Latin,** the Latin language current in Europe in the Middle Ages, from about 700 A.D. to about 1500: also called *Middle Latin.*
**Me·di·na** (me-dē'nä), *n.* a city in W Saudi Arabia: pop., c. 50,000: site of Mohammed's tomb.
**me·di·o·cre** (mē'di-ō'kēr, mē'di-ō'-), *adj.* [< Fr. < L. *mediocris* < *medius,* middle + *ocris,* a peak], of middle quality, neither very good nor very bad; ordinary; average; commonplace.
**me·di·oc·ri·ty** (mē'di-ok'rə-ti), *n.* [*pl.* -TIES], 1. a being mediocre. 2. mediocre ability or attainment. 3. a person of mediocre abilities, etc.
**Medit.,** Mediterranean.
**med·i·tate** (med'ə-tāt'), *v.t.* [-TATED, -TATING], [< L. pp. of *meditari*], 1. [Rare], to think about; contemplate. 2. to plan; intend. *v.i.* to think deeply and continuously; reflect. —**med'i·ta'tive,** *adj.* —**med'i·ta'tive·ly,** *adv.* —**med'i·ta'tor,** *n.*
**med·i·ta·tion** (med'ə-tā'shən), *n.* 1. act of meditating; reflection. 2. solemn reflection on sacred matters as a devotional act.
**Med·i·ter·ra·ne·an** (med'ə-tə-rā'ni-ən), *adj.* [< L. < *medius,* middle + *terra,* land], of the Mediterranean Sea or near-by regions. *n.* 1. the Mediterranean Sea. 2. a person who lives near this sea.
**Mediterranean fever,** undulant fever.
**Mediterranean Sea,** a large sea surrounded by Europe, Africa, and Asia: area, 1,145,000 sq. mi.
**me·di·um** (mē'di-əm), *n.* [*pl.* -DIUMS, -DIA], [L., neut. of *medius,* middle], 1. *a)* something intermediate. *b)* a middle state or degree; mean. 2. an intervening thing through which a force acts. 3. any means, agency, etc.: as, radio is a *medium* of communication. 4. any surrounding substance in which bodies exist. 5. environment. 6. a nutritive substance, as agar, for cultivating bacteria, etc. 7. one through whom communications are supposedly sent from the spirits of the dead. 8. a liquid mixed with pigments to give fluency. *adj.* intermediate in quantity, quality, place, etc.
**med·lar** (med'lēr), *n.* [< OFr. < L. < Gr. *mespilon*], 1. a small tree of the rose family, growing in Europe and Asia. 2. its small, brown, applelike fruit, eaten when partly decayed.
**med·ley** (med'li), *n.* [*pl.* -LEYS], [< OFr. < pp. of *medler,* to mix; see MEDDLE], 1. a mixture of things not usually placed together. 2. a musical composition made up of passages or sections from various other compositions. *adj.* mixed; made up of heterogeneous parts.
**me·dul·la** (mi-dul'ə), *n.* [*pl.* -LAE (-ē)], [L., the marrow], 1. in *anatomy, a)* the marrow of bones. *b)* the medulla oblongata. *c)* the inner substance of an organ. 2. in *botany,* the pith.
**medulla ob·lon·ga·ta** (ob'lôŋ-gä'tə), [Mod. L., oblong medulla], the widening continuation of the spinal cord forming the lowest part of the brain: it controls breathing, circulation, etc.
**med·ul·lar·y** (med'ə-ler'i, mi-dul'ēr-i), *adj.* of or like the medulla or the medulla oblongata.
**Me·du·sa** (mə-dōō'sə, -dū'zə), *n.* 1. in *Gr. mythology,* one of the three Gorgons, who was slain by Perseus. 2. [m-], [*pl.* -SAS, -SAE (-sē, -zē)], in *zoology,* a jellyfish. —**me·du'san, me·du'soid,** *adj. & n.*
**meed** (mēd), *n.* [AS. *med*], [Poetic], a merited recompense or reward.
**meek** (mēk), *adj.* [< ON. *miukr,* gentle], 1. patient and mild; not inclined to anger or resentment. 2. *a)* tamely submissive. *b)* too submissive; spiritless. —**meek'ly,** *adv.* —**meek'ness,** *n.*
**meer·schaum** (mêr'shəm, -shôm'), *n.* [G. < *meer,* sea + *schaum,* foam], 1. a soft, white, claylike, heat-resistant mineral used for tobacco pipes, etc. 2. a tobacco pipe made of this.
**meet** (mēt), *v.t.* [MET, MEETING], [AS. *metan*], 1. to come upon; come across (a person). 2. to come face to face with; confront. 3. to be present at the arrival of: as, he *met* the bus. 4. to come into contact, connection, etc. with: as, her hand *met* his. 5. *a)* to come into the presence of. *b)* to be introduced to; get acquainted with. 6. *a)* to fight with. *b)* to face: as, he *met* angry words with a laugh. *c)* to oppose; deal with effectively: as, to *meet* an objection. 7. to experience: as, he will *meet* disaster. 8. to come within the perception of (the eye, ear, etc.). 9. *a)* to comply with; satisfy (a demand, etc.). *b)* to pay (a bill, etc.). *v.i.* 1. to come together, as from different directions. 2. to come into contact, connection, etc. 3. to become acquainted; be introduced. 4. to be opposed in or as in battle; fight. 5. to be united. 6. to assemble. *n.* 1. a meeting, gathering, etc.: as, a track *meet.* 2. the people who meet or assemble. 3. the place of meeting. —**meet with,** 1. to experience. 2. to receive.
**meet** (mēt), *adj.* [< AS. (*ge*)*mæte,* fitting], suitable; appropriate; fitting: as, it is *meet* that you should go. —**meet'ly,** *adv.*
**meet·ing** (mēt'iŋ), *n.* 1. a coming together of persons or things. 2. an assembly; gathering of people. 3. an assembly or place of assembly for

purposes of worship. 4. a point of contact or intersection; junction. 5. a duel.
**meet·ing·house** (mēt′iŋ-hous′), *n.* a building used for public worship; church.
**meg·a-,** [Gr. < *megas*, great], a combining form meaning: 1. *large, great, powerful*, as in *megaphone*. 2. *a million (of)*, as in *megacycle*. Also **meg-.**
**meg·a·cy·cle** (meg′ə-sī′k'l), *n.* [*mega-* + *cycle*], in *physics*, one million cycles.
**meg·a·lo-,** [Gr. < *megas*, large], a combining form meaning: 1. *large, great, powerful*, as in *megalomania*. 2. *abnormal enlargement*, as in *megalocephaly*. Also **megal-.**
**meg·a·lo·ceph·a·ly** (meg′ə-lō-sef′ə-li), *n.* [< *megalo-* + Gr. *kephalē*, a head], a condition in which the head is unusually large. —**meg′a·lo·ce·phal′ic** (-sə-fal′ik), **meg′a·lo·ceph′a·lous,** *adj.*
**meg·a·lo·ma·ni·a** (meg′ə-lə-mā′ni-ə), *n.* [*megalo-* + *mania*], a mental disorder characterized by delusions of grandeur, wealth, power, etc. —**meg′a·lo·ma′ni·ac** (-ak), *adj. & n.*
**meg·a·lop·o·lis** (meg′ə-lop′ə-lis), *n.* [Gr., great city], a vast, populous, continuously urban area.
**meg·a·phone** (meg′ə-fōn′), *n.* [*mega-* + *-phone*], a large, funnel-shaped device for increasing the volume of the voice and directing it. *v.t. & v.i.* [-PHONED, -PHONING], to magnify or direct (the voice) through a megaphone.
**meg·a·ton** (meg′ə-tun′), *n.* [*mega-* + *ton*], the explosive force of a million tons of TNT.
**meg·ohm** (meg′ōm′), *n.* one million ohms.
**me·grim** (mē′grim), *n.* [< OFr.; see MIGRAINE], 1. migraine. 2. a whim; fancy. 3. *pl.* low spirits.
**Meis·ter·sing·er** (mīs′tēr-siŋ′ēr), *n.* [*pl.* -SINGER], [G., lit., master singer], a member of one of the German guilds organized in the 14th to 16th centuries for cultivating music and poetry.
**Mé·ji·co** (me′hi-kô′), *n.* Mexico: Spanish spelling.
**Me·kong** (mā′koŋ′), *n.* a river flowing through Tibet and SW China into the South China Sea.
**mel·an·cho·li·a** (mel′ən-kō′li-ə), *n.* a mental disorder characterized by extreme depression of spirits, brooding, etc. —**mel′an·cho′li·ac,** *adj. & n.*
**mel·an·chol·y** (mel′ən-kol′i), *n.* [*pl.* -CHOLIES], [< OFr. < LL. < Gr. *melancholia* < *melas*, black + *cholē*, bile: orig. referring to black bile as the humor causing this], 1. *a)* sadness and depression of spirits. *b)* a tendency to be sad or depressed. 2. pensiveness. *adj.* 1. sad and depressed; gloomy. 2. causing sadness or depression. 3. pensive. —**mel′an·chol′ic,** *adj.* —**mel′an·chol′i·cal·ly,** *adv.*
**Mel·a·ne·sia** (mel′ə-nē′zhə, -shə), *n.* a group of islands in the South Pacific, east of Australia.
**Mel·a·ne·sian** (mel′ə-nē′zhən, -shən), *adj.* of Melanesia, its people, or their languages. *n.* 1. a member of the dark-skinned native people of Melanesia. 2. their Austronesian languages.
‡**mé·lange** (mā′länzh′), *n.* [Fr. < *mêler*, to mix], a mixture; medley; hodgepodge.
**mel·a·nin** (mel′ə-nin), *n.* [< Gr. *melas*, black], a brownish-black pigment found in skin, hair, etc.
**Mel·ba toast** (mel′bə), [after Nellie *Melba* (1861?–1931), Australian soprano], slightly stale bread sliced thin and toasted until crisp.
**Mel·bourne** (mel′bērn), *n.* a seaport in SE Australia: pop., 1,912,000.
**meld** (meld), *v.t. & v.i.* [G. *melden*, to announce], in *pinochle*, etc., to declare (a combination of cards in one's hand) for inclusion in one's score. *n.* 1. a melding. 2. the cards melded. 3. the score made by melding.
**me·lee, mê·lée** (mā-lā′, mā′lā, mel′ā), *n.* [Fr. *mêlée* < OFr.; see MEDLEY], a confused, general hand-to-hand fight between groups.
**mel·io·rate** (mēl′yə-rāt′), *v.t. & v.i.* [-RATED, -RATING], [< LL. pp. < L. *melior*, better], to make or become better; improve. —**mel′io·ra′tion,** *n.* —**mel′io·ra′tive,** *adj.* —**mel′io·ra′tor,** *n.*
**mel·lif·er·ous** (mə-lif′ēr-əs), *adj.* [< L. < *mel*, honey; + *-ferous*], producing honey.
**mel·lif·lu·ent** (mə-lif′lōō-ənt), *adj.* mellifluous. —**mel·lif′lu·ence,** *n.* —**mel·lif′lu·ent·ly,** *adv.*
**mel·lif·lu·ous** (mə-lif′lōō-əs), *adj.* [< L. < *mel*, honey + *fluere*, to flow], flowing sweetly and smoothly; honeyed: said of words, sounds, etc. —**mel·lif′lu·ous·ly,** *adv.* —**mel·lif′lu·ous·ness,** *n.*
**mel·low** (mel′ō), *adj.* [prob. < AS. *melu*, meal (ground grain)], 1. soft, sweet, and juicy because ripe: said of fruit. 2. full-flavored; matured: said of wine, etc. 3. full, rich, soft, and pure: said of sound, light, etc. 4. moist and rich: said of soil. 5. made soft, gentle, and understanding by experience. *v.t. & v.i.* to make or become mellow. —**mel′low·ly,** *adv.* —**mel′low·ness,** *n.*
**me·lo·de·on** (mə-lō′di-ən), *n.* [pseudo-Gr. form < *melody*], a small keyboard organ in which air is drawn through metal reeds by means of a bellows.
**me·lod·ic** (mə-lod′ik), *adj.* 1. of or like melody. 2. melodious. —**me·lod′i·cal·ly,** *adv.*
**me·lo·di·ous** (mə-lō′di-əs), *adj.* 1. containing or producing melody. 2. pleasing to hear; tuneful. —**me·lo′di·ous·ly,** *adv.* —**me·lo′di·ous·ness,** *n.*
**mel·o·dist** (mel′ə-dist), *n.* a singer or composer of melodies.
**mel·o·dra·ma** (mel′ə-drä′mə, -dram′ə), *n.* [< Fr. < Gr. *melos*, a song + *drama*, drama], 1. originally, a sensational or romantic stage play with interspersed songs. 2. now, a drama with sensational, romantic action, extravagant emotions, and, generally, a happy ending. 3. any sensational, emotional action, utterance, etc.
**mel·o·dra·mat·ic** (mel′ə-drə-mat′ik), *adj.* of, like, or fit for melodrama; sensational, violent, and extravagantly emotional. —**mel′o·dra·mat′i·cal·ly,** *adv.* —**mel′o·dra·mat′ics,** *n.pl.*
**mel·o·dy** (mel′ə-di), *n.* [*pl.* -DIES], [< OFr. < LL. < Gr. *melōidia* < *melos*, song + *aedein*, to sing], 1. pleasing sounds or arrangement of sounds in sequence. 2. in *music*, *a)* a sequence of single tones to produce a rhythmic whole; often, a tune, song, etc. *b)* the leading part in a harmonic composition.
**mel·on** (mel′ən), *n.* [< OFr. < LL. *melo* for L. *melopepo* < Gr. < *mēlon*, apple + *pepōn*, melon], the large, juicy, many-seeded fruit of certain trailing plants of the gourd family, as the watermelon, muskmelon, and cantaloupe. —**cut a melon,** [Slang], to distribute profits, etc., as among stockholders.
**Mel·pom·e·ne** (mel-pom′ə-nē′), *n.* in *Gr. mythology*, the Muse of tragedy.
**melt** (melt), *v.t. & v.i.* [MELTED, MELTING; *archaic* pp. MOLTEN], [AS. *m(i)eltan*], 1. to change from a solid to a liquid state, generally by heat. 2. to dissolve; disintegrate. 3. to disappear or cause to disappear gradually (often with *away*). 4. to merge gradually; blend: as, the sea seems to *melt* into the sky. 5. to soften: as, her grief *melted* our hearts. *n.* a melting or being melted. —**melt′a·ble,** *adj.* —**melt′er,** *n.*
**melting point,** the temperature at which a specified solid becomes liquid.
**melting pot,** a country, etc. in which people of various nationalities and races are assimilated.
**mel·ton** (mel′t'n), *n.* [< *Melton* Mowbray, England], a heavy woolen cloth with a short nap.
**Mel·ville, Herman** (mel′vil), 1819–1891; U.S. novelist.
**mem.,** 1. member. 2. memorandum.
**mem·ber** (mem′bēr), *n.* [< OFr. < L. *membrum*], 1. a limb or other part or organ of a person, animal, or plant. 2. a distinct part of a whole, as of a series, an equation, a structure, etc. 3. any of the persons constituting an organization or group.
**mem·ber·ship** (mem′bēr-ship′), *n.* 1. the state of being a member. 2. all the members of a group. 3. the number of members.
**mem·brane** (mem′brān′), *n.* [< L. *membrana* < *membrum*, member], a thin, soft, pliable layer of animal or plant tissue, that covers or lines an organ or part. —**mem′bra·nous** (-brə-nəs), *adj.*
**me·men·to** (mi-men′tō), *n.* [*pl.* -TOS, -TOES], [L., imperative of *meminisse*, to remember], an object serving as a reminder, warning, or souvenir.
‡**me·men·to mo·ri** (mi-men′tō mō′rī), [L., remember that you must die], any reminder of death.
**mem·o** (mem′ō), *n.* [*pl.* -OS], [Colloq.], a memorandum.
**mem·oir** (mem′wär), *n.* [< Fr. *mémoire*, memory < L. *memoria*], 1. a biography. 2. a monograph, as on scientific study. 3. *pl.* *a)* a record of happenings that is based on the writer's personal experience and knowledge. *b)* an autobiography.
**mem·o·ra·bil·i·a** (mem′ēr-ə-bil′i-ə), *n.pl.* [*sing.* -ORABILE (-ə-rab′ə-lē′)], [L.], noteworthy events.
**mem·o·ra·ble** (mem′ēr-ə-b'l), *adj.* worth remembering; notable. —**mem′o·ra·bil′i·ty, mem′o·ra·ble·ness,** *n.* —**mem′o·ra·bly,** *adv.*
**mem·o·ran·dum** (mem′ə-ran′dəm), *n.* [*pl.* -DUMS, -DA (-də)], [L.], 1. *a)* a short note written to help one remember something. *b)* a record, as of events, for future use. 2. an informal written communication, as in a business office. 3. a short written statement of the terms of a contract or transaction, as of the goods and terms of a consignment

**me·mo·ri·al** (mə-môr′i-əl, -mō′ri-), *adj.* [see MEMORY], serving to help people remember some person or event. *n.* 1. anything meant to help people remember some person or event, as a statue, holiday, etc. 2. a statement of facts, often with a petition for action, sent to a government, official, etc.

**Memorial Day,** a U.S. holiday, observed in most States on May 30, for honoring the dead of the armed forces: also called *Decoration Day.*

**me·mo·ri·al·ize** (mə-môr′i-ə-līz′, -mō′ri-), *v.t.* [-IZED, -IZING], 1. to commemorate. 2. to present a memorial to; petition. **—me·mo′ri·al·i·za′tion,** *n.* **—me·mo′ri·al·iz′er,** *n.*

**mem·o·rize** (mem′ə-rīz′), *v.t.* [-RIZED, -RIZING], to commit to memory; learn by heart. **—mem′o·ri·za′tion,** *n.* **—mem′o·riz′er,** *n.*

**mem·o·ry** (mem′ēr-i), *n.* [*pl.* -RIES], [< OFr. < L. *memoria* < *memor,* mindful], 1. the power, act, or process of remembering. 2. the total of what one remembers. 3. someone or something remembered. 4. the period over which remembering extends: as, not within the *memory* of living men. 5. commemoration or remembrance: as, in *memory* of his father. 6. fame after death.

**Mem·phis** (mem′fis), *n.* 1. an ancient city in Egypt, near the mouth of the Nile. 2. a city in SW Tennessee, on the Mississippi: pop., 498,000.

**mem·sa·hib** (mem′sä′ib), *n.* [Anglo-Ind.; *mem* for Eng. *ma'am* + Ar. *sāhib,* a master], lady; mistress: title used, until recently, by natives in India when addressing a European woman.

**men** (men), *n.* pl. of **man.**

**men·ace** (men′is), *n.* [< OFr. < L. *minacia* < *minax,* threatening < *minari,* to threaten], 1. a threat or threatening. 2. anything threatening harm or evil. *v.t. & v.i.* [-ACED, -ACING], to threaten. **—men′ac·ing·ly,** *adv.*

**me·nad** (mē′nad), *n.* a maenad.

**mé·nage, me·nage** (mə-näzh′, mā-), *n.* [< Fr. < OFr. *manaige* < LL. < L. *mansio,* a house], 1. a household. 2. the management of a household.

**me·nag·er·ie** (mə-naj′ēr-i, -nazh′-), *n.* [< Fr. < *ménage;* see MÉNAGE], 1. a collection of wild animals kept in cages, etc., especially for exhibition. 2. a place where such animals are kept.

**Men·cken, H. L.** (meŋ′k′n), (*Henry Louis Mencken*), 1880–1956; U.S. writer, editor, and critic.

**mend** (mend), *v.t.* [ME. *menden;* see AMEND], 1. to repair; restore to good condition. 2. to make better; improve; reform: as, *mend* your manners. 3. to atone for: now only in *least said, soonest mended.* *v.i.* to improve, especially in health. *n.* 1. a mending; improvement. 2. a mended place. **—on the mend,** improving, especially in health. **—mend′a·ble,** *adj.* **—mend′er,** *n.*

**men·da·cious** (men-dā′shəs), *adj.* [< L. *mendax*], lying; untruthful; false. **—men·da′cious·ly,** *adv.* **—men·dac′i·ty** (-das′ə-ti), **men·da′cious·ness,** *n.*

**Men·del, Gre·gor Jo·hann** (grā′gôr yō′hän men′dəl), 1822–1884; Austrian monk and botanist. **—Men·de·li·an** (men-dē′li-ən), *adj.* **—Men′del·ism, Men·de′li·an·ism,** *n.*

**Men·de·le·ev, Dmi·tri I·va·no·vich** (d'mē′tri i-vä′nə-vich men′də-lā′ef), 1834–1907; Russian chemist: also spelled **Mendelyeev,** etc. **—Mendeleev's law,** the periodic law.

**men·de·le·vi·um** (men′də-lē′vi-əm), *n.* a transuranic, radioactive chemical element: symbol, Mv; at. wt., 256 (?); at. no., 101.

**Mendel's laws,** the principles of hereditary phenomena discovered and formulated by Mendel, holding that characteristics, as height, color, etc., are inherited in definite, predictable combinations.

**Men·dels·sohn, Felix** (men′d'l-s'n, -sōn′), 1809–1847; German composer.

**men·di·cant** (men′di-kənt), *adj.* [< L. ppr. of *mendicare,* to beg < *mendicus,* needy], begging; asking for alms: as, *mendicant* friars. *n.* 1. a beggar. 2. a mendicant friar. **—men′di·can·cy, men·dic·i·ty** (men-dis′ə-ti), *n.*

**Men·e·la·us** (men′ə-lā′əs), *n.* in *Gr. legend,* a king of Sparta, brother of Agamemnon, and husband of Helen.

**men·folk** (men′fōk′), *n.pl.* [Dial.], men: also **menfolks.**

**men·ha·den** (men-hā′d'n), *n.* [< Am. Ind.], a sea fish of the herring family, common along the Atlantic coast: used for making oil and fertilizer.

**me·ni·al** (mē′ni-əl, mēn′yəl), *adj.* [< Anglo-Fr. < OFr. *meisniee,* household; ult. < L. *mansio;* see MANSION], 1. of or fit for servants; hence, 2. servile; low; mean. *n.* 1. a domestic servant. 2. a servile, low person. **—me′ni·al·ly,** *adv.*

**me·nin·ges** (mə-nin′jēz), *n.pl.* [< Gr. *mēninx,* a membrane], the three membranes that envelop the brain and spinal cord. **—me·nin′ge·al (-ji-əl),** *adj.*

**men·in·gi·tis** (men′in-jī′tis), *n.* inflammation of the meninges, especially as the result of infection. **—men′in·git′ic** (-jit′ik), *adj.*

**me·nis·cus** (mi-nis′kəs), *n.* [*pl.* -CUSES, -CI (-nis′ī)], [Gr. *mēniskos,* dim. of *mēnē,* the moon], 1. a crescent-shaped thing. 2. a lens convex on one side and concave on the other. 3. in *physics,* the curved upper surface of a column of liquid.

**Men·non·ite** (men′ən-īt), *n.* [after *Menno* Simons (1492–1559), a leader], a member of an evangelical Christian sect: Mennonites oppose the taking of oaths, infant baptism, and military service, and favor plain dress and plain living.

‡**me·no** (me′nô), *adv.* [It.], in *music,* less.

**men·o·pause** (men′ə-pôz′), *n.* [< Gr. *mēn,* month + *pauein,* to cause to cease], the permanent, natural cessation of menstruation; change of life.

**men·ses** (men′sēz), *n.pl.* [L., pl. of *mensis,* month], the periodic flow of blood from the uterus: it normally occurs in women about every four weeks, from puberty to menopause.

**Men·she·vik, men·she·vik** (men′shə-vik′), *n.* [*pl.* -VIKS, -VIKI (-vē′ki)], [Russ. < *menshe,* the smaller], a member of the minority faction of the Social Democratic Party of Russia before 1917, who opposed the Bolsheviks. **—Men′she·vism, men′she·vism,** *n.* **—Men′she·vist, men′she·vist,** *n.*

**men·stru·al** (men′strōō-əl), *adj.* 1. of the menses. 2. in *astronomy,* monthly.

**men·stru·ate** (men′strōō-āt′), *v.i.* [-ATED, -ATING], [< L. pp. of *menstruare* < *mensis,* month], to have a discharge of the menses. **—men′stru·a′tion,** *n.*

**men·stru·um** (men′strōō-əm), *n.* [*pl.* -STRUUMS, -STRUA (-ə)], [from alchemists' notion of the function of menstrual blood], a solvent.

**men·sur·a·ble** (men′shēr-ə-b'l), *adj.* measurable. **—men′sur·a·bil′i·ty,** *n.*

**men·su·ra·tion** (men′shə-rā′shən, -soo-), *n.* [< LL. < *mensuratus,* pp. < L. *mensura,* measure], 1. a measuring. 2. the branch of mathematics dealing with the determination of length, area, or volume.

**-ment** (mənt, mint), [Fr. < L. *-mentum*], a suffix meaning: 1. *a result* or *product of,* as in *improvement.* 2. *a means* or *instrument for,* as in *adornment.* 3. *the act, process,* or *art of,* as in *movement.* 4. *the state, fact,* or *degree of being,* as in *bereavement.*

**men·tal** (men′t'l), *adj.* [< OFr. < LL. *mentalis* < L. *mens,* the mind], 1. of or for the mind: as, *mental* aids. 2. done by or in the mind: as, *mental* arithmetic. 3. mentally ill: as, a *mental* patient. 4. for the mentally ill: as, a *mental* hospital.

**mental deficiency,** subnormality of intelligence.

**mental healing,** the treatment of diseases by mental concentration or hypnotic suggestion.

**men·tal·i·ty** (men-tal′ə-ti), *n.* [*pl.* -TIES], mental capacity, power, or activity; mind.

**men·tal·ly** (men′t'l-i), *adv.* 1. in, with, or by the mind. 2. as regards the mind.

**mental reservation,** a qualification (of a statement) that one thinks but does not express.

**men·thol** (men′thol, -thōl, -thôl), *n.* [G. < L. *mentha,* mint; + *-ol* (sense 1)], a white, waxy, crystalline alcohol, $C_{10}H_{19}OH$, obtained from oil of peppermint and used in medicine and perfumery.

**men·tho·lat·ed** (men′thə-lā′tid), *adj.* containing or impregnated with menthol.

**men·tion** (men′shən), *n.* [OFr. < L. *mentio* < stem of *mens,* the mind], a brief reference (to) or statement (about). *v.t.* to refer to or speak about briefly or incidentally. **—make mention of,** to mention. **—not to mention,** without even mentioning. **—men′tion·a·ble,** *adj.* **—men′tion·er,** *n.*

**men·tor** (men′tēr), *n.* 1. [M-], in *Gr. legend,* the loyal friend and wise adviser of Odysseus (Ulysses). 2. a wise, loyal adviser.

**men·u** (men′ū, mā′nū), *n.* [*pl.* -US], [Fr., small, detailed < L. *minutus;* see MINUTE, *adj.*], 1. a detailed list of the foods served at a meal; bill of fare. 2. the foods served.

**me·ow, me·ou** (mi-ou′, myou), *n.* [echoic], the characteristic vocal sound made by a cat. *v.i.* to make this sound. Also **miaow, mew,** etc.

**Me·phis·to** (mi-fis′tō), *n.* Mephistopheles.

**Meph·i·stoph·e·les** (mef′ə-stof′ə-lēz′), *n.* 1. in *medieval legend,* a devil to whom Faust sells his soul for riches and power. 2. a diabolical person. **—Me·phis·to·phe·le·an, Me·phis·to·phe·li·an** (mef′is-tə-fē′li-ən, mə-fis′-), *adj.*

**me·phit·ic** (me-fit′ik), *adj.* [< L. *mephitis,* a stench], 1. bad-smelling. 2. poisonous; noxious.

**mer·can·tile** (mũr′kən-til, -tīl′), *adj.* [Fr. < It. < *mercante,* a merchant < L. *mercans;* see MERCHANT], 1. of or characteristic of merchants or trade; commercial. 2. of mercantilism.

**mer·can·til·ism** (mũr′kən-til-iz′m, -tīl-), *n.* 1. the doctrine or policy that a balance of exports over imports is desirable, and that industry, agriculture, and commerce should be directed toward this objective. 2. the practice of this policy. Also **mercantile system. —mer′can·til·ist,** *n.*

**Mer·ca·tor's projection** (mẽr-kā′tẽrz), [< G. *Mercator* (1512–1594), Flemish cartographer], a method of making flat maps in which the lines of longitude and latitude are parallel straight lines (cf. illus. for spacing): areas on such maps become increasingly distorted toward the poles.

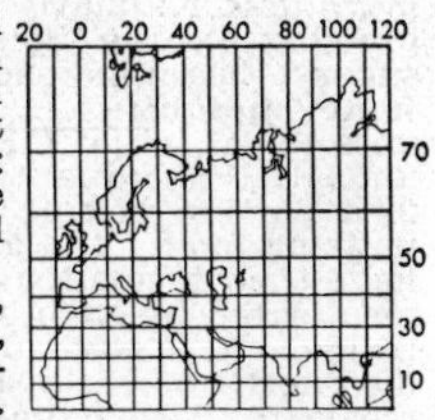

MERCATOR'S PROJECTION

**mer·ce·nar·y** (mũr′sə-ner′i), *adj.* [< L. < *merces,* wages], 1. working or done for payment only; venal; greedy. 2. designating a soldier serving for pay in a foreign army. *n.* [*pl.* -NARIES], 1. a mercenary soldier. 2. [Archaic], a hireling. **—mer′ce·nar′i·ly,** *adv.* **—mer′ce·nar′i·ness,** *n.*

**mer·cer** (mũr′sẽr), *n.* [< OFr. < *merz* (< L. *merx*), wares], [Brit.], a dealer in textiles.

**mer·cer·ize** (mũr′sə-rīz′), *v.t.* [-IZED, -IZING], [after J. *Mercer* (1791–1866), Eng. calico dealer], to treat (cotton thread or fabric) with a caustic alkali solution in order to strengthen it, give it a silky gloss, and make it more receptive to dyes.

**mer·cer·y** (mũr′sẽr-i), *n.* [*pl.* -IES], [Brit.], 1. goods sold by a mercer. 2. the business or shop of a mercer.

**mer·chan·dise** (mũr′chən-dīz′; *for n., also* -dīs′), *n.* [< OFr.; see MERCHANT], things bought and sold; goods; wares. *v.t. & v.i.* [-DISED, -DISING], to buy and sell; trade in (some kind of goods). Also sp. **merchandize. —mer′chan·dis′er,** *n.*

**mer·chant** (mũr′chənt), *n.* [OFr. *marchant* < LL. < L. *mercari,* to trade < *merx,* wares], 1. one whose business is buying and selling goods for profit. 2. one who sells goods at retail; storekeeper. *adj.* 1. of or used in trade; mercantile. 2. of the merchant marine.

**mer·chant·a·ble** (mũr′chən-tə-b'l), *adj.* marketable.

**mer·chant·man** (mũr′chənt-mən), *n.* [*pl.* -MEN], a vessel used in commerce; merchant ship.

**merchant marine,** 1. all the ships of a nation that are used in commerce. 2. their personnel.

**merchant prince,** a rich merchant.

**‡mer·ci** (mâr′sē′), *interj.* [Fr.], thank you.

**Mer·ci·a** (mũr′shi-ə, -shə), *n.* a former Anglo-Saxon kingdom of central England.

**Mer·ci·an** (mũr′shi-ən, -shən), *adj.* of Mercia, its people, etc. *n.* 1. a native or inhabitant of Mercia. 2. the Anglo-Saxon dialects of the Mercians.

**‡mer·ci beau·coup** (mâr′sē′ bō′kōō′), [Fr.], thanks very much.

**mer·ci·ful** (mũr′si-fəl), *adj.* full of mercy; having, feeling, or showing mercy; lenient; clement. **—mer′ci·ful·ly,** *adv.* **—mer′ci·ful·ness,** *n.*

**mer·ci·less** (mũr′si-lis), *adj.* without mercy; having, feeling, or showing no mercy; pitiless. **—mer′ci·less·ly,** *adv.* **—mer′ci·less·ness,** *n.*

**mer·cu·rate** (mũr′kyoo-rāt′), *v.t.* [-RATED, -RATING], to treat or combine with mercury or a compound of mercury.

**mer·cu·ri·al** (mẽr-kyoor′-i-əl), *adj.* 1. [M-], of Mercury (the god or planet). 2. of or containing mercury. 3. caused by the use of mercury. 4. having qualities suggestive of mercury; quick, quick-witted, changeable, fickle, etc. *n.* a drug or preparation containing mercury. **—mer·cu′ri·al·ly,** *adv.* **—mer·cu′ri·al·ness,** *n.*

**mer·cu·ri·al·ism** (mẽr-kyoor′i-əl-iz'm), *n.* chronic poisoning caused by mercury or its compounds.

**mer·cu·ri·al·ize** (mẽr-kyoor′iə-līz′), *v.t.* [-IZED, -IZING], 1. to make mercurial. 2. to treat with mercury or a compound of mercury.

**mer·cu·ric** (mẽr-kyoor′ik), *adj.* of or containing mercury, especially with a valence of two.

**mercuric chloride,** a very poisonous, white crystalline compound, $HgCl_2$, used as an antiseptic.

**mer·cu·ro·chrome** (mẽr-kyoor′ə-krōm′), *n.* [see MERCURY & -CHROME], 1. a crystalline dye, $C_{20}H_8O_6Br_2Na_2Hg$. 2. an aqueous solution of this, used as an antiseptic. A trade-mark (**Mercurochrome).**

**mer·cu·rous** (mẽr-kyoor′əs, mũr′kyoo-rəs), *adj.* of or containing mercury, especially with a valence of one.

**Mer·cu·ry** (mũr′kyoo-ri), *n.* [L. *Mercurius*], 1. in *Roman mythology,* the messenger of the gods, god of commerce, manual skill, eloquence, and cleverness: identified with the Greek Hermes. 2. the smallest planet in the solar system and the nearest to the sun: diameter, c. 3,000 mi.

MERCURY

**mer·cu·ry** (mũr′kyoo-ri), *n.* [*pl.* -RIES], [< *Mercury*], 1. a heavy, silver-white metallic chemical element, liquid at ordinary temperatures; quicksilver: it is used in thermometers, dentistry, etc.: symbol, Hg; at. wt., 200.61; at. no., 80. 2. the mercury column in a thermometer or barometer.

**mer·cy** (mũr′si), *n.* [*pl.* -CIES], [< OFr. < L. *merces,* payment, reward], 1. a refraining from harming or punishing offenders, enemies, etc.; kindness in excess of what may be expected. 2. a disposition to forgive or be kind. 3. the power to forgive or be kind; clemency. 4. kind or compassionate treatment. 5. a fortunate thing; blessing. *interj.* a mild exclamation of surprise, annoyance, etc. **—at the mercy of,** completely in the power of.

**mere** (mêr), *adj.* [superl. MEREST], [OFr. *mier;* L. *merus,* unmixed, pure], nothing more or other than; only (as said to be): as, he's a *mere* boy.

**mere** (mêr), *n.* [AS.], [Archaic, Poetic, or Brit. Dial.], 1. the sea. 2. a lake or pond.

**-mere** (mêr), [< Gr. *meros,* a part], a combining form meaning *part.*

**Mer·e·dith, George** (mer′ə-dith), 1828–1909; English novelist and poet.

**mere·ly** (mêr′li), *adv.* 1. no more than; and nothing else; only; simply. 2. [Obs.], wholly.

**mer·e·tri·cious** (mer′ə-trish′əs), *adj.* [< L. < *meretrix,* a prostitute < *mereri,* to serve for hire], alluring by false, showy charms; speciously attractive; flashy; tawdry. **—mer′e·tri′cious·ly,** *adv.* **—mer′e·tri′cious·ness,** *n.*

**mer·gan·ser** (mẽr-gan′sẽr), *n.* [*pl.* -SERS, -SER; see PLURAL, II, D, 1], [Mod. L. < L. *mergus,* diver + *anser,* goose], a large, fish-eating, diving duck with a long, slender, toothed beak and, usually, a crested head.

**merge** (mũrj), *v.i. & v.t.* [MERGED, MERGING], [L. *mergere,* to dip], to lose or cause to lose identity by being absorbed, swallowed up, or combined.

**merg·er** (mũr′jẽr), *n.* 1. a merging; specif., the combination of several companies, corporations, etc. in one. 2. something formed by merging.

**me·rid·i·an** (mə-rid′i-ən), *adj.* [< OFr. < L. < *meridies,* noon; ult. < *medius,* middle + *dies,* day], 1. of or at noon. 2. of or passing through the highest point in the daily course of any heavenly body. 3. of or along a meridian. 4. of or at the highest point, as of power. *n.* 1. the highest point reached by a heavenly body in its course. 2. the highest point of power, prosperity, etc.; zenith. 3. a great circle of the celestial sphere passing through the poles of the heavens and the zenith and nadir of any given point. 4. *a*) a great circle of the earth passing through the geographical poles and any given point on the earth's surface. *b*) the half of such a circle between the poles. *c*) any of the lines of longitude on a globe or map, representing such a circle or half circle.

**me·ringue** (mə-raŋ′), *n.* [Fr.], 1. egg whites beaten stiff and mixed with sugar, often browned in the oven and used as a covering for pies, cakes, etc. 2. a small cake made of this.

**me·ri·no** (mə-rē′no), *n.* [*pl.* -NOS], [< Sp. *merino,* shepherd < ML. *majorinus,* steward < L. *major,* greater], 1. one of a hardy breed of sheep with long, fine wool. 2. the wool. 3. a fine, soft yarn made from this wool, used for stockings, underwear, etc. 4. a soft, thin cloth made of this wool. *adj.* designating or of this sheep, wool, etc.

**mer·it** (mer′it), *n.* [< OFr. < L. *meritum* < pp. of *mereri,* to earn], 1. *sometimes pl.* the state, fact, or quality of deserving well or ill; desert. 2. worth; value; excellence. 3. something deserving reward, praise, etc. 4. a mark, badge, etc. awarded for excellence. 5. *pl.* actual qualities or facts, good or bad: as, decide the question on its *merits.* *v.t.* to deserve. **—mer′it·ed,** *adj.*

**mer·i·to·ri·ous** (mer′ə-tôr′i-əs, -tō′ri-), *adj.* having merit; deserving reward, praise, or honor. **—mer′i·to′ri·ous·ly,** *adv.* **—mer′i·to′ri·ous·ness,** *n.*

**merit system,** in civil service, a system of hiring

and promoting people on the basis of merit as determined by competitive examinations.

**merl, merle** (mũrl), *n.* [< OFr. < L. *merula*], [Archaic or Poetic], the European blackbird.

**Mer·lin** (mũr′lin), *n.* in *medieval legend*, a magician and seer, helper of King Arthur.

**mer·maid** (mũr′mād′), *n.* [see MERE (sea) & MAID], 1. a legendary sea creature with the head and trunk of a beautiful woman and the tail of a fish. 2. a girl or woman who swims well. **—mer′-man′** [*pl.* -MEN], *n.masc.*

**-mer·ous** (mẽr-əs), [< Gr. *meros*, a part], a suffix that means *having* (a specified number of) *parts.*

**Mer·o·vin·gi·an** (mer′ə-vin′ji-ən), *adj.* designating or of the Frankish line of kings who reigned in Gaul (ancient France) from c. 500 to 752 A.D. *n.* a king of this line.

**mer·ri·ment** (mer′i-mənt), *n.* merrymaking; gaiety and fun; mirth; hilarity.

**mer·ry** (mer′i), *adj.* [-RIER, -RIEST], [AS. *myrge*], 1. full of fun and laughter; gay; mirthful. 2. festive: as, the *merry* month of May. 3. [Archaic], *a*) pleasant. *b*) amusing. **—make merry,** to be hilarious or festive. **—mer′ri·ly,** *adv.* **—mer′ri·ness,** *n.*

**mer·ry-an·drew** (mer′i-an′drōō), *n.* [*merry* + *Andrew*, given name], a buffoon; clown.

**mer·ry-go-round** (mer′i-gō-round′), *n.* 1. a circular, revolving platform with wooden animals and seats on it, used as an amusement ride: it is turned by machinery, usually to music; carrousel. 2. a whirl; swift round, as of social life.

**mer·ry·mak·ing** (mer′i-māk′iŋ), *n.* 1. a making merry and having fun; festivity. 2. a cheerful festival or entertainment. *adj.* taking part in merrymaking; gay and festive. **—mer′ry·mak′er,** *n.*

**mer·thi·o·late** (mẽr-thī′ə-lāt′), *n.* [< sodium ethyl-*mer*curi-*thio*salicy*late*], a red or colorless liquid used as an antiseptic and germicide: a trade-mark (**Merthiolate**).

**me·sa** (mā′sə), *n.* [Sp. < L. *mensa*, a table], a small, high plateau or flat tableland with steep sides and, often, a layer of rock covering it.

**mé·sal·li·ance** (mā-zal′i-əns; Fr. mā′zȧ′lyäns′), *n.* [Fr.], marriage with one of lower social status.

**mes·cal** (mes-kal′), *n.* [Sp. *mezcal* < Nahuatl *mexcalli*], 1. a colorless alcoholic liquor made from the fermented juice of an agave. 2. the agave plant. 3. a small cactus whose buttonlike tops (**mescal buttons**) are chewed by the Indians for their stimulating effect.

**mes·dames** (mā-däm′), *n.pl.* [Fr.], plural of **madame, madam** (sense 1), or **Mrs.**: abbrev. **Mmes.**

**‡mes·de·moi·selles** (mād′mwȧ′zel′), *n.pl.* [Fr.], plural of **mademoiselle**: abbrev. **Mlles.**

**me·seems** (mē-sēmz′), *impersonal v.* [pt. -SEEMED], [Archaic], it seems to me: also **me·seem′eth.**

**mes·en·ter·y** (mes′′n-ter′i), *n.* [*pl.* -IES], [< ML. < Gr. < *mesos*, middle + *enteron*, intestine], a supporting membrane or membranes enfolding some internal organ and attaching it to the body wall or to another organ. **—mes′en·ter′ic,** *adj.*

**mesh** (mesh), *n.* [prob. < MD. *maesche*], 1. any of the open spaces of a net, screen, sieve, etc. 2. *pl.* the threads, cords, etc. forming these openings. 3. a net or network. 4. anything that snares or entangles. *v.t. & v.i.* 1. to entangle or become entangled. 2. to engage or become engaged: said of gears or gear teeth. **—in mesh,** with the gears engaged.

**mesh·work** (mesh′wũrk′), *n.* meshes; network.

**mes·mer·ism** (mes′mẽr-iz′m, mez′-), *n.* [after F. A. *Mesmer* (1734–1815), G. physician], hypnotism. **—mes·mer·ic** (mes-mer′ik, mez-), *adj.* **—mes·mer′i·cal·ly,** *adv.* **—mes′mer·ist,** *n.*

**mes·mer·ize** (mes′mə-rīz′, mez′-), *v.t.* [-IZED, -IZING], to hypnotize. **—mes′mer·iz′a·ble,** *adj.* **—mes′mer·i·za′tion,** *n.* **—mes′mer·iz′er,** *n.*

**mes·o-,** [< Gr. *mesos*, middle], a combining form meaning *in the middle, intermediate:* also **mes-.**

**mes·o·blast** (mes′ə-blast′), *n.* [*meso-* + *-blast*], the mesoderm. **—mes′o·blas′tic,** *adj.*

**mes·o·carp** (mes′ə-kärp′), *n.* [*meso-* + *-carp*], the middle layer of a pericarp.

**mes·o·derm** (mes′ə-dũrm′), *n.* [*meso-* + *-derm*], the middle layer of cells of an embryo. **—mes′o·der′mal,** *adj.*

**mes·on** (mes′on, mē′son), *n.* [< *mesotron*], an unstable particle, between the electron and the proton in mass, first observed in cosmic rays.

**Mes·o·po·ta·mi·a** (mes′ə-pə-tā′mi-ə), *n.* 1. an ancient country in SW Asia, between the Tigris and Euphrates rivers. 2. Iraq: the former name. **—Mes′o·po·ta′mi·an,** *adj. & n.*

**mes·o·tron** (mes′ə-tron′), *n.* [*meso* + elec*tron*], a meson.

**Mes·o·zo·ic** (mes′ə-zō′ik), *adj.* [*meso-* + *zo-* + *-ic*], designating or of the geological era after the Paleozoic and before the Cenozoic: see **geology,** chart. *n.* the Mesozoic Era.

**mes·quite, mes·quit** (mes-kēt′, mes′kēt), *n.* [Sp. *mezquite* < Nahuatl *mizquitl*], a spiny tree or shrub growing in the Southwest and in Mexico: its sugary, beanlike pods are eaten by cattle: also **honey mesquite.**

**mess** (mes), *n.* [< OFr. < L. *missus*, a course (at a meal)], 1. a quantity of food for a meal or dish. 2. a portion of soft food, as porridge. 3. unappetizing food. 4. a group of people who regularly have their meals together, as in the army. 5. the meal eaten by such a group. 6. a jumble; hodge-podge. 7. a state of trouble or difficulty. 8. a disorderly or dirty condition. *v.t.* 1. to supply meals to. 2. to make dirty or untidy. 3. to bungle; botch. *v.i.* 1. to eat as one of a mess (sense 4). 2. to make a mess. 3. to putter or meddle. **—mess around** (or **about**), to putter around. **—mess up,** to mess (*v.t.* 2 & 3).

**mes·sage** (mes′ij), *n.* [OFr. < ML. < pp. of L. *mittere*, to send], 1. any communication sent between persons. 2. a formal, official communication: as, the President's *message* to Congress. 3. an inspired communication, as of a poet.

**mes·sa·line** (mes′ə-lēn′, mes′ə-lēn′), *n.* [Fr.], a thin, soft, lustrous twilled silk cloth.

**mes·sen·ger** (mes′′n-jẽr), *n.* [< OFr. *messagier* (see MESSAGE)], 1. a person who carries a message or is sent on an errand. 2. [Archaic], a harbinger; forerunner.

**mess hall,** a room or building where a group, as of soldiers, regularly have their meals.

**Mes·si·ah** (mə-sī′ə), *n.* [< LL. < Gr. *Messias* < Aram. < Heb. *māshīah*, lit., anointed], 1. in *Judaism*, the promised and expected deliverer of the Jews. 2. in *Christianity*, Jesus. 3. [m-], any expected savior or liberator. Also **Messias** (-əs). **—Mes·si′ah·ship′, mes·si′ah·ship′,** *n.* **—Mes·si·an·ic, mes·si·an·ic** (mes′i-an′ik), *adj.*

**mes·sieurs** (mes′ẽrz; Fr. mā′syö′), *n.pl.* [Fr.], plural of **monsieur**: abbrev. **MM.**: see also **Messrs.**

**Mes·si·na** (mə-sē′nə, me-), *n.* a seaport in NE Sicily: pop., 221,000.

**mess jacket,** a man's fitted, waist-length jacket for semiformal wear in warm weather.

**mess kit,** the compactly arranged metal plates and eating utensils carried by a soldier or camper for use in the field: also **mess gear.**

**mess·mate** (mes′māt′), *n.* a person with whom one regularly has meals, as in the army.

**Messrs.** (mes′ẽrz), Messieurs: now used chiefly as the plural of **Mr.**

**mess·y** (mes′i), *adj.* [-IER, -IEST], in or like a mess; untidy, disordered, dirty, etc. **—mess′i·ly** *adv.* **—mess′i·ness,** *n.*

**mes·ti·zo** (mes-tē′zō), *n.* [*pl.* -ZOS, -ZOES], [Sp. < LL. *misticius*, of mixed race < L. pp. of *miscere*, to mix], a person of mixed parentage; esp., in the western U.S. and in Latin American countries, the offspring of a Spaniard or Portuguese and an American Indian. **—mes·ti′za** (-zə), *n.fem.*

**met** (met), pt. and pp. of **meet.**

**met.,** metropolitan.

**met·a-** (met′ə), [< Gr. *meta*, along with, after, between], a prefix meaning: 1. *changed, transposed*, as in *metamorphosis, metathesis.* 2. *after, beyond, higher*, as in *metaphysics*. Also **met-.**

**me·tab·o·lism** (mə-tab′ə-liz′m), *n.* [< Gr. *metabolē*, change < *meta*, beyond + *ballein*, to throw], the continuous processes in living organisms and cells, comprising those by which food is built up into protoplasm and those by which protoplasm is broken down into simpler substances or waste matter, with the release of energy for all vital functions. **—met·a·bol·ic** (met′ə-bol′ik), *adj.*

**me·tab·o·lize** (mə-tab′ə-līz′), *v.t. & v.i.* [-LIZED, -LIZING], to change by metabolism.

**met·a·car·pus** (met′ə-kär′pəs), *n.* [*pl.* -PI (-pī), -PUSES], [< Gr. < *meta*, beyond + *karpos*, the wrist], 1. the part of the hand, especially the five bones, between the wrist and the fingers. 2. the part of an animal's forelimb between the carpus and the phalanges. **—met′a·car′pal,** *adj. & n.*

**met·al** (met′′l), *n.* [OFr. < L. *metallum* < Gr. *metallon*, mine], 1. *a*) any of a class of chemical elements, as iron, gold, aluminum, etc., generally characterized by ductility, luster, conductivity of heat and electricity, and the ability to replace the hydrogen of an acid to form a salt. *b*) an alloy of such elements, as brass, bronze, etc. 2. any substance consisting of metal. 3. material; substance. 4. molten material for making glassware. 5. [Brit.], broken stone, cinders, etc. used as in making roads.

*adj.* made of metal. *v.t.* [-ALED or -ALLED, -ALING or -ALLING], to cover or supply with metal.
**metal.,** 1. metallurgical. 2. metallurgy.
**me·tal·lic** (mə-tal′ik), *adj.* 1. of, or having the nature of, metal. 2. containing, yielding, or producing metal. 3. like or suggestive of metal: as, a *metallic* sound. —**me·tal′li·cal·ly,** *adv.*
**met·al·lif·er·ous** (met′'l-if′ẽr-əs), *adj.* [< L. < *metallum*, metal + *ferre*, to bear], containing, yielding, or producing metal or ore.
**met·al·lur·gy** (met′'l-ũr′ji), *n.* [< Gr. < *metallon*, metal, mine + *-ergos*, working], the art or science of separating metals from their ores and preparing them for use, by refining, etc. —**met′al·lur′gi·cal, met′al·lur′gic,** *adj.* —**met′al·lur′gi·cal·ly,** *adv.* —**met′al·lur′gist,** *n.*
**met·al·work** (met′'l-wũrk′), *n.* 1. things made out of metal. 2. the making of such things: also **met′al·work′ing.** —**met′al·work′er,** *n.*
**met·a·mor·phic** (met′ə-môr′fik), *adj.* of, characterized by, causing, or formed by metamorphism or metamorphosis: also **met′a·mor′phous.**
**met·a·mor·phism** (met′ə-môr′fiz'm), *n.* 1. metamorphosis; change of form. 2. change in the structure of rocks under pressure, heat, etc., which makes limestone into marble, etc.
**met·a·mor·phose** (met′ə-môr′fōz, -fōs), *v.t. & v.i.* [-PHOSED, -PHOSING], to change in form; transform.
**met·a·mor·pho·sis** (met′ə-môr′fə-sis, -môr-fō′-), *n.* [*pl.* -SES (-sēz′)], [L. < Gr. *metamorphoun*, to transform < *meta*, over + *morphē*, form], 1. *a*) change of form or structure, especially by magic or sorcery. *b*) the form resulting from this. 2. a marked change of character, appearance, etc. 3. in *biology*, a change in form or function as a result of development; specif., the physical transformation undergone by various animals after the embryonic state, as of the tadpole to the frog.
**met·a·phor** (met′ə-fẽr, -fôr′), *n.* [< Fr. < L. < Gr.; ult. < *meta*, over + *pherein*, to carry], a figure of speech in which one thing is likened to another, different thing by being spoken of as if it were that other (e.g., "all the world's a stage"): cf. *simile.* —**mix metaphors,** to use two or more inconsistent metaphors in a single expression (e.g., the storm of protest was nipped in the bud). —**met′a·phor′i·cal** (-fôr′i-k'l, -for′-), **met′a·phor′ic,** *adj.* —**met′a·phor′i·cal·ly,** *adv.*
**met·a·phys·i·cal** (met′ə-fiz′i-k'l), *adj.* 1. of, or having the nature of, metaphysics. 2. very abstract or abstruse. 3. designating or of the school of early 17th-century English poets, whose verse is characterized by subtle, highly intellectualized imagery. —**met′a·phys′i·cal·ly,** *adv.*
**met·a·phys·ics** (met′ə-fiz′iks), *n.pl.* [construed as sing.], [< ML. < Gr. *meta ta physika*, after the *Physics* (of Aristotle)], 1. the branch of philosophy that deals with first principles and seeks to explain the nature of being and of the origin and structure of the world. 2. speculative philosophy in general. —**met′a·phy·si′cian** (-fə-zish′ən), *n.*
**me·tas·ta·sis** (mə-tas′tə-sis), *n.* [*pl.* -SES (-sēz′)], [LL. < Gr. < *meta*, after + *histanai*, to place], the shifting of disease from one part or organ of the body to another unrelated to it, as by the transfer of the cells of a malignant tumor. —**met·a·stat·ic** (met′ə-stat′ik), *adj.*
**me·tas·ta·size** (mə-tas′tə-sīz′), *v.i.* [-SIZED, -SIZING], in *medicine*, to spread to some other part or parts of the body by metastasis.
**met·a·tar·sus** (met′ə-tär′səs), *n.* [*pl.* -SI (-sī)], [*meta-*, after + *tarsus*], 1. the part of the foot between the ankle and toes. 2. the part of an animal's hind limb, between the tarsus and phalanges. —**met′a·tar′sal,** *adj. & n.*
**me·tath·e·sis** (mə-tath′ə-sis), *n.* [*pl.* -SES (-sēz′)], [LL. < Gr. < *meta*, over + *tithenai*, to place], transposition or interchange; specif., *a*) the transposition of letters or sounds in a word, as in *clasp* (from Middle English *clapse*). *b*) in *chemistry*, the interchange of elements or radicals between compounds. —**met·a·thet·ic** (met′ə-thet′ik), **met′a·thet′i·cal,** *adj.* —**met′a·thet′i·cal·ly,** *adv.*
**Met·a·zo·a** (met′ə-zō′ə), *n.pl.* [< *meta-* + Gr. *zōion*, animal], the large zoological division made up of all animals whose bodies are composed of many cells: cf. *Protozoa.* —**met′a·zo′an,** *adj. & n.* —**met′a·zo′ic,** *adj.*
**mete** (mēt), *v.t.* [METED, METING], [AS. *metan*], to allot; distribute; portion (*out*).
**mete** (mēt), *n.* [OFr. < L. *meta*], a boundary.
**met·em·psy·cho·sis** (met′əm-si-kō′sis, mi-temp′-si-), *n.* [*pl.* -SES (-sēz′)], [LL. < Gr. < *meta*, over + *empsychoun*, to put a soul into < *en*, in + *psychē*, soul], the supposed passing of the soul at death into another body; transmigration of souls.
**me·te·or** (mē′ti-ẽr), *n.* [< ML. < Gr. < *meteōra*, things in the air < *meta*, beyond + *eōra*, a hovering in the air], a meteoroid entering the atmosphere of the earth at very great speed and made white-hot by air friction; shooting star.
**me·te·or·ic** (mē′ti-ôr′ik, -or′-), *adj.* 1. atmospheric or meteorological. 2. of a meteor or meteors. 3. like a meteor; momentarily brilliant, flashing, or swift. —**me′te·or′i·cal·ly,** *adv.*
**me·te·or·ite** (mē′ti-ẽr-īt′), *n.* a mass of metal or stone that has fallen to earth from outer space; fallen meteor. —**me′te·or·it′ic** (-ə-rit′ik), *adj.*
**me·te·or·oid** (mē′ti-ẽr-oid′), *n.* any of the many small, solid bodies traveling through outer space.
**me·te·or·o·log·i·cal** (mē′ti-ẽr-ə-loj′i-k'l), *adj.* 1. of weather or climate. 2. of meteorology. Also **me′te·or·o·log′ic.** —**me′te·or·o·log′i·cal·ly,** *adv.*
**me·te·or·ol·o·gy** (mē′ti-ə-rol′ə-ji), *n.* [< Gr.; see METEOR & -LOGY], the science of the atmosphere and its phenomena; study of weather and climate. —**me′te·or·ol′o·gist,** *n.*
**me·ter** (mē′tẽr), *n.* [< OFr. < L. < Gr. *metron*, measure], 1. *a*) rhythm in verse; measured, patterned arrangement of syllables, primarily according to stress and length. *b*) the specific rhythmic pattern of a stanza. 2. rhythm in music; esp., the division into measures, or bars, having a uniform number of beats. 3. the basic unit of length in the metric system, equal to 39.37 inches. Also sp. **metre.**
**me·ter** (mē′tẽr), *n.* [< *mete* (to measure)], 1. a person who measures. 2. an apparatus for measuring and recording the quantity or rate of flow of gas, electricity, or water passing through it. *v.t.* to measure or record with a meter.
**-me·ter** (mē′tẽr, mi-), [Fr. *-mètre* or Mod. L. *-metrum*, both < Gr. *metron*, a measure], a suffix meaning: 1. *a device for measuring*, as in *barometer.* 2. *a*) (a specified number of) *meters*, as in *kilometer.* *b*) (a specified fraction of) *a meter*, as in *centimeter.* 3. *having* (a specified number of) *metrical feet*, as in *pentameter.*
**me·ter·age** (mē′tẽr-ij), *n.* 1. measurement. 2. the charge for measurement.
**Meth.,** Methodist.
**meth·ane** (meth′ān), *n.* [< *methyl* + *-ane*], a colorless, odorless, inflammable gas, $CH_4$, formed by the decomposition of vegetable matter, as in marshes: used as a fuel and for illumination.
**methane series,** a series of saturated hydrocarbons having the general formula $C_nH_{2n+2}$.
**meth·a·nol** (meth′ə-nōl′, -nol′), *n.* [< *methane* + *-ol* (alcohol)], a colorless, inflammable, poisonous liquid, $CH_3OH$, obtained by the distillation of wood and used as a fuel and in the manufacture of paints, etc.: also called *wood alcohol.*
**me·thinks** (mi-thiŋks′), *impersonal v.* [pt. -THOUGHT], [< AS. < *me*, to me + *thyncth*, it seems < *thyncan*, to seem], [Archaic], it seems to me: also **me·think′eth.**
**meth·od** (meth′əd), *n.* [< Fr. < L. < Gr. *methodos*, pursuit < *meta*, after + *hodos*, a way], 1. a way of doing anything; mode; process; esp., a regular, orderly procedure or way of teaching, investigating, etc. 2. system in doing things or handling ideas. 3. regular, orderly arrangement.
**me·thod·i·cal** (mə-thod′i-k'l), *adj.* characterized by method; orderly; systematic: also **me·thod′ic.** —**me·thod′i·cal·ly,** *adv.*
**Meth·od·ism** (meth′əd-iz'm), *n.* 1. the doctrines, organization, etc. of the Methodists. 2. [m-], excessive adherence to systematic procedure.
**Meth·od·ist** (meth′əd-ist), *n.* 1. a member of a Protestant Christian denomination that developed from the evangelistic teachings of John and Charles Wesley. 2. [m-], one who adheres to systematic procedure. *adj.* of or characteristic of the Methodists or Methodism. —**Meth′od·is′tic,** *adj.*
**meth·od·ize** (meth′ə-dīz′), *v.t.* [-IZED, -IZING], to make methodical; systematize. —**meth′od·iz′er,** *n.*
**meth·od·ol·o·gy** (meth′ə-dol′ə-ji), [< Gr. *methodos*, method; + *-logy*], 1. the science of method, or orderly arrangement. 2. a system of methods, as in any particular science. —**meth′od·o·log′i·cal** (-əd-ə-loj′i-k'l), *adj.*
**me·thought** (mi-thôt′), [Archaic], pt. of **methinks.**
**Me·thu·se·lah** (mə-thōō′z'l-ə, -thū′-), *n.* 1. in the

*Bible*, one of the patriarchs, said to have lived 969 years: Gen. 5:27. 2. a very old man.

**meth·yl** (meth′əl), *n.* [< Fr. or G.; ult. < Gr. *methy*, wine + *hylē*, wood], the monovalent hydrocarbon radical $CH_3$, found only in combination. **—me·thyl·ic** (me-thil′ik), *adj.*

**methyl alcohol,** methanol.

**meth·yl·ate** (meth′ə-lāt′), *v.t.* [-ATED, -ATING], to mix with methyl alcohol, often in order to make the resulting mixture undrinkable.

**methyl chloride,** a gas, $CH_3Cl$, which when compressed becomes a sweet, colorless liquid: it is used as a refrigerant and local anesthetic.

**me·tic·u·lous** (mə-tik′yoo-ləs), *adj.* [< Fr. < L. *meticulosus*, fearful < *metus*, fear], extremely or excessively careful about details; scrupulous; finical. **—me·tic′u·los′i·ty** (-los′ə-ti), *n.* **—me·tic′u·lous·ly,** *adv.*

**mé·tier** (mā-tyā′), *n.* [Fr. < OFr. *mestier* < L.; see MINISTRY], a trade, profession, or occupation.

**me·ton·y·my** (mə-ton′ə-mi), *n.* [*pl.* -MIES], [< LL. < Gr. < *meta*, change + *onyma*, name], use of the name of one thing for that of another associated with it (e.g., "the White House has decided" for "the President has decided"). **—met·o·nym·i·cal** (met′ə-nim′i-k'l), **met′o·nym′ic,** *adj.*

**me·tre** (mē′tēr), *n.* meter: chiefly Brit. spelling.

**met·ric** (met′rik), *adj.* 1 of or used in measurement. 2. *a*) of the meter (unit of length). *b*) designating or of the system of measurement based on the meter and the gram. 3. metrical.

**met·ri·cal** (met′ri-k'l), *adj.* 1. of or composed in meter or verse. 2. of, involving, or used in measurement; metric. **—met′ri·cal·ly,** *adv.*

**metric system,** a decimal system of weights and measures in which the gram (.0022046 pound), the meter (39.37 inches), and the liter (61.025 cubic inches) are the basic units of weight, length, and capacity, respectively.

**metric ton,** a measure of weight equal to 1,000 kilograms or 2,204.6 pounds.

**met·ro·nome** (met′rə-nōm′), *n.* [< Gr. *metron*, measure + *nomos*, law], 1. a clockwork device with an inverted pendulum that beats time, as in setting musical tempo, at a rate determined by the position of a sliding weight on the pendulum. 2. an electrical device that makes an intermittent sound or flashing light for similar use. **—met′ro·nom′ic** (-nom′ik), *adj.*

METRONOME

**me·trop·o·lis** (mə-trop′'l-is), *n.* [*pl.* -LISES], [L. < Gr. < *mētēr*, a mother + *polis*, a city], 1. the main city, often the capital, of a country, state, etc. 2. any large city or center of population, culture, etc. 3. the main diocese of an ecclesiastical province.

**met·ro·pol·i·tan** (met′rə-pol′ə-t'n), *adj.* 1. of or constituting a metropolis (senses 1 & 2). 2. designating or of a metropolitan (sense 2) or metropolis (sense 3). *n.* 1. a person who lives in and is wise in the ways of a metropolis (senses 1 & 2). 2. an archbishop having authority over the bishops of a church province.

**-me·try** (-mə-tri), [< Gr. < *metron*, measure], a terminal combining form meaning *the process, art,* or *science of measuring*, as in *geometry*.

**Met·ter·nich,** Prince **von** (met′ēr-nik), 1773–1859; Austrian statesman and diplomat.

**met·tle** (met′'l), *n.* [var. of *metal*, used figuratively], quality of character; spirit; courage; ardor. **—on one's mettle,** prepared to do one's best.

**met·tle·some** (met′'l-səm), *adj.* full of mettle; spirited, brave, etc.: also **met′tled** (-'ld).

**Meuse** (möz; Eng. mūz), *n.* a river in NE France, Belgium, and the Netherlands, flowing into the North Sea.

**mev, Mev** (mev), *n.* [*pl.* MEV, MEV], [*m*illion *e*lectron-*v*olts], a unit of energy equal to one million electron-volts.

**mew** (mū), *n.* [< OFr. < *muer* (< L. *mutare*), to change], 1. a cage, as for hawks while molting. 2. a secret place or den. See also **mews.** *v.t.* to confine in or as in a cage.

**mew** (mū), *n.* [echoic], the characteristic vocal sound made by a cat. *v.i.* to make this sound.

**mew** (mū), *n.* [AS. *mæw*], a sea gull or other gull: also **mew gull.**

**mewl** (mūl), *v.i.* [freq. of *mew* (to make the sound of a cat)], to cry weakly, like a baby; whimper.

**mews** (mūz), *n.pl.* [construed as sing.], [< *mew* (a cage)], a group of stables, as around a court.

**Mex.,** 1. Mexican. 2. Mexico.

**Mex·i·can** (mek′si-kən), *adj.* of Mexico, its people, their language, or their culture. *n.* 1. a native or inhabitant of Mexico. 2. Nahuatl.

**Mexican War,** a war between the U.S. and Mexico (1846–1848).

**Mex·i·co** (mek′si-kō′), *n.* a country in North America, south of the U.S.: area, 761,000 sq. mi.; pop., 34,626,000; capital, Mexico City. Mexican spelling, **México**; Spanish spelling, **Méjico.**

**Mexico, Gulf of,** a gulf of the Atlantic, east of Mexico and south of the U.S.

**Mexico City,** the capital of Mexico: pop., 3,302,000; officially **México, D.F.**

**mez·za·nine** (mez′ə-nēn′, -nin), *n.* [Fr. < It. < *mezzano*, middle < L.; see MEDIAN], a low-ceilinged story between two main stories in a building, sometimes in the form of a balcony projecting partly over the main floor: also **mezzanine floor.**

**mez·zo** (met′sō, med′zō, mez′ō), *adj.* [It. < L. *medius*, middle], in *music*, medium; moderate; half. *adv.* in *music*, moderately; somewhat.

**mez·zo-so·pra·no** (met′sō-sə-pran′ō, med′zō-sə-prä′nō, mez′ō-), *n.* [*pl.* -NOS, -NI (-i, -ni)], [It.], 1. a voice or part between soprano and contralto. 2. a singer with such a voice. *adj.* designating or of such a voice, part, etc.

**mez·zo·tint** (met′sə-tint′, med′zə-, mez′ə-), *n.* [< It.; see MEZZO & TINT], 1. a method of engraving on a copper or steel plate by scraping or polishing parts of a roughened surface to produce impressions of light and shade. 2. an engraving so produced. *v.t.* to engrave by this method.

**mf.,** in *music*, mezzo forte.

**mfd.,** manufactured.

**mfg.,** manufacturing.

**MFr., MF.,** Middle French.

**mfr.** [*pl.* MFRS.], manufacturer.

**Mg,** in *chemistry*, magnesium.

**mg.,** milligram; milligrams.

**MGr.,** 1. Medieval Greek. 2. Middle Greek.

**Mgr.,** 1. Manager. 2. Monseigneur. 3. Monsignor.

**MHG., M.H.G.,** Middle High German.

**mi** (mē), *n.* [It.], in *music*, a syllable representing the third tone of the diatonic scale.

**mi.,** 1. mile; miles. 2. mill; mills.

**Mi·am·i** (mī-am′i, -ə), *n.* a resort city on the SE coast of Florida: pop., 292,000.

**Miami Beach,** a resort city in SE Florida, on an island opposite Miami: pop., 63,000.

**mi·aow, mi·aou** (mi-ou′, myou), *n.* & *v.i.* meow.

**mi·as·ma** (mī-az′mə, mi-), *n.* [*pl.* -MAS, -MATA (-mə-tə)], [< Gr. < *miainein*, to pollute], poisonous vapor formerly supposed to arise from decomposing animal or vegetable matter, swamps, etc. **—mi·as′mal, mi′as·mat′ic, mi·as′mic,** *adj.*

**mibs** (mibs), *n.pl.* [Dial.], the game of marbles.

**Mic.,** Micah.

**mi·ca** (mī′kə), *n.* [L., a crumb; infl. by *micare*, to shine], any of a group of minerals that crystallize in thin, somewhat flexible, easily separated layers, resistant to heat and electricity: a transparent variety is often called *isinglass.* **—mi·ca·ceous** (mī-kā′shəs), *adj.*

**Mi·cah** (mī′kə), *n.* 1. a Hebrew prophet of the 8th century B.C. 2. a book of the Old Testament.

**mice** (mīs), *n.* pl. of **mouse.**

**Mich.,** 1. Michaelmas. 2. Michigan.

**Mi·chael** (mī′k'l), *n.* in the *Bible*, the archangel who victoriously warred with the rebel angel Lucifer: Rev. 12:7-9.

**Mich·ael·mas** (mik′'l-məs), *n.* the feast of the archangel Michael, celebrated September 29.

**Mi·chel·an·ge·lo** (mī′k'l-an′jə-lō′, mik′'l-), *n.* (*Michelangelo Buonarroti*), Italian painter, sculptor, architect, and poet; 1475–1564.

**Mi·chel·son, Albert Abraham** (mī′k'l-sən), 1852–1931; American physicist, born in Germany.

**Mich·i·gan** (mish′ə-gən), *n.* 1. a Middle Western State of the U.S.: area, 58,216 sq. mi.; pop., 7,823,000; capital, Lansing: abbrev. **Mich.** 2. one of the Great Lakes, between Michigan and Wisconsin: usually **Lake Michigan.**

**Mich·i·gan·der** (mish′ə-gan′dēr), *n.* a native or inhabitant of Michigan: also **Mich′i·gan·ite′** (-gən-īt′).

**mick·ey finn, Mick·ey Finn** (mik′i fin′), [Slang], a drink of liquor to which a narcotic or purgative has been secretly added: also **mickey, Mickey.**

**mick·le** (mik′'l), *adj., adv., n.* [AS. *micel*], [Archaic or Scot.], much.

**Mic·mac** (mik′mak), *n.* [*pl.* -MAC, -MACS], a member of a tribe of Algonquian Indians in Newfoundland and the Maritime Provinces of Canada.

**mi·cra** (mī′krə), *n.* pl. of **micron.**

**mi·cro-,** [< Gr. < *mikros*, small], a combining form meaning: 1. *little, small*, as in *microfilm.* 2. *en-*

*larging what is small*, as in *microscope*. 3. *microscopic*, as in *microchemistry*. 4. in the *metric system*, etc., *one millionth part of* (a specified unit), as in *microgram*. Also **micr-**.
**mi·crobe** (mī′krōb), *n.* [Fr. < Gr. *mikros*, small + *bios*, life], a very minute living thing, whether plant or animal; microorganism; esp., any of the bacteria that cause disease; germ. —**mi·cro′bic** (-krō′bik, -krob′ik), **mi·cro′bi·al**, *adj.*
**mi·cro·bi·ol·o·gy** (mī′krō-bī-ol′ə-ji), *n.* the branch of biology that deals with microorganisms.
**mi·cro·ceph·a·ly** (mī′krə-sef′ə-li), *n.* [*micro-* + *cephal-* + *-y*], a condition in which the head or cranial capacity is abnormally small. —**mi′cro-ceph′a·lous, mi′cro·ce·phal′ic** (-sə-fal′ik), *adj.*
**mi·cro·chem·is·try** (mī′krō-kem′is-tri), *n.* the chemistry of microscopic quantities or objects.
**mi·cro·cop·y** (mī′krə-kop′i), *n.* a photographic copy on microfilm.
**mi·cro·cosm** (mī′krə-koz′m), *n.* a little world; miniature universe; specif., man, a community, etc. regarded as a miniature of the world. —**mi′-cro·cos′mic, mi′cro·cos′mi·cal**, *adj.*
**mi·cro·film** (mī′krə-film′), *n.* film on which documents, printed pages, etc. are photographed in a reduced size for convenience in storage and use. *v.t. & v.i.* to photograph on microfilm.
**mi·cro·gram, mi·cro·gramme** (mī′krə-gram′), *n.* one millionth of a gram.
**mi·cro·groove** (mī′krə-grōōv′), *n.* a very narrow needle groove, as in a long-playing phonograph record: a trade-mark (**Microgroove**).
**mi·crom·e·ter** (mī-krom′ə-tẽr), *n.* [< Fr.; see MICRO- & -METER], 1. an instrument for measuring very small distances, angles, etc., used on a telescope or microscope. 2. micrometer calipers.
**micrometer calipers** (or **caliper**), calipers with a micrometer screw, for extremely accurate measurement.
**micrometer screw,** a finely threaded screw of definite pitch, with a head graduated to show how much the screw has been moved in or out.

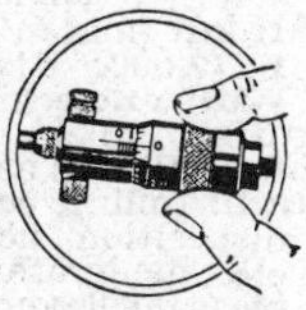

MICROMETER CALIPERS

**mi·crom·e·try** (mī-krom′ə-tri), *n.* measurement by means of micrometers. —**mi′cro·met′ric**, *adj.*
**mi·cron** (mī′kron), *n.* [*pl.* -CRONS, -CRA (-krə)], [< Gr. *mikros*, small], one millionth of a meter; one thousandth of a millimeter: symbol, *μ*.
**Mi·cro·ne·sia** (mī′krə-nē′zhə, -shə), *n.* the groups of islands in the Pacific north of the equator and east of the Philippines.
**Mi·cro·ne·sian** (mī′krə-nē′zhən, -shən), *adj.* of Micronesia, its people, their languages, etc. *n.* 1. a native of Micronesia. 2. any of the Austronesian languages spoken in Micronesia.
**mi·cro·or·gan·ism, mi·cro·ör·gan·ism, mi-cro-or·gan·ism** (mī′krō-ôr′gən-iz′m), *n.* any microscopic animal or vegetable organism; esp., any of the bacteria, protozoa, etc.
**mi·cro·phone** (mī′krə-fōn′), *n.* [*micro-* + *-phone*], an instrument for intensifying weak sounds or for transforming sound waves into electrical impulses, as for transmission by radio. —**mi′cro·phon′ic** (-fon′ik), *adj.*
**mi·cro·print** (mī′krə-print′), *n.* a photographic copy so greatly reduced that it can be read only through a magnifying device.
**mi·cro·scope** (mī′krə-skōp′), *n.* [see MICRO- & -SCOPE], an instrument consisting essentially of a lens or combination of lenses, for making very small objects, as microorganisms, look larger.
**mi·cro·scop·ic** (mī′krə-skop′ik), *adj.* 1. so small as to be invisible or obscure except through a microscope; minute. 2. of or with a microscope. 3. like or suggestive of a microscope. Also **mi′-cro·scop′i·cal**. —**mi′cro·scop′i·cal·ly**, *adv.*
**mi·cros·co·py** (mī-kros′kə-pi, mī′krə-skō′-), *n.* the use of a microscope; investigation by means of a microscope. —**mi·cros′co·pist**, *n.*
**mi·cro·wave** (mī′krə-wāv′), *n.* an extremely short electromagnetic wave, less than ten meters long.
**mic·tu·rate** (mik′choo-rāt′), *v.i.* [-RATED, -RATING], [< L. pp. of *micturire* < *mingere*, to urinate], to urinate. —**mic′tu·ri′tion** (-rish′ən), *n.*
**mid** (mid), *adj.* [*superl.* MIDMOST], [< AS. *midd*], middle. *n.* [Archaic], the middle.
**mid, ′mid** (mid), *prep.* [Poetic], amid.
**mid-**, a combining form meaning *middle* or *middle part of*, as in *midbrain, mid-Atlantic.*
**Mi·das** (mī′dəs), *n.* in *Gr. legend*, a king of Phrygia to whom Dionysus granted the power of turning everything that he touched into gold.
**mid·brain** (mid′brān′), *n.* the middle part of the brain.
**mid·day** (mid′dā′), *n.* [AS. *middæg*], the middle part of the day; noon. *adj.* of midday.
**mid·den** (mid′′n), *n.* [prob. < ON.], 1. [Brit. Dial.], a dunghill or refuse heap. 2. in *archaeology*, a heap of bones, shells, etc. marking the site of a prehistoric dwelling: also **kitchen midden.**
**mid·dle** (mid′′l), *adj.* [AS. *middel*], 1. halfway between two given points, times, etc.; equally distant from the ends, etc.; in the center. 2. intermediate; in between. 3. [M-], in *geology*, designating a division, as of a period, between *Upper* and *Lower*. 4. [M-], in *linguistics*, designating a stage in language development intermediate between *Old* and *Modern*: as, *Middle* English. *n.* 1. a point or part halfway between extremes; central point, time, etc. 2. something intermediate. 3. the middle part of the body; waist. *v.t. & v.i.* [-DLED, -DLING], to put in the middle.
**middle age,** the time of life between youth and old age: now usually applied to the years from about 40 to about 60. —**mid′dle-aged′**, *adj.*
**Middle Ages,** the period of European history between ancient and modern times, c. 500 A.D.–1450 A.D.
**middle C,** the musical note on the first ledger line below the treble staff and the first above the bass staff.
**middle class,** the social class between the aristocracy or very wealthy and the working class, or proletariat. —**mid′dle-class′**, *adj.*
**middle ear,** the tympanum.
**Middle East,** 1. the area including Iraq, Iran, Afghanistan, and, sometimes, India, Tibet, and Burma. 2. [Brit.], the Near East (sense 1), excluding the Balkans. —**Middle Eastern.**
**Middle English,** the English language as written and spoken between about 1125 and about 1475.
**Middle Greek,** Medieval Greek.
**Middle High German,** the language of the highlands of south and central Germany as it was written and spoken between about 1100 and about 1500.
**Middle Irish,** the Irish language as it developed in the later Middle Ages.
**Middle Latin,** Medieval Latin.
**Middle Low German,** the Germanic language of the NW European lowlands, as written and spoken between about 1100 and about 1450.
**mid·dle·man** (mid′′l-man′), *n.* [*pl.* -MEN], 1. a trader who buys commodities from the producer and sells them to the retailer or, sometimes, directly to the consumer. 2. a go-between.
**mid·dle·most** (mid′′l-mōst′), *adj.* midmost.
**middle school,** a school between elementary school and high school, usually having three or four grades, variously between 5 and 9.
**mid·dle·weight** (mid′′l-wāt′), *n.* a boxer or wrestler who weighs between 148 and 160 pounds. *adj.* of middleweights.
**Middle West, middle west,** that part of the U.S. between the Rocky Mountains and the Allegheny Mountains, north of the Ohio River and the southern borders of Kansas and Missouri. —**Middle Western.** —**Middle Westerner.**
**mid·dling** (mid′liŋ), *adj.* of middle size, quality, grade, state, etc.; medium. *adv.* [Colloq.], moderately; somewhat. *n.* 1. *pl.* products of medium quality, size, or price. 2. *pl.* particles of coarsely ground wheat mixed with bran.
**mid·dy** (mid′i), *n.* [*pl.* -DIES], a loose, hip-length blouse with a sailor collar, worn by women and children: in full, **middy blouse.**
**Mid·gard** (mid′gärd′), *n.* in *Norse mythology*, the earth, regarded as midway between heaven and hell: also **Mid′garth′** (-gärth′).
**midge** (mij), *n.* [AS. *mycg*], 1. a small gnat or gnatlike insect. 2. a very small person.
**midg·et** (mij′it), *n.* 1. a very small person. 2. anything very small of its kind. *adj.* very small of its kind; miniature.
‡**Mi·di** (mē′dē′), *n.* [Fr.], southern France.
**mid·i-** (mid′i), [< *mid* (middle), after *mini-*], a combining form meaning *of a length to the middle of the calf*, as in *midiskirt*.
**Mid·i·an·ite** (mid′i-ən-īt′), *n.* in the *Bible*, a member of a nomadic tribe of Arabs that fought the Israelites: Ex. 2:15-22, Numb. 31.
**mid·i·ron** (mid′ī′ẽrn), *n.* in *golf*, a club with a steel

or iron head, used for fairway shots of medium distance: now usually called *number 2 iron*.

**mid·land** (mid′lənd), *n.* 1. the middle region of a country; interior. 2. [M-], the English dialects of the Midlands. 3. [M-], a city in west central Texas: pop., 63,000. *adj.* 1. in or of the midland; inland. 2. [M-], of the Midlands. — **the Midlands,** the middle counties of England.

**mid·most** (mid′mōst′), *adj.* exactly in the middle, or nearest the middle. *adv.* in the middle or midst. *prep.* in the middle or midst of.

**mid·night** (mid′nīt′), *n.* the middle of the night; twelve o'clock at night. *adj.* 1. of or at midnight. 2. like midnight; very dark. —**burn the midnight oil,** to study or work very late at night.

**midnight sun,** the sun visible at midnight in the arctic or antarctic regions during the summer.

**mid·noon** (mid′no͞on′), *n.* [Rare], noon; midday.

**mid·rib** (mid′rib′), *n.* the central vein of a leaf.

**mid·riff** (mid′rif), *n.* [< AS. < *midd*, mid + *hrif*, belly], 1. the diaphragm; hence, 2. the middle part of the body, between the abdomen and the chest. *adj.* designating or of a garment that bares this part.

**mid·ship** (mid′ship′), *adj.* of the middle of a ship.

**mid·ship·man** (mid′ship′mən), *n.* [*pl.* -MEN], 1. a student in training for the rank of ensign in the U.S. Navy, especially at the Naval Academy at Annapolis. 2. a junior British naval officer ranking just below sublieutenant. 3. formerly, one of a class of ship's boys assigned to British naval vessels to be trained as officers.

**mid·ships** (mid′ships′), *adv.* amidships.

**midst** (midst, mitst), *n.* the middle; central part: now mainly in phrases. —**in our** (or **your, their**) **midst,** among or with us (or you, them). —**in the midst of,** 1. in the middle of. 2. during.

**midst, 'midst** (midst, mitst), *prep.* [Poetic], in the midst of; amidst; amid.

**mid·stream** (mid′strēm′), *n.* the middle of a stream.

**mid·sum·mer** (mid′sum′ẽr), *n.* 1. the middle of summer. 2. the time of the summer solstice, about June 21. *adj.* of, in, or like midsummer.

**mid·term** (mid′tũrm′), *adj.* at the middle of the term. *n.* [Colloq.], a midterm examination, as in a college course.

**mid-Vic·to·ri·an** (mid′vik-tôr′i-ən, -tō′ri-), *adj.* 1. of or characteristic of the middle part of Queen Victoria's reign in Great Britain (c. 1850–1890). 2. old-fashioned, prudish, morally strict, etc. *n.* 1. a person who lived during this period. 2. a person of mid-Victorian ideas, manners, etc. —**mid′-Vic·to′ri·an·ism,** *n.*

**mid·way** (mid′wā′, -wā′), *n.* 1. originally, a middle way or course. 2. that part of a fair or exposition where side shows and other amusements are located. *adj.* & *adv.* in the middle; halfway.

**Midway Islands,** a group of islands in the North Pacific, part of the Hawaiian group, about halfway between the U.S. mainland and the Philippines.

**mid·week** (mid′wēk′), *n.* & *adj.* (in) the middle of the week. —**mid′week′ly,** *adj.* & *adv.*

**Mid·west** (mid′west′), *n.* the Middle West. *adj.* Midwestern.

**Mid·west·ern** (mid′wes′tẽrn), *adj.* of, in, or characteristic of the Middle West.

**Mid·west·ern·er** (mid′wes′tẽr-nẽr), *n.* a native or inhabitant of the Middle West.

**mid·wife** (mid′wīf′), *n.* [*pl.* -WIVES], [AS. *mid*, with + *wif*, wife], a woman who helps women in childbirth.

**mid·wife·ry** (mid′wīf′ẽr-i, -wif′ri), *n.* the work of a midwife; obstetrics.

**mid·win·ter** (mid′win′tẽr), *n.* 1. the middle of the winter. 2. the time of the winter solstice, about December 22. *adj.* of, in, or like midwinter.

**mid·year** (mid′yêr′), *adj.* at the middle of the (calendar or academic) year. *n.* [Colloq.], a midyear examination, as in a college course.

**mien** (mēn), *n.* [short for *demean;* associated with Fr. *mine*, look, air], way of carrying and conducting oneself; bearing; manner.

**miff** (mif), *n.* [cf. G. *muffen*, to sulk], [Colloq.], a trivial quarrel or fit of the sulks; tiff or huff. *v.t.* & *v.i.* [Colloq.], to offend or take offense.

**might** (mīt), *v.* [AS. *mihte*], 1. pt. of **may.** 2. an auxiliary with present or future sense, generally equivalent to *may* (e.g., it *might* rain).

**might** (mīt), *n.* [AS. *miht*], great strength, power, force, or vigor. —**with might and main,** with strength and vigor.

**might·y** (mīt′i), *adj.* [-IER, -IEST], 1. having might; powerful; strong. 2. great; remarkably large, extensive, etc. *adv.* [Colloq.], very; extremel —**might′i·ly,** *adv.* —**might′i·ness,** *n.*

**mi·gnon** (min′yon; Fr. mē′nyōn′), *adj.* [fem. MIGNONNE (-yən; Fr. -nyôn′)], [Fr.], small, delicately formed, and pretty.

**mi·gnon·ette** (min′yə-net′), *n.* [< Fr. dim. of *mignon*], a plant with wedge-shaped leaves, and spikes of small, fragrant, greenish-white flowers.

**mi·graine** (mī′grān, mi-grān′), *n.* [Fr. < LL. *hemicrania* < Gr. < *hēmi-*, half + *kranion*, skull], a type of periodically returning headache, usually limited to one side of the head.

**mi·grant** (mī′grənt), *adj.* migrating. *n.* a person, bird, or other animal that migrates.

**mi·grate** (mī′grāt), *v.i.* [-GRATED, -GRATING], [< L. pp. of *migrare*, to migrate], 1. to move from one place to another; esp., to settle in another country. 2. to move from one region to another with the change in seasons, as many birds. —**mi′gra·tor,** *n.*

**mi·gra·tion** (mī-grā′shən), *n.* 1. a migrating. 2. a group of people or birds, fishes, etc. migrating together. 3. in *chemistry*, *a*) the shifting of position of one or more atoms within a molecule. *b*) the movement of ions toward an electrode. —**mi·gra′tion·al,** *adj.*

**mi·gra·to·ry** (mī′grə-tôr′i, -tō′ri), *adj.* 1. migrating; characterized by migration. 2. of migration. 3. roving; wandering.

**mi·ka·do** (mi-kä′dō), *n.* [*pl.* -DOS], [Japan. < *mi*, exalted + *kado*, gate], [often M-], the emperor of Japan: title used by non-Japanese.

**mike** (mīk), *n.* [Slang], a microphone.

**mil** (mil), *n.* [< L. *mille*, thousand], 1. a unit of length, equal to .001 of an inch, used in measuring the diameter of wire. 2. in *military usage*, a unit of angle measurement for artillery fire, equal to 1/6400 of the circumference of a circle.

**mil.,** 1. military. 2. militia.

**mi·la·dy, mi·la·di** (mi-lā′di), *n.* [Fr. < Eng. *my lady*], an English gentlewoman: Continental term.

**Mi·lan** (mi-lan′, mil′ən), *n.* a city in N Italy: pop., 1,277,000: Italian name, **Mi·la·no** (mē-lä′nô). —**Mil·a·nese** (mil′ə-nēz′), [*pl.* -NESE], *adj.* & *n.*

**milch** (milch), *adj.* [AS. *-milce*], giving milk; kept for milking: as, *milch* cows.

**mild** (mīld), *adj.* [AS. *milde*], 1. gentle or kind in disposition, action, or effect; not severe, harsh, etc.; moderate: as, a *mild* nature. 2. having a soft, pleasant flavor; not strong, bitter, etc.: said of tobacco, cheese, etc. —**mild′ly,** *adv.* —**mild′ness,** *n.*

**mil·dew** (mil′do͞o′, -dū′), *n.* [AS. *meledeaw*, lit., honeydew], 1. a fungus that attacks various plants or appears on damp cloth, paper, etc. as a furry, whitish coating. 2. any coating or discoloration so caused; mold. *v.t.* & *v.i.* to affect or be affected with mildew. —**mil′dew′y,** *adj.*

**mile** (mīl), *n.* [*pl.* MILES, *dial.* MILE], [< AS. < L. *milia* (*passuum*), thousand (paces)], a unit of linear measure, equal to 1,760 yards (5,280 feet or 1,609.35 meters), used in the U.S., Great Britain, etc.: in full, **statute mile.** The **geographical** (or **nautical, sea, or air**) **mile** is 1/60 of one degree of the earth's equator, by international agreement (1954), 6,076.10333 feet.

**mile·age** (mīl′ij), *n.* 1. an allowance for traveling expenses at a specified amount per mile. 2. total number of miles traveled. 3. expense or charge per mile, as for travel. Also sp. **milage.**

**mile·post** (mīl′pōst′), *n.* a signpost showing the distance in miles from a specified place.

**mil·er** (mīl′ẽr), *n.* one trained to run a mile race.

**mile·stone** (mīl′stōn′), *n.* 1. a stone or pillar set up to show the distance in miles from a specified place. 2. a significant event in history, in one's career, etc.

**mi·lieu** (mēl-yoo′; Fr. mē′lyö′), *n.* [Fr. < OFr. *mi*, middle + *lieu*, a place], surroundings; environment.

**mil·i·tant** (mil′i-tənt), *adj.* [< L. ppr. of *militare*, to serve as a soldier < *miles*, a soldier], 1. fighting. 2. ready and willing to fight. *n.* a militant person. —**mil′i·tan·cy,** *n.* —**mil′i·tant·ly,** *adv.*

**mil·i·ta·rism** (mil′i-tə-riz′m), *n.* 1. military spirit or its dominance in a nation. 2. a continuous and belligerent maintenance of strong armed forces. —**mil′i·ta·rist,** *n.* —**mil′i·ta·ris′tic,** *adj.* —**mil′i·ta·ris′ti·cal·ly,** *adv.*

**mil·i·ta·rize** (mil′i-tə-rīz′), *v.t.* [-RIZED, -RIZING], 1. to equip and prepare for war. 2. to fill with militarism; make warlike. —**mil′i·ta·ri·za′tion,** *n.*

**mil·i·tar·y** (mil′ə-ter′i), *adj.* [< Fr. < L. *militaris*, < *miles*, a soldier], 1. of, characteristic of, for, fit for, or done by soldiers. 2. of, for, or fit for war. 3. of the army. *n.* soldiers; the army; troops (with *the*). —**mil′i·tar′i·ly,** *adv.*

**military attaché,** an army officer attached to his nation's embassy or legation in a foreign land.

**military intelligence,** 1. information of military value to a nation. 2. the military branch whose work is getting and analyzing such information.

**military police,** troops assigned to carry on police duties for the army.
**mil·i·tate** (mil′ə-tāt′), *v.i.* [-TATED, -TATING], [< L. pp. of *militare*, to be a soldier], to be directed (*against*); operate or work (*against* or, rarely, *for*): said of facts, actions, etc.
**mi·li·tia** (mə-lish′ə), *n.* [L., soldiery < *miles*, a soldier], any army composed of citizens rather than professional soldiers, called out in time of emergency. **—mi·li′tia·man** [*pl.* -MEN], *n.*
**milk** (milk), *n.* [AS. *meolc*], 1. a white liquid secreted by the mammary glands of female mammals for suckling their young; esp., cow's milk. 2. any liquid like this, as coconut milk. *v.t.* 1. to draw milk from the mammary glands of (a cow, etc.). 2. to extract as if by milking. 3. to extract money, ideas, information, etc. from as if by milking. 4. to extract sap, venom, etc. from. *v.i.* 1. to give milk. 2. to draw milk. **—milk′er,** *n.* **—milk′ing,** *n.*
**milk-and-wa·ter** (milk′ən-wô′tẽr, -wät′ẽr), *adj.* insipid; weak; wishy-washy; namby-pamby.
**milk leg,** a painful swelling of the legs, caused by clotting of the femoral veins, as in childbirth.
**milk·maid** (milk′mād′), *n.* a girl or woman who milks cows or works in a dairy; dairymaid.
**milk·man** (milk′man′), *n.* [*pl.* -MEN], a man who sells or delivers milk.
**milk of human kindness,** natural feelings of sympathy, generosity, etc.
**milk of magnesia,** a milky-white fluid, a suspension of magnesium hydroxide, $Mg(OH)_2$, in water, used as a laxative and antacid.
**milk shake,** a drink made of milk, flavoring, and, usually, ice cream, mixed until frothy.
**milk·shed** (milk′shed′), *n.* [after *watershed*], all the dairy farms supplying milk for a given city.
**milk snake,** a small, harmless snake, gray with black markings: also **milk adder, house snake.**
**milk·sop** (milk′sop′), *n.* an effeminate man or boy; mollycoddle; sissy.
**milk sugar,** lactose, a sugar obtained from milk.
**milk tooth,** any of the temporary, first set of teeth in a young child or other mammal: also called *baby tooth, deciduous tooth.*
**milk·weed** (milk′wēd′), *n.* any of a group of plants with a milky juice.
**milk·y** (mil′ki), *adj.* [-IER, -IEST], 1. like milk; white as milk. 2. of or containing milk. 3. mild, timid, or effeminate. **—milk′i·ness,** *n.*
**Milky Way,** a broad, faintly luminous band seen across the sky at night, consisting of very distant stars and nebulae; the Galaxy.
**mill** (mil), *n.* [AS. *mylen* < LL. *molina* < L. *mola*, millstone], 1. a building with machinery for grinding grain into flour or meal. 2. a machine for grinding grain. 3. a machine for grinding or crushing any solid material: as, a coffee *mill.* 4. any of various machines for cutting, stamping, shaping, etc. 5. a factory: as, a textile *mill.* 6. a raised edge, ridged surface, etc. made by milling. *v.t.* 1. to grind, work, form, etc. by, in, or as in a mill. 2. to raise and ridge the edge of (a coin). *v.i.* to move (*around*) slowly in a circle, as cattle or a confused crowd. **—through the mill,** [Colloq.], through a hard, painful, instructive experience. **—milled,** *adj.*
**mill** (mil), *n.* [for L. *millesimus*, thousandth < *mille*, thousand], one tenth of a cent; $.001: a unit used in calculating but not as a coin.
**Mill, John Stuart** (mil), 1806–1873; English philosopher and political economist.
**Mil·lay, Edna St. Vincent** (mi-lā′), 1892–1950; U.S. poet.
**mill·dam** (mil′dam′), *n.* a dam built across a stream to raise its level enough to provide water power for turning a mill wheel.
**mil·len·ni·um** (mi-len′i-əm), *n.* [*pl.* -NIUMS, -NIA (-ə)], [< L. *mille*, thousand + *annus*, year], 1. a period of a thousand years. 2. in *theology*, the period of a thousand years during which Christ will reign on earth (with *the*): Rev. 20:1-5. 3. any period of great happiness, peace, prosperity, etc. **—mil·len′ni·al,** *adj.*
**mil·le·pede** (mil′ə-pēd′), *n.* [< L. < *mille*, thousand + *pes*, a foot], a wormlike arthropod with two pairs of legs on each of most of its segments: also **mil′li·pede, mil′li·ped′** (-ped′).
**mil·le·pore** (mil′ə-pôr′, -pōr′), *n.* [< Fr. < *mille*, thousand + *pore*, a pore], any of a group of hydrozoans that form leaflike masses of coral.
**mill·er** (mil′ẽr), *n.* 1. one who owns or operates a mill, especially a flour mill. 2. a tool used for milling. 3. a moth with wings that look dusty, suggesting a miller's clothes.
**Mill·er, Joe** (mil′ẽr), 1684–1738; English comedian: a book of jokes attributed to him was published in 1739.
**mill·er's-thumb** (mil′ẽrz-thum′), *n.* any of several small fresh-water fishes with spiny fins.
**mil·let** (mil′it), *n.* [see PLURAL, II, D, 3], [Fr., dim. of *mil* < L. *milium*, millet], 1. a cereal grass whose small grain is used for food in Europe and Asia. 2. the grain. Millet is used for hay in both the U.S. and Europe.
**Mil·let, Jean Fran·çois** (zhän′ frän′swȧ′ mē′le′; Eng. mi-lā′), 1814–1875; French painter.
**mil·li-,** [< L. *mille*, thousand], a combining form meaning: 1. *one thousandth part of* (a specified unit), as in *millimeter.* 2. *one thousand.*
**mil·li·am·pere** (mil′i-am′pêr), *n.* one thousandth of an ampere.
**mil·liard** (mil′yẽrd, -yärd), *n.* [Fr. < Pr. *milhar*, thousand; ult. < L. *mille*, thousand], [Brit.], one thousand millions; billion.
**mil·li·gram, mil·li·gramme** (mil′ə-gram′), *n.* one thousandth of a gram.
**mil·li·li·ter, mil·li·li·tre** (mil′ə-lē′tẽr), *n.* one thousandth of a liter.
**mil·li·me·ter, mil·li·me·tre** (mil′ə-mē′tẽr), *n.* one thousandth of a meter (.03937 inch).
**mil·li·mi·cron** (mil′ə-mī′kron), *n.* [*pl.* -CRONS, -CRA], one thousandth of a micron, or ten angstroms: a unit of length for measuring waves of light, etc.
**mil·li·ner** (mil′ə-nẽr), *n.* [< *Milaner*, importer of silks, etc. from Milan], a person who designs, makes, or sells women's hats, etc.
**mil·li·ner·y** (mil′ə-ner′i, -nẽr-), *n.* 1. women's hats, headdresses, etc. 2. the work or business of making or selling women's hats, etc.
**mill·ing** (mil′iŋ), *n.* 1. the process or business of grinding grain into flour. 2. the grinding, cutting, or working of metal, cloth, etc. in a mill.
**milling machine,** a power tool for cutting and grinding metal parts.
**mil·lion** (mil′yən), *n.* [OFr. < It. *milione* < *mille* (< L. *mille*), thousand], 1. a thousand thousands; 1,000,000. 2. an indefinite but very large number. *adj.* 1. one thousand thousand. 2. very many. **—mil′lionth,** *adj. & n.*
**mil·lion·aire** (mil′yən-âr′), *n.* 1. a person whose wealth comes to at least a million dollars, pounds, francs, etc. 2. a very wealthy person. Also sp. **millionnaire.**
**mil·lion·fold** (mil′yən-fōld′), *adj. & adv.* [see -FOLD], a million times as much or as many.
**mil·li·pede** (mil′ə-pēd′), *n.* a millepede: also **mil′li·ped′** (-ped′).
**mill·pond** (mil′pond′), *n.* a pond from which water flows for driving a mill wheel.
**mill·race** (mil′rās′), *n.* 1. the current of water that drives a mill wheel. 2. the channel in which it runs.
**mill·stone** (mil′stōn′), *n.* 1. either of a pair of large, flat, round stones used for grinding grain, etc. 2. a heavy burden: Matt. 18:6. 3. something that grinds, pulverizes, or crushes.
**mill·stream** (mil′strēm′), *n.* the water flowing in a millrace.
**mill wheel,** the wheel, usually a water wheel, that drives the machinery in a mill.
**mill·work** (mil′wũrk′), *n.* 1. doors, windows, etc. made in a planing mill. 2. work done in a mill. **—mill′work′er,** *n.*
**mill·wright** (mil′rīt′), *n.* 1. one who designs, builds, or installs mills or their machinery. 2. a worker who installs or repairs the machinery in a mill.
**mi·lord** (mi-lôrd′), *n.* [Fr. < Eng. *my lord*], an English nobleman or gentleman: Continental term.
**milque·toast** (milk′tōst′), *n.* [< Caspar *Milquetoast*, comic-strip character by H. T. Webster (1885–1952)], any timid, shrinking, apologetic person.
**mil·reis** (mil′rās′), *n.* [*pl.* -REIS], [Port. *mil reis*, a thousand reis], 1. a former Brazilian monetary unit and silver coin. 2. a former Portuguese monetary unit and gold coin.
**milt** (milt), *n.* [AS. *milte*], 1. the reproductive glands of male fishes, especially when filled with the milky fluid containing the germ cells. 2. such fish sperm. *adj.* breeding: said of male fishes. *v.t.* to fertilize (fish roe) with milt.
**Mil·ton, John** (mil′t'n), 1608–1674; English poet. **—Mil·ton′ic** (-ton′ik), **Mil·to′ni·an** (-tō′ni-ən), *adj.*

**Mil·wau·kee** (mil-wô'ki), *n.* a city in SE Wisconsin, on Lake Michigan: pop., 744,000.

**mime** (mīm), *n.* [< L. < Gr. *mimos*], 1. an ancient Greek or Roman farce, in which people and events were mimicked and burlesqued. 2. an actor in such a farce. 3. a clown or mimic. *v.t.* [MIMED, MIMING], to mimic or act out as a mime. *v.i.* to act as a mime, usually without speaking. —**mim'er,** *n.*

**mim·e·o·graph** (mim'i-ə-graf', -gräf'), *n.* [< Gr. *mimeisthai,* to imitate; + *-graph*], a machine for making copies of written or typewritten matter by means of a stencil: formerly a trade-mark (**Mimeograph**). *v.t.* 1. to make copies of on such a machine. 2. to make (copies) on such a machine.

**mi·met·ic** (mi-met'ik, mī-), *adj.* [< Gr. < *mimeisthai,* to imitate], 1. imitative; of or characterized by imitation. 2. make-believe. 3. of or characterized by mimicry. —**mi·met'i·cal·ly,** *adv.*

**mim·ic** (mim'ik), *adj.* [< L. < Gr. < *mimos,* a mime], 1. imitative. 2. of, or having the nature of, mimicry or imitation. 3. make-believe; mock. *n.* a person or thing that imitates; esp., an actor skilled in mimicry. *v.t.* [-ICKED, -ICKING], 1. to imitate in speech or action, as in ridicule. 2. to copy closely. 3. to exhibit mimicry (sense 2). —**mim'ick·er,** *n.*

**mim·ic·ry** (mim'ik-ri), *n.* [*pl.* -RIES], 1. the practice, art, instance, or way of mimicking. 2. close resemblance of one organism to another or to some object in its environment.

**mi·mo·sa** (mi-mō'sə, -zə), *n.* [< L. *mimus;* see MIME], a tree, shrub, or herb of the pea family, growing in warm regions and usually having feathery leaves and spikes of small white or pink flowers.

**min.,** 1. mineralogy. 2. minim(s). 3. minimum. 4. mining. 5. minor. 6. minute(s).

**mi·na, mi·nah** (mī'nə), *n.* a myna.

**min·a·ret** (min'ə-ret', min'ə-ret'), *n.* [< Sp. < Turk. < Ar. *manārah,* lamp, lighthouse], a high, slender tower attached to a Moslem mosque, with balconies from which a muezzin cries the call to prayer.

MINARET

**min·a·to·ry** (min'ə-tôr'i, -tō'ri), *adj.* [< OFr. < LL. < L. *minari,* to threaten], menacing; threatening: also **min'a·to'ri·al.** —**min'a·to'ri·ly,** *adv.*

**mince** (mins), *v.t.* [MINCED, MINCING], [OFr. *mincier* < LL. < L. *minutus,* small], 1. to cut up (meat, etc.) into very small pieces. 2. to express or do with affected elegance or daintiness. 3. to lessen the force of; weaken: as, I *minced* no words. *v.i.* 1. to speak or behave with affected elegance or daintiness. 2. to walk with short steps or in an affected, dainty manner. *n.* mincemeat. —**not mince matters,** to speak frankly. —**minc'er,** *n.*

**mince·meat** (mins'mēt'), *n.* a mixture of chopped apples, spices, suet, raisins, and (now rarely) meat, used as a pie filling. —**make mincemeat of,** to defeat or refute completely.

**mince pie,** a pie with a filling of mincemeat.

**minc·ing** (min'siŋ), *adj.* 1. affectedly elegant or dainty. 2. with short steps or affected daintiness: as, a *mincing* walk. —**minc'ing·ly,** *adv.*

**mind** (mīnd), *n.* [AS. (*ge*)*mynd*], 1. memory or remembrance: as, this brings to *mind* a story. 2. *a*) what one thinks; opinion: as, speak your *mind.* *b*) what one intends or wills; purpose or desire: as, to change one's *mind.* 3. *a*) that which thinks, perceives, feels, etc.; the seat of consciousness. *b*) the intellect. *c*) the psyche (sense 2*b*). 4. reason; sanity: as, to lose one's *mind.* 5. a person having intelligence: as, the great *minds* of today. 6. way, state, or direction of thinking and feeling: as, the reactionary *mind.* 7. in *religion,* a Mass in memory of a dead person: a *month's mind* is said one month after death. *v.t.* 1. to direct one's mind to; specif., *a*) to perceive; observe. *b*) to pay attention to; heed. *c*) to obey: as, the dog *minds* his master. *d*) to take care of; look after: as, *mind* the baby. *e*) to be careful about: as, *mind* those rickety stairs. 2. *a*) to care about; feel concern about. *b*) to object to; dislike: as, I don't *mind* the cold. 3. [Dial.], to remember. 4. [Dial. or Archaic], to remind. *v.i.* 1. to pay attention; give heed. 2. to be obedient. 3. to be careful. 4. *a*) to care; feel concern. *b*) to object. —**bear** (or **keep**) **in mind,** to remember. —**be in one's right mind,** to be sane. —**be out of one's mind,** 1. to be mentally ill. 2. to be frantic (*with* worry, grief, etc.). —**call to mind,** 1. to remember. 2. to be a reminder of. —**give a person a piece of one's mind,** to criticize or rebuke sharply. —**have a (good** or **great) mind to,** to feel (strongly) inclined to. —**have half a mind to,** to be somewhat inclined to. —**have in mind,** 1. to remember. 2. to think of. 3. to intend; purpose. —**keep one's mind on,** to pay attention to. —**know one's mind,** to know one's real thoughts, feelings, etc. —**make up one's mind,** to form a definite opinion or decision. —**meeting of minds,** an agreement. —**never mind,** don't concern yourself; it doesn't matter. —**on one's mind,** 1. occupying one's thoughts. 2. worrying one. —**put in mind,** to remind. —**set one's mind on,** to be determinedly desirous of. —**take one's mind off,** to turn one's thoughts or attention from. —**to one's mind,** in one's opinion. —**mind'er,** *n.*

**Min·da·na·o** (min'dä-nou'), *n.* the southernmost large island of the Philippine Islands.

**mind·ed** (mīn'did), *adj.* 1. having a (specified kind of) mind: as, *high-minded, weak-minded.* 2. inclined; disposed: as, I am *minded* to go.

**mind·ful** (mīnd'fəl), *adj.* having in mind; aware or careful (*of*): as, I am *mindful* of the danger. —**mind'ful·ly,** *adv.* —**mind'ful·ness,** *n.*

**mind·less** (mīnd'lis), *adj.* 1. lacking a mind; without intelligence. 2. taking no thought; heedless (*of*). —**mind'less·ly,** *adv.* —**mind'less·ness,** *n.*

**Min·do·ro** (min-dō'rō), *n.* one of the Philippine Islands, south of Luzon.

**mind reader,** one who professes to be able to perceive another's thoughts. —**mind reading.**

**mind's eye,** the imagination.

**mine** (mīn), *pron.* [AS. *min*], that or those belonging to me: the absolute form of *my,* used without a following noun, as, a friend of *mine,* this is *mine.* *possessive pronominal adj.* [Mainly Archaic & Poetic], my: formerly used before a vowel or *h* (e.g., *mine* eyes, *mine* honor), now used after a noun in direct address (e.g., son *mine*).

**mine** (mīn), *n.* [OFr.; ? < Celt.], 1. a large excavation made in the earth, from which to extract metallic ores, coal, etc. 2. a deposit of ore, coal, etc. 3. any great source of supply: as, a *mine* of information. 4. a firework that explodes in the air and scatters a number of smaller fireworks. 5. in *military science, a*) a tunnel dug under an enemy's trench, fort, etc., in which an explosive is placed to destroy the enemy fortifications. *b*) an explosive charge in a container, buried in the ground (see **land mine**), or placed in the sea for destroying enemy ships, and set off by direct contact, by a time fuse, etc. *v.i.* [MINED, MINING], 1. to dig a mine; specif., to dig ores, coal, etc. from the earth. 2. to place explosive mines on land or in water. *v.t.* 1. *a*) to dig in (the earth) for ores, coal, etc. *b*) to dig (ores, coal, etc.) from the earth. 2. to destroy, or try to destroy, with explosive mines. 3. to undermine slowly by secret methods.

**mine detector,** an electromagnetic device for locating the position of buried explosive mines.

**mine field,** an area on land or in water where explosive mines have been set.

**mine-lay·er** (mīn'lā'ēr), *n.* a ship especially equipped to lay explosive mines in the water.

**min·er** (mīn'ēr), *n.* a person whose work is digging coal, ore, etc. in a mine.

**min·er·al** (min'ēr-əl, min'rəl), *n.* [OFr. < ML. neut. of *mineralis* < *minera,* a mine], 1. an inorganic substance occurring naturally in the earth and having distinctive physical properties and a composition that can be expressed by a chemical formula: sometimes applied to similar organic substances, as coal. 2. any naturally occurring substance that is neither vegetable nor animal. *adj.* of, like, or containing a mineral or minerals.

**mineral.,** mineralogy.

**min·er·al·ize** (min'ēr-ə-līz', min'rə-), *v.t.* [-IZED, -IZING], 1. to convert (a metal) into an ore. 2. to petrify (organic matter). 3. to impregnate (water, etc.) with minerals. —**min'er·al·i·za'tion,** *n.* —**min'er·al·iz'er,** *n.*

**min·er·al·o·gy** (min'ēr-al'ə-ji, -äl'-), *n.* 1. the science of minerals. 2. [*pl.* -GIES], a book or treatise on minerals. —**min'er·a·log'i·cal,** *adj.* —**min'er·a·log'i·cal·ly,** *adv.* —**min'er·al'o·gist,** *n.*

**mineral oil,** any oil of mineral origin; specif., *a*) petroleum. *b*) a colorless, tasteless oil derived from petroleum and used as a laxative.

**mineral water,** water naturally or artificially impregnated with mineral salts or gases.

**mineral wool,** a fibrous material made from melted slag and used as wall insulation.

**Mi·ner·va** (mi-nũr'və), *n.* the ancient Roman goddess of wisdom, technical skill, and invention: identified with the Greek Athena.

**mi·ne·stro·ne** (min'ə-strō'ni), *n.* [It.; ult. < L. *ministrare,* to serve], a thick vegetable soup containing vermicelli, barley, etc. in a meat broth.

**mine sweeper,** a ship especially equipped for destroying or removing enemy mines at sea.

**Ming** (miŋ), *n.* a Chinese dynasty ruling from 1368 to 1644. *adj.* of this dynasty: as, a *Ming* vase.

**min·gle** (miŋ′g'l), *v.t.* [-GLED, -GLING], [< AS. *mengan*, to mix], to mix together; combine; blend. *v.i.* 1. to be or become mixed, blended, etc. 2. to join or unite with others. **—min′gler,** *n.*

**min·i-** (min′i), [< *mini*ature], a combining form meaning *smaller, shorter, lesser,* etc. *than usual*, as in *miniskirt.*

**min·i·a·ture** (min′i-ə-chẽr, -i-chẽr), *n.* [Fr. < It. *miniatura* < ML. < L. *miniare*, to paint red < *minium*, red lead], 1. *a)* a small painting, especially a portrait. *b)* the art of making these. 2. a copy or model on a very small scale. *adj.* done on a very small scale; minute. **—in miniature,** on a small scale; greatly reduced. **—min′i·a·tur·ist,** *n.*

**min·i·a·tur·ize** (min′i-ə-chẽr-īz′, -i-chẽr-), *v.t.* [-IZED, -IZING], to design and build (industrial and military devices) in a small, compact form.

**min·im** (min′im), *n.* [< L. *minimus*, least, superl. of *minor*, lesser], 1. the smallest liquid measure, 1/60 fluid dram, or about a drop. 2. a tiny portion. 3. in *music*, a half note (𝅗𝅥). *adj.* smallest.

**min·i·mize** (min′ə-mīz′), *v.t.* [-MIZED, -MIZING], to reduce to or estimate at a minimum, or the least possible amount, degree, etc. **—min′i·mi·za′tion,** *n.* **—min′i·miz′er,** *n.*

**min·i·mum** (min′ə-məm), *n.* [*pl.* -MUMS, -MA (-mə)], [L., neut. of *minimus*, least], 1. the smallest quantity, number, or degree possible or permissible. 2. the lowest degree or point reached or recorded. *adj.* 1. smallest possible, permissible, or reached. 2. of, marking, or setting a minimum or minimums. Opposed to *maximum.* **—min′i·mal,** *adj.*

**minimum wage,** a wage established by contract or by law as the lowest that may be paid to employees doing a specified type of work.

**min·ing** (mīn′iŋ), *n.* the act, process, or work of removing ores, coal, etc. from a mine.

**min·ion** (min′yən), *n.* [Fr. *mignon*, darling], 1. a favorite, especially one who is a servile follower: term of contempt. 2. in *printing*, a size of type, 7 point. *adj.* [Rare], dainty, pretty, etc.

**minion of the law,** a policeman.

**min·is·ter** (min′is-tẽr), *n.* [< OFr. < L. *minister*, a servant < *minor*, lesser], 1. a person appointed to take charge of some governmental department. 2. a diplomatic officer sent to a foreign nation to represent his government. 3. anyone authorized to carry out the spiritual functions of a church, conduct worship, preach, etc.; pastor. 4. any person or thing thought of as serving as the agent of some power, force, etc.: as, a *minister* of evil. *v.t.* to administer. *v.i.* 1. to act as an agent. 2. to give help; esp., to serve as a nurse.

**min·is·te·ri·al** (min′is-têr′i-əl), *adj.* 1. of a minister or (the) ministry. 2. subordinate or instrumental. 3. administrative; executive. **—min′is·te′ri·al·ly,** *adv.*

**minister plenipotentiary,** [*pl.* MINISTERS PLENIPOTENTIARY], a diplomatic representative with full authority to negotiate.

**min·is·trant** (min′is-trənt), *adj.* serving as a minister; ministering. *n.* one who ministers.

**min·is·tra·tion** (min′is-trā′shən), *n.* 1. the act of serving as a minister or clergyman. 2. help; care.

**min·is·try** (min′is-tri), *n.* [*pl.* -TRIES], 1. the act of ministering, or serving. 2. the office or function of a minister of religion. 3. ministers collectively; the clergy. 4. *a)* the department under a minister of government. *b)* his term of office. *c)* such ministers collectively.

**min·i·track** (min′i-track′), *n.* a system for tracking the path of a satellite in orbit by signals from miniature transmitters in the satellite.

**min·i·ver** (min′ə-vẽr), *n.* [< OFr. < *menu*, small + *vair*, kind of fur < L. *varius*, variegated], 1. in medieval times, a kind of white or gray fur used for trimming garments. 2. any fine white fur.

**mink** (miŋk), *n.* [*pl.* MINKS, MINK; see PLURAL, II, D, 1], [< Scand.], 1. a mammal somewhat like a large weasel, living on land and in water. 2. its valuable fur, soft, brown, and lustrous.

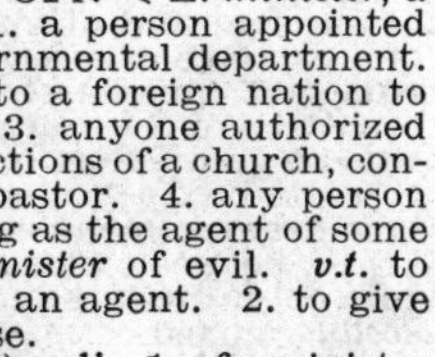

MINK (2 ft. long)

**Minn.,** Minnesota.

**Min·ne·ap·o·lis** (min′i-ap′'l-is), *n.* a city in E Minnesota, on the Mississippi: pop., 483,000.

**min·ne·sing·er** (min′i-siŋ′ẽr), *n.* [G.; *minne*, love + *singer*, singer], any of a number of German lyric poets and singers of the 12th to 14th centuries.

**Min·ne·so·ta** (min′i-sō′tə), *n.* a Middle Western State of the U.S.: area, 84,068 sq. mi.; pop., 3,414,000; capital, St. Paul: abbrev. **Minn. —Min′ne·so′tan,** *adj. & n.*

**min·now** (min′ō), *n.* [*pl.* -NOWS, -NOW; see PLURAL, II, D, 1], [prob. merging of AS. *myne* with OFr. *menu*, small], 1. any of various species of very small fresh-water fish of the carp family, used commonly as bait. 2. any small fish like these.

**min·ny** (min′i), *n.* [*pl.* -NIES], [Dial.], a minnow.

**Mi·no·an** (mi-nō′ən), *adj.* [< *Minos*], designating or of an advanced prehistoric culture that flourished in Crete from c. 3000 to 1100 B.C.

**mi·nor** (mī′nẽr), *adj.* [L.], 1. *a)* lesser in size, amount, or extent. *b)* lesser in importance or rank. 2. under full legal age. 3. constituting the minority. 4. in a minor key; sad; melancholy. 5. in *education*, designating a field of study in which a student specializes, but to a lesser degree than in his major. 6. in *music*, *a)* designating an interval lower than the corresponding major interval by a half tone. *b)* designating a tone distant from another by a minor interval. *c)* designating or of a mode characterized by minor intervals. *v.i.* in *education*, to specialize to a secondary degree (*in* some field of study): as, to *minor* in art. *n.* 1. a person under full legal age. 2. in *education*, a minor field of study. 3. in *music*, a minor interval, key, etc.

**Mi·nor·ca** (mi-nôr′kə), *n.* one of the Balearic Islands, east of Majorca.

**mi·nor·i·ty** (mə-nôr′ə-ti, mī-nor′-), *n.* [*pl.* -TIES], 1. the lesser part or smaller number; less than half. 2. a racial, religious, or political group that is part of, but differs from, a larger, controlling group. 3. the period or state of being under full legal age.

**minor league,** any of the leagues of professional baseball clubs, etc. other than the major leagues. **—mi′nor-league′,** *adj.* **—mi′nor-lea′guer,** *n.*

**minor scale,** one of the two standard diatonic scales, consisting of eight tones with half steps, in ascending, after the second and seventh tones (*melodic minor scale*) or after the second, fifth, and seventh tones (*harmonic minor scale*).

**minor suit,** in *bridge*, diamonds or clubs.

**Mi·nos** (mī′nəs, -nos), *n.* in *Gr. mythology*, 1. a king of Crete who after he died became a judge of the dead in the lower world. 2. his grandson, for whom Daedalus built the labyrinth in Crete.

**Min·o·taur** (min′ə-tôr′), *n.* in *Gr. mythology*, a monster with the body of a man and the head of a bull, confined by Minos in a labyrinth and annually fed young Athenians, until killed by Theseus.

MINOTAUR

**Minsk** (minsk), *n.* the capital of the Byelorussian S.S.R.: pop., 717,000.

**min·ster** (min′stẽr), *n.* [AS. *mynster* < LL.; see MONASTERY], 1. the church of a monastery. 2. any of various large churches or cathedrals.

**min·strel** (min′strəl), *n.* [< OFr. < LL. *ministerialis*, servant < L.; see MINISTER], 1. any of a class of lyric poets and singers of the Middle Ages, who traveled from place to place singing and reciting. 2. [Poetic], a poet; singer; musician. 3. a performer in a minstrel show.

**minstrel show,** a comic variety show presented by a company of performers in blackface, who sing songs, tell jokes, etc.

**min·strel·sy** (min′strəl-si), *n.* [*pl.* -SIES], 1. the art or occupation of a minstrel. 2. a group of minstrels. 3. a collection of their songs.

**mint** (mint), *n.* [AS. *mynet*, coin < L. < *Moneta*, surname of Juno, in whose temple money was coined], 1. a place where money is coined by the government. 2. a large amount: as, a *mint* of ideas. 3. a source of manufacture or invention. *adj.* new, as if freshly minted: as, a stamp in *mint* condition. *v.t.* 1. to coin (money). 2. to invent or create; fabricate. **—mint′er,** *n.*

**mint** (mint), *n.* [< AS. < L. < Gr. *mintha*], 1. any of various aromatic plants whose leaves are used for flavoring and in medicine: as, pepper*mint*. 2. a piece of candy flavored with mint.

**mint·age** (min′tij), *n.* 1. the act or process of minting money. 2. money so produced. 3. a fee paid for coining. 4. the stamp impressed on a coin.

**mint julep,** see **julep.**

**min·u·end** (min'ū-end'), *n.* [< L. gerundive of *minuere*, to lessen], in *arithmetic*, the number or quantity from which another is to be subtracted.
**min·u·et** (min'ū-et'), *n.* [Fr. *menuet* < *menu*, small], 1. a slow, stately dance for groups of couples. 2. the music for this, in 3/4 time.
**mi·nus** (mī'nəs), *prep.* [L., neut. sing. of *minor*, less], 1. less; reduced by the subtraction of: as, four *minus* two. 2. [Colloq.], without: as, *minus* a finger. *adj.* 1. involving subtraction: as, a *minus* sign. 2. negative: as, a *minus* quantity. 3. somewhat less than: as, a grade of A *minus*. *n.* 1. a minus sign. 2. a negative quantity.
**minus sign,** in *mathematics*, a sign (−), indicating subtraction or negative quantity.
**min·ute** (min'it), *n.* [< OFr. < ML. *minuta* < L.; see MINUTE, *adj.*], 1. the sixtieth part of any of certain units; specif., *a*) 1/60 of an hour. *b*) 1/60 of a degree of an arc. 2. a moment; instant. 3. a specific point in time. 4. a note or memorandum; specif., *pl.* an official record of what was said and done at a meeting, etc. *v.t.* [-UTED, -UTING], to make minutes of; record. —**the minute (that)**, just as soon as. —**up to the minute**, in the latest style, fashion, etc.
**mi·nute** (mī-nōōt', mi-nūt'), *adj.* [< L. < pp. of *minuere*, to lessen < *minor*, less], 1. very small; tiny. 2. of little importance; trifling. 3. of or attentive to tiny details; precise. —**mi·nute'ly,** *adv.* —**mi·nute'ness,** *n.*
**minute hand,** the long hand of a clock or watch, which indicates the minutes and moves around the dial once every hour.
**min·ute·man** (min'it-man'), *n.* [*pl.* -MEN], a member of the American citizen army at the time of the Revolution who volunteered to be ready for military service at a minute's notice.
**min·ute steak** (min'it), a small steak, often cubed, that can be cooked quickly.
**mi·nu·ti·ae** (mi-nū'shi-ē'), *n.pl.* [*sing.* -TIA (-shi-ə)], [L. < *minutus*; see MINUTE, *adj.*], small or relatively unimportant details.
**minx** (miŋks), *n.* [< LG.], a pert, saucy girl.
**Mi·o·cene** (mī'ə-sēn'), *adj.* [< Gr. *meiōn*, less + *kainos*, recent], designating or of the third epoch of the Tertiary Period in the Cenozoic Era: see **geology**, chart. *n.* the Miocene Epoch or its rocks.
**MIr.,** Middle Irish.
**Mi·ra·beau,** Comte **de** (də mir'ə-bō'), 1749–1791; French revolutionist and statesman.
**mir·a·cle** (mir'ə-k'l), *n.* [OFr. < L. *miraculum* < *mirus*, wonderful], 1. an event or action that apparently contradicts known scientific laws: as, the *miracles* in the Bible. 2. a remarkable thing; marvel. 3. a wonderful example: as, a *miracle* of fortitude. 4. a miracle play.
**miracle play,** 1. any of a class of medieval religious dramas based on miracles worked by the saints. 2. in medieval England, a mystery play.
**mi·rac·u·lous** (mi-rak'yoo-ləs), *adj.* 1. having the nature of a miracle; supernatural. 2. like a miracle; marvelous. 3. able to work miracles. —**mi·rac'u·lous·ly,** *adv.* —**mi·rac'u·lous·ness,** *n.*
**mi·rage** (mi-räzh'), *n.* [Fr. < (*se*) *mirer*, to be reflected < LL. *mirare*, to look at], 1. an optical illusion caused by the reflection of light through layers of air of different temperatures and densities, by which a ship, oasis in the desert, etc. appears to be very near. 2. anything that falsely appears to be real.
**mire** (mīr), *n.* [< ON. *myrr*], 1. an area of wet, soggy ground; bog. 2. deep mud or slush. *v.t.* [MIRED, MIRING], 1. to cause to get stuck in or as in mire. 2. to soil with mud or dirt. *v.i.* to sink or stick in mud.
**Mir·i·am** (mir'i-əm), *n.* in the *Bible*, the sister of Moses and Aaron: Ex. 15:20.
**mirk** (mũrk), *n.* & *adj.* murk.
**mirk·y** (mũr'ki), *adj.* [-IER, -IEST], murky.
**mir·ror** (mir'ẽr), *n.* [< OFr. *mirour* < LL. *mirare*, to look at < L. *mirari*, to wonder at], 1. a smooth surface that reflects images; esp., a looking glass. 2. anything that gives a true representation or description. 3. something to be imitated; model. *v.t.* to reflect, as in a mirror.
**mirth** (mũrth), *n.* [AS. *mirgth* < *myrig*, pleasant], joyfulness, gaiety, or merriment, especially when marked by laughter or hilarity. —**mirth'less,** *adj.* —**mirth'less·ly,** *adv.* —**mirth'less·ness,** *n.*
**mirth·ful** (mũrth'fəl), *adj.* full of, expressing, or causing mirth; merry. —**mirth'ful·ly,** *adv.* —**mirth'ful·ness,** *n.*
**mir·y** (mīr'i), *adj.* [-IER, -IEST], 1. boggy; swampy. 2. muddy; dirty. —**mir'i·ness,** *n.*
**mis-,** [< AS. *mis-* or OFr. *mes-*], a prefix meaning *wrong(ly)*, *bad(ly)*, as in *misplace*, *misadventure*.
**mis·ad·ven·ture** (mis'əd-ven'chẽr), *n.* a mishap; bad luck; mischance.
**mis·ad·vise** (mis'əd-vīz'), *v.t.* [-VISED, -VISING], to advise wrongly.
**mis·al·li·ance** (mis'ə-lī'əns), *n.* an improper alliance; esp., an unsuitable marriage.
**mis·al·ly** (mis'ə-lī'), *v.t.* [-LIED, -LYING], to ally unsuitably or inappropriately.
**mis·an·thrope** (mis'ən-thrōp'), *n.* [< Gr. < *misein*, to hate + *anthrōpos*, a man], one who hates or distrusts all people: also **mis·an'thro·pist** (-an'thrə-pist). —**mis'an·throp'ic** (-throp'ik), **mis'an·throp'i·cal,** *adj.* —**mis'an·throp'i·cal·ly,** *adv.*
**mis·an·thro·py** (mis-an'thrə-pi), *n.* [see MISANTHROPE], hatred or distrust of all people.
**mis·ap·ply** (mis'ə-plī'), *v.t.* [-PLIED, -PLYING], to apply badly or improperly, as one's energies, a trust fund, etc. —**mis'ap·pli·ca'tion,** *n.*
**mis·ap·pre·hend** (mis'ap-ri-hend'), *v.t.* to misunderstand. —**mis'ap·pre·hen'sion** (-hen'shən), *n.*
**mis·ap·pro·pri·ate** (mis'ə-prō'pri-āt'), *v.t.* [-ATED, -ATING], to appropriate to a wrong or dishonest use. —**mis'ap·pro'pri·a'tion,** *n.*
**mis·be·come** (mis'bi-kum'), *v.t.* [-CAME, -COME, -COMING], to be unbecoming to; be unsuitable for.
**mis·be·got·ten** (mis'bi-got''n), *adj.* wrongly or unlawfully begotten; illegitimate: also **mis'be·got'.**
**mis·be·have** (mis'bi-hāv'), *v.i.* [-HAVED, -HAVING], to behave wrongly. *v.t.* to conduct (oneself) improperly. —**mis'be·hav'ior** (-yẽr), *n.*
**mis·be·lief** (mis'bə-lēf'), *n.* wrong, false, or unorthodox belief.
**mis·be·lieve** (mis'bə-lēv'), *v.i.* [-LIEVED, -LIEVING], to hold wrong, false, or unorthodox beliefs, especially in religion. *v.t.* [Rare], to disbelieve. —**mis'be·liev'er,** *n.*
**misc.,** 1. miscellaneous. 2. miscellany.
**mis·cal·cu·late** (mis-kal'kyoo-lāt'), *v.t.* & *v.i.* [-LATED, -LATING], to calculate incorrectly; miscount or misjudge. —**mis'cal·cu·la'tion,** *n.*
**mis·call** (mis-kôl'), *v.t.* to call by a wrong name.
**mis·car·riage** (mis-kar'ij), *n.* 1. failure to reach a proper end. 2. failure of mail, freight, etc. to reach its destination. 3. the premature birth of a fetus, so that it does not live; abortion.
**mis·car·ry** (mis-kar'i), *v.i.* [-RIED, -RYING], 1. to go wrong; fail: said of a plan, project, etc. 2. to fail to arrive: said of mail, freight, etc. 3. to suffer a miscarriage of a fetus.
**mis·cast** (mis-kast', -käst'), *v.t.* [-CAST, -CASTING], to cast (an actor or a play) unsuitably.
**mis·ce·ge·na·tion** (mis'i-jə-nā'shən), *n.* [< L. *miscere*, to mix + *genus*, race], marriage or interbreeding between members of different races; esp., in the U.S., between whites and Negroes.
**mis·cel·la·ne·ous** (mis''l-ā'ni-əs), *adj.* [< L. < *miscellus*, mixed < *miscere*, to mix], 1. consisting of various kinds; varied; mixed. 2. having various qualities, etc.; many-sided. —**mis'cel·la'ne·ous·ly,** *adv.* —**mis'cel·la'ne·ous·ness,** *n.*
**mis·cel·la·ny** (mis''l-ā'ni), *n.* [*pl.* -NIES], [see MISCELLANEOUS], 1. a collection of various kinds, especially of literary works. 2. *often pl.* a book made up of such a collection.
**mis·chance** (mis-chans', -chäns'), *n.* bad luck; misadventure.
**mis·chief** (mis'chif), *n.* [< OFr. < *meschever*, to come to grief < *mes-*, mis- + *chief*, end], 1. harm or damage, especially that done by a person. 2. *a*) action that causes damage or trouble. *b*) a person causing damage or annoyance. 3. a tendency to vex with playful tricks. 4. *a*) a prank; playful, vexing trick. *b*) gay teasing.
**mis·chief-mak·er** (mis'chif-māk'ẽr), *n.* one who causes mischief; esp., one who causes quarrels by gossiping. —**mis'chief-mak'ing,** *adj.* & *n.*
**mis·chie·vous** (mis'chi-vəs), *adj.* 1. causing mischief; specif., *a*) injurious; harmful. *b*) prankish; teasing. 2. inclined to annoy with playful tricks; naughty. —**mis'chie·vous·ly,** *adv.* —**mis'chie·vous·ness,** *n.*
**mis·ci·ble** (mis'ə-b'l), *adj.* [< L. *miscere*, to mix], that can be mixed. —**mis'ci·bil'i·ty,** *n.*
**mis·con·ceive** (mis'kən-sēv'), *v.t.* & *v.i.* to conceive or interpret wrongly; misunderstand. —**mis'con·ceiv'er,** *n.* —**mis'con·cep'tion,** *n.*
**mis·con·duct** (mis'kən-dukt'; *for n.*, mis-kon'dukt), *v.t.* 1. to manage badly or dishonestly. 2. to conduct (oneself) improperly. *n.* 1. bad or dishonest management. 2. improper behavior.
**mis·con·strue** (mis'kən-strōō', mis-kon'strōō), *v.t.* [-STRUED, -STRUING], to construe wrongly; misinterpret. —**mis'con·struc'tion,** *n.*
**mis·count** (mis-kount'), *v.t.* & *v.i.* to count incorrectly. *n.* (mis'kount'), an incorrect count.
**mis·cre·ant** (mis'kri-ənt), *adj.* [< OFr. < *mes-*,

mis- + ppr. of *creire*, to believe], 1. villainous; evil. 2. [Archaic], unbelieving. *n.* 1. a criminal; villain. 2. [Archaic], an unbeliever.

**mis·cue** (mis-kū′), *n.* 1. in *billiards*, a shot spoiled by the cue's slipping off the ball. 2. [Colloq.], a mistake; error. *v.i.* [-CUED, -CUING], 1. to make a miscue. 2. in the *theater*, to miss one's cue.

**mis·date** (mis-dāt′), *v.t.* [-DATED, -DATING], to date (a letter, etc.) incorrectly. *n.* a wrong date.

**mis·deal** (mis-dēl′), *v.t. & v.i.* [-DEALT (-delt′), -DEALING], to deal (playing cards) wrongly. *n.* a wrong deal. **—mis·deal′er,** *n.*

**mis·deed** (mis-dēd′), *n.* a wrong or wicked act; crime, sin, etc.

**mis·de·mean** (mis′di-mēn′), *v.t. & v.i.* [Rare], to conduct (oneself) badly; misbehave.

**mis·de·mean·or** (mis′di-mēn′ẽr), *n.* 1. [Rare], a misbehaving. 2. in *law*, any minor offense, as the breaking of a municipal ordinance, for which statute provides a lesser punishment than for a felony. Brit. sp. **mis′de·mean′our.**

**mis·di·rect** (mis′də-rekt′, -dī-), *v.t.* to direct wrongly or badly. **—mis′di·rec′tion,** *n.*

**mis·do** (mis-do͞o′), *v.t.* [-DID, -DONE, -DOING], to do wrongly; bungle. **—mis·do′er,** *n.* **—mis·do′ing,** *n.*

**mis·doubt** (mis-dout′), *v.t.* [Archaic], 1. to have doubt about; distrust. 2. to fear. *n.* [Archaic], suspicion; doubt.

**mis·em·ploy** (mis′em-ploi′), *v.t.* to employ wrongly or badly; misuse. **—mis′em·ploy′ment,** *n.*

**mi·ser** (mī′zẽr), *n.* [L., wretched], a greedy, stingy person who hoards money for its own sake, even at the expense of his own comfort.

**mis·er·a·ble** (miz′ẽr-ə-b'l, miz′rə-), *adj.* [< Fr. < L. *miserabilis*], 1. in a condition of misery; wretched. 2. causing misery, discomfort, etc.: as, *miserable* weather. 3. bad, poor, inadequate, etc.: a generalized term of disapproval. 4. pitiable. *n.* [Obs.], a miserable person. **—mis′er·a·ble·ness,** *n.* **—mis′er·a·bly,** *adv.*

**Mis·e·re·re** (miz′ə-râr′i, -rêr′-), *n.* [L., have mercy: first word of the psalm], 1. the 51st Psalm (50th in the Douay Version). 2. a musical setting for this.

**mi·ser·ly** (mī′zẽr-li), *adj.* like or characteristic of a miser; greedy and stingy. **—mi′ser·li·ness,** *n.*

**mis·er·y** (miz′ẽr-i), *n.* [*pl.* -IES], [< OFr. < L. < *miser*, wretched], 1. a condition of great wretchedness or suffering, because of pain, poverty, etc.; distress. 2. a cause of such suffering; pain, ache, poverty, etc.

**mis·fea·sance** (mis-fē′z'ns), *n.* [< OFr. < *mes-*, mis- + *faire* (< L. *facere*), to do], in *law*, wrongdoing; specif., the doing of a lawful act in an unlawful manner: cf. *malfeasance, nonfeasance.*

**mis·fire** (mis-fīr′), *v.i.* [-FIRED, -FIRING], 1. to fail to ignite properly: said of an internal-combustion engine. 2. to fail to be discharged: said of a firearm. *n.* a misfiring.

**mis·fit** (mis-fit′; *for n.* 3, mis′fit′), *v.t. & v.i.* to fail to fit properly. *n.* 1. a misfitting. 2. anything that misfits. 3. a person not suited to his position, status, etc.

**mis·for·tune** (mis-fôr′chən), *n.* 1. bad luck; ill fortune; trouble; adversity. 2. an instance of this; unlucky accident; mishap.

**mis·give** (mis-giv′), *v.t.* [-GAVE, -GIVEN, -GIVING], to cause fear, doubt, or suspicion in: as, his heart *misgave* him. *v.i.* to feel fear, etc.

**mis·giv·ing** (mis-giv′iŋ), *n. often in pl.* a disturbed feeling of fear, doubt, apprehension, etc.

**mis·gov·ern** (mis-guv′ẽrn), *v.t.* to govern or administer badly. **—mis·gov′ern·ment,** *n.*

**mis·guide** (mis-gīd′), *v.t.* [-GUIDED, -GUIDING], to guide wrongly; lead into error or misconduct; mislead. **—mis·guid′ance,** *n.* **—mis·guid′ed,** *adj.*

**mis·han·dle** (mis-han′d'l), *v.t.* [-DLED, -DLING], to handle badly or roughly; abuse, maltreat, etc.

**mis·hap** (mis′hap′, mis-hap′), *n.* 1. bad luck; adversity; misfortune. 2. an unlucky accident.

**mish·mash** (mish′mash′), *n.* a hodgepodge.

**Mish·nah, Mish·na** (mish′nə), *n.* [*pl.* -NAYOTH (-nä-yōth′)], [< Mod. Heb. < Heb. *shānāh*, to repeat, learn], the first part of the Talmud, containing interpretations of scriptural ordinances, compiled by the rabbis about 200 A.D.

**mis·in·form** (mis′in-fôrm′), *v.t. & v.i.* to supply (with) false or misleading information. **—mis′in·form′ant, mis′in·form′er,** *n.* **—mis′in·for·ma′tion,** *n.*

**mis·in·ter·pret** (mis′in-tũr′prit), *v.t.* to interpret wrongly; understand or explain incorrectly. **—mis′in·ter′pre·ta′tion,** *n.*

**mis·judge** (mis-juj′), *v.t. & v.i.* [-JUDGED, -JUDGING], to judge wrongly or unfairly. **—mis·judg′ment, mis·judge′ment,** *n.*

**mis·lay** (mis-lā′), *v.t.* [-LAID, -LAYING], 1. to put in a place afterward forgotten. 2. to misplace (sense 1). **—mis·lay′er,** *n.*

**mis·lead** (mis-lēd′), *v.t.* [-LED, -LEADING], 1. to lead in a wrong direction; lead astray. 2. to deceive or delude. 3. to lead into wrongdoing. **—mis·lead′ing,** *adj.* **—mis·lead′ing·ly,** *adv.*

**mis·like** (mis-līk′), *v.t.* [-LIKED, -LIKING], 1. to displease. 2. to dislike. *n.* dislike; disapproval.

**mis·man·age** (mis-man′ij), *v.t. & v.i.* [-AGED, -AGING], to manage or administer badly. **—mis·man′age·ment,** *n.*

**mis·match** (mis-mach′), *v.t.* to match badly or unsuitably. *n.* a bad match.

**mis·mate** (mis-māt′), *v.t. & v.i.* [-MATED, -MATING], to mate badly or unsuitably.

**mis·name** (mis-nām′), *v.t.* [-NAMED, -NAMING], to call by a wrong name.

**mis·no·mer** (mis-nō′mẽr), *n.* [< OFr. < *mes-*, mis- + *nomer* (< L. *nominare*), to name], 1. a name or epithet wrongly applied. 2. an error in naming a person or place in a legal document.

**mis·o-,** [< Gr. < *misein*, to hate], a combining form meaning *hatred*, as in *misogyny*: also **mis-.**

**mi·sog·a·my** (mi-sog′ə-mi), *n.* [< *miso-* + Gr. *gamos*, marriage], hatred of marriage. **—mi·sog′a·mist,** *n.*

**mi·sog·y·ny** (mi-soj′ə-ni), *n.* [< Gr. < *misein*, to hate + *gynē*, woman], hatred of women. **—mi·sog′y·nist,** *n.* **—mi·sog′y·nous,** *adj.*

**mis·place** (mis-plās′), *v.t.* [-PLACED, -PLACING], 1. to put in a wrong place. 2. to bestow (one's trust, affection, etc.) unwisely. 3. [Colloq.], to mislay (sense 1). **—mis·place′ment,** *n.*

**mis·play** (mis-plā′), *v.t. & v.i.* to play wrongly or badly, as in a game. *n.* a wrong or bad play.

**mis·print** (mis-print′; *also, for n.,* mis′print′), *v.t.* to print incorrectly. *n.* an error in printing.

**mis·pri·sion** (mis-prizh′ən), *n.* [< OFr. < pp. of *mesprendre*, to take wrongly < LL. < L. *minus*, less + *prehendere*, to take], misconduct or neglect of duty, especially by a public official.

**misprision of felony** (or **treason**), the offense of concealing knowledge of another's felony (or treason).

**mis·prize** (mis-prīz′), *v.t.* [-PRIZED, -PRIZING], [< OFr. < *mes-*, mis- + LL. *pretiare*, to value < L. *pretium*, a price], to despise or undervalue: also **mis·prise′** [-PRISED, -PRISING].

**mis·pro·nounce** (mis′prə-nouns′), *v.t. & v.i.* [-NOUNCED, -NOUNCING], to give (a word) a pronunciation different from any of the accepted standard pronunciations. **—mis′pro·nun′ci·a′tion** (-nun′si-ā′shən), *n.*

**mis·quote** (mis-kwōt′), *v.t. & v.i.* [-QUOTED, -QUOTING], to quote incorrectly. **—mis′quo·ta′tion,** *n.*

**mis·read** (mis-rēd′), *v.t. & v.i.* [-READ (-red′), -READING], to read wrongly, especially so as to misinterpret or misunderstand.

**mis·rep·re·sent** (mis′rep-ri-zent′), *v.t.* to represent falsely; give an untrue idea of. **—mis′rep·re·sen·ta′tion,** *n.* **—mis′rep·re·sent′er,** *n.*

**mis·rule** (mis-ro͞ol′), *v.t.* [-RULED, -RULING], to misgovern. *n.* 1. misgovernment. 2. disorder or riot. **—mis·rul′er,** *n.*

**miss** (mis), *v.t.* [AS. *missan*], 1. to fail to hit, meet, catch, do, see, hear, etc. 2. to let (an opportunity, etc.) go by. 3. to escape; avoid: as, he *missed* being hit. 4. to fail or forget to do, keep, attend, etc.: as, he *missed* a class. 5. to notice, feel, or regret the absence or loss of. *v.i.* 1. to fail to hit something aimed at. 2. to fail to be successful. *n.* a failure to hit, obtain, etc.

**miss** (mis), *n.* [*pl.* MISSES], [contr. of *mistress*], 1. [M-], a title used in speaking to or of an unmarried woman or girl, placed before the name: as, *Miss* Smith, the *Misses* Smith. 2. a young unmarried woman or girl: now usually humorous or in trade jargon, as, coats in *misses'* sizes.

**Miss.,** Mississippi.

**miss.,** 1. mission. 2. missionary.

**mis·sal** (mis′'l), *n.* [< ML. < LL. *missa*, Mass], in the *R.C. Church*, a book containing all the prayers for celebrating Mass throughout the year.

**mis·shape** (mis-shāp′), *v.t.* [-SHAPED, -SHAPED or *archaic* -SHAPEN, -SHAPING], to shape badly; deform; misform. **—mis·shap′en,** *adj.*

**mis·sile** (mis′'l), *adj.* [< L. *missilis* < pp. of *mittere*, to send], that can be, or is, thrown or shot.

*n.* a weapon or other object, as a spear, bullet, rocket, etc., designed to be thrown or launched toward a target; often, specif., a guided missile.

**mis·sile·ry, mis·sil·ry** (mis′'l-ri), *n.* the science of building and launching guided missiles.

**miss·ing** (mis′iŋ), *adj.* absent; lost; lacking; specif., absent after combat, but not definitely known to be dead or taken prisoner.

**missing link,** something necessary for completing a series; specif., a hypothetical form of animal believed to have existed in the evolutionary process intermediate between man and the apes.

**mis·sion** (mish′ən), *n.* [< L. *missio* < pp. of *mittere*, to send], 1. a sending out or being sent out with authority to perform a special duty, as by a church, government, etc. 2. *a*) a group of persons sent by a church to spread its religion, especially in a foreign land. *b*) its headquarters. 3. a diplomatic delegation; embassy. 4. the special duty or function on which someone is sent. 5. the special task for which a person is apparently destined in life; calling. 6. any charitable or religious organization for doing welfare work for the needy. 7. *pl.* organized missionary work. 8. in *military usage*, an assigned combat operation; esp., a single combat flight by an airplane or group of airplanes. *adj.* of a mission or missions. *v.t.* to send on a mission.

**mis·sion·ar·y** (mish′ən-er′i), *adj.* of or characteristic of religious missions or missionaries. *n.* [*pl.* -IES], a person sent on a mission; specif., a person sent out by his church to preach, teach, and proselytize in a foreign country, especially in one considered heathen: also **mis′sion·er.**

**mis·sis** (mis′əz), *n.* [var. of *Mrs.*], [Colloq. or Dial.], one's wife: also used with *the:* also sp. **missus.**

**Mis·sis·sip·pi** (mis′ə-sip′i), *n.* 1. a river in the U.S., flowing from N Minnesota to the Gulf of Mexico. 2. a Southern State of the U.S., on the Gulf of Mexico: area, 47,716 sq. mi.; pop., 2,178,000; capital, Jackson: abbrev. **Miss.**

**Mis·sis·sip·pi·an** (mis′ə-sip′i-ən), *adj.* 1. of the Mississippi River. 2. of the State of Mississippi. 3. designating or of the first coal-forming period of the Paleozoic Era in North America: see **geology,** chart. *n.* 1. a native or inhabitant of Mississippi. 2. the Mississippian Period or its rocks.

**mis·sive** (mis′iv), *n.* [Fr. < ML. < L. pp. of *mittere*, to send], a letter or written message.

**Mis·sour·i** (mi-zoor′i, -ə), *n.* 1. a Middle Western State of the U.S.: area, 69,674 sq. mi.; pop., 4,320,000; capital, Jefferson City: abbrev. **Mo.** 2. a river flowing from Montana to the Mississippi. **—from Missouri,** [Slang], not easily convinced. **—Mis·sour′i·an,** *adj. & n.*

**mis·speak** (mis-spēk′), *v.t. & v.i.* [-SPOKE, -SPOKEN, -SPEAKING], to speak or say incorrectly.

**mis·spell** (mis-spel′), *v.t. & v.i.* [-SPELLED or -SPELT, -SPELLING], to spell incorrectly.

**mis·spell·ing** (mis-spel′iŋ), *n.* incorrect spelling.

**mis·spend** (mis-spend′), *v.t.* [-SPENT, -SPENDING], to spend improperly or wastefully.

**mis·state** (mis-stāt′), *v.t.* [-STATED, -STATING], to state incorrectly or falsely. **—mis·state′ment,** *n.*

**mis·step** (mis-step′), *n.* 1. a wrong or awkward step. 2. a mistake in conduct; faux pas.

**mist** (mist), *n.* [AS.], 1. a large mass of water vapor like a fog, but less dense. 2. a cloud of dust, gas, etc. 3. a cloudiness before the eyes, blurring the vision: as, she smiled in a *mist* of tears. 4. anything that dims or obscures the understanding, memory, etc. *v.t. & v.i.* to dim or obscure with or as with a mist.

**mis·tak·a·ble** (mis-tāk′ə-b'l), *adj.* that can be mistaken or misunderstood. **—mis·tak′a·bly,** *adv.*

**mis·take** (mis-tāk′), *v.t.* [-TOOK, -TAKEN or *obs.* -TOOK, -TAKING], [< ON. *mistaka*, to take wrongly], 1. to understand or perceive wrongly. 2. to take to be another: as, he *mistook* me for my brother. *v.i.* to make a mistake. *n.* a fault in understanding, interpretation, etc.; blunder; error. **—and no mistake,** [Colloq.], certainly.

**mis·tak·en** (mis-tāk′'n), *adj.* 1. wrong; having an incorrect understanding, perception, etc.: said of persons. 2. incorrect; misunderstood: said of ideas, etc. **—mis·tak′en·ly,** *adv.*

**mis·ter** (mis′tẽr), *n.* [weakened form of *master*], 1. [M-], a title used in speaking to or of a man, placed before his name or office and usually written *Mr.*: as, *Mr.* Stein, *Mr.* Secretary. 2. [Colloq.], sir: as, what time is it, *mister?*

**mis·tle·toe** (mis′'l-tō′), *n.* [< AS. < *mistel*, mistletoe + *tan*, a twig], 1. a parasitic evergreen plant with yellowish flowers and waxy white berries, growing on certain trees. 2. a sprig of this, hung as a Christmas decoration.

**mis·took** (mis-took′), pt. and obs. pp. of **mistake.**

**mis·tral** (mis′trəl), *n.* [Fr.; Pr., lit., master-wind < L. < *magister*, a master], a cold, dry, north wind that blows over the Mediterranean coast of France and near-by regions.

**mis·treat** (mis-trēt′), *v.t.* to treat wrongly or badly. **—mis·treat′ment,** *n.*

**mis·tress** (mis′tris), *n.* [< OFr. fem. of *maistre*, master], 1. a woman who rules others or controls something; specif., *a*) a woman who is head of a household or institution. *b*) [Chiefly Brit.], a woman schoolteacher. 2. [sometimes M-], something regarded as feminine that has control, power, etc.: as, England was *Mistress* of the seas. 3. a woman who lives as a wife with a man to whom she is not married; paramour. 4. [Archaic], a sweetheart. 5. [M-], formerly, a title prefixed to the name of a woman: now replaced by **Mrs.** or **Miss.**

**mis·tri·al** (mis-trī′əl), *n.* in *law*, a trial made void because of an error in the proceedings, or because the jury cannot reach a verdict.

**mis·trust** (mis-trust′), *n.* lack of trust or confidence; suspicion. *v.t. & v.i.* to have no trust or confidence in; doubt. **—mis·trust′er,** *n.* **—mis·trust′ful,** *adj.* **—mis·trust′ful·ly,** *adv.* **—mis·trust′ful·ness,** *n.* **—mis·trust′ing·ly,** *adv.*

**mist·y** (mis′ti), *adj.* [-IER, -IEST], 1. of or like mist. 2. characterized by or covered with mist. 3. blurred or dimmed, as by mist; obscure; vague. **—mist′i·ly,** *adv.* **—mist′i·ness,** *n.*

**mis·un·der·stand** (mis′un-dẽr-stand′, mis-un′-), *v.t.* [-STOOD, -STANDING], to understand incorrectly; miscomprehend or misinterpret.

**mis·un·der·stand·ing** (mis′un-dẽr-stan′diŋ), *n.* 1. a failure to understand correctly. 2. a quarrel; disagreement.

**mis·un·der·stood** (mis′un-dẽr-stood′, mis-un′-), *adj.* 1. incorrectly understood. 2. not properly appreciated.

**mis·us·age** (mis-ūs′ij, -ūz′-), *n.* 1. incorrect usage, as of words. 2. bad or harsh treatment.

**mis·use** (mis-ūz′; *for n.*, -ūs′), *v.t.* [-USED, -USING], 1. to use improperly; misapply. 2. to treat badly or harshly; abuse. *n.* 1. incorrect or improper use. 2. [Rare], abuse. **—mis·us′er,** *n.*

**mis·val·ue** (mis-val′ū), *v.t.* [-UED, -UING], to value wrongly.

**mis·word** (mis-wūrd′), *v.t.* to word incorrectly.

**mite** (mīt), *n.* [AS.], any of a large number of tiny arachnids, many of which live as parasites upon animals or plants, or in prepared foods.

**mite** (mīt), *n.* [< MD.; ult. same as prec.], 1. *a*) a very small sum of money. *b*) a coin of very small value. 2. a very small creature or object.

**mi·ter** (mī′tẽr), *n.* [< OFr. < L. < Gr. *mitra*, a headband], 1. a tall, ornamented cap with peaks in front and back, worn by bishops and abbots as a mark of office. 2. the office or rank of a bishop. *v.t.* to invest with the office of bishop by placing a miter on. Also sp. **mitre.** **—mi′tered,** *adj.*

MITER

**mi·ter** (mī′tẽr), *n.* [? < *miter* (headdress)], in *carpentry*, 1. a kind of joint formed by fitting together two pieces, each of which has been beveled so that they form a corner (usually a right angle): also **miter joint.** 2. either of the facing surfaces of such a joint. *v.t.* to fit together in a miter. Also sp. **mitre.** **—mi′tered,** *adj.*

**mit·i·gate** (mit′ə-gāt′), *v.t. & v.i.* [-GATED, -GATING], [< L. pp. of *mitigare*, to make mild < *mitis*, mild], to make or become milder, less severe, or less painful; moderate. **—mit′i·ga·ble** (-i-gə-b'l), *adj.* **—mit′i·ga′tion,** *n.* **—mit′i·ga′tive,** *adj. & n.* **—mit′i·ga′tor,** *n.* **—mit′i·ga·to′ry** (-gə-tôr′i, -tō′ri), *adj.*

**mi·to·sis** (mi-tō′sis, mī-), *n.* [< Gr. *mitos*, thread], in *biology*, the indirect method of cell division, in which the nuclear chromatin is formed into a long thread which in turn breaks into chromosomes that are split lengthwise. **—mi·tot′ic** (-tot′ik), *adj.* **—mi·tot′i·cal·ly,** *adv.*

**mi·tral** (mī′trəl), *adj.* of or like a miter.

**mitral valve,** the valve between the left auricle and left ventricle of the heart.

**mi·tre** (mī′tẽr), *n. & v.t.* [-TRED, -TRING], miter.

**mitt** (mit), *n.* [abbrev. of *mitten*], 1. a glove covering the forearm, hand, and, sometimes, part of the fingers. 2. a mitten. 3. [Slang], a hand. 4. in *sports*, *a*) a glove padded on the palm and fingers, worn by baseball players in the field. *b*) *usually in pl.* a padded mitten worn by boxers.

**mit·ten** (mit′'n), *n.* [< OFr. *mitaine*], 1. a glove with a thumb but no separately divided fingers. 2. a mitt (senses 1 & 4*b*).

**mix** (miks), *v.t.* [MIXED or MIXT, MIXING], [prob.

< *mixt*, mixed < Fr. < L. pp. of *miscere*, to mix], 1. to blend together in a single mass or compound. 2. to make by blending ingredients: as, she's *mixing* a cake. 3. to join; combine: as, to *mix* work and play. 4. to cause to associate: as, we *mix* the boys with the girls in our school. *v.i.* 1. to be mixed; blend; mingle. 2. to associate or get along together. *n.* 1. a mixing or being mixed. 2. a muddle; state of confusion. 3. a mixture. 4. soda, ginger ale, etc. for mixing with alcoholic liquor. **—mix up,** 1. to mix thoroughly. 2. to confuse. 3. to involve (*in* some matter).

**mixed** (mikst), *adj.* 1. joined or mingled in a single mass or compound; blended. 2. made up of different parts, elements, classes, races, etc 3. consisting of or involving both sexes: as, *mixed* company. 4. confused; muddled.

**mixed marriage,** marriage between persons of different religions or races.

**mixed number,** a number consisting of a whole number and a fraction, as 3 $^2/_3$.

**mix·er** (mik′sẽr), *n.* 1. one that mixes; specif., *a*) a device for mixing foods. *b*) a person with reference to his sociability. 2. [Slang], a social gathering for getting people acquainted.

**mixt** (mikst), alt. pt. and pp. of **mix.**

**mix·ture** (miks′chẽr), *n.* 1. a mixing or being mixed. 2. something mixed, as a cloth made of differently colored threads. 3. in *chemistry*, a substance containing two or more elements: distinguished from *compound* in that the constituents are not in fixed proportions and do not lose their individual characteristics.

**mix-up** (miks′up′), *n.* 1. confusion; tangle. 2. [Colloq.], a fight.

**miz·zen, miz·en** (miz′'n), *adj.* [< OFr. < It. fem. of *mezzano*, middle < L. *medianus*; see MEDIAN], of the mizzenmast. *n.* 1. a fore-and-aft sail set on the mizzenmast. 2. a mizzenmast.

**miz·zen·mast, miz·en·mast** (miz′'n-məst, -mast′, -mäst′), *n.* the mast closest to the stern in a ship with two or three masts.

**mkt.,** market.

**ML., M.L.,** 1. Medieval Latin. 2. Middle Latin.

**MLG., M.L.G.,** Middle Low German.

**Mlle.,** [*pl.* MLLES.], Mademoiselle.

**MM.,** Messieurs.

**mm.,** millimeter; millimeters.

**Mme.,** [*pl.* MMES.], Madame.

**Mn,** in *chemistry*, manganese.

**mne·mon·ic** (ni-mon′ik), *adj.* [< Gr. < *mnēmōn*, mindful < *mnasthai*, to remember], 1. helping, or meant to help, the memory. 2. of the memory.

**mne·mon·ics** (ni-mon′iks), *n.pl.* [construed as sing.], the science or art of improving the memory, as by the use of certain formulas.

**-mo** (mō), [< L. abl. ending], a suffix meaning *having* (a specified number of) *leaves as a result of folding a sheet of paper*, as in *12mo*.

**Mo,** in *chemistry*, molybdenum.

**Mo.,** 1. Missouri. 2. Monday.

**mo.,** [*pl.* MOS.], month.

**M.O.,** 1. Medical Officer. 2. money order: also **m.o.**

**mo·a** (mō′ə), *n.* [< native (Maori) name], any of an extinct group of large, flightless birds of New Zealand, related to the ostrich.

**Mo·ab** (mō′ab), *n.* in the *Bible*, an ancient kingdom east of the Dead Sea. **—Mo′ab·ite′,** *adj. & n.*

**moan** (mōn), *n.* [prob. < base of AS. *mænen*, to complain], 1. [Rare], a lamentation. 2. a low, mournful sound of sorrow or pain. 3. any sound like this: as, the *moan* of the wind. *v.i.* 1. to utter a moan. 2. to complain, grieve, etc. *v.t.* 1. to say with a moan. 2. to bewail: as, he *moaned* his fate. **—moan′ing·ly,** *adv.*

**moat** (mōt), *n.* [OFr. *mote*], a deep, broad ditch dug around a fortress or castle, and often filled with water, for protection against invasion. *v.t.* to surround with or as with a moat.

**mob** (mob), *n.* [< L. *mobile* (*vulgus*), movable (crowd)], 1. a disorderly and lawless crowd; rabble. 2. any crowd. 3. the masses: a contemptuous term. 4. [Slang], a gang of criminals. *v.t.* [MOBBED, MOBBING], to crowd around and attack, annoy, etc. **—mob′ber,** *n.* **—mob′bish,** *adj.*

**mob·cap** (mob′kap′), *n.* [< MD. *mop*, woman's cap; + *cap*], formerly, a woman's full, loose cap, often tied under the chin, worn indoors.

**Mo·bile** (mō-bēl′), *n.* a city in SW Alabama, on Mobile Bay; pop., 203,000.

**mo·bile** (mō′b'l; *also, and for adj. 4 and n. usually*, -bēl), *adj.* [Fr.; L. neut. of *mobilis* < *movere*, to move], 1. movable. 2. very fluid, as mercury. 3. easily expressing changes in emotion: as, *mobile* features. 4. designating abstract sculpture which aims to depict movement, as by an arrangement of thin forms, rings, etc. suspended in mid-air. 5. in *military usage*, capable of being moved quickly and easily. *n.* a piece of mobile sculpture. **—mo·bil′i·ty** (-bil′ə-ti), *n.*

**Mobile Bay** (mō′bēl), a part of the Gulf of Mexico, extending 35 mi. into SW Alabama.

**mo·bil·ize** (mō′b'l-īz′), *v.t.* [-IZED, -IZING], 1. *a*) to make movable. *b*) to put into motion, circulation, or use. 2. to make (armed forces or a nation) ready for war. 3. to organize and make ready for use. *v.i.* to become organized and ready, as for war. **—mo′bil·iz′a·ble,** *adj.* **—mo′bil·i·za′tion,** *n.* **—mo′bil·iz′er,** *n.*

**mob·ster** (mob′stẽr), *n.* [Slang], a gangster.

**moc·ca·sin** (mok′ə-s'n), *n.* [< Am. Ind. (Algonquian)], 1. a heelless slipper of soft, flexible leather, worn by North American Indians. 2. any slipper like this. 3. the water moccasin (sense 1).

**moccasin flower,** a variety of pink or yellow orchid shaped like a slipper.

**mo·cha** (mō′kə), *n.* 1. [also M-], a variety of coffee grown originally in Arabia. 2. [Colloq.], any coffee. 3. a soft, velvety leather used for gloves. *adj.* flavored with coffee or coffee and chocolate.

**mock** (mok), *v.t.* [OFr. *mocquer*, to mock], 1. to hold up to scorn or contempt; ridicule. 2. to mimic, as in fun or derision. 3. to lead on and disappoint; deceive. 4. to defy and make futile. *v.i.* to express scorn, ridicule, etc. *n.* 1. an act of mocking. 2. a person or thing receiving or deserving ridicule or derision. 3. an imitation. *adj.* false; imitation. **—mock′er,** *n.* **—mock′ing,** *adj.* **—mock′ing·ly,** *adv.*

**mock·er·y** (mok′ẽr-i), *n.* [*pl.* -IES], 1. a mocking. 2. a person or thing receiving or deserving ridicule. 3. a false, derisive, or impertinent imitation. 4. vain effort; futility.

**mock-he·ro·ic** (mok′hi-rō′ik), *adj.* mocking, or burlesquing, heroic manner, action, or character.

**mock·ing·bird** (mok′iŋ-bũrd′), *n.* a small bird of the thrush family, found in the southern U.S.: it imitates the calls of other birds.

**mock orange,** a shrub with fragrant white flowers resembling those of the orange; syringa.

**mock turtle soup,** a soup made from calf's head, veal, etc., spiced to taste like green turtle soup.

**mock-up** (mok′up′), *n.* a full-sized model, in wood, canvas, etc., of a structure or weapon, used for instructional purposes, to test the design, etc.

**mod, Mod** (mod), *n.* [< *mod*ern], a young person in England who, in his rebellion against conventional society, wears flamboyant clothes, long hair, etc. *adj.* of or characteristic of such a person.

**mod.,** 1. moderate. 2. modern.

**mo·dal** (mō′d'l), *adj.* of or indicating a mode or mood; specif., in *grammar*, of or expressing a mood: as, a *modal* verb. **—mo·dal′i·ty** (-dal′ə-ti), *n.* **—mo′dal·ly,** *adv.*

**modal auxiliary,** an auxiliary verb used with another to indicate its mood: *may, might, must, can, would,* and *should* are modal auxiliaries.

**mode** (mōd), *n.* [< L. *modus*; in sense 2, Fr. < L.], 1. a manner or way of acting, doing, or being. 2. customary usage, or current fashion or style. 3. in *grammar*, mood. 4. in *music*, any of the various forms of octave arrangement: the *major mode* is characterized by major intervals and the *minor mode* by minor intervals. 5. in *statistics*, the value, number, etc. most frequent in a given series.

**mod·el** (mod′'l), *n.* [< Fr. < It. *modello*, dim. of *modo* < L. *modus*, a measure], 1. *a*) a small copy or representation of an existing or planned object, as a ship, building, etc. *b*) a piece of sculpture in wax or clay from which a finished work in bronze, marble, etc. is to be made. 2. a person or thing considered as a standard of excellence to be imitated. 3. a style or design: as, last year's *model* of automobile. 4. *a*) a person who poses for an artist or photographer. *b*) a person, especially a woman, employed to display clothes by wearing them. *adj.* serving as a model, or standard of excellence. *v.t.* [-ELED or -ELLED, -ELING or -ELLING], 1. *a*) to make a model of. *b*) to plan or form after a model. *c*) to make conform to a standard of excellence: as, I *model* my behavior on yours. 2. to display (a dress, etc.) by wearing. *v.i.* 1. to make a model or models: as, she *models* in clay. 2. to serve as a model (sense 4). **—mod′el·er, mod′el·ler,** *n.*

**mod·er·ate** (mod′ẽr-it; *for v.*, -ə-rāt′), *adj.* [< L.

pp. of *moderare*, to restrain], 1. within reasonable limits; avoiding extremes; temperate. 2. mild; not violent: as, *moderate* weather. 3. of medium quality; mediocre: as, a *moderate* success. *n.* a person holding moderate views in politics or religion. *v.i. & v.t.* [-ATED, -ATING], 1. to become or cause to become moderate. 2. to preside over (a meeting, etc.). —**mod'er·ate·ly,** *adv.* —**mod'er·ate·ness,** *n.*

**mod·er·a·tion** (mod'ə-rā'shən), *n.* 1. a moderating, or bringing within bounds. 2. avoidance of extremes. 3. absence of violence; calmness. —**in moderation,** to a moderate degree; without excess.

**mod·e·ra·to** (mod'ə-rä'tō), *adj. & adv.* [It.], in *music,* with moderation in tempo.

**mod·er·a·tor** (mod'ə-rā'tēr), *n.* a person or thing that moderates; specif., a person who presides at an assembly, debate, etc. —**mod'er·a'tor·ship',** *n.*

**mod·ern** (mod'ērn), *adj.* [< Fr. < LL. *modernus* < L. *modo* (abl. of *modus*), just now], 1. of or characteristic of the present or recent times: often designating certain contemporary tendencies in art, music, literature, etc. 2. up-to-date; not old-fashioned. 3. [often M-], designating the form of a language in current use. *n.* 1. a person living in modern times. 2. a person having modern ideas, standards, etc. 3. in *printing,* a type characterized by heavy down strokes contrasting with narrow cross strokes. —**mod'ern·ly,** *adv.* —**mod'ern·ness,** *n.*

**Modern English,** the English language since about 1500.

**mod·ern·ism** (mod'ērn-iz'm), *n.* 1. (a) modern usage, practice, or thought; sympathy with modern ideas. 2. [M-], in *Christianity,* a movement attempting to redefine Biblical and Christian dogma and teachings in the light of modern science. —**mod'ern·ist, Mod'ern·ist,** *n.*

**mod·ern·is·tic** (mod'ērn-is'tik), *adj.* 1. of or characteristic of modernism or modernists. 2. modern (sense 1). —**mod'ern·is'ti·cal·ly,** *adv.*

**mo·der·ni·ty** (mo-dūr'nə-ti, mō-), *n.* 1. a being modern. 2. [*pl.* -TIES], something modern.

**mod·ern·ize** (mod'ērn-īz'), *v.t.* [-IZED, -IZING], to make modern; cause to conform to present-day practice, standards, or taste. *v.i.* to become modern. —**mod'ern·i·za'tion,** *n.* —**mod'ern·iz'er,** *n.*

**Modern Latin,** the Latin that has come into use since the Renaissance, or about 1500, chiefly in scientific literature: also called *New Latin.*

**mod·est** (mod'ist), *adj.* [< Fr. < L. *modestus* < *modus,* measure], 1. having or showing a moderate or humble opinion of one's own value, abilities, etc.; not vain. 2. not forward; shy or reserved. 3. decorous; chaste; decent; now, esp., not displaying one's body. 4. not extreme or excessive: as, a *modest* request. 5. quiet and humble in appearance, style, etc. —**mod'est·ly,** *adv.*

**mod·es·ty** (mod'is-ti), *n.* a being modest; specif., *a*) unassuming or humble behavior. *b*) moderation. *c*) decency; decorum.

**Mod. Gr.,** Modern Greek.

**mod·i·cum** (mod'i-kəm), *n.* [L., neut. of *modicus,* moderate], a small amount or portion; bit.

**mod·i·fi·ca·tion** (mod'ə-fi-kā'shən), *n.* a modifying or being modified; specif., *a*) a partial or slight change in form. *b*) a product of such a change. *c*) a slight reduction; moderation. *d*) a qualification or limitation of meaning.

**mod·i·fi·er** (mod'ə-fī'ēr), *n.* a person or thing that modifies; esp., a word, phrase, or clause that limits the meaning of another word or phrase: as, adjectives and adverbs are *modifiers.*

**mod·i·fy** (mod'ə-fī'), *v.t.* [-FIED, -FYING], [< L. *modificare,* to limit < *modus,* measure + *facere,* to make], 1. to change slightly or partially in character, form, etc. 2. to limit or reduce slightly: as, the judge *modified* her penalty. 3. in *grammar,* to limit in meaning; qualify: as, "large" *modifies* "house" in *large house.* 4. in *linguistics,* to change (a vowel) by umlaut. *v.i.* to be modified. —**mod'i·fi'a·ble,** *adj.*

**mod·ish** (mōd'ish), *adj.* in the latest style; fashionable. —**mod'ish·ly,** *adv.* —**mod'ish·ness,** *n.*

**mo·diste** (mō-dēst'), *n.* [Fr. < *mode;* see MODE], a woman who makes or deals in fashionable clothes, hats, etc. for women.

**Mod. L.,** Modern Latin.

**mod·u·late** (moj'oo-lāt'), *v.t.* [-LATED, -LATING], [< L. pp. of *modulari* < dim. of *modus,* measure], 1. to regulate, adjust, or adapt. 2. to vary the pitch, intensity, etc. of (the voice). 3. to sing; intone (a song). 4. in *music,* to cause to shift to another key. 5. in *radio,* to vary the frequency of (a radio wave, etc.), as by superimposing a lower frequency. *v.i.* 1. in *music,* to shift from one key to another. 2. in *radio,* to produce modulation. —**mod'u·la'tor,** *n.* —**mod'u·la·to'ry** (-lə-tôr'i, -tō'-ri), *adj.*

**mod·u·la·tion** (moj'oo-lā'shən), *n.* a modulating or being modulated; specif., *a*) in *music,* a shifting from one key to another. *b*) in *radio,* a variation in the frequency of a radio wave in accordance with some other impulse.

**mod·ule** (moj'ōōl), *n.* [ult. < L. dim. of *modus,* measure], 1. a standard or unit of measurement; specif., in *architecture,* any of several used in the construction of building materials, etc. 2. *a*) any of a set of units, as cabinets, shelves, etc., designed to be arranged or joined in a variety of ways. *b*) a detachable section or unit with a specific function, as in a spacecraft. —**mod'u·lar** (-oo-lēr), *adj.*

‡**mo·dus o·per·an·di** (mō'dəs op'ə-ran'dī), [L.], manner of working; procedure.

‡**modus vi·ven·di** (vi-ven'dī), [L., manner of living], a temporary compromise in a dispute.

**Mo·gul** (mō'gul, mō-gul'), *n.* [Per. *Mughul*], 1. a Mongol; Mongolian; esp., any of the Mongolian conquerors of India or their descendants. 2. [m-], a powerful or important person.

**mo·hair** (mō'hâr'), *n.* [< It. < Ar. *mukhayyar*], 1. the hair of the Angora goat. 2. any of several fabrics made from this. *adj.* made of mohair.

**Mo·ham·med** (mō-ham'id), *n.* Arabian founder and prophet of the Moslem religion; lived 570–632 A.D.: also **Mahomet, Muhammad.**

**Mo·ham·med·an** (mō-ham'ə-dən), *adj.* of Mohammed or the Moslem religion. *n.* an adherent of the Moslem religion. Also **Muhammadan.**

**Mo·ham·med·an·ism** (mō-ham'ə-dən-iz'm), *n.* the Moslem religion, founded by Mohammed; Islam.

**Mo·ha·ve** (mō-hä'vi), *n.* a member of a tribe of Indians that lived around the Colorado River. *adj.* of this people. Also sp. **Mojave.**

**Mo·hawk** (mō'hôk), *n.* [*pl.* -HAWK, -HAWKS], a member of a tribe of Iroquoian Indians that lived in the Mohawk Valley, New York. *adj.* of the Mohawks.

**Mo·he·gan** (mō-hē'gən), *n.* 1. a member of a Mahican tribe of Algonquian Indians that lived in Connecticut. 2. Mahican. *adj.* of the Mohegans.

**Mo·hi·can** (mō-hē'kən), *n. & adj.* Mahican.

**moi·dore** (moi'dôr, -dōr), *n.* [Port. *moeda d'ouro,* coin of gold], a former gold coin of Portugal or Brazil.

**moi·e·ty** (moi'ə-ti), *n.* [*pl.* -TIES], [< OFr. < L. < *medius,* middle], 1. a half. 2. an indefinite part.

**moil** (moil), *v.i.* [< OFr. *moillier,* to moisten < L. *mollis,* soft], to toil; drudge. *n.* 1. drudgery; hard work. 2. confusion; turmoil. —**moil'er,** *n.*

**moire** (mwär, mwôr, môr, mōr), *n.* [Fr., watered silk < Eng. *mohair*], a fabric, especially silk, having a watered, or wavy, pattern.

‡**moi·ré** (mwȧ'rā'; Eng. mō'rā'), *adj.* [Fr.], having a watered, or wavy, pattern. *n.* 1. a watered, or wavy, pattern pressed into textiles. 2. moire.

**moist** (moist), *adj.* [OFr. *moiste* < L. *mucidus,* moldy < *mucus,* mucus], 1. damp; slightly wet. 2. suggestive of the presence of liquid. —**moist'ly,** *adv.* —**moist'ness,** *n.*

**mois·ten** (mois''n), *v.t. & v.i.* to make or become moist. —**mois'ten·er,** *n.*

**mois·ture** (mois'chēr), *n.* water or other liquid causing a slight wetness or dampness.

**Mo·ja·ve Desert** (mō-hä'vi), a desert in S California: also sp. **Mohave Desert.**

**mo·lar** (mō'lēr), *adj.* [< L. < *mola,* millstone], 1. used for or capable of grinding. 2. designating or of a tooth or teeth adapted for grinding. *n.* a molar tooth: in man there are twelve molars.

**mo·las·ses** (mə-las'iz), *n.* [*pl.* -LASSES], [< Port. *melaço* < LL. *mellaceum,* must < L. < *mel,* honey], a thick, dark-colored sirup, especially that produced during the refining of sugar.

**mold** (mōld), *n.* [OFr. *molle* < L. *modulus;* see MODULE], 1. a hollow form or matrix for giving a certain form to something in a plastic or molten state. 2. a frame, shaped core, etc. on or around which something is modeled. 3. a pattern after which something is formed. 4. something formed in or on, or as if in or on, a mold. 5. the form given by a mold. 6. distinctive character or nature. *v.t.* 1. to make or shape in or on, or as if in or on, a mold. 2. to work into a certain form. 3. in *founding,* to make a mold of or from in order to make a casting. Also sp. **mould.** —**mold'a·ble,** *adj.* —**mold'er,** *n.*

**mold** (mōld), *n.* [ME. *moul;* sp. prob. infl. by *molde,* earth], 1. a furry growth on the surface of organic matter, caused by fungi, especially in the presence of dampness or decay. 2. any fungus producing such a growth. *v.t. & v.i.* to make or become moldy. Also sp. **mould.**

**mold** (mōld), *n.* [AS. *molde,* earth], 1. loose, soft soil, especially when rich with decayed organic matter and good for growing plants. 2. the material that a thing is made of. Also sp. **mould.**

**Mol·da·vi·an Soviet Socialist Republic** (mol-dā′vi-ən), a republic of the U.S.S.R. in SW European Russia, on the Black Sea: area, 13,680 sq. mi.; pop., 2,700,000; capital, Kishinev.

**mold·board** (mōld′bôrd′, -bōrd′), ***n.*** a curved plate of iron attached to a plowshare, for turning over the soil: also sp. **mouldboard.**

**mold·er** (mōl′dẽr), ***v.i. & v.t.*** [see MOLD (soil)], to crumble into dust; decay. Also sp. **moulder.**

**mold·ing** (mōl′diŋ), ***n.*** 1. the act of a person or thing that molds. 2. something molded. 3. a cornice or other ornamental projection, etc., as on a surface of a structure. 4. a shaped strip of wood, etc., as around the upper part of the walls of a room. Also sp. **moulding.**

**mold·y** (mōl′di), ***adj.*** [-IER, -IEST], 1. covered or overgrown with mold (fungous growth). 2. musty or stale. Also sp. **mouldy.** —**mold′i·ness,** ***n.***

**mole** (mōl), ***n.*** [AS. *mal*], a small, congenital spot on the human skin, usually dark-colored and slightly raised, sometimes hairy.

**mole** (mōl), ***n.*** [ME. *molle*], a small, burrowing, insect-eating mammal with very small eyes and ears and soft fur: moles live mainly underground.

MOLE (7 in. long)

**mole** (mōl), ***n.*** [< Fr. < L. *moles*, a mass], a breakwater.

**Mo·lech** (mō′lek), ***n.*** Moloch.

**mo·lec·u·lar** (mə-lek′yoo-lẽr), ***adj.*** of, consisting of, produced by, or existing between, molecules. —**mo·lec′u·lar·ly,** ***adv.***

**molecular weight,** the relative average weight of a molecule of a substance: cf. **atomic weight.**

**mol·e·cule** (mol′ə-kūl′), ***n.*** [< Fr. < Mod.L. *molecula*, dim. of L. *moles*, a mass], 1. the smallest particle of an element or compound that can exist in the free state and still retain the characteristics of the substance. 2. a small particle.

**mole·hill** (mōl′hil′), ***n.*** a small ridge or mound of earth, formed by a burrowing mole. —**make a mountain out of a molehill,** to regard a trivial difficulty as a great one.

**mole·skin** (mōl′skin′), ***n.*** 1. the soft skin of the mole, used as fur. 2. a strong cotton fabric with a soft nap, used for work clothes, etc. 3. *pl.* trousers made of this fabric.

**mo·lest** (mə-lest′), ***v.t.*** [< OFr. < L. < *molestus*, troublesome < *moles*, a burden], to annoy or meddle with so as to trouble or harm. —**mo·les·ta·tion** (mō′les-tā′shən, mol′əs-), ***n.*** —**mo·lest′er,** ***n.***

**Mo·lière** (mô′lyâr′), ***n.*** (pseudonym of *Jean Baptiste Poquelin*), French dramatist; lived 1622–1673.

**moll** (mol), ***n.*** [after fem. name, dim. of *Mary*], [Slang], [sometimes M-], 1. the mistress of a gangster, thief, or vagrant. 2. a prostitute.

**mol·li·fy** (mol′ə-fī′), ***v.t.*** [-FIED, -FYING], [< OFr. < LL. < L. *mollis*, soft + *facere*, to make], 1. to soothe; pacify; appease. 2. to make less severe or violent. —**mol′li·fi·ca′tion,** ***n.*** —**mol′li·fi′er,** ***n.*** —**mol′li·fy′ing·ly,** ***adv.***

**mol·lusk, mol·lusc** (mol′əsk), ***n.*** [< Fr. < L. *molluscus*, soft < *mollis*, soft], any of a large group (*Mollusca*) of invertebrates comprising the oysters, clams, snails, squids, octopi, etc., characterized by a soft, unsegmented body enclosed, in most instances, in a calcareous shell. —**mol·lus·can** (mə-lus′kən), ***adj. & n.***

**mol·ly·cod·dle** (mol′i-kod′′l), ***n.*** [< *Molly*, dim. of *Mary* + *coddle*], a man or boy used to being coddled or protected; milksop. ***v.t.*** [-DLED, -DLING], to pamper; coddle. —**mol′ly·cod′dler,** ***n.***

**Mo·loch** (mō′lok), ***n.*** 1. in the *Bible*, a god of the ancient Phoenicians and Ammonites, to whom children were sacrificed by burning. 2. anything regarded as demanding terrible sacrifice.

**Mo·lo·kai** (mō′lō-kī′), ***n.*** one of the Hawaiian Islands: site of a leper colony.

**Mo·lo·tov, Vya·che·slav Mi·khai·lo·vich** (vyä′chi-släf′ mi-khī′lô-vich mô′lô-tôf), 1890– ; Soviet statesman.

**molt** (mōlt), ***v.i.*** [AS. (*be*)*mutian*, to exchange < L. *mutare*, to change], to shed the hair, outer skin, horns, etc. prior to replacement by a new growth, as reptiles, birds, etc. ***v.t.*** to shed and replace by molting. ***n.*** 1. the act or process of molting. 2. the parts so shed. Also sp. **moult.** —**molt′er,** ***n.***

**mol·ten** (mōl′t'n), archaic pp. of **melt.** ***adj.*** 1. melted or liquefied by heat. 2. made by being melted and cast in a mold.

‡**mol·to** (môl′tô), ***adv.*** [It.], in *music*, very; much.

**Mo·luc·ca Islands** (mō-luk′ə), a group of islands of Indonesia, between Celebes and New Guinea: also called *Moluccas, Spice Islands.*

**mo·lyb·de·nite** (mə-lib′də-nīt′, mol′ib-dē′nīt), ***n.*** a scaly, lead-gray ore of molybdenum, $MoS_2$.

**mo·lyb·de·num** (mə-lib′də-nəm, mol′ib-dē′-), ***n.*** [< L. *molybdaena* (< Gr. < *molybdos*), lead], a silver-white metallic chemical element, used in alloys: symbol, Mo; at. wt., 95.95; at. no., 42.

**mom** (mom), ***n.*** [Colloq.], mother.

**mo·ment** (mō′mənt), ***n.*** [< L. *momentum*, movement < *movere*, to move], 1. an indefinitely brief period of time; instant. 2. a definite point in time. 3. importance; consequence: as, business of great *moment.* 4. in *mechanics, a*) the tendency to cause rotation about a point or axis. *b*) a measure of this. —**the moment,** the present time.

**mo·men·tar·i·ly** (mō′mən-ter′ə-li, mō′mən-ter′-), ***adv.*** 1. for a short time. 2. from instant to instant; every moment.

**mo·men·tar·y** (mō′mən-ter′i), ***adj.*** lasting for only a moment; transitory. —**mo′men·tar′i·ness,** ***n.***

**mo·ment·ly** (mō′mənt-li), ***adv.*** 1. from moment to moment. 2. instantly. 3. for a single instant.

**mo·men·tous** (mō-men′təs), ***adj.*** of great moment; very important: as, a *momentous* decision. —**mo·men′tous·ly,** ***adv.*** —**mo·men′tous·ness,** ***n.***

**mo·men·tum** (mō-men′təm), ***n.*** [*pl.* -TUMS, -TA (-tə)], [L.; see MOMENT], 1. the impetus of a moving object. 2. in *mechanics*, the quantity of motion of a moving object, equal to the product of its mass and its linear velocity.

**Mon.,** 1. Monday. 2. Monsignor.

**Mon·a·co** (mon′ə-kō′), ***n.*** a principality on the Mediterranean, geographically in SE France: area, ⅛ sq. mi.; pop., 20,000.

**mon·ad** (mon′ad, mō′nad), ***n.*** [< LL. *monas* < Gr. < *monos*, alone], 1. a unit. 2. in *biology*, any simple, single-celled organism. 3. in *chemistry*, an atom, element, or radical with a valence of one. —**mon·ad′ic, mon·ad′i·cal,** ***adj.***

**mon·arch** (mon′ẽrk), ***n.*** [< LL. < Gr. < *monos*, alone + *archein*, to rule], 1. the hereditary ruler of a state; king, queen, emperor, etc. 2. a person or thing that surpasses others of the same kind. 3. a species of large butterfly of North America, having reddish-brown wings with a black margin.

**mo·nar·chal** (mə-när′k'l), ***adj.*** of, like, suitable for, or characteristic of a monarch; royal: also **mo·nar′chi·al** (-ki-əl). —**mo·nar′chal·ly,** ***adv.***

**mo·nar·chi·cal** (mə-när′ki-k'l), ***adj.*** 1. of or like a monarch or monarchy. 2. favoring a monarchy. Also **mo·nar′chic** (-kik). —**mo·nar′chi·cal·ly,** ***adv.***

**mon·arch·ism** (mon′ẽr-kiz'm), ***n.*** 1. monarchical principles. 2. advocacy of such principles. —**mon′arch·ist,** ***n. & adj.*** —**mon′arch·is′tic,** ***adj.***

**mon·arch·y** (mon′ẽr-ki), ***n.*** [*pl.* -IES], 1. a state headed by a king, queen, or emperor. 2. government by a monarch.

**mon·as·ter·y** (mon′əs-ter′i), ***n.*** [*pl.* -IES], [< LL. < Gr. *monastērion* < *monazein*, to be alone < *monos*, alone], a place of residence occupied by a group of people, especially monks, who have retired from the world under religious vows. —**mon·as·te·ri·al** (mon′ə-stêr′i-əl), ***adj.***

**mo·nas·tic** (mə-nas′tik), ***adj.*** 1. of or characteristic of monasteries. 2. of or characteristic of monks or nuns; ascetic; self-denying. Also **mo·nas′ti·cal.** ***n.*** a monk. —**mo·nas′ti·cal·ly,** ***adv.***

**mo·nas·ti·cism** (mə-nas′tə-siz'm), ***n.*** the monastic system, state, or way of life.

**mon·au·ral** (mon-ô′rəl), ***adj.*** [*mon*(*o*)- + *aural*], designating or of sound reproduction that uses only one source of sound, giving a monophonic effect.

**Mon·day** (mun′di), ***n.*** [AS. *mon*(*an*)*dæg*, moon's day], the second day of the week.

‡**monde** (mōnd), ***n.*** [Fr.], the world; society.

‡**mon Dieu** (mōn′dyö′), [Fr.], my God.

**mo·ne·cious** (mə-nē′shəs, mō-), ***adj.*** monoecious.

**Mo·nel (metal)** (mō-nel′), [after A. *Monell*, U.S. manufacturer], an alloy of nickel, copper, iron, manganese, silicon, and carbon, very resistant to corrosion: a trade-mark: also sp. **Monell.**

**Mo·net, Claude** (klōd mô′ne′; Eng. mō-nā′), 1840–1926; French impressionist painter.

**mon·e·tar·y** (mon′ə-ter′i, mun′-), ***adj.*** [< L. < *moneta;* see MINT (place for coining money)], 1. of the coinage or currency of a country. 2. of money; pecuniary. —**mon′e·tar′i·ly,** ***adv.***

---

fat, āpe, bâre, cär; ten, ēven, hêre, ovẽr; is, bīte; lot, gō, hôrn, tōōl, look; oil, out; up, ūse, fũr; get; joy; yet; chin; she; thin, *th*en; zh, leisure; ŋ, ring; ə for *a* in *ago*, *e* in *agent*, *i* in *sanity*, *o* in *comply*, *u* in *focus;* ′ in *able* (ā′b'l); Fr. bål; ë, Fr. coeur; ö, Fr. feu; Fr. mon; ô, Fr. coq; ü, Fr. duc; H, G. ich; kh, G. doch. ‡ foreign; < derived from.

**mon·e·tize** (mon′ə-tīz′, mun′-), *v.t.* [-TIZED, -TIZING], [see MONETARY], 1. to coin into money. 2. to legalize as money. —**mon′e·ti·za′tion,** *n.*

**mon·ey** (mun′i), *n.* [*pl.* -EYS, -IES], [< OFr. < L. *moneta*, a mint; see MINT (place for coining money)], 1. *a*) pieces of gold, silver, etc. stamped by government authority and used as a medium of exchange; coin or coins. *b*) any paper note authorized to be so used; bank notes; bills. 2. anything used as a medium of exchange. 3. property; wealth. 4. any form or denomination of legally current money. 5. a money of account. —**for one's money,** for one's choice. —**in the money,** [Slang], prosperous; wealthy. —**make money,** to gain profits; become wealthy. —**put money into,** to invest money in. —**put money on,** to bet on.

**mon·ey·bag** (mun′i-bag′), *n.* 1. a bag for money. 2. *pl.* [Colloq.], [construed as sing.], a rich person.

**mon·ey·chang·er** (mun′i-chān′jēr), *n.* 1. one whose business is exchanging money of different countries. 2. a device holding stacked coins for making change quickly.

**mon·eyed** (mun′id), *adj.* 1. having much money; wealthy. 2. consisting of or representing money.

**mon·ey·lend·er** (mun′i-len′dēr), *n.* one whose business is lending money at interest.

**mon·ey-mak·ing** (mun′i-māk′iŋ), *n.* the gaining of money; acquisition of wealth. *adj.* profitable; lucrative. —**mon′ey-mak′er,** *n.*

**money of account,** a monetary denomination used in keeping accounts, etc., especially one not issued as a coin (e.g., the U.S. mill).

**money order,** an order for the payment of a specified sum of money, as one issued at one post office or bank and payable at another.

**mon·ger** (muŋ′gēr), *n.* [AS. *mangere* < *mangian*, to trade], [Chiefly Brit.], a dealer or trader (in a specified commodity): as, *fishmonger.*

**Mon·gol** (moŋ′gəl, -gol, -gōl), *adj.* Mongolian. *n.* 1. a native of Mongolia or near-by regions. 2. a member of the Mongolian race. 3. any of the Mongolian languages.

**Mongol.,** Mongolian.

**Mon·go·li·a** (moŋ-gō′li-ə, mon-gōl′yə), *n.* a region in central Asia, consisting of the Mongolian People's Republic and Inner Mongolia.

**Mon·go·li·an** (moŋ-gō′li-ən, mon-gōl′yən), *adj.* 1. of Mongolia or its people, language, or culture. 2. designating or of one of the three principal races of mankind, including most of the peoples of Asia, the Eskimos, etc., who are generally characterized by yellowish skins, slanting eyes, etc. 3. having Mongolism. *n.* 1. a native of Mongolia. 2. a member of the Mongolian race. 3. any of the Mongolian languages.

**Mongolian** (or **Mongoloid**) **idiot,** a person having Mongolism. —**Mongolian idiocy.**

**Mongolian People's Republic,** a country in central Asia: area, 600,000 sq. mi.; pop., 1,174,000; capital, Ulan Bator: formerly **Outer Mongolia.**

**Mon·gol·ism** (moŋ′gəl-iz′m), *n.* a type of congenital mental deficiency, accompanied with a flattened forehead, slanting eyes, etc.

**Mon·gol·oid** (moŋ′gəl-oid′), *adj.* 1. of or characteristic of the natives of Mongolia or the members of the Mongolian race. 2. having Mongolism. *n.* a member of the Mongolian race.

**mon·goose, mon·goos** (moŋ′gōōs, muŋ′-), *n.* [*pl.* -GOOSES], [< native name], a ferretlike, flesh-eating animal of India, known for its ability to kill rats, poisonous snakes, etc.

**mon·grel** (muŋ′grəl, moŋ′-), *n.* [< base of AS. *mengan*, to mix], 1. an animal or plant produced by the crossing of different breeds or varieties; esp., a dog of this kind. 2. anything produced by the mixture of incongruous things. *adj.* of mixed breed, race, origin, or character.

**mon·ies** (mun′iz), *n.* alt. pl. of **money.**

**mon·i·ker, mon·ick·er** (mon′i-kēr), *n.* [prob. < thieves' slang], [Slang], one's name or nickname.

**mon·ism** (mon′iz′m, mō′niz′m), *n.* [< Gr. *monos*, single], in *philosophy*, the doctrine that there is only one ultimate substance or principle, whether mind (*idealism*), matter (*materialism*), or something that is the basis of both. —**mon′ist,** *n.* —**mo·nis·tic** (mō-nis′tik), **mo·nis′ti·cal,** *adj.*

**mo·ni·tion** (mō-nish′ən), *n.* [OFr. < L. < pp. of *monere*, to warn], 1. admonition; warning; caution. 2. an official or legal notice.

**mon·i·tor** (mon′ə-tēr), *n.* [L. < pp. of *monere*, to warn], 1. [Rare], one who advises or warns. 2. in some schools, a student chosen to help keep order, record attendance, etc. 3. something that reminds or warns. 4. a flesh-eating lizard of Africa, S Asia, and Australia. 5. formerly, an armored warship with a low flat deck and heavy guns fitted in revolving turrets. 6. any of various devices for checking or regulating the performance of machines, aircraft, etc. 7. in *radio & television*, a receiver for reproducing transmission, used for checking on the operation of a transmitter. *v.t. & v.i.* 1. to watch or check on (a person or thing) as a monitor. 2. to check on or regulate the performance of (a machine, etc.). 3. to listen in on (a foreign broadcast, telephone conversation, etc.) as for gathering information. 4. in *radio & television*, to receive or check on (transmission, a transmitter, etc.) with a monitor. —**mon′i·to′ri·al** (-tôr′i-əl, -tō′ri-), *adj.* —**mon′i·tor·ship′,** *n.*

**mon·i·to·ry** (mon′ə-tôr′i, -tō′ri), *adj.* giving monition; admonishing. *n.*[*pl.* -RIES], a monitory letter.

**monk** (muŋk), *n.* [AS. *munuc* < LL. < Late Gr. < Gr. *monos*, alone], 1. originally, a man who retired to live in solitary self-denial for religious reasons. 2. a man who joins a religious order living in retirement according to a rule and under vows of poverty, obedience, and chastity.

**mon·key** (muŋ′ki), *n.* [*pl.* -KEYS], [prob. < MLG. *Moneke*, the son of Martin the Ape in the medieval beast epic *Reynard the Fox*], 1. any of the primates except man and the lemurs; specif., any of the smaller, long-tailed primates. 2. a person regarded as like a monkey, as a mischievous child. *v.i.* [Colloq.], to play, fool, trifle, or meddle.

**monkey business,** [Slang], foolish, mischievous, or deceitful tricks or behavior.

**mon·key·shine** (muŋ′ki-shīn′), *n. usually in pl.* [Slang], a mischievous trick or prank.

**monkey wrench,** a wrench with a movable jaw, adjustable to fit various sizes of nuts, etc.

**monk·ish** (muŋk′ish), *adj.* of, like, or characteristic of a monk or monks: often used in contempt. —**monk′ish·ly,** *adv.* —**monk′ish·ness,** *n.*

**monk's cloth,** a heavy cotton cloth with a basket weave, used for drapes, etc.

**monks·hood** (muŋks′hood′), *n.* the aconite plant.

**mon·o** (mon′ō), *adj.* [Colloq.], monophonic, *n.* [Colloq.], mononucleosis.

**mon·o-,** [Gr. < *monos*, single], a prefix meaning: *one, alone, single*, as in *monograph*. Also **mon-.**

**mon·o·bas·ic** (mon′ə-bā′sik), *adj.* in *chemistry*, designating an acid the molecule of which contains one hydrogen atom replaceable by a metal or positive radical.

**mon·o·chrome** (mon′ə-krōm′), *n.* [Fr. < Gr. < *monos*, single + *chrōma*, color], a painting or drawing in one color or different shades of one color. —**mon′o·chro·mat′ic,** *adj.* —**mon′o·chro′mic, mon′o·chro′mi·cal,** *adj.* —**mon′o·chrom′ist,** *n.*

**mon·o·cle** (mon′ə-k′l), *n.* [Fr. < LL. *monoculus*, one-eyed < Gr. *monos*, single + L. *oculus*, eye], an eyeglass for one eye. —**mon′o·cled,** *adj.*

**mon·o·cli·nal** (mon′ə-klī′n′l), *adj.* in *geology*, designating or of strata dipping in one direction.

**mon·o·cline** (mon′ə-klīn′), *n.* [< *mono-* + Gr. *klinein*, to incline], in *geology*, a monoclinal rock fold or structure.

**mon·o·cli·nous** (mon′ə-klī′nəs), *adj.* [< *mono-* + Gr. *klinē*, a bed], in *botany*, having the stamens and pistils in the same flower.

**mon·o·cot·y·le·don** (mon′ə-kot′′l-ē′d′n), *n.* in *botany*, any plant with only one cotyledon. —**mon′o·cot′y·le′don·ous** (-ē′d′n-əs, -ed′′n-), *adj.*

**mon·o·dy** (mon′ə-di), *n.* [*pl.* -DIES], [< LL. < Gr. *monōidia* < *monos*, alone + *aeidein*, to sing], 1. a solo lament or dirge, as in an ancient Greek tragedy. 2. a poem mourning someone's death. 3. in *music*, *a*) a style of composition in which the melody is carried by one part, or voice. *b*) a composition in this style. —**mo·nod·ic** (mə-nod′ik), **mo·nod′i·cal,** *adj.* —**mo·nod′i·cal·ly,** *adv.*

**mo·noe·cious** (mə-nē′shəs, mō-), *adj.* [< *mon*(*o*)- + Gr. *oikos*, a house], in *botany*, having the stamens and pistils in separate flowers on the same plant, as the oak: also sp. **monecious.**

**mo·nog·a·my** (mə-nog′ə-mi), *n.* [<Fr. < LL. < Gr. < *monos*, single + *gamos*, marriage], 1. the practice or state of being married to only one person at a time. 2. in *zoology*, the habit of having only one mate. —**mo·nog′a·mist,** *n.* —**mo·nog′a·mous, mon·o·gam·ic** (mon′ə-gam′ik), *adj.*

**mon·o·gram** (mon′ə-gram′), *n.* [< LL. < Gr. < *monos*, single + *gramma*, letter], the initials of a name, combined in a single design. *v.t.* [-GRAMMED, -GRAMMING] to decorate with a monogram.

**mon·o·graph** (mon′ə-graf′, -gräf′), *n.* [*mono-* + *-graph*], a book, article, or paper written about a particular subject. —**mo·nog·ra·pher** (mə-nog′rə-fēr), *n.* —**mon′o·graph′ic,** *adj.*

**mon·o·lith** (mon′ə-lith′), *n.* [< Fr. < L. < Gr. < *monos*, single + *lithos*, stone], 1. a single large block or piece of stone. 2. a pillar, statue, monument, etc. made of a single block of stone.

**mon·o·lith·ic** (mon'ə-lith'ik), *adj.* 1. of or like a monolith. 2. massively solid, single, and uniform.

**mon·o·logue, mon·o·log** (mon'ə-lôg', -log'), *n.* [Fr. < Gr. < *monos*, alone + *legein*, to speak], 1. a long speech, as one monopolizing a conversation. 2. a poem, etc. in the form of a soliloquy. 3. a part of a play in which one character speaks alone; soliloquy. 4. a play, skit, or recitation for one actor only. **—mon'o·logu'ist, mon'o·log'ist,** *n.*

**mon·o·ma·ni·a** (mon'ə-mā'ni-ə), *n.* 1. an excessive interest in or enthusiasm for some one thing; craze. 2. a mental disorder characterized by irrationality on one subject. **—mon'o·ma'ni·ac'** (-ak'), *n.* **—mon'o·ma·ni'a·cal** (-ō-mə-nī'ə-k'l), *adj.*

**mon·o·met·al·lism** (mon'ə-met''l-iz'm), *n.* the use of one metal, usually gold or silver, as the monetary standard. **—mon'o·me·tal'lic** (-ō-mə-tal'ik), *adj.*

**mo·no·mi·al** (mō-nō'mi-əl), *adj.* [< *mono-*, after *binomial*], in *algebra*, consisting of only one term. *n.* a monomial expression, quantity, etc.

**Mo·non·ga·he·la** (mə-noŋ'gə-hē'lə), *n.* a river in Pennsylvania: see **Allegheny.**

**mon·o·nu·cle·o·sis** (mon'ə-nōō'kli-ō'sis, -nū'-), *n.* a disease in which there is present in the blood an excessive number of cells with a single nucleus, characterized by enlargement of the lymph nodes: also **infectious mononucleosis.**

**mon·o·phon·ic** (mon'ə-fon'ik), *adj.* [*mono-* + *phonic*], designating or of sound reproduction using a single channel to carry and reproduce sounds: cf. *stereophonic.*

**mon·o·plane** (mon'ə-plān'), *n.* an airplane with only one pair of wings.

**mo·nop·o·list** (mə-nop'ə-list), *n.* 1. a person who has a monopoly. 2. a person who favors monopoly. *adj.* monopolistic. **—mo·nop'o·lism,** *n.*

**mo·nop·o·lis·tic** (mə-nop'ə-lis'tik), *adj.* 1. of monopolies or monopolists. 2. having a monopoly. **—mo·nop'o·lis'ti·cal·ly,** *adv.*

**mo·nop·o·lize** (mə-nop'ə-līz'), *v.t.* [-LIZED, -LIZING], 1. to get, have, or exploit a monopoly of. 2. to get or occupy the whole of. **—mo·nop'o·li·za'tion,** *n.* **—mo·nop'o·liz'er,** *n.*

**mo·nop·o·ly** (mə-nop'ə-li), *n.* [*pl.* -LIES], [< L. < Gr. < *monopōlia*, exclusive sale < *monos*, single + *pōlein*, to sell], 1. exclusive control of a commodity or service in a given market, or control that makes possible the fixing of prices. 2. such exclusive control granted by a government. 3. exclusive possession or control of something. 4. something that is the subject of a monopoly. 5. a company that has a monopoly.

**mon·o·rail** (mon'ə-rāl'), *n.* 1. a single rail serving as a track for cars suspended from it or balanced on it. 2. a railway with such a track.

**mon·o·syl·lab·ic** (mon'ə-si-lab'ik), *adj.* 1. having only one syllable. 2. consisting of, using, or speaking in, monosyllables. **—mon'o·syl·lab'i·cal·ly,** *adv.*

**mon·o·syl·la·ble** (mon'ə-sil'ə-b'l), *n.* a word of one syllable, as *cat.*

**mon·o·the·ism** (mon'ə-thē-iz'm), *n.* [< *mono-* + *theism*], the doctrine or belief that there is only one God. **—mon'o·the'ist,** *n.* **—mon'o·the·is'tic, mon'o·the·is'ti·cal,** *adj.*

**mon·o·tone** (mon'ə-tōn'), *n.* 1. utterance of successive words without change of pitch or key. 2. monotony of tone, style, color, etc. 3. a single, unchanging tone. 4. recitation, singing, etc. in such a tone. *adj.* monotonous.

**mo·not·o·nous** (mə-not'ə-nəs), *adj.* [see MONOTONE, & -OUS], 1. going on in the same tone without variation. 2. having little or no variety. 3. tiresome because unvarying. **—mo·not'o·nous·ly,** *adv.*

**mo·not·o·ny** (mə-not'ə-ni), *n.* 1. continuance of the same tone without variation. 2. lack of variety. 3. tiresome sameness.

**mon·o·treme** (mon'ə-trēm'), *n.* [< Gr. *monos*, single + *trema*, hole], any of the lowest order of mammals (the duckbill and echidnas), which have a single opening for the excretory and genital organs. **—mon'o·trem'a·tous** (-trem'ə-təs, -trē'mə-), *adj.*

**mon·o·type** (mon'ə-tīp'), *n.* [*mono-* + *-type*], 1. in *biology*, the only type of its group. 2. in *printing*, either of a pair of machines for casting and setting up type in separate characters: one, a casting machine, is controlled by a paper tape perforated on the other, a keyboard machine: a trade-mark (**Monotype**).

**mon·o·va·lent** (mon'ə-vā'lənt), *adj.* in *chemistry*, *a*) having a valence of one. *b*) univalent. **—mon'o·va'lence, mon'o·va'len·cy,** *n.*

**mon·ox·ide** (mon-ok'sīd, mə-nok'-), *n.* an oxide with one atom of oxygen in each molecule.

**Mon·roe, James** (mən-rō'), 1758–1831; fifth president of the U.S. (1817–1825).

**Monroe Doctrine,** the doctrine, stated by President Monroe, that the U.S. would regard as an unfriendly act any move by a European nation to interfere in the affairs of, or increase its possessions in, the Americas.

**Mon·ro·vi·a** (mon-rō'vi-ə), *n.* seaport and capital of Liberia, Africa: pop., 60,000.

**Mon·sei·gneur, mon·sei·gneur** (mon'sen-yūr'; Fr. mōn'se'nyër'), *n.* [*pl.* MESSEIGNEURS (mes'en-yūrz'; Fr. mā'se'nyër')], [Fr., lit., my lord], 1. a French title of honor given to persons of high birth or rank, as princes, bishops, etc. 2. a person who has this title.

**mon·sieur** (mə-syūr'; Fr. mə-syö'), *n.* [*pl.* MESSIEURS (mes'ērz; Fr. mā'syö')], [Fr., lit., my lord], a man; gentleman: French title [M-], equivalent to *Mr.* or *Sir:* abbrev. **M., Mons.**

**Monsig.,** 1. Monseigneur. 2. Monsignor.

**Mon·si·gnor, mon·si·gnor** (mon-sēn'yēr; It. môn'sē-nyôr'), *n.* [*pl.* -GNORS; It. -GNORI (-nyô'rē)], [It., lit., my lord], 1. a title given to Roman Catholic prelates. 2. a person who has this title.

**mon·soon** (mon-sōōn'), *n.* [< MD. < Port. < Ar. *mausim*, a season], 1. a seasonal wind of the Indian Ocean and S Asia, blowing from the southwest from April to October, and from the opposite direction the rest of the year. 2. the rainy season during which this wind blows from the southwest.

**mon·ster** (mon'stēr), *n.* [< OFr. < L. *monstrum*, divine portent < *monere*, to warn], 1. any plant or animal of abnormal shape or structure; monstrosity. 2. any imaginary creature with striking incongruities in form, as a centaur or griffin. 3. something monstrous. 4. any very cruel or wicked person. 5. any huge animal or thing. *adj.* huge; monstrous.

**mon·strance** (mon'strəns), *n.* [OFr. < ML. < L. *monstrare*, to show], in the *R.C. Church*, a receptacle in which the consecrated Host is exposed.

**mon·stros·i·ty** (mon-stros'ə-ti), *n.* 1. the state or quality of being monstrous. 2. [*pl.* -TIES], a monstrous thing or creature; monster.

**mon·strous** (mon'strəs), *adj.* 1. having the character or appearance of a monster. 2. horrible; hideous. 3. hideously wrong or evil; atrocious. 4. huge; enormous. 5. very unnatural in shape, type, or character. *adv.* [Colloq.], very; extremely. **—mon'strous·ly,** *adv.* **—mon'strous·ness,** *n.*

**mon·tage** (mon-täzh', mōn-), *n.* [Fr. < *monter*, to mount], 1. *a*) the art or process of making a composite picture of a number of different pictures. *b*) a picture so made. 2. in *motion pictures*, a kaleidoscope of images or scenes to show a rapid succession of associated ideas.

**Mon·taigne, Mi·chel Ey·quem de** (mē'shel' e'kem' də mōn'ten'y'; Eng. mon-tān'), 1533–1592; French essayist.

**Mon·tan·a** (mon-tan'ə), *n.* a Western State of the U.S.: area, 147,138 sq. mi.; pop., 675,000; capital, Helena: abbrev. **Mont. —Mon·tan'an,** *adj. & n.*

**Mont Blanc** (mōn blän'; Eng. mont blaŋk), a mountain in E France, on the Italian border: height, 15,781 ft.: highest peak of the Alps.

**Mont·calm** (mont-käm'), *n.* (*Louis Joseph, Marquis de Montcalm*), French field marshal; 1712–1759; defeated by the British at Quebec (1759).

**mon·te** (mon'ti, mōn'tā), *n.* [Sp., lit., mountain (of cards)], a Spanish gambling game in which players bet on the color of cards to be turned up.

**Mon·te Car·lo** (mon'ti kär'lō), a town in Monaco: gambling resort.

**Mon·te·ne·gro** (mon'tə-nē'grō), *n.* a former kingdom north of Albania, now a federated republic of Yugoslavia. **—Mon'te·ne'grin** (-grin), *adj. & n.*

**Mon·ter·rey** (mon'tə-rā'), *n.* a city in NE Mexico: pop., 564,000.

**Mon·tes·quieu** (mon'təs-kū'), *n.* (*Baron de la Brède et de Montesquieu*), French jurist and writer on history and government; lived 1689–1755.

**Mon·tes·so·ri, Maria** (mon'tə-sôr'i, -sō'ri), 1870–1952; Italian educator.

**Mon·te·vid·e·o** (mon'tə-vi-dā'ō, -vid'i-ō'), *n.* capital of Uruguay, on the Plata River: pop., 923,000.

**Mon·te·zu·ma II** (mon'tə-zōō'mə), 1480?–1520; last Aztec emperor of Mexico (1502–1520); conquered by Cortés.

**Mont·gom·er·y** (mont-gum′ẽr-i, mən-gum′ri), *n.* the capital of Alabama, in the central part: pop., 134,000.

**month** (munth), *n.* [AS. *monath* < base of *mona*, moon], 1. any of the twelve parts into which the calendar year is divided: also **calendar month.** 2. *a)* the time from any day of one month to the corresponding day of the next. *b)* a period of four weeks or 30 days. 3. the period of a complete revolution of the moon (in full, **lunar month**). 4. one twelfth of the solar year (in full, **solar month**). —**month after month,** every month. —**month by month,** each month. —**month in, month out,** every month.

**month·ly** (munth′li), *adj.* 1. continuing or lasting for a month. 2. done, happening, payable, etc. every month. 3. of the menses. *n.* [*pl.* -LIES], 1. a periodical published once a month. 2. *pl.* the menses. *adv.* once a month; every month.

**Mon·ti·cel·lo** (mon′tə-sel′ō; *occas.* -chel′ō), *n.* the home of Thomas Jefferson, in central Virginia.

**Mont·mar·tre** (mōn′mȧr′tr′), *n.* a section of the N part of Paris, famous for its night life.

**Mont·pel·ier** (mont-pēl′yẽr), *n.* the capital of Vermont, in the central part: pop., 9,000.

**Mont·re·al** (mont′ri-ôl′, munt′-), *n.* a city in S Quebec, Canada, on an island in the St. Lawrence River: pop., 1,109,000 (with suburbs, 1,621,000).

**Mont St. Mi·chel** (mōn′ san′ mē′shel′), a small island off the NW coast of France, noted for its fortress and abbey: also **Mont-Saint-Michel.**

**mon·u·ment** (mon′yoo-mənt), *n.* [OFr. < L. *monumentum* < *monere*, to remind], 1. something set up to keep alive the memory of a person or event, as a tablet, statue, building, etc. 2. a writing, etc. serving as a memorial. 3. a work of enduring significance: as, *monuments* of learning. 4. a stone boundary marker. 5. [Obs.], a tomb.

**mon·u·men·tal** (mon′yoo-men′t′l), *adj.* 1. of, suitable for, or serving as a monument. 2. like a monument; massive, enduring, etc. 3. of lasting importance: as, a *monumental* book. 4. great; colossal: as, *monumental* ineptitude. —**mon′u·men′tal·ly,** *adv.*

**-mo·ny** (mō′ni), [< Fr. *-monie* or L. *-monia*], a suffix used to form nouns that mean *a resulting thing, condition,* or *state,* as in *patrimony.*

**moo** (mo͞o), *n.* [*pl.* MOOS], [echoic], the vocal sound made by a cow; lowing sound. *v.i.* [MOOED, MOOING], to make this sound; low.

**mooch** (mo͞och), *v.i.* [ult. < OFr. *muchier*, to hide], [Slang], 1. to skulk or sneak. 2. to loiter. *v.t.* [Slang], 1. to steal. 2. to get by begging or asking; cadge. —**mooch′er,** *n.*

**mood** (mo͞od), *n.* [AS. *mod*, mind], 1. a particular state of mind or feeling; humor, or temper. 2. *pl.* fits of morose, sullen, or uncertain temper.

**mood** (mo͞od), *n.* [< *mode*, infl. by prec. *mood*], in *grammar,* that aspect of verbs which indicates whether the action or state expressed is regarded as a fact (*indicative mood*), as a matter of supposal, desire, etc. (*subjunctive mood*), as a command (*imperative mood*) etc.: also **mode.**

**mood·y** (mo͞od′i), *adj.* [-IER, -IEST], 1. subject to or characterized by gloomy, sullen, or changing moods. 2. resulting from or indicating such a mood. 3. gloomy; sullen. —**mood′i·ly,** *adv.* —**mood′i·ness,** *n.*

**moon** (mo͞on), *n.* [AS. *mona*], 1. the satellite of the earth, that revolves around it once every 29½ days and shines at night by reflecting the sun's light. 2. this body as it appears at a particular time of the month: see **new moon, half-moon, full moon,** and **old moon.** 3. a month; esp., a lunar month. 4. moonlight. 5. anything shaped like the moon (i.e., orb or crescent). 6. any planetary satellite. *v.i.* to wander or gaze about in an idle, listless, or abstracted manner. *v.t.* to pass (time) in mooning. —**moon′like′,** *adj.*

**moon·beam** (mo͞on′bēm′), *n.* a ray of moonlight.

**moon·calf** (mo͞on′kaf′, -käf′), *n.* an idiot; fool.

**moon-faced** (mo͞on′fāst′), *adj.* round-faced.

**moon·light** (mo͞on′līt′), *n.* the light of the moon. *adj.* 1. of moonlight. 2. moonlit. 3. done or occurring by moonlight, or at night.

**moon·light·ing** (mo͞on′līt′iŋ), *n.* [from night hours usual for second job], the practice of holding another regular job in addition to one's main job.

**moon·lit** (mo͞on′lit), *adj.* lighted by the moon.

**moon·shine** (mo͞on′shīn′), *n.* 1. moonlight. 2. foolish or empty talk, notions, etc. 3. [Colloq.], whisky, etc. unlawfully made or smuggled.

**moon·shin·er** (mo͞on′shīn′ẽr), *n.* [Colloq.], a person who makes alcoholic liquor unlawfully.

**moon·stone** (mo͞on′stōn′), *n.* a translucent feldspar with a pearly luster, used as a gem.

**moon·struck** (mo͞on′struk′), *adj.* crazed; lunatic; dazed: also **moon′-strick′en** (-strik′ən).

**moon·y** (mo͞on′i), *adj.* [-IER, -IEST], mooning; listless, dreamy, or silly. —**moon′i·ly,** *adv.*

**Moor** (moor), *n.* 1. a member of a Moslem people of mixed Arab and Berber descent living in NW Africa. 2. a member of a group of this people that invaded and occupied Spain in the 8th century A.D. —**Moor′ish,** *adj.*

**moor** (moor), *n.* [AS. *mor*], [Brit.], a tract of open wasteland, usually covered with heather and often marshy; heath.

**moor** (moor), *v.t.* [cf. AS. *mærels*, mooring rope], 1. to hold (a ship, etc.) in place by cables or chains fastened on shore, or by anchors, etc. 2. to secure. *v.i.* 1. to moor a ship, etc. 2. to be secured by cables, anchors, etc. —**moor′age** (-ij), *n.*

**moor cock,** [Brit.], the male moorfowl.

**Moore, Thomas** (moor, môr, mōr), 1779–1852; Irish poet.

**moor·fowl** (moor′foul′), *n.* [Brit.], the red grouse, a ptarmigan of the moors.

**moor hen,** [Brit.], 1. the female moorfowl. 2. the common European gallinule.

**moor·ing** (moor′iŋ), *n.* 1. *often in pl.* the lines, cables, etc. by which a ship, etc. is moored. 2. *pl.* a place where a ship, etc. is moored.

**mooring mast** (or **tower**), a mast (or tower) to which an airship is moored.

**moor·land** (moor′land′), *n.* [Brit.], uncultivated land covered with heather; moor.

**moose** (mo͞os), *n.* [*pl.* MOOSE], [< Am. Ind. (Algonquian)], 1. the largest animal of the deer family, native to the northern U.S. and Canada: the male has huge palmate antlers. 2. the European elk.

**moot** (mo͞ot), *n.* [AS. (*ge*)*mot*, a meeting], 1. an early English assembly of freemen to administer justice, etc. 2. a discussion or argument. *adj.* debatable. *v.t.* 1. to debate or discuss. 2. to propose for discussion or debate. —**moot′er,** *n.*

**moot court,** a mock court in which hypothetical cases are tried, as to give law students practice.

**mop** (mop), *n.* [Early Mod. Eng. *mappe*], 1. a bundle of loose rags, yarns, a sponge, etc. at the end of a stick, as for washing floors. 2. anything suggestive of this, as a thick head of hair. *v.t.* [MOPPED, MOPPING], to wash, wipe, or remove with or as with a mop (sometimes with *up*). —**mop up,** [Colloq.], to finish.

**mop** (mop), *n.* & *v.i.* [MOPPED, MOPPING], [< dial. phr. *mop and mow*], grimace.

**mope** (mōp), *v.i.* [MOPED, MOPING], [? akin to *mop* (grimace)], to be gloomy and apathetic. *n.* 1. one who mopes. 2. *pl.* low spirits. —**mop′er,** *n.* —**mop′ish,** *adj.* —**mop′ish·ly,** *adv.* —**mop′ish·ness,** *n.*

**mop·pet** (mop′it), *n.* [< ME. *moppe*, rag doll], [Archaic], a little child: a term of affection.

**Mor.,** Morocco.

**mo·raine** (mə-rān′, mō-), *n.* [Fr.], a mass of rocks, gravel, sand, etc. deposited by a glacier, either along its side (**lateral moraine**) or at its lower end (**terminal moraine**). —**mo·rain′ic,** *adj.*

**mor·al** (môr′əl, mor′-), *adj.* [< L. < *mos*, pl. *mores*, manners, morals], 1. relating to, dealing with, or capable of distinguishing between, right and wrong in conduct. 2. of, teaching, or in accordance with, the principles of right and wrong. 3. good or right in conduct or character; often, specif., sexually virtuous. 4. designating support, etc. that involves sympathy without action. 5. being virtually such because of its general results: as, a *moral* victory. 6. based on strong probability: as, a *moral* certainty. *n.* 1. a moral implication or lesson taught by a fable, event, etc. 2. a maxim. 3. *pl.* principles, standards, or habits with respect to right or wrong in conduct; ethics.

**mo·rale** (mə-ral′, mô-räl′), *n.* [Fr., fem. of *moral;* see MORAL], moral or mental condition with respect to courage, discipline, confidence, etc.

**mor·al·ist** (môr′əl-ist, mor′-), *n.* 1. a person who moralizes. 2. one who lives virtuously. —**mor′al·is′tic,** *adj.* —**mor′al·is′ti·cal·ly,** *adv.*

**mo·ral·i·ty** (mô-ral′ə-ti, mə-), *n.* [*pl.* -TIES], 1. moral quality or character; rightness or wrongness, as of an action. 2. a being in accord with the principles or standards of right conduct; virtue. 3. principles of right and wrong in conduct; ethics. 4. moral instruction or lesson. 5. a morality play.

**morality play,** any of a class of allegorical dramas of the 15th and 16th centuries, whose characters were personifications, as Everyman, Vice, etc.

**mor·al·ize** (môr′ə-līz′, mor′-), *v.i.* [-IZED, -IZING], to consider or discuss matters of right and wrong. *v.t.* 1. *a)* to explain in terms of right and wrong. *b)* to draw a moral from. 2. to improve the morals of. —**mor′al·i·za′tion,** *n.* —**mor′al·iz′er,** *n.*

**mor·al·ly** (môr′əl-i, mor′-), *adv.* 1. in a moral manner. 2. as regards morals. 3. virtually.
**moral philosophy,** ethics.
**mo·rass** (mô-ras′, mə-, mō-), *n.* [< D. < OFr. *maresc* < Frank.], a tract of low, soft, watery ground; bog; swamp: used figuratively of a difficulty, etc.
**mor·a·to·ri·um** (môr′ə-tôr′i-əm, mor′ə-tō′ri-), *n.* [*pl.* -RIUMS, -RIA (-ri-ə)], [< LL. < L. < *mora*, a delay], 1. a legal authorization, usually by an emergency law, to delay payment of money due. 2. the effective period of such an authorization.
**Mo·ra·vi·a** (mô-rā′vi-ə, mō-), *n.* a former province of Austria: now a part of Czechoslovakia.
**Mo·ra·vi·an** (mô-rā′vi-ən, mō-), *adj.* 1. of Moravia, its people, etc. 2. of the Moravians (sense 3). *n.* 1. a native or inhabitant of Moravia. 2. the Czech dialect of Moravia. 3. a member of a Protestant sect founded in Moravia c. 1722.
**mo·ray** (môr′ā, mō-rā′), *n.* [< Port. < L. *muraena*, kind of fish], a voracious, brilliantly colored eel, found especially among coral reefs.
**mor·bid** (môr′bid), *adj.* [< L. *morbidus*, sickly < *morbus*, disease], 1. of, having, or caused by disease. 2. resulting from or as from a diseased state of mind. 3. gruesome; horrible. 4. of diseased parts; pathological: as, *morbid* anatomy. **—mor·bid′i·ty, mor′bid·ness,** *n.* **—mor′bid·ly,** *adv.*
**mor·dant** (môr′d'nt), *adj.* [< OFr. pp. of *mordre* (< L. *mordere*), to bite], 1. biting, caustic, or sarcastic: as, *mordant* wit. 2. acting to fix colors in dyeing, etc. *n.* 1. a substance used in dyeing to fix the colors. 2. an acid, etc. used in etching to bite lines, etc. into a metal surface. **—mor′dan·cy,** *n.* **—mor′dant·ly,** *adv.*
**more** (môr, mōr), *adj.* [superl. MOST], [AS. *mara*], 1. greater in amount, quantity, or degree: used as the comparative of *much*. 2. greater in number: used as the comparative of *many*. 3. additional; further: as, there is *more* tea. *n.* 1. a greater amount, quantity, or degree. 2. [construed as pl.], a greater number (*of*): as, *more* of us are going. 3. something additional or further: as, *more* cannot be said. *adv.* 1. [superl. MOST], in or to a greater degree or extent: used with many adjectives and adverbs (always with those of three or more syllables) to form comparatives. 2. in addition; further. **—more and more,** 1. increasingly. 2. a constantly increasing amount, quantity, etc. **—more or less,** 1. somewhat. 2. approximately.
**More,** Sir **Thomas** (môr, mōr), 1478–1535; English statesman and author; executed; canonized in 1935: also **Saint Thomas More.**
**more·o·ver** (môr-ō′vẽr, mōr-), *adv.* in addition to what has been said; besides; further; also.
**mo·res** (mō′rēz, môr′ēz), *n.pl.* [*sing.* MOS (mōs)], [L., customs], folkways that, through general observance, develop the force of law.
**Mor·gan, John Pier·pont** (pêr′pont môr′gən), 1837–1913; U.S. financier.
**mor·ga·nat·ic** (môr′gə-nat′ik), *adj.* [< ML. < *morganaticum*; altered < OHG. *morgengeba*, morning gift (given to the wife on the day after marriage in lieu of a dower)], designating or of a form of marriage in which a man of high rank marries a woman of inferior social status with the stipulation that neither she nor their offspring may lay claim to his rank or property. **—mor′ga·nat′i·cal·ly,** *adv.*
**morgue** (môrg), *n.* [Fr.], 1. a place where the bodies of accident victims and unknown dead are kept prior to identification. 2. a newspaper office's reference library of back numbers, clippings, etc.
**mor·i·bund** (môr′ə-bund′, mor′ə-bənd), *adj.* [< L. *moribundus* < *mori*, to die], 1. dying. 2. coming to an end. **—mor′i·bun′di·ty,** *n.* **—mor′i·bund·ly,** *adv.*
**mo·ri·on** (môr′i-on′, mō′ri-), *n.* [Fr. < Sp. < *morra*, crown of the head], a crested, visorless helmet of the 16th and 17th centuries.
**Mo·ris·co** (mə-ris′kō), *adj.* [Sp. < *Moro*, Moor], Moorish. *n.* [*pl.* -COS, -COES], a Moor; esp., one of the Moors of Spain.
**Mor·mon** (môr′mən), *n.* a member of the Church of Jesus Christ of Latter-day Saints (commonly called the **Mormon Church**), founded in the U.S. in 1830 by Joseph Smith. *adj.* of the Mormons or their religion. **—Mor′mon·ism,** *n.*
**morn** (môrn), *n.* [AS. *morne*], [Poetic], morning.
**morn·ing** (môr′niŋ), *n.* [ME. *morweninge* (by analogy with *evening*) < AS. *morgen*], 1. the first or early part of the day, from midnight, or especially dawn, to noon. 2. the first or early part: as, the *morning* of life. 3. dawn; daybreak. *adj.* of, suited to, or occurring, appearing, etc. in the morning.
**morn·ing-glo·ry** (môr′niŋ-glôr′i, -glō′ri), *n.* [*pl.* -RIES], a twining plant with heart-shaped leaves and trumpet-shaped flowers of lavender, blue, pink, or white.
**morning star,** a planet, especially Venus, visible in the eastern sky before sunrise.
**Mo·ro** (môr′ō, mō′rō), *n.* [*pl.* -ROS], [Sp., a Moor], 1. a member of a group of Moslem Malay tribes living in the S Philippines. 2. their Malay language. *adj.* of the Moros.
**Mo·roc·co** (mə-rok′ō), *n.* 1. a country of NW Africa, formerly divided into a French zone, a Spanish zone, and Tangier: area, 174,471 sq. mi.; pop., 11,598,000; capital, Rabat. 2. Marrakech. 3. [m-], a fine, soft leather made, originally in Morocco, from goatskins tanned with sumac: also **morocco leather.** **—Mo·roc′can,** *adj.* & *n.*
**mo·ron** (môr′on, mō′ron), *n.* [< Gr. neut. of *mōros*, foolish], 1. a mentally deficient person with an intelligence quotient of from 50 to 75: *moron* is the highest classification of mental deficiency: cf. *idiot*, *imbecile*. 2. loosely, a very stupid person. **—mo·ron′ic,** *adj.* **—mo·ron′i·ty, mo′ron·ism,** *n.*
**mo·rose** (mə-rōs′), *adj.* [L. *morosus*, fretful < *mos*, manner], gloomy, sullen, surly, etc. **—mo·rose′ly,** *adv.* **—mo·rose′ness,** *n.*
**-morph** (môrf), [< Gr. *morphē*, form], a combining form meaning *one having a* (specified) *form*.
**mor·pheme** (môr′fēm), *n.* [< Gr. *morphē*, form], any word or part of a word, as an affix, that conveys meaning and cannot be further divided into smaller elements conveying meaning.
**Mor·pheus** (môr′fi-əs, -fūs), *n.* in *Gr. mythology*, the god of dreams, son of the god of sleep.
**mor·phi·a** (môr′fi-ə), *n.* [Mod. L.], morphine.
**-mor·phic** (môr′fik), [< Gr. *morphē*, form], a combining form meaning *having a* (specified) *form* or *shape*, as in *anthropomorphic*: also **-mor′phous** (-fəs).
**mor·phine** (môr′fēn), *n.* [< G. or Fr. < L. *Morpheus*, Morpheus], a bitter, white, crystalline alkaloid derived from opium and used to induce sleep and relieve pain: also **mor′phin** (-fin).
**mor·phin·ism** (môr′fin-iz'm), *n.* addiction to the use of morphine.
**mor·phol·o·gy** (môr-fol′ə-ji), *n.* [< Gr. *morphē*, form; + *-logy*], 1. the branch of biology dealing with the form and structure of animals and plants. 2. the branch of linguistics dealing with the internal structure and forms of words. **—mor′pho·log′i·cal** (-fə-loj′i-k'l), **mor′pho·log′ic,** *adj.* **—mor′pho·log′i·cal·ly,** *adv.* **—mor·phol′o·gist,** *n.*
**mor·ris** (môr′is, mor′-), *adj.* [earlier *morys*, Moorish], designating or of an old English folk dance for which costumes were worn. *n.* this dance.
**Mor·ris, William** (môr′is, mor′-), 1834–1896; English poet, artist, craftsman, and socialist.
**Morris chair,** [after Wm. *Morris*, who popularized it], a large armchair with an adjustable back.
**mor·ro** (mor′ō), *n.* [*pl.* -ROS], [Sp.], a rounded hill, bluff, or point of land.
**mor·row** (mor′ō, môr′ō), *n.* [< AS. *morgen*, morning], [Poetic], 1. morning. 2. the following day. 3. the time just after some particular event.
**Morse** (môrs), *adj.* [after S. F. B. *Morse*, the inventor], designating or of a code, or alphabet, consisting of a system of dots, dashes, and spaces, used in telegraphy, etc. *n.* the Morse code.
**Morse, Samuel F. B.** (môrs), 1791–1872; U.S. inventor of the telegraph.
**mor·sel** (môr's'l), *n.* [< OFr. dim. of *mors* < L. *morsum*, a bite < pp. of *mordere*, to bite], 1. a small bite or mouthful of food. 2. a small piece or amount. *v.t.* to divide into small portions.
**mor·tal** (môr't'l), *adj.* [< OFr. < L. *mortalis* < *mors*, death], 1. that must eventually die. 2. of man as a being who must eventually die. 3. of this world. 4. of death. 5. causing death; fatal. 6. very grave: said of certain sins. 7. to the death: as, *mortal* combat. 8. dire; grievous: as, *mortal* terror. 9. [Colloq.], *a*) extreme; very great. *b*) very long and tedious. *n.* a being who must eventually die; esp., a human being. *adv.* [Dial.], extremely. **—mor′tal·ly,** *adv.*
**mor·tal·i·ty** (môr-tal′ə-ti), *n.* 1. the mortal nature of man. 2. death on a large scale, as from disease or war. 3. the proportion of deaths to the population of a region, nation, etc.; death rate. 4. human beings collectively.

**mor·tar** (môr′tẽr), *n.* [< AS. & OFr. < L. *mortarium*], 1. a very hard bowl in which substances are ground or pounded to a powder with a pestle. 2. a short-barreled cannon with a low muzzle velocity, which throws shells in a high trajectory. 3. a mixture of cement or lime with sand and water, used between bricks, etc., or as plaster. *v.t.* to plaster together with mortar.

MORTAR AND PESTLE

**mor·tar·board** (môr′tẽr-bôrd′, -bōrd′), *n.* 1. a square board with a handle beneath, on which mortar is carried. 2. an academic cap with a square, flat top, worn at commencements, etc.

**mort·gage** (môr′gij), *n.* [< OFr. < *mort*, dead + *gage*, pledge], in *law*, 1. the pledging of property to a creditor as security for the payment of a debt. 2. the deed by which this pledge is made. *v.t.* [-GAGED, -GAGING], 1. in *law*, to pledge (property) by a mortgage. 2. to put an advance claim or liability on: as, he *mortgaged* his future.

**mort·ga·gee** (môr′gi-jē′), *n.* a person to whom property is mortgaged.

**mort·ga·gor, mort·ga·ger** (môr′gi-jẽr), *n.* a person who mortgages property.

**mor·tice** (môr′tis), *n.* & *v.t.* [-TICED, -TICING], mortise.

**mor·ti·cian** (môr-tish′ən), *n.* [< L. *mors*, death; + *-ician*], a funeral director; undertaker.

**mor·ti·fi·ca·tion** (môr′tə-fi-kā′shən), *n.* 1. a mortifying or being mortified; specif., *a*) the control of physical desires by self-denial, fasting, etc. *b*) shame, humiliation, etc. *c*) gangrene. 2. something causing shame, humiliation, etc.

**mor·ti·fy** (môr′tə-fī′), *v.t.* [-FIED, -FYING], [< OFr. < LL. *mortificare*, to kill < L. *mors*, death + *facere*, to make], 1. to punish (one's body) or control (one's physical desires) by self-denial, fasting, etc. 2. to shame, humiliate, etc. 3. to make gangrenous. *v.i.* to become gangrenous. —**mor′ti·fi′er,** *n.*

**mor·tise** (môr′tis), *n.* [< OFr. *mortaise* < Ar. *murtazza*, joined], a notch or hole cut, as in a piece of wood, to receive a projecting part (*tenon*) shaped to fit. *v.t.* [-TISED, -TISING], 1. to join securely, especially with a mortise and tenon. 2. to cut a mortise in.

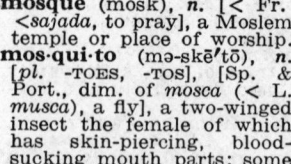

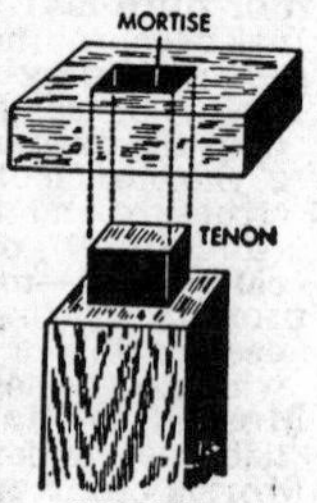

MORTISE

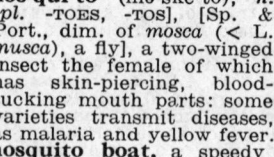

**mort·main** (môrt′mān), *n.* [< Anglo-Fr. < OFr. < ML. < L. *mortuus*, pp. of *mori*, to die + *manus*, hand], in *law*, a transfer of lands or houses to a corporate body for perpetual ownership.

**mor·tu·ar·y** (môr′chōō-er′i), *n.* [*pl.* -IES], [< ML. < LL. < L. *mortuus*, dead], a place where dead bodies are kept before burial or cremation, as a morgue. *adj.* 1. of the burial of the dead. 2. of death.

**mos** (mōs), *n.* sing. of **mores.**

**mos.,** months.

**Mo·sa·ic** (mō-zā′ik), *adj.* of Moses or the writings, laws, etc. attributed to him.

**mo·sa·ic** (mō-zā′ik), *n.* [< OFr. < It. < ML. *mosaicus* < Gr. *mouseios*, of the Muses < *Mousa*, a Muse], 1. the process of making pictures or designs by inlaying small bits of colored stone, glass, etc. in mortar. 2. a picture or design so made. 3. anything resembling this. *adj.* of, like, or forming a mosaic. *v.t.* [-ICKED, -ICKING], to make by or as by mosaic. —**mo·sa′i·cist** (-ə-sist), *n.*

**Mosaic law,** the ancient Hebrew law, ascribed to Moses and contained mainly in the Pentateuch.

**Mos·cow** (mos′kou, -kō), *n.* a city in central European Russia: capital of the R.S.F.S.R. and the U.S.S.R.: pop., 4,137,000.

**Mo·selle** (mō-zel′), *n.* a river flowing through NE France and Germany into the Rhine.

**Mo·ses** (mō′ziz, -zəs), *n.* in the *Bible*, the leader and lawgiver who brought the Israelites out of slavery in Egypt and into the Promised Land, and who received the Ten Commandments.

**mo·sey** (mō′zi), *v.i.* [-SEYED, -SEYING], [< *vamose*, var. of *vamoose*], [Slang], 1. to amble along. 2. to go away.

**Mos·lem** (moz′ləm, mos′-), *n.* [*pl.* -LEMS, -LEM], [< Ar. *muslim*, true believer < *aslama*, to resign oneself (to God)], an adherent of Islam, or follower of Mohammed. *adj.* of Islam or the Moslems. Also **Muslem, Muslim.** —**Mos′lem·ism,** *n.*

**mosque** (mosk), *n.* [< Fr. < It. < Ar. *masjid* <*sajada*, to pray], a Moslem temple or place of worship.

MOSQUE

**mos·qui·to** (mə-skē′tō), *n.* [*pl.* -TOES, -TOS], [Sp. & Port., dim. of *mosca* (< L. *musca*), a fly], a two-winged insect the female of which has skin-piercing, blood-sucking mouth parts: some varieties transmit diseases, as malaria and yellow fever.

**mosquito boat,** a speedy motorboat equipped with torpedoes and small guns: now called *PT Boat.*

**mosquito net** (or **netting**), a fine curtain for keeping mosquitoes out of a bed, etc.

**moss** (môs, mos), *n.* [AS. *mos*, a swamp], 1. a very small, green plant that grows in velvety clusters on rocks, trees, moist ground, etc. 2. any of various similar plants, as some lichens. *v.t.* to cover with moss. —**moss′like′,** *adj.*

**moss agate,** agate with mosslike markings.

**moss·back** (môs′bak′, mos′-), *n.* [Colloq.], an old-fashioned or very conservative person.

**moss rose,** 1. a variety of rose with a roughened, mossy stem. 2. its flower.

**moss·y** (môs′i, mos′i), *adj.* [-SIER, -SIEST], 1. full of or covered with moss or a mosslike growth. 2. like moss. —**moss′i·ness,** *n.*

**most** (mōst), *adj.* [compar. MORE], [AS. *mast*, *mæst*], 1. greatest in amount, quantity, or degree: used as the superlative of *much.* 2. greatest in number: used as the superlative of *many.* 3. in the greatest number of instances: as, *most* fame is fleeting. *n.* 1. the greatest amount, quantity, or degree. 2. the greatest number (*of*): as, *most* of us are going. *adv.* 1. [compar. MORE], in or to the greatest degree or extent: used with many adjectives and adverbs (always with those of three or more syllables) to form superlatives. 2. very: as, a *most* beautiful morning. 3. [Colloq.], almost; nearly. —**at (the) most,** at the very limit; not more than. —**for the most part,** in most instances; mainly. —**make the most of,** to take fullest advantage of.

**-most** (mōst), [AS. *-mest*], a suffix used in forming superlatives, as *foremost, hindmost.*

**most·ly** (mōst′li), *adv.* 1. for the most part; in the main. 2. chiefly; principally.

**Mo·sul** (mō-sōōl′), *n.* a city in N Iraq, on the Tigris River: pop., 203,000.

**mot** (mō), *n.* [Fr., a word < L. *muttum*, a grunt], a witticism or pithy remark.

**mote** (mōt), *n.* [AS. *mot*], a speck, as of dust.

**mo·tel** (mō-tel′), *n.* [*motorist* + *hotel*], a roadside hotel for motorists, usually with private cabins.

**mo·tet** (mō-tet′), *n.* [< OFr. dim. of *mot*, a word], a contrapuntal polyphonic song of a sacred nature.

**moth** (môth, moth), *n.* [*pl.* MOTHS (môthz, moths)], [AS. *moththe*], 1. a four-winged, chiefly night-flying insect related to the butterfly but generally smaller and less brightly colored. 2. a species of moth (**clothes moth**) whose larvae eat holes in woolens, furs, etc.

**moth ball,** a small ball of naphthalene, the fumes of which repel moths, as from woolens, furs, etc.

**moth-eat·en** (môth′ē′t'n, moth′-), *adj.* 1. gnawed away in patches by moths, as cloth; hence, 2. worn out. 3. out-dated.

**moth·er** (muth′ẽr), *n.* [AS. *modor*], 1. a woman who has borne a child. 2. the female parent of a plant or animal. 3. that which is the origin, source, or nurturer of something. 4. *a*) a woman having the responsibility and authority of a mother. *b*) a woman who is the head (**mother superior**) of a religious establishment. 5. an elderly woman: used as a title of affectionate respect. *adj.* 1. being, or being like, a mother. 2. of or characteristic of a mother: as, *mother* love. 3. native: as, *mother* tongue. *v.t.* 1. to be the mother of. 2. to care for as a mother does. —**moth′er·less,** *adj.*

**moth·er** (muth′ẽr), *n.* [prob., by folk etymology, < MD. *moeder*], a stringy, gummy, slimy substance formed by bacteria in vinegar or on the surface of fermenting liquids: also **mother of vinegar.**

**Mother Car·ey's chicken** (kâr′iz), 1. the stormy petrel. 2. any of various other petrels.

**mother country,** a motherland.

**Mother Goose,** the imaginary creator of a collection of English nursery rhymes.

**moth·er·hood** (muth′ẽr-hood′), *n.* 1. the state of being a mother. 2. the qualities or character of a mother. 3. mothers collectively.

**Mother Hub·bard** (hub′ẽrd), a full, loose gown for women.

**moth·er-in-law** (muth′ẽr-'n-lô′), *n.* [*pl.* MOTHERS-IN-LAW], the mother of one's husband or wife.

**moth·er·land** (muth′ẽr-land′), *n.* 1. the country of one's birth. 2. the country of one's ancestors.

**mother lode,** the main vein of ore in a mine.

**moth·er·ly** (muth′ẽr-li), *adj.* of, like, or befitting a mother; maternal. *adv.* in a motherly manner. **—moth′er·li·ness,** *n.*

**moth·er-of-pearl** (muth′ẽr-əv-pũrl′), *n.* the hard, pearly internal layer of certain marine shells, as of the pearl oyster, used for making pearl buttons, etc.; nacre. *adj.* of mother-of-pearl.

**Mother's Day,** the second Sunday in May, a day set aside (in the U.S.) in honor of mothers.

**mother tongue,** 1. one's native language. 2. a language from which another derives.

**mother wit,** native intelligence; common sense.

**moth·y** (môth′i, moth′i), *adj.* [-IER, -IEST], 1. infested with moths. 2. moth-eaten.

**mo·tif** (mō-tēf′), *n.* [Fr.; see MOTIVE], a main element, idea, etc.; specif., in *art, literature, & music,* a main theme or subject for development.

**mo·tile** (mō′t'l, -til), *adj.* [< L. *motus,* pp. of *movere,* to move], in *biology,* capable of or exhibiting spontaneous motion. **—mo·til′i·ty,** *n.*

**mo·tion** (mō′shən), *n.* [< L. *motio* < pp. of *movere,* to move], 1. a moving from one place to another; movement. 2. a moving of the body or any of its parts. 3. a meaningful movement of the hand, eyes, etc.; gesture. 4. a suggestion; esp., a proposal formally made in an assembly or meeting. *v.i.* to make a meaningful movement of the hand, head, etc. *v.t.* to direct or command by a meaningful gesture: as, he *motioned* me toward him. **—in motion,** moving, or in operation.

**mo·tion·less** (mō′shən-lis), *adj.* without, or incapable of, motion; not moving. **—mo′tion·less·ly,** *adv.* **—mo′tion·less·ness,** *n.*

**motion picture,** a sequence of photographs or drawings projected on a screen in such rapid succession as to create the optical illusion of moving persons and objects: also called *moving picture, movie.* **—mo′tion-pic′ture,** *adj.*

**mo·ti·vate** (mō′tə-vāt′), *v.t.* [-VATED, -VATING], to provide with, or affect as, a motive or motives; incite. **—mo′ti·va′tion,** *n.*

**mo·tive** (mō′tiv), *n.* [< OFr. *motif* < ML. < L. pp. of *movere,* to move], 1. an inner drive, impulse, etc. that causes one to act in a certain way; incentive; goal. 2. in *art, literature, & music,* a motif. *adj.* of, causing, or tending to cause motion. *v.t.* [-TIVED, -TIVING], to motivate.

**-mo·tive** (mō′tiv), [< *motive*], a suffix meaning *moving, of motion,* as in *automotive, locomotive.*

**mot·ley** (mot′li), *adj.* [prob. < OFr.], 1. of many colors. 2. wearing many-colored garments: as, a *motley* fool. 3. of many different elements: as, a *motley* group. *n.* 1. cloth of mixed colors. 2. a garment of various colors, worn by a jester.

**mo·tor** (mō′tẽr), *n.* [L., a mover < *motus,* pp. of *movere,* to move], 1. anything that produces or imparts motion. 2. an engine; esp., an internal-combustion engine for propelling a vehicle. 3. an automobile. 4. in *electricity,* a machine for converting electrical energy into mechanical energy. *adj.* 1. producing motion. 2. of or powered by a motor: as, a *motor* vehicle. 3. of, by, or for motor vehicles: as, a *motor* trip. 4. in *physiology,* designating or of a nerve carrying impulses from the central nervous system to a muscle producing motion. *v.i.* to travel by automobile.

**mo·tor·bike** (mō′tẽr-bīk′), *n.* [Colloq.], 1. a bicycle propelled by a motor. 2. a motorcycle.

**mo·tor·boat** (mō′tẽr-bōt′), *n.* a boat propelled by a motor.

**mo·tor·bus** (mō′tẽr-bus′), *n.* a passenger bus propelled by a motor: also **motor coach.**

**mo·tor·cade** (mō tẽr-kād′), *n.* [*motor*car + caval*cade*], a procession of automobiles.

**mo·tor·car** (mō′tẽr-kär′), *n.* an automobile.

**motor court,** a motel.

**mo·tor·cy·cle** (mō′tẽr-sī′k'l), *n.* a two-wheeled vehicle, like a bicycle, propelled by an internal-combustion engine. *v.i.* [-CLED, -CLING], to ride a motorcycle. **—mo′tor·cy′clist,** *n.*

**mo·tor·ist** (mō′tẽr-ist), *n.* one who drives an automobile or travels by automobile.

**mo·tor·ize** (mō′tẽr-īz′), *v.t.* [-IZED, -IZING], 1. to equip with motor-driven vehicles: as, they *motorized* the cavalry. 2. to equip (a vehicle, etc.) with a motor. **—mo′tor·i·za′tion,** *n.*

**mo·tor·man** (mō′tẽr-mən), *n.* [*pl.* -MEN], 1. one who drives an electric streetcar or electric locomotive. 2. one who operates a motor.

**motor truck,** a motor-driven truck for hauling loads.

**mot·tle** (mot′'l), *v.t.* [-TLED, -TLING], [< *mottled*], to mark with blotches or streaks of different colors. *n.* a mottled pattern, as of marble.

**mot·tled** (mot′'ld), *adj.* [< *motley* + *-ed*], marked with blotches or spots of different colors or shades.

**mot·to** (mot′ō), *n.* [*pl.* -TOES, -TOS], [It., a word; see MOT], 1. a word, phrase, or sentence inscribed on something, as expressive of its character. 2. a maxim adopted as a principle of behavior.

**mouch** (mōōch), *v.i. & v.t.* to mooch.

**‡moue** (mōō), *n.* [Fr.; see MOW (grimace)], a pouting grimace.

**‡mou·jik** (mōō-zhēk′, mōō′zhik), *n.* a muzhik.

**Mouk·den** (mook′den′, mōōk′- mook′dən), *n.* Mukden.

**mould** (mōld), *n., v.t. & v.i.* mold (growth).

**mould** (mōld), *n.* mold (soil).

**mould** (mōld), *n. & v.t.* mold (form). **—mould′er,** *n.*

**mould·board** (mōld′bôrd′, -bōrd′), *n.* a moldboard.

**mould·er** (mōl′dẽr), *v.t. & v.i.* to molder.

**mould·ing** (mōl′diŋ), *n.* molding.

**mould·y** (mōl′di), *adj.* [-IER, -IEST], moldy.

**moult** (mōlt), *n., v.t. & v.i.* molt.

**mound** (mound), *n.* [prob. < MD. *mond,* protection; infl. by *mount,* hill], 1. a heap or bank of earth, sand, etc., whether built or natural; small hill. 2. in *baseball,* the slightly raised area in which the pitcher must stand when pitching. *v.t.* 1. to enclose with a mound. 2. to heap up in a mound.

**Mound Builders,** any of various early Indian peoples who built mounds and embankments found in the Middle West and the Southeast.

**mount** (mount), *n.* [< AS. *munt* & OFr. *mont;* both < L. *mons*], a mountain or hill: now poetic or [M-] before a proper name, as, *Mount* McKinley.

**mount** (mount), *v.i.* [< OFr. *munter;* ult. < L. *mons,* mountain], 1. to climb; ascend (often with *up*). 2. to climb up on something; esp., to get on a horse for riding. 3. to increase in amount: as, profits are *mounting.* *v.t.* 1. to go up; ascend; climb: as, to *mount* stairs. 2. to get up on (a platform, stool, etc.). 3. *a*) to get on (a horse) for riding. *b*) to set on or provide with a horse. 4. to place on something raised (with *on*): as, *mount* the statue on a pedestal. 5. to place or fix on or in the proper support, backing, etc., as a gem in a setting, a specimen on a microscope slide, a picture on a mat, etc. 6. to arrange (a skeleton, dead animal, etc.) for exhibition. 7. to furnish the costumes, settings, etc. for producing (a play). 8. in *military & naval usage, a*) to place (a gun) into position ready for use. *b*) to be armed with (cannon): as, this ship *mounts* six cannon. *c*) to post (a guard) on sentry duty. *d*) to go on (guard) as a sentry. *n.* 1. the act or manner of mounting (a horse, etc.). 2. a horse, bicycle, etc. for riding. 3. the support, setting, etc. on or in which something is mounted. **—mount′a·ble,** *adj.* **—mount′er,** *n.*

**moun·tain** (moun′t'n), *n.* [< OFr. *montaigne;* ult. < L. *mons*], 1. a natural raised part of the earth's surface, larger than a hill. 2. *pl.* a chain or group of such elevations: also **mountain chain, mountain range.** 3. a large pile, heap, or mound. *adj.* 1. of mountains. 2. situated, living, or used in the mountains. 3. like a mountain.

**mountain ash,** any of various small trees with clusters of white flowers and red berries.

**mountain cat,** 1. a cougar. 2. a bobcat.

**moun·tain·eer** (moun′t'n-êr′), *n.* 1. a person who lives in a mountainous region. 2. a mountain climber. *v.i.* to climb mountains, as for sport.

**mountain goat,** a long-haired, goatlike mammal of the Rocky Mountains: also **Rocky Mountain goat.**

**mountain laurel,** an evergreen shrub of the eastern U.S., with pink and white flowers and shiny leaves.

**mountain lion,** the cougar; puma.

**moun·tain·ous** (moun′t'n-əs), *adj.* 1. full of mountains. 2. like a mountain; esp., very large.

**mountain sheep,** any of various wild sheep found in mountain regions; esp., the bighorn.

**Mountain Standard Time,** see **standard time.**

**moun·te·bank** (moun′tə-baŋk′), *n.* [< It. < *montare,* to mount + *in,* on + *banco,* a bench], 1. one who sells quack medicines in a public place, attracting an audience by tricks, stories, etc. 2. any charlatan, or quack. *v.i.* to act as a mountebank.

**mount·ed** (moun′tid), *adj.* serving on horseback: as, *mounted* police.
**Mount·ie** (moun′ti), *n.* [Colloq.], a member of the Royal Canadian Mounted Police.
**mount·ing** (moun′tiŋ), *n.* something serving as a backing, support, setting, etc.
**Mount Ver·non** (vūr′nən), 1. the home of George Washington in Virginia, on the Potomac. 2. a city in New York, near New York City: pop., 76,000.
**mourn** (môrn, mōrn), *v.i. & v.t.* [AS. *murnan*], 1. to feel or express sorrow for (something regrettable); lament. 2. to grieve for (someone who has died). —**mourn′er,** *n.*
**mourners' bench,** in some revivalist churches, a front row of seats reserved for those who are to make public professions of penitence.
**mourn·ful** (môrn′fəl, mōrn′-), *adj.* 1. of or characterized by mourning; feeling or expressing grief or sorrow. 2. causing sorrow; melancholy. —**mourn′ful·ly,** *adv.* —**mourn′ful·ness,** *n.*
**mourn·ing** (môr′niŋ, mōr′-), *n.* 1. a sorrowing or lamenting; specif., the expression of grief at someone's death. 2. black clothes, drapery, etc., worn or displayed as a sign of grief for the dead. 3. the period during which one mourns for the dead. *adj.* of or expressing mourning. —**mourn′ing·ly,** *adv.*
**mourning dove,** a wild dove of the U.S.: so called because of its cooing, regarded as mournful.
**mouse** (mous; *for v.,* mouz), *n.* [*pl.* MICE (mīs)], [AS. *mus*], 1. any of various small rodents found throughout the world; esp., the house mouse, which infests human dwellings. 2. a timid or spiritless person. 3. [Slang], a dark, swollen bruise under the eye. *v.i.* [MOUSED, MOUSING], 1. to hunt for mice; hence, 2. to search for something busily and stealthily. *v.t.* to hunt for.
**mous·er** (mou′zẽr), *n.* a cat, dog, etc. with reference to its ability to catch mice.
**mous·ey** (mou′si, -zi), *adj.* mousy.
**mousse** (mo͞os), *n.* [Fr., foam < L. *mulsa,* kind of mead], a light frozen dessert, made from whipped cream, gelatin, etc., sweetened and flavored.
**mous·tache** (məs-tash′, mus′tash), *n.* a mustache.
**mous·y** (mou′si, -zi), *adj.* [-IER, -IEST], 1. of, characteristic of, or like a mouse; quiet, timid, etc. 2. infested with mice.
**mouth** (mouth; *for v.,* mouth), *n.* [*pl.* MOUTHS (mouthz)], [AS. *muth*], 1. the opening through which an animal takes in food; specif., the cavity in the head which contains the teeth and tongue and through which sounds are uttered. 2. the mouth regarded as the organ of eating and speaking. 3. a grimace. 4. any opening regarded as like the mouth: as, the *mouth* of a river, of a jar, of a cavern, etc. *v.t.* 1. to say; esp., to say in an affected or oratorical manner. 2. to caress or rub with the mouth or lips. *v.i.* 1. to speak in an oratorical manner; declaim. 2. to grimace. —**down in** (or **at**) **the mouth,** [Colloq.], depressed; unhappy. —**have a big mouth,** [Slang], to talk loudly, excessively, etc. —**mouth′er** (mouth′ẽr), *n.*
**-mouthed** (mouthd), a combining form used in hyphenated compounds, meaning *having a* (specified kind of) *mouth* or (specified number of) *mouths.*
**mouth·ful** (mouth′fool′), *n.* [*pl.* -FULS], 1. as much as the mouth can hold. 2. the usual amount taken into the mouth. 3. a small amount. 4. [Slang], a pertinent remark: usually in **say a mouthful.**
**mouth organ,** a harmonica.
**mouth·piece** (mouth′pēs′), *n.* 1. a part placed at, or forming, a mouth: as, the *mouthpiece* of a telephone. 2. the part of a musical instrument held in or to the mouth. 3. a person, periodical, etc. serving as a spokesman for others. 4. [Slang], a criminal's lawyer.
**mouth·y** (mouth′i, mouth′i), *adj.* [-IER, -IEST], very talkative; bombastic. —**mouth′i·ly,** *adv.* —**mouth′i·ness,** *n.*
**mou·ton** (mo͞o′ton′), *n.* [Fr., sheep], the fur of any of certain sheep, made water-repellent and dyed to resemble other furs, especially beaver.
**mov·a·ble, move·a·ble** (mo͞ov′ə-b'l), *adj.* 1. that can be moved from one place to another. 2. changing in date from one year to the next: as, *movable* holidays. *n.* 1. something movable. 2. *usually pl.* in *law,* personal property, especially furniture. —**mov′a·bil′i·ty, move′a·bil′i·ty, mov′a·ble·ness, move′a·ble·ness,** *n.* —**mov′a·bly, move′a·bly,** *adv.*
**move** (mo͞ov), *v.t.* [MOVED, MOVING], [< Anglo-Fr. < OFr. < L. *movere*], 1. to change the place or position of. 2. to set or keep in motion; stir. 3. to cause (*to act, do, say,* etc.); prompt. 4. to arouse the emotions, passions, etc. of. 5. to propose; esp., to propose formally, as in a meeting. 6. to cause (the bowels) to evacuate. 7. in *commerce,* to dispose of (goods) by selling. *v.i.* 1. to change place or position. 2. to change one's residence. 3. to be active: as, we *move* in good society. 4. to make progress; advance. 5. to take action. 6. to be, or be set, in motion; turn, revolve, etc. 7. to make formal application (*for*): as, *move* for a new trial. 8. to be evacuated: said of the bowels. 9. [Colloq.], to depart: as, let's *move* on. 10. in *chess, checkers,* etc., to change the position of a piece. 11. in *commerce,* to be disposed of by sale: said of goods. *n.* 1. act of moving; movement. 2. one of a series of actions toward some goal. 3. a change of residence. 4. in *chess, checkers,* etc., the act of moving or one's turn to move. —**get a move on,** [Slang], 1. to start moving. 2. to hurry. —**on the move,** [Colloq.], moving about from place to place.
**move·ment** (mo͞ov′mənt), *n.* 1. a moving or manner of moving; specif., *a*) an action of a person or group. *b*) an evacuation of the bowels. *c*) a change in the location of troops, ships, etc., as part of a maneuver. 2. organized action by people working concertedly toward some goal. 3. the progress of events in a literary work; action. 4. the effect of motion in painting, sculpture, etc. 5. in *mechanics,* the moving parts of a mechanism: as, the *movement* of a clock. 6. in *music, a*) tempo. *b*) rhythm. *c*) any of the principal divisions of a symphony or other extended composition. 7. in *prosody,* rhythmic flow; cadence.
**mov·er** (mo͞ov′ẽr), *n.* a person or thing that moves; specif., a person whose work or business is moving furniture, etc. for those changing residence.
**mov·ie** (mo͞ov′i), *n.* [contr. < *moving picture*], [Colloq.], 1. a motion picture. 2. a motion-picture theater. —**the movies,** [Colloq.], motion pictures or the motion-picture industry.
**mov·ing** (mo͞ov′iŋ), *adj.* that moves; specif., *a*) changing, or causing to change, place or position. *b*) causing motion or action. *c*) stirring the emotions. —**mov′ing·ly,** *adv.*
**moving picture,** a motion picture.
**moving staircase** (or **stairway**)**,** an escalator.
**mow** (mō), *v.t.* [MOWED (mōd), MOWED or MOWN (mōn), MOWING], [AS. *mawan*], 1. to cut down (standing grass or grain) with a sickle, lawn mower, etc. 2. to cut grass or grain from (a lawn, field, etc.). 3. to cause to fall like cut grass or grain; kill: as, we *mowed* down the enemy. *v.i.* to cut down standing grass or grain. —**mow′er,** *n.*
**mow** (mou), *n.* [AS. *muga*], 1. a stack or heap of hay, grain, etc., especially in a barn. 2. the part of a barn where hay or grain is stored.
**mow, mowe** (mou, mō), *n. & v.i.* [< OFr. *mo(u)e,* a mouth, pout < MD. *mouwe*], [Archaic], grimace.
**Mo·zam·bique** (mō′zəm-bēk′), *n.* a Portuguese colony on the coast of SE Africa.
**Mo·zart, Wolf·gang A·ma·de·us** (vôlf′gäŋk ä′mä-dā′oos mō′tsärt), 1756–1791; Austrian composer.
**MP, M.P.,** Military Police.
**mp.,** *mezzo piano,* [It.], in *music,* moderately soft.
**M.P.,** Member of Parliament.
**M.P., m.p.,** melting point.
**mph, m.p.h.,** miles per hour.
**Mr.** (mis′tẽr), [*pl.* MESSRS. (mes′ẽrz)], mister: used before the name or title of a man.
**Mrs.** (mis′iz), mistress: now used as a title before the name of a married woman.
**MS., ms.,** [*pl.* MSS., MSS.], manuscript.
**M.S., M.Sc.,** Master of Science.
**MScand.,** Middle Scandinavian.
**MScot.,** Middle Scottish.
**Msgr.,** Monsignor.
**M.Sgt., M/Sgt,** Master Sergeant.
**m'sieur** (mə-syūr′; Fr. mə-syö′), *n.* monsieur.
**M.S.T.,** Mountain Standard Time.
**Mt., mt.,** [*pl.* MTS., MTS.], 1. mount. 2. mountain.
**M.T.,** metric ton.
**mtg.,** 1. meeting. 2. mortgage: also **mtge.**
**mtn.,** mountain.
**mu** (mū, mo͞o), *n.* [< Gr.], the twelfth letter of the Greek alphabet (M, $\mu$).
**much** (much), *adj.* [MORE, MOST], [< AS. *mycel*], great in quantity, amount, degree, etc. *adv.* 1. to a great degree or extent: as, *much* relieved. 2. just about; nearly: as, *much* the same. *n.* 1. a great amount or quantity: as, *much* can be done. 2. something great, important, etc.: as, is he *much* of a scholar? —**make much of,** to treat or consider as of great importance. —**much′ness,** *n.*
**mu·ci·lage** (mū′s'l-ij), *n.* [< OFr. < LL. *mucilago,* musty juice < L. < *mucus,* mucus], 1. any of various thick, sticky substances found in certain plants. 2. any watery solution of gum, glue, etc. used as an adhesive.

**mu·ci·lag·i·nous** (mū'sə-laj'i-nəs), *adj.* 1. of or like mucilage; sticky. 2. producing mucilage.
**muck** (muk), *n.* [< Anglo-N. < ON. *myki*], 1. moist manure. 2. black earth containing decaying matter, used as a fertilizer. 3. anything unclean or degrading; dirt; filth. *v.t.* 1. to fertilize with muck. 2. [Colloq.], to dirty as with muck. —**muck'y** [-IER, -IEST], *adj.*
**muck·er** (muk'ēr), *n.* [prob. < G. < *mucken*, to grumble], [Slang], a coarse or vulgar person.
**muck·rake** (muk'rāk'), *v.i.* [-RAKED, -RAKING], [coined c. 1906; see MUCK & RAKE], to search for and either charge or expose corruption by public officials, businessmen, etc. —**muck'rak'er,** *n.*
**mu·cous** (mū'kəs), *adj.* 1. of, containing, or secreting mucus. 2. like mucus or covered with or as with mucus; slimy.
**mucous membrane,** a mucus-secreting membrane lining body cavities and canals, as the mouth, etc., connecting with the external air.
**mu·cus** (mū'kəs), *n.* [L.], the slimy secretion that moistens and protects the mucous membranes.
**mud** (mud), *n.* [prob. < a LG. source], wet, soft, sticky earth. *v.t.* [MUDDED, MUDDING], to cover or soil with or as with mud.
**mud·der** (mud'ēr), *n.* a race horse that runs especially well on a wet, muddy track.
**mud·dle** (mud''l), *v.t.* [-DLED, -DLING], [< *mud*], 1. to mix up; jumble; bungle. 2. to confuse; befuddle, as with liquor. *v.i.* to act or think in a confused way. *n.* mess, confusion, etc. —**muddle through,** [Chiefly Brit.], to succeed in spite of confusion.
**mud·dler** (mud'lēr), *n.* a stick to stir mixed drinks.
**mud·dy** (mud'i), *adj.* [-DIER, -DIEST], 1. full of or spattered with mud. 2. not clear; cloudy: as, *muddy* coffee. 3. confused, obscure, etc.: as, *muddy* thinking. *v.t. & v.i.* [-DIED, -DYING], to make or become muddy. —**mud'di·ly,** *adv.* —**mud'di·ness,** *n.*
**mud·fish** (mud'fish'), *n.* [*pl.* see FISH], any of various fishes that live in mud or muddy water.
**mud·guard** (mud'gärd'), *n.* a cover or shield over the wheel of a bicycle, automobile, etc., to protect from mud thrown up by the wheel.
**mud hen,** any of various birds that live in marshes, as the coot, rail, gallinule, etc.
**mud puppy,** a North American salamander that lives in mud under water.
**mud·sling·ing** (mud'sliŋ'iŋ), *n.* unscrupulous attacks against an opponent, as in a political campaign. —**mud'sling'er,** *n.*
**mud turtle,** a small turtle of North and Central America that lives in muddy ponds, streams, etc.
**mu·ez·zin** (mū-ez'in), *n.* [< Ar. *mu'adhdhin* < *adhana*, to proclaim], a Moslem crier who calls the people to prayer at the proper hours.
**muff** (muf), *n.* [D. *mof* < Walloon < Fr. *moufle*, a mitten], 1. a cylindrical covering of fur, etc. into which the hands are placed from either end for warmth. 2. *a*) in *baseball*, etc., a failure to hold a ball when catching it; hence, *b*) any bungling action. *v.t. & v.i.* to do badly or awkwardly; specif., in *baseball*, etc., to bungle (a play).
**muf·fin** (muf'in), *n.* [? akin to OFr. *moufflet*, soft], a quick bread made with eggs or yeast and baked in a cup-shaped mold, usually eaten hot.
**muf·fle** (muf''l), *v.t.* [-FLED, -FLING], [prob. < OFr *enmoufle* < *moufle*, a mitten], 1. to wrap in a shawl, blanket, etc. so as to hide, keep warm, etc.: often with *up*. 2. to keep (a person) from seeing or speaking by wrapping up the head. 3. to wrap or cover in order to deaden or prevent sound. 4. to deaden (a sound). *n.* a wrap, covering, etc. used for muffling.
**muf·fler** (muf'lēr), *n.* 1. a scarf, shawl, etc. worn around the throat, as for warmth. 2. a device for silencing noises, as a baffle in the exhaust pipe of an internal-combustion engine.
**muf·ti** (muf'ti), *n.* [*pl.* -TIS], [Ar. < *āftā*, to judge; sense 2 ? < fancied resemblance to Moslem dress of early 19th c.], 1. in Moslem countries, an expounder of religious law. 2. civilian clothes, especially when worn by one who has worn a uniform.
**mug** (mug), *n.* [prob. < ON.], 1. a heavy drinking cup of earthenware or metal with a handle. 2. as much as such a cup will hold. 3. [Slang], *a*) the face. *b*) the mouth. *c*) a rough, uncouth person. *v.t.* [MUGGED, MUGGING], [Slang], 1. to photograph, as for police records. 2. to assault from behind by strangling: also sp. **mugg.** *v.i.* [Slang], to grimace, especially in overacting. —**mug'ger,** *n.*
**mug·gy** (mug'i), *adj.* [-GIER, -GIEST], [< ME. *muggen*, to drizzle < ON.], hot, damp, and close: as, *muggy* weather. —**mug'gi·ness,** *n.*
**mug·wump** (mug'wump'), *n.* [< Algonquian *mugquomp*, great man], an independent, especially in politics.
**Mu·ham·mad** (moo-ham'əd), *n.* Mohammed.
**Mu·ham·mad·an, Mu·ham·med·an** (moo-ham'əd-ən), *adj. & n.* Mohammedan.
**mu·jik** (mōō-zhēk', mōō'zhik), *n.* a muzhik.
**Muk·den** (mook'den', mŏŏk'- mook'dən), *n.* the capital of Manchuria: pop., 1,551,000: also sp. **Moukden.**
**mu·lat·to** (mə-lat'ō, myoo-), *n.* [*pl.* -TOES], [Sp. & Port. *mulato*, of mixed breed < *mulo* (< L. *mulus*), a mule], 1. a person one of whose parents is a Negro and the other a Caucasian. 2. popularly, any person of mixed Negro and Caucasian ancestry. *adj.* of the light-brown color of a mulatto's skin.
**mul·ber·ry** (mul'ber'i, -bēr-i), *n.* [*pl.* -RIES], [AS. *morberie* < L. *morum*, mulberry + AS. *berie*, a berry], 1. the purplish-red, edible, berrylike fruit of any of a group of trees on whose leaves silkworms feed. 2. this tree. 3. purplish-red.
**mulch** (mulch), *n.* [ME. *molsh*, soft], leaves, straw, peat, etc. spread on the ground around plants to prevent evaporation of water from the soil, freezing of roots, etc. *v.t.* to apply mulch to.
**mulct** (mulkt), *v.t.* [< L. < *mul(c)ta*, a fine], 1. to punish by a fine. 2. to deprive of something, as by fraud. *n.* a fine or similar penalty. —**mulct'er,** *n.*
**mule** (mūl), *n.* [< OFr. < L. *mulus*], 1. the (usually sterile) offspring of a donkey and a horse, especially of a jackass and a mare. 2. a machine that draws and spins cotton fibers into yarn and winds the yarn. 3. [Colloq.], a stubborn person.
**mule** (mūl), *n.* [Fr. < D. < L. *mulleus*, red shoe], a lounging slipper that does not cover the heel.
**mule deer,** a long-eared deer of the western U.S.
**mule skinner,** [Colloq.], a mule driver.
**mu·le·teer** (mū'lə-têr'), *n.* [< Fr.], a mule driver.
**mul·ish** (mūl'ish), *adj.* like a mule; stubborn; obstinate. —**mul'ish·ly,** *adv.* —**mul'ish·ness,** *n.*
**mull** (mul), *v.t. & v.i.* [ME. *mullen*, to grind], [Colloq.], to cogitate or ponder (*over*).
**mull** (mul), *v.t.* [prob. < Fr. *mollir*, to soften < *mol*, soft < L. *mollis*], to heat, sweeten, and flavor with spices, as beer, cider, wine, etc.
**mul·lah, mul·la** (mul'ə, mool'ə), *n.* [Turk., Per. & Hind. *mulla* < Ar. *mawla*], a Moslem teacher or interpreter of the religious law: used as a general title of respect for a learned man.
**mul·lein, mul·len** (mul'in), *n.* [< OFr. *moleine*], a tall plant of the figwort family, with downy leaves and spikes of variously colored flowers.
**mul·let** (mul'it), *n.* [*pl.* -LETS, -LET; see PLURAL, II, D, 1], [< OFr. *mulet*, dim. < L. *mullus*, red mullet], any of a group of edible fishes found in fresh and salt waters; specif., *a*) the *gray mullet*, with silvery scales. *b*) the *red mullet*, with reddish or golden scales.
**mul·li·gan (stew)** (mul'i-g'n), *n.* [prob. < personal name], [Slang], a stew made of odd bits of meat and vegetables, especially as prepared by hoboes.
**mul·li·ga·taw·ny** (mul'i-gə-tô'ni), *n.* [Tamil *milagutannir*, pepper water], an East Indian soup of meat, etc., flavored with curry.
**mul·lion** (mul'yən), *n.* [prob. < OFr. *moienel* < L. *medianus*, middle], a slender vertical dividing bar between the lights of windows, screens, etc. *v.t.* to furnish with mullions. —**mul'lioned,** *adj.*

MULLIONS

**mul·ti-** (mul'ti, -tə), [L. < *multus*, much, many], a combining form meaning: 1. *having many*, as in *multicolored*. 2. *more than two*, as in *multilateral*. 3. *many times more than*, as in *multimillionaire*. Also **mult-**. The meanings of the following words can be determined by combining the meanings of their component elements:

| | | |
|---|---|---|
| **multiangular** | **multilobate** | **multirooted** |
| **multicellular** | **multilocular** | **multispeed** |
| **multicolored** | **multinuclear** | **multispiral** |
| **multiflorous** | **multiphase** | **multistoried** |
| **multifold** | **multipinnate** | **multistriate** |
| **multifoliate** | **multipolar** | **multitubular** |
| **multilinear** | **multiradial** | **multivalved** |
| **multilingual** | **multiramose** | **multivoiced** |

**mul·ti·far·i·ous** (mul′tə-fâr′i-əs), *adj.* [L. *multifarius* < *multus*, many], having many kinds of parts or elements; of great variety. —**mul′ti·far′i·ous·ly,** *adv.* —**mul′ti·far′i·ous·ness,** *n.*
**mul·ti·form** (mul′tə-fôrm′), *adj.* having many forms, shapes, etc. —**mul′ti·for′mi·ty,** *n.*
**mul·ti·graph** (mul′tə-graf′, -gräf′), *n.* a type of rotary printing machine used for reproducing typewritten matter: a trade-mark (**Multigraph**). *v.t.* to reproduce with such a machine.
**mul·ti·lat·er·al** (mul′ti-lat′ẽr-əl), *adj.* 1. many-sided. 2. involving more than two nations: as, a *multilateral* treaty. —**mul′ti·lat′er·al·ly,** *adv.*
**mul·ti·mil·lion·aire** (mul′ti-mil′yən-âr′), *n.* a person whose wealth amounts to several millions of dollars, francs, pounds, etc.
**mul·tip·a·rous** (mul-tip′ə-rəs), *adj.* [see MULTI- & -PAROUS], in *zoology*, normally bearing more than one offspring at a delivery.
**mul·ti·par·tite** (mul′ti-pär′tīt), *adj.* 1. divided into many parts. 2. multilateral (sense 2).
**mul·ti·ple** (mul′tə-p′l), *adj.* [Fr. < LL. *multiplus*, for L. *multiplex;* see MULTIPLEX], 1. having or consisting of many parts, elements, etc.; manifold. 2. in *electricity*, designating or of a circuit with two or more conductors in parallel. *n.* a number that is a product of some specified number and another number: as, 10 is a *multiple* of 5 and 2.
**multiple sclerosis,** a disease in which there is sclerosis in various parts of the nervous system.
**mul·ti·plex** (mul′tə-pleks), *adj.* [L., manifold < *multus*, many + base of *plaga*, surface], 1. multiple. 2. *a)* designating a system of telegraphy or telephony in which two or more messages can be sent simultaneously in either or both directions over the same wire or on the same wave. *b)* in *radio*, designating or of a system in which two or more signals can be transmitted simultaneously on the same wave, as for stereophonic broadcasting. *n.* a multiplex system. *v.t.* to transmit by multiplex.
**mul·ti·pli·cand** (mul′tə-pli-kand′), *n.* [< L. *multiplicandus*, to be multiplied], in *mathematics*, the number that is, or is to be, multiplied by another (the *multiplier*).
**mul·ti·pli·ca·tion** (mul′tə-pli-kā′shən), *n.* a multiplying or being multiplied; specif., in *mathematics*, the process of finding the quantity obtained by repeating a specified quantity a specified number of times.
**mul·ti·plic·i·ty** (mul′tə-plis′ə-ti), *n.* [< LL. < L. *multiplex*, manifold], 1. a being manifold or various. 2. a great number.
**mul·ti·pli·er** (mul′tə-plī′ẽr), *n.* 1. a person or thing that multiplies or increases. 2. in *mathematics*, the number by which another number (the *multiplicand*) is, or is to be, multiplied.
**mul·ti·ply** (mul′tə-plī′), *v.t.* [-PLIED, -PLYING], [< OFr. < L. *multiplicare* < *multiplex*, manifold], 1. to cause to increase in number, amount, or degree. 2. in *mathematics*, to find the product of by multiplication. *v.i.* 1. to increase in number, degree, etc. 2. in *mathematics*, to perform multiplication.
**mul·ti·tude** (mul′tə-tōōd′, -tūd′), *n.* [OFr. < L. *multitudo* < *multus*, many], 1. a large number of persons or things; crowd, host, myriad, etc. 2. the common people (preceded by *the*).
**mul·ti·tu·di·nous** (mul′tə-tōō′d′n-əs, -tū′-), *adj.* 1. very numerous; many. 2. consisting of many parts, elements, etc.; manifold. —**mul′ti·tu′di·nous·ly,** *adv.* —**mul′ti·tu′di·nous·ness,** *n.*
**mul·ti·va·lent** (mul′ti-vā′lənt, mul-tiv′ə-lənt), *adj.* in *chemistry*, having a valence of more than two. —**mul′ti·va′lence,** *n.*
**mul·ti·ver·si·ty** (mul′tə-vũr′sə-ti), *n.* [*pl.* -TIES], the modern large and complex university with its many colleges, extensions, etc., regarded as being impersonal, bureaucratic, etc.
**mum** (mum), *v.i.* [MUMMED, MUMMING], [prob. < MD. *mommen*, to mask < OFr. < *momon*, a mask], to wear a mask or costume in fun; specif., to act as a mummer at Christmas time: also sp. **mumm.**
**mum** (mum), *n.* [Colloq.], a chrysanthemum.
**mum** (mum), *adj.* [ME. *momme;* imitative], silent; not speaking. *interj.* be silent! do not speak! —**mum's the word,** say nothing.
**mum·ble** (mum′b'l), *v.t. & v.i.* [-BLED, -BLING], [ME. *momelen*], 1. to speak or say indistinctly, as with the mouth partly closed; mutter. 2. [Rare], to chew gently and ineffectively. *n.* a mumbled utterance. —**mum′bler,** *n.* —**mum′bling·ly,** *adv.*
**mum·ble·ty·peg** (mum′b'l-ti-peg′), *n.* a boy's game in which a jackknife is tossed in various ways to make it land with the blade in the ground.
**Mum·bo Jum·bo** (mum′bō jum′bō), [orig. *mama dyambo*, in a W African dialect], 1. among certain African tribes of W Sudan, a medicine man who is supposed to protect his people from evil. 2. [m- j-], an idol or fetish. 3. [m- j-], meaningless ritual, etc.
**mum·mer** (mum′ẽr), *n.* [see MUM, *v.*], 1. one who wears a mask or disguise for fun; specif., in England, any of the masked and costumed persons who act out pantomimes at Christmas time. 2. any actor.
**mum·mer·y** (mum′ẽr-i), *n.* [*pl.* -IES], 1. performance by mummers. 2. any show or ceremony regarded as pretentious or hypocritical.
**mum·mi·fy** (mum′ə-fī′), *v.t.* [-FIED, -FYING], to make into or like a mummy. *v.i.* to shrivel up; dry. —**mum′mi·fi·ca′tion,** *n.*
**mum·my** (mum′i), *n.* [*pl.* -MIES], [< Fr. < ML. < Ar. *mūmiyā* < *mum*, wax], 1. a dead body preserved by embalming, as by the ancient Egyptians. 2. any well-preserved dead body.
**mumps** (mumps), *n.pl.* [construed as sing.], [*pl.* of obs. *mump*, a grimace], an acute communicable disease, caused by a virus and characterized by swelling of the salivary glands.
**mun.,** municipal.
**munch** (munch), *v.t. & v.i.* [ME. *munchen;* echoic], to chew vigorously, often with a crunching sound.
**Mun·chau·sen,** Baron (mun-chô′zən, mun′chou-), 1720–1797; German adventurer and soldier; known for the exaggerated tales allegedly told by him.
**Mun·cie** (mun′si), *n.* a city in E Indiana: pop., 69,000.
**mun·dane** (mun′dān), *adj.* [< Fr. < L. < *mundus*, world], of the world; esp., worldly, as distinguished from heavenly, etc. —**mun′dane·ly,** *adv.*
**Mu·nich** (mū′nik), *n.* the capital of Bavaria, Germany: pop., 1,215,000.
**Munich Pact** (or **Agreement**), a pact signed September 29, 1938, at Munich by Great Britain, France, Italy, and Germany, which provided that Germany was to get the Sudetenland: used allusively of any appeasement of an aggressor.
**mu·nic·i·pal** (mū-nis′ə-p'l), *adj.* [< L. < *municeps*, citizen of a free town < *munia*, official duties + *capere*, to take], 1. of or characteristic of a city, town, etc. or its local government. 2. having local self-government. —**mu·nic′i·pal·ly,** *adv.*
**mu·nic·i·pal·i·ty** (mū-nis′ə-pal′ə-ti), *n.* [*pl.* -TIES], [see MUNICIPAL], a city, town, etc. having its own incorporated government.
**mu·nic·i·pal·ize** (mū-nis′ə-p'l-īz′), *v.t.* [-IZED, -IZING], 1. to bring under the control or ownership of a municipality. 2. to make a municipality of.
**mu·nif·i·cent** (mū-nif′ə-s'nt), *adj.* [< L. < *munificus*, bountiful < *munus*, a gift + *facere*, to make], 1. very generous in giving; lavish. 2. given with great generosity. —**mu·nif′i·cence,** *n.*
**mu·ni·tion** (mū-nish′ən), *v.t.* to provide with munitions.
**mu·ni·tions** (mū-nish′ənz), *n.pl.* [< Fr. < L. pp. of *munire*, to fortify], military supplies; esp., weapons and ammunition. *adj.* of or producing munitions.
**mu·ral** (myoor′əl), *adj.* [Fr. < L. *muralis* < *murus*, a wall], 1. of, on, in, or for a wall. 2. like a wall. *n.* a picture, especially a large one, painted directly on a wall. —**mu′ral·ist,** *n.*
**mur·der** (mũr′dẽr), *n.* [AS. *morthor*], the unlawful and malicious or premeditated killing of one human being by another. *v.t.* 1. to kill unlawfully and with malice. 2. to spoil or botch, as in performance: as, she *murdered* that song. *v.i.* to commit murder. —**get away with murder,** [Slang], to escape detection or punishment for a blameworthy act. —**mur′der·er,** *n.* —**mur′der·ess,** *n.fem.*
**mur·der·ous** (mũr′dẽr-əs), *adj.* 1. of, having the nature of, or characteristic of murder; brutal. 2. capable or guilty of, or intending, murder.
**mu·ri·at·ic acid** (myoor′i-at′ik), [< L. < *muria*, brine], hydrochloric acid: a commercial term.
**Mu·ril·lo, Bar·to·lo·mé Es·te·ban** (bär′tô-lô-me′ es-te′bän mōō-rē′lyô), 1617–1682; Spanish painter.
**murk** (mũrk), *n.* [< ON. *myrkr*, dark], darkness; gloom. *adj.* dark or dim. Also sp. **mirk.**
**murk·y** (mũr′ki), *adj.* [-IER, -IEST], 1. dark or gloomy. 2. heavy and obscure with smoke, etc. Also sp. **mirky.** —**murk′i·ly,** *adv.* —**murk′i·ness,** *n.*
**Mur·mansk** (mōōr-mänsk′), *n.* an arctic seaport in NW Soviet Russia: pop., 279,000.
**mur·mur** (mũr′mẽr), *n.* [< OFr. < L.; echoic word], 1. a low, indistinct, continuous sound, as of a stream, far-off voices, etc. 2. a mumbled complaint. 3. in *medicine*, any abnormal sound heard by auscultation; esp., such a sound in the region of the heart, resulting from lesions of the heart valves. *v.i.* 1. to make a murmur. 2. to mumble a complaint. *v.t.* to say in a murmur. —**mur′mur·er,** *n.* —**mur′mur·ing,** *adj.*
**mur·rain** (mũr′in), *n.* [< OFr. *morine* < L. *mori*, to die], 1. any of various infectious diseases of cattle. 2. [Archaic], a pestilence; plague.

**Mur·ray** (mũr'i), *n.* a river in SE Australia.

**mur·ther** (mũr'thẽr), *n., v.t. & v.i.* [Obs. or Dial.], murder.

**mus.,** 1. museum. 2. music. 3. musical.

**mus·ca·dine** (mus'kə-din, -dīn'), *n.* [< Pr. *muscade,* fem. of *muscat;* see MUSCAT], a variety of grape grown in the southern U.S.

**mus·cat** (mus'kət, -kat), *n.* [Fr. < Pr. < It. *moscato,* musky < LL. *muscus,* musk], 1. a variety of sweet European grape from which muscatel (wine) is made. 2. muscatel (wine).

**Mus·cat and Oman** (mus-kat'), an independent sultanate in SE Arabia, on the Arabian Sea: area, 82,000 sq. mi.; pop., 600,000; capital, Muscat.

**mus·ca·tel** (mus'kə-tel'), *n.* [OFr.; see MUSCAT], 1. a rich, sweet wine made from the muscat. 2. the muscat. Also **mus'ca·del'** (-del').

**mus·cle** (mus''l), *n.* [Fr. < L. *musculus,* lit., dim. of *mus,* a mouse], 1. any of the body organs consisting of bundles of fibers that can be contracted and expanded to produce bodily movements. 2. the tissue making up such an organ. 3. muscular strength; brawn. *v.i.* [-CLED, -CLING], [Colloq.], to make one's way by sheer force (usually with *in*).

**mus·cle-bound** (mus''l-bound'), *adj.* having some of the muscles enlarged and less elastic, as from too much exercise.

**Mus·co·vite** (mus'kə-vīt'), *n. & adj.* Russian.

**Mus·co·vy** (mus'kə-vi), *n.* Russia: ancient name.

**Muscovy duck,** [altered < *musk duck*], a common domesticated duck of tropical America, with a large crest and red wattles.

**mus·cu·lar** (mus'kyoo-lẽr), *adj.* 1. of, consisting of, or accomplished by a muscle or muscles. 2. having well-developed muscles; strong; brawny. **—mus'cu·lar'i·ty,** *n.* **—mus'cu·lar·ly,** *adv.*

**muscular dys·tro·phy** (dis'trə-fi), a chronic disease characterized by a progressive wasting of the muscles.

**mus·cu·la·ture** (mus'kyoo-lə-chẽr), *n.* [Fr.], the arrangement of the muscles of a body or of some part of the body; muscular system.

**Muse** (mūz), *n.* [Fr. < L. < Gr. *mousa*], 1. in *Gr. mythology,* any of the nine goddesses who presided over literature and the arts and sciences. 2. [m-], the spirit regarded as inspiring a poet or artist.

**muse** (mūz), *v.t. & v.i.* [MUSED, MUSING], [< OFr. *muser,* to loiter], to think or consider deeply; meditate; ponder. *n.* a musing. **—mus'er,** *n.*

**muse·ful** (mūz'fəl), *adj.* [*muse* + *-ful*], meditative.

**mu·se·um** (mū-zē'əm), *n.* [L. < Gr. *mouseion,* place for the Muses < *mousa,* a Muse], a building, room, etc. for preserving and exhibiting artistic, historical, or scientific objects.

**mush** (mush), *n.* [var. of *mash* (mixture)], 1. a thick porridge of boiled corn meal. 2. any thick, soft mass. 3. [Colloq.], maudlin sentimentality.

**mush** (mush), *interj.* [? < Fr. *marche,* imperative of *marcher,* to go], in Canada and Alaska, a shout commanding sled dogs to start or to go faster. *v.i.* to travel on foot over snow, usually with a dog sled. *n.* a journey by mushing. **—mush'er,** *n.*

**mush·room** (mush'rōōm, -room), *n.* [OFr. *mouscheron* < *mousse,* moss], 1. any of various rapid-growing, fleshy fungi having a stalk with an umbrellalike top; popularly, any edible variety, as distinguished from the poisonous ones (*toadstools*). 2. anything like a mushroom in shape or rapid growth. *adj.* 1. of or made with mushrooms. 2. like a mushroom in shape or rapid growth. *v.i.* 1. to grow or spread rapidly. 2. to flatten out at the end so as to resemble a mushroom.

**mush·y** (mush'i), *adj.* [-IER, -IEST], 1. like mush; thick and soft. 2. [Colloq.], sentimental and maudlin. **—mush'i·ly,** *adv.* **—mush'i·ness,** *n.*

**mu·sic** (mū'zik), *n.* [< OFr. < L.; Gr. *mousikē* (*technē*), musical (art) < *mousa,* a Muse], 1. the art and science of combining tones in varying melody, harmony, etc., especially so as to form complete and expressive compositions. 2. the tones so arranged, or their arrangement. 3. any rhythmic sequence of pleasing sounds, as of birds, etc. 4. a musical composition or compositions; esp., the written or printed score. 5. ability to respond to or take pleasure in music. **—face the music,** [Colloq.], to accept the consequences, however unpleasant. **—set to music,** to compose music for (a poem, etc.).

**mu·si·cal** (mū'zi-k'l), *adj.* 1. of or for the creation or performance of music. 2. melodious or harmonious. 3. fond of or skilled in music. 4. set to music: as, a *musical* comedy. *n.* 1. a musical comedy. 2. [Colloq.], a musicale. **—mu'si·cal·ly,** *adv.* **—mu'si·cal·ness,** *n.*

**musical comedy,** a theatrical production consisting of musical numbers, dances, and humorous skits, centered upon some slight plot.

**mu·si·cale** (mū'zi-kal'), *n.* [Fr.], a party or social affair featuring a musical program.

**music box,** a mechanical musical instrument containing a bar with tuned steel teeth that are struck by pins so arranged on a revolving cylinder as to produce a certain tune or tunes.

**music hall,** 1. an auditorium for musical productions. 2. [Brit.], a vaudeville theater.

**mu·si·cian** (mū-zish'ən), *n.* a person skilled in music; esp., a professional performer of music. **—mu·si'cian·ly,** *adv.* **—mu·si'cian·ship',** *n.*

**mu·si·col·o·gy** (mū'zi-kol'ə-ji), *n.* [see -LOGY], the systematized study of the science, history, and methods of music. **—mu'si·col'o·gist,** *n.*

**mus·ing** (mūz'iŋ), *adj.* meditative; reflective. *n.* meditation; reflection. **—mus'ing·ly,** *adv.*

**musk** (musk), *n.* [< OFr. < LL. < Gr. < Ar. *mushk* < Sans. *mushka,* testicle], 1. a substance with a strong, penetrating odor, obtained from a small sac (*musk bag*) under the skin of the abdomen in the male musk deer: used as the basis of numerous perfumes. 2. the odor of this substance, now often created synthetically. **—musk'like',** *adj.*

**musk deer,** a small, hornless deer of central Asia: the male secretes musk.

**mus·kel·lunge, mus·kal·lunge** (mus'kə-lunj'), *n.* [*pl.* -LUNGE], [< Algonquian *maskinonge*], a very large pike of the Great Lakes and Mississippi Valley: also **mus'kal·longe'** (-lonj'), [*pl.* -LONGE].

**mus·ket** (mus'kit), *n.* [< Fr. < OFr. < It. *moschetto,* orig. sparrow hawk < L. *musca,* a fly], a smooth-bore, long-barreled firearm, used, as by infantry soldiers, before the invention of the rifle.

**mus·ket·eer** (mus'kə-têr'), *n.* formerly, a soldier armed with a musket.

**mus·ket·ry** (mus'kit-ri), *n.* 1. the art or practice of firing muskets or other small arms. 2. muskets or musketeers, collectively.

**Mus·kho·ge·an** (mus-kō'gi-ən, mus'kō-gē'ən), *adj.* designating or of a linguistic stock of North American Indians of the southeastern U.S.

**musk·mel·on** (musk'mel'ən), *n.* [*musk* + *melon*], any of several roundish fruits of the melon family, as the cantaloupe, with sweet, juicy flesh.

**musk ox,** a hardy ox of arctic America and Greenland, with a long, shaggy coat, large, curved horns, and a musklike odor.

**musk·rat** (musk'rat'), *n.* [*pl.* -RATS, -RAT; see PLURAL, II, D, 1], 1. a North American rodent living in water and having a long-haired, glossy brown fur and a musklike odor. 2. its fur.

MUSKRAT (20 in. long)

**musk·y** (mus'ki), *adj.* [-IER, -IEST], of, like, or smelling of musk. **—musk'i·ness,** *n.*

**Mus·lem, Mus·lim** (muz'ləm), *n. & adj.* Moslem.

**mus·lin** (muz'lin), *n.* [< Fr. < It. *mussolino* < *Mussolo,* Mosul, city in Iraq], a fine cotton cloth of plain weave: a heavy variety is used for sheets, pillowcases, etc.

**muss** (mus), *n.* [prob. var. of *mess*], [Colloq. or Dial.], 1. a mess; disorder. 2. a squabble. *v.t.* [Colloq. or Dial.], to make messy (often with *up*).

**mus·sel** (mus''l), *n.* [< AS. < LL. < L. *musculus,* orig. dim. of *mus,* a mouse], any of various bivalve mollusks; specif., *a*) a salt-water variety used as food. *b*) a fresh-water variety whose shell is made into buttons, etc.

**Mus·so·li·ni, Be·ni·to** (be-nē'tō moos'ə-lē'ni, mus'-), 1883–1945; Fascist dictator of Italy (1922–1943).

**Mus·sul·man** (mus''l-mən), *n.* [*pl.* -MANS], [< Turk. & Per. < Ar. *muslim*], a Moslem.

**muss·y** (mus'i), *adj.* [-IER, -IEST], [Colloq.], messy; disordered, rumpled, etc. **—muss'i·ness,** *n.*

**must** (must), *v.aux.* [pt. MUST], [AS. *moste,* pt. of *motan,* may], an auxiliary used with the infinitive of various verbs (without *to*) to express: 1. *compulsion, obligation,* or *necessity*: as, I *must* pay her. 2. *probability*: as, there *must* have been 500 people there. 3. *certainty*: as, all men *must* die. *Must* is sometimes used with the verb understood: as, I

*must* away. *n.* something that must be done, had, seen, etc.: as, this book is a *must.* *adj.* that must be done, etc.
**must** (must), *n.* [< AS. < L. *mustum,* new wine < *mustus,* fresh], the juice pressed from grapes or other fruit before it has fermented.
**mus·tache** (məs-tash′, mus′tash), *n.* [< Fr. < It. *mostacchio* < Gr. *mystax,* upper lip < *mastax,* a mouth], 1. the hair on the upper lip of men. 2. the hair or bristles growing around an animal's mouth. Also sp. **moustache.**
**mus·ta·chio** (məs-tä′shō), *n.* [*pl.* -CHIOS], [< Sp. or It.], a mustache. —**mus·ta′chioed** (-shōd), *adj.*
**mus·tang** (mus′taŋ), *n.* [< Sp. < *mestengo,* belonging to the graziers, wild], a small wild or half-wild horse of the Southwest plains.
**mus·tard** (mus′tẽrd), *n.* [< OFr. *moustarde* < L. *mustum,* must (orig. added to the condiment)], 1. any of several plants with yellow flowers and slender pods. 2. the yellow powder made from the ground seeds of this plant, often prepared as a paste, used as a pungent seasoning. 3. a dark yellow.
**mustard gas,** [from its mustardlike odor], a volatile liquid, $(CH_2ClCH_2)_2S$, used in warfare as a poison gas: it has blistering and disabling effects.
**mustard plaster,** a plaster made with powdered mustard, applied to the skin as a counterirritant.
**mus·ter** (mus′tẽr), *v.t.* [< OFr. < L. *monstrare,* to show < *monere,* to warn], 1. to assemble (troops, etc.). 2. to gather together and display; summon (often with *up*): as, he *mustered* up strength. *v.i.* to assemble: said of troops, etc. *n.* 1. a gathering or assembling, especially of troops for inspection, service, etc. 2. the persons or things assembled. 3. the number of these. 4. the list of men in a military or naval unit: also **muster roll.** —**muster in** (or **out**), to enlist in (or discharge from) military service. —**pass muster,** to measure up to the required standard.
**must·n't** (mus′'nt), must not.
**mus·ty** (mus′ti), *adj.* [-TIER, -TIEST], [prob. ult. < *moist*], 1. having a stale, moldy smell or taste. 2. stale or trite: as, *musty* scholarship. 3. dull; apathetic. —**mus′ti·ly,** *adv.* —**mus′ti·ness,** *n.*
**mut.,** 1. mutilated. 2. mutual.
**mu·ta·ble** (mū′tə-b'l), *adj.* [< L. < *mutare,* to change], 1. that can be changed. 2. tending to frequent change; fickle. —**mu′ta·bil′i·ty, mu′ta·ble·ness,** *n.* —**mu′ta·bly,** *adv.*
**mu·tant** (mū′tənt), *n.* [< L. ppr. of *mutare,* to mutate], an animal or plant with inheritable characteristics that differ from those of the parents.
**mu·tate** (mū′tāt), *v.i. & v.t.* [-TATED, -TATING], [< L. pp. of *mutare,* to change], to change; specif., to undergo or cause to undergo mutation.
**mu·ta·tion** (mū-tā′shən), *n.* 1. a changing or being changed. 2. a change, as in form, nature, etc. 3. in *biology, a*) a sudden variation in some inheritable characteristic of an animal or plant. *b*) an individual resulting from such variation; mutant. —**mu·ta′tion·al,** *adj.*
**mute** (mūt), *adj.* [< LL. < L. *mutus*], 1. not speaking; voluntarily silent. 2. unable to speak; dumb. 3. in *law,* refusing to plead when arraigned. 4. in *linguistics,* not pronounced; silent, as the *e* in *mouse.* *n.* 1. one who does not speak; specif., one who cannot speak because deaf; deaf-mute. 2. in *law,* a defendant who refuses to plead when arraigned. 3. in *linguistics,* a silent letter. 4. in *music,* a device used to soften the tone of an instrument. *v.t.* [MUTED, MUTING], to soften the sound of (a musical instrument, etc.) as with a mute. —**mute′ly,** *adv.* —**mute′ness,** *n.*
**mu·ti·late** (mū′t'l-āt′), *v.t.* [-LATED, -LATING], [< L. pp. < *mutilus,* maimed], 1. to cut off or damage a limb, etc. of (a person or animal). 2. to damage or otherwise make imperfect, as by removing an essential part or parts. —**mu′ti·la′tion,** *n.* —**mu′ti·la′tive,** *adj.* —**mu′ti·la′tor,** *n.*
**mu·ti·neer** (mū′t'n-êr′), *n.* one guilty of mutiny.
**mu·ti·nous** (mū′t'n-əs), *adj.* 1. of, engaged in, or inclined to mutiny. 2. like or characteristic of mutiny. —**mu′ti·nous·ly,** *adv.* —**mu′ti·nous·ness,** *n.*
**mu·ti·ny** (mū′t'n-i), *n.* [*pl.* -NIES], [< Fr. < OFr. *mutin,* riotous < *meute,* a revolt < L. *movere,* to move], forcible revolt against constituted authority; esp., rebellion of soldiers or sailors against their officers. *v.i.* [-NIED, -NYING], to participate in a mutiny; revolt.
**mutt** (mut), *n.* [Slang], 1. a stupid person; blockhead. 2. a mongrel dog; cur. Also sp. **mut.**
**mut·ter** (mut′ẽr), *v.i.* [ME. *materen*], 1. to speak in low, indistinct tones, as in complaining. 2. to complain or grumble. 3. to make a low, rumbling sound, as thunder. *v.t.* to say in low, indistinct tones. *n.* 1. a muttering. 2. something muttered. —**mut′ter·er,** *n.* —**mut′ter·ing·ly,** *adv.*
**mut·ton** (mut′'n), *n.* [< OFr. *moton,* a ram < ML. *multo,* sheep], the flesh of (grown) sheep used as food. —**mut′ton·y,** *adj.*
**mutton chop,** 1. a piece cut from the rib of a sheep for broiling or frying. 2. *pl.* side whiskers shaped like mutton chops.
**mu·tu·al** (mū′cho͞o-əl), *adj.* [< Fr. < LL. < L. *mutuus,* reciprocal < *mutare,* to change], 1. *a*) done, felt, etc. by each of two or more for or toward the other or others; reciprocal: as, *mutual* love. *b*) of each other: as, *mutual* enemies. 2. shared in common; joint: as, our *mutual* friend. —**mu′tu·al′i·ty** (-al′ə-ti), [*pl.* -TIES], *n.* —**mu′tu·al·ly,** *adv.*
**mutual fund,** a trust or corporation formed to invest the funds it obtains from its shareholders.
**mu·tu·el** (mū′cho͞o-əl), *n.* [Slang], parimutuel.
‡**mu·zhik, muz·jik** (mo͞o-zhēk′, mo͞o′zhik), *n.* [Russ.], in czarist Russia, a peasant.
**muz·zle** (muz′'l), *n.* [< OFr. < ML. dim. of *musus*], 1. the part of the head of a dog, horse, etc. including the mouth, nose, and jaws. 2. a device, as of wire or straps, put over the mouth of an animal to prevent its biting or eating. 3. the front end of the barrel of a firearm. *v.t.* [-ZLED, -ZLING], 1. to put a muzzle on (an animal). 2. to prevent from talking or expressing an opinion. —**muz′zler,** *n.*
**muz·zle-load·er** (muz′'l-lōd′ẽr), *n.* any firearm loaded through the muzzle.
**Mv,** in *chemistry,* mendelevium.
**my** (mī), *pron.* [AS. *min,* of me, my, mine], possessive form of **I.** *possessive pronominal adj.* of, belonging to, or done by me. *interj.* an exclamation of surprise, dismay, etc.
**my·ce·li·um** (mī-sē′li-əm), *n.* [*pl.* -LIA (-li-ə)], [Mod. L. < Gr. *mykēs,* a mushroom], the thallus, or vegetative part, of a fungus, made of threadlike tubes. —**my·ce′li·al,** *adj.*
**My·ce·nae** (mī-sē′nē), *n.* an ancient Greek city in the NE Peloponnesus.
**My·ce·nae·an** (mī′si-nē′ən), *adj.* 1. of Mycenae. 2. designating or of the civilization that existed in Greece, Asia Minor, etc. from 1500 to 1100 B.C.
**-my·cete** (mī-sēt′), [< Gr. < *mykēs,* mushroom], a combining form meaning *one of a* (specified) *group of fungi.*
**my·co-,** [< Gr. *mykēs,* fungus], a combining form meaning *fungus:* also **myc-.**
**my·col·o·gy** (mī-kol′ə-ji), *n.* [*myco-* + *-logy*], the branch of botany dealing with fungi. —**my′co·log′i·cal** (-kə-loj′i-k'l), *adj.* —**my·col′o·gist,** *n.*
**my·co·sis** (mī-kō′sis), *n.* [*pl.* -SES (-sēz)], [*myc-* + *-osis*], 1. the growth of parasitic fungi in any part of the body. 2. a disease caused by such fungi. —**my·cot′ic** (-kot′ik), *adj.*
**my·e·li·tis** (mī′ə-lī′tis), *n.* [< Gr. *myelos,* marrow; + *-itis*], inflammation of the spinal cord or the bone marrow.
**my·na, my·nah** (mī′nə), *n.* [Hind. *mainā*], any of a group of tropical birds of SE Asia related to the starling: often kept as a pet: also sp. **mina.**
**Myn·heer** (mīn-hâr′, -hêr′), *n.* [D. *mijn heer,* lit., my lord], Sir; Mr.: a Dutch title of address.
**my·o-,** [< Gr. *mys, myos,* a muscle], a combining form meaning *muscle:* also **my-.**
**my·o·car·di·um** (mī′ō-kär′di-əm), *n.* [see MYO- & CARDIO-], the muscular substance of the heart.
**my·o·pi·a** (mī-ō′pi-ə), *n.* [< LL. < Gr. < *myein,* to close + *ōps,* an eye], the condition of being nearsighted. —**my·op′ic** (-op′ik), *adj.*
**myr·i·ad** (mir′i-əd), *n.* [< Gr. *myrias,* ten thousand < *myrios,* countless], 1. ten thousand. 2. any indefinitely large number. 3. a large number of persons or things. *adj.* very many; countless.
**myr·i·a·pod** (mir′i-ə-pod′), *adj.* [see MYRIAD & -POD], having many legs; specif., of a large group of arthropods having long bodies of many segments, each bearing one or more pairs of jointed legs, as the centipedes. *n.* any animal of this group.
**Myr·mi·don** (mũr′mi-don′, -dən), *n.* [*pl.* -DONS, -DONES (mẽr-mid′ə-nēz′)], 1. in *Gr. legend,* any of a tribe of Thessalian warriors who fought under Achilles, their king, in the Trojan War. 2. [m-], an unquestioning follower or subordinate.
**myrrh** (mũr), *n.* [< AS. & OFr. < L. < Gr. *myrrha* < Ar. *murr*], 1. a fragrant, bitter-tasting gum resin exuded from any of several shrubs of Arabia and E Africa, used in making incense, perfume, etc. 2. any of these shrubs.
**myr·tle** (mũr′t'l), *n.* [< OFr. < ML. dim. of L. *myrtus* < Gr. *myrtos*], 1. a shrub with evergreen leaves, white or pink flowers, and dark berries. 2. any of various other plants, as the periwinkle.
**my·self** (mī-self′, mə-), *pron.* a form of the first person singular pronoun, used: *a*) as an intensive:

as, I went *myself*. *b*) as a reflexive: as, I hurt *myself*. *c*) as a quasi-noun meaning "my real or true self" (e.g., I am not *myself* today).

**My·sore** (mī-sôr′, -sōr′), *n.* a city in S India: pop., 254,000.

**mys·te·ri·ous** (mis-têr′i-əs), *adj.* of, containing, implying, or characterized by mystery. **—mys·te′ri·ous·ly,** *adv.* **—mys·te′ri·ous·ness,** *n.*

**mys·ter·y** (mis′tēr-i, -tri), *n.* [*pl.* -IES], [< L. < Gr. *mystērion;* ult. < *myein,* to initiate into the mysteries, lit., to shut the mouth or eyes], 1. something unexplained, unknown, or kept secret. 2. *a*) anything that remains so secret or obscure as to excite curiosity: as, a murder *mystery*. *b*) a novel or play involving such an event. 3. obscurity or secrecy. 4. *pl.* secret rites or doctrines known only to the initiated: as, the Eleusinian *mysteries*. 5. a mystery play. 6. in *theology,* any assumed truth that cannot be comprehended by the human mind.

**mys·ter·y** (mis′tēr-i), *n.* [*pl.* -IES], [< ML. < L. *ministerium,* office, by confusion with *mysterium,* mystery], [Archaic], a craft or trade.

**mystery play,** [orig. presented by *mysteries* (guilds)], any of a class of medieval dramatic representations of Biblical events.

**mys·tic** (mis′tik), *adj.* [< L. < Gr. *mystikos* < *mystēs,* one initiated], 1. of mystics or mysticism. 2. of occult character or meaning. 3. mysterious or enigmatic. *n.* one who professes to undergo mystical experiences by which he intuitively comprehends truths beyond human understanding.

**mys·ti·cal** (mis′ti-k'l), *adj.* 1. spiritually symbolic; allegorical: as, the *mystical* rose, a symbol of the Virgin Mary. 2. mystic (senses 1 & 2). **—mys′ti·cal·ly,** *adv.* **—mys′ti·cal·ness,** *n.*

**mys·ti·cism** (mis′tə-siz'm), *n.* 1. doctrines or beliefs of mystics. 2. any doctrine that asserts the possibility of knowledge of spiritual truths through intuition acquired by fixed meditation. 3. vague thinking or belief.

**mys·ti·fy** (mis′tə-fī′), *v.t.* [-FIED, -FYING], [< Fr.; cf. MYSTIC & -FY], 1. to puzzle or perplex; esp., to bewilder deliberately. 2. to involve in mystery; make obscure. **—mys′ti·fi·ca′tion,** *n.*

**mys·tique** (mis-tēk′), *n.* [Fr., mystic], a complex of quasi-mystical attitudes and feelings surrounding some person, institution, activity, etc.

**myth** (mith), *n.* [< LL. < Gr. *mythos,* a word, legend], 1. a traditional story of unknown authorship, serving usually to explain some phenomenon of nature, the origin of man, or the customs, institutions, etc. of a people: cf. *legend*. 2. such stories collectively; mythology. 3. any fictitious story. 4. any imaginary person or thing.

**myth·i·cal** (mith′i-k'l), *adj.* 1. of, or having the nature of, a myth or myths. 2. existing only in a myth or myths. 3. imaginary or fictitious. Also **myth′ic. —myth′i·cal·ly,** *adv.*

**my·thol·o·gy** (mi-thol′ə-ji), *n.* [*pl.* -GIES], [< LL. < Gr. *mythologia;* cf. -LOGY], 1. the science or study of myths. 2. myths collectively; esp., all the myths of a specific people or about a specific being. **—myth·o·log·i·cal** (mith′ə-loj′i-k'l), **myth′o·log′ic,** *adj.* **—myth′o·log′i·cal·ly,** *adv.* **—my·thol′o·gist,** *n.*

**Myt·i·le·ne, Myt·i·le·ni** (mit′ə-lē′nē), *n.* a Greek island in the Aegean: ancient name, *Lesbos*.

# N

**N, n** (en), *n.* [*pl.* N's, n's, Ns, ns], 1. the fourteenth letter of the English alphabet. 2. the sound of N or n. 3. in *printing,* an en (half an em). *adj.* fourteenth in a sequence or group.

**N** (en), *n.* in *chemistry, the symbol for* nitrogen. *adj.* shaped like N.

**n** (en), *n.* 1. in *mathematics, the symbol for* an indefinite number. 2. in *physics, the symbol for* neutron.

**N.,** 1. Norse. 2. November.

**N., n.,** 1. *natus,* [L.], born. 2. navy. 3. neuter. 4. new. 5. nominative. 6. noon. 7. noun.

**N, N., n, n.,** 1. North. 2. northern.

**n.,** 1. note. 2. number.

**Na,** *natrium,* [L.], in *chemistry,* sodium.

**N.A.,** 1. National Army. 2. North America.

**N.A.A.C.P., NAACP,** National Association for the Advancement of Colored People.

**nab** (nab), *v.t.* [NABBED, NABBING], [prob. var. of dial. *nap,* to snatch], [Colloq.], 1. to snatch or seize suddenly. 2. to arrest or catch (a felon or wrongdoer). **—nab′ber,** *n.*

**na·bob** (nā′bob), *n.* [< Hind. < Ar. *nuwwāb,* pl. of *nā'ib,* deputy], 1. a native provincial deputy or governor of the old Mogul Empire in India. 2. a very rich man. **—na′bob·ish,** *adj.* **—na′bob·ism,** *n.*

**na·celle** (nə-sel′), *n.* [Fr. < LL. *navicella,* dim. of L. *navis,* a ship], an enclosed part in an aircraft, for housing the engine, cargo, etc.

**na·cre** (nā′kēr), *n.* [Fr., of Ar. origin], mother-of-pearl.

**na·cre·ous** (nā′kri-əs), *adj.* 1. of or like nacre. 2. yielding nacre. 3. iridescent; lustrous.

**na·dir** (nā′dēr, -dêr), *n.* [< OFr. < Ar. *nazīr* (*as-samt*), opposite (to the zenith)], 1. that point of the celestial sphere directly opposite to the zenith; point directly beneath the observer. 2. the lowest point.

**nae** (nā), *adj. & adv.* [Scot.], 1. no. 2. not.

**nag** (nag), *v.t.* [NAGGED, NAGGING], [of Scand. origin], to annoy by continual scolding, faultfinding, etc. *v.i.* to urge, scold, etc. constantly; vex; pester. *n.* 1. the act of nagging. 2. [Colloq.], a person who nags. **—nag′ger,** *n.* **—nag′ging·ly,** *adv.* **—nag′gy** [-GIER, -GIEST], *adj.*

**nag** (nag), *n.* [ME. *nagge*], 1. a small saddle horse; pony; sometimes, any horse. 2. a mediocre horse.

**Na·ga·sa·ki** (nä′gä-sä′kē), *n.* a seaport on the W coast of Kyushu, Japan: pop., 242,000 (1950): on August 9, 1945, it was largely destroyed by an American atomic bomb.

**Na·go·ya** (nä′gô-yä′), *n.* a coastal city in S Honshu, Japan: pop., 1,031,000.

**Nag·pur** (näg′poor), *n.* a city in central India: pop., 449,000.

**Na·hua·tl** (nä′wä-t'l), *n.* a group of languages spoken by various tribes of North and Central American Indians, including the Aztecs, Toltecs, etc. *adj.* of this group of languages.

**Na·hua·tlan** (nä-wät′lan), *adj. & n.* Nahuatl.

**Na·hum** (nā′əm, -hum), *n.* in the *Bible,* 1. a Hebrew prophet of the 7th century B.C. 2. a book of the Old Testament containing his prophecies. Abbrev. **Nah.**

**nai·ad** (nā′ad, nī′-), *n.* [*pl.* -ADS, -ADES (-ə-dēz′)], [< Fr. < L. < Gr. *Naïas* < *naein,* to flow], 1. in *Gr. & Rom. mythology,* any of the nymphs who lived in and gave life to springs, fountains, rivers, etc. 2. a girl or woman swimmer.

**na·if, na·ïf** (nä-ēf′), *adj.* [Fr.], naive.

**nail** (nāl), *n.* [AS. *nægl*], 1. the thin, horny plate at the ends of the fingers and toes: cf. *claw*. 2. a tapered piece of metal, commonly pointed and with a head, driven with a hammer to hold pieces of wood together, serve as a peg, etc. *v.t.* 1. to attach, fasten together, or fasten shut with nails. 2. to secure; make sure: as, he *nailed* the bargain. 3. to fix (the eyes, attention, etc.) steadily on an object. 4. to discover or expose, as a lie. 5. [Colloq.], to catch, capture, etc. **—hit the nail on the head,** to do or say whatever is exactly right. **—on the nail,** [Colloq.], 1. immediately. 2. at the exact spot or time. **—nail′er,** *n.*

**nail file,** a small file for trimming the fingernails.

**nail set,** a tool for sinking a nail so that it is level with, or below, the surface of the wood.

**nain·sook** (nān′sook, nan′-), *n.* [< Hind. < *nain,* the eye + *sukh,* pleasure], a thin, plain-woven, lightweight cotton, sometimes striped.

**Nai·ro·bi** (nī-rō′bi), *n.* the capital of Kenya, Africa: pop., 119,000.

**na·ive, na·ïve** (nä-ēv′), *adj.* [Fr., fem. of *naïf* < L. *nativus,* natural], unaffectedly or foolishly simple;

artless; unsophisticated. —**na·ive′ly, na·ïve′ly,** *adv.* —**na·ive′ness, na·ïve′ness,** *n.*
**na·ïve·té, na·ive·te** (nä-ēv′tā′, -ēv′tā), *n.* 1. a being naive. 2. a naive action or remark.
**na·ive·ty** (nä-ēv′ti), *n.* [*pl.* -TIES], naïveté.
**na·ked** (nā′kid), *adj.* [AS. *nacod*], 1. *a*) completely unclothed; nude. *b*) uncovered; exposed: said of parts of the body. 2. destitute. 3. without protection or defense. 4. without its usual covering; specif., *a*) out of its sheath: as, a *naked* sword. *b*) without furnishing, decoration, etc.: as, a *naked* wall. 5. without additions, disguises, etc.; plain: as, the *naked* truth. —**na′ked·ly,** *adv.* —**na′ked·ness,** *n.*
**naked eye,** the unaided eye; eye without the help of any optical device.
**N.A.M., NAM,** National Association of Manufacturers.
**nam·ay·cush** (nam′i-kush′, -ā-), *n.* [Algonquian *namekus*], a large, light-spotted lake trout, of northern U.S., Canada, and Alaska: also called *Great Lakes trout, lake trout.*
**nam·by-pam·by** (nam′bi-pam′bi), *adj.* [< nickname of *Ambrose* Philips, 18th-c. Eng. poet], weakly sentimental; insipidly pretty. *n.* [*pl.* -BIES], 1. namby-pamby talk or writing. 2. a namby-pamby person.
**name** (nām), *n.* [AS. *nama*], 1. a word or phrase by which a person, thing, or class of things is known; title. 2. a word or phrase expressing some quality considered descriptive; epithet: as, they called him *names.* 3. *a*) fame or reputation. *b*) good reputation. 4. a family or clan. 5. appearance only, not reality; semblance: as, chief in *name* only. 6. a noted person. *adj.* well-known. *v.t.* [NAMED, NAMING], 1. to give a name to (anything). 2. to designate or mention (a person or object) by name. 3. to identify by the right name: as, he *named* all the States. 4. to nominate or appoint to a post or office. 5. to specify (a date, price, etc.). 6. to speak about; mention. —**call names,** to swear at. —**in the name of,** 1. in appeal to. 2. by the authority of. —**to one's name,** belonging to one. —**nam′a·ble, name′a·ble,** *adj.* —**nam′er,** *n.*
**name·less** (nām′lis), *adj.* 1. not having a name. 2. left unnamed. 3. not publicly known; obscure. 4. illegitimate. 5. that cannot be named; indescribable. 6. unfit for mention. —**name′less·ly,** *adv.* —**name′less·ness,** *n.*
**name·ly** (nām′li), *adv.* that is to say; to wit.
**name·sake** (nām′sāk′), *n.* a person with the same name as another; esp., one named after another.
**nan·keen, nan·kin** (nan-kēn′), *n.* [< *Nankin(g)*, China], 1. a buff-colored, durable cotton cloth, originally from China. 2. *pl.* trousers made of this cloth.
**Nan·king** (nan′kiŋ′), *n.* a city in east central China, on the Yangtze River: pop., 1,085,000.
**nan·ny** (nan′i), *n.* [*pl.* -NIES], [< *Nan*, dim. of *Ann(a)*], [Brit.], a child's nurse.
**nanny goat,** [see prec.], [Colloq.], a female goat.
**Nan·sen, Fridt·jof** (frit′yof nän′sən), 1861–1930; Norwegian arctic explorer and writer.
**Nantes** (nänt; Eng. nants), *n.* a city in W France, on the Loire: pop., 200,000.
**Nantes, Edict of,** a decree issued (1598) in France, giving political equality to the Huguenots.
**Nan·tuck·et** (nan-tuk′it), *n.* an island and summer resort off Massachusetts, south of Cape Cod.
**Na·o·mi** (nā-ō′mi, na-, nā′ə-mi′), *n.* in the *Bible*, the mother-in-law of Ruth: Ruth 1.
**nap** (nap), *v.i.* [NAPPED, NAPPING], [AS. *hnappian*], 1. to sleep lightly for a short time; hence, 2. to be off one's guard: as, he was caught *napping.* *n.* a brief, light sleep; doze.
**nap** (nap), *n.* [AS. *-cnoppa*], the downy or hairy surface of cloth formed by short hairs or fibers, raised by brushing, etc. —**nap′less,** *adj.*
**na·palm** (nā′päm), *n.* [*na*phthenic and *palm*itic acids], jellied gasoline used in flame throwers and incendiary bombs.
**nape** (nāp, nap), *n.* [ME.], the back of the neck.
**na·per·y** (nā′pẽr-i), *n.* [< OFr. < *nappe;* see NAPKIN], table linen; napkins, doilies, etc.
**naph·tha** (naf′thə, nap′-), *n.* [L. < Gr. < Per. *naft*], 1. an inflammable, volatile liquid produced by distilling petroleum, coal tar, wood, etc.: it is used as a fuel, solvent, etc. 2. petroleum.
**naph·tha·lene, naph·tha·line** (naf′thə-lēn′, nap′-), *n.* [*naphtha* + *al*cohol + *-ene*], a white, crystalline hydrocarbon, $C_{10}H_8$, produced from coal tar: it is used in moth repellents and in certain dyes, etc.: also **naph′tha·lin** (-lin).
**naph·thol** (naf′thōl, -thol, nap′thôl), *n.* [*naphtha*lene + *-ol* (-ole)], either of two white, crystalline compounds, $C_{10}H_7OH$, derived from naphthalene and used as antiseptics and in dyes.
**nap·kin** (nap′kin), *n.* [< OFr. *nap(p)e* (< L. *mappa*), cloth], 1. a small piece of cloth or paper used at table for protecting the clothes and wiping the fingers or lips. 2. a small towel. 3. [Chiefly Brit.], a baby's diaper.
**Na·ples** (nā′p′lz), *n.* a seaport in SW Italy: pop., 1,028,000.
**na·po·le·on** (nə-pō′li-ən, -pōl′yən), *n.* [after *Napoleon*], 1. a former gold coin of France, equivalent to 20 francs. 2. a card game. 3. a French pastry with a cream filling.
**Na·po·le·on I** (nə-pō′li-ən, -pōl′yən), (*Napoléon Bonaparte*), 1769–1821; French general and emperor (1804–1815). —**Na·po′le·on′ic** (-on′-ik), *adj.*
**Napoleon III,** (*Louis Napoleon*), 1808–1873; nephew of Napoleon; emperor of France (1852–1870).
**Na·po·li** (nä′pô-lē′), *n.* Naples: the Italian name.
**nap·py** (nap′i), *adj.* [-PIER, -PIEST], having or covered with nap; hairy or downy.
**Nar·bad·a** (nur-bud′ä), *n.* a river in central India, flowing westward into the Arabian Sea.
**nar·cism** (när′siz′m), *n.* narcissism. —**nar′cist,** *n.* —**nar·cis′tic** (-sis′tik), *adj.*
**nar·cis·sism** (när-sis′iz′m), *n.* [see NARCISSUS & -ISM], 1. self-love. 2. in *psychoanalysis*, that stage, normal in infancy, in which the self is an object of sexual pleasure. —**nar·cis′sist,** *n.* —**nar′cis·sis′tic** (-sə-sis′tik), *adj.*
**Nar·cis·sus** (när-sis′əs), *n.* 1. in *Gr. mythology*, a beautiful youth who pined away for love of his own reflection in a spring and was changed into the narcissus: cf. *Echo.* 2. [n-], [*pl.* -SUSES, -SI (-ī)], [L. < Gr. *narkissos* < *narkē* (see NARCOTIC): in reference to the sedative effect], a bulbous plant with smooth leaves and clusters of white, yellow, or orange flowers.
**nar·co·sis** (när-kō′sis), *n.* a condition of deep unconsciousness caused by a narcotic.
**nar·co·syn·the·sis** (när′kō-sin′thə-sis), *n.* a method of treating a neurosis by working with a patient while he is under the influence of a narcotic, as pentothal sodium.
**nar·cot·ic** (när-kot′ik), *adj.* [< OFr. < Gr. < *narkoun*, to benumb < *narkē*, numbness], 1. of, like, or capable of producing narcosis. 2. of or having to do with addiction to narcotics. *n.* 1. a drug, as morphine, that induces profound sleep, lethargy, and relief of pain. 2. a person addicted to narcotics. 3. anything that causes drowsiness, lethargy, etc.
**nar·co·tism** (när′kə-tiz′m), *n.* 1. narcosis. 2. addiction to narcotics.
**nar·co·tize** (när′kə-tīz′), *v.t.* [-TIZED, -TIZING], to subject to a narcotic. —**nar′co·ti·za′tion,** *n.*
**nard** (närd), *n.* [< OFr. < L. < Gr. *nardos;* ult. < Sans.], 1. spikenard. 2. an ointment made from the roots of these plants.
**na·res** (nâr′ēz), *n.pl.* [*sing.* -RIS (-is)], [L.], the nasal passages; esp., the nostrils.
**nar·ghi·le** (när′gə-li, -lā′), *n.* [< Turk. & Per. < Per. *nargīl*, coconut tree: orig. made of coconut shell], an Oriental pipe with a long tube so arranged that it draws the smoke through water in a vase to cool it; hookah: also sp. **nargile, nargileh.**
**Nar·ra·gan·sett Bay** (nar′ə-gan′sit), an inlet of the Atlantic, extending into Rhode Island.
**nar·rate** (na-rāt′, nar′āt), *v.t. & v.i.* [-RATED, -RATING], [< L. pp. of *narrare*, to relate], 1. to tell (a story). 2. to give an account of (events).
**nar·ra·tion** (na-rā′shən), *n.* 1. a narrating. 2. a narrative. 3. writing or speaking that narrates, as history, biography, and fiction.
**nar·ra·tive** (nar′ə-tiv), *adj.* 1. in story form. 2. concerned with narration. *n.* 1. a story; account; tale. 2. the art or practice of relating stories or accounts. —**nar′ra·tive·ly,** *adv.*
**nar·ra·tor, nar·rat·er** (na-rā′tẽr, nar′ā-tẽr), *n.* 1. one who narrates a story, etc. 2. one who reads narrative passages between the scenes of a play.
**nar·row** (nar′ō), *adj.* [AS. *nearu*], 1. small in width; not wide. 2. limited in meaning, size, amount, or extent: as, a *narrow* majority. 3. limited in outlook; not liberal; prejudiced. 4. close; careful: as, a *narrow* inspection. 5. with limited margin; close: as, a *narrow* escape. 6. limited in means: as, *narrow* circumstances. 7. in *phonetics*, tense: said of the tongue. *v.i. & v.t.* to decrease or limit in width, extent, or scope. *n.* 1. a narrow part of a valley, pass, road, etc. 2. *usually pl.* a narrow passage; strait. —**nar′row·ly,** *adv.* —**nar′row·ness,** *n.*
**narrow gauge,** 1. a width (between the rails) of less than 56½ inches. 2. a railroad having such a gauge. —**nar′row-gauge′,** *adj.*

**nar·row-mind·ed** (nar′ō-mīn′did), ***adj.*** limited in outlook; not liberal; bigoted; prejudiced. **—nar′row-mind′ed·ly,** ***adv.*** **—nar′row-mind′ed·ness,** ***n.***

**nar·whal** (när′wəl, -hwəl), ***n.*** [prob. < D. *narwal* or Dan. & Sw. *narhval*], an arctic cetacean valued for its oil and ivory: the male has a long, spiral tusk extending from the upper jaw: also **nar′wal** (-wəl), **nar′whale** (-hwāl).

NARWHAL (15–20 ft. long)

**nar·y** (nâr′i), ***adj.*** [< *ne'er a,* never a], [Dial. & Colloq.], not any; no (with *a* or *an*).

**NASA,** National Aeronautics and Space Administration.

**na·sal** (nā′z'l), ***adj.*** [< L. *nasus,* a nose], 1. of the nose. 2. produced by causing the breath to pass through the nose, as the sounds of *m, n, ng* (ŋ). 3. characterized by such production of sounds: as, a *nasal* voice. ***n.*** a nasal sound. **—na·sal′i·ty** (-zal′ə-ti), ***n.*** **—na′sal·ly,** ***adv.***

**na·sal·ize** (nā′z'l-īz′), ***v.t. & v.i.*** [-IZED, -IZING], to pronounce or speak with a nasal sound or sounds. **—na′sal·i·za′tion,** ***n.***

**nas·cent** (nas′'nt, nā′s'nt), ***adj.*** [< L. ppr. of *nasci,* to be born], 1. coming into being; being born. 2. beginning to form, grow, or develop: said of ideas, cultures, etc. **—nas′cen·cy, nas′cence,** ***n.***

**nascent state,** in *chemistry,* the earliest state of an element at liberation from a compound.

**Nash·ville** (nash′vil), ***n.*** the capital of Tennessee, on the Cumberland River: pop., 171,000.

**Nas·sau** (nas′ô), ***n.*** the capital of the Bahama Islands: pop., 50,000.

**Nas·ser, Ga·mal Ab·del** (gä-mäl′ äb′dəl nä′sẽr), 1918– ; Egyptian president of the United Arab Republic (1958– ).

**na·stur·tium** (nə-stũr′shəm), ***n.*** [L. < *nasus,* nose + pp. of *torquere,* to twist: from its pungent odor], 1. a plant with shield-shaped leaves and red, orange, or yellow flowers. 2. the flower.

**nas·ty** (nas′ti), ***adj.*** [-TIER, -TIEST], [? < ON.], 1. filthy; foul. 2. nauseating. 3. morally offensive; obscene. 4. very unpleasant: as, *nasty* weather. 5. mean: as, a *nasty* temper. 6. harmful: as, a *nasty* bruise. **—nas′ti·ly,** ***adv.*** **—nas′ti·ness,** ***n.***

**nat.,** 1. national. 2. native. 3. natural.

**Na·tal** (nə-tal′, -täl′), ***n.*** a province of the Union of South Africa, on the Indian Ocean.

**na·tal** (nā′t'l), ***adj.*** [L. *natalis* < pp. of *nasci,* to be born], 1. of or connected with one's birth. 2. [Poetic], native.

**na·tant** (nā′t'nt), ***adj.*** [< L. ppr. of *natare,* to swim], swimming or floating.

**na·ta·to·ri·um** (nā′tə-tôr′i-əm, -tō′ri-), ***n.*** [*pl.* -RIUMS, -RIA (-ri-ə)], [LL.], a swimming pool.

**na·ta·to·ry** (nā′tə-tôr′i, -tō′ri), ***adj.*** [< LL. < L.; see NATANT], of, characterized by, or adapted for swimming: also **na′ta·to′ri·al.**

**nathe·less** (nāth′lis, nath′-), ***adv.*** [< AS. < *na,* never + *the,* the + *læs,* less], [Archaic], nevertheless. ***prep.*** [Archaic], notwithstanding. Also **nath′less** (nath′-).

**na·tion** (nā′shən), ***n.*** [< OFr. < L. *natio* < pp. of *nasci,* to be born], 1. a stable, historically developed community of people with a territory, economic life, culture, and language in common. 2. the people of a territory united under a single government; country. 3. a people or tribe.

**Na·tion, Carry** (nā′shən), (born *Carry Amelia Moore*), 1846–1911; U.S. agitator for temperance.

**na·tion·al** (nash′ən-'l), ***adj.*** of a nation or the nation; affecting the nation as a whole. ***n.*** a citizen of a nation. **—na′tion·al·ly,** ***adv.***

**national bank,** 1. a bank that manages and controls the finances of a nation. 2. in the U.S., a bank chartered by the Federal government and controlled by a centralized banking system.

**National Guard,** in the U.S., that part of the militia consisting of the organized forces of the individual States, supported in part by the Federal government: it becomes part of the Army of the U.S. when called into active Federal service.

**na·tion·al·ism** (nash′ən-'l-iz'm), ***n.*** 1. *a)* devotion to one's nation; patriotism. *b)* chauvinism. 2. the putting of national interests, aims, etc. above international considerations. 3. national quality or character. 4. the advocacy of national independence. 5. the policy of nationalizing all industry. **—na′tion·al·ist,** ***adj. & n.*** **—na′tion·al·is′tic,** ***adj.*** **—na′tion·al·is′ti·cal·ly,** ***adv.***

**na·tion·al·i·ty** (nash′ə-nal′ə-ti), ***n.*** [*pl.* -TIES], 1. national quality or character. 2. the condition or fact of belonging to a nation by birth or naturalization. 3. the condition or fact of being a nation. 4. a nation or national group.

**na·tion·al·ize** (nash′ən-'l-īz′), ***v.t.*** [-IZED, -IZING], 1. to make national. 2. to transfer ownership or control of land, resources, industries, etc. to the nation. 3. to make into a nation. **—na′tion·al·i·za′tion,** ***n.*** **—na′tion·al·iz′er,** ***n.***

**na·tion-wide** (nā′shən-wīd′), ***adj.*** by or through the whole nation; national.

**na·tive** (nā′tiv), ***adj.*** [< OFr. < L. *nativus* < pp. of *nasci,* to be born], 1. inborn; innate. 2. belonging to a locality or country by birth, production, or growth: as, a *native* Bostonian, *native* plants. 3. *a)* being the place of one's birth: as, one's *native* land. *b)* belonging to one because of the place of one's birth: as, one's *native* language. 4. as found in nature; natural. 5. occurring in a pure state in nature: as, *native* gold. 6. of or characteristic of the inhabitants of any given region. 7. of or characteristic of the indigenous inhabitants, particularly nonwhites, of a region. ***n.*** 1. a person born or thing produced in the region indicated. 2. *a)* an indigenous inhabitant of a region, as distinguished from an invader, colonist, etc. *b)* an indigenous plant or animal. 3. a permanent resident, as distinguished from a visitor, etc. **—go native,** to adopt a primitive mode of life. **—na′tive·ly,** ***adv.*** **—na′tive·ness,** ***n.***

**na·tive-born** (nā′tiv-bôrn′), ***adj.*** born in a specified place or country.

**na·tiv·i·ty** (nə-tiv′ə-ti, nā-), ***n.*** [*pl.* -TIES], [see NATIVE], 1. birth. 2. one's horoscope. **—the Nativity,** 1. the birth of Jesus. 2. Christmas Day.

**natl.,** national.

**NATO** (nā′tō), North Atlantic Treaty Organization.

**nat·ty** (nat′i), ***adj.*** [-TIER, -TIEST], [? < *neat, adj.*], trim and smart in appearance or dress; spruce. **—nat′ti·ly,** ***adv.*** **—nat′ti·ness,** ***n.***

**nat·u·ral** (nach′ẽr-əl), ***adj.*** [< OFr. < L. *naturalis,* by birth], 1. of, forming a part of, or arising from nature. 2. produced or existing in nature; not artificial or manufactured. 3. dealing with nature: as, a *natural* science. 4. in a state provided by nature, without man-made changes; uncultivated. 5. *a)* innate; not acquired: as, *natural* abilities. *b)* having certain qualities, abilities, etc. innately: as, a *natural* comedian. 6. innately felt to be right: as, *natural* rights. 7. true to nature; lifelike: as, a *natural* likeness. 8. normal; in the ordinary course of events: as, a *natural* outcome. 9. customarily expected: as, a *natural* courtesy. 10. free from affectation or restraint. 11. illegitimate: as, a *natural* child. 12. in *music, a)* without flats or sharps. *b)* neither sharped nor flatted. ***n.*** 1. an idiot. 2. [Colloq.], one who is naturally expert. 3. [Colloq.], a thing that is, or promises to be, immediately successful. 4. in *music, a)* the sign (♮), used to remove the effect of a preceding sharp or flat: in full, **natural sign.** *b)* the note so changed. *c)* a white key on a piano. **—nat′u·ral·ness,** ***n.***

**natural gas,** a mixture of gaseous hydrocarbons, chiefly methane, occurring naturally in the earth in certain places: it is used as a fuel.

**natural history,** 1. formerly, zoology, botany, geology, and other subjects dealing with nature. 2. the nontechnical study of these subjects.

**nat·u·ral·ism** (nach′ẽr-əl-iz'm), ***n.*** 1. action or thought based on natural desires or instincts. 2. in *literature, painting,* etc., faithful adherence to nature and life: specifically applied to the realism of a group of 19th-century French writers. 3. in *philosophy,* the belief that the natural world is the whole of reality.

**nat·u·ral·ist** (nach′ẽr-əl-ist), ***n.*** 1. one who studies animals and plants. 2. one who believes in or practices naturalism in art, literature, etc.

**nat·u·ral·is·tic** (nach′ẽr-ə-lis′tik), ***adj.*** 1. of natural history or naturalists. 2. of or characterized by naturalism in art, literature, etc. 3. in accordance with, or in imitation of, nature.

**nat·u·ral·ize** (nach′ẽr-ə-līz′), ***v.t.*** [-IZED, -IZING], 1. to confer citizenship upon (an alien). 2. to adopt and make common (a custom, word, etc.) from another locality. 3. to adapt (a plant or animal) to a new environment. ***v.i.*** to become naturalized. **—nat′u·ral·i·za′tion,** ***n.***

**nat·u·ral·ly** (nach′ẽr-əl-i), ***adv.*** 1. in a natural manner. 2. by nature; innately. 3. as one might expect; of course.

**natural philosophy,** 1. the study of the physical universe. 2. physics.
**natural resources,** those forms of wealth supplied by nature, as coal, oil, waterpower, etc.
**natural science,** the systematized knowledge of nature, including biology, chemistry, geology, etc.
**natural selection,** in Darwinism, the process by which those individuals with characteristics that help them become adapted to their environment tend to survive (*survival of the fittest*) and transmit their characteristics.
**na·ture** (nā′chẽr), *n.* [< OFr. < L. *natura* < pp. of *nasci*, to be born], 1. the quality or qualities that make something what it is; essence. 2. inherent tendencies of a person. 3. the vital functions and activities of the organs. 4. kind; type: as, things of that *nature*. 5. the desires, drives, etc. of a person. 6. the sum total of all things in the physical universe. 7. [sometimes N-], the power, force, etc. that seems to regulate this. 8. the primitive state of man. 9. natural scenery. —**by nature,** naturally; inherently. —**of** (or **in**) **the nature of,** having the essential character of; like.
**-na·tured** (nā′chẽrd), a combining form meaning *having* or *showing a* (specified kind of) *nature, disposition*, or *temperament*, as *good-natured*.
**naught** (nôt), *n.* [< AS. < *na*, no + *wiht*, a person], 1. nothing. 2. in *arithmetic*, the figure zero (0). *adj. & adv.* [Obs.], nought.
**naugh·ty** (nô′ti), *adj.* [-TIER, -TIEST], [< obs. *naught*, wicked], 1. not behaving properly; disobedient: usually of children. 2. improper; obscene. —**naught′i·ly,** *adv.* —**naught′i·ness,** *n.*
**Na·u·ru** (nä-ōō′rōō), *n.* a country on an island in Micronesia, in the W Pacific: area, 8 sq. mi.; pop., 6,000.
**nau·se·a** (nô′shə, -shi-ə, -zi-ə, -zhə, -si-ə), *n.* [L. < Gr. *nausia*, seasickness < *naus*, a ship], 1. a feeling of sickness at the stomach, with an impulse to vomit. 2. any stomach disorder causing this, as seasickness. 3. disgust; loathing.
**nau·se·ate** (nô′shi-āt′, -zi-, -zhi-, -si-), *v.i. & v.t.* [-ATED, -ATING], to feel or cause to feel nausea; make or become sick. —**nau′se·a′tion,** *n.*
**nau·seous** (nô′shəs, -shi-əs, -zi-əs, -zhəs, -si-əs), *adj.* causing nausea; specif., *a*) sickening. *b*) disgusting. —**nau′seous·ly,** *adv.* —**nau′seous·ness,** *n.*
**naut.,** nautical.
**nautch** (nôch), *n.* [< Hind. < Prakrit < Sans. *nrtya*, dancing < *nrt*, to dance], in India, a performance by professional dancing girls (**nautch girls**).
**nau·ti·cal** (nô′ti-k'l), *adj.* [< Fr. < L. < Gr. < *nautēs*, sailor < *naus*, a ship], of sailors, ships, or navigation. —**nau′ti·cal·ly,** *adv.*
**nautical mile,** a unit of linear measure for ships and aircraft, equal to about 6,076 ft.
**nau·ti·lus** (nô′t'l-əs), [*pl.* -LUSES, -LI (-ī′)], [L. < Gr. *nautilos*, sailor < *naus*, a ship], 1. a tropical mollusk with a many-chambered, spiral shell, having a pearly interior: also **pearly nautilus.** 2. the paper nautilus.
**nav.,** 1. naval. 2. navigation.
**Nav·a·ho, Nav·a·jo** (nav′ə-hō′), *n.* [*pl.* -HOS, -JOS; -HOES, -JOES], a member of a tribe of Athapascan Indians now living on a reservation in Arizona, New Mexico, and Utah.
**na·val** (nā′v'l), *adj.* [< Fr. < L. *navalis* < *navis*, a ship], of, having, characteristic of, or for a navy, its ships, personnel, etc.
**Na·varre** (nə-vär′), *n.* a former kingdom of N Spain and SW France.
**nave** (nāv), *n.* [OFr. < L. *navis*, a ship], the main part of a church, between the side aisles, extending from the chancel to the principal entrance.
**nave** (nāv), *n.* [AS. *nafu*], the hub of a wheel.
**na·vel** (nā′v'l), *n.* [AS. *nafela*], 1. the small scar or depression in the abdomen, marking the place where the umbilical cord was attached to the fetus. 2. any point centrally located on something.
**navel orange,** a seedless orange having a navellike depression containing a small, secondary fruit.
**nav·i·cert** (nav′i-sũrt′), *n.* [*navigation certificate*], a document issued by a nation at war authorizing a ship of a friendly or neutral nation to move through a belligerent's blockade.
**navig.,** 1. navigation. 2. navigator.
**nav·i·ga·ble** (nav′i-gə-b'l), *adj.* 1. wide or deep enough to be traveled on by ships: as, a *navigable* river. 2. that can be steered, or directed: as, a *navigable* balloon. —**nav′i·ga·bil′i·ty, nav′i·ga·ble·ness,** *n.* —**nav′i·ga·bly,** *adv.*
**nav·i·gate** (nav′ə-gāt′), *v.i.* [-GATED, -GATING], [< L. pp. of *navigare* < *navis*, a ship + *agere*, to lead], 1. to travel by ship. 2. to steer a ship or aircraft. *v.t.* 1. to travel through or on (land, air, sea, etc.) in a boat or aircraft. 2. to steer, or direct the course of (a ship or aircraft).
**nav·i·ga·tion** (nav′ə-gā′shən), *n.* the act or practice of navigating; esp., the science of locating the position and plotting the course of ships and aircraft. —**nav′i·ga′tion·al,** *adj.*
**nav·i·ga·tor** (nav′ə-gā′tẽr), *n.* 1. one who navigates; esp., one skilled in the navigation of a ship or aircraft. 2. [Brit.], a navvy.
**nav·vy** (nav′i), *n.* [*pl.* -VIES], [abbrev. of *navigator*], [Brit.], an unskilled laborer, as on canals, roads, etc.
**na·vy** (nā′vi), *n.* [*pl.* -VIES], [< OFr. *navie* < LL. *navia* (for L. *navis*, a ship)], 1. [Archaic], a fleet of ships. 2. all the warships of a nation. 3. [often N-], *a*) the entire sea force of a nation, including vessels, personnel, stores, etc. *b*) the governmental department in charge of this. 4. very dark blue: also **navy blue.**
**navy bean,** [from common use in the U.S. Navy], a small, white bean related to the kidney bean, dried for use as a food.
**navy yard,** a dockyard for building and repairing naval ships, storing supplies, etc.
**na·wab** (nə-wôb′), *n.* [Hind. *navāb*; see NABOB], in India, 1. a native ruler under the Mogul government. 2. [N-], a title of courtesy for a Moslem prince. 3. a rich, retired Anglo-Indian; nabob.
**nay** (nā), *adv.* [< ON. < *ne*, not + *ei*, ever], 1. [Archaic], no. 2. not that only, but also: as, I permit, *nay*, encourage it. *n.* 1. a refusal or denial. 2. a negative vote or voter. 3. a negative answer.
**Naz·a·rene** (naz′ə-rēn′, naz′ə-rēn′), *adj.* of Nazareth or the Nazarenes. *n.* 1. a native or inhabitant of Nazareth; esp., Jesus (*the Nazarene*). 2. any member of an early sect of Jewish Christians.
**Naz·a·reth** (naz′ə-rəth, naz′rith), *n.* a town in N Palestine, where Jesus lived as a child.
**Naz·a·rite** (naz′ə-rit′), *n.* [< LL. < Gr. < Heb. *nāzar*, to consecrate], among the ancient Hebrews, a person (as Samson) who voluntarily assumed certain strict religious vows: also sp. **Nazirite.**
**Na·zi** (nä′tsi, na′tsi), *adj.* [G., contr. of *National-sozialistische*, in party name], designating, of, or characteristic of the German fascist political party (*National Socialist German Workers' Party*), which ruled Germany under Hitler (1933–1945). *n.* 1. a member of this party. 2. [often n-], a supporter of this party or its doctrines; fascist.
**Na·zi·fy** (nä′tsi-fī′, na′-), *v.t.* [-FIED, -FYING], to place under Nazi control or influence: also **nazify.** —**Na′zi·fi·ca′tion, na′zi·fi·ca′tion,** *n.*
**Na·zism** (nä′tsiz'm, na′-), *n.* the philosophy, aims, or characteristics of the Nazi Party; German fascism: also **Na′zi·ism** (-tsi-iz'm).
**Nb,** in *chemistry*, niobium.
**N.B.,** New Brunswick.
**N.B., n.b.,** *nota bene*, [L.], note well.
**N.B.C., NBC,** National Broadcasting Company.
**N.C.,** 1. New Caledonia. 2. North Carolina.
**N.C.O.,** noncommissioned officer.
**Nd,** in *chemistry*, neodymium.
**N.D., n.d.,** no date.
**N.D., N. Dak.,** North Dakota.
**Ne,** in *chemistry*, neon.
**NE, N.E., n.e.,** 1. northeast. 2. northeastern.
**N.E.,** New England.
**N.E.A.,** National Education Association.
**Ne·an·der·thal** (ni-an′dẽr-täl′, -thôl′), *adj.* [name of German valley where remains were found], designating or of a race of early man of the paleolithic period in Europe.
**neap** (nēp), *adj.* [AS. *nep-* in *nepflod*, neap tide], designating either of the two lowest monthly tides, occurring just after the first and third quarters of the lunar month. *n.* neap tide.
**Ne·a·pol·i·tan** (nē′ə-pol′ə-t'n), *adj.* of Naples. *n.* a native or inhabitant of Naples.
**near** (nêr), *adv.* [AS. *near*, compar. of *neah*, *adv.*, nigh], 1. at a short distance in space or time: as, summer draws *near*. 2. relatively close in degree; almost: as, you are *near* right: now usually *nearly*. 3. closely; intimately. *adj.* 1. close in distance or time; not far. 2. close in relationship; akin. 3. close in friendship; intimate. 4. close in degree: as, a *near* escape. 5. on the left side: said of animals, vehicles, etc., as, the *near* horse. 6. short or quick: as, take the *near* way. 7. stingy. 8. somewhat resembling; approximating: as, *near* beer. *prep.* close to in space, time, degree, etc. *v.t. & v.i.* to draw near (to); approach. —**near at hand,** very close in time or space. —**near′ness,** *n.*
**near-by, near·by** (nêr′bī′), *adj. & adv.* near; close at hand.
**Near East,** 1. the countries near or east of the E

Mediterranean, including those in SW Asia and, sometimes, the Balkans. 2. [Brit.], the Balkans.

**near·ly** (nêr'li), *adv.* 1. almost; not quite: as, I'm *nearly* finished. 2. closely: as, *nearly* related.

**near·sight·ed** (nêr'sīt'id), *adj.* seeing only near objects distinctly; myopic. —**near'sight'ed·ly,** *adv.* —**near'sight'ed·ness,** *n.*

**neat** (nēt), *adj.* [< Fr. < L. *nitidus,* shining, trim < *nitere,* to shine], 1. unmixed with anything; pure: said of liquor drunk without a chaser. 2. [Rare], free of deductions; net. 3. *a)* trim; tidy; clean. *b)* skillful and precise: as, a *neat* worker. 4. well proportioned; shapely. 5. cleverly phrased or done; adroit. —**neat'ly,** *adv.* —**neat'ness,** *n.*

**neat** (nēt), *n.* [*pl.* NEAT], [AS. *neat*], [Now Rare], an animal of the ox family; cow, steer, etc.: also **neat cow** (or **steer,** etc.).

**'neath, neath** (nēth, nē*th*), *prep.* [Poetic], beneath.

**neat·herd** (nēt'hūrd'), *n.* [Obs.], a cowherd.

**neat's-foot oil** (nēts'foot'), a light-yellow oil obtained from the feet, etc. of cattle, used as a dressing for leather.

**neb** (neb), *n.* [AS. *nebb*], 1. *a)* the beak of a bird. *b)* the snout of an animal. 2. the nose or mouth of a person. 3. a nib; tip.

**Ne·bras·ka** (nə-bras'kə), *n.* a Middle Western State of the U.S.: area, 77,237 sq. mi.; pop. 1,411,,000; capital, Lincoln: abbrev. **Neb., Nebr.** —**Ne·bras'·kan,** *adj. & n.*

**Neb·u·chad·nez·zar** (neb'yoo-kəd-nez'ẽr, neb'ə-), *n.* Chaldean king of Babylon (604?–562? B.C.) who conquered Jerusalem: Dan. 1–4, II Kings 24: also **Neb'u·chad·rez'zar** (-rez'ẽr).

**neb·u·la** (neb'yoo-lə), *n.* [*pl.* -LAE (-lē'), -LAS], [L.], any of the cloudlike patches seen in the night sky, consisting of far-distant groups of stars or of masses of gaseous matter. —**neb'u·lar,** *adj.*

**nebular hypothesis,** the theory that the solar system was formed by the condensation of a nebula.

**neb·u·los·i·ty** (neb'yoo-los'ə-ti), *n.* 1. a nebulous quality or condition. 2. [*pl.* -TIES], a nebula.

**neb·u·lous** (neb'yoo-ləs), *adj.* 1. of or like a nebula or nebulae. 2. cloudy; misty. 3. unclear; vague; indefinite. —Also **neb'u·lose'** (-lōs'). —**neb'u·lous·ly,** *adv.* —**neb'u·lous·ness,** *n.*

**nec·es·sar·i·ly** (nes'ə-ser'ə-li, nes'ə-sâr'-), *adv.* 1. because of necessity. 2. as a necessary result.

**nec·es·sar·y** (nes'ə-ser'i), *adj.* [< L. < *necesse,* unavoidable < *ne-,* not + *cedere,* to give way], 1. essential; indispensable. 2. inevitable. 3. not voluntary; required. 4. undeniable; unavoidable from the premises. *n.* [*pl.* -IES], a thing necessary to life, to some purpose, etc.

**ne·ces·si·tate** (nə-ses'ə-tāt'), *v.t.* [-TATED, -TATING], 1. to make (something) necessary or unavoidable. 2. to compel; require; force: usually in passive. —**ne·ces'si·ta'tion,** *n.*

**ne·ces·si·tous** (nə-ses'ə-təs), *adj.* in great need; destitute; indigent; needy. —**ne·ces'si·tous·ly,** *adv.* —**ne·ces'si·tous·ness,** *n.*

**ne·ces·si·ty** (nə-ses'ə-ti), *n.* [*pl.* -TIES], [< L. < *necesse;* see NECESSARY], 1. natural causation; fate. 2. that which is necessary in natural sequence: as, death is a *necessity* to life. 3. what is required by social or legal compulsion: as, a passport is a *necessity.* 4. such compulsion. 5. great need: as, call me in case of *necessity.* 6. *often in pl.* something that cannot be done without. 7. want; poverty. —**of necessity,** necessarily.

**neck** (nek), *n.* [AS. *hnecca*], 1. that part of man or animal joining the head to the body. 2. a narrow part between the head or end and the body of any object, as of a violin. 3. that part of a garment which covers or is nearest the neck. 4. a narrow, necklike part; specif., *a)* a narrow strip of land. *b)* the narrowest part of a bottle, vase, etc. *c)* a strait. ***v.t. & v.i.*** [Slang], to kiss and caress in making love. —**get it in the neck,** [Slang], to be severely punished. —**neck and neck,** very close or even, as in a contest or election. —**risk one's neck,** to put one's life in danger.

**neck·band** (nek'band'), *n.* 1. a band worn around the neck. 2. the part of a garment that encircles the neck; esp., the part fastened to the collar.

**neck·cloth** (nek'klôth'), *n.* a neckerchief; cravat.

**neck·er·chief** (nek'ẽr-chif), *n.* [*neck* + *kerchief*], a handkerchief or scarf worn around the neck.

**neck·lace** (nek'lis), *n.* [*neck* + *lace* (string)], a string or chain of gold, silver, jewels, shells, etc., worn around the neck as an ornament.

**neck·piece** (nek'pēs'), *n.* a decorative scarf, often of fur, worn around the neck.

**neck·tie** (nek'tī'), *n.* a band to be worn around the neck, tied in a bow or knotted in front.

**neck·wear** (nek'wâr'), *n.* articles worn about the neck; esp., neckties, scarfs, and collars.

**nec·ro-,** [< Gr. *nekros,* dead body], a combining form meaning *death, corpse:* also **necr-.**

**ne·crol·o·gy** (ne-krol'ə-ji), *n.* [*pl.* -GIES], [*necro-* + *-logy*], 1. a list of people who have died. 2. a death notice; obituary. —**nec·ro·log·i·cal** (nek'rə-loj'i-k'l), *adj.* —**nec'ro·log'i·cal·ly,** *adv.*

**nec·ro·man·cy** (nek'rə-man'si), *n.* [< OFr. < ML. *nigromantia* (infl. by L. *niger,* black) < L. *necromantia* < Gr. < *nekros,* corpse + *manteia,* divination], 1. divination by alleged communication with the dead. 2. black magic. —**nec'ro·man'cer,** *n.*

**ne·crop·o·lis** (ne-krop'ə-lis), *n.* [*pl.* -LISES, -LEIS (-līs')], [< Gr. < *nekros,* dead body + *polis,* city], a cemetery.

**ne·cro·sis** (ne-krō'sis), *n.* [*pl.* -SES (-sēz)], [< Gr. < *nekroun,* to make dead < *nekros,* dead body], 1. the death or decay of tissue in a part of the body. 2. in *botany,* gradual decay of trees or plants. —**ne·crot'ic** (-krot'ik), *adj.*

**nec·tar** (nek'tẽr), *n.* [L. < Gr. *nektar,* lit., death-overcoming], 1. in *Gr. mythology,* the drink of the gods. 2. any very delicious beverage. 3. the sweetish liquid in many flowers, used by bees for the making of honey. —**nec·tar'e·an** (-târ'i-ən), **nec·tar'e·ous,** *adj.*

**nec·tar·ine** (nek'tə-rēn', nek'tə-rēn'), *n.* [< *nectar*], a kind of peach that has a smooth skin.

**nec·ta·ry** (nek'tə-ri), *n.* [*pl.* -RIES], an organ or part (of a flower) that secretes nectar.

**nee, née** (nā), *adj.* [Fr., fem. pp. of *naître* (< L. *nasci*), to be born], born: used to introduce the maiden name of a married woman, as, Mrs. Helen Jones, *nee* Smith.

**need** (nēd), *n.* [AS. *nied*], 1. necessity; obligation: as, no *need* to worry. 2. a lack of something required or desired: as, the *need* of a long rest. 3. something required or desired that is lacking: as, what are his daily *needs?* 4. *a)* a time or condition when help is required: as, a friend in *need.* *b)* poverty; extreme want. *v.t.* to have need of; require. *Need* is often used as an auxiliary followed by an infinitive with or without *to,* meaning "to be obliged, must": as, he *need* not come, he *needs* to be careful. ***v.i.*** 1. [Archaic], to be necessary: as, it *needs* not. 2. to be in need. See also **needs.** —**have need to,** to be required to; must. —**if need be,** if it is required. —**need'er,** *n.*

**need·ful** (nēd'fəl), *adj.* 1. necessary; needed; required. 2. [Archaic], needy. —**need'ful·ly,** *adv.* —**need'ful·ness,** *n.*

**nee·dle** (nē'd'l), *n.* [AS. *nædl*], 1. a small, slender, sharp-pointed piece of steel with a hole for thread, used for sewing. 2. *a)* a slender rod of steel, bone, etc. with a hook at one end, used for crocheting. *b)* a similar rod without a hook, used in knitting. 3. the short, pointed piece of metal, etc. that moves in the grooves of a phonograph record and transmits vibrations. 4. the pointer of a compass, gauge, meter, etc. 5. the thin, short, pointed leaf of the pine, spruce, etc. 6. the thin rod that opens or closes a passage in a valve (**needle valve**) and permits close adjustment. 7. the sharp, very slender metal tube at the end of a hypodermic syringe. 8. a slender, pointed electrode (**electric needle**) used in hair electrolysis, as a cautery, etc. ***v.t.*** [-DLED, -DLING], 1. to sew, puncture, etc. with a needle. 2. [Colloq.], *a)* to provoke into doing something; goad. *b)* to tease or heckle. —**nee'dle-like',** *adj.*

**nee·dle-point** (nē'd'l-point'), *adj.* designating a kind of lace made on a pattern with a needle.

**needle point,** 1. an embroidery of woolen threads upon canvas, used as a covering in upholstery. 2. needle-point lace.

**need·less** (nēd'lis), *adj.* not needed; unnecessary. —**need'less·ly,** *adv.* —**need'less·ness,** *n.*

**nee·dle·wom·an** (nē'd'l-woom'ən), *n.* [*pl.* -WOMEN], a woman who does needlework; esp., a seamstress.

**nee·dle·work** (nē'd'l-wūrk'), *n.* work done with a needle; embroidery; sewing.

**need·n't** (nēd''nt), need not.

**needs** (nēdz), *adv.* [AS. *nedes*], of necessity; necessarily (with *must*): as, he must *needs* obey.

**need·y** (nēd'i), *adj.* [-IER, -IEST], in need; very poor; destitute; indigent. —**need'i·ness,** *n.*

**ne'er** (nâr), *adv.* [Poetic], never.

**ne'er-do-well** (nâr'doo-wel'), *n.* a shiftless, irresponsible person. *adj.* good-for-nothing.

**ne·far·i·ous** (ni-fâr′i-əs), *adj.* [< L. < *nefas*, crime < *ne-*, not + *fas*, lawful], very wicked; iniquitous. —**ne·far′i·ous·ly,** *adv.* —**ne·far′i·ous·ness,** *n.*

**neg.,** 1. negative. 2. negatively.

**ne·gate** (ni-gāt′, nē′gāt), *v.t.* [-GATED, -GATING], [see NEGATION], 1. to deny the existence or truth of. 2. to make ineffective; nullify.

**ne·ga·tion** (ni-gā′shən), *n.* [< Fr. < L. pp. of *negare*, to deny], 1. act or instance of denying; denial. 2. the lack or opposite of something positive; annihilation, nullity, etc.

**neg·a·tive** (neg′ə-tiv), *adj.* [see NEGATION], 1. expressing denial or refusal; saying "no." 2. opposite to or lacking in that which is positive: as, *negative* forces, a *negative* personality. 3. not indicating the presence of symptoms, bacteria, etc. 4. in *mathematics*, designating a quantity less than zero, or one to be subtracted; minus. 5. in *photography*, reversing the light and shade of the original subject. 6. in *physics*, of negative electricity. *n.* 1. a word, term, or phrase that denies, refuses, etc. (e.g., *no, not*). 2. a statement of denial, refusal, etc. 3. the point of view that opposes the positive or affirmative. 4. the right of veto. 5. the plate in a voltaic battery where the lower potential is. 6. in *mathematics*, a negative quantity. 7. in *photography*, an exposed and developed photographic film or plate on which the light and shadow of the original subject are reversed. *v.t.* [-TIVED, -TIVING], 1. to refuse; reject; veto (a candidate, bill, etc.). 2. to deny. 3. to disprove. 4. to neutralize. —**in the negative,** 1. in refusal or denial of a plan, etc. 2. with a denial. —**neg′a·tive·ly,** *adv.* —**neg′a·tive·ness, neg′a·tiv′i·ty,** *n.*

**negative electricity,** 1. electricity made by friction on resin or wax, rather than on glass. 2. electricity appearing at the pole of the plate having the lower potential in a voltaic cell.

**neg·a·tiv·ism** (neg′ə-tiv-iz′m), *n.* in *psychology*, an attitude characterized by ignoring or opposing suggestions or orders from others. —**neg′a·tiv·ist,** *adj.* & *n.* —**neg′a·tiv·is′tic,** *adj.*

**neg·lect** (ni-glekt′), *v.t.* [< L. pp. of *negligere* < *neg-*, not + *egere*, to gather], 1. to ignore or disregard (something). 2. not to attend to (something) properly: as, he *neglected* his clothes. 3. to leave undone. *n.* 1. a neglecting. 2. negligence; disregard. 3. a being neglected. —**neg·lect′er, neg·lec′tor,** *n.*

**neg·lect·ful** (ni-glekt′fəl), *adj.* careless; negligent. —**neg·lect′ful·ly,** *adv.* —**neg·lect′ful·ness,** *n.*

‡**né·gli·gé** (nā′glē′zhā′), *n.* & *adj.* [Fr.], negligee.

**neg·li·gee** (neg′li-zhā′, neg′li-zhā′), *n.* [< Fr., fem. pp. of *négliger*, to neglect], 1. a woman's loosely fitting dressing gown. 2. any informal attire. *adj.* informally or incompletely dressed.

**neg·li·gence** (neg′li-jəns), *n.* [see NEGLIGENT], 1. *a*) habitual failure to do the required thing. *b*) carelessness; indifference. 2. an instance of such failure or carelessness.

**neg·li·gent** (neg′li-jənt), *adj.* [< OFr. < L. ppr. of *negligere;* see NEGLECT], 1. habitually failing to do the required thing; neglectful. 2. careless, inattentive, or indifferent. —**neg′li·gent·ly,** *adv.*

**neg·li·gi·ble** (neg′li-jə-b'l), *adj.* that can be neglected or disregarded; trifling. —**neg′li·gi·bil′i·ty, neg′li·gi·ble·ness,** *n.* —**neg′li·gi·bly,** *adv.*

**ne·go·ti·a·ble** (ni-gō′shi-ə-b'l, -shə-b'l), *adj.* 1. that can be sold or transferred to a third person: said of bonds, checks, etc. 2. that can be passed, crossed, etc. —**ne·go′ti·a·bil′i·ty,** *n.*

**ne·go·ti·ate** (ni-gō′shi-āt′), *v.i.* [-ATED, -ATING], [< L. pp. < *negotium*, business < *nec-*, not + *otium*, ease], to confer or discuss with a view to reaching agreement. *v.t.* 1. to settle or conclude (a transaction, treaty, etc.). 2. to transfer or sell (negotiable paper). 3. [Colloq.], to succeed in crossing, surmounting, etc. —**ne·go′ti·a′tor,** *n.*

**ne·go·ti·a·tion** (ni-gō′shi-ā′shən), *n.* a negotiating; specif., *often in pl.*, a conferring, bargaining, etc. to reach agreement.

**Ne·gress** (nē′gris), *n.* [sometimes n-], a Negro woman or girl: often a contemptuous term.

**Ne·gri·to** (ni-grē′tō), *n.* [*pl.* -TOS, -TOES], [Sp., dim. of *negro*, black], a member of any of various groups of dwarfish Negroid peoples of the East Indies, the Philippines, and Africa.

**Ne·gro** (nē′grō), *n.* [*pl.* -GROES], [< Sp. & Port. *negro* (< L. *niger*), black], 1. *a*) a member of the dominant black race of Africa, living chiefly in the Congo and Sudan regions. *b*) a member of any of the other black races of Africa, as a Bantu, etc. 2. any person with some Negro ancestors. *adj.* of or for a Negro or Negroes. Less often **negro.**

**Ne·groid** (nē′groid), *adj.* [sometimes n-], of, like, or characteristic of Negroes. *n.* [sometimes n-], a member of any dominantly Negro people.

**ne·gus** (nē′gəs), *n.* [after Col. Francis *Negus* (d. 1732), who first made it], a beverage of hot water, wine, and lemon juice, sweetened and spiced.

**Ne·he·mi·ah** (nē′ə-mī′ə), *n.* in the *Bible*, 1. a Hebrew leader of about the 5th century B.C. 2. a book of the Old Testament describing his work.

**Neh·ru, Ja·wa·har·lal** (jə-wä′hēr-läl′ nā′rōō), 1889–1964; prime minister of India (1947–1964).

**neigh** (nā), *v.i.* [AS. *hnægan*], to utter the characteristic cry of a horse; whinny. *n.* this cry.

**neigh·bor** (nā′bēr), *n.* [< AS. < *neah* (see NIGH) + hyp. *gebur*, farmer], 1. one who lives near another. 2. a person or thing situated near another. 3. a fellow man. *adj.* near-by; adjacent. *v.t.* & *v.i.* to live or be situated near or near-by. —**neigh′bor·er,** *n.* —**neigh′bor·ing,** *adj.*

**neigh·bor·hood** (nā′bēr-hood′), *n.* 1. a being neighbors. 2. a community, region, etc. with regard to some characteristic: as, a friendly *neighborhood.* 3. the people living near one another; community. —**in the neighborhood of,** [Colloq.], 1. near; close to (a place). 2. about; roughly.

**neigh·bor·ly** (nā′bēr-li), *adj.* like or appropriate to neighbors; friendly. —**neigh′bor·li·ness,** *n.*

**neigh·bour** (nā′bēr), *n., v.t.* & *v.i.* neighbor: Brit. sp. —**neigh′bour·er,** *n.* —**neigh′bour·hood′,** *n.* —**neigh′bour·ing,** *adj.* —**neigh′bour·li·ness,** *n.* —**neigh′bour·ly,** *adj.*

**nei·ther** (nē′thēr, nī′-), *adj.* [AS. *na-hwæther*, lit., not whether], not either: as, use *neither* hand. *pron.* not one or the other (of two): as, *neither* of the boys is well. *conj.* 1. not either: the first element of the pair of correlatives *neither . . . nor*: as, I can *neither* go nor stay. 2. nor yet: as, he doesn't smoke, *neither* does he drink. *adv.* [Dial. or Colloq.], any more than the other.

**Nejd** (nezhd), *n.* an inland state of Saudi Arabia.

**Nel·son, Horatio** (nel′s'n), Viscount Nelson, 1758–1805; English admiral.

**nem·a·tode** (nem′ə-tōd′), *adj.* [< Gr. *nēma*, thread; + *-ode*], designating or of a group of worms with a long, cylindrical, unsegmented body, as the hookworm, pinworm, etc. *n.* a nematode worm.

**Nem·e·sis** (nem′ə-sis), *n.* [Gr. < *nemein*, to deal out], 1. in *Gr. mythology*, the goddess of retribution or vengeance. 2. [usually n-], [*pl.* -SES (-sēz′)], *a*) just punishment. *b*) one who imposes it.

**N. Eng.,** 1. New England. 2. North England.

**ne·o-,** [< Gr. *neos*], [sometimes N-], a combining form meaning *new, recent*, as in *neoclassic.*

**ne·o·clas·sic** (nē′ō-klas′ik), *adj.* designating or of a revival of classic style and form in art, literature, etc.: also **ne′o·clas′si·cal.**

**ne·o·dym·i·um** (nē′ə-dim′i-əm), *n.* a metallic chemical element of the rare-earth group: symbol, Nd; at. wt., 144.27; at. no., 60

**ne·o·lith·ic** (nē′ə-lith′ik), *adj.* [*neo-* + *-lith* + *-ic*], designating or of the later part of the Stone Age, during which man developed polished stone tools.

**ne·ol·o·gism** (nē-ol′ə-jiz′m), *n.* [< Fr.; see NEO-, -LOGY, & -ISM], 1. a new word or a new meaning for an established word. 2. the use of such words and meanings. Also **ne·ol′o·gy** [*pl.* -GIES]. —**ne·ol′o·gist,** *n.* —**ne·ol′o·gis′tic, ne·ol′o·gis′ti·cal,** *adj.*

**ne·ol·o·gize** (nē-ol′ə-jiz′), *v.i.* [-GIZED, -GIZING], to invent or use neologisms.

**ne·o·my·cin** (nē′ə-mī′sin), *n.* [< *neo-* + Gr. *mykēs*, fungus], an antibiotic drug similar to streptomycin, used in treating various infections and as an intestinal antiseptic.

**ne·on** (nē′on), *n.* [< Gr. *neon*, neut. of *neos*, new], a rare, colorless, and inert gaseous chemical element, found in the earth's atmosphere: symbol, Ne; at. wt., 20.183; at. no., 10.

**neon lamp,** a glass tube filled with neon, which glows when an electric current is sent through it.

**ne·o·phyte** (nē′ə-fīt′), *n.* [< LL. < Gr. < *neos*, new + *phytos* < *phyein*, to produce], 1. a new convert; esp., a newly baptized member of the early Christian Church. 2. any beginner; novice.

**ne·o·plasm** (nē′ə-plaz′m), *n.* [*neo-* + *-plasm*], any abnormal growth of tissue; tumor, etc.

**ne·o·prene** (nē′ə-prēn′), *n.* a synthetic rubber, highly resistant to oil, heat, light, and oxidation.

**Ne·pal** (ni-pôl′), *n.* a country in the Himalaya Mountains, between India and Tibet: area, 54,000 sq. mi.; pop., 9,388,000; capital, Katmandu.

**Nep·a·lese** (nep′ə-lēz′), *adj.* of Nepal, its people, or their culture. *n.* [*pl.* -LESE], a native of Nepal.

**ne·pen·the** (ni-pen′thi), *n.* [L. < Gr. < *nē-*, not + *penthos*, sorrow], 1. a drug supposed by the ancient Greeks to cause forgetfulness of sorrow. 2. anything that causes this. Also **ne·pen′thes** (-thēz). —**ne·pen′the·an,** *adj.*

**neph·ew** (nef′ū; *esp.* Brit., nev′ū), *n.* [< OFr. < L. *nepos*], 1. the son of one's brother or sister. 2. the son of one's brother-in-law or sister-in-law.
**ne·phrid·i·um** (ne-frid′i-əm), *n.* [*pl.* -IA (-ə)], [< Gr. dim. of *nephros*, kidney], 1. the waste-discharging organ of some invertebrates, as worms, mollusks, etc. 2. the waste-discharging organ of vertebrate embryos.
**ne·phrit·ic** (ne-frit′ik), *adj.* [< LL. < Gr. < *nephros*, kidney], 1. of a kidney or the kidneys; renal. 2. of or having nephritis.
**ne·phri·tis** (ne-frī′tis), *n.* [see NEPHRO- & -ITIS], disease of the kidneys, characterized by inflammation, degeneration, etc.: certain types are called *Bright's disease.*
**neph·ro-,** [< Gr. *nephros*, kidney], a combining form meaning *kidney:* also **nephr-.**
‡**ne plus ul·tra** (nē plus ul′trə), [L., no more beyond], the highest point of perfection.
**nep·o·tism** (nep′ə-tiz′m), *n.* [< Fr. < It. < L. *nepos*, nephew], favoritism shown to relatives, especially in appointment to desirable positions. —**nep′o·tist,** *n.*
**Nep·tune** (nep′tōōn, -chōōn), *n.* 1. the Roman god of the sea: identified with the Greek Poseidon. 2. the third largest planet in the solar system: diameter, 33,000 mi. —**Nep·tu′ni·an,** *adj.*
**nep·tu·ni·um** (nep-tōō′ni-əm, -chōō′-), *n.* a chemical element produced by the irradiation of ordinary uranium atoms with neutrons: symbol, Np; at. wt., 239; at. no., 93.
**Ne·re·id** (nêr′i-id), *n.* in *Gr. mythology*, a sea nymph, one of the fifty daughters of Nereus.
**Ne·reus** (nêr′ōōs, -yōōs), *n.* in *Gr. mythology*, a sea god, father of the fifty Nereids.
**Ne·ro** (nêr′ō), *n.* emperor of Rome (54–68 A.D.); lived 37 A.D.–68 A.D. —**Ne·ro′ni·an,** *adj.*
**ner·va·tion** (nūr-vā′shən), *n.* the arrangement of nerves, or veins, in a leaf or insect's wing.
**nerve** (nūrv), *n.* [< OFr. < L. *nervus*], 1. a tendon: now poetic except in *strain every nerve.* 2. any of the cordlike fibers carrying impulses between the body organs and the central nervous system. 3. emotional control; courage: as, a man of *nerve.* 4. strength; energy; vigor. 5. [Colloq.], impudent boldness; audacity. 6. in *biology*, a vein in a leaf or insect's wing. *v.t.* [NERVED, NERVING], to give strength or courage to. —**get on one's nerves,** [Colloq.], to make one irritable. —**nerves,** 1. nervousness. 2. an attack of this; hysteria. —**strain every nerve,** to try as hard as possible.
**nerve block,** a method of anesthesia by stopping the impulses through a particular nerve.
**nerve cell,** a cell which with its processes forms the structural and functional unit of the nervous system.
**nerve center,** any group of nerve cells that function together in controlling some specific sense or bodily activity, as breathing.
**nerve·less** (nūrv′lis), *adj.* 1. without strength, vigor, courage, etc.; weak; unnerved. 2. in *anatomy*, *botany & zoology*, having no nerve or nerves. —**nerve′less·ly,** *adv.* —**nerve′less·ness,** *n.*

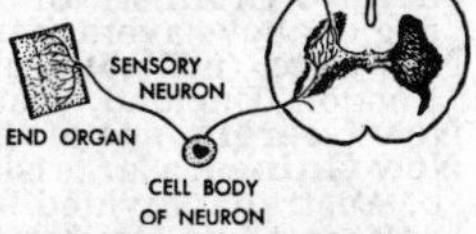

NERVE CELL

**nerve-rack·ing, nerve-wrack·ing** (nūrv′rak′iŋ), *adj.* very trying to one's patience or equanimity.
**nerv·ous** (nūr′vəs), *adj.* 1. originally, strong; sinewy. 2. vigorous in expression; animated. 3. of the nerves. 4. made up of or containing nerves. 5. characterized by or having a disordered state of the nerves. 6. emotionally tense, restless, etc. 7. fearful; apprehensive. —**nerv′ous·ly,** *adv.* —**nerv′ous·ness,** *n.*
**nervous prostration,** neurasthenia.
**nervous system,** all the nerve cells and nervous tissues in an organism, including, in the vertebrates, the brain, spinal cord, nerves, etc.
**ner·vure** (nūr′vyoor), *n.* [Fr.; see NERVE & -URE], a vein or rib in a leaf or insect's wing.
**nerv·y** (nūr′vi), *adj.* [-IER, -IEST], 1. [Rare], strong; sinewy. 2. [Brit.], nervous; jittery. 3. courageous; bold. 4. [Slang], brazen; impudent.
**nes·ci·ent** (nesh′ənt, -i-ənt), *adj.* [< L. *nesciens*, ppr. < *ne-*, not + *scire*, to know], 1. ignorant. 2. agnostic. —**nes′ci·ence,** *n.*
**-ness** (nis, nəs), [AS. *-nes(s)*, *-nis(s)*], a noun-forming suffix meaning: 1. *condition, quality* or *state of being*, as in *sadness.* 2. *a single instance of such a condition, quality*, or *state.*
**nest** (nest), *n.* [AS.], 1. the structure made or the place chosen by birds for laying their eggs and sheltering their young. 2. the place used by insects, fish, etc. for spawning or breeding. 3. a cozy place to live; retreat. 4. a resort, haunt, or den or its frequenters: as, a *nest* of thieves. 5. a swarm or colony of birds, insects, etc. 6. a set of similar things, each fitting within the one next larger. *v.i.* to build or live in a nest. *v.t.* 1. to make a nest for. 2. to place in or as in a nest.
‡**n'est-ce pas?** (nes′pä′), [Fr.], isn't that so?
**nest egg,** 1. an artificial or real egg left in a nest to induce a hen to lay more eggs. 2. money, etc. put aside as a reserve or to set up a fund.
**nes·tle** (nes′'l), *v.i.* [-TLED, -TLING], [AS. *nestlian*], 1. to settle down comfortably and snugly. 2. to press close for comfort or in affection. 3. to lie sheltered or partly hidden, as a house among trees. *v.t.* 1. to rest or press in a snug, affectionate manner. 2. to house as in a nest; shelter. —**nes′tler,** *n.*
**nest·ling** (nest′liŋ, nes′liŋ), *n.* 1. a young bird not yet ready to leave the nest. 2. a baby.
**Nes·tor** (nes′tẽr), *n.* in *Gr. legend*, a wise old counselor who fought with the Greeks at Troy.
**net** (net), *n.* [AS. *nett*], 1. a fabric of string, cord, etc., loosely knotted in an openwork pattern and used to snare birds, fish, etc. 2. a trap; snare. 3. a meshed fabric used to hold, protect, or mark off something: as, a hair *net*, tennis *net.* 4. a fine, meshed, lacelike cloth. 5. a network. *v.t.* [NETTED, NETTING], 1. to make into a net. 2. to snare as with a net. 3. to shelter or enclose as with a net. *v.i.* to make nets or network. *adj.* 1. of or like net. 2. caught in a net. —**net′like′,** *adj.*
**net** (net), *adj.* [Fr.; see NEAT, *adj.*], left over after certain deductions or allowances have been made, as for expenses, weight of containers, etc. *n.* a net amount, profit, weight, price, etc. *v.t.* [NETTED, NETTING], to gain: as, to *net* a profit.
**Neth.,** Netherlands.
**neth·er** (neth′ẽr), *adj.* [AS. *neothera*], lower or under: as, the *nether* world, *nether* garments.
**Neth·er·lands** (neth′ẽr-ləndz), *n.* 1. a country in W Europe, on the North Sea: area, 12,868 sq. mi.; pop., 11,861,000; commercial capital, Amsterdam; political capital, The Hague: also called *Holland.* 2. a kingdom consisting of the independent states of the Netherlands, Surinam, and Netherlands Antilles. —**Neth′er·land′er** (-lan′dẽr, -lən-), *n.*
**Netherlands Antilles,** a group of islands in the West Indies: part of the Netherlands (sense 2).
**Netherlands Guiana,** Surinam.
**Netherlands Indies,** see **Indonesia.**
**Netherlands New Guinea,** a former territory of the Netherlands, comprising the W part of New Guinea: see **West Irian.**
**neth·er·most** (neth′ẽr-mōst′, -məst), *adj.* lowest.
**nether world,** the supposed world of the dead or of punishment after death; hell.
**net·ting** (net′iŋ), *n.* 1. the act or process of making nets or fishing with them. 2. netted material.
**net·tle** (net′'l), *n.* [AS. *netele*], any of a number of related weeds with stinging hairs. *v.t.* [-TLED, -TLING], 1. to sting with or as with nettles. 2. to irritate; annoy; vex.
**net ton,** a short ton.
**net·work** (net′wūrk′), *n.* 1. any arrangement or fabric of parallel wires, threads, etc. crossed at regular intervals by others so as to leave open spaces. 2. a thing resembling this; specif., *a)* a system of crossed roads, canals, etc. *b)* in *radio & television*, a chain of transmitting stations controlled and operated as a unit. *adj.* broadcast simultaneously over all or most stations of a network.
**Neuf·châ·tel** (nōō′shə-tel′, nū′-), *n.* [after a town in N France], a soft, white cheese prepared from sweet milk: also **Neufchâtel cheese.**
**neu·ral** (noor′əl, nyoor′-), *adj.* [*neur(o)-* + *-al*], of a nerve, nerves, or the nervous system.
**neu·ral·gia** (noo-ral′jə, nyoo-), *n.* [*neur(o)-* + *-algia*], a severe pain along the course of a nerve. —**neu·ral′gic,** *adj.*
**neu·ras·the·ni·a** (noor′əs-thē′ni-ə, nyoor′-), *n.* [< *neur(o)-* + Gr. *astheneia*, weakness], 1. formerly, exhaustion of the nervous system. 2. a type of neurosis, usually the result of emotional conflicts, characterized by fatigue, depression, worry, etc. —**neu′ras·then′ic** (-then′ik), *adj. & n.*
**neu·ri·tis** (noo-rī′tis, nyoo-), *n.* [*neur(o)-* + *-itis*],

inflammation of a nerve or nerves, with pain and muscle tenderness. **—neu·rit'ic** (-rit'ik), ***adj.***

**neu·ro-,** [< Gr. *neuron*, nerve], a combining form meaning *of a nerve, nerves*, or *the nervous system*, as in *neuropathy:* also **neur-.**

**neu·rol·o·gy** (noo-rol'ə-ji, nyoo-), ***n.*** [*neuro-* + *-logy*], the branch of medicine dealing with the nervous system and its diseases. **—neu·ro·log·i·cal** (noor'ə-loj'i-k'l, nyoor'-), ***adj.*** **—neu·rol'o·gist,** ***n.***

**neu·ron** (noor'on, nyoor'-), ***n.*** [< Gr. *neuron*, nerve], the structural and functional unit of the nervous system, consisting of the nerve cell body and all its processes: also **neu'rone** (-ōn). **—neu·ron'ic,** ***adj.***

**neu·rop·a·thy** (noo-rop'ə-thi, nyoo-), ***n.*** [*neuro-* + *-pathy*], any disease of the nervous system. **—neu·ro·path·ic** (noor'ə-path'ik, nyoor'-), ***adj. & n.***

**neu·ro·psy·chi·a·try** (noor'ō-si-kī'ə-tri, nyoor'-), ***n.*** the branch of medicine dealing with disorders of both the mind and nervous system.

**neu·rop·ter·ous** (noo-rop'tēr-əs, nyoo-), ***adj.*** [< *neuro-* + Gr. *pteron*, wing], of a group of insects with four membranous wings, having a lacelike framework of ribs. **—neu·rop'ter·an,** ***adj. & n.***

**neu·ro·sis** (noo-rō'sis, nyoo-), ***n.*** [*pl.* -SES (-sēz)], [< Gr. *neuron*, nerve], a psychic, or mental, disorder characterized by combinations of anxieties, compulsions, obsessions, and phobias without apparent organic or structural injury or change.

**neu·rot·ic** (noo-rot'ik, nyoo-), ***adj.*** 1. of or having a neurosis. 2. neural. ***n.*** a neurotic person.

**neut.,** neuter.

**neu·ter** (no͞o'tēr, nū'-), ***adj.*** [< Fr. < L. < *ne-*, not + *uter*, either], 1. [Archaic], neutral. 2. in *biology*, *a*) having no sexual organs; asexual. *b*) having undeveloped sexual organs in the adult, as the worker bee. 3. in *grammar*, designating or of the gender that refers to things regarded as neither male nor female. ***n.*** 1. in *biology*, a neuter plant or animal. 2. in *grammar*, *a*) neuter gender. *b*) a neuter word.

**neu·tral** (no͞o'trəl, nū'-), ***adj.*** [< L.; see NEUTER], 1. not taking part in either side of a quarrel or war. 2. of or characteristic of a nation not taking part in a war. 3. not one thing or the other; indifferent. 4. having little or no decided color. 5. in *botany*, without stamens or pistils. 6. in *chemistry*, neither acid nor alkaline. 7. in *electricity*, neither negative nor positive. 8. in *phonetics*, reduced in quality so as to become (ə) or (i): said of unstressed vowels. 9. in *zoology*, neuter. ***n.*** 1. a nation not taking part in a war. 2. a neutral person. 3. a neutral color. 4. in *mechanics*, the position of disengaged gears, when they do not transmit power from the engine. **—neu'tral·ly,** ***adv.***

**neu·tral·ism** (no͞o'trəl-iz'm, nū'-), ***n.*** a policy, or the advocacy of a policy, of remaining neutral, as in foreign affairs. **—neu'tral·ist,** ***n. & adj.***

**neu·tral·i·ty** (no͞o-tral'ə-ti, nū-), ***n.*** 1. the quality, state, or character of being neutral. 2. the status or policy of a nation not participating in a war between other nations.

**neu·tral·ize** (no͞o'trə-līz', nū'-), ***v.t.*** [-IZED, -IZING], 1. to declare (a nation, etc.) neutral in war. 2. to destroy or counteract the effectiveness, force, etc. of. 3. in *chemistry*, to destroy the active properties of: as, an alkali *neutralizes* an acid. 4. in *electricity*, to make electrically neutral. **—neu'tral·i·za'tion,** ***n.*** **—neu'tral·iz'er,** ***n.***

**neu·tri·no** (no͞o-trē'nō, nū-), ***n.*** [*pl.* -NOS], [< L. *neuter* + It. dim. suffix *-ino*], in *physics*, a hypothetical neutral particle smaller than a neutron.

**neu·tron** (no͞o'tron, nū'-), ***n.*** [< *neutral* + *-on* as in *electron*], one of the fundamental particles of an atom: neutrons are uncharged and have approximately the same mass as protons.

**Ne·vad·a** (nə-vad'ə, -vä'də), ***n.*** a Western State of the U.S.: area, 110,540 sq. mi.; pop., 285,000; capital, Carson City: abbrev. **Nev.** **—Ne·vad'an,** ***adj. & n.***

**nev·er** (nev'ēr), ***adv.*** [AS. *næfre; ne*, not + *æfre*, ever], 1. not ever; at no time. 2. not at all; in no case; under no conditions; to no degree.

**nev·er·more** (nev'ēr-môr', -mōr'), ***adv.*** never again.

**nev·er·the·less** (nev'ēr-*th*ə-les'), ***adv.*** none the less; in spite of that; however.

**ne·vus** (nē'vəs), ***n.*** [*pl.* -VI (-vī)], [L.], a colored spot on the skin, usually congenital; birthmark or mole: also sp. **naevus.** **—ne'void, nae'void,** ***adj.***

**new** (no͞o, nū), ***adj.*** [AS. *niwe*], 1. appearing, thought of, developed, discovered, made, etc. for the first time. 2. *a*) different from (the) one in the past: as, she has a *new* hair-do. *b*) strange; unfamiliar. 3. not yet familiar or accustomed: as, *new* to the job. 4. designating the more or most recent of two or more things of the same class: as, the *new* library. 5. recently grown; fresh: as, *new* potatoes. 6. not worn out; not previously used. 7. modern; recent; fashionable. 8. more; additional. 9. starting as a repetition of a cycle, series, etc.: as, the *new* moon. 10. having just reached a position, rank, place, etc.: as, a *new* arrival. 11. refreshed in spirits, health, etc.: as, a *new* man. 12. [N-], modern; in use since the Middle Ages: said of languages. ***n.*** something new. ***adv.*** 1. again. 2. newly; recently. **—new'ish,** ***adj.*** **—new'ness,** ***n.***

**New Amsterdam,** the Dutch colonial town on Manhattan Island which became New York City.

**New·ark** (no͞o'ērk, nū'-), ***n.*** a city in NE New Jersey: pop., 405,000.

**New Bed·ford** (bed'fērd), a seaport in SE Massachusetts: pop., 102,000.

**new·born** (no͞o'bôrn', nū'-), ***adj.*** 1. recently born; just born. 2. reborn.

**New Britain,** a city in central Connecticut: pop., 82,000.

**New Brunswick,** a province of Canada, on the SE coast: area, 28,354 sq. mi.; pop., 621,000; capital, Fredericton.

**New·burg** (no͞o'bērg, nū'-), ***n.*** see **à la Newburg.**

**New Caledonia,** a French island in Melanesia, in the Coral Sea.

**New·cas·tle** (no͞o'kas''l, nū'käs''l), ***n.*** a city in NE England: pop., 263,000: also **New'cas'tle-u·pon'-Tyne'** (-tīn'). **—carry coals to Newcastle,** to do that which is superfluous or unneeded.

**new·com·er** (no͞o'kum'ēr, nū'-), ***n.*** a person who has come recently; recent arrival.

**New Deal,** the economic and political principles and policies adopted by President Franklin D. Roosevelt to advance the economic and social welfare of the American people. **—New Dealer.**

**New Delhi,** the capital of India, adjacent to Delhi: pop., 276,000.

**new·el** (no͞o'əl, nū'-), ***n.*** [< OFr. < LL. *nucalis*, like a nut < L. *nux*, nut], 1. the upright pillar around which the steps of a winding staircase turn. 2. the post at the top or bottom of a flight of stairs, supporting the handrail: also **newel post.**

**New England,** the six northeastern States of the U.S.; Maine, Vermont, New Hampshire, Massachusetts, Rhode Island, and Connecticut. **—New Englander.**

**Newf.,** Newfoundland.

**new·fan·gled** (no͞o'faŋ'g'ld, nū'-), ***adj.*** [< ME. < *newe*, new + *-fangel* < base of AS. *fon*, to take], 1. new; novel. 2. fond of new things or ideas. A contemptuous term.

**New·found·land** (no͞o'fənd-land', nū'fənd-lənd; *officially* nū-found'land'), ***n.*** 1. an island off the E coast of Canada. 2. a province of Canada comprising Newfoundland and Labrador: area, 156,185 sq. mi.; pop., 494,000; capital, St. John's. **—New·found'land·er,** ***n.***

**New·found·land dog** (no͞o-found'lənd, nū-), any of a North American breed of large, shaggy-haired dog of above average intelligence.

**New·gate** (no͞o'gāt', nū'-), ***n.*** a former prison in London, England, destroyed in 1902.

**New Georgia,** one of the British Solomon Islands.

**New Guinea,** a large island in the East Indies, north of Australia: divided between Indonesia, in the W half, and two territories (*Territories of Papua* and *New Guinea*), jointly administered by Australia, in the E half: also called *Papua.*

**New Guinea, Territory of,** an Australian trust territory on NE New Guinea and near-by islands.

**New Hamp·shire** (hamp'shir), a New England State of the U.S.: area, 9,304 sq. mi.; pop., 607,000; capital, Concord: abbrev. **N.H.**

**New Ha·ven** (hā'v'n), a city in S Connecticut, on Long Island Sound: pop., 152,000.

**New Hebrides,** a group of Melanesian islands in the South Pacific, under the joint control of Britain and France.

**New High German,** see **German, High German.**

**New Jersey,** an Eastern State of the U.S.: area, 7,836 sq. mi.; pop., 6,067,000; capital, Trenton: abbrev. **N.J.** **—New Jer·sey·ite** (jūr'zi-īt').

**New Jerusalem,** in the *Bible*, heaven: Rev. 22:2.

**New Latin,** Modern Latin.

**new·ly** (no͞o'li, nū'li), ***adv.*** 1. recently; lately. 2. anew; afresh.

**new·ly·wed** (no͞o'li-wed', nū'-), ***n.*** a recently married person.

**New·man, John Henry** (no͞o'mən, nū'-), Cardinal, 1801–1890; English theologian and writer.

**New Mexico,** a Southwestern State of the U.S. on the Mexican border: area, 121,666 sq. mi.; pop., 951,000; capital, Santa Fe: abbrev. **N. Mex.** **—New Mexican.**

**new moon,** the moon when it is between the earth

and the sun: it appears as a thin crescent curving toward the right.
**new-mown** (nōō′mōn′, nū′-), *adj.* freshly mown; just cut: said of hay or grass.
**New Netherland,** a former Dutch colony (1613–1664), later comprising the British colonies of New York, New Jersey, and Delaware.
**New Or·le·ans** (ôr′li-ən*z*; *esp. formerly,* ôr-lēnz′; *esp. Southern,* ôr′lənz), a city in SE Louisiana, on the Mississippi: pop., 628,000.
**New·port News** (nōō′pôrt′, nū′pōrt′), a seaport in SE Virginia, on the James River: pop., 114,000.
**New Ro·chelle** (rə-shel′), a city in New York, north of New York City: pop., 77,000.
**news** (nōōz, nūz), *n.pl.* [construed as sing.], [after OFr. *noveles* or ML. *nova,* pl. of *novum,* what is new], 1. new information about anything; information previously unknown: as, that's *news* to me. 2. recent happenings. 3. reports of such events, collectively.
**news·boy** (nōōz′boi′, nūz′-), *n.* a boy who sells or delivers newspapers.
**news·cast** (nōōz′kast′, nūz′käst′), *n.* [*news* + broad*cast*], a radio or television news broadcast. *v.t. & v.i.* to broadcast (news). —**news′cast′er,** *n.*
**news·deal·er** (nōōz′dēl′ẽr, nūz′-), *n.* a person who sells newspapers, magazines, etc.
**news·let·ter** (nōōz′let′ẽr, nūz′-), *n.* a bulletin issued at regular intervals to subscribers, containing recent political and economic news.
**news·man** (nōōz′man′, nūz′mən), *n.* [*pl.* -MEN], 1. one who sells newspapers. 2. a newspaper reporter.
**news·mon·ger** (nōōz′muŋ′gẽr, nūz′-), *n.* one who spreads news; esp., a gossip.
**New South Wales,** a state of SE Australia.
**news·pa·per** (nōōz′pā′pẽr, nūz′-), *n.* a regular publication, usually daily or weekly, containing news, opinions, advertisements, etc.
**news·print** (nōōz′print′, nūz′-), *n.* a cheap, thin paper, mainly from wood pulp, for newspapers, etc.
**news·reel** (nōōz′rēl′, nūz′-), *n.* a motion picture of current news events.
**news·stand** (nōōz′stand′, nūz′-), *n.* a stand at which newspapers, magazines, etc. are sold.
**New Style,** the method of reckoning time in accordance with the Gregorian calendar.
**news·wor·thy** (nōōz′wũr′*th*i, nūz′-), *adj.* timely, important, and interesting.
**news·y** (nōōz′i, nūz′i), *adj.* [-IER, -IEST], [Colloq.], containing much news. *n.* [*pl.* -IES], [Colloq.], a newsboy.
**newt** (nōōt, nūt), *n.* [by syllabic merging of ME. *an eute* < AS. *efete*], any of various small amphibious salamanders.

SMOOTH NEWT
(3–6 in. long)

**New Testament,** the part of the Bible that contains the life and teachings of Jesus and his followers.
**New·ton** (nōō′t'n, nū′-), *n.* a city in Massachusetts, near Boston: pop., 92,000.
**New·ton,** Sir **Isaac** (nōō′t'n, nū′-), 1642–1727; English mathematician and philosopher. —**New·to′ni·an** (-tō′ni-ən), *adj. & n.*
**New World,** the Western Hemisphere. —**new′-world′,** *adj.*
**new year,** 1. the year just about to begin or just begun (usually with *the*). 2. the first day or days of the new year (with *the* or *a*): also **New Year's.**
**New Year's Day,** January 1, usually celebrated as a legal holiday: also **New Year's.**
**New Year's Eve,** the evening before New Year's Day.
**New York,** 1. an Eastern State of the U.S.: area, 49,576 sq. mi.; pop., 16,782,000; capital, Albany. 2. the largest city in the U.S., in SE New York State, at the mouth of the Hudson: area, 309 sq. mi.; pop., 7,782,000 (metropolitan area,10,695,000): often **New York City.** Abbrev. **N.Y.** —**New York′er.**
**New York State Barge Canal,** 1. the New York State canal system. 2. the canal from Buffalo, on Lake Erie, to Troy, on the Hudson.
**New Zea·land** (zē′lənd), a British dominion made up of two large and several small islands in the Pacific, southeast of Australia: total area, 103,934 sq. mi.; pop., 2,174,000; capital, Wellington: abbrev. **N.Z.** —**New Zea′land·er.**
**next** (nekst), *adj.* [older superl. of *nigh*], [AS. *neahst,* superl. of *neah,* nigh], nearest; immediately preceding or following. *adv.* 1. in the time, place, degree, or rank immediately preceding or following. 2. on the first subsequent occasion: as, when *next* we meet. *prep.* beside; nearest to: as, sit *next* the tree. —**get next to,** [Slang], to become friendly or close to. —**next door (to),** in or at the next house, building, etc. (adjacent to).
**next-door** (neks′dôr′, -dōr′), *adj.* in or at the next house, building, etc.
**next of kin,** one's nearest blood relative(s).
**nex·us** (nek′səs), *n.* [*pl.* -USES, -US], [L. < pp. of *nectere,* to bind], 1. a connection, tie, or link between individuals of a group, members of a series, etc. 2. the group or series connected.
**Nez Per·cé** (nā′ pâr′sā′; Eng. nez′ pũrs′), *n.* [*pl.* NEZ PERCÉS (pâr′sā′; Eng. pũr′siz)], [Fr., lit., pierced nose: from the false notion that they pierced the nose], a member of a tribe of North American Indians who lived in the Northwest.
**Nfld., N.F., Nfd.,** Newfoundland.
**N.G.,** 1. National Guard. 2. New Guinea.
**N.G., n.g.,** [Slang], no good.
**N.H.,** New Hampshire.
**Ni,** in *chemistry,* nickel.
**N.I.,** Northern Ireland.
**ni·a·cin** (nī′ə-s'n), *n.* [*ni*cotinic *ac*id + *-in*], nicotinic acid.
**Ni·ag·a·ra** (nī-ag′rə, -ag′ə-rə), *n.* a river between New York and Ontario, Canada, flowing from Lake Erie into Lake Ontario.
**Niagara Falls,** 1. the waterfall of the Niagara River: it is divided into two great falls (*Horseshoe,* or *Canadian, Falls* and *American Falls*). 2. a city in New York, near Niagara Falls: pop., 102,000.
**nib** (nib), *n.* [var. of *neb*], 1. the bill or beak of a bird. 2. the split end of a pen point or the pen point itself. 3. the projecting end of anything; point; sharp prong. *v.t.* [NIBBED, NIBBING], to put a point on (a pen).
**nib·ble** (nib′'l), *v.t. & v.i.* [-BLED, -BLING], [cf. MLG. *nibbelen*], 1. to eat (food) with quick, small bites, as a mouse does. 2. to bite at (food) lightly and intermittently. *n.* 1. a small bite or morsel. 2. a nibbling. —**nib′bler,** *n.*
**Ni·be·lung** (nē′bə-looŋ′), *n.* [G.], in *Norse mythology,* any of a race of dwarfs who owned a magic ring and a hoard of gold, taken from them by Siegfried.
**Ni·be·lung·en·lied** (nē′bə-looŋ′ən-lēt′), *n.* a Middle High German epic poem of the 13th century, by an unknown author: cf. *Siegfried.*
**nib·lick** (nib′lik), *n.* [? < D. < *kneppel,* a club], a heavy, iron-headed golf club used, as in sand traps, for short lofts: also called *number 9 iron.*
**Nic·a·ra·gua** (nik′ə-rä′gwə), *n.* a country in Central America, on the Caribbean and Pacific: area, 57,000 sq. mi.; pop., 1,471,000; capital, Managua: abbrev. **Nicar.** —**Nic′a·ra′guan,** *adj. & n.*
**Nicaragua, Lake,** a lake in SW Nicaragua.
**Nice** (nēs), *n.* a seaport and resort in SE France, on the Mediterranean: pop., 244,000.
**nice** (nīs), *adj.* [NICER, NICEST], [OFr., stupid < L. *nescius,* ignorant < *ne-,* not + *scire,* to know: etym. reflected in obs. senses], 1. difficult to please; fastidious. 2. delicate; precise; discriminative; subtle: as, a *nice* distinction. 3. calling for accuracy, care, tact, etc.: as, a *nice* problem. 4. *a)* finely discriminating. *b)* minutely accurate. 5. morally scrupulous. 6. *a)* agreeable; pleasant. *b)* attractive; pretty. *c)* kind; thoughtful. *d)* modest; well-mannered. *e)* good; excellent. A generalized term of approval. —**nice′ly,** *adv.* —**nice′ness,** *n.*
**Ni·cene Creed** (nī-sēn′, nī′sēn′), [< *Nicaea,* ancient city in Asia Minor where it was formulated], a confession of faith for Christians, originally adopted in 325 A.D.: now accepted in various forms by most Christian denominations.
**ni·ce·ty** (nī′sə-ti), *n.* [*pl.* -TIES], 1. a being nice; specif., *a)* coyness; modesty. *b)* precision; accuracy, as of discrimination or perception. *c)* fastidiousness; refinement. 2. the quality of calling for delicacy or precision in handling. 3. a subtle or minute detail, distinction, etc. 4. something choice or dainty. —**to a nicety,** exactly.
**niche** (nich), *n.* [Fr. < OFr.; ult. < L. *nidus,* a nest], 1. a recess in a wall, for a statue, bust, or vase. 2. a place or position particularly suitable for the person or thing in it. *v.t.* [NICHED, NICHING], to place in or as in a niche.
**Nich·o·las I** (nik′'l-əs), 1796–1855; czar of Russia (1825–1855).
**Nicholas II,** 1868–1918; czar of Russia (1894–1917); forced to abdicate; executed.

**Nicholas,** Saint, ?–342 A.D.; patron saint of Russia and of young people, sailors, etc.: cf. *Santa Claus.*

**Nick** (nik), *n.* the Devil: usually **Old Nick.**

**nick** (nik), ***v.t.*** [prob. < MLG. *knicken*], 1. to make a small cut, indention, or chip on (the edge or surface of wood, china, etc.). 2. to cut through or into. 3. to strike or catch at the exact or proper time. 4. [Slang], to trick; cheat. ***n.*** a cut, chip, etc. made by nicking. **—in the nick of time,** at the critical moment.

**nick·el** (nik''l), ***n.*** [Sw. < G. *kupfernickel*, copper demon: so called because the copperlike ore contains no copper], 1. a hard, silver-white, malleable metallic chemical element, used in alloys and for plating: symbol, Ni; at. wt., 58.69; at. no., 28. 2. a U.S. or Canadian coin made of an alloy of nickel and copper and equal to five cents. ***v.t.*** [-ELED or -ELLED, -ELING or -ELLING], to plate with nickel.

**nick·el·o·de·on** (nik''l-ō'di-ən), ***n.*** [< *nickel* + Fr. *odéon*, concert hall], 1. formerly, a motion-picture theater, etc. where admission was five cents. 2. a player piano or phonograph operated by the insertion of a nickel in a slot.

**nickel plate,** a thin layer of nickel deposited by electroplating on metallic objects to prevent rust. **—nick'el-plate'** [-PLATED, -PLATING], ***v.t.***

**nickel silver,** a hard, tough, ductile, malleable alloy composed essentially of nickel, copper, and zinc: also called *German silver.*

**nick·er** (nik'ēr), ***n.*** **& *v.i.*** [prob. < freq. of *neigh*], [Brit. Dial.], 1. neigh. 2. laugh; snicker.

**nick·nack** (nik'nak'), ***n.*** a knickknack.

**nick·name** (nik'nām'), ***n.*** [by syllabic merging of ME. *an ekename*, a surname], 1. substitute, often descriptive name given to a person or thing, as in fun, affection, etc. (e.g., "Shorty"). 2. a familiar form of a proper name (e.g., "Tommy" for "Thomas"). ***v.t.*** [-NAMED, -NAMING], 1. to give a nickname to. 2. to call by a wrong name.

**nic·o·tine** (nik'ə-tēn', -tin), ***n.*** [Fr. < J. *Nicot*, 16th-c. Fr. diplomat who introduced tobacco into France], a poisonous alkaloid, $C_{10}H_{14}N_2$, extracted from tobacco leaves as an oily, acrid liquid and used as an insecticide: also **nic'o·tin** (-tin).

**nic·o·tin·ic acid** (nik'ə-tin'ik), a white, odorless substance, $C_6H_5O_2N$, found in protein foods like lean meat, eggs, etc.: it is a member of the vitamin B complex, used in treating pellagra: also called *niacin.*

**nic·tate** (nik'tāt), ***v.i.*** [-TATED, -TATING], to nictitate.

**nic·ti·tate** (nik'tə-tāt'), ***v.i.*** [-TATED, -TATING], [< ML. pp. of *nictitare*, freq. < L. *nictare*, to wink], to wink or blink rapidly, as birds and animals with a nictitating membrane. **—nic'ti·ta'tion,** ***n.***

**nictitating membrane,** a transparent third eyelid hinged at the inner side or lower lid of the eye of various animals: also **nictating membrane.**

**niece** (nēs), ***n.*** [< OFr. < LL. < L. *neptis*], 1. the daughter of one's brother or sister. 2. the daughter of one's brother-in-law or sister-in-law.

**Nie·men** (nē'mən), ***n.*** a river in Byelorussia and Lithuania, flowing into the Baltic Sea.

**Nie·tzsche, Frie·drich Wil·helm** (frē'driH vil'-helm nē'chə), 1844–1900; German philosopher. **—Nie'tzsche·an** (-chi-ən), ***adj.* & *n.***

**Ni·fl·heim, Ni·fel·heim** (niv''l-hām'), ***n.*** [< ON.], in *Norse mythology*, the regions of darkness and cold, or the realm of the dead; hell.

**nif·ty** (nif'ti), ***adj.*** [-TIER, -TIEST], [prob. < *magnificent*], [Slang], attractive, smart, stylish, enjoyable, etc.: a generalized term of approval. ***n.*** [-TIES], [Slang], a clever remark.

**Ni·ger** (nī'jēr), ***n.*** 1. a river in west central Africa, flowing through Nigeria into the Gulf of Guinea. 2. a country in central Africa: a member of the French Community: area, 459,000 sq. mi.; pop., 2,850,000; capital, Niamey.

**Ni·ge·ri·a** (nī-jêr'i-ə), ***n.*** a country in W Africa, on the Gulf of Guinea: a member of the British Commonwealth of Nations: area, 356,670 sq. mi.; pop., 30,500,000; capital, Lagos. **—Ni·ge'ri·an,** ***adj.* & *n.***

**nig·gard** (nig'ērd), ***n.*** [prob. ult. < ON.], a stingy person; miser. ***adj.*** stingy; miserly.

**nig·gard·ly** (nig'ērd-li), ***adj.*** 1. stingy; miserly. 2. small, few, or scanty: as, a *niggardly* sum. ***adv.*** stingily. **—nig'gard·li·ness,** ***n.***

**nig·ger** (nig'ēr), ***n.*** [< Fr. *nègre* < Sp. *negro;* see NEGRO], 1. a Negro. 2. a member of any dark-skinned people. A vulgar, offensive term of hostility and contempt, as used by racists.

**nig·gle** (nig''l), ***v.i.*** [-GLED, -GLING], [prob. < ON.], to work fussily; be finical; putter. **—nig'gler,** ***n.*** **—nig'gling,** ***adj.* & *n.***

**nigh** (nī), ***adv.*** [AS. *neah*], [Chiefly Archaic or Dial.], 1. near in time, place, etc. 2. almost. ***adj.*** [NIGHER, NIGHEST or, *older*, NEXT], [Chiefly Archaic or Dial.], 1. near; close. 2. direct or short. 3. on the left: said of animals, vehicles, etc. ***prep.*** [Chiefly Archaic or Dial.], near. ***v.i.* & *v.t.*** [Archaic], to approach.

**night** (nīt), ***n.*** [AS. *niht*], 1. the period of darkness between sunset and sunrise. 2. the darkness of this period. 3. any period or condition of darkness or gloom; specif., *a)* a period of intellectual or moral degeneration. *b)* a time of grief. *c)* death. ***adj.*** of or for the night. **—make a night of it,** to celebrate all night. **—night and day,** continuously or continually.

**night blindness,** imperfect vision in the dark or in dim light: a sign of vitamin A deficiency.

**night-bloom·ing ce·re·us** (nīt'blōōm'iŋ sêr'i-əs), a tropical American cactus with large, white flowers that open at night.

**night·cap** (nīt'kap'), ***n.*** 1. a cap worn in bed to protect the head from cold. 2. [Colloq.], an alcoholic drink taken just before going to bed.

**night clothes,** clothes worn in bed, as pajamas.

**night club,** a place of entertainment open at night for eating, drinking, dancing, etc.

**night·dress** (nīt'dres'), ***n.*** a nightgown.

**night·fall** (nīt'fôl'), ***n.*** the close of the day.

**night·gown** (nīt'goun'), ***n.*** a loose gown, usually long, worn in bed by women or girls.

**night·hawk** (nīt'hôk'), ***n.*** 1. any of a group of night birds related to the whippoorwill; goatsucker. 2. a night owl.

**night·in·gale** (nīt''n-gāl', -iŋ-), ***n.*** [< AS. < *niht*, night + base of *galan*, to sing], a small European thrush with a russet back and buff underparts, characterized by the melodious singing of the male, especially at night.

**Night·in·gale, Florence** (nīt''n-gāl', -iŋ-), 1820–1910; English pioneer in modern nursing.

**night·jar** (nīt'jär'), ***n.*** [*night* + *jar*, *v.*], the European goatsucker; nighthawk.

**night letter,** a long telegram sent at night at a cheaper rate than a regular telegram.

**night·long** (nīt'lôŋ'), ***adj.*** lasting the entire night. ***adv.*** during the entire night.

**night·ly** (nīt'li), ***adj.*** 1. of, like, or characteristic of the night. 2. done or occurring every night. ***adv.*** 1. at night. 2. every night.

**night·mare** (nīt'mâr'), ***n.*** [< ME. < *niht*, night + *mare*, demon], 1. a frightening dream, often accompanied by a sensation of oppression and helplessness. 2. any frightening experience. **—night'-mar'ish,** ***adj.*** **—night'mar'ish·ness,** ***n.***

**night owl,** a person who works at night or otherwise stays up late.

**nights** (nīts), ***adv.*** [Colloq.], at or by night.

**night school,** a school held in the evening, as for adults unable to attend by day.

**night·shade** (nīt'shād'), ***n.*** any of a group of flowering plants related to the potato and tomato; esp., any of various poisonous varieties, including the belladonna (*deadly nightshade*).

**night·shirt** (nīt'shũrt'), ***n.*** a long, loose, shirtlike garment, worn in bed by men or boys.

**night·spot** (nīt'spot'), ***n.*** [Colloq.], a night club.

**night stick,** a long, heavy club carried by a policeman, especially at night.

**night·time** (nīt'tīm'), ***n.*** the period of darkness from sunset to sunrise.

**night·walk·er** (nīt'wôk'ēr), ***n.*** 1. a large earthworm that comes out of the earth at night: also **night crawler.** 2. [Rare], a person who goes about at night, as a thief, prostitute, etc.

**night·wear** (nīt'wâr'), ***n.*** night clothes.

**night·y** (nīt'i), ***n.*** [*pl.* -IES], [Colloq.], a nightgown.

**ni·hil·ism** (nī'ə-liz'm), ***n.*** [< L. *nihil*, nothing], 1. in *philosophy*, *a)* the denial of the existence of any basis for knowledge. *b)* the general rejection of customary beliefs in morality, religion, etc. 2. in *politics*, *a)* the doctrine that all existing social, political, and economic institutions must be completely destroyed. *b)* [N-], a movement in Russia (c. 1860–1917) which advocated such revolutionary reform. 3. loosely, any use of terrorism against a government. **—ni'hil·ist,** ***n.*** **—ni'hil·is'tic,** ***adj.***

**Ni·jin·sky, Vas·lav** (vàs-lâf' ni-zhēn'ski; Eng. nə-jin'ski), 1890–1950; Russian ballet dancer.

**Ni·ke** (nī'kē), ***n.*** 1. in *Gr. mythology*, the winged goddess of victory. 2. a U. S. Army automatically guided missile for launching from the ground against enemy aircraft.

**nil** (nil), ***n.*** [L., contr. of *nihil*], nothing.

**Nile** (nīl), ***n.*** a river in E Africa, flowing through Egypt into the Mediterranean.

**Nile green,** yellowish green. **—Nile'-green',** ***adj.***

**nil·gai, nil·ghai** (nil'gī), ***n.*** [*pl.* -GAIS, -GHAIS, -GAI, -GHAI; see PLURAL, II, D, 1], [< Hind. & Per. *nīlgāw*, blue cow], a large, slate-blue antelope of India.

**nil·gau, nil·ghau** (nil′gô), *n.* [*pl.* -GAUS, -GHAUS, -GAU, -GHAU; see PLURAL, II, D, 1], a nilgai.

**nim·ble** (nim′b'l), *adj.* [-BLER, -BLEST], [< AS. *numol* < *niman*, to take], 1. quick-witted; alert: as, a *nimble* mind. 2. showing mental quickness: as, a *nimble* reply. 3. moving quickly and lightly; agile. —**nim′ble·ness,** *n.* —**nim′bly,** *adv.*

**nim·bo-stra·tus** (nim′bō-strā′təs), *n.* [*nimbo-* (see NIMBUS) + *stratus*], a low, gray cloud layer that covers the sky and brings rain or snow.

**nim·bus** (nim′bəs), *n.* [*pl.* -BUSES, -BI (-bī)], [L., rain cloud], 1. a bright cloud surrounding gods or goddesses when they appeared on earth. 2. an aura of splendor about any person or thing. 3. a halo surrounding the heads of saints, etc., as on pictures or medals. 4. a nimbo-stratus.

**Nim·rod** (nim′rod), *n.* 1. in the *Bible*, a mighty hunter: Gen. 10:8-9; hence, 2. a hunter.

**nin·com·poop** (nin′kəm-po͞op′), *n.* [< ?], a stupid, silly person; fool; simpleton.

**nine** (nīn), *adj.* [AS. *nigon*], totaling one more than eight. *n.* 1. the cardinal number between eight and ten; 9; IX. 2. any group of nine persons or things; esp., a baseball team. —**the Nine,** the nine Muses.

**nine·fold** (nīn′fōld′), *adj.* [see -FOLD], 1. having nine parts. 2. having nine times as much or as many. *adv.* nine times as much or as many.

**nine·pins** (nīn′pinz′), *n.pl.* [construed as sing.], a game like tenpins, in which nine wooden pins are set up at one end of an alley and bowled at.

**nine·teen** (nīn′tēn′), *adj.* [AS. *nigontyne*], nine more than ten. *n.* the cardinal number between eighteen and twenty; 19; XIX.

**nine·teenth** (nīn′tēnth′), *adj.* 1. preceded by eighteen others in a series; 19th. 2. designating any of the nineteen equal parts of something. *n.* 1. the one following the eighteenth. 2. any of the nineteen equal parts of something; 1/19.

**nine·ti·eth** (nīn′ti-ith), *adj.* 1. preceded by eighty-nine others in a series; 90th. 2. designating any of the ninety equal parts of something. *n.* 1. the one following the eighty-ninth. 2. any of the ninety equal parts of something; 1/90.

**nine·ty** (nīn′ti), *adj.* [AS. *nigontig*], nine times ten. *n.* [*pl.* -TIES], the cardinal number between eighty-nine and ninety-one; 90; XC (or LXXXX). —**the nineties,** the years from ninety through ninety-nine (of a century or a person's age).

**Nin·e·veh** (nin′ə-və), *n.* a city in ancient Assyria.

**nin·ny** (nin′i), *n.* [*pl.* -NIES], [prob. by syllabic merging and contr. of *an innocent*], a fool; dolt.

**ninth** (nīnth), *adj.* [AS. *nigonthe*], 1. preceded by eight others in a series; 9th. 2. designating any of the nine equal parts of something. *n.* 1. the one following the eighth. 2. any of the nine equal parts of something; 1/9. —**ninth′ly,** *adv.*

**Ni·o·be** (nī′ə-bi), *n.* in *Gr. mythology*, a mother whose children were slain by Artemis and Apollo when she boastfully compared herself to their mother: the weeping Niobe was changed by Zeus into a stone from which tears continued to flow.

**ni·o·bi·um** (nī-ō′bi-əm), *n.* [< L. *Niobe*, Niobe, daughter of Tantalus], a rare metallic chemical element with properties like those of tantalum: symbol, Nb; at. wt., 92.91; at. no., 41: formerly also called *columbium*.

**nip** (nip), *v.t.* [NIPPED, NIPPING], [prob. < MLG. *nippen* or ON. *hnippa*], 1. to pinch or squeeze, as between two surfaces; bite. 2. to sever (shoots, etc.), as by clipping. 3. to check the growth of. 4. to have a painful or injurious effect on: said of cold, as, frost *nipped* the plants. *v.i.* to give a nip or nips. *n.* 1. a nipping; pinch; bite. 2. a piece nipped off. 3. a stinging quality, as in cold air. 4. stinging cold; frost. —**nip and tuck,** so close or critical as to leave the outcome in doubt. —**nip in the bud,** to check (something) at the start.

**nip** (nip), *n.* [prob. < D. < base of *nippen*, to sip], a small drink of liquor. *v.t. & v.i.* [NIPPED, NIPPING], to drink (liquor) in nips.

**nip·per** (nip′ẽr), *n.* 1. anything that nips, or pinches. 2. *pl.* any of certain tools for grasping or severing, as pliers, pincers, or forceps. 3. the pincerlike claw of a crab or lobster. 4. [Brit. Colloq.], a small boy.

**nip·ple** (nip′'l), *n.* [prob. < dim. of *neb*], 1. the small protuberance on a breast or udder, through which the milk passes in suckling the young; teat. 2. a rubber cap with a teatlike part, for a baby's bottle. 3. any projection or thing resembling a nipple in shape or function.

**Nip·pon** (nip on, ni-pon′), *n.* Japan: the Japanese name. —**Nip′pon·ese′** (-ə-nēz′), *adj. & n. sing. & pl.*

**nip·py** (nip′i), *adj.* [-PIER, -PIEST], sharp; biting.

**nir·va·na** (nẽr-van′ə, nir-vä′nə), *n.* [< Sans.], [also N-], in *Buddhism*, the state of perfect blessedness achieved by the extinction of the self and by the absorption of the soul into the supreme spirit.

**Ni·san** (nī′san, nis′ən; Heb. ni-sän′), *n.* [Heb.], the seventh month of the Jewish year: see **Jewish calendar.**

**ni·sei** (nē′sā′), *n.* [*pl.* -SEI, -SEIS], [Japan., lit., second generation], [also N-], a native U.S. citizen born of immigrant Japanese parents.

**Nis·sen hut** (nis′'n), [after its Canadian designer], a prefabricated shelter made of a half cylinder of corrugated metal resting on its flat surface, first used by the British Army in World War II: see also **Quonset hut.**

**nit** (nit), *n.* [AS. *hnitu*], 1. the egg of a louse or similar insect. 2. the young insect.

**ni·ter, ni·tre** (nī′tẽr), *n.* [< Fr. < L. < Gr. *nitron*], 1. potassium nitrate, a crystalline salt found in nature and used in making gunpowder, etc.; saltpeter. 2. sodium nitrate, a crystalline salt, used as a fertilizer, etc.; Chile saltpeter.

**ni·ton** (nī′ton), *n.* [< L. *nitere*, to shine; + *-on* as in *argon*], radon: symbol, Nt: former name.

**ni·trate** (nī′trāt, -trit), *n.* 1. a salt or ester of nitric acid. 2. potassium nitrate or sodium nitrate, used as a fertilizer. *v.t.* [-TRATED, -TRATING], to treat or combine with nitric acid or a nitrate. —**ni·tra′tion,** *n.*

**ni·tric** (nī′trik), *adj.* 1. of or containing nitrogen. 2. designating or of compounds in which nitrogen has a higher valence than in the corresponding nitrous compounds.

**nitric acid,** a colorless, fuming acid, $HNO_3$, that is highly corrosive: also called *aqua fortis*.

**ni·tri·fy** (nī′trə-fī′), *v.t.* [-FIED, -FYING], [< Fr.; see NITER & -FY], 1. to impregnate (soil, etc.) with nitrates. 2. to cause the oxidation of (ammonium salts, etc.) to nitrates and nitrites, as by the action of soil bacteria, etc. —**ni′tri·fi·ca′tion,** *n.* —**ni′tri·fi′er,** *n.*

**ni·trite** (nī′trīt), *n.* a salt or ester of nitrous acid.

**ni·tro-,** [< L. < Gr. *nitron*, niter], a combining form used to indicate: 1. *the presence of nitrogen compounds made as by the action of nitric* or *nitrous acid*, as in *nitrocellulose*. 2. *the presence of the $NO_2$ radical*, as in *nitrobenzene*. Also **nitr-.**

**ni·tro·ben·zene** (nī′trə-ben′zēn), *n.* a poisonous yellow liquid, $C_6H_5NO_2$, prepared by treating benzene with nitric acid, used in dyes, etc.

**ni·tro·cel·lu·lose, ni·tro·cel·lu·lose** (nī′trə-sel′yoo-lōs′), *n.* a substance obtained by treating cellulose with nitric acid, used in making explosives, lacquers, etc.

**ni·tro·gen** (nī′trə-jən), *n.* [< Fr.; see NITRO- & -GEN], a colorless, tasteless, odorless gaseous chemical element forming nearly four fifths of the atmosphere: it is a component of all living things: symbol, N; at. wt., 14.008; at. no., 7. —**ni·trog′e·nous** (-troj′ə-nəs), *adj.*

**nitrogen fixation,** the conversion of atmospheric nitrogen into nitrates by soil bacteria (**nitrogen fixers**), found in the nodules of certain legumes. —**ni′tro·gen-fix′ing,** *adj.*

**ni·trog·e·nize** (nī-troj′ə-nīz′, nī′trə-jə-), *v.t.* [-NIZED, -NIZING], to combine with nitrogen or nitrogen compounds.

**ni·tro·glyc·er·in, ni·tro·glyc·er·ine** (nī′trə-glis′ẽr-in), *n.* a thick, explosive oil, $C_3H_5(NO_3)_3$, prepared by treating glycerin with a mixture of nitric and sulfuric acids: it is used in dynamite.

**ni·trous** (nī′trəs), *adj.* 1. of, like, or containing niter. 2. designating or of compounds in which nitrogen has a lower valence than in the corresponding nitric compounds.

**nitrous acid,** an acid, $HNO_2$, known only in solution: it forms salts called *nitrites*.

**nitrous oxide,** a colorless gas, $N_2O$, used as an anesthetic: also called *laughing gas*.

**nit·ty** (nit′i), *adj.* [-TIER, -TIEST], full of nits.

**nit·wit** (nit′wit′), *n.* [*nit* (< G. dial. for G. *nicht*, not) or *nit* (louse) + *wit*], a stupid person.

**nix** (niks), *n.* [*pl.* NIXES; G. NIXE (nik′sə)], [G.], in *Germanic mythology*, a water sprite.

**nix** (niks), *adv.* [G. *nichts*], [Slang], 1. nothing. 2. no. 3. not at all. *interj.* an exclamation meaning: 1. stop! 2. I forbid, refuse, disagree, etc.

**nix·ie** (nik′si), *n.* [G. *nixe*], a female nix.

**Nix·on, Richard M.** (nik's'n), 1913– ; 37th president of the U.S. (1969– ).
**Ni·zam** (ni-zäm', ni-zam'), *n.* [< Hind. & Per. < Ar. < *nazama*, to govern], 1. the former title of the native ruler in Hyderabad, India. 2. [n-], [*pl.* -ZAM], a soldier in the Turkish regular army.
**N.J.,** New Jersey.
**NLRB, N.L.R.B.,** National Labor Relations Board.
**N.M.,** New Mexico: also **N. Mex.**
**NNE, N.N.E., n.n.e.,** north-northeast.
**NNW, N.N.W., n.n.w.,** north-northwest.
**no** (nō), *adv.* [AS. *na* < *ne a*, lit., not ever], 1. [Scot. or Rare], not: as, whether or *no*. 2. not in any degree: as, he is *no* worse. 3. nay; not so: the opposite of *yes*, used to deny, refuse, or disagree. *adj.* not any; not a: as, he is *no* fool. *n.* [*pl.* NOES], 1. refusal or denial. 2. a negative vote or voter.
**No,** in *chemistry*, nobelium.
**No.,** 1. north. 2. northern.
**No., no.,** 1. number. 2. *numero*, [L.], by number.
**No·ah** (nō'ə), *n.* in the *Bible*, the patriarch commanded by God to build the ark on which he, his family, and two of every kind of creature survived the Flood: Gen. 5:28-10.
**nob** (nob), *n.* [later form of *knob*], 1. a knob. 2. [Slang], the head.
**nob·by** (nob'i), *adj.* [-BIER, -BIEST], [? ult. < *nabob*], [Slang], 1. stylish. 2. excellent.
**No·bel, Al·fred Bern·hard** (äl'fred bâr'närd nō-bel'), 1833-1896; Swedish inventor of dynamite; established Nobel prizes.
**no·bel·i·um** (nō-bel'i-əm), *n.* [< *Nobel* Inst., Stockholm, where discovered], a radioactive chemical element produced by the nuclear bombardment of curium: symbol, No; at. wt., 255(?); at. no., 102.
**Nobel prizes,** the five annual prizes given by the Nobel Foundation for distinction in physics, chemistry, medicine, and literature, and for the promotion of peace.
**no·bil·i·ty** (nō-bil'ə-ti), *n.* [*pl.* -TIES], 1. a being noble. 2. high station or rank in society. 3. the class of people of noble rank; in Great Britain, the peerage (usually with *the*).
**no·ble** (nō'b'l), *adj.* [OFr. < L. *nobilis*, lit., well-known], 1. famous or renowned. 2. having or showing high moral qualities. 3. having excellent qualities. 4. grand; stately; magnificent: as, a *noble* view. 5. of high rank or title; aristocratic. *n.* one having hereditary rank or title; nobleman; peer. **—no'ble·ness,** *n.* **—no'bly,** *adv.*
**no·ble·man** (nō'b'l-mən), *n.* [*pl.* -MEN], a member of the nobility; peer; titled person. **—no'ble·wom'an** [*pl.* -WOMEN], *n.fem.*
**‡no·blesse o·blige** (nô'bles' ô'blēzh'), [Fr., lit., nobility obliges], people of high social position should behave nobly toward others.
**no·bod·y** (nō'bəd-i, -bod'i), *pron.* not anybody; no one. *n.* [*pl.* -IES], a person of no importance.
**nock** (nok), *n.* [prob. < ON.], 1. a notch for holding the string at either end of a bow. 2. the notch in the end of an arrow, for the bowstring.
**noc·tu·id** (nok'chōō-id), *n.* [< L. *noctua*, night owl < *nox*, night], any of a large group of moths which fly at night, including most of those attracted to light. *adj.* of this group.
**noc·tur·nal** (nok-tũr'n'l), *adj.* [LL. *nocturnalis* < L. < *nox*, night], 1. of the night. 2. functioning at night. 3. done or happening in the night. **—noc·tur'nal·ly,** *adv.*
**noc·turne** (nok'tẽrn, nok-tũrn'), *n.* [Fr.], 1. in *art*, a painting of a night scene. 2. in *music*, a composition of a romantic or dreamy character thought appropriate to night.
**nod** (nod), *v.i.* [NODDED, NODDING], [ME. *nodden*], 1. to bend the head forward quickly, as in agreement, greeting, command, etc. 2. to have the head fall forward involuntarily because of drowsiness. 3. to be careless; make a slip. 4. to sway back and forth or up and down, as plumes. *v.t.* 1. to bend (the head) forward quickly. 2. to signify (assent, approval, etc.) by doing this. *n.* 1. a nodding. 2. [N-], the imaginary realm of sleep and dreams: usually **land of Nod. —nod'der,** *n.*
**nodding acquaintance,** a slight, not intimate acquaintance with a person or thing.
**nod·dle** (nod''l), *n.* [ME. *nodle*], [Colloq.], the head; pate: a humorous term.
**nod·dy** (nod'i), *n.* [*pl.* -DIES], [? < *nod*], 1. a fool; simpleton. 2. a tame tropical sea bird, easily caught and hence considered stupid.
**node** (nōd), *n.* [L. *nodus*, knot], 1. a knot; knob; swelling. 2. a central point. 3. in *astronomy*, *a*) either point at which the orbit of a planet intersects the apparent path of the sun. *b*) either point at which the orbit of a satellite intersects the plane of the orbit of its planet. 4. in *botany*, that part of a stem from which a leaf starts to grow. 5. in *physics*, the point, line, or surface of a vibrating object where there is comparatively no vibration. **—nod'al** (nō'd'l), *adj.*
**nod·ule** (noj'ōōl, nod'ūl), *n.* [L. *nodulus*, dim. of *nodus*, a knot], 1. a small knot or rounded lump. 2. in *botany*, a small knot or joint on a stem or root. **—nod·u·lar** (noj'oo-lẽr, nod'yoo-lẽr), *adj.* **—nod'u·lose'** (-lōs'), **nod'u·lous** (-ləs), *adj.*
**no·el, no·ël** (nō-el', nō'el), *n.* [< Fr. *noël* < L. *natalis*, a birthday < *natus*, born], 1. an expression of joy used in Christmas carols. 2. a Christmas carol. 3. [N-], Christmas.
**nog, nogg** (nog), *n.* [< East Anglian dial.], 1. [Brit.], a kind of strong ale. 2. eggnog.
**nog·gin** (nog'in), *n.* [prob. < *nog*], 1. a small cup or mug. 2. one fourth of a pint: a measure for ale or liquor. 3. [Colloq.], the head.
**No·gu·chi, Hi·de·yo** (hi'de-yō' nō-gōō'chi), 1876–1928; Japanese bacteriologist in U.S.
**no·how** (nō'hou'), *adv.* in no manner; not at all: generally regarded as substandard.
**noise** (noiz), *n.* [OFr.; prob. < L.; see NAUSEA], 1. loud shouting; clamor; din. 2. sound; esp., any loud, disagreeable sound. *v.t.* [NOISED, NOISING], to spread (a report, rumor, etc.). *v.i.* 1. to talk much or loudly. 2. to make noise or a noise.
**noise·less** (noiz'lis), *adj.* 1. without noise; silent. 2. with much less noise than is expected: as, a *noiseless* typewriter. **—noise'less·ly,** *adv.* **—noise'less·ness,** *n.*
**noi·some** (noi'səm), *adj.* [see ANNOY & -SOME], 1. injurious to health; harmful. 2. foul-smelling; offensive. **—noi'some·ly,** *adv.* **—noi'some·ness,** *n.*
**nois·y** (noiz'i), *adj.* [-IER, -IEST], 1. making noise. 2. making more sound than is expected or customary. 3. full of noise; turbulent: as, the *noisy* city. **—nois'i·ly,** *adv.* **—nois'i·ness,** *n.*
**‡no·lens vo·lens** (nō'lenz vō'lenz), [L.], unwilling (or) willing; whether or not one wishes to.
**‡nol·le pros·e·qui** (nol'i pros'i-kwī'), [L., to be unwilling to prosecute], in *law*, formal notice that prosecution in a criminal case or civil suit will be partly or entirely ended.
**‡no·lo con·ten·de·re** (nō'lō kən-ten'də-ri), [L., I do not wish to contest (it)], in *law*, a plea by the defendant in a criminal case declaring that he will not make a defense, but not admitting guilt.
**nol-pros** (nol'pros'), *v.t.* [-PROSSED, -PROSSING], [< abbrev. of *nolle prosequi*], to abandon (all or part of a suit) by entering a *nolle prosequi* on the court records.
**nom.,** nominative.
**no·mad** (nō'mad, nom'ad), *n.* [< L. < Gr. < *nemein*, to pasture], 1. a member of a tribe or people having no permanent home, but moving about constantly as in search of pasture. 2. a wanderer. *adj.* wandering.
**no·mad·ic** (nō-mad'ik), *adj.* of or like nomads or their way of life. **—no·mad'i·cal·ly,** *adv.* **—no·mad·ism** (nō'mad-iz'm, nom'ad-), *n.*
**no man's land,** 1. a piece of land to which no one has a recognized title. 2. the area on a battlefield separating the combatants.
**‡nom de guerre** (nōn'də gâr'), [Fr., lit., a war name], a pseudonym.
**nom de plume** (nom' də plōōm'; Fr. nōn'də plüm'), [Eng. formation < Fr.], a pen name; pseudonym.
**Nome** (nōm), *n.* a seaport and mining town in W Alaska, on the Bering Strait: pop., 2,300.
**no·men·cla·ture** (nō'mən-klā'chẽr), *n.* [< L. < *nomen*, name + pp. of *calare*, to call], the system of names used in a branch of learning, for the parts of a mechanism, etc.
**nom·i·nal** (nom'ə-n'l), *adj.* [< L. < *nomen*, a name], 1. of, or having the nature of, a name. 2. of or having to do with a noun. 3. in name only, not in fact: as, the *nominal* leader. 4. relatively very small: as, a *nominal* fee. *n.* in *linguistics*, a nounlike word. **—nom'i·nal·ly,** *adv.*
**nom·i·nate** (nom'ə-nāt'), *v.t.* [-NATED, -NATING], [< L. < pp. of *nominare* < *nomen*, a name], 1. to name or appoint (a person) to an office or position. 2. to name (a person) as a candidate for election or appointment. **—nom'i·na'tor,** *n.*
**nom·i·na·tion** (nom'ə-nā'shən), *n.* a nominating or being nominated; esp., a being named for office, or as a candidate.
**nom·i·na·tive** (nom'i-nə-tiv; *for adj. 1*, usually nom'ə-nā'tiv), *adj.* 1. named or appointed to a position or office. 2. in *grammar*, designating or of the case of the subject of a finite verb and the words (appositives, predicate adjectives, etc.) that agree with it; active case. *n.* 1. the nominative case. 2. a word in this case.

**nom·i·nee** (nom′ə-nē′), *n.* a person who is nominated, especially a candidate for election.

**-nomy** (nə-mi), [< Gr. < *nomos*, law], a combining form meaning *systematized knowledge of*, as in *astronomy*.

**non-**, [< L. *non*, not], a prefix meaning *not*, used to give a negative force, especially to nouns, adjectives, and adverbs: *non-* is less emphatic than *in-* and *un-*, which often give a word an opposite meaning (e.g., *non-American*, *un-American*). The list below includes the more common compounds formed with *non-* that do not have special meanings; they will be understood if *not* is used before the meaning of the base word.

**non·age** (non′ij, nō′nij), *n.* [< OFr.; see NON- & AGE], 1. in *law*, the state of being under full legal age (usually twenty-one). 2. the period of immaturity; early stage.

**non·a·ge·nar·i·an** (non′ə-ji-nâr′i-ən, nō′nə-), *adj.* [< L. < *nonaginta*, ninety], ninety years old, or between the ages of ninety and one hundred. *n.* a person of this age.

**non·ag·gres·sion pact** (non′ə-gresh′ən), an agreement between two nations in which each guarantees not to aggress against the other.

**non·a·gon** (non′ə-gon′), *n.* [< L. *nonus*, ninth; + *-gon*], a polygon with nine angles and nine sides.

**nonce** (nons), *n.* [ME. (*for the*) *nones*, formed by syllabic merging < (*for then*) *ones*, lit., for the once], the present use, occasion, or time; time being: chiefly in *for the nonce*.

**nonce word**, a word coined and used for a single occasion.

**non·cha·lant** (non′shə-lənt, non′shə-länt′), *adj.* [Fr. < *non*, not + *chaloir*, to care for < L. *calere*, to be warm], 1. without warmth or enthusiasm. 2. showing cool lack of concern; casually indifferent. —**non′cha·lance** (-ləns, -läns′), **non′cha·lant·ness**, *n.* —**non′cha·lant·ly**, *adv.*

**non·com** (non′kom′), *n.* [Colloq.], a noncommissioned officer.

**non·com·bat·ant** (non-kom′bə-tənt, -kum′-), *n.* 1. a civilian in wartime. 2. a member of the armed forces whose activities do not include actual combat, as a chaplain. *adj.* of noncombatants.

**non·com·mis·sioned officer** (non′kə-mish′ənd) an enlisted person in the armed forces appointed to any of the ranks above private first class and below warrant officer.

**non·com·mit·tal** (non′kə-mit′'l), *adj.* not committing one to any point of view or course of action; not taking or disclosing a definite stand. —**non′com·mit′tal·ly**, *adv.*

**non·com·pli·ance** (non′kəm-plī′əns), *n.* failure or refusal to comply. —**non′com·pli′ant**, *adj.*

‡**non com·pos men·tis** (non kom′pəs men′tis), [L.], in *law*, not of sound mind; mentally incapable of handling one's affairs: often **non compos.**

**non·con·duc·tor** (non′kən-duk′tẽr), *n.* a substance that does not readily transmit certain forms of energy, as electricity, sound, heat, etc.

**non·con·form·ist** (non′kən-fôr′mist), *n* one who does not conform to an established church; esp., [N-], a Protestant in England who is not a member of the Anglican Church. —**non′con·form′i·ty**, **non′con·form′ance** (-məns), *n.*

**non-co-op·er·a·tion** (non′kō-op′ə-rā′shən), *n.* 1. failure to work together or act jointly. 2. refusal to perform civic duties, pay taxes, etc., often as a means of protest against a government.

**non·de·script** (non′di-skript′), *adj.* [< L. *non*, not + *descriptus*, described], belonging to no definite class or type; hard to classify or describe. *n.* a nondescript person or thing.

---

**nonabsorbent**
**nonabstainer**
**nonacceptance**
**nonacid**
**nonactinic**
**nonactive**
**nonadhesive**
**nonadjacent**
**nonadjectival**
**nonadministrative**
**nonadmission**
**nonadvantageous**
**nonadverbial**
**nonaesthetic**
**non-African**
**nonaggression**
**nonaggressive**
**nonagreement**
**nonagricultural**
**nonalcoholic**
**nonalgebraic**
**nonallegorical**
**nonalliterative**
**nonalphabetic**
**nonamendable**
**non-American**
**non-Anglican**
**nonantagonistic**
**nonapologetic**
**nonapostolic**
**nonappearance**
**nonappearing**
**nonapprehension**
**nonaquatic**
**non-Arab**
**non-Arabic**
**nonaristocratic**
**nonarithmetical**
**non-Aryan**
**non-Asiatic**
**nonassertive**
**nonassessable**
**nonassignable**
**nonassimilable**
**nonassimilation**
**nonassociable**
**nonathletic**
**nonatmospheric**
**nonattendance**
**nonattributive**
**nonauricular**
**nonautomatic**
**nonbacterial**
**nonbasic**
**nonbeliever**
**nonbelligerent**
**nonbenevolent**
**non-Biblical**
**nonblooming**
**non-Bolshevist**
**nonbreakable**
**non-British**
**non-Buddhist**
**nonbudding**
**nonbureaucratic**
**nonburnable**
**nonbusiness**
**non-Calvinist**
**noncanonical**
**noncapitalistic**
**noncarnivorous**
**noncategorical**
**non-Catholic**
**non-Caucasian**
**noncelestial**
**noncellular**
**non-Celtic**
**noncentral**
**noncereal**
**noncertified**
**nonchargeable**
**nonchemical**
**non-Chinese**
**non-Christian**
**noncivilized**
**nonclassifiable**
**nonclerical**
**nonclinical**
**noncoagulating**
**noncoalescing**
**noncoercive**
**noncoherent**
**noncohesive**
**noncollapsible**
**noncollectable**
**noncollegiate**
**noncombat**
**noncombining**
**noncombustible**
**noncommercial**
**noncommunicant**
**noncommunicating**
**non-Communist**
**noncompensating**
**noncompetency**
**noncompeting**
**noncompetitive**
**noncomplaisant**
**noncompletion**
**noncomplying**
**noncompressible**
**noncompression**
**noncompulsion**
**nonconcealment**
**nonconciliating**
**nonconcordant**
**nonconcurrence**
**noncondensing**
**nonconducive**
**nonconducting**
**nonconferrable**
**nonconfidential**
**nonconflicting**
**nonconforming**
**noncongealing**
**noncongenital**
**non-Congressional**
**nonconnective**
**nonconsecutive**
**nonconsent**
**nonconservative**
**nonconspiring**
**nonconstitutional**
**nonconstructive**
**nonconsultative**
**noncontagious**
**noncontemplative**
**noncontemporary**
**noncontentious**
**noncontiguous**
**noncontinental**
**noncontinuance**
**noncontinuous**
**noncontraband**
**noncontradictory**
**noncontributory**
**noncontroversial**
**nonconventional**
**nonconvergent**
**nonconversant**
**nonconvertible**
**nonconviction**
**non-co-operative**
**non-co-ordinating**
**noncorrective**
**noncorresponding**
**noncorroding**
**noncorrosive**
**noncreative**
**noncreditor**
**noncriminal**
**noncritical**
**noncrucial**
**noncrystalline**
**nonculpable**
**noncumulative**
**nondamageable**
**nondecaying**
**nondeceptive**
**nondeciduous**
**nondefamatory**
**nondefensive**
**nondefilement**
**nondefining**
**nondehiscent**
**nondelineation**
**nondelivery**
**nondemand**
**nondemocratic**
**nondepartmental**
**nondeparture**
**nondependence**
**nondepositor**
**nondepreciating**
**nonderivative**
**nonderogatory**
**nondestructive**
**nondetachable**
**nondetonating**
**nondevelopment**
**nondevotional**
**nondialectal**
**nondictatorial**
**nondidactic**
**nondifferentiation**
**nondiffractive**
**nondiffusing**
**nondiplomatic**
**nondirigible**
**nondisappearing**
**nondischarging**
**nondisciplinary**
**nondiscountable**
**nondiscrimination**
**nondisparaging**
**nondisposal**
**nondistinctive**
**nondivergent**
**nondivisible**
**nondoctrinal**
**nondocumentary**
**nondogmatic**
**nondramatic**
**nondrying**
**nondutiable**
**nondynastic**

---

fat, āpe, bâre, cär; ten, ēven, hêre, ovẽr; is, bīte; lot, gō, hôrn, tōōl, look; **oil**, **out**; up, ūse, fũr; get; joy; yet; **chin**; **she**; thin, *th*en; **zh**, leisure; ŋ, ring; ə for *a* in *ago*, *e* in *agent*, *i* in *sanity*, *o* in *comply*, *u* in *focus*; ′ in *able* (ā′b'l); Fr. bál; **ë**, Fr. coeur; **ö**, Fr. feu; Fr. mon; **ô**, Fr. coq; **ü**, Fr. duc; **H**, G. ich; **kh**, G. doch. ‡ foreign; < derived from.

**none** (nun), *pron.* [AS. *nan* < *ne*, not + *an*, one], 1. no one; not anyone: as, *none* but Jack can do it. 2. no persons or things; not any: usually used with a plural verb, as, there are *none* on the table. *n.* no part; nothing: as, I want *none* of it. *adv.* in no way; not at all: as, he came *none* too soon. —**none the less,** nevertheless.

**non·en·ti·ty** (non-en′tə-ti), *n.* [*pl.* -TIES], 1. the state of not existing. 2. something without existence. 3. a person considered of little importance.

**nones** (nōnz), *n.pl.* [< L. < *nonus*, ninth < *novem*, nine], 1. in the ancient Roman calendar, the ninth day before the ides of a month. 2. the fifth of the seven canonical hours.

**non·es·sen·tial** (non′i-sen′shəl), *adj.* not essential; unnecessary. *n.* a nonessential person or thing.

**none·such** (nun′such′), *n.* a person or thing unrivaled or unequaled; paragon: also sp. **nonsuch.**

**non·fea·sance** (non-fē′z'ns), *n.* in *law*, failure to do what duty requires to be done.

**no·nil·lion** (nō-nil′yən), *n.* [Fr. < L. *nonus*, ninth + Fr. *million*], 1. in the U.S. and France, the number represented by 1 followed by 30 zeros. 2. in Great Britain and Germany, the number represented by 1 followed by 54 zeros. *adj.* amounting to one nonillion in number.

**non·in·ter·ven·tion** (non′in-tẽr-ven′shən), *n.* refusal or failure to intervene; esp., a refraining by one nation from interference in another's affairs.

**non·ju·ror** (non-joor′ẽr), *n.* one who refuses to take an oath of allegiance, as to his ruler.

**non·met·al** (non-met′'l, non′met′'l), *n.* an element lacking the characteristics of a metal; specif., any of the elements (e.g., oxygen, carbon, nitrogen, fluorine) whose oxides are not basic. —**non′me·tal′lic,** *adj.*

**non·mor·al** (non-môr′əl, -mor′-), *adj.* not connected in any way with morality; not moral and not immoral. —**non′mo·ral′i·ty,** *n.*

**non·ob·jec·tive** (non′ob-jek′tiv), *adj.* nonrepresentational.

**non·pa·reil** (non′pə-rel′), *adj.* [Fr. < *non*, not + *pareil*, equal < LL. dim. of *par*, equal], unequaled; peerless. *n.* 1. someone or something unequaled or unrivaled. 2. in *printing*, a size of type between agate and minion; 6 point.

**non·par·ti·san, non·par·ti·zan** (non-pär′tə-z'n), *adj.* not partisan; esp., not controlled by, or supporting, any single political party.

**non·plus** (non-plus′, non′plus), *n.* [L. *non*, not + *plus*, more], a condition of perplexity in which one is unable to go, speak, or act further. *v.t.* [-PLUSED or -PLUSSED, -PLUSING or -PLUSSING], to cause to be in a nonplus.

**non·pro·duc·tive** (non′prə-duk′tiv), *adj.* 1. not productive. 2. not directly related to the production of goods: as, *nonproductive* personnel. —**non′pro·duc′tive·ly,** *adv.* —**non′pro·duc′tive·ness,** *n.*

---

**nonearning**
**nonecclesiastical**
**nonedible**
**noneditorial**
**noneducable**
**noneducational**
**noneffective**
**nonefficient**
**nonelastic**
**nonelective**
**nonelectric**
**nonelementary**
**nonemotional**
**nonemphatic**
**nonencyclopedic**
**nonendemic**
**non-English**
**nonentailed**
**nonepiscopal**
**nonequal**
**nonequivalent**
**nonerotic**
**noneternal**
**nonethical**
**non-Euclidean**
**noneugenic**
**non-European**
**nonevangelical**
**nonevolutionary**
**nonexchangeable**
**nonexclusive**
**nonexcusable**
**nonexecutive**
**nonexempt**
**nonexistence**
**nonexistent**
**nonexisting**
**nonexpansive**
**nonexperienced**
**nonexperimental**
**nonexplosive**
**nonexportable**
**nonextended**
**nonextension**
**nonextraditable**
**nonextraneous**
**nonfactual**
**nonfading**
**nonfanciful**
**non-Fascist**
**nonfatal**
**nonfatalistic**
**nonfederal**
**nonfederated**
**nonfermentable**
**nonfermented**
**nonfertile**
**nonfestive**
**nonfeudal**
**nonfiction**
**nonfictional**
**nonfigurative**
**nonfinancial**
**nonfireproof**
**nonfiscal**
**nonflowering**
**nonflowing**
**nonfluctuating**
**nonflying**
**nonfocal**
**nonforfeiting**
**nonforfeiture**
**nonformal**
**nonfreezing**
**non-French**
**nonfulfillment**
**nonfunctional**
**nonfundamental**
**nongaseous**
**nongenetic**
**non-German**
**non-Germanic**
**nongovernmental**
**nongranular**
**non-Greek**
**nongregarious**
**nonhabitable**
**nonhabitual**
**nonhazardous**
**non-Hellenic**
**nonhereditary**
**nonheritable**
**nonhistoric**
**nonhostile**
**nonhuman**
**nonhumorous**
**nonidentical**
**nonidentity**
**nonidiomatic**
**nonimaginary**
**nonimitative**
**nonimmune**
**nonimmunized**
**nonimperial**
**nonimportation**
**nonimpregnated**
**noninclusive**
**nonindependent**
**non-Indian**
**nonindictable**
**nonindividualistic**
**noninductive**
**nonindustrial**
**noninfected**
**noninfectious**
**noninfinite**
**noninflammable**
**noninflammatory**
**noninflectional**
**noninformative**
**noninheritable**
**noninjurious**
**noninstructional**
**noninstrumental**
**nonintellectual**
**nonintelligent**
**nonintercourse**
**noninterference**
**noninternational**
**nonintersecting**
**nonintoxicant**
**nonintoxicating**
**nonintuitive**
**noniodized**
**nonionized**
**non-Irish**
**nonirradiated**
**nonirritant**
**nonirritating**
**non-Islamic**
**non-Italian**
**non-Japanese**
**non-Jew**
**nonjudicial**
**non-Latin**
**nonlegal**
**nonlicensed**
**nonliquefying**
**nonliquidating**
**nonliterary**
**nonlustrous**
**nonmagnetic**
**nonmaintenance**
**nonmalignant**
**nonmalleable**
**nonmarital**
**nonmaritime**
**nonmarriageable**
**nonmarrying**
**nonmartial**
**nonmaterial**
**nonmaterialistic**
**nonmaternal**
**nonmathematical**
**nonmatrimonial**
**nonmechanical**
**nonmedicinal**
**nonmelodious**
**nonmember**
**nonmercantile**
**nonmetaphysical**
**nonmetropolitan**
**nonmigratory**
**nonmilitant**
**nonmilitary**
**nonmineral**
**nonministerial**
**nonmiraculous**
**non-Mormon**
**nonmortal**
**non-Moslem**
**nonmotile**
**nonmunicipal**
**nonmuscular**
**nonmystical**
**nonmythical**
**nonnational**
**nonnative**
**nonnatural**
**nonnavigable**
**nonnecessity**
**nonnegotiable**
**non-Negro**
**nonneutral**
**non-Norse**
**nonnucleated**
**nonnutritious**
**nonnutritive**
**nonobedience**
**nonobligatory**
**nonobservance**
**nonobservant**
**nonobstructive**
**nonoccupational**
**nonoccurrence**
**nonodorous**
**nonofficial**
**nonoperative**
**nonoriental**
**non-Oriental**
**nonorthodox**
**nonoxidizing**
**nonoxygenated**
**nonpacific**
**nonpagan**
**nonpalatal**
**nonpapal**
**nonpapist**
**nonparallel**
**nonparasitic**
**nonparental**
**nonparishioner**
**nonparliamentary**
**nonparochial**
**nonparticipation**
**nonpartisanship**
**nonpaying**
**nonpayment**
**nonpensionable**
**nonperceptual**
**nonperforated**
**nonperformance**
**nonperiodical**
**nonperishing**
**nonpermanent**
**nonpermeable**
**nonpermissible**
**nonperpendicular**
**nonpersecution**
**nonpersistent**
**nonphilosophical**
**nonphysical**
**nonphysiological**
**nonplastic**
**nonpoetic**
**nonpoisonous**
**nonpolarizable**
**non-Polish**
**nonpolitical**
**nonporous**
**non-Portuguese**
**nonpredatory**
**nonpredictable**
**nonpreferential**
**nonprejudicial**
**nonprepositional**
**non-Presbyterian**
**nonprescriptive**
**nonpreservative**
**nonpresidential**
**nonpriestly**
**nonproducer**
**nonprofessional**
**nonprofessorial**

**non·prof·it** (non-prof'it), *adj.* not intending or intended to earn a profit.
**non·pro·lif·er·a·tion** (non'prō-lif'ə-rā'shən), *n.* a not proliferating; specif., the limitation of the production of nuclear weapons.
**non-pros** (non'pros'), *v.t.* [-PROSSED, -PROSSING], to enter a judgment of *non prosequitur* against.
**‡non pro·se·qui·tur** (non prō-sek'wi-tẽr), [L., he does not prosecute], in *law,* a judgment entered against a plaintiff who fails to appear at the court proceedings of his suit.
**non·rep·re·sen·ta·tion·al** (non'rep-ri-zen-tā'shən-'l), *adj.* designating or of art that does not attempt to represent in recognizable form any object in nature; abstract.
**non·res·i·dent** (non-rez'ə-dənt), *adj.* not residing in a specified place; esp., not residing in the locality where one works, attends school, etc. *n.* a nonresident person. **—non·res'i·dence,** *n.*
**non·re·sist·ant** (non'ri-zis'tənt), *adj.* not resistant; submitting to force or arbitrary authority. *n.* one who believes that force and violence should not be used to oppose arbitrary authority, however unjust. **—non're·sist'ance,** *n.*
**non·re·stric·tive** (non'ri-strik'tiv), *adj.* in *grammar,* designating a clause, phrase, or word felt as not essential to the sense, or purely descriptive, and hence usually set off by commas (e.g., John, *who is six feet tall,* is younger than Bill).
**non·sec·tar·i·an** (non'sek-târ'i-ən), *adj.* not sectarian; not confined to any specific religion.
**non·sense** (non'sens, -səns), *n.* [*non-* + *sense*], 1. words or actions that convey an absurd meaning or no meaning at all. 2. things of relatively no importance or value. 3. impudent or foolish behavior. *interj.* how foolish! how absurd!
**non·sen·si·cal** (non-sen'si-k'l), *adj.* unintelligible, foolish, absurd, etc. **—non·sen'si·cal·ly,** *adv.* **—non·sen'si·cal·ness,** *n.*
**‡non se·qui·tur** (non sek'wi-tẽr), [L., lit., it does not follow], a conclusion or inference that does not follow from the premises or evidence upon which it is based: abbrev. **non seq.**
**non·skid** (non'skid'), *adj.* constructed so as to reduce skidding: said of tire tread, etc.
**non·stop** (non'stop'), *adj.* & *adv.* without a stop.
**non·suit** (non'sōōt', -sūt'), *n.* [< Anglo-Fr.; see NON- & SUIT], in *law,* a judgment against a plaintiff because of his failure to establish a valid case or to produce adequate evidence. *v.t.* to bring a nonsuit against (a plaintiff or his case).
**non·sup·port** (non'sə-pôrt', -pōrt'), *n.* failure to provide for a legal dependent.
**‡non trop·po** (nôn trôp'pô), [It.], in *music,* not too much; moderately.
**non·un·ion** (non-ūn'yən), *n.* failure to mend or unite: said of a broken bone. *adj.* 1. not belonging to a labor union. 2. not made or serviced under conditions required by a labor union. 3. refusing to recognize a labor union.
**non·un·ion·ism** (non-ūn'yən-iz'm), *n.* theories and practices of those who oppose labor unions. **—non·un'ion·ist,** *n.*
**non·vot·er** (non-vōt'ẽr), *n.* a person who does not vote or is not permitted to vote.
**noo·dle** (nōō'd'l), *n.* [< ?], [Slang], the head.
**noo·dle** (nōō'd'l), *n.* [G. *nudel,* macaroni], a flat, narrow strip of dry dough, usually containing egg and served in soup, etc.
**nook** (nook), *n.* [ME. *nok*], 1. a corner, especially of a room. 2. a small recess or secluded spot.
**noon** (nōōn), *n.* [AS. *non* < L. *nona* (*hora*), ninth (hour); cf. NONES, now recited at midday], 1. twelve o'clock in the daytime; midday. 2. the highest point or culmination: as, in the *noon* of his life. 3. [Rare], midnight: now only in *noon of night.* *adj.* of or occurring at noon (midday).
**noon·day** (nōōn'dā'), *n.* & *adj.* noon (midday).
**no-one** (nō'wun', nō'ən), *pron.* no one.
**no one,** no person; not anybody; nobody.
**noon·tide** (nōōn'tīd'), *n.* & *adj.* noon (midday).
**noon·time** (nōōn'tīm'), *n.* & *adj.* noon (midday).

**nonprofitable**
**nonprofiteering**
**nonprogressive**
**nonprohibitive**
**nonprolific**
**nonprophetic**
**nonproportional**
**nonproprietary**
**nonproscriptive**
**nonprotective**
**non-Protestant**
**nonpsychic**
**nonpuncturable**
**nonpunishable**
**nonpurulent**
**nonracial**
**nonradiating**
**nonradical**
**nonratable**
**nonrational**
**nonreactive**
**nonreality**
**nonreciprocal**
**nonreciprocating**
**nonrecognition**
**nonrecoverable**
**nonrecurring**
**nonrefillable**
**nonrefueling**
**nonregenerating**
**nonregimented**
**nonregistered**
**nonregistrable**
**nonreigning**
**nonrelative**
**nonreligious**
**nonremunerative**
**nonrenewable**
**nonrepayable**
**nonrepentance**
**nonreprehensible**
**nonrepresentative**
**nonreproductive**
**nonresidential**
**nonresidual**
**nonresonant**
**nonrestraint**
**nonrestricted**
**nonretentive**
**nonretiring**
**nonretraceable**
**nonretractile**
**nonreturnable**
**nonrevealing**
**nonreversible**
**nonrevertible**
**nonreviewable**
**nonrevolving**
**nonrhetorical**
**nonrhyming**
**nonrhythmic**
**nonrigid**
**nonritualistic**
**nonrival**
**non-Roman**
**nonromantic**
**nonrotating**
**nonroyal**
**nonrural**
**non-Russian**
**nonrustable**
**nonsacred**
**nonsacrificial**
**nonsalable**
**nonsalaried**
**nonsalutary**
**nonsaturated**
**nonscholastic**
**nonscientific**
**nonscoring**
**nonseasonal**
**nonsecret**
**nonsecretory**
**nonsectional**
**nonsecular**
**nonsedentary**
**nonseditious**
**nonselective**
**non-Semitic**
**nonsensitive**
**nonsensitized**
**nonserious**
**nonservile**
**non-Shakespearean**
**nonsharing**
**nonshattering**
**nonshrinkable**
**nonsinkable**
**nonslaveholding**
**non-Slavic**
**nonsmoker**
**nonsocial**
**nonsocialist**
**nonsolid**
**nonsolvent**
**non-Spanish**
**nonsparing**
**nonspecializing**
**nonspectral**
**nonspeculative**
**nonspherical**
**nonspiritual**
**nonspirituous**
**nonspottable**
**nonstaining**
**nonstandardized**
**nonstarting**
**nonstatic**
**nonstationary**
**nonstatistical**
**nonstatutory**
**nonstrategic**
**nonstretchable**
**nonstriated**
**nonstriker**
**nonstriking**
**nonstructural**
**nonsubmissive**
**nonsubscriber**
**nonsuccessive**
**nonsupporting**
**nonsuppurative**
**nonsustaining**
**non-Swedish**
**non-Swiss**
**nonsymbolic**
**nonsymmetrical**
**nonsympathizer**
**nonsymphonic**
**nonsymptomatic**
**nonsynchronous**
**nonsyntactic**
**nonsynthesized**
**nonsystematic**
**nontarnishable**
**nontaxable**
**nontechnical**
**nonterritorial**
**nontestamentary**
**nontheatrical**
**nontheological**
**nontherapeutic**
**nonthinking**
**nontitular**
**nontoxic**
**nontragic**
**nontransferable**
**nontransitional**
**nontransparent**
**nontreasonable**
**nontributary**
**nontropical**
**nontuberculous**
**non-Turkish**
**nontypical**
**nontyrannical**
**nonulcerous**
**nonunderstandable**
**non-Unitarian**
**nonuniversal**
**nonuser**
**nonuterine**
**nonutilitarian**
**nonutilized**
**nonvascular**
**nonvegetative**
**nonvenereal**
**nonvenomous**
**nonvenous**
**nonverminous**
**nonvernacular**
**nonvertical**
**nonviable**
**nonvibratory**
**nonvicarious**
**nonviolation**
**nonviolent**
**nonvirulent**
**nonviscous**
**nonvisiting**
**nonvisual**
**nonvitreous**
**nonvocal**
**nonvocational**
**nonvolatile**
**nonvolcanic**
**nonvoluntary**
**nonvoting**
**nonworker**
**nonyielding**

**noose** (nōōs), *n.* [< Pr. < L. *nodus*], 1. a loop formed in a rope, cord, etc. by means of a slip knot so that the loop tightens as the rope is pulled. 2. anything that restricts one's freedom; tie, bond, etc. *v.t.* [NOOSED, NOOSING], 1. to catch or hold as in a noose. 2. to form a noose in (a rope, etc.).

**no-par** (nō′pär′), *adj.* having no stated par value: as, a *no-par* certificate of stock.

**nope** (nōp), *adv.* [Slang], no: negative reply.

**nor** (nôr; *unstressed* nẽr), *conj.* [ME., contr. of *nother*, neither], and not; and not either: used as the second of the correlatives *neither . . . nor* or after some other negative: as, I can neither go *nor* stay; I don't smoke *nor* drink.

**nor', nor** (nôr), north: used especially in compounds, as in *nor'western.*

**Nor.,** 1. North. 2. Norway. 3. Norwegian.

**Nor·dic** (nôr′dik), *adj.* [< ML. < G. or Fr. *nord*, north], designating or of a division of the Caucasian race, denoting typically any of the long-headed, blond peoples of N Europe, as the Scandinavians. *n.* a Nordic person.

**Nor·folk** (nôr′fək), *n.* a seaport in SE Virginia, on Hampton Roads: pop., 305,000.

**Norfolk jacket,** a loose-fitting, single-breasted, belted jacket with box pleats: also **Norfolk coat.**

**Nor·ge** (nôr′gə), *n.* Norway: the Norwegian name.

**no·ri·a** (nō′ri-ə), *n.* [Sp. < Ar. *nā'ūrah*], in Spain and the Orient, a water wheel with buckets at its circumference to raise and discharge water.

**norm** (nôrm), *n.* [< L. *norma*, rule], a standard, model, or pattern for a group; esp., such a standard of achievement as represented by the average achievement of a large group.

**Norm.,** Norman.

**nor·mal** (nôr′m'l), *adj.* [< L. < *norma*, a rule], 1. conforming with or constituting an accepted standard or norm; esp., corresponding to the average of a large group; natural; usual; regular. 2. in *chemistry*, designating or of a salt formed by replacing all the replaceable hydrogen of an acid. 3. in *mathematics*, perpendicular; at right angles. 4. in *psychology*, average in intelligence or emotional stability. *n.* 1. anything normal. 2. the usual state, amount, degree, etc. 3. in *mathematics*, a perpendicular. —**nor′mal·cy, nor·mal′i·ty** (-mal′ə-ti), *n.*

**nor·mal·ize** (nôr′m'l-īz′), *v.t.* [-IZED, -IZING], to make normal; bring into conformity with a standard. —**nor′mal·i·za′tion,** *n.* —**nor′mal·iz′er,** *n.*

**nor·mal·ly** (nôr′m'l-i), *adv.* 1. in a normal manner. 2. under normal circumstances; ordinarily.

**normal school,** a school for training high-school graduates to become teachers.

**Nor·man** (nôr′mən), *n.* [< OFr. < early ON.], 1. any of the Northmen who occupied Normandy in the 10th century A.D. 2. a descendant of the Normans and French who conquered England in 1066. 3. Norman French. 4. a native or inhabitant of Normandy. 5. the modern French dialect of Normandy. *adj.* of Normandy, the Normans, their language, or culture.

**Norman Conquest,** the conquest of England (1066) by the Normans under William the Conqueror.

**Nor·man·dy** (nôr′mən-di), *n.* a district, formerly a province, of France, on the English Channel.

**Norman French,** the French spoken in England by the Norman conquerors; Anglo-French. —**Nor′man-French′,** *adj. & n.*

**Nor·ris, Frank** (nôr′is, nor′-), (*Benjamin Franklin Norris*), 1870–1902; U.S. novelist and journalist.

**Norris, George William,** 1861–1944; U.S. senator from Nebraska (1913–1943).

**Norse** (nôrs), *adj.* [prob. < D. *Noorsch*, a Norwegian < *noord*, north], Scandinavian, especially of those languages spoken in western Scandinavia. *n.* the Scandinavian, especially the West Scandinavian, group of languages. —**the Norse,** 1. the Scandinavians. 2. the West Scandinavians.

**Norse·man** (nôrs′mən), *n.* [*pl.* -MEN], a member of the ancient Scandinavian people; Northman.

**north** (nôrth), *n.* [AS.], 1. the direction to the right of a person facing the sunset (0° or 360° on the compass, opposite south). 2. a region or district in or toward this direction. 3. [often N-], the northern part of the earth, especially the arctic regions. *adj.* 1. in, of, to, or toward the north. 2. from the north: as, a *north* wind. 3. [N-], designating the northern part of a continent, country, etc. *adv.* in or toward the north. —**the North,** that part of the U.S. which is bounded on the south by Maryland, the Ohio River, and Missouri.

**North America,** the northern continent in the Western Hemisphere: area, 8,500,000 sq. mi.; pop., 276,000,000. —**North American.**

**North Cape,** a cape on an island in Norway, the northernmost part of Europe.

**North Carolina,** a Southern State of the U.S.: area, 52,712 sq. mi.; pop., 4,556,000; capital, Raleigh: abbrev. **N.C.** —**North Carolinian.**

**North Dakota,** a Middle Western State of the U.S.: area, 70,665 sq. mi.; pop., 632,000; capital, Bismarck: abbrev. **N. Dak., N.D.** —**North Dakotan.**

**north·east** (nôrth′ēst′; *in nautical usage,* nôr-), *n.* 1. the direction halfway between north and east (45° east of due north). 2. a region or district in or toward this direction. *adj.* 1. in, of, to, or toward the northeast. 2. from the northeast, as a wind. *adv.* in, toward, or from the northeast. —**the Northeast,** the northeastern part of the U.S., especially New England.

**north·east·er** (nôrth′ēs′tẽr; *in nautical usage,* nôr-), *n.* a storm or wind from the northeast.

**north·east·er·ly** (nôrth′ēs′tẽr-li; *in nautical usage,* nôr-), *adj. & adv.* 1. toward the northeast. 2. from the northeast.

**north·east·ern** (nôrth′ēs′tẽrn; *in nautical usage,* nôr-), *adj.* 1. in, of, or toward the northeast. 2. from the northeast. 3. [N-], of or characteristic of the Northeast or New England.

**north·east·ward** (nôrth′ēst′wẽrd; *in nautical usage,* nôr-), *adv. & adj.* toward the northeast: also **northeastwards,** *adv.* *n.* a northeastward direction, point, or region.

**north·east·ward·ly** (nôrth′ēst′wẽrd-li; *in nautical usage,* nôr-), *adj. & adv.* 1. toward the northeast. 2. from the northeast, as a wind.

**north·er** (nôr′*th*ẽr), *n.* a storm or strong wind from the north.

**north·er·ly** (nôr′*th*ẽr-li), *adj. & adv.* 1. toward the north. 2. from the north. —**north′er·li·ness,** *n.*

**north·ern** (nôr′*th*ẽrn), *adj.* 1. in, of, or toward the north. 2. from the north. 3. [N-], of or characteristic of the North. *n.* a northerner. —**north′ern-most′,** *adj.*

**north·ern·er** (nôr′*th*ẽr-nẽr, -*th*ən-ẽr), *n.* 1. a native or inhabitant of the north. 2. [N-], a native or inhabitant of the N part of the U.S.

**Northern Hemisphere,** that half of the earth north of the equator.

**Northern Ireland,** a division of the United Kingdom, in NE Ireland: it consists of most of the former province of Ulster: area, 5,241 sq. mi.; pop., 1,437,000; capital, Belfast.

**northern lights,** the aurora borealis.

**Northern Rhodesia,** Zambia: the former name.

**Northern Spy,** a yellowish-red winter apple.

**North Island,** the northern of the two chief islands of New Zealand.

**north·land** (nôrth′lənd, -land′), *n.* the northern region of a country, etc. —**north′land·er,** *n.*

**North Little Rock,** city in central Arkansas: pop., 58,000.

**North·man** (nôrth′mən), *n.* [*pl.* -MEN], 1. a Norseman. 2. an inhabitant of northern Europe.

**north-north·east** (nôrth′nôrth′ēst′; *in nautical usage,* nôr′nôr-), *n.* the direction halfway between due north and northeast (22° 30′ east of due north). *adj. & adv.* 1. in or toward this direction. 2. from this direction.

**north-north·west** (nôrth′nôrth′west′; *in nautical usage,* nôr′nôr-), *n.* the direction halfway between due north and northwest (22° 30′ west of due north). *adj. & adv.* 1. in or toward this direction. 2. from this direction.

**North Pole,** the northern end of the earth's axis.

**North Sea,** an arm of the Atlantic, between Great Britain on the west and Norway and Denmark on the east.

**North Star,** Polaris, the bright star almost directly above the North Pole; polestar.

**North·um·bri·a** (nôr-thum′bri-ə), *n.* a former Anglo-Saxon kingdom of NE England.

**North·um·bri·an** (nôr-thum′bri-ən), *adj.* of Northumbria, its people, or their dialect. *n.* 1. a native or inhabitant of Northumbria. 2. the Anglo-Saxon dialect of Northumbria.

**north·ward** (nôrth′wẽrd; *in nautical usage,* nôr′*th*ẽrd), *adv. & adj.* toward the north: also **northwards,** *adv.* *n.* a northward direction, point, etc.

**north·ward·ly** (nôrth′wẽrd-li; *in nautical usage,* nôr′*th*ẽrd-li), *adj. & adv.* 1. toward the north. 2. from the north.

**north·west** (nôrth′west′; *in nautical usage,* nôr-), *n.* 1. the direction halfway between north and west (45° west of due north). 2. a district or region in or toward this direction. *adj.* 1. in, of, or toward the northwest. 2. from the northwest. *adv.* in, toward, or from the northwest. —**the Northwest,** the northwestern part of the U.S., especially Washington, Oregon, and Idaho.

**north·west·er** (nôrth′wes′tẽr; *in nautical usage,* nôr-), *n.* a storm or wind from the northwest.

**north·west·er·ly** (nôrth′wes′tẽr-li; *in nautical usage,* nôr-), ***adj. & adv.*** 1. toward the northwest. 2. from the northwest.

**north·west·ern** (nôrth′wes′tẽrn; *in nautical usage,* nôr-), ***adj.*** 1. in, of, or toward the northwest. 2. from the northwest. 3. [N-], of or characteristic of the Northwest.

**Northwest Territories,** a division of N Canada: area, 1,305,000 sq. mi.; pop., 19,000.

**Northwest Territory,** a region ceded (1783) by England to the U.S.: it now forms Ohio, Indiana, Illinois, Michigan, Wisconsin, and part of Minnesota.

**north·west·ward** (nôrth′west′wẽrd; *in nautical usage,* nôr-), ***adv. & adj.*** toward the northwest: also **northwestwards, *adv.*** ***n.*** a northwestward direction, point, or region.

**north·west·ward·ly** (nôrth′west′wẽrd-li; *in nautical usage,* nôr-), ***adj. & adv.*** 1. toward the northwest. 2. from the northwest, as a wind.

**Norw.,** 1. Norway. 2. Norwegian.

**Nor·walk** (nôr′wôk), ***n.*** 1. a city in SW California: suburb of Los Angeles: pop., 89,000. 2. a city in SW Connecticut: pop., 68,000.

**Nor·way** (nôr′wā), ***n.*** a country in N Europe, in the western part of the Scandinavian Peninsula: area, 124,556 sq. mi.; pop., 3,572,000; capital, Oslo.

**Nor·we·gian** (nôr-wē′jən), ***adj.*** of Norway, its people, their language, or culture. ***n.*** 1. a native or inhabitant of Norway. 2. the Scandinavian language of the Norwegians.

**Nor·wich** (nôr′ij, nor′ich), ***n.*** a city in E England: pop., 118,000.

**Nos., nos.,** numbers.

**nose** (nōz), ***n.*** [AS. *nosu*], 1. the part of the face between the mouth and the eyes, having two openings for breathing and smelling; in animals, the snout, or muzzle. 2. the sense of smell. 3. *a*) scent. *b*) power of perceiving as by scent. 4. anything like a nose in shape or position; foremost part, as a nozzle, prow of a ship, etc. ***v.t.*** [NOSED, NOSING], 1. to discover or perceive as by smell; scent. 2. to rub with the nose. 3. to push (a way, etc.) with the front forward: as, the ship *nosed* its way into port. 4. to defeat by a very small margin (with *out*). ***v.i.*** 1. to smell; sniff. 2. to pry inquisitively. 3. to advance; move forward. —**by a nose,** 1. in horse racing, etc., by the length of the animal's nose. 2. by a very small margin. —**lead by the nose,** to dominate completely. —**look down one's nose at,** [Colloq.], to be disdainful of. —**nose over,** to turn over on the ground nose first: said of an airplane, etc. —**on the nose,** [Slang], 1. in horse-race betting, that will finish first. 2. precisely; exactly. —**pay through the nose,** to pay an unreasonable price. —**poke one's nose into,** to pry into. —**turn up one's nose at,** to sneer at; scorn. —**under one's (very) nose,** in plain view.

**nose bag,** a canvas bag for holding feed for a horse, etc., hung over the animal's head.

**nose·band** (nōz′band′), ***n.*** that part of a bridle or halter which passes over the animal's nose.

**nose·bleed** (nōz′blēd′), ***n.*** a bleeding from the nose.

**nose dive,** 1. a swift, downward plunge of an airplane, nose first. 2. any sudden, sharp drop. —**nose′-dive′** [-DIVED, -DIVING], ***v.i.***

**nose·gay** (nōz′gā′), ***n.*** [*nose* + *gay* (in obs. sense of "gay object")], a bunch of flowers.

**nose·piece** (nōz′pēs′), ***n.*** 1. that part of a helmet which protects the nose. 2. a noseband. 3. anything like a nose in form or position, as a nozzle.

**nos·tal·gi·a** (nos-tal′jə, -ji-ə), ***n.*** [< Gr. *nostos,* a return; + *-algia*], 1. homesickness. 2. a longing for something far away or long ago. —**nos·tal′gic, *adj.*** —**nos·tal′gi·cal·ly, *adv.***

**nos·tril** (nos′trəl), ***n.*** [AS. *nosthyrl* < *nosu,* nose + *thyrel,* hole], either of the openings into the nose.

**nos·trum** (nos′trəm), ***n.*** [*pl.* -TRUMS], [L., ours], 1. *a*) a medicine prepared by the person selling it. *b*) a quack medicine. *c*) a patent medicine. 2. a pet scheme for solving some problem.

**nos·y, nos·ey** (nōz′i), ***adj.*** [-IER, -IEST], [Colloq.], given to prying; inquisitive.

**not** (not), ***adv.*** [ME., unstressed form of *nought*], in no manner, to no degree, etc.: a particle of negation, or word expressing the idea of *no.*

**‡no·ta be·ne** (nō′tə bē′ni), [L.], note well; take particular notice: abbrev. **N.B., n.b.**

**no·ta·ble** (nō′tə-b'l), ***adj.*** [OFr. < L. *notabilis* < *notare,* to note], worthy of notice; remarkable; eminent. ***n.*** a person of distinction. —**no′ta·ble·ness, no′ta·bil′i·ty, *n.*** —**no′ta·bly, *adv.***

**no·ta·rize** (nō′tə-rīz′), ***v.t.*** [-RIZED, -RIZING], to certify or attest (a document) as a notary. —**no′ta·ri·za′tion, *n.***

**no·ta·ry** (nō′tẽr-i), ***n.*** [*pl.* -RIES], [< OFr. < L. < *notare,* to note], an official authorized to certify or attest documents, take affidavits, etc. —**no·tar′i·al** (-târ′i-əl), ***adj.***

**notary public,** [*pl.* NOTARIES PUBLIC], a notary.

**no·ta·tion** (nō-tā′shən), ***n.*** [< L. < *notare,* to note], 1. the use of signs or symbols to represent words, quantities, etc. 2. any such system of signs or symbols, as in algebra, music, etc. 3. a noting. 4. a note; annotation. —**no·ta′tion·al, *adj.***

**notch** (noch), ***n.*** [by syllabic merging of ME. *an oche* (< OFr. *oche*), a notch], 1. a V-shaped cut in an edge or surface. 2. a narrow pass with steep sides; defile; gap. 3. [Colloq.], a step; grade; degree: as, his average dropped a *notch.* ***v.t.*** 1. to cut a notch or notches in. 2. to record or tally, as by means of notches. —**notched, *adj.*** —**notch′er, *n.***

**note** (nōt), ***n.*** [OFr. < L. *nota,* a mark, sign < pp. of (*g*)*noscere,* to know], 1. a distinguishing feature: as, a *note* of sadness. 2. importance, distinction, or eminence: as, a person of *note.* 3. *a*) a brief statement, as of a fact, written down as an aid to memory; memorandum. *b*) *pl.* a record of experiences, etc.: as, the *notes* of a journey. 4. a comment or explanation; annotation. 5. notice; heed: as, take *note* of this. 6. *a*) a short informal letter. *b*) a formal diplomatic communication. 7. any of certain commercial papers relating to debts or payment of money: as, a promissory *note,* a bank *note.* 8. a cry or call, as of a bird. 9. a signal or intimation: as, a *note* of admonition. 10. [Archaic], a melody or tune. 11. in *music, a*) a tone of definite pitch. *b*) a symbol for a tone, indicating the duration and the pitch. *c*) a key of a piano or similar instrument. ***v.t.*** [NOTED, NOTING], 1. to heed; notice; observe. 2. to set down in writing; make a note of. 3. to mention specially. 4. to denote or signify. —**compare notes,** to exchange views; discuss. —**strike the right note,** to say or do what is specially suitable. —**take notes,** to write down facts for later reference. —**note′less, *adj.*** —**not′er, *n.***

MUSICAL NOTES
A, whole note; B, half notes; C, quarter notes; D, eighth notes; E, sixteenth notes; F, thirty-second notes; G, sixty-fourth notes; H, double notes

**note·book** (nōt′book′), ***n.*** 1. a book in which notes, or memorandums, are kept. 2. a record book for registering promissory notes.

**not·ed** (nōt′id), ***adj.*** distinguished; renowned; eminent. —**not′ed·ly, *adv.*** —**not′ed·ness, *n.***

**note paper,** paper for writing notes (letters).

**note·wor·thy** (nōt′wũr′thi), ***adj.*** worthy of note; deserving notice; outstanding; remarkable. —**note′wor′thi·ly, *adv.*** —**note′wor′thi·ness, *n.***

**noth·ing** (nuth′iŋ), ***n.*** [AS. *na thing*], 1. no thing; not anything; nought. 2. nothingness. 3. a thing that does not exist. 4. *a*) something of little or no value, importance, etc. *b*) a person considered of no importance. 5. in *mathematics,* zero. ***adv.*** not at all; in no manner or degree. —**for nothing,** 1. free; at no cost. 2. in vain. 3. without reason. —**make nothing of,** 1. to treat as of little importance. 2. to fail to understand. 3. to fail to use or do. —**nothing but,** only; nothing other than. —**nothing less than,** no less than: also **nothing short of.** —**think nothing of,** to regard as easy, unimportant, etc.

**noth·ing·ness** (nuth′iŋ-nis), ***n.*** 1. nonexistence. 2. insignificance. 3. unconsciousness. 4. anything that is nonexistent, worthless, etc.

**no·tice** (nō′tis), ***n.*** [Fr. < L. *notitia* < *notus;* see NOTE], 1. announcement or warning. 2. a short article about a book, play, etc. 3. a written or printed sign giving some public information, warning, or rule. 4. *a*) attention; heed. *b*) civility. 5. a formal warning of intention to end an agreement or contract at a certain time: as, the tenant gave *notice.* ***v.t.*** [-TICED, -TICING], 1. *a*) to mention; refer to. *b*) to review briefly. 2. to observe; pay attention to. 3. [Rare], to serve with a notice. —**serve notice,** to announce; warn. —**take notice,** to pay attention; observe.

---

**no·tice·a·ble** (nō′tis-ə-b'l), *adj.* 1. easily seen; conspicuous. 2. significant. —**no′tice·a·bly,** *adv.*

**no·ti·fi·ca·tion** (nō′tə-fi-kā′shən), *n.* 1. a notifying or being notified. 2. the notice given or received. 3. a letter, etc. notifying.

**no·ti·fy** (nō′tə-fī′), *v.t.* [-FIED, -FYING], [< OFr. < L. < *notus* (see NOTE) + *facere*, to make], 1. to give notice to; inform. 2. [Chiefly Brit.], to give notice of; announce. —**no′ti·fi′er,** *n.*

**no·tion** (nō′shən), *n.* [OFr. < L. < *notus;* see NOTE], 1. *a*) a general idea. *b*) a vague thought. 2. a belief; opinion; view. 3. an inclination; whim. 4. an intention. 5. *pl.* small, useful articles, as needles, thread, etc., sold in a store.

**no·tion·al** (nō′shən-'l), *adj.* 1. of, expressing, or consisting of notions, or concepts. 2. imaginary; not actual. 3. having visionary ideas; fanciful. —**no′tion·al·ly,** *adv.*

**no·to·ri·e·ty** (nō′tə-rī′ə-ti), *n.* [*pl.* -TIES], 1. a being notorious. 2. a well-known person.

**no·to·ri·ous** (nō-tôr′i-əs, -tō′ri-), *adj.* [ML. *notorius* < L. *notus;* see NOTE], 1. [Rare], well-known. 2. widely but unfavorably known or talked about. —**no·to′ri·ous·ly,** *adv.* —**no·to′ri·ous·ness,** *n.*

**no-trump** (nō′trump′), *adj.* in *bridge*, with no suit being trumps. *n.* 1. a bid to play with no suit being trumps. 2. the hand so played.

**Not·ting·ham** (not′iŋ-əm), *n.* a city in central England: pop., 311,000.

**not·with·stand·ing** (not′with-stan′diŋ, -with-), *prep.* in spite of: as, he drove on, *notwithstanding* the storm. *adv.* all the same; nevertheless: as, he will go, *notwithstanding. conj.* although.

**nou·gat** (nōō′gət, -gä), *n.* [Fr. < Pr. < *noga* < L. *nux*, nut], a confection of sugar paste with nuts.

**nought** (nôt), *n.* [AS. *nowiht* < *ne*, not + *awiht*, aught], naught. *adj.* worthless; useless. *adv.* [Archaic], in no way; not at all.

**noun** (noun), *n.* [< OFr. < L. *nomen*, a name], in *grammar*, 1. any of a class of words naming or denoting a person, thing, action, quality, etc.: as, *boy, water,* and *truth* are *nouns.* 2. any word, phrase, or clause similarly used; substantive. *adj.* of or like a noun: also **noun′al.**

**nour·ish** (nũr′ish), *v.t.* [< OFr. *nurir* < L. *nutrire*], 1. to feed or sustain with substances necessary to life and growth. 2. to stimulate; foster; develop; support: as, to *nourish* good will. —**nour′ish·er,** *n.* —**nour′ish·ing,** *adj.* —**nour′ish·ing·ly,** *adv.*

**nour·ish·ment** (nũr′ish-mənt), *n.* 1. a nourishing or being nourished. 2. food; nutriment.

‡**nou·veau riche** (nōō′vō′rēsh′), [*pl.* NOUVEAUX RICHES (nōō′vō′rēsh′)], [Fr., newly rich], one who has only recently become rich: often implying tasteless ostentation, lack of culture, etc.

**Nov.,** November.

**no·va** (nō′və), *n.* [*pl.* -VAS, -VAE (-vē)], [L. *nova* (*stella*), new (star)], in *astronomy*, a star that suddenly increases greatly in brilliance and then gradually grows fainter.

**No·va Sco·tia** (nō′və skō′shə), a peninsular maritime province of SE Canada: pop., 761,000; capital, Halifax. —**No′va Sco′tian.**

**nov·el** (nov′'l), *adj.* [< OFr. < L. *novellus*, dim. of *novus*, new], new; recent; strange; unusual. *n.* [< Fr. or It.; both < L. *novella*, new things < *novellus*], 1. a relatively long fictional prose narrative with a more or less complex plot. 2. the type of literature represented by such narratives (with *the*). —**nov′el·is′tic,** *adj.* —**nov′el·is′ti·cal·ly,** *adv.*

**nov·el·ette** (nov′ə-let′), *n.* a short novel.

**nov·el·ist** (nov′'l-ist), *n.* one who writes novels.

**nov·el·ize** (nov′'l-īz′), *v.t.* [-IZED, -IZING], to make into or like a novel. —**nov′el·i·za′tion,** *n.*

**no·vel·la** (nō-vel′ə), *n.* [*pl.* -LAS, -LE (-ē)], [It.], 1. a short prose narrative, usually with a moral, as any of the tales in Boccaccio's *Decameron.* 2. a novelette.

**nov·el·ty** (nov′'l-ti), *n.* [*pl.* -TIES], 1. the quality of being novel; newness. 2. something new, fresh, or unusual; innovation. 3. *usually in pl.* a small, often cheap, cleverly made article, usually for play or adornment.

**No·vem·ber** (nō-vem′bẽr), *n.* [< L. < *novem*, nine: the early Romans reckoned from March], the eleventh month of the year, having 30 days: abbrev. **Nov.**

**no·ve·na** (nō-vē′nə), *n.* [*pl.* -NAS, -NAE (-nē)], [ML. < L. < *novem*, nine], in the *R. C. Church*, special prayers and devotions during a nine-day period for a particular object or occasion.

**nov·ice** (nov′is), *n.* [OFr. < L. *novicius* (< *novus*), new], 1. a person on probation in a religious group or order before taking the final vows; neophyte. 2. a person new to a particular activity, etc.; apprentice; beginner; tyro.

**no·vi·ti·ate, no·vi·ci·ate** (nō-vish′i-it, -āt′), *n.* 1. the period of probation of a novice in a religious order. 2. the state of being a novice. 3. a novice. 4. the quarters of religious novices.

**no·vo·cain, no·vo·caine** (nō′və-kān′), *n.* [*novo-* (< L. *novus*, new) + *cocaine*], procaine: a trademark (**Novocain**).

**now** (nou), *adv.* [AS. *nu*], 1. *a*) at the present time. *b*) at once. 2. at the time referred to; then; next: as, *now* the tide began to turn. 3. very recently: as, he left just *now.* 4. very soon: as, he's leaving just *now.* 5. with things as they are: as, *now* we'll never know. *Now* is often used in transition or emphasis: as, come *now*, don't be absurd. *conj.* since; seeing that: as, *now* (that) the rain has come, we won't starve. *n.* the present time. *interj.* an exclamation of warning, reproach, etc. *adj.* of the present time: as, the *now* generation. —**now and then,** occasionally: also **now and again.**

**now·a·days** (nou′ə-dāz′), *adv.* in these days; at the present time. *n.* the present time.

**no·way** (nō′wā′), *adv.* in no manner; by no means; not at all; nowise: also **no′ways′** (-wāz′).

**no·where** (nō′hwâr′), *adv.* not in, at, or to any place; not anywhere. *n.* a nonexistent place. —**be** (or **get**) **nowhere,** to have no success; fail. —**nowhere near,** not nearly.

**no·wheres** (nō′hwârz′), *adv.* [Dial.], nowhere.

**no·wise** (nō′wīz′), *adv.* in no manner; noway.

**nox·ious** (nok′shəs), *adj.* [< L. < *noxa*, injury < *nocere*, to hurt], harmful to health or morals; injurious; unwholesome. —**nox′ious·ly,** *adv.* —**nox′ious·ness,** *n.*

**noz·zle** (noz′'l), *n.* [dim. of *nose*], 1. the small spout of a hose, pipe, etc. 2. [Slang], the nose.

**Np,** in *chemistry*, neptunium.

**N.P., n.p.,** Notary Public.

**N.S.,** 1. New Style. 2. Nova Scotia.

**N.S.W.,** New South Wales.

**-n't,** a contracted form of *not*, as in *aren't.*

**Nt,** in *chemistry*, niton.

**NT., N.T.,** New Testament.

**nth** (enth), *adj.* 1. expressing the ordinal equivalent to *n;* hence, 2. of the indefinitely large or small quantity represented by *n.* —**to the nth degree,** 1. to an indefinite degree. 2. to an extreme.

**nt. wt.,** net weight.

**nu** (nōō, nū), *n.* [Gr.], the thirteenth letter of the Greek alphabet (Ν, ν).

**nu·ance** (nōō-äns′, nū′äns), *n.* [Fr. < *nuer*, to shade], a slight variation in tone, color, meaning, expression, etc.; shade of difference.

**nub** (nub), *n.* [ult. var. of *knob*], 1. a knob; lump. 2. [Colloq.], the point of a story, etc.; gist.

**nub·bin** (nub′in), *n.* [dim. of *nub*], 1. a small lump. 2. a small or imperfect ear of corn.

**nub·by** (nub′i), *adj.* [-BIER, -BIEST], covered with small lumps: said of a fabric with a rough, knotted weave.

**Nu·bi·a** (nōō′bi-ə, nū′-), *n.* a former kingdom of NE Africa: now part of Egypt and Sudan. —**Nu′bi·an,** *adj. & n.*

**nu·bile** (nōō′b'l, nū′bil), *adj.* [< Fr. or L.; ult. < L. *nubere*, to marry], marriageable: said of women, with reference to their age or physical development. —**nu·bil′i·ty,** *n.*

**nu·cle·ar** (nōō′kli-ẽr, nū′-), *adj.* 1. of, like, or forming a nucleus. 2. of, involving, or using atomic nuclei or atomic energy, bombs, power, etc.

**nuclear fission,** the splitting of the nuclei of atoms, accompanied by conversion of part of the mass into energy, as in the atomic bomb.

**nuclear fusion,** the fusion of atomic nuclei, as of heavy hydrogen or tritium, into a nucleus of heavier mass, as of helium, with a resultant loss in the combined mass, which is converted into energy: the principle of the hydrogen bomb.

**nuclear physics,** the branch of physics dealing with the structure of atomic nuclei and the energies involved in nuclear changes.

**nu·cle·ate** (nōō′kli-it, nū′kli-āt′), *adj.* having a nucleus. *v.t.* (nōō′kli-āt′, nū′-), [-ATED, -ATING], to form into or around a nucleus. *v.i.* to form a nucleus. —**nu′cle·a′tion,** *n.* —**nu′cle·a′tor,** *n.*

**nu·cle·o·lus** (nōō-klē′ə-ləs, nū-), *n.* [*pl.* -LI (-lī′)], [LL., dim. of *nucleus*], a conspicuous, spherical body found in the nucleus of most cells: also **nu′cle·ole′** (-ōl′). —**nu·cle′o·lar,** *adj.*

**nu·cle·on** (nōō′kli-on, nū′-), *n.* a proton or neutron in the nucleus of an atom.

**nu·cle·on·ics** (nōō′kli-on′iks, nū′-), *n.pl.* [construed as sing.], the branch of physics dealing with nucleons or with nuclear action.

**nu·cle·us** (nōō′kli-əs, nū′-), *n.* [*pl.* -CLEI (-kli-ī′), -CLEUSES], [L., a kernel < *nux*, nut], 1. a central thing or part around which other parts or things are grouped. 2. any center of growth or development. 3. in *astronomy*, the bright central part of the head of a comet. 4. in *biology*, the central, spherical mass of protoplasm in most plant and animal cells, necessary to growth, reproduction, etc. 5. in *chemistry & physics*, the central part of an atom, the fundamental particles of which are the proton and neutron: it carries a positive charge. 6. in *organic chemistry*, a stable arrangement of atoms that may occur in many compounds.

**nude** (nōōd, nūd), *adj.* [L. *nudus*], naked; bare; unclothed. *n.* a nude figure, especially as in painting, sculpture, etc. —**the nude,** 1. the nude human figure. 2. the representation of this in art. 3. a nude condition. —**nude′ly,** *adv.* —**nude′ness,** *n.*

**nudge** (nuj), *v.t.* [NUDGED, NUDGING], [? < AS. hyp. *nycgan*], to push gently, especially with the elbow, in order to get attention. *n.* a gentle push with the elbow, etc.; jog.

**nud·ism** (nōōd′iz′m, nūd′-), *n.* the practice or cult of going nude for hygienic reasons. —**nud′ist,** *adj. & n.*

**nu·di·ty** (nōōd′ə-ti, nūd′-), *n.* 1. a being nude; nakedness. 2. [*pl.* -TIES], anything nude.

**nu·ga·to·ry** (nōō′gə-tôr′i, nū′gə-tō′ri), *adj.* [< L. < *nugari*, to trifle], 1. trifling; worthless. 2. not operative; ineffectual; invalid.

**nug·get** (nug′it), *n.* [prob. dim. of dial. *nug*, lump], a lump; esp., a lump of native gold.

**nui·sance** (nōō′s'ns, nū′-), *n.* [OFr. < *nuisir* < L. *nocere*, to annoy], an act, thing, person, etc. causing trouble, annoyance, or inconvenience.

**nuisance tax,** a tax considered a nuisance because paid in very small amounts by the consumer.

**null** (nul), *adj.* [< Fr. < L. *nullus*, none < *ne-*, not + *ullus*, any], 1. without legal force; void; invalid. 2. amounting to nought; nil. 3. of no value, effect, etc.; insignificant. —**null and void,** without legal force; invalid.

**nul·li·fi·ca·tion** (nul′ə-fi-kā′shən), *n.* 1. a nullifying or being nullified. 2. in U.S. history, the refusal of a State to enforce any act of Congress held to be an infringement on its sovereignty.

**nul·li·fy** (nul′ə-fī′), *v.t.* [-FIED, -FYING], [< LL. < L. *nullus*, none + *facere*, to make], 1. to make legally null; make void. 2. to make valueless or useless; bring to nothing. —**nul′li·fi′er,** *n.*

**nul·li·ty** (nul′ə-ti), *n.* 1. a being null. 2. [*pl.* -TIES], anything that is null.

**Num.,** Numbers, a book of the Old Testament.

**num.,** 1. number. 2. numeral; numerals.

**numb** (num), *adj.* [< ME. *numen*, pp. of *nimen*, to take], weakened in or deprived of the power of feeling or moving; deadened; insensible: as, *numb* with grief. *v.t.* to make numb. —**numb′ing·ly,** *adv.* —**numb′ly,** *adv.* —**numb′ness,** *n.*

**num·ber** (num′bẽr), *n.* [< OFr. < L. *numerus*], 1. a symbol or word, or a group of either of these, showing how many or what place in a sequence (e.g., 2, 27, four, fifth, etc.): see also **cardinal number, ordinal.** 2. *pl.* arithmetic. 3. the sum of any collection of persons or things; total. 4. a collection of persons or things; assemblage. 5. *a*) *also pl.* a considerable collection; many. *b*) *pl.* numerical superiority. 6. quantity, as consisting of units. 7. *a*) a single issue of a periodical: as, the June *number* of a magazine. *b*) a distinct part of a program of entertainment. 8. [Colloq.], a person or thing singled out: as, this hat is a smart *number.* 9. in *grammar*, *a*) a difference of word form to show whether one or more than one person or thing is meant. *b*) the form itself. See **plural, singular.** 10. *pl.* in *music*, measures. 11. *pl.* in *poetry*, metrical feet, verses, or verse. *v.t.* 1. to count; enumerate. 2. to give a number to; designate by number. 3. to include as one of a group, class, etc. 4. to limit the number of: as, his days are *numbered.* 5. to comprise in number. 6. to total; equal. *v.i.* 1. to total; count. 2. to be numbered. —**a number of,** several or many. —**beyond** (or **without**) **number,** too numerous to be counted. —**get one's number,** [Slang], to discover one's true character or motives. —**one's number is up,** [Slang], one's time to die, suffer, etc. has arrived. —**the numbers,** numbers pool. —**num′bẽr·er,** *n.*

**num·ber·less** (num′bẽr-lis), *adj.* 1. without number; countless. 2. without a number or numbers.

**Num·bers** (num′bẽrz), *n.pl.* [construed as sing.], [so named from containing the census of the Hebrews after the Exodus], the fourth book of the Old Testament.

**numbers pool** (or **game, racket**), an illegal lottery in which people place small bets on the order of certain numbers in a tabulation, as of financial reports, published in the daily newspapers.

**nu·mer·a·ble** (nōō′mẽr-ə-b'l, nū′-), *adj.* that can be numbered or counted.

**nu·mer·al** (nōō′mẽr-əl, nū′-), *adj.* [< LL. < L. *numerus*, number], of, expressing, or denoting number or numbers. *n.* a figure, letter, or word, or a group of any of these, expressing a number: see **Arabic numerals, Roman numerals.**

**nu·mer·ate** (nōō′mə-rāt′, nū′-), *v.t.* [-ATED, -ATING], 1. to count; enumerate. 2. to read (numbers expressed in figures).

**nu·mer·a·tion** (nōō′mə-rā′shən, nū′-), *n.* 1. a numbering or counting. 2. a system of numbering or of reading numbers expressed in figures.

**nu·mer·a·tor** (nōō′mə-rā′tẽr, nū′-), *n.* 1. that term of a fraction, written above the line, which shows how many of the specified parts of a unit are taken. 2. a person or thing that numbers.

**nu·mer·i·cal** (nōō-mer′i-k'l, nū-), *adj.* 1. of, or having the nature of, number. 2. in or by numbers. 3. denoting (a) number. 4. expressed by numbers, not letters. Also **nu·mer′ic.** —**nu·mer′i·cal·ly,** *adv.*

**nu·mer·ol·o·gy** (nōō′mə-rol′ə-ji, nū′-), *n.* [< L. *numerus*, a number; + *-logy*], a system of occultism involving divination by numbers.

**nu·mer·ous** (nōō′mẽr-əs, nū′-), *adj.* [< L. < *numerus*, a number], 1. consisting of a great number. 2. very many. —**nu′mer·ous·ly,** *adv.* —**nu′mer·ous·ness,** *n.*

**Nu·mid·i·a** (nōō-mid′i-ə, nū-), *n.* an ancient kingdom in N Africa. —**Nu·mid′i·an,** *adj. & n.*

**nu·mis·mat·ic** (nōō′miz-mat′ik, nū mis-), *adj.* [< Fr. < L. *numisma*, a coin < Gr. < *nomizein*, to sanction < *nomos*, law], 1. of coins or medals. 2. of numismatics. Also **nu′mis·mat′i·cal.** —**nu′mis·mat′i·cal·ly,** *adv.*

**nu·mis·mat·ics** (nōō′miz-mat′iks, nū′mis-), *n.pl.* [construed as sing.], the study or collection of coins and medals. —**nu·mis·ma·tist** (nōō-miz′mə-tist, nū-mis′-), *n.*

**num·skull** (num′skul′), *n.* [< *numb* + *skull*], a stupid person; dolt; blockhead; dunce.

**nun** (nun), *n.* [< AS. < LL. *nonna*], a woman devoted to a religious life; esp., a member of a convent under vows of chastity, poverty, etc.

**Nunc Di·mit·tis** (nuŋk di-mit′is), [L., now thou lettest depart: first words of the L. version], the song of Simeon, sung as a hymn or canticle in various liturgies: Luke 2:29-32. 2. [n- d-], *a*) departure or farewell. *b*) dismissal.

**nun·ci·o** (nun′shi-ō′), *n.* [*pl.* -IOS], [< It. < L. *nuntius*, messenger], the permanent ambassador of the Pope to a foreign government.

**nun·ner·y** (nun′ẽr-i), *n.* [*pl.* -IES], a community of nuns and the place in which they live; convent.

**nun's veiling,** a soft, loosely woven woolen material, used for veils, light dresses, etc.

**nup·tial** (nup′shəl, -chəl), *adj.* [< Fr. or L.; ult. < L. *nubere*, to marry], of marriage or a wedding. *n. pl.* a wedding; marriage ceremony.

**Nu·rem·berg** (nyoor′əm-būrg′ noor′-), *n.* a city in Bavaria, Germany: pop., 362,000: site of trials (1945–1946) of Nazi war criminals: German name **Nürn·berg** (nür′'n-berkh′).

**nurse** (nũrs), *n.* [< OFr. < LL. < L. < *nutrix* < *nutrire*, to nourish], 1. a woman hired to take full care of another's young child or children. 2. a person trained to take care of the sick or aged, assist surgeons, etc. 3. a person or thing that nourishes, fosters, or protects. *v.t.* [NURSED, NURSING], 1. to suckle (an infant). 2. to take care of (a child or children). 3. to tend (the sick or aged). 4. to nourish, foster, or develop: as, she's *nursing* her anger. 5. to treat; try to cure: as, he is *nursing* a cold. 6. *a*) to use or handle carefully, so as to avoid injury, pain, etc.: as, he's *nursing* his injured leg. *b*) to drink slowly, so as to conserve: as, she *nursed* her highball. 7. to clasp; fondle. *v.i.* 1. to feed at the breast. 2. to suckle a child. 3. to serve as a nurse.

**nurse·maid** (nũrs′mād′), *n.* a girl or woman hired to take care of a child or children.

**nurs·er·y** (nũr′sẽr-i, nũrs′ri), *n.* [*pl.* -IES], 1. *a*) a room in a home, set aside for the children. *b*) a nursery school. 2. a place where young trees or plants are raised for transplanting. 3. anything that nourishes, protects, or fosters.

**nurs·er·y·maid** (nũr′sẽr-i-mād′, nũrs′ri-), *n.* a nursemaid.
**nurs·er·y·man** (nũr′sẽr-i-mən, nũrs′ri-), *n.* [*pl.* -MEN], one who owns, operates, or works in a nursery for growing trees, plants, etc.
**nursery rhyme,** a short poem for children.
**nursery school,** a prekindergarten school for young children, as between the ages of 3 and 5.
**nursing home,** a residence providing needed care for persons who are infirm, chronically ill, etc.
**nurs·ling, nurse·ling** (nũrs′liŋ), *n.* 1. a young baby still being nursed. 2. anything that is being carefully tended or cared for.
**nur·ture** (nũr′chẽr), *n.* [< OFr. < LL. < L. *nutrire,* to nourish], 1. food; nutriment. 2. training; rearing; upbringing. *v.t.* [-TURED, -TURING], 1. to feed or nourish; foster. 2. to train; educate; rear. **—nur′tur·er,** *n.*
**nut** (nut), *n.* [AS. *hnutu*], 1. a dry, one-seeded fruit, consisting of a kernel, often edible, in a woody or leathery shell: walnuts, pecans, acorns, etc. are *nuts.* 2. the kernel of such a fruit. 3. loosely, any hard-shelled fruit, as the peanut and cashew, that will keep more or less indefinitely. 4. a person, problem, or thing difficult to understand or handle. 5. a small metal block with a threaded hole through the center, for screwing onto a bolt, etc. 6. [Slang], the head. 7. [Slang], an eccentric or demented person. *v.i.* [NUTTED, NUTTING], to hunt for or gather nuts. **—off one's nut,** [Slang], insane; crazy.
**nut·crack·er** (nut′krak′ẽr), *n.* 1. *sometimes pl.* an instrument for cracking the shells of nuts. 2. *a*) a white-spotted, dark-brown European bird of the crow family, that feeds on nuts. *b*) a similar bird of W North America, with grayish plumage.
**nut·gall** (nut′gôl′), *n.* a small, nut-shaped gall on the oak and other trees.
**nut·hatch** (nut′hach′), *n.* a small, nut-eating bird having a sharp beak and a short tail.
**nut·meat** (nut′mēt′), *n.* the kernel of a nut.
**nut·meg** (nut′meg), *n.* [< ME. < *nut,* nut + OFr. *mugue* (< L. *muscus*), musk], 1. the hard, aromatic kernel of the seed of an East Indian tree: it is grated and used as a spice. 2. the tree itself.
**nut·pick** (nut′pik′), *n.* a small, sharp instrument for digging out the kernels of cracked nuts.
**nu·tri·a** (nōō′tri-ə, nū′-), *n.* [Sp. < L. *lutra,* otter], 1. the coypu. 2. its short-haired, soft, brown fur, often dyed to look like beaver.
**nu·tri·ent** (nōō′tri-ənt, nū′-), *adj.* [< L. ppr. of *nutrire,* to nourish], nutritious; nourishing. *n.* anything nutritious.
**nu·tri·ment** (nōō′trə-mənt, nū′-), *n.* [< L. < *nutrire,* to nourish], anything that nourishes; food.
**nu·tri·tion** (nōō-trish′ən, nū-), *n.* [< L. *nutrire,* to nourish], 1. a nourishing or being nourished; esp., the series of processes by which an organism takes in and assimilates food for promoting growth and repairing tissues. 2. anything that nourishes; food. **—nu·tri′tion·al,** *adj.* **—nu·tri′tion·al·ly,** *adv.* **—nu·tri′tion·ist,** *n.*
**nu·tri·tious** (nōō-trish′əs, nū-), *adj.* providing or promoting nutrition; nourishing. **—nu·tri′tious·ly,** *adv.* **—nu·tri′tious·ness,** *n.*
**nu·tri·tive** (nōō′trə-tiv, nū′-), *adj.* 1. having to do with nutrition. 2. nutritious. **—nu′tri·tive·ly,** *adv.*
**nuts** (nuts), *adj.* [Slang], crazy; foolish. *interj.* [Slang], an exclamation of disgust, scorn, disapproval, refusal, etc. **—be nuts about,** [Slang], to be extremely fond of.
**nut·shell** (nut′shel′), *n.* the shell enclosing the kernel of a nut. **—in a nutshell,** in brief or concise form; in a few words.
**nut·ting** (nut′iŋ), *n.* the gathering of nuts.
**nut·ty** (nut′i), *adj.* [-TIER, -TIEST], 1. containing or producing many nuts. 2. having a nutlike flavor. 3. [Slang], *a*) very enthusiastic. *b*) queer, foolish, demented, etc. **—nut′ti·ness,** *n.*
**nux vom·i·ca** (nuks′ vom′i-kə), [ML. < L. *nux,* nut + *vomere,* to vomit], 1. the poisonous seed of an Asiatic tree, containing strychnine. 2. the tree itself. 3. a medicine made from the seed.
**nuz·zle** (nuz′'l), *v.t.* [-ZLED, -ZLING], [< *nose*], to push against or rub with the nose, snout, etc. *v.i.* 1. to push or rub with the nose, etc. against or into something. 2. to lie close; nestle; snuggle.
**NW, N.W., n.w.,** 1. northwest. 2. northwestern.
**N.Y.,** New York.
**Nya·sa·land** (nyä′sä-land′, nī-as′ə-), *n.* Malawi: the former name.
**N.Y.C.,** New York City.
**ny·lon** (nī′lon), *n.* [arbitrary formation], 1. an elastic, very strong, synthetic material made into thread, bristles, etc. 2. *pl.* stockings made of this.
**nymph** (nimf), *n.* [< OFr. < L. < Gr. *nymphē*], 1. in *Gr. & Rom. mythology,* any of a group of minor nature goddesses, represented as beautiful maidens living in rivers, mountains, trees, etc. 2. a lovely young woman. 3. the young of an insect without complete metamorphosis: also **nym·pha** (nim′fə), [*pl.* -PHAE (-fē)]. **—nymph′al,** *adj.*
**nym·pho·ma·ni·a** (nim′fə-mā′ni-ə), *n.* excessive and uncontrollable sexual desire in a woman. **—nym′pho·ma′ni·ac′** (-ak′), *adj. & n.*
**Nyx** (niks), *n.* [Gr.], in *Gr. mythology,* the goddess of night.
**N.Z., N. Zeal.,** New Zealand.

# O

**O, o** (ō), *n.* [*pl.* O's, o's, Os, os, oes], 1. the fifteenth letter of the English alphabet. 2. the sound of O or o. 3. the numeral zero; a cipher. 4. an object shaped like O or o. 5. in *physics, the symbol for* ohm. *adj.* 1. circular or oval in shape. 2. fifteenth in a sequence or group.
**O** (ō), *interj.* an exclamation variously used: 1. in direct address: as, *O* God, save us! 2. to express surprise, fear, etc.: now usually *oh.* *n.* [*pl.* O's], any instance of this exclamation.
**o′** (ō; *unstressed* ə), *prep.* an abbreviated form of: 1. *of.* 2. [Archaic or Dial.], *on.*
**O,** 1. in **chemistry,** oxygen. 2. in **linguistics,** Old.
**O.,** 1. Ocean. 2. October. 3. Ohio.
**O., o.,** 1. *octarius,* [L.], in **pharmacy,** a pint. 2. old.
**oaf** (ōf), *n.* [*pl.* OAFS, OAVES (ōvz)], [< ON. *alfr,* elf], 1. a misshapen or idiotic child. 2. a stupid, clumsy fellow; lout. **—oaf′ish,** *adj.* **—oaf′ish·ly,** *adv.* **—oaf′ish·ness,** *n.*
**O·a·hu** (ō-ä′hōō), *n.* the chief island of the Hawaiian Islands: area, 595 sq. mi.; pop., 500,000; chief city, Honolulu.
**oak** (ōk), *n.* [see PLURAL, II, D, 3], [AS. *ac*], 1. a large hardwood tree or bush bearing nuts called *acorns.* 2. its wood. 3. any of various plants resembling this tree: as, poison *oak.* *adj.* of oak. **—oak′en,** *adj.*
**oak apple,** an applelike gall on oak trees: also **oak gall.**
**Oak·land** (ōk′lənd), *n.* a city in W California, on San Francisco Bay: pop., 368,000.
**Oakley, Annie,** see **Annie Oakley.**
**Oak Park,** a city (legally, a village) in NE Illinois: suburb of Chicago: pop., 61,000.
**Oak Ridge,** a city in E Tennessee, near Knoxville: a center of atomic research: pop., 27,000.
**oa·kum** (ō′kəm), *n.* [AS. *acumba* < *a-,* out + *camb,* a comb], stringy, hemp fiber got by taking apart old ropes: used to pack the seams of boats, etc.
**oar** (ôr, ōr), *n.* [AS. *ar*], 1. a long pole with a broad blade at one end, used in rowing. 2. a person who uses an oar; rower. *v.t. & v.i.* to row. **—put one's oar in,** to meddle; interfere. **—rest on one's oars,** to stop one's work in order to rest. **—oared,** *adj.* **—oar′less,** *adj.*
**OAr.,** Old Arabic.
**oar·lock** (ôr′lok′, ōr′-), *n.* a U-shaped device for holding the oar in place in rowing; rowlock.
**oars·man** (ôrz′mən, ōrz′-), *n.* [*pl.* -MEN], a man who rows; esp., an expert at rowing. **—oars′man·ship′,** *n.*
**OAS, O.A.S.,** Organization of American States: see **Pan American Union.**
**o·a·sis** (ō-ā′sis, ō′ə-), *n.* [*pl.* -SES (-sēz, -sēz′)], [L. < Gr. *ōasis;* orig. < Coptic], a fertile place in a desert, due to the presence of water.
**oat** (ōt), *n.* [AS. *ate*], 1. *usually in pl. a*) a hardy

cereal grass. *b*) its edible grain. 2. any related grass; esp., the wild oat. 3. [Obs. or Poetic], a musical pipe made of an oat stalk. —**feel one's oats,** [Slang], 1. to be frisky. 2. to feel and act important. —**oat′en,** *adj.*

**oat·cake** (ōt′kāk′), *n.* a thin, flat, hard cake made of oatmeal.

**oath** (ōth), *n.* [*pl.* OATHS (ōthz, ōths)], [AS. *ath*], 1. *a*) a ritualistic declaration, based on an appeal to God or to some revered person or object, that one will speak the truth, keep a promise, etc. *b*) the ritual form used in such a declaration. *c*) the thing so promised or declared. 2. the profane use of the name of God or of a sacred thing in anger or emphasis. 3. a swearword; curse. —**take oath,** to promise or declare with an oath.

**oat·meal** (ōt′mēl′), *n.* 1. oats crushed into meal or flakes; rolled or ground oats. 2. a porridge made from such oats.

**ob-,** [< L. *ob, prep.*], a prefix meaning: 1. *to, toward, before,* as in *object.* 2. *opposed to, against,* as in *obnoxious.* 3. *upon, over,* as in *obfuscate.* 4. *completely, totally,* as in *obsolete.* 5. *inversely, oppositely,* as in *objurgate.* In words of Latin origin, *ob-* assimilates to *o-, oc-, of-,* and *op-.*

**Ob., Obad.,** Obadiah.

**ob.,** *obiit,* [L.], he (or she) died.

**O.B.,** obstetrics.

**O·ba·di·ah** (ō′bə-dī′ə), *n.* in the *Bible,* 1. one of the minor Hebrew prophets. 2. a book of the Old Testament containing his prophecies.

**ob·bli·ga·to** (ob′li-gä′tō), *adj.* [It. < L. pp. of *obligare;* see OBLIGE], in *music,* indispensable: said of an elaborate accompaniment that is necessary to the proper performance of a piece. *n.* [*pl.* -TOS, -TI (-ti)], an accompaniment of this kind.

**ob·du·rate** (ob′doo-rit, -dyoo-), *adj.* [< L. *obduratus,* pp. < ob-, intens. + *durare,* to harden], 1 hardhearted. 2. hardened and unrepenting. 3. not giving in readily; stubborn. —**ob′du·ra·cy** (-rə-si), **ob′du·rate·ness,** *n.* —**ob′du·rate·ly,** *adv.*

**o·be·di·ence** (ō-bē′di-əns), *n.* the state or fact of being obedient; a doing what is ordered.

**o·be·di·ent** (ō-bē′di-ənt), *adj.* [< L. ppr. of *obedire;* see OBEY], obeying or willing to obey; docile. —**o·be′di·ent·ly,** *adv.* —**o·be′di·ent·ness,** *n.*

**o·bei·sance** (ō-bā′s'ns, ō-bē′-), *n.* [< OFr. < ppr. of *obeir,* to obey], 1. a gesture of respect or reverence, as a bow or curtsy. 2. homage; deference. —**o·bei′sant,** *adj.* —**o·bei′sant·ly,** *adv.*

**ob·e·lisk** (ob′'l-isk′), *n.* [< L. < Gr. *obeliskos,* dim. of *obelos,* a needle], 1. a tall, four-sided stone pillar tapering toward its pyramidal top. 2. in *printing,* a reference mark (†), used to indicate footnotes, etc.; dagger: also **ob′e·lus** (-əs), [*pl.* -LI (-ī′)].

**O·ber·am·mer·gau** (ō′bēr-äm′ēr-gou′, -am′-), *n.* a town in S Bavaria, Germany, where the Passion play is normally presented every ten years.

**O·ber·on** (ō′bə-ron′), *n.* in early folklore, the king of fairyland and husband of Titania.

**o·bese** (ō-bēs′), *adj.* [< L. *obesus,* pp. < *ob-* (see OB-) + *edere,* to eat], very fat; stout. —**o·bese′ly,** *adv.* —**o·bes′i·ty** (ō-bēs′ə-ti, -bes′-), **o·bese′ness,** *n.*

**o·bey** (ō-bā′), *v.t.* [< OFr. < L. *obedire* < *ob-* (see OB-) + *audire,* to hear], 1. to carry out the orders of. 2. to carry out (an order, etc.). 3. to be guided by: as, *obey* your common sense. *v.i.* to be obedient. —**o·bey′er,** *n.* —**o·bey′ing·ly,** *adv.*

**ob·fus·cate** (ob-fus′kāt, ob′fəs-kāt′), *v.t.* [-CATED, -CATING], [< L. *obfuscatus,* pp. < *ob-* (see OB-) + *fuscare,* to obscure < *fuscus,* dark], 1. to darken; obscure. 2. to confuse; bewilder. —**ob′fus·ca′tion,** *n.* —**ob·fus′ca·tor** (-kā-tēr), *n.*

**o·bi** (ō′bi), *n.* [Japan.], a broad sash worn by Japanese women and children.

**o·bit** (ō′bit, ob′it), *n.* an obituary.

**ob·i·ter dic·tum** (ob′i-tēr dik′təm), [*pl.* OBITER DICTA (-tə)], [L.], 1. an incidental opinion expressed by a judge. 2. any incidental remark.

**o·bit·u·ar·y** (ō-bich′ōō-er′i), *n.* [*pl.* -IES], [< ML. < L. *obitus,* death; ult. < *ob-* (see OB-) + *ire,* to go], a notice of someone's death, usually with a short biography of the deceased. *adj.* of or recording a death or deaths.

**obj.,** 1. object. 2. objective.

**ob·ject** (ob′jikt; *for v.,* əb-jekt′, ob-), *n.* [< ML. < L. *objectum,* something thrown in the way; ult. < *ob-* (see OB-) + *jacere,* to throw], 1. a thing that can be seen or touched; material thing. 2. *a*) a person or thing to which action, thought, or feeling is directed. *b*) [Colloq.], a person or thing that excites pity or ridicule. 3. what is aimed at; purpose; goal. 4. in *grammar,* a noun or substantive that receives the action of the verb (cf. *direct object, indirect object*), or one that is governed by a preposition. 5. in *philosophy,* anything that can be perceived by the mind. *v.t.* to state in opposition or disapproval. *v.i.* 1. to put forward an objection; be opposed. 2. to feel or express disapproval. —**ob′ject·less,** *adj.* —**ob·jec′tor** (-jek′tēr), *n.*

**object glass,** an objective (*n.* sense 4).

**ob·jec·ti·fy** (əb-jek′tə-fī′, ob-), *v.t.* [-FIED, -FYING], to make objective. —**ob·jec′ti·fi·ca′tion,** *n.*

**ob·jec·tion** (əb-jek′shən, ob-), *n.* 1. a feeling or expression of opposition, disapproval, or dislike. 2. a cause or reason for objecting.

**ob·jec·tion·a·ble** (əb-jek′shən-ə-b'l, ob-), *adj.* 1. open to objection. 2. disagreeable; offensive. —**ob·jec′tion·a·bly,** *adv.* —**ob·jec′tion·a·ble·ness,** *n.*

**ob·jec·tive** (əb-jek′tiv, ob-), *adj.* 1. of or having to do with a known or perceived object, not a mental image or idea. 2. being, or regarded as being, independent of the mind; real. 3. concerned with the actual characteristics of the thing dealt with rather than the thoughts, feelings, etc. of the artist, writer, or speaker: as, an *objective* description. 4. without bias or prejudice; impersonal. 5. being the aim or goal: as, an *objective* point. 6. in *grammar,* designating or of the case of an object of a preposition or verb. *n.* 1. anything external to or independent of the mind; reality. 2. something aimed at or striven for. 3. in *grammar,* *a*) the objective case. *b*) a word in this case. 4. in *optics,* the lens or lenses nearest to the object observed, in a microscope, telescope, etc. —**ob·jec′tive·ly,** *adv.* —**ob·jec′tive·ness,** *n.*

**ob·jec·tiv·i·ty** (ob′jek-tiv′ə-ti), *n.* 1. an objective state or quality. 2. objective reality.

**object lesson,** an actual or practical demonstration or exemplification of some principle.

‡**ob·jet d art** (ôb′zhe′dàr′), [*pl.* OBJETS D'ART (ôb′zhe′dàr′)], [Fr.], a relatively small object of artistic value, as a figurine, vase, etc.

**ob·jur·gate** (ob′jēr-gāt′, əb-jūr′gāt), *v.t.* [-GATED, -GATING], [< L. < *objurgatus,* pp. < *ob-* (see OB-) + *jurgare,* to chide], to chide vehemently; upbraid sharply; rebuke. —**ob′jur·ga′tion,** *n.* —**ob′jur·ga′tor,** *n.* —**ob·jur′ga·to′ry** (-gə-tôr′i, -tō′ri), *adj.* —**ob·jur′ga·to′ri·ly,** *adv.*

**ob·late** (ob′lāt, ob-lāt′), *adj.* [Mod. L. *oblatus; ob-* (see OB-) + *-latus* as in *prolatus;* see PROLATE], in *geometry,* flattened at the poles: as, an *oblate* spheroid. —**ob′late·ly,** *adv.* —**ob′late·ness,** *n.*

**ob·la·tion** (ob-lā′shən), *n.* [OFr. < L. < *oblatus,* pp. of *offerre;* see OFFER], 1. an offering of a sacrifice, thanksgiving, etc. to God or a god. 2. the thing offered; esp., the bread and wine of the Eucharist. —**ob·la′tion·al, ob·la·to·ry** (ob′lə-tôr′i, -tō′ri), *adj.*

**ob·li·gate** (ob′lə-gāt′; *for adj.,* -gət), *v.t.* [-GATED -GATING], [< L. pp. of *obligare;* see OBLIGE], to bind by a contract, promise, sense of duty, etc. *adj.* bound; obliged.

**ob·li·ga·tion** (ob′lə-gā′shən), *n.* 1. an obligating or being obligated. 2. the contract, promise, responsibility, etc. binding one. 3. a thing, duty, etc. to which one is so bound. 4. the binding power of a contract, promise, responsibility, etc. 5. *a*) a being indebted to another for a favor or service received. *b*) a favor or service. —**ob′li·ga′tion·al,** *adj.* —**ob′li·ga′tor,** *n.*

**ob·li·ga·to** (ob′li-gä′tō), *adj. & n.* [*pl.* -TOS, -TI (-ti)], obbligato.

**ob·lig·a·to·ry** (ə-blig′ə-tôr′i, ob′li-gə-tō′ri), *adj.* legally or morally binding; required. —**ob·lig′a·to′ri·ly,** *adv.* —**ob·lig′a·to′ri·ness,** *n.*

**o·blige** (ə-blīj′, ō-), *v.t.* [OBLIGED, OBLIGING], [< OFr. < L. *obligare* < *ob-* (see OB-) + *ligare,* to bind], 1. to compel by moral, legal, or physical force; constrain. 2. to make indebted for a favor or kindness done; do a favor for. —**o·blig′er,** *n.*

**o·blig·ing** (ə-blij′iŋ, ō-), *adj.* ready to do favors; helpful; accommodating. —**o·blig′ing·ly,** *adv.* —**o·blig′ing·ness,** *n.*

**ob·lique** (ə-blēk′; *esp. in military use,* ō-blik′), *adj.* [< L. *obliquus* < *ob-* (see OB-) + *liquis,* awry], 1. having a slanting position or direction; neither perpendicular nor horizontal. 2. not straight to the point; indirect. 3. evasive, underhand, etc. 4. indirectly aimed at or attained. 5. in *grammar,* designating or of any case except the nominative and the vocative. 6. in *rhetoric,* indirect: said of discourse. *v.i.* [-LIQUED, -LIQUING], to veer from the perpendicular; slant. —**ob·lique′ly,** *adv.* —**ob·liq·ui·ty** (ə-blik′wə-ti), [*pl.* -TIES], **ob·lique′ness,** *n.*

**oblique angle,** any angle other than a right angle; acute or obtuse angle.

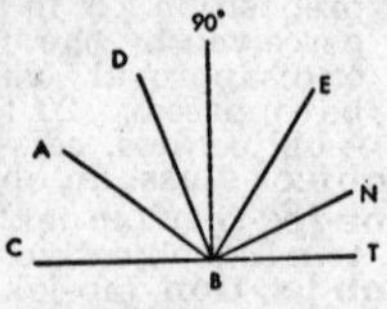

OBLIQUE ANGLES (ABC, DBA, DBC, DBE, EBN, NBC, ABT, etc.)

**ob·lit·er·ate** (ə-blit′ə-rāt′), *v.t.* [-ATED, -ATING], [< L. pp. of *obliterare,* to blot out < *ob-* (see OB-) + *litera,* a letter], 1. to blot out, leaving no traces; efface. 2. to do away with; destroy. —**ob·lit′er·a′tion,** *n.* —**ob·lit′er·a′tive,** *adj.* —**ob·lit′er·a′tor,** *n.*

**ob·liv·i·on** (ə-bliv′i-ən), *n.* [< OFr. < L. < *oblivisci,* to forget], 1. a forgetting or having forgotten; forgetfulness. 2. a being forgotten.

**ob·liv·i·ous** (ə-bliv′i-əs), *adj.* 1. forgetful; unmindful (with *of* or *to*). 2. causing forgetfulness. —**ob·liv′i·ous·ly,** *adv.* —**ob·liv′i·ous·ness,** *n.*

**ob·long** (ob′lôŋ), *adj.* [< L. < *ob-* (see OB-) + *longus,* long], longer than broad; elongated; specif., rectangular and longer in one direction than in the other. *n.* anything oblong in form.

**ob·lo·quy** (ob′lə-kwi), *n.* [*pl.* -QUIES], [< LL. < *obloqui,* to speak against; *ob-* (see OB-) + *loqui,* to speak], 1. verbal abuse of a person or thing; esp., widespread censure. 2. disgrace or infamy resulting from this.

**ob·nox·ious** (əb-nok′shəs, ob-), *adj.* [< L. < *obnoxius,* in danger < *ob-* (see OB-) + *noxa,* a harm], very unpleasant; objectionable; offensive. —**ob·nox′ious·ly,** *adv.* —**ob·nox′ious·ness,** *n.*

**o·boe** (ō′bō, ō′boi), *n.* [It. < Fr. *hautbois;* see HAUTBOY], a double-reed woodwind instrument having a high, penetrating, melancholy tone. —**o′bo·ist,** *n.*

OBOE

**Obs., obs.,** obsolete.

**ob·scene** (ob-sēn′, əb-), *adj.* [< Fr. < L. *obscenus,* filthy, repulsive], 1. offensive to modesty or decency; lewd. 2. disgusting; repulsive. —**ob·scene′ly,** *adv.* —**ob·scen·i·ty** (-sen′ə-ti, -sē′nə-), [*pl.* -TIES], **ob·scene′ness,** *n.*

**ob·scur·ant·ism** (əb-skyoor′ən-tiz'm, ob-), *n.* [< L. *obscurans,* obscuring], principles or practices in opposition to human progress and enlightenment. —**ob·scur′ant, ob·scur′ant·ist,** *n. & adj.*

**ob·scure** (əb-skyoor′, ob-), *adj.* [< OFr. < L. *obscurus,* lit., covered over], 1. dim; dark; gloomy: as, an *obscure* corner. 2. not easily seen; not clear or distinct: as, an *obscure* figure. 3. not easily understood; vague; ambiguous: as, an *obscure* answer. 4. in an inconspicuous position; hidden. 5. not well known: as, an *obscure* scientist. *v.t.* [-SCURED, -SCURING], 1. to make obscure; specif., *a*) to darken; make dim. *b*) to conceal from view. *c*) to overshadow: as, his success *obscured* his failures. *d*) to confuse: as, his testimony *obscured* the issue. 2. in *phonetics,* to decrease the quality of (a vowel) to a more or less neutral sound. —**ob·scure′ly,** *adv.* —**ob·scure′ness,** *n.*

**ob·scu·ri·ty** (əb-skyoor′ə-ti, ob-), *n.* 1. the quality or condition of being obscure. 2. [*pl.* -TIES], an obscure person or thing.

**ob·se·qui·ous** (əb-sē′kwi-əs, ob-), *adj.* [< Fr. < L. < *obsequi,* to comply with], excessively willing to serve or obey; overly submissive; servile. —**ob·se′qui·ous·ly,** *adv.* —**ob·se′qui·ous·ness,** *n.*

**ob·se·quy** (ob′si-kwi), *n.* [*pl.* -QUIES], [< OFr. < ML. *obsequiae* (by confusion with *exsequiae,* funeral) < L. *obsequium,* complaisance], *usually in pl.* a funeral rite or ceremony.

**ob·serv·a·ble** (əb-zũr′və-b'l, ob-), *adj.* 1. that can be observed, or perceived; noticeable. 2. that can or should be observed, or kept, as a holiday, a rule, etc. —**ob·serv′a·ble·ness,** *n.* —**ob·serv′a·bly,** *adv.*

**ob·serv·ance** (əb-zũr′vəns, ob-), *n.* 1. the act or practice of observing a law, duty, custom, etc. 2. a customary act, rite, etc. 3. observation. 4. in the *R.C. Church,* the rule to be observed by a religious order.

**ob·serv·ant** (əb-zũr′vənt, ob-), *adj.* 1. strict in observing a rule, custom, etc. (often with *of*). 2. paying careful attention. 3. perceptive or alert. —**ob·serv′ant·ly,** *adv.*

**ob·ser·va·tion** (ob′zẽr-vā′shən), *n.* 1. *a*) the act, practice, or power of observing, or noticing. *b*) something noticed. 2. a being seen or noticed. 3. *a*) a noting and recording of facts and events, as for some scientific study. *b*) the data so noted and recorded. 4. a comment based on something observed. 5. in *navigation,* the act of determining the altitude of the sun, a star, etc., in order to find the ship's position at sea. *adj.* for observing. —**ob′ser·va′tion·al,** *adj.* —**ob′ser·va′tion·al·ly,** *adv.*

**ob·serv·a·to·ry** (əb-zũr′və-tôr′i, ob-zũr′və-tō′ri), *n.* [*pl.* -RIES], 1. a building equipped for scientific observation, especially for astronomical or meteorological research. 2. any place or building providing an extensive view of the surrounding terrain. —**ob·serv′a·to′ri·al,** *adj.*

**ob·serve** (əb-zũrv′, ob-), *v.t.* [-SERVED, -SERVING], [< OFr. < L. *observare,* to watch < *ob-* (see OB-) + *servare,* to keep], 1. to adhere to or keep (a law, custom, duty, etc.). 2. to celebrate (a holiday, etc.) according to custom. 3. *a*) to notice or perceive (something). *b*) to pay special attention to. 4. to say casually; remark. 5. to examine scientifically. *v.i.* 1. to take notice or make observations. 2. to comment (*on* or *upon*). —**ob·serv′er,** *n.* —**ob·serv′ing,** *adj.* —**ob·serv′ing·ly,** *adv.*

**ob·sess** (əb-ses′, ob-), *v.t.* [< L. *obsessus,* pp. of *obsidere,* to besiege < *ob-* (see OB-) + *sedere,* to sit], to haunt or trouble in mind; harass; preoccupy. —**ob·ses′sive,** *adj.* —**ob·ses′sor,** *n.*

**ob·ses·sion** (əb-sesh′ən, ob-), *n.* the fact or state of being obsessed with an idea, desire, emotion, etc. 2. such an idea, desire, etc.

**ob·sid·i·an** (əb-sid′i-ən, ob-), *n.* [after *Obsius,* who, according to Pliny, discovered it], a dark, hard, glassy volcanic rock.

**ob·so·les·cent** (ob′sə-les′'nt), *adj.* [see -ESCENT], becoming obsolete; passing out of general use, etc. —**ob′so·les′cence,** *n.* —**ob′so·les′cent·ly,** *adv.*

**ob·so·lete** (ob′sə-lēt′), *adj.* [< L. pp. of *obsolescere* < *ob-* (see OB-) + *solere,* to become accustomed], 1. no longer in use or practice; discarded: cf. *archaic.* 2. out of date; passé: as, *obsolete* styles. —**ob′so·lete′ly,** *adv.* —**ob′so·lete′ness,** *n.*

**ob·sta·cle** (ob′sti-k'l), *n.* [OFr. < L. *obstaculum* < *ob-* (see OB-) + *stare,* to stand], anything that stands in the way or hinders; obstruction.

**ob·stet·ric** (ob-stet′rik, əb-), *adj.* [< L. < *obstetrix,* midwife < *ob-* (see OB-) + *stare,* to stand], of childbirth or obstetrics: also **ob·stet′ri·cal.** —**ob·stet′ri·cal·ly,** *adv.*

**ob·ste·tri·cian** (ob′stə-trish′ən), *n.* a doctor who specializes in obstetrics.

**ob·stet·rics** (ob-stet′riks, əb-), *n.pl.* [construed as sing.], the branch of medicine concerned with the care and treatment of women in pregnancy, childbirth, and the period immediately following.

**ob·sti·na·cy** (ob′sti-nə-si), *n.* 1. the state or quality of being obstinate; stubbornness. 2. [*pl.* -CIES], an instance of this. Also **ob′sti·nance.**

**ob·sti·nate** (ob′sti-nit), *adj.* [< L. pp. of *obstinare,* to resolve on < *ob-* (see OB-) + *stare,* to stand], 1. unreasonably determined to have one's own way; stubborn; dogged. 2. resisting treatment: as, an *obstinate* fever. 3. not easily subdued, ended, etc. —**ob′sti·nate·ly,** *adv.* —**ob′sti·nate·ness,** *n.*

**ob·strep·er·ous** (əb-strep′ẽr-əs, ob-), *adj.* [< L.; ult. < *ob-* (see OB-) + *strepere,* to make a noise, roar], noisy, boisterous, or unruly, especially in resisting or opposing. —**ob·strep′er·ous·ly,** *adv.* —**ob·strep′er·ous·ness,** *n.*

**ob·struct** (əb-strukt′, ob-), *v.t.* [< L. *obstructus,* pp.; ult. < *ob-* (see OB-) + *struere,* to pile up], 1. to block (a passage) with obstacles; bar. 2. to hinder (progress, an activity, etc.); impede; hamper. 3. *a*) to get in the way of. *b*) to block (the view). —**ob·struct′er, ob·struct′or,** *n.* —**ob·struct′ing·ly,** *adv.* —**ob·struc′tive,** *adj.* —**ob·struc′tive·ly,** *adv.* —**ob·struc′tive·ness,** *n.*

**ob·struc·tion** (əb-struk′shən, ob-), *n.* 1. an obstructing or being obstructed. 2. anything that obstructs; hindrance; obstacle.

**ob·struc·tion·ist** (əb-struk′shən-ist, ob-), *n.* one who obstructs progress; esp., a member of a legislature who hinders legislation by technical maneuvers. *adj.* of obstructionists. —**ob·struc′tion·ism,** *n.*

**ob·tain** (əb-tān′, ob-), *v.t.* [< OFr. < L. < *ob-* (see OB-) + *tenere,* to hold], to get possession of by trying; procure. *v.i.* to be in force or in general usage; prevail: as, peace will *obtain.* —**ob·tain′a·ble,** *adj.* —**ob·tain′er,** *n.* —**ob·tain′ment,** *n.*

**ob·trude** (əb-trōōd′, ob-), *v.t.* [-TRUDED, -TRUDING], [< L. < *ob-* (see OB-) + *trudere,* to thrust], 1. to thrust forward; push out; eject. 2. to force (oneself, one's opinions, etc.) upon others without being asked or wanted. *v.i.* to obtrude oneself (*on* or *upon*). —**ob·trud′er,** *n.* —**ob·tru′sion,** *n.*

**ob·tru·sive** (əb-trōō′siv, ob-), *adj.* 1. inclined to obtrude. 2. obtruding itself. —**ob·tru′sive·ly,** *adv.* —**ob·tru′sive·ness,** *n.*

**ob·tuse** (əb-to͞os′, ob-tūs′), *adj.* [< L. pp. of *obtundere*, to blunt < *ob-* (see OB-) + *tundere*, to strike], 1. not sharp or pointed; blunt. 2. greater than 90 degrees: said of an angle. 3. slow to understand or perceive; insensitive. 4. not acute; dull, as pain, etc. —**ob·tuse′ly,** *adv.* —**ob·tuse′ness, ob·tu′si·ty,** *n.*

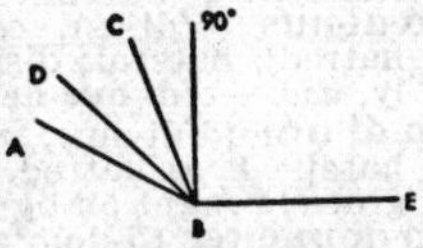

OBTUSE ANGLES (ABE, DBE, CBE)

**ob·verse** (əb-vũrs′; *also, & for n. always,* ob′vẽrs), *adj.* [L. *obversus*, pp.; ult. < *ob-* (see OB-) + *vertere*, to turn], 1. turned toward the observer: opposed to *reverse*. 2. narrower at the base than at the top: as, an *obverse* leaf. 3. forming a counterpart. *n.* 1. the side, as of a coin or medal, bearing the main design. 2. the front or main surface of anything. 3. a counterpart. —**ob·verse′ly,** *adv.*

**ob·vi·ate** (ob′vi-āt′), *v.t.* [-ATED, -ATING], [< L. *obviatus*, pp. < *obvius;* see OBVIOUS], to do away with or prevent by effective measures; make unnecessary. —**ob′vi·a′tion,** *n.* —**ob′vi·a′tor,** *n.*

**ob·vi·ous** (ob′vi-əs), *adj.* [L. *obvius*, in the way; see OB- & VIA], easy to see or understand; evident. —**ob′vi·ous·ly,** *adv.* —**ob′vi·ous·ness,** *n.*

**oc-,** ob-: used before *c*, as in *occur*.

**Oc., oc.,** ocean.

**oc·a·ri·na** (ok′ə-rē′nə), *n.* [It., dim. of *oca* (< L. *auca*), a goose: from its shape], a small, simple wind instrument with finger holes and a mouthpiece: it produces soft, hollow tones.

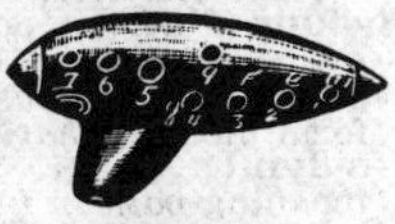
OCARINA

**O'Ca·sey, Sean** (shôn ō-kā′si), 1880–1964; Irish dramatist.

**occas.,** 1. occasion. 2. occasional. 3. occasionally.

**oc·ca·sion** (ə-kā′zhən), *n.* [< OFr. < L. < pp. of *occidere* < *ob-* (see OB-) + *cadere*, to fall], 1. a favorable time; opportunity. 2. a fact or event that is the immediate cause of something. 3. *a)* a happening; occurrence. *b)* a particular time: as, on the *occasion* of our last meeting. 4. a special time or event. 5. need arising from circumstances. *v.t.* to give occasion to; cause. —**on occasion,** once in a while; sometimes. —**rise to the occasion,** to meet an emergency. —**take occasion,** to choose a favorable time.

**oc·ca·sion·al** (ə-kā′zhən-'l), *adj.* 1. occurring on a particular occasion. 2. of or for a special occasion. 3. acting only on special occasions. 4. happening now and then; infrequent. —**oc·ca′sion·al·ly,** *adv.*

**oc·ci·dent** (ok′sə-dənt), *n.* [< L. *occidens*, direction of the setting sun < *occidere*, to fall], 1. [Poetic], the west. 2. [O-], the countries west of Asia; specif., *a)* formerly, Europe. *b)* now, also, the Western Hemisphere. Opposed to *orient*. —**oc′ci·den′tal, Oc′ci·den′tal,** *adj. & n.*

**oc·cip·i·tal** (ok-sip′ə-t'l), *adj.* of the occiput or the occipital bone. *n.* the occipital bone. —**oc·cip′i·tal·ly,** *adv.*

**occipital bone,** the bone that forms the back part of the skull.

**oc·ci·put** (ok′si-put′), *n.* [*pl.* OCCIPITA (ok-sip′ə-tə)], [L. < *ob-* (see OB-) + *caput*, head], the back part of the skull or head.

**oc·clude** (ə-klo͞od′), *v.t.* [-CLUDED, -CLUDING], [< L. < *ob-* (see OB-) + *claudere*, to shut], 1. to close or block (a passage). 2. to shut in or out. 3. in *chemistry*, to absorb (a gas or liquid): as, palladium *occludes* hydrogen. *v.i.* in *dentistry*, to meet with the cusps fitting closely. —**oc·clud′ing·ly,** *adv.* —**oc·clu′sion** (-klo͞o′zhən), *n.* —**oc·clu′sive,** *adj.* —**oc·clu′sive·ly,** *adv.*

**oc·cult** (ə-kult′, ok′ult), *adj.* [< L. pp. of *occulere*, to conceal], 1. hidden. 2. secret; esoteric. 3. beyond human understanding; mysterious. 4. designating or of such mystic studies as alchemy, astrology, etc. *v.t. & v.i.* to hide or become hidden. —**the occult,** anything occult. —**oc·cult′ism,** *n.* —**oc·cult′ist,** *n.* —**oc·cult′ly,** *adv.* —**oc·cult′ness,** *n.*

**oc·cul·ta·tion** (ok′ul-tā′shən), *n.* 1. concealment. 2. in *astronomy*, the disappearance of one heavenly body behind another.

**oc·cu·pan·cy** (ok′yoo-pən-si), *n.* [*pl.* -CIES], 1. an occupying; a taking or keeping in possession. 2. in *law*, the taking possession of a previously unowned object.

**oc·cu·pant** (ok′yoo-pənt), *n.* 1. one who occupies. 2. one who acquires possession by occupancy.

**oc·cu·pa·tion** (ok′yoo-pā′shən), *n.* 1. an occupying or being occupied. 2. what occupies, or engages, one's time; business; employment; vocation. —**oc′cu·pa′tion·al,** *adj.* —**oc′cu·pa′tion·al·ly,** *adv.*

**occupational disease,** a disease commonly acquired by people in a particular occupation: as, silicosis is an *occupational disease* of miners.

**occupational therapy,** the treatment of mental or physical ailments by work designed to divert the mind or to correct a physical defect.

**oc·cu·py** (ok′yoo-pi′), *v.t.* [-PIED, -PYING], [< OFr. < L. *occupare*, to possess < *ob-* (see OB-) + *capere*, to seize], 1. to take possession of by settlement or seizure. 2. to hold possession of by tenure; specif., *a)* to dwell in. *b)* to hold (a position or office). 3. to take up or fill up (space, time, etc.). 4. to employ or busy (oneself, one's mind, etc.). —**oc′cu·pi′er,** *n.*

**oc·cur** (ə-kũr′), *v.i.* [-CURRED, -CURRING], [< L. < *ob-* (see OB-) + *currere*, to run], 1. to be or be met with; exist: as, fish *occur* in most waters. 2. to present itself; come to mind: as, an idea *occurred* to him. 3. to take place; happen.

**oc·cur·rence** (ə-kũr′əns), *n.* 1. the act or fact of occurring. 2. something that occurs; event; incident. —**oc·cur′rent,** *adj.*

**o·cean** (ō′shən), *n.* [< L. *oceanus* < Gr. *ōkeanos*], 1. the great body of salt water that covers more than two thirds of the earth's surface. 2. any of its five principal divisions; the Atlantic, Pacific, Indian, Arctic, or Antarctic Ocean. 3. a great expanse or quantity. —**o·ce·an·ic** (ō′shi-an′ik), *adj.* —**o′ce·an′i·cal·ly,** *adv.*

**O·ce·an·i·a** (ō′shi-an′i-ə), *n.* the islands in the Pacific, including Melanesia, Micronesia, and Polynesia, and sometimes New Zealand, Australia, and the Malay Archipelago: also **O′ce·an′i·ca** (-i-kə). —**O′ce·an′i·an,** *adj. & n.*

**o·ce·a·nog·ra·phy** (ō′shi-ə-nog′rə-fi, ō′shən-og′-), *n.* the branch of geography dealing with the ocean. —**o′ce·a·nog′ra·pher,** *n.* —**o·ce·a·no·graph·ic** (ō′shi-ən-ə-graf′ik, ō′shən-), **o′ce·a·no·graph′i·cal,** *adj.*

**o·cel·lus** (ō-sel′əs), *n.* [*pl.* -LI (-ī)], [L., dim. of *oculus*, an eye], a small eye; esp., the simple, or rudimentary, eye of certain invertebrates.

**o·ce·lot** (ō′sə-lot′, os′ə-lət), *n.* [*pl.* -LOTS, -LOT; see PLURAL, II, D, 1], [Fr.; contr. < Mex. *tlalocelotl* < *tlalli*, a field + *ocelotl*, jaguar], a large wild cat of North and South America, with a yellow or gray hide marked with black spots.

**OCelt.,** Old Celtic.

**o·cher** (ō′kẽr), *n.* [< L. < Gr. < *ōchros*, pale-yellow], 1. a yellow or reddish-brown clay containing iron, used as a pigment. 2. the color of ocher; esp., dark yellow. *v.t.* to color with ocher. —**o′cher·ous, o′cher·y,** *adj.*

**o·chre** (ō′kẽr), *n. & v.t.* [OCHRED, OCHRING], ocher. —**o·chre·ous** (ō′kẽr-əs, ō′kri-), **o·chry** (ō′kri), *adj.*

**-ock,** [AS. *-oc*, *-uc*, dim.], a suffix used originally to form the diminutive, as in *hillock*.

**o'clock** (ə-klok′, ō-), of or according to the clock.

**Oct.,** October.

**oct.,** octavo.

**oc·ta-,** [Gr. *okta-* < *oktō*], a combining form meaning *eight*, as in *octagon*: also **octo-, oct-.**

**oc·ta·gon** (ok′tə-gon′, -gən), *n.* [< L. < Gr. < *okta-*, eight + *gōnia*, an angle], a plane figure with eight angles and eight sides. —**oc·tag′o·nal** (-tag′ə-n'l), *adj.* —**oc·tag′o·nal·ly,** *adv.*

**oc·ta·he·dron** (ok′tə-hē′drən), *n.* [*pl.* -DRONS, -DRA (-drə)], [< Gr.; see OCTA- & -HEDRON], a solid figure with eight plane surfaces. —**oc′ta·he′dral,** *adj.*

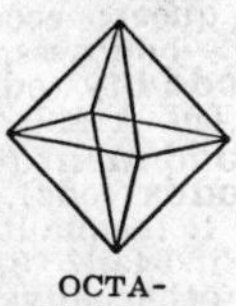
OCTAHEDRON

**oc·tane** (ok′tān), *n.* [*oct-* + *-ane*], an oily hydrocarbon, $C_8H_{18}$, occurring in petroleum.

**octane number** (or **rating**), a number representing the antiknock quality of a gasoline, etc: the higher the number, the greater this quality.

**oc·tave** (ok′tāv, ok′tiv), *n.* [< L. *octavus*, eighth < *octo*, eight], 1. *a)* the eighth day inclusive following a church festival. *b)* the entire period including the festival and this day. 2. the first eight lines of a sonnet: also called *octet*. 3. any group of eight. 4. in *music*, *a)* the eighth full tone above or below a given tone. *b)* the interval of eight diatonic degrees between a tone and either of its octaves. *c)* the series of tones (a full scale) within this interval, or the keys of an instrument producing such a series. *d)* a tone and either of its octaves sounded together. *adj.* consisting of eight, or an octave. —**oc·ta·val** (ok-tā′v'l, ok′ti-), *adj.*

**Oc·ta·vi·an** (ok-tā′vi-ən), *n.* see **Augustus.**
**oc·ta·vo** (ok-tā′vō, -tä′-), *n.* [*pl.* -vos], [< L. *in octavo*, in eight], 1. the page size (from 5 by 8 to 6 by 9½ inches) of a book made up of printer's sheets folded into eight leaves. 2. a book consisting of pages of this size: also written *8vo* or *8°*. *adj.* consisting of pages of this size.
**oc·tet, oc·tette** (ok-tet′), *n.* [< L. *octo*, eight; + du*et*], 1. any group of eight; esp., an octave (sense 2). 2. in *music*, *a*) a composition for eight voices or eight instruments. *b*) the eight performers of this.
**oc·to-,** [Gr. *oktō-* < *oktō*, eight], a combining form meaning *eight*: also **octa-, oct-.**
**Oc·to·ber** (ok-tō′bẽr), *n.* [AS. < L. < *octo*, eight: it was the eighth month to the early Romans], the tenth month of the year, having 31 days: abbrev. **Oct., O.**
**oc·to·dec·i·mo** (ok′tō-des′ə-mō′), *n.* [*pl.* -mos], [< L. *in octodecimo*, in eighteen], 1. the page size (about 4 by 6¼ inches) of a book made up of printer's sheets folded into eighteen leaves. 2. a book consisting of pages of this size: also called *eighteenmo*, and written *18mo* or *18°*. *adj.* consisting of pages of this size.
**oc·to·ge·nar·i·an** (ok′tə-ji-nâr′i-ən), *adj.* [< L. < *octoginta*, eighty], eighty years old, or between the ages of eighty and ninety. *n.* a person of this age. **—oc·tog·e·nar·y** (ok-toj′ə-ner′i), *adj.* & *n.* [*pl.* -ies].
**oc·to·pus** (ok′tə-pəs), *n.* [*p.* -puses, -podes (ok-top′ə-dēz′), -pi (-pī′)], [< Gr. < *oktō*, eight + *pous*, a foot], 1. a mollusk with a soft body and eight arms covered with suckers. 2. anything suggesting an octopus; esp., an organization with branches that reach out in a powerful and influential manner.
**oc·to·roon** (ok′tə-rōōn′), *n.* [*octo-* + quad*roon*], the offspring of a white and a quadroon.
**oc·tu·ple** (ok′too-p'l, -tyoo-), *adj.* [< L. < *octo*, eight + *plicare*, to fold], eightfold. *n.* something eight times as great as something else. *v.t.* [-pled, -pling], to multiply by eight. **—oc′tu·ply,** *adv.*
**oc·u·lar** (ok′yoo-lẽr), *adj.* [< L. < *oculus*, the eye], 1. of, for, or like the eye. 2. by eyesight: as, an *ocular* demonstration. *n.* the lens or lenses constituting the eyepiece of an optical instrument. **—oc′u·lar·ly,** *adv.*
**oc·u·list** (ok′yoo-list), *n.* [< Fr. < L. *oculus*, the eye], a physician specializing in the treatment of diseases of the eye; ophthalmologist.
**O.D.,** Officer of the Day.
**O.D., OD.,** Old Dutch.
**O.D., o.d.,** 1. olive drab. 2. outside diameter.
**o·da·lisque, o·da·lisk** (ō′də-lisk′), *n.* [< Fr. < Turk. *ōdaliq*, chambermaid], a female slave or concubine in an Oriental harem.
**ODan.,** Old Danish.
**odd** (od), *adj.* [< ON. < *oddi*, triangle, hence (from the third angle) odd number], 1. being one of a pair of which the other is missing: as, an *odd* glove. 2. having a remainder of one when divided by two; not even: said of numbers. 3. characterized by an odd number: as, an *odd* month. 4. left over after taking a round number: as, *odd* change. 5. with a relatively small number over that specified: as, thirty *odd* years ago. 6. extra; occasional; incidental: as, *odd* jobs. 7. being one or more of a set or series separated from the others: as, a few *odd* volumes of Dickens. 8. *a*) singular; peculiar. *b*) queer; eccentric. **—odd′ish,** *adj.* **—odd′ly,** *adv.* **—odd′ness,** *n.*
**odd·i·ty** (od′ə-ti), *n.* 1. queerness; peculiarity. 2. [*pl.* -ties], an odd person or thing.
**odd·ment** (od′mənt), *n.* something left over; scrap.
**odds** (odz), *n.pl.* [sometimes construed as sing.], 1. inequalities. 2. difference: as, what's the *odds* if I fail? 3. difference in favor of one side over the other; advantage. 4. advantage given to a bettor or competitor in proportion to the assumed chances against him. **—at odds,** in disagreement; quarreling. **—by (all) odds,** by far. **—the odds are,** the likelihood is; the chances are.
**odds and ends,** scraps; remnants.
**ode** (ōd), *n.* [Fr. < LL. < Gr. *ōidē*, song < *aeidein*, to sing], a lyric poem usually addressed to some person or thing and characterized by lofty feeling and dignified style. **—od′ic,** *adj.*
**-ode,** [< Gr. *hodos*], a suffix meaning *way, path.*
**O·der** (ō′dẽr), *n.* a river forming part of the boundary between Poland and Germany, flowing into the Baltic Sea.
**O·des·sa** (ō-des′ə, ə-), *n.* 1. a city in the Ukrainian S.S.R., on the Black Sea: pop., 667,000. 2. a city in west central Texas: pop., 80,000.
**O·din** (ō′din), *n.* in *Norse mythology*, the supreme deity, god of art, culture, war, and the dead: identified with the Teutonic Woden.
**o·di·ous** (ō′di-əs), *adj.* [< OFr. < L. < *odium*, hatred], hateful; disgusting; offensive. **—o′di·ous·ly,** *adv.* **—o′di·ous·ness,** *n.*
**o·di·um** (ō′di-əm), *n.* [L. *odium*, hatred < *odi*, I hate], 1. *a*) hatred. *b*) a being hated. 2. the disgrace brought on by hateful action; opprobrium.
**o·dom·e·ter** (ō-dom′ə-tẽr), *n.* [< Gr. < *hodos*, way + *metron*, a measure], an instrument for measuring distance traveled, as by an automobile.
**-o·dont** (ə-dont′), [< Gr. *odōn*], a combining form meaning *tooth.*
**o·dont·o-,** [< Gr. *odōn*], a combining form meaning *tooth* or *teeth*: also **odont-.**
**o·don·tol·o·gy** (ō′don-tol′ə-ji), *n.* [*odonto-* + *-logy*], the science dealing with the structure, growth, and diseases of the teeth. **—o·don·to·log·i·cal** (ō-don′tə-loj′i-k'l), *adj.*
**o·dor** (ō′dẽr), *n.* [ME. via OFr. < L.], 1. a smell, whether pleasant or unpleasant; scent; aroma. 2. a perfume. **—be in bad (or ill) odor,** to be in ill repute. **—o′dored,** *adj.* **—o′dor·less,** *adj.*
**o·dor·if·er·ous** (ō′də-rif′ẽr-əs), *adj.* [< L. < *odor*, odor + *ferre*, to bear], giving off an odor, especially a fragrant odor. **—o′dor·if′er·ous·ly,** *adv.* **—o′dor·if′er·ous·ness,** *n.*
**o·dor·ous** (ō′dẽr-əs), *adj.* having an odor; esp., sweet-smelling; fragrant. **—o′dor·ous·ly,** *adv.* **—o′dor·ous·ness,** *n.*
**o·dour** (ō′dẽr), *n.* odor: British spelling. **—o′doured,** *adj.* **—o′dour·less,** *adj.*
**-o·dus,** [Gr. *-odous* < *odōn*, tooth], a combining form meaning *having teeth, toothed.*
**-o·dyn·i·a,** [< Gr. < *odynē*, pain], a combining form meaning *pain in* (a specified organ or part).
**O·dys·seus** (ō-dis′ūs, -i-əs), *n.* the hero of the *Odyssey*, a king of Ithaca and one of the Greek leaders in the Trojan War; Ulysses.
**Od·ys·sey** (od′ə-si), *n.* 1. an ancient Greek epic poem, generally attributed to Homer, describing the wanderings of Odysseus during the ten years after the fall of Troy. 2. [sometimes o-], [*pl.* -seys (-sēz′)], any extended wandering or journey.
**oe-** (ē), e-: most words beginning with *oe-* are now more commonly written with *e-*.
**OE., O.E.,** Old English (Anglo-Saxon).
**oec·u·men·i·cal** (ek′yoo-men′i-k'l, ē′kyoo-), *adj.* ecumenical: also **oec′u·men′ic. —oec′u·men′i·cal·ly,** *adv.*
**O.E.D., OED,** Oxford English Dictionary.
**Oed·i·pus** (ed′ə-pəs, ē′də-), *n.* in *Gr. legend*, a king of Thebes who unwittingly killed his father and married his mother.
**Oedipus complex,** in *psychoanalysis*, the unconscious tendency of a child, sometimes unresolved in adulthood, to be attached to the parent of the opposite sex and hostile toward the other parent.
**o'er** (ôr, ōr), *prep.* & *adv.* [Poetic], over.
**oe·soph·a·gus** (i-sof′ə-gəs), *n.* esophagus.
**oes·trus** (es′trəs, ēs′-), *n.* estrus.
**of** (uv, ov; *unstressed* əv), *prep.* [AS., unstressed var. of *af*, *æf*, away (from)], 1. from; specif., *a*) derived or coming from: as, men *of* Ohio. *b*) resulting from; through: as, he died *of* starvation. *c*) at a distance from: as, a mile east *of* the river. *d*) proceeding as a product from; by: as, the stories *of* Poe. *e*) separated from: as, robbed *of* his money. *f*) from the whole constituting: as, he gave *of* his time. *g*) made from: as, a house *of* wood. 2. belonging to: as, the leaves *of* the book. 3. *a*) possessing: as, a man *of* property. *b*) containing: as, a bag *of* peanuts. 4. specified as: as, a height *of* six feet. 5. with (something specified) as object, goal, etc.: as, a reader *of* books. 6. characterized by: as, a man *of* honor. 7. having to do with; concerning: as, don't think ill *of* me. 8. set aside for: as, a week *of* festivities. 9. during: as, *of* recent years. 10. before: used in telling time, as, ten *of* twelve. *Of* is also used in various idiomatic expressions, many of which are entered in this dictionary under the key words.
**of-,** ob-: used before *f*, as in *offer.*
**OF., O.F.,** Old French.
**off** (ôf), *adv.* [ME. variant of *of*], 1. so as to be away, at a distance, etc.: as, move *off* toward the door. 2. so as to be no longer on, attached, etc.: as, take *off* his coat. 3. (a specified distance) away in space or time: as, 200 yards *off*, two weeks *off*. 4. so as to be no longer in operation, function, etc.: as, turn the motor *off*. 5. so as to be less, smaller, etc.: as, production dropped *off*. 6. away from one's work: as, take the day *off*. *prep.* 1. no longer (or not) on, attached, etc.: as, the car is *off* the road. 2. from the substance of; on: as, to live *off* the land. 3. branching out from: as, a

lane *off* the main road. 4. free or relieved from: as, *off* duty. 5. not up to the usual level, standard, etc. of: as, *off* one's game. 6. [Colloq.], no longer using, supporting, etc.: as, he's *off* liquor for life. 7. in *nautical usage*, away from (shore): as, a mile *off* the coast. ***adj.*** 1. not on, attached, etc.: as, his hat is *off*. 2. not in operation, function, etc.: as, the motor is *off*. 3. on the way: as, he is *off* to school. 4. away from work, etc.: as, the office force is *off* today. 5. not up to the usual level, standard, etc.: as, an *off* season. 6. more remote; further: as, on the *off* chance. 7. on the right: said of a horse in double harness, etc. 8. in (specified) circumstances: as, they are well *off*. 9. wrong; in error: as, you are *off* by a cent. 10. in *nautical usage*, toward the sea. ***interj.*** go away! stay away! —**be** (or **take**) **off,** to go away; depart. —**off and on,** now and then. —**off with,** take off! remove! —**off with you!** go away! depart!

**off.,** 1. office. 2. officer. 3. official.

**of·fal** (ôf′'l, of′-), ***n.*** [ME. *ofall*, lit., off-fall], 1. [construed as sing. or pl.], the entrails, etc. of a butchered animal. 2. rubbish; refuse; garbage.

**off·beat** (ôf′bēt′), ***adj.*** [< a rhythm in jazz music], [Colloq.], not conforming to the usual pattern or trend; unconventional, unusual, etc.

**off-col·or** (ôf′kul′ẽr), ***adj.*** 1. varying from the usual or standard color. 2. not quite proper; risqué: as, an *off-color* joke.

**of·fence** (ə-fens′), ***n.*** offense: Brit. spelling. —**of·fence′less,** ***adj.*** —**of·fence′less·ly,** ***adv.***

**of·fend** (ə-fend′), ***v.i.*** [< OFr. < L. < *ob-* (see OB-) + OL. *fendere*, to hit], 1. to commit an offense; sin. 2. to create resentment, anger, etc. ***v.t.*** 1. to hurt the feelings of; make resentful, angry, etc. 2. to be displeasing to (the taste, sense, etc.). —**of·fend′er,** ***n.*** —**of·fend′ing·ly,** ***adv.***

**of·fense** (ə-fens′), ***n.*** 1. an offending; specif., *a*) a breaking of the law; sin; crime. *b*) a creating of resentment, anger, etc. 2. a being offended; esp., a feeling hurt, resentful, or angry. 3. something that causes wrongdoing. 4. something that causes resentment, anger, etc. 5. the act of attacking. 6. the person, team, army, etc. that is attacking. —**give offense,** to offend; anger, insult, etc. —**take offense,** to become offended; feel hurt, angry, etc. —**of·fense′less,** ***adj.*** —**of·fense′less·ly,** ***adv.***

**of·fen·sive** (ə-fen′siv), ***adj.*** 1. attacking. 2. of or for attack. 3. unpleasant; disgusting; revolting: as, an *offensive* odor. 4. causing resentment, anger, etc.; insulting. ***n.*** attitude, position, or operation of attack. —**of·fen′sive·ly,** ***adv.*** —**of·fen′sive·ness,** ***n.***

**of·fer** (ôf′ẽr, of′-), ***v.t.*** [AS. *offrian* < L. < *ob-* (see OB-) + *ferre*, to bring], 1. to present to God or a god in an act of worship: as, to *offer* prayers. 2. to present for acceptance: as, I *offered* my services. 3. to present for consideration; suggest; propose. 4. to indicate intention of: as, they *offered* resistance. 5. to bid (a price, etc.). ***v.i.*** 1. to make a presentation in worship. 2. to occur; present itself: as, opportunity *offered*. ***n.*** the act of offering or thing offered. —**of′fer·er, of′fer·or,** ***n.***

**of·fer·ing** (ôf′ẽr-iŋ, of′-), ***n.*** 1. the act of making an offer. 2. something offered; specif., *a*) a contribution. *b*) presentation in worship; sacrifice.

**of·fer·to·ry** (ôf′ẽr-tôr′i, of′ẽr-tō′ri), ***n.*** [*pl.* -RIES], [< OFr. < LL. *offertorium*, place for offerings], 1. that part of the Eucharist during which the unconsecrated bread and wine are offered to God. 2. the prayers recited or hymn sung at this time. 3. money collected at a church service or a hymn sung during the collection.

**off·hand** (ôf′hand′), ***adv.*** without prior preparation; extemporaneously. ***adj.*** 1. said or done offhand; extemporary. 2. casual, curt, etc. Also **off′hand′ed,** ***adj.*** —**off′hand′ed·ly,** ***adv.*** —**off′hand′ed·ness,** ***n.***

**of·fice** (ôf′is, of′-), ***n.*** [< OFr. < L. *officium;* prob. < *opus*, a work + *facere*, to make], 1. something done for another; (specified kind of) service: as, this was done through his good (or ill) *offices*. 2. an assigned duty, especially as an essential part of one's work. 3. a position of authority or trust, especially in a government, corporation, etc. 4. any of the branches of the U.S. Government ranking next below the departments: as, the Printing *Office*. 5. *a*) the room or rooms in which the affairs of a business, professional person, etc. are carried on. *b*) the people working in such a place; staff. 6. a religious or social ceremony, as *a*) the daily service of the Roman Catholic breviary: also **Divine Office.** *b*) the service of Holy Communion. *c*) any special rites: as, the *Office* of the Dead.

**office boy,** a boy doing small tasks in an office.

**of·fice·hold·er** (ôf′is-hōl′dẽr, of′-), ***n.*** a person holding an office; esp., a government official.

**of·fi·cer** (ôf′ə-sẽr, of′-), ***n.*** 1. anyone holding an office, or position of authority, in a government, business, club, etc. 2. a policeman. 3. a person holding a position of authority in the armed forces; esp., a commissioned officer. 4. the captain or any of the mates of a ship. ***v.t.*** 1. to provide with officers. 2. to command; direct. —**of′fi·cer·ship′,** ***n.***

**officer of the day,** the military officer in over-all charge of the interior guard and security of his garrison for any given day.

**of·fi·cial** (ə-fish′əl), ***adj.*** 1. of or holding an office, or position of authority. 2. coming from the proper authority; authorized: as, an *official* ruling. 3. formal; ceremonious. ***n.*** a person holding office. —**of·fi′cial·ly,** ***adv.***

**of·fi·cial·dom** (ə-fish′əl-dəm), ***n.*** 1. officials collectively. 2. excessive adherence to official routine; red tape. 3. the domain or position of officials. Also, in senses 1 & 2, **of·fi′cial·ism.**

**of·fi·ci·ate** (ə-fish′i-āt′), ***v.i.*** [-ATED, -ATING], 1. to perform the duties of an office. 2. to perform the functions of a priest, minister, etc. —**of·fi′ci·a′tion,** ***n.*** —**of·fi′ci·a′tor,** ***n.***

**of·fic·i·nal** (ə-fis′i-n'l), ***adj.*** [< ML. < L. *officina*, workshop; ult. < *opus*, a work + *facere*, to do], authorized and kept in stock in a pharmacy: said of drugs, etc. ***n.*** an officinal drug, etc.

**of·fi·cious** (ə-fish′əs), ***adj.*** [< L. *officiosus;* see OFFICE], offering unwanted advice or services; meddlesome. —**of·fi′cious·ly,** ***adv.*** —**of·fi′cious·ness,** ***n.***

**of·fing** (ôf′iŋ), ***n.*** [< *off*], 1. the distant part of the sea visible from the shore. 2. distance, or position at a distance, from the shore. —**in the offing,** 1. barely visible from shore. 2. far but in sight. 3. at some vague future time.

**off·ish** (ôf′ish), ***adj.*** [Colloq.], inclined to remain aloof. —**off′ish·ly,** ***adv.*** —**off′ish·ness,** ***n.***

**off·scour·ing** (ôf′skour′iŋ), ***n.*** *usually pl.* something scoured off; refuse; rubbish; filth.

**off·set** (ôf′set′; *for v.*, ôf-set′), ***n.*** 1. an offshoot; branch; spur; extension. 2. anything that balances or compensates for something else. 3. a ledge formed in a wall by a reduction in its thickness above. 4. in *mechanics*, a bend in a pipe, etc. to permit it to pass an obstruction. 5. *a*) offset printing. *b*) an impression made by this process. ***v.t.*** [-SET, -SETTING], 1. to balance, compensate for, etc. 2. to make an offset in. 3. to make (an impression) by offset printing. ***v.i.*** to project or develop as an offset.

**offset printing,** a printing process in which the inked impression is first made on a rubber-covered roller, then transferred to paper.

**off·shoot** (ôf′shōōt′), ***n.*** anything that derives from a main source; specif., a shoot or stem growing from the main stem of a plant.

**off·shore** (ôf′shôr′, -shōr′), ***adj.*** 1. moving away from the shore. 2. at some distance from the shore. ***adv.*** away from the shore; seaward.

**off·side** (ôf′sīd′), ***adj.*** not in the proper position for play, as, in football, ahead of the ball before play has begun. ***n.*** an offside play. Also **off side.**

**off·spring** (ôf′spriŋ′), ***n.*** [sometimes construed as pl.], 1. a child or children; descendant or descendants; issue. 2. a product; result.

**off-stage** (ôf′stāj′), ***n.*** that part of a stage not seen by the audience. ***adj.*** in or from the off-stage. ***adv.*** to the off-stage.

**OFr.,** Old French.

**oft** (ôft), ***adv.*** [AS.], [Rare or Poetic], often.

**of·ten** (ôf′'n; *frequently* ôf′t'n), ***adv.*** [ME. var. of *oft(e)*], many times; frequently: also **oft′en·times′, oft′times′.** ***adj.*** [Archaic], frequent.

**Og·den** (og′dən, ôg′-), ***n.*** a city in N Utah: pop., 70,000.

**o·gee** (ō-jē′, ō′jē), ***n.*** [< OFr. *ogive*], 1. an S-shaped curve, line, molding, etc. 2. a pointed arch formed with the curve of an ogee on each side: also **ogee arch.**

OGEE ARCH

**o·gle** (ō′g'l), ***v.i.*** & ***v.t.*** [OGLED, OGLING], [prob. < LG. *oegeln* < *oog*, the eye], to keep looking (at) with fondness or desire; make eyes (at). ***n.*** an ogling look. —**o′gler,** ***n.***

**o·gre** (ō′gẽr), ***n.*** [Fr.] 1. in fairy tales and folklore, a man-eating monster or giant. 2. a hideous or cruel man. —**o′gre·ish, o′grish** (ō′grish), ***adj.*** —**o′gress** (-gris), ***n.fem.***

**oh** (ō), *interj.* an exclamation of surprise, fear, wonder, pain, etc. *n.* [*pl.* OH'S, OHS], any instance of this exclamation. Also **O.**
**O. Henry,** see **Henry, O.**
**OHG., O.H.G.,** Old High German.
**O·hi·o** (ō-hī'ō), *n.* 1. a Middle Western State of the U.S.: area, 41,222 sq. mi.; pop., 9,706,000; capital, Columbus. 2. a river flowing southwest from W Pennsylvania into the Mississippi. **—O·hi'o·an,** *adj. & n.*
**ohm** (ōm), *n.* [after G. S. *Ohm* (1787–1854), G. physicist], the unit of electrical resistance, equal to the resistance of a circuit in which an electromotive force of one volt maintains a current of one ampere. **—ohm'age,** *n.* **—ohm'ic,** *adj.*
**ohm·me·ter** (ōm'mē'tẽr), *n.* an instrument for measuring electrical resistance in ohms.
**-oid** (oid), [< Gr. < *eidos*, a form, shape], a suffix meaning *like, resembling*, as in *anthropoid.*
**oil** (oil), *n.* [< OFr. < L. *oleum*], 1. any of various greasy, combustible substances obtained from animal, vegetable, and mineral matter: oils are liquid at ordinary temperatures and soluble in certain organic solvents, as ether, but not in water. 2. petroleum. 3. any of various substances with the consistency of oil. 4. an oil color. 5. an oil painting. *v.t.* 1. to lubricate or supply with oil. 2. to bribe. *v.i.* to turn into oil by melting. *adj.* of, from, or like oil, or having to do with the production or use of oil. **—oil'er,** *n.*
**oil cake,** a mass of crushed linseed, cottonseed, etc. from which the oil has been extracted: it is used as feed for cattle and as a fertilizer.
**oil·cloth** (oil'klôth'), *n.* cloth made waterproof by being coated with paint or treated with oil.
**oil color,** paint made by grinding a pigment in oil.
**oil of vitriol,** sulfuric acid.
**oil painting,** 1. a picture painted in oil colors. 2. the art of painting in oil colors.
**oil·pa·per** (oil'pā'pẽr), *n.* paper made transparent and waterproof by treatment with oil.
**oil·skin** (oil'skin'), *n.* 1. cloth made waterproof by treatment with oil. 2. *often in pl.* a garment made of this.
**oil·stone** (oil'stōn'), *n.* a whetstone used with oil.
**oil well,** a well bored through layers of rock, etc. to a supply of petroleum.
**oil·y** (oil'i), *adj.* [-IER, -IEST], 1. of, like, or containing oil. 2. covered with oil; greasy. 3. too suave or smooth; unctuous. **—oil'i·ly,** *adv.* **—oil'i·ness,** *n.*
**oint·ment** (oint'mənt), *n.* [< OFr.; ult. < L. *unguentum;* see UNGUENT], a fatty substance applied to the skin as a salve or cosmetic; unguent.
**Oise** (wȧz), *n.* a river in Belgium and France, flowing into the Seine.
**O·jib·wa** (ō-jib'wā), *adj. & n.* [*pl.* -WA, -WAS], Ojibway.
**O·jib·way** (ō-jib'wā), *n.* [*pl.* -WAY, -WAYS], 1. a member of a tribe of Algonquian Indians who lived in an area between western Lake Erie and North Dakota. 2. their language. *adj.* of this tribe. Also called *Chippewa.*
**O.K., OK** (ō'kā'; *for the v.*, ō'kā'), *adj., adv., interj.* [prob. from Democratic *O.K.* Club < *O(ld) K(inderhook)*, birthplace of Martin Van Buren, whom the Club supported], all right; correct. *n.* approval. *v.t.* [O.K.'D, OK'D, O.K.'ING, OK'ING], to put an O.K. on; approve. Also sp. **okay.**
**o·ka·pi** (ō-kä'pi), *n.* [*pl.* -PIS, -PI; see PLURAL, II, D, 1], [native name], an African animal related to the giraffe, but having a short neck.
**o·kay** (ō'kā'; *for the v.*, ō'kā'), *adj., adv., interj., n., v.t.* [Colloq.], O.K.
**O·khotsk, Sea of** (ō-kotsk'; Russ. ô-khôtsk'), an arm of the Pacific, east of Siberia.
**O·kie** (ō'ki), *n.* a migratory farm worker, especially one forced from Oklahoma by drought, farm foreclosure, etc., in the late 1930's.
**O·ki·na·wa** (ō'ki-nä'wä), *n.* one of the Ryukyu Islands, in the North Pacific.
**O·kla·ho·ma** (ō'klə-hō'mə), *n.* a Southern State of the U.S.: area, 69,919 sq. mi.; pop., 2,328,000; capital, Oklahoma City: abbrev. **Okla. —O'kla·ho'man,** *adj. & n.*
**Oklahoma City,** the capital of Oklahoma: pop., 324,000.
**o·kra** (ō'krə), *n.* [< W. Afr. name], 1. a tall plant with sticky green pods, used in soups, stews, etc. 2. the pod of this plant. Also called *gumbo.*
**-ol** (ōl, ol), a suffix used in chemistry to mean: 1. [< alcohol], *an alcohol* or *phenol*, as in *menthol, thymol.* 2. [< L. *oleum*, oil], *-ole.*
**OL., O.L.,** Old Latin.
**old** (ōld), *adj.* [OLDER OR ELDER, OLDEST OR ELDEST], [AS. *ald*], 1. having lived or existed for a long time; aged. 2. of or characteristic of aged people. 3. of a certain age: as, he's five years *old.* 4. made some time ago; not new. 5. worn out by age or use; shabby. 6. former; quondam. 7. experienced: as, an *old* hand. 8. having existed long ago; ancient: as, an *old* civilization. 9. of long standing: as, an *old* joke. 10. designating the earlier or earliest of two or more: as, the *Old* Testament. 11. [Colloq.], dear: a familiar term of cordiality, as, *old* boy. 12. [Colloq.], good; fine; excellent: as, a gay *old* time. *n.* 1. time long past; yore: as, days of *old.* 2. a person of a specified age: used in hyphenated compounds, as a *six-year-old.* **—the old,** old people. **—old'ish,** *adj.* **—old'ness,** *n.*
**old age,** the advanced years of life, when strength and vigor decline: cf. **middle age.**
**Old Celtic,** any of the Celtic languages supposedly spoken at the close of the 4th century A.D.
**old country,** the country from which an immigrant came, especially a country in Europe.
**old·en** (ōl'd'n), *adj.* [Poetic], (of) old; ancient.
**Old English,** 1. the West Germanic, Low German language of the Anglo-Saxons, spoken in England from the 5th century A.D. until shortly after the Norman Conquest (1066); Anglo-Saxon. 2. a style of black letter.
**old-fash·ioned** (ōld'fash'ənd), *adj.* in accordance with or favoring the methods, ideas, etc. of past times; out-of-date. *n.* [also O-F-], a cocktail made with whisky, a dash of soda, bitters, sugar, and fruit.
**old fogy, old fogey,** an old-fashioned or overly conservative person. **—old'-fo'gy, old'-fo'gey,** or **old'-fo'gy·ish, old'-fo'gey·ish,** *adj.*
**Old French,** the French language as spoken from the 9th century A.D. to the 16th.
**Old Frisian,** a West Germanic language spoken from the 11th century A.D. to the 16th, closely related to Anglo-Saxon and Old Saxon.
**Old Glory,** the flag of the U.S.
**Old Guard,** [after Napoleon's imperial guard (1804)] 1. any old group of defenders of a cause. 2. the conservative element of a group, party, etc.
**old hat,** [Slang], old-fashioned; outmoded.
**Old High German,** the German language as spoken in S Germany from the 8th century A.D. to the 12th.
**Old Icelandic,** 1. Old Norse as spoken and written in Iceland. 2. loosely, Old Norse.
**Old Irish,** the Gaelic Celtic of Ireland as spoken from the 8th century A.D. to the 12th.
**old lady,** [Slang], 1. one's mother. 2. one's wife.
**Old Latin,** the Latin language from about the 6th to the 1st century B.C.
**old-line** (ōld'lin'), *adj.* 1. old and well-established. 2. following tradition; conservative.
**Old Low German,** the language of N Germany and the Netherlands from the 8th century A.D. to the 12th.
**old maid,** 1. a woman who is unmarried and seems likely to remain so. 2. a prim, prudish, fussy person. **—old'-maid'ish,** *adj.*
**old man,** [Slang], 1. one's father. 2. one's husband. 3. any man in a position of authority, as the captain of a vessel, etc.
**old master,** 1. any of the great painters before the 18th century. 2. a painting by any of these.
**old moon,** the phase of the moon in which it appears as a crescent curving to the left.
**Old Nick,** the Devil; Satan: also **Old Harry.**
**Old Norman French,** Norman French.
**Old Norse,** the language spoken in Norway, Denmark, and Iceland from the 8th century A.D. to the 14th: also called *Old Icelandic.*
**Old Persian,** the oldest form of Persian, dating from the 7th to the 4th century B.C.
**Old Prussian,** a Baltic language spoken from the 15th century A.D. to the early 18th.
**old rose,** grayish or purplish red. **—old'-rose',** *adj.*
**Old Saxon,** a Low Germanic dialect of part of N Germany in the 9th and 10th centuries A.D.
**old school,** a group of people who cling to traditional or conservative ideas, methods, etc.
**Old South,** the South before the Civil War.
**old·ster** (ōld'stẽr), *n.* [Colloq.], one who is no longer a youngster; old or elderly person.
**old style,** 1. an old style of type, still in use. 2. [O-S-], the old method of reckoning time by the Julian calendar, which was off one day every 128 years. **—old'-style',** *adj.*
**Old Testament,** the Bible of Judaism or the first of the two divisions of the Bible of Christianity, containing the history of the Hebrews, the Mosaic law, the writings of the prophets, etc.
**old-time** (ōld'tīm'), *adj.* of or like past times.

**old-tim·er** (ōld′tīm′ẽr), *n.* [Colloq.], 1. one who has been a resident, employee, member, etc. for a long time. 2. one who is old-fashioned.
**old wives' tale,** a silly story or superstition such as gossipy old women might pass around.
**old-wom·an·ish** (ōld′woom′ən-ish), *adj.* like or suitable for an old woman; fussy.
**old-world** (ōld′wũrld′), *adj.* 1. of or belonging to the ancient world or former times. 2. of the Old World: often **Old-World.**
**Old World,** Europe, Asia, and Africa.
**-ole** (ōl), [< L. *oleum*, oil], a suffix used in chemistry: 1. to indicate a closed-chain compound with five members. 2. to form the names of certain aldehydes and ethers. Also **-ol.**
**o·le·a·ceous** (ō′li-ā′shəs), *adj.* [< L. *olea*, olive tree], designating or belonging to the olive family of trees and shrubs, as the lilac.
**o·le·ag·i·nous** (ō′li-aj′i-nəs), *adj.* [< Fr. < L. < *olea*, the olive], oily; unctuous. **—o′le·ag′i·nous·ly,** *adv.* **—o′le·ag′i·nous·ness,** *n.*
**o·le·an·der** (ō′li-an′dẽr), *n.* [ML.], a poisonous evergreen shrub with fragrant white or red flowers.
**o·le·ate** (ō′li-āt′), *n.* a salt or ester of oleic acid.
**o·le·ic acid** (ō-lē′ik, ō′li-), an oily acid, $C_{17}H_{33}COOH$, present as the glyceryl ester in most fats and oils, used in making soap, etc.
**o·le·in** (ō′li-in), *n.* [< Fr. < L. *oleum*, an oil], 1. a liquid glyceride of oleic acid. 2. the liquid part of any fat.
**o·le·o** (ō′li-ō′), *n.* oleomargarine.
**o·le·o-,** [< L. *oleum*, an oil], a combining form meaning *oil* or *olein*, as in *oleomargarine.*
**o·le·o·mar·ga·rine** (ō′li-ō-mär′jə-rin, -rēn′), *n.* margarine: also **oleomargarin** (-rin).
**o·le·o·res·in** (ō′li-ō-rez′'n), *n.* a solution of a resin in an essential oil, as turpentine, occurring naturally in various plants or prepared.
**ol·fac·tion** (ol-fak′shən, ōl-), *n.* [see OLFACTORY], 1. the sense of smell. 2. the act of smelling.
**ol·fac·to·ry** (ol-fak′tẽr-i, ōl-), *adj.* [< L. pp. of *olfacere*, to smell < *olere*, to have a smell + *facere*, to make], of the sense of smell: also **ol·fac′tive.** *n.* [*pl.* -RIES], *usually in pl.* an organ of smell.
**ol·i·garch** (ol′i-gärk′), *n.* any of the rulers of an oligarchy.
**ol·i·garch·y** (ol′i-gär′ki), *n.* [*pl.* -IES], [Gr. *oligarchia;* see OLIGO- & -ARCHY], 1. a form of government in which a few persons have the ruling power. 2. a state so governed or the persons ruling it. **—ol′i·gar′chic, ol′i·gar′chi·cal,** *adj.*
**ol·i·go-,** [Gr. < *oligos*, small], a combining form meaning *few, small, a deficiency of*: also **olig-.**
**Ol·i·go·cene** (ol′ig-ə-sēn′), *adj.* [< *oligo-* + Gr. *kainos*, new], designating or of the second epoch of the Tertiary Period in the Cenozoic Era: see **geology,** chart. *n.* the Oligocene Epoch.
**ol·i·gop·o·ly** (ol′ə-gop′ə-li) *n.* [*pl.* -LIES], [*olig-* (see OLIGO-) + *monopoly*], control of a commodity or service in a given market by a few companies.
**o·li·o** (ō′li-ō′), *n.* [*pl.* -OS], [< Sp. *olla;* see OLLA], 1. a stew; olla. 2. a medley; miscellany.
**ol·ive** (ol′iv), *n.* [OFr. < L. *oliva*], 1. an evergreen tree of S Europe and the Near East, with leathery leaves and an edible fruit. 2. the small oval fruit, eaten green or ripe, or pressed to extract its oil. 3. the wood of this tree. 4. an olive branch. 5. the dull yellowish-green color of the unripe olive fruit. *adj.* 1. of the olive. 2. dull yellowish-green.
**olive branch,** 1. the branch of the olive tree, a symbol of peace. 2. any peace offering.
**olive drab,** 1. a shade of greenish brown used as a camouflage color in the armed forces. 2. woolen cloth dyed this color.
**olive oil,** a light-yellow oil pressed from ripe olives, used in cooking, soap, etc.
**ol·la** (ol′ə, Sp. ôl′yä), *n.* [Sp. < L.], 1. a large-mouthed pot or jar. 2. a highly spiced stew.
**ol·o·gy** (ol′ə-ji), *n.* [*pl.* -GIES], [< *-logy*], a branch of learning; science: humorous usage.
**O·lym·pi·a** (ō-lim′pi-ə, ə-), *n.* 1. a plain in ancient Greece: site of Olympic games. 2. the capital of Washington, on Puget Sound: pop., 18,000.
**O·lym·pi·ad** (ō-lim′pi-ad′, ə-), *n.* 1. in ancient Greece, any of the four-year periods between Olympic games. 2. a celebration of the modern Olympic games.
**O·lym·pi·an** (ō-lim′pi-ən, ə-), *n.* 1. in *Gr. mythology*, any of the gods on Mount Olympus. 2. a native of Olympia. 3. a participant in the Olympic games. *adj.* 1. of Olympia or Mount Olympus. 2. god-like; majestic. 3. of the ancient Olympic games.
**O·lym·pic** (ō-lim′pik, ə-), *adj.* Olympian. *n. pl.* the Olympic games (preceded by *the*).
**Olympic games,** 1. an ancient Greek festival with contests in athletics, poetry, and music, held every four years at Olympia in honor of Zeus: also **Olympian games.** 2. an international athletic competition of modern times, held at a chosen city, generally every four years, since 1896.
**O·lym·pus** (ō-lim′pəs, ə-), *n.* 1. a mountain in N Greece: height, 9,793 ft.: in *Gr. mythology*, the home of the gods. 2. heaven; the sky.
**-o·ma,** [Gr. *-ōma*], a suffix meaning *morbid growth, tumor*, as in *sarcoma.*
**O·ma·ha** (ō′mə-hô′, -hä′), *n.* a city in E Nebraska: pop., 302,000.
**O·man** (ō-män′), *n.* see **Muscat and Oman.**
**O·mar Khay·yám** (ō′mär kī-yäm′, ō′mẽr kī-yam′), ?–1123; Persian poet.
**o·ma·sum** (ō-mā′səm), *n.* [*pl.* -SA (-sə)], [L., paunch], the third division in the stomach of a cud-chewing animal, as the cow.
**om·buds·man** (om′bədz-mən), *n.* [*pl.* -MEN], [Swed.], an appointed public official who investigates activities of government agencies that may infringe on the rights of individuals.
**o·me·ga** (ō-meg′ə, -mē′gə, -mā′-), *n.* [Gr. *o mega*, lit., great *o*], 1. the twenty-fourth and final letter of the Greek alphabet (Ω, ω). 2. the last (of a series); end.
**om·e·let, om·e·lette** (om′lit, om′ə-let), *n.* [< Fr.; ult. < L. *lamella*, small plate], eggs beaten up, often with milk or water, and cooked as a pancake in a frying pan.
**o·men** (ō′mən), *n.* [L.], a thing or happening supposed to foretell a future (good or evil) event; portent. *v.t.* to be an omen of; presage.
**om·i·cron, om·i·kron** (om′i-kron′, ō′mi-), *n.* [Gr. *o mikron*, lit., small *o*], the fifteenth letter of the Greek alphabet (O, ο).
**om·i·nous** (om′ə-nəs), *adj.* [L. *ominosus*], of or serving as an evil omen; threatening; sinister. **—om′i·nous·ly,** *adv.* **—om′i·nous·ness,** *n.*
**o·mis·si·ble** (ō-mis′ə-b'l), *adj.* that can be omitted.
**o·mis·sion** (ō-mish′ən), *n.* [< LL. *omissio*], 1. an omitting or being omitted. 2. anything omitted.
**o·mit** (ō-mit′), *v.t.* [OMITTED, OMITTING], [< L. *omittere* < *ob-* (see OB-) + *mittere*, to send], 1. to leave out; fail to include. 2. to neglect; fail to do. **—o·mit′ter,** *n.*
**om·ni-,** [L. < *omnis*, all], a combining form meaning *all, everywhere*, as in *omniscient.*
**om·ni·bus** (om′ni-bus′, -nə-bəs), *n.* [*pl.* -BUSES], [Fr. < L., lit., for all], a large motor coach; bus. *adj.* providing for many things at once.
**om·ni·far·i·ous** (om′ni-fâr′i-əs), *adj.* [< L. *omnifarius* < *omnis*, all + *fari*, to speak], of all kinds, varieties, or forms. **—om′ni·far′i·ous·ly,** *adv.*
**om·nip·o·tence** (om-nip′ə-təns), *n.* 1. the state or quality of being omnipotent. 2. [O-], God.
**om·nip·o·tent** (om-nip′ə-tənt), *adj.* [OFr. < L. < *omnis*, all + *potens*, able], having unlimited power or authority; all-powerful. **—the Omnipotent,** God. **—om·nip′o·tent·ly,** *adv.*
**om·ni·pres·ent** (om′ni-prez′'nt), *adj.* [< ML.; see OMNI- & PRESENT], present in all places at the same time. **—om′ni·pres′ence,** *n.*
**om·nis·cient** (om-nish′ənt), *adj.* [< *omni-* + L. *sciens*, ppr. of *scire*, to know], knowing all things. **—the Omniscient,** God. **—om·nis′cience,** *n.* **—om·nis′cient·ly,** *adv.*
**om·ni·um-gath·er·um** (om′ni-əm-gath′ẽr-əm), *n.* [L. *omnium*, all + Latinized form of Eng. *gather*], a miscellaneous collection of persons or things.
**om·niv·o·rous** (om-niv′ẽr-əs), *adj.* [< L. < *omnis*, all + *vorare*, to devour], 1. eating any sort of food, especially both animal and vegetable food. 2. taking in everything indiscriminately: as, an *omnivorous* reader. **—om·niv′o·rous·ly,** *adv.* **—om·niv′o·rous·ness,** *n.*
**Omsk** (ômsk), *n.* a city in NW Siberia, U.S.S.R.: pop., 746,000.
**on** (on, ôn), *prep.* [AS. *on, an*], 1. above, but in contact with and supported by. 2. in contact with or covering. 3. near to: as, *on* my right. 4. at the time of: as, *on* entering. 5. indicating the basis of: as, *on* purpose. 6. connected with; engaged in: as, *on* the faculty, *on* a trip. 7. in a state of: as, *on* parole. 8. as a result of: as, a profit *on* the sale. 9. toward: as, light shone *on* us. 10. through the use of: as, to live *on* bread. 11. concerning: as, an essay *on* war. 12. [Colloq.], at the expense of: as, a drink *on* the house. *adv.* 1. in a situation of

contacting, being supported by, or covering: as, put your shoes *on*. 2. in a direction toward something: as, he looked *on*. 3. forward; ahead: as, move *on*. 4. continuously: as, she sang *on*. 5. into operation or action: as, turn *on* the light. *adj.* 1. in action or operation: as, the play is *on*. 2. near or nearer. *n.* the fact or state of being on. **—and so on,** and more like the preceding. **—on and off,** intermittently. **—on and on,** continuously.

**ON., O.N.,** Old Norse.

**o·nan·ism** (ō′nən-iz′m), *n.* [< *Onan* (Gen. 38:9)], 1. withdrawal in coition before ejaculation. 2. masturbation. **—o′nan·ist,** *n.*

**once** (wuns), *adv.* [AS. *anes*, genit. of *an*, one], 1. one time; one time only: as, he eats *once* a day. 2. at any time; ever. 3. formerly: as, a *once* famous man. *conj.* as soon as; whenever: as, *once* he is tired, he will quit. *adj.* former. *n.* one time: as, I'll go this *once*. **—all at once,** 1. all at the same time. 2. suddenly. **—at once,** 1. immediately. 2. at the same time. **—for once,** for at least one time. **—once and again,** repeatedly. **—once (and) for all,** conclusively. **—once in a while,** occasionally. **—once or twice,** not often. **—once upon a time,** a long time ago.

**once-o·ver** (wuns′ō′vẽr), *n.* [Slang], a quick, comprehensive look or examination.

**on·com·ing** (on′kum′iŋ), *adj.* coming nearer in position or time; approaching. *n.* an approach.

**one** (wun), *adj.* [AS. *an*], 1. being a single thing. 2. characterized by unity: as, with *one* accord. 3. designating a person or thing as contrasted with another: as, from *one* day to another. 4. a certain but indefinite or unspecified: as, *one* day we'll win. 5. single in kind; the same. *n.* 1. the number expressing unity: it is the first and lowest cardinal number; 1; I. 2. a single person or thing. *pron.* 1. some or a certain person or thing. 2. any person or thing. 3. the same person or thing. **—all one,** 1. united or agreed. 2. immaterial. **—at one,** in accord. **—make one,** 1. to join or take part in something. 2. to unite (a couple) in marriage. **—one and all,** everybody. **—one another,** each the other: as, they love *one another*. **—one by one,** individually in succession.

**-one,** [Gr. *ōnē*], a suffix used in chemistry, meaning *a ketone*, as in *acetone*.

**one-horse** (wun′hôrs′), *adj.* 1. drawn by or using a single horse. 2. [Colloq.], limited in resources, scope, etc.; inferior.

**O·nei·da** (ō-nī′də), *n.* [*pl.* -DA, -DAS], one of a tribe of Iroquoian Indians who lived in New York State.

**O'Neill, Eugene** (ō-nēl′), 1888–1953; U.S. dramatist.

**one·ness** (wun′nis), *n.* 1. singleness; unity. 2. unity of mind, feeling, etc. 3. sameness; identity.

**one-night stand** (wun′nīt′), a single night performance of a show, lecture, etc. at a given town.

**on·er·ous** (on′ẽr-əs), *adj.* [< OFr. < L. *onerosus* < *onus*, a load], burdensome; oppressive. **—on′er·ous·ly,** *adv.* **—on′er·ous·ness,** *n.*

**one·self** (wun′self′, wunz′-), *pron.* a person's own self: also, **one's self. —be oneself,** 1. to function normally. 2. to be natural. **—by oneself,** alone; withdrawn. **—come to oneself,** to recover one's senses or capacity for judgment.

**one-sid·ed** (wun′sīd′id), *adj.* 1. on, having, or involving only one side. 2. larger on one side. 3. unequal: as, a *one-sided* race. 4. favoring one side; partial; prejudiced. **—one′-sid′ed·ness,** *n.*

**one-step** (wun′step′), *n.* a ballroom dance with quick walking steps in 2/4 time. *v.i.* [-STEPPED, -STEPPING], to dance the one-step.

**one-time** (wun′tīm′), *adj.* at a past time; former.

**one-track** (wun′trak′), *adj.* 1. having a single track. 2. [Colloq.], able to deal with only one thing at a time: as, a *one-track* mind.

**one-way** (wun′wā′), *adj.* moving, or allowing movement, in one direction only: as, a *one-way* street.

**on·ion** (un′yən), *n.* [< OFr. < L. *unio* < *unus*, one], 1. a plant of the lily family with an edible bulb of concentric layers. 2. this bulb, having a sharp smell and taste. **—on′ion·like′,** *adj.*

**on·ion·skin** (un′yən-skin′), *n.* a tough, thin, translucent paper with a glossy surface.

**on·look·er** (on′look′ẽr), *n.* one who looks on; spectator. **—on′look′ing,** *n.* & *adj.*

**on·ly** (ōn′li), *adj.* [AS. *anlic* < *an*, one + *-lic*, -ly], 1. alone of its or their kind; sole. 2. alone in superiority; best. *adv.* 1. and no other; and no more; solely. 2. merely. *conj.* [Colloq.], except that; but: as, I'd have gone, *only* it rained. **—only too,** very.

**on·o·mat·o·poe·ia** (on′ə-mat′ə-pē′ə, ō-nom′ə-tə-), *n.* [LL. < Gr. < *onoma*, a name + *poiein*, to make], 1. the formation of a word by imitating the sound associated with an object or action (e.g., *chickadee*, *buzz*). 2. such a word. 3. the use of such words, as in poetry. **—on′o·mat′o·poe′ic, on′o·mat′o·po·et′ic** (-pō-et′ik), *adj.*

**On·on·da·ga** (on′ən-dô′gə, -dä′-), *n.* [*pl.* -GA, -GAS], a member of a tribe of Iroquoian Indians who lived in New York State.

**ONorm.Fr.,** Old Norman French.

**on·rush** (on′rush′), *n.* a headlong dash forward; strong onward flow. **—on′rush′ing,** *adj.*

**on·set** (on′set′), *n.* 1. an attack. 2. a beginning.

**on·shore** (on′shôr′, -shōr′), *adj.* 1. moving onto or toward the shore. 2. situated or operating on land. *adv.* toward the shore; landward.

**on·slaught** (on′slôt′), *n.* [prob. < D. *annslag* < *slagen*, to strike], a violent, intense attack.

**On·tar·i·o** (on-târ′i-ō′), *n.* 1. the smallest of the Great Lakes, between New York and Ontario, Canada: usually **Lake Ontario.** 2. a province of Canada, on the Great Lakes: pop., 6,668,000; capital, Toronto. Abbrev. **Ont., O. —On·tar′i·an,** *adj.* & *n.*

**on·to** (on′tōō, -tə), *prep.* 1. to a position on. 2. [Slang], aware of: as, *onto* his tricks. Also **on to.**

**on·to-,** [< Gr. ppr. of *einai*, to be], a combining form meaning *being, existence.*

**on·tog·e·ny** (on-toj′ə-ni), *n.* [*onto-* + *-geny*], the life cycle of a single organism: cf. *phylogeny.* **—on·to·ge·net·ic** (on′tō-jə-net′ik), *adj.* **—on′to·ge·net′i·cal·ly,** *adv.*

**on·tol·o·gy** (on-tol′ə-ji), *n.* the study of the nature of being or reality. **—on′to·log′i·cal,** *adj.*

**o·nus** (ō′nəs), *n.* [L.], a burden; responsibility.

**on·ward** (on′wẽrd), *adv.* toward or at a position ahead; forward: also **onwards.** *adj.* moving or directed ahead; advancing.

**on·yx** (on′iks, ō′niks), *n.* [< OFr. < L. < Gr. *onyx*, nail, claw: the stone resembles these in color], a type of agate with alternate layers of color.

**o·ö-,** [< Gr. *ōion*], a combining form meaning *egg* or *ovum.*

**oo·dles** (ōō′d'lz), *n.pl.* [? dial. form of *huddle*], [Slang], a great amount.

**o·ö·lite** (ō′ə-līt′), *n.* [see OÖ- & -LITE], a limestone formed of small grains of carbonate of lime cemented together like fish eggs. **—o′ö·lit′ic** (-lit′ik), *adj.*

**o·öl·o·gy** (ō-ol′ə-ji), *n.* the study of birds' eggs. **—o·ö·log·i·cal** (ō′ə-loj′i-k'l), *adj.*

**oo·long** (ōō′lôŋ, -loŋ), *n.* [< Chin. *wulung*, lit., black dragon], a Chinese black tea that is partly fermented before being dried.

**oo·mi·ac, oo·mi·ak** (ōō′mi-ak′), *n.* an umiak.

**o·öph·o·ro-** (ō-of′ə-rə), [< Gr. *ōion*, an egg + *-phoros*, bearing], a combining form meaning *ovary* or *ovaries*: also **oöphor-.**

**ooze** (ōōz), *n.* [AS. *wos*, sap], an oozing or something that oozes. *v.i.* [OOZED, OOZING], 1. to flow out slowly or give forth moisture, as through small holes. 2. to disappear gradually: as, his hope *oozed* away. *v.t.* to exude (a fluid).

**ooze** (ōōz), *n.* [AS. *wase*], 1. soft mud or slime; esp., the sediment at the bottom of an ocean, lake, etc. 2. a muddy area; bog; marsh.

**oo·zy** (ōō′zi), *adj.* [-ZIER, -ZIEST], oozing moisture. **—oo′zi·ly,** *adv.* **—oo′zi·ness,** *n.*

**oo·zy** (ōō′zi), *adj.* [-ZIER, -ZIEST], full of or like ooze; slimy. **—oo′zi·ly,** *adv.* **—oo′zi·ness,** *n.*

**op-,** ob-: used before *p*, as in *oppose.*

**op.,** 1. opera. 2. opposite. 3. opus.

**o·pac·i·ty** (ō-pas′ə-ti), *n.* 1. an opaque state or quality. 2. [*pl.* -TIES], an opaque thing.

**o·pal** (ō′p'l), *n.* [< L. < Gr. *opalios* < Sans. *upala*, precious stone], a glassy, translucent silica of various colors that can refract light and then reflect it in a play of colors: some types are semiprecious stones. **—o′pal·ine** (-in, -īn′), *adj.*

**o·pal·esce** (ō′pə-les′), *v.i.* [-ESCED, -ESCING], to show a play of colors like an opal. **—o′pal·es′cence,** *n.* **—o′pal·es′cent,** *adj.*

**o·paque** (ō-pāk′, ə-), *adj.* [L. *opacus*, shady], 1. not transparent. 2. not reflecting light; dull; dark. 3. hard to understand; obscure. 4. slow in understanding; obtuse. *n.* anything opaque. **—o·paque′ly,** *adv.* **—o·paque′ness,** *n.*

**op (art)** (op), a style of abstract painting utilizing geometrical patterns or figures to create various optical effects and illusions.

**op. cit.,** *opere citato*, [L.], in the work cited.

**ope** (ōp), *adj., v.t. & v.i.* [OPED, OPING], [Poetic], open.

**o·pen** (ō′p'n), *adj.* [AS.; a semantic extension of *up*], 1. not closed, covered, clogged, or shut: as, *open* doors. 2. not enclosed, sheltered, etc.; clear: as, *open* fields. 3. unsealed; unwrapped. 4. without covering or protection: as, an *open* boat, *open* flank. 5. unfolded; spread out: as, an *open* book.

6. having spaces, gaps, etc.: as, *open* ranks. 7. free from ice: as, the lake is *open*. 8. free to be entered, used, etc. by all: as, an *open* meeting. 9. free to argument; not settled: as, an *open* question. 10. not closed to new ideas, etc.: as, an *open* mind. 11. generous. 12. free from restrictions or effective regulation: as, *open* season, the city is wide *open*. 13. in force or operation: as, an *open* account. 14. *a*) not already taken, engaged, etc.: as, the job is *open*. *b*) free to be accepted or rejected. 15. accessible; available. 16. not secret; public: as, an *open* quarrel. 17. frank; candid: as, an *open* manner. 18. in *music*, *a*) not stopped by the finger: said of a string. *b*) not closed at the top: said of an organ pipe. *c*) produced by an open string or pipe, or without a slide or key: said of a tone. 19. in *phonetics*, *a*) low: said of a vowel. *b*) fricative: said of a consonant. *c*) ending in a vowel sound: said of a syllable. ***v.t.*** 1. to cause to be open (senses 1, 2, 3); unfasten. 2. to make an opening in. 3. to spread out; expand: as, to *open* ranks. 4. to make available for use, participation, etc. without restriction. 5. to make liberal and generous. 6. to make known; reveal. 7. to begin; start. 8. to start operating: as, to *open* a store. ***v.i.*** 1. to become open. 2. to spread out; expand; unfold. 3. to become liberal and generous. 4. to be revealed, disclosed, etc. 5. to be an opening: as, it *opens* to the east. 6. to begin; start. 7. to start operating. **—open out,** 1. to make or become extended. 2. to develop. 3. to reveal. **—open to,** 1. willing to receive, discuss, etc. 2. liable to. 3. available to. **—open up,** 1. to make or become open. 2. to unfold. 3. to start; begin. 4. [Colloq.], to speak freely. **—the open,** 1. any open, clear space. 2. the outdoors. 3. public knowledge. **—o′pen·a·ble,** ***adj.*** **—o′pened,** ***adj.*** **—o′pen·er,** ***n.*** **—o′pen·ly,** ***adv.*** **—o′pen·ness,** ***n.***

**open air,** out of doors. **—o′pen-air′,** ***adj.***

**o·pen-and-shut** (ō′p'n-'n-shut′), ***adj.*** easily decided; obvious: as, an *open-and-shut* case.

**open city,** a city left undefended against enemy capture to gain immunity, under international law, from bombardment and attack.

**open door,** 1. unrestricted admission. 2. free and equal opportunity for all nations to trade with a given nation. **—o′pen-door′,** ***adj.***

**o·pen-eyed** (ō′p'n-īd′), ***adj.*** 1. with open eyes; awake, watchful, etc. 2. done with open eyes.

**o·pen-faced** (ō′p'n-fāst′), ***adj.*** 1. with the face uncovered. 2. having a frank, honest face.

**o·pen·hand·ed** (ō′p'n-han′did), ***adj.*** generous. **—o′pen·hand′ed·ly,** ***adv.*** **—o′pen·hand′ed·ness,** ***n.***

**o·pen·heart·ed** (ō′p'n-här′tid), ***adj.*** 1. not reserved; frank. 2. kindly; generous. **—o′pen·heart′ed·ly,** ***adv.*** **—o′pen·heart′ed·ness,** ***n.***

**o·pen-hearth** (ō′p'n-härth′), ***adj.*** designating or using a furnace with a wide hearth and low roof, for making steel.

**open house,** 1. a house extending welcome to all. 2. a time when an institution is open to visitors.

**o·pen·ing** (ō′p'n-iŋ), ***n.*** 1. a becoming or making open. 2. an open place; hole; gap. 3. a clearing. 4. a beginning; commencement. 5. formal beginning. 6. a favorable chance; opportunity. 7. an unfilled job. 8. the first moves, as of a chess game.

**open letter,** a letter written as to a specific person, but published for all to read.

**o·pen-mind·ed** (ō′p'n-mīn′did), ***adj.*** having a mind open to new ideas; unprejudiced. **—o′pen-mind′ed·ly,** ***adv.*** **—o′pen-mind′ed·ness,** ***n.***

**o·pen-mouthed** (ō′p'n-mouthd′, -moutht′), ***adj.*** 1. having the mouth open. 2. gaping, as in surprise. 3. greedy; ravenous. 4. clamorous.

**open season,** a period during which it is legal to kill or capture specified game, fish, etc.

**open secret,** something supposed to be secret but known by almost everyone.

**open sesame,** 1. magic words spoken to open the door of the thieves' den in the story of Ali Baba. 2. any unfailing means of gaining admission.

**open shop,** a factory, business, etc. employing workers regardless of union membership.

**open stock,** merchandise sold in sets, the individual pieces of which are kept in stock in quantity so that replacements or additions are available.

**o·pen·work** (ō′p'n-wũrk′), ***n.*** ornamental work in cloth, metal, etc. with openings in the material.

**OPer.,** Old Persian.

**op·er·a** (op′ẽr-ə), ***n.*** [It. < L. *opera*, a work], 1. a play having all or most of its text set to music and sung to orchestral accompaniment, usually characterized by elaborate costuming, scenery, etc. 2. the branch of art represented by such plays. 3. the score, libretto, or performance of such a play.

**op·er·a** (op′ẽr-ə), ***n.*** pl. of **opus.**

**op·er·a·ble** (op′ẽr-ə-b'l), ***adj.*** [< L. *operari*, to work; + *-able*], 1. practicable. 2. that can be treated by a surgical operation. **—op′er·a·ble·ness,** ***n.*** **—op′er·a·bly,** ***adv.***

‡**o·pé·ra bouffe** (ô′pā′rà′ bōōf′; Eng. op′ẽr-ə bōōf′), [Fr.], comic opera, especially if farcical.

**opera glasses,** a small binocular telescope used at the opera, in theaters, etc.

**opera hat,** a man's tall, collapsible silk hat.

**opera house,** a theater where operas are performed.

**op·er·ate** (op′ə-rāt′), ***v.i.*** [-ATED, -ATING], [< L. pp. of *operari*, to work < *opus*, a work], 1. to be in action; act; work. 2. to bring about a certain effect. 3. to carry on military movements (usually with *against*). 4. to perform a surgical operation. ***v.t.*** 1. to bring about as an effect. 2. to put or keep in action; conduct; manage. **—op′er·ant,** ***adj. & n.*** **—op′er·at′a·ble,** ***adj.***

**op·er·at·ic** (op′ə-rat′ik), ***adj.*** of or like the opera. **—op′er·at′i·cal·ly,** ***adv.***

**op·er·a·tion** (op′ə-rā′shən), ***n.*** 1. the act, process, or method of operating. 2. the condition of being in action or at work. 3. a procedure that is part of a series in some work or plan, as in manufacturing, business, military maneuvers, etc. 4. any surgical procedure performed, usually with instruments, to remedy a physical ailment or defect. 5. in *mathematics*, a process, as addition, involving a change in a quantity. **—in operation,** 1. in the act or process of working. 2. in force.

**op·er·a·tion·al** (op′ə-rā′shən-'l), ***adj.*** 1. of or having to do with the operation of a device, system, process, etc. 2. capable of operation. 3. of or ready to be used in a military operation.

**op·er·a·tive** (op′ə-rā′tiv, -ẽr-ə-tiv), ***adj.*** 1. in operation; active. 2. effective; efficient. 3. connected with physical work or mechanical action. 4. of or resulting from a surgical operation. ***n.*** 1. a worker; esp., a skilled industrial worker. 2. a detective. **—op′er·a′tive·ly,** ***adv.*** **—op′er·a′tive·ness,** ***n.***

**op·er·a·tor** (op′ə-rā′tẽr), ***n.*** one who operates; specif., *a*) a person who effects something; agent. *b*) a person who works a machine: as, a telephone *operator*. *c*) a person engaged in business or industrial operations or enterprises.

**o·per·cu·lum** (ō-pũr′kyoo-ləm), ***n.*** [*pl.* -LA (-lə), -LUMS], [L. < *operire*, to close], any of various covering flaps or lidlike structures in plants and animals, as the bony covering protecting the gills of fishes. **—o·per′cu·lar,** ***adj.*** **—o·per′cu·late** (-lit, -lāt′), **o·per′cu·lat′ed,** ***adj.***

**op·er·et·ta** (op′ə-ret′ə), ***n.*** [It., dim. of *opera*], a short, amusing musical play.

**oph·thal·mi·a** (of-thal′mi-ə), ***n.*** [< LL. < Gr. < *ophthalmos*, the eye], a severe inflammation of the eyeball or conjunctiva.

**oph·thal·mic** (of-thal′mik), ***adj.*** of or connected with the eyes.

**oph·thal·mo-,** [< Gr. *ophthalmos*, the eye], a combining form meaning *the eye*: also **ophthalm-.**

**oph·thal·mol·o·gy** (of′thal-mol′ə-ji), ***n.*** the branch of medicine dealing with the structure, functions, and diseases of the eye. **—oph·thal′mo·log′i·cal** (-mə-loj′i-k'l), ***adj.*** **—oph′thal·mol′o·gist,** ***n.***

**oph·thal·mo·scope** (of-thal′mə-skōp′), ***n.*** [*ophthalmo-* + *-scope*], an instrument for examining the interior of the eye. **—oph·thal′mo·scop′ic** (-skop′ik), ***adj.*** **—oph′thal·mos′co·py** (-mos′kə-pi), ***n.***

**-o·pi·a** (ō′pi-ə), [< Gr. < *ōps*, an eye], a combining form meaning *a* (specified kind of) *eye defect.*

**o·pi·ate** (ō′pi-it, -āt′), ***n.*** 1. any medicine containing opium or any of its derivatives and acting as a sedative and narcotic. 2. anything quieting or soothing. ***adj.*** 1. containing opium. 2. bringing sleep, quiet, etc.; narcotic.

**o·pine** (ō-pīn′), ***v.t. & v.i.*** [OPINED, OPINING], [< Fr. < L. *opinari*, to think], to think; suppose: now usually humorous. **—o·pin′er,** ***n.***

**o·pin·ion** (ə-pin′yən), ***n.*** [< OFr. < L. < *opinari*, to think], 1. a belief not based on certainty or knowledge but on what seems true or probable; judgment. 2. an evaluation, estimation, etc. 3. the formal judgment of an expert. 4. a judge's formal statement of the law bearing on a decision. **—o·pin′ion·a·ble,** ***adj.*** **—o·pin′ioned,** ***adj.***

**o·pin·ion·at·ed** (ə-pin′yən-ā′tid), ***adj.*** holding unreasonably or obstinately to one's opinions. **—o·pin′ion·at′ed·ly,** ***adv.*** **—o·pin′ion·at′ed·ness,** ***n.***

**o·pin·ion·a·tive** (ə-pin′yən-ā′tiv), *adj.* 1. of or consisting in opinion. 2. opinionated. —**o·pin′ion·a′tive·ly,** *adv.* —**o·pin′ion·a′tive·ness,** *n.*

**o·pi·um** (ō′pi-əm), *n.* [L. < Gr. < *opos*, vegetable juice], a narcotic drug prepared from the seed capsules of the opium poppy, used as an intoxicant and medicinally to relieve pain and produce sleep.

**opium poppy,** a plant with large white or purple flowers, the source of opium.

**O·por·to** (ō-pôr′tō), *n.* a seaport in N Portugal: pop., 280,000: Portuguese name, *Porto.*

**o·pos·sum** (ə-pos′əm), *n.* [*pl.* -SUMS, -SUM; see PLURAL, II, D, 1], [N.Am. Ind.], a small tree-dwelling mammal, the female of which carries its young in a pouch: it is active at night and pretends to be dead when trapped: also **possum.**

OPOSSUM
(15 in. long)

**opp.,** 1. opposed. 2. opposite.

**op·po·nent** (ə-pō′nənt), *adj.* [< L. ppr. < *ob-* (see OB-) + *ponere*, to set], 1. opposite, as in position. 2. opposing; antagonistic. *n.* one who opposes, as in a fight, game, etc.; adversary.

**op·por·tune** (op′ẽr-tōōn′, -tūn′), *adj.* [< L. *opportunus*, lit., before the port < *ob-* (see OB-) + *portus*, a port], 1. right for the purpose: said of time. 2. happening at the right time; timely. —**op′portune′ly,** *adv.* —**op′por·tune′ness,** *n.*

**op·por·tun·ism** (op′ẽr-tōōn′iz'm, -tūn′-), *n.* the adapting of one's actions, thoughts, etc. to circumstances, as in politics, without regard for principles or consequences. —**op′por·tun′ist,** *n.* —**op′portun·is′tic,** *adj.* —**op′por·tun·is′ti·cal·ly,** *adv.*

**op·por·tu·ni·ty** (op′ẽr-tōō′nə-ti, -tū′-), *n.* [*pl.* -TIES], a combination of circumstances favorable for the purpose; good chance.

**op·pos·a·ble** (ə-pōz′ə-b'l), *adj.* 1. that can be opposed. 2. that can be placed opposite something else. —**op·pos′a·bil′i·ty,** *n.* —**op·pos′a·bly,** *adv.*

**op·pose** (ə-pōz′), *v.t.* [-POSED, -POSING], [< Fr. < *poser;* see POSE, *v.*], 1. to set against; place opposite, in balance or contrast. 2. to resist; contend with in speech or action. —**op·posed′,** *adj.* —**oppos′er,** *n.* —**op·pos′ing,** *adj.* —**op·pos′ing·ly,** *adv.*

**op·po·site** (op′ə-zit), *adj.* [OFr. < L. pp. of *opponere;* see OPPONENT], 1. opposed to. 2. set against; in a contrary direction (often with *to*). 3. hostile or resistant. 4. entirely different; exactly contrary. 5. in *botany*, growing in pairs, but separated by a stem. *n.* anything opposed. *adv.* on opposing sides; in opposite positions. *prep.* fronting; across from. —**op′po·site·ly,** *adv.* —**op′po·site·ness,** *n.*

**op·po·si·tion** (op′ə-zish′ən), *n.* 1. an opposing or being opposed. 2. resistance; hostility. 3. anything that opposes. 4. [sometimes O-], a political party serving as a check on the party in power. 5. the position of two heavenly bodies 180° apart in longitude. —**op′po·si′tion·al,** *adj.*

**op·press** (ə-pres′), *v.t.* [< OFr. < ML. < L. pp. of *opprimere* < *ob-* (see OB-) + *primere*, to press], 1. to weigh heavily on the mind, spirits, etc. of; burden. 2. to keep down by the cruel or unjust use of authority; tyrannize over. —**op·pres′sor,** *n.*

**op·pres·sion** (ə-presh′ən), *n.* 1. an oppressing or being oppressed. 2. a thing that oppresses. 3. physical or mental distress.

**op·pres·sive** (ə-pres′iv), *adj.* 1. hard to put up with; burdensome. 2. cruelly overbearing; tyrannical. 3. causing physical or mental distress. —**op·pres′sive·ly,** *adv.* —**op·pres′sive·ness,** *n.*

**op·pro·bri·ous** (ə-prō′bri-əs), *adj.* 1. expressing opprobrium; abusive; scornful. 2. deserving opprobrium; infamous. —**op·pro′bri·ous·ly,** *adv.* —**op·pro′bri·ous·ness,** *n.*

**op·pro·bri·um** (ə-prō′bri-əm), *n.* [L. < *opprobare*, to reproach < *ob-* (see OB-) + *probrum*, a disgrace], 1. the disgrace attached to shameful conduct; scorn. 2. anything bringing shame.

**-op·sis,** [< Gr. < *opsis*, a sight], a combining form meaning *sight* or *view*, as in *synopsis.*

**opt** (opt), *v.i.* [< Fr. < L. *optare*], to make a choice.

**opt.,** 1. optative. 2. optician. 3. optics.

**op·ta·tive** (op′tə-tiv), *adj.* [< Fr. < LL. < L. *optare*, to desire], expressing wish or desire, as the mood in Greek grammar. *n.* the optative mood or a verb in this mood. —**op′ta·tive·ly,** *adv.*

**op·tic** (op′tik), *adj.* [< Fr. < ML. < Gr. *optikos* < base *op-* (as in *opsomai*, I shall see)], of the eye or sense of sight. *n.* [Colloq.], the eye.

**op·ti·cal** (op′ti-k'l), *adj.* 1. of the sense of sight; visual. 2. of optics. 3. made to give help in seeing: as, *optical* instruments. —**op′ti·cal·ly,** *adv.*

**op·ti·cian** (op-tish′ən), *n.* a person who makes or sells eyeglasses and other optical instruments.

**op·tics** (op′tiks), *n.pl.* [construed as sing.], [< *optic*], the branch of physics dealing with the nature and properties of light and vision.

**op·ti·mism** (op′tə-miz'm), *n.* [< Fr. < L. *optimus*, best], 1. in *philosophy*, *a*) the doctrine that the existing world is the best possible. *b*) the belief that good ultimately prevails over evil. 2. the tendency to take the most hopeful or cheerful view of matters: cf. *pessimism.* —**op′ti·mist,** *n.* —**op′ti·mis′tic, op′ti·mis′ti·cal,** *adj.* —**op′ti·mis′ti·cal·ly,** *adv.*

**op·ti·mum** (op′tə-məm), *n.* [*pl.* -MUMS, -MA (-mə)], [L., neut. of *optimus*, best], the best or most favorable degree, condition, amount, etc. *adj.* best; most favorable: also **op′ti·mal.**

**op·tion** (op′shən), *n.* [Fr. < L. *optio* < *optare*, to wish], 1. a choosing; choice. 2. the right or liberty of choosing. 3. something that is or can be chosen. 4. the right to buy or sell something at a fixed price within a specified time.

**op·tion·al** (op′shən-'l), *adj.* left to one's option, or choice; elective. —**op′tion·al·ly,** *adv.*

**op·tom·e·try** (op-tom′ə-tri), *n.* [see OPTIC & -METRY], 1. measurement of the range and power of vision. 2. the science or profession of testing the vision and fitting glasses to correct eye defects. —**op·to·met·ric** (op′tə-met′rik), **op′to·met′ri·cal,** *adj.* —**op·tom′e·trist,** *n.*

**op·u·lence** (op′yoo-ləns), *n.* [see OPULENT], 1. wealth; riches. 2. abundance. Also **op′u·len·cy.**

**op·u·lent** (op′yoo-lənt), *adj.* [< L. < *ops*, wealth], 1. wealthy; rich. 2. abundant. —**op′u·lent·ly,** *adv.*

**o·pus** (ō′pəs), *n.* [*pl.* OPERA (op′ẽr-ə); *now also* OPUSES], [L., a work], a work; composition; esp., any of the chronologically numbered musical works of a composer.

**-o·py** (ō-pi), -opia.

**or** (ôr; *unstressed* ẽr), *conj.* [ME., in form a contr. of *other*, either, but actually < AS. *oththe*], a coordinating conjunction introducing: *a*) an alternative (coffee *or* milk) or the last of a series of choices (apples, pears, *or* plums). *b*) a synonymous word or phrase (botany, *or* the science of plants). *c*) the second of two choices when the first is introduced by *either* or *whether.*

**or** (ôr), *n.* [Fr. < L. *aurum*, gold], in heraldry, gold.

**-or** (ẽr; *rarely* ôr), [< OFr. < L. *-or*], a noun-forming suffix meaning: *a*) *a person* or *thing that*, as in *inventor, tractor. b*) *quality* or *condition*, as in *horror, favor:* in Brit. usage, often *-our.*

**or·a·cle** (ôr′ə-k'l, or′i-), *n.* [OFr. < L. *oraculum* < *orare*, to pray < *os*, the mouth], 1. in ancient Greece and Rome, the place where or medium by which deities were consulted. 2. the revelation of a medium or priest. 3. *a*) any person or agency believed to be in communication with a deity. *b*) any person of great knowledge or wisdom. *c*) opinion or statements of such a person.

**o·rac·u·lar** (ô-rak′yoo-lẽr, ō-), *adj.* 1. of or like an oracle. 2. very wise; prophetic; mysterious. —**o·rac′u·lar·ly,** *adv.*

**o·ral** (ôr′əl, ō′rəl), *adj.* [< L. *os*, the mouth], 1. uttered; spoken. 2. of or using speech. 3. of, at, or near the mouth. *n.* an oral examination, as in a university. —**o′ral·ly,** *adv.* —**o′ral·ness,** *n.*

**Or·ange** (ôr′ənj, or′inj), *n.* 1. a river in the Union of South Africa, flowing into the Atlantic. 2. a former principality of W Europe, now in France.

**or·ange** (ôr′ənj, or′inj), *n.* [< OFr. < Pr. *auranja* (after L. *aurum*, gold) < Sp. *naranja* < Ar. & Per.], 1. a reddish-yellow, round citrus fruit with a sweet juicy pulp. 2. the evergreen tree producing this or a shrub resembling this tree. 3. reddish yellow. *adj.* 1. of oranges. 2. reddish-yellow.

**or·ange·ade** (ôr′ənj-ād′, or′inj-), *n.* a drink made of orange juice, water, and sugar.

**Or·ange·man** (ôr′ənj-mən, or′inj-), *n.* [pl. -MEN], [after William III of England, Prince of *Orange*], a member of a secret society organized in northern Ireland in 1795 to support Protestantism.

**orange pekoe,** a black tea from Ceylon or India.

**orange stick,** a pointed stick of orangewood, used in manicuring.

**orange·wood** (ôr′ənj-wood′, or′inj-), *n.* the wood of the orange tree. *adj.* of orangewood.

**o·rang·u·tan** (ō-raŋ′oo-tan′), *n.* [< Malay < *oran*, man + *utan*, forest], a large ape, smaller than the gorilla, with shaggy, reddish hair, long arms, and a hairless face: it is found only in the jungles of Borneo and Sumatra: also **o·rang′, o·rang′ou·tang′** (-taŋ′).

**o·rate** (ôr′āt, ō-rāt′), *v.i.* & *v.t.* [ORATED, ORATING], [< *oration*], to make (an oration); say in a pompous manner: a humorously derogatory term.

**o·ra·tion** (ô-rā′shən, ō-), *n.* [< L. *oratio* < *orare*

to speak], a formal speech, as at a ceremony.
**or·a·tor** (ôr′ə-tẽr, or′-), *n.* 1. one who delivers an oration. 2. an eloquent public speaker.
**or·a·to·ri·o** (ôr′ə-tôr′i-ō′, or′ə-tō′ri-), *n.* [*pl.* -os], [It., small chapel: from performances at a chapel in Rome], a long, dramatic musical work, usually on a religious theme, consisting of arias, recitatives, choruses, etc. with orchestral accompaniment.
**or·a·to·ry** (ôr′ə-tôr′i, or′ə-tō′ri), *n.* [*pl.* -RIES], [L. *oratoria*], 1. the art of an orator; skill in public speaking. 2. [< L. *oratorius* < *orare*, to pray], a small chapel, as for private prayer. —**or′a·tor′i·cal,** *adj.* —**or′a·tor′i·cal·ly,** *adv.*
**orb** (ôrb), *n.* [< Fr. < L. *orbis*, a circle], 1. a globe; sphere. 2. any heavenly sphere, as the sun or moon. 3. [Poetic], the eye or eyeball. *v.t.* 1. to form into a sphere or circle. 2. [Poetic], to enclose. *v.i.* to move in an orbit. —**orbed,** *adj.* —**orb′y,** *adj.*
**or·bic·u·lar** (ôr-bik′yoo-lẽr), *adj.* [< LL. < L. dim. of *orbis*, a circle], 1. in the form of an orb. 2. in *botany*, round and flat, as a leaf. Also **or·bic′u·late** (-lit). —**or·bic′u·lar′i·ty,** *n.* —**or·bic′u·lar·ly,** *adv.*
**or·bit** (ôr′bit), *n.* [< Fr. < L. *orbita* < *orbis*, a circle], 1. the eye socket. 2. the path of a heavenly body in its revolution around another. 3. the range of one's experience or activity. *v.t.* & *v.i.* to put or go in an orbit (sense 2), as an artificial satellite. —**or′bit·al,** *adj.*
**or·chard** (ôr′chẽrd), *n.* [< AS. < *ort*, a garden + *geard*, enclosure], 1. an area of land where fruit trees, nut trees, etc. are grown. 2. such trees.
**or·ches·tra** (ôr′kis-trə), *n.* [L. < Gr. *orchēstra*, space for the chorus in front of the stage < *orcheisthai*, to dance], 1. in modern theaters, the space in front of and below the stage, where the musicians sit: also *orchestra pit.* 2. *a*) the section of seats near the pit on the main floor of a theater. *b*) the main floor of a theater. 3. *a*) a group of musicians playing together; esp., a symphony orchestra. *b*) the instruments of such a group. —**or·ches′tral** (-kes′trəl), *adj.* —**or·ches′tral·ly,** *adv.*
**or·ches·trate** (ôr′kis-trāt′), *v.t.* & *v.i.* [-TRATED, -TRATING], to compose or arrange (music) for an orchestra. —**or′ches·tra′tion,** *n.*
**or·chid** (ôr′kid), *n.* [< L.; see ORCHIS], 1. any of several related plants having flowers with three petals, one of which is enlarged and irregularly shaped. 2. the flower of such a plant. 3. a light bluish red. *adj.* light bluish-red.
**or·chis** (ôr′kis), *n.* [L. < Gr. *orchis*, testicle: from the shape of the roots], an orchid; specif., a variety with small flowers growing in spikes.
**ord.,** 1. order. 2. ordinance. 3. ordinary.
**or·dain** (ôr-dān′), *v.t.* [< OFr. < L. *ordinare* < *ordo*, an order], 1. to appoint; decree; establish; enact. 2. to appoint or admit to the position of minister, priest, etc. 3. to qualify (a man) as a rabbi. —**or·dain′er,** *n.* —**or·dain′ment,** *n.*
**or·deal** (ôr-dēl′, -dē′əl, ôr′dēl), *n.* [AS. *ordal* < *or-*, out + *dæl*, what is dealt], 1. an old method of trial in which the accused was exposed to dangers, which were supposed to be harmless to him if he was innocent. 2. any difficult or painful experience.
**or·der** (ôr′dẽr), *n.* [< OFr. < L. *ordo*, straight row], 1. social position. 2. a state of peace; orderly conduct. 3. arrangement of things or events; series. 4. a fixed or definite plan; system. 5. a group set off from others by some quality. 6. *a*) a military or monastic brotherhood: as, the Franciscan *Order.* *b*) an organized group of persons united by common interests, often in the form of a lodge: as, the *Order* of the Eastern Star. 7. *a*) a group of persons distinguished by having received a certain award: as, the *Order* of the Purple Heart. *b*) the badge of such a group. 8. a condition in which everything is in its right place and functioning properly. 9. condition in general: as, the car is in poor *order.* 10. a command, instruction, etc. usually backed by authority. 11. a class; kind; sort: as, sentiments of a high *order.* 12. an established method, as of conduct in meetings, court, etc. 13. *a*) a request or commission to supply something: as, my *order* for books. *b*) the goods so supplied: as, the grocery *order* is here. *c*) a single portion of some food, as in a restaurant. 14. in *architecture*, any of several classical styles of structure, determined chiefly by the type of column. 15. in *biology*, a group of plants or animals next larger than the family and smaller than the class. 16. in *finance*, written instructions to pay money or surrender property. 17. in *law*, a decision of a court, usually not final. 18. in *theology*, *a*) any of the nine grades of angels. *b*) any rank in the Christian clergy. *c*) *pl.* the position of ordained minister; as, he took holy *orders.* *v.t.* 1. to put or keep in order; arrange. 2. to command. 3. to request (something to be supplied): as, *order* a meal. 4. in *theology*, to ordain. *v.i.* 1. to give a command. 2. to request that something be supplied. —**by order,** in observance of an order. —**call to order,** to request to be quiet, as in order to start (a meeting). —**in** (or **out of**) **order,** 1. in (or out of) proper sequence or position. 2. in (or not in) good condition. 3. in (or not in) accordance with the rules. 4. (not) suitable. —**in order that,** so that. —**in order to,** for the purpose of. —**in short order,** without delay. —**on order,** requested but not yet supplied. —**on the order of,** similar to. —**to order,** as specified by the purchaser. —**or′der·er,** *n.* —**or′der·less,** *adj.*
**or·der·ly** (ôr′dẽr-li), *adj.* 1. neat; well-arranged. 2. well-behaved; law-abiding. *n.* [*pl.* -LIES], 1. a soldier assigned to an officer for carrying messages, performing personal services, etc. 2. a male hospital attendant. —**or′der·li·ness,** *n.*
**or·di·nal** (ôr′d'n-əl), *adj.* [< LL. *ordinalis* < L. *ordo*, an order], 1. expressing order, specifically of a number in a series: the ordinal numbers are *first, second, third*, etc., or *1st, 2d, 3d*, etc.: cf. *cardinal.* 2. of an order of animals or plants. *n.* 1. an ordinal number. 2. [often O-], a book of prescribed forms used in church services. —**or′di·nal·ly,** *adv.*
**or·di·nance** (ôr′di-nəns), *n.* [< OFr. < *ordener;* see ORDAIN], 1. an authoritative command. 2. an established religious rite, as the Communion. 3. a statute enacted by a city government.
**or·di·nar·i·ly** (ôr′d'n-er′ə-li, ôr′də-nâr′-), *adv.* usually; generally; as a rule.
**or·di·nar·y** (ôr′d'n-er′i), *n.* [*pl.* -IES], [< L. *ordinarius* < *ordo*, an order], 1. an official of church or court whose power is original and not that of a deputy. 2. a book containing the form for divine service. 3. a set meal served daily at a fixed price. 4. a tavern. *adj.* 1. customary; usual; regular. 2. familiar; unexceptional; common. —**in ordinary,** in regular service. —**out of the ordinary,** unusual. —**or′di·nar′i·ness,** *n.*
**or·di·nate** (ôr′d'n-āt′, -it), *n.* [< L. pp. of *ordinare*, to order < *ordo*, an order], one of two lines used in fixing a point on a geometric graph.

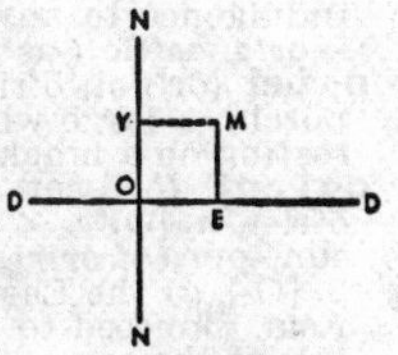

ORDINATE
ME or YO, ordinate of point M; OE or YM, abscissa of M; NN, axis of ordinates; DD, axis of abscissas

**or·di·na·tion** (ôr′də-nā′shən), *n.* [see ORDINATE], an ordaining or being ordained.
**ord·nance** (ôrd′nəns), *n.* [< *ordinance*], 1. artillery. 2. *a*) all weapons and ammunition used in warfare. *b*) equipment used in servicing weapons.
**Or·do·vi·cian** (ôr′də-vish′ən), *adj.* [< L. *Ordovices*, a tribe in Wales], designating or of the second period of the Paleozoic Era: see **geology**, chart. *n.* the Ordovician Period.
**or·dure** (ôr′jẽr, -dyoor), *n.* [OFr. < *ord*, filthy; L. *horridus*, horrid], dung; excrement.
**ore** (ôr, ōr), *n.* [AS. *ar*, brass, copper], 1. any natural combination of minerals, especially one from which a metal or metals can be profitably extracted. 2. a natural substance from which a nonmetallic material, as sulfur, can be extracted.
**Or·e·gon** (ôr′i-gon′, or′i-gən), *n.* a Northwestern State of the U.S.: area, 96,981 sq. mi.; pop., 1,769,000; capital, Salem: abbrev. **Ore., Oreg.** —**Or′e·go′ni·an** (-gō′ni-ən), *adj.* & *n.*
**O·res·tes** (ô-res′tēz, ō-), *n.* in *Gr. legend*, brother of Electra: see **Electra.**
**or·gan** (ôr′gən), *n.* [< OFr. & AS. < L. *organum* < Gr. *organon*, an instrument], 1. any of several musical instruments, especially one consisting of various sets of pipes which, as they are opened by corresponding keys on a keyboard, allow passage to a column of compressed air that causes sound by vibration. 2. in animals and plants, a part composed of several tissues, adapted to perform a specific function or functions. 3. a means

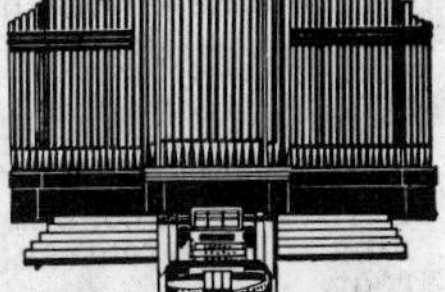
PIPE ORGAN

for performing some action. 4. a means of communicating ideas or opinions, as a periodical.

**or·gan·dy, or·gan·die** (ôr'gən-di), *n.* [*pl.* -DIES], [Fr. *organdi*], a very sheer, stiff cotton fabric, used for blouses, etc. *adj.* made of organdy.

**organ grinder,** a person who makes a living by playing a barrel organ in the street.

**or·gan·ic** (ôr-gan'ik), *adj.* 1. of or having to do with an organ. 2. inherent; constitutional. 3. systematically arranged. 4. *a*) designating or of any chemical compound containing carbon. *b*) designating or of the branch of chemistry dealing with carbon compounds. 5. of, like, or derived from living organisms. 6. in *law*, fundamental: as, the *organic* law of the U.S. is the Constitution. 7. in *medicine*, involving alteration in the structure of an organ. 8. in *philosophy*, having a complex but necessary interrelationship of parts, like that in living things. —**or·gan'i·cal·ly,** *adv.*

**organic disease,** a disease accompanied by visible structural changes in the tissues or organs.

**or·gan·ism** (ôr'gən-iz'm), *n.* 1. any living thing. 2. anything like a living thing in its complexity of structure or functions.

**or·gan·ist** (ôr'gən-ist), *n.* one who plays the organ.

**or·gan·i·za·tion** (ôr'gən-i-zā'shən, -ī-zā'-), *n.* 1. an organizing or being organized. 2. organic structure. 3. any unified group or systematized whole; esp., a body of persons organized for some purpose, as a club, union, etc. 4. the administrative or executive structure of a business or political party. —**or'gan·i·za'tion·al,** *adj.*

**or·gan·ize** (ôr'gən-īz'), *v.t.* [-IZED, -IZING], 1. to provide with an organic structure; systematize. 2. to arrange; bring into being. 3. to enlist in, or cause to form, a labor union. *v.i.* 1. to become organic or organized. 2. to form or join in a labor union. —**or'gan·iz'a·bil'i·ty,** *n.* —**or'gan·iz'a·ble,** *adj.* —**or'gan·iz'er,** *n.*

**or·gasm** (ôr'gaz'm), *n.* [< Fr. < Gr. *orgasmos* < *organ*, to swell with moisture], a frenzy; esp., the climax of a sexual act. —**or·gas'mic,** *adj.*

**or·gy** (ôr'ji), *n.* [*pl.* -GIES], [< Fr. < L. < Gr. *orgia*, *pl.*, secret rites], 1. *usually in pl.* in ancient Greece and Rome, wild celebration in worship of certain gods. 2. any wild merrymaking. 3. an overindulgence in any activity: as, an *orgy* of work. —**or'gi·as'tic** (-as'tik), *adj.* —**or'gi·as'ti·cal·ly,** *adv.*

**o·ri·el** (ôr'i-əl, ō'ri-), *n.* [< OFr. < ML. *oriolum*, porch], a large window built out from a wall and resting on a bracket or corbel.

**o·ri·ent** (ôr'i-ənt, ō'ri-; *for v., usually* ôr'i-ent', ō'ri-), *n.* [OFr. < L. *oriens*, direction of the rising sun, ppr. of *oriri*, to arise], 1. [Poetic], the east. 2. [O-], *a*) the East; Asia. *b*) the Far East; eastern Asia. Opposed to *Occident*. *adj.* 1. [Poetic], oriental; of the east. 2. shining, as pearls. 3. [Chiefly Poetic], rising, as the sun. *v.t.* 1. to cause to face the east. 2. *a*) to set, as a map, in agreement with the points of the compass. *b*) figuratively, to adjust to a particular situation (often used reflexively). *v.i.* 1. to face the east. 2. to become adjusted to a situation.

**o·ri·en·tal** (ôr'i-en't'l, ō'ri-), *adj.* 1. eastern. 2. [O-], of the Orient, its people, or their culture. *n.* [usually O-], a native of the Orient or a member of a people native to that region. —**o'ri·en'tal·ly, O'ri·en'tal·ly,** *adv.*

**O·ri·en·tal·ism** (ôr'i-en't'l-iz'm, ō'ri-), *n.* [also o-], 1. any trait, quality, etc. associated with people of the East. 2. study of Eastern culture. —**O'ri·en'tal·ist, o'ri·en'tal·ist,** *n.*

**o·ri·en·tate** (ôr'i-en-tāt', ō'ri-en'tāt), *v.t. & v.i.* [-TATED, -TATING], to orient.

**o·ri·en·ta·tion** (ôr'i-en-tā'shən, ō'ri-), *n.* 1. an orienting or being oriented. 2. recognition of and adaptation to a situation or environment.

**or·i·fice** (ôr'ə-fis, or'-), *n.* [Fr. < LL. *orificium* < L. *os*, mouth + *facere*, to make], an opening; mouth or outlet. —**or'i·fi'cial** (-fish'əl), *adj.*

**or·i·flamme** (ôr'ə-flam', or'-), *n.* [Fr. < OFr. < L. *aurum*, gold + *flamma*, flame], 1. the ancient royal standard of France, a red silk banner with flame-shaped streamers. 2. any battle standard.

**orig.,** 1. origin. 2. original. 3. originally.

**or·i·gin** (ôr'ə-jin, or'-), *n.* [< Fr. < L. *origo* < *oriri*, to rise], 1. a coming into existence or use; beginning. 2. parentage; birth; lineage. 3. source; root.

**o·rig·i·nal** (ə-rij'ə-n'l), *adj.* 1. having to do with an origin; first; earliest. 2. never having been before; new; novel. 3. capable of creating something new; inventive; ingenious. 4. coming from someone as the originator, maker, author, etc. 5. being that from which copies are made. *n.* 1. a primary type that has given rise to varieties. 2. an original work, as of art or literature, as distinguished from a copy, etc. 3. the person or thing depicted in a painting or the like. 4. a person of original mind, character, etc. 5. an eccentric person. —**o·rig'i·nal·ly,** *adv.*

**o·rig·i·nal·i·ty** (ə-rij'ə-nal'ə-ti), *n.* 1. a being original. 2. [*pl.* -TIES], anything original.

**original sin,** in *Christian theology*, sinfulness and depravity regarded as innate in man as a direct result of Adam's sin.

**o·rig·i·nate** (ə-rij'ə-nāt'), *v.t.* [-NATED, -NATING], to bring into being; esp., to create (something original); invent. *v.i.* to come into being; begin; start. —**o·rig'i·na'tion,** *n.* —**o·rig'i·na'tive,** *adj.* —**o·rig'i·na'tor,** *n.*

**O·ri·no·co** (ôr'ə-nō'kō, ō'ri-), *n.* a river in Venezuela, flowing into the Atlantic.

**o·ri·ole** (ôr'i-ōl', ō'ri-), *n.* [< OFr. < ML. < L. *aureolus*, golden < *aurum*, gold], 1. any of a group of yellow and black birds found from Europe to Australia. 2. any of a group of American birds, including the Baltimore oriole, which have orange and black plumage and build hanging nests.

**O·ri·on** (ō-rī'ən), *n.* an equatorial constellation near Taurus, supposedly outlining a hunter with a belt and sword.

**or·i·son** (ôr'i-z'n, or'-), *n.* [< OFr. < L. < *orare*, to pray], *usually in pl.* a prayer.

**Ork·ney Islands** (ôrk'ni), a group of Scottish islands north of Scotland.

**Or·lan·do** (ôr-lan'dō), *n.* a city in central Florida: pop., 88,000.

**Or·lé·ans** (ôr'lā'än'; Eng. ôr'li-ənz), *n.* a city in north central France: pop., 76,000.

**or·lon** (ôr'lon), *n.* a synthetic acrylic fiber somewhat similar to nylon, or a fabric made from this fiber: a trade-mark (**Orlon**).

**or·mo·lu** (ôr'mə-lōō'), *n.* [< Fr. *or moulu*, ground gold], an imitation gold consisting of an alloy of copper and tin.

**or·na·ment** (ôr'nə-mənt; *for v.*, -ment'), *n.* [< OFr. < L. *ornamentum* < *ornare*, to adorn], 1. anything that adorns; decoration; embellishment. 2. one whose character or talent adds luster to his surroundings, society, etc. 3. an adorning or being adorned. 4. mere external display. 5. in *music*, an embellishing trill, arpeggio, etc. *v.t.* to decorate; furnish with ornaments or be an ornament to. —**or'na·ment'er,** *n.*

**or·na·men·tal** (ôr'nə-men't'l), *adj.* serving as an ornament; decorative. *n.* something ornamental. —**or'na·men'tal·ly,** *adv.*

**or·na·men·ta·tion** (ôr'nə-men-tā'shən), *n.* 1. an ornamented appearance. 2. an ornamenting or being ornamented. 3. ornaments collectively; decoration.

**or·nate** (ôr-nāt'), *adj.* [< L. pp. of *ornare*, to adorn], 1. heavily ornamented; overadorned. 2. flowery; showy: said of literary style. —**or·nate'ly,** *adv.* —**or·nate'ness,** *n.*

**or·ner·y** (ôr'nēr-i), *adj.* [-IER, -IEST], [altered < *ordinary*], [Chiefly Dial.], 1. having an ugly or mean disposition. 2. obstinate. 3. base; low. —**or'ner·i·ness,** *n.*

**or·ni·thol·o·gy** (ôr'ni-thol'ə-ji), *n.* [< Gr. *ornis*, bird; + *-logy*], the branch of zoology dealing with birds. —**or'ni·tho·log'i·cal** (-thə-loj'i-k'l), *adj.* —**or'ni·thol'o·gist,** *n.*

**o·ro·tund** (ôr'ə-tund', ō'rə-), *adj.* [< L. *os*, mouth + *rotundus*, round], 1. full; resonant; clear: said of the voice. 2. showy; bombastic; pompous, as speaking or writing. —**o'ro·tun'di·ty,** *n.*

**O·roz·co, Jo·sé Cle·men·te** (hô-se' kle-men'te ô-rôs'kô), 1883–1949; Mexican painter.

**or·phan** (ôr'fən), *n.* [< LL. < Gr. *orphanos*], a child whose parents are dead. *adj.* 1. being an orphan. 2. of or for orphans. *v.t.* to cause to become an orphan. —**or'phan·hood',** *n.*

**or·phan·age** (ôr'fən-ij), *n.* 1. the condition of being an orphan. 2. an institution for orphans.

**Or·pheus** (ôr'fi-əs, -fūs), *n.* in *Gr. mythology*, a musician with magic ability on the lyre: when his wife Eurydice died, he obtained her release from Hades, but when he violated an agreement not to look at her as they left, she vanished. —**Or·phe'an** (-fē'ən), *adj.*

**Or·phic** (ôr'fik), *adj.* 1. of or characteristic of Orpheus. 2. like the music attributed to Orpheus; entrancing. 3. [also o-], mystic; occult.

**or·pine, or·pin** (ôr'pin), *n.* [Fr. *orpin*], a plant with fleshy leaves and white or purple flowers.

**Or·ping·ton** (ôr'piŋ-tən), *n.* [< *Orpington*, village in England], a breed of large, heavy chickens.

**or·ris, or·rice** (ôr'is, or'-), *n.* [prob. < MIt. < L. *iris*, iris], a plant of the iris family, having fragrant roots.

**or·ris·root** (ôr′is-ro͞ot′, -root′), *n.* the rootstock of the orris, ground and used in perfumery or as a powder to whiten the hair in stage make-up.

**or·tho-,** [< Gr. *orthos*, straight], a combining form meaning: 1. *straight*, as in *orthodontia*. 2. *right angle*, as in *orthoclase*. 3. *proper, correct*, as in *orthography*. 4. in *medicine, correction of deformities*, as in *orthopedics*. Also **orth-**.

**or·tho·clase** (ôr′thə-klās′, -klāz′), *n.* [< *ortho-* + Gr. *klasis*, a breaking < *klan*, to break], a mineral of the feldspar family, having perfect cleavage. —**or′tho·clas′tic** (-klas′tik), *adj.*

**or·tho·don·ti·a** (ôr′thə-don′shə, -shi-ə), *n.* the branch of dentistry concerned with correcting and preventing irregularities of the teeth. —**or′tho·don′tic,** *adj.* —**or′tho·don′tist,** *n.*

**or·tho·dox** (ôr′thə-doks′), *adj.* [< Fr. < LL. < Gr. < *orthos*, correct + *doxa*, opinion < *dokein*, to think], 1. conforming to the usual beliefs or practices or established doctrines, especially in religion; conventional. 2. conforming to the Christian faith as formulated in the early Church creeds. 3. [O-], designating or of any church in the Orthodox Eastern Church. —**or′tho·dox′y** [*pl.* -IES], *n.*

**Orthodox Eastern Church,** the dominant Christian church in E Europe, W Asia, and N Africa: it now includes churches recognizing the primacy of the patriarchs of Constantinople, Alexandria, Antioch, and Jerusalem, and also autonomous churches of the Soviet Union, Greece, Yugoslavia, etc.: also called *Eastern Church, Orthodox Church.*

**or·tho·ë·py** (ôr-thō′i-pi, ôr′thō-), *n.* [< Gr. < *orthos*, right + *epos*, a word], 1. the study dealing with pronunciation; phonology. 2. standard pronunciation. —**or′tho·ë·p′ic** (-ep′ik), **or′tho·ë·p′i·cal,** *adj.* —**or·tho′ë·pist,** *n.*

**or·thog·ra·phy** (ôr-thog′rə-fi), *n.* [*pl.* -PHIES], [< OFr. < L. < Gr.; see ORTHO- & -GRAPHY], 1. correct spelling. 2. any method of spelling. 3. spelling as a subject or science. —**or·thog′ra·pher,** *n.* —**or·tho·graph·ic** (ôr′thə-graf′ik), **or′tho·graph′i·cal,** *adj.* —**or′tho·graph′i·cal·ly,** *adv.*

**or·tho·pe·dics, or·tho·pae·dics** (ôr′thə-pē′diks), *n.pl.* [construed as sing.], [< *ortho-* + Gr. *paideia*, training of children < *pais*, child], the branch of surgery dealing with the treatment of deformities, diseases, and injuries of the bones and joints: also **or′tho·pe′dy.** —**or′tho·pe′dic, or′tho·pae′dic,** *adj.* —**or′tho·pe′dist, or′tho·pae′dist,** *n.*

**or·thop·ter·on** (ôr-thop′tẽr-on′), *n.* [*pl.* -TERA (-ə)], [< *ortho-* + Gr. *pteron*, wing], any of an order of insects, including crickets, grasshoppers, etc., having biting mouth parts and hard forewings covering membranous hind wings. —**or·thop′ter·an,** *adj.* & *n.* —**or·thop′ter·ous,** *adj.*

**or·to·lan** (ôr′tə-lən), *n.* [Fr. < Pr. < It. < L. *hortulanus*, dim. of *hortus*, a garden], an Old World bunting, prized as a table delicacy.

**-o·ry** (ôr′i; *for* 2, *also* ẽr-i), [< OFr. < L. *-orius, -oria, -orium*], 1. an adjective-forming suffix meaning *of, having the nature of*, as in *commendatory*. 2. a noun-forming suffix meaning *a place* or *thing for*, as in *directory*.

**o·ryx** (ôr′iks, or′-, ō′riks), *n.* [*pl.* ORYXES, ORYX; see PLURAL, II, D, 1], [L. < Gr. *oryx*], a large African antelope with long, straight horns projecting backward; gemsbok.

‡**os** (os), *n.* [*pl.* OSSA (os′ə)], [L.], a bone.

‡**os** (os), *n.* [*pl.* ORA (ō′rə)], [L.], a mouth; opening.

**Os,** in *chemistry*, osmium.

**O.S.,** Old Style.

**OS., O.S.,** Old Saxon.

**O·sage orange** (ō′sāj′), [< *Osage*, Am. Ind. tribe], 1. a spiny tree with orange-colored wood, used for hedges, etc. 2. its orangelike, inedible fruit.

**O·sa·ka** (ō-sä′kə), *n.* a city on the S coast of Honshu, Japan: pop., 1,956,000.

**Os·car** (os′kẽr), *n.* [Slang], any of the statuettes awarded annually in the U.S. for outstanding contributions to the motion-picture industry.

**os·cil·late** (os′ə-lāt′), *v.i.* [-LATED, -LATING], [< L. pp. of *oscillare*, to swing], 1. to swing to and fro. 2. to be indecisive; fluctuate; vacillate. 3. in *physics*, to vary between maximum and minimum values, as an electric current. *v.t.* to cause to oscillate. —**os′cil·la′tor,** *n.* —**os′cil·la·to′ry** (-lə-tôr′i, -tō′ri), *adj.*

**os·cil·la·tion** (os′ə-lā′shən), *n.* 1. an oscillating. 2. a single swing of an oscillating object. 3. fluctuation; instability. 4. in *electricity*, variation between maximum and minimum values, as of current or voltage.

**os·cil·lo·graph** (ə-sil′ə-graf′, -gräf′), *n.* [< L. *oscillare*, to swing; + *-graph*], an instrument which registers oscillations of an electric current.

**os·cil·lo·scope** (ə-sil′ə-skōp′), *n.* [< L. *oscillare*, to swing; + *-scope*], a type of oscillograph that visually records an electrical wave on a fluorescent screen, as of a cathode-ray tube.

**os·cine** (os′in, -īn), *adj.* [< L. *oscen*, singing bird], designating a group of perching birds, as the finches, larks, etc., with highly developed vocal organs: most species sing. *n.* an oscine bird.

**os·cu·late** (os′kyoo-lāt′), *v.t.* & *v.i.* [-LATED, -LATING], [L. *osculari* < *osculum*, kiss, dim. of *os*, a mouth], 1. to kiss. 2. to touch closely. 3. in *biology*, to have (characteristics) in common. —**os′cu·lant** (-lənt), *adj.* —**os′cu·la′tion,** *n.* —**os′cu·la·to′ry** (-lə-tôr′i, -tō′ri), *adj.*

**-ose** (ōs), [Fr. < *glucose;* see GLUCOSE], a suffix meaning: 1. *a carbohydrate*, as in *sucrose*. 2. *the product of a protein hydrolysis*, as in *proteose*.

**-ose** (ōs), [Fr. < L. *-osus*], a suffix meaning *full of, having the qualities of*, as in *bellicose, morose.*

**OSerb.,** Old Serbian.

**o·sier** (ō′zhẽr), *n.* [< OFr. < ML. *ausaria*, bed of willows], any of several willows whose wood is used for baskets and furniture.

**O·si·ris** (ō-sī′ris), *n.* the ancient Egyptian god of the lower world, husband and brother of Isis.

**-o·sis** (ō′sis), [L. < Gr. *-osis*], a suffix meaning: 1. *state, condition, action*, as in *osmosis*. 2. *an abnormal* or *diseased condition*, as in *neurosis*.

**-os·i·ty** (os′ə-ti), [< Fr. < L. *-ositas*], a suffix used to form nouns corresponding to adjectives ending in *-ose* or *-ous*.

**OSlav.,** Old Slavic.

**Os·lo** (os′lō, oz′-; Norw. oos′loo), *n.* the capital of Norway, a seaport in the SE part: pop., 434,000: formerly called *Christiania*.

**Os·man·li** (oz-man′li, os-), *n.* [Turk. < *Osman* (1259–1326), founder of Ottoman Empire], 1. [*pl.* -LIS], an Ottoman Turk. 2. the language of the Ottoman Turks. *adj.* Ottoman.

**os·mi·um** (oz′mi-əm, os′-), *n.* [< Gr. *osmē*, odor], a bluish-white, amorphous, metallic chemical element of the platinum group: it occurs in the form of an alloy with platinum and iridium: symbol, Os; at. wt., 190.2; at. no., 76.

**os·mose** (oz′mōs, os′-), *v.i.* [-MOSED, -MOSING], to undergo osmosis.

**os·mo·sis** (oz-mō′sis, os-), *n.* [ult. < Gr. *osmos*, an impulse < *ōthein*, to push], 1. the tendency of fluids to pass through a separating semipermeable membrane, as the wall of a living cell, so as to equalize concentrations on both sides of the membrane. 2. the diffusion of fluids through a porous partition. —**os·mot′ic** (-mot′ik), *adj.* —**os·mot′i·cal·ly,** *adv.*

**OSp.,** Old Spanish.

**os·prey** (os′pri), *n.* [*pl.* -PREYS], [< L. *osifrago*, lit., the bone-breaker < *os*, a bone + *frangere*, to break], a large bird of the hawk family with a brown back and white breast, which feeds solely on fish: also called *fish hawk*.

**Os·sa** (os′ə), *n.* a mountain in NE Greece: in *Gr. mythology*, the Titans, in a futile attempt to attack the gods in heaven, piled Ossa on Pelion and both on Olympus.

**os·se·ous** (os′i-əs), *adj.* [< L. < *os*, a bone], composed of, containing, or like bone; bony.

**Os·sian** (osh′ən, os′i-ən), *n.* in *Gaelic folklore*, a bard and hero of the 3d century A.D.

**os·sif·er·ous** (o-sif′ẽr-əs), *adj.* [< L. *os*, a bone; + *-ferous*], containing bones, as a geological deposit.

**os·si·fi·ca·tion** (os′ə-fi-kā′shən), *n.* 1. an ossifying or being ossified. 2. the abnormal conversion of soft tissue into bone.

**os·si·fy** (os′ə-fī′), *v.t.* & *v.i.* [-FIED, -FYING], [< L. *os*, a bone; + *-fy*], 1. in *physiology*, to change or develop into bone. 2. to settle or fix rigidly in a practice, custom, etc.

**Os·si·ning** (os′ə-niŋ), *n.* a town in SE New York, on the Hudson: site of Sing Sing, State prison.

**os·te·al** (os′ti-əl), *adj.* osseous; bony.

**Ost·end** (os-tend′), *n.* a seaport and summer resort in NW Belgium: pop., 50,000.

**os·ten·si·ble** (os-ten′sə-b'l), *adj.* [Fr. < LL. < L. *ostendere*, to show < *ob(s)-*, against + *tendere*, to stretch], apparent; seeming; professed. —**os·ten′si·bil′i·ty,** *n.* —**os·ten′si·bly,** *adv.*

**os·ten·sive** (os-ten′siv), *adj.* ostensible; exhibiting; revealing. —**os·ten′sive·ly,** *adv.*

**os·ten·ta·tion** (os′tən-tā′shən), *n.* [< L.; ult. <

*ostendere;* see OSTENSIBLE], outright display; showiness; boastful exhibition. —**os′ten·ta′tious,** *adj.* —**os′ten·ta′tious·ly,** *adv.* —**os′ten·ta′tious·ness,** *n.*
**os·te·o-,** [< Gr. *osteon*], a combining form meaning *a bone* or *bones*, as in *osteopath*: also **oste-.**
**os·te·ol·o·gy** (os′ti-ol′ə-ji), *n.* [*osteo-* + *-logy*], the study of the bones of vertebrates. —**os′te·o·log′i·cal** (-ə-loj′i-k′l), *adj.* —**os′te·ol′o·gist,** *n.*
**os·te·o·ma** (os′ti-ō′mə), *n.* [*pl.* -MAS, -MATA (-mə-tə)], [< *osteo-* + *-oma*], a tumor composed of bony tissue.
**os·te·o·my·e·li·tis** (os′ti-ō-mī′ə-lī′tis), *n.* [*osteo-* + *myelitis*], inflammation of the bone marrow.
**os·te·op·a·thy** (os′ti-op′ə-thi), *n.* [*osteo-* + *-pathy*], a system of treating ailments based on the belief that they generally result from the pressure of displaced bones on nerves, etc. and are curable by manipulation. —**os′te·o·path′** (-ə-path′), **os′te·op′a·thist,** *n.* —**os′te·o·path′ic,** *adj.* —**os′te·o·path′i·cal·ly,** *adv.*
**Ös·ter·reich** (ös′tĕr-rīH′), *n.* Austria: the German name.
**ost·ler** (os′lĕr), *n.* a hostler; stableman.
**os·tra·cism** (os′trə-siz′m), *n.* [see OSTRACIZE], 1. in ancient Greece, the temporary banishment of a citizen by popular vote. 2. an exclusion by general consent, as from society.
**os·tra·cize** (os′trə-sīz′), *v.t.* [-CIZED, -CIZING], [< Gr. *ostrakizein* < *ostrakon*, a shell (cast as a ballot)], to banish, shut out, etc. by ostracism. —**os′tra·ciz′a·ble,** *adj.* —**os′tra·ciz′er,** *n.*
**os·trich** (ôs′trich, os′-), *n.* [*pl.* OSTRICHES, OSTRICH; see PLURAL, II, D, 1], [< OFr. < LL. < L. *avis*, bird + *struthio*, ostrich], 1. a swift-running, nonflying bird of Africa and the Near East, the largest bird extant, with a long neck and legs and small wings. 2. a smaller related bird of South America; rhea.
**Os·tro·goth** (os′trə-goth′), *n.* an East Goth; esp., a member of the tribe which conquered Italy in the 5th century A.D. —**Os′tro·goth′ic,** *adj.*
**O.T., OT, OT.,** Old Testament.
**O·thel·lo** (ə-thel′ō, ō-), *n.* a tragedy by Shakespeare in which the title character, made madly jealous by the villainous Iago, kills his faithful wife, Desdemona.
**oth·er** (*uth*′ĕr), *adj.* [AS.], 1. being the remaining one or ones of two or more: as, the *other* foot, his *other* books. 2. different or distinct from that or those implied: as, any *other* girl. 3. different: as, I wouldn't want it *other* than it is. 4. additional: as, he has no *other* coat. 5. former: as, in *other* times. *pron.* 1. the other one: as, each loved the *other.* 2. some other person or thing: as, to do as *others* do. *adv.* otherwise; differently: as, he can't do *other* than go. —**every other,** every second; every alternate. —**of all others,** above all others. —**the other day** (or **night**), not long ago.
**oth·er·wise** (*uth*′ĕr-wīz′), *adv.* 1. in another manner; differently: as, she believed *otherwise.* 2. in all other respects: as, he is *otherwise* intelligent. 3. in other circumstances. *adj.* different: as, his answer could not be *otherwise.*
**other world,** the supposed world after death.
**oth·er·world·ly** (*uth*′ĕr-wŭrld′li), *adj.* being apart from earthly interests; concerned with life in a future world. —**oth′er·world′li·ness,** *n.*
**Oth·man** (oth′mən), *n.* [*pl.* -MANS], an Ottoman.
**-ot·ic** (ot′ik), [Gr. *-ōtikos*], a suffix meaning: 1. *of* or *affected with*, as in *sclerotic.* 2. *producing*, as in *narcotic.*
**o·ti·ose** (ō′shi-ōs′, -ti-), *adj.* [< L. < *otium*, leisure], 1. idle; indolent. 2. futile; ineffective. 3. useless; superfluous. —**o′ti·ose·ly,** *adv.* —**o′ti·os′i·ty** (-os′ə-ti), **o′ti·ose·ness,** *n.*
**o·ti·tis** (ō-tī′tis), *n.* [see OTO- & -ITIS], inflammation of the ear.
**o·to-,** [< Gr. *ous, ōtos*, the ear], a combining form meaning *the ear*, as in *otology*: also **ot-.**
**o·tol·o·gy** (ō-tol′ə-ji), *n.* [*oto-* + *-logy*], the branch of medicine dealing with the ear and its diseases. —**o·to·log·i·cal** (ō′tə-loj′i-k′l), *adj.* —**o·tol′o·gist,** *n.*
**O·tran·to, Strait of** (ō-trän′tō), the strait between Albania and Italy.
**Ot·ta·wa** (ot′ə-wə, -wä′), *n.* 1. a member of a tribe of Algonquian Indians that lived in SE Ontario and SW Quebec. 2. the capital of Canada, in E Ontario: pop., 202,000.
**ot·ter** (ot′ĕr), *n.* [*pl.* -TERS, -TER; see PLURAL, II, D, 1], [AS. *otor*], 1. a furry, flesh-eating, swimming mammal related to the weasel and mink, with webbed feet and a long tail. 2. its fur.
**Ot·to·man** (ot′ə-mən), *adj.* [ult. < Ar. *'Uthmāni*, of Osman; see OSMANLI], Turkish. *n.* [*pl.* -MANS], 1. a Turk. 2. [o-], *a*) a low, cushioned seat or couch without a back or arms. *b*) a cushioned footstool.
**Ottoman Empire,** the empire (c. 1300–1919) of the Turks in SE Europe, SW Asia, and NE Africa: also called *Turkish Empire.*
**ouch** (ouch), *interj.* an exclamation of pain.
**ought** (ôt), *v. aux.* [orig., pt. of *owe* < AS. pp. of *agan*, to owe], an auxiliary used with infinitives to express: 1. *obligation* or *duty*: as, he *ought* to pay his debts. 2. *desirability*: as, you *ought* to eat more. 3. *probability*: as, I *ought* to be through soon.
**ought** (ôt), *n.* anything whatever; aught. *adv.* to any degree; in any way; aught.
**ought** (ôt), *n.* a nought; cipher; zero.
‡**oui** (wē), *adv.* [Fr.], yes.
**oui·ja** (wē′jə), *n.* [Fr. *oui*, yes + G. *ja*, yes], a device consisting of a small three-cornered board moved over a larger board (**ouija board**) bearing the alphabet and other symbols, used in fortunetelling, etc.: a trademark (**Ouija**).

OUIJA BOARD

**ounce** (ouns), *n.* [< OFr. < L. *uncia*, a twelfth], 1. a unit of weight equal to 1/16 pound avoirdupois, or 1/12 pound troy. 2. any small amount. 3. a fluid ounce. Abbrev. **oz.** (*sing.* & *pl.*).
**ounce** (ouns), *n.* [< OFr. *l'once* < LL. < L. *lynx;* see LYNX], the snow leopard of Central Asia, having woolly, gray-white fur marked with black.
**our** (our; *often* är), *pron.* [< AS. *ure*], possessive form of **we.** *poss. pronominal adj.* of, belonging to, or done by us.
**ours** (ourz; *often* ärz), *pron.* that or those belonging to us: used without a following noun, often after *of*, as, a friend of *ours.*
**our·self** (our-self′), *pron.* a form corresponding to *ourselves*, used, as in royal proclamations, by one person.
**our·selves** (our-selvz′; *often* är-), *pron.* a form of the first person plural pronoun, used: *a*) as an intensive: as, we went *ourselves.* *b*) as a reflexive: as, we hurt *ourselves.* *c*) as a quasi-noun meaning "our true selves" (e.g., we are not *ourselves* today).
**-ous** (əs), [< OFr. < L. *-osus*], a suffix meaning: 1. *having, full of, characterized by*, as in *outrageous.* 2. in chemistry, *having a lower valence than is indicated by the suffix -ic*, as in *nitrous.*
**ou·sel** (o͞o′z'l), *n.* the ouzel.
**oust** (oust), *v.t.* [< Anglo-Fr. < OFr. *ouster;* said to be < L. < *ob-*, against + *stare*, to stand], to force out; expel; drive out; dispossess.
**oust·er** (ous′tĕr), *n.* 1. a person or thing that ousts. 2. in *law*, an ousting or being ousted, especially from real property by illegal means.
**out** (out), *adv.* [< AS. *ut*], 1. *a*) away or forth from a place, position, etc.: as, *out* of the house. *b*) away from home. *c*) on strike. 2. into the open air: as, come *out* and play. 3. into existence or activity: as, disease broke *out.* 4. *a*) to a conclusion: as, argue it *out.* *b*) completely: as, tired *out.* 5. into sight or notice: as, the moon came *out.* 6. *a*) into or in circulation: as, they put *out* a new style. *b*) into or in society: as, she has just come *out.* 7. from existence or activity: as, fade *out.* 8. aloud: as, sing *out.* 9. beyond a regular surface, condition, etc.: as, stand *out*, eke *out.* 10. away from the interior or midst: as, spread *out.* 11. from one state, as of composure, into another, as of annoyance: as, friends may fall *out.* 12. into disuse or retirement: as, long skirts went *out.* 13. from a number or stock: as, pick *out.* 14. [Colloq.], out on or along: as, *out* our way. 15. [Slang], into unconsciousness: as, he passed *out.* 16. in *baseball*, etc., in a manner producing an out: as, he struck *out.* *adj.* 1. external: usually in combination, as in *outpost.* 2. irregular: said of sizes of clothes, etc. 3. beyond regular limits. 4. outlying. 5. away from work, etc.: as, *out* because of sickness. 6. deviating from what is accurate: as, *out* in my estimates. 7. having suffered a loss: as, *out* five dollars. 8. not in operation, use, etc. 9. in *baseball, a*) not at bat; fielding. *b*) failing to get on base. *prep.* forth from: usually after *from.* *n.* 1. something that is out. 2. [Slang], a way out; excuse. 3. in *baseball*, retirement of a batter or of a player who has reached base. 4. *pl.* in *politics*, the party not in office. 5. in *tennis*, a return that lands outside the court. *v.i.* to go out; come out. *v.t.* to put out. *interj.* get out! —**at** (or **on**) **the outs,** [Colloq.], on unfriendly terms. —**out and away,** by far; without comparison. —**out and out,** completely; thoroughly. —**out for,** making a determined effort to get or do. —**out of,** 1. from inside of. 2. from the number of. 3. beyond. 4. from (material, etc.): as, made *out of* stone. 5. because of: as, *out of* spite. 6. so as to deprive: as, cheat *out of* money. —**out to,** making a determined effort to.

**out-** (out), a combining form meaning: 1. *at* or *from a point away, outside,* as in *outbuilding, outpatient.* 2. *going away* or *forth, outward,* as in *outbound.* 3. *better* or *more than,* as in *outdo.*
**out-and-out** (out′'n-out′), *adj.* complete; thorough.
**out·back** (out′bak′), *n.* [also O-], the sparsely settled, flat, arid inland region of Australia.
**out·bal·ance** (out-bal′əns), *v.t.* [-ANCED, -ANCING], to be greater than in weight, value, etc.
**out·bid** (out-bid′), *v.t. & v.i.* [-BID, -BIDDING], to bid more than (another).
**out·board** (out′bôrd′, -bōrd′), *adj.* located on the outer surface of a water craft. *adv.* away from the center of a craft. *n.* an outboard motor.
**outboard motor,** a portable gasoline engine attached to a small craft for propelling it.
**out·bound** (out′bound′), *adj.* outward bound.
**out·break** (out′brāk′), *n.* a breaking out; sudden occurrence, as of disease, looting, anger, etc.
**out·build·ing** (out′bil′diŋ), *n.* a structure, as a garage, separate from the main building.
**out·burst** (out′bũrst′), *n.* an outbreak; eruption.
**out·cast** (out′kast′, -käst′), *adj.* driven out; rejected. *n.* a person or thing cast out or rejected.
**out·class** (out-klas′, -kläs′), *v.t.* to surpass.
**out·come** (out′kum′), *n.* result; consequence.
**out·crop** (out′krop′; *for v.,* out-krop′), *n.* the emergence of a mineral so as to be exposed on the surface of the ground. *v.i.* [-CROPPED, -CROPPING], to emerge from the earth in this way.
**out·cry** (out′krī′), *n.* [*pl.* -CRIES], 1. a crying out. 2. a strong protest or objection.
**out·dat·ed** (out-dāt′id), *adj.* 1. old-fashioned. 2. no longer popular.
**out·dis·tance** (out-dis′təns), *v.t.* [-TANCED, -TANCING], to leave behind, as in a race; outstrip.
**out·do** (out-do͞o′), *v.t.* [-DID, -DONE, -DOING], to exceed; surpass. **—outdo oneself,** to do one's best or better than expected. **—out·do′er,** *n.*
**out·door** (out′dôr′, -dōr′), *adj.* 1. being outside of a building; open-air. 2. used or done outside.
**out·doors** (out′dôrz′, -dōrz′; *for n.,* out-dôrz′, -dōrz′), *adv.* in or into the open; outside. *n.* 1. any area outside a building. 2. the outdoor world.
**out·er** (out′ẽr), *adj.* 1. located farther out; exterior. 2. relatively far removed: as, the *outer* regions.
**out·er·most** (out′ẽr-mōst′, -məst), *adj. & adv.* in a position farthest from the inside or center.
**out·face** (out-fās′), *v.t.* [-FACED, -FACING], 1. to subdue with a look or stare. 2. to defy or resist.
**out·field** (out′fēld′), *n.* in *baseball,* 1. the playing area beyond the base lines. 2. the outfielders.
**out·field·er** (out′fēl′dẽr), *n.* in *baseball,* a player whose position is in the outfield.
**out·fit** (out′fit), *n.* 1. *a*) a set of articles for equipping. *b*) the equipment used in any craft or activity. 2. articles of clothing worn together; ensemble: as, a spring *outfit.* 3. a group of people associated in some activity; esp., a military unit. *v.t.* [-FITTED, -FITTING], to equip. **—out′fit′ter,** *n.*
**out·flank** (out-flaŋk′), *v.t.* 1. to maneuver so as to go beyond or cut off the flank of (a body of enemy troops). 2. to thwart; outwit. **—out·flank′er,** *n.*
**out·flow** (out′flō′), *n.* 1. the act of flowing out. 2. *a*) that which flows out. *b*) amount flowing out.
**out·fox** (out′foks′), *v.t.* to outwit.
**out·gen·er·al** (out-jen′ẽr-əl), *v.t.* [-ALED or -ALLED, -ALING or -ALLING], to surpass, as in leadership.
**out·go** (out-gō′; *for n.,* out′gō′), *v.t.* [-WENT, -GONE, -GOING], to go beyond; surpass. *n.* [*pl.* -GOES], 1. a going out. 2. that which goes or is paid out.
**out·go·ing** (out′gō′iŋ), *adj.* 1. going out; leaving. 2. sociable; friendly. *n.* the act of going out.
**out·grow** (out-grō′), *v.t.* [-GREW, -GROWN, -GROWING], 1. to exceed in growing. 2. to lose or get rid of by becoming mature. 3. to grow too large for.
**out·growth** (out′grōth′), *n.* 1. a growing out. 2. consequence; development; result. 3. an offshoot.
**out·guess** (out-ges′), *v.t.* to outwit.
**out·house** (out′hous′), *n.* a separate building near a main building; specif., an outdoor latrine.
**out·ing** (out′iŋ), *n.* 1. a pleasure trip or a holiday spent outdoors. 2. a walk in the open air.
**out·land·er** (out′lan′dẽr), *n.* a foreigner; stranger.
**out·land·ish** (out-lan′dish), *adj.* 1. strange; alien. 2. fantastic; bizarre. 3. remote; out-of-the-way. **—out·land′ish·ly,** *adv.* **—out·land′ish·ness,** *n.*
**out·last** (out-last′, -läst′), *v.t.* 1. to endure longer than. 2. to outlive.
**out·law** (out′lô′), *n.* [AS. *utlaga* < ON. *utlagi*], 1. originally, a person deprived of legal rights and protection. 2. a notorious criminal; fugitive from the law. *v.t.* 1. originally, to declare to be an outlaw. 2. to remove the legal force of (contracts, etc.). 3. to declare illegal. **—out′law·ry** [*pl.* -RIES], *n.*
**out·lay** (out′lā′), *n.* 1. a spending (of money). 2. money spent.
**out·let** (out′let′), *n.* 1. a passage for letting something out. 2. a means of expression: as, an *outlet* for rage. 3. *a*) a market for goods. *b*) a store, etc. that sells the goods of a specific manufacturer or wholesaler. 4. a point in a wiring system at which electric current is available.
**out·line** (out′lin′), *n.* 1. a line bounding the limits of an object. 2. a sketch showing only the contours of an object. 3. an undetailed general plan. 4. a systematic listing of the most important points of some subject. *v.t.* [-LINED, -LINING], 1. to draw in outline. 2. to list the main points of. **—out′lin′er,** *n.*
**out·live** (out-liv′), *v.t.* [-LIVED, -LIVING], to live or endure longer than; survive or outlast.
**out·look** (out′look′), *n.* 1. a place for looking out. 2. the view from such a place. 3. a looking out. 4. viewpoint. 5. prospect; probability.
**out·ly·ing** (out′lī′iŋ), *adj.* relatively far out from a certain point or center; remote.
**out·man** (out-man′), *v.t.* [-MANNED, -MANNING], to outnumber in men.
**out·ma·neu·ver, out·ma·noeu·vre** (out′mə-no͞o′vẽr), *v.t.* [-VERED or -VRED, -VERING or -VRING], to maneuver with better effect than; outwit.
**out·match** (out-mach′), *v.t.* to surpass; outdo.
**out·mod·ed** (out-mōd′id), *adj.* no longer in fashion or accepted; obsolete.
**out·most** (out′mōst′), *adj.* outermost.
**out·num·ber** (out-num′bẽr), *v.t.* to be more numerous than.
**out-of-date** (out′əv-dāt′), *adj.* not current; obsolete; old-fashioned.
**out-of-doors** (out əv-dôrz′), *adj.* open-air; outdoor: also **out-of-door.** *n. & adv.* outdoors.
**out-of-the-way** (out′əv-*th*ə-wā′), *adj.* 1. secluded. 2. unusual. 3. not conventional.
**out·pa·tient** (out′pā′shənt), *n.* a patient, not an inmate, receiving treatment at a hospital.
**out·play** (out-plā′), *v.t.* to play better than.
**out·point** (out-point′), *v.t.* 1. to score more points than. 2. in *nautical usage,* to get into a position closer to the wind than (another vessel).
**out·post** (out′pōst′), *n.* 1. *a*) a small group of troops stationed at a distance from the main force, to prevent a surprise attack. *b*) the station so occupied. 2. a settlement on a frontier.
**out·pour** (out′pôr′, -pōr′; *for the v.,* out-pôr′, -pōr′), *n.* a pouring out. *v.t. & v.i.* to pour out. **—out′pour′ing,** *n.*
**out·put** (out′poot′), *n.* 1. the work done or the amount produced, especially over a given period. 2. information delivered by a computer. 3. in *electronics,* the useful voltage, current, or power delivered by amplifiers, generators, etc.
**out·rage** (out′rāj′), *n.* [OFr. *oultrage* < L. *ultra,* beyond], 1. an extremely violent or vicious act. 2. a deep insult or offense. 3. any serious breach of legal or moral codes. *v.t.* [-RAGED, -RAGING], 1. to commit an outrage upon. 2. to rape. 3. to cause great anger, indignation, etc. in.
**out·ra·geous** (out-rā′jəs), *adj.* 1. involving or doing great injury or wrong. 2. very offensive or shocking. 3. violent in action or disposition. **—out·ra′geous·ly,** *adv.* **—out·ra′geous·ness,** *n.*
**out·rank** (out-raŋk′), *v.t.* to exceed in rank.
**‡ou·tré** (o͞o′trā′; Eng. *also* o͞o′trā), *adj.* [Fr.], 1. exaggerated. 2. eccentric; bizarre.
**out·reach** (out-rēch′), *v.t. & v.i.* 1. to reach farther (than); surpass. 2. to reach out; extend.
**out·ride** (out-rīd′), *v.t.* [-RODE, -RIDDEN, -RIDING], to surpass or outstrip in riding.
**out·rid·er** (out′rīd′ẽr), *n.* an attendant on horseback who rides ahead of or beside a carriage.
**out·rig·ger** (out′rig′ẽr), *n.* 1. any framework extended beyond the rail of a ship; as, *a*) a projecting brace for an oarlock. *b*) a timber rigged out from the side of a native canoe to prevent tipping. 2. a canoe of this type.
**out·right** (out′rīt′; *for adv.,* out′rīt′), *adj.* 1. without reservation; downright. 2. straightforward. 3. complete; whole. *adv.* 1. entirely. 2. openly. 3. at once. **—out′right′ness,** *n.*

OUTRIGGER

**out·run** (out-run′), *v.t.* [-RAN, -RUN, -RUNNING], 1. to run faster or longer than. 2. to exceed. 3. to escape (a pursuer) as by running.
**out·sell** (out-sel′), *v.t.* [-SOLD, -SELLING], 1. to sell more easily or in greater volume than. 2. to have a higher price than.
**out·set** (out′set′), *n.* a setting out; beginning.
**out·shine** (out-shīn′), *v.t.* [-SHONE, -SHINING], 1. to shine brighter or longer than (another). 2. to surpass; excel. *v.i.* to shine forth.
**out·side** (out′sīd′; *for prep., usually* out-sīd′), *n.* 1. the exterior; outer side or surface. 2. the unenclosed part of anything partly enclosed. 3. *a*) that part which can be seen. *b*) what is obvious or superficial. 4. the most; absolute limit (with *the*). *adj.* 1. outer. 2. coming from or situated beyond the stated limits: as, he accepted no *outside* help. 3. extreme: as, an *outside* estimate. 4. mere; slight: as, an *outside* chance. *adv.* 1. externally. 2. to or toward the exterior. 3. beyond certain limits. 4. in or into the open air. *prep.* 1. on or to the outer side of. 2. outside the limits of. —**at the outside,** at the most. —**outside of,** 1. outside. 2. [Colloq.], other than.
**out·sid·er** (out-sīd′ēr), *n.* one who is outside, or not included; esp., one not a member of or in sympathy with a given group; alien.
**out·sit** (out-sit′), *v.t.* [-SAT, -SITTING], to sit longer than or beyond the time of.
**out·size** (out′sīz′), *n.* 1. an odd size; esp., unusually large size. 2. a garment of such size.
**out·skirt** (out′skũrt′), *n. usually in pl.* a district remote from the center, as of a city.
**out·smart** (out-smärt′), *v.t.* [Colloq.], to overcome by cunning or cleverness; to outwit.
**out·spo·ken** (out′spō′kən), *adj.* 1. unrestrained in speech; frank. 2. spoken boldly or candidly. —**out′spo′ken·ly,** *adv.* —**out′spo′ken·ness,** *n.*
**out·spread** (out-spred′; *also for adj., and for n. usually,* out′spred′), *v.t. & v.i.* [-SPREAD, -SPREADING], to spread out; expand; extend. *n.* a spreading out. *adj.* extended; expanded.
**out·stand·ing** (out′stan′diŋ), *adj.* 1. projecting. 2. distinguished; prominent. 3. unpaid; unsettled. —**out′stand′ing·ly,** *adv.* —**out′stand′ing·ness,** *n.*
**out·stare** (out-stâr′), *v.t.* [-STARED, -STARING], 1. to stare down. 2. to stare at.
**out·stay** (out-stā′), *v.t.* [-STAYED or *archaic* -STAID, -STAYING], to stay longer than or beyond.
**out·stretch** (out-strech′), *v.t.* 1. to extend. 2. to stretch beyond. —**out·stretched′,** *adj.*
**out·strip** (out-strip′), *v.t.* [-STRIPPED, -STRIPPING], 1. to go at a faster pace than; get ahead of. 2. to excel; surpass.
**out·talk** (out-tôk′), *v.t.* to talk more skillfully, loudly, or forcibly than; surpass in talking.
**out·vote** (out-vōt′), *v.t.* [-VOTED, -VOTING], to defeat in voting.
**out·ward** (out′wẽrd), *adj.* 1. having to do with the outside; outer. 2. obvious; visible. 3. away from the interior. 4. having to do with the physical nature as opposed to the spirit or mind. 5. superficial. *adv.* 1. externally; on the outside. 2. toward the outside. 3. visibly; publicly. Also **out′wards.** —**out′ward·ness,** *n.*
**out·ward·ly** (out′wẽrd-li), *adv.* 1. toward or on the outside. 2. in regard to external appearance.
**out·wear** (out-wâr′), *v.t.* [-WORE, -WORN, -WEARING], 1. to wear out. 2. to be more lasting than.
**out·weigh** (out-wā′), *v.t.* 1. to weigh more than. 2. to be more important, valuable, etc. than.
**out·wit** (out-wit′), *v.t.* [-WITTED, -WITTING], to get the better of by cunning or cleverness.
**out·work** (out′wũrk′), *n.* a lesser fortification built out beyond the main defenses. *v.t.* (out-wũrk′), to work better or harder than.
**ou·zel** (ōō′z′l), *n.* [AS. *osle*], 1. the European blackbird. 2. any of several thrushes or related birds. Also sp. **ousel.**
**o·va** (ō′və), *n.* pl. of **ovum.**
**o·val** (ō′v′l), *adj.* [< Fr. < L. *ovum*, an egg], 1. egg-shaped. 2. elliptical. *n.* anything oval in form. —**o′val·ly,** *adv.* —**o′val·ness,** *n.*
**o·va·ry** (ō′vẽr-i), *n.* [*pl.* -RIES], [< L. *ovum*, an egg], 1. in *anatomy & zoology*, the female reproductive gland, in which ova are formed. 2. in *botany*, the enlarged hollow part of the pistil, containing ovules. —**o·var·i·an** (ō-vâr′i-ən), *adj.*
**o·vate** (ō′vāt), *adj.* [< L. < *ovum*, an egg], 1. egg-shaped. 2. shaped like the longitudinal section of an egg: *ovate* leaves have the broader end at the base. —**o′vate·ly,** *adv.* —**o′vate·ness,** *n.*
**o·va·tion** (ō-vā′shən), *n.* [L. *ovatio* < *ovare*, to celebrate a triumph], an enthusiastic outburst of applause or an enthusiastic public welcome.
**ov·en** (uv′ən), *n.* [AS. *ofen*], a receptacle or compartment for baking, drying, etc. by means of heat.
**ov·en·bird** (uv′ən-bũrd′), *n.* a North American warbler that builds a domelike nest on the ground.
**o·ver** (ō′vẽr), *prep.* [AS. *ofer*], 1. in, at, or to a position up from; above: as, stars hung *over* us. 2. so as to cover: as, put a board *over* the well. 3. while engaged in: as, we'll discuss it *over* dinner. 4. upon the surface of: as, spread the jam *over* bread. 5. upon, as an effect or influence: as, he cast a spell *over* us. 6. above in authority, power, etc.: as, preside *over* the meeting. 7. along the length of: as, drive *over* this route. 8. to or on the other side of: as, fly *over* the lake, a city *over* the border. 9. through all or many parts of: as, *over* the whole state. 10. during: as, *over* a decade. 11. more than: as, *over* five dollars. 12. up to and including: as, stay *over* Easter. 13. in preference to. 14. concerning. *adv.* 1. *a*) above, across, or to the other side. *b*) across the brim or edge. 2. more; beyond: as, he stayed three hours or *over.* 3. covering the whole area: as, the wound healed *over.* 4. from start to finish: as, count the money *over.* 5. *a*) from an upright position: as, the tree fell *over.* *b*) into an inverted position: as, turn the plank *over.* 6. again: as, do it *over.* 7. at or on the other side, as of an intervening space: as, *over* in Spain. 8. from one side, viewpoint, person, etc. to another: as, we'll win him *over.* *adj.* 1. upper, outer, superior, excessive, or extra: often in combination, as in *overcoat, overseer, oversupply.* 2. finished; past: as, the game is *over.* 3. having reached the other side. 4. [Colloq.], having a surplus: as, he is three hours *over* this week. *n.* something in addition; surplus. —**all over,** 1. on or in every part (of). 2. throughout. 3. ended: also **all over with.** —**over again,** another time; anew. —**over against,** in contrast with. —**over all,** from end to end. —**over and above,** more than. —**over and over (again),** repeatedly.
**o·ver-,** a combining form meaning: 1. *above in position, rank, etc., superior,* as in *overhead, overlord.* 2. *excessive, beyond the normal,* as in *overrate, oversleep.* 3. *passing across* or *beyond,* as in *overrun.* 4. *causing a change to a lower position,* as in *overwhelm.* The list below includes some common compounds formed with *over-;* they will be understood if *too much* or *excessively* is used with the meaning of the base word.

| | |
|---|---|
| **overactive** | **overindulge** |
| **overabundance** | **overindulgence** |
| **overambitious** | **overinflate** |
| **overanxious** | **overinflation** |
| **overattentive** | **overinvest** |
| **overbuild** | **overjudicious** |
| **overburden** | **overladen** |
| **overbusy** | **overlong** |
| **overbuy** | **overmeasure** |
| **overcareful** | **overnegligent** |
| **overcareless** | **overnervous** |
| **overcaution** | **overnice** |
| **overcautious** | **overobedient** |
| **overcompensate** | **overpay** |
| **overconfident** | **overpayment** |
| **overconscientious** | **overpeopled** |
| **overconservative** | **overpopulate** |
| **overconsiderate** | **overpraise** |
| **overcook** | **overprecise** |
| **overcritical** | **overrefined** |
| **overcrowd** | **overrefinement** |
| **overdecorate** | **overreligious** |
| **overdye** | **overripe** |
| **overeager** | **oversensitive** |
| **overeat** | **oversentimental** |
| **overemotional** | **overspecialize** |
| **overemphasize** | **overstimulate** |
| **overenthusiastic** | **overstretch** |
| **overexercise** | **overstrict** |
| **overexert** | **overstudy** |
| **overexpansion** | **oversufficient** |
| **overexpose** | **oversuspicious** |
| **overexposure** | **overthrifty** |
| **overfond** | **overtire** |
| **overgenerous** | **overuse** |
| **overgreedy** | **overvehement** |
| **overhasty** | **overwind** |
| **overheat** | **overzealous** |

**o·ver·act** (ō′vẽr-akt′), *v.t. & v.i.* to act with exaggeration.
**o·ver·age** (ō′vẽr-āj′), *adj.* over the age fixed as a standard.
**o·ver·age** (ō′vẽr-ij), *n.* a surplus, as of goods.
**o·ver-all, o·ver·all** (ō′vẽr-ôl′), *adj.* 1. from end to end. 2. total; including everything.
**o·ver·alls** (ō′vẽr-ôlz′), *n.pl.* loose-fitting trousers, often with an attached bib, worn over other clothing as a protection against dirt, etc.

**o·ver·awe** (ō′vẽr-ô′), *v.t.* [-AWED, -AWING], to overcome or subdue by inspiring awe.

**o·ver·bal·ance** (ō′vẽr-bal′əns), *v.t.* [-ANCED, -ANCING], 1. to weigh more than. 2. to throw off balance. *n.* something that overbalances.

**o·ver·bear** (ō′vẽr-bâr′), *v.t.* [-BORE, -BORNE, -BEARING], 1. to press down by weight or physical power. 2. to dominate or subdue. *v.i.* to be too fruitful.

**o·ver·bear·ing** (ō′vẽr-bâr′iŋ), *adj.* disregarding the wishes of others; arrogant; domineering.

**o·ver·bid** (ō′vẽr-bid′), *v.t. & v.i.* [-BID, -BIDDING], 1. to outbid (another person). 2. to bid more than the worth of (a thing). *n.* (ō′vẽr-bid′), a higher or excessive bid.

**o·ver·blown** (ō′vẽr-blōn′), *adj.* 1. past the stage of full bloom. 2. blown down or over.

**o·ver·board** (ō′vẽr-bôrd′, -bōrd′), *adv.* 1. over a ship's side. 2. from a ship into the water.

**o·ver·cap·i·tal·ize** (ō′vẽr-kap′ə-t'l-īz′), *v.t.* [-IZED, -IZING], to establish the capital stock of (a business) beyond what is warranted by its prospects. **—o′ver·cap′i·tal·i·za′tion,** *n.*

**o·ver·cast** (ō′vẽr-kast′, -käst′), *n.* a covering, especially of clouds. *adj.* 1. covered over. 2. cloudy: said of the sky or weather. 3. in *sewing*, made with overcasting. *v.t.* [-CAST, -CASTING], 1. (ō′vẽr-kast′, -käst′), *a*) to overspread. *b*) to overcloud. 2. to sew over (an edge) with long, loose stitches to prevent raveling.

**o·ver·charge** (ō′vẽr-chärj′; *for n.*, ō′vẽr-chärj′), *v.t.* [-CHARGED, -CHARGING], 1. to charge too much for. 2. to overload. 3. to exaggerate. *n.* 1. an excessive charge. 2. too full or heavy a load.

**o·ver·cloud** (ō′vẽr-kloud′), *v.t.* 1. to cover over with clouds; obscure. 2. to make gloomy, angry, etc. in appearance: as, grief *overclouded* his face. *v.i.* to become cloudy, gloomy, etc.

**o·ver·coat** (ō′vẽr-kōt′), *n.* a coat worn over the usual clothing; topcoat or greatcoat.

**o·ver·come** (ō′vẽr-kum′), *v.t.* [-CAME, -COME, -COMING], 1. to get the better of in competition, etc.; conquer. 2. to suppress, prevail over, overwhelm, etc.: as, *overcome* obstacles. *v.i.* to win.

**o·ver·de·vel·op** (ō′vẽr-di-vel′əp), *v.t.* to develop, as a photographic film, too long or too much.

**o·ver·do** (ō′vẽr-do͞o′), *v.t.* [-DID, -DONE, -DOING], 1. to do too much, or to excess. 2. to spoil the effect of by exaggeration. 3. to cook too long. 4. to exhaust; tire. *v.i.* to do too much.

**o·ver·dose** (ō′vẽr-dōs′; *for v.*, ō′vẽr-dōs′), *n.* too large a dose. *v.t.* [-DOSED, -DOSING], to dose to excess.

**o·ver·draft, o·ver·draught** (ō′vẽr-draft′, -dräft′), *n.* 1. an overdrawing of money from a bank. 2. the amount overdrawn.

**o·ver·draw** (ō′vẽr-drô′), *v.t.* [-DREW, -DRAWN, -DRAWING], 1. to spoil the effect of by exaggeration. 2. in *banking*, to draw on in excess of the amount credited to the drawer.

**o·ver·dress** (ō′vẽr-dres′), *v.t. & v.i.* to dress extravagantly or beyond the limits of good taste.

**o·ver·drive** (ō′vẽr-drīv′), *n.* a gear that automatically reduces an engine's power output without reducing its driving speed.

**o·ver·due** (ō′vẽr-do͞o′, -dū′), *adj.* past or delayed beyond the time set for payment, arrival, etc.

**o·ver·es·ti·mate** (ō′vẽr-es′tə-māt′; *for n.*, *usually* -mit), *v.t.* to set too high an estimate on or for. *n.* an estimate that is too high.

**o·ver·flight** (ō′vẽr-flīt′), *n.* the flight of an aircraft over a site or territory, especially one over foreign territory for reconnaissance.

**o·ver·flow** (ō′vẽr-flō′; *for n.*, ō′vẽr-flō′), *v.t.* 1. to flow or spread across; flood. 2. to flow over the brim or edge of. 3. to fill beyond capacity. *v.i.* 1. to run over. 2. to be superabundant. *n.* 1. an overflowing or being overflowed. 2. the amount that overflows. 3. a vent for overflowing liquids. **—o′ver·flow′ing,** *adj.* **—o′ver·flow′ing·ly,** *adv.*

**o·ver·grow** (ō′vẽr-grō′), *v.t.* [-GREW, -GROWN, -GROWING], 1. to overspread so as to cover, as with foliage. 2. to outgrow. *v.i.* 1. to grow too large or too fast. 2. to grow beyond normal size. **—o′ver·grown′,** *adj.* **—o′ver·growth′,** *n.*

**o·ver·hand** (ō′vẽr-hand′; *for adv.*, *also* ō′vẽr-hand′), *adj.* 1. done with the hand raised above the elbow: as, an *overhand* pitch. 2. designating or of sewing in which the stitches are passed over two edges to sew them together. *adv.* in an overhand manner. *v.t.* to sew overhand. *n.* in *sports*, skill or style in performing overhand strokes. **—o′ver·hand′ed,** *adj.*

**o·ver·hang** (ō′vẽr-haŋ′; *for n.*, ō′vẽr-haŋ′), *v.t.* [-HUNG, -HANGING], 1. to hang over; to project beyond. 2. to impend; threaten. *v.i.* to project or jut out over something. *n.* the projection of one thing over or beyond another.

**o·ver·haul** (ō′vẽr-hôl′), *v.t.* 1. to haul over, as for examination. 2. *a*) to check thoroughly for needed repairs, adjustments, etc. *b*) to make such repairs, etc., as on a motor. 3. to catch up with. **—o′ver·haul′ing,** *n.*

**o·ver·head** (ō′vẽr-hed′; *for adv.*, ō′vẽr-hed′), *adj.* 1. located or operating above the level of the head. 2. in the sky. 3. on a higher level, with reference to related objects. *n.* the general, continuing costs of running a business, as of rent, maintenance, etc. *adv.* aloft; above the head.

**o·ver·hear** (ō′vẽr-hêr′), *v.t.* [-HEARD, -HEARING], to hear (something spoken or a speaker) without the speaker's knowledge or intention.

**o·ver·joy** (ō′vẽr-joi′), *v.t.* to give great joy to; delight. **—o′ver·joyed′,** *adj.*

**o·ver·land** (ō′vẽr-land′), *adv. & adj.* by, on, or across land.

**o·ver·lap** (ō′vẽr-lap′; *for n.*, ō′vẽr-lap′), *v.t. & v.i.* [-LAPPED, -LAPPING], to lap over; to extend over (something or each other) so as to coincide in part. *n.* 1. an overlapping. 2. a part that overlaps. 3. the extent or place of overlapping.

**o·ver·lay** (ō′vẽr-lā′; *for n.*, ō′vẽr-lā′), *v.t.* [-LAID, -LAYING], 1. to lay or spread over. 2. to cover, as with a decorative layer. 3. to weigh down; burden. *n.* 1. a covering. 2. a decorative layer or the like.

**o·ver·leap** (ō′vẽr-lēp′), *v.t.* [-LEAPED or -LEAPT, -LEAPING], 1. to leap over or across. 2. to omit; pass over. 3. to leap farther than. 4. to overreach (oneself) by leaping too far.

**o·ver·lie** (ō′vẽr-lī′), *v.t.* [-LAY, -LAIN, -LYING], to lie on or over.

**o·ver·load** (ō′vẽr-lōd′; *for n.*, ō′vẽr-lōd′), *v.t.* to put too great a load upon. *n.* too great a load.

**o·ver·look** (ō′vẽr-look′; *for n.*, ō′vẽr-look′), *v.t.* 1. to look at from above. 2. to give a view of from above. 3. to rise above. 4. *a*) to look beyond and not see. *b*) to ignore; neglect. 5. to pass over indulgently; excuse. 6. to supervise; manage. *n.* a height or the view from it. **—o′ver·look′er,** *n.*

**o·ver·lord** (ō′vẽr-lôrd′), *n.* a lord ranking over other lords. **—o′ver·lord′ship′,** *n.*

**o·ver·ly** (ō′vẽr-li), *adv.* too much; excessively.

**o·ver·man** (ō′vẽr-man′), *v.t.* [-MANNED, -MANNING], to supply with more men than necessary.

**o·ver·mas·ter** (ō′vẽr-mas′tẽr, -mäs′-), *v.t.* to overcome; conquer. **—o′ver·mas′ter·ing,** *adj.* **—o′ver·mas′ter·ing·ly,** *adv.*

**o·ver·match** (ō′vẽr-mach′), *v.t.* to exceed; surpass.

**o·ver·much** (ō′vẽr-much′), *adj. & adv.* too much. *n.* too great a quantity; excessive amount.

**o·ver·night** (ō′vẽr-nīt′), *adv.* 1. during the night. 2. on or during the previous evening. *adj.* 1. done or lasting during the night. 2. of the previous evening. 3. for one night: as, an *overnight* guest. 4. of or for a short trip: as, an *overnight* bag.

**o·ver·pass** (ō′vẽr-pas′, -päs′; *for v.*, ō′vẽr-pas′, -päs′), *n.* a bridge or other passageway over a road, railway, etc. *v.t.* [-PASSED, -PASSED or, *rare*, -PAST, -PASSING], 1. to pass over. 2. to surpass. 3. to overlook. 4. to transgress.

**o·ver·play** (ō′vẽr-plā′), *v.t.* 1. to overact or overdo. 2. in *cards*, to overestimate the strength of (one's hand).

**o·ver·pow·er** (ō′vẽr-pou′ẽr), *v.t.* 1. to subdue; overwhelm. 2. to furnish with too much power. **—o′ver·pow′er·ing,** *adj.* **—o′ver·pow′er·ing·ly,** *adv.*

**o·ver·print** (ō′vẽr-print′; *for n.*, ō′vẽr-print′), *v.t.* to print over (a previously printed surface). *n.* anything overprinted, as (on) a stamp.

**o·ver·pro·duce** (ō′vẽr-prə-do͞os′, -dūs′), *v.t. & v.i.* [-DUCED, -DUCING], to produce more than is needed or in a quantity that exceeds demand. **—o·ver·pro·duc·tion** (ō′vẽr-prə-duk′shən), *n.*

**o·ver·rate** (ō′vẽr-rāt′), *v.t.* [-RATED, -RATING], to rate or estimate too highly.

**o·ver·reach** (ō′vẽr-rēch′), *v.t.* 1. to reach beyond or above. 2. to extend beyond in time. 3. to spread over and cover. 4. to reach too far for and miss. 5. to cheat. *v.i.* 1. to reach too far. 2. to cheat. 3. to stretch beyond something. **—overreach oneself,** 1. to fail because of trying more than one can do. 2. to fail because of being too crafty or eager. **—o′ver·reach′er,** *n.*

**o·ver·ride** (ō′vẽr-rīd′), *v.t.* [-RODE, -RIDDEN, -RIDING], 1. to ride over. 2. to trample down. 3. to suppress, oppress, or domineer over. 4. to disregard; nullify: as, he *overrode* their pleas. 5. to fatigue (a horse, etc.) by riding too long.

**o·ver·rule** (ō′vẽr-rōōl′), *v.t.* [-RULED, -RULING], 1. to rule out or set aside, as by higher authority; annul. 2. to prevail over. —**o′ver·rul′ing,** *adj.* —**o′ver·rul′ing·ly,** *adv.*

**o·ver·run** (ō′vẽr-run′; *for n.*, ō′vẽr-run′), *v.t.* [-RAN, -RUN, -RUNNING], 1. to spread out over so as to cover. 2. to swarm over, as vermin, or ravage, as an army. 3. to spread swiftly throughout, as ideas. 4. to extend beyond (certain limits): as, the program *overran* its schedule. *v.i.* 1. to overflow. 2. to run beyond certain limits. *n.* 1. an overrunning. 2. the amount that overruns, or by which something overruns. —**o′ver·run′ner,** *n.*

**o·ver·seas** (ō′vẽr-sēz′), *adv.* over or beyond the sea. *adj.* 1. foreign. 2. from beyond the sea. 3. over or across the sea. Also **oversea.**

**o·ver·see** (ō′vẽr-sē′), *v.t.* [-SAW, -SEEN, -SEEING], 1. to supervise; superintend. 2. to survey; watch.

**o·ver·se·er** (ō′vẽr-sē′ẽr), *n.* one who directs the work of others; supervisor. —**o′ver·se′er·ship,** *n.*

**o·ver·sell** (ō′vẽr-sel′), *v.t.* [-SOLD, -SELLING], 1. to sell more than can be supplied. 2. to sell to an excessive degree.

**o·ver·set** (ō′vẽr-set′; *for n.*, ō′vẽr-set′), *v.t.* [-SET, -SETTING], 1. to upset. 2. to overturn or overthrow. *v.i.* to tip over. *n.* an overturning.

**o·ver·shad·ow** (ō′vẽr-shad′ō), *v.t.* 1. to cast a shadow over. 2. to darken. 3. to be more significant or important than by comparison.

**o·ver·shoe** (ō′vẽr-shōō′), *n.* a kind of boot of rubber or fabric worn over the regular shoe as a protection from cold or dampness; galosh.

**o·ver·shoot** (ō′vẽr-shōōt′), *v.t.* [-SHOT, -SHOOTING], 1. to shoot or pass over or beyond. 2. to go farther than (an intended or normal limit); exceed. 3. to cause to exceed. *v.i.* to shoot or go too far.

**o·ver·shot** (ō′vẽr-shot′), *adj.* 1. with the upper part or half extending past the lower: as, an *overshot* jaw. 2. driven by water flowing onto the upper part: as, an *overshot* water wheel.

**o·ver·sight** (ō′vẽr-sīt′), *n.* 1. failure to see or notice. 2. a careless mistake or omission.

**o·ver·size** (ō′vẽr-sīz′; *for n.*, ō′vẽr-sīz′), *adj.* 1. too large. 2. larger than the normal or usual. *n.* a size larger than regular sizes.

**o·ver·skirt** (ō′vẽr-skũrt′), *n.* an outer skirt.

**o·ver·sleep** (ō′vẽr-slēp′), *v.i.* [-SLEPT, -SLEEPING], to sleep longer than intended.

**o·ver·spread** (ō′vẽr-spred′), *v.t. & v.i.* [-SPREAD, -SPREADING], to spread over or cover over.

**o·ver·state** (ō′vẽr-stāt′), *v.t.* [-STATED, -STATING], to give a magnified account of (facts, truth, etc.); exaggerate. —**o′ver·state′ment,** *n.*

**o·ver·stay** (ō′vẽr-stā′), *v.t.* to stay beyond the time, duration, or limits of.

**o·ver·step** (ō′vẽr-step′), *v.t.* [-STEPPED, -STEPPING], to go beyond; usually figurative.

**o·ver·stock** (ō′vẽr-stok′; *for n.*, -stok′), *v.t.* to stock more of than is needed. *n.* too large a stock.

**o·ver·strung** (ō′vẽr-struŋ′), *adj.* tense; jittery.

**o·ver·stuff** (ō′vẽr-stuf′), *v.t.* 1. to stuff with too much of something. 2. to upholster (furniture) with deep stuffing.

**o·ver·sub·scribe** (ō′vẽr-səb-skrīb′), *v.t. & v.i.* [-SCRIBED, -SCRIBING], to subscribe for more (of) than is available or asked.

**o·ver·sup·ply** (ō′vẽr-sə-plī′), *v.t.* [-SUPPLIED, -SUPPLYING], to supply in excess. *n.* [-PLIES], too great a supply.

**o·vert** (ō′vẽrt, ō-vũrt′), *adj.* [< OFr. pp. of *ovrir* < L. *aperire*, to open], 1. open; public. 2. in *law*, done outwardly, without attempt at concealment. —**o·vert′ly,** *adv.* —**o·vert′ness,** *n.*

**o·ver·take** (ō′vẽr-tāk′), *v.t.* [-TOOK, -TAKEN, -TAKING], 1. to catch up with. 2. to come upon unexpectedly or suddenly. —**o′ver·tak′er,** *n.*

**o·ver·tax** (ō′vẽr-taks′), *v.t.* 1. to tax too heavily. 2. to make excessive demands on.

**o·ver-the-count·er** (ō′vẽr-*thə*-koun′tẽr), *adj.* 1. sold directly rather than through an exchange, as bonds. 2. sold in stores rather than by mail.

**o·ver·throw** (ō′vẽr-thrō′; *for n.*, ō′vẽr-thrō′), *v.t.* [-THREW, -THROWN, -THROWING], 1. to throw or turn over; upset. 2. to conquer; bring to an end. *n.* 1. an overthrowing or being overthrown. 2. destruction; end. —**o′ver·throw′er,** *n.*

**o·ver·time** (ō′vẽr-tīm′; *for v.*, ō′vẽr-tīm′), *n.* 1. time beyond the established limit, as of working hours. 2. pay for work done in such time. 3. in *sports*, an extra period added to the game to decide a tie. *adj. & adv.* of, for, or during (an) overtime. *v.t.* [-TIMED, -TIMING], to exceed the proper limit in timing (a photographic exposure, etc.).

**o·ver·tone** (ō′vẽr-tōn′), *n.* 1. any of the higher tones which faintly accompany the fundamental tone produced by a musical instrument. 2. *pl.* implications; nuances: as, a reply full of *overtones.*

**o·ver·top** (ō′vẽr-top′), *v.t.* [-TOPPED, -TOPPING], 1. to rise beyond or above. 2. to excel; surpass.

**o·ver·train** (ō′vẽr-trān′), *v.t. & v.i.* to train too long or too hard.

**o·ver·ture** (ō′vẽr-chẽr), *n.* [< OFr.; see OVERT], 1. an introductory offer or proposal. 2. a musical introduction to an opera, oratorio, etc.

**o·ver·turn** (ō′vẽr-tũrn′; *for n.*, ō′vẽr-tũrn′), *v.t.* 1. to turn over; upset. 2. to conquer. *v.i.* to tip over; capsize. *n.* an overturning or being overturned. —**o′ver·turn′er,** *n.*

**o·ver·ween·ing** (ō′vẽr-wēn′iŋ), *adj.* [< AS. < *ofer*, over + *wenan*, to hope], arrogant; conceited. —**o′ver·ween′ing·ly,** *adv.* —**o′ver·ween′ing·ness,** *n.*

**o·ver·weigh** (ō′vẽr-wā′), *v.t.* 1. to outweigh. 2. to burden; oppress.

**o·ver·weight** (ō′vẽr-wāt′; *for adj. & v.*, ō′vẽr-wāt′), *n.* 1. extra or surplus weight. 2. a greater amount of importance; preponderance. *adj.* above normal or legal weight. *v.t.* to overweigh.

**o·ver·whelm** (ō′vẽr-hwelm′), *v.t.* [see OVER- & WHELM], 1. to pour down on and bury beneath. 2. to crush; overpower. —**o′ver·whelm′ing,** *adj.* —**o′ver·whelm′ing·ly,** *adv.*

**o·ver·work** (ō′vẽr-wũrk′), *v.t.* to work or use to excess. *v.i.* to work too hard or too long. *n.* work that is severe or burdensome.

**o·ver·write** (ō′vẽr-rīt′), *v.t. & v.i.* [-WROTE, -WRITTEN, -WRITING], 1. to write over (other writing). 2. to write too much, or in too labored a style, about (some subject).

**o·ver·wrought** (ō′vẽr-rôt′), *adj.* 1. overworked. 2. strained; too excited. 3. too elaborate.

**o·vi-** (ō′vi), [< L. *ovum*, an egg], a combining form meaning *egg* or *ovum*, as in *oviduct, oviform.*

**Ov·id** (ov′id), *n.* (*Publius Ovidius Naso*), Roman poet; lived 43 B.C.–17? A.D.

**o·vi·duct** (ō′vi-dukt′), *n.* [*ovi-* + *duct*], a duct or tube through which the ova pass from the ovary to the uterus or to the outside.

**o·vi·form** (ō′vi-fôrm′), *adj.* [*ovi-* + *-form*], egg-shaped.

**o·vip·a·rous** (ō-vip′ẽr-əs), *adj.* [< L. < *ovum*, egg + *parere*, to produce], producing eggs which hatch after leaving the body. —**o′vi·par′i·ty** (-vi-par′ə-ti), **o·vip′a·rous·ness,** *n.* —**o·vip′a·rous·ly,** *adv.*

**o·vi·pos·i·tor** (ō′vi-poz′i-tẽr), *n.* [*ovi-* + L. *positor*, one who places < *ponere*, to place], 1. a tubular organ of insects for depositing eggs, usually situated at the end of the abdomen.

**o·void** (ō′void), *adj.* [< *ovi-* + *-oid*], egg-shaped: also **o·voi′dal.** *n.* anything of ovoid form.

**o·vu·late** (ō′vyoo-lāt′), *v.i.* [-LATED, -LATING], [< *ovule* + *-ate*], to produce ova; discharge ova from the ovary. —**o′vu·la′tion,** *n.*

**o·vule** (ō′vūl), *n.* [Fr. < Mod. L. dim. of L. *ovum*, egg], 1. in *zoology*, an immature ovum. 2. in *botany*, the part of a plant which develops into a seed. —**o′vu·lar,** *adj.*

**o·vum** (ō′vəm), *n.* [*pl.* OVA (ō′və)], [L., an egg], in *biology*, an egg; female germ cell.

**owe** (ō), *v.t.* [OWED, OWING], [AS. *agan*, to own], 1. to be indebted to (someone) for (a specified amount or thing). 2. to be morally obligated to give: as, I *owe* him my thanks. 3. to cherish (a feeling) toward another; bear: as, he *owed* her ill will. *v.i.* to be in debt.

**ow·ing** (ō′iŋ), *adj.* 1. that owes. 2. due; unpaid: as, there are three dollars *owing.* —**owing to,** resulting from; caused by; on account of.

**owl** (oul), *n.* [AS. *ule*], a night bird of prey found throughout the world, having a large head, large eyes, a short hooked beak, and feathered legs with sharp talons: applied figuratively to a person of nocturnal habits, solemn appearance, etc. —**owl′ish,** *adj.* —**owl′ish·ly,** *adv.* —**owl′ish·ness,** *n.* —**owl′like′,** *adj.*

**owl·et** (oul′it), *n.* a young or small owl.

**own** (ōn), *adj.* [AS. *agen*, pp. of *agan*, to possess], belonging or relating to oneself or itself: used to strengthen a preceding possessive, as, he mows his *own* lawn. *n.* that which belongs to oneself: as, that is his *own.* *v.t.* 1. to possess; have. 2. to admit; acknowledge. *v.i.* to confess (with *to*). —**come into one's own,** to receive what properly belongs to one, especially recognition. —**hold one's own,** to maintain one's place or condition in spite of attack, illness, etc. —**of one's own,** belonging strictly to oneself. —**on one's own,** [Colloq.], on one's own resources, responsibility, etc.

**own·er** (ōn′ẽr), *n.* a person who owns; proprietor. —**own′er·less,** *adj.* —**own′er·ship′,** *n.*

**ox** (oks), *n.* [*pl.* OXEN, *rarely* OX; see PLURAL II, D, 1], [AS. *oxa*], 1. any animal of the bovine family. 2. a castrated bull. —**ox′like′**, *adj.*
**ox·al·ic** (ok-sal′ik), *adj.* [< Fr. < L. < Gr. *oxalis*, sorrel < *oxys*, acid], designating or of a colorless, poisonous, crystalline acid, $(COOH)_2$, found in many plants: used in dyeing, bleaching, etc.
**ox·blood** (oks′blud′), *n.* a deep red color.
**ox·bow** (oks′bō′), *n.* 1. the U-shaped part of an ox yoke which passes under and around the animal's neck. 2. a crescent-shaped bend in a river.

YOKE WITH OXBOWS

**ox·en** (ok′s'n), *n.* pl. of **ox.**
**ox·eye** (oks′ī′), *n.* any of various daisylike plants; esp., the common American daisy: in full, **oxeye daisy.**
**ox-eyed** (oks′īd′), *adj.* with eyes large and full like those of an ox.
**Ox·ford** (oks′fẽrd), *n.* a city in S England: pop., 107,000: home of Oxford University.
**ox·ford** (oks′fẽrd), *n.* [after *Oxford*], [sometimes O-], 1. a low shoe laced over the instep: also **oxford shoe.** 2. a cotton cloth with a basketlike weave, used for shirts, etc.: also **oxford cloth.**
**Oxford gray,** a very dark gray, nearly black.
**ox·heart** (oks′härt′), *n.* a large cherry shaped like a heart. 2. a kind of cabbage.
**ox·i·da·tion** (ok′sə-dā′shən), *n.* an oxidizing or being oxidized. —**ox′i·da′tive,** *adj.*
**ox·ide** (ok′sīd, -sid), *n.* [Fr. < Gr. *oxys*, sour + Fr. *acide*, acid], a binary compound of oxygen with another element or a radical: also **ox′id** (-sid).
**ox·i·dize** (ok′sə-dīz′), *v.t.* [-DIZED, -DIZING], 1. to unite with oxygen; hence, to rust. 2. to increase the positive valence or decrease the negative valence of (an element or ion). *v.i.* to become oxidized. —**ox′i·diz′a·ble,** *adj.* —**ox′i·diz′er,** *n.*
**ox·lip** (oks′lip′), *n.* [< AS. < *oxa*, ox + *slyppe*, dropping], a plant of the primrose family, having yellow flowers.
**Ox·o·ni·an** (ok-sō′ni-ən), *adj.* of Oxford or Oxford University. *n.* 1. a student or alumnus of Oxford University. 2. a native or inhabitant of Oxford.
**ox·tail** (oks′tāl′), *n.* the tail of an ox, especially when skinned and used to make soup.
**ox·y-,** [< *oxygen*], a combining form meaning *containing oxygen*: also **ox-.**
**ox·y-,** [< Gr. *oxys*, sharp], a combining form meaning *sharp, pointed,* or *acid*, as in *oxygen, oxymoron.*
**ox·y·a·cet·y·lene** (ok′si-ə-set′'l-ēn′), *adj.* of or using a mixture of oxygen and acetylene.
**oxyacetylene torch** (or **blowpipe**), a blowpipe whose hot oxyacetylene flame is used for cutting and welding steel.
**ox·y·gen** (ok′si-jən), *n.* [< Fr.; see OXY- (sharp) & -GEN], a colorless, odorless, tasteless gaseous chemical element, the most abundant of all elements: it occurs free in the atmosphere, forming one fifth of its volume, and is able to combine with nearly all other elements; it is essential to life processes and to combustion: symbol O; at. wt., 16; at. no., 8.
**ox·y·gen·ate** (ok′si-jə-nāt′), *v.t.* [-ATED, -ATING], to mix or combine with oxygen; oxidize: also **ox′y·gen·ize′** [-IZED, -IZING]. —**ox′y·gen·a′tion,** *n.*
**oxygen tent,** a boxlike enclosure supplied with oxygen, used, as in cases of pneumonia and cardiac disease, to facilitate breathing.

OXYGEN TENT

**ox·y·hy·dro·gen** (ok′si-hī′drə-jən), *adj.* of or using a mixture of oxygen and hydrogen. *n.* oxyhydrogen gas.
**oxyhydrogen torch** (or **blowpipe**), a blowpipe that burns oxyhydrogen, used as for welding steel.
**ox·y·mo·ron** (ok′si-môr′on, -mō′ron), *n.* [*pl.* -RA], [< Gr. < *oxys*, sharp + *moros*, dull], a figure of speech in which contradictory ideas or terms are combined (e.g., sweet sorrow).
**o·yez, o·yes** (ō′yes, -yez), *interj.* [Anglo-Fr., hear ye; ult. < L. *audire*, to hear], hear ye! attention!: usually cried out three times by an official to command attention before making an announcement.
**oys·ter** (ois′tẽr), *n.* [< OFr. < L. *ostrea* < Gr. *ostreon*], 1. a marine mollusk with an irregular, hinged shell, found especially on the ocean floor and widely used as food. 2. any of numerous similar bivalve mollusks, as the scallop, pearl oyster, etc. Applied figuratively to a thing from which profit or advantage can be extracted.
**oyster bed,** a natural or artificially prepared place on the ocean floor for breeding oysters.
**oyster crab,** any of a group of nonparasitic crabs that live in the gill cavities of oysters.
**oyster cracker,** a small, round soda cracker.
**oyster plant,** salsify: also **oys′ter-root′,** *n.*
**oz.,** [*pl.* oz., ozs.], ounce.
**O·zark Mountains** (ō′zärk), a low mountain range in SW Missouri, NW Arkansas, and NE Oklahoma: also **Ozarks.**
**o·zone** (ō′zōn, ō-zōn′), *n.* [Fr. < Gr. *ozein*, to smell], 1. a blue gas, $O_3$, with a strong odor: it is an allotropic form of oxygen, formed by a silent electrical discharge in air and used as a bleaching agent, water purifier, etc. 2. [Slang], pure air. —**o·zon′ic** (-zon′ik), **o′zo·nous** (-zə-nəs), *adj.* —**o′zo·nif′er·ous** (-nif′ẽr-əs), *adj.*
**o·zo·nize** (ō′zə-nīz′), *v.t.* [-NIZED, -NIZING], 1. to make ozone of (oxygen). 2. to treat with ozone.

# P

**P, p** (pē), *n.* [*pl.* P's, p's, Ps, ps], 1. the sixteenth letter of the English alphabet. 2. the sound of P or p. *adj.* sixteenth in a sequence or group. —**mind one's p's and q's,** to be careful of what one does.
**P** (pē), *n.* 1. in *chemistry, the symbol for* phosphorus. 2. in *mechanics, the symbol for: a*) power. *b*) pressure. *adj.* shaped like P.
**P,** in *chess*, pawn.
**p.,** 1. [*pl.* PP.], page. 2. participle. 3. past. 4. per. 5. pint. 6. pitcher. 7. in *music*, piano.
**Pa,** in *chemistry*, protactinium.
**pa** (pä; *dial., often* pô), *n.* [Colloq.], father; papa.
**Pa.,** Pennsylvania.
**P.A.,** [Slang], public address (system).
**pab·u·lum** (pab′yoo-ləm), *n.* [L.], food.
**pace** (pās), *n.* [< OFr. *pas* < L. *passus*, a step], 1. a step in walking, running, etc. 2. the length of a step or stride (usually, 2½–3 feet). 3. the rate of speed in walking, etc. 4. *a*) rate of progress, development, etc. *b*) an equal rate or speed: as, try to keep *pace* with me. 5. a particular way of stepping; gait. 6. a gait of a horse in which both legs on the same side are raised together. *v.t.* [PACED, PACING], 1. to walk back and forth across. 2. to measure by paces. 3. to train or guide the pace of (a horse). 4. to set the pace for (a runner, etc.). *v.i.* 1. to walk with regular steps. 2. to raise both legs on the same side at the same time in moving: said of a horse. —**put one through his paces,** test one's abilities. —**set the pace,** 1. to go at a speed that others try to equal. 2. to do or be something for others to emulate. —**pac′er,** *n.*
**pace·mak·er** (pās′mā′kẽr), *n.* 1. a runner, horse, automobile, etc. that sets the pace for others, as in a race. 2. an electronic device implanted into the body, designed to stimulate contraction of the heart muscles and restore normalcy to the heartbeat. —**pace′mak′ing,** *n.*
**pach·y·derm** (pak′ə-dũrm′), *n.* [< Fr. < Gr. < *pachys*, thick + *derma*, a skin], 1. a large thick-skinned, hoofed animal, as the elephant, rhinoceros, or hippopotamus. 2. a stolid, insensitive person. —**pach′y·der′ma·tous,** *adj.* —**pach′y·der′mous,** *adj.*
**Pa·cif·ic** (pə-sif′ik), *n.* the largest of the earth's oceans, between Asia and the American continents. *adj.* of, in, on, or near this ocean.

**pa·cif·ic** (pə-sif′ik), *adj.* [< Fr. < L. < *pacificare*; see PACIFY], 1. making or tending to make peace. 2. of a peaceful nature; calm; tranquil. Also **pa-cif′i·cal.** —**pa·cif′i·cal·ly,** *adv.*

**pa·cif·i·cate** (pə-sif′i-kāt′), *v.t.* [-CATED, -CATING], to pacify. —**pac·i·fi·ca·tion** (pas′ə-fi-kā′shən), *n.* —**pa·cif′i·ca′tor,** *n.* —**pa·cif′i·ca·to′ry** (-kə-tôr′i, -tō′ri), *adj.*

**Pacific Standard Time,** see **standard time.**

**pac·i·fi·er** (pas′ə-fī′ẽr), *n.* 1. a person or thing that pacifies. 2. a nipple or teething ring for babies.

**pac·i·fism** (pas′ə-fiz′m), *n.* belief that international disputes should be settled by peaceful means rather than by force or war. —**pac′i·fist,** *n.* —**pac′i-fis′tic,** *adj.* —**pac′i·fis′ti·cal·ly,** *adv.*

**pac·i·fy** (pas′ə-fī′), *v.t.* [-FIED, -FYING], [< Fr. < L. < *pax*, peace + *facere*, to make], 1. to make peaceful or calm; appease; tranquilize. 2. to secure peace in (a nation, etc.). —**pac′i·fi′a·ble,** *adj.* —**pac′i-fy′ing·ly,** *adv.*

**pack** (pak), *n.* [ME. *pakke* < LG.], 1. a bundle of things tied up for carrying, as on the back; load; burden. 2. a number of related persons or things: as, a *pack* of lies; specif., *a*) a package of a standard number: as, a *pack* of cigarettes. *b*) a set of playing cards, usually 52. *c*) a set of hunting hounds. *d*) a number of wild animals living together: as, a *pack* of wolves. 3. a mass of floating pieces of ice driven together. 4. *a*) treatment by wrapping a patient in sheets, etc. that are wet or dry and hot or cold. *b*) the sheets so used. 5. a cosmetic paste applied to the skin and left to dry. 6. the amount of fish, meat, etc. put in cans, etc. *v.t.* 1. to make a pack of. 2. *a*) to put together in a box, trunk, etc. *b*) to fill (a box, trunk, etc.). 3. to put, as food, in (cans, etc.) for preservation. 4. *a*) to crowd; cram: as, the hall was *packed*. *b*) to crowd (people) together. 5. to fill in tightly, as for prevention of leaks: as, to *pack* a joint. 6. to load (an animal) with a pack. 7. to carry (goods, etc.) in a pack: said of an animal. 8. to carry or wear as part of one's equipment: as, he *packs* a gun. 9. to send (*off*): as, they *packed* him off to school. 10. [Slang], to deliver (a blow, punch, etc.) with force. *v.i.* 1. to make up packs. 2. to put one's clothes, etc. into luggage for a trip. 3. to crowd together in a small space. 4. to admit of being folded compactly, put in a container, etc.: as, this suit *packs* well. 5. to settle into a compact mass. *adj.* 1. used in or suitable for packing. 2. formed into packs. 3. used for carrying packs, loads, etc. —**send packing,** to dismiss (a person) without delay.

**pack** (pak), *v.t.* to choose (a jury, committee, etc.) dishonestly so as to get desired results.

**pack·age** (pak′ij), *n.* 1. the act or process of packing. 2. a wrapped or boxed thing; parcel; bundle. 3. a box, case, etc. in which things are packed. *v.t.* [-AGED, -AGING], to put into a package.

**package store,** a store where alcoholic liquor is sold by the bottle to be drunk off the premises.

**pack animal,** an animal used for carrying packs.

**pack·er** (pak′ẽr), *n.* a person or thing that packs; specif., *a*) one who packs goods for shipping, sale, etc. *b*) one who owns or manages a packing house.

**pack·et** (pak′it), *n.* 1. a small package. 2. a packet boat. *v.t.* to make up into a packet.

**packet boat,** a boat that travels a regular route carrying passengers, freight, and mail.

**pack horse,** 1. a horse used to carry packs, luggage, etc. 2. a drudge.

**pack·ing** (pak′iŋ), *n.* 1. the act or process of a person or thing that packs; specif., the canning of meats, fruits, etc. 2. any material used in packing, as to make watertight, etc.

**packing house,** a place where meats, fruits, vegetables, etc., are prepared for future sale.

**pack·sad·dle** (pak′sad′'l), *n.* a saddle designed to support the load carried by a pack animal.

**pack·thread** (pak′thred′), *n.* strong, thick thread or twine for tying bundles, packages, etc.

**pack train,** a procession of pack animals.

**pact** (pakt), *n.* [< OFr. < L. < pp. of *paciscere*, to agree < *pax*, peace], a compact or agreement.

**pad** (pad), *n.* [chiefly echoic but partly < D. *pad*, path], the dull sound made by a footstep or staff on the ground. *v.i.* [PADDED, PADDING], 1. to travel on foot; walk. 2. to walk or run with a soft step.

**pad** (pad), *n.* [prob. var. of *pod*], 1. a soft, stuffed saddle. 2. anything made of soft material and used to fill hollow places or protect from friction, blows, etc.: as, a shoulder *pad*. 3. the foot of certain animals, as the wolf, fox, etc. 4. the cushion-like part of the foot of some animals. 5. the floating leaf of a water plant, as the water lily. 6. a number of sheets of paper fastened along one edge; tablet. 7. a cushion soaked with ink for inking a rubber stamp. *v.t.* [PADDED, PADDING], 1. to stuff or cover with soft material. 2. to lengthen (a speech, etc.) with unnecessary material. 3. to fill (an expense account, etc.) with fraudulent entries. —**pad′der,** *n.*

**pad** (pad), *n.* [D. *pad*, path], 1. a horse with an easy, slow pace. 2. [Rare], a highwayman.

**pad·ding** (pad′iŋ), *n.* 1. the action of one who pads. 2. any soft material used to pad, as cotton, straw, etc. 3. unnecessary material inserted in a speech, writing, etc. to make it longer.

**pad·dle** (pad′'l), *n.* [prob. ult. < L. *patella*, small pan], 1. a short oar with a wide blade at one or both ends, used without an oarlock. 2. any of various implements shaped like this and used as in washing clothes, working butter, flogging, etc. 3. any of the propelling boards in a water wheel or paddle wheel. *v.t. & v.i.* [-DLED, -DLING], 1. to propel (a canoe, etc.) by a paddle. 2. to punish by beating with a paddle; spank. 3. to stir, work, etc. with a paddle. —**paddle one's own canoe,** to depend entirely on oneself. —**pad′dler,** *n.*

**pad·dle** (pad′'l), *v.i.* [-DLED, -DLING], [prob. < *pad*, *v.i.*], 1. to move the feet in shallow water; dabble. 2. to walk like a small child; toddle. —**pad′dler,** *n.*

**pad·dle·fish** (pad′'l-fish′), *n.* [*pl.* see FISH], a large fish of the Mississippi, with a snout shaped somewhat like a paddle.

**paddle wheel,** a wheel with boards, or paddles, around it for propelling a steamboat.

**pad·dock** (pad′ək), *n.* [< AS. *pearruc*, enclosure], 1. a small enclosure near a stable, in which horses are exercised. 2. an enclosure near a race track, where horses are assembled before a race.

**pad·dy** (pad′i), *n.* [*pl.* -DIES], [Malay *padi*], 1. rice in the husk, growing or cut. 2. rice in general. 3. loosely, a rice field.

**paddy wagon,** [Slang], a police wagon in which arrested persons are taken into custody.

**Pa·de·rew·ski, I·gnace Jan** (ē′nyàs′ yän pä′de-ref′ski; Eng. pad′ə-), 1860–1941; Polish pianist, composer, and statesman.

**pa·di·shah** (pä′di-shä′), *n.* [< Per. < *pati*, master + *shāh*, shah], 1. a great king; emperor. 2. [often P-], the shah of Iran.

**pad·lock** (pad′lok′), *n.* [? < ME. *padde*, toad, with reference to the shape], a removable lock with a hinged link to be passed through a staple, chain, or eye. *v.t.* to fasten as with a padlock.

**pa·dre** (pä′dri; It. -dre; Sp. -*th*re), *n.* [*pl.* -DRES (-driz; Sp. -*th*res); It. -DRI (-drē)], [Sp.; It.; Port. < L. *pater*, a father], 1. father: the title of a priest in Italy, Spain, Portugal, and Latin America. 2. [Military Slang], a chaplain.

**Pad·u·a** (paj′oo-ə, pad′ū-ə), *n.* a city in NE Italy: pop., 173,000.

**pae·an** (pē′ən), *n.* [L.; Gr. < *Paian*, Apollo], a song of joy, triumph, etc.: also sp. **pean.**

**pae·do-,** pedo-: also **paed-.**

**pa·gan** (pā′gən), *n.* [< L. *paganus* (in LL., a pagan), a peasant < *pagus*, country], 1. *a*) formerly, a person who was not a Christian. *b*) now, a person who is not a Christian, Moslem, or Jew; heathen. 2. a person who has no religion. *adj.* 1. of pagans or paganism. 2. not religious; heathen. —**pa′gan·dom,** *n.* —**pa′gan·ish,** *adj.* —**pa′gan·ism,** *n.*

**Pa·ga·ni·ni, Ni·co·lò** (nē′kô-lô′ pä′gä-nē′nē), 1782–1840; Italian violinist and composer.

**pa·gan·ize** (pā′gən-īz′), *v.t. & v.i.* [-IZED, -IZING], to make or become pagan. —**pa′gan·i·za′tion,** *n.*

**page** (pāj), *n.* [Fr. < L. *pagina* < *pangere*, to fasten], 1. *a*) one side of a leaf of a book, newspaper, etc. *b*) the printing or writing on it. Often loosely applied to the entire leaf. 2. *often pl.* a record; writing: as, the *pages* of history. 3. an event or series of events that might fill a page: as, a colorful *page* in his life. *v.t.* [PAGED, PAGING], to number the pages of.

**page** (pāj), *n.* [OFr. < It. < ML. *pagius*; ? < Gr. dim. of *pais*, child], 1. formerly, a boy training for knighthood. 2. a boy attendant, especially one serving a person of high rank, as in court. 3. a boy who runs errands, carries messages, etc., as in a hotel. 4. an attendant in Congress or a legislature. *v.t.* [PAGED, PAGING], 1. to attend as a page. 2. to try to find (a person) by calling his name, as a hotel page does. *v.i.* to serve as a page.

**pag·eant** (paj′ənt), *n.* [< Anglo-L.; prob. < ME. *pagend*, stage (as for medieval mystery plays) < L. *pangere*, to fix], 1. a spectacular exhibition, elaborate parade, etc. 2. an outdoor drama celebrating a historical event or events. 3. empty pomp or display.

**pag·eant·ry** (paj′ən-tri), *n.* [*pl.* -RIES], 1. pageants collectively. 2. grand spectacle; gorgeous display. 3. empty show or display.

**pag·i·nate** (paj′ə-nāt′), *v.t.* [-NATED, -NATING], to number the pages of (a book, etc.); page.

**pag·i·na·tion** (paj′ə-nā′shən), *n.* 1. the act of numbering the pages of a book, etc. 2. the figures, etc. with which pages are numbered.

**pa·go·da** (pə-gō′də), *n.* [< Port.; prob. < Per. < *but*, idol + *kadah*, house; ? infl. by Tamil *pagavadi*, temple], in India, China, Japan, etc., a temple in the form of a pyramidal tower of several stories.

PAGODA

**Pa·go Pa·go** (päŋ′ō päŋ′ō, pä′gō pä′gō), the main seaport of American Samoa, on Tutuila Island.

**paid** (pād), pt. and pp. of **pay.** *adj.* 1. receiving pay; hired: as, a *paid* advisor. 2. *a*) given in payment, as money (also with *out*). *b*) settled, as a debt (also with *up*).

**pail** (pāl), *n.* [< AS. & OFr. < L. *patella*, a pan], 1. a cylindrical container, usually with a handle, for holding liquids, etc.; bucket. 2. a pailful.

**pail·ful** (pāl′fool′), *n.* [*pl.* -FULS], as much as a pail will hold.

**pail·lasse** (pal-yas′, pal′yəs), *n.* [Fr. < It. < LL. < L. *palea*, straw], a mattress filled with straw, sawdust, etc.: also sp. **pal·liasse′.**

**pain** (pān), *n.* [< OFr. < L. *poena* (< Gr. *poinē*), penalty], 1. originally, penalty. 2. the physical or mental sensations one feels when hurt; distress, suffering, anguish, etc. 3. a sensation of hurting caused by injury, disease, etc., transmitted by the nervous system. 4. *pl.* the labor of childbirth. 5. *pl.* great care: as, he took *pains* with his work. *v.t.* to cause pain to; hurt. —**on** (or **upon, under**) **pain of,** with the threat of (death, punishment, etc.) unless a specified thing is done. —**pain′less,** *adj.* —**pain′less·ly,** *adv.* —**pain′less·ness,** *n.*

**Paine, Thomas** (pān), 1737–1809; American Revolutionary patriot and writer, born in England.

**pained** (pānd), *adj.* 1. hurt or distressed; offended. 2. showing hurt feelings or resentment.

**pain·ful** (pān′fəl), *adj.* 1. causing pain; hurting. 2. having pain; aching. 3. requiring trouble and care; irksome. —**pain′ful·ly,** *adv.* —**pain′ful·ness,** *n.*

**pains·tak·ing** (pānz′tāk′iŋ), *n.* great care or diligence. *adj.* 1. very careful; diligent. 2. characterized by great care. —**pains′tak′ing·ly,** *adv.*

**paint** (pānt), *v.t.* [< OFr. pp. of *peindre* < L. *pingere*], 1. *a*) to make (a picture, etc.) in colors by means of pigments, brushes, etc. *b*) to depict with paints: as, he *painted* a hill. 2. to describe colorfully; picture in words. 3. to cover or decorate with paint: as, he *painted* the walls. 4. to decorate with colors, cosmetics, etc.; adorn. 5. to apply (a medicine, etc.) like paint. *v.i.* 1. to practice the art of painting pictures. 2. to use cosmetics. *n.* 1. a mixture of colored pigment with oil, water, etc. used as a covering or coloring, or for making pictures on canvas, etc. 2. a dried coat of paint. 3. coloring matter, as lipstick, rouge, etc., used on the face or body. —**paint out,** to cover up as with a coat of paint. —**paint′a·ble,** *adj.* —**paint′y** [-IER, -IEST], *adj.*

**paint·brush** (pānt′brush′), *n.* a brush used for applying paint.

**paint·ed** (pān′tid), *adj.* 1. represented in colors as a picture, etc. 2. coated with paint. 3. pretended; feigned.

**paint·er** (pān′tẽr), *n.* 1. an artist who paints pictures. 2. a person whose work is covering surfaces, as walls, with paint.

**paint·er** (pān′tẽr), *n.* [< OFr.; ult. < L. *pendere*, to hang], a rope attached to the bow of a boat for tying it to a dock, etc.

**paint·er** (pān′tẽr), *n.* [var. of *panther*], [Dial.], the American panther; mountain lion; cougar.

**paint·ing** (pān′tiŋ), *n.* 1. the act of one who paints or the occupation of a painter. 2. a picture in paint, as an oil, water color, etc.

**pair** (pâr), *n.* [*pl.* PAIRS; *sometimes, after a number,* PAIR], [< OFr. < L. neut. pl. of *par*, equal], 1. two similar or corresponding things associated or used together: as, a *pair* of shoes. 2. a single unit of two corresponding parts that must be used together: as, a *pair* of pants. 3. *a*) a married or engaged couple. *b*) two mated animals. *c*) two people with something in common: as, a *pair* of thieves. *d*) a brace; span: as, a *pair* of oxen. *e*) two members of opposing parties in a legislature who agree to withhold their vote on a given question; also, this agreement. 4. two playing cards of the same denomination. *v.t.* 1. to make a pair of (two persons or things) by matching, joining, etc. 2. to arrange in pairs. *v.i.* 1. to form a pair; match. 2. to mate. —**pair off,** 1. to join (two people or things) in a pair. 2. to make a pair.

**pais·ley** (pāz′li), *adj.* [after *Paisley*, a city in Scotland where originally made], 1. [also P-], designating a shawl of soft wool with an elaborate, colorful pattern. 2. designating or made of cloth having such a pattern. *n.* a paisley shawl or cloth.

**pa·ja·mas** (pə-jam′əz, -jä′məz), *n.pl.* [< Hind. < Per. *pāi*, a leg + *jāmah*, garment], 1. in the Orient, a pair of loose silk or cotton trousers. 2. a loosely fitting sleeping or lounging suit consisting of jacket and trousers. Also sp. **pyjamas.**

**Pa·ki·stan** (pä′ki-stän′, pak′i-stan′), *n.* a country on the peninsula of India, consisting of two provinces, *West Pakistan* in the NW part and *East Pakistan* in the NE part: a member of the British Commonwealth of Nations: area, 364,737 sq. mi.; pop., 86,823,000; capital, Rawalpindi.

**Pa·ki·stan·i** (pä′ki-stän′i, pak′i-stan′i), *adj.* of Pakistan or its people. *n.* a native or inhabitant of Pakistan.

**pal** (pal), *n.* [< Eng. Gypsy < Sans. *bhrātr*, brother], [Colloq.], an intimate friend; comrade; chum. *v.i.* [PALLED, PALLING], [Colloq.], to associate as pals.

**pal·ace** (pal′is), *n.* [< OFr. < L. < *Palatium*, one of the seven hills of Rome, where Augustus lived], 1. the official residence of a king, bishop, etc. 2. any large, magnificent house or building.

**pal·a·din** (pal′ə-din), *n.* [< Fr. < It. < L. *palatinus*, a palace officer; see PALACE], 1. any of the twelve peers of Charlemagne's court. 2. a knight.

**pal·an·quin, pal·an·keen** (pal′ən-kēn′), *n.* [< Port. < Jav. < Sans. *palyanka*], in the Orient, a covered litter for one person, carried by poles on men's shoulders.

PALANQUIN

**pal·at·a·ble** (pal′i-tə-b′l), *adj.* 1. pleasant to the taste; savory. 2. pleasing to the mind; agreeable. —**pal′at·a·bil′i·ty, pal′at·a·ble·ness,** *n.* —**pal′at·a·bly,** *adv.*

**pal·a·tal** (pal′i-t′l), *adj.* 1. of the palate. 2. pronounced with the tongue raised against or near the hard palate, as *y* in *young*. *n.* a palatal sound.

**pal·a·tal·ize** (pal′i-t′l-īz′), *v.t.* [-IZED, -IZING], to pronounce as a palatal sound: as, the *t* in *nature* is *palatalized* to *ch*. —**pal′a·tal·i·za′tion,** *n.*

**pal·ate** (pal′it), *n.* [< OFr. < L. *palatum*], 1. the roof of the mouth, consisting of a hard bony forward part (the *hard palate*) and a soft fleshy back part (the *soft palate*). 2. taste.

**pa·la·tial** (pə-lā′shəl), *adj.* [see PALACE], 1. of, suitable for, or like a palace. 2. large and ornate; magnificent. —**pa·la′tial·ly,** *adv.*

**pa·lat·i·nate** (pə-lat′'n-āt′, -it), *n.* the territory ruled by a palatine.

**pal·a·tine** (pal′ə-tīn′, -tin), *adj.* [< L. < *palatium*, palace], 1. of a palace. 2. designating or of a nobleman (*count palatine*) having royal privileges in his own territory (*county palatine*, or *palatinate*). *n.* 1. a count palatine. 2. [P-], one of the seven hills of Rome.

**Pa·la·u (Islands)** (pä-lou′), a group of islands in the Pacific, west of the Caroline Islands.

**pa·lav·er** (pə-lav′ẽr), *n.* [Port. *palavra*, a word < L. *parabola*, a speech], 1. a conference, especially among or with African tribes. 2. talk; esp., profuse or idle talk. 3. flattery; cajolery. *v.i.* to talk glibly or flatteringly. *v.t.* to flatter.

**pale** (pāl), *adj.* [OFr. < L. *pallere*, to be pale], 1. of a whitish or colorless complexion; pallid; wan. 2. lacking intensity; faint: said of color, light, etc. 3. feeble; weak: as, a *pale* imitation. *v.i.* & *v.t.* [PALED, PALING], to become or make pale. —**pale′ly,** *adv.* —**pale′ness,** *n.* —**pal′ish,** *adj.*

**pale** (pāl), *n.* [< OFr. < L. *palus*, a stake], 1. a pointed stake used in fences; picket. 2. a fence; enclosure; boundary: now chiefly figurative. 3. a district enclosed within bounds.

**pa·le-** (pā′li; *occas.* pal′i), paleo-: words beginning with *pale-* are also spelled **palae-.**

**pale·face** (pāl′fās′), *n.* a white person: a term allegedly first used by American Indians.

**pa·le·o-,** [< Gr. *palaios*, ancient], a combining form meaning: 1. *ancient, prehistoric*, as in *Paleozoic*. 2. *primitive*, as in *paleolithic*. Also **palaeo-.**

**Pa·le·o·cene** (pā′li-ə-sēn′), *adj.* [< *paleo-* + Gr.

*kainos*, recent], designating or of an epoch preceding the Eocene in the Tertiary Period: see **geology**, chart. *n.* the Paleocene Epoch.

**pa·le·og·ra·phy** (pā'li-og'rə-fi), *n.* 1. ancient writing or forms of writing. 2. the study of describing or deciphering ancient writings, etc. —**pa'le·og'ra·pher,** *n.* —**pa'le·o·graph'ic** (-ə-graf'ik), **pa'le·o·graph'i·cal,** *adj.*

**pa·le·o·l** ⁊**h·ic** (pā'li-ə-lith'ik), *adj.* designating or of the middle period of the Stone Age, characterized by the use of stone tools.

**pa·le·on·tol·o·gy** (pā'li-ən-tol'ə-ji), *n.* [< *paleo-* + Gr. *ōn*, a being; + *-logy*], the branch of geology dealing with prehistoric life through the study of fossils. —**pa'le·on'to·log'ic** (-on'tə-loj'ik), **pa'le·on'to·log'i·cal,** *adj.* —**pa'le·on·tol'o·gist,** *n.*

**Pa·le·o·zo·ic** (pā'li-ə-zō'ik), *adj.* [*paleo-* + *zo-* + *-ic*], designating or of the era between the Proterozoic and the Mesozoic: see **geology**, chart. *n.* the Paleozoic Era.

**Pa·ler·mo** (pə-lūr'mō; It. pä-ler'mô), *n.* a seaport in N Sicily: pop., 501,000.

**Pal·es·tine** (pal'əs-tīn'), *n.* 1. a territory on the E coast of the Mediterranean, the country of the Jews in Biblical times. 2. part of this territory under a British mandate after World War I: divided into independent Arab and Jewish states by the UN in 1947: cf. **Israel.** —**Pal'es·tin'i·an** (-tin'i-ən, -tin'yən), *adj. & n.*

**Pal·es·tri·na, Gio·van·ni** (jô-vän'nē pä'les-trē'nä; Eng. pal'ə-strē'nə), 1526?–1594; Italian composer.

**pal·ette** (pal'it), *n.* [Fr. < L. *pala*, a shovel], 1. a thin oblong board with a hole at one end for the thumb, on which an artist arranges and mixes his paints: also **pallet.** 2. the colors used, as by a particular artist.

PALETTE

**pal·frey** (pôl'fri), *n.* [*pl.* -FREYS], [< OFr. < LL.; ult. < Gr. *para*, beside + L. *veredus*, post horse], [Archaic], a saddle horse, especially one for a woman.

**Pa·li** (pä'lē), *n.* the Old Indic dialect which has become the religious language of Buddhism.

**pal·imp·sest** (pal'imp-sest'), *n.* [< L. < Gr. < *palin*, again + *psēn*, to rub smooth], a parchment, tablet, etc. that has been written upon several times, with previous, erased texts still partly visible. *adj.* written upon more than once.

**pal·ing** (pā'liŋ), *n.* 1. the action of making a fence of pales. 2. a fence so made. 3. a pale, or pales collectively.

**pal·i·sade** (pal'ə-sād'), *n.* [< Fr. < Pr. < L. *palus*, a stake], 1. any of a row of large pointed stakes set in the ground to form a fence as for fortification. 2. such a fence. 3. *pl.* a line of steep cliffs. *v.t.* to surround or fortify with a palisade.

**pall** (pôl), *v.t.* [PALLED, PALLING], [ME. *pallen*] to satiate; disgust. *v.i.* 1. to become cloying, insipid, etc. 2. to become cloyed or satiated.

**pall** (pôl), *n.* [< AS. < L. *pallium*, a cover], 1. a piece of velvet, etc. used to cover a coffin, hearse, or tomb. 2. a dark or gloomy covering: as, a *pall* of smoke. 3. in *Christian churches*, a cloth, or cardboard covered with cloth, used to cover the chalice. *v.t.* [PALLED, PALLING], to cover as with a pall.

**Pal·la·di·um** (pə-lā'di-əm), *n.* [*pl.* -DIA (-di-ə)], 1. the statue of the Greek goddess Pallas Athena in Troy on which the safety of the city was supposed to depend. 2. [p-], any safeguard.

**pal·la·di·um** (pə-lā'di-əm), *n.* [ult. < Gr. *Pallas*, the goddess], a rare, silvery-white, metallic chemical element of the platinum group: it is used as a catalyst, or in alloys with gold, silver, etc.: symbol, Pd; at. wt., 106.7; at. no., 46.

**Pal·las** (pal'əs), *n.* in *Gr. mythology*, Athena, goddess of wisdom: also **Pallas Athena.** —**Pal·la·di·an** (pə-lā'di-ən), *adj.*

**pall·bear·er** (pôl'bâr'ēr), *n.* [*pall* (cover) + *bearer*], one of the persons who attend the coffin at a funeral.

**pal·let** (pal'it), *n.* [< Fr.; see PALETTE], 1. a wooden tool consisting of a flat blade with a handle; esp., such a tool for smoothing pottery. 2. a palette. 3. any of the clicks or pawls in the escapement of a clock which engage the ratchet wheel to regulate the speed.

**pal·let** (pal'it), *n.* [< OFr. < *paille*, straw < L. *palea*, chaff], a straw bed or mattress: often connoting a poor or inferior bed.

**pal·li·ate** (pal'i-āt'), *v.t.* [-ATED, -ATING], [< L. pp. < *pallium*, a cloak], 1. to lessen the pain or severity of without curing; alleviate. 2. to make (a crime, offense, etc.) appear less serious than it is; excuse. —**pal'li·a'tion,** *n.* —**pal'li·a'tive** (-ā'tiv, -ə-tiv), *adj. & n.* —**pal'li·a'tor,** *n.*

**pal·lid** (pal'id), *adj.* [< L. < *pallere*, to become pale], faint in color; pale; wan. —**pal'lid·ly,** *adv.* —**pal'lid·ness,** *n.*

**Pall Mall** (pel mel, pal mal), a London street, noted for its clubs.

**pal·lor** (pal'ēr), *n.* [L. < *pallere*, to be pale], lack of color; unnatural paleness, as of the face.

**palm** (päm), *n.* [AS. < L. *palma*: from its *handlike* fronds], 1. any of several tropical or subtropical trees with a tall branchless trunk and a bunch of huge leaves at the top. 2. a leaf of this tree carried as a symbol of victory, triumph, etc. 3. victory; triumph. —**bear** (or **carry off**) **the palm,** to be the winner. —**pal·ma·ceous** (pal-mā'shəs), *adj.*

PALM (60–80 ft. high)

**palm** (päm), *n.* [< OFr. < L. *palma*], 1. the inner surface of the hand between the fingers and wrist. 2. the part of a glove, etc. covering the palm. 3. the broad, flat part of an antler, as of a moose, etc. 4. a unit of measure equal to either the width (3 to 4 inches) or the length (7 to 9 inches) of the hand. 5. any broad, flat part at the end of an armlike part, handle, etc. *v.t.* to hide (something) in the palm or about the hand, as in a sleight-of-hand trick. —**grease the palm of,** to bribe. —**have an itching palm,** [Colloq.], to desire money greedily. —**palm off,** to manage to get (a thing) accepted, sold, etc. by fraud or deceit. —**pal·mar** (pal'mēr), *adj.*

**Pal·ma** (päl'mä), *n.* a city on Majorca, capital of the Balearic Islands, Spain: pop., 137,000: also called *Palma de Mallorca.*

**pal·mate** (pal'māt, -mit), *adj.* [see PALM (of hand)], shaped like a hand with the fingers spread; specif., *a*) in *botany*, having veins or lobes radiating from a common center, as some leaves. *b*) in *zoology*, web-footed. Also **pal'mat·ed.** —**pal'mate·ly,** *adv.* —**pal·ma'tion,** *n.*

**Palm Beach,** a resort town in SE Florida.

**palm·er** (päm'ēr), *n.* 1. a pilgrim who carried a palm leaf as a sign that he had been to the Holy Land. 2. any pilgrim.

**pal·met·to** (pal-met'ō), *n.* [*pl.* -TOS, -TOES], [< Sp. *palmito*, dim. < L. *palma*, the palm], any of several small palm trees with fan-shaped leaves.

**palm·is·try** (päm'is-tri), *n.* [< ME.; prob. contr. < *paume*, the palm + *maistrie*, mastery], the pretended art of telling a person's fortune by the lines, etc. on the palm of his hand. —**palm'ist,** *n.*

**palm leaf,** the leaf of a palm tree, especially of a palmetto, used to make fans, hats, etc.

**palm oil,** a fat obtained from the fruit of certain palms, used in making soap, candles, etc.

**Palm Sunday,** the Sunday before Easter, commemorating Jesus' entry into Jerusalem, when palm branches were strewn before him.

**palm·y** (päm'i), *adj.* [-IER, -IEST], 1. abounding in or shaded by palm trees. 2. of or like a palm. 3. flourishing; successful: as, *palmy* days.

**pal·my·ra** (pal-mī'rə), *n.* [< Port. < L. *palma*, the palm], a kind of palm tree of India and Ceylon, with large, fan-shaped leaves used to make matting, hats, etc.: also **palmyra palm** (or **tree**).

**pal·o·mi·no** (pal'ə-mē'nō), *n.* [Am. Sp. dim. of *paloma*, dove; ult. < L. *palumbes*, ringdove: orig. applied to horses of a dovelike color], a pale-yellow horse with a white mane and tail.

**pa·loo·ka** (pə-lōō'kə), *n.* [Slang], in *sports*, an incompetent or easily defeated player.

**palp** (palp), *n.* a palpus.

**pal·pa·ble** (pal'pə-b'l), *adj.* [< LL. < L. *palpare*, to touch], 1. that can be touched, felt, etc.; tangible. 2. easily perceived by the senses; perceptible, recognizable, etc. 3. obvious; plain. —**pal'pa·bil'i·ty,** *n.* —**pal'pa·bly,** *adv.*

**pal·pate** (pal'pāt), *v.t.* [-PATED, -PATING], [< L. pp. of *palpare*, to touch], to examine by touching, as for medical diagnosis. —**pal·pa'tion,** *n.*

**pal·pi·tate** (pal'pə-tāt'), *v.i.* [-TATED, -TATING], [< L. pp. of *palpitare*, freq. of *palpare*, to feel], 1. to beat rapidly or flutter, as the heart. 2. to throb; quiver; tremble. —**pal'pi·tant,** *adj.* —**pal'pi·ta'tion,** *n.*

**pal·pus** (pal'pəs), *n.* [*pl.* -PI (-pī)], [< L. *palpus*, the soft palm of the hand], a jointed organ or feeler for touching or tasting, attached to the mouth of insects, lobsters, etc.: also **palp.**

**pal·sied** (pôl'zid), *adj.* 1. having palsy; paralyzed. 2. shaking; trembling.

**pal·sy** (pôl'zi), *n.* [*pl.* -SIES], [< OFr. < L. *paralysis;*

see PARALYSIS], paralysis in any part of the body, sometimes accompanied by involuntary tremors. *v.t.* [-SIED, -SYING], 1. to afflict with palsy. 2. to make helpless, as with fear.

**pal·ter** (pôl′tẽr), *v.i.* [freq. < dial. *palt*, rag], 1. to talk or act insincerely; prevaricate. 2. to trifle. 3. to haggle.

**pal·try** (pôl′tri), *adj.* [-TRIER, -TRIEST], [prob. < LG. < *palte*, a rag], trifling; worthless; petty. —**pal′tri·ly**, *adv.* —**pal′tri·ness**, *n.*

**pam·pas** (pam′pəz; *for adj.*, -pəs), *n.pl.* [Sp. < Quechua *pampa*, plain], the extensive treeless plains of South America, esp. of Argentina. *adj.* of the pampas. —**pam·pe·an** (pam′pi-ən, pam-pē′-), *adj. & n.*

**pam·per** (pam′pẽr), *v.t.* [prob. < LG.], 1. originally, to feed too much; glut. 2. to be overindulgent with; coddle: as, to *pamper* a baby. —**pam′per·er**, *n.*

**pam·phlet** (pam′flit), *n.* [< OFr. *Pamphilet*, popular name of a ML. poem], 1. a small, unbound booklet, usually with a paper cover. 2. a treatise in this form, as on some topic of current interest.

**pam·phlet·eer** (pam′fli-têr′), *n.* a writer of pamphlets. *v.i.* to write or publish pamphlets.

**Pan** (pan), *n.* in *Gr. mythology*, a god of fields, forests, wild animals, flocks, and shepherds, represented with the legs of a goat.

**pan** (pan), *n.* [AS. *panne*], 1. any broad, shallow dish, usually of metal and without a cover, used in cooking, etc.: often in combination, as, a *saucepan*. 2. a pan-shaped part or object; specif., *a*) a container for washing out gold, etc. from gravel. *b*) either receptacle in a pair of scales. 3. hardpan. 4. the part holding the powder in a flintlock. 5. [Slang], a face. *v.t.* [PANNED, PANNING], 1. to cook in a pan. 2. [Colloq.], to criticize unfavorably, as a play or book. 3. in *mining*, *a*) to wash (gravel) in a pan. *b*) to separate (gold, etc.) from gravel in this way. *v.i.* in *mining*, 1. to wash gravel in a pan. 2. to yield gold in this process. —**pan out**, 1. in *mining*, to yield gold, as gravel, a mine, etc. 2. [Colloq.], to turn out; esp., to turn out well.

**pan** (pan), *v.t. & v.i.* [PANNED, PANNING], [abbrev. < *panorama*], to move (a motion-picture or television camera) to get a panoramic effect or to follow a moving object.

**pan-**, [< Gr. *pan*, neut. of *pas*, all, every], a combining form meaning: 1. *all*, as in *pantheism*. 2. [P-], *a*) *of, comprising*, or *common to every*, as in *Pan-American*. *b*) (*belief in*) *the union of all members of* (a certain nationality, race, etc.), as in *Pan-Americanism*. In sense 2, used with a hyphen, as in the following words:

| | |
|---|---|
| **Pan-Asiatic** | **Pan-Islamic** |
| **Pan-European** | **Pan-Islamism** |
| **Pan-German** | **Pan-Slavic** |
| **Pan-Germanic** | **Pan-Slavism** |
| **Pan-Germanism** | **Pan-Teutonism** |

**pan·a·ce·a** (pan′ə-sē′ə), *n.* [L. < Gr. < *pan*, all + *akeisthai*, to cure], a supposed remedy or cure for all diseases or ills; cure-all.

**Pan·a·ma** (pan′ə-mä′, pan′ə-mô′), *n.* 1. a Central American republic on the Isthmus of Panama: area, 32,000 sq. mi.; pop., 1,053,000. 2. its capital, on the Pacific: pop., 200,000: also **Panama City.** Abbrev. **Pan.** —**Pan′a·ma′ni·an** (-mā′ni-ən), *adj. & n.*

**Panama, Isthmus of,** an isthmus connecting North and South America.

**Panama Canal,** a ship canal across the Isthmus of Panama, connecting the Atlantic and Pacific Oceans: length, 50.7 mi.

**Panama Canal Zone,** see **Canal Zone.**

**Panama hat,** [< *Panama* (city)], a fine, hand-plaited hat made from select leaves of a Central and South American palm tree.

**Pan-A·mer·i·can** (pan′ə-mer′ə-kən), *adj.* of North, Central, and South America, or their peoples.

**Pan-A·mer·i·can·ism** (pan′ə-mer′ə-kən-iz′m), *n.* a policy of political and economic co-operation, mutual cultural understanding, etc. among the Pan-American nations.

**Pan American Union,** the official agency of the Organization of American States (OAS) through which the 21 member republics work to further Pan-Americanism.

**Pa·nay** (pä-nī′; Eng. pə-nī′), *n.* one of the central Philippine Islands.

**pan·cake** (pan′kāk′, paŋ′-), *n.* 1. a thin, flat cake of batter fried on a griddle or in a pan; griddlecake; flapjack. 2. a landing in which the airplane in a horizontal position drops almost vertically to the ground. *v.i. & v.t.* [-CAKED, -CAKING], to make or cause (an airplane) to make such a landing.

**pan·chro·mat·ic** (pan′krō-mat′ik), *adj.* sensitive to light of all colors: as, *panchromatic* film. —**pan-chro·ma·tism** (pan-krō′mə-tiz′m), *n.*

**pan·cre·as** (pan′kri-əs, paŋ′-), *n.* [< Gr. < *pan*, all + *kreas*, flesh], a large, elongated gland that secretes an alkaline digestive juice (*pancreatic juice*) into the small intestine: the pancreas of a calf, etc., when used as food, is called *sweetbread*. —**pan′cre·at′ic** (-at′ik), *adj.*

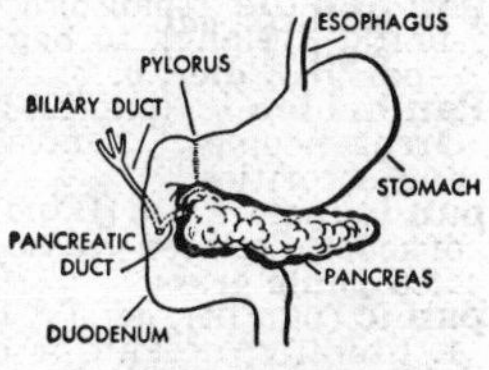

PANCREAS

**pan·da** (pan′də), *n.* [< native name], 1. a small, reddish-brown, raccoon-like animal of the Himalayas. 2. a white-and-black, bearlike animal of Asia: also called *giant panda*.

**pan·dem·ic** (pan-dem′ik), *adj.* [< Gr. < *pan*, all + *dēmos*, the people], epidemic over a large region.

**Pan·de·mo·ni·um** (pan′di-mō′ni-əm), *n.* [< *pan-* + Gr. *daimōn*, demon], 1. the abode of all demons, as in Milton's *Paradise Lost*. 2. hell. 3. [p-], wild disorder, noise, or confusion, or a place where this exists.

**pan·der** (pan′dẽr), *n.* [< *Pandarus*, who, in the story of Troilus and Cressida, acts as their go-between], 1. a go-between in a sexual intrigue; pimp. 2. one who provides the means of helping to satisfy the ambitions, vices, etc. of another. Also **pan′der·er.** *v.i.* to act as a pander (with *to*).

**pan·dit** (pun′dit, pan′-), *n.* [var. of *pundit*], in India, a learned man: used [P-] as a title of respect.

**Pan·do·ra** (pan-dôr′ə, -dō′rə), *n.* [L. < Gr. < *pan*, all + *dōron*, a gift], in *Gr. mythology*, the first mortal woman, sent by Zeus as a punishment to mankind for the theft of fire from heaven: Zeus gave her a box which she opened, letting out all human ills into the world.

**pan·dow·dy** (pan-dou′di), *n.* [*pl.* -DIES], [< *pan*: 2d element prob. < obs. Eng. dial.], deep-dish apple pie, having a top crust only.

**pane** (pān), *n.* [< OFr. < L. *pannus*, piece of cloth], 1. a flat piece, side, or face. 2. *a*) a single division of a window, etc., consisting of a sheet of glass, etc. in a frame. *b*) this sheet of glass. 3. a panel, as of a door.

**pan·e·gyr·ic** (pan′ə-jir′ik), *n.* [< Fr. < L. < Gr. *panēgyris*, public meeting < *pan*, all + *ageirein*, to bring together], 1. a formal speech or writing praising a person or event. 2. high praise; eulogy. —**pan′e·gyr′i·cal**, *adj.* —**pan′e·gyr′i·cal·ly**, *adv.* —**pan′e·gyr′ist**, *n.* —**pan′e·gy·rize′** (-ji-rīz′), [-RIZED, -RIZING], *v.t. & v.i.*

**pan·el** (pan′'l), *n.* [< OFr. < ML. dim. of L. *pannus*, piece of cloth], 1. a section or division of a surface; specif., *a*) a flat piece, usually rectangular, forming part of the surface of a wall, door, etc., usually set off by being recessed, raised, framed, etc. *b*) a pane of a window. *c*) a board, or flat surface, for instruments or controls. 2. *a*) a thin board for an oil painting. *b*) a painting on such a board. *c*) a picture much longer than it is wide. 3. a group of persons selected for a specific purpose, as judging, discussing, etc. 4. a lengthwise strip, as of contrasting material, in a skirt or dress. 5. *a*) a list of persons summoned for jury duty. *b*) the jurors as a whole. *v.t.* [-ELED or -ELLED, -ELING or -ELLING], to provide, decorate, etc. with panels.

**panel discussion,** a discussion carried on by a selected group of speakers before an audience.

**pan·el·ing, pan·el·ling** (pan′'l-iŋ), *n.* panels collectively; series of panels in a wall, etc.

**pan·el·ist** (pan′'l-ist), *n.* 1. a participant in a panel discussion. 2. a person who serves on a panel, as on a radio quiz program.

**pan·e·tel·a, pan·e·tel·la** (pan′ə-tel′ə), *n.* [Sp.], a long, slender cigar.

**pan fish,** any small fish that can be fried whole in a pan.

**pan-fry** (pan′frī′), *v.t.* [-FRIED, -FRYING], to fry with fat in a shallow skillet or frying pan.

**pang** (paŋ), *n.* [< ME. *prong*; prob. a special use of *prong*, a point], a sudden, sharp, brief pain, physical or emotional; spasm of distress.

**pan·go·lin** (paŋ-gō′lin), *n.* [Malay *pĕngulin*, roller

<*gulin*, to roll], any of various toothless, scaly mammals of Asia and Africa, able to roll into a ball when attacked: also called *scaly anteater.*

**pan·han·dle** (pan′han′d'l), ***n.*** 1. the handle of a pan. 2. [often P-], a strip of land like the handle of a pan, as the northern extension of Texas.

**pan·han·dle** (pan′han′d'l), ***v.t.* & *v.i.*** [-DLED, -DLING], [Slang], to beg, especially on the streets. **—pan′han′dler, *n.***

**Pan·hel·len·ic** (pan′hə-len′ik), ***adj.*** 1. of all the Greek peoples. 2. of all Greek-letter fraternities and sororities.

**pan·ic** (pan′ik), ***n.*** [L. *panicum*, kind of millet], any of several related grasses, as millet, used as fodder: also **panic grass.**

**pan·ic** (pan′ik), ***adj.*** [< Fr. < Gr. *panikos*, of Pan], 1. literally, of Pan or of sudden fear supposedly inspired by him. 2. like, showing, or resulting from panic. ***n.*** 1. a sudden, unreasoning, hysterical fear, often spreading quickly. 2. a widespread fear of the collapse of the financial system. 3. [Slang], a very comical person or thing. ***v.t.*** [-ICKED, -ICKING], 1. to affect with panic. 2. [Slang], to delight: as, the clown *panicked* the audience. **—pan′ick·y, *adj.***

**pan·i·cle** (pan′i-k'l), ***n.*** [< L. dim. of *panus*, a swelling, ear of millet], a loose, irregularly branched flower cluster; compound raceme. **—pan′i·cled, *adj.***

**pan·ic-strick·en** (pan′ik-strik″'n), ***adj.*** stricken with panic; badly frightened: also **panic-struck.**

**pa·nic·u·late** (pə-nik′yoo-lāt′, -lit), ***adj.*** growing or arranged in panicles: also **pa·nic′u·lat′ed.**

**pan·jan·drum** (pan-jan′drəm), ***n.*** [arbitrary coinage], a self-important, pompous official.

**pan·nier** (pan′yēr, -i-ēr), ***n.*** [< OFr. < L. *panarium*, breadbasket < *panis*, bread], 1. a large basket; specif., *a*) a wicker basket for carrying loads on the back. *b*) either of a pair of baskets hung across the back of a mule, horse, etc. 2. *a*) a framework, as of wire, etc., used to puff out a skirt at the hips. *b*) a skirt so puffed.

PANNIERS

**pan·ni·kin** (pan′ə-kin), ***n.*** a small pan or cup.

**pa·no·cha** (pə-nō′chə), ***n.*** [Sp. < L. *panucula;* see PANICLE], 1. a coarse Mexican sugar. 2. a candy made of brown sugar, milk, butter, and nuts.

**pan·o·ply** (pan′ə-pli), ***n.*** [*pl.* -PLIES], [< Gr. < *pan*, all + *hopla*, arms], 1. a complete suit of armor. 2. any complete or magnificent covering or array. **—pan′o·plied, *adj.***

**pan·o·ra·ma** (pan′ə-ram′ə, -rä′mə), ***n.*** [< *pan-* + Gr. *horama*, a view], 1. *a*) a picture unrolled in such a way as to give the impression of a continuous view. *b*) a cyclorama. 2. an unlimited view in all directions. 3. a comprehensive survey of a subject. 4. a constantly changing scene: as, the *panorama* of the waterfront. **—pan′o·ram′ic, *adj.* —pan′o·ram′i·cal·ly, *adv.* —pan′o·ram′ist, *n.***

**panoramic sight,** a kind of periscopic gun sight that provides a greatly enlarged field of view.

**Pan·pipe** (pan′pīp′), ***n.*** a primitive musical instrument made of a row of reeds or tubes of graduated lengths, played by blowing across the open ends: also called **Panpipes, Pan's pipes, syrinx.**

**pan·sy** (pan′zi), ***n.*** [*pl.* -SIES], [< Fr. *pensée*, a thought < *penser*, to think], 1. a small plant of the violet family, with flat, velvety petals in many colors. 2. [Slang], a male homosexual.

**pant** (pant), ***v.i.*** [prob. < OFr. *pantaisier;* ult. < L. *phantasia*, nightmare], 1. to breathe rapidly and heavily, as from running fast. 2. to throb; pulsate, as the heart. 3. to gasp with desire (with *for* or *after*). ***v.t.*** to gasp out (often with *out* or *forth*). ***n.*** 1. any of a series of rapid, heavy breaths; gasp. 2. a throb, as of the heart. 3. a puff of an engine.

**pan·ta·lets, pan·ta·lettes** (pan′tə-lets′), ***n.pl.*** [dim. of *pantaloon*], 1. long, loose drawers showing below the skirt, worn by women in the 19th century. 2. detachable ruffles for the legs of drawers.

**pan·ta·loon** (pan′tə-lōōn′), ***n.*** [< Fr. < It.; ult. after the Venetian patron saint *Pantolone*], 1. [P-], *a*) a character in an old Italian comedy, usually a foolish old man conventionally dressed in tight trousers. *b*) a similar buffoon in modern pantomime. 2. *pl.* trousers.

**pan·the·ism** (pan′thē-iz'm), ***n.*** [*pan-* + *theism*], 1. the belief that God is not a personality, but that all forces, manifestations, etc. of the universe are God. 2. the worship of all gods. **—pan′the·ist, *n.* —pan′the·is′tic, pan′the·is′ti·cal, *adj.* —pan′the·is′ti·cal·ly, *adv.***

**pan·the·on** (pan′thē-on′, -thi-ən, pan-thē′-), ***n.*** [< L. < Gr. < *pan*, all + *theos*, a god], 1. a temple for all the gods; esp., [P-], a temple built in Rome in 27 B.C.: used since 609 A.D. as a Christian church. 2. all the gods of a people. 3. [often P-], a building in which the famous dead of a nation are entombed or commemorated.

**pan·ther** (pan′thēr), ***n.*** [*pl.* -THERS, -THER; see PLURAL, II, D, 1], [< L. < Gr. *panthēr*], 1. a puma; cougar; mountain lion. 2. a leopard. 3. a jaguar. **—pan′ther·ess, *n.fem.* —pan′ther·like′, *adj.***

**pan·ties** (pan′tiz), ***n.pl.*** women's or children's short underpants.

**pan·to-,** [< Gr. *pantos*, genit. of *pan*, all, every], a combining form meaning *all* or *every*: also **pant-.**

**pan·to·graph** (pan′tə-graf′, -gräf′), ***n.*** [*panto-* + *graph*], a mechanical device for reproducing a drawing on the same or a different scale.

**pan·to·mime** (pan′tə-mīm′), ***n.*** [Fr. < L. < Gr. < *pas*, all + *mimos*, a mimic], 1. in ancient Rome, an actor who used gestures and action without words. 2. a drama without words, using actions and gestures only. 3. actions or gestures without words. ***adj.*** of or like pantomime. ***v.t.* & *v.i.*** [-MIMED, -MIMING], to express or act in pantomime. **—pan′to·mim′ic** (-mim′ik), ***adj.*** **—pan′to·mim′ist** (-mīm′ist), ***n.***

**pan·try** (pan′tri), ***n.*** [*pl.* -TRIES], [< OFr. < ML. *panetaria* < L. *panis*, bread], 1. a small room off the kitchen, where cooking ingredients and utensils, china, etc. are kept. 2. a butler's pantry.

**pants** (pants), ***n.pl.*** [abbrev. of *pantaloons*], 1. trousers. 2. drawers or panties.

**pan·ty·waist** (pan′ti-wāst′), ***n.*** 1. originally, a child's two-piece undergarment. 2. [Slang], a weakling; sissy.

**pan·zer** (pan′zēr; G. pän′tsēr), ***adj.*** [G., armor], armored: as, a *panzer* division.

**pap** (pap), ***n.*** [< ON.], [Archaic], a nipple or teat.

**pap** (pap), ***n.*** [? echoic of infant's cry for food], any soft food for babies or invalids.

**pa·pa** (pä′pə; *less freq.*, pə-pä′), ***n.*** [like Fr. & L. *papa* < baby talk], father: a child's word.

**pa·pa·cy** (pā′pə-si), ***n.*** [*pl.* -CIES], [< ML. < *papa*, pope], 1. the position or authority of the Pope. 2. the period during which a pope rules. 3. the succession of popes. 4. [also P-], the government of the Roman Catholic Church, headed by the Pope.

**pa·pal** (pā′p'l), ***adj.*** [< OFr. < ML. *papa*, pope], 1. of the Pope. 2. of the papacy. 3. of the Roman Catholic Church.

**Papal States,** the lands in central Italy that belonged to the Roman Catholic Church and were ruled by the Pope until 1870.

**pa·paw** (pô′pô, pə-pô′), ***n.*** [< Sp. *papaya* < Carib. name], 1. a papaya. 2. *a*) a tree of the central and southern U.S., having a yellowish, edible fruit with many seeds. *b*) its fruit. Also **pawpaw.**

**pa·pa·ya** (pə-pä′yə), ***n.*** [Sp., fruit of the papaw], 1. a palmlike tropical tree having a bunch of large leaves at the top, and bearing a large, yellowish-orange, edible fruit like a melon. 2. its fruit.

**pa·per** (pā′pēr), ***n.*** [< OFr. < L. *papyrus;* see PAPYRUS, sense 2], 1. a thin, flexible material in sheets, made from rags, wood pulp, etc., and used to write or print on, wrap, decorate, etc. 2. a single piece or sheet of this. 3. a printed or written paper; specif., *a*) an official document. *b*) an essay, dissertation, etc. *c*) a written examination, report, etc. 4. *a*) checks, promissory notes, and similar negotiable papers. *b*) paper money. 5. a newspaper. 6. a small wrapper of paper, usually including its contents: as, a *paper* of pins. 7. wallpaper. 8. any material like paper, as papyrus. 9. *pl.* *a*) documents proving one's identity; credentials. *b*) a collection of letters, writings, etc. ***adj.*** 1. of, or made of, paper. 2. like paper; thin. 3. existing only in written form; theoretical: as, *paper* profits. ***v.t.*** 1. to cover with paper, especially wallpaper. 2. to wrap in paper. **—on paper,** 1. in written or printed form. 2. in theory. **—pa′per·er, *n.* —pa′per·like′, pa′per·y, *adj.***

**pa·per·back** (pā′pēr-bak′), ***n.*** a book bound in paper. **—pa′per·backed′, *adj.***

**pa·per·boy** (pā′pēr-boi′), ***n.*** a boy or man who sells or delivers newspapers.

**paper cutter,** 1. a paper knife. 2. a machine used to cut and trim paper to required dimensions.

**paper hanger,** a person whose work is to cover walls with wallpaper. **—paper hanging.**

**paper knife,** a dull knife of metal, wood, etc. used to cut open sealed envelopes or uncut pages.

**paper money,** noninterest-bearing notes issued by a government as a substitute for metallic money: as, a dollar bill is *paper money.*

**paper nautilus,** an eight-armed mollusk related to the octopus: the female has a paperlike shell.

**pa·per·weight** (pā′pēr-wāt′), *n.* any small, heavy object to be placed on papers to keep them from being scattered.

**paper work,** the keeping of records, filing of reports, etc. that is incidental to some work or task.

**‡pa·pier-mâ·ché** (pā′pēr-mə-shā′; Fr. på′pyā′må′-shā′), *n.* [Fr. < *papier*, paper + *mâché*, pp. of *mâcher*, to chew], a material made of paper pulp mixed with rosin, oil, etc. and molded into various objects when moist. *adj.* made of papier-mâché.

**pa·pil·la** (pə-pil′ə), *n.* [*pl.* -LAE (-ē)], [L., dim. of *papula*, pimple], 1. *a*) any small nipplelike projection of connective tissue, as at the root of a developing tooth, hair, etc., or on the surface of the tongue. *b*) the nipple. 2. in *botany*, a tiny, protruding cell. —**pap·il·lar·y** (pap′ə-ler′i, pə-pil′ēr-i), *adj.*

**pap·il·lo·ma** (pap′ə-lō′mə), *n.* [*pl.* -MATA (-mə-tə), -MAS], [Mod. L. < *papilla* + *-oma*], a tumor of the skin or mucous membrane, consisting of a thickened and enlarged papilla, as a corn or wart.

**pap·il·lose** (pap′ə-lōs′), *adj.* having many papillae. —**pap·il·los·i·ty** (pap′ə-los′ə-ti), *n.*

**pa·pist** (pā′pist), *n.* [< Fr. < ML. < L. *papa*, pope], 1. one who believes in papal supremacy. 2. a Roman Catholic. *adj.* Roman Catholic. A hostile term. —**pa·pis′tic, pa·pis′ti·cal,** *adj.* —**pa′pist·ry,** *n.*

**pa·poose** (pa-po͞os′), *n.* [< Am. Ind. *papoos*], a North American Indian baby.

**pap·pus** (pap′əs), *n.* [*pl.* -PI (-ī)], [< Gr. *pappos*, old man], in *botany*, a downy tuft of bristles on certain fruits, as on the seeds of the dandelion. —**pap′pose** (-ōs), **pap′pous** (-əs), *adj.*

**pap·py** (pap′i), *n.* [Dial. or Colloq.], papa; father.

**pap·ri·ka, pap·ri·ca** (pa-prē′kə, pap′ri-), *n.* [G.; Hung. < Gr. *peperi*, a pepper], a mild red condiment ground from the fruit of certain peppers.

**Pap·u·a** (pä′po͞o-ə; Eng. pap′ū-ə), *n.* 1. New Guinea. 2. the Territory of Papua. —**Pap·u·an** (pap′ū-ən), *adj. & n.*

**Papua, Territory of,** a territory on SE New Guinea and near-by islands, under UN trusteeship and administered, with the Territory of New Guinea, by Australia: area, 90,540 sq. mi.; pop., 374,000.

**pap·ule** (pap′ūl), *n.* [L.], a pimple. —**pap′u·lar** (-yoo-lēr), *adj.*

**pa·py·rus** (pə-pī′rəs), *n.* [*pl.* -RI (-rī), -RUSES], [L. < Gr. *papyros*], 1. a tall water plant of the sedge family, formerly abundant in Egypt. 2. a writing material made from the pith of this plant by the ancient Egyptians, Greeks, and Romans. 3. any ancient document or manuscript on papyrus.

**par** (pär), *n.* [L., an equal], 1. the established value of the money of one country in terms of the money of another. 2. an equal status, footing, level, etc. (with *on* or *upon*): as, they are on a *par* in ability. 3. the average state, condition, etc.: as, his work is above *par*. 4. in *commerce*, the face value of stocks, bonds, etc.: as, this stock is selling at *par*. 5. in *golf*, the number of strokes established as an expert score for a hole or course. *adj.* 1. of or at par. 2. average; normal.

**par.,** 1. [*pl.* PARS.], paragraph. 2. parallel. 3. [*pl.* PARENS.], parenthesis. 4. parish.

**Pa·rá** (pä-rä′), *n.* Belém.

**par·a-,** [< Gr. < *para*, at the side of], a prefix meaning: 1. *by the side of, beside*, as in *parallel*. 2. in *medicine*, *a*) *functionally disordered, abnormal*, as in *parafunctional*. *b*) *like* or *resembling*, as in *paracholera*. Also **par-.**

**par·a·ble** (par′ə-b′l), *n.* [< OFr. < L. < Gr. *parabolē*, a comparing; ult. < *para-*, beside + *ballein*, to throw], a short, simple story teaching a moral lesson: it is usually an allegory.

**pa·rab·o·la** (pə-rab′ə-lə), *n.* [*pl.* -LAS], [< Gr. *parabolē*; see PARABLE], in *geometry*, a plane curve shaped as the curve formed by the intersection of a cone with a plane parallel to its side.

**par·a·bol·ic** (par′ə-bol′ik), *adj.* 1. of, like, or expressed by a parable; allegorical: also **par′a·bol′i·cal.** 2. of or like a parabola. —**par′a·bol′i·cal·ly,** *adv.*

**pa·rab·o·lize** (pə-rab′ə-līz′), *v.t.* [-LIZED, -LIZING], 1. to tell in a parable or parables. 2. to make parabolic in shape. —**pa·rab′o·liz′er,** *n.*

**Par·a·cel·sus, Phi·lip·pus Au·re·o·lus** (fi-lip′əs ô-rē′ə-ləs par′ə-sel′səs), 1493?–1541; German physician and alchemist, born in Switzerland.

**par·a·chute** (par′ə-sho͞ot′), *n.* [Fr. < *para-* (< It. < L. *parare*, to prepare) + *chute*, fall], 1. a large cloth contrivance, shaped like an umbrella when unfolded, used to retard the speed of a person or thing dropping from an airplane, etc. 2. something shaped like or having the effect of a parachute. *v.t. & v.i.* [-CHUTED, -CHUTING], to drop or descend by a parachute. —**par′a·chut′ist,** *n.*

**pa·rade** (pə-rād′), *n.* [Fr. < Sp. *parada* < L. *parare*, to prepare], 1. ostentatious display. 2. *a*) a military assembly; review of troops. *b*) a place where troops assemble regularly for parade. 3. any organized procession or march, as for display. 4. *a*) a public walk or promenade. *b*) persons promenading. *v.t.* [-RADED, -RADING], 1. to bring together (troops, etc.) for inspection or display. 2. to march or walk through (the streets, etc.), as for display. 3. to show off: as, he *parades* his knowledge. *v.i.* 1. to march in a parade. 2. to walk about ostentatiously. 3. to assemble in military formation for review or display. —**on parade,** on display. —**pa·rad′er,** *n.*

**par·a·digm** (par′ə-dim, -dīm′), *n.* [< Fr. < LL. < Gr. < *para*, beside + *deigma*, example < *deiknynai*, to show], 1. a pattern, example, or model. 2. in *grammar*, an example of a declension or conjugation, giving all the inflectional forms of a word. —**par′a·dig·mat′ic** (-dig-mat′ik), *adj.*

**par·a·dise** (par′ə-dīs′), *n.* [< OFr. < L. < Gr. *paradeisos*, a garden < Per.], 1. [P-], the garden of Eden. 2. heaven. 3. any place or state of perfection, happiness, etc. —**par′a·dis′i·ac′** (-dis′i-ak′), **par′a·di·si′a·cal** (-di-sī′ə-k′l), **par′a·dis′ic** (-dis′ik), *adj.*

**par·a·dox** (par′ə-doks′), *n* [< Fr. < L. < Gr. < *para-*, beyond + *doxa*, opinion < *dokein*, to think], 1. a statement that seems contradictory, absurd, etc. but may be true in fact. 2. a statement that is self-contradictory in fact and, hence, false. 3. a person or thing seeming inconsistent and full of contradictions. —**par′a·dox′i·cal,** *adj.* —**par′a·dox′i·cal·ly,** *adv.* —**par′a·dox′i·cal·ness,** *n.*

**par·af·fin** (par′ə-fin), *n.* [G. < L. *parum*, too little + *affinis*, akin: from its chemical inertness], 1. a white, waxy substance consisting of a mixture of hydrocarbons, distilled from petroleum and used for making candles, sealing jars, etc. 2. in *chemistry*, any member of the methane series. *v.t.* to coat or impregnate with paraffin.

**par·af·fine** (par′ə-fin, -fēn′), *n. & v.t.* [-FINED, -FINING], paraffin.

**paraffin series,** the methane series.

**paraffin wax,** solid paraffin.

**par·a·gon** (par′ə-gon′, -gən), *n.* [< OFr. < It. *paragone*, touchstone < Gr. < *para-*, against + *akonē*, whetstone], a model of perfection or excellence.

**par·a·graph** (par′ə-graf′, -gräf′), *n.* [< Fr. < ML. < Gr. *paragraphē*, marginal note < *para-*, beside + *graphein*, to write], 1. a distinct section of a chapter, letter, etc. dealing with a particular point: it is begun on a new line, often indented. 2. a sign (¶ or ⁋) used to indicate the beginning of a paragraph, as in proofreading. 3. a brief item in a magazine or newspaper. *v.t.* 1. to write about in paragraphs. 2. to arrange in paragraphs. —**par′a·graph′er,** *n.* —**par′a·graph′ic, par′a·graph′i·cal,** *adj.* —**par′a·graph′i·cal·ly,** *adv.*

**Par·a·guay** (par′ə-gwā′, -gwī′), *n.* 1. a country in central South America: area, 157,039 sq. mi.; pop., 1,768,000; capital, Asunción. 2. a river flowing through S Brazil and Paraguay. —**Par′a·guay′an,** *adj. & n.*

**Paraguay tea,** 1. a beverage made from the leaves of the maté. 2. this plant.

**par·a·keet** (par′ə-kēt′), *n.* [OFr. *paroquet* (prob. < *perrot*); see PARROT], any of certain small, slender parrots with long, tapering tails: also **parrakeet, parroket, paroquet, parroquet.**

**par·al·lax** (par′ə-laks′), *n.* [< Fr. < Gr. < *para-*, beyond + *allassein*, to change], 1. the apparent change in the position of an object resulting from a change in the viewer's position. 2. the amount of such change; specif., in *astronomy*, the apparent difference in the position of a heavenly body with reference to some point on the surface of the earth and some other point, as the center of the earth. —**par′al·lac′tic** (-lak′tik), *adj.*

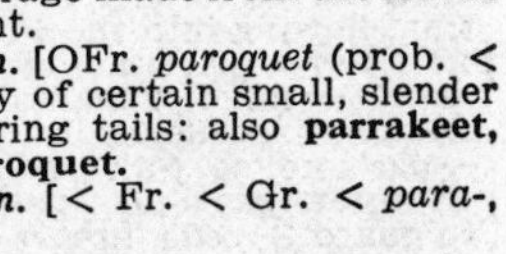


PARALLAX
P, star; R, point on earth's surface; A, center of the earth; angle RPA, parallax

**par·al·lel** (par′ə-lel′), *adj.* [< Fr. < L. < Gr. < *para-*, side by side + *allēlos*, one another], 1. extending in the same direction and at a constant distance apart, so as never to meet, as lines, planes, etc. 2. having parallel parts or movements, as some machines. 3. similar or corresponding, as in purpose, time, or essential parts. *n.* 1. a parallel line, surface, etc. 2. any person or thing similar or corresponding to another; counterpart. 3. a being parallel. 4. any comparison showing likeness. 5. *a)* any of the imaginary lines parallel to the equator and representing degrees of latitude. *b)* such a line drawn on a map or globe. Also *parallel of latitude.* 6. in *electricity*, a hookup in which all positive poles are connected in one conductor and all negatives in another: also called *multiple circuit.* 7. *pl.* in *printing*, a sign (||) marking material referred to in a note. *v.t.* [-LELED or -LELLED, -LELING or -LELLING], 1. *a)* to make (one thing) parallel to another. *b)* to make parallel to each other. 2. to be parallel with: as, the road *parallels* the river. 3. to compare (things) in order to show likeness. 4. to find or be a counterpart for.

**parallel bars,** two parallel, horizontal bars set on adjustable upright posts: used in gymnastics.

**par·al·lel·e·pi·ped** (par′ə-lel′ə-pī′pid, -pip′id), *n.* [< Gr. *parallēlos*, parallel + *epipedos*, plane], a solid with six faces, each of which is a parallelogram: also **par′al·lel′e·pip′e·don′** (-pip′ə-don′).

**par·al·lel·ism** (par′ə-lel-iz′m), *n.* 1. the state of being parallel. 2. close resemblance; correspondence; similarity.

**par·al·lel·o·gram** (par′ə-lel′ə-gram′), *n.* [< Fr. < L. < Gr.; see PARALLEL & -GRAM], a four-sided plane figure having the opposite sides parallel and equal.

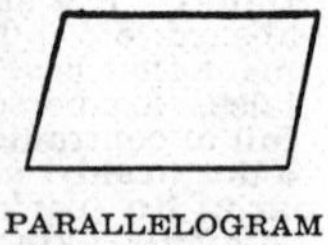

PARALLELOGRAM

**par·a·lyse** (par′ə-līz′), *v.t.* [-LYSED, -LYSING], to paralyze: Brit. spelling. **—par′a·ly·sa′tion,** *n.* **—par′a·lys′er,** *n.*

**pa·ral·y·sis** (pə-ral′ə-sis), *n.* [*pl.* -SES (-sēz′)], [L. < Gr. < *paralyein*, to loosen at the side < *para-*, beside + *lyein*, to loose], 1. (partial or complete) loss of the power of motion or sensation, especially voluntary motion, in part or all of the body. 2. a condition of helpless inactivity; crippling of activities: as, a *paralysis* of industry. **—par·a·lyt·ic** (par′ə-lit′ik), *adj. & n.*

**par·a·lyze** (par′ə-līz′), *v.t.* [-LYZED, -LYZING]. 1. to cause paralysis in. 2. to make ineffective, powerless, or inactive. **—par′a·ly·za′tion,** *n.* **—par′a·lyz′er,** *n.*

**Par·a·mar·i·bo** (par′ə-mar′i-bō′), *n.* seaport and capital of Surinam: pop., 123,000.

**par·a·me·ci·um** (par′ə-mē′shi-əm, -si-əm), *n.* [*pl.* -CIA (-shi-ə, -si-ə)], [< Gr. *paramēkēs*, oval], a one-celled, elongated animal having a large mouth in a fold at the side and moving by means of cilia.

**par·a·mil·i·tar·y** (par′ə-mil′ə-ter′i), *adj.* [*para-* + *military*], 1. designating or of forces working along with, or in place of, a regular military organization. 2. designating or of a private, often secret, quasi-military organization.

**par·a·mount** (par′ə-mount′), *adj.* [< OFr. *paramont* < *par* (L. *per*) by + *amont*, uphill < L. *ad montem*, to the hill], ranking higher than any other; chief; supreme. *n.* a person having supreme power. **—par′a·mount′cy,** *n.* **—par′a·mount′ly,** *adv.*

**par·a·mour** (par′ə-moor′), *n.* [< OFr. *par amour*, with love], the illicit sexual partner of a man or woman, especially of a married man or woman.

**Pa·ra·ná** (pä′rä-nä′), *n.* a river in Brazil and Argentina, flowing into the Plata River.

**par·a·noi·a** (par′ə-noi′ə), *n.* [Gr. < *para-*, beside + *nous*, the mind], a mental disorder characterized by systematized delusions, especially of persecution. **—par′a·noi′ac** (-ak), *adj. & n.* **—par′a·noid′,** *adj.*

**par·a·pet** (par′ə-pit, -pet′), *n.* [Fr. < It. < *parare*, to guard + *petto*, breast < L. *pectus*], 1. a wall or bank for screening troops from enemy fire. 2. a low wall or railing, as on a balcony or bridge.

**par·a·pher·na·li·a** (par′ə-fēr-nā′li-ə, -fə-nāl′yə), *n.pl.* [ML. < LL. *parapherna* < Gr. < *para-*, beyond + *phernē*, a dowry], 1. personal belongings. 2. equipment; apparatus; gear.

**par·a·phrase** (par′ə-frāz′), *n.* [Fr. < L. < Gr. *paraphrasis;* ult. < *para-*, beyond + *phrazein*, to tell], a rewording of the meaning of something spoken or written. *v.t. & v.i.* [-PHRASED, -PHRASING], to explain or express in a paraphrase. **—par′a·phras′er,** *n.* **—par′a·phras′tic** (-fras′tik), *adj.* **—par′a·phras′ti·cal·ly,** *adv.*

**par·a·ple·gi·a** (par′ə-plē′ji-ə), *n.* [< Gr. *paraplēgia*, a stroke at one side < *para-*, beside + *plēssein*, to strike], paralysis of the entire lower half of the body. **—par′a·pleg′ic** (-plej′ik, -plē′jik), *adj. & n.*

**Pará rubber,** crude rubber obtained from several South American trees.

**par·a·site** (par′ə-sīt′), *n.* [Fr. < L. < Gr. *parasitos*, one who eats at the table of another < *para-*, beside + *sitos*, food], 1. a person who lives at others' expense without making any useful return. 2. a plant or animal that lives on or within another from which it derives sustenance. **—par′a·sit′ic** (-sit′ik), **par′a·sit′i·cal,** *adj.* **—par′a·sit′i·cal·ly,** *adv.* **—par′a·sit·ism** (-sīt-iz′m), *n.*

**par·a·sol** (par′ə-sôl′, -sol′), *n.* [Fr. < It. < *parare*, to ward off + *sole*, the sun], a light umbrella carried by women as a sunshade.

**par·a·thy·roid** (par′ə-thī′roid), *adj.* [*para-* + *thyroid*], designating or of any of four small glands located on or embedded in the thyroid gland: their secretions increase the calcium content of the blood. *n.* a parathyroid gland.

**par·a·troops** (par′ə-tro͞ops′), *n.pl.* a unit of soldiers trained to land behind enemy lines from airplanes, using parachutes. **—par′a·troop′er,** *n.*

**par·a·ty·phoid** (par′ə-tī′foid), *adj.* [*para-* + *typhoid*], designating, of, or causing a disease similar to typhoid fever but usually milder and caused by a different bacillus. *n.* paratyphoid fever.

‡**par a·vi·on** (pȧr′ ȧ′vyōn′), [Fr.], by air mail.

**par·boil** (pär′boil′), *v.t.* [< OFr. < *par* (< L. *per*), through + *boullir* (< L. *bullire*), to boil: meaning infl. by Eng. *part*], 1. to boil until partly cooked, as before roasting. 2. to make uncomfortably hot.

**par·buck·le** (pär′buk′'l), *n.* [earlier *parbunkel*, altered after *buckle*], a sling for a log, barrel, etc. made by passing a doubled rope around the object and pulling the ends through the loop. *v.t.* [-LED, -LING], to raise or lower by using a parbuckle.

PARBUCKLE

**Par·cae** (pär′sē), *n.pl.* in *Rom. mythology*, the three Fates.

**par·cel** (pär′s'l), *n.* [< OFr. < LL. < L. *particula;* see PARTICLE], 1. a small, wrapped bundle; package. 2. a quantity of items put up for sale. 3. a group; pack: as, a *parcel* of fools. 4. a piece, as of land. *v.t.* [-CELED or -CELLED, -CELING or -CELLING], 1. to separate into parts and distribute (with *out*). 2. to make up in or as a parcel. *adj. & adv.* part; partly.

**parcel post,** the branch of the post office which carries and delivers parcels.

**parch** (pärch), *v.t.* [< ME. contr. of *perischen* (see PERISH)], 1. to expose to great heat so as to dry or roast, as corn. 2. to make hot and dry. 3. to make very thirsty. 4. to dry up and shrivel with cold. *v.i.* to become very dry and hot.

**par·chee·si, par·che·si, par·chi·si** (pär-chē′zi), *n.* [Hind. *pacīsī* < *pacīs*, twenty-five: highest throw in the game, as orig. played in India], a game in which the moves of pieces around a board are determined by the throwing of dice.

**parch·ment** (pärch′mənt), *n.* [< OFr.; ult. < LL. (*charta*) *Pergamenum*, (paper) of Pergamum, city in Asia Minor], 1. an animal skin, as of a sheep or goat, prepared as a surface for writing or painting. 2. a manuscript on parchment. 3. a fine paper having a texture like parchment.

**pard** (pärd), *n.* [< OFr. < L. < Gr. *pardos*], [Archaic or Poetic], a leopard, or panther.

**pard** (pärd), *n.* [contr. of *pardner* < *partner*], [Slang], a partner; companion.

**par·don** (pär′d'n), *v.t.* [< OFr. < LL. < L. *per-*, through + *donare*, to give], 1. to release (a person) from punishment. 2. to cancel penalty for (an offense); forgive. 3. to excuse (a person) for (a minor fault, discourtesy, etc.). *n.* 1. a pardoning or being pardoned; forgiveness. 2. an official document granting a pardon. 3. in the *R.C. Church*, an indulgence. **—par′don·a·ble,** *adj.* **—par′don·a·bly,** *adv.*

**par·don·er** (pär′d'n-ēr), *n.* 1. in the *R.C. Church*, historically, a person authorized to grant or sell ecclesiastical pardons. 2. one who pardons.

**pare** (pâr), *v.t.* [PARED, PARING], [< OFr. < L. *parare*, to prepare], 1. to cut or trim away the rind, skin, covering, etc. of; peel. 2. to cut or trim away (rind, skin, etc.) of anything. 3. to reduce gradually. **—par′er,** *n.*

**par·e·gor·ic** (par′ə-gôr′ik, -gor′-), *adj.* [< LL. < Gr. < *parēgoros*, mitigating < *para-*, beside + *agora*, assembly], lessening pain. *n.* a paregoric medicine; esp., camphorated tincture of opium.

**pa·ren·chy·ma** (pə-reŋ′ki-mə), *n.* [< Gr. *para-*, beside + *en-*, in + *chein*, to pour], 1. in *anatomy*, the functional tissue of an organ, as distinguished from its connective tissue, etc. 2. in *botany*, a soft tissue of thin-walled cells in a plant stem or fruit pulp. **—par·en·chym·a·tous** (par′eŋ-kim′ə-təs), *adj.*

**par·ent** (pâr′ənt), *n.* [OFr. < L. *parens* (orig. ppr. of *parere*, to beget)], 1. a father or mother. 2. any organism in relation to one that it has produced. 3. a source or cause. —**pa·ren·tal** (pə-ren′t'l), *adj.* —**pa·ren′tal·ly**, *adv.* —**par′ent·hood′**, *n.*

**par·ent·age** (pâr′ənt-ij), *n.* 1. descent or derivation from parents or ancestors; family. 2. the fact or state of being a parent.

**pa·ren·the·sis** (pə-ren′thə-sis), *n.* [*pl.* -SES (-sēz′)], [ML. < Gr. *para-*, beside + *entithenai*, to insert], 1. a word, clause, etc. added as an explanation or comment within a complete sentence, usually marked off by curved lines, commas, etc. 2. *usually in pl.* either or both of the curved lines ( ) used to mark this off. 3. an irrelevant episode.

**pa·ren·the·size** (pə-ren′thə-sīz′), *v.t.* [-SIZED, -SIZING], 1. to insert (a word, etc.) as a parenthesis. 2. to put into parentheses (sense 2).

**par·en·thet·i·cal** (par′ən-thet′i-k'l), *adj.* 1. *a*) of or like a parenthesis. *b*) placed within parentheses. 2. giving qualifying information or explanation. 3. containing parentheses. Also **par′en·thet′ic.** —**par′en·thet′i·cal·ly**, *adv.*

**pa·re·sis** (pə-rē′sis, par′ə-), *n.* [Gr. < *parienai*, to relax], 1. partial paralysis. 2. a brain disease caused by syphilis of the central nervous system, characterized by mental instability, paralytic attacks, etc.: also called *general paralysis* (or *paresis*). —**pa·ret′ic** (-ret′ik, -rē′tik), *adj.* & *n.*

**par ex·cel·lence** (pär ek′sə-läns′; Fr. pȧr′ ek′se′läns′), [Fr.], in the greatest degree of excellence; beyond comparison.

**par·fait** (pär-fā′), *n.* [Fr., perfect], a frozen dessert of rich cream and eggs, or ice cream, sirup, crushed fruit, etc., served in a tall, narrow glass.

**par·he·li·on** (pär-hē′li-ən, -hēl′yən), *n.* [*pl.* -LIA (-ə, -yə)], [< L. < Gr. < *para-*, beside + *hēlios*, the sun], a bright spot of light on a solar halo. —**par·he′lic, par′he·li′a·cal** (-hi-lī′ə-k'l), *adj.*

**par·i-** (par′i), [< L. *par*, equal], a combining form used in biology to mean *equal*.

**pa·ri·ah** (pə-rī′ə, par′i-, pä′ri-), *n.* [< Tamil *paraiyan*, a drummer: the pariah was a hereditary drumbeater], 1. in the former caste system of India, a member of one of the oppressed social castes. 2. any outcast; a despised person.

**pa·ri·e·tal** (pə-rī′ə-t'l), *adj.* [< Fr. < LL. < L. *paries*, a wall], in *anatomy*, of the walls of a cavity, etc.; esp., designating either of two bones forming part of the top and sides of the skull.

**par·i-mu·tu·el** (par′i-mū′choo-əl), *n.* [Fr., lit., mutual bets], 1. a system of betting on races in which the winning bettors share the total amount bet minus a percentage to the operators. 2. a machine that registers such bets.

**par·ing** (pâr′iŋ), *n.* a piece or strip pared off.

**Par·is** (par′is), *n.* in *Gr. legend*, a son of Priam, king of Troy: his kidnaping of Helen, wife of Menelaus, caused the Trojan War.

**Par·is** (par′is; Fr. pȧ′rē′), *n.* the capital of France, on the Seine: pop., 2,850,000. —**Pa·ri·sian** (pə-rizh′ən), *adj.* & *n.*

**Paris green,** a poisonous, bright-green powder used as an insecticide and pigment.

**par·ish** (par′ish), *n.* [< OFr. < LL. < Gr. *paroikia*, diocese < *para-*, beside + *oikos*, dwelling], 1. a district of British local government. 2. *a*) a part of a diocese under the charge of a priest or minister. *b*) the congregation of a church or the territory in which its members live. 3. a civil division in Louisiana, corresponding to a county.

**pa·rish·ion·er** (pə-rish′ən-ēr), *n.* a member of a parish.

**par·i·ty** (par′ə-ti), *n.* [< Fr. < L. *par*, equal], 1. a being the same in power, value, etc.; equality. 2. resemblance; similarity. 3. the equivalent in value of a sum of money in terms of another country's currency. 4. equality of value at a given ratio between different kinds of money, commodities, etc.

**park** (pärk), *n.* [< OFr. < ML. *parricus* < Gmc.; cf. PADDOCK], 1. land containing woods, lakes, etc. held as part of a private estate or as a hunting preserve. 2. an area of public land; specif., *a*) an area for public recreation, usually with walks, playgrounds, etc. *b*) an open square in a city, with benches, trees, etc. *c*) a large area with natural scenery, preserved by a government. 3. a space for leaving vehicles temporarily. 4. in *military usage*, *a*) an area for vehicles, supplies, etc. *b*) things kept in such an area. *v.t.* 1. to enclose as in a park. 2. to place (military equipment) in a park. 3. to leave (a vehicle) in a certain place temporarily. 4. to maneuver (a vehicle) into a space for parking. 5. [Slang], to put or leave in a certain place; deposit. *v.i.* to park a vehicle.

**par·ka** (pär′kə), *n.* [Aleutian], a fur or woolen jacket with an attached hood for the head.

**parking meter,** a coin-operated timing device installed near a parking space for indicating the length of time that a vehicle has been parked.

**parking ticket,** a police summons given for violating regulations on the parking of vehicles.

**park·way** (pärk′wā′), *n.* a broad roadway edged or divided with plantings of trees, bushes, etc.

**Parl.,** 1. Parliament. 2. Parliamentary.

**parl·ance** (pär′ləns), *n.* [OFr. < *parler*, to speak], 1. conversation; speech. 2. a style of speaking or writing; idiom: as, military *parlance*.

**par·lay** (pär′li, pär-lā′), *v.t.* & *v.i.* [Fr. & It. *paroli* < *paro*, an equal], 1. to bet (an original wager plus its winnings) on another race, etc. 2. to exploit (an asset) successfully: as, he *parlayed* his voice into fame. *n.* a parlayed bet or series of bets.

**par·ley** (pär′li), *v.i.* [< Fr. pp. of *parler*, to speak < LL. < L. *parabola*, parable], to confer, especially with an enemy. *n.* [*pl.* -LEYS], a conference, as to settle a dispute; esp., a conference with an enemy to discuss terms.

**par·lia·ment** (pär′lə-mənt), *n.* [< OFr. *parlement* < *parler*, to speak], 1. an official conference or council concerned with government. 2. [P-], the national legislative body of Great Britain, composed of the House of Commons and the House of Lords. 3. [P-], a similar body in other countries.

**par·lia·men·tar·i·an** (pär′lə-men-târ′i-ən), *n.* one skilled in parliamentary rules or debate.

**par·lia·men·ta·ry** (pär′lə-men′tə-ri), *adj.* 1. of, like, or established by a parliament. 2. conforming to the rules of a parliament or other public assembly. 3. governed by a parliament.

**par·lor** (pär′lēr), *n.* [< OFr. < ML. < *parlare*, to speak], 1. *a*) originally, a formal sitting room. *b*) now, any living room. 2. a semiprivate sitting room in a hotel, etc. 3. a business establishment, often with special equipment for personal services: as, a beauty *parlor*. Brit. sp., **parlour.**

**parlor car,** a railroad car for daytime travel, having comfortable individual chairs.

**par·lous** (pär′ləs), *adj.* [ME. < *perilous*], [Chiefly Archaic], 1. dangerous. 2. cunning, shrewd, etc. *adv.* [Chiefly Archaic], extremely; very.

**Par·ma** (pär′mä, -mə), *n.* 1. a city in N Italy: pop., 124,000. 2. (pär′mə), a city in NE Ohio: suburb of Cleveland: pop., 83,000.

**Par·me·san (cheese)** (pär′mə-zan′), [Fr. < It. < *Parma*, city in Italy], a dry, hard, yellow Italian cheese, usually grated for use as a flavoring.

**Par·nas·sus** (pär-nas′əs), *n.* 1. a mountain in S Greece: in ancient times it was sacred to Apollo and the Muses; hence, 2. *a*) poetry or poets collectively. *b*) any center of poetic or artistic activity. —**Par·nas′si·an** (-i-ən), *adj.*

**Par·nell, Charles Stewart** (pär′n'l, pär-nel′), 1846–1891; Irish statesman and nationalist leader.

**pa·ro·chi·al** (pə-rō′ki-əl), *adj.* [OFr. < ML. < *parochia*; see PARISH], 1. of or in a parish or parishes. 2. narrow; limited; provincial. —**pa·ro′chi·al·ism**, *n.* —**pa·ro′chi·al·ly**, *adv.*

**parochial school,** a school supported and controlled by a church.

**par·o·dy** (par′ə-di), *n.* [*pl.* -DIES], [< Fr. < L. < Gr. *parōidia* < *para-*, beside + *ōidē*, song], 1. a musical or literary composition imitating the style of some other work or of a writer or composer, but treating a serious subject in a nonsensical or humorous manner. 2. a weak imitation. *v.t.* [-DIED, -DYING], to make a parody of. —**par′o·dist**, *n.*

**pa·role** (pə-rōl′), *n.* [Fr. < It. < LL. *parabola*, a word], 1. word of honor; esp., the promise of a military prisoner that, if released, he will fight no further. 2. a being on parole. 3. the release of a prisoner before his sentence has expired, on condition of future good behavior. 4. the conditional freedom granted by such release, or its duration. *v.t.* [-ROLED, -ROLING], to release on parole. —**on parole,** at liberty under conditions of parole.

**pa·rol·ee** (pə-rō′lē′), *n.* a person who has been released from prison on parole.

**par·o·quet** (par′ə-ket′), *n.* a parakeet.

**pa·rot·id** (pə-rot′id), *adj.* [< Fr. < L. < Gr. *parōtis* < *para-*, beside + *ous*, ear], designating or of either of the salivary glands below and in front of each ear. *n.* a parotid gland.

**-par·ous,** [< L. < *parere,* to bear], a combining form meaning *bearing, producing,* as in *viviparous.*

**par·ox·ysm** (par′ək-siz'm), *n.* [< Fr. < ML. < Gr. < *para-,* beyond + *oxynein,* to sharpen < *oxys,* sharp], 1. a sudden attack, or intensification of the symptoms, of a disease, usually recurring periodically. 2. a sudden outburst, as of laughter. —**par′ox·ys′mal,** *adj.*

**par·quet** (pär-kā′, -ket′), *n.* [Fr., dim. of *parc,* a park], 1. the main floor of a theater: usually called *orchestra.* 2. a flooring of parquetry. *v.t.* [-QUETED (-kād′, -ket′id), -QUETING], 1. to use parquetry to make (a floor, etc.). 2. to decorate the floor of (a room) with parquetry.

**parquet circle,** the part of a theater beneath the balcony and behind the parquet.

**par·quet·ry** (pär′kit-ri), *n.* inlaid woodwork in geometric forms: used especially in flooring.

**parr** (pär), *n.* [*pl.* PARRS, PARR; see PLURAL, II, D, 1], a young salmon before it enters salt water.

**par·ra·keet** (par′ə-kēt′), *n.* a parakeet.

**par·ri·cide** (par′ə-sīd′), *n.* [Fr. < L. *parri-* (< ? *pater,* father) + *caedere,* to kill], 1. one who murders his parent or parents. 2. the act of a parricide. —**par′ri·cid′al,** *adj.*

**par·ro·ket, par·ro·quet** (par′ə-ket′), *n.* a parakeet.

**par·rot** (par′ət), *n.* [Fr. *perrot*], 1. any of several birds with hooked bills, brightly colored feathers, and feet having two toes pointing forward and two backward: some parrots can learn to repeat words. 2. a person who mechanically mimics others without full understanding. *v.t.* to repeat or imitate without understanding.

**parrot fever,** psittacosis.

**parrot fish,** any of various brightly colored fishes found in warm seas, with parrotlike jaws.

**par·ry** (par′i), *v.t.* [-RIED, -RYING], [< Fr. < It. *parare,* to parry < L. *parare,* to prepare], 1. to ward off, as a blow. 2. to evade, as a question. *v.i.* to make a parry. *n.* [*pl.* -RIES], 1. a warding off or turning aside of an attack, etc., as in fencing. 2. an evasion.

**parse** (pärs), *v.t.* [PARSED, PARSING], [< L. *pars* (*orationis*), part (of speech)], 1. to break (a sentence) down into parts, explaining the grammatical form and function of each part. 2. to describe the form, part of speech, and function of (a word) in a sentence.

**Par·see, Par·si** (pär′sē, pär-sē′), *n.* [Per., a Persian], a member of a Zoroastrian religious sect in India descended from Persian refugees who fled from the Moslem persecutions of the 7th and 8th centuries. —**Par′see·ism, Par′si·ism,** *n.*

**Par·si·fal** (pär′si-fäl′, -sə-f'l), *n.* the title character in Wagner's music drama (1882) of the knights of the Holy Grail.

**par·si·mo·ny** (pär′sə-mō′ni), *n.* [< L. *parcimonia* < *parcere,* to spare], stinginess; extreme frugality. —**par′si·mo′ni·ous** (-ni-əs), *adj.* —**par′si·mo′ni·ous·ly,** *adv.* —**par′si·mo′ni·ous·ness,** *n.*

**pars·ley** (pärs′li), *n.* [< AS. & OFr. < LL. *petrosilium* < L. < Gr. < *petros,* a rock + *selinon,* parsley], a plant with finely divided curled or flat leaves used to flavor or garnish some foods.

**pars·nip** (pärs′nip), *n.* [< OFr. < L. *pastinaca* < *pastinare,* to dig up: infl. by ME. *nepe,* turnip], 1. a plant with a long, thick, sweet, white root used as a vegetable. 2. the root.

**par·son** (pär′s'n), *n.* [see PERSON], 1. a minister in charge of a parish. 2. [Colloq.], any clergyman.

**par·son·age** (pär′s'n-ij), *n.* the dwelling provided by a church for the use of its parson.

**part** (pärt), *n.* [< L. *pars*], 1. a portion of a whole; specif., *a*) any of several equal quantities, numbers, pieces, etc. into which something can be divided. *b*) an essential, separable element: as, an automobile *part.* *c*) a portion detached from a whole; fragment. *d*) a certain amount but not all: as, he lost *part* of his fortune. *e*) a section, segment, or member of a whole: as, a novel in two *parts,* the *parts* of the body. 2. a portion assigned or given; share; specif., *a*) duty: as, we do our *part.* *b*) interest; concern: as, it's not my *part* to interfere. *c*) *usually pl.* talent; ability: as, a man of *parts.* *d*) a role in a play. *e*) in *music,* any of the voices or instruments in a musical ensemble, or the score for this. 3. a region; esp., *usually pl.* a portion of a country; district: as, he left these *parts.* 4. one of the sides in a transaction, conflict, etc. 5. the dividing line formed by combing the hair in opposite directions. *v.t.* [< OFr. < L. *partire* < the *n.*], 1. to break or divide into parts. 2. to comb (the hair) so as to leave a part. 3. to break or hold apart; put asunder. 4. [Archaic], to apportion. *v.i.* 1. to break or divide into parts. 2. to separate and go different ways. 3. to cease associating. 4. to go away; leave. 5. to die. *adj.* less than a whole: as, *part* interest. *adv.* partly; in part. —**for (or on) one's part,** so far as one is concerned. —**for the most part,** mostly; generally. —**in good part,** good-naturedly. —**in part,** to a certain extent; partly. —**part and parcel,** a necessary part: used emphatically. —**part from,** to separate from; leave. —**part with,** to give up; relinquish. —**play a part,** 1. to behave unnaturally in trying to deceive. 2. to participate: also **take part.** —**take one's part,** to side with one. —**part′er,** *n.*

**part.,** 1. participial. 2. participle.

**par·take** (pär-tāk′), *v.i.* [-TOOK, -TAKEN, -TAKING], [< *partaker,* contr. of *part taker*], 1. to take part in an activity; participate. 2. to eat or drink something, especially with others. —**partake of,** 1. *a*) to take or have a share in, as a meal. *b*) to take some of. 2. to have some of the qualities or nature of. —**par·tak′er,** *n.*

**part·ed** (pär′tid), *adj.* divided; separated; split.

**par·terre** (pär-târ′), *n.* [Fr. < *par,* on + *terre,* earth], 1. an ornamental garden area. 2. the part of a theater under the balcony and behind the parquet: also *orchestra* (or *parquet*) *circle.*

**par·the·no·gen·e·sis** (pär′thə-nō-jen′ə-sis), *n.* [< Gr. *parthenos,* virgin + *genesis,* origin], reproduction by the development of an unfertilized ovum, seed, or spore, as in certain insects, algae, etc. —**par′the·no·ge·net′ic** (-jə-net′ik), *adj.* —**par′the·no·ge·net′i·cal·ly,** *adv.*

**Par·the·non** (pär′thə-non′, -nən), *n.* [L. < Gr. < *parthenos,* a virgin (i.e., Athena)], the Doric temple of Athena built in the 5th century B.C. on the Acropolis in Athens.

**Par·thi·a** (pär′thi-ə), *n.* an ancient kingdom southeast of the Caspian Sea. —**Par′thi·an,** *n.* & *adj.*

**Parthian shot,** any hostile gesture or remark made in leaving: Parthian cavalrymen shot at the enemy while retreating or pretending to retreat.

**par·tial** (pär′shəl), *adj.* [< LL. < L. *pars,* a part], 1. favoring one person, faction, etc. more than another; biased; prejudiced. 2. not complete or total. —**partial to,** fond of. —**par′tial·ly,** *adv.* —**par′tial·ness,** *n.*

**par·ti·al·i·ty** (pär′shi-al′ə-ti, pär-shal′-), *n.* [*pl.* -TIES], 1. the state or quality of being partial. 2. strong liking; particular fondness.

**par·tial·ly** (pär′shəl-i), *adv.* 1. with partiality or bias. 2. in part; partly.

**partial tone,** in *acoustics* & *music,* any of the pure, or harmonic, tones forming a complex tone.

**par·tic·i·pant** (pär-tis′ə-pənt, pẽr-), *adj.* participating. *n.* one who participates.

**par·tic·i·pate** (pär-tis′ə-pāt′, pẽr-), *v.i.* [-PATED, -PATING], [< L. pp. of *participare* < *pars,* a part + *capere,* to take], to have or take a share with others (*in* some activity). —**par·tic′i·pa′tion,** *n.* —**par·tic′i·pa′tor,** *n.*

**par·ti·cip·i·al** (pär′tə-sip′i-əl, -sip′yəl), *adj.* of, based on, or used as a participle. *n.* a verbal derivative, as a gerund or infinitive, used as a noun or adjective. —**par′ti·cip′i·al·ly,** *adv.*

**par·ti·ci·ple** (pär′tə-si-p'l), *n.* [OFr. < L. *particeps,* partaking < *pars,* a part + *capere,* to take], a word derived from a verb and having the qualities of both verb and adjective: a participle has voice and tense and may take an object or be modified by an adverb (e.g., I was *asked* to leave; softly *humming* a tune).

**par·ti·cle** (pär′ti-k'l), *n.* [< OFr. < L. *particula,* dim. of *pars,* a part], 1. a tiny fragment or trace. 2. a clause or article in a document. 3. in *grammar,* *a*) a short, indeclinable part of speech, as an article, preposition, conjunction, or interjection. *b*) a prefix or suffix. 4. in *physics,* a piece of matter so small as to be considered without magnitude.

**par·ti-col·ored** (pär′ti-kul′ẽrd), *adj.* [*parti-* < Fr. *parti;* see PARTY], 1. having different colors in different parts; hence, 2. diversified. Also sp. **party-colored.**

**par·tic·u·lar** (pẽr-tik′yoo-lẽr, pär-), *adj.* [< OFr. < LL. < L. *particula;* see PARTICLE], 1. of or belonging to a single, definite group, person, or thing. 2. regarded separately; specific: as, why that *particular* hat? 3. unusual; special. 4. itemized; detailed. 5. exacting; hard to please. *n.* 1. a distinct fact, item, or instance. 2. a detail: as, the full *particulars.* —**in particular,** especially.

**par·tic·u·lar·i·ty** (pẽr-tik′yoo-lar′ə-ti, pär-), *n.* [*pl.* -TIES], 1. the state, quality, or fact of being particular; esp., individuality or attention to detail. 2. something particular; specif., *a*) a peculiarity. *b*) a minute detail.

**par·tic·u·lar·ize** (pẽr-tik′yoo-lẽr-īz′, pär-), *v.t.* [-IZED, -IZING], to specify; itemize. *v.i.* to give particulars or details. —**par·tic′u·lar·i·za′tion,** *n.*

**par·tic·u·lar·ly** (pẽr-tik′yoo-lẽr-li, pär-), *adv.* 1. so as to be particular; in detail. 2. especially; unusually. 3. specifically.

**part·ing** (pär′tiŋ), *adj.* [ppr. of *part*], 1. dividing; separating. 2. departing. 3. dying. 4. given, spoken, done, etc. at parting. *n.* 1. a breaking or separating. 2. a dividing point or line. 3. something that separates or divides. 4. a leavetaking. 5. a departure. 6. death.

**par·ti·san** (pär′tə-z'n), *n.* [Fr. < It. *partigiano* < L. *pars*, part], 1. a strong supporter of a faction, party, or person; esp., an unreasoning, emotional adherent. 2. any of a group of guerrilla fighters. *adj.* of or like a partisan. Also sp. **partizan.** —**par′ti·san·ship′, par′ti·zan·ship′,** *n.*

**par·tite** (pär′tīt), *adj.* [< L. pp. of *partire*, to part], divided into parts: often in compounds, as *tripartite.*

**par·ti·tion** (pär-tish′ən, pẽr-), *n.* [< L. *partitio*], 1. division into parts; separation. 2. something that divides, as a wall separating rooms. 3. a part or section. *v.t.* 1. to divide into parts or shares. 2. to divide by a partition. —**par·ti′tion·er,** *n.* —**par·ti′tion·ment,** *n.*

**par·ti·tive** (pär′tə-tiv), *adj.* [Fr. < L. pp. of *partire*, to part], 1. making a division. 2. in *grammar*, restricting to or involving only a part of a whole. *n.* a partitive word (e.g., *few, some, any*). —**par′ti·tive·ly,** *adv.*

**part·ly** (pärt′li), *adv.* not fully or completely.

**part·ner** (pärt′nẽr), *n.* [< ME. < *parcener*, infl. by *part*], one who takes part in an activity with another or others; specif., *a*) one of two or more persons in the same business enterprise, sharing its profits and risks. *b*) a husband or wife. *c*) either of two persons dancing together. *d*) a player on the same side or team. *v.t.* 1. to join (others) together as partners. 2. to join with (another) as a partner. —**part′ner·less,** *adj.*

**part·ner·ship** (pärt′nẽr-ship′), *n.* 1. the state of being a partner. 2. the relationship of partners; joint interest. 3. *a*) an association of two or more people who carry on a joint business and who share profits or losses. *b*) a contract by which such an association is created.

**part of speech,** in *grammar*, 1. any of the traditional form classes to which the words of a language are assigned according to their function (e.g., noun, verb, pronoun, adjective, adverb, preposition, conjunction, and interjection). 2. any word considered as belonging to one of these classes.

**par·took** (pär-took′), pt. of **partake.**

**par·tridge** (pär′trij), *n.* [*pl.* -TRIDGES, -TRIDGE; see PLURAL, II, D, 1], [< OFr. < L. < Gr. *perdix*], any of several game birds resembling domestic fowls, as the ruffed grouse, quail, etc.

**part song,** a song for several voices singing in harmony, generally without accompaniment.

**part-time** (pärt′tīm′), *adj.* for, during, or by part time: as, *part-time* work.

**part time,** a part of the customary time.

**par·tu·ri·ent** (pär-tyoor′i-ənt, -toor′-), *adj.* [< L. ppr. of *parturire*, to be in labor < *parere*, to produce], 1. giving birth or about to give birth to young. 2. of childbirth. —**par·tu′ri·en·cy,** *n.*

**par·tu·ri·tion** (pär′choo-rish′ən, -tyoo-), *n.* [< L.; see PARTURIENT], the act of giving birth; childbirth.

**par·ty** (pär′ti), *n.* [*pl.* -TIES], [< OFr. < *partir*, to divide < L. *pars*, part], 1. a group of people working to establish or promote some kind of government, cause, etc.; esp., a political group which tries to elect its candidates to office. 2. a group of persons acting together to accomplish a task: as, a surveying *party.* 3. *a*) a group assembled for recreation or social entertainment: as, a card *party*, a cocktail *party. b*) the entertainment itself. 4. one who is concerned in an action, plan, etc. (often with *to*): as, I'll not be a *party* to the affair. 5. either of the persons or sides concerned in a legal matter. 6. [Colloq.], a person.

**party line,** 1. a single circuit connecting two or more telephone users with the exchange. 2. the line of policy followed by a political party.

**party politics,** political acts and principles directed toward the interests of one political party without reference to the common good.

**par value,** the value of a stock, bond, etc. fixed at the time of its issue; face value.

**par·ve·nu** (pär′və-nōō′, -nū′), *n.* [*pl.* -NUS], [Fr., pp. of *parvenir* < L. *parvenire*, to arrive], one who has suddenly acquired wealth or power and is considered an upstart. *adj.* like or characteristic of a parvenu.

‡**pas** (pä), *n.* [Fr. < L. *passus*, a step], a step or series of steps in dancing.

**Pas·a·de·na** (pas′ə-dē′nə), *n.* a city in California, near Los Angeles: pop., 116,000.

**Pas·cal, Blaise** (blez pȧs′kȧl′; Eng. pas′k'l), 1623–1662; French mathematician and philosopher.

**Pasch** (pask), *n.* [< OFr. < LL. < LGr. *pascha* < Heb. *pesah*, the Passover], [Chiefly Archaic], 1. the Passover. 2. Easter.

**pas·chal** (pas′k'l), *adj.* [see PASCH], 1. of or connected with the Passover. 2. of or connected with Easter.

**pa·sha** (pə-shä′, pash′ə, pä′shə), *n.* [< Turk. *bāshā*; prob. < *bāsh*, a head], in Turkey, 1. a title of rank or honor placed after the name. 2. a high civil or military official. Also sp. **pacha.**

**pa·sha·lik, pa·sha·lic** (pə-shä′lik), *n.* the jurisdiction of a pasha: also sp. **pachalic.**

**pasque·flow·er** (pask′flou′ẽr), *n.* [< Fr. < *passer*, to surpass + *fleur*, a flower; altered after Fr. *pasque*, Pasch], any of several related plants with hairy leaves and blue or purplish flowers shaped like cups: also **paschal flower.**

**pass** (pas, päs), *n.* [see PACE], a narrow passage, opening, etc., especially between mountains.

**pass** (pas, päs), *v.i.* [PASSED, PASSED or, *rare*, PAST, PASSING], [< OFr. *passer* < LL. < L. *passus*, a step], 1. to go; move forward; proceed. 2. to extend; lead: as, the road *passes* around the hill. 3. to go from one to another; circulate. 4. to go, shift, or be conveyed from one place, form, condition, possession, etc. to another. 5. to be exchanged between persons, as greetings. 6. *a*) to cease: as, the fever *passed. b*) to go away; depart. 7. to die. 8. to go by or past. 9. to slip by or elapse: as, an hour *passed.* 10. to make a way (with *through* or *by*). 11. to take place or be accepted without question. 12. to be sanctioned or approved, as by a legislative body. 13. to go through a trial, test, course, etc. successfully; satisfy requirements. 14. to happen; occur. 15. to give a judgment, sentence, etc.: as, the jury *passed* upon the case. 16. to be rendered or pronounced: as, the judgment *passed* against us. 17. in *card games*, to decline a chance to bid, play a round, etc. 18. in *sports*, to make a pass. *v.t.* 1. to go by, beyond, over, or through; specif., *a*) to leave behind. *b*) to undergo. *c*) to disregard. *d*) to omit the payment of (a regular dividend). *e*) to go through (a trial, test, course, etc.) successfully. *f*) to surpass; excel. 2. to cause or allow to go, move, or proceed; specif., *a*) to send; dispatch. *b*) to direct the movement of: as, he *passed* his hand through his hair. *c*) to guide into position: as, he *passed* the rope around his waist. *d*) to cause to penetrate. *e*) to cause to move past: as, the troops were *passed* in review. *f*) to cause or allow to get by an obstacle or through a test, course, etc. successfully. *g*) to ratify; sanction; enact. *h*) to spend: as, we *passed* an hour there. *i*) to excrete; void. *j*) in *baseball*, to walk (a batter). 3. to cause to move from place to place or person to person; specif., *a*) to hand to another: as, *pass* the salt. *b*) to cause (money, etc.) to circulate: as, to *pass* a bad check. *c*) to hand, throw, or hit (a ball, etc.) from one player to another. 4. to give as an opinion or judgment. *n.* 1. an act of passing; passage. 2. the successful completion of a scholastic course or test, often, specifically, without honors. 3. a mark indicating this. 4. state; situation: as, a strange *pass.* 5. *a*) a ticket, etc. giving permission to come or go freely or without charge. *b*) a leave of absence for a brief period, given to a soldier. 6. sleight of hand. 7. a motion of the hand, as in hypnotism. 8. [Slang], an attempt to embrace or kiss, often an improper or overfamiliar one. 9. in *card games*, a declining of a chance to bid or play a round, etc. 10. in *sports*, *a*) an intentional transfer of the ball, etc. to another player during play. *b*) a thrust, as in fencing. *c*) a walk in baseball. —**a pretty pass,** [Colloq.], a difficult or critical situation. —**bring to pass,** to cause to happen. —**come to pass,** to happen. —**pass away,** 1. to cease. 2. to die. —**pass for,** to be accepted as: usually said of an imitation. —**pass off,** 1. to come to an end; cease. 2. to take place, as a transaction. 3. to be or cause to be accepted as genuine, etc., especially by using deceit. —**pass out,** [Slang], to faint. —**pass over,** to disregard; ignore; omit. —**pass through,** to experience, as the phases of an illness. —**pass up,** [Slang], to reject, refuse, or let go, as an opportunity. —**pass′er,** *n.*

**pass.,** 1. passenger. 2. passive. 3. passim.

**pass·a·ble** (pas′ə-b'l, päs′-), *adj.* 1. that can be passed, traveled over, or crossed. 2. that can be circulated, as coin. 3. moderate; adequate. 4. that can be enacted, as a law. —**pass′a·ble·ness,** *n.* —**pass′a·bly,** *adv.*

**pas·sage** (pas′ij), *n.* [OFr. < *passer*], 1. the act of passing; specif., *a*) migration: as, birds of *passage*. *b*) transition. *c*) the enactment of a law by a legislature. 2. permission, right, or a chance to pass. 3. a journey by water; voyage. 4. passenger accommodations on a ship. 5. a way or means of passing; specif., *a*) a road; opening. *b*) a passageway. 6. interchange, as of blows or vows. 7. a portion of something written or spoken: as, a *passage* from *Hamlet*. 8. a bowel movement. 9. a short section of a musical composition. *v.i.* [-SAGED, -SAGING], 1. to journey. 2. to take part in a fight or quarrel.

**passage of arms,** 1. a fight. 2. a quarrel.

**pas·sage·way** (pas′ij-wā′), *n.* a narrow way for passage, as a hall, corridor, or alley; passage.

**Pas·sa·ic** (pə-sā′ik, pa-), *n.* a city in NE New Jersey: pop., 58,000.

**pass·book** (pas′book′, päs′-), *n.* a bankbook.

**pas·sé** (pa-sā′, pas′ā; Fr. pȧ′sā′), *adj.* [Fr.], past; out of date; old-fashioned.

**passed ball,** in *baseball*, a pitch that gets by the catcher and allows a base runner to advance.

**pas·sen·ger** (pas′'n-jẽr), *n.* [< OFr. *passager* < *passage*, passage], a person traveling in a train, boat, etc., especially one having no part in the operation of the conveyance.

**passe par·tout** (pas pär-to͞o′), [Fr., pass everywhere], 1. a picture mounting in which glass, picture, and backing are bound together by gummed paper along the edges. 2. the gummed paper so used.

**pass·er-by** (pas′ẽr-bī′, päs′-), *n.* [*pl.* PASSERS-BY], a person who passes by.

**pas·ser·ine** (pas′ẽr-in, -īn′), *adj.* [< L. < *passer*, a sparrow], of the group of perching songbirds to which most birds belong. *n.* a bird of this group.

‡**pas·sim** (pas′im), *adv.* [L.], throughout; in various parts (of a book, etc.).

**pass·ing** (pas′iŋ, päs′-), *adj.* 1. going by, beyond, over, or through. 2. fleeting. 3. casual; incidental: as, a *passing* remark. 4. bringing one through a test, etc. successfully: as, a *passing* grade. 5. that is happening; current. *adv.* [Archaic], very. *n.* 1. the act of one that passes. 2. a means or place of passing. —**in passing,** incidentally.

**pas·sion** (pash′ən), *n.* [OFr. < LL. < L. pp. of *pati*, to suffer], 1. originally, suffering, as of a martyr. 2. [P-], the sufferings of Jesus during the Crucifixion or after the Last Supper. 3. *a*) any emotion, as hate, love, grief, joy, etc. *b*) *pl.* all of these emotions. 4. intense emotional excitement; specif., *a*) rage; fury. *b*) enthusiasm, as for music. *c*) strong love or affection. *d*) sexual desire; lust. 5. the object of any strong desire or fondness. —**pas′sion·less,** *adj.* —**pas′sion·less·ly,** *adv.* —**pas′sion·less·ness,** *n.*

**pas·sion·ate** (pash′ən-it), *adj.* [see PASSION], 1. having or showing strong emotions. 2. hot-tempered. 3. intense; ardent; rousing: as, a *passionate* speech. 4. lustful; amorous. 5. strong; vehement: said of an emotion. —**pas′sion·ate·ly,** *adv.* —**pas′sion·ate·ness,** *n.*

**pas·sion·flow·er** (pash′ən-flou′ẽr), *n.* a plant with variously colored flowers and yellow, egglike fruit (**passion fruit**): so called because parts of the flower are supposed to resemble Jesus' wounds, crown of thorns, etc.

**Passion play,** a religious play representing the Passion of Jesus.

**pas·sive** (pas′iv), *adj.* [< L. *passivus* < pp. of *pati*, to suffer], 1. inactive, but acted upon. 2. offering no resistance; submissive; patient. 3. taking no part; inactive; inert. 4. in *grammar*, indicating that the subject is the receiver (object) of the action (e.g., in "I was struck by the ball," *was struck* is in the passive voice). *n.* 1. *usually pl.* a passive thing, trait, etc. 2. in *grammar*, *a*) the passive voice. *b*) a verb in this voice. —**pas′sive·ly,** *adv.* —**pas′sive·ness, pas·siv′i·ty,** *n.*

**passive resistance,** opposition to a law, tax, etc. by refusal to comply or by such nonviolent acts as voluntary fasting.

**pass·key** (pas′kē′, päs′-), *n.* 1. a master key fitting all of a group of locks. 2. a private key.

**Pass·o·ver** (pas′ō′vẽr, päs′-), *n.* [*pass* + *over*], a Jewish holiday (*Pesach*) commemorating the deliverance of the ancient Hebrews from slavery in Egypt: Ex. 12: see **Jewish holidays.**

**pass·port** (pas′pôrt′, päs′pōrt′), *n.* [< Fr. < *passer*, to pass + *port*, a port], 1. a government document carried by a citizen traveling abroad, certifying his identity and citizenship and entitling him to the protection of his own country and the countries visited. 2. anything that enables one to be accepted, admitted, or successful.

**pass·word** (pas′wũrd′, päs′-), *n.* a secret word or phrase used by the members of a group to identify themselves, as in passing a guard.

**past** (past, päst), rare pp. of **pass.** *adj.* 1. gone by; ended: as, his worries are *past*. 2. of a former time. 3. immediately preceding: as, the *past* week. 4. having served formerly: as, a *past* chairman. 5. in *grammar*, indicating a time or state gone by or an action completed or in progress at a former time. *n.* 1. the history or former life of a person, group, etc. 2. a personal background that is hidden or questionable: as, a woman with a *past*. 3. in *grammar*, *a*) the past tense. *b*) a verb form in this tense. *prep.* 1. later than. 2. farther on than. 3. beyond in amount or degree. 4. beyond the extent, power, scope, etc. of: as, this is *past* belief. *adv.* to and beyond a point in time or space. —**the past,** past time, state, or happenings.

**pas·ta** (päs′tə), *n.* [It.; LL.; see PASTE], 1. the flour paste of which spaghetti, macaroni, etc. is made. 2. any food made of this paste.

**paste** (pāst), *n.* [OFr. < LL. *pasta* < Gr. *pastē*, barley porridge], 1. dough used in making rich pastry. 2. any soft, moist, smooth-textured substance: as, tooth *paste*. 3. a foodstuff, pounded or ground until creamy: as, almond *paste*. 4. a mixture of flour or starch, water, resin, etc. used as an adhesive for paper, etc. 5. *a*) a hard, brilliant glass used in making artificial gems. *b*) such a gem or gems. 6. [Slang], a blow or punch. *v.t.* [PASTED, PASTING], 1. to make adhere, as with paste. 2. to cover with pasted material. 3. [Slang], to hit; punch. —**past′er,** *n.*

**paste·board** (pāst′bôrd′, -bōrd′), *n.* 1. a stiff material made of layers of paper pasted together or of pressed and dried paper pulp. 2. [Slang], something made of pasteboard, as a ticket. *adj.* 1. of pasteboard. 2. flimsy; sham.

**pas·tel** (pas-tel′, pas′tel), *n.* [Fr. < It. *pastello* < LL. *pasta*, a paste], 1. *a*) ground coloring matter formed into a crayon. *b*) a crayon so made. 2. a picture drawn with such crayons. 3. drawing with pastels as an art form. 4. a soft, pale shade of some color. *adj.* 1. soft and pale: said of colors. 2. of pastel. —**pas′tel·ist, pas′tel·list,** *n.*

**pas·tern** (pas′tẽrn), *n.* [< OFr. < *pasture*, tether < LL. < L. *pastor*, shepherd], the part of a horse's foot between the fetlock and the hoof.

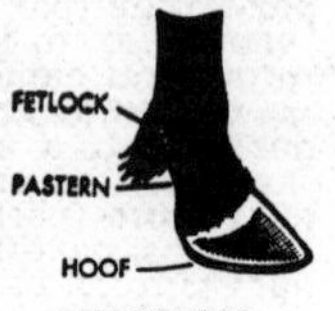

PASTERN

**Pas·teur, Lou·is** (lwē päs′tẽr′; Eng. pas-tũr′), 1822–1895; French chemist and bacteriologist.

**pas·teur·i·za·tion** (pas′tẽr-i-zā′shən, -chẽr-i-), *n.* a method of destroying or checking bacteria in milk, beer, etc. by heating the liquid to 142°–145°F. for thirty minutes.

**pas·teur·ize** (pas′tẽr-īz′, -chẽr-), *v.t.* [-IZED, -IZING], [after L. *Pasteur*], to subject (milk, beer, etc.) to pasteurization.

**pas·tille** (pas-tēl′), *n.* [Fr. < L. *pastillus*, lozenge < *pascere*, to feed], 1. a small tablet or lozenge containing medicine, flavoring, etc. 2. an aromatic pellet burned for fumigating, etc.

**pas·time** (pas′tīm′, päs′-), *n.* [< *pass* + *time*], a way of spending spare time; amusement; diversion.

**past master,** 1. a former master, as in a lodge or club. 2. one who has had long experience in some occupation, art, etc.; expert.

**pas·tor** (pas′tẽr, päs′-), *n.* [OFr.; L., a shepherd < *pascere*, to feed], a clergyman in charge of a church or congregation. —**pas′tor·ship′,** *n.*

**pas·to·ral** (pas′tẽr-əl, päs′-), *adj.* [< L. < *pastor*, a shepherd], 1. of shepherds, their work, way of life, etc. 2. of or depicting (conventionalized) rustic life. 3. peaceful; simple; natural. 4. of a pastor or his duties. *n.* 1. a poem, play, etc. with a pastoral or rustic setting. 2. a pastoral picture or scene. 3. a letter from a pastor or bishop. —**pas′to·ral·ism,** *n.* —**pas′to·ral·ist,** *n.* —**pas′to·ral·ly,** *adv.*

**pas·tor·ate** (pas′tẽr-it, päs′-), *n.* 1. the position, rank, duties, or term of office of a pastor. 2. a group of pastors.

**past participle,** a participle used usually with an auxiliary to indicate a time or state gone by or an action completed in the past (e.g., *grown* in "the garden has grown well").

**past perfect,** in *grammar*, 1. expressing action completed before a given or implied time; pluperfect (e.g., *had locked* in "he had locked the door before he left"). 2. a past perfect tense or form.

**pas·tra·mi** (pə-strä′mi), ***n.*** [Yid. < Hung.], rolled beef, highly spiced and smoked.

**pas·try** (pās′tri), ***n.*** [*pl.* -TRIES], [< *paste*], 1. flour dough made with shortening and used for pie crust, etc. 2. food made with this, as pies, tarts, etc. 3. all fancy baked goods.

**pas·tur·age** (pas′chēr-ij, päs′-), ***n.*** [OFr.], pasture.

**pas·ture** (pas′chēr, päs′-), ***n.*** [OFr. < LL. *pastura* < L. *pascere*, to feed], 1. grass or growing plants used as food by grazing animals. 2. ground suitable, or a field set aside, for grazing. ***v.t.*** [-TURED, -TURING], 1. to put (cattle, etc.) out to graze in a pasture. 2. to feed on (grass, etc.). 3. to provide with pasture: said of land. ***v.i.*** to graze. **—pas′tur·a·ble,** ***adj.*** **—pas′tur·er,** ***n.***

**past·y** (pās′ti), ***adj.*** [-IER, -IEST], of or like paste in color or texture. **—past′i·ness,** ***n.***

**past·y** (pas′ti, päs′-; *now often* pās′-), ***n.*** [*pl.* -IES], [< OFr. < LL. *pasta*, a paste], [Chiefly Brit.], a pie; esp., a meat pie.

**pat** (pat), ***n.*** [prob. echoic], 1. a gentle tap or stroke with a hand or flat surface. 2. a sound made by this. 3. a small lump, as of butter. ***v.t.*** [PATTED, PATTING], 1. *a*) to tap or stroke gently with the hand as in affection, sympathy, etc. *b*) to tap lightly with a flat surface. 2. to give a certain shape to, as mud, by patting. ***v.i.*** to make a patting sound, as in running.

**pat** (pat), ***adj.*** [prob. < prec.], 1. apt; opportune; timely. 2. exactly suitable: as, a *pat* hand in poker. ***adv.*** aptly; suitably. **—have** (or **know**) **pat,** [Colloq.], to know thoroughly. **—stand pat,** [Colloq.], to refuse to change an opinion, course of action, etc. **—pat′ly,** ***adv.*** **—pat′ness,** ***n.***

**pat.,** 1. patent. 2. patented. 3. pattern.

**Pat·a·go·ni·a** (pat′ə-gō′ni-ə, -gōn′yə), ***n.*** a region in S Argentina and Chile. **—Pat′a·go′ni·an,** ***adj. & n.***

**patch** (pach), ***n.*** [ME. *pacche*], 1. a piece of material applied to mend a hole or tear or strengthen a weak spot. 2. a dressing for a wound. 3. a shield worn over an injured eye. 4. a beauty spot (sense 1). 5. an area or spot: as, *patches* of blue sky. 6. a small plot of ground: as, a potato *patch*. 7. a scrap; bit; remnant. ***v.t.*** 1. to put a patch on. 2. to be a patch for. 3. to make (a quilt, etc.) out of patches. 4. to produce crudely or hurriedly (often with *up*). **—patch up,** to make right; settle, as a quarrel. **—patch′er,** ***n.***

**patch·ou·li, patch·ou·ly** (pach′oo-li, pə-chōō′li), ***n.*** [Fr. < Tamil < *paccu*, green + *ilai*, leaf], 1. an East Indian plant of the mint family. 2. a perfume made from its fragrant oil.

**patch pocket,** a pocket made by sewing a patch of material to the outside of a garment.

**patch·work** (pach′wūrk′), ***n.*** 1. anything formed of odd, miscellaneous parts; jumble. 2. needlework, as a quilt, made of odd patches of cloth. 3. any design or surface like this.

**patch·y** (pach′i), ***adj.*** [-IER, -IEST], 1. *a*) made up of or characterized by patches. *b*) forming or like patches. 2. not consistent or uniform in quality. **—patch′i·ly,** ***adv.*** **—patch′i·ness,** ***n.***

**pate** (pāt), ***n.*** [? < L. *patina*, a pan], 1. the head or top of the head. 2. intelligence. A humorous use.

‡**pâ·té de foie gras** (pä-tā′ də fwȧ′ grä′), [Fr.], a paste made of the livers of fattened geese.

**pa·tel·la** (pə-tel′ə), ***n.*** [*pl.* -LAS, -LAE (-ē)], [L., dim. of *patina*, a pan], the kneecap. **—pa·tel′lar** (-ēr), ***adj.*** **—pa·tel′late** (-it, -āt), ***adj.***

**pat·en** (pat′'n), ***n.*** [< OFr. < L. *patina*, a pan], 1. a metal dish; esp., the plate holding the Eucharistic bread. 2. a thin, flat piece of metal; disk. Also sp. **patin, patine.**

**pat·ent** (pat′'nt; *also, esp. Brit., & for adj. 1, 2, & 3, usually,* pā′t'nt), ***adj.*** [ult. < L. ppr. of *patere*, to be open], 1. open to all; generally accessible. 2. obvious; plain; evident. 3. unobstructed, as a tube. 4. protected by a patent, or letters patent. ***n.*** 1. a document granting a certain right or privilege; letters patent; esp., a document granting the exclusive right to produce, use, or sell an invention, etc. for a certain time. 2. *a*) the right so granted. *b*) the thing protected by such a right. 3. any exclusive right, title, or license: as, she had no *patent* on charm. ***v.t.*** to secure a patent for. **—pa′ten·cy** (pā′-), ***n.*** **—pat′ent·a·ble** (pat′-), ***adj.*** **—pat·ent·ee** (pat″n-tē′), ***n.*** **—pa′tent·ly** (pā′-, pat′-), ***adv.*** **—pat′en·tor** (pat′-), ***n.***

**patent leather,** leather having a hard, glossy, usually black finish: formerly patented.

**patent medicine,** a trade-marked medical preparation usually made by secret formula.

**pa·ter** (pā′tēr), ***n.*** [L.], [Brit. Colloq.], father.

**pa·ter·fa·mil·i·as** (pā′tēr-fə-mil′i-əs), ***n.*** [*pl.* PATRESFAMILIAS (pā′trēz-)], [L.], the father of a family.

**pa·ter·nal** (pə-tūr′n'l), ***adj.*** [< ML. < L. < *pater*, father], 1. of, like, or characteristic of a father; fatherly. 2. received or inherited from a father. 3. on the father's side of the family: as, *paternal* grandparents. **—pa·ter′nal·ly,** ***adv.***

**pa·ter·nal·ism** (pə-tūr′n'l-iz′m), ***n.*** the system of governing a country, a group of employees, etc. in a manner suggesting a father's relationship with his children. **—pa·ter′nal·is′tic,** ***adj.***

**pa·ter·ni·ty** (pə-tūr′nə-ti), ***n.*** 1. the state of being a father; fatherhood. 2. male parentage; paternal origin.

**pa·ter·nos·ter** (pā′tēr-nos′tēr, pat′ēr-), ***n.*** [L., our father], 1. the Lord's Prayer, especially in Latin: often **Pater Noster.** 2. every eleventh bead of a rosary on which this prayer is said.

**Pat·er·son** (pat′ēr-s'n), ***n.*** a city in NE New Jersey: pop., 144,000.

**path** (path, päth), ***n.*** [AS. *pæth*], 1. a way worn by footsteps; trail. 2. a walk for the use of people on foot, as in a garden. 3. a line of movement: as, the *path* of the meteor. 4. a course of conduct or procedure. **—path′less,** ***adj.***

**path., pathol.,** 1. pathological. 2. pathology.

**Pa·than** (pə-tän′, pət-hän′), ***n.*** a member of a Moslem, Indo-Iranian people of Afghanistan.

**pa·thet·ic** (pə-thet′ik), ***adj.*** [< LL. < Gr. *pathētikos* < *pathos*, suffering], 1. arousing or intended to arouse pity, sorrow, sympathy, etc.; pitiful. 2. of the emotions. **—pa·thet′i·cal·ly,** ***adv.***

**pathetic fallacy,** the ascribing of human attributes to nonhuman things (e.g., a stubborn door).

**path·find·er** (path′fīn′dēr, päth′-), ***n.*** one who makes a way for the first time, as in a jungle.

**-path·i·a** (path′i-ə), -pathy.

**-path·ic** (path′ik), a suffix forming adjectives corresponding to nouns ending in *-pathy*.

**path·o-,** [< Gr. *pathos*, suffering], a combining form meaning *suffering, disease, feeling*, as in *pathology*: also **path-.**

**path·o·gen·e·sis** (path′ə-jen′ə-sis), ***n.*** [see PATHO- & GENESIS], the development of a disease: also **pa·thog·e·ny** (pə-thoj′ə-ni).

**path·o·gen·ic** (path′ə-jen′ik), ***adj.*** causing disease: also **path′o·ge·net′ic** (-jə-net′ik).

**pa·thol·o·gy** (pə-thol′ə-ji), ***n.*** [< Fr.; see PATHO- & -LOGY], 1. the branch of medicine that deals with the nature of disease, especially with the structural and functional changes caused by disease. 2. [*pl.* -GIES], all the conditions, results, etc. of a particular disease. **—path·o·log·i·cal** (path′ə-loj′i-k'l), **path′o·log′ic,** ***adj.*** **—path′o·log′i·cal·ly,** ***adv.*** **—pa·thol′o·gist,** ***n.***

**pa·thos** (pā′thos), ***n.*** [Gr., suffering], the quality in something (in life or art) which arouses pity, sorrow, sympathy, etc.

**path·way** (path′wā′, päth′-), ***n.*** a path.

**-pa·thy** (pə-thi), [< Gr. *pathos*, suffering], a combining form meaning *feeling, disease, treatment of disease*, as in *antipathy, osteopathy*.

**pa·tience** (pā′shəns), ***n.*** [< OFr. < L. *patientia* < *pati*, to suffer], 1. a being patient; specif., *a*) the will or ability to endure without complaint. *b*) endurance, perseverance, etc. in performing a task. 2. [Chiefly Brit.], solitaire (sense 2).

**pa·tient** (pā′shənt), ***adj.*** [< OFr. < L. ppr. of *pati*, to suffer], 1. enduring pain, trouble, etc. with composure and without complaining. 2. refusing to be provoked, as by an insult; forbearing. 3. calmly tolerating delay, confusion, etc. 4. characterized by patience: as, a *patient* face. 5. diligent; persevering, as a worker. ***n.*** one who is receiving medical care. **—pa′tient·ly,** ***adv.***

**pat·in, pat·ine** (pat′'n), ***n.*** a paten.

**pat·i·na** (pat′i-nə), ***n.*** [*pl.* -NAE (-nē′)], [L.], a paten.

**pat·i·na** (pat′'n-ə), ***n.*** [< It.], 1. a fine greenish crust on bronze or copper, formed by oxidation and valued as being ornamental. 2. any color change due to age, as on the surface of old woodwork.

**pa·ti·o** (pä′ti-ō′, pa′-), ***n.*** [*pl.* -OS], [Sp.], 1. a courtyard or inner area open to the sky: common in Spanish and Spanish-American architecture. 2. a terrace (sense 4).

**pat·ois** (pat′wä; Fr. pȧ′twȧ′), ***n.*** [*pl.* -OIS (-wäz; Fr. -twȧ′)], [Fr.], a form of a language differing from the accepted standard, as a provincial dialect.

**pat. pend.,** patent pending.
**pat·ri-,** [L. < Gr. *patēr*, father], a combining form meaning *father.*
**pa·tri·arch** (pā′tri-ärk′), *n.* [< OFr. < LL. < Gr. < *patēr*, father + *archein*, to rule], 1. the father and ruler of a family or tribe: in the *Bible*, Abraham, Isaac, Jacob, and Jacob's twelve sons were patriarchs. 2. one regarded as the founder of a religion, business, etc. 3. *a*) a bishop in the early Christian Church. *b*) in the *Orthodox Eastern Church*, the highest ranking bishop at Constantinople, Alexandria, Jerusalem, Moscow, etc. 4. a man of great age and dignity. **—pa′tri·arch′al,** *adj.* **—pa′tri·arch′al·ly,** *adv.*
**pa·tri·arch·ate** (pā′tri-är′kit), *n.* the position, rank, jurisdiction, etc. of a patriarch.
**pa·tri·arch·y** (pā′tri-är′ki), *n.* [*pl.* -IES], 1. a form of social organization in which the father is the head of the family or tribe, descent being traced through the male line. 2. government by men.
**pa·tri·cian** (pə-trish′ən), *adj.* [< OFr. < L. *patricius;* ult. < *pater*, father], 1. of or characteristic of patricians. 2. noble; aristocratic. *n.* 1. in ancient Rome, *a*) originally, a member of any of the Roman citizen families. *b*) later, a member of the nobility. 2. an aristocrat.
**pat·ri·cide** (pat′rə-sīd′), *n.* [< L. *pater*, father; + *-cide*], 1. the act of killing one's own father. 2. one who kills his own father. **—pat′ri·cid′al,** *adj.*
**Pat·rick,** Saint (pat′rik), 389?–461? A.D.; British bishop who converted the Irish to Christianity.
**pat·ri·mo·ny** (pat′rə-mō′ni), *n.* [*pl.* -NIES], [< OFr. < L. *patrimonium* < *pater*, father], 1. property inherited from one's father or ancestors. 2. property endowed to a church, etc. 3. anything inherited, as a trait. **—pat′ri·mo′ni·al,** *adj.*
**pa·tri·ot** (pā′tri-ət, -ot′; *esp. Brit.*, pat′ri-ət), *n.* [< Fr. < LL. < Gr. *patris*, fatherland], one who loves and zealously supports his own country. **—pa′tri·ot′ic** (-ot′ik), *adj.* **—pa′tri·ot′i·cal·ly,** *adv.*
**pa·tri·ot·ism** (pā′tri-ət-iz′m), *n.* love and loyal or zealous support of one's own country.
**pa·tris·tic** (pə-tris′tik), *adj.* [< L. *pater*, father; + *-istic*], of the early leaders, or fathers, of the Christian Church or their writings, etc.: also **pa·tris′ti·cal.** **—pa·tris′ti·cal·ly,** *adv.*
**pa·trol** (pə-trōl′), *v.t.* & *v.i.* [-TROLLED, -TROLLING], [Fr. *patrouiller* < *patouiller*, to paddle], to make a regular, repeated circuit of (an area, camp, etc.) in guarding. *n.* 1. a patrolling. 2. a person or group patrolling. 3. a group of ships, airplanes, etc. used in patrolling. 4. a subdivision of a troop of boy scouts. **—pa·trol′ler,** *n.*
**pa·trol·man** (pə-trōl′mən), *n.* [*pl.* -MEN], a policeman assigned to patrol a certain area.
**patrol wagon,** a small, enclosed truck used by the police in transporting prisoners.
**pa·tron** (pā′trən), *n.* [OFr. < L. *patronus* < *pater*, father], 1. one who is like a father in some respects; protector; benefactor. 2. a patron saint. 3. *a*) a rich or influential person who sponsors and supports some person, activity, etc. *b*) a champion; advocate. 4. a regular customer. **—pa′tron·al,** *adj.* **—pa′tron·ess,** *n.fem.*
**pa·tron·age** (pā′trən-ij, pat′rən-), *n.* 1. *a*) the status or function of a patron. *b*) support, favor, etc. given by a patron. 2. favor, courtesy, etc. shown to people considered inferior; condescension. 3. *a*) clientele; customers. *b*) trade; business. 4. *a*) the power to appoint to office or grant other political favors. *b*) such offices or favors.
**pa·tron·ize** (pā′trə-nīz′, pat′rə-), *v.t.* [-IZED, -IZING], 1. to act as a patron toward; sponsor; support. 2. to show favor to in a condescending manner. 3. to be a regular customer of (a store, etc.). **—pa′tron·iz′er,** *n.* **—pa′tron·iz′ing,** *adj.* **—pa′tron·iz′ing·ly,** *adv.*
**patron saint,** a saint looked upon as the special guardian of a person, place, or institution.
**pat·ro·nym·ic** (pat′rə-nim′ik), *n.* [< LL. < Gr. < *patēr*, father + *onoma*, a name], a name showing descent from a given person as by the addition of a prefix or suffix (e.g., *Stevenson*, son of Steven, *O'Brien*, descendant of Brien).
**pa·troon** (pə-tro͞on′), *n.* [D. < Fr.; see PATRON], one who held an estate with manorial rights under the old Dutch governments of New York and New Jersey.
**pat·ten** (pat′'n), *n.* [< OFr. *patin*, a clog < *patte*, a paw], a shoe with a thick wooden sole.
**pat·ter** (pat′ēr), *v.i.* [< *pat*, to tap gently], to make, or move so as to make, a patter. *v.t.* to cause to patter. *n.* a series of light, rapid taps: as, the *patter* of rain on dry leaves.
**pat·ter** (pat′ēr), *v.t.* & *v.i.* [< *pater*, in *paternoster*], to speak rapidly or glibly; recite mechanically. *n.* 1. language peculiar to a group, class, etc.; jargon. 2. the glib, rapid speech of salesmen, magicians, etc. 3. [Colloq.], idle, meaningless chatter. **—pat′ter·er,** *n.*
**pat·ter** (pat′ēr), *n.* a person or thing that pats.
**pat·tern** (pat′ērn), *n.* [< OFr. *patron*, patron, pattern], 1. a person or thing so ideal as to be worthy of imitation. 2. a model, guide, plan, etc. used in making things. 3. something representing a class or type; sample. 4. an arrangement of form; design or decoration: as, wallpaper *patterns.* 5. definite direction, tendency, or characteristics: as, behavior *patterns.* *v.t.* to make or do (something) in imitation of a pattern (with *on*, *upon*, or *after*). **—pat′tern·mak′er,** *n.*
**patter song,** a musical comedy song with a simple tune and comic lyrics sung with great rapidity.
**pat·ty** (pat′i), *n.* [*pl.* -TIES], [Fr. *pâté*, a pie], 1. a small pie. 2. a small, flat cake of ground meat, fish, etc., usually fried. 3. any disk-shaped piece of food.
**pau·ci·ty** (pô′sə-ti), *n.* [< Fr. < L. < *paucus*, few], 1. fewness; small number. 2. scarcity; insufficiency.
**Paul,** Saint (pôl), ?–67? A.D.; a Jew of Tarsus, apostle of Christianity to the Gentiles; author of many Epistles. **—Paul′ine** (-īn, -ēn), *adj.*
**Paul VI,** 1897– ; Pope (1963– ).
**Paul Bun·yan** (bun′yən), in *American legend*, a giant lumberjack who, with the help of his blue ox, Babe, performed various superhuman feats.
**paul·dron** (pôl′drən), *n.* [< OFr. < *espaule*, the shoulder], a piece of plate armor to protect the shoulder: see **armor,** illus.
**paunch** (pônch), *n.* [< OFr. < L. *pantex*, belly], the abdomen, or belly; esp., a potbelly. **—paunch′y,** *adj.* **—paunch′i·ly,** *adv.* **—paunch′i·ness,** *n.*
**pau·per** (pô′pēr), *n.* [L., poor person], 1. a person who lives on charity, especially public charity. 2. an extremely poor person. **—pau′per·ism,** *n.*
**pau·per·ize** (pô′pēr-īz′), *v.t.* [-IZED, -IZING], to make a pauper of. **—pau′per·i·za′tion,** *n.*
**pause** (pôz), *n.* [Fr. < L. < Gr. *pausis*, a stopping < *pauein*, to stop], 1. a temporary stop or rest, as in working or speaking. 2. hesitation; delay: as, pursuit without *pause.* 3. in *music*, a sign (𝄐 or 𝄑) placed below or above a note or rest that is to be prolonged. 4. in *prosody*, a rhythm break or caesura. *v.i.* [PAUSED, PAUSING], 1. to make a pause; stop; hesitate. 2. to dwell or linger (*on* or *upon*). **—give one pause,** to make one hesitant or uncertain. **—paus′er,** *n.*
**pave** (pāv), *v.t.* [PAVED, PAVING], [< OFr. *paver;* ult. < L. *pavire*, to beat], 1. to cover the surface of (a road, etc.), as with concrete, asphalt, etc. 2. to be the top surface of. **—pave the way (for),** to prepare the way (for). **—pav′er,** *n.*
**pave·ment** (pāv′mənt), *n.* 1. a paved surface, as of concrete, brick, etc. 2. a paved street or road. 3. the material used in paving.
**pa·vil·ion** (pə-vil′yən), *n.* [< OFr. < L. *papilio*, butterfly, also tent], 1. a large tent, usually with a peaked top. 2. a building, often open-air, for exhibits, etc., as at a fair or park. 3. part of a building jutting out. 4. any of the separate or connected parts of a group of related buildings, as of a hospital. *v.t.* to furnish with or shelter in a pavilion.
**pav·ing** (pāv′iŋ), *n.* 1. a pavement. 2. material for a pavement.
**Pav·lov, I·van Pe·tro·vich** (i-vän′ pye-trô′vich päv′lôf), 1849–1936; Russian physiologist.
**Pav·lo·va, An·na** (än′ä päv′lô-vä; Eng. päv-lō′və), 1885–1931; Russian ballet dancer.
**paw** (pô), *n.* [< OFr. *poue;* prob. < Gmc.], 1. the foot of a four-footed animal having claws. 2. [Colloq.], a hand. *v.t.* & *v.i.* 1. to touch, dig, strike, etc. with paws or feet: as, the horse *pawed* the air. 2. to handle clumsily, roughly, or overintimately; maul. **—paw′er,** *n.*
**pawl** (pôl), *n.* [? < Fr. *épaule*, a shoulder; or ? < D. *pal*, pawl], a mechanical device allowing or imparting motion in only one direction, as a hinged tongue which engages the notches of a cog-wheel, preventing backward motion.

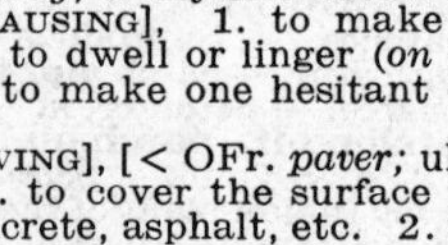

PAWL

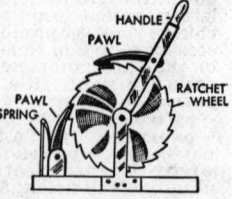

**pawn** (pôn), *n.* [< OFr. *pan*], 1. anything given as security, as for a debt; pledge. 2. the state of being pledged: as, his ring was in *pawn.* 3. the act of pawning. *v.t.* 1. to put in pawn. 2. to wager or risk. **—pawn′age,** *n.* **—pawn′er, pawn′or,** *n.*

**pawn** (pôn), *n.* [< OFr. < LL. *pedo,* foot soldier < L. *pes,* foot], 1. a chessman of the lowest value. 2. a person subject to the will of another; tool.
**pawn·bro·ker** (pôn'brō'kẽr), *n.* a person licensed to lend money at interest on personal property left with him as security. —**pawn'bro'king,** *n.*
**Paw·nee** (pô-nē'), *n.* 1. [*pl.* -NEE, -NEES], a member of an Indian tribe formerly living in Nebraska, and now in N Oklahoma. 2. their language. *adj.* of this tribe or their language.
**pawn·shop** (pôn'shop'), *n.* a pawnbroker's shop.
**pawn ticket,** a receipt for goods in pawn.
**paw·paw** (pô'pô'), *n.* the papaw.
**Paw·tuck·et** (pô-tuk'it), *n.* a city in Rhode Island: pop., 81,000.
‡**pax vo·bis·cum** (paks vō-bis'kəm), [L.], peace (be) with you.
**pay** (pā), *v.t.* [PAID or *obs.* (except in phrase *pay out,* sense 2) PAYED, PAYING], [< OFr. < L. *pacare,* to pacify < *pax,* peace], 1. to give to (a person) what is due, as for goods or services; remunerate. 2. to make recompense for; repay: as, she *paid* kindness with evil. 3. to give (what is due) in return, as for goods or services. 4. to settle (a debt, etc.). 5. *a*) to give (a compliment, respects, etc.). *b*) to make (a visit, etc.). 6. to yield, as a recompense: as, this job *pays* $50. 7. to be profitable to: as, it *paid* me to come. *v.i.* 1. to give due compensation; make payment. 2. to be profitable. *n.* 1. a paying or being paid: said of wages. 2. compensation; esp., wages or salary. *adj.* 1. rich enough in minerals, etc. to make mining profitable: as, *pay* gravel. 2. operated by inserting a specified coin: as, a *pay* telephone. —**in the pay of,** employed and paid by. —**pay as you go,** to pay expenses as they arise. —**pay back,** to repay. —**pay for,** 1. to undergo punishment because of. 2. to atone for. —**pay off,** 1. to pay all that is owed. 2. to take revenge on (a wrongdoer) for (a wrong done). 3. in *nautical usage,* to allow the bow of (a vessel) to veer to leeward. —**pay out,** 1. to give out (money, etc.). 2. to let out (a rope, cable, etc.). —**pay up,** to pay in full or on time. —**pay'er,** *n.*
**pay** (pā), *v.t.* [PAYED, PAYING], [ONorm. Fr. *peier* < L. < *pix,* pitch], to coat with tar, etc. in order to make waterproof.
**pay·a·ble** (pā'ə-b'l), *adj.* 1. that can be paid. 2. that is to be paid (on a specified date); due.
**pay·day** (pā'dā'), *n.* the day when wages are paid.
**pay dirt,** soil, gravel, ore, etc. rich enough in minerals to make mining profitable.
**pay·ee** (pā-ē'), *n.* the person to whom a check, note, money, etc. is payable.
**pay·load** (pā'lōd'), *n.* 1. the cargo, or the part of a cargo, producing income: also **pay load.** 2. *a*) the war head of a guided missile, the artificial satellite launched by a rocket, etc. *b*) the weight of such a load.
**pay·mas·ter** (pā'mas'tẽr, -mäs'-), *n.* the official in charge of paying wages to employees. —**pay'mis'tress,** *n.fem.*
**pay·ment** (pā'mənt), *n.* 1. a paying or being paid. 2. something paid. 3. penalty or reward.
**pay·nim** (pā'nim), *n.* [< OFr. < LL. *paganismus,* paganism], [Archaic], 1. a pagan or the pagan world. 2. a non-Christian; esp., a Moslem. *adj.* [Archaic], 1. pagan. 2. non-Christian.
**pay-off** (pā'ôf'), *n.* [Colloq.], 1. originally, the act or time of payment. 2. settlement or reckoning. 3. something unexpected or almost incredible, especially when coming as a climax.
**pay roll,** 1. a list of employees to be paid, with the amount due to each. 2. the total amount needed for this for a given period.
**payt., pay't.,** payment.
**Pb,** *plumbum,* [L.], in *chemistry,* lead.
**pc.,** 1. piece. 2. prices.
**p.c., pct.,** per cent.
**Pd,** in *chemistry,* palladium.
**pd.,** paid.
**P.D.,** 1. Police Department. 2. postal district.
**P.D., p.d.,** per diem.
**pea** (pē), *n.* [*pl.* PEAS, or *archaic* or *Brit. dial.* PEASE], [< ME. *pese* (later misunderstood as pl. form) < AS. < L. < Gr. *pison*], 1. a climbing plant with white or pinkish flowers and green seed pods. 2. its small round seed, eaten as a vegetable. 3. any related plant. —**as like as two peas,** exactly alike.
**peace** (pēs), *n.* [< OFr. *pais* < L. *pax*], 1. freedom from war or civil strife. 2. an agreement to end war. 3. freedom from public disturbance; law and order. 4. harmony; concord. 5. an undisturbed state of mind; serenity. 6. calm; quiet. *v.i.* [PEACED, PEACING], [Obs. except in imperative], to be or become quiet. —**at peace,** free from war, conflict, etc. —**hold** (or **keep**) **one's peace,** to be silent. —**keep the peace,** to maintain law and order. —**make peace,** to end hostilities.
**peace·a·ble** (pēs'ə-b'l), *adj.* 1. fond of or promoting peace; not quarrelsome. 2. at peace; peaceful. —**peace'a·ble·ness,** *n.* —**peace'a·bly,** *adv.*
**Peace Corps,** an agency of the U.S., established to provide volunteers skilled in teaching, construction, etc. to assist underdeveloped areas abroad.
**peace·ful** (pēs'fəl), *adj.* 1. not quarrelsome; peaceable. 2. free from disturbance; calm. 3. of or characteristic of a time of peace. —**peace'ful·ly,** *adv.*
**peace·mak·er** (pēs'māk'ẽr), *n.* one who makes peace, as by settling the quarrels of others.
**peace pipe,** a ceremonial pipe smoked by American Indians as part of a peace conference.
**peace·time** (pēs'tīm'), *n.* a time of peace. *adj.* of or characteristic of such a time.
**peach** (pēch), *n.* [< OFr. < LL. < L. *Persicum* (*malum*), Persian (apple)], 1. a small tree with pink blossoms and round, juicy, orange-yellow fruit having a fuzzy skin and a rough pit. 2. its fruit. 3. the color of this fruit. 4. [Slang], any person or thing well-liked. *adj.* 1. of the peach. 2. orange-yellow. —**peach'like',** *adj.*
**peach** (pēch), *v.i.* [< OFr.; see IMPEACH], [Slang], to give evidence against another; turn informer.
**peach·y** (pē'chi), *adj.* [-IER, -IEST], 1. peachlike, as in color or texture. 2. [Slang], fine; excellent.
**pea·cock** (pē'kok'), *n.* [*pl.* -COCKS, -COCK; see PLURAL, II, D, 1], [AS. *pawa, pea* (L. *pavo*), peafowl + *cok,* a cock], 1. any of a number of related large birds, especially the male with a crest and a long tail which has rainbow-colored, eyelike spots and can spread out like a fan: regarded as a symbol of vanity. 2. a vain person. —**pea'cock'ish,** *adj.*
**pea·fowl** (pē'foul'), *n.* [*pl.* -FOWLS, -FOWL; see PLURAL, II, D, 1], a peacock or peahen.
**pea green,** a light yellowish green. —**pea'-green',** *adj.*
**pea·hen** (pē'hen'), *n.* the female of the peacock.
**pea jacket,** [prob. < D. *pij,* warm jacket], a short, heavy woolen coat worn by sailors.
**peak** (pēk), *n.* [var. of *pike* (summit)], 1. a pointed end or top, as of a cap, roof, etc. 2. the summit of a hill or mountain ending in a point. 3. a mountain with such a summit. 4. the highest or utmost point of anything; maximum: as, the *peak* of activity. 5. in *nautical usage, a*) the top rear corner of a fore-and-aft sail. *b*) the narrowed part of a hull, front or rear. *adj.* maximum: as, *peak* production. *v.t. & v.i.* 1. to bring or come to a vertical position; tilt up, as a sail yard. 2. to reach or bring to a high, or the highest, point.
**peaked** (pēkt, pēk'id), *adj.* having a peak; pointed.
**peak·ed** (pēk'id), *adj.* having sharp features; thin and drawn, as from illness.
**peal** (pēl), *n.* [< ME. < *apele,* appeal], 1. the loud ringing of a bell or bells. 2. a set of bells; chimes. 3. any loud, prolonged sound, as of gunfire, laughter, etc. *v.t. & v.i.* to sound in a peal; ring or resound.
**pe·an** (pē'ən), *n.* a paean.
**pea·nut** (pē'nut'), *n.* 1. a vine of the pea family, with brittle pods ripening underground and containing edible seeds. 2. the pod or its seeds.

PEANUT PLANT
(1–2 ft. high)

**peanut butter,** a paste or spread made by grinding roasted peanuts.
**pear** (pâr), *n.* [< AS. < LL. < L. *pirum*], 1. a tree with glossy leaves, white blossoms, and greenish-yellow fruit. 2. the soft, juicy fruit, round at the base and narrowing toward the stem. —**pear'-shaped',** *adj.*
**pearl** (pũrl), *n.* [< OFr. < ML. *perla* < L. *perna,* kind of shellfish], 1. a smooth, hard, usually white or bluish-gray, roundish growth, formed around a foreign body within the shell of some oysters and other mollusks: it is used as a gem. 2. mother-of-pearl. 3. anything pearl-like in size, color, value, beauty, etc. 4. the color of pearl, a bluish gray. 5. in *printing,* a size of type, 5 point. *v.i.* to fish for pearl-bearing mollusks. *adj.* 1. of, like, or having pearls. 2. like a pearl in shape or color. —**pearl'er,** *n.* —**pearl'i·ness,** *n.* —**pearl'y** [-IER, -IEST], *adj.*

**pearl** (pũrl), *v.t. & v.i., n.* purl.

**pearl·ash** (pũrl′ash′), *n.* a refined potash.

**pearl diver** (or **fisher**), a person who dives for pearl-bearing mollusks.

**pearl gray,** a pale bluish gray. —**pearl′-gray′,** *adj.*

**Pearl Harbor,** an inlet on the S coast of Oahu, Hawaii, near Honolulu: site of the U. S. naval base attacked by Japan, December 7, 1941.

**peart** (pêrt, pũrt), *adj.* [Dial.], 1. pert. 2. clever. —**peart′ly,** *adv.* —**peart′ness,** *n.*

**Pear·y, Robert Edwin** (pêr′i), 1856–1920; U.S. arctic explorer; discovered the North Pole.

**peas·ant** (pez′'nt), *n.* [< Anglo-Fr. < OFr. < *païs,* country < LL. < *pagus,* district], 1. in Europe, a worker who farms the land; farmer. 2. [Obs.], a person considered inferior.

**peas·ant·ry** (pez′'n-tri), *n.* peasants collectively.

**pease** (pēz), *n.* 1. [*pl.* PEASES, PEASEN], [Obs.], a pea. 2. archaic or Brit. dial. pl. of **pea.**

**pease·cod, peas·cod** (pēz′kod′), *n.* the pod of the pea plant.

**peat** (pēt), *n.* [< ML. *peta,* piece of turf], 1. partly decayed plant matter found in ancient swamps. 2. a dried block of this used as fuel. —**peat′y** [-IER, -IEST], *adj.*

**peat moss,** a certain moss found especially in the peat of N Europe, used as a mulch.

**pea·vey** (pē′vi), *n.* [*pl.* -VEYS], [after J. *Peavey,* its inventor], a heavy wooden lever with a pointed tip and hinged hook near the end: used by lumbermen in handling logs: also sp. **peavy** [*pl.* -VIES].

**peb·ble** (peb′'l), *n.* [< AS. *papol(stan),* pebble (stone)], 1. a small stone worn smooth and round, as by the action of water. 2. clear, transparent quartz or a lens made from it. *v.t.* [-BLED, -BLING], to stamp (leather) so as to produce a pebbly appearance. —**peb′bled,** *adj.*

**peb·bly** (peb′li), *adj.* [-BLIER, -BLIEST], 1. having many pebbles. 2. having a pebbled surface.

**pe·can** (pi-kan′, -kän′, pē′kan), *n.* [< Am. Ind. name], 1. an olive-shaped nut with a thin shell. 2. the tree it grows on, related to the hickory.

**pec·ca·dil·lo** (pek′ə-dil′ō), *n.* [*pl.* -LOES, -LOS], [Sp., dim. < L. < *peccare,* to sin], a minor or petty sin.

**pec·cant** (pek′ənt), *adj.* [< L. ppr. of *peccare,* to sin], sinful; sinning. —**pec′can·cy** [*pl.* -CIES], *n.* —**pec′cant·ly,** *adv.*

**pec·ca·ry** (pek′ə-ri), *n.* [*pl.* -RIES, -RY; see PLURAL, II, D, 1], [< Sp. < Carib. *pakira*], a piglike wild animal of tropical America, with sharp tusks.

‡**pec·ca·vi** (pe-kā′vi, -kä′vē), [L.], I have sinned. *n.* [*pl.* -VIS], a confession of guilt.

**peck** (pek), *v.t.* [< ME. var. of *pikken,* to pick], 1. to strike with a pointed object, as with a beak. 2. to make by doing this: as, to *peck* a hole. 3. to pick up or get by pecking. *v.i.* to make strokes with a pointed object. *n.* 1. a stroke made with a pointed object. 2. a mark made by pecking. 3. [Colloq.], a quick, casual kiss. —**peck at,** 1. to make a pecking motion at. 2. [Colloq.], to eat very little of. 3. [Colloq.], to criticize constantly. —**peck′er,** *n.*

**peck** (pek), *n.* [< Anglo-Fr. *pek*], 1. a unit of dry measure equal to ¼ bushel or eight quarts. 2. any container that will hold a peck. 3. [Colloq.], a large quantity or amount, as of trouble.

**pec·tin** (pek′tin), *n.* [< Gr. *pēktos,* congealed], a water-soluble carbohydrate obtained from certain ripe fruits, which yields a gel that is the basis of fruit jellies. —**pec′tic,** *adj.*

**pec·to·ral** (pek′tə-rəl), *adj.* [< Fr. < L. < *pectus,* breast], 1. of or located in or on the breast or chest. 2. of or used in treating diseases of the chest or lungs. *n.* 1. a pectoral medicine. 2. a pectoral fin or muscle.

**pectoral fin,** either of a pair of fins just behind the head of a fish.

**pec·u·late** (pek′yoo-lāt′), *v.t. & v.i.* [-LATED, -LATING], [< L. pp. of *peculari,* to embezzle], to steal or misuse (money or property in one's care); embezzle. —**pec′u·la′tion,** *n.* —**pec′u·la′tor,** *n.*

**pe·cul·iar** (pi-kūl′yẽr), *adj.* [< L. *peculiaris* < *peculium,* private property], 1. of only one person, thing, group, etc.; exclusive. 2. particular; special: as, a *peculiar* talent for lying. 3. odd; strange. —**pe·cul′iar·ly,** *adv.*

**pe·cu·li·ar·i·ty** (pi-kū′li-ar′ə-ti, pi-kūl′yar′-), *n.* 1. a being peculiar. 2. [*pl.* -TIES], something that is peculiar, as a trait.

**pe·cu·ni·ar·y** (pi-kū′ni-er′i), *adj.* [< L. < *pecunia,* money], 1. of or involving money. 2. involving a money penalty, or fine. —**pe·cu′ni·ar′i·ly,** *adv.*

**ped·a·gog·ic** (ped′ə-goj′ik), *adj.* [see PEDAGOGUE], of or characteristic of teachers or teaching: also **ped′a·gog′i·cal.** —**ped′a·gog′i·cal·ly,** *adv.*

**ped·a·gog·ism** (ped′ə-gog-iz'm, -gôg-), *n.* 1. the practices, beliefs, etc. of a pedagogue. 2. the state of being a pedagogue. Also **ped′a·gogu·ism.**

**ped·a·gogue** (ped′ə-gog′, -gôg′), *n.* [< OFr. < L. < Gr. < *pais,* a child + *agein,* to lead], a teacher; esp., a pedantic, dogmatic teacher: also **ped′a·gog′.**

**ped·a·go·gy** (ped′ə-gō′ji, -goj′i), *n.* [see PEDAGOGUE], 1. teaching. 2. the art or science of teaching; esp., instruction in teaching methods.

**ped·al** (ped′'l; *also, for adj. 1,* pē′d'l), *adj.* [< L. < *pes,* a foot], 1. of the foot or feet. 2. of or operated by a pedal. *n.* a lever operated by the foot to transmit motion, as in a bicycle, or to change the tone or volume of an organ, harp, etc. *v.t. & v.i.* [-DALED or -DALLED, -DALING or -DALLING], to operate by a pedal or pedals; use the pedals (of). —**ped′al·ist,** *n.*

**pedal pushers,** knee-length trousers for women or girls, used originally for bicycle riding.

**ped·ant** (ped′'nt), *n.* [< Fr. < It. *pedante;* ult. prob. < L. < *paedagogare,* to educate], 1. one who emphasizes trivial points of learning, showing a scholarship lacking in judgment. 2. a narrow-minded teacher who insists on exact adherence to rules. —**pe·dan·tic** (pi-dan′tik), *adj.* —**pe·dan′ti·cal·ly,** *adv.*

**ped·ant·ry** (ped′'n-tri), *n.* 1. the characteristics, beliefs, etc. of a pedant; narrow-minded scholarship or arbitrary adherence to rules. 2. [*pl.* -RIES], a pedantic act, idea, etc.: also **pe·dan·ti·cism** (pi-dan′tə-siz'm).

**ped·ate** (ped′āt), *adj.* [< L. < *pes,* foot], 1. having feet. 2. footlike. 3. in *botany,* in a fanlike arrangement with subdivided leaves. —**ped′ate·ly,** *adv.*

**ped·dle** (ped′'l), *v.i.* [-DLED, -DLING], [back-formation < *peddler;* ult. < ME. *ped,* a basket], to go from place to place selling small articles. *v.t.* 1. to carry from place to place and offer for sale. 2. to deal in or dispense, as in small amounts. —**ped′dler, ped′lar,** *n.*

**-pede** (pēd), [< L. *pes,* a foot], a combining form meaning *foot* or *feet,* as in *centipede:* also **-ped.**

**ped·er·as·ty** (ped′ə-ras′ti, pē′də-), *n.* [< Gr. < *pais,* boy + *eran,* to love], sodomy between men, especially between a man and a boy: also sp. **paederasty.** —**ped′er·ast′, paed′er·ast′,** *n.*

**ped·es·tal** (ped′is-t'l), *n.* [< Fr. < It. < *piè* (< L. *pes*), a foot + *di,* of + *stal* (< OHG. *stal*), a rest], 1. the bottom support of a column, statue, etc. 2. any foundation, base, etc. *v.t.* [-TALED or -TALLED, -TALING or -TALLING], to furnish with a pedestal. —**to put** (or **set**) **on a pedestal,** to idolize.

**pe·des·tri·an** (pə-des′tri-ən), *adj.* [< L. *pedester* < *pes,* a foot], 1. going or done on foot. 2. lacking interest or imagination; prosaic; dull. *n.* one who goes on foot; walker. —**pe·des′tri·an·ism,** *n.*

**ped·i-,** [< L. *pes,* a foot], a combining form meaning *foot* or *feet,* as in *pedicure:* also **ped-.**

**pe·di·a·tri·cian** (pē′di-ə-trish′ən, ped′i-), *n.* a specialist in pediatrics: also **pe′di·at′rist** (-at′rist).

**pe·di·at·rics** (pē′di-at′riks, ped′i-), *n.pl.* [construed as sing.], [see PEDO- & -IATRICS], the branch of medicine dealing with the care of infants and children and the treatment of their diseases. —**pe′di·at′ric,** *adj.*

**ped·i·cel** (ped′i-s'l), *n.* [< L. *pediculus,* dim. of *pes,* a foot], in *botany & zoology,* a small, stalklike structure; peduncle: also **ped′i·cle** (-k'l). —**ped′i·cel′lar** (-sel′ẽr), *adj.*

**pe·dic·u·lo·sis** (pi-dik′yoo-lō′sis), *n.* [< L. dim. of *pedis,* a louse], infestation with lice; condition of being lousy. —**pe·dic′u·lous** (-ləs), *adj.*

**ped·i·cure** (ped′i-kyoor′), *n.* [< Fr. < L. *pes,* a foot + *cura,* care], 1. a chiropodist. 2. chiropody. 3. a trimming, cleaning, and polishing of the toenails. —**ped′i·cur′ist,** *n.*

**ped·i·gree** (ped′ə-grē′), *n.* [< OFr. *pié de grue,* lit., crane's foot: after the lines in the genealogical tree], 1. a list of ancestors; family tree. 2. descent; lineage 3. a known line of descent, as of a pure-bred animal. —**ped′i·greed′,** *adj.*

**ped·i·ment** (ped′ə-mənt), *n.* [< *periment* (alteration of *pyramid*), infl. by L. *pes,* a foot], 1. a low-pitched gable on the front of some buildings of Grecian architecture. 2. any similar, decorative triangular piece, as over a doorway, etc. —**ped′i·men′tal** (-men′t'l), *adj.* —**ped′i·ment′ed,** *adj.*

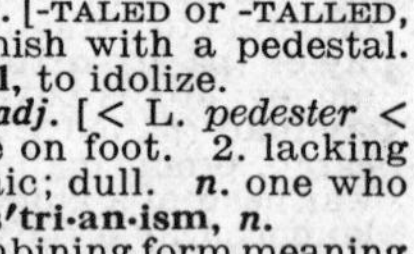

PEDIMENT

**ped·lar** (ped′lẽr), *n.* a peddler.

**pe·do-,** [< Gr. *pais,* a child], a combining form meaning *child, children:* also sp. **paedo-:** also **ped-.**

**pe·dom·e·ter** (pi-dom′ə-tẽr), *n.* [< Fr. < L. *pes,* a

foot + Gr. *metron*, a measure], an instrument which measures the distance covered in walking by recording the number of steps taken.
**pe·dun·cle** (pi-duŋ′k'l), *n.* [< dim. of L. *pes*, foot], 1. a flower stalk. 2. in *anatomy & zoology*, a slender stalklike part. —**pe·dun′cu·lar** (-kyoo-lẽr), *adj.* —**pe·dun′cu·late** (-lit, -lāt′), **pe·dun′cu·lat′ed,** *adj.*
**peek** (pēk), *v.i.* [< ME. *piken*, prob. var. of *kiken*, to peer], to glance or peer quickly and furtively, as through an opening. *n.* a glance or look.
**peek·a·boo** (pēk′ə-bo͞o′), *n.* a child's game in which someone hides his face, as behind his hands, and then suddenly reveals it, calling "peekaboo!"
**peel** (pēl), *v.t.* [< OFr. < L. *pilare*, to make bald < *pilus*, a hair], 1. to cut away the skin, rind, surface, etc. of. 2. to trim away (skin, rind, etc.) of anything. *v.i.* 1. to shed skin or the outer surface. 2. to come off: as, sunburned skin will *peel*. 3. [Slang], to undress. *n.* the rind or skin of fruit. —**keep one's eyes peeled,** [Colloq.], to keep on the watch. —**peel off,** in *aviation*, to veer away from a flight formation so as to dive at a target or to land. —**peel′er,** *n.*
**peel** (pēl), *n.* [< OFr. < L. *pala*, a spade], a long shovellike tool used by bakers for moving bread into and out of ovens.
**Peel, Sir Robert** (pēl), 1788–1850; prime minister of England (1834–1835; 1841–1846).
**peel·ing** (pēl′iŋ), *n.* anything peeled off, as an apple skin.
**peen** (pēn), *n.* [prob. < ON.], the part of a hammer head opposite the flat striking surface: often rounded or wedgelike. *v.t.* to hammer with a peen.
**peep** (pēp), *v.i.* [prob. echoic], 1. to make the short, high-pitched cry of a young bird. 2. to speak in a weak voice, as from fear. *n.* a peeping sound like that of a young bird. —**peep′er,** *n.*
**peep** (pēp), *v.i.* [ME. *pepen*], 1. to look through a small opening or from a place of hiding. 2. to peer slyly or secretly. 3. to show or appear gradually or partially: as, stars *peeped* through clouds. *v.t.* to cause to protrude slightly. *n.* 1. a brief look; secret or furtive glimpse. 2. the first appearance, as of dawn.
**peep·er** (pēp′ẽr), *n.* 1. a person who peeps or pries. 2. [Slang], an eye.
**peep·hole** (pēp′hōl′), *n.* a hole to peep through.
**Peeping Tom,** 1. in *English legend*, the tailor who was struck blind after peeping at Lady Godiva. 2. [p-T-], a person who gets pleasure, especially sexual pleasure, from furtively watching others.
**peer** (pêr), *n.* [< OFr. *per* < L. *par*, an equal], 1. a person or thing of the same rank, value, ability, etc.; specif., an equal before the law. 2. a noble; esp., a British duke, marquis, earl, viscount, or baron. *v.t.* to match or equal. —**peer of the realm,** any British peer entitled to a seat in the House of Lords.
**peer** (pêr), *v.i.* [prob. < *appear*], 1. to look closely, as in trying to see more clearly. 2. [Poetic], to appear. 3. to show slightly; come partly into sight.
**peer·age** (pêr′ij), *n.* 1. all the peers of a particular country. 2. the rank or dignity of a peer. 3. a list of peers with their lineage.
**peer·ess** (pêr′is), *n.* 1. the wife of a peer. 2. a woman having the rank of peer in her own right.
**peer·less** (pêr′lis), *adj.* without equal; unrivaled. —**peer′less·ly,** *adv.* —**peer′less·ness,** *n.*
**peeve** (pēv), *v.t. & v.i.* [PEEVED, PEEVING], [Colloq.], to make or become peevish. *n.* [Colloq.], an object of dislike; annoyance.
**pee·vish** (pēv′ish), *adj.* [ME. *pevische* < ?], 1. irritable; fretful. 2. showing ill humor or impatience, as a remark. —**pee′vish·ly,** *adv.* —**pee′vish·ness,** *n.*
**pee·wee** (pē′wē′), *n.* [prob. < Am. Ind. *pewe*, little], [Colloq.], an unusually small person or thing.
**peg** (peg), *n.* [ME. *pegge*], 1. a short pin or bolt used to hold parts together, close an opening, hang things on, fasten ropes to, mark the score in a game, etc. 2. any of the pins that regulate the tension of the strings of a violin, guitar, etc. 3. the distance between pegs. 4. a step or degree. 5. a point or prong for tearing, hooking, etc. 6. [Colloq.], the foot or leg. 7. [Brit.], an alcoholic drink. *v.t.* [PEGGED, PEGGING], 1. to put a peg or pegs into so as to fasten, mark, etc. 2. to mark, as a score, with pegs. 3. [Colloq.], to throw, as a ball. *v.i.* 1. to work, progress, etc. steadily: as, he *pegs* away at Latin. 2. to keep score with pegs, as in cribbage. —**round peg in a square hole,** one in a position, situation, etc. for which he is unfitted: also **square peg in a round hole.** —**take down a peg,** to lower the pride or conceit of. —**peg′ger,** *n.*
**Peg·a·sus** (peg′ə-səs), *n.* 1. in *Gr. mythology*, a winged horse, symbol of poetic inspiration. 2. a northern constellation.
**peg leg,** [Colloq.], 1. a wooden leg. 2. a person with a wooden leg.
**peg-top** (peg′top′), *adj.* designating trousers that are full at the hips and narrow at the cuffs.
**peg top,** 1. a child's spinning toy, pear-shaped with a metal tip; top. 2. *pl.* peg-top trousers.
**peign·oir** (pān-wär′, pān′wär), *n.* [Fr. < *peigner*, to comb < L. *pecten*, a comb], a negligee.
**Pei·ping** (pā′piŋ′; Chin. bā′piŋ′), *n.* Peking.
**pe·jo·ra·tion** (pē′jə-rā′shən, pej′ə-), *n.* [< L.; ult. < *pejor*, worse], 1. a worsening. 2. in *linguistics*, a change of meaning for the worse: cf. etymology and definition of *cretin*. —**pe·jo·ra·tive** (pē′jə-rā′tiv, pej′ə-, pi-jôr′ə-tiv), *adj. & n.*
**Pe·kin·ese** (pē′kə-nēz′), *adj. & n.* [*pl.* PEKINESE], Pekingese.
**Pe·king** (pē′kiŋ′; Chin. bā′jiŋ′), *n.* the capital of China: pop., 1,603,000.
**Pe·king·ese** (pē′kiŋ-ēz′), *adj.* of Peking or its people. *n.* [*pl.* PEKINGESE], 1. a native or inhabitant of Peking, China. 2. the Chinese dialect of Peking. 3. a small dog with long, silky hair, short legs, and a pug nose.
**Peking man,** a type of primitive man of about 475,000 B.C. whose fossil remains were found near Peking, China.
**pe·koe** (pē′kō; Brit. pek′ō), *n.* [< Chin. *pek-ho*, lit., white down (on the young leaves used)], a black, small-leaved tea of Ceylon and India.
**pe·lag·ic** (pə-laj′ik), *adj.* [< L. < Gr. *pelagos*, the sea], of the open sea or ocean.
**pel·ar·go·ni·um** (pel′är-gō′ni-əm), *n.* [< Gr. *pelargos*, stork], any of various related plants with deeply cut leaves and variously colored flowers; geranium.
**pelf** (pelf), *n.* [ult. < OFr. *pelfre*, plunder], 1. [Rare], booty. 2. mere wealth: a term of contempt.
**pel·i·can** (pel′i-kən), *n.* [< AS. < LL. < Gr. *pelekan*], a large water bird with webbed feet and a distensible pouch in the lower bill for scooping up fish.
**Pe·li·on** (pē′li-ən), *n.* a mountain in E Thessaly, Greece: see **Ossa.**
**pe·lisse** (pə-lēs′), *n.* [Fr. < L. *pellicius*, made of skins < *pellis*, a skin], a long cloak or outer coat, especially one made or lined with fur.
**pel·la·gra** (pə-lā′grə, -lag′rə), *n.* [It. < *pelle* (< L. *pellis*), the skin + *agra*, hard], a chronic disease caused by a deficiency of nicotinic acid in the diet and characterized by skin eruptions and nervous disorders. —**pel·la′grous,** *adj.*
**pel·let** (pel′it), *n.* [< OFr. *pelote* < ML. dim. of L. *pila*, a ball], 1. a little ball, as of clay, paper, medicine, etc. 2. a crude projectile, as used in a catapult. 3. a bullet. 4. a small lead shot. *v.t.* to shoot or hit with pellets.
**pell-mell, pell·mell** (pel′mel′), *adv.* [< Fr. < OFr. *pesle mesle*, redupl. < *mesler*, to mix], 1. in a jumbled mass or manner. 2. in reckless haste. *adj.* 1. confused. 2. headlong. *n.* confusion; disorder.
**pel·lu·cid** (pə-lo͞o′sid), *adj.* [< L. < *per*, intens. + *lucidus*, bright], 1. transparent; clear. 2. clear and simple: as, a *pellucid* style. —**pel′lu·cid′i·ty, pel·lu′cid·ness,** *n.* —**pel·lu′cid·ly,** *adv.*
**Pel·o·pon·ne·sus, Pel·o·pon·ne·sos** (pel′ə-pə-nē′səs), *n.* the peninsula of S Greece. —**Pel′o·pon·ne′sian** (-shən, -zhən), *n. & adj.*
**pelt** (pelt), *v.t.* [prob. ult. < L. *pillare*, to drive], 1. to throw things at. 2. to beat heavily and repeatedly. 3. to throw (missiles). *v.i.* 1. to strike heavily or steadily, as hard rain. 2. to hurry. *n.* 1. a blow. 2. speed: as, at full *pelt*. —**pelt′er,** *n.*
**pelt** (pelt), *n.* [prob. < *peltry*], 1. the skin of a fur-bearing animal, especially when prepared for tanning. 2. humorously, the human skin.
**pel·tate** (pel′tāt), *adj.* [< L. *pelta*, light shield], having the stalk attached to the center of the lower surface: said of a leaf.
**pelt·ry** (pel′tri), *n.* [*pl.* -RIES], [< OFr. < *peletier*, furrier < *pel*, a skin], 1. pelts, or fur-bearing skins, collectively. 2. a pelt.
**pel·vis** (pel′vis), *n.* [*pl.* -VES (-vēz)], [L., a basin], in *anatomy & zoology*, any basinlike structure; specif.,

*a*) the basinlike cavity in the posterior part of the trunk in man and many other vertebrates. *b*) the bones forming this cavity: also **pelvic arch** (or **girdle**). —**pel'vic,** *adj.*

**pem·mi·can, pem·i·can** (pem'i-kən), *n.* [< Am. Ind. *pemikkân*, fat meat < *pimiy*, fat], 1. dried lean meat, pounded into a paste with fat and preserved as pressed cakes. 2. a concentrated food of dried beef, suet, sugar, etc., as for explorers.

**pen** (pen), *n.* [< AS. *penn*], 1. a small yard or enclosure for domestic animals. 2. the animals kept in this. 3. any small enclosure: as, a play *pen* for babies. *v.t.* [PENNED or PENT, PENNING], to enclose or confine as in a pen.

**pen** (pen), *n.* [< OFr. < L. *penna*, a feather], 1. originally, a heavy quill trimmed to a split point, for writing with ink. 2. any of various devices used in writing or drawing with ink, often with a metal point split into two nibs. 3. the metal point for this device. 4. *a*) writing as a profession. *b*) literary style. *v.t.* [PENNED, PENNING], to write as with a pen.

**pen** (pen), *n.* [Slang], a penitentiary.

**Pen., pen.,** peninsula.

**pe·nal** (pē'n'l), *adj.* [< L. < *poena*, punishment], 1. of, for, or constituting punishment, especially legal punishment. 2. making one liable to punishment, as an offense. —**pe'nal·ly,** *adv.*

**penal code,** a body of law dealing with various crimes or offenses and their legal penalties.

**pe·nal·ize** (pē'n'l-īz', pen''l-), *v.t.* [-IZED, -IZING], 1. to make punishable, as an offense. 2. to impose a penalty on, as for the infraction of a rule. —**pe'nal·i·za'tion,** *n.*

**penal servitude,** imprisonment, usually at hard labor: the legal punishment for certain crimes.

**pen·al·ty** (pen''l-ti), *n.* [*pl.* -TIES], 1. a punishment fixed by law, as for a crime. 2. the handicap, etc. imposed on an offender, as a fine. 3. any unfortunate consequence of an act or condition.

**pen·ance** (pen'əns), *n.* [< OFr. < L. < *paenitens;* see PENITENT], 1. in the *R.C. Church*, a sacrament involving the confession of sin, repentance, and submission to penalties imposed, followed by absolution. 2. any voluntary suffering to show repentance for wrongdoing. *v.t.* [-ANCED, -ANCING], to impose a penance on.

**Pe·nang** (pi-naŋ'), *n.* a state of the Federation of Malaya.

**pe·na·tes** (pi-nā'tēz), *n.pl.* [L.], the household gods of the ancient Romans: see **lares.**

**pence** (pens), *n.* [Brit.], pl. of **penny**: used also in compounds, as *twopence.*

**pen·chant** (pen'chənt; Fr. pän'shän'), *n.* [Fr. < *pencher*, to incline; ult. < L. *pendere*, to hang], a strong liking or fondness; inclination.

**pen·cil** (pen's'l), *n.* [< OFr. < L. *penicillus* < dim. of *penis*, a tail], 1. originally, an artist's brush. 2. the style of a given artist. 3. a pointed, rod-shaped instrument with a core of graphite or crayon, used for writing, drawing, etc. 4. something shaped or used like a pencil: as, a styptic *pencil.* 5. a series of lines coming to or spreading out from a point. *v.t.* [-CILED or -CILLED, -CILING or -CILLING], 1. to write, draw, etc. as with a pencil. 2. to use a pencil on. —**pen'cil·er, pen'cil·ler,** *n.* —**pen'cil·ing, pen'cil·ling,** *n.*

**pend** (pend), *v.i.* [< Fr. < L. *pendere*, to hang], to await judgment or decision.

**pend·ant** (pen'dənt), *n.* [< OFr., ppr. of *pendre* < L. *pendere*, to hang], 1. a hanging object, as an earring, used as an ornament. 2. anything hanging, as the chain on a lamp. 3. a decorative piece suspended from a ceiling or roof. Also sp. **pendent.** *adj.* pendent.

**pend·ent** (pen'dənt), *adj.* [< L. ppr. of *pendere*, to hang], 1. suspended. 2. overhanging. 3. undecided; pending. Also sp. **pendant.** *n.* pendant. —**pend'en·cy,** *n.* —**pend'ent·ly,** *adv.*

**pend·ing** (pen'diŋ), *adj.* 1. not decided or established: as, a *pending* patent. 2. impending. *prep.* 1. throughout the course of; during. 2. while awaiting; until: as, *pending* his arrival.

**pen·drag·on** (pen-drag'ən), *n.* [W. *pen*, head + *dragon*, leader], supreme chief or leader: a title used in ancient Britain.

**pen·du·lous** (pen'joo-ləs), *adj.* [L. *pendulus* < *pendere*, to hang], 1. hanging freely without a rigid attachment. 2. swinging. —**pen'du·lous·ly,** *adv.* —**pen'du·lous·ness,** *n.*

**pen·du·lum** (pen'joo-ləm, -d'l-əm), *n.* [*pl.* -LUMS], [< L.; see PENDULOUS], a body hung from a fixed point so that it can swing freely to and fro under the combined forces of gravity and momentum: often used to regulate clock movements.

**Pe·nel·o·pe** (pə-nel'ə-pi), *n.* the faithful wife of Ulysses: during his long absence she cleverly postponed answering her many suitors.

**pen·e·tra·ble** (pen'i-trə-b'l), *adj.* that can be penetrated. —**pen'e·tra·bil'i·ty, pen'e·tra·ble·ness,** *n.* —**pen'e·tra·bly,** *adv.*

**pen·e·trate** (pen'ə-trāt'), *v.t.* [-TRATED, -TRATING], [< L. pp. of *penetrare* < base of *penitus*, inward], 1. to find or force a way into or through; enter by piercing. 2. to have an effect throughout; permeate. 3. to affect or move deeply; imbue. 4. to discover; understand. *v.i.* 1. to make a way into and through something; pierce. 2. to have a marked effect on the mind.

**pen·e·trat·ing** (pen'ə-trāt'iŋ), *adj.* 1. that can penetrate; sharp; piercing: as, a *penetrating* smell. 2. that has entered deeply: as, a *penetrating* wound. 3. showing keenness of mind; acute. Also **pen'e·tra'tive.** —**pen'e·trat'ing·ly, pen'e·trat'ive·ly,** *adv.*

**pen·e·tra·tion** (pen'ə-trā'shən), *n.* 1. a penetrating. 2. the depth to which something enters. 3. sharp discernment; insight.

**pen·guin** (peŋ'gwin, pen'-), *n.* [prob. first applied by Bret. fisherman (cf. Bret. *pen*, head + *gouin*, white) to the great auk], any of a group of flightless birds of the Southern Hemisphere, having webbed feet and paddle-like flippers for swimming.

KING PENGUIN (36 in. tall)

**pen·hold·er** (pen'hōl'dēr), *n.* 1. the holder into which a pen point fits. 2. a container for a pen.

**pen·i·cil·lin** (pen'ə-sil'in), *n.* a powerful antibiotic obtained from some penicilliums and used in the treatment and prevention of some infections.

**pen·i·cil·li·um** (pen'ə-sil'i-əm), *n.* [*pl.* -UMS, -A (-ə)], [< L. *penicillus*, a brush: from the tuftlike ends], any of a group of fungi growing as green mold on stale bread, decaying fruit, etc.

**pen·in·su·la** (pə-nin'sə-lə, -syoo-lə), *n.* [< L. < *paene*, almost + *insula*, an isle], 1. a land area almost entirely surrounded by water, connected with the mainland by an isthmus. 2. any land area projecting into the water. —**pen·in'su·lar,** *adj.*

**pe·nis** (pē'nis), *n.* [*pl.* -NES (-nēz), -NISES], [L., orig., a tail], the male organ of sexual intercourse: in mammals it is also the organ through which urine is ejected.

**pen·i·tent** (pen'ə-tənt), *adj.* [< OFr. < L. ppr. of *paenitere*, to repent], sorry for having done wrong and willing to atone; repentant. *n.* 1. a penitent person. 2. in the *R.C. Church*, a person undergoing penance. —**pen'i·tence,** *n.* —**pen'i·tent·ly,** *adv.*

**pen·i·ten·tial** (pen'ə-ten'shəl), *adj.* of, constituting, or expressing penitence or penance. *n.* 1. a penitent. 2. a list or book of rules governing religious penance. —**pen'i·ten'tial·ly,** *adv.*

**pen·i·ten·tia·ry** (pen'ə-ten'shə-ri), *adj.* [see PENITENT], 1. of or for penance. 2. used in punishing and reforming. 3. that makes one liable to imprisonment in a penitentiary. *n.* [*pl.* -RIES], a prison; esp., a State or Federal prison for persons convicted of serious crimes.

**pen·knife** (pen'nīf'), *n.* [*pl.* -KNIVES], a small pocketknife: originally used in making quill pens.

**pen·man** (pen'mən), *n.* [*pl.* -MEN], 1. a person employed to write or copy; scribe. 2. a person skilled in penmanship. 3. an author; writer.

**pen·man·ship** (pen'mən-ship'), *n.* 1. handwriting as an art or skill. 2. a style of handwriting.

**Penn, William** (pen), 1644–1718; English Quaker; founder of Pennsylvania.

**Penn., Penna.,** Pennsylvania.

**pen name,** a name used by an author in place of his true name; pseudonym.

**pen·nant** (pen'ənt), *n.* [< *pennon;* infl. by *pendant*], 1. any long, narrow flag or banner. 2. such a flag symbolizing a championship, as in baseball.

**pen·ni·less** (pen'i-lis), *adj.* without even a penny; extremely poor.

**Pen·nine Alps** (pen'īn, -in), a range of the Alps between Switzerland and NW Italy.

**pen·non** (pen'ən), *n.* [< OFr. < L. *penna*, a quill], 1. a long, narrow, triangular or swallow-tailed flag used as an ensign by knights or lancers. 2. any flag or pennant. 3. a pinion; wing.

**Penn·syl·va·ni·a** (pen's'l-vān'yə, -vā'ni-ə), *n.* an Eastern State of the U.S.: area, 45,333 sq. mi.; pop., 11,319,000; capital, Harrisburg: abbrev. **Pa., Penn., Penna.**

**Pennsylvania Dutch,** 1. the descendants of early German immigrants to Pennsylvania. 2. their German dialect. Also called **Pennsylvania German.** —**Penn'syl·va'ni·a-Dutch',** *adj.*

**Penn·syl·va·ni·an** (pen′s'l-vān′yən, -vā′ni-ən), ***adj.*** 1. of Pennsylvania. 2. designating or of the second coal-forming period of the Paleozoic Era in North America: see **geology,** chart. ***n.*** 1. a native or inhabitant of Pennsylvania. 2. the Pennsylvanian Period.

**pen·ny** (pen′i), ***n.*** [*pl.* -NIES; for 1 (esp. collective), PENCE], [< AS. *pening*], 1. *a*) a British coin equal to 1/12 shilling: abbrev. **d.** *b*) a British coin, in the new decimal system, equal to 1/100 pound: in full, **new penny:** abbrev. **p.** 2. a cent (U.S. or Canadian). 3. a sum of money. **—a pretty penny,** [Colloq.], a large sum of money.

**-pen·ny,** a combining form meaning *costing* (a specified number of) *pennies,* as in *fourpenny:* as applied to nails, now a measure of their length.

**pen·ny·roy·al** (pen′i-roi′əl), ***n.*** [< OFr. *pouliel* (< L. *pulegium,* fleabane) + *real,* royal], 1. a hairy plant of the mint family. 2. the oil it yields.

**pen·ny·weight** (pen′i-wāt′), ***n.*** a unit of weight, equal to 24 grains or 1/20 ounce troy weight.

**pen·ny-wise** (pen′i-wiz′), ***adj.*** careful or thrifty in small matters. **—penny-wise and pound-foolish,** thrifty in small matters but wasteful in major ones.

**pen·ny·worth** (pen′i-wũrth′), ***n.*** 1. the amount that can be bought for a penny. 2. the value of something bought, with regard to price paid: as, a good *pennyworth.* 3. a small amount.

**pe·nol·o·gy** (pē-nol′ə-ji), ***n.*** [Gr. *poinē,* penalty; + *-logy*], the study of the reformation and rehabilitation of criminals and the management of prisons. **—pe′no·log′i·cal** (-nə-loj′ə-k'l), ***adj.*** **—pe·nol′o·gist,** ***n.***

**pen·sile** (pen′sil), ***adj.*** [L. *pensilis* < *pendere,* to hang], 1. hanging. 2. building a hanging nest.

**pen·sion** (pen′shən), ***n.*** [< OFr. < L. *pensio* < *pendere,* to pay], 1. a regular payment, not wages, to one who has fulfilled certain requirements, as of service, age, disability, etc. 2. a regular payment, not a fee, given to artists, etc. by their patrons; subsidy. 3. (pon′si-on′; Fr. pän′syōn′), in France, etc., a boarding school or boardinghouse. ***v.t.*** to grant a pension to. **—pension off,** to dismiss from service with a pension. **—pen′sion·a·ble,** ***adj.*** **—pen′sion·ar′y,** ***adj.* & *n.*** **—pen′sion·er,** ***n.***

**pen·sive** (pen′siv), ***adj.*** [< OFr. < L. *pensare,* to consider, freq. of *pendere,* to weigh], 1. thinking deeply, often of sad or melancholy things. 2. expressing deep thoughtfulness, often with some sadness. **—pen′sive·ly,** ***adv.*** **—pen′sive·ness,** ***n.***

**pen·stock** (pen′stok′), ***n.*** [*pen* (enclosure) + *stock*], a sluice for controlling the flow of water.

**pent** (pent), alt. pt. and pp. of **pen** (to shut in). ***adj.*** held or kept in; penned (often with *up*).

**pen·ta-,** [Gr. *penta-* < *pente,* five], a combining form meaning *five:* also **pent-.**

**pen·ta·gon** (pen′tə-gon′), ***n.*** [< LL. < Gr. < *penta-,* five + *gōnia,* an angle], 1. a plane figure with five angles and five sides. 2. [P-], the pentagonal building in Arlington, Virginia, containing offices of the Defense Department. **—pen·tag′o·nal** (-tag′ə-n'l), ***adj.*** **—pen·tag′o·nal·ly,** ***adv.***

**pen·ta·he·dron** (pen′tə-hē′drən), ***n.*** [*pl.* -DRONS, -DRA (-drə)], [see PENTA- & -HEDRON], a solid figure with five plane surfaces. **—pen′ta·he′dral,** ***adj.***

**pen·tam·er·ous** (pen-tam′ẽr-əs), ***adj.*** [*penta-* + *-merous*], in *biology,* made up of five parts: also written **5-merous.** **—pen·tam′er·ism,** ***n.***

**pen·tam·e·ter** (pen-tam′ə-tẽr), ***n.*** [< L. < Gr.; see PENTA- & METER], 1. a line of verse containing five metrical feet. 2. verse consisting of pentameters. ***adj.*** consisting of five metrical feet.

**pen·tan·gu·lar** (pen-taŋ′gyoo-lẽr), ***adj.*** [*pent*(*a*)- + *angular*], having five angles.

**Pen·ta·teuch** (pen′tə-tōōk′, -tūk′), ***n.*** [< Gr. < *penta-,* five + *teuchos,* a book], the first five books of the Old Testament.

**pen·tath·lon** (pen-tath′lən, -lon), ***n.*** [< Gr. < *penta-,* five + *athlon,* a contest], an athletic contest in which each contestant takes part in five track and field events.

**pen·ta·va·lent** (pen′tə-vā′lənt, pen-tav′ə-), ***adj.*** 1. having a valence of five. 2. having five valences.

**Pen·te·cost** (pen′ti-kôst′, -kost′), ***n.*** [< L. < Gr. *pentēkostē* (*hēmera*), the fiftieth (day)], 1. Shabuoth. 2. a Christian festival on the seventh Sunday after Easter, celebrating the descent of the Holy Spirit upon the Apostles; Whitsunday. **—Pen′te·cos′tal,** ***adj.***

**pent·house** (pent′hous′), ***n.*** [< OFr. *apentis;* ult. < L. *appendere,* to append], a house or apartment built on the roof of a building.

**pen·to·thal sodium** (pen′tə-thal′), [< *pento-* for *penta-* + *thi*obarbiturate + *-al*], a barbiturate drug injected intravenously as an anesthetic and hypnotic: a trade-mark (**Pentothal Sodium**).

**pent-up** (pent′up′), ***adj.*** held in check; curbed; confined: as, *pent-up* emotion.

**pe·nult** (pē′nult, pi-nult′), ***n.*** [< L. < *paene,* almost + *ultimus,* last], the one next to the last; specif., the next to the last syllable in a word.

**pe·nul·ti·mate** (pi-nul′tə-mit), ***adj.*** 1. next to the last. 2. of the penult. ***n.*** the penult.

**pe·num·bra** (pi-num′brə), ***n.*** [*pl.* -BRAE (-brē), -BRAS], [< L. *paene,* almost + *umbra,* shade], 1. the partly lighted area surrounding the complete shadow of a body, as the moon, in full eclipse. 2. a partly lighted area around a full shadow, as of a sunspot. **—pe·num′bral,** ***adj.***

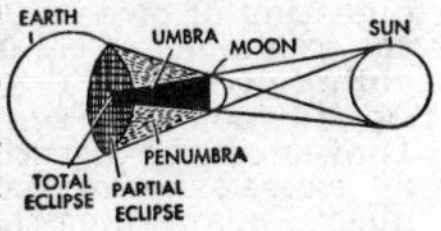


PENUMBRA

**pe·nu·ri·ous** (pə-nyoor′i-əs, -noor′-), ***adj.*** [see PENURY], 1. unwilling to part with money or possessions; miserly; stingy. 2. scanty; barren. **—pe·nu′ri·ous·ly,** ***adv.*** **—pe·nu′ri·ous·ness,** ***n.***

**pen·u·ry** (pen′yoo-ri), ***n.*** [< L. *penuria,* want], lack of money or property; extreme poverty.

**pe·on** (pē′ən), ***n.*** [< Sp. < ML. *pedo,* foot soldier], 1. in Latin America, a member of the laboring class. 2. in the southwestern U.S., a person forced into servitude to work off a debt.

**pe·on·age** (pē′ən-ij), ***n.*** 1. the condition of a peon. 2. the system by which debtors or legal prisoners are forced to labor for their creditors or for persons who lease their services from the state.

**pe·o·ny** (pē′ə-ni), ***n.*** [*pl.* -NIES], [< AS. & OFr. < L. < Gr. *Paiōn,* name for Apollo, god of medicine from its former medicinal use], 1. any of a group of plants with large pink, white, red, or yellow, showy flowers. 2. the flower.

**peo·ple** (pē′p'l), ***n.*** [*pl.* -PLE; for 1 & 9, -PLES], [< Anglo-Fr. < OFr. < L. *populus,* nation], 1. all the persons of a racial, cultural, historical, religious, or linguistic group; nation, race, ethnic group, etc. 2. the persons belonging to a certain place, community, or class: as, *people* of Ohio, *people* of wealth. 3. the persons under the leadership or control of a particular person or body. 4. the members of one's class, set, race, etc.: as, the miner spoke for his *people.* 5. one's family; relatives; ancestry. 6. persons without wealth, privilege, etc.; populace. 7. the electorate of a state. 8. persons considered indefinitely: as, what will *people* say? 9. a group of creatures: as, the ant *people.* 10. human beings. ***v.t.*** [-PLED, -PLING], to fill with people; populate.

**people's front,** popular front.

**Pe·or·i·a** (pi-ôr′i-ə, -ō′ri-), ***n.*** a city in central Illinois: pop., 103,000.

**pep** (pep), ***n.*** [< *pepper*], [Slang], energy; briskness; vigor; spirit. ***v.t.*** [PEPPED, PEPPING], [Slang], to fill with pep; invigorate; encourage (with *up*). **—pep′py** [-PIER, -PIEST], ***adj.***

**pep·lum** (pep′ləm), ***n.*** [*pl.* -LUMS, -LA (-lə)], [L. < Gr. *peplos,* a shawl], 1. a flounce attached at the waist of a dress, coat, etc., extending around the hips. 2. a large scarf worn draped about the body by women in ancient Greece.

**pep·per** (pep′ẽr), ***n.*** [see PLURAL, II, D, 3], [< AS. < L. *piper* < Gr. *peperi*], 1. *a*) any of various tropical shrubs of the capsicum family, especially a variety with a many-seeded, red or green, sweet or hot fruit. *b*) the fruit. 2. *a*) a pungent condiment prepared from the dried berries of an East Indian plant: see **black pepper, white pepper.** *b*) this plant. 3. cayenne; red pepper. ***v.t.*** 1. to season with ground pepper. 2. to sprinkle thickly. 3. to shower with many small objects: as, the lawn was *peppered* with hailstones. 4. to beat or thrash.

**pep·per-and-salt** (pep′ẽr-'n-sôlt′), ***adj.*** consisting of a mixture of black with white, so as to be grayish: said of cloth.

**pep·per·corn** (pep′ẽr-kôrn′), ***n.*** [< AS. *piporcorn*], the dried berry of the black pepper.

**pep·per·grass** (pep′ẽr-gras′, -gräs′), ***n.*** a plant of the mustard family with pungent leaves that are used in salads: also **pep′per·wort′** (-wũrt′).

**pep·per·mint** (pep′ẽr-mint′), ***n.*** 1. a plant of the mint family, with lance-shaped leaves and pink flowers. 2. the pungent oil it yields, used for flavoring. 3. a candy flavored with this oil.

**pepper pot,** any of various stews or soups of vegetables, meat, etc. flavored with hot spices.
**pepper tree,** a tree with loose-hanging branches and reddish berries: also **pepper shrub.**
**pep·per·y** (pep′ēr-i), *adj.* [-IER, -IEST], 1. of, like, or highly seasoned with pepper. 2. sharp; fiery; hot, as speech or writing. 3. hot-tempered; irritable. **—pep′per·i·ness,** *n.*
**pep·py** (pep′i), *adj.* [-PIER, -PIEST], [Slang], full of pep, or energy; brisk; vigorous; spirited. **—pep′pi·ly,** *adv.* **—pep′pi·ness,** *n.*
**pep·sin** (pep′sin), *n.* [G. < Gr. < *peptein,* to digest], 1. an enzyme secreted in the stomach, aiding in the digestion of proteins. 2. an extract of pepsin from the stomachs of calves, etc., used as a medicine in aiding digestion: also sp. **pepsine.**
**pep·tic** (pep′tik), *adj.* [< Gr. < *peptein,* to digest], 1. of or aiding digestion. 2. that can digest. 3. of or caused by digestive secretions: as, a *peptic* ulcer. *n.* anything that aids digestion.
**pep·tone** (pep′tōn), *n.* [< G. < Gr. *peptos,* digested], any of a group of soluble and diffusible simple proteins formed by the action of pepsin on albuminous substances, as in digestion. **—pep·ton′ic** (-ton′ik), *adj.*
**Pepys, Samuel** (pēps; *occas.* peps, pep′is), 1633–1703; English diarist and government official.
**Pe·quot** (pē′kwot), *n.* a member of a tribe of Algonquian Indians that settled in Connecticut. *adj.* of this tribe.
**per** (pũr, pēr), *prep.* [L.], 1. through; by; by means of. 2. for each: as, fifty cents *per* yard.
**per-,** [< L. *per,* through], a prefix meaning: 1. *through, throughout,* as in *perceive, percolate.* 2. *thoroughly, very,* as in *persuade.* 3. in *chemistry, containing* (a specified element or radical) *in its maximum,* or *a higher, valence,* as in *peroxide.*
**Per.,** 1. Persia. 2. Persian.
**per.,** 1. period. 2. person.
**per·ad·ven·ture** (pũr′əd-ven′chēr), *adv.* [< OFr. *par,* by + *aventure,* chance], [Archaic], 1. possibly. 2. by chance. *n.* [Archaic], chance; doubt.
**per·am·bu·late** (pēr-am′byoo-lāt′), *v.t.* [-LATED, -LATING], [< L. pp. < *per,* through + *ambulare,* to walk], to walk through, over, around, etc., as in inspecting. *v.i.* to stroll. **—per·am′bu·la′tion,** *n.* **—per·am′bu·la·to′ry** (-lə-tôr′i, -tō′ri), *adj.*
**per·am·bu·la·tor** (pēr-am′byoo-lā′tēr), *n.* 1. one who perambulates. 2. [Chiefly Brit.], a baby carriage.
**per an·num** (pēr an′əm), [L.], by the year; yearly.
**per·cale** (pēr-kāl′, -kal′), *n.* [Fr. < Per. *pargāl*], closely woven cotton cloth, used for sheets, etc.
**per cap·i·ta** (pēr kap′ə-tə), [L., lit., by heads], for each person.
**per·ceive** (pēr-sēv′), *v.t. & v.i.* [-CEIVED, -CEIVING], [< OFr. < L. *per,* through + *capere,* to take], 1. to grasp or take in mentally. 2. to become aware (of) through the senses. **—per·ceiv′a·ble,** *adj.* **—per·ceiv′a·bly,** *adv.*
**per·cent** (pēr-sent′), *n.* per cent.
**per cent,** [L. *per centum*], in, to, or for every hundred: as, 10 *per cent* of 50 = $^{10}/_{100}$ of 50 = 5: symbol, %. *n.* 1. [Colloq.], percentage. 2. *pl.* bonds, etc. bearing regular interest of a (stated) per cent: as, the three *per cents.*
**per·cent·age** (pēr-sen′tij), *n.* 1. a given rate or proportion in every hundred. 2. any quantity stated in per cent. 3. part; portion: as, only a small *percentage* won. 4. [Colloq.], use; advantage.
**per·cen·tile** (pēr-sen′til, -tīl), *n.* in *statistics,* 1. any value in a series dividing the distribution of its members into 100 groups of equal frequency. 2. any of these groups. *adj.* of a percentile.
**per cen·tum** (pēr sen′təm), [L.], by the hundred: abbrev. **per cent.**: symbol, %.
**per·cept** (pũr′sept), *n.* [< L. < *percipere,* to perceive], a recognizable sensation or impression received by the mind through the senses.
**per·cep·ti·ble** (pēr-sep′tə-b'l), *adj.* that can be perceived. **—per·cep′ti·bil′i·ty,** *n.* **—per·cep′ti·bly,** *adv.*
**per·cep·tion** (pēr-sep′shən), *n.* 1. consciousness. 2. the awareness of objects or other data through the senses. 3. the process or faculty of perceiving. 4. knowledge, etc. gained by perceiving. 5. insight; intuition. **—per·cep′tion·al,** *adj.*
**per·cep·tive** (pēr-sep′tiv), *adj.* 1. of perception. 2. capable of perceiving; esp., perceiving readily. **—per·cep′tive·ly,** *adv.* **—per·cep′tive·ness, per′cep·tiv′i·ty** (pũr′-), *n.*
**perch** (pũrch), *n.* [*pl.* PERCH, PERCHES; see PLURAL, II, D, 2], [< OFr. < L. < Gr. < *perknos,* dark], 1. a small, spiny-finned, fresh-water food fish. 2. any of several similar marine fishes.
**perch** (pũrch), *n.* [< OFr. < L. *pertica,* a pole], 1. a horizontal pole, branch, etc. serving as a roost for birds. 2. any resting place, especially a high or insecure one. 3. a measure of length, equal to 5½ yards. 4. a measure of area, equal to 30¼ square yards. *v.i. & v.t.* to alight and rest, or place, on or as on a perch. **—perch′er,** *n.*
**per·chance** (pēr-chans′, -chäns′), *adv.* [< OFr. *par,* by + *chance,* chance], [Archaic or Poetic], 1. by chance. 2. perhaps; possibly.
**Per·che·ron** (pũr′chə-ron′, -shə-), *n.* [Fr. < Le *Perche,* district of France], a breed of large, fast-trotting draft horses: also **Percheron Norman.**
**per·cip·i·ent** (pēr-sip′i-ənt), *adj.* perceiving, especially keenly or readily. *n.* one who perceives. **—per·cip′i·ence, per·cip′i·en·cy,** *n.*
**Per·ci·vale, Per·ci·val** (pũr′sə-v'l), *n.* in *Arthurian legend,* a knight who glimpsed the Holy Grail.
**per·co·late** (pũr′kə-lāt′), *v.t.* [-LATED, -LATING], [< L. pp. < *per,* through + *colare,* to strain], 1. to pass (a liquid) gradually through a porous substance; filter. 2. to drain or ooze through (a porous substance); permeate. 3. to brew (coffee) in a percolator. *v.i.* to ooze through a porous substance. **—per′co·la′tion,** *n.*
**per·co·la·tor** (pũr′kə-lā′tēr), *n.* a coffeepot in which boiling water bubbles up through a tube and filters back down through the coffee grounds.
**per·cus·sion** (pēr-kush′ən), *n.* [< L. < *percussus,* pp. of *percutere,* to strike], 1. the hitting of one body against another, as the hammer of a firearm against a powder cap (**percussion cap**). 2. the impact of sound waves on the ear. 3. in *medicine,* the tapping of the chest, back, etc. with the fingers to determine from the sound produced the state of any of the internal organs. **—per·cus′sive,** *adj.* **—per·cus′sor,** *n.*
**percussion instrument,** a musical instrument in which the tone is produced when some part is struck, as the drums, cymbals, xylophone, etc.
**per diem** (pēr dī′əm), [L.], daily; by the day.
**per·di·tion** (pēr-dish′ən), *n.* [< OFr. < L. < pp. of *perdere,* to lose], 1. complete and irreparable loss; ruin. 2. in *theology, a*) the loss of the soul or of hope for salvation; damnation. *b*) hell.
‡**père** (pâr), *n.* [Fr.], father: often used after the surname, like English *Senior,* as, Dumas *père.*
**per·e·gri·nate** (per′ə-gri-nāt′), *v.t. & v.i.* [-NATED, -NATING], [< L. pp. of *peregrinari* < *peregrinus;* see PILGRIM], to travel (along); journey. **—per′e·gri·na′tion,** *n.* **—per′e·gri·na′tor,** *n.*
**per·e·grine (falcon)** (per′ə-grin, -grīn′), [see prec. entry], a large, swift falcon.
**per·emp·to·ry** (pēr-emp′tēr-i; *occas.* per′əmp-tôr′i, -tō′ri), *adj.* [< Fr. < L. pp. of *perimere,* to destroy < *per-,* intens. + *emere,* to take], 1. in *law,* barring further action, debate, etc.; final; decisive. 2. that cannot be denied, delayed, etc., as a command. 3. intolerantly positive; dogmatic: as, a *peremptory* manner. **—per·emp′to·ri·ly,** *adv.* **—per·emp′to·ri·ness,** *n.*
**per·en·ni·al** (pə-ren′i-əl), *adj.* [< L. < *per,* through + *annus,* a year], 1. lasting or active throughout the whole year. 2. continuing for a long time: as, a *perennial* youth. 3. becoming active again and again; perpetual. 4. having a life cycle of more than two years: said of plants. *n.* a perennial plant. **—per·en′ni·al·ly,** *adv.*
**perf.,** 1. perfect. 2. perforated.
**per·fect** (pũr′fikt; *for v., usually* pēr-fekt′), *adj.* [< OFr. < L. *perfectus,* finished; ult. < *per,* through + *facere,* to do], 1. complete in all respects; flawless. 2. in a condition of excellence, as in skill or quality. 3. completely accurate; exact: as, a *perfect* copy. 4. sheer; utter: as, a *perfect* fool. 5. in *grammar,* expressing a state or action completed at the time of speaking or at the time indicated: verbs have three perfect tenses; present perfect, past perfect, and future perfect. 6. in *music,* designating an interval, as an octave, whose character is not altered by inversion. *v.t.* 1. to bring to completion. 2. to make perfect or more nearly perfect according to a given standard, as by training, etc. *n.* 1. the perfect tense. 2. a verb form in this tense. **—per·fect′er,** *n.* **—per′fect·ly,** *adv.* **—per′fect·ness,** *n.*
**per·fect·i·ble** (pēr-fek′tə-b'l), *adj.* that can become, or be made, perfect. **—per·fect′i·bil′i·ty,** *n.*
**per·fec·tion** (pēr-fek′shən), *n.* 1. the act or process of perfecting. 2. a being perfect. 3. a person or thing that is the perfect embodiment of some quality. **—to perfection,** completely; perfectly.
**per·fec·tion·ist** (pēr-fek′shən-ist), *n.* a person who strives for perfection.
**per·fec·tive** (pēr-fek′tiv), *adj.* tending to bring to perfection. **—per·fec′tive·ly,** *adv.* **—per·fec′tive·ness,** *n.*

**per·fec·to** (pẽr-fek'tō), *n.* [*pl.* -TOS], [Sp., perfect], a cigar of standard shape, thick in the center and tapering to a point at either end.

**perfect participle,** the past participle.

**per·fer·vid** (pẽr-fũr'vid), *adj.* extremely fervid.

**per·fi·dy** (pũr'fə-di), *n.* [*pl.* -DIES], [< Fr. < L. *perfidia* < *per*, through +*fides*, faith], betrayal of trust; treachery. —**per·fid'i·ous** (pẽr-fid'i-əs), *adj.* —**per·fid'i·ous·ly,** *adv.*

**per·fo·li·ate** (pẽr-fō'li-it, -āt'), *adj.* [< *per*, through + L. *folium*, a leaf; + *-ate*], having a stem that seems to pass through it: said of a leaf.

**per·fo·rate** (pũr'fə-rāt'; *for adj., usually* -rit), *v.t. & v.i.* [-RATED, -RATING], [< L. pp. < *per*, through + *forare*, to bore], 1. to make a hole or holes through, as by boring or punching. 2. to pierce with holes in a row, as a pattern, etc. *adj.* pierced with holes: also **per'fo·rat'ed.** —**per'fo·ra'tive,** *adj.* —**per'fo·ra'tor,** *n.*

**per·fo·ra·tion** (pũr'fə-rā'shən), *n.* 1. a perforating or being perforated. 2. a hole or any of a series of holes, as between postage stamps on a sheet.

**per·force** (pẽr-fôrs', -fōrs'), *adv.* [< OFr.; see PER & FORCE], of or through necessity; necessarily. *n.* [Rare], necessity.

**per·form** (pẽr-fôrm'), *v.t.* [< OFr. *parfournir*, to consummate < *par* (< L. *per-*, intens.) + *fornir*, to accomplish], 1. to do, as a task, process, etc. 2. to fulfill, as a promise. 3. to render or enact, as a piece of music, dramatic role, etc. *v.i.* to execute an action or process; esp., to give a public exhibition of skill. —**per·form'er,** *n.*

**per·form·ance** (pẽr-fôr'məns), *n.* 1. the act of performing; accomplishment. 2. functioning, usually with regard to effectiveness, as of an airplane. 3. deed or feat. 4. a formal exhibition of skill or talent, as a play, etc.; show.

**per·fume** (pẽr-fūm'; *for n., usually* pũr'fūm), *v.t.* [-FUMED, -FUMING], [< Fr. < It. < L. *per-*, intens. + *fumare*, to smoke], to scent with perfume. *n.* 1. a sweet scent; fragrance. 2. a substance producing a pleasing odor, as a liquid extract of the scent of flowers.

**per·fum·er** (pẽr-fūm'ẽr), *n.* 1. one who makes or sells perfumes. 2. one who or that which perfumes.

**per·fum·er·y** (pẽr-fūm'ẽr-i), *n.* [*pl.* -IES], 1. the trade of a perfumer. 2. perfumes collectively. 3. a place where perfume is made or sold.

**per·func·to·ry** (pẽr-fuŋk'tẽr-i), *adj.* [< LL. < L. pp. < *per-*, intens. + *fungi*, to perform], 1. done merely as a routine; superficial: as, a *perfunctory* examination. 2. without concern; indifferent: as, a *perfunctory* speaker. —**per·func'to·ri·ly,** *adv.* —**per·func'to·ri·ness,** *n.*

**per·go·la** (pũr'gə-lə), *n.* [It., arbor < L. < *pergere*, to proceed], a tunnel-shaped structure of latticework, on which climbing plants are grown.

**per·haps** (pẽr-haps', -aps'), *adv.* [*per-* + pl. of *hap*, chance], 1. possibly; probably. 2. by chance.

**pe·ri** (pêr'i), *n.* [Per. *parī*], in *Persian mythology*, a fairy or elf.

**per·i-,** [< Gr. *peri-*], a prefix meaning: 1. *around, about*, as in *periscope*. 2. *near*, as in *perigee*.

**per·i·anth** (per'i-anth'), *n.* [Fr. < Gr. *peri-*, around + *anthos*, a flower], the envelope of a flower, especially one in which the calyx and corolla are indistinguishable.

**per·i·car·di·tis** (per'i-kär-dī'tis), *n.* inflammation of the pericardium.

**per·i·car·di·um** (per'ə-kär'di-əm), *n.* [*pl.* -DIA (-di-ə)], [< Gr. < *peri-*, around + *kardia*, heart], the thin, membranous sac around the heart. —**per'i·car'di·al, per'i·car'di·ac,** *adj.*

**per·i·carp** (per'ə-kärp'), *n.* [< Fr. < Gr. < *peri-*, around + *karpos*, a fruit], in *botany*, the wall of a ripened ovary. —**per'i·car'pi·al,** *adj.*

**Per·i·cles** (per'ə-klēz'), *n.* Athenian statesman and general; ?-429 B.C. —**Per'i·cle'an** (-klē'ən), *adj.*

**per·i·cra·ni·um** (per'ə-krā'ni-əm), *n.* [*pl.* -NIA (-ni-ə)], [< Gr. < *peri-*, around + *kranion*, skull], the tough membrane covering the skull.

**per·i·gee** (per'ə-jē'), *n.* [< Fr.; ult. < Gr. *peri-*, around + *gē*, the earth], the point nearest to the earth in the orbit of the moon or of a man-made satellite: cf. *apogee*. —**per'i·ge'an, per'i·ge'al,** *adj.*

**per·i·he·li·on** (per'ə-hē'li-ən), *n.* [*pl.* -LIA (-li-ə)], [< Gr. *peri-*, around + *hēlios*, the sun], that point in the orbit of a planet or comet nearest the sun: cf. *aphelion*.

**per·il** (per'əl), *n.* [OFr. < L. *periculum*, danger], exposure to harm or injury; risk. *v.t.* [-ILED or -ILLED, -ILING or -ILLING], to expose to danger; risk.

**per·il·ous** (per'ə-ləs), *adj.* involving peril or risk; dangerous. —**per'il·ous·ly,** *adv.*

**per·im·e·ter** (pə-rim'ə-tẽr), *n.* [< L. < Gr. < *peri-*, around + *metron*, a measure], 1. the outer boundary of a figure or area. 2. the total length of this. —**per·i·met·ric** (per'ə-met'rik), **per'i·met'ri·cal,** *adj.*

**per·i·ne·um** (per'ə-nē'əm), *n.* [*pl.* -NEA (-nē'ə)], [< LL. < Gr. < *peri-*, around + *inaō*, I discharge], the small triangular region between the thighs, including the anus and the vulva or the base of the penis. —**per'i·ne'al,** *adj.*

**pe·ri·od** (pêr'i-əd), *n.* [< Fr. < L. < Gr. *periodos*, a cycle < *peri-*, around + *hodos*, way], 1. the interval between the successive occurrences of an astronomical event, as between two full moons. 2. a portion of time distinguished by certain processes, characteristics, etc.; stage: as, a *period* of change. 3. any of the portions of time into which a game, school day, etc. is divided. 4. the full course or one of the stages of a disease. 5. the menses. 6. an end or conclusion: as, death put a *period* to his plans. 7. in *geology*, a subdivision of a geological era. 8. in *grammar*, *a*) a complete sentence. *b*) the pause in speaking or the mark of punctuation (.) used at the end of a sentence. *c*) the dot (.) following most abbreviations. 9. in *physics*, the interval of time necessary for a complete cycle of a regularly recurring motion. *adj.* of or like that of a certain period or age: as, *period* furniture.

**pe·ri·od·ic** (pêr'i-od'ik), *adj.* 1. appearing or recurring at regular intervals: as, a *periodic* fever. 2. occurring from time to time; intermittent. 3. of or characterized by periods. 4. of a sentence (**periodic sentence**) in which the essential elements are withheld until the end.

**pe·ri·od·i·cal** (pêr'i-od'i-k'l), *adj.* 1. periodic. 2. of a periodical. 3. published at regular intervals of more than one day. *n.* a publication appearing at such intervals. —**pe'ri·od'i·cal·ly,** *adv.*

**pe·ri·o·dic·i·ty** (pêr'i-ə-dis'ə-ti), *n.* [*pl.* -TIES], a tendency to recur at regular intervals.

**periodic law,** the law that properties of chemical elements recur periodically when the elements are arranged in order of their atomic numbers.

**periodic table,** an arrangement of the chemical elements according to their atomic numbers, to exhibit the periodic law by their groupings.

**per·i·o·don·tics** (per'i-ə-don'tiks), *n.pl.* [construed as sing.] [*peri* + *-odont* + *-ics*], the branch of dentistry concerned with diseases of the bone and tissue supporting the teeth.

**per·i·os·te·um** (per'i-os'ti-əm), *n.* [*pl.* -TEA (-ti-ə)], [< L. < Gr. < *peri-*, around + *osteon*, a bone], the membrane of connective tissue covering all bones except at the joints. —**per'i·os'te·al,** *adj.*

**per·i·pa·tet·ic** (per'i-pə-tet'ik), *adj.* [< L. < Gr.; ult. < *peri-*, around + *patein*, to walk], 1. [P-], of the philosophy or followers of Aristotle, who walked about while he was teaching. 2. walking or moving about; itinerant. *n.* 1. [P-], a follower of Aristotle. 2. one who walks from place to place. —**per'i·pa·tet'i·cal·ly,** *adv.*

**pe·riph·er·al** (pə-rif'ẽr-əl), *adj.* 1. of or forming a periphery. 2. lying at the outside or away from the central part; outer. —**pe·riph'er·al·ly,** *adv.*

**pe·riph·er·y** (pə-rif'ẽr-i), *n.* [*pl.* -IES], [< Fr. < LL. < Gr. < *peri-*, around + *pherein*, to bear], 1. a boundary line or outside surface, especially of a rounded object. 2. surrounding space or area.

**pe·riph·ra·sis** (pə-rif'rə-sis), *n.* [*pl.* -SES (-sēz')], [L. < Gr. < *peri-*, around + *phrazein*, to speak], the use of many words where a few would do; roundabout way of speaking.

**per·i·phras·tic** (per'ə-fras'tik), *adj.* 1. of, like, or expressed in periphrasis. 2. in *grammar*, formed with a particle or auxiliary verb instead of by inflection (e.g., "she did sing" for "she sang"). —**per'i·phras'ti·cal·ly,** *adv.*

**pe·rique** (pə-rēk'), *n.* [Fr.] a strong, black tobacco grown in Louisiana: used in blending.

**per·i·scope** (per'ə-skōp'), *n.* [*peri-* + *-scope*], an optical instrument consisting of a tube equipped with prisms or mirrors arranged in series so that a person looking through one end can see objects in range of the other end: used especially on submerged submarines to scan the surface. —**per'i·scop'ic** (-skop'ik), **per'i·scop'i·cal,** *adj.*

**per·ish** (per'ish), *v.i.* [< OFr. < L. *perire*, to perish < *per-*, intens. + *ire*, to go], to be utterly destroyed or ruined; specif., to die a violent or untimely death. —**perish the thought!** do not even consider such a possibility!

**per·ish·a·ble** (per′ish-ə-b'l), *adj.* that may perish; liable to spoil, as some foods. *n.* something, as a food, liable to spoil or deteriorate. —**per′ish·a·ble·ness, per′ish·a·bil′i·ty,** *n.*

**per·i·stal·sis** (per′ə-stal′sis), *n.* [*pl.* -SES (-sēz)], [< Gr. < *peri-*, around + *stellein*, to place], the wavelike muscular contractions and dilations of the walls of the alimentary canal and certain other hollow organs, that move the contents onward. —**per′i·stal′tic,** *adj.*

**per·i·style** (per′ə-stil′), *n.* [< Fr. < L. < Gr. < *peri-*, around + *stylos*, a column], 1. a row of columns forming an enclosure or supporting a roof. 2. any space, as a court, so formed. —**per′i·sty′lar,** *adj.*

**per·i·to·ne·um, per·i·to·nae·um** (per′i-tə-nē′əm), *n.* [*pl.* -NEA, -NAEA (-nē′ə)], [< LL. < Gr. < *peri-*, around + *teinein*, to stretch], the serous membrane lining the abdominal cavity and covering the visceral organs. —**per′i·to·ne′al, per′i·to·nae′al,** *adj.*

**per·i·to·ni·tis** (per′i-tə-nī′tis), *n.* inflammation of the peritoneum.

**per·i·wig** (per′ə-wig′), *n.* [earlier *perwyke;* altered < Fr. *perruque;* see PERUKE], a wig.

**per·i·win·kle** (per′ə-wiŋ′k'l), *n.* [< AS. < L. *pervinca*], a creeping plant with evergreen leaves and white or blue flowers; myrtle.

**per·i·win·kle** (per′ə-wiŋ′k'l), *n.* [AS. *perwynke*], 1. any of various small salt-water snails having a thick, cone-shaped shell. 2. such a shell.

**per·jure** (pũr′jẽr), *v.t.* [-JURED, -JURING], [< OFr. < L. < *per*, through + *jurare*, to swear], to make (oneself) guilty of perjury by speaking falsely under oath. —**per′jur·er,** *n.*

**per·jured** (pũr′jẽrd), *adj.* guilty of perjury.

**per·ju·ry** (pũr′jẽr-i), *n.* [*pl.* -RIES], [< OFr. < L. < *perjurus*, false], 1. the willful telling of a lie while under oath. 2. the breaking of any oath.

**perk** (pũrk), *v.t.* [ME. *perken;* prob. < ONorm. Fr. *perquer*, to perch], 1. to raise, as the head, briskly (often with *up*). 2. to make (oneself) smart in appearance (often with *up* or *out*). *v.i.* 1. to straighten one's posture, as in acting jaunty. 2. to become lively or animated (with *up*).

**perk** (pũrk), *v.t. & v.i.* [Colloq.], to percolate.

**perk·y** (pũr′ki), *adj.* [-IER, -IEST], 1. spirited; aggressive. 2. brisk; gay; saucy. —**perk′i·ly,** *adv.* —**perk′i·ness,** *n.*

**per·ma·nence** (pũr′mə-nəns), *n.* the state or quality of being permanent.

**per·ma·nen·cy** (pũr′mə-nən-si), *n.* 1. permanence. 2. [*pl.* -CIES], something permanent.

**per·ma·nent** (pũr′mə-nənt), *adj.* [OFr. < L. ppr. < *per*, through + *manere*, to remain], lasting or intended to last indefinitely or for a relatively long time. *n.* [Colloq.], a permanent wave. —**per′ma·nent·ly,** *adv.*

**permanent wave,** a hair wave produced by use of chemicals or heat and lasting for months.

**per·man·ga·nate** (pẽr-maŋ′gə-nāt′), *n.* a salt of permanganic acid, generally dark purple.

**per·man·gan·ic acid** (pũr′man-gan′ik), an unstable acid, $HMnO_4$, that is an oxidizing agent.

**per·me·a·ble** (pũr′mi-ə-b'l), *adj.* that can be permeated, as by liquids. —**per′me·a·bil′i·ty,** *n.*

**per·me·ate** (pũr′mi-āt′), *v.t.* [-ATED, -ATING], [< L. pp. < *per*, through + *meare*, to glide], to pass into and affect every part of; spread through: as, water *permeates* blotting paper. *v.i.* to spread or diffuse (with *through* or *among*). —**per′me·a′tion, per′me·ance,** *n.* —**per′me·a′tive,** *adj.*

**Per·mi·an** (pũr′mi-ən), *adj.* [after *Perm*, former province of Russia], designating or of the geological period following the Pennsylvanian in the Paleozoic Era: see **geology,** chart. *n.* the Permian Period.

**per·mis·si·ble** (pẽr-mis′ə-b'l), *adj.* that can be permitted; allowable. —**per·mis′si·bil′i·ty,** *n.* —**per·mis′si·bly,** *adv.*

**per·mis·sion** (pẽr-mish′ən), *n.* the act of permitting; formal consent; leave.

**per·mis·sive** (pẽr-mis′iv), *adj.* 1. giving permission; allowing. 2. permitted; allowable. —**per·mis′sive·ly,** *adv.* —**per·mis′sive·ness,** *n.*

**per·mit** (pẽr-mit′; *for n., usually* pũr′mit), *v.t.* [-MITTED, -MITTING], [< L. < *per*, through + *mittere*, to send], 1. to allow to be done; consent to: as, smoking is not *permitted.* 2. to authorize; give leave: as, he *permitted* me to go. 3. to give opportunity for: as, an intermission *permits* conversation. *v.i.* to give opportunity: as, if time *permits.* *n.* 1. permission. 2. a document granting permission; license. —**per·mit′ter,** *n.*

**per·mu·ta·tion** (pũr′myoo-tā′shən), *n.* 1. a change; alteration. 2. any one of the combinations or changes in position possible within a group: as, the *permutations* of *1, 2,* and *3* are *123, 132, 213, 231, 312, 321.*

**per·mute** (pẽr-mūt′), *v.t.* [-MUTED, -MUTING], [< L. < *per-*, intens. + *mutare*, to change], 1. to make different; alter. 2. to rearrange the order or sequence of. —**per·mut′a·ble,** *adj.*

**Per·nam·bu·co** (pũr′nəm-bōō′kō; Port. per′nȧm-bōō′koo), *n.* Recife, a city of Brazil.

**per·ni·cious** (pẽr-nish′əs), *adj.* [< Fr. < L. < *per*, thoroughly + *necare*, to kill < *nex*, death], 1. causing injury, destruction, etc.; fatal. 2. [Rare], wicked; evil. —**per·ni′cious·ly,** *adv.* —**per·ni′cious·ness,** *n.*

**pernicious anemia,** a severe form of anemia characterized by a reduction of the red blood cells, weakness, nervous disturbances, etc.

**per·nick·e·ty** (pẽr-nik′ə-ti), *adj.* [< Scot. dial.], [Colloq.], 1. too particular or precise; fussy. 2. showing or requiring extremely careful treatment.

**per·o·rate** (per′ə-rāt′), *v.i.* [-RATED, -RATING], [see PERORATION], 1. to give an oration; declaim. 2. to sum up or conclude a speech.

**per·o·ra·tion** (per′ə-rā′shən), *n.* [< L. pp. < *per*, through + *orare*, to speak], the concluding part of a speech, including a summing up.

**per·ox·ide** (pẽr-ok′sid), *n.* [*per-* + *oxide*], any oxide containing the oxygen ($O_2$) group linked by a single bond; specif., hydrogen peroxide: also **per·ox′id** (-sid). *v.t.* [-IDED, -IDING], to bleach with hydrogen peroxide. *adj.* bleached with hydrogen peroxide: as, *peroxide* hair.

**per·pen·dic·u·lar** (pũr′pən-dik′yoo-lẽr), *adj.* [< OFr. < L. < *perpendiculum*, plumb line < *per-*, intens. + *pendere*, to hang], 1. at right angles to a given line or plane. 2. exactly upright; vertical. *n.* 1. a line at right angles to the plane of the horizon, or to another line or plane. 2. a perpendicular position. —**per′pen·dic′u·lar′i·ty** (-lar′ə-ti), *n.* —**per′pen·dic′u·lar·ly,** *adv.*

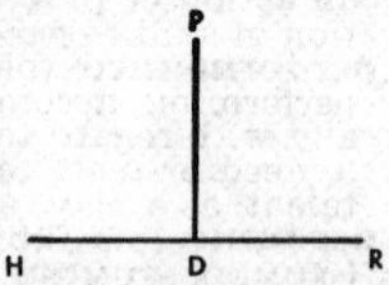

PERPENDICULAR
PD, perpendicular to HR

**per·pe·trate** (pũr′pə-trāt′), *v.t.* [-TRATED, -TRATING], [< L. pp. < *per*, thoroughly + *patrare*, to effect], to do (something evil, criminal, or offensive); commit (a blunder), impose (a hoax), etc. —**per′pe·tra′tion,** *n.* —**per′pe·tra′tor,** *n.*

**per·pet·u·al** (pẽr-pech′ōō-əl), *adj.* [< OFr. < L. < *perpetuus*, constant], 1. lasting forever or for an indefinitely long time. 2. continuing indefinitely without interruption; constant: as, a *perpetual* nuisance. —**per·pet′u·al·ly,** *adv.*

**perpetual motion,** the motion of a hypothetical device which, once set in motion, would operate indefinitely by creating its own energy.

**per·pet·u·ate** (pẽr-pech′ōō-āt′), *v.t.* [-ATED, -ATING], to make perpetual; cause to continue or be remembered. —**per·pet′u·a′tion,** *n.* —**per·pet′u·a′tor,** *n.*

**per·pe·tu·i·ty** (pũr′pə-tōō′ə-ti, -tū′-), *n.* [*pl.* -TIES], 1. a being perpetual. 2. something perpetual, as a pension to be paid indefinitely. 3. unlimited time; eternity. —**in perpetuity,** forever.

**per·plex** (pẽr-pleks′), *v.t.* [< OFr. < L. *perplexus*, confused < *per*, through + pp. of *plectere*, to twist], 1. to make (a person) uncertain, hesitant, etc.; bewilder. 2. to make intricate or complicated. —**per·plexed′,** *adj.* —**per·plex′ed·ly,** *adv.* —**per·plex′ing,** *adj.* —**per·plex′ing·ly,** *adv.*

**per·plex·i·ty** (pẽr-plek′sə-ti), *n.* 1. the state of being perplexed; bewilderment. 2. [*pl.* -TIES], something that perplexes or is perplexed.

**per·qui·site** (pũr′kwə-zit), *n.* [< ML. < L. pp. < *per-*, intens. + *quaerere*, to seek], 1. something additional to regular profit or pay, resulting from one's employment. 2. a prerogative or right, by virtue of status, position, etc.

**Per·ry, Matthew Cal·braith** (kal′breth per′i), 1794–1858; brother of *Oliver;* U.S. commodore.

**Perry, Oliver Haz·ard** (haz′ẽrd), 1785–1819; U.S. naval officer.

**Pers.,** 1. Persia. 2. Persian.

**pers.,** 1. person. 2. personal.

**per se** (pũr′sē′), [L.], by (or in) itself; inherently.

**per·se·cute** (pũr′sə-kūt′), *v.t.* [-CUTED, -CUTING], [< Fr. < L. *persequi*, to pursue < *per*, through + *sequi*, to follow], 1. to afflict constantly so as to injure or distress, especially for reasons of religion, politics, or race. 2. to annoy constantly: as, *persecuted* by mosquitoes. —**per′se·cu′tion,** *n.* —**per′se·cu′tive,** *adj.* —**per′se·cu′tor,** *n.*

**Per·seph·o·ne** (pẽr-sef′ə-ni), *n.* in *Gr. mythology*, the daughter of Zeus and Demeter, abducted by Hades (Pluto) and made his wife: identified by the Romans with Proserpina.

**Per·seus** (pũr′sūs, -si-əs), *n.* 1. in *Gr. mythology*, the son of Zeus and slayer of Medusa: he married

Andromeda after rescuing her from a sea monster. 2. a northern constellation.

**per·se·ver·ance** (pũr′sə-vêr′əns), *n.* 1. the act of persevering. 2. persistence; steadfastness.

**per·se·vere** (pũr′sə-vêr′), *v.i.* [-VERED, -VERING], [< OFr. < L. *perseverus* < *per-*, intens. + *severus*, severe], to continue doing something in spite of difficulty, opposition, etc.; persist. —**per′se·ver′ing,** *adj.* —**per′se·ver′ing·ly,** *adv.*

**Per·shing, John Joseph** (pũr′shiŋ), 1860–1948; U.S. commanding general in World War I.

**Per·sia** (pũr′zhə, -shə), *n.* 1. the Persian Empire. 2. Iran, a country in W Asia: the former name.

**Per·sian** (pũr′zhen, -shən), *adj.* of Persia, its people, their language, etc.; Iranian. *n.* 1. a native or inhabitant of Persia. 2. the Iranian language of the Persians.

**Persian Empire,** an empire of SW Asia, from the Indus River to the Mediterranean: it was destroyed by Alexander the Great in 331 B.C.

**Persian Gulf,** an arm of the Arabian Sea, between Arabia and Iran.

**Persian lamb,** 1. the lamb of certain Asiatic sheep. 2. its black, gray, or brown curly fleece.

**Persian rug** (or **carpet**), an Oriental rug made in Persia, with a richly colored, intricate pattern.

**per·si·flage** (pũr′si-fläzh′), *n.* [Fr. < *persifler*, to banter < L. *per* + Fr. *siffler*, to whistle], 1. a light, frivolous style of writing or speaking. 2. talk or writing of this kind; banter.

**per·sim·mon** (pẽr-sim′ən), *n.* [< Am. Ind.], 1. any of various trees with white flowers, hard wood, and plumlike fruit. 2. the fruit, sour and astringent when green, but sweet and edible when ripe.

**per·sist** (pẽr-sist′, -zist′), *v.i.* [< Fr. < L. < *per*, through + *sistere*, to cause to stand], 1. to refuse to give up, especially when faced with opposition. 2. to continue insistently, as in repeating a question. 3. to endure; remain; last.

**per·sist·ence** (pẽr-sis′təns, -zis′-), *n.* 1. a persisting; stubborn continuance. 2. a persistent quality; resoluteness. 3. continuous existence; endurance, as of a headache. Also **per·sist′en·cy.**

**per·sist·ent** (pẽr-sis′tənt, -zis′-), *adj.* 1. continuing, especially in the face of opposition, etc.; stubborn. 2. continuing to exist or endure. 3. constantly repeated; continued. —**per·sist′ent·ly,** *adv.*

**per·snick·e·ty** (pẽr-snik′ə-ti), *adj.* [Colloq.], pernickety.

**per·son** (pũr′s'n), *n.* [< OFr. < L. *persona*, lit., actor's mask, hence a person], 1. a human being; individual man, woman, or child: as, no *person* saw it. 2. *a*) a living human body. *b*) bodily appearance: as, she was clean about her *person*. 3. personality; self. 4. in *grammar*, *a*) division into three classes of pronouns (**personal pronouns**), and, usually, corresponding verb forms, to identify the subject, thus: the *first person* (*I* or *we*) is used for the speaker; the *second person* (*you*) for the subject spoken to; the *third person* (*he, she, it,* or *they*) for the subject spoken of. *b*) any of these classes. 5. in *law*, any individual or incorporated group having certain legal rights and responsibilities. —**in person,** in the flesh; in bodily presence.

**per·so·na** (pẽr-sō′nə), *n.* [*pl.* -NAE (-nē)], [L.], 1. a person 2. *pl.* the characters of a novel, play, etc.

**per·son·a·ble** (pũr′s'n-ə-b'l), *adj.* having an attractive personal appearance; handsome; comely.

**per·son·age** (pũr′s'n-ij), *n.* 1. an important person; notable. 2. a person. 3. a character in history, a book, play, etc.

**‡per·so·na gra·ta** (pẽr-sō′nə grā′tə, grä′-), [L.], one who is acceptable, or always welcome.

**per·son·al** (pũr′s'n-əl), *adj.* 1. private; individual. 2. done in person or by oneself: as, a *personal* interview. 3. of the body or physical appearance. 4. having to do with the character, conduct, etc. of a certain person: as, a *personal* remark. 5. tending to be inquisitive about the private affairs of others. 6. of or like a person or rational being: as, a *personal* God. 7. in *grammar*, indicating person: see **person** (sense 4). 8. in *law*, of property (**personal property**) that is movable or not attached to the land. *n.* 1. a local news item about a person or persons. 2. a newspaper advertisement about a personal matter.

**per·son·al·i·ty** (pũr′sə-nal′ə-ti), *n.* [*pl.* -TIES], 1. the quality or fact of being a person. 2. the quality or fact of being a particular person; individuality. 3. distinctive individual qualities of a person, collectively. 4. the sum of such qualities as impressing others: as, she has *personality*. 5. a person; esp., a notable person. 6. *usually pl.* any offensive remark aimed at a person.

**per·son·al·ize** (pũr′s'n-əl-īz′), *v.t.* [-IZED, -IZING], 1. to make personal; apply to a specific person. 2. to personify. 3. to have printed with one's name: as, *personalized* checks.

**per·son·al·ly** (pũr′s'n-əl-i), *adv.* 1. without the use of others; in person. 2. as a person: as, I dislike him *personally*. 3. in one's own opinion: as, *personally*, I'd rather not go. 4. as though directed at oneself: as, to take a remark *personally*.

**per·son·al·ty** (pũr′s'n-əl-ti), *n.* [*pl.* -TIES], personal property: see **personal** (sense 8).

**‡per·so·na non gra·ta** (pẽr-sō′nə non grā′tə, grä′-), [L.], a person who is not acceptable.

**per·son·ate** (pũr′s'n-āt′), *v.t.* [-ATED, -ATING], 1. to act the part of, as in a drama. 2. in *law*, to assume the identity of with intent to defraud. —**per′son·a′tion,** *n.* —**per′son·a′tive,** *adj.* —**per′son·a′tor,** *n.*

**per·son·i·fi·ca·tion** (pẽr-son′ə-fi-kā′shən), *n.* 1. a personifying or being personified. 2. a person or thing thought of as representing some quality, idea, etc.; perfect example: as, Cupid is the *personification* of love. 3. a figure of speech in which a thing or idea is represented as a person.

**per·son·i·fy** (pẽr-son′ə-fī′), *v.t.* [-FIED, -FYING], 1. to think or speak of (a thing) as a person: as, we *personify* a ship by referring to it as "she." 2. to symbolize (an abstract idea) by a human figure, as in art. 3. to be a perfect example of (something); typify. —**per·son′i·fi′er,** *n.*

**per·son·nel** (pũr′sə-nel′), *n.* [Fr.], persons employed in any work, enterprise, service, etc. *adj.* of or in charge of personnel.

**per·spec·tive** (pẽr-spek′tiv), *adj.* [< LL. *perspectivus* < L. < *per*, through + *specere*, to look], 1. of perspective. 2. drawn in perspective. *n.* 1. the art of picturing objects or a scene as they appear to the eye with reference to relative distance or depth. 2. *a*) the appearance of objects as determined by their relative distance and positions. *b*) the effect of relative distance and position. 3. the relationship of the parts of a whole, regarded from a particular standpoint or point in time. 4. a proper evaluation with proportional importance given to the component parts.

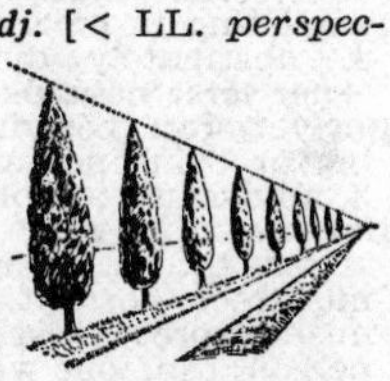
PERSPECTIVE

**per·spi·ca·cious** (pũr′spi-kā′shəs), *adj.* [< L. < *perspicere*, to see through], having keen judgment or understanding; discerning. —**per′spi·ca′cious·ly,** *adv.* —**per′spi·cac′i·ty** (-kas′ə-ti), *n.*

**per·spic·u·ous** (pẽr-spik′ū-əs), *adj.* [L. *perspicuus*, transparent < *perspicere*, to see through], clear in statement or expression; easily understood; lucid. —**per·spi·cu·i·ty** (pũr′spi-kū′ə-ti), **per·spic′u·ous·ness,** *n.* —**per·spic′u·ous·ly,** *adv.*

**per·spi·ra·tion** (pũr′spə-rā′shən), *n.* [Fr.], 1. a perspiring, or sweating. 2. sweat. —**per·spir·a·to·ry** (pẽr-spīr′ə-tôr′i, -tō′ri), *adj.*

**per·spire** (pẽr-spīr′), *v.t. & v.i.* [-SPIRED, -SPIRING], [< Fr. < L. < *per*, through + *spirare*, to breathe], to give forth (a characteristic salty moisture) through the pores of the skin; sweat.

**per·suade** (pẽr-swād′), *v.t.* [-SUADED, -SUADING], [< Fr. < L. < *per-*, intens. + *suadere*, to urge], to cause (someone) to do or believe something, especially by reasoning, urging, etc.; induce; convince. —**per·suad′a·ble,** *adj.* —**per·suad′er,** *n.*

**per·sua·sion** (pẽr-swā′zhən), *n.* 1. a persuading or being persuaded. 2. power of persuading. 3. a strong belief; conviction. 4. a particular religious belief. 5. a particular sect, group, etc. 6. [Colloq.], kind, sex, etc.: used humorously.

**per·sua·sive** (pẽr-swā′siv), *adj.* having the power, or tending, to persuade. —**per·sua′sive·ly,** *adv.* —**per·sua′sive·ness,** *n.*

**pert** (pũrt), *adj.* [contr. < ME. & OFr. *apert* < L. *apertus*, open], 1. bold or impudent in speech or behavior; saucy. 2. [Dial.], lively; brisk. —**pert′ly,** *adv.* —**pert′ness,** *n.*

**per·tain** (pẽr-tān′), *v.i.* [< OFr. < L. *pertinere*, to reach < *per-*, intens. + *tenere*, to hold], 1. to belong; be connected or associated; be a part. 2. to be appropriate: as, conduct that *pertains* to a gentleman. 3. to have reference: as, his remark did not *pertain* to the question.

**Perth** (pũrth), *n.* seaport and capital of Western Australia: pop., 351,000.

**per·ti·na·cious** (pũr′tə-nā′shəs), *adj.* [< L. *pertinax*, firm < *per-*, intens. + *tenax*, holding fast], 1. holding firmly or stubbornly to some purpose, belief, or action. 2. hard to get rid of; persistent. —**per′ti·na′cious·ly,** *adv.* —**per′ti·nac′i·ty** (-nas′ə-ti), **per′ti·na′cious·ness,** *n.*

**per·ti·nent** (pũr′t'n-ənt), *adj.* [< L. ppr. of *pertinere;* see PERTAIN], of or connected with the matter at hand; relevant. —**per′ti·nence, per′ti·nen·cy,** *n.* —**per′ti·nent·ly,** *adv.*

**per·turb** (pẽr-tũrb′), *v.t.* [< OFr. < L. < *per-*, intens. + *turbare*, to disturb], to cause to be alarmed, agitated, or upset; disturb or trouble greatly. —**per·turb′a·ble,** *adj.* —**per·tur·ba·tion** (pũr′tẽr-bā′shən), *n.* —**per·turb′ed·ly,** *adv.*

**Pe·ru** (pə-rōō′), *n.* a country in South America, on the Pacific: area, 482,133 sq .mi.; pop., 12,385,000; capital, Lima. —**Pe·ru′vi·an** (-vi-ən), *adj. & n.*

**pe·ruke** (pə-rook′), *n.* [< Fr. *perruque*], a wig.

**pe·rus·al** (pə-rōō′z'l), *n.* a perusing.

**pe·ruse** (pə-rōōz′), *v.t.* [-RUSED, -RUSING], [prob. < L. *per-*, intens.; + *use, v.*], 1. to read carefully; study. 2. to read. —**pe·rus′a·ble,** *adj.* —**pe·rus′er,** *n.*

**Peruvian bark,** cinchona.

**per·vade** (pẽr-vād′), *v.t.* [-VADED, -VADING], [< L. < *per*, through + *vadere*, to go], 1. to pass through; spread throughout. 2. to be prevalent throughout. —**per·vad′er,** *n.* —**per·va′sion** (-vā′zhən), *n.*

**per·va·sive** (pẽr-vā′siv), *adj.* tending to pervade or spread throughout. —**per·va′sive·ly,** *adv.* —**per·va′sive·ness,** *n.*

**per·verse** (pẽr-vũrs′), *adj.* [< OFr. < L. pp. of *pervertere;* see PERVERT], 1. deviating from what is considered right or acceptable. 2. wicked. 3. persisting in error or fault; stubbornly contrary. 4. obstinately disobedient. —**per·verse′ly,** *adv.* —**per·verse′ness, per·ver′si·ty** [*pl.* -TIES], *n.*

**per·ver·sion** (pẽr-vũr′zhən, -shən), *n.* 1. a perverting or being perverted. 2. something perverted. 3. any sexual act or practice considered abnormal.

**per·vert** (pẽr-vũrt′; *for n.*, pũr′vẽrt), *v.t.* [< L. < *per-*, intens. + *vertere*, to turn], 1. to lead astray; misdirect; corrupt. 2. to misuse. 3. to distort; misinterpret; twist. 4. to debase. *n.* a perverted person; esp., one who practices sexual perversions. —**per·vert′ed,** *adj.* —**per·vert′er,** *n.* —**per·vert′i·ble,** *adj.*

**per·vi·ous** (pũr′vi-əs), *adj.* [< L. < *per*, through + *via*, way], 1. allowing passage through; permeable. 2. having a mind open to influence, argument, etc. —**per′vi·ous·ly,** *adv.* —**per′vi·ous·ness,** *n.*

**Pe·sach** (pā′säkh), *n.* [Heb. *pēsah*, a passing over], the Passover: see **Jewish holidays.**

**pe·se·ta** (pə-sā′tə; Sp. pe-se′tä), *n.* [Sp., dim. of *pesa*, a weight], a monetary unit and coin of Spain.

**pes·ky** (pes′ki), *adj.* [-KIER, -KIEST], [prob. var. of *pesty*], [Colloq.], annoying; troublesome. —**pes′ki·ness,** *n.*

**pe·so** (pā′sō; Sp. pe′sô), *n.* [*pl.* -SOS], [Sp. < L. *pensum*, something weighed], any of the monetary units and silver coins of some Spanish-speaking countries, as Mexico, Cuba, Uruguay, etc.

**pes·sa·ry** (pes′ə-ri), *n.* [*pl.* -RIES], [< ML. < L. < Gr. *pessos*, pebble], a device worn in the vagina to support the uterus or to prevent conception.

**pes·si·mism** (pes′ə-miz'm), *n.* [< L. *pessimus*, superl. of *pejor*, worse], 1. *a*) the belief that the existing world is the worst possible. *b*) the belief that the evil in life outweighs the good. 2. the tendency to expect the worst outcome in any circumstances; a looking on the dark side of things: cf. *optimism.* —**pes′si·mist,** *n.* —**pes′si·mis′tic, pes′si·mis′ti·cal,** *adj.* —**pes′si·mis′ti·cal·ly,** *adv.*

**pest** (pest), *n.* [< Fr. < L. *pestis*, a plague], 1. a person or thing that causes trouble, annoyance, etc.; nuisance; specif., any destructive insect or other small animal; vermin. 2. [Now Rare], a fatal epidemic disease; esp., the plague.

**pes·ter** (pes′tẽr), *v.t.* [< OFr. *empestrer*, orig., to entangle with foot shackles: meaning infl. by *pest*], to annoy repeatedly with petty irritations; bother; vex. —**pes′ter·er,** *n.*

**pest·hole** (pest′hōl′), *n.* a place infested or likely to be infested with an epidemic disease.

**pest·house** (pest′hous′), *n.* [Archaic], a hospital for people with contagious diseases.

**pes·ti·cide** (pes′tə-sīd′), *n.* any chemical used for killing insects, weeds, etc.

**pes·tif·er·ous** (pes-tif′ẽr-əs), *adj.* [< L. < *pestis*, a plague + *ferre*, to bear], 1. *a*) bringing or carrying disease. *b*) infected with an epidemic disease. 2. dangerous to the welfare of society; evil. 3. [Colloq.], annoying; bothersome. —**pes·tif′er·ous·ly,** *adv.* —**pes·tif′er·ous·ness,** *n.*

**pes·ti·lence** (pes′tə-ləns), *n.* [see PESTILENT], 1. any virulent or fatal contagious disease. 2. an epidemic of such disease; esp., the bubonic plague. 3. anything, as a doctrine, regarded as harmful. —**pes′ti·len′tial** (-len′shəl), *adj.*

**pes·ti·lent** (pes′tə-lənt), *adj.* [< L. < *pestis*, plague], 1. likely to cause death; deadly. 2. dangerous to morals or to the welfare of society; pernicious. 3. annoying; troublesome.

**pes·tle** (pes′'l, -t'l), *n.* [< OFr. < L. *pistillum* < *pinsere*, to pound], 1. a tool used to pound or grind substances, as in a mortar: see **mortar,** illus. 2. a heavy bar used in pounding or stamping, as in a mill. *v.t. & v.i.* [-TLED, -TLING], to pound, grind, crush, etc. as with a pestle.

**pet** (pet), *n.* [orig. Scot. dial.], 1. an animal that is domesticated and kept as a companion or treated with affection. 2. a person who is treated with particular indulgence; darling. *adj.* 1. kept or treated as a pet. 2. especially liked; favorite. 3. greatest; particular: as, a *pet* peeve. *v.t.* [PETTED, PETTING], to stroke or pat gently; fondle; caress. *v.i.* [Colloq.], to make love; kiss, embrace, etc.

**pet** (pet), *n.* [< obs. phr. *to take the pet*], a state of sulky peevishness or ill-humor.

**Pet.,** Peter.

**pet·al** (pet′'l), *n.* [< Gr. < *petalos*, outspread], any of the component parts, or leaves, of a corolla. —**pet′aled, pet′alled,** *adj.*

**pe·tard** (pi-tärd′), *n.* [< Fr. < *péter* (< L. *pedere*), to break wind], a metal cone filled with explosives: formerly fastened to walls and gates and exploded to force an opening.

**pet·cock** (pet′kok′), *n.* [? < obs. *pett*, breaking wind + *cock* (valve)], a small valve for draining excess water or air from pipes, etc.: also **pet cock.**

**Pe·ter** (pē′tẽr), *n.* 1. in the *Bible*, one of the twelve Apostles, a fisherman; ?–67 A.D.; reputed author of two books of the New Testament that bear his name: also called *Simon Peter, Saint Peter.* 2. either of the two Epistles of Peter. —**Pe·trine** (pē′trīn, -trin), *adj.*

**pe·ter** (pē′tẽr), *v.i.* [< ?], [Colloq.], to become gradually smaller, weaker, etc. and then disappear (with *out*).

**Peter I,** 1672–1725; czar of Russia (1682–1725): called *Peter the Great.*

**pet·i·ole** (pet′i-ōl′), *n.* [< L. *petiolus*, dim. of *pes*, a foot], 1. in *botany*, the stalk to which a leaf is attached. 2. in *zoology*, a slender, stalklike part; peduncle. —**pet′i·o·lar** (-ə-lẽr), *adj.* —**pet′i·o·late′** (-ə-lāt′), **pet′i·o·lat′ed,** *adj.*

**pet·it** (pet′i), *adj.* [< OFr.; var. of *petty*], petty; minor: now used only in law.

**pe·tite** (pə-tēt′), *adj.* [Fr., fem. of *petit*], small and trim in figure: said of a woman.

**pe·ti·tion** (pə-tish′ən), *n.* [< L. *petitio* < *petere*, to ask], 1. a solemn, earnest plea or request to a superior or to those in authority; entreaty. 2. a formal document embodying such a request, often signed by a number of persons. 3. something that is asked or entreated. 4. in *law*, a written plea in which specific court action is sought. *v.t.* 1. to address a petition to. 2. to ask for; solicit. *v.i.* to make a petition: as, he *petitioned* for a pardon. —**pe·ti′tion·ar′y** (-er′i), *adj.* —**pe·ti′tion·er,** *n.*

**petit jury,** a group of twelve citizens picked to weigh the evidence in and decide the issues of a trial in court: cf. **grand jury.**

**pe·tits fours** (pet′i fôrz′, fōrz′; Fr. pə-tē′ fōōr′), [Fr. pl. < *petit*, small + *four*, lit., oven], cupcakes made of spongecake, etc., usually frosted.

**Pe·trarch** (pē′trärk), *n.* (*Francesco Petrarca*), Italian poet and humanist; 1304–1374.

**pet·rel** (pet′rəl), *n.* [? a dim. of *Peter*, in allusion to Saint Peter's walking on the sea], any of various related small, dark sea birds with long wings; esp., the stormy petrel.

**pet·ri·fy** (pet′rə-fī′), *v.t.* [-FIED, -FYING], [< Fr. < L. (< Gr.) *petra*, a rock + *facere*, to make], 1. to replace the normal cells of (organic matter) with silica, etc. so as to change into a stony substance. 2. to make stiff; deaden; harden. 3. to stupefy; stun, as with fear. *v.i.* to change into stone. —**pet′ri·fac′tion** (-fak′shən), **pet′ri·fi·ca′tion,** *n.* —**pet′ri·fac′tive,** *adj.*

**pet·ro-,** [< Gr. *petra* or *petros*], a combining form meaning *rock* or *stone:* also **petr-.**

**Pet·ro·grad** (pet′rə-grad), *n.* Leningrad: the name from 1914 to 1924.

**pe·trog·ra·phy** (pi-trog′rə-fi), *n.* [*petro-* + *-graphy*], the science of the description or classification of rocks. —**pe·trog′ra·pher,** *n.* —**pet·ro·graph·ic** (pet′rə-graf′ik), **pet′ro·graph′i·cal,** *adj.*

**pet·rol** (pet′rəl), *n.* [< Fr. < ML. *petroleum;* see PETROLEUM], [Brit.], gasoline.

**pet·ro·la·tum** (pet′rə-lā′təm), *n.* [< *petroleum*], a greasy, jellylike substance consisting of a mixture of semisolid hydrocarbons obtained from petroleum: used as a base for ointments, etc.

**pe·tro·le·um** (pə-trō′li-əm), *n.* [ML. < L. *petra*, a rock + *oleum*, oil], an oily, liquid solution of hydrocarbons, yellowish-green to black in color, occurring naturally in certain rock strata: it yields paraffin, kerosene, fuel oil, gasoline, etc.

**petroleum jelly,** petrolatum.

**pe·trol·o·gy** (pi-trol′ə-ji), *n.* [*petro-* + *-logy*], the study of the composition, structure, and origin of rocks. —**pet·ro·log·ic** (pet′rə-loj′ik), **pet′ro·log′i·cal,** *adj.* —**pet′ro·log′i·cal·ly,** *adv.* —**pe·trol′o·gist,** *n.*

**pet·ti·coat** (pet′i-kōt′), *n.* [< *petty* + *coat*], 1. a skirt, now especially an underskirt, worn by women and young children. 2. [Colloq.], a woman or girl. *adj.* 1. feminine; womanly. 2. of or by women.

**pet·ti·fog** (pet′i-fog′, -fôg′), *v.i.* [-FOGGED, -FOGGING], [< *pettifogger*], to act as a pettifogger.

**pet·ti·fog·ger** (pet′i-fog′ẽr, -fôg′-), *n.* [cf. *petty* & obs. D. *focker*, cheater], a lawyer who handles petty cases, especially by using unethical methods.

**pet·ti·fog·ging** (pet′i-fog′iŋ, -fôg′-), *adj.* tricky or dishonest, especially in petty matters. *n.* petty dishonesty; trickery: also **pet′ti·fog′ger·y.**

**pet·tish** (pet′ish), *adj.* [< *pet* (a fit)], peevish; petulant; cross. —**pet′tish·ly,** *adv.*

**pet·ty** (pet′i), *adj.* [-TIER, -TIEST], [< OFr. *petit*], 1. relatively unimportant; trivial. 2. narrow-minded; mean. 3. relatively low in rank; subordinate. —**pet′ti·ly,** *adv.* —**pet′ti·ness,** *n.*

**petty cash,** a cash fund for incidental expenses.

**petty jury,** a petit jury.

**petty larceny,** see **larceny.**

**petty officer,** an enlisted man in the navy holding the rank of a noncommissioned officer.

**pet·u·lant** (pech′oo-lənt), *adj.* [< Fr. < L. *petulans;* ult. < *petere*, to attack], impatient or irritable, especially over a petty annoyance; peevish. —**pet′u·lance, pet′u·lan·cy,** *n.* —**pet′u·lant·ly,** *adv.*

**pe·tu·ni·a** (pə-tōōn′yə, -tū′ni-ə), *n.* [< Fr. < Braz. *petun*, tobacco], 1. a plant of the nightshade family, with variously colored, funnel-shaped flowers. 2. the flower.

**pew** (pū), *n.* [< OFr. *puie* < L. pl. of *podium*, balcony < Gr. *podion* < *pous*, a foot], 1. any of the rows of fixed benches with a back, in a church. 2. any of the boxlike enclosures with seats, in a church, for the use of one family, etc.

**pe·wee** (pē′wē), *n.* [echoic of its call], 1. the phoebe. 2. any of several other small flycatchers.

**pe·wit** (pē′wit, pū′it), *n.* [echoic of its call], 1. the lapwing. 2. the phoebe. 3. the European black-headed gull.

**pew·ter** (pū′tẽr), *n.* [< OFr. *peutre*], 1. an alloy of tin with lead, brass, or copper: it has a grayish, silvery luster when polished. 2. articles made of pewter collectively. *adj.* made of pewter.

**pf.,** 1. perfect. 2. pianoforte. 3. preferred: also **pfd.** 4. pfennig.

**Pfc.,** Private First Class.

**pfen·nig** (fen′ig; G. pfen′iH), *n.* [*pl.* -NIGS; G. -NIGE (-i-gə)], [G.], a minor bronze coin of Germany, equal to 1/100 mark.

**Pg.,** 1. Portugal. 2. Portuguese.

**Phae·dra** (fē′drə), *n.* in *Gr. legend*, the wife of Theseus: she caused the death of her stepson, who had rejected her advances.

**Pha·ë·thon** (fā′ə-thən, -t′n), *n.* in *Gr. & Rom. mythology*, son of Helios: he borrowed his father's sun chariot and would have set the world on fire had not Zeus struck him down with a thunderbolt.

**pha·e·ton, pha·ë·ton** (fā′ə-t′n), *n.* [< Fr. < L.; see PHAETHON], 1. a light, four-wheeled carriage, with front and back seats and, usually, a folding top. 2. a kind of touring car.

**-phage** (fāj), [< Gr. *phagein*, to eat], a combining form meaning *eating* or *destroying*.

**phag·o-,** [< Gr. *phagein*, to eat], a combining form meaning: 1. *eating* or *destroying*, as in *phagocyte*. 2. *phagocyte*. Also **phag-.**

**phag·o·cyte** (fag′ə-sīt′), *n.* [*phago-* + *-cyte*], any leucocyte that ingests and destroys other cells, bacteria, etc. in the blood and tissues. —**phag′o·cyt′ic** (-sit′ik), *adj.*

**-pha·gous** (fə-gəs), [< Gr. *phagein*, to eat], a combining form used to form adjectives corresponding to nouns ending in *-phage*.

**-pha·gy** (fə-ji), [< Gr. *phagein*, to eat], a combining form meaning *the practice of eating* (something specified): also **-pha·ji·a** (fā′ji-ə).

**pha·lan·ger** (fə-lan′jẽr), *n.* [< Gr. *phalanx*, bone between two joints: with reference to the structure of its hind feet], any of various small, pouched Australian animals with a long tail.

**pha·lanx** (fā′laŋks, fal′aŋks), *n.* [*pl.* PHALANXES, PHALANGES (fə-lan′jēz)], [L. < Gr., line of battle], 1. an ancient military formation of infantry in close ranks with shields together and spears overlapping. 2. a massed group of individuals. 3. a group of individuals united for a common purpose. 4. [*pl.* -LANGES], any of the bones of the fingers or toes: also **phal′ange** (fal′ənj, fə-lanj′). —**pha·lan′ge·al** (-lan′-ji-əl), **pha·lan′gal** (-laŋ′g′l), *adj.*

**phal·li·cism** (fal′ə-siz′m), *n.* worship of the phallus as a symbol of the male generative power: also **phal′lism.** —**phal′li·cist, phal′list,** *n.*

**phal·lus** (fal′əs), *n.* [*pl.* -LI (-ī)], [L. < Gr. *phallos*], 1. an image of the penis as a symbol of generative power. 2. the penis or clitoris. —**phal′lic,** *adj.*

**phan·tasm** (fan′taz′m), *n.* [< OFr. < L. < Gr. *phantasma* < *phantazein*, to show], 1. a figment of the mind; esp., a ghost, or specter. 2. a deceptive likeness (*of* something). —**phan·tas′mal, phan·tas′mic,** *adj.* —**phan·tas′mal·ly,** *adv.*

**phan·tas·ma·go·ri·a** (fan-taz′mə-gôr′i-ə, -gō′ri-ə), *n.* [< Gr. *phantasma*, phantasm + (prob.) *agora*, assembly], a rapidly changing series of things seen or imagined, as in a dream: also **phan·tas′ma·go′ry** [*pl.* -RIES]. —**phan·tas′ma·go′ri·al, phan·tas′ma·gor′ic** (-gôr′ik, -gor′-), *adj.*

**phan·ta·sy** (fan′tə-si, -zi), *n.* [*pl.* -SIES], a fantasy.

**phan·tom** (fan′təm), *n.* [see PHANTASM], 1. an apparition; vision; specter. 2. an illusion. 3. a person or thing that is something in appearance but not in fact: as, a *phantom* of a leader. 4. any mental image or representation. *adj.* of, like, or constituting a phantom; unreal.

**Phar·aoh** (fâr′ō), *n.* the title of the rulers of ancient Egypt. —**Phar′a·on′ic** (-ā-on′ik), **Phar′a·on′i·cal,** *adj.*

**Phar·i·sa·ic** (far′ə-sā′ik), *adj.* 1. of the Pharisees. 2. [p-], *a*) observing the letter but not the spirit of religious law; self-righteous. *b*) hypocritical. Also **phar′i·sa′i·cal.** —**phar′i·sa′i·cal·ly,** *adv.*

**Phar·i·sa·ism** (far′ə-sā-iz′m), *n.* 1. the beliefs and practices of the Pharisees. 2. [p-], pharisaic behavior, character, etc.; hypocrisy.

**Phar·i·see** (far′ə-sē′), *n.* 1. a member of an ancient Jewish sect that rigidly observed the written and oral (or traditional) law: cf. *Sadducee*. 2. [p-], a pharisaic person. —**Phar′i·see·ism** (-sē-iz′m), *n.*

**Pharm.,** 1. pharmaceutical. 2. pharmacopoeia. 3. pharmacy. Also **Phar.**

**phar·ma·ceu·ti·cal** (fär′mə-sōō′ti-k′l, -sū′-), *adj.* [< LL. < Gr. < *pharmakon*, a medicine], 1. of pharmacy or pharmacists. 2. of or by drugs. Also **phar′ma·ceu′tic.** —**phar′ma·ceu′ti·cal·ly,** *adv.*

**phar·ma·ceu·tics** (fär′mə-sōō′tiks, -sū′-), *n.pl.* [construed as sing.], pharmacy (sense 1).

**phar·ma·cist** (fär′mə-sist), *n.* one licensed to practice pharmacy.

**phar·ma·col·o·gy** (fär′mə-kol′ə-ji), *n.* [< Gr. *pharmakon*, a drug; + *-logy*], the study of the preparation, qualities, and uses of drugs. —**phar′ma·co·log′i·cal** (-kə-loj′i-k′l), *adj.* —**phar′ma·col′o·gist,** *n.*

**phar·ma·co·poe·ia** (fär′mə-kə-pē′ə), *n.* [< Gr. < *pharmakon*, a drug + *poiein*, to make], 1. an official book with a list of drugs and medicines and a description of their properties, preparation, etc. 2. a stock of drugs. —**phar′ma·co·poe′ial,** *adj.*

**phar·ma·cy** (fär′mə-si), *n.* [*pl.* -CIES], [< OFr. < ML. < Gr. *pharmakon*, drug], 1. the art or profession of preparing and dispensing drugs and medicines. 2. a place where this is done; drugstore.

**phar·yn·gi·tis** (far′in-jī′tis), *n.* inflammation of the mucous membrane of the pharynx; sore throat.

**phar·ynx** (far′iŋks), *n.* [*pl.* PHARYNXES, PHARYNGES (fə-rin′jēz)], [< Gr. *pharynx*], the cavity leading from the mouth and nasal passages to the larynx and esophagus. —**pha·ryn·ge·al** (fə-rin′ji-əl, far′in-jē′-), **pha·ryn·gal** (fə-riŋ′g′l), *adj.*

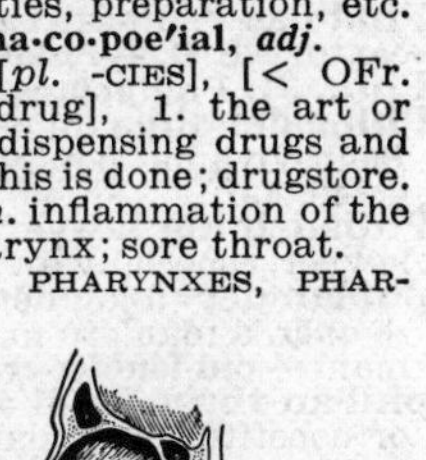

PHARYNX

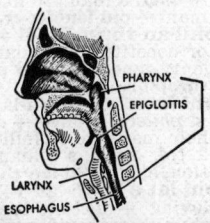

**phase** (fāz), *n.* [< Gr. *phasis* < *phainesthai*, to appear], 1. any stage in the illumination or appearance of the moon or a planet. 2. any stage or form in a series of changes, as in development. 3. aspect; side; part: as, the subject has many *phases*. 4. a solid, liquid, or gaseous homogeneous form: as, ice is a *phase* of $H_2O$. 5. the stage or progress of any cyclic movement, as of sound or light waves, alternating electric current, etc., with reference to a standard position. 6. a characteristic variation in the color of an animal's fur or plumage, according to season, age, etc. —**phase out,** to terminate (an activity) by stages.

**Ph.D.,** *Philosophiae Doctor,* [L.], Doctor of Philosophy.

**pheas·ant** (fez′'nt), *n.* [*pl.* -ANTS, -ANT; see PLURAL, II, D, 1], [< Anglo-Fr. < OFr. < L. < Gr. *phasianos,* lit., (bird) of *Phasis,* river in Asia], 1. a chickenlike game bird with a long tail and brilliant feathers. 2. any of various birds resembling the pheasant, as the ruffed grouse.

**phen-,** [< Fr. < Gr. *phainein,* to show], a combining form meaning *of* or *derived from benzene:* also **pheno-.**

**phe·nac·e·tin, phe·nac·e·tine** (fi-nas′ə-tin), *n.* [*phen-* + *acet(o)-* + *-in*], a coal-tar preparation of white crystals or powder, $C_{10}H_{13}O_2N$, used in medicine to reduce fever.

**phe·nix** (fē′niks), *n.* phoenix.

**phe·no·bar·bi·tal** (fē′nə-bär′bi-tal′, fen′ə-bär′bi-tôl′), *n.* [*pheno-* + *barbital*], an odorless, white crystalline powder, $C_{12}O_3N_2H_{12}$, used as a sedative and soporific.

**phe·no·cryst** (fē′nə-krist, fen′ə-), *n.* [< Fr. < Gr. *phainein,* to show + *krystallos,* crystal], a conspicuous crystal embedded in porphyritic rock.

**phe·nol** (fē′nôl, -nol, -nōl), *n.* [*phen-* + *-ol*] a white crystalline compound, $C_6H_5OH$, produced from coal tar and used in making explosives, etc.: its dilute aqueous solution is commonly called *carbolic acid.* —**phe·nol′ic** (-nol′ik, -nō′lik), *adj.*

**phe·nol·phthal·ein, phe·nol·phthal·ein** (fē′nôl-thal′ēn, -nōl-fthal′i-in), *n.* [*phenol* + *phthalein*], a white to pale-yellow, crystalline powder, $C_{20}H_{14}O_4$, used as a laxative, in making dyes, and as an acid-base indicator in chemical analysis.

**phe·nom·e·na** (fi-nom′ə-nə), *n.* pl. of **phenomenon.**

**phe·nom·e·nal** (fi-nom′ə-n'l), *adj.* 1. of or constituting a phenomenon or phenomena. 2. extremely unusual; extraordinary. —**phe·nom′e·nal′ly,** *adv.*

**phe·nom·e·non** (fi-nom′ə-non′), *n.* [*pl.* -NA; also, esp. for 3 & 4, -NONS], [< LL. < Gr. *phainomenon,* neut. ppr. of *phainesthai,* to appear], 1. any fact or event that is apparent to the senses and can be scientifically described: as, an eclipse is a *phenomenon.* 2. the appearance of something experienced as distinguished from the thing itself. 3. anything extremely unusual. 4. [Colloq.], a person with some extraordinary quality, etc.; prodigy.

**phen·yl** (fen′il, fē′nil), *n.* [*phen-* + *-yl*], a monovalent radical, $C_6H_5$, forming the basis of phenol, benzene, aniline, and some other compounds.

**phew** (fū: *conventionalized pronun.*), *interj.* an exclamation of disgust, surprise, relief, etc.

**phi** (fī, fē), *n.* [Gr.], the twenty-first letter of the Greek alphabet (Φ, φ).

**phi·al** (fī′əl), *n.* [< OFr. < Pr. < LL. < L. < Gr. *phialē,* shallow bowl], a small glass bottle; vial.

**Phi Be·ta Kap·pa** (fī bā′tə kap′ə, bē′-), an honorary society composed of American college students of high scholastic rank.

**Phid·i·as** (fid′i-əs), *n.* Greek sculptor; lived 5th century B.C. —**Phid′i·an,** *adj.*

**Phil.,** 1. Philippians. 2. Philippine.

**Phil·a·del·phi·a** (fil′ə-del′fi-ə, -fyə), *n.* a city in SE Pennsylvania: pop., 2,003,000 (metropolitan area, 4,343,000).

**Philadelphia lawyer,** [Slang], a clever or shrewd lawyer, especially an unscrupulous one.

**phi·lan·der** (fi-lan′dēr), *v.i.* [< Gr. < *philos,* loving + *anēr,* a man], to make love insincerely: said of a man. —**phi·lan′der·er,** *n.*

**phil·an·throp·ic** (fil′ən-throp′ik), *adj.* of, showing, or constituting philanthropy; charitable; benevolent; generous: also **phil′an·throp′i·cal** —**phil′an·throp′i·cal·ly,** *adv.*

**phi·lan·thro·py** (fi-lan′thrə-pi), *n.* [< LL. < Gr. < *philein,* to love + *anthrōpos,* man], 1. desire to help mankind as indicated by acts of charity, etc. 2. [*pl.* -PIES], a philanthropic service, gift, institution, etc. —**phi·lan′thro·pist,** *n.*

**phi·lat·e·ly** (fi-lat′'l-i), *n.* [< Fr. < Gr. *philos,* loving + *ateleia,* exemption from (further) tax: stamps are evidence of prepayment by sender], the collection and study of postage stamps, postmarks, etc. —**phil·a·tel·ic** (fil′ə-tel′ik), **phil′a·tel′i·cal,** *adj.* —**phi·lat′e·list,** *n.*

**-phile** (fil, fil), [< Gr. *philos,* loving], a combining form meaning *loving, liking, favorably disposed to,* as in *Anglophile:* also **-phil** (fil).

**Phi·le·mon** (fi-lē′mən, fī-), *n.* a book of the New Testament: the Epistle of the Apostle Paul to his convert Philemon: abbrev. **Philem.**

**phil·har·mon·ic** (fil′här-mon′ik, fil′ēr-), *adj.* [< Fr. < Gr. *philos,* loving + *harmonia,* harmony], 1. loving or devoted to music. 2. of or by a philharmonic society. *n.* 1. [P-], a society that sponsors a symphony orchestra. 2. [P-], [Colloq.], the orchestra or any of its concerts.

**Phil·ip** (fil′əp), *n.* one of the twelve Apostles.

**Philip II,** 1. 382–336 B.C.; king of Macedonia (359–336 B.C.); father of *Alexander the Great.* 2. 1527–1598; king of Spain (1556–1598); sent the Armada against England.

**Phi·lip·pi** (fi-lip′ī), *n.* an ancient city in Macedonia. —**Phi·lip′pi·an,** *adj. & n.*

**Phi·lip·pi·ans** (fi-lip′i-ənz), *n.pl.* [construed as sing.], a book of the New Testament: an Epistle from Paul to the Christians at Philippi.

**Phi·lip·pic** (fi-lip′ik), *n.* 1. any of the orations of Demosthenes against Philip, king of Macedonia. 2. [p-], any bitter verbal attack.

**Phil·ip·pine** (fil′ə-pēn′), *adj.* of the Philippine Islands or their people.

**Philippine Islands,** a group of 7,083 islands in the Pacific, northeast of Borneo, comprising a republic (*Republic of the Philippines*): area, 114,830 sq. mi.; pop., 34,656,000; capital, Quezon City: also **Phil′ip·pines′.**

**Phi·lis·ti·a** (fə-lis′ti-ə), *n.* an ancient country on the southern coast of Palestine.

**Phi·lis·tine** (fə-lis′tin, fil′əs-tēn′, -tīn′), *n.* 1. a member of a non-Semitic people who lived in SW Palestine from c. 1200 B.C. on. 2. a person regarded as smugly conventional, indifferent to cultural values, etc. *adj.* 1. of the ancient Philistines. 2. smugly conventional, indifferent to culture, etc. —**Phi·lis′tin·ism,** *n.*

**phil·o-,** [< Gr. *philos,* loving], a combining form meaning *loving, liking, having a predilection for,* as in *philology:* also **phil-.**

**phil·o·den·dron** (fil′ə-den′drən), *n.* [< Gr. *philos,* loving + *dendron,* a tree], a tropical American plant of the arum family, usually climbing, with tough, leathery leaves.

**phi·log·y·ny** (fi-loj′ə-ni), *n.* [< Gr. < *philein,* to love + *gynē,* woman], love of or fondness for women. —**phi·log′y·nist,** *n.* —**phi·log′y·nous,** *adj.*

**phi·lol·o·gy** (fi-lol′ə-ji), *n.* [< Fr. < L. < Gr. *philologia,* love of literature < *philein,* to love + *logos,* a word], 1. the study of literary texts, etc. in order to determine their authenticity, meaning, etc. 2. linguistics: a former term. —**phil·o·log·i·cal** (fil′ə-loj′i-k'l), **phil′o·log′ic,** *adj.* —**phi·lol′o·gist, phi·lol′o·ger,** *n.*

**phil·o·mel** (fil′ə-mel′), *n.* [< OFr. < L. < Gr. < *philein,* to love + *melos,* song], [Poetic], the nightingale: also **Phil′o·me′la** (-mē′lə).

**philos.** philosophy.

**phi·los·o·pher** (fi-los′ə-fēr), *n.* [< OFr. < L. < Gr. < *philos,* loving + *sophos,* wise], 1. a person who studies or is learned in philosophy. 2. a person who lives by a system of philosophy. 3. a person who meets all events with calmness and composure.

**philosophers'** (or **philosopher's**) **stone,** an imaginary substance that alchemists believed would change base metals into gold or silver.

**phil·o·soph·ic** (fil′ə-sof′ik), *adj.* 1. of a philosophy or a philosopher. 2. devoted to or learned in philosophy. 3. rational; calm, as in a difficult situation. Also **phil′o·soph′i·cal.** —**phi′lo·soph′i·cal·ly,** *adv.*

**phi·los·o·phize** (fi-los′ə-fīz′), *v.i.* [-PHIZED, -PHIZING], to deal philosophically with abstract matter; think or reason like a philosopher. —**phi·los′o·phiz′er,** *n.*

**phi·los·o·phy** (fi-los′ə-fi), *n.* [*pl.* -PHIES], [< OFr. < L. < Gr.; see PHILOSOPHER], 1. a study of the processes governing thought and conduct; investigation of the principles that regulate the universe and underlie all reality. 2. the general principles of a field of knowledge: as, the *philosophy* of economics. 3. a particular system of principles for the conduct of life. 4. a study of human morals, character, etc. 5. calmness; composure.

**-phi·lous** (fi-ləs), [< Gr. *philos,* loving], a combining form meaning *loving, having a liking for.*

**phil·ter** (fil′tēr), *n.* [< Fr. < L. < Gr. *philtron* < *philein,* to love], 1. a potion or charm thought to make a person fall in love. 2. any magic potion. *v.t.* [-TERED, -TERING], to charm with a philter.

**phil·tre** (fil′tēr), *n. & v.t.* [-TRED, -TRING], philter.

**phle·bi·tis** (fli-bī′tis), *n.* [*phleb(o)-* + *-itis*], inflammation of a vein. —**phle·bit′ic** (-bit′ik), *adj.*

**phleb·o-,** [< Gr. *phleps,* a vein], a combining form meaning *vein:* also **phleb-.**

**phle·bot·o·my** (fli-bot′ə-mi), ***n.*** [< OFr. < LL. < Gr. < *phleps*, a vein + *temnein*, to cut], the formerly common practice of bloodletting as a therapeutic measure. —**phle·bot′o·mist, *n.*** —**phle·bot′o·mize′** [-MIZED, -MIZING], ***v.t. & v.i***

**phlegm** (flem), ***n.*** [< OFr. < LL. < Gr. *phlegma*, inflammation < *phlegein*, to burn], 1. the thick secretion of the mucous glands of the respiratory tract, discharged from the throat, as during a cold. 2. in *early physiology*, that one of the four humors believed to cause sluggishness. 3. *a*) sluggishness; apathy. *b*) calmness; equanimity.

**phleg·mat·ic** (fleg-mat′ik), ***adj.*** [< OFr. < LL. < Gr. *phlegmatikos;* see PHLEGM], hard to rouse to action; specif., *a*) sluggish; dull. *b*) calm; cool: also **phleg·mat′i·cal.** —**phleg·mat′i·cal·ly, *adv.***

**phlo·em, phlo·ëm** (flō′em), ***n.*** [G. < Gr. *phloos*, the bark], the cell tissue serving as a path for the distribution of food material in a plant; bast.

**phlo·gis·ton** (flō-jis′ton, -tən), ***n.*** [< Gr. *phlogistos;* ult. < *phlegein*, to burn], an imaginary element formerly believed to cause combustion; principle of fire. —**phlo·gis′tic, *adj.***

**phlox** (floks), ***n.*** [< L. < Gr. *phlox*, a flame < *phlegein*, to burn], any of various plants with small leaves and clusters of flowers of various colors.

**-phobe** (fōb), [< Fr. < L. < Gr. < *phobos*, fear], a combining form meaning *fearing* or *hating*, as in *Francophobe.*

**pho·bi·a** (fō′bi-ə), ***n.*** [< Gr. *phobos*, a fear], an irrational, persistent fear of some particular thing or situation. —**pho·bic** (fō′bik, fob′ik), ***adj.***

**-pho·bi·a** (fō′bi-ə), [< Gr. < *phobos*, a fear], a combining form meaning *fear, dread, hatred*, as in *claustrophobia.*

**Phoe·be** (fē′bi), ***n.*** 1. in *Gr. mythology*, Artemis, goddess of the moon: identified by the Romans with Diana. 2. [Poetic], the moon.

**phoe·be** (fē′bi), ***n.*** [echoic of its call; sp. influenced by *Phoebe*], a small bird, one of the flycatchers, with a greenish-brown back, light-yellow breast, and a short crest.

**Phoe·bus** (fē′bəs), ***n.*** 1. in *Gr. mythology*, Apollo, god of the sun. 2. [Poetic], the sun.

**Phoe·ni·ci·a** (fə-nish′ə, -nish′i-ə, -nē′shə), ***n.*** an ancient kingdom on the Mediterranean in modern Syria and Palestine: also sp. **Phe·ni′ci·a.**

**Phoe·ni·cian** (fə-nish′ən, fə-nē′shən), ***adj.*** of Phoenicia, its people, their language, etc. ***n.*** 1. a native of Phoenicia. 2. the extinct Northwest Semitic language of the Phoenicians.

**Phoe·nix** (fē′niks), ***n.*** the capital of Arizona: pop., 439,000.

**phoe·nix** (fē′niks), ***n.*** [< AS. & OFr. *fenix;* ult. < L. *phoenix* < Gr. *phoinix*], in *Egyptian mythology*, a beautiful bird which lived for 500 years and then consumed itself in fire, rising renewed from the ashes: a symbol of immortality: also sp. **phe′nix.**

**pho·nate** (fō′nāt), ***v.i.*** [-NATED, -NATING], [< Gr. *phōnē*, a voice; + *-ate*], to utter a voiced sound; vocalize. —**pho·na′tion, *n.***

**phone** (fōn), ***n.*** [Gr. *phōnē*, a sound], any single speech sound: a phoneme is composed of *phones.*

**phone** (fōn), ***n., v.t. & v.i.*** [PHONED, PHONING], [abbrev. of *telephone*], [Colloq.], telephone.

**-phone** (fōn), [< Gr. *phōnē*, a sound], a combining form meaning *producing*, or *connected with, sound*, as in *megaphone.*

**pho·neme** (fō′nēm), ***n.*** [< Fr. < Gr. *phōnēma*, a sound < *phōnē*, a voice], in *linguistics*, a family of closely related speech sounds (*phones*) regarded as a single sound and represented in phonetic transcription by the same symbol, as the sounds of *r* in *bring, red*, and *car.* —**pho·ne′mic, *adj.***

**pho·ne·mics** (fō-nē′miks), ***n.pl.*** [construed as sing.], the branch of linguistics dealing with a system of phonemes. —**pho·ne′mi·cist** (-mə-sist), ***n.***

**pho·net·ic** (fə-net′ik, fō-), ***adj.*** [< Gr. < *phōnētos*, to be spoken; ult. < *phōnē*, a sound], 1. of speech sounds. 2. of phonetics. 3. conforming to pronunciation: as, *phonetic* spelling. Also **pho·net′i·cal.** —**pho·net′i·cal·ly, *adv.***

**pho·net·ics** (fə-net′iks, fō-), ***n.pl.*** [construed as sing.], 1. the branch of linguistics dealing with speech sounds, their production and combination, and their representation by written symbols. 2. the phonetic system of a particular language. —**pho·ne·ti·cian** (fō′nə-tish′ən), **pho·net′i·cist, pho·ne·tist** (fō′nə-tist), ***n.***

**pho·ney** (fō′ni), ***adj. & n.*** [Slang], phony.

**phon·ic** (fon′ik, fō′nik), ***adj.*** [< Gr. *phōnē*, a sound], 1. of, or having the nature of, sound; esp., of speech sounds. 2. [Rare], voiced.

**phon·ics** (fon′iks, fō′niks), ***n.pl.*** [construed as sing.], [< *phonic*], the use of elementary phonetics in teaching beginners to read or enunciate.

**pho·no-,** [< Gr. *phōnē*, a sound], a combining form meaning *sound, speech*, as in *phonology:* also **phon-.**

**pho·no·gram** (fō′nə-gram′), ***n.*** [*phono-* + *-gram*], a symbol representing a word, syllable, or sound, as in shorthand. —**pho′no·gram′ic, pho′no·gram′mic, *adj.***

**pho·no·graph** (fō′nə-graf′, -gräf′), ***n.*** [*phono-* + *-graph*], an instrument that reproduces sound from tracings made on a flat disk. —**pho′no·graph′ic, *adj.*** —**pho′no·graph′i·cal·ly, *adv.***

**pho·nog·ra·phy** (fō-nog′rə-fi), ***n.*** [*phono-* + *-graphy*], 1. a written representation of the sounds of speech; phonetic spelling or transcription. 2. any system of shorthand based on a phonetic transcription of speech.

**pho·nol·o·gy** (fō-nol′ə-ji), ***n.*** [*phono-* + *-logy*], 1. *a*) phonetics. *b*) phonemics. 2. the study of the evolution of speech sounds, especially within a particular language. —**pho·no·log·i·cal** (fō′nə-loj′i-k′l), **pho′no·log′ic, *adj.*** —**pho·nol′o·gist, *n.***

**pho·ny** (fō′ni), ***adj.*** [-NIER, -NIEST], [? < *Forney* (*rings*), cheap brass rings made by a person named *Forney*], [Slang], not genuine; false; counterfeit; fake. ***n.*** [*pl.* -NIES], [Slang], 1. something not genuine; a fake. 2. one who pretends to be what he is not; charlatan. Also sp. **phoney.**

**-pho·ny** (fō′ni, fə-), [< Gr. *phōnē*, a sound], a combining form meaning *a* (specified kind of) *sound*, as in *cacophony:* also **-pho·ni·a** (fō′ni-ə).

**-phore** (fôr, fōr), [< Gr. *-phoros* < *pherein*, to bear], a combining form meaning *bearer, producer.*

**-phor·ous** (fôr′əs, fō′rəs), [see -PHORE], a combining form meaning *bearing, producing.*

**phos·gene** (fos′jēn), ***n.*** [< Gr. *phōs*, a light; + *-gene* (for *-gen*)], a colorless gas, $COCl_2$, used as a lung irritant in warfare.

**phos·phate** (fos′fāt), ***n.*** [Fr.], 1. a salt or ester of phosphoric acid. 2. a fertilizer containing phosphates. 3. a soft drink made with soda water, sirup, and, sometimes, a few drops of phosphoric acid. —**phos·phat′ic** (-fat′ik), ***adj.***

**phos·phide** (fos′fīd, -fid), ***n.*** a compound consisting of trivalent phosphorus with another element or a radical: also **phos′phid** (-fid).

**phos·phite** (fos′fīt), ***n.*** [Fr.], a salt or ester of phosphorous acid.

**phos·pho-,** [< *phosphorus*], a combining form meaning *phosphorus:* also **phosph-.**

**phos·phor** (fos′fẽr), ***n.*** [see PHOSPHORUS], 1. [P-], [Poetic], the morning star, especially Venus. 2. [Archaic & Poetic], phosphorus or any other phosphorescent substance. ***adj.*** [Rare], phosphorescent.

**phos·pho·rate** (fos′fə-rāt′), ***v.t.*** [-RATED, -RATING] to combine or impregnate with phosphorus.

**phos·pho·resce** (fos′fə-res′), ***v.i.*** [-RESCED, -RESCING], to exhibit phosphorescence.

**phos·pho·res·cence** (fos′fə-res′′ns), ***n.*** 1. the condition or property of giving off light without noticeable heat or combustion, as shown by phosphorus, etc. 2. such a light. —**phos′pho·res′cent, *adj.***

**phos·pho·ret·ed, phos·pho·ret·ted** (fos′fə-ret′id), ***adj.*** combined or impregnated with phosphorus: also **phos′phu·ret′ed, phos′phu·ret′ted** (-fyoo-).

**phos·phor·ic** (fos-fôr′ik, -for′-, -fō′rik), ***adj.*** 1. of, like, or containing phosphorus, especially with a valence of five. 2. designating any of three oxygen acids of phosphorus, especially a colorless crystalline acid, $H_3PO_4$, soluble in water and used as a reagent.

**phos·pho·ro-,** a combining form meaning *phosphorus* or *phosphorescence:* also **phosphor-.**

**phos·pho·rous** (fos′fẽr-əs, fos-fôr′-, -fō′rəs), ***adj.*** 1. of, like, or containing phosphorus, especially with a valence of three. 2. designating a white or yellowish crystalline acid, $H_3PO_3$, that absorbs oxygen readily.

**phos·pho·rus** (fos′fẽr-əs), ***n.*** [*pl.* -RI (-ī′)], [< L. *Phosphorus*, morning star < Gr. < *phōs*, a light + *pherein*, to bear], 1. any phosphorescent substance or object. 2. a nonmetallic chemical element, normally a white, phosphorescent, waxy solid, becoming yellow when exposed to light: it is poisonous and ignites spontaneously at room temperature:

when heated in sealed tubes it becomes red, nonpoisonous, and less inflammable: symbol, P; at. wt., 30.98; at. no., 15.
**pho·to** (fō'tō), *n.* [*pl.* -TOS], [Colloq.], a photograph.
**pho·to-,** [< Gr. *phōs*, a light], a combining form meaning: 1. *of* or *produced by light*, as in *photograph*. 2. *of a photograph* or *photography*.
**pho·to·chem·is·try** (fō'tō-kem'is-tri), *n.* the branch of chemistry having to do with the effect of light, etc. in producing chemical action, as in photography. —**pho'to·chem'i·cal,** *adj.*
**pho·to·cop·y** (fō'tō-kop'i), *n.* [*pl.* -COPIES], a copy of printed or other graphic material made by a device (**photocopier**) which photographically reproduces the original.
**pho·to·e·lec·tric** (fō'tō-i-lek'trik), *adj.* [*photo-* + *electric*], of or having to do with the electric effects produced by light, especially as in the emission of electrons by certain substances when subjected to radiation of suitable wave length.
**photoelectric cell,** any device in which light controls the electron emission from a cathode, the electrical resistance of an element, etc.: it is usually used in an electric circuit for controlling mechanical devices, as for opening doors: also called *electric eye*.
**pho·to·en·grave** (fō'tō-in-grāv'), *v.t.* [-GRAVED, -GRAVING], to reproduce by the process of photoengraving. —**pho'to·en·grav'er,** *n.*
**pho·to·en·grav·ing** (fō'tō-in-grāv'iŋ), *n.* 1. a process by which photographs are reproduced in relief on printing plates. 2. a plate so made. 3. a print from such a plate.
**photo finish,** a race so close that the winner can be determined only from a photograph of the finish.
**pho·to·flash** (fō'tə-flash'), *adj.* 1. designating an electric bulb which when lighted gives off a single bright flash of light: used in photography. 2. *a*) of or for such a bulb. *b*) made by using such a bulb. *n.* a photoflash bulb or photograph.
**pho·to·flood** (fō'tə-flud'), *adj.* 1. designating an electric bulb which burns with a sustained intense light: used in photography. 2. *a*) of or for such a bulb. *b*) made with the aid of such a bulb. *n.* a photoflood bulb or photograph.
**photog.,** 1. photograph. 2. photography.
**pho·to·gen·ic** (fō'tə-jen'ik), *adj.* [*photo-* + *-genic*], 1. artistically suitable for being photographed, as a person. 2. in *biology*, phosphorescent. —**pho'to·gen'i·cal·ly,** *adv.*
**pho·to·graph** (fō'tə-graf', -gräf'), *n.* a picture made by means of photography. *v.t.* to take a photograph of. *v.i.* 1. to practice photography. 2. to undergo being photographed, with reference to photogenic qualities: as, she *photographs* well. —**pho·tog·ra·pher** (fə-tog'rə-fēr), *n.*
**pho·to·graph·ic** (fō'tə-graf'ik), *adj.* 1. of or like a photograph or photography. 2. used in or made by photography. Also **pho'to·graph'i·cal.** —**pho'to·graph'i·cal·ly,** *adv.*
**pho·tog·ra·phy** (fə-tog'rə-fi), *n.* [*photo-* + *-graphy*], the art or process of producing images of objects upon a photosensitive surface by the chemical action of light or other radiant energy.
**pho·to·gra·vure** (fō'tō-grə-vyoor', -tə-grā'vyoor), *n.* [Fr.], 1. a photoengraving process by which photographs are reproduced on intaglio printing plates from which they may be transferred to paper. 2. a print so made.
**pho·to·lith·o·graph** (fō'tə-lith'ə-graf', -gräf'), *n.* a lithograph produced by photoengraving. —**pho'to·lith'o·graph'ic,** *adj.* —**pho·to·li·thog·ra·phy** (fō'tō-li-thog'rə-fi), *n.*
**pho·tol·y·sis** (fō-tol'ə-sis), *n.* [see PHOTO- & -LYSIS], chemical decomposition due to the action of light. —**pho'to·lyt'ic** (-tə-lit'ik), *adj.*
**pho·tom·e·ter** (fō-tom'ə-tēr), *n.* [*photo-* + *-meter*], an instrument used to measure the intensity of light: also called *light meter*.
**pho·tom·e·try** (fō-tom'ə-tri), *n.* 1. the measurement of the intensity of light. 2. the branch of optics dealing with this. —**pho'to·met'ric** (-tə-met'rik), **pho'to·met'ri·cal,** *adj.* —**pho·tom'e·trist,** *n.*
**pho·to·mon·tage** (fō'tō-mon-täzh', -mōn-), *n.* montage done in photographs.
**pho·to·mu·ral** (fō'tə-myoor'əl), *n.* a large photograph used as a mural.
**pho·ton** (fō'ton), *n.* [< *photo-* + *-on*, as in *electron*], a quantum of light energy.
**pho·to-off·set** (fō'tō-ôf'set'), *n.* a method of offset printing in which the text or pictures are photographically transferred to a metal plate from which inked impressions are made on a rubber-surfaced cylinder to be transferred to the paper.
**pho·to·play** (fō'tə-plā'), *n.* a play presented in motion pictures; screenplay.
**pho·to·sen·si·tive** (fō'tə-sen'sə-tiv), *adj.* sensitive to radiant energy, especially to light.
**pho·to·stat** (fō'tə-stat'), *n.* [*photo-* + *-stat*], 1. a device for making inexpensive photographic reproductions of printed matter, drawings, etc. directly as a positive upon special paper: a trademark (**Photostat**). 2. a reproduction so made. *v.t.* [-STATED or -STATTED, -STATING or -STATTING], to make a photostat of. —**pho'to·stat'ic,** *adj.*
**pho·to·syn·the·sis** (fō'tə-sin'thə-sis), *n.* the formation of carbohydrates in plants from water and carbon dioxide, by the action of sunlight on the chlorophyll. —**pho'to·syn·thet'ic** (-thet'ik), *adj.*
**pho·to·tel·e·graph** (fō'tə-tel'ə-graf', -gräf'), *v.t.* & *v.i.* to send by phototelegraphy. *n.* something sent by phototelegraphy.
**pho·to·te·leg·ra·phy** (fō'tō-tə-leg'rə-fi), *n.* 1. communication by means of light, as by flashing reflections of the sun's rays. 2. the sending of photograph facsimiles by telegraphy. —**pho'to·tel'e·graph'ic** (-tə-tel'ə-graf'ik, -gräf'ik), *adj.*
**pho·tot·ro·pism** (fō-tot'rə-piz'm), *n.* in *biology*, tropism toward or away from light. —**pho'to·trop'ic** (-tə-trop'ik), *adj.* —**pho'to·trop'i·cal·ly,** *adv.*
**pho·to·type** (fō'tə-tīp'), *n.* 1. a printing block or plate upon which a photograph is reproduced. 2. the process used in producing such a block: also **pho'to·typ'y.** 3. a print from such a block. —**pho'to·typ'ic** (-tip'ik), *adj.*
**phrase** (frāz), *n.* [Fr. < L. *phrasis*, diction < Gr. < *phrazein*, to speak], 1. a manner or style of speech; expression; phraseology. 2. a short, colorful, or forceful expression. 3. in *grammar*, a group of two or more words conveying a single thought or forming a separate part of a sentence but not containing a subject and predicate (e.g., *of mine, giving parties, fresh milk*). 4. in *music*, a short, distinct passage, usually of two, four, or eight measures. *v.t.* & *v.i.* [PHRASED, PHRASING], 1. to express in words or in a phrase. 2. in *music*, to mark off (notes) into phrases. —**phras'al,** *adj.* —**phras'ing,** *n.*
**phra·se·ol·o·gy** (frā'zi-ol'ə-ji), *n.* [*pl.* -GIES], [see PHRASE & -LOGY], choice or pattern of words; way of speaking or writing. —**phra'se·o·log'i·cal** (-ə-loj'i-k'l), *adj.* —**phra'se·ol'o·gist,** *n.*
**phre·net·ic** (fri-net'ik), *adj.* [< OFr. < L. < Gr. *phrenētikos*, mad], 1. wild; insane; frenetic. 2. excessively excited; fanatic. Also **phre·net'i·cal.** *n.* a phrenetic person. —**phre·net'i·cal·ly,** *adv.*
**phre·nol·o·gy** (fri-nol'ə-ji), *n.* [< Gr. *phrēn*, mind; + *-logy*], a system by which an analysis of character and mental faculties is allegedly made by studying the shape and protuberances of the skull. —**phren·o·log·ic** (fren'ə-loj'ik), **phren'o·log'i·cal,** *adj.* —**phren'o·log'i·cal·ly,** *adv.* —**phre·nol'o·gist,** *n.*
**Phryg·i·a** (frij'i-ə), *n.* an ancient country in central Asia Minor. —**Phryg'i·an,** *adj.* & *n.*
**PHS, P.H.S.,** Public Health Service.
**phthal·ein** (thal'ēn, fthal'ē-in), *n.* [< *naphthalene*], any of a group of synthetic dyes manufactured from phenols, etc.
**phthi·sis** (thī'sis), *n.* [L. < Gr. < *phthiein*, to waste away], a wasting away of the body or any of its parts; esp., tuberculosis of the lungs: also **phthis·ic** (tiz'ik). —**phthis'i·cal, phthis'ick·y,** *adj.*
**phy·co·my·ce·tous** (fī'kō-mī-sē'təs), *adj.* [< Gr. *phykos*, seaweed + *mykēs*, fungus], of a group of fungi closely resembling the algae.
**Phyfe, Duncan** (fīf), 1768–1854; U.S. cabinetmaker and furniture designer, born in Scotland.
**phy·la** (fī'lə), *n.* pl. of **phylum.**
**phy·lac·ter·y** (fi-lak'tēr-i), *n.* [*pl.* -IES], [< LL. < Gr. *phylaktērion*, a fort < *phylassein*, to guard], 1. a small leather case holding slips inscribed with Scripture passages: one is worn on the forehead and one on the left arm by orthodox Jewish men during morning prayer. 2. a reminder.
**-phyll** (fil), [< Gr. *phyllon*, a leaf], a combining form meaning *leaf*, as in *chlorophyll*.
**phyl·lo-,** [< Gr. *phyllon*, a leaf], a combining form meaning *leaf*: also **phyll-.**
**phyl·lo·tax·y** (fil'ə-tak'si), *n.* [*phyllo-* + *-taxy*], 1. the arrangement of leaves on a stem. 2. the principles of such arrangement: also **phyl'lo·tax'is.**
**-phyl·lous** (fil'əs), [see PHYLLO- & -OUS], a combining form meaning *having* (a specified number or kind of) *leaves, leaflets*, etc.
**phyl·lox·er·a** (fil'ək-sēr'ə, fi-lok'sēr-ə), *n.* [< Gr. *phyllon*, a leaf + *xeros*, dry], any of various plant lice that attack the leaves and roots of certain grapevines.
**phy·lo-,** [< Gr. *phylon*, tribe], a combining form meaning *tribe, race*, etc., as in *phylogeny:* also **phyl-.**

**phy·log·e·ny** (fī-loj′ə-ni), *n.* [*pl.* -NIES], [< G.; see PHYLO- & -GENY], the evolutionary development of any plant or animal species: also **phy·lo·gen·e·sis** (fī′lə-jen′ə-sis). —**phy′lo·ge·net′ic** (-jə-net′ik), **phy′lo·gen′ic,** *adj.* —**phy′lo·ge·net′i·cal·ly,** *adv.*

**phy·lum** (fī′ləm), *n.* [*pl.* -LA (-lə)], [< Gr. *phylon*, tribe], any of the broad, basic divisions of the plant or animal kingdom: also **phy′lon** (-lon), [*pl.* -LA].

**phys.,** 1. physical. 2. physician. 3. physics.

**phys. ed.,** physical education.

**phys·ic** (fiz′ik), *n.* [< OFr. < L. *physica*, natural science < Gr. < *physis*, nature < *phyein*, to produce], 1. [Rare], physics. 2. [Archaic], medical science. 3. a medicine, especially a cathartic. *v.t.* [-ICKED, -ICKING], 1. to dose with medicine, especially with a cathartic. 2. to cause to have a bowel movement. 3. to cure; heal; relieve.

**phys·i·cal** (fiz′i-k′l), *adj.* [< ML. < L.; see PHYSIC], 1. of nature and all matter; natural; material. 2. of natural science or natural philosophy. 3. of or according to the laws of nature. 4. of, or produced by the forces of, physics. 5. of the body as opposed to the mind: as, *physical* exercise. *n.* [Colloq.], a physical examination. —**phys′i·cal·ly,** *adv.*

**physical chemistry,** the branch of chemistry dealing with the physical properties of substances as they relate to the chemical properties.

**physical education,** instruction in the exercise, care, and hygiene of the human body; esp., a course in gymnastics, etc., as in a school.

**physical geography,** the study of the features and nature of the earth's surface, climate, distribution of plant and animal life, etc.

**physical science,** any of the sciences that deal with inanimate matter or energy, as physics, chemistry, geology, etc.

**physical therapy,** the treatment of disease, injury, etc. by physical means rather than with drugs, as by massage, infrared light, electrotherapy, etc.

**phy·si·cian** (fə-zish′ən), *n.* [< OFr. < L.; see PHYSIC], 1. a doctor of medicine. 2. a general medical practitioner, as distinguished from a surgeon. 3. any person or thing that heals or relieves.

**phys·i·cist** (fiz′ə-sist), *n.* an expert in physics.

**phys·ics** (fiz′iks), *n.pl.* [construed as sing. in senses 1 & 2], [< *physic*], 1. originally, natural science. 2. the science dealing with the properties, changes, interaction, etc. of matter and energy: physics is subdivided into mechanics, thermodynamics, optics, acoustics, etc. 3. physical properties or processes: as, the *physics* of flight.

**phys·i·o-,** [< Gr. *physis*, nature], a combining form meaning *nature, natural*: also **physi-.**

**phys·i·og·no·my** (fiz′i-og′nə-mi, -on′ə-mi), *n.* [*pl.* -MIES], [< OFr. < ML. < Gr. < *physis*, nature + *gnōmōn*, one who knows], 1. the practice of trying to judge character by observation of bodily, especially facial, features. 2. the face; facial expression, especially as supposedly indicative of character. 3. external features. —**phys′i·og·nom′ic** (-og-nom′ik, -ə-nom′ik), **phys′i·og·nom′i·cal,** *adj.* —**phys′i·og·nom′i·cal·ly,** *adv.* —**phys′i·og′no·mist** *n.*

**phys·i·og·ra·phy** (fiz′i-og′rə-fi), *n.* [*physio-* + *-graphy*], 1. a description of the features and phenomena of nature. 2. physical geography. —**phys′i·og′ra·pher,** *n.* —**phys′i·o·graph′ic** (-ə-graf′ik), **phys′i·o·graph′i·cal,** *adj.*

**physiol.,** 1. physiological. 2. physiology.

**phys·i·ol·o·gy** (fiz′i-ol′ə-ji), *n.* [Fr. < L. < Gr. *physis*, nature + *logos*, a discourse], 1. the branch of biology dealing with the functions and vital processes of living organisms or their parts and organs. 2. the functions and vital processes, collectively (*of* an organism). —**phys′i·o·log′i·cal** (-ə-loj′i-k′l), **phys′i·o·log′ic,** *adj.* —**phys′i·o·log′i·cal·ly,** *adv.* —**phys′i·ol′o·gist,** *n.*

**phys·i·o·ther·a·py** (fiz′i-ō-ther′ə-pi), *n.* physical therapy. —**phys′i·o·ther′a·pist,** *n.*

**phy·sique** (fi-zēk′), *n.* [Fr.], the structure, strength, form, or appearance of the body.

**-phyte** (fīt), [< Gr. *phyton*, a plant], a combining form meaning *a plant growing in a* (specified) *way* or *place*.

**phy·to-,** [< Gr. *phyton*, a plant], a combining form meaning *a plant, vegetation*: also **phyt-.**

**pi** (pī), *n.* [var. of *pie* (baked dish)], 1. a mixed, disordered collection of printing type. 2. any jumble or mixture. *v.t.* [PIED, PIEING], to make jumbled or disordered. Also sp. **pie.**

**pi** (pī, pē), *n.* [Gr.], 1. the sixteenth letter of the Greek alphabet (Π, π). 2. the symbol (π) designating the ratio of the circumference of a circle to its diameter: π equals 3.14159265+.

**P. I.,** Philippine Islands.

**pi·a ma·ter** (pī′ə mā′tēr), [ML. < L., lit., gentle mother], the vascular membrane enveloping the brain and spinal cord, the innermost of the three surrounding membranes.

**pi·a·nis·si·mo** (pē′ə-nis′ə-mō′), *adj. & adv.* [It., superl. of *piano*, soft], in *music*, very soft: cf. *fortissimo*. *n.* [*pl.* -MOS, -MI (-mē′)], a passage to be performed pianissimo.

**pi·an·ist** (pi-an′ist, pyan′-, pē′ə-nist), *n.* one who plays the piano, especially as a profession.

**pi·an·o** (pi-an′ō, pyan′-), *n.* [*pl.* -OS], [It., contr. < *pianoforte*], a large, stringed, percussion instrument played from a keyboard: each key operates a small, felt-covered hammer that strikes and vibrates a corresponding steel wire.

**pi·an·o** (pi-ä′nō, pyä′-), *adj. & adv.* [It., soft, smooth < L. *planus*, smooth], in *music*, soft. *n.* [*pl.* -OS], a passage to be performed piano.

**pi·an·o·for·te** (pi-an′ə-fôrt′, pyan′ə-fōr′ti), *n.* [It. < *piano*, soft + *forte*, strong], a piano.

**pi·as·ter, pi·as·tre** (pi-as′tēr), *n.* [Fr. < It. & Sp.; ult. < L. *emplastrum*, plaster], 1. [Rare], the Spanish dollar. 2. a monetary unit and coin of Turkey and Egypt.

**pi·az·za** (pi-az′ə; It. pyät′tsä), *n.* [It. < L. *platea*; see PLACE], 1. in Italy, an open public square, especially one surrounded by buildings. 2. a covered gallery or arcade. 3. a large, covered porch; veranda.

**pi·broch** (pē′brok), *n.* [< Gael. *piobaireachd*; ult. < *piob*, bagpipe], a piece of music for the bagpipe, usually martial but sometimes dirgelike.

**pi·ca** (pī′kə), *n.* [ML., directory, hence prob. applied to the type used in printing it], 1. a size of type, 12 point. 2. the length of this type, about $^1/_6$ inch: used as a measure.

**pic·a·dor** (pik′ə-dôr′), *n.* [Sp. < *picar*, to prick], any of the horsemen who irritate the bull by pricking him with a lance to start a bullfight.

**Pic·ar·dy** (pik′ēr-di), *n.* a former province of N France, once a part of Flanders.

**pic·a·resque** (pik′ə-resk′), *adj.* [< Sp. < *picaro*, a rascal], of or dealing with sharp-witted vagabonds and their adventures: as, a *picaresque* novel.

**Pi·cas·so, Pa·blo** (pä′blô pē-kä′sô), 1881–; Spanish painter and sculptor in France.

**pic·a·yune** (pik′i-ūn′), *n.* [Fr. *picaillon*, farthing], 1. any coin of small value. 2. anything trivial or worthless. *adj.* trivial; cheap; petty; contemptible: also **pic′a·yun′ish.**

**Pic·ca·dil·ly** (pik′ə-dil′i), *n.* a fashionable street in London.

**pic·ca·lil·li** (pik′ə-lil′i), *n.* [prob. < *pickle*], a relish of vegetables, mustard, spices, etc.

**pic·co·lo** (pik′ə-lō′), *n.* [*pl.* -LOS], [It., small], a small flute, pitched an octave above the ordinary flute. —**pic′co·lo′ist,** *n.*

**pick** (pik), *n.* [var. of *pike* (weapon)], 1. a heavy, pointed metal tool used in breaking up soil, rock, etc. 2. any of several pointed tools for picking: as, an ice *pick*. 3. a plectrum.

**pick** (pik), *v.t.* [ME. *picken*, akin to AS. *picung*, a pricking], 1. to break up, pierce, or dig up (soil, rock, etc.) with something pointed. 2. to form, as a hole, with something pointed. 3. *a*) to probe, scratch at, etc. in an attempt to remove, as a scab. *b*) to clear something from (the teeth, etc.) in this way. 4. to remove by pulling; specif., to gather (flowers, berries, etc.). 5. to pluck clean in this way, as a fowl of its feathers or a tree of its fruit. 6. to eat sparingly or daintily. 7. to pull apart. 8. to choose; select. 9. to look for purposefully and find: as, to *pick* a fight, to *pick* flaws. 10. *a*) to pluck (guitar strings, etc.). *b*) to play (a guitar, etc.) in this way. 11. to open (a lock) with a wire, etc. instead of a key. 12. to steal from (one's purse, etc.). *v.i.* 1. to eat sparingly or in a fussy manner. 2. to thieve. 3. to use a pick. 4. to gather berries, flowers, etc. 5. to select, especially in a fussy manner. *n.* 1. a stroke or blow with something pointed. 2. the act of choosing or a thing chosen. 3. the most desirable; best. 4. the amount of a crop gathered at one time. —**pick at,** 1. to eat small portions of. 2. [Colloq.], to nag at. 3. to meddle with; finger. —**pick off,** 1. to remove by picking or plucking. 2. to hit with a carefully aimed shot. —**pick on,** 1. to choose. 2. [Colloq.], *a*) to single out for criticism. *b*) to annoy; tease.

—**pick out,** 1. to choose. 2. to single out among a group; distinguish. 3. to make out (meaning). —**pick over,** to examine item by item. —**pick up,** 1. to grasp and lift. 2. to get; find; learn, especially by chance or in a casual manner. 3. to stop for and take along. 4. to gain (speed). 5. to regain (health, power, etc.); improve. 6. to bring into range of sight, hearing, etc. 7. to make a room, etc. tidy. 8. [Colloq.], to become acquainted with casually, usually for purposes of love-making. —**pick′er,** *n.* —**pick′y** [-IER, -IEST], *adj.*

**pick·a·back** (pik′ə-bak′), *adv.* [var. of *pickapack*, redupl. of *pack*], on the shoulders or back: as, to carry *pickaback*: also **piggyback.**

**pick·a·nin·ny** (pik′ə-nin′i), *n.* [*pl.* -NIES], [dim. < Sp. *pequeño*, little], a Negro baby or child: a patronizing or contemptuous term.

**pick·ax** (pik′aks′), *n.* [alt. (after *ax*) < OFr. *picquois*], a pick with a point at one end of the head and a chiselllike edge at the other. *v.t. & v.i.* to use a pickax (on).

PICKAX

**pick·axe** (pik′aks′), *n., v.t. & v.i.* [-AXED, -AXING], pickax.

**picked** (pikt), *adj.* [< *pick*, to pierce], 1. selected with care: as, *picked* men. 2. gathered directly from plants, as berries, apples, etc.

**pick·er·el** (pik′ẽr-əl, pik′rəl), *n.* [*pl.* -EL, -ELS; see PLURAL, II, D, 2], [dim. of *pike* (fish)], any of various fresh-water fishes of the pike family, often having a narrow, pointed snout.

**pick·er·el·weed** (pik′ẽr-əl-wēd′, pik′rəl-), *n.* any of various water plants with large, arrow-shaped leaves and blue-violet flowers.

**pick·et** (pik′it), *n.* [< Fr. dim. of *pic*, a pike], 1. a stake, usually pointed, used as an upright in a fence, as a hitching post, etc. 2. a soldier or soldiers used to guard troops from surprise attack. 3. a person, as a member of a labor union on strike, stationed outside a factory, store, etc. to demonstrate protest, keep strikebreakers out, etc. *v.t.* 1. to enclose, protect, etc. with a picket fence. 2. to hitch (an animal) to a picket. 3. *a*) to post as a military picket. *b*) to guard (troops) with a picket. 4. to place pickets, or serve as a picket, at (a factory, etc.). *v.i.* to serve as a picket (sense 3). —**pick′et·er,** *n.* —**pick′et·ing,** *n.*

**picket fence,** a fence made of upright stakes.

**picket line,** a line of people serving as pickets.

**pick·ing** (pik′iŋ), *n.* 1. the act of one who picks. 2. *usually pl.* something picked, or the amount of this; specif., *a*) small scraps that may be gleaned. *b*) something got by dishonest means; spoils.

**pick·le** (pik′'l), *n.* [< MD. *pekel*], 1. any brine, vinegar, or spicy solution used to preserve or flavor food. 2. a vegetable, specifically a cucumber, preserved in such a solution. 3. a chemical bath used to clear metal of scale, preserve wood, etc. 4. [Colloq.], an awkward or difficult situation. *v.t.* [-LED, -LING], to treat or preserve in a pickle solution. —**pick′ler,** *n.*

**pick·led** (pik′'ld), *adj.* [Slang], intoxicated.

**pick-me-up** (pik′mi-up′), *n.* [Colloq.], an alcoholic drink taken for quick stimulation.

**pick·pock·et** (pik′pok′it), *n.* a person who steals from pockets.

**pick·up** (pik′up′), *n.* 1. the act of picking up. 2. the process or power of increasing in speed. 3. a small truck used in collecting and delivering parcels, etc. 4. [Colloq.], a casual acquaintance, as one formed for purposes of love-making. 5. [Colloq.], improvement, as in trade. 6. [Colloq.], *a*) a stimulant; bracer. *b*) stimulation. 7. *a*) in an electric phonograph, a device that produces audio-frequency currents from the vibrations of the needle moving over the record. *b*) the arm holding the needle and this device. 8. in *radio & television*, *a*) the reception of sound or light for conversion into electrical energy in the transmitter. *b*) the apparatus used for this. *c*) any place outside a studio where a broadcast originates. *d*) the electrical system connecting this place to the broadcasting station.

**pic·nic** (pik′nik), *n.* [< Fr.; prob. < *piquer*, to pick], 1. a pleasure outing at which a meal is eaten outdoors. 2. [Slang], any pleasant experience. *v.i.* [-NICKED, -NICKING], to hold or attend a picnic. —**pic′nick·er,** *n.*

**pi·cot** (pē′kō), *n.* [*pl.* -COTS (-kōz)], [Fr., dim. of *pic*, a point], any of the small loops forming an ornamental edging on lace, ribbon, etc. *v.t. & v.i.* [-COTED (-kōd), -COTING], to trim with these.

**pic·ric acid** (pik′rik), [< Gr. *pikros*, bitter], a yellow, crystalline, bitter acid, $C_6H_3O_7N_3$, used in making dyes and explosives.

**Pict** (pikt), *n.* one of an ancient people of Great Britain, driven into Scotland by the Britons and Romans. —**Pic′tish,** *adj. & n.*

**pic·to·graph** (pik′tə-graf′, -gräf′), *n.* [< L. *pictus* (see PICTURE); + *-graph*], 1. a picture representing an idea; hieroglyph. 2. writing of this kind. —**pic′to·graph′ic,** *adj.* —**pic′to·graph′i·cal·ly,** *adv.* —**pic·tog′ra·phy** (-tog′rə-fi), *n.*

**pic·to·ri·al** (pik-tôr′i-əl, -tō′ri-), *adj.* 1. [Rare], of a painter or painting. 2. of, containing, or expressed in pictures. 3. suggesting a mental image; vivid. *n.* a magazine or newspaper featuring many pictures. —**pic·to′ri·al·ly,** *adv.*

**pic·ture** (pik′chẽr), *n.* [< L. *pictura* < *pictus*, pp. of *pingere*, to paint], 1. a likeness of an object, person, etc. produced by drawing, painting, photography, etc. 2. a printed reproduction of this. 3. anything resembling or typifying something else: as, he's the *picture* of laziness. 4. anything admired for beauty. 5. a mental image; idea. 6. a description. 7. all the pertinent facts of an event. 8. a tableau. 9. a motion picture. *v.t.* [-TURED, -TURING], 1. to make a picture of by drawing, photographing, etc. 2. to show visibly: as, hate was *pictured* in his face. 3. to describe or explain. 4. to imagine. —**pic′tur·a·ble,** *adj.* —**pic′tur·a·ble·ness,** *n.* —**pic′tured,** *adj.*

**picture show,** a motion picture or motion-picture theater.

**pic·tur·esque** (pik′chẽr-esk′), *adj.* 1. like a picture; specif., *a*) having a natural beauty, as mountain scenery. *b*) pleasantly unfamiliar; quaint. 2. suggesting a mental picture; vivid. —**pic′tur·esque′ly,** *adv.* —**pic′tur·esque′ness,** *n.*

**picture window,** a large window, as in a living room, that seems to frame the outside view.

**picture writing,** 1. writing consisting of pictures or figures representing ideas. 2. the pictures, etc. so used; pictographs.

EGYPTIAN PICTURE WRITING

**pid·dle** (pid′'l), *v.i. & v.t.* [-DLED, -DLING], [child's word for *urinate*], to dawdle; trifle: as, he *piddles* the time away. —**pid′dler,** *n.* —**pid′dling,** *adj.*

**pidg·in** (pij′in), *n.* [Chin. pronun. of *business*], a jargon, as pidgin English, incorporating the vocabulary of one or more languages: also sp. **pigeon.**

**pidgin English,** a simplified form of English, with Chinese or Melanesian syntax, used by Chinese, etc. in dealing with foreigners.

**pie** (pī), *n.* [prob. same word as *pie* (magpie), from the magpie's habit of collecting oddments], 1. a baked dish consisting of fruit, meat, etc. with an upper or under crust, or both. 2. a layer cake filled with custard, jelly, etc. 3. [Slang], something very good or easy.

**pie** (pī), *n. & v.t.* [PIED, PIEING], pi (jumble).

**pie** (pī), *n.* [OFr. < L. *pica*], a magpie.

**pie·bald** (pī′bôld′), *adj.* [*pie* (magpie) + *bald*], covered with patches of two colors, often white and black. *n.* a piebald horse or other animal.

**piece** (pēs), *n.* [OFr. *pece*; prob. < Celt.], 1. a part broken or separated from the whole. 2. a section or quantity of a whole regarded as complete in itself. 3. any single thing, specimen, etc.; specif., *a*) an artistic work, as of music, etc. *b*) a firearm. *c*) a coin. *d*) one of a set, as of china. *e*) a counter, as used in various games. 4. the quantity, as of cloth, that is manufactured as a unit. 5. an amount of work constituting a single job. *v.t.* [PIECED, PIECING], 1. to add pieces to, as in repairing or enlarging. 2. to join (*together*) the pieces of, as in mending. 3. to unite. —**a piece of one's mind,** a severe reprimand or criticism. —**go to pieces,** 1. to fall apart. 2. to lose all self-control. —**of a** (or **one**) **piece,** of the same sort; alike. —**piec′er,** *n.* —**piec′ing,** *n.*

‡**pièce de ré·sis·tance** (pyes′ də rā′zēs′täns′), [Fr., piece of resistance], 1. the principal dish of a meal. 2. the main item or event in a series.

**piece goods,** textiles sold in standard sizes.

**piece·meal** (pēs′mēl′), *adv.* [< ME. < *pece*, piece + *-mele*, a part], 1. piece by piece; in small amounts or degrees. 2. into pieces. *adj.* made or done in pieces or one piece at a time.

**piece of eight,** the obsolete Spanish dollar.

**piece·work** (pēs′wũrk′), *n.* work paid for at a fixed rate (**piece rate**) per piece of work done. —**piece′work′er,** *n.*

**pied** (pīd), *adj.* covered with spots of two or more colors; piebald; variegated.

**Pied·mont** (pēd′mont), *n.* 1. a plateau between the Atlantic coast and the Appalachians in the southeastern U.S. 2. a region in NW Italy.

**pied·mont** (pēd′mont), *adj.* [< *Piedmont*, Italy], at the base of mountains. *n.* a piedmont area, etc.

**pie·plant** (pī′plant′), *n.* the rhubarb: so called from its use in pies.

**pier** (pêr), *n.* [OFr. *pere* < ML. *pera*], 1. a heavy structure supporting the spans of a bridge. 2. a structure built out over the water and supported by pillars: used as a landing place, pavilion, etc. 3. in *architecture*, *a*) a heavy column used to support weight. *b*) the part of a wall between windows or other openings. *c*) a buttress.

**pierce** (pêrs), *v.t.* [PIERCED, PIERCING], [OFr. *percer*; cf. PERISH], 1. to pass into or through as a pointed instrument does; stab. 2. to affect sharply the senses of. 3. to make a hole in; perforate; bore. 4. to make (a hole), as by boring. 5. to force a way into; break through. 6. to sound sharply through: as, a shriek *pierced* the air. 7. to penetrate with the sight or mind. *v.i.* to penetrate. **—pierc′er,** *n.* **—pierc′ing,** *adj.* **—pierc′ing·ly,** *adv.*

**Pierce, Franklin** (pêrs), 1804–1869; 14th president of the U.S. (1853–1857).

**pier glass,** a tall mirror such as was formerly set in the pier, or wall section, between windows.

**Pi·er·i·an** (pī-êr′i-ən), *adj.* 1. of Pieria, in ancient Macedonia, where the Muses were worshiped. 2. of the Muses or the arts.

**Pierre** (pêr), *n.* the capital of South Dakota, on the Missouri: pop., 10,000.

**Pi·er·rot** (pē′ĕr-ō′; Fr. pye′rō′), *n.* [Fr., dim. of *Pierre*, Peter], a comedy character having a whitened face and wearing loose white pantaloons: originally a stock figure in French pantomime.

**pi·e·tism** (pī′ə-tiz′m), *n.* 1. a system which stresses devotion in religion. 2. exaggerated pious feeling. **—pi′e·tist,** *n.* **—pi′e·tis′tic, pi′e·tis′ti·cal,** *adj.*

**pi·e·ty** (pī′ə-ti), *n.* [*pl.* -TIES], [< OFr. < L. *pietas* < *pius*, pious], 1. devotion to religious duties, etc. 2. loyalty and devotion to parents, family, etc. 3. a pious act, statement, etc.

**pi·e·zo·e·lec·tric·i·ty** (pī-ē′zō-i-lek′tris′ə-ti), *n.* [< Gr. *piezein*, to press; + *electricity*], charges of electricity induced in crystalline substances by pressure. **—pi·e′zo·e·lec′tric,** *adj.* **—pi·e′zo·e·lec′tri·cal·ly,** *adv.*

**pif·fle** (pif′'l), *n.* [Colloq.], anything regarded as insignificant or nonsensical. *v.i.* [-FLED, -FLING], [Colloq.], to talk nonsense.

**pig** (pig), *n.* [*pl.* PIGS, PIG; see PLURAL, II, D, 1], [ME. *pigge*, orig., young pig], 1. a domesticated animal with a long, broad snout and a thick, fat body covered with bristles; swine; hog. 2. a young hog. 3. pork. 4. [Colloq.], a person regarded as like a pig; greedy or filthy person. 5. *a*) an oblong casting of metal poured from the smelting furnace. *b*) pig iron collectively. *v.i.* [PIGGED, PIGGING], to bear pigs. **—pig′like′** *adj.*

**pi·geon** (pij′ən), *n.* [*pl.* -GEONS, -GEON; see PLURAL, II, D, 1], [< OFr. < LL. *pipio*, chirping bird < *pipire*, to peep], 1. any of various related birds with a small head, plump body, and short legs; dove. 2. [Slang], a person easily deceived; dupe.

**pi·geon** (pij′in), *n.* pidgin.

**pigeon breast,** a deformity of the human chest characterized by a sharply projecting sternum. **—pi′geon-breast′ed,** *adj.*

**pigeon hawk,** a small variety of hawk.

**pi·geon·hole** (pij′ən-hōl′), *n.* 1. a small recess for pigeons to nest in. 2. a small open compartment, as in a desk, for filing papers, etc. *v.t.* [-HOLED, -HOLING], 1. to put in the pigeonhole of a desk, etc. 2. to put aside indefinitely; shelve. 3. to arrange systematically.

**pi·geon-toed** (pij′ən-tōd′), *adj.* having the toes or feet turned in.

**pig·ger·y** (pig′ēr-i), *n.* [*pl.* -IES], a place where pigs are raised; pigpen.

**pig·gish** (pig′ish), *adj.* like a pig; gluttonous; filthy. **—pig′gish·ly,** *adv.* **—pig′gish·ness,** *n.*

**pig·gy** (pig′i), *n.* [*pl.* -GIES], a little pig: also sp. **piggie.** *adj.* piggish.

**pig·gy·back** (pig′i-bak′), *adv.* & *adj.* 1. pickaback. 2. designating or by means of a transportation system in which loaded truck trailers are carried on railroad flatcars: usually **piggy-back.**

**piggy bank,** a small savings bank, especially one shaped like a pig, with a slot for receiving coins.

**pig·head·ed** (pig′hed′id), *adj.* stubborn; obstinate.

**pig iron,** [from being cast in molds, or pigs], crude iron, as it comes from the blast furnace.

**pig Latin,** a playful code in which each word is begun with its first vowel, preceding consonants being moved to the end to form a new syllable with the vowel sound (ā): as "oybay" for *boy.*

**pig·let** (pig′lit), *n.* a little pig.

**pig·ment** (pig′mənt), *n.* [< L. *pigmentum* < base of *pingere*, to paint], 1. coloring matter, usually in the form of an insoluble powder, mixed with oil, water, etc. to make paints. 2. any coloring matter in the cells and tissues of plants or animals. **—pig′men·tar′y** (-mən-ter′i), *adj.*

**pig·men·ta·tion** (pig′mən-tā′shən), *n.* coloration in plants or animals due to pigment in the tissue.

**pig·ment·ed** (pig′mən-tid), *adj.* having pigmentation.

**Pig·my** (pig′mi), *adj.* & *n.* [*pl.* -MIES], Pygmy.

**pig·nut** (pig′nut′), *n.* 1. a kind of hickory nut. 2. the tree it grows on. 3. a variety of earthnut.

**pig·pen** (pig′pen′), *n.* a pen where pigs are kept.

**pig·skin** (pig′skin′), *n.* 1. the skin of a pig. 2. leather made from this. 3. [Colloq.], a football.

**pig·stick·ing** (pig′stik′iŋ), *n.* the hunting of wild boars with spears. **—pig′stick′er,** *n.*

**pig·sty** (pig′stī′), *n.* [*pl.* -STIES], a pigpen.

**pig·tail** (pig′tāl′), *n.* 1. tobacco in a twisted roll. 2. a braid of hair hanging at the back of the head.

**pike** (pīk), *n.* [short for *turnpike*], a toll road.

**pike** (pīk), *n.* [< Fr. < *piquer*, to pierce < *pic*, a pike], a weapon formerly used by foot soldiers, consisting of a metal spearhead on a long wooden shaft. *v.t.* [PIKED, PIKING], to pierce or kill with a pike. **—pike′man** (-mən), [*pl.* -MEN], *n.*

**pike** (pīk), *n.* [*pl.* PIKE, PIKES; see PLURAL, II, D, 2], [ME. *pik* for *pikefish*: from the pointed head], a slender, fresh-water fish with a pointed snout, projecting lower jaw, and sharp teeth.

**pike** (pīk), *n.* [AS. *piic*, a pickax], a spike or point, as the tip of a spear.

**pik·er** (pī′kēr), *n.* [< dial. var. of *pick*, in sense "petty pilferer"], [Slang], a person who does things in a petty or niggardly way.

**Pikes Peak** (pīks), a mountain in central Colorado: height, 14,110 ft.: also **Pike's Peak.**

**pike·staff** (pīk′staf′, -stäf′), *n.*[*pl.* -STAVES (-stāvz′)], the shaft of a pike (spear).

**pi·laf, pi·laff** (pi-läf′), *n.* pilau.

**pi·las·ter** (pi-las′tēr), *n.* [< Fr. < It. *pilastro* < L. *pila*, a pile], a rectangular support projecting slightly from the wall and treated architecturally as a column, with a base, shaft, and capital.

**Pi·late, Pon·tius** (pon′shəs, -chəs, *or* -ti-əs pī′lət), the Roman governor of Judea (26–36? A.D.) when Jesus was crucified.

**pi·lau, pi·law** (pi-lô′), *n.* [Per. *pilāw*], an Oriental dish of rice boiled with meat or fish and spiced.

**pil·chard** (pil′chērd), *n.* [? < ME. *pilken*, to pluck], any of various small fishes of the herring family; sardine: also **pil′cher** (-chēr), **pil′cherd** (-chērd).

**pile** (pīl), *n.* [< OFr. < L. *pila*, a pillar], 1. a mass of things heaped together. 2. a heap of wood, etc. on which a corpse or sacrifice is burned. 3. a large building or group of buildings. 4. [Colloq.], a large amount. 5. [Slang], a fortune. 6. in *electricity*, *a*) originally, a series of alternate plates of dissimilar metals with acid-saturated cloth or paper between them, for making an electric current. *b*) any similar arrangement that produces an electric current; battery. 7. in *physics*, a device for controlling the nuclear chain reaction in the production of atomic energy, consisting of a latticework arrangement of uranium and some moderating material, as graphite. *v.t.* [PILED, PILING], 1. to put in a pile; heap up. 2. to accumulate (with *up*). 3. to cover with a pile. *v.i.* 1. to form a pile. 2. to move confusedly in a mass (with *in*, *out*, etc.). 3. to accumulate (with *up*).

**pile** (pīl), *n.* [< L. *pilus*, a hair], 1. a raised surface on material, produced by making yarn loops on the cloth and, often, shearing them to produce a velvety surface. 2. soft, fine hair; down, wool, fur, etc. **—piled,** *adj.*

**pile** (pīl), *n.* [< AS. < L. *pilum*, a javelin], 1. a long, heavy beam driven into the ground, sometimes under water, to support a bridge, etc. 2. any similar support. *v.t.* [PILED, PILING], 1. to drive piles into. 2. to support with piles.

**pi·le·ate** (pī′li-it, pil′i-āt′), *adj.* [< L. < *pileus*, cap], having a crest extending from the bill to the nape, as some birds: also **pi′le·at′ed.**

**pileated woodpecker,** a North American woodpecker, black and white with a red crest.
**pile driver** (or **engine**), a machine with a drop hammer for driving piles.
**pi·le·ous** (pī′li-əs), *adj.* [< L. *pilus*, a hair], hairy.
**piles** (pīlz), ***n.pl.*** [< L. *pila*, a ball], hemorrhoids.
**pi·le·um** (pī′li-əm, pil′i-), *n.* [*pl.* -A (-ə)], [< L. *pilleum* (or *pilleus*), felt cap], the top of a bird's head from the bill to the nape.
**pi·le·us** (pī′li-əs, pil′i-), *n.* [*pl.* -I (-ī′)], [see prec. entry], in *botany*, the cap of a mushroom.
**pil·fer** (pil′fẽr), *v.t. & v.i.* [OFr. *pelfrer*, to plunder < *pelfre*, goods, booty], to steal (especially small sums or petty objects); filch. **—pil′fer·age,** *n.* **—pil′fer·er,** *n.*

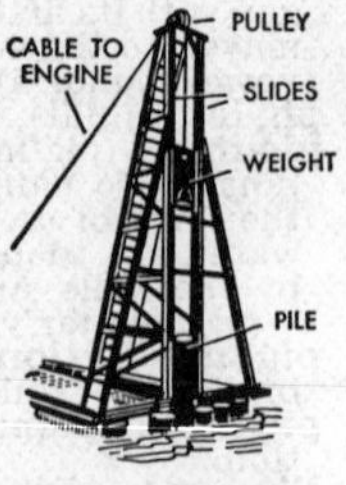

PILE DRIVER

**pil·grim** (pil′grim), *n.* [< L. *peregrinus*, foreigner < *per*, through + *ager*, country], 1. a wanderer; sojourner. 2. one who travels to a shrine or holy place. 3. [P-], one of the band of English Puritans who founded Plymouth Colony in 1620.
**pil·grim·age** (pil′grə-mij), *n.* 1. a journey made by a pilgrim, especially to a shrine or holy place. 2. any long journey.
**Pilgrim Fathers,** the Pilgrims.
**Pilgrim's Progress, The,** a religious allegory by John Bunyan (1678).
**pil·ing** (pil′iŋ), *n.* 1. a supplying with piles. 2. piles collectively. 3. a structure of piles.
**pill** (pil), *n.* [prob. < MD. < L. dim. of *pila*, a ball], 1. a small ball or pellet of medicine to be swallowed whole. 2. anything unpleasant but unavoidable. 3. [Colloq.], an oral contraceptive for women (usually with *the*). 4. [Slang], a baseball, golf ball, etc. 5. [Slang], an unpleasant person. *v.t.* 1. to dose with pills. 2. to form into pills.
**pil·lage** (pil′ij), *n.* [< Late OFr. < *piller*, to rob], 1. a plundering. 2. that which is plundered; booty; loot. *v.t.* [-LAGED, -LAGING], 1. to deprive of money or property by violence; loot. 2. to take as booty or loot. *v.i.* to engage in plunder; take loot. **—pil′lag·er,** *n.*
**pil·lar** (pil′ẽr), *n.* [< OFr. < L. *pila*, a column], 1. a slender, vertical structure used as a support; column. 2. such a column standing alone as a monument. 3. anything like a pillar in form or function, as one who is a main support of an institution, movement, etc. *v.t.* to support as with pillars. **—from pillar to post,** from one predicament to another. **—pil′lared,** *adj.*
**Pillars of Hercules,** the two points of land on either side of the Strait of Gibraltar.
**pill·box** (pil′boks′), *n.* 1. a small, shallow box for holding pills. 2. an enclosed gun emplacement of concrete and steel.
**pil·lion** (pil′yən), *n.* [< Gael. < *peall* (< L. *pellis*), a skin], 1. a cushion behind a saddle for an extra rider, especially a woman. 2. an extra seat behind the driver's saddle on a motorcycle.
**pil·lo·ry** (pil′ə-ri), *n.* [*pl.* -RIES], [< OFr. < Pr. *espilori*], 1. a device with holes for the head and hands, in which petty offenders were formerly locked and exposed to public scorn. 2. any exposure to public scorn, etc. *v.t.* [-RIED, -RYING], 1. to punish by placing in a pillory. 2. to lay open to public scorn or abuse.
**pil·low** (pil′ō), *n.* [AS. *pyle;* ult. < L. *pulvinus*, a cushion], 1. a cloth case filled with feathers, down, air, etc., to support the head, as in sleeping. 2. anything like this, as a pad on which certain laces are made. 3. the block supporting the inner end of a bowsprit. *v.t.* 1. to rest as on a pillow. 2. to be a pillow for. *v.i.* to rest the head as on a pillow. **—pil′low·y,** *adj.*
**pil·low·case** (pil′ō-kās′), *n.* a removable cotton, linen, etc. covering for a pillow: also **pil′low·slip′.**
**pillow lace,** lace made by interlacing thread from bobbins around pins set into a pillow.
**pi·lose** (pī′lōs), *adj.* [< L. *pilus*, a hair], covered with hair, especially fine, soft hair: also **pi′lous** (-ləs). **—pi·los′i·ty** (-los′ə-ti), *n.*
**pi·lot** (pī′lət), *n.* [< Fr. < It. *pilota* < Gr. *pēdon*, an oar], 1. a steersman; specif., a person licensed to steer ships into or out of a harbor or through difficult waters. 2. a person who flies an airplane, airship, etc. 3. a guide; leader. 4. a device that guides the action of a machine or machine part. 5. a pilot light. *v.t.* 1. to act as a pilot of, on, in, or over. 2. to guide; lead. *adj.* that serves as a trial unit on a small scale for experimentation or testing.
**pi·lot·age** (pī′lət-ij), *n.* 1. a piloting. 2. the fee paid to a pilot.
**pilot balloon,** a small balloon sent up to determine the direction and velocity of the wind.
**pilot biscuit** (or **bread**), hardtack.
**pilot fish,** a narrow, spiny-finned fish with a widely forked tail, often seen near sharks.
**pi·lot·house** (pī′lət-hous′), *n.* an enclosed place for the helmsman on the upper deck of a ship.
**pilot lamp,** an electric lamp placed in an electric circuit to indicate when the current is on.
**pilot light,** 1. a small gas burner which is kept lighted to rekindle the principal burner when needed: also **pilot burner.** 2. a pilot lamp.
**pilot plant,** a small factory for making experimental tests in production.
**Pilt·down man** (pilt′doun′), a supposed species of prehistoric man whose existence was presumed on the basis of bone fragments found in Piltdown (Sussex, England) in 1911. These were exposed as a hoax in 1953.
**pi·men·to** (pi-men′tō), *n.* [*pl.* -TOS], [< Sp. < ML. *pigmentum*, a spice, spiced drink < L., pigment], 1. the pimiento. 2. allspice, or the tropical tree it comes from.
**pimento cheese,** a cheese containing pimientos.
**pi·mien·to** (pi-myen′tō), *n.* [*pl.* -TOS], [Sp.; see PIMENTO], a variety of garden pepper or its sweet, red fruit, used as a relish, etc.
**pimp** (pimp), *n.* [? < OFr. *pimper*, to entice], a prostitute's agent; pander. *v.i.* to act as a pimp.
**pim·per·nel** (pim′pẽr-nel′, -nəl), *n.* [<OFr. < ML. < L. *piperinus*, like peppercorns (cf. the pimpernel's fruit) < *piper*, pepper], a plant of the primrose family, with red, white, or blue, starlike flowers which close in bad weather.
**pim·ple** (pim′p'l), *n.* [? < AS. *piplian*, to be pimpled], any small, often inflamed, swelling of the skin. **—pim′pled, pim′ply** [-PLIER, -PLIEST], *adj.*
**pin** (pin), *n.* [AS. *pinn*], 1. a peg of wood, metal, etc., used for fastening things together, as a support for hanging things, etc. 2. a little piece of stiff wire with a pointed end and flattened or rounded head, for fastening things together. 3. something worthless or insignificant; trifle. 4. a clothespin, hairpin, cotter pin, rolling pin, etc. 5. anything like a pin in form, use, etc. 6. an ornament or badge with a pin or clasp for fastening it to the clothing. 7. a peg for holding a string in a violin, etc. and regulating its tension. 8. *usually pl.* [Colloq.], the leg. 9. in *bowling*, one of the wooden clubs at which the ball is rolled. 10. in *golf*, the pole for the flag at the hole of a green. 11. in *nautical usage*, *a*) a thole. *b*) a peg or bolt used in fastening the rigging. *v.t.* [PINNED, PINNING], 1. to fasten as with a pin. 2. to pierce with a pin. 3. to hold firmly in one position. 4. [College Slang], to give one's fraternity pin to, as an informal token of betrothal. **—on pins and needles,** filled with anxiety. **—pin one down,** to get one to commit himself as to his opinion, plans, etc. **—pin (something) on one,** [Colloq.], to lay the blame of (something) on one. **—pin′like′,** *adj.* **—pin′ner,** *n.*
**pin·a·fore** (pin′ə-fôr′, -fōr′), *n.* [*pin* + *afore*], a sleeveless, apronlike garment worn by girls.
**pin·ball** (pin′bôl′), *n.* a game played on an inclined board containing holes, pins, etc. and marked with scores credited to the player if he makes a ball hit the pins or roll into the holes.
**pin boy,** in *bowling*, a boy or man who sets up the pins after each frame and returns the balls.
**pince-nez** (pans′nā′, pins′-), *n.* [*pl.* PINCE-NEZ], [Fr., nose-pincher], eyeglasses kept in place by a spring gripping the bridge of the nose.
**pin·cers** (pin′sẽrz), ***n.pl.*** [occas. construed as sing.], [<OFr. *pincier*, to pinch], 1. a tool formed of two pivoted parts, used in gripping or nipping things. 2. in *zoology*, a grasping claw, as of a crab; chela. **—pin′cer·like′,** *adj.*

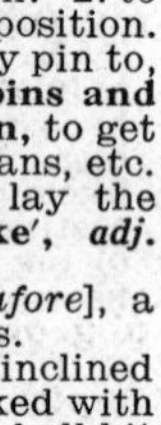
PINCERS

**pinch** (pinch), *v.t.* [< ONorm. Fr. *pincher;* prob. < Gmc.], 1. to squeeze as between a finger and the thumb or between two edges. 2. to press painfully upon (a part of the body). 3. to cause distress or discomfort to. 4. to cause to become thin, cramped, etc., as by hunger, cold, etc. 5. to restrict closely; stint (often in the passive). 6. [Slang], to steal. 7. [Slang], to arrest. *v.i.* 1. to squeeze painfully. 2. to be stingy or niggardly. *n.* 1. a pinching; squeeze or nip. 2. the quantity that may be grasped between the finger and thumb; small amount. 3. hardship; difficulty. 4. an emergency; urgent situation. 5. [Slang], a theft. 6. [Slang], an arrest. **—pinched,** *adj.* **—pinch′er,** *n.*
**pinch·beck** (pinch′bek), *n.* [< C. *Pinchbeck*, Eng. jeweler who invented it], 1. a gold-colored alloy of

copper and zinc. 2. anything cheap or imitation. *adj.* 1. made of pinchbeck. 2. cheap; imitation.

**pinch·ers** (pin′chẽrz), ***n.pl.*** pincers.

**pinch-hit** (pinch′hit′), ***v.i.*** [-HIT, -HITTING], 1. in *baseball,* to bat in place of the regular player when a hit is especially needed. 2. to act as a substitute in an emergency (*for*). —**pinch hitter.**

**pin·cush·ion** (pin′koosh′ən), ***n.*** a small cushion in which pins and needles are stuck to keep them handy for use.

**Pin·dar** (pin′dẽr), ***n.*** Greek lyric poet; 522?–443 B.C. —**Pin·dar′ic** (-dar′ik), ***adj.***

**pine** (pīn), ***n.*** [see PLURAL, II, D, 3], [AS. *pin* < L. *pinus,* pine tree], 1. any of various evergreen trees having cones and clusters of needle-shaped leaves: many pines are valuable for their wood and their resin, which yields turpentine, tar, etc. 2. the wood of such a tree.

**pine** (pīn), ***v.i.*** [PINED, PINING], [AS. *pinian,* to torment < *pin* (L. *poena*), a pain], 1. to waste (*away*) through grief, pain, hunger, etc. 2. to have an intense longing or desire; yearn.

**pin·e·al body** (or **gland**) (pin′i-əl), [< Fr. < L. *pinea,* a pine cone], a small cone-shaped structure in the brain of all vertebrates having a cranium: it has no known function.

**pine·ap·ple** (pīn′ap′'l), ***n.*** [ME. *pinappel,* pine cone], 1. a juicy, edible tropical fruit somewhat resembling a pine cone. 2. the plant it grows on, having spiny-edged leaves. 3. [Slang], a small bomb or hand grenade.

**pine cone,** the cone (sense 3) of a pine tree.

**pine needle,** the needlelike leaf of a pine tree.

**pine tar,** a viscid, dark liquid obtained from pine wood and used in disinfectants, tar paints, etc.

**pin·ey** (pīn′i), ***adj.*** [-IER, -IEST], piny.

**pin·feath·er** (pin′feth′ẽr), ***n.*** an undeveloped feather that is just emerging through the skin.

**pin·fold** (pin′fōld′), ***n.*** [< AS. < *pund,* a pound + *fald,* a pen], a place where stray animals are confined. ***v.t.*** to confine in a pinfold.

**ping** (piŋ), ***n.*** [echoic], the sound made by a bullet striking something sharply. ***v.i. & v.t.*** to strike with a ping.

**ping-pong** (piŋ′poŋ′, -pôŋ′), ***n.*** [echoic], a game somewhat like tennis, played on a table with a small, celluloid ball and small racket-shaped paddles; table tennis: a trade-mark (**Ping-pong**).

**pin·head** (pin′hed′), ***n.*** 1. the head of a pin. 2. anything very small or trifling. 3. a stupid or foolish person.

**pin·hole** (pin′hōl′), ***n.*** 1. a tiny hole made as by a pin. 2. a hole into which a pin goes.

**pin·ion** (pin′yən), ***n.*** [< Fr.; ult. < L. *pinna,* a pinnacle], a small cogwheel which meshes with a larger gearwheel or a rack.

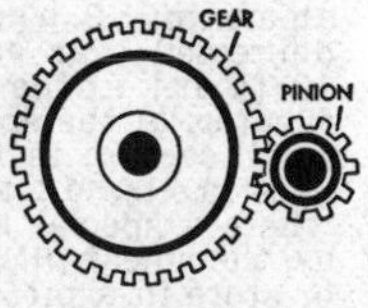

PINION

**pin·ion** (pin′yən), ***n.*** [< OFr. < L. *pinna,* a feather], 1. the end joint of a bird's wing. 2. a wing. 3. any wing feather. ***v.t.*** 1. to cut off or bind the pinions of (a bird) to keep it from flying. 2. to bind (the wings). 3. to disable by binding the arms of. 4. to confine or shackle.

**pink** (piŋk), ***n.*** [? < *pinkeye,* lit., little eye], 1. any of various plants with five-petaled, pale-red flowers and sticky stems. 2. the flower. 3. its pale-red color. 4. the highest or finest condition, example, etc. 5. [often P-], one whose political views are somewhat radical: a derogatory term. ***adj.*** 1. pale-red. 2. mildly radical. —**pink′ish,** ***adj.***

**pink** (piŋk), ***v.t.*** [? form of *pick, v.;* ? < AS. *pyngan,* to prick], 1. to ornament (cloth, paper, etc.) by making perforations in a pattern. 2. to cut a saw-toothed edge on (cloth, etc.) to prevent unraveling or for decoration. 3. to prick; stab. 4. to adorn; embellish. —**pink′er,** ***n.***

**pink·eye** (piŋk′ī′), ***n.*** an acute, contagious form of conjunctivitis in which the eyeball and the conjunctiva become inflamed: also **pink eye.**

**pink·ie, pink·y** (piŋk′i), ***n.*** [*pl.* -IES], the fifth, or smallest, finger.

**pink·ing shears** (piŋk′iŋ), shears with notched blades, used for pinking the edges of cloth, etc.

**pink tea,** [Colloq.], a frivolous social gathering, especially one attended largely by women.

**pin money,** 1. an allowance of money given to a wife for her personal use. 2. any small sum of money, as for incidental minor expenses.

**pin·na** (pin′ə), ***n.*** [*pl.* -NAE (-ē), -NAS], [L., a feather], 1. in *anatomy,* the external ear. 2. in *botany,* a leaflet. 3. in *zoology,* a feather, wing, fin, etc. —**pin′nal,** ***adj.***

**pin·nace** (pin′is), ***n.*** [< Fr. < It. < L. *pinus,* pine (tree)], 1. a small sailing ship. 2. a ship's boat.

**pin·na·cle** (pin′ə-k'l), ***n.*** [< OFr. < LL. dim. of L. *pinna,* a wing], 1. a small turret or spire as on a buttress. 2. a slender, pointed formation, as a mountain peak. 3. the highest point; acme. ***v.t.*** [-CLED, -CLING], 1. to set on a pinnacle. 2. to furnish with pinnacles. 3. to form the pinnacle of.

**pin·nate** (pin′āt, -it), ***adj.*** [< L. < *pinna,* a feather], 1. resembling a feather. 2. in *botany,* with leaflets on each side of a common stem. Also **pin′nat·ed.** —**pin′nate·ly,** ***adv.*** —**pin·na′tion,** ***n.***

**pi·noch·le, pi·noc·le** (pē′nuk′'l), ***n.*** [prob. < Fr.], a game of cards played with a special deck of 48 cards, consisting of a double deck of all cards above the eight. Also sp. **pe′nuch′le, pe′nuck′le.**

**pi·ñon** (pin′yən, pēn′yōn), ***n.*** [Sp. < L. *pinea,* pine cone < *pinus,* a pine], 1. any of certain pine trees with large, edible seeds. 2. the seed.

**pin·point** (pin′point′), ***v.t.*** 1. to show the location of by sticking a pin into, as on a map. 2. to show the precise location of. ***n.*** 1. the point of a pin. 2. something trifling or insignificant.

**pin stripe,** a slender, light-colored stripe, about the width of a pin, as in some suits.

**pint** (pīnt), ***n.*** [< OFr. *pinte* < MD.], a measure of capacity (liquid or dry) equal to ½ quart.

**pin·tail** (pin′tāl′), ***n.*** [*pl.* -TAILS, -TAIL; see PLURAL, II, D, 1], 1. a variety of duck with long, pointed tail feathers. 2. a variety of grouse with a long, pointed tail.

**pin·tle** (pin′t'l), ***n.*** [AS. *pintel,* penis], a pin or bolt on which some other part turns.

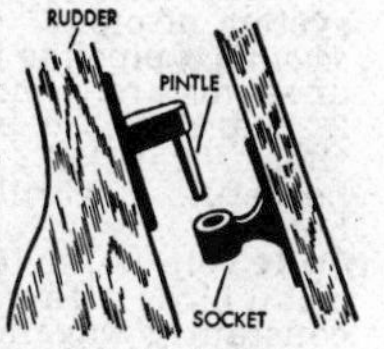

PINTLE

**pin·to** (pin′tō), ***adj.*** [Sp.; ult. < L. pp. of *pingere,* to paint], marked with spots of two or more colors; mottled; piebald. ***n.*** [*pl.* -TOS], 1. a pinto horse or pony. 2. the pinto bean.

**pinto bean,** a kind of mottled kidney bean that grows in the SW United States.

**pin-up** (pin′up′), ***adj.*** 1. that is or can be pinned up on or fastened to a wall: as, a *pin-up* lamp. 2. [Slang], designating a girl whose sexual attractiveness makes her a suitable subject for a picture to be displayed on a wall. ***n.*** [Slang], a pin-up girl, picture, etc.

**pin·wheel** (pin′hwēl′), ***n.*** 1. a small wheel with colored vanes of paper, etc. pinned to a stick so as to revolve in the wind. 2. a firework that revolves when set off. Also **pin wheel.**

**pin·worm** (pin′wũrm′), ***n.*** a small, threadlike worm, sometimes parasitic in the human rectum.

**pin·y** (pīn′i), ***adj.*** [-IER, -IEST], 1. abounding in pines. 2. of or like pines. Also sp. **piney.**

**pi·o·neer** (pī′ə-nêr′), ***n.*** [< Fr. < OFr. *peonier,* foot soldier < *peon;* see PEON], 1. a member of a military unit that builds bridges, roads, etc.; military engineer. 2. one who goes before, preparing the way for others, as an early settler. ***v.i.*** to act as a pioneer. ***v.t.*** 1. to open (a way, etc.). 2. to be a pioneer in or of.

**pi·ous** (pī′əs), ***adj.*** [< Fr. *pieux* or L. *pius*], 1. having or showing religious devotion; devout. 2. springing from actual or pretended religious devotion. 3. sacred. —**pi′ous·ly,** ***adv.*** —**pi′ous·ness,** ***n.***

**pip** (pip), ***n.*** [abbrev. of *pippin*], a small seed, as of an apple, pear, orange, etc.

**pip** (pip), ***n.*** [earlier *peep* < ?], any of the figures or spots on playing cards, dice, etc.

**pip** (pip), ***v.i.*** [PIPPED, PIPPING], [prob. var. of *peep* (to cry)], to peep or chirp, as a bird. ***v.t.*** to break through (the shell), as a hatching bird.

**pip** (pip), ***n.*** [< MD. < LL. *pipita* for L. *pituita,* phlegm], 1. a contagious disease of fowl, characterized by the secretion of mucus in the throat. 2. any minor human ailment: a humorous usage.

**pipe** (pīp), ***n.*** [AS. < LL. < L. *pipare,* to chirp], 1. a cylindrical tube, as of reed, wood, metal, etc., for making musical sounds; specif., *pl. a)* the Panpipe. *b)* the bagpipe. 2. any of the tubes in an organ that produce the tones. 3. *a)* a boatswain's whistle. *b)* the sounding of it as a signal. 4. *often pl.* the singing voice. 5. the call or note of a bird. 6. a long tube for conveying water, gas, oil, etc.

7. a tubular organ of the body; esp., *pl.* the respiratory organs. 8. anything tubular in form. 9. *a*) a tube with a small bowl at one end in which tobacco, etc. is smoked. *b*) enough tobacco to fill such a bowl. 10. a large cask, holding about two hogsheads, for wine, oil, etc. 11. this volume as a unit of measure. ***v.i.*** [PIPED, PIPING], 1. to play on a pipe. 2. to utter shrill sounds. 3. in *nautical usage*, to signal the crew by a boatswain's pipe. ***v.t.*** to play (a tune, etc.) on a pipe. 2. to utter in a shrill voice. 3. to bring, call, etc. by piping. 4. to convey (water, gas, etc.) by pipes. 5. to provide with pipes. 6. to trim with piping, as a dress. **—pipe down,** [Slang], to become quiet. **—pipe up,** 1. to begin to play (music). 2. to speak up in a piping voice.

**pipe clay,** a white, plastic clay used for whitening, making clay pipes, etc.

**pipe dream,** [Colloq.], a fantastic idea or vain hope, such as in the mind of an opium smoker.

**pipe·ful** (pīp′fool′), ***n.*** [*pl.* -FULS], the amount (of tobacco, etc.) put in a pipe at one time.

**pipe-line** (pīp′lin′), ***v.t.*** [-LINED, -LINING], to convey by, or supply with, a pipe line.

**pipe line,** 1. a line of pipes for conveying water, gas, oil, etc. 2. any means whereby something is conveyed: as, a *pipe line* of information.

**pipe of peace,** a peace pipe; calumet.

**pipe organ,** an organ (sense 1).

**pip·er** (pīp′ēr), ***n.*** a person who plays on a pipe; esp., a bagpiper.

**pipe·stem** (pīp′stem′), ***n.*** 1. the slender stem of a tobacco pipe. 2. anything like this in form.

**pi·pette, pi·pet** (pi-pet′, pi-), ***n.*** [Fr., dim. of *pipe*, a tube], a slender glass tube for transferring or measuring small amounts of liquids.

**pip·ing** (pīp′iŋ), ***n.*** 1. the act of one who pipes. 2. music made by pipes. 3. a shrill sound. 4. a system of pipes. 5. material used for pipes. 6. in *sewing*, a pipelike fold of material with which edges or seams are trimmed. ***adj.*** 1. playing on a pipe. 2. characterized by "peaceful" pipe music rather than "warlike" drums, trumpets, etc.; hence, peaceful. 3. shrill. ***adv.*** so as to sizzle: as, *piping* hot.

**pip·it** (pip′it), ***n.*** [echoic of its cry], any of various small birds with a slender bill, streaked breast, and constantly wagging tail.

**pip·kin** (pip′kin), ***n.*** [dim. of *pipe*], 1. a small earthenware pot. 2. a piggin.

**pip·pin** (pip′in), ***n.*** [< OFr. *pepin*, seed, pip], any of a number of varieties of apple.

**pip·sis·se·wa** (pip-sis′ə-wə), ***n.*** [< Am. Ind.], any of various plants with pink or white flowers and jagged, leathery leaves, used in medicine.

**pip-squeak** (pip′skwēk′), ***n.*** anything or anyone regarded as small or insignificant.

**pi·quant** (pē′kənt), ***adj.*** [Fr., ppr. of *piquer*, to prick], 1. agreeably pungent to the taste; pleasantly sharp. 2. exciting interest; stimulating. **—pi′quan·cy, pi′quant·ness,** ***n.*** **—pi′quant·ly,** ***adv.***

**pique** (pēk), ***n.*** [Fr. < *piquer*, to prick], 1. resentment at being slighted; ruffled pride. 2. a fit of displeasure. ***v.t.*** [PIQUED, PIQUING], 1. to arouse resentment in, as by slighting; offend. 2. to excite; arouse. **—pique oneself on** (or **upon**), to be proud of.

**pi·qué** (pi-kā′), ***n.*** [Fr., pp. of *piquer*, to prick], a firmly woven cotton fabric with vertical cords.

**pi·quet** (pi-ket′), ***n.*** [Fr., spade at cards], a game of cards for two persons, played with 32 cards.

**pi·ra·cy** (pī′rə-si), ***n.*** [*pl.* -CIES], [see PIRATE], 1. robbery of ships on the high seas. 2. the unauthorized publication or use of a copyrighted or patented work.

**Pi·rae·us** (pī-rē′əs), ***n.*** a city in Greece; seaport of Athens: pop., 185,000: also sp. **Pei·rae′us.**

**Pi·ran·del·lo, Lu·i·gi** (lōō-ē′ji pē′rän-del′lô; Eng. pir′ən-del′ō), 1867–1936; Italian dramatist and novelist.

**pi·rate** (pī′rit), ***n.*** [< L. < Gr. *peiratēs* < *peiran*, to attack], 1. one who practices piracy; esp., a robber of ships on the high seas. 2. a pirates' ship. ***v.t. & v.i.*** [-RATED, -RATING], 1. to practice piracy (upon). 2. to publish or use (a literary work, etc.) in violation of a copyright or patent. **—pi·rat′i·cal** (-rat′i-k'l), **pi·rat′ic,** ***adj.*** **—pi·rat′i·cal·ly,** ***adv.***

**pi·rogue** (pi-rōg′), ***n.*** [< Fr. < Sp. *piragua* < W. Ind. name], a canoe made by hollowing out a log.

**pir·ou·ette** (pir′ōō-et′), ***n.*** [Fr., spinning top; prob. < dial. *piroue*, a top], in *dancing*, a whirling on the toes. ***v.i.*** [-ETTED, -ETTING], to do a pirouette. **—pir′ou·et′ter, pir′ou·et′tist,** ***n.***

**Pi·sa** (pē′zə; It. pē′sä), ***n.*** a city in NW Italy: famous for its Leaning Tower: pop., 82,000.

**pis·ca·to·ri·al** (pis′kə-tôr′i-əl, -tō′ri-əl), ***adj.*** [< L. < *piscator*, fisherman], of fishermen or fishing: also **pis′ca·to′ry.** **—pis′ca·to′ri·al·ly,** ***adv.***

**Pis·ces** (pis′ēz), ***n.*** 1. a constellation south of Andromeda, supposedly resembling a fish in shape. 2. the twelfth sign of the zodiac (♓), entered by the sun about February 21.

**pis·ci-,** [< L. *piscus*, a fish], a combining form meaning *fish*, as in *pisciculture*.

**pis·ci·cul·ture** (pis′i-kul′chēr), ***n.*** [*pisci-* + *culture*], the breeding of fish as an art or industry.

**pish** (pish, psh), ***interj. & n.*** an exclamation of disgust or impatience. ***v.i. & v.t.*** to make this exclamation (at); express disgust, etc. (at).

**pis·mire** (pis′mīr′), ***n.*** [< ME. < *pisse*, urine + *mire*, ant], an ant.

**pis·ta·chi·o** (pis-tä′shi-ō′, -tash′i-ō′), ***n.*** [*pl.* -os], [< It. < L. < Gr. *pistakē*], 1. a small tree of the cashew family. 2. its edible, greenish seed (**pistachio nut**). 3. the flavor of this nut. 4. a light yellow-green color.

**pis·til** (pis′til, -t'l), ***n.*** [Fr. < L. *pistillum*, a pestle], the seed-bearing organ of a flower, consisting of the ovary, stigma, and style.

**pis·til·late** (pis′tə-lit, -lāt′), ***adj.*** having a pistil or pistils; esp., having pistils but no stamens.

**pis·tol** (pis′t'l), ***n.*** [< Fr. & G. < Czech *pist'al* < *pisk*, a whistling sound], a small firearm held and fired with one hand. ***v.t.*** [-TOLED or -TOLLED, -TOLING or -TOLLING], to shoot with a pistol.

**pis·tole** (pis-tōl′), ***n.*** [Fr.], 1. a former Spanish gold coin. 2. any similar obsolete European coin.

**pis·ton** (pis′t'n), ***n.*** [< Fr. < It. < *pestone*, a pestle < *pistare*, to beat; ult. < L. *pi(n)sere*, to pound], 1. a disk or short cylinder closely fitted in a hollow cylinder and moved back and forth by the pressure of a fluid so as to transmit reciprocating motion to a rod (**piston rod**) or moved by the rod so as to exert pressure on the fluid. 2. a sliding valve moved in the cylinder of a brass-wind instrument to change the pitch.

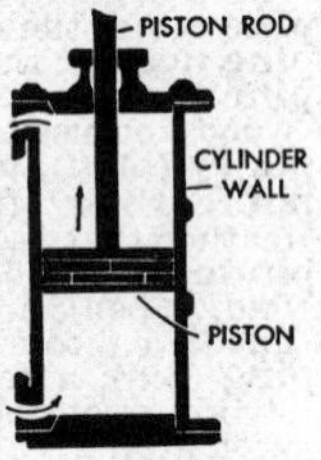

PISTON

**piston ring,** a split metal ring placed around a piston to make it fit the cylinder closely.

**pit** (pit), ***n.*** [D., kernel], the hard stone, as of the plum, peach, etc., which contains the seed. ***v.t.*** [PITTED, PITTING], to remove the pit from.

**pit** (pit), ***n.*** [AS. *pytt* < L. *puteus*, a well], 1. a hole in the ground. 2. an abyss. 3. hell. 4. a covered hole used to trap wild animals; pitfall. 5. any concealed danger; trap. 6. an enclosed area in which animals are kept or made to fight: as, a bear *pit*. 7. *a*) the shaft of a coal mine. *b*) the mine itself. 8. an indentation on a part of the human body: as, an arm*pit*. 9. a small hollow in a surface; specif., a depressed scar as that resulting from smallpox. 10. [Brit.], *a*) the rear part of the ground floor of a theater. *b*) the spectators in that section. 11. the small section in front of the stage where the orchestra sits. 12. the part of the floor of an exchange where a special branch of business is transacted: as, the wheat *pit*. ***v.t.*** [PITTED, PITTING], 1. to put or store in a pit. 2. to make pits in. 3. to mark with small scars: as, *pitted* by smallpox. 4. to set (cocks, etc.) in a pit to fight. 5. to set in competition (*against*). ***v.i.*** to become marked with pits. **—pit′ted,** ***adj.***

**pit·a·pat** (pit′ə-pat′), ***adv.*** with rapid and strong beating; palpitatingly. ***n.*** a rapid succession of beats. ***v.i.*** [-PATTED, -PATTING], to go pitapat.

**pitch** (pich), ***n.*** [AS. *pic* < L. *pix*], 1. a black, sticky substance formed in the distillation of coal tar, petroleum, etc. and used for waterproofing, pavements, etc. 2. any of certain bitumens, as asphalt. 3. a resin found in certain evergreen trees. ***v.t.*** to cover or smear with pitch.

**pitch** (pich), ***v.t.*** [ME. *picchen*], 1. to set up: as, *pitch* a tent. 2. to throw; fling; toss. 3. to fix or set at a particular point, level, degree, etc. 4. in *baseball*, to throw (the ball) to the batter. 5. in *music*, to set the key of (a tune, an instrument, or the voice). ***v.i.*** 1. to encamp. 2. to take up one's position; settle. 3. to pitch anything, as hay, a ball, etc. 4. to plunge forward or headlong. 5. to incline downward; dip. 6. to toss with the bow and stern rising and falling: said of a ship. ***n.*** 1. act or manner of pitching. 2. a throw; toss. 3. the pitching of a ship in a rough sea. 4. anything pitched. 5. the amount pitched. 6. a point or degree: as, feelings were at a high *pitch*. 7. the degree of slope or inclination. 8. [Slang], a line of talk, such as a hawker uses. 9. in *machinery*, the distance between corresponding points, as on two adjacent gear teeth or on two adjacent threads of a screw.

10. in *music*, etc. *a*) that quality of a tone or sound determined by the frequency of vibration of the sound waves: the greater the frequency the higher the pitch. *b*) a standard of pitch for tuning instruments. —**pitch in,** [Colloq.], to set to work energetically. —**pitch into,** [Colloq.], to attack physically or verbally. —**pitch on** (or **upon**), to select; decide on.

**pitch-black** (pich′blak′), *adj.* very black.

**pitch·blende** (pich′blend′), *n.* [< G. < *pech*, pitch + *blende;* see BLENDE], a brown to black lustrous mineral containing radium, uranium, etc.

**pitch-dark** (pich′därk′), *adj.* very dark.

**pitched battle** (picht), a battle in which the arrangement of troops and the line of combat have been planned beforehand.

**pitch·er** (pich′ẽr), *n.* [< OFr.; ult. < LL. *bicarium*, a jug < Gr. *bikos*, wine jar], a container, usually with a handle and lip, for holding and pouring liquids. —**pitch′er·ful** [*pl.* -FULS], *n.*

**pitch·er** (pich′ẽr), *n.* one who pitches; esp., in *baseball*, the player who pitches the ball to the batter.

**pitcher plant,** a plant with pitcherlike leaves which attract and trap insects.

**pitch·fork** (pich′fôrk′), *n.* a large, long-handled fork for lifting and tossing hay, etc. *v.t.* to lift and toss with a pitchfork.

PITCHER PLANT
(2 ft. high)

**pitch·man** (pich′mən), *n.* [*pl.* -MEN], [Slang], one who makes his living by hawking novelties, jewelry, etc. from small stands, as at carnivals.

**pitch pine,** a resinous pine from which pitch or turpentine is obtained.

**pitch pipe,** a small pipe which produces a fixed tone as a standard for tuning instruments, etc.

**pitch·y** (pich′i), *adj.* [-IER, -IEST], 1. full of or smeared with pitch. 2. like pitch in consistency; sticky. 3. black. —**pitch′i·ness,** *n.*

**pit·e·ous** (pit′i-əs), *adj.* arousing or deserving pity. —**pit′e·ous·ly,** *adv.* —**pit′e·ous·ness,** *n.*

**pit·fall** (pit′fôl′), *n.* [< *pit* + AS. *fealle*, a trap], 1. a covered pit used as a trap for animals. 2. any concealed danger for an unwary person.

**pith** (pith), *n.* [AS. *pitha*], 1. the soft, spongy tissue in the center of certain plant stems. 2. any soft core, as of a bone. 3. the essential part; gist. 4. strength; vigor. *v.t.* to remove the pith from (a plant stem).

**Pith·e·can·thro·pus (e·rec·tus)** (pith′ə-kan′thrə-pəs, -kan-thrō′pəs i-rek′təs), [< Gr. *pithēkos*, an ape + *anthrōpos*, man; see ERECT], Java man.

**pith·y** (pith′i), *adj.* [-IER, -IEST], 1. of, like, or full of pith. 2. full of meaning, substance, or force. —**pith′i·ly,** *adv.* —**pith′i·ness,** *n.*

**pit·i·a·ble** (pit′i-ə-b'l), *adj.* 1. arousing or deserving pity. 2. deserving contempt; despicable. —**pit′i·a·ble·ness,** *n.* —**pit′i·a·bly,** *adv.*

**pit·i·ful** (pit′i-fəl), *adj.* 1. full of pity. 2. exciting or deserving pity. 3. deserving contempt; despicable. —**pit′i·ful·ly,** *adv.* —**pit′i·ful·ness,** *n.*

**pit·i·less** (pit′i-lis), *adj.* without pity; merciless. —**pit′i·less·ly,** *adv.* —**pit′i·less·ness,** *n.*

**pit·man** (pit′mən), *n.* [*pl.* -MEN], 1. one who works in a pit; esp., a coal miner. 2. [*pl.* -MANS], in *machinery*, a connecting rod.

**Pitt, William** (pit), 1. 1708–1778; English statesman. 2. 1759–1806; son of the above; British prime minister (1783–1801; 1804–1806).

**pit·tance** (pit′əns), *n.* [< OFr. *pitance*, food allowed a monk; ult. < L. *pietas*, piety], 1. a meager allowance of money. 2. a small amount or share.

**pit·ter-pat·ter** (pit′ẽr-pat′ẽr), *n.* [echoic], a rapid succession of light beating or tapping sounds. *adv.* with a pitter-patter.

**Pitts·burgh** (pits′bẽrg), *n.* a city in W Pennsylvania: pop., 604,000 (metropolitan area, 2,405,000).

**Pitts·field** (pits′fēld), *n.* a city in W Massachusetts: pop., 58,000.

**pi·tu·i·tar·y** (pi-tōō′ə-ter′i, pi-tū′-), *adj.* [< L. *pituita*, phlegm], of the pituitary gland. *n.* 1. the pituitary gland. 2. a preparation made from extracts of the pituitary gland.

**pituitary gland** (or **body**), a small, oval endocrine gland attached to the base of the brain: it secretes hormones influencing body growth, etc.

**pit·y** (pit′i), *n.* [*pl.* -IES], [< OFr. < L. *pietas*, piety < *pius*, pious], 1. sorrow for another's suffering or misfortune; compassion. 2. a cause for sorrow or regret. *v.t. & v.i.* [-IED, -YING], to feel pity (for). —**have** (or **take**) **pity on,** to show pity for. —**pit′i·er,** *n.* —**pit′y·ing·ly,** *adv.*

‡**più** (pū), *adv.* [It.], more: a direction in music, as in *più allegro*, more quickly.

**Pi·us XII** (pī′əs), 1876–1958; Pope (1939–1958).

**piv·ot** (piv′ət), *n.* [Fr.; cf. It. *pivolo*, peg], 1. a point, shaft, etc. on which something turns. 2. a person or thing on which something turns or depends; central point. 3. a pivoting movement. *adj.* pivotal. *v.t.* to provide with or mount on a pivot. *v.i.* to turn as on a pivot. —**piv′ot·al,** *adj.* —**piv′ot·al·ly,** *adv.*

**pix·i·lat·ed** (pik′sə-lā′tid), *adj.* [< *pixy* + *titillated*], 1. slightly unbalanced mentally. 2. [Slang], drunk.

**pix·y** (pik′si), *n.* [*pl.* -IES], [< Brit. dial.], a fairy; sprite: also sp. **pixie.**

**piz·za** (pēt′sə), *n.* [It.], an Italian dish consisting of a breadlike crust covered with a spiced preparation of tomatoes, cheese, etc. and baked.

**piz·ze·ri·a** (pēt′sə-rē′ə), *n.* [It.], a place where pizzas are prepared and sold.

**piz·zi·ca·to** (pit′sə-kä′tō), *adj.* [It.], in *music*, plucked: a direction to pluck the strings of a violin, etc. with the fingers. *n.* 1. the act or art of plucking the strings on a violin, etc. 2. [*pl.* -TI (-tē)], a note or passage so played.

**pk.,** [*pl.* PKS.], 1. pack. 2. park. 3. peak. 4. peck.

**pkg.,** [*pl.* PKGS.], package.

**pl.,** 1. place. 2. plate. 3. plural.

**pla·ca·ble** (plā′kə-b'l, plak′ə-), *adj.* [< OFr. < L. < *placare*, to soothe], capable of being placated; forgiving. —**pla′ca·bil′i·ty,** *n.* —**pla′ca·bly,** *adv.*

**plac·ard** (plak′ärd; *for v., usually* plə-kärd′), *n.* [< OFr. < Pr. *placa*, plaque], a notice for display in a public place. *v.t.* 1. to place placards on or in. 2. to advertise by means of placards. 3. to display as a placard. *v.i.* to set up placards.

**pla·cate** (plā′kāt, plak′āt), *v.t.* [-CATED, -CATING], [< L. pp. of *placare*, to appease], to appease; pacify. —**pla′cat·er,** *n.* —**pla·ca′tion,** *n.* —**pla′ca·tive,** *adj.* —**pla′ca·to′ry** (-tôr′i, -tō′ri), *adj.*

**place** (plās), *n.* [OFr. < L. *platea* < Gr. *plateia*, a street < *platys*, broad], 1. a square or court in a city. 2. a short street. 3. space; room. 4. a region. 5. *a*) the part of space occupied by a person or thing. *b*) situation. 6. a city, town, or village. 7. a residence; house and grounds. 8. a building or space devoted to a special purpose: as, a *place* of amusement. 9. a particular spot on or part of something: as, a sore *place* in the back. 10. a particular passage or page in a book, etc. 11. position or standing as determined by others: as, his *place* in history is sure. 12. a step or point in a sequence: as, in the first *place*. 13. the customary or proper position, time, or character. 14. a space reserved or occupied by a person, as a seat in a theater, etc. 15. the position formerly occupied by another: as, he ruled in *place* of the king. 16. (another's) situation or state: as, if I were in his *place*. 17. an office; employment. 18. official position. 19. the duties of any position. 20. the duty (of a person). 21. in *arithmetic*, the position of an integer, as in noting decimals: as, the third decimal *place*. 22. in *racing*, the first, second, or third position at the finish; esp., the second. *v.t.* [PLACED, PLACING], 1. to put in a particular place, condition, or relation. 2. to find employment for. 3. to repose (trust, etc.) *in* a person or thing. 4. to identify by connecting with some place, circumstance, etc. *v.i.* to finish among the first three in a race; specif., to finish second. —**give place,** 1. to make room. 2. to yield. —**go places,** [Slang], to achieve success. —**in place,** 1. in the customary or proper place. 2. fitting; timely. —**out of place,** 1. not in the customary or proper place. 2. not fitting or timely. —**put one in one's place,** to humble one who is overstepping bounds. —**take place,** to occur. —**take the place of,** to be a substitute for. —**plac′er,** *n.*

**pla·ce·bo** (plə-sē′bō), *n.* [-BOS, -BOES], [L., I shall please], a medicine given merely to humor the patient.

**place card,** a small card with the name of a guest, placed at the seat that he is to occupy at table.

**place kick,** in *football*, a kick performed while the ball is held in place on the ground, as in attempting a field goal. —**place′-kick′,** *v.i.*

**place mat,** a small mat serving as an individual table cover for each person at a meal.

**place·ment** (plās'mənt), *n.* 1. a placing or being placed. 2. the finding of employment for a person. 3. location or arrangement. 4. in *football, a*) the setting of the ball on the ground in position for a place kick. *b*) this position of the ball.

**pla·cen·ta** (plə-sen'tə), *n.* [*pl.* -TAE (-tē), -TAS], [L., lit., a cake; ult. < Gr. *plax*, a flat object], a vascular organ within the uterus, connected to the fetus by the umbilical cord: it is the structure through which the fetus is nourished. —**pla·cen'tal, pla·cen'tate,** *adj.*

**plac·er** (plas'ēr), *n.* [Sp. < *plaza*, a place], a water-borne or glacial deposit of gravel or sand containing small particles of gold, platinum, etc. that can be washed out.

**placer mining,** mining of placers (deposits) by washing, dredging, or other hydraulic methods.

**plac·id** (plas'id), *adj.* [< L. < *placere*, to please], calm; quiet; undisturbed. —**pla·cid·i·ty** (plə-sid'ə-ti), **plac'id·ness,** *n.* —**plac'id·ly,** *adv.*

**plack·et** (plak'it), *n.* [< *placard*, in related obs. sense], a slit at the top of a skirt to make it easy to put on and take off: also **placket hole.**

**pla·gi·a·rism** (plā'jə-riz'm, -ji-ə-), *n.* [< L. *plagiarius*, kidnaper], 1. the act of plagiarizing. 2. an idea, passage, etc. that has been plagiarized. —**pla'gi·a·rist,** *n.* —**pla'gi·a·ris'tic,** *adj.* —**pla'gi·a·ris'ti·cal·ly,** *adv.*

**pla·gi·a·rize** (plā'jə-rīz', -ji-ə-), *v.t.* & *v.i.* [-RIZED, -RIZING], [see PLAGIARISM], to take (ideas, writings, etc.) from (another) and pass them off as one's own. —**pla'gi·a·riz'er,** *n.*

**pla·gi·a·ry** (plā'jə-ri, -ji-ə-), *n.* [*pl.* -RIES], 1. a plagiarist. 2. plagiarism.

**pla·gi·o·clase** (plā'ji-ə-klās'), *n.* [< G. < Gr. *plagios*, oblique + *klasis*, a cleaving], a feldspar containing calcium and sodium and having oblique cleavage. —**pla'gi·o·clas'tic** (-klas'tik), *adj.*

**plague** (plāg), *n.* [< OFr. < L. *plaga* < Gr. *plēgē*, misfortune], 1. anything that afflicts or troubles; calamity. 2. any deadly epidemic disease; specif., the bubonic plague. 3. [Colloq.], a nuisance. *v.t.* [PLAGUED, PLAGUING], 1. to afflict with a plague. 2. to vex; torment. —**pla'guer,** *n.*

**pla·guy** (plā'gi), *adj.* [Colloq.], annoying; vexatious. *adv.* [Colloq.], in an annoying manner. Also sp. **plaguey.** —**pla'gui·ly,** *adv.*

**plaice** (plās), *n.* [*pl.* PLAICE, PLAICES; see PLURAL, II, D, 2], [< OFr. < LL. *platessa*, flatfish], a fish having a flat, olive-brown body with white spots.

**plaid** (plad), *n.* [Gael. *plaide*, a blanket], 1. a long woolen cloth with a checkered or crossbarred pattern, worn over the shoulder by Scottish Highlanders. 2. cloth with such a pattern. 3. any pattern of this kind. —**plaid, plaid'ed,** *adj.*

**plain** (plān), *adj.* [OFr. < L. *planus*, flat], 1. flat; level. 2. not obstructed; open: as, in *plain* view. 3. clearly understood; obvious: as, a *plain* prose style. 4. outspoken; straightforward: as, *plain* talk. 5. not luxurious: as, a *plain* meal. 6. not complicated; simple: as, *plain* sewing. 7. homely: as, a *plain* face. 8. unfigured, undyed, etc.: as, *plain* cloth. 9. not of high rank; ordinary: as, a *plain* man. *n.* an extent of level country. *adv.* in a plain manner; clearly. —**the (Great) Plains,** the broad expanse of level land stretching westward from the Mississippi Valley. —**plain'ish,** *adj.* —**plain'ly,** *adv.* —**plain'ness,** *n.*

**plain-clothes man** (plān'klōz', -klōthz'), a police detective who wears civilian clothes on duty.

**plains·man** (plānz'mən), *n.* [*pl.* -MEN], a person who lives on the plains.

**plain song,** the early Christian church music used in Roman Catholic and Anglican services, in free rhythm and sung in unison without accompaniment: also **plain chant.**

**plain-spo·ken** (plān'spō'k'n), *adj.* speaking or spoken plainly or frankly.

**plaint** (plānt), *n.* [< OFr. < LL. < L. < *plangere*, to lament], 1. [Poetic], lament. 2. a complaint.

**plain·tiff** (plān'tif), *n.* [< OFr. < *plaindre*, to complain < L. *plangere*, to lament], one who brings a suit into a court of law; complainant.

**plain·tive** (plān'tiv), *adj.* [< OFr.; see PLAINTIFF], expressing sorrow or melancholy; sad. —**plain'tive·ly,** *adv.* —**plain'tive·ness,** *n.*

**plait** (plāt; *occas.* plēt; *for n. 2 and v. 2, occas.* plat), *n.* [< OFr. < L. pp. of *plicare*, to fold], 1. a flattened fold, as of cloth doubled back on itself; pleat. 2. a braid of hair, ribbon, etc. *v.t.* 1. to pleat. 2. to braid. —**plait'er,** *n.*

**plan** (plan), *n.* [Fr. < It. < L. *planta*, sole of the foot, or *planus*, level], 1. an outline; draft; map. 2. a diagram showing the arrangement in horizontal section of a structure, piece of ground, etc. 3. a scheme for making, doing, or arranging something; project; program. *v.t.* [PLANNED, PLANNING], 1. to make a plan of (a structure, etc.). 2. to devise a scheme for doing, making, etc. 3. to have in mind as a project or purpose. *v.i.* to make plans. —**plan'ner,** *n.*

**Planck, Max** (mäks plänk), 1858–1947; German physicist; formulated the quantum theory.

**plane** (plān), *n.* [< OFr. < L. < Gr. < *platys*, broad: from its broad leaves], any of various trees with large leaves and streaky bark that sheds, as the sycamore: also **plane tree.**

**plane** (plān), *adj.* [< L. *planus*], 1. flat; level. 2. in *mathematics, a*) on a surface that is a plane. *b*) of such surfaces. *n.* 1. a surface that wholly contains every straight line joining any two points lying on it. 2. a flat or level surface. 3. a level of achievement, existence, etc.: as, a low *plane* of culture. 4. an airplane. 5. an airfoil; esp., a wing of an airplane.

**plane** (plān), *n.* [Fr. < LL. < *planare*, to plane < L. *planus*, level], a carpenter's tool for leveling, smoothing, or removing wood. *v.t.* [PLANED, PLANING], 1. to smooth or level with a plane. 2. to remove with a plane (with *off* or *away*). *v.i.* 1. to work with a plane. 2. to do the work of a plane. —**plan'er,** *n.*

PLANE

**plane** (plān), *v.i.* [PLANED, PLANING], [< Fr. *plan*, a plane], 1. to soar; glide. 2. to rise from the water, as a hydroplane, while moving at high speed.

**plane geometry,** the branch of geometry dealing with plane figures.

**plan·et** (plan'it), *n.* [< OFr. < LL. < Gr. *planētēs*, wanderer < *planan*, to wander], 1. originally, any heavenly body with apparent motion, including the sun, moon, Venus, Mars, etc. 2. now, any heavenly body that shines by reflected sunlight and revolves about the sun: the major planets, in their order from the sun, are Mercury, Venus, Earth, Mars, Jupiter, Saturn, Uranus, Neptune, and Pluto. 3. in *astrology*, any heavenly body supposed to influence a person's life.

**plan·e·tar·i·um** (plan'ə-târ'i-əm), *n.* [*pl.* -UMS, -A (-ə)], 1. an arrangement for projecting the images of the sun, moon, planets, and stars inside a large dome by means of a complex optical instrument that revolves to show the celestial motions. 2. the room or building containing this.

**plan·e·tar·y** (plan'ə-ter'i), *adj.* 1. of a planet or the planets. 2. terrestrial; worldly. 3. wandering; erratic. 4. in *machinery*, designating or of an epicyclic train of gears in an automobile transmission. 5. in *physics*, moving in an orbit, as a planet.

**plan·e·tes·i·mal** (plan'ə-tes'i-m'l), *adj.* [< *planet* + *infinitesimal*], of very small bodies in space moving in planetary orbits. *n.* any of these bodies.

**planetesimal hypothesis,** a hypothesis that the planets were formed by the uniting of planetesimals created by eruptions on the sun.

**plan·et·oid** (plan'ə-toid'), *n.* [*planet* + *-oid*], an asteroid.

**plan·ish** (plan'ish), *v.t.* [< OFr. < L. *planus*, smooth], to toughen, smooth, or polish (metal) by hammering or rolling. —**plan'ish·er,** *n.*

**plank** (plaŋk), *n.* [< ONorm.Fr. < OFr. < LL. *planca*], 1. a long, broad, thick board. 2. timber cut into planks; planking. 3. something that supports. 4. any of the principles in a platform, as of a political party. *v.t.* 1. to cover, lay, etc. with planks. 2. to broil and serve on a board, as steak. 3. [Colloq.], *a*) to lay or set down with force. *b*) to pay (usually with *down* or *out*). —**walk the plank,** to walk off a plank projecting out from a ship's side, as pirates' victims were forced to do.

**plank·ing** (plaŋk'iŋ), *n.* 1. the act of laying planks. 2. planks collectively.

**plank·ton** (plaŋk'tən), *n.* [G. < Gr. *planktos*, wandering < *plazesthai*, to wander], the microscopic animal and plant life found floating in bodies of water, used as food by fish.

**plan·ner** (plan'ēr), *n.* a person who plans.

**pla·no-,** [< L. *planus*, flat], a combining form meaning *plane, plane and*, as in *plano-convex*.

**pla·no-con·cave** (plā'nō-kon'kāv), *adj.* having one side plane and the other concave: see **concave.**

**pla·no-con·vex** (plā'nō-kon'veks), *adj.* having one side plane and the other convex: see **convex.**

**plant** (plant, plänt), *n.* [AS. *plante* < L. *planta*], 1. a young tree, shrub, or herb, ready to put into other soil to mature. 2. any living thing that cannot move voluntarily, has no sense organs, and generally makes its own food by photosynthesis; vegetable organism. 3. a soft-stemmed organism of this kind, as distinguished from a tree or shrub. 4. the machinery, buildings, etc. of a factory. 5. the equipment, buildings, etc. of an institution, as a school. 6. the apparatus for a certain mechanical operation: as, a ship's power *plant.* 7. [Slang], *a*) a swindle; trick. *b*) a person or thing used to trick or trap. ***v.t.*** 1. to put into the ground to grow. 2. to set firmly in position. 3. to fix in the mind; implant. 4. to settle; found; establish. 5. to furnish; stock. 6. to put a stock of (fish, etc.) in a body of water. 7. [Slang], to deliver (a punch, etc.) accurately. 8. [Slang], to place (a person or thing) in such a way as to trick, trap, etc. **—plant′ing,** ***n.*** **—plant′like′,** ***adj.***

**Plan·tag·e·net** (plan-taj′ə-nit), ***n.*** the ruling family of England (1154–1399) or any member of this family.

**plan·tain** (plan′tin), ***n.*** [OFr. < L. *plantago*], 1. any of various related plants with leaves at the bottom of the stem and spikes of tiny, greenish flowers. 2. a weed with broad, ribbed leaves.

**plan·tain** (plan′tin), ***n.*** [< Sp. *plá(n)tano* < W.Ind. native name], 1. a tropical plant yielding a kind of banana. 2. its fruit.

**plan·tar** (plan′tẽr), ***adj.*** [< L. < *planta,* sole of the foot], of the sole of the foot.

**plan·ta·tion** (plan-tā′shən), ***n.*** [< L. < *plantare,* to plant], 1. formerly, a colony. 2. an area growing cultivated crops. 3. an estate, as in the South, cultivated by workers living on it. 4. a cultivated planting of trees.

**plant·er** (plan′tẽr, plän′-), ***n.*** 1. the owner of a plantation. 2. a person or machine that plants. 3. a decorative container for plants.

**plan·ti·grade** (plan′tə-grād′), ***adj.*** [Fr. < L. *planta,* sole + *gradi,* to walk], walking on the whole sole of the foot, as a bear, man, etc. ***n.*** a plantigrade animal.

**plant louse,** an aphid.

**plaque** (plak), ***n.*** [Fr. < D. *plak,* a disk], 1. any thin, flat piece of metal, wood, porcelain, etc., used for ornamentation, as on a wall. 2. a platelike brooch or pin worn as a badge or ornament.

**plash** (plash), ***n.*** [AS. *plæsc;* prob. echoic], a pool or puddle. **—plash′y** [-IER, -IEST], ***adj.***

**plash** (plash), ***n., v.t. & v.i.*** [echoic], splash.

**-pla·si·a** (plā′zhə, -zhi-ə), [< Gr. < *plassein,* to mold], a combining form meaning *change, development*: also **-plasis, -plasy.**

**-plasm** (plaz′m), [see PLASMA], a combining form meaning: 1. *the fluid substances of an animal or vegetable cell.* 2. *protoplasm,* as in *ectoplasm.*

**plas·ma** (plaz′mə), ***n.*** [LL., something molded < Gr. *plasma* < *plassein,* to mold], 1. the fluid part of blood, without the corpuscles. 2. the fluid part of lymph, milk, or intramuscular liquid. 3. protoplasm. Also **plasm. —plas·mat′ic** (-mat′ik), **plas′mic,** ***adj.***

**plas·ter** (plas′tẽr, pläs′-), ***n.*** [< AS. & OFr. < LL. *plastrum* < L. *emplastrum* < Gr. < *emplassein,* to daub over], 1. a pasty mixture of lime, sand, and water, hard when dry, for coating walls, ceilings, etc. 2. plaster of Paris. 3. a pasty preparation spread on cloth and applied to the body as a medicine. ***v.t.*** 1. to cover, smear, etc. as with plaster. 2. to apply or affix like a plaster: as, a wall *plastered* with posters. **—plas′ter·er,** ***n.*** **—plas′ter·ing,** ***n.*** **—plas′ter·y,** ***adj.***

**plas·ter·board** (plas′tẽr-bôrd′, pläs′tẽr-bōrd′), ***n.*** a thin board formed of layers of plaster and paper.

**plas·tered** (plas′tẽrd, pläs′-), ***adj.*** [Slang], intoxicated; drunk.

**plaster of Paris,** [from use of gypsum from Paris, France], a heavy white powder, calcined gypsum, which, when mixed with water, forms a thick paste that sets quickly: used for casts, statuary, etc.

**plas·tic** (plas′tik), ***adj.*** [< L. < Gr. *plastikos* < *plassein,* to form], 1. molding or shaping matter; formative. 2. that can be molded or shaped. 3. impressionable; easily influenced. 4. dealing with molding or modeling. ***n.*** any of various nonmetallic compounds, as Bakelite, Lucite, etc., synthetically produced, which can be molded and hardened for commercial use. **—plas′ti·cal·ly,** ***adv.*** **—plas·tic′i·ty** (-tis′ə-ti), ***n.***

**-plas·tic,** [< Gr.; see PLASTIC], a combining form meaning *forming, developing.*

**plastic surgery,** surgery dealing with the repair of injured, deformed, or destroyed parts of the body, especially by transferring skin, bone, etc., as from other parts.

**plastic wood,** a synthetic product which, when it hardens, resembles wood: used in repairing wooden articles or as a filler in cracks, etc.

**plas·tid** (plas′tid), ***n.*** [< G. < Gr. < *plastēs,* molder < *plassein,* to form], 1. a unit of protoplasm; cell. 2. a granule of specialized protoplasm occurring in some cytoplasm.

**plas·tron** (plas′trən), ***n.*** [Fr. < It. < *piastra;* see PIASTER], 1. a metal breastplate. 2. the under shell of a turtle.

**-plas·ty** (plas′ti), [< Gr. < *plastos,* formed < *plassein,* to mold], a combining form meaning: 1. *the act* or *means of forming, growth, development.* 2. *plastic surgery,* as in *rhinoplasty.*

**plat** (plat), ***v.t.*** [PLATTED, PLATTING], [see PLAIT], to braid; plait. ***n.*** [Dial.], a braid; plait.

**plat** (plat), ***n.*** [var. of *plot*], 1. a small piece of ground. 2. a map; plan. ***v.t.*** [PLATTED, PLATTING], to make a map or plan of.

**Pla·ta, Ri·o de la** (rē′ô de lä plä′tä), the estuary of the Paraná and Uruguay rivers, between Argentina and Uruguay: English name, *River Plate.*

**plate** (plāt), ***n.*** [OFr. < ML. *platta;* ult. < Gr. *platys,* broad], 1. a smooth, flat, thin piece of metal, etc. 2. sheet metal. 3. any of the thin pieces of metal used in armor. 4. armor made of these. 5. *a*) a thin, flat piece of metal on which an engraving is cut. *b*) an impression taken from this. *c*) loosely, a print of a woodcut, lithograph, etc.; esp., a full-page book illustration printed on special paper. 6. dishes, utensils, etc. of, or plated with, silver or gold. 7. a shallow dish from which food is eaten. 8. a plateful. 9. the food in a dish; course: as, a fruit *plate.* 10. food and service for an individual at a meal: as, lunch at a dollar a *plate.* 11. a receptacle passed in churches, etc. for donations of money. 12. a thin cut of beef from the forequarter, just below the short ribs. 13. in *anatomy & zoology,* a thin layer or scale, as of horny tissue, etc. 14. in *architecture,* a horizontal wooden girder that supports the trusses of a roof. 15. in *baseball,* home plate. 16. in *dentistry, a*) that part of a set of false teeth which fits to the mouth and holds the teeth. *b*) loosely, a set of false teeth. 17. in *electricity,* the anode of an electron tube, a flat plate or cylinder toward which the stream of electrons flows. 18. in *photography,* a sheet of glass, metal, etc. coated with a film sensitive to light, upon which the image is formed. 19. in *printing,* a cast, to be printed from, made from a mold of set type by electrotypy or stereotypy. ***v.t.*** [PLATED, PLATING], 1. to coat with gold, tin, etc. 2. to cover with metal plates for protection. 3. in *printing,* to make a stereotype or electrotype plate of. **—plate′like′,** ***adj.***

**pla·teau** (pla-tō′), ***n.*** [*pl.* -TEAUS, -TEAUX], [Fr. < OFr. < *plat,* piece of ground; ult. < Gr. *platys,* broad], 1. an elevated tract of more or less level land. 2. figuratively, a period of relatively little progress, as represented by a flat extent in a graph, etc.

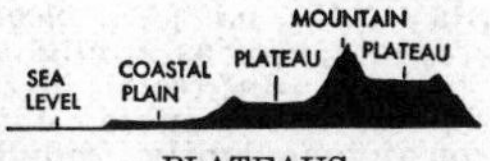

PLATEAUS

**plat·ed** (plāt′id), ***adj.*** 1. protected with plates, as of armor. 2. coated with a metal: as, *silver-plated.*

**plate·ful** (plāt′fool′), ***n.*** [*pl.* -FULS], as much as a plate will hold.

**plate glass,** polished, clear glass in thick sheets, used for shop windows, mirrors, etc.

**plate·let** (plāt′lit), ***n.*** [*plate* + *-let*], any of certain roundish disks, smaller than a red blood cell, found in the blood of mammals and associated with blood clotting: in full, *blood platelet.*

**plat·en** (plat′'n), ***n.*** [< OFr. *platine,* flat plate < *plat,* flat], 1. in a printing press, a flat metal plate or rotating cylinder that presses the paper against the inked type. 2. in a typewriter, the roller against which the keys strike.

**plat·er** (plāt′ẽr), ***n.*** 1. a person or thing that plates. 2. an inferior race horse.

**plat·form** (plat′fôrm′), ***n.*** [Fr. *plateforme,* lit., flat form], 1. a raised horizontal surface; specif., *a*) a raised flooring beside railroad tracks, etc. *b*) a vestibule at the end of a railway car, etc. *c*) a raised stage for performers, speakers, etc. 2. the statement of policy of a political party, etc. ***adj.***

fat, āpe, bâre, cär; ten, ēven, hêre, ovẽr; is, bīte; lot, gō, hôrn, tōōl, look; oil, out; up, ūse, fũr; get; joy; yet; chin; she; thin, *th*en; zh, leisure; ŋ, ring; ə for *a* in *ago, e* in *agent, i* in *sanity, o* in *comply, u* in *focus;* ′ in *able* (ā′b'l); Fr. bål; ë, Fr. coeur; ö, Fr. feu; Fr. mo*n*; ô, Fr. coq; ü, Fr. duc; H, G. ich; kh, G. doch. ‡ foreign; < derived from.

1. designating a thick shoe sole, as of cork or wood. 2. designating a shoe with such a sole.

**plat·ing** (plāt'iŋ), *n.* 1. the act or process of one that plates. 2. an external layer of metal plates. 3. a thin coating of gold, silver, etc.

**plat·i·nize** (plat''n-īz'), *v.t.* [-NIZED, -NIZING], to coat or combine with platinum.

**plat·i·num** (plat''n-əm), *n.* [< Sp. *platina* < *plata*, silver], a steel-gray, ductile metallic chemical element, resistant to corrosion and electricity: used for chemical and dental equipment, jewelry, etc.: symbol, Pt; at. wt., 195.23; at. no., 78.

**platinum blonde,** a girl or woman who has very light pale-yellow hair.

**plat·i·tude** (plat'ə-tōōd', -tūd'), *n.* [Fr. < *plat*, flat, after *latitude*, etc.], 1. commonplaceness; dullness. 2. a trite remark, especially one uttered as if it were fresh. **—plat'i·tu'di·nous,** *adj.* **—plat'i·tu'di·nous·ly,** *adv.*

**plat·i·tu·di·nize** (plat'ə-tōō'd'n-īz', -tū'-), *v.i.* [-NIZED, -NIZING], to write or speak platitudes.

**Pla·to** (plā'tō), *n.* Greek philosopher; lived 427–347 B.C.

**Pla·ton·ic** (plə-ton'ik, plā-), *adj.* 1. of or characteristic of Plato or his philosophy. 2. idealistic or impractical. 3. [also p-], not amorous but purely spiritual: as, *Platonic* love. **—Pla·ton'i·cal·ly, pla·ton'i·cal·ly,** *adv.*

**Pla·ton·ism** (plā't'n-iz'm), *n.* 1. the philosophy of Plato or his school: see **idealism.** 2. [also p-], the theory or practice of Platonic love. **—Pla'to·nist,** *adj.* & *n.* **—Pla'to·nis'tic,** *adj.*

**pla·toon** (plə-tōōn'), *n.* [Fr. *peloton*, a ball, group < *pelote*, a ball], 1. a military unit composed of two or more squads. 2. a group like this: as, a *platoon* of police.

**Platt·deutsch** (plät'doich'), *n.* [G.; *platt*, lit., flat, low + *deutsch*, German], the Low German vernacular language of N Germany.

**Platte** (plat), *n.* a river in Nebraska, flowing eastward into the Missouri.

**plat·ter** (plat'ẽr), *n.* [< OFr. *plat*, flat], 1. a large, shallow dish, usually oval, for serving food. 2. [Slang], a phonograph record.

**plat·y-,** [< Gr. *platys*, flat], a combining form meaning *broad* or *flat*, as in *platypus*: also **plat-.**

**plat·y·pus** (plat'ə-pəs), *n.* [*pl.* -PUSES, -PI (-pī')], [< *platy-* + Gr. *pous*, a foot], a duckbill.

**plau·dit** (plô'dit), *n.* [< L. imperative of *plaudere*, to applaud], *usually in pl.* 1. a round of applause. 2. any expression of approval or praise.

**plau·si·ble** (plô'zə-b'l), *adj.* [< L. *plausibilis* < *plaudere*, to applaud], 1. seemingly true, acceptable, etc.: often implying disbelief. 2. seemingly honest, trustworthy, etc.: as, a *plausible* rogue. **—plau'si·bil'i·ty, plau'si·ble·ness,** *n.* **—plau'si·bly,** *adv.*

**Plau·tus** (plô'təs), *n.* (*Titus Maccius Plautus*), Roman writer of comedies; lived 254?–184 B.C.

**play** (plā), *v.i.* [AS. *pleg(i)an*], 1. to move lightly, rapidly, etc.: as, sunlight *plays* on the waves. 2. *a*) to have fun; frolic. *b*) to take part in a game or sport. 3. to gamble. 4. to handle or treat anything or anyone lightly; trifle (*with*). 5. to perform on a musical instrument. 6. to give out musical sounds: said of an instrument. 7. to act in a specified way: as, to *play* fair. 8. to perform on the stage. 9. to be performed in a theater, on the radio, etc. 10. to be directed repeatedly or continuously, as a fountain, a spotlight, etc. (with *on*, *over*, or *along*). *v.t.* 1. to take part in (a game or sport). 2. to engage in a game against. 3. to use (a player, etc.) in a game: as, the coach *played* Jones at center. 4. to do (something), often in fun or to deceive: as, to *play* tricks. 5. *a*) to bet. *b*) to bet on: as, to *play* the horses. 6. to put into or keep in action; wield. 7. to cause; effect: as, to *play* havoc. 8. to perform (music, a drama, etc.). 9. to perform on (an instrument). 10. to act the part of: as, to *play* Iago. 11. to imitate for amusement: as, to *play* soldier. 12. to give performances in: as, they *played* New York. 13. to direct repeatedly or continuously, as a light, etc. (with *on*, *over*, or *along*). 14. to let (a hooked fish) tire itself by tugging at the line. *n.* 1. motion or activity, especially when free and rapid: as, the *play* of light. 2. freedom for motion or action. 3. action for amusement; recreation; sport. 4. fun; joking: as, to do a thing in *play*. 5. the playing of, or the way of playing, a game. 6. a move or act in a game. 7. gambling. 8. a dramatic composition or performance; drama. **—in** (or **out of**) **play,** in *sports*, in (or not in) a position or condition that play may legitimately be continued: said of a ball, etc. **—make a play for,** [Colloq.], to employ one's arts or talents to obtain, win, etc. **—play at,** 1. to pretend to be engaged in. 2. to work at halfheartedly. **—play down,** to attach little importance to; minimize. **—played out,** 1. finished. 2. exhausted. **—play into (someone's) hands,** to act so as to give the advantage to (someone). **—play off,** 1. to pit (one against another). 2. to palm off. 3. in *games*, to break (a tie) by playing once more. **—play on** (or **upon**), to make adroit use of (a person's feelings) for one's own purposes. **—play out,** 1. to play to the finish; end. 2. to pay out (a rope, etc.). **—play up,** [Colloq.], to give prominence to. **—play up to,** [Colloq.], to try to please by flattery, etc. **—play'a·ble,** *adj.*

**play·back** (plā'bak'), *n.* a playing back.

**play·bill** (plā'bil'), *n.* 1. a poster or circular advertising a play. 2. a program of a play.

**play·boy** (plā'boi'), *n.* [Colloq.], a man, usually well-to-do, who spends much time and energy in pleasure-seeking and dissipation.

**play·er** (plā'ẽr), *n.* 1. one who plays a specified game. 2. an actor. 3. one who plays a musical instrument. 4. a gambler. 5. an apparatus for playing a musical instrument mechanically.

**player piano,** a piano played mechanically.

**play·fel·low** (plā'fel'ō), *n.* a playmate.

**play·ful** (plā'fəl), *adj.* 1. fond of play or fun; sportive; frisky. 2. humorous; joking; merry. **—play'ful·ly,** *adv.* **—play'ful·ness,** *n.*

**play·go·er** (plā'gō'ẽr), *n.* a person who goes to the theater frequently or regularly.

**play·ground** (plā'ground'), *n.* a place, often near a schoolhouse, for outdoor recreation.

**play hooky,** [prob. < *hook it*, to run away], to stay away from school without permission.

**play·house** (plā'hous'), *n.* 1. a theater. 2. a small house for children to play in. 3. a doll house.

**playing cards,** cards used in playing various games, arranged in decks of four suits (spades, clubs, diamonds, and hearts).

**play·let** (plā'lit), *n.* a short drama.

**play·mate** (plā'māt'), *n.* a companion in games and recreation; playfellow.

**play-off** (plā'ôf'), *n.* in *games*, a match played to break a tie.

**play on words,** a pun or punning.

**play·thing** (plā'thiŋ'), *n.* a toy.

**play·time** (plā'tīm'), *n.* time for play.

**play·wright** (plā'rīt'), *n.* a person who writes plays; dramatist.

**pla·za** (plaz'ə, plä'zə), *n.* [Sp. < L.; see PLACE], a public square or market place in a city or town.

**plea** (plē), *n.* [< OFr. < L. *placitum*, an opinion < pp. of *placere*, to please], 1. a statement in defense; excuse. 2. an appeal; request. 3. in *law*, a defendant's statement, answering the charges against him or showing why he should not answer.

**plead** (plēd), *v.i.* [PLEADED, PLEADING; *colloq.* or *dial.* pt. & pp. PLEAD, PLED (pled)], [< OFr.; see PLEA], 1. to present a plea in a law court. 2. to make an appeal; beg: as, *plead* for mercy. *v.t.* 1. to argue (a law case). 2. to declare oneself to be (guilty or not guilty) in answer to a charge. 3. to offer as an excuse: as, *plead* ignorance. **—plead'er,** *n.* **—plead'ing,** *adj.* **—plead'ing·ly,** *adv.*

**plead·ings** (plēd'iŋz), *n.pl.* the statements setting forth to the court the claims of the plaintiff and the answer of the defendant.

**pleas·ance** (plez''ns), *n.* [< OFr. < *plaisir*, to please], a pleasure ground or garden, usually part of an estate.

**pleas·ant** (plez''nt), *adj.* [< OFr. ppr. of *plaisir*, to please], 1. agreeable to the mind or senses; pleasing. 2. having an agreeable manner, appearance, etc. 3. *a*) gay; merry. *b*) jesting; playful. **—pleas'ant·ly,** *adv.* **—pleas'ant·ness,** *n.*

**pleas·ant·ry** (plez''n-tri), *n.* [*pl.* -RIES], 1. pleasant jocularity in conversation. 2. a humorous remark; jest.

**please** (plēz), *v.t.* [PLEASED, PLEASING], [< OFr. < L. *placere*], 1. to be agreeable to; satisfy. 2. to be the will or wish of: as, it *pleased* him to remain. *v.i.* 1. to be agreeable; satisfy: as, we aim to *please*. 2. to have the will or wish; like: as, I'll do as I *please*. *Please* is also used for politeness, as in requests, to mean "be obliging enough": as, *please* (to) do it now. **—if you please,** if you wish or like. **—pleased,** *adj.*

**pleas·ing** (plēz'iŋ), *adj.* giving pleasure; agreeable. **—pleas'ing·ly,** *adv.* **—pleas'ing·ness,** *n.*

**pleas·ur·a·ble** (plezh'ẽr-ə-b'l), *adj.* pleasant; enjoyable. **—pleas'ur·a·ble·ness,** *n.* **—pleas'ur·a·bly,** *adv.*

**pleas·ure** (plezh'ẽr), *n.* 1. a pleased feeling; enjoyment; delight. 2. one's wish, will, or choice:

as, what is his *pleasure?* 3. a thing that gives delight or satisfaction. 4. sensual satisfaction.

**pleat** (plēt), *n.* [ME. *pleten;* cf. PLAIT], a flat double fold, as in cloth, pressed or stitched in place. *v.t.* to lay and press (cloth) in a pleat or series of pleats. —**pleat′er,** *n.*

**plebe** (plēb), *n.* [short for *plebeian*], a member of the lowest class at the U.S. Military Academy at West Point or the Naval Academy at Annapolis.

**ple·be·ian** (pli-bē′ən), *n.* [< L. < *plebs,* common people], 1. a member of the ancient Roman lower class. 2. one of the common people. 3. a vulgar, coarse person. *adj.* 1. of or characteristic of the Roman lower class or the common people. 2. vulgar; coarse. —**ple·be′ian·ism,** *n.*

**pleb·i·scite** (pleb′ə-sīt′, -sit), *n.* [< Fr. < L. < *plebs,* common people + *scitum,* decree], an expression of the people's will on a political issue by direct ballot of all eligible voters. —**pleb′i·scit′ic** (-sit′ik), *adj.*

**plec·trum** (plek′trəm), *n.* [*pl.* -TRUMS, -TRA (-trə)], [< L. < Gr. *plēktron* < *plēssein,* to strike], a small, thin piece of metal, bone, etc. used for plucking the strings of a guitar, mandolin, etc.

**pled** (pled), colloq. or dial. pt. and pp. of **plead.**

**pledge** (plej), *n.* [< OFr. < ML. *plegium* < base of AS. *plegian,* to play], 1. the condition of being given or held as security for a contract, payment, etc. 2. a person or thing given or held as such security; something pawned; hostage. 3. a token. 4. a drinking of one's health; toast. 5. a promise or agreement. 6. one who has promised to join a fraternity. *v.t.* [PLEDGED, PLEDGING], 1. to present as security, especially for the repayment of a loan; pawn. 2. to drink a toast to. 3. to bind by a promise. 4. to promise to join (a fraternity). —**take the pledge,** to vow not to drink alcoholic liquor. —**pledg′er,** *n.*

**pledg·ee** (plej′ē′), *n.* a person with whom a pledge is deposited.

**pledg·or, pledge·or** (plej′ôr′), *n.* in *law,* a person who deposits something as security.

**-ple·gi·a** (plē′ji-ə), [< Gr. < *plēgē,* a stroke], a combining form meaning *paralysis,* as in *paraplegia:* also **-ple′gy** (-ji).

**Ple·ia·des** (plē′ə-dēz′, plī′-), *n.pl.* [*sing.* PLEIAD (plē′əd, plī′ad)], 1. in *Gr. mythology,* the seven daughters of Atlas who were placed by Zeus among the stars. 2. in *astronomy,* a large group of stars in the constellation Taurus.

**Plei·o·cene** (plī′ə-sēn′), *adj.* Pliocene.

**Pleis·to·cene** (plīs′tə-sēn′), *adj.* [< Gr. *pleistos,* most + *kainos,* new], designating or of the first epoch of the Quaternary Period in the Cenozoic Era: see **geology,** chart. *n.* the Pleistocene Epoch or its rocks.

**ple·na·ry** (plē′nə-ri, plen′ə-), *adj.* [< LL. < L. *plenus,* full], 1. full; complete. 2. attended by all members, as an assembly. —**ple′na·ri·ly,** *adv.*

**plenary indulgence,** in the *R.C. Church,* an indulgence remitting in full the temporal punishment incurred by a sinner.

**plen·i·po·ten·ti·ar·y** (plen′i-pə-ten′shi-er′i, -shə-ri), *adj.* [< ML. < L. *plenus,* full + *potens,* powerful], having or conferring full authority. *n.* [*pl.* -IES], one given full authority to act as representative of a government; ambassador.

**plen·i·tude** (plen′ə-to͞od′, -tūd′), *n.* [OFr. < L. < *plenus,* full], 1. fullness; completeness. 2. abundance; plenty. —**plen′i·tu′di·nous,** *adj.*

**plen·te·ous** (plen′ti-əs), *adj.* 1. abundant; plentiful. 2. producing abundantly. —**plen′te·ous·ly,** *adv.* —**plen′te·ous·ness,** *n.*

**plen·ti·ful** (plen′ti-fəl), *adj.* 1. having or yielding plenty. 2. sufficient; abundant. —**plen′ti·ful·ly,** *adv.* —**plen′ti·ful·ness,** *n.*

**plen·ty** (plen′ti), *n.* [*pl.* -TIES], [< OFr. < L. *plenitas* < *plenus,* full], 1. prosperity; opulence. 2. a sufficient supply; enough. *adj.* plentiful; ample. *adv.* [Colloq.], very: as, *plenty* good.

**ple·o·nasm** (plē′ə-naz′m), *n.* [< LL. < Gr. < *pleonazein,* to be in excess < *pleōn,* more, compar. of *polys,* much], 1. the use of more words than are necessary for the meaning; redundancy. 2. a redundant word or expression. —**ple′o·nas′tic,** *adj.* —**ple′o·nas′ti·cal·ly,** *adv.*

**pleth·o·ra** (pleth′ə-rə), *n.* [ML. < Gr. < *plēthos,* fullness], 1. the state of being too full; overabundance. 2. an abnormal condition characterized by an excess of blood in the circulatory system. —**ple·thor·ic** (ple-thôr′ik, -thor′ik, pleth′ə-rik), *adj.* —**ple·thor′i·cal·ly,** *adv.*

**pleu·ra** (ploor′ə), *n.* [*pl.* -RAE (-ē)], [ML. < Gr. *pleura,* a rib], a thin serous membrane lining each half of the chest cavity and enveloping the lungs. —**pleu′ral,** *adj.*

**pleu·ri·sy** (ploor′ə-si), *n.* [< OFr. < LL. < L. < Gr. < *pleura,* a rib], inflammation of the pleura, characterized by painful breathing, fever, and a dry cough. —**pleu·rit·ic** (ploo-rit′ik), *adj.*

**pleu·ro-,** [< Gr. *pleura,* a rib], a combining form meaning: 1. *on* or *near the side.* 2. *of* or *near the pleura.* Also **pleur-.**

**plex·i·glass** (plek′si-glas′, -gläs′), *n.* [< L. *plexus,* a twining; + *glass*], a lightweight, transparent, thermoplastic substance, used as a cockpit cover for aircraft, etc.: a trade-mark (**Plexiglas**).

**plex·us** (plek′səs), *n.* [*pl.* -USES, -US], [L. < pp. of *plectere,* to twine], a network; specif., in *anatomy,* a network of blood vessels, nerves, etc.

**pli·a·ble** (plī′ə-b′l), *adj.* [Fr. < *plier,* to bend < L. *plicare,* to fold], 1. easily bent; flexible. 2. easily influenced or persuaded. —**pli′a·bil′i·ty, pli′a·ble·ness,** *n.* —**pli′a·bly,** *adv.*

**pli·ant** (plī′ənt), *adj.* 1. easily bent; pliable. 2. adaptable; compliant. —**pli′an·cy, pli′ant·ness,** *n.* —**pli′ant·ly,** *adv.*

**pli·cate** (plī′kāt), *adj.* [< L. pp. of *plicare,* to fold], folded in pleats, as a fan: also **pli′cat·ed.** —**pli·ca′tion, plic·a·ture** (plik′ə-chẽr), *n.*

**pli·er** (plī′ẽr), *n.* a person or thing that plies.

**pli·ers** (plī′ẽrz), *n.pl.* [< *ply* (to bend)], small pincers for handling small objects, cutting wire, etc.

PLIERS

**plight** (plīt), *n.* [< Anglo-Fr. *plit,* for OFr. *ploit,* a fold], a condition, situation, etc.; esp., a dangerous or awkward situation.

**plight** (plīt), *v.t.* [< AS. *pliht,* danger], 1. to pledge or engage: as, *plight* one's troth. 2. to bind (oneself) by a promise; betroth. —**plight one's troth,** 1. to give one's word. 2. to make a promise of marriage.

**Plim·soll mark (or line),** (plim′səl, -sol), [after S. *Plimsoll* (1824–1898), Brit. statesman], a line on the outside of British merchant ships showing the lawful submergence level: also **Plimsoll's mark** (or **line**).

**plinth** (plinth), *n.* [< L. < Gr. *plinthos,* a brick, tile], 1. the square block at the base of a column, pedestal, etc. 2. the base on which a statue is placed. —**plinth′less,** *adj.* —**plinth′like′,** *adj.*

**Plin·y** (plin′i), *n.* 1. (*Gaius Plinius Secundus*), Roman naturalist and writer; lived 23–79 A.D.: called *the Elder.* 2. (*Gaius Plinius Caecilius Secundus*), nephew of the above; lived 62–113 A.D.; Roman statesman and writer: called *the Younger.*

**Pli·o·cene** (plī′ə-sēn′), *adj.* [< Gr. *pleōn,* more + *kainos,* new], designating or of the last epoch of the Tertiary Period in the Cenozoic Era: see **geology,** chart. *n.* the Pliocene Epoch.

**plod** (plod), *v.i.* [PLODDED, PLODDING], [prob. echoic], 1. to walk or move heavily and laboriously; trudge. 2. to work steadily and monotonously; drudge. *v.t.* to walk heavily and laboriously along. *n.* 1. a plodding. 2. a heavy step. 3. the sound of this. —**plod′der,** *n.* —**plod′ding,** *adj.* —**plod′ding·ly,** *adv.*

**plop** (plop), *v.t. & v.i.* [PLOPPED, PLOPPING], [echoic], to drop with a sound like that of something flat falling into water. *n.* 1. such a sound. 2. a plopping. *adv.* with a plop.

**plo·sive** (plō′siv), *adj.* [< *explosive*], designating or of a speech sound produced by the stoppage and sudden release of the breath, as the sounds *k, p,* and *t* used initially. *n.* a plosive sound.

**plot** (plot), *n.* [? < OFr. *pelote,* clod], 1. a small area of ground; plat. 2. a diagram or map, as of an estate. 3. a secret, usually evil, scheme. 4. the plan of action of a play, novel, etc. *v.t.* [PLOTTED, PLOTTING], 1. to draw a map, plan, etc. of (a building, ship's course, etc.). 2. to make secret plans for. 3. to plan the action of (a story, etc.). 4. to represent (an equation) by joining points on a graph to form (a curve). *v.i.* to scheme; conspire. —**plot′less,** *adj.* —**plot′less·ness,** *n.* —**plot′ter,** *n.*

**plough** (plou), *n., v.t. & v.i.* plow.

**plov·er** (pluv′ẽr, plō′vẽr), *n.* [*pl.* -ERS, -ER; see PLURAL, II, D, 1], [< OFr. < L. *pluvia,* rain], a shore bird of North America with a short tail and long, pointed wings.

**plow** (plou), *n.* [AS. *ploh*], 1. a farm implement used to cut and turn up the soil. 2. any implement like this, as a snow-plow. 3. [P-], the Big Dipper. *v.t.* 1. to cut and turn up (soil) with a plow. 2. to make furrows in (the earth, one's face, etc.). 3. to make as if by plowing: as, he *plowed* his way in. 4. to remove with a plow (with *up*). 5. to cut a way through (water). *v.i.* 1. to use a plow in tilling the soil. 2. to be in a specified condition for plowing: as, the field *plows* well. 3. to cut a way (*through* water, etc.). 4. to plod. Also sp. **plough.** —**plow into,** to begin work vigorously on (a job, etc.). —**plow′er, plough′er,** *n.* —**plow′ing, plough′ing,** *adj.*

PLOW

**plow·man, plough·man** (plou′mən), *n.* [*pl.* -MEN], 1. one who plows. 2. a farm worker.
**plow·share, plough·share** (plou′shâr′), *n.* the share, or cutting blade, of a moldboard plow.
**ploy** (ploi), *n.* [? < em*ploy*], an action or maneuver intended to outwit or disconcert another person.
**pluck** (pluk), *v.t.* [AS. *pluccian*], 1. to pull off or out; pick. 2. to drag or snatch. 3. to pull out the feathers of (a fowl). 4. to pull at and release quickly, as the strings of a musical instrument. 5. [Slang], to rob or swindle. *v.i.* to pull; tug; snatch (with *at*). *n.* 1. a pulling. 2. courage; spirit. —**pluck up,** to take heart. —**plucked,** *adj.*
**pluck·y** (pluk′i), *adj.* [-IER, -IEST], brave; resolute; spirited. —**pluck′i·ly,** *adv.* —**pluck′i·ness,** *n.*
**plug** (plug), *n.* [MD. *plugge*], 1. an object used to stop up a hole, outlet, etc. 2. *a*) a cake of pressed tobacco. *b*) a piece of chewing tobacco. 3. an electrical device fitted into an outlet, etc. for making contact or closing the circuit. 4. a spark plug. 5. a fireplug. 6. [Slang], a plug hat. 7. [Slang], an inferior animal or thing; esp., a worn-out horse. 8. [Slang], an advertisement; esp., a recommendation for someone or something, as in a radio program. *v.t.* [PLUGGED, PLUGGING], 1. to fill (a hole, etc.) by inserting a plug (usually with *up*). 2. to insert as a plug. 3. [Slang], to shoot a bullet into. 4. [Slang], to hit with the fist. 5. [Slang], to advertise or publicize insistently. *v.i.* 1. [Colloq.], to work doggedly; plod. 2. [Slang], to shoot or hit (*at*). —**plug in,** to connect (an electrical device) with an outlet, etc. by inserting a plug in a socket. —**plug′ger,** *n.* —**plug′ging·ly,** *adv.* —**plug′like′,** *n.*
**plug hat,** [Slang], a man's high silk hat.
**plug-ug·ly** (plug′ug′li), *n.* [*pl.* -LIES], [cf. PLUG, *v.t.* 4], [Slang], a ruffian or gangster.
**plum** (plum), *n.* [AS. *plume* < L. *prunum* < Gr. < *proumnon*], 1. any of several trees having smooth-skinned fruit with a smooth pit. 2. the fruit. 3. a raisin, when used in pudding or cake. 4. the dark bluish-red color of some plums. 5. a choice or desirable object. —**plum′my,** *adj.*
**plum·age** (plōōm′ij), *n.* [OFr. < *plume*, a feather], a bird's feathers.
**plumb** (plum), *n.* [< OFr. < L. *plumbum*, lead (metal)], a lead weight (**plumb bob**) hung at the end of a line (**plumb line**), used to determine how deep water is or whether a wall, etc. is vertical. *adj.* exactly perpendicular. *adv.* 1. straight down; directly. 2. [Colloq.], entirely; absolutely: as, *plumb* crazy. *v.i.* 1. to sink straight down. 2. to hang vertically. *v.t.* 1. to test or sound with a plumb. 2. to discover the facts of; solve. 3. to make vertical. —**out of plumb,** not vertical: also **off plumb.**

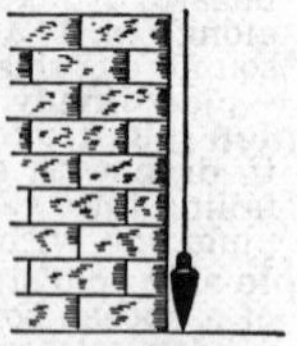

PLUMB

**plumb·er** (plum′ẽr), *n.* [< OFr. < L. < *plumbarius*, lead-worker < *plumbum*, lead (metal)], a skilled worker who fits and repairs the pipes, fixtures, etc. of gas and water systems.
**plumb·ing** (plum′iŋ), *n.* [< *plumber*], 1. the using of a plumb. 2. the work of a plumber. 3. the pipes and fixtures with which a plumber works.
**plum·bum** (plum′bəm), *n.* [L.], lead: symbol, Pb.
**plume** (plōōm), *n.* [OFr. < L. *pluma*], 1. *a*) a feather, especially a large, wavy one. *b*) a group of these. 2. an ornament made of such a feather or feathers, or a feathery tuft of hair, especially when worn on a helmet. 3. a token of worth or achievement; prize. 4. something like a plume in shape or lightness: as, a *plume* of smoke. *v.t.* [PLUMED, PLUMING], 1. to provide or adorn with plumes. 2. to smooth its feathers: used reflexively, of a bird. 3. to pride (oneself). 4. to preen. —**plume′let,** *n.*
**plum·met** (plum′it), *n.* [< OFr. dim. of *plom;* see PLUMB], 1. a plumb bob. 2. a plumb line and plumb bob together. 3. a thing that weighs heavily. *v.i.* to fall straight downward.
**plu·mose** (plōō′mōs), *adj.* [< L. < *pluma*, a feather], 1. feathered. 2. like a feather. —**plu′mose·ly,** *adv.* —**plu·mos·i·ty** (-mos′ə-ti), *n.*
**plump** (plump), *adj.* [< MD. *plomp*, bulky], full and rounded in form; chubby. *v.t. & v.i.* to fatten or fill out (sometimes with *up* or *out*). —**plump′ly,** *adv.* —**plump′ness,** *n.*
**plump** (plump), *v.i.* [< MD. *plompen;* echoic], to fall or bump (*against*) suddenly or heavily. *v.t.* to put down heavily or all at once. *n.* 1. a falling, bumping, etc. suddenly or heavily. 2. the sound of this. *adv.* 1. suddenly; heavily. 2. straight down. 3. in plain words; bluntly. *adj.* blunt; straightforward. —**plump for,** 1. to vote for. 2. to support strongly. —**plump′er,** *n.*
**plum pudding,** [orig. made with *plums*], a rich pudding made of suet, raisins, currants, etc., boiled or steamed, as in a linen bag.
**plum·y** (plōō′mi), *adj.* 1. made of or adorned with plumes; feathered. 2. like a plume; feathery.
**plun·der** (plun′dẽr), *v.t.* [< G. < *plunder*, baggage], 1. to rob (a person or place) by force, especially in warfare. 2. to take (property) by force or fraud. *v.i.* to steal. *n.* 1. the act of plundering; pillage. 2. goods taken by force or fraud; loot; booty.
**plunge** (plunj), *v.t.* [PLUNGED, PLUNGING], [< OFr. *plongier* < LL. < L. *plumbum*, lead (metal)], to thrust or throw suddenly (*into* a liquid, hole, condition, etc.). *v.i.* 1. to dive or rush, as into water, a fight, etc. 2. to move violently and rapidly downward or forward. 3. to pitch, as a ship. 4. [Colloq.], to spend or gamble heavily. *n.* 1. a place for plunging; swimming pool. 2. *a*) a dive or downward leap. *b*) a swim. 3. any sudden, violent plunging motion. 4. [Colloq.], a heavy, rash investment. —**take the plunge,** to start on some new and uncertain enterprise.
**plung·er** (plun′jẽr), *n.* 1. one who plunges. 2. [Colloq.], one who acts hastily or recklessly; esp., a rash gambler. 3. any cylindrical device that operates with a plunging motion, as a piston, etc.
**plunk** (pluŋk), *v.t.* [echoic], 1. to pluck or strum (a banjo, etc.). 2. to throw or put down heavily; plump. *v.i.* 1. to give out a twanging sound, as a banjo. 2. to fall heavily. *n.* 1. a plunking. 2. the sound made by plunking. 3. [Colloq.], a hard blow. *adv.* with a twang or thud.
**plu·per·fect** (plōō-pũr′fikt, plōō′pũr′-), *adj.* [abbrev. of L. *plus quam perfectum*, more than perfect], in *grammar*, past perfect. *n.* a pluperfect tense or form.
**plu·ral** (ploor′əl), *adj.* [< OFr. < L. *pluralis* < *plus*, more], 1. of or including more than one. 2. of or involving a plurality of persons or things: as, *plural* marriage. 3. in *grammar*, designating or of more than one (of what is referred to). *n.* in *grammar*, 1. the plural number. 2. a plural form of a word. 3. a word in plural form.

NOUN PLURALS IN ENGLISH.—The regular plural suffix is -(*e*)*s*. Borrowed foreign words often have alternative plurals in this form, in addition to their original plurals. Words with alternative plurals in the regular -(*e*)*s* form are marked (*).

I. Regular English Plurals.
  A. Add *-s* in all cases except as noted below.
  B. Add *-es* after final *-ss*, *-sh*, and *-ch*: *glass-es*, *ash-es*, *witch-es*.
  C. Add *-es* after *-y* preceded by a consonant or by *-qu-*, and change the *-y* to *-i*: *fly*, *fli-es; soliloquy*, *soliloqui-es*. (Add *-s* after *-y* preceded by a vowel: *day*, *day-s; monkey*, *monkey-s*.)
  D. Add *-es* to some words ending in *-o* preceded by a consonant: **buffalo-es*, **domino-es*, *echo-es*, *hero-es*, *potato-es*. (Add *-s* to most words ending in *-o* preceded by a consonant, and to all words ending in *-o* preceded by a vowel: *piano-s*, *radio-s*, *studio-s*.)
II. Minor English Plurals.
  A. Change *f* to *v* in many words, and add -(*e*)*s*: *half*, *self*, *life*, **scarf*, **wharf*.
  B. Regular plural replaced:
    1. By *-en: ox-en*.
    2. By *-ren: child-ren*.
    3. By vowel change: *man*, *men; foot*, *feet; mouse*, *mice*.
  C. Plural the same as the singular: *alms*, *barracks*, *Chinese*, *deer* (occas. *deers*), *forceps*, *gallows*, *gross*, *means*, *salmon*, *Swiss*.
  D. Plural either different from or the same as the singular:
    1. Plural usually different, but sometimes

the same, especially in the usage of hunters and fishermen:

**albacore**
**albatross**
**anchovy**
**antelope**
**argali**
**badger**
**bear**
**beaver**
**bighorn**
**bittern**
**blackcock**
**blenny**
**boar**
**bobcat**
**bobwhite**
**bonito**
**brant**
**buck**
**buffalo**
**canvasback**
**carabao**
**caribou**
**cat**
**char**
**chub**
**clam**
**coot**
**cougar**
**coyote**
**coypu**
**crake**
**crane**
**crappie**
**croppie**
**curlew**
**dhole**
**doe**
**dog**
**duck**
**dunlin**
**eel**
**egret**
**eider**
**elephant**
**ermine**
**fisher**
**flounder**
**fowl**
**fox**
**gadwall**
**gannet**
**gazelle**
**giraffe**
**gnu**
**goat**
**goby**
**goldeneye**
**goose**
**grebe**
**grouper**
**gull**
**gurnard**
**hare**
**hart**
**hartebeest**
**heron**
**herring**
**hind**
**hippopotamus**
**hog**
**horse**
**ibex**
**ibis**
**jack**
**jackal**
**jaguar**
**kangaroo**
**killdee**
**killdeer**
**kittiwake**
**kudu**
**lemming**
**leopard**
**lion**
**llama**
**lobster**
**lynx**
**mallard**
**marten**
**meadow lark**
**merganser**
**mink**
**minnow**
**mullet**
**muskrat**
**nilgai, nilghai**
**nilgau, nilghau**
**ocelot**
**okapi**
**opossum**
**oryx**
**ostrich**
**otter**
**ox**
**panther**
**parr**
**partridge**
**peacock**
**peafowl**
**peccary**
**pheasant**
**pig**
**pigeon**
**plover**
**polecat**
**porcupine**
**porgy**
**porpoise**
**pronghorn**
**ptarmigan**
**puma**
**quail**
**rabbit**
**raccoon**
**rail**
**rhinoceros**
**roebuck**
**sable**
**sandpiper**
**sardine**
**scaup**
**seal**
**sheldrake**
**shiner**
**shrimp**
**skate**
**skunk**
**smelt**
**snapper**
**snipe**
**squid**
**squirrel**
**stag**
**stoat**
**stork**
**sturgeon**
**swan**
**tapir**
**tarpon**
**teal**
**tiger**
**tortoise**
**tunny**
**turkey**
**turtle**
**vicuña**
**wallaby**
**walrus**
**wapiti**
**waterfowl**
**weasel**
**whale**
**whippoorwill**
**whiting**
**widgeon**
**wigeon**
**wildcat**
**wildebeest**
**wolverine**
**woodcock**
**yak**
**zebra**
**zebu**

2. Plural usually the same, but different if referring to different kinds, species, varieties, etc.: as, the *fishes* of the South Pacific:

**barracuda**
**bass**
**beluga**
**bream**
**burbot**
**capelin**
**carp**
**cod**
**codling**
**cusk**
**dace**
**eelpout**
**eland**
**elk**
**fish** (and its compounds, as, *bluefish*)
**gar**
**gemsbok**
**grayling**
**grilse**
**haddock**
**hake**
**halibut**
**holibut**
**ling**
**mackerel**
**perch**
**pickerel**
**pike**
**plaice**
**roach**
**roe**
**salmon**
**scup**
**shad**
**sole**
**springbok**
**steenbok**
**steinbock**
**trout**
**tuna**
**turbot**

3. Plural usually lacking, but given in -(*e*)*s* form when different kinds are referred to: as, the many *steels* produced.

**barley**
**brass**
**coffee**
**fruit**
**iron**
**linen**
**millet**
**oak**
**pepper**
**pine**
**rye**
**silk**
**steel**
**tea**
**wheat**
**wool**

4. Plural and collective singular interchangeable: *cannons, cannon.*

III. Forms Singular or Plural Only.

A. Singular only (or when a generalized abstraction): *chess, clearness, fishing, information, knowledge, luck, music, nonsense, truth.*

B. Plural only (even when singular in meaning). This includes certain senses of nouns otherwise singular: *Balkans, blues* (depression), *bowels, glasses, lodgings, overalls, pliers, remains* (corpse), *scissors, tongs, trousers.*

C. Plural in form but construed as singular: *cards* (game), *checkers* (game), *measles, news.*

D. Nouns ending in *-ics* are singular when they denote scientific subjects, as *mathematics, physics,* and plural when they denote activities or qualities, as *acrobatics, acoustics.*

IV. Latin and Greek Plurals.

A. With suffix *-a* and loss of singular ending: 1. Latin nouns in *-um: agendum, agend-a; datum, dat-a; *medium, medi-a.* 2. Greek nouns in *-on: criterion, criteri-a; phenomenon, phenomen-a.*

B. With Latin suffix *-i* and loss of singular ending *-us: alumnus, alumn-i; *focus, foc-i; *radius, radi-i.*

C. With Latin suffix *-ae* and loss of singular ending *-a: alumna, alumn-ae; *formula, formul-ae.*

D. With suffix *-es:* 1. Latin nouns in *-ex* or *-ix* change the ending to *-ic* and add *-es: *appendix, appendices; *index, ind-ices.* 2. Latin or Greek nouns in *-is* change *-is* to *-es: analysis, analys-es; axis, ax-es.*

E. Miscellaneous Latin plurals: **phalanx, phalang-es; *stigma, stigma-ta.*

V. Foreign Plurals.

A. Hebrew: **cherub, cherub-im; *seraph, seraph-im.*

B. Italian: **bandit, bandit-ti; *prima donna, prim-e donn-e; *dilettante, dilettant-i; *virtuoso, virtuos-i.*

C. French: *bijou, bijou-x; *château, château-x; *portmanteau, portmanteau-x.*

VI. Plurals of Numbers, Letters, Signs, Words (when thought of as things), etc. add *-'s: 8's, B's, &'s, whereas's.*

**plu·ral·ism** (ploor'əl-iz'm), *n.* 1. existence in more than one part or form. 2. the holding by one person of more than one office or church benefice at the same time. —**plu'ral·ist,** *n.* —**plu'ral·is'tic,** *adj.*

**plu·ral·i·ty** (ploo-ral'ə-ti), *n.* [*pl.* -TIES], 1. a being plural or numerous. 2. a great number; multitude. 3. a majority. 4. the excess of votes in an election that the leading candidate has over his nearest rival.

**plu·ral·ize** (ploor'əl-īz'), *v.t.* [-IZED, -IZING], to make plural; put into plural form.

**plu·ral·ly** (ploor'əl-i), *adv.* in the plural.

**plu·ri-** (ploor′ə), [L. < *plus*, several], a combining form meaning *several* or *many*.

**plus** (plus), *prep.* [L., more], 1. added to: as, two *plus* two equals four: opposed to *minus*. 2. and in addition: as, a suit with coat *plus* vest. *adj.* 1. designating a sign (**plus sign**) indicating addition: as, + is a *plus sign*. 2. positive: as, a *plus* quantity. 3. somewhat higher than: as, a grade of B *plus*. 4. [Colloq.], and more: as, she has personality *plus*. 5. in *electricity*, positive: opposed to *negative*. *n.* 1. a plus sign. 2. an added quantity or thing. 3. a plus quantity. *adv.* in *electricity*, positively.

**plus fours,** [orig. indicating added length of material for overlap below the knee], loose knickerbockers worn for active sports.

**plush** (plush), *n.* [< Fr. < *peluche;* ult. < L. *pilus*, hair], a fabric having a soft pile over one eighth of an inch long. *adj.* 1. of plush. 2. [Slang], luxurious, as in furnishings. **—plush′like′,** *adj.* **—plush′y** [-IER, -IEST], *adj.* **—plush′i·ness,** *n.*

**Plu·tarch** (plo͞o′tärk), *n.* Greek biographer and moralist; lived 46?–120? A.D.

**Plu·to** (plo͞o′tō), *n.* 1. in *Gr. & Rom. mythology*, the god of the lower world: also called *Hades* by the Greeks and *Dis* by the Romans. 2. the outermost planet of the solar system: diameter, 7,600 mi. **—Plu·to′ni·an, Plu·ton′ic** (-ton′ik), *adj.*

**plu·toc·ra·cy** (plo͞o-tok′rə-si), *n.* [*pl.* -CIES], [< Gr. < *ploutos*, wealth + *kratein*, to rule], 1. government by the wealthy. 2. a state so ruled. 3. the class of wealthy people who control a government.

**plu·to·crat** (plo͞o′tə-krat′), *n.* 1. a member of a wealthy ruling class. 2. one whose wealth gives him control or great influence. 3. [Colloq.], any wealthy person. **—plu′to·crat′ic, plu′to·crat′i·cal,** *adj.* **—plu′to·crat′i·cal·ly,** *adv.*

**plu·to·ni·um** (plo͞o-tō′ni-əm), *n.* [after *Pluto* (planet)], a radioactive chemical element formed by the transformation of neptunium: symbol, Pu; at. wt., 239; at. no., 94.

**Plu·tus** (plo͞o′təs), *n.* in *Gr. mythology*, the blind god of wealth.

**plu·vi·al** (plo͞o′vi-əl), *adj.* [< L. < *pluvia*, rain], 1. of or having to do with rain; rainy: also **plu′vi·ous.** 2. in *geology*, formed by rain.

**ply** (plī), *v.t.* [PLIED, PLYING], [< OFr. < L. *plicare*, to fold], to bend, twist, fold, or mold. *n.* [*pl.* PLIES], 1. a single thickness or layer, as of doubled cloth, plywood, etc. 2. one of the twisted strands in rope, yarn, etc. 3. bent, bias, or inclination. *adj.* having (a specified number of) layers, strands, etc.: as, three-*ply*.

**ply** (plī), *v.t.* [PLIED, PLYING], [contr. < *apply*], 1. to use; work with; wield (a tool, faculty, etc.). 2. to work at (a trade); keep working on (*with* a tool, process, etc.). 3. to address (someone) urgently (*with* questions, etc.). 4. to keep supplying (*with* presents, food, etc.). 5. to sail back and forth across: as, boats *ply* the channel. *v.i.* 1. to keep busy; work (*at* something). 2. to travel regularly (*between* places), as a ship or bus.

**Plym·outh** (plim′əth), *n.* 1. a city in SW England, on the English Channel: pop., 221,000. 2. a town on the coast of Massachusetts: settled by the Pilgrims (1620).

**Plymouth Rock,** 1. a rock at Plymouth, Massachusetts, where the Pilgrims are said to have landed. 2. one of a breed of American chickens.

**ply·wood** (plī′wood′), *n.* [*ply* (*n.*) + *wood*], a construction material made of thin layers of wood glued and pressed together, usually with their grains at right angles to one another.

**Pm,** in *chemistry*, promethium.

**P.M.,** 1. Paymaster. 2. Postmaster.

**P.M., p.m.,** *post meridiem*, [L.], after noon.

**p.m.,** *post-mortem*, [L.], after death.

**pmk.,** postmark.

**pneu·mat·ic** (no͞o-mat′ik, nū-), *adj.* [< L. < Gr. *pneuma*, air, wind], 1. of or containing wind, air, or gases. 2. worked by or filled with compressed air. 3. equipped with pneumatic tires. *n.* a pneumatic tire. **—pneu·mat′i·cal·ly,** *adv.*

**pneu·mat·ics** (no͞o-mat′iks, nū-), *n.pl.* [construed as sing.], the branch of physics that deals with the properties, such as pressure, density, etc., of air and other gases.

**pneumatic tire,** a rubber tire inflated with compressed air.

**pneu·mo·coc·cus** (no͞o′mə-kok′əs, nū′-), *n.* [*pl.* -COCCI (-kok′sī)], a bacterium that is the causative agent of lobar pneumonia and some other diseases. **—pneu′mo·coc′cal, pneu′mo·coc′cic** (-sik), *adj.*

**pneu·mo·ni·a** (no͞o-mō′nyə, nū-mō′ni-ə), *n.* [< Gr. < *pneumōn*, a lung < *pnein*, to breathe], a disease of the lungs in which tissue becomes inflamed, hardened, and watery. **—pneu·mon′ic** (-mon′ik), *adj.*

**Pnom-Penh** (pnoom′pen′y′; Eng. nom′pen′), *n.* the capital of Cambodia: pop., 103,000.

**Po** (pō), *n.* a river in N Italy, flowing eastward into the Adriatic: length, 415 mi.

**Po,** in *chemistry*, polonium.

**P.O., p.o.,** 1. petty officer. 2. post office.

**poach** (pōch), *v.t.* [< OFr. < *poche*, a pocket: the yolk is "pocketed" in the white], to cook the unbroken contents of (an egg) in or over boiling water, until the white of the egg coagulates.

**poach** (pōch), *v.t.* [< Fr. < OFr. *pochier*, to tread upon < MHG. *puchen*, to plunder], 1. to trample. 2. to trespass on (private property), especially for hunting or fishing. 3. to hunt or catch (game or fish) illegally. 4. to steal. *v.i.* to hunt or fish on another's property; trespass. **—poach′er,** *n.*

**Po·ca·hon·tas** (pō′kə-hon′təs), *n.* 1595?–1617; American Indian princess; said to have saved Captain John Smith from execution.

**pock** (pok), *n.* [AS. *pocc*], 1. a pimple or pustule caused by smallpox and some other diseases. 2. a scar or pit in the skin left by such a pustule. **—pocked,** *adj.* **—pock′y** [-IER, -IEST], *adj.*

**pock·et** (pok′it), *n.* [< Anglo-Fr. < ONorm.Fr. dim. of *poque*, a bag], 1. a little bag or pouch, especially when sewed into clothing for carrying money and small articles. 2. any cavity or enclosure for holding something. 3. an air pocket. 4. an open pouch at the side or corner of a pool table. 5. in *mining*, *a*) a cavity filled with ore. *b*) a small deposit of ore. *adj.* 1. that can be carried in a pocket; hence, 2. small. *v.t.* 1. to put into a pocket. 2. to envelop; enclose. 3. to take dishonestly; appropriate, as money. 4. to submit to (an insult, etc.) without answering or showing anger. 5. to hide or suppress: as, to *pocket* one's pride. **—line one's pockets,** to gain much money.

**pocket battleship,** a type of small battleship carrying heavier guns than a cruiser.

**pock·et·book** (pok′it-book′), *n.* 1. a case, as of leather, for carrying money and papers in one's pocket; billfold. 2. a woman's purse.

**pocket book,** a book small enough to be carried in one's pocket.

**pock·et·ful** (pok′it-fool′), *n.* [*pl.* -FULS], as much as a pocket will hold.

**pock·et·knife** (pok′it-nīf′), *n.* [*pl.* -KNIVES], a small knife whose blades fold into the handle.

**pocket money,** cash for small expenses.

**pocket veto,** the method whereby the President of the U.S. can veto a bill passed by Congress within ten days of its adjournment by failing to sign and return the bill by the time of adjournment.

**pock·mark** (pok′märk′), *n.* a scar or pit left by a pustule, as in smallpox. **—pock′-marked′,** *adj.*

**‡po·co** (pô′kô; Eng. pō′kō), *adv.* [It.], in *music*, somewhat. *n.* a little.

**pod** (pod), *n.* [prob. < LG.], the seedcase of peas, beans, etc. *v.i.* [PODDED, PODDING], 1. to bear pods. 2. to swell out into a pod. *v.t.* to take (peas, etc.) out of pods; shell. **—pod′like′,** *adj.*

**-pod,** [*pl.* -PODA], [< Gr. *pous*, a foot], a combining form meaning: 1. *foot.* 2. (*one*) *having* (a specified number or kind of) *feet*, as in *tripod:* also **-pode.**

**podg·y** (poj′i), *adj.* [-IER, -IEST], [var. of *pudgy*], short and thick; pudgy. **—podg′i·ness,** *n.*

**po·di·a·try** (pō-dī′ə-tri), *n.* [< Gr. *pous*, foot; + *-iatry*], the branch of medicine dealing with disorders of the feet. **—po·di′a·trist,** *n.*

**po·di·um** (pō′di-əm), *n.* [*pl.* -DIA (-di-ə)], [L. < Gr. *podion*, dim. of *pous*, a foot], 1. a raised platform for the conductor of an orchestra; dais. 2. in *zoology*, a structure serving as a foot.

**-pod·ous,** [< Gr. < *pous*, a foot], a combining form meaning *having* (a specified number or kind of) *feet.*

**Po·dunk** (pō′duŋk′), *n.* [Colloq.], an imaginary typical small town in the U.S.: humorous usage.

**Poe, Edgar Allan** (pō), 1809–1849; American poet, critic, and fiction writer.

**po·em** (pō′im), *n.* [< Fr. < L. < Gr. *poiēma* < *poiein*, to compose], 1. an arrangement of words in verse; esp., a rhythmical composition, sometimes rhymed, in language more concentrated and imaginative than ordinary speech. 2. anything likened to a poem in its beauty.

**po·e·sy** (pō′i-si, -zi), *n.* [*pl.* -SIES], [< OFr. < L. < Gr. *poiēsis*], 1. [Archaic], poetry. 2. [Obs.], a poem.

**po·et** (pō′it), *n.* [< OFr. < L. < Gr. *poiētēs*], 1. one who writes poems. 2. one who expresses himself with beauty of thought and language. **—po′et·ess,** *n.fem.*

**poet.,** 1. poetic. 2. poetry.

**po·et·as·ter** (pō′it-as′tẽr), *n.* [see POET & -ASTER], a writer of mediocre verse; rhymester.

**po·et·ic** (pō-et′ik), *adj.* 1. of, like, or fit for a poet or poetry. 2. written in verse. 3. having the beauty, imagination, etc. of poetry. 4. imaginative. Also **po·et′i·cal.** —**po·et′i·cal·ly,** *adv.*

**poetic justice,** justice, as in some plays, etc., in which good is rewarded and evil punished.

**poetic license,** the right to deviate, for artistic effect, from literal fact or rigid form.

**po·et·ics** (pō-et′iks), *n.pl.* [construed as sing.], 1. the part of literary criticism that has to do with poetry. 2. a treatise on poetry.

**po·et·ize** (pō′it-īz′), *v.i.* & *v.t.* [-IZED, -IZING], to write, or express in, poetry.

**poet laureate,** [*pl.* POETS LAUREATE, POET LAUREATES], 1. the court poet of England, appointed by the monarch to write poems celebrating official occasions, national events, etc. 2. any official poet of a State, nation, etc.

**po·et·ry** (pō′it-ri), *n.* [< OFr. < ML. < L. *poeta*, a poet], 1. the writing of poems; art of writing poems. 2. poems. 3. something having the quality or effect of poetry. 4. poetic quality or spirit.

**po·go stick** (pō′gō), [< ?], a stilt with two pedals attached by a spring, on which one can propel himself in a series of short jumps.

**po·grom** (pō′grəm, pō-grom′), *n.* [Russ., devastation], 1. an organized massacre of Jews, as in Czarist Russia. 2. any similar attack.

**po·i** (poi, pō′i), *n.* [Haw.], a Hawaiian food made of mashed, fermented taro root.

**-poi·et·ic,** [< Gr. *poiēsis*, a creating], a combining form meaning *making, producing, forming.*

**poign·ant** (poin′ənt, -yənt), *adj.* [OFr., ppr. of *poindre* < L. *pungere*, to prick], 1. sharp to the smell or taste; tart; pungent. 2. sharply painful to the feelings; piercing. 3. keen: as, *poignant* wit. —**poign′an·cy,** *n.* —**poign′ant·ly,** *adv.*

**poi·lu** (pwä′lo͞o; Fr. pwȧ′lü′), *n.* [Fr., lit., hairy], [Slang], in World War I, a French soldier.

**poin·ci·a·na** (poin′si-ā′nə, -an′ə), *n.* [after M. de *Poinci*, a governor of the French West Indies], any of various related small tropical trees with showy red, orange, or yellow flowers.

**poin·set·ti·a** (poin-set′i-ə, -set′ə), *n.* [after J. R. *Poinsett* (d. 1851), U.S. ambassador to Mexico], a Mexican and South American shrub with small flowers surrounded by petallike red leaves.

**point** (point), *n.* [< OFr. *point*, a dot, and *pointe*, a sharp end; both ult. < L. *punctus*, pp. of *pungere*, to prick], 1. a speck or dot. 2. a dot in print or writing, as a period, decimal point, etc. 3. something having position in space, but no size or shape; location. 4. *a*) the position of a certain player, as in cricket. *b*) the player. 5. the exact moment: as, the *point* of death. 6. a stage or condition reached: as, boiling *point.* 7. a part of something; item: as, explain it *point* by *point.* 8. *a*) a distinguishing characteristic. *b*) a physical characteristic of an animal, used in judging breeding. 9. a unit, as of measurement, value, game scores, etc. 10. *a*) a sharp end. *b*) something with a sharp end. 11. needle-point lace. 12. a projecting piece of land; cape. 13. a branch of a deer's antler: as, a ten-*point* buck. 14. the essential fact or idea under consideration (preceded by *the*): as, the *point* of a joke. 15. a purpose; object: as, there's no *point* in going. 16. an impressive argument or fact: as, you have a *point* there! 17. in *commerce*, a standard unit of value, as $1, used in quoting prices, as of stocks. 18. in *craps*, the number that the thrower must make to win. 19. in *electricity*, either of the two tungsten or platinum contacts that make or break the circuit in a distributor. 20. in *navigation*, *a*) one of the thirty-two marks showing direction on a compass card. *b*) the angle between two successive compass points. 21. in *printing*, a unit measure for type bodies, equal to about $^{1}/_{72}$ of an inch. 22. *usually in pl.* [Brit.], in *railroading*, a tapering rail in a switch. *v.t.* 1. to put punctuation marks in: as, to *point* a sentence. 2. to mark off (a sum, etc.) with (decimal) points (with *off*). 3. to sharpen to a point, as a pencil. 4. to give (a story, remark, etc.) emphasis (sometimes with *up*). 5. to show (often with *out*): as, *point* the way. 6. to aim or direct (a gun, finger, etc.). 7. to show the location of (game) by standing still and facing toward it: said of hunting dogs. 8. in *masonry*, to fill the joints of (brickwork) with mortar. *v.i.* 1. to direct one's finger (*at* or *to*). 2. to call attention (*to*); hint (*at*). 3. to aim or be directed (*to* or *toward*); face. 4. to point game: said of hunting dogs. —**at the point of,** very close to. —**beside the point,** not pertinent; irrelevant. —**in point of,** in the matter of. —**make a point of,** to insist on. —**on the point of,** on the verge of. —**stretch** (or **strain**) **a point,** to make an exception or concession. —**to the point,** pertinent; apt: also **in point.** —**point′a·ble,** *adj.*

**point-blank** (point′blaŋk′), *adj.* [*point* + *blank* (white center of the target)], 1. aimed horizontally, straight at a mark. 2. straightforward; plain: as, a *point-blank* answer. *adv.* 1. straight: as, to fire a gun *point-blank.* 2. without quibbling; bluntly: as, she refused *point-blank.*

**point·ed** (poin′tid), *adj.* 1. having a sharp end; tapering. 2. sharp; incisive, as an epigram. 3. aimed at someone, as a remark. 4. very evident; emphasized. —**point′ed·ly,** *adv.* —**point′ed·ness,** *n.*

**point·er** (poin′tẽr), *n.* 1. a person or thing that points. 2. a long, tapered rod for pointing to things, as on a map. 3. an indicator on a clock, meter, etc. 4. a large, lean hunting dog with a smooth coat: it smells out game and then points. 5. [Colloq.], a hint; clue. 6. [P-], *pl.* in *astronomy*, the two stars in the Big Dipper that are almost in a direct line with the North Star.

POINTER (26 in. high at shoulder)

**point lace,** needle-point lace.

**point·less** (point′lis), *adj.* 1. without a point. 2. without meaning, relevance, or force; senseless. —**point′less·ly,** *adv.* —**point′less·ness,** *n.*

**point of honor,** a matter affecting one's honor.

**point of order,** a question as to whether parliamentary procedure is being observed.

**point of view,** 1. the place from which, or way in which, something is viewed; standpoint. 2. a mental attitude or opinion.

**poise** (poiz), *n.* [< OFr. < LL. < L. *pensum*, something weighed < *pendere*, to weigh], 1. balance; stability. 2. ease and dignity of manner. 3. carriage; bearing, as of the body. 4. a suspension of activity in a condition of balance. 5. suspense; indecision. *v.t.* [POISED, POISING], 1. to balance; keep steady. 2. to suspend (usually passive or reflexive): as, the earth is *poised* in space. *v.i.* 1. to be suspended or balanced. 2. to hover.

**poi·son** (poi′z'n), *n.* [< OFr. < L. *potio*, potion], 1. a substance, usually a drug, causing illness or death when eaten, drunk, or absorbed in small quantities. 2. anything harmful to happiness or welfare. *v.t.* 1. to harm or destroy by means of poison. 2. to put poison on or into. 3. to influence wrongfully: as, they *poisoned* his mind. *adj.* poisonous. —**poi′son·er,** *n.* —**poi′son·ing,** *n.*

**poison dogwood** (or **elder**), poison sumac.

**poison ivy,** any of several American sumacs with grayish berries and leaves that grow in groups of three and can cause a skin rash if touched.

**poison oak,** 1. a shrubby western variety of poison ivy. 2. poison sumac.

**poi·son·ous** (poi′z'n-əs), *adj.* that can injure or kill by or as by poison; full of poison; venomous. —**poi′son·ous·ly,** *adv.* —**poi′son·ous·ness,** *n.*

**poison sumac,** a swamp shrub with clusters of grayish fruit and leaves made up of 7 to 13 gray leaflets which can cause a rash if touched.

POISON IVY

**poke** (pōk), *v.t.* [POKED, POKING], [MD. or LG. *poken*], 1. to push; prod, as with a stick, an elbow, etc. 2. [Slang], to hit with the fist. 3. to make (a hole, etc.) by poking. 4. to stir up (a fire). 5. to thrust; intrude: as, don't *poke* your nose into my affairs. *v.i.* 1. to jab with a stick, poker, etc. (*at*). 2. to intrude; meddle. 3. to search (sometimes with *about* or *around*). 4. to move slowly or lazily; loiter (often with *along*). *n.* 1. a poking; jab; thrust. 2. [Slang], a blow with the fist. 3. a slow-moving person; dawdler. 4. a poke bonnet. —**poke fun** (**at**), to ridicule or deride.

**poke** (pōk), *n.* [OFr. *poke, poque*], [Archaic & Dial.], 1. a sack; bag. 2. a pocket.

**poke** (pōk), *n.* [< Am. Ind. *pakon*], pokeweed.

**poke·ber·ry** (pōk′ber′i, -bẽr-i), *n.* [*pl.* -RIES], 1. the berry of the pokeweed. 2. the pokeweed.

**poke bonnet,** a bonnet with a wide front brim.

**pok·er** (pō′kẽr), *n.* [akin to G. *pochspiel* < *pochen*, to brag], a card game in which the players bet on the value of their hands, forming a pool to be taken by the winner: see **draw poker, stud poker.**

**pok·er** (pō′kẽr), *n.* 1. a person or thing that pokes. 2. a bar, as of iron, for stirring a fire.

**poker face,** [Colloq.], an expressionless face, as of a poker player hiding the nature of his hand.

**poke·weed** (pōk′wēd′), *n.* [see POKE (weed)], a North American weed with purplish-white flowers, reddish-purple berries, and poisonous roots.

**pok·y, pok·ey** (pō′ki), *adj.* [-IER, -IEST], [< *poke* (to push)], 1. slow; dull. 2. small and uncomfortable, as a room. 3. shabbily dressed.

**Pol.,** 1. Poland. 2. Polish.

**Po·land** (pō′lənd), *n.* a country in central Europe, on the Baltic Sea: area, 120,360 sq. mi.; pop., 29,480,000; capital, Warsaw.

**Poland China,** an American breed of large hog, usually black and white.

**po·lar** (pō′lẽr), *adj.* [< ML. < L. *polus;* see POLE], 1. of or near the North or South Pole. 2. of a pole or poles. 3. having polarity. 4. having two opposite natures, directions, etc.

**polar bear,** a large white bear of arctic regions.

**Po·la·ris** (pō-lâr′is), *n.* [short for ML. *stella polaris*, polar star], the North Star; polestar.

**po·lar·i·scope** (pō-lar′ə-skōp′), *n.* an instrument for demonstrating the polarization of light.

**po·lar·i·ty** (pō-lar′ə-ti), *n.* 1. the condition of having magnetic poles (one positive and attracting, one negative and repelling). 2. the having of two contrary qualities, powers, etc. 3. in *electricity*, the condition of being positive or negative in relation to a magnetic pole.

**po·lar·i·za·tion** (pō′lẽr-i-zā′shən), *n.* 1. the producing or acquiring of polarity. 2. the production of a reverse electromotive force at the electrodes of a cell, by the depositing on them of gases produced during electrolysis. 3. in *optics*, a condition, or the production of a condition, of light in which the rays assume different forms in different planes.

**po·lar·ize** (pō′lẽr-īz′), *v.t.* [-IZED, -IZING], [< Fr. < *polaire*, polar], to give polarity to; produce polarization in. *v.i.* to acquire polarity. **—po′lar·iz′a·bil′i·ty,** *n.* **—po′lar·iz′a·ble,** *adj.* **—po′lar·iz′er,** *n.*

**po·lar·oid** (pō′lẽr-oid′), *n.* [*polar* + *-oid*], a thin, transparent, filmlike material capable of polarizing light, used in optics, photography, etc.: a trademark (**Polaroid**).

**Pole** (pōl), *n.* a native or inhabitant of Poland.

**pole** (pōl), *n.* [AS. < L. *palus*, a stake], 1. a long, slender piece of wood, metal, etc.: as, a tent *pole.* 2. a unit of measure, equal to one rod or one square rod. *v.t. & v.i.* [POLED, POLING], to propel (a boat or raft) with a pole. **—pol′er,** *n.*

**pole** (pōl), *n.* [OFr. < L. < Gr. *polos*], 1. either end of any axis, as of the earth, of the celestial sphere, etc. 2. the region contiguous to either end of the earth's axis: cf. **North Pole, South Pole.** 3. either of two opposed forces, parts, etc., such as the ends of a magnet, the terminals of a battery, etc. **—poles apart,** widely separated.

**pole·ax, pole·axe** (pōl′aks′), *n.* [< ME. < *pol*, head + *ax*], 1. a long-handled battle-ax. 2. any ax with a spike, hook, etc. opposite the blade. *v.t.* [-AXED, -AXING], to attack with a poleax.

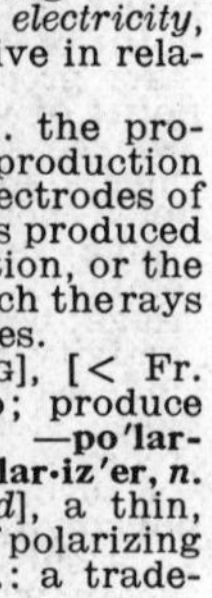

POLEAX

**pole·cat** (pōl′kat′), *n.* [*pl.* -CATS, -CAT; see PLURAL, II, D, 1], [prob. < OFr. *po(u)le*, a hen; + *cat*], 1. a small, bad-smelling, weasellike carnivore of Europe. 2. a skunk.

**po·lem·ic** (pō-lem′ik), *adj.* [< Gr. *polemikos* < *polemos*, a war], of or involving dispute; controversial: also **po·lem′i·cal.** *n.* 1. an argument or controversial discussion. 2. a person inclined to argument. **—po·lem′i·cal·ly,** *adv.*

**po·lem·ics** (pō-lem′iks), *n.pl.* [construed as sing.], 1. the art or practice of disputation. 2. a dispute. **—po·lem′i·cist** (-ə-sist), *n.*

**pole·star** (pōl′stär′), *n.* the North Star.

**pole-vault** (pōl′vôlt′), *v.i.* to perform in the pole vault. **—pole′-vault′er,** *n.* **—pole′-vault′ing,** *n.*

**pole vault,** in *track & field*, 1. an event in which the contestant leaps for height, vaulting over a bar with the aid of a long pole. 2. such a leap.

**po·lice** (pə-lēs′), *n.* [Fr. < LL. < Gr. *politeia*, the state < *politēs*, citizen < *polis*, city], 1. the regulation of morals, safety, etc.; law enforcement. 2. the governmental department (of a city, state, etc.) for keeping order and preventing or detecting crimes. 3. [construed as pl.], the members of such a department. 4. in the *U.S. Army, a)* the act of maintaining order or cleanliness in a camp, etc. *b)* the soldiers charged with this. *v.t.* [-LICED, -LICING], 1. to control, protect, etc. with police or the like: as, *police* the street. 2. to keep (a military camp, etc.) clean and orderly (sometimes with *up*).

**police dog,** a dog specially trained to assist police, etc.; esp., the German shepherd.

**po·lice·man** (pə-lēs′mən), *n.* [*pl.* -MEN], a member of a police force. **—po·lice′wom′an** [*pl.* -WOMEN], *n.fem.*

**police state,** a government that seeks to intimidate and suppress political opposition by means of a secret police force.

**pol·i·clin·ic** (pol′i-klin′ik), *n.* [< G. < Gr. *polis*, city + G. *klinik*, clinic], the department of a hospital where outpatients are treated.

**pol·i·cy** (pol′ə-si), *n.* [*pl.* -CIES], [< OFr. < L. < Gr. *politeia;* see POLICE], 1. political wisdom; diplomacy; prudence. 2. wise or crafty management. 3. any governing principle, plan, etc.

**pol·i·cy** (pol′ə-si), *n.* [*pl.* -CIES], [< Fr. < It. *polizza* < ML. < Gr. *apodeixis*, proof < *apodeiknynai*, to display], a written contract in which one party guarantees to insure another against a specified loss or misfortune.

**policy game** (or **racket**), a numbers pool.

**pol·i·cy·hold·er** (pol′ə-si-hōl′dẽr), *n.* a person to whom an insurance policy is issued.

**pol·i·o** (pō′li-ō′, pol′i-), *n.* [Colloq.], poliomyelitis.

**pol·i·o·my·e·li·tis** (pol′i-ō-mī′ə-lī′tis), *n.* [< Gr. *polios*, gray + *myelos*, marrow], an acute infectious disease, especially of children, caused by a virus inflammation of the gray matter of the spinal cord, often resulting in muscular paralysis; esp., infantile paralysis.

**Pol·ish** (pō′lish), *adj.* of Poland, its people, their language, or culture. *n.* the West Slavic language of the Poles.

**pol·ish** (pol′ish), *v.t.* [< OFr. < L. *polire*], 1. to smooth and brighten, as by rubbing. 2. to remove crudity from; refine (manners, style, etc.). 3. to complete or embellish; perfect. *v.i.* to take a polish; become glossy, elegant, etc. *n.* 1. surface gloss. 2. elegance; refinement. 3. a substance used to polish. 4. a polishing or being polished. **—polish off,** [Colloq.], 1. to finish (a meal, job, etc.) completely. 2. to get rid of (a competitor, enemy, etc.). **—polish up,** [Colloq.], to improve. **—pol′ished,** *adj.* **—pol′ish·er,** *n.*

**Polish Corridor,** formerly, the narrow strip of Poland between Germany and East Prussia.

**Po·lit·bu·ro** (pə-lit′byoor′ō), *n.* [< Russ. *Politicheskoe Buro*, political bureau], the former leading committee of the Communist Party of the Soviet Union, replaced by the Presidium in 1952.

**po·lite** (pə-līt′), *adj.* [< L. pp. of *polire*, to polish], 1. polished; cultured; refined: as, *polite* society. 2. having good manners; courteous. **—po·lite′ly,** *adv.* **—po·lite′ness,** *n.*

**pol·i·tesse** (pol′ə-tes′), *n.* [Fr.], politeness.

**pol·i·tic** (pol′ə-tik), *adj.* [< L. < Gr. < *politēs;* see POLICE], 1. having practical wisdom; prudent; diplomatic. 2. crafty; unscrupulous. 3. artful; expedient, as a plan, action, etc. 4. [Rare], political: see **body politic.** **—pol′i·tic·ly,** *adv.*

**po·lit·i·cal** (pə-lit′i-k'l), *adj.* 1. of or concerned with government, politics, etc. 2. having a definite governmental organization. 3. engaged in politics: as, *political* parties. 4. of or characteristic of political parties or politicians. **—po·lit′i·cal·ly,** *adv.*

**political economy,** economics. **—political economist.**

**political science,** the science of the principles, organization, and methods of government.

**pol·i·ti·cian** (pol′ə-tish′ən), *n.* one actively engaged in politics, often one holding or seeking political office: often used derogatorily, with implications of seeking personal or partisan gain, scheming, etc., as distinguished from *statesman.*

**po·lit·i·co** (pə-lit′i-kō′), *n.* [It.], a politician.

**pol·i·tics** (pol′ə-tiks), *n.pl.* [construed as sing. except in sense 5], 1. the science of government; political science. 2. political affairs. 3. participation in political affairs. 4. political methods, tactics, etc. 5. political opinions, principles, etc.

**pol·i·ty** (pol′ə-ti), *n.* [*pl.* -TIES], [< OFr. < L. *politia;* see POLICY (wisdom)], 1. the governmental organization of a state, church, etc. 2. a society or institution with a government; state.

**Polk, James Knox** (pōk), 1795–1849; 11th president of the United States (1845–1849).
**pol·ka** (pōl′kə), *n.* [Fr. & G.; prob. < Czech *pulka*, half step], 1. a fast dance for couples. 2. the basic step of this dance. 3. music for this dance, in fast duple time. *v.i.* to dance the polka.
**pol·ka dot** (pō′kə), 1. any of a grouping of small round dots forming a pattern on cloth. 2. a cloth with such dots. —**pol′ka-dot′ted,** *adj.*
**poll** (pōl), *n.* [< MD. *polle,* head], 1. the head; esp., the crown, back, or hair of the head. 2. a counting, listing, etc. of persons, especially of voters. 3. the amount of voting; number of votes recorded. 4. *usually in pl.* a place where votes are cast and recorded. 5. a canvassing of a selected sample group of people to try to discover public opinion on some question. *v.t.* 1. to cut off or cut short. 2. to trim the wool, hair, etc. of. 3. to register the votes of: as, *poll* a county. 4. to receive (a certain number of votes): said of a candidate. 5. to cast (a vote). 6. to canvass in a poll (sense 5). *v.i.* to vote in an election.
**pol·len** (pol′ən), *n.* [L., dust], the yellow, powderlike male sex cells on the stamens of a flower.
**pollen count,** the number of grains of a specified kind of pollen, usually ragweed, present in a given volume of air at a specified time and place.
**pol·li·nate** (pol′ə-nāt′), *v.t.* [-NATED, -NATING], to place pollen on the pistil of. —**pol′li·na′tion,** *n.*
**pol·li·wog** (pol′i-wog′), *n.* [cf. POLL (head) & WIGGLE], a tadpole: also sp. **pollywog.**
**poll·ster** (pōl′stẽr), *n.* a person who conducts polls (sense 5).
**poll tax,** a tax per head: in some States payment of a poll tax is a prerequisite for voting.
**pol·lu·tant** (pə-lo͞o′tənt), *n.* something that pollutes; esp., a harmful chemical or waste material discharged into the water or atmosphere.
**pol·lute** (pə-lo͞ot′), *v.t.* [-LUTED, -LUTING], [< L. pp. of *polluere*], to make unclean, impure, or corrupt; defile. —**pol·lut′er,** *n.* —**pol·lu′tion,** *n.*
**Pol·lux** (pol′əks), *n.* 1. in *Gr. & Rom. mythology,* one of the twin sons of Zeus. 2. the brightest star in the constellation Gemini. Cf. **Castor.**
**Pol·ly·an·na** (pol′i-an′ə), *n.* [the heroine of a novel by Eleanor H. Porter (1868–1920), U.S. writer], a persistently optimistic person.
**po·lo** (pō′lō), *n.* [prob. < Tibet. *pulu,* the ball], a game played on horseback by two teams who try to drive a small wooden ball through the opponents' goal with long-handled mallets.
**Po·lo, Mar·co** (mär′kō pō′lō), 1254?–1324?; Venetian traveler in Asia.
**po·lo·naise** (pol′ə-nāz′, pō′lə-), *n.* [Fr., fem. of *polonais,* Polish], 1. a stately Polish dance in triple time. 2. music for this dance.
**po·lo·ni·um** (pə-lō′ni-əm), *n.* [< ML. *Polonia,* Poland: coinage of Marie Curie, its co-discoverer], a radioactive chemical element formed by the disintegration of radium: symbol, Po; at. wt., 210; at. no., 84.
**polo shirt,** a short-sleeved, usually knitted, pullover sport shirt with a buttoned collar.
**Pol·ska** (pôl′skä), *n.* Poland: the Polish name.
**pol·troon** (pol-tro͞on′), *n.* [< Fr. < It. *poltrone,* idler, coward < OHG. *polstar,* a bed], a thorough coward. —**pol·troon′er·y,** *n.* —**pol·troon′ish,** *adj.*
**pol·y-,** [< Gr. < *polys*], a combining form meaning: *much, many, more than one,* as in *polyandry.*
**pol·y·an·dry** (pol′i-an′dri, pol′i-an′-), *n.* [< Gr. < *poly-,* many + *anēr,* a man], the state or practice of having two or more husbands at the same time. —**pol′y·an′drist,** *n.* —**pol′y·an′drous,** *adj.*
**pol·y·an·thus** (pol′i-an′thəs), *n.* [< Gr. < *poly-,* many + *anthos,* a flower], 1. the oxlip. 2. a kind of narcissus with many star-shaped flowers.
**pol·y·clin·ic** (pol′i-klin′ik), *n.* [*poly-* + *clinic*], a clinic or hospital for the treatment of various kinds of diseases.
**pol·y·es·ter** (pol′i-es′ter), *n.* [*poly*mer + *ester*], any of several polymeric resins used in making plastics, fibers, etc.
**pol·y·eth·yl·ene** (pol′i-eth′ə-lēn′), *n.* [*poly*mer + *ethylene*], any of several thermoplastic resins, $(C_2H_4)_n$, used in making plastics, films, etc.
**po·lyg·a·my** (pə-lig′ə-mi), *n.* [< Fr. < Gr. < *poly-,* many + *gamos,* marriage], the practice of having two or more wives (or husbands) at the same time. —**po·lyg′a·mist,** *n.* —**po·lyg′a·mous,** *adj.*
**pol·y·glot** (pol′i-glot′), *adj.* [< Gr. < *poly-,* many + *glōtta,* the tongue], 1. speaking or writing several languages. 2. containing or written in several languages. *n.* a polyglot person, book, etc.
**pol·y·gon** (pol′i-gon′), *n.* [< LL. < Gr.; see POLY- & -GON], a plane figure with several angles and sides, usually more than four. —**po·lyg·o·nal** (pə-lig′ə-n'l), *adj.* —**po·lyg′o·nal·ly,** *adv.*
**pol·y·graph** (pol′i-graf′, -gräf′), *n.* [see POLY- & -GRAPH], a device measuring changes in respiration, pulse rate, etc., used on persons suspected of lying. —**pol′y·graph′ic,** *adj.*
**po·lyg·y·ny** (pə-lij′ə-ni), *n.* [< *poly-* + Gr. *gynē,* a female], the practice of having two or more wives or concubines at the same time. —**po·lyg′y·nous,** *adj.*
**pol·y·he·dron** (pol′i-hē′drən), *n.* [*pl.* -DRONS, -DRA (-drə)], [< Gr.; see POLY- & -HEDRON], a solid figure with several plane surfaces, usually over six. —**pol′y·he′dral,** *adj.*
**Pol·y·hym·ni·a** (pol′i-him′ni-ə), *n.* in *Gr. mythology,* the Muse of sacred poetry.
**pol·y·mer** (pol′i-mẽr), *n.* any of two or more polymeric compounds.
**pol·y·mer·ic** (pol′i-mer′ik), *adj.* [< *poly-* + Gr. *meros,* a part], composed of the same chemical elements in the same proportions by weight, but differing in molecular weight. —**po·lym·er·ism** (pə-lim′ẽr-iz'm, pol′i-mẽr-), *n.*
**pol·y·mer·i·za·tion** (pol′i-mẽr-i-zā′shən, pə-lim′-ẽr-i-), *n.* the process of joining two or more like molecules to form a more complex molecule whose molecular weight is a multiple of the original and whose physical properties are different. —**pol′y·mer·ize′** (-īz′), [-IZED, -IZING], *v.t. & v.i.*
**pol·y·mor·phous** (pol′i-môr′fəs), *adj.* [< Gr. < *poly-,* many + *morphē,* a form], having, occurring in, or passing through several or various forms: also **pol′y·mor′phic.** —**pol′y·mor′phism,** *n.*
**Pol·y·ne·sia** (pol′ə-nē′zhə, -shə), *n.* a group of islands in the Pacific, east of Micronesia.
**Pol·y·ne·sian** (pol′ə-nē′zhən, -shən), *adj.* of Polynesia, its people, their language, etc. *n.* 1. a member of the brown people of Polynesia, including the Hawaiians, Tahitians, Maoris, etc. 2. the group of Austronesian languages of Polynesia.
**pol·y·no·mi·al** (pol′i-nō′mi-əl), *n.* [*poly-* + *binomial*], 1. in *algebra,* an expression consisting of two or more terms, as $x^2 - 2xy + y^2$. 2. in *biology,* a species name consisting of more than two terms. *adj.* consisting of polynomials.
**pol·yp** (pol′ip), *n.* [< Fr. < L. < Gr. < *poly-,* many + *pous,* a foot], 1. a small, flowerlike water animal having a mouth fringed with tentacles at the top of a tubelike body, as the sea anemone, hydra, etc. 2. a projecting growth of mucous membrane, as in the bladder, etc. —**pol′y·pous** (-i-pəs), *adj.*
**pol·y·pet·al·ous** (pol′i-pet′'l-əs), *adj.* [*poly-* + *petal* + *-ous*], having separate petals.
**pol·y·phon·ic** (pol′i-fon′ik), *adj.* [< Gr. < *poly-,* many + *phōnē,* a sound], 1. having or making many sounds. 2. in *music,* of, having, or in polyphony; contrapuntal. Also **po·lyph·o·nous** (pə-lif′ə-nəs).
**po·lyph·o·ny** (pə-lif′ə-ni, pol′i-fō′ni), *n.* 1. multiplicity of sounds, as in an echo. 2. in *music,* a combining of a number of individual but harmonious melodies; counterpoint.
**pol·y·syl·lab·ic** (pol′i-si-lab′ik), *adj.* 1. having more than three syllables. 2. characterized by polysyllables. —**pol′y·syl·lab′i·cal·ly,** *adv.*
**pol·y·syl·la·ble** (pol′i-sil′ə-b'l), *n.* a word of more than three syllables.
**pol·y·tech·nic** (pol′i-tek′nik), *adj.* [< Fr. < Gr. < *poly-,* many + *technē,* an art], of or providing instruction in many scientific and technical subjects. *n.* a polytechnic school.
**pol·y·the·ism** (pol′i-thē-iz'm), *n.* [< Fr. < Gr. < *poly-,* many + *theos,* god], belief in more than one god. —**pol′y·the′ist,** *n.* —**pol′y·the·is′tic,** *adj.*
**pol·y·un·sat·u·rat·ed** (pol′i-un-sach′ə-rāt′id), *adj.* [*poly-* + *unsaturated*], designating any of certain plant and animal fats and oils thought to reduce the cholesterol content of the blood.
**pol·y·u·re·thane** (pol′i-yoor′ə-thān′), *n.* [*poly-* + *urethane,* a urea derivative], any of certain synthetic rubber polymers used in cushions, insulation, molded products, etc.
**pol·y·va·lent** (pol′i-vā′lənt, pə-liv′ə-lənt), *adj.* in *chemistry,* having more than one valence. —**pol′y·va′lence,** *n.*
**pom·ace** (pum′is), *n.* [ML. *pomacium,* cider < L. *pomum,* apple], 1. the crushed pulp of apples or other fruit pressed for juice. 2. the crushed matter of anything pressed, as seeds for oil.
**po·ma·ceous** (pō-mā′shəs), *adj.* 1. [Poetic], having to do with apples. 2. of or like the pomes.

**po·made** (pō-mād′, pə-mäd′), *n.* [< Fr. < It. *pomata;* ult. < L. *pomum,* apple (originally an ingredient)], a perfumed ointment, usually for the hair. *v.t.* [-MADED, -MADING], to apply pomade to.
**po·ma·tum** (pō-mā′təm, -mä′-), *n.* pomade.
**pome** (pōm), *n.* [OFr. < L. *pomum,* apple], any fleshy fruit containing a core and seeds, as an apple, quince, pear, etc.
**pome·gran·ate** (pom′gran′it, pum′-, pum-gran′it), *n.* [< OFr. < *pome,* apple + *granade* < L. *granatum,* lit., having seeds], 1. a round, red, pulpy fruit with a hard rind and many seeds. 2. the bush or small tree that bears it.
**Pom·er·a·ni·a** (pom′ə-rā′ni-ə), *n.* a former province of Prussia, on the Baltic Sea: divided between Germany and Poland (1945).
**Pom·er·a·ni·an** (pom′ə-rā′ni-ən), *adj.* of Pomerania or its people. *n.* 1. a native or inhabitant of Pomerania. 2. a dog of a small breed with long, silky hair, pointed ears, and a bushy tail.
**pom·mel** (pum′'l, pom′-), *n.* [< OFr. dim. < L. *pomum,* apple], 1. a round knob on the end of the hilt of a sword, etc. 2. the rounded, upward-projecting front part of a saddle. *v.t.* [-MELED or -MELLED, -MELING or -MELLING], to beat, as with the fists. **—pom′mel·er, pom′mel·ler,** *n.*
**po·mol·o·gy** (pō-mol′ə-ji), *n.* [see POME & -LOGY], the science of fruit cultivation. **—po′mo·log′i·cal** (-mə-loj′i-k'l), *adj.* **—po·mol′o·gist,** *n.*
**Po·mo·na** (pə-mō′nə), *n.* a city in SW California, near Los Angeles: pop., 67,000.
**pomp** (pomp), *n.* [< OFr. < L. < Gr. *pompē,* solemn procession], 1. stately display; splendor. 2. ostentatious or vain show.
**pom·pa·dour** (pom′pə-dôr′, -door′, -dōr′), *n.* [after de *Pompadour*], a hairdo in which the hair is brushed or swept up high from the forehead.
**Pom·pa·dour, Marquise de** (də pom′pə-dôr′, -door′, -dōr′), 1721–1764; mistress of Louis XV.
**pom·pa·no** (pom′pə-nō′), *n.* [*pl.* -NOS], [Sp. *pámpano*], a spiny-finned food fish of North America and the West Indies.
**Pom·pe·ii** (pom-pā′ē, -pā′), *n.* an ancient city on the SW coast of Italy: destroyed by the eruption of Mount Vesuvius (79 A.D.). **—Pom·pei′an** (-pā′ən, -pē′-), *adj. & n.*
**Pom·pey the Great** (pom′pi), 106–48 B.C.; Roman general and statesman.
**pom·pon** (pom′pon), *n.* [Fr.], 1. an ornamental ball or tuft as of silk or wool, worn on hats, dresses, etc. 2. *a)* a kind of chrysanthemum with small, round flowers. *b)* its flower.
**pom·pous** (pom′pəs), *adj.* 1. full of pomp; magnificent. 2. characterized by exaggerated stateliness; pretentious, as in speech or manner; self-important. **—pom·pos′i·ty** (-pos′ə-ti), [*pl.* -TIES], **pom′pous·ness,** *n.* **—pom′pous·ly,** *adv.*
**Pon·ce de Le·ón, Juan** (hwän pôn′the *the* le-ôn′; Eng. pons′ də lē′ən), 1460?–1521; Spanish explorer who discovered Florida.
**pon·cho** (pon′chō), *n.* [*pl.* -CHOS], [Sp. < S. Am. Ind.], a cloak like a blanket with a hole in the middle for the head, especially one of rubber, etc., worn as a raincoat.
**pond** (pond), *n.* [< ME. var. of *pound,* enclosure], a body of standing water smaller than a lake, often artificially formed.
**pon·der** (pon′dēr), *v.t. & v.i.* [< OFr. < L. *ponderare,* to weigh < *pondus,* a weight], to think deeply (about); deliberate. **—pon′der·a·bil′i·ty,** *n.* **—pon′der·a·ble,** *adj.* **—pon′der·er,** *n.*
**pon·der·ous** (pon′dēr-əs), *adj.* [< L. < *pondus,* a weight], 1. very heavy. 2. unwieldy because of weight. 3. bulky; massive. 4. labored; dull: as, a *ponderous* style. **—pon′der·ous·ly,** *adv.* **—pon′der·ous·ness, pon′der·os′i·ty** (-os′ə-ti), *n.*
**pond lily,** the water lily.
**pond scum,** a mass of one-celled plants floating as green scum on the surface of ponds, etc.
**pond·weed** (pond′wēd′), *n.* any of various related plants with straplike or long, grasslike leaves.
**pone** (pōn), *n.* [< Algonquian], in the southern U.S., 1. bread made of corn meal. 2. a loaf or cake of this.
**pon·gee** (pon-jē′), *n.* [< Chin. dial. *pen-chi,* domestic loom], 1. a soft, thin silk cloth, usually left in its natural light-brown color. 2. a cloth like this. *adj.* made of pongee.
**pon·iard** (pon′yērd), *n.* [< Fr. < *poing* < L. *pugnus,* fist], a dagger. *v.t.* to stab with a poniard.
**pons** (ponz), *n.* [*pl.* PONTES (pon′tēz)], [L., a bridge], in *anatomy & zoology,* a narrow piece of tissue connecting two parts of an organ.
**Pon·ti·ac** (pon′ti-ak′), *n.* 1. an Ottawa Indian chief; died 1769. 2. a city in SE Michigan: pop., 82,000.
**pon·ti·fex** (pon′tə-feks′), *n.* [*pl.* PONTIFICES (pon-tif′ə-sēz′)], [L.; see PONTIFF], in ancient Rome, a member of the supreme college of priests.
**pon·tiff** (pon′tif), *n.* [< Fr. < L. *pontifex,* high priest; prob. < Old Italic dial. *puntis,* sacrifice + L. *facere,* to make], 1. a bishop. 2. the Pope. 3. a high priest.
**pon·tif·i·cal** (pon-tif′i-k'l), *adj.* 1. having to do with a high priest or a bishop. 2. papal. 3. having the pomp, dogmatism, etc. of a pontiff: often used to imply arrogance. *n. pl.* a pontiff's vestments and insignia. **—pon·tif′i·cal·ly,** *adv.*
**pon·tif·i·cate** (pon-tif′i-kit; *also, and for v.i. always,* -kāt′), *n.* the office or tenure of a pontiff. *v.i.* [-CATED, -CATING], 1. to officiate as a pontiff. 2. to be dogmatic; speak pompously.
**Pon·tine** (pon′tin, -tīn), *adj.* designating or of a formerly swampy region **(Pontine Marshes)** in central Italy, now largely reclaimed.
**pon·ton** (pon′t'n), *n.* in the *U.S. Army,* a pontoon.
**pon·toon** (pon-to͞on′), *n.* [Fr. < L. *pons,* a bridge], 1. a flat-bottomed boat. 2. any of a number of these, or of hollow, floating cylinders, etc., used to support a temporary bridge. 3. either of two boatlike floats on the landing gear of small airplanes to allow them to land on water.
**pontoon bridge,** a temporary bridge on pontoons: in military usage, usually **ponton bridge.**
**po·ny** (pō′ni), *n.* [*pl.* -NIES], [< Scot.; prob. < OFr. dim. of *poulain,* a colt < L. *pullus,* foal], 1. a horse of any of several small breeds, usually not over 14 hands high. 2. something small of its kind. 3. [Colloq.], a small liqueur glass or its contents. 4. [Colloq.], a literal translation of a foreign work, used in doing schoolwork, often dishonestly. *v.t. & v.i.* [-NIED, -NYING], [Slang], to pay (money), as to settle an account (with *up*).
**pony express,** a former system of carrying and delivering mail by riders on swift ponies.
**pooch** (po͞och), *n.* [Slang], a dog; esp., a mongrel.
**poo·dle** (po͞o′d'l), *n.* [G. *pudel* < LG. < *pudeln,* to splash], any of a breed of variously colored, curly-haired dogs.

POODLE (15 in. high at shoulder)

**pooh** (po͞o, poo, pə), *interj.* an exclamation of contempt, disbelief, or impatience.
**pooh** (po͞o), *v.t.* [Slang], to tire; exhaust.
**pooh-pooh** (po͞o′po͞o′), *v.t.* to express contempt for; make light of. *n.* a pooh-poohing.
**pool** (po͞ol), *n.* [AS. *pol*], 1. a small pond, as in a garden. 2. a puddle. 3. a swimming pool. 4. a deep, still spot in a river.
**pool** (po͞ol), *n.* [Fr. *poule* < LL. *pulla,* hen; infl. by *pool* (of water)], 1. the total stakes played for in a card game, etc. 2. a game of billiards played with numbered object balls and a cue ball, on a table with six pockets. 3. a combination of resources, funds, etc. for some common purpose. 4. the parties forming such a combination. 5. a combination of business firms for control of a common market; monopoly. *v.t. & v.i.* to contribute to a pool, or common fund; form a pool (of).
**pool·room** (po͞ol′ro͞om′, -room′), *n.* a room or establishment where pool is played.
**Poo·na** (po͞o′nə), *n.* a city in W India: pop., 481,000.
**poop** (po͞op), *n.* [< OFr. < It. < L. *puppis*], 1. originally, the stern of a ship. 2. on sailing ships, a raised deck at the stern, sometimes forming the roof of a cabin: also **poop deck.** *v.t.* to break over the poop or stern of: said of waves.

POOP

**poop** (po͞op), *v.t.* [Slang], to tire: usually in the passive voice: also **pooh.**
**poor** (poor), *adj.* [< OFr. < L. *pauper,* poor], 1. having little or no means of support; needy. 2. indicating or characterized by poverty. 3. lacking in some quality. 4. scanty; inadequate: as, *poor* crops. 5. barren; sterile: as, *poor* soil. 6. lacking nourishment; feeble. 7. lacking excellence; inferior. 8. mean-spirited; contemptible. 9. lacking pleasure, comfort, etc.: as, we had a *poor* time. 10. worthy of pity; unfortunate. **—the poor,** poor, or needy, people. **—poor′ly,** *adv.* **—poor′ness,** *n.*
**poor·house** (poor′hous′), *n.* a house or institution for paupers, supported from public funds.
**poor white,** a white, usually rural Southerner who lives in poverty and ignorance: also, collectively, **poor white trash**: contemptuous term.
**pop** (pop), *n.* [echoic], 1. a sudden, short, light

explosive sound. 2. a shot with a revolver, rifle, etc. 3. any carbonated, nonalcoholic beverage. *v.i.* [POPPED, POPPING], 1. to make a pop. 2. to burst with a pop. 3. to move, go, come, etc. suddenly and quickly: as, he *popped* into view. 4. to open wide suddenly, or protrude: said of the eyes. 5. to shoot a pistol, etc. *v.t.* 1. to cause to pop, as corn by roasting, etc. 2. to fire (a pistol, etc.). 3. to shoot. 4. to put suddenly or quickly: as, he *popped* his head in the door. *adv.* with or like a pop. —**pop the question,** [Colloq.], to propose marriage.
**pop** (pop), *n.* [< *papa*], [Slang], father: often a familiar term of address for any elderly man.
**pop.,** 1. popular. 2. popularly. 3. population.
**pop (art)** (pop), a realistic style of painting and sculpture, using techniques and popular subjects from commercial art and mass communications media, such as comic strips, posters, etc.
**pop concert,** a popular concert, chiefly of semi-classical and light classical music.
**pop·corn** (pop′kôrn′), *n.* 1. a variety of Indian corn with small ears and hard grains which pop open into a white, puffy mass when heated. 2. the popped grains, eaten as a confection.
**pope** (pōp), *n.* [AS. *papa* < LL. < Gr. *pappas*, father], [usually P-], in the *R.C. Church*, the bishop of Rome and head of the Church. —**pope′dom,** *n.*
**Pope, Alexander** (pōp), 1688–1744; English poet.
**pop·er·y** (pōp′ēr-i), *n.* the doctrines and rituals of the Roman Catholic Church: a hostile term.
**pop·eyed** (pop′īd′), *adj.* having protruding eyes.
**pop·gun** (pop′gun′), *n.* a toy gun that shoots pellets by air compression, with a pop.
**pop·in·jay** (pop′in-jā′), *n.* [< OFr. *papagai* < Ar. *babaghā*, parrot], a talkative, vain person; fop.
**pop·ish** (pōp′ish), *adj.* Roman Catholic: a hostile term. —**pop′ish·ly,** *adj.* —**pop′ish·ness,** *n.*
**pop·lar** (pop′lēr), *n.* [< OFr. *poplier* < L. *populus*], 1. any of various tall, fast-growing trees with small leaves. 2. the wood of any of these.
**pop·lin** (pop′lin), *n.* [< Fr. < It. *papalino*, lit., papal: orig. made in Avignon, a papal town], a silk, cotton, or woolen cloth with a ribbed surface.
**Po·po·ca·te·petl** (pô-pô′kä-te′pet′l; Eng. pō′pə-kat′ə-pet″l), *n.* a volcanic mountain in S Mexico.
**pop·o·ver** (pop′ō′vēr), *n.* a puffy, hollow muffin.
**pop·per** (pop′ēr), *n.* 1. one that pops. 2. a covered wire basket or pan for popping corn.
**pop·pet** (pop′it), *n.* [form of *puppet*], a valve that moves up out of and down into its port, as in a gasoline engine: also **poppet valve.**
**pop·py** (pop′i), *n.* [*pl.* -PIES], [AS. *popæg*; ult. < L. *papaver*], 1. any of certain related plants with deeply cut leaves, milky or colored juice, and variously colored flowers. 2. the flower of any of these. 3. a pharmaceutical extract made from poppy juice. 4. opium. 5. yellowish red, the color of some poppies: also **poppy red.**
**pop·py·cock** (pop′i-kok′), *n.* [Colloq.], nonsense.
**poppy seed,** the small, dark seed of the poppy, used in baking, etc. as a flavoring.
**pop·u·lace** (pop′yoo-lis), *n.* [Fr. < It. < L. *populus*, the people], the common people; the masses.
**pop·u·lar** (pop′yoo-lēr), *adj.* [< L. < *populus*, the people], 1. of or carried on by people generally. 2. suitable or intended for the people at large: as, *popular* music. 3. within the means of the ordinary person: as, *popular* prices. 4. common; prevalent: as, a *popular* misconception. 5. liked by the people or by many people: as, a *popular* magazine. 6. having many friends. —**pop′u·lar′i·ty** (-lar′ə-ti), *n.* —**pop′u·lar·ly,** *adv.*
**popular front,** a political coalition of leftist and centrist groups, as in France (1936–1939), to combat fascism and promote reforms.
**pop·u·lar·ize** (pop′yoo-lə-rīz′), *v.t.* [-IZED, -IZING], to make popular. —**pop′u·lar·i·za′tion,** *n.* —**pop′u·lar·iz′er,** *n.*
**pop·u·late** (pop′yoo-lāt′), *v.t.* [-LATED, -LATING], [< ML. *populatus*, pp. of *populare* < L. *populus*, the people], 1. to inhabit. 2. to supply with inhabitants. —**pop′u·la′tor,** *n.*
**pop·u·la·tion** (pop′yoo-lā′shən), *n.* 1. all the people in a country, region, etc. 2. the number of these. 3. a (specified) part of the people in a given area: as, the Japanese *population* of Hawaii. 4. a populating or being populated. 5. in *statistics*, a group of items or individuals.
**Pop·u·lism** (pop′yoo-liz'm), *n.* [< L. *populus*, the people], the theory and policies of an American political party (**People's party,** 1891–1904) advocating free coinage of gold and silver, public ownership of utilities, an income tax, etc. —**Pop′u·list,** *n. & adj.* —**Pop′u·lis′tic,** *adj.*
**pop·u·lous** (pop′yoo-ləs), *adj.* full of people; thickly populated. —**pop′u·lous·ly,** *adv.* —**pop′u·lous·ness,** *n.*
**por·ce·lain** (pôr′s'l-in, pōrs′lin), *n.* [< Fr. < It. < *porcella*, little pig: from its resemblance to a shell curved like a pig's back], 1. a fine, white, translucent, hard earthenware; china. 2. porcelain dishes or ornaments, collectively. *adj.* made of porcelain. —**por′ce·la′ne·ous** (-sə-lā′ni-əs), **por′-cel·la′ne·ous,** *adj.*
**porch** (pôrch, pōrch), *n.* [< OFr. < L. *porticus* < *porta*, a gate], 1. a covered entrance to a building, usually projecting from the wall. 2. an open or screened-in room on the outside of a building.
**por·cine** (pôr′sīn, -sin), *adj.* [< Fr. < L. < *porcus*, a hog], of or like pigs or hogs.
**por·cu·pine** (pôr′kyoo-pīn′), *n.* [*pl.* -PINES, -PINE; see PLURAL, II, D, 1], [< OFr. < L. *porcus*, a pig + *spina*, a spine], a gnawing animal having coarse hair mixed with long, stiff, sharp spines.

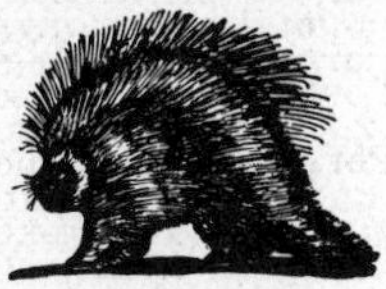
PORCUPINE (3 ft. long)

**pore** (pôr, pōr), *v.i.* [PORED, PORING], [ME. *pouren*], 1. to gaze intently. 2. to study minutely (with *over*): as, he *pored* over the book. 3. to ponder (with *on*, *upon*, or *over*). —**por′er,** *n.*
**pore** (pôr, pōr), *n.* [< L. < Gr. *poros*, a passage], 1. a tiny opening, as in plant leaves, the skin, etc., through which fluids may be absorbed or discharged. 2. a similar tiny opening in rock, etc.
**por·gy** (pôr′gi, -ji), *n.* [*pl.* -GIES, -GY; see PLURAL, II, D, 1], [? ult. < Am. Ind.], a salt-water food fish having spiny fins and a wide body.
**pork** (pôrk, pōrk), *n.* [< OFr. < L. *porcus*, a pig], 1. the flesh of a pig used, fresh or cured, as food. 2. [Slang], money, position, etc. received from the government through political patronage. —**pork′like′,** *adj.*

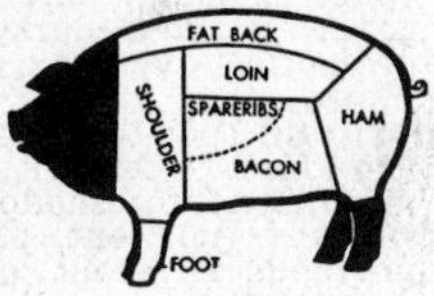

PORK

**pork barrel,** [Slang], government appropriations for political patronage, as for local improvements to please legislators' constituents.
**pork·er** (pôr′kēr, pōr′-), *n.* a hog, especially a young one, fattened for use as food.
**pork pie,** 1. a meat pie made of chopped pork, usually eaten cold. 2. a man's soft hat with a round, flat crown: now often **pork′pie′,** *n.*
**pork·y** (pôr′ki, pōr′-), *adj.* [-IER, -IEST], 1. of or like pork. 2. fat, as though overfed.
**por·nog·ra·phy** (pôr-nog′rə-fi), *n.* [< Gr. *pornē*, a prostitute; + *-graphy*], writings, pictures, etc. intended to arouse sexual desire. —**por′no·graph′ic** (-nə-graf′ik), *adj.* —**por′no·graph′i·cal·ly,** *adv.*
**po·rous** (pôr′əs, pō′rəs), *adj.* full of pores, or tiny holes through which fluids, air, or light may pass. —**po·ros·i·ty** (pô-ros′ə-ti), **po′rous·ness,** *n.* —**po′-rous·ly,** *adv.*
**por·phy·ry** (pôr′fə-ri), *n.* [*pl.* -RIES], [< OFr. < ML. < Gr. *porphyros*, purple], 1. originally, a hard Egyptian rock having red and white feldspar crystals embedded in a fine-grained, dark-red or purplish rock mass. 2. any igneous rock of similar texture. —**por′phy·rit′ic,** *adj.*
**por·poise** (pôr′pəs), *n.* [*pl.* -POISES, -POISE; see PLURAL, II, D, 1], [< OFr. *porpeis* < L. *porcus*, a pig + *piscis*, a fish], 1. a small cetacean, dark above and white below, with a blunt snout and many teeth. 2. any of several other small cetaceans, as the dolphin.
**por·ridge** (pôr′ij, por′-), *n.* [< *pottage* by confusion with ME. *porrey* < OFr. < LL. *porrata*, leek broth < L. *porrum*, leek], [Chiefly Brit.], a soft food made of cereal or meal boiled in water or milk.
**por·rin·ger** (pôr′in-jēr, por′-), *n.* [< Fr. *potager*, soup dish; infl. by *porridge*], a bowl for porridge, children's food, etc.
**port** (pôrt, pōrt), *n.* [OFr. & AS. < L. *portus*, a haven], 1. a harbor. 2. a city with a harbor where ships load or unload cargoes. 3. a port of entry.
**port** (pôrt, pōrt), *n.* [< *Oporto*, city in Portugal], a sweet, dark-red wine, originally from Portugal.
**port** (pôrt, pōrt), *v.t.* [< OFr. < L. *portare*, to carry], to hold or place (a rifle or sword) diagonally in front of one, as for inspection. *n.* one's deportment, or carriage.

**port** (pôrt, pōrt), *n.* [< *port* (harbor)], the left-hand side of a ship, etc. as one faces forward, toward the bow. *adj.* of or on the port. *v.t. & v.i.* to move or turn (the helm) to the left.

**port** (pôrt, pōrt), *n.* [< OFr. < L. *porta*, a door], 1. *a*) a porthole. *b*) the covering for this. 2. an opening, as in a valve face, for the passage of steam, gas, etc.

**Port.,** 1. Portugal. 2. Portuguese.

**port·a·ble** (pôr′tə-b'l, pōr′-), *adj.* [LL. *portabilis* < L. *portare*, to carry], 1. that can be carried. 2. easily carried. —**port′a·bil′i·ty,** *n.*

**por·tage** (pôr′tij, pōr′-), *n.* [OFr. < ML. < L. *portare*, to carry], 1. the act of carrying. 2. its cost. 3. a carrying of boats and supplies overland between navigable rivers, lakes, etc. 4. any route over which this is done. *v.t. & v.i.* [-TAGED, -TAGING], to carry (boats, etc.) over a portage.

**por·tal** (pôr′t'l, pōr′-), *n.* [OFr. < ML. < L. *porta*, a gate], a doorway, gate, or entrance, especially a large and imposing one.

**Port Arthur,** 1. a seaport in NE China: see **Dairen.** 2. a city in E Texas: pop., 67,000.

**Port-au-Prince** (pôrt′ō-prins′, pōrt′-), *n.* seaport and capital of Haiti: pop., c.250,000.

**port·cul·lis** (pôrt-kul′is, pōrt-), *n.* [< OFr. *porte*, a gate + *coleïce*, sliding < L. *colare*, to strain], a large, heavy iron grating suspended by chains and lowered between grooves to bar the gateway of a castle or fortified town.

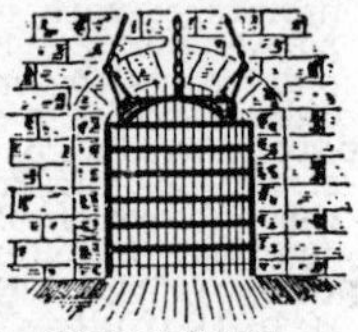
PORTCULLIS

**Porte** (pôrt, pōrt), *n.* [< Fr. *porte*, gate: from gate of palace at which justice was administered], the Ottoman Turkish government.

**porte-co·chere, porte-co·chère** (pôrt′kō-shâr′), *n.* [Fr., coach gate], 1. a large gateway into a courtyard. 2. a kind of porch roof projecting over a driveway at an entrance to a house, etc.

**por·tend** (pôr-tend′, pōr-), *v.t.* [< L. *portendere* < *pro-*, forth + *tendere*, to stretch], to be an omen or warning of; foreshadow; presage.

**por·tent** (pôr′tent, pōr′-), *n.* 1. something that portends an event, usually evil, about to occur; omen. 2. a portending; significance. 3. a marvel.

**por·ten·tous** (pôr-ten′təs, pōr-), *adj.* 1. portending evil; ominous. 2. marvelous; amazing. —**por·ten′tous·ly,** *adv.* —**por·ten′tous·ness,** *n.*

**por·ter** (pôr′tẽr, pōr′-), *n.* [< OFr. < LL. *portarius* < L. *porta*, a gate], a doorman; gatekeeper.

**por·ter** (pôr′tẽr, pōr′-), *n.* [< OFr. < LL. < L. *portare*, to carry], 1. a man who carries luggage, etc. for hire, as at a hotel, railroad station, etc. 2. a man who sweeps, cleans, does errands, etc. in a bank, store, etc. 3. a railroad employee who waits on passengers in a parlor car or sleeper. 4. [abbrev. of *porter's ale*], a dark-brown beer.

**Por·ter, Katherine Anne** (pôr′tẽr, pōr′-), 1890– ; U.S. short-story writer, essayist, and novelist.

**Porter, William Sydney,** see **Henry, O.**

**por·ter·house** (pôr′tẽr-hous′, pōr′-), *n.* 1. formerly, a place where beer, porter, etc. (and sometimes steaks and chops) were served. 2. a choice cut of beef from between the tenderloin and the sirloin: in full, **porterhouse steak.**

**port·fo·li·o** (pôrt-fō′li-ō′, pōrt-fōl′yō), *n.* [*pl.* -os], [< It. *portafoglio* < L. *portare*, to carry + *folium*, a leaf], 1. a flat, portable case for carrying loose papers, drawings, etc.; brief case. 2. such a case for state documents; hence, 3. the office of a minister of state. 4. a list of an investor's stocks, bonds, etc.

**port·hole** (pôrt′hōl′, pōrt′-), *n.* 1. an opening in a ship's side to admit light and air, load cargo, or fire a gun through. 2. any similar opening.

**por·ti·co** (pôr′ti-kō′, pōr′-), *n.* [*pl.* -COES, -COS], [It. < L. *porticus*; see PORCH], a porch or covered walk, consisting of a roof supported by columns.

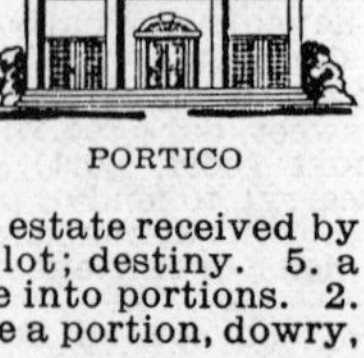
PORTICO

**por·tiere, por·tière** (pôr-tyâr′, pōr′ti-âr′), *n.* [Fr. < *porte*, a door], a curtain hung in a doorway.

**por·tion** (pôr′shən, pōr′-), *n.* [< OFr. < L. *portio*], 1. a part, especially as allotted to a person; share. 2. the part of an estate received by an heir. 3. a dowry. 4. one's lot; destiny. 5. a helping of food. *v.t.* 1. to divide into portions. 2. to give as a portion to. 3. to give a portion, dowry, etc. to. —**por′tion·less,** *adj.*

**Port·land** (pôrt′lənd, pōrt′-), *n.* 1. a city on the coast of S Maine: pop. 73,000. 2. a city in NW Oregon: pop., 373,000.

**portland cement,** [concrete made from it resembles stone from the Isle of *Portland*, England], [also P-], a kind of cement that hardens under water, made by burning limestone and clay or similar materials.

**port·ly** (pôrt′li, pōrt′-), *adj.* [-LIER, -LIEST], 1. having a dignified and stately port or demeanor. 2. stout; obese. —**port′li·ness,** *n.*

**port·man·teau** (pôrt-man′tō, pōrt-), *n.* [*pl.* -TEAUS, -TEAUX (-tōz)], [< Fr. < *porter*, to carry + *manteau*, a cloak], a stiff leather suitcase that opens like a book into two compartments.

**portmanteau word,** a compact blend of two words (e.g., *smog*, from *smoke* and *fog*).

**Por·to** (pôr′too), *n.* Oporto: Portuguese name.

**port of entry,** any place where customs officials check the entry of foreign goods into a country.

**Port of Spain** (pôrt′əv-spān′, pōrt′-), the capital of Trinidad and Tobago, on Trinidad: pop., 94,000.

**Por·to Ri·co** (pôr′tə rē′kō, pōr′-), Puerto Rico: former name. —**Por′to Ri′can.**

**por·trait** (pôr′trāt, pōr′trit), *n.* [Fr., pp. of *portraire*; see PORTRAY], 1. a painting, photograph, etc. of a person, especially of his face. 2. a description, portrayal, etc. of a person. —**por′trait·ist,** *n.*

**por·trai·ture** (pôr′tri-chẽr, pōr′-), *n.* 1. the process, practice, or art of portraying. 2. a portrait.

**por·tray** (pôr-trā′, pōr-), *v.t.* [< OFr. *po(u)rtraire* < L. < *pro-*, forth + *trahere*, to draw], 1. to make a portrait of; depict; delineate. 2. to make a word picture of; describe graphically. 3. to represent on the stage. —**por·tray′al,** *n.* —**por·tray′er,** *n.*

**Port Sa·id** (pôrt sä-ēd′, pōrt sä′id), a seaport in Egypt, at the Mediterranean end of the Suez Canal: pop., 244,000.

**Ports·mouth** (pôrts′məth, pōrts′-), *n.* 1. a seaport in S England: pop., 225,000. 2. a seaport in SE Virginia, near Norfolk: pop., 115,000.

**Por·tu·gal** (pôr′chə-g'l, pōr′choo-gəl), *n.* a country in SW Europe, on the Atlantic: area, 35,490 sq. mi.; pop., 9,073,000; capital, Lisbon.

**Por·tu·guese** (pôr′chə-gēz′, pōr′choo-), *adj.* of Portugal, its people, their language, etc. *n.* 1. [*pl.* -GUESE], a native or inhabitant of Portugal. 2. the Romance language of Portugal and Brazil.

**Portuguese East Africa,** Mozambique.

**Portuguese Guinea,** a Portuguese overseas territory on the coast of W Africa.

**Portuguese India,** a former Portuguese overseas territory on the west coast of India.

**Portuguese man-of-war,** a large, tubelike, warm-sea animal having a large, bladderlike sac, which enables it to float on the water.

**Portuguese West Africa,** Angola.

**por·tu·lac·a** (pôr′choo-lak′ə, pōr′-), *n.* [L., purslane], any of various fleshy plants with yellow, pink, or purple flowers.

**pose** (pōz), *v.t.* [POSED, POSING], [< OFr. *poser* < L. *pausare*, to pause, confused with LL. *positus*, pp. of *ponere*, to place], 1. to put forth; assert, as a claim, argument, etc. 2. to introduce, as a question, problem, etc. 3. to put (an artist's model, etc.) in a certain attitude. *v.i.* 1. to assume a certain attitude, as in being photographed. 2. to strike attitudes for effect: as, look at her *posing*. 3. to assume a mental attitude; set oneself up: as, he *poses* as a scholar. *n.* 1. a bodily attitude, especially one held for an artist, photographer, etc. 2. a mental attitude assumed for effect; pretense.

**pose** (pōz), *v.t.* [POSED, POSING], [< *oppose* or *appose*], to puzzle or disconcert, as by a difficult question.

**Po·sei·don** (pō-sī′d'n), *n.* in *Gr. mythology*, god of the sea: identified with the Roman Neptune.

**pos·er** (pōz′ẽr), *n.* one who poses; affected person: also **po·seur** (pō-zũr′).

**pos·er** (pōz′ẽr), *n.* a baffling question or problem.

**posh** (posh), *adj.* [< obs. Brit. slang *posh*, a dandy], [Colloq.], luxurious and fashionable; elegant.

**pos·it** (poz′it), *v.t.* [< L. *positus*, pp. of *ponere*, to place], 1. to set in place or position; situate. 2. to set down as fact; assume; postulate.

**po·si·tion** (pə-zish′ən), *n.* [Fr. < L. *positio* < pp. of *ponere*, to place], 1. the way in which a person or thing is placed or arranged; attitude. 2. one's mental attitude toward or opinion on a subject; stand. 3. the place where a person or thing is; location; site. 4. the usual or proper place; station: as, the players are in *position*. 5. a location or condition of advantage: as, jockey for *position*. 6. one's relative place, as in society; rank; status. 7. a place high in society, business, etc.: as, a man of *position*. 8. a post of employment; job; office. *v.t.* to put in a particular position; place. —**po·si′tion·al,** *adj.*

**pos·i·tive** (poz′ə-tiv), *adj.* [< OFr. < L. *positivus* < pp. of *ponere*, to place], 1. definitely set; explicitly laid down; specific: as, *positive* instructions. 2. having the mind set or settled; confident; assured: as, a *positive* person. 3. overconfident; dogmatic. 4. showing resolution or agreement; affirmative: as, a *positive* answer. 5. tending in the direction regarded as that of increase, progress, etc. 6. making a definite contribution; constructive: as, *positive* criticism. 7. unrelated to anything else; absolute; unqualified. 8. regarded as having real existence; characterized by the presence of certain attributes, not their absence: as, a *positive* evil. 9. based on reality or facts: as, *positive* proof. 10. concerned only with real things and experience; practical. 11. showing the presence of a specific disease, condition, etc. 12. [Colloq.], complete; downright: as, a *positive* rogue. 13. in *biology*, directed toward the source of a stimulus: as, *positive* tropism. 14. in *electricity*, *a*) designating or of the kind of electricity generated on a glass rod rubbed with a piece of silk. *b*) of, generating, or charged with such electricity. 15. in *grammar*, of an adjective or adverb in its simple, uncompared degree: cf. *comparative*, *superlative*. 16. in *mathematics*, greater than zero; plus. 17. in *photography*, with the lights and shades corresponding to those of the subject. *n.* something positive, as a degree, quality, quantity, battery terminal, photographic print, etc. —**pos′i·tive·ly**, *adv.* —**pos′i·tive·ness**, *n.*

**pos·i·tiv·ism** (poz′ə-tiv-iz′m), *n.* 1. a being positive; certainty; assurance. 2. dogmatism. 3. [also P-], the system of philosophy of Auguste Comte, based solely on positive observable scientific facts: it rejects speculation on ultimate origins. —**pos′i·tiv·ist**, *n.* & *adj.* —**pos′i·tiv·is′tic**, *adj.*

**pos·i·tron** (poz′ə-tron′), *n.* [*positive* + elec*tron*], the positive counterpart of an electron, having about the same mass and magnitude of charge.

**poss.**, 1. possession. 2. possessive. 3. possibly.

**pos·se** (pos′i), *n.* [ML., power; L. inf., to be able], the body of men summoned by a sheriff to assist him in keeping the peace, etc.

**pos·sess** (pə-zes′), *v.t.* [< OFr. < L. *possessus*, pp. of *possidere*], 1. to have as belonging to one; own. 2. to have as an attribute, quality, etc.: as, he *possesses* wisdom. 3. to gain or maintain control over; dominate: as, the idea *possessed* him. 4. [Archaic], to seize; win. —**pos·ses′sor**, *n.*

**pos·sessed** (pə-zest′), *adj.* 1. owned. 2. controlled by a demon. —**possessed of**, in possession of.

**pos·ses·sion** (pə-zesh′ən), *n.* 1. a possessing or being possessed; ownership; occupancy. 2. anything possessed. 3. *pl.* property; wealth. 4. territory held by an outside country. 5. self-possession.

**pos·ses·sive** (pə-zes′iv), *adj.* 1. of possession, or ownership. 2. showing or desiring possession: as, a *possessive* person. 3. in *grammar*, designating or of a case, form, or construction indicating possession and expressed: *a*) by a final *s* preceded or followed by an apostrophe, or by an apostrophe only following a final *s* sound (e.g., *John's* book, *boys'* games, *conscience'* sake; *b*) by change of form of pronouns (**possessive pronouns**: *my, mine, your, yours, his, her, hers, its, our, ours, their, theirs, whose*); *c*) by *of* with the objective case (e.g., lives *of men*) or with the possessive case (e.g., a book *of John's*—called a *double possessive*). *n.* in *grammar*, the possessive case, form, or construction. —**pos·ses′sive·ly**, *adv.* —**pos·ses′sive·ness**, *n.*

**pos·set** (pos′it), *n.* [ME. *poshote*], a hot drink made of milk and ale, wine, etc., usually spiced.

**pos·si·bil·i·ty** (pos′ə-bil′ə-ti), *n.* 1. a being possible. 2. [*pl.* -TIES], something that is possible.

**pos·si·ble** (pos′ə-b'l), *adj.* [OFr. < L. < *posse*, to be able], 1. that can be or exist. 2. that may or may not happen. 3. that can be done, known, acquired, etc. by a person or thing expressed or implied. 4. potential: as, a *possible* location. 5. permissible.

**pos·si·bly** (pos′ə-bli), *adv.* 1. by any possible means: as, it can't *possibly* work. 2. perhaps; maybe: as, *possibly* it's true.

**pos·sum** (pos′əm), *n.* [Colloq.], an opossum. —**play possum**, to feign ignorance, illness, etc.

**post** (pōst), *n.* [AS. < L. *postis*], 1. a piece of wood, metal, etc. set upright, as to support a building, sign, gate, etc.; pillar; pole. 2. the starting point in a horse race. *v.t.* 1. to put up (a poster, etc.) on a wall, post, etc. 2. to announce by posting notices, etc.: as, to *post* a reward. 3. to put posters, etc. on. 4. to warn against trespassing on (grounds, etc.) by posted notices. 5. to put (a name) on a posted or published list.

**post** (pōst), *n.* [< Fr. < It. < LL. *postum* < L. pp. of *ponere*, to place], 1. the place where a soldier is stationed. 2. a place where troops are stationed. 3. the troops at such a place; garrison. 4. a local unit of a veterans' organization. 5. the place or station assigned to one. 6. a position or job. 7. a trading post. *v.t.* to station at or assign to a post.

**post** (pōst), *n.* [< Fr. < It. < LL. *posta* < L. pp. of *ponere*, to place], 1. formerly, *a*) one of a number of riders or runners posted at intervals to carry mail in relays or stages along a route. *b*) a stage of a post route. *c*) a post horse. 2. [Chiefly Brit.], *a*) (the) mail. *b*) a post office. *c*) a mailbox. *v.i.* 1. formerly, to travel in posts or stages. 2. to travel fast; hasten. *v.t.* 1. formerly, to send by post. 2. [Chiefly Brit.], to mail. 3. to inform, as of events: as, he is well *posted*. 4. in *bookkeeping*, *a*) to transfer (an item) to the ledger. *b*) to enter all necessary items in (a ledger, etc.). *adv.* posthaste. —**post′ed**, *adj.*

**post-**, [L. < *post*, after], a prefix meaning: 1. *after in time, later, following*, as in *postgraduate*. 2. *after in space, behind.*

**post·age** (pōs′tij), *n.* the amount charged for mailing a letter or package.

**postage stamp**, a government stamp to be put on a letter or package as a sign that the proper postage has been prepaid.

**post·al** (pōs′t'l), *adj.* having to do with mail or post offices. *n.* [Colloq.], a postal card.

**postal card**, 1. a card with a printed postage stamp, issued by a government for use in the mails. 2. loosely, a post card.

**post-bel·lum** (pōst′bel′əm), *adj.* [< L.], after the war; specif., after the American Civil War.

**post·box** (pōst′boks′), *n.* a mailbox.

**post card**, 1. a postal card. 2. an unofficial card, often a picture card, that can be sent through the mail when a postage stamp is affixed.

**post chaise**, a closed, four-wheeled carriage drawn by fast horses, formerly used to carry mail and passengers.

**post·date** (pōst′dāt′), *v.t.* [-DATED, -DATING], 1. to assign or affix a later date to than the actual date. 2. to be subsequent to.

**post·er** (pōs′tẽr), *n.* 1. a person who posts notices, etc. 2. a large advertisement or notice, often illustrated, posted publicly.

**pos·te·ri·or** (pos-têr′i-ẽr), *adj.* [L., compar. of *posterus*, following < *post*, after], 1. later; following after. 2. coming after in order; succeeding. 3. located behind; hinder; rear. *n. sometimes pl.* the buttocks. —**pos·te′ri·or′i·ty** (-ôr′ə-ti), *n.* —**pos·te′ri·or·ly**, *adv.*

**pos·ter·i·ty** (pos-ter′ə-ti), *n.* [< MFr. < L. < *posterus;* see POSTERIOR], 1. all of a person's descendants. 2. all future generations.

**pos·tern** (pōs′tẽrn, pos′-), *n.* [< OFr. < LL. *posterula* < *posterus;* see POSTERIOR], a back door or gate; private entrance or exit. *adj.* of or like a postern; rear, lesser, private, etc.

**Post Exchange**, a nonprofit general store at an army post, for the sale of small personal articles, refreshments, etc.: abbrev. **PX** (no period).

**post·gla·cial** (pōst′glā′shəl), *adj.* existing or happening after the glacial, or Pleistocene, Epoch.

**post·grad·u·ate** (pōst′graj′ōō-it, -āt′), *adj.* of or taking a course of study after graduation. *n.* a student taking such courses.

**post·haste** (pōst′hāst′), *n.* [Archaic], great haste, as of a postrider. *adv.* with great haste.

**post horse**, formerly, a horse kept at a post house, as for couriers or for hire to travelers.

**post house**, formerly, an inn or other place where post horses were kept.

**post·hu·mous** (pos′choo-məs), *adj.* [LL. < L. *postumus*, last, superl. of *posterus* (see POSTERIOR); altered after *humare*, to bury], 1. born after the father's death. 2. published after the author's death. 3. arising or continuing after one's death. —**post′hu·mous·ly**, *adv.*

**pos·til·ion, pos·til·lion** (pōs-til′yən, pos-), *n.* [Fr.; It. < *posta*, a post], a person who rides the left-hand horse of the leaders of a carriage.

**post·im·pres·sion·ism** (pōst′im-presh′ən-iz′m), *n.* the theory or practice of a group of late 19th-century painters who, in reaction to impressionism, emphasized the subjective viewpoint of the artist. —**post′im·pres′sion·ist**, *adj.* & *n.* —**post′im·pres′sion·is′tic**, *adj.*

**post·lude** (pōst′lōōd′), *n.* [*post-* + pre*lude*], 1. an organ voluntary at the end of a church service. 2. a concluding movement of a musical composition.
**post·man** (pōst′mən), *n.* [*pl.* -MEN], a person who collects and delivers mail; letter carrier.
**post·mark** (pōst′märk′), *n.* a post-office mark stamped on a piece of mail, canceling the postage stamp and recording the date, time, and place. *v.t.* to stamp with a postmark.
**post·mas·ter** (pōst′mas′tẽr, -mäs′-), *n.* a person in charge of a post office. **—post′mas′ter·ship′,** *n.*
**postmaster general,** [*pl.* POSTMASTERS GENERAL, POSTMASTER GENERALS], the head of a government's postal system.
**post·me·rid·i·an** (pōst′mə-rid′i-ən), *adj.* [< L.; see POST- & MERIDIAN], of or occurring after the sun has passed the meridian; afternoon.
‡**post me·ri·di·em** (pōst mə-rid′i-em′), [L.], after noon: abbrev. **P.M., PM, p.m.**
**post·mis·tress** (pōst′mis′tris), *n.* a woman postmaster.
**post-mor·tem** (pōst′môr′təm), *adj.* [L., after death], 1. happening or done after death. 2. designating or of an examination of a human body after death. *n.* a post-mortem examination; autopsy.
**post·na·tal** (pōst′nā′t'l), *adj.* after birth.
**post office,** 1. the governmental department in charge of the mails. 2. an office or building where mail is sorted, postage stamps are sold, etc. **—post′-of′fice,** *adj.*
**post·op·er·a·tive** (pōst′op′ə-rā′tiv, -op′ẽr-ə-tiv), *adj.* of or occurring in the period after a surgical operation.
**post·paid** (pōst′pād′), *adj.* with the postage prepaid.
**post·pone** (pōst-pōn′), *v.t.* [-PONED, -PONING], [< L. *post*, after + *ponere*, to put], to put off until later; defer; delay. **—post·pon′a·ble,** *adj.* **—post·pone′·ment,** *n.* **—post·pon′er,** *n.*
**post·pran·di·al** (pōst′pran′di-əl), *adj.* [< *post-* + L. *prandium*, noonday meal], after-dinner.
**post·rid·er** (pōst′rīd′ẽr), *n.* a person who carries the post, or mail, on horseback.
**post road,** a road over which the post, or mail, is or formerly was carried.
**post·script** (pōst′skript′, pōs′-), *n.* [< L. pp. < *post-*, after + *scribere*, to write], a note, paragraph, etc. added below the signature of a letter, or to a book or article, as an afterthought or to give supplementary information.
**pos·tu·late** (pos′choo-lāt′; *for n., usually* -lit), *v.t.* [-LATED, -LATING], [< L. pp. of *postulare*, to demand], 1. to claim; demand; require. 2. to assume without proof to be true, real, or necessary, especially as a basis for argument. 3. to take as axiomatic. *n.* 1. something postulated (senses 2 & 3). 2. a prerequisite. 3. a basic principle. **—pos′tu·la′tion,** *n.* **—pos′tu·la′tor,** *n.*
**pos·ture** (pos′chẽr), *n.* [Fr. < L. *positura* < *ponere*, to place], 1. the position of the body or its parts; carriage; bearing. 2. a position assumed as in posing, etc. 3. the way things stand; condition: as, the *posture* of foreign affairs. 4. an attitude or frame of mind. *v.t.* [-TURED, -TURING], to place in a posture; pose. *v.i.* to assume a bodily or mental posture, as for effect; pose; attitudinize. **—pos′·tur·al,** *adj.* **—pos′tur·er,** *n.*
**pos·tur·ize** (pos′chẽr-īz′), *v.t. & v.i.* [-IZED, -IZING], to posture.
**post·war** (pōst′wôr′), *adj.* after the (or a) war.
**po·sy** (pō′zi), *n.* [*pl.* -SIES], [contr. < *poesy*], 1. originally, a verse or motto inscribed inside a ring. 2. a flower or bouquet.
**pot** (pot), *n.* [AS. *pott*], 1. a round vessel, as of metal or earthenware, for holding liquids, cooking, etc. 2. a pot with its contents; amount in a pot. 3. a pot of liquor. 4. something like a pot in shape or use: as, a chimney *pot*, lobster *pot*. 5. [Colloq.], *a*) all the money bet at a single time. *b*) a large amount of money. 6. [Slang], marijuana. *v.t.* [POTTED, POTTING], 1. to put into a pot. 2. to cook or preserve in a pot. 3. to shoot (game) for food instead of for sport. 4. to hit with a pot shot. **—go to pot,** to go to ruin. **—pot′ful′,** *n.*
**po·ta·ble** (pō′tə-b'l), *adj.* [Fr. < LL. < L. *potare*, to drink], drinkable. *n. usually in pl.* something drinkable; beverage. **—po′ta·bil′i·ty,** *n.*
‡**po·tage** (pô′tȧzh′), *n.* [Fr.], soup; broth.
**pot·ash** (pot′ash), *n.* [< D. < *pot*, pot + *asch*, ash], 1. an oxide, $K_2O$, derived from wood ashes, natural brines, etc. and used in fertilizer, soaps, etc. 2. potassium carbonate. Cf. **caustic potash.**
**po·tas·si·um** (pə-tas′i-əm), *n.* [Mod. L.; see POTASH], a soft, silver-white, waxlike metallic chemical element: its native salts are used in fertilizers, glass, etc.: symbol, K; at. wt., 39.096; at. no., 19. **—po·tas′sic,** *adj.*
**potassium bromide,** a white, crystalline compound, KBr, used in photography, medicine, etc.
**potassium carbonate,** an alkaline, crystalline compound, $K_2CO_3$, used in making soap, glass, etc.
**potassium chlorate,** a crystalline salt, $KClO_3$, a strong oxidizing agent.
**potassium chloride,** a colorless, crystalline salt, KCl, used in fertilizers, explosives, etc.
**potassium cyanide,** an extremely poisonous, white, crystalline compound, KCN: cf. *cyanide.*
**potassium hydroxide,** a white, strongly alkaline compound, KOH, used in making soap, glass, etc.: also called *caustic potash.*
**potassium nitrate,** a colorless, crystalline salt, $KNO_3$, used in fertilizers, gunpowder, etc. and as an oxidizing agent: also called *niter, saltpeter.*
**potassium permanganate,** a dark-purple, crystalline compound, $KMnO_4$, used as an oxidizing agent, disinfectant, antiseptic, etc.
**po·ta·tion** (pō-tā′shən), *n.* [< OFr. < L. *potare*, to drink], 1. the act of drinking. 2. a drink or draft. 3. excessive drinking. 4. a liquor.
**po·ta·to** (pə-tā′tō), *n.* [*pl.* -TOES], [Sp. *patata* < Haitian], 1. the starchy tuber of a widely cultivated plant of the nightshade family, used as a vegetable. 2. this plant. 3. a sweet potato.
**po·ta·to beetle** (or **bug**), a black-striped, yellow beetle that eats the leaves of potatoes.
**potato chip,** a very thin slice of potato fried crisp and then salted.
**pot·bel·ly** (pot′bel′i), *n.* [*pl.* -LIES], a protruding belly. **—pot′bel′lied,** *adj.*
**pot·boil·er** (pot′boil′ẽr), *n.* a book, painting, etc., often inferior, produced only to make money.
**po·teen** (pō-tēn′), *n.* [< Ir. dim. of *poite*, a pot], in Ireland, illicitly distilled whisky: also **po·theen** (pō-thēn′, -tēn′).
**po·tent** (pō′t'nt), *adj.* [< L. *potens*, ppr. of *posse*, to be able], 1. having authority or power; powerful. 2. convincing; cogent. 3. effective or powerful in action, as a drug. 4. able to perform sexual intercourse: said of a male. **—po′ten·cy** [*pl.* -CIES], **po′tence,** *n.* **—po′tent·ly,** *adv.*
**po·ten·tate** (pō′t'n-tāt′), *n.* a potent, or powerful, person; ruler; monarch.
**po·ten·tial** (pə-ten′shəl), *adj.* [see POTENT], 1. that can, but has not yet, come into being; possible; latent. 2. in *grammar*, expressing possibility, capability, etc.: as, "I can go" is in the *potential* mood. *n.* 1. something potential. 2. the relative voltage or degree of electrification at a point in an electric circuit or field, as referred to some other point in the same circuit or field. **—po·ten′tial·ly,** *adv.*
**potential energy,** energy that is a result of relative position instead of motion, as in a coiled spring, a raised weight, etc.
**po·ten·ti·al·i·ty** (pə-ten′shi-al′ə-ti), *n.* [*pl.* -TIES], (a) possibility of becoming, developing, etc.; potential state, quality, or fact.
**poth·er** (poth′ẽr), *n.* [< ?], 1. a choking cloud of dust, smoke, etc. 2. an uproar; fuss; commotion. *v.t. & v.i.* to bother; worry.
**pot·herb** (pot′ũrb′, -hũrb′), *n.* any herb whose fleshy leaves and stems are boiled and eaten, or used to flavor food.
**pot·hold·er** (pot′hōl′dẽr), *n.* a small pad or piece of cloth for handling hot pots, etc.
**pot·hook** (pot′hook′), *n.* 1. an S-shaped hook for hanging a pot or kettle over a fire. 2. a hooked rod for lifting hot pots, etc. 3. an S-shaped mark, as one made by children learning to write.
**pot·house** (pot′hous′), *n.* [Brit.], an alehouse or tavern, especially a disreputable one.
**po·tion** (pō′shən), *n.* [< L. < *potare*, to drink], a drink, especially of medicine or poison; dose.
**pot·luck** (pot′luk′), *n.* whatever the family meal happens to be: as, take *potluck* with us.
**Po·to·mac** (pə-tō′mək), *n.* a river forming the boundaries of West Virginia, Virginia, and Maryland, flowing into Chesapeake Bay.
**pot·pie** (pot′pī′), *n.* 1. a meat pie made in a pot or deep dish. 2. a stew with dumplings.
**pot·pour·ri** (pō′poo-rē′, pot-poor′i), *n.* [Fr.; *pot*, a pot + pp. of *pourrir*, to rot], 1. a mixture, as of dried flower petals with spices, kept in a jar for its fragrance. 3. a medley or miscellany.
**pot roast,** meat, usually beef, cooked by braising.
**Pots·dam** (pots′dam′), *n.* a city in Germany, near Berlin: pop., 115,000: scene of a conference (1945) of Truman, Churchill (later Attlee), and Stalin.
**pot·sherd** (pot′shũrd′), *n.* [< *pot* + *shard*], a piece of broken pottery.
**pot shot,** 1. an easy shot, as one at close range. 2. a random shot. 3. a haphazard try at something.

**pot·tage** (pot′ij), *n.* [OFr. *potage* < *pot*, a pot], a kind of stew or thick soup.
**pot·ted** (pot′id), *adj.* 1. put into a pot. 2. cooked or preserved in a pot or can. 3. [Slang], drunk.
**pot·ter** (pot′ẽr), *n.* one who makes earthenware pots, dishes, etc.
**pot·ter** (pot′ẽr), *v.i. & v.t.*, *n.* [< AS. *potian*, to push], [Chiefly Brit.], putter. —**pot′ter·er,** *n.* —**pot′ter·ing·ly,** *adv.*
**potter's field,** [cf. Matt. 27:7], a burial ground for persons who die impoverished or unknown.
**potter's wheel,** a rotating horizontal disk, usually operated by a treadle or motor, upon which clay is molded into bowls, etc.
**pot·ter·y** (pot′ẽr-i), *n.* [*pl.* -IES], [< Fr. < *potier*, a potter < *pot*, a pot], 1. a potter's workshop or factory. 2. the art of a potter. 3. pots, dishes, etc. made of clay hardened by heat; earthenware.
**pot·tle** (pot′'l), *n.* [< OFr. dim. of *pot*, a pot], 1. formerly, a liquid measure equal to a half gallon. 2. a pot having this capacity. 3. the contents of such a pot. 4. alcoholic liquor.
**pot·ty** (pot′i), *adj.* [-TIER, -TIEST], [Brit. Colloq.], 1. trivial; petty. 2. slightly crazy.
**pouch** (pouch), *n.* [OFr. *po(u)che;* cf. POKE], 1. a small sack or bag, as for ammunition, pipe tobacco, etc. 2. a mailbag. 3. a pouchlike cavity or part. 4. *a*) a saclike structure on the abdomen of some animals, as the kangaroo, used to carry young. *b*) a baglike part, as of a gopher's cheeks, used to carry food. *v.t.* 1. to put in a pouch. 2. to make into a pouch. *v.i.* to form a pouch. —**pouched,** *adj.* —**pouch′y** [-IER, -IEST], *adj.*
**Pough·keep·sie** (pə-kip′si), *n.* a city in SE New York, on the Hudson: pop., 38,000.
**poul·ter·er** (pōl′tẽr-ẽr), *n.* [Chiefly Brit.], one who deals in poultry.
**poul·tice** (pōl′tis), *n.* [ML. *pultes*, orig. pl. of L. *puls*, pap], a hot, soft, moist mass, as of mustard, etc., applied to a sore part of the body. *v.t.* [-TICED, -TICING], to apply a poultice to.
**poul·try** (pōl′tri), *n.* [< OFr. < *poulet;* see PULLET], domestic fowls; chickens, ducks, geese, etc.
**pounce** (pouns), *n.* [? < OFr. *pounson;* see PUNCHEON], 1. a claw or talon of a bird of prey. 2. the act of pouncing. *v.i.* [POUNCED, POUNCING], to swoop down or leap (*on*, *upon*, or *at*) as if to seize.
**pounce** (pouns), *n.* [< Fr. < L. *pumex*, pumice], 1. a fine powder, as of cuttlefish bone, formerly used to prevent ink from blotting, etc. 2. powdered charcoal, etc. sprinkled over a stencil to make a design, as on cloth. *v.t.* [POUNCED, POUNCING], 1. to sprinkle, rub, etc. with pounce. 2. to stencil with pounce.
**pound** (pound), *n.* [*pl.* POUNDS, collectively POUND], [AS. *pund* < L. *pondo*, abl. of *pondus*, weight], 1. a unit of weight, equal to 16 ounces (7,000 grains) avoirdupois or 12 ounces (5,760 grains) troy: abbrev. **lb.** 2. the monetary unit of the United Kingdom, equal to 20 shillings or 100 (new) pennies: symbol, £. 3. the monetary unit of various other countries, as Ireland, Israel, Nigeria, Syria, and Turkey.
**pound** (pound), *v.t.* [AS. *punian*], 1. to beat to a pulp, powder, etc. 2. to hit hard. *v.i.* 1. to deliver repeated, heavy blows (*at* or *on* a door, etc.). 2. to move with heavy steps. 3. to throb. *n.* 1. a pounding. 2. a hard blow. 3. the sound of this; thud. —**pound out,** 1. to flatten by pounding. 2. to play with a heavy touch, as on a piano. —**pound′er,** *n.*
**pound** (pound), *n.* [< AS. *pund-*], 1. a municipal enclosure for confining stray animals until claimed. 2. an enclosure for trapping animals. 3. a place of confinement, as for arrested persons. 4. an enclosed area for catching or keeping fish. *v.t.* to impound.
**pound·age** (poun′dij), *n.* a tax, rate, or commission, etc. per pound (sterling or weight).
**pound·al** (poun′d'l), *n.* [< *pound* (weight)], a unit of force that, acting on a one-pound mass for one second, will give it a velocity of one foot per second.
**pound·cake** (pound′kāk′), *n.* a rich cake made with a pound each of flour, butter, sugar, etc.
**pound·er** (poun′dẽr), *n.* something weighing, worth, or having to do with a pound or (a specified number of) pounds: as, a ten-*pounder.*
**pound-fool·ish** (pound′fōōl′ish), *adj.* foolish in handling large sums of money: cf. **penny-wise.**
**pound sterling,** a pound (British monetary unit).
**pour** (pôr, pōr), *v.t.* [ME. *pouren*], 1. to cause to flow in a continuous stream. 2. to emit, utter, etc. profusely or steadily. *v.i.* 1. to flow freely, continuously, or copiously. 2. to rain heavily. 3. to swarm. *n.* 1. a pouring. 2. a downpour; heavy rain. —**pour′er,** *n.* —**pour′ing·ly,** *adv.*
‡**pour·boire** (pōōr′bwär′), *n.* [Fr.; *pour*, for + *boire*, to drink], a tip, or gratuity.
**pout** (pout), *v.i.* [ME. *pouten*], 1. to thrust out the lips, as in sullenness. 2. to sulk. 3. to protrude, as the lips. *v.t.* 1. to thrust out (the lips or mouth). 2. to utter with a pout. *n.* 1. a pouting. 2. *pl.* a fit of sulking. —**pout′ing·ly,** *adv.* —**pout′y** [-IER, -IEST], *adj.*
**pout** (pout), *n.* [AS. (*æl*)*pute*], [*pl.* POUT, POUTS; see PLURAL, II, D, 2], any of several fishes, as the horned pout or eelpout.
**pout·er** (pout′ẽr), *n.* 1. one who pouts. 2. a breed of long-legged pigeon that can distend its crop.
**pov·er·ty** (pov′ẽr-ti), *n.* [< OFr. < L. < *pauper*, poor], 1. the condition or quality of being poor; need. 2. inferiority; inadequacy. 3. scarcity.
**pov·er·ty-strick·en** (pov′ẽr-ti-strik′'n), *adj.* stricken with poverty; very poor.
**POW,** prisoner of war: also **P.O.W.**
**pow·der** (pou′dẽr), *n.* [< OFr. *poudre* < L. *pulvis*], 1. any dry substance in the form of fine, dustlike particles, produced by crushing, grinding, etc. 2. a specific kind of powder: as, bath *powder.* 3. gunpowder. *v.t.* 1. to sprinkle, dust, or cover with or as with powder. 2. to make into powder; pulverize. *v.i.* 1. to be made into powder. 2. to use powder as a cosmetic. —**pow′der·er,** *n.*
**powder blue,** pale blue. —**pow′der-blue′,** *adj.*
**powder burn,** a skin burn caused by exploding gunpowder.
**powder horn,** a container for carrying gunpowder, especially one made of an animal's horn.
**powder puff,** a soft pad for applying cosmetic powder.
**powder room,** a toilet or lavatory for women.
**pow·der·y** (pou′dẽr-i), *adj.* [-IER, -IEST], 1. of, like, or in the form of, powder. 2. easily crumbled into powder. 3. covered with powder; dusty.
**pow·er** (pou′ẽr), *n.* [< OFr. *poeir*, earlier *poter*, inf. < LL. *potere*, to be able, for L. *posse*, to be able], 1. ability to do; capacity to act. 2. a specific faculty: as, the *power* of hearing. 3. great ability to do, act, etc.; vigor; force. 4. *a*) the ability to control others; authority; influence. *b*) legal authority. 5. *a*) physical force or energy: as, electric *power.* *b*) the capacity to exert such force, in terms of the rate or results of its use: as, 60-watt *power.* 6. a person or thing having great influence, force, or authority. 7. a nation, especially one with influence over other nations: as, the big *powers.* 8. national might or political strength. 9. a spirit or divinity. 10. the product of the multiplication of a quantity by itself: as, 32 is the fifth *power* of 2 ($2^5$). 11. the degree of magnification of a lens, microscope, etc. *adj.* 1. operated by electricity, etc.: as, *power* tools. 2. served by an auxiliary, engine-driven system that reduces the effort of the operation: as, *power* steering in an automobile. —**in power,** 1. in authority or control. 2. in office. —**the powers that be,** the persons in control. —**pow′ered,** *adj.*
**pow·er·boat** (pou′ẽr-bōt′), *n.* a motorboat.
**pow·er·ful** (pou′ẽr-fəl), *adj.* having power; strong; mighty; influential. *adv.* [Dial.], very. —**pow′er·ful·ly,** *adv.* —**pow′er·ful·ness,** *n.*
**pow·er·house** (pou′ẽr-hous′), *n.* a building where power, especially electric power, is generated.
**pow·er·less** (pou′ẽr-lis), *adj.* without power; weak, impotent, unable, etc. —**pow′er·less·ly,** *adv.* —**pow′er·less·ness,** *n.*
**power of attorney,** a written statement legally authorizing a person to act for one.
**power politics,** international political relations in which each nation attempts to advance its interests by using military force or the threat of it.
**pow·wow** (pou′wou′), *n.* [< Am. Ind.], 1. a North American Indian ceremony to conjure the cure of disease, success in war, etc., marked by magic, feasting, etc. 2. a conference of or with North American Indians. 3. [Colloq.], any conference. *v.i.* 1. to hold a powwow. 2. [Colloq.], to confer.
**pox** (poks), *n.* [for *pocks;* see POCK], 1. any of various diseases characterized by skin eruptions, as smallpox. 2. syphilis.
**Poz·nan** (pôz′nän′y′), *n.* a city in W Poland: pop., 395,000: German name, *Posen* (pō′zən).
**pp, pp.,** in *music*, pianissimo.

**pp.,** 1. pages. 2. past participle.

**P.P., p.p.,** 1. parcel post. 2. past participle. 3. postpaid.

**ppr., p.pr.,** present participle.

**P.P.S., p.p.s.,** *post postscriptum,* [L.], an additional postscript.

**Pr,** in *chemistry,* praseodymium.

**Pr.,** Provençal.

**pr.,** 1. [*pl.* PRS.], pair. 2. present. 3. price.

**P.R.,** Puerto Rico.

**prac·ti·ca·ble** (prak′ti-kə-b'l), *adj.* [< Fr. < *pratiquer;* see PRACTICE], 1. that can be done or put into practice; feasible: as, a *practicable* plan. 2. that can be used; usable: as, a *practicable* tool. —**prac′ti·ca·bil′i·ty, prac′ti·ca·ble·ness,** *n.* —**prac′ti·ca·bly,** *adv.*

**prac·ti·cal** (prak′ti-k'l), *adj.* [obs. *practic* < LL. *practicus;* see PRACTICE], 1. of or obtained through practice or action: as, *practical* knowledge. 2. that can be used; useful. 3. designed for use: as, a *practical* dress. 4. concerned with the application of knowledge to useful ends, rather than with speculation, etc.: as, a *practical* mind. 5. given to actual practice: as, a *practical* farmer. 6. that is so in practice, if not in theory, law, etc.; virtual. 7. matter-of-fact; realistic. —**prac′ti·cal′i·ty** [*pl.* -TIES], **prac′ti·cal·ness,** *n.*

**practical joke,** a trick played on someone in fun.

**prac·ti·cal·ly** (prak′tik-li, -ti-k'l-i), *adv.* 1. in a practical manner. 2. from a practical viewpoint. 3. for all practical purposes; virtually. 4. [Colloq.], almost; nearly.

**practical nurse,** an experienced nurse, neither a nursing school graduate nor a registered nurse.

**prac·tice** (prak′tis), *v.t.* [-TICED, -TICING], [< OFr. < *pratiquer;* ult. < LL. *practicus* < Gr. *praktikos,* practical < *prassein,* to do], 1. to do or perform frequently; make a habit of. 2. to do repeatedly in order to become proficient: as, to *practice* batting. 3. to work at, especially as a profession: as, to *practice* medicine. 4. to teach through practice; exercise. *v.i.* 1. to do something repeatedly in order to become proficient, as in music, etc. 2. to work at a profession, as medicine, law, etc. Also sp. **practise.** *n.* 1. a practicing; specif., *a)* a frequent action; habit: as, make a *practice* of coming early. *b)* a usual method; custom. 2. repeated action for the purpose of acquiring proficiency: as, *practice* makes perfect. 3. proficiency so acquired: as, he's out of practice. 4. the doing of something, often as an application of knowledge: as, theory is useless without *practice.* 5. the exercise of a profession: as, the *practice* of law. 6. a business based on this. 7. *a)* a scheme; intrigue. *b)* a stratagem. 8. in *law,* an established method of court procedure. —**prac′tic·er,** *n.*

**prac·ticed** (prak′tist), *adj.* 1. proficient through practice; skilled. 2. learned or perfected by practice. Also sp. **practised.**

**prac·tise** (prak′tis), *v.t. & v.i.* [-TISED, -TISING], to practice. —**prac′tis·er,** *n.*

**prac·ti·tion·er** (prak-tish′ən-ẽr), *n.* 1. one who practices a profession, art, etc.: as, a medical *practitioner.* 2. a Christian Science healer.

**prae-,** [L. < *prae,* before], pre-, as in *praenomen.*

**prae·fect** (prē′fekt), *n.* a prefect.

**prae·no·men** (prē-nō′men), *n.* [*pl.* -NOMINA (-nom′i-nə)], [L.; *prae-,* before + *nomen,* a name], in ancient Rome, a person's first, or personal, name. —**prae·nom′i·nal** (-nom′i-n'l), *adj.*

**prae·tor** (prē′tẽr, -tôr), *n.* [L.; ult. < *prae-,* before + *ire,* to go], a magistrate of ancient Rome, next below a consul in rank. —**prae·to·ri·al** (pri-tôr′i-əl, -tō′ri-), *adj.*

**prae·to·ri·an** (pri-tôr′i-ən, -tō′ri-), *adj.* 1. of a praetor. 2. [often P-], designating or of the bodyguard (**Praetorian Guard**) of a Roman emperor.

**prag·mat·ic** (prag-mat′ik), *adj.* [< Fr. < L. < Gr. *pragmatikos* < *pragma,* business < *prassein,* to do], 1. *a)* busy; active. *b)* practical. 2. *a)* officious; meddlesome. *b)* conceited. 3. having to do with the affairs of a state or community. 4. of or relating to pragmatism. Also, and for 2 usually, **prag·mat′i·cal.** —**prag·mat′i·cal·ly,** *adv.* —**prag·mat′i·cal·ness,** *n.*

**prag·ma·tism** (prag′mə-tiz'm), *n.* 1. quality, condition, or instance of being pragmatic. 2. a system of philosophy which tests the validity of all concepts by their practical results. —**prag′ma·tist,** *n.*

**Prague** (präg), *n.* the capital of Czechoslovakia, in the western part: pop., 922,000: Czech name, **Pra·ha** (prä′hä).

**prai·rie** (prâr′i), *n.* [Fr. < ML. < L. *pratum,* meadow], a large area of level or rolling grassland.

**prairie chicken,** a large, brown and white, henlike grouse with a rounded tail, found on the North American prairies: also **prairie hen.**

**prairie dog,** any of various small, squirrellike animals of North America, having a barking cry.

**prairie schooner,** a large covered wagon used by pioneers to cross the American prairies.

PRAIRIE SCHOONER

**prairie wolf,** a wolflike animal of the western plains of North America; coyote.

**praise** (prāz), *v.t.* [PRAISED, PRAISING], [< OFr. < LL. < L. *pretium,* worth], 1. to commend the worth of; express approval of. 2. to laud the glory of (God, etc.), as in song; glorify. *n.* a praising or being praised; commendation; glorification. —**sing one's praise** (or **praises**), to praise one highly. —**prais′er,** *n.*

**praise·wor·thy** (prāz′wũr′*thi*), *adj.* worthy of praise; laudable. —**praise′wor′thi·ly,** *adv.* —**praise′wor′thi·ness,** *n.*

**Pra·krit** (prä′krit), *n.* [Sans. *prakrtā,* natural < *pra-,* before + *kr,* to do], any of several vernacular Indic languages used in India, chiefly in the period B.C.

**pra·line** (prä′lēn, prā′-), *n.* [Fr. < Marshal Duplessis-*Praslin* (1598–1675), whose cook invented it], a crisp candy made of nuts, as pecans, browned in boiling sugar.

**pram** (pram), *n.* [Brit. Colloq.], a perambulator.

**prance** (prans, präns), *v.i.* [PRANCED, PRANCING], [ME. *prauncen;* prob. < OFr.], 1. to rise up on the hind legs; esp., to move along in this way: said of a horse. 2. to ride on a prancing horse. 3. to caper; gambol. 4. to move or ride gaily or arrogantly; strut. *v.t.* to cause (a horse) to prance. *n.* a prancing. —**pranc′er,** *n.* —**pranc′ing·ly,** *adv.*

**prank** (praŋk), *n.* [? < *prank, v.*], a mischievous trick; practical joke. —**prank′ish,** *adj.* —**prank′ish·ly,** *adv.* —**prank′ish·ness,** *n.* —**prank′ster,** *n.*

**prank** (praŋk), *v.t.* [prob. < a LG. source], to dress showily; adorn (also with *up* or *out*). *v.i.* to dress up; make a show.

**pra·se·o·dym·i·um** (prā′zi-ə-dim′i-əm, prā′si-), *n.* [< Gr. *prasios,* green; + *didymium,* a rare mineral < Gr. *didymos,* twin], a metallic chemical element of the rare-earth group: symbol, Pr; at. wt., 140.92; at. no., 59.

**prat** (prat), *n. sometimes pl.* [Slang], the buttocks.

**prate** (prāt), *v.i. & v.t.* [PRATED, PRATING], [< MD. *praten;* prob. echoic], to talk on and on, foolishly; chatter. *n.* foolish talk; chatter. —**prat′er,** *n.* —**prat′ing·ly,** *adv.*

**prat·fall** (prat′fôl′), *n.* [Slang], a fall on the buttocks.

**prat·tle** (prat′'l), *v.i. & v.t.* [-TLED, -TLING], [MLG. *pratelen;* see PRATE], 1. to prate. 2. to speak childishly; babble. *n.* 1. prate. 2. babble. —**prat′tler,** *n.* —**prat′tling·ly,** *adv.*

**prawn** (prôn), *n.* [ME. *prayne*], any of various edible, shrimplike animals having a thin shell.

**Prax·it·e·les** (prak-sit′ə-lēz′), *n.* Athenian sculptor of the 4th century B.C.

**pray** (prā), *v.t.* [< OFr. < LL. < L. *precari* < *prex,* prayer], 1. to implore; beseech: used elliptically, as, (I) *pray* (you) tell me. 2. to ask for by prayer; beg for imploringly. 3. to bring about, get, etc. by praying. *v.i.* to make supplication; say prayers, as to God. —**pray′er,** *n.*

**prayer** (prâr), *n.* [< OFr. < ML. < L. *precarius,* got by begging < *precari,* to entreat], 1. the act of praying. 2. an earnest request; entreaty. 3. *a)* a humble entreaty made to God, to a god, etc. *b)* any set formula for praying, as to God. 4. *often pl.* a devotional service consisting chiefly of prayers. 5. something prayed for. —**prayer′ful,** *adj.* —**prayer′ful·ly,** *adv.* —**prayer′ful·ness,** *n.*

**prayer book,** a book of formal religious prayers.

**praying mantis,** a mantis.

**pre-,** [< Fr. *pré-* or L. *prae-* < L. *prae,* before], a prefix meaning: 1. *before in time, place, rank, etc.,* as in *prewar, pre-eminent.* 2. *preliminary to,* as in *preschool.* Words formed with *pre-* are generally written without a hyphen unless the prefix is followed by *e* or a capital letter.

**preach** (prēch), *v.i.* [< OFr. < L. < *prae-,* before + *dicare,* to proclaim], 1. to speak in public on religious matters; give a sermon. 2. to give moral or religious advice, especially in a tiresome manner. *v.t.* 1. to urge or expound as by preaching. 2. to deliver (a sermon). —**preach′ing,** *n.* —**preach′ing·ly,** *adv.*

**preach·er** (prē′chẽr), *n.* a person who preaches; esp., a clergyman.

**preach·i·fy** (prē′chə-fī′), *v.i.* [-FIED, -FYING], [Colloq.], to preach in a tiresome manner.
**preach·ment** (prēch′mənt), *n.* a preaching or sermon, especially a long, tiresome one.
**preach·y** (prē′chi), *adj.* [-IER, -IEST], [Colloq.], given to or resembling preaching.
**pre·am·ble** (prē′am′b'l, prē-am′-), *n.* [< Fr.; ult. < L. < *prae-*, before + *ambulare*, to go], 1. an introduction, especially one to a constitution, statute, etc., stating its purpose. 2. an introductory fact, event, etc.; preliminary.
**pre·ar·range** (prē′ə-rānj′), *v.t.* [-RANGED, -RANGING], to arrange beforehand. —**pre′ar·range′ment,** *n.*
**preb·end** (preb′ənd), *n.* [< OFr. < ML. *praebenda*, things to be supplied < L. *praebere*, to give], 1. the allotment of a cathedral or collegiate church for a clergyman's salary. 2. a prebendary or his benefice. —**pre·ben·dal** (pri-ben′d'l), *adj.*
**preb·en·dar·y** (preb′ən-der′i), *n.* [*pl.* -IES], a person receiving a prebend.
**prec.,** preceding.
**Pre-Cam·bri·an** (prē′kam′bri-ən), *adj.* designating or of all the geologic time before the Cambrian Era: see **geology,** chart. *n.* the Pre-Cambrian Era.
**pre·can·cel** (prē-kan′s'l), *v.t.* [-CELED or -CELLED, -CELING or -CELLING], to cancel (a postage stamp) before use in mailing. *n.* a precanceled stamp.
**pre·car·i·ous** (pri-kâr′i-əs), *adj.* [L. *precarius;* see PRAYER], 1. dependent upon the will or favor of another: as, a *precarious* allowance. 2. dependent upon circumstances or chance; uncertain; risky. —**pre·car′i·ous·ly,** *adv.* —**pre·car′i·ous·ness,** *n.*
**pre·cau·tion** (pri-kô′shən), *n.* [< Fr. < LL. < L. *praecautus*, pp. < *prae-*, before + *cavere*, to take care], 1. care taken beforehand. 2. a measure taken beforehand against possible danger, failure, etc. —**pre·cau′tion·ar′y,** *adj.* —**pre·cau′tious,** *adj.*
**pre·cede** (pri-sēd′, prē-), *v.t.* & *v.i.* [-CEDED, -CEDING], [< L. < *prae-*, before + *cedere*, to move], to be, come, or go before in time, place, rank, etc.
**pre·ced·ence** (pri-sē′d'ns, pres′ə-dəns), *n.* 1. the act, privilege, or fact of preceding in time, place, order, etc. 2. superiority in rank. Also **pre·ced′en·cy** (-ən-si), [*pl.* -CIES].
**pre·ced·ent** (pri-sē′d'nt; *for n.*, pres′ə-dənt), *adj.* preceding. *n.* an act, statement, etc. that may serve as an example, reason, or justification for a later one. —**prec·e·den·tial** (pres′ə-den′shəl), *adj.* —**pre·ced′ent·ly,** *adv.*
**pre·ced·ing** (pri-sēd′iŋ, prē-), *adj.* that precedes.
**pre·cen·tor** (pri-sen′tẽr), *n.* [< LL. < L. *prae*, before + *canere*, to sing], one who directs a choir or congregation in singing. —**pre·cen′tor·ship′,** *n.*
**pre·cept** (prē′sept), *n.* [< OFr. < L. < *praecipere*, to teach < *prae-*, before + *capere*, to take], 1. a direction meant as a rule of action or conduct. 2. a rule of moral conduct; maxim.
**pre·cep·tor** (pri-sep′tẽr), *n.* a teacher. —**pre·cep·to·ri·al** (prē′sep-tôr′i-əl, -tō′ri-), **pre·cep′tor·al,** *adj.* —**pre·cep′tor·ship′,** *n.* —**pre·cep′tress,** *n.fem.*
**pre·ces·sion** (pri-sesh′ən, prē-), *n.* a preceding; precedence. —**pre·ces′sion·al,** *adj.*
**pre·cinct** (prē′siŋkt), *n.* [< ML. < L. < *praecingere*, to encompass < *prae-*, before + *cingere*, to surround], 1. an enclosure between buildings, walls, etc., as the grounds surrounding a church. 2. *usually pl.* environs; neighborhood. 3. a subdivision of a city, ward, etc.: as, a police *precinct.* 4. any limited area. 5. a boundary.
**pre·ci·os·i·ty** (presh′i-os′ə-ti), *n.* [*pl.* -TIES], [see PRECIOUS], great fastidiousness, affectation, etc., especially in language.
**pre·cious** (presh′əs), *adj.* [< OFr. < L. *pretiosus* < *pretium*, a price], 1. of great price or value; costly. 2. of great desirability: as, freedom is *precious.* 3. beloved; dear. 4. very fastidious, affected, etc. 5. [Colloq.], very great: as, a *precious* liar. *adv.* [Colloq.], very. —**pre′cious·ly,** *adv.* —**pre′cious·ness,** *n.*
**precious stone,** a rare and costly gem.
**prec·i·pice** (pres′ə-pis), *n.* [< Fr. < L. < *praeceps*, headlong < *prae-*, before + *caput*, a head], 1. a vertical, almost vertical, or overhanging rock face; steep cliff. 2. a hazardous situation.
**pre·cip·i·tant** (pri-sip′ə-tənt), *adj.* [< Fr. < L. *praecipitans*, ppr. < *praeceps;* see PRECIPICE], 1. falling steeply or rushing headlong. 2. acting very hastily or rashly. 3. very abrupt or unexpected. *n.* a substance which, when added to a solution, causes the formation of a precipitate. —**pre·cip′i·tance, pre·cip′i·tan·cy** [*pl.* -CIES], *n.* —**pre·cip′i·tant·ly,** *adv.*
**pre·cip·i·tate** (pri-sip′ə-tāt′; *also, for adj.* & *n.*, -tit), *v.t.* [-TATED, -TATING], [< L. *praecipitatus*, pp. < *praeceps;* see PRECIPICE], 1. to throw headlong; hurl downward. 2. to cause to happen before expected, needed, etc.; hasten. 3. in *chemistry*, to separate (a soluble substance) out from a solution. 4. in *meteorology*, to condense (vapor, etc.) and cause to fall as rain, snow, etc. *v.i.* 1. in *chemistry*, to be precipitated. 2. in *meteorology*, to condense and fall, as rain, snow, etc. *adj.* 1. falling steeply, rushing headlong, etc. 2. acting, happening, etc. very hastily or rashly; impetuous. 3. very sudden; unexpected. *n.* a substance separated out from a solution as a solid by chemical reagents, etc. —**pre·cip′i·tate·ly,** *adv.* —**pre·cip′i·ta′tor,** *n.*
**pre·cip·i·ta·tion** (pri-sip′ə-tā′shən), *n.* 1. a precipitating or being precipitated; specif., a headlong fall or rush. 2. rash haste; impetuosity. 3. a bringing on suddenly; acceleration. 4. in *chemistry*, *a*) a precipitating or being precipitated from a solution. *b*) a precipitate. 5. in *meteorology*, *a*) a depositing of rain, snow, etc. *b*) rain, snow, etc. *c*) the amount of this. —**pre·cip′i·ta′tive,** *adj.*
**pre·cip·i·tous** (pri-sip′ə-təs), *adj.* 1. steep like a precipice. 2. having precipices. 3. rash. —**pre·cip′i·tous·ly,** *adv.* —**pre·cip′i·tous·ness,** *n.*
**pré·cis** (prā-sē′, prā′sē), *n.* [*pl.* -CIS (-sēz′, -sēz)], [Fr.; see PRECISE], a concise abridgment; summary. *v.t.* to make a précis of.
**pre·cise** (pri-sis′), *adj.* [< Fr. < L. < *praescidere*, to cut off < *prae-*, before + *caedere*, to cut], 1. accurately stated; definite. 2. speaking definitely or distinctly. 3. minutely exact. 4. *a*) that strictly conforms to usage, etc.; scrupulous. *b*) overnice. —**pre·cise′ly,** *adv.* —**pre·cise′ness,** *n.*
**pre·ci·sion** (pri-sizh′ən), *n.* the quality of being precise; exactness. —**pre·ci′sion·ist,** *n.*
**pre·clude** (pri-klōōd′), *v.t.* [-CLUDED, -CLUDING] [< L. < *prae-*, before + *claudere*, to shut], to shut out; hinder; make impossible, especially in advance. —**pre·clu′sion** (-klōō′zhən), *n.* —**pre·clu′sive,** *adj.* —**pre·clu′sive·ly,** *adv.*
**pre·co·cious** (pri-kō′shəs), *adj.* [L. *praecox;* ult. < *prae-*, before + *coquere*, to cook], 1. developed earlier than usual, as a child. 2. of or showing premature development. —**pre·co′cious·ly,** *adv.* —**pre·co′cious·ness, pre·coc·i·ty** (-kos′ə-ti), *n.*
**pre·con·ceive** (prē′kən-sēv′), *v.t.* to form a conception or opinion of beforehand; conceive in advance. —**pre·con·cep·tion** (-sep′shən), *n.*
**pre·con·cert** (prē′kən-sũrt′), *v.t.* to arrange or settle beforehand. —**pre′con·cert′ed·ly,** *adv.*
**pre·cur·sor** (pri-kũr′sẽr), *n.* [< L. < *praecurrere*, to run ahead], 1. a forerunner. 2. a predecessor.
**pre·cur·so·ry** (pri-kũr′sə-ri), *adj.* 1. serving as a precursor. 2. introductory; preliminary.
**pred.,** predicate.
**pre·da·ceous, pre·da·cious** (pri-dā′shəs), *adj.* [< L. *praeda*, a prey], preying on other animals. —**pre·dac′i·ty** (-das′ə-ti), **pre·da′ceous·ness, pre·da′cious·ness,** *n.*
**pred·a·to·ry** (pred′ə-tôr′i, -tō′ri), *adj.* [< L. < *praeda*, a prey], 1. of, living by, or characterized by plundering or robbing. 2. predaceous. —**pred′a·to′ri·ly,** *adv.* —**pred′a·to′ri·ness,** *n.*
**pre·de·cease** (prē′di-sēs′), *v.t.* [-CEASED, -CEASING], [*pre-* + *decease*], to die before.
**pred·e·ces·sor** (pred′ə-ses′ẽr, pred′ə-ses′ẽr), *n.* [< OFr. < LL. < L. *prae-*, before + *decessor*, retiring officer < *decessus;* see DECEASE], 1. a person preceding another, as in office. 2. a thing replaced by another thing, as in use. 3. an ancestor.
**pre·des·ti·nate** (pri-des′tə-nit; *for v.*, -nāt′), *adj.* [< L. pp. of *praedestinare*, to foretell], foreordained. *v.t.*[-NATED, -NATING], 1. in *theology*, to foreordain by divine decree. 2. to predestine. —**pre·des′ti·na′tor,** *n.*
**pre·des·ti·na·tion** (pri-des′tə-nā′shən), *n.* 1. in *theology*, *a*) the act by which God foreordained everything that would happen. *b*) God's predestinating of souls to damnation or to salvation. 2. a predestinating or being predestinated; destiny.
**pre·des·tine** (pri-des′tin), *v.t.* [-TINED, -TINING], to destine or decree beforehand; foreordain.
**pre·de·ter·mine** (prē′di-tũr′min), *v.t.* [-MINED, -MINING], 1. to determine or decide beforehand. 2. to give a tendency to beforehand; prejudice. —**pre′de·ter′mi·na·ble,** *adj.* —**pre′de·ter′mi·nate** (-mə-nit), *adj.* —**pre′de·ter′mi·na′tion,** *n.*
**pred·i·ca·ble** (pred′i-kə-b'l), *adj.* that can be predicated. *n.* something predicable. —**pred′i·ca·bil′i·ty, pred′i·ca·ble·ness,** *n.* —**pred′i·ca·bly,** *adv.*

**pre·dic·a·ment** (pri-dik′ə-mənt), *n.* [< LL. *praedicamentum* < L. *praedicare;* see PREACH], a condition or situation, especially one that is distressing or embarrassing. —**pre·dic′a·men′tal** (-men′t'l), *adj.*

**pred·i·cate** (pred′i-kāt′; *for n. and adj.,* -kit), *v.t.* [-CATED, -CATING], [< ML. < L. pp. of *praedicare;* see PREACH], 1. [Rare], to proclaim; affirm. 2. to affirm as a quality, attribute, etc.: as, to *predicate* greenness of grass. 3. to imply: as, grass *predicates* greenness. 4. to base upon facts, conditions, etc. *v.i.* to make an affirmation. *n.* 1. in *grammar,* the word or words that make a statement about the subject of a clause or sentence: e.g., *a*) a verb (the wind *blows*). *b*) a verb and adverb (the wind *blows hard*). *c*) a transitive verb and object (John *hit me*). *d*) a linking verb and complement (grass *is green*). 2. in *logic,* something that is affirmed or denied about the subject of a proposition (e.g., *green* in "grass is green"). *adj.* 1. predicated. 2. in *grammar,* of, or having the nature of, a predicate. —**pred′i·ca′tion,** *n.* —**pred′i·ca′tive,** *adj.* —**pred′i·ca′tive·ly,** *adv.*

**pre·dict** (pri-dikt′), *v.t. & v.i.* [< L. < *prae-,* before + *dicere,* to tell], to make known beforehand; foretell; prophesy. —**pre·dict′a·ble,** *adj.* —**pre·dic′tive,** *adj.* —**pre·dic′tive·ly,** *adv.* —**pre·dic′tor,** *n.*

**pre·dic·tion** (pri-dik′shən), *n.* 1. a predicting or being predicted. 2. something predicted.

**pre·di·gest** (prē′di-jest′, -dī-), *v.t.* to make (food) more digestible by an artificial process before it is eaten. —**pre′di·ges′tion,** *n.*

**pre·di·lec·tion** (prē′də-lek′shən, pred′'l-ek′-), *n.* [< Fr. < ML. < L. *prae-,* before + *diligere,* to prefer], a preconceived liking; partiality.

**pre·dis·pose** (prē′dis-pōz′), *v.t.* [-POSED, -POSING], to make receptive beforehand; make susceptible; incline. —**pre′dis·po·si′tion,** *n.*

**pre·dom·i·nant** (pri-dom′ə-nənt), *adj.* 1. having influence or authority over others; superior. 2. most frequent; prevailing. —**pre·dom′i·nance, pre·dom′i·nan·cy,** *n.* —**pre·dom′i·nant·ly,** *adv.*

**pre·dom·i·nate** (pri-dom′ə-nāt′), *v.i.* [-NATED, -NATING], 1. to have influence or authority (*over* others); be superior. 2. to prevail; preponderate. —**pre·dom′i·nat′ing·ly,** *adv.* —**pre·dom′i·na′tion,** *n.* —**pre·dom′i·na′tor,** *n.*

**pre-em·i·nent, pre·ëm·i·nent** (prē-em′ə-nənt), *adj.* eminent above others; prominent; surpassing. —**pre-em′i·nence, pre·ëm′i·nence,** *n.* —**pre-em′i·nent·ly, pre·ëm′i·nent·ly,** *adv.*

**pre-empt, pre·ëmpt** (prē-empt′), *v.t.* [< *pre-emption*], 1. to settle on (public land) to establish pre-emption. 2. to seize before anyone else can; appropriate. —**pre-emp′tor, pre·ëmp′tor,** *n.*

**pre-emp·tion, pre·ëmp·tion** (prē-emp′shən), *n.* [< ML. < L. *prae-,* before + *emere,* to buy] the act or right of buying land, etc. before, or in preference to, others. —**pre-emp′tive, pre·ëmp′tive, pre-emp′to·ry** (-tə-ri), **pre·ëmp′to·ry,** *adj.*

**preen** (prēn), *v.t.* [var. of *prune* (to trim)], 1. to clean and trim (the feathers) with the beak: said of birds. 2. to dress up or adorn (oneself). 3. to show satisfaction with or vanity in (oneself). *v.i.* to primp. —**preen′er,** *n.*

**pre-ex·ist, pre·ëx·ist** (prē′ig-zist′), *v.i. & v.t.* to exist previously or before (another person or thing). —**pre′-ex·ist′ence, pre′ëx·ist′ence,** *n.* —**pre′-ex·ist′ent, pre′ëx·ist′ent,** *adj.*

**pref.,** 1. preface. 2. preferred. 3. prefix.

**pre·fab** (prē′fab′), *n.* a prefabricated building.

**pre·fab·ri·cate** (prē-fab′ri-kāt′), *v.t.* [-CATED, -CATING], 1. to fabricate beforehand. 2. to build in standardized sections for shipment and quick assembly, as a house. —**pre′fab·ri·ca′tion,** *n.*

**pref·ace** (pref′is), *n.* [< OFr. < L. < *prae-,* before + *fari,* to speak], 1. a statement introductory to an article, book, or speech, telling its subject, purpose, etc. 2. something introductory. *v.t.* [-ACED, -ACING], 1. to furnish or introduce with a preface. 2. to be or serve as a preface to.

**pref·a·to·ry** (pref′ə-tôr′i, -tō′ri), *adj.* of, like, or serving as a preface; introductory: also **pref′a·to′ri·al.** —**pref′a·to′ri·ly,** *adv.*

**pre·fect** (prē′fekt), *n.* [< OFr. < L. pp. of *praeficere,* to set over < *prae-,* before + *facere,* to make], 1. in ancient Rome, any of various officials in charge of governmental or military departments. 2. any of various administrators; specif., the head of a department of France. Also sp. **praefect.**

**pre·fec·ture** (prē′fek-chēr), *n.* the office, authority, territory, or residence of a prefect. —**pre·fec·tur·al** (pri-fek′chēr-əl), *adj.*

**pre·fer** (pri-fũr′), *v.t.* [-FERRED, -FERRING], [< L. < *prae-,* before + *ferre,* to bear], 1. to put before a magistrate, court, etc. for consideration or redress. 2. to promote; advance. 3. to choose before something else; like better. —**pre·fer′rer,** *n.*

**pref·er·a·ble** (pref′ēr-ə-b'l, pref′rə-), *adj.* to be preferred; more desirable. —**pref′er·a·bil′i·ty, pref′er·a·ble·ness,** *n.* —**pref′er·a·bly,** *adv.*

**pref·er·ence** (pref′ēr-əns, pref′rəns), *n.* 1. a preferring or being preferred. 2. the right, power, etc. of prior choice or claim. 3. something preferred. 4. a giving of advantage to one person, country, etc. over others, as in tariff rates.

**pref·er·en·tial** (pref′ə-ren′shəl), *adj.* 1. of, giving, or receiving preference. 2. offering a preference. —**pref′er·en′tial·ly,** *adv.*

**preferential shop,** a union shop in which the management gives preference to union members, as in hiring, layoffs, promotions, etc.

**pre·fer·ment** (pri-fũr′mənt), *n.* 1. an advancement in rank or office; promotion. 2. an office, rank, or honor to which a person is advanced.

**preferred stock,** stock on which dividends must be paid before those of common stock.

**pre·fig·ure** (prē-fig′yēr), *v.t.* [-URED, -URING], [< LL. < L. *prae-,* before + *figurare,* to fashion], 1. to suggest or represent beforehand; foreshadow. 2. to imagine beforehand. —**pre′fig·u·ra′tion** (-yoo-rā′shən), *n.* —**pre·fig′ur·a·tive** (-yēr-ə-tiv), *adj.*

**pre·fix** (prē-fiks′; *for n.,* prē′fiks), *v.t.* [< OFr. < L. pp. < *prae-,* before + *figere,* to fix], to fix to the beginning of a word, etc.; place before. *n.* a syllable or group of syllables joined to the beginning of a word to alter its meaning (e.g., *non*profit, *pre*date). —**pre′fix·al,** *adj.* —**pre·fix′ion,** *n.*

**preg·na·ble** (preg′nə-b'l), *adj.* [< Late OFr. < *prendre,* to take], that can be assailed or captured; vulnerable. —**preg′na·bil′i·ty,** *n.*

**preg·nant** (preg′nənt), *adj.* [< L. *pregnans* < *prae-,* before + base of OL. *gnasci,* to be born], 1. having a fetus or fetuses growing in the uterus; with young or with child. 2. mentally fertile; inventive. 3. productive of results; fruitful. 4. full of meaning, significance, etc. 5. filled (*with*) or rich (*in*); abounding. —**preg′nan·cy** [*pl.* -CIES], *n.* —**preg′nant·ly,** *adv.*

**pre·hen·sile** (pri-hen′sil, -s'l), *adj.* [< Fr. < L. pp. of *prehendere,* to take], adapted for seizing or grasping, especially by wrapping around something, as a monkey's tail. —**pre·hen·sil·i·ty** (prē′hen-sil′ə-ti), *n.*

**pre·his·tor·ic** (prē′his-tôr′ik, -tor′-), *adj.* of the period before recorded history: also **pre′his·tor′i·cal.** —**pre′his·tor′i·cal·ly,** *adv.*

**pre·judge** (prē-juj′), *v.t.* [< Fr. < L.; see PRE- & JUDGE], to judge beforehand, or without all the evidence. —**pre·judg′ment, pre·judge′ment,** *n.*

**prej·u·dice** (prej′oo-dis), *n.* [< OFr. < L. < *prae-,* before + *judicium,* judgment], 1. an opinion formed before the facts are known; preconceived, usually unfavorable, idea. 2. an opinion held in disregard of facts that contradict it; unreasonable bias. 3. hatred or intolerance of other races, creeds, etc. 4. injury resulting as from some judgment or action of another. *v.t.* [-DICED, -DICING], 1. to injure, as by some judgment or action. 2. to cause to have prejudice; bias.

**prej·u·di·cial** (prej′oo-dish′əl), *adj.* causing prejudice, or harm; injurious; detrimental. —**prej′u·di′cial·ly,** *adv.*

**prel·a·cy** (prel′ə-si), *n.* [*pl.* -CIES], 1. the office or rank of a prelate. 2. prelates collectively. 3. church government by prelates: often a hostile term: also **prel′a·tism** (-it-iz'm).

**prel·ate** (prel′it), *n.* [< OFr. < ML. < L. *praelatus,* pp. < *prae-,* before + *ferre,* to bear], a high-ranking ecclesiastic, as a bishop. —**prel′ate·ship′,** *n.*

**prelim.,** preliminary.

**pre·lim·i·nar·y** (pri-lim′ə-ner′i), *adj.* [< *pre-* + L. *liminaris* < *limen,* threshold], leading up to the main action, business, etc.; introductory; preparatory. *n.* [*pl.* -IES], *often in pl.* 1. a preliminary step, procedure, etc. 2. a preliminary examination. —**pre·lim′i·nar′i·ly,** *adv.*

**prel·ude** (prel′ūd, prē′lo͞od), *n.* [< Fr. < ML. < L. < *prae-,* before + *ludere,* to play], 1. a preliminary part; preface; opening. 2. in *music, a*) an introductory section of a suite, fugue, etc. *b*) since the 19th century, any short romantic composition. *v.i. & v.t.* [-UDED, -UDING], 1. to serve as or be a prelude (to). 2. to provide a prelude (for).

**pre·ma·ture** (prē′mə-tyoor′, -choor′, prē′mə-toor′), *adj.* [< L. < *prae-,* before + *maturus,* ripe], happening, done, arriving, or existing before the proper or usual time; too early or too hasty. —**pre′ma·ture′ly,** *adv.* —**pre′ma·ture′ness, pre′ma·tu′ri·ty,** *n.*

**pre·med·i·cal** (prē-med′i-k'l), *adj.* of the studies preparatory to the study of medicine.

**pre·med·i·tate** (prē-med′ə-tāt′), *v.t.* [-TATED, -TAT-

ING], to think out or plan beforehand. *v.i.* to meditate beforehand. **—pre·med'i·tat'ed,** *adj.* **—pre·med'i·tat'ed·ly,** *adv.* **—pre·med'i·ta'tive,** *adj.* **—pre·med'i·ta'tor,** *n.*

**pre·med·i·ta·tion** (prē'med-ə-tā'shən), *n.* a premeditating; specif., in *law,* a degree of forethought sufficient to show intent to commit an act.

**pre·mi·er** (prē'mi-ēr, prem'yēr; *for n., usually* pri-mêr'), *adj.* [Fr. < L. *primarius* < *primus,* first], 1. first in importance; chief; foremost. 2. first in time; earliest. *n.* a chief official; specif., a prime minister. **—pre·mier'ship,** *n.*

**pre·mière** (pri-mêr'; Fr. prə-myâr'), *n.* [Fr., fem. of *premier*], a first performance of a play, etc.

**prem·ise** (prem'is; *for v., usually* pri-mīz'), *n.* [< ML. < L. *praemissus,* pp. < *prae-,* before + *mittere,* to send], 1. a previous statement serving as the basis for an argument. 2. *pl. a*) the part of a deed that states its reason, the property involved, etc. *b*) the property so mentioned. *c*) a piece of real estate: as, keep off the *premises.* 3. either of the two propositions of a syllogism from which the conclusion is drawn. Also **premiss.** *v.t.* [-MISED, -MISING], 1. to state as a premise. 2. to preface, as with explanatory remarks. *v.i.* to make a premise.

**pre·mi·um** (prē'mi-əm), *n.* [*pl.* -UMS], [< L. < *prae-,* before + *emere,* to take], 1. a reward or prize, especially as an added inducement to win, buy, etc. 2. an amount paid in addition to the regular charge, interest, etc. 3. a payment, as for an insurance policy. 4. very high value: as, he put a *premium* on honesty. 5. the amount by which one form of money exceeds another (of the same nominal value), as in exchange value. **—at a premium,** 1. at a value or price higher than normal. 2. very valuable, usually because hard to get.

**pre·mo·lar** (prē-mō'lēr), *adj.* designating or of any of the (bicuspid) teeth situated in front of the molars. *n.* a premolar tooth.

**pre·mo·ni·tion** (prē'mə-nish'ən), *n.* [< OFr. < LL. < L. < *prae-,* before + *monere,* to warn], 1. a forewarning. 2. a foreboding. **—pre·mon·i·to·ry** (pri-mon'ə-tôr'i, -tō'ri), *adj.* **—pre·mon'i·to'ri·ly,** *adv.*

**pre·na·tal** (prē-nā't'l), *adj.* [*pre-* + *natal*], before birth. **—pre·na'tal·ly,** *adv.*

**pre·oc·cu·py** (prē-ok'yoo-pī'), *v.t.* [-PIED, -PYING], [< L. < *prae-,* before + *occupare,* to seize], 1. to occupy the thoughts of; engross; absorb. 2. to occupy or take possession of before someone else or beforehand. **—pre·oc'cu·pan·cy** (-pən-si), *n.* **pre·oc'cu·pa'tion** (-pā'shən), *n.* **—pre·oc'cu·pied',** *adj.*

**pre·or·dain** (prē'ôr-dān'), *v.t.* to ordain or decree beforehand. **—pre'or·di·na'tion** (-d'n-ā'shən), *n.*

**prep** (prep), *adj.* [Colloq.], preparatory.

**prep.,** 1. preparatory. 2. preposition.

**pre·paid** (prē-pād'), pt. and pp. of **prepay.**

**prep·a·ra·tion** (prep'ə-rā'shən), *n.* 1. a preparing. 2. a being prepared; readiness. 3. a preparatory measure. 4. something prepared for a special purpose, as a medicine, cosmetic, etc.

**pre·par·a·to·ry** (pri-par'ə-tôr'i, -tō'ri), *adj.* 1. that prepares or serves to prepare; introductory. 2. undergoing preparation, or instruction, especially for college entrance: as, a *preparatory* student. **—pre·par'a·to'ri·ly,** *adv.*

**preparatory school,** a private school for preparing students to enter college.

**pre·pare** (pri-pâr'), *v.t.* [-PARED, -PARING], [< Fr. < L. < *prae-,* before + *parare,* to get ready], 1. to make ready or suitable. 2. to make receptive; dispose. 3. to equip or furnish; fit out. 4. to put together; compound; construct: as, *prepare* dinner. *v.i.* 1. to make things ready. 2. to make oneself ready. **—pre·par'ed·ly,** *adv.* **—pre·par'er,** *n.*

**pre·par·ed·ness** (pri-pâr'id-nis, -pârd'-), *n.* the state of being prepared; specif., possession of sufficient armed forces, etc. for waging war.

**pre·pay** (prē-pā'), *v.t.* [-PAID, -PAYING], to pay or pay for in advance. **—pre·pay'ment,** *n.*

**pre·pense** (pri-pens'), *adj.* [< OFr. < *pur-,* pro- + *penser,* to think], planned beforehand.

**pre·pon·der·ant** (pri-pon'dēr-ənt), *adj.* that preponderates; greater in amount, weight, power, etc.; predominant. **—pre·pon'der·ance, pre·pon'der·an·cy,** *n.* **—pre·pon'der·ant·ly,** *adv.*

**pre·pon·der·ate** (pri-pon'də-rāt'), *v.i.* [-ATED, -ATING], [< L. pp. < *prae-,* before + *ponderare,* to weigh < *pondus,* a weight], 1. to weigh more than something else. 2. to surpass in amount, power, influence, etc.; predominate. **—pre·pon'der·a'tion,** *n.* **—pre·pon'der·at'ing·ly,** *adv.*

**prep·o·si·tion** (prep'ə-zish'ən), *n.* [< L. *praepositus* < *prae-,* before + pp. of *ponere,* to place], 1. a relation word, as *in, by, for, with, to,* etc., that connects a noun, pronoun, or noun phrase (called its *object*) to another element, as to a verb (e.g., he went *to* the store), to a noun (e.g., the sound *of* rain), or to an adjective (e.g., old *in* years). 2. any construction of similar function (e.g., *in back of,* equivalent to *behind*). **—prep'o·si'tion·al,** *adj.* **—prep'o·si'tion·al·ly,** *adv.*

**prepositional phrase,** a preposition and its object.

**pre·pos·sess** (prē'pə-zes'), *v.t.* 1. [Rare], to take possession of beforehand. 2. to preoccupy to the exclusion of later thoughts, feelings, etc. 3. to prejudice. 4. to impress favorably beforehand or at once. **—pre'pos·ses'sion,** *n.*

**pre·pos·sess·ing** (prē'pə-zes'iŋ), *adj.* that prepossesses, or impresses favorably; pleasing. **—pre'pos·sess'ing·ly,** *adv.* **—pre'pos·sess'ing·ness,** *n.*

**pre·pos·ter·ous** (pri-pos'tēr-əs), *adj.* [< L. < *prae-,* before + *posterus,* coming after], contrary to nature, reason, etc.; absurd; ridiculous. **—pre·pos'ter·ous·ly,** *adv.* **—pre·pos'ter·ous·ness,** *n.*

**pre·puce** (prē'pūs), *n.* [< Fr. < L. *praeputium*], the foreskin. **—pre·pu·tial** (pri-pū'shəl), *adj.*

**Pre-Raph·a·el·ite** (prē-raf'i-ə-līt', -raf'ə-, -rā'fi-ə-), *n.* 1. a member of a society of artists (*the Pre-Raphaelite Brotherhood*) formed in England in 1848 to revive the qualities of Italian art before the time of Raphael. 2. any artist with similar aims. *adj.* of or like the Pre-Raphaelites.

**pre·req·ui·site** (prē-rek'wə-zit), *adj.* required beforehand, especially as a necessary condition for something following. *n.* something prerequisite.

**pre·rog·a·tive** (pri-rog'ə-tiv), *n.* [< OFr. < L. *praerogativa,* called upon to vote first; ult. < *prae-,* before + *rogare,* to ask], 1. a prior or exclusive privilege, especially one peculiar to a rank, class, etc. 2. priority or precedence. 3. a superior advantage. *adj.* of or having a prerogative.

**Pres.,** 1. Presbyterian. 2. President.

**pres.,** 1. present. 2. presidency.

**pres·age** (pres'ij; *for v.,* pri-sāj'), *n.* [< L. < *prae-,* before + *sagire,* to perceive], 1. a sign or warning of a future event; portent. 2. a foreboding. 3. meaning; import: as, of ominous *presage.* *v.t.* [-AGED, -AGING], 1. to give presage of; portend. 2. to have a foreboding of. 3. to predict. *v.i.* 1. to have a foreboding. 2. to make a prediction. **—pre·sag'er,** *n.* **—pre·sag'ing·ly,** *adv.*

**pres·by·ter** (prez'bi-tēr, pres'-), *n.* [LL.; see PRIEST], 1. in the early Christian church and in the Presbyterian Church, an elder. 2. in the Episcopal Church, a priest or minister. **—pres'by·te'ri·al** (-bə-têr'i-əl), **pres·byt'er·al** (-bit'ēr-əl), *adj.*

**Pres·by·te·ri·an** (prez'bə-têr'i-ən, pres'-), *adj.* 1. [p-], having to do with church government by presbyters. 2. designating or of a church of a Calvinistic Protestant denomination governed by presbyters, or elders. *n.* a member of a Presbyterian church. **—Pres'by·te'ri·an·ism,** *n.*

**pres·by·ter·y** (prez'bi-ter'i, pres'-), *n.* [*pl.* -IES], 1. in Presbyterian churches, an ecclesiastical court made up of all the ministers and certain presbyters from each parish in a given district. 2. the district of such a court. 3. the part of a church reserved for the officiating clergy.

**pre·school** (prē'sko͞ol'), *adj.* designating, of, or for a child between infancy and school age.

**pre·sci·ence** (prē'shi-əns, presh'i-), *n.* [< OFr. < L.; ult. < *prae-,* before + *scire,* to know], knowledge of things before they happen; foresight. **—pre'sci·ent,** *adj.* **—pre'sci·ent·ly,** *adv.*

**pre·scribe** (pri-skrib'), *v.t.* [-SCRIBED, -SCRIBING], [< L. < *prae-,* before + *scribere,* to write], 1. to set down as a rule or direction; order. 2. to order or advise as a medicine or treatment: said of physicians, etc. *v.i.* 1. to set down rules, directions, etc. 2. to give medical advice or prescriptions. **—pre·scrib'er,** *n.*

**pre·script** (pri-skript'; *also, and for n. always,* prē'skript), *adj.* prescribed. *n.* something prescribed; order; direction.

**pre·scrip·tion** (pri-skrip'shən), *n.* 1. a prescribing. 2. something prescribed; order. 3. a doctor's written direction for the preparation and use of a medicine. 4. a medicine so prescribed. **—pre·scrip'tive,** *adj.* **—pre·scrip'tive·ly,** *adv.*

**pres·ence** (prez''ns), *n.* 1. the fact or state of being present. 2. immediate surroundings: as, I was admitted to his *presence.* 3. attendance; company. 4. one who is present, especially a royal person. 5. one's bearing or appearance: as, he has a poor *presence.* 6. pleasing deportment; dignity. 7. a spirit or ghost felt to be present.

**presence of mind,** ability to think clearly and act quickly and intelligently in an emergency.

**pres·ent** (prez''nt; *for v.*, pri-zent'), ***adj.*** [OFr. < L. *praesens*, ppr. < *prae-*, before + *esse*, to be], 1. being at the specified place; in attendance. 2. existing or happening now. 3. now being discussed, considered, etc.: as, the *present* writer. 4. in *grammar*, designating or of a tense or verb form expressing action as now taking place or state as now existing (e.g., he *goes*), action that is habitual (e.g., he *speaks* softly), or action that is always true (e.g., two and two *is* four). ***n.*** 1. the present time. 2. the present occasion. 3. the present tense or a verb in it. 4. a gift. ***v.t.*** [< OFr. < L. *praesentare* < *praesens;* see the *adj.*], 1. to introduce (a person), especially formally. 2. to offer to view or notice; exhibit; show. 3. to offer for consideration. 4. to make a gift of (or to). 5. to point or aim, as a weapon. **—by these presents,** in *law*, by this document. **—present arms,** 1. to hold a rifle vertically in front of the body: a position of salute. 2. *a*) this position. *b*) the command to assume it. **—pre·sent'er, *n.***

**pre·sent·a·ble** (pri-zen'tə-b'l), ***adj.*** 1. suitable for presentation. 2. suitably attired, groomed, etc. for meeting people. **—pre·sent'a·bil'i·ty, pre·sent'a·ble·ness, *n.* —pre·sent'a·bly, *adv.***

**pres·en·ta·tion** (prez''n-tā'shən, prē'zen-), ***n.*** 1. a presenting or being presented. 2. something presented, as a theatrical performance, a gift, etc. **—pres'en·ta'tion·al, *adj.* —pre·sent'a·tive, *adj.***

**pres·ent-day** (prez''nt-dā'), ***adj.*** of the present time.

**pre·sen·ti·ment** (pri-zen'tə-mənt), ***n.*** [< L.; see PRE- & SENTIMENT], a feeling that something, especially of an unfortunate nature, is about to take place; foreboding. **—pre·sen'ti·men'tal, *adj.***

**pres·ent·ly** (prez''nt-li), ***adv.*** 1. in a little while; soon. 2. at present; now. 3. [Archaic or Dial.], at once; instantly.

**pre·sent·ment** (pri-zent'mənt), ***n.*** 1. presentation. 2. an exhibition; thing presented to view.

**present participle,** in *grammar*, a participle of present meaning (e.g., *running* water).

**present perfect,** in *grammar*, 1. expressing action or state as completed at some indefinite time in the past. 2. the present perfect tense, formed with the present tense of *have* and a past participle (e.g., he *has gone*).

**pre·serv·a·tive** (pri-zũr'və-tiv), ***adj.*** preserving. ***n.*** anything that preserves; esp., a substance added to food to keep it from spoiling.

**pre·serve** (pri-zũrv'), ***v.t.*** [-SERVED, -SERVING], [< LL. < L. *prae-*, before + *servare*, to keep], 1. to keep from harm, damage, etc.; protect; save. 2. to keep from spoiling or rotting. 3. to prepare (food), as by canning, salting, etc., for future use. 4. to carry on; maintain. ***v.i.*** to preserve fruit, etc. ***n.*** 1. *usually pl.* fruit preserved whole by cooking with sugar. 2. a place where game, fish, etc. are maintained for hunting and fishing. **—pre·serv'a·ble, *adj.* —pres·er·va·tion** (prez'ẽr-vā'shən), ***n.*** **—pre·serv'er, *n.***

**pre-shrunk** (prē'shruŋk'), ***adj.*** shrunk by a special process in manufacture so as to minimize shrinkage in laundering or dry cleaning.

**pre·side** (pri-zīd'), ***v.i.*** [-SIDED, -SIDING], [< Fr. < L. < *prae-*, before + *sedere*, to sit], 1. to be in charge of a meeting; act as chairman. 2. to have control or authority. **—pre·sid'er, *n.***

**pres·i·den·cy** (prez'i-dən-si), ***n.*** [*pl.* -CIES], 1. the office, function, or term of president. 2. [often P-], the office of President of the U.S.

**pres·i·dent** (prez'i-dənt), ***n.*** [< L. ppr. of *praesidere;* see PRESIDE], 1. the highest officer of a company, society, university, club, etc. 2. [often P-], the chief executive, or sometimes formal head, of a republic. **—pres'i·den'tial** (-den'shəl), ***adj.*** **—pres'i·den'tial·ly, *adv.* —pres'i·dent·ship', *n.***

**pres·i·dent-e·lect** (prez'i-dənt-i-lekt'), ***n.*** an elected president who has not yet taken office.

**pre·sid·i·o** (pri-sid'i-ō'), ***n.*** [*pl.* -OS], [Sp. < L. *praesidium*], military post; fort; garrison. **—pre·sid'i·al, pre·sid'i·ar'y, *adj.***

**pre·sid·i·um** (pri-sid'i-əm), ***n.*** [L. *praesidium*, a presiding over], in the Soviet Union, 1. any of a number of permanent administrative committees. 2. [P-], the permanent administrative committee of the Supreme Soviet.

**pre·sig·ni·fy** (prē-sig'nə-fī'), ***v.t.*** [-FIED, -FYING], to signify beforehand; foreshadow.

**press** (pres), ***v.t.*** [< OFr. < L. *pressare*, freq. of *premere*, to press], 1. to act on with steady force or weight; push steadily against; squeeze. 2. to squeeze (juice, etc.) from (olives, etc.); express. 3. *a*) to squeeze so as to make smooth, compact, etc.; compress. *b*) to iron, as clothes. 4. to embrace closely. 5. to force; compel; constrain. 6. to urge persistently; entreat; importune. 7. to try to force: as, she *pressed* the gift on us. 8. to lay stress on; emphasize. 9. to distress; embarrass: as, they were *pressed* with want. 10. to urge on; drive on. 11. [Archaic], to crowd; throng. 12. [Obs.], to oppress. ***v.i.*** to exert pressure; specif., *a*) to weigh down; bear heavily. *b*) to go forward with determined effort. *c*) to force one's way. *d*) to crowd; throng. *e*) to be urgent or insistent; try too hard. ***n.*** 1. a pressing or being pressed; pressure, urgency, etc. 2. a crowd; throng. 3. any instrument or machine by which something is crushed, stamped, smoothed, etc. by pressure. 4. *a*) a printing press. *b*) a printing establishment. *c*) the art or business of printing. *d*) newspapers, magazines, etc., or the persons who write for them. *e*) publicity, criticism, etc., as in newspapers. 5. an upright closet for storing clothes, etc. **—go to press,** to start to be printed. **—press'er, *n.***

**press** (pres), ***v.t.*** [altered (after prec. *press*) < obs. *prest*, to lend < OFr. < L. *prae-*, before + *stare*, to stand], 1. to force into service, especially military or naval service. 2. to use in a way different from the ordinary.

**press agent,** one whose work is to get publicity for a person, organization, etc.

**press box,** a place reserved for reporters at sports events, etc.

**press conference,** a collective interview granted to journalists, as by a celebrity or personage.

**press gang,** [for *prest gang;* see PRESS (to force into service)], a group of men who round up other men and force them into naval or military service.

**press·ing** (pres'iŋ), ***adj.*** calling for immediate attention; urgent. **—press'ing·ly, *adv.***

**press·man** (pres'mən), ***n.*** [*pl.* -MEN], an operator of a printing press.

**press of sail** (or **canvas**), in *nautical usage*, the maximum amount of sail that a ship can safely carry under given conditions.

**pres·sure** (presh'ẽr), ***n.*** [OFr. < L. < *pressus*, pp. of *premere*, to press], 1. a pressing or being pressed; compression; squeezing. 2. a state of distress; oppression. 3. a compelling influence; constraining force: as, social *pressure.* 4. urgent demands; urgency. 5. electromotive force. 6. in *physics*, force exerted against an opposing body, expressed in weight per unit of area. ***v.t.*** [-SURED, -SURING], [Colloq.], to exert pressure, or constraint, on.

**pressure cooker,** an airtight metal container for quick cooking by means of steam under pressure.

**pressure group,** any group exerting pressure upon legislators and the public through lobbies, propaganda, etc., as in order to affect legislation.

**pressure point,** any of a number of points on the body where pressure on an artery will check bleeding from a distal injured part.

**pres·sur·ize** (presh'ẽr-īz'), ***v.t.*** [-IZED, -IZING], to keep nearly normal atmospheric pressure inside of (an airplane, etc.), as at high altitudes.

**press·work** (pres'wũrk'), ***n.*** 1. the operation of a printing press. 2. work done by a printing press.

**pres·ti·dig·i·ta·tion** (pres'tə-dij'i-tā'shən), ***n.*** [Fr. < It. *presto*, quick + L. *digitus*, a finger], the doing of tricks by quick, skillful use of the hands; sleight of hand. **—pres'ti·dig'i·ta'tor, *n.***

**pres·tige** (pres-tēzh', pres'tij), ***n.*** [Fr. < L. *praestigium*, delusion < *praestingere*, to blindfold], 1. the power to command esteem. 2. reputation based on high achievement, character, etc.; renown.

**pres·ti·gious** (pres-tij'əs), ***adj.*** having or imparting prestige or distinction.

**pres·tis·si·mo** (pres-tis'ə-mō'), ***adv. & adj.*** [It., superl. of *presto*, quick], in *music*, very fast.

**pres·to** (pres'tō), ***adv. & adj.*** [It., quick < LL. *praestus*, ready], 1. fast. 2. in *music*, in fast tempo. ***n.*** a presto musical passage or movement.

**pre·sume** (pri-zōōm', -zūm'), ***v.t.*** [-SUMED, -SUMING], [< OFr. < L. < *prae-*, before + *sumere*, to take], 1. to take upon oneself without permission or authority; venture. 2. to take for granted, lacking proof; suppose. 3. to constitute reasonable evidence for supposing: as, a signed invoice *presumes* receipt of goods. ***v.i.*** 1. to act presumptuously; take liberties. 2. to rely too much (*on* or *upon*), as in taking liberties. **—pre·sum'a·ble, *adj.* —pre·sum'a·bly, *adv.* —pre·sum'ed·ly, *adv.* —pre·sum'er, *n.***

**pre·sump·tion** (pri-zump'shən), ***n.*** 1. a presuming; specif., *a*) an overstepping of proper bounds;

effrontery. *b*) a taking of something for granted. 2. the thing presumed; supposition. 3. ground for presuming. 4. in *law*, the inference that a fact exists, based on other known facts.

**pre·sump·tive** (pri-zump′tiv), **adj.** 1. giving reasonable ground for belief: as, *presumptive* evidence. 2. based on probability; presumed: as, an heir *presumptive*. —**pre·sump′tive·ly, adv.**

**pre·sump·tu·ous** (pri-zump′choo-əs), **adj.** too bold or forward; showing overconfidence, effrontery, etc.; taking liberties. —**pre·sump′tu·ous·ly, adv.** —**pre·sump′tu·ous·ness, n.**

**pre·sup·pose** (prē′sə-pōz′), **v.t.** [-POSED, -POSING], 1. to suppose or assume beforehand; take for granted. 2. to require or imply as a preceding condition. —**pre′sup·po·si′tion** (-sup-ə-zish′ən), **n.**

**pret.,** preterit.

**pre·tend** (pri-tend′), **v.t.** [< OFr. < L. < *prae-*, before + *tendere*, to reach], 1. to claim; profess: as, to *pretend* ignorance of the law. 2. to claim or profess falsely; feign: as, he *pretended* illness. 3. to suppose in play; make believe: as, she *pretended* to be a queen. **v.i.** 1. to lay claim (with *to*). 2. to make believe in play or deception. —**pre·tend′ed, adj.** —**pre·tend′ing·ly, adv.**

**pre·tend·er** (pri-ten′dẽr), **n.** 1. one who pretends. 2. a claimant to a throne.

**pre·tense** (pri-tens′, prē′tens), **n.** [< Anglo-Fr. < ML. < *praetensus*, alleged < L. pp. of *praetendere;* see PRETEND], 1. a claim; pretension: as, he made no *pretense* to being infallible. 2. a false claim or profession: as, a *pretense* of friendship. 3. a false show of something. 4. something said or done for show. 5. a pretending, as at a play; make-believe. 6. a false reason; pretext. 7. pretentiousness. Also, Brit. spelling, **pretence.**

**pre·ten·sion** (pri-ten′shən), **n.** [< ML.; see PRETENSE], 1. a pretext or allegation. 2. a claim, as to a right, title, distinction, etc. 3. assertion of a claim. 4. pretentiousness.

**pre·ten·tious** (pri-ten′shəs), **adj.** [< Fr. < L. pp. of *praetendere;* see PRETEND], 1. making claims, explicit or implicit, to some distinction, importance, dignity, etc. 2. showy; ostentatious. —**pre·ten′tious·ly, adv.** —**pre·ten′tious·ness, n.**

**pret·er·it, pret·er·ite** (pret′ẽr-it), **adj.** [< OFr. < L. *praeteritus*, gone by < *praeter-*, beyond + *ire*, to go], in *grammar*, expressing past action or state. **n.** the past tense. 2. a verb in it.

**pre·ter·mit** (prē′tẽr-mit′), **v.t.** [-MITTED, -MITTING], [< L. < *praeter-*, beyond + *mittere*, to send], to neglect, omit, or overlook.

**pre·ter·nat·u·ral** (prē′tẽr-nach′ẽr-əl), **adj.** [< ML. < L. *praeter-*, beyond + *naturalis*, natural], 1. differing from or beyond what is natural; out of the ordinary. 2. supernatural. —**pre′ter·nat′u·ral·ism, n.** —**pre′ter·nat′u·ral·ly, adv.**

**pre·text** (prē′tekst), **n.** [< Fr. < L. pp. of *praetexere*, to pretend < *prae-*, before + *texere*, to weave], a false reason or motive put forth to hide the real one; excuse.

**pre·tor** (prē′tẽr, -tôr), **n.** a praetor. —**pre·to′ri·an** (-tôr′i-ən, -tō′ri-), **adj.**

**Pre·to·ri·a** (pri-tôr′i-ə, -tō′ri-ə), **n.** the capital of Transvaal and seat of government of the Union of South Africa, in S Transvaal: pop., 283,000.

**pret·ti·fy** (prit′i-fī′), **v.t.** [-FIED, -FYING], to make pretty, especially in a finical way.

**pret·ty** (prit′i, pūr′ti), **adj.** [-TIER, -TIEST], [< AS. *prættig*, crafty < *prætt*, a trick], 1. pleasing; attractive in a dainty, graceful way. 2. fine; good; nice: often used ironically. 3. foppish. 4. [Colloq.], considerable; rather large. **adv.** somewhat; to some degree. **n.** [*pl.* -TIES], a pretty person or thing. —**sitting pretty,** [Slang], in a favorable position. —**pret′ti·ly, adv.** —**pret′ti·ness, n.** —**pret′ty·ish, adj.**

**pret·zel** (pret′s'l), **n.** [< G. *brezel* < OHG.; prob. ult. < L. *brachium*, an arm; basic sense "bracelet"], a hard, brittle biscuit usually in the form of a loose knot, sprinkled with salt.

**pre·vail** (pri-vāl′), **v.i.** [< L. < *prae-*, before + *valere*, to be strong], 1. to gain the advantage or mastery; be victorious (*over* or *against*). 2. to be effective; succeed. 3. to be or become stronger or more widespread; predominate. 4. to exist widely; be prevalent. —**prevail on** (or **upon, with**), to persuade; induce. —**pre·vail′er, n.**

**pre·vail·ing** (pri-vāl′iŋ), **adj.** 1. being superior in strength or influence. 2. predominant. 3. widely existing; prevalent. —**pre·vail′ing·ly, adv.**

**prev·a·lent** (prev′ə-lənt), **adj.** [see PREVAIL], 1. [Rare], predominant. 2. widely existing; generally practiced, occurring, or accepted. —**prev′a·lence, n.** —**prev′a·lent·ly, adv.**

**pre·var·i·cate** (pri-var′ə-kāt′), **v.i.** [-CATED, -CATING], [< L. pp. of *praevaricari*, lit., to walk crookedly < *prae-*, before + *varicare*, to straddle; ult. < *varus*, bent], 1. to turn aside from or evade the truth; equivocate. 2. loosely, to lie. —**pre·var′i·ca′tion, n.** —**pre·var′i·ca′tor, n.**

**pre·vent** (pri-vent′), **v.t.** [< L. *praeventus*, pp. < *prae-*, before + *venire*, to come], 1. to stop or keep from doing something. 2. to keep from happening; make impossible by prior action; hinder. —**pre·vent′a·ble, pre·vent′i·ble, adj.** —**pre·vent′er, n.**

**pre·ven·tion** (pri-ven′shən), **n.** 1. a preventing. 2. a means of preventing; hindrance.

**pre·ven·tive** (pri-ven′tiv), **adj.** preventing or serving to prevent; specif., in *medicine*, preventing disease. **n.** anything that prevents; specif., in *medicine*, anything that prevents disease. Also **pre·ven′ta·tive** (-tə-tiv). —**pre·ven′tive·ly, adv.** —**pre·ven′tive·ness, n.**

**pre·view** (prē-vū′; *also, and for* n. *always*, prē′vū′), **v.t.** to view or show beforehand. **n.** 1. a previous view or survey. 2. *a*) a private showing, as of a motion picture, before exhibition to the public. *b*) a showing of scenes from a motion picture to advertise its coming appearance.

**pre·vi·ous** (prē′vi-əs, prēv′yəs), **adj.** [< L. < *prae-*, before + *via*, a way], 1. occurring before in time or order; preceding; prior. 2. [Colloq.], premature. —**previous to,** before. —**pre′vi·ous·ly, adv.** —**pre′vi·ous·ness, n.**

**previous question,** the question whether a matter under consideration by a parliamentary body should be voted on immediately.

**pre·vi·sion** (prē-vizh′ən), **n.** [< Fr. < ML. < L. *praevisus*, pp. < *prae-*, before + *videre*, to see], 1. foresight; knowledge of the future. 2. a prognostication. —**pre·vi′sion·al, adj.**

**pre·vue** (prē′vū′), **n.** a preview (sense 2*b*).

**pre·war** (prē′wôr′), **adj.** before the war.

**prex·y** (prek′si), **n.** [*pl.* -IES], [Slang], a president, especially of a college or university.

**prey** (prā), **n.** [OFr. *preie* < L. *praeda*], 1. originally, plunder; booty. 2. an animal hunted for food by another animal. 3. a person or thing that falls victim to someone or something. 4. the act of seizing other animals for food: as, a bird of *prey*. **v.i.** 1. to plunder; rob. 2. to hunt other animals for food. 3. to engage in swindling, blackmail, etc. 4. to have a wearing or destructive influence. Usually used with *on* or *upon.*

**Pri·am** (prī′əm), **n.** in *Gr. legend*, the last king of Troy, who reigned during the Trojan War, father of Hector and Paris.

**price** (prīs), **n.** [< OFr. < L. *pretium*], 1. the amount of money, etc. asked or given for something; cost. 2. value; worth. 3. a reward for the capture or death of a person. 4. the cost, as in life, labor, etc., of obtaining some benefit. **v.t.** [PRICED, PRICING], 1. to fix the price of. 2. [Colloq.], to ask or find out the price of. —**at any price,** no matter what the cost. —**beyond** (or **without**) **price,** priceless; invaluable. —**priced, adj.** —**pric′er, n.**

**price control,** the establishment of ceiling prices on basic commodities by a government to prevent or combat inflation.

**price·less** (prīs′lis), **adj.** 1. of too great worth to be measured by price; invaluable. 2. [Colloq.], very amusing or absurd. —**price′less·ness, n.**

**prick** (prik), **n.** [AS. *prica*, a dot], 1. a very small puncture or dot made by a sharp point. 2. [Archaic], a pointed object, as a thorn. 3. a pricking. 4. a sharp pain caused as by being pricked. **v.t.** 1. to pierce slightly with a sharp point. 2. to make (a hole) with a sharp point. 3. to pain sharply or sting: as, *pricked* by remorse. 4. to mark by dots or points. 5. [Archaic], to spur or urge on; goad. **v.i.** 1. to give or feel a slight piercing pain. 2. to have a prickly sensation; tingle. 3. [Archaic], to spur a horse on. —**prick up,** to rise erect or stick up. —**prick up one's** (or **its**) **ears,** 1. to raise the ears with the points upward. 2. to listen closely. —**prick′er, n.** —**prick′ing, n.**

**prick·le** (prik′'l), **n.** [AS. *pricel* < *prica*, prick], 1. a small, sharply pointed growth; spine; thorn. 2. a prickly sensation; tingling. **v.t.** [-LED, -LING], 1. to prick as with a thorn. 2. to cause to feel a tingling sensation. **v.i.** to tingle.

**prick·ly** (prik′li), **adj.** [-LIER, -LIEST], 1. full of prickles, or sharp points. 2. stinging; tingling. —**prick′li·ness, n.**

**prickly heat,** an itching skin eruption caused by inflammation of the sweat glands.
**prickly pear,** 1. the pear-shaped fruit of a species of flat-stemmed cactus. 2. this cactus.
**pride** (prīd), *n.* [AS. *pryte* < *prut*, proud], 1. an overhigh opinion of oneself; exaggerated self-esteem. 2. haughtiness; arrogance. 3. a sense of one's own dignity; self-respect. 4. delight or satisfaction in one's achievements, children, etc. 5. a person or thing in which pride is taken. 6. the best of a class, group, etc.; pick. 7. the best part; prime: as, in the *pride* of manhood. *v.t.* [PRIDED, PRIDING], [Rare], to make proud. **—pride oneself on,** to be proud of. **—pride'ful,** *adj.* **—pride'ful·ly,** *adv.* **—pride'ful·ness,** *n.* **—pride'less,** *adj.*
**pri·er** (prī'ẽr), *n.* one who pries: also sp. **pryer.**
**priest** (prēst), *n.* [AS. *preost* < LL. *presbyter*, an elder < Gr. compar. of *presbys*, old], 1. in hierarchical Christian churches, a clergyman authorized to administer the sacraments and pronounce absolution. 2. any clergyman. 3. a minister of any religion. 4. a person whose function is to make sacrificial offerings and perform other religious rites. **—priest'hood,** *n.* **—priest'like',** *adj.*
**priest·craft** (prēst'kraft', -kräft'), *n.* the craft, policies, methods, etc. of priests.
**priest·ess** (prēs'tis), *n.* a girl or woman priest, as of a pagan religion.
**Priest·ley, Joseph** (prēst'li), 1733–1804; English theologian and chemist; discoverer of oxygen.
**priest·ly** (prēst'li), *adj.* [-LIER, -LIEST], of, like, or suitable for a priest. **—priest'li·ness,** *n.*
**priest-rid·den** (prēst'rid''n), *adj.* dominated or tyrannized by priests.
**prig** (prig), *n.* [< 16th-c. cant], one who annoyingly affects great preciseness or propriety in matters of learning or morals. **—prig'gish,** *adj.* **—prig'gish·ly,** *adv.* **—prig'gish·ness,** *n.*
**prig·ger·y** (prig'ẽr-i), *n.* the character or behavior of a prig: also **prig'gism.**
**prim** (prim), *adj.* [PRIMMER, PRIMMEST], [prob. < OFr. *prim*, prime, sharp, neat < L. *primus*, first], stiffly formal, precise, or correct; proper. *v.t.* [PRIMMED, PRIMMING], to get a prim look on (one's face or mouth). **—prim'ly,** *adv.* **—prim'ness,** *n.*
**prim.,** 1. primary. 2. primitive.
**pri·ma·cy** (prī'mə-si), *n.* [*pl.* -CIES], [< OFr. < ML. < LL. *primas;* see PRIMATE], 1. the state of being first in time, rank, importance, etc.; supremacy. 2. the rank or duties of a primate. 3. in the *R.C.Church*, the supreme authority of the Pope.
**pri·ma don·na** (prē'mə don'ə), [*pl.* PRIMA DONNAS], [It., lit., first lady], 1. the principal woman singer, as in an opera. 2. [Colloq.], a temperamental or vain person; esp., such a woman.
**pri·ma fa·ci·e** (prī'mə fā'shi-ē', fā'shi), [L.], at first view: used adjectivally (**prima-facie**) of evidence adequate to establish a fact unless refuted.
**pri·mal** (prī'm'l), *adj.* [< ML. < L. *primus*, first], 1. first in time; original; primitive. 2. first in importance; chief; primary. **—pri'mal·ly,** *adv.*
**pri·ma·ri·ly** (prī'mer'ə-li, prī'mẽr-; *esp. when emphatic* prī-mâr'-), *adv.* 1. at first; originally. 2. in the first place; principally.
**pri·ma·ry** (prī'mer'i, -mẽr-i), *adj.* [< L. *primarius* <*primus*, first], 1. first in time or order of development; primitive; original. 2. *a*) from which others are derived; fundamental. *b*) designating the colors regarded as basic, from which all others may be derived, as red, green, and blue in color photography or red, yellow, and blue in painting: cf. *color.* 3. first in importance; chief: as, a *primary* policy. 4. in *electricity*, designating or of an inducing current, circuit, or coil in an induction coil, etc. 5. in *zoology*, of the large feathers on the end joint of a bird's wing. *n.* [*pl.* -RIES], 1. something first in order, quality, etc. 2. in the U.S., a local meeting of voters of a given political party to select delegates to a nominating convention. 3. *often in pl.* a direct primary election. 4. one of the primary colors. 5. in *electricity*, a primary coil. 6. in *zoology*, a primary feather. **—pri'ma·ri·ness,** *n.*
**primary accent,** 1. the heaviest accent in pronouncing a word. 2. the mark for this (').
**primary election,** see **direct primary election.**
**primary school,** a school providing elementary instruction.
**pri·mate** (prī'mit, -māt), *n.* [< OFr. < LL. *primas*, chief < L. *primus*, first], 1. an archbishop, or the highest-ranking bishop in a province, etc. 2. any member of the most highly developed order of animals, composed of man, the apes, etc. **—pri'mate·ship',** *n.* **—pri·ma·tial** (prī-mā'shəl), *adj.*
**prime** (prīm), *adj.* [OFr. < L. *primus*, first], 1. first in time; original; primitive. 2. first in rank; chief: as, *prime* minister. 3. first in importance; principal: as, a *prime* advantage. 4. first in quality; first-rate: as, *prime* beef. 5. from which others are derived; fundamental. 6. in *mathematics*, *a*) that can be divided by no other whole number than itself or 1, as 3, 5, or 7. *b*) that cannot be divided by the same whole number except 1: as, 9 and 16 are *prime* to one another. *n.* 1. the first daylight canonical hour. 2. the first or earliest part; dawn, springtime, youth, etc. 3. the best or most vigorous period or stage of a person or thing. 4. the best part; pick. 5. any of a number of equal parts, usually sixty, into which a unit, as a degree, is divided. 6. the mark indicating this ('): it is also used to distinguish a letter, etc. from another of the same kind, as *A'*. 7. in *arithmetic*, a prime number. 8. in *music*, unison. *v.t.* [PRIMED, PRIMING], 1. to make ready; prepare. 2. to prepare (a gun) for firing, as by providing a primer. 3. to get (a pump) into operation by pouring water into it. 4. to undercoat, size, etc. (a surface) for painting. 5. to provide (a person) beforehand with information, answers, etc. *v.i.* to prime a gun, pump, surface, etc. **—prime'ness,** *n.*
**prime meridian,** the meridian from which longitude is measured both east and west; 0°: it passes through Greenwich, England.
**prime minister,** in some countries, the chief executive of the government and head of the cabinet.
**prim·er** (prim'ẽr), *n.* [< ML. < L. *primus*, first], 1. a book for teaching children how to spell or read. 2. a textbook that gives the first principles of any subject. 3. in *printing*, either of two type sizes: *a*) **great primer,** or 18 point. *b*) **long primer,** or 10 point.
**prim·er** (prīm'ẽr), *n.* 1. a person or thing that primes. 2. a small cap, tube, etc. containing explosive, used to fire the main charge of a gun.
**pri·me·val** (prī-mē'v'l), *adj.* [< L. *primaevus* < *primus*, first + *aevum*, an age], of the first age or ages; primitive: as, *primeval* forests. **—pri·me'val·ly,** *adv.* **—pri·me'val·ness,** *n.*
**prim·ing** (prīm'iŋ), *n.* 1. the explosive used to fire a charge, as in a gun. 2. an undercoat or first coat of paint, sizing, etc.
**prim·i·tive** (prim'ə-tiv), *adj.* [< L. *primitivus* < *primus*, first], 1. of or existing in the earliest time or ages; original. 2. characteristic of the earliest ages; crude; simple. 3. underived; primary. *n.* 1. a primitive person or thing. 2. an artist or a work of art belonging to an early period. **—prim'i·tive·ly,** *adv.* **—prim'i·tive·ness,** *n.*
**prim·i·tiv·ism** (prim'ə-tiv-iz'm), *n.* belief in or practice of primitive ways, living, etc.
**pri·mo·gen·i·tor** (prī'mə-jen'i-tẽr), *n.* [ML. < L. *primus*, first + *genitor*, a father], 1. an ancestor; forefather. 2. the earliest ancestor of a family, race, etc.
**pri·mo·gen·i·ture** (prī'mə-jen'i-chẽr), *n.* [< ML. < L. *primus*, first + *genitura*, a begetting <*gignere*, to beget], 1. the condition or fact of being the first-born of the same parents. 2. in *law*, the right of inheritance of the eldest son.
**pri·mor·di·al** (prī-môr'di-əl), *adj.* [< LL. < L. *primordium*, the beginning <*primus*, first + *ordiri*, to begin], 1. existing at or from the beginning; primitive. 2. fundamental; original. **—pri·mor'di·al·ism,** *n.* **—pri·mor'di·al·ly,** *adv.*
**primp** (primp), *v.t. & v.i.* [dial. extension of *prim*], to dress overcarefully or showily; prink.
**prim·rose** (prim'rōz'), *n.* [alt. (after *rose*) < OFr. *primerole* < ML. < L. *primus*, first], 1. any of a number of related plants having variously colored, tubelike flowers. 2. the flower of any of these plants. 3. the light yellow of some primroses. *adj.* 1. of the primrose. 2. light-yellow.
**prin.,** 1. principal. 2. principle.
**prince** (prins), *n.* [OFr. < L. *princeps*, chief < *primus*, first + *capere*, to take], 1. a monarch; esp., a king. 2. a ruler whose rank is below that of a king. 3. a nonreigning male member of a royal family. 4. in Great Britain, a son or grandson of the sovereign. 5. a pre-eminent person in any class or group: as, a *merchant* prince. **—prince'dom,** *n.* **—prince'like',** *adj.* **—prince'ship,** *n.*
**Prince Albert,** a long, double-breasted frock coat.
**prince consort,** the husband of a queen or empress who reigns in her own right.
**Prince Edward Island,** an island province of Canada, in the Gulf of St. Lawrence: pop., 98,000; capital, Charlottetown.
**prince·ling** (prins'liŋ), *n.* a young, small, or subordinate prince: also **prince'kin, prince'let.**
**prince·ly** (prins'li), *adj.* [-LIER, -LIEST], 1. of a prince; royal. 2. characteristic or worthy of a prince; magnificent; generous. **—prince'li·ness,** *n.*

**Prince of Darkness,** the Devil; Satan.
**Prince of Peace,** Jesus Christ.
**Prince of Wales,** the oldest son and heir apparent of a British king or queen.
**prin·cess** (prin′sis, -ses), ***n.*** 1. originally, a woman sovereign. 2. a nonreigning female member of a royal family. 3. in Great Britain, a daughter or granddaughter of the sovereign. 4. the wife of a prince. —**prin′cess·ly,** ***adj.***
**prin·cesse, prin·cess** (prin-ses′, prin′sis), ***adj.*** [Fr., a princess], of or designating a woman's one-piece, closefitting, gored dress, etc.
**prin·ci·pal** (prin′sə-p'l), ***adj.*** [OFr. < L. *principalis* < *princeps;* see PRINCE], first in rank, authority, importance, etc. ***n.*** 1. a principal person or thing; specif., *a*) a chief; head. *b*) a governing officer, as of a school. *c*) a main actor or performer. 2. one of the main end rafters of a roof. 3. in *finance*, *a*) the amount of a debt, investment, etc. minus the interest. *b*) the face value of a stock or bond. *c*) the main body of an estate, etc. 4. in *law*, *a*) one who employs another to act as his agent. *b*) the one primarily responsible for an obligation: cf. *surety*. *c*) one who commits a crime: cf. *accessory*. —**prin′ci·pal·ship′,** ***n.***
**prin·ci·pal·i·ty** (prin′sə-pal′ə-ti), ***n.*** [*pl.* -TIES], 1. the rank, dignity, or jurisdiction of a prince. 2. the territory ruled by a prince. 3. a country with which a prince's title is identified.
**prin·ci·pal·ly** (prin′sə-p'l-i, -sip-li), ***adv.*** chiefly; mainly; for the most part.
**principal parts,** the principal inflected forms of a verb from which the other forms may be derived: in English, they are the present infinitive, the past tense, the past participle, and sometimes the present participle (e.g., *drink, drank, drunk, drinking; add, added, added, adding*).
**prin·ci·ple** (prin′sə-p'l), ***n.*** [< L. *principium* < *princeps;* see PRINCE], 1. the ultimate source or cause. 2. a natural or original tendency, faculty, etc. 3. a fundamental truth, law, etc., upon which others are based. 4. a rule of conduct: as, the *principle* of equality. 5. *a*) such rules collectively. *b*) adherence to them; integrity: as, a person of *principle*. 6. an essential element or quality: as, the active *principle* of a medicine. 7. the law of nature by which a thing operates: as, capillary attraction is the *principle* of a blotter. 8. the method of a thing's operation. —**in principle,** theoretically or in essence.
**prin·ci·pled** (prin′sə-p'ld), ***adj.*** having principles, as of conduct.
**prink** (priŋk), ***v.t.*** [? akin to *prank*], to dress (oneself) up. ***v.i.*** 1. to dress up; preen. 2. to fuss over one's appearance; primp. —**prink′er,** ***n.***
**print** (print), ***n.*** [< OFr. < *prient*, pp. of *preindre* < L. *premere*, to press], 1. a mark made on a surface by pressing or hitting with an object; imprint: as, the *print* of a heel. 2. an object for making such a mark, as a stamp, die, etc. 3. a cloth printed with a design, or a dress made of this. 4. the condition of being printed. 5. printed letters, words, etc.; the impression made by inked type. 6. a picture or design printed from a plate, block, etc., as an etching or lithograph. 7. a photograph made by exposing sensitized paper to light passed through a negative. ***v.t.*** 1. to make a print on or in. 2. to stamp (a mark, letter, etc.) on or in a surface. 3. to produce on (paper, etc.) the impression of inked type, plates, etc. by means of a printing press. 4. to produce (a book, etc.) by typesetting, presswork, binding, etc. 5. to publish (a manuscript, etc.) in print. 6. to write in letters resembling printed ones. 7. to produce (a photograph), by exposing sensitized paper to light passed through a negative. 8. to impress upon the mind, memory, etc. ***v.i.*** 1. to practice the trade of a printer. 2. to produce an impression, photograph, etc. 3. to draw letters resembling printed ones. —**in** (or **out of**) **print,** still (or no longer) procurable for purchase from the publisher: said of books, etc. —**print′a·ble,** ***adj.*** —**print′er,** ***n.***
**printed circuit,** an electrical circuit formed by applying conductive material in fine lines or other shapes to an insulating surface.
**printer's devil,** a printer's apprentice or helper.
**print·ing** (prin′tiŋ), ***n.*** 1. the act of a person or thing that prints. 2. the production of printed matter. 3. this as an art; typography. 4. something printed. 5. all the copies of a book, etc. printed at one time. 6. letters made like printed ones.
**printing press,** a machine for printing from inked type, plates, etc.
**print·out** (print′out′), ***n.*** the output of a computer in printed or typewritten form.
**print shop,** 1. a shop where printing is done. 2. a shop where prints, etchings, etc. are sold.
**pri·or** (prī′ẽr), ***adj.*** [L., former, superior], 1. preceding in time; earlier. 2. preceding in order or importance: as, a *prior* choice. —**prior to,** before.
**pri·or** (prī′ẽr), ***n.*** [< AS. & OFr. < ML. < L.; see PRIOR, *adj.*] 1. the head of a priory. 2. in an abbey, the person in charge next below an abbot. —**pri′or·ate, pri′or·ship′,** ***n.*** —**pri′or·ess,** ***n.fem.***
**pri·or·i·ty** (prī-ôr′ə-ti, -or′-), ***n.*** [*pl.* -TIES], 1. a being prior; precedence. 2. *a*) a prior right in getting travel reservations, buying certain things, etc. *b*) an order granting this.
**pri·o·ry** (prī′ẽr-i), ***n.*** [*pl.* -RIES], a monastery governed by a prior, or a nunnery governed by a prioress, sometimes as a branch of an abbey.
**prise** (prīz), ***v.t.*** [PRISED, PRISING], to prize (pry).
**prism** (priz′m), ***n.*** [< LL. < Gr. *prisma*, lit., something sawed < *prizein*, to saw], 1. a solid figure whose ends are equal and parallel polygons and whose faces are parallelograms. 2. anything that refracts light, as a drop of water. 3. in *optics*, *a*) a transparent body, as of glass, whose ends are equal and parallel triangles, and whose three sides are parallelograms: used for refracting or dispersing light, as into the spectrum. *b*) any similar body of three or more sides. —**pris′mal,** ***adj.***

PRISM

**pris·mat·ic** (priz-mat′ik), ***adj.*** 1. of or like a prism. 2. that reflects light as a prism. 3. that forms prismatic colors. 4. many-colored; brilliant. Also **pris·mat′i·cal.** —**pris·mat′i·cal·ly,** ***adv.***
**prismatic colors,** [see PRISM, sense 3*a*], the colors of the visible spectrum; red, orange, yellow, green, blue, indigo, and violet.
**pris·on** (priz′'n), ***n.*** [OFr. < L. *pre(he)nsio* < *prendere*, to take], 1. a place where persons are confined. 2. a building, usually with cells, where persons convicted by, or awaiting, trial are confined; jail. 3. in the U.S., a State or Federal prison.
**pris·on·er** (priz′'n-ẽr, priz′nẽr), ***n.*** 1. a person confined in prison, as for some crime. 2. a person held in custody. 3. a person who is captured or held captive: as, a *prisoner* of war.
**pris·sy** (pris′i), ***adj.*** [-SIER, -SIEST], [< *precise* or *prim* + *sissy*], [Colloq.], 1. very prim or fussy. 2. prudish. —**pris′si·ly,** ***adv.*** —**pris′si·ness,** ***n.***
**pris·tine** (pris′tēn, -tin), ***adj.*** [< L. *pristinus*], 1. characteristic of the earliest period or condition; original. 2. uncorrupted; unspoiled.
**prith·ee** (prith′i), ***interj.*** [< *pray thee*], [Archaic], I pray thee; please: also sp. **prythee.**
**pri·va·cy** (prī′və-si), ***n.*** [*pl.* -CIES], 1. the quality or condition of being private; seclusion. 2. secrecy.
**pri·vate** (prī′vit), ***adj.*** [< L. *privatus*, pp. < *privus*, separate], 1. of or concerning a particular person or group; not general: as, *private* property, a *private* joke. 2. not open to or controlled by the public: as, a *private* school. 3. not holding public office: as, a *private* citizen. 4. away from public view; secluded: as, a *private* dining room. 5. secret; confidential: as, my *private* opinion. ***n.*** in the *U.S. armed forces*, the lowest rank (in the Army, the two lowest ranks) of enlisted man: abbrev. **Pvt.** —**in private,** not publicly. —**pri′vate·ly,** ***adv.***
**pri·va·teer** (prī′və-têr′), ***n.*** [< *private*, after *buccaneer*], 1. a privately owned and manned armed ship commissioned in a war to attack and capture enemy ships, especially merchant ships. 2. a commander or crew member of a privateer: also **pri′va·teers′man** [*pl.* -MEN]. ***v.i.*** to sail as a privateer.
**pri·va·tion** (prī-vā′shən), ***n.*** [< L. *privatio;* see PRIVATE], 1. the absence or loss of some quality or condition: as, cold is the *privation* of heat. 2. the lack of usual necessities or comforts.
**priv·a·tive** (priv′ə-tiv), ***adj.*** 1. depriving or tending to deprive. 2. in *grammar*, changing a positive term to give it a negative meaning. ***n.*** a privative prefix or suffix, as *a-*, *un-*, *non-*, or *-less*.
**priv·et** (priv′it), ***n.*** [< ?], any of various shrubs of the olive family, with bluish-black berries and white flowers, often grown for hedges.
**priv·i·lege** (priv′'l-ij), ***n.*** [< OFr. < L. *privilegium*, a law for or against an individual < *privus*, separate + *lex*, a law], 1. a special right, advantage, favor, etc. granted to some person or group. 2. a

basic civil right, guaranteed by a government: as, the *privilege* of equality. ***v.t.*** [-LEGED, -LEGING], to grant a privilege to. —**priv'i·leged,** ***adj.***

**priv·y** (priv'i), ***adj.*** [< OFr. < L. *privatus;* see PRIVATE], 1. originally, confidential; private. 2. [Archaic], secret; furtive. ***n.*** [*pl.* -IES], 1. a toilet; esp., an outhouse with a toilet. —**privy to,** privately informed about. —**priv'i·ly,** ***adv.***

**privy council,** a group of confidential counselors appointed by a ruler to advise him.

**privy seal,** in Great Britain, the seal placed on documents which later receive the great seal or which are not important enough to receive it.

**prize** (prīz), ***v.t.*** [PRIZED, PRIZING], [var. of *price*], 1. to appraise; price. 2. to value highly; esteem. ***n.*** 1. something offered or given to a person winning a contest, lottery, etc. 2. anything worth striving for; any highly valued possession. ***adj.*** 1. that has received a prize. 2. that could win a prize: as, a *prize* answer. 3. given as a prize.

**prize** (prīz), ***n.*** [< OFr. *prise,* fem. pp. of *prendre* (< L. *prehendere*), to take], something taken by force, as in war; esp., a captured enemy warship. ***v.t.*** [PRIZED, PRIZING], 1. to seize as a prize of war. 2. to pry, as with a lever: also sp. **prise.**

**prize court,** a military court having authority over the disposition of prizes, or property captured at sea in wartime.

**prize fight,** a professional boxing match. —**prize fighter.** —**prize fighting.**

**prize ring,** 1. a square platform, enclosed by ropes, where prize fights are held. 2. prize fighting.

**pro** (prō), ***adv.*** [L., for], on the affirmative side; favorably. ***adj.*** favorable. ***n.*** [*pl.* PROS], 1. one who favors the affirmative side of some debatable question. 2. an argument or vote for something.

**pro** (prō), ***adj. & n.*** [*pl.* PROS], [contr. < *professional*], [Colloq.], professional.

**pro-,** [< Gr. < *pro,* before], a prefix meaning: 1. *before in place* or *position,* as in *prostrate.* 2. *before in time,* as in *prophet.*

**pro-,** [L. < *pro,* forward], a prefix meaning: 1. *moving forward* or *ahead of,* as in *progress.* 2. *substituting* or *acting for,* as in *pronoun.* 3. *acting in behalf of.* 4. *favoring,* as in *pro-German.*

**pro·a** (prō'ə), ***n.*** [Malay *prau*], a Malayan canoe equipped with a lateen sail and an outrigger.

**prob.,** 1. probable. 2. probably. 3. problem.

**prob·a·bil·i·ty** (prob'ə-bil'ə-ti), ***n.*** [*pl.* -TIES], 1. likelihood; chance stronger than possibility; the quality or state of being probable. 2. something probable. —**in all probability,** very likely.

**prob·a·ble** (prob'ə-b'l), ***adj.*** [< L. < *probare,* to prove], 1. likely to occur or to be so; that can reasonably be expected or believed, though not certain. 2. such as to establish a probability: said of evidence, etc. —**prob'a·bly,** ***adv.***

**pro·bate** (prō'bāt), ***n.*** [< L. pp. of *probare;* see PROBE], the official establishing of the genuineness or validity of a will. ***adj.*** having to do with such action: as, a *probate* judge. ***v.t.*** [-BATED, -BATING], 1. to establish officially the genuineness or validity of (a will). 2. to put on probation. 3. to certify in a probate court as mentally unsound. —**pro'ba·tive** (-bə-tiv), **pro'ba·to'ry** (-tôr'i, -tō'ri), ***adj.***

**probate court,** a court for probating wills and, when necessary, administering estates.

**pro·ba·tion** (prō-bā'shən), ***n.*** [< OFr. < L. < *probare;* see PROBE], 1. a testing or trial, as of a person's character, ability, etc. 2. the conditional suspension of a sentence of a person convicted but not yet imprisoned. 3. the status of a person being tested or on trial. 4. the period of testing or trial. —**pro·ba'tion·al, pro·ba'tion·ar'y,** ***adj.***

**pro·ba·tion·er** (prō-bā'shən-ēr), ***n.*** a person on probation.

**probation officer,** an officer appointed by a court to supervise a person placed on probation.

**probe** (prōb), ***n.*** [LL. *proba,* proof < L. *probare,* to test], 1. a slender, blunt surgical instrument for exploring a wound or the like. 2. the act of probing. 3. a searching investigation, as by a legislative committee, of alleged corrupt practices, etc. ***v.t.*** [PROBED, PROBING], 1. to explore (a wound, etc.) with a probe. 2. to investigate thoroughly. ***v.i.*** to search (with *into*). —**prob'er,** ***n.*** —**prob'ing,** ***adj. & n.*** —**prob'ing·ly,** ***adv.***

PROBE

**prob·i·ty** (prō'bə-ti, prob'ə-), ***n.*** [< Fr. < L. < *probus,* good], integrity; uprightness; honesty.

**prob·lem** (prob'ləm), ***n.*** [< L. < Gr. *problēma* < *pro-,* forward + *ballein,* to throw], 1. a question proposed for solution or consideration. 2. a matter, person, etc. that is perplexing or difficult. 3. in *mathematics,* anything required to be done. ***adj.*** 1. depicting a social problem: as, a *problem* play. 2. very difficult to train or discipline: as, a *problem* child.

**prob·lem·at·i·cal** (prob'lə-mat'i-k'l), ***adj.*** 1. having the nature of a problem. 2. uncertain. Also **prob'lem·at'ic.** —**prob'lem·at'i·cal·ly,** ***adv.***

‡**pro bo·no pu·bli·co** (prō bō'nō pub'li-kō'), [L.], for the public good; for the commonweal.

**pro·bos·cis** (prō-bos'is), ***n.*** [*pl.* -BOSCISES (-is-iz), -BOSCIDES (-ə-dēz')], [L. < Gr. < *pro-,* before + *boskein,* to feed], 1. an elephant's trunk, or a long, flexible snout, as of a tapir. 2. a tubular sucking organ, as of some insects, worms, and mollusks. 3. a person's nose: humorously so called.

**pro·caine** (prō-kān', prō'kān), ***n.*** [*pro-* + *cocaine*], a crystalline compound resembling, but less toxic than, cocaine, used as a local anesthetic.

**pro·ce·dure** (prə-sē'jēr, prō-), ***n.*** 1. the act, method, or manner of proceeding in some action. 2. a particular course or method of action. 3. the established way of carrying on the business of a legislature, law court, etc. —**pro·ce'dur·al,** ***adj.***

**pro·ceed** (prə-sēd', prō-), ***v.i.*** [< L. < *pro-,* forward + *cedere,* to go], 1. to advance or go on, especially after stopping. 2. to go on speaking, especially after an interruption. 3. to undertake and carry on some action or process. 4. to take legal action (often with *against*). 5. to issue; come forth. —**pro·ceed'er,** ***n.*** See also **proceeds.**

**pro·ceed·ing** (prə-sēd'iŋ, prō-), ***n.*** 1. an advancing or going on with what one has been doing. 2. action or course of action. 3. *pl.* transactions. 4. *pl.* a record of the business transacted by a learned society, etc. 5. *pl.* legal action.

**pro·ceeds** (prō'sēdz), ***n.pl.*** the sum derived from a sale, venture, etc.

**proc·ess** (pros'es; *mainly Brit.* prō'ses), ***n.*** [< OFr. < L. *processus,* pp.; see PROCEED], 1. the course of being done: chiefly in *in process.* 2. course, as of time. 3. a continuing development involving many changes: as, the *process* of digestion. 4. a particular method of doing something, with all the steps involved. 5. in *biology,* a projecting part of a structure or organism. 6. in *law, a*) an action or suit. *b*) a written order, as a summons to appear in court. ***v.t.*** to prepare by or subject to a special process. ***adj.*** 1. prepared by a special process. —**in (the) process of,** in or during the course of.

**pro·ces·sion** (prə-sesh'ən, prō-), ***n.*** [OFr. < L. *processio;* see PROCEED], 1. the act of proceeding, especially in an orderly manner. 2. a number of persons or things moving forward, usually in a long line, in orderly fashion.

**pro·ces·sion·al** (prə-sesh'ən-'l, prō-), ***adj.*** of or relating to a procession. ***n.*** 1. a hymn sung at the beginning of a church service during the entrance of the clergy. 2. any musical composition to accompany a procession. —**pro·ces'sion·al·ly,** ***adv.***

**pro·claim** (prō-klām'), ***v.t.*** [< OFr. < L. < *pro-,* before + *clamare,* to cry out], 1. to announce officially; announce to be. 2. to outlaw, ban, etc. by a proclamation. 3. to show to be: as, her acts *proclaimed* her a snob. —**pro·claim'er,** ***n.***

**proc·la·ma·tion** (prok'lə-mā'shən), ***n.*** 1. a proclaiming or being proclaimed. 2. something that is proclaimed. —**pro·clam·a·to·ry** (prō-klam'ə-tôr'i, -tō'-ri), ***adj.***

**pro·cliv·i·ty** (prō-kliv'ə-ti), ***n.*** [*pl.* -TIES], [< Fr. < L. *proclivitas* < *pro-,* before + *clivus,* a slope], a natural tendency in human nature; inclination.

**pro·con·sul** (prō-kon's'l), ***n.*** [L. < *pro,* for + *consul,* a consul], a Roman official with consular authority who commanded an army in the provinces, often acting as provincial governor. —**pro·con'su·lar,** ***adj.*** —**pro·con'su·late, pro·con'sul·ship',** ***n.***

**pro·cras·ti·nate** (prō-kras'tə-nāt'), ***v.i.*** [-NATED, -NATING], [< L. pp.; ult. < *pro-,* forward + *cras,* tomorrow], to put off doing something until later; defer taking action. ***v.t.*** to postpone. —**pro·cras'ti·na'tion,** ***n.*** —**pro·cras'ti·na'tive, pro·cras'ti·na·to'ry** (-nə-tôr'i, -tō'ri), ***adj.*** —**pro·cras'ti·na'tor,** ***n.***

**pro·cre·ate** (prō'kri-āt'), ***v.t. & v.i.*** [-ATED, -ATING], [< L. pp. < *pro-,* before + *creare,* to create], 1. to produce (young); beget. 2. to produce; bring into existence. —**pro'cre·ant,** ***adj.*** —**pro'cre·a'tion,** ***n.*** —**pro'cre·a'tive,** ***adj.*** —**pro'cre·a'tor,** ***n.***

**Pro·crus·te·an** (prō-krus'ti-ən), ***adj.*** 1. of Procrustes or his bedstead. 2. designed to secure conformity at any cost; drastic.

**Pro·crus·tes** (prō-krus'tēz), ***n.*** in *Gr. mythology,* a giant who seized travelers, tied them to an iron bedstead, and either cut off their legs or stretched his victims till they fitted it.

**proc·tol·o·gy** (prok-tol'ə-ji), *n.* [< Gr. *prōktos*, anus; + *-logy*], the branch of medicine dealing with the rectum and its diseases. —**proc·tol'o·gist,** *n.*

**proc·tor** (prok'tẽr), *n.* [< ME.; akin to *procurator*], 1. a person employed to manage another's affairs. 2. a college or university official who maintains order, supervises examinations, etc. *v.t.* to supervise (an examination). —**proc·to'ri·al** (-tôr'i-əl, -tō'ri-), *adj.* —**proc'tor·ship',** *n.*

**pro·cum·bent** (prō-kum'bənt), *adj.* [< L. ppr.; ult. < *pro-*, forward + *cubare*, to lie down], 1. lying face down. 2. in *botany*, trailing along the ground.

**proc·u·ra·tor** (prok'yoo-rā'tẽr), *n.* [< OFr. < L. < *procurare;* see PROCURE], 1. in the Roman Empire, an official who managed the financial affairs of a province or acted as governor of a territory. 2. a person employed to manage another's affairs. —**proc'u·ra·to'ri·al** (-rə-tôr'i-əl, -tō'ri-), *adj.* —**proc'u·ra'tor·ship',** *n.*

**pro·cure** (prō-kyoor'), *v.t.* [-CURED, -CURING], [< OFr. < L. < *pro*, for + *curare*, to attend to < *cura*, a care], 1. to obtain or secure. 2. [Rare], to cause. 3. to obtain (women) for the purpose of prostitution. —**pro·cur'a·ble,** *adj.* —**pro·cure'ment,** *n.* —**pro·cur'er,** *n.* —**pro·cur'ess,** *n.fem.*

**Pro·cy·on** (prō'si-on'), *n.* [L. < Gr. < *pro-*, before + *kyōn*, dog: it rises before the Dog Star], a star of the first magnitude in Canis Minor.

**prod** (prod), *n.* [prob. merging of *prog* & *brod*, both meaning "to stab"], 1. a thrust with something pointed. 2. something that serves to goad or urge on. *v.t.* [PRODDED, PRODDING], 1. to jab as with a pointed stick. 2. to urge or rouse. —**prod'der,** *n.*

**prod·i·gal** (prod'i-g'l), *adj.* [obs. Fr.; ult. < L. *prodigere*, to waste < *pro-*, forth + *agere*, to drive], 1. exceedingly or recklessly wasteful. 2. extremely generous (often with *of*). 3. extremely abundant. *n.* a spendthrift. —**prod'i·gal·ly,** *adv.*

**prod·i·gal·i·ty** (prod'i-gal'ə-ti), *n.* [*pl.* -TIES], 1. reckless wastefulness. 2. abundant generosity. 3. extreme abundance.

**pro·di·gious** (prə-dij'əs), *adj.* [see PRODIGY], 1. wonderful; amazing. 2. enormous. 3. monstrous. —**pro·di'gious·ly,** *adv.* —**pro·di'gious·ness,** *n.*

**prod·i·gy** (prod'ə-ji), *n.* [*pl.* -GIES], [< L. *prodigium*, omen], 1. a person or thing, especially a child, so extraordinary as to inspire wonder. 2. something monstrous.

**pro·duce** (prə-dōōs', -dūs'; *for n.*, prod'ōōs, prō'-dūs), *v.t.* [-DUCED, -DUCING], [< L. < *pro-*, forward + *ducere*, to lead], 1. to bring to view; offer for inspection: as, he *produced* his license. 2. to bear; bring forth; yield: as, a well that *produces* oil. 3. to make or manufacture. 4. to cause; give rise to: as, floods *produce* misery. 5. to get (a play, motion picture, etc.) ready for exhibition. 6. in *economics*, to create (anything having exchange value). 7. in *geometry*, to extend (a line or plane). *v.i.* to yield, manufacture, etc. the customary product. *n.* something produced; yield; esp., farm products collectively. —**pro·duc'i·ble,** *adj.*

**pro·duc·er** (prə-dōōs'ẽr, -dūs'-), *n.* 1. one who produces; specif., in *economics*, one who produces goods or services: cf. *consumer.* 2. one who supervises the production of a play, motion picture, etc.

**prod·uct** (prod'əkt), *n.* [< L. *productus*, pp.; see PRODUCE], 1. something produced by nature or made by industry or art. 2. result; outgrowth. 3. in *chemistry*, any substance resulting from a chemical change. 4. in *mathematics*, the number obtained by multiplying two or more numbers together.

**pro·duc·tion** (prə-duk'shən), *n.* 1. the act or process of producing. 2. the rate of producing. 3. *a*) something produced. *b*) a work of art, literature, the theater, etc. 4. the creation of economic value; producing of goods or services.

**pro·duc·tive** (prə-duk'tiv), *adj.* 1. fertile. 2. marked by abundant production. 3. bringing as a result (with *of*): as, waste is *productive* of many evils. 4. of or engaged in the creating of economic value. —**pro·duc'tive·ly,** *adv.* —**pro·duc·tiv·i·ty** (prō'duk-tiv'ə-ti), **pro·duc'tive·ness,** *n.*

**pro·em** (prō'em), *n.* [< OFr. < L. < Gr. < *pro-*, before + *oimē*, song], a brief introduction. —**pro·e'mi·al** (-ē'mi-əl), *adj.*

**prof** (prof), *n.* [Colloq.], a professor.

**Prof., prof.,** Professor.

**prof·a·na·tion** (prof'ə-nā'shən), *n.* a profaning or being profaned; desecration. —**pro·fan·a·to·ry** (prə-fan'ə-tôr'i, prō-fan'ə-tō'ri), *adj.*

**pro·fane** (prə-fān', prō-), *adj.* [Fr. < L. < *pro-*, before + *fanum*, a temple], 1. not concerned with religion; secular: as, *profane* art. 2. not hallowed. 3. showing disregard or contempt for sacred things; irreverent. *v.t.* [-FANED, -FANING], 1. to treat (sacred things) with irreverence or contempt. 2. to put to a base or improper use. —**pro·fane'ly,** *adv.* —**pro·fane'ness,** *n.* —**pro·fan'er,** *n.*

**pro·fan·i·ty** (prə-fan'ə-ti, prō-), *n.* 1. the state or quality of being profane. 2. [*pl.* -TIES], something profane, especially profane language.

**pro·fess** (prə-fes'), *v.t.* [< OFr. < L. *professus*, pp. < *pro-*, before + *fateri*, to avow], 1. to make an open declaration of; affirm: as, he *professed* ignorance. 2. to lay claim to (some feeling) insincerely: as, she *professed* gratitude. 3. to practice as one's profession: as, to *profess* law. 4. to declare one's belief in: as, to *profess* Christ.

**pro·fessed** (prə-fest'), *adj.* 1. openly declared; avowed: as, a *professed* liberal. 2. insincerely avowed; pretended: as, *professed* neutrality. 3. having made one's profession (sense 5). —**pro·fess'ed·ly** (-fes'id-li), *adv.*

**pro·fes·sion** (prə-fesh'ən), *n.* 1. a professing, or declaring; avowal, as of religious belief. 2. a faith or religion professed. 3. an occupation requiring advanced training in some liberal art or science, as teaching, engineering, medicine, law, or theology. 4. the body of persons in a particular occupation. 5. the avowal made on entering a religious order.

**pro·fes·sion·al** (prə-fesh'ən-'l), *adj.* 1. of, engaged in, or worthy of the standards of, a profession. 2. making some activity not usually followed for gain, as a sport, the source of one's livelihood. 3. engaged in by professional players: as, *professional* hockey. 4. engaged in a specific occupation for pay: as, a *professional* writer. 5. pursuing an activity in an intensive, calculating manner: as, a *professional* rabble-rouser. *n.* a person who is professional (esp. in sense 2). —**pro·fes'sion·al·ism,** *n.* —**pro·fes'sion·al·ly,** *adv.*

**pro·fes·sion·al·ize** (prə-fesh'ən-'l-īz'), *v.t. & v.i.* [-IZED, -IZING], to make or become professional. —**pro·fes'sion·al·i·za'tion,** *n.*

**pro·fes·sor** (prə-fes'ẽr), *n.* 1. a person who professes something. 2. a teacher; specif., a college teacher of the highest rank. —**pro·fes·so·ri·al** (prō'fə-sôr'i-əl, prof'ə-sō'ri-), *adj.* —**pro'fes·so'ri·al·ly,** *adv.* —**pro·fes'sor·ship', pro·fes'sor·ate,** *n.*

**prof·fer** (prof'ẽr), *v.t.* [< Anglo-Fr. & OFr. < *por-*, pro- + *offrir* (< L. *offerre*), to offer], to offer (usually something intangible): as, to *proffer* friendship. *n.* an offer. —**prof'fer·er,** *n.*

**pro·fi·cien·cy** (prə-fish'ən-si), *n.* [*pl.* -CIES], a being proficient; expertness; skill.

**pro·fi·cient** (prə-fish'ənt), *adj.* [< L. ppr. of *proficere*, to advance < *pro-*, forward + *facere*, to make], highly competent; skilled. *n.* an expert. —**pro·fi'cient·ly,** *adv.*

**pro·file** (prō'fīl), *n.* [< It. < *profilare*, to outline < *pro-* (< L. *pro-*), before + *filo* (< L. *filum*), a thread], 1. a side view of the face. 2. a drawing of this. 3. outline: as, the *profile* of a hill. 4. a short, vivid biography. 5. in *architecture*, a side or sectional elevation of a building, etc. *v.t.* [-FILED, -FILING], 1. to draw or write a profile of. 2. to form as a profile. —**pro'fil·ist,** *n.*

**prof·it** (prof'it), *n.* [OFr. < L. pp. of *proficere*, to profit < *pro-*, toward + *facere*, to make], 1. advantage; gain; benefit. 2. *often pl.* financial gain obtained from the use of capital in transactions. 3. *often pl.* in *economics*, the net income, as of a business, or the difference between the income and the costs. *v.i.* 1. to be of advantage or benefit. 2. to benefit. *v.t.* to be of advantage or benefit to. —**prof'it·er,** *n.* —**prof'it·less,** *adj.* —**prof'it·less·ly,** *adv.*

**prof·it·a·ble** (prof'it-ə-b'l), *adj.* yielding profit, gain, or benefit. —**prof'it·a·ble·ness,** *n.* —**prof'it·a·bly,** *adv.*

**prof·it·eer** (prof'ə-têr'), *n.* a person who makes excessive profits by taking advantage of a shortage of supply to charge high prices. *v.i.* to be a profiteer. —**prof'it·eer'ing,** *n.*

**profit sharing,** the practice of giving employees a share in the profits of a business, in addition to their wages. —**prof'it-shar'ing,** *adj.*

**prof·li·ga·cy** (prof'lə-gə-si), *n.* [*pl.* -CIES], profligate state, quality, act, etc.

**prof·li·gate** (prof'lə-git), *adj.* [< L. pp. of *profligare*, to rout, ruin < *pro-*, forward + *fligere*, to drive], 1. abandoned to vice; dissolute. 2. recklessly wasteful. *n.* a profligate person. —**prof′li·gate·ly,** *adv.* —**prof′li·gate·ness,** *n.*

**pro·found** (prə-found′), *adj.* [< OFr. < L. *profundus* < *pro-*, forward + *fundus*, bottom], 1. [Poetic], very deep or low: as, a *profound* abyss. 2. marked by intellectual depth: as, a *profound* discussion. 3. deeply or intensely felt: as, *profound* grief. 4. thoroughgoing: as, *profound* changes. 5. unbroken: as, *profound* silence. —**pro·found′ly,** *adv.* —**pro·found′ness,** *n.*

**pro·fun·di·ty** (prə-fun′də-ti), *n.* [*pl.* -TIES], 1. depth. 2. something profound, as a thought.

**pro·fuse** (prə-fūs′), *adj.* [< L. *profusus*, pp. < *pro-*, forth + *fundere*, to pour], 1. giving freely; generous: as, she was *profuse* in her apologies. 2. given or poured forth freely and abundantly. —**pro·fuse′ly,** *adv.* —**pro·fuse′ness,** *n.*

**pro·fu·sion** (prə-fū′zhən), *n.* 1. a pouring forth with great liberality or wastefulness. 2. great liberality or wastefulness. 3. abundance.

**pro·gen·i·tor** (prō-jen′ə-tẽr), *n.* [< Fr. < L. < *pro-*, forth + *gignere*, to beget], a forefather; ancestor in direct line.

**prog·e·ny** (proj′ə-ni), *n.* [*pl.* -NIES], [< OFr. < L. < *progignere;* see PROGENITOR], children, descendants, or offspring collectively; issue.

**pro·ges·ter·one** (prō-jes′tə-rōn′), *n.* [*pro-* + *ges*tation + *ster*ol + *-one*], an ovarian hormone, $C_{21}H_{30}O_2$, preparing the uterus for the fertilized ovum: also, earlier, **pro·ges′tin** (-tin).

**prog·na·thous** (prog′nə-thəs, prog-nā′-), *adj.* [< *pro-* + Gr. *gnathos*, a jaw], having either or both jaws projecting abnormally.

**prog·no·sis** (prog-nō′sis), *n.* [*pl.* -SES (-sēz)], [< LL. < Gr. < *pro-*, before + *gignōskein*, to know], a forecast or forecasting; esp., in *medicine*, a prediction of the probable course of a disease.

**prog·nos·tic** (prog-nos′tik), *n.* [see PROGNOSIS], 1. a sign; omen. 2. a forecast. 3. in *medicine*, a symptom indicating the probable course of a disease. *adj.* 1. foretelling. 2. in *medicine*, of, or serving as a basis for, prognosis.

**prog·nos·ti·cate** (prog-nos′tə-kāt′), *v.t.* [-CATED, -CATING], 1. to foretell; predict. 2. to indicate beforehand. —**prog·nos′ti·ca′tion,** *n.* —**prog·nos′ti·ca′tive,** *adj.* —**prog·nos′ti·ca′tor,** *n.*

**pro·gram, pro·gramme** (prō′gram, -grəm), *n.* [< LL. & Fr. < Gr. *programma*, an edict < *pro-*, before + *graphein*, to write], 1. *a)* a list of the events, pieces, performers, etc., as of an entertainment or ceremony. *b)* the events or pieces collectively. 2. a plan of procedure. 3. *a)* a logical sequence of operations to be performed by an electronic computer, as in solving a problem. *b)* the coded instructions and data for this. *v.t.* [-GRAMMED or -GRAMED, -GRAMMING or -GRAMING], 1. to schedule in a program. 2. to furnish (a computer) with a program. —**pro′gram·mer, pro′gram·er,** *n.* —**pro′-gram·mat′ic** (-grə-mat′ik), *adj.*

**program music,** instrumental music that suggests a particular scene, story, etc.

**prog·ress** (prog′res, prō′gres; *for v.*, prə-gres′), *n.* [< OFr. < L. pp. < *pro-*, before + *gradi*, to step], 1. a moving forward or onward. 2. forward course; development. 3. improvement; advance toward perfection. *v.i.* 1. to move forward or onward. 2. to continue toward completion. 3. to improve; advance toward perfection.

**pro·gres·sion** (prə-gresh′ən), *n.* 1. a moving forward or onward. 2. a succession, as of acts, happenings, etc. 3. in *mathematics*, a series of numbers increasing or decreasing by proportional differences: see **arithmetic progression, geometric progression.** —**pro·gres′sion·al,** *adj.*

**pro·gres·sive** (prə-gres′iv), *adj.* 1. moving forward or onward. 2. continuing by successive steps. 3. marked by progress, reform, or improvement. 4. favoring progress, as through political reform. 5. in *grammar*, indicating continuing action: said of certain verb forms, as *am working*. 6. in *medicine*, becoming more severe: said of a disease. *n.* 1. one who is progressive; esp., one who favors political progress. 2. [P-], a member of a Progressive Party. —**pro·gres′sive·ly,** *adv.* —**pro·gres′sive·ness,** *n.*

**Progressive Party,** in American politics, 1. a party organized in 1912 by followers of Theodore Roosevelt. 2. a party formed in 1924 under the leadership of Robert M. LaFollette. 3. a party formed in 1948, originally led by Henry A. Wallace.

**pro·hib·it** (prō-hib′it, prə-), *v.t.* [< L. *prohibitus*, pp. < *pro-*, before + *habere*, to have], 1. to refuse to permit; forbid, as by law. 2. to prevent; hinder. —**pro·hib′it·ed,** *adj.*

**pro·hi·bi·tion** (prō′ə-bish′ən), *n.* 1. a prohibiting or being prohibited. 2. an order or law that forbids. 3. the forbidding by law of the manufacture or sale of alcoholic liquors; specif. [P-], in the U.S., the period (1920–1933) of prohibition by Federal law. —**pro′hi·bi′tion·ist,** *n.*

**pro·hib·i·tive** (prō-hib′ə-tiv, prə-), *adj.* 1. prohibiting or tending to prohibit something. 2. such as to prevent purchase, use, etc.: as, *prohibitive* prices. Also **pro·hib′i·to′ry** (-tôr′i, -tō′ri). —**pro·hib′i·tive·ly,** *adv.* —**pro·hib′i·tive·ness,** *n.*

**proj·ect** (proj′ekt, -ikt; *for v.*, prə-jekt′), *n.* [< L. < *projectus*, pp. < *pro-*, before + *jacere*, to throw], 1. a proposal; scheme. 2. an undertaking. *v.t.* 1. to propose (a plan of action). 2. to throw forward. 3. to send forth in one's imagination: as, to *project* oneself into tomorrow. 4. to cause to stick out. 5. to cause (a shadow, image, etc.) to fall upon a surface. 6. in *geometry*, to represent (a solid, etc.) on a plane surface by lines of correspondence. *v.i.* to stick out. —**pro·ject′ed,** *adj.* —**pro·ject′ing,** *adj.*

**pro·jec·tile** (prə-jek′t'l), *n.* 1. an object, as a bullet, shell, etc., designed to be shot forward, as from a gun. 2. anything thrown forward. *adj.* 1. designed to be hurled forward, as a javelin. 2. hurling forward: as, *projectile* energy.

**pro·jec·tion** (prə-jek′shən), *n.* 1. a projecting or being projected. 2. something that projects, or sticks out. 3. something that is projected; specif., in *map making*, the representation on a plane of all or part of the earth's surface or of the celestial sphere. 4. in *psychiatry*, the unconscious act of ascribing to others one's own ideas or impulses. 5. in *photography*, *a)* the process of causing an image to appear upon a screen, etc. *b)* the representation thus produced. —**pro·jec′tive,** *adj.*

**pro·jec·tor** (prə-jek′tẽr), *n.* a person or thing that projects; specif., a machine for throwing an image on a screen: as, a motion-picture *projector*.

**Pro·kof·iev, Ser·ge·i** (syer-gyā′ prô-kôf′yef), 1891–1953; Russian composer.

**pro·lapse** (prō-laps′), *n.* [< L. *prolapsus*, pp. < *pro-*, forward + *labi*, to fall], in *medicine*, the slipping out of place of an internal organ, as the uterus. *v.i.* [-LAPSED, -LAPSING], to suffer prolapse.

**pro·late** (prō′lāt, prō-lāt′), *adj.* [< L. *prolatus*, pp. of *proferre*, to bring forward], extended or elongated at the poles: as, a *prolate* spheroid.

**pro·le·tar·i·at** (prō′lə-târ′i-ət), *n.* [< Fr. < L. *proletarius*, a Roman citizen of the poorest class, who served the state only by having children < *proles*, offspring], 1. [Rare], the class of lowest status in any society. 2. the working class; esp., the industrial working class: the current sense. —**pro′le·tar′i·an,** *adj. & n.*

**pro·lif·er·ate** (prō-lif′ə-rāt′), *v.t. & v.i.* [-ATED, -ATING], [< ML. < L. *proles*, offspring + *ferre*, to bear], in *biology*, to reproduce (new parts) in quick succession. —**pro·lif′er·a′tion,** *n.* —**pro·lif′er·ous,** *adj.*

**pro·lif·ic** (prə-lif′ik), *adj.* [< Fr. < ML. < L. *proles*, offspring + *facere*, to make], 1. producing many young or much fruit. 2. creating many products of the mind: as, a *prolific* poet. 3. fruitful; abounding (often with *in* or *of*). —**pro·lif′i·ca·cy** (-i-kə-si), **pro·lif′ic·ness,** *n.* —**pro·lif′i·cal·ly,** *adv.*

**pro·lix** (prō-liks′, prō′liks), *adj.* [< L. *prolixus*, extended], so wordy as to be tiresome; verbose or long-winded. —**pro·lix′i·ty** [*pl.* -TIES], **pro·lix′ness,** *n.* —**pro·lix′ly,** *adv.*

**pro·logue** (prō′lôg, -log), *n.* [< OFr. < L. < Gr. < *pro-*, before + *logos*, a discourse], 1. an introduction to a poem, play, etc.; esp., introductory lines or verses spoken before a dramatic performance. 2. the person who speaks such lines. 3. any preliminary act, event, etc. Also sp. **prolog.**

**pro·long** (prə-lôŋ′), *v.t.* [< OFr. < LL. < L. *pro-*, forth + *longus*, long], to lengthen in time or space: also **pro·lon·gate** (prə-lôŋ′gāt), [-GATED, -GATING]. —**pro·long′a·ble,** *adj.* —**pro′lon·ga′tion** (prō′-), **pro·long′ment,** *n.* —**pro·long′er,** *n.*

**prom** (prom), *n.* [contr. < *promenade*], [Colloq.], a ball or dance, as given by a particular class of students at a college, high school, etc.

**prom·e·nade** (prom′ə-nād′, -näd′), *n.* [Fr. < *se promener*, to go for a walk < LL. < L. *pro-*, forth + *minare*, to herd], 1. a leisurely walk taken for pleasure, to display one's finery, etc. 2. a public place for walking, as an avenue. 3. in *dancing*, *a)* a ball. *b)* a march, usually by all guests, beginning a formal ball. *v.i. & v.t.* [-NADED, -NADING], to take a promenade (along or through); parade. —**prom′e·nad′er,** *n.*

**Pro·me·theus** (prə-mē′thūs, -thi-əs), *n.* in *Gr. mythology*, a Titan who taught mankind the use of fire, which he had stolen from heaven: he was punished by being chained to a rock where a vulture ate away at his liver. —**Pro·me′the·an** (-thi-ən), *adj. & n.*

**pro·me·thi·um** (prō-mē'thi-əm), ***n.*** [< *Prometheus*], a metallic chemical element of the rare-earth group: symbol, Pm; at. wt., 147(?); at. no., 61: formerly designated as *illinium.*

**prom·i·nence** (prom'ə-nəns), ***n.*** 1. a being prominent. 2. something prominent or projecting. Also **prom'i·nen·cy** [*pl.* -CIES].

**prom·i·nent** (prom'ə-nənt), ***adj.*** [< L. ppr. of *prominere,* to project], 1. sticking out; projecting: as, a *prominent* chin. 2. noticeable at once; conspicuous. 3. widely and favorably known: as, a *prominent* man. **—prom'i·nent·ly, *adv.***

**pro·mis·cu·ous** (prə-mis'kū-əs), ***adj.*** [< L. < *pro-,* forth + *miscere,* to mix], 1. consisting of different elements mixed together without discrimination. 2. characterized by a lack of discrimination; specif., engaging in sexual liaisons indiscriminately. 3. [Colloq.], without plan or purpose. **—prom·is·cu·i·ty** (prom'is-kū'ə-ti, prō'mis-), [*pl.* -TIES], **pro·mis'cu·ous·ness, *n.* —pro·mis'cu·ous·ly, *adv.***

**prom·ise** (prom'is), ***n.*** [< L. *promissum;* ult < *pro-,* forth + *mittere,* to send], 1. an agreement to do or not to do something; vow. 2. indication, as of a successful future; basis for expectation. 3. anything promised. ***v.i.*** [-ISED, -ISING], 1. to make a promise. 2. to give a basis for expectation. ***v.t.*** 1. to make a promise of (something) to somebody. 2. to engage or pledge (with an infinitive or clause): as, *promise* to go. 3. to give as a basis for expecting. **—prom'is·ee', *n.* —prom'is·er, prom'i·sor'** (in *law*), ***n.***

**Promised Land,** Land of Promise.

**prom·is·ing** (prom'is-iŋ), ***adj.*** likely to be successful; showing promise. **—prom'is·ing·ly, *adv.***

**prom·is·so·ry** (prom'ə-sôr'i, -sō'ri), ***adj.*** containing, or having the nature of, a promise.

**promissory note,** a written promise to pay a certain sum of money to a certain person or bearer on demand or on a specified date.

**prom·on·to·ry** (prom'ən-tôr'i, -tō'ri), ***n.*** [*pl.* -RIES], [< LL. < L. *promunturium;* prob. < *prominere,* to project], a peak of high land that juts out over an expanse of water; headland.

**pro·mote** (prə-mōt'), ***v.t.*** [-MOTED, -MOTING], [< L. *promotus,* pp. < *pro-,* forward + *movere,* to move], 1. to raise (a person) to a higher or better position: as, *promoted* to manager. 2. to further the growth or establishment of (something). 3. to work actively and stir up interest for: as, *promote* a new law. 4. in *education,* to move forward a grade in school. **—pro·mot'a·ble, *adj.* —pro·mo'tive, *adj.***

**pro·mot·er** (prə-mōt'ēr), ***n.*** 1. a person or thing that promotes. 2. a person who begins and furthers the organization of a new enterprise.

**pro·mo·tion** (prə-mō'shən), ***n.*** 1. a promoting; furtherance. 2. the result of promoting. 3. the stirring up of interest in an enterprise. **—pro·mo'tion·al, *adj.***

**prompt** (prompt), ***adj.*** [< OFr. < L. < *promptus,* pp. < *pro-,* forth + *emere,* to take], 1. ready; quick; instantly at hand. 2. done, spoken, etc. at once or without delay. ***n.*** a notice of payment due. ***v.t.*** 1. to urge into action. 2. to remind (a person) of something he has forgotten; help with a cue. 3. to move or inspire by suggestion. **—prompt'ly, *adv.* —prompt'ness, *n.***

**prompt·er** (prompt'ēr), ***n.*** 1. one who prompts. 2. the person in a theatrical company who cues the performers when they forget their lines, etc.

**promp·ti·tude** (promp'tə-to͞od', -tūd'), ***n.*** the quality of being prompt.

**pro·mul·gate** (prō-mul'gāt, prom'əl-gāt'), ***v.t.*** [-GATED, -GATING], [< L. pp. of *promulgare,* to publish; prob. ult. < *pro-,* before + *vulgus,* the people], 1. to publish or make known officially (a decree, law, dogma, etc.). 2. to make widespread: as, to *promulgate* culture. **—pro'mul·ga'tion, *n.* —pro·mul'ga·tor, *n.***

**pron.,** 1. pronominal. 2. pronoun. 3. pronounced. 4. pronunciation.

**prone** (prōn), ***adj.*** [< L. *pronus* < *pro,* before], 1. lying or leaning face downward. 2. lying flat or prostrate: as, he fell *prone* on the floor. 3. having a natural bent toward; disposed or inclined (with *to*): as, *prone* to error. 4. groveling: as, *prone* before tyranny. **—prone'ness, *n.***

**prong** (prôŋ), ***n.*** [prob. < MLG. *prange,* a pinching instrument], 1. one of the pointed ends of a fork; tine. 2. any pointed projecting part, as the tip of an antler. ***v.t.*** 1. to pierce with a prong. 2. to break up (clods) with a prong. **—pronged, *adj.* —prong'like', *adj.***

**prong·horn** (prôŋ'hôrn'), ***n.*** [-HORNS, -HORN; see PLURAL, II, D, 1], an antelopelike deer having forked horns, found in the western U.S.

**pro·nom·i·nal** (prō-nom'ə-n'l), ***adj.*** in *grammar,* of, or having the function of, a pronoun. **—pro·nom'i·nal·ly, *adv.***

**pro·noun** (prō'noun), ***n.*** [< Fr. < L. *pronomen; pro,* for + *nomen,* noun], in *grammar,* a word used in the place of or as a substitute for a noun: *I, you, he, she, it, we, they,* etc. are *pronouns.*

**pro·nounce** (prə-nouns'), ***v.t.*** [-NOUNCED, -NOUNCING], [< OFr. < L. < *pro-,* before + *nuntiare,* to announce < *nuntius,* messenger], 1. to say officially, solemnly, etc.: as, the judge *pronounced* sentence. 2. to declare to be as specified: as, the coroner *pronounced* him dead. 3. *a*) to utter or articulate (a sound or word): as, I *pronounce* it differently. *b*) to utter in the required or standard manner: as, he couldn't *pronounce* my name. ***v.i.*** 1. to make a pronouncement (with *on*). 2. to pronounce words, etc. **—pro·nounce'a·ble, *adj.* —pro·nounc'er, *n.***

**pro·nounced** (prə-nounst'), ***adj.*** 1. spoken or uttered. 2. clearly marked; unmistakable. 3. decided: as, *pronounced* opinions. **—pro·nounc'ed·ly, *adv.***

**pro·nounce·ment** (prə-nouns'mənt), ***n.*** 1. a pronouncing. 2. a formal statement of a fact, opinion, or judgment.

**pron·to** (pron'tō), ***adv.*** [Sp. < L. *promptus;* see PROMPT], [Slang], at once; quickly; immediately.

**pro·nun·ci·a·men·to** (prə-nun'si-ə-men'tō, -shi-ə-), ***n.*** [*pl.* -TOS], [Sp. < L.; see PRONOUNCE], 1. a public declaration; proclamation. 2. a manifesto.

**pro·nun·ci·a·tion** (prə-nun'si-ā'shən, -shi-), ***n.*** 1. the act or manner of pronouncing words. 2. the transcription in phonetic symbols of the accepted or standard pronunciation(s) of a word.

**proof** (pro͞of), ***n.*** [*pl.* PROOFS], [< OFr. *prueve* < LL.; see PROBE], 1. a proving, testing, or trying of something. 2. anything serving to establish the truth of something; conclusive evidence. 3. the establishment of the truth of something: as, to complete the *proof* of a theory. 4. a test or trial of the truth, worth, quality, etc. of something. 5. the state of having been tested or proved. 6. tested or proved strength, as of armor. 7. the relative strength of an alcoholic liquor with reference to the arbitrary standard for proof spirit, taken as 100 proof. 8. in *law,* all the facts, admissions, etc. which together operate to determine a verdict. 9. in *photography,* a trial print of a negative. 10. in *printing,* a trial impression, as from composed type, for checking to correct errors, make changes, etc. ***adj.*** 1. of tested and proved strength; impervious to (with *against*): as, *proof* against criticism. 2. used in proving or testing: as, a printer's *proof* sheet. 3. of standard strength: said of alcoholic liquors.

**-proof** (pro͞of), a suffix meaning: 1. *impervious to,* as in *waterproof.* 2. *protected from,* as in *weatherproof.* 3. *resistive to,* as in *pityproof.*

**proof·read** (pro͞of'rēd'), ***v.t. & v.i.*** [-READ (-red'), -READING], to read (printers' proofs, etc.) in order to make corrections. **—proof'read'er, *n.* —proof'read'ing, *n.***

**proof spirit,** an alcoholic liquor containing 50% of its volume of alcohol having a specific gravity of .7939 at 60° F.

**prop** (prop), ***n.*** [< MD. *proppe,* a prop], a support, as a stake or pole, placed under or against a structure or part: often used figuratively. ***v.t.*** [PROPPED, PROPPING], 1. to support or hold up, as with a prop (often with *up*). 2. to lean (something) *against* a support. 3. to sustain or bolster.

**prop** (prop), ***n.*** a property (sense 5).

**prop.,** 1. proper(ly). 2. proposition.

**prop·a·gan·da** (prop'ə-gan'də), ***n.*** [< L. *congregatio de propaganda fide,* the congregation for propagating the faith], 1. [P-], in the *R.C. Church,* a committee of cardinals in charge of the foreign missions. 2. any organization or movement for the propagation of particular ideas, doctrines, etc. 3. the ideas, etc. spread in this way. 4. any systematic, widespread indoctrination: now often connoting deception or distortion. **—prop'a·gan'dism, *n.* —prop'a·gan'dist, *n.* & *adj.* —prop'a·gan'dize** [-DIZED, -DIZING], ***v.t. & v.i.***

**prop·a·gate** (prop'ə-gāt'), ***v.t.*** [-GATED, -GATING], [< L. pp. of *propagare* < *propago,* slip (of a plant)], 1. to cause (a plant or animal) to reproduce itself; raise or breed. 2. to reproduce (itself): said of a plant or animal. 3. to spread (ideas, customs, etc.). 4. to extend or transmit through space, as light. *v.i.* to reproduce, as plants or animals. —**prop′a·ga·bil′i·ty** (-gə-bil′ə-ti), *n.* —**prop′a·ga·ble,** *adj.* —**prop′a·ga′tion,** *n.* —**prop′a·ga′tive,** *adj.* —**prop′a·ga′tor,** *n.*

**pro·pane** (prō′pān), *n.* [*propyl* + *methane*], a gaseous hydrocarbon of the methane series, $C_3H_8$.

‡**pro pa·tri·a** (prō pā′tri-ə), [L.], for (one's) country.

**pro·pel** (prə-pel′), *v.t.* [-PELLED, -PELLING], [< L. < *pro-*, forward + *pellere*, to drive], to push or impel onward or forward. —**pro·pel′la·ble,** *adj.* —**pro·pel′lant,** *n.* —**pro·pel′lent,** *adj. & n.*

**pro·pel·ler** (prə-pel′ẽr), *n.* a person or thing that propels; specif., a device consisting typically of a series of blades mounted at an angle in a revolving hub and serving to propel a ship or aircraft forward.

**pro·pen·si·ty** (prə-pen′sə-ti), *n.* [*pl.* -TIES], [< L. pp. of *propendere*, to hang forward], a natural inclination or tendency; bent.

**prop·er** (prop′ẽr), *adj.* [< OFr. < L. *proprius*, one's own], 1. specially adapted or suitable; appropriate: as, the *proper* tool for this job. 2. naturally belonging or peculiar (*to*): as, this weather is *proper* to Florida. 3. conforming to an accepted standard or to good usage; correct. 4. fitting; seemly; right. 5. decent; decorous: often connoting exaggerated respectability. 6. in the most restricted sense; strictly so called: as, Cleveland *proper* (i.e., apart from its suburbs). 7. [Now Dial.], *a*) fine; excellent. *b*) handsome. 8. [Brit. Colloq.], complete; thorough: as, a *proper* scoundrel. 9. in *grammar*, used to designate a specific individual, place, etc.: *Alan*, *Boston*, etc. are *proper* nouns, written with an initial capital letter. —**prop′er·ly,** *adv.* —**prop′er·ness,** *n.*

**proper fraction,** a fraction in which the numerator is less than the denominator, as $^2/_5$.

**prop·er·tied** (prop′ẽr-tid), *adj.* owning property.

**prop·er·ty** (prop′ẽr-ti), *n.* [*pl.* -TIES], [< OFr. < L. *proprietas* < *proprius*, one's own], 1. the right to possess, use, and dispose of something; ownership. 2. a thing or things owned; holdings or possessions; esp., land or real estate owned. 3. a specific piece of land or real estate. 4. any trait or attribute proper to a thing; characteristic or essential quality: as, the *properties* of a chemical compound. 5. any of the movable articles used as part of a stage setting or in a piece of stage business, except the costumes, backdrops, etc.

**proph·e·cy** (prof′ə-si), *n.* [*pl.* -CIES], [< OFr. < LL. < Gr. < *prophētēs*; see PROPHET], 1. prediction of the future under the influence of divine guidance; act or practice of a prophet. 2. any prediction. 3. something prophesied or predicted.

**proph·e·sy** (prof′ə-sī′), *v.t. & v.i.* [-SIED, -SYING], 1. to declare or predict (something) by or as by the influence of divine guidance; utter (prophecies). 2. to predict (a future event) in any way. —**proph′e·si′er,** *n.*

**proph·et** (prof′it), *n.* [< OFr. < LL. < Gr. *prophētēs* <*pro-*, before + *phanai*, to speak], 1. one who speaks for God or a god, or as though under divine guidance. 2. a religious leader regarded as, or claiming to be, divinely inspired. 3. a spokesman for some cause, group, etc. 4. one who predicts the future. —**the Prophet,** 1. in *Islam*, Mohammed. 2. in *Mormonism*, Joseph Smith. —**the Prophets,** 1. the writers of the prophetic books of the Old Testament. 2. these books. —**proph′et·ess,** *n.fem.* —**proph′et·hood′,** *n.*

**pro·phet·ic** (prə-fet′ik), *adj.* 1. of, or having the powers of, a prophet. 2. of, or having the nature of, prophecy. 3. containing a prophecy. Also **pro·phet′i·cal.** —**pro·phet′i·cal·ly,** *adv.*

**pro·phy·lac·tic** (prō′fə-lak tik, prof′ə-), *adj.* [< Gr.; ult. < *pro-*, before + *phylassein*, to guard], preventive or protective; esp., preventing disease. *n.* a prophylactic medicine, device, etc. —**pro′phy·lac′ti·cal·ly,** *adv.*

**pro·phy·lax·is** (prō′fə-lak′sis, prof′ə-), *n.* [*pl.* -LAXES (-lak′sēz)], the prevention of or protection from disease; prophylactic treatment.

**pro·pin·qui·ty** (prō-piŋ′kwə-ti), *n.* [< OFr. < L. < *propinquus*, near], 1. nearness in time or place. 2. nearness of relationship; kinship.

**pro·pi·ti·ate** (prə-pish′i-āt′), *v.t.* [-ATED, -ATING], [< L. *propitiatus*, pp.; see PROPITIOUS], to win or regain the good will of; appease or conciliate. —**pro·pi′ti·a·ble,** *adj.* —**pro·pi′ti·a′tion,** *n.* —**pro·pi′ti·a′tive,** *adj.* —**pro·pi′ti·a′tor,** *n.* —**pro·pi′ti·a·to′ry** (-tôr′i, -tō′ri), *adj.*

**pro·pi·tious** (prə-pish′əs), *adj.* [< OFr. < L. *propitius* < *pro-*, before + *petere*, to seek], 1. favorably inclined; gracious: as, the gods were *propitious.* 2. favorable; auspicious: as, a *propitious* omen. 3. that favors or furthers; advantageous: as, *propitious* winds. —**pro·pi′tious·ly,** *adv.* —**pro·pi′tious·ness,** *n.*

**pro·po·nent** (prə-pō′nənt), *n.* [< L. ppr. < *pro-*, forth + *ponere*, to place], 1. one who makes a proposal or proposition. 2. one who supports a cause.

**pro·por·tion** (prə-pôr′shən, -pōr′-), *n.* [< OFr. < L. < *pro-*, before + *portio*, a part], 1. a part, share, etc. in its relation to the whole; quota. 2. the comparative relation between things with respect to size, amount, etc.; ratio. 3. balance or symmetry. 4. size, degree, etc. relative to a standard. 5. *pl.* dimensions. 6. in *mathematics*, *a*) an equality between ratios (e.g., 2 is to 6 as 3 is to 9): also **geometrical proportion.** *b*) a method for finding the fourth quantity in such a relationship when three are given. *v.t.* 1. to cause to be in proper relation with something else: as, *proportion* the penalty to the crime. 2. to arrange the parts of (a whole) so as to be harmonious. —**pro·por′tion·a·ble,** *adj.* —**pro·por′tion·a·bly,** *adv.* —**pro·por′tioned,** *adj.* —**pro·por′tion·er,** *n.* —**pro·por′tion·ment,** *n.*

**pro·por·tion·al** (prə-pôr′shən-'l, -pōr′-), *adj.* 1. of or determined by proportion; relative. 2. in proportion: as, his work was *proportional* to his strength. 3. in *mathematics*, having the same ratio. *n.* a quantity in a mathematical proportion. —**pro·por′tion·al′i·ty,** *n.* —**pro·por′tion·al·ly,** *adv.*

**pro·por·tion·ate** (prə-pôr′shən-it, -pōr′-; *for v.*, -shə-nāt′), *adj.* in proper proportion; proportional. *v.t.* [-ATED, -ATING], to make proportionate. —**pro·por′tion·ate·ly,** *adv.*

**pro·pos·al** (prə-pō′z'l), *n.* 1. a proposing. 2. a proposed plan or scheme. 3. an offer of marriage.

**pro·pose** (prə-pōz′), *v.t.* [-POSED, -POSING], [< Fr. < *pro-* (< L. *pro-*), forth + *poser* < L. pp. of *ponere*, to place], 1. to put forth for consideration or acceptance. 2. to plan; intend. 3. to present as a toast in drinking. 4. to nominate for membership, office, etc. *v.i.* 1. to make a proposal; form a plan, purpose, etc. 2. to offer marriage. —**pro·pos′a·ble,** *adj.* —**pro·pos′er,** *n.*

**prop·o·si·tion** (prop′ə-zish′ən), *n.* 1. a proposing. 2. something proposed; plan. 3. [Colloq.], a project; business undertaking. 4. [Colloq.], a person, problem, etc. to be dealt with. 5. a subject to be debated. 6. in *logic*, an expression in which the predicate affirms or denies something about the subject. 7. in *mathematics*, a theorem to be demonstrated or a problem to be solved. —**prop′o·si′tion·al,** *adj.* —**prop′o·si′tion·al·ly,** *adv.*

**pro·pound** (prə-pound′), *v.t.* [earlier *propone;* L. *proponere;* see PROPONENT], to put forward for consideration; propose. —**pro·pound′er,** *n.*

**pro·pri·e·tar·y** (prə-prī′ə-ter′i), *n.* [*pl.* -IES], [< LL. < L. *proprietas;* see PROPERTY], 1. a proprietor. 2. a group of proprietors. 3. proprietorship. *adj.* 1. belonging to a proprietor. 2. holding property. 3. of property or proprietorship. 4. held under patent, trade-mark, or copyright: as, a *proprietary* medicine.

**pro·pri·e·tor** (prə-prī′ə-tẽr), *n.* [< *proprietary* + *-or*], a person who has an exclusive right to some property; owner. —**pro·pri′e·tor·ship′,** *n.* —**pro·pri′e·tress,** *n.fem.*

**pro·pri·e·ty** (prə-prī′ə-ti), *n.* [*pl.* -TIES], [< Fr. < OFr.; see PROPERTY], 1. the quality of being proper, fitting, etc.; fitness. 2. conformity with what is proper or fitting or with accepted standards of behavior. —**the proprieties,** accepted standards of behavior in polite society.

**pro·pul·sion** (prə-pul′shən), *n.* [Fr. < L. pp.; see PROPEL], 1. a propelling or being propelled. 2. something that propels. —**pro·pul′sive,** *adj.*

**pro·pyl** (prō′pil), *n.* [< *proto-* + Gr. *piōn*, fat; + *-yl*], the monovalent radical $C_3H_7$, derived from propane.

**pro ra·ta** (prō rā′tə; *occas.*, rä′tə), [L. *pro rata* (*parte*), according to the calculated (share)], in proportion; proportionately.

**pro·rate** (prō′rāt′, prō′rāt′), *v.t. & v.i.* [-RATED, -RATING], [< *pro rata*], to divide, assess, or distribute proportionally. —**pro·rat′a·ble,** *adj.*

**pro·rogue** (prō-rōg′), *v.t.* [-ROGUED, -ROGUING], [< Fr. < L. *prorogare*, to defer < *pro-*, for + *rogare*, to ask], to discontinue or end a session of (a legislative assembly). —**pro′ro·ga′tion** (-rō-gā′shən), *n.* —**pro·ro′guer,** *n.*

**pro·sa·ic** (prō-zā′ik), *adj.* [< ML. < L. *prosa*, prose], 1. of or like prose; unpoetic. 2. commonplace; dull. —**pro·sa′i·cal·ly,** *adv.* —**pro·sa′ic·ness,** *n.*

**pro·sce·ni·um** (prō-sē′ni-əm), *n.* [*pl.* -NIA (-ni-ə)], [L. < Gr. < *pro-*, before + *skēnē*, a tent], 1. the area of a theater stage in front of the curtain. 2. the curtain and the framework around it.

**pro·scribe** (prō-skrīb′), *v.t.* [-SCRIBED, -SCRIBING], [< L. < *pro-*, before + *scribere*, to write], 1. in ancient Rome, to publish the name of (a person) condemned to death, banishment, etc. 2. to deprive of the protection of the law; outlaw. 3. to banish; exile. 4. to denounce and forbid; interdict. —**pro·scrib′er,** *n.* —**pro·scrip′tion** (-skrip′shən), *n.* —**pro·scrip′tive,** *adj.*

**prose** (prōz), *n.* [OFr. < L. *prosa*, for *prorsa* (*oratio*), direct (speech) < *pro-*, forward + pp. of *vertere*, to turn], 1. the ordinary form of language, without rhyme or meter: cf. *verse, poetry*. 2. dull, commonplace talk. *adj.* 1. of or in prose. 2. dull; prosaic. *v.t. & v.i.* [PROSED, PROSING], to speak or write in prose. —**pros′er,** *n.*

**pros·e·cute** (pros′i-kūt′), *v.t.* [-CUTED, -CUTING], [< L. *prosecutus*, pp. < *pro-*, before + *sequi*, to follow], 1. to pursue (something) so as to complete it: as, *prosecute* a war. 2. to carry on; practice: as, *prosecute* your studies. 3. to conduct legal proceedings against, especially for a crime. 4. to try to get, enforce, etc. by legal process. *v.i.* to institute and carry on a legal suit. —**pros′e·cut′a·ble,** *adj.* —**pros′e·cu′tor,** *n.*

**prosecuting attorney,** a public official who conducts criminal prosecutions on behalf of the State.

**pros·e·cu·tion** (pros′i-kū′shən), *n.* 1. a prosecuting, or following up. 2. the conducting of a lawsuit. 3. the party who institutes and carries on criminal proceedings in court.

**pros·e·lyte** (pros′′l-īt′), *n.* [< ML. < Gr. *prosēlytos*], a person who has been converted from one religion, opinion, etc. to another. *v.t. & v.i.* [-LYTED, -LYTING], to proselytize. —**pros′e·lyt′er,** *n.* —**pros′e·lyt·ism** (-i-tiz′m, -īt-iz′m), *n.*

**pros·e·lyt·ize** (pros′′l-i-tīz′, -īt-īz′), *v.i. & v.t.* [-IZED, -IZING], to make proselytes, or converts, (of). —**pros′e·lyt′i·za′tion,** *n.* —**pros′e·lyt·iz′er,** *n.*

**Pro·ser·pi·na** (prō-sũr′pi-nə), *n.* in *Rom. mythology*, Persephone: also **Pro·ser′pi·ne′** (-nē′, pros′ẽr-pīn′).

‡**pro·sit** (prō′sit), *interj.* [L., 3d pers. sing. subj. of *prodesse*, to do good], to your health: a toast, especially among Germans.

**pro·slav·er·y** (prō-slāv′ẽr-i), *adj.* in *U.S. history*, in favor of preserving Negro slavery.

**pros·o·dy** (pros′ə-di), *n.* [*pl.* -DIES], [< L. < Gr. *prosōidia*, tone, accent < *pros*, to + *ōidē*, song], 1. the science or art of versification, including the study of metrical structure, rhyme, etc. 2. a system of versification: as, Dryden's *prosody*. —**pro·sod·ic** (prə-sod′ik), **pros′o·di′a·cal** (-dī′ə-k′l), *adj.* —**pro·sod′i·cal·ly,** *adv.* —**pros′o·dist,** *n.*

**pros·pect** (pros′pekt), *n.* [< L. *prospectus*, lookout; ult. < *pro-*, forward + *specere*, to look], 1. a broad view; scene. 2. the view from any particular point; outlook. 3. a looking forward; anticipation. 4. *a*) something expected; probable outcome. *b*) *usually in pl.* apparent chance for success, gain, etc. 5. a likely customer, candidate, etc. *v.t. & v.i.* to explore or search (*for*): as, to *prospect* for gold. —**in prospect,** expected.

**pro·spec·tive** (prə-spek′tiv), *adj.* 1. looking to the future. 2. expected; likely. —**pro·spec′tive·ly,** *adv.* —**pro·spec′tive·ness,** *n.*

**pros·pec·tor** (pros′pek-tẽr), *n.* a person who prospects for precious minerals, oil, etc.

**pro·spec·tus** (prə-spek′təs), *n.* [L.; see PROSPECT], a statement outlining the main features of a new work, business enterprise, etc.

**pros·per** (pros′pẽr), *v.i.* [< Fr. < L. < *prosperus*, favorable], to succeed; be prosperous; thrive. *v.t.* to cause to prosper. —**pros′per·ing,** *adj.*

**pros·per·i·ty** (pros-per′ə-ti), *n.* [*pl.* -TIES], prosperous condition; good fortune; wealth.

**pros·per·ous** (pros′pẽr-əs), *adj.* 1. prospering; successful; flourishing. 2. well-to-do; well-off. 3. conducive to success; favorable. —**pros′per·ous·ly,** *adv.* —**pros′per·ous·ness,** *n.*

**pros·tate** (pros′tāt), *adj.* [< ML. < Gr. *prostatēs*, one standing before; ult. < *pro-*, before + *histanai*, to set], designating or of a muscular gland surrounding the urethra at the base of the bladder in the male. *n.* the prostate gland. —**pro·stat·ic** (prō-stat′ik), *adj.*

**pros·the·sis** (pros′thə-sis), *n.* [< LL. < Gr. < *pros*, to + *tithenai*, to place], in *medicine*, 1. the replacement of a missing limb, eye, etc. by an artificial substitute. 2. such a substitute. —**pros·thet·ic** (pros-thet′ik), *adj.*

**pros·ti·tute** (pros′tə-tōōt′, -tūt′), *v.t.* [-TUTED, -TUTING], [< L. *prostitutus*, pp. < *pro*, before + *statuere*, to cause to stand], 1. to sell the services of (oneself or another) for purposes of sexual intercourse. 2. to sell (oneself, one's integrity, etc.) for unworthy purposes. *adj.* debased; corrupt. *n.* 1. a woman who engages in promiscuous sexual intercourse for pay. 2. a writer, artist, etc. who sells his services for unworthy purposes. —**pros′ti·tu′tion,** *n.* —**pros′ti·tu′tor,** *n.*

**pros·trate** (pros′trāt), *adj.* [< L. *prostratus*, pp. < *pro-*, before + *sternere*, to stretch out], 1. lying with the face downward in humility or submission. 2. lying flat, prone, or supine. 3. thrown or fallen to the ground. 4. laid low; overcome. 5. in *botany*, trailing on the ground. *v.t.* [-TRATED, -TRATING], 1. to lay flat on the ground. 2. to lay low; exhaust or subjugate. —**pros·tra′tion,** *n.*

**pro·style** (prō′stīl), *adj.* [< L. < Gr. < *pro*, before + *stylos*, pillar], having a portico with columns across the front only. *n.* such a portico.

**pros·y** (prō′zi), *adj.* [-IER, -IEST], 1. like, or having the nature of, prose. 2. prosaic; dull, tedious, etc. —**pros′i·ly,** *adv.* —**pros′i·ness,** *n.*

**Prot.,** Protestant.

**pro·tac·tin·i·um** (prō′tak-tin′i-əm), *n.* [< *proto-* + *actinium*], a rare radioactive chemical element: symbol, Pa; at. wt., 231; at. no., 91: formerly called **pro′to·ac·tin′i·um** (prō′tō-ak-).

**pro·tag·o·nist** (prō-tag′ə-nist), *n.* [< Gr. *prōtos*, first + *agōnistēs*, actor], 1. the main character in a drama, novel, or story. 2. a person who plays a leading or active part.

**prot·a·sis** (prot′ə-sis), *n.* [LL. < Gr. < *pro-*, before + *teinein*, to stretch], in *grammar*, the clause that expresses the condition in a conditional sentence: opposed to *apodosis*.

**pro·te·an** (prō′ti-ən, prō-tē′-), *adj.* 1. [P-], of or like Proteus. 2. very changeable; readily taking on different shapes and forms.

**pro·tect** (prə-tekt′), *v.t.* [< L. *protectus*, pp. < *pro-*, before + *tegere*, to cover], 1. to shield from injury, danger, or loss; defend. 2. to set aside funds for paying (a note, draft, etc.) at maturity. 3. in *economics*, to guard (domestic industry) by tariffs on imported products. —**pro·tect′ing,** *adj.* —**pro·tect′ing·ly,** *adv.*

**pro·tec·tion** (prə-tek′shən), *n.* 1. a protecting or being protected. 2. a person or thing that protects. 3. a passport. 4. [Colloq.], *a*) money extorted by racketeers as insurance against threatened violence. *b*) such extortion. 5. in *economics*, the system of protecting domestic products by taxing imports: opposed to *free trade*.

**pro·tec·tion·ism** (prə-tek′shən-iz′m), *n.* in *economics*, the system, theory, or policy of protection. —**pro·tec′tion·ist,** *n.*

**pro·tec·tive** (prə-tek′tiv), *adj.* 1. protecting or intended to protect. 2. intended to protect domestic products, industries, etc. in competition with foreign ones: as, a *protective* tariff. —**pro·tec′tive·ly,** *adv.* —**pro·tec′tive·ness,** *n.*

**protective coloration** (or **coloring**), the natural coloration of any of certain organisms by means of which it is blended in with its normal environment and is thus protected from detection.

**pro·tec·tor** (prə-tek′tẽr), *n.* 1. one that protects. 2. *a*) one who rules a kingdom during the minority, absence, etc. of the sovereign. *b*) [P-], the title (in full, *Lord Protector*) held by Oliver Cromwell (1653–1658) and his son Richard (1658–1659), during the Commonwealth. —**pro·tec′tor·al,** *adj.* —**pro·tec′tor·ship′,** *n.* —**pro·tec′tress,** *n.fem.*

**pro·tec·tor·ate** (prə-tek′tẽr-it), *n.* 1. government by a protector. 2. the office or term of a protector. 3. [P-], the government of England under the Protectors (1653–1659). 4. the relation of a strong state to a weaker state under its control and protection. 5. a state so controlled.

**pro·té·gé** (prō′tə-zhā′), *n.* [Fr., pp. of *protéger* < L.; see PROTECT], a person under the patronage or protection of another. —**pro′té·gée′** (-zhā′), *n.fem.*

**pro·te·in** (prō′tē-in, -tēn), *n.* [G. < Gr. *prōteios*, prime < *prōtos*, first], any of a class of complex nitrogenous substances occurring in all animal and vegetable matter and essential to the diet of animals. *adj.* containing proteins. Also **pro′te·ide′** (-ti-īd′), **pro′te·id** (-ti-id).

**pro tem·po·re** (prō tem′pə-rē′), [L.], for the time being; temporarily: shortened to **pro tem.**

**Prot·er·o·zo·ic** (prot′ẽr-ə-zō′ik), *adj.* [< Gr. *proteros*, former; + *zo*(*o*)- + *-ic*], designating or of the geological era following the Archeozoic and preceding the Paleozoic: see **geology,** chart. *n.* the Proterozoic Era.

**pro·test** (prə-test′; *for n.*, prō′test), ***v.t.*** [< L. < *pro-*, forth + *testari*, to affirm < *testis*, a witness], 1. to state positively; assert. 2. to speak strongly against. 3. to make a written declaration of the nonpayment of (a promissory note, check, etc.). ***v.i.*** 1. to make a solemn affirmation. 2. to express disapproval; object. ***n.*** 1. an objection; remonstrance. 2. a document formally objecting to something. 3. in *law*, a formal declaration that a bill or note has not been honored by the drawer. **—under protest,** having first expressed one's objections. **—pro·test′er, *n.* —pro·test′ing·ly, *adv.***

**prot·es·tant** (prot′is-tənt; *also for n. 2 & adj. 2*, prə-tes′tənt), ***n.*** [Fr. < L. ppr. of *protestari;* see PROTEST], 1. [P-], any Christian not belonging to the Roman Catholic or Orthodox Eastern Church: cf. *Reformation*. 2. one who protests. ***adj.*** 1. [P-], of Protestants or Protestantism. 2. protesting.

**Protestant Episcopal Church,** the Protestant church in the U.S. that conforms to the practices and principles of the Church of England.

**Prot·es·tant·ism** (prot′is-tənt-iz′m), ***n.*** 1. the religion of Protestants. 2. a being Protestant. 3. Protestants or Protestant churches, collectively.

**prot·es·ta·tion** (prot′əs-tā′shən), ***n.*** 1. a protesting; strong declaration. 2. a protest; objection.

**Pro·teus** (prō′tūs, -ti-əs), ***n.*** in *Gr. mythology*, a sea god who could change his own form at will.

**pro·to-,** [< Gr. < *prōtos*, first], a combining form meaning: 1. *first in time, original, primitive,* as in *protocol, proto-Arabic.* 2. *first in importance, chief,* as in *protagonist.* Also **prot-**.

**pro·to·ac·tin·i·um** (prō′tō-ak-tin′i-əm), ***n.*** protactinium: the former name.

**pro·to·col** (prō′tə-kol′), ***n.*** [< OFr. < ML. < Late Gr. *prōtokollon*, first leaf glued to a manuscript (noting the contents) < Gr. *prōtos*, first + *kolla*, glue], 1. an original draft or record of a document, negotiation (preliminary to a treaty), etc. 2. the established ceremonial forms and courtesies used in official dealings, as between heads of states and their ministers. ***v.i.*** to draw up a protocol. **—pro′to·col′ist, *n.***

**pro·ton** (prō′ton), ***n.*** [< Gr. neut. of *prōtos*, first], a fundamental particle of the nuclei of all atoms, carrying a unit positive charge of electricity: cf. **neutron.**

**pro·to·plasm** (prō′tə-plaz′m), ***n.*** [< G. < Gr. *prōtos*, first + *plasma*, anything molded < *plassein*, to mold], a semifluid, viscous, translucent colloid, the essential living matter of all animal and plant cells. **—pro′to·plas′mic, *adj.***

**pro·to·type** (prō′tə-tīp′), ***n.*** [see PROTO-], the first thing or being of its kind; archetype; original. **—pro′to·typ′al, pro′to·typ′ic** (-tip′ik), ***adj.***

**Pro·to·zo·a** (prō′tə-zō′ə), ***n.pl.*** [< Gr. *prōtos*, first + *zōion*, an animal], the phylum of protozoans.

**pro·to·zo·an** (prō′tə-zō′ən), ***n.*** any of a number of one-celled animals, usually microscopic, belonging to the lowest division of the animal kingdom: also **pro′to·zo′on** (-on). ***adj.*** of or belonging to the Protozoa: also **pro′to·zo′ic, pro′to·zo′al.**

**pro·tract** (prō-trakt′), ***v.t.*** [< L. *protractus*, pp. < *pro-*, forward + *trahere*, to draw], 1. to draw out in time; prolong. 2. to draw to scale, using a protractor and scale. 3. in *zoology*, to extend; thrust out. **—pro·tract′ed, *adj.* —pro·tract′ed·ly, *adv.* —pro·tract′ed·ness, *n.* —pro·tract′i·ble, *adj.* —pro·trac′tion, *n.* —pro·trac′tive, *adj.***

**pro·trac·tile** (prō-trak′t'l), ***adj.*** that can be protracted or thrust out; extensible.

**pro·trac·tor** (prō-trak′tẽr), ***n.*** 1. one who protracts. 2. a graduated, semicircular instrument for drawing and measuring angles.

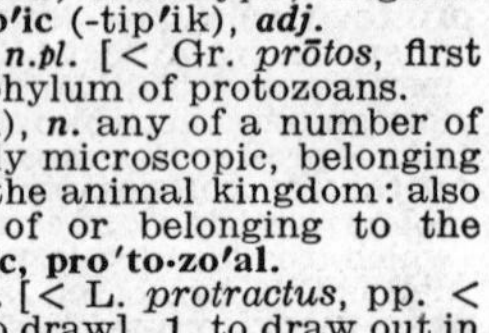

PROTRACTOR
DAC, angle measured

**pro·trude** (prō-trōōd′), ***v.t. & v.i.*** [-TRUDED, -TRUDING], [< L. < *pro-*, forth + *trudere*, to thrust], to thrust or jut out; project. **—pro·tru′dent, *adj.* —pro·tru′sion** (-trōō′zhən), ***n.***

**pro·tru·sile** (prō-trōō′s'l), ***adj.*** that can be protruded, or thrust out, as a tentacle, etc.

**pro·tru·sive** (prō-trōō′siv), ***adj.*** 1. protruding; jutting or bulging out. 2. obtrusive. **—pro·tru′sive·ly, *adv.* —pro·tru′sive·ness, *n.***

**pro·tu·ber·ance** (prō-tōō′bẽr-əns, -tū′-), ***n.*** 1. a being protuberant. 2. a part or thing that protrudes; projection; bulge. Also **pro·tu′ber·an·cy** (-ən-si), [*pl.* -CIES].

**pro·tu·ber·ant** (prō-tōō′bẽr-ənt, -tū′-), ***adj.*** [< LL. < *protuberare*, to bulge out < L. *pro-*, forth + *tuber*, a bump], bulging out; protruding; prominent. **—pro·tu′ber·ant·ly, *adv.***

**proud** (proud), ***adj.*** [AS. *prud*], 1. having or showing a proper pride in oneself, one's position, etc. 2. having or showing an overweening opinion of oneself; haughty. 3. feeling or showing great pride or joy. 4. that is a cause of pride; highly gratifying. 5. caused by pride; presumptuous. 6. stately; splendid: as, a *proud* fleet. 7. spirited: as, a *proud* stallion. **—do oneself proud,** [Colloq.], to do extremely well. **—proud of,** highly pleased with. **—proud′ly, *adv.***

**proud flesh,** [< the notion of swelling up], an abnormal growth of flesh around a healing wound.

**Proust, Mar·cel** (mär′sel′ prōōst′), 1871–1922; French novelist.

**Prov.,** 1. Provençal. 2. Proverbs. 3. Province.

**prov.,** 1. provincial. 2. provisional. 3. provost.

**prove** (prōōv), ***v.t.*** [PROVED, PROVED or PROVEN, PROVING], [< AS. < OFr. *prover* < L.; see PROBE], 1. to test by experiment, standard, etc.; try out. 2. to establish as true. 3. to establish the validity of (a will, etc.). 4. in *mathematics*, to test the correctness of (a calculation, etc.). ***v.i.*** to be found by experience or trial; turn out to be. **—the exception proves the rule,** the exception puts the rule to the test. **—prov′a·ble, *adj.* —prov′a·ble·ness, *n.* —prov′a·bly, *adv.* —prov′er, *n.***

**Pro·ven·çal** (prō′vən-säl′, prov′ən-), ***adj.*** of Provence, its people, their language, etc. ***n.*** 1. the vernacular of southern France, a distinct Romance language which, in its medieval form, was an important literary language. 2. a native or inhabitant of Provence.

**Pro·vence** (prov′ens; Fr. prô′väns′), ***n.*** a former province of SE France, on the Mediterranean.

**prov·en·der** (prov′ən-dẽr), ***n.*** [< OFr. < L. *praebenda;* see PREBEND], 1. dry food for livestock, as hay, corn, etc. 2. [Colloq.], food: used humorously.

**Prov. Eng.,** Provincial English.

**prov·erb** (prov′ẽrb), ***n.*** [< OFr. < L. < *pro-*, before + *verbum*, a word], 1. a short, popular saying that expresses some obvious truth. 2. a person or thing that has become commonly recognized as a type; byword. ***v.t.*** 1. to make a proverb of. 2. to describe in a proverb.

**pro·ver·bi·al** (prə-vũr′bi-əl), ***adj.*** 1. of, or having the nature of, a proverb. 2. expressed in a proverb. 3. that has become an object of common reference, as in a proverb. **—pro·ver′bi·al·ly, *adv.***

**Prov·erbs** (prov′ẽrbz), ***n.pl.*** [construed as sing.], a book of the Old Testament, containing various maxims ascribed to Solomon and others.

**pro·vide** (prə-vīd′), ***v.t.*** [-VIDED, -VIDING], [< L. < *pro-*, before + *videre*, to see], 1. to get ready beforehand. 2. to make available; supply. 3. to furnish (*with*). ***v.i.*** 1. to prepare (*for* or *against*) a possible situation, event, etc. 2. to make a condition; stipulate. 3. to furnish the means of support (*for*). **—pro·vid′a·ble, *adj.* —pro·vid′er, *n.***

**pro·vid·ed** (prə-vīd′id), ***conj.*** on the condition or understanding; if (often with *that*).

**Prov·i·dence** (prov′ə-dəns), ***n.*** capital of Rhode Island, on Narragansett Bay: pop., 207,000.

**prov·i·dence** (prov′ə-dəns), ***n.*** [< L. < *providere;* see PROVIDE], 1. a looking to, or preparation for, the future; provision. 2. skill in management; prudence. 3. the benevolent guidance of God or nature. 4. an instance of this. 5. [P-], God.

**prov·i·dent** (prov′ə-dənt), ***adj.*** 1. providing for future needs or events. 2. prudent; economical. **—prov′i·dent·ly, *adv.***

**prov·i·den·tial** (prov′ə-den′shəl), ***adj.*** 1. of providence. 2. decreed by Providence. 3. fortunate; lucky. **—prov′i·den′tial·ly, *adv.***

**pro·vid·ing** (prə-vīd′iŋ), ***conj.*** on the condition or understanding (that); provided.

**prov·ince** (prov′ins), ***n.*** [< OFr. < L. *provincia*], 1. a territory, outside Italy, governed by ancient Rome. 2. an administrative division of a country, especially of Canada. 3. *a)* a region; district. *b) pl.* the parts of a country removed from the capital and the major cities. 4. proper duties or functions. 5. a department; branch of learning. 6. a division of a country under the jurisdiction of an archbishop or metropolitan.

**pro·vin·cial** (prə-vin′shəl), ***adj.*** 1. of or belonging to the provinces. 2. having the ways, speech, attitudes, etc. of people in a province. 3. countrified; rustic. 4. narrow; limited. ***n.*** 1. a native of a province. 2. a provincial person. **—pro·vin′cial·ly, *adv.***

**pro·vin·cial·ism** (prə-vin′shəl-iz′m), ***n.*** 1. a being provincial. 2. narrowness of outlook. 3. a provincial custom, characteristic, etc. 4. a word, phrase, etc. peculiar to a province. Also **pro·vin'ci·al'i·ty** [pl. -TIES]. **—pro·vin'cial·ist,** ***n.***

**pro·vi·sion** (prə-vizh'ən), ***n.*** [< L. *provisus*, pp.; see PROVIDE], 1. a providing or preparing. 2. something provided for the future; specif., *pl.* a stock of food. 3. preparatory measures taken in advance. 4. a clause, as in a legal document, stipulating some specific thing. ***v.t.*** to supply with provisions. **—pro·vi'sion·er,** ***n.***

**pro·vi·sion·al** (prə-vizh'ən-'l), ***adj.*** conditional or temporary, pending permanent arrangement: as, a *provisional* government: also **pro·vi'sion·ar'y** (-er'i). **—pro·vi'sion·al·ly,** ***adv.***

**pro·vi·so** (prə-vī'zō), ***n.*** [*pl.* -SOS, -SOES], [L., it being provided, abl. of pp. of *providere;* see PROVIDE], 1. a clause, as in a document, making some condition. 2. a condition; stipulation.

**pro·vi·so·ry** (prə-vī'zẽr-i), ***adj.*** 1. conditional. 2. provisional. **—pro·vi'so·ri·ly,** ***adv.***

**prov·o·ca·tion** (prov'ə-kā'shən), ***n.*** 1. a provoking. 2. something that provokes; incitement.

**pro·voc·a·tive** (prə-vok'ə-tiv), ***adj.*** provoking or tending to provoke, as to action, thought, anger, etc. ***n.*** something that provokes. **—pro·voc'a·tive·ly,** ***adv.*** **—pro·voc'a·tive·ness,** ***n.***

**pro·voke** (prə-vōk'), ***v.t.*** [-VOKED, -VOKING], [< OFr. < L. < *pro-*, forth + *vocare*, to call], 1. to excite to some action or feeling. 2. to anger; irritate. 3. to stir up (action or feeling). 4. to call forth; evoke. **—pro·vok'er,** ***n.*** **—pro·vok'ing,** ***adj.*** **—pro·vok'ing·ly,** ***adv.***

**prov·ost** (prov'əst; *in military usage,* prō'vō), ***n.*** [< AS. & OFr. < LL. *propositus*, for L. *praepositus*, chief; ult. < *prae-*, before + *ponere*, to put], 1. a superintendent; official in charge. 2. the chief magistrate in a Scottish burgh. 3. the head of, or an administrator in, some colleges. **—prov'ost·ship',** ***n.***

**pro·vost marshal** (prō'vō), 1. in the *army*, an officer in charge of military police. 2. in the *navy*, an officer charged with the custody of prisoners on trial by court-martial.

**prow** (prou), ***n.*** [< Fr. < L. < Gr. *prōira*], 1. the forward part of a ship. 2. something like this.

**prow·ess** (prou'is), ***n.*** [< OFr. *prouesse* < *prou*, brave; ult. < L. *prodesse*, to be of use], 1. bravery; gallantry. 2. a valorous act. 3. superior ability, skill, technique, etc.

**prowl** (proul), ***v.i. & v.t.*** [ME. *prollen*], to roam about furtively in search of prey. ***n.*** a prowling. **—on the prowl,** prowling about. **—prowl'er,** ***n.*** **—prowl'ing·ly,** ***adv.***

**prowl car,** a squad car.

**prox.,** proximo.

**prox·i·mal** (prok'sə-m'l), ***adj.*** 1. proximate; next or nearest. 2. situated nearest the point of attachment of a limb, etc. **—prox'i·mal·ly,** ***adv.***

**prox·i·mate** (prok'sə-mit), ***adj.*** [< LL. pp. < L. *proximus*, superl. of *prope*, near], 1. next or nearest in space, order, time, etc. 2. approximate. **—prox'i·mate·ly,** ***adv.***

**prox·im·i·ty** (prok-sim'ə-ti), ***n.*** [< Fr. < L. < *proximus;* see PROXIMATE], nearness in space, time, etc.

**prox·i·mo** (prok'sə-mō'), ***adv.*** [L. *proximo* (*mense*), in the next (month)], in or of the next month.

**prox·y** (prok'si), ***n.*** [*pl.* -IES], [< ME. < *procuracie*, office of a proctor], 1. the function of a deputy. 2. the authority to act for another, as in voting. 3. a document so authorizing one or a person so authorized.

**prude** (prōōd), ***n.*** [Fr.; prob. < *prudefemme*, excellent woman], one who is overly modest or proper in behavior, speech, dress, etc. **—prud'ish,** ***adj.*** **—prud'ish·ly,** ***adv.*** **—prud'ish·ness,** ***n.***

**pru·dence** (prōō'd'ns), ***n.*** 1. the quality or fact of being prudent. 2. careful management; economy.

**pru·dent** (prōō'd'nt), ***adj.*** [OFr. < L. *prudens*, for *providens*, provident], 1. exercising sound judgment in practical matters. 2. cautious in conduct; sensible; not rash. **—pru'dent·ly,** ***adv.***

**pru·den·tial** (prōō-den'shəl), ***adj.*** 1. characterized by or exercising prudence. 2. discretionary or advisory. **—pru·den'tial·ly,** ***adv.***

**prud·er·y** (prōōd'ẽr-i), ***n.*** 1. a being prudish, or overly proper. 2. [*pl.* -IES], an instance of this.

**prune** (prōōn), ***n.*** [OFr. < L. < Gr. *prounon*, plum], a dried plum.

**prune** (prōōn), ***v.t.*** [PRUNED, PRUNING], [< OFr.; prob. ult. < *provain* (< L. *propago*), a slip], 1. to remove dead or living parts from (a plant), as for increasing fruit or flower production. 2. to cut out, as unnecessary parts. ***v.i.*** to remove unnecessary branches or parts. **—prun'er,** ***n.***

**pruning hook,** a pair of shears with one hooked blade, used for pruning branches, vines, etc.

**pru·ri·ent** (proor'i-ənt), ***adj.*** [< L. *pruriens* < *prurire*, to itch or long for], 1. having lustful ideas or desires. 2. lustful; lewd. **—pru'ri·ence, pru'ri·en·cy,** ***n.*** **—pru'ri·ent·ly,** ***adv.***

**Prus.,** 1. Prussia. 2. Prussian.

**Prus·sia** (prush'ə), ***n.*** a former state of N Germany, once a kingdom. **—Prus'sian,** ***adj. & n.***

**Prussian blue,** any of a group of dark-blue powders, cyanogen compounds of iron, used as dyes, etc.

**prus·sic acid** (prus'ik), hydrocyanic acid.

**pry** (prī), ***n.*** [*pl.* PRIES], [back-formation < *prize*, a lever], 1. a lever, crowbar, etc. 2. leverage. ***v.t.*** [PRIED, PRYING], 1. to raise or move with a lever, etc. 2. to draw forth with difficulty.

**pry** (prī), ***v.i.*** [PRIED, PRYING], [ME. *prien*, to peer], to look closely or inquisitively. ***n.*** [*pl.* PRIES], 1. a prying. 2. a person who is improperly curious.

**pry·er** (prī'ẽr), ***n.*** a prier.

**pry·ing** (prī'iŋ), ***adj.*** improperly curious; inquisitive; peering. **—pry'ing·ly,** ***adv.***

**ps.,** pieces.

**P.S.,** 1. Privy Seal. 2. Public School.

**PS., P.S., p.s.,** [*pl.* P.SS.], postscript.

**Ps., Psa.,** Psalm; Psalms.

**psalm** (säm), ***n.*** [< AS. & OFr. < LL. < Gr. *psalmos* < *psallein*, to pluck (a harp)], 1. a sacred song or poem. 2. any of the songs or hymns composing the Book of Psalms in the Old Testament.

**psalm·book** (säm'book'), ***n.*** a collection of psalms for use in religious worship.

**psalm·ist** (säm'ist), ***n.*** a composer of psalms. **—the Psalmist,** King David, to whom all or certain of the Psalms are attributed.

**psal·mo·dy** (säm'ə-di, sal'mə-), ***n.*** [*pl.* -DIES], [< LL. < Gr. < *psalmos* (see PSALM) + *ōdē*, a song], 1. the singing of psalms. 2. psalms collectively. 3. the arrangement of psalms for singing. **—psal'mo·dic,** ***adj.*** **—psal'mo·dist,** ***n.***

**Psalms** (sämz), ***n.pl.*** [construed as sing.], a book of the Old Testament, consisting of 150 psalms.

**Psal·ter** (sôl'tẽr), ***n.*** [< L. < Gr. *psaltērion*, psaltery], 1. the Book of Psalms. 2. [also p-], a version of the Psalms for use in religious services.

**psal·ter·y** (sôl'tẽr-i, -tri), ***n.*** [*pl.* -IES], [< OFr. < L. < Gr. *psaltērion* < *psallein*, to pull], an ancient stringed instrument with a shallow sound box, played by plucking the strings.

**pseud.,** pseudonym.

**pseu·do** (sōō'dō, sū'-), ***adj.*** [see PSEUDO-], sham; false; spurious; pretended; counterfeit.

**pseu·do-,** [< Gr. < *pseudēs*, false < *pseudein*, to deceive], a combining form meaning: 1. *fictitious*, *sham*, as in *pseudonym*. 2. *counterfeit*, *spurious*. 3. *closely* or *deceptively similar to* (a specified thing).

**pseu·do·nym** (sōō'də-nim', sū'-), ***n.*** [< Fr. < Gr. < *pseudēs*, false + *onyma*, a name], a fictitious name, as assumed by an author; pen name. **—pseu'do·nym'i·ty,** ***n.*** **—pseu·don'y·mous** (-don'ə-məs), ***adj.***

**pseu·do·po·di·um** (sōō'də-pō'di-əm, sū'-), ***n.*** [*pl.* -DIA (-di-ə)], [*pseudo-* + Gr. dim. of *pous*, a foot], a temporary projection of the protoplasm of certain protozoa, serving as a means of moving about or for taking in food: also **pseu'do·pod'** (-pod').

**pshaw** (shô), ***interj. & n.*** an exclamation of impatience, disgust, etc. ***v.i. & v.t.*** to express impatience, contempt, etc. (at) by saying "pshaw."

**psi** (sī; Gr. psē), ***n.*** [Gr.], the twenty-third letter of the Greek alphabet (Ψ, ψ).

**psit·ta·co·sis** (sit'ə-kō'sis), ***n.*** [< Gr. *psittakos*, a parrot; + *-osis*], an acute infectious virus disease of birds of the parrot family, often transmitted to man: also called *parrot fever.*

**pso·ri·a·sis** (sō-rī'ə-sis, sə-), ***n.*** [< Gr. < *psōra*, an itch], a chronic skin disease with scaly, reddish patches. **—pso·ri·at·ic** (sôr'i-at'ik, sō'ri-), ***adj.***

**P.S.T., PST,** Pacific Standard Time.

**psych.,** 1. psychological. 2. psychology.

**Psy·che** (sī'ki), ***n.*** [L. < Gr. < *psychē*, the soul], 1. in *Gr. & Rom. mythology*, a maiden who becomes the wife of Cupid and is made immortal: she personifies the soul. 2. [p-], *a*) the soul. *b*) the mind, especially as an organic system serving to adjust the total organism to the environment.

**psy·che·del·ic** (sī'ki-del'ik), ***adj.*** [< *psyche* + Gr. *delein*, to make manifest], of or causing extreme changes in the conscious mind, as hallucinations, delusions, etc.

**psy·chi·a·try** (sī-kī′ə-tri), *n.* [< *psych(o)-* + Gr. *iatreia*, healing], the branch of medicine dealing with disorders of the mind, including psychoses and neuroses. —**psy′chi·at′ric** (-ki-at′rik), **psy′chi·at′ri·cal,** *adj.* —**psy′chi·at′ri·cal·ly,** *adv.* —**psy·chi′a·trist,** *n.*

**psy·chic** (sī′kik), *adj.* [< Gr. < *psychē*, the soul], 1. of the psyche, or mind. 2. beyond natural or known physical processes. 3. apparently sensitive to forces beyond the physical world. Also **psy′chi·cal.** *n.* one who is supposedly psychic (sense 3). —**psy′chi·cal·ly,** *adv.*

**psy·cho** (sī′kō), *adj.* & *n.* [Colloq.], psychoneurotic.

**psy·cho-,** [< Gr. *psychē*, soul], a combining form meaning *the mind* or *mental processes*, as in *psychology*: also **psych-.**

**psy·cho·a·nal·y·sis** (sī′kō-ə-nal′ə-sis), *n.* [*psycho-* + *analysis*], 1. a method of treating neuroses and some other mental disorders by analyzing emotional conflicts, repressions, etc. through the use of free association, dream analysis, etc. 2. the theory or practice of this. —**psy′cho·an′a·lyst** (-an′əl-ist), *n.* —**psy′cho·an′a·lyt′ic** (-ə-lit′ik), **psy′cho·an′a·lyt′i·cal,** *adj.* —**psy′cho·an′a·lyt′ical·ly,** *adv.*

**psy·cho·an·a·lyze** (sī′kō-an′ə-līz′), *v.t.* [-LYZED, -LYZING], to treat by means of psychoanalysis.

**psy·cho·gen·ic** (sī′kə-jen′ik), *adj.* [*psycho-* + *-genic*], of psychic origin; caused by mental conflicts.

**psy·cho·log·i·cal** (sī′kə-loj′i-k'l), *adj.* 1. of psychology. 2. of the mind; mental. Also **psy′cho·log′ic.** —**psy′cho·log′i·cal·ly,** *adv.*

**psychological moment,** 1. the most propitious time to act. 2. the critical moment.

**psy·chol·o·gist** (sī-kol′ə-jist), *n.* a student of or specialist in psychology.

**psy·chol·o·gize** (sī-kol′ə-jīz′), *v.i.* [-GIZED, -GIZING], 1. to study psychology. 2. to reason psychologically. *v.t.* to analyze psychologically.

**psy·chol·o·gy** (sī-kol′ə-ji), *n.* [*pl.* -GIES], [see PSYCHO- & -LOGY], 1. *a*) the science dealing with the mind and mental processes, feelings, desires, etc. *b*) the science of human and animal behavior. 2. the sum of a person's actions, traits, thoughts, etc. 3. a system of psychology.

**psy·cho·neu·ro·sis** (sī′kō-nyoo-rō′sis, -noo-rō′-), *n.* [*pl.* -SES (-sēz)], [see PSYCHO- + NEUROSIS], a neurosis. —**psy′cho·neu·rot′ic** (-rot′ik), *adj.* & *n.*

**psy·cho·path** (sī′kə-path′), *n.* a psychopathic personality (sense 1).

**psy·cho·path·ic** (sī′kə-path′ik), *adj.* of or characterized by psychopathy. —**psy′cho·path′i·cal·ly,** *adv.*

**psychopathic personality,** 1. a person with serious personality defects, as emotional immaturity, impulsive (often criminal) behavior, asocial feelings, etc. 2. the personality of such a person.

**psy·cho·pa·thol·o·gy** (sī′kō-pə-thol′ə-ji), *n.* the pathology of the psyche, or mind.

**psy·chop·a·thy** (sī-kop′ə-thi), *n.* [*psycho-* + *-pathy*], 1. mental disorder. 2. loosely, psychotherapy.

**psy·cho·sis** (sī-kō′sis), *n.* [*pl.* -SES (-sēz)], [< Gr. < *psychē*, soul], any mental disorder in which the personality is very seriously disorganized: psychoses may be functional, as in schizophrenia, or organic, as in paresis.

**psy·cho·so·mat·ic** (sī′kō-sō-mat′ik), *adj.* [*psycho-* + *somatic*], 1. designating or of a physical disorder originating in or aggravated by one's psychic or emotional processes. 2. designating the branch of medicine using a psychological approach toward such disorders. —**psy′cho·so·mat′i·cal·ly,** *adv.*

**psy·cho·ther·a·py** (sī′kō-ther′ə-pi), *n.* [*psycho-* + *therapy*], the treatment of nervous and mental disorders by hypnosis, psychoanalysis, etc. —**psy′cho·ther′a·pist,** *n.*

**psy·chot·ic** (sī-kot′ik), *adj.* of, like, or having a psychosis. *n.* a person who has a psychosis. —**psy·chot′i·cal·ly,** *adv.*

**Pt,** in *chemistry*, platinum.

**pt.,** [*pl.* PTS.], 1. part. 2. pint. 3. point.

**pt.,** past tense: also **p.t.**

**P.T.A.,** Parent-Teacher Association.

**ptar·mi·gan** (tär′mə-gən), *n.* [*pl.* -GANS, -GAN; see PLURAL II, D, 1], [< Scot. *tarmachan;* the *p* is from its supposed Gr. origin], any of several varieties of northern grouse, having feathered legs and undergoing seasonal color changes.

**PT boat,** patrol torpedo boat.

**pter·i·do·phyte** (ter′ə-dō-fīt′), *n.* [< Gr. *pteris*, a fern; + *-phyte*], a fern or related plant having no seeds. —**pter′i·do·phyt′ic** (-fit′ik), *adj.* —**pter′i·doph′y·tous** (-dof′ə-təs), *adj.*

**ptero-,** [< Gr. *pteron*], a combining form meaning *feather, wing*, as in *pterodactyl.*

**pter·o·dac·tyl** (ter′ə-dak′til), *n.* [see PTERO- & DACTYL], an extinct flying reptile, having wings of skin stretched between the hind limb and a long digit of the forelimb.

PTERODACTYL (18 ft. across wings)

**-pter·ous** (tēr-əs), [see PTERO- & -OUS], a combining form meaning *having* (a specified number or kind of) *wings*, as in *homopterous.*

**Ptol·e·ma·ic** (tol′ə-mā′ik), *adj.* of Ptolemy or his astronomical theory (**Ptolemaic system**), according to which the earth was the center of the universe, around which the heavenly bodies moved.

**Ptol·e·my** (tol′ə-mi), *n.* Alexandrian astronomer and geographer; lived 2d century A.D.

**Ptolemy I,** 367?–285 B.C.; king of Egypt (323–285 B.C.); first of the Greco-Egyptian dynasty.

**Ptolemy II,** 309–246 B.C.; son of Ptolemy I; king of Egypt (289–246 B.C.).

**pto·maine, pto·main** (tō′mān, tō-mān′), *n.* [< It. < Gr. *ptōma*, a corpse < *piptein*, to fall], any of a class of alkaloid substances, some of which are poisonous, found in decaying matter.

**ptomaine poisoning,** an acute digestive disorder caused by eating putrid food containing certain toxic bacilli (once believed to be ptomaines).

**pty·a·lin** (tī′ə-lin), *n.* [< Gr. < *ptyein*, to spit], an enzyme in the saliva of man (and some animals) that converts starch to dextrin and maltose.

**Pu,** in *chemistry*, plutonium.

**pub** (pub), *n.* [contr. < *public* (*house*)], [Brit. Slang], 1. a bar; tavern. 2. a hotel; inn.

**pub.,** 1. public. 2. published. 3. publisher.

**pu·ber·ty** (pū′bēr-ti), *n.* [< Fr. < L. < *pubes*, adult], the state of physical development when it is first possible to beget or bear children: the usual legal age of puberty is 14 for boys and 12 for girls.

**pu·bes** (pū′bēz), *n.* [L., adult], 1. the hair appearing at puberty; esp., the hair surrounding the genitals. 2. the region of the abdomen covered by such hair.

**pu·bes·cent** (pū-bes′'nt), *adj.* [Fr. < L. ppr. of *pubescere*, to reach puberty < *pubes*, adult], 1. reaching or having reached puberty. 2. covered with a soft down, as many plants and insects. —**pu·bes′cence,** *n.*

**pu·bic** (pū′bik), *adj.* of or in the region of the pubes.

**pu·bis** (pū′bis), *n.* [*pl.* -BES (-bēz)], [see PUBES], either of two bones that, with a third bone between them, make up the front arch of the pelvis.

**pub·lic** (pub′lik), *adj.* [< L. *publicus* (infl. by *pubes*, adult) < *poplicus;* ult. < *populus*, the people], 1. of, belonging to, or concerning the people as a whole; of the community at large. 2. for the use or benefit of all: as, a *public* building. 3. acting in an official capacity for the people as a whole: as, a *public* prosecutor. 4. known by all or most people: as, a *public* scandal. *n.* 1. the people as a whole; community at large. 2. a specific part of the people: as, the sporting *public.* —**in public,** in open view; not in private or in secrecy. —**pub′lic·ly,** *adv.*

**pub·li·can** (pub′li-kən), *n.* 1. in ancient Rome, a tax collector. 2. [Brit.], a saloonkeeper; innkeeper.

**pub·li·ca·tion** (pub′li-kā′shən), *n.* [< L. < *publicare;* see PUBLISH], 1. a publishing or being published; public notification. 2. the printing and distribution of books, magazines, newspapers, etc. 3. something published, as a book, periodical, etc.

**public domain,** 1. public lands. 2. the condition of being free from copyright or patent.

**public enemy,** a hardened criminal or other person who is a menace to society.

**public house,** [Brit.], 1. a saloon. 2. an inn.

**pub·li·cist** (pub′li-sist), *n.* 1. a specialist in international law. 2. a journalist who writes about public affairs. 3. a publicity agent.

**pub·lic·i·ty** (pub-lis′ə-ti), *n.* 1. a being public, or commonly known. 2. any information which brings a person, place, thing, etc. to the notice of the public. 3. notice by the public. 4. any procedure or act seeking to gain this.

**pub·li·cize** (pub′li-sīz′), *v.t.* [-CIZED, -CIZING], to give publicity to.

**public opinion,** the opinion of the people generally, especially as a force in determining social conduct and political action.

**public relations,** relations of an organization with the general public through publicity intended to create favorable public opinion.

**public school,** 1. in the U.S., an elementary or secondary school that is part of a system of schools maintained by public taxes and supervised by local or State authorities. 2. in England, any of several private, expensive, endowed boarding schools for boys, offering college-preparatory education, as Eton. —**pub′lic-school′,** *adj.*

**public servant,** a person who serves the people, as in civil service or elective office.

**pub·lic-spir·it·ed** (pub′lik-spir′i-tid), ***adj.*** having or showing zeal for the public welfare.

**public utility,** an organization supplying water, electricity, transportation, etc. to the public, operated by a private corporation under a government franchise, or by the government directly.

**public works,** works constructed by the government for the public use, as highways or dams

**pub·lish** (pub′lish), ***v.t.*** [< OFr. < L. *publicare* < *publicus;* see PUBLIC], 1. to make publicly known; announce; proclaim. 2. to issue (a printed work) to the public, as for sale. —**pub′lish·a·ble,** ***adj.***

**pub·lish·er** (pub′lish-ẽr), ***n.*** a person or firm that publishes books, magazines, newspapers, etc.

**Puc·ci·ni, Gia·co·mo** (jä′kô-mô′ po͞ot-chē′nē), 1858–1924; Italian operatic composer.

**puck** (puk), ***n.*** [akin to POKE], the hard rubber disk used in ice hockey: cf. *hockey.*

**puck** (puk), ***n.*** [AS. *puca*], 1. a mischievous sprite; goblin; elf. 2. [P-], the mischievous sprite in Shakespeare's *Midsummer Night's Dream.* —**puck′ish,** ***adj.*** —**puck′ish·ly,** ***adv.*** —**puck′ish·ness,** ***n.***

**puck·a** (puk′ə), ***adj.*** [Hind. *pakkā*, ripe, cooked], [Anglo-Indian], 1. good or first-rate of its kind. 2. genuine; real. Also sp. **pukka.**

**puck·er** (puk′ẽr), ***v.t. & v.i.*** [freq. of *poke* (bag)], to draw up or gather into wrinkles or small folds. ***n.*** a wrinkle or small fold, or a number of these running together. —**puck′er·y,** ***adj.***

**pud·ding** (po͝od′iŋ), ***n.*** [prob. a blend of MFr. *boudin,* black pudding & AS. *puduc,* a swelling], 1. [Scot. & Dial.], a sausage made of intestine stuffed with meat, suet, etc. and boiled. 2. a soft, sweetened food, usually made with flour or some cereal and variously containing eggs, milk, fruit, etc. 3. any similar but nonsweetened soft food.

**pud·dle** (pud′'l), ***n.*** [dim. of AS. *pudd,* a ditch], 1. a small pool of water, especially stagnant or spilled water. 2. a thick mixture of clay, and sometimes sand, with water. ***v.t.*** [-DLED, -DLING], 1. to make muddy. 2. to make a thick mixture of (wet clay and sand). 3. to waterproof with such a mixture. 4. to treat (iron) by puddling. ***v.i.*** to dabble or wallow in muddy water. —**pud′dler,** ***n.*** —**pud′dly** [-DLIER, -DLIEST], ***adj.***

**pud·dling** (pud′liŋ), ***n.*** the process of making wrought iron from pig iron by heating and stirring it in the presence of oxidizing agents.

**pudg·y** (puj′i), ***adj.*** [-IER, -IEST], [prob. < Scot. *pud,* belly], short and stocky or fat; dumpy. —**pudg′i·ly,** ***adv.*** —**pudg′i·ness,** ***n.***

**pueb·lo** (pweb′lō), ***n.*** [*pl.* -LOS; *also, for 2,* -LO], [Sp. (< L. *populus*), people], 1. a type of communal village built by certain Indians of the Southwest, consisting of stone or adobe terraced structures housing a number of families. 2. [P-], any Indian of the tribes inhabiting such villages, as the Hopi. 3. [P-], a city in central Colorado: pop., 91,000. ***adj.*** [P-], of the Pueblo Indians.

**pu·er·ile** (pū′ẽr-il), ***adj.*** [< Fr. < L. < *puer,* boy], childish; silly; immature. —**pu′er·ile·ly,** ***adv.*** —**pu′er·il′i·ty** [*pl.* -TIES], **pu′er·ile·ness,** ***n.***

**pu·er·per·al** (pū-ūr′pẽr-əl), ***adj.*** [< L. < *puer,* boy + *parere,* to bear], of or connected with childbirth.

**puerperal fever,** septic poisoning sometimes occurring during childbirth.

**Puer·to Ri·co** (pwer′tə rē′kō), a commonwealth associated with the U.S., on an island in the West Indies: area, 3,421 sq. mi.; pop., 2,350,000: capital, San Juan: formerly *Porto Rico.* —**Puer′to Ri′can.**

**puff** (puf), ***n.*** [ME. *puf*], 1. *a*) a short, sudden gust, as of wind, or expulsion, as of breath. *b*) a bit of vapor, smoke, etc. expelled at one time. 2. a draw at a cigarette, etc. 3. a swelling, or a protuberance caused by swelling. 4. a shell of light pastry filled with whipped cream, etc. 5. a soft, bulging mass of material, gathered in at the edges. 6. a soft roll of hair on the head. 7. a soft pad as for dabbing powder on the skin. 8. a bed quilt filled with wool, down, etc. 9. exaggerated praise, as of a book, etc. ***v.i.*** [AS. *pyffan*], 1. to blow in puffs. 2. *a*) to give forth puffs of smoke, steam, etc. *b*) to breath rapidly and hard. 3. to move (*away, out,* or *in*), giving forth puffs. 4. to inflate with air or pride; swell (with *out* or *up*). 5. to take a puff or puffs at a cigarette, etc. ***v.t.*** 1. to blow, drive, etc. in or with a puff or puffs. 2. to swell; inflate. 3. to praise unduly, as in a book review. 4. to smoke (a cigarette, etc.). 5. to set in soft rolls, as the hair. —**puff′i·ly,** ***adv.*** —**puff′i·ness,** ***n.*** —**puff′y** [-IER, -IEST], ***adj.***

**puff adder,** 1. a large, poisonous African snake which swells out its body when irritated. 2. the hognose snake. Also **puffing adder.**

**puff·ball** (puf′bôl′), ***n.*** any of various round, white-fleshed, mushroomlike plants that burst at the touch and discharge a brown powder.

**puff·er** (puf′ẽr), ***n.*** 1. a person or thing that puffs. 2. any of various fishes capable of expanding by swallowing air, as the globefish.

**puf·fin** (puf′in), ***n.*** [ME. *poffin*], a northern sea bird with a ducklike body, short neck, and brightly colored triangular beak.

**pug** (pug), ***n.*** [prob. var. of *puck*], 1. a small, short-haired dog with a wrinkled face, snub nose, and curled tail. 2. a pug nose.

**pug** (pug), ***v.t.*** [PUGGED, PUGGING], [< dial.; prob. echoic of pounding], to mix or fill in with wet, plastic clay. ***n.*** such clay used for bricks, etc.

**pug** (pug), ***n.*** [Slang], a pugilist.

**Pu·get Sound** (pū′jit), an inlet of the Pacific, extending southward into Washington State.

**pu·gil·ism** (pū′jə-liz'm), ***n.*** [< L. *pugil,* boxer < base of *pugnare;* cf. PUGNACIOUS], the art or practice of fighting with the fists. —**pu′gil·ist,** ***n.*** —**pu′gil·is′tic,** ***adj.*** —**pu′gil·is′ti·cal·ly,** ***adv.***

**pug·na·cious** (pug-nā′shəs), ***adj.*** [< L. < *pugnare,* to fight < *pugnus,* a fist], given to fighting; quarrelsome; combative. —**pug·na′cious·ly,** ***adv.*** —**pug·nac′i·ty** (-nas′ə-ti), **pug·na′cious·ness,** ***n.***

**pug nose,** a short, thick, turned-up nose. —**pug′-nosed′,** ***adj.***

**puis·ne** (pū′ni), ***adj.*** [< OFr. < *puis,* since + *né,* born], in *law,* of lower rank; junior.

**pu·is·sant** (pū′i-s'nt, pū-is′'nt, pwis′'nt), ***adj.*** [OFr.; ult. < L. *posse,* to be able], [Archaic or Poetic], powerful; strong. —**pu′is·sance,** ***n.*** —**pu′is·sant·ly,** ***adv.***

**puke** (pūk), ***n., v.i. & v.t.*** [PUKED, PUKING], [prob. akin to G. *spucken,* to spit], vomit.

**puk·ka** (puk′ə), ***adj.*** pucka.

**Pu·las·ki, Cas·i·mir** (kaz′i-mir poo-las′ki, -kī), Count, 1748?–1779; Polish soldier and patriot; general in the American Revolutionary army.

**pul·chri·tude** (pul′krə-to͞od′, -tūd′), ***n.*** [< L. < *pulcher,* beautiful], physical beauty. —**pul′chri·tu′di·nous** (-to͞o′d'n-əs, -tū′-), ***adj.***

**pule** (pūl), ***v.i.*** [PULED, PULING], [echoic], to whine or whimper, as a sick child. —**pul′ing,** ***adj.***

**Pul·it·zer, Joseph** (pool′it-sẽr; *now commonly* pū′lit-sẽr), 1847–1911; American journalist and philanthropist, born in Hungary.

**Pulitzer Prize,** any of a number of yearly prizes for outstanding work in journalism and literature, established by Joseph Pulitzer.

**pull** (pool), ***v.t.*** [< AS. *pullian,* to pluck], 1. to exert force on so as to cause to move toward the source of the force. 2. *a*) to draw, or pluck, out: as, to *pull* a tooth. *b*) to pluck and gather: as, she *pulled* six roses. 3. to draw apart; tear. 4. to stretch (taffy, etc.) back and forth repeatedly. 5. to strain to the point of injury: as, to *pull* a muscle. 6. [Colloq.], to perform; do: as, the police *pulled* a raid. 7. [Colloq.], to hold back; restrain: as, he's *pulling* his punches. 8. in *baseball, golf,* etc., to hit (the ball) so that it curves to the left or, if one is left-handed, to the right. 9. in *printing,* to take (a proof) on a hand press. 10. in *rowing, a*) to work (an oar) by drawing it toward one. *b*) to be rowed normally by: as, this boat *pulls* four oars. ***v.i.*** 1. to exert force in or for dragging, tugging, or attracting something. 2. to take a deep draft of a drink or puff at a cigarette, etc. 3. to be capable of being pulled. 4. to move (*away, ahead,* etc.). ***n.*** 1. the act or force of pulling; specif., *a*) a dragging, tugging, attracting, etc. *b*) a drink, puff at a cigarette, etc. *c*) any difficult, continuous effort, as in climbing. 2. something to be pulled, as the handle of a drawer, etc. 3. [Slang], influence or special advantage. —**pull apart,** find fault with. —**pull down,** to degrade; humble. —**pull for,** [Colloq.], to cheer on, or hope for the success of. —**pull off,** [Colloq.], to accomplish. —**pull oneself together,** to collect one's faculties; regain one's poise, etc. —**pull over,** [Colloq.], to move to the curb, as a motor vehicle. —**pull through,** [Colloq.], to get over (an illness, difficulty, etc.). —**pull up,** 1. to bring or come to a stop. 2. to move ahead. —**pull′er,** ***n.***

**pul·let** (pool′it), ***n.*** [< OFr. dim. of *poule,* hen <

L. *pullus*, chicken], a young hen, usually not more than a year old.

**pul·ley** (pool′i), *n.* [*pl.* -LEYS], [< OFr. < ML. *poleia;* prob. < Gr. dim. of *polos*, axis], 1. a small wheel with a grooved rim in which a rope runs, as to raise weights by being pulled down. 2. a combination of such wheels, used to increase the applied power. 3. a wheel that turns or is turned by a belt so as to transmit or apply power.

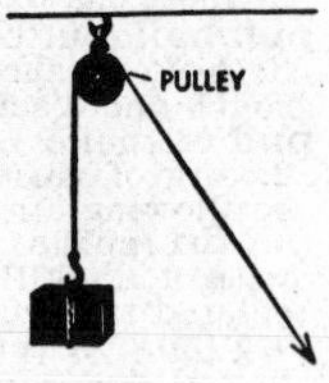

PULLEY

**Pull·man car** (pool′mən), [after G. M. *Pullman* (1831–1897), Am. inventor], a railroad car with private compartments or chairs that can be made up into berths for sleeping: also **Pullman,** *n.*

**pull-o·ver** (pool′ō′vēr), *adj.* that is pulled on over the head. *n.* a pull-over sweater, shirt, etc.

**pul·mo·nar·y** (pul′mə-ner′i), *adj.* [< L. < *pulmo*, a lung], 1. of, like, or affecting the lungs. 2. having lungs or lunglike organs. 3. designating the artery conveying blood from the heart to the lungs, and the vein conveying blood from the lungs to the heart. Also **pul·mon′ic** (-mon′ik).

**pul·mo·tor** (pul′mō′tēr, pool′-), *n.* [< L. *pulmo*, a lung; + *motor*], an apparatus for applying artificial respiration to those who have nearly drowned, suffocated, etc.: a trade-mark **(Pulmotor).**

**pulp** (pulp), *n.* [< Fr. < L. *pulpa*, flesh], 1. a soft, moist, sticky mass. 2. the soft, juicy part of a fruit. 3. the soft pith of a plant stem. 4. the soft, sensitive substance underneath the dentine of a tooth. 5. ground-up, moistened fibers of wood, linen, rags, etc., from which paper is made. 6. *usually in pl.* [Slang], a magazine printed on rough, inferior paper, usually containing sensational stories of love, crime, etc. *v.t.* to reduce to pulp. *v.i.* to become pulp. —**pulp′er,** *n.* —**pulp′i·ness,** *n.* —**pulp′y** [-IER, -IEST], *adj.*

**pul·pit** (pool′pit), *n.* [< OFr. < L. *pulpitum*, a stage], 1. a raised platform from which a clergyman preaches in a church. 2. preachers collectively; (*the*) ministry. 3. preaching.

**pulp·wood** (pulp′wood′), *n.* 1. soft wood used in making paper. 2. wood ground to pulp for paper.

**pul·que** (pool′ki; Sp. pōōl′ke), *n.* [Sp.; prob. < Mex. Ind.], a fermented drink, popular in Mexico, made from the juice of an agave.

**pul·sate** (pul′sāt), *v.i.* [-SATED, -SATING], [< L. pp. of *pulsare*, to beat], 1. to beat or throb rhythmically, as the heart. 2. to vibrate; quiver. —**pul·sa′tion,** *n.* —**pul′sa·tive** (-sə-tiv), *adj.* —**pul·sa′tor,** *n.* —**pul′sa·to′ry** (-tôr′i, -tō′ri), *adj.*

**pulse** (puls), *n.* [< OFr. < L. *pulsus*, pp. of *pellere*, to beat], 1. the regular beating in the arteries, caused by the contractions of the heart. 2. any beat that is regular or rhythmical. 3. the perceptible underlying feelings, as of the public. *v.i.* [PULSED, PULSING], to pulsate; beat; throb.

**pulse** (puls), *n.* [< OFr. < L. *puls*, a pottage], 1. the edible seeds of peas, beans, lentils, and similar plants having pods. 2. any such plant.

**pulse·jet** (puls′jet′), *n.* an aeropulse.

**pul·ver·ize** (pul′və-riz′), *v.t.* [-IZED, -IZING], [< Fr. < LL. < L. *pulvis*, dust], 1. to crush, grind, etc. into a powder or dust. 2. to demolish. *v.i.* to be crushed, ground, etc. into powder or dust. —**pul′ver·iz′a·ble, pul′ver·a·ble,** *adj.* —**pul′ver·i·za′tion,** *n.* —**pul′ver·iz′er,** *n.*

**pu·ma** (pū′mə), *n.* [*pl.* -MAS, -MA; see PLURAL, II, D, 1], [Sp. < Peruv.], 1. the cougar. 2. its fur.

**pum·ice** (pum′is), *n.* [< OFr. < L. *pumex*], a light, porous, volcanic rock, used, often as a powder, for removing stains, polishing, etc.: also **pumice stone.** *v.t.* [-ICED, -ICING], to clean, polish, etc. with pumice. —**pu·mi·ceous** (pyoo-mish′əs), *adj.*

**pum·mel** (pum′'l), *n.* & *v.t.* [-MELED or -MELLED, -MELING or -MELLING], pommel. —**pum′mel·er,** *n.*

**pump** (pump), *n.* [< MD. *pompe* < Sp. *bomba*; prob. of echoic origin], any of various machines that force a liquid or gas into, or draw it out of, something, as by pressure. *v.t.* 1. to move (fluids) with a pump. 2. to remove water, etc. from. 3. to inflate (a rubber tire) with air. 4. to draw out, move up and down, pour forth, etc. in the manner of a pump. 5. to question closely and persistently. 6. to get (information) in this way. *v.i.* 1. to work a pump. 2. to move water, etc. with a pump. 3. to move up and down like a pump handle or piston. —**pump′er,** *n.*

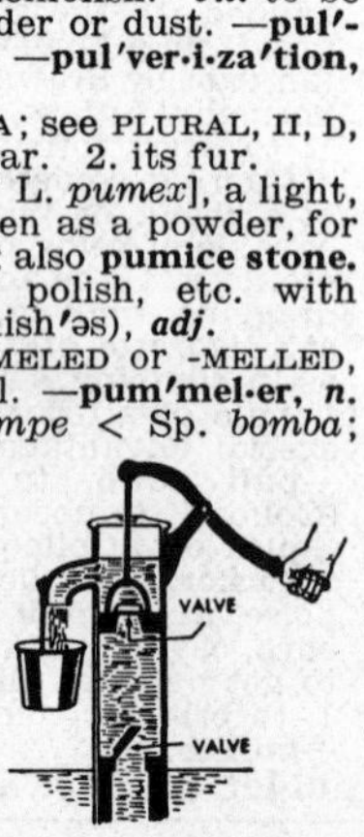

PUMP

**pump** (pump), *n.* [prob. < Fr. *pompe*, an ornament], a low-cut shoe without straps or ties.

**pump·er·nick·el** (pum′pēr-nik′'l), *n.* [G.], a coarse, dark bread made of unsifted rye.

**pump·kin** (pump′kin; *also commonly* puŋ′kin), *n.* [< MFr. < L. < Gr. *pepōn*, lit., ripe], 1. a large, round, orange-yellow, edible gourdlike fruit with many seeds. 2. the vine on which it grows.

**pun** (pun), *n.* [? < It. *puntiglio*, fine point], the humorous use of a word, or of different words which sound alike, so as to play on two or more of the possible meanings. *v.i.* [PUNNED, PUNNING], to make puns. —**pun′ner,** *n.* —**pun′ning·ly,** *adv.*

**Punch** (punch), *n.* [< *Punchinello*], the hero of the puppet show **Punch and Judy,** a hook-nosed, humpbacked figure constantly fighting with his wife, Judy. —**pleased as Punch,** greatly pleased.

**punch** (punch), *n.* [see PUNCHEON (a die)], a tool driven or pressed against a surface that is to be pierced, shaped, or stamped, or a nail, bolt, etc. that is to be worked in or out. *v.t.* to pierce, shape, stamp, etc. with a punch. —**punch′er,** *n.*

**punch** (punch), *v.t.* [ME. *punchen*], 1. to prod or poke with a stick. 2. to herd (cattle) as by prodding. 3. to strike with the fist. 4. to pierce or perforate with a punch. 5. to make (a hole) with a punch. 6. to cut *out* (a piece) by punching. *n.* 1. a thrusting blow with the fist. 2. [Colloq.], effective force; vigor. —**pull one's punches,** [Colloq.], to deliver blows, criticisms, etc. that are intentionally ineffective. —**punch′er,** *n.*

**punch** (punch), *n.* [< Hind. *pāc*, five: it orig. had five ingredients], a sweet drink flavored with fruit juices, spices, etc., often mixed with wine or liquor.

**pun·cheon** (pun′chən), *n.* [< OFr. < LL.; ult. < L. pp. of *pungere*, to prick], 1. a short, upright wooden post used in framework. 2. a heavy, broad piece of roughly dressed timber. 3. a figured die or punch used by goldsmiths, etc. 4. a large cask of varying capacity (72–120 gallons), as for beer. 5. as much as such a cask will hold.

**pun·chi·nel·lo** (pun′chə-nel′ō), *n.* [*pl.* -LOS, -LOES], [< the name of a character in a Neapolitan puppet play], a buffoon; clown.

**punching bag,** a stuffed or inflated leather bag hung up so that it can be punched for exercise.

**punch press,** a press in which dies are fitted for cutting, shaping, or stamping metal.

**punc·til·i·o** (puŋk-til′i-ō′), *n.* [*pl.* -OS], [< Sp. < It. *puntiglio* < *punto* < L. *punctum*, a point], 1. a nice point of conduct, manners, ceremony, etc. 2. observance of petty formalities.

**punc·til·i·ous** (puŋk-til′i-əs), *adj.* 1. careful in the observance of the nice points of behavior and ceremony. 2. very exact; scrupulous. —**punc·til′i·ous·ly,** *adv.* —**punc·til′i·ous·ness,** *n.*

**punc·tu·al** (puŋk′chōō-əl), *adj.* [< ML. *punctualis* < L. *punctus*, a point], 1. punctilious. 2. on time; prompt. —**punc′tu·al′i·ty** [*pl.* -TIES], **punc′tu·al·ness,** *n.* —**punc′tu·al·ly,** *adv.*

**punc·tu·ate** (puŋk′chōō-āt′), *v.t.* [-ATED, -ATING], [< ML. pp. of *punctuare* < L. *punctus*, a point], 1. to insert punctuation marks in (written or printed matter) in order to clarify the meaning. 2. to interrupt from time to time. 3. to emphasize. *v.i.* to use punctuation marks. —**punc′tu·a′tor,** *n.*

**punc·tu·a·tion** (puŋk′chōō-ā′shən), *n.* 1. the use of certain standardized marks to separate sentences, clauses, etc. in order to make the meaning clearer. 2. punctuation marks.

**punctuation mark,** any of the marks used in punctuation, chiefly the period, comma, colon, semicolon, interrogation mark, exclamation mark, apostrophe, quotation marks, parentheses, dash, hyphen, and brackets.

**punc·ture** (puŋk′chēr), *n.* [< LL. < L. *pungere*, to pierce], 1. a perforating or piercing. 2. a hole made by a sharp point, as in a tire, the skin, etc. *v.t.* [-TURED, -TURING], 1. to pierce with a sharp point. 2. to reduce or injure, as if by a puncture: as, his pride was *punctured.* *v.i.* to be punctured. —**punc′tur·a·ble,** *adj.*

**pun·dit** (pun′dit), *n.* [< Hind. < Sans. *paṇḍita*], 1. in India, one who is learned in Sanskrit, Hindu law, etc. 2. a person of great learning.

**pun·gent** (pun′jənt), *adj.* [< L. ppr. of *pungere*, to prick], 1. producing a sharp sensation of taste and smell; acrid. 2. sharp and piercing; poignant. 3. sharply penetrating; biting: as, *pungent* language. 4. keenly clever; stimulating. —**pun′gen·cy,** *n.* —**pun′gent·ly,** *adv.*

**Pu·nic** (pū′nik), *adj.* [< L. *Punicus* < *Poeni*, the Carthaginians], 1. of ancient Carthage or its people. 2. like the Carthaginians, regarded by the Romans as faithless and treacherous.

**pun·ish** (pun′ish), ***v.t.*** [< OFr. < L. *punire*, to punish < *poena*, punishment], 1. to cause (a person) to undergo pain, loss, or suffering, as for a crime. 2. to impose a penalty for (an offense). 3. [Colloq.], to treat in a harsh, severe, or greedy manner. ***v.i.*** to deal out punishment. —**pun′ish·a·bil′i·ty, pun′ish·a·ble·ness,** ***n.*** —**pun′ish·a·ble,** ***adj.*** —**pun′ish·er,** ***n.***

**pun·ish·ment** (pun′ish-mənt), ***n.*** 1. a punishing or being punished. 2. a penalty imposed on an offender. 3. [Colloq.], rough handling.

**pu·ni·tive** (pū′nə-tiv), ***adj.*** 1. inflicting punishment. 2. concerned with punishment. Also **pu′ni·to′ry** (-tôr′i, -tō′ri). —**pu′ni·tive·ly,** ***adv.*** —**pu′ni·tive·ness,** ***n.***

**Pun·jab** (pun-jäb′, pun′jäb), ***n.*** a former province of British India, now divided between India and Pakistan.

**punk** (puŋk), ***n.*** [< Am. Ind.], 1. decayed wood or dried fungus used for tinder. 2. any substance that smolders when ignited, usually in the form of a stick used to light fireworks, etc.

**punk** (puŋk), ***n.*** [Slang], 1. a young gangster. 2. any person regarded as inexperienced, insignificant, etc. ***adj.*** [Slang], poor or bad in quality.

**pun·kah, pun·ka** (puŋ′kə), ***n.*** [Hind. *pankhā*], in India, a large fan made from the palmyra leaf, or a large, swinging fan hung from the ceiling.

**punk·ie** (puŋ′ki), ***n.*** [D. *punki* < Am. Ind.], a tiny fly of the U.S., with sucking mouth parts.

**pun·ster** (pun′stẽr), ***n.*** a person who is fond of making puns.

**punt** (punt), ***n.*** [< slang of Rugby School, England], in *football*, a kick in which the ball is dropped from the hands and kicked before it strikes the ground. ***v.t. & v.i.*** to kick (a football) in a punt. —**punt′er,** ***n.***

**punt** (punt), ***n.*** [AS. < L. < *pons*, a bridge], a flat-bottomed boat with square ends, usually propelled by a long pole. ***v.t.*** to propel (a punt) by pushing with a pole against the bottom of a river or lake. ***v.i.*** to go in a punt. —**punt′er,** ***n.***

**punt** (punt), ***v.i.*** [< Fr. < Sp. < L. *punctum*, a point], 1. in certain card games, to bet against the dealer or banker. 2. to gamble. —**punt′er,** ***n.***

**pu·ny** (pū′ni), ***adj.*** [-NIER, -NIEST], [< Fr. < OFr. *puis*, after + *né*, born], of inferior size, strength, or importance; weak. —**pu′ni·ly,** ***adv.*** —**pu′ni·ness,** ***n.***

**pup** (pup), ***n.*** 1. a young dog; puppy. 2. a young seal. ***v.i.*** [PUPPED, PUPPING], to give birth to pups.

**pu·pa** (pū′pə), ***n.*** [*pl.* -PAE (-pē), -PAS], [L., a girl, doll], an insect in the stage between the larval and adult forms. —**pu′pal,** ***adj.***

PUPA OF MOTH

**pu·pil** (pū′p'l), ***n.*** [< OFr. < L. *pupillus* (< *pupus*, boy), *pupilla* (< *pupa*, girl), ward], a person being taught under the supervision of a teacher or tutor, as in school. —**pu′pil·age,** ***n.***

**pu·pil** (pū′p'l), ***n.*** [< Fr. < L. *pupilla*, figure reflected in the eye; see PUPIL (learner)], the contractile circular opening in the center of the iris of the eye: see **eye,** illus.

**pup·pet** (pup′it), ***n.*** [< OFr. < LL. < L. *pupa*, a girl, doll], 1. a small figure humanlike in form; doll. 2. such a figure moved by strings, wires, or the hands, in a puppet show. 3. a person whose actions, ideas, etc. are controlled by another.

**pup·pet·eer** (pup′i-têr′), ***n.*** a person who operates puppets or produces puppet shows.

**puppet show,** a performance with puppets.

**pup·py** (pup′i), ***n.*** [*pl.* -PIES], [< Fr. *poupée*, a doll < LL.; see PUPPET], 1. a young dog. 2. a silly, conceited, or insolent young man. —**pup′py·hood,** ***n.*** —**pup′py·ish,** ***adj.***

**puppy love,** calf love.

**pup tent,** a small, portable tent large enough to shelter two men: it consists of two sections (*shelter halves*), each of which is carried by a soldier as part of his field equipment.

**pur** (pũr), ***n., v.t. & v.i.*** [PURRED, PURRING], purr.

**pur·blind** (pũr′blīnd′), ***adj.*** [ME. *pur blind*, quite blind], 1. partly blind. 2. slow in perceiving or understanding. —**pur′blind′ly,** ***adv.*** —**pur′blind′ness,** ***n.***

**Pur·cell, Henry** (pũr′s'l), 1659–1695; English composer.

**pur·chase** (pũr′chis), ***v.t.*** [-CHASED, -CHASING], [< OFr. < *pour*, for + *chacier*, to chase], 1. to obtain for money; buy. 2. to obtain at a cost or sacrifice. 3. to move or raise by applying mechanical power. ***n.*** 1. anything obtained by buying. 2. the act of buying. 3. a fast hold applied to move something mechanically or to keep from slipping. 4. any apparatus for applying such a hold. —**pur′chas·a·ble,** ***adj.*** —**pur′chas·er,** ***n.***

**purchasing power,** the value of a monetary unit in terms of what can be bought with it.

**pur·dah** (pũr′də), ***n.*** [Hind. & Per. *pardah*, a veil], in India, a curtain used to screen off the part of the house where women are secluded.

**pure** (pyoor), ***adj.*** [< OFr. < L. *purus*], 1. free from anything that adulterates, taints, etc.; unmixed. 2. simple; mere. 3. utter; absolute. 4. free from defects; faultless. 5. free from sin or guilt; blameless. 6. virgin or chaste. 7. of unmixed stock; pure-blooded. 8. abstract or theoretical: as, *pure* physics: contrasted with *applied.* ***n.*** [Poetic], that which is pure (with *the*). —**pure′ly,** ***adv.*** —**pure′ness,** ***n.***

**pu·rée** (pyoo-rā′, pyoor′ā), ***n.*** [Fr. < OFr. < L. < *purus*, pure], 1. food prepared by straining the boiled pulp through a sieve. 2. a thick soup. ***v.t.*** [-RÉED, -RÉING], to prepare a purée from.

**pur·ga·tion** (pũr-gā′shən), ***n.*** a purging.

**pur·ga·tive** (pũr′gə-tiv), ***adj.*** 1. purging. 2. causing bowel movement. ***n.*** 1. a substance that purges. 2. a cathartic. —**pur′ga·tive·ly,** ***adv.*** —**pur′ga·tive·ness,** ***n.***

**pur·ga·to·ry** (pũr′gə-tôr′i, -tō′ri), ***n.*** [*pl.* -RIES], [< OFr. & ML. < LL. < L. *purgare;* see PURGE], 1. in *R.C. theology*, a state or place in which those who have died in the grace of God expiate their sins by suffering. 2. any state or place of temporary suffering. ***adj.*** purgative. —**pur′ga·to′ri·al,** ***adj.***

**purge** (pũrj), ***v.t.*** [PURGED, PURGING], [< OFr. < L. *purgare* < *purus*, clean + *agere*, to do], 1. to cleanse of impurities, foreign matter, etc. 2. to cleanse of guilt, sin, etc. 3. to remove by cleansing. 4. to rid (a nation, political party, etc.) of individuals held to be undesirable. 5. in *medicine*, *a)* to empty (the bowels). *b)* to cause (a person) to empty his bowels. ***v.i.*** 1. to become clean, clear, or pure. 2. to have or effect a bowel movement. ***n.*** 1. a purging. 2. that which purges; esp., a cathartic. —**purge′a·ble,** ***adj.*** —**purg′er,** ***n.***

**pu·ri·fy** (pyoor′ə-fī′), ***v.t.*** [-FIED, -FYING], [< OFr. < L. < *purus*, pure + *facere*, to make], 1. to rid of impurities, pollution, or corruptions. 2. to free from guilt, sin, etc. ***v.i.*** to be purified. —**pu′ri·fi·ca′tion,** ***n.*** —**pu′ri·fi′er,** ***n.***

**Pu·rim** (po͞o-rēm′, poor′im, pyoor′-), ***n.pl.*** [construed as sing.], a Jewish holiday, the Feast of Lots, commemorating the deliverance of the Jews by Esther from a massacre: see **Jewish holidays.**

**pur·ism** (pyoor′iz'm), ***n.*** 1. strict observance of or insistence upon precise usage or purity in language, style, etc. 2. an instance of this. —**pur′ist,** ***n.*** —**pu·ris′tic, pu·ris′ti·cal,** ***adj.***

**Pu·ri·tan** (pyoor′ə-t'n), ***n.*** [see PURITY], 1. a member of a group in England and the American colonies who, in the 16th and 17th centuries, wanted to purify the Church of England from elaborate ceremonies and forms. 2. [p-], a person regarded as excessively strict in morals and religion. ***adj.*** 1. of the Puritans or Puritanism. 2. [p-], puritanical. —**Pu′ri·tan·ism, pu′ri·tan·ism,** ***n.***

**pu·ri·tan·i·cal** (pyoor′ə-tan′i-k'l), ***adj.*** 1. [P-], of the Puritans or their doctrines. 2. excessively strict in morals and religion: also **pu′ri·tan′ic.** —**pu′ri·tan′i·cal·ly,** ***adv.*** —**pu′ri·tan′i·cal·ness,** ***n.***

**pu·ri·ty** (pyoor′ə-ti), ***n.*** [< OFr. < LL. < L. *purus*, pure], a being pure; specif., *a)* freedom from adulterating matter. *b)* cleanness; clearness. *c)* freedom from sin; innocence; chastity. *d)* freedom from errors, corruptions, etc.: said of language, style, etc.

**purl** (pũrl), ***v.i.*** [echoic], 1. to move in ripples or with a murmuring sound. 2. to move in eddies; swirl. ***n.*** 1. a purling stream. 2. the murmuring sound of purling water.

**purl** (pũrl), ***v.t. & v.i.*** [< a Romance source], 1. to edge (lace) with a chain of small loops. 2. to invert (stitches) in knitting. Also sp. **pearl.** 3. to decorate the border of. ***n.*** 1. a small loop, or a chain of loops, made on the edge of lace. 2. twisted metal thread used in embroidery. 3. an inversion of stitches in knitting to produce a ribbed effect. Also sp. **pearl** (in senses 1 & 3).

**pur·lieu** (pũr′lo͞o), ***n.*** [< Anglo-Fr. < OFr. < *pur-*, through + *aler*, to go], 1. an outlying part of a forest, exempted from forest laws and returned to private owners. 2. a place that one visits often or habitually. 3. *pl.* bounds; limits. 4. an outlying part, as of a city.

**pur·lin, pur·line** (pũr′lin), *n.* [prob. < OFr.], a horizontal timber supporting the rafters of a roof.
**pur·loin** (pũr-loin′), *v.t. & v.i.* [< OFr. < *pur-*, for + *loin*, far], to steal; filch. —**pur·loin′er,** *n.*
**pur·ple** (pũr′p'l), *n.* [< AS. < L. *purpura* < Gr. *porphyra*, shellfish yielding purple dye], 1. a dark color that is a blend of red and blue. 2. crimson cloth or clothing, especially as a former emblem of royalty or high rank. 3. the rank or office of a cardinal. *adj.* 1. of the color purple. 2. imperial; royal. 3. ornate; elaborate: as, a *purple* passage in a book. *v.t. & v.i.* [-PLED, -PLING], to make or become purple. —**born to (or in) the purple,** of high or royal birth. —**pur′plish, pur′ply** [-PLIER, -PLIEST], *adj.*
**Purple Heart,** a United States military decoration awarded to soldiers wounded in action.
**purple martin,** a large American swallow with bluish-black plumage.
**pur·port** (pũr-pôrt′, -pōrt′; *also, and for n. always,* pũr′pôrt, -pōrt), *v.t.* [< Anglo-Fr. < OFr. < *pur-*, forth + *porter*, to bear], 1. to profess or claim as its meaning. 2. to give the appearance, often falsely, of being, intending, etc. *n.* 1. meaning; sense. 2. intention; object. —**pur′port·less,** *adj.*
**pur·pose** (pũr′pəs), *v.t. & v.i.* [-POSED, -POSING], [< OFr. < *por*, for + *poser*, to place], to aim, intend, plan, etc. *n.* 1. something one intends to get or do; aim. 2. resolution; determination. 3. the object for which something exists or is done. —**of set purpose,** with determination. —**on purpose,** intentionally. —**to good purpose,** with good effect. —**to little (or no) purpose,** with little or no effect. —**pur′pose·ful,** *adj.* —**pur′pose·ful·ly,** *adv.* —**pur′pose·ful·ness,** *n.* —**pur′pose·less,** *adj.* —**pur′pose·less·ly,** *adv.* —**pur′pose·less·ness,** *n.*
**pur·pose·ly** (pũr′pəs-li), *adv.* with a definite purpose; intentionally; deliberately.
**purr** (pũr), *n.* [echoic], 1. a low, vibratory sound made by a cat when it seems to be pleased. 2. any sound like this. *v.i.* to utter such a sound. *v.t.* to express by purring. Also sp. **pur.**
**purse** (pũrs), *n.* [< AS. < LL. < Gr. *byrsa*, a skin], 1. a small bag or pouch for carrying money. 2. finances; money. 3. a sum of money given as a present or prize. 4. a woman's handbag. *v.t.* [PURSED, PURSING], to gather into small folds; pucker.
**purs·er** (pũr′sẽr), *n.* [ME., a purse bearer], a ship's officer in charge of the accounts, freight, tickets, etc., especially on a passenger vessel.
**purse strings,** strings drawn to close a purse. —**hold the purse strings,** to be in control of the money. —**tighten (or loosen) the purse strings,** to reduce (or increase) the amount spent.
**purs·lane** (pũrs′lin, -lān), *n.* [< OFr. < L. *porcilaca*], any of various weeds with pink, fleshy stems and small, round leaves.
**pur·su·ance** (pẽr-sōō′əns, -sū′-), *n.* a pursuing, or carrying out, as of a project, plan, etc.
**pur·su·ant** (pẽr-sōō′ənt, -sū′-), *adj.* carrying out; following. —**pursuant to,** 1. following upon. 2. in accordance with. —**pur·su′ant·ly,** *adv.*
**pur·sue** (pẽr-sōō′, -sū′), *v.t.* [-SUED, -SUING], [< OFr. < LL. < L. *pro-*, forth + *sequi*, to follow], 1. to follow in order to overtake or capture; chase. 2. to follow, as a specified course, action, etc. 3. to try to find; seek. 4. to follow as an occupation, profession, etc. 5. to continue to annoy or distress. *v.i.* 1. to go in pursuit. 2. to go on. —**pur·su′a·ble,** *adj.* —**pur·su′er,** *n.*
**pur·suit** (pẽr-sōōt′, -sūt′), *n.* 1. a pursuing. 2. an occupation or the like ordinarily followed.
**pursuit plane,** a fast, maneuverable military plane.
**pur·sui·vant** (pũr′swi-vənt), *n.* [< OFr. ppr. < *poursuir;* see PURSUE], 1. in England, an officer ranking below a herald. 2. a follower; attendant.
**pur·sy** (pũr′si), *adj.* [-SIER, -SIEST], [< Anglo-Fr. *pursif*, for OFr. *polsif* < *poulser*, to push < L. *pulsare*, to beat], 1. short-winded. 2. fat. —**pur′si·ly,** *adv.* —**pur′si·ness,** *n.*
**pu·ru·lent** (pyoor′ə-lənt, -yoo-lənt), *adj.* [< L. < *pus*, pus], of, like, containing, or discharging pus. —**pu′ru·lence, pu′ru·len·cy,** *n.* —**pu′ru·lent·ly,** *adv.*
**pur·vey** (pẽr-vā′), *v.t.* [< Anglo-Fr. < OFr. < L. *providere;* see PROVIDE], to supply, as food or provisions. —**pur·vey′a·ble,** *adj.* —**pur·vey′or,** *n.*
**pur·vey·ance** (pẽr-vā′əns), *n.* 1. a purveying. 2. the things purveyed; provisions.
**pur·view** (pũr′vū), *n.* [Anglo-Fr. for OFr. *pourveü* provided], 1. the body and scope of an act or bill. 2. the extent of control, activity, etc.; province. 3. range of sight or understanding.
**pus** (pus), *n.* [L.], the yellowish-white matter produced by an infection, consisting of bacteria, white corpuscles, serum, etc. —**pus′sy,** *adj.*
**push** (poosh), *v.t.* [< OFr. < L. *pulsare*, to beat], 1. to press against (a thing) so as to move it away. 2. to move in this way. 3. to thrust or drive up, down, in, out, etc. 4. to urge forward or on. 5. to follow up vigorously, as a claim. 6. to extend; expand. 7. to press hard upon: as, *pushed* for time. 8. to urge the use, sale, success, etc. of. *v.i.* 1. to press against a thing to move it. 2. to press or thrust forward vigorously. 3. to put forth great effort. 4. to advance against opposition. *n.* 1. a pushing; shove, thrust, etc. 2. a vigorous effort. 3. an advance against opposition. 4. pressure of affairs or of circumstances. 5. an emergency. 6. [Colloq.], aggressiveness. —**push off,** [Colloq.], to depart. —**push on,** to proceed. —**push′er,** *n.*
**push button,** a small knob or button which when pushed makes or breaks an electric circuit.
**push·cart** (poosh′kärt′), *n.* a cart pushed by hand.
**push·ing** (poosh′iŋ), *adj.* 1. aggressive; enterprising. 2. forward; officious. —**push′ing·ly,** *adv.*
**Push·kin, A·le·ksan·dr Ser·ge·ye·vich** (ȧ′lyek-sän′dẽr syer-gyā′ye-vich pōōsh′kin; Eng. poosh′-kin), 1799–1837; Russian poet.
**push-o·ver** (poosh′ō′vẽr), *n.* [Slang], 1. anything very easy to accomplish. 2. a person, group, etc. easily persuaded, defeated, seduced, etc.
**Push·tu** (push′tōō), *n.* an Iranian language, the principal one spoken in Afghanistan.
**pu·sil·lan·i·mous** (pū′s'l-an′ə-məs), *adj.* [< LL. < L. *pusillus*, tiny + *animus*, the mind], 1. cowardly; fainthearted. 2. proceeding from or showing a lack of courage. —**pu′sil·la·nim′i·ty** (-ə-nim′ə-ti), *n.* —**pu′sil·lan′i·mous·ly,** *adv.*
**puss** (poos), *n.* [echoic of the spitting of a cat], 1. a cat: pet name. 2. a girl: term of affection.
**puss** (poos), *n.* [Slang], the face or mouth.
**puss·y** (poos′i), *n.* [*pl.* -IES], [dim. of *puss*], a cat.
**puss·y·foot** (poos′i-foot′), *v.i.* [Slang], 1. to move with stealth or caution, as a cat does. 2. to avoid committing oneself or making one's position clear. *n.* [Slang], a person who pussyfoots: also **puss′y·foot′er.** —**puss′y·foot′ing,** *n.*
**pussy willow,** a willow having silvery velvetlike catkins, which appear before the leaves.
**pus·tu·late** (pus′choo-lāt′), *v.t. & v.i.* [-LATED, -LATING], [< L. pp. < *pustula*, a pustule], to form into pustules. *adj.* covered with pustules. —**pus′tu·lant,** *adj. & n.* —**pus′tu·la′tion,** *n.*
**pus·tule** (pus′chool), *n.* [L. *pustula*], 1. a small elevation of the skin containing pus. 2. any elevation like a blister or pimple. —**pus′tu·lar,** *adj.*
**put** (poot), *v.t.* [PUT, PUTTING], [< AS. *putian*, to push], 1. to thrust; push; drive. 2. to throw with an overhand thrust from the shoulder: as, *put* the shot. 3. to cause to be in a specified position or place; place; set; lay. 4. to cause to be in a specified condition, relation, etc.: as, *put* her at ease. 5. to impose: as, *put* a tax on luxuries. 6. to bring to bear; apply: as, *put* your heart into your work. 7. to attribute; ascribe: as, *put* the proper interpretation on that clause. 8. to express; state: as, *put* it plainly. 9. to present for consideration, decision, etc.: as, *put* the question. 10. to appraise. 11. to adapt, as words to music. 12. to wager. *v.i.* to take one's course; go (with *in, out, for,* etc.). *n.* a throw; cast. *adj.* [Colloq.], fixed: as, stay *put.* —**put about,** 1. to change a vessel's course to another tack. 2. to move in another direction. —**put across,** [Slang], 1. to cause to be understood or accepted. 2. to carry out with success. —**put aside,** 1. to reserve for later use: also **put away (or by).** 2. to give up; discard. —**put away,** 1. [Colloq.], to consume (food or drink). 2. [Slang], to kill. —**put down,** 1. to crush; repress. 2. to write down. 3. to attribute (to). 4. [Slang], to belittle, reject, or humiliate. —**put forth,** 1. to grow (leaves, shoots, etc.). 2. to set out from port. —**put in,** 1. to enter a port or haven. 2. [Colloq.], to spend (time) in a specified manner. —**put it on,** [Slang], to make a pretentious show; exaggerate. —**put it (or something) over on,** [Colloq.], to deceive; trick. —**put off,** 1. to delay; postpone. 2. to discard. 3. to evade; divert. —**put on,** 1. to clothe or adorn oneself with. 2. to assume or pretend. 3. to apply, as a brake. 4. to stage (a play). 5. [Slang], to fool (someone) by a trick; hoax. —**put out,** 1. to expel; dismiss. 2. to gouge out (an eye). 3. to extinguish (a fire or light). 4. to disconcert; confuse. 5. to distress; vex. 6. to inconvenience. 7. to publish. 8. in *baseball*, to retire (a batter or runner). —**put over,** 1. to postpone; delay. 2. [Colloq.], to accomplish (something) against odds or by craft. —**put through,** 1. to carry out. 2. to cause to do or undergo. —**put (up) to,** to present to for consideration or decision. —**put to it,** to place in a difficult

situation. **—put up,** 1. to offer; show. 2. to offer as a candidate. 3. to preserve, as fruits, etc. 4. to erect; build. 5. to lodge, or provide lodgings for. 6. to advance, provide, etc. (money). 7. to pack in containers. 8. [Colloq.], to incite (a person) *to* some action. **—put upon,** to impose on; victimize. **—put up with,** to tolerate. **—put′ter,** *n.*

**pu·ta·tive** (pū′tə-tiv), *adj.* [< L. < *putare,* to suppose], reputed; supposed. **—pu′ta·tive·ly,** *adv.*

**put-out** (poot′out′), *n.* in *baseball,* a play in which the batter or runner is retired or put out.

**pu·tre·fac·tion** (pū′trə-fak′shən), *n.* [see PUTREFY], 1. a rotting. 2. rotting or putrid matter. **—pu′tre·fac′tive,** *adj.*

**pu·tre·fy** (pū′trə-fī′), *v.t. & v.i.* [-FIED, -FYING], [< L. < *putris,* putrid + *facere,* to make], to make or become putrid or rotten. **—pu′tre·fi′er,** *n.*

**pu·tres·cent** (pū-tres′′nt), *adj.* [L. *putrescens,* ppr. of *putrescere,* to be rotten < *putris,* rotten], 1. putrefying; rotting. 2. of or connected with putrefaction. **—pu·tres′cence,** *n.*

**pu·trid** (pū′trid), *adj.* [< Fr. < L. *putridus* < *putrere,* to be rotten], 1. rotten and foul-smelling. 2. causing, showing, or proceeding from decay. 3. depraved. 4. [Colloq.], very unpleasant. **—pu·trid′i·ty, pu′trid·ness,** *n.* **—pu′trid·ly,** *adv.*

**‡Putsch** (pooch), *n.* [G.], an uprising or rebellion, especially a minor one.

**putt** (put), *n.* [< *put, v.*], in *golf,* a light stroke made on the putting green to get the ball into the hole. *v.t. & v.i.* to hit (the ball) with a putt.

**put·tee** (pu-tē′, put′i), *n.* [< Hind. *paṭṭī,* a bandage < Sans. *paṭṭa,* a strip of cloth], a covering for the lower leg in the form of a cloth or leather gaiter or a cloth strip wound spirally: also **puttie, putty** [*pl.* -TIES].

**putt·er** (put′ēr), *n.* 1. a short, straight-faced golf club used in putting. 2. one who putts.

**put·ter** (put′ēr), *v.i.* [var. of *potter*], to busy oneself in an ineffective or aimless way (often with *along, around,* etc.). *v.t.* to fritter (with *away*). *n.* a puttering. Also **potter. —put′ter·er,** *n.*

**putt·ing green** (put′iŋ), in *golf,* the area of smooth, closely mowed turf around the hole.

**put·ty** (put′i), *n.* [< Fr. *potée,* lit., potful < *pot,* a pot], 1. a soft, plastic mixture of powdered chalk and linseed oil, used to fix glass panes, fill cracks, etc. 2. any substance like this in consistency, use, etc. *v.t.* [-TIED, -TYING], to cement, fix, or fill with putty. **—put′ti·er,** *n.*

**put-up** (poot′up′), *adj.* [Colloq.], planned beforehand in a secret manner: as, a *put-up* job.

**puz·zle** (puz′′l), *v.t.* [-ZLED, -ZLING], [prob. freq. < ME. *posen,* to pose (a question, etc.)], to perplex; bewilder. *v.i.* 1. to be perplexed, etc. 2. to exercise one's mind, as over the solution of a problem. *n.* 1. bewilderment. 2. a question, problem, etc. that puzzles. 3. a toy or problem for exercising mental ingenuity. **—puzzle out,** to solve by deep study, etc. **—puzzle over,** to concentrate on. **—puz′zle·ment,** *n.* **—puz′zler,** *n.*

**Pvt.,** Private.

**PWA, P.W.A.,** Public Works Administration.

**pwt.,** pennyweight.

**PX** (pē′eks′), post exchange.

**py·e·mi·a, py·ae·mi·a** (pī-ē′mi-ə), *n.* [< *pyo-* + Gr. *haima,* blood], an infection caused by the presence in the blood of pus-producing microorganisms. **—py·e′mic, py·ae′mic,** *adj.*

**Pyg·ma·li·on** (pig-māl′yən, -mā′li-ən), *n.* in *Gr. legend,* a sculptor, who fell in love with his statue of a maiden, Galatea, later brought to life by Aphrodite.

**Pyg·my** (pig′mi), *n.* [*pl.* -MIES], [< L. < Gr. *pygmaios,* of the length of the *pygmē,* forearm and fist], 1. a person belonging to any of several races of African and Asiatic dwarfs. 2. [p-], any abnormally undersized or insignificant person or thing. *adj.* 1. of the Pygmies. 2. [p-], dwarfish. 3. [p-], insignificant. Also sp. **Pigmy.**

**py·ja·mas** (pə-jam′əz, -jä′məz), *n.pl.* pajamas: Brit. spelling.

**py·lon** (pī′lon), *n.* [Gr. *pylōn,* gateway], 1. a gateway, as of an Egyptian temple. 2. a towerlike structure flanking an entranceway, supporting telegraph wires, marking a flight course, etc.

**py·lo·rus** (pī-lôr′əs, pə-lō′rəs), *n.* [*pl.* -RI (-ī, -rī)], [LL. < Gr. *pylōros,* gatekeeper < *pylē,* a gate + *ouros,* watchman], the opening from the stomach into the duodenum, the first part of the small intestine. **—py·lor′ic,** *adj.*

**py·o-,** [< Gr. *pyon,* pus], a combining form meaning: 1. *pus.* 2. *suppurative.* Also **py-.**

**Pyong·yang** (pyôŋ′yäŋ′), *n.* the capital of North Korea: pop., 343,000.

**py·or·rhe·a, py·or·rhoe·a** (pī′ə-rē′ə), *n.* [see PYO- & -RRHEA], a discharge of pus; esp., pyorrhea alveolaris. **—py′or·rhe′al, py′or·rhoe′al,** *adj.*

**pyorrhea al·ve·o·la·ris** (al-vē′ə-lâr′is), an infection of the gums and tooth sockets, characterized by formation of pus and loosening of the teeth.

**pyr·a·mid** (pir′ə-mid), *n.* [< Fr. < L. < Gr. *pyramis*], 1. a huge structure with a square base and four triangular sides meeting at a point, built by the ancient Egyptians as a royal tomb. 2. anything shaped like this. 3. in *geometry,* a solid figure having a polygonal base, the sides of which form the bases of triangular surfaces meeting at a common vertex. *v.t. & v.i.* 1. to build up as in the form of a pyramid. 2. to engage in (a series of buying or selling operations) in the stock market, working on margin with profits made in the transactions. **—the (Great) Pyramids,** the three large pyramids near Cairo, Egypt. **—py·ram·i·dal** (pi-ram′ə-d′l), **pyr′a·mid′ic, pyr′a·mid′i·cal,** *adj.* **—py·ram′i·dal·ly,** *adv.*

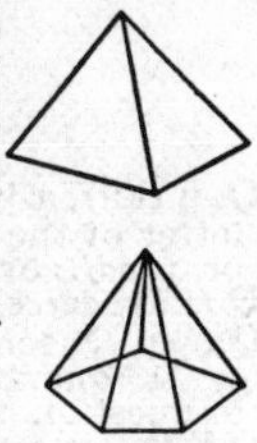

PYRAMIDS

**pyre** (pīr), *n.* [< L. < Gr. *pyr,* a fire], a pile of wood on which a dead body is burned; funeral pile.

**Pyr·e·nees** (pêr′ə-nēz′), *n.pl.* a mountain range between France and Spain. **—Pyr′e·ne′an,** *adj.*

**py·re·thrum** (pī-rē′thrəm), *n.* [L. < Gr. *pyrethron,* feverfew], 1. a kind of chrysanthemum. 2. an insecticide made from certain chrysanthemums.

**py·ret·ic** (pī-ret′ik), *adj.* [< Gr. *pyretos,* fever < *pyr,* a fire], 1. of or causing fever. 2. feverish.

**py·rex** (pī′reks), *n.* [< *pie* + L. *rex,* king; spelled as if < Gr. *pyr,* a fire], a heat-resistant glassware for cooking, etc.: a trade-mark (**Pyrex**).

**pyr·i·dox·ine** (pir′ə-dok′sēn, -sin), *n.* a B complex vitamin used in treating irradiation sickness, etc.: also called *vitamin* $B_6$.

**py·rite** (pī′rīt), *n.* [*pl.* -RITES (pə-rī′tēz, pī-, pī′rīts)], [< L. < Gr. *pyritēs,* flint < *pyr,* a fire], iron sulfide, $FeS_2$, a lustrous, yellow mineral: also called *iron pyrites, fool's gold.*

**py·ri·tes** (pə-rī′tēz, pī-, pī′rīts), *n.* any of various native metallic sulfides, as pyrite. **—py·rit·ic** (pī-rit′ik), **py·rit′i·cal,** *adj.*

**py·ro-,** [< Gr. *pyr,* a fire], a combining form meaning *fire, heat,* as in *pyromania:* also **pyr-.**

**py·rog·ra·phy** (pī-rog′rə-fi), *n.* [*pyro-* + *-graphy*], 1. the art of burning designs on wood or leather by the use of heated tools. 2. a design so made. **—py·rog′ra·pher,** *n.* **—py′ro·graph′ic** (-rə-graf′ik), *adj.*

**py·ro·ma·ni·a** (pī′rə-mā′ni-ə), *n.* [*pyro-* + *-mania*], a persistent compulsion to start destructive fires. **—py′ro·ma′ni·ac′,** *n.* & *adj.* **—py′ro·ma·ni′a·cal** (-rō-mə-nī′ə-k′l), *adj.*

**py·rom·e·ter** (pī-rom′ə-tēr), *n.* [*pyro-* + *-meter*], a thermometer for measuring unusually high temperatures. **—py′ro·met′ric** (-rə-met′rik), **py′ro·met′ri·cal,** *adj.* **—py·rom′e·try,** *n.*

**py·ro·tech·nics** (pī′rə-tek′niks), *n.pl.* [construed as sing.], [< Fr. < *pyro-* + Gr. *technē,* art], 1. the art of making and using fireworks. 2. a display of fireworks. Also **py′ro·tech′ny.** 3. a dazzling display, as of eloquence, wit, etc. **—py′ro·tech′nic, py′ro·tech′ni·cal,** *adj.* **—py′ro·tech′nist,** *n.*

**py·rox·y·lin, py·rox·y·line** (pī-rok′sə-lin), *n.* [< Fr. < Gr. *pyr,* a fire + *xylon,* wood], nitrocellulose, especially in less explosive forms than guncotton, used in making paints, lacquers, celluloid, etc.

**Pyr·rhic victory** (pir′ik), [after *Pyrrhus,* a Greek king who defeated the Romans in 279 B.C., suffering extremely heavy losses], a too costly victory.

**Py·thag·o·ras** (pi-thag′ēr-əs), *n.* Greek philosopher and mathematician; lived 6th century B.C. **—Py·thag′o·re′an** (-ə-rē′ən), *n.* & *adj.*

**Pyth·i·an** (pith′i-ən), *adj.* [< L. < Gr. *Pythios,* of *Pytho,* older name for Delphi], 1. of Apollo as patron of Delphi and the oracle located there. 2. designating or of the games held at Delphi every four years in ancient Greece in honor of Apollo.

**Pythias,** *n.* see **Damon and Pythias.**

**py·thon** (pī′thən, -thon), *n.* [< L. < Gr. *Pythōn,* a serpent slain by Apollo], 1. any of various large, nonpoisonous snakes of SE Asia that crush their prey to death. 2. any large snake that crushes its prey, as the boa.

fat, āpe, bâre, cär; ten, ēven, hêre, ovēr; is, bīte; lot, gō, hôrn, tōōl, look; oil, out; up, ūse, fūr; get; joy; yet; chin; she; thin, *th*en; zh, leisure; ŋ, ring; ə for *a* in *ago,* *e* in *agent,* *i* in *sanity,* *o* in *comply,* *u* in *focus;* ′ in *able* (ā′b′l); Fr. bál; ë, Fr. coeur; ö, Fr. feu; Fr. mo*n*; ô, Fr. coq; ü, Fr. duc; H, G. ich; kh, G. doch. ‡ foreign; < derived from.

**py·tho·ness** (pī′thə-nis), ***n.*** [< OFr. < ML. < LL. < Gr. *Pytho;* see PYTHIAN], 1. the priestess of Apollo at Delphi. 2. any woman soothsayer; prophetess.

**pyx** (piks), ***n.*** [< L. < Gr. *pyxis*, a box < *pyxos*, the box tree], the container in which the consecrated wafer of the Eucharist is kept or carried.

**pyx·id·i·um** (pik-sid′i-əm), ***n.*** [*pl.* -IA (-i-ə)], [< Gr. dim. of *pyxis;* see PYX], in *botany*, a seedcase with two parts, the upper acting as a lid.

# Q

**Q, q** (kū), ***n.*** [*pl.* Q's, q's, Qs, qs], 1. the seventeenth letter of the English alphabet. 2. the sound of Q or q. ***adj.*** seventeenth in a sequence or group.

**Q** (kū), ***adj.*** shaped like Q.

**Q.**, 1. Queen. 2. Question.

**q.**, 1. quart. 2. quarter. 3. quarto. 4. queen. 5. question. 6. quintal: also **ql.** 7. quire.

**Q.E.D.**, *quod erat demonstrandum*, [L.], which was to be proved.

**Q.M.**, Quartermaster.

**qr.**, [*pl.* QRS.], 1. quarter: also **qtr.** 2. quire.

**qt.**, [*pl.* QTS.], 1. quantity. 2. quart.

**Q.T.**, [Slang], quiet: in *on the Q.T.*, in secret.

**qto.**, quarto.

**quack** (kwak), ***v.i.*** [echoic], to utter the sound or cry made by a duck, or a sound like it. ***n.*** the sound made by a duck, or any sound like it.

**quack** (kwak), ***n.*** [short for *quacksalver*], 1. an untrained person who practices medicine fraudulently. 2. a person who, with little or no foundation, pretends to have knowledge or skill in a particular field; charlatan. ***adj.*** 1. characterized by pretentious claims with little or no foundation. 2. dishonestly claiming to effect a cure. **—quack′ish,** ***adj.*** **—quack′ish·ly,** ***adv.***

**quack·er·y** (kwak′ēr-i), ***n.*** [*pl.* -IES], the actions, claims, or methods of a quack.

**quack·sal·ver** (kwak′sal′vēr), ***n.*** [Late MD. < *quacken*, to brag + *zalf*, salve], a quack; charlatan.

**quad** (kwäd), ***n.*** [Colloq.], a quadrangle (of a college).

**quad** (kwäd), ***n.*** in *printing*, a quadrat.

**quad** (kwäd), ***n.*** a quadruplet.

**Quad·ra·ges·i·ma** (kwäd′rə-jes′i-mə), ***n.*** [LL. < L. *quadragesimus*, fortieth], the first Sunday in Lent: also **Quadragesima Sunday.**

**quad·ran·gle** (kwäd′raŋ′g'l), ***n.*** [Fr. < LL. < L.; see QUADRI- & ANGLE], 1. a plane figure with four angles and four sides. 2. an area surrounded on its four sides by buildings. 3. the buildings themselves. **—quad·ran′gu·lar** (-gyoo-lēr), ***adj.***

**quad·rant** (kwäd′rənt), ***n.*** [ML. < L. *quadrans*, fourth part], 1. a fourth part of the circumference of a circle; an arc of 90°. 2. a quarter section of a circle. 3. an instrument for measuring altitudes or angular elevations in astronomy and navigation. **—quad·ran′tal** (-ran′t'l), ***adj.***

**quad·rat** (kwäd′rat), ***n.*** [var. of *quadrate, n.*], in *printing*, a piece of type metal lower than the face of the type, used for spacing, etc.

**quad·rate** (kwäd′rāt; *also, for adj. & n.*, -rit), ***adj.*** [< L. pp. of *quadrare*, to make square], square or nearly square; rectangular. ***n.*** 1. a square or rectangle. 2. a square or rectangular space, thing, etc. ***v.i.*** [-RATED, -RATING], to conform (*to*); square (*with*).

**quad·rat·ic** (kwäd-rat′ik), ***adj.*** 1. square. 2. in *algebra*, involving a quantity or quantities that are squared but none that are raised to a higher power. ***n.*** in *algebra*, a quadratic term, expression, or equation. **—quad·rat′i·cal·ly,** ***adv.***

**quadratic equation,** in *algebra*, an equation in which the second power, or square, is the highest to which the unknown quantity is raised.

**quad·rat·ics** (kwäd-rat′iks), ***n.pl.*** [construed as sing.], algebra dealing with quadratic equations.

**quad·ra·ture** (kwäd′rə-chēr), ***n.*** [< LL. < L. *quadratus*, pp.; see QUADRATE], 1. the act of squaring. 2. the determining of the dimensions of a square equal in area to a given surface, as in "the *quadrature* (or squaring) of the circle," a geometrically insoluble problem.

**quad·ren·ni·al** (kwäd-ren′i-əl), ***adj.*** [< L. < *quadri-* (see QUADRI-) + *annus*, a year], 1. lasting four years. 2. occurring once every four years. ***n.*** a quadrennial event. **—quad·ren′ni·al·ly,** ***adv.***

**quad·ri-,** [L. < *quattuor*, four], a combining form meaning *four times, fourfold*: also **quadr-.**

**quad·ri·lat·er·al** (kwäd′rə-lat′ēr-əl), ***adj.*** [< L.; see QUADRI- & LATERAL], four-sided. ***n.*** 1. in *geometry*, a plane figure having four sides and four angles. 2. a four-sided area. **—quad′ri·lat′er·al·ly,** ***adv.***

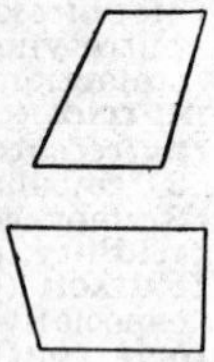

QUADRI-LATERALS

**qua·drille** (kwə-dril′, kə-), ***n.*** [Fr. < Sp. *cuadrilla*, dim. < *cuadro*, a square; ult. < L. *quattuor*, four], 1. a square dance performed by four couples. 2. music for this dance.

**quad·ril·lion** (kwäd-ril′yən), ***n.*** [Fr.; *quadri-* (see QUADRI-) + *million*], 1. in the U.S. and France, the number represented by 1 followed by 15 zeros. 2. in Great Britain and Germany, the number represented by 1 followed by 24 zeros. ***adj.*** amounting to one quadrillion in number.

**quad·ri·va·lent** (kwäd′rə-vā′lənt, kwäd-riv′ə-), ***adj.*** 1. having four valences. 2. having a valence of four. Also, esp. for 2, **tetravalent. —quad′ri·va′lence, quad′ri·va′len·cy,** ***n.***

**quad·roon** (kwäd-ro͞on′), ***n.*** [< Sp. < *cuarto* (< L. *quartus*), a fourth], a person who has one Negro grandparent; child of a mulatto and a white.

**quad·ru·ped** (kwäd′roo-ped′), ***n.*** [< L. *quadru-* (for *quadri-*), four + *pes*, a foot], an animal, especially a mammal, with four feet. ***adj.*** having four feet. **—quad·ru′pe·dal** (-ro͞o′pi-d'l, kwäd′roo-ped′'l), ***adj.***

**quad·ru·ple** (kwäd′roo-p'l, kwäd-ro͞o′-), ***adj.*** [Fr. < L. *quadru-*, four + *-plus*, -fold], 1. consisting of four. 2. four times as much or as many; fourfold. 3. in *music*, having four beats to the measure, the first and third accented. ***adv.*** fourfold. ***n.*** an amount four times as much or as many. ***v.t. & v.i.*** [-PLED, -PLING], to make or become four times as much or as many.

**quad·ru·plet** (kwäd′roo-plit, kwäd-ro͞o′-), ***n.*** 1. *a*) any of four offspring born at a single birth. *b*) *pl.* four offspring born at a single birth. 2. a group of four, usually of one kind.

**quad·ru·pli·cate** (kwäd-ro͞o′plə-kāt′; *for adj. & n., usually* -kit), ***v.t.*** [-CATED, -CATING], [< L. pp. < *quadru-*, four + *plicare*, to fold], to make four identical copies of. ***adj.*** fourfold. ***n.*** any of four identical copies. **—quad·ru′pli·ca′tion,** ***n.***

**quaes·tor** (kwes′tēr, kwēs′-), ***n.*** [L. < pp. of *quaerere*, to inquire], in ancient Rome, 1. originally, a judge in certain criminal cases. 2. later, any of certain state treasurers. **—quaes′tor·ship′,** ***n.***

**quaff** (kwäf, kwaf), ***v.t. & v.i.*** [prob. < LG. *quassen*, to overindulge, printed *ss* being misread as *ff*], to drink in large quantities and with pleasure. ***n.*** a quaffing or what is quaffed. **—quaff′er,** ***n.***

**quag·gy** (kwag′i, kwäg′i), ***adj.*** [-GIER, -GIEST], 1. like a quagmire; boggy; miry. 2. soft; flabby.

**quag·mire** (kwag′mīr′, kwäg′-), ***n.*** [< earlier *quag*, var. of *quake* + *mire*], 1. wet, boggy ground, yielding under the feet. 2. a difficult position, as of one sinking in a quagmire.

**qua·hog, qua·haug** (kwô′hôg, kwə-hôg′), ***n.*** [Am. Ind.], a kind of clam with a hard, solid shell.

**quail** (kwāl), ***v.i.*** [prob. < OFr. *coaillier* (< L. *coagulare*), to coagulate], to draw back in fear; lose heart or courage; cower. **—quail′er,** ***n.***

**quail** (kwāl), ***n.*** [*pl.* QUAILS, QUAIL; see PLURAL, II, D, 1], [< OFr.; prob. < Gmc. echoic name], any of various migratory game birds, resembling domestic fowl: also called *partridge* or *bobwhite*.

**quaint** (kwānt), ***adj.*** [< OFr. *cointe* < L. *cognitus*, known; see COGNITION], 1. pleasingly odd and antique. 2. singular; unusual; curious. 3. fanciful; whimsical. **—quaint′ly,** ***adv.*** **—quaint′ness,** ***n.***

**quake** (kwāk), ***v.i.*** [QUAKED, QUAKING], [< AS. *cwacian*], 1. to tremble; shake; quiver, as land in an earthquake. 2. to shudder or shiver, as with fear or cold. ***n.*** 1. a shaking or tremor. 2. an earthquake.

**Quak·er** (kwāk′ēr), ***n.*** [orig. derisive: from founder's

admonition to "quake" at the word of the Lord], a member of the Society of Friends: a popular name: see **Society of Friends.** —**Quak′er·ish,** *adj.* —**Quak′er·ism,** *n.* —**Quak′er·ly,** *adj. & adv.*
**quaking aspen,** a poplar with small, flat-stemmed leaves that tremble with the gentlest breeze.
**quak·y** (kwāk′i), *adj.* [-IER, -IEST], inclined to quake; shaky. —**quak′i·ly,** *adv.* —**quak′i·ness,** *n.*
**qual·i·fi·ca·tion** (kwäl′ə-fi-kā′shən), *n.* 1. a qualifying or being qualified. 2. a modification; restriction; limiting condition. 3. any ability, experience, etc. that fits a person for a position, office, etc.; requisite.
**qual·i·fied** (kwäl′ə-fīd′), *adj.* 1. having met conditions or requirements set. 2. having the necessary or desirable qualities; fit; competent. 3. limited; modified: as, *qualified* approval. —**qual′i·fied·ly,** *adv.* —**qual′i·fied·ness,** *n.*
**qual·i·fy** (kwäl′ə-fī′), *v.t.* [-FIED, -FYING], [< Fr. < ML. < L. *qualis*, of what kind + *facere*, to make], 1. to describe by giving the qualities or characteristics of. 2. to make fit for a position, office, etc. 3. to make legally capable. 4. to modify; restrict; limit. 5. to moderate; soften. 6. to change the strength of (a liquor, etc.). 7. in *grammar*, to modify the meaning of (a word), as with an adjective. *v.i.* to be or become qualified. —**qual′i·fi′a·ble,** *adj.* —**qual′i·fi′er,** *n.* —**qual′i·fy′ing·ly,** *adv.*
**qual·i·ta·tive** (kwäl′ə-tā′tiv), *adj.* having to do with quality or qualities. —**qual′i·ta′tive·ly,** *adv.*
**qualitative analysis,** the branch of chemistry dealing with the determination of the elements or ingredients of which a substance is composed.
**qual·i·ty** (kwäl′ə-ti), *n.* [*pl.* -TIES], [< OFr. < L. < *qualis*, of what kind], 1. that which makes something what it is; characteristic; attribute. 2. basic nature; character; kind. 3. the degree of excellence which a thing possesses. 4. excellence; superiority. 5. [Archaic], *a*) position in society. *b*) people of high social position. 6. the property of a tone or sound, determined by its overtones; timbre.
**qualm** (kwäm, kwôm), *n.* [AS. *cwealm*, disaster], 1. a sudden fit of sickness, faintness, or nausea. 2. a sudden feeling of uneasiness or doubt; misgiving. 3. a scruple; twinge of conscience. —**qualm′ish,** *adj.* —**qualm′ish·ly,** *adv.* —**qualm′ish·ness,** *n.*
**quan·da·ry** (kwän′dri, -də-ri), *n.* [*pl.* -RIES], [? < L. *quando*, when], a state of perplexity; dilemma.
**quan·ti·ta·tive** (kwän′tə-tā′tiv), *adj.* 1. having to do with quantity. 2. capable of being measured. —**quan′ti·ta′tive·ly,** *adv.*
**quantitative analysis,** the branch of chemistry dealing with the measurement of the amounts of the various components of a substance.
**quan·ti·ty** (kwän′tə-ti), *n.* [*pl.* -TIES], [< OFr. < L. < *quantus*, how much], 1. an amount; portion. 2. any indeterminate, often great, bulk, weight, or number. 3. that property of anything which can be determined by measurement. 4. the relative length of a vowel, syllable, musical tone, etc. 5. in *mathematics*, *a*) a thing that has the property of being measurable in dimensions, amounts, etc. *b*) a number or symbol used to express a quantity.
**quan·tum** (kwän′təm), *n.* [*pl.* -TA (-tə)], [L., neut. sing. of *quantus*, how much], in *physics*, an (or the) elemental unit of energy: the **quantum theory** states that energy is not absorbed nor radiated continuously but discontinuously, in quanta.
**quar·an·tine** (kwôr′ən-tēn′, kwär′-), *n.* [< It. < *quaranta* (< L. *quadraginta*), forty], 1. the period, originally forty days, during which a vessel suspected of carrying contagious disease is detained in port in isolation. 2. the place where such a vessel is stationed. 3. any isolation or restriction on travel imposed to keep contagious diseases, insect pests, etc. from spreading. 4. a place where persons, animals, or plants having such diseases, etc. are isolated. *v.t.* [-TINED, -TINING], 1. to place under quarantine. 2. to isolate politically, commercially, etc. —**quar′an·tin′a·ble,** *adj.*
**quark** (kwôrk), *n.* [arbitrary use of a word coined by James Joyce], any of three hypothetical particles postulated as forming the building blocks of baryons and mesons.
**quar·rel** (kwôr′əl, kwär′-), *n.* [< OFr. < L. *quadrus*, square], a square-headed arrow for a crossbow.
**quar·rel** (kwôr′əl, kwär′-), *n.* [< OFr. < L. *querella*, complaint < *queri*, to complain], 1. a cause for dispute. 2. a dispute, especially one marked by anger and resentment. 3. a breaking up of friendly relations. *v.i.* [-RELED or -RELLED or -RELING or -RELLING], 1. to find fault; complain. 2. to dispute heatedly. 3. to have a breach in friendship. —**quar′rel·er, quar′rel·ler,** *n.*
**quar·rel·some** (kwôr′əl-səm, kwär′-), *adj.* inclined to quarrel. —**quar′rel·some·ly,** *adv.* —**quar′rel·some·ness,** *n.*
**quar·ry** (kwôr′i, kwär′i), *n.* [*pl.* -RIES], [< OFr. *cuiree*; alt. (after *cuir*, a hide) < pp. of *curer*, to eviscerate], 1. an animal that is being hunted down. 2. anything being hunted or pursued.
**quar·ry** (kwôr′i, kwär′i), *n.* [*pl.* -RIES], [< ML.; ult. < L. *quadrare*, to square], a place where stone or slate is excavated for building purposes, etc. *v.t.* [-RIED, -RYING], 1. to excavate from a quarry. 2. to make a quarry in (land). —**quar′ri·er, quar′ry·man** [*pl.* -MEN], *n.* —**quar′ry·ing,** *n.*
**quart** (kwôrt), *n.* [< OFr. < L. *quartus*, fourth < *quattuor*, four], 1. a liquid measure, equal to 1/4 gallon (57.75 cubic inches). 2. a dry measure, equal to 1/8 peck. 3. any container with a capacity of one quart. Abbrev. **qt., q., qu.**
**quar·ter** (kwôr′tẽr), *n.* [< OFr. < L. *quartarius*, a fourth < *quartus*, fourth], 1. any of the four equal parts of something; fourth. 2. one fourth of a year; three months. 3. a school or college term of instruction, usually one fourth of a school year. 4. *a*) one fourth of an hour; 15 minutes. *b*) the moment marking the end of each fourth of an hour. 5. *a*) one fourth of a dollar; 25 cents. *b*) a silver coin of the United States and Canada equal to 25 cents. 6. one leg of a four-legged animal, with the adjoining parts. 7. *a*) any of the four main points of the compass. *b*) any of the regions of the earth thought of as under these; any part of the earth. 8. a particular district in a city: as, the Chinese *quarter*. 9. *pl.* lodgings; place of abode. 10. a particular or previously identified source, as a person, place, point, etc.: as, this news comes from the highest *quarters*. 11. the period of time in which the moon makes one fourth of its revolution around the earth. 12. mercy granted to a surrendering foe. 13. *a*) the after part of a ship's side. *b*) the station assigned to one on a ship. 14. in *football*, etc., any of the four periods into which a game is divided. 15. in *heraldry*, *a*) any of the four equal divisions into which a shield is divided. *b*) the charge occupying such a division. *v.t.* 1. to divide into four equal parts. 2. loosely, to separate into any number of parts. 3. to dismember (a person put to death) into four parts. 4. to provide lodgings for; specif., to assign (soldiers) to lodgings. 5. to pass over (an area) in many directions, as hounds searching for game. 6. in *heraldry*, to place, as different coats of arms, on the quarters of a shield, or add (a coat of arms) to a shield thus. *v.i.* 1. to be lodged or stationed (with *at* or *with*). 2. to range over a field, etc., as hounds in hunting. 3. in *nautical usage*, to blow, as a wind, on the quarter of a ship. *adj.* constituting or equal to a quarter. —**at close quarters,** at close range. —**cry quarter,** to beg for mercy. —**quar′ter·ing,** *n.*
**quar·ter·back** (kwôr′tẽr-bak′), *n.* in *football*, the back who generally calls the signals and receives the ball from the center.
**quarter day,** any of the four days regarded as beginning a new quarter of the year, when quarterly payments on rents, etc. are due.
**quar·ter-deck, quar·ter·deck** (kwôr′tẽr-dek′), *n.* the after part of the upper deck of a ship, usually reserved for officers.

QUARTER-DECK

**quar·tered** (kwôr′tẽrd), *adj.* 1. divided into fourths. 2. provided with quarters, or lodgings. 3. quartersawed. 4. in *heraldry*, divided into quarters.
**quar·ter·ly** (kwôr′tẽr-li), *adj.* 1. occurring or appearing at regular intervals four times a year. 2. consisting of a quarter. *adv.* once every quarter of the year. *n.* [*pl.* -LIES], a publication issued every three months.
**quar·ter·mas·ter** (kwôr′tẽr-mas′tẽr, -mäs′-), *n.* 1. in *military usage*, an officer whose duty is to provide troops with quarters, clothing, equipment, etc. 2. in *nautical usage*, a petty officer who attends to the steering, signals, etc. Abbrev. **Q.M.**
**quar·tern** (kwôr′tẽrn), *n.* [< OFr.; see QUART], a fourth part; esp., a quarter of a pint; gill.
**quarter note,** in *music*, a note (♩) having one fourth the duration of a whole note; crotchet.
**quar·ter·saw** (kwôr′tẽr-sô′), *v.t.* [-SAWED, -SAWED or

-SAWN, -SAWING], to saw (a log) into quarters lengthwise and then into boards, in order to show the grain of the wood to advantage.
**quarter section,** one fourth of a section of land, approximately 1/4 sq. mi., or 160 acres.
**quarter sessions,** 1. in England, a court that sits quarterly in civil proceedings and has limited criminal jurisdiction. 2. in the U.S., any of various courts that sit every three months.
**quar·ter·staff** (kwôr'tẽr-staf', -stäf'), *n.* [*pl.* -STAVES (-stāvz')], a stout, iron-tipped wooden staff, six to eight feet long, formerly used in England as a weapon.
**quar·tet, quar·tette** (kwôr-tet'), *n.* [< Fr. < It. dim. of *quarto* (< L. *quartus*), a fourth], 1. any group of four. 2. in *music, a*) a composition for four voices or four instruments. *b*) the four performers of such a composition.
**quar·to** (kwôr'tō), *n.* [*pl.* -TOS], [< L. (*in*) *quarto*, (in) the fourth], 1. the page size (about 9 by 12 inches) of a book made up of sheets each of which is folded into four leaves, or eight pages. 2. a book of this size of page. Abbrev. **4to, 4°, qto., q.** *adj.* having four (quarto) leaves to the sheet.
**quartz** (kwôrts), *n.* [G. *quarz*], a brilliant, crystalline mineral, silicon dioxide, $SiO_2$, occurring most often in a colorless, transparent form, but also as variously colored semiprecious stones.
**quartz lamp,** a mercury-vapor lamp with a quartz tube for transmitting ultraviolet rays.
**qua·sar** (kwā'sär, -sər), *n.* [*quas*i-stell*ar* radio source], any of a number of distant, starlike celestial objects that emit immense quantities of light or of powerful radio waves.
**quash** (kwäsh), *v.t.* [< OFr. < LL. *cassare*, to destroy < L. *cassus*, empty], in *law*, to annul or set aside, as an indictment. —**quash'er,** *n.*
**quash** (kwäsh), *v.t.* [< OFr. < L. *quassare*, to shatter < pp. of *quatere*, to break], to quell; put down; suppress, as an uprising. —**quash'er,** *n.*
**qua·si** (kwā'sī, -zī, kwä'si), *adv.* [L. < *quam*, as + *si*, if], as if; seemingly. *adj.* seeming. Often hyphenated as a prefix, as in *quasi-judicial*.
**quas·si·a** (kwäsh'i-ə, kwäsh'ə), *n.* [< Graman *Quassi*, Surinam Negro who prescribed it as a remedy for fever, c. 1730], 1. any of a number of related tropical plants. 2. the wood of any of these. 3. a bitter drug extracted from this wood.
**qua·ter·na·ry** (kwə-tũr'nə-ri), *adj.* [< L. < *quaterni*, four each], 1. consisting of four. 2. [Q-], designating or of the geological period following the Tertiary in the Cenozoic Era: see **geology,** chart. *n.* [Q-], the Quaternary Period.
**quat·rain** (kwät'rān), *n.* [Fr. < *quatre* < L. *quattuor*, four], a stanza or poem of four lines.
**quat·re·foil** (kat'ẽr-foil', kat'rə-), *n.* [< OFr. < *quatre* (< L. *quattuor*), four + *feuille* (< L. *folium*), a leaf], 1. a flower with four petals. 2. a leaf with four leaflets. 3. in *architecture*, a leaflike ornament having four lobes.
**qua·ver** (kwā'vẽr), *v.i.* [ME. *cwaflen*], 1. to shake or tremble. 2. to be tremulous: said of the voice. 3. to make a trill in singing or playing. *v.t.* 1. to utter in a tremulous voice. 2. to sing or play with a trill. *n.* 1. a tremulous quality in a voice or tone. 2. in *music*, an eighth note; half of a crotchet. —**qua'ver·ing·ly,** *adv.* —**qua'ver·y,** *adj.*
**quay** (kē), *n.* [< OFr. *cai* < Celt.], a wharf, usually of concrete or stone, with facilities for loading and unloading ships.
**quean** (kwēn), *n.* [AS. *cwene*], 1. a bold or impudent girl or woman. 2. an immoral woman; slut.
**quea·sy** (kwē'zi), *adj.* [-SIER, -SIEST], [ME. *qwesye;* prob. < ON. or LG.], 1. causing or feeling nausea. 2. squeamish; easily nauseated. 3. uneasy. —**quea'si·ly,** *adv.* —**quea'si·ness,** *n.*
**Que·bec** (kwi-bek'), *n.* 1. a province of E Canada: pop., 4,628,000: abbrev. **Que., Q.** 2. its capital, on the St. Lawrence River: pop., 171,000.
**Quech·ua** (kech'wä), *n.* 1. a member of any of a group of South American Indian tribes dominant in the former Inca Empire. 2. the language of these tribes. —**Quech'uan** (-wən), *adj. & n.*
**queen** (kwēn), *n.* [AS. *cwen*], 1. the wife of a king. 2. a woman who rules over a monarchy in her own right. 3. a woman who is noted, as for her beauty or accomplishments. 4. a place or thing regarded as the finest of its kind: as, Cuba is called the *Queen* of the Antilles. 5. the fully developed, reproductive female in a colony of bees, ants, etc. 6. in *cards*, a playing card with a picture of a queen on it. 7. in *chess*, the most powerful piece: it can move in any straight or diagonal direction. *v.t.* to make (a girl or woman) a queen. *v.i.* to reign as a queen. —**queen it,** to act like a queen; domineer. —**queen'dom, queen'hood',** *n.* —**queen'like',** *adj.*
**Queen Anne's lace,** a wild plant of the carrot family, with delicate, white flowers in flat-topped clusters.
**queen consort,** the wife of a reigning king.
**queen dowager,** the widow of a king.
**queen·ly** (kwēn'li), *adj.* [-LIER, -LIEST], 1. of or like a queen. 2. suitable to a queen. *adv.* in a queenly manner. —**queen'li·ness,** *n.*
**queen mother,** a queen dowager who is mother of a reigning sovereign.
**queen post,** in *carpentry*, either of two vertical posts set between the rafters and the base of a truss, at equal distances from the apex.
**Queens** (kwēnz), *n.* a borough of New York City, on W Long Island: pop., 1,810,000.
**Queens·land** (kwēnz'land', -lənd), *n.* a state of E Australia.
**queer** (kwêr), *adj.* [prob. < G. *quer*, crosswise], 1. differing from what is usual or ordinary; odd; strange. 2. slightly ill; giddy. 3. [Colloq.], doubtful; suspicious. 4. [Colloq.], having mental quirks; eccentric. 5. [Slang], counterfeit; not genuine. 6. [Slang], homosexual. *v.t.* [Slang], 1. to spoil the success of. 2. to put (oneself) into an unfavorable position. *n.* [Slang], 1. counterfeit money. 2. a homosexual. —**queer'ly,** *adv.* —**queer'ness,** *n.*
**quell** (kwel), *v.t.* [< AS. *cwellan*, to kill], 1. to crush; subdue. 2. to quiet; allay. —**quel'ler,** *n.*
**quench** (kwench), *v.t.* [AS. *cwencan*, caus. of *cwincan*, to go out], 1. to extinguish; put out: as, water *quenched* the fire. 2. to satisfy; slake: as, he *quenched* his thirst. 3. to cool suddenly, as hot steel, by plunging into water, oil, etc. —**quench'a·ble,** *adj.* —**quench'er,** *n.* —**quench'less,** *adj.* —**quench'less·ly,** *adv.* —**quench'less·ness,** *n.*
**quer·u·lous** (kwer'ə-ləs, -yoo-), *adj.* [< LL. < L. < *queri*, to complain], 1. inclined to find fault; fretful. 2. characterized by complaining. —**quer'u·lous·ly,** *adv.* —**quer'u·lous·ness,** *n.*
**que·ry** (kwêr'i), *n.* [*pl.* -RIES], [< L. *quaere*, 2d pers. sing., imperative of *quaerere*, to ask], 1. a question; inquiry. 2. a doubt. 3. a question mark (?). *v.t.* [-RIED, -RYING], 1. to call in question; ask about. 2. to question (a person). 3. to question the accuracy of (written or printed matter) by marking with a question mark. *v.i.* 1. to ask questions. 2. to express doubt. —**que'rist,** *n.*
**quest** (kwest), *n.* [< OFr. < ML. < L. < pp. of *quaerere*, to seek], 1. a seeking; hunt. 2. a journey in search of adventure, etc., as those undertaken by knights-errant in medieval times. 3. the persons participating in a quest. *v.i.* [Rare], to go in search or pursuit. —**quest'er,** *n.* —**quest'ful,** *adj.*
**ques·tion** (kwes'chən), *n.* [< Anglo-Fr. < OFr. < L. < pp. of *quaerere*, to ask], 1. an asking; inquiry. 2. something asked; interrogative sentence. 3. doubt; uncertainty. 4. something in controversy before a court. 5. a problem; matter open to discussion. 6. a matter or case of difficulty: as, it's not a *question* of money. 7. a point being debated or a resolution brought up before an assembly. 8. the putting of such a matter to a vote. *v.t.* 1. to ask questions of; interrogate. 2. to doubt; express uncertainty about. 3. to dispute; challenge. *v.i.* to ask a question or questions. —**beside the question,** irrelevant. —**beyond (all) question,** beyond dispute. —**call in question,** 1. to challenge. 2. to cast doubt on. —**in question,** under consideration. —**out of the question,** impossible; not to be considered. —**ques'tion·er,** *n.* —**quest'ion·ing,** *adj.* —**ques'tion·ing·ly,** *adv.*
**ques·tion·a·ble** (kwes'chən-ə-b'l), *adj.* 1. that can be questioned. 2. of dubious repute; suspected of being immoral, not respectable, etc. —**ques'tion·a·ble·ness,** *n.* —**ques'tion·a·bly,** *adv.*
**question mark,** the interrogation mark (?).
**ques·tion·naire** (kwes'chən-âr'), *n.* a written or printed list of questions used in gathering information from one or more persons.
**quet·zal** (ket-säl'), *n.* [Sp. < Nahuatl < *quetzalli*, tail feather], 1. a Central American bird, usually brilliant green above and red below, with long, streaming tail feathers (in the male). 2. [*pl.* -ZALES (-sä'les)], the gold monetary unit of Guatemala. Also **que·zal** (ke-säl').
**queue** (kū), *n.* [Fr. < OFr. *coue* < L. *cauda*, tail], 1. a pigtail. 2. a line, as of persons waiting to be served. *v.i.* [QUEUED, QUEUING], [Chiefly Brit.], to form in a queue, or line (often with *up*).
**Que·zon, Ma·nuel Lu·is** (mä-nwel' lōō-ēs' ke'sôn; Eng. kā'zon), 1878–1944; Philippine statesman.
**Quezon City,** the capital of the Philippine Islands, on Luzon, adjoining Manila: pop., 398,000.
**quib·ble** (kwib''l), *n.* [< L. *quibus* (formerly common in legal documents), abl. pl. of *qui*, who], a petty evasion or cavil. *v.i.* [-BLED, -BLING], to

evade the truth of a point under discussion by caviling. —**quib′bler,** *n.* —**quib′bling·ly,** *adv.*

**quick** (kwik), *adj.* [< AS. *cwicu,* living], 1. [Archaic], living. 2. a) rapid; swift: as, a *quick* walk. b) prompt: as, a *quick* reply. 3. prompt to understand or learn. 4. sensitive: as, a *quick* sense of smell. 5. easily stirred; fiery: as, a *quick* temper. 6. fresh; invigorating. *adv.* quickly; rapidly. *n.* 1. the living: as, the *quick* and the dead. 2. the sensitive flesh under a toenail or fingernail. 3. the center of the feelings: as, her sarcasm cut him to the *quick.* —**quick′ish,** *adj.* —**quick′ly,** *adv.* —**quick′ness,** *n.*

**quick bread,** any bread, as muffins, corn bread, etc., leavened with baking powder, soda, etc., and baked as soon as the batter is mixed.

**quick·en** (kwik′ən), *v.t.* 1. to animate; enliven. 2. to arouse, stimulate. 3. to cause to move more rapidly; hasten. *v.i.* 1. to become enlivened; revive. 2. to move or beat more rapidly: as, the pulse *quickens* with fear. —**quick′en·er,** *n.*

**quick-freeze** (kwik′frēz′), *v.t.* [-FROZE, -FROZEN, -FREEZING], to subject (food) to such sudden freezing that the flavor and natural juices are retained and the food can be stored at low temperatures for a long time. —**quick freezing.**

**quick·ie** (kwik′i), *n.* [Slang], anything done or made quickly and cheaply.

**quick·lime** (kwik′līm′), *n.* unslaked lime.

**quick·sand** (kwik′sand′), *n.* [prob. < MD. or MLG.], a loose, wet, deep sand deposit in which a person or heavy object may easily be engulfed.

**quick·set** (kwik′set′), *n.* 1. a live slip, especially of hawthorn, planted, as for a hedge. 2. any plant growing in a hedge. 3. a hedge.

**quick·sil·ver** (kwik′sil′vẽr), *n.* mercury (the metal). *v.t.* to cover with mercury.

**quick·step** (kwik′step′), *n.* 1. the step used for marching in quick time. 2. a march in the rhythm of quick time. 3. a spirited dance step.

**quick-tem·pered** (kwik′tem′pẽrd), *adj.* easily aroused to anger.

**quick time,** the normal rate of marching (in the U.S. Army), 120 paces a minute.

**quick-wit·ted** (kwik′wit′id), *adj.* nimble of mind. —**quick′-wit′ted·ly,** *adv.* —**quick′-wit′ted·ness,** *n.*

**quid** (kwid), *n.* [var. of *cud*], a piece, as of tobacco, to be chewed.

**quid** (kwid), *n.* [*pl.* QUID], [Brit. Slang], a sovereign, or one pound sterling.

**quid·di·ty** (kwid′ə-ti), *n.* [*pl.* -TIES], [< ML. < L. *quid,* what], 1. essential quality. 2. a quibble.

**quid·nunc** (kwid′nuŋk′), *n.* [L., lit., what now?], one who is inquisitive about gossip; busybody.

‡**quid pro quo** (kwid′ prō kwō′), [L.], 1. one thing in return for another. 2. a substitute.

**qui·es·cent** (kwī-es′′nt), *adj.* [< L. ppr. of *quiescere,* to become quiet], quiet; still; inactive. —**qui·es′cence, qui·es′cen·cy,** *n.* —**qui·es′cent·ly,** *adv.*

**qui·et** (kwī′ət), *adj.* [< OFr. < L. *quietus,* pp. of *quiescere,* to keep quiet < *quies,* rest], 1. still; calm; motionless. 2. *a*) not noisy; hushed. *b*) not speaking; silent. 3. not agitated; gentle: as, a *quiet* sea. 4. not easily excited: as, a *quiet* disposition. 5. not ostentatious: as, *quiet* furnishings. 6. not forward; unobtrusive: as, a *quiet* manner. 7. secluded: as, a *quiet* den. 8. serving to relax: as, a *quiet* evening. 9. in *commerce,* not busy: as, a *quiet* market. *n.* 1. a quiet state; calmness, stillness, etc. 2. a quiet or peaceful quality. *v.t. & v.i.* to make or become quiet. *adv.* in a quiet manner. —**qui′et·er,** *n.* —**qui′et·ly,** *adv.* —**qui′et·ness,** *n.*

**qui·et·en** (kwī′ə-t′n), *v.t. & v.i.* [Brit. or Dial.], to make or become quiet.

**qui·e·tude** (kwī′ə-tōōd′, -tūd′), *n.* a state of being quiet; rest; calmness.

**qui·e·tus** (kwī-ē′təs), *n.* [< ML. *quietus est,* he is quit], 1. discharge or release from debt, obligation, etc. 2. discharge or release from life; death. 3. anything that kills.

**quill** (kwil), *n.* [prob. < MLG. or MD.], 1. any of the large, stiff wing or tail feathers of a bird. 2. *a*) the hollow, horny stem of a feather. *b*) anything made from this, as a pen or plectrum. 3. any of the spines of a porcupine or hedgehog.

**quilt** (kwilt), *n.* [< OFr. < L. *culcit(r)a,* a bed], 1. a bedcover made of two layers of cloth filled with down, wool, etc. and stitched together in lines or patterns. 2. anything used as a quilt. 3. any material made up like a quilt. *v.t.* 1. to stitch together with a soft material between. 2. to stitch in lines or patterns like those in quilts. *v.i.* to make a quilt. —**quilt′ed,** *adj.* —**quilt′er,** *n.*

**quilt·ing** (kwilt′iŋ), *n.* 1. the act of making quilts. 2. material for quilts. 3. a quilting bee.

**quilting bee,** a social gathering of women at which they work together sewing quilts.

**quince** (kwins), *n.* [orig. pl. of ME. *quyne* < OFr. < L. < Gr. *kydōnion*], 1. a golden or greenish-yellow, apple-shaped fruit, used in preserves. 2. the tree that bears it.

**Quin·cy** (kwin′zi), *n.* a city in Massachusetts, near Boston: pop., 87,000.

**Quin·cy, Josiah** (kwin′zi, -si), 1744–1775; American patriot.

**qui·nine** (kwī′nīn, kwi-nēn′), *n.* [< *quina,* cinchona bark (< Sp. < Quechua *quinquina*) + *-ine*], 1. a bitter, crystalline alkaloid, $C_{20}H_{24}N_2O_2$, extracted from cinchona bark. 2. any compound of this used in medicine for various purposes, especially in treating malaria. Also **quin·i·a** (kwin′i-ə), **quin′in** (-in), **qui·ni·na** (ki-nē′nə).

**quin·nat salmon** (kwin′at), [< the Am. Ind. name], chinook salmon.

**quin·qua·ge·nar·i·an** (kwiŋ′kwə-ji-nâr′i-ən), *adj.* [< L. < *quinquaginta,* fifty], fifty years old, or between the ages of fifty and sixty. *n.* a person of this age.

**Quin·qua·ges·i·ma** (kwiŋ′kwə-jes′ə-mə), *n.* [< LL. fem. of L. *quinquagesimus,* fiftieth], the Sunday before Lent: also **Quinquagesima Sunday.**

**quin·quen·ni·al** (kwiŋ-kwen′i-əl), *adj.* [< L. < *quinque,* five + *annus,* year], 1. lasting five years. 2. taking place every five years. *n.* a quinquennial event. —**quin·quen′ni·al·ly,** *adv.*

**quin·sy** (kwin′zi), *n.* [< ML. *quinancia* < LL. *cynanche* < Gr. *kynanchē,* lit., dog-choking < *kyōn,* dog + *anchein,* to choke], an inflammation of the tonsils, accompanied by the formation of pus.

**quint** (kwint), *n.* [Colloq.], a quintuplet.

**quin·tal** (kwin′t'l), *n.* [Fr. < ML. < Ar. *qinṭār* < L. < *centum;* see CENTENARY], a hundredweight.

**quin·tes·sence** (kwin-tes′′ns), *n.* [< ML. *quinta essentia,* fifth essence, or ultimate substance], 1. the pure, concentrated essence of anything. 2. the most perfect manifestation of a quality or thing. —**quin′tes·sen′tial** (-tə-sen′shəl), *adj.*

**quin·tet, quin·tette** (kwin-tet′), *n.* [< Fr. < It. dim. of *quinto* (< L. *quintus*), a fifth], 1. any group of five. 2. in *music, a*) a composition for five voices or five instruments. *b*) the five performers of such a composition.

**Quin·til·ian** (kwin-til′yən, -i-ən), *n.* Roman rhetorician and critic; lived 1st century A.D.

**quin·til·lion** (kwin-til′yən), *n.* [< L. *quintus,* a fifth; + *million*], 1. in the U.S. and France, the number represented by 1 followed by 18 zeros. 2. in Great Britain and Germany, the number represented by 1 followed by 30 zeros. *adj.* amounting to one quintillion in number.

**quin·tu·ple** (kwin′too-p'l, kwin-tū′-), *adj.* [Fr. < L. < *quintus,* a fifth + *-plus,* -fold], 1. consisting of five. 2. five times as much or as many; fivefold. *n.* an amount five times as much or as many. *v.t. & v.i.* [-PLED, -PLING], to make or become five times as much or as many.

**quin·tu·plet** (kwin′too-plit, kwin-tū′-, -tup′lit), *n.* 1. *a*) any of five offspring born at a single birth. *b*) *pl.* five offspring born at a single birth. 2. a group of five, usually of one kind.

**quip** (kwip), *n.* [< earlier *quippy* < L. *quippe,* indeed], 1. a witty or sarcastic expression; jest. 2. a quibble. 3. something curious or odd. *v.t. & v.i.* [QUIPPED, QUIPPING], to make quips (at). —**quip′pish, quip′py,** *adj.* —**quip′ster,** *n.*

**quire** (kwīr), *n., v.t. & v.i.* [QUIRED, QUIRING], [Archaic], choir.

**quire** (kwīr), *n.* [< OFr. < LL. *quaternum,* paper in sets of four < L. *quattuor,* four], a set of 24 or 25 sheets of paper of the same size and stock.

**Quir·i·nal** (kwir′i-n'l), *n.* [L.], 1. one of the seven hills on which Rome was built: site of a papal palace later used as a royal residence of Italy. 2. the Italian civil government.

**quirk** (kwũrk), *n.* [? < ON. *kuerk,* a bird's neck], 1. a sudden twist, turn, etc., as a flourish in writing. 2. a quibble. 3. a witticism. 4. a peculiarity or mannerism. —**quirk′y** [-IER, -IEST], *adj.*

**quirt** (kwũrt), *n.* [< Mex. Sp. *cuarta*], a riding whip with a braided leather lash and a short handle. *v.t.* to strike with a quirt.

**quis·ling** (kwiz′liŋ), *n.* [after Vidkun *Quisling,* Norw. collaborationist with the Nazis], a person who betrays his own country by helping an enemy to invade and occupy it.

**quit** (kwit), ***v.t.*** [QUIT, QUITTED, QUITTING], [< OFr. < ML. < LL. *quietare*, to set free < L. *quietus*, quiet], 1. to free (oneself) *of*. 2. to discharge (a debt); repay. 3. to give up. 4. to let go (something held). 5. to leave; depart from. 6. to stop, as work. ***v.i.*** 1. to go away. 2. to stop doing something. 3. [Colloq.], to give up one's job; resign. ***adj.*** clear; free; rid.

**quit·claim** (kwit'klām'), ***n.*** [< OFr. < *quite*, quit + *clamer*, to call], 1. the relinquishment of a claim. 2. a legal paper in which a person relinquishes to another a claim to some property or right. ***v.t.*** to give up a claim to (some property, etc.).

**quite** (kwit), ***adv.*** [ME. form of *quit, adj.*], 1. completely; entirely. 2. really; truly; positively. 3. [Colloq.], to a considerable degree or extent. **—quite a few,** [Colloq.], more than a few.

**Qui·to** (kē'tō), ***n.*** the capital of Ecuador: pop., 213,000.

**quit·rent** (kwit'rent'), ***n.*** a rent paid in lieu of feudal services: also **quit rent.**

**quits** (kwits), ***adj.*** [< *quit, adj.*], on even terms, as by discharge of a debt, retaliation in vengeance, etc. **—cry quits,** to declare oneself even with another; agree to stop competing.

**quit·tance** (kwit''ns), ***n.*** [see QUIT], 1. discharge from a debt or obligation. 2. a document certifying this; receipt. 3. recompense; repayment.

**quit·ter** (kwit'ẽr), ***n.*** [Colloq.], a person who quits or gives up easily, without trying hard.

‡**qui va là?** (kē' vȧ' lȧ'), [Fr.], who goes there?: a sentry's challenge.

**quiv·er** (kwiv'ẽr), ***v.i.*** [prob. < base of *quaver*], to shake with a tremulous motion; tremble. ***n.*** the act or condition of quivering; tremor. **—quiv'er·ing,** ***adj.*** **—quiv'er·ing·ly,** ***adv.***

**quiv·er** (kwiv'ẽr), ***n.*** [< Anglo-Fr. *quiveir* < Gmc.], 1. a case for holding arrows. 2. its contents.

‡**qui vive?** (kē'vēv'), [Fr., lit., who lives?], who goes there?: a sentry's challenge. **—on the qui vive,** on the lookout; on the alert.

**Quixote, Don,** see **Don Quixote.**

**quix·ot·ic** (kwik-sot'ik), ***adj.*** 1. [sometimes Q-], like or befitting Don Quixote. 2. extravagantly chivalrous or romantically idealistic; visionary; impractical. Also **quix·ot'i·cal. —quix·ot'i·cal·ly,** ***adv.*** **—quix'ot·ism** (-sə-tiz'm), ***n.***

**quiz** (kwiz), ***n.*** [*pl.* QUIZZES], [? < L. *quis*, who, which, what], 1. a practical joke; hoax. 2. a questioning; esp., an informal examination to test one's knowledge. ***v.t.*** [QUIZZED, QUIZZING], 1. to make fun of. 2. to ask questions of (a person) to test his knowledge. **—quiz'zer,** ***n.*** **—quiz'zing,** ***adj.*** **—quiz'zing·ly,** ***adv.***

**quiz program,** a type of radio or television program in which a group of experts or members of the audience compete in answering questions.

**quiz section,** in some colleges, etc., a small group of students who meet with an instructor to discuss and be examined on lectures.

**quiz·zi·cal** (kwiz'i-k'l), ***adj.*** 1. odd; comical. 2. teasing; bantering. 3. perplexed. **—quiz'zi·cal·ly,** ***adv.*** **—quiz'zi·cal·ness,** ***n.***

**quod** (kwod), ***n.*** [< *quadrangle*], [Chiefly Brit. Slang], prison: also sp. **quad.**

**quoin** (koin, kwoin), ***n.*** [var. of *coin*], 1. the external corner of a building; esp., any of the stones by which the corner of a building is marked. 2. a wedgelike piece of stone, etc., such as the keystone of an arch. 3. a wedge-shaped wooden or metal block.

QUOINS

**quoit** (kwoit, koit), ***n.*** [< Anglo-Fr.; prob. < OFr. *coite*, a cushion], 1. a ring of rope or metal thrown, in a game, at an upright peg, the object being to encircle it. 2. *pl.* the game so played.

**quon·dam** (kwon'dəm), ***adj.*** [L.], that was at one time; former: as, my *quondam* companion.

**Quon·set hut** (kwon'sit), [< *Quonset*, R.I., where first manufactured], a prefabricated, metal shelter shaped like the longitudinal half of a cylinder resting on its flat surface.

**quo·rum** (kwôr'əm, kwō'rəm), ***n.*** [L., genit. pl. of *qui*, who], the minimum number of members required to be present at an assembly before it can validly proceed to transact business.

**quot.,** quotation.

**quo·ta** (kwō'tə), ***n.*** [*pl.* -TAS], [L., fem. of *quotus*, how many], a share which each of a number is to contribute or receive; proportional share.

**quot·a·ble** (kwō'tə-b'l), ***adj.*** that can be quoted; suited for quotation. **—quot'a·bil'i·ty, quot'a·ble·ness,** ***n.*** **—quot'a·bly,** ***adv.***

**quo·ta·tion** (kwō-tā'shən), ***n.*** 1. a quoting. 2. the words or passage quoted. 3. in *commerce*, *a*) a statement of the current price of a stock, bond, etc. *b*) the price itself. **—quo·ta'tion·al,** ***adj.*** **—quo·ta'tion·al·ly,** ***adv.***

**quotation mark,** either of a pair of punctuation marks (". . .") used to enclose a direct quotation: a quotation within a quotation is enclosed in single marks ('. . .').

**quote** (kwōt), ***v.t.*** [QUOTED, QUOTING], [< OFr. < ML. *quotare*, to number (chapters, etc.) < L. *quotus*, of what number], 1. to repeat a passage from or statement of. 2. to repeat (a passage, statement, etc.). 3. to cite as an example or authority. 4. to state (the price of something). ***n.*** [Colloq.], 1. a quotation. 2. a quotation mark. **—quot'er,** ***n.***

**quoth** (kwōth), ***v.t.*** [< AS. < *cwethan*, to speak], [Archaic], said: used in the past tense, followed by a subject of the first or third person.

**quoth·a** (kwōth'ə), ***interj.*** [phonetic alteration of *quoth he*], [Archaic], indeed! forsooth!

**quo·tid·i·an** (kwō-tid'i-ən), ***adj.*** [< OFr. < L. < *quotidie*, daily < *quotus*, how many + *dies*, day], daily; recurring every day. ***n.*** anything, especially a fever or ague, that recurs daily.

**quo·tient** (kwō'shənt), ***n.*** [< L. *quoties*, how often < *quot*, how many], in *arithmetic*, the number obtained when one quantity is divided by another.

**quo war·ran·to** (kwō wô-ran'tō), [*pl.* -TOS], [ML., by what warrant], a legal proceeding undertaken to recover an office, franchise, or privilege from the person in possession.

**q.v.,** [L.], *quod vide*, which see.

# R

**R, r** (är), ***n.*** [*pl.* R's, r's, Rs, rs], 1. the eighteenth letter of the English alphabet. 2. the sound of R or r. ***adj.*** eighteenth in a sequence or group.

**R** (är), ***n.*** 1. in *electricity, the symbol for* resistance. 2. in *mathematics, the symbol for* radius. ***adj.*** shaped like R. **—the three R's,** reading, writing, and arithmetic, regarded as the basic studies.

**R.,** 1. Radical. 2. Republic. 3. Republican.

**R., r.,** 1. rabbi. 2. radius. 3. railroad. 4. railway. 5. *Regina*, [L.], queen. 6. *Rex*, [L.], king. 7. right. 8. river. 9. road. 10. ruble. 11. rupee.

**r.,** 1. rare. 2. rod; rods. 3. in *baseball*, run; runs. 4. in *law*, rule.

**Ra** (rä), ***n.*** the sun god, principal god of the ancient Egyptians: also **Re.**

**Ra,** in *chemistry*, radium.

**Ra·bat** (rä-bät', rə-), ***n.*** the capital of Morocco, on the west coast: pop., 156,000.

**rab·bet** (rab'it), ***n.*** [< OFr. < *rabattre;* see REBATE], 1. a groove or cut made in the edge of a board, etc. so that another piece may be fitted into it. 2. a joint made in this way. ***v.t.*** 1. to cut a rabbet in. 2. to join in a rabbet (joint). ***v.i.*** to be joined by a rabbet.

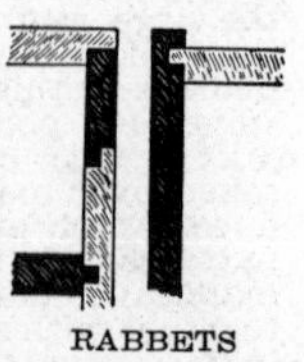

RABBETS

**rab·bi** (rab'ī), ***n.*** [*pl.* -BIS, -BIES], [< LL. < Gr. < Heb. *rabbī*, my master], an ordained teacher of the Jewish law, now usually the spiritual head of a congregation.

**Rab·bin·ic** (rə-bin'ik), ***n.*** the Hebrew language as used by rabbis in the Middle Ages.

**rab·bin·i·cal** (rə-bin'i-k'l), ***adj.*** of the rabbis, their doctrines, learning, language, etc.: also **rab·bin'ic. —rab·bin'i·cal·ly,** ***adv.***

**rab·bit** (rab′it), *n.* [*pl.* -BITS, -BIT; see PLURAL, II, D, 1], [ME. *rabette*], 1. a burrowing rodent of the hare family, having soft fur, long ears, and a bobbed tail. 2. its fur. *v.i.* to hunt rabbits.

**rabbit fever,** tularemia.

**rabbit punch,** in *boxing,* a short, sharp blow to the back of the neck.

**rabbit's** (or **rabbit**) **foot,** the hind foot of a rabbit, used as a good-luck charm.

**rab·ble** (rab′'l), *n.* [prob. < *rabble,* a puddling bar], a noisy, disorderly crowd; mob. —**the rabble,** the common people: a term of contempt.

**rabble rouser,** one who tries to stir up people by appeals to their emotions, prejudices, etc.

**Rab·e·lais, Fran·çois** (frän′swȧ′ rȧ′ble′; Eng. rab′ə-lā′), 1494?–1533; French writer known for his broad, coarse humor, satire, etc. —**Rab·e·lai·si·an** (rab′ə-lā′zhən, -zi-ən), *adj.* & *n.*

**rab·id** (rab′id), *adj.* [< L. < *rabere,* to rage], 1. violent; raging. 2. fanatical in beliefs or opinions. 3. of or having rabies. —**ra·bid·i·ty** (rə-bid′ə-ti), **rab′id·ness,** *n.* —**rab′id·ly,** *adv.*

**ra·bies** (rā′bēz, -bi-ēz′), *n.* [L., madness], an infectious virus disease of dogs, wolves, etc. that can be transmitted to man by the bite of an infected animal and is characterized by choking, convulsions, etc.: also called *hydrophobia.*

**rac·coon** (ra-ko͞on′), *n.* [*pl.* -COONS, -COON; see PLURAL, II, D, 1], [< Am. Ind. *arakunem,* lit., hand-scratcher], 1. a small, tree-climbing, flesh-eating mammal of North America, active at night and having long, yellow-black fur and a long, black-ringed tail. 2. its fur. Also sp. **racoon.**

RACCOON
(34 in. long)

**race** (rās), *n.* [< ON. *rās,* a running], 1. a competition of speed in running, riding, etc. 2. *pl.* a series of such competitions for horses, on a regular course. 3. any contest likened to a race: as, the *race* for mayor. 4. a steady onward movement. 5. *a*) a swift current of water. *b*) the channel for a current of water, especially for industrial use: as, a mill*race.* *v.i.* [RACED, RACING], 1. to take part in a race. 2. to go or move swiftly. 3. to move too swiftly because of less resistance or a lighter load: said of machinery. *v.t.* 1. to compete with in a race. 2. to cause (a horse, etc.) to engage in a race. 3. *a*) to cause to go swiftly. *b*) to cause (an engine) to run too swiftly without engaging the gears.

**race** (rās), *n* [Fr. < It. *razza*], 1. *a*) any of the three major biological divisions of mankind, distinguished by color of hair and skin, stature, etc. *b*) mankind. 2. any geographical, national, or tribal ethnic grouping. 3. *a*) the state of belonging to a certain ethnic group. *b*) the characteristics or features of such a group. 4. any group of people having the same ancestry. 5. any group of people regarded as a distinct class: as, the *race* of dramatists. 6. a group of plants or animals with distinguishing traits passed on to the offspring. *adj.* Negro.

**race·course** (rās′kôrs′, -kōrs′), *n.* a race track, especially one for horse races.

**ra·ceme** (rā-sēm′, rə-), *n.* [L. *racemus,* cluster of grapes], a variety of flower cluster in which single flowers grow on small stems arranged at intervals along a single larger stem, as in the lily of the valley. —**rac·e·mose** (ras′ə-mōs′), *adj.*

**rac·er** (rās′ẽr), *n.* 1. a person, animal, airplane, etc. that takes part in races. 2. any of several snakes; esp., the American blacksnake.

**race riot,** fighting between different groups in a community, resulting from racist hostility.

**race suicide,** the gradual dying out of a people as a result of deliberate failure to maintain a birth rate equal to the death rate.

**race track,** a course prepared for racing.

**Ra·chel** (rā′chəl), *n.* in the *Bible,* the younger of the two wives of Jacob.

**ra·chi·tis** (rə-kī′tis), *n.* [< Gr. *rhachitis,* inflammation of the spine < *rhachis,* spine], rickets. —**ra·chit′ic** (-kit′ik), *adj.*

**Rach·ma·ni·noff, Ser·ge·i** (syer-gyā′i räkh-mä′ni-nôf), 1873–1943; Russian composer, conductor, and pianist: also sp. **Rachmaninov.**

**ra·cial** (rā′shəl), *adj.* of or characteristic of a race (ethnic group) or races. —**ra′cial·ly,** *adv.*

**ra·cial·ism** (rā′shəl-iz'm), *n.* a doctrine or feeling of racial antagonisms, with reference to supposed racial superiority or purity; racial prejudice, hatred, or discrimination.

**Ra·cine** (rə-sēn′), *n.* a city in SE Wisconsin, on Lake Michigan: pop., 89,000.

**Ra·cine, Jean Bap·tiste** (zhän bȧ′tēst′ rȧ′sēn′), 1639–1699; French poet and writer of tragedies.

**rac·ism** (rās′iz'm), *n.* 1. racialism. 2. the practice of racial discrimination, persecution, etc., based on racialism. —**rac′ist,** *adj.* & *n.*

**rack** (rak), *n.* [prob. < MD. *rek* < *recken,* to stretch], 1. a framework, case, etc. for holding or displaying things; specif., *a*) a grating for holding hay, etc. to feed cattle. *b*) a frame for holding hay, straw, etc. on a wagon. *c*) a frame with hooks for hanging clothes. 2. a toothed bar into which a toothed gearwheel, etc. meshes. 3. an instrument of torture which stretches the victim's limbs out of place. 4. any great mental or physical torment, or its cause. 5. a wrenching or upheaval, as by a storm. *v.t.* 1. to arrange as in a rack. 2. to torture on a rack. 3. to torment. 4. to oppress, as by exacting exorbitant rents. —**on the rack,** in a difficult or painful situation. —**rack one's brains** (or **memory,** etc.), to try very hard to remember or think of something.

**rack** (rak), *n.* [? var. of *track*], either of two gaits used by horses, the single-foot or the pace. *v.i.* to move with either of these.

**rack** (rak), *n.* [var. of *wrack*], destruction: now only in *go to rack and ruin,* to become ruined.

**rack** (rak), *n.* [prob. < ON.], a broken mass of clouds blown by the wind: also sp. **wrack.**

**rack·et** (rak′it), *n.* [prob. echoic], 1. a noisy confusion; uproar. 2. a period of gay merrymaking. 3. [Slang], *a*) an obtaining of money illegally, as by bootlegging, threats of violence, etc. *b*) any dishonest scheme. *c*) any business, profession, etc.: used humorously. —**rack′et·y,** *adj.*

**rack·et** (rak′it), *n.* [Fr. *raquette* < Ar. *rāhah,* palm of the hand], 1. a light bat for tennis, etc., with a network of catgut, silk, etc. in a frame attached to a handle. 2. *pl.* a variety of tennis played in a walled enclosure. Also sp. **racquet.**

**rack·et·eer** (rak′ə-têr′), *n.* [see RACKET (uproar) & -EER], one who obtains money illegally, as by fraud, threats of violence, etc. *v.i.* to obtain money in such a way. —**rack′et·eer′ing,** *n.* & *adj.*

**rac·on·teur** (rak′on-tũr′; Fr. rȧ′kōn′tẽr′), *n.* [Fr. < *raconter,* to recount], a person skilled at telling stories or anecdotes.

**ra·coon** (ra-ko͞on′), *n.* a raccoon.

**rac·y** (rās′i), *adj.* [-IER, -IEST], [< *race* (tribe) + *-y*], 1. having the taste or quality associated with the genuine type: as, *racy* fruit. 2. lively; spirited. 3. piquant; pungent. 4. somewhat indecent; risqué —**rac′i·ly,** *adv.* —**rac′i·ness,** *n.*

**rad.,** 1. radical. 2. radius.

**ra·dar** (rā′där), *n.* [*ra*dio *d*etecting *a*nd *r*anging], an instrument that sends out radio waves and picks them up after they have been reflected by a land mass, ship, etc.: used to indicate the direction and distance of the reflecting object.

**ra·di·al** (rā′di-əl), *adj.* [Fr. < L.; see RADIUS], 1. of or like a ray or rays; branching out in all directions from a common center. 2. of or situated like a radius. 3. in *anatomy,* of or near the radius or forearm. —**ra′di·al·ly,** *adv.*

**radial engine,** an internal-combustion engine with cylinders arranged like wheel spokes.

**ra·di·ant** (rā′di-ənt), *adj.* [< L. ppr. of *radiare;* see RADIATE], 1. shining brightly. 2. filled with light; bright. 3. showing joy, well-being, etc.; beaming: as, a *radiant* smile. 4. issuing (from a source) in or as in rays: as, *radiant* energy. —**ra′di·ance, ra′di·an·cy,** *n.* —**ra′di·ant·ly,** *adv.*

**radiant energy,** any form of energy radiating from a source, as sound, heat, X rays, etc.

**ra·di·ate** (rā′di-āt′), *v.i.* [-ATED, -ATING], [< L. pp. of *radiare* < *radius;* see RADIUS], 1. to send out rays of heat, light, etc. 2. to spread out in rays. 3. to branch out in lines from a center. *v.t.* 1. to send out (heat, light, etc.) in rays. 2. to give forth (love, happiness, etc.). *adj.* having rays or parts like rays; radial. —**ra′di·ate′ly,** *adv.*

**ra·di·a·tion** (rā′di-ā′shən), *n.* 1. a radiating; specif., the process in which energy in the form of rays of light, heat, etc. is sent out from atoms and molecules as they undergo internal change. 2. the rays sent out. 3. the treatment of disease by radioactive material. —**ra′di·a′tive,** *adj.*

---

**fat, āpe, bâre, cär; ten, ēven, hêre, ovẽr; is, bīte; lot, gō, hôrn, to͞ol, look; oil, out; up, ūse, fũr; get; joy; yet; chin; she; thin, *th*en; zh,** leisure; **ŋ,** ring; **ə** for *a* in *ago, e* in *agent, i* in *sanity, o* in *comply, u* in *focus;* ′ in *able* (ā′b'l); Fr. bȧl; **ë,** Fr. coeur; **ö,** Fr. feu; Fr. mo*n*; **ô,** Fr. coq; **ü,** Fr. duc; **H,** G. ich; **kh,** G. doch. ‡ foreign; < derived from.

**ra·di·a·tor** (rā′di-ā′tẽr), *n.* anything that radiates; specif., *a*) a series of pipes through which hot water or steam circulates so as to radiate heat into a room, etc. *b*) a water-filled apparatus, as in an automobile, for radiating superfluous heat and thus cooling the engine.

**rad·i·cal** (rad′i-k'l), *adj.* [< LL. < L. *radix*, a root], 1. of or from the root; fundamental; basic. 2. *a*) favoring extreme change, as of the social structure. *b*) [R-], designating any of various modern political parties, ranging from leftist to conservative in program. *n.* 1. *a*) a basic part of something. *b*) a fundamental. 2. *a*) a person having radical views. *b*) [R-], a member of a Radical party. 3. in *chemistry*, a group of two or more atoms that acts as a single atom and goes through a reaction unchanged, or is replaced by a single atom. 4. in *linguistics*, a word, or part of a word, serving as a root. 5. in *mathematics*, the radical sign. —**rad′i·cal·ly**, *adv.*

**rad·i·cal·ism** (rad′i-k'l-iz'm), *n.* 1. the quality or state of being radical, especially in politics. 2. radical principles, methods, or practices.

**rad·i·cal·ize** (rad′i-k'l-iz′), *v.t.* & *v.i.* [-IZED, -IZING], to make or become politically radical.

**radical sign,** in *mathematics*, the sign ($\surd$ or $\sqrt{\ }$) used before a quantity to indicate that its root is to be extracted.

**rad·i·cle** (rad′i-k'l), *n.* [< L. *radix*, a root], in *botany*, the lower part of the axis of an embryo seedling.

**ra·di·i** (rā′di-ī′), *n.* alt. pl. of **radius.**

**ra·di·o** (rā′di-ō′), *n.* [*pl.* -OS], [< *radiotelegraphy*, etc.], 1. the practice or science of communicating over a distance by converting sounds or signals into electromagnetic waves and transmitting these through space, without wires, to a receiving set, which changes them into sounds. 2. such a receiving set. 3. broadcasting by radio as a business, entertainment, etc. 4. a radiogram. *adj.* 1. of, using, used in, or sent by radio. 2. having to do with electric frequencies of more than 15,000 cycles per second. *v.t.* & *v.i.* [-OED, -OING], to send (a message, etc.) to (a person, etc.) by radio.

**ra·di·o-,** [see RADIUS], a combining form meaning: 1. *radial.* 2. *by radio*, as in *radiotelegraphy.* 3. *by means of radiant energy*, as in *radiotherapy.* 4. *radioactive*, as in *radioisotope.*

**ra·di·o·ac·tive, ra·di·o-ac·tive** (rā′di-ō-ak′tiv), *adj.* giving off radiant energy in the form of particles or rays, as alpha, beta, and gamma rays, by the disintegration of atomic nuclei: as, *radioactive* chemical elements. —**ra′di·o·ac′tive·ly, ra′di·o-ac′tive·ly,** *adv.* —**ra′di·o·ac·tiv′i·ty, ra′di·o-ac·tiv′i·ty,** *n.*

**radio beacon,** a radio transmitter that gives off special signals to help ships or aircraft determine their position or come in safely, as at night.

**radio beam,** a beam (sense 12*a*).

**ra·di·o·broad·cast** (rā′di-ō-brôd′kast′, -käst′), *n.* & *v.t.* [-CAST or -CASTED, -CASTING], broadcast by radio.

**radio frequency,** in *electricity*, a frequency of more than 10,000 vibrations per second.

**ra·di·o·gram** (rā′di-ō-gram′), *n.* 1. a message sent by radio: also **ra′di·o·tel′e·gram′.** 2. a radiograph.

**ra·di·o·graph** (rā′di-ō-graf′, -gräf′), *n.* a picture produced on a sensitized film or plate by rays other than light rays, especially by X rays. —**ra′di·og′ra·pher** (-og′rə-fẽr), *n.* —**ra′di·o·graph′ic,** *adj.* —**ra′di·o·graph′i·cal·ly,** *adv.* —**ra′di·og′ra·phy,** *n.*

**ra·di·o·i·so·tope** (rā′di-ō-ī′sə-tōp′), *n.* an artificially created radioactive isotope of a chemical element that is normally nonradioactive.

**ra·di·ol·o·gy** (rā′di-ol′ə-ji), *n.* [*radio-* + *-logy*], the science dealing with radiant energy and its uses, as in X-ray therapy. —**ra′di·ol′o·gist,** *n.*

**ra·di·o·phone** (rā′di-ō-fōn′), *n.* a telephone operated by radio.

**ra·di·os·co·py** (rā′di-os′kə-pi), *n.* [*radio-* + *-scopy*], the direct examination of the inside structure of opaque objects by radiation, as by X rays.

**ra·di·o·sonde** (rā′di-ō-sond′), *n.* [Fr.; *radio* + *sonde*, depth sounding], a miniature radio transmitter with instruments, sent aloft by balloon and dropped by parachute, for transmitting signals giving temperature, pressure, and humidity readings from the upper atmosphere.

**radio spectrum,** the complete range of frequencies or wave lengths of electromagnetic waves, specifically those used in radio and television.

**ra·di·o·tel·e·graph** (rā′di-ō-tel′ə-graf′, -gräf′), *n.* an instrument for sending radiograms. *v.t.* & *v.i.* to send (a message) by a radiotelegraph. —**ra′di·o·tel′e·graph′ic,** *adj.* —**ra′di·o·te·leg′ra·phy** (-tə-leg′rə-fi), *n.*

**ra·di·o·tel·e·phone** (rā′di-ō-tel′ə-fōn′), *n.* a radiophone.

**ra·di·o·te·leph·o·ny** (rā′di-ō-tə-lef′ə-ni), *n.* telephony by radio, without connecting wires. —**ra′di·o·tel′e·phon′ic** (-tel′ə-fon′ik), *adj.*

**ra·di·o·tel·e·scope** (rā′di-ō-tel′ə-skōp′), *n.* a radio antenna or an array of antennae, designed to intercept radio waves from celestial sources.

**ra·di·o·ther·a·py** (rā′di-ō-ther′ə-pi), *n.* the treatment of disease by the use of X rays or rays from a radioactive substance, as radium.

**rad·ish** (rad′ish), *n.* [< Fr. < L. *radix*, a root], 1. a plant of the mustard family, with an edible red or white root. 2. the pungent root, eaten raw as a relish or in a salad.

**ra·di·um** (rā′di-əm), *n.* [< L. *radius*, a ray], a radioactive metallic chemical element, found in very small amounts in pitchblende and certain other uranium minerals, which undergoes spontaneous atomic disintegration: it is used in the treatment of cancer and some skin diseases: symbol, Ra; at. wt., 226.05; at. no., 88.

**ra·di·um·ther·a·py** (rā′di-əm-ther′ə-pi), *n.* the treatment of cancer or other diseases by the use of radium: also **radium therapy.**

**ra·di·us** (rā′di-əs), *n.* [*pl.* -DII (-di-ī′), -DIUSES], [L., a spoke (of a wheel), hence ray], 1. a ray or raylike part, as any of the rays of a composite flower. 2. any straight line from the center to the periphery of a circle or sphere. 3. the circular area or distance limited by the sweep of such a line: as, no house within a *radius* of five miles. 4. any limited extent, scope, etc.: as, within the *radius* of my experience. 5. the shorter and thicker of the two bones of the forearm on the same side as the thumb.

**ra·don** (rā′don), *n.* [*rad*ium + *-on* as in *neon*], a radioactive gaseous chemical element formed in the atomic disintegration of radium: symbol, Rn; at. wt., 222; at. no., 86.

**R.A.F., RAF,** Royal Air Force.

**raf·fi·a** (raf′i-ə), *n.* [< Malagasy native name], 1. a palm tree of Madagascar with large, pinnate leaves: also **raffia palm.** 2. fiber from its leaves, woven into baskets, hats, etc. 3. a related palm.

**raff·ish** (raf′ish), *adj.* [rif*fraff* + *-ish*], 1. disreputable; disgraceful. 2. tawdry; flashy; cheap.

**raf·fle** (raf′'l), *n.* [< OFr. *rafle*, dice game; ult. < D. *rafelen*, to snatch away], a lottery in which each participant buys a chance to win the prize. *v.t.* [-FLED, -FLING], to offer as a prize in a raffle (often with *off*). *v.i.* to conduct a raffle.

**raft** (raft, räft), *n.* [< ON. *raptr*, a log], a number of logs, boards, barrels, etc. fastened together into a platform and floated on water as a means of transportation. *v.t.* 1. to transport on a raft. 2. to make into a raft. —**raft′like′,** *adj.* —**rafts′man** [*pl.* -MEN], *n.*

**raft** (raft, räft), *n.* [< Scot. *raff*, rubbish], [Colloq.], a large number, collection, etc.; lot.

**raft·er** (raf′tẽr, räf′-), *n.* [AS. *ræfter*], any of the beams that slope from the ridge of a roof to the eaves and serve to support the roof.

**rag** (rag), *n.* [ult. < ON. *rögg*, tuft of hair], 1. a waste piece of cloth, especially one torn or uneven. 2. a small piece of cloth for dusting, cleaning, etc. 3. anything suggesting a rag, as in worthlessness. 4. *pl.* old, worn clothes. 5. *pl.* any clothes: used humorously. *adj.* made of rags: as, a *rag* doll. —**chew the rag,** [Slang], to chat.

**rag** (rag), *v.t.* [RAGGED, RAGGING], [Slang], 1. to tease. 2. to scold. *n.* [Slang], a ragging.

**rag** (rag), *n.* [Slang], ragtime. *v.t.* [RAGGED, RAGGING], [Slang], to play in ragtime style.

**rag·a·muf·fin** (rag′ə-muf′in), *n.* [ME. *Ragamofin*, name of a demon in mystery plays: demons were often described as *ragged*, i.e., shaggy], a dirty, ragged person; esp., a dirty, ragged child.

**rage** (rāj), *n.* [< OFr. < LL. < L. *rabies*, madness], 1. a furious, uncontrolled anger. 2. a great violence or intensity, as of the wind. 3. strong emotion, enthusiasm, or desire. 4. anything arousing general enthusiasm; fad. *v.i.* [RAGED, RAGING], 1. to show violent anger in action or speech. 2. to be forceful, violent, etc.: as, the sea *raged.* 3. to spread unchecked, as a disease.

**rag·ged** (rag′id), *adj.* 1. shabby or torn from wear. 2. wearing shabby or torn clothes. 3. uneven: rough. 4. shaggy; unkempt: as, *ragged* hair. 5. not finished; imperfect: as, a *ragged* style. 6. harsh; strident. —**rag′ged·ly,** *adv.* —**rag′ged·ness,** *n.*

**ragged edge,** the extreme edge; verge. —**on the ragged edge,** precariously close to loss of self-control, mental stability, etc.

**rag·lan** (rag′lən), *n.* [after Lord *Raglan* (1788–1855), Brit. general], a loose overcoat or topcoat with sleeves that continue in one piece to the collar, so that there are no shoulder seams. *adj.* designating or of such a sleeve.

**rag·man** (rag'man , -mən), *n.* [*pl.* -MEN], a man who collects, buys, and sells rags, old paper, etc.

**Rag·na·rok** (räg'nə-rok'), *n.* [< ON. < genit. pl. of *regin*, god + *rök*, judgment], in *Norse mythology*, the destruction of the world in the last great conflict between the gods and the forces of evil: also **Rag'na·rök'** (-na-rök').

**ra·gout** (ra-gōō'), *n.* [< Fr. < *ragoûter*, to revive the appetite of], a stew of highly seasoned meat and vegetables. *v.t.* [-GOUTED (-gōōd'), -GOUTING (-gōō'iŋ)], to make into a ragout.

**rag·pick·er** (rag'pik'ẽr), *n.* one who makes his living by picking up and selling rags and junk.

**rag·time** (rag'tīm'), *n.* [< *ragged time*], 1. a type of American music, an early form of jazz first popular from about 1890 to 1915, characterized by strong syncopation in fast, even time. 2. its syncopated rhythm.

**rag·weed** (rag'wēd'), *n.* [after the tattered appearance of the leaves], a common weed with divided leaves and small, yellow-green flowers: the pollen is a cause of hay fever.

**rag·wort** (rag'wũrt'), *n.* [see RAGWEED], any of various tall plants with irregularly toothed leaves and yellow flowers.

**rah** (rä, rô), *interj.* hurrah.

**raid** (rād), *n.* [North Eng. form of *road*, in etym. sense "a riding"], 1. a sudden, hostile attack, as by troops, aircraft, bandits, etc. 2. any sudden invasion of some place by police, for discovering violations of the law. *v.t.* to make a raid on. *v.i.* to take part in a raid. **—raid'er,** *n.*

**rail** (rāl), *n.* [< OFr. < L. *regula*, a rule], 1. a bar of wood, metal, etc. placed horizontally between posts as a guard or support. 2. a fence or railing. 3. any of a series of parallel metal bars laid as upon crossties to make a track for railroad cars, streetcars, etc. 4. a railroad as a means of transportation: as, he went by *rail*. 5. a narrow wooden piece at the top of a ship's bulwarks. *v.t.* to supply with rails or a railing; fence.

**rail** (rāl), *v.i.* [< Fr. *railler*, to banter], to speak bitterly or reproachfully (with *against* or *at*). **—rail'er,** *n.* **—rail'ing·ly,** *adv.*

**rail** (rāl), *n.* [*pl.* RAILS, RAIL; see PLURAL, II, D, 1], [< OFr. *raale*], any of a number of small wading birds living in marshes, characterized by short wings and tail, long toes, and a harsh cry.

**rail·ing** (rāl'iŋ), *n.* 1. material for rails. 2. rails collectively. 3. a fence or balustrade made of rails and posts.

**rail·ler·y** (rāl'ẽr-i), *n.* [*pl.* -IES], [Fr. *raillerie;* see RAIL, *v.i.*], 1. light, good-natured ridicule or satire. 2. a teasing act or remark.

**rail·road** (rāl'rōd'), *n.* 1. a road laid with parallel steel rails along which cars are drawn by locomotives. 2. a complete system of such roads, including land, rolling stock, stations, etc. 3. the corporation owning such a system. *v.t.* 1. to transport by railroad. 2. to furnish with railroads. 3. [Colloq.], to rush through quickly, so as to prevent careful consideration. 4. [Slang], to cause to go to prison on a trumped-up charge. *v.i.* to work on a railroad. **—rail'road'er,** *n.* **—rail'road'ing,** *n.*

**rail-split·ter** (rāl'split'ẽr), *n.* a person who splits logs into rails, as for fences. **—the Rail-Splitter,** Abraham Lincoln.

**rail·way** (rāl'wā'), *n.* 1. a railroad for light vehicles: as, a street *railway*. 2. [Brit.], a railroad. 3. any track with rails for guiding wheels.

**rai·ment** (rā'mənt), *n.* [contr. of *arrayment;* see ARRAY], [Archaic or Poetic], clothing; attire.

**rain** (rān), *n.* [AS. *regn*], 1. water falling in drops condensed from the moisture in the atmosphere. 2. the falling of such drops; shower. 3. *a)* rainy weather. *b) pl.* seasonal rainfalls (preceded by *the*). 4. a rapid falling or propulsion of many small objects: as, a *rain* of ashes. *v.i.* 1. to fall: said of rain, as, it is *raining*. 2. to fall like rain: as, bullets *rained* about him. 3. to cause rain to fall. *v.t.* 1. to pour down (rain or something likened to rain). 2. to give in large quantities: as, they *rained* praises on him. **—rain'less,** *adj.*

**rain·bow** (rān'bō'), *n.* the arc containing the colors of the spectrum in consecutive bands, formed in the sky by the refraction, reflection, and dispersion of the sun's rays in falling rain or mist. *adj.* of many colors.

**rain check,** the stub of a ticket to a baseball game, etc., entitling the holder to be admitted at a future date if the event is halted because of rain: also used figuratively.

**rain·coat** (rān'kōt'), *n.* a waterproof coat for giving protection from rain.

**rain·drop** (rān'drop'), *n.* a single drop of rain.

**rain·fall** (rān'fôl'), *n.* 1. a falling of rain; shower. 2. the amount of water falling as rain, snow, etc. over a given area in a given period of time: measured in inches of depth.

**Rai·nier, Mount** (rā-nêr', rā'nir), a mountain of the Cascade Range, in the State of Washington.

**rain·proof** (rān'prōōf'; *for v.*, -prōōf'), *adj.* [see -PROOF], not permitting rain to come through; shedding rain. *v.t.* to make rainproof.

**rain·storm** (rān'stôrm'), *n.* a storm with a heavy rain.

**rain·y** (rān'i), *adj.* [-IER, -IEST], 1. characterized by rain, especially by much rain. 2. wet with rain. 3. bringing rain. **—rain'i·ness,** *n.*

**rainy day,** a possible future time of need.

**raise** (rāz), *v.t.* [RAISED, RAISING], [< ON. *reisa*], 1. to cause to rise; lift. 2. to construct (a building, etc.). 3. to stir up; incite: as, to *raise* a revolt. 4. to increase in size, value, amount, etc.: as, to *raise* prices. 5. to increase in degree, intensity, strength, etc.: as, she *raised* her voice. 6. to improve the position or rank of: as, hard work *raised* the man from poverty. 7. to cause to appear, arise, etc.; esp., to reanimate: as, her cries could *raise* the dead. 8. to provoke; inspire: as, the remark *raised* a laugh. 9. to bring forward for consideration: as, he *raised* a question. 10. to collect or procure (an army, money, etc.). 11. to utter (a cry, shout, etc.). 12. to bring (a siege) to an end. 13. to leaven (bread, etc.). 14. *a)* to cause to grow; breed, as corn. *b)* to rear (children). 15. in *nautical usage*, to come within sight of. 16. in *poker*, etc., to bet more than (a preceding bet or better). *v.i.* 1. [Dial.], to rise or arise. 2. in *poker*, etc., to increase the bet. *n.* 1. an act of raising. 2. an increase in amount; specif., an increase in salary or wages. **—raise Cain** (or **the devil, hell, a rumpus, the roof,** etc.), [Slang], to cause trouble; create a disturbance. **—rais'a·ble,** *adj.* **—rais'er,** *n.*

**raised** (rāzd), *adj.* [pp. of *raise*], 1. made in low relief; embossed. 2. made light and fluffy with yeast or other leavening agent: said of bread, etc.

**rai·sin** (rā'z'n), *n.* [< OFr. < L. *racemus*, cluster of grapes], a sweet, dried grape, usually seedless.

**‡rai·son d'être** (re'zōn' de'tr'; Eng. rā'zôn det'), [Fr.], reason for being; justification for existence.

**raj** (räj), *n.* [see RAJAH], in India, rule; sovereignty.

**ra·jah, ra·ja** (rä'jə), *n.* [< Hind. < Sans. *rājan* < *rāj*, to rule], a prince or chief in India, etc. **—ra'jah·ship, ra'ja·ship,** *n.*

**rake** (rāk), *n.* [AS. *raca*], a long-handled tool with teeth at one end, used for gathering hay, leaves, etc., or for smoothing broken ground. *v.t.* [RAKED, RAKING], 1. to gather with a rake. 2. to gather with great care. 3. to scratch with a rake, as in leveling broken ground. 4. to search through minutely. 5. to direct gunfire along the length of (a line of troops, etc.): often used figuratively. *v.i.* 1. to use a rake. 2. to search as if with a rake.

**rake** (rāk), *n.* [contr. of earlier *rakehell*], a dissolute, debauched man; roué.

**rake** (rāk), *v.i.* [RAKED, RAKING], [akin to Sw. *raka*, to project], to be slightly inclined; slant, as a ship's masts, etc. *v.t.* to give a slant to. *n.* a slanting from the perpendicular.

**rake-off** (rāk'ôf'), *n.* [Slang], a commission, rebate, or share, especially when received in an illegitimate transaction.

**rak·ish** (rāk'ish), *adj.* [< *rake* (to slant) + *-ish*], 1. having a trim, neat appearance, suggesting speed: said of a ship. 2. dashing; jaunty. **—rak'ish·ly,** *adv.* **—rak'ish·ness,** *n.*

**rak·ish** (rāk'ish), *adj.* like a rake; dissolute. **—rak'ish·ly,** *adv.* **—rak'ish·ness,** *n.*

**Ra·leigh** (rô'li), *n.* the capital of North Carolina: pop., 94,000.

**Ra·leigh,** Sir **Walter** (rô'li, rä'-), 1552?–1618; English explorer, courtier, historian, and poet: also sp. **Ralegh.**

**ral·len·tan·do** (räl'en-tän'dō, ral'ən-tan'-), *adj. & adv.* [It., ppr. of *rallentare*, to slow down], in *music*, gradually slower: abbrev. **rall.**

**ral·ly** (ral'i), *v.t.* [-LIED, -LYING], [< Fr. < *re-*, again + *allier*, to join; see ALLY], 1. to bring back together in a state of order, as retreating troops. 2. to bring together for a common purpose. 3. to revive: as, he *rallied* his energy. *v.i.* 1. to come back to a state of order: as, the soldiers *rallied*. 2. to come together for a common purpose. 3. to come in order to help: as, he *rallied* to his defeated friend. 4. to revive; recover: as, she *rallied* from her coma. 5. to rise in price after having fallen: said of stocks, etc. 6. in *tennis*, etc., to take part in a rally. *n.* [*pl.* -LIES], a rallying or being rallied; specif., *a*) a gathering of people for a common purpose. *b*) in *tennis*, etc., an exchange of several strokes before the point is won. —**ral'li·er,** *n.*

**ral·ly** (ral'i), *v.t.* & *v.i.* [-LIED, -LYING], [Fr. *rallier;* see RAIL (to complain)], to tease; ridicule; banter. —**ral'li·er,** *n.* —**ral'ly·ing·ly,** *adv.*

**ram** (ram), *n.* [AS. *ramm*], 1. a male sheep. 2. a battering-ram. 3. a pump that raises water by the force of the water itself falling through a pipe: also called **hydraulic ram.** 4. the striking part of a pile driver. 5. the plunger of a force pump. 6. [R-], Aries. *v.t.* [RAMMED, RAMMING], 1. to strike against with great force. 2. to force into place; press or drive down. 3. to stuff or cram (*with* something). —**ram'mer,** *n.*

**Ram·a·dan** (ram'ə-dän'), *n.* [Ar. *ramaḍān*, lit., the hot month < *ramaḍa*, to be hot], 1. the ninth month of the Moslem year, a period of daily fasting from sunrise to sunset. 2. the fasting.

**ram·ble** (ram'b'l), *v.i.* [-BLED, -BLING], [< ME. *romblen*, freq. of *romen*, to roam], 1. to move, especially to walk, about idly; stroll; roam. 2. to talk or write aimlessly. 3. to spread in all directions, as vines. *n.* a rambling; an aimless stroll.

**ram·bler** (ram'blẽr), *n.* a person or thing that rambles; esp., any of certain climbing roses.

**ram·bunc·tious** (ram-buŋk'shəs), *adj.* [altered < *robustious* < *robust*], [Colloq.], disorderly, boisterous, wild, unruly, etc. —**ram·bunc'tious·ly,** *adv.* —**ram·bunc'tious·ness,** *n.*

**ram·e·kin, ram·e·quin** (ram'ə-kin), *n.* [Fr. *ramequin* < D. < G. *rahm*, cream], 1. a food mixture, as of bread crumbs, cheese, and eggs, baked in individual baking dishes. 2. such a baking dish.

**ram·i·fi·ca·tion** (ram'ə-fi-kā'shən), *n.* 1. a ramifying or being ramified. 2. the result of this; specif., *a*) a branch or offshoot. *b*) a subdivision or consequence.

**ram·i·fy** (ram'ə-fī'), *v.t.* & *v.i.* [-FIED, -FYING], [< Fr. < L. *ramus*, a branch + *facere*, to make], to separate into branches or branchlike divisions.

**ram·jet** (ram'jet'), *n.* a jet engine in which the air is continuously compressed by being rammed into the open front end: also called *athodyd.*

**ra·mose** (rā'mōs, rə-mōs'), *adj.* [< L. < *ramus*, a branch], 1. bearing many branches. 2. branching.

**ra·mous** (rā'məs), *adj.* 1. ramose. 2. branchlike.

**ramp** (ramp), *n.* [< Fr.; see RAMP, *v.*], a sloping passage, sometimes curved, joining different levels of a building, road, etc.

**ramp** (ramp), *v.i.* [< OFr. *ramper*, to climb], 1. to be rampant, as a lion in heraldry. 2. to move or rush threateningly, violently, or with fury; rampage. *n.* a ramping.

**ram·page** (ram-pāj'; *also, and for n. always,* ram'pāj), *v.i.* [-PAGED, -PAGING], [< *ramp, v.* + *rage*], to rush violently about; rage; act wildly. *n.* an outbreak of violent, raging behavior: usually in *on the* (or *a*) *rampage.* —**ram·pa'geous,** *adj.*

**ramp·ant** (ram'pənt), *adj.* [< OFr.; see RAMP, *v.*], 1. growing or spreading unchecked; rife. 2. violent in action, speech, etc. 3. in *heraldry*, rearing up on the hind legs with one forepaw raised above the other, as a lion, etc. —**ramp'an·cy,** *n.* —**ramp'ant·ly,** *adv.*

**ram·part** (ram'pärt, -pẽrt), *n.* [Fr. < *re-*, again + *emparer*, to prepare < L. *ante*, before + *parare*, to prepare], 1. an embankment of earth surmounted by a parapet and encircling a castle, fort, etc., for defending it. 2. anything that defends or protects. *v.t.* to protect as with a rampart.

**ram·rod** (ram'rod'), *n.* 1. a metal rod for ramming down the charge in a muzzle-loading gun. 2. a rod for cleaning a rifle bore.

**Ram·ses** (ram'sēz'), *n.* any of twelve Egyptian monarchs who ruled from 1500 to 1000 B.C.: also **Ram·e·ses** (ram'ə-sēz').

**ram·shack·le** (ram'shak''l), *adj.* [< freq. of *ransack*], loose and rickety; likely to fall to pieces.

**ran** (ran), pt. of **run.**

**ranch** (ranch), *n.* [< Sp. *rancho*, a group eating together], 1. a large farm, especially in the western U.S., with its buildings, lands, workers, etc., for raising cattle, horses, or sheep. 2. any large farm for raising a particular crop or livestock: as, a fruit *ranch.* *v.i.* to work on or manage a ranch. —**ranch'er, ranch'man** [*pl.* -MEN], *n.*

**ran·cho** (ran'chō, rän'-), *n.* [*pl.* -CHOS], [Sp.], in Spanish America, a ranch.

**ran·cid** (ran'sid), *adj.* [< L. < *rancere*, to be rank], having the bad smell or taste of stale fats or oils; spoiled. —**ran'cid·ly,** *adv.* —**ran·cid'i·ty, ran'cid·ness,** *n.*

**ran·cor** (raŋ'kẽr), *n.* [OFr. < L. < *rancere*, to be rank], a continuing and bitter hate or ill will; deep spite: Brit. sp. **rancour.** —**ran'cor·ous,** *adj.* —**ran'cor·ous·ly,** *adv.* —**ran'cor·ous·ness,** *n.*

**ran·dom** (ran'dəm), *n.* [< OFr. *randon*, violence, speed], haphazard movement: now only in *at random*, without careful choice, aim, plan, etc. *adj.* lacking aim or method; haphazard.

**ra·nee** (rä'ni), *n.* a rani.

**rang** (raŋ), pt. of **ring** (to sound, as a bell).

**range** (rānj), *v.t.* [RANGED, RANGING], [< OFr. var. of *reng(i)er* < OHG. *hring*, a ring], 1. to arrange in a certain order; esp., to set in a row or rows. 2. to place (oneself or another) with others in a cause, party, etc. 3. to travel through; roam about: as, they *ranged* the woods. *v.i.* 1. to extend or lie in a given direction: as, the hills *range* toward the east. 2. to wander about; roam. 3. to roam through an area, as in searching. 4. to vary between stated limits: as, they *ranged* in age from two to five years. 5. in *biology*, to live or grow in a specified region. *n.* 1. a row, line, or series; rank. 2. a class, kind, or order. 3. a series of connected mountains considered as a single system. 4. a line of direction: as, a tree in *range* with the house. 5. *a*) the maximum effective horizontal distance that a gun can fire its projectile. *b*) the distance from a gun to its target. 6. a place for shooting practice. 7. the full extent over which something moves or is heard, seen, understood, etc.; scope. 8. a wandering or roaming. 9. a large, open area on which livestock graze. 10. the limits of possible variations of amount, degree, etc.: as, a wide *range* in price. 11. a cooking stove. 12. in *biology*, the region in which a plant or animal is normally found. *adj.* of a range(open grazing place): as, *range* livestock.

**range finder,** an instrument for determining the distance of a target, photographic subject, etc.

**rang·er** (rān'jẽr), *n.* 1. a wanderer. 2. *a*) any of a group of mounted troops for patrolling a region. *b*) [often R-], any of a group of U.S. soldiers trained for raiding behind enemy lines. 3. in England, the chief official of a royal park or forest. 4. in the U.S., a warden who patrols government forests.

**Ran·goon** (raŋ-go͞on'), *n.* a seaport and the capital of Burma: pop., 400,000.

**rang·y** (rān'ji), *adj.* [-IER, -IEST], 1. able or inclined to range about; hence, 2. long-limbed and slender. —**rang'i·ness,** *n.*

**ra·ni** (rä'ni), *n.* [< Hind. < Sans. fem. of *rājan;* see RAJAH], in India, 1. the wife of a rajah or prince. 2. a reigning queen or princess. Also sp. **ranee.**

**rank** (raŋk), *n.* [OFr. *ranc* < OHG. *hring*, a ring], 1. a row, line, or series; range. 2. an orderly arrangement. 3. a social class: as, men from all *ranks* of life. 4. a high position in society: as, a man of *rank.* 5. an official grade: as, the *rank* of major. 6. a relative position; degree of quality: as, a first *rank* poet. 7. in *military usage*, *a*) a row of soldiers, vehicles, etc. placed side by side: opposed to *file.* *b*) *pl.* an army. *c*) *pl.* the body of soldiers of an army, as opposed to the officers. *v.t.* 1. to place in a rank or ranks. 2. to assign a certain position to: as, he *ranks* music above painting. 3. to outrank. *v.i.* 1. to hold a certain position: as, he *ranks* third. 2. to hold the highest rank: as, the *ranking* man on the staff. —**rank and file,** 1. the body of soldiers of an army, as opposed to the officers; hence, 2. the common people, as opposed to leaders, etc.

**rank** (raŋk), *adj.* [AS. *ranc*, strong], 1. growing vigorously and coarsely; overly luxuriant as, *rank* grass. 2. producing a luxuriant crop, often to excess; extremely fertile: as, *rank* soil. 3. strong and offensive in smell or taste; rancid. 4. in bad taste; coarse; indecent. 5. extreme; utter: as, *rank* deceit. —**rank'ly,** *adv.* —**rank'ness,** *n.*

**ran·kle** (raŋ'k'l), *v.i.* [-KLED, -KLING], [< OFr. < *draoncle* < ML. *dracunculus*, a fester < L. dim. of *draco*, dragon], 1. to fester; become inflamed or cause inflammation. 2. to cause continual mental pain, resentment, etc.: as, the speech *rankled.*

**ran·sack** (ran'sak), *v.t.* [< ON. < *rann*, a house + *sækja*, to search], 1. to search thoroughly. 2. to search for plunder; pillage. —**ran'sack·er,** *n.*

**ran·som** (ran'səm), *n.* [< OFr. *raençon* < L. pp. of *redimere;* see REDEEM], 1. the redeeming of a captive or of seized property by payment of money or compliance with demands. 2. the price thus paid or demanded. *v.t.* 1. to obtain the release of (a captive, etc.) by paying the price demanded. 2. in *theology*, to free from sin. —**ran'som·er,** *n.*

**rant** (rant), *v.i.* [MD. *ranten*, to rave], to talk in a loud, wild, extravagant way; declaim violently; rave. *v.t.* to say or declaim in a ranting manner (often with *out*): as, to *rant* out a speech. *n.* loud, wild, extravagant speech. —**rant′er,** *n.* —**rant′ing,** *n.* —**rant′ing·ly,** *adv.*

**rap** (rap), *v.t.* [RAPPED, RAPPING], [prob. < Gmc.], 1. to strike quickly and sharply; tap. 2. to say sharply (with *out*): as, he *rapped* out an oath. 3. [Slang], to criticize sharply. *v.i.* 1. to knock sharply. 2. [Slang], to talk; chat. *n.* 1. a quick, sharp knock; tap. 2. [Slang], blame or punishment; specif., a prison sentence: usually in *beat* (escape) or *take* (receive) *the rap*. —**rap′per,** *n.* —**rap′ping,** *n.*

**rap** (rap), *n.* [Colloq.], the least bit: now usually in *not care* (or *give*) *a rap*, not care (or give) anything at all.

**ra·pa·cious** (rə-pā′shəs), *adj.* [< L. *rapax* < *rapere*, to seize], 1. taking by force; plundering. 2. greedy; voracious. 3. living on captured prey: said of animals or birds. —**ra·pa′cious·ly,** *adv.* —**ra·pa′cious·ness, ra·pac′i·ty** (-pas′ə-ti), *n.*

**rape** (rāp), *n.* [< Anglo-Fr.; prob. < L. *rapere*, to seize], 1. the crime of having sexual intercourse with a woman or girl forcibly and without her consent. 2. the act of seizing and carrying away by force. *v.t.* [RAPED, RAPING], 1. to commit rape on (a woman or girl); ravish; violate. 2. to seize and carry away by force. —**rap′ist,** *n.*

**rape** (rāp), *n.* [< L. *rapa*, *rapum*, turnip], a plant of the mustard family whose leaves are used for fodder and whose seeds (**rapeseed**) yield an oil (**rape oil** or **rapeseed oil**) used for lubricating.

**Raph·a·el** (raf′i-əl, rā′fi-), *n.* 1. an archangel mentioned in the Apocrypha. 2. (*Raffaello Santi*), Italian painter and architect; lived 1483–1520.

**rap·id** (rap′id), *adj.* [< Fr. < L. *rapidus* < *rapere*, to rush], 1. swift; quick; moving, progressing, or done with speed. 2. steep; abrupt: as, a *rapid* rise in the road. *n. usually in pl.* a part of a river where the water moves swiftly. —**ra·pid·i·ty** (rə-pid′ə-ti), **rap′id·ness,** *n.* —**rap′id·ly,** *adv.*

**rap·id-fire** (rap′id-fīr′), *adj.* 1. capable of firing shots in rapid succession: said of guns. 2. done, delivered, or carried on swiftly and sharply: as, a *rapid-fire* talk. Also **rapid-firing.**

**ra·pi·er** (rā′pi-ẽr, rāp′yẽr), *n.* [Fr. *rapière*], 1. originally, a slender, two-edged sword with a large cup hilt, used chiefly for thrusting. 2. later, a light, sharp-pointed sword used only for thrusting.

**rap·ine** (rap′in), *n.* [Fr. < L. *rapina* < *rapere*, to seize], the act of seizing and carrying off by force the property of others; plunder; pillage.

**rap·port** (ra-pôrt′, -pōrt′; Fr. rȧ′pôr′), *n.* [Fr. < *re-*, again + *apporter* < L. < *ad-*, to + *portare*, to carry], sympathetic relationship; agreement; harmony: see also **en rapport.**

‡**rap·proche·ment** (rȧ′prôsh′män′), *n.* [Fr.], an establishing or restoring of friendly relations.

**rap·scal·lion** (rap-skal′yən), *n.* [< earlier *rascallion*, extension of *rascal*], a rascal; rogue.

**rapt** (rapt), *adj.* [< L. pp. of *rapere*, to seize], 1. carried away in body or spirit (*to* heaven, etc.). 2. carried away with joy, love, etc.; enraptured. 3. completely absorbed or engrossed (*in* meditation, study, etc.). 4. resulting from or showing rapture. —**rapt′ly,** *adv.* —**rapt′ness,** *n.*

**rap·to·ri·al** (rap-tôr′i-əl, -tō′ri-), *adj.* [< L. < pp. of *rapere*, to seize], 1. adapted for seizing prey: as, *raptorial* claws. 2. of or belonging to a group of birds of prey with a strong notched beak and sharp talons, as the eagle, hawk, etc.

**rap·ture** (rap′chẽr), *n.* [*rapt* + *-ure*], 1. the state of being carried away with joy, love, etc.; ecstasy. 2. an expression of great joy, pleasure, etc. *v.t.* [-TURED, -TURING], [Poetic], to enrapture. —**rap′tur·ous,** *adj.* —**rap′tur·ous·ly,** *adv.*

**rare** (râr), *adj.* [RARER, RAREST], [Fr. < L. *rarus*], 1. not frequently found; scarce; uncommon; unusual. 2. unusually good; excellent. 3. thin; not dense: as, *rare* atmosphere. —**rare′ness,** *n.*

**rare** (râr), *adj.* [RARER, RAREST], [AS. *hrere*], not completely cooked; partially raw: as, *rare* beef.

**rare·bit** (râr′bit), *n.* Welsh rabbit.

**rare earth,** any of certain similar basic oxides; specif., any of the oxides of the rare-earth metals.

**rare-earth metals** (or **elements**) (râr′ũrth′), a group of rare metallic chemical elements with consecutive atomic numbers of 57 to 71 inclusive.

**rar·e·fy** (râr′ə-fī′), *v.t.* & *v.i.* [-FIED, -FYING], [< Fr. < L. < *rarus*, rare + *facere*, to make], 1. to make or become thin, or less dense. 2. to make or become purer, or more refined. —**rar′e·fac′tion** (-fak′shən), *n.* —**rar′e·fac′tive,** *adj.*

**rare·ly** (râr′li), *adv.* 1. infrequently; seldom. 2. beautifully, excellently, etc. 3. uncommonly.

**rar·i·ty** (râr′ə-ti), *n.* 1. a being rare; specif., *a*) uncommonness; scarcity. *b*) excellence. *c*) lack of density; thinness. 2. [*pl.* -TIES], something remarkable or valuable because of its scarcity.

**ras·cal** (ras′k'l), *n.* [< OFr. < *rasque*, filth; prob. < LL. *rasicare* (< L. *radere*), to scrape], a scoundrel; rogue; scamp: often used playfully, as of a mischievous child. *adj.* [Rare], low; base. —**ras·cal′i·ty** (-kal′ə-ti), *n.* —**ras′cal·ly,** *adj.* & *adv.*

**rase** (rāz), *v.t.* [RASED, RASING], to raze.

**rash** (rash), *adj.* [ME. *rasch*], 1. too hasty in acting or speaking; reckless. 2. resulting from such recklessness. —**rash′ly,** *adv.* —**rash′ness,** *n.*

**rash** (rash), *n.* [OFr. *rasche*, *rasque;* see RASCAL], an eruption of red spots on the skin.

**rash·er** (rash′ẽr), *n.* [? < Fr. *raser;* see RAZE], a thin slice of bacon, etc. to be fried or broiled.

**rasp** (rasp, räsp), *v.t.* [< OFr. < OHG. *raspon*, to scrape together], 1. to scrape or rub as with a file. 2. to utter in a rough, grating tone. 3. to grate upon; irritate. *v.i.* 1. to scrape; grate. 2. to make a rough, grating sound. *n.* 1. a type of rough file with raised points instead of lines. 2. a rough, grating sound. —**rasp′ing, rasp′y** [-IER, -IEST], *adj.* —**rasp′ing·ly,** *adv.*

**rasp·ber·ry** (raz′ber′i, -bẽr-), *n.* [*pl.* -RIES], [earlier *raspis berry* < *rasp*(*is*), raspberry], 1. any of a group of prickly shrubs of the rose family. 2. its small, juicy, edible fruit, consisting of a cluster of red, purple, or black drupelets. 3. [Slang], a sound of derision made by expelling air so as to vibrate the tongue between the lips.

**ras·sle** (ras′'l), *n.*, *v.i.* & *v.t.* [-SLED, -SLING], [Dial. or Colloq.], wrestle: also sp. **rassel, wrassle.**

**rat** (rat), *n.* [AS. *ræt*], 1. any of various black, brown, or gray, long-tailed rodents, resembling, but larger than, the mouse. 2. [Colloq.], a small pad used by women to puff out the hair. 3. [Slang], a sneaky, contemptible person; an informer, stool pigeon, deserter, etc. *v.i.* [RATTED, RATTING], 1. to hunt for rats. 2. [Slang], *a*) to act as a stool pigeon. *b*) to desert or betray one's companions. —**rats!** [Slang], an exclamation of disgust, disappointment, etc. —**smell a rat,** to suspect a trick, plot, etc. —**rat′tish,** *adj.*

**rat·a·ble** (rāt′ə-b'l), *adj.* 1. that can be rated, or estimated, etc. 2. figured at a certain rate; proportional. 3. [Brit.], taxable. Also sp. **rateable.** —**rat′a·bly, rate′a·bly,** *adv.*

**ra·tan** (ra-tan′), *n.* rattan.

**ratch·et** (rach′it), *n.* [< Fr. < It. *rocchetto*, dim. of *rocca*, distaff], 1. a hinged catch, or pawl, that engages with a toothed wheel or bar whose teeth slope in one direction, thus preventing backward movement. 2. such a wheel or bar. 3. such a catch and wheel (or bar) as a unit. Also **ratch.**

**ratchet wheel,** a toothed wheel with a catch, or pawl, that keeps it from turning backward.

**rate** (rāt), *n.* [OFr. < L. *rata* (*pars*), reckoned (part) < pp. of *reri*, to reckon], 1. the amount, degree, etc. of anything in relation to units of something else: as, the *rate* of pay per month. 2. a fixed ratio; proportion: as, the *rate* of exchange. 3. a price or value; specif., the cost per unit of some commodity, service, etc. 4. speed of movement or action. 5. a class; rank: as, of the first *rate*. 6. [Brit.], a local property tax. *v.t.* [RATED, RATING], 1. to estimate the value of; appraise. 2. to put into a particular class or rank. 3. to consider; esteem. 4. to determine the rates for shipping (goods), as by rail. 5. [Colloq.], to deserve: as, he *rates* the best. *v.i.* 1. to be classed or ranked. 2. to have value, status, or rating. —**at any rate,** 1. in any event. 2. at least; anyway. —**rat′er,** *n.*

**rate** (rāt), *v.t.* & *v.i.* [RATED, RATING], [ME. *raten*], to scold; chide. —**rat′ing,** *n.*

**rate·pay·er** (rāt′pā′ẽr), *n.* [Brit.], one who pays rates, or local taxes.

**-rat·er** (rāt′ẽr), a combining form used in hyphenated compounds, meaning *one of a* (specified) *rate*, or *class*, as in *first-rater*.

**rath·er** (rath′ẽr, rä′thẽr), *adv.* [< AS. *hrathor*, compar. of *hrathe*, quickly], 1. more willingly; preferably. 2. with more justice, reason, etc.: as, I, *rather* than you, should pay. 3. more accurately; more precisely: as, my brother or, *rather*, stepbrother. 4. on the contrary: as, we won't go; *rather*, we'll stay. 5. somewhat; to some degree: as, I *rather* liked it. 6. [Chiefly Brit. Colloq.], certainly; assuredly: used as an answer. —**had rather,** would choose to; would prefer that.

**raths·kel·ler** (räts′kel′ẽr, rath′skel′-), *n.* [G. < *rat*, council + *keller*, cellar], a restaurant that serves beer, wine, etc., usually below street level.

**rat·i·fy** (rat′ə-fī′), *v.t.* [-FIED, -FYING], [< Fr. < ML. < L. *ratus* (see RATE, *n.*) + *facere*, to make], to approve or confirm; esp., to give formal sanction to. —**rat′i·fi·ca′tion,** *n.* —**rat′i·fi′er,** *n.*

**ra·ti·né** (rat′ə-nā′), *n.* [Fr., frizzed: of the nap], a loosely woven fabric of cotton, wool, rayon, etc., with a nubby or knotty surface.

**rat·ing** (rāt′iŋ), *n.* 1. a rank, or grade, as of enlisted men in an army. 2. a placement in a certain rank or class. 3. an evaluation of the credit or financial standing of a business, etc. 4. an amount determined as a rate, or grade.

**ra·tio** (rā′shō, -shi-ō′), *n.* [*pl.* -TIOS], [L.; see REASON], 1. a fixed relation in degree, number, etc. between two similar things; proportion: as, a *ratio* of one boy to two girls. 2. in *mathematics*, the quotient of one quantity divided by another of the same kind: usually expressed as a fraction.

**ra·ti·oc·i·nate** (rash′i-os′ə-nāt′), *v.i.* [-NATED, -NATING], [< L. pp. of *ratiocinari* < *ratio;* see REASON], to reason, especially using formal logic. —**ra′ti·oc′i·na′tion,** *n.* —**ra′ti·oc′i·na′tive,** *adj.* —**ra′ti·oc′i·na′tor,** *n.*

**ra·tion** (rash′ən, rā′shən), *n.* [Fr. < ML. < L. *ratio;* see REASON], 1. a fixed portion; share; allowance. 2. a fixed allowance of food or provisions, as a daily allowance for one soldier, etc. *v.t.* 1. to give rations to. 2. to distribute (food, clothing, etc.) in rations, as in times of scarcity. —**ra′tion·ing,** *n.*

**ra·tion·al** (rash′ən-'l), *adj.* [L. *rationalis* < *ratio;* see REASON], 1. of or based on reasoning. 2. able to reason; reasoning. 3. showing reason; sensible: as, a *rational* plan. 4. in *mathematics*, designating a number or quantity expressible without a radical sign. —**ra′tion·al′i·ty** (-al′ə-ti), *n.* —**ra′tion·al·ly,** *adv.*

**ra·tion·a·le** (rash′ə-nal′, -nä′li, -nā′-), *n.* [L.; see RATIONAL], 1. the rational basis of something. 2. an explanation of reasons or principles.

**ra·tion·al·ism** (rash′ən-'l-iz'm), *n.* the principle or practice of accepting reason as the only authority in determining one's opinions or course of action. —**ra′tion·al·ist,** *n.* —**ra′tion·al·is′tic,** *adj.* —**ra′tion·al·is′ti·cal·ly,** *adv.*

**ra·tion·al·ize** (rash′ən-'l-īz′), *v.t.* [-IZED, -IZING], 1. to make rational; make conform to reason. 2. to explain on rational grounds. 3. in *psychology*, to devise plausible explanations for (one's acts, beliefs, etc.), usually without being aware that these are not the real motives. *v.i.* 1. to think in a rational or rationalistic manner. 2. to rationalize one's acts, beliefs, etc. —**ra′tion·al·i·za′tion,** *n.* —**ra′tion·al·iz′er,** *n.*

**rat·ite** (rat′īt), *adj.* [< L. *ratis*, a raft], of a group of large, flightless birds having a flat breastbone without the keellike ridge of flying birds. *n.* any bird of this group, as the ostrich.

**rat·line** (rat′lin), *n.* [folk-etym. form.; prob. < ME. *raddle* (to interlace)], 1. any of the small pieces of rope which join the shrouds of a ship and serve as a ladder. 2. the light, tarred rope used for this. Also sp. **ratlin.**

**rat race,** [Slang], a frantic scurry or mad scramble.

**rats·bane** (rats′bān′), *n.* [see BANE], rat poison.

**rat·tan** (ra-tan′), *n.* [Malay *rotan* < *raut*, to strip], 1. a climbing palm with long, slender, tough stems. 2. these stems, used in wickerwork, etc. 3. a cane or switch made from such a stem. Also sp. **ratan.**

**rat·ter** (rat′ẽr), *n.* 1. a dog skilled at catching rats. 2. [Slang], a betrayer or deserter.

**rat·tle** (rat′'l), *v.i.* [-TLED, -TLING], [ME. *ratelen;* prob. echoic], 1. to make a series of sharp, short sounds: as, the shutter *rattled.* 2. to move with such sounds: as, the wagon *rattled* over the stones. 3. to chatter (often with *on*). *v.t.* 1. to cause to rattle: as, he *rattled* the handle. 2. to utter or perform rapidly. 3. [Colloq.], to confuse or upset: as, applause *rattled* the speaker. *n.* 1. a quick succession of sharp, short sounds. 2. a rattling noise in the throat, as of a dying person. 3. a noisy uproar. 4. the series of horny rings at the end of a rattlesnake's tail. 5. a device, as a baby's toy, intended to rattle when shaken. —**rat′tly** (-'l-i, -li), *adj.*

**rat·tle·brain** (rat′'l-brān′), *n.* a silly, talkative person. —**rat′tle·brained′,** *adj.*

**rat·tle·pate** (rat′'l-pāt′), *n.* a rattlebrain. —**rat′tle·pat′ed,** *adj.*

**rat·tler** (rat′lẽr), *n.* a person or thing that rattles; specif., a rattlesnake.

**rat·tle·snake** (rat′'l-snāk′), *n.* any of various poisonous American snakes having a series of horny rings at the end of the tail that produce a rattling sound when shaken.

RATTLESNAKE (2–8 ft. long)

**rat·tle·trap** (rat′'l-trap′), *n.* [*rattle* + *trap* (carriage)], anything worn out or rattling, especially such a wagon, automobile, etc.

**rat·ty** (rat′i), *adj.* [-TIER, -TIEST], 1. of, like, or full of rats. 2. [Slang], shabby, mean, despicable, etc.

**rau·cous** (rô′kəs), *adj.* [L. *raucus*], hoarse; rough-sounding: as, a *raucous* shout. —**rau′cous·ly,** *adv.* —**rau′cous·ness, rau′ci·ty** (-sə-ti), *n.*

**rav·age** (rav′ij), *n.* [Fr. < *ravir;* see RAVISH], 1. the act or practice of violently destroying. 2. ruin; devastating damage. *v.t.* [-AGED, -AGING], to destroy violently; devastate; ruin. *v.i.* to commit ravages. —**rav′ag·er,** *n.*

**rave** (rāv), *v.i.* [RAVED, RAVING], [OFr. *raver*], 1. to talk incoherently or wildly, as a delirious person. 2. to talk with excessive enthusiasm (*about*). 3. to rage, as a storm. *v.t.* to utter incoherently. *n.* 1. a raving. 2. [Slang], an excessively enthusiastic commendation: often used attributively, as, *rave* reviews. —**rav′er,** *n.*

**rav·el** (rav′'l), *v.t.* [-ELED or -ELLED, -ELING or -ELLING], [MD. *ravelen*], 1. originally, to make complicated or tangled. 2. to separate the parts, especially threads, of; untwist. 3. to make clear; disentangle. *v.i.* 1. to become separated into its parts, as threads; fray (usually with *out*). *n.* a raveled part, especially a thread; a raveling. —**rav′el·er, rav′el·ler,** *n.*

**Ra·vel, Mau·rice Jo·seph** (mô′rēs′ zhō′zef′ rȧ′vel′), 1875–1937; French composer.

**rav·el·ing, rav·el·ling** (rav′'l-iŋ, rav′liŋ), *n.* anything raveled; esp., a thread raveled from a knitted or woven material.

**ra·ven** (rā′vən), *n.* [AS. *hræfn*], a large bird of the crow family, with lustrous black feathers and a sharp beak. *adj.* black and lustrous.

**rav·en·ing** (rav′ən-iŋ), *adj.* [see RAVENOUS], 1. greedily searching for prey. 2. demented; mad.

**rav·e·nous** (rav′ən-əs), *adj.* [< OFr. < *ravine* (< L. *rapina*); see RAPINE], 1. greedily hungry. 2. greedy: as, *ravenous* for praise. 3. rapacious. —**rav′e·nous·ly,** *adv.* —**rav′e·nous·ness,** *n.*

**ra·vine** (rə-vēn′), *n.* [Fr., flood < OFr.; ult. < L. *rapina;* see RAPINE], a long, deep hollow in the earth's surface, worn by a stream; gorge.

**rav·ing** (rāv′iŋ), *adj.* 1. raging; delirious. 2. [Colloq.], exciting raving admiration: as, a *raving* beauty. *adv.* so as to cause raving: as, *raving* mad. *n.* wild, incoherent speech. —**rav′ing·ly,** *adv.*

**ra·vi·o·li** (rav′i-ō′li), *n.pl.* [construed as sing.], [It.], small casings of dough containing highly seasoned chopped meat, cooked and served usually in a savory sauce.

**rav·ish** (rav′ish), *v.t.* [< stem of OFr. *ravir* < L. *rapere*, to seize], 1. to seize and carry away forcibly. 2. to rape. 3. to fill with great joy; enrapture. —**rav′ish·er,** *n.* —**rav′ish·ment,** *n.*

**rav·ish·ing** (rav′ish-iŋ), *adj.* causing great joy or delight. —**rav′ish·ing·ly,** *adv.*

**raw** (rô), *adj.* [AS. *hreaw*], 1. uncooked. 2. in its natural condition; not changed by art, manufacture, etc.; unprocessed: as, *raw* silk. 3. inexperienced: as, a *raw* recruit. 4. with the skin rubbed off; sore and inflamed: as, a *raw* cut. 5. uncomfortably cold and damp: as, a *raw* wind. 6. [Colloq.], indecent; bawdy. 7. [Slang], harsh or unfair: as, *raw* treatment. *n.* a raw or inflamed spot on the body. —**in the raw,** 1. in the natural state. 2. naked. —**raw′ly,** *adv.* —**raw′ness,** *n.*

**raw·boned** (rô′bōnd′), *adj.* lean; gaunt.

**raw·hide** (rô′hīd′), *n.* 1. an untanned or only partially tanned cattle hide. 2. a whip made of this.

**ray** (rā), *n.* [< OFr. < L. *radius;* see RADIUS], 1. any of the thin lines, or beams, of light that appear to come from a bright source. 2. any of several lines radiating from a center. 3. a tiny amount: as, a *ray* of hope. 4. in *botany* & *zoology*, any of the elements of a radial structure, as the petals of certain flowers, the limbs of a starfish, etc. 5. in *physics*, *a*) a stream of particles given off by a radioactive substance. *b*) a straight line along which any part of a wave of radiant energy is regarded as traveling. *v.i.* 1. to shine forth in rays. 2. to radiate. *v.t.* 1. to send out in rays. 2. to subject to the action of X rays, radium rays, etc. —**ray′less,** *adj.* —**ray′like′,** *adj.*

**ray** (rā), *n.* [< OFr. < L. *raia*], any of several fishes, as the electric ray, skate, etc., with a horizontally flat body, widely expanded fins at each side, and a slender, whiplike tail.

STING RAY
(3 ft. wide)

**ray flower,** any of the flowers around the margin of the head of certain composite flowers, as the daisy: also **ray floret.**

**ray·on** (rā′on), *n.* [arbitrary coinage < *ray*], 1. any of various textile fibers produced by pressing a cellulose solution through very small holes and solidifying it in the form of filaments. 2. any of various fabrics woven from such fibers.

**raze** (rāz), *v.t.* [RAZED, RAZING], [< Fr. *raser* < L. *rasus*, pp. of *radere*, to scrape], 1. to scrape off; erase. 2. to tear down completely; demolish: the current sense. Also sp. **rase.**

**ra·zor** (rā′zẽr), *n.* [< OFr. < *raser;* see RAZE], a sharp-edged cutting instrument for shaving.

**ra·zor·back** (rā′zẽr-bak′), *n.* 1. a wild or semiwild hog of the southern U.S., with a ridged back and long legs. 2. a finback.

**razz** (raz), *v.t. & v.i.* [contr. < *raspberry*], [Slang], to tease, ridicule, deride, etc. *n.* [Slang], a raspberry (derisive sound).

**raz·zle-daz·zle** (raz′′l-daz′′l), *n.* [Slang], a state or event of confusion, bustling, etc.

**Rb,** in *chemistry,* rubidium.

**r.b.i., rbi, RBI,** in *baseball,* run(s) batted in.

**R. C.,** 1. Red Cross. 2. Roman Catholic.

**R. C. Ch.,** Roman Catholic Church.

**Rd., rd.,** 1. road. 2. rod; rods. 3. round.

**R.D.,** Rural Delivery.

**re** (rā), *n.* [It. < L. *resonare;* see GAMUT], in *music,* a syllable representing the second tone of the diatonic scale.

**re** (rē), *prep.* [L., abl. of *res,* thing], in the case or matter of; as regards.

**re-,** [< Fr. *re-, ré-* or L. *re-, red-,* back], a prefix meaning: 1. *back,* as in *repay.* 2. *again, anew,* as in *reappear.* When hyphenated, it is used: 1) to distinguish between a word in which the prefix means *again* or *anew* and a word having a special meaning (e.g., *re-sound, resound*); 2) to avoid ambiguity in forming nonce words, as in *re-urge;* 3) before elements beginning with *e,* as in *re-edit* (also written *reëdit*). The following list contains some of the more common words in which *re-* means *again* or *anew.* The syllabification and pronunciation of the base word in each instance remains unaltered.

**reabsorb**
**reabsorption**
**reaccommodate**
**reaccompany**
**reaccusation**
**reaccuse**
**reacquire**
**readapt**
**readdress**
**readjust**
**readjustment**
**readmission**
**readmit**
**readopt**
**reaffirm**
**reaffirmation**
**reappear**
**reappearance**
**reapplication**
**reapply**
**reappoint**
**reappointment**
**reapportion**
**reascend**
**reassemble**
**reassembly**
**reassert**
**reassertion**
**reassess**
**reassign**
**reassignment**
**reassume**
**reassumption**
**reattach**
**reattack**
**reattempt**
**reawaken**
**rebaptism**
**rebaptize**
**rebind**
**reborn**
**rebuild**
**rebuilt**
**recapitalize**
**recharge**
**recharter**
**recheck**
**recircle**
**recirculate**
**reclasp**
**reclothe**
**recoin**
**recolor**
**recombine**
**recommence**
**recompose**
**reconcentrate**
**recondense**
**reconduct**
**reconfirm**
**reconquer**
**reconquest**
**reconsecrate**
**reconsign**
**reconsolidate**
**reconstitute**
**reconstitution**
**reconvene**
**reconvey**
**reconveyance**
**recopy**
**recross**
**recrown**
**recrystallize**
**recultivate**
**redamage**
**redecorate**
**rededicate**
**redeliver**
**redemand**
**redemonstrate**
**redeny**
**redeposit**
**redescend**
**redescribe**
**redetermine**
**redevelop**
**redigest**
**rediscover**
**rediscovery**
**redistribute**
**redistribution**
**redivide**
**redo**
**redraft**
**redraw**
**re-dress**
**redry**
**re-edit**
**re-elect**
**re-election**
**re-elevate**
**re-embark**
**re-embody**
**re-embrace**
**re-emerge**
**re-emergence**
**re-emigrate**
**re-emphasize**
**re-enact**
**re-enaction**
**re-enactment**
**re-encourage**
**re-engage**
**re-engrave**
**re-enjoy**
**re-enlist**
**re-enlistment**
**re-enter**
**re-entrance**
**re-establish**
**re-establishment**
**re-examination**
**re-examine**
**re-experience**
**re-explain**
**re-export**
**refashion**
**refasten**
**refold**
**reforge**
**reformulate**
**reformulation**
**refortification**
**refortify**
**refreeze**
**refuel**
**refurnish**
**regather**
**regild**
**regird**
**regive**
**reglaze**
**reglorify**
**reglue**
**regrade**
**regrant**
**regrasp**
**rehandle**
**rehear**
**reheat**
**reheel**
**rehire**
**reignite**
**reimpose**
**reimpress**
**reimprint**
**reimprison**
**reimprisonment**
**reincorporate**
**reincur**
**reinduce**
**reinfect**
**reinfection**
**reinflate**
**reinform**
**reinfuse**
**reinoculate**
**reinsert**
**reinspect**
**reinspire**
**reinstall**
**reinstruct**
**reinsurance**
**reinsure**
**reintegrate**
**reinter**
**reinterment**
**reinterrogate**
**reintroduce**
**reintroduction**
**reinvent**
**reinvest**
**reinvestigate**
**reinvigorate**
**reinvite**
**reinvolve**
**reissue**
**rekindle**
**relabel**
**relaunder**
**relearn**
**relend**
**relet**
**relight**
**reline**
**relive**
**reload**
**reloan**
**relocate**
**remarriage**
**remarry**
**rematch**
**remeasure**
**remelt**
**remerge**
**remigrate**
**remilitarize**
**remix**
**remodify**
**remold**
**rename**
**renegotiate**
**renominate**
**renotify**
**renumber**
**reobtain**
**reoccupation**
**reoccupy**
**reoffer**
**reopen**
**reoppose**
**reorient**
**reorientation**
**repack**
**repaint**
**repaper**
**repartition**
**repass**
**repave**
**re-pay**
**repenalize**
**rephotograph**
**replant**
**replaster**
**replay**
**repledge**
**repolish**
**repopularize**
**repopulate**
**re-pose**
**repour**
**re-present**
**re-press**
**reprocess**
**reproclaim**
**re-prove**
**republication**
**republish**
**repurchase**
**repurify**
**repursue**
**requicken**
**reread**
**reroll**
**resaddle**
**reseal**
**re-search**
**reseed**
**reseek**
**reseize**
**resell**
**resend**
**re-serve**
**resettle**
**resettlement**
**reshape**
**resharpen**
**reshuffle**
**resift**
**re-sign**
**resolder**
**resolidify**
**re-solve**
**re-sort**
**re-sound**
**respace**
**respray**
**respread**
**restack**
**restamp**
**restart**
**restipulate**
**re-strain**
**restrengthen**
**restrike**
**restring**
**restrive**
**restudy**
**resummon**
**resupply**
**resurvey**
**reteach**
**retell**
**retest**
**rethink**
**retie**
**retold**
**retrain**
**retransfer**
**retranslate**
**re-treat**
**retrial**
**retry**
**retune**
**retwist**
**re-use**
**revaluate**
**revaluation**
**revalue**
**revarnish**
**reverify**
**revibrate**
**revindicate**
**revisit**
**revitalize**
**revoice**
**revote**
**rewarm**
**rewash**
**rewater**
**reweigh**
**rewind**
**rework**

**Re,** in *chemistry,* rhenium.

**reach** (rēch), *v.t.* [AS. *ræcan*], 1. to thrust out; extend (the hand, etc.). 2. to touch; extend to by thrusting out, etc. 3. to obtain and hand over: as, *reach* me the salt. 4. to go as far as; attain. 5. to carry as far as: as, the news *reached* me late. 6. to influence; affect. 7. to get in touch with, as by telephone. *v.i.* 1. to thrust out the hand, foot, etc. 2. to stretch, or extend, in amount, influence, space, time, etc. 3. to carry, as sight, sound, etc. 4. to try to obtain something. 5. in *nautical usage,* to sail on a reach. *n.* 1. a stretching or thrusting out. 2. the power of stretching, obtaining, etc. 3. the distance or extent covered in stretching, obtaining, etc. 4. a continuous extent or stretch, as of water. 5. in *nautical usage,* a tack sailed with the wind coming from abeam. **—reach′a·ble,** *adj.* **—reach′er,** *n.*

**re·act** (ri-akt′), *v.i.* 1. to act in return or recipro-

fat, āpe, bâre, cär; ten, ēven, hêre, ovẽr; is, bīte; lot, gō, hôrn, tōōl, look; oil, out; up, ūse, fũr; get; joy; yet; chin; she; thin, *th*en; zh, leisure; ŋ, ring; ə for *a* in *ago*, *e* in *agent*, *i* in *sanity*, *o* in *comply*, *u* in *focus;* ′ in *able* (ā′b'l); Fr. bål; ë, Fr. coeur; ö, Fr. feu; Fr. mo*n*; ô, Fr. coq; ü, Fr. duc; H. G. ich; kh, G. doch. ‡ foreign; < derived from.

cally. 2. to act in opposition. 3. to go back to a former condition, stage, etc. 4. to respond to a stimulus. 5. in *chemistry*, to act with another substance in producing a chemical change.

**re-act** (rē'akt'), *v.t.* to act or do again.

**re·act·ance** (ri-ak'təns), *n.* in *electricity*, the opposition to the flow of alternating current made by an induction coil or a condenser.

**re·act·ant** (ri-ak'tənt), *n.* any of the substances involved in a chemical reaction.

**re·ac·tion** (ri-ak'shən), *n.* 1. a return or opposing action, influence, etc. 2. a response, as to a stimulus. 3. a movement back to a former or less advanced condition, stage, etc.; esp., such a movement in politics. 4. a chemical change. 5. in *medicine*, *a*) an action induced by resistance to another action. *b*) depression or exhaustion following nervous tension, overstimulation, etc. *c*) increased activity following depression. —**re·ac'tive,** *adj.*

**re·ac·tion·ar·y** (ri-ak'shən-er'i), *adj.* of, characterized by, or advocating reaction. *n.* [*pl.* -IES], an advocate of reaction, especially in politics.

**re·ac·tor** (ri-ak'tẽr), *n.* 1. one that reacts. 2. in *nuclear physics*, an atomic pile in which there is control of the atomic energy produced.

**read** (rēd), *v.t.* [READ (red), READING], [< AS. *rædan*, to counsel], 1. to get the meaning of (something written, printed, etc.) by interpreting its characters or signs. 2. to utter aloud (printed or written matter). 3. to learn the true meaning of: as, I *read* the answer in his face. 4. to interpret, as dreams. 5. to foretell (the future). 6. to interpret (a printed passage, etc.) as having a particular meaning. 7. to give as a reading in a certain passage: as, for "shew" *read* "show." 8. to study: as, to *read* law. 9. to register: as, the speedometer *reads* 50 mph. 10. to put into a (specified) state by reading. *v.i.* 1. to read something written, printed, etc. 2. to learn by reading (with *about* or *of*). 3. to study. 4. to give a particular meaning when read. 5. to be drawn up in certain words: as, the sentence *reads* as follows. 6. to admit of being read: as, it *reads* well. —**read into** (or **in**), to interpret in a certain way. —**read out of,** to expel from (a political party, society, etc.).

**read** (red), *adj.* [pt. & pp. of *read*], full of knowledge got from reading: as, well-*read*.

**read·a·ble** (rēd'ə-b'l), *adj.* 1. that can be read; legible. 2. interesting to read. —**read'a·bil'i·ty, read'a·ble·ness,** *n.* —**read'a·bly,** *adv.*

**read·er** (rēd'ẽr), *n.* 1. one who reads. 2. a reciter of literary works in public. 3. one who reads manuscripts for a publisher, etc. and advises as to their merit. 4. a proofreader. 5. a book with selected passages for instruction in reading.

**Read·ing** (red'iŋ), *n.* a city in SE Pennsylvania: pop., 98,000.

**read·ing** (rēd'iŋ), *adj.* 1. inclined to read. 2. of, or for use in, reading. *n.* 1. the act or practice of one who reads. 2. the uttering aloud of printed or written matter, as for public entertainment. 3. the study of books. 4. any material printed or written to be read. 5. a recording of information by figures, signs, etc., as on a barometer. 6. the form of a specified word, sentence, etc. in a particular edition of a literary work. 7. a particular interpretation.

**read·out** (rēd'out'), *n.* 1. the retrieving of information from storage in a computer. 2. such information displayed visually or recorded, as by typewriter or on tape.

**read·y** (red'i), *adj.* [-IER, -IEST], [AS. (*ge*)*ræde*], 1. prepared to act or be used immediately: as, she is *ready* to sing, your bath is *ready*. 2. prepared in mind; willing. 3. *a*) likely or liable immediately. *b*) apt; inclined: as, he's always *ready* to quibble. 4. dexterous. 5. done without delay; prompt: as, a *ready* reply. 6. available immediately: as, *ready* cash. *v.t.* [-IED, -YING], to make ready (often used reflexively). *n.* the position of a rifle just before aiming and firing. —**make ready,** to prepare. —**read'i·ly,** *adv.* —**read'i·ness,** *n.*

**read·y-made** (red'i-mād'), *adj.* made so as to be ready for use or sale at once; not custom-made.

**re·a·gent** (rē-ā'jənt), *n.* in *chemistry*, a substance used to detect or measure another substance or to convert one substance into another.

**re·al** (rē'əl, rēl), *adj.* [OFr. < ML. *realis* < L. *res*, thing], 1. existing or happening as or in fact; actual, true, etc. 2. authentic; genuine. 3. in *law*, of or relating to permanent, immovable things: as, *real* property. 4. in *philosophy*, existing objectively. *adv.* [Colloq. or Dial.], very. —**re'al·ness,** *n.*

**re·al** (rē'əl; Sp. re-äl'), *n.* [*pl.* -ALS; Sp. -ALES (-ä'les)], [Sp. & Port., lit., royal < L. *regalis;* see REGAL], a former silver coin of Spain.

**re·al** (re-äl'), *n.* sing. of **reis.**

**real estate,** land, including the buildings or improvements on it and its natural assets, as minerals, water, etc. —**re'al-es·tate',** *adj.*

**re·al·ism** (rē'əl-iz'm), *n.* 1. a tendency to face facts and be practical. 2. in *art & literature*, the picturing of people and things as they really are. 3. in *philosophy*, *a*) the doctrine that universals have objective reality. *b*) the doctrine that material objects exist in themselves apart from the mind's consciousness of them. —**re'al·ist,** *n.* —**re'al·is'tic,** *adj.* —**re'al·is'ti·cal·ly,** *adv.*

**re·al·i·ty** (ri-al'ə-ti), *n.* [*pl.* -TIES], 1. the quality or state of being real. 2. a person or thing that is real; fact. 3. the quality of being true to life. —**in reality,** in fact; actually.

**re·al·ize** (rē'ə-liz'), *v.t.* [-IZED, -IZING], 1. to make real; bring into being. 2. to make appear real. 3. to understand fully. 4. to convert (assets, rights, etc.) into money. 5. to gain; obtain: as, to *realize* a profit. 6. to be sold for; bring as profit: said of property. *v.i.* to sell property, etc. for ready money. —**re'al·iz'a·ble,** *adj.* —**re'al·i·za'tion,** *n.* —**re'al·iz'er,** *n.*

**re·al·ly** (rē'əl-i, rēl'i), *adv.* 1. in reality; actually. 2. indeed: as, *really*, you mustn't say that. 3. truly or genuinely: as, a *really* hot day.

**realm** (relm), *n.* [< OFr. *reaume;* ult. < L. *regalis;* see REGAL], 1. a kingdom. 2. a region; sphere; territory: as, the *realm* of thought.

**re·al·tor** (rē'əl-tẽr, -tôr'), *n.* [*realty* + *-or*], a real-estate broker who is a member of the National Association of Real Estate Boards.

**re·al·ty** (rē'əl-ti), *n.* [*real* + *-ty*], real estate.

**real wages,** wages measured by how much they can buy, rather than by monetary value.

**ream** (rēm), *n.* [< OFr. < Sp. *resma* < Ar. *rizmah*, a bale], 1. a quantity of paper varying from 480 sheets (20 quires) to 516 sheets (*printer's ream*). 2. *pl.* [Colloq.], a great amount.

**ream** (rēm), *v.t.* [prob. < AS. *ryman*, lit., to make roomy < base of *rum;* see ROOM], 1. *a*) to enlarge or taper (a hole). *b*) to enlarge the bore of (a gun, etc.). Often with *out*. 2. to get rid of (a defect) by reaming (with *out*). 3. to remove the juice from (a lemon, etc.).

**ream·er** (rēm'ẽr), *n.* a person or thing that reams; specif., *a*) a sharp-edged tool for enlarging or tapering holes. *b*) a device for squeezing juice from lemons, oranges, etc.

REAMER

**re·an·i·mate** (rē-an'ə-māt'), *v.t.* [-MATED, -MATING], 1. to animate again; restore to life. 2. to give new courage, power, etc. to. —**re·an'i·ma'tion,** *n.*

**reap** (rēp), *v.t.* [AS. *ripan*], 1. to cut (grain) with a scythe, machine, etc. 2. to gather (a harvest). 3. to harvest grain from (a field). 4. to obtain as the reward of action, work, etc. *v.i.* 1. to reap a harvest. 2. to get a return or reward.

**reap·er** (rēp'ẽr), *n.* 1. one who reaps. 2. a reaping machine. —**the (Grim) Reaper,** death.

**reaping machine,** a machine for reaping grain: it often has an attached binder.

**rear** (rêr), *n.* [< *arrear*], 1. the back part. 2. the position behind or at the back. 3. the part of an army, etc. farthest from the battle front. *adj.* of, at, or in the rear. —**bring up the rear,** to come at the end (of a procession).

**rear** (rêr), *v.t.* [AS. *ræran*, caus. of *risan*, to rise], 1. to put upright; elevate. 2. to build; erect. 3. to grow; breed, as animals or plants. 4. to bring to maturity by educating, nourishing, etc.: as, to *rear* children. *v.i.* 1. to rise on the hind legs, as a horse. 2. to rise in anger, etc. (usually with *up*).

**rear admiral,** a naval officer next in rank above a captain.

**rear guard,** in *military science*, a detachment of troops to protect an army's rear.

**re·arm** (rē-ärm'), *v.t. & v.i.* 1. to arm again. 2. to arm with new or more effective weapons. —**re·ar'ma·ment** (-är'mə-mənt), *n.*

**rear·most** (rêr'mōst'), *adj.* farthest in the rear.

**re·ar·range** (rē'ə-rānj'), *v.t.* [-RANGED, -RANGING], 1. to arrange again. 2. to arrange in a different manner. —**re'ar·range'ment,** *n.*

**rear·ward** (rêr'wẽrd), *adj.* at, in, or toward the rear. *adv.* toward the rear: also **rear'wards.**

**rea·son** (rē'z'n), *n.* [< OFr. < L. *ratio*, a reckoning < pp. of *reri*, to think], 1. an explanation or justification of an act, idea, etc. 2. a cause; motive. 3. the ability to think, draw conclusions, etc. 4. sound thought; good sense. 5. normal mental powers; sanity. *v.i.* 1. to think logically; draw conclusions from facts known or assumed. 2. to argue or talk in a logical way. *v.t.* 1. to analyze;

think logically about. 2. to argue; discuss. 3. to justify with reasons. 4. to persuade by reasoning (with *into* or *out of*). —**by reason of,** because of. —**out of all reason,** unreasonable. —**reason that,** to conclude or infer that. —**stand to reason,** to be logical. —**with reason,** justifiably; rightly. —**rea′son·er,** *n.* —**rea′son·less,** *adj.*

**rea·son·a·ble** (rē′z'n-ə-b'l), *adj.* 1. able to reason. 2. amenable to reason; just. 3. not extreme; sensible. 4. not expensive. —**rea′son·a·bil′i·ty, rea′son·a·ble·ness,** *n.* —**rea′son·a·bly,** *adv.*

**rea·son·ing** (rē′z'n-iŋ), *n.* 1. the drawing of inferences or conclusions from known or assumed facts. 2. the reasons resulting from this.

**re·as·sure** (rē′ə-shoor′), *v.t.* [-SURED, -SURING], 1. to assure again or anew. 2. to restore to confidence. 3. to reinsure. —**re′as·sur′ance,** *n.* —**re′as·sur′ing·ly,** *adv.*

**re·bate** (rē′bāt, ri-bāt′), *v.t.* [-BATED, -BATING], [< OFr. < *re-*, re- + *abattre;* see ABATE], 1. to give back (part of an amount paid). 2. to make a deduction from (a bill). *n.* a deduction; return of part of an amount paid, as for goods. —**re′bat·er,** *n.*

**re·bec, re·beck** (rē′bek), *n.* [Fr. < OFr. *rebebe* < Ar. *rabāb*], a medieval violinlike instrument played with a bow.

**Re·bec·ca, Re·bek·ah** (ri-bek′ə), *n.* in the *Bible,* the wife of Isaac and mother of Jacob and Esau.

**reb·el** (reb′'l; *for v.,* ri-bel′), *n.* [< OFr. < L. < *re-*, again + *bellare,* to war < *bellum,* war], one who openly resists authority or opposes any control. *adj.* 1. rebellious. 2. of rebels. *v.i.* [-ELLED, -ELLING], 1. to resist, oppose, or combat authority, government, etc. 2. to feel or show strong aversion: as, his mind *rebels* at the thought.

**re·bel·lion** (ri-bel′yən), *n.* [see REBEL], 1. an act or state of armed, open resistance to authority, government, etc. 2. defiance of any control.

**re·bel·lious** (ri-bel′yəs), *adj.* 1. resisting authority; engaged in rebellion. 2. of or like rebels or rebellion. 3. opposing any control; defiant. 4. in medicine, difficult to treat. —**re·bel′lious·ly,** *adv.* —**re·bel′lious·ness,** *n.*

**re·birth** (rē-bũrth′, rē′bũrth′), *n.* 1. a new or second birth. 2. a reawakening; revival.

**re·bound** (ri-bound′; *for n., usually* rē′bound′), *v.i.* to bound or spring back, as upon impact. *v.t.* [Rare], to make bound back. *n.* a rebounding; recoil: sometimes used figuratively.

**re·broad·cast** (rē-brôd′kast′, -käst′), *v.t. & v.i.* [-CAST or, *in radio,* -CASTED, -CASTING], 1. to broadcast again. 2. to broadcast (a program, etc. received in a relay system from another station). *n.* 1. a rebroadcasting. 2. a rebroadcasted program.

**re·buff** (ri-buf′), *n.* [< MFr. < It. *rabbuffo;* ult. < OHG.], 1. a blunt refusal of offered advice, help, etc. 2. any check or repulse. *v.t.* 1. to refuse bluntly; snub. 2. to check; repulse.

**re·buke** (ri-būk′), *v.t.* [-BUKED, -BUKING], [< Anglo-Fr. < OFr. < *re-*, back + *bu(s)chier,* to beat], to address in sharp disapproval; reprimand. *n.* a sharp reprimand. —**re·buk′er,** *n.* —**re·buk′ing·ly,** *adv.*

**re·bus** (rē′bəs), *n.* [L., lit., by things], a kind of puzzle consisting of pictures of things whose names suggest words or phrases: as, a picture of a bee plus the figure 4 is a *rebus* for *before.*

**re·but** (ri-but′), *v.t.* [-BUTTED, -BUTTING], [< Anglo-Fr. < OFr. < *re-*, back + *bouter,* to push], to contradict or oppose, especially in a formal manner by argument, proof, etc. —**re·but′ter,** *n.*

**re·but·tal** (ri-but′'l), *n.* a rebutting, as in law.

**rec.,** 1. receipt. 2. recipe. 3. record(ed).

**re·cal·ci·trant** (ri-kal′si-trənt), *adj.* [< L. ppr. < *re-*, back + *calcitrare,* to kick < *calx,* a heel], refusing to obey authority, regulation, etc.; stubbornly defiant. *n.* a recalcitrant person. —**re·cal′ci·trance, re·cal′ci·tran·cy,** *n.*

**re·call** (ri-kôl′; *for n., usually* rē′kôl′), *v.t.* 1. to call back; bid return. 2. to remember. 3. to take back; revoke. 4. to bring back in awareness or attention. *n.* 1. a recalling. 2. the process of removing, or the right to remove, a public official from office by popular vote. —**re·call′a·ble,** *adj.*

**re·cant** (ri-kant′), *v.t. & v.i.* [< L. < *re-*, back + *cantare,* freq. of *canere,* to sing], to withdraw or renounce formally or publicly (former beliefs, statements, etc.). —**re·can·ta·tion** (rē′kan-tā′shən), *n.* —**re·cant′er,** *n.*

**re·cap** (rē-kap′; *also, and for n. always,* rē′kap′), *v.t.* [-CAPPED, -CAPPING], [*re-* + *cap*], to cement, mold, and vulcanize a strip of rubber on the outer surface of (a worn pneumatic tire): cf. **retread.** *n.* a recapped tire. —**re·cap′pa·ble,** *adj.*

**re·ca·pit·u·late** (rē′kə-pich′oo-lāt′), *v.i. & v.t.* [-LATED, -LATING], [see RE- & CAPITULATE], to summarize; restate briefly. —**re′ca·pit′u·la′tor,** *n.*

**re·ca·pit·u·la·tion** (rē′kə-pich′oo-lā′shən), *n.* 1. a recapitulating. 2. a summary, or brief restatement. —**re′ca·pit′u·la′tive, re′ca·pit′u·la·to′ry** (-lə-tôr′i, -tō′ri), *adj.*

**re·cap·ture** (rē-kap′chẽr), *v.t.* [-TURED, -TURING], 1. to capture again; retake; reacquire. 2. to remember. *n.* a recapturing or being recaptured.

**re·cast** (rē-kast′, -käst′; *for n.,* rē′kast′, -käst′), *v.t.* [-CAST, -CASTING], 1. to cast again or anew. 2. to improve the form of; reconstruct: as, he *recast* the sentence. *n.* a recasting.

**recd., rec'd.,** received.

**re·cede** (ri-sēd′), *v.i.* [-CEDED, -CEDING], [< L.; see RE- & CEDE], 1. to go or move back: as, the flood *receded.* 2. to withdraw: as, he *receded* from his bargain. 3. to slope backward.

**re·cede** (rē′sēd′), *v.t.* [-CEDED, -CEDING], to cede back.

**re·ceipt** (ri-sēt′), *n.* [< OFr. < L. < pp. of *recipere;* see RECEIVE], 1. a recipe. 2. a receiving or being received. 3. a written acknowledgment that something has been received, as money, goods, etc. 4. *a)* something received. *b) pl.* the amount received. *v.t.* 1. to mark (a bill) paid. 2. to write a receipt for, as goods, etc.

**re·ceiv·a·ble** (ri-sēv′ə-b'l), *adj.* 1. that can be received. 2. due; requiring payment. 3. suitable for acceptance. *n. pl.* accounts or bills receivable. —**re·ceiv′a·bil′i·ty,** *n.*

**re·ceive** (ri-sēv′), *v.t.* [-CEIVED, -CEIVING], [< OFr. < L. *recipere* < *re-*, back + *capere,* to take], 1. to take into one's possession (something given, sent, etc.); get. 2. to encounter; experience: as, she *received* much acclaim. 3. to undergo; submit to; suffer: as, he *received* punishment. 4. to bear; take the effect or force of: as, all wheels *received* equal weight. 5. to take from another by listening: as, a confession *received* by the priest. 6. to get knowledge of; learn: as, he *received* the news. 7. to accept as authentic, valid, etc. 8. *a)* to let enter; admit. *b)* to have room for; contain. 9. to greet (visitors, etc.). *v.i.* 1. to be a recipient. 2. to greet guests or visitors. 3. in *radio & television,* to convert incoming electromagnetic waves into sound or light, thus reproducing the sounds or images being transmitted.

**re·ceiv·er** (ri-sēv′ẽr), *n.* 1. one who receives; specif., *a)* a collector; treasurer. *b)* in *baseball,* a catcher. *c)* in *law,* a person appointed by a court to administer or hold in trust property in bankruptcy or in a lawsuit. 2. a thing that receives; specif., *a)* a receptacle. *b)* an apparatus for receiving electrical waves, signals, etc. and converting them into sound or light, as a radio or television receiving set, or that part of a telephone held to the ear.

**re·ceiv·er·ship** (ri-sēv′ẽr-ship′), *n.* in *law,* 1. the duties or office of a receiver. 2. the state of being administered or held by a receiver.

**receiving set,** in *radio & television,* an apparatus for converting incoming electromagnetic waves into sound or light; a receiver.

**re·cent** (rē′s'nt), *adj.* [< Fr. < L. *recens*], 1. done, made, etc. just before the present time; modern; new. 2. of a time just before the present. 3. [R-], in *geology,* designating or of the present epoch, extending from the close of the Pleistocene: see **geology,** chart. *n.* [R-], the Recent Epoch. —**re′cen·cy, re′cent·ness,** *n.* —**re′cent·ly,** *adv.*

**re·cep·ta·cle** (ri-sep′tə-k'l), *n.* [L. *receptaculum* < freq. of *recipere;* see RECEIVE], 1. anything used to contain or hold something else; container. 2. in *botany,* that part of the stalk from which the flower grows.

**re·cep·tion** (ri-sep′shən), *n.* [OFr. < L. pp. of *recipere;* see RECEIVE], 1. a receiving or being received. 2. the manner of this: as, a hearty *reception.* 3. a social function, often formal, for the receiving of guests. 4. in *radio & television,* the receiving of signals with reference to the quality of reproduction: as, storms can affect *reception.*

**re·cep·tion·ist** (ri-sep′shən-ist), *n.* an office employee who receives callers, gives information, etc.

**re·cep·tive** (ri-sep′tiv), *adj.* 1. receiving or tending to receive, admit, contain, etc. 2. able or ready to receive requests, suggestions, new ideas, etc. 3. of reception or receptors. —**re·cep′tive·ly,** *adv.* —**re·cep′tiv′i·ty, re·cep′tive·ness,** *n.*

**re·cep·tor** (ri-sep′tẽr), *n.* a sense organ; nerve ending specialized for the reception of stimuli.
**re·cess** (ri-ses′; *also, for n., esp. sense* 3, rē′ses), *n.* [< L. pp. of *recedere*, to recede], 1. a receding or hollow place, as in a wall; niche. 2. *usually in pl.* a secluded or withdrawn place: as, the *recesses* of the subconscious. 3. *a*) a temporary halting of work or business, as at school. *b*) the state or time of this. *v.t.* 1. to place in a recess. 2. to form a recess in. *v.i.* to take a recess.
**re·ces·sion** (ri-sesh′ən), *n.* [L. *recessio* < pp. of *recedere*, to recede], 1. a going backward; withdrawal. 2. the procession of the clergy and choir to the vestry at the end of the service. 3. a receding part, as of a wall. 4. in *economics*, a temporary falling off of business activity, as during the upsurge following a depression.
**re·ces·sion** (rē′sesh′ən), *n.* [*re-* + *cession*], a ceding, or giving, back, as to a former owner.
**re·ces·sion·al** (ri-sesh′ən-'l), *adj.* of a recession. *n.* 1. a hymn (**recessional hymn**) sung at the end of a church service during the recession (sense 2). 2. music for such a hymn.
**re·ces·sive** (ri-ses′iv), *adj.* 1. receding or tending to recede. 2. in *genetics*, designating or of that one of any pair of opposite Mendelian characters which, when factors for both are present, remains latent: cf. *dominant*. **—re·ces′sive·ly,** *adv.*
**re·cher·ché** (rə-shâr′shā, -shâr′shā′), *adj.* [Fr., pp. of *rechercher;* see RESEARCH], 1. sought out with care; choice. 2. having refinement or studied elegance. 3. too refined; too studied.
**Re·ci·fe** (re-sē′fə), *n.* a seaport in central Brazil: pop., 512,000: also called *Pernambuco*.
**rec·i·pe** (res′ə-pi), *n.* [L., imperative of *recipere;* see RECEIVE], 1. a medical prescription. 2. a list of materials and directions for preparing a dish or drink. 3. anything proposed for producing a desired result.
**re·cip·i·ent** (ri-sip′i-ənt), *n.* [< L. ppr. of *recipere;* see RECEIVE], a person or thing that receives. *adj.* receiving, or ready or able to receive. **—re·cip′i·ence, re·cip′i·en·cy,** *n.*
**re·cip·ro·cal** (ri-sip′rə-k'l), *adj.* [< L. *reciprocus*, returning], 1. done, felt, given, etc. in return: as, *reciprocal* tolerance. 2. on both sides; mutual. 3. corresponding but reversed. 4. equivalent or interchangeable; complementary. 5. in *grammar*, expressing mutual action or relation: as, *each other* is a *reciprocal* pronoun. 6. in *mathematics*, of reciprocals. *n.* 1. anything that has a reciprocal relation to another; counterpart. 2. in *mathematics*, the quantity (with reference to a given quantity) resulting from the division of 1 by the given quantity: as, the *reciprocal* of 7 is 1/7. **—re·cip′ro·cal′i·ty** (-kal′ə-ti), *n.* **—re·cip′ro·cal·ly,** *adv.*
**re·cip·ro·cate** (ri-sip′rə-kāt′), *v.t. & v.i.* [-CATED, -CATING], [< L. pp.; see RECIPROCAL], 1. to move alternately back and forth. 2. to give and get reciprocally. 3. to give, do, feel, etc. (something similar) in return. **—re·cip′ro·ca′tion,** *n.* **—re·cip′ro·ca′tive, re·cip′ro·ca·to′ry** (-kə-tôr′i, -tō′ri), *adj.* **—re·cip′ro·ca′tor,** *n.*
**rec·i·proc·i·ty** (res′ə-pros′ə-ti), *n.* [< Fr.], 1. reciprocal state or relationship. 2. mutual exchange; esp., exchange of special privileges between two countries, as mutual reduction of tariffs.
**re·cit·al** (ri-sī′t'l), *n.* 1. a reciting; specif., a telling in detail. 2. the account, story, etc. told. 3. a musical program given by a soloist, soloists, or small ensemble. **—re·cit′al·ist,** *n.*
**rec·i·ta·tion** (res′ə-tā′shən), *n.* 1. a recital (in senses 1 & 2). 2. *a*) the speaking aloud in public of something memorized. *b*) the piece so presented. 3. a reciting by pupils of answers to questions on a prepared lesson, etc.
**rec·i·ta·tive** (res′ə-tə-tēv′), *n.* [It. *recitativo* < L. *recitare;* see RECITE], in *music*, 1. a type of declamatory singing, free in rhythm and tempo, as in the prose parts of operas. 2. a work or passage in this style. 3. music for such passages. Abbrev. **recit.**
**re·cite** (ri-sīt′), *v.t.* [-CITED, -CITING], [< Fr. < L. *recitare;* see RE- & CITE], 1. to speak aloud as from memory, as lessons in class or a poem, etc. before an audience. 2. to give an account of; narrate. *v.i.* to speak aloud something memorized. 2. to recite a lesson, or answer questions orally, in class. **—re·cit′er,** *n.*
**reck** (rek), *v.i. & v.t.* [AS. *reccan*], [Archaic], 1. to have care or concern (for) or take heed (of). 2. to concern or be of concern; matter (to).
**reck·less** (rek′lis), *adj.* [see RECK & -LESS], 1. careless; heedless. 2. not regarding consequences; rash. **—reck′less·ly,** *adv.* **—reck′less·ness,** *n.*
**reck·on** (rek′ən), *v.t.* [AS. *-recenian*], 1. to count; figure up; compute. 2. to consider as; regard as being: as, I *reckon* him an enemy. 3. to judge; estimate. 4. [Colloq. or Dial.], to suppose: as, I *reckon* he's tired. *v.i.* 1. to count up; figure. 2. to depend; rely (with *on*). **—reckon with,** 1. to settle accounts with. 2. to take into consideration. **—reck′on·er,** *n.*
**reck·on·ing** (rek′ən-iŋ), *n.* 1. the act of one who reckons; count or computation. 2. a calculated guess. 3. the settlement of an account. 4. a bill, as at an inn. 5. *a*) the determination of the position of a ship. *b*) the position so determined. See **dead reckoning. —day of reckoning,** 1. a time for settling accounts. 2. the Last Judgment.
**re·claim** (ri-klām′), *v.t.* [< OFr. < L. *reclamare;* see RE- & CLAIM], 1. to rescue or bring back (someone) from error, vice, etc. 2. to make (desert, etc.) capable of being cultivated or lived in, as by irrigating, etc. 3. to obtain (useful material, etc.) from waste products. *n.* reclamation: as, he's past *reclaim*. **—re·claim′a·ble,** *adj.* **—re·claim′ant, re·claim′er,** *n.*
**re-claim** (rē′klām′), *v.t.* to claim back; demand the return of; try to get back.
**rec·la·ma·tion** (rek′lə-mā′shən), *n.* a reclaiming or being reclaimed, as of wasteland.
**re·cline** (ri-klīn′), *v.t. & v.i.* [-CLINED, -CLINING], [<L. < *re-*, back + *clinare*, to lean], to lie or cause to lie back or down; lean back. **—re·clin′er,** *n.*
**re·cluse** (ri-klo͞os′; *for n., usually* rek′lo͞os), *adj.* [< OFr. < L. *reclusus*, pp.; ult. < *re-*, back + *claudere*, to shut], secluded; solitary. *n.* 1. one who lives apart from the world for religious contemplation. 2. one who lives a secluded, solitary life. **—re·clu′sion** (-klo͞o′zhən), *n.* **—re·clu′sive,** *adj.*
**rec·og·ni·tion** (rek′əg-nish′ən), *n.* [< Fr. < L. pp. of *recognoscere;* see RECOGNIZANCE], 1. a recognizing or being recognized; acknowledgment and approval, gratitude, etc.: as, in *recognition* of your services. 2. formal acceptance by a government of the sovereignty of a newly established state or government. 3. identification of a person or thing as being known to one; hence, greeting.
**re·cog·ni·zance** (ri-kog′ni-zəns, ri-kon′i-), *n.* [< OFr. < L. < *re-*, again + *cognoscere*, to know; see COGNITION], in *law*, *a*) a bond or obligation of record binding a person to some act, as to appear in court. *b*) the money subject to forfeit if this obligation is not fulfilled.
**rec·og·nize** (rek′əg-nīz′), *v.t.* [-NIZED, -NIZING], [back-formation < *recognizance*], 1. to identify as known before. 2. to know by some detail, as of appearance. 3. to perceive; identify: as, *recognize* the omens of defeat. 4. to acknowledge the existence, validity, etc. of, as a claim. 5. to accept as a fact; admit: as, to *recognize* defeat. 6. to acknowledge as worthy of appreciation or approval. 7. to acknowledge the sovereignty of (a government or state) by dealing with it. 8. to show acquaintance with (a person) by greeting. 9. to grant (a person) the right of speaking in a meeting, etc. **—rec′og·niz′a·ble,** *adj.* **—rec′og·niz′a·bly,** *adv.* **—rec′og·niz′er,** *n.*
**re·coil** (ri-koil′; *for n. 1, of weapons, usually* rē′koil′), *v.i.* [< OFr. < L. *re-*, back + *culus*, the buttocks], 1. to draw, start, or shrink back, as in fear, surprise, etc. 2. to fly back when released, as a spring, or kick back when fired, as a gun. 3. to return as to the starting point or source; react: as, our acts *recoil* upon ourselves. *n.* 1. a recoiling. 2. the state of having recoiled; reaction. **—re·coil′er,** *n.*
**re-coil** (rē′koil′), *v.t. & v.i.* to coil anew or again.
**rec·ol·lect** (rek′ə-lekt′), *v.t.* [< L.; see RE- & COLLECT], 1. to call back to mind; remember, especially with some effort. 2. to recall to (oneself) something temporarily forgotten. *v.i.* to remember. **—rec′ol·lec′tion,** *n.* **—rec′ol·lec′tive,** *adj.*
**re-col·lect** (rē′kə-lekt′), *v.t.* 1. to collect again (what has been scattered). 2. to recover or compose (oneself, one's thoughts, etc.): in this sense sometimes written **recollect.**
**rec·om·mend** (rek′ə-mend′), *v.t.* [< ML.; see RE- & COMMEND], 1. to give in charge; entrust: as, I *recommend* him to your care. 2. to name or speak of favorably as suited for some function, position, etc. 3. to make acceptable or pleasing: as, his diligence *recommends* him. 4. to advise; counsel. **—rec′om·mend′a·ble,** *adj.* **—rec′om·mend′a·to′ry** (-tôr′i, -tō′ri), *adj.* **—rec′om·mend′er,** *n.*
**rec·om·men·da·tion** (rek′ə-men-dā′shən), *n.* 1. a recommending. 2. anything that recommends; specif., a letter recommending a person or thing. 3. qualities, abilities, etc. that make a person or thing acceptable or pleasing. 4. advice; counsel.
**re·com·mit** (rē′kə-mit′), *v.t.* [-MITTED, -MITTING], 1. to commit again. 2. to refer to a committee, as a

question, bill, etc. —**re'com·mit'ment, re'com·mit'tal,** *n.*
**rec·om·pense** (rek'əm-pens'), *v.t.* [-PENSED, -PENSING], [< OFr. < LL.; see RE- & COMPENSATE], 1. to repay (a person, etc.); reward. 2. to compensate, as a loss. *n.* 1. something given or done in return for something else; requital, reward, etc. 2. something given or done to make up for a loss, injury, etc.; compensation.
**rec·on·cile** (rek'ən-sil'), *v.t.* [-CILED, -CILING], [< OFr. < L.; see RE- & CONCILIATE], 1. to make friendly again. 2. to settle (a quarrel, etc.). 3. to make (facts, ideas, texts, etc.) consistent or compatible. 4. to make content or acquiescent (*to*). —**rec'on·cil'a·bil'i·ty, rec'on·cil'a·ble·ness,** *n.* —**rec'on·cil'a·ble,** *adj.* —**rec'on·cil'a·bly,** *adv.* —**rec'on·cil'i·a'tion** (-sil'i-ā'shən), **rec'on·cile'ment,** *n.* —**rec'on·cil'er,** *n.* —**rec'on·cil'i·a·to'ry** (-sil'i-ə-tôr'i, -tō'ri), *adj.*
**rec·on·dite** (rek'ən-dīt', ri-kon'dīt), *adj.* [< L. pp. < *re-*, back + *condere*, to store up, hide], 1. beyond the grasp of ordinary understanding; profound. 2. dealing with abstruse or difficult subjects. 3. obscure; concealed. —**rec'on·dite'ly,** *adv.* —**rec'on·dite'ness,** *n.*
**re·con·di·tion** (rē'kən-dish'ən), *v.t.* to put back in good condition by cleaning, repairing, etc.
**re·con·nais·sance, re·con·nois·sance** (ri-kon'ə-səns), *n.* [Fr.; see RECOGNIZANCE], the examination or survey of a region, especially, in *military science*, for obtaining information about the enemy.
**rec·on·noi·ter** (rek'ə-noi'tēr, rē'kə-), *v.t.* [< Fr. < OFr.; see RECOGNIZANCE], 1. in *military science*, to observe or scout (an enemy position, etc.). 2. to make an examination or survey of (an area, region, etc.). *v.i.* to make a reconnaissance. —**rec'on·noi'ter·er,** *n.*
**rec·on·noi·tre** (rek'ə-noi'tēr, rē'kə-), *v.t. & v.i.* [-TRED, -TRING], to reconnoiter. —**rec'on·noi'trer,** *n.*
**re·con·sid·er** (rē'kən-sid'ēr), *v.t. & v.i.* to consider again; think over, as with a view to changing a decision. —**re'con·sid'er·a'tion,** *n.*
**re·con·struct** (rē'kən-strukt'), *v.t.* 1. to construct again; make over. 2. to build up, as from remaining parts, an image of what something was in its original form. —**re'con·struc'tive,** *adj.*
**re·con·struc·tion** (rē'kən-struk'shən), *n.* 1. a reconstructing. 2. [R-], *a*) the process, after the Civil War, of reorganizing the Southern States and re-establishing them in the Union. *b*) the period of this (1867–1877). 3. something reconstructed.
**re·con·vert** (rē'kən-vũrt'), *v.t. & v.i.* [*re-* + *convert*], 1. to change back, as to a former status, religion, etc. 2. to change back from a wartime to a peacetime basis. —**re'con·ver'sion,** *n.*
**re·cord** (ri-kôrd'; *for n. & adj.*, rek'ērd), *v.t.* [< OFr. < L. *recordari*, to remember < *re-*, again + *cor*, heart, mind], 1. to set down, as in writing; preserve an account of. 2. to register, as on a graph, an indication of (a motion or event) as it occurs. 3. to serve as evidence of; tell of. 4. to transform (sound) by electrical or mechanical means and register it, as on a grooved disk or magnetized wire, so that it can be reproduced at will 5. to show; indicate. 6. to set down in a register: as, *record* a vote. *v.i.* 1. to record something. 2. to admit of being recorded. *n.* 1. a recording or being recorded. 2. anything that serves as evidence of an event, etc. 3. anything that the written evidence is put on or in, as a register, monument, etc. 4. an official report of public proceedings, as in a court. 5. the known facts about anything, as about conduct, one's career, etc. 6. a flat disk, etc. on which sound has been recorded. 7. the best performance attained, as the highest speed, greatest amount, etc. *adj.* being the largest, fastest, etc. of its kind: as, a *record* crop. —**break a record,** to excel the best previous performance. —**go on record,** to state one's opinions publicly. —**off the record,** not for publication. —**on record,** publicly declared.
**re·cord·er** (ri-kôr'dēr), *n.* 1. a public officer who keeps records of deeds or other official papers. 2. a person, machine, etc. that records. 3. an early form of flute. —**re·cord'er·ship',** *n.*
**re·cord·ing** (ri-kôr'diŋ), *adj.* that records. *n.* 1. the act of one that records. 2. what is recorded, as on a phonograph record. 3. the record itself.
**re·count** (ri-kount'), *v.t.* [< Anglo-Fr.; see RE- & COUNT], to tell in detail; narrate; enumerate.
**re-count** (rē'kount'; *for n., usually* rē'kount'), *v.t.* to count again. *n.* a second or additional count, as of votes: also written **recount.**
**re·coup** (ri-kōōp'), *v.t.* [< Fr. < *re-*, again + *couper*, to cut], 1. to make up for: as, *recoup* a loss. 2. to repay. *n.* a recouping. —**re·coup'ment,** *n.*
**re·course** (rē'kôrs, ri-kōrs'), *n.* [< OFr. < L. *recursus*, a running back; see RE- & COURSE], 1. a turning for aid, protection, etc.: as, he had *recourse* to the law. 2. that to which one turns seeking aid, etc.: as, his one *recourse* was the law.
**re·cov·er** (ri-kuv'ēr), *v.t.* [< OFr. < L. *recuperare;* see RECUPERATE], 1. to get back (something lost, stolen, etc.); regain (health, etc.). 2. to compensate for: as, *recover* losses. 3. to save (oneself) from a fall, loss of poise or control, etc. 4. to reclaim, as land from the sea, useful substances from waste, etc. 5. in *law*, to get or get back by final judgment in a court. *v i.* 1. to get back to a healthy or normal condition, former position, etc. 2. to save oneself from a slip, self-betrayal, etc. 3. in *law*, to receive judgment in one's favor. —**re·cov'er·a·ble,** *adj.* —**re·cov'er·er,** *n.*
**re-cov·er** (rē'kuv'ēr), *v.t.* to cover again or anew.
**re·cov·er·y** (ri-kuv'ēr-i), *n.* [*pl.* -IES], 1. a recovering, regaining, reclaiming, etc. 2. a regaining of health, former position or condition, something lost, etc. 3. the time needed for recovering. 4. the amount gained in recovering.
**rec·re·ant** (rek'ri-ənt), *adj.* [OFr. ppr. of *recreire*, to surrender allegiance < ML. < L. *re-*, back + *credere*, to believe], 1. *a*) crying for mercy. *b*) cowardly. 2. disloyal; traitorous. *n.* 1. a coward. 2. a disloyal person; traitor. —**rec're·ance, rec're·an·cy,** *n.* —**rec're·ant·ly,** *adv.*
**rec·re·ate** (rek'ri-āt'), *v.t.* [-ATED, -ATING], [< L. pp.; see RE- & CREATE], to refresh in body or mind. *v.i.* to take recreation. —**rec're·a'tive,** *adj.*
**re-cre·ate** (rē'kri-āt'), *v.t.* [-ATED, -ATING], to create anew. —**re'-cre·a'tion,** *n.*
**rec·re·a·tion** (rek'ri-ā'shən), *n.* [see RECREATE], 1. refreshment in body or mind, as after work, by some form of play, amusement, or relaxation. 2. any form of play, amusement, etc. used for this purpose. —**rec're·a'tion·al,** *adj.*
**re·crim·i·nate** (ri-krim'ə-nāt'), *v.i.* [-NATED, -NATING], [< ML.; see RE- & CRIMINATE], to reply to an accusation by accusing, or charging some fault, in return. —**re·crim'i·na'tion,** *n.* —**re·crim'i·na'tive, re·crim'i·na·to'ry** (-nə-tôr'i, -tō'ri), *adj.*
**re·cru·des·cence** (rē'krōō-des''ns), *n.* [< L. *re-*, again + *crudescere*, to become harsh < *crudus*, raw], a breaking out afresh; renewal of activity: also **re'cru·des'cen·cy.** —**re'cru·des'cent,** *adj.*
**re·cruit** (ri-krōōt'), *v.t.* [< Fr. < pp. of *recroître*, to grow again < L. *re-*, again + *crescere*, to grow], 1. to raise or strengthen (an army, navy, etc.) by enlisting personnel. 2. to enlist (personnel) into an army or navy. 3. to enlist (new members) for a party, organization, etc. *v.i.* 1. to enlist new personnel for a military force. 2. to get new supplies of something, as in replacement. *n.* 1. a recently enlisted soldier, sailor, etc. 2. a new member of any group, etc. —**re·cruit'er,** *n.* —**re·cruit'ment,** *n.*
**Rec. Sec., rec. sec.,** recording secretary.
**rec·tal** (rek't'l), *adj.* of, for, or near the rectum. —**rec'tal·ly,** *adv.*
**rec·tan·gle** (rek'taŋ'g'l), *n.* [Fr. < LL.; see RECTI- & ANGLE (a corner)], any four-sided plane figure with four right angles.
**rec·tan·gu·lar** (rek-taŋ'gyoo-lēr), *adj.* 1. shaped like a rectangle. 2. right-angled. —**rec·tan'gu·lar'i·ty,** *n.* (-lar'ə-ti), *n.* —**rec·tan'gu·lar·ly,** *adv.*
**rec·ti-,** [< L. *rectus*], a combining form meaning *straight, right*, as in *rectilinear*: also **rect-.**
**rec·ti·fi·er** (rek'tə-fī'ēr), *n.* 1. a person or thing that rectifies. 2. in *electricity*, a device for changing alternating current into direct current.
**rec·ti·fy** (rek'tə-fī'), *v.t.* [-FIED, -FYING], [< OFr. < LL. < L. *rectus*, right + *facere*, to make], 1. to put right; correct. 2. in *chemistry*, to refine or purify by distilling. 3. in *electricity*, to change (alternating current) into direct current. —**rec'ti·fi'a·ble,** *adj.* —**rec'ti·fi·ca'tion,** *n.*
**rec·ti·lin·e·ar** (rek'tə-lin'i-ēr), *adj.* [*recti-* + *linear*], 1. in or forming a straight line. 2. bounded, formed, or characterized by straight lines. Also **rec'ti·lin'e·al.** —**rec'ti·lin'e·ar·ly,** *adv.*
**rec·ti·tude** (rek'tə-tōōd', -tūd'), *n.* [Fr. < LL. < L. *rectus*, straight], 1. honesty; uprightness of character. 2. correctness of judgment or method.
**rec·tor** (rek'tēr), *n.* [L. < pp. of *regere*, to rule], 1. in the *Protestant Episcopal Church* and the *Church of England*, a clergyman in charge of a

parish. 2. in the *R.C. Church*, *a*) the head priest of a parish. *b*) the head of a religious institution or school. 3. in certain schools, colleges, etc., the headmaster. **—rec′tor·ate** (-it), **rec′tor·ship′**, *n.* **—rec·to·ri·al** (rek-tôr′i-əl, -tō′ri-), *adj.*
**rec·to·ry** (rek′tēr-i), *n.* [*pl.* -RIES], 1. a rector's residence. 2. in the *Church of England*, a rector's benefice.
**rec·tum** (rek′təm), *n.* [*pl.* -TA (-tə)], [L. *rectum* (*intestinum*), straight (intestine)], the lowest segment of the large intestine, ending at the anus.
**re·cum·bent** (ri-kum′bənt), *adj.* [< L. < *re-*, back + *cumbere*, to lie down], 1. lying down; reclining. 2. resting; inactive. **—re·cum′ben·cy,** *n.* **—re·cum′bent·ly,** *adv.*
**re·cu·per·ate** (ri-kōō′pə-rāt′, -kū′-), *v.t.* [-ATED, -ATING], [< L. pp. of *recuperare*, to recover], 1. to restore to health, strength, etc. 2. to recover (losses, health, etc.). *v.i.* 1. to get well again. 2. to recover losses, etc. **—re·cu′per·a′tion,** *n.* **—re·cu′per·a′tive, re·cu′per·a·to′ry** (-pēr-ə-tôr′i, -tō′ri), *adj.* **—re·cu′per·a′tor,** *n.*
**re·cur** (ri-kũr′), *v.i.* [-CURRED, -CURRING], [< L. *re-*, back + *currere*, to run], 1. to return in thought, talk, etc.: as, to *recur* to a topic. 2. to occur again, as in memory. 3. to happen or appear again or at intervals.
**re·cur·rent** (ri-kũr′ənt), *adj.* 1. recurring; appearing again or periodically. 2. turning back in the opposite direction, as some nerves. **—re·cur′rence,** *n.* **—re·cur′rent·ly,** *adv.*
**re·curve** (ri-kũrv′), *v.t. & v.i.* [-CURVED, -CURVING], to curve or bend back or backward. **—re·cur′vate** (-kũr′vit, -vāt), *adj.*
**red** (red), *n.* [AS. *read*], 1. a primary color varying in hue from that of blood to pale pink. 2. a pigment producing this color. 3. [often R-], *a*) a political radical; esp., a communist. *b*) a citizen of the Soviet Union. *c*) *pl.* North American Indians. 4. a red object, as a red chessman. *adj.* [REDDER, REDDEST], 1. of the color red. 2. having red hair. 3. [often R-], *a*) politically radical; esp., communist. *b*) of the Soviet Union. **—in the red,** losing money; in debt. **—paint the town red,** [Slang], to have a noisy good time, as by visiting bars, etc. **—see red,** [Colloq.], to be or become angry. **—red′dish,** *adj.* **—red′ness,** *n.*
**re·dact** (ri-dakt′), *v.t.* [< L. pp. of *redigere*, to reduce to order], to arrange in proper form for publication; edit. **—re·dac′tion,** *n.* **—re·dac′tor,** *n.*
**red algae,** a group of red, brownish-red, purple, or greenish seaweeds.
**red·bait** (red′bāt′), *v.t. & v.i.* to make indiscriminate attacks on (a person or group) as being red, or communist.
**red·bird** (red′bũrd′), *n.* 1. the American cardinal. 2. the scarlet tanager.
**red blood cell,** a red corpuscle.
**red-blood·ed** (red′blud′id), *adj.* 1. high-spirited; vigorous: said of persons. 2. full of action; exciting: said of novels, etc.
**red·breast** (red′brest′), *n.* the robin.
**red·bud** (red′bud′), *n.* a tree with small, pink, budlike flowers; Judas tree.
**red·cap** (red′kap′), *n.* a porter in a railroad station, bus station, etc.
**red·coat** (red′kōt′), *n.* a British soldier (when a red coat was part of the British uniform).
**Red Cross,** 1. a red cross on a white ground, emblem of neutrality in war for hospitals, ambulances, etc. 2. *a*) an international society for the relief of suffering in time of war or disaster. *b*) any national branch of this.
**red deer,** 1. a deer native to Europe and Asia. 2. the American deer (in its summer coloring).
**red·den** (red′'n), *v.t.* to make red. *v.i.* to become red; esp., to blush or flush.
**re·deem** (ri-dēm′), *v.t.* [< Fr. < L. *redimere* < *re*(*d*)-, back + *emere*, to get], 1. to get or buy back; recover. 2. to pay off (a mortgage, etc.). 3. to convert (paper money) into coin. 4. to turn in (coupons) for premiums. 5. *a*) to set free; rescue. *b*) to deliver from sin and its penalties. 6. to fulfill, as a promise. 7. to make amends for; atone for. **—re·deem′a·ble,** *adj.*
**re·deem·er** (ri-dēm′ēr), *n.* 1. one who redeems. 2. [R-], Jesus Christ.
**re·demp·tion** (ri-demp′shən), *n.* [OFr. < L. < pp. of *redimere;* see REDEEM], 1. a redeeming or being redeemed. 2. something that redeems. **—re·demp′tive, re·demp′to·ry** (-tə-ri), *adj.*
**re·de·ploy** (rē′di-ploi′), *v.t.* to move (troops) from one front to another. **—re′de·ploy′ment,** *n.*
**red·eye** (red′ī′), *n.* [Slang], strong whisky, especially if inferior: also **red eye.**
**red flag,** 1. the flag symbolizing revolution, revolutionary socialism, etc.: often figurative. 2. a danger signal. 3. anything that arouses anger.
**red-hand·ed** (red′han′did), *adj.* 1. having hands stained with blood. 2. in the act, or fresh from the scene, of a crime. **—red′-hand′ed·ly,** *adv.* **—red′-hand′ed·ness,** *n.*
**red·head** (red′hed′), *n.* 1. a person with red hair. 2. a North American duck related to the canvasback: the male has a red head. **—red′head′ed,** *adj.*
**redheaded woodpecker,** a North American woodpecker with a bright-red head and neck.
**red herring,** 1. a smoked herring. 2. something used to confuse, or to divert attention from something else: from the act of drawing a herring across the trace in hunting, to divert the hounds.
**red-hot** (red′hot′), *adj.* 1. hot enough to glow; very hot. 2. very excited, as with anger, etc. 3. very new; up-to-the-minute: said of news, etc.
**red·in·gote** (red′iŋ-gōt′), *n.* [Fr. < Eng. *riding coat*], 1. formerly, a man's full-skirted, double-breasted overcoat. 2. a long, unlined, lightweight coat, open down the front, worn by women.
**red·in·te·grate** (ri-din′tə-grāt′), *v.t.* [-GRATED, -GRATING], [< L. pp.; see RE- & INTEGRATE], to make whole or perfect again; reunite; re-establish. **—red·in′te·gra′tion,** *n.*
**re·di·rect** (rē′də-rekt′, -dī-), *v.t.* to direct again. *adj.* in *law*, of the questioning of one's own witness again, after his cross-examination by the opposing lawyer. **—re′di·rec′tion,** *n.*
**re·dis·count** (rē-dis′kount), *v.t.* to discount again. *n.* 1. a rediscounting. 2. *usually pl.* rediscounted commercial paper.
**re·dis·trict** (rē-dis′trikt), *v.t.* to divide anew into districts.
**red lead,** red oxide of lead, $Pb_3O_4$, used in making paint, in glassmaking, etc.
**red-let·ter** (red′let′ēr), *adj.* memorable; happy: as, a *red-letter* day: from the custom of marking church holidays on the calendar in red ink.
**red light,** 1. a danger signal. 2. the red phase of a traffic light, a direction to stop.
**red-light district** (red′līt′), a district containing many houses of prostitution, sometimes indicated by red lights.
**red man,** a North American Indian.
**red meat,** beef or mutton, as distinguished from pork, veal, etc.
**red·o·lent** (red′ə-lənt), *adj.* [OFr. < L. ppr. < *re*(*d*)-, intens. + *olere*, to smell], 1. sweet-smelling; fragrant. 2. smelling (*of*): as, *redolent* of tar. 3. suggestive (*of*). **—red′o·lence, red′o·len·cy,** *n.*
**re·dou·ble** (rē-dub′'l), *v.t. & v.i.* [-BLED, -BLING], [Fr. *redoubler*], 1. to increase or be increased twofold; double. 2. to echo or re-echo. 3. to refold; double back. 4. in *bridge*, to double the doubled bid of (one's opponent). *n.* in *bridge*, a redoubling.
**re·doubt** (ri-dout′), *n.* [< Fr. < It. *ridotto* < ML. *reductus*, orig. pp. of L. *reducere;* see REDUCE], 1. a temporary fortification used to secure a hilltop, pass, etc. 2. a stronghold.
**re·doubt·a·ble** (ri-dout′ə-b'l), *adj.* [< OFr. < *redouter*, to fear < L. *re-*, intens. + *dubitare*, to doubt], 1. formidable. 2. deserving of respect. **—re·doubt′a·ble·ness,** *n.* **—re·doubt′a·bly,** *adv.*
**re·dound** (ri-dound′), *v.i.* [< Fr. < L. *redundare*, to overflow < *re*(*d*)-, intens. + *undare*, to surge], 1. to have a result (*to* the credit or discredit of someone or something). 2. to come back; react; recoil (*upon*): said of honor, etc.
**red pepper,** 1. a plant with a red, many-seeded fruit, as the cayenne. 2. the fruit. 3. the ground fruit or seeds, used for seasoning.
**red·poll** (red′pōl′), *n.* any of a number of finches the males of which usually have a red crown.
**re·dress** (ri-dres′; *for n., usually* rē′dres), *v.t.* [< OFr.; see RE- & DRESS], 1. to compensate for, as an evil. 2. to remedy, as a fault. 3. to make amends to. 4. to adjust: as, *redress* the balances. *n.* 1. compensation, as for a wrong. 2. a redressing. **—re·dress′a·ble,** *adj.* **—re·dress′er, re·dress′or,** *n.*
**Red River,** 1. a river flowing through Texas and Louisiana into the Mississippi. 2. a river of the northern U.S. flowing into Lake Winnipeg, Canada: also **Red River of the North.**
**Red Sea,** a sea between Africa and Arabia, connected with the Mediterranean by the Suez Canal.
**red·skin** (red′skin′), *n.* a North American Indian.
**red snapper,** a salt-water food fish with a reddish, oblong body, found off the coasts of Florida and Georgia.
**red·start** (red′stärt′), *n.* [*red* + *start*, tail], 1. a small European warbler with a reddish tail. 2. an American fly-catching warbler.
**red tape,** [< a tape used to tie official papers], rigid

adherence to routine and regulations, causing delay and exasperation. —**red′-tape′**, *adj.*

**red·top** (red′top′), *n.* a grass grown in E North America for hay and pasturage.

**re·duce** (ri-dōōs′, -dūs′), *v.t.* [-DUCED, -DUCING], [< L. < *re-*, back + *ducere*, to lead], 1. to lessen in any way, as in size, value, price, etc. 2. to bring into a certain order; classify. 3. to change to a different form, as by melting, grinding, etc. 4. to lower, as in rank; degrade. 5. to bring to order, attention, etc., as by persuasion or force. 6. to subdue or conquer. 7. *a*) to bring into a difficult state: as, *reduced* to poverty. *b*) to compel by need: used in the passive, as, he was *reduced* to stealing. 8. in *arithmetic*, to change in denomination or form without changing in value: as, to *reduce* fractions. 9. in *chemistry*, *a*) to decrease the positive valence or increase the negative valence of (an element or radical). *b*) to remove the oxygen from. *c*) to combine with hydrogen. *d*) to bring into the metallic state by removing nonmetallic elements. 10. in *photography*, to make less dense, as a negative. *v.i.* 1. to become reduced. 2. to lose weight, as by dieting. —**re·duc′er,** *n.* —**re·duc′i·ble,** *adj.* —**re·duc′i·bil′i·ty,** *n.* —**re·duc′i·bly,** *adv.*

**reducing agent,** in *chemistry*, any substance that reduces another substance, or brings about reduction, and is itself oxidized in the process.

‡**re·duc·ti·o ad ab·sur·dum** (ri-duk′shi-ō′ ad ab-sũr′dəm), [L., lit., reduction to absurdity], in *logic*, the disproof of a proposition by showing its logical conclusions to be absurd.

**re·duc·tion** (ri-duk′shən), *n.* 1. *a*) a reducing or being reduced. *b*) the amount of this. 2. anything made or brought about by reducing, as a smaller copy. —**re·duc′tion·al,** *adj.* —**re·duc′tive,** *adj.*

**re·dun·dan·cy** (ri-dun′dən-si), *n.* 1. a being redundant. 2. [*pl.* -CIES], something redundant. 3. the use of redundant words. Also **re·dun′dance.**

**re·dun·dant** (ri-dun′dənt), *adj.* [< L. ppr. of *redundare;* see REDOUND], 1. more than enough; excessive. 2. excess; superfluous. 3. wordy: as, a *redundant* literary style. 4. unnecessary to the meaning: said of words. —**re·dun′dant·ly,** *adv.*

**re·du·pli·cate** (ri-dōō′plə-kāt′, -dū′-; *for adj. & n., usually* -kit), *v.t.* [-CATED, -CATING], [see RE- & DUPLICATE], 1. to redouble, double, or repeat. 2. to double (a syllable or word), sometimes with changes, to form a new word (e.g., *chitchat*). *v.i.* to become reduplicated. *adj.* reduplicated; doubled. *n.* something reduplicated. —**re·du′pli·ca′tion,** *n.* —**re·du′pli·ca′tive,** *adj.*

**red·wing** (red′wiŋ′), *n.* 1. a small European thrush with an orange-red patch on the underside of the wings. 2. a North American blackbird (**red-winged blackbird**) with a bright-red patch on the top surface of the wings.

**red·wood** (red′wood′), *n.* 1. a giant evergreen of the Pacific coast; sequoia. 2. its reddish wood.

**re-ech·o, re·ëch·o** (rē-ek′ō), *v.t. & v.i.* [-OED, -OING], to echo back or again; resound. *n.* [*pl.* -OES], the echo of an echo.

**reed** (rēd), *n.* [AS. *hreod*], 1. any of various grasses with jointed, hollow stems. 2. a mass of these. 3. a rustic musical pipe made from such a stem. 4. [Poetic], an arrow. 5. in *music*, *a*) a thin strip of some flexible substance, placed against the opening of the mouthpiece as of a clarinet: when vibrated by the breath, it produces a musical tone. *b*) an instrument with a reed. *c*) in a reed organ, a similar contrivance that vibrates in a current of air.

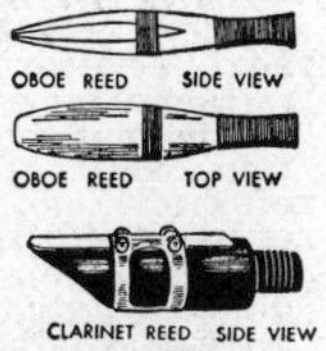

REEDS

**reed organ,** an organ with a set of free metal reeds instead of pipes to make tones.

**re-ed·u·cate, re·ëd·u·cate** (rē-ej′oo-kāt′), *v.t.* [-CATED, -CATING], to educate anew; esp., to rehabilitate (a handicapped person, etc.) by special training. —**re′-ed·u·ca′tion, re′ëd·u·ca′tion,** *n.*

**reed·y** (rēd′i), *adj.* [-IER, -IEST], 1. full of reeds. 2. made of reed or reeds. 3. like a reed. 4. sounding like a reed instrument; thin; piping. —**reed′i·ly,** *adv.* —**reed′i·ness,** *n.*

**reef** (rēf), *n.* [< ON. *rif*, a rib], a ridge of rock or sand at or near the surface of the water.

**reef** (rēf), *n.* [ME. *riff;* akin to prec. entry], 1. a part of a sail which can be folded together and tied down to reduce the area exposed to the wind. 2. the act of reefing. *v.t. & v.i.* 1. to reduce (a sail) by taking in part of it. 2. to lower or shorten (a spar).

**reef·er** (rēf′ẽr), *n.* 1. one who reefs. 2 a short, thick, double-breasted coat, worn especially by sailors. 3. [from the rolled appearance of a *reef* (of a sail)], [Slang], a marijuana cigarette.

**reef knot,** a common square knot.

**reek** (rēk), *n.* [AS. *rec*], 1. vapor; fume. 2. a strong, unpleasant smell. *v.i.* 1. to fume. 2. to have a strong, offensive smell. 3. to be permeated with anything very unpleasant. *v.t.* to emit or exude (vapor, fumes, etc.). —**reek′er,** *n.* —**reek′y** [-IER, -IEST], *adj.*

**reel** (rēl), *v.i.* [< *reel* (spool)], 1. to give way; sway, swing, or stagger from shock: as, the line of battle *reeled.* 2. to stagger; lurch, as from drunkenness. 3. to go around and around; whirl. 4. to be dizzy. *v.t.* to cause to reel. *n.* a reeling; whirl; stagger.

**reel** (rēl), *n.* [< prec. *reel*, *n.* (a whirl)], 1. a lively Scottish dance. 2. the Virginia reel. 3. music for either of these.

**reel** (rēl), *n.* [AS. *hreol*], 1. any frame or spool on which thread, wire, film, etc. may be wound. 2. such a frame for winding line on a fishing rod. 3. the quantity of wire, thread, motion-picture film, etc. usually wound on one reel. *v.t.* 1. to wind on or off a reel (with *in* or *out*). 2. to pull in (a fish) by winding a line on a reel (with *in*). 3. to narrate, write, etc. fluently and easily (with *off*). —**off the reel,** fluently; easily.

**re-en·force, re·ën·force** (rē′in-fôrs′, -fōrs′), *v.t.* reinforce. —**re′-en·force′ment, re′ën·force′ment,** *n.* —**re′-en·forc′er, re′ën·forc′er,** *n.*

**re-en·try, re·ën·try** (rē-en′tri), *n.* 1. a re-entering; specif., a coming back, as of a space vehicle, into the earth's atmosphere. 2. a second entry. 3. in *bridge & whist*, a card that will win a trick and recover the lead.

**reeve** (rēv), *n.* [AS. *gerefa*], in *English history*, *a*) the chief officer of a town or district. *b*) the overseer of a manor; steward.

**reeve** (rēv), *v.t.* [REEVED or ROVE; also, for pp., ROVEN; REEVING], [prob. < D. *reven*], in *nautical usage*, 1. to slip (a rope, etc.) through a block, ring, etc. 2. *a*) to pass in, through, or around something. *b*) to fasten by so doing. 3. to pass a rope through (a block or pulley).

**ref.,** 1. referee. 2. reference. 3. reformed.

**re·fec·tion** (ri-fek′shən), *n.* [OFr. < L. *refectio* < pp. < *re-*, again + *facere*, to make], 1. food or drink taken to refresh oneself. 2. a light meal.

**re·fec·to·ry** (ri-fek′tə-ri), *n.* [*pl.* -RIES], a dining hall in a monastery, convent, college, etc.

**re·fer** (ri-fũr′), *v.t.* [-FERRED, -FERRING], [< OFr. < L. < *re-*, back + *ferre*, to bear], 1. to assign (*to*); regard as caused by: as, he *referred* his troubles to the war. 2. to assign or regard as belonging (*to* a kind, class, etc.). 3. to submit (a quarrel, etc.) for settlement. 4. to direct (a person) *to* someone or something for aid, information, etc. *v.i.* 1. to be concerned (with): with *to*, as, the book *referred* only to fish. 2. to direct attention, or make reference (with *to*). 3. to turn for information, aid, etc. (with *to*): as, *refer* to a map. —**ref·er·a·ble** (ref′ẽr-ə-b'l), **re·fer′ra·ble,** *adj.* —**re·fer′rer,** *n.*

**ref·er·ee** (ref′ə-rē′), *n.* 1. a person to whom anything is referred for decision. 2. in *law*, a person appointed by a court to study, and report on, a matter. 3. in *sports*, a judge of a game, as of a boxing match. *v.t. & v.i.* [-EED, -EEING], to act as referee (in).

**ref·er·ence** (ref′ẽr-əns), *n.* 1. a referring or being referred. 2. relation; regard: as, with *reference* to his reply. 3. the directing of attention to a person or thing. 4. a mention or allusion. 5. an indication, as in a book, of some other work to be consulted. 6. the work so indicated. 7. *a*) the giving of the name of a person who can offer information or recommendation. *b*) the person so indicated. 8. a written statement of character, qualification, etc. 9. a source of information: often attributive, as, *reference* books. —**make reference to,** to refer to; mention. —**ref′er·en′tial** (-ə-ren′shəl), *adj.* —**ref′er·en′tial·ly,** *adv.*

**ref·er·en·dum** (ref′ə-ren′dəm), *n.* [*pl.* -DUMS, -DA (-də)], [L., gerund of *referre;* see REFER], 1. the submission of a law, proposed or already in effect, to a direct vote of the people. 2. the right of the people to vote on such laws, overruling the legislature. 3. the vote itself.

**ref·er·ent** (ref′ẽr-ənt), *n.* what is referred to; esp., in *semantics*, the thing referred to by a term.

**re·fer·ral** (ri-fũr′əl), *n.* a referring or being referred, as for professional service, etc.

**re·fill** (rē-fil′; *for n.*, rē′fil′), *v.t.* to fill again. *n.* a new filling; esp., a unit made to replace the contents of a container. —**re·fill′a·ble,** *adj.*

**re·fine** (ri-fīn′), *v.t. & v.i.* [*re-* + *fine*, to make fine], 1. to free or become freed from impurities, dross, etc.; purify. 2. to free or become freed from imperfection, vulgarity, etc.; make or become more polished, as language. —**refine on** (or **upon**), to improve. —**re·fin′er,** *n.*

**re·fined** (ri-fīnd′), *adj.* 1. made free from impurities; purified. 2. cultivated or elegant; free from vulgarity: said of manners, speech, etc. 3. characterized by great subtlety, exactness, etc.

**re·fine·ment** (ri-fīn′mənt), *n.* 1. a refining or being refined. 2. the result of this. 3. delicacy or elegance of language, speech, etc.; polish. 4. a development; improvement. 5. a fine distinction.

**re·fin·er·y** (ri-fīn′ēr-i), *n.* [*pl.* -IES], an establishment or plant for purifying materials such as oil, metal, sugar, fats, etc.

**re·fit** (rē-fit′; *also, for n*, rē′fit′), *v.t. & v.i.* [-FITTED, -FITTING], to make or be made ready or fit for use again, as by repairing, re-equipping, etc. *n.* a refitting.

**refl.,** 1. reflection. 2. reflex. 3. reflexive.

**re·flect** (ri-flekt′), *v.t.* [< OFr. < L. < *re-*, back + *flectere*, to bend], 1. to bend or throw back, as light, heat, or sound. 2. to give back an image of; mirror or reproduce. 3. to bring back as a consequence: as, his deeds *reflect* honor on the nation. *v.i.* 1. to be thrown back: as, the light *reflected* into his eyes. 2. to throw back light, heat, etc. 3. *a*) to give back an image. *b*) to be mirrored. 4. to think seriously; contemplate (with *on* or *upon*). 5. to cast blame or discredit (*on* or *upon*). —**re·flect′er,** *n.* —**re·flect′i·ble,** *adj.*

**re·flec·tion** (ri-flek′shən), *n.* 1. a reflecting or being reflected. 2. the throwing back by a surface of sound, light, etc. 3. anything reflected. 4. an image; likeness. 5. serious thought: contemplation. 6. the result of such thought; idea or remark. 7. blame; discredit. 8. a remark imputing, or an action bringing, discredit. 9. in *anatomy & zoology*, a bending back on itself. Also sp. **re·flex′ion.** —**re·flec′tion·al,** *adj.*

**re·flec·tive** (ri-flek′tiv), *adj.* 1. reflecting. 2. of or produced by reflection. 3. meditative; thoughtful. —**re·flec′tive·ly,** *adv.* —**re·flec·tiv·i·ty** (rē′flek-tiv′ə-ti), **re·flec′tive·ness,** *n.*

**re·flec·tor** (ri-flek′tēr), *n.* a person or thing that reflects; esp., a surface, object, or device that reflects light, sound, heat, etc.

**re·flex** (rē′fleks; *for v.*, ri-fleks′), *n.* [< L. pp. of *reflectere;* see REFLECT], 1. reflection, as of light. 2. a reflected image or reproduction. 3. in *physiology*, a reflex action. *adj.* 1. turned or bent back. 2. coming in reaction; esp., designating or of an involuntary action, as a sneeze, resulting when a stimulus carried to a nerve center is directly transmitted to the muscle or gland that responds. *v.t.* to bend, turn, or fold back. —**re·flex′i·bil′i·ty,** *n.* —**re·flex′i·ble,** *adj.* —**re′flex·ly,** *adv.*

**re·flex·ive** (ri-flek′siv), *adj.* 1. reflex. 2. in *grammar*, *a*) designating a verb whose subject and direct object are identical (e.g., *wash* in "I wash myself"). *b*) designating a pronoun used as the direct object of such a verb, as *myself* in the above example. *n.* a reflexive verb or pronoun. —**re·flex′ive·ly,** *adv.* —**re·flex′ive·ness, re·flex·iv·i·ty** (rē′flek-siv′ə-ti), *n.*

**ref·lu·ent** (ref′lo͞o-ənt), *adj.* [< L. ppr. of *refluere*, to flow back], flowing back; ebbing, as the tide.

**re·flux** (rē′fluks′), *n.* [< L. pp. of *refluere;* see REFLUENT], a flowing back; ebbing, as of a tide.

**re·for·est** (rē-fôr′ist, -for′-), *v.t. & v.i.* to plant new trees on (land once forested). —**re′for·est·a′tion,** *n.*

**re·form** (ri-fôrm′), *v.t.* [< OFr. < L.; see RE- & FORM], 1. to make better by removing faults; correct. 2. to make better by stopping abuses, introducing better procedures, etc. 3. to put a stop to (abuses). 4. to bring (a person) to give up misconduct and behave better. *v.i.* to become or behave better. *n.* 1. an improvement; correction of faults or evils, as in social problems. 2. an improvement in character and conduct. —**re·form′a·ble,** *adj.* —**re·form′a·tive,** *adj.* —**re·formed′,** *adj.* —**re·form′ist,** *adj. & n.*

**re-form** (rē′fôrm′), *v.t. & v.i.* to form again.

**ref·or·ma·tion** (ref′ēr-mā′shən), *n.* 1. a reforming or being reformed. 2. [R-], the 16th-century religious movement that aimed at reforming the Roman Catholic Church and resulted in establishing the Protestant churches. —**ref′or·ma′tion·al,** *adj.*

**re·form·a·to·ry** (ri-fôr′mə-tôr′i, -tō′ri), *adj.* reforming or aiming at reform. *n.* [*pl.* -RIES], an institution to which young law offenders are sent for training and discipline intended to reform them: also **reform school.**

**re·form·er** (ri-fôr′mēr), *n.* one who reforms, or tries to reform, morals, customs, institutions, etc.

**re·fract** (ri-frakt′), *v.t.* [< L. *refractus*, pp. < *re-*, back + *frangere*, to break], 1. to bend (a ray of light, etc.) as it passes from one medium into another: as, glass *refracts* light. 2. in *optics*, to measure the degree of refraction of (an eye or lens). —**re·frac′tive,** *adj.* —**re·frac′tive·ly,** *adv.* —**re·frac·tiv·i·ty** (rē′frak-tiv′ə-ti), **re·frac′tive·ness,** *n.* —**re·frac′tor,** *n.*

**re·frac·tion** (ri-frak′shən), *n.* 1. a refracting or being refracted; bending of a ray or wave of light, heat, etc., as it passes obliquely from one medium to another of different density. 2. in *optics*, the ability of the eye to refract light entering it, so as to form an image on the retina. —**re·frac′tion·al,** *adj.*

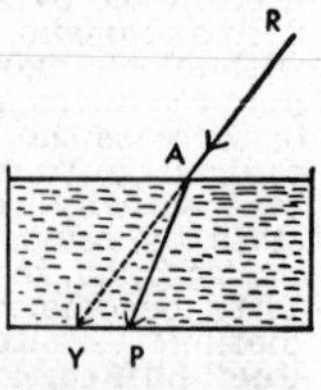


REFRACTION OF LIGHT RAY

RAY, light ray in straight line; RAP, refracted light ray

**re·frac·to·ry** (ri-frak′tə-ri), *adj.* [< L. < *refractus;* see REFRACT], 1. stubborn; obstinate; hard to manage. 2. resistant to heat; hard to melt or work: said of ores or metals. 3. not yielding to treatment, as a disease. —**re·frac′to·ri·ly,** *adv.* —**re·frac′to·ri·ness,** *n.*

**re·frain** (ri-frān′), *v.i.* [< OFr. < L. < *re-*, back + *frenare*, to curb < *frenum*, a rein], to hold back; keep oneself (*from*); forbear (often with *from*).

**re·frain** (ri-frān′), *n.* [< OFr. < L. *re-*, back + *frangere*, to break], 1. a phrase or verse repeated at intervals in a song or poem. 2. music for this.

**re·fran·gi·ble** (ri-fran′jə-b′l), *adj.* [< *re-* + L. *frangere*, to break; + *-ible*], that can be refracted, as light rays. —**re·fran′gi·bil′i·ty,** *n.*

**re·fresh** (ri-fresh′), *v.t.* [< OFr.; see RE- & FRESH], 1. to make fresh by cooling, airing, etc., as a room. 2. to make (a person) feel cooler, stronger, etc., as by food, drink, or sleep. 3. to renew; replenish, as by new supplies; revive, as the memory. *v.i.* 1. to become fresh again; revive. 2. to take refreshment, as food or drink. —**re·fresh′er,** *n.* —**re·fresh′ing,** *adj.* —**re·fresh′ing·ly,** *adv.*

**refresher course,** a course of study reviewing material previously studied.

**re·fresh·ment** (ri-fresh′mənt), *n.* 1. a refreshing or being refreshed. 2. something that refreshes, as food, drink, etc. 3. *pl.* food or drink or both.

**re·frig·er·ant** (ri-frij′ēr-ənt), *adj.* 1. refrigerating; cooling or freezing. 2. reducing heat or fever. *n.* 1. a medicine used to reduce fever. 2. a substance used in refrigeration, as ice. 3. any of various liquids that vaporize at a low temperature, used in mechanical refrigeration.

**re·frig·er·ate** (ri-frij′ə-rāt′), *v.t.* [-ATED, -ATING], [< L. pp. < *re-*, intens. + *frigerare*, to cool < *frigus*, cold], 1. to make or keep cool or cold; chill. 2. to preserve (food, etc.) by keeping cold or freezing. —**re·frig′er·a′tion,** *n.* —**re·frig′er·a′tive, re·frig′er·a·to′ry** (-ēr-ə-tôr′i, -tō′ri), *adj*

**re·frig·er·a·tor** (ri-frij′ə-rā′tēr), *n.* something that refrigerates; esp., a box or room in which food, etc. is kept cool, as by ice or mechanical refrigeration.

**reft** (reft), *adj.* robbed or bereft (*of* something).

**ref·uge** (ref′ūj), *n.* [< OFr. < L.; ult. < *re-*, back + *fugere*, to flee], 1. shelter or protection from danger, difficulty, etc. 2. a place of safety; shelter; safe retreat.

**ref·u·gee** (ref′yoo-jē′, ref′yoo-jē′), *n.* a person who flees from his home or country to seek refuge elsewhere, as in a time of war, persecution, etc.

**re·ful·gent** (ri-ful′jənt), *adj.* [< L. ppr.; see RE- & FULGENT], shining; radiant; glowing. —**re·ful′gence, re·ful′gen·cy,** *n.*

**re·fund** (ri-fund′; *for n.*, rē′fund′), *v.t. & v.i.* [< OFr. < L. < *re-*, back + *fundere*, to pour], to give back (money, etc.); repay. *n.* a refunding or the amount refunded; repayment. —**re·fund′a·ble,** *adj.* —**re·fund′er,** *n.* —**re·fund′ment,** *n.*

**re·fund** (rē′fund′), *v.t.* to fund again or anew; specif., in *finance*, to use borrowed money, as from the sale of a bond issue, to pay back (a loan).

**re·fur·bish** (rē-fūr′bish), *v.t.* [*re-* + *furbish*], to brighten, freshen, or polish up again; renovate.

**re·fus·al** (ri-fū′z′l), *n.* 1. a refusing. 2. the right or chance to accept or refuse something before it is offered to another; option.

**re·fuse** (ri-fūz′), *v.t.* [-FUSED, -FUSING], [< OFr. *refuser* < L. pp. < *re-*, back + *fundere*, to pour], 1. to decline to accept; reject. 2. *a*) to decline to do or grant. *b*) to decline (*to* do something): as, *refuse* to go. 3. to decline to obey (a command, etc.). 4. to stop short at (a fence, etc.), without jumping it: said of a horse. ***v.i.*** to decline to accept or agree. **—re·fus′a·ble, *adj.* —re·fus′er, *n.***

**ref·use** (ref′ūs, -ūz), ***n.*** [< OFr. pp. of *refuser;* see REFUSE, *v.*], anything thrown away or rejected as worthless or useless; waste; rubbish. ***adj.*** thrown away or rejected as worthless or useless.

**re·fute** (ri-fūt′), ***v.t.*** [-FUTED, -FUTING], [< L. *refutare,* to repel; see RE- & CONFUTE], 1. to prove (a person) to be wrong; confute. 2. to prove (an argument or statement) to be false or wrong, by argument or evidence. **—ref·u·ta·ble** (ref′yoo-tə-b'l, ri-fū′-), ***adj.* —ref′u·ta·bly, *adv.* —ref′u·ta′tion, re·fut′al, *n.* —re·fut′er, *n.***

**reg.,** 1. regiment. 2. region. 3. register. 4. registered. 5. regular. 6. regulation.

**re·gain** (ri-gān′), ***v.t.*** 1. to get back again; recover. 2. to get back to; succeed in reaching again. **—re·gain′a·ble, *adj.***

**re·gal** (rē′g'l), ***adj.*** [< OFr. < L. *regalis* < *rex,* a king], 1. of a king; royal. 2. characteristic of, like, or fit for a king; splendid, stately, etc. **—re′gal·ly, *adv.* —re′gal·ness, *n.***

**re·gale** (ri-gāl′), ***v.t.*** [-GALED, -GALING], [< Fr. < *ré-* (see RE-) + OFr. *gale,* joy], 1. to entertain, as with a feast. 2. to delight with something pleasing. ***v.i.*** to feast. **—re·gale′ment, *n.* —re·gal′er, *n.***

**re·ga·li·a** (ri-gā′li-ə, -gāl′yə), ***n.pl.*** [L., neut. pl. of *regalis;* see REGAL], 1. the emblems and insignia of kingship, as a crown, scepter, etc. 2. the insignia or decorations of any rank, society, etc. 3. splendid clothes; finery.

**re·gard** (ri-gärd′), ***n.*** [Fr. < *regarder;* see RE- & GUARD], 1. a firm, fixed look; gaze. 2. consideration; concern: as, have *regard* for your health. 3. respect and affection; esteem: as, he has high *regard* for teachers. 4. reference; relation: as, in *regard* to your question. 5. *pl.* good wishes; respects: as, give my *regards* to Bill. ***v.t.*** 1. to look at with a firm, steady gaze. 2. to take into account; consider. 3. to give attentive heed or respect to. 4. to hold in affection and respect. 5. to consider in a certain light: as, I *regard* this as a bother. 6. to have relation to; concern: as, this *regards* your welfare. ***v.i.*** 1. to look; gaze. 2. to pay heed or attention. **—as regards,** concerning. **—without regard to,** not taking into account.

**re·gard·ful** (ri-gärd′fəl), ***adj.*** 1. observant; heedful; mindful (*of*). 2. showing regard; respectful. **—re·gard′ful·ly, *adv.* —re·gard′ful·ness, *n.***

**re·gard·ing** (ri-gär′diŋ), ***prep.*** in (or with) regard to; concerning; about.

**re·gard·less** (ri-gärd′lis), ***adj.*** without regard; heedless; careless (often with *of*). ***adv.*** [Colloq.], without regard for objections, difficulties, etc. **—re·gard′less·ly, *adv.* —re·gard′less·ness, *n.***

**re·gat·ta** (ri-gat′ə), ***n.*** [It.], 1. a boat race. 2. a series of boat races.

**re·gen·cy** (rē′jən-si), ***n.*** [*pl.* -CIES], 1. the position, function, or authority of a regent or group of regents. 2. a group of regents governing a country. 3. a country so governed. 4. the time during which a regent or regency governs.

**re·gen·er·ate** (ri-jen′ēr-it; *for v.,* -ə-rāt′), ***adj.*** [< L.; see RE- & GENERATE], 1. spiritually reborn. 2. renewed; restored; reformed. ***v.t.*** [-ATED, -ATING], 1. to cause to be spiritually reborn, as by a religious conversion. 2. to cause to be completely reformed or improved. 3. to bring into existence again; reestablish. 4. in *electricity & radio,* to amplify by feeding energy back from the output into the input circuit. 5. in *biology,* to grow (a part) anew, as a replacement for one hurt or lost. ***v.i.*** 1. to form again; be made anew. 2. to be regenerated. **—re·gen′er·a·cy, *n.* —re·gen′er·a′tion, *n.* —re·gen′er·a′tive, *adj.* —re·gen′er·a′tive·ly, *adv.* —re·gen′er·a′tor, *n.***

**re·gent** (rē′jənt), ***adj.*** [< Fr. < L. ppr. of *regere,* to rule], acting in place of a king or ruler: as, prince *regent.* ***n.*** 1. a person appointed to rule while a king, etc. is absent, too young, or incapacitated. 2. a member of a governing board, as of a university. **—re′gent·ship′, *n.***

**reg·i·cide** (rej′ə-sīd′), ***n.*** [< L. *rex,* a king; + *-cide*], 1. one who kills a king. 2. the killing of a king. **—reg′i·cid′al, *adj.***

**re·gime, ré·gime** (ri-zhēm′, rā-), ***n.*** [< Fr. < L. *regimen;* see REGIMEN], 1. a political or ruling system. 2. a social system. 3. a regimen.

**reg·i·men** (rej′ə-men′, -mən), ***n.*** [L., rule < *regere,* to rule], a regulated system of diet, exercise, rest, etc. for promoting the health.

**reg·i·ment** (rej′ə-mənt; *for v.,* -ment′), ***n.*** [< Fr. <OFr. < LL. *regimentum,* government < L. *regere,* to rule], 1. a military unit, now usually consisting of three battalions: it is the basic component of a division. 2. a large number (of persons, etc.). ***v.t.*** 1. to form into regiments. 2. to assign to a regiment. 3. to organize systematically, as into uniform groups. 4. to organize and subject to strict discipline and conformity. **—reg′i·men′tal, *adj.* —reg′i·men·ta′tion, *n.***

**reg·i·men·tals** (rej′ə-men′t'lz), ***n.pl.*** 1. a regiment's uniform and insignia. 2. military uniform.

**Re·gi·na** (ri-jī′nə), ***n.*** the capital of Saskatchewan, Canada: pop., 71,000.

**re·gion** (rē′jən), ***n.*** [< OFr. < L. *regio* < *regere,* to rule], 1. a large and indefinite part of the surface of the earth. 2. an area; place; space. 3. a sphere; realm, as of art. 4. a division or part of an organism: as, the abdominal *region.*

**re·gion·al** (rē′jən-'l), ***adj.*** 1. of a whole region, not just a locality. 2. of some particular region, district, etc. **—re′gion·al·ly, *adv.***

**reg·is·ter** (rej′is-tēr), ***n.*** [< OFr. < ML. *registrum* < LL. < L. pp. of *regerere,* to record], 1. *a*) a record or list of names, events, items, etc. *b*) a book in which this is kept. 2. an entry in such a record. 3. a registration; registry. 4. a device for recording; meter or counter: as, a cash *register.* 5. an opening into a room by which the amount of air passing, as from a furnace, can be controlled. 6. in *music,* the range or compass of a voice or instrument, or a specific portion of this: as, head *register.* 7. in *printing,* exact placing of lines, pages, colors, etc. ***v.t.*** 1. to enter in a record or list; enroll. 2. to indicate as on a scale: as, the thermometer *registers* 50°. 3. to show, as by facial expression: as, to *register* surprise. 4. to safeguard (mail) by having its committal to the postal system recorded, for a fee. 5. in *printing,* to cause to be in register. ***v.i.*** 1. to enter one's name, as in a hotel register, a list of eligible voters, etc. 2. [Colloq.], to make an impression. **—reg′is·tra·ble** (-trə-b'l), ***adj.* —reg′is·trant, *n.***

**reg·is·tered** (rej′is-tērd), ***adj.*** 1. officially recorded or enrolled. 2. legally certified or authenticated: as, a *registered* nurse.

**reg·is·trar** (rej′i-strär′, rej′i-strär′), ***n.*** a person charged with keeping a register; esp., one responsible for the records in a college, court, etc.

**reg·is·tra·tion** (rej′i-strā′shən), ***n.*** 1. a registering or being registered. 2. an entry in a register. 3. the number of persons registered. **—reg′is·tra′tion·al, *adj.***

**reg·is·try** (rej′is-tri), ***n.*** [*pl.* -TRIES], 1. registration. 2. an office where registers are kept. 3. a register.

**reg·nant** (reg′nənt), ***adj.*** [< L. ppr. of *regnare,* to reign], 1. reigning; ruling. 2. predominant. 3. prevalent; widespread. **—reg′nan·cy, *n.***

**re·gorge** (ri-gôrj′), ***v.t.*** [-GORGED, -GORGING], [< Fr.; see RE- & GORGE, *v.*], to throw up or back; vomit.

**re·gress** (rē′gres; *for v.,* ri-gres′), ***n.*** [< L. *regressus,* pp. < *re-,* back + *gradi,* to go], 1. a going or coming back. 2. backward movement; retrogression. ***v.i.*** to go back; move backward. **—re·gres′sion, *n.* —re·gres′sive, *adj.* —re·gres′sive·ly, *adv.* —re·gres′sor, *n.***

**re·gret** (ri-gret′), ***v.t.*** [-GRETTED, -GRETTING], [< OFr. *regreter,* to mourn], 1. to mourn for (a person or thing gone, lost, etc.). 2. to feel sorrow or remorse over (an occurrence, one's acts, etc.). ***n.*** 1. sorrow or remorse, especially over one's acts or omissions. 2. sorrow over a person or thing gone, lost, etc. **—regrets,** a polite expression of regret, as at declining an invitation. **—re·gret′ful, *adj.* —re·gret′ful·ly, *adv.* —re·gret′ful·ness, *n.* —re·gret′ta·ble, *adj.* —re·gret′ta·bly, *adv.* —re·gret′ter, *n.***

**re·group** (rē-grōōp′), ***v.t. & v.i.*** to group again; specif., in *military usage,* to reorganize (one's forces), as after a battle.

**reg·u·lar** (reg′yoo-lēr), ***adj.*** [< OFr. < L. < *regula;* see RULE], 1. conforming in form or arrangement to a rule, principle, type, etc.; orderly; symmetrical. 2. characterized by conformity to a fixed principle or procedure. 3. usual; customary. 4. consistent or habitual: as, a *regular* customer. 5. unchanging; uniform: as, a *regular* pulse. 6. conforming to a generally accepted rule of conduct; proper. 7. properly qualified: as, a *regular* doctor. 8. [Colloq.], thorough; complete: as, a *regular* nuisance. 9. [Colloq.], pleasant, amiable, etc. 10. in *botany,* having all similar parts of the same shape and size: said of flowers. 11. in *ecclesiastical usage*, being of a religious order, etc. and adhering to its rule. 12. in *grammar*, conforming to the usual type as in inflection: said mainly of verbs. 13. in *international law*, designating soldiers recognized as legitimate combatants in warfare. 14. in *mathematics*, having all angles and sides equal, as a polygon, or all faces equal, as a polyhedron. 15. in *military usage*, designating or of the standing army of a country. 16. in *politics*, designating, of, or loyal to the party leadership, candidates, etc. ***n.*** 1. one of the regular clergy. 2. a regular soldier. 3. in *politics*, one who is loyal to the party leadership, candidates, etc. **—reg'u·lar'i·ty** (-lar'ə-ti), [*pl.* -TIES], ***n.*** **—reg'u·lar·ize'** [-IZED, -IZING], ***v.t.*** **—reg'u·lar·ly,** ***adv.***

**reg·u·late** (reg'yoo-lāt'), ***v.t.*** [-LATED, -LATING], [< L. pp. < *regula;* see RULE], 1. to control or direct according to a rule, principle, etc. 2. to adjust to a standard, rate, degree, etc.: as, *regulate* the heat. 3. to adjust so as to make operate accurately, as a clock. 4. to make uniform, methodical, etc. **—reg'u·la·ble** (-lə-b'l), ***adj.*** **—reg'u·la'tive,** ***adj.*** **—reg'u·la·to'ry** (-lə-tôr'i, -tō'ri), ***adj.***

**reg·u·la·tion** (reg'yoo-lā'shən), ***n.*** 1. a regulating or being regulated. 2. a rule or law by which conduct, etc. is regulated. ***adj.*** 1. required by regulation: as, a *regulation* uniform. 2. usual; normal.

**reg·u·la·tor** (reg'yoo-lā'tẽr), ***n.*** a person or thing that regulates; specif., *a*) a mechanism for controlling the movement of machinery, etc.; governor. *b*) the device in a watch or clock by which its speed is adjusted.

**re·gur·gi·tate** (rē-gũr'jə-tāt'), ***v.i. & v.t.*** [-TATED, -TATING], [< ML. pp. < *re-*, back + LL. *gurgitare*, to surge], to surge or flow back or cause to do this; specif., to bring (partly digested food) from the stomach back to the mouth. **—re·gur'gi·tant,** ***adj.*** **—re·gur'gi·ta'tion,** ***n.***

**re·ha·bil·i·tate** (rē'hə-bil'ə-tāt', rē'ə-), ***v.t.*** [-TATED, -TATING], [< ML.; see RE- & HABILITATE], 1. to restore to rank, privileges, reputation, etc. which one has lost. 2. to put back in good condition. 3. to restore (a defective, criminal, etc.) to a healthy, working state by training, etc. **—re'ha·bil'i·ta'tion,** ***n.***

**re·hash** (rē-hash'; *for n.*, rē'hash'), ***v.t.*** [*re-* + *hash*], to work up again, as old materials for publication, or go over again, as old, familiar arguments. ***n.*** 1. a rehashing. 2. a thing rehashed.

**re·hears·al** (ri-hũr's'l), ***n.*** 1. a rehearsing. 2. a practice performance of a play, concert, etc.

**re·hearse** (ri-hũrs'), ***v.t.*** [-HEARSED, -HEARSING], [< OFr. < *re-*, again + *herser*, to harrow < *herse*, a harrow], 1. to repeat aloud as heard or read; recite. 2. to tell in detail. 3. to perform for practice, as a play, etc., in preparation for a public performance. 4. to drill (a person) in what he is to do. ***v.i.*** to rehearse a play, etc. **—re·hears'er,** ***n.***

**Reich** (rīk; G. rīH), ***n.*** [G.], formerly, Germany or the German government.

**reichs·mark** (rīks'märk'; G. rīHs'-), ***n.*** [*pl.* -MARKS, -MARK], [G.], the former monetary unit of Germany: see **mark.**

**Reichs·tag** (rīks'täg'; G. rīHs'täkh'), ***n.*** [G.], formerly, the legislative assembly of Germany.

**reign** (rān), ***n.*** [< OFr. < L. *regnum* < *regere*, to rule], 1. royal power or rule. 2. dominance; prevalence: as, the *reign* of fashion. 3. the period of a sovereign's rule. ***v.i.*** 1. to rule as a king or queen. 2. to prevail: as, peace *reigns.*

**Reign of Terror,** the period of the French Revolution from 1793 to 1794, during which many persons were executed.

**re·im·burse** (rē'im-bũrs'), ***v.t.*** [-BURSED, -BURSING], [*re-* + archaic *imburse*, after Fr. *rembourser*], 1. to pay back (money spent). 2. to compensate (a person) for money spent, time lost, damages, etc. **—re'im·burse'ment,** ***n.*** **—re'im·burs'er,** ***n.***

**re·im·port** (rē'im-pôrt', -pōrt'; *for n.*, rē-im'pôrt, -pōrt), ***v.t.*** to import again; esp., to import as finished products (goods previously exported as raw materials). ***n.*** 1. a reimporting. 2. something reimported. Also **re'im·por·ta'tion,** ***n.***

**Reims** (rēmz; Fr. rans), ***n.*** a city in N France: pop., 134,000: also sp. **Rheims.**

**rein** (rān), ***n.*** [< OFr. *resne* < LL. < L. *retinere;* see RETAIN], 1. *usually in pl.* a narrow strap of leather attached to each end of a horse's bit and held by the rider or driver to control the animal. 2. *pl.* a means of guiding, controlling, etc.: as, the *reins* of government. ***v.t.*** 1. to put reins on. 2. to guide or control as with reins. ***v.i.*** to stop or slow down by using the reins (with *in* or *up*). **—draw rein,** to slacken speed; stop: also **draw in the reins.** **—give (free) rein to,** to allow to act without restraint.

**re·in·car·nate** (rē'in-kär'nāt), ***v.t.*** [-NATED, -NATING], to incarnate again; give another or different body to (a soul or spirit).

**re·in·car·na·tion** (rē'in-kär-nā'shən), ***n.*** 1. rebirth (of the soul) in another body. 2. a new incarnation. 3. the doctrine that the soul reappears after death in another and different bodily form.

**rein·deer** (rān'dêr'), ***n.*** [*pl.* -DEER; *occas.*, -DEERS], [< ON. < *hreinn*, reindeer + *dȳr*, deer], a large deer with branching antlers, found in northern regions, and domesticated there as beasts of burden and as a source of milk, meat, etc.

**re·in·force** (rē'in-fôrs', -fōrs'), ***v.t.*** [-FORCED, -FORCING], [*re-* + var. of *enforce*], 1. to strengthen (a military or naval force) by sending new troops or ships. 2. to strengthen, as by propping, adding new material, etc.: as, to *reinforce* an argument. Also sp. **re-enforce, reënforce.** **—re'in·forc'er,** ***n.***

**reinforced concrete,** concrete masonry containing steel bars or mesh to increase its strength.

**re·in·force·ment** (rē'in-fôrs'mənt, -fōrs'-), ***n.*** 1. a reinforcing or being reinforced. 2. anything that reinforces; specif., *pl.* additional troops, ships, etc. to reinforce those already sent.

**re·in·state** (rē'in-stāt'), ***v.t.*** [-STATED, -STATING], to instate again; restore to a former condition, position, etc. **—re'in·state'ment,** ***n.***

**reis** (rās), ***n.pl.*** [*sing.* REAL (re-äl')], [Port.], a former Portuguese and Brazilian money of account.

**re·it·er·ate** (rē-it'ə-rāt'), ***v.t.*** [-ATED, -ATING], [< L. pp. < *re-*, again + *itare*, to repeat < *iterum*, again], to say or do again or repeatedly. **—re·it'er·a'tion,** ***n.*** **—re·it'er·a'tive,** ***adj.*** **—re·it'er·a'tive·ly,** ***adv.***

**re·ject** (ri-jekt'; *for n.*, rē'jekt), ***v.t.*** [< L. pp. < *re-*, back + *jacere*, to throw], 1. to refuse to take, agree to, use, believe, etc. 2. to discard; throw away as worthless. 3. to vomit. 4. to rebuff. ***n.*** something rejected. **—re·ject'a·ble,** ***adj.*** **—re·ject'er,** ***n.*** **—re·ject'ing·ly,** ***adv.*** **—re·jec'tion,** ***n.***

**re·joice** (ri-jois'), ***v.i.*** [-JOICED, -JOICING], [< OFr. < *re-* + *ĕjouir* (< L. *ex-*, out + *gaudere*, to rejoice)], to be glad or happy (often with *at* or *in*). ***v.t.*** to make glad; delight. **—re·joic'er,** ***n.*** **—re·joic'ing,** ***n.*** **—re·joic'ing·ly,** ***adv.***

**re·join** (rē-join'), ***v.t.*** [prob. *re-* + *join*], 1. to come into the company of again: as, I will *rejoin* you soon. 2. to join together again; reunite. ***v.i.*** to become joined together again.

**re·join** (rē-join'), ***v.t.*** [prob. < Anglo-Fr.; see RE- & JOIN], to say in answer. ***v.i.*** to answer.

**re·join·der** (ri-join'dẽr), ***n.*** [< Anglo-Fr.; noun use of Fr. *rejoindre*, to rejoin], 1. *a*) an answer to a reply. *b*) any answer. 2. in *law*, the defendant's answer to the plaintiff's replication.

**re·ju·ve·nate** (ri-jōō'və-nāt'), ***v.t.*** [-NATED, -NATING], [< *re-* + L. *juvenis*, young], to make young again; bring back to youthful strength, appearance, etc.: also **re·ju've·nize'** [-NIZED, -NIZING]. **—re·ju've·na'tion,** ***n.*** **—re·ju've·na'tor,** ***n.***

**re·lapse** (ri-laps'), ***v.i.*** [-LAPSED, -LAPSING], [< L. pp. of *relabi*, to slip back; see RE- & LAPSE], to slip back into a former condition, especially after improvement or seeming improvement. ***n.*** 1. a relapsing. 2. the recurrence of a disease after apparent recovery. **—re·laps'er,** ***n.***

**re·late** (ri-lāt'), ***v.t.*** [-LATED, -LATING], [< Fr. < L. *relatus*, pp. of *referre*, to bring back; see REFER], 1. to tell the story of; narrate. 2. to connect, as in thought or meaning; show a relation between: as, *relate* theory and practice. ***v.i.*** 1. to have some connection (*to*). 2. to have reference (*to*). **—re·lat'or, re·lat'er,** ***n.***

**re·lat·ed** (ri-lāt'id), ***adj.*** 1. narrated; told. 2. connected; associated. 3. connected by origin, kinship, marriage, etc. **—re·lat'ed·ness,** ***n.***

**re·la·tion** (ri-lā'shən), ***n.*** [< OFr. < L.; see RELATE], 1. a narrating, telling, etc. 2. what is narrated; recital. 3. connection, as in thought, meaning, etc.: as, the *relation* of theory and practice. 4. the connection of persons by origin or marriage; kinship. 5. a person as so connected with others; relative. 6. *pl.* the connections between or among persons, groups, nations, etc.: as, trade *relations.* **—in (or with) relation to,** concerning; regarding; with reference to. **—re·la'tion·al,** ***adj.***

**re·la·tion·ship** (ri-lā'shən-ship'), ***n.*** 1. a being related. 2. connection by origin or marriage; kinship.

**rel·a·tive** (rel'ə-tiv), ***adj.*** 1. related each to the other; referring to each other. 2. having to do with; relevant. 3. regarded in relation to something else; comparative. 4. meaningful only in relationship: as, "cold" is a *relative* term. 5. in *grammar*, *a*) designating a word that introduces a subordinate clause and refers to an antecedent: as, *which* is a *relative* pronoun in "the hat which you bought." *b*) introduced by such a word: as, a *relative* clause. *n.* 1. a relative word or thing. 2. a person connected by origin or marriage. —**relative to,** 1. concerning; about. 2. corresponding to; in proportion to. —**rel′a·tive·ness,** *n.*

**rel·a·tive·ly** (rel′ə-tiv-li), *adv.* 1. in a relative manner; in relation to or compared with something else: as, a *relatively* unimportant matter. 2. in relation or proportion (*to*).

**rel·a·tiv·i·ty** (rel′ə-tiv′ə-ti), *n.* 1. a being relative. 2. in *physics*, the fact, principle, or theory of the relative, rather than absolute, character of motion, velocity, mass, etc., and the interdependence of matter, time, and space: as developed especially by Albert Einstein in two separate theories, the theory includes the statements that: 1) motion is relative, not absolute; 2) the velocity of light is constant; 3) the mass of a body in motion varies with the velocity; 4) space and time are interdependent and form a four-dimensional continuum.

**re·lax** (ri-laks′), *v.t. & v.i.* [< L. < *re-*, back + *laxare*, to loosen < *laxus*, loose], 1. to make or become looser, or less firm, stiff, or tense. 2. to make or become less strict, severe, or intense, as discipline, effort, etc. 3. to rest, as from work or application. —**re·laxed′,** *adj.* —**re·lax′ed·ly** (-lak′-sid-li), *adv.* —**re·lax′er,** *n.*

**re·lax·a·tion** (rē′lak-sā′shən), *n.* 1. a relaxing or being relaxed; a loosening, lessening of severity, etc. 2. a lessening of or rest from work or effort. 3. recreation; amusement.

**re·lay** (rē′lā; *also, and for v. usually,* ri-lā′), *n.* [OFr. *relais, pl.*, orig., relays of hunting hounds < *re-*, back + *laier*, to leave], 1. a fresh supply of horses, etc. ready to relieve others, as for a stage of a journey. 2. a crew of workers relieving others; shift. 3. in *electricity*, a device by means of which a variation in conditions of an electric circuit causes a change in conditions of another circuit or operates another device in either circuit: used in telegraphy, etc. 4. in *sports*, a relay race, or any lap of it. *v.t.* [-LAYED, -LAYING], 1. to convey by or as if by relays: as, to *relay* news. 2. in *electricity*, to control, operate, or send on by a relay.

**re-lay** (rē′lā′), *v.t.* [-LAID, -LAYING], to lay again or anew: also written **relay.**

**relay race,** a race between teams, each member of which goes a certain part of the distance.

**re·lease** (ri-lēs′), *v.t.* [-LEASED, -LEASING], [< OFr. < *re-*, again + *laisser*, to leave < L. *laxare;* see RELAX], 1. to set free, as from prison, work, an obligation, suffering, etc. 2. to let go, as a missile, something caught or snagged, etc. 3. to permit to be issued, published, etc. 4. in *law*, to give up to someone else (a claim, right, etc.). *n.* 1. a freeing or being freed, as from prison, work, an obligation, etc. 2. a written discharge, as from prison. 3. a letting go of something caught or held. 4. a device used to release some other device, as on a machine. 5. *a*) a releasing to the public, as of a book, news, etc. *b*) the book, news, etc. released. 6. in *law*, *a*) a giving up of a claim or right. *b*) the document by which this is done. —**re·leas′a·ble,** *adj.* —**re·leas′er,** *n.*

**re-lease** (rē′lēs′), *v.t.* [-LEASED, -LEASING], to lease again.

**rel·e·gate** (rel′ə-gāt′), *v.t.* [-GATED, -GATING], [< L. *relegatus*, pp. < *re-*, away + *legare*, to send], 1. to exile; banish (*to*). 2. to consign or assign to an inferior position. 3. to assign to a class, sphere, realm, etc. 4. to refer, commit, or hand over for decision, as to a person. —**rel′e·ga·ble** (-gə-b'l), *adj.* —**rel′e·ga′tion,** *n.*

**re·lent** (ri-lent′), *v.i.* [< L. *relentescere*, to become soft < *re-*, again + *lentus*, pliant], to soften in temper, resolution, etc.; become less severe, stern, or stubborn. —**re·lent′ing·ly,** *adv.*

**re·lent·less** (ri-lent′lis), *adj.* 1. not relenting; harsh; pitiless. 2. persistent; unremitting. —**re·lent′less·ly,** *adv.* —**re·lent′less·ness,** *n.*

**rel·e·vant** (rel′ə-vənt), *adj.* [< ML. ppr. of *relevare;* see RELIEVE], bearing upon or relating to the matter in hand; pertinent. —**rel′e·vance, rel′e·van·cy,** *n.* —**rel′e·vant·ly,** *adv.*

**re·li·a·ble** (ri-lī′ə-b'l), *adj.* that can be relied on; dependable. —**re·li′a·bil′i·ty, re·li′a·ble·ness,** *n.* —**re·li′a·bly,** *adv.*

**re·li·ance** (ri-lī′əns), *n.* 1. a relying. 2. trust, dependence, or confidence. 3. what is relied on.

**re·li·ant** (ri-lī′ənt), *adj.* 1. having or showing trust, dependence, or confidence. 2. self-reliant.

**rel·ic** (rel′ik), *n.* [< OFr. < L. *reliquiae, pl.* < *relinquere;* see RELINQUISH], 1. an object, custom, etc. that has survived from the past. 2. a keepsake or souvenir. 3. *pl.* remaining fragments; ruins. 4. bodily remains of a saint, martyr, etc., or an object associated with him, reverenced as a memorial.

**rel·ict** (rel′ikt), *n.* [L. *relicta*, fem. pp. of *relinquere;* see RELINQUISH], [Rare], a widow.

**re·lief** (ri-lēf′), *n.* [< OFr. *relever;* see RELIEVE], 1. an easing, as of pain, anxiety, a burden, etc. 2. anything that eases tension, or offers a pleasing change. 3. aid in the form of goods or money given, as by a public agency, to the unemployed or needy. 4. any aid given in times of need or danger, as troops sent to replace tired forces. 5. *a*) release from work or duty. *b*) the person or persons bringing such release by taking over a post. 6. *a*) the projection of sculptured figures and forms from a flat surface, so that they stand wholly or partly free. *b*) a work of art so made. 7. *a*) the differences in height, collectively, of land forms in any particular area. *b*) these differences as shown by lines or colors on a map (**relief map**). 8. in *painting*, the apparent solidity or projection of objects. 9. distinctness of outline; contrast. —**in relief,** carved or molded so as to project from a surface.

**re·lieve** (ri-lēv′), *v.t.* [-LIEVED, -LIEVING], [< OFr. < L. < *re-*, again + *levare*, to raise < *levis*, light], 1. to ease; lighten; reduce, as pain, anxiety, etc. 2. to free from pain, distress, etc. 3. to give or bring aid or assistance to: as, to *relieve* a besieged city. 4. *a*) to set free from a burden, obligation, etc. *b*) to remove (a burden, etc.). 5. to set free from duty or work by replacing with another or oneself: as, she *relieved* the nurse. 6. to make less tedious, etc. by providing a pleasing change. 7. to set off by contrast; make distinct or prominent. 8. to ease (oneself) by passing bodily waste matter. —**re·liev′a·ble,** *adj.* —**re·liev′er,** *n.*

**re·li·gion** (ri-lij′ən), *n.* [< OFr. < L. *religio;* ? ult. < *re-*, back + *ligare*, to bind], 1. belief in a superhuman power or powers to be obeyed and worshiped as the creator(s) and ruler(s) of the universe. 2. expression of this belief in conduct and ritual. 3. any specific system of belief, worship, etc., often involving a code of ethics: as, the Christian *religion*. 4. a state of mind or way of life expressing love for and trust in God: as, he achieved *religion*. 5. any object of conscientious pursuit: as, cleanliness was a *religion* to him.

**re·lig·i·os·i·ty** (ri-lij′i-os′ə-ti), *n.* 1. a being extremely religious. 2. an affectation of this.

**re·li·gious** (ri-lij′əs), *adj.* 1. characterized by adherence to religion; pious. 2. of or concerned with religion: as, *religious* books. 3. of or belonging to a monastic order. 4. conscientiously exact; scrupulous: as, he worked with *religious* care. *n.* [*pl.* RELIGIOUS], a person belonging to a monastic order. —**re·li′gious·ly,** *adv.* —**re·li′gious·ness,** *n.*

**re·lin·quish** (ri-liŋ′kwish), *v.t.* [< OFr. < L. < *re-*, from + *linquere*, to leave], 1. to give up, as a plan, policy, etc. 2. to surrender (property, a right, etc.). 3. to release (one's grasp, etc). —**re·lin′quish·er,** *n.* —**re·lin′quish·ment,** *n.*

**rel·i·quar·y** (rel′ə-kwer′i), *n.* [*pl.* -IES], [< Fr. < L.; see RELIC], a small box, casket, etc. in which a relic or relics are kept and shown.

**rel·ique** (rel′ik, ri-lēk′), *n.* [Archaic], a relic.

**rel·ish** (rel′ish), *n.* [< OFr. *reles*, something remaining < *relaisser;* see RELEASE], 1. *a*) a flavor; taste. *b*) characteristic flavor. 2. a trace (of some quality). 3. an appetizing flavor; pleasing taste. 4. enjoyment; zest: as, he eats with *relish*. 5. anything that gives pleasure, zest, etc. 6. pickles, chutney, etc. served with meat, etc. to make it more appetizing. *v.t.* 1. to give flavor to. 2. to like; enjoy. *v.i.* 1. to have the flavor (*of* something). 2. to have a pleasing taste. 3. to please. —**rel′ish·a·ble,** *adj.* —**rel′ish·ing·ly,** *adv.*

**re·luc·tance** (ri-luk′t'ns), *n.* 1. a being reluctant; a not wanting to do or agree to something. 2. in *electricity*, resistance to the passage of magnetic lines of force. Also **re·luc′tan·cy.**

**re·luc·tant** (ri-luk′t'nt), *adj.* [< L. *reluctans*, ppr. < *re-*, against + *luctari*, to struggle], 1. unwilling; disinclined. 2. marked by unwillingness: as, a *reluctant* answer. —**re·luc′tant·ly,** *adv.*

**re·ly** (ri-lī′), *v.i.* [-LIED, -LYING], [< OFr. < L. *religare;* see RELIGION], to trust; depend; have confidence (with *on* or *upon*).

**re·main** (ri-mān′), *v.i.* [< OFr. < L. < *re-*, back + *manere*, to stay], 1. to be left over when the rest has been taken away, destroyed, etc. 2. to stay on as while others go: as, he *remained* at home. 3. to go on being: as, he *remained* a cynic. 4. to continue to exist; persist: as, her hope *remains*. 5. to be left to be dealt with, done, etc.

**re·main·der** (ri-mān′dēr), *n.* 1. those remaining. 2. what is left when a part is taken away. 3. a copy or copies of a book still held by a publisher when the sale has fallen off. 4. in *mathematics*, what is left when a smaller number is subtracted from a larger. *adj.* left over.

**re·mains** (ri-mānz′), *n.pl.* 1. what is left after use, destruction, etc. 2. the dead body of a person. 3. surviving works, as of an ancient writer.

**re·make** (rē-māk′; *for n.*, rē′māk′), *v.t.* [-MADE, -MAKING], to make again or anew. *n.* 1. a remaking. 2. something remade, as a motion picture.

**re·mand** (ri-mand′), *v.t.* [< OFr.; ult. < L. *re-*, back + *mandare*, to order], 1. to send back. 2. in *law*, to send (a prisoner or accused person) back to jail, as to investigate the charges against him further. *n.* 1. a remanding or being remanded. 2. a person remanded. **—re·mand′ment,** *n.*

**re·mark** (ri-märk′), *v.t.* [Fr. *remarquer;* see RE- & MARK, *v.*], 1. to notice; observe; perceive. 2. to comment; say or write as an observation. *v.i.* to make an observation or comment (with *on* or *upon*). *n.* 1. a noticing or observing: as, a person worthy of *remark*. 2. a brief comment; casual observation.

**re·mark·a·ble** (ri-mär′kə-b'l), *adj.* 1. worthy of remark; noticeable. 2. unusual; extraordinary. **—re·mark′a·ble·ness,** *n.* **—re·mark′a·bly,** *adv.*

**Rem·brandt** (rem′bränt; Eng. rem′brant), *n.* (*Rembrandt Harmenszoon van Rijn* or *Ryn*), Dutch painter and etcher; lived 1606–1669.

**rem·e·di·a·ble** (ri-mē′di-ə-b'l), *adj.* that can be remedied. **—re·me′di·a·bly,** *adv.*

**re·me·di·al** (ri-mē′di-əl), *adj.* providing, or intended to provide, a remedy. **—re·me′di·al·ly,** *adv.*

**rem·e·dy** (rem′ə-di), *n.* [*pl.* -DIES], [< OFr. < L. *remedium* < *re-*, again + *mederi*, to heal], 1. any medicine or treatment that cures, heals, or relieves a disease, deadens pain, etc. 2. something that corrects or counteracts an evil or wrong; relief. 3. legal means by which violation of a right is prevented or compensated for. *v.t.* [-DIED, -DYING], to act as a remedy for; cure, correct, counteract, etc. **—rem′e·di·less,** *adj.*

**re·mem·ber** (ri-mem′bēr), *v.t.* [< OFr. < LL. < L. *re-*, again + *memorare*, to bring to mind < *memor*, mindful], 1. to have (an event, thing, person, etc.) come to mind again; think of again. 2. to bring back to mind by an effort; recall. 3. to bear in mind; be careful not to forget. 4. to keep (a person) in mind for a present, legacy, etc. 5. to mention (a person) to another as sending regards: as, *remember* me to her. *v.i.* 1. to bear in mind or call back to mind. 2. to have memory. **—re·mem′ber·a·ble,** *adj.* **—re·mem′ber·er,** *n.*

**re·mem·brance** (ri-mem′brəns), *n.* 1. a remembering or being remembered. 2. the power to remember. 3. the extent of time over which one can remember. 4. a souvenir; keepsake. 5. *pl.* greetings.

**re·mind** (ri-mīnd′), *v.t. & v.i.* [*re-* + *mind*, *v.*], to put (a person) in mind (*of* something); cause to remember. **—re·mind′er,** *n.* **—re·mind′ful,** *adj.*

**rem·i·nisce** (rem′ə-nis′), *v.i.* [-NISCED, -NISCING], [< *reminiscence*], 1. to call past events to mind. 2. to talk or write about remembered events.

**rem·i·nis·cence** (rem′ə-nis′'ns), *n.* [Fr. < L. ppr. of *reminisci* < *re-*, again + *memini*, to remember], 1. a remembering. 2. memory; recollection. 3. *pl.* an account, written or spoken, of remembered events. **—rem′i·nis′cent,** *adj.* **—rem′i·nis′cent·ly,** *adv.*

**re·miss** (ri-mis′), *adj.* [see REMIT], 1. careless or negligent at work; irresponsible. 2. showing carelessness or negligence. **—re·miss′ness,** *n.*

**re·mis·si·ble** (ri-mis′ə-b'l), *adj.* that can be remitted. **—re·mis′si·bil′i·ty,** *n.*

**re·mis·sion** (ri-mish′ən), *n.* [see REMIT], 1. pardon; forgiveness, as of sins. 2. release from a debt, tax, etc. 3. an abating, as of heat or pain.

**re·mit** (ri-mit′), *v.t.* [-MITTED, -MITTING], [< L. *remittere* (pp. *remissus*) < *re-*, back + *mittere*, to send], 1. to forgive or pardon (sins, etc.). 2. to refrain from exacting (a payment, tax, etc.), inflicting (a punishment), or enforcing (a sentence). 3. to let slacken, as effort. 4. to submit or refer (a matter) for consideration or action. 5. to send or pay (money). 6. [Rare], to send back to jail. 7. to send back (a case) to a lower court for further action. *v.i.* 1. to slacken. 2. to send money, as in payment for goods. **—re·mit′ta·ble,** *adj.* **—re·mit′tal,** *n.* **—re·mit′ter,** *n.*

**re·mit·tance** (ri-mit′'ns), *n.* 1. the sending of money, as by mail. 2. the money sent.

**re·mit·tent** (ri-mit′'nt), *adj.* remitting; slackening for a while or at intervals, as a fever. **—re·mit′tent·ly,** *adv.*

**rem·nant** (rem′nənt), *n.* [< OFr. ppr. of *remaindre;* see REMAIN], 1. what is left over. 2. a small remaining part or quantity. 3. a piece of cloth, ribbon, etc. left over, as at the end of a bolt.

**re·mod·el** (rē-mod′'l), *v.t.* [-ELED or -ELLED, -ELING or -ELLING], 1. to model again. 2. to make over; rebuild. **—re·mod′el·er,** *n.*

**re·mon·e·tize** (rē-mon′ə-tīz′, -mun′-), *v.t.* [-TIZED, -TIZING], to reinstate (silver, etc.) as legal tender. **—re·mon′e·ti·za′tion,** *n.*

**re·mon·strance** (ri-mon′strəns), *n.* a remonstrating; protest, complaint, or expostulation.

**re·mon·strant** (ri-mon′strənt), *adj.* remonstrating; expostulatory. *n.* one who remonstrates. **—re·mon′strant·ly,** *adv.*

**re·mon·strate** (ri-mon′strāt), *v.t.* [-STRATED, -STRATING], [< ML. pp. < L. *re-*, again + *monstrare*, to show], to say or plead in protest, objection, etc. *v.i.* to urge reasons in opposition or complaint; protest. **—re·mon·stra·tion** (rē′mon-strā′shən, rem′ən-), *n.* **—re·mon′stra·tive** (-strə-tiv), *adj.* **—re·mon′stra·tive·ly,** *adv.* **—re·mon′stra·tor,** *n.*

**re·morse** (ri-môrs′), *n.* [< OFr. < LL. < L. *remorsus*, pp. < *re-*, again + *mordere*, to bite], 1. a deep, torturing sense of guilt for one's actions; repentance. 2. pity: now only in *without remorse*, pitilessly. **—re·morse′ful,** *adj.* **—re·morse′ful·ly,** *adv.* **—re·morse′ful·ness,** *n.* **—re·morse′less,** *adj.* **—re·morse′less·ly,** *adv.* **—re·morse′less·ness,** *n.*

**re·mote** (ri-mōt′), *adj.* [< L. *remotus*, pp. of *removere*, to remove], 1. distant in space or time; far off. 2. far off and hidden; secluded. 3. distant in relation, connection, etc. (*from*): as, a question *remote* from the subject. 4. distantly related: as, a *remote* cousin. 5. distant in manner; aloof; withdrawn. 6. slight; faint: as, a *remote* chance. **—re·mote′ly,** *adv.* **—re·mote′ness,** *n.*

**remote control,** control of aircraft, missiles, etc. from a distance, as by radio waves.

**re·mount** (rē-mount′; *for n., usually* rē′mount′), *v.t. & v.i.* to mount again. *n.* a fresh horse to replace another.

**re·mov·a·ble** (ri-mōōv′ə-b'l), *adj.* that can be removed. **—re·mov′a·bil′i·ty, re·mov′a·ble·ness,** *n.* **—re·mov′a·bly,** *adv.*

**re·mov·al** (ri-mōōv′'l), *n.* a removing or being removed; esp., *a*) a taking away. *b*) dismissal, as from an office. *c*) a change of residence, etc.

**re·move** (ri-mōōv′), *v.t.* [-MOVED, -MOVING], [< OFr. < L. *removere;* see RE- & MOVE], 1. to move (something) from where it is; take away. 2. to take off: as, *remove* your hat. 3. to dismiss, as from an office. 4. to wipe out; get rid of: as, *remove* the causes of war. 5. to kill. 6. to separate (*from*). *v.i.* 1. [Poetic], to go away. 2. to move away, as to another residence. *n.* 1. a removing. 2. the space or time in which a move is made. 3. a step; interval: as, but one *remove* from war. **—re·mov′er,** *n.*

**re·moved** (ri-mōōvd′), *adj.* 1. distant by (a specified number of degrees of relationship): as, one's cousin once *removed* is the child of one's first cousin. 2. remote; distant (with *from*).

**re·mu·ner·ate** (ri-mū′nə-rāt′), *v.t.* [-ATED, -ATING], [< L. pp. of *remunerari*, to reward < *re-*, again + *munus*, a gift], to pay (a person) for work done, loss incurred, etc.; reward. **—re·mu′ner·a′tion,** *n.* **—re·mu′ner·a′tive** (-nə-rā′tiv, -nēr-ə-tiv), *adj.* **—re·mu′ner·a′tive·ly,** *adv.* **—re·mu′ner·a′tor,** *n.*

**Re·mus** (rē′məs), *n.* [L.], see **Romulus.**

**ren·ais·sance** (ren′ə-säns′, -zäns′, ri-nā′s'ns), *n.* [Fr. < *re-*, again + *naître* (ult. < L. *nasci*), to be born], 1. a rebirth; revival. 2. [R-], *a*) the great revival of art, literature, and learning in Europe in the 14th, 15th, and 16th centuries. *b*) the period of this. *c*) the style of art, literature, etc. of this period. *d*) any similar revival. *adj.* [R-], of, or in the style of, the Renaissance.

**re·nal** (rē′n'l), *adj.* [< Fr. < L. *renalis* < *renes*, kidneys], of or near the kidneys.

**re·nas·cence** (ri-nas′'ns), *n.* 1. a rebirth; revival. 2. [R-], the Renaissance.

**re·nas·cent** (ri-nas′'nt), *adj.* [< L.; see RE- & NASCENT], being reborn; springing up again.

**rend** (rend), *v.t.* [RENT, RENDING], [AS. *rendan*], 1. to tear or pull with violence (with *from, off*, etc.). 2. to tear apart or split with violence: often figurative, as, a roar *rends* the air. *v.i.* to tear; split apart. **—rend′er,** *n.*

**rend·er** (ren′dẽr), ***v.t.*** [<Anglo-Fr. < OFr.; ult. < L. < *re(d)*-, back + *dare*, to give], 1. to hand over, or submit, as for approval, consideration, etc.: as, *render* an account of your actions. 2. to surrender (often with *up*). 3. to give in return: as, *render* good for evil. 4. to give back; restore (often with *back*). 5. to give or pay as due: as, *render* thanks. 6. to cause to be; make: as, to *render* someone safe. 7. *a)* to give (aid, etc.). *b)* to do (a service, etc.). 8. to represent; depict. 9. to recite (a poem, etc.), play (music), act (a role), etc. 10. to translate. 11. to melt down; clarify, as lard. —**ren′der·a·ble,** ***adj.*** —**ren′der·er,** ***n.***

**ren·dez·vous** (rän′də-vōō′), ***n.*** [*pl.* -VOUS (-vōōz′)], [< Fr. *rendez vous*, betake yourself], 1. a place for a meeting, as of troops, ships, etc. 2. a place where people gather; meeting place. 3. *a)* an agreement to meet at a certain time or place. *b)* the meeting itself. ***v.i. & v.t.*** [-VOUSED (-vood′), -VOUSING], to assemble, as troops, at a certain time or place.

**ren·di·tion** (ren-dish′ən), ***n.*** a rendering or result of rendering; specif., *a)* a performance (of a piece of music, a role, etc.). *b)* a translation.

**ren·e·gade** (ren′ə-gād′), ***n.*** [< Sp. pp. of *renegar*, to deny; ult. < L. *re*-, again + *negare*, to deny], one who abandons his religion, party, principles, etc. to join the opposition; apostate; traitor.

**re·nege** (ri-nig′, -nēg′), ***v.i.*** [-NEGED, -NEGING], [ML. *renegare;* see RENEGADE], 1. in *card games*, to play a card of another suit, against the rules, when holding any of the suit called for. 2. [Colloq.], to go back on a promise. ***n.*** in *card games*, a failure to follow suit. —**re·neg′er,** ***n.***

**re·new** (ri-nōō′, -nū′), ***v.t.*** 1. to make new or as if new again; make fresh or strong again. 2. to cause to exist again; re-establish. 3. to begin again; resume. 4. to go over again; repeat: as, *renew* a promise. 5. to replace by something new of the same kind: as, *renew* provisions. 6. to give or get an extension of: as, *renew* a lease. ***v.i.*** 1. to become new again. 2. to begin again. —**re·new′a·ble,** ***adj.*** —**re·new′al,** ***n.*** —**re·new′ed·ly,** ***adv.***

**ren·i-,** [< L. *ren*], a combining form meaning *kidney, kidneys*, as in *reniform*: also **ren·o-.**

**ren·i·form** (ren′i-fôrm′, rē′ni-), ***adj.*** [see RENI- & FORM], shaped like a kidney.

**ren·net** (ren′it), ***n.*** [ME. <*rennen*, to run (dial., to curdle)], 1. the membrane that lines the fourth stomach of young ruminants, as a calf. 2. an extract of this membrane, used to curdle milk, as in making cheese. 3. a substance containing rennin.

**ren·nin** (ren′in), ***n.*** [*rennet* + *-in*], a milk-curdling enzyme in the gastric juice of the calf, etc.

**Re·no** (rē′nō), ***n.*** a city in W Nevada: pop., 51,000.

**Re·noir, Pierre Au·guste** (pyâr ô′güst′ rə-nwär′), 1841–1919; French painter.

**re·nounce** (ri-nouns′), ***v.t.*** [-NOUNCED, -NOUNCING], [< OFr. < L. < *re*-, back + *nuntiare*, to tell < *nuntius*, messenger], 1. to give up formally (a claim, right, etc.). 2. to give up, as a habit, practice, etc. 3. to cast off; disown, as a son. —**re·nounce′ment,** ***n.*** —**re·nounc′er,** ***n.***

**ren·o·vate** (ren′ə-vāt′), ***v.t.*** [-VATED, -VATING], [< L. pp. < *re*-, again + *novare*, to make new < *novus*, new], to make new or like new; clean up, repair, restore, etc. —**ren′o·va′tion,** ***n.*** —**ren′o·va′tor,** ***n.***

**re·nown** (ri-noun′), ***n.*** [< Anglo-Fr. < OFr. < *re*-, again + *nom(m)er*, to name < L. < *nomen*, a name], fame; great reputation. —**re·nowned′,** ***adj.***

**rent** (rent), ***n.*** [< OFr. < LL. hyp. form for L. *reddita (pecunia)*, paid (money)], 1. a stated payment at fixed intervals for the use of a house, land, etc. 2. in *economics*, income from the ownership of real estate. ***v.t.*** to get or give use of (a house, land, automobile, etc.) in return for stated payments at fixed intervals. ***v.i.*** to be let for rent: as, this house *rents* for $75. —**for rent,** available to be rented. —**rent′a·ble,** ***adj.*** —**rent′er,** ***n.***

**rent** (rent), pt. and pp. of **rend.** ***adj.*** torn or split.

**rent** (rent), ***n.*** [n. use of obs. var. of *rend*], 1. a hole or gap made by tearing or splitting. 2. a split in an organization; schism.

**rent·al** (ren′t'l), ***n.*** 1. an amount paid or received as rent. 2. a house, automobile, etc. for rent. ***adj.*** of, in, or for rent.

**re·nun·ci·a·tion** (ri-nun′si-ā′shən), ***n.*** [see RENOUNCE], a renouncing, as of a right, claim, etc. —**re·nun′ci·a·to′ry** (-ə-tôr′i, -tō′ri), ***adj.***

**re·or·der** (rē-ôr′dẽr), ***n.*** a repeated order for the same goods. ***v.t.*** 1. to order again. 2. to put in order again. ***v.i.*** to order goods again.

**re·or·gan·i·za·tion** (rē′ôr-gən-i-zā′shən), ***n.*** 1. a reorganizing or being reorganized. 2. a thorough reconstruction of a business corporation as effected after, or in anticipation of, a failure.

**re·or·gan·ize** (rē-ôr′gə-nīz′), ***v.t. & v.i.*** [-IZED, -IZING], to organize again or anew; effect a reorganization (of). —**re·or′gan·iz′er,** ***n.***

**rep** (rep), ***n.*** [Fr. *reps* < Eng. *ribs*], a ribbed fabric of silk, wool, rayon, etc.: also **repp.**

**Rep.,** 1. Representative. 2. Republican.

**re·paid** (ri-pād′), pt. and pp. of **repay.**

**re·pair** (ri-pâr′), ***v.t.*** [< OFr. < L. < *re*-, again + *parare*, to prepare], 1. to put back in good condition after damage, decay, etc.; fix. 2. to renew; restore, as one's health. 3. to set right; remedy, as a mistake. 4. to make amends for (a wrong, etc.). ***n.*** 1. a repairing. 2. *usually in pl.* an instance or result of repairing. 3. the state of being repaired: as, to keep a car in *repair*. 4. state with respect to repairing: as, in bad *repair*. —**re·pair′a·ble,** ***adj.*** —**re·pair′er,** ***n.***

**re·pair** (ri-pâr′), ***v.i.*** [< OFr. < LL. < L. *re*-, back + *patria*, one's native country], to go (*to* a place); betake oneself.

**re·pair·man** (ri-pâr′man′, -mən), ***n.*** [*pl.* -MEN], a man whose work is repairing things.

**rep·a·ra·ble** (rep′ẽr-ə-b'l), ***adj.*** that can be repaired, remedied, etc. —**rep′a·ra·bly,** ***adv.***

**rep·a·ra·tion** (rep′ə-rā′shən), ***n.*** [< OFr. < LL. < pp. of L. *reparare;* see REPAIR (to fix)], 1. a repairing or being repaired. 2. repairs. 3. a making up for a wrong or injury. 4. compensation; specif., *usually pl.*, compensation by a defeated nation for damage done in a war, payable in money, labor, etc. —**re·par·a·tive** (ri-par′ə-tiv), ***adj.***

**rep·ar·tee** (rep′ẽr-tē′, -är-). ***n.*** [< Fr. pp. of *repartir*, to reply < *re*-, back + *partir*, to part], 1. a quick, witty reply. 2. quick, witty conversation. 3. skill in making such replies.

**re·past** (ri-past′, -päst′), ***n.*** [OFr. < ML. < LL. < *re*-, again + *pascere*, to feed], food and drink; a meal.

**re·pa·tri·ate** (rē-pā′tri-āt′), ***v.t. & v.i.*** [-ATED, -ATING], [< LL. pp. < L. *re*-, back + *patria*, native land], to send back or return to the country of birth, citizenship, etc.: as, to *repatriate* prisoners of war. —**re·pa′tri·a′tion,** ***n.***

**re·pay** (ri-pā′), ***v.t.*** [-PAID, -PAYING], [OFr. *repaier*], 1. to pay back (money); refund. 2. to pay back (a person). 3. to make some return for: as, *repay* a kindness. 4. to make some return to (a person), as for some service. ***v.i.*** to pay back something or make some return. —**re·pay′a·ble,** ***adj.*** —**re·pay′er,** ***n.*** —**re·pay′ment,** ***n.***

**re·peal** (ri-pēl′), ***v.t.*** [< OFr. *rapeler;* see RE- & APPEAL], to revoke; cancel; annul: as, the law was *repealed*. ***n.*** revocation, abrogation, etc. —**re·peal′a·ble,** ***adj.*** —**re·peal′er,** ***n.***

**re·peat** (ri-pēt′), ***v.t.*** [< OFr. < L. < *re*-, again + *petere*, to seek], 1. to say or utter again. 2. to say over; recite, as a poem. 3. to say after someone else. 4. to tell to someone else: as, *repeat* a secret. 5. to do or make again: as, *repeat* an operation. 6. to say again what has been said before by (oneself): as, he *repeats* himself. ***v.i.*** 1. to say or do again what has been said or done before. 2. to vote more than once in an election. ***n.*** 1. a repeating. 2. anything said or done again. 3. in *music*, *a)* a passage to be repeated. *b)* the symbol indicating this. —**re·peat′a·ble,** ***adj.***

**re·peat·ed** (ri-pēt′id), ***adj.*** said, made, or done again, or again and again. —**re·peat′ed·ly,** ***adv.***

**re·peat·er** (ri-pēt′ẽr), ***n.*** 1. a person or thing that repeats. 2. a repeating rifle or pistol. 3. a person who fraudulently votes more than once in the same election. 4. a student who repeats a course or grade in school.

**repeating rifle** (or **pistol**), a rifle or pistol that can fire a number of shots without reloading.

**re·pel** (ri-pel′), ***v.t.*** [-PELLED, -PELLING], [< L. < *re*-, back + *pellere*, to drive], 1. to drive back; force back: as, *repel* an attack. 2. to refuse; reject; spurn, as advances or a suitor. 3. to cause dislike in; disgust: as, the odor *repels* me. 4. to be resistant to: as, the plastic *repels* moisture. 5. to fail to mix with: as, water *repels* oil. ***v.i.*** to cause distaste, dislike, etc. —**re·pel′ler,** ***n.***

**re·pel·lent** (ri-pel′ənt), ***adj.*** 1. repelling; driving back. 2. causing distaste, dislike, etc. 3. waterproof. ***n.*** something that repels, as a mosquito repellent. —**re·pel′lence, re·pel′len·cy,** ***n.***

**re·pent** (ri-pent′), ***v.i. & v.t.*** [< OFr. < L. *re*-, again + *poenitere*, to make repent < *poena*, punishment],

1. to feel sorry for (a past error, sin, omission, etc.). 2. to feel such regret over (some past action, intention, etc.) as to change one's mind. —**re·pent′er,** *n.*

**re·pent·ance** (ri-pen′təns), *n.* a repenting; feeling of sorrow, regret, etc., especially for wrongdoing; remorse. —**re·pent′ant,** *adj.* —**re·pent′ant·ly,** *adv.*

**re·peo·ple** (rē-pē′p'l), *v.t.* [-PLED, -PLING], to people anew; provide with new inhabitants.

**re·per·cus·sion** (rē′pēr-kush′ən), *n.* [< Fr. < L. pp.; see RE- & PERCUSSION], 1. a driving back or being driven back by something resistant; rebound. 2. reflection, as of sound; echo. 3. a reaction set in motion by an event or action: as, the war had *repercussions* around the world. —**re′per·cus′sive,** *adj.*

**rep·er·toire** (rep′ēr-twär′, -twôr′), *n.* [< Fr. < LL. *repertorium;* see REPERTORY], the stock of plays, operas, songs, etc. that a company, actor, singer, etc. is prepared to perform.

**rep·er·to·ry** (rep′ēr-tôr′i, -tō′ri), *n.* [*pl.* -RIES], [LL. *repertorium* < L. pp. of *reperire,* to discover], 1. a storehouse. 2. the things stored; stock. 3. a repertoire.

**rep·e·ti·tion** (rep′ə-tish′ən), *n.* [< Fr. < L. *repetitio*], 1. a repeating; a doing or saying again. 2. something repeated. —**re·pet·i·tive** (ri-pet′ə-tiv), *adj.* —**re·pet′i·tive·ly,** *adv.*

**rep·e·ti·tious** (rep′ə-tish′əs), *adj.* full of or characterized by repetition, especially tiresome repetition. —**rep′e·ti′tious·ly,** *adv.* —**rep′e·ti′tious·ness,** *n.*

**re·phrase** (rē-frāz′), *v.t.* [-PHRASED, -PHRASING], to phrase again, anew, or in a different way.

**re·pine** (ri-pīn′), *v.i.* [-PINED, -PINING], [*re-* + *pine,* *v.*], to feel or express discontent; fret (*at*).

**re·place** (ri-plās′), *v.t.* [-PLACED, -PLACING], 1. to put back in a former place, condition, etc. 2. to take the place of; supplant. 3. to provide an equivalent for: as, *replace* a worn tire. 4. to put back or pay back; restore: as, *replace* embezzled funds. —**re·place′a·ble,** *adj.* —**re·plac′er,** *n.*

**re·place·ment** (ri-plās′mənt), *n.* 1. a replacing or being replaced. 2. a person or thing that replaces another that is lost, worn out, etc.

**re·plen·ish** (ri-plen′ish), *v.t.* [< OFr. < L. *re-,* again + *plenus,* full], 1. to make full or complete again, as with a new supply. 2. to supply or stock again. —**re·plen′ish·er,** *n.* —**re·plen′ish·ment,** *n.*

**re·plete** (ri-plēt′), *adj.* [< OFr. < L. *repletus,* pp. < *re-,* again + *plere,* to fill], 1. well-filled; plentifully supplied. 2. stuffed, as with food; gorged. —**re·plete′ly,** *adv.* —**re·ple′tion,** *n.*

**re·plev·in** (ri-plev′in), *n.* [< OFr. *re-,* again + *plevir,* to pledge], in *law,* 1. the recovery by a person of goods claimed to be his, on his promise to test the matter in court and give up the goods if defeated. 2. the writ by which this is done. *v.t.* to recover (goods) under a writ of replevin: also **re·plev′y** [-IED, -YING].

**rep·li·ca** (rep′li-kə), *n.* [It. < It. & L. *replicare;* see REPLY], a reproduction or copy; esp., a copy of a work of art made by the original artist.

**rep·li·ca·tion** (rep′li-kā′shən), *n.* [< OFr. < L. < pp. of *replicare;* see REPLY], in *law,* the plaintiff's answer to the plea of the defendant.

**re·ply** (ri-plī′), *v.i.* [-PLIED, -PLYING], [< OFr. < L. < *re-,* back + *plicare,* to fold], 1. to answer in speech or writing. 2. to respond by some action: as, they *replied* with applause. 3. in *law,* to answer a defendant's plea. *v.t.* to say in answer: as, she *replied* that she would. *n.* [*pl.* -PLIES], 1. an answer in speech or writing. 2. a response by some action. —**re·pli′er,** *n.*

**re·port** (ri-pôrt′, -pōrt′), *v.t.* [< OFr. < L. < *re-,* back + *portare,* to carry], 1. to give an account of; give information about; say. 2. to carry and repeat (a message, etc.). 3. to write an account of for publication, as in a newspaper. 4. to give a formal account of; announce formally. 5. to present (something referred for study, etc.) with conclusions, recommendations, etc.: as, the committee *reported* the bill out. 6. to denounce (an offense or offender) to a person in authority. *v.i.* 1. to make a report. 2. to work as a reporter. 3. to present oneself or make one's presence known: as, *report* for duty. *n.* 1. rumor; gossip: as, *report* has it that he is married. 2. reputation: as, a man of good *report.* 3. a statement or account brought in and presented, often for publication. 4. a formal or official presentation of facts or of the record of something. 5. the noise made by an explosion: as, the *report* of a gun. —**re·port′a·ble,** *adj.* —**re·port′ed·ly,** *adv.* —**re·port′ing,** *n.*

**report card,** a written report of a pupil's grades, etc. sent to his home at regular intervals.

**re·port·er** (ri-pôr′tēr, -pōr′-), *n.* one who reports; esp., *a*) a person who reports legal or legislative proceedings: as, a court *reporter.* *b*) a person who gathers information and writes reports for publication in a newspaper, magazine, etc. —**rep·or·to·ri·al** (rep′ēr-tôr′i-əl, -tō′ri-), *adj.*

**re·pose** (ri-pōz′), *v.t.* [-POSED, -POSING], [< OFr. < LL. < L. *re-,* again + *pausare,* to rest], to lay to rest: as, *repose* yourself on the bed. *v.i.* 1. to lie at rest. 2. to rest from work, travel, etc. 3. to depend; rely (with *in*). 4. to rest or be supported: as, the shale *reposes* on bedrock. *n.* 1. a reposing or resting. 2. *a*) rest. *b*) sleep. 3. ease of manner; composure. 4. calm; peace. —**re·pose′ful,** *adj.* —**re·pose′ful·ly,** *adv.*

**re·pose** (ri-pōz′), *v.t.* [-POSED, -POSING], [< L. *repositus* (see REPOSITORY)], to place (trust, etc. *in* someone). —**re·pos′al,** *n.*

**re·pos·i·to·ry** (ri-poz′ə-tôr′i, -tō′ri), *n.* [*pl.* -RIES], [< L. < *repositus,* pp. < *re-,* back + *ponere,* to place], a box, room, place, etc. in which things may be put for safekeeping: often used figuratively.

**re·pos·sess** (rē′pə-zes′), *v.t.* 1. to get possession of again. 2. to put in possession again. —**re′pos·ses′sion,** *n.* —**re′pos·ses′sor,** *n.*

**repp** (rep), *n.* rep (fabric).

**rep·re·hend** (rep′ri-hend′), *v.t.* [< L. < *re-,* back + *prehendere,* to take], 1. to reprimand; rebuke. 2. to find fault with; blame.

**rep·re·hen·si·ble** (rep′ri-hen′sə-b'l), *adj.* deserving to be reprehended. —**rep′re·hen′si·bil′i·ty, rep′re·hen′si·ble·ness,** *n.* —**rep′re·hen′si·bly,** *adv.*

**rep·re·hen·sion** (rep′ri-hen′shən), *n.* a reprehending; reproof or censure.

**rep·re·sent** (rep′ri-zent′), *v.t.* [< OFr. < L.; see RE- & PRESENT, *v.*], 1. to present or picture to the mind. 2. to present a likeness of; portray. 3. to describe or set forth, often in order to influence, persuade, etc.: as, he *represented* the war as lost. 4. *a*) to be a sign for; stand for: as, x *represents* the unknown. *b*) to express by symbols, characters, etc. 5. to be the equivalent of; correspond to: as, a cave *represented* home to them. 6. to play (a role), as in a drama. 7. to act in place of; be a substitute for. 8. to speak and act for by conferred authority, as a legislator for his constituents. 9. to serve as a specimen, example, type, etc. of. —**rep′re·sent′a·ble,** *adj.*

**rep·re·sen·ta·tion** (rep′ri-zen-tā′shən), *n.* 1. a representing or being represented. 2. a likeness, picture, etc. 3. *often in pl.* an account of facts, allegations, etc., especially one intended to influence action, make protest, etc. 4. presentation, production, etc. as of a play. 5. representatives collectively. —**rep′re·sen·ta′tion·al,** *adj.* —**rep′re·sen·ta′tion·al·ly,** *adv.*

**rep·re·sent·a·tive** (rep′ri-zen′tə-tiv), *adj.* 1. representing; specif., *a*) picturing; portraying. *b*) acting in the place of another or others; serving as a delegate, as in a legislative body. 2. of or based on representation of the people by elected delegates: as, *representative* government. 3. typical. *n.* 1. a type; example. 2. a person authorized to act or speak for others, as an elected legislator. 3. [R-], a member of the lower house of Congress or of a State legislature. —**rep′re·sent′a·tive·ly,** *adv.* —**rep′re·sent′a·tive·ness,** *n.*

**re·press** (ri-pres′), *v.t.* [< L. pp.; see RE- & PRESS (to squeeze)], 1. to hold back; restrain: as, *repress* a sigh. 2. to put down; subdue. 3. to prevent the natural development or expression of: as, the parents *repressed* their child. 4. in *psychiatry,* *a*) to force (painful ideas, impulses, etc.) into the unconscious. *b*) to prevent (unconscious ideas, etc.) from becoming conscious. —**re·press′er,** *n.* —**re·press′i·ble,** *adj.* —**re·pres′sive,** *adj.* —**re·pres′sive·ly,** *adv.* —**re·pres′sive·ness,** *n.*

**re·pres·sion** (ri-presh′ən), *n.* 1. a repressing or being repressed. 2. in *psychiatry,* what is repressed.

**re·prieve** (ri-prēv′), *v.t.* [-PRIEVED, -PRIEVING], [ult. < Fr. pp. of *reprendre,* to take back], 1. to postpone the punishment of; esp., to postpone the execution of (a condemned person). 2. to give temporary relief to, as from pain. *n.* a reprieving or being reprieved; specif., *a*) postponement of a penalty, especially of execution. *b*) a temporary relief, as from pain or evil.

**rep·ri·mand** (rep′rə-mand′, -mänd′), *n.* [< Fr. < L. *reprimendus,* that is to be repressed < *reprimere,* to repress], a severe or formal rebuke. *v.t.* to rebuke severely or formally.

**re·print** (rē-print′; *for n., usually* rē′print′), *v.t.* to print again; print a new impression of. *n.* something reprinted; specif., a new impression or edition, as of an earlier book, pamphlet, etc.

**re·pris·al** (ri-prī′z'l), *n.* [< OFr. < pp. of *reprendre* (< L. *reprehendere*), to take back; see REPREHEND]

1. the use of force, short of war, against another nation to obtain redress of grievances. 2. injury done in return for injury received; retaliation, especially in war, as the killing of prisoners.

**re·proach** (ri-prōch'), *v.t.* [OFr. *reprochier;* ult. < L. *re-*, back + *prope*, near], 1. to accuse of a fault; rebuke; reprove. 2. to bring disgrace upon: as, this crime will *reproach* him. *n.* 1. a cause of shame, disgrace, etc. 2. shame, disgrace, etc. incurred. 3. a reproaching; censure; rebuke: as, he was above *reproach.* 4. an object of blame, censure, etc. —**re·proach'a·ble,** *adj.* —**re·proach'er,** *n.* —**re·proach'ing·ly,** *adv.* —**re·proach'less,** *adj.*

**re·proach·ful** (ri-prōch'fəl), *adj.* full of or expressing reproach. —**re·proach'ful·ly,** *adv.* —**re·proach'ful·ness,** *n.*

**rep·ro·bate** (rep'rə-bāt'), *adj.* [< LL. pp. of *reprobare;* see REPROVE], 1. depraved; unprincipled. 2. in *theology*, rejected by God. *n.* a depraved, corrupt person. *v.t.* [-BATED, -BATING], to disapprove; condemn. —**rep'ro·ba'tion,** *n.* —**rep'ro·ba'tive,** *adj.*

**re·pro·duce** (rē'prə-dōōs', -dūs'), *v.t.* [-DUCED, -DUCING], to produce again; specif., *a)* to produce by generation or propagation. *b)* to make grow again, as a lost organ. *c)* to make a copy, imitation, etc. of (a picture, sound, etc.). *d)* to repeat. *v.i.* to produce offspring. —**re'pro·duc'er,** *n.* —**re'pro·duc'i·ble,** *adj.*

**re·pro·duc·tion** (rē'prə-duk'shən), *n.* 1. a reproducing or being reproduced. 2. something made by reproducing; copy. 3. the process by which animals and plants produce new individuals.

**re·pro·duc·tive** (rē'prə-duk'tiv), *adj.* 1. reproducing. 2. of or for reproduction. —**re'pro·duc'tive·ly,** *adv.* —**re'pro·duc'tive·ness,** *n.*

**re·proof** (ri-prōōf'), *n.* 1. a reproving; rebuking. 2. a censure; rebuke. Also **re·prov'al** (-prōōv''l).

**re·prove** (ri-prōōv'), *v.t.* [-PROVED, -PROVING], [< OFr. < LL. *reprobare;* see RE- & PROVE], 1. to speak to in disapproval; rebuke. 2. to express disapproval of; censure. —**re·prov'a·ble,** *adj.* —**re·prov'er,** *n.* —**re·prov'ing·ly,** *adv.*

**rep·tile** (rep'til, -tīl), *n.* [LL., neut. of L. *reptilis*, crawling < pp. of *repere*, to creep], 1. any of a group of cold-blooded vertebrates that crawl on their bellies, as snakes, or creep on short, stubby legs, as lizards, alligators, turtles, etc. 2. a mean, sneaky person. *adj.* 1. of or like reptiles. 2. creeping or crawling. 3. sneaky, mean, etc.

**rep·til·i·an** (rep-til'i-ən), *adj.* 1. of the reptiles. 2. like or characteristic of a reptile. 3. sneaky, mean, groveling, etc. *n.* a reptile.

**re·pub·lic** (ri-pub'lik), *n.* [< Fr. < L. < *res publica*, public thing], 1. a state or nation in which the supreme power rests in all the citizens entitled to vote and is exercised by representatives elected by them. 2. the government of such a state.

**re·pub·li·can** (ri-pub'li-kən), *adj.* 1. of, like, or characteristic of, a republic. 2. favoring a republic. 3. [R-], of the Republican Party. *n.* 1. one who favors a republican form of government. 2. [R-], a member of the Republican Party.

**re·pub·li·can·ism** (ri-pub'li-kən-iz'm), *n.* 1. republican government. 2. republican principles, etc. 3. adherence to these. 4. [R-], the principles, policies, etc. of the Republican Party.

**Republican Party,** one of the two major political parties in the U.S.: it was organized in 1854.

**re·pu·di·ate** (ri-pū'di-āt'), *v.t.* [-ATED, -ATING], [< L. pp. of *repudiare*, to divorce < *repudium*, separation], 1. to disown, as a son. 2. to refuse to accept or acknowledge, as a policy. 3. to refuse to acknowledge or pay, as a debt. —**re·pu'di·a'tion,** *n.* —**re·pu'di·a'tive,** *adj.* —**re·pu'di·a'tor,** *n.*

**re·pug·nance** (ri-pug'nəns), *n.* [< OFr. < L. ppr. < *re-*, back + *pugnare*, to fight], extreme dislike or distaste; aversion. Also **re·pug'nan·cy.**

**re·pug·nant** (ri-pug'nənt), *adj.* 1. contradictory or opposed. 2. causing repugnance; distasteful; offensive. —**re·pug'nant·ly,** *adv.*

**re·pulse** (ri-puls'), *v.t.* [-PULSED, -PULSING], [< L. *repulsus*, pp. of *repellere;* see REPEL], 1. to drive back; repel, as an attack. 2. to repel with discourtesy, coldness, etc.; refuse; rebuff. *n.* 1. a repelling or being repelled. 2. a refusal or rebuff. —**re·puls'er,** *n.*

**re·pul·sion** (ri-pul'shən), *n.* 1. a repelling or being repelled; repulse. 2. strong dislike, distaste, etc. 3. in *physics*, the mutual action by which bodies, particles, etc. repel each other.

**re·pul·sive** (ri-pul'siv), *adj.* 1. tending to repel. 2. causing strong dislike or aversion; disgusting. —**re·pul'sive·ly,** *adv.* —**re·pul'sive·ness,** *n.*

**rep·u·ta·ble** (rep'yoo-tə-b'l), *adj.* 1. having a good reputation; well thought of; respectable. 2. in good usage: said of words. —**rep'u·ta·bil'i·ty,** **rep'u·ta·ble·ness,** *n.* —**rep'u·ta·bly,** *adv.*

**rep·u·ta·tion** (rep'yoo-tā'shən), *n.* [< L. < pp. of *reputare;* see REPUTE], 1. estimation in which a person or thing is commonly held. 2. such estimation when favorable; good name. 3. fame.

**re·pute** (ri-pūt'), *v.t.* [-PUTED, -PUTING], [< OFr. < L. < *re-*, again + *putare*, to think], to consider or esteem to be as specified: as, he is *reputed* to be rich. *n.* 1. reputation. 2. good reputation.

**re·put·ed** (ri-pūt'id), *adj.* generally accounted or supposed to be such: as, the *reputed* owner of the house. —**re·put'ed·ly,** *adv.*

**re·quest** (ri-kwest'), *n.* [< OFr. < ML. < L. pp. of *requirere;* see REQUIRE], 1. an asking for something; solicitation. 2. what is asked for: as, he granted the *request.* 3. the state of being asked for; demand: as, this style is in great *request.* *v.t.* 1. to ask for, usually in a polite or formal way. 2. to ask (a person) to do something. —**by request,** in response to a request.

**Re·qui·em, re·qui·em** (rē'kwi-əm, rek'wi-), *n.* [L., acc. of *requies*, rest: first word of the Mass], 1. in the *R.C. Church*, *a)* a Mass for the repose of the dead. *b)* its musical setting. 2. a dirge.

‡**re·qui·es·cat in pa·ce** (rek'wi-es'kat in pā'si), [L.], may he (or she) rest in peace.

**re·quire** (ri-kwīr'), *v.t.* [-QUIRED, -QUIRING], [< OFr. < L. < *re-*, again + *quaerere*, to ask], 1. to ask or insist upon, as by right or authority; demand. 2. to order; command: as, he *required* us to be present. 3. to demand as necessary; need: as, a hungry man *requires* food. —**re·quir'er,** *n.*

**re·quire·ment** (ri-kwīr'mənt), *n.* 1. a requiring. 2. something required, or demanded, as a condition. 3. something needed; a necessity.

**req·ui·site** (rek'wə-zit), *adj.* [< L. pp. of *requirere;* see REQUIRE], required, as by circumstances; necessary; indispensable: as, qualities *requisite* for success. *n.* something requisite. —**req'ui·site·ly,** *adv.* —**req'ui·site·ness,** *n.*

**req·ui·si·tion** (rek'wə-zish'ən), *n.* 1. a requiring; demanding, as by right or authority. 2. a formal written order, request, etc., as for equipment. 3. the state of being demanded or put to service or use: as, horses were in *requisition.* 4. a requirement; indispensable condition. *v.t.* 1. to demand or take, as by authority. 2. to demand from: as, *requisition* a town for food.

**re·quite** (ri-kwīt'), *v.t.* [-QUITED, -QUITING], [*re-* + *quite*, obs. var. of *quit*], 1. to repay or make return for (a benefit, service, etc., or an injury, wrong, etc.). 2. to make return to for a benefit, injury, etc. 3. to make up for. 4. to give or do in return. —**re·quit'al** (-kwīt''l), *n.* —**re·quit'er,** *n.*

**rere·dos** (rêr'dos), *n.* [< Anglo-Fr. *rere-* (see REAR) + *dos*, back], an ornamental screen or partition wall behind an altar in a church.

**re·route** (rē-rōōt', -rout'), *v.t.* [-ROUTED, -ROUTING], to send by a new or different route.

**re·run** (rē-run'; *for n., usually* rē'run'), *v.t.* [-RAN, -RUN, -RUNNING], to run again. *n.* a rerunning; esp., a return showing of a motion picture.

**res.,** 1. reserve. 2. residence. 3. resides.

**re·sale** (rē-sāl', rē'sāl'), *n.* a selling again. —**re·sal'a·ble,** *adj.*

**re·scind** (ri-sind'), *v.t.* [< OFr. < L. *re-*, back + *scindere*, to cut], to abrogate; annul; cancel, as a law. —**re·scind'a·ble,** *adj.* —**re·scind'er,** *n.*

**re·scis·sion** (ri-sizh'ən, -sish'-), *n.* a rescinding. —**re·scis'si·ble** (-sis'-), *adj.* —**re·scis'so·ry,** *adj.*

**re·script** (rē'skript), *n.* [< L. pp. < *re-*, back + *scribere*, to write], 1. a decree issued by a Roman emperor or by the Pope, answering some point of law and having the force of law. 2. any official decree.

**res·cue** (res'kū), *v.t.* [-CUED, -CUING], [< OFr. < *re-*, again + *escorre*, to shake < L. < *ex-*, off + *quatere*, to shake], 1. to free or save from danger, evil, etc. 2. in *law*, to take out of legal custody by force. *n.* 1. a freeing or saving from danger, evil, etc. 2. removal by force from legal custody. —**res'cu·er,** *n.*

**re·search** (ri-sūrch', rē'sūrch), *n.* [< MFr.; see RE- & SEARCH], *often in pl.* careful, systematic study and investigation in some field of knowledge, undertaken to establish facts or principles. *v.i.* to do research; study. —**re·search'er,** *n.*

**re·seat** (rē-sēt ), *v.t.* 1. to seat again. 2. to supply with a new seat or seats.
**re·sect** (ri-sekt′), *v.t.* [< L. pp. < *re-*, back + *secare*, to cut], in *surgery*, to remove part of (an organ, bone, etc.). —**re·sec′tion,** *n.*
**re·sem·blance** (ri-zem′bləns), *n.* 1. the state or quality of resembling; likeness. 2. a point, degree, or sort of likeness.
**re·sem·ble** (ri-zem′b'l), *v.t.* [-BLED, -BLING], [< OFr. < *re-*, again + *sembler* < L. *simulare;* see SIMULATE], to be like or similar to in appearance or nature.
**re·sent** (ri-zent′), *v.t.* [< Fr. < L. *re-*, again + *sentire*, to feel], to feel or show displeasure and indignation at (a person, act, etc.), as from a sense of being offended. —**re·sent′ful,** *adj.* —**re·sent′ful·ly,** *adv.* —**re·sent′ful·ness,** *n.*
**re·sent·ment** (ri-zent′mənt), *n.* a feeling of displeasure and indignation, from a sense of being injured or offended.
**res·er·va·tion** (rez′ẽr-vā′shən), *n.* 1. a reserving; withholding. 2. something reserved or withheld. 3. a limiting condition or qualification, tacit or expressed: as, mental *reservations*. 4. public land set aside for some special use, as for Indians. 5. *a*) an arrangement by which a hotel room, train ticket, etc. is set aside and held until called for. *b*) anything so reserved in advance.
**re·serve** (ri-zũrv′), *v.t.* [-SERVED, -SERVING], [< OFr. < L.; see RE- & SERVE], 1. to keep back; set apart for later use or for some special purpose. 2. to hold over to a later time. 3. to set aside or have set aside for someone: as, *reserve* a hotel room. 4. to keep back or retain for oneself: as, I *reserve* the right to refuse. *n.* 1. something kept back or stored up, as for later use or for a special purpose. 2. a limitation; reservation. 3. the practice of keeping one's thoughts, feelings, etc. to oneself. 4. reticence; silence. 5. restraint in artistic expression; freedom from exaggeration. 6. *pl.* in *military usage*, *a*) troops held out of action for later use as needed. *b*) troops not on active duty but subject to call; militia. 7. cash, or assets easily turned into cash, held out of use by a bank or company to meet demands. 8. land set apart for a special purpose. *adj.* being, or having the nature of, a reserve. —**in reserve,** reserved for later use, etc. —**without reserve,** subject to no limitation.
**re·served** (ri-zũrvd′), *adj.* 1. kept in reserve; set apart or kept back for some purpose, use, person, etc. 2. keeping one's thoughts, feelings, etc. to oneself; reticent. 3. characterized by reticence, etc. —**re·serv′ed·ly** (-zũr′vid-li), *adv.* —**re·serv′ed·ness,** *n.*
**re·serv·ist** (ri-zũr′vist), *n.* a member of a country's military reserves, or militia.
**res·er·voir** (rez′ẽr-vwär′, -vwôr′, -vôr′), *n.* [< Fr. < *réserver;* see RESERVE], 1. a place where anything is collected and stored; esp., a natural or artificial lake in which water is stored for use. 2. a receptacle (in an apparatus) for holding a fluid, as oil. 3. a large supply or store of something.
**re·set** (rē-set′; *for n.*, rē′set′), *v.t.* [-SET, -SETTING], to set again, as a broken arm, type, a gem, etc. *n.* 1. a resetting. 2. something reset.
**re·ship** (rē-ship′), *v.t.* [-SHIPPED, -SHIPPING], 1. to ship again. 2. to transfer to another ship. *v.i.* 1. to embark again. 2. to go back to sea (on a ship's crew) for another voyage. —**re·ship′ment,** *n.*
**re·side** (ri-zīd′), *v.i.* [-SIDED, -SIDING], [< Fr. < L. < *re-*, back + *sedere*, to sit], 1. to dwell for some time; live (*in* or *at*): as, he *resides* at a hotel. 2. to be present or inherent (*in*): said of qualities, etc. 3. to be vested (*in*): said of rights, powers, etc. —**re·sid′er,** *n.*
**res·i·dence** (rez′i-dəns), *n.* 1. a residing; esp., the fact or status of living or staying in a place while working, going to school, etc.: as, a surgeon in *residence* at a hospital. 2. the place where one resides; abode; esp., a house. 3. the time during which one resides in a place.
**res·i·den·cy** (rez′i-dən-si), *n.* [*pl.* -CIES], residence, especially of a physician at a hospital.
**res·i·dent** (rez′i-dənt), *adj.* 1. residing; having a residence (*in*). 2. living or staying in a place while working, carrying on official duties, etc.: as, a *resident* physician of a hospital. 3. present; inherent. 4. not migratory: said of birds, etc. *n.* 1. one who lives in a place, as distinguished from a visitor or transient. 2. a diplomatic representative living at a foreign court or capital, as in a protectorate.
**res·i·den·tial** (rez′i-den′shəl), *adj.* 1. of or connected with residence: as, a *residential* requirement for students. 2. of or suitable for residences, or homes: as, a *residential* area.
**re·sid·u·al** (ri-zij′o͞o-əl), *adj.* 1. of, or having the nature of, a residue; remaining. 2. in *mathematics*, left by the subtraction of one number from another. *n.* a residue or remainder.
**re·sid·u·ar·y** (ri-zij′o͞o-er′i), *adj.* 1. residual; remaining. 2. in *law*, receiving the residue of an estate: as, a *residuary* legatee.
**res·i·due** (rez′ə-do͞o′, -dū′), *n.* [< OFr. < L. neut. of *residuus*, remaining < *residere;* see RESIDE], 1. that which is left after part is taken away; remainder. 2. a residuum (sense 2). 3. in *law*, that part of a testator's estate left after all claims, charges, and bequests have been satisfied.
**re·sid·u·um** (ri-zij′o͞o-əm), *n.* [*pl.* -SIDUA (-ə)], [L.], 1. residue. 2. in *chemistry*, the matter remaining after combustion, filtration, etc.
**re·sign** (ri-zīn′), *v.t.* [< OFr. < L. < *re-*, back + *signare*, to sign], 1. to give up; relinquish, as a claim. 2. to give up (an office, position, etc.). *v.i.* to withdraw (*from* an office, etc.), especially by formal notice. —**resign oneself,** to submit.
**res·ig·na·tion** (rez′ig-nā′shən), *n.* 1. the act of resigning. 2. formal notice of this, especially in writing. 3. patient submission; acquiescence.
**re·signed** (ri-zīnd′), *adj.* feeling or showing resignation; submissive; yielding and uncomplaining. —**re·sign·ed·ly** (-zīn′id-li), *adv.*
**re·sil·i·ence** (ri-zil′i-əns, -zil′yəns), *n.* 1. a being resilient; elasticity. 2. the ability to recover strength, spirits, etc. quickly; buoyancy. Also **re·sil′i·en·cy.**
**re·sil·i·ent** (ri-zil′i-ənt, -zil′yənt), *adj.* [< L. *resiliens*, ppr. < *re-*, back + *salire*, to jump], 1. bouncing or springing back into shape, position, etc.; elastic. 2. recovering strength, spirits, good humor, etc. quickly; buoyant.
**res·in** (rez′'n), *n.* [< OFr. < L. *resina*], 1. a solid or semisolid organic substance exuded from various plants and trees, as the pines: resins are soluble in ether, alcohol, etc. and are used in medicines, varnish, etc. 2. rosin. *v.t.* to treat or rub with resin. —**res′in·ous, res′in·y,** *adj.*
**re·sist** (ri-zist′), *v.t.* [< OFr. < L. < *re-*, back + *sistere*, to set], 1. to withstand; fend off; stand firm against. 2. to oppose actively; fight or work against. 3. to keep from yielding to: as, to *resist* temptation. *v.i.* to oppose or withstand something; offer resistance. —**re·sist′er,** *n.* —**re·sist′i·bil′i·ty,** *n.* —**re·sist′i·ble,** *adj.* —**re·sist′i·bly,** *adv.*
**re·sist·ance** (ri-zis′təns), *n.* 1. a resisting. 2. power or capacity to resist; specif., the ability of an organism to ward off disease. 3. opposition of some force, thing, etc. to another. 4. in *electricity*, *a*) the property of opposing the passage of a current, causing electric energy to be transformed into heat: also called *true* (or *ohmic*) *resistance*. *b*) something that offers such resistance, as a coil of wire; resistor. *c*) impedance: also called *apparent resistance*. —**re·sist′ant,** *adj.*
**re·sist·less** (ri-zist′lis), *adj.* 1. that cannot be resisted; irresistible. 2. without power to resist. —**re·sist′less·ly,** *adv.* —**re·sist′less·ness,** *n.*
**re·sis·tor** (ri-zis′tẽr), *n.* in *electricity*, a device used in a circuit to provide resistance.
**re·sole** (rē-sōl′), *v.t.* [-SOLED, -SOLING], to put a new sole on (a shoe, etc.).
**res·o·lute** (rez′ə-lo͞ot′), *adj.* [< L. pp. of *resolvere;* see RE- & SOLVE], having or showing a fixed, firm purpose; determined; resolved. —**res′o·lute′ly,** *adv.* —**res′o·lute′ness,** *n.*
**res·o·lu·tion** (rez′ə-lo͞o′shən), *n.* 1. *a*) the act of resolving something. *b*) the result of this. 2. *a*) a determining. *b*) the thing determined upon; decision as to future action. 3. a resolute quality of mind. 4. a formal statement of opinion or determination adopted by a group of persons. 5. a solving or answering; solution.
**re·solve** (ri-zolv′), *v.t.* [-SOLVED, -SOLVING], [< L.; see RE- & SOLVE], 1. to break up into separate parts; analyze. 2. to change; transform: as, the talk *resolved* itself into an argument. 3. to cause to decide: as, the flood *resolved* him to sell. 4. to determine; reach as a decision: as, we *resolved* to go. 5. to solve or explain, as a problem. 6. to decide by vote; decide formally, as a legislature. 7. in *music*, to cause (a dissonant chord) to pass to a consonant one. *v.i.* 1. to be resolved, as by analysis (with *into* or *to*). 2. to determine; come to a decision. *n.* 1. fixed purpose or intention. 2. a formal resolution, as of an assembly. —**re·solv′a·bil′i·ty,** *n.* —**re·solv′a·ble,** *adj.* —**re·solv′er,** *n.*
**re·solved** (ri-zolvd′), *adj.* firm and fixed in purpose; determined. —**re·solv′ed·ly** (-zol′vid-li), *adv.* —**re·solv′ed·ness,** *n.*
**res·o·nance** (rez′ə-nəns), *n.* 1. a being resonant. 2. intensification and prolongation of a sound by reflection or by vibration of a near-by object. 3. in *electricity*, that adjustment of a circuit which al-

lows the greatest flow of current of a certain frequency. 4. in *physics*, the reinforced vibration of a body caused by the vibration of another body.

**res·o·nant** (rez'ə-nənt), ***adj.*** [< L. ppr. of *resonare*, to resound], 1. resounding; re-echoing: as, a *resonant* sound. 2. increasing the intensity of sounds: as, *resonant* walls. 3. of, full of, or intensified by, resonance: as, a *resonant* voice. **—res'o·nant·ly, *adv.***

**res·o·na·tor** (rez'ə-nā'tẽr), ***n.*** [< L. *resonare*, to resound], 1. a device for producing resonance or increasing sound by resonance. 2. in *radio*, the high-frequency circuits of a receiving set.

**res·or·cin·ol** (rez-ôr'si-nōl', -nol), ***n.*** [ <*resin* + It. *orcello*, a kind of lichen], a colorless, crystalline compound, $C_6H_4(OH)_2$, used in dyes, celluloid, and hair tonics: also **res·or'cin.**

**re·sort** (ri-zôrt'), ***v.i.*** [< OFr. < *re-*, again + *sortir*, to go out], 1. to go; esp., to go often: as, people *resort* to parks in summer. 2. to have recourse; turn for use, help, etc.: as, he *resorted* to threats. ***n.*** 1. a place to which people go often, as for rest or relaxation. 2. a frequent or customary going or assembling: as, a place of general *resort*. 3. a person or thing that one turns to for help, support, etc. 4. a turning for help, support, etc.; recourse. **—re·sort'er, *n.***

**re·sound** (ri-zound'), ***v.i.*** [< OFr. < L. *resonare*; see RE- & SOUND], 1. to echo; reverberate: said of places, etc. 2. to make a loud, echoing sound. 3. to be echoed or repeated: said of sounds. ***v.t.*** 1. to give back (sound); echo. 2. to give forth or repeat loudly. 3. to celebrate (someone's praises, etc.). **—re·sound'er, *n.* —re·sound'ing, *adj.* —re·sound'ing·ly, *adv.***

**re·source** (ri-sôrs', rē'sōrs), ***n.*** [< Fr. < OFr. < *re-*, again + *sourdre*, to spring up < L. *surgere;* see SURGE], 1. something that lies ready for use or can be drawn upon for aid. 2. *pl.* wealth; assets. 3. *usually in pl.* something that a country, state, etc. has and can use to its advantage: as, natural *resources*. 4. an emergency measure; expedient. 5. ability to deal effectively with problems, etc.

**re·source·ful** (ri-sôrs'fəl, -sōrs'-), ***adj.*** full of resource; able to deal effectively with problems, etc. **—re·source'ful·ly, *adv.* —re·source'ful·ness, *n.***

**re·spect** (ri-spekt'), ***v.t.*** [< L.; ult. < *re-*, back + *specire*, to look at], 1. to feel or show honor or esteem for. 2. to show consideration for: as, *respect* his privacy. 3. to concern; relate to. ***n.*** 1. a feeling of honor or esteem. 2. a state of being held in honor or esteem. 3. consideration: as, have *respect* for her feelings. 4. *pl.* expressions of respect; regards: as, to pay one's *respects*. 5. a particular point or detail: as, in this *respect* he's wrong. 6. reference; relation: as, with *respect* to your problem. **—in respect of,** with reference to. **—re·spect'er, *n.***

**re·spect·a·ble** (ri-spek'tə-b'l), ***adj.*** 1. worthy of respect or esteem. 2. having good social status, reputation, etc.; decent, honest, etc.: as, a *respectable* hotel. 3. fairly good in quality. 4. fairly large in size, number, etc. 5. good enough to be seen, used, etc.; presentable. **—re·spect'a·bil'i·ty, re·spect'a·ble·ness, *n.* —re·spect'a·bly, *adv.***

**re·spect·ful** (ri-spekt'fəl), ***adj.*** full of or characterized by respect; showing deference. **—re·spect'ful·ly, *adv.* —re·spect'ful·ness, *n.***

**re·spect·ing** (ri-spek'tiŋ), ***prep.*** concerning; about.

**re·spec·tive** (ri-spek'tiv), ***adj.*** relating individually to each of two or more: as, the *respective* weaknesses of his arguments. **—re·spec'tive·ness, *n.***

**re·spec·tive·ly** (ri-spek'tiv-li), ***adv.*** with respect to each in the order named: as, the first and second prizes went to John and Mary *respectively*.

**re·spell** (rē-spel'), ***v.t.*** to spell again; specif., to spell (a word) in a different, usually phonetic, system so as to indicate the pronunciation.

**res·pi·ra·tion** (res'pə-rā'shən), ***n.*** 1. act or process of respiring; breathing. 2. the processes by which a living organism or cell takes in oxygen, distributes and utilizes it in oxidation, and gives off products, especially carbon dioxide.

**res·pi·ra·tor** (res'pə-rā'tẽr), ***n.*** 1. a device of gauze, etc. worn over the mouth and nose, as to prevent the inhaling of harmful substances. 2. an apparatus for giving artificial respiration.

**re·spir·a·to·ry** (ri-spīr'ə-tôr'i, res'pẽr-ə-tō'ri), ***adj.*** of or for respiration.

**re·spire** (ri-spīr'), ***v.t. & v.i.*** [-SPIRED, -SPIRING], [< OFr. < L. < *re-*, back + *spirare*, to breathe], to breathe; inhale and exhale (air).

**res·pite** (res'pit), ***n.*** [< OFr. < L. *respectus*, pp.; see RESPECT], 1. a delay or postponement; specif., in *law*, postponement of an execution; reprieve. 2. temporary relief, as from pain, work, etc.; rest. ***v.t.*** [-PITED, -PITING], to give a respite to.

**re·splend·ent** (ri-splen'dənt), ***adj.*** [< L. ppr.; see RE- & SPLENDENT], shining brightly; dazzling. **—re·splend'ence, re·splend'en·cy, *n.* —re·splend'ent·ly, *adv.***

**re·spond** (ri-spond'), ***v.i.*** [< OFr. < L. < *re-*, back + *spondere*, to pledge], 1. to answer; reply. 2. to act in return, as if in answer; react, as to a stimulus. 3. in *law*, to be answerable or liable. ***v.t.*** to say in answer; reply.

**re·spond·ent** (ri-spon'dənt), ***adj.*** responding; answering. ***n.*** 1. a person who responds. 2. in *law*, a defendant.

**re·sponse** (ri-spons'), ***n.*** [< OFr. < L. pp.; see RESPOND], 1. something said or done in answer; reply. 2. words, phrases, etc. sung or spoken by the congregation or choir in answer to the officiating clergyman. 3. in *physiology & psychology*, any reaction to a stimulus.

**re·spon·si·bil·i·ty** (ri-spon'sə-bil'ə-ti), ***n.*** [*pl.* -TIES], 1. a being responsible; obligation. 2. a thing or person for whom one is responsible.

**re·spon·si·ble** (ri-spon'sə-b'l), ***adj.*** 1. expected or obliged to account (*for*); answerable (*to*): as, he is *responsible* for the car. 2. involving obligation or duties: as, a *responsible* position. 3. accountable as being the cause of something. 4. able to think and act rationally, and hence accountable for one's behavior. 5. trustworthy; dependable: as, a *responsible* person. **—re·spon'si·ble·ness, *n.* —re·spon'si·bly, *adv.***

**re·spon·sive** (ri-spon'siv), ***adj.*** 1. answering. 2. reacting readily, as to appeal: as, a *responsive* audience. 3. containing responses: as, a *responsive* prayer. **—re·spon'sive·ly, *adv.* —re·spon'sive·ness, *n.***

**rest** (rest), ***n.*** [< AS. *rest(e)*], 1. sleep or repose. 2. refreshing ease after work or exertion. 3. a period of inactivity, as during work. 4. *a*) relief from anything distressing, tiring, etc. *b*) peace of mind. 5. the repose of death. 6. absence of motion. 7. a resting place; shelter, as for travelers, sailors, etc. 8. a support, as for a gun, billiard cue, etc. 9. in *music*, *a*) an interval of silence between tones. *b*) a symbol indicating this. ***v.i.*** 1. *a*) to get ease and refreshment by sleeping, lying down, etc. *b*) to sleep. 2. to get ease by ceasing from work or exertion. 3. to be at ease or at peace. 4. to be dead. 5. to be or become quiet or still. 6. to remain without change: as, let the matter *rest*. 7. to be supported; specif., *a*) to lie, sit, or lean. *b*) to be placed or based (*in*, *on*, etc.). 8. to be or lie (where specified): as, the fault *rests* with him. 9. to be fixed (*on* or *upon*): as, his eyes *rested* on her. 10. to rely (*on* or *upon*); depend. 11. in *law*, to end voluntarily the introduction of evidence in a case. ***v.t.*** 1. to give rest to; refresh by rest. 2. to put or lay for ease, support, etc.: as, *rest* your head on the pillow. 3. to base; ground: as, he *rested* his argument on facts. 4. in *law*, to end voluntarily the introduction of evidence in (a case). **—at rest,** 1. asleep. 2. immobile. 3. free from care, worry, etc. 4. dead. **—lay to rest,** to bury.

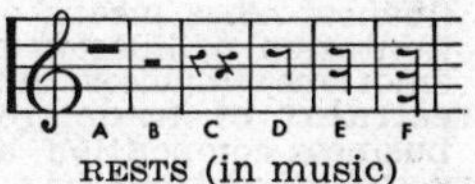


RESTS (in music) A, whole; B, half; C, quarter rests; D, eighth; E, sixteenth; F, thirty-second.

**rest** (rest), ***n.*** [< OFr. < L. *restare*, to remain < *re-*, back + *stare*, to stand], 1. *a*) what is left; remainder. *b*) [construed as pl.], those that are left. ***v.i.*** to go on being: as, *rest* assured.

**re·state** (rē-stāt'), ***v.t.*** [-STATED, -STATING], 1. to state again. 2. to state (something previously stated) in a new form. **—re·state'ment, *n.***

**res·tau·rant** (res'tə-rənt, -ränt'), ***n.*** [Fr. < ppr. of *restaurer;* see RESTORE], a place where meals can be bought and eaten.

**res·tau·ra·teur** (res'tə-rə-tũr'; Fr. -tô'rȧ'tër'), ***n.*** [Fr.], one who owns or operates a restaurant.

**rest·ful** (rest'fəl), ***adj.*** 1. full of or giving rest. 2. at rest; quiet; peaceful; tranquil. **—rest'ful·ly, *adv.* —rest'ful·ness, *n.***

**res·ti·tu·tion** (res'tə-tōō'shən, -tū'-), ***n.*** [OFr. < L. < pp. of *restituere*, to restore < *re-*, again + *statuere*, to set up], 1. a giving back to the rightful owner of something that has been lost or taken away; restoration. 2. a making good for loss or damage.

**res·tive** (res′tiv), *adj.* [< OFr. < *rester;* see REST (to remain)], 1. refusing to go forward; balky: said of a horse, etc. 2. hard to control; unruly. 3. nervous or impatient under restraint; restless. **—res′tive·ly,** *adv.* **—res′tive·ness,** *n.*

**rest·less** (rest′lis), *adj.* 1. unable to rest or relax; uneasy. 2. giving no rest or relaxation; disturbed: as, a *restless* sleep. 3. never or rarely quiet or still; active. 4. seeking change; discontented. **—rest′less·ly,** *adv.* **—rest′less·ness,** *n.*

**re·stock** (rē-stok′), *v.t. & v.i.* to provide with new stock, as a store or farm.

**res·to·ra·tion** (res′tə-rā′shən), *n.* 1. a restoring or being restored; reinstatement. 2. a putting back into a former or normal state. 3. a representation of the original form, as of a building, fossil animal, etc.; reconstruction. 4. something restored. **—the Restoration,** 1. the re-establishment of the monarchy in England under Charles II. 2. the period of his reign (1660–1685).

**re·stor·a·tive** (ri-stôr′ə-tiv, -stō′rə-), *adj.* 1. of restoration. 2. tending to restore or capable of restoring health, strength, consciousness, etc. *n.* something that restores.

**re·store** (ri-stôr′, -stōr′), *v.t.* [-STORED, -STORING], [< OFr. < L. < *re-*, again + *staurare,* to make strong], 1. to give back (something taken away, lost, etc.). 2. to bring back to a former or normal state, as by repairing, rebuilding, etc. 3. to put back in a position, rank, etc.: as, *restore* a king. 4. to bring back to health, strength, etc. 5. to re-establish, as a former custom, etc. **—re·stor′a·ble,** *adj.* **—re·stor′er,** *n.*

**re·strain** (ri-strān′), *v.t.* [< OFr. < L. < *re-*, back + *stringere,* to draw tight], 1. to hold back from action; check; curb. 2. to keep under control. 3. to deprive of physical liberty, as by imprisoning. 4. to limit; restrict. **—re·strain′a·ble,** *adj.* **—re·strain′ed·ly,** *adv.* **—re·strain′er,** *n.*

**re·straint** (ri-strānt′), *n.* 1. a restraining or being restrained. 2. something that restrains, as an influence. 3. a means of restraining. 4. a loss or limitation of liberty; confinement. 5. control of emotions, impulses, etc.; reserve.

**restraint of trade,** restriction or prevention of business competition, as by monopoly.

**re·strict** (ri-strikt′), *v.t.* [< L. pp. of *restringere;* see RESTRAIN], to keep within limits; hold down; limit; confine. **—re·strict′a·ble,** *adj.*

**re·strict·ed** (ri-strik′tid), *adj.* 1. limited; confined. 2. limited to certain groups; esp., limited to white Christians. **—re·strict′ed·ly,** *adv.*

**re·stric·tion** (ri-strik′shən), *n.* 1. a restricting or being restricted. 2. something that restricts.

**re·stric·tive** (ri-strik′tiv), *adj.* 1. restricting or tending to restrict; limiting. 2. in *grammar,* designating a subordinate clause or phrase felt as limiting the application of the word or words that it modifies, and usually not set off by commas (e.g., a man *with money* is needed).

**rest-room** (rest′rōōm′, -room′), *n.* a room or rooms (in a public building) equipped with toilets, washbowls, etc.; lavatory: also **rest room.**

**re·sult** (ri-zult′), *v.i.* [< ML. < L. *resultare,* to rebound; ult. < *re-*, back + *salire,* to jump], 1. to happen as a consequence or effect of some cause (often with *from*). 2. to end as a consequence (*in* something). *n.* 1. anything that issues as a consequence of some action, process, etc. 2. the number, quantity, etc. obtained by mathematical calculation. **—re·sult′ing,** *adj.* **—re·sult′ing·ly,** *adv.*

**re·sult·ant** (ri-zul′t′nt), *adj.* resulting; being a result. *n.* 1. a result. 2. in *physics,* a force with an effect equal to that of two or more such forces acting together. **—re·sult′ant·ly,** *adv.*

**re·sume** (ri-zōōm′, -zūm′), *v.t.* [-SUMED, -SUMING], [< L. < *re-*, again + *sumere,* to take], 1. *a)* to take or occupy again: as, *resume* your seat. *b)* to take on again: as, *resume* a former name. 2. to begin again or continue after interruption: as, *resume* talking. *v.i.* to begin again after interruption. **—re·sum′a·ble,** *adj.* **—re·sum′er,** *n.*

**ré·su·mé** (rā′zoo-mā′, rez′yoo-, rez′ōō-mā′), *n.* [Fr., pp.; see RESUME], a summing up; summary.

**re·sump·tion** (ri-zump′shən), *n.* [< L. < pp. of *resumere*], a resuming. **—re·sump′tive,** *adj.*

**re·sur·face** (rē-sūr′fis), *v.t.* [-FACED, -FACING], to put a new or different surface on.

**re·surge** (ri-sūrj′), *v.i.* [-SURGED, -SURGING], 1. to rise again; revive. 2. to surge back again.

**re·sur·gent** (ri-sūr′jənt), *adj.* rising or tending to rise again. **—re·sur′gence,** *n.*

**res·ur·rect** (rez′ə-rekt′), *v.t.* [< *resurrection*], 1. to raise from the dead; bring back to life. 2. to bring back into notice, use, etc.: as, *resurrect* an old custom. **—res′ur·rect′or,** *n.*

**res·ur·rec·tion** (rez′ə-rek′shən), *n.* [< OFr. < LL. < L. *resurrectus,* pp. of *resurgere,* to rise again], 1. a rising from the dead, or coming back to life. 2. a coming back into notice, use, etc.; revival. 3. the state of having risen from the dead. **—the Resurrection,** in *Christian theology,* 1. the rising of Jesus from the dead. 2. the rising of all the dead at the Last Judgment. **—res′ur·rec′tion·al, res′ur·rec′tion·ar′y,** *adj.*

**re·sus·ci·tate** (ri-sus′ə-tāt′), *v.t. & v.i.* [-TATED, -TATING], [< L. pp. < *re-*, again + *suscitare,* to revive], to revive, as a person apparently dead, in a faint, etc. **—re·sus′ci·ta′tion,** *n.* **—re·sus′ci·ta′tive,** *adj.* **—re·sus′ci·ta′tor,** *n.*

**ret** (ret), *v.t.* [RETTED, RETTING], [< MD. *reten*], to dampen or soak (flax, hemp, etc.) in water.

**ret.,** 1. retired. 2. returned.

**re·tail** (rē′tāl; *also, for v.t. 2,* ri-tāl′), *n.* [< OFr. *retailler,* to cut up < *re-*, again + *tailler,* to cut], the sale of goods in small quantities directly to the consumer: cf. *wholesale.* *adj.* of, connected with, or engaged in the sale of goods at retail. *v.t.* 1. to sell in small quantities directly to the consumer. 2. to repeat to others, as gossip. *v.i.* to be retailed. **—re′tail·er,** *n.*

**re·tain** (ri-tān′), *v.t.* [< OFr. < L. < *re-*, back + *tenere,* to hold], 1. to hold or keep in possession, use, etc. 2. to keep in a fixed state or condition. 3. to keep in mind. 4. to engage the services of (a lawyer) by paying a fee. **—re·tain′a·ble,** *adj.* **—re·tain′ment,** *n.*

**re·tain·er** (ri-tān′ẽr), *n.* 1. a person or thing that retains. 2. a person serving someone of rank or wealth; a vassal, attendant, or servant.

**re·tain·er** (ri-tān′ẽr), *n.* [n. use of OFr. *retenir,* to retain], 1. the act of engaging the services of a lawyer, etc. 2. a fee paid in advance for this.

**retaining wall,** a wall built to keep a bank of earth from sliding or water from flooding.

**re·take** (rē-tāk′; *for n.,* rē′tāk′), *v.t.* [-TOOK, -TAKEN, -TAKING], 1. to take again, take back, or recapture. 2. to photograph again. *n.* 1. a retaking. 2. a scene, sequence, etc. photographed again.

**re·tal·i·ate** (ri-tal′i-āt′), *v.i.* [-ATED, -ATING], [< L. pp. < *re-*, back + *talio,* punishment in kind < *talis,* such], to return like for like; esp., to pay back injury for injury. *v.t.* to return (an injury, wrong, etc.) in kind. **—re·tal′i·a′tion,** *n.* **—re·tal′i·a·to′ry** (-ə-tôr′i, -tō′ri), **re·tal′i·a′tive,** *adj.*

**re·tard** (ri-tärd′), *v.t.* [< Fr. < L. < *re-*, back + *tardare,* to hinder < *tardus,* slow], to hinder, delay, or slow the advance or progress of. *v.t.* to be delayed. *n.* a retarding; delay. **—re·tar·da·tion** (rē′tär-dā′shən), *n.* **—re·tard′er,** *n.*

**retch** (rech) *v.i.* [AS. *hræcan,* to hawk, spit], to make a straining, involuntary effort to vomit.

**retd.,** 1. retained. 2. returned.

**re·ten·tion** (ri-ten′shən), *n.* 1. a retaining or being retained. 2. power of or capacity for retaining. 3. *a)* memory. *b)* ability to remember.

**re·ten·tive** (ri-ten′tiv), *adj.* 1. having the power of or capacity for retaining. 2. *a)* tenacious: as, a *retentive* memory. *b)* having a good memory. **—re·ten′tive·ly,** *adv.* **—re·ten′tive·ness,** *n.*

**ret·i·cence** (ret′ə-s′ns), *n.* quality, state, or instance of being reticent; reserve: also **ret′i·cen·cy.**

**ret·i·cent** (ret′ə-s′nt), *adj.* [< L. ppr. < *re-*, again + *tacere,* to be silent], disinclined to speak readily; habitually uncommunicative; reserved; taciturn. **—ret′i·cent·ly,** *adv.*

**re·tic·u·lar** (ri-tik′yoo-lẽr), *adj.* [see RETICULE], 1. netlike. 2. intricate; entangled.

**re·tic·u·late** (ri-tik′yoo-lit; *also, and for v. always,* -lāt′), *adj.* [< L. < *reticulum;* see RETICULE], like a net or network; netlike, as the veins of some leaves. *v.t. & v.i.* [-LATED, -LATING], to divide or mark so as to look like network. **—re·tic′u·late·ly,** *adv.* **—re·tic′u·la′tion,** *n.*

**ret·i·cule** (ret′i-kūl′), *n.* [< Fr. < L. *reticulum,* double dim. of *rete,* a net], a small handbag carried by women, originally made of network.

**re·tic·u·lum** (ri-tik′yoo-ləm), *n.* [*pl.* -LA (-lə)], [L.; see RETICULE], 1. network. 2. the second division of the stomach of cud-chewing animals, as cows.

**ret·i·na** (ret′′n-ə), *n.* [*pl.* -NAS, -NAE (-ē′)], [prob. < L. *rete,* a net], the innermost coat of the back part of the eyeball, on which the image is formed by the lens: see **eye,** illus. **—ret′i·nal,** *adj.*

**ret·i·nue** (ret′′n-ōō′, -i-nū′), *n.* [< OFr. pp. of *retenir;* see RETAIN], a group of persons in attendance on a person of rank; escort.

**re·tire** (ri-tīr′), *v.i.* [-TIRED, -TIRING], [< Fr. < *re-*, back + *tirer,* to draw], 1. to withdraw to a private or secluded place. 2. to go to bed. 3. to retreat; withdraw, as in battle. 4. to withdraw oneself from business, active service, etc., especially because of advanced age. 5. to move back or away. ***v.t.*** 1. to take or lead away; withdraw, as troops. 2. to take out of circulation, as money, bonds, etc. 3. to remove from a position or office: as, to *retire* a general. 4. in *baseball*, etc., to cause (a batter, side, etc.) to be out.

**re·tired** (ri-tīrd′), ***adj.*** 1. in seclusion; secluded. 2. withdrawn from business, active service, etc. 3. of or for a person or persons so withdrawn.

**re·tire·ment** (ri-tīr′mənt), ***n.*** 1. a retiring or being retired; withdrawal. 2. privacy; seclusion. 3. a place of privacy or seclusion.

**re·tir·ing** (ri-tīr′iŋ), ***adj.*** 1. that retires. 2. reserved; modest; shy. **—re·tir′ing·ly, *adv.***

**re·tool** (rē-tōōl′), ***v.t. & v.i.*** to adapt the machinery of (a factory) to the manufacture of a different product by changing the tools and dies.

**re·tort** (ri-tôrt′), ***v.t.*** [< L. *retortus*, pp. < *re-*, back + *torquere*, to twist], 1. to turn (an insult, deed, etc.) back upon the person from whom it came. 2. to answer (an argument, etc.) in kind. ***v.i.*** to make a sharp or witty reply. ***n.*** a sharp or witty reply, especially one that retorts the words of the previous speaker. **—re·tort′er, *n.***

**re·tort** (ri-tôrt′), ***n.*** [< Fr. < ML. *retorta* < L. *retortus;* see prec.], a glass container with a long tube, in which substances are distilled or decomposed by heat.

RETORT
A, retort; B, Bunsen burner; C, flask for receiving distilled liquids.

**re·touch** (rē-tuch′; *also, for n.*, rē′tuch′), ***v.t.*** 1. to touch up details in (a painting, writing, etc.) so as to improve it. 2. in *photography*, to change (a negative or print) by adding details or removing blemishes. ***n.*** 1. a retouching. 2. a photograph, etc. that has been retouched. **—re·touch′er, *n.***

**re·trace** (ri-trās′), ***v.t.*** [-TRACED, -TRACING], [Fr. *retracer;* see RE- & TRACE], 1. to go back over again, especially in the reverse direction: as, he *retraced* his steps. 2. to trace again the story of, from the beginning. **—re·trace′a·ble, *adj.***

**re-trace, re·trace** (rē′trās′), ***v.t.*** [-TRACED, -TRACING], to trace over again, as a drawing.

**re·tract** (ri-trakt′), ***v.t. & v.i.*** [< L.; ult. < *re-*, back + *trahere*, to draw], 1. to draw back or in. 2. to withdraw (a statement, charge, etc.); recant or revoke. **—re·tract′a·bil′i·ty, *n.* —re·tract′a·ble, *adj.***

**re·trac·tile** (ri-trak′t'l), ***adj.*** [Fr.], that can be retracted, or drawn back or in, as claws. **—re·trac·til·i·ty** (rē′trak-til′ə-ti), ***n.***

**re·trac·tion** (ri-trak′shən), ***n.*** 1. a retracting or being retracted; specif., *a*) withdrawal, as of a statement, etc. *b*) a drawing or being drawn back or in. 2. power of retracting.

**re·trac·tor** (ri-trak′tẽr), ***n.*** one that retracts; esp., *a*) a muscle that retracts an organ, etc. *b*) a surgical device for retracting a part or organ.

**re·tread** (rē′tred′; *for n.*, rē′tred′), ***v.t. & n.*** recap.

**re-tread, re·tread** (rē-tred′), ***v.t.*** [-TROD, -TROD or -TRODDEN, -TREADING], to tread again.

**re·treat** (ri-trēt′), ***n.*** [< OFr. pp.; ult. < L. *re-*, back + *trahere*, to draw], 1. a going back or backward; withdrawal, as to a safe place; a giving ground before opposition. 2. a safe, quiet, or secluded place. 3. a period of seclusion, especially for religious contemplation. 4. in *military usage*, *a*) the forced withdrawal of troops under attack by the enemy. *b*) a signal for such a withdrawal. *c*) a signal by drum or bugle at sunset for lowering the national flag. *d*) the ceremony of this. ***v.i.*** to withdraw; go back. **—beat a retreat**, 1. to signal for retreat by beating a drum. 2. to retreat.

**re·trench** (ri-trench′), ***v.t.*** [< MFr.; see RE- & TRENCH, *v.*], 1. to cut down; curtail; reduce, as expenses. 2. to delete, as part of a book. ***v.i.*** to reduce expenses; economize. **—re·trench′ment, *n.***

**ret·ri·bu·tion** (ret′rə-bū′shən), ***n.*** [< OFr. < L.; ult. < *re-*, back + *tribuere*, to pay], deserved punishment for evil done, or, sometimes, reward for good done. **—re·trib·u·tive** (ri-trib′yoo-tiv), **re·trib′u·to′ry** (-tôr′i, -tō′ri), ***adj.* —re·trib′u·tive·ly, *adv.***

**re·triev·al** (ri-trēv′'l), ***n.*** 1. a retrieving; recovery. 2. possibility of recovery.

**re·trieve** (ri-trēv′), ***v.t.*** [-TRIEVED, -TRIEVING], [< OFr. < *re-*, again + *trouver*, to find], 1. to get back; recover. 2. to restore; revive: as, he *retrieved* his spirits. 3. to set right; make amends for (a loss, error, etc.). 4. to recall to mind. 5. to find and bring back (killed or wounded game): said of hunting dogs. ***v.i.*** in *hunting*, to retrieve game. ***n.*** retrieval. **—re·triev′a·ble, *adj.***

**re·triev·er** (ri-trēv′ẽr), ***n.*** 1. a person who retrieves. 2. a dog trained to retrieve game.

**ret·ro-,** [< L. *retro*, backward], a combining form meaning *backward, back, behind*, as in *retrocede*.

**ret·ro·ac·tive** (ret′rō-ak′tiv), ***adj.*** having effect on things done prior to its enactment or effectuation: as, a *retroactive* law. **—ret′ro·ac′tive·ly, *adv.***

**ret·ro·cede** (ret′rō-sēd′), ***v.i.*** [-CEDED, -CEDING], [< L. < *retro-*, back + *cedere*, to go], to go back; recede. **—ret′ro·ces′sion** (-sesh′ən), ***n.***

**ret·ro·fire** (ret′rə-fīr′), ***v.t.*** [-FIRED, -FIRING], to ignite (a retrorocket). ***v.i.*** to become ignited: said of a retrorocket. ***n.*** the igniting of a retrorocket.

**ret·ro·flex** (ret′rə-fleks′), ***adj.*** [see RETRO- & FLEX], in *phonetics*, *a*) having the tip bent backward: said of the tongue. *b*) formed thus, as a sound.

**ret·ro·grade** (ret′rə-grād′), ***adj.*** [< L.; see RETRO- & GRADE], 1. moving or directed backward. 2. going back to an earlier or worse condition. ***v.i.*** [-GRADED, -GRADING], 1. to go, or seem to go, backward. 2. to become worse; decline.

**ret·ro·gress** (ret′rə-gres′, ret′rə-gres′), ***v.i.*** [< L. pp. of *retrogradi;* see RETROGRADE], to move backward, especially into an earlier or worse condition; decline. **—ret′ro·gres′sion, *n.* —ret′ro·gres′sive, *adj.* —ret′ro·gres′sive·ly, *adv.***

**ret·ro·rock·et** (ret′rō-rok′it), ***n.*** a small rocket, as on a spacecraft, producing thrust opposite to the direction of flight in order to reduce speed, as for landing.

**ret·ro·spect** (ret′rə-spekt′), ***n.*** [< L. pp. of *retrospicere*, to look back < *retro-*, back + *specere*, to look], a looking back on or thinking about things past. **—in retrospect**, in reviewing the past. **—ret′ro·spec′tion, *n.* —ret′ro·spec′tive, *adj.* —ret′ro·spec′tive·ly, *adv.***

**ret·rous·sé** (ret′rōō-sā′), ***adj.*** [Fr., turned up], turned up at the tip: said of a nose.

**re·turn** (ri-tũrn′), ***v.i.*** [< OFr. *returner;* see RE- & TURN], 1. to go or come back. 2. to answer; reply. ***v.t.*** 1. to bring, send, carry, or put back. 2. to give, send, or do in requital or reciprocation: as, to *return* a visit. 3. to produce, as a profit; yield. 4. to report officially or formally. 5. to elect or re-elect, as to a legislature. 6. to turn back. 7. in *card games*, to respond to (a partner's lead). ***n.*** 1. a coming or going back. 2. a bringing, sending, carrying, or putting back. 3. something returned. 4. a coming back again; recurrence: as, many happy *returns*. 5. repayment; requital; reciprocation. 6. *a*) profit made on an exchange of goods. *b*) *often in pl.* yield or profit, as from investments. 7. an answer; reply. 8. *a*) an official or formal report. *b*) *usually in pl.* a report on a count of votes: as, election *returns*. 9. in *tennis*, etc., *a*) a batting back of a ball. *b*) a ball so returned. ***adj.*** 1. of or for a return: as, a *return* ticket. 2. given, sent, done, etc. in return: as, a *return* visit. 3. returning. 4. returned. **—in return**, as a return; as an equivalent, etc. **—re·turn′a·ble, *adj.***

**re·type** (rē-tīp′; *for n.*, rē′tīp′), ***v.t.*** [-TYPED, -TYPING], to type over again. ***n.*** copy retyped.

**Reu·ben** (rōō′bin), ***n.*** in the *Bible*, 1. the eldest son of Jacob. 2. the tribe of Israel descended from him.

**re·un·ion** (rē-ūn′yən), ***n.*** 1. a bringing or coming together again. 2. a gathering of persons after separation, as of members of a family.

**re·u·nite** (rē′yoo-nīt′), ***v.t. & v.i.*** [-NITED, -NITING], to unite again; bring or come together again. **—re′u·nit′a·ble, *adj.* —re′u·nit′er, *n.***

**rev** (rev), ***n.*** [Colloq.], a revolution, as of an engine. ***v.t. & v.i.*** [REVVED, REVVING], [Colloq.], to change the speed of (an engine, motor, etc.): usually in *rev up*, to accelerate.

**Rev.,** 1. Revelation. 2. [*pl.* REVS.], Reverend.

**rev.,** 1. revenue. 2. reverse. 3. review. 4. revised. 5. revision. 6. [*pl.* REVS.], revolution.

**re·vamp** (rē-vamp′), ***v.t.*** to vamp again or anew; specif., to renovate; patch up; redo.

**re·veal** (ri-vēl′), ***v.t.*** [< OFr. < L. *revelare*, lit., to draw back the veil < *re-*, back + *velum*, veil], 1. to make known (something hidden or secret); disclose. 2. to expose to view; show. **—re·veal′a·ble, *adj.* —re·veal′er, *n.* —re·veal′ment, *n.***

**re·veil·le** (rev′ə-li), ***n.*** [< Fr. imper. of (*se*) *réveiller*, to wake up; ult. < L. *re-*, again + *vigilare*, to watch], in *military usage*, 1. a signal on a bugle, drum, etc. in the morning to waken soldiers or sailors or call them to first assembly. 2. the first assembly of the day.

**rev·el** (rev′'l), *v.i.* [-ELED or -ELLED, -ELING or -ELLING], [< OFr. < L. *rebellare;* see REBEL], 1. to make merry; be noisily festive. 2. to take much pleasure (*in*): as, he *revels* in sports. *n.* 1. merrymaking; revelry. 2. *often pl.* an occasion of merrymaking; celebration. —**rev′el·er, rev′el·ler,** *n.*

**rev·e·la·tion** (rev′ə-lā′shən), *n.* 1. a revealing, or disclosing. 2. something disclosed; esp., a striking disclosure. 3. in *Christian theology,* God's disclosure to man of himself and his will. 4. [R-], *also pl.* the last book of the New Testament (in full, **The Revelation of Saint John the Divine**).

**rev·el·ry** (rev′'l-ri), *n.* [*pl.* -RIES], a reveling; noisy merrymaking; boisterous festivity.

**re·venge** (ri-venj′), *v.t.* [-VENGED, -VENGING], [< OFr. < *re-*, again + *vengier,* to take vengeance < L. *vindicare;* see VINDICATE], 1. to inflict injury or punishment in return for (an injury, insult, etc.). 2. to avenge (a person, oneself, etc.). *n.* 1. a revenging; vengeance. 2. what is done in revenging. 3. desire to take vengeance. 4. a chance to retaliate, as by a return match after a defeat. —**be revenged,** to get revenge. —**re·veng′er,** *n.*

**re·venge·ful** (ri-venj′fəl), *adj.* full of or desiring revenge; vindictive. —**re·venge′ful·ly,** *adv.* —**re·venge′ful·ness,** *n.*

**rev·e·nue** (rev′ə-nōō′, -nū′), *n.* [< OFr. pp. < *re-*, back + *venir* (< L. *venire*), to come], 1. the return from property or investment; income. 2. a source of income. 3. the income of a government from taxes, duties, etc.

**re·ver·ber·ant** (ri-vūr′bēr-ənt), *adj.* reverberating.

**re·ver·ber·ate** (ri-vūr′bə-rāt′), *v.t.* [-ATED, -ATING], [< L. < *re-*, again + *verberare,* to beat < *verber,* a lash], 1. to throw back (sound); cause to re-echo. 2. to reflect (light, heat, etc.). *v.i.* 1. to re-echo; resound. 2. to be reflected, as light or sound waves. 3. to recoil; rebound.

**re·ver·ber·a·tion** (ri-vūr′bə-rā′shən), *n.* 1. a reverberating or being reverberated; specif., a reflection, as of light or sound waves. 2. something reverberated, as re-echoed sound. —**re·ver′ber·a′tive** (-bə-rā′tiv, -bēr-ə-tiv), *adj.* —**re·ver′ber·a·to′ry** (-bēr-ə-tôr′i, -tō′ri), *adj.*

**re·vere** (ri-vêr′), *v.t.* [-VERED, -VERING], [< Fr. < L. < *re-*, again + *vereri,* to fear], to regard with deep respect, love, and awe; venerate.

**re·vere** (ri-vêr′), *n.* a revers.

**Re·vere, Paul** (ri-vêr′), 1735–1818; U.S. silversmith and patriot.

**rev·er·ence** (rev′ēr-əns), *n.* 1. a feeling or attitude of deep respect, love, and awe; veneration. 2. a manifestation of this; specif., a bow or curtsy. 3. [R-], a title used in speaking to or of a clergyman: preceded by *your* or *his.* *v.t.* [-ENCED, -ENCING], to regard with reverence; revere.

**rev·er·end** (rev′ēr-ənd), *adj.* [L. *reverendus,* gerundive of *revereri;* see REVERE], worthy of reverence: used [usually R-], as a title of respect for a clergyman. *n.* [Colloq.], a clergyman.

**rev·er·ent** (rev′ēr-ənt), *adj.* feeling or showing reverence. —**rev′er·ent·ly,** *adv.*

**rev·er·en·tial** (rev′ə-ren′shəl), *adj.* reverent. —**rev′er·en′tial·ly,** *adv.* —**rev′er·en′tial·ness,** *n.*

**rev·er·ie** (rev′ēr-i), *n.* [< Fr. < *rêver,* to dream], 1. dreamy thinking, especially of agreeable things; daydreaming. 2. a fanciful notion. Also sp. **revery.**

**re·vers** (rə-vêr′, -vâr′), *n.* [*pl.* -VERS (-vêrz′, -vârz′)], [Fr. < L. *reversus;* see REVERSE], a part (of a garment) turned back to show the reverse side or facing, as a lapel: also **revere.**

**re·ver·sal** (ri-vūr′s'l), *n.* a reversing or being reversed.

**re·verse** (ri-vūrs′), *adj.* [< OFr. < L. *reversus,* pp. of *revertere;* see REVERT], 1. turned backward; opposite or contrary, as in position, direction, etc. 2. acting in a way opposite or contrary to the usual. 3. causing movement backward or in the opposite direction. *n.* 1. the opposite or contrary. 2. the back, as of a coin, medal, etc. 3. a reversing; esp., a change from good fortune to bad; defeat; check. 4. a mechanism, etc. for reversing, as a gear that causes a machine to run backward. *v.t.* [-VERSED, -VERSING], 1. to turn in an opposite position or direction, upside down, or inside out. 2. to change to the opposite. 3. to cause to go in an opposite direction. 4. in *law,* to revoke or annul (a decision, etc.). *v.i.* 1. to go or turn in the opposite direction. 2. to put a motor, etc. in reverse. —**re·verse′ly,** *adv.* —**re·vers′er,** *n.*

**re·vers·i·ble** (ri-vūr′sə-b'l), *adj.* 1. that can be reversed, as cloth, coats, etc. with both sides finished as possible outer surfaces. 2. that can reverse, as a chemical reaction. *n.* a reversible coat, jacket, etc. —**re·vers′i·bil′i·ty, re·vers′i·ble·ness,** *n.* —**re·vers′i·bly,** *adv.*

**re·ver·sion** (ri-vūr′zhən, -shən), *n.* 1. a return, as to a former state, custom, etc. 2. in *biology,* a return to a former or primitive type; atavism. 3. in *law, a*) the right of succession, future possession, etc. *b*) the return of an estate to the grantor and his heirs after a grant terminates. —**re·ver′sion·ar′y** (-er′i), **re·ver′sion·al,** *adj.*

**re·vert** (ri-vūrt′), *v.i.* [< OFr. < L. < *re-*, back + *vertere,* to turn], 1. to go back; return, as to a former state, practice, etc. 2. in *biology,* to return to an earlier type. 3. in *law,* to go back to a former owner or his heirs. —**re·vert′i·ble,** *adj.*

**rev·er·y** (rev′ēr-i), *n.* [*pl.* -IES], a reverie.

**re·vet·ment** (ri-vet′mənt), *n.* [< Fr. < OFr. < L. < *re-*, again + *vestire,* to clothe], a facing of stone, cement, etc., as to protect an embankment, etc.

**re·view** (ri-vū′), *n.* [< Fr. < L. < *re-*, again + *videre,* to see], 1. a viewing or studying again. 2. a general survey or report. 3. a looking back, as on past events. 4. re-examination, as of the decision of a lower court. 5. a critical discussion, as in a newspaper, of a book, play, etc. 6. a magazine containing articles of criticism and appraisal: as, a scientific *review.* 7. act of going over a lesson again, as in recitation. 8. a revue. 9. a formal inspection, as of troops on parade. Also **re·view′al.** *v.t.* 1. to look at or study again. 2. to look back on; view in retrospect. 3. to survey in thought, speech, or writing. 4. to inspect formally, as troops. 5. to give or write a critical discussion of (a book, etc.). 6. to re-examine, as a lower court's decision. 7. to go over (lessons, etc.) again. *v.i.* to review books, plays, etc. —**re·view′a·ble,** *adj.*

**re·view·er** (ri-vū′ēr), *n.* one who reviews; esp., one who reviews books, etc. for a periodical.

**re·vile** (ri-vil′), *v.t.* & *v.i.* [-VILED, -VILING], [< OFr. *reviler,* to treat as vile; see RE- & VILE], to use abusive language (to or about). —**re·vile′ment,** *n.* —**re·vil′er,** *n.* —**re·vil′ing·ly,** *adv.*

**re·vise** (ri-vīz′), *v.t.* [-VISED, -VISING], [< Fr. < L. < *re-*, back + *visere,* to survey, freq. of *videre,* to see], 1. to read over carefully, as a manuscript, etc., to correct and improve. 2. to change or amend. *n.* 1. a revision. 2. in *printing,* a proof taken after corrections have been made. —**re·vis′er, re·vis′or,** *n.* —**re·vi′so·ry,** *adj.*

**Revised Standard Version,** a revised translation of the Bible in contemporary English: the complete version was published in the U.S. in 1952.

**Revised Version,** a revision of the Authorized Version of the Bible: the New Testament was published in 1881, the Old Testament in 1885.

**re·vi·sion** (ri-vizh′ən), *n.* 1. act, process, or work of revising. 2. a revised form, as of a book, etc. —**re·vi′sion·al,** *adj.*

**re·viv·al** (ri-vī′v'l), *n.* 1. a reviving or being revived. 2. a bringing or coming back into use, being, etc. 3. a new presentation of an earlier play, motion picture, etc. 4. restoration to vigor or activity. 5. a bringing or coming back to life or consciousness. 6. a stirring up of religious faith. 7. a meeting characterized by fervid preaching, public confessions, etc. aimed at arousing religious belief: in full, **revival meeting.**

**re·viv·al·ist** (ri-vī′v'l-ist), *n.* one who promotes or conducts religious revivals.

**re·vive** (ri-vīv′), *v.i.* [-VIVED, -VIVING], [< OFr. < L. < *re-*, again + *vivere,* to live], 1. to come back to life or consciousness. 2. to come back to health and vigor. 3. to flourish again. 4. to come back into use or attention. *v.t.* 1. to bring back to life or consciousness. 2. to bring back to a healthy, vigorous condition. 3. to bring back into use or attention. 4. to bring to mind again. 5. to produce (a play, etc.) again after an interval. —**re·viv′er,** *n.*

**re·viv·i·fy** (ri-viv′ə-fī′), *v.t.* & *v.i.* [-FIED, -FYING], to give or acquire new life or vigor; revive. —**re·viv′i·fi·ca′tion,** *n.* —**re·viv′i·fi′er,** *n.*

**rev·o·ca·ble** (rev′ə-kə-b'l), *adj.* that can be revoked. —**rev′o·ca·bil′i·ty,** *n.* —**rev′o·ca·bly,** *adv.*

**rev·o·ca·tion** (rev′ə-kā′shən), *n.* a revoking or being revoked; repeal; annulment.

**rev·o·ca·to·ry** (rev′ə-kə-tôr′i, -tō′ri), *adj.* revoking or tending to revoke.

**re·voke** (ri-vōk′), *v.t.* [-VOKED, -VOKING], [< OFr. < L. < *re-*, back + *vocare,* to call], to withdraw, repeal, or cancel, as a law, etc. *v.i.* in *card games,* to fail to follow suit when required and able to do so; renege. *n.* in *card games,* a revoking. —**re·vok′a·ble,** *adj.* —**re·vok′er,** *n.*

**re·volt** (ri-vōlt′), *n.* [< Fr. < It.; ult. < L. *revolvere;* see REVOLVE], 1. a rising up against the government; rebellion. 2. any refusal to submit to authority. 3. the state of a person or persons revolting. *v.i.* 1. to rise up against the government. 2. to refuse to submit to authority; rebel. 3. to be disgusted; feel repugnance (with *at, against,* or *from*). *v.t.* to disgust. **—re·volt′er,** *n.*

**re·volt·ing** (ri-vōl′tiŋ), *adj.* 1. rebellious. 2. causing revulsion; disgusting. **—re·volt′ing·ly,** *adv.*

**rev·o·lu·tion** (rev′ə-lo͞o′shən), *n.* [< OFr. < LL. < pp. of *revolvere;* see REVOLVE], 1. movement of a body in an orbit or circle. 2. the time taken for a body to go around an orbit. 3. a turning motion of a body around its center or axis; rotation. 4. a complete cycle of events. 5. a complete change of any kind. 6. overthrow of a government or social system, with another taking its place.

**rev·o·lu·tion·ar·y** (rev′ə-lo͞o′shən-er′i), *adj.* 1. of, characterized by, or causing a revolution, especially in a government. 2. revolving or rotating. *n.* [*pl.* -IES], a revolutionist.

**Revolutionary War,** the war (1775–1783), by which the American colonies won their independence from England; American Revolution.

**rev·o·lu·tion·ist** (rev′ə-lo͞o′shən-ist), *n.* one who favors or engages in a revolution.

**rev·o·lu·tion·ize** (rev′ə-lo͞o′shən-īz′), *v.t.* [-IZED, -IZING], 1. to make a complete change in; alter drastically. 2. [Rare], to bring about a political revolution in.

**re·volve** (ri-volv′), *v.t.* [-VOLVED, -VOLVING], [< OFr. < L. < *re-,* back + *volvere,* to roll], 1. to turn over in the mind; reflect on. 2. to cause to travel in a circle or orbit. 3. to cause to rotate. *v.i.* 1. to move in a circle or orbit. 2. to rotate. 3. to recur at intervals. **—re·volv′a·ble,** *adj.* **—re·volv′ing,** *adj.*

**re·volv·er** (ri-vol′vẽr), *n.* a pistol with a revolving cylinder containing several cartridges: it can be fired in quick succession without reloading.

**revolving door,** a door consisting of four vanes hung on a central axle: a person using it turns it around by pushing on one of the vanes.

**re·vue** (ri-vū′), *n.* [Fr.; see REVIEW], a musical show consisting of skits, songs, and dances, often parodying recent events, etc.: also sp. **review.**

**re·vul·sion** (ri-vul′shən), *n.* [< Fr. < L. < *revulsus,* pp. < *re-,* back + *vellere,* to pull], a sudden, complete, and violent change of feeling; abrupt, strong reaction; esp., disgust.

**Rev. Ver.,** Revised Version.

**re·ward** (ri-wôrd′), *n.* [< OFr. *regarde;* see REGARD], 1. something given in return for something done, especially for something good. 2. money offered, as for the capture of a criminal, etc. 3. profit; return. *v.t.* 1. to give a reward to. 2. to give a reward for (service, etc.). **—re·ward′er,** *n.*

**re·ward·ing** (ri-wôrd′iŋ), *adj.* giving a sense of reward, or return: as, a *rewarding* experience.

**re·wire** (rē-wīr′), *v.t. & v.i.* [-WIRED, -WIRING], to wire again; specif., *a*) to put new wires in or on (a house, etc.). *b*) to telegraph again.

**re·word** (rē-wũrd′), *v.t.* 1. to change the wording of. 2. to state again; repeat.

**re·write** (rē-rīt′; *for n.,* rē′rīt′), *v.t. & v.i.* [-WROTE, -WRITTEN, -WRITING], 1. to write again. 2. to revise. 3. in *journalism,* to write (news turned in by a reporter) in a form suitable for publication. *n.* an article written this way.

**Rex** (reks), *n.* [*pl.* REGES (rē′jēz)], [L.], king: the official title of a reigning king, as George *Rex.*

**Rey·kja·vik** (rā′kyȧ-vēk′), *n.* seaport and capital of Iceland: pop., 78,000.

**Reyn·ard** (ren′ẽrd, rā′nẽrd, -närd), *n.* [OFr. *Renard* < OHG.], the fox in the medieval beast epic *Reynard the Fox;* hence, a name for any fox.

**Reyn·olds,** Sir **Joshua** (ren′əldz), 1723–1792; English portrait painter.

**R.F., r.f.,** 1. radio-frequency. 2. rapid-fire.

**RFC, R.F.C.,** Reconstruction Finance Corporation.

**RFD, R.F.D.,** Rural Free Delivery.

**Rh,** in *chemistry,* rhodium.

**Rhad·a·man·thus** (rad′ə-man′thəs), *n.* in *Gr. mythology,* a son of Zeus, rewarded for his justice on earth by being made, after his death, a judge in the lower world. **—Rhad′a·man′thine** (-thin), *adj.*

**rhap·sod·i·cal** (rap-sod′i-k'l), *adj.* of, or having the nature of, rhapsody; extravagantly enthusiastic: also **rhap·sod′ic. —rhap·sod′i·cal·ly,** *adv.*

**rhap·so·dize** (rap′sə-dīz′), *v.i. & v.t.* [-DIZED, -DIZING], to speak, write, or recite in a rhapsodical manner or form. **—rhap′so·dist,** *n.*

**rhap·so·dy** (rap′sə-di), *n.* [*pl.* -DIES], [< Fr. < L. < Gr. *rhapsōidia;* ult. < *rhaptein,* to stitch together + *ōidē,* song], 1. any ecstatic or extravagantly enthusiastic speech or writing. 2. in *music,* an instrumental composition of free, irregular form, suggesting improvisation.

**Rhe·a** (rē′ə), *n.* 1. in *Gr. mythology,* the daughter of Uranus and Gaea, wife of Cronus, and mother of Zeus, Hera, etc.: called *Mother of the Gods.* 2. [r-], a large South American nonflying bird, resembling the African ostrich but smaller and having three toes instead of two.

**Rheims** (rēmz; rans), *n.* Reims.

**Rhein** (rīn), *n.* the Rhine: the German name.

**Rhein·gold** (rīn′gōld′; G. -gôlt′), *n.* [G., Rhine gold], in *Germanic mythology,* the hoard of gold guarded by the Rhine maidens and afterward owned by the Nibelungs and Siegfried.

**Rhen·ish** (ren′ish), *adj.* of the Rhine or the regions around it. *n.* Rhine wine.

**rhe·ni·um** (rē′ni-əm), *n.* [< L. *Rhenus,* Rhine], a rare metallic chemical element resembling manganese: symbol, Re; at. wt., 186.31; at. no., 75. **—rhe′nic** (-nik), *adj.*

**rhe·o-,** [< Gr. *rheos,* current], a combining form meaning *a flow, current,* as in *rheostat.*

**rhe·o·stat** (rē′ə-stat′), *n.* [< *rheo-* + Gr. *statos,* standing still], a device for regulating strength of an electric current by varying the resistance without opening the circuit. **—rhe′o·stat′ic,** *adj.*

**Rhe·sus factor** (rē′səs), Rh factor.

**rhe·sus (monkey)** (rē′səs), [< L. < Gr. proper name], a small, short-tailed, brownish-yellow monkey of India: often used in medical experiments.

**rhet·o·ric** (ret′ə-rik), *n.* [< OFr. < L. < Gr. *rhētorikē* (*technē*), oratorical (art) < *rhētōr,* orator], 1. the art of using words effectively in speaking or writing; esp., now, the art of prose composition. 2. a book on this. 3. artificial eloquence; showiness in literary style.

**rhe·tor·i·cal** (ri-tôr′i-k'l, -tor′-), *adj.* 1. of, having the nature of, or according to rhetoric. 2. artificially eloquent; showy and elaborate in literary style. **—rhe·tor′i·cal·ly,** *adv.*

**rhetorical question,** a question asked only for rhetorical effect, no answer being expected.

**rhet·o·ri·cian** (ret′ə-rish′ən), *n.* 1. one skilled in rhetoric. 2. one who is artificially eloquent.

**rheum** (ro͞om), *n.* [< OFr. < L. < Gr. *rheuma,* a flow], 1. any watery discharge from the mucous membranes, as of the eyes, nose, etc. 2. a cold; rhinitis. **—rheum′ic,** *adj.* **—rheum′y** [-IER, -IEST], *adj.*

**rheu·mat·ic** (ro͞o-mat′ik), *adj.* 1. of or caused by rheumatism. 2. having or subject to rheumatism. *n.* one who has rheumatism.

**rheumatic fever,** an infectious disease that most commonly attacks children and is characterized by fever, inflammation of the heart valves, etc.

**rheu·ma·tism** (ro͞o′mə-tiz'm), *n.* [< L. < Gr. *rheumatismos;* see RHEUM], 1. a painful condition of the joints and muscles; esp., a disease believed to be caused by a microorganism, with inflammation and pain of the joints. 2. rheumatic fever. **—rheu′ma·toid′** (-toid′), **rheu′ma·toi′dal,** *adj.*

**rheumatoid arthritis,** a chronic disease characterized by inflammation, stiffness, and often deformity, of the joints.

**Rh factor,** [first discovered in *rh*esus monkeys], an agglutinating factor, usually present in human blood, which may cause hemolytic reactions during pregnancy or after transfusion of blood containing this factor into someone lacking it: people who have this factor are *Rh positive;* those who do not are *Rh negative:* also called **Rhesus factor.**

**rhi·nal** (rī′n'l), *adj.* [< *rhin*(*o*)- + *-al*], of the nose; nasal.

**Rhine** (rīn), *n.* a river flowing through Switzerland and Germany into the North Sea.

**Rhine·gold** (rīn′gōld′), *n.* Rheingold.

**Rhine·land** (rīn′land′, -lənd), *n.* that part of Germany west of the Rhine.

**rhine·stone** (rīn′stōn′), *n.* [transl. of Fr. *caillou du Rhin:* so called because orig. made at Strasbourg], an artificial gem of colorless, bright glass or paste, often cut to imitate a diamond.

**Rhine wine,** 1. any of various wines produced in the Rhine Valley; esp., any such light, dry white wine. 2. a wine like this produced elsewhere.

**rhi·ni·tis** (rī-nī′tis), *n.* [see RHINO- & -ITIS], inflammation of the nasal mucous membrane.

**rhi·no** (rī′nō), *n.* [*pl.* -NOS], [Colloq.], a rhinoceros.

**rhi·no-,** [< Gr. *rhis,* the nose], a combining form meaning *nose:* also **rhin-.**

**rhi·noc·er·os** (rī-nos′ēr-əs), *n.* [*pl.* -OSES, -OS; see PLURAL, II, D, 1], [< LL. < Gr. < *rhis*, the nose + *keras*, horn], any of various large, thick-skinned, plant-eating mammals of Africa and Asia, with one or two upright horns on the snout.

INDIAN RHINOCEROS ($5\text{-}5\frac{3}{4}$ ft. high at shoulder)

**rhi·zo-,** [< Gr. *rhiza*, a root], a combining form meaning *root:* also **rhiz-.**

**rhi·zoid** (rī′zoid), *adj.* rootlike: also **rhi·zoi′dal.** *n.* any of the rootlike filaments in a moss, fern, etc. that attach it to the substratum.

**rhi·zome** (rī′zōm), *n.* [< Gr. < *rhiza*, a root], a horizontal, rootlike stem under or along the ground, which usually sends out roots from its lower surface and leafy shoots from its upper surface. —**rhi·zom′a·tous** (-zom′ə-təs, -zō′mə-), *adj.*

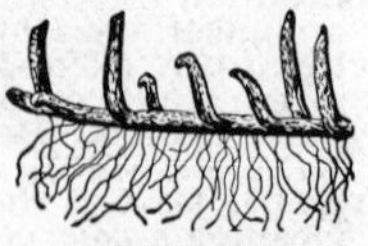
RHIZOME (of sensitive fern)

**rhi·zo·pod** (rī′zə-pod′), *n.* [*rhizo-* + *-pod*], any of various one-celled animals with rootlike pseudopods.

**rho** (rō), *n.* [Gr.], the seventeenth letter of the Greek alphabet (Ρ, ρ).

**Rhode Island** (rōd), a New England State of the U.S.: area, 1,214 sq. mi.; pop., 859,000; capital, Providence: abbrev. **R.I.** —**Rhode Islander.**

**Rhode Island Red,** any of a breed of American chicken with reddish feathers and a black tail.

**Rhodes** (rōdz), *n.* one of the Dodecanese Islands SW of Turkey. —**Rho′di·an,** *adj.* & *n.*

**Rho·de·si·a** (rō-dē′zhi-ə, -zhə), *n.* a country in S Africa: area, 150,333 sq. mi.; pop., 4,530,000; capital, Salisbury. —**Rho·de′sian,** *adj.* & *n.*

**Rhodesian man,** [< Northern *Rhodesia*, where cranial remains have been found], a type of early man similar to Neanderthal man.

**rho·di·um** (rō′di-əm), *n.* [< Gr. *rhodon*, a rose: from the color of its salts], a hard, gray-white metallic chemical element, used as an alloy with platinum and gold: symbol, Rh; at. wt., 102.91; at. no., 45. —**rho′dic,** *adj.*

**rho·do-,** [< Gr. *rhodon*, a rose], a combining form meaning *rose, rose-red:* also **rhod-.**

**rho·do·den·dron** (rō′də-den′drən), *n.* [L. < Gr. < *rhodon*, a rose + *dendron*, a tree], any of various trees and shrubs, mainly evergreen, with showy flowers of pink, white, or purple.

**rhom·boid** (rom′boid), *n.* [< Fr. < LL. < Gr.; see RHOMBUS & -OID], a parallelogram with oblique angles and only the opposite sides equal. *adj.* shaped like a rhomboid or rhombus: also **rhom·boi′dal.**

RHOMBOID

**rhom·bus** (rom′bəs), *n.* [*pl.* -BUSES, -BI (-bī)], [L. < Gr. *rhombos*], an equilateral parallelogram with oblique angles: also **rhomb.** —**rhomb′ic, rhom′bi·cal,** *adj.*

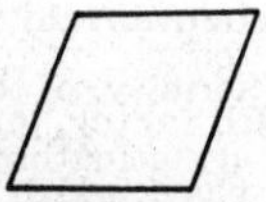
RHOMBUS

**Rhone, Rhône** (rōn), *n.* a river flowing through S Switzerland and SE France into the Mediterranean.

**rhu·barb** (rōō′bärb), *n.* [< OFr. < ML. < LL. < Gr. *rhēon*, plant from the *Rha*, (the Volga River) + *barbaron*, foreign], 1. any of various plants with large leaves and fleshy, acid leafstalks used as food. 2. the leafstalks made into a sauce or baked in a pie. 3. [Slang], a heated argument.

**rhumb** (rum, rumb), *n.* [< Fr. *rumb* or Port. & Sp. *rumbo*], 1. any of the points of a mariner's compass. 2. a course keeping a constant compass direction, charted as a line: in full, **rhumb line.**

**rhum·ba** (rum′bə), *n.* a rumba.

**rhyme** (rīm), *n.* [< OFr. *rime;* prob. < L. *rhythmus*, rhythm], 1. correspondence of end sounds in lines of verse or in words. 2. a word that corresponds with another in end sound (e.g., *love* & *above*, *witty* & *pretty*). 3. poetry or (a) verse employing such correspondence. *v.i.* [RHYMED, RHYMING], 1. to make verse, especially with rhymes. 2. to form a rhyme: as, "more" *rhymes* with "door." 3. to be composed with rhymes: said of verses. *v.t.* 1. to put into rhyme. 2. to compose in metrical form with rhymes. 3. to use (a word) as a rhyme. Also sp. **rime.** —**neither rhyme nor reason,** neither order nor sense. —**rhyme′less,** *adj.* —**rhym′er,** *n.*

**rhyme·ster** (rīm′stēr), *n.* a maker of mediocre rhymes or poems; poetaster.

**rhythm** (rith′'m, -əm), *n.* [< Fr. < L. < Gr. *rhythmos*, measure < *rheein*, to flow], 1. *a*) flow, movement, etc. characterized by a regular recurrence, as of beat, rise and fall, etc.: as, the *rhythm* of the heart, the seasons, etc. *b*) the pattern of such flow. 2. in *music*, *a*) regular recurrence of grouped strong and weak beats, or heavily and lightly accented tones, in alternation. *b*) form or pattern of this: as, waltz *rhythm*. Cf. **time, meter.** 3. in *prosody*, *a*) regular recurrence of stressed and unstressed or long and short syllables in alternation. *b*) form or pattern of this: as, iambic *rhythm*.

**rhyth·mi·cal** (rith′mi-k'l), *adj.* of or having rhythm: also **rhyth′mic.** —**rhyth′mi·cal·ly,** *adv.*

**rhythm method,** a method of birth control involving abstinence from sexual intercourse during the woman's probable monthly ovulation period.

**R.I.,** Rhode Island.

**ri·al** (rī′əl), *n.* [OFr., lit., royal], the monetary unit and a silver coin of Iran.

**Ri·al·to** (ri-al′tō), *n.* 1. an island in Venice, formerly the business center. 2. the theater district in New York City. 3. [r-], a trading place.

**rib** (rib), *n.* [AS. *rib*], 1. any of the arched bones attached posteriorly to the vertebral column and enclosing the chest cavity: in man there are twelve pairs of such bones. 2. a cut of meat having one or more ribs. 3. a raised ridge in cloth, especially in knitted material. 4. any riblike piece used to form or strengthen something: as, a *rib* of an umbrella, the *ribs* of an arch, etc. 5. any of the main veins of a leaf. *v.t.* [RIBBED, RIBBING], 1. to provide, form, or strengthen with ribs. 2. [Slang], to tease. —**ribbed,** *adj.* —**rib′ber,** *n.* —**rib′less,** *adj.*

**rib·ald** (rib′əld), *adj.* [OFr. *ribauld;* prob. < Gmc.], characterized by coarse joking; offensive, irreverent, or vulgar in language. *n.* a ribald person.

**rib·ald·ry** (rib′əld-ri), *n.* ribald language.

**rib·and** (rib′ənd, -ən), *n.* [Archaic], a ribbon.

**rib·bing** (rib′iŋ), *n.* ribs collectively; arrangement of ribs, as in cloth, a ship, etc.

**rib·bon** (rib′ən), *n.* [< OFr. *riban*], 1. a narrow strip as of silk or rayon, used for decorating or tying, for badges, etc. 2. anything suggesting such a strip: as, a *ribbon* of blue sky. 3. *pl.* torn, ribbonlike shreds: as, a sleeve torn to *ribbons*. 4. a narrow strip of cloth inked for use on a typewriter, etc. *v.t.* 1. to decorate, trim, or mark with or as with ribbons. 2. to tear into ribbonlike shreds. *v.i.* to extend in a ribbonlike strip. —**rib′boned,** *adj.* —**rib′bon·like′,** *adj.* —**rib′bon·y,** *adj.*

**ri·bo·fla·vin** (rī′bə-flā′vin), *n.* [< *ribose*, a sugar + *flavin*], a factor of the vitamin B complex, found in milk, eggs, liver, fruits, leafy vegetables, etc.: lack of riboflavin in the diet causes stunted growth, loss of hair, etc.: also called *lactoflavin, vitamin* $B_2$.

**-ric** (rik), [AS. *rice*, reign], a combining form meaning *jurisdiction, realm*, as in *bishopric*.

**rice** (rīs), *n.* [OFr. *ris* < It. < L. < Gr. *oryza;* of Oriental origin], 1. a cereal grass grown widely in warm climates, especially in the Orient. 2. the starchy grain of this grass, used as food. *v.t.* [RICED, RICING], to reduce (potatoes, etc.) to a rice-like consistency.

**rice paper,** 1. a thin paper made from the straw of the rice grass. 2. a fine, delicate paper made in China from the pith of other plants.

**ric·er** (rīs′ēr), *n.* a utensil for ricing cooked potatoes, etc. by forcing them through small holes.

**rich** (rich), *adj.* [< AS. *rice*, noble], 1. having much money or property; wealthy. 2. having abundant natural resources: as, a *rich* country. 3. well supplied; abounding (with *in* or *with*). 4. valuable: as, a *rich* prize. 5. costly and elegant; sumptuous: as, *rich* gifts. 6. full of choice ingredients, as butter, sugar, cream, etc.: as, *rich* pastries. 7. *a*) full and mellow: said of sound, the voice, etc. *b*) deep; vivid: said of colors. *c*) very fragrant: said of odors. 8. abundant; ample: as, a *rich* fund of stories. 9. yielding in abundance, as soil, etc. 10. [Colloq.], *a*) very amusing. *b*) absurd. —**the rich,** wealthy people collectively. —**rich′ly,** *adv.* —**rich′ness,** *n.*

**Rich·ard I** (rich′ērd), 1157–1199; king of England (1189–1199): called **Richard the Lion-Hearted** (Fr., *Richard Coeur de Lion*).

**Rich·ard·son, Samuel** (rich′ērd-s'n), 1689–1761; English novelist.

**Ri·che·lieu, Duc de** (də rē′shə-lyö′; Eng. rish′ə-lōō′), 1585–1642; French cardinal and statesman.

**rich·es** (rich′iz), *n.pl.* [orig. sing.], [< OFr. *richesse*], wealth; money, real estate, etc.

**Rich·mond** (rich′mənd), *n.* 1. the capital of Virginia: port on the James River: pop., 220,000. 2. a borough of New York City, including all of Staten Island: pop., 222,000. 3. a city in California, near San Francisco: pop., 72,000.

**rick** (rik), *n.* [AS. *hreac*], a stack of hay, straw, etc.

especially one covered for protection from rain. *v.t.* to form into a rick or ricks.

**rick·ets** (rik′its), *n.* [? alteration of *rachitis*], a disease, chiefly of children, resulting from a lack of calcium, vitamin D, or sunlight, and characterized by a softening and, often, bending of the bones.

**rick·ett·si·a** (ri-ket′si-ə), *n.* [*pl.* -SIAE (-si-ē′)], [< H. T. *Ricketts* (1871–1910), Am. pathologist], any of a genus of microorganisms that cause certain diseases, as typhus: they are transmitted by the bite of certain lice and ticks. **—rick·ett′si·al,** *adj.*

**rick·et·y** (rik′i-ti), *adj.* 1. having rickets. 2. of or like rickets. 3. weak in the joints; feeble. 4. liable to fall or break down because weak; shaky. **—rick′et·i·ness,** *n.*

**rick·ey** (rik′i), *n.* [said to be < a Col. *Rickey*], a drink made of carbonated water, lime juice, and an alcoholic liquor, especially gin (*gin rickey*).

**rick·rack** (rik′rak′), *n.* [redupl. of *rack* (to stretch)], 1. flat, zigzag braid used as trimming for dresses, etc. 2. trimming made with this.

**rick·shaw, rick·sha** (rik′shô), *n.* a jinrikisha.

**ric·o·chet** (rik′ə-shā′, -shet′), *n.* [Fr.], the motion made by an object that rebounds or skips one or more times, as a pebble thrown along the surface of a pond. *v.i.* [-CHETED (-shād′) or -CHETTED (-shet′id), -CHETING (-shā′iŋ) or -CHETTING (-shet′iŋ)], to move with such a motion.

**rid** (rid), *v.t.* [RID or RIDDED, RIDDING], [< ON. *rythja*, to empty], to free, clear, or relieve, as of something undesirable: as, *rid* yourself of fear. **—be rid of,** to be freed from. **—get rid of,** 1. to get free from. 2. to do away with; dispose of.

**rid·dance** (rid′′ns), *n.* a ridding or being rid; clearance or removal, as of something undesirable. **—good riddance!** welcome relief or deliverance!

**rid·den** (rid′′n), pp. of **ride.** *adj.* dominated or obsessed (by the thing specified): as, fear-*ridden*.

**rid·dle** (rid′′l), *n.* [AS. *rædels* < *rædan*, to guess], 1. a puzzle in the form of a question, statement, etc., requiring some ingenuity to solve or answer it; conundrum. 2. any puzzling or perplexing person or thing; enigma. *v.t.* [-DLED, -DLING], to solve or explain (a riddle). *v.i.* to propound riddles. **—rid′dler,** *n.*

**rid·dle** (rid′′l), *n.* [AS. *hriddel*], a coarse sieve for cinders, gravel, etc. *v.t.* [-DLED, -DLING], 1. to sift through a riddle. 2. to make holes in; perforate: as, bullets *riddled* the wall. 3. to show many flaws in, as a theory. **—rid′dler,** *n.*

**ride** (rīd), *v.i.* [RODE or *archaic* RID, RIDDEN or *archaic* RID or RODE, RIDING], [AS. *ridan*], 1. to sit on and control a horse or other animal in motion. 2. to be carried along in a vehicle, etc. 3. to be carried on something as if on a horse, etc. 4. to be carried or supported in motion (*on* or *upon*): as, tanks *ride* on treads. 5. to move, lie, or float on the water. 6. to admit of being ridden: as, the car *rides* smoothly. 7. to move out of place (with *up*): as, his collar *rode* up constantly. 8. [Slang], to continue undisturbed, with no action taken: as, let the matter *ride*. *v.t.* 1. to sit on or in and control so as to move along: as, *ride* a horse. 2. to move along on or be carried or supported on: as, the ship *rides* the waves, he *rode* the bus. 3. to move over, along, or through (a road, area, etc.) by horse, car, etc. 4. to engage in by riding: as, to *ride* a race. 5. to cause to ride. 6. to control, dominate, or oppress: as, *ridden* by fear. 7. [Colloq.], to torment or tease, as with ridicule, criticism, etc. *n.* 1. a riding; esp., a journey by horseback, automobile, etc. 2. a road, etc. for riding. **—ride down,** 1. to knock down by riding against. 2. to overtake by riding. 3. to overcome. 4. to exhaust (a horse, etc.) by riding. **—ride out,** to withstand or endure (a storm, crisis, etc.) successfully. **—take for a ride,** [Slang], 1. to take somewhere (as in an automobile) and kill. 2. to hoax; deceive. **—rid′a·ble,** *adj.*

**rid·er** (rīd′ẽr), *n.* 1. a person who rides. 2. an addition or amendment to a document, etc. 3. a clause, usually dealing with an unrelated matter, added to a legislative bill when it is up for passage. 4. any of various pieces moving or resting on something else. **—rid′er·less,** *adj.*

**ridge** (rij), *n.* [AS. *hrycg*], 1. the long, narrow top or crest of something, as of an animal's back, a wave, etc. 2. a long, narrow elevation of land or range of hills or mountains. 3. any narrow raised strip, as on fabric. 4. the horizontal line formed by the meeting of two sloping surfaces: as, the *ridge* of a roof. *v.t. & v.i.* [RIDGED, RIDGING], 1. to mark as with ridges. 2. to form into or furnish with a ridge or ridges. **—ridge′like′,** *adj.* **—ridg′y** [-IER, -IEST], *adj.*

**ridge·pole** (rij′pōl′), *n.* the horizontal timber or beam at the ridge of a roof: also **ridge′piece′, ridge pole, ridge beam,** etc.

**rid·i·cule** (rid′i-kūl′), *n.* [Fr. < L. *ridiculus*, laughable < *ridere*, to laugh], 1. the act or practice of making someone or something the object of contemptuous laughter by mocking, caricaturing, etc.; derision. 2. words or actions intended to produce such laughter. *v.t.* [-CULED, -CULING], to make fun of with ridicule; deride. **—rid′i·cul′er,** *n.*

**ri·dic·u·lous** (ri-dik′yoo-ləs), *adj.* deserving ridicule; absurd; preposterous. **—ri·dic′u·lous·ly,** *adv.* **—ri·dic′u·lous·ness,** *n.*

**rid·ing** (rīd′iŋ), *n.* [AS. *-thrithing*, a third part], any of the three administrative divisions of Yorkshire, England.

**Rie·ka** (rye′kä), *n.* Fiume: Yugoslavian name.

**Rif** (rif), *n.* a hilly region along the Mediterranean coast of Morocco: also Er Rif (er), **Riff.**

**rife** (rīf), *adj.* [AS. *rife*], 1. frequently or commonly occurring; widespread: as, gossip was *rife*. 2. abounding; replete (followed by *with*): as, a thesis *rife* with error. **—rife′ness,** *n.*

**Riff** (rif), *n.* 1. a Berber living in or near the Rif. 2. the Rif. **—Rif′fi·an** (-i-ən), *adj. & n.*

**rif·fle** (rif′′l), *n.* [< the *v.*], 1. *a*) a shoal, reef, etc. in a stream, producing a ripple. *b*) such a ripple. 2. the act or method of riffling cards. *v.t. & v.i.* [-FLED, -FLING], [prob. var. of *ripple*], 1. to flow over a riffle. 2. to shuffle (playing cards) by holding part of the deck in each hand, raising the edges slightly, and letting the cards fall alternately together.

**riff·raff** (rif′raf′), *n.* [< OFr. *rif et raf;* see RIFLE (to rob) & RAFFLE], 1. those people regarded as of no consequence or merit; rabble. 2. [Dial.], trash.

**ri·fle** (rī′f′l), *v.t.* [-FLED, -FLING], [Fr. *rifler*, to scrape; prob. < OLG. < *rive*, a groove], to cut spiral grooves within (a gun barrel, etc.). *n.* 1. a firearm having spiral grooves in the barrel to spin the bullet and so give it greater accuracy and distance; esp., such a firearm to be fired from the shoulder. 2. *pl.* troops armed with rifles.

**ri·fle** (rī′f′l), *v.t.* [-FLED, -FLING], [< OFr. *rifler;* of Gmc. origin], 1. to ransack and rob; pillage: as, the troops *rifled* the city. 2. to strip bare: as, thieves *rifled* the safe. 3. to take as plunder; steal. **—ri′fler,** *n.*

**ri·fle·man** (rī′f′l-mən), *n.* [*pl.* -MEN], 1. a soldier armed with a rifle. 2. a man who uses a rifle.

**rifle range,** a place for target practice with a rifle.

**ri·fling** (rī′fliŋ), *n.* 1. the act or operation of cutting spiral grooves within a gun barrel. 2. a system of such grooves.

**rift** (rift), *n.* [< Dan. < ON. < *ripta*, to break (a bargain)], an opening caused by splitting; cleft. *v.t. & v.i.* to burst open; split.

**rig** (rig), *v.t.* [RIGGED, RIGGING], [? < ON. *rigga*, to wrap around], 1. *a*) to fit (a ship, mast, etc.) with sails, shrouds, etc. *b*) to fit (a ship's sails, shrouds, etc.) to the masts, yards, etc. 2. to fit out; equip (often with *out* or *up*). 3. to prepare for use, especially in a hurried fashion (often with *up*). 4. to arrange in a dishonest way for selfish advantage. 5. [Colloq.], to dress; clothe (often with *out* or *up*). *n.* 1. the arrangement of sails, masts, etc. on a vessel. 2. apparatus; equipment; gear. 3. a carriage, etc. with its horse or horses. 4. [Colloq.], dress; costume. **—rigged,** *adj.* **—rig′ger,** *n.*

**Ri·ga** (rē′gə), *n.* seaport and capital of the Latvian S.S.R.: pop., 393,000.

**rig·ger** (rig′ẽr), *n.* one who rigs; specif., one whose work is fitting the rigging of ships.

**rig·ging** (rig′iŋ), *n.* 1. the chains, ropes, etc. used for supporting and working the masts, sails, etc. of a vessel. 2. equipment; tackle.

**right** (rīt), *adj.* [AS. *riht*], 1. straight: as, a *right* line. 2. *a*) formed by a straight line perpendicular to a base: as, a *right* angle. *b*) having the axis perpendicular to the base: as, a *right* cylinder. 3. in accordance with justice, law, etc.; virtuous: as, *right* conduct. 4. in accordance with fact, reason, etc.; correct: as, the *right* answer. 5. *a*) fitting; suitable. *b*) most convenient or favorable. 6. designating the side meant to be seen: as, the *right* side of cloth. 7. having sound physical or mental health. 8. *a*) designating or of that side of one's body which is toward the east when one faces north.

*b*) designating or of the corresponding side of anything. *c*) closer to the right side of a person facing the thing mentioned. 9. of the political right; conservative or reactionary. 10. [Archaic], genuine; real. ***n.*** 1. what is right, or just, lawful, proper, etc. 2. a power, privilege, etc. that belongs to a person by law, nature, etc.; as, his *right* to speak. 3. all or part of the right side. 4. in *boxing*, *a*) the right hand. *b*) a blow delivered with the right hand. 5. [often R-], in *politics*, a conservative or reactionary position, party, etc. (often with *the*): from the location of their seats in some European legislatures. ***adv.*** 1. in a straight line; directly: as, go *right* home. 2. *a*) properly; fittingly. *b*) favorably; conveniently. 3. completely; thoroughly. 4. exactly; precisely: as, *right* here. 5. immediately: as, come *right* now. 6. according to law, justice, etc. 7. correctly. 8. on or toward the right hand. 9. very; extremely: as, he knows *right* well: dialectal or colloquial except in certain titles, as, the *right* honorable. ***v.t.*** 1. to put in an upright position: as, we *righted* the boat. 2. to correct. 3. to put in order: as, she *righted* the room. 4. to do justice to (a person). 5. to make amends for. ***v.i.*** to resume an upright position. —**by right** (or **rights**), in justice; properly. —**in the right,** right; correct. —**right away** (or **off**), at once; immediately. —**to rights,** [Colloq.], in or into proper condition or order. —**right′a·ble,** ***adj.*** —**right′er,** ***n.*** —**right′ness,** ***n.***

**right·a·bout** (rīt′ə-bout′), ***n.*** a rightabout-face. ***adv. & adj.*** with, in, or by a rightabout-face.

**right·a·bout-face** (rīt′ə-bout′fās′), ***n.*** 1. a turning directly about to face in the opposite direction. 2. a complete reversal, as of belief. ***interj.*** a military command to perform a rightabout-face.

**right angle,** an angle of 90 degrees, made by the meeting of two lines perpendicular to each other.

**right-an·gled** (rīt′aŋ′g'ld), ***adj.*** having or forming one or more right angles; rectangular.

**right·eous** (rī′chəs), ***adj.*** [altered < AS. *rihtwis;* see RIGHT & -WISE], 1. acting in a just, upright manner; virtuous: as, a *righteous* man. 2. morally right or justifiable: as, a *righteous act.* —**right′eous·ly,** ***adv.*** —**right′eous·ness,** ***n.***

**right·ful** (rīt′fəl), ***adj.*** 1. right; just; fair. 2. having a just, lawful claim, or right: as, the *rightful* owner. 3. belonging or owned by just or lawful claim: as, a *rightful* rank. —**right′ful·ly,** ***adv.*** —**right′ful·ness,** ***n.***

**right-hand** (rīt′hand′), ***adj.*** 1. on or toward the right. 2. of, for, or with the right hand. 3. most helpful or reliable: as, my *right-hand* man.

**right-hand·ed** (rīt′han′did), ***adj.*** 1. using the right hand more skillfully than the left. 2. done with the right hand. 3. made for use with the right hand. 4. turning from left to right; clockwise. —**right′-hand′ed·ness,** ***n.***

**right·ist** (rīt′ist), ***n.*** in *politics*, one who is conservative or reactionary; member of the right. ***adj.*** in *politics*, conservative or reactionary.

**right·ly** (rīt′li), ***adv.*** 1. with justice; fairly. 2. properly; suitably. 3. correctly.

**right-mind·ed** (rīt′mīn′did), ***adj.*** thinking what is right; having correct views or principles. —**right′-mind′ed·ly,** ***adv.*** —**right′mind′ed·ness,** ***n.***

**right·o** (rīt′ō′), ***interj.*** [Brit. Colloq.], all right.

**right of way,** 1. the right to move first, as at traffic intersections. 2. right of passage, as over another's property. 3. a strip of land used by a railroad for its tracks. 4. land over which a road, an electric-power line, etc. passes. Also **right′-of-way′.**

**right triangle,** a triangle with one right angle.

**right whale,** a large-headed whalebone whale without teeth or dorsal fin.

**right wing,** in *politics*, the more conservative or reactionary section of a party, group, etc. —**right′-wing′,** ***adj.*** —**right′-wing′er,** ***n.***

**rig·id** (rij′id), ***adj.*** [< L. < *rigere*, to be stiff], 1. not bending or flexible; stiff: as, a *rigid* metal girder. 2. not moving; set. 3. severe; strict: as, a *rigid* taskmaster, rule, etc. 4. in *aeronautics*, having a rigid framework that encloses containers for the gas, as a dirigible. —**ri·gid′i·ty** [*pl.* -TIES], **rig′id·ness,** ***n.*** —**rig′id·ly,** ***adv.***

**rig·ma·role** (rig′mə-rōl′), ***n.*** [< *ragman roll* < ME. *rageman*, a document], silly, meaningless, or confused talk; nonsense.

**rig·or** (rig′ẽr), ***n.*** [< OFr. < L. < *rigere*, to be rigid], 1. extreme harshness or severity; specif., *a*) strictness: as, the *rigor* of martial law. *b*) hardship: as, the *rigors* of life. 2. a severe, harsh, or oppressive act, etc. 3. stiffness; rigidity.

‡**ri·gor mor·tis** (rī′gôr môr′tis, rig′ẽr), [L., stiffness of death], the stiffening of the muscles after death.

**rig·or·ous** (rig′ẽr-əs), ***adj.*** 1. very strict or harsh, as rules. 2. very severe or sharp, as climate. 3. rigidly precise: as, *rigorous* scholarship. —**rig′or·ous·ly,** ***adv.*** —**rig′or·ous·ness,** ***n.***

**rig·our** (rig′ẽr), ***n.*** rigor: Brit. spelling.

**rile** (rīl), ***v.t.*** [RILED, RILING], [pronun. var. of *roil*], [Colloq.], 1. to make (a liquid) muddy by stirring the dregs. 2. to anger; irritate.

**Ri·ley, James Whit·comb** (hwit′kəm rī′li), 1853?–1916; U.S. poet: called the *Hoosier poet.*

**rill** (ril), ***n.*** [cf. D. *ril* & G. *rille*], a little brook.

**rim** (rim), ***n.*** [AS. *rima*, an edge], 1. the edge, border, or margin, especially of something circular. 2. *a*) the outer part of a wheel. *b*) a circular strip of metal on which the tire is mounted on the wheel of an automobile, etc. ***v.t.*** [RIMMED, RIMMING], 1. to put a rim on or around. 2. to roll around the rim of: as, the golf ball *rimmed* the hole. —**rim′less,** ***adj.*** —**rimmed,** ***adj.***

**rime** (rīm), ***n., v.t. & v.i.*** [RIMED, RIMING], rhyme. —**rim′er,** ***n.***

**rime** (rīm), ***n.*** [< AS. *hrim*], white frost on grass, leaves, etc.; hoarfrost. ***v.t.*** [RIMED, RIMING], to coat with rime. —**rim′y** [-IER, -IEST], ***adj.***

**Rim·ski-Kor·sa·kov, Ni·ko·lai** (nik′ə-lī′ rim′ski-kôr′sə-kôf′), 1844–1908; Russian composer.

**rind** (rīnd), ***n.*** [AS.], a hard or firm outer layer or coating: as, the *rind* of cheese or fruit.

**rin·der·pest** (rin′dẽr-pest′), ***n.*** [< G. *rinder*, cattle + *pest*, a plague], an acute infectious disease of cattle and, often, sheep and goats.

**ring** (riŋ), ***v.i.*** [RANG or *rarely* RUNG, RUNG, RINGING], [< AS. *hringan*], 1. to give forth the resonant sound of a bell. 2. to produce, as by sounding, a specified impression: as, her promises *rang* false. 3. to cause a bell to sound. 4. to sound a bell as a summons: as, she *rang* for the maid. 5. to sound loudly; resound: as, the room *rang* with merriment. 6. to have a sensation as of ringing, etc.: said of the ears or head. ***v.t.*** 1. to cause (a bell, etc.) to ring. 2. to sound (a peal, etc.) as by ringing a bell. 3. to signal or announce (*in* or *out*), etc. as by ringing. 4. to call by telephone. ***n.*** 1. the sound of a bell. 2. any similar sound, especially when loud and continued: as, the *ring* of an ovation. 3. a characteristic sound or quality: as, the *ring* of pride. 4. act of ringing a bell, etc. 5. a telephone call. —**ring down the curtain,** 1. to signal for a theater curtain to be lowered. 2. to end something. —**ring up,** to record (a specified amount) in a cash register. —**ring up the curtain,** 1. to signal for a theater curtain to be raised. 2. to begin something.

**ring** (riŋ), ***n.*** [AS. *hring*], 1. a small, circular band, especially of precious metal, to be worn on the finger. 2. any circular object used for some special purpose: as, a key *ring.* 3. a circular line, mark, or figure. 4. the outer edge, or rim, as of a wheel. 5. any of the circular marks seen in the cross section of a tree trunk, resulting from the yearly addition of layers of wood: in full, **annual ring.** 6. a number of people or things grouped in a circle. 7. a group of people working together to advance their own selfish interests, as in politics, etc. 8. an enclosed area, often circular, for contests, exhibitions, etc.: as, the *ring* of a circus. 9. an enclosure, now a square, in which boxing and wrestling matches are held; hence, prize fighting (with *the*). 10. a political contest: now usually in *toss one's hat in the ring*, to announce publicly that one is a candidate for political nomination. ***v.t.*** [RINGED, RINGING], 1. to encircle as with a ring. 2. to form into, or furnish with, a ring or rings. 3. in some games, to toss a ring, horseshoe, etc. so that it encircles (a peg). 4. to cut a circle of bark from (a tree). ***v.i.*** to form in a ring or rings. —**run rings around,** [Colloq.], 1. to run much faster than. 2. to excel greatly. —**ringed,** ***adj.***

**ring-bolt** (riŋ′bōlt′), ***n.*** a bolt with a ring at the head.

**ring·dove** (riŋ′duv′), ***n.*** 1. the European wood pigeon. 2. a European and Asiatic dove resembling the turtledove: also **ringed turtledove.**

**rin·gent** (rin′jənt), ***adj.*** [< L. ppr. of *ringi*, to gape], 1. gaping. 2. in *botany*, having the lips widely separated, as some corollas.

**ring·er** (riŋ′ẽr), ***n.*** a person or thing that rings, or encircles, etc.; specif., a horseshoe, quoit, etc. thrown so that it encircles the peg.

**ring·er** (riŋ′ẽr), ***n.*** 1. one that rings a bell, chime, etc. 2. [Slang], *a*) a player, horse, etc. dishonestly entered in some competition. *b*) a person or thing that very much resembles another.

**ring·lead·er** (riŋ′lēd′ẽr), ***n.*** a person who leads others, especially in unlawful acts, etc.

**ring·let** (riŋ′lit), *n.* 1. a little ring. 2. a curl, especially a long one. —**ring′let·ed,** *adj.*
**ring·mas·ter** (riŋ′mas′tẽr, -mäs′-), *n.* a man who directs the performances in a circus ring.
**ring·side** (riŋ′sīd′), *n.* 1. the place just outside the ring, as at a boxing match or circus. 2. any place that provides a close view.
**ring·worm** (riŋ′wũrm), *n.* a contagious skin disease, as athlete's foot, caused by a fungus and characterized by ring-shaped patches.
**rink** (riŋk), *n.* [< Scot. < OFr. *renc,* rank, course], 1. a smooth expanse of ice for skating. 2. a smooth floor, usually of wood, for roller skating. 3. an enclosure for either of these.
**rinse** (rins), *v.t.* [RINSED, RINSING], [< OFr. *rincer;* ult. < L. *recens,* fresh], 1. to wash lightly. 2. to remove soap, dirt, etc. from by washing lightly with clean water. 3. to remove (soap, dirt, etc.) in this way. *v.i.* to admit of being rinsed. *n.* 1. a rinsing. 2. the water used in rinsing. —**rins′er,** *n.*
**Ri·o de Ja·nei·ro** (rē′ō də jə-nêr′ō, dā zhə-nā′rō), the capital, a seaport, of Brazil: pop., 2,303,000: often shortened to **Rio.**
**Ri·o Grande** (rē′ō grand′, gran′di, grän′dā), a river flowing from S Colorado to the Gulf of Mexico: the boundary between Texas and Mexico.
**ri·ot** (rī′ət), *n.* [< OFr. < *rioter* < L. *rugire,* to roar], 1. wild or violent disorder, confusion, etc.; tumult. 2. a violent disturbance of the peace by a number of persons assembled together. 3. a brilliant display (*of* color). 4. *a*) debauchery. *b*) unrestrained revelry. *v.i.* 1. to take part in a violent disturbance of the peace. 2. to revel. —**read the riot act to,** to command on pain of punishment to stop doing something. —**run riot,** 1. to act in a wild, unrestrained manner. 2. to grow in profusion. —**ri′ot·er,** *n.*
**ri·ot·ous** (rī′ət-əs), *adj.* 1. having the nature of a riot. 2. engaging in a riot. 3. *a*) loud and disorderly; boisterous. *b*) hilarious. —**ri′ot·ous·ly,** *adv.* —**ri′ot·ous·ness,** *n.*
**rip** (rip), *v.t.* [RIPPED, RIPPING], [prob. < MD. or LG.], 1. *a*) to cut or tear apart roughly. *b*) to sever the threads of (a seam). 2. to remove as by cutting or tearing roughly (with *off, out,* etc.). 3. to produce a rip in; tear. 4. to saw or split (wood) along the grain. *v.i.* 1. to become torn or split apart. 2. [Colloq.], to move with speed or violence. *n.* a torn place or burst seam, as in cloth. —**rip into,** [Colloq.], to attack violently, often with words. —**rip out,** [Colloq.], to utter sharply. —**rip′per,** *n.*
**rip** (rip), *n.* [prob. < *rip, v.*], an extent of rough water caused by cross currents or tides meeting.
**rip** (rip), *n.* [var. of *rep* (< *reprobate*)], [Colloq.], a dissolute, dissipated person.
**R.I.P.,** [L.], *Requiescat in pace,* may he (or she) rest in peace.
**ri·par·i·an** (ri-pâr′i-ən, rī-), *adj.* [< L. < *ripa,* a bank], of, relating to, or living on the bank of a river, lake, etc: as, *riparian* land.
**rip cord,** a cord, etc. for opening a parachute during descent.
**ripe** (rīp), *adj.* [AS.], 1. ready to be harvested for food, as grain or fruit. 2. like ripe fruit, as in being ruddy and full: as, *ripe* lips. 3. sufficiently advanced to be ready for use: as, *ripe* wine. 4. fully or highly developed; mature: as, *ripe* wisdom. 5. advanced in years: as, the *ripe* age of ninety. 6. fully prepared: as, *ripe* for trouble. 7. ready to be lanced, as a boil. 8. sufficiently advanced (*for*): said of time. —**ripe′ly,** *adv.* —**ripe′ness,** *n.*
**rip·en** (rīp′ən), *v.i.* & *v.t.* to become or make ripe; mature. —**rip′en·er,** *n.*
**ri·poste, ri·post** (ri-pōst′), *n.* [< Fr. < It. *risposta* < L. *respondere;* see RESPOND], 1. in *fencing,* a sharp, swift thrust made after parrying an opponent's lunge. 2. a sharp, swift retort. *v.i.* [-POSTED, -POSTING], to make a riposte.
**rip·ping** (rip′iŋ), *adj.* 1. that rips. 2. [Chiefly Brit. Slang], excellent; fine. —**rip′ping·ly,** *adv.*
**rip·ple** (rip′'l), *v.i.* [-PLED, -PLING], [prob. < *rip, v.* + *-le,* freq. suffix], 1. to form little waves on the surface, as water stirred by a breeze. 2. to flow with such waves on the surface. 3. to make a sound like that of rippling water. *v.t.* to cause to have ripples. *n.* 1. a small wave or undulation, as on the surface of water. 2. a movement, appearance, etc. like this. 3. the sound of rippling water. —**rip′pler,** *n.* —**rip′pling·ly,** *adv.* —**rip′ply** [-PLIER -PLIEST], *adj.*
**rip-roar·ing** (rip′rôr′iŋ, -rōr′-), *adj.* [Slang], very lively and noisy; boisterous; uproarious.
**rip·saw** (rip′sô′), *n.* a saw with coarse teeth, for cutting wood along the grain.
**rip·tide** (rip′tīd′), *n.* [see RIP (rough water)], a tide opposing another tide, producing rough waters.
**rise** (rīz), *v.i.* [ROSE, RISEN (riz′'n), RISING], [AS. *risan*], 1. to stand or assume a more nearly erect position after sitting, lying, etc. 2. to get up after sleeping or resting. 3. to return to life after dying. 4. to rebel; revolt: as, to *rise* against a king. 5. to end an official assembly, hearing, etc.: as, the court *rose.* 6. to go to a higher place or position; ascend. 7. to appear above the horizon: as, the moon *rose.* 8. to attain a higher level: as, the river is *rising.* 9. to advance in status, rank, etc.; become rich, famous, etc. 10. to become erect or rigid. 11. to extend or incline upward: as, the hills *rise* steeply. 12. to go up in pitch (of sound). 13. to increase in amount, degree, etc. 14. to become louder. 15. to become stronger, more vivid, etc.: as, his spirits *rose.* 16. to become larger and puffier, as dough with yeast. 17. to protrude; stand out. 18. to originate; begin. 19. to have a source: said of a stream. 20. to happen; occur. 21. to become apparent to the mind or senses: as, land *rose* ahead of them. 22. to be built: as, the house *rose* quickly. *v.t.* to cause to rise, as birds from cover. *n.* 1. the appearance of the sun, moon, etc. above the horizon. 2. upward motion; ascent. 3. an advance in status, rank, etc. 4. the appearance of a fish at the water's surface. 5. a return to life. 6. a piece of rising ground; hill. 7. a slope upward. 8. the vertical height of something, as a staircase. 9. an increase in height, as of water level. 10. an increase in pitch of a sound. 11. an increase in degree, amount, etc. 12. a beginning, origin, etc. 13. [Brit.], a raise (in wages). —**give rise to,** to bring about; begin. —**rise to,** to show oneself capable of coping with: as, he *rose to* the occasion.
**ris·er** (rīz′ẽr), *n.* 1. a person or thing that rises. 2. a vertical piece between the steps in a stairway.
**ris·i·bil·i·ty** (riz′ə-bil′ə-ti), *n.* [*pl.* -TIES], 1. the quality or state of being risible. 2. *usually pl.* sense of the ridiculous or amusing.
**ris·i·ble** (riz′ə-b'l), *adj.* [Fr. < LL. < L. *risus,* pp. of *ridere,* to laugh], 1. able or inclined to laugh. 2. of or connected with laughter. 3. causing laughter; laughable; funny. —**ris′i·bly,** *adv.*
**ris·ing** (rīz′iŋ), *adj.* 1. that rises; ascending, advancing, etc. 2. growing; maturing: as, the *rising* generation. *prep.* [Colloq.], somewhat more than. *n.* 1. the act of one that rises; esp., an uprising; revolt. 2. something that rises; projection.
**risk** (risk), *n.* [< Fr. *risque* < It. *risco*], 1. the chance of injury, damage, or loss; dangerous chance; hazard. 2. in *insurance, a*) the chance of loss. *b*) the degree of probability of loss. *v.t.* 1. to expose to risk; hazard: as, to *risk* one's life. 2. to incur the risk of: as, to *risk* a war. —**run** (or **take**) **a risk,** to expose oneself to a risk; take a chance. —**risk′er,** *n.*
**risk·y** (ris′ki), *adj.* [-IER, -IEST], involving risk; hazardous. —**risk′i·ly,** *adv.* —**risk′i·ness,** *n.*
**ris·qué** (ris-kā′; Fr. rēs′-), *adj.* [Fr., pp. of *risquer,* to risk; see RISK], very close to being improper or indecent; daring; suggestive.
**ris·sole** (ris′ōl; Fr. rē′sôl′), *n.* [Fr.; ult. < LL. *russeolus* < L. *russus,* red], a small ball or roll of minced meat or fish mixed with bread crumbs, egg, etc., enclosed in a thin pastry and fried.
**ri·tar·dan·do** (rē′tär-dän′dō), *adj.* [It., gerund of *ritardare,* to delay; see RETARD], in *music,* becoming gradually slower.
**rite** (rīt), *n.* [L. *ritus*], 1. a solemn, ceremonial act or observance in accordance with prescribed rule, as in a religion. 2. any formal, customary observance or procedure: as, the *rites* of courtship. 3. *a*) a particular system of ceremonial procedure; ritual. *b*) [often R-], liturgy; esp., any of the forms of the Eucharistic service.
**rit·u·al** (rich′ōō-əl), *adj.* [L. *ritualis*], of, having the nature of, or done as a rite. *n.* 1. a system of rites, religious or otherwise. 2. the observance of set forms or rites, as in worship. 3. a book containing rites. 4. a ritual service or procedure. —**rit′u·al·ly,** *adv.*
**rit·u·al·ism** (rich′ōō-əl-iz'm), *n.* 1. the observance of, or insistence on, ritual. 2. the study of religious ritual. —**rit′u·al·ist,** *n.* —**rit′u·al·is′tic,** *adj.* —**rit′u·al·is′ti·cal·ly,** *adv.*
**ritz·y** (rit′si), *adj.* [-IER, -IEST], [< the *Ritz-* Carlton

Hotel, New York City], [Slang], luxurious, fashionable, elegant, etc. —**ritz′i·ness,** *n.*

**ri·val** (rī′v'l), *n.* [Fr. < L. *rivalis,* orig., one using the same stream as another < *rivus,* a brook], 1. a person who is trying to get the same thing as another or to equal or surpass another; competitor. 2. a person or thing that can be said to equal or surpass another: as, plastics are *rivals* of many metals. *adj.* acting as a rival; competing. *v.t.* [-VALED or -VALLED, -VALING or -VALLING], 1. to try to equal or surpass. 2. to equal: as, he *rivals* his teacher in ability. *v.i.* [Archaic], to be a rival.

**ri·val·ry** (rī′v'l-ri), *n.* [*pl.* -RIES], act of rivaling or fact or state of being a rival; competition.

**rive** (rīv), *v.t. & v.i.* [RIVED, RIVED or RIVEN (riv′'n), RIVING], [ON. *rifa*], 1. to tear apart; rend. 2. to split; cleave. —**riv′er,** *n.*

**riv·er** (riv′ẽr), *n.* [< OFr. < LL. < L. *riparius;* see RIPARIAN], 1. a natural stream of water larger than a creek, emptying into an ocean, lake, etc. 2. any plentiful stream or flow. —**sell down the river,** to betray, deceive, etc. —**up the river,** [Slang], (sent) to or confined in a penitentiary. —**riv′er·less,** *adj.* —**riv′er·like′,** *adj.*

**Ri·ve·ra, Die·go** (dye′gô rē-ve′rä), 1886–1957; Mexican painter, known especially for murals.

**river basin,** the area drained by a river and its tributaries.

**Riv·er·side** (riv′ẽr-sīd′), *n.* a city in S California: pop., 84,000.

**riv·er·side** (riv′ẽr-sīd′), *n.* the bank of a river. *adj.* on or near the bank of a river.

**riv·et** (riv′it), *n.* [< OFr. < *river,* to clinch], a metal bolt with a head on one end, used to fasten together heavy beams by being inserted through holes and then having the plain end hammered into a head. *v.t.* 1. to fasten with rivets. 2. to hammer the end of (a bolt, etc.) into a head. 3. to fasten or fix firmly. —**riv′et·er,** *n.*

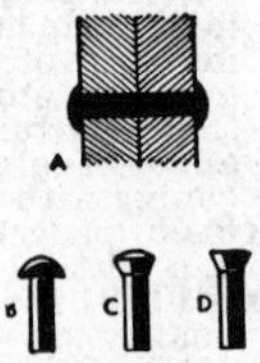


RIVET
A, rivet holding steel beams together; B, C, D, rivets

**Riv·i·er·a** (riv′i-âr′ə), *n.* a part of the Mediterranean coast of SE France and NW Italy: site of a famous resort area.

**riv·u·let** (riv′yoo-lit), *n.* [< It. *rivoletto* < L. *rivus,* a brook], a little stream.

**rm.,** [*pl.* RMS.], 1. ream. 2. room.

**Rn,** in *chemistry,* radon.

**R.N.,** 1. registered nurse. 2. Royal Navy.

**roach** (rōch), *n.* a cockroach.

**roach** (rōch), *n.* [*pl.* ROACH, ROACHES; see PLURAL, II, D, 2], [< OFr. *roche*], 1. a fresh-water fish of the carp family, found in N Europe. 2. any of various similar fishes, as the American sunfish.

**road** (rōd), *n.* [< AS. *rad,* a ride < *ridan,* to ride], 1. a way made for traveling between places by automobile, horseback, etc.; highway. 2. a way; path; course: as, the *road* to fortune. 3. a railroad. 4. *often in pl.* a protected place near shore where ships can ride at anchor. —**on the road,** 1. traveling, as a salesman. 2. on tour, as actors. —**take to the road,** to start traveling. —**the road,** the cities visited by touring theatrical companies.

**road agent,** a highwayman, especially as on former stagecoach routes in the western U.S.

**road·bed** (rōd′bed′), *n.* 1. the foundation laid to support the ties and rails of a railroad. 2. the foundation and surface of a road, or highway.

**road·block** (rōd′blok′), *n.* a blockade set up in a road to prevent movement of vehicles.

**road·house** (rōd′hous′), *n.* a tavern, inn, or night club at the side of a road in the country.

**road metal,** crushed rock, cinders, etc., used for making and repairing roads and roadbeds.

**road runner,** a long-tailed desert bird of the southwestern U.S., that can run swiftly.

**road·side** (rōd′sīd′), *n.* the side of a road. *adj.* on or at the side of a road.

**road·stead** (rōd′sted′), *n.* [*road* + *stead* (a place)], a road (sense 4).

**road·ster** (rōd′stẽr), *n.* an open automobile with a single seat and, often, a rumble seat.

**road·way** (rōd′wā′), *n.* 1. a road. 2. that part of a road used by cars, trucks, etc.

**roam** (rōm), *v.i.* [ME. *romen*], to travel without purpose, direction, or plan; wander; rove. *v.t.* to wander over or through: as, to *roam* the streets. *n.* a roaming; aimless travel. —**roam′er,** *n.*

**roan** (rōn), *adj.* [OFr. < Sp. *ruano*], grayish-yellow or reddish-brown with a thick sprinkling of gray or white: said chiefly of horses. *n.* 1. a roan color. 2. a roan horse or other animal.

**Ro·a·noke** (rō′ə-nōk′), *n.* 1. a city in SW Virginia: pop., 97,000. 2. an island off the NE coast of North Carolina: site of Raleigh's colony (1585–1587).

**roar** (rôr, rōr), *v.i.* [AS. *rarian*], 1. to utter a loud, deep, often rumbling, sound, as a lion. 2. to talk or laugh loudly and boisterously. 3. to operate with a loud noise, as a motor or gun. *v.t.* 1. to utter with a roar: as, he *roared* a welcome. 2. to make, put, etc. by roaring: as, he *roared* himself hoarse. *n.* 1. a loud, deep sound, as of a bull, lion, person shouting, etc. 2. a loud noise, as of waves, a motor, etc.; din. —**roar′er,** *n.*

**roast** (rōst), *v.t.* [< OFr. < OHG. < *rost,* gridiron], 1. to cook (meat, etc.) over an open fire or in an oven with little moisture; bake. 2. to dry, parch, or brown, as coffee, by exposure to heat. 3. to expose to great heat. 4. to heat (ore, etc.) in a furnace in order to remove impurities or cause oxidation. 5. [Colloq.], to criticize or ridicule severely. *v.i.* 1. to undergo roasting. 2. to become very hot. *n.* 1. roasted meat. 2. a cut of meat for roasting. 3. a roasting or being roasted. 4. [Colloq.], a picnic at which food is roasted: as, a steak *roast. adj.* roasted: as, *roast* pork.

**roast·er** (rōs′tẽr), *n.* 1. a person or thing that roasts. 2. a pan, oven, etc. for roasting meat. 3. a young chicken, pig, etc. suitable for roasting.

**rob** (rob), *v.t.* [ROBBED, ROBBING], [< OFr. < OHG. *roubon*], 1. to take property from unlawfully by using or threatening force. 2. to deprive of something legally belonging or due, as by stealth or fraud. *v.i.* to commit robbery. —**rob′ber,** *n.*

**rob·ber·y** (rob′ẽr-i), *n.* [*pl.* -IES], a robbing; specif., in *law,* the felonious taking of another's property from his person or in his immediate presence, by violence or intimidation.

**robe** (rōb), *n.* [< OFr. < OHG. *roub,* plunder], 1. a long, loose, usually outer, garment; specif., *a)* such a garment worn on formal occasions, to show rank or office, as by a judge. *b)* a bathrobe or dressing gown. 2. *pl.* clothes; costume. 3. a covering or wrap: as, a lap *robe. v.t. & v.i.* [ROBED, ROBING], to dress in a robe. —**robed,** *adj.*

**Rob·ert I** (rob′ẽrt), Robert the Bruce: see **Bruce.**

**Ro·bes·pierre, Max·i·mi·lien de** (mȧk′sē′mē′lyan′ də rô′bes′pyâr′; Eng. rōbz′pyer, -pêr), 1758–1794; French revolutionist; Jacobin leader.

**rob·in** (rob′in), *n.* [< OFr. dim. of *Robert*], 1. a large North American thrush with a dull-red breast. 2. a small European thrush with a yellowish-red breast. Also **robin redbreast.**

**Robin Good·fel·low** (good′fel′ō), in *English folklore,* a mischievous elf; Puck.

**Robin Hood,** in *English legend,* an outlaw who lived with his followers in Sherwood Forest and robbed the rich to help the poor.

**rob·in's-egg blue** (rob′inz-eg′), a light greenish blue.

**Rob·in·son, Edwin Arlington** (rob′in-s'n), 1869–1935; U.S. poet.

**Robinson Cru·soe** (krōō′sō), the hero of Defoe's novel (1719) of the same name, a sailor who is shipwrecked on a tropical island.

**ro·bot** (rō′bət, rob′ət), *n.* [< Czech *robotnik,* serf < *robotiti,* to drudge], 1. any of the manlike mechanical beings in Karel Capek's play *R.U.R.* (1923). 2. *a)* an automaton. *b)* a person who acts or works mechanically.

**robot bomb,** a small, jet-propelled airplane steered by a gyropilot and loaded with explosives: it falls as a bomb when its fuel is used up.

**ro·bust** (rō-bust′, rō′bust), *adj.* [< L. *robustus* < *robur,* hard variety of oak], 1. *a)* strong and healthy; hardy. *b)* strongly built; muscular. 2. suited to or requiring physical strength: as, *robust* work. 3. rough; rude; coarse: as, *robust* actions. —**ro·bust′ly,** *adv.* —**ro·bust′ness,** *n.*

**roc** (rok), *n.* [< Ar. < Per. *rukh*], in *Arabian & Persian legend,* a fabulous bird, so huge and strong that it could carry off the largest animal.

**Ro·chelle salt** (rō-shel′), [after *Rochelle,* France], a colorless, crystalline compound used as a laxative.

**Roch·es·ter** (ro′ches′tẽr; roch′is-), *n.* a city in W New York: pop., 319,000.

**rock** (rok), *n.* [< OFr. *roche*], 1. a large mass of stone. 2. *a)* stone in the mass. *b)* broken pieces of such stone. 3. *a)* mineral matter formed in masses in the earth's crust. *b)* a particular kind or mass of this. 4. anything like a rock, as in strength; esp., a firm support, basis, etc. 5. [Colloq. or Dial.], a stone. 6. [Slang], a diamond or other gem. —**on the rocks,** [Colloq.], 1. in a condition of ruin or catastrophe. 2. bankrupt. 3. served over ice cubes, as whisky.

**rock** (rok), *v.t.* [< AS. *roccian*], 1. to move back and forth or from side to side, as a cradle. 2. to make or put by moving in this way: as, *rock* the baby asleep. 3. to sway strongly; shake: as, the explosion *rocked* the house. *v.i.* 1. to move back and forth or from side to side. 2. to sway strongly; shake. *n.* 1. a rocking. 2. a rocking motion. 3. popular music evolved from rock-and-roll, containing elements of folk music, etc.

**rock-and-roll, rock 'n' roll** (rok′'n-rōl′), *n.* a kind of commercial jazz music based on the blues and having a strong, regular beat.

**rock bottom,** the lowest level; very bottom. **—rock′-bot′tom,** *adj.*

**rock-bound** (rok′bound′), *adj.* surrounded or hemmed in by rocks: as, a *rock-bound* inlet.

**rock candy,** large, hard, clear crystals of sugar.

**rock crystal,** a transparent, colorless quartz.

**Rock·e·fel·ler, John Da·vi·son** (dā′vi-s'n rok′ə-fel′ẽr), 1839–1937; U.S. capitalist and philanthropist.

**rock·er** (rok′ẽr), *n.* 1. either of the curved pieces on the bottom of a cradle, rocking chair, etc. 2. a rocking chair. 3. any of various devices that work with a rocking motion.

**rock·et** (rok′it), *n.* [It. *rocchetta,* a spool, orig. dim. of *rocca,* a distaff < OHG.], a projectile in which the combustion of a substance within produces gases that escape in the rear, driving the projectile forward by the principle of reaction: rockets are used in fireworks, weapons, aircraft, etc. *v.i.* to dart ahead swiftly like a rocket.

**rock·et·ry** (rok′ə-tri), *n.* 1. the science of designing, building, and launching rockets. 2. rockets collectively.

**Rock·ford** (rok′fẽrd), *n.* a city in N Illinois: pop., 127,000.

**rock garden,** a garden with flowers and plants growing among rocks variously arranged.

**Rock·ies** (rok′iz), *n.pl.* the Rocky Mountains.

**rocking chair,** a chair mounted on rockers or springs, so as to allow a rocking movement.

**rocking horse,** a toy horse of wood, etc., arranged on rockers or springs, for a child to ride.

**rock-ribbed** (rok′ribd′), *adj.* 1. having rocky ridges: as, *rock-ribbed* coasts. 2. firm; unyielding.

**rock salt,** common salt in solid masses.

**rock wool,** a fibrous material that looks like spun glass, made from molten rock or slag: it is used for insulation, especially in buildings.

**rock·y** (rok′i), *adj.* [-IER, -IEST], 1. full of rocks. 2. consisting of rock. 3. like a rock; firm, hard, unfeeling, etc. **—rock′i·ness,** *n.*

**rock·y** (rok′i), *adj.* [-IER, -IEST], 1. inclined to rock, or sway; unsteady. 2. [Slang], weak and dizzy, as from dissipation. **—rock′i·ness,** *n.*

**Rocky Mountain goat,** see **mountain goat.**

**Rocky Mountains,** a mountain system in W North America, extending from New Mexico to Alaska.

**Rocky Mountain sheep,** the bighorn.

**ro·co·co** (rə-kō′kō; *occas.* rō′kə-kō′), *n.* [Fr. < *rocaille,* shellwork], a style of architecture and decoration characterized by elaborate ornamentation imitating foliage, shellwork, scrolls, etc.: popular in the 18th century. *adj.* 1. of or in rococo. 2. too elaborate; florid and tasteless.

**rod** (rod), *n.* [AS. *rodd*], 1. in Biblical use, stock or race: as, the *rod* of Isaiah. 2. any straight stick or bar, as of wood, metal, etc. 3. *a*) a stick for beating as punishment. *b*) punishment. 4. *a*) a staff, scepter, etc. carried as a symbol of office or rank. *b*) power; authority. 5. a pole for fishing. 6. a stick used to measure something. 7. *a*) a measure of length equal to 5½ yards. *b*) a square rod; 30¼ square yards. 8. [Slang], a pistol. 9. in *biology,* a rod-shaped cell, microorganism, etc. **—spare the rod,** to refrain from punishing.

**rode** (rōd), pt. and archaic pp. of **ride.**

**ro·dent** (rō′d'nt), *adj.* [< L. *rodens,* ppr. of *rodere,* to gnaw], 1. gnawing. 2. of or like the rodents. *n.* any of several mammals, as rats, mice, rabbits, squirrels, etc., characterized by incisors adapted for gnawing; esp., a rat or mouse.

**ro·de·o** (rō′di-ō′, rō-dā′ō), *n.* [*pl.* -DEOS], [Sp. < *rodear,* to surround < L. *rotare;* see ROTATE], 1. a roundup of cattle. 2. a public exhibition of the skills of cowboys, as horsemanship, lassoing, etc.

**Ro·din, Au·guste** (ô′güst′ rô′dan′; Eng. rō-dan′), 1840–1917; French sculptor.

**rod·o·mon·tade** (rod′ə-mon-tād′, -täd′), *n.* [< Fr. < It. < *Rodomonte,* boastful leader in a 16th-century Italian play], arrogant boasting or blustering, ranting talk. *adj.* arrogantly boastful.

**roe** (rō), *n.* [prob. < ON. *hrogn*], 1. fish eggs, especially when still massed in the ovarian membrane. 2. fish sperm. 3. the spawn of certain crustaceans, as of the lobster.

**roe** (rō), *n.* [*pl.* ROE, ROES; see PLURAL, II, D, 2], [< AS. *ra, raha*], a small, agile, graceful European and Asiatic deer: also **roe deer.**

**roe·buck** (rō′buk′), *n.* [*pl.* -BUCKS, -BUCK; see PLURAL, II, D, 1], the male of the roe (deer).

**Roent·gen rays** (rent′gən), [after W. K. *Roentgen,* 1845–1923, German physicist who discovered them], [also r-], X rays: also sp. **Röntgen rays.**

**ro·ga·tion** (rō-gā′shən), *n.* [< OFr. < L. < *rogare,* to ask], *usually in pl.* a prayer or supplication, especially as chanted during the three days **(Rogation days)** before Ascension Day.

**Rog·er** (roj′ẽr), *interj.* [< conventional name of international signal flag for *R*], [also r-], 1. received: term used in radiotelephony to indicate reception of a message. 2. [Slang], right! O.K.!

**rogue** (rōg), *n.* [? ult. < L. *rogare,* to ask], 1. formerly, a vagabond. 2. a scoundrel. 3. a fun-loving, mischievous person. 4. an animal that wanders apart from the herd and is fierce and wild. *v.t.* [ROGUED (rōgd), ROGUING], to cheat. *v.i.* to live or act like a rogue.

**ro·guer·y** (rō′gə-ri), *n.* [*pl.* -IES], the behavior of a rogue; specif., *a*) cheating. *b*) playful mischief.

**rogue's gallery,** a collection of photographs of criminals, as used by police in identification.

**ro·guish** (rō′gish), *adj.* of or like a rogue; specif., *a*) dishonest; unscrupulous. *b*) playfully mischievous. **—ro′guish·ly,** *adv.* **—ro′guish·ness,** *n.*

**roil** (roil), *v.t.* [< Fr. < OFr. *rouil,* rust; ult. < L. *robigo,* rust], 1. to make (a liquid) cloudy, muddy, etc. by stirring up the sediment. 2. to displease; vex. **—roil′y** [-IER, -IEST], *adj.*

**roist·er** (rois′tẽr), *v.i.* [< OFr. < L. *rusticus;* see RUSTIC], 1. to swagger. 2. to be lively and noisy; revel. **—roist′er·er,** *n.* **—roist′er·ous,** *adj.*

**Ro·land** (rō′lənd), *n.* a legendary hero of the Charlemagne cycle, killed while fighting the Saracens.

**role, rôle** (rōl), *n.* [Fr. *rôle,* a roll: < the roll containing the actor's part], 1. a part, or character, assumed by an actor in a play. 2. a function assumed by someone: as, an advisory *role.*

**roll** (rōl), *v.i.* [< OFr. < LL. < L. *rotula,* dim. of *rota,* a wheel], 1. to move by turning over and over. 2. to move on wheels. 3. to pass: as, the years *rolled* by. 4. to move in a periodical revolution, as stars, etc. 5. to flow, as water, in a full, sweeping motion. 6. to extend in gentle swells. 7. to make a loud, rising and falling sound: as, thunder *rolls.* 8. to rise and fall in a full, mellow cadence, as speech. 9. to be wound into a ball or cylinder, as string. 10. to turn in a circular motion: as, her eyes *rolled.* 11. to move in a rocking motion, as a ship. 12. to walk by swaying. 13. to become spread under a roller. 14. to make progress; advance. *v.t.* 1. to move by turning over and over. 2. to move on wheels or rollers. 3. to beat (a drum) with light, rapid blows. 4. to utter with full, flowing sound. 5. to say with a trill: as, he *rolls* his r's. 6. to give a swaying motion to. 7. to move around or from side to side: as, she *rolled* her eyes. 8. to wind into a ball or cylinder: as, *roll up* the carpet. 9. to wrap or enfold. 10. to make flat, or spread out, by using a roller, etc. 11. to iron (sleeves, etc.) without forming a crease. 12. [Slang], to rob (a drunk or helpless person). 13. in *printing,* to spread ink on, as type, with a roller. *n.* 1. a rolling. 2. a scroll. 3. a register; catalogue. 4. a list of names for checking attendance. 5. a measure of something rolled into a cylinder: as, a *roll* of wallpaper. 6. a cylindrical mass of something. 7. any of various small cakes of bread, etc. 8. a roller. 9. a swaying motion. 10. a rapid succession of light blows on a drum. 11. a loud, reverberating sound, as of thunder. 12. a slight swell on the surface of something, as land. 13. a maneuver in which an airplane in flight performs a rotation around its axis. 14. [Slang], money; esp., a wad of paper money. **—roll back,** to reduce (prices) to a previous level by government action. **—roll in,** 1. to arrive, usually in large numbers. 2. [Colloq.], to abound in. **—roll round,** to recur, as in a cycle. **—roll up,** 1. to accumulate; increase. 2. [Colloq.], to arrive as in an automobile, etc. **—strike off the rolls,** to expel from membership. **—roll′a·ble,** *adj.*

**roll·a·way** (rōl′ə-wā′), *adj.* having rollers for easy moving and storing when not in use, as a bed.

**roll call,** the reading aloud of a roll, as in military formations, to find out who is absent.
**roll·er** (rōl′ẽr), *n.* 1. one that rolls. 2. *a*) a cylinder of metal, wood, etc. on which something is rolled or wound. *b*) a rolling cylinder used to crush, smooth, or spread something. 3. a long bandage in a roll. 4. a heavy, swelling wave that breaks on the shoreline. 5. a canary that trills its notes.
**roller bearing,** a bearing in which the shaft turns on rollers in a ringlike track.
**roller coaster,** an amusement ride in which small cars move on tracks that curve and dip sharply.
**roller skate,** a skate having four small wheels, instead of a runner, for use on a smooth surface. **—roll′er-skate′** [-SKATED, -SKATING], *v.i.*
**rol·lick** (rol′ik), *v.i.* [prob. blend of *romp* & *frolic*], to be gay, carefree, and hilarious in play; romp. **—rol′lick·ing, rol′lick·some,** *adj.*
**roll·ing** (rōl′iŋ), *adj.* 1. moving by turning over and over. 2. moving on wheels or rollers. 3. rotating or revolving. 4. folded over or back: as, a *rolling* collar. 5. swaying: as, a *rolling* walk. 6. surging; billowing, as waves. 7. reverberating, as thunder. 8. trilled: as, a *rolling* note. 9. dipping up and down in gentle slopes, as land. *n.* the action, motion, or sound of something that rolls.
**rolling mill,** 1. a factory in which metal bars, sheets, etc. are rolled out. 2. a machine used for such rolling.

ROLLING MILL

**rolling pin,** a heavy, smooth cylinder of wood, glass, etc. used to roll out dough.
**rolling stock,** locomotives, freight and passenger cars, and other wheeled railroad vehicles.
**roll-top** (rōl′top′), *adj.* made with a flexible top of parallel slats that slides back, as a desk.
**ro·ly-po·ly** (rō′li-pō′li), *adj.* [redupl. on *roll*], short and plump; pudgy. *n.* [*pl.* -LIES], 1. a roly-poly person or thing. 2. [Chiefly Brit.], a pudding made of rich dough spread with fruit or jam, rolled up, and boiled, steamed, etc.
**Rom.,** 1. Roman. 2. Romance. 3. Romanic. 4. Romans (Epistle to the Romans).
**rom.,** roman (type).
**Ro·ma·ic** (rō-mā′ik), *adj.* designating or of the language of modern Greece. *n.* Modern Greek.
**ro·maine** (rō-mān′), *n.* [Fr., fem. adj., Roman], a kind of lettuce with leaves that form a long, slender head: also **romaine lettuce.**
**Ro·man** (rō′mən), *adj.* 1. of or characteristic of ancient or modern Rome, its people, etc. 2. of the Roman Catholic Church, or the Latin Rite. 3. [usually r-], designating or of the usual style (upright and with serifs) of printing types. *n.* 1. a native, citizen, or inhabitant of ancient or modern Rome. 2. Latin. 3. loosely, a Roman Catholic. 4. [usually r-], roman type or characters.
**Roman arch,** a semicircular arch.
**Roman candle,** a firework consisting of a long tube that sends out balls of fire, sparks, etc.
**Roman Catholic,** 1. of the Roman Catholic Church. 2. a member of the Roman Catholic Church.
**Roman Catholic Church,** the Christian church headed by the Pope. **—Roman Catholicism.**
**Ro·mance** (rō-mans′, rō′mans), *adj.* [< Fr. < OFr. *romanz*; see ROMANCE (tale)], designating or of any of the languages derived from Low Latin, as French, Spanish, Italian, etc. *n.* these languages.
**ro·mance** (rō-mans′; *also, for n.*, rō′mans), *n.* [< OFr. *romanz*, Roman (i.e., the vernacular, not Latin); ult. < L. *Romanicus*, Roman], 1. a long, verse or prose narrative, originally written in one of the Romance dialects, about knights and chivalric deeds, adventure, and love. 2. a novel of love, adventure, etc. 3. the quality of excitement, love, etc. found in such literature. 4. real happenings having this quality. 5. the tendency to enjoy romantic adventures. 6. an exaggeration or falsehood. 7. a love affair. *v.i.* [-MANCED, -MANCING], 1. to write or tell romances. 2. to be fanciful or imaginative. 3. [Colloq.], to make love; woo. *v.t.* [Colloq.], to make love to. **—ro·manc′er,** *n.*
**Roman Curia,** the papal court: see **Curia Romana.**
**Roman Empire,** the empire of ancient Rome, existing from 27 B.C. until 395 A.D.
**Ro·man·esque** (rō′mə-nesk′), *adj.* designating or of a style of European architecture of the 11th and 12th centuries, using round arches and vaults, massive walls, etc. *n.* this style of architecture.
**Roman holiday,** entertainment or gain at the expense of others' suffering or loss: so called from the gladiatorial contests in ancient Rome.
**Ro·ma·ni·a, Ro·mâ·ni·a** (rō-mā′ni-ə, -mān′yə), *n.* a country in south central Europe, on the Black Sea: area, 91,669 sq. mi.; pop., c. 18,360,000; capital, Bucharest: also **Rumania, Roumania.**
**Ro·ma·ni·an** (rō-mā′ni-ən, -mān′yən), *adj.* of Romania, its people, language, etc. *n.* 1. a native or inhabitant of Romania. 2. the Romance language of the Romanians. Also **Rumanian, Roumanian.**
**Ro·man·ic** (rō-man′ik), *adj.* derived from ancient Rome or from vernacular Latin. *n.* in *linguistics*, Romance.
**Ro·man·ism** (rō′mən-iz′m), *n.* Roman Catholicism: hostile usage. **—Ro′man·ist,** *n.*
**Ro·man·ize** (rō′mən-iz′), *v.t. & v.i.* [-IZED, -IZING], 1. to make or become Roman in character, spirit, etc. 2. to convert or be converted to Roman Catholicism. **—Ro′man·i·za′tion,** *n.*
**Roman nose,** a nose with a prominent bridge.
**Roman numerals,** the Roman letters used as numerals until the 10th century A.D.: in Roman numerals, I = 1, V = 5, X = 10, L = 50, C = 100, D = 500, and M = 1,000. The value of a symbol following another of the same or greater value is added (e.g., XV = 15); the value of a symbol preceding one of greater value is subtracted (e.g., IX = 9).
**Ro·ma·nov** (rô-mä′nôf; Eng. rō′mə-nôf′), *n.* the Russian ruling family (1613–1917): also sp. **Romanoff.**
**Roman rite,** in the *R. C. Church*, 1. the authentic form or use of the Latin Rite. 2. the Latin Rite.
**Ro·mans** (rō′mənz), *n.pl.* [construed as sing.], a book of the New Testament, Epistle from the Apostle Paul to the Christians of Rome: abbrev. **Rom.**
**ro·man·tic** (rō-man′tik), *adj.* 1. of, like, or characterized by romance. 2. without a basis in fact; fanciful; fictitious. 3. not practical; visionary. 4. full of thoughts, feelings, etc. of romance. 5. of or characteristic of the Romantic Movement: now often used with derogatory implications of unrestrained sensuousness, escape from reality, etc. 6. suitable for romance. *n.* a romantic person. **—ro·man′ti·cal·ly,** *adv.*
**ro·man·ti·cism** (rō-man′tə-siz′m), *n.* 1. romantic spirit, outlook, etc. 2. *a*) the Romantic Movement. *b*) the spirit, style, etc. of, or adherence to, the Romantic Movement: contrasted with *classicism*, *realism*, etc. **—ro·man′ti·cist,** *n.*
**ro·man·ti·cize** (rō-man′tə-siz′), *v.t.* [-CIZED, -CIZING], to treat or regard romantically.
**Romantic Movement,** the revolt in the 18th and 19th centuries against the principles of neoclassicism: characterized in the arts by liberalism in form and subject matter, emphasis on feeling and imagination, etc.
**Rom·a·ny** (rom′ə-ni), *n.* [< Gypsy < *rom*, man], 1. [*pl.* -NY, -NIES], a gypsy. 2. the Indic language of the gypsies. *adj.* of the gypsies, their language, etc.
**Rom. Cath.,** Roman Catholic.
**Rome** (rōm), *n.* 1. the capital of Italy, on the Tiber River: pop., 1,702,000: formerly the capital of the Roman Empire. 2. the Roman Catholic Church.
**Ro·me·o** (rō′mi-ō′), *n.* 1. the hero of Shakespeare's tragedy *Romeo and Juliet* (c. 1595), lover of Juliet. 2. [*pl.* -OS], a lover.
**Rom·ma·ny** (rom′ə-ni), *n.* [*pl.* -NY, -NIES], & *adj.* Romany.
**romp** (romp), *n.* [< earlier *ramp*, hussy, prob. < OFr. *ramper*; see RAMP, *v.*], 1. one who romps, especially a girl. 2. boisterous, lively play. 3. [Slang], an easy, winning gait in a race: as, the horse won in a *romp*. *v.i.* 1. to play in a boisterous, lively way. 2. [Slang], to win with ease in a race, etc. **—romp′ish,** *adj.*
**romp·er** (rom′pẽr), *n.* 1. one who romps. 2. *pl.* a young child's loose-fitting outer garment, combining a waist with bloomerlike pants.
**Rom·u·lus** (rom′yoo-ləs), *n.* in *Rom. mythology*, the founder and first king of Rome: he and his twin brother Remus were reared by a she-wolf; later Romulus killed Remus.
**ron·deau** (ron′dō, ron-dō′), *n.* [*pl.* -DEAUX (-dōz, -dōz′)], [Fr. < *rondel* < *rond*, round], a short lyrical poem of thirteen (or ten) lines with an unrhymed refrain that consists of the opening words and is used in two places.
**ron·del** (ron′d'l, -del), *n.* [OFr.; see RONDEAU], a kind of rondeau, usually with fourteen lines, two rhymes, and the first two lines used as a refrain in the middle and at the end.
**ron·do** (ron′dō, ron-dō′), *n.* [*pl.* -DOS], [It. < Fr.; see

RONDEAU], in *music*, a composition or movement having its principal theme stated three or more times, interposed with subordinate themes.

**Röntgen rays,** [also r-], Roentgen rays; X rays.

**rood** (rōōd), *n.* [AS. *rod*], 1. originally, the cross on which Jesus was crucified. 2. any cross representing this; crucifix. 3. a measure of area usually equal to ¼ acre (40 square rods).

**roof** (rōōf, roof), *n.* [*pl.* ROOFS], [AS. *hrof*], 1. the outside top covering of a building. 2. anything like a roof: as, the *roof* of the mouth. *v.t.* to cover as with a roof. —**raise the roof,** [Slang], to be very noisy, as in applause, anger, etc. —**roof′less,** *adj.*

**roof·er** (rōōf′ẽr, roof′-), *n.* a person who builds or repairs roofs.

**roof garden,** 1. a garden on the flat roof of a building. 2. the roof or top floor of a building, decorated as a garden and used as a restaurant, etc.

**roof·ing** (rōōf′iŋ, roof′-), *n.* 1. the act of covering with a roof. 2. material for roofs. 3. a roof.

**roof·tree** (rōōf′trē′, roof′-), *n.* 1. the ridgepole. 2. a roof. 3. a home or shelter.

**rook** (rook), *n.* [AS. *hroc*], 1. a European crow that builds its nest in trees around buildings. 2. a cheat, especially in gambling. *v.t. & v.i.* to swindle; cheat.

**rook** (rook), *n.* [< OFr. *roc* < Per. *rukh*], in *chess*, a castle.

**rook·er·y** (rook′ẽr-i), *n.* [*pl.* -IES], 1. a breeding place or colony of rooks, or of some other animals or birds, as seals, penguins, etc. 2. a shabby, overcrowded tenement house or district.

**rook·ie** (rook′i), *n.* [< *recruit*], [Slang], 1. an inexperienced recruit in the army. 2. any novice.

**room** (rōōm, room), *n.* [AS. *rum*], 1. space that holds or can hold something: as, *room* for one more. 2. opportunity: as, *room* for doubt. 3. an interior space enclosed or set apart by walls. 4. *pl.* living quarters; lodgings. 5. the people in a room: as, the whole *room* was silent. *v.i.* to have lodgings. *v.t.* to provide with lodgings.

**room and board,** lodging and meals.

**room·er** (rōōm′ẽr, room′-), *n.* a person who rents a room or rooms to live in; lodger.

**room·ette** (rōōm-et′, room-), *n.* a small, private bedroom in some railroad sleeping cars.

**room·ful** (rōōm′fool′, room′-), *n.* [*pl.* -FULS], 1. as much or as many as will fill a room. 2. the people or objects in a room, collectively.

**rooming house,** a house with furnished rooms for renting; lodging house.

**room·mate** (rōōm′māt′, room′-), *n.* a person with whom one shares a room or rooms.

**room·y** (rōōm′i, room′i), *adj.* [-IER, -IEST], having plenty of room; spacious. —**room′i·ly,** *adv.* —**room′i·ness,** *n.*

**roor·back, roor·bach** (roor′bak), *n.* [after a (nonexistent) book, *Roorback's Tour,* containing spurious charges against presidential candidate James K. Polk] a slanderous story spread to damage the reputation of a political candidate.

**Roo·se·velt, Franklin Del·a·no** (del′ə-nō′ rō′zə-velt′, rōz′velt), 1882–1945; 32nd president of the U.S. (1933–1945).

**Roosevelt, Theodore,** 1858–1919; 26th president of the U.S. (1901–1909).

**roost** (rōōst), *n.* [AS. *hrost*], 1. a perch on which birds, especially domestic fowls, can rest or sleep. 2. a place with perches for birds. 3. a place for resting, sleeping, etc. *v.i.* 1. to sit, sleep, etc. on a perch. 2. to settle down, as for the night. —**come home to roost,** to have repercussions; boomerang. —**rule the roost,** to be master.

**roost·er** (rōōs′tẽr), *n.* the male of the chicken.

**root** (rōōt, root), *n.* [AS. *rote* < ON. *rot*], 1. the part of a plant, usually below the ground, that anchors the plant, draws water and nourishment from the soil, and stores food. 2. any underground part of a plant. 3. the embedded part of a bodily structure, as of the teeth, hair, etc. 4. the source of an action, quality, etc. 5. an ancestor. 6. a supporting part; base. 7. an essential part; core: as, the *root* of the matter. 8. in *mathematics*, *a*) a quantity that, multiplied by itself a specified number of times, produces a given quantity: cf. *square root, cube root.* *b*) a quantity that, when substituted for an unknown quantity, will satisfy an equation. 9. in *music*, the basic tone of a chord. 10. in *linguistics*, a base to which prefixes, suffixes, etc. are added. *v.i.* 1. to begin to grow by putting out roots. 2. to become fixed, etc. *v.t.* 1. to fix the roots of in the ground. 2. to establish; settle. —**root up** (or **out, away**), to pull out by the roots; remove completely. —**take root,** 1. to begin growing by putting out roots. 2. to become settled. —**root′less,** *adj.* —**root′y** [-IER, -IEST], *adj.*

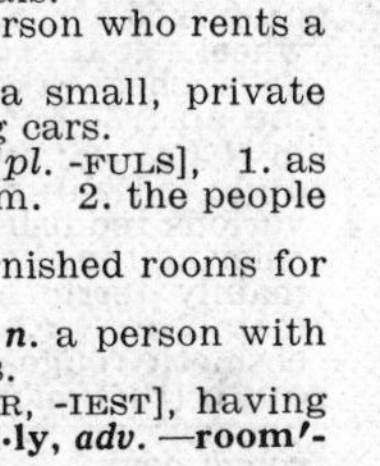

ROOT

**root** (rōōt, root), *v.t.* [AS. *wrotan* < *wrot*, snout], to dig up with the snout, as a pig. *v.i.* 1. to search by rummaging. 2. [Slang], to encourage a contestant or team, as by cheering. —**root′er,** *n.*

**root beer,** a carbonated drink made of root extracts from certain plants, as sassafras, etc.

**root hair,** in *botany*, one of the hairlike tubular outgrowths from a growing root, which absorb water and minerals from the soil.

**root·let** (rōōt′lit, root′-), *n.* a little root.

**root·stock** (rōōt′stok′, root′-), *n.* a rhizome: also **root′stalk′** (-stôk′).

**rope** (rōp), *n.* [AS. *rap*], 1. a thick, strong cord made of intertwisted strands of fiber, wires, etc. 2. a noose for hanging a person. 3. death by hanging. 4. a lasso. 5. a ropelike string of things: as, a *rope* of pearls. 6. a ropelike, sticky formation, as in wine. *v.t.* [ROPED, ROPING], 1. to fasten or tie with a rope. 2. to connect by a rope. 3. to mark off or enclose with a rope (usually with *in*, *off*, etc.). 4. to catch with a lasso. *v.i.* to become ropelike and sticky, as candy. —**know the ropes,** [Colloq.], to be acquainted with the details of a business or procedure. —**rope in,** [Slang], to entice; persuade; lure. —**the end of one's rope,** the end of one's actions, means, etc. in a desperate situation.

**rope·walk** (rōp′wôk′), *n.* a long, low, narrow shed, etc. in which ropes are made.

**rope·walk·er** (rōp′wôk′ẽr), *n.* an acrobat who performs on a rope stretched high above the ground: also **rope′danc′er.**

**rop·y** (rōp′i), *adj.* [-IER, -IEST], 1. forming sticky threads, as some liquids. 2. like a rope or ropes. —**rop′i·ly,** *adv.* —**rop′i·ness,** *n.*

**Roque·fort (cheese)** (rōk′fẽrt), [< *Roquefort*, France, where orig. made], a strong cheese with a bluish mold, made from goats' and ewes' milk.

**ror·qual** (rôr′kwəl), *n.* [Fr. < Norw. *röyrkval* < ON. *reytharhvalr*, lit., red whale], any of the whalebone whales with a dorsal fin; finback.

**Ror·schach test** (rôr′shäkh), [after H. *Rorschach* (1884–1922), Swiss psychiatrist], in *psychology*, a test for personality analysis, in which the one being tested tells what various ink-blot designs suggest to him: his responses are then interpreted.

**ro·sa·ceous** (rō-zā′shəs), *adj.* [L. *rosaceus*], 1. of the rose family of plants, as the strawberry, blackberry, etc. 2. like a rose. 3. rose-colored.

**Ro·sa·ri·o** (rō-sä′ryô), *n.* a city in east central Argentina: pop., 522,000.

**ro·sa·ry** (rō′zə-ri), *n.* [*pl.* -RIES], [L. *rosarium*, ult. < *rosa*, a rose], 1. a rose garden. 2. in the *R. C. Church*, *a*) a string of beads used to keep count in saying prayers. *b*) [also R-], the prayers said with these beads.

**rose** (rōz), *n.* [AS. < L. *rosa* < Gr. *rhodon*], 1. any of various plants with prickly stems and five-petaled, usually fragrant, flowers of red, pink, white, yellow, etc. 2. the flower of any of these. 3. any of several related plants. 4. pinkish red or purplish red: also **rose color.** 5. a rosette. 6. a perforated nozzle, as for a hose. 7. a form in which gems are often cut. 8. a gem, especially a diamond, cut in this way. *v.t.* [ROSED, ROSING], to make rose-colored; flush. *adj.* rose-colored. —**bed of roses,** luxury or idleness. —**under the rose,** secretly.

**rose** (rōz), pt. of **rise.**

**ro·se·ate** (rō′zi-it, -āt′), *adj.* 1. rose-colored; rosy. 2. made or consisting of roses. 3. cheerful or optimistic. —**ro′se·ate·ly,** *adv.*

**rose beetle,** a copper-colored beetle destructive to rosebushes: also called *rose bug, rose chafer.*

**rose·bud** (rōz′bud′), *n.* the bud of a rose.

**rose·bush** (rōz′boosh′), *n.* a shrub that bears roses.

**rose cold** (or **fever**), a kind of hay fever believed to be caused by the pollen of roses.

**rose-col·ored** (rōz′kul′ẽrd), *adj.* 1. pinkish-red or purplish-red. 2. cheerful or optimistic.

**rose·mar·y** (rōz′mâr′i, -mẽr-), *n.* [altered (after *rose & Mary*) ult. < L. *ros marinus*, lit., dew of the sea], an evergreen shrub of the mint family, with small, light-blue flowers and fragrant leaves used in perfumery, cooking, etc.

**rose of Sharon,** 1. the althea. 2. a St.-John's-wort, with evergreen leaves and yellow flowers.

**ro·se·o·la** (rō-zē′ə-lə), *n.* [< L. *roseus*, rose], German measles.

**Ro·set·ta stone** (rō-zet′ə), a stone tablet, found in 1799 at Rosetta, Egypt, bearing inscriptions that provided a key for deciphering Egyptian hieroglyphics.

**ro·sette** (rō-zet′), *n.* [Fr., dim. of *rose*, a rose], an ornament, arrangement, etc. suggesting a rose: as, a *rosette* of ribbon.

**rose water,** a preparation of water and oil of roses, used as a perfume. —**rose′-wa′ter,** *adj.*

**rose window,** a circular window with roselike tracery or spokelike mullions.

**rose·wood** (rōz′wood′), *n.* [so called from its odor], 1. any of various valuable hard, reddish, black-streaked woods, used in making furniture, etc. 2. a tropical tree yielding such wood.

**Rosh Ha·sha·na** (rōsh′ hä-shä′nə), the Jewish New Year: also sp. **Rosh Hashona**: see **Jewish holidays.**

**ros·in** (roz′'n, -in), *n.* [< OFr. var. of *resine;* see RESIN], resin; specif., the hard, brittle, light-yellow to almost black, resin left after the distillation of crude turpentine: it is rubbed on violin bows, used in making varnish, etc. *v.t.* to put rosin on. —**ros′in·y,** *adj.*

**Ross, Betsy** (rôs), 1752–1836; American woman who made the first American Flag.

**Ros·set·ti, Christina Georgina** (rō-set′i, -zet′i), 1830–1894; sister of *D.G.*; English poet.

**Rossetti, Dante Gabriel,** 1828–1882; English Pre-Raphaelite poet and painter.

**Ros·si·ni, Gio·ac·chi·no An·to·nio** (jô′ä-kē′nô än-tô′nyô rôs-sē′nē; Eng. rō-sē′ni), 1792–1868; Italian composer of operas.

**ros·ter** (ros′tẽr), *n.* [D. *rooster*, orig., gridiron, hence a list (from ruled paper used for lists)], 1. a list of military or naval personnel, with their assignments, duties, etc. 2. any list; roll.

**Ros·tov** (rô-stôf′; Eng. ros′tov), *n.* a seaport in S Soviet Russia, at the mouth of the Don: pop., 510,000: also **Rostov-on-Don.**

**ros·trum** (ros′trəm), *n.* [*pl.* -TRUMS, -TRA (-trə)], [L., (ship's) beak, hence the speakers' platform in the Forum, decorated with ramming beaks taken from captured ships], 1. a platform for public speaking. 2. public speaking, or public speakers collectively. —**ros′tral,** *adj.*

**ros·y** (rō′zi), *adj.* [-IER, -IEST], 1. like a rose, especially in color; rose-red or pink: as, *rosy* cheeks. 2. made of, or adorned with, roses. 3. bright, promising, etc.: as, a *rosy* future. —**ros′i·ly,** *adv.* —**ros′i·ness,** *n.*

**rot** (rot), *v.i.* [ROTTED, ROTTING], [AS. *rotian*], 1. to decompose gradually; decay. 2. to decay morally; degenerate. *v.t.* 1. to cause to decay. 2. to soften the fibers of (flax, etc.) by soaking; ret. *n.* 1. a rotting or being rotten; decay. 2. something rotting or rotten. 3. any of various plant and animal diseases, especially of sheep, characterized by decay. 4. [Slang], nonsense. *interj.* an exclamation of disgust, annoyance, etc.

**ro·ta·ry** (rō′tə-ri), *adj.* [< LL. < L. *rota*, a wheel], 1. turning around a central point or axis, as a wheel; rotating. 2. having a rotating part or parts. *n.* [*pl.* -RIES], a rotary machine or engine.

**Rotary Club,** any local organization of an international association (*Rotary International*) of business and professional men with the aim of community service, etc. —**Ro·tar·i·an** (rō-târ′i-ən), *n.* & *adj.* —**Ro·tar′i·an·ism,** *n.*

**rotary engine,** an internal-combustion engine, as in many airplanes, with radially arranged cylinders rotating around a stationary crankshaft.

**rotary press,** a printing press with curved plates mounted on rotating cylinders: often used for printing on a continuous sheet of paper.

**ro·tate** (rō′tāt, rō-tāt′), *v.i. & v.t.* [-TATED, -TATING], [< L. pp. of *rotare* < *rota*, a wheel], 1. to move or turn around, as a wheel. 2. to go or cause to go in a regular and recurring succession of changes: as, to *rotate* crops. —**ro′tat·a·ble,** *adj.* —**ro′ta·tive** (-tə-tiv), *adj.* —**ro′ta·tor,** *n.*

**ro·ta·tion** (rō-tā′shən), *n.* 1. a rotating or being rotated. 2. regular and recurring succession of changes. —**ro·ta′tion·al,** *adj.*

**rotation of crops,** a system of rotating in a fixed order the kinds of crops grown in the same field, to maintain fertility.

**ro·ta·to·ry** (rō′tə-tôr′i, -tō′ri), *adj.* 1. of, or having the nature of, rotation. 2. rotary. 3. going or following in rotation. 4. causing rotation.

**R.O.T.C.,** Reserve Officers' Training Corps.

**rote** (rōt), *n.* [ME., var. of *route* (road)], a fixed, mechanical way of doing something; routine. —**by rote,** by memory alone, without thought.

**rot·gut** (rot′gut′), *n.* [*rot* + *gut* (bowel)], [Slang], raw, low-grade whisky

**ro·ti·fer** (rō′ti-fẽr), *n.* [< L. *rota*, a wheel + *ferre*, to bear], any of various microscopic water animals with rings of cilia on an anterior disc: also called **wheel animalcule.** —**ro·tif′er·al** (rō-tif′ẽr-əl), **ro·tif′er·ous,** *adj.*

**ro·tis·ser·ie** (rō-tis′ẽr-i), *n.* [Fr. < *rôtir*, to roast], 1. a shop where roasted meats are sold. 2. a portable electric grill with a turning spit.

**ro·to·gra·vure** (rō′tə-grə-vyoor′, -grā′vyoor), *n.* [< L. *rota*, a wheel; + *gravure*], 1. a process of printing pictures, etc. on a rotary press using copper cylinders etched from photographic plates. 2. a print so made. 3. a newspaper pictorial section printed by this process: also **roto section.**

**ro·tor** (rō′tẽr), *n.* [contr. of *rotator*], 1. the rotating part of a motor, dynamo, etc. 2. a system of rotating airfoils (**rotor blades**), as of a helicopter.

**rot·ten** (rot′'n), *adj.* [ON. *rotinn*], 1. decayed; decomposed; spoiled. 2. smelling of decay; putrid. 3. morally corrupt or offensive; dishonest, etc. 4. unsound or weak, as if decayed within. 5. [Slang], very bad, disagreeable, etc.: as, a *rotten* show. —**rot′ten·ly,** *adv.* —**rot′ten·ness,** *n.*

**rot·ter** (rot′ẽr), *n.* [< *rot*], [Chiefly Brit. Slang], a despicable or objectionable person.

**Rot·ter·dam** (rot′ẽr-dam′; D. rôt′ẽr-däm′), *n.* a seaport in the SW Netherlands: pop., 697,000.

**ro·tund** (rō-tund′), *adj.* [L. *rotundus;* akin to *rota*, a wheel], 1. round or rounded out; plump: as, a *rotund* little man. 2. full-toned; sonorous: as, *rotund* speech. —**ro·tun′di·ty** [*pl.* -TIES], **ro·tund′ness,** *n.* —**ro·tund′ly,** *adv.*

**ro·tun·da** (rō-tun′də), *n.* [< It. < L. fem. of *rotundus*, rotund], a round building, hall, or room, especially one with a dome.

**rou·ble** (rōō′b'l), *n.* a ruble.

**rouche** (rōōsh), *n.* a ruche.

**rou·é** (rōō-ā′), *n.* [Fr., pp. of *rouer*, to break on the wheel < L. *rota*, a wheel], a dissipated man; debauchee; rake.

**Rou·en** (rōō-än′; Fr. rwän), *n.* a city on the Seine, in N France: pop., 108,000.

**rouge** (rōōzh), *n.* [Fr., red < L. *rubeus*], 1. any of various reddish cosmetic powders, pastes, etc. for coloring the cheeks and lips. 2. a reddish powder, mainly ferric oxide, used for polishing jewelry, metal, etc. *v.t. & v.i.* [ROUGED, ROUGING], to use cosmetic rouge (on).

**rough** (ruf), *adj.* [AS. *ruh*], 1. not smooth or level; uneven: as, a *rough* surface. 2. shaggy: as, a *rough* coat. 3. *a*) moving violently; agitated: as, *rough* waters. *b*) stormy; tempestuous: as, *rough* weather. 4. disorderly or riotous: as, *rough* play. 5. harsh; rude; coarse; not gentle or mild: as, *rough* manners, temper, etc. 6. sounding, feeling, or tasting harsh. 7. lacking comforts and conveniences: as, the *rough* life of pioneers. 8. not refined or polished; natural, crude, etc.: as, *rough* jewels. 9. not finished, perfected, etc.: as, a *rough* sketch, a *rough* estimate. 10. needing strength instead of skill, intelligence, etc.: as, *rough* labor. 11. [Colloq.], difficult or severe: as, he had a *rough* time. 12. in *phonetics*, pronounced with an aspirate; having the sound of *h*. *n.* 1. rough ground. 2. rough material, condition, or part. 3. [Chiefly Brit.], a rough person; rowdy. 4. in *golf*, any part of the course where grass, weeds, etc. grow uncut. *adv.* in a rough manner. *v.t.* 1. to make rough; roughen. 2. to treat roughly (often with *up*). 3. to make or shape roughly (usually with *in* or *out*): as, *rough* out a scheme. *v.i.* 1. to become rough. 2. to behave roughly. —**in the rough,** in a rough or crude state. —**rough it,** to live without comforts and conveniences. —**rough′er,** *n.* —**rough′ish,** *adj.* —**rough′ness,** *n.*

**rough·age** (ruf′ij), *n.* rough or coarse substance; specif., coarse food or fodder, as bran, straw, etc., serving as a stimulus to peristalsis.

**rough-and-ready** (ruf′'n-red′i), *adj.* 1. rough, or crude, rude, etc., but effective: as, *rough-and-ready* methods. 2. characterized by rough vigor rather than refinement, formality, etc.

**rough-and-tum·ble** (ruf′'n-tum′b'l), *adj.* violent and disorderly, with little or no concern for rules. *n.* a fight or struggle of this kind; brawl.

**rough·cast** (ruf′kast′, -käst′), *n.* 1. a coarse plaster for covering outside surfaces, as walls. 2. a rude pattern or model. *v.t.* [-CAST, -CASTING], 1. to cover (walls, etc.) with roughcast. 2. to make, shape, draft, etc. in a rough form.

**rough-dry** (ruf′drī′), *v.t.* [-DRIED, -DRYING], to dry

(washed laundry) without ironing: also **roughdry.** *adj.* washed and dried but not ironed.

**rough·en** (ruf′'n), *v.t. & v.i.* to make or become rough.

**rough-hew** (ruf′hū′), *v.t.* [-HEWED, -HEWED or -HEWN, -HEWING], 1. to hew (timber, stone, etc.) roughly, or without finishing or smoothing. 2. to form roughly. Also **roughhew.**

**rough·house** (ruf′hous′), *n.* [Slang], rough or boisterous play, fighting, etc. *v.t.* [-HOUSED, -HOUSING], [Slang], to treat roughly and boisterously. *v.i.* [Slang], to take part in roughhouse.

**rough·ly** (ruf′li), *adv.* 1. in a rough manner. 2. approximately.

**rough·neck** (ruf′nek′), *n.* [Slang], a rowdy.

**rough·rid·er** (ruf′rīd′ẽr), *n.* 1. a person who breaks horses for riding. 2. a person who does much rough, hard riding. 3. [R-], a member of Theodore Roosevelt's volunteer cavalry regiment in the Spanish-American War: also **Rough Rider.**

**rough·shod** (ruf′shod′), *adj.* shod with horseshoes that have calks to prevent slipping. **—ride roughshod over,** to treat in a harsh, arrogant manner.

**rou·lette** (ro͞o-let′), *n.* [Fr., dim. of *rouelle,* a small wheel; ult. < L. *rota,* a wheel], 1. a gambling game played with a small ball in a whirling shallow bowl (*roulette wheel*) with red and black numbered compartments. 2. a small toothed wheel for making rows of marks, dots, or slits, as between postage stamps. *v.t.* [-LETTED, -LETTING], to make marks, slits, etc. in with a roulette.

**Rou·ma·ni·a** (ro͞o-mā′ni-ə, -mān′yə), *n.* Romania. **—Rou·ma′ni·an,** *adj. & n.*

**round** (round), *adj.* [< OFr. < L. *rotundus,* rotund], 1. shaped like a ball; spherical. 2. shaped like a circle, ring, etc.; circular or curved. 3. shaped like a cylinder; cylindrical. 4. plump: as, a *round* figure. 5. with or involving a circular motion: as, a *round* dance. 6. pronounced with the lips forming an oval: as, a *round* vowel. 7. full; complete: as, a *round* dozen. 8. expressed by a whole number, or in tens, hundreds, etc. 9. large in amount, size, etc.: as, a *round* sum. 10. mellow and full in tone, as a sound or the voice. 11. brisk; vigorous: as, a *round* pace. *n.* 1. something round; thing that is spherical, circular, curved, etc. 2. a rung of a ladder. 3. the part of a beef animal between the rump and the leg: in full, **round of beef.** 4. sculpture in which the figures are full, not projecting from a background (with *the*). 5. a being round. 6. a group of people. 7. movement in a circular course. 8. a round dance. 9. a course or series of actions, events, etc.: as, a *round* of parties. 10. the complete extent: as, the *round* of human beliefs. 11. *often in pl.* a regular, customary circuit: as, the watchman made his *rounds.* 12. a single shot from a rifle, etc. or from a number of rifles fired together. 13. ammunition for such a shot. 14. a single outburst, as of applause. 15. in *games & sports,* a single division of action: as, a *round* of golf; specif., in *boxing,* any of the timed periods of a fight. 16. in *music,* a short song, repeated several times, in which one group begins singing when another has reached the second phrase, etc. *v.t.* 1. to make round. 2. to pronounce with rounded lips. 3. to make plump. 4. to complete; finish. 5. to make a circuit of: as, we *rounded* the island. 6. to encircle; surround. *v.i.* 1. to make a complete or partial circuit. 2. to turn; reverse direction. 3. to become round or plump. *adv.* 1. in a circle; along a circular course. 2. through a recurring period of time: as, when autumn comes *round.* 3. from one person or place to another: as, the peddler went *round.* 4. for each of several: as, not enough candy to go *round.* 5. in circumference: as, forty inches *round.* 6. on all sides: as, the meadows extended *round.* 7. about; near: as, visit all the people *round.* 8. in a roundabout way. 9. here and there: as, the child played *round.* 10. with a rotating movement. 11. in the opposite direction: as, he turned *round.* *prep.* 1. so as to encircle or surround: as, tie the rope *round* the tree. 2. on the circumference or border of. 3. on all sides of. 4. in the vicinity of. 5. in a circuit or course through: as, we went *round* the museum. 6. here and there in: as, walk *round* the room. 7. so as to turn to the other side of: as, to flow *round* an obstruction. *Round* (*adv. & prep.*) and *around* are used interchangeably in colloquial and informal usage; formal usage tends to prefer *round* for "in a circle," etc. and *around* for "on all sides", "here and there." **—go the round** (or **rounds**), to be circulated widely, as a story, rumor, etc. **—round about,** in or to the opposite direction. **—round off** (or **out**), 1. to make or become round. 2. to complete; finish. **—round up,** 1. to drive together in a herd, group, etc. 2. [Colloq.], to gather or assemble. **—round′ish,** *adj.* **—round′ish·ness,** *n.* **—round′ness,** *n.*

**round·a·bout** (round′ə-bout′), *adj.* 1. indirect; circuitous: as, *roundabout* methods. 2. encircling; enclosing. *n.* 1. a path, speech, etc. that is indirect. 2. a short, tight jacket worn by men and boys. 3. [Chiefly Brit.], a merry-go-round.

**round·ed** (roun′did), *adj.* made round.

**roun·de·lay** (roun′də-lā′), *n.* [< OFr. dim. of *rondel,* a rondel], a simple song in which some phrase, line, etc. is continually repeated.

**round·er** (roun′dẽr), *n.* 1. a person or thing that rounds, as a tool for rounding edges. 2. [Colloq.], a dissolute spendthrift or drunkard.

**Round·head** (round′hed′), *n.* a member of the Parliamentary, or Puritan, party in England during the English civil war (1642–1652).

**round·house** (round′hous′), *n.* 1. a building, generally circular, with a turntable in the center, for storing and repairing locomotives. 2. a cabin on the after part of a ship's quarter-deck.

**round·ly** (round′li), *adv.* 1. in a round form. 2. in a round manner; specif., *a*) vigorously, severely, etc. *b*) fully; completely.

**round robin,** 1. a petition, protest, etc. with the signatures written in a circle to conceal the order of signing. 2. a tournament in which every entrant is matched with every other one.

**round-shoul·dered** (round′shōl′dẽrd), *adj.* having the shoulders bent forward.

**round steak,** a cut from a round of beef: see **round,** *n.* (sense 3).

**Round Table,** 1. the table around which King Arthur and his knights sat. 2. King Arthur and his knights, collectively. 3. [r- t-], *a*) a group of persons gathered together for an informal discussion. *b*) such a discussion. **—round′-ta′ble,** *adj.*

**round trip,** a trip to a place and back to the starting point: also **return trip. —round′-trip′,** *adj.*

**round·up** (round′up′), *n.* 1. the act of driving cattle, etc. together on the range, as for branding. 2. the cowboys, horses, etc. that do this work. 3. any similar driving or collecting.

**round·worm** (round′wũrm′), *n.* any of a group of round, unsegmented worms, as the hookworm; nematode, especially one parasitic in the intestines of man or other animals.

**rouse** (rouz), *v.t.* [ROUSED, ROUSING], [prob. < Anglo-Fr. or OFr.], 1. to stir up (game) to flight or attack from cover. 2. to stir up, as to anger or action; excite. 3. to wake. *v.i.* 1. to leave cover: said of game. 2. to wake. 3. to become active. *n.* a rousing. **—rous′er,** *n.* **—rous′ing·ly,** *adv.*

**Rous·seau, Hen·ri** (äN′rē′ ro͞o′sō′), 1844–1910; French painter.

**Rousseau, Jean Jacques** (zhäN zhåk), 1712–1778; French social philosopher and writer.

**roust·a·bout** (roust′ə-bout′), *n.* [*roust,* dial. var. of *rouse* + *about*], an unskilled or transient laborer on wharves, in circuses, on ranches, etc.

**rout** (rout), *n.* [< OFr. < L. *rupta;* see ROUTE], 1. a disorderly crowd. 2. the rabble. 3. a disorderly flight, as of defeated troops. 4. an overwhelming defeat. 5. [Archaic], an assemblage; company; band. *v.t.* 1. to put to disorderly flight. 2. to defeat overwhelmingly.

**rout** (rout), *v.i.* [var. of *root* (to dig)], 1. to dig for food with the snout, as a pig. 2. to search by poking and rummaging. *v.t.* 1. to dig up with the snout. 2. to get by turning up, poking about, etc. (with *out*). 3. to scoop, gouge, or hollow out. 4. to force out. **—rout′er,** *n.*

**route** (ro͞ot, rout), *n.* [OFr. < L. *rupta* (*via*), broken (path) < pp. of *rumpere,* to break], 1. a road, course, etc. traveled or to be traveled in going from place to place, as in delivering milk, mail, etc. 2. a set of customers to whom one regularly delivers something. *v.t.* [ROUTED, ROUTING], 1. to send by a specified route: as, *route* the goods via Albany. 2. to arrange the route for, or direct.

**rou·tine** (ro͞o-tēn′), *n.* [Fr. < *route;* see ROUTE], a regular, unvarying procedure, customary, prescribed, or habitual, as of work. *adj.* having the nature of or using routine: as, *routine* tasks. **—rou·tine′ly,** *adv.* **—rou·tin′ism,** *n.*

**rove** (rōv), *v.i.* [ROVED, ROVING], [prob. < base of

AS. *arafian*, to set free], to wander about; roam. *v.t.* to wander over; roam through: as, he *roved* the woods. *n.* a roving; ramble. —**rov′er,** *n.*

**rove** (rōv), alternative pt. and pp. of **reeve.**

**rov·en** (rōv′'n), alternative pp. of **reeve.**

**row** (rō), *n.* [AS. *raw*], 1. a number of people or things arranged in a line. 2. any of the lines of seats in a theater, etc. 3. a street with a line of buildings on either side. *v.t.* to arrange or put in rows (often with *up*). —**hard** (or **long**) **row to hoe,** anything difficult or wearisome to do.

**row** (rō), *v.t.* [AS. *rowan*], 1. to propel (a boat, etc.) on water by using oars. 2. to carry in a boat propelled by oars. 3. to use (a specified number of oars): said of a boat. 4. to use in rowing: as, he *rowed* a powerful stroke. 5. to engage in (a race) by rowing. *v.i.* 1. to use oars in propelling a boat. 2. to be propelled by oars: said of a boat. *n.* 1. a rowing. 2. a trip made by rowboat. —**row′er,** *n.*

**row** (rou), *n.* [prob. < *rouse*], [Colloq.], 1. a noisy quarrel, dispute, etc.; squabble; brawl. 2. noise; clamor. *v.i.* [Colloq.], to quarrel noisily. *v.t.* [Colloq.], to scold or criticize severely.

**row·an** (rō′ən, rou′-), *n.* [< Scand.], 1. the mountain ash, a tree with white flowers and reddish berries. 2. its fruit: also **row′an·ber′ry** [*pl.* -RIES].

**row·boat** (rō′bōt′), *n.* a boat designed to be rowed.

**row·dy** (rou′di), *n.* [*pl.* -DIES], [? < *row* (quarrel)], a person whose behavior is rough, quarrelsome, and disorderly; hoodlum. *adj.* [-DIER, -DIEST], of, or like that of, a rowdy. —**row′di·ly,** *adv.* —**row′di·ness,** *n.* —**row′dy·ish,** *adj.* —**row′dy·ism,** *n.*

**row·el** (rou′əl), *n.* [< OFr. *rouelle;* see ROULETTE], a small wheel with sharp projecting points, forming the end of a spur. *v.t.* [-ELED or -ELLED, -ELING or -ELLING], to spur or prick with a rowel.

**row·lock** (rō′lok′, rul′ək), *n.* [altered (after *row, v.t.*) < *oarlock*], [Chiefly Brit.], an oarlock.

**roy·al** (roi′əl), *adj.* [OFr. *real* < L. *regalis;* see REGAL], 1. of a king or queen: as, a *royal* edict. 2. being a king or queen. 3. of a kingdom, its government, etc.: as, the *royal* fleet. 4. founded or supported by a king or queen: as, the *Royal* Society. 5. like or suitable for a king or queen; magnificent; majestic; stately. 6. unusually large, fine, etc. *n.* a small sail set on the royal mast. —**roy′al·ly,** *adv.*

**royal blue,** a deep, vivid reddish blue.

**royal flush,** the highest poker hand; the ace, king, queen, jack, and ten of the same suit.

**roy·al·ist** (roi′əl-ist), *n.* one who supports a monarch or monarchy, especially in times of revolution, etc., as [R-], in the American Revolution. —**roy′al·ism,** *n.*

**Royal Oak,** a city in SE Michigan: pop., 81,000.

**royal mast,** the mast above the topgallant mast.

**royal palm,** a tall, ornamental palm tree.

**roy·al·ty** (roi′əl-ti), *n.* [*pl.* -TIES], 1. the rank, status, or power of a king or queen. 2. a royal person or, collectively, royal persons. 3. a kingdom. 4. royal quality or character; nobility, magnanimity, etc. 5. *usually pl.* a right, privilege, etc. of a monarch. 6. a share of the proceeds paid to the owner of a right, as a patent, for its use. 7. a share of the proceeds from his work paid to an author, composer, etc.

**r.p.m.,** revolutions per minute.

**R.R.,** 1. railroad. 2. Right Reverend.

**-rrha·gi·a** (rā′ji-ə), [Gr. < *rhēgnynai*, to burst], a combining form meaning *abnormal discharge* or *flow*: also **-rhagia, -rrhage, -rhage, -rrhagy.**

**-rrhe·a, -rrhoe·a** (rē′ə), [< Gr. < *rhein*, to flow], a combining form meaning *a flow, discharge*: also **-rhea, -rhoea.**

**Rs.,** 1. reis. 2. rupees: also **Rs, rs.**

**R.S.F.S.R., RSFSR,** Russian Soviet Federated Socialist Republic.

**RSV, R.S.V.,** Revised Standard Version.

**R.S.V.P., r.s.v.p.,** *répondez s'il vous plaît*, [Fr.], please reply.

**rt.,** right.

**Ru,** in *chemistry*, ruthenium.

**Ru·an·da-U·run·di** (rōō-än′dä-oo-roon′di), *n.* a former Belgian trust territory in central Africa.

**rub** (rub), *v.t.* [RUBBED, RUBBING], [ME. *rubben;* prob. < MLG. or MD.], 1. to move one's hand, a cloth, etc. over (something) with pressure and friction. 2. to move (one's hand, a cloth, etc.) over, or spread (polish, etc.) on something. 3. to move (a thing) against something else, or move (things) over each other with pressure and friction. 4. to put into a specified condition by applying pressure and friction: as, *rub* it dry. 5. to make sore by rubbing. 6. to remove by rubbing (with *out, off,* etc.). *v.i.* 1. to move with pressure and friction (*against*). 2. to rub something. 3. to admit of being rubbed or removed by rubbing (often with *out, off,* etc.). *n.* 1. a rubbing. 2. an obstacle or difficulty. 3. something that irritates, annoys, etc., as a jeer. —**rub down,** 1. to massage. 2. to smooth, polish, etc. by rubbing. —**rub it in,** [Slang], to keep mentioning someone's failure or mistake. —**rub the wrong way,** to irritate or annoy.

**ru·ba·to** (rōō-bä′tō), *adj.* [It. < (*tempo*) *rubato*, stolen (time)], in *music*, intentionally and temporarily deviating from a strict tempo. *n.* [*pl.* -TOS], 1. rubato execution. 2. a rubato passage, phrase, etc. *adv.* with rubato.

**rub·ber** (rub′ēr), *n.* 1. a person or thing that rubs, as a masseur. 2. [from use as an eraser], an elastic substance produced from the milky sap of various tropical plants, or synthetically. 3. something made of this substance, as, *a*) an elastic band: in full, **rubber band.** *b*) an eraser. *c*) *usually in pl.* an overshoe. *adj.* made of rubber. —**rub′ber·like′, rub′ber·y,** *adj.*

**rub·ber** (rub′ēr), *n.* [? < OFr. *a rebours*, backward], 1. in *bridge, whist*, etc., a series of games, usually three, the majority of which must be won to win the whole series. 2. the deciding game in a series.

**rub·ber·ize** (rub′ēr-īz′), *v.t.* [-IZED, -IZING], to coat or impregnate with rubber.

**rub·ber·neck** (rub′ēr-nek′), *n.* [Slang], a person who gazes about in curiosity, as a sightseer. *v.i.* [Slang], to gaze about in this way.

**rubber plant,** 1. any plant yielding latex from which crude rubber is formed. 2. a house plant with large, glossy, leathery leaves.

**rubber stamp,** 1. a stamp made of rubber, inked on a pad and used for printing signatures, dates, etc. 2. [Colloq.], a person, bureau, etc. that approves something in a routine manner, without thought. —**rub′ber-stamp′,** *v.t.*

**rub·bish** (rub′ish), *n.* [< Anglo-Fr. *rubbous*, rubble], 1. any material rejected or thrown away as worthless; trash. 2. worthless, foolish ideas, statements, etc.; nonsense. —**rub′bish·y,** *adj.*

**rub·ble** (rub′'l), *n.* [prob. akin to *rubbish*], 1. rough, irregularly broken pieces of stone, brick, etc. 2. masonry made of such pieces: also **rub′ble·work′.** —**rub′bly** [-BLIER, -BLIEST], *adj.*

**rub·down** (rub′doun′), *n.* a massage.

**rube** (rōōb), *n.* [< *Reuben*], [Slang], a country person, regarded as simple, uncouth, etc.; rustic.

**ru·bel·la** (rōō-bel′ə), *n.* [< L. *rubellus* < *ruber*, red], German measles.

**Ru·bens, Peter Paul** (rōō′bənz), 1577–1640; Flemish painter.

**Ru·bi·con** (rōō′bi-kon′), *n.* a small river in N Italy crossed by Caesar on his return from Gaul to seize power in Rome. —**cross** (or **pass**) **the Rubicon,** to make a decisive, irrevocable move.

**ru·bi·cund** (rōō′bi-kund′), *adj.* [< Fr. < L. < *ruber*, red], reddish; ruddy. —**ru′bi·cun′di·ty,** *n.*

**ru·bid·i·um** (rōō-bid′i-əm), *n.* [< L. *rubidus*, red (from red lines in its spectrum)], a soft, silvery-white metallic chemical element, resembling potassium: symbol, Rb; at. wt., 85.48; at. no., 37.

**ru·ble** (rōō′b'l), *n.* [Russ. *rubl′*], the monetary unit and a silver coin of the Soviet Union.

**ru·bric** (rōō′brik), *n.* [< OFr. < L. *rubrica*, red earth (for coloring) < *ruber*, red], 1. in early books and manuscripts, a chapter heading, initial letter, etc., printed or written in red or in decorative lettering. 2. a heading, title, etc., as of a chapter. 3. a direction in a prayer book, usually printed in red. —**ru′bri·cal,** *adj.* —**ru′bri·cal·ly,** *adv.*

**ru·by** (rōō′bi), *n.* [*pl.* -BIES], [< OFr. *rubi;* ult. < L. *rubeus*, red], 1. a clear, deep-red variety of corundum, valued as a precious stone: also called *Oriental ruby, true ruby.* 2. deep red. *adj.* deep-red. —**ru′by·like′,** *adj.*

**ruche** (rōōsh), *n.* [Fr., lit., beehive < OFr. < ML. *rusca*, bark], a frilling or pleating of lace, ribbon, net, etc. for trimming women's dresses.

**ruch·ing** (rōōsh′iŋ), *n.* 1. ruches collectively. 2. material used to make a ruche.

**ruck·sack** (ruk′sak′), *n.* [G. < *rucken*, the back + *sack*, a sack], a knapsack strapped on the back.

**ruck·us** (ruk′əs), *n.* [prob. a merging of *rumpus* & *ruction*, an uproar], [Dial. or Colloq.], noisy confusion; uproar; row; disturbance.

**rud·der** (rud′ēr), *n.* [AS. *rother*, a paddle], 1. a broad, flat, movable piece of wood or metal hinged vertically at the stern of a boat or ship, used for steering. 2. a piece like this in an aircraft, etc. —**rud′der·less,** *adj.*

**rud·dy** (rud′i), *adj.* [-DIER, -DIEST], [AS. *rudig*], 1. having a healthy red color. 2. red or reddish. —**rud′di·ly,** *adv.* —**rud′di·ness,** *n.*

**ruddy duck,** a North American duck the adult male of which has a brownish-red upper body.

**rude** (ro͞od), ***adj.*** [OFr. < L. *rudis*], 1. coarse or rough in form; crude. 2. barbarous or ignorant: as, *rude* savages. 3. lacking refinement; uncouth. 4. discourteous; impolite: as, a *rude* reply. 5. rough; violent: as, *rude* winds. 6. harsh in sound; discordant. 7. having little skill, accuracy, etc. **—rude′ly, *adv.* —rude′ness, *n.***

**ru·di·ment** (ro͞o′də-mənt), ***n.*** [L. *rudimentum* < *rudis*, rude], 1. a first principle or element, as of a subject to be learned: as, the *rudiments* of language. 2. a first slight beginning of something. 3. in *biology*, an incompletely developed or vestigial organ or part.

**ru·di·men·ta·ry** (ro͞o′də-men′tẽr-i, -tri), ***adj.*** 1. elementary. 2. incompletely developed. 3. vestigial. Also **ru′di·men′tal. —ru′di·men′ta·ri·ly, *adv.* —ru′di·men′ta·ri·ness, *n.***

**rue** (ro͞o), ***v.t.*** [RUED, RUING], [AS. *hreowan*], 1. to feel remorse for (a sin, fault, etc.). 2. to wish (an act, etc.) undone; regret. ***v.i.*** to feel sorrow or regret. ***n.*** [Archaic], sorrow or regret.

**rue** (ro͞o), ***n.*** [< OFr. < L. *ruta* < Gr. *rhytē*], a strong-scented herb with yellow flowers and bitter-tasting leaves formerly used in medicine.

**rue·ful** (ro͞o′fəl), ***adj.*** 1. causing sorrow or pity. 2. feeling or showing sorrow or pity; mournful. **—rue′ful·ly, *adv.* —rue′ful·ness, *n.***

**ruff** (ruf), ***n.*** [contr. of *ruffle* (a pleat)], 1. a high, frilled, starched collar worn by men and women in the 16th and 17th centuries. 2. a stripe of colored feathers or fur around the neck of a bird or beast. 3. a European sandpiper the male of which grows a ruff during the breeding season. **—ruffed, *adj.***

**ruff** (ruf), ***n.*** [< OFr. *roffle*], in *card games*, the act of trumping. ***v.t. & v.i.*** to trump.

**ruffed grouse,** a North American game bird with a feathered ruff: also called *partridge* (in northern U.S.), *pheasant* (in southern U.S.).

**ruf·fi·an** (ruf′i-ən, -yən), ***n.*** [< Fr. < It. *ruffiano*, a pander], a brutal, violent, lawless person. ***adj.*** brutal, violent, and lawless. **—ruf′fi·an·ism, *n.* —ruf′fi·an·ly, *adj.***

**ruf·fle** (ruf′′l), ***v.t.*** [-FLED, -FLING], [< ON. or MLG.], 1. to disturb the smoothness of; ripple: as, wind *ruffles* the water. 2. to fold into ruffles. 3. to put ruffles on. 4. to make (feathers, etc.) stand up as in a ruff. 5. to disturb or annoy. 6. to shuffle (cards). ***v.i.*** 1. to become uneven. 2. to become disturbed, irritated, etc. ***n.*** 1. a narrow, pleated or puckered trimming of cloth, lace, etc. 2. a bird's ruff. 3. a disturbance; irritation. 4. a ripple. **—ruf′fler, *n.***

**ruf·fle** (ruf′′l), ***n.*** [prob. echoic], a low, continuous beating of a drum. ***v.t. & v.i.*** [-FLED, -FLING], to beat (a drum, etc.) with a ruffle.

**ruf·fly** (ruf′li), ***adj.*** [-FLIER, -FLIEST], of, in, or like a ruffle or ruffles.

**ru·fous** (ro͞o′fəs), ***adj.*** [< L. *rufus*, red], brownish-red or yellowish-red; rust-colored.

**rug** (rug), ***n.*** [of Scand. origin], 1. a piece of thick, often napped fabric, woven strips of rag, etc. used as a floor covering. 2. [Chiefly Brit.], a heavy, warm cloth used as a lap robe, etc.

**Rug·by** (rug′bi), ***n.*** 1. a town in central England: pop., 45,000. 2. a famous boys' school there. 3. a kind of football first played at this school: in full, **Rugby football.**

**rug·ged** (rug′id), ***adj.*** [< Scand. < base of *rug*], 1. having an irregular surface; uneven; rough: as, *rugged* ground. 2. heavy, strong, and irregular, as facial features. 3. stormy: as, *rugged* weather. 4. sounding harsh. 5. severe; hard: as, a *rugged* life. 6. not polished or refined; rude: as, *rugged* manners. 7. strong; robust; vigorous. **—rug′ged·ly, *adv.* —rug′ged·ness, *n.***

**Ruhr** (roor; G. ro͞or), ***n.*** 1. a river in W Germany, flowing into the Rhine. 2. the important mining and industrial region along this river.

**ru·in** (ro͞o′in, -′n), ***n.*** [< OFr. < L. *ruina* < *ruere*, to fall], 1. *pl.* the remains of a fallen building, city, etc., or of something destroyed, decayed, etc. 2. anything that has been destroyed, etc.: as, the city was a *ruin*. 3. the state of being destroyed, decayed, etc. 4. downfall, destruction, decay, etc., as of a thing or person. 5. anything that causes downfall, destruction, etc.: as, gambling was his *ruin*. ***v.t.*** to bring to ruin; specif., *a*) to destroy, damage greatly, etc. *b*) to make bankrupt. *c*) to deprive (a woman) of chastity. ***v.i.*** to go or come to ruin. **—ru′in·a·ble, *adj.* —ru′in·er, *n.***

**ru·in·a·tion** (ro͞o′ə-nā′shən), ***n.*** 1. a ruining or being ruined. 2. anything that ruins.

**ru·in·ous** (ro͞o′in-əs, -′n-), ***adj.*** 1. falling or fallen into ruin. 2. bringing ruin; disastrous. **—ru′in·ous·ly, *adv.* —ru′in·ous·ness, *n.***

**rule** (ro͞ol), ***n.*** [< OFr. < L. *regula*, straight stick < *regere*, to lead straight], 1. an established guide or regulation for conduct, procedure, etc. 2. a set of regulations in a religious order. 3. custom; usage: as, morning prayer was his *rule*. 4. a criterion or standard. 5. the customary course of events: as, famine is the *rule* following war. 6. government; reign: as, the *rule* of Elizabeth. 7. a ruler (sense 2). 8. in *law*, a decision made by a court or judge. 9. in *printing*, a thin strip of metal as high as type, used to print lines. ***v.t.*** [RULED, RULING], 1. to have an influence over; guide. 2. to lessen; restrain: as, reason *ruled* his fear. 3. to exercise authority over; govern. 4. to settle by decree; determine officially. 5. to mark lines on as with a ruler. ***v.i.*** 1. to govern. 2. to issue a formal decree: as, the court will *rule* later. **—as a rule,** usually. **—rule out,** to exclude by decision. **—rul′a·ble, *adj.***

**rule of thumb,** 1. a rule based on experience or practice rather than on scientific knowledge. 2. any practical, though crude, method.

**rul·er** (ro͞ol′ẽr), ***n.*** 1. one who governs. 2. a thin strip of wood, metal, etc. with a straight edge, used in drawing lines, measuring, etc.

**rul·ing** (ro͞ol′iŋ), ***adj.*** 1. that rules; governing. 2. predominant. ***n.*** 1. a governing. 2. a decision made by a court. 3. the act of drawing with a ruler. 4. a line so drawn. **—rul′ing·ly, *adv.***

**rum** (rum), ***n.*** [short for *rumbullion*, associated with Fr. place name *Rambouillet*], 1. an alcoholic liquor distilled from fermented molasses, sugar cane, etc. 2. any alcoholic liquor.

**rum** (rum), ***adj.*** [< obs. *rum*, good], [Chiefly Brit. Slang], odd; strange; queer.

**Rum.,** 1. Rumania. 2. Rumanian.

**rum** (rum), ***n.*** rummy (card game).

**Ru·ma·ni·a** (ro͞o-mā′ni-ə, -mān′yə), ***n.*** Romania. **—Ru·ma′ni·an, *adj. & n.***

**rum·ba** (rum′bə; Sp. ro͞om′bä), ***n.*** [Sp.; prob. of Afr. origin], 1. a dance of Cuban Negro origin. 2. a ballroom adaptation of this, characterized by rhythmic movements of the lower part of the body. 3. music for this dance. Also sp. **rhumba.**

**rum·ble** (rum′b′l), ***v.i.*** [-BLED, -BLING], [prob. < MD. *rommelen*], 1. to make a deep, heavy, continuous, rolling sound: as, thunder *rumbles*. 2. to move with such a sound. ***v.t.*** 1. to cause to make, or move with, such a sound. 2. to utter with such a sound. ***n.*** 1. a deep, heavy, continuous, rolling sound. 2. a space for luggage or a small extra seat **(rumble seat)** in the rear of a carriage or automobile. 3. [Slang], a gang fight. **—rum′bler, *n.* —rum′bling, rum′bly, *adj.***

**ru·men** (ro͞o′min), ***n.*** [*pl.* -MINA (-mi-nə)], [L., gullet], the first stomach of a ruminant.

**ru·mi·nant** (ro͞o′mə-nənt), ***adj.*** [< L. ppr. of *ruminare*, to ruminate], 1. chewing the cud. 2. of the cud-chewing animals. 3. meditative. ***n.*** any of a group of four-footed, hoofed, even-toed, and cud-chewing mammals, as the cattle, sheep, goat, deer, camel, etc. **—ru′mi·nant·ly, *adv.***

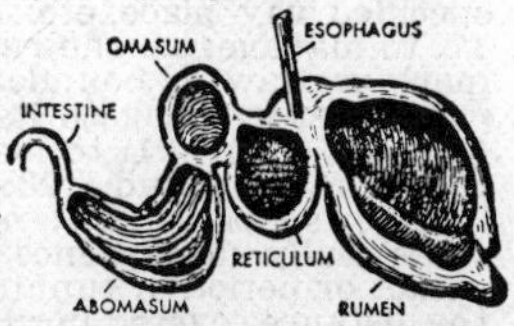

STOMACH OF A RUMINANT

**ru·mi·nate** (ro͞o′mə-nāt′), ***v.i. & v.t.*** [-NATED, -NATING], [< L. pp. of *ruminare*], 1. to chew (the cud), as a cow does. 2. to meditate or reflect (on). **—ru′mi·nat′ing·ly, *adv.* —ru′mi·na′tion, *n.* —ru′mi·na′tive, *adj.* —ru′mi·na′tor, *n.***

**rum·mage** (rum′ij), ***n.*** [< MFr. < *arrumer*, to stow cargo < *run*, ship's hold < AS. *rum*, room], 1. odds and ends. 2. a rummaging search. ***v.t.*** [-MAGED, -MAGING], 1. to search through (a place, etc.) thoroughly by moving the contents about. 2. to get or turn up by searching thoroughly (with *up* or *out*). ***v.i.*** to search thoroughly, as through the contents of a receptacle. **—rum′mag·er, *n.***

**rummage sale,** a sale of miscellaneous articles.

**rum·my** (rum′i), ***adj.*** [-MIER, -MIEST], [*rum* (queer) + *-y*], [Chiefly Brit. Slang], odd; strange; queer. ***n.*** any of certain card games in which the object is to match cards into sets of the same denomination or sequences of the same suit.

**rum·my** (rum′i), ***n.*** [*pl.* -MIES], [Slang], a drunkard. ***adj.*** of or like rum.

**ru·mor** (rōō′mẽr), *n.* [< OFr. < L., noise], 1. general talk not based on definite knowledge; hearsay. 2. an unconfirmed report, story, etc. in general circulation. *v.t.* to tell or spread by rumor.
**ru·mour** (rōō′mẽr), *n. & v.t.* rumor: British sp.
**rump** (rump), *n.* [< ON. *rumpr*], 1. the hind part of an animal, where the legs and back join. 2. a cut of beef from this part. 3. the buttocks. 4. the last and unimportant part; remnant.
**rum·ple** (rum p'l), *n.* [< MD. < *rompe*, a wrinkle], an uneven fold or crease; wrinkle. *v.t. & v.i.* [-PLED, -PLING], to fold or crease unevenly; wrinkle; muss. —**rum′ply,** *adj.*
**rum·pus** (rum′pəs), *n.* [prob. < Swiss G. student slang], [Colloq.], noisy disturbance; uproar.
**rum·run·ner** (rum′run′ẽr), *n.* a person, ship, etc. smuggling alcoholic liquor across a border.
**run** (run), *v.i.* [RAN or *dial.* RUN, RUN, RUNNING], [ME. *rinnen* < AS. (*ge*)*rinnan* < ON.], 1. to go by moving the legs faster than in walking. 2. to move swiftly: as, we *ran* to her aid. 3. to go, move, etc. easily and freely, without hindrance. 4. to flee. 5. to make a quick trip (*up to, down to,* etc.) for a brief stay. 6. *a*) to take part in a contest or race. *b*) to be a candidate in an election. 7. to swim in migration: said of fish. 8. to ply (between two points): as, the bus *runs* between Chicago and New York. 9. to pass lightly and rapidly: as, a breeze *ran* through the trees. 10. to be current; circulate: as, the story *runs* that he is rich. 11. to climb or creep, as a vine. 12. to extend in time: as, its history *runs* back 500 years. 13. to ravel: as, her stocking *ran.* 14. to move with parts that revolve, slide, etc.; operate, as a machine. 15. to flow: as, blood *runs* in the veins. 16. to melt and flow, as butter. 17. to spread over cloth, etc. when moistened, as colors. 18. to be wet with a flow: as, her eyes *ran* with tears. 19. to discharge pus, mucus, etc. 20. to appear continuously: as, the play *ran* for a year. 21. to continue in effect: as, the law *runs* for ten years. 22. to extend in a continuous line: as, the fence *runs* through the woods. 23. to pass into a specified condition, etc.: as, he *ran* into trouble. 24. to be written, expressed, etc. in a specified way: as, the proverb *runs* like this. 25. to be at a specified size, price, etc.: as, eggs still *run* high. *v.t.* 1. to follow (a specified course). 2. to travel over: as, wild horses *ran* the range. 3. to perform as by running: as, he *ran* a race. 4. to incur (a risk, etc.). 5. to get past: as, to *run* a blockade. 6. to sew with a continuous succession of stitches. 7. to hunt (game, etc.). 8. to compete with as in a race. 9. to put up as a candidate for election. 10. to make run, move, etc. 11. to bring into a specified condition, etc. as by running: as, he *ran* me breathless. 12. to convey, as in a vehicle. 13. to smuggle. 14. to drive (an object) into or against (something). 15. to allow to continue in force: as, he *ran* a bill at the store. 16. to make flow in a specified way, place, etc.: as, *run* water into a glass. 17. to manage: as, she *runs* the household. 18. to mark or draw, as boundary lines. 19. to trace: as, *run* the story back to its source. 20. to undergo (a fever, etc.). 21. to melt or smelt (ore). 22. to cast or mold; found. 23. to publish (a story, etc.) in a newspaper. 24. in *billiards*, etc., to complete successfully (a sequence of shots, etc.). *n.* 1. *a*) an act or period of running. *b*) a running pace. 2. the distance covered in running. 3. a trip; journey. 4. a route: as, the milkman finished his *run.* 5. *a*) movement onward; progression. *b*) the tendency, as of events. 6. a continuous course or period: as, a *run* of good luck. 7. a continuous course of performances, etc., as of a play. 8. a continued series of demands, as on a bank. 9. a continuous extent of something. 10. a flow or rush of water, etc., as of the tide. 11. a brook. 12. *a*) a period in which some fluid flows readily. *b*) the amount of flow. 13. *a*) a period of operation of a machine. *b*) the amount produced in such a period. 14. *a*) a kind or class, as of goods. *b*) the usual or average kind. 15. an enclosed area for domestic animals: as, a chicken *run.* 16. freedom to move about at will: as, we had the *run* of the house. 17. *a*) a large number of fish migrating together. *b*) such migration. 18. a ravel, as in a stocking. 19. in *aviation*, the approach to the target made by a bombing plane: in full, **bombing run.** 20. in *baseball*, a scoring point, made by a successful circuit of the bases. 21. in *billiards*, etc., a sequence of successful shots, etc. 22. in *music*, a rapid succession of tones. *adj.* 1. melted. 2. poured while in a melted state: as, *run* metal. —**a run for one's money,** 1. powerful competition. 2. satisfaction for what one has expended. —**in the long run,** in the final outcome; ultimately. —**on the run,** running or running away. —**run across,** to encounter by chance. —**run away with,** 1. to deprive of self-control, etc. 2. to outdo all others in (a contest, etc.). —**run down,** 1. to stop operating. 2. to run or drive against so as to knock down. 3. to pursue and capture or kill. 4. to speak of disparagingly. 5. to make or become run-down. —**run for it,** to run to escape something. —**run in,** 1. to include, as something additional. 2. [Slang], to arrest. —**run into,** 1. to encounter by chance. 2. to collide with. —**run off,** 1. to print, typewrite, etc. 2. to cause to be run, played, etc. —**run on,** 1. to continue or be continued. 2. to talk continuously. —**run out,** to come to an end; expire. —**run out of,** to use up. —**run over,** 1. to ride over. 2. to overflow. 3. to examine, rehearse, etc. rapidly. —**run through,** 1. to use up or spend quickly or recklessly. 2. to pierce. —**run up,** to raise, rise, or make rapidly.
**run·a·bout** (run′ə-bout′), *n.* 1. one who runs about from place to place. 2. a light, one-seated, open carriage or automobile. 3. a light motorboat.
**run-a·round** (run′ə-round′), *n.* [Slang], a series of evasions: also **run′round′.**
**run·a·way** (run′ə-wā′), *n.* 1. a fugitive. 2. a horse, etc. that runs away. 3. a running away. *adj.* 1. running away or having run away. 2. of or done by runaways. 3. easily won, as a race. 4. rising rapidly, as prices.
**run-down** (run′doun′), *adj.* 1. not wound and therefore not running, as a watch. 2. in poor physical condition, as from overwork. 3. fallen into disrepair; dilapidated. *n.* a quick summary.
**rune** (rōōn), *n.* [AS. *run*], 1. any of the characters of an ancient Germanic alphabet. 2. something inscribed in such characters. 3. any similar mark having mysterious or magic meaning. 4. loosely, an ancient Scandinavian poem.
**rung** (ruŋ), *n.* [AS. *hrung*, a staff], any sturdy stick, bar, or rod used as a crossbar, support, etc.; specif., *a*) any of the steps of a ladder. *b*) a crosspiece between the legs of a chair, or across the back, etc. *c*) a spoke of a wheel.
**rung** (ruŋ), pp. and rare pt. of **ring** (to sound).
**ru·nic** (rōō′nik), *adj.* 1. of, consisting of, or characterized by runes. 2. like or suggestive of runes in decorative interlaced effect.
**run-in** (run′in′), *adj.* in *printing*, that is run in. *n.* 1. in *printing*, run-in matter. 2. [Colloq.], a quarrel, fight, etc.
**run·nel** (run′'l), *n.* [AS. *rynel* < *rinnan*, to run], a small stream; little brook: also **run′let** (-lit).
**run·ner** (run′ẽr), *n.* 1. one that runs, as a racer. 2. a messenger or agent, as for a bank or broker. 3. a smuggler. 4. one who operates a machine, etc. 5. a long, narrow cloth or rug. 6. a long ravel, as in hose; run. 7. a long, trailing stem, as of a strawberry, that puts out roots along the ground, thus producing new plants. 8. something on or in which something else moves. 9. either of the long, narrow pieces on which a sled or sleigh slides. 10. the blade of a skate.
**run·ner-up** (run′ẽr-up′), *n.* a person or team that finishes second in a race, contest, etc.
**run·ning** (run′iŋ), *n.* 1. the act of one that runs; racing, management, etc. 2. that which runs, or flows. *adj.* 1. moving or advancing rapidly. 2. flowing: as, *running* water. 3. cursive: said of handwriting. 4. melting; becoming liquid. 5. discharging pus: as, a *running* sore. 6. creeping or climbing: said of plants. 7. in operation, as machinery. 8. measured in a straight line: as, a *running* foot. 9. continuous: as, a *running* commentary. 10. successive: as, for five days *running.* 11. prevalent. 12. current: as, a *running* account. 13. moving easily or smoothly. 14. slipping or sliding easily, as a knot. 15. moving when pulled, as a rope. 16. done in or by a run: as, a *running* jump. 17. of the run (of a train, bus, etc.): as, the *running* time is two hours. —**in** (or **out of**) **the running,** having (or having lost) a chance to win.
**running board,** a footboard along the lower part of the side of some automobiles, etc.
**running fire,** a rapid succession of fired shots, remarks, questions, etc.
**running head** (or **title**), a heading or title printed at the top of every, or every other, page.
**running knot,** a knot so tied as to slide along the rope, thus forming a noose (*running noose*).
**running mate,** a candidate for a lesser office, as for the vice-presidency, regarded as running together with his party's candidate for the greater.
**Run·ny·mede** (run′i-mēd′), *n.* a meadow west of London where King John is thought to have signed the Magna Charta in 1215.
**run-off** (run′ôf′), *n.* 1. something that runs off,

as rain in excess of the amount absorbed by the ground. 2. a deciding, final race, game, etc.

**run-of-the-mill** (run′əv-*th*ə-mil′), *adj.* [see RUN, *n.*, 14*b*], not selected or special; ordinary.

**run-on** (run′on′), *adj.* in *printing*, that is run on. *n.* run-on matter.

**runt** (runt), *n.* [prob. akin to AS. *hrindan*, to thrust], 1. *a*) a stunted animal, plant, or (in a contemptuous sense) person. *b*) the smallest animal of a litter. 2. an ox or cow of a small breed. —**runt′y** [-IER, -IEST], **runt′ish**, *adj.* —**runt′i·ness**, *n.*

**run·way** (run′wā′), *n.* 1. a channel, track, strip, etc. in, on, or along which something moves; specif., *a*) a strip of leveled ground used by airplanes in taking off and landing. *b*) a beaten path made by deer, etc. 2. a run (*n.* 15) for chickens.

**ru·pee** (ro͞o-pē′), *n.* [< Hind. < Sans. *rūpya*, wrought silver], 1. the monetary unit and a silver coin of India. 2. the monetary unit of Pakistan.

**rup·ture** (rup′chẽr), *n.* [Fr. < L. pp. of *rumpere*, to break], 1. a breaking apart or being broken apart; breach. 2. a breaking off of peaceful relations, as between countries. 3. hernia. *v.t.* & *v.i.* [-TURED, -TURING], 1. to break; burst. 2. to affect with or undergo a rupture. —**rup′tur·a·ble**, *adj.*

**ru·ral** (roor′əl), *adj.* [< LL. *ruralis* < L. *rus*, the country], 1. of or like the country (as distinguished from the city), country folk, etc.; rustic. 2. living in the country. —**ru′ral·ly**, *adv.*

**rural free delivery,** free delivery of mail by carriers on routes in rural areas.

**ru·ral·ism** (roor′əl-iz′m), *n.* 1. rural quality or character. 2. a rural idiom. —**ru′ral·ist**, *n.*

**ru·ral·ize** (roor′əl-īz′), *v.t.* [-IZED, -IZING], to make rural. *v.i.* to live for a time in the country; rusticate. —**ru′ral·i·za′tion**, *n.*

**ruse** (ro͞oz), *n.* [< OFr. < *ruser*, to dodge], a stratagem, trick, or artifice.

**rush** (rush), *v.i.* [< OFr. *reüsser*, to get out of the way], 1. to move swiftly or impetuously. 2. to make a sudden attack (*on* or *upon*). 3. to dash rashly. 4. to pass, come, go, etc. swiftly or suddenly: as, the stars *rushed* out. 5. in *football*, to advance the ball by rushes. *v.t.* 1. to move, send, push, etc. violently or hastily: as, they *rushed* him out of the room. 2. to do, make, etc. with unusual haste; hurry: as, *rush* this order. 3. to make a sudden attack on. 4. [Slang], to lavish attentions on, as in courting. *n.* 1. a rushing. 2. an eager movement of many people to get to a place. 3. busyness; haste: as, the *rush* of modern life. 4. a sudden, swift attack. 5. a kind of scrimmage between groups of college students, held as a contest. 6. a press, as of business, necessitating unusual haste. 7. in *football*, an attempt to advance the ball by plunging through the line. 8. *usually in pl.* in *motion pictures*, a first print of a scene, projected for inspection by the director, etc. *adj.* necessitating haste: as, *rush* orders. —**with a rush**, suddenly and forcefully. —**rush′er**, *n.* —**rush′ing**, *adj.* —**rush′ing·ly**, *adv.*

**rush** (rush), *n.* [AS. *rysce*], 1. a grasslike plant with a hollow or pithy stem, growing usually in wet places. 2. such a stem, used for making baskets, mats, etc. 3. something of little value. —**rush′like′**, *adj.* —**rush′y** [-IER, -IEST], *adj.*

**rush candle,** a candle made with the pith of a rush as the wick: also **rush′light′**, **rush light.**

**rush hour,** a time of the day when business, traffic, etc. are especially heavy.

**rusk** (rusk), *n.* [< Sp. *rosca*, twisted bread roll], 1. a piece of sweet, raised bread or cake toasted in an oven. 2. a light, soft, sweetened biscuit.

**Rus·kin, John** (rus′kin), 1819–1900; English writer on social reform and art critic.

**Russ** (rus), *adj.* & *n.* [*pl.* RUSS], Russian.

**Russ.,** 1. Russia. 2. Russian.

**Rus·sell, Bertrand** (rus′'l), third Earl Russell, 1872–1970; English philosopher, mathematician, and writer.

**rus·set** (rus′it), *n.* [< OFr. < L. *russus*, reddish], 1. yellowish (or reddish) brown. 2. a coarse, brownish cloth, formerly used for clothing by country people. 3. a winter apple with a mottled skin. *adj.* yellowish-brown or reddish-brown. —**rus′set·y**, *adj.*

**Rus·sia** (rush′ə), *n.* 1. before 1917, an empire (*Russian Empire*) in E Europe and N Asia, ruled by a czar: capital, St. Petersburg. 2. now, the Union of Soviet Socialist Republics.

**Russia leather,** a fine, smooth leather, usually dark red, originally made in Russia.

**Rus·sian** (rush′ən), *adj.* of Russia, its people, their language, etc. *n.* 1. a native or inhabitant of Russia. 2. a member of the chief Slavic people of Russia. 3. the East Slavic language of the Russians, the principal language of the U.S.S.R.

**Russian dressing,** mayonnaise mixed with chili sauce, chopped pickles, etc.: used on salads.

**Rus·sian·ize** (rush′ən-īz′), *v.t.* [-IZED, -IZING], to make Russian in character.

**Russian Revolution,** the revolution of 1917 in which the czarist government was overthrown by Russian workers, peasants, soldiers, etc.

**Russian Soviet Federated Socialist Republic,** a republic in Europe and Asia, forming the largest division of the Soviet Union: area, 6,322,350 sq. mi.; pop., 126,600,000; capital, Moscow.

**Russian thistle,** a large weed with spiny branches, which matures into a tumbleweed.

**Russian wolfhound,** any of a breed of large dog with a narrow head, long legs, and silky coat.

**Rus·so-,** a combining form meaning: 1. *Russia* or *Russian*. 2. *Russian and*, as in *Russo-Japanese*.

**rust** (rust), *n.* [AS.], 1. the reddish-brown coating (mainly ferric oxide) formed on iron and steel by oxidation, as during exposure to air and moisture: also **iron rust.** 2. any similar coating formed on other metals. 3. any stain resembling iron rust. 4. any habit, influence, etc. injurious to usefulness, to the mind, etc. 5. inactivity; idleness. 6. a reddish brown. 7. in *botany*, a plant disease caused by parasitic fungi (*rust fungi*), spotting stems and leaves. *v.i.* & *v.t.* 1. to have or cause to have such a disease. 2. to become or cause to be coated with rust. 3. to deteriorate, as through disuse. 4. to become or make rust-colored. —**rust′a·ble**, *adj.* —**rust′-col′ored**, *adj.* —**rust′less**, *adj.*

**rus·tic** (rus′tik), *adj.* [L. *rusticus* < *rus*, the country], 1. of or living in the country; rural. 2. lacking sophistication; simple; artless. 3. rough; uncouth; awkward. 4. made of bark-covered branches or roots: as, *rustic* furniture. *n.* a country person, especially one regarded as unsophisticated, simple, etc. —**rus′ti·cal·ly**, *adv.*

**rus·ti·cate** (rus′ti-kāt′), *v.i.* [-CATED, -CATING], 1. to go to the country. 2. to lead a rural life. *v.t.* 1. to send to live in the country. 2. [Brit.], to suspend (a student) from a college as punishment. 3. to make (a person, etc.) rustic. —**rus′ti·ca′tion**, *n.* —**rus′ti·ca′tor**, *n.*

**rus·tic·i·ty** (rus-tis′ə-ti), *n.* [*pl.* -TIES], 1. rustic quality or state; awkwardness, ignorance, etc. 2. rural life. 3. a rural characteristic.

**rus·tle** (rus′'l), *v.i.* & *v.t.* [-TLED, -TLING], [< ME. *rouslen*, etc.], to make, or move so as to produce, irregular, soft, rubbing sounds, as of moving leaves, paper, etc. *n.* a series of such sounds. —**rus′tling**, *adj.* & *n.* —**rus′tling·ly**, *adv.*

**rus·tle** (rus′'l), *v.i.* & *v.t.* [-TLED, -TLING], [? < *rush*, *v.* + *hustle*], [Colloq.], 1. to work or proceed with energetic action. 2. to steal (cattle, etc.). —**rustle up**, [Colloq.], to collect or get together, as by foraging around.

**rus·tler** (rus′lẽr), *n.* one that rustles; esp., [Colloq.], *a*) an energetic person. *b*) a cattle thief.

**rust·proof** (rust′pro͞of′), *adj.* resistant to rust.

**rust·y** (rus′ti), *adj.* [-TIER, -TIEST], 1. coated with rust, as a metal, or affected by rust, as a plant. 2. caused by rust. 3. not working freely because of, or as if because of, rust. 4. *a*) impaired by disuse, neglect, etc. *b*) having lost facility through lack of practice. 5. rust-colored. 6. faded, old-looking, etc. —**rust′i·ly**, *adv.* —**rust′i·ness**, *n.*

**rut** (rut), *n.* [OFr. *route*; see ROUTE], 1. a groove, track, etc., especially one made by wheeled vehicles. 2. a fixed, routine procedure, course of action, etc. *v.t.* [RUTTED, RUTTING], to make ruts in.

**rut** (rut), *n.* [< OFr. < L. < *rugire*, to roar], 1. the periodic sexual excitement of many male mammals. 2. the period of this. *v.i.* [RUTTED, RUTTING], to be in rut. —**rut′tish**, *adj.*

**ru·ta·ba·ga** (ro͞o′tə-bā′gə), *n.* [Sw. dial. *rotabagge*], a turnip with a large, yellow root.

**Ruth** (ro͞oth), *n.* in the *Bible*, *a*) a Moabite woman, celebrated for her devotion to her mother-in-law, Naomi. *b*) a book of the Old Testament that tells the story of Ruth.

**ruth** (ro͞oth), *n.* [< AS. *hreowian*, to rue; + *-th*], [Archaic], 1. pity; compassion. 2. sorrow; grief.

**Ruth, George Herman** (ro͞oth), ("*Babe*" *Ruth*), 1895–1948; U.S. baseball player.

**ru·the·ni·um** (ro͞o-thē′ni-əm), *n.* [< ML. *Ruthenia*,

Russia, where first found], a rare, very hard, silvery-gray, metallic chemical element of the platinum group: symbol, Ru; at. wt., 101.7; at. no., 44.
**ruth·less** (rōōth′lis), ***adj.*** without ruth; pitiless. **—ruth′less·ly,** ***adv.*** **—ruth′less·ness,** ***n.***
**rut·ty** (rut′i), ***adj.*** [-TIER, -TIEST], full of ruts.
**R.V.,** Revised Version (of the Bible).
**Rwan·da** (ẽr-wän′dä), ***n.*** a country in east central Africa: area, 10,169 sq. mi.; pop., 2,780,000; capital, Kigali.
**Rwy., Ry.,** Railway.
**-ry** (ri), -ery: shortened form, as in *dentistry*.
**rye** (rī), ***n.*** [see PLURAL, II, D, 3], [AS. *ryge*], 1. a hardy cereal grass widely grown for its grain and straw. 2. the grain or seeds of this plant, used for making flour and whisky, and as feed for livestock. 3. whisky distilled from this grain.
**rye grass,** any of various quick-growing grasses.
**Ryu·kyu** (rū′kū′), ***n.*** a chain of islands in the W Pacific, between Kyushu and Taiwan.

# S

**S, s** (es), ***n.*** [*pl.* S's, s's, Ss, ss], 1. the nineteenth letter of the English alphabet. 2. a sound of S or s. ***adj.*** nineteenth in a sequence or group.
**S** (es), ***n.*** 1. an object shaped like S. 2. in *chemistry, the symbol for* sulfur. ***adj.*** shaped like S.
**-s,** [alt. form of *-es*], 1. the plural ending of most nouns, as in *hips, shoes*, etc. 2. the ending of the third person singular, present indicative, of verbs, as in *gives, runs*, etc. 3. a suffix used to form some adverbs, as in *betimes*, etc.
**-'s,** [AS. *-es*], the ending of the possessive singular of nouns (and some pronouns) and of the possessive plural of nouns not ending in *s*: as, boy'*s*, one'*s*, women'*s*.
**-'s,** the unstressed and assimilated form of: 1. *is*, as in *he's here*. 2. *has*, as in *she's spoken*. 3. *us*, as in *let's go*.
**S.,** 1. Saturday. 2. September. 3. Sunday
**S, S., s, s.,** 1. south. 2. southern.
**S., s.,** 1. [*pl.* SS., ss.], saint. 2. school.
**s.,** 1. second(s). 2. shilling(s). 3. singular.
**Sa,** in *chemistry*, samarium.
**S.A.,** 1. Salvation Army. 2. South Africa. 3. South America. 4. South Australia.
**Saar** (sär; G. zär), ***n.*** 1. a river in France and Germany flowing northward into the Moselle River. 2. a state of West Germany, in the valley of the Saar River: from 1948 to 1957, an autonomous government having a customs union with France: area, 991 sq. mi.; pop., 1,106,000: also called *Saarland*.
**Saar·land** (zär′länt), ***n.*** the Saar.
**Sa·ba** (sā′bə), ***n.*** an ancient kingdom of S Arabia: Biblical name, *Sheba*.
**Sab·ba·tar·i·an** (sab′ə-târ′i-ən), ***adj.*** of the Sabbath and its observance. ***n.*** 1. one who observes the Sabbath (Saturday). 2. one who favors rigid observance of Sunday as the Sabbath. **—Sab′ba·tar′i·an·ism,** ***n.***
**Sab·bath** (sab′əth), ***n.*** [< OFr. & AS. < L. < Gr. < Heb. < *shābath*, to rest], 1. the seventh day of the Jewish week, set aside for rest and worship; Saturday. 2. Sunday: so called by most Protestants. 3. [s-], a period of rest. ***adj.*** of the Sabbath.
**Sab·bat·i·cal** (sə-bat′i-k'l), ***adj.*** [< Fr. < Gr. *sabbatikos;* see SABBATH], 1. of or suited to the Sabbath. 2. [s-], bringing a period of rest that recurs in regular cycles: as, a *sabbatical* leave. ***n.*** [s-], a sabbatical year. Also **Sab·bat′ic. —Sab·bat′i·cal·ly, sab·bat′i·cal·ly,** ***adv.***
**sabbatical year,** a leave of absence for rest, study, etc. given every seven years to teachers, in some colleges and universities.
**sa·ber, sa·bre** (sā′bẽr), ***n.*** [< Fr. < MHG. *sabel;* of Slav. origin], a heavy cavalry sword with a slightly curved blade. ***v.t.*** [-BERED or -BRED, -BERING or -BRING], to strike, wound, or kill with a saber. **—sa′ber·like′, sa′bre·like′,** ***adj.***
**saber rattling,** a threatening of war, or a menacing show of armed force.
**Sa·bine** (sā′bīn), ***n.*** a member of an ancient tribe living in central Italy, conquered by the Romans in the 3d century B.C. ***adj.*** of the Sabines.
**sa·ble** (sā′b'l), ***n.*** [*pl.* -BLES, -BLE; see PLURAL, II, D, 1], [OFr. < ML. *sabelum;* of Oriental origin], 1. a flesh-eating, weasellike mammal of N Europe and Asia, related to the marten and valued for its glossy, dark fur. 2. a related animal of North America. 3. the costly fur or pelt of the sable. 4. in *heraldry*, the color black. ***adj.*** 1. made of the fur of the sable. 2. black; dark.
**sa·bot** (sab′ō; Fr. sȧ′bō′), ***n.*** [Fr.; ult. < Ar. *sabbât*, sandal], 1. a kind of shoe shaped and hollowed from a single piece of wood, worn by peasants in Europe. 2. a heavy leather shoe with a wooden sole.

SABOT

**sab·o·tage** (sab′ə-täzh′, -tij), ***n.*** [Fr. < *saboter*, to damage < *sabot;* from damage done to machinery by wooden shoes], 1. intentional destruction of machines, waste of materials, etc., as during labor disputes. 2. destruction of railroads, bridges, etc., as by enemy agents or an underground resistance, in time of war. 3. any deliberate obstruction of an effort, as of a nation's war work. ***v.t. & v.i.*** (sab′ə-täzh′), [-TAGED, -TAGING], to commit sabotage (on).
**sab·o·teur** (sab′ə-tūr′), ***n.*** [Fr.], a person who engages in sabotage.
**sac** (sak), ***n.*** [Fr. < L. *saccus;* see SACK (bag)], a pouchlike part in a plant or animal, often filled with fluid. **—sac′like′,** ***adj.***
**SAC,** Strategic Air Command.
**sac·cha·rin** (sak′ə-rin), ***n.*** [< ML. < L. < Gr. *sakcharon*], a white, crystalline coal-tar compound, about 400 times sweeter than cane sugar, used as a sugar substitute in diabetic diets, etc.
**sac·cha·rine** (sak′ə-rin, -rin′), ***adj.*** 1. of, like, or producing sugar. 2. very sweet or sirupy: as, a *saccharine* voice: used derisively. ***n.*** saccharin. **—sac′cha·rine·ly,** ***adv.*** **—sac′cha·rin′i·ty,** ***n.***
**Sac·co, Ni·co·la** (nē-kō′lä säk′kō; Eng. sak′ō), 1891–1927; Italian anarchist in U.S.; with B. Vanzetti charged with murder in 1920 and executed; their conviction, regarded as the result of political bias, aroused international protest.
**sac·er·do·tal** (sas′ẽr-dō′t'l), ***adj.*** [< OFr. < L. < *sacerdos*, priest], of priests or the office of priest; priestly. **—sac′er·do′tal·ly,** ***adv.***
**sac·er·do·tal·ism** (sas′ẽr-dō′t'l-iz'm), ***n.*** the character, system, methods, etc. of the priesthood.
**sa·chem** (sā′chəm), ***n.*** [< Algonquian *sâchimau*], among some American Indian tribes, the chief.
**sa·chet** (sa-shā′; *also, esp.* Brit., sash′ā), ***n.*** [Fr., dim. of *sac*, a bag], 1. a small bag, pad, etc. filled with perfumed powder, used to scent clothing. 2. such powder: also **sachet powder.**
**sack** (sak), ***n.*** [AS. *sacc* < L. *saccus* < Gr. < Heb. *saq*], 1. a bag; esp., a large bag of coarse cloth, for holding grain, foodstuffs, etc. 2. such a bag with its contents. 3. a varying measure of weight. 4. a short, loose-fitting jacket: also sp. **sacque.** 5. [Slang], dismissal; discharge (with *the*). 6. [Slang], a bed. 7. in *baseball*, a base. ***v.t.*** 1. to put into sacks. 2. [Slang], to discharge (a person).
**sack** (sak), ***n.*** [Fr. *sac* < It.; ult. < L. *saccus;* see prec. entry], the plundering or looting of a captured city or town. ***v.t.*** to plunder; pillage. **—sack′er,** ***n.***
**sack** (sak), ***n.*** [< Fr. (*vin*) *sec*, dry (wine) < L. *siccus*, dry], any of various dry white wines from Spain or the Canary Islands.
**sack·but** (sak′but′), ***n.*** [Fr. *saquebute* < OFr. *saquer*, to pull + *bouter*, to push], 1. a medieval wind instrument, forerunner of the trombone. 2. [false transl. of Aram. *sabbekha*], in the *Bible*, a stringed instrument like a lyre.
**sack·cloth** (sak′klôth′, -kloth′), ***n.*** 1. sacking. 2. coarse, rough cloth worn as a symbol of penitence or mourning. **—in sackcloth and ashes,** in a state of great mourning, penitence, etc.
**sack coat,** a man's short, loose-fitting, straight-backed coat, usually part of a business suit.

**sack·ful** (sak′fool′), *n.* [*pl.* -FULS], 1. as much as a sack will hold. 2. a large quantity.
**sack·ing** (sak′iŋ), *n.* coarse cloth woven of flax, hemp, jute, etc., used for sacks and bags.
**sac·ra·ment** (sak′rə-mənt), *n.* [< OFr. < L. *sacramentum;* ult. < *sacer*, sacred], 1. any of certain rites variously observed by Christians as ordained by Jesus, as baptism, the Eucharist (or Lord's Supper), confirmation, etc. 2. [occas. S-], the Eucharist: often with *the.* 3. the consecrated bread, or bread and wine, of the Eucharist. 4. something regarded as sacred. 5. a symbol or token. 6. a solemn oath. —**sac′ra·men′tal,** *adj.* —**sac′ra·men′tal·ly,** *adv.*
**Sac·ra·men·to** (sak′rə-men′tō), *n.* 1. a river in California, flowing into San Francisco Bay. 2. the capital of California, on this river: pop., 192,000.
**sa·cred** (sā′krid), *adj.* [pp. of ME. *sacren*, to consecrate < OFr. < L. < *sacer*, holy], 1. consecrated to a god or deity; holy. 2. of a religion or religious rites and practices: opposed to *profane, secular.* 3. granted the respect accorded holy things; venerated; hallowed. 4. dedicated to some person, place, purpose, etc.: as, *sacred* to his memory. 5. secured by a religious feeling against violation; inviolate. —**sa′cred·ly,** *adv.* —**sa′cred·ness,** *n.*
**Sacred College,** see **College of Cardinals.**
**sac·ri·fice** (sak′rə-fīs′), *n.* [< OFr. < L. *sacrificium* < *sacer*, sacred + *facere*, to make], 1. *a*) an offering of the life of a person or animal, or of an object, in homage to a deity. *b*) something so offered. 2. *a*) a giving up, destroying, etc. of one thing for the sake of another of higher value. *b*) a thing so given up. 3. the loss incurred in selling something at less than its supposed value. 4. in *baseball*, a play (in full, **sacrifice hit**) in which the batter bunts so as to be put out but so as to advance a runner: cf. **sacrifice fly.** *v.t.* [-FICED, -FICING], 1. to offer to a deity in homage or propitiation. 2. to give up, destroy, etc. (one thing) for the sake of another of greater value. 3. to incur a loss in selling. 4. in *baseball*, to advance (a runner) by a sacrifice. *v.i.* to offer or make a sacrifice. —**the supreme sacrifice,** the giving of one's life, as for a cause.
**sacrifice fly,** in *baseball*, a play in which the batter intentionally flies out in order to score a runner from third.
**sac·ri·fi·cial** (sak′rə-fish′əl), *adj.* of, having the nature of, or used in a sacrifice. —**sac′ri·fi′cial·ly,** *adv.*
**sac·ri·lege** (sak′rə-lij), *n.* [< OFr. < L. < *sacrilegus*, temple robber < *sacer*, sacred + *legere*, to take away], 1. the crime of misappropriating what is consecrated to God or religion. 2. the disrespectful treatment of persons, things, or ideas held sacred.
**sac·ri·le·gious** (sak′ri-lē′jəs, -lij′əs), *adj.* injurious or disrespectful to things held sacred. —**sac′ri·le′gious·ly,** *adv.* —**sac′ri·le′gious·ness,** *n.*
**sac·ris·tan** (sak′ris-tən), *n.* an official in charge of a sacristy: also **sa·crist** (sā′krist).
**sac·ris·ty** (sak′ris-ti), *n.* [*pl.* -TIES], [< Fr. < ML. < L. *sacer*, sacred], a room in a church where the sacred vessels, vestments, etc. are kept.
**sac·ro·il·i·ac** (sā′krō-il′i-ak′), *adj.* [< *sacrum* + *iliac*], of the sacrum and the ilium; esp., designating the joint between them.
**sac·ro·sanct** (sak′rō-saŋkt′), *adj.* [< L. < *sacer*, sacred + *sanctus*, holy], very sacred, holy, or inviolable. —**sac′ro·sanc′ti·ty, sac′ro·sanct′ness,** *n.*
**sa·crum** (sā′krəm), *n.* [*pl.* -CRA (-krə), -CRUMS], [< L. (*os*) *sacrum*, sacred (bone): ? anciently used in sacrifices], a thick, triangular bone, consisting of fused vertebrae, at the lower end of the spinal column, forming the dorsal part of the pelvis.
**sad** (sad), *adj.* [SADDER, SADDEST], [AS. *sæd*, sated], 1. having or expressing low spirits or sorrow; unhappy; sorrowful. 2. causing or characterized by sorrow, dejection, etc. 3. dark-colored; dull. 4. [Colloq.], very bad; deplorable. 5. [Dial.], heavy, soggy, etc.: said of earth, pastry, etc. —**sad′ly,** *adv.* —**sad′ness,** *n.*
**sad·den** (sad′'n), *v.t. & v.i.* to make or become sad.
**sad·dle** (sad′'l), *n.* [AS. *sadol*], 1. a padded leather seat for a rider on a horse, bicycle, etc. 2. the position of one riding in such a seat. 3. a padded part of a harness worn over a horse's back. 4. the part of an animal's back where a saddle is placed. 5. anything suggestive of a saddle. 6. a ridge between two peaks. 7. a cut of mutton, etc. including part of the backbone and the two loins. *v.t.* [-DLED, -DLING], 1. to put a saddle upon. 2. to encumber, as with a burden. 3. to impose as a burden, obligation, etc. —**in the saddle,** in a position of control.
**sad·dle·bag** (sad′'l-bag′), *n.* a large bag, usually one of a pair, carried on either side of the back of a horse, etc., just behind the saddle.
**sad·dle·bow** (sad′'l-bō′), *n.* the arched front part of a saddle, the top of which is the pommel.
**sad·dle·cloth** (sad′'l-klôth′, -kloth′), *n.* a thick cloth placed under a saddle on an animal's back.
**saddle horse,** a horse trained for riding.
**sad·dler** (sad′lẽr), *n.* a person whose work is making, repairing, or selling saddles.
**saddle roof,** a roof with two gables and a ridge.
**sad·dler·y** (sad′lẽr-i), *n.* [*pl.* -IES], 1. the work of a saddler. 2. the harnesses, saddles, etc. made by a saddler. 3. a shop where these are sold.
**saddle shoes,** flat-heeled sport shoes with a band of different-colored leather across the instep.
**saddle soap,** a mild soap for cleaning leather, containing neat's-foot oil.
**saddle stitch,** a simple overcasting stitch.
**Sad·du·cee** (saj′oo-sē′, sad′yoo-), *n.* a member of an ancient Jewish sect that denied resurrection of the dead and adhered strictly to the written law: cf. *Pharisee.* —**Sad′du·ce′an,** *adj.*
**sad·i·ron** (sad′ī′ẽrn), *n.* a heavy flatiron.
**sad·ism** (sad′iz'm, sā′diz'm), *n.* [after Count de *Sade* (1740–1814), French writer], 1. the getting of sexual pleasure from dominating, mistreating, or hurting one's partner. 2. the getting of pleasure of any sort from mistreating others. —**sad′ist,** *n.* —**sa·dis′tic,** *adj.* —**sa·dis′ti·cal·ly,** *adv.*
**sad sack,** [Slang], a person who means well but is incompetent and consistently in trouble.
**sa·fa·ri** (sə-fä′ri, suf′ə-rē′), *n.* [*pl.* -RIS], [Swahili < Ar. *safara*, to travel], a journey or hunting expedition, especially in eastern Africa.
**safe** (sāf), *adj.* [SAFER, SAFEST], [< OFr. *sauf* < L. *salvus*], 1. free from damage, danger, etc.; secure. 2. having escaped injury; unharmed. 3. *a*) giving protection. *b*) trustworthy. 4. unable to cause trouble or damage: as, *safe* in jail. 5. taking or involving no risks; cautious. 6. in *baseball*, designating a player who reaches a base without being put out. *n.* 1. a locking metal container in which to store valuables. 2. any place for keeping articles safe. —**safe′ly,** *adv.* —**safe′ness,** *n.*
**safe-con·duct** (sāf′kon′dukt), *n.* 1. permission to travel through foreign or enemy regions, protected against arrest or harm. 2. a written pass giving such permission.
**safe-crack·er** (sāf′krak′ẽr), *n.* a person who breaks open safes to rob them: also **safe′break′er.**
**safe-de·pos·it box** (sāf′di-poz′it), a box for storing valuables, as in a bank's vault.
**safe·guard** (sāf′gärd′), *n.* any person or thing that protects or guards against loss or injury; protection; precaution. *v.t.* to protect or guard.
**safe·keep·ing** (sāf′kēp′iŋ), *n.* a keeping or being kept in safety; protection.
**safe·ty** (sāf′ti), *n.* [*pl.* -TIES], 1. a being safe; security. 2. any of certain devices for preventing accident. 3. in *football*, a play in which a player grounds the ball behind his own goal line when the ball was caused to pass the goal line by his own team: it scores two points for the opponents. *adj.* giving safety; reducing danger.
**safety belt,** 1. a life belt. 2. a belt worn by telephone linesmen, window washers, etc. and attached, as to the telephone pole or window sill, to prevent falling. 3. a seat belt securing a passenger in an airplane or automobile to give protection against jolting or in a collision.
**safety glass,** 1. shatterproof glass made of two sheets of glass with a transparent, plastic substance between. 2. glass reinforced with wire.
**safety lamp,** a miner's lamp, etc. constructed to avoid explosion or fire.
**safety match,** a match that will light only when it is struck on a prepared surface.
**safety pin,** a pin bent back on itself so as to form a spring, and having the point held with a guard.
**safety razor,** a razor with a detachable blade fitted at an angle into a holder with guards.
**safety valve,** 1. an automatic valve for a steam boiler, etc., which opens and releases steam if the pressure becomes excessive. 2. anything which serves as an outlet for emotion, anxiety, etc.
**saf·fron** (saf′rən), *n.* [< OFr. *safran;* ult. < Ar. *za'farān*], 1. a plant with purplish flowers and orange stigmas yielding a dye and seasoning. 2. its

dried stigmas. 3. orange yellow: also **saffron yellow.** *adj.* orange-yellow.

**S. Afr.,** 1. South Africa. 2. South African.

**S. Afr. D.,** South African Dutch.

**sag** (sag), *v.i.* [SAGGED, SAGGING], [prob. < ON. nautical language], 1. to sink or bend, especially in the middle, from weight or pressure. 2. to hang down unevenly. 3. to lose firmness or strength; weaken through weariness, age, etc. 4. to decline in price or value. *v.t.* to cause to sag. *n.* 1. a sagging. 2. a sagging or sunken place.

**sa·ga** (sä′gə), *n.* [ON., a tale], 1. a medieval Scandinavian story of battles, legends, etc., generally telling the traditional history of a Norse family. 2. any long story of heroic deeds.

**sa·ga·cious** (sə-gā′shəs), *adj.* [< L. *sagax*, wise], keenly perceptive or discerning; shrewd. —**sa·ga′cious·ly,** *adv.* —**sa·ga′cious·ness,** *n.*

**sa·gac·i·ty** (sə-gas′ə-ti), *n.* [*pl.* -TIES], quality or instance of being sagacious; penetrating intelligence and sound judgment.

**sag·a·more** (sag′ə-môr′, -mōr′), *n.* [< Algonquian; see SACHEM], a chief, especially of second rank among certain American Indian tribes.

**sage** (sāj), *adj.* [SAGER, SAGEST], [< OFr.; ult. < L. *sapiens*, orig. ppr. of *sapere*, to know], 1. wise and perceptive. 2. based upon wisdom; showing judgment: as, a *sage* comment. *n.* a very wise man; esp., an old man respected for his wisdom, experience, etc. —**sage′ly,** *adv.* —**sage′ness,** *n.*

**sage** (sāj), *n.* [< OFr. < L. < *salvus*, safe: it reputedly had healing powers], 1. a plant of the mint family with grayish-green leaves used for flavoring meats, etc. 2. sagebrush.

**sage·brush** (sāj′brush′), *n.* any of various shrubs with small flowers and a sagelike odor, found chiefly on the western plains of the U.S.

**sage grouse,** any of a variety of large grouse living on the sagebrush plains of W North America.

**sage hen,** the sage grouse, especially the female.

**Sag·i·naw** (sag′ə-nô′), *n.* a city in central Michigan: pop., 98,000.

**Sag·it·ta·ri·us** (saj′i-târ′i-əs), *n.* [L., archer], 1. a southern constellation supposedly outlining a centaur shooting an arrow. 2. the ninth sign of the zodiac (♐), entered by the sun about November 23.

**sag·it·tate** (saj′i-tāt′), *adj.* [< L. *sagitta*, arrow], in the shape of an arrowhead, as some leaves.

**sa·go** (sā′gō), *n.* [*pl.* -GOS], [Malay *sāgū*], 1. a starch made from the pith of certain palm trees, used in puddings, etc. 2. any of these trees.

**sa·gua·ro** (sə-gwä′rō, sə-wä′-), *n.* [*pl.* -ROS], [Sp.], a giant spiny cactus with white flowers.

**Sa·ha·ra** (sə-hâr′ə, -hä′rə), *n.* [Ar. *ṣaḥra*, a desert], a vast desert extending over N Africa.

**sa·hib** (sä′ib), *n.* [< Hind. < Ar. *ṣāḥib*, master], master: title formerly used by natives in India when speaking to or of a European: also **sa′heb** (-eb).

**said** (sed), pt. and pp. of **say.** *adj.* aforesaid.

**Saï·gon** (sī-gōn′, -gon′), *n.* seaport in South Vietnam: pop. (with near-by city of *Cholon*), 1,300,000.

**sail** (sāl), *n.* [AS. *segl*], 1. any of the shaped sheets, as of canvas, spread to catch the wind, by means of which some vessels are driven forward. 2. sails collectively. 3. a sailing vessel. 4. a trip in any vessel. 5. anything like a sail, as an arm of a windmill. *v.i.* 1. to be moved forward by means of sails. 2. to travel on water. 3. to begin a trip by water. 4. to navigate a sailboat, as for pleasure. 5. to glide through the air. 6. to move smoothly, like a ship in full sail. 7. [Colloq.], to move quickly or vigorously. *v.t.* 1. to move through or upon (a body of water) in a boat or ship. 2. to manage (a boat or ship). —**sail into,** [Colloq.], 1. to begin vigorously. 2. to attack or criticize severely. —**set** (or **make**) **sail,** 1. to hoist the sails for departure. 2. to begin a trip by water. —**take in sail,** to lower sails. —**under sail,** with sails set. —**sail′ing,** *n.*

**sail·boat** (sāl′bōt′), *n.* a boat having a sail or sails by means of which it is propelled.

**sail·cloth** (sāl′klôth′, -kloth′), *n.* canvas or similar heavy cloth used in making sails, etc.

**sail·er** (sāl′ēr), *n.* 1. a sailboat, with reference to speed: as, a swift *sailer.* 2. any fast vessel.

**sail·fish** (sāl′fish′), *n.* [*pl.* see FISH], a large tropical marine fish related to the swordfish, with a large saillike dorsal fin.

**sail·or** (sāl′ēr), *n.* 1. one who makes his living by sailing; seaman. 2. an enlisted man in the navy. 3. a voyager on water, as affected by seasickness: as, a bad *sailor.* 4. a straw hat with a flat crown and flat brim. *adj.* like a sailor's: as, a *sailor* suit. —**sail′or·ly,** *adj.*

**saint** (sānt), *n.* [< OFr. < L. *sanctus*, holy], 1. a holy person. 2. a person who is exceptionally patient, charitable, etc. 3. [S-], a member of any of certain religious groups calling themselves *Saints.* 4. in certain churches, a person officially recognized as having lived an exceptionally holy life, and so canonized. *adj.* holy; sacred. *v.t.* to make a saint of. See also given names (e.g. **Jerome,** Saint) and entries with **St.** —**saint′hood, saint′ship,** *n.* —**saint′like′,** *adj.*

**Saint Agnes's Eve,** the night of January 20, when a girl's future husband was supposed to be revealed to her if she performed certain rites.

**Saint Ber·nard** (bēr-närd′), a large, brown and white dog of a breed formerly kept at St. Bernard hospice in the Swiss Alps to rescue lost travelers.

**saint·ed** (sān′tid), *adj.* 1. of or fit for a saint; saintly. 2. regarded as a saint. 3. holy; sacred.

**Saint-Gau·dens, Augustus** (sānt-gô′d′nz), 1848–1907; U.S. sculptor, born in Ireland.

**saint·ly** (sānt′li), *adj.* [-LIER, -LIEST], like or suitable for a saint. —**saint′li·ness,** *n.*

**Saint Patrick's Day,** March 17, observed by the Irish in honor of the patron saint of Ireland.

**Saint-Saëns, Charles Ca·mille** (shȧrl′ kȧ′mē′y′ san′sän′), 1835–1921; French composer.

**Saint Valentine's Day,** February 14, observed in honor of a martyr of the 3d century, now a day for sending valentines, candy, etc. to sweethearts.

**Sai·pan** (sī′pän′, -pan′), *n.* one of the Marianas Islands, in the W Pacific: formerly Japanese, it became a U.S. trust territory in 1946.

**saith** (seth), archaic 3d pers. sing., pres. indic. of **say.**

**sake** (sāk), *n.* [AS. *sacu*, suit at law], 1. motive; purpose; cause: as, for the *sake* of money. 2. advantage; behalf; account: as, for my *sake.*

**sa·ke** (sä′ki), *n.* [Japan.], a Japanese alcoholic beverage made from fermented rice.

**Sa·kha·lin** (sä-khä-lēn′; Eng. sak′ə-lēn′), *n.* a Russian island off E Siberia, north of Japan.

**sal** (sal), *n.* [L.], in *pharmacy*, etc., salt.

**sa·laam** (sə-läm′), *n.* [Ar. *salām*, peace], 1. an Oriental greeting, etc. made by bowing low with the palm of the right hand placed on the forehead. 2. a respectful greeting. *v.t.* to greet with a salaam. *v.i.* to make a salaam.

**sal·a·ble** (sāl′ə-b′l), *adj.* that can be sold; marketable: also sp. **saleable.** —**sal′a·bil′i·ty, sal′a·ble·ness,** *n.* —**sal′a·bly,** *adv.*

**sa·la·cious** (sə-lā′shəs), *adj.* [< L. < *salire*, to leap], 1. lecherous; lustful. 2. pornographic; obscene. —**sa·la′cious·ly,** *adv.* —**sa·la′cious·ness, sa·lac′i·ty** (-las′ə-ti), *n.*

**sal·ad** (sal′əd), *n.* [< OFr. < Pr. < L. pp. of *salare*, to salt < *sal*, salt], 1. a dish, usually cold, of fruits, vegetables (especially lettuce), meat, eggs, etc. in various combinations, prepared with a dressing of oil and vinegar, or mayonnaise, etc. 2. any green plant used raw for such a dish.

**salad days,** time of youth and inexperience.

**salad dressing,** a preparation of oil, vinegar, spices, etc. served with a salad.

**sal·a·man·der** (sal′ə-man′dēr), *n.* [< OFr. < L. *salamandra* < Gr.], 1. a mythological reptile supposedly able to live in fire. 2. any of a group of scaleless, lizardlike amphibians, with a soft, moist skin and a tail. —**sal′a·man′drine** (-man′drin), *adj.*

SALAMANDER (about 4 in. long)

**sa·la·mi** (sə-lä′mi), *n.* [It., *pl.*, preserved meat < L. *sal*, salt], a highly spiced, salted sausage.

**sal ammoniac,** ammonium chloride: also **sal′-am·mo′ni·ac,** *n.*

**sal·a·ried** (sal′ə-rid), *adj.* 1. receiving a salary. 2. yielding a salary: as, a *salaried* position.

**sal·a·ry** (sal′ə-ri), *n.* [*pl.* -RIES], [< OFr. < L. *salarium*, orig., part of a soldier's pay for buying salt < *sal*, salt], a fixed payment at regular intervals for services, usually other than manual.

**sale** (sāl), *n.* [< AS. < ON. *sala*], 1. a selling; the exchange of property or a service for money, etc. 2. a market; opportunity to sell. 3. an auction. 4. a special offering of goods at reduced prices: as, a rummage *sale.* —**for** (or **on**) **sale,** to be sold.

**sale·a·ble** (sāl′ə-b′l), *adj.* salable. —**sale′a·bil′i·ty, sale′a·ble·ness,** *n.* —**sale′a·bly,** *adv.*

**Sa·lem** (sā′ləm), *n.* 1. a city on the coast of N Massachusetts: pop., 39,000. 2. a city in NW Oregon: the capital: pop., 49,000.

**sal·e·ra·tus** (sal′ə-rā′təs), *n.* [Mod. L. *sal aeratus*, aerated salt], sodium bicarbonate.

**Sa·ler·no** (sä-ler′nô; Eng. sə-lūr′nō), *n.* an Italian seaport near Naples: pop., 87,000.

**sales·girl** (sālz′gũrl′), *n.* a saleswoman.
**sales·la·dy** (sālz′lā′di), *n.* [*pl.* -DIES], [Colloq.], a saleswoman.
**sales·man** (sālz′mən), *n.* [*pl.* -MEN], a man employed to sell goods, either in a store or as a traveling agent.
**sales·man·ship** (sālz′mən-ship′), *n.* 1. the work of a salesman. 2. ability or skill at selling.
**sales·peo·ple** (sālz′pē′p'l), *n.pl.* salespersons.
**sales·per·son** (sālz′pũr′s'n), *n.* a person employed to sell goods, especially in a store.
**sales resistance,** resistance of potential customers to efforts aimed at getting them to buy.
**sales·room** (sālz′rōōm′, -room′), *n.* a room in which goods are offered for sale.
**sales talk,** 1. persuasion used in an attempt to sell something. 2. any argument aimed at persuading one to do something.
**sales tax,** a tax on sales or on receipts from sales, usually added to the price by the seller.
**sales·wom·an** (sālz′woom′ən), *n.* [*pl.* -WOMEN], a woman employed to sell goods, especially in a store.
**Sal·ic law** (sal′ik, sā′lik), [< Fr. < ML. < LL. *Salii*, a tribe of Franks], 1. a code of laws of Germanic tribes; esp., the provision of this code excluding women from inheriting land. 2. the law excluding women from succeeding to the throne in the French and Spanish monarchies.
**sal·i·cyl·ate** (sal′ə-sil′āt, sə-lis′ə-lāt′), *n.* any salt or ester of salicylic acid.
**sal·i·cyl·ic acid** (sal′ə-sil′ik), [< *salicin* (a glucoside obtained from the bark of certain willows) + *-yl* + *-ic*], a white, crystalline compound, $C_7H_6O_3$, used in the form of its salts, as in aspirin, to treat rheumatism, relieve pain, etc.
**sa·li·ent** (sā′li-ənt, sāl′yənt), *adj.* [< L. ppr. of *salire*, to leap], 1. leaping. 2. pointing outward; jutting. 3. prominent; conspicuous: as, the *salient* facts. *n.* 1. the part of a battle line, fort, etc. which projects farthest toward the enemy. 2. a salient angle, part, etc. —**sa′li·ence, sa′li·en·cy** [*pl.* -CIES], *n.* —**sa′li·ent·ly,** *adv.*
**sa·line** (sā′līn), *adj.* [< Fr. < L. *sal*, salt], of, like, or containing salt; salty. *n.* 1. a salt spring, lick, etc. 2. a metallic salt, as of magnesium, used in medicine as a cathartic. 3. a saline solution. —**sa·lin′i·ty** (sə-lin′ə-ti), *n.*
**Salis·bur·y steak** (sôlz′ber′i, -bẽr-), Hamburg steak.
**sa·li·va** (sə-lī′və), *n.* [L.], the thin, watery, slightly viscid fluid secreted by the salivary glands: it aids digestion by moistening and softening food, and converts starch to maltose.
**sal·i·var·y** (sal′ə-ver′i), *adj.* of or secreting saliva.
**sal·i·vate** (sal′ə-vāt′), *v.t.* [-VATED, -VATING], [< L. pp. of *salivare*], to produce excessive flow of saliva in. *v.i.* to secrete saliva. —**sal′i·va′tion,** *n.* —**sal′i·va′tor** (-tẽr), *n.*
**Salk, Jonas Edward** (sôlk), 1914–; U.S. physician; developed a vaccine to prevent poliomyelitis.
**sal·low** (sal′ō), *adj.* [AS. *salu*], of a sickly pale-yellowish complexion. *v.t.* to make sallow. —**sal′low·ish,** *adj.* —**sal′low·ness,** *n.*
**sal·ly** (sal′i), *n.* [*pl.* -LIES], [< Fr. *saillie* < L. *salire*, to leap], 1. a sudden rushing forth, as of troops to attack besiegers. 2. any sudden start into activity. 3. a quick witticism; quip. 4. an excursion; jaunt. *v.i.* [-LIED, -LYING], to rush or start (*out* or *forth*) on a sally.
**sal·ma·gun·di** (sal′mə-gun′di), *n.* [< Fr. *salmigondis;* prob. < It. *salome conditi*, pickled meat], 1. a dish of chopped meat, eggs, onions, anchovies, pepper, etc. 2. any mixture or medley.
**salm·on** (sam′ən), *n.* [*pl.* -ON, -ONS; see PLURAL, II, D, 2], [< OFr. *saumon* < L. *salmo*], 1. a game and food fish of the North Atlantic, with silver scales and yellowish-pink flesh: it lives in salt water and spawns in fresh water. 2. any of several closely related varieties, as of the North Pacific or of landlocked lakes. 3. yellowish pink: also **salmon pink.** *adj.* yellowish-pink: also **salmon-pink.**
**salmon trout,** 1. a European sea trout. 2. a namaycush. 3. any trout resembling a salmon.
**Sa·lo·me** (sə-lō′mi), *n.* in the *Bible*, the stepdaughter of Herod Antipas: her dancing pleased Herod so much that he granted her request for the head of John the Baptist: Matt. 14:8.
**Sa·lo·mé** (så′lô′mā′), *n.* [Fr.], Salome.
**sa·lon** (sə-lon′; Fr. så′lōn′), *n.* [*pl.* -LONS (-lonz′; Fr. -lōn′)], [Fr.; see SALOON], 1. a large reception hall. 2. a drawing room of a French private home. 3. a regular gathering of distinguished guests, as in a celebrity's home. 4. a gallery for the exhibition of works of art. 5. a commercial establishment for performing some service: as, a beauty *salon*.
**Sa·lo·ni·ka** (sal′ə-nē′kə, -nī′kə, sə-lon′i-kə), *n.* a seaport in Macedonia, Greece: pop., 217,000.
**sa·loon** (sə-lōōn′), *n.* [< Fr. *salon* < It. < *sala*, a hall], 1. any large room or hall for receptions, exhibitions, etc., as the main social cabin of a passenger ship. 2. a place where alcoholic drinks are sold to be drunk on the premises; public bar.
**sa·loon·keep·er** (sə-lōōn′kēp′ẽr), *n.* a person who operates a saloon (sense 2).
**sal·si·fy** (sal′sə-fī′), *n.* [< Fr. < It. *sassefrica*], a plant with long, white, fleshy roots having an oysterlike flavor: also called *oyster plant*.
**sal soda,** crystallized sodium carbonate.
**salt** (sôlt), *n.* [AS. *sealt*], 1. sodium chloride, NaCl, a white, crystalline substance found in natural beds, in sea water, etc., and used for seasoning and preserving food, etc. 2. a chemical compound derived from an acid by replacing hydrogen, wholly or partly, with a metal or an electropositive radical. 3. that which gives a tang or piquancy to anything. 4. sharp, pungent humor. 5. something that preserves, purifies, etc. 6. a saltcellar. 7. *pl.* *a)* mineral salts used medicinally as a cathartic. *b)* smelling salts. 8. [Colloq.], a sailor. *adj.* 1. containing salt. 2. preserved with salt. 3. tasting or smelling of salt. 4. pungent; witty. 5. *a)* flooded with salt water. *b)* growing in salt water. *v.t.* 1. to sprinkle or season with salt. 2. to preserve with salt. 3. to season or give tang to. 4. to give artificial value to; specif., to scatter ores in (a mine), put oil in (a well), etc. in order to deceive prospective buyers. —**salt away** (or **down**), 1. to pack and preserve with salt. 2. [Colloq.], to store or save (money, etc.). —**salt of the earth,** any person or persons regarded as the finest, etc. —**with a grain** (or **pinch**) **of salt,** with allowance for exaggeration, etc. —**worth one's salt,** worth one's wages, etc. —**salt′er,** *n.* —**salt′ish,** *adj.* —**salt′less,** *adj.*
**salt·cel·lar** (sôlt′sel′ẽr), *n.* [*salt* + Fr. *salière* < L. *sal*, salt], a small dish, or a container with a perforated top, for holding salt.
**salt·ed** (sôl′tid), *adj.* 1. seasoned or preserved with salt. 2. [Colloq.], experienced, as in some work.
**Salt Lake City,** the capital of Utah, near Great Salt Lake: pop., 189,000: center of Mormonism.
**salt lick,** an exposed natural deposit of mineral rock salt which animals come to lick.
**salt·pe·ter, salt·pe·tre** (sôlt′pē′tẽr), *n.* [< OFr. < ML. < L. *sal*, salt + *petra*, a rock], 1. potassium nitrate. 2. sodium nitrate: also *Chile saltpeter*.
**salt pork,** pork cured in salt.
**salt shaker,** a container for salt, with a perforated top.
**salt-wat·er** (sôlt′wô′tẽr, -wät′ẽr), *adj.* of, consisting of, or living in salt water.
**salt water,** water containing much salt; sea water.
**salt·works** (sôlt′wũrks′), *n.* [*pl.* -WORKS], a place where salt is prepared, as by evaporation.
**salt·wort** (sôlt′wũrt′), *n.* the glasswort.
**salt·y** (sôl′ti), *adj.* [-IER, -IEST], 1. of, tasting of, or containing salt. 2. pungent; sharp; witty. —**salt′i·ly,** *adv.* —**salt′i·ness,** *n.*
**sa·lu·bri·ous** (sə-lōō′bri-əs), *adj.* [L. *salubris* < *salus*, health], healthful; wholesome. —**sa·lu′bri·ous·ly,** *adv.* —**sa·lu′bri·ous·ness, sa·lu′bri·ty** (-brə-ti), *n.*
**sal·u·tar·y** (sal′yoo-ter′i), *adj.* [< Fr. < L. < *salus*, health], 1. conducive to health; healthful. 2. promoting some good purpose; beneficial. —**sal′u·tar′i·ly,** *adv.* —**sal′u·tar′i·ness,** *n.*
**sal·u·ta·tion** (sal′yoo-tā′shən), *n.* [< OFr. < L. *salutatis* < pp. of *salutare;* see SALUTE], 1. the act of greeting, paying respect, etc. by gestures or words. 2. a form of words serving as a greeting; esp., the "Dear Sir," etc. of a letter.
**sa·lu·ta·to·ri·an** (sə-lōō′tə-tôr′i-ən, -tō′ri-ən), *n.* in some schools and colleges, the student, usually second highest in scholastic rank, who gives the salutatory.
**sa·lu·ta·to·ry** (sə-lōō′tə-tôr′i, -tō′ri), *adj.* of or expressing a salutation. *n.* [*pl.* -RIES], an opening address, as at school commencement exercises.
**sa·lute** (sə-lōōt′), *v.t.* [-LUTED, -LUTING], [< L. *salutare* < *salus*, health, greeting], 1. to greet in a friendly manner, as by bowing, tipping the hat, etc. 2. to honor ceremonially by firing cannon, raising the hand, etc. as a mark of official respect.

3. to present itself to, as if in greeting: as, laughter *saluted* us. ***v.i.*** to make a salute. ***n.*** an act, words, etc. expressing welcome, honor, respect, etc.; specif., a prescribed formal gesture, such as raising the hand to the head, in military and naval practice. —**sa·lut′er, *n.***

**Sal·va·do·ran** (sal′və-dôr′ən, -dō′rən), ***adj.*** of El Salvador, its people, or culture. ***n.*** a native or inhabitant of El Salvador. Also **Sal′va·do′ri·an.**

**sal·vage** (sal′vij), ***n.*** [Fr. < OFr. *salver*, to save; see SAVE], 1. the rescue of a ship, crew, and cargo from fire, shipwreck, etc. 2. compensation paid for such rescue. 3. the ship, cargo, etc. so rescued. 4. the restoration of a sunken ship by divers and special apparatus. 5. in *insurance*, *a*) the rescue of property from fire. *b*) the property so rescued. ***v.t.*** [-VAGED, -VAGING], 1. to save from shipwreck, fire, etc. 2. to restore (sunken ships) by divers and special apparatus. 3. to utilize (damaged goods, etc.). —**sal′vag·er, *n.***

**sal·var·san** (sal′vẽr-san′), ***n.*** [G. < L. *salvare*, to save + G. *arsen*, arsenic], arsphenamine, a compound of arsenic used in the treatment of syphilis, etc.: a trade-mark (**Salvarsan**).

**sal·va·tion** (sal-vā′shən), ***n.*** [< OFr. < L. pp. of *salvare*, to save], 1. a saving or being saved. 2. a person or thing that saves or rescues. 3. in *theology*, the saving of the soul from sin and death, as, in Christianity, by the atonement of Jesus.

**Salvation Army,** a religious and charitable organization founded in 1865 to aid the very poor.

**salve** (sav, säv), ***n.*** [AS. *sealf*], 1. any soothing or healing ointment applied to wounds, burns, sores, etc. 2. something that soothes or heals; balm. ***v.t.*** [SALVED, SALVING], 1. to apply salve to. 2. to soothe; smooth over; assuage.

**sal·ve** (sal′vi), ***interj.*** [L.], hail!

**salve** (salv), ***v.t.*** [SALVED, SALVING], [< *salvage*], to salvage.

**sal·ver** (sal′vẽr), ***n.*** [< Fr. < Sp. *salva* < *salvar*, to taste (so as to prove food wholesome) < L. *salvare*, to save], a tray on which letters, visiting cards, refreshments, etc. are presented.

**sal·vi·a** (sal′vi-ə), ***n.*** [L.], any of various plants of the mint family; esp., the scarlet sage.

**sal·vo** (sal′vō), ***n.*** [*pl.* -VOS, -VOES], [< It. < L. *salve*, hail!], 1. a discharge of a number of guns in succession or at the same time, either in salute or at a target. 2. a burst of cheers or applause.

**sal vo·la·ti·le** (vō-lat′′l-ē′), [Mod. L., volatile salt], a mixture of ammonium bicarbonate and ammonium carbonate, used as smelling salts.

**Salz·burg** (sôlz′bẽrg), ***n.*** a city in central Austria: pop., 103,000.

**Sam.,** Samuel.

**S. Am., S. Amer.,** South America(n).

**Sa·mar** (sä′mär), ***n.*** one of the Philippine Islands, southeast of Luzon.

**sam·a·ra** (sam′ə-rə, sə-mâr′ə), ***n.*** [L., elm seed], a dry, hard, winged fruit, as of the elm or ash.

**Sa·mar·i·a** (sə-mâr′i-ə), ***n.*** 1. an ancient kingdom of Palestine, between Judea and Galilee. 2. a city in Samaria: the ancient capital of Israel.

**Sa·mar·i·tan** (sə-mar′ə-t′n), ***n.*** 1. a native or inhabitant of Samaria. 2. a good Samaritan: see **good Samaritan.** ***adj.*** of Samaria or its people.

**sa·ma·ri·um** (sə-mâr′i-əm), ***n.*** [< *samarskite*, a mineral < Col. *Samarski*, Russ. mining official], a metallic chemical element of the rare-earth group: symbols, Sm, Sa; at. wt., 150.43; at. no., 62.

**Sam·ar·kand, Sam·ar·cand** (sam′ẽr-kand′), ***n.*** a city of the Uzbek S.S.R., in central Asia: pop., 195,000.

**sam·ba** (sam′bə, säm′-), ***n.*** [Port.], a Brazilian dance of African origin. ***v.i.*** to dance the samba.

**Sam Browne belt** (broun), [after 19th-c. Brit. Gen., *Samuel J. Browne*], a military belt with one or two diagonal shoulder straps, worn by officers.

**same** (sām), ***adj.*** [< ON. *samr, sami*], 1. being the very one; identical. 2. alike, in kind, quality, amount, etc.; corresponding. 3. unchanged; not different: as, he looks the *same*. 4. before-mentioned; just spoken of. ***pron.*** the same person or thing. ***adv.*** in like manner. The *adj.* and *pron.* are usually used with *the, this,* or *that;* the *adv.*, with *the.* —**all the same,** 1. nevertheless. 2. of no importance. —**just the same,** 1. in the same way. 2. nevertheless. —**same′ness, *n.***

**Sam Hill** (sam hil), [Slang], hell: a euphemism.

**sam·i·sen** (sam′i-sen′), ***n.*** [Japan. < Chin. *san hsien*, three strings], a three-stringed Japanese musical instrument, somewhat like a banjo.

**sam·ite** (sam′īt, sā′mīt), ***n.*** [< OFr. < ML. < MGr. < *hexamitos*, woven with six threads], a heavy silk fabric worn in the Middle Ages: it was sometimes interwoven with gold.

**Sa·mo·a** (sə-mō′ə), ***n.*** a group of islands in the South Pacific, six of which constitute a possession of the U.S. (**American Samoa**): see also **Western Samoa.** —**Sa·mo′an, *adj.* & *n.***

**Sa·mos** (sā′mos), ***n.*** a Greek island off Asia Minor. —**Sa′mi·an** (-mi-ən), ***adj.* & *n.***

**Sam·o·thrace** (sam′ə-thrās′), ***n.*** a Greek island in the N Aegean.

**sam·o·var** (sam′ə-vär′, säm′ə-vär′), ***n.*** [Russ., lit., self-boiler], a Russian metal urn with an internal tube for heating water in making tea.

SAMOVAR

**Sam·o·yed, Sam·o·yede** (sam′ə-yed′), ***n.*** [Russ.], 1. any of a Uralic people of Siberia. 2. their language. 3. any of a powerful breed of Siberian dog, with a thick, white coat. ***adj.*** of the Samoyeds (sense 1) or Samoyed: also **Sam′o·yed′ic.**

**samp** (samp), ***n.*** [< Algonquian *nasaump*, softened by water], coarse corn meal or a porridge of this.

**sam·pan** (sam′pan), ***n.*** [Chin. *san-pan* < Port. < Sp. *champán*, canoe], any of various small boats used in China and Japan, rowed with a scull from the stern, and often having a sail.

**sam·ple** (sam′p'l, säm′-), ***n.*** [< OFr.; see EXAMPLE], 1. a part or piece taken as representative of a whole thing, group, etc.; specimen. 2. an example: as, a *sample* of your skill. ***adj.*** being a sample. ***v.t.*** [-PLED, -PLING], to take or test a sample of.

**sam·pler** (sam′plẽr, säm′-), ***n.*** 1. one who prepares samples for inspection. 2. a piece of cloth embroidered with designs, letters, etc., formerly made to display skill in needlework.

**Sam·son** (sam′s'n), ***n.*** 1. in the *Bible*, an Israelite with great strength: he was betrayed to the Philistines by Delilah, his mistress: Judges 13–16. 2. any very strong man.

**Sam·u·el** (sam′ū-əl, -yool), ***n.*** in the *Bible*, 1. a Hebrew judge and prophet. 2. either of two books (*I Samuel, II Samuel*) of the Old Testament.

**sam·u·rai** (sam′oo-rī′), ***n.*** [*pl.* -RAI], [Japan.], 1. a member of a military caste in feudal Japan. 2. ***pl.*** this class.

**San** (san, sän), ***n.*** [Sp. & It.], Saint.

**San An·to·ni·o** (san′ ən-tō′ni-ō′, san′ an-), a city in S Texas: pop, 588,000: site of the Alamo.

**san·a·tive** (san′ə-tiv), ***adj.*** [< OFr. < ML. < L. pp. of *sanare*, to heal], [Rare], healing; curative.

**san·a·to·ri·um** (san′ə-tôr′i-əm, -tō′ri-), ***n.*** [*pl.* -UMS, -A (-ə)], [< LL. *sanatorius*, giving health < L. *sanare*, to heal], a sanitarium.

**san·a·to·ry** (san′ə-tôr′i, -tō′ri), ***adj.*** [< LL.; see SANATORIUM], conducive to health; healing.

**San Ber·nar·di·no** (san′ bũr′nẽr-dē′nō), a city in S California: pop., 92,000.

**sanc·ti·fied** (saŋk′tə-fīd′), ***adj.*** 1. dedicated; consecrated. 2. sanctimonious.

**sanc·ti·fy** (saŋk′tə-fī′), ***v.t.*** [-FIED, -FYING], [< OFr. < LL. < L. *sanctus*, holy + *facere*, to make], 1. to make holy; specif., *a*) to make free from sin; purify. *b*) to set apart as holy; consecrate. 2. to give sanction to; make sacred, or inviolable. —**sanc′ti·fi·ca′tion, *n.*** —**sanc′ti·fi′er, *n.***

**sanc·ti·mo·ni·ous** (saŋk′tə-mō′ni-əs), ***adj.*** pretending to be very pious; affecting sanctity. —**sanc′ti·mo′ni·ous·ly, *adv.*** —**sanc′ti·mo′ni·ous·ness, *n.***

**sanc·ti·mo·ny** (saŋk′tə-mō′ni), ***n.*** [< OFr. < L. *sanctimonia* < *sanctus*, holy], assumed holiness; pretended piety; religious hypocrisy.

**sanc·tion** (saŋk′shən), ***n.*** [< Fr. < L. < pp. of *sancire*, to make sacred], 1. the confirming or ratifying of an action by authority; authorization. 2. support; approval. 3. something that gives binding force to a law as the penalty for breaking it, or a reward for carrying it out. 4. a principle, influence, etc. which makes a moral law binding. 5. *usually in pl.* a coercive measure, usually by several nations, for attempting to enforce international law. ***v.t.*** to give sanction to; specif., *a*) to authorize; confirm. *b*) to approve; encourage; support. —**sanc′tion·a·ble, *adj.*** —**sanc′tion·er, *n.***

**sanc·ti·ty** (saŋk′tə-ti), ***n.*** [*pl.* -TIES], [< L. < *sanctus*, holy], 1. saintliness; holiness. 2. a being consecrated to a deity; sacredness. 3. binding force; inviolability. 4. anything held sacred.

**sanc·tu·ar·y** (saŋk′chōō-er′i), ***n.*** [*pl.* -IES], [< OFr. < LL. < L. *sanctus*, sacred], 1. a holy place; place set aside for worship; specif., *a*) the Temple at Jerusalem. *b*) a church, temple, etc. *c*) a holy place within a church or temple, as the part around the altar, the holy of holies, etc. 2. a place of refuge or protection; esp., a reservation where animals or birds may not be hunted or molested. 3. refuge; protection; immunity from punishment.

**sanc·tum** (saŋk′təm), *n.* [*pl.* -TUMS, -TA (-tə)], [L., neut. of *sanctus*, pp. of *sancire*, to consecrate], 1. a sacred or private place. 2. a study or private room where one is not to be disturbed.

**sanctum sanc·to·rum** (saŋk-tôr′əm, -tō′rəm), [L.], 1. the holy of holies. 2. a most holy place.

**sand** (sand), *n.* [AS.], 1. loose, gritty grains of disintegrated rock, as on beaches, in deserts, etc. 2. *usually pl.* a tract of sand. 3. the sand in an hourglass. 4. *pl.* particles of time. 5. [Slang], grit; courage. *v.t.* 1. to sprinkle, mix, or fill with sand. 2. to smooth or polish with sand or sandpaper. **—sand′ed,** *adj.* **—sand′er,** *n.*

**Sand, George** (sand; Fr. säṅd), (pseudonym of *Baronne Dudevant*), 1803–76; French woman novelist.

**san·dal** (san′d'l), *n.* [< L. < Gr. dim. of *sandalon*], 1. a kind of shoe made of a sole fastened to the foot by straps. 2. a kind of slipper having the upper slashed with openwork or made of straps. **—san′daled, san′dalled,** *adj.*

**san·dal·wood** (san′d'l-wood′), *n.* [< OFr. < ML. < Ar. *çandal;* ult. < Sans.], 1. the hard, sweet-smelling heartwood of any of certain Asiatic trees, used for carving and cabinetmaking or burned as incense. 2. any of these trees. Also **sandal.**

**sand·bag** (sand′bag′), *n.* 1. a bag filled with sand and used for ballast in ships, fortifications, etc. 2. a small bag filled with sand and used as a weapon. *v.t.* [-BAGGED, -BAGGING], 1. to place sandbags in or around. 2. to strike with a sandbag.

**sand bar,** a ridge of sand formed in a river or along a shore by the action of currents or tides.

**sand·blast** (sand′blast′, -bläst′), *n.* 1. a current of air or steam carrying sand at a high velocity, used in etching glass and in cleaning the surfaces of stone, buildings, etc. 2. the machine used to apply this blast. *v.t.* to engrave or clean with a sandblast. **—sand′blast′er,** *n.*

**sand·box** (sand′boks′), *n.* a box filled with sand, as for children to play in.

**Sand·burg, Carl** (sand′bẽrg, san′-), 1878–1967; U.S. poet, writer, and ballad collector.

**sand flea,** 1. any of various fleas that live in sandy places. 2. the chigoe. Also **sand hopper.**

**sand·hog** (sand′hôg′, -hog′), *n.* a laborer in underground or underwater construction: also **sand hog.**

**San Diego** (san′ di-ā′gō), a seaport in S California: pop., 573,000.

**sand-lot** (sand′lot′), *adj.* of, having to do with, or played in a sandy lot or field in or near a city: as, *sand-lot* baseball.

**sand·man** (sand′man′), *n.* a mythical person, as in fairy tales, supposed to make children sleepy by dusting sand on their eyes.

**sand·pa·per** (sand′pā′pẽr), *n.* paper coated on one side with sand, used for smoothing and polishing. *v.t.* to smooth or polish with sandpaper.

**sand·pip·er** (sand′pīp′ẽr), *n.* [*pl.* -ERS, -ER; see PLURAL, II, D, 1], a shore bird with a long, soft-tipped bill, related to the plovers and snipes.

**sand·stone** (sand′stōn′), *n.* a common sedimentary rock consisting of sand grains cemented together by silica, lime, etc.: much used for building.

**sand·storm** (sand′stôrm′), *n.* a windstorm in which sand is blown about in large clouds.

**sand·wich** (sand′wich, san′-), *n.* [< 4th Earl of *Sandwich* (1718–1792)], two or more slices of bread with a filling of meat, cheese, etc. between them. *v.t.* to place between other persons, things, etc.

**Sandwich Islands,** the Hawaiian Islands: the former name.

**sandwich man,** a man who walks the street displaying two advertising boards hung from his shoulders, one in front and one behind.

**sand·y** (san′di), *adj.* [-IER, -IEST], 1. composed of, full of, or covered with sand. 2. like sand; shifting; unstable. 3. pale reddish-yellow: as, *sandy* hair. **—sand′i·ness,** *n.*

**sane** (sān), *adj.* [L. *sanus*, healthy], 1. mentally healthy; sound of mind; rational. 2. sound; not diseased: said of the mind. 3. showing good sense; sound; sensible. **—sane′ly,** *adv.* **—sane′ness,** *n.*

**San·for·ize** (san′fə-rīz′), *v.t.* [-IZED, -IZING], [back-formation from *Sanforized*, a trade-mark applied to fabrics so treated; after *Sanford* L. Cluett, Am. inventor of the process], to preshrink (cotton or linen cloth) permanently by a patented process before making it into clothes.

**San Fran·cis·co** (san′ frən-sis′kō), a city on the coast of central California: pop., 740,000 (with Oakland and suburbs, 2,783,000).

**San Francisco Bay,** an arm of the Pacific, off San Francisco and Oakland.

**sang** (saŋ), pt. of **sing.**

**‡sang-froid** (säṅ′frwå′), *n.* [Fr., lit., cold blood], composure; imperturbability.

**san·gui-** (saŋ′gwi), [< L. *sanguis*, blood], a combining form meaning *blood.*

**san·gui·nar·y** (saŋ′gwi-ner′i), *adj.* [< L. < *sanguis*, blood], 1. accompanied by much bloodshed, or murder. 2. bloodstained. 3. bloodthirsty. **—san′gui·nar′i·ly,** *adv.* **—san′gui·nar′i·ness,** *n.*

**san·guine** (saŋ′gwin), *adj.* [< OFr. < L. < *sanguis*, blood], 1. of the color of blood; ruddy. 2. cheerful; confident; optimistic. 3. sanguinary. Also **sanguin·e·ous** (saŋ-gwin′i-əs). **—san′guine·ly,** *adv.*

**San·he·drin** (san′hi-drin, san′i-; Heb. sän-hed′rin), *n.* [< L.Heb. < Gr. < *syn-*, together + *hedra*, seat], the highest court and council of the ancient Jewish nation, having religious and civil functions: also **Great Sanhedrin, San′he·drim** (-drim).

**san·i·tar·i·an** (san′ə-târ′i-ən), *adj.* sanitary. *n.* an expert in public health and sanitation.

**san·i·tar·i·um** (san′ə-târ′i-əm), *n.* [*pl.* -UMS, -A (-ə)], [Mod. L. < *sanitas*, health], 1. a quiet resort where people go to rest and regain health. 2. an institution for the care of invalids or convalescents, as for those recuperating from tuberculosis.

**san·i·tar·y** (san′ə-ter′i), *adj.* [< Fr. < L. *sanitas*, health], 1. of health or the rules and conditions of health; esp., of absence of dirt and agents of disease. 2. in a clean, healthy condition; hygienic. *n.* [*pl.* -IES], a public toilet. **—san′i·tar′i·ly,** *adv.*

**sanitary napkin,** an absorbent pad of cotton, etc. worn by women during menstruation.

**san·i·ta·tion** (san′ə-tā′shən), *n.* 1. the science and practice of effecting healthful and hygienic conditions. 2. drainage and disposal of sewage.

**san·i·tize** (san′ə-tīz′), *v.t.* [-TIZED, -TIZING], to make sanitary.

**san·i·ty** (san′ə-ti), *n.* [< L. *sanitas*, health], 1. the condition of being sane; soundness of mind; mental health. 2. soundness of judgment.

**San Joa·quin** (san′ wô-kēn′, wä-), a river in California flowing into the Sacramento River.

**San Jo·se** (san′ hō-zā′, ə-zā′), a city in west central California: pop., 204,000.

**San Jo·sé** (sän hô-se′), the capital of Costa Rica: pop., 174,000.

**San Jo·se scale** (san′ hō-zā′), [< *San Jose*, Calif., where first observed in the U.S.], a scale insect very destructive to fruit trees.

**San Juan** (san hwän′, wôn′; Sp. sän hwän′), seaport and capital of Puerto Rico: pop., 432,000.

**sank** (saŋk), alt. pt. of **sink.**

**San Le·an·dro** (san′ li-an′drō), a city in central California, near Oakland: pop., 66,000.

**San Ma·ri·no** (san′ mə-rē′nō), an independent republic within E Italy: area, 38 sq. mi.; pop., 18,000.

**San Mar·tin, Jo·sé de** (hô-se′ de sän′ mär-tēn′), 1778–1850; South American liberator.

**San Ma·te·o** (san′ mə-tā′ō), a city in central California, near San Francisco: pop., 70,000.

**sans** (sanz; Fr. säṅ), *prep.* [< OFr. < L. *absentia*, absence (infl. by *sine*, without)], [Archaic], without.

**San Sal·va·dor** (san sal′və-dôr′), 1. the capital of El Salvador: pop., 256,000. 2. one of the E Bahama Islands: first land sighted by Columbus.

**sans-cu·lotte** (sanz′koo-lot′, -kyoo-), *n.* [Fr., without breeches], 1. a revolutionary: term of contempt applied by the aristocrats to the republicans of the poorly clad French Revolutionary army. 2. any radical or revolutionary. **—sans′-cu·lot′tic,** *adj.*

**san·se·vi·e·ri·a** (san′sə-vi-ē′ri-ə), *n.* [< the Prince of *Sanseviero* (1710–1771)], any of various plants of the lily family, with thick, lance-shaped leaves.

**San·skrit, San·scrit** (san′skrit), *n.* the classical Old Indic literary language: it has provided the chief clue in the charting of Indo-European languages. *adj.* of or written in Sanskrit. Abbr. **Sans.**

**sans-ser·if** (san-ser′if, sanz′-), *n.* [see SANS], a style of printing with no serifs.

**‡sans sou·ci** (säṅ′ sōō′sē′), [Fr.], without worry.

**San·ta** (san′tə, -ti; *for adj., also* sän′tä), *n.* Santa Claus. *adj.* [Sp. & It., saint, fem.], holy or saint: used in combinations, as *Santa Fe.*

**San·ta An·a** (san′tə an′ə), a city in SW California, near Los Angeles: pop., 100,000.

**San·ta Cat·a·li·na** (san′tə kat′ə-lē′nə), an island off the coast of S California: a tourist resort.

**San·ta Claus, San·ta Klaus** (san′tə klôz′, san′ti), [< dial. D. < *Sant Nikolaas*, St. Nicholas], in *folklore*, a fat, white-bearded, jolly old man in a red suit, who distributes gifts at Christmas time: also called *Saint Nicholas, Saint Nick*.

**San·ta Fe** (san′tə fā′, fē′), the capital of New Mexico: pop., 35,000.

**Santa Fe Trail,** a former trade route between Santa Fe, New Mexico, and Independence, Missouri.

**San·ta Mon·i·ca** (san′tə mon′i-kə), a suburb of Los Angeles, California, on the coast: pop., 83,000.

**San·ti·a·go** (sän′tē-ä′gô; Eng. san′ti-ā′gō), *n.* the capital of Chile: pop., 2,093,000.

**San·to Do·min·go** (san′tō də-miŋ′gō), 1. the Dominican Republic: the former name. 2. the capital of the Dominican Republic: pop., 478,000.

**São Pau·lo** (soun pou′loo), a city in SE Brazil: pop., 3,825,000.

**São Sal·va·dor** (soun säl′və-dôr′), Bahía.

**sap** (sap), *n.* [AS. *sæp*], 1. the juice which circulates through a plant, especially a woody plant, bearing water, food, etc. 2. any fluid considered vital to life or health. 3. vigor; energy. 4. sapwood. 5. [Slang], a stupid person; fool. *v.t.* [SAPPED, SAPPING], to drain of sap. **—sap′less,** *adj.*

**sap** (sap), *n.* [< Fr. *sappe* & It. *zappe*, a spade], a trench for approaching or undermining an enemy position. *v.t.* [SAPPED, SAPPING], 1. to undermine by digging away foundations. 2. to undermine in any way; weaken; exhaust. *v.i.* 1. to dig saps. 2. to approach an enemy's position by saps.

**sap·head** (sap′hed′), *n.* [Colloq.], a stupid person; fool. **—sap′head′ed,** *adj.*

**sa·pi·ent** (sā′pi-ənt), *adj.* [< L. *sapiens*, ppr. of *sapere*, to taste, know], wise; full of knowledge; discerning: often ironical. **—sa′pi·ence, sa′pi·en·cy,** *n.* **—sa′pi·ent·ly,** *adv.*

**sap·ling** (sap′liŋ), *n.* 1. a young tree. 2. a youth.

**sap·o·dil·la** (sap′ə-dil′ə), *n.* [< Sp. < Nahuatl *tzapotl*], 1. a tropical American evergreen tree yielding chicle and having a brown fruit with a yellowish pulp. 2. the fruit: also **sapodilla plum.**

**sap·o·na·ceous** (sap′ə-nā′shəs), *adj.* [< L. *sapo*, soap], soapy. **—sap′o·na′ceous·ness,** *n.*

**sa·pon·i·fy** (sə-pon′ə-fi′), *v.t.* [-FIED, -FYING], [< Fr. < L. *sapo*, soap + *facere*, to make], to convert (a fat) into soap by reaction with an alkali. *v.i.* to be made into soap. **—sa·pon′i·fi′a·ble,** *adj.* **—sa·pon′i·fi·ca′tion,** *n.* **—sa·pon′i·fi′er,** *n.*

**sap·per** (sap′ẽr), *n.* a soldier employed in digging saps, repairing fortifications, etc.

**sap·phire** (saf′īr), *n.* [< OFr. < L. < Gr. *sappheiros*], 1. a hard, transparent precious stone of a clear, deep-blue corundum. 2. its color. 3. a hard variety of corundum, varying in color. 4. a gem made of this: as, white *sapphire*. *adj.* deep-blue.

**Sap·pho** (saf′ō), *n.* a woman poet of ancient Greece; fl. c. 600 B.C.: known for love lyrics. **—Sap′phic** (saf′ik), *adj.*

**sap·py** (sap′i), *adj.* [-PIER, -PIEST], 1. full of sap; juicy. 2. energetic; vigorous. 3. [Slang], foolish; silly. **—sap′pi·ly,** *adv.* **—sap′pi·ness,** *n.*

**sap·ro·phyte** (sap′rə-fīt′), *n.* [< Gr. *sapros*, rotten; + *-phyte*], any organism that lives on decaying organic matter, as some fungi and bacteria. **—sap′ro·phyt′ic** (-fit′ik), *adj.*

**sap·suck·er** (sap′suk′ẽr), *n.* any of a group of small American woodpeckers that drill holes in certain trees and drink the sap.

**sap·wood** (sap′wood′), *n.* the soft wood just beneath the bark of a tree; alburnum.

**sar·a·band** (sar′ə-band′), *n.* [< Fr. < Sp.; ult. < Per. *sarband*, kind of dance], 1. a stately, slow Spanish dance in triple time, developed from an earlier lively dance. 2. music for this dance.

**Sar·a·cen** (sar′ə-s′n), *n.* formerly, *a)* a Moslem, especially as opposed to the Crusaders. *b)* an Arab. *adj.* of the Saracens. **—Sar′a·cen′ic** (-sen′ik), **Sar′a·cen′i·cal,** *adj.*

**Sar·ah** (sâr′ə), *n.* in the *Bible*, the wife of Abraham and mother of Isaac: also **Sa·rai** (sâr′ī).

**Sa·ra·je·vo** (sä′rə-yā′vō), *n.* a city in central Yugoslavia: pop., 143,000: scene of the assassination of an Austrian archduke, which precipitated World War I.

**sa·ran** (sə-ran′), *n.* any of various thermoplastic resins obtained, as by polymerization, from certain vinyl compounds: it is used in making various fabrics, as wrapping film, etc.

**sar·casm** (sär′kaz′m), *n.* [< Fr. < L. < Gr. < *sarkazein*, to tear flesh like dogs < *sarx*, flesh], 1. a taunting or caustic remark; gibe or jeer, generally ironical. 2. the making of such remarks. 3. sarcastic or caustic quality.

**sar·cas·tic** (sär-kas′tik), *adj.* 1. of, like, or characterized by sarcasm; sneering; caustic. 2. using sarcasm. **—sar·cas′ti·cal·ly,** *adv.*

**sarce·net** (särs′net), *n.* [Anglo-Fr. *sarzinett*, dim. < ME. *Sarsin*, Saracen], a soft silk cloth.

**sar·co-,** [< Gr. *sarx*, flesh], a combining form meaning *flesh*, as in *sarcocarp*: also **sarc-.**

**sar·co·carp** (sär′kə-kärp′), *n.* [*sarco-* + *-carp*], the fleshy part of a stone fruit, as the plum.

**sar·co·ma** (sär-kō′mə), *n.* [*pl.* -MAS, -MATA (-mə-tə)], [Mod. L. < Gr. < *sarx*, flesh], any of various malignant tumors that begin in connective tissue. **—sar·co′ma·tous** (-kō′mə-təs, -kom′ə-təs), **sar·co′ma·toid′** (-kō′mə-toid′), *adj.*

**sar·coph·a·gus** (sär-kof′ə-gəs), *n.* [*pl.* -GI (-jī′), -GUSES], [L. < Gr. < *sarx*, flesh + *phagein*, to eat: limestone, anciently used for coffins, hastened disintegration], a stone coffin, especially an ornamented one exposed to view, as in a tomb.

**sard** (särd), *n.* [< L. < Gr. < *Sardeis*, Sardis, capital of Lydia], a very hard, deep orange-red variety of chalcedony, used in jewelry, etc.

**sar·dine** (sär-dēn′), *n.* [*pl.* -DINES, -DINE; see PLURAL, II, D, 1], [Fr. < L. < Gr. *sardēnē* < *sarda*, kind of fish], 1. a small pilchard suitable for eating when preserved in oil. 2. any of various small fishes preserved in cans for eating.

**Sar·din·i·a** (sär-din′i-ə, -din′yə), *n.* an Italian island in the Mediterranean, south of Corsica: area, 9,300 sq. mi. **—Sar·din′i·an,** *adj.* & *n.*

**sar·don·ic** (sär-don′ik), *adj.* [< Fr. < L. < Gr. < *sardanios*, bitter: alt. after *Sardō*, Sardinia (habitat of a plant whose bitterness caused grimaces)], disdainfully or bitterly sneering or sarcastic: as, a *sardonic* smile. **—sar·don′i·cal·ly,** *adv.*

**sar·do·nyx** (sär′də-niks), *n.* [L. < Gr. < *sardios*, sard + *onyx*, onyx], a variety of onyx made up of layers of white chalcedony and sard, used as a gem.

**sar·gas·so** (sär-gas′ō), *n.* [< Port. < *sarga*, kind of grape], any of various floating, brown seaweeds with berrylike air sacs: also **sargasso weed, sar·gas′sum** (-əm).

**Sar·gent, John Singer** (sär′jənt), 1856–1925; U.S. painter.

**sa·ri** (sä′rē), *n.* [*pl.* -RIS], [< Hind. < Sans.], an outer garment of Hindu women, a long cloth wrapped around the body with one end over the head.

**sa·rong** (sə-rôŋ′, sä′-), *n.* [Malay *sāroŋ*], a garment of men and women in the Malay Archipelago, East Indies, etc., consisting of a cloth, often brightly colored and printed, worn like a skirt.

**sar·sa·pa·ril·la** (särs′pə-ril′ə, sär′sə-pə-, sas′pə-), *n.* [< Sp. < *zarza*, bramble + dim. of *parra*, vine], 1. a tropical American plant with fragrant roots. 2. its dried roots, used as a tonic or flavoring. 3. a carbonated drink flavored with sarsaparilla.

**Sar·to, An·dre·a del** (än-dre′ä del sär′tô), (born *Andrea d'Agnolo*), 1486–1531; Florentine painter.

**sar·to·ri·al** (sär-tôr′i-əl, -tō′ri-), *adj.* [< LL. *sartor*, a tailor], 1. of tailors or their work. 2. of men's clothing or dress. **—sar·to′ri·al·ly,** *adv.*

**sash** (sash), *n.* [Ar. *shāsh*, turban], an ornamental band, ribbon, or scarf worn over the shoulder or around the waist.

**sash** (sash), *n.* [taken as sing. of earlier *shashes* < Fr. *châssis*, a frame], a frame for holding the glass pane of a window or door, especially a sliding frame. *v.t.* to furnish with sashes.

**sa·shay** (sa-shā′), *v.i.* [altered < *chassé* (dance)], [Colloq.], to glide, move around, or go.

**sash cord** (or **line**), a cord attached to either side of a sliding sash, having balancing weights for raising or lowering the window easily.

**Sas·katch·e·wan** (sas-kach′ə-wän′), *n.* a province of SW Canada: pop., 925,000; capital, Regina.

**sass** (sas), *n.* [var. of *sauce*], [Colloq.], impudent talk. *v.t.* [Colloq.], to talk impudently to.

**sas·sa·fras** (sas′ə-fras′), *n.* [Sp. *sasafras*], 1. a slender tree with yellow flowers and bluish fruit. 2. its dried root bark, used in medicine and for flavoring. 3. the flavor.

**sass·y** (sas′i), *adj.* [-IER, -IEST], [dial. var. of *saucy*], [Dial. or Colloq.], impudent; saucy. **—sass′i·ly,** *adv.* **—sass′i·ness,** *n.*

**sat** (sat), pt. and pp. of **sit.**

**Sat.,** 1. Saturday. 2. Saturn.

**Sa·tan** (sā′t'n), *n.* [< Heb. < *ṣāṭān*, enemy], in *Christian theology*, the great enemy of man and goodness; the Devil. **—Sa·tan·ic** (sā-tan′ik, sə-), *adj.*

**sa·tan·ic** (sā-tan′ik, sə-), *adj.* like Satan; devilish wicked: also **sa·tan′i·cal. —sa·tan′i·cal·ly,** *adv.*

**satch·el** (sach′əl), *n.* [< OFr. < L. dim. of *saccus*, a sack], a small bag for carrying clothes, books, etc., sometimes having a shoulder strap.

**sate** (sāt), *v.t.* [SATED, SATING], [prob. < L. *satiare*, to satisfy], 1. to satisfy (an appetite, desire, etc.) to the full. 2. to gratify with more than enough, so as to weary or disgust; satiate.

**sate** (sat, sāt), archaic pt. and pp. of **sit**.

**sa·teen** (sa-tēn′), *n.* [< *satin*], a smooth, glossy, cotton cloth, made to imitate satin.

**sat·el·lite** (sat′ə-līt′), *n.* [< Fr. < L. *satelles*, an attendant], 1. an attendant of some important person. 2. an obsequious follower. 3. a small planet revolving around a larger one. 4. a man-made object put into orbit around the earth, the sun, or some other heavenly body. 5. a small state that is economically dependent on a larger state.

**sa·ti·a·ble** (sā′shi-ə-b'l, -shə-b'l), *adj.* that can be sated or satiated. **—sa′ti·a·bil′i·ty, sa′ti·a·ble·ness,** *n.* **—sa′ti·a·bly,** *adv.*

**sa·ti·ate** (sā′shi-āt′), *adj.* [< L. pp. of *satiare*, to satisfy < *satis*, sufficient], having had enough or more than enough; sated. *v.t.* [-ATED, -ATING], 1. [Rare], to satisfy to the full. 2. to gratify with more than enough, so as to weary or disgust; sate; glut. **—sa′ti·a′tion,** *n.*

**sa·ti·e·ty** (sə-tī′ə-ti), *n.* a being satiated.

**sat·in** (sat′'n), *n.* [OFr. < Sp. < Ar. *zaitūnī*, of *Zaitūn*, former name of a Chinese seaport], a silk, nylon, or rayon cloth with a smooth, glossy finish on one side. *adj.* of or like satin; smooth and glossy. **—sat′in·like′,** *adj.* **—sat′in·y,** *adj.*

**sat·i·net, sat·i·nette** (sat′'n-et′), *n.* 1. thin or inferior satin. 2. cloth made to resemble satin.

**sat·in·wood** (sat′'n-wood′), *n.* 1. a smooth wood used in fine furniture. 2. a tree, especially an East Indian mahogany, yielding such a wood.

**sat·ire** (sat′īr), *n.* [Fr. < L. *satira*, orig. a dish of fruits < *satur*, full], 1. a literary work in which vices, follies, etc. are held up to ridicule and contempt. 2. the use of ridicule, sarcasm, irony, etc. to attack vices, follies, etc.

**sa·tir·i·cal** (sə-tir′i-k'l), *adj.* 1. of, like, or containing satire. 2. indulging in satire. Also **sa·tir′ic. —sa·tir′i·cal·ly,** *adv.* **—sa·tir′i·cal·ness,** *n.*

**sat·i·rist** (sat′ə-rist), *n.* 1. a writer of satires. 2. one who is fond of indulging in satire.

**sat·i·rize** (sat′ə-rīz′), *v.t.* [-RIZED, -RIZING], to attack or criticize with satire. **—sat′i·riz′er,** *n.*

**sat·is·fac·tion** (sat′is-fak′shən), *n.* 1. a satisfying or being satisfied. 2. something that satisfies; specif., *a*) reparation for injury or insult. *b*) settlement of debt. *c*) anything that brings pleasure or contentment. **—give satisfaction,** 1. to satisfy. 2. to accept a challenge to duel.

**sat·is·fac·to·ry** (sat′is-fak′tēr-i), *adj.* satisfying; fulfilling all needs, desires, etc. **—sat′is·fac′to·ri·ly,** *adv.* **—sat′is·fac′to·ri·ness,** *n.*

**sat·is·fy** (sat′is-fī′), *v.t.* [-FIED, -FYING], [< OFr. < L. < *satis*, enough + *facere*, to make], 1. to fulfill the needs or desires of; content. 2. to fulfill the requirements of. 3. to comply with (rules or obligations). 4. *a*) to free from doubt; convince. *b*) to answer (a doubt, etc.) adequately. 5. *a*) to give what is due to. *b*) to discharge (a debt, etc.). 6. to make reparation to or for. *v.i.* to give satisfaction. **—sat′is·fi′a·ble,** *adj.* **—sat′is·fi′er,** *n.*

**sa·trap** (sā′trap, sat′rəp), *n.* [< L. < Gr. *satrapēs* < OPer.], 1. the governor of a province in ancient Persia. 2. a ruler of a dependency, often a despotic, subordinate official.

**sa·trap·y** (sā′trə-pi, sat′rə-), *n.* [*pl.* -IES], 1. the government or authority of a satrap. 2. the province ruled by a satrap.

**sat·u·ra·ble** (sach′ēr-ə-b'l), *adj.* that can be saturated. **—sat′u·ra·bil′i·ty,** *n.*

**sat·u·rate** (sach′oo-rāt′), *v.t.* [-RATED, -RATING], [< L. pp. of *saturare*, to fill up < *satur*, full], 1. to cause to be thoroughly soaked. 2. to cause to be so completely filled or charged that no more can be taken up. 3. in *chemistry*, to cause (a substance) to combine to its full capacity with another. **—sat′u·rat′er, sat′u·ra′tor,** *n.* **—sat′u·ra′tion,** *n.*

**saturation point,** the point at which the maximum amount of something has been absorbed.

**Sat·ur·day** (sat′ēr-di), *n.* [< AS. *Sæterdæg*, Saturn's day], the seventh and last day of the week: abbrev. **Sat., S.**

**Sat·urn** (sat′ērn), *n.* 1. in *Roman mythology*, the god of agriculture: identified with the Greek Cronus. 2. the second largest planet in the solar system, notable for the three rings which revolve around it: diameter, 72,000 mi. **—Sa·tur·ni·an** (sə-tūr′ni-ən), *adj.*

**Sat·ur·na·li·a** (sat′ēr-nā′li-ə), *n.pl.* 1. the ancient Roman festival of Saturn, held about December 17, with general feasting and revelry. 2. [s-], a period of unrestrained revelry. **—Sat′ur·na′li·an, sat′ur·na′li·an,** *adj.*

**sat·ur·nine** (sat′ēr-nīn′), *adj.* 1. in *astrology*, born under the supposed influence of the planet Saturn. 2. reserved, sluggish, grave, etc. **—sat′ur·nine′ly,** *adv.* **—sat′ur·nine′ness,** *n.*

**sat·yr** (sat′ēr, sā′tēr), *n.* [< Fr. < L. < Gr. *satyros*], 1. in *Gr. mythology*, a lecherous woodland deity, attendant on Bacchus: satyrs are represented as men with a goat's legs, pointed ears, and short horns. 2. a lecherous man. **—sa·tyr·ic** (sə-tir′ik), **sa·tyr′i·cal,** *adj.*

**sat·y·ri·a·sis** (sat′ə-rī′ə-sis), *n.* [see SATYR], excessive, uncontrollable sexual desire in a man.

**sauce** (sôs), *n.* [< OFr. < LL. < L. *salsus*, salted < *sal*, salt], 1. a liquid or soft dressing served with food as a seasoning. 2. mashed, stewed fruit. 3. something that adds interest or zest. 4. [Colloq.], impudence; sauciness. *v.t.* [SAUCED, SAUCING], 1. to flavor with sauce. 2. [Colloq.], to be saucy to.

**sauce·pan** (sôs′pan′), *n.* a small metal pot with a long handle, used for cooking.

**sau·cer** (sô′sēr), *n.* [< OFr. *saussier* < *sauce;* see SAUCE], 1. *a*) a shallow dish designed to hold a cup. *b*) any small, shallow dish. 2. anything like a saucer in shape. **—sau′cer·like′,** *adj.*

**sau·cy** (sô′si), *adj.* [-CIER, -CIEST], [*sauce* + *-y*], 1. rude; impudent. 2. pert; sprightly: as, a *saucy* smile. **—sau′ci·ly,** *adv.* **—sau′ci·ness,** *n.*

**Sa·u·di Arabia** (sä-ōō′di), a kingdom in central Arabia: area, c. 597,000 sq. mi.; pop., c. 6,000,000; capitals, Riyadh and Mecca.

**sauer·kraut** (sour′krout′), *n.* [G.; *sauer*, sour + *kraut*, cabbage], chopped cabbage fermented in a brine of its own juice with salt.

**Saul** (sôl), *n.* in the *Bible*, 1. the first king of Israel. 2. the original name of the Apostle Paul.

**Sault Sainte Ma·rie Canals** (sōō′sānt′mə-rē′), three ship canals in the waterway connecting Lake Superior with Lake Huron: also **the Soo (Canals).**

**saun·ter** (sôn′tēr), *v.i.* [< ME. *santre(n)*, to muse], to walk about idly; stroll. *n.* 1. a leisurely and aimless walk. 2. a careless, slow gait. **—saun′ter·er,** *n.* **—saun′ter·ing·ly,** *adv.*

**sau·ri·an** (sô′ri-ən), *adj.* [< Gr. *saura*, a lizard], of, or having the characteristics of, lizards, crocodiles, or dinosaurs. *n.* any of a group of reptiles including the lizards, dinosaurs, etc.

**-sau·rus** (sô′rəs), [< Gr. *sauros*, a lizard], a combining form meaning *lizard*.

**sau·sage** (sô′sij), *n.* [< ONorm.Fr. < OFr. *saulsage* < LL. < L. *salsus;* see SAUCE], meat, usually pork, chopped fine, seasoned, and ordinarily stuffed into a tubular casing.

**sau·té** (sō-tā′), *adj.* [Fr., pp. of *sauter*, to leap], fried quickly and turned frequently in a little fat. *v.t.* [-TÉED, -TÉING], to fry quickly and turn frequently in a little fat. *n.* a sautéed dish.

**sau·terne** (sō-tūrn′), *n.* [< *Sauternes*, town in France], a white table wine, usually sweet.

**sav·age** (sav′ij), *adj.* [< OFr. < LL. < L. *silvaticus*, wild < *silva*, a wood], 1. wild; uncultivated: as, a *savage* forest. 2. fierce; untamed: as, a *savage* tiger. 3. without civilization; barbarous: as, a *savage* tribe. 4. crude; rude. 5. cruel; ferocious. *n.* 1. a human being living in an uncivilized, primitive way. 2. a fierce, brutal person. **—sav′age·ly,** *adv.* **—sav′age·ness,** *n.*

**sav·age·ry** (sav′ij-ri), *n.* [*pl.* -RIES], 1. the condition of being savage, wild, or primitive. 2. savage act or behavior; barbarity. 3. savage creatures collectively. Also **sav′ag·ism.**

**sa·van·na, sa·van·nah** (sə-van′ə), *n.* [< Sp. < *zavana* < the Carib name], a treeless plain or flat, open region, especially near the tropics.

**Sa·van·nah** (sə-van′ə), *n.* a seaport in E Georgia: pop., 149,000.

**sa·vant** (sə-vänt′, sav′ənt), *n.* [Fr., orig. ppr. of *savoir* (< L. *sapere*), to know], a learned person.

**save** (sāv), *v.t.* [SAVED, SAVING], [< OFr. *salver* < L. < *salvus*, safe], 1. to rescue or preserve from harm or danger. 2. to preserve for future use (often with *up*). 3. to prevent loss or waste of: as, this train *saves* hours. 4. to prevent or lessen: as, *save* expense. 5. to treat carefully in order to preserve, lessen wear, etc. 6. in *theology*, to deliver from sin; redeem. *v.i.* 1. to avoid expense, loss, waste, etc.

2. to keep something or someone from danger, harm, etc. 3. to store up money or goods. 4. to keep; last. —**sav′a·ble, save′a·ble,** *adj.* —**sav′er,** *n.*

**save** (sāv), *prep.* [< OFr. < L. *salvus*, safe], except; but. *conj.* 1. except; but. 2. [Archaic], unless.

**sav·ing** (sāv′iŋ), *adj.* that saves; specif., *a*) rescuing. *b*) economical. *c*) containing an exception: as, a *saving* clause. *d*) compensating; redeeming. *n.* 1. the act of one that saves. 2. any reduction in time, expense, etc.: as, a *saving* of 10%. 3. what is saved; esp., *pl.* sums of money saved. —**sav′ing·ly,** *adv.* —**sav′ing·ness,** *n.*

**sav·ing** (sāv′iŋ), *prep.* 1. with due respect for. 2. except; save. *conj.* save.

**savings account,** an account in a bank (**savings bank**) which receives and invests depositors' savings, on which it pays interest.

**sav·ior, sav·iour** (sāv′yẽr), *n.* [< OFr. *sauveour;* ult. < L. *salvare*, to save], 1. a person who saves. 2. [usually Saviour], Jesus Christ: with *the.*

**sa·voir-faire** (sav′wär-fâr′), *n.* [Fr., to know (how) to do], ready knowledge of how and when to do or say the correct thing; tact.

**sa·vor** (sā′vẽr), *n.* [< OFr. < L. *sapor*], 1. *a*) that quality of something which acts on the sense of taste or of smell. *b*) a particular taste or smell. 2. characteristic quality. 3. perceptible trace. 4. power to excite interest, zest, etc. *v.i.* to have the particular taste or smell, or the characteristic quality (*of*). *v.t.* 1. to season or flavor. 2. to have the flavor or quality of. 3. to taste or smell, especially with relish. 4. to relish. Also, Brit. sp., **savour.** —**sa′vored, sa′voured,** *adj.* —**sa′vor·er, sa′vour·er,** *n.* —**sa′vor·less, sa′vour·less,** *adj.* —**sa′vor·ous, sa′vour·ous,** *adj.*

**sa·vor·y** (sā′vẽr-i), *adj.* [-IER, -IEST], [< OFr. pp. of *savourer*, to taste; see SAVOR], 1. pleasing to the taste or smell. 2. agreeable; pleasing. 3. morally pleasing; respectable. *n.* [*pl.* -IES], [Brit.], a small, seasoned portion of food served at the end or beginning of dinner. Also, Brit. sp., **savoury.** —**sa′vor·i·ly, sa′vour·i·ly,** *adv.* —**sa′vor·i·ness, sa′vour·i·ness,** *n.*

**sa·vor·y** (sā′vẽr-i), *n.* [< OFr. *savoreie* (prob. infl. by *savour*, savor) < L. *satureia*], an aromatic variety of mint, used in cooking.

**Sa·voy** (sə-voi′), *n.* a ruling family of Italy (1861–1946).

**sa·voy** (sə-voi′), *n.* [Fr., after *Savoy*, a part of France], a kind of cabbage with crinkled leaves and a compact head.

**Sa·voy·ard** (sə-voi′ẽrd), *n.* [< the *Savoy*, London theater], an actor, producer, or admirer of Gilbert and Sullivan operas.

**sav·vy** (sav′i), *v.i.* [-VIED, -VYING], [alt. < Sp. *sabe* (*usted*), do (you) know? < *saber* (< L. *sapere*), to know], [Slang], to understand; get the idea. *n.* [Slang], common sense; understanding.

**saw** (sô), *n.* [AS. *saga*], 1. a cutting tool consisting of a thin, metal blade or disk edged with sharp teeth. 2. a machine that operates such a tool. *v.t.* [SAWED, SAWED or SAWN, SAWING], 1. to cut or shape with a saw. 2. to make sawlike cutting motions through (the air, etc.) or with. *v.i.* 1. to cut with a saw. 2. to cut, as a saw. 3. to be cut with a saw: as, this plank *saws* easily. —**saw′er,** *n.*

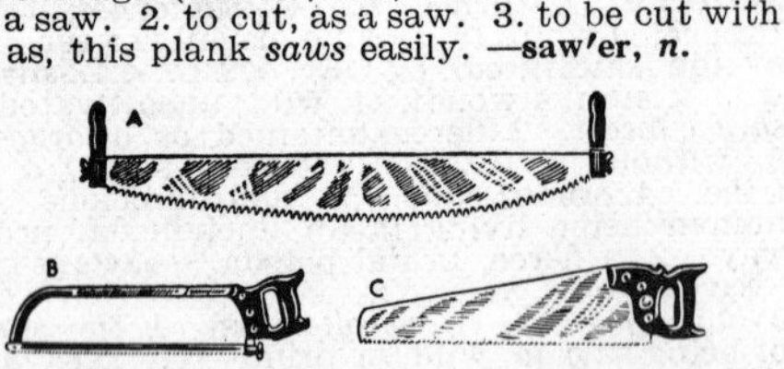


SAWS
A, crosscut saw; B, butcher's saw; C, handsaw

**saw** (sô), *n.* [AS. *sagu*], a saying; maxim.

**saw** (sô), pt. of **see.**

**saw·bones** (sô′bōnz′), *n.* [Slang], a surgeon.

**saw·buck** (sô′buk′), *n.* [D. *zaagbuk*], 1. a sawhorse. 2. [from resemblance of the crossed legs of a sawbuck to an X (Roman numeral for 10)], [Slang], a ten-dollar bill.

**saw·dust** (sô′dust′), *n.* minute particles of wood resulting as a by-product of sawing wood.

**saw·fish** (sô′fish′), *n.* [*pl.* see FISH], any of a group of tropical giant rays having a long, flat, sawlike snout edged with teeth on both sides.

**saw·fly** (sô′flī′), *n.* [*pl.* -FLIES], any of a group of four-winged insects the female of which has a pair of sawlike organs that cut into plants, the eggs being then deposited in the cuts.

**saw·horse** (sô′hôrs′), *n.* a rack on which wood is placed for sawing: see **bucksaw,** illus.

**saw·mill** (sô′mil′), *n.* 1. a place where logs are sawed into boards. 2. a large sawing machine.

**sawn** (sôn), alt. pp. of **saw.**

**saw-toothed** (sô′tōōtht′), *adj.* having teeth like those of a saw; serrate.

**saw·yer** (sô′yẽr), *n.* a person whose work is sawing wood, as into planks and boards.

**sax** (saks), *n.* [Colloq.], a saxophone.

**sax·horn** (saks′hôrn′), *n.* [< A. J. *Sax* (1814–1894), Belgian inventor], any of a group of valved brass-wind instruments, with a full, even tone.

**sax·i·frage** (sak′si-frij), *n.* [OFr. < L. < *saxum*, a rock + *frangere*, to break: the plant grows in rock crevices], any of a group of plants with white, yellow, purple, or pinkish, small flowers, and leaves massed usually at the base of the plant.

**Sax·on** (sak′s'n), *n.* 1. a member of an ancient Germanic people that lived in N Germany: some Saxons conquered parts of England in the 5th and 6th centuries A.D. 2. an Anglo-Saxon (senses 1 & 3). 3. a native or inhabitant of modern Saxony. 4. Old Saxon. *adj.* of the early Continental Saxons, their language, etc.

**Sax·o·ny** (sak′sə-ni), *n.* 1. a former kingdom of Germany. 2. a division of central Germany.

**sax·o·phone** (sak′sə-fōn′), *n.* [< A. J. *Sax* (see SAXHORN) + Gr. *phōnē*, sound], a single-reed, keyed wind instrument having a curved metal body and a deep, mellow tone. —**sax′o·phon′ist,** *n.*

SAXOPHONE

**say** (sā), *v.t.* [SAID, SAYING; 3d pers. sing., pres. indic., SAYS (sez), *archaic* SAITH], [AS. *secgan*], 1. to utter; speak. 2. to state; express in words; declare; tell. 3. to state positively or as an opinion: as, I cannot *say* who will win. 4. to recite; repeat: as, *say* your prayers. 5. to estimate; assume: as, he is, *say*, forty. 6. to allege; report: as, they *say* he is guilty. *v.i.* to make a statement; speak; express an opinion. *n.* 1. what a person says. 2. a chance to speak: as, you've had your *say*. 3. authority, as to make a final decision: often with *the.* —**go without saying,** to be too obvious to need explanation. —**that is to say,** in other words; that means. —**say′er,** *n.*

**say·ing** (sā′iŋ), *n.* something said; esp., an adage, proverb, or maxim.

**say-so** (sā′sō′), *n.* [Colloq.], 1. an unsupported statement. 2. right of decision. 3. a dictum.

**Sb,** *stibium*, [L.], in *chemistry*, antimony.

**'sblood** (zblud), *interj.* [Archaic], God's blood: a euphemistic oath expressing anger, surprise, etc.

**Sc,** in *chemistry*, scandium.

**Sc.,** 1. Scotch. 2. Scots. 3. Scottish.

**sc.,** 1. scene. 2. science. 3. scilicet.

**S.C.,** 1. Signal Corps. 2. South Carolina.

**s.c.,** in *printing*, small capitals.

**scab** (skab), *n.* [AS. *sceabb*], 1. a crust which forms over a sore or wound during healing. 2. mange, especially in sheep. 3. a plant disease caused by certain fungi, forming roundish, roughened spots. 4. [Slang], a scoundrel. 5. *a*) a worker who refuses to join a union. *b*) a worker who refuses to strike, or who takes the place of a striking worker. *v.i.* [SCABBED, SCABBING], 1. to become covered with a scab. 2. to act as a scab.

**scab·bard** (skab′ẽrd), *n.* [< OFr. *escalberc;* prob. < OHG. *scar*, sword + *bergan*, to hide], a sheath or case to hold the blade of a sword, dagger, or bayonet. *v.t.* to put into a scabbard.

**scab·by** (skab′i), *adj.* [-BIER, -BIEST], 1. covered with or consisting of scabs. 2. low; base; mean. —**scab′bi·ly,** *adv.* —**scab′bi·ness,** *n.*

**sca·bi·es** (skā′bi-ēz′, -bēz), *n.* [L., itch < *scabere*, to scratch], a contagious skin disease caused by mites that burrow under the skin and deposit eggs, causing intense itching; the itch. —**sca·bi·et·ic** (skā′bi-et′ik), *adj.*

**sca·bi·o·sa** (skā′bi-ō′sə), *n.* [< ML. < L.; see SCABIES: it was considered a remedy for scabies], any of various related plants having showy flowers with protruding stamens: also **sca′bi·ous** (-əs).

**sca·brous** (skā′brəs), *adj.* [< LL. < L. *scabere*, to scratch], 1. rough, like a file; scaly; scabby. 2. full of difficulties. 3. lacking in delicacy; risqué. —**sca′brous·ly,** *adv.* —**sca′brous·ness,** *n.*

**scads** (skadz), *n.pl.* [prob. for *scat*, a tax], [Colloq.], a very large number or amount.

**scaf·fold** (skaf′'ld, -ōld), *n.* [< OFr. *escafalt* < LL.; akin to *catafalque*], 1. a temporary framework for supporting workmen during the erecting, repairing, or painting of a building, etc. 2. a raised platform on which criminals are executed, as by hanging.

3. any raised framework. *v.t.* to furnish or support with a scaffold.
**scaf·fold·ing** (skaf′'l-diŋ), *n.* 1. the materials which form a scaffold. 2. a scaffold or scaffolds.
**scal·a·wag** (skal′ə-wag′), *n.* 1. a scamp; rascal. 2. a white Southerner who was a Republican during the Reconstruction: an opprobrious term. Also sp. **scallawag, scallywag.**
**scald** (skôld), *v.t.* [< ONorm.Fr. < OFr. < LL. < L. *ex-*, intens. + *caldus*, hot], 1. to burn with hot liquid or steam. 2. to heat almost to the boiling point. 3. to use boiling liquid on, as in sterilizing, etc. *v.i.* to be or become scalded. *n.* 1. a burn caused by scalding. 2. a discoloring of plant tissues, caused by certain fungi or too much sun.
**scald** (skôld, skäld), *n.* a skald. **—scald′ic,** *adj.*
**scale** (skāl), *n.* [< It. or L. *scala*, a ladder], 1. originally, a ladder; flight of stairs. 2. a series of marks along a line, as at regular intervals, used in measuring: as, the *scale* of a thermometer. 3. any instrument so marked. 4. the proportion that a map, model, etc. bears to the thing that it represents: as, a *scale* of one inch to a mile. 5. *a*) a system of classifying in a series of degrees according to relative size, amount, importance, etc.: as, a wage *scale*. *b*) any point, level, or degree in such a series. 6. in *music*, a sequence of tones, rising or falling in pitch, in accordance with any of various systems of intervals. *v.t.* [SCALED, SCALING], 1. to climb up or over. 2. to make according to a scale. 3. to reduce according to a fixed ratio: as, prices were *scaled* down 5 per cent. *v.i.* 1. to climb; go up. 2. to go up in a graduated series. **—on a large** (or **small**) **scale,** to a relatively large (or small) degree or extent. **—scal′a·ble,** *adj.* **—scal′er,** *n.*
**scale** (skāl), *n.* [< OFr. *escale*, husk & *escaille*, fish scale], 1. any of the thin, flat, overlapping, horny plates forming the outer covering of many fishes and reptiles. 2. any thin, flaky, or platelike layer or piece, as of skin. 3. a coating that forms on metals when heated or rusted, as on the inside of a boiler. 4. any scalelike leaf or bract; esp., such a leaf covering the bud of a seed plant. 5. a scale insect. *v.t.* [SCALED, SCALING], 1. to strip or scrape scales from. 2. to remove in thin layers; pare down. 3. to cause scales to form on. *v.i.* 1. to flake or peel off in scales. 2. to become covered with scale. **—scale′less,** *adj.* **—scale′like′,** *adj.*
**scale** (skāl), *n.* [< ON. *skāl*, bowl], 1. either of the shallow dishes or pans of a balance. 2. *usually pl.* *a*) a balance. *b*) any weighing machine. *v.t.* [SCALED, SCALING], 1. to weigh in scales. 2. to have a weight of: as, it *scales* 20 pounds. 3. to balance; compare. *v.i.* to be weighed. **—the Scales,** Libra. **—turn the scales,** to determine; decide.
**scale insect,** any of various small insects destructive to plants: the females secrete a round scale under which they live and lay their eggs.
**sca·lene** (skā-lēn′, skā′lēn′), *adj.* [< LL. < Gr. *skalēnos*, uneven], in *geometry*, *a*) having unequal sides and angles: said of a triangle. *b*) having the axis not perpendicular to the base: said of a cone, etc.
**scaling ladder,** a ladder used for climbing walls of fortified places, etc.
**scal·la·wag** (skal′ə-wag′), *n.* a scalawag.
**scal·lion** (skal′yən), *n.* [< ONorm.Fr. < LL. < L. (*caepa*) *Ascalonia*, (onion of) Ascalon (in Philistia)], any of three varieties of onion; specif., *a*) the shallot. *b*) the leek. *c*) a green onion with a thick stem and an almost bulbless root.
**scal·lop** (skäl′əp, skal′-), *n.* [OFr. *escalope*; of Gmc. origin], 1. any of numerous mollusks with two curved, deeply grooved shells hinged together. 2. the large muscle of such a mollusk, used as food. 3. one of the two shells; specif., one used as a baking dish. 4. one of a series of curves, angles, etc. forming an ornamental edge as on cloth or lace. *v.t.* 1. to cut the edge of in scallops. 2. to bake with a milk sauce and bread crumbs; escalop. Also **scollop.**
**scal·ly·wag** (skal′ə-wag′), *n.* a scalawag.
**scalp** (skalp), *n.* [prob. < ON. *skālpr*, sheath], 1. the skin on the top and back of the head, usually covered with hair. 2. a part of this, cut or torn from the head of an enemy as a trophy by North American Indians. *v.t.* 1. to cut or tear the scalp from. 2. to cheat, defeat, etc. 3. [Colloq.], to buy and sell in order to make small, quick profits. 4. [Colloq.], to buy (theater tickets, etc.) and resell them at prices in excess of established rates. *v.i.* [Colloq.], to scalp tickets, etc. **—scalp′er,** *n.*
**scal·pel** (skal′pəl), *n.* [< L. dim. of *scalprum*, a knife], a small, light, straight knife with a very sharp blade, used in surgery and anatomical dissections.

SCALPEL

**scal·y** (skāl′i), *adj.* [-IER, -IEST], having, covered with, or resembling scales. **—scal′i·ness,** *n.*
**scamp** (skamp), *n.* [< obs. *scamp*, to roam, contr. of *scamper*], a worthless fellow; rogue; rascal. **—scamp′ish,** *adj.* **—scamp′ish·ness,** *n.*
**scamp** (skamp), *v.t.* [cf. ON. *skemma*, to shorten], to do in a careless, inadequate way. **—scamp′er,** *n.*
**scam·per** (skam′pēr), *v.i.* [< ONorm.Fr. *escamper*, to decamp; ult. < L. *ex*, out + *campus*, a field], to run or go hurriedly or quickly. *n.* a scampering. **—scam′per·er,** *n.*
**scan** (skan), *v.t.* [SCANNED, SCANNING], [< L. *scandere*, to climb, scan], 1. to analyze (verse) by marking off the metrical feet and showing the rhythmic structure. 2. to look at closely; scrutinize. 3. to glance at quickly. 4. in *television*, to traverse (a surface) rapidly with a beam of light or electrons in transmitting or reproducing a picture. *v.i.* 1. to scan verse. 2. to conform to metrical principles: said of verse. *n.* a scanning. **—scan′na·ble,** *adj.* **—scan′ner,** *n.*
**Scan., Scand.,** 1. Scandinavia. 2. Scandinavian.
**scan·dal** (skan′d'l), *n.* [< Fr. or OFr. < LL. *scandalum*, cause for stumbling < Gr. *skandalon*, a snare], 1. any act, person, or thing that offends moral feelings and leads to disgrace. 2. a reaction of shame, outrage, etc. caused by this. 3. ignominy; disgrace. 4. malicious gossip; backbiting.
**scan·dal·ize** (skan′d'l-īz′), *v.t.* [-IZED, -IZING], to outrage the moral feelings of by improper conduct. **—scan′dal·i·za′tion,** *n.* **—scan′dal·iz′er,** *n.*
**scan·dal·mon·ger** (skan′d'l-muŋ′gēr), *n.* a person who gossips maliciously and spreads scandal.
**scan·dal·ous** (skan′d'l-əs), *adj.* 1. causing scandal; shocking to people's moral feelings; shameful. 2. spreading slander; libelous; defamatory. **—scan′dal·ous·ly,** *adv.* **—scan′dal·ous·ness,** *n.*
**Scan·di·na·vi·a** (skan′də-nā′vi-ə), *n.* 1. the ancient Norse lands: now, Sweden, Norway, Denmark, and Iceland. 2. the Scandinavian Peninsula.
**Scan·di·na·vi·an** (skan′də-nā′vi-ən), *adj.* of Scandinavia, its people, their languages, etc. *n.* 1. one of the people of Scandinavia. 2. the subbranch of the Germanic languages spoken by them; North Germanic; Norse.
**Scandinavian Peninsula,** a large peninsula of N Europe, containing Norway and Sweden.
**scan·di·um** (skan′di-əm), *n.* [< ML. < L. *Scandia*, Scandinavia], a rare metallic chemical element: symbol, Sc; at. wt., 45.10; at. no., 21. **—scan′dic,** *adj.*
**scan·sion** (skan′shən), *n.* the act of scanning verse.
**scant** (skant), *adj.* [< ON. < *skammr*, short], 1. inadequate in size or amount; not enough; meager. 2. not quite up to full measure. *v.t.* 1. to limit in size or amount; stint. 2. to fail to give full measure of. 3. to treat in an inadequate manner. *adv.* [Dial.], scarcely; barely. **—scant of,** short of. **—scant′ly,** *adv.* **—scant′ness,** *n.*
**scant·ling** (skant′liŋ), *n.* [< OFr. *eschantillon*, specimen], 1. a small beam or timber; esp., a small upright timber, as in the frame of a structure. 2. small beams or timbers collectively.
**scant·y** (skan′ti), *adj.* [-IER, -IEST], [< *scant*], 1. barely sufficient; not ample.; meager. 2. insufficient; not enough. **—scant′i·ly,** *adv.* **—scant′i·ness,** *n.*
**Scap·a Flow** (skap′ə, skä′pə), a channel in the Orkney Islands, N Scotland: British naval base.
**'scape, scape** (skāp), *n., v.t.* & *v.i.* ['SCAPED, 'SCAPING; SCAPED, SCAPING], [Archaic], escape.
**scape·goat** (skāp′gōt′), *n.* [see prec. entry], 1. a goat over which the high priest of the ancient Jews confessed the sins of the people, after which it was allowed to escape: Lev. 16:8-22. 2. a person, group, or thing that bears the blame for the mistakes or crimes of others.
**scape·grace** (skāp′grās′), *n.* [see SCAPEGOAT], a graceless, unprincipled fellow; scamp; rogue.
**scap·u·la** (skap′yoo-lə), *n.* [*pl.* -LAE (-lē′), -LAS], [L.], the shoulder blade.
**scap·u·lar** (skap′yoo-lēr), *adj.* of the shoulder or scapula. *n.* 1. a sleeveless outer garment falling from the shoulders, worn by monks. 2. two small pieces of cloth joined by strings, worn on the chest

and back, under the clothes, by some Roman Catholics as a token of religious devotion. Also **scap′u·lar′y** (-ler′i), [*pl.* -IES].

**scar** (skär), *n.* [< OFr. < L. < Gr. *eschara*, fireplace, scar of a burn], 1. a mark left after a wound, burn, ulcer, etc. has healed. 2. any mark resembling this. 3. the result left on the mind by suffering. *v.t.* [SCARRED, SCARRING], to mark as with a scar. *v.i.* to form a scar in healing.

**scar·ab** (skar′əb), *n.* [< Fr. < L. *scarabeus*], 1. a beetle, especially the black beetle held sacred by the ancient Egyptians 2. an image of this beetle, cut from a stone or gem and formerly worn as a charm.

EGYPTIAN SCARAB

**scar·a·bae·us** (skar′ə-bē′əs), *n.* [*pl.* -BAEUSES, -BAEI (-bē′ī)], [L.], a scarab.

**Scar·a·mouch** (skar′ə-mouch′, -mo͞osh′), *n.* [< Fr. < It. *Scaramuccia*, lit., a skirmish], 1. a stock character in old Italian comedy, depicted as a braggart and poltroon. 2. [s-], a boastful coward.

**scarce** (skârs), *adj.* [< ONorm.Fr. *escars*; ult. < L. pp. of *excerpere*, to pick out], 1. not common; rarely seen. 2. not plentiful; hard to get. *adv.* scarcely: a literary usage. —**make oneself scarce,** [Colloq.], to go or stay away. —**scarce′ness,** *n.*

**scarce·ly** (skârs′li), *adv.* 1. hardly; not quite. 2. probably not or certainly not: as, *scarcely* true.

**scar·ci·ty** (skâr′sə-ti), *n.* [*pl.* -TIES], 1. the condition or quality of being scarce; inadequate supply; lack. 2. rarity; uncommonness.

**scare** (skâr), *v.t.* [SCARED, SCARING], [< ON. *skiarr*, shy], 1. to fill with sudden fear or terror. 2. to drive (*away* or *off*) by frightening. *v.i.* to be frightened. *n.* a sudden fear; panic. —**scare up,** [Colloq.], to produce or gather quickly. —**scar′er,** *n.*

**scare·crow** (skâr′krō′), *n.* 1. the roughly dressed figure of a man, etc. put in a field to scare crows, etc. away from crops. 2. anything harmless that frightens one. 3. a person in ragged clothes.

**scare·head** (skâr′hed′), *n.* [Colloq.], a large newspaper headline, for sensational news.

**scarf** (skärf), *n.* [*pl.* SCARFS, SCARVES], [< OFr. *escreppe*, a purse hung from the neck < ON. *skreppa*, wallet], 1. a long, broad piece of cloth worn about the neck, head, etc. as an ornament or to give warmth. 2. any necktie with hanging ends. 3. a long, narrow covering for a table, etc. 4. in *military usage*, a sash. *v.t.* to cover as with a scarf.

**scarf** (skärf), *n.* [prob. < ON. *skarfr*], 1. a joint made by cutting the ends of two pieces and fastening them so that they join firmly into one continuous piece: also **scarf joint.** 2. the ends of a piece so cut. *v.t.* 1. to join by a scarf. 2. to make a scarf in the end of.

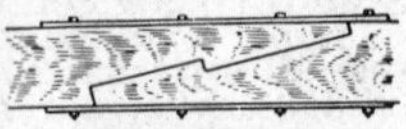
SCARF JOINT

**scar·i·fy** (skar′ə-fī′), *v.t.* [-FIED, -FYING], [< Fr. < L. < Gr. *skariphasthai*, to scratch < *skariphos*, a stylus], 1. to make a series of small cuts or punctures in (the skin), as in surgery. 2. to criticize sharply. 3. in *agriculture*, to loosen or stir (the topsoil). —**scar′i·fi·ca′tion,** *n.* —**scar′i·fi′er,** *n.*

**scar·la·ti·na** (skär′lə-tē′nə), *n.* [< It.], scarlet fever, especially in a mild form.

**Scar·lat·ti** (skär-lä′ti), *n.* the name of an Italian family of composers including Alessandro (1659–1725) and his son Domenico (1683–1757).

**scar·let** (skär′lit), *n.* [< OFr. < ML. *scarlatum*; of Per. or Ar. origin], 1. very bright red with a slightly orange tinge. 2. cloth or clothing of this color. *adj.* 1. of this color. 2. sinful.

**scarlet fever,** an acute contagious disease characterized by sore throat, fever, and a scarlet rash.

**scarlet letter,** a scarlet letter A, which condemned adulteresses were formerly forced to wear.

**scarlet runner,** a climbing bean plant of tropical America, having scarlet flowers, and pods with red-and-black seeds: also **scarlet runner bean.**

**scarlet tanager,** any of a group of songbirds related to the finch and native to the U.S., with a scarlet body and black wings and tail.

**scarp** (skärp), *n.* [< Fr. < It. *scarpa*], 1. a steep slope. 2. ground formed into a steep slope as part of a fortification. *v.t.* to make into a steep slope.

**scarves** (skärvz), *n.* alt. pl. of **scarf** (cloth).

**scar·y** (skâr′i), *adj.* [-IER, -IEST], [< *scare* + *-y*], [Colloq.], 1. causing alarm; frightening. 2. easily frightened. —**scar′i·ly,** *adv.*

**scat** (skat), *v.i.* [SCATTED, SCATTING], [? a hiss + *cat*], [Colloq.], to go away: usually imperative.

**scathe** (skāth), *v.t.* [SCATHED, SCATHING], [< ON. < *skathi*, harm], 1. [Archaic or Dial.], *a*) to injure. *b*) to sear. 2. to denounce fiercely. *n.* [Archaic or Dial.], injury or harm. —**scathe′less,** *adj.*

**scath·ing** (skāth′iŋ), *adj.* searing; blasting: usually figurative, as, *scathing* remarks. —**scath′ing·ly,** *adv.*

**sca·tol·o·gy** (skə-tol′ə-ji), *n.* [< Gr. *skōr*, excrement; + *-logy*], the study of or obsession with excrement. —**scat·o·log·i·cal** (skat′ə-loj′i-k′l), *adj.*

**scat·ter** (skat′ēr), *v.t.* [ME. *sc(h)ateren*], 1. to throw about; sprinkle here and there; strew. 2. to separate and drive in several directions; disperse. *v.i.* to separate and go in several directions: as, the crowd *scattered*. *n.* 1. a scattering. 2. what is scattered. —**scat′ter·er,** *n.*

**scat·ter·brain** (skat′ēr-brān′), *n.* a person who is flighty and incapable of concentrated thinking: also **scat′ter·brains′.** —**scat′ter·brained′,** *adj.*

**scatter rug,** any of various types of small rug for covering only part of a floor.

**scaup** (skôp), *n.* [*pl.* SCAUPS, SCAUP; see PLURAL, II, D, 1], [< obs. var. of *scalp*], any of several northern wild ducks related to the canvasback and redhead: also **scaup duck.**

**scav·enge** (skav′inj), *v.t.* [-ENGED, -ENGING], [< *scavenger*], to clean up (streets, etc.) as a scavenger. *v.i.* 1. to act as a scavenger. 2. to look for food.

**scav·eng·er** (skav′in-jēr), *n.* [< Anglo-Fr.; ult. < Fl. *scauwen*, to see], 1. a person who cleans the streets, removing filth, garbage, etc. 2. any animal that eats refuse and decaying matter.

**Sc. B.,** *Scientiae Baccalaureus*, [L.], Bachelor of Science.

**sce·na·ri·o** (si-nâr′i-ō′, -nä′ri-), *n.* [*pl.* -OS], [It. < LL. < L. *scena*; see SCENE], 1. a synopsis of the plot of a drama, opera, etc. 2. the outline of a motion picture, indicating the action, the scenes, the cast of characters, etc.

**sce·na·rist** (si-nâr′ist, -nä′rist), *n.* one who writes scenarios for motion pictures.

**scene** (sēn), *n.* [< Fr. < L. < Gr. *skēnē*, tent, stage], 1. the place in which any event occurs: as, the *scene* of the crime. 2. the setting of the action of a play, story, etc.: as, the *scene* of *Hamlet* is Denmark. 3. a division of a play, usually part of an act. 4. a part of a play, story, etc. that constitutes a unit of action: as, a flash-back *scene*. 5. the painted screens, backdrops, and properties which represent the locale of a play, motion picture, etc. 6. a view of people or places. 7. a display of strong feeling before others: as, she made a *scene* in court. 8. an episode or event, real or imaginary, especially as described.

**scen·er·y** (sēn′ēr-i), *n.* [*pl.* -IES], 1. painted screens, backdrops, hangings, etc. used on the stage to represent places. 2. the general appearance of a place; features of a landscape.

**sce·nic** (sē′nik, sen′ik), *adj.* 1. *a*) of the stage; theatrical. *b*) relating to stage effects or stage scenery. 2. of natural scenery; picturesque. 3. representing an action, event, etc. Also **sce′ni·cal.** —**sce′ni·cal·ly,** *adv.*

**scent** (sent), *v.t.* [< OFr. < L. *sentire*, to feel], 1. to smell. 2. to have a suspicion of. 3. to fill with an odor; perfume. *v.i.* to hunt by the sense of smell. *n.* 1. a smell; odor. 2. the sense of smell. 3. a perfume. 4. an odor left by an animal, by which it is tracked. 5. a track followed in hunting. 6. any clue by which something is followed or detected. —**scent′less,** *adj.*

**scep·ter, scep·tre** (sep′tēr), *n.* [< OFr. < L. < Gr. *skēptron*, staff], 1. a staff held by rulers on ceremonial occasions as a symbol of sovereignty. 2. royal authority; sovereignty. *v.t.* [-TERED, -TERING; -TRED, -TRING], to furnish with a scepter; invest with royal authority. —**scep′tered, scep′tred,** *adj.*

**scep·tic** (skep′tik), *n.* & *adj.* skeptic.

**scep·ti·cal** (skep′ti-k′l), *adj.* skeptical.

**scep·ti·cism** (skep′tə-siz′m), *n.* skepticism.

**sched·ule** (skej′ool; Brit. shed′yool), *n.* [< OFr. < LL. dim. of L. *sceda*, a leaf of paper < Gr. *shidē*, splinter of wood], 1. a list or catalogue of details, as of a bill of sale. 2. a list of times of recurring events, arriving and departing trains, etc.; timetable. 3. a timed plan for a project. *v.t.* [-ULED, -ULING], 1. to place in a schedule. 2. to make a schedule of. 3. to plan for a certain time.

**Scheldt** (skelt), *n.* a river in France, Belgium, and the Netherlands, flowing into the North Sea: also **Schel·de** (skhel′də).

**sche·ma** (skē′mə), *n.* [*pl.* -MATA (-mə-tə)], [L., see SCHEME], an outline, diagram, plan, etc.

**sche·mat·ic** (skē-mat′ik), *adj.* of, or having the nature of, a scheme or schema; diagrammatic. —**sche·mat′i·cal·ly,** *adv.*

**scheme** (skēm), *n.* [< L. < Gr. *schēma*, a form], 1. an systematic plan for attaining some object. 2. an orderly combination of things on a definite plan; system. 3. a plot; underhand intrigue. 4. an outline showing different parts of an object or system. *v.t.* [SCHEMED, SCHEMING], to plan as a scheme; devise; contrive; plot. *v.i.* 1. to make schemes. 2. to plot; intrigue. —**schem'er,** *n.*

**schem·ing** (skēm'iŋ), *adj.* crafty; tricky; given to forming crafty schemes. —**schem'ing·ly,** *adv.*

**Sche·nec·ta·dy** (skə-nek'tə-di), *n.* a city in east central New York: pop., 82,000.

**scher·zan·do** (sker-tsän'dō, -tsan'-), *adj.* [It. < *scherzo;* see SCHERZO], in *music,* playful; sportive. *adv.* in *music,* playfully; sportively.

**scher·zo** (sker'tsō), *n.* [*pl.* -ZOS, -ZI (-tsē)], [It. < G. *scherz,* a jest], a lively, playful movement, as of a sonata or symphony, in ¾ time.

**Schick test** (shik), [after B. *Schick* (1877–); U.S. pediatrician], a test for immunity to diphtheria, made by injecting diphtheria toxin under the skin.

**Schil·ler, Jo·hann Frie·drich von** (yō'hän frē'-driH fôn shil'ēr), 1759–1805; German dramatist.

**schil·ling** (shil'iŋ), *n.* [G.], 1. the monetary unit of Austria. 2. a former minor coin of Germany.

**schism** (siz''m), *n.* [< OFr. < LL. < Gr. *schisma* < *schizein,* to cleave], 1. a split in an organization because of difference of opinion, of doctrine, etc.; esp., a split in the Christian church. 2. the offense of trying to cause a split in a church.

**schis·mat·ic** (siz-mat'ik), *adj.* 1. of, or characteristic of, schism. 2. tending to cause, or guilty of, schism. Also **schis·mat'i·cal.** *n.* one who participates in a schism. —**schis·mat'i·cal·ly,** *adv.*

**schist** (shist), *n.* [< Fr. < L. < Gr. *schistos,* easily cleft < *schizein,* to cleave], a crystalline rock that can be easily split into layers. —**schist·ose** (shis'-tōs), **schist·ous** (shis'təs), *adj.*

**schiz·o-,** [< Gr. *schizein,* to cleave], a combining form meaning *split, cleavage, division:* also **schiz-.**

**schiz·o·carp** (skiz'ə-kärp'), *n.* [*schizo-* + *-carp*], in *botany,* a dry fruit, as of the maple, that splits into one-seeded carpels. —**schiz'o·car'pous,** *adj.*

**schiz·oid** (skiz'oid), *n.* one who has schizophrenia. *adj.* of, like, or having schizophrenia.

**schiz·o·phre·ni·a** (skiz'ə-frē'ni-ə), *n.* [< *schizo-* + Gr. *phrēn,* mind], a mental disorder characterized by indifference, withdrawal, hallucinations, etc. —**schiz'o·phren'ic** (-fren'ik), *adj. & n.*

**schle·mihl, schle·miel** (shlə-mēl'), *n.* [Yid. < Heb. proper name *Shelumiēl*], [Slang], a bungling person who habitually fails or is easily victimized.

**Schles·wig-Hol·stein** (shles'wig-hōl'stīn), *n.* a state of West Germany, on the border of Denmark.

**schmaltz** (shmälts), *n.* [via Yid. < G. *schmalz,* lit., melted fat], [Slang], anything very sentimental and unctuous, as some music, writing, etc.

**schnapps, schnaps** (shnäps, shnaps), *n.* [G., a dram], 1. Holland gin. 2. any strong liquor.

**schnau·zer** (shnou'zēr), *n.* [G. < *schnauzen,* to snarl], any of a breed of small active terrier with a wiry coat: also called *wire-haired pinscher.*

SCHNAUZER (18–20 in. high at shoulder)

**schnoz·zle** (shnoz''l), *n.* [via Yid. < G. *schnauze*], [Slang], the nose.

**schol·ar** (skol'ēr), *n.* [< AS. or OFr. < LL. < L. *schola,* a school], 1. a learned person; one who has had advanced training in literature, the arts, etc. 2. a student who has a scholarship (sense 3). 3. any student or pupil.

**schol·ar·ly** (skol'ēr-li), *adj.* 1. of or characteristic of scholars. 2. showing much knowledge and critical ability. 3. studious; devoted to learning. *adv.* like a scholar. —**schol'ar·li·ness,** *n.*

**schol·ar·ship** (skol'ēr-ship'), *n.* 1. the quality of knowledge and learning shown by a student. 2. the systematized knowledge of a learned man. 3. a gift of money or other aid to help a student.

**scho·las·tic** (skə-las'tik), *adj.* [< L. < Gr. < *scholazein,* to be at leisure < *scholē;* see SCHOOL], 1. of schools, colleges, students, teachers, etc.; academic. 2. of or characteristic of scholasticism. Also **scho·las'ti·cal.** *n.* 1. a schoolman (sense 1). 2. one who favors scholasticism. Also **Scholastic** (for *n.* 1 & 2, *adj.* 2). —**scho·las'ti·cal·ly,** *adv.*

**scho·las·ti·cism** (skə-las'tə-siz'm), *n.* 1. [often S-], the system of logic, philosophy, and theology of medieval schoolmen. 2. an insistence upon traditional doctrines and methods.

**scho·li·ast** (skō'li-ast'), *n.* [< LL. < LGr. < Gr. *scholion,* a comment < *scholē;* see SCHOOL], an ancient interpreter and annotator of the classics. —**scho'li·as'tic,** *adj.*

**Schön·berg, Arnold** (shōn'bērg), 1874–1951; Austrian composer in the U.S.

**school** (skōōl), *n.* [< AS. < L. *schola* < Gr. *scholē,* leisure, school], 1. a place or institution for teaching and learning, as a public school, dancing school, college or university, etc. 2. *a*) the building or buildings, classrooms, etc. of a school. *b*) all of its students and teachers. *c*) a regular session of teaching at a school. 3. the process of being educated: as, he never finished *school.* 4. any situation or experience through which one gains knowledge, training, etc.: as, the *school* of hard knocks. 5. a particular division of a college or university: as, the law *school.* 6. a group following the same teachings, beliefs, methods, etc.: as, the French Impressionist *school.* 7. a way of life: as, a gentleman of the old *school.* *v.t.* 1. to train; teach; educate. 2. to discipline; control. *adj.* of a school or schools.

**school** (skōōl), *n.* [D., a crowd], a large number of fish or water animals of the same kind swimming together. *v.i.* to swim together in such a school.

**school board,** a group of people, elected or appointed, who are in charge of local public schools.

**school·book** (skōōl'book'), *n.* a book used for study in schools; textbook.

**school·boy** (skōōl'boi'), *n.* a boy attending school. *adj.* characteristic of a boy attending school.

**school·fel·low** (skōōl'fel'ō), *n.* a schoolmate.

**school·girl** (skōōl'gūrl'), *n.* a girl attending school. *adj.* characteristic of a girl attending school.

**school·house** (skōōl'hous'), *n.* a building used as a school.

**school·ing** (skōōl'iŋ), *n.* 1. formal instruction at school; education. 2. cost of instruction and living at school. 3. training.

**school·man** (skōōl'mən; *for* 2, -man'), *n.* [*pl.* -MEN (-mən; *for* 2, -men')], 1. [often S-], one of the medieval university teachers of philosophy, logic, and theology. 2. a teacher or educator.

**school·marm** (skōōl'mäm', -märm'), *n.* [Colloq.], a woman schoolteacher, especially one regarded as old-fashioned and prudish: also **school'ma'am'** (-mäm', -mam').

**school·mas·ter** (skōōl'mas'tēr, -mäs'-), *n.* a man who teaches in, or is head of, a school. —**school'-mis'tress** (-mis'tris), *n.fem.*

**school·mate** (skōōl'māt'), *n.* one educated at the same school and at the same time as another.

**school·room** (skōōl'rōōm', -room'), *n.* a room in which pupils are instructed, as in a school.

**school·teach·er** (skōōl'tēch'ēr), *n.* a person who teaches in a school.

**school year,** the part of a year when school is in session, usually from September to June.

**schoon·er** (skōōn'ēr), *n.* [< New England *scoon,* to skim upon the water], 1. a ship with two or more masts, rigged fore and aft. 2. [Colloq.], a prairie schooner. 3. a large beer glass.

**Scho·pen·hau·er, Ar·thur** (är'toor shō'pən-hou'-ēr), 1788–1860; German philosopher.

**schot·tische, schot·tish** (shot'ish), *n.* [< G. (*der*) *schottische* (*tanz*), (the) Scottish (dance)], 1. a form of round dance in 2/4 time, similar to the polka. 2. music for this dance.

**Schu·bert, Franz Peter** (fränts shōō'bērt), 1797–1828; Austrian composer.

**Schu·mann, Robert** (shōō'män), 1810–1856; German composer.

**schwa** (shwä), *n.* [G. < Heb. *sh'wa*], 1. the neutralized vowel sound of most unstressed syllables in English; sound of *a* in *ago, e* in *agent,* etc. 2. the symbol (ə) representing this sound.

**Schweit·zer, Al·bert** (äl'bert shvīt'sēr; Eng. shwīt'sēr), 1875–1965; Alsatian theologian, musician, and medical missionary in Africa.

**sci.,** 1. science. 2. scientific.

**sci·at·ic** (sī-at'ik), *adj.* [< Fr. < ML. < L. < Gr. *ischiadikos* < *ischion,* the hip], of, near, or affecting the hip or its nerves: also **sci·at'i·cal.**

**sci·at·i·ca** (sī-at'i-kə), *n.* any painful condition in the region of the hip and thighs; esp., neuritis of the long nerve (**sciatic nerve**) passing down the back of the thigh.

**sci·ence** (sī'əns), *n.* [< OFr. < L. < *sciens,* ppr. of *scire,* to know], 1. originally, knowledge. 2. systematized knowledge derived from observation, study, and experimentation. 3. a branch of knowledge, especially one concerned with establishing and systematizing facts, principles, and methods: as, the *science* of music. 4. *a*) the systematized knowledge of nature. *b*) any branch of this. See **natural science.** 5. skill, technique, or ability: as, the *science* of boxing. 6. [S-], Christian Science.

**science fiction,** highly imaginative novels and stories centered about some projected, often fantastic, scientific development.

**sci·en·tif·ic** (sī′ən-tif′ik), ***adj.*** 1. of or dealing with science. 2. used in or for natural science. 3. based on, or using, the principles and methods of science; systematic and exact. 4. *a*) done according to methods gained by training and experience: as, *scientific* boxing. *b*) highly trained; skillful. **—sci′en·tif′i·cal·ly, *adv.***

**sci·en·tist** (sī′ən-tist), ***n.*** 1. a specialist in science, especially natural science. 2. [S-], a Christian Scientist.

**scil·i·cet** (sil′i-set′), ***adv.*** [L., contr. of *scire licet,* it is permitted to know], namely; to wit.

**scim·i·tar, scim·i·ter** (sim′ə-tēr), ***n.*** [It. *scimitarra*], a short, curved sword with an edge on the convex side, used by Turks, Arabs, etc.

**scin·til·la** (sin-til′ə), ***n.*** [L.], 1. a spark. 2. a particle; the least trace: used figuratively.

**scin·til·late** (sin′tə-lāt′), ***v.i.*** [-LATED, -LATING], [< L. pp. < *scintilla,* a spark], 1. to give off sparks; flash. 2. to sparkle intellectually; be brilliant and witty. 3. to twinkle, as a star. ***v.t.*** to give off (sparks, etc.). **—scin′til·lat′ing, scin′til·lant, *adj.* —scin′til·la′tion, *n.***

**sci·o·lism** (sī′ə-liz'm), ***n.*** [< L. dim. of *scius,* knowing < *scire,* to know], surface knowledge; shallow learning. **—sci′o·list, *n.* —sci′o·lis′tic, *adj.***

**sci·on** (sī′ən), ***n.*** [OFr. *cion;* prob. < L. *sectio*; see SECTION], 1. a shoot or bud of a plant, used for grafting: also sp. **cion.** 2. a descendant.

**scis·sion** (sizh′ən, sish′-), ***n.*** [Fr. < L. pp. of *scindere,* to cut], a cutting or splitting, or the state of being cut or split; division.

**scis·sor** (siz′ēr), ***v.t.*** to cut with scissors.

**scis·sors** (siz′ērz), ***n.pl.*** [< OFr. < LL. pl. of *cisorium,* cutting tool < *caedere,* to cut], 1. a cutting instrument, smaller than shears, with two opposing blades which are pivoted together so that they slide over each other: also *pair of scissors.* 2. [construed as sing.], *a*) a gymnastic feat in which the legs are moved in a way suggestive of scissors. *b*) a scissors hold.

**scissors hold,** a wrestling hold in which one contestant clasps the other with his legs.

**scissors kick,** a swimming kick in which one leg is bent back at the knee, the other swung forward, then both brought together with a snap.

**scis·sor·tail** (siz′ēr-tāl′), ***n.*** a variety of flycatcher found in the southern U.S. and Mexico, having a forked tail: also **scissor-tailed flycatcher.**

**scle·ra** (sklêr′ə), ***n.*** [< Gr. *sklēros,* hard], a tough, white, fibrous membrane covering all of the eyeball except the area covered by the cornea.

**scle·ren·chy·ma** (skli-reŋ′ki-mə), ***n.*** [< Gr. *sklēros,* hard + *enchyma,* infusion], in *botany,* plant tissue of thick-walled cells, as in nut shells.

**scle·ro-,** [< Gr. *sklēros,* hard], a combining form meaning: 1. *hard.* 2. *of the sclera.* Also **scler-.**

**scle·ro·sis** (skli-rō′sis), ***n.*** [*pl.* -SES (-sēz)], [< Gr. < *sklēros,* hard], a hardening of body tissues, as by an excessive growth of fibrous connective tissue. **—scle·ro′sal, *adj.***

**scle·rot·ic** (skli-rot′ik), ***adj.*** 1. of, characterized by, or having sclerosis. 2. of the sclera. ***n.*** the sclera.

**scoff** (skôf, skof), ***n.*** [prob. < ON.], 1. an expression of scorn or derision; jeer. 2. an object of mocking contempt, scorn, etc. ***v.t.*** to mock at or deride. ***v.i.*** to show scorn or derision; jeer (*at*). **—scoff′er, *n.* —scoff′ing·ly, *adv.***

**scold** (skōld), ***n.*** [prob. < ON. *skald,* poet (in allusion to satirical verses)], a person, especially a woman, who habitually uses abusive language. ***v.t.*** to find fault with angrily; rebuke. ***v.i.*** 1. to find fault angrily; chide. 2. to use angry, abusive language. **—scold′er, *n.* —scold′ing, *adj. & n.* —scold′ing·ly, *adv.***

**scol·lop** (skol′əp), ***n. & v.t.*** scallop.

**sconce** (skons), ***n.*** [< OFr. < ML. *sconsa;* ult. < L. pp. of *abscondere,* to hide], a bracket attached to a wall for holding a candle, etc.

**sconce** (skons), ***n.*** [D. *schans,* a fortress, orig. wickerwork], a shelter, protection, etc.; specif., a small fort. ***v.t.*** [SCONCED, SCONCING], to provide with a sconce; fortify, shelter, etc.

**scone** (skōn), ***n.*** [Scot., contr. < MD. *schoonbrot,* fine bread], a kind of tea cake, often resembling a baking powder biscuit, usually baked over a hot fire on a griddle.

**scoop** (sko͞op), ***n.*** [< MD. *schope,* bailing vessel & *schoppe,* a shovel], 1. any of various small, shovel-like utensils; specif., *a*) a kitchen utensil used to take up sugar or flour. *b*) a ladle. *c*) a small, hemispherical utensil for dishing up ice cream. 2. the deep shovel of a dredge or steam shovel, which takes up sand, etc. 3. the act of taking up with a scoop. 4. the amount taken up at one time by a scoop. 5. a hollowed-out place. 6. a motion as of scooping. 7. [Colloq.], a large profit made by speculation. 8. [Newspaper Slang], a beat. ***v.t.*** 1. to take up or out as with a scoop. 2. to dig out; hollow out. 3. to make by digging out. 4. [Colloq.], to gather (*in*) as if with a scoop. 5. [Newspaper Slang], to publish an item of news before (a rival). **—scoop′er, *n.***

**scoop·ful** (sko͞op′fool′), ***n.*** [*pl.* -FULS], as much as a scoop will hold.

**scoot** (sko͞ot), ***v.i.*** [prob. < ON. *skiōta,* to shoot], [Colloq.], to go quickly; scurry off; dart. ***n.*** [Colloq.], a scurrying off.

**scoot·er** (sko͞ot′ēr), ***n.*** [< *scoot*], 1. a child's vehicle, consisting of a low footboard with a wheel at each end and a handlebar for steering: it is moved by pushing one foot against the ground. 2. a similar vehicle with a seat, propelled by a motor: in full, **motor scooter.** 3. a sailboat with runners, for use on water or ice.

**scoot·er** (sko͞ot′ēr), ***n.*** a scoter.

**scope** (skōp), ***n.*** [< It. < L. < Gr. *skopos,* object, watcher], 1. the area that the mind can cover; range of view. 2. range or extent of action, observation, inclusion, etc.: as, the *scope* of a dictionary. 3. room for achievement; opportunity.

**-scope** (skōp), [< Gr. < *skopein,* to see], a combining form meaning (an instrument, etc. for) *seeing* or *observing,* as in *telescope.*

**sco·pol·a·mine** (skō-pol′ə-mēn′), ***n.*** [< Mod. L. *Scopolia,* a genus of plants (after G. A. *Scopoli* (1723–1788), It. naturalist + G. *amin,* amine], an alkaloid, $C_{17}H_{21}O_4N$, used in producing twilight sleep: also **sco·pol′a·min** (-min).

**-sco·py** (skə-pi), [< Gr. *skopein,* to see], a combining form meaning *a seeing, observing,* as in *bioscopy.*

**scor·bu·tic** (skôr-bū′tik), ***adj.*** [< ML. *scorbutus,* scurvy < MD. *scorft*], of, like, or having scurvy: also **scor·bu′ti·cal.**

**scorch** (skôrch), ***v.t.*** [< OFr. *escorcher,* to flay < L. < *ex-* + *cortex,* bark], 1. to burn slightly; char the surface of. 2. to parch or shrivel by heat. 3. to affect painfully by verbal attack or sarcasm. ***v.i.*** to be burned slightly; be singed. ***n.*** a superficial burn. **—scorch′ing, *adj.***

**scorched-earth policy** (skôrcht′ûrth′), the policy of burning and destroying all property in a given area before giving it up to an enemy.

**scorch·er** (skôr′chēr), ***n.*** one that scorches; specif., [Colloq.], *a*) an extremely hot day. *b*) a severe rebuke, etc. *c*) one who drives very fast.

**score** (skôr, skōr), ***n.*** [< AS. < ON. *skor*], 1. *a*) a scratch, mark, incision, etc. *b*) a drawn line, as one to mark a starting point. *c*) notches, marks, etc. made to keep tally or account. 2. an amount due; debt. 3. a grudge: as, pay off an old *score.* 4. a reason; motive. 5. the number of points made in a game or contest: as, the *score* is 2 to 0. 6. grade or rating, as on a test. 7. *a*) twenty people or objects. *b*) *pl.* very many. 8. [Colloq.], a successful move, remark, etc. 9. [Colloq.], the actual facts: often in *know the score.* 10. in *music, a*) a written or printed composition, showing all parts for the instruments or voices. *b*) the music for a musical comedy or motion picture. ***v.t.*** [SCORED, SCORING], 1. to mark or mark out with notches, lines, etc. 2. to keep account of by lines or notches. 3. *a*) to make (runs, hits, etc.) in a game: as, he *scored* a hit. *b*) to record the score of. *c*) to add (points) to one's score: as, he *scores* two for that play. 4. *a*) to scourge. *b*) to upbraid. 5. to evaluate, as in testing. 6. to achieve, as a success. 7. in *music,* to arrange in a score. ***v.i.*** 1. to make points, as in a game. 2. to run up a score. 3. to keep score in a game. 4. *a*) to gain an advantage. *b*) to achieve success. **—scor′er, *n.***

**score card,** 1. a card recording the score of a game, match, etc. 2. a card printed with players' names, positions, etc. at a sports event.

**sco·ri·a** (skôr′i-ə, skō′ri-ə), ***n.*** [*pl.* -AE (-ē′)], [L. < Gr. < *skōr,* dung], 1. the refuse left after the metal has been smelted from the ore. 2. loose, cinderlike lava. **—sco′ri·a′ceous** (-ā′shəs), ***adj.***

**scorn** (skôrn), ***n.*** [< OFr. < *escarnir,* to scorn], 1. a feeling of anger and disdain; extreme contempt. 2. the expression of this feeling. 3. an object of this feeling. ***v.t.*** 1. to regard with scorn; treat disdainfully. 2. to refuse or reject as contemptible. ***v.i.***

[Obs.], to scoff; mock. —**laugh to scorn,** to treat derisively. —**scorn'er,** *n.*

**scorn·ful** (skôrn'fəl), *adj.* full of scorn; having or showing contempt and disdain. —**scorn'ful·ly,** *adv.* —**scorn'ful·ness,** *n.*

**Scor·pi·o** (skôr'pi-ō'), *n.* [L.], 1. a southern constellation, supposedly resembling a scorpion in shape. 2. the eighth sign of the zodiac (♏), which the sun enters about October 24.

**scor·pi·on** (skôr'pi-ən), *n.* [OFr. < L. < Gr. *skorpios*], 1. any of various arachnids found in warm regions, with a long tail ending in a curved, poisonous sting. 2. in the *Bible*, a whip or scourge: I Kings 12:11. 3. [S-], Scorpio.

**Scot** (skot), *n.* 1. one of a Gaelic tribe of N Ireland that migrated to Scotland in the 5th century A.D. 2. a native or inhabitant of Scotland.

**scot** (skot), *n.* [merging of ON. *skot* & OFr. *escot*], money assessed or paid; tax; levy.

SCORPION (1–8 in. long)

**Scot.,** 1. Scotch. 2. Scotland. 3. Scottish.

**Scotch** (skoch), *adj.* Scottish. *n.* 1. any of the dialects of English spoken by the people of Scotland. 2. Scotch whisky. Cf. **Scottish.**

**scotch** (skoch), *v.t.* [prob. < Anglo-Fr. < OFr.; akin to Fr. *coche*, a notch], 1. to cut; scratch; notch. 2. to wound without killing; maim. 3. to put down; stifle: as, he *scotched* the rumor.

**Scotch-I·rish** (skoch'i'rish), *adj.* 1. designating or of a group of people of Northern Ireland who are descended from Scottish settlers. 2. of Scottish and Irish descent.

**Scotch·man** (skoch'mən), *n.* [*pl.* -MEN], a Scot; Scotsman: often considered an opprobrious form.

**Scotch tape,** a thin, paperlike adhesive tape: a trade-mark.

**Scotch terrier,** a Scottish terrier.

**Scotch whisky,** whisky, often having a smoky flavor, distilled in Scotland from malted barley.

**sco·ter** (skō'tēr), *n.* [*pl.* -TERS, -TER; see PLURAL, II, D, 1], [prob. dial. var. < *scoot*], any of several large sea ducks found along arctic coasts.

**scot-free** (skot'frē'), *adj.* 1. free from payment of scot, or tax. 2. unharmed or unpunished; safe.

**Sco·tia** (skō'shə, -shi-ə), *n.* [Poetic], Scotland.

**Scot·land** (skot'lənd), *n.* a division of Great Britain, north of England: area, 30,405 sq. mi.; pop., 5,241,000; capital, Edinburgh.

**Scotland Yard,** 1. the headquarters of the London police: in full, **New Scotland Yard.** 2. the London police, especially the detective bureau.

**Scots** (skots), *adj.* Scottish. *n.* the Scottish dialect of English. Cf. **Scottish.**

**Scots·man** (skots'mən), *n.* [*pl.* -MEN], a Scot: the current term in Scotland.

**Scott,** Sir **Walter** (skot), 1771–1832; Scottish poet and novelist.

**Scot·ti·cism** (skot'ə-siz'm), *n.* a Scottish idiom, expression, pronunciation, etc.

**Scot·tish** (skot'ish), *adj.* of Scotland, its people, their English dialect, etc. *n.* the English spoken in Scotland. —**the Scottish,** the Scottish people. *Scottish* is preferred in formal usage, but with some words, *Scotch* is almost invariably used (e.g., tweed, whisky), with others, *Scots* (e.g., law).

**Scottish Gaelic,** see **Gaelic.**

**Scottish terrier,** any of a breed of terrier with short legs, a squarish muzzle, rough, wiry hair, and erect, pointed ears.

**scoun·drel** (skoun'drəl), *n.* [prob. < Anglo-Fr. *escoundre*, to hide; ult. < L. *ex-*, from + *condere*, to hide], a person without principles or moral scruples; rascal; villain. *adj.* characteristic of a scoundrel; base. —**scoun'drel·ly,** *adj.*

**scour** (skour), *v.t.* [< MD. < OFr. < L. *ex-*, intens. + *curare*, to take care of < *cura*, care], 1. to clean by vigorous rubbing, as with abrasives. 2. to remove dirt and grease from (wool, etc.). 3. *a*) to wash by flowing through or over; flush. *b*) to wash away. 4. to remove from as if by cleaning. *v.i.* 1. to clean things by rubbing and polishing. 2. to become clean and bright by rubbing. *n.* 1. the act of scouring. 2. a cleansing agent used in scouring. 3. *pl.* dysentery in cattle, etc. —**scour'er,** *n.* —**scour'ing,** *n.*

**scour** (skour), *v.t.* [prob. < OFr. < L. < *ex-*, out + *currere*, to run], to pass over quickly, or range over or through, as in search or pursuit: as, he *scoured* the library for the book. *v.i.* to move quickly, or range about, as in search or pursuit.

**scourge** (skūrj), *n.* [< OFr. < L. *ex*, off + *corrigia*, a whip], 1. a whip. 2. any means of inflicting severe punishment, suffering, etc. 3. a punishment or affliction. *v.t.* [SCOURGED, SCOURGING], 1. to whip; flog severely. 2. to punish or afflict severely. —**scourg'er,** *n.*

**scout** (skout), *n.* [< OFr. < *escouter*, to hear < L. *auscultare*, to listen], 1. a person, plane, etc. sent out to discover the enemy's strength, actions, etc. 2. a member of the Boy Scouts or Girl Scouts. 3. the act of scouting. 4. [Slang], fellow; guy. 5. in *sports*, a person sent out to learn the tactics of a competitor, to find new talent, etc. *v.t.* 1. to spy upon; follow closely. 2. to look for; watch. *v.i.* 1. to go in search of information about the enemy; reconnoiter. 2. to go in search of something: as, *scout* around for some firewood. 3. to be a member of the Boy Scouts or Girl Scouts. —**scout'er,** *n.* —**scout'ing,** *n.*

**scout** (skout), *v.t.* [< ON. *skúta*, a taunt], to reject as absurd; flout; scoff at.

**scout·mas·ter** (skout'mas'tēr, -mäs'-), *n.* the adult leader of a troop of Boy Scouts.

**scow** (skou), *n.* [< D. *schouw*], a large, flat-bottomed boat with square ends, used for carrying freight, generally towed by a tug.

**scowl** (skoul), *v.i.* [prob. < ON.], 1. to wrinkle the forehead and lower the eyebrows in displeasure; look angry, sullen, etc. 2. to look threatening; lower. *v.t.* to affect or express with a scowl. *n.* 1. a scowling; angry frown. 2. a threatening or gloomy look. —**scowl'er,** *n.* —**scowl'ing·ly,** *adv.*

**scrab·ble** (skrab''l), *v.i.* [-BLED, -BLING], [< D. freq. of *schrabben*, to scrape], 1. to scratch, scrape, or paw as though looking for something. 2. to struggle. 3. to scribble. *v.t.* 1. to scrape together quickly. 2. to scribble. *n.* a scrabbling; a scramble, scribble, etc. —**scrab'bler,** *n.*

**scrag** (skrag), *n.* [prob. < ON.], 1. a thin, scrawny person, animal, or plant. 2. [Slang], the human neck. *v.t.* [SCRAGGED, SCRAGGING], [Slang], to twist or wring the neck of.

**scrag·gly** (skrag'li), *adj.* [-GLIER, -GLIEST], [see SCRAGGY & -LY], unkempt; rough; jagged.

**scrag·gy** (skrag'i), *adj.* [-GIER, -GIEST], [< *scrag*], 1. scraggly. 2. lean; bony; skinny. —**scrag'gi·ly,** *adv.* —**scrag'gi·ness,** *n.*

**scram** (skram), *v.t.* [SCRAMMED, SCRAMMING], [contr. of *scramble*], [Slang], to go away or out.

**scram·ble** (skram'b'l), *v.i.* [-BLED, -BLING], [? a fusion of *scamper* + *scrabble*], 1. to climb, crawl, etc. with the hands and feet. 2. to scuffle and fight for something. 3. to struggle to get something prized: as, they *scrambled* for office. *v.t.* 1. to throw together haphazardly. 2. to cook (eggs) after mixing the white and yolk together. *n.* 1. a hard climb or advance, as over difficult ground. 2. a disorderly struggle, as for something prized. —**scram'bler,** *n.*

**Scran·ton** (skran'tən), *n.* a city in NE Pennsylvania: pop., 111,000.

**scrap** (skrap), *n.* [< ON. *skrap*], 1. a small piece; fragment. 2. a fragment of something written. 3. discarded metal suitable only for reprocessing. 4. discarded articles of rubber, leather, paper, etc. 5. *pl.* bits of food. *adj.* 1. in the form of pieces, leftovers, etc. 2. used and discarded. *v.t.* [SCRAPPED, SCRAPPING], 1. to make into scraps. 2. to discard; junk. —**scrap'pa·ble,** *adj.* —**scrap'per,** *n.*

**scrap** (skrap), *n.* [prob. < *scrape*], [Slang], a fight or quarrel. *v.i.* [SCRAPPED, SCRAPPING], [Slang], to fight or quarrel. —**scrap'per,** *n.*

**scrap·book** (skrap'book'), *n.* a book of blank pages for pasted clippings, pictures, etc.

**scrape** (skrāp), *v.t.* [SCRAPED, SCRAPING], [< ON. *skrapa*], 1. to rub over the surface of with something rough or sharp. 2. to make smooth or clean with a tool or abrasive. 3. to remove by rubbing with something sharp or rough (with *off*, *out*, etc.). 4. to scratch, abrade, or graze. 5. to rub with a harsh sound: as, the bow *scrapes* the fiddle. 6. to gather slowly and with difficulty: as, to *scrape* up some money. *v.i.* 1. to rub against something harshly; grate. 2. to give out a harsh, grating noise. 3. to gather goods or money slowly and with difficulty. 4. to manage to get along, but with difficulty. 5. to draw the foot back along the floor when bowing. *n.* 1. a scraping. 2. a scraped place; abrasion. 3. a harsh, grating sound. 4. a disagreeable situation; predicament. —**scrap'er,** *n.*

**scrap·ing** (skrāp′iŋ), *n.* 1. the act of a person or thing that scrapes. 2. the sound of this. 3. *usually pl.* something scraped off, together, or up.
**scrap iron,** discarded or waste pieces of iron, to be recast or reworked.
**scrap·ple** (skrap′'l), *n.* [dim. of *scrap*], corn meal boiled with scraps of pork to form a loaf that is then sliced and fried.
**scrap·py** (skrap′i), *adj.* [-PIER, -PIEST], 1. made of scraps. 2. disconnected: as, *scrappy* thinking. —**scrap′pi·ly,** *adv.* —**scrap′pi·ness,** *n.*
**scrap·py** (skrap′i), *adj.* [-PIER, -PIEST], [< *scrap* (fight) + *-y*], [Slang], fond of fighting. —**scrap′pi·ly,** *adv.* —**scrap′pi·ness,** *n.*
**Scratch** (skrach), *n.* [< ON. *skratti,* devil; alt. after *scratch*], the Devil: usually **Old Scratch.**
**scratch** (skrach), *v.t.* [prob. a fusion of ME. *scratten* & *cracchen*], 1. to mark or cut the surface of slightly with something pointed or sharp. 2. to tear or dig with the nails or claws. 3. *a)* to scrape lightly to relieve itching, etc. *b)* to chafe. 4. to rub or scrape with a grating noise. 5. to write or draw hurriedly or carelessly. 6. to strike out (writing, etc.). 7. to gather with difficulty (with *up*). 8. in *sports,* to withdraw a contestant, entry, etc. *v.i.* 1. to use nails or claws in digging or wounding. 2. to scrape the skin lightly to relieve itching, etc. 3. to get along with difficulty. 4. to give out a harsh, scraping noise. 5. in *billiards & pool,* to commit a scratch. *n.* 1. the act of scratching. 2. a mark, tear, or slight wound made by scratching. 3. a grating sound; scraping. 4. a scribble. 5. a line indicating the starting point of a race. 6. in *billiards & pool, a)* a shot that results in a penalty. *b)* a miss. 7. in *sports,* the starting point or time of a contestant who receives no handicap. *adj.* 1. used for hasty notes, preliminary figuring, etc.: as, *scratch* paper. 2. having no handicap, as a contestant. 3. done or made by chance, as a shot. 4. put together hastily, without selection. —**from** (or **at, on**) **scratch,** 1. from the starting line, as in a race. 2. from nothing; without advantage. —**up to scratch,** [Colloq.], up to a standard. —**scratch′a·ble,** *adj.* —**scratch′er,** *n.*
**scratch hit,** in *baseball,* a chance hit credited to the batter, which normally would have been an out.
**scratch·y** (skrach′i), *adj.* [-IER, -IEST], 1. made with scratches. 2. making a scratching noise. 3. scratched together; haphazard. 4. itching: as, *scratchy* cloth. —**scratch′i·ly,** *adv.* —**scratch′i·ness,** *n.*
**scrawl** (skrôl), *v.t. & v.i.* [prob. alt. form of *crawl*], to write, draw, or mark hastily, carelessly, or awkwardly. *n.* 1. shapeless, sprawling, often illegible handwriting. 2. something scrawled. —**scrawl′er,** *n.* —**scrawl′y** [-IER, -IEST], *adj.*
**scraw·ny** (skrô′ni), *adj.* [-NIER, -NIEST], [prob. < ON.], lean; thin; scraggy; scrubby. —**scraw′ni·ly,** *adv.* —**scraw′ni·ness,** *n.*
**scream** (skrēm), *v.i.* [< ON. *skraema,* to terrify], 1. to utter a shrill, piercing cry as in pain or fright. 2. to laugh loudly or hysterically. 3. to use intense or hysterical language. *v.t.* 1. to utter with or as with a scream. 2. to bring into a specified state by screaming: often reflexive. *n.* 1. a sharp, piercing cry or sound; shriek. 2. [Colloq.], a hilariously entertaining person or thing.
**scream·er** (skrēm′ẽr), *n.* 1. one who screams. 2. [Slang], a person or thing that makes one scream with laughter. 3. [Slang], a sensational headline. 4. any of various long-toed South American birds.
**scream·ing** (skrēm′iŋ), *adj.* 1. that screams. 2. violent or startling in effect. 3. causing screams of laughter; hilarious. —**scream′ing·ly,** *adv.*
**screech** (skrēch), *v.i.* [< ON. *skraekja,* of Gmc. echoic origin], to utter a shrill, high-pitched, harsh cry or shriek. *v.t.* to utter with a shriek. *n.* a shrill, high-pitched, harsh cry or shriek. —**screech′er,** *n.* —**screech′y** [-IER, -IEST], *adj.* —**screech′i·ly,** *adv.* —**screech′i·ness,** *n.*
**screech owl,** 1. a small owl with feathered ear tufts and an eerie, wailing screech. 2. a barn owl.
**screed** (skrēd), *n.* [ME. *screde;* var. of *shred*], a long, tiresome speech or writing; harangue.
**screen** (skrēn), *n.* [< OFr.; prob. < OHG. *scerm,* a guard], 1. a curtain or movable partition, as a covered frame, used to separate, conceal, protect, etc. 2. anything serving to shield, conceal, etc.: as, a smoke *screen.* 3. a coarse mesh of wire, etc., used as a sieve, as for grading coal. 4. a frame covered with a mesh, as of wire, used, as on a window, to keep insects out. 5. a large surface upon which lantern slides, motion pictures, etc. are projected. 6. the motion-picture industry: with *the.* *v.t.* 1. to shut off from view, shelter, or protect, as with a screen. 2. to sift through a screen. 3. to interview or test in order to separate according to skills, personality, etc. 4. to show (a motion picture, etc.) upon a screen. 5. to photograph with a motion-picture camera. 6. to adapt (a story, play, etc.) for motion pictures. *v.i.* to be screened or suitable for screening, as in motion pictures. —**screen′a·ble,** *adj.* —**screen′er,** *n.* —**screen′less,** *adj.*
**screen·ings** (skrēn′iŋz), *n.pl.* 1. refuse left after screening. 2. material that has been screened.
**screen·play** (skrēn′plā′), *n.* a story written in a form suitable to production as a motion picture.
**screw** (skrōō), *n.* [< OFr. *escroue,* hole in which a screw turns < L. *scrofa,* sow, infl. by *scrobis,* vulva], 1. a naillike cylinder of metal for fastening things by being turned: it is grooved in an advancing spiral, and usually has a slotted head: **male** (or **external**) **screw.** 2. any spiral thing like this. 3. a hollow, threaded cylinder into which the male screw fits: **female** (or **internal**) **screw.** 4. a turning or twisting, as of a screw. 5. a screw propeller. 6. [Chiefly Brit.], a stingy person; skinflint. 7. [Slang], a prison guard. 8. [Brit. Slang], salary. *v.t.* 1. to twist; turn; tighten. 2. to fasten, tighten, press, etc. as with a screw. 3. to contort; twist out of shape. 4. to force to do something, as if by using screws. 5. to extort or practice extortion on. *v.i.* 1. to come apart or go together by being turned like a screw: as, the lid *screws* on. 2. to be fitted for screws: as, the hinge *screws* on to the door. 3. to twist; turn; wind. 4. to practice extortion. —**have a screw loose,** [Slang], to be eccentric, odd, etc. —**put the screws on** (or **to**), to subject to force or great pressure. —**screw′er,** *n.*

SCREWS

**screw·ball** (skrōō′bôl′), *n.* [Slang], an erratic, irrational, or unconventional person. *adj.* [Slang], erratic, irrational, etc.
**screw·driv·er** (skrōō′drīv′ẽr), *n.* a tool with a blunt end which fits into the slotted head of a screw, used for turning screws: also **screw driver.**
**screw eye,** a screw with a loop instead of a head.
**screw hook,** a screw with a hook instead of a head.
**screw propeller,** a revolving hub fitted with radiating blades arranged in a spiral, used for propelling ships, aircraft, etc.
**screw thread,** the spiral edge of a screw.
**screw·y** (skrōō′i), *adj.* [-IER, -IEST], [Slang], irrational, peculiar, absurd, impractical, etc. —**screw′i·ly,** *adv.* —**screw′i·ness,** *n.*
**scrib·ble** (skrib′'l), *v.t. & v.i.* [-BLED, -BLING], [< ML. < L. *scribere,* to write], 1. to write carelessly, hastily, or illegibly. 2. to cover with or make meaningless or illegible marks. *n.* scribbled writing, marks, etc.; scrawl. —**scrib′bler,** *n.* —**scrib′bly,** *adj.*
**scribe** (skrīb), *n.* [Early Fr. < L. < *scribere,* to write], 1. a writer; author. 2. a person who copied manuscripts before the invention of printing. 3. a public writer or copyist. 4. formerly, a teacher of the Jewish law. *v.i.* [SCRIBED, SCRIBING], to work as a scribe. —**scrib′al,** *adj.*
**scrim** (skrim), *n.* [prob. a cognate of G. *schirm,* a screen], a light, loosely woven cotton or linen cloth, used for curtains, etc.
**scrim·mage** (skrim′ij), *n.* [altered < *skirmish*], 1. a tussle; confused struggle. 2. in *football, a)* the play that follows the pass from center. *b)* football practice in the form of actual play. *v.i.* [-MAGED, -MAGING], to take part in a scrimmage. —**line of scrimmage,** in *football,* an imaginary line along which the two teams line up for each play.
**scrimp** (skrimp), *v.t.* [prob. < AS. *scrimman,* to shrink], 1. to make too small, short, etc.; skimp. 2. to treat stingily; stint. *v.i.* to be sparing and frugal. —**scrimp′er,** *n.* —**scrimp′ing·ly,** *adv.*
**scrimp·y** (skrim′pi), *adj.* [-IER, -IEST], 1. skimpy; scanty; meager. 2. stingy. —**scrimp′i·ly,** *adv.* —**scrimp′i·ness,** *n.*
**scrip** (skrip), *n.* [altered < *script*], 1. a writing; list, receipt, etc. 2. a certificate of a right to receive something, as stocks, bonds, land, money, etc. 3. paper money in amounts of less than a dollar, formerly issued in the U.S.
**script** (skript), *n.* [< OFr. < L. *scriptum,* neut. pp. of *scribere,* to write], 1. handwriting. 2. printing type that imitates handwriting. 3. a style of handwriting. 4. an original manuscript. 5. a working copy of a play, radio or television show, etc.
**Scrip·ture** (skrip′chẽr), *n.* [< OFr. < L. < *scriptus;* see SCRIPT], 1. *usually pl.* the Bible; books of the Old and New Testaments or of either: also **(the) Holy Scripture, (the) Holy Scriptures.** 2.

[s-], any sacred writing. —**Scrip′tur·al, scrip′tur·al,** *adj.* —**Scrip′tur·al·ly, scrip′tur·al·ly,** *adv.*

**scrive·ner** (skriv′nẽr, -′n-ẽr), *n.* [< OFr. < It. *scrivano;* ult. < L. *scribere,* to write], [Archaic], 1. a public clerk, copyist, etc. 2. a notary.

**scrod** (skrod), *n.* [prob. < MD. *schrode,* strip], a young codfish, split and prepared for cooking.

**scrof·u·la** (skrof′yoo-lə), *n.* [ML. < L. < *scrofa,* a sow], tuberculosis of the lymphatic glands, especially of the neck, with enlargement of the glands; king's evil. —**scrof′u·lous,** *adj.* —**scrof′u·lous·ly,** *adv.* —**scrof′u·lous·ness,** *n.*

**scroll** (skrōl), *n.* [alt. (after *roll*) < ME. *scrowe* < OFr. *escroue* < Gmc.], 1. a roll of parchment or paper, usually with writing upon it. 2. anything having the form of a loosely rolled sheet of paper; specif., an ornamental design in coiled or spiral form. *v.t. & v.i.* to form into or roll up into a scroll.

**scroll saw,** a thin, ribbonlike saw for cutting thin wood into spiral or ornamental designs.

**Scrooge** (skrōōj), *n.* the hard, miserly old man in Dickens' story *A Christmas Carol.*

**scro·tum** (skrō′təm), *n.* [*pl.* -TA (-tə), -TUMS], [L.], in most male mammals, the pouch of skin containing the testicles. —**scro′tal,** *adj.*

**scrounge** (skrounj), *v.t. & v.i.* [SCROUNGED, SCROUNGING], [< ?], [Slang], to take (something) without permission; pilfer. —**scroung′er,** *n.*

**scrub** (skrub), *n.* [dial. var. of *shrub,* infl. by ON.], 1. *a*) short, stunted trees or bushes growing thickly together. *b*) land covered with such growth. 2. any person or thing smaller than the usual, or inferior in quality, breed, etc. 3. in *sports,* a player not on the regular team. *adj.* 1. mean; poor; inferior. 2. undersized; small. 3. of or for players not on the regular team.

**scrub** (skrub), *v.t. & v.i.* [SCRUBBED, SCRUBBING], [prob. < ON.], 1. to clean or wash by rubbing hard. 2. to rub hard. *n.* 1. the act of scrubbing. 2. a drudge. —**scrub′ber,** *n.*

**scrub·by** (skrub′i), *adj.* [-BIER, -BIEST], 1. undersized or inferior; stunted. 2. covered with brushwood. 3. paltry, shabby, etc. —**scrub′bi·ly,** *adv.* —**scrub′bi·ness,** *n.*

**scrub oak,** any of various American dwarf oaks.

**scruff** (skruf), *n.* [alt. < earlier *scuff,* after *scruff,* var. of *scurf*], the nape of the neck.

**scrum·mage** (skrum′ij), *n.* [dial. var. of *scrimmage*], in *Rugby,* a formation around the ball in which the two sets of forwards try to push their opponents away from the ball and restart the play. *v.t. & v.i.* [-MAGED, -MAGING], to play or place (the ball) in a scrummage. —**scrum′mag·er,** *n.*

**scrump·tious** (skrump′shəs), *adj.* [alt. < *sumptuous*], [Slang], very fine; first-rate; splendid. —**scrump′tious·ly,** *adv.* —**scrump′tious·ness,** *n.*

**scru·ple** (skrōō′p'l), *n.* [< OFr. < L. *scrupulus,* small sharp stone], 1. a very small quantity. 2. an apothecaries' weight, equal to 1/3 dram (20 grains). 3. a doubt arising from difficulty in deciding what is right, proper, etc.; qualm. *v.t. & v.i.* [-PLED, -PLING], to hesitate (at) from doubt; have scruples (about): usually with an infinitive.

**scru·pu·lous** (skrōō′pyoo-ləs), *adj.* 1. having or showing scruples; conscientiously honest and upright. 2. careful of details; precise, accurate, and correct. —**scru′pu·los′i·ty** (-los′ə-ti), [*pl.* -TIES], **scru′pu·lous·ness,** *n.* —**scru′pu·lous·ly,** *adv.*

**scru·ti·nize** (skrōō′t'n-īz′), *v.t.* [-NIZED, -NIZING], to look at carefully or examine. —**scru′tiniz′er,** *n.*

**scru·ti·ny** (skrōō′t'n-i), *n.* [*pl.* -NIES], [< OFr. < LL < L. *scrutari,* to search into carefully], a close examination; careful, lengthy look.

**scu·ba** (skōō′bə), *n.* [*s*elf-*c*ontained *u*nderwater *b*reathing *a*pparatus], a diver's apparatus with compressed-air tanks for breathing under water.

**scud** (skud), *v.i.* [SCUDDED, SCUDDING], [orig. of a hare; hence prob. < dial *scut,* a tail], 1. to move swiftly. 2. to be driven before the wind. *n.* 1. a scudding. 2. clouds or spray driven by the wind.

**scuff** (skuf), *v.t.* [prob. < ON. *skūfa,* to shove], 1. to scrape (the ground, etc.) with the feet. 2. to wear a rough place on the surface of. *v.i.* to walk without lifting the feet; shuffle. *n.* 1. a noise or act of scuffing. 2. a worn or rough spot.

**scuf·fle** (skuf′'l), *v.i.* [-FLED, -FLING], [< *scuff* + *-le,* freq. suffix], 1. to struggle or fight in rough confusion. 2. to drag the feet; shuffle. *n.* 1. a rough, confused fight. 2. a shuffling: as, the *scuffle* of feet.

**scull** (skul), *n.* [ME. *skulle;* prob. < ON.], 1. an oar twisted from side to side over the stern of a boat to move it forward. 2. either of a pair of light oars used by a single rower. 3. a light rowboat for racing. *v.t. & v.i.* to propel (a boat) with a scull or sculls. —**scull′er,** *n.*

**scul·ler·y** (skul′ẽr-i), *n.* [*pl.* -IES], [< OFr.; ult. < *escuelle,* a dish < L. *scutella,* a tray], a room adjoining the kitchen, where pots and pans are cleaned, etc.

**scul·lion** (skul′yən), *n.* [< OFr. < *escouve* (< L. *scopa*), a broom], [Archaic], 1. a servant who does rough kitchen work. 2. a miserable wretch.

**scul·pin** (skul′pin), *n.* [prob. alt. < Fr. *scorpene* < L. *scorpaena,* sea scorpion], any of a group of spiny sea fishes with a large head and wide mouth.

**sculp·tor** (skulp′tẽr), *n.* [L. < *sculpere,* to carve], an artist who models or carves figures of clay, stone, wood, etc. —**sculp′tress,** *n.fem.*

**sculp·ture** (skulp′chẽr), *n.* [< OFr. < L. < pp. of *sculpere,* to carve], 1. the art of chiseling stone, modeling clay, carving wood, etc. into statues, figures, or the like. 2. a work or works of sculpture. *v.t.* [-TURED, -TURING], 1. to cut, carve, chisel, etc. into statues, figures, etc. 2. to represent or make by means of sculpture. 3. to decorate with sculpture. —**sculp′tur·al,** *adj.* —**sculp′tur·al·ly,** *adv.* —**sculp′tured,** *adj.*

**sculp·tur·esque** (skulp′chə-resk′), *adj.* like or suggesting sculpture; shapely, statuelike, etc.

**scum** (skum), *n.* [< MD. *schum*], 1. a thin layer of impurities which forms on the top of a liquid. 2. refuse; worthless parts of anything. 3. low, despicable person or people. *v.t.* [SCUMMED, SCUMMING], to skim. *v.i.* to become covered with scum.

**scum·my** (skum′i), *adj.* [-MIER, -MIEST], 1. of, like, or covered with, scum. 2. low; despicable. —**scum′mi·ly,** *adv.* —**scum′mi·ness,** *n.*

**scup** (skup), *n.* [*pl.* SCUP, SCUPS; see PLURAL, II, D, 2], [< Am. Ind.], any of a group of food fishes found on the Atlantic coast of the U.S.; porgy.

**scup·per** (skup′ẽr), *n.* [prob. for *scupper hole* < OFr. *escope,* bailing scoop], an opening in a ship's side to allow water to run off the deck.

**scup·per·nong** (skup′ẽr-nôŋ′, -noŋ′), *n.* [< the *Scuppernong* River, North Carolina], 1. a yellowish-green grape. 2. the wine made from this grape.

**scurf** (skũrf), *n.* [AS. < Scand.], 1. little, dry scales shed by the skin, as dandruff. 2. any scaly coating. —**scurf′y** [-IER, -IEST], *adj.*

**scur·ril·ous** (skũr′i-ləs), *adj.* [< L. < *scurra,* buffoon], 1. coarse; vulgar; abusive. 2. containing coarse vulgarisms or abuse. —**scur·ril·i·ty** (skə-ril′ə-ti), [*pl.* -TIES], —**scur′ril·ous·ly,** *adv.*

**scur·ry** (skũr′i), *v.i.* [-RIED, -RYING], [? a fusion of *scour* + *hurry*], to run hastily; scamper. *n.* a hasty running; scampering.

**scur·vy** (skũr′vi), *adj.* [-VIER, -VIEST], [< *scurf*], low; mean; vile. *n.* a disease resulting from a deficiency of vitamin C in the body, characterized by weakness, anemia, spongy gums, bleeding from the mucous membranes, etc. —**scur′vi·ly,** *adv.* —**scur′vi·ness,** *n.*

**scut** (skut), *n.* [prob. < ON.], a short, stumpy tail, especially of a rabbit or deer.

**scu·tate** (skū′tāt), *adj.* [< L. < *scutum,* a shield], 1. in *botany,* peltate: said of a leaf. 2. in *zoology,* covered by bony or horny plates or scales.

**scutch·eon** (skuch′ən), *n.* an escutcheon.

**scu·tel·late** (skū′t'l-āt′, skū-tel′it), *adj.* covered with scutella, or small scales or plates.

**scu·tel·lum** (skū-tel′əm), *n.* [*pl.* -LA (-ə)], [< L. dim. of *scutum,* a shield], in *botany & zoology,* any shieldlike scale, plate, etc.

**scut·tle** (skut′'l), *n.* [AS. *scutel,* a dish < L. *scutella*], a kind of bucket used for pouring coal on a fire.

**scut·tle** (skut′'l), *v.i.* [-TLED, -TLING], [< dial. *scut,* var. of *scud* + *-le,* freq. suffix], to scurry; scamper. *n.* a scamper. —**scut′tler,** *n.*

**scut·tle** (skut′'l), *n.* [< OFr. < Sp. *escotilla*], 1. an opening in a wall or roof, fitted with a cover. 2. an opening in the hull or deck of a ship, fitted with a cover. *v.t.* [-TLED, -TLING], 1. to cut a hole or holes through the hull of (a ship) below the water line. 2. to sink (a ship) by this means. —**scut′tler,** *n.*

**scut·tle·butt** (skut′'l-but′), *n.* [orig. < *scuttled butt,* lidded cask], [Slang], 1. a drinking fountain on shipboard. 2. rumor or gossip.

**scu·tum** (skū′təm), *n.* [*pl.* -TA (-tə)], [L.], 1. the long, leather-covered, wooden shield of Roman infantrymen. 2. in *zoology,* a heavy, horny scale, as on certain reptiles: also **scute** (skūt).

**Scyl·la** (sil′ə), *n.* a dangerous rock on the Italian coast: see **Charybdis.**

**scythe** (sīth), *n.* [alt. (after L. *scindere*, to cut) < AS. *sithe*], a tool with a long, single-edged blade on a bent wooden shaft, used in cutting grass, grain, etc. by hand. *v.t.* [SCYTHED, SCYTHING], to cut with a scythe.

SCYTHE

**Scyth·i·a** (sith′i-ə), *n.* an ancient region in SE Europe and Asia. —**Scyth′i·an,** *adj. & n.*
**S. Dak., S.D.,** South Dakota.
**'sdeath** (zdeth), *interj.* [Archaic], God's death: a euphemistic oath.
**Se,** in *chemistry*, selenium.
**SE, S.E., s.e.,** 1. southeast. 2. southeastern.
**sea** (sē), *n.* [< AS. *sæ*], 1. the ocean. 2. a large body of salt water wholly or partly enclosed by land: as, the Red *Sea.* 3. a large body of fresh water: as, the *Sea* of Galilee. 4. the state of the surface of the ocean: as, a calm *sea.* 5. a heavy wave: as, swamped by the *seas.* 6. a very great amount: as, lost in a *sea* of debt. —**at sea,** 1. on the open sea. 2. uncertain; bewildered. —**follow the sea,** to be a sailor. —**go to sea,** to become a sailor. —**put to sea,** to sail away from land.
**sea anemone,** a sea polyp having a firm, gelatinous body topped with colored, petallike tentacles.
**sea bass,** 1. a marine food fish with large scales and a wide mouth, found along the Atlantic coast. 2. any of various similar fishes.
**Sea·bee** (sē′bē′), *n.* [< *C*onstruction *B*attalion], a member of any of the construction and engineering battalions of the U.S. Navy.
**sea·board** (sē′bôrd′, -bōrd′), *n.* land bordering on the sea; seacoast. *adj.* bordering on the sea.
**sea-born** (sē′bôrn′), *adj.* 1. born in or of the sea. 2. produced by or originating in the sea.
**sea-borne, sea·borne** (sē′bôrn′, -bōrn′), *adj.* 1. carried on or by the sea. 2. afloat: said of ships.
**sea bread,** ship biscuit; hardtack.
**sea breeze,** a breeze blowing inland from the sea.
**sea calf,** the common seal; harbor seal.
**sea·coast** (sē′kōst′), *n.* land on or near the sea.
**sea cow,** 1. any of several sea mammals, as the dugong and manatee. 2. the walrus.
**sea cucumber,** an echinoderm with a cucumber-shaped body and long tentacles around the mouth.
**sea dog,** 1. the dogfish. 2. the common seal. 3. a sailor, especially an experienced one.
**sea eagle,** any of several fish-eating birds related to the bald eagle.
**sea elephant,** any of several very large seals that are hunted for oil: the male has a short trunk.
**sea·far·er** (sē′fâr′ẽr), *n.* one who travels on the sea.
**sea·far·ing** (sē′fâr′iŋ), *adj.* of or engaged in life at sea. *n.* 1. the profession of a sailor. 2. travel by sea.
**sea food,** food prepared from or consisting of salt-water fish or shellfish.
**sea·fowl** (sē′foul′), *n.* any bird living on or near the sea.
**sea·girt** (sē′gũrt′), *adj.* surrounded by the sea.
**sea·go·ing** (sē′gō′iŋ), *adj.* 1. made for use on the open sea: as, a *seagoing* schooner. 2. seafaring.
**sea green,** a pale bluish green. —**sea′-green′,** *adj.*
**sea gull,** a bird with long wings and webbed feet, living near the water; gull.
**sea horse,** 1. the walrus. 2. a small, semitropical fish with a slender tail, plated body, and a head somewhat like that of a horse. 3. a mythical sea creature, half fish and half horse.

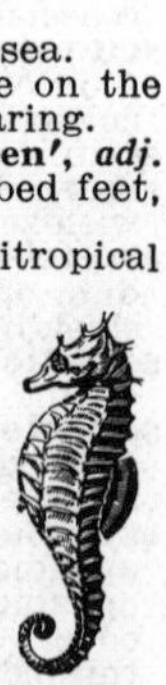

SEA HORSE (3–10 in. long)

**sea king,** a Norse pirate chief of the Middle Ages.
**seal** (sēl), *n.* [< OFr. < L. *sigillum*, a seal < *signum*, a sign], 1. a design or initial placed on a letter, document, etc. as a proof of authenticity: letters were formerly sealed with a molten wax wafer impressed with such a design. 2. a stamp or ring for making such an impression. 3. a wax wafer, piece of paper, etc. bearing an impressed design recognized as official. 4. something that seals or closes tightly. 5. something that guarantees; pledge: as, his fear is a *seal* of secrecy. 6. a sign; token: as, a *seal* of friendship. 7. an ornamental paper stamp: as, a Christmas *seal.* *v.t.* 1. to mark with a seal. 2. to secure the contents of (a letter, etc.) by closing with a wax wafer, mucilage, etc. 3. to confirm the genuineness of (a promise, etc.). 4. to ratify or authenticate (a document, etc.). 5. to certify as being accurate, exact, etc. by fixing a seal to. 6. to assign (an estate, etc.) with a seal, or pledge. 7. to settle or determine finally: as, it *sealed* his fate. 8. to close or shut with or as with a seal: as, *seal* the cracks in the wall. —**set one's seal to,** 1. to mark with one's seal. 2. to endorse. —**the seals,** [Brit.], symbols of (public) office. —**seal′a·ble,** *adj.* —**seal′er,** *n.*
**seal** (sēl), *n.* [*pl.* SEALS, SEAL; see PLURAL, II, D, 1], [< AS. *seolh*], 1. a sea mammal with a torpedo-shaped body and four flippers: it lives in cold waters and eats fish; *fur seals* are hunted for the valuable fur. 2. this fur. 3. leather made from sealskin. *v.i.* to hunt seals. —**seal′er,** *n.*
**sea legs,** the ability to walk without loss of balance on board ship, especially in a rough sea.
**seal·er·y** (sēl′ẽr-i), *n.* [*pl.* -IES], 1. the hunting of seals. 2. a place where seals are hunted.
**sea level,** the level of the surface of the sea, when halfway between high and low tide: used as a standard in measuring heights and depths.
**sea lily,** a crinoid.
**sealing wax,** a hard mixture of resin and turpentine used for sealing letters, dry batteries, etc.: it softens when heated.
**sea lion,** a large, eared seal of the North Pacific.
**seal ring,** a signet ring.
**seal·skin** (sēl′skin′), *n.* 1. the skin of the seal; esp., the soft undercoat dyed dark-brown or black. 2. a garment made of this. *adj.* made of sealskin.
**Sea·ly·ham terrier** (sē′li-ham′, -əm), [< *Sealyham*, an estate in Wales], any of a breed of terrier with short legs and a shaggy white coat.
**seam** (sēm), *n.* [< AS. *seam*], 1. a line formed by sewing together two pieces of material. 2. any line marking joining edges, as of boards. 3. a mark, line, etc. like this, as a scar, wrinkle, etc. 4. a thin layer or stratum of ore, coal, etc. *v.t.* 1. to join together so as to form a seam. 2. to mark with a seamlike line, crack, etc. *v.i.* to crack open. —**seam′less,** *adj.*
**sea·man** (sē′mən), *n.* [*pl.* -MEN], 1. a sailor. 2. an enlisted man ranking below a petty officer in the navy. —**sea′man·like′, sea′man·ly,** *adj.*
**sea·man·ship** (sē′mən-ship′), *n.* skill in sailing or working a ship; ability of a good seaman.
**sea mew,** a sea gull.
**seam·stress** (sēm′stris), *n.* a woman who sews expertly or who makes her living by sewing.
**seam·y** (sēm′i), *adj.* [-IER, -IEST], having or showing seams. —**the seamy side,** the least attractive aspect. —**seam′i·ness,** *n.*
**sé·ance** (sā′äns; Fr. sā′äns′), *n.* [Fr. < OFr. *seoir* (< L. *sedere*), to sit], 1. a meeting or session. 2. a meeting at which spiritualists try to communicate with the spirits of the dead.
**sea·plane** (sē′plān′), *n.* any airplane designed to land on or take off from water.
**sea·port** (sē′pôrt′, -pōrt′), *n.* 1. a port or harbor used by ocean ships. 2. a town or city having such a port or harbor.
**sea purse,** a horny case produced by certain skates, sharks, etc., serving to hold their eggs.
**sear** (sêr), *adj.* [AS.], sere; withered. *v.t.* 1. to dry up; wither. 2. to scorch or burn the surface of. 3. to brand with a hot iron. 4. to make callous or unfeeling. *v.i.* to become sear. *n.* a mark produced by searing. —**sear′ing·ly,** *adv.*
**search** (sũrch), *v.t.* [< OFr. *cercher* < L. *circare*, to go about < *circus*, ring], 1. to go over and look through in order to find something; explore: as, *search* the house. 2. to examine (a person) for something concealed. 3. to examine carefully; probe: as, he *searched* his soul. 4. to pierce; penetrate. *v.i.* to make a search. *n.* 1. a searching; scrutiny or examination. 2. the act of stopping and searching a neutral ship for contraband. —**in search of,** making a search for. —**search out,** to seek or find by searching. —**search′a·ble,** *adj.* —**search′er,** *n.*
**search·ing** (sũr′chiŋ), *adj.* 1. examining thoroughly. 2. keen; piercing. —**search′ing·ly,** *adv.*
**search·light** (sũrch′līt′), *n.* 1. an apparatus, as on a swivel, that projects a strong beam of light in any direction. 2. the beam of light.
**search warrant,** a legal document authorizing a police search, as for stolen articles, suspected criminals, etc.
**sea·scape** (sē′skāp′), *n.* [*sea* + land*scape*], 1. a view of the sea. 2. a picture of this.
**sea shell,** the shell of any salt-water mollusk.
**sea·shore** (sē′shôr′, -shōr′), *n.* land along the sea; seacoast.
**sea·sick·ness** (sē′sik′nis), *n.* nausea, dizziness, etc. caused by the rolling of a ship at sea. —**sea′sick′,** *adj.*
**sea·side** (sē′sīd′), *n.* land along the sea; seashore; seacoast. *adj.* at or of the seaside.

**sea·son** (sē′z'n), *n.* [< OFr. < LL. *satio*, sowing time < base of L. *serere*, to sow], 1. any one of the four arbitrary divisions of the year; spring, summer, fall, or winter. 2. the time when something specified takes place, is popular, permitted, etc.: as, the planting *season*, fishing *season*. 3. a period of time. 4. the fitting or convenient time. 5. the time of a specified festival: as, the Easter *season*. *v.t.* 1. to add to or change the flavor of (food); flavor. 2. to add zest or interest to. 3. to make more usable, as by aging or curing. 4. to make used to; accustom. 5. to temper; soften: as, *season* your criticism. *v.i.* to become seasoned, or more usable. —**for a season,** for a while. —**in season,** 1. available fresh for use as food. 2. at the legally established time for being hunted or caught: said of game, etc. 3. in or at the proper time. 4. early enough: also **in good season.** —**in season and out of season,** at all times. —**out of season,** not in season. —**sea′son·er,** *n.* —**sea′son·less,** *adj.*

**sea·son·a·ble** (sē′z'n-ə-b'l), *adj.* 1. suitable to or usual for the season. 2. opportune; timely. —**sea′son·a·ble·ness,** *n.* —**sea′son·a·bly,** *adv.*

**sea·son·al** ((sē′z'n-əl), *adj.* 1. of or characteristic of the season or seasons. 2. affected by or depending on a season. 3. coming at regular intervals. —**sea′son·al·ly,** *adv.*

**sea·son·ing** (sē′z'n-iŋ), *n.* 1. any flavoring added to food. 2. anything adding zest, variety, etc.

**season ticket,** a ticket entitling the holder to service, etc. for a given period or series of events.

**seat** (sēt), *n.* [ON. *sæti*], 1. the manner of sitting, as on horseback. 2. a place to sit. 3. a thing to sit on; chair, bench, etc. 4. the buttocks. 5. the part of a garment covering the buttocks. 6. the part of a chair, etc. that supports the buttocks. 7. the right to sit as a member; membership: as, a *seat* on the council. 8. a surface upon which the base of something rests. 9. the chief location, or center: as, the *seat* of government. 10. a residence, especially on a large estate. *v.t.* 1. to put or set in or on a seat. 2. to have seats for: as, the car *seats* six people. 3. to put a seat in or on; reseat. 4. to put in a certain place, position, etc. —**be seated,** 1. to sit down. 2. to be sitting. 3. to be located. —**seat′less,** *adj.*

**seat·er** (sēt′ẽr), *n.* something having (a specified number of) seats: as, a *two-seater*.

**seat·ing** (sēt′iŋ), *n.* 1. a providing with a seat or seats. 2. material for covering chair seats, etc. 3. the arrangement of seats.

**SEATO** (sē′tō), Southeast Asia Treaty Organization.

**Se·at·tle** (sē-at′'l), *n.* a seaport on Puget Sound, in Washington: pop., 557,000.

**sea urchin,** any of several sea animals, having a flattened globular body covered with a spiny skin.

**sea wall,** a wall made to break the force of the waves and to protect the shore from erosion.

**sea·ward** (sē′wẽrd), *n.* a direction or position toward the sea. *adj.* 1. directed or situated toward the sea. 2. from the sea: said of a wind. *adv.* toward the sea: also **sea′wards.**

**sea·way** (sē′wā′), *n.* 1. a way or route by sea. 2. the movement of a ship through the water. 3. the open sea. 4. a rough sea. 5. an inland waterway to the sea for ocean-going ships.

**sea·weed** (sē′wēd′), *n.* any sea plant or plants; esp., any marine alga.

**sea·wor·thy** (sē′wūr′*th*i), *adj.* fit for travel in on the open sea; safe in rough weather; sturdy: said of a ship. —**sea′wor′thi·ness,** *n.*

**se·ba·ceous** (si-bā′shəs), *adj.* [< L. *sebum*, tallow], of or like fat, tallow, or sebum; esp., designating certain skin glands that secrete sebum.

**Se·bas·to·pol** (si-bas′tə-pōl′), *n.* Sevastopol.

**se·bum** (sē′bəm), *n.* [L., tallow], the semiliquid, greasy secretion of the sebaceous glands.

‡**sec** (sek), *adj.* [Fr.], dry; not sweet: said of wine.

**SEC, S.E.C.,** Securities and Exchange Commission.

**sec.,** 1. secant. 2. second(s). 3. secondary. 4. secretary. 5. section(s). 6. security.

**se·cant** (sē′kənt, -kant), *adj.* [< L. ppr. of *secare*, to cut], cutting; intersecting. *n.* 1. any straight line intersecting a curve at two or more points. 2. in *trigonometry*, *a*) a line from the center of a circle through the circumference to another line tangent to the circle. *b*) the ratio of the length of this line to the length of the radius of the circle. *c*) the ratio of the hypotenuse of a right triangle to either of the other two sides with reference to the enclosed angle.

**se·cede** (si-sēd′), *v.i.* [-CEDED, -CEDING], [< L. < *se-*, apart + *cedere*, to go], to withdraw formally from a group, organization, etc. —**se·ced′er,** *n.*

**se·ces·sion** (si-sesh′ən), *n.* 1. a seceding. 2. [often S-], the withdrawal of the Southern States from the Federal Union in 1860–1861. —**se·ces′sion·al,** *adj.* —**se·ces′sion·ist,** *n.*

**Seck·el** (sek′'l), *n.* [after the Penn. fruitgrower who originated it], a small, sweet, juicy, reddish-brown variety of pear: also **Seckel pear.**

**se·clude** (si-klōōd′), *v.t.* [-CLUDED, -CLUDING], [< L. < *se-*, apart + *claudere*, to shut], 1. to keep away or shut off from others; isolate. 2. to make private or hidden; screen.

**se·clud·ed** (si-klōōd′id), *adj.* shut off or kept apart from others; isolated; withdrawn. —**se·clud′ed·ly,** *adv.* —**se·clud′ed·ness,** *n.*

**se·clu·sion** (si-klōō′zhən), *n.* 1. a secluding or being secluded; retirement; isolation; privacy. 2. a secluded spot. —**se·clu′sive,** *adj.* —**se·clu′sive·ly,** *adv.* —**se·clu′sive·ness,** *n.*

**sec·ond** (sek′ənd), *adj.* [OFr. < L. *secundus* < *sequi*, to follow], 1. coming next after the first in order; 2d. 2. another; other; additional: as, a *second* chance. 3. being of the same kind as another: as, a *second* Caesar. 4. next below the first in rank, value, merit, etc. 5. inferior; subordinate. 6. in *music*, *a*) lower in pitch. *b*) performing a part lower in pitch. *n.* 1. a person or thing that is second. 2. the next after the first. 3. an article of merchandise that is not of first quality. 4. a person who acts as an aid or assistant, as to a duelist or boxer. *v.t.* 1. to act as an aid to; assist. 2. to give support or encouragement to; reinforce. 3. to indicate formal support of (a motion) so that it may be discussed or voted on. *adv.* in the second place, group, etc. —**sec′ond·er,** *n.*

**sec·ond** (sek′ənd), *n.* [< Fr. < ML. *secunda minuta*, lit., second minute (i.e., the minute divided)], 1. 1/60 of a minute of time. 2. a very short time; instant. 3. 1/60 of a minute of angular measure.

**sec·ond·ar·y** (sek′ən-der′i), *adj.* 1. second, or below the first, in rank, importance, place, etc.; subordinate; minor. 2. derived from something considered primary or original; derivative. 3. coming after the first in a series of processes, stages, events, etc. 4. in *electricity*, designating or of an induced current or its circuit. *n.* [*pl.* -IES], 1. a person or thing that is secondary, subordinate, etc. 2. in *electricity*, a secondary circuit or coil. —**sec′ond·ar′i·ly,** *adv.* —**sec′ond·ar′i·ness,** *n.*

**secondary accent,** 1. in a word with two or more syllables accented, any accent that is weaker than the primary accent. 2. a symbol (in this dictionary, ′) indicating such an accent.

**secondary school,** a school, especially a high school, giving education (**secondary education**) between the primary and collegiate levels.

**second childhood,** senility; dotage.

**sec·ond-class** (sek′ənd-klas′, -kläs′), *adj.* 1. of the class, rank, etc. next below the highest. 2. designating or of travel accommodations next below the best. 3. designating or of a class of mail consisting of newspapers, periodicals, etc. 4. inferior, inadequate, etc. *adv.* 1. with second-class travel accommodations. 2. as or by second-class mail.

**second cousin,** the child of one's parent's cousin.

**second growth,** tree growth on land stripped of virgin forest.

**sec·ond-guess** (sek′ənd-ges′), *v.t. & v.i.* [Colloq.], to use hindsight in criticizing (someone), remaking (a decision), etc.

**sec·ond·hand** (sek′ənd-hand′), *adj.* 1. not direct from the original source; not original. 2. used or worn previously by another; not new. 3. of or dealing in merchandise that is not new.

**second hand,** the hand (of a clock or watch) that indicates the seconds and moves around the dial once every minute.

**second lieutenant,** a commissioned officer of the lowest rank in the U.S. Army, Marine Corps, or Air Force.

**sec·ond·ly** (sek′ənd-li), *adv.* in the second place; second: used chiefly in enumerating topics.

**second nature,** an acquired habit, etc. fixed so deeply as to seem part of one's nature.

**second person,** that form of a pronoun or verb which refers to the person spoken to: in *you do*, *you* and *do* are in the second person.

**sec·ond-rate** (sek′ənd-rāt′), *adj.* 1. second in

quality or other rating; second-class. 2. inferior; mediocre. —**sec′ond-rat′er,** *n.*
**second sight,** the supposed ability to see what cannot normally be seen, as future events, etc.
**second wind,** 1. the return of normal breathing following the exhaustion of severe exertion. 2. the recovered capacity for continuing any effort.
**se·cre·cy** (sē′krə-si), *n.* [*pl.* -CIES], 1 a being secret. 2. the ability or a tendency to keep secrets.
**se·cret** (sē′krit), *adj.* [< OFr. < L. *secretus,* pp. < *se-,* apart + *cernere,* to sift, discern], 1. kept from the knowledge of others. 2. remote; secluded. 3. secretive; reticent. 4. beyond general understanding; mysterious. 5. concealed from sight or notice; hidden: as, a *secret* drawer. 6. acting in secret: as, a *secret* society. *n.* 1. something known only to some and kept from the knowledge of others. 2. something not understood or explained; mystery. 3. the true explanation, regarded as not obvious: as, the *secret* of success. —**in secret,** without the knowledge of others; secretly. —**se′cret·ly,** *adv.* —**se′cret·ness,** *n.*
**secret agent,** one who carries on espionage or work of a highly secret nature, as for a government.
**sec·re·tar·i·at, sec·re·tar·i·ate** (sek′rə-târ′i-it), *n.* 1. the office or position of a secretary. 2. the place where a secretary does his work. 3. a staff headed by a secretary. 4. a staff of secretaries.
**sec·re·tar·y** (sek′rə-ter′i), *n.* [*pl.* -IES], [< ML. *secretarius,* one entrusted with secrets < L. *secretum,* secret], 1. one employed to keep records, handle correspondence, etc. for an organization or individual. 2. an official in over-all charge of such work. 3. an official in charge of a department of government. 4. a writing desk, especially one topped with a small bookcase. —**sec′re·tar′i·al** (-târ′i-əl), *adj.* —**sec′re·tar′y·ship′,** *n.*
**secretary bird,** [so named because its crest resembles pens stuck over the ear], a large African bird of prey with long legs and a long neck.
**sec·re·tar·y-gen·er·al** (sek′rə-ter′i-jen′ẽr-əl), *n.* [*pl.* SECRETARIES-GENERAL], head of a secretariat.
**se·crete** (si-krēt′), *v.t.* [-CRETED, -CRETING], [< L. *secretus,* pp.; see SECRET], 1. to hide; conceal. 2. in *biology,* to separate (a substance) from the blood or sap and elaborate as a new substance to be used or excreted. —**se·cre′tor** (-krē′tẽr), *n.*
**se·cre·tion** (si-krē′shən), *n.* 1. a secreting; specif., *a*) a hiding or concealing. *b*) the separation and elaboration of a substance from the blood or sap. 2. a substance so secreted by an animal or plant. —**se·cre′tion·ar′y, se·cre′tion·al,** *adj.*
**se·cre·tive** (si-krē′tiv; *for 1, often* sē′krə-), *adj.* 1. reticent; not frank or open. 2. secretory. —**se·cre′tive·ly,** *adv.* —**se·cre′tive·ness,** *n.*
**se·cre·to·ry** (si-krē′tə-ri), *adj.* of, or having the function of, secretion. *n.* a secretory gland, etc.
**secret service,** 1. a government service that carries on secret investigations, etc. 2. [S- S-], a division of the U.S. Treasury Department for uncovering counterfeiters, guarding the President, etc. 3. espionage service, as conducted by the armed forces. —**se′cret-serv′ice,** *adj.*
**sect** (sekt), *n.* [< Fr. < L. < *sequi,* to follow], 1. a group of people having a common leadership, philosophy, etc.; school; party. 2. a religious denomination, especially one that has broken away from an established church.
**sec·tar·i·an** (sek-târ′i-ən), *adj.* 1. of or characteristic of a sect. 2. devoted to some sect. 3. narrow-minded. *n.* 1. a member of a sect. 2. one who is blindly devoted to a sect. —**sec·tar′i·an·ism,** *n.*
**sec·ta·ry** (sek′tə-ri), *n.* [*pl.* -RIES], 1. a sectarian. 2. [often S-], a dissenter from an established church; esp., a Protestant nonconformist.
**sec·tion** (sek′shən), *n.* [Fr. < L. < pp. of *secare,* to cut], 1. a cutting or separating by cutting. 2. a part separated by cutting; slice; portion. 3. a division of something written. 4. any distinct or separate part: as, a bookcase in *sections.* 5. a division of public lands (640 acres). 6. a drawing, etc. of something as it would appear if cut straight through in a given plane. 7. in *railroading, a*) part of a sleeping car containing an upper and lower berth. *b*) a division of the right of way maintained by a single crew. *v.t.* 1. to divide into sections. 2. to represent in sections.
**sec·tion·al** (sek′shən-'l), *adj.* 1. of or characteristic of a given section or district. 2. made up of sections. —**sec′tion·al·ly,** *adv.*
**sec·tion·al·ism** (sek′shən-'l-iz'm), *n.* undue concern for the interests of a particular section of the country; sectional bias. —**sec′tion·al·ist,** *n.*
**sec·tor** (sek′tẽr), *n.* [LL.; L., cutter < *secare,* to cut], 1. part of a circle bounded by any two radii and the included arc. 2. a mathematical instrument, as for measuring angles, consisting of two scaled rulers jointed together at one end. 3. any of the districts into which an area is divided for military operations. *v.t.* to divide into sectors. —**sec·to′ri·al** (-tôr′i-əl, -tō′ri-), *adj.*
**sec·u·lar** (sek′yoo-lẽr), *adj.* [< OFr. < LL. < L. *saeculum,* age, generation], 1. not sacred or religious; not connected with a church; temporal: as, *secular* schools. 2. living in the outside world; not bound by a monastic vow: as, the *secular* clergy. *n.* a secular clergyman. —**sec′u·lar·ly,** *adv.*
**sec·u·lar·ism** (sek′yoo-lẽr-iz'm), *n.* 1. secular spirit, views, etc.; esp., rejection of any form of religious faith. 2. the belief that religion should not enter into public education or other state functions. —**sec′u·lar·ist,** *n.* —**sec′u·lar·is′tic,** *adj.*
**sec·u·lar·ize** (sek′yoo-lə-rīz′), *v.t.* [-IZED, -IZING], 1. to convert from religious to civil ownership or use. 2. to remove any religious character, influence, etc. from. —**sec′u·lar·i·za′tion,** *n.* —**sec′u·lar·iz′er,** *n.*
**se·cure** (si-kyoor′), *adj.* [< L. < *se-,* free from + *cura,* care], 1. free from fear, care, or doubt; not worried, troubled, etc. 2. free from danger; safe. 3. in safekeeping. 4. firm; stable: as, make the knot *secure.* 5. sure; certain; to be relied upon. *v.t.* [-CURED, -CURING], 1. to make secure, or safe; protect. 2. to make sure or certain; guarantee, as with a pledge: as, to *secure* a loan. 3. to make firm, fast, etc.: as, *secure* the catch on the window. 4. to obtain; acquire: as, to *secure* a book. *v.i.* to be or become secure; have or give security. —**se·cur′a·ble,** *adj.* —**se·cure′ly,** *adv.* —**se·cure′ness,** *n.* —**se·cur′er,** *n.*
**se·cu·ri·ty** (si-kyoor′ə-ti), *n.* [*pl.* -TIES], 1. the state or feeling of being free from fear, care, danger, etc. 2. freedom from doubt; certainty. 3. protection; safeguard. 4. something given as a pledge of repayment, etc.; guarantee. 5. one who agrees to make good the failure of another to pay, etc. 6. *pl.* bonds, stocks, debentures, etc.
**Security Council,** the organ of the UN responsible for maintaining international peace and security.
**secy., sec'y.,** secretary.
**se·dan** (si-dan′), *n.* [prob. < L. *sedere,* to sit], 1. a type of closed automobile with two or four doors, and front and rear seats. 2. a sedan chair.
**sedan chair,** an enclosed chair for one person, carried on poles by two men.
**se·date** (si-dāt′), *adj.* [< L. pp. of *sedare,* to settle], 1. calm; composed. 2. serious; sober; dignified. —**se·date′ly,** *adv.* —**se·date′ness,** *n.*
**se·da·tion** (si-dā′shən), *n.* in *medicine,* the act or process of reducing excitement, irritation, or pain, especially by means of a sedative.
**sed·a·tive** (sed′ə-tiv), *adj.* [see SEDATE], tending to soothe or quiet; specif., in *medicine,* having the property of lessening excitement, irritation, or pain. *n.* a sedative medicine or treatment.
**sed·en·tar·y** (sed′'n-ter′i), *adj.* [< Fr. < L. < ppr. of *sedere,* to sit], 1. characterized by sitting: as, a *sedentary* task. 2. accustomed to sit much of the time. 3. not migratory, as some birds. 4. in *zoology,* fixed to one spot, as a barnacle. —**sed′en·tar′i·ly,** *adv.* —**sed′en·tar′i·ness,** *n.*
**Se·der** (sā′dẽr), *n.* [Heb. *sedher,* arrangement], in *Judaism,* the Passover feast commemorating the exodus of the Jews from Egypt.
**sedge** (sej), *n.* [AS. *secg*], any of several coarse, grasslike plants usually growing in clumps in wet ground. —**sedg′y** [-IER, -IEST], *adj.*
**sed·i·ment** (sed′ə-mənt), *n.* [< Fr. < L. < *sedere,* to sit], 1. any matter that settles to the bottom of a liquid. 2. in *geology,* any matter deposited by water or wind. —**sed′i·men·ta′tion** (-men-tā′shən), *n.*
**sed·i·men·ta·ry** (sed′ə-men′tẽr-i), *adj.* 1. of, having the nature of, or containing sediment. 2. formed by the deposit of sediment, as rocks. Also **sed′i·men′tal.** —**sed′i·men′ta·ri·ly,** *adv.*
**se·di·tion** (si-dish′ən), *n.* [OFr. < L. < *sed-,* apart + *itio,* a going], a stirring up of rebellion against the government. —**se·di′tion·ist,** *n.*
**se·di·tious** (si-dish′əs), *adj.* 1. of or constituting sedition. 2. stirring up rebellion. —**se·di′tious·ly,** *adv.* —**se·di′tious·ness,** *n.*
**se·duce** (si-dōōs′, -dūs′), *v.t.* [-DUCED, -DUCING], [< L. < *se-,* apart + *ducere,* to lead], 1. to persuade to do something disloyal, disobedient, etc. 2. to tempt to evil or wrongdoing; lead astray. 3. to induce to give up one's chastity. —**se·duc′er,** *n.* —**se·duc′i·ble,** *adj.* —**se·duc′ing·ly,** *adv.*
**se·duc·tion** (si-duk′shən), *n.* 1. a seducing or being seduced. 2. something that seduces. Also **se·duce′ment** (-dōōs′mənt, -dūs′-).

**se·duc·tive** (si-duk′tiv), *adj.* tending to seduce, or lead astray; tempting; enticing. —**se·duc′tive·ly,** *adv.* —**se·duc′tive·ness,** *n.*
**sed·u·lous** (sej′oo-ləs), *adj.* [L. *sedulus*], working hard and steadily; diligent. —**se·du·li·ty** (si-dū′lə-ti, -dōō′-), **sed′u·lous·ness,** *n.* —**sed′u·lous·ly,** *adv.*
**se·dum** (sē′dəm), *n.* [L.], any of a large group of mainly perennial herbs with fleshy stalks and leaves, and white, yellow, or pink flowers.
**see** (sē), *v.t.* [SAW, SEEN, SEEING], [AS. *seon*], 1. to get knowledge of through the eyes; look at; view. 2. to perceive mentally; understand: as, I *see* your point. 3. to learn; find out: as, *see* who's there. 4. to experience; witness: as, I've *seen* better days. 5. to inspect; examine: as, did you *see* the report? 6. to take care; make sure: as, *see* that he goes. 7. to escort: as, *see* her to the door. 8. to encounter; meet: as, have you *seen* him recently? 9. to call on; consult: as, *see* a lawyer. 10. to receive: as, he is too ill to *see* you. 11. to be a spectator at; attend (a show, etc.). 12. in *card games*, to meet (a bet) of (another) by staking an equal sum. *v.i.* 1. to have the power of sight. 2. to discern objects, etc. by using the eyes: as, I can't *see* that far. 3. to understand. 4. to look in order to find out something. 5. to think: as, let me *see*, where did I put it? *in′erj.* behold! look! —**see about,** 1. to investigate. 2. to attend to. —**see after,** to take care of. —**see off,** to escort (a traveler) to the train, ship, etc. —**see through,** 1. to understand the true meaning or nature of: also **see into.** 2. to carry out to the end. 3. to help out through a time of difficulty. —**see to,** to attend to. —**see′a·ble,** *adj.*
**see** (sē), *n.* [< OFr. *sie* < L. *sedes*, a seat], 1. the official seat, or center of authority, of a bishop. 2. the authority or jurisdiction of a bishop.
**seed** (sēd), *n.* [*pl.* SEEDS, SEED], [AS. *sæd*], 1. the part of a flowering plant that contains the embryo and will develop into a new plant if sown. 2. any part from which a new plant will grow. 3. seeds collectively. 4. the source or origin of anything. 5. family stock; ancestry. 6. descendants; posterity. 7. sperm; semen. *v.t.* 1. to plant with seed. 2. to remove the seeds from. 3. to sprinkle particles of dry ice, silver iodide, etc. into (clouds) in an attempt to induce rainfall. 4. in *sports*, to distribute the names of (contestants in a tournament) so that the best players are not matched together in the early rounds. *v.i.* 1. to become ripe and produce seed. 2. to shed seeds. 3. to sow seed. —**go to seed,** 1. to shed seeds after flowering. 2. to deteriorate; weaken, wane, etc. —**seed′er,** *n.* —**seed′less,** *adj.* —**seed′like′,** *adj.*
**seed·bed** (sēd′bed′), *n.* a bed of soil in which small plants are grown from seed for transplanting.
**seed bud,** a plant bud that develops into a seed.
**seed·case** (sēd′kās′), *n.* a seed vessel.
**seed coat,** the skin or coating of a seed.
**seed leaf,** a cotyledon.
**seed·ling** (sēd′liŋ), *n.* 1. a plant grown from a seed, rather than from a cutting, bud graft, etc. 2. a young tree less than three feet high.
**seed oysters,** very young oysters, especially at the stage suitable for transplanting.
**seed pearl,** a very small pearl, often imperfect.
**seed plant,** any seed-bearing plant.
**seed vessel,** any dry, hollow fruit, as a pod, containing seeds; pericarp.
**seed·y** (sēd′i), *adj.* [-IER, -IEST], 1. containing much seed: as, a *seedy* orange. 2. gone to seed. 3. shabby, unkempt, etc. 4. [Colloq.], feeling or looking physically bad or low in spirits. —**seed′i·ly,** *adv.* —**seed′i·ness,** *n.*
**see·ing** (sē′iŋ), *n.* 1. the sense of sight; vision. 2. the use of the eyes to see. *adj.* having the sense of sight. *conj.* in view of the fact; considering.
**Seeing Eye,** an institution near Morristown, New Jersey, which breeds and trains dogs (**Seeing Eye dogs**) as guides for blind people.
**seek** (sēk), *v.t.* [SOUGHT, SEEKING], [AS. *secan*], 1. to try to find; search for. 2. to go to; resort to: as, he *sought* the woods for peace. 3. to search; explore. 4. to ask or inquire for; try to discover. 5. to try to get; aim at. 6. to try; attempt: as, he *sought* to appease his enemies. *v.i.* to make a search or investigation. —**seek′er,** *n.*
**seem** (sēm), *v.i.* [prob. < ON. *sæma*, to conform to], 1. to appear to be; appear: as, he *seems* glad to see us. 2. to appear to one's own mind: as, I *seem* to hear voices. 3. to appear to exist: as, there *seems* no point in going. 4. to be apparently true: as, it *seems* he was not there.
**seem·ing** (sēm′iŋ), *adj.* apparent; not actual. *n.* outward appearance; esp., deceptive appearance. —**seem′ing·ly,** *adv.* —**seem′ing·ness,** *n.*
**seem·ly** (sēm′li), *adj.* [-LIER, -LIEST], [< ON. < *sæmr*, fitting], 1. [Archaic or Dial.], fair; handsome. 2. suitable; proper; becoming. *adv.* in a seemly manner; properly. —**seem′li·ness,** *n.*
**seen** (sēn), pp. of **see.**
**seep** (sēp), *v.i.* [< AS. *sipian*, to soak], to leak through small openings; ooze. —**seep′y,** *adj.*
**seep·age** (sēp′ij), *n.* 1. the act or process of seeping; leakage; oozing. 2. liquid that seeps.
**seer** (*for 1*, sē′ēr; *for 2*, sêr), *n.* 1. one who sees. 2. one who foretells the future; prophet.
**seer·ess** (sêr′is), *n.* a woman seer; prophetess.
**seer·suck·er** (sêr′suk′ēr), *n.* [< Hind. < Per. *shir u shakar*, lit., milk and sugar], a light, crinkled fabric of linen or cotton, usually striped.
**see·saw** (sē′sô′), *n.* [redupl. of *saw*], 1. a plank balanced at the middle, used by children at play, who ride the ends, causing them to rise and fall alternately. 2. this play. 3. any back-and-forth or up-and-down motion, tendency, etc. *adj.* moving back and forth or up and down. *v.t. & v.i.* to move in such a way.
**seethe** (sēth), *v.t.* [SEETHED, SEETHING], [AS. *sēothan*], 1. to cook by boiling. 2. to soak, steep, or saturate in liquid. *v.i.* 1. to boil. 2. to surge or bubble, as boiling liquid. 3. to be violently agitated. —**seeth′ing·ly,** *adv.*
**seg·ment** (seg′mənt), *n.* [L. *segmentum* < *secare*, to cut], 1. any of the parts into which something is separated; section. 2. in *geometry*, a section, as of a circle or sphere, cut off by a line or plane. *v.t. & v.i.* to divide into segments. —**seg·men′tal** (-men′t'l), **seg′men·tar′y,** *adj.* —**seg·men′tal·ly,** *adv.*
**seg·men·ta·tion** (seg′mən-tā′shən), *n.* 1. a dividing or being divided into segments. 2. in *biology*, the progressive growth and cleavage of a single cell into others to form a new organism.
**se·go** (sē′gō), *n.* [< Am. Ind.], a perennial bulb plant with trumpet-shaped flowers, found in the western U.S.: also **sego lily.**
**seg·re·gate** (seg′ri-gāt′; *for adj., usually* -git), *adj.* [< L. pp. of *segregare* < *se-*, apart + *grex*, a flock], separate; set apart. *v.t.* [-GATED, -GATING], to set apart from others; isolate; specif., to compel (racial groups) to live, go to school, etc. apart from each other. *v.i.* to separate from the main mass and collect together in a new body: said of crystals. —**seg′re·ga′tion,** *n.* —**seg′re·gat′ive,** *adj.* —**seg′re·ga′tor,** *n.*
**seg·re·gat·ed** (seg′ri-gāt′id), *adj.* conforming to a system that segregates racial groups.
**sei·del** (zī′d'l, sī′-), *n.* [*pl.* SEIDEL], [G.], [often S-], a large beer mug, sometimes with a hinged lid.
**Seid·litz powder(s)** (sed′lits), [after *Seidlitz*, a village in Czechoslovakia], a laxative composed of two powders separately dissolved in water, combined, and drunk while effervescing.
**sei·gneur** (sān′yēr; Fr. sān′yër′), *n.* [Fr. < L. *senior;* see SENIOR], a feudal lord; seignior.
**seign·ior** (sēn′yēr), *n.* [< Anglo-Fr. < OFr. < L. *senior;* see SENIOR], 1. originally, the lord of a manor. 2. a lord; gentleman. 3. a title of respect corresponding to *Sir.* —**sei·gno′ri·al** (-yôr′i-əl, -yō′ri-), **seign′ior·al** (-yēr-əl), *adj.*
**seign·ior·y** (sēn′yēr-i), *n.* [*pl.* -IES], the dominion, rights, or authority of a seignior, or feudal lord.
**Seine** (sān; Fr. sen), *n.* a river in N France, flowing through Paris into the English Channel.
**seine** (sān), *n.* [AS. *segne* < L. < Gr. *sagēnē*], a large fishing net having floats along the top edge and weights along the bottom. *v.t. & v.i.* [SEINED, SEINING], to catch or fish with a seine.
**seis·mic** (sīz′mik, sīs′-), *adj.* [< Gr. *seismos*, an earthquake < *seiein*, to shake], 1. of or relating to an earthquake or earthquakes. 2. caused by an earthquake. Also **seis′mal** (-məl), **seis′mi·cal.**
**seis·mo-,** [< Gr. *seismos;* see SEISMIC], a combining form meaning *earthquake*, as in *seismogram.*
**seis·mo·gram** (sīz′mə-gram′, sīs′-), *n.* the chart of an earthquake as recorded on a seismograph.
**seis·mo·graph** (sīz′mə-graf′, sīs′mə-gräf′), *n.* [*seismo-* + *-graph*], an instrument that records the direction, intensity, and time of earthquakes. —**seis·mog′ra·pher** (-mog′rə-fēr), *n.* —**seis′mo·graph′ic,** *adj.* —**seis·mog′ra·phy,** *n.*
**seis·mol·o·gy** (sīz-mol′ə-ji, sīs-), *n.* [*seismo-* + *-logy*], the study of earthquakes and related matters. —**seis′mo·log′i·cal** (-mə-loj′i-k'l), **seis′mo-**

log'ic, *adj.* —seis'mo·log'i·cal·ly, *adv.* —seis·mol'o·gist, *n.*

**seize** (sēz), *v.t.* [SEIZED, SEIZING], [< OFr. < LL. *sacire*], 1. to take legal possession of. 2. to take possession of suddenly and by force. 3. to attack; strike: as, *seized* with paralysis. 4. to capture; take prisoner; arrest. 5. to grasp suddenly with the hand. 6. to grasp with the mind; understand. 7. to take advantage of (an opportunity, etc.) quickly. 8. in *nautical usage*, to fasten together (ropes, etc.); bind; lash. —**seize on** (or **upon**), 1. to take hold of suddenly; grasp. 2. to take possession of. —**seiz'a·ble,** *adj.* —**seiz'er,** *n.*

**sei·zure** (sē'zhẽr), *n.* 1. a seizing or being seized. 2. a sudden attack, as of a disease.

**sel.,** 1. selected. 2. selection. 3. selections.

**se·lah** (sē'lə), *n.* a Hebrew word found frequently in the Psalms, interpreted as an indication of a musical pause.

**sel·dom** (sel'dəm), *adv.* [AS. *seldum*], rarely; infrequently; not often. —**sel'dom·ness,** *n.*

**se·lect** (sə-lekt'), *adj.* [< L. *selectus*, pp. < *se-*, apart + *legere*, to choose], 1. chosen in preference to others; specially picked. 2. choice; excellent. 3. careful in choosing; fastidious. 4. exclusive: as, a *select* company of critics. *v.t.* to choose from among others, as for excellence, etc. *v.i.* to make a selection; choose. —**se·lect'ly,** *adv.* —**se·lect'ness,** *n.* —**se·lec'tor,** *n.*

**se·lect·ee** (sə-lek'tē'), *n.* a person inducted into the armed forces under selective service.

**se·lec·tion** (sə-lek'shən), *n.* 1. a selecting or being selected. 2. that or those selected. 3. in *biology*, natural selection: see **natural selection.**

**se·lec·tive** (sə-lek'tiv), *adj.* 1. of, having to do with, or characterized by selection. 2. having the power of selecting. 3. in *radio*, excluding oscillations on all frequencies except the one desired. —**se·lec'tive·ly,** *adv.* —**se·lec'tive·ness,** *n.*

**selective service,** compulsory military training and service according to age, physical fitness, etc.

**se·lec·tiv·i·ty** (sə-lek'tiv'ə-ti), *n.* 1. the state or quality of being selective. 2. the degree to which a radio receiver is selective.

**se·lect·man** (sə-lekt'mən), *n.* [*pl.* -MEN], one of a board of officers chosen annually in New England towns to manage municipal affairs.

**Se·le·ne** (si-lē'nē), *n.* the Greek goddess of the moon.

**sel·e·nite** (sel'ə-nīt', si-lē'nīt), *n.* [< L. < Gr. *selēnitēs* (*lithos*), lit., moon (stone) < *selēnē*, the moon: it was thought to wax and wane with the moon], a kind of gypsum found in crystallized or foliated form.

**se·le·ni·um** (si-lē'ni-əm), *n.* [< Gr. *selēnē*, the moon], a chemical element of the sulfur group: it is used in photoelectric devices because its electrical conductivity varies with the intensity of light: symbol, Se; at. wt., 78.96; at. no., 34.

**self** (self), *n.* [*pl.* SELVES], [AS. *se(o)lf*], 1. the identity, character, etc. of any person or thing. 2. one's own identity, personality, etc. 3. one's own welfare or interest; selfishness. *pron.* [Colloq.], myself, himself, herself, yourself: as, tickets for *self* and wife. *adj.* 1. being uniform throughout. 2. of the same kind, material, color, etc. as the rest: as, a *self* lining.

**self-,** a prefix used in hyphenated compounds, meaning: 1. *of oneself* or *itself*, as in *self-appraisal*. 2. *by oneself* or *itself*, as in *self-starting*. 3. *in oneself* or *itself*, as in *self-centered*. 4. *to* or *with oneself* or *itself*, as in *self-addressed*.

**self-a·base·ment** (self'ə-bās'mənt), *n.* abasement or humiliation of oneself.

**self-ab·ne·ga·tion** (self'ab-ni-gā'shən), *n.* lack of consideration for oneself; self-denial.

**self-ab·sorp·tion** (self'əb-sôrp'shən, -zôrp'-), *n.* absorption in one's own interests, affairs, etc.

**self-a·buse** (self'ə-būs'), *n.* 1. misuse of one's own talents, etc. 2. masturbation: a euphemism.

**self-act·ing** (self'ak'tiŋ), *adj.* acting without outside influence or stimulus; automatic. —**self'-ac'tive,** *adj.* —**self'-ac'tor,** *n.*

**self-ad·dressed** (self'ə-drest'), *adj.* addressed to oneself: as, enclose a *self-addressed* envelope.

**self-ap·point·ed** (self'ə-poin'tid), *adj.* appointed or chosen by oneself and not by others.

**self-as·ser·tion** (self'ə-sũr'shən), *n.* the act of demanding recognition for oneself or of insisting upon one's rights, etc. —**self'-as·ser'tive,** *adj.*

**self-as·sur·ance** (self'ə-shoor'əns), *n.* confidence in oneself. —**self'-as·sured',** *adj.*

**self-cen·tered** (self'sen'tẽrd), *adj.* 1. being a center about which other things move. 2. concerned only with one's own affairs; selfish. Also, esp. Brit., **self'-cen'tred.** —**self'-cen'tered·ly, self'-cen'tred·ly,** *adv.* —**self'-cen'tered·ness, self'-cen'tred·ness,** *n.*

**self-col·ored** (self'kul'ẽrd), *adj.* 1. having only one color. 2. having the natural color, as a fabric.

**self-com·mand** (self'kə-mand', -mänd'), *n.* self-control.

**self-com·pla·cent** (self'kəm-plā's'nt), *adj.* self-satisfied; pleased with oneself. —**self'-com·pla'cence, self'-com·pla'cen·cy,** *n.* —**self'-com·pla'cent·ly,** *adv.*

**self-con·ceit** (self'kən-sēt'), *n.* too high an opinion of oneself; conceit. —**self'-con·ceit'ed,** *adj.*

**self-con·fi·dent** (self'kon'fə-dənt), *adj.* confident of one's own ability; sure of oneself. —**self'-con'fi·dence,** *n.* —**self'-con'fi·dent·ly,** *adv.*

**self-con·scious** (self'kon'shəs), *adj.* 1. unduly conscious of oneself as an object of notice; ill-at-ease; shy. 2. showing embarrassment, etc.: as, a *self-conscious* cough. —**self'-con'scious·ly,** *adv.* —**self'-con'scious·ness,** *n.*

**self-con·sist·ent** (self'kən-sis'tənt), *adj.* consistent with oneself or itself. —**self'-con·sist'en·cy,** *n.* —**self'-con·sist'ent·ly,** *adv.*

**self-con·tained** (self'kən-tānd'), *adj.* 1. keeping one's affairs to oneself; reserved. 2. showing self-control. 3. having all working parts in an enclosed unit: said of machinery. 4. having within oneself or itself all that is necessary; self-sufficient, as a community. —**self'-con·tain'ment,** *n.*

**self-con·tent** (self'kən-tent'), *adj.* content with what one has or is. *n.* self-satisfaction: also **self'-con·tent'ment.**

**self-con·tra·dic·tion** (self'kon'trə-dik'shən), *n.* 1. contradiction of oneself or itself. 2. any statement containing elements that contradict each other. —**self'-con'tra·dic'to·ry,** *adj.*

**self-con·trol** (self'kən-trōl'), *n.* control of one's emotions, desires, etc. —**self'-con·trolled',** *adj.*

**self-de·ceit** (self'di-sēt'), *n.* a deceiving of oneself or being deceived by oneself: also **self'-de·cep'tion** (-sep'shən). —**self'-de·cep'tive,** *adj.*

**self-de·fense** (self'di-fens'), *n.* 1. defense of oneself or of one's property, security, rights, etc. 2. the art of boxing: usually in *manly art of self-defense*. —**self'-de·fen'sive,** *adj.*

**self-de·ni·al** (self'di-nī'əl), *n.* denial or sacrifice of one's own desires or pleasures. —**self'-de·ny'ing,** *adj.* —**self'-de·ny'ing·ly,** *adv.*

**self-de·struc·tion** (self'di-struk'shən), *n.* destruction of oneself or itself; specif., suicide.

**self-de·ter·mi·na·tion** (self'di-tũr'mə-nā'shən), *n.* 1. determination according to one's own mind, without outside influence; free will. 2. the right of a people to decide upon its own form of government, without outside influence. —**self'-de·ter'mined,** *adj.* —**self'-de·ter'min·ing,** *adj.*

**self-de·vo·tion** (self'di-vō'shən), *n.* devotion of oneself to the interests of others; self-sacrifice.

**self-dis·ci·pline** (self'dis'ə-plin), *n.* control and training of oneself for the sake of development.

**self-ed·u·cat·ed** (self'ej'oo-kāt'id), *adj.* educated or trained by oneself, with little or no formal schooling. —**self'-ed'u·ca'tion,** *n.*

**self-ef·face·ment** (self'i-fās'mənt), *n.* modest, retiring behavior. —**self'-ef·fac'ing,** *adj.*

**self-es·teem** (self'ə-stēm'), *n.* 1. belief in oneself; self-respect. 2. undue pride in oneself; conceit.

**self-ev·i·dent** (self'ev'i-dənt), *adj.* evident without explanation or proof. —**self'-ev'i·dent·ly,** *adv.*

**self-ex·am·i·na·tion** (self'ig-zam'ə-nā'shən), *n.* examination of one's own qualities, thoughts, conduct, etc.; introspection.

**self-ex·ist·ent** (self'ig-zis'tənt), *adj.* having independent existence; existing of or by itself without external cause. —**self'-ex·ist'ence,** *n.*

**self-ex·plan·a·to·ry** (self'ik-splan'ə-tôr'i, -tō'ri), *adj.* explaining itself; obvious: also **self'-ex·plain'ing.**

**self-ex·pres·sion** (self'ik-spresh'ən), *n.* the expression of one's own personality, as through art.

**self-fer·til·i·za·tion** (self'fũr't'l-i-zā'shən), *n.* fertilization by its own pollen or sperm cells.

**self-gov·ern·ment** (self'guv'ẽr-mənt), *n.* 1. [Rare], self-control. 2. government of a group by the action of its own members, as in electing representatives, etc. —**self'-gov'ern·ing** (-ẽrn-iŋ), *adj.*

**self·heal** (self'hēl'), *n.* a plant with purple or blue flowers, supposed to have healing properties.

**self-help** (self'help'), *n.* a helping or improving oneself, as through study.

**self-im·por·tance** (self'im-pôr't'ns), *n.* an exaggerated opinion of one's own importance; officious conceit. —**self'-im·por'tant,** *adj.*

**self-im·posed** (self'im-pōzd'), *adj.* imposed or inflicted on oneself by oneself, as a penalty.

**self-im·prove·ment** (self'im-prōōv'mənt), *n.* improvement of one's condition, mind, etc. through one's own efforts. —**self'-im·prov'ing,** *adj.*
**self-in·duced** (self'in-dōōst', -dūst'), *adj.* 1. induced by oneself or itself. 2. produced by self-induction.
**self-in·duc·tion** (self'in-duk'shən), *n.* the induction of an electric current in a circuit by the variation of current in that circuit.
**self-in·dul·gence** (self'in-dul'jəns), *n.* indulgence of one's own desires, impulses, etc. —**self'-in·dul'gent,** *adj.* —**self'-in·dul'gent·ly,** *adv.*
**self-in·flict·ed** (self'in-flik'tid), *adj.* inflicted on oneself by oneself, as an injury.
**self-in·ter·est** (self'in'tēr-ist, -trist), *n.* 1. one's own interest or advantage. 2. an exaggerated regard for this, usually at the expense of others; selfishness. —**self'-in'ter·est·ed,** *adj.*
**self·ish** (sel'fish), *adj.* 1. having such regard for one's own interests and advantage that the welfare of others becomes of less concern than is considered just. 2. showing or caused by such regard. —**self'ish·ly,** *adv.* —**self'ish·ness,** *n.*
**self-knowl·edge** (self'nol'ij), *n.* knowledge of one's own qualities, character, abilities, etc.
**self·less** (self'lis), *adj.* without regard for oneself or one's own interests; unselfish. —**self'less·ly,** *adv.* —**self'less·ness,** *n.*
**self-load·ing** (self'lōd'iŋ), *adj.* loading again by its own action, as a gun.
**self-love** (self'luv'), *n.* love of self; self-conceit or selfishness. —**self'-lov'ing,** *adj.*
**self-made** (self'mād'), *adj.* 1. made by oneself or itself. 2. successful through one's own efforts.
**self-o·pin·ion·at·ed** (self'ə-pin'yən-āt'id), *adj.* 1. stubborn in holding to one's own opinions. 2. conceited.
**self-pit·y** (self'pit'i), *n.* pity for oneself.
**self-pol·li·nat·ed** (self'pol'ə-nāt'id), *adj.* fertilized by its own pollen: said of a flower.
**self-pos·ses·sion** (self'pə-zesh'ən), *n.* the full control of one's faculties or feelings; self-control; composure. —**self'-pos·sessed',** *adj.*
**self-pres·er·va·tion** (self'prez-ēr-vā'shən), *n.* 1. preservation of oneself from injury or death. 2. the instinctive urge to preserve oneself.
**self-pro·nounc·ing** (self'prə-noun'siŋ), *adj.* having marks of pronunciation directly applied to the original spelling instead of being rewritten in phonetic symbols.
**self-pro·pelled** (self'prə-peld'), *adj.* producing its own power of movement: also **self'-pro·pel'ling.**
**self-pro·tec·tion** (self'prə-tek'shən), *n.* self-defense.
**self-re·cord·ing** (self'ri-kôr'diŋ), *adj.* making an automatic record of its own operations.
**self-re·gard** (self'ri-gärd'), *n.* regard or concern for oneself and one's interests.
**self-re·li·ance** (self'ri-lī'əns), *n.* reliance upon one's own judgment, abilities, etc. —**self'-re·li'ant,** *adj.* —**self'-re·li'ant·ly,** *adv.*
**self-re·proach** (self'ri-prōch'), *n.* blame of oneself; guilt feeling. —**self'-re·proach'ful,** *adj.*
**self-re·spect** (self'ri-spekt'), *n.* a proper respect for oneself, one's character, etc. —**self'-re·spect'ing, self'-re·spect'ful,** *adj.*
**self-re·straint** (self'ri-strānt'), *n.* restraint imposed on oneself by oneself; self-control. —**self'-re·strained',** *adj.*
**self-right·eous** (self'rī'chəs), *adj.* 1. righteous, moral, etc. in one's own opinion; pharisaical. 2. characteristic of a self-righteous person. —**self'-right'eous·ly,** *adv.* —**self'-right'eous·ness,** *n.*
**self-ris·ing** (self'rīz'iŋ), *adj.* rising by itself; specif., rising without the aid of a ferment, as certain flour.
**self-sac·ri·fice** (self'sak'rə-fīs'), *n.* the sacrifice of oneself or one's interests, usually for the advantage of others. —**self'-sac'ri·fic'ing,** *adj.*
**self·same** (self'sām'), *adj.* identical; (the) very same. —**self'same'ness,** *n.*
**self-sat·is·fied** (self'sat'is-fīd'), *adj.* feeling or showing satisfaction with oneself or one's accomplishments. —**self'-sat·is·fac'tion,** *n.*
**self-seal·ing** (self'sēl'iŋ), *adj.* made with a substance that automatically seals punctures, etc.
**self-seek·er** (self'sēk'ēr), *n.* one who seeks mainly to further his own interests. —**self'-seek'ing,** *n. & adj.*
**self-serv·ice** (self'sūr'vis), *n.* the practice of serving oneself in a cafeteria, store, etc. *adj.* designating an establishment with such a practice.
**self-sown** (self'sōn'), *adj.* sown by wind, water, or other natural agency, as some weeds.
**self-start·er** (self'stär'tēr), *n.* a device for automatically starting an internal-combustion engine.
**self-styled** (self'stīld'), *adj.* named (as such) by oneself: as, he is a *self-styled* patriot.
**self-suf·fi·cient** (self'sə-fish'ənt), *adj.* 1. able to get along without help; independent. 2. smug; conceited. Also **self'-suf·fic'ing** (-fīs'iŋ). —**self'-suf·fi'cien·cy,** *n.* —**self'-suf·fi'cient·ly,** *adv.*
**self-sup·port** (self'sə-pôrt', -pōrt'), *n.* support of oneself or itself without aid or reinforcement. —**self'-sup·port'ed,** *adj.* —**self'-sup·port'ing,** *adj.*
**self-sus·tain·ing** (self'sə-stān'iŋ), *adj.* supporting or able to support oneself or itself.
**self-taught** (self'tôt'), *adj.* taught through one's own efforts with little or no help from others.
**self-will** (self'wil'), *n.* a persistent carrying out of one's own wishes, especially when in conflict with others; stubbornness. —**self'-willed',** *adj.*
**self-wind·ing** (self'wīn'diŋ), *adj.* wound automatically, as some wrist watches, clocks, etc.
**sell** (sel), *v.t.* [SOLD, SELLING], [AS. *sellan,* to give], 1. to exchange (goods, services, etc.) for money or its equivalent. 2. to have or offer regularly for sale: as, this store *sells* radios. 3. *a*) to deliver (a person) to his enemies or into slavery, etc. *b*) to betray (a country, cause, etc.). 4. to give up (one's honor, etc.) for profit. 5. to promote the sale of: as, radio *sells* many products. 6. [Colloq.], *a*) to establish faith or belief in: as, to *sell* an idea. *b*) to persuade (a person) of the value of (with *on*): as, I'm *sold* on the idea. 7. [Slang], to cheat; dupe; hoax. *v.i.* 1. to engage in selling. 2. to attract buyers: as, will it *sell?* 3. [Colloq.], to be widely approved: as, his plan didn't *sell.* *n.* [Slang], 1. a trick or hoax. 2. salesmanship: usually in *hard sell,* high-pressure salesmanship. —**sell oneself,** 1. to do something, especially something dishonorable, for a price. 2. [Colloq.], to convince another of one's worth. —**sell out,** 1. to get rid of completely by selling. 2. [Colloq.], to sell or betray (someone, one's trust, etc.). —**sell'ing,** *n. & adj.*
**sell·er** (sel'ēr), *n.* 1. one who sells. 2. something with reference to its rate of sale: as, a good *seller.*
**sell·out, sell-out** (sel'out'), *n.* [Colloq.], 1. a selling out. 2. an entertainment for which all the seats or tickets are sold.
**Selt·zer** (selt'sēr), *n.* [< *Nieder Selters,* a town near Wiesbaden, Germany], 1. a spring water of high mineral content and effervescent quality. 2. [often s-], carbonated water. Also **Seltzer water.**
**sel·vage, sel·vedge** (sel'vij), *n.* [< *self* + *edge,* after MD. *selfegge*], a specially woven edge which prevents cloth or fabric from raveling.
**selves** (selvz), *n.* pl. of **self.**
**Sem.,** 1. Seminary. 2. Semitic.
**se·man·tic** (sə-man'tik), *adj.* [Gr. *sēmantikos,* significant < *sēmainein,* to show], 1. of meaning, especially meaning in language. 2. of or according to semantics. —**se·man'ti·cal·ly,** *adv.*
**se·man·tics** (sə-man'tiks), *n.pl.* [construed as sing.], 1. the branch of linguistics concerned with the nature, structure, and, especially, the development and changes, of the meanings of words. 2. the scientific study of the relations between signs, or symbols, and their meanings, and of their influence on human behavior. —**se·man'ti·cist,** *n.*
**sem·a·phore** (sem'ə-fôr', -fōr'), *n.* [< Fr. < Gr. *sēma,* a sign + *pherein,* to bear], 1. any apparatus for signaling, as by an arrangement of lights, flags, and mechanical arms on railroads. 2. any system of signaling with such apparatus. *v.t. & v.i.* [-PHORED, -PHORING], to signal by semaphore. —**sem'a·phor'ic,** *adj.*
**Se·ma·rang** (sə-mä'räŋ), *n.* a city on the N coast of Java: pop., 218,000: also sp. **Sa·ma'rang.**
**se·ma·si·ol·o·gy** (si-mā'si-ol'ə-ji), *n.* [< Gr. *sēmasia,* signification; + *-logy*], in *linguistics,* semantics. —**se·ma'si·o·log'i·cal** (-ə-loj'i-k'l), *adj.*
**sem·blance** (sem'bləns), *n.* [< OFr. < *sembler,* to seem; ult. < L. *similis,* like], 1. outward form or appearance; aspect. 2. resemblance. 3. a likeness, image, or copy. 4. false, assumed, or deceiving appearance. 5. mere empty show; pretense.
**se·men** (sē'mən), *n.* [*pl.* SEMINA (sem'i-nə)], [L., a seed], the fluid secreted by the male reproductive organs, containing the spermatozoa.
**se·mes·ter** (sə-mes'tēr), *n.* [G. < L. *semestris,* half-yearly < *sex,* six + *mensis,* month], either of the

two terms which generally make up a school year. —**se·mes′tral,** *adj.*

**sem·i-,** [L.], a prefix meaning: 1. *half,* as in *semicircle.* 2. *partly, not fully,* as in *semiskilled.* 3. *twice in a* (specified period), as in *semiannual.*

**sem·i·an·nu·al** (sem′i-an′ū-əl), *adj.* 1. happening, coming, etc. every half year. 2. lasting half a year, as some plants. —**sem′i·an′nu·al·ly,** *adv.*

**sem·i·breve** (sem′ə-brēv′), *n.* [It.], in *music,* a whole note ( 𝅝 ), equal to four quarter notes.

**sem·i·cir·cle** (sem′ə-sũr′k'l), *n.* a half circle. —**sem′i·cir′cu·lar** (-kyoo-lẽr), *adj.* —**sem′i·cir′cu·lar·ly,** *adv.*

**semicircular canal,** any of the three loop-shaped, tubular structures of the inner ear that serve to maintain balance in the organism: see **ear,** illus.

**sem·i·civ·i·lized** (sem′ə-siv′'l-īzd′), *adj.* partly civilized. —**sem′i·civ′i·li·za′tion,** *n.*

**sem·i·co·lon** (sem′ə-kō′lən), *n.* a mark of punctuation (;) indicating a degree of separation greater than that marked by the comma and less than that marked by the period, etc.: chiefly used between units containing elements separated by commas.

**sem·i·con·duc·tor** (sem′i-kən-duk′tẽr), *n.* a substance, as germanium, whose conductivity is improved by minute additions of certain other substances or by the application of heat, light, or voltage: used in transistors, rectifiers, etc.

**sem·i·con·scious** (sem′ə-kon′shəs), *adj.* not fully conscious or awake. —**sem′i·con′scious·ly,** *adv.* —**sem′i·con′scious·ness,** *n.*

**sem·i·de·tached** (sem′i-di-tacht′), *adj.* partly detached, as a pair of houses joined with a common wall but not connected with other buildings.

**sem·i·fi·nal** (sem′ə-fī′n'l), *adj.* coming just before the final: said of the divisions of a contest. *n.* a semifinal round, match, etc. —**sem′i·fi′nal·ist,** *n.*

**sem·i·flu·id** (sem′ə-flōō′id), *adj.* neither liquid nor solid; viscous but fluid. *n.* a substance of this nature. —**sem′i·flu·id′i·ty,** *n.*

**sem·i·month·ly** (sem′ə-munth′li), *adj.* coming, happening, etc. twice a month. *n.* something coming, appearing, etc. twice a month, as a magazine. *adv.* twice monthly.

**sem·i·nal** (sem′ə-n'l), *adj.* [< OFr. < L. < *semen,* a seed], 1. of or containing seed or semen. 2. of reproduction. 3. like seed; capable of future development; germinal. —**sem′i·nal·ly,** *adv.*

**sem·i·nar** (sem′ə-när′), *n.* 1. a group of supervised students doing research. 2. *a)* a course for such a group. *b)* the room where it meets.

**sem·i·nar·y** (sem′ə-ner′i), *n.* [*pl.* -IES], [< L. neut. of *seminarius,* of seed < *semen,* a seed], 1. a school, especially a private school for young women. 2. a school for training men to be clergymen.

**sem·i·na·tion** (sem′ə-nā′shən), *n.* [< L. < *seminare,* to sow < *semen,* seed], 1. a spreading or propagation; dissemination. 2. a sowing of seed.

**sem·i·nif·er·ous** (sem′ə-nif′ẽr-əs), *adj.* [< L. *semen,* a seed; + *-ferous*], 1. seed-bearing. 2. containing or conveying semen.

**Sem·i·nole** (sem′ə-nōl′), *n.* [*pl.* -NOLE, -NOLES], a member of a tribe of Muskhogean Indians who settled in Florida. *adj.* of this tribe.

**sem·i·of·fi·cial** (sem′i-ə-fish′'l), *adj.* having some official authority; partly official. —**sem′i·of·fi′cial·ly,** *adv.*

**sem·i·per·me·a·ble** (sem′ə-pũr′mi-ə-b'l), *adj.* permeable to smaller molecules but not to larger ones.

**sem·i·pre·cious** (sem′ə-presh′əs), *adj.* designating gems of lower value than those classified as precious: said of the garnet, turquoise, etc.

**sem·i·pri·vate** (sem′ə-prī′vit), *adj.* not completely private; specif., designating or of a hospital room having two, or sometimes three or four, beds.

**sem·i·pro** (sem′i-prō′), *n.* [< *semiprofessional*], [Colloq.], a person who engages in a sport for pay but not as a regular occupation.

**sem·i·qua·ver** (sem′ə-kwā′vẽr), *n.* in *music,* a sixteenth note ( 𝅘𝅥𝅯 ).

**sem·i·rig·id** (sem′ə-rij′id), *adj.* designating an airship having a rigid internal keel.

**sem·i·skilled** (sem′ə-skild′), *adj.* partly skilled.

**sem·i·sol·id** (sem′ə-sol′id), *adj.* partly solid, as jelly. *n.* a semisolid substance.

**Sem·ite** (sem′īt, sē′mīt), *n.* [< LL. < Gr. < Heb. *shēm;* see SHEM], a member of any of the peoples whose language is Semitic, including the Hebrews, Arabs, Phoenicians, etc.; now, specif., a Jew.

**Se·mit·ic** (sə-mit′ik), *adj.* 1. of, characteristic of, or like the Semites. 2. designating or of a major group of languages of SW Asia and N Africa, including Aramaic, Hebrew, Arabic, etc.

**Sem·i·tism** (sem′ə-tiz'm, sē′mə-), *n.* 1. a Semitic word or idiom. 2. Semitic characteristics; esp., the ideas, qualities, etc. originating with the Jews.

**sem·i·tone** (sem′ə-tōn′), *n.* 1. in *music,* a tone at an interval of a half step from another. 2. such an interval. —**sem′i·ton′ic** (-ton′ik), *adj.*

**sem·i·trop·i·cal** (sem′ə-trop′i-k'l), *adj.* having some of the characteristics of the tropics.

**sem·i·vow·el** (sem′ə-vou′əl), *n.* a vowel used as a consonant: *w* and *y* are phonetically vowels (ōō, ē) used as consonants, as in *wall, yoke.*

**sem·i·week·ly** (sem′ə-wēk′li), *adj.* coming, happening, done, etc. twice a week. *n.* something that comes, happens, etc. twice weekly, as a newspaper published twice a week. *adv.* twice weekly.

**sem·i·year·ly** (sem′ə-yêr′li), *adj.* coming, happening, etc. twice a year. *n.* something that comes, happens, etc. twice yearly. *adv.* twice yearly.

**sem·o·li·na** (sem′ə-lē′nə), *n.* [< It. dim. of *semola,* bran], meal consisting of the hard kernels of wheat, a by-product in the manufacture of flour: used in making macaroni, puddings, etc.

‡**sem·per fi·de·lis** (sem′pẽr fi-dē′lis, -dā′-), [L.], always faithful: the motto of the U.S. Marine Corps.

‡**semper par·a·tus** (pə-rā′təs), [L.], always prepared: the motto of the U.S. Coast Guard.

**sem·pi·ter·nal** (sem′pi-tũr′n'l), *adj.* [< OFr. < L. < *semper,* always + *eternus,* eternal], everlasting; perpetual; eternal. —**sem′pi·ter′ni·ty,** *n.*

**sen** (sen), *n.* [*pl.* SEN], [Japan. < Chin. *ch'ien,* coin], a Japanese coin equal to 1/100 of a yen.

**Sen., sen.,** 1. Senate. 2. Senator. 3. senior.

**sen·ate** (sen′it), *n.* [< OFr. < L. *senatus* < *senex,* old], 1. the supreme council of the ancient Roman state. 2. a lawmaking assembly. 3. [S-], a legislative group, usually the smaller (and called the *upper*) of the two houses forming certain national and State legislatures. 4. a governing body of some colleges.

**sen·a·tor** (sen′ə-tẽr), *n.* a member of a senate. —**sen′a·to′ri·al** (-tôr′i-əl, -tō′ri-), *adj.* —**sen′a·to′ri·al·ly,** *adv.* —**sen′a·tor·ship′,** *n.*

**send** (send), *v.t.* [SENT, SENDING], [AS. *sendan*], 1. *a)* to cause to go; transmit: as, food was *sent* by plane. *b)* to dispatch (a letter, etc.) by mail or messenger. 2. to cause (a person) to go: as, *send* the man to me, his father *sent* him to college. 3. to cause to move, as by releasing, throwing, etc.: as, he *sent* the ball over the trees. 4. to drive into some state or condition: as, to *send* one out of his mind. 5. to cause to happen, come, etc.: as, a crop *sent* to reward our toil. 6. [Slang], to play jazz music in such a way as to excite (the listener). *v.i.* to send a message or messenger. —**send for,** 1. to summon. 2. to place an order for. —**send forth,** to cause to appear; produce; emit. —**send off,** 1. to mail or dispatch, as a letter. 2. to dismiss. —**send packing,** to dismiss abruptly. —**send up,** [Colloq.], to sentence to imprisonment. —**send′er,** *n.*

**send-off** (send′ôf′), *n.* [Colloq.], 1. a demonstration of friendly feeling toward someone starting out on a trip, career, etc. 2. a start given to something.

**Sen·e·ca** (sen′i-kə), *n.* a member of a tribe of Iroquoian Indians who lived in W New York.

**Sen·e·gal, Sé·né·gal** (sen′i-gôl′; Fr. sā′nā′gàl′), *n.* 1. a country in W Africa, on the Atlantic: a member of the French Community: area, 76,124 sq. mi.; pop., 3,280,000; capital, Dakar. 2. river in W Africa, flowing into the Atlantic. —**Sen′e·gal·ese′** (-i-gô-lēz′, -gə-lēz′), *adj. & n. sing. & pl.*

**se·nes·cent** (sə-nes′'nt), *adj.* [< L. ppr. of *senescere,* to grow old], growing old. —**se·nes′cence,** *n.*

**sen·es·chal** (sen′ə-shəl), *n.* [< OFr. < OHG. *siniskalk,* oldest servant], an official in the household of a medieval noble, who administered justice and managed the estate. —**sen′es·chal·ship′,** *n.*

**se·nile** (sē′nīl, -nil), *adj.* [L. *senilis* < *senex,* old], 1. of old age. 2. showing signs of old age; weak in mind and body. 3. resulting from old age. —**se·nil·i·ty** (sə-nil′ə-ti, sē-), *n.*

**sen·ior** (sēn′yẽr), *adj.* [L., compar. of *senex,* old], 1. older: often indicating the older of two having the same name, as a father and son: abbrev. **Sr.** 2. of higher rank or longer service. 3. of or belonging to the graduating class of a school or college. *n.* 1. a person older than another or others. 2. a person of greater rank or length of service. 3. a person in the graduating class.

**senior high school,** high school: usually the tenth, eleventh, and twelfth grades.

**sen·ior·i·ty** (sēn-yôr′ə-ti, -yor′-), *n.* [*pl.* -TIES], 1. a being senior, as in age or rank. 2. status or priority achieved by length of service in a given job.

**sen·na** (sen′ə), *n.* [< ML. < Ar. *sanā*], 1. any of various cassia plants. 2. the dried leaves of some of these plants, used as a laxative.

‡**se·ñor** (se-nyôr′), *n.* [*pl.* -NORES (-nyô′res)], [Sp. < L. *senior;* see SENIOR], a man; gentleman: Spanish title equivalent to *Mr.* or *Sir.*

‡**se·ño·ra** (se-nyô′rä), *n.* [Sp.], a married woman; lady: Spanish title equivalent to *Mrs.* or *Madam.*

‡**se·ño·ri·ta** (se′nyô-rē′tä), *n.* [Sp.], an unmarried woman or girl; young lady: Spanish title corresponding to *Miss.*

**sen·sa·tion** (sen-sā′shən), *n.* [< ML. < LL. *sensatus*, intelligent < L. *sensus*, sense], 1. the power or process of receiving conscious sense impressions through stimulation of the sense organs; hearing, seeing, touching, tasting, or smelling. 2. a conscious feeling or sense impression: as, a *sensation* of cold. 3. a generalized feeling in an individual: as, a *sensation* of joy. 4. a feeling of excitement among people: as, the play caused a *sensation.* 5. the cause of such a feeling.

**sen·sa·tion·al** (sen-sā′shən-'l), *adj.* 1. of the senses or sensation. 2. arousing intense interest and excitement; exciting. 3. using or having effects intended to excite, shock, thrill, etc. **—sen·sa′tion·al·ize′** [-IZED, -IZING], *v.t.* **—sen·sa′tion·al·ly,** *adv.*

**sen·sa·tion·al·ism** (sen-sā′shən-'l-iz'm), *n.* 1. the use of subject matter, language, etc. that is intended to shock, excite, thrill, etc. 2. in *philosophy*, the belief that all knowledge is acquired through the senses. **—sen·sa′tion·al·ist,** *n.* **—sen·sa′tion·al·is′tic,** *adj.*

**sense** (sens), *n.* [< Fr. < L. *sensus* < *sentire*, to feel], 1. the ability to receive stimuli; specif., any of five faculties of receiving impressions through body organs and their associated nerves (sight, hearing, touch, smell, and taste): cf. **sixth sense.** 2. the senses considered as a total bodily function, as distinguished from intellect, movement, etc. 3. feeling, perception, or discrimination, through either the senses or the intellect; awareness: as, a *sense* of warmth, of guilt, of direction, etc. 4. an ability to feel or understand some quality, as humor, honor, etc. 5. sound intelligence and judgment. 6. meaning; esp., any of several meanings of the same word or phrase. 7. wisdom or reason: as, there's no *sense* in going. 8. the general opinion, sentiment, etc. of a group. 9. direction; tendency. *v.t.* [SENSED, SENSING], 1. to be or become aware of; perceive. 2. [Colloq.], to understand. **—in a sense,** to some extent or degree. **—make sense,** to be intelligible or logical. **—senses,** normal ability to think or reason soundly.

**sense·less** (sens′lis), *adj.* 1. unconscious. 2. stupid or foolish. 3. unreasonable; meaningless. **—sense′less·ly,** *adv.* **—sense′less·ness,** *n.*

**sense organ,** any organ or structure, as an eye or taste bud, that receives specific stimuli and transmits them as sensations to the brain.

**sen·si·bil·i·ty** (sen′sə-bil′ə-ti), *n.* [*pl.* -TIES], [see SENSIBLE], 1. the capacity for physical sensation; ability to feel. 2. *often pl.* the capacity for being affected emotionally or intellectually. 3. *often pl.* sensitive awareness or responsiveness; keen perception, as of moral or aesthetic values. 4. [Archaic], acutely delicate feelings.

**sen·si·ble** (sen′sə-b'l), *adj.* [< OFr. < L. *sensibilis* < pp. of *sentire*, to feel], 1. that can cause physical sensation. 2. perceptible to the intellect. 3. easily perceived; appreciable. 4. capable of sensation; sensitive. 5. aware; emotionally or intellectually conscious. 6. having or showing good sense; wise. **—sen′si·ble·ness,** *n.* **—sen′si·bly,** *adv.*

**sen·si·tive** (sen′sə-tiv), *adj.* [< OFr. < ML. *sensitivus* < L. pp. of *sentire*, to feel], 1. of the senses or sensation; sensory. 2. receiving and responding to stimuli. 3. very keenly susceptible to stimuli: as, a *sensitive* ear. 4. tender; raw; easily hurt: as, a *sensitive* bruise. 5. having or showing keen sensibilities. 6. easily offended, disturbed, etc.; touchy. 7. very responsive to external conditions: as, a *sensitive* thermometer. **—sen′si·tive·ly,** *adv.* **—sen′si·tiv′i·ty, sen′si·tive·ness,** *n.*

**sensitive plant,** a tropical American plant with purplish flowers, whose leaflets fold and leafstalks droop at the slightest touch.

**sen·si·tize** (sen′sə-tīz′), *v.t.* [-TIZED, -TIZING], to make sensitive; specif., in *photography*, to make (a film or plate) sensitive to light, etc. **—sen′si·ti·za′tion,** *n.* **—sen′si·tiz′er,** *n.*

**sen·so·ri·um** (sen-sôr′i-əm, -sō′ri-), *n.* [*pl.* -UMS, -A (-ə)], [LL. < L. *sensus*, sense], the supposed seat of sensation in the brain.

**sen·so·ry** (sen′sẽr-i), *adj.* 1. of the senses or sensation. 2. connected with the reception and transmission of sense impressions. Also **sen·so′ri·al** (-sôr′i-əl, -sō′ri-).

**sen·su·al** (sen′sho͞o-əl), *adj.* [< Fr. < L. *sensualis* < *sensus*, sense], 1. [Rare], sensory or sensuous. 2. of the body and the senses as distinguished from the intellect. 3. *a*) connected or preoccupied with bodily or sexual pleasures; voluptuous. *b*) lustful; lewd. **—sen′su·al·ly,** *adv.*

**sen·su·al·ism** (sen′sho͞o-əl-iz'm), *n.* 1. frequent or excessive indulgence in sexual pleasure. 2. the belief that sensual pleasures constitute the greatest good. **—sen′su·al·ist,** *n.* **—sen′su·al·is′tic,** *adj.*

**sen·su·al·i·ty** (sen′sho͞o-al′ə-ti), *n.* 1. a being sensual; fondness for or indulgence in sensual pleasures. 2. lewdness.

**sen·su·al·ize** (sen′sho͞o-əl-īz′), *v.t.* [-IZED, -IZING], to make sensual. **—sen′su·al·i·za′tion,** *n.*

**sen·su·ous** (sen′sho͞o-əs), *adj.* 1. of, derived from, affecting, or perceived by the senses. 2. readily susceptible through the senses; enjoying sensation. **—sen′su·ous·ly,** *adv.* **—sen′su·ous·ness,** *n.*

**sent** (sent), pt. and pp. of **send.**

**sen·tence** (sen′təns), *n.* [< OFr. < L. *sententia*, opinion; ult. < ppr. of *sentire*, to feel], 1. a decision or judgment, as of a court. 2. *a*) the determination by a court of the punishment of a convicted person. *b*) the punishment. 3. a group of words stating something, usually containing a subject and predicate, beginning with a capital letter, and ending with an end mark (a period, etc.). 4. in *music*, a period. *v.t.* [-TENCED, -TENCING], to pronounce punishment upon (a convicted person). **—sen·ten·tial** (sen-ten′shəl), *adj.* **—sen′ten·cer,** *n.*

**sen·ten·tious** (sen-ten′shəs), *adj.* [< L. < *sententia*; see SENTENCE], 1. expressing much in few words; short and pithy. 2. full of, or fond of using, maxims, proverbs, etc.; often, ponderously trite. **—sen·ten′tious·ly,** *adv.* **—sen·ten′tious·ness,** *n.*

**sen·tient** (sen′shənt, -shi-ənt), *adj.* [< L. ppr. of *sentire*, to feel], of or capable of feeling or perception; conscious. *n.* a sentient person or thing. **—sen′tience, sen′tien·cy,** *n.* **—sen′tient·ly,** *adv.*

**sen·ti·ment** (sen′tə-mənt), *n.* [< OFr. < ML. < L. < *sentire*, to feel], 1. a complex combination of feelings and opinions as a basis for judgment. 2. an opinion, judgment, etc., often colored by emotion. 3. sensibility; susceptibility to emotional appeal. 4. appeal to the emotions in literature or art. 5. sentimentality; maudlin emotion. 6. the meaning of something said, as distinct from the words used. 7. a brief, trite expression, as in a toast.

**sen·ti·men·tal** (sen′tə-men′t'l), *adj.* 1. having or showing tenderness, emotion, etc. 2. affectedly or superficially emotional; maudlin; mawkish. 3. influenced more by emotion than reason. 4. of or caused by sentiment. **—sen′ti·men′tal·ly,** *adv.*

**sen·ti·men·tal·i·ty** (sen′tə-men-tal′ə-ti), *n.* 1. the quality or state of being sentimental. 2. [*pl.* -TIES], any expression of this. Also **sen′ti·men′tal·ism. —sen′ti·men′tal·ist,** *n.*

**sen·ti·men·tal·ize** (sen′tə-men′t'l-īz′), *v.i.* [-IZED, -IZING], to be sentimental. *v.t.* 1. to make sentimental. 2. to be sentimental about.

**sen·ti·nel** (sen′ti-n'l), *n.* [< Fr. < It. *sentinella*; prob. < L. *sentire*, to feel], one guarding a group against surprise; sentry. *v.t.* [-NELED or -NELLED, -NELING or -NELLING], 1. to guard as a sentinel. 2. to furnish with a sentinel. 3. to post as a sentinel. **—stand sentinel,** to serve as a sentinel.

**sen·try** (sen′tri), *n.* [*pl.* -TRIES], [prob. < ME. *centry* (sanctuary), infl. by *centrenel* (sentinel)], 1. a sentinel; esp., a member of a military guard. 2. guard or watch: as, to keep *sentry.*

**Se·oul** (sā-o͞ol′, sōl; Kor. syō-ool′), *n.* a capital of Korea (see **Korea**): pop., 1,142,000.

**se·pal** (sē′p'l, sep′'l), *n.* [< Fr. < Mod. L. *sepalum*, coined < L. *separatus*, separate + *petalum*, petal], in *botany*, any of the leaf divisions of the calyx.

**-sep·al·ous** (sep′'l-əs), a combining form meaning *having* (a specified number or kind of) *sepals.*

**sep·a·ra·ble** (sep′ẽr-ə-b'l), *adj.* that can be separated. **—sep′a·ra·bil′i·ty, sep′a·ra·ble·ness,** *n.* **—sep′a·ra·bly,** *adv.*

**sep·a·rate** (sep′ə-rāt′; *for adj. & n.*, -ẽr-it, sep′rit), *v.t.* [-RATED, -RATING], [< L. pp. < *se-*, apart + *parare*, to arrange], 1. to set apart (two or more things) into parts, groups, etc.; divide; sever. 2. to see the differences between. 3. to cause (two people) to cease living together: as, the Parkers are *separated.* 4. to keep apart by being between: as, a wall *separates* the yards. 5. to set apart from others for a special purpose; sort. 6. to take away (a part) from a mixture. 7. to discharge from the armed forces. *v.i.* 1. to withdraw or secede (with *from*). 2. to part, become disconnected, etc. 3. to part company; go in different directions. 4. to stop being together as man and wife. 5. to become distinct or disengaged: as, cream *separates* from milk. ***adj.*** 1. set apart or divided from the rest or others. 2. not associated with others; distinct; individual. 3. having its own individual form or function: as, the *separate* parts of the body. 4. withdrawn from the association of others; solitary; isolated. 5. not shared or held in common: as, *separate* lockers. ***n.*** anything separate. —**sep′a·rate·ly,** ***adv.*** —**sep′a·rate·ness,** ***n.*** —**sep′a·ra′tive, sep′a·ra·to′ry** (-ə-tôr′i, -tō′ri), ***adj.*** —**sep′a·ra′tor,** ***n.***

**sep·a·ra·tion** (sep′ə-rā′shən), ***n.*** 1. a separating or being separated. 2. the place where this occurs; break; division. 3. something that separates. 4. a divorce. 5. an arrangement by which a man and wife live apart by agreement.

**sep·a·ra·tist** (sep′ə-rā′tist), ***n.*** 1. one who withdraws or secedes; esp., a member of a group that has seceded from a larger group; nonconformer. 2. one who advocates political or religious separation. Also **sep′a·ra′tion·ist.**

**se·pi·a** (sē′pi-ə), ***n.*** [L. < Gr. *sēpia*], 1. any of several cuttlefishes with an internal shell. 2. a dark-brown pigment prepared from the inky secretion of cuttlefish. 3. a dark reddish-brown color. 4. a photographic print in this color. ***adj.*** 1. of sepia. 2. dark reddish-brown.

**se·poy** (sē′poi), ***n.*** [< Port. *sipae* < Hind. & Per. *sipāhī* < *sipāh*, army], formerly, a native of India serving in the British army.

**sep·pu·ku** (se′po͞o′koo), ***n.*** in Japan, hara-kiri.

**sep·sis** (sep′sis), ***n.*** [< Gr. < *sēpein*, to make putrid], poisoning caused by the absorption into the blood of pathogenic microorganisms.

**Sept.,** 1. September. 2. Septuagint.

**sep·ta** (sep′tə), ***n.*** pl. of **septum.**

**Sep·tem·ber** (sep-tem′bẽr, səp-), ***n.*** [< L. < *septem*, seven: the early Romans reckoned from March], the ninth month of the year, having 30 days.

**sep·te·nar·y** (sep′tə-ner′i), ***adj.*** [< L. < *septem*, seven], consisting of seven. ***n.*** [*pl.* -IES], a group or set of seven.

**sep·ten·ni·al** (sep-ten′i-əl), ***adj.*** [< L. < *septem*, seven + *annus*, year], 1. lasting seven years. 2. coming, happening, etc. every seven years. —**sep·ten′ni·al·ly,** ***adv.***

**sep·tet, sep·tette** (sep-tet′), ***n.*** [G. < L. *septem*, seven + G. *duett*], 1. a group of seven persons or things. 2. in *music*, *a*) a composition for seven voices or instruments. *b*) the performers of this.

**sep·tic** (sep′tik), ***adj.*** [< L. < Gr. *sēptikos* < *sēpein*, to make putrid], 1. causing sepsis or putrefaction; infective. 2. of or resulting from sepsis or putrefaction. ***n.*** a septic substance or agent. —**sep·tic′i·ty** (-tis′ə-ti), ***n.***

**sep·ti·ce·mi·a, sep·ti·cae·mi·a** (sep′tə-sē′mi-ə), ***n.*** [< Gr. *sēptikos*, putrefactive + *haima*, blood], blood poisoning caused by the presence of pathogenic microorganisms and their toxic products in the blood. —**sep′ti·ce′mic, sep′ti·cae′mic,** ***adj.***

**septic tank,** a tank in which waste matter is putrefied and decomposed through bacterial action.

**sep·til·lion** (sep-til′yən), ***n.*** [Fr. < L. *septem*, seven + Fr. *million*], 1. in the U.S. and France, the number represented by 1 followed by 24 zeros. 2. in Great Britain and Germany, the number represented by 1 followed by 42 zeros. ***adj.*** amounting to one septillion in number.

**sep·tu·a·ge·nar·i·an** (sep′cho͞o-ə-ji-nâr′i-ən), ***adj.*** [< L. < *septuageni*, seventy each < *septuaginta*, seventy], seventy years old or between seventy and eighty. ***n.*** a person of this age.

**sep·tu·ag·e·nar·y** (sep′cho͞o-aj′ə-ner′i), ***adj. & n.*** [*pl.* -IES], septuagenarian.

**Sep·tu·a·gint** (sep′to͞o-ə-jint′, sep′cho͞o-), ***n.*** [< L. *septuaginta*, seventy: in tradition, done by 72 translators in 70 days], a Greek translation of the Old Testament.

**sep·tum** (sep′təm), ***n.*** [*pl.* -TA (-tə)], [< L. < *sepire*, to enclose < *saepes*, a hedge], a part that separates; partition: as, the nostrils are divided by a *septum*. —**sep′tal,** ***adj.***

**sep·tu·ple** (sep′to͞o-p′l, sep-tū′-), ***adj.*** [< LL. *septuplus* < L. *septem*, seven], 1. consisting of seven. 2. seven times as much or as many. ***v.t.*** [-PLED, -PLING], to multiply by seven.

**sep·ul·cher** (sep′'l-kẽr), ***n.*** [< OFr. < L. *sepulcrum* < *sepelire*, to bury], a vault for burial; tomb. ***v.t.*** [-CHERED, -CHERING], to bury in a sepulcher.

**se·pul·chral** (sə-pul′krəl), ***adj.*** 1. of sepulchers, burial, etc. 2. suggestive of the grave or burial; dismal; gloomy. 3. deep and melancholy: said of sound. —**se·pul′chral·ly,** ***adv.***

**sep·ul·chre** (sep′'l-kẽr), ***n. & v.t.*** [-CHRED, -CHRING], sepulcher: Brit. spelling.

**sep·ul·ture** (sep′'l-chẽr), ***n.*** 1. burial; interment. 2. [Archaic], a sepulcher.

**seq.,** *sequentes* or *sequentia*, [L.], the following.

**se·quel** (sē′kwəl), ***n.*** [< OFr. < L. < *sequi*, to follow], 1. something that follows; continuation. 2. something coming as a result of something else; consequence. 3. any literary work complete in itself but continuing a story begun in an earlier work.

**se·quence** (sē′kwəns), ***n.*** [< Fr. < LL. < L. *sequens;* see SEQUENT], 1. the coming of one thing after another; succession. 2. the order in which this occurs. 3. a continuous or related series. 4. a resulting event; consequence. 5. in a motion picture, radio play, etc., a part treating an episode without interruptions of continuity.

**se·quent** (sē′kwənt), ***adj.*** [< L. *sequens*, ppr. of *sequi*, to follow], 1. following in time or order; subsequent. 2. following as a result; consequent. ***n.*** something that follows; consequence.

**se·quen·tial** (si-kwen′shəl), ***adj.*** 1. sequent. 2. characterized by or forming a regular sequence of parts. —**se·quen′tial·ly,** ***adv.***

**se·ques·ter** (si-kwes′tẽr), ***v.t.*** [< OFr. < LL. *sequestrare*, to remove < L. *sequester*, trustee], 1. to set apart; separate. 2. to take possession of (property) as security for a debt, claim, etc. 3. to confiscate; seize, especially by authority. 4. [Rare], to withdraw; seclude. —**se·ques′tered,** ***adj.***

**se·ques·trate** (si-kwes′trāt), ***v.t.*** [-TRATED, -TRATING], 1. to confiscate. 2. [Archaic], to sequester. —**se·ques·tra·tor** (sē′kwes-trā′tẽr, si-kwes′-), ***n.***

**se·ques·tra·tion** (sē′kwes-trā′shən, si-kwes′-), ***n.*** 1. a sequestering or being sequestered; seclusion. 2. *a*) the legal seizure of property for security. *b*) confiscation of property, as by court action.

**se·quin** (sē′kwin), ***n.*** [Fr. < It. *zecchino* < *zecca*, a mint < Ar. *sikkah*, a stamp], 1. an obsolete Italian gold coin. 2. a small, shiny spangle, especially one of many sewn on fabric for decoration.

**se·quoi·a** (si-kwoi′ə), ***n.*** [Mod. L. < *Sikwâyi*, Indian inventor of the Cherokee syllabary], either of two species of related giant evergreen trees, found in California.

**se·ra** (sêr′ə), ***n.*** alt. pl. of **serum.**

**se·rag·lio** (si-ral′yō, se-räl′-), ***n.*** [*pl.* -LIOS], [< It. *serraglio*, enclosure (infl. by Turk. *serai*, palace); ult. < L. *serare*, to lock < *sera*, a lock], 1. the place where a Moslem keeps his wives or concubines; harem. 2. the palace of a Turkish sultan.

**se·ra·pe** (se-rä′pi), ***n.*** [Mex. Sp.], a woolen blanket, often brightly colored, used as a garment in Spanish-American countries.

**ser·aph** (ser′əf), ***n.*** [*pl.* -APHS, -APHIM (-ə-fim′)], [< ML. < LL. < Heb. *ṣerāphīm, pl.*], in *theology*, a member of the highest order of angels. —**se·raph·ic** (sə-raf′ik), **se·raph′i·cal,** ***adj.*** —**se·raph′i·cal·ly,** ***adv.***

**Serb** (sũrb), ***n.*** 1. one of a Slavic people of the Balkans. 2. their language. ***adj.*** Serbian.

**Ser·bi·a** (sũr′bi-ə), ***n.*** a former kingdom in the Balkans: now a federated republic of Yugoslavia.

**Ser·bi·an** (sũr′bi-ən), ***adj.*** of Serbia, the Serbs, or their language. ***n.*** 1. a native or inhabitant of Serbia. 2. Serbo-Croatian as spoken in Serbia.

**Ser·bo-Cro·a·tian** (sũr′bō-krō-ā′shən), ***n.*** the South Slavic language spoken in Yugoslavia. ***adj.*** of this language or the people who speak it.

**sere** (sêr), ***adj.*** [var. of *sear*], [Poetic], withered.

**ser·e·nade** (ser′ə-nād′), ***n.*** [< Fr. < It. *serenata;* ult. < L. *serenus*, clear], 1. a performance of vocal or instrumental music outdoors at night, especially by a lover under the window of his sweetheart. 2. music suitable for this. ***v.t. & v.i.*** [-NADED, -NADING], to play or sing a serenade (to). —**ser′e·nad′er,** ***n.***

**se·rene** (sə-rēn′), ***adj.*** [L. *serenus*], 1. clear; unclouded: as, a *serene* sky. 2. undisturbed; calm; quiet. 3. [S-], honorable: in titles, as, His *Serene* Highness. —**se·rene′ly,** ***adv.*** —**se·rene′ness,** ***n.***

**se·ren·i·ty** (sə-ren′ə-ti), ***n.*** [*pl.* -TIES], [< Fr. < L. *serenitas*], 1. a being serene; calmness; tranquillity. 2. clearness; brightness. 3. [S-], a title of honor for members of certain royal families.

**serf** (sũrf), ***n.*** [OFr. < L. *servus*, a slave], 1. originally, a slave. 2. a person in feudal servitude, bound to his master's land and transferred with it to a new owner. 3. any person who is oppressed. —**serf′dom, serf′age, serf′hood′,** ***n.***

**serge** (sũrj), ***n.*** [< OFr.; ult. < L. *serica* (*lana*), (wool of the) *Seres*, prob. the Chinese], 1. a twilled, worsted fabric used for suits, etc. 2. a twilled silk, rayon, etc., used for linings.

**ser·geant** (sär′jənt), ***n.*** [< OFr. < L. *serviens*, ppr. of *servire*, to serve], 1. a sergeant-at-arms. 2. a police officer ranking next below a captain or lieutenant. 3. in the *U.S. armed forces*, a noncommissioned officer ranking just above a corporal. Abbrev. **Sgt.**, **Sergt.** —**ser′gean·cy** [*pl.* -CIES], **ser′geant·ship′**, *n.*

**ser·geant-at-arms** (sär′jənt-ət-ärmz′), *n.* [*pl.* SERGEANTS-AT-ARMS], an officer appointed to keep order in a legislature, court, social club, etc.

**sergeant first class,** in the *U.S. Army*, an enlisted man ranking just above sergeant.

**sergeant major,** [*pl.* SERGEANTS MAJOR], 1. in the *U.S. Army*, a sergeant who is assistant to an adjutant, as of a regiment. 2. in the *U.S. Marine Corps*, the highest ranking noncommissioned officer.

**se·ri·al** (sêr′i-əl), *adj.* [< L. *series*, a row, order], 1. of, arranged in, or forming a series: as, *serial* numbers. 2. appearing, published, etc. in a series of continuous parts at regular intervals. 3. of a serial or serials. *n.* any novel, story, etc. presented in serial form. —**se′ri·al·ly**, *adv.*

**se·ri·al·ize** (sêr′i-ə-līz′), *v.t.* [-IZED, -IZING], to put or publish in serial form, as a story. —**se′ri·al·i·za′tion**, *n.*

**serial number,** any one of a series of numbers used to identify, as those given to soldiers.

**se·ri·a·tim** (sêr′i-ā′tim, ser′-), *adv.* [ML. < L. *series*], one after another in order; serially.

**se·ries** (sêr′iz), *n.* [*pl.* SERIES], [L. < *serere*, to join together], 1. a number of similar things arranged in a row: as, a *series* of arches. 2. a number of similar persons, things, or events coming one after another; sequence. 3. a number of things produced as a related group; set. 4. in *mathematics*, *a*) a succession of terms, each related to a preceding term by some law. *b*) the sum of such terms. —**in series,** connected in a series circuit.

**series circuit,** an electrical circuit in which the parts are connected end to end, positive pole to negative successively.

**ser·if** (ser′if), *n.* [< D. *schreef*, a stroke < *schrijve*, to write < L. *scribere*], in *printing*, a fine cross stroke projecting from a main stroke of a letter, especially at the top or bottom.

**se·ri·o·com·ic** (sêr′i-ō-kom′ik), *adj.* partly serious and partly comic: also **se′ri·o·com′i·cal.** —**se′ri·o·com′i·cal·ly**, *adv.*

**se·ri·ous** (sêr′i-əs), *adj.* [< Fr. < ML. *seriosus* < L. *serius*], 1. earnest, grave, sober, or solemn: as, a *serious* man. 2. of a grave aspect: as, a *serious* face. 3. not joking or trifling; sincere. 4. concerned with grave matters, problems, etc.; important. 5. requiring careful consideration. 6. giving cause for anxiety; dangerous: as, a *serious* wound. —**se′ri·ous·ly**, *adv.* —**se′ri·ous·ness**, *n.*

**se·ri·ous-mind·ed** (sêr′i-əs-mīn′did), *adj.* having or showing earnestness of purpose, etc. —**se′ri·ous-mind′ed·ly**, *adv.* —**se′ri·ous-mind′ed·ness**, *n.*

**ser·jeant** (sär′jənt), *n.* [Esp. British], sergeant. —**ser′jean·cy** [*pl.* -CIES], **ser′jeant·ship′**, *n.*

**ser·mon** (sũr′mən), *n.* [OFr. < L. *sermo*], 1. a speech given as instruction in religion or morals, especially by a clergyman. 2. any serious talk on behavior, responsibility, etc., especially a long, tedious one. —**ser·mon′ic** (-mon′ik), *adj.*

**ser·mon·ize** (sũr′mə-nīz′), *v.i.* & *v.t.* [-IZED, -IZING], 1. to preach (to); lecture. —**ser′mon·iz′er**, *n.*

**Sermon on the Mount,** the sermon delivered by Jesus to his disciples: Matt. 5–7, Luke 6:20-49.

**se·rol·o·gy** (si-rol′ə-ji), *n.* [< *serum* + *-logy*], the science dealing with the properties or use of serums. —**se·ro·log·ic** (sêr′ə-loj′ik), **se′ro·log′i·cal**, *adj.* —**se·rol′o·gist**, *n.*

**se·rous** (sêr′əs), *adj.* 1. of or containing serum. 2. like serum; thin and watery. —**se·ros·i·ty** (si-ros′ə-ti), [*pl.* -TIES], *n.*

**ser·pent** (sũr′pənt), *n.* [OFr. < L. < ppr. of *serpere*, to creep], 1. a snake; esp., a large or poisonous one. 2. a sly, treacherous person.

**ser·pen·tine** (sũr′pən-tēn′; *for adj., also* -tīn′), *adj.* of or like a serpent; esp., *a*) evilly cunning; treacherous. *b*) coiled or twisted; winding. *n.* a green or brownish-red mineral, magnesium silicate.

**ser·rate** (ser′āt, -it), *adj.* [< L. *serratus* < *serra*, a saw], having sawlike teeth or notches along the edge, as some leaves: also **ser′rat·ed.**

**ser·ra·tion** (se-rā′shən), *n.* 1. the condition of being serrate. 2. a single tooth in a serrate edge. 3. a set of these. Also **ser·ra·ture** (ser′ə-chẽr).

**ser·ried** (ser′id), *adj.* [pp. of obs. *serry* < Fr. *serrer*, to crowd; ult. < LL. *sera*, a bar], placed close together; compact, as soldiers in ranks.

**se·rum** (sêr′əm), *n.* [*pl.* SERUMS, SERA (-ə)], [L., whey], 1. any watery animal fluid, especially blood serum, the yellowish fluid which separates from the clot when blood coagulates. 2. blood serum used as an antitoxin, taken from an animal made immune to a specific disease by inoculation. 3. whey. 4. watery vegetable fluid.

**ser·vant** (sũr′vənt), *n.* [OFr., ppr. of *servir* (< L. *servire*), to serve], 1. a person employed by another, especially to perform household duties. 2. a slave. 3. a person employed by a government. 4. a person ardently devoted to another or to a cause, creed, etc. —**ser′vant·less**, *adj.* —**ser′vant·like′**, *adj.*

**serve** (sũrv), *v.t.* [SERVED, SERVING], [< OFr. < L. *servire*, to serve], 1. to work for; be a servant to. 2. *a*) to do services for; help; aid: as, he *served* his country well. *b*) to give reverence to, as God. 3. to do military or naval service for. 4. to go through (a term of imprisonment, service, etc.): as, he *served* four years. 5. to carry out the duties of (a position, office, etc.). 6. to provide (customers) with (goods or services). 7. to prepare and offer (food, etc.) to others: as, she *served* cocktails. 8. to set food, etc. before (a person). 9. to be sufficient for: as, one nail *served* my purpose. 10. to be used by: as, one hospital *serves* the city. 11. to function for: as, my memory *serves* me well. 12. to treat: as, she was cruelly *served.* 13. to deliver (a summons, etc.) to (someone). 14. to hit (a ball, etc.) to one's opponent in order to start play, as in tennis, etc. 15. to operate (a large gun). 16. in *animal husbandry*, to copulate with (a female). 17. in *nautical usage*, to put a binding around in order to strengthen (rope, etc.). *v.i.* 1. to work as a servant. 2. to be in service: as, he *served* in the navy. 3. to carry out the duties of an office. 4. to be of service; function. 5. to be adequate or sufficient: as, this nail won't *serve.* 6. to wait on table. 7. to be suitable: as, when the opportunity *serves.* 8. to start play by hitting the ball, etc., as in tennis. *n.* in *tennis*, etc., the act or manner of, or one's turn at, serving the ball, etc. —**serve one right,** to give one his just deserts.

**serv·er** (sũr′vẽr), *n.* 1. one who serves, as a waiter, etc. 2. a thing used in serving, as a tray.

**serv·ice** (sũr′vis), *n.* [< OFr. < L. *servitium* < *servus*, a slave], 1. the occupation or condition of a servant. 2. employment, especially public employment. 3. a branch of this, including the people in it. 4. the U.S. armed forces: with *the.* 5. work done or duty performed for others: as, professional *services*, repair *service.* 6. a religious ceremony; esp., public worship. 7. helpful or friendly action or conduct. 8. the result of this; benefit. 9. the act or manner of serving food. 10. a set of articles used in serving: as, a silver tea *service.* 11. the act or method of providing people with the use of something, as electric power, water, transportation, etc. 12. anything useful, as maintenance, supplies, etc., provided to customers by a dealer, etc. 13. *a*) an act, manner, or turn of serving in tennis, etc. *b*) the ball, etc. as served. 14. in *law*, notification of legal action, as by the serving of a writ, etc. 15. in *nautical usage*, any material, as wire, used in serving (ropes, etc.). *adj.* 1. of, for, or in service. 2. of, for, or used by servants, tradespeople, etc.: as, a *service* entrance. *v.t.* [-ICED, -ICING], 1. to furnish with a service; supply. 2. to make fit for service, as by adjusting, repairing, etc. —**at one's service,** 1. ready to serve one. 2. ready for one's use. —**of service,** helpful; useful.

**serv·ice·a·ble** (sũr′vis-ə-b'l), *adj.* 1. that can be of service; useful. 2. that will give good service; durable. 3. beneficial; helpful. 4. [Archaic], willing to serve. —**serv′ice·a·bil′i·ty**, **serv′ice·a·ble·ness**, *n.* —**ser′vice·a·bly**, *adv.*

**serv·ice·man** (sũr′vis-man′), *n.* [*pl.* -MEN (-men′)], a member of the armed forces: also **service man.**

**service station,** a place providing fuel, maintenance service, parts, etc. for automotive vehicles; gas station.

**ser·vi·ette** (sũr′vi-et′), *n.* [Fr. < *servir*, to serve], a table napkin.

**ser·vile** (sũr′v'l), *adj.* [< L. < *servus*, a slave], 1. of a slave or slaves. 2. like that of slaves or servants: as, *servile* employment. 3. humbly submissive; slavish; cringing. —**ser′vile·ly**, *adv.* —**ser·vil′i·ty** (-vil′ə-ti), [*pl.* -TIES], **ser′vile·ness**, *n.*

**ser·vi·tor** (sũr′və-tẽr), *n.* a servant, attendant, or follower. —**ser′vi·to′ri·al** (-tôr′i-əl, -tō′ri-), *adj.*

**ser·vi·tude** (sũr′və-tōōd′, -tūd′), *n.* [Fr. < L. < *servus*, a slave], 1. the condition of a slave; slavery. 2. work imposed as punishment for crime.

**ser·vo·mech·a·nism** (sũr′vō-mek′ə-niz'm), ***n.*** [< L. *servus*, slave; + *mechanism*], in *automation*, the device, as an electric motor, pump, etc., activated as by electrical impulses, that automatically operates a machine, tool, etc.
**ses·a·me** (ses′ə-mē′), ***n.*** [< Fr. < L. < Gr. *sēsamon*], 1. an East Indian plant whose edible seeds yield an oil. 2. its seeds. See also **open sesame.**
**ses·qui-** (ses′kwi), [< L. < *semis*, half + *que*, and], a combining form meaning *one and a half.*
**ses·qui·cen·ten·ni·al** (ses′kwi-sen-ten′i-əl), ***adj.*** [*sesqui-* + *centennial*], of or ending a period of 150 years. ***n.*** a 150th anniversary or its celebration.
**ses·sile** (ses′il), ***adj.*** [< L. < *sessus*, pp. of *sedere*, to sit], 1. in *anatomy & zoology*, attached directly by its base. 2. in *botany*, attached directly to the main stem.

SESSILE LEAVES

**ses·sion** (sesh′ən), ***n.*** [Fr. < L. *sessio* < pp. of *sedere*, to sit], 1. the sitting of a court, council, legislature, etc. to carry on its work. 2. a continuous series of such sittings. 3. the period of either of these. 4. a school term or period of study, classes, etc. 5. [Colloq.], a period of activity of any kind, especially one that is trying. —**in session,** meeting. —**ses′sion·al,** ***adj.***
**ses·tet** (ses-tet′, ses′tet), ***n.*** [< It. dim. of *sesto*, sixth < L. < *sex*, six], 1. in *music*, a sextet. 2. the last six lines of a sonnet.
**set** (set), ***v.t.*** [SET, SETTING], [AS. *settan*], 1. to cause to sit; seat. 2. *a*) to cause (a fowl) to sit on eggs to hatch them. *b*) to put (eggs) under a fowl to hatch them. 3. to put in the specified or required place or position: as, *set* the book on the table, he *set* the wheel on the axle. 4. to cause to be next or applied to something: as, she *set* a match to the paper. 5. to write down; record. 6. to cause to be in the condition specified: as, he *set* the house on fire. 7. to cause to be in working or proper condition; arrange; fix; specif., *a*) to fix (a net, trap, etc.) to catch animals. *b*) to fix (a sail) to catch the wind. *c*) to adjust; regulate: as, *set* a clock, dial, etc. *d*) to arrange (a table) with tableware for a meal. *e*) to put (a dislocated or fractured bone) into normal position. 8. to cause to be in a settled, rigid, or fixed position or condition: as, he *set* his jaw, we *set* our minds to the task, pectin *sets* jelly, to *set* a color in dyeing. 9. *a*) to mount (gems) in rings, bracelets, etc. *b*) to decorate (gold, watches, etc.) with gems. 10. to cause to take a particular direction; direct: as, he *set* his face toward home. 11. to appoint; establish; specif., *a*) to post (a person) for certain duties. *b*) to fix (limits or boundaries). *c*) to fix (a time) for (an event). *d*) to establish (a rule, form, law, etc.). *e*) to furnish (an example) for others. *f*) to introduce (a fashion, etc.). *g*) to fix (a quota) for a given period. *h*) to begin to apply (oneself) to a task, etc. 12. *a*) to fix (the amount of a price, fine, etc.). *b*) to have (a certain estimate of a person or thing): as, I *set* little store by him. 13. to point toward the position of (game): said of dogs. 14. in *baking*, to put aside (leavened dough) to rise. 15. in *music*, to write or fit (words) to music or (music) to words. 16. in *printing*, *a*) to compose (type). *b*) to put (manuscript) into type. 17. in the *theater*, *a*) to place (a scene) in a given locale. *b*) to arrange the scenery and properties on (the stage). ***v.i.*** 1. to sit on eggs: said of a fowl. 2. to become firm or hard: as, is the cement *set?* 3. to become fast, as a dye. 4. to begin to move, travel, etc. (with *out*, *forth*, *on*, *off*, etc.). 5. to have a certain direction; tend: as, the wind *sets* to the south. 6. to sink below the horizon; hence, 7. to wane; decline. 8. to hang or fit in a certain way: as, the jacket *sets* well. 9. [Now Dial.], to sit. 10. in *botany*, to form fruit in the blossom. ***adj.*** 1. fixed in advance: as, a *set* time. 2. established, as by authority. 3. deliberate; intentional. 4. conventional: as, a *set* speech. 5. fixed; rigid. 6. resolute; obstinate. 7. firm in consistency. 8. ready: as, get *set*. 9. formed; built. ***n.*** 1. a setting or being set; specif., the act of a dog in setting game. 2. the way or position in which a thing is set; specif., *a*) direction, as of a current. *b*) tendency; inclination. *c*) warp; bend. *d*) the way in which an article of clothing fits. *e*) the position of a part of the body: as, the *set* of her head. 3. something which is set; specif., *a*) a twig or slip for planting. *b*) the constructed scenery for a play, motion picture, etc. 4. a group of persons or things classed or belonging together: as, the social *set*, a *set* of tools, books, china, etc. 5. assembled equipment for radio or television reception, record playing, etc. 6. in *tennis*, a group of six or more games won by a margin of at least two. —**all set,** [Colloq.], prepared; ready. —**set about,** to begin; start doing. —**set against,** 1. to balance. 2. to compare. 3. to make hostile toward. —**set aside,** 1. to separate and keep for a purpose: also **set apart.** 2. to discard; dismiss; reject. 3. to annul. —**set back,** to reverse or hinder the progress of. —**set down,** 1. to put down; let alight. 2. to put in writing or print. 3. to consider; estimate; ascribe. —**set forth,** 1. to publish. 2. to state. —**set in,** 1. to begin. 2. to blow or flow shoreward. —**set off,** 1. to start (a person) doing something. 2. to make prominent by contrast. 3. to enhance. 4. to cause to explode. —**set on** (or **upon**), 1. to incite to attack. 2. to attack. —**set out,** 1. to display, as for sale. 2. to plant. —**set to,** 1. to get to work; begin. 2. to begin fighting. —**set up,** 1. to raise to power, a high position, etc. 2. to put together or erect (a tent, machine, etc.). 3. to establish; found. 4. to start. 5. to put (drinks, etc.) before customers.
**se·ta** (sē′tə), ***n.*** [*pl.* -TAE (-tē)], [L.], in *botany & zoology*, a bristle or bristlelike part or organ.
**se·ta·ceous** (si-tā′shəs), ***adj.*** [< L. *seta*, a bristle], 1. having bristles. 2. bristlelike. Also **se′tose.**
**set·back** (set′bak′), ***n.*** 1. a reversal or check in progress; relapse. 2. a steplike indentation or recessed section, as in the upper part of a wall.
**Seth** (seth), ***n.*** in the *Bible*, the third son of Adam.
**set·off** (set′ôf′), ***n.*** 1. a thing that makes up for something else; counterbalance. 2. *a*) the settlement of a debt through the debtor's establishment of a counterclaim against his creditor. *b*) a claim so established.
**set·screw** (set′skrōō′), ***n.*** a machine screw passing through one part and against or into another to prevent movement, as of a ring around a shaft.
**set·tee** (se-tē′), ***n.*** [< *set*], 1. a seat or bench with a back. 2. a small or medium-sized sofa.
**set·ter** (set′ẽr), ***n.*** 1. one who sets or a thing used in setting. 2. any of a breed of long-haired bird dog of which there are three varieties (*English*, *Irish*, and *Gordon setters*): they are trained to find game and point out its position by standing rigid.
**set·ting** (set′iŋ), ***n.*** 1. the act of one that sets. 2. a thing in or on which something, as a gem, is set. 3. time and place, environment, etc., as of a story or poem. 4. actual physical surroundings or scenery, whether real or artificial. 5. the music composed for a set of words. 6. the eggs in the nest of a setting hen.
**set·tle** (set′'l), ***n.*** [AS. *setl*], a long wooden bench with a back and arm rests.
**set·tle** (set′'l), ***v.t.*** [-TLED, -TLING], [< AS. < *setl*, a seat], 1. to put in order; arrange, as a room, one's affairs, etc. 2. to set in place so as to be firmly or comfortably situated. 3. to establish as a resident: as, the firm *settled* him in a near-by house. 4. to set up residence in; colonize: as, New York was *settled* by the Dutch. 5. to cause to sink and become more compact: as, the rain *settled* the dust. 6. to clarify (a liquid) by settling the sediment. 7. to free from disturbance, as the mind, nerves, stomach, etc. 8. to establish in business, marriage, etc. 9. to fix definitely; decide (something in doubt). 10. to end (a dispute). 11. to pay (a bill, debt, etc.). 12. to decide (a legal dispute) by agreement without court action. ***v.i.*** 1. to stop moving and stay in one place: as, his gaze *settled* on her. 2. to cast itself over a landscape, as fog, or over a person, as gloom. 3. to become localized in a given area, as a pain. 4. to take up permanent residence. 5. to move downward; sink: as, the car *settled* in the mud. 6. to become more dense by sinking, as sediment. 7. to become clearer by the settling of dregs. 8. to become more stable; settle down. 9. to reach a decision (usually with *with*, *on*, or *upon*). 10. to pay what is owing. —**settle down,** 1. to take up permanent residence, a regular job, etc. 2. to become less nervous, erratic, etc. 3. to apply oneself steadily. —**settle upon** (or **on**), to make over (property, etc.) to by legal action.
**set·tle·ment** (set′'l-mənt), ***n.*** 1. a settling or being settled. 2. establishment in life, business, etc. 3. an inhabiting or colonizing, as of a new land. 4. a colony. 5. a small community; village. 6. an agreement, understanding, etc. 7. payment, as of a claim. 8. the disposition of property for the benefit of a person. 9. the amount of such property. 10. a community center for the underprivileged, offering social and educational activities: also **settlement house.**
**set·tler** (set′lẽr), ***n.*** 1. a person or thing that settles. 2. one who settles in a new country.
**set·tlings** (set′liŋz), ***n.pl.*** sediment; dregs.
**set-to** (set′tōō′), ***n.*** [*pl.* -TOS], [Colloq.], 1. a fight or struggle. 2. any sharp contest.

**set·up** (set′up′), *n.* 1. the way in which something is set up; plan, make-up, etc., as of equipment, an organization, etc. 2. bodily posture; carriage. 3. soda water, ice, etc. for mixing with alcoholic liquor. 4. [Slang], *a*) a contest deliberately arranged to result in an easy victory. *b*) any undertaking that is very easy.

**Se·vas·to·pol** (si-vas′tə-pōl′), *n.* a city in the Crimea, on the Black Sea: pop., 112,000: also **Sebastopol.**

**sev·en** (sev′'n), *adj.* [AS. *seofon*], totaling one more than six. *n.* 1. the cardinal number between six and eight; 7; VII. 2. a person or thing numbered seven, as a contestant, playing card, etc.

**sev·en·fold** (sev′'n-fōld′), *adj.* [see -FOLD], 1. having seven parts. 2. having seven times as much or as many. *adv.* seven times as much or as many.

**Seven Hills of Rome,** the seven hills on and about which the city of Rome was built.

**seven seas,** all the oceans of the world.

**sev·en·teen** (sev′'n-tēn′), *adj.* [AS. *seofentyne*], seven more than ten. *n.* the cardinal number between sixteen and eighteen; 17; XVII.

**sev·en·teenth** (sev′'n-tēnth′), *adj.* 1. preceded by sixteen others in a series; 17th. 2. designating any of the seventeen equal parts of something. *n.* 1. the one following the sixteenth. 2. any of the seventeen equal parts of something; 1/17.

**sev·enth** (sev′'nth), *adj.* [AS. *seofande*], 1. preceded by six others in a series; 7th. 2. designating any of the seven equal parts of something. *n.* 1. the one following the sixth. 2. any of the seven equal parts of something; 1/7. 3. in *music, a*) a note seven degrees above or below another in the diatonic scale. *b*) the interval between these. —**sev′enth·ly,** *adv.*

**seventh heaven,** 1. the highest sphere of heaven according to ancient astronomy and certain theologies. 2. a condition of perfect happiness.

**sev·en·ti·eth** (sev′'n-ti-ith), *adj.* 1. preceded by sixty-nine others in a series; 70th. 2. designating any of the seventy equal parts of something. *n.* 1. the one following the sixty-ninth. 2. any of the seventy equal parts of something; 1/70.

**sev·en·ty** (sev′'n-ti), *adj.* seven times ten. *n.* [*pl.* -TIES], the cardinal number between sixty-nine and seventy-one; 70; LXX. —**the seventies,** the years from seventy through seventy-nine (of a century or a person's age).

**sev·er** (sev′ẽr), *v.t.* & *v.i.* [< OFr. < LL. < L. *separare*], 1. to separate; divide. 2. to part or break off; cut in two: as, *sever* the cable, to *sever* a relationship. —**sev′er·a·ble,** *adj.* —**sev′er·er,** *n.*

**sev·er·al** (sev′ẽr-əl, sev′rəl), *adj.* [OFr. < LL. < L. *separ*, separate], 1. separate; distinct. 2. different; respective: as, the *several* opinions of the different people. 3. more than two but not many; few. *n.* several persons or things; a few.

**sev·er·al·ly** (sev′ẽr-əl-i, sev′rəl-i), *adv.* 1. separately; distinctly. 2. respectively.

**sev·er·ance** (sev′ẽr-əns), *n.* a severing or being severed.

**severance pay,** extra pay given to an employee leaving his job, based on his length of service.

**se·vere** (sə-vêr′), *adj.* [< Fr. < L. *severus*], 1. harsh or strict, as in treatment; stern. 2. serious; grave, as in expression. 3. rigidly accurate or exact. 4. extremely plain; unornamented: said of style. 5. violent; intense, as pain. 6. difficult; rigorous, as a rule or test. —**se·vere′ly,** *adv.* —**se·vere′ness,** *n.*

**se·ver·i·ty** (sə-ver′ə-ti), *n.* 1. a being severe; specif., *a*) strictness; harshness. *b*) gravity; seriousness. *c*) rigid accuracy. *d*) extreme plainness, as in style. *e*) violence; intensity. *f*) rigorousness; difficulty. 2. [*pl.* -TIES], something severe.

**Sev·ern** (sev′ẽrn), *n.* a river in Wales and England, flowing into the Bristol Channel.

**Se·ville** (sə-vil′), *n.* a city in S Spain: pop., 377,000: Spanish name, **Se·vil·la** (sā-vē′lyä).

**Sè·vres** (sev′rə, sev′ẽrz), *n.* 1. a town in France, near Paris. 2. a fine porcelain made there.

**sew** (sō), *v.t.* [SEWED, SEWED or SEWN, SEWING], [AS. *si(o)wan*], 1. to join or fasten with stitches made with needle and thread. 2. to make, mend, etc. by sewing. *v.i.* to work with needle and thread or at a sewing machine. —**sew up,** 1. to close together the edges of with stitches. 2. [Colloq.], to get or have absolute control of; monopolize. —**sew′a·ble,** *adj.* —**sew′er,** *n.*

**sew·age** (sōō′ij, sū′-), *n.* the waste matter carried off by sewers or drains.

**Sew·ard, William Henry** (sōō′ẽrd, sū′-), 1801–1872; U.S. secretary of state (1861–1869).

**sew·er** (sōō′ẽr, sū′-), *n.* [< OFr. *seuwiere* < LL. < L. *ex*, out + *aqua*, water], an underground pipe or drain for carrying off water and waste matter.

**sew·er·age** (sōō′ẽr-ij, sū′-), *n.* 1. removal of surface water and waste matter by sewers. 2. a system of sewers. 3. sewage.

**sew·ing** (sō′iŋ), *n.* 1. the act of one who sews. 2. material for sewing. *adj.* of or for sewing.

**sewing circle,** a group of women who make a social event of sewing.

**sewing machine,** a machine with a mechanically driven needle used for sewing and stitching.

**sewn** (sōn), alt. pp. of **sew.**

**sex** (seks), *n.* [< OFr. < L. *sexus;* prob. < base of *secare*, to divide], 1. either of the two divisions of organisms distinguished as male or female. 2. the character of being male or female. 3. anything connected with sexual gratification or reproduction; esp., the attraction of one sex for the other. —**the fair** (or **gentle, weaker**) **sex,** women. —**the sterner** (or **stronger**) **sex,** men.

**sex-,** [< L. *sex*, six], a combining form meaning *six*: also **sex′i-.**

**sex·a·ge·nar·i·an** (sek′sə-ji-nâr′i-ən), *adj.* [< L. < *sexageni*, sixty each], sixty years old or between sixty and seventy. *n.* a person of this age.

**sex·ag·e·nar·y** (seks-aj′ə-ner′i), *adj.* & *n.* [*pl.* -IES], sexagenarian.

**sex appeal,** the physical attractiveness and charm that attract members of the opposite sex.

**sex chromosome,** a sex-determining chromosome in the germ cells of most plants and animals.

**sexed** (sekst), *adj.* 1. of or having sex. 2. having (a specified degree of) sexuality.

**sex·less** (seks′lis), *adj.* 1. lacking sexual characteristics; asexual. 2. apparently lacking in normal sexual drive. —**sex′less·ly,** *adv.* —**sex′less·ness,** *n.*

**sex-linked** (seks′liŋkt′), *adj.* in *genetics*, designating or of any factor linked to the sex chromosomes of either parent.

**sex·ol·o·gy** (sek-sol′ə-ji), *n.* the science dealing with sexual behavior. —**sex·ol′o·gist,** *n.*

**sext** (sekst), *n.* [< LL. < L. *sexta* (*hora*), sixth (hour)], [often S-], in *ecclesiastical usage*, 1. the fourth of the seven canonical hours: it falls near noon, the sixth hour of the day. 2. a service held daily at this time.

**sex·tant** (seks′tənt), *n.* [< L. *sextans*, a sixth (part of a circle)], an instrument for measuring angular distance: used chiefly by navigators in determining position by measurement of the angle between a heavenly body and the horizon.

**sex·tet, sex·tette** (seks-tet′), *n.* [alt. (after L. *sex*, six) < *sestet*], 1. any group of six. 2. in *music, a*) a composition for six voices or instruments. *b*) the performers of this. Also **sestet.**

**sex·til·lion** (seks-til′yən), *n.* [Fr. < L. *sex*, six + Fr. *septillion*], 1. in the U.S. and France, the number represented by 1 followed by 21 zeros. 2. in England and Germany, the number represented by 1 followed by 36 zeros. *adj.* amounting to one sextillion in number.

**sex·to·dec·i·mo** (seks′tō-des′ə-mō′), *n.* [*pl.* -MOS], [< L. (*in*) *sextodecimo*, (in) sixteen], 1. the page size of a book made up of printer's sheets folded into sixteen leaves, each leaf being about 4½ by 6¾ inches. 2. a book consisting of pages of this size: also called *sixteenmo*, and written *16mo* or *16°*. *adj.* consisting of pages of this size.

**sex·ton** (seks′tən), *n.* [< OFr. < ML. *sacristanus;* see SACRISTAN], a church official in charge of the maintenance of church property.

**sex·tu·ple** (seks′too-p'l, seks-tū′-), *adj.* [< L. *sextus*, sixth, after Eng. *quintuple*], 1. consisting of six. 2. six times as much or as many; sixfold. 3. in *music*, having six beats to the measure. *n.* an amount six times as much or as many. *v.t.* & *v.i.* [-PLED, -PLING], to multiply by six.

**sex·tu·plet** (seks′too-plit, seks-tū′-, -tup′lit), *n.* 1. *a*) one of six offspring born of a single birth. *b*) *pl.* six offspring born at a single birth. 2. a group of six, usually of one kind.

**sex·u·al** (sek′shōō-əl), *adj.* 1. of or affecting sex, the sexes, the sex organs, etc. 2. in *biology, a*) having sex. *b*) designating or of reproduction by the union of male and female germ cells. —**sex′u·al′i·ty** (-al′ə-ti), *n.* —**sex′u·al·ly,** *adv.*

**sex·y** (sek′si), *adj.* [-IER, -IEST], [Slang], exciting or intended to excite sexual desire; erotic; lascivious. —**sex′i·ly,** *adv.* —**sex′i·ness,** *n.*

‡**sfor·zan·do** (sfôr-tsän′dô), *adj. & adv.* [It. < *sforzare*, to force], in *music*, with emphasis: symbol, >, ∧: abbrev. **sf., sfz.**: also **sfor·za′to** (-tsä′tô).
**s.g.,** specific gravity.
**sgd.,** signed.
**Sgt., sgt.,** Sergeant.
**sh.,** shilling; shillings.
**shab·by** (shab′i), *adj.* [-BIER, -BIEST], [< dial. var. *shab* < AS. *sceabb*, a scab], 1. worn out; deteriorated. 2. showing much wear; threadbare: said of clothing. 3. wearing such clothing. 4. beggarly; mean: as, a *shabby* reward. 5. shameful: as, *shabby* treatment. —**shab′bi·ly,** *adv.* —**shab′bi·ness,** *n.*
**shab·by-gen·teel** (shab′i-jen-tēl′), *adj.* shabby but giving or trying to give an appearance of dignity, self-respect, etc.
**Sha·bu·oth** (shä-vōō′ōth, shə-vōō′ōs), *n.pl.* [construed as sing.], a Jewish holiday, the Feast of Weeks, or Pentecost: see **Jewish holidays.**
**shack** (shak), *n.* [? < Mex. *jacal* < Aztec *xacalli*, wooden hut, or ? < contr. of *ramshackle*], a small, crudely built cabin; hut; shanty.
**shack·le** (shak′'l), *n.* [AS. *sceacul*], 1. a metal fastening, usually one of a linked pair, for the wrist or ankle of a prisoner; fetter; manacle. 2. anything that restrains freedom, as of expression. 3. a device for fastening or coupling. *v.t.* [-LED, -LING], 1. to put shackles on. 2. to fasten or connect with a shackle. 3. to restrain in freedom, as of expression. —**shack′ler,** *n.*

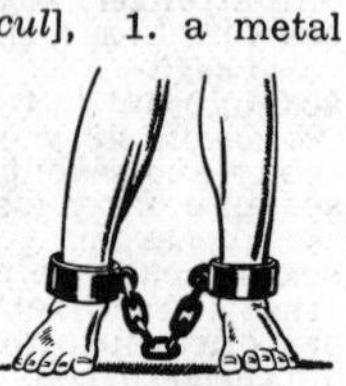
SHACKLES

**shad** (shad), *n.* [*pl.* SHAD, SHADS; see PLURAL, II, D, 2], [AS. *sceadd*], any of several salt-water fishes related to the herring but spawning in rivers.
**shad·ber·ry** (shad′ber′i, -bēr-i), *n.* [*pl.* -RIES], 1. a shadbush. 2. its fruit.
**shad·bush** (shad′boosh′), *n.* [from its flowering when shad spawn], a shrub of the rose family, with white flowers and purplish berries.
**shade** (shād), *n.* [AS. *sceadu*], 1. comparative darkness caused by an object cutting off rays of light, as from the sun. 2. an area less brightly lighted than its surroundings, as an open place sheltered from sunlight. 3. [Archaic or Poetic], a shadow. 4. *chiefly pl.* a secluded place. 5. a representation of darkness in painting, etc. 6. degree of darkness of a color. 7. *a*) a small difference: as, *shades* of opinion. *b*) a slight amount or degree; trace. 8. [Poetic], a phantom; ghost; spirit. 9. a device used to protect or screen from light: as, a window *shade*. *v.t.* [SHADED, SHADING], 1. to protect or screen from light or heat. 2. to hide, as with a shadow. 3. to darken; dim. 4. *a*) to represent the effects of shade in (a painting, etc.). *b*) to mark with gradations of light or color. 5. to change by very slight degrees or gradations. 6. to lessen slightly. *v.i.* to change or vary slightly or by degrees. —**in** (or **into**) **the shade,** 1. in darkness or shadow. 2. in comparative obscurity. —**the shades,** 1. the increasing darkness, as of evening. 2. the world of the dead; Hades. —**shade′less,** *adj.* —**shad′er,** *n.*
**shad·ing** (shād′iŋ), *n.* 1. a shielding against light. 2. the representation of light or shade in a picture. 3. any small variation, as in quality.
**shad·ow** (shad′ō), *n.* [< dat. & genit. of AS. *sceadu*, shade], 1. darkness cast upon a surface by a body intercepting the light rays; shade. 2. the specific image made by such a body. 3. *pl.* the growing darkness after sunset. 4. *a*) gloom; sadness. *b*) that which casts gloom, etc. over something. 5. the shaded area of a picture. 6. a mirrored image; reflection. 7. *a*) an imaginary vision. *b*) a ghost; apparition. 8. a vague indication; symbol; omen. 9. *a*) a slight amount; trace. *b*) a remnant; vestige. 10. a constant companion. 11. one who trails another closely, as a spy. 12. [Rare], protection or shelter. *v.t.* 1. [Archaic], to shelter, as from light. 2. to throw a shadow upon. 3. to make dark or gloomy. 4. to foreshadow (often with *forth*). 5. to shade in painting, etc. 6. to follow closely, especially in secret. —**in the shadow of,** very close to. —**under the shadow of,** 1. very close to. 2. in danger of. —**shad′ow·er,** *n.* —**shad′ow·less,** *adj.*
**shad·ow·box·ing** (shad′ō-bok′siŋ), *n.* sparring with an imaginary opponent: an exercise used by boxers. —**shad′ow·box′,** *v.i.*
**shad·ow·y** (shad′ō-i), *adj.* 1. resembling, or of the nature of, a shadow; specif., *a*) fleeting or illusory. *b*) dim; indistinct. 2. shaded or giving shade or shadow. —**shad′ow·i·ness,** *n.*
**Sha·drach, Me·shach, and A·bed·ne·go** (shā′drak mē′shak 'nd a-bed′ni-gō′), in the *Bible*, three Jewish captives in Babylonia who were cast into a blazing furnace by Nebuchadnezzar and came out miraculously unharmed: Dan. 3.
**shad·y** (shād′i), *adj.* [-IER, -IEST], 1. giving shade. 2. shaded, as from the sun; full of shade. 3. [Colloq.], of questionable character or honesty. —**on the shady side of,** beyond (a given age). —**shad′i·ly,** *adv.* —**shad′i·ness,** *n.*
**shaft** (shaft), *n.* [AS. *sceaft*], 1. the stem or body of an arrow or spear. 2. an arrow or spear. 3. a missile or something like a missile: as, *shafts* of light, wit, etc. 4. a long, slender part or object; specif., *a*) [Rare], a plant stem or tree trunk. *b*) the stem of a feather. *c*) a column or obelisk; also, the main, usually cylindrical, part between the ends of a column. *d*) a flagpole. *e*) the long handle of some tools. *f*) either of the two poles between which an animal is harnessed to a vehicle. *g*) a bar supporting, or transmitting motion to, a mechanical part, as of an engine. 5. a long, narrow opening sunk into the earth. 6. a vertical opening through the floors of a building, as for an elevator.
**shag** (shag), *n.* [< AS. *sceacga*], 1. [Rare], heavily matted wool or hair. 2. a heavy, rough nap, as on some cloth. 3. cloth with such a nap. 4. any disordered mass. 5. coarsely shredded tobacco. *v.t.* [SHAGGED, SHAGGING], to make shaggy or rough.
**shag·bark** (shag′bärk′), *n.* 1. a hickory tree with gray, shredding bark and roundish nuts. 2. its wood. 3. its nut. Also **shellbark.**
**shag·gy** (shag′i), *adj.* [-GIER, -GIEST], 1. covered with long, coarse hair or wool. 2. carelessly groomed: said of a person. 3. of tangled, coarse growth; straggly. 4. having a rough nap or surface. —**shag′gi·ly,** *adv.* —**shag′gi·ness,** *n.*
**shaggy dog,** [< an anecdote involving a shaggy dog], [Slang], a humorous anecdote with a surprise ending involving ludicrously unreal behavior.
**sha·green** (shə-grēn′), *n.* [< Fr. < Venetian *sagrin* < Turk. *saghri*, hide], 1. rough, granular rawhide, made from the skin of the horse, camel, etc. 2. the hard, rough skin of the shark or dogfish.
**shah** (shä), *n.* [Per. *shāh*], a title of the ruler of certain Eastern lands, especially Iran.
**Shak., Shaks.,** Shakespeare.
**shake** (shāk), *v.t.* [SHOOK, SHAKEN, SHAKING], [AS. *sceacan*], 1. to cause to move up and down, back and forth, or from side to side with short, quick movements. 2. to bring, force, throw, etc. by abrupt, brisk movements. 3. to cause to tremble; vibrate. 4. *a*) to cause to totter or become unsteady. *b*) to unnerve: as, he was *shaken* by the news. 5. to brandish; wave. 6. to clasp (another's hand), as in greeting. 7. [Slang], to get away from: as, he *shook* his pursuers. 8. in *music*, to trill. *v.i.* 1. to move quickly up and down, back and forth, etc.; vibrate. 2. to tremble, quiver, etc., as from cold or fear. 3. to become unsteady; totter. 4. to shake hands, as in greeting. 5. in *music*, to trill. *n.* 1. an act of shaking. 2. an unsteady movement; tremor. 3. a natural fissure in rock or timber. 4. [Colloq.], an earthquake. 5. [Slang], a moment: as, I'll finish in a *shake*. 6. in *music*, a trill. —**no great shakes,** [Colloq.], not outstanding or unusual. —**shake down,** 1. to bring down or cause to fall by shaking. 2. to cause to settle by shaking. 3. to condition (new equipment, etc.). 4. [Slang], to extort money from. —**shake off,** to get away from or rid of. —**shake out,** 1. to cause to fall out by shaking. 2. to empty by shaking. 3. to straighten out by shaking, as a folded cloth. —**shake up,** 1. to shake, especially so as to mix. 2. to disturb or rouse by shaking. 3. to jar or shock. 4. to reorganize as by shaking. —**the shakes,** [Colloq.], a convulsive trembling.
**shake·down** (shāk′doun′), *n.* [Slang], an extortion of money, as by blackmail. *adj.* [Colloq.], for testing the performance, acclimating the personnel, etc.: as, the *shakedown* cruise of a ship.
**shak·en** (shāk′ən), pp. of **shake.**
**shak·er** (shāk′ēr), *n.* 1. a person or thing that shakes. 2. a device used in shaking, as in mixing. 3. [S-], [from movements of a dance in their ritual], a member of a religious sect practicing celibacy, communal living, etc. —**Shak′er·ism,** *n.*
**Shake·speare, William** (shāk′spêr′), 1564–1616; English poet and dramatist: called the *Bard of Avon*: also sp. **Shakspere, Shaksper, Shakespere,** etc. —**Shake·spear′e·an, Shake·spear′i·an,** *adj. & n.*
**Shakespearean sonnet,** a sonnet composed of three quatrains and a final couplet: also called *Elizabethan sonnet.*
**shake-up** (shāk′up′), *n.* a shaking up; specif., an extensive reorganization, as in personnel.

**shak·o** (shak′ō), *n.* [*pl.* -os], [< Fr. < Hung. *csákó* < G. *zacke*, a peak], a stiff, cylindrical military dress hat, usually with a flat top and a plume.

SHAKO

**shak·y** (shāk′i), *adj.* [-IER, -IEST], 1. not firm, substantial, etc.; unsound, as a structure. 2. shaking; trembling. 3. not dependable or reliable; questionable. —**shak′i·ly,** *adv.* —**shak′i·ness,** *n.*

**shale** (shāl), *n.* [< AS. *scealu*, a shell], a fine-grained rock formed of hardening clay: it splits into thin layers. —**shal′y** [-IER, -IEST], *adj.*

**shall** (shal), *v.* [pt. SHOULD (shood)], [< AS. *sceal*, inf. *sceolan*], an auxiliary used in formal speech: 1. to express futurity in the first person, and determination, obligation, etc. in the second and third persons. 2. in a question expecting *shall* in the answer. 3. in laws and resolutions: as, the fine *shall* not exceed $100. 4. in subordinate clauses introduced by *if*, *when*, etc. These formal conventions, however, do not reflect prevailing usage in which *shall* and *will* are used interchangeably, with *will* predominating in all persons.

**shal·lop** (shal′əp), *n.* [< Fr. < D. *sloep*], a small open boat fitted with oars or sails or both.

**shal·lot** (shə-lot′), *n.* [obs. Fr. *eschalotte*, alt. < *eschaloigne*, scallion], 1. an onionlike plant whose clustered bulbs, resembling garlic, are used for flavoring. 2. a small onion.

**shal·low** (shal′ō), *adj.* [prob. < AS. *sceald*], 1. not deep: as, a *shallow* stream. 2. lacking depth of character or intellect; superficial. *n.* a shallow place in water; shoal. *v.t. & v.i.* to make or become shallow. —**shal′low·ly,** *adv.* —**shal′low·ness,** *n.*

**shalt** (shalt), archaic 2d pers. sing., pres. indic. of **shall.**

**sham** (sham), *n.* [prob. < a dial. var. of *shame*], 1. formerly, a fraud. 2. an imitation; counterfeit; fake. 3. one who falsely affects a certain character. *adj.* not genuine or real; false. *v.t. & v.i.* [SHAMMED, SHAMMING], to pretend; counterfeit; feign. —**sham′mer,** *n.*

**sha·man** (shä′mən, shā′-, sham′ən), *n.* [*pl.* -MANS], [Russ.; ult. < Prakrit *samana*, Buddhist monk < Sans.], a priest or medicine man of Shamanism. —**sha·man·ic** (shə-man′ik), *adj.*

**sha·man·ism** (shä′mən-iz′m, shā′-, sham′ən-), *n.* 1. a religion of northeast Asia based on a belief in spirits who are influenced only by shamans. 2. a similar religion of some American Indians.

**sham·ble** (sham′b'l), *v.i.* [-BLED, -BLING], [orig. *adj.* referring to the legs of a *shamble*, bench; see SHAMBLES], to walk in a clumsy manner, barely lifting the feet. *n.* a shambling walk.

**sham·bles** (sham′b'lz), *n.pl.* [construed as sing.], [< AS. *scamel*, a bench < L. *scamellum*, dim. < *scamnum*: from early sense, butcher's bench or stall], 1. a slaughterhouse. 2. a place where much killing has been done; sometimes, any scene or condition of great destruction or disorder.

**shame** (shām), *n.* [< AS. *scamu*], 1. a painful feeling of guilt, incompetence, indecency, etc. 2. the capacity for such feelings. 3. dishonor; disgrace. 4. a person or thing that brings dishonor. 5. something unfortunate or outrageous: as, what a *shame!* *v.t.* [SHAMED, SHAMING], 1. to cause to feel shame. 2. to dishonor; disgrace. 3. to force by a sense of shame: as, he was *shamed* out of his prejudice. —**for shame!** you ought to be ashamed! —**put to shame,** 1. to cause to feel shame. 2. to do much better than; surpass. —**sham′er,** *n.*

**shame·faced** (shām′fāst′), *adj.* [alt. < AS. *scam*, shame + *fæst*, fast], 1. shy; bashful. 2. showing shame or guilt; ashamed. —**shame′fac′ed·ly** (-fās′id-li, -fāst′li), *adv.* —**shame′fac′ed·ness,** *n.*

**shame·ful** (shām′fəl), *adj.* 1. bringing or causing shame or disgrace; disgraceful. 2. violating what is considered to be just or decent; offensive. —**shame′ful·ly,** *adv.* —**shame′ful·ness,** *n.*

**shame·less** (shām′lis), *adj.* having or showing no shame, modesty, or decency; brazen. —**shame′less·ly,** *adv.* —**shame′less·ness,** *n.*

**sham·my** (sham′i), *n.* [*pl.* -MIES], chamois.

**sham·poo** (sham-pōō′), *v.t.* [-POOED, -POOING], [< Hind. imperative of *chāmpnā*, to press], 1. to massage. 2. to wash (the hair and scalp). 3. to wash the hair and scalp of. 4. to wash (a carpet, upholstery, etc.). *n.* 1. a washing of the hair, or of a carpet, etc. 2. a preparation used for this. —**sham·poo′er,** *n.*

**sham·rock** (sham′rok), *n.* [< Ir. dim. of *seamar*, clover], any of certain clovers or cloverlike plants with leaflets in groups of three: the emblem of Ireland.

SHAMROCK

**Shang·hai** (shaŋ′hī′, shäŋ′-), *n.* a seaport in east central China, near the mouth of the Yangtze River: pop., 6,000,000.

**shang·hai** (shaŋ′hī, shaŋ-hī′), *v.t.* [-HAIED, -HAIING], [< *Shanghai*, China: in allusion to such kidnapping for crews on the China run], 1. to kidnap, usually by drugging, for service aboard ship. 2. [Slang], to induce (another) to do something through force or underhanded methods.

**Shan·gri-La** (shaŋ′gri-lä′), *n.* [< the scene of J. Hilton's novel, *Lost Horizon*], any imaginary, idyllic utopia or hidden paradise.

**shank** (shaŋk), *n.* [< AS. *scanc*], 1. the part of the leg between the knee and the ankle in man, or a corresponding part in animals. 2. the whole leg. 3. a cut of beef from the upper leg. 4. the part between the handle and the working part; shaft (of a tool, etc.). 5. the body of a piece of type. 6. the narrow part of a shoe sole in front of the heel. 7. [Colloq.], the latter part of anything: as, the *shank* of a journey. —**ride (or go) on shank's mare,** to walk. —**shank of the evening,** [Colloq.], the early part of the evening. —**shanked,** *adj.*

**Shan·non** (shan′ən), *n.* a river in Ireland, flowing southwestward into the Atlantic.

**shan't** (shant, shänt), shall not.

**shant·ey** (shan′ti, shän′-), *n.* [*pl.* -IES], a chantey; sailor's work song; also sp. **shant′y** [*pl.* -IES].

**Shan·tung** (shan′tuŋ′, shän′dooŋ′), *n.* 1. a province of NE China, on the Yellow Sea. 2. [often s-], *a*) a fabric made from the silk of wild silkworms. *b*) a similar rayon or cotton fabric.

**shan·ty** (shan′ti), *n.* [*pl.* -TIES], [< Canad. Fr. *chantier*, workshop], a small, shabby dwelling; hut.

**shape** (shāp), *n.* [< AS. < *scieppan*, to create], 1. the quality of a thing that depends on the relative position of all points on its outline or surface; physical form. 2. the form of a particular person or thing. 3. the contour of the body; figure. 4. assumed appearance; guise: as, an enemy in the *shape* of a friend. 5. a phantom. 6. a mold used for shaping; form, as for making hats. 7. definite or regular form: as, his story is taking *shape*. 8. [Colloq.], condition; state: as, the victim was in bad *shape*. *v.t.* [SHAPED, SHAPED or *archaic* SHAPEN, SHAPING], 1. to give definite shape to; make. 2. to arrange, devise, or express in definite form, as an answer. 3. to adapt: as, *shape* your plans to your abilities. 4. to direct or conduct, as one's life. *v.i.* [Colloq.], to take shape. —**shape up,** [Colloq.], 1. to develop to a definite form, condition, etc. 2. to develop satisfactorily. —**take shape,** to show distinct development. —**shap′er,** *n.*

**shape·less** (shāp′lis), *adj.* 1. without distinct or regular form. 2. not pleasing to the eye; unshapely. —**shape′less·ly,** *adv.* —**shape′less·ness,** *n.*

**shape·ly** (shāp′li), *adj.* [-LIER, -LIEST], having good shape; well-proportioned. —**shape′li·ness,** *n.*

**shard** (shärd), *n.* [AS. *sceard*], 1. a fragment or broken piece, especially of pottery; potsherd. 2. the thin, hard wing cover of a beetle.

**share** (shâr), *n.* [< AS. < *sceran*, to cut], 1. a part or portion which belongs to an individual. 2. a just or full portion: as, we had our *share* of laughs. 3. any of the parts into which the ownership of a property is divided; esp., any of the equal parts of capital stock of a corporation. *v.t.* [SHARED, SHARING], 1. to distribute in shares. 2. to have a share of with others: as, to *share* expenses. *v.i.* to have a share; participate (often with *in*). —**go shares,** to take part jointly, as in an enterprise. —**shar′er,** *n.*

**share** (shâr), *n.* [AS. *scear*], a plowshare.

**share·crop** (shâr′krop′), *v.i. & v.t.* [-CROPPED, -CROPPING], to work (land) for a share of the crop. —**share′crop′per,** *n.* —**share′crop′ping,** *n.*

**share·hold·er** (shâr′hōl′dẽr), *n.* a person who holds or owns a share or shares.

**shark** (shärk), *n.* [prob. < G. *schurke*, scoundrel], 1. a viciously dishonest person; swindler. 2. [Slang], a person having great ability in a given activity; expert. *v.i.* to live by fraud.

**shark** (shärk), *n.* [prob. same word as prec.], any of several large fishes, mostly marine, with a tough, slate-gray skin: most sharks are fish-eaters and the larger ones will attack man.

**shark·skin** (shärk'skin'), *n.* 1. leather made from the skin of a shark. 2. a cloth of cotton or rayon with a smooth, silky surface. 3. a worsted woven with a small, pebbly pattern.

**sharp** (shärp), *adj.* [< AS. *scearp*], 1. having a thin edge or fine point, suitable for cutting or piercing; keen. 2. having a point or edge; not rounded: as, a *sharp* ridge. 3. not gradual; abrupt: as, a *sharp* turn. 4. clearly defined; distinct: as, a *sharp* difference. 5. quick or acute in perception or intellect; clever. 6. attentive; vigilant: as, *sharp* eyes. 7. crafty; underhanded. 8. harsh; severe, as language, temper, etc. 9. violent, as an attack. 10. brisk; active: as, a *sharp* run. 11. cold, as the wind. 12. severe; intense, as pain, grief, etc. 13. strong; pungent, as in taste. 14. high-pitched; shrill: said of sound. 15. [Slang], attractively groomed; handsome. 16. in *music*, *a*) raised in pitch by a half step: as, C *sharp*. *b*) above true pitch. *c*) with the signature in sharps. 17. in *phonetics*, voiceless. *n.* 1. [Colloq.], *a*) an expert. *b*) a sharper. 2. in *music*, *a*) a tone one half step above another. *b*) the symbol (♯) indicating this. *v.t.* in *music*, to raise a half step. *v.i.* in *music*, to sing or play above true pitch. *adv.* 1. in a sharp manner; specif., *a*) abruptly or briskly. *b*) attentively or alertly. *c*) so as to have a sharp point or edge. *d*) keenly; piercingly. *e*) in *music*, above true pitch. 2. precisely: as, one o'clock *sharp*. —**sharp'ly,** *adv.* —**sharp'ness,** *n.*

**sharp·en** (shär'p'n), *v.t. & v.i.* to make or become sharp or sharper. —**sharp'en·er,** *n.*

**sharp·er** (shär'pẽr), *n.* a person, as a gambler, who is dishonest in dealing with others; swindler.

**sharp·ie** (shär'pi), *n.* [< *sharp*], a long, narrow, flat-bottomed fishing boat with one or two masts, each with a triangular sail.

**sharp·shoot·er** (shärp'shōōt'ẽr), *n.* a person who shoots with great accuracy; good marksman. **sharp'shoot'ing,** *n.*

**sharp-tongued** (shärp'tuŋd'), *adj.* using or characterized by sharp or harshly critical language.

**sharp-wit·ted** (shärp'wit'id), *adj.* having or showing keen intelligence or discernment. —**sharp'-wit'ted·ly,** *adv.* —**sharp'-wit'ted·ness,** *n.*

**Shas·ta, Mount** (shas'tə), a mountain in N California.

**Shasta daisy,** [after Mt. *Shasta*], 1. a daisylike chrysanthemum. 2. its flower.

**shat·ter** (shat'ẽr), *v.t.* [ME. *sc(h)ateren*, to scatter], 1. to break into pieces suddenly, as with a blow. 2. to damage severely, as a structure, one's health, etc.; destroy. *v.i.* to burst into pieces; smash. *n. pl.* broken pieces. —**shat'ter·er,** *n.*

**shave** (shāv), *v.t.* [SHAVED, SHAVED or SHAVEN, SHAVING], [< AS. *sceafan*], 1. to cut away thin slices from, as the edge of a plank. 2. to scrape into thin sections, as ice. 3. *a*) to cut off (hair, as the beard) at the surface of the skin (often with *off* or *away*). *b*) to cut the hair to the surface of (the face, legs, etc.). *c*) to cut the beard of (a person). 4. to skim the surface of; graze. 5. to trim closely, as grass. *v.i.* to cut off hair with a razor; shave oneself. *n.* 1. a tool used for shaving thin slices, etc. 2. something shaved off; shaving. 3. the act or result of shaving the beard. 4. [Colloq.], a narrow escape: as, a *close* shave.

**shav·en** (shāv''n), alt. pp. of **shave.** *adj.* 1. shaved or tonsured. 2. closely trimmed.

**shav·er** (shāv'ẽr), *n.* 1. a person who shaves. 2. an instrument used in shaving: as, an electric *shaver*. 3. [Colloq.], a boy; youngster.

**shave·tail** (shāv'tāl'), *n.* [orig., an unbroken mule], [Slang], a newly appointed second lieutenant.

**Sha·vi·an** (shā'vi-ən), *adj.* of or characteristic of George Bernard Shaw or his work. *n.* an admirer of Shaw or his work.

**shav·ing** (shāv'iŋ), *n.* 1. the act of one who shaves. 2. a thin piece of wood, metal, etc. shaved off.

**Shaw, George Bernard** (shô), 1856–1950; Irish dramatist and critic.

**shawl** (shôl), *n.* [< Per. *shāl*], an oblong or square cloth worn, especially by women, as a covering for the head and shoulders.

**Shaw·nee** (shô-nē', shô'nē), *n.* [*pl.* -NEE, -NEES], a member of a tribe of Algonquian Indians that migrated from South Carolina and Tennessee into Ohio and now live in Oklahoma.

**shay** (shā), *n.* [back-formation < *chaise*, assumed as pl.], [Colloq.], a light carriage; chaise.

**she** (shē; *unstressed* shi), *pron.* [for *pl.* see THEY], [prob. after AS. *seo*, fem. def. article; replacing AS. *heo*, she], the girl, woman, or female animal (or the object regarded as female) previously mentioned: *she* is the nominative case form, *her* the objective, *her* or *hers* the possessive, and *herself* the intensive and reflexive, of the feminine third personal pronoun. *n.* a girl, woman, or female animal: as, our dog is a *she*.

**sheaf** (shēf), *n.* [*pl.* SHEAVES], [< AS. *sceaf*], 1. a bunch of cut stalks of grain, etc. bound together. 2. a collection, as of papers, bound in a bundle. *v.t.* to bind in a sheaf, as grain.

**shear** (shêr), *v.t.* [SHEARED, SHEARED or SHORN, SHEARING], [< AS. *sceran*], 1. to cut as with shears. 2. to remove (the hair, wool, etc.) by cutting. 3. to clip the hair, wool, etc. from. 4. to strip (*of* a power, right, etc.). *v.i.* 1. to use shears, etc. as in cutting wool or metal. 2. to break under a shearing stress. 3. to move as if by cutting: as, the plane *sheared* through the clouds. *n.* 1. *a*) [Rare], shears. *b*) a single blade of a pair of shears. 2. a machine used in cutting metal. 3. the act or result of shearing. 4. something shorn, as a sheep or its wool. 5. a shearing: as, a sheep of three *shears*. 6. shearing stress. —**shear'er,** *n.*

**shearing stress,** the force tending to make two contacting parts slide upon each other in opposite directions parallel to their plane of contact.

**shears** (shêrz), *n.pl.* 1. large scissors. 2. any of several large tools or machines with two opposed blades, used to cut metal, etc.

**shear·wa·ter** (shêr'wô'tẽr, -wot'ẽr), *n.* any of several black-and-white sea birds, related to the petrels, that skim the water in flight.

**sheath** (shēth), *n.* [*pl.* SHEATHS (shēthz, shēths)], [< AS. *sceath*], 1. a case for the blade of a knife, sword, etc. 2. a covering resembling this, as the membrane around a muscle, etc. *v.t.* to sheathe. —**sheath'less,** *adj.*

**sheathe** (shēth), *v.t.* [SHEATHED, SHEATHING], 1. to put into a sheath or scabbard. 2. to enclose in a case or covering. —**sheathed,** *adj.* —**sheath'er,** *n.*

**sheath·ing** (shēth'iŋ), *n.* 1. the act of placing in a sheath. 2. something that sheathes; specif., *a*) the inner covering of boards or waterproof material on the roof or outside wall of a frame house. *b*) the protective covering of a ship's hull. *c*) the material for either of these.

**sheave** (shiv), *n.* [< ME. *schive*], a wheel with a grooved rim, as in a pulley block.

**sheave** (shēv), *v.t.* [SHEAVED, SHEAVING], to gather (grain, papers, etc.) in a sheaf or sheaves.

**sheaves** (shēvz), *n.* pl. of **sheaf** and of **sheave.**

**She·ba** (shē'bə), *n.* Saba: the Biblical name.

**Sheba, Queen of,** in the *Bible*, the queen who visited King Solomon to investigate his reputed wisdom: I Kings 10:1-13.

**she·bang** (shə-baŋ'), *n.* [Slang], a particular matter of concern; affair, business, thing, etc.

**She·bat** (shə-bät', -vät'), *n.* [Heb.], the fifth month of the Jewish year: see **Jewish calendar.**

**shed** (shed), *n.* [var. of *shade* < AS. *scead*], 1. a small, roughly built shelter or storage place. 2. any barnlike structure for storage.

**shed** (shed), *v.t.* [SHED, SHEDDING], [< AS. *sceadan*, to separate], 1. to pour out; emit. 2. to cause to flow; let drop: as, she *shed* tears. 3. to send forth or spread about; radiate: as, to shed confidence. 4. to throw off; repel: as, oilskin *sheds* water. 5. to cast off (a natural growth, as leaves, hair, etc.). *v.i.* to shed hair, etc.: as, our dog is *shedding* badly. *n.* a watershed. —**shed blood,** to kill by violent means.

**she'd** (shēd), 1. she had. 2. she would.

**shed·der** (shed'ẽr), *n.* one that sheds; specif., a lobster, crab, etc. that is shedding its shell.

**sheen** (shēn), *n.* [< AS. *scene*, beautiful], 1. brightness; luster. 2. bright or shining attire. *adj.* [Poetic], of shining beauty; bright. *v.i.* [Poetic], to shine; gleam. —**sheen'y** [-IER, -IEST], *adj.*

**sheep** (shēp), *n.* [*pl.* SHEEP], [AS. *sceap*], 1. a cud-chewing mammal related to the goats, with heavy wool and edible flesh called mutton. 2. leather made from sheepskin. 3. a person who is meek, stupid, timid, etc. —**make sheep's eyes at,** to look shyly and lovingly at.

**sheep·cote** (shēp'kōt'), *n.* [cf. COTE], a sheepfold: also **sheep'cot'** (-kot').

**sheep·dip** (shēp'dip'), *n.* a chemical preparation used as a bath to free sheep from vermin, etc.

**sheep dog,** a dog trained to herd sheep; specif., *a*) a collie. *b*) a large, gentle dog with long, rough hair: also called **old English sheep dog.**

**sheep·fold** (shēp'fōld'), *n.* an enclosure for sheep.

**sheep·herd·er** (shēp'hũr'dẽr), *n.* a person who herds or tends a large flock of grazing sheep.

**sheep·ish** (shēp'ish), *adj.* 1. bashful; shy; awkward. 2. resembling sheep in meekness, timidity, etc. —**sheep'ish·ly,** *adv.* —**sheep'ish·ness,** *n.*

**sheep·man** (shēp'man'), *n.* [*pl.* -MEN (-men')], 1.

a person whose business is raising sheep. 2. a sheepherder or shepherd.
**sheep·shank** (shēp′shaŋk′), *n.* a knot used for shortening a rope.
**sheep·skin** (shēp′skin′), *n.* 1. the skin of a sheep, especially one dressed with the fleece on it. 2. parchment or leather made from the skin of a sheep. 3. [Colloq.], a diploma.
**sheep sorrel,** a weed with fleshy, acid-tasting leaves, found in dry places.
**sheep·walk** (shēp′wôk′), *n.* a pasture for sheep: also **sheep run.**
**sheer** (shêr), *v.i.* [a form of *shear*], to turn aside from a course; swerve; deviate. *v.t.* to cause to turn. *n.* 1. deviation from a course. 2. the oblique heading of a ship riding at a single bow anchor. 3. the upward curve of a ship's deck lines as seen from the side.
**sheer** (shêr), *adj.* [< ON. *skiær*, bright], 1. very thin; transparent: said of textiles. 2. not mixed with anything else; pure. 3. absolute; downright: as, *sheer* persistence. 4. extremely steep, as the face of a cliff. *adv.* 1. completely; utterly. 2. very steeply. *n.* thin, fine material, or a garment made of it. —**sheer′ly,** *adv.* —**sheer′ness,** *n.*
**sheet** (shēt), *n.* [AS. *sceat*], 1. a large piece of cotton, linen, etc., used as bedding. 2. [Poetic], a sail. 3. *a*) a single piece of paper. *b*) *pl.* the leaves of a book, magazine, etc., especially when unbound. *c*) a newspaper. 4. a broad, continuous surface or layer, as of flame, water, etc. 5. a broad, thin piece of any material, as glass, tin, etc. *v.t.* to cover or provide with a sheet.
**sheet** (shēt), *n.* [< AS. *sceatline*], 1. a rope for controlling the set of a sail, attached to a lower corner. 2. *pl.* the spaces not occupied by thwarts, at the bow and stern of an open boat.
**sheet anchor,** 1. a large anchor used only in emergencies. 2. a person or thing to be relied upon in emergency.
**sheet bend,** a knot used in fastening a rope to the bight of another rope or to an eye.
**sheet·ing** (shēt′iŋ), *n.* 1. cotton or linen material used for making sheets. 2. material used in covering or lining a surface: as, copper *sheeting.*
**sheet metal** (or **iron, copper,** etc.), metal (or iron, copper, etc.) rolled thin to the form of a sheet.
**sheet music,** music printed on unbound sheets of paper.
**Shef·field** (shef′ēld), *n.* a city in NE England: pop., 508,000.
**sheik, sheikh** (shēk), *n.* [< Ar. *shaikh*, old man], 1. the chief of an Arab family, tribe, or village: a title of respect. 2. an official in the Moslem religious organization. 3. [Slang], a man irresistible to women. —**sheik′dom, sheikh′dom,** *n.*
**shek·el** (shek′'l), *n.* [< Heb. < *shāqal*, to weigh], 1. among the ancient Hebrews, Babylonians, etc., a weight unit (about ½ oz.), or a gold or silver coin of this weight. 2. *pl.* [Slang], money; coins.
**shel·drake** (shel′drāk′), *n.* [*pl.* -DRAKES, -DRAKE; see PLURAL, II, D, 1], [< ME. *sheld*, a shield, hence varicolored; + *drake*], 1. a large European wild duck that feeds on fish, etc. and nests in burrows: the plumage is variegated. 2. a merganser.
**shelf** (shelf), *n.* [*pl.* SHELVES], [< MLG. *schelf*, set of shelves], 1. a thin, flat length of wood, metal, etc. set horizontally against a wall, or in a cupboard, etc., used for holding things. 2. the contents or capacity of a shelf. 3. something like a shelf, as a flat ledge of rock. 4. a sandbar or reef. —**on the shelf,** out of use, circulation, etc.
**shell** (shel), *n.* [AS. *sciel*], 1. a hard outer covering, as of an animal, egg, nut, etc. 2. material of or like animal shell, used in making or decorating articles. 3. something like a shell in being hollow, empty, a covering, etc., as the hull of a ship, an unfilled pie crust, etc. 4. mere outward appearance. 5. a light, long, narrow racing boat rowed by a team of oarsmen. 6. a missile fired from a large gun, containing high explosives, shrapnel, etc. 7. a small arms cartridge. *v.t.* 1. to remove the shell or covering from: as, to *shell* peas. 2. to separate (kernels of corn, etc.) from the ear. 3. to fire shells at from large guns; bombard. *v.i.* 1. to separate from the shell or covering. 2. to fall or peel off, as a shell. —**come out of** (or **retire into**) **one's shell,** to become less (or more) shy or reserved. —**shell out,** [Colloq.], to pay out (money). —**shelled,** *adj.* —**shell′er,** *n.* —**shell′-less,** *adj.* —**shell′y** [-IER, -IEST], *adj.*
**she'll** (shēl, shil), 1. she shall. 2. she will.
**shel·lac, shel·lack, shell-lac** (shə-lak′), *n.* [*shell* + *lac*, transl. of Fr. *laque en écailles*, lac in fine sheets], 1. refined lac, a resin usually produced in thin, flaky layers, used in making varnish, phonograph records, etc. 2. a thin varnish containing shellac resin and alcohol. *v.t.* [SHELLACKED or SHELL-LACKED, SHELLACKING or SHELL-LACKING], 1. to apply shellac to; cover with shellac. 2. [Slang], *a*) to beat; flog. *b*) to defeat decisively. —**shel·lack′er,** *n.* —**shel·lack′ing,** *n.*
**shell·back** (shel′bak′), *n.* [prob. in allusion to sea turtle], 1. an old, experienced sailor. 2. anyone who has crossed the equator by ship.
**shell·bark** (shel′bärk′), *n.* the shagbark.
**-shelled** (sheld), a combining form meaning: *having a* (specified kind of) *shell*, as in *soft-shelled.*
**Shel·ley, Per·cy Bysshe** (pũr′si bish shel′i), 1792–1822; English poet.
**shell·fire** (shel′fīr′), *n.* bombardment with shells.
**shell·fish** (shel′fish′), *n.* [*pl.* see FISH], any aquatic animal with a shell, as the oyster or clam.
**shell game,** 1. a swindling game in which the victim bets on the location of a pea ostensibly concealed under one of three shells. 2. any scheme for victimizing people.
**shell·proof** (shel′prōōf′), *adj.* proof against damage from shells or bombs.
**shell shock,** combat fatigue: formerly so called because thought to be caused by continued concussion of artillery fire. —**shell′shocked′,** *adj.*
**shel·ter** (shel′tẽr), *n.* [< AS. *sceldtruma*, troop protected by interlocked shields < *sceld*, shield + *truma*, a troop], 1. something that covers or protects; place of protection against the elements, danger, etc. 2. a being covered, protected, etc.; refuge. *v.t.* to provide shelter or refuge for; protect. *v.i.* to find shelter or refuge. —**shel′ter·er,** *n.* —**shel′ter·less,** *adj.*
**shelve** (shelv), *v.i.* [SHELVED, SHELVING], to slope gradually. *v.t.* 1. to furnish with shelves. 2. to put on a shelf or shelves. 3. *a*) to put away as if on a shelf; lay aside: as, to *shelve* a discussion. *b*) to retire from active service.
**shelves** (shelvz), *n.* pl. of **shelf.**
**shelv·ing** (shel′viŋ), *n.* 1. material for shelves: as, wood *shelving.* 2. shelves collectively.
**Shem** (shem), *n.* in the *Bible*, the eldest son of Noah: traditional ancestor of the Semitic people.
**Shem·ite** (shem′īt), *n.* Semite. —**Shem·it′ic** (-it′ik), *adj.*
**Shen·an·do·ah** (shen′ən-dō′ə), *n.* a river in Virginia flowing into the Potomac River.
**she·nan·i·gan** (shi-nan′i-gən), *n.* [? < Ir. *sionnachuighim*, I play the fox; ? < G. dial. *schinageln*, to use trickery to avoid work], *usually pl.* [Colloq.], nonsense; trickery; mischief.
**She·ol** (shē′ōl), *n.* [< Heb. < *shā'al*, to dig], 1. in the *Bible*, the abode of the dead, in the depths of the earth; underworld. 2. [s-], [Colloq.], hell.
**shep·herd** (shep′ẽrd), *n.* [AS. *sceaphyrde;* see SHEEP & HERD], 1. one who herds sheep. 2. a religious leader; minister. *v.t.* to herd, guard, lead, etc. as a shepherd. —**the Good Shepherd,** Jesus. —**shep′herd·ess,** *n.fem.*
**shepherd dog,** a sheep dog.
**shep·herd's-purse** (shep′ẽrdz-pũrs′), *n.* a weed with small, white flowers and pouchlike pods.
**Sher·a·ton** (sher′ə-t'n), *adj.* [after T. *Sheraton* (1751–1806), Eng. cabinetmaker], designating or of furniture characterized by simplicity and lightness of form, straight lines, etc.
**sher·bet** (shũr′bət), *n.* [< Turk. < Ar. *sharbah*, a drink], 1. [Brit.], a beverage made of watered fruit juice and sugar. 2. a frozen dessert of fruit juice, sugar, and water, milk, or egg white.
**Sher·i·dan, Philip Henry** (sher′i-d'n), 1831–1888; Union general in the Civil War.
**Sheridan, Richard Brins·ley** (brinz′li), 1751–1816; Irish dramatist and politician.
**she·rif** (shə-rēf′), *n.* [Ar. *sharif*, noble], 1. a descendant of Mohammed through his daughter Fatima. 2. an Arab prince or chief. Also sp. **shereef.**
**sher·iff** (sher′if), *n.* [< AS. < *scir*, shire + *gerefa*, reeve], the chief law-enforcement officer of a county, charged with the keeping of the peace and the execution of court orders. —**sher′iff·dom,** *n.*
**Sher·man, William Te·cum·seh** (ti-kum′sə shũr′mən), 1820–1891; Union general in the Civil War.
**sher·ry** (sher′i), *n.* [< earlier *sherris* < *Xeres* (now

Jerez), Spain], 1. a strong, yellow or brownish Spanish wine. 2. any similar wine.

**Sher·wood Forest** (shūr′wood), a forest near Nottingham, England, famous in Robin Hood legends.

**she's** (shēz), 1. she is. 2. she has.

**Shet·land Islands** (shet′lənd), a group of Scottish islands northeast of the Orkney Islands.

**Shetland pony,** any of a breed of sturdy pony with a rough coat and long tail and mane, originally from the Shetland Islands.

**She·vu·oth** (shə-vōō′ōth, -ōs), *n.* [Heb.], Shabuoth.

**shew** (shō), *n., v.t. & v.i.* [SHEWED, SHEWN, SHEWING], [Brit. or Archaic], show.

**shew·bread** (shō′bred′), *n.* [*shew* + *bread;* transl. of Heb. *lehem pānīm*, presence bread], the unleavened bread placed at the altar before Jehovah every Sabbath by the ancient Hebrew priests: also sp. **showbread.**

**shib·bo·leth** (shib′ə-ləth), *n.* [< L. < Heb. *shibbōleth*, a stream], 1. in the *Bible*, the test word used by the Gileadites to distinguish the escaping Ephraimites, who could not pronounce the *sh*: Judg. 12:6; hence, 2. any password. 3. any distinctive phrase, formula, etc., as of a party or class.

**shied** (shīd), pt. and pp. of **shy.**

**shield** (shēld), *n.* [AS. *scield*], 1. a piece of armor carried in the hand or worn on the forearm to ward off blows or missiles. 2. any person or thing that guards, protects, etc. 3. a heraldic escutcheon. 4. anything shaped like a shield. 5. a safety guard, as over the moving parts of machinery. 6. a device worn under the armpit, to prevent soiling a garment by perspiration. *v.t. & v.i.* to be a shield (for); defend; protect. —**shield′er,** *n.*

**shift** (shift), *v.t.* [AS. *sciftan*, to divide], 1. to move or transfer as from one person or place to another. 2. to put another or others in place of; change. 3. to change the arrangement of (gears). *v.i.* 1. to change position, direction, etc. 2. to get along; manage: as, to *shift* for oneself. 3. to use tricky or fraudulent methods. 4. to change from one gear to another. *n.* 1. a plan of conduct, especially for an emergency; stratagem. 2. a fraudulent scheme; trick. 3. the act of shifting; transfer; substitution. 4. a group of employees working in relay with another. 5. the daily work period of such a group. 6. a change in direction, as of the wind. 7. [Now Rare], a chemise. 8. in *football*, a regrouping of the players just before the ball is put in play. —**make shift,** 1. to do as well as one can under difficulties. 2. to do one's best (*with*). —**shift′a·ble,** *adj.* —**shift′er,** *n.*

**shift·less** (shift′lis), *adj.* 1. lacking the will or ability to do or accomplish; inefficient, lazy, etc. 2. showing such lack. —**shift′less·ly,** *adv.* —**shift′less·ness,** *n.*

**shift·y** (shif′ti), *adj.* [-IER, -IEST], 1. full of shifts or expedients; resourceful. 2. of a tricky nature; evasive. —**shift′i·ly,** *adv.* —**shift′i·ness,** *n.*

**Shi·ko·ku** (shē′kō-kōō′), *n.* an island of Japan, south of Honshu.

**shill** (shil), *n.* [Slang], a confederate, as of a gambler or peddler at a carnival, who pretends to buy, bet, etc. in order to lure others.

**shil·le·lagh, shil·la·lah** (shi-lā′lə, shə-lā′li), *n.* [< *Shillelagh*, Irish village famous for oaks], a club or cudgel: also sp. **shillelah, shillala.**

**shil·ling** (shil′iŋ), *n.* [AS. *scylling*], 1. a British money of account and silver coin, equal to 12 pence: symbol, /. 2. a coin of colonial America, of varying value.

**shil·ly-shal·ly** (shil′i-shal′i), *adv.* [a redupl. of *shall I?*], in a vacillating manner; hesitantly. *adj.* vacillating; irresolute. *n.* indecision; vacillation, especially of a trifling kind. *v.i.* [-LIED, -LYING], 1. to be irresolute; vacillate. 2. to concern oneself with trifles. —**shil′ly-shal′ly·er, shil′ly-shal′li·er,** *n.*

**Shi·loh** (shī′lō), *n.* 1. a national military park in SW Tennessee: scene of a battle (1862) of the Civil War. 2. an ancient town in Palestine.

**shi·ly** (shī′li), *adv.* shyly.

**shim** (shim), *n.* [< ?], a thin piece of wood, metal, etc., used for filling space, leveling, etc. *v.t.* [SHIMMED, SHIMMING], to fit with a shim or shims.

**shim·mer** (shim′ēr), *v.i.* [AS. *scymrian*], to shine with an unsteady light; glimmer. *n.* a shimmering light; glimmer. —**shim′mer·y,** *adj.*

**shim·my, shim·mey** (shim′i), *n.* [*pl.* -MIES or -MEYS], [< Fr. *chemise*, a chemise], 1. a jazz dance of the 1920's, with much shaking of the body. 2. a marked vibration or wobble, as in automobile wheels. *v.i.* [-MIED, -MYING; MEYED, -MEYING], to shake, vibrate, or wobble.

**shin** (shin), *n.* [AS. *scinu*], 1. the front part of the leg between the knee and the ankle. 2. the lower part of the foreleg in beef cattle. *v.t. & v.i.* [SHINNED, SHINNING], to climb (a rope, pole, etc.), gripping with both hands and legs.

**shin·bone** (shin′bōn′), *n.* the inner bone of the lower leg; tibia: also **shin bone.**

**shin·dig** (shin′dig), *n.* [folk-etym. form of colloq. *shindy*, commotion], [Colloq.], a dance, party, or other social affair.

**shine** (shīn), *v.i.* [SHONE or, esp. for *v.t.* 2, SHINED, SHINING], [AS. *scinan*], 1. to emit or reflect light; gleam; glow. 2. to excel; be eminent. 3. to exhibit itself clearly: as, love *shone* from her face. *v.t.* 1. to cause to shine: as, to *shine* a flashlight. 2. to make shiny by polishing. *n.* 1. brightness; radiance. 2. luster; polish; gloss. 3. a shoeshine. 4. splendor; brilliance. 5. [Slang], a trick or prank. —**rain or shine,** whether it is raining or fair weather. —**shine up to,** [Slang], to try to become friendly with. —**take a shine to,** [Slang], to develop a liking for.

**shin·er** (shīn′ēr), *n.* 1. a person or thing that shines. 2. [*pl.* -ERS, -ER; see PLURAL, II, D, 1], a minnow with silvery scales. 3. [Slang], a black eye.

**shin·gle** (shiŋ′g'l), *n.* [Norw. *singel*], 1. coarse, waterworn gravel, as on a beach. 2. an area covered with this. —**shin′gly** [-GLIER, -GLIEST], *adj.*

**shin·gle** (shiŋ′g'l), *n.* [ME. < *schindle* < L. < *scindere*, to split], 1. a thin, wedge-shaped tile of wood, slate, etc. laid with others in a series of overlapping rows as a covering for roofs, etc. 2. a short haircut with the hair in back cropped close. 3. [Colloq.], a small signboard, as that of a doctor or lawyer. *v.t.* [-GLED, -GLING], 1. to cover (a roof, etc.) with shingles. 2. to cut (hair) in shingle style. —**shin′gler,** *n.*

**shin·gles** (shiŋ′g'lz), *n.* [< ML. < L. *cingulum*, a girdle < *cingere*, to gird], an acute virus disease with eruption of small blisters on the skin along the course of a nerve; herpes zoster.

**shin·ing** (shīn′iŋ), *adj.* 1. giving off or reflecting light; bright. 2. brilliant; eminent: as, a *shining* example. —**shin′ing·ly,** *adv.*

**shin·ny, shin·ney** (shin′i), *n.* [*pl.* -NIES or -NEYS], [? < *shin*], 1. a simple form of hockey played by children. 2. the crooked stick used in this game. *v.i.* [-NIED, -NYING; -NEYED, -NEYING], to play shinny.

**shin·ny** (shin′i), *v.i.* [-NIED, -NYING], [Colloq.], to climb (*up*) using the shins for gripping.

**shin·plas·ter** (shin′plas′tēr, -pläs′-), *n.* 1. any plaster or poultice used on sore shins. 2. a piece of paper money depreciated by inflation or, formerly, one having a face value of less than a dollar.

**Shin·to** (shin′tō), *n.* [Japan. < Chin. *shin*, god + *tao*, way], a religion of Japan, emphasizing ancestor worship and, formerly, the divinity of the emperor: also **Shin′to·ism.** —**Shin′to·ist,** *n. & adj.*

**shin·y** (shīn′i), *adj.* [-IER, -IEST], 1. bright; shining. 2. smoothly polished; glossy. —**shin′i·ness,** *n.*

**ship** (ship), *n.* [AS. *scip*], 1. any large vessel navigating deep water: cf. *boat.* 2. a sailing vessel with a bowsprit and at least three square-rigged masts. 3. a ship's officers and crew. 4. any aircraft. *v.t.* [SHIPPED, SHIPPING], 1. to put or take on board a ship. 2. to send or transport by any carrier: as, to *ship* coal by rail. 3. to take in (water) over the side, as in a heavy sea. 4. to put or fix in its proper place on a ship or boat: as, *ship* the oars. 5. to engage for work on a ship. 6. [Colloq.], to send away; get rid of. *v.i.* 1. to go aboard ship; embark. 2. to engage to serve on a ship. —**when one's ship comes home** (or **in**), when one's fortune has been made. —**ship′pa·ble,** *adj.*

**-ship,** [AS. *-scipe*], a suffix meaning: 1. *the quality* or *state of*, as in *friendship.* 2. *a*) *the rank* or *office of*, as in *governorship.* *b*) *one having the rank of*, as in *lordship.* 3. *ability in*, as in *leadership.*

**ship biscuit,** a kind of hard biscuit that will not spoil easily, used on long voyages; hardtack.

**ship·board** (ship′bôrd′, -bōrd′), *n.* a ship. —**on shipboard,** on or in a ship.

**ship·build·er** (ship′bil′dēr), *n.* one whose business is building ships. —**ship′build′ing,** *n. & adj.*

**ship canal,** a canal large enough for ships.

**ship·load** (ship′lōd′), *n.* the load of a ship.

**ship·mas·ter** (ship′mas′tēr, -mäs′-), *n.* the officer in command of a merchant ship; captain.

**ship·mate** (ship′māt′), *n.* a sailor on the same ship; fellow sailor.

**ship·ment** (ship′mənt), *n.* 1. the shipping of goods; consignment. 2. goods shipped.

**ship of the desert,** a camel.

**ship of the line,** formerly, a warship of the largest class, carrying at least seventy-four guns.

**ship·own·er** (ship′ōn′ēr), *n.* an owner of a ship or ships.

**ship·per** (ship′ẽr), *n.* a person who ships goods.
**ship·ping** (ship′iŋ), *n.* 1. the act or business of transporting goods. 2. ships collectively, as of a nation or port, with reference to tonnage.
**ship·shape** (ship′shāp′), *adj.* having everything neatly in place, as on board ship; trim. *adv.* in a shipshape manner.
**ship·worm** (ship′wũrm′), *n.* any of various small, wormlike mollusks that burrow into submerged wood.
**ship·wreck** (ship′rek′), *n.* 1. the remains of a wrecked ship. 2. the loss or destruction of a ship through storm, collision, etc. 3. any ruin or destruction. *v.t.* 1. to cause to undergo shipwreck (sense 2). 2. to destroy, ruin, or wreck.
**ship·wright** (ship′rīt′), *n.* a man whose work is the construction and repair of ships.
**ship·yard** (ship′yärd′), *n.* a place where ships are built and repaired.
**shire** (shīr), *n.* [AS. *scire*, office], 1. formerly, a district in Great Britain, coinciding with the modern county. 2. any of the counties of Great Britain with a name containing the suffix *-shire.*
**shirk** (shũrk), *v.t.* [prob. < G. *schurke*, rascal], to neglect or evade doing (something that should be done). *v.i.* to neglect an obligation. *n.* a person who shirks: also **shirk′er.**
**shirr** (shũr), *n.* [< ?], a series of parallel rows of short, running stitches with gatherings between rows. *v.t.* 1. to make shirrs in (cloth). 2. to bake (eggs) with crumbs in small buttered dishes.
**shirt** (shũrt), *n.* [AS. *scyrte*], 1. any of various garments worn by men on the upper part of the body, often under a suit coat. 2. an undershirt. —**keep one's shirt on,** [Slang], to be patient or calm. —**lose one's shirt,** [Slang], to lose everything.
**shirt·ing** (shũr′tiŋ), *n.* material for making shirts.
**shirt-sleeve** (shũrt′slēv′), *adj.* 1. plain; informal. 2. homespun: as, *shirt-sleeve* philosophy.
**shirt·waist** (shũrt′wāst′), *n.* a woman's tailored blouse, worn with a separate skirt.
**Shi·va** (shē′və), *n.* Siva.
**shiv·a·ree** (shiv′ə-rē′), *n.* [< *charivari*], a mock serenade, as to newlyweds, with kettles, horns, etc. *v.t.* [-REED, -REEING], to serenade with a shivaree.
**shiv·er** (shiv′ẽr), *n.* [ME. *schivere*], a fragment or splinter of something broken, as glass. *v.t. & v.i.* to break into many fragments or splinters; shatter. —**shiv′er·y,** *adj.*
**shiv·er** (shiv′ẽr), *v.i.* [prob. < ME. *cheveren* < AS. *ceafl*, a jaw], to shake, tremble, etc., as from fear or cold. *n.* a shaking, trembling, etc., as from fear or cold. —**shiv′er·er,** *n.* —**shiv′er·y,** *adj.*
**shoal** (shōl), *n.* [AS. *scolu*], 1. a large group; mass; crowd. 2. a large school of fish. *v.i.* to come together in or move about as a shoal.
**shoal** (shōl), *n.* [< AS. *sceald*, shallow], 1. a place in a river, sea, etc. where the water is shallow. 2. a sand bar, etc. forming a shallow place, especially one visible at low water. *v.t. & v.i.* to make or become shallow. —**shoal′y,** *adj.*
**shoat** (shōt), *n.* [prob. < LG.], a young pig, especially when able to feed alone: also sp. **shote.**
**shock** (shok), *n.* [< Fr. < *choquer* < MD. *schokken*, to collide], 1. *a*) a sudden, powerful blow, shake, disturbance, etc. *b*) the effect of this. 2. *a*) any sudden emotional disturbance, as through great surprise. *b*) something causing this. 3. an extreme stimulation of the nerves by the passage of electric current through the body. 4. [Colloq.], a paralytic stroke. 5. in *medicine*, a disorder of the circulatory system, caused by injury or sudden psychic disturbance, and characterized by a decrease in blood pressure, a weak and rapid pulse, etc. *v.t.* 1. to disturb emotionally; astonish, horrify, etc. 2. to affect with physical shock. 3. to produce electrical shock in. —**shock′er,** *n.*
**shock** (shok), *n.* [prob. < MD. or MLG.], a bunch of grain sheaves stacked together to cure and dry. *v.t. & v.i.* to gather in shocks. —**shock′er,** *n.*
**shock** (shok), *n.* [< obs. *shock dog*, poodlelike dog], a thick, bushy or tangled mass, as of hair.
**shock absorber,** a device that lessens or absorbs the force of shocks, as on automobile springs.
**shock·ing** (shok′iŋ), *adj.* 1. causing great surprise and distress; staggering. 2. offensive or revolting: sometimes used to mean merely "very bad." —**shock′ing·ly,** *adv.* —**shock′ing·ness,** *n.*
**shock therapy,** in *psychiatry*, a method of treating patients by injecting drugs or by applying electric current to the brain, in order to induce shock artificially: also **shock treatment.**
**shock troops,** troops especially chosen, trained, and equipped to lead an attack.
**shod** (shod), pt. and pp. of **shoe.**
**shod·dy** (shod′i), *n.* [*pl.* -DIES], [< Yorkshire dial., orig. inferior stone or coal < *shode*, loose pieces], 1. an inferior woolen yarn or cloth made from fibers of used fabrics. 2. anything of less worth than it appears to have. *adj.* [-DIER, -DIEST], 1. made of shoddy or of inferior material. 2. lacking the required or claimed quality. —**shod′di·ly,** *adv.* —**shod′di·ness,** *n.*
**shoe** (sho͞o), *n.* [*pl.* SHOES, *archaic* or *dial.* SHOON], [< AS. *scoh*], 1. an outer covering for the foot, usually of leather and with a stiff sole and heel. 2. a horseshoe. 3. something like a shoe in shape or use; specif., *a*) the curved part of a brake that presses against a wheel. *b*) the metal strip along the bottom of a sled runner. *c*) the outer casing of a pneumatic tire. *v.t.* [SHOD, SHOEING], to furnish with shoes. —**fill one's shoes,** to take one's place. —**in another's shoes,** in another position.
**shoe·black** (sho͞o′blak′), *n.* a bootblack.
**shoe·horn** (sho͞o′hôrn′), *n.* an implement of metal, horn, etc. with a troughlike blade, inserted at the back of a shoe to aid in slipping it on.
**shoe·lace** (sho͞o′lās′), *n.* a length of cord, leather, etc. used for lacing and fastening a shoe.
**shoe·mak·er** (sho͞o′māk′ẽr), *n.* one whose business is making or repairing shoes. —**shoe′mak′ing,** *n.*
**sho·er** (sho͞o′ẽr), *n.* one who shoes horses.
**shoe·shine** (sho͞o′shīn′), *n.* 1. the cleaning and polishing of a pair of shoes. 2. a bootblack.
**shoe·string** (sho͞o′striŋ′), *n.* a shoelace. —**on a shoestring,** with little capital and resources, as in starting a business.
**shoe tree,** a shoe-shaped form inserted in a shoe to stretch it or preserve its shape.
**sho·gun** (shō′go͞on′, -gun′), *n.* [Japan. < Chin. *chiang-chun*, leader of an army], any of the military governors of Japan who, until 1868, exercised absolute rule. —**sho′gun·ate′** (-āt′, -it), *n.*
**shone** (shōn), alt. pt. and pp. of **shine.**
**shoo** (sho͞o), *interj.* 1. an exclamation used in scaring away chickens or other animals. 2. go away! get out! *v.i.* [SHOOED, SHOOING], to cry "shoo." *v.t.* to drive away abruptly, as by crying "shoo."
**shook** (shook), pt. of **shake.**
**shoon** (sho͞on), *n.pl.* [Archaic or Dial.], shoes.
**shoot** (sho͞ot), *v.t.* [SHOT, SHOT or *obs.* SHOTTEN, SHOOTING], [< AS. *sceotan*], 1. to pass swiftly over, by, etc.: as, he *shot* the rapids in his canoe. 2. to pour or empty out. 3. to cast (an anchor, net, etc.). 4. to slide (a door bolt) into or out of its fastening. 5. to variegate with another color or substance: as, blue *shot* with orange. 6. to thrust forth, as a branch, bud, etc. 7. *a*) to discharge (a bullet, arrow, etc.) or fire (a gun, bow, etc.). *b*) to discharge (rays) with force. 8. to send forth swiftly, or with force, as a question, fist, etc. 9. to take the altitude of, as a star. 10. to hit, wound, or kill with a missile discharged from a weapon. 11. to photograph. 12. in *games & sports, a*) to throw or drive (a ball, etc.) toward the objective. *b*) to score (a goal, points, etc.). *c*) to play, as pool, craps, etc. *v.i.* 1. to move swiftly, as an arrow from a bow. 2. to be felt suddenly and keenly, as pain, etc. 3. to grow rapidly; sprout. 4. to project; jut out. 5. to fire a missile, as from a gun. 6. to be discharged, as a gun. 7. *a*) to photograph a scene. *b*) to start motion picture cameras working. 8. to hunt game with a gun. 9. in *sports, a*) to propel a ball, etc. toward the objective. *b*) to play golf, pool, etc. *n.* 1. a shooting trip, party, or contest. 2. the act of sprouting. 3. a new growth; sprout. 4. a sloping trough; chute. 5. a spasm of pain. *interj.* [Slang], an exclamation of disgust, disappointment, etc. —**shoot at,** [Colloq.], to strive for. —**shoot off one's** (or **at the**) **mouth,** [Slang], to speak without discretion; blab. —**shot through with,** filled with (something unwanted, dangerous, etc.). —**shoot′er,** *n.* —**shoot′ing,** *n.*
**shooting star,** a meteor.
**shop** (shop), *n.* [< AS. *sceoppa*, booth], 1. a place where things are offered for sale; store. 2. a place where a particular kind of work is done: as, a machine *shop.* *v.i.* [SHOPPED, SHOPPING], to visit shops in order to examine or buy merchandise. —**set up shop,** to start a business. —**talk shop,** to discuss one's work. —**shop′ping,** *n.*
**shop·girl** (shop′gũrl′), *n.* a young woman who works as a clerk in a store.

**shop·keep·er** (shop′kēp′ẽr), *n.* one who operates a shop, or store.

**shop·lift·er** (shop′lif′tẽr), *n.* one who steals articles exposed for sale in a shop. —**shop′lift′ing,** *n.*

**shop·man** (shop′mən), *n.* [*pl.* -MEN], 1. a shopkeeper. 2. a salesperson in a store; clerk.

**shop·per** (shop′ẽr), *n.* 1. one who shops; esp., one hired by a store to shop for others. 2. one hired by a store to compare competitors' merchandise.

**shop steward,** a union member elected to represent his local in dealing with the employer.

**shop·talk** (shop′tôk′), *n.* 1. the specialized vocabulary of a particular occupation, etc. 2. conversation about one's work, especially after hours.

**shop·walk·er** (shop′wôk′ẽr), *n.* a floorwalker.

**shop·win·dow** (shop′win′dō), *n.* a show window.

**shop·worn** (shop′wôrn′, -wōrn′), *adj.* soiled, worn, etc. from having been displayed in a shop.

**Shor·an, shor·an** (shôr′an, shōr′an), *n.* [< *Sh*ort *R*ange *N*avigation], a system for locating positions on the earth's surface in relation to an airplane by means of radar.

**shore** (shôr, shōr), *n.* [prob. < MLG. or MD. *schore*], 1. land at the edge of a body of water. 2. land as opposed to water. —**in shore,** near or toward shore. —**off shore,** in the water but close to shore.

**shore** (shôr, shōr), *n.* [< MD. or MLG.; prob. < base of SHEAR], a beam, etc. placed under or against something as a prop. *v.t.* [SHORED, SHORING], to support with shores; prop (usually with *up*).

SHORES

**shore** (shôr, shōr), archaic and dial. pt. and pp. of **shear.**

**shore dinner,** a meal of freshly caught sea food.

**shore·less** (shôr′lis, shōr′-), *adj.* [Poetic], having no shore; extending without end; boundless.

**shore line,** the edge of a body of water.

**shore patrol,** a detail of the U.S. Navy, Coast Guard, or Marine Corps serving as military police.

**shore·ward** (shôr′wẽrd, shōr′-), *adv. & adj.* toward the shore: also **shore′wards,** *adv.*

**shor·ing** (shôr′iŋ, shōr′-), *n.* 1. the act of propping with shores. 2. a system of shores, or props.

**shorn** (shôrn, shōrn), alt. pp. of **shear.**

**short** (shôrt), *adj.* [< AS. *sc(e)ort*]. 1. not extending far from end to end; not long. 2. not great in range or scope, as a journey, view, etc. 3. low in height; not tall. 4. lasting but a little time; brief. 5. not retentive: as, a *short* memory. 6. concise; brief: as, a *short* tale. 7. brief to the point of rudeness; curt. 8. less than a sufficient or correct amount: as, a *short* measure. 9. not far enough to reach the objective: as, a shot that fell *short.* 10. having a tendency to crumble, as pastry. 11. in *commerce, a*) not possessing at the time of sale the commodities or securities one is selling. *b*) designating or of a sale of commodities or securities which the seller does not yet have but expects to buy at a lower price before date of delivery. 12. in *phonetics & prosody,* comparatively brief in duration, as sounds, syllables, etc. *n.* 1. something short; specif., *a*) a short sound or syllable. *b*) a motion-picture short subject. 2. *a*) a person making a short sale. *b*) a short sale. 3. *pl. a*) knee breeches. *b*) short trousers reaching part way to the knee. *c*) a man's undergarment of similar form. 4. *pl.* a by-product of wheat milling that consists of bran, germ, and coarse meal. 5. in *baseball,* shortstop. 6. in *electricity,* a short circuit. *adv.* 1. abruptly; suddenly. 2. rudely; curtly. 3. briefly; concisely. 4. so as to be short: as, cut it off *short.* 5. on the near side of a given point: as, we stopped *short* of danger. 6. without possessing (that which is being sold). *v.t. & v.i.* in *electricity,* to short-circuit. —**fall** (or **come**) **short,** 1. to be insufficient. 2. to fail to reach. —**in short,** 1. in summing up. 2. briefly. —**make short work of,** to deal with or dispose of quickly. —**run short,** to have less than enough. —**short for,** being an abbreviation for. —**short of,** not equaling; less than or lacking. —**short′ish,** *adj.* —**short′ness,** *n.*

**short·age** (shôr′tij), *n.* a deficiency in the quantity or amount needed; deficit.

**short·bread** (shôrt′bred′), *n.* a rich, crumbly cake or cooky made with shortening.

**short·cake** (shôrt′kāk′), *n.* a light biscuit or a sweet cake served with fruit, etc. as a dessert.

**short·change** (shôrt′chānj′), *v.t. & v.i.* [-CHANGED, -CHANGING], [Colloq.], 1. to give less money than is due in change. 2. to cheat. —**short′chang′er,** *n.*

**short-cir·cuit** (shôrt′sũr′kit), *v.t. & v.i.* to make a short circuit (in).

**short circuit,** 1. a side circuit of very low relative resistance connecting two points in an electric circuit of higher resistance so as to deflect most of the current. 2. loosely, a disrupted electric circuit resulting from this.

**short·com·ing** (shôrt′kum′iŋ), *n.* a coming short of what is expected or required; fault; defect.

**short cut,** 1. a shorter way to get to the same place. 2. any way of saving time, effort, etc.

**short·en** (shôr′t'n), *v.t.* 1. to make short or shorter. 2. to furl or reef (a sail). 3. to add shortening to (pastry, etc.). *v.i.* to become short or shorter —**short′en·er,** *n.*

**short·en·ing** (shôr′t'n-iŋ, shôrt′niŋ), *n.* 1. a making or becoming short or shorter. 2. fat used in baked goods to make them crisp or flaky.

**short·hand** (shôrt′hand′), *n.* any system of speed writing using symbols for letters, words, and phrases. *adj.* written in or using shorthand.

**short-hand·ed** (shôrt′han′did), *adj.* short of workers or helpers. —**short′-hand′ed·ness,** *n.*

**short-head·ed, short·head·ed** (shôrt′hed′id), *adj.* having a relatively short skull; brachycephalic. —**short′-head′ed·ness, short′head′ed·ness,** *n.*

**short·horn** (shôrt′hôrn′), *n.* any of a breed of heavy cattle with short, curved horns: they are raised for both beef and milk.

**short-lived** (shôrt′līvd′; *also, esp. Brit.,* -livd′) *adj.* living, lasting, or continuing only a short time.

**short·ly** (shôrt′li), *adv.* 1. in a few words; briefly. 2. in a short time; soon. 3. abruptly or curtly.

**short order,** any food quickly prepared after it has been ordered in a restaurant. —**in short order,** quickly. —**short′-or′der,** *adj.*

**short shrift,** 1. very little care or attention, as from lack of patience. 2. little or no mercy or respite. —**make short shrift of,** to make short work of; dismiss summarily: also **give short shrift.**

**short·sight·ed** (shôrt′sīt′id), *adj.* 1. unable to see clearly at a distance; nearsighted. 2. having or showing a lack of foresight. —**short′sight′ed·ly,** *adv.* —**short′sight′ed·ness,** *n.*

**short·stop** (shôrt′stop′), *n.* in *baseball,* the infielder stationed between second and third base.

**short story,** a kind of story shorter than the novel or novelette and more limited in scope, number of characters, etc.

**short subject,** any short film presentation added to the feature in a motion-picture program.

**short-tem·pered** (shôrt′tem′pẽrd), *adj.* having a tendency to lose one's temper; easily angered.

**short-term** (shôrt′tũrm′), *adj.* requiring payment or coming due in a short time, as a loan.

**short ton,** 2,000 pounds avoirdupois.

**short wave,** a radio wave sixty meters or less in length. —**short-wave** (shôrt′wāv′), *adj.*

**short-wind·ed** (shôrt′win′did), *adj.* 1. easily put out of breath by exercise. 2. breathing with quick, labored breaths. —**short′wind′ed·ness,** *n.*

**short·y** (shôr′ti), *n.* [*pl.* -IES], [Colloq.], a person or thing of less than average height or size.

**Sho·sho·ne** (shō-shō′ni), *n.* a member of a group of Shoshonean Indians originally scattered over Montana, Wyoming, and Oregon: also sp. **Shoshoni.**

**Sho·sho·ne·an** (shō-shō′ni-ən, shō′shə-nē′-), *adj.* designating a subbranch of the Uto-Aztecan linguistic family of North American Indians.

**Sho·sta·ko·vich, Dmi·tri** (d′mē′tri shô′stä-kô′-vich), 1906– ; Russian composer.

**shot** (shot), *n.* [< AS. *sceot*], 1. the act of shooting; discharge of a missile. 2. *a*) the distance a missile travels; hence, *b*) range; scope. 3. an attempt to hit with a missile. 4. *a*) any attempt; try. *b*) a guess. 5. a pointed, critical remark. 6. a stroke, throw, etc. in any of several games. 7. *a*) a projectile to be discharged from a gun, especially a solid ball or bullet. *b*) such projectiles collectively. 8. a small pellet or pellets of lead, used for a charge of a shotgun. 9. a heavy metal ball cast overhand for distance by contestants: in phrase *to put the shot.* 10. a blast. 11. a marksman: as, he's a fair *shot.* 12. a film sequence or a photograph. 13. [Slang], a dose, as of morphine. 14. [Colloq.], a bet with reference to the odds given: as, that horse is a two-to-one *shot.* 15. [Slang], a drink of liquor. *v.t.* [SHOTTED, SHOTTING], to load or weight with shot. —**a long shot,** an attempt not likely to succeed. —**have** (or **take**) **a shot at,** [Colloq.], to make a try at. —**like a shot,** quickly or suddenly. —**not by a long shot,** improbably or not at all.

**shot** (shot), pt. and pp. of **shoot,** *adj.* 1. variegated, streaked, etc. with another color or substance. 2. [Colloq.], ruined; worn out.

**shote** (shōt), *n.* a shoat.

**shot·gun** (shot'gun'), *n.* a smoothbore gun for firing a charge of small shot at short range.
**shot-put** (shot'poot'), *n.* 1. a contest in which athletes put the shot. 2. a throw of the shot.
**should** (shood), *v.* [< AS. *sc(e)olde*, pt. of *sc(e)al*, I am obliged], 1. pt. of **shall.** 2. an auxiliary used to express *a*) obligation, duty, etc.: e.g., you *should* help him. *b*) expectation or probability: e.g., he *should* be here by Monday: equivalent to *ought to.* *c*) futurity from the standpoint of the past in indirect quotations: replaceable by *would*: e.g., I said I *should* (or *would*) be home late. *d*) futurity in polite requests or in statements of uncertainty: replaceable by *would:* e.g., *should* (or *would*) you like some tea? *e*) a future condition: e.g., if I *should* go, would you care? *f*) a past condition: replaceable by *would:* e.g., I *should* (or *would*) have gone had you asked me. In formal usage the distinctions between *should* and *would* are the same as those between *shall* and *will.*
**shoul·der** (shōl'dẽr), *n.* [AS. *sculdor*], 1. *a*) the joint connecting the arm or forelimb with the body. *b*) the part of the body including this joint, extending to the base of the neck. 2. *pl.* the two shoulders and the part of the back between them. 3. a cut of meat consisting of the upper foreleg and attached parts. 4. the part of a garment that covers the shoulder. 5. a shoulderlike projection. 6. the edge of a road or highway. *v.t.* 1. to push along or through, as with the shoulder: as, he *shouldered* his way through the crowd. 2. to carry upon the shoulder. 3. to assume the burden of. *v.i.* to push with the shoulder. **—cry on someone's shoulder,** to tell one's troubles to someone in seeking sympathy. **—put one's shoulder to the wheel,** to set to work vigorously. **—shoulder arms,** to rest a rifle against the shoulder, supporting the butt with the hand. **—shoulder to shoulder,** 1. side by side and close together. 2. working together. **—straight from the shoulder,** 1. moving straight forward from the shoulder: said of a blow. 2. without reserve; frankly. **—turn** (or **give**) **a cold shoulder to,** to treat with disdain; avoid.
**shoulder blade,** either of the two flat bones in the upper back articulated with the humerus.
**shoulder knot,** a knot of ribbon or lace worn on the shoulder as an insigne, decoration, etc.
**shoulder strap,** a strap worn over the shoulder to support the garment, etc. to which it is attached.
**should·n't** (shood''nt), should not.
**shouldst** (shoodst), archaic 2d pers. sing. of **should**: also **should·est** (shood'ist).
**shout** (shout), *n.* [ME. *schoute*], a loud, sudden cry, call, or outburst. *v.t. & v.i.* to utter or cry out in a loud voice. **—shout (someone) down,** to silence (someone) by shouting. **—shout'er,** *n.*
**shove** (shuv), *v.t. & v.i.* [SHOVED, SHOVING], [AS. *scufan*], 1. to push, as along a surface. 2. to push roughly. *n.* a push or thrust. **—shove off,** 1. to push (a boat) away from shore. 2. [Colloq.], to start off; leave. **—shov'er,** *n.*
**shov·el** (shuv''l), *n.* [AS. *sceofol*], 1. a tool with a broad scoop or blade and a long handle: used in lifting and moving loose material. 2. a shovelful. *v.t.* [-ELED or -ELLED, -ELING or -ELLING], 1. to lift and move with a shovel. 2. to dig out with a shovel, as a path. 3. to put in large quantities: as, he *shoveled* sugar into his coffee.
**shov·el·board** (shuv''l-bôrd', -bōrd'), *n.* shuffleboard.
**shov·el·er, shov·el·ler** (shuv''l-ẽr), *n.* 1. one that shovels. 2. a kind of river duck with a very long, broad bill: also **shov'el·bill'.**
**shov·el·ful** (shuv''l-fool'), *n.* [*pl.* -FULS], as much as a shovel will hold.
**show** (shō), *v.t.* [SHOWED, SHOWN or SHOWED, SHOWING], [< AS. *sceawian*, to look], 1. to bring or put in sight; make visible; exhibit. 2. to guide; conduct: as, *show* him to his room. 3. to direct attention to; point out: as, we *showed* him the sights. 4. to reveal, manifest, etc.: as, *show* no anger, she *shows* herself to be clever. 5. to prove; demonstrate: as, *show* that it is possible. 6. to register: as, a barometer *shows* air pressure. 7. to grant or bestow (favor, grace, etc.). *v.i.* 1. to be or become seen; appear. 2. to be noticeable: as, the scratch won't *show.* 3. to finish third or better in a horse or dog race. 4. in the *theater,* to give a performance; appear. *n.* 1. a showing or demonstration: as, a *show* of passion. 2. a display or exhibition, especially in public or for the public. 3. a spectacular, pompous display. 4. an indication or trace, as of metal, coal, etc. in the earth. 5. something false; pretense: as, her sorrow was mere *show.* 6. one looked upon as peculiar, ridiculous, etc. 7. a presentation of entertainment: as, a television *show.* **—for show,** in order to attract attention. **—show off,** 1. to make a display of. 2. to make a vain display of (one's skills, etc.). **—show up,** 1. to expose. 2. to be clearly seen. 3. to come; arrive, as for an appointment. 4. [Colloq.], to be far superior to. **—show'er,** *n.*
**show·boat** (shō'bōt'), *n.* a boat with a theater and actors who play river towns.
**show·bread** (shō'bred'), *n.* shewbread.
**show business,** the theater, vaudeville, motion pictures, etc. as a business or industry.
**show·case** (shō'kās'), *n.* a glass-enclosed case for protecting things on display, as in a store.
**show·down** (shō'doun'), *n.* [Colloq.], 1. in *poker,* the laying down of the cards face up. 2. a disclosure, as of the true nature of a situation.
**show·er** (shou'ẽr), *n.* [AS. *scur*], 1. a brief fall of rain, hail, or sleet. 2. a sudden, abundant fall or flow, as of sparks, tears, praise, etc. 3. a party during which gifts are presented to the guest of honor: as, a bridal *shower.* 4. a shower bath. *v.t.* 1. to spray with water or other liquid. 2. to pour forth in a shower; give abundantly. *v.i.* 1. to fall or come in a shower. 2. to take a shower bath. **—show'er·y,** *adj.*
**shower bath,** 1. a bath in which the body is sprayed with fine streams of water from small jets. 2. an apparatus or room used for such a bath.
**show·ing** (shō'iŋ), *n.* an exhibition; formal display.
**show·man** (shō'mən), *n.* [*pl.* -MEN], 1. a person who makes a business of producing shows. 2. a person skilled at this or at presenting anything in a striking manner. **—show'man·ship',** *n.*
**shown** (shōn), alt. pp. of **show.**
**show-off** (shō'ôf'), *n.* 1. a showing off; vain display. 2. [Colloq.], one who shows off.
**show·piece** (shō'pēs'), *n.* 1. something exhibited. 2. something that is a fine example of its kind.
**show place,** 1. a place that is exhibited to the public for its beauty, etc. 2. any place that is beautiful, lavishly furnished, etc.
**show·room** (shō'rōōm', -room'), *n.* a room where merchandise is displayed for advertising or sale.
**show window,** a store window for displaying goods.
**show·y** (shō'i), *adj.* [-IER, -IEST], 1. of striking appearance. 2. attracting attention in a cheap way; flashy. **—show'i·ly,** *adv.* **—show'i·ness,** *n.*
**shrank** (shraŋk), alt. pt. of **shrink.**
**shrap·nel** (shrap'nəl), *n.* [after Brit. Gen. H. *Shrapnel* (1761–1842), its inventor], 1. an artillery shell filled with an explosive charge and many small metal balls, set to explode in the air. 2. the metal balls scattered on explosion. 3. shell fragments scattered by any exploding shell.
**shred** (shred), *n.* [AS. *screada*], 1. an irregular strip or long, narrow piece cut or torn off. 2. a very small piece or amount; fragment: as, not a *shred* of truth. *v.t.* [SHREDDED or SHRED, SHREDDING], to cut or tear into shreds. **—shred'der,** *n.*
**Shreve·port** (shrēv'pôrt', -pōrt'), *n.* a city in NW Louisiana, on the Red River: pop., 164,000.
**shrew** (shrōō), *n.* [AS. *screawa*], 1. a small, mouselike mammal with soft, brown fur and a long snout: also **shrew'mouse'** [*pl.* -MICE]. 2. a nagging, evil-tempered woman. **—shrew'ish,** *adj.* **—shrew'ish·ly,** *adv.* **—shrew'ish·ness,** *n.*
**shrewd** (shrōōd), *adj.* [< ME. pp. of *schrewen,* to curse < *schrewe,* shrew], keen-witted, clever, or sharp in practical affairs; astute. **—shrewd'ly,** *adv.* **—shrewd'ness,** *n.*
**shriek** (shrēk), *v.i.* [prob. < ON.], to make a loud, sharp, piercing cry or sound; screech; scream. *v.t.* to utter with a shriek. *n.* a loud, sharp, piercing cry or sound. **—shriek'er,** *n.*
**shrift** (shrift), *n.* [AS. *scrift;* ult. < L. *scribere,* to write], [Archaic], 1. confession to and absolution by a priest. 2. the act of shriving.
**shrike** (shrīk), *n.* [< AS. *scric*], any of several shrill-voiced birds with hooked beaks: most types feed on insects, some on small birds, frogs, etc., hanging them on thorns after the kill.
**shrill** (shril), *adj.* [ME. *schril(le);* echoic], 1. having or producing a high, thin, piercing tone; high-pitched. 2. characterized or accompanied by shrill sounds. *adv.* in or with a shrill tone, voice, etc. *v.t. & v.i.* to utter with or make a shrill sound. **—shrill'ness,** *n.* **—shril'ly,** *adv.*

**shrimp** (shrimp), *n.* [*pl.* SHRIMPS, SHRIMP; see PLURAL, II, D, 1], [< base of AS. *scrimman*, to shrink], 1. a small, long-tailed crustacean, valued as food. 2. [Colloq.], a small or insignificant person.

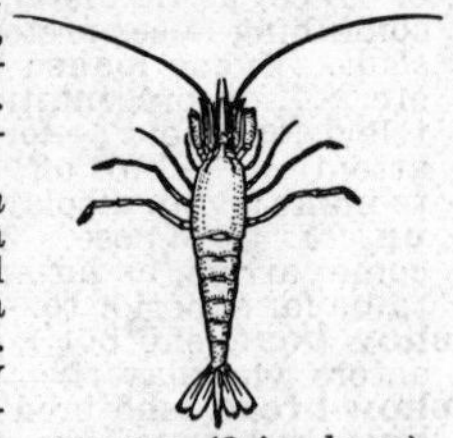

SHRIMP (2 in. long)

**shrine** (shrīn), *n.* [AS. *scrin* < L. *scrinium*, box], 1. a container holding sacred relics. 2. the tomb of a saint or revered person. 3. a place of worship, usually one centered around a sacred object or scene. 4. a place or thing endowed with a sacred character because of its history or associations. *v.t.* [SHRINED, SHRINING], to enshrine.

**shrink** (shriŋk), *v.i.* [SHRANK or SHRUNK, SHRUNK or SHRUNKEN, SHRINKING], [AS. *scrincan*], 1. to contract, as from heat, cold, wetting, etc. 2. to lessen, as in amount, worth, etc. 3. to draw back; flinch, as from fear. *v.t.* to cause to shrink or contract. *n.* a shrinking. —**shrink'a·ble,** *adj.* —**shrink'er,** *n.* —**shrink'ing·ly,** *adv.*

**shrink·age** (shriŋk'ij), *n.* 1. the act or process of shrinking. 2. decrease in value; depreciation. 3. the amount of shrinking, decrease, etc.

**shrive** (shrīv), *v.t.* [SHRIVED or SHROVE, SHRIVEN (shriv''n) or SHRIVED, SHRIVING], [AS. *scrifan* < L. *scribere*, to write], [Archaic], to hear the confession of and, usually after penance, give absolution to. *v.i.* [Archaic], 1. to make confession. 2. to hear confessions.

**shriv·el** (shriv''l), *v.t. & v.i.* [-ELED or -ELLED, -ELING or -ELLING], [cf. Sw. *skryvla*, to wrinkle], 1. to curl up or wrinkle; wither. 2. to make or become helpless, useless, or inefficient.

**Shrop·shire** (shrop'shir), *n.* a county of England, on the border of Wales.

**shroud** (shroud), *n.* [AS. *scrud*], 1. a cloth used to wrap a corpse for burial. 2. something that covers, protects, etc.; veil. 3. any of the ropes stretched from a ship's side to a masthead to offset lateral strain on the mast. *v.t.* 1. to hide; cover. 2. to wrap (a corpse) in a shroud.

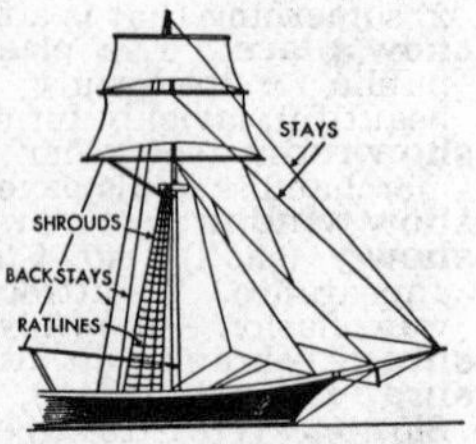


SHROUDS

**shrove** (shrōv), alt. pt. of **shrive.**

**Shrove·tide** (shrōv'tīd'), *n.* the three days before Ash Wednesday (Shrove Sunday, Monday, and Tuesday), formerly set aside as a period for confession and festivity just before Lent.

**shrub** (shrub), *n.* [prob. < AS. *scrybb*, brushwood], a bushy, woody plant with several permanent stems instead of a single trunk; bush.

**shrub·ber·y** (shrub'ẽr-i), *n.* [*pl.* -IES], shrubs collectively; a heavy growth of shrubs.

**shrub·by** (shrub'i), *adj.* [-BIER, -BIEST], 1. covered with shrubs. 2. like a shrub. —**shrub'bi·ness,** *n.*

**shrug** (shrug), *v.t. & v.i.* [SHRUGGED, SHRUGGING], [ME. *schruggen*, orig., to shiver], to draw up (the shoulders), as in expressing indifference, doubt, disdain, etc. *n.* the gesture so made.

**shrunk** (shruŋk), alt. pt. and pp. of **shrink.**

**shrunk·en** (shruŋk''n), alt. pp. of **shrink.** *adj.* contracted in size; shriveled.

**shuck** (shuk), *n.* [? a metathesis of *husk*], 1. a shell, pod, or husk. 2. the shell of an oyster or clam. *v.t.* 1. to remove the shucks of. 2. to remove like a shuck: as, he *shucked* his clothes. —**shuck'er,** *n.*

**shucks** (shuks), *interj.* an exclamation expressing disappointment or disgust.

**shud·der** (shud'ẽr), *v.i.* [ME. *schoderen*, freq. < base of AS. *scudan*, to hurry], to shake or tremble suddenly and violently, as in horror. *n.* a shuddering; convulsive tremor. —**shud'der·ing·ly,** *adv.*

**shuf·fle** (shuf''l), *v.t.* [-FLED, -FLING], [prob. < LG. *schuffeln* < base of *shove*], 1. to move (the feet) with a dragging gait. 2. to mix (playing cards) so as to change their order. 3. to mix together in a disordered mass. 4. to shift from one place to another. 5. to bring, put, or thrust (*into* or *out of*) clumsily or trickily. *v.i.* 1. to move or slide the feet with a slow, dragging gait, as in walking or dancing. 2. to act in a tricky, evasive, or dishonest manner. 3. to shift repeatedly from one position or place to another. 4. to shuffle cards. *n.* 1. the act of shuffling. 2. a deceptive action; evasion; trick. 3. a shuffling of the feet. 4. a gait, dance, etc. characterized by this. 5. *a*) a shuffling of playing cards. *b*) the right of, or one's turn at, this. —**shuffle off,** to get rid of. —**shuf'fler,** *n.*

**shuf·fle·board** (shuf''l-bôrd', -bōrd'), *n.* [prob. for *shovel board*, after the shape of the cues], 1. a game in which disks are slid, with a push from a cue, along a flat surface toward numbered squares. 2. the surface on which it is played.

**shun** (shun), *v.t.* [SHUNNED, SHUNNING], [AS. *scunian*], to keep away from; avoid scrupulously or consistently. —**shun'ner,** *n.*

**shunt** (shunt), *v.t. & v.i.* [prob. < AS. *scyndan*, to hasten], 1. to move or turn to one side; turn out of the way. 2. to switch, as a train, from one track to another. 3. in *electricity*, to divert or be diverted by a shunt. *n.* 1. a shunting. 2. a railroad switch. 3. in *electricity*, a conductor connecting two points in a circuit and diverting part of the current from the main circuit. —**shunt'er,** *n.*

**shush** (shush), *interj.* [echoic], hush! be quiet! *v.t.* to say "shush" to; tell (another) to be quiet.

**shut** (shut), *v.t.* [SHUT, SHUTTING], [AS. *scyttan* < base of *sceotan*, to cast], 1. to move (a door, lid, etc.) so as to close the opening to which it is fitted. 2. to fasten (a door, etc.) securely, as with a bolt. 3. to close (an opening, container, etc.). 4. to prevent entrance to or exit from; bar. 5. to fold up or close the parts of, as an umbrella, the fist, etc. *v.i.* to be or become shut. *adj.* closed, fastened, etc. *n.* the act or time of shutting. —**shut down,** 1. to close by lowering. 2. to cease operating, usually temporarily, as a factory. 3. [Colloq.], to bring to an end (with *on* or *upon*). —**shut in,** to surround or enclose. —**shut off,** 1. to prevent the passage of (water, etc.). 2. to prevent passage through (a road, etc.). —**shut out,** 1. to deny entrance to; exclude (sound, a view, etc.). 2. to prevent (the opposition) from scoring. —**shut up,** 1. to enclose or confine; imprison. 2. to close all the entrances to. 3. [Colloq.], to stop or cause to stop talking.

**shut·down** (shut'doun'), *n.* a stoppage of activity, especially in a factory temporarily.

**shut-eye** (shut'ī'), *n.* [Slang], sleep.

**shut-in** (shut'in'), *n.* an invalid who is unable to go out. *adj.* unable to go out; confined.

**shut·off** (shut'ôf'), *n.* 1. something that shuts off a flow, etc., as of a liquid. 2. a stoppage.

**shut·out** (shut'out'), *n.* 1. a lockout. 2. in *sports*, *a*) a preventing of the opposing team from scoring. *b*) a game in which this occurs.

**shut·ter** (shut'ẽr), *n.* 1. a person or thing that shuts. 2. a movable, usually hinged cover for a window. 3. anything used to cover an opening; specif., a device for opening and closing the aperture of a camera lens to expose the film or plate. *v.t.* to close or furnish with shutters.

**shut·tle** (shut''l), *n.* [AS. *scytel*, missile: from being cast back and forth], 1. an instrument that carries the woof thread back and forth between the warp threads in weaving. 2. any of several devices having a similar use or motion, as the device that carries the lower thread back and forth on a sewing machine. 3. a bus (**shuttle bus**) or train (**shuttle train**) that makes regular and frequent trips back and forth over a very short route. *v.t. & v.i.* [-TLED, -TLING], to move rapidly to and fro. —**shut'tler,** *n.*

**shut·tle·cock** (shut''l-kok'), *n.* 1. a rounded piece of cork having a flat end stuck with feathers: it is struck back and forth across a net by players in badminton or in battledore and shuttlecock. 2. the game of battledore and shuttlecock.

SHUTTLECOCK

**shy** (shī), *adj.* [SHIER or SHYER, SHIEST or SHYEST], [< AS. *sceoh*], 1. easily frightened or startled; timid. 2. uncomfortable in the presence of, and avoiding contact with, others; bashful. 3. distrustful; wary. 4. [Slang], lacking; short in amount, etc. *v.i.* [SHIED, SHYING], 1. to move suddenly as though startled; start; recoil. 2. to be or become cautious, hesitant, etc. (often with *at*). *n.* [*pl.* SHIES], an act of shying; start, as of a horse. —**fight shy of,** to keep from; avoid. —**shi'er, shy'er,** *n.* —**shy'ly,** *adv.* —**shy'ness,** *n.*

**shy** (shī), *v.t. & v.i.* [SHIED, SHYING], [prob. < *shy* cock, one that will not fight unless tormented by missiles], to fling, especially sidewise with a jerk. *n.* [*pl.* SHIES], a shying; fling.

**Shy·lock** (shī'lok'), *n.* 1. the relentless money-lender in Shakespeare's *Merchant of Venice.* 2. an exacting creditor.

**shy·ster** (shī′stẽr), *n.* [? ult. < G. *scheisser*, defecator], [Slang], a person, especially a lawyer, who uses unethical or tricky methods.

**si** (sē), *n.* in *music*, ti: the former name.

**‡sí** (sē), *adv.* [Sp.], yes: also [It.] **si.**

**Si,** in *chemistry*, silicon.

**S.I.,** Staten Island.

**Si·am** (sī-am′, sī′am), *n.* Thailand: former name.

**Siam, Gulf of,** an arm of the South China Sea, South of Thailand and East of the Malay Peninsula.

**Si·a·mese** (sī′ə-mēz′), *n.* 1. [*pl.* -MESE], a native of Siam, or Thailand. 2. the Sino-Tibetan language of the Siamese; Thai. *adj.* of Siam (or Thailand), its people, their language, etc.

**Siamese twins,** [after such a pair born in Siam], any pair of twins born joined to each other.

**sib** (sib), *n.* [AS. *sib(b)*], 1. a person's blood relatives; kin. 2. a blood relative; esp., a brother or sister. *adj.* related by blood.

**Si·be·li·us, Jean** (zhän si-bā′li-oos), 1865–1957; Finnish composer.

**Si·ber·i·a** (sī-bêr′i-ə), *n.* the region of the Soviet Union in N Asia extending from the Ural Mountains to the Pacific. —**Si·ber′i·an,** *adj. & n.*

**sib·i·lant** (sib′'l-ənt), *adj.* [< L. < *sibilare*, to hiss], having or making a hissing sound. *n.* a hissing sound or the symbol for it: *s, sh, z, zh, j,* and *ch* are sibilants. —**sib′i·lance, sib′i·lan·cy** [*pl.* -CIES], *n.* —**sib′i·lant·ly,** *adv.*

**sib·ling** (sib′liŋ), *n.* [< AS. *sib(b)*; + *-ling*], *often in pl.* one of two or more persons born at different times of the same parents; brother or sister.

**sib·yl** (sib′'l), *n.* [< L. < Gr. *sibylla*], 1. any of certain women consulted as prophetesses or oracles by the ancient Greeks and Romans. 2. a witch; fortuneteller. —**sib′yl·line′** (-'l-īn′, -in), **si·byl·ic, sy·byl·lic** (si-bil′ik), *adj.*

**‡sic** (sik), *adv.* [L.], thus; so: used within brackets, [*sic*], to show that a quoted passage, often containing some error, is precisely reproduced.

**sic** (sik), *v.t.* [SICKED, SICKING], to sick.

**Sic·i·ly** (sis′'l-i), *n.* an island of Italy, off its SW tip: area, 9,926 sq. mi.; pop., 4,462,000. —**Si·cil·i·an** (si-sil′i-ən, -yən), *adj. & n.*

**sick** (sik), *adj.* [AS. *seoc*], 1. suffering from disease; ill. 2. having nausea; vomiting or ready to vomit. 3. characteristic of sickness: as, a *sick* expression. 4. of or for sick people: as, *sick* leave. 5. deeply disturbed, as by grief, failure, etc. 6. disgusted by reason of excess: as, he is *sick* of their puns. 7. unsound. 8. having a great longing (*for*): as, he is *sick* for the hills. 9. of sickly color; pale. *n.* sick people (with *the*).

**sick** (sik), *v.t.* [var. of *seek*], 1. to pursue and attack: said of or to a dog. 2. to urge to attack: as, he *sicked* his dog on us. Also sp. **sic.**

**sick bay,** a ship's hospital or dispensary.

**sick·bed** (sik′bed′), *n.* the bed of a sick person.

**sick·en** (sik′'n), *v.t. & v.i.* to make or become sick. —**sick′en·er,** *n.*

**sick·en·ing** (sik′'n-iŋ), *adj.* 1. causing sickness or nausea. 2. disgusting. —**sick′en·ing·ly,** *adv.*

**sick headache,** 1. any headache accompanied by or resulting from nausea. 2. migraine.

**sick·ish** (sik′ish), *adj.* 1. somewhat sick or nauseated. 2. somewhat nauseating. —**sick′ish·ly,** *adv.*

**sick·le** (sik′'l), *n.* [< AS. < L. *secula* < *secare*, to cut], a tool consisting of a crescent-shaped blade with a short handle, for cutting tall grass, etc.

SICKLE

**sick·ly** (sik′li), *adj.* [-LIER, -LIEST], 1. in poor health; chronically sick. 2. of or produced by sickness: as, a *sickly* pallor. 3. producing illness; unhealthy. 4. sickening, as an odor. 5. faint; pale, as light or color. 6. weak; insipid. *adv.* in a sick manner. *v.t.* [-LIED, -LYING], to make sickly, as in color, vigor, etc. —**sick′li·ness,** *n.*

**sick·ness** (sik′nis), *n.* 1. a being sick or diseased; illness. 2. a malady. 3. nausea.

**sick·room** (sik′rōōm′, -room′), *n.* a room in which a person lies sick.

**side** (sīd), *n.* [AS.], 1. the right or left half of a human or animal body. 2. a position beside one: as, he left my *side.* 3. *a*) any of the lines or surfaces that bound something: as, a square has four *sides.* *b*) either of the two opposed vertical surfaces of an object that are not the front or back. 4. either of the two surfaces of paper, cloth, etc. 5. a surface having a specified aspect: as, the inner *side* of a vase. 6. an aspect or phase: as, his cruel *side.* 7. the slope of a hill, bank, etc. 8. any location, space, etc. with reference to a central point. 9. the position or attitude of one person or faction opposing another: as, explain your *side* of the argument. 10. one of the parties in a contest, conflict, etc. 11. line of descent through either parent. 12. [Brit.], in *billiards*, English. *adj.* 1. of, at, or on a side: as, a *side* entrance. 2. to or from one side: as, a *side* glance. 3. minor; secondary: as, a *side* interest. *v.t.* [SIDED, SIDING], to furnish with sides or siding. —**on the side,** [Colloq.], 1. as a part-time occupation. 2. extra. —**side by side,** beside each other. —**side with,** to support (one faction, etc.) in opposition to another. —**take sides,** to support one of the parties in a dispute, etc.

**side arms,** weapons of the kind that may be worn at the side or at the waist, as sword, pistol, etc.

**side·board** (sīd′bôrd′, -bōrd′), *n.* a piece of furniture for holding table linen, china, etc.

**side·burns** (sīd′bũrnz′), *n.pl.* [< *burnsides*], 1. short whiskers grown only on the cheeks. 2. the hair growing on the face, near the ears.

**side·car** (sīd′kär′), *n.* a small car attached to the side of a motorcycle, for carrying a passenger.

**sid·ed** (sīd′id), *adj.* having sides: usually in combination, as, six-*sided.*

**side-kick** (sīd′kik′), *n.* [Slang], 1. a companion; close friend. 2. a partner; confederate.

**side light,** 1. a light coming from the side. 2. chance or incidental knowledge or information.

**side line,** a line along the side; specif., *a*) either of two lines marking the side limits of a playing area, as in tennis, football, etc. *b*) *pl.* the space just outside such lines, usually for spectators. *c*) a line, as of merchandise, maintained in addition to one's main line.

**side·line** (sīd′līn′), *v.t.* [-LINED, -LINING], to remove from some activity, as because of injury.

**side·long** (sīd′lôŋ′), *adv.* 1. toward the side; obliquely. 2. side downward. *adj.* 1. inclined; slanting. 2. directed to the side, as a glance.

**side·piece** (sīd′pēs′), *n.* a piece forming or attached to the side of something.

**si·de·re·al** (sī-dêr′i-əl), *adj.* [< L. *sidereus* < *sidus*, a star], 1. of the stars or constellations; astral. 2. measured by the apparent motion of fixed stars: a *sidereal day* equals 23 hours, 56 minutes, 4.09 seconds of mean solar time.

**sid·er·ite** (sid′ẽr-īt′), *n.* [< Fr. or L. < Gr. < *sidēros*, iron], a yellowish to light-brown iron ore, $FeCO_3$. —**sid′er·it′ic** (-ə-rit′ik), *adj.*

**side·sad·dle** (sīd′sad′'l), *n.* a kind of saddle, for women wearing skirts, upon which the rider sits with both legs on the same side of the animal.

**side show,** 1. a small show apart from the main show, as of a circus. 2. something of minor importance.

**side·slip** (sīd′slip′), *v.i.* [-SLIPPED, -SLIPPING], 1. to slip sideways, as on skis. 2. in *aeronautics*, to perform a sideslip. *v.t.* to cause to sideslip. *n.* 1. a slip or skid to the side. 2. in *aeronautics*, a maneuver in which an airplane is made to fall sideways and slightly forward.

**side·split·ting** (sīd′split′iŋ), *adj.* designating, of, or causing very hearty laughter.

**side-step** (sīd′step′), *v.t.* [-STEPPED, -STEPPING], to avoid as by stepping aside; dodge: as, to *side-step* a difficulty. *v.i.* to step to one side.

**side step,** 1. a step to one side, as to avoid something. 2. a step or stair located at the side.

**side·swipe** (sīd′swīp′), *v.t. & v.i.* [-SWIPED, -SWIPING], to hit along the side in passing. *n.* a glancing blow of this kind.

**side·track** (sīd′trak′), *v.t. & v.i.* 1. to switch (a train) to a siding. 2. to turn away from the main issue. *n.* a railroad siding.

**side·walk** (sīd′wôk′), *n.* a path or area, usually paved, at the side of a street, for pedestrians.

**side·ward** (sīd′wẽrd), *adv. & adj.* directed or moving toward one side: also **side′wards,** *adv.*

**side·way** (sīd′wā′), *adj. & adv.* sideways. *n.* a byway: also **side way.**

**side·ways** (sīd′wāz′), *adv.* 1. from the side. 2. with one side forward. 3. toward one side; obliquely. *adj.* turned or moving toward or from one side.

**side-wheel** (sīd′hwēl′), *adj.* designating a steamboat having a paddle wheel on each side. —**side′-wheel′er,** *n.*

**side whiskers,** whiskers at the side of the face.

**side·wise** (sīd′wīz′), *adj.* & *adv.* sideways.
**sid·ing** (sīd′iŋ), *n.* 1. boarding, etc. forming the outside covering of a frame building. 2. a short railway track connected with a main track by a switch and used for unloading, bypassing, etc.
**si·dle** (sī′d'l), *v.i.* [-DLED, -DLING], [prob. < *sideling*, sideways], to move sideways, as in a shy or stealthy manner. *n.* a sidling movement.
**Sid·ney,** Sir **Philip** (sid′ni), 1554–1586; English soldier, poet, and statesman.
**siege** (sēj), *n.* [OFr. < LL. < L. *sedere*, to sit], 1. the encirclement of a fortified place by an enemy intending to take it, usually by blockade. 2. any persistent attempt to gain control, overcome opposition, etc. 3. [Colloq.], a long, distressing period: as, a *siege* of illness. *v.t.* [SIEGED, SIEGING], to lay siege to; besiege. **—lay siege to,** to subject to a siege.
**Sieg·fried** (sēg′frēd), *n.* the hero of various Germanic legends: in the *Nibelungenlied*, he wins a treasure, kills a dragon, and rescues Brunhild.
**Sien·kie·wicz, Hen·ryk** (hen′rik shen-kye′vich), 1846–1916; Polish novelist.
**si·en·na** (si-en′ə), *n.* [It. *terra di Siena*, lit., earth of Siena (a city in Italy)], 1. a yellowish-brown earth pigment containing iron and manganese. 2. a reddish-brown pigment made by burning this. 3. the color of either of these.
**si·er·ra** (si-er′ə), *n.* [Sp. < L. *serra*, a saw], a range of mountains with a saw-toothed appearance.
**Si·er·ra Le·on·e** (si-er′ə lē-ō′ni), a country in W Africa, on the Atlantic: a member of the British Commonwealth of Nations: area, 27,925 sq. mi.; pop., 2,500,000; capital, Freetown.
**Sierra Nevada,** a mountain range in E California.
**si·es·ta** (si-es′tə), *n.* [Sp. < L. *sexta* (*hora*), sixth (hour), noon], a brief nap or rest, especially as taken at midday or in the afternoon in Spain, some Latin American countries, etc.
**‡sieur** (syẽr), *n.* [Fr.; contr. < *seigneur*], [Archaic], sir: a French title of respect.
**sieve** (siv), *n.* [< AS. *sife*], a utensil having many small openings allowing passage only to liquids or fine particles of matter; strainer. *v.t.* & *v.i.* [SIEVED, SIEVING], to sift.
**sift** (sift), *v.t.* [AS. *siftan*], 1. to pass through a sieve so as to separate the coarse from the fine particles. 2. to scatter as by the use of a sieve. 3. to examine with care, as evidence. 4. to separate; screen: as, he *sifted* fact from fable. *v.i.* 1. to sift something. 2. to pass through or as through a sieve. **—sif′ter,** *n.*
**sigh** (sī), *v.i.* [< AS. *sican*], 1. to take in and let out a long, deep, audible breath, as in sorrow, relief, fatigue, etc. 2. to make a similar sound, as trees in the wind. 3. to feel longing or grief (often with *for*). *v.t.* 1. to express with a sigh. 2. to spend in sighing: as, he *sighed* his life away. *n.* the act or sound of sighing. **—sigh′er,** *n.* **—sigh′ing·ly,** *adv.*
**sight** (sīt), *n.* [AS. (ge)*siht* < base of *seon*, to see], 1. *a*) something seen; view. *b*) a remarkable view; spectacle. *c*) *chiefly in pl.* a thing worth seeing: as, the *sights* of the city. 2. the act of seeing. 3. inspection or examination. 4. a look; glimpse. 5. aim or an observation taken as with a gun or telescope. 6. the power of seeing; eyesight. 7. range of vision. 8. a device used to aid the eyes in lining up a gun, telescope, etc. on its objective. 9. [Colloq.], anything with an unpleasant or unusual appearance: as, my hair is a *sight*. 10. [Colloq.], a large amount: as, it'll need a *sight* of fixing. *v.t.* 1. to observe or examine by taking a sight. 2. to catch sight of; see. 3. to furnish with a sighting device. 4. to adjust the sights of (a gun, etc.). *v.i.* 1. to take aim with a sight. 2. to look carefully: as, *sight* along the line. **—a sight for sore eyes,** [Colloq.], a person or thing that is pleasant to see. **—at** (or **on**) **sight,** as soon as seen. **—by sight,** by appearance. **—catch sight of,** to discern; see; glimpse. **—lose sight of,** 1. to see no longer. 2. to forget. **—not by a long sight,** 1. not nearly. 2. not at all. **—out of sight (of),** 1. not in sight (of). 2. far off (from). 3. [Colloq.], beyond reach (of). **—out of sight, out of mind,** persons or things not present are forgotten or neglected.
**sight draft,** a draft payable on presentation.
**sight·less** (sīt′lis), *adj.* 1. blind. 2. unseen. **—sight′less·ly,** *adv.* **—sight′less·ness,** *n.*
**sight·ly** (sīt′li), *adj.* [-LIER, -LIEST], 1. pleasant to the sight. 2. providing a fine view. **—sight′li·ness,** *n.*
**sight-see·ing** (sīt′sē′iŋ), *n.* the act of going to visit places and things of interest. *adj.* for or engaged in seeing sights. **—sight′-se′er,** *n.*
**sig·ma** (sig′mə), *n.* [Gr.], the eighteenth letter of the Greek alphabet (Σ, σ, ς).
**sig·moid** (sig′moid), *adj.* having a double curve like the letter S: also **sig·moi′dal.**
**sign** (sīn), *n.* [< OFr. < L. *signum*], 1. something that indicates a fact, quality, etc.: as, black is a *sign* of mourning. 2. a gesture that conveys information, etc.: as, his nod is a *sign* of approval. 3. a mark or symbol having a specific meaning: as, the *sign* ? indicates a question. 4. a publicly displayed board, etc. bearing information or advertisement. 5. any visible trace or indication: as, no *sign* of friendship. 6. an omen. 7. in *astrology*, any of the twelve divisions of the zodiac. *v.t.* 1. to mark with a sign (as of the cross) in blessing, etc. 2. to write one's name on, as in agreement, authorization, etc. 3. to write (one's name) as a signature. 4. to hire by written contract. 5. to express, signify, etc. with a gesture: as, he *signed* his approval. *v.i.* 1. to write one's signature, as in confirming something. 2. to make a sign; signal. **—sign away** (or **over**), to transfer title to (something) by signing a document. **—sign off,** in *radio* & *television*, to stop broadcasting after making station identification. **—sign on,** to hire or be hired. **—sign up,** 1. to sign on. 2. to enlist.
**sig·nal** (sig′n'l), *n.* [< OFr. < LL. < L. *signum*, a sign], 1. a sign; token. 2. any sign, event, etc. which incites to action: as, a *signal* for a fire drill. 3. a sign given by gesture, a device, etc. to convey command, warning, etc.: as, a red light is a stop *signal*. 4. in *card games*, a bid or play designed to give information to one's partner. 5. in *radio*, *telegraphy*, etc., the electrical impulses, sound, etc. received or transmitted. *adj.* 1. not average; conspicuous; notable. 2. used as a signal. *v.t.* & *v.i.* [-NALED or -NALLED, -NALING or -NALLING], 1. to make a signal or signals (to). 2. to communicate by signals. **—sig′nal·er, sig′nal·ler,** *n.*
**Signal Corps,** in the *U.S. Army*, the combat arm in charge of communication and certain other services, as photography, meteorology, etc.
**sig·nal·ize** (sig′n'l-īz′), *v.t.* [-IZED, -IZING], 1. to make signal, or noteworthy. 2. to point out.
**sig·nal·ly** (sig′nəl-i), *adv.* remarkably; notably.
**sig·nal·man** (sig′n'l-man′, -mən), *n.* [*pl.* -MEN], a man who operates, sends, or receives signals.
**sig·na·to·ry** (sig′nə-tôr′i, -tō′ri), *adj.* taking part in the signing of something. *n.* [*pl.* -IES], a person, agency, etc., usually one of several, whose signature is attached to a document.
**sig·na·ture** (sig′nə-chẽr), *n.* [< ML. < L. *signare*, to sign], 1. a person's name written by himself. 2. the act of signing one's name. 3. a song, sound effect, etc. that regularly opens or closes a radio or television program. 4. in *music*, signs placed at the beginning of a staff to show key or time. 5. in *printing*, *a*) a large sheet upon which is printed four, or some multiple of four, pages and which, when folded and bound, forms one section of a book. *b*) a letter or number on the first page of such a sheet indicating the sequence of the section.
**sign·board** (sīn′bôrd′, -bōrd′), *n.* a board bearing a sign, especially one advertising a business.
**sig·net** (sig′nit), *n.* [< OFr. dim. of *signe*, a sign], 1. a small seal used in marking documents as official, etc. 2. a mark made by a signet.
**signet ring,** a finger ring containing a signet, often in the form of an initial.
**sig·nif·i·cance** (sig-nif′ə-kəns), *n.* 1. that which is signified; meaning. 2. the quality of being significant; suggestiveness; expressiveness. 3. importance; consequence. Also **sig·nif′i·can·cy.**
**sig·nif·i·cant** (sig-nif′ə-kənt), *adj.* [< L. ppr. of *significare*, to signify], 1. *a*) having or expressing a meaning. *b*) full of meaning. 2. important; momentous. 3. having or conveying a special or hidden meaning. Also **sig·nif′i·ca′tive** (-kā′tiv). **—sig·nif′i·cant·ly,** *adv.*
**sig·ni·fi·ca·tion** (sig′nə-fi-kā′shən), *n.* 1. significance; meaning. 2. a signifying; indication.
**sig·ni·fy** (sig′nə-fī′), *v.t.* [-FIED, -FYING], [< OFr. < L. *significare* < *signum*, a sign + *facere*, to make], 1. to be an indication of; mean. 2. to show or make known, as by a sign, words, etc. *v.i.* to be significant; matter. **—sig′ni·fi′er,** *n.*
**sign language,** communication of thoughts or ideas by means of manual signs and gestures.
**sign of the zodiac,** any of the twelve divisions of the zodiac, each represented by a symbol.
**‡si·gnor** (sē-nyôr′), *n.* [It.], 1. [S-], Mr.: Italian title of respect, used before the name. 2. a gentleman; man. Abbrev. **Sig., sig., S.**
**‡si·gno·ra** (sē-nyô′rä), *n.* [*pl.* -RE (-re)], [It.], woman; lady: Italian title equivalent to *Mrs.*
**si·gno·re** (sē-nyô′re), *n.* [*pl.* -RI (-rē)], [It.], 1. a gentleman; man. 2. sir: Italian title of respect, not used before the name.

**si·gno·ri·na** (sē′nyô-rē′nä), ***n.*** [*pl.* -NE (-ne)], [It.], an unmarried woman or girl; young lady: Italian title equivalent to *Miss.*

**sign·post** (sīn′pōst′), ***n.*** 1. a post bearing a sign. 2. a clear indication; obvious clue, symptom, etc.

**Si·gurd** (sig′ẽrd), ***n.*** in *Norse legend,* a hero identified with Siegfried: cf. *Brynhild.*

**Sikh** (sēk), ***n.*** [Hind., a disciple], a member of a religious sect and militaristic group of the Punjab in India. ***adj.*** of the Sikhs. —**Sikh′ism, *n.***

**si·lage** (sī′lij), ***n.*** [< *ensilage,* after *silo*], in *agriculture,* green fodder preserved in a silo.

**si·lence** (sī′ləns), ***n.*** 1. the state or fact of keeping silent or still. 2. absence of any sound or noise; stillness. 3. a withholding of knowledge; omission of mention. 4. failure to communicate, write, etc. ***v.t.*** [-LENCED, -LENCING], 1. to cause to be silent. 2. to put down; repress. 3. to put (enemy guns) out of action. ***interj.*** be silent!

**si·lenc·er** (sī′lən-sẽr), ***n.*** 1. one that silences. 2. a device for deadening the sound of a gun. 3. [Chiefly Brit.], a muffler (sense 2).

**si·lent** (sī′lənt), ***adj.*** [< L. ppr. of *silere,* to be silent], 1. making no vocal sound; mute. 2. seldom speaking; not talkative. 3. free from noise; quiet; still. 4. not spoken, expressed, etc.; tacit: as, *silent* longing. 5. withholding knowledge; omitting mention. 6. inactive: as, the machines were *silent* for six days. 7. designating or of motion pictures not accompanied by synchronized sound. —**si′lent·ly, *adv.*** —**si′lent·ness, *n.***

**silent butler,** an ornamental dish with a hinged cover and handle, in which to empty ash trays, etc.

**silent partner,** a partner who shares in financing but not in managing a business, firm, etc.

**Si·le·sia** (sī-lē′shi-ə, sə-lē′shə), ***n.*** a region of central Europe divided, since 1945, between Poland and Czechoslovakia. —**Si·le′sian, *adj.* & *n.***

**si·lex** (sī′leks), ***n.*** [L.], 1. silica, especially in the form of quartz. 2. heat-resistant glass made of fused quartz. 3. a device of such glass used for making coffee: a trade-mark **(Silex).**

**sil·hou·ette** (sil′oo-et′), ***n.*** [after E. de *Silhouette,* 18th-c. Fr. statesman], 1. an outline drawing, especially a profile, filled in with a solid color, usually black, on a light background. 2. any dark shape seen against a light background. ***v.t.*** [-ETTED, -ETTING], to show or project in a silhouette.

SILHOUETTE

**sil·i·ca** (sil′i-kə), ***n.*** [< L. *silex,* flint], the dioxide of silicon, $SiO_2$, a hard, glassy mineral found in a variety of forms, as quartz, sand, etc.

**sil·i·cate** (sil′i-kit, -kāt′), ***n.*** a salt or ester derived from silica or a silicic acid.

**si·li·ceous** (sə-lish′əs), ***adj.*** of, containing, or like silica: also sp. **si·li′cious.**

**si·lic·ic** (sə-lis′ik), ***adj.*** of, like, or derived from silica or silicon.

**silicic acid,** any of several hypothetical acids, of which the silicates may be regarded as salts.

**sil·i·con** (sil′i-kən), ***n.*** [< L. *silex,* flint], a nonmetallic chemical element found always in combination: it combines with oxygen to form silica: symbol, Si; at. wt., 28.06; at. no., 14.

**sil·i·cone** (sil′ə-kōn′), ***n.*** any of a group of synthetic resins, oils, plastics, etc. in which the carbon has been replaced by silicon: used in lubricants, polishes, salves, etc.

**sil·i·co·sis** (sil′ə-kō′sis), ***n.*** [< *silicon* + *-osis*], a chronic disease of the lungs caused by continued inhaling of silica dust, as in quarrying stone.

**silk** (silk), ***n.*** [see PLURAL, II, D, 3], [AS. *seoluc;* ult. < L. *sericus,* fabric of the *Seres,* the Chinese], 1. the fine, soft, shiny fiber produced by silkworms. 2. thread or fabric made from this. 3. a garment made of this fabric. 4. any silklike substance, as that within a milkweed pod, etc. ***adj.*** of or like silk; silken. —**hit the silk,** [Slang], to jump from an aircraft using a parachute.

**silk cotton,** the silky fibers covering the seeds of various trees, used to stuff cushions, etc.

**silk·en** (sil′k'n), ***adj.*** 1. made of silk. 2. dressed in silk. 3. silklike in appearance, texture, etc. 4. *a)* smooth and ingratiating: as, *silken* flattery. *b)* luxurious: as, *silken* ease. *c)* soft; gentle.

**silk hat,** a tall, cylindrical hat covered with silk or satin, worn by men in dress clothes.

**silk-screen process,** a stencil method of printing a flat color design through a screen of silk, etc.

**silk-stock·ing** (silk′stok′iŋ), ***adj.*** 1. richly dressed; elegant. 2. wealthy; aristocratic. ***n.*** a member of the wealthy, aristocratic class.

**silk·worm** (silk′wũrm′), ***n.*** any of certain moth caterpillars that produce cocoons of silk fiber.

**silk·y** (sil′ki), ***adj.*** [-IER, -IEST], 1. of or like silk; soft; smooth. 2. having silklike hairs, as some leaves. —**silk′i·ly, *adv.*** —**silk′i·ness, *n.***

**sill** (sil), ***n.*** [AS. *syl(l)*], 1. a heavy, horizontal timber or line of masonry supporting a house wall, etc. 2. a horizontal piece forming the bottom frame of a door or window.

**sil·ly** (sil′i), ***adj.*** [-LIER, -LIEST], [< AS. *sælig,* happy; hence innocent, foolish], 1. having or showing little sense or judgment; foolish, absurd, etc. 2. [Colloq.], dazed; senseless, as from a blow. 3. [Archaic], *a)* feeble; infirm. *b)* simple; innocent. ***n.*** [*pl.* -LIES], [Colloq.], a silly person. —**sil′li·ly, *adv.*** —**sil′li·ness, *n.***

**si·lo** (sī′lō), ***n.*** [*pl.* -LOS], [Fr. < Sp. < L. < Gr. *siros*], 1. an airtight pit or tower in which green fodder is preserved. 2. an underground structure for storing and launching a large ballistic missile. ***v.t.*** [-LOED, -LOING], to store in a silo.

**silt** (silt), ***n.*** [prob. < ON.], fine particles of any earthy material, as soil or sand, suspended in or deposited by water. ***v.t.* & *v.i.*** to fill or choke up with silt. —**silt′y** [-IER, -IEST], ***adj.***

**Si·lu·ri·an** (sə-loor′i-ən, sī-lyoor′-), ***adj.*** designating or of the geological period after the Ordovician in the Paleozoic Era: see **geology,** chart. ***n.*** the Silurian Period.

**sil·va** (sil′və), ***n.*** [*pl.* -VAS, -VAE (-vē)], [L., forest], the forest trees of a region: also sp. **syl′va.**

**sil·van** (sil′vən), ***adj.* & *n.*** sylvan.

**sil·ver** (sil′vẽr), ***n.*** [< AS. *seolfer*], 1. a white, precious, metallic chemical element that is extremely ductile and malleable: symbol, Ag; at. wt., 107.880; at. no., 47. 2. silver coin; hence, 3. money; wealth. 4. silverware. 5. the lustrous, grayish-white color of silver. 6. something like silver, as in color, value, etc. ***adj.*** 1. made of, containing, or plated with silver: as, *silver* thread. 2. of or having to do with silver: as, the *silver* standard. 3. of or advocating the adoption of silver as a standard of currency. 4. having the color of silver. 5. having a silvery tone. 6. eloquent: as, a *silver* tongue. 7. marking the twenty-fifth year: as, a *silver* anniversary. ***v.t.*** to cover with silver or something like silver. ***v.i.*** to become silvery in color. —**sil′ver·er, *n.*** —**sil′ver·like′, *adj.*** —**sil′ver·ly, *adv.***

**silver certificate,** a piece of paper money issued on the basis of a government's possession of silver in the amount of its face value, payable on demand.

**sil·ver·fish** (sil′vẽr-fish′), ***n.*** [*pl.* see FISH], a wingless insect with silvery scales, found in damp, dark places.

**silver fox,** 1. a fox with black fur in which the hairs are white near the tips. 2. the fur.

**silver-gray** (sil′vẽr-grā′), ***adj.* & *n.*** gray with a silvery luster.

**sil·ver-haired** (sil′vẽr-hârd′), ***adj.*** having silvery-white or gray hair.

**silver lining,** some basis for hope in the midst of despair, misfortune, etc.

**silver nitrate,** a colorless crystalline salt, $AgNO_3$, prepared by dissolving silver in nitric acid and used in photography, as an antiseptic, etc.

**sil·ver·smith** (sil′vẽr-smith′), ***n.*** a skilled worker who makes articles of silver.

**silver standard,** a monetary standard in which the basic unit equals a specified quantity of silver.

**sil·ver-tongued** (sil′vẽr-tuŋd′), ***adj.*** eloquent.

**sil·ver·ware** (sil′vẽr-wâr′), ***n.*** articles, especially tableware, made of or plated with silver.

**silver wedding,** a 25th wedding anniversary.

**sil·ver·y** (sil′vẽr-i), ***adj.*** 1. having the appearance of silver. 2. softly and clearly ringing: as, a *silvery* tone. 3. covered with or containing silver. —**sil′ver·i·ness, *n.***

**‡s'il vous plaît** (sēl′ vōō′ ple′), [Fr.], if you please.

**Sim·chath To·rah** (sim-khäth′ tō-rä′, sim′khäs tō′rô), a Jewish holiday: also sp. **Simhath Torah:** see **Jewish holidays.**

**Sim·e·on** (sim′i-ən), ***n.*** in the *Bible,* 1. a son of Jacob. 2. a tribe of Israel descended from him.

**sim·i·an** (sim′i-ən), ***adj.*** [< L. *simia,* an ape], of or like an ape or monkey. ***n.*** an ape or monkey.

**sim·i·lar** (sim'ə-lẽr), *adj.* [< Fr. < L. *similis*], 1. nearly but not exactly the same or alike. 2. in *geometry*, having the same shape, but not the same size or position. —**sim'i·lar·ly,** *adv.*

**sim·i·lar·i·ty** (sim'ə-lar'ə-ti), *n.* 1. a being similar. 2. [*pl.* -TIES], a point, feature, or instance in which things are similar.

**sim·i·le** (sim'ə-lē'), *n.* [*pl.* -LES], [L. < *similis*, like], a figure of speech in which one thing is likened to another, dissimilar thing by the use of *like, as*, etc. (e.g., a heart as big as a whale): cf. **metaphor.**

**si·mil·i·tude** (sə-mil'ə-tood', -tūd'), *n.* [OFr. < L. *similitudo*], 1. a person or thing resembling another; counterpart. 2. form; image. 3. [Rare], a simile. 4. similarity; likeness.

**sim·mer** (sim'ẽr), *v.i.* [of echoic origin], 1. to boil gently with a low, murmuring sound. 2. to be about to break out, as in anger, revolt, etc. *v.t.* to keep close to the boiling point. *n.* the state of simmering. —**simmer down,** 1. to simmer, as a liquid, until the volume is reduced. 2. to cease simmering; subside.

**si·mo·le·on** (sə-mō'li-ən), *n.* [Slang], a dollar.

**Si·mon** (sī'mən), *n.* Peter, the apostle: also called **Simon Peter.**

**Si·mon·ize** (sī'mə-nīz'), *v.t.* [-IZED, -IZING], [< the trade-mark *Simoniz*], to clean and wax the enameled surface of (an automobile body, etc.).

**Simon Le·gree** (lə-grē'), 1. the villainous slave overseer in H. B. Stowe's *Uncle Tom's Cabin;* hence, 2. any relentless taskmaster.

**Simon Ma·gus** (mā'gəs), in the *Bible*, a Samaritan magician who offered money for instruction in the rite of imparting the Holy Ghost: Acts 8:9-24.

**si·mon-pure** (sī'mən-pyoor'), *adj.* [after *Simon Pure*, a Quaker in S. Centlivre's play *A Bold Stroke for a Wife* (1718)], genuine; authentic.

**sim·o·ny** (sī'mə-ni, sim'ə-), *n.* [< ML. *simonia* < *Simon Magus*], the buying or selling of sacred things, as church pardons, offices, etc. —**si'mon·ist,** *n.*

**si·moom** (si-mōōm'), *n.* [< Ar. < *samma*, to poison], a hot, violent, sand-laden wind of the African and Asiatic deserts: also **si·moon'** (-mōōn').

**simp** (simp), *n.* [Slang], a simpleton.

**sim·per** (sim'pẽr), *v.i.* [cf. MD. *simper*, dainty, affected], to smile in a silly, affected way; smirk. *v.t.* to say with a simper. *n.* a silly, affected smile; smirk. —**sim'per·er,** *n.* —**sim'per·ing·ly,** *adv.*

**sim·ple** (sim'p'l), *adj.* [-PLER, -PLEST], [OFr. < L. *simplex*], 1. having but one or a few parts or features; uncomplicated; not compounded or complex: as, a *simple* pattern. 2. easy to do or understand, as a task, problem, etc. 3. without additions; bare: as, the *simple* facts. 4. *a*) not ornate; unadorned: as, *simple* clothes. *b*) not luxurious; plain: as, *simple* tastes. 5. without guile or deceit; innocent. 6. without ostentation; natural. 7. of low rank or position; humble; common. 8. unimportant. 9. having or showing little sense; foolish; stupid. 10. in *chemistry*, elementary or unmixed. 11. in *law*, unconditional: as, in fee *simple*. 12. in *zoology*, not divided into parts; not compounded. *n.* 1. an ignorant or foolish person. 2. a medicinal herb, or a medicine made from it. 3. something having only one part, substance, etc. —**sim'ple·ness,** *n.*

**simple fraction,** a fraction in which both numerator and denominator are whole numbers, as ½.

**sim·ple-heart·ed** (sim'p'l-här'tid), *adj.* artless or unsophisticated in nature; sincere. —**sim'ple-heart'ed·ly,** *adv.* —**sim'ple-heart'ed·ness,** *n.*

**simple interest,** interest paid only on the principal lent and not on accumulated interest.

**simple machine,** any one of the simple devices, including the lever, wheel and axle, pulley, wedge, screw, and inclined plane, once believed to constitute the basic features of all machines.

**sim·ple-mind·ed** (sim'p'l-mīn'did), *adj.* 1. simple-hearted. 2. foolish; stupid. 3. feeble-minded. —**sim'ple-mind'ed·ly,** *adv.* —**sim'ple-mind'ed·ness,** *n.*

**simple sentence,** a sentence having one main clause and no subordinate clauses.

**sim·ple·ton** (sim'p'l-tən), *n.* [< *simple*], a person who is stupid or easily deceived; fool.

**sim·plic·i·ty** (sim-plis'ə-ti), *n.* [*pl.* -TIES], 1. a being simple; freedom from complexity, difficulty, etc. 2. absence of luxury, elegance, etc. 3. sincerity; artlessness. 4. plainness, as of way of life. 5. lack of sense; foolishness.

**sim·pli·fy** (sim'plə-fī'), *v.t.* [-FIED, -FYING], to make more simple; make easy or easier. —**sim'pli·fi·ca'tion,** *n.* —**sim'pli·fi'er,** *n.*

**sim·plis·tic** (sim-plis'tik), *adj.* simplified to an unrealistic degree; oversimplified.

**sim·ply** (sim'pli), *adv.* 1. in a simple manner; with simplicity. 2. merely; just: as, his reply was *simply* this. 3. completely: as, it is *simply* absurd.

**sim·u·la·crum** (sim'yoo-lā'krəm), *n.* [*pl.* -CRA (-krə), -CRUMS], [L. < *simulare*, to feign], 1. an image. 2. a mere semblance; vague representation; sham.

**sim·u·late** (sim'yoo-lāt'), *v.t.* [-LATED, -LATING], [< L. pp. of *simulare*, to feign < *simul*, likewise], 1. to give a false appearance of; feign: as, *simulate* an interest. 2. to look or act like: as, the insect *simulated* a twig. *adj.* pretended; feigned. —**sim'u·la'tion,** *n.* —**sim'u·la'tive,** *adj.* —**sim'u·la'tive·ly,** *adv.* —**sim'u·la'tor,** *n.*

**si·mul·cast** (sī'məl-kast', -käst'), *v.t.* [-CAST, -CASTING], [*simul*taneous + broad*cast*], to transmit simultaneously by radio and television. *n.* a program, etc. so transmitted.

**si·mul·ta·ne·ous** (sī'm'l-tā'ni-əs, sim''l-), *adj.* [< L. *simul*, at the same time], occurring, done, etc. together or at the same time. —**si'mul·ta'ne·ous·ly,** *adv.* —**si'mul·ta'ne·ous·ness, si'mul·ta·ne'i·ty** (-tə-nē'ə-ti), *n.*

**sin** (sin), *n.* [< AS. *synne*], 1. the breaking of religious or moral law, especially through a willful act. 2. any offense or fault: as, a social *sin*. *v.i.* [SINNED, SINNING], to commit a sin.

**Si·nai, Mount** (sī'nī), in the *Bible*, the mountain where Moses received the law from God: Ex. 19.

**since** (sins), *adv.* [< AS. *siththan;* ult. < *sith*, after + *thon*, instrumental form of *thæt*, that], 1. from then until now: as, he came Monday and has been here ever *since*. 2. at some or any time between then and now: as, he was ill last week but has *since* recovered. 3. before now; ago: as, he disappeared long *since*. *prep.* 1. continuously from (the time given) until now: as, I've walked *since* one o'clock. 2. during the period between (the time given) and now: as, he's written twice *since* Sunday. *conj.* 1. during the period following the time when: as, he's died *since* they met. 2. continuously from the time when: as, she's been unhappy *since* she left. 3. because: as, *since* I can, I will.

**sin·cere** (sin-sêr'), *adj.* [-CERER, -CEREST], [< Fr. < L. *sincerus*, clean < *sine*, without + base of *caries*, decay], 1. without deceit or pretense; truthful; honest. 2. genuine; real: as, *sincere* grief. —**sin·cere'ly,** *adv.* —**sin·cere'ness,** *n.*

**sin·cer·i·ty** (sin-ser'ə-ti), *n.* [*pl.* -TIES], a being sincere; honesty; good faith; truth.

**Sin·clair, Up·ton** (up't'n sin-klâr'), 1878– ; U.S. novelist and socialist.

**sine** (sīn), *n.* [L. *sinus*, a curve, used as transl. of Ar. *jaib*, bosom of a garment], in *mathematics*, the ratio of the side opposite an acute angle of a right triangle to the hypotenuse.

‡**si·ne** (sī'ni), *prep.* [L.], without.

**si·ne·cure** (sī'ni-kyoor', sin'ə-), *n.* [< L. *sine*, without + *cura*, cure], 1. a church benefice not involving cure (care) of souls. 2. any position that brings profit without involving much work, responsibility, etc. —**si'ne·cur'ism,** *n.* —**si'ne·cur'ist,** *n.*

**si·ne di·e** (sī'ni dī'ē), [L.], without (a) day (being set for meeting again); for an indefinite period: as, the assembly adjourned *sine die*.

‡**si·ne qua non** (sī'ni kwā non'), [L., without which not], an indispensable or essential thing.

**sin·ew** (sin'ū), *n.* [< AS. *seonwe*, oblique form < nom. *sinu*], 1. a tendon. 2. muscular power; strength. 3. any source of power or strength. *v.t.* to strengthen as with sinews. —**sin'ew·less,** *adj.*

**sin·ew·y** (sin'yoo-wi), *adj.* 1. of or like sinew; tough. 2. having many sinews, as meat. 3. having good muscular development: as, *sinewy* shoulders. 4. vigorous; powerful. —**sin'ew·i·ness,** *n.*

**sin·ful** (sin'fəl), *adj.* full of or characterized by sin; wicked. —**sin'ful·ly,** *adv.* —**sin'ful·ness,** *n.*

**sing** (siŋ), *v.i.* [SANG or *now rarely* SUNG, SUNG, SINGING], [< AS. *singan*], 1. *a*) to produce musical sounds with the voice. *b*) to deliver musical selections vocally. 2. to use song in description, praise, etc.: as, of thee I *sing*. 3. to produce musical notes, as a songbird, wind, etc. 4. to hum, buzz, etc., as an insect. 5. to admit of being sung. 6. to rejoice: as, my heart *sings* in me. *v.t.* 1. to utter or perform by singing. 2. to chant (Mass, etc.). 3. to celebrate in song or verse: as, we *sing* his praises. 4. to bring or put, as to sleep, by singing. *n.* 1. a shrill, whistling or humming sound: as, the *sing* of arrows. 2. [Colloq.], *a*) group singing. *b*) a gathering for this purpose. —**sing out,** [Colloq.], to call out loudly; shout. —**sing'a·ble,** *adj.*

**sing.**, singular.

**Sin·ga·pore** (siŋ'gə-pôr', siŋ'gə-pōr'), *n.* 1. an island off the tip of the Malay Peninsula. 2. a country on this island and near-by islets: area, 225 sq. mi.; pop., 1,713,000. 3. its capital, a seaport: pop., 925,000.

**singe** (sinj), *v.t.* [SINGED, SINGEING], [< AS. *sengan*], 1. to burn superficially or slightly. 2. to expose (a carcass) to flame in removing bristles or feathers. *n.* 1. a singeing. 2. a slight burn. —**sing'er**, *n.*

**sing·er** (siŋ'ēr), *n.* 1. a person who sings. 2. a bird that sings.

**Sin·gha·lese** (siŋ'gə-lēz'), *adj.* of Ceylon, its principal race, their language, etc. *n.* 1. [*pl.* -LESE], a member of the Singhalese people. 2. their Indic language. Abbrev. **Singh.**

**sin·gle** (siŋ'g'l), *adj.* [< OFr. < LL. *singulus*], 1. one only; one and no more. 2. without another; alone. 3. of or for one person or family, as a room, house, etc. 4. between two persons only: as, *single* combat. 5. unmarried. 6. having only one part; not double, multiple, etc. 7. having only one set of petals: said of flowers. 8. honest; sincere. *v.t.* [-GLED, -GLING], to select from others (usually with *out*). *v.i.* in *baseball*, to make a single. *n.* 1. a single person or thing. 2. in *baseball*, a hit by which the batter reaches first base only. 3. in *cricket*, a hit by which one run is scored. 4. *pl.* in *tennis*, etc., a game with only one player on each side. —**sin'gle·ness**, *n.*

**sin·gle-breast·ed** (siŋ'g'l-bres'tid), *adj.* covering the front of the body with only one thickness, overlapping just enough to fasten, as a coat.

**single file,** a single column of persons or things, one directly behind another.

**sin·gle-foot** (siŋ'g'l-foot'), *n.* the gait of a horse in which the legs move in lateral pairs, each foot falling singly. *v.i.* to move with this gait.

**sin·gle-hand·ed** (siŋ'g'l-han'did), *adj.* 1. having only one hand or one person. 2. using or requiring the use of only one hand. 3. without help; done or working alone. —**sin'gle-hand'ed·ly**, *adv.*

**sin·gle-heart·ed** (siŋ'g'l-här'tid), *adj.* honest; faithful; sincere. —**sin'gle-heart'ed·ly**, *adv.* —**sin'gle-heart'ed·ness**, *n.*

**sin·gle-mind·ed** (siŋ'g'l-mīn'did), *adj.* 1. single-hearted. 2. with only one aim or purpose. —**sin'gle-mind'ed·ly**, *adv.* —**sin'gle-mind'ed·ness**, *n.*

**single standard,** a moral code setting one standard of sexual behavior for men and women alike.

**sin·gle-stick** (siŋ'g'l-stik'), *n.* 1. a swordlike stick used for fencing. 2. fencing with such sticks.

**single tax,** 1. taxation in which all revenue derives from a tax on a single object, specifically land. 2. a tax of this kind. —**sin'gle-tax'**, *adj.*

**sin·gle·ton** (siŋ'g'l-tən), *n.* 1. a playing card that is the only one of a suit held by a player. 2. a single thing, not one of a pair or of several.

**sin·gle-track** (siŋ'g'l-trak'), *adj.* 1. having only one set of rails, as a railroad. 2. having a limited scope: as, a *single-track* mind.

**sin·gle·tree** (siŋ'g'l-trē'), *n.* [< earlier *swingletree* < ME. *swingle*, a rod + *tre*, a tree], the pivoted crossbar at the front of a wagon, etc. to which the traces of a horse's harness are hooked: also called *whiffletree, whippletree.*

**sin·gly** (siŋ'gli), *adv.* 1. as a single, separate person or thing; alone. 2. one by one. 3. unaided.

**Sing Sing** (siŋ'siŋ'), a New York State penitentiary at Ossining.

**sing·song** (siŋ'sôŋ', -soŋ'), *n.* 1. a rising and falling tone in a monotonous cadence. 2. verse, sound, voice, etc. having such tone or cadence. *adj.* characterized by such tone or cadence. *v.t. & v.i.* to speak, sing, etc. in a singsong manner.

**sin·gu·lar** (siŋ'gyoo-lēr), *adj.* [< OFr. < L. < *singulus*, single], 1. being the only one of its kind; sole; unique. 2. individual; separate. 3. strange; unusual: as, a *singular* remark. 4. exceptional; remarkable: as, *singular* beauty. 5. in *grammar*, of or denoting only one: opposed to *plural*. *n.* in *grammar*, *a)* the singular number. *b)* the singular form of a word. —**sin'gu·lar'i·ty** (-lar'ə-ti), **sin'gu·lar·ness**, *n.* —**sin'gu·lar·ly**, *adv.*

**sin·gu·lar·ize** (siŋ'gyoo-lə-rīz'), *v.t.* [-IZED, -IZING], to make singular.

**Sin·ha·lese** (sin'hə-lēz'), *adj. & n.* Singhalese.

**sin·is·ter** (sin'is-tēr), *adj.* [< OFr. < L. *sinister*, left (hand)], 1. originally, on, to, or toward the left-hand side (in *heraldry*, the left of the bearer). 2. suggesting the approach of disaster, misfortune, etc.; threatening. 3. wicked, evil, or dishonest, especially in a mysterious way. 4. disastrous; unfortunate. —**sin'is·ter·ly**, *adv.* —**sin'is·ter·ness**, *n.*

**sin·is·tral** (sin'is-trəl), *adj.* 1. of, on, or toward the left. 2. left-handed. —**sin'is·tral'i·ty** (-tral'ə-ti), *n.* —**sin'is·tral·ly**, *adv.*

**sin·is·trorse** (sin'is-trôrs'), *adj.* [< L. < *sinister*, left + pp. of *vortere*, to turn], in *botany*, turning upward to the left, as the stems of some vines.

**sink** (siŋk), *v.i.* [SANK or SUNK, SUNK or *obs.* SUNKEN, SINKING], [AS. *sincan*], 1. to go beneath the surface of water, etc. so as to be partly or completely covered. 2. to go down slowly: as, the balloon *sank* to earth. 3. to appear to descend, as the sun or moon. 4. to become lower in level: as, the lake is *sinking*. 5. to become less intense; subside, as wind, flames, a voice, etc. 6. to become lower in value or amount, as prices. 7. to become hollow or shrunken, as the cheeks. 8. to pass gradually (*into* sleep, despair, etc.). 9. to approach death; fail: as, he is *sinking* rapidly. 10. to undergo decline in social, moral, or economic state. 11. to penetrate: as, water *sinks* into soil. *v.t.* 1. to cause to sink or go down; submerge, lower, lessen, etc. 2. to make (a well, design, etc.) by digging, drilling, cutting, etc. 3. to invest. 4. to lose by investing. 5. to suppress or conceal (evidence, identity, etc.). 6. to defeat; undo: as, if they see us we're *sunk*. *n.* 1. a cesspool, drain, or sewer. 2. any place or thing considered morally filthy. 3. a basin, as in a kitchen, connected with a drainpipe and, usually, a water supply. 4. an area of sunken land, especially one in which water collects without a natural outlet. —**sink in**, [Colloq.], to be grasped by the mind, especially with difficulty. —**sink'a·ble**, *adj.*

**sink·er** (siŋk'ēr), *n.* 1. a person or thing that sinks (in various senses). 2. a lead weight used on a fishing line. 3. [Colloq.], a doughnut.

**Sin·kiang** (sin'kyaŋ'), *n.* a large province of NW China.

**sinking fund,** a fund made up of sums of money set aside at intervals, usually invested at interest, to pay a debt, meet depreciation, etc.

**sin·less** (sin'lis), *adj.* without sin; innocent. —**sin'less·ly**, *adv.* —**sin'less·ness**, *n.*

**sin·ner** (sin'ēr), *n.* one who sins; wrongdoer.

**Sinn Fein** (shin fān), [Ir., we ourselves], a revolutionary society and movement founded in Ireland about 1905 to establish Irish independence.

**Sin·o-,** [< Gr. *Sinai*, an oriental people], a combining form meaning: 1. *of the Chinese people or language*. 2. *Chinese and.*

**Sin·o-Ti·bet·an** (sī'nō-ti-bet''n, sin'ō-), *adj.* designating or of a family of Eastern Asiatic languages spoken in Tibet, China, Burma, and Thailand.

**sin·u·ate** (sin'ū-it, -āt'), *adj.* [< L. pp. of *sinuare*, to bend < *sinus*, a bend], 1. bending or winding in or out; wavy. 2. in *botany*, having a wavy margin, as some leaves. —**sin'u·a'tion** (-ā'shən), *n.*

**sin·u·ous** (sin'ū-əs), *adj.* [< L. < *sinus*, a bend], 1. bending or winding in and out; wavy. 2. devious; crooked; not honest. —**sin'u·os'i·ty** (-os'ə-ti), **sin'u·ous·ness**, *n.* —**sin'u·ous·ly**, *adv.*

**si·nus** (sī'nəs), *n.* [*pl.* -NUSES, -NUS], [L., a bent surface], 1. a bend or curve. 2. a cavity, hollow, etc.; specif., *a)* any of the air cavities in the skull opening into the nasal cavities. *b)* a channel for venous blood. *c)* a narrow channel leading from a pus-filled cavity. 3. popularly, sinusitis.

**si·nus·i·tis** (sī'nəs-ī'tis), *n.* inflammation of a sinus or sinuses, especially of the skull.

**Si·on** (sī'ən), *n.* Zion.

**-sion** (shən, zhən), [< L. *-sio*], a suffix meaning *the act, quality, state, or result of*, as in *fusion.*

**Siou·an** (sōō'ən), *adj.* designating or of a linguistic family of North American Indians formerly inhabiting the west central U.S., including Dakota, Crow, etc.

**Sioux** (sōō), *n.* [*pl.* SIOUX (sōō, sōōz)], a member of a confederation of Siouan Indian tribes that lived in the northern U.S. *adj.* of these tribes.

**Sioux City,** a city in W Iowa: pop., 89,000.

**Sioux Falls,** a city in SE South Dakota: pop., 65,000.

**sip** (sip), *v.t. & v.i.* [SIPPED, SIPPING], [prob. < AS. *sypian*, to drink in], to drink only a little at a time. *n.* 1. the act of sipping. 2. a small quantity sipped. —**sip'per**, *n.*

**si·phon** (sī'fən), *n.* [Fr. < L. < Gr. *siphōn*, a tube], 1. a bent tube for carrying liquid out over the edge of a container to a lower level, through the atmospheric pressure on the surface of the liquid. 2. a siphon bottle. 3. a tubelike organ, as in a cuttlefish, for drawing in or ejecting liquids. ***v.t.* & *v.i.*** to draw off, or pass, through a siphon. Also sp. **syphon.** —**si′phon·al, si·phon·ic** (sī-fon′-ik), ***adj.***

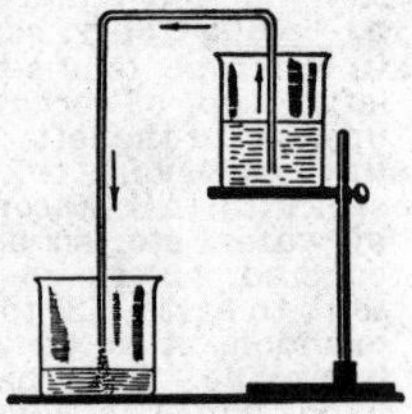
SIPHON

**siphon bottle,** a sealed bottle with a tube on the inside which, when opened by a valve, releases pressurized, carbonated water contained within.

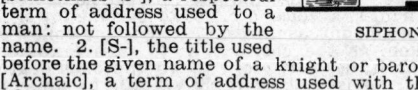

**sir** (sũr), ***n.*** [see SIRE], 1. [sometimes S-], a respectful term of address used to a man: not followed by the name. 2. [S-], the title used before the given name of a knight or baronet. 3. [Archaic], a term of address used with the title of a man's office, etc.: as, *sir* judge.

**sire** (sīr), ***n.*** [< OFr. < L. *senior;* see SENIOR], 1. a title of respect now used only in addressing a king. 2. [Poetic], a father or forefather. 3. the male parent of a quadruped. ***v.t.*** [SIRED, SIRING], to beget: said especially of quadrupeds.

**si·ren** (sī′rən), ***n.*** [< L. < Gr. *seirēn*], 1. in *Gr. & Rom. mythology,* any of several sea nymphs whose seductive singing lured sailors to their death on rocky coasts. 2. a seductive woman. 3. a device in which steam or air driven against a rotating, perforated disk produces a wailing sound: used as a warning signal, etc. ***adj.*** seductive.

**Sir·i·us** (sir′i-əs), ***n.*** [L. < Gr. *Seirios,* the scorcher], the brightest star in the heavens, in the constellation Canis Major: also called *Dog Star.*

**sir·loin** (sũr′loin), ***n.*** [< OFr. < *sur,* over + *longe,* loin], a choice cut of beef from the loin end between the rump and the porterhouse.

**si·roc·co** (sə-rok′ō), ***n.*** [*pl.* -COS], [It. < Ar. *sharq,* the east], 1. a hot, oppressive wind blowing from the Libyan deserts into S Europe, sometimes with rain. 2. any hot, oppressive wind.

**sir·rah** (sir′ə), ***n.*** [< *sir*], [Archaic], a contemptuous term of address used to a man.

**sir·up** (sir′əp, sũr′-), ***n.*** [< OFr. < ML. < Ar. < *shariba,* to drink], any sweet, thick liquid; specif., *a*) a solution made by boiling sugar with water, fruit juices, etc.: often used in pharmacy as a vehicle for medicines. *b*) maple sirup, etc. Also sp. **syrup.** —**sir′up·y,** ***adj.***

**sis** (sis), ***n.*** [contr. of *sister*], [Colloq.], sister.

**si·sal** (sī′s′l, sis′′l), ***n.*** [< *Sisal,* Yucatán, a former seaport], 1. a strong fiber obtained from the leaves of an agave, used for making rope. 2. the plant yielding this fiber. Also **sisal hemp.**

**sis·si·fy** (sis′ə-fī′), ***v.t.*** [-FIED, -FYING], [Colloq.], to cause (a boy or man) to be a sissy.

**sis·sy** (sis′i), ***n.*** [*pl.* -SIES], [dim. of *sis*], [Colloq.], a boy or man whose behavior, tastes, etc. seem more feminine than masculine. —**sis′sy·ish,** ***adj.***

**sis·ter** (sis′tẽr), ***n.*** [< ON. *systir*], 1. *a*) a female related to one by having the same parents. *b*) a half sister, stepsister, or foster sister. 2. a female member of the same race, organization, etc. 3. a member of a female religious order; nun. 4. one of the same kind, model, etc. 5. [Brit.], a nurse. ***adj.*** related or seeming to be related as sisters.

**sis·ter·hood** (sis′tẽr-hood′), ***n.*** 1. the relationship of sisters. 2. a group of women having the same interests, status, etc. 3. an association of women, as one forming a religious order.

**sis·ter-in-law** (sis′tẽr-in-lô′), ***n.*** [*pl.* SISTERS-IN-LAW], 1. the sister of one's husband or wife. 2. the wife of one's brother. 3. the wife of the brother of one's husband or wife.

**sis·ter·ly** (sis′tẽr-li), ***adj.*** of, like, or befitting a sister. ***adv.*** as a sister should.—**sis′ter·li·ness,** ***n.***

**Sis·y·phus** (sis′ə-fəs), ***n.*** in *Gr. mythology,* a greedy king doomed forever in Hades to roll uphill a boulder which always rolled down again.

**sit** (sit), ***v.i.*** [SAT or *archaic* SATE, SITTING], [< AS. *sittan*], 1. to rest oneself upon the buttocks, as on a chair, etc. 2. to rest on the haunches with the forelegs braced, as a dog. 3. to perch, as a bird. 4. to cover eggs for hatching, as a hen. 5. to occupy a seat as a judge, legislator, etc. 6. to be in session, as a court. 7. to pose, as for a portrait. 8. to be inactive. 9. to be located: as, that chair *sits* here. 10. to fit: as, this hat *sits* well. 11. to rest or lie: as, his duties *sit* lightly on him. 12. to baby-sit. ***v.t.*** 1. to cause to sit: as, *sit* yourself here. 2. to keep one's seat on (a horse, etc.). —**sit down,** to take a seat. —**sit in,** to participate; attend (often with *on*). —**sit on** (or **upon**), 1. to be on (a jury, committee, etc.). 2. to confer on. 3. [Colloq.], to suppress, rebuke, etc. —**sit out,** 1. to stay until the end of. 2. to be a nonparticipant temporarily in (a dance, game, etc.). —**sit up,** 1. to rise to a sitting position. 2. to sit erect. 3. to stay up past one's bedtime. 4. [Colloq.], to be startled. —**sit′ter,** ***n.***

**si·tar** (si-tär′), ***n.*** [Hindi *sitār*], a lutelike instrument of India, with a long, fretted neck.

**sit-down strike** (sit′doun′), a strike in which the strikers stay inside a factory, etc., refusing to work until agreement is reached: also **sit-down.**

**site** (sīt), ***n.*** [OFr. < L. *situs,* position], 1. a piece of land considered for a certain purpose: as, a poor *site* for a picnic. 2. the place or scene of anything.

**sith** (sith), ***adv., conj., prep.*** [Archaic], since.

**sit-in** (sit′in′), ***n.*** the organized act of occupying seats in a restaurant, etc. that practices racial discrimination, in seeking to integrate it.

**sit·ting** (sit′iŋ), ***n.*** 1. the act or position of one that sits. 2. a meeting or session, as of a court. 3. a period of being seated at some activity. 4. *a*) a clutch of eggs being hatched. *b*) a brooding upon eggs. ***adj.*** that sits; seated.

**Sit·ting Bull** (sit′iŋ bool), 1834?–1890: Sioux Indian chief; defeated General Custer (1876).

**sitting room,** a living room.

**sit·u·ate** (sich′ōō-āt′), ***v.t.*** [-ATED, -ATING], [< ML. pp. of *situare,* to place < L. *situs,* position], to put in a certain place or position; locate.

**sit·u·at·ed** (sich′ōō-āt′id), ***adj.*** 1. placed; located. 2. subject to certain circumstances.

**sit·u·a·tion** (sich′ōō-ā′shən), ***n.*** 1. location; position. 2. a place; locality. 3. condition with regard to circumstances. 4. *a*) a state of affairs. *b*) any significant combination of circumstances, as in a novel or play. 5. a position of employment.

**sit-up, sit·up** (sit′up′), ***n.*** an exercise in which a person lying flat on the back rises to a sitting position without using the hands.

**Si·va** (sē′və, shē′-), ***n.*** Hindu god of destruction and reproduction, a member of the Supreme Hindu trinity (Brahma, Vishnu, and Siva): also **Shiva.**

**Si·van** (si-vän′, siv′ən), ***n.*** [Heb.], the ninth month of the Jewish year: see **Jewish calendar.**

**six** (siks), ***adj.*** [AS. *sex*], totaling one more than five. ***n.*** 1. the cardinal number between five and seven; 6; VI. 2. something having six units or members. —**at sixes and sevens,** [Colloq.], 1. in confusion or disorder. 2. at odds; disagreeing.

**six·fold** (siks′fōld′), ***adj.*** 1. having six parts. 2. having six times as much or as many. ***adv.*** six times as much or as many.

**six·pence** (siks′pəns), ***n.*** 1. the sum of six pence (pennies). 2. a British silver coin of this value.

**six·pen·ny** (siks′pen′i, -pən-i), ***adj.*** 1. worth or costing sixpence. 2. of small worth; cheap. 3. designating a size of nails, usually two inches.

**six-shoot·er** (siks′shōōt′ẽr), ***n.*** [Colloq.], a revolver firing six shots without reloading.

**six·teen** (siks′tēn′), ***adj.*** [AS. *syxtene*], six more than ten. ***n.*** the cardinal number between fifteen and seventeen; 16; XVI.

**six·teenth** (siks′tēnth′), ***adj.*** 1. preceded by fifteen others in a series; 16th. 2. designating any of the sixteen equal parts of something. ***n.*** 1. the one following the fifteenth. 2. any of the sixteen equal parts of something; 1/16.

**sixteenth note,** in *music,* a note (♬) having one sixteenth the duration of a whole note.

**sixth** (siksth), ***adj.*** [AS. *sixta*], 1. preceded by five others in a series; 6th. 2. designating any of the six equal parts of something. ***n.*** 1. the one following the fifth. 2. any of the six equal parts of something; 1/6. 3. in *music, a*) an interval of six degrees in a diatonic scale. *b*) a tone six degrees above or below a given tone. *c*) the combination of two tones separated by this interval. —**sixth′ly,** ***adv.***

**sixth sense,** a power of perception which seems as strong as any of the five senses; intuition.

**six·ti·eth** (siks′ti-ith), ***adj.*** 1. preceded by fifty-nine others in a series; 60th. 2. designating any of the sixty equal parts of something. ***n.*** 1. the one following the fifty-ninth. 2. any of the sixty equal parts of something; 1/60.

**six·ty** (siks′ti), ***adj.*** [AS. *sixtig*], six times ten. ***n.*** [*pl.* -TIES], the cardinal number between fifty-nine and sixty-one; 60; LX. —**the sixties,** the years from sixty through sixty-nine (of a century or a person's age).

**six·ty-fourth note** (siks′ti-fôrth′, -fōrth′), in *music,* a note (♪) having one sixty-fourth the duration of a whole note.

**siz·a·ble** (sīz′ə-b′l), ***adj.*** quite large or bulky: also sp. **sizeable.** —**siz′a·ble·ness,** ***n.*** —**siz′a·bly,** ***adv.***

**size** (sīz), ***n.*** [< OFr. contr. of *assise;* see ASSIZE], 1. that quality of a thing which determines how much space it occupies; dimensions. 2. any of a series of graded classifications according to this:

as, *size* nine shoes. 3. *a*) extent, magnitude, etc.: as, a plan of great *size*. *b*) sizable amount, dimensions, etc. 4. ability to meet requirements: as, a job too big for the *size* of him. 5. [Colloq.], true state of affairs: as, that's the *size* of it. *v.t.* [SIZED, SIZING], 1. to make in accordance with a given size. 2. to arrange according to size. **—of a size,** of one or the same size. **—size up,** [Colloq.], 1. to make an estimate or judgment of. 2. to meet requirements.

**size** (sīz), *n.* [contr. of Fr. *assise*, layer; see ASSIZE], any thin, pasty substance used as a glaze or filler on porous materials, as on paper, cloth, etc. *v.t.* [SIZED, SIZING], to apply size to; fill, stiffen, or glaze with size. **—siz′y,** *adj.*

**-sized** (sīzd), a combining form meaning *having* (a specified) *size*, as in *small-sized*: also **-size.**

**siz·ing** (sīz′iŋ), *n.* 1. size (glaze or filler). 2. the act or process of applying this.

**siz·zle** (siz′'l), *v.i.* [-ZLED, -ZLING], [echoic], to make a hissing sound when in contact with heat, as water on hot metal. *n.* such a sound.

**S.J.,** Society of Jesus.

**skald** (skôld, skäld), *n.* [ON. *skāld*], any ancient Scandinavian poet writing in the late Old Norse style: also sp. **scald. —skald′ic,** *adj.*

**skate** (skāt), *n.* [assumed sing. < D. *schaats*, skate < OFr. *escache*, stilt; of Gmc. origin], 1. *a*) a bladelike metal runner mounted in a frame to be fastened to a shoe, used for gliding on ice. *b*) a shoe with such a runner attached. Also **ice skate.** 2. a roller skate. *v.i.* [SKATED, SKATING], to move along or glide on skates. **—skate on thin ice,** to be in a precarious situation. **—skat′er,** *n.*

**skate** (skāt), *n.* [*pl.* SKATES, SKATE; see PLURAL, II, D, 1], [< ON. *skata*], a salt-water food fish of the ray family, with a broad, flat body.

**ske·dad·dle** (ski-dad′'l), *v.i.*[-DLED, -DLING], [coinage of Civil War period], [Colloq.], to scurry away. *n.* [Colloq.], a scurrying away.

**skeet** (skēt), *n.* trapshooting in which the shooter fires from different angles at clay pigeons.

**skein** (skān), *n.* [< OFr. *esca(i)gne*], 1. a quantity of thread or yarn wound in a coil. 2. something resembling this, as a coil of hair.

**skel·e·ton** (skel′ə-t'n), *n.* [< Gr. *skeleton* (*sōma*), dried (body) < *skeletos*, dried up], 1. the hard framework of an animal for supporting the tissues and protecting the organs; specif., all the bones of a body, collectively. 2. anything like a skeleton; specif., *a*) a very lean person or animal. *b*) a supporting framework, as of a ship. *c*) an outline, as of a book. *adj.* of or like a skeleton; having the essential outline, framework, etc.: as, a *skeleton* force. **—skeleton in the closet,** some fact about a relative, etc. kept secret because of shame. **—skel′e·tal,** *adj.*

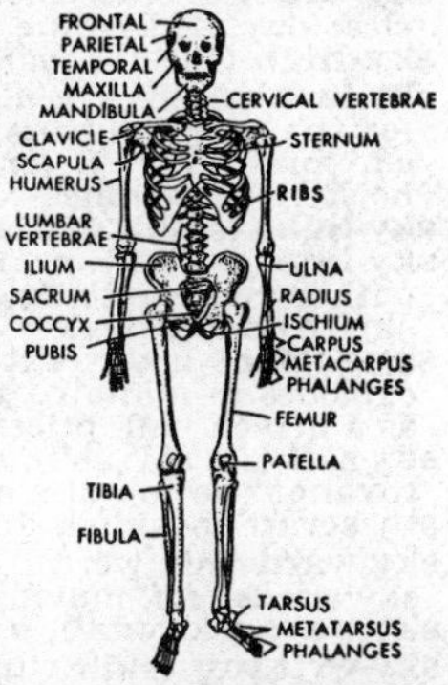

HUMAN SKELETON

**skel·e·ton·ize** (skel′ə-t'n-īz′), *v.t.* [-IZED, -IZING], 1. to reduce to a skeleton. 2. to outline. 3. to reduce greatly in number or size.

**skeleton key,** a key with a slender bit that can open many simple locks.

**skep·tic** (skep′tik), *adj.* [< OFr. < L. < Gr. *skeptikos*, inquiring], skeptical. *n.* 1. [S-], a member of any of the ancient Greek philosophical schools which denied the possibility of real knowledge. 2. a believer in philosophical skepticism. 3. one who habitually doubts or questions matters generally accepted. 4. one who doubts religious doctrines. Also sp. **sceptic.**

**skep·ti·cal** (skep′tə-k'l), *adj.* 1. of or characteristic of skeptics or skepticism. 2. not easily convinced; doubting; questioning. 3. doubting the fundamental doctrines of religion. Also sp. **sceptical. —skep′ti·cal·ly,** *adv.* **—skep′ti·cal·ness,** *n.*

**skep·ti·cism** (skep′tə-siz'm), *n.* 1. the philosophical doctrine that the truth of all knowledge must always be in question. 2. skeptical or doubting attitude or state of mind. 3. doubt or disbelief of religious doctrines. Also sp. **scepticism.**

**sketch** (skech), *n.* [D. *schets* < It. *schizzo* < L. < Gr. *schedios*, extempore], 1. a simple, rough drawing or design, done rapidly. 2. a brief plan; outline. 3. a short, light, informal story, description, play, etc. *v.t. & v.i.* to make a sketch (of). **—sketch′a·ble,** *adj.* **—sketch′er,** *n.*

**sketch·book** (skech′book′), *n.* 1. a book of drawing paper for making sketches. 2. a book of literary sketches. Also **sketch book.**

**sketch·y** (skech′i), *adj.* [-IER, -IEST], 1. having the form of a sketch; not detailed. 2. lacking completeness or thoroughness; rough; inadequate. **—sketch′i·ly,** *adv.* **—sketch′i·ness,** *n.*

**skew** (skū), *v.i.* [< ONorm.Fr. *eskiuer*, varied < OFr. < OHG.; see ESCHEW], to move at a slant; swerve or twist. *v.t.* 1. to make slanting or oblique. 2. to bias or distort. *adj.* 1. turned to one side; slanting; oblique. 2. having such a part, as gearing. 3. not symmetrical. *n.* 1. a slant or twist. 2. a slanting part or movement. **—skew′ness,** *n.*

**skew·er** (skū′ẽr), *n.* [formerly *skiver* < ON. *skifa*, a slice], 1. a long wooden or metal pin used to hold meat together while cooking. 2. anything like a skewer. *v.t.* to fasten or pierce as with skewers.

**ski** (skē; *also* Norw., shē), *n.* [*pl.* SKIS, SKI], [Norw. < ON. *skith*, snowshoe], one of a pair of long, thin, wood runners fastened to the feet for gliding over snow. *v.i.* [SKIED, SKIING], to glide on skis, as down snow-covered inclines. **—ski′er,** *n.* **—ski′ing,** *n.*

**skid** (skid), *n.* [< ON. *skith*, wooden billet], 1. a plank, log, etc. used as a support or as a track upon which to slide a heavy object. 2. a low, wooden platform for holding loads. 3. a runner used in place of a wheel on an aircraft landing gear. 4. a sliding wedge or drag used to check the motion of a vehicle by pressure against a wheel. 5. the act of skidding. *v.t.* [SKIDDED, SKIDDING], 1. to brake (a wheel) with a skid. 2. to support with or slide on a skid or skids. 3. to cause (a wheel, vehicle, etc.) to skid. *v.i.* 1. to slide without turning, as a wheel when skids or brakes are applied on a slippery surface. 2. to slide or slip sideways, as a vehicle on an icy road. **—on the skids,** [Slang], falling from power, losing prestige, etc. **—skid′der,** *n.* **—skid′ding·ly,** *adv.*

**skid row,** [Slang], a section of a city frequented by hobos, vagrants, derelicts, etc.

**skiff** (skif), *n.* [< OFr. < It. *schifo* < OHG. *scif*], 1. any light rowboat. 2. a long, narrow rowboat, especially one with a small sail.

**skill** (skil), *n.* [< ON. *skil*, distinction], 1. great ability or proficiency; expertness. 2. an art, craft, or science, especially one involving the use of the hands or body. 3. ability in such an art, craft, or science.

**skilled** (skild), *adj.* 1. skillful. 2. having or requiring an ability, as in an industrial occupation, gained by special experience or apprenticeship.

**skil·let** (skil′it), *n.* [? < OFr. dim. of *escuelle*, basin < L. *scutella*, dim. of *scutra*, a dish], 1. a deep, heavy stewing pan with a long handle. 2. a frying pan.

**skill·ful, skil·ful** (skil′fəl), *adj.* having or showing skill; accomplished. **—skill′ful·ly, skil′ful·ly,** *adv.* **—skill′ful·ness, skil′ful·ness,** *n.*

**skim** (skim), *v.t.* [SKIMMED, SKIMMING], [< OFr. *escumer* < OHG. *scum*, scum], 1. to clear (a liquid) of floating matter. 2. to remove (floating matter) from a liquid. 3. to coat with a thin layer: as, a pond *skimmed* with ice. 4. to look through (a book, etc.) in a cursory manner. 5. to glide swiftly and lightly over. 6. to cause to move in this way: as, to *skim* a stone across water. *v.i.* 1. to move along swiftly and lightly; glide. 2. to read (*through* or *over* a book, etc.) in a cursory manner. 3. to become thinly coated, as with scum. *n.* 1. something skimmed off. 2. the act of skimming. **—skim′mer,** *n.*

**skim milk,** milk from which the cream is removed.

**skimp** (skimp), *v.i.* [prob. altered < *scrimp*], [Colloq.], 1. to give or allow too little; scrimp. 2. to keep expenses very low. *v.t.* [Colloq.], 1. to do poorly or carelessly. 2. to be stingy in or toward. **—skimp′er,** *n.* **—skimp′ing·ly,** *adv.*

**skimp·y** (skim′pi), *adj.* [-IER, -IEST], [Colloq.], 1. barely or not quite enough; scanty. 2. stingy. **—skimp′i·ly,** *adv.* **—skimp′i·ness,** *n.*

**skin** (skin), *n.* [< ON. *skinn*], 1. the outer covering or integument of the animal body. 2. such a covering, as of a small animal, when removed from the body and prepared for use; pelt. 3. something like skin in appearance or function, as fruit rind, a film or scum, etc. 4. a container for liquids, made of skin. *v.t.* [SKINNED, SKINNING], 1. to cover as with skin. 2. to remove the skin from. 3. [Colloq.], to defraud; swindle. *v.i.* to shed the skin. **—by the skin of one's teeth,** [Colloq.], by the narrowest margin. **—get under one's skin,** [Slang], to anger or irritate one. **—have a thick (or thin) skin,** to be insensitive (or sensitive) to criticism, insults, etc. **—save one's skin,** [Colloq.], to avoid death or injury. **—skin'less,** *adj.*

**skin-deep** (skin'dēp'), *adj.* 1. penetrating no deeper than the skin. 2. without real significance; superficial. *adv.* so as to be skin-deep.

**skin diving,** underwater diving in which the swimmer, without lines to the surface, is variously equipped with goggles, portable compressed-air equipment, etc. **—skin diver.**

**skin·flint** (skin'flint'), *n.* [lit., one who would skin a flint for economy], a niggardly person; miser.

**skin grafting,** the surgical transplanting of skin to replace skin destroyed, as by burning.

**skink** (skiŋk), *n.* [< L. < Gr. *skinkos*], a tropical lizard with a thick, shiny body and short legs.

**skinned** (skind), *adj.* having a (specified kind of) skin: usually in compounds, as *dark-skinned.*

**skin·ner** (skin'ẽr), *n.* 1. one who strips skins or processes them for market. 2. a swindler.

**skin·ny** (skin'i), *adj.* [-NIER, -NIEST], 1. of or like skin. 2. without much flesh; emaciated; thin. **—skin'ni·ness,** *n.*

**skin·ny-dip** (skin'i-dip'), *v.i.* [-DIPPED, -DIPPING], [Colloq.], to swim in the nude.

**skin·tight** (skin'tīt'), *adj.* clinging closely to the skin; tight-fitting, as a garment.

**skip** (skip), *v.i.* [SKIPPED, SKIPPING], [prob. < ON.], 1. to leap, jump, etc. lightly and quickly. 2. to be deflected from a surface; ricochet. 3. to pass from one point to another, omitting what lies between. 4. to be promoted in school beyond the next regular grade. 5. [Colloq.], to leave hurriedly; abscond. *v.t.* 1. to leap lightly over. 2. to pass over without noticing, reading, doing, etc. 3. to cause to skip. 4. [Colloq.], to leave (a place) hurriedly. *n.* 1. *a)* an act of skipping; leap; spring. *b)* a skipping gait in which hops and steps are alternated. 2. a passing over or omitting.

**ski pants,** loose-cut slack trousers that fit tightly around the ankle: used in winter sports.

**skip·jack** (skip'jak'), *n.* [*pl.* -JACKS, -JACK; see PLURAL, II, D, 1], any of several kinds of fish that play at the surface of the water.

**skip·per** (skip'ẽr), *n.* 1. a person or thing that skips. 2. any of various skipping insects.

**skip·per** (skip'ẽr), *n.* [MD. *schipper* < *schip*, a ship], 1. the captain of a ship. 2. anyone who leads or directs. *v.t.* to act as skipper of.

**skirl** (skũrl), *v.t.* & *v.i.* [prob. < ON.], [Scot. & Dial.], to sound out in shrill, piercing tones, as a bagpipe. *n.* a shrill sound, as of a bagpipe.

**skir·mish** (skũr'mish), *n.* [< OFr. < *eskirmir* < Gmc.], 1. a brief fight between small groups, usually part of a battle or war. 2. any slight, unimportant conflict. *v.i.* to take part in a skirmish.

**skir·mish·er** (skũr'mish-ẽr), *n.* 1. a person who skirmishes. 2. any of a group of soldiers spread out in extended order for attack.

**skirt** (skũrt), *n.* [< ON. *skyrt*, shirt], 1. that part of a robe, dress, coat, etc. that hangs below the waist. 2. a woman's separate garment that hangs from the waist. 3. something like a skirt, as a flap hanging from a saddle. 4. *pl.* the outer parts; outskirts, as of a city. 5. [Slang], a girl or woman. *v.t.* 1. to lie along or form the edge of. 2. to move along the border or edge of: as, *skirt* the woods. 3. to border or edge (*with*). *v.i.* to be on, or move along, the edge: as, the path *skirts* along the pond. **—skirt'ed,** *adj.* **—skirt'er,** *n.*

**skit** (skit), *n.* [prob. ult. < ON. *skjota*, to shoot], 1. a verbal slap; gibe. 2. a short, satirical or humorous sketch, as in the theater.

**skit·ter** (skit'ẽr), *v.i.* [freq. of dial. *skit*, to dart about; of Scand. origin], to skip or move along quickly and lightly, especially over water. *v.t.* to cause to skitter.

**skit·tish** (skit'ish), *adj.* [< base of *skit* + *-ish*], 1. spirited; lively; playful; coy. 2. easily frightened; nervous; jumpy. 3. fickle; undependable. **—skit'tish·ly,** *adv.* **—skit'tish·ness,** *n.*

**skit·tle** (skit''l), *n.* [prob. < the ON. cognate of *shuttle*], 1. *pl.* the game of ninepins. 2. any of the pins used in this game. **—(not) all beer and skittles,** (not) pure pleasure and enjoyment.

**skiv·vy** (skiv'i), *n.* [*pl.* -VIES], [< dial. *skivie*, silly, awry], [Slang], a man's, especially a sailor's, undershirt or, *pl.*, underwear.

**skoal** (skōl), *interj.* [< Dan. & Norw. *skaal*, a cup < ON. *skāl*, a bowl], to your health!: a toast.

**Skr., Skrt., Skt.,** Sanskrit.

**sku·a** (skū'ə), *n.* [ult. < ON. *skūfr*], any of several large, brown, northern sea birds related to the gulls; jaeger: also **skua gull.**

**skul·dug·ger·y** (skul-dug'ẽr-i), *n.* [< OFr. < *escoulourgier*, to slip], [Colloq.], mean trickery; craftiness.

**skulk** (skulk), *v.i.* [prob. < ON.], 1. to move about in a stealthy, craven manner; slink. 2. to avoid work or responsibility; shirk. *n.* one who skulks. **—skulk'er,** *n.* **—skulk'ing·ly,** *adv.*

**skull** (skul), *n.* [< Scand.], 1. the bony framework of the head, enclosing the brain. 2. the mind.

**skull and crossbones,** a representation of a human skull on crossbones, used to label poisons, etc.

**skull·cap** (skul'kap'), *n.* a light, closefitting, brimless cap, usually worn indoors.

**skunk** (skuŋk), *n.* [contr. < Am. Ind. *segonku*], 1. [*pl.* SKUNKS, SKUNK; see PLURAL, II, D, 1], a bushy-tailed mammal about the size of a cat: it has black fur with white stripes down its back, and ejects an offensive-smelling liquid when molested. 2. its fur. 3. [Colloq.], a despicable, offensive person. *v.t.* [Slang], to defeat overwhelmingly in a game or contest.

SKUNK (about 2 ft. long)

**skunk cabbage,** a plant with thick roots, wide leaves, and a disagreeable smell: also **skunk'-weed'.**

**sky** (skī), *n.* [*pl.* SKIES], [< ON. *sky̅*, cloud], 1. *often pl.* the upper atmosphere, especially with reference to its appearance: as, blue *skies*, a cloudy *sky*. 2. the heavens, apparently arching over the earth; firmament. 3. heaven. *v.t.* [SKIED or SKYED (skīd), SKYING], [Colloq.], to hit, throw, etc. high in the air. **—out of a clear sky,** without warning; suddenly. **—to the skies,** without reserve; extravagantly.

**sky blue,** a blue color like that of the sky on a clear day. **—sky-blue** (skī'blo͞o'), *adj.*

**sky-high** (skī'hī'), *adj.* & *adv.* very high.

**sky·lark** (skī'lärk'), *n.* the Old World lark, famous for the song it utters as it soars toward the sky. *v.i.* [prob. *sky* + *lark*, to play], to play about boisterously; frolic.

**sky·light** (skī'līt'), *n.* a window in a roof or ceiling.

**sky·line** (skī'līn'), *n.* 1. the visible horizon. 2. the outline of something, as a city, seen against the sky. Also **sky line.**

**sky·rock·et** (skī'rok'it), *n.* a firework rocket that explodes in mid-air. *v.i.* [Colloq.], to rise rapidly, as a driven ball, prices, etc.

**sky·sail** (skī'sāl', -s'l), *n.* the small sail set above the royal at the top of a square-rigged mast.

**sky·scrap·er** (skī'skrāp'ẽr), *n.* a very tall building.

**sky·ward** (skī'wẽrd), *adv.* toward the sky: also **sky'wards.** *adj.* moving or leading toward the sky.

**sky·ways** (skī'wāz'), *n.pl.* routes of air travel.

**sky·writ·ing** (skī'rīt'iŋ), *n.* the tracing of words, figures, etc. in the sky by trailing smoke from an airplane in flight. **—sky'writ'er,** *n.*

**slab** (slab), *n.* [ME. *sclabbe*], 1. a piece that is flat, broad, and fairly thick: as, a *slab* of concrete. 2. a half-curved piece cut from the outside of a log. *v.t.* [SLABBED, SLABBING], to cut the slabs from (a log).

**slack** (slak), *adj.* [< AS. *slæc*], 1. slow; sluggish. 2. barely moving, as a current of air. 3. not busy or active; dull: as, a *slack* period. 4. loose; not tight or taut. 5. careless; neglectful: as, a *slack* workman. *v.t.* 1. to make slack. 2. to slake. *v.i.* to be or become slack; slacken. *adv.* in a slack manner. *n.* 1. a part that is slack or hangs loose. 2. a lack of tension: as, *slack* in a rope. 3. a stoppage of movement in a current. 4. a dull period; lull. **—slack off,** to slacken. **—slack up,** to go more slowly. **—slack'ly,** *adv.* **—slack'ness,** *n.*

**slack** (slak), *n.* [< MLG. or MD.], a mixture of small pieces of coal, coal dust, and dirt left from the screening of coal.

**slack·en** (slak'ən), *v.t.* & *v.i.* 1. to make or become less active, brisk, intense, etc. 2. to loosen or relax, as rope. **—slack'en·er,** *n.*

**slack·er** (slak'ẽr), *n.* one who evades duties, work, etc.; esp., one who evades military service.

**slacks** (slaks), *n.pl.* full-cut trousers for casual wear by men and women.

**slag** (slag), *n.* [< MLG. *slagge*], 1. the fused refuse separated from a metal in smelting. 2. lava resembling this. ***v.t. & v.i.*** [SLAGGED, SLAGGING], to change into slag. —**slag′gy** [-GIER, -GIEST], ***adj.***
**slain** (slān), pp. of **slay.**
**slake** (slāk), ***v.t.*** [SLAKED, SLAKING], [< AS. < *slæc*, slack], 1. to make less intense by satisfying, as thirst, desire, etc. 2. to put out (a fire). 3. to produce a chemical change in (lime) by combination with water. ***v.i.*** 1. to become slaked. 2. to slacken.
**slaked lime** (slākt), calcium hydroxide.
‡**sla·lom** (slä′lôm), ***n.*** [Norw.], a downhill skiing race over a zigzag course. ***v.i.*** to ski in a slalom.
**slam** (slam), ***v.t.*** [SLAMMED, SLAMMING], [prob. < ON.], 1. to shut with force and noise: as, to *slam* a door. 2. to hit, put, etc. with force and noise: as, he *slammed* the book on the table. 3. [Colloq.], to criticize severely. ***v.i.*** to shut, go into place, etc. with force and noise. ***n.*** 1. a heavy impact, shutting, etc. 2. the noise made by this. 3. [Colloq.], severe criticism.
**slam** (slam), ***n.*** [< prec.], in *card games*, the winning of all the tricks in one deal: in *bridge*, called **grand slam**, or if one trick short of this, **little slam.**
**slan·der** (slan′dẽr), ***n.*** [< Anglo-Fr. < LL. *scandalum;* see SCANDAL], 1. the oral utterance or spreading of a falsehood, harmful to another's reputation: cf. *libel*. 2. such a falsehood. ***v.t.*** to make a slanderous statement about. —**slan′der·er,** ***n.***
**slan·der·ous** (slan′dẽr-əs), ***adj.*** 1. characterized by slander. 2. uttering or spreading slander. —**slan′der·ous·ly,** ***adv.*** —**slan′der·ous·ness,** ***n.***
**slang** (slaŋ), ***n.*** [< 18th-c. cant; ? akin to *sling*], 1. originally, the specialized vocabulary of criminals, tramps, etc.: now usually called *cant*. 2. the specialized vocabulary of those in the same work, way of life, etc.: usually called *shoptalk*, *argot*, *jargon*. 3. colloquial language, usually short-lived and of a vigorous or pungent nature, that is outside of formal usage: it consists of both coined words (*hep*, *rube*) and those with new meanings (*square*, *sap*). ***v.t. & v.i.*** to address with or use slang.
**slang·y** (slaŋ′i), ***adj.*** [-IER, -IEST], 1. of, like, or containing slang. 2. given to using slang. —**slang′i·ly,** ***adv.*** —**slang′i·ness,** ***n.***
**slank** (slaŋk), archaic pt. of **slink.**
**slant** (slant), ***v.t. & v.i.*** [prob. < ON.], 1. to incline from a direct line or level; slope. 2. [Colloq.], to tell so as to express a particular attitude or bias. ***n.*** 1. an oblique or inclined surface, line, etc.; slope. 2. [Colloq.], a point of view; attitude. ***adj.*** oblique; sloping. —**slant′ing,** ***adj.*** —**slant′ing·ly,** ***adv.***
**slant·wise** (slant′wīz′), ***adv.*** slantingly; obliquely: also **slant′ways′** (-wāz′). ***adj.*** slanting; oblique.
**slap** (slap), ***n.*** [LG. *sklapp;* echoic], 1. a blow with something flat, as the palm of the hand. 2. an insult; rebuff. ***v.t.*** [SLAPPED, SLAPPING], 1. to strike with something flat. 2. to put, hit, etc. carelessly or with force. ***adv.*** [Colloq.], 1. suddenly. 2. directly. —**slap′per,** ***n.***
**slap·dash** (slap′dash′), ***n.*** 1. carelessness. 2. something done carelessly and hastily. ***adv.*** in a hasty, careless manner. ***adj.*** hasty, careless, etc.
**slap-hap·py** (slap′hap′i), ***adj.*** [Slang], 1. dazed, as by blows on the head. 2. foolish; silly.
**slap·jack** (slap′jak′), ***n.*** a pancake or griddlecake.
**slap·stick** (slap′stik′), ***n.*** 1. a device, formerly used by stage comedians, made of two wooden slats that slap together loudly when hit against something. 2. crude comedy full of violent activity, horseplay, etc. ***adj.*** characterized by such comedy.
**slash** (slash), ***v.t.*** [? < OFr. *esclachier*, to break], 1. to cut or wound with sweeping strokes, as of a knife. 2. to gash: as, he fell and *slashed* his arm. 3. to whip viciously; lash. 4. to cut slits in (a fabric, dress, etc.), especially so as to expose underlying material. 5. to reduce drastically, as prices. 6. to criticize severely. ***v.i.*** to make a sweeping stroke with something sharp. ***n.*** 1. a sweeping stroke made with a knife, etc. 2. a cut made by such a stroke; gash. 3. a slit in a fabric, dress, etc. 4. *a)* an open place in a forest, cluttered with branches, chips, etc., as from the cutting of timber. *b)* such debris. —**slash′er,** ***n.***
**slash·ing** (slash′iŋ), ***adj.*** 1. severe; violent. 2. dashing; spirited. ***n.*** a slash. —**slash′ing·ly,** ***adv.***
**slat** (slat), ***n.*** [< OFr. *esclat*, fragment], a thin, narrow strip of wood, metal, etc.; lath: as, *slats* of a bedstead, Venetian blind, etc. ***v.t.*** [SLATTED, SLATTING], to provide with slats.
**slate** (slāt), ***n.*** [< OFr. fem. of *esclat;* see SLAT], 1. a hard, fine-grained rock that cleaves naturally into thin, smooth layers. 2. its bluish-gray color. 3. a thin piece of slate, especially one used as a roofing tile or as a tablet for writing on with chalk. 4. a list of candidates proposed for nomination or election. ***v.t.*** [SLATED, SLATING], 1. to cover with slate. 2. to designate, as for candidacy, appointment, etc. —**a clean slate,** a clean record. —**slat′er,** ***n.*** —**slat′y** [-IER, -IEST], ***adj.***
**slat·tern** (slat′ẽrn), ***n.*** [prob. < dial. *slatter*, to slop], a woman who is careless and untidy in her habits, appearance, etc. —**slat′tern·li·ness,** ***n.*** —**slat′tern·ly,** ***adj. & adv.***
**slaugh·ter** (slô′tẽr), ***n.*** [< ON. *slātr*, lit., slain flesh], 1. the killing of animals for food; butchering. 2. the brutal killing of a human being. 3. the killing of people in large numbers, as in battle. ***v.t.*** 1. to kill (animals) for food; butcher. 2. to kill (people) brutally or in large numbers. —**slaugh′ter·er,** ***n.*** —**slaugh′ter·ous,** ***adj.***
**slaugh·ter·house** (slô′tẽr-hous′), ***n.*** a place where animals are butchered for food.
**Slav** (släv, slav), ***n.*** a member of any of a group of peoples of E and SE Europe, including the Russians, Ukrainians, Poles, Czechs, Slovaks, Serbs, Croats, Bulgars, etc. ***adj.*** Slavic.
**Slav.,** 1. Slavic. 2. Slavonian. 3. Slavonic.
**slave** (slāv), ***n.*** [< OFr. < ML. *S(c)lavus*, Slav < LGr. *Sklabos*: first applied to captive Slavs], 1. a human being who is owned by and absolutely subject to another human being, as by capture, purchase, etc. 2. one who is dominated by some influence, habit, etc.: as, *slaves* to fashion. 3. one who works like a slave; drudge. 4. any ant captured by and forced to work for ants of other species: also **slave ant.** ***v.i.*** [SLAVED, SLAVING], to work like a slave; toil. —**slave′like′,** ***adj.***
**slave driver,** 1. a person who oversees the work of slaves. 2. any merciless taskmaster.
**slave·hold·ing** (slāv′hōl′diŋ), ***adj.*** owning slaves. ***n.*** ownership of slaves. —**slave′hold′er,** ***n.***
**slav·er** (slav′ẽr), ***v.i.*** [prob. < ON. *slafra*], to let saliva, etc. run from the mouth; drool. ***v.t.*** to cover with saliva. ***n.*** 1. saliva drooling from the mouth. 2. nonsense; drivel. —**slav′er·er,** ***n.***
**slav·er** (slāv′ẽr), ***n.*** 1. a ship in the slave trade. 2. a person who deals in slaves; slave trader.
**slav·er·y** (slāv′ẽr-i), ***n.*** 1. the owning of slaves as a practice or institution. 2. the condition of a slave; bondage. 3. a condition of domination by some influence, habit, etc. 4. drudgery; toil.
**slave trade,** traffic in slaves; specif., the former transportation of African Negroes to America for sale as slaves.
**slav·ey** (slāv′i), ***n.*** [*pl.* -EYS], [Brit. Colloq.], a female domestic who does menial work.
**Slav·ic** (släv′ik, slav′-), ***adj.*** of the Slavs, their languages, etc. ***n.*** a major subbranch of the Indo-European family of languages, including Polish, Serbian, Czech, and Slovak **(West Slavic)**; Bulgarian, Serbo-Croatian, and Slovene **(South Slavic)**; and Russian, Ukrainian, and Byelorussian **(East Slavic).**
**slav·ish** (slāv′ish), ***adj.*** 1. of or characteristic of slaves; servile. 2. of or characteristic of slavery; oppressive. 3. blindly dependent: as, *slavish* imitation. —**slav′ish·ly,** ***adv.*** —**slav′ish·ness,** ***n.***
**Sla·vo·ni·a** (slə-vō′ni-ə), ***n.*** a region of the Balkans, now in N Yugoslavia.
**Sla·vo·ni·an** (slə-vō′ni-ən), ***adj.*** 1. of Slavonia or its people. 2. Slavic. ***n.*** 1. a native of Slavonia. 2. a Slav. 3. the Slavic language group. Also, for *adj.* & *n.* 3, **Sla·von′ic** (-von′ik).
**slaw** (slô), ***n.*** [D. *sla*, contr. of Fr. *salade*, salad], shredded cabbage served as a salad.
**slay** (slā), ***v.t.*** [SLEW, SLAIN, SLAYING], [< AS. *slean*], to kill by violent means. —**slay′er,** ***n.***
**sleave** (slēv), ***n.*** [< AS. *-slæfan*, to separate], 1. untwisted silk that tends to tangle; floss. 2. any tangle. ***v.t.*** [SLEAVED, SLEAVING], to separate or pull apart, as tangled threads.
**slea·zy** (slē′zi, slā′-), ***adj.*** [-ZIER, -ZIEST], [< obs. *Sleasie*, cloth made in Silesia, Germany], flimsy or thin in substance: as, a *sleazy* fabric. —**slea′zi·ly,** ***adv.*** —**slea′zi·ness,** ***n.***
**sled** (sled), ***n.*** [< MLG. or MFl. *sledde*], a vehicle mounted on runners for coasting or for carrying loads on snow, ice, etc. ***v.t. & v.i.*** [SLEDDED, SLEDDING], to carry or ride on a sled. —**sled′der,** ***n.***
**sled·ding** (sled′iŋ), ***n.*** 1. a riding or carrying on a

sled. 2. the condition of the ground for this: often figurative, as, the work was hard *sledding*.

**sledge** (slej), *n.* [< AS. *slecge* < base of *slean*, to strike], a long, heavy hammer, usually used with both hands: also **sledge hammer.** ***v.t. & v.i.*** [SLEDGED, SLEDGING], to strike with a sledge.

**sledge** (slej), *n.* [MD. *sleedse*], a sled or sleigh for carrying people or loads over snow. ***v.i. & v.t.*** [SLEDGED, SLEDGING], to go or take by sledge.

**sleek** (slēk), ***adj.*** [var. of *slick*], 1. smooth and shiny; glossy. 2. of well-fed or well-groomed appearance. 3. polished in speech and behavior. Also **sleek'y** [-IER, -IEST]. ***v.t.*** to make sleek; smooth. **—sleek'ly, *adv.* —sleek'ness, *n.***

**sleep** (slēp), *n.* [AS. *slæp*], 1. *a*) a natural, regularly recurring condition of rest for the body and mind, during which there is little or no conscious thought. *b*) a period of sleeping. 2. any condition resembling sleep, as death, a coma, etc. ***v.i.*** [SLEPT, SLEEPING], 1. to be in the state of sleep; slumber. 2. to be in a condition like sleep, as in death, hibernation, etc. ***v.t.*** 1. to slumber in (a specified sleep): as, he *slept* the sleep of the just. 2. [Colloq.], to provide sleeping accommodations for: as, this boat *sleeps* four. **—last sleep,** death. **—sleep away,** to spend in sleep. **—sleep off,** to rid oneself of by sleeping. **—sleep'ing, *adj. & n.***

**sleep·er** (slēp'ẽr), *n.* 1. a sleeping person or animal. 2. a beam laid horizontally to support something above it. 3. [Brit.], a tie supporting a railroad track. 4. a sleeping car. 5. something that achieves an unexpected success.

**sleeping bag,** a large, warmly lined bag made to sleep in, especially out of doors.

**sleeping car,** a railway car with berths, compartments, etc. for passengers to sleep in.

**sleeping sickness,** 1. an infectious disease, especially of tropical Africa, transmitted as by the bite of the tsetse fly: it is characterized by fever, lethargy, and coma, usually ending in death. 2. inflammation of the brain, caused by a virus and inducing drowsiness, etc.

**sleep·less** (slēp'lis), ***adj.*** 1. with little or no sleep; wakeful; restless. 2. alert at all times. 3. never at rest: as, the *sleepless* wind. **—sleep'less·ly, *adv.* —sleep'less·ness, *n.***

**sleep·walk·ing** (slēp'wôk'iŋ), *n.* the act or practice of walking while asleep. **—sleep'walk'er, *n.***

**sleep·y** (slēp'i), ***adj.*** [-IER, -IEST], 1. ready or inclined to sleep; drowsy. 2. dull; idle; lethargic: as, a *sleepy* little town. 3. causing or exhibiting drowsiness. **—sleep'i·ly, *adv.* —sleep'i·ness, *n.***

**sleet** (slēt), *n.* [< AS. hyp. *sliete*], 1. partly frozen rain. 2. a mixture of rain with snow. 3. the icy coating formed when rain freezes on trees, streets, etc. ***v.i.*** to shower in the form of sleet. **—sleet'y** [-IER, -IEST], ***adj.*** **—sleet'i·ness, *n.***

**sleeve** (slēv), *n.* [< AS. *sl(i)efe*], 1. that part of a garment that covers the arm. 2. a tube or tubelike part fitting around another part. ***v.t.*** [SLEEVED, SLEEVING], to provide with a sleeve. **—laugh up (or in) one's sleeve,** to be secretly amused. **—up one's sleeve,** hidden but ready at hand. **—sleeved, *adj.* —sleeve'less, *adj.***

**sleigh** (slā), *n.* [D. *slee* < *slede*, sled], a light vehicle on runners, for travel on snow and ice. ***v.i.*** to ride in or drive a sleigh. **—sleigh'ing, *n.***

**sleight** (slīt), *n.* [< ON. *slægth* < *slægr*, crafty], 1. a skillful trick or stratagem. 2. skill; dexterity.

**sleight of hand,** 1. skill with the hands, especially in deceiving onlookers, as in magic. 2. a trick or series of tricks thus performed.

**slen·der** (slen'dẽr), ***adj.*** [ME. *s(c)lendre*], 1. long and thin; slim. 2. small in amount, size, etc.; meager: as, *slender* earnings. 3. of little force or validity; feeble: as, *slender* hope. **—slen'der·ly, *adv.* —slen'der·ness, *n.***

**slen·der·ize** (slen'dẽr-īz'), ***v.t. & v.i.*** [-IZED, -IZING], to make or become slender.

**slept** (slept), pt. and pp. of **sleep.**

**sleuth** (slōōth), *n.* [< ON. *sloth*, a track], 1. a bloodhound. 2. [Colloq.], a detective. Also **sleuth'-hound'.** ***v.i.*** to act as a detective.

**slew** (slōō), *n.* a slough (swamp).

**slew** (slōō), ***n., v.t. & v.i.*** slue (turn).

**slew** (slōō), *n.* [? akin to Ir. *sluagh*, a host], [Colloq.], a large number, group, or quantity; lot: also sp. **slue.**

**slew** (slōō), pt. of **slay.**

**slice** (slīs), *n.* [OFr. *esclice;* ult. < OHG. *slizan*, to split], 1. a relatively thin, broad piece cut from something. 2. a part or share: as, a *slice* of the profits. 3. a spatula or knife with a flat, broad blade. 4. in *golf*, a sliced stroke. ***v.t.*** [SLICED, SLICING], 1. to cut into slices. 2. *a*) to cut as a slice (with *off, from*, etc.). *b*) to cut through like a knife. 3. to separate into parts or shares. 4. to use a slice (spatula) to work at, spread, etc. 5. in *golf*, to cause (a ball) to curve off, as to the right for a right-handed player, by a glancing stroke. ***v.i.*** in *golf*, to slice a ball. **—slic'er, *n.***

**slick** (slik), ***v.t.*** [prob. < AS. *-slician*, lit., to smooth by hammering], 1. to make sleek or smooth. 2. [Colloq.], to make smart, neat, etc. (usually with *up*). ***adj.*** 1. sleek; smooth. 2. slippery; oily, as a surface. 3. adept; clever; ingenious. 4. [Colloq.], clever in deception; smooth: as, a *slick* alibi. 5. [Colloq.], having or showing skill in composition but little depth: as, a *slick* book. 6. [Slang], excellent, fine, attractive, etc. *n.* 1. a smooth area on the surface of water, as resulting from a film of oil. 2. [Slang], a magazine printed on paper with a glossy finish: cf. **pulp.** ***adv.*** smoothly, cleverly, deftly, etc. **—slick'ly, *adv.* —slick'ness, *n.***

**slick·er** (slik'ẽr), *n.* 1. a loose, waterproof coat. 2. [Colloq.], a smooth, tricky person.

**slide** (slīd), ***v.i.*** [SLID (slid), SLID or SLIDDEN (slid''n), SLIDING], [AS. *slidan*], 1. to move along in constant contact with a smooth surface, as on ice. 2. to move quietly and smoothly; glide. 3. to move stealthily or secretly. 4. to slip: as, it *slid* from his grasp. 5. to pass gradually into or out of some condition, habit, etc. ***v.t.*** 1. to cause to slide. 2. to move or place quietly or dexterously (usually with *in* or *into*). *n.* 1. an act of sliding. 2. a smooth, usually inclined track, surface, etc. used for sliding. 3. something that operates by sliding. 4. a transparent plate bearing a picture for projection on a screen. 5. a small glass plate on which objects are mounted for microscopic study. 6. *a*) the fall of a mass of rock, snow, etc. down a slope. *b*) the mass that falls. 7. in *music*, a U-shaped section of tubing which is moved to change the pitch of a trombone, etc. **—let slide,** to neglect. **—slid'a·ble, *adj.* —slid'er, *n.***

**slide fastener,** a device used to fasten and unfasten two edges of material: it consists of two rows of small interlocking tabs worked by a part that slides up and down: also called *zipper*.

**slide rule,** an instrument consisting of a ruler with a central sliding piece, both marked with logarithmic scales: used for rapid mathematical calculations.

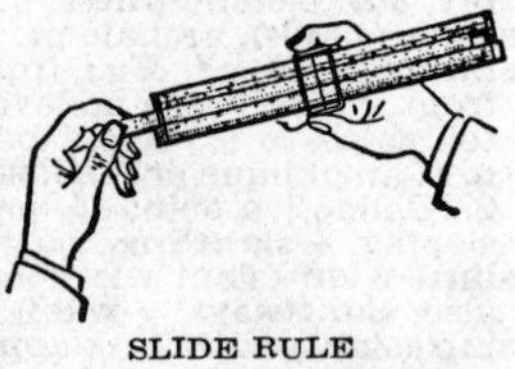

SLIDE RULE

**sliding scale,** 1. a standard or schedule, as of rates, wages, etc., which varies with other conditions or standards. 2. a slide rule.

**slight** (slīt), ***adj.*** [ME. *sliht*], 1. light in form or build; slender. 2. frail; fragile. 3. lacking weight, strength, significance, etc. 4. small in amount or extent: as, a *slight* fever. ***v.t.*** 1. to do carelessly or poorly; neglect. 2. to treat with disrespect or pointed indifference. 3. to treat as unimportant. *n.* a slighting or being slighted (in sense 2 of the v.). **—slight'er, *n.* —slight'ing·ly, *adv.* —slight'ly, *adv.* —slight'ness, *n.***

**sli·ly** (slī'li), ***adv.*** slyly.

**slim** (slim), ***adj.*** [SLIMMER, SLIMMEST], [< D. *slim*, bad], 1. small in girth in proportion to height or length; slender. 2. small in amount, degree, or extent; slight; scant; meager. ***v.t. & v.i.*** [SLIMMED, SLIMMING], to make or become slim. **—slim'ly, *adv.* —slim'ness, *n.***

**slime** (slīm), *n.* [AS. *slim*], 1. any soft, moist, slippery, often sticky matter, as thin mud, the mucous coating on fish, etc. 2. any such substance considered disgusting. ***v.t.*** [SLIMED, SLIMING], 1. to cover with slime. 2. to clean slime from.

**slim·y** (slīm'i), ***adj.*** [-IER, -IEST], 1. of or like slime. 2. covered with slime. 3. disgusting; filthy. **—slim'i·ly, *adv.* —slim'i·ness, *n.***

**sling** (sliŋ), *n.* [< AS. *slingan*, to twist oneself], 1. a primitive instrument for throwing stones, etc., consisting of a piece of leather tied to cords that are whirled for releasing the missile. 2. a slingshot. 3. a throwing as with a sling; cast; fling. 4. a device, as a supporting band or strap, used in raising or lowering a heavy object, carrying a rifle from the shoulder, etc. 5. a wide piece of cloth looped from the neck under an injured arm for support. ***v.t.*** [SLUNG, SLINGING], 1. to throw (stones, etc.) with a sling. 2. to throw, cast, fling, etc. 3. to raise, lower, etc. in a sling. 4. to hang loosely or in a sling; suspend. **—sling'er, *n.***

**sling** (sliŋ), *n.* [cf. G. *schlingen*, to swallow], an iced drink made with alcoholic liquor, water, and sugar.

**sling·shot** (sliŋ′shot′), *n.* a Y-shaped piece of wood, metal, etc. with an elastic band attached to the upper tips for shooting stones, etc.

**slink** (sliŋk), *v.i.* [SLUNK or *archaic* SLANK, SLUNK, SLINKING], [AS. *slincan,* to creep], to move in a furtive or sneaking manner, as from fear or guilt. —**slink′ing·ly,** *adv.* —**slink′y** [-IER, -IEST], *adj.*

**slip** (slip), *v.i.* [SLIPPED or *archaic* or *poetic* SLIPT, SLIPPING], [MLG. *slippen*], 1. to go quietly or secretly: as, he *slipped* away. 2. to move or pass smoothly, quickly, or easily. 3. to pass gradually into or out of some condition, habit, etc. 4. to escape from one's mind, power, etc.: as, his one chance *slipped* by. 5. to shift or slide from position: as, it *slipped* out of his hand. 6. to slide accidentally, lose footing, etc. 7. to make a mistake; err. 8. to become worse; lose strength, keenness, etc.: as, my memory is *slipping.* 9. [Colloq.], to decline slightly: as, the market has *slipped.* *v.t.* 1. to cause to slip or move smoothly: as, *slip* the bolt through the hole. 2. to put (*on*) or take (*off*) quickly, as an article of clothing. 3. to put, pass, etc. quickly or deftly: as, she *slipped* a pill into her mouth. 4. *a*) to escape from (the mind). *b*) to overlook; miss. 5. to get loose from (a restraining device). 6. to let loose: said of hunting dogs. *n.* 1. *a*) an inclined plane leading down to water, on which ships are built or repaired. *b*) a dock for ships between piers or wharves. 2. a leash for a dog, etc. 3. a woman's undergarment, about the length of a dress. 4. a pillowcase. 5. a slipping or falling down. 6. an error or mistake. 7. an accident or mishap. 8. a cleavage and displacement in a rock strata. —**give one the slip,** to escape from one. —**let slip,** to say without intending to. —**slip one over on,** [Colloq.], to trick; hoodwink; cheat. —**slip up,** [Colloq.], to make a mistake.

**slip** (slip), *n.* [< MD. < *slippen,* to cut], 1. a stem, root, twig, etc. of a plant, used for planting or grafting; scion. 2. a young, slender person. 3. a long, thin piece or strip, as of wood. 4. a small piece of paper, often for a specific use: as, an order *slip.* *v.t.* [SLIPPED, SLIPPING], to take a slip from (a plant) for planting or grafting.

**slip cover,** a removable, fitted cloth cover, as for an armchair, sofa, etc.

**slip·knot** (slip′not′), *n.* a knot made so that it will slip along the rope around which it is tied: also **slip knot.**

**slip-on** (slip′on′), *adj.* to be put on and taken off over the head: said of garments. *n.* a slip-on garment, as a sweater. Also **slip′o′ver** (-ō′vẽr).

**slip·per** (slip′ẽr), *n.* a kind of light, low shoe that may be easily slipped on. —**slip′pered,** *adj.*

**slip·per·y** (slip′ẽr-i, slip′ri), *adj.* [-IER, -IEST], [< AS. *slipur*], 1. causing or liable to cause slipping, as a wet surface. 2. tending to slip away, as from a hold. 3. evasive; shifty; unreliable. —**slip′per·i·ness,** *n.*

**slippery elm,** 1. a wide-spreading hardwood tree with fragrant, sticky inner bark. 2. the bark.

**slip·py** (slip′i), *adj.* [-PIER, -PIEST], [Colloq.], slippery.

**slip·shod** (slip′shod′), *adj.* [after obs. *slip-shoe,* a slipper], 1. wearing shoes with worn-down heels. 2. generally careless; slovenly.

**slip stream,** the current of air thrust backward by the spinning propeller of an aircraft.

**slipt** (slipt), archaic or poetic pt. of **slip.**

**slip-up** (slip′up′), *n.* [Colloq.], an error; oversight.

**slit** (slit), *v.t.* [SLIT, SLITTING], [< AS. *slitan,* to cut], 1. to cut or split open, especially by a straight, lengthwise incision. 2. to cut lengthwise into strips. *n.* 1. a long, straight cut or tear. 2. a narrow opening. —**slit′ter,** *n.*

**slith·er** (sli*th*′ẽr), *v.i.* [< AS. *sliderian,* freq. < base of *slidan,* to slide], 1. to slip or slide on a loose, broken surface, as a gravelly slope. 2. to move along by sliding or gliding, as a snake. *v.t.* to cause to slide or slither. *n.* a slithering motion. —**slith′er·y,** *adj.*

**sliv·er** (sliv′ẽr), *n.* [< dial. *slive,* to cut < AS. *slifan*], 1. a thin, often pointed piece that has been cut, split, or broken off; splinter. 2. a loose, thin, continuous fiber, as of flax, ready to be drawn and twisted. *v.t.* & *v.i.* to cut, split, or break into slivers. —**sliv′er·y,** *adj.*

**slob** (slob), *n.* [Ir. *slab*], 1. [Dial.], mud. 2. [Colloq.], a sloppy, stupid, clumsy person.

**slob·ber** (slob′ẽr), *v.i.* [prob. < D. *slobberen*], 1. to let saliva run from the mouth; slaver. 2. to speak with excessive sentimentality. *v.t.* to smear or dribble on with saliva. *n.* 1. saliva running from the mouth; slaver. 2. excessive sentimentality. —**slob′ber·er,** *n.* —**slob′ber·y,** *adj.*

**sloe** (slō), *n.* [AS. *sla*], 1. the small, blue-black, plumlike fruit of the blackthorn. 2. this plant.

**sloe-eyed** (slō′īd′), *adj.* having large, dark eyes.

**sloe gin,** alcoholic liquor distilled from grain and flavored with fresh sloes.

**slog** (slog), *v.t.* & *v.i.* [SLOGGED, SLOGGING], [var. of *slug, v.*], to hit hard; slug. —**slog′ger,** *n.*

**slog** (slog), *v.t.* & *v.i.* [SLOGGED, SLOGGING], [prob. < ON.], to make (one's way) heavily and with great effort; plod; toil. —**slog′ger,** *n.*

**slo·gan** (slō′gən), *n.* [< Gael. < *sluagh,* a host + *gairm,* a call], 1. a battle cry of Scottish Highland and Irish clans. 2. a catchword or motto associated with a political party or other group. 3. a catch phrase used to advertise a product.

**sloid, slojd** (sloid), *n.* sloyd.

**sloop** (sl͞oop), *n.* [< D. < LG. *slupen,* to glide], a small boat with a single mast and a jib.

**slop** (slop), *n.* [AS. *sloppe* (only in comp.)], 1. watery snow or mud; slush. 2. a splash or puddle of spilled liquid. 3. liquid or semiliquid food that is unappetizing or of poor quality. 4. *often pl.* *a*) liquid waste of any kind. *b*) kitchen swill, used for feeding pigs, etc. 5. [Slang], a sloppy person. *v.i.* [SLOPPED, SLOPPING], 1. to spill or splash. 2. to walk or splash through slush. *v.t.* 1. to spill liquid on. 2. to spill. —**slop over,** 1. to overflow or spill. 2. [Colloq.], to make a display of sentimentality; gush.

**slope** (slōp), *n.* [< AS. *aslopen,* pp. < *slupan,* to glide], 1. rising or falling ground. 2. any inclined line, surface, position, etc.; slant. 3. the amount or degree of this. 4. the land area that drains into a given ocean. *v.i.* [SLOPED, SLOPING], to have an upward or downward inclination; incline; slant. *v.t.* to cause to slope. —**slop′er,** *n.* —**slop′ing·ly,** *adv.*

**slop·py** (slop′i), *adj.* [-PIER, -PIEST], [see SLOP], 1. wet and splashy; muddy; slushy. 2. splashed or spotted with liquids. 3. [Colloq.], *a*) very untidy; slovenly; messy. *b*) careless; slipshod. —**slop′pi·ly,** *adv.* —**slop′pi·ness,** *n.*

**slops** (slops), *n.pl.* [< AS. *oferslop,* loose upper garment], 1. loose-fitting garments, especially trousers. 2. cheap, ready-made clothing. 3. the clothes, bedding, etc. issued to a ship's crew.

**slosh** (slosh), *v.t.* [var. of *slush*], to shake or agitate (a liquid or something in it). *v.i.* to splash clumsily through water, mud, etc. *n.* slush.

**slot** (slot), *n.* [< OFr. *esclot,* the hollow between the breasts], 1. a narrow notch, groove, or opening, as a slit for a coin in a vending machine. *v.t.* [SLOTTED, SLOTTING], to make a slot in.

**sloth** (slōth, slôth, sloth), *n.* [AS. *slæwth* < *slaw,* slow], 1. disinclination to work or exert oneself; indolence; laziness. 2. slowness. 3. any of several slow-moving, tree-dwelling South American mammals.

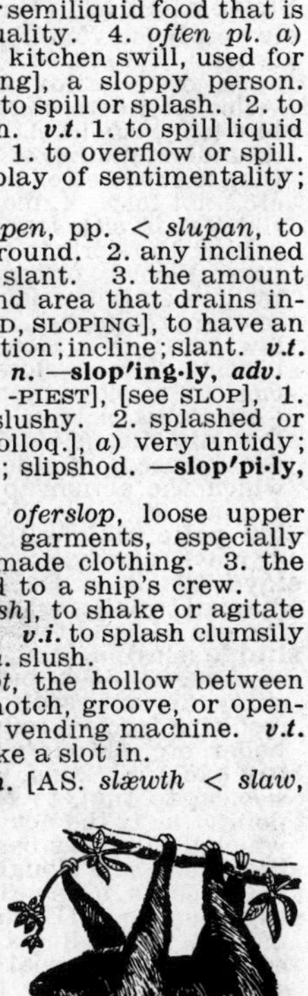
SLOTH (24 in. long)

**sloth·ful** (slōth′fəl, slôth′-, sloth′-), *adj.* characterized by sloth; indolent; lazy. —**sloth′ful·ly,** *adv.* —**sloth′ful·ness,** *n.*

**slot machine,** a vending machine, gambling device, etc. fitted with a slot in which a coin must be inserted before the mechanism will work.

**slouch** (slouch), *n.* [akin to ON. *slōkr,* lazy fellow], 1. *a*) one who is awkward or lazy. *b*) [Colloq.], one who is incompetent: as, he's no *slouch* at golf. 2. *a*) a drooping or bending forward of the head and shoulders. *b*) slovenly posture in general. 3. a drooping, as of a hat brim. *v.i.* 1. to have a drooping, slovenly posture. 2. to hang down or droop, as a hat brim. *v.t.* to cause to slouch. —**slouch′i·ly,** *adv.* —**slouch′i·ness,** *n.* —**slouch′y** [-IER, -IEST], *adj.*

**slough** (sluf), *n.* [ME. *slouh*], 1. the skin of a snake, especially the outer, castoff layer. 2. any castoff layer or covering: often used figuratively. 3. in *medicine,* the dead tissue that separates from surrounding tissue. *v.i.* 1. to be shed, cast off, etc.; fall away. 2. to shed skin or other covering: often used figuratively. 3. in *medicine,* to separate from the surrounding tissue. Often with *off* or *away.* *v.t.* 1. to throw off; discard. 2. in *bridge,* to discard

(a valueless card). Often with *off.* —**slough'y** [-IER, -IEST], *adj.*
**slough** (slou), *n.* [AS. *sloh*], 1. a place full of soft, deep mud. 2. [< *slough of despond,* in Bunyan's *Pilgrim's Progress*], deep, hopeless discouragement. 3. moral degradation. 4. (slōō), a swamp, bog, etc., especially as part of an inlet: also sp. **slew, slue.** —**slough'y** [-IER, -IEST], *adj.*
**Slo·vak** (slō'vak, slō-vak', slō'väk), *n.* 1. any of a Slavic people living chiefly in Slovakia. 2. their West Slavic language, related to Czech. *adj.* of Slovakia, the Slovaks, their language, etc.
**Slo·va·ki·a** (slō-vä'ki-ə, -vak'i-), *n.* a province in E Czechoslovakia.
**Slo·va·ki·an** (slō-vä'ki-ən, -vak'i-), *n. & adj.* Slovak.
**slov·en** (sluv'ən), *n.* [prob. < MD. *slof*], one who is careless in his habits, appearance, work, etc.; untidy person.
**Slo·vene** (slō-vēn', slō'vēn), *n.* 1. any of a Slavic people living chiefly in Slovenia. 2. their South Slavic language. *adj.* of Slovenia, the Slovenes, their language, etc.
**Slo·ve·ni·a** (slō-vē'ni-ə), *n.* a federated republic in NW Yugoslavia.
**Slo·ve·ni·an** (slō-vē'ni-ən), *adj. & n.* Slovene.
**slov·en·ly** (sluv'ən-li), *adj.* [-LIER, -LIEST], 1. characteristic of a sloven. 2. careless in habits, appearance, etc.; untidy. *adv.* in a slovenly manner. —**slov'en·li·ness,** *n.*
**slow** (slō), *adj.* [< AS. *slaw*], 1. not quick or clever in understanding; obtuse. 2. taking a longer time than is expected or usual. 3. marked by low speed, etc.; not fast. 4. making speed difficult or impossible: as, a *slow* track. 5. showing a time that is behind the correct time: said of a timepiece. 6. passing slowly or tediously; dull. 7. characterized by little activity; slack: as, *slow* trading. 8. lacking in energy; sluggish. 9. burning so as to give off a low heat: as, a *slow* fire. *v.t. & v.i.* to make or become slow or slower (often with *up* or *down*). *adv.* in a slow manner; slowly. —**slow'ly,** *adv.* —**slow'ness,** *n.*
**slow-mo·tion** (slō'mō'shən), *adj.* 1. moving below usual speed. 2. denoting a motion picture in which the action appears much slower than the original.
**slow·poke** (slō'pōk'), *n.* [Slang], a person who acts or moves slowly.
**sloyd** (sloid), *n.* [< Sw. *slöjd*, skill], a system of manual training originating in Sweden, based upon the use of hand tools in wood carving.
**sludge** (sluj), *n.* [dial. var. of *slutch*], 1. mud, mire, or ooze. 2. finely broken drift ice. 3. any heavy, slimy deposit, sediment, or mass, as the waste resulting from oil refining, the sediment in a steam boiler, etc. —**sludg'y** [-IER, -IEST], *adj.*
**slue** (slōō), *v.t. & v.i.* [SLUED, SLUING], [? < obs. D. *slooien*, to tug], to turn or swing around a fixed point. *n.* 1. the act of sluing. 2. the position to which a thing has been slued. Also sp. **slew.**
**slue** (slōō), *n.* a slough (swamp).
**slue** (slōō), *n.* a slew (large number).
**slug** (slug), *n.* [ME. *slugge*, clumsy one], 1. a small mollusk resembling a land snail, but having only a rudimentary internal shell or none at all. 2. any of several caterpillars that resemble slugs. 3. an animal, vehicle, etc. that moves sluggishly.
**slug** (slug), *n.* [prob. < LG.], 1. a small piece of metal; specif., a bullet. 2. a piece of metal used in place of a coin in automatic coin machines. 3. in *printing, a*) a strip of nonprinting metal used to space between lines. *b*) a line of type made in one piece, as by a linotype machine.
**slug** (slug), *n.* [D. *sluck*, a swallow], [Slang], a single drink, especially of alcoholic liquor.
**slug** (slug), *v.t.* [SLUGGED, SLUGGING], [< dial.], [Colloq.], to hit hard, especially with the fist. *n.* [Colloq.], a hard blow or hit. —**slug'ger,** *n.*
**slug·gard** (slug'ẽrd), *n.* [< ME. < *sluggen*, to be lazy], a person who is habitually lazy or idle. *adj.* lazy; idle. —**slug'gard·ly,** *adv.*
**slug·gish** (slug'ish), *adj.* [< *slug* (mollusk)], 1. lacking in energy or alertness; lazy. 2. slow or slow-moving. 3. lacking normal vigor: as, a *sluggish* appetite. —**slug'gish·ly,** *adv.* —**slug'gish·ness,** *n.*
**sluice** (slōōs), *n.* [< OFr. *escluse* < LL. pp. < L. < *ex-*, out + *claudere*, to shut], 1. an artificial channel for water, with a gate at its head to regulate the flow, as in a canal. 2. the water held back by such a gate. 3. such a gate: also **sluice gate.** 4. any channel, especially one for excess water. 5. a sloping trough through which water is run, as in carrying logs, etc. *v.t.* [SLUICED, SLUICING], 1. to draw off by means of a sluice. 2. to wash with water flowing from or as from a sluice. 3. to carry (logs, etc.) in a sluice. *v.i.* to run or flow as in a sluice.
**slum** (slum), *n.* [< cant; orig. sense, a room], a heavily populated area in which housing and other living conditions are extremely poor. *v.i.* [SLUMMED, SLUMMING], to visit slums: as, they *slummed* out of curiosity. —**slum'mer,** *n.*
**slum·ber** (slum'bẽr), *v.i.* [< AS. < *sluma*, *n.*], 1. to sleep. 2. to be dormant or inactive. *v.t.* to spend in sleeping. *n.* 1. sleep. 2. an inactive state. —**slum'ber·er,** *n.* —**slum'ber·ing,** *adj. & n.*
**slum·ber·ous** (slum'bẽr-əs), *adj.* 1. inclined to slumber; sleepy. 2. suggestive of or characterized by slumber. 3. causing sleep. 4. calm; quiet: as, a *slumberous* town. Also **slum'brous** (-brəs).
**slump** (slump), *v.i.* [prob. < LG. *slumpen*, to come about by accident], 1. to fall or sink suddenly. 2. to decline suddenly, as in value, etc. 3. to have a drooping posture. *n.* a sudden or sharp fall.
**slung** (sluŋ), pt. and pp. of **sling.**
**slunk** (sluŋk), pt. and pp. of **slink.**
**slur** (slũr), *v.t.* [SLURRED, SLURRING], [prob. < MD. *sleuren*, to drag], 1. to pass (*over*) quickly and carelessly. 2. to pronounce (a syllable, etc.) indistinctly. 3. to disparage or discredit. 4. in *music, a*) to sing or play (successive notes) by gliding from one to another without a break. *b*) to mark (notes) with a slur. *n.* 1. a slurring. 2. something slurred, as a pronunciation. 3. a remark that is harmful to a person's reputation; aspersion. 4. in *music, a*) a combination of slurred notes. *b*) a mark, (‿) or (⁀), connecting such notes. —**slur'ring·ly,** *adv.*
**slush** (slush), *n.* [prob. < ON.], 1. partly melted snow or ice. 2. soft mud; mire. 3. grease. 4. overly sentimental talk or writing. —**slush'i·ness,** *n.* —**slush'y** [-IER, -IEST], *adj.*
**slush fund,** money used for bribery, political pressure, or other corrupt purposes.
**slut** (slut), *n.* [cf. MLG. *slōt*, a puddle], 1. a dirty, slovenly woman; slattern. 2. a disreputable or promiscuous woman. 3. a female dog; bitch. —**slut'tish,** *adj.* —**slut'tish·ly,** *adv.* —**slut'tish·ness,** *n.*
**sly** (slī), *adj.* [SLIER or SLYER, SLIEST or SLYEST], [< ON. *slægr*], 1. [Dial.], skillful or clever. 2. skillful at trickery; crafty; wily. 3. cunningly underhanded. 4. mischievous in a playful way; roguish. —**on the sly,** secretly; stealthily. —**sly'ly, sli'ly,** *adv.* —**sly'ness,** *n.*
**Sm,** in *chemistry*, samarium.
**smack** (smak), *n.* [< AS. *smæc*], 1. a slight but distinctive taste or flavor. 2. a small amount; bit; trace. *v.i.* to have a smack (usually with *of*): as, diction that *smacks* of the stage.
**smack** (smak), *n.* [of Gmc. echoic origin], 1. a sharp noise made by parting the lips suddenly. 2. a loud kiss. 3. a sharp blow with a flat object; slap. 4. the sound of such a blow. *v.t.* 1. to move (the lips) suddenly so as to make a smack. 2. to kiss or slap loudly. *v.i.* to make a loud, sharp noise: as, with *smacking* lips. *adv.* 1. with a smack; violently. 2. directly; fully.
**smack** (smak), *n.* [prob. < D. & LG. *smak*], 1. a small sailboat rigged as a sloop. 2. a fishing vessel fitted with a well for keeping fish alive.
**smack·ing** (smak'iŋ), *adj.* brisk; sharp; lively.
**small** (smôl), *adj.* [< AS. *smæl*], 1. comparatively little in size; not large: as, a *small* city. 2. *a*) little in quantity, extent, value, duration, etc.: as, a *small* income. *b*) consisting of relatively few members: as, a *small* class. 3. of little importance; trivial. 4. having only a little investment, capital, etc.: as, a *small* tradesman. 5. small-minded; petty. 6. of common or humble rank. 7. gentle and low; soft, as a sound. *adv.* 1. in small pieces. 2. in a low tone; softly. 3. in a small manner. *n.* something small; small part: as, the *small* of the back. —**feel small,** to feel shame or humiliation. —**small'ish,** *adj.* —**small'ness,** *n.*
**small arms,** firearms of small caliber, carried by hand, as pistols, carbines, rifles, etc.
**small·clothes** (smôl'klōz' -klōthz'), *n.pl.* [Archaic], closefitting knee breeches of the 18th century.
**small fry,** 1. small fish. 2. small children. 3. persons or things regarded as unimportant.
**small hours,** the first few hours after midnight.
**small-mind·ed** (smôl'mīn'did), *adj.* petty, mean, prejudiced, etc. —**small'-mind'ed·ness,** *n.*
**small potatoes,** [Colloq.], 1. a person or thing of little importance. 2. petty people or things.
**small·pox** (smôl'poks'), *n.* an acute, infectious virus disease characterized by fever, vomiting, and pustular eruptions that often leave pitted scars.

**small talk,** light conversation about common, everyday things.
**small-time** (smôl′tīm′), *adj.* [Slang], limited, minor, or petty; not large-scale or significant.
**smart** (smärt), *v.i.* [< AS. *smeortan*], 1. *a*) to cause sharp, stinging pain, as a slap, wound, etc. *b*) to feel such pain. 2. to feel mental distress, as in grief, remorse, etc.; suffer. *v.t.* to cause to smart. *n.* a smarting sensation. *adj.* 1. causing keen pain: as, a *smart* blow. 2. sharp; intense, as pain. 3. brisk; lively: as, a *smart* pace. 4. *a*) alert; clever; capable; witty. *b*) shrewd or sharp, as in one's dealings. 5. neat; clean; fresh. 6. stylish. 7. [Dial.], quite strong, intense, etc.; considerable: as, a right *smart* rain. **—smart′ly,** *adv.* **—smart′ness,** *n.*
**smart al·eck** (al′ik), [*smart* + *Aleck*, for *Alexander*], [Colloq.], an impertinent, conceited person.
**smart·en** (smär′t'n), *v.t.* 1. to make smart; improve in appearance. 2. to make brisk or alert.
**smart set,** sophisticated, fashionable people.
**smart·weed** (smärt′wēd′), *n.* any of several plants growing in wet places, with leaves which cause the skin to smart on contact.
**smash** (smash), *n.* [prob. < *mash*], 1. a hard, heavy hit; specif., a hard, overhand tennis stroke. 2. *a*) a violent, noisy breaking. *b*) the sound of this. 3. *a*) a violent collision. *b*) a wreck. 4. total failure, especially in business. *adj.* [Colloq.], highly successful: as, the play is a *smash* hit: also **smash′ing.** *v.t.* 1. to break into pieces with noise or violence. 2. to hit (a tennis ball) with a hard, overhand stroke. 3. to hit with a hard, heavy blow. 4. to ruin completely; destroy. *v.i.* 1. to break into pieces. 2. to be destroyed. 3. to move or collide with force. **—go** (or **come**) **to smash,** [Colloq.], 1. to become smashed. 2. to fail utterly. **—smash′er,** *n.*
**smash·up** (smash′up′), *n.* 1. a violent wreck or collision. 2. total failure; ruin. 3. any disaster.
**smat·ter** (smat′ẽr), *v.t.* [< ON.], to speak, study, or learn superficially. *n.* a smattering.
**smat·ter·ing** (smat′ẽr-iŋ), *n.* slight or superficial knowledge (usually with *of*).
**smear** (smêr), *v.t.* [< AS. *smerian*, to anoint], 1. to cover or soil with something greasy, sticky, etc. 2. to apply (something greasy, sticky, etc.). 3. to make a smear with (the hand, a rag, etc.). 4. to harm the reputation of; slander. 5. [Slang], to overwhelm or defeat decisively. *v.i.* to be or become smeared. *n.* 1. a mark made by smearing. 2. a small quantity of some substance smeared on a slide for microscopic study, etc. 3. slander.
**smear·case** (smêr′kās′), *n.* [< G. *schmierkäse* < *schmieren*, to spread + *käse*, cheese], cottage cheese.
**smear·y** (smêr′i), *adj.* [-IER, -IEST], 1. covered with smears; smeared. 2. tending to smear, as wet ink. **—smear′i·ness,** *n.*
**smell** (smel), *v.t.* [SMELLED or SMELT, SMELLING], [< ME. *smellen*], 1. to be aware of by means of the nose and the olfactory nerves; catch the odor of. 2. to sense the presence of: as, to *smell* trouble. 3. to test by the odor of; sniff: as, *smell* the milk to see if it's sour. *v.i.* 1. to use the sense of smell; sniff (often with *at* or *of*). 2. *a*) to have a scent or odor: as, to *smell* fresh. *b*) to have an unpleasant odor. 3. to have the odor or a suggestion (*of* something specified): as, it *smells* of garlic. 4. [Slang], to lack ability, worth, etc. *n.* 1. that one of the five senses by which a substance is perceived through the stimulation of nerves (*olfactory nerves*) in the nasal cavity. 2. the stimulation of any specific substance upon the olfactory nerves; odor; scent. 3. an act of smelling. 4. that which suggests the presence of something; trace. **—smell out,** to look for or find as by smelling. **—smell up,** to cause to smell bad. **—smell′a·ble,** *adj.* **—smell′er,** *n.*
**smelling salts,** carbonate of ammonium, inhaled to relieve faintness, etc.
**smell·y** (smel′i), *adj.* [-IER, -IEST], giving off an unpleasant odor. **—smell′i·ness,** *n.*
**smelt** (smelt), *n.* [*pl.* SMELTS, SMELT; see PLURAL, II, D, 1], [AS.], a small, silvery, troutlike food fish found in northern seas.
**smelt** (smelt), *v.t.* [< MD. or MLG. *smelten*], 1. to melt or fuse (ore, etc.) so as to separate impurities from pure metal. 2. to refine (metal) in this way. *v.i.* to undergo smelting.
**smelt·er** (smel′tẽr), *n.* 1. a person engaged in the work of smelting. 2. an apparatus in which, or a place where, smelting is done.
**smidg·en** (smij′in), *n.* [? related to *midge*], [Dial. or Colloq.], a small amount; a bit.
**smi·lax** (smī′laks), *n.* [L. < Gr. *smilax*, bindweed], 1. any of various related, usually prickly, woody vines, as the sarsaparilla. 2. a greenhouse vine popular for its bright-green leaves.
**smile** (smīl), *v.i.* [SMILED, SMILING], [ME. *smilen*], to show pleasure, amusement, affection, irony, etc. by an upward curving of the mouth and a sparkling of the eyes. *v.t.* 1. to express with a smile. 2. to affect by smiling. *n.* 1. the act or facial expression of smiling. 2. a favorable or agreeable appearance. **—smile away,** to get rid of by smiling: as, he *smiled away* his tears. **—smile on** (or **upon**), to regard with favor or approval. **—smil′er,** *n.* **—smil′ing,** *adj.* **—smil′ing·ly,** *adv.*
**smirch** (smũrch), *v.t.* [prob. < OFr. *esmorcher*, to hurt], 1. to soil or smear as with grime. 2. to dishonor (a reputation). *n.* 1. a smudge; smear. 2. a stain on reputation. **—smirch′er,** *n.*
**smirk** (smũrk), *v.i.* [< AS. *smercian*, to smile], o smile in a conceited or complacent way. *n.* such a smile. **—smirk′er,** *n.* **—smirk′ing·ly,** *adv.*
**smite** (smīt), *v.t.* [SMOTE, SMITTEN or SMIT (smit) or SMOTE, SMITING], [AS. *smitan*], 1. to hit or strike hard. 2. to defeat, punish, or kill. 3. to attack with disastrous effect: as, *smitten* by disease. 4. to affect strongly and suddenly (*with*): as, *smitten* with dread. 5. to distress: as, *smitten* by conscience. 6. to impress favorably; enamor: as, *smitten* by her charms. *v.i.* 1. to strike hard. 2. to fall, come, etc. with sudden force. **—smit′er,** *n.*
**smith** (smith), *n.* [AS.], 1. one who makes or repairs metal objects; metalworker: usually in combination, as *silversmith*. 2. a blacksmith.
**Smith, Adam** (smith), 1723–1790; Scottish economist.
**Smith,** Captain **John,** 1580–1631; English colonist in Virginia.
**Smith, Joseph,** 1805–1844; American founder of the Mormon Church.
**smith·er·eens** (smith′ə-rēnz′), *n.pl.* [Ir. *smidirin*], [Colloq.], fragments; bits: also **smith′ers** (-ẽrz).
**smith·y** (smith′i), *n.* [*pl.* -IES], the workshop of a smith, especially a blacksmith; forge.
**smit·ten** (smit′'n), alt. pp. of **smite.** *adj.* 1. struck with great force. 2. disastrously or deeply affected; afflicted. 3. [Colloq.], deeply in love.
**smock** (smok), *n.* [< AS. *smoc* or ON. *smokkr*], a loose, shirtlike, outer garment worn to protect the clothes. *v.t.* 1. to dress in a smock. 2. to decorate with smocking.
**smock·ing** (smok′iŋ), *n.* [from use in smocks], decorative stitching used in gathering cloth to make it hang in folds.
**smog** (smog), *n.* [*smoke* + *fog*], a mixture of fog and smoke.
**smoke** (smōk), *n.* [< AS. *smoca*], 1. the vaporous matter, with suspended particles of carbon, arising from something burning. 2. any vapor, fume, etc. resembling smoke. 3. an act or period of smoking tobacco, etc.: as, time for a *smoke*. 4. something fleeting, insubstantial, or beclouding: as, our plans went up in *smoke*. 5. something to smoke, as a cigarette. *v.i.* [SMOKED, SMOKING], 1. to give off smoke or a smokelike substance. 2. to discharge smoke excessively or improperly, as a fuel, a fireplace, etc. 3. to draw in the smoke of tobacco and blow it out again; use cigarettes, etc. *v.t.* 1. to stain or color with smoke. 2. to cure (meats, etc.) with smoke. 3. to force out with smoke: as, we *smoked* the woodchuck from his hole. 4. to use (a pipe, cigar, or cigarette) in smoking. **—smoke out,** to force out of hiding, secrecy, etc.
**smoke·house** (smōk′hous′), *n.* a place where meats, fish, etc. are cured or flavored with smoke.
**smoke·less** (smōk′lis), *adj.* having or making little or no smoke. **—smoke′less·ly,** *adv.* **—smoke′less-ness,** *n.*
**smo·ker** (smōk′ẽr), *n.* 1. something that smokes. 2. one who smokes tobacco. 3. a railroad compartment or car in which smoking is allowed: also **smoking car.** 4. an informal social gathering for men only.
**smoke screen,** a cloud of artificial smoke spread to screen the movements of troops, ships, etc.
**smoke·stack** (smōk′stak′), *n.* a pipe for the discharge of smoke from a steamship, factory, etc.
**smoking jacket,** a man's lounging jacket made of velvet, satin brocade, or the like.
**smok·y** (smōk′i), *adj.* [-IER, -IEST], 1. giving off smoke, especially to excess. 2. like, of, or as of smoke: as, a *smoky* haze. 3. filled with smoke. 4. having the color of smoke. 5. colored or soiled by smoke. **—smok′i·ly,** *adv.* **—smok′i·ness,** *n.*

**Smoky Mountains,** Great Smoky Mountains.

**smol·der** (smōl'dẽr), *v.i.* [ME. *smoldren*], 1. to burn and smoke without flame. 2. to exist in a suppressed state. 3. to show suppressed anger or hate: as, his glance *smoldered*. *n.* a smoldering. Also sp. **smoulder.** —**smol'der·ing·ly,** *adv.*

**Smol·lett, To·bi·as George** (tō-bī'əs smol'it), 1721–1771; British novelist.

**smolt** (smōlt), *n.* [< dial. *smolt*, shining: its scales are silvery], a young salmon at the stage when it leaves fresh water to descend to the sea.

**smooch** (smōōch), *v.t.* & *n.* smutch.

**smooth** (smōōth), *adj.* [AS. *smoth*], 1. having an even surface, with no roughness or projections. 2. without lumps: as, a *smooth* paste. 3. even or gentle in flow or movement: as, a *smooth* voyage. 4. free from interruptions, difficulties, etc.: as, *smooth* progress. 5. calm; serene, as a disposition, etc. 6. free from hair: as, a *smooth* cheek. 7. pleasing to the taste; bland. 8. having an easy, flowing rhythm or sound. 9. suave or ingratiating, especially in an insincere way. 10. [Slang], very pleasant, attractive, etc. 11. [Slang], polished; competent: as, a *smooth* dancer. 12. in *phonetics*, not aspirated. *v.t.* 1. to make level or even. 2. to remove the lumps from. 3. to free from interruptions, difficulties, etc. 4. to make calm; soothe. 5. to make less crude; refine. *adv.* in a smooth manner. *n.* 1. a smooth part. 2. an act of smoothing. —**smooth away,** to remove (difficulties, etc.). —**smooth down,** to calm; soothe. —**smooth over,** to make light of; palliate; minimize, as faults. —**smooth'er,** *n.* —**smooth'ly,** *adv.* —**smooth'ness,** *n.*

**smooth·bore** (smōōth'bôr', -bōr'), *adj.* having no rifling: said of guns. *n.* a smoothbore gun.

**smooth·en** (smōōth''n), *v.t.* & *v.i.* to make or become smooth.

**smooth muscle,** muscle controlled by the involuntary nervous system, as in the uterus, intestines, etc.

**smooth-shav·en** (smōōth'shāv''n), *adj.* wearing no beard or mustache.

**smooth-spo·ken** (smōōth'spō'k'n), *adj.* speaking in a pleasing, persuasive, or polished manner.

**smooth-tongued** (smōōth'tuŋd'), *adj.* smooth-spoken, especially in a plausible or pleasing way.

**smör·gås·bord, smor·gas·bord** (smôr'gəs-bôrd', smũr'gəs-bôrd'), *n.* [Sw.], 1. hors d'oeuvres, especially as served buffet style. 2. a meal composed of these. 3. a restaurant serving smörgasbord.

**smote** (smōt), pt. and alt. pp. of **smite.**

**smoth·er** (smuth'ẽr), *v.t.* [< ME. < *smorther*, dense smoke], 1. *a*) to prevent (a person) from getting air; suffocate. *b*) to kill by smothering. 2. to cover (a fire), causing it to smolder or go out. 3. to cover over thickly: as, liver *smothered* in onions. 4. to hide or suppress as by covering; stifle, as a yawn. *v.i.* 1. to be suffocated. 2. to be hidden or suppressed. *n.* dense, suffocating smoke, dust, etc. —**smoth'er·er,** *n.* —**smoth'er·y,** *adj.*

**smoul·der** (smōl'dẽr), *v.i.* & *n.* smolder.

**smudge** (smuj), *n.* [var. of *smutch*], 1. a stain, smear, etc.; dirty spot. 2. a fire made to produce dense smoke. 3. such smoke, as used in driving away insects or protecting plants from frost. *v.t.* [SMUDGED, SMUDGING], 1. to protect (an orchard, etc.) by a smudge. 2. to soil; make dirty. *v.i.* 1. to blur or smear. 2. to be smudged.

**smudg·y** (smuj'i), *adj.* [-IER, -IEST], covered with smudges; stained, blurred, or smeared. —**smudg'i·ly,** *adv.* —**smudg'i·ness,** *n.*

**smug** (smug), *adj.* [SMUGGER, SMUGGEST], [prob. < LG. *smuk*, trim], 1. originally, neat; trim. 2. fatuously content with one's own accomplishments, abilities, morality, etc.; self-satisfied. —**smug'ly,** *adv.* —**smug'ness,** *n.*

**smug·gle** (smug''l), *v.t.* [-GLED, -GLING], [< D. *smuckeln* or LG. *smuggeln*], 1. to bring into or take out of a country secretly or illegally. 2. to bring, take, etc. secretly. *v.i.* to practice smuggling. —**smug'gler,** *n.*

**smut** (smut), *n.* [< LG. *smutt*], 1. *a*) sooty matter. *b*) a particle of this. 2. a soiled spot. 3. obscene talk or writing. 4. *a*) a plant disease characterized by masses of black spores that break up into a fine powder. *b*) any of various fungi causing this disease. *v.t.* & *v.i.* [SMUTTED, SMUTTING], to make or become smutty.

**smutch** (smuch), *v.t.* [< ME. hyp. *smuchchen*], to make dirty; smudge. *n.* 1. a dirty mark; smudge. 2. soot, smut, dirt, etc.

**smutch·y** (smuch'i), *adj.* [-IER, -IEST], smudgy.

**Smuts, Jan Chris·ti·aan** (yän kris'ti-än smuts), 1870–1950; South African statesman and general.

**smut·ty** (smut'i), *adj.* [-TIER, -TIEST], 1. soiled with smut. 2. affected with plant smut. 3. obscene. —**smut'ti·ly,** *adv.* —**smut'ti·ness,** *n.*

**Smyr·na** (smũr'nə), *n.* a city in Turkey, on the Aegean Sea: pop., 231,000: Turkish name, *Izmir.* —**Smyr'ne·an** (-ni-ən), *adj.*

**Sn,** *stannum*, [L.], in *chemistry*, tin.

**snack** (snak), *n.* [prob. < MD. *snacken*, to snap], 1. a share or part. 2. a light, quick meal.

**snaf·fle** (snaf''l), *n.* [prob. < D. < OD. dim. of *snabbe*, bill of a bird], a light, jointed bit attached to a bridle and having no curb. *v.t.* [-FLED, -FLING], to fit with or control by a snaffle.

**sna·fu** (sna-fōō', snaf'ōō), *adj.* [< *s*ituation *n*ormal, *a*ll *f*ouled (euphemism) *u*p], [Military Slang], in characteristic disorder or confusion. *v.t.* [-FUED, -FUING], [Military Slang], to throw into confusion.

**snag** (snag), *n.* [< ON.], 1. a part, point, etc. that sticks out, especially one that is sharp or rough. 2. an underwater tree stump or branch that is dangerous to navigation. 3. a snaggletooth. 4. a tear, as in cloth, made by a snag, etc. 5. an unexpected or hidden difficulty. *v.t.* [SNAGGED, SNAGGING], 1. to tear, damage, etc. on a snag. 2. to impede with a snag. —**snag'gy** [-GIER, -GIEST], *adj.*

**snag·gle·tooth** (snag''l-tōōth'), *n.* [*pl.* -TEETH], [< *snag*], 1. a projecting tooth. 2. a crooked or broken tooth. —**snag'gle·toothed',** *adj.*

**snail** (snāl), *n.* [AS. *snegl*], 1. a slow-moving gastropod mollusk living on land or in water and having a short, thick, wormlike body and a protective, usually spiral shell. 2. any lazy, slow-moving person or animal.

**snake** (snāk), *n.* [AS. *snaca*], 1. any of various long, scaly, limbless reptiles with a tapering tail. 2. a treacherous or deceitful person. 3. a long, flexible metal rod used by a plumber in removing obstructions from pipes, etc. *v.i.* [SNAKED, SNAKING], to move, twist, etc. like a snake. *v.t.* [Colloq.], to drag, pull, or jerk. —**snake'like',** *adj.*

**snake dance,** an informal parade in which the celebrants join hands in a long winding line.

**snake in the grass,** a seemingly harmless person or thing that is really evil or dangerous.

**snake·root** (snāk'rōōt', -root'), *n.* 1. any of various plants reputed to be remedies for snake bites. 2. the roots of any of these plants.

**snak·y** (snāk'i), *adj.* [-IER, -IEST], 1. of or like a snake or snakes. 2. sinuous; winding; twisting. 3. cunningly treacherous or evil. 4. infested with snakes.

**snap** (snap), *v.i.* & *v.t.* [SNAPPED, SNAPPING], [< MD. or MLG. *snappen*], 1. to bite suddenly (often with *at*). 2. to snatch or grasp quickly or eagerly (often with *at*): as, we *snapped* (at) the invitation. 3. to shout (*at*) or utter sharply, irritably, etc. 4. to break or sever suddenly, especially with a sharp, cracking sound. 5. to break down suddenly under strain, as nerves, resistance, etc. 6. to make or cause to make a sudden, sharp, cracking sound. 7. to close, fasten, etc. with this sound, as a lock. 8. to move or cause to move suddenly and smartly: as, the men *snapped* to attention, he *snapped* the ball to me. 9. to take a snapshot (of). *n.* 1. a sudden bite, grasp, snatch, etc. 2. a sudden breaking or parting. 3. a sudden, sharp cracking or clicking sound. 4. a short, angry utterance. 5. a brief period or spell: said of cold weather. 6. any clasp or fastening that closes with a click. 7. a hard, thin cooky: as, ginger *snaps*. 8. a snapshot. 9. [Colloq.], alertness, vigor, etc.: as, the performers had no *snap*. 10. [Slang], something easy, as a job, problem, etc. *adj.* 1. made or done quickly without deliberation: as, a *snap* decision. 2. that fastens with a snap. 3. [Slang], simple; easy. *adv.* with a snap. —**not a snap,** not at all. —**snap (a person's) head off,** to speak sharply or harshly to. —**snap one's fingers at,** to show lack of concern for. —**snap out of it,** to improve or recover quickly.

**snap·drag·on** (snap'drag'ən), *n.* [< *snap* + *dragon*: from the mouth-shaped flowers], any of various plants with white, yellow, red, or purplish, saclike, two-lipped flowers.

**snap·per** (snap'ẽr), *n.* [*pl.* -PERS, -PER; see PLURAL, II, D, 1], 1. a person or thing that snaps. 2. a snapping turtle. 3. any of various tropical basslike food fishes; esp., the red snapper.

**snapping turtle,** a large, fresh-water turtle of the eastern and southern U.S., having powerful jaws which snap with great force.

**snap·pish** (snap'ish), *adj.* 1. likely to snap or bite. 2. cross; irritable; sharp-tongued. —**snap'pish·ly,** *adv.* —**snap'pish·ness,** *n.*

**snap·py** (snap'i), *adj.* [-PIER, -PIEST], 1. snappish. 2. that snaps; snapping. 3. [Colloq.], full of vigor; brisk; strong: as, a *snappy* pace. 4. [Colloq.], stylish; smart. **—make it snappy,** [Slang], hurry. **—snap′pi·ly,** *adv.* **—snap′pi·ness,** *n.*

**snap·shot** (snap′shot′), *n.* 1. a hurried shot fired with little or no aim. 2. a photograph taken in an instant with a hand camera. *v.t. & v.i.* [-SHOTTED, -SHOTTING], to take a snapshot (of): now usually **snap.**

**snare** (snâr), *n.* [sense 1 < ON. *snara;* others < MD. & MLG. *snare*], 1. a trap for small animals, usually consisting of a noose which jerks tight upon the release of a spring trigger. 2. anything dangerous, risky, etc. that tempts or attracts; trap. 3. a length of wire or gut across the bottom of a snare drum. *v.t.* [SNARED, SNARING], 1. to catch in a snare; trap. 2. to lure into a situation that is dangerous, risky, etc. **—snar′er,** *n.*

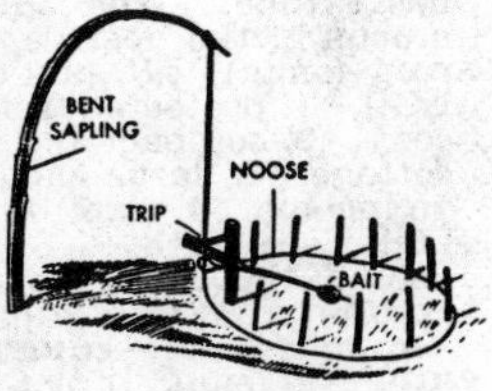

SNARE

**snare drum,** a small, double-headed drum with snares across the bottom for increased resonance.

**snarl** (snärl), *v.i.* [< earlier *snar,* to growl], 1. to growl fiercely, baring the teeth, as a threatening dog. 2. to speak sharply, as in anger. *v.t.* to utter with a snarl. *n.* 1. a fierce, angry growl. 2. a harsh, angry utterance. **—snarl′er,** *n.* **—snarl′ing·ly,** *adv.* **—snarl′y** [-IER, -IEST], *adj.*

**snarl** (snärl), *v.t.* [< *snare*], 1. to make knotted or tangled, as thread. 2. to make disordered or confused: as, traffic is *snarled.* *v.i.* to become knotted or tangled. *n.* 1. a tangled mass; tangle. 2. a confused, disordered state or situation; confusion. **—snarl′y** [-IER, -IEST], *adj.*

**snatch** (snach), *v.t.* [prob. var. of ME. *snakken,* to seize], 1. to grasp or seize suddenly, eagerly, or without right, warning, etc.; grab. 2. to remove abruptly or hastily. 3. to take, get, etc. hastily or while there is a chance. 4. [Slang], to kidnap. *n.* 1. a snatching. 2. a brief period; short time. 3. a fragment; bit: as, *snatches* of gossip. **—snatch at,** 1. to try to seize. 2. to take advantage of (a chance, etc.) quickly. **—snatch′er,** *n.*

**snatch·y** (snach′i), *adj.* [-IER, -IEST], done in snatches; irregular; disconnected; incomplete.

**sneak** (snēk), *v.i.* [AS. *snican*], 1. to move quietly and stealthily so as to avoid notice. 2. to act in an underhand or cowardly manner. *v.t.* 1. to give, put, etc. secretly or in a stealthy manner. 2. [Colloq.], to steal. *n.* 1. one who sneaks; stealthy, underhand, contemptible person. 2. an act of sneaking. **—sneak out of,** to avoid (duty, etc.) craftily. **—sneak′y** [-IER, -IEST], *adj.* **—sneak′i·ly,** *adv.* **—sneak′i·ness,** *n.*

**sneak·er** (snēk′ẽr), *n.* 1. a person or animal that sneaks. 2. *pl.* [< their noiseless tread], [Colloq.], canvas shoes with heelless, soft rubber soles.

**sneak·ing** (snēk′iŋ), *adj.* 1. cowardly; stealthy; furtive. 2. not admitted; secret: as, a *sneaking* fondness for jazz. **—sneaking suspicion,** a slight or increasing suspicion. **—sneak′ing·ly,** *adv.*

**sneer** (snêr), *v.i.* [ME. *sneren*], 1. to show scorn or contempt by a derisive smile. 2. to express derision, scorn, etc. in speech or writing. *v.t.* to utter in a sneering manner. *n.* 1. an act of sneering. 2. a sneering expression, utterance, etc. **—sneer′er,** *n.* **—sneer′ing,** *adj.* **—sneer′ing·ly,** *adv.*

**sneeze** (snēz), *v.i.* [SNEEZED, SNEEZING], [ME. *snesen;* altered < *fnesen*], to exhale breath from the nose and mouth in an involuntary, explosive action, caused by an irritation of the nasal mucous membrane. *n.* an act of sneezing. **—not to be sneezed at,** not to be disregarded. **—sneez′er,** *n.*

**snell** (snel), *n.* [prob. < D.], a short length of gut, etc. used to attach a fishhook to a fish line.

**snick** (snick), *n.* [prob. < *snick and snee,* combat with knives], a small cut or notch; nick. *v.t.* to make a snick in; nick.

**snick** (snik), *n., v.t. & v.i.* [echoic], click.

**snick·er** (snik′ẽr), *v.i.* [echoic], to laugh in a sly, partly stifled manner; giggle; titter. *v.t.* to utter with a snicker. *n.* a sly, partly stifled laugh. **—snick′er·ing·ly,** *adv.*

**snide** (snīd), *adj.* [orig., counterfeit < thieves' slang; prob. < D. dial. or G.], [Slang], sly and malicious: as, a *snide* remark. **—snide′ly,** *adv.*

**sniff** (snif), *v.i.* [ME. *sniffen;* echoic], 1. to draw in air audibly through the nose. 2. to express contempt, skepticism, etc. by sniffing. *v.t.* 1. to breathe in forcibly through the nose. 2. to test the smell of by sniffing. 3. to detect, perceive, etc. as by sniffing; smell: as, we *sniffed* danger. *n.* 1. an act or sound of sniffing. 2. something sniffed. **—sniff′er,** *n.* **—sniff′y** [-IER, -IEST], *adj.*

**snif·fle** (snif′'l), *v.i.* [-FLED, -FLING], to sniff repeatedly so as to check mucus running from the nose. *n.* an act or sound of sniffling. **—the sniffles,** [Colloq.], 1. a head cold. 2. the sniffling that accompanies a crying spell. **—snif′fler,** *n.*

**snig·ger** (snig′ẽr), *n., v.t. & v.i.* [echoic], snicker.

**snip** (snip), *v.t.* [SNIPPED, SNIPPING], [D. *snippen*], 1. to cut with scissors, etc. in a short, quick stroke or strokes. 2. to remove by such cutting. *v.i.* to make a short, quick cut or cuts. *n.* 1. a small cut made with scissors, etc. 2. the sound of this. 3. a small piece cut off. 4. *pl.* heavy hand shears for cutting sheet metal, etc. 5. [Colloq.], a small, young, or insignificant person. **—snip′per,** *n.*

**snipe** (snīp), *n.* [*pl.* SNIPES, SNIPE; see PLURAL, II, D, 1], [ON. *snipa*], a wading bird living chiefly in marshes and having a long, flexible bill. *v.i.* [SNIPED, SNIPING], 1. to hunt or shoot snipe. 2. to shoot from a hidden position at individuals of an enemy force. **—snip′er,** *n.*

**snip·pet** (snip′it), *n.* [dim. of *snip*], 1. a small fragment, especially one snipped off. 2. [Colloq.], a small or young person; snip. **—snip′pet·y,** *adj.*

**snip·py** (snip′i), *adj.* [-PIER, -PIEST], 1. made up of small scraps or snips; fragmentary. 2. [Colloq.], curt, sharp, etc., especially in an insolent way. **—snip′pi·ly,** *adv.* **—snip′pi·ness,** *n.*

**snitch** (snich), *v.t.* [< 18th-c. thieves' slang; orig. sense "a nose"], [Slang], to steal (usually something of little value). *v.i.* [Slang], 1. to steal. 2. to be an informer; tell (usually with *on*). *n.* [Slang], an informer. **—snitch′er,** *n.*

**sniv·el** (sniv′'l), *v.i.* [-ELED or -ELLED, -ELING or -ELLING], [ME. *snivelen* < AS.], 1. to have mucus running from the nose. 2. to cry and sniffle. 3. to complain in a whining, tearful manner. 4. to make a tearful, often false display of grief, sympathy, etc. *n.* 1. nasal mucus. 2. a sniffling. 3. a whining display of grief, etc. **—sniv′el·er,** *n.*

**snob** (snob), *n.* [? ult. < ON. *snāpr,* dolt], 1. one who attaches great importance to wealth, social position, etc., having contempt for those he considers inferior. 2. one who regards himself as superior to others in some way: as, an intellectual *snob.* **—snob′ber·y** [*pl.* -IES], *n.* **—snob′bish,** *adj.* **—snob′bish·ly,** *adv.* **—snob′bish·ness,** *n.*

**snood** (snōōd), *n.* [< AS. *snod*], 1. a ribbon formerly worn around the hair, especially by young unmarried women. 2. a netlike bag worn at the back of a woman's head to hold the hair. 3. a hat resembling this. *v.t.* to bind (the hair) with a snood.

**snoop** (snōōp), *v.i.* [D. *snoepen*], [Colloq.], to pry about in a sneaking way. *n.* [Colloq.], 1. one who snoops. 2. a snooping. **—snoop′er,** *n.* **—snoop′y** [-IER, -IEST], *adj.*

**snoot** (snōōt), *n.* [see SNOUT], [Colloq.], 1. the nose. 2. the face. 3. a grimace.

**snoot·y** (snōōt′i), *adj.* [-IER, -IEST], [Colloq.], [*snoot* + *-y*], haughty; snobbish. **—snoot′i·ly,** *adv.* **—snoot′i·ness,** *n.*

**snooze** (snōōz), *n.* [prob. < LG. *snūsen,* to snore], [Colloq.], a brief sleep; nap; doze. *v.i.* [SNOOZED, SNOOZING], [Colloq.], to take a brief sleep; nap.

**snore** (snôr, snōr), *v.i.* [SNORED, SNORING], [echoic], to breathe with a harsh, vibrating sound while asleep, usually with the mouth open. *n.* the act or sound of snoring. **—snor′er,** *n.*

**snor·kel** (snôr′k'l), *n.* [G. *schnörkel,* spiral], 1. a device for submarines, with air intake and exhaust tubes, permitting submergence for long periods. 2. a breathing tube extending above the surface of the water, used in swimming just below the surface.

**snort** (snôrt), *v.i.* [prob. < *snore*], 1. to force breath violently and audibly through the nostrils. 2. to express anger, contempt, etc. by a snort. 3. to make a noise like a snort: as, the motor *snorted.* 4. [Colloq.], to laugh roughly. *v.t.* to express or utter with a snort. *n.* 1. the act or sound of snorting. 2. a small drink of liquor. **—snort′er,** *n.*

**snot** (snot), *n.* [AS. (*ge*)*snot,* mucus], 1. nasal mucus: vulgar term. 2. [Slang], an offensive or impudent young person.

**snot·ty** (snot′i), *adj.* [-TIER, -TIEST], 1. of, like, or dirtied with snot. 2. [Slang], *a*) offensive or contemptible. *b*) impudent or condescendingly smug. **—snot′ti·ly,** *adv.* **—snot′ti·ness,** *n.*

**snout** (snout), ***n.*** [prob. < MD. *snute*], 1. the projecting nose and jaws, or muzzle, of an animal. 2. something like an animal's snout, as a nozzle or spout. 3. [Colloq.], a human nose, especially a large one.

**snout beetle,** a small weevil with a long beak.

**snow** (snō), ***n.*** [AS. *snaw*], 1. particles of water vapor which when frozen in the upper air fall to earth as soft, white, crystalline flakes. 2. a falling of snow. 3. a mass of fallen snow. 4. [Poetic], whiteness. 5. [Slang], cocaine or heroin. ***v.i.*** to fall as or like snow. ***v.t.*** 1. to shower or let fall as or like snow. 2. to cover, enclose, etc. with or as with snow (with *in*, *under*, etc.).

**snow·ball** (snō'bôl'), ***n.*** 1. a mass of snow packed together into a ball. 2. a variety of cranberry bush with large, round clusters of small, white flowers. ***v.i.*** 1. to increase rapidly like a rolling ball of snow. 2. to throw snowballs. ***v.t.*** to throw snowballs at.

**snow·bank** (snō'baŋk'), ***n.*** a large mound of snow.

**snow·ber·ry** (snō'ber'i, -bẽr-), ***n.*** [*pl.* -RIES], 1. any of various plants with white berries. 2. the berry.

**snow·bird** (snō'bũrd'), ***n.*** 1. an American bird of the finch family, with a gray back and white breast; junco. 2. the snow bunting.

**snow-blind** (snō'blind'), ***adj.*** blinded temporarily by exposure to the rays of the sun reflected from snow. **—snow blindness.**

**snow-bound** (snō'bound'), ***adj.*** confined by snow.

**snow bunting,** a small finch inhabiting cold regions in the Northern Hemisphere.

**snow·cap** (snō'kap'), ***n.*** a cap of snow, as on a mountain, tree, etc. **—snow'-capped',** ***adj.***

**snow-clad** (snō'klad'), ***adj.*** covered with snow.

**snow·drift** (snō'drift'), ***n.*** 1. a pile of snow heaped up by the wind. 2. snow borne along by the wind.

**snow·drop** (snō'drop'), ***n.*** 1. a low-growing bulb plant with drooping white flowers which appear in early spring. 2. its bulb or flower.

**snow·fall** (snō'fôl'), ***n.*** 1. a fall of snow. 2. the amount of snow falling in a given area or time.

**snow·flake** (snō'flāk'), ***n.*** 1. a single crystal of snow. 2. a plant resembling the snowdrop.

SNOW-FLAKES

**snow line** (or **limit**), the lower boundary of a high region in which snow never melts.

**snow·mo·bile** (snō'mō-bēl'), ***n.*** a motor vehicle for traveling over snow, usually one with steerable runners at the front and tractor treads at the rear.

**snow·plow** (snō'plou'), ***n.*** any plowlike machine used to clear snow off a road, railroad, etc.

**snow·shoe** (snō'shōō'), ***n.*** a racket-shaped frame of wood crisscrossed with leather, etc., worn on the feet to prevent sinking in deep snow. ***v.i.*** [-SHOED, -SHOEING], to use snowshoes in walking.

**snow·storm** (snō'stôrm'), ***n.*** a snow accompanied by a strong wind.

**snow-white** (snō'hwit'), ***adj.*** white as snow.

**snow·y** (snō'i), ***adj.*** [-IER, -IEST], 1. of or characterized by snow. 2. covered or filled with snow. 3. like snow; specif., *a*) pure; spotless. *b*) white. **—snow'i·ly,** ***adv.*** **—snow'i·ness,** ***n.***

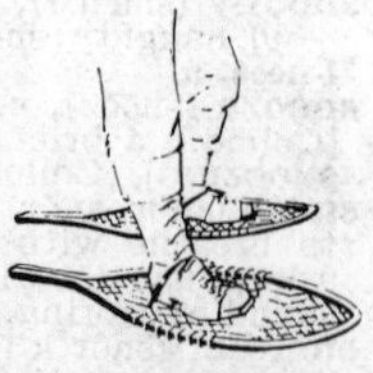

SNOWSHOES

**snub** (snub), ***v.t.*** [SNUBBED, SNUBBING], [< ON. *snubba*, to chide], 1. originally, to check with sharp words. 2. to treat with scorn, disregard, etc.; slight. 3. to check the movement of suddenly: said as of a rope or a boat, etc. attached to it. ***n.*** 1. scornful action or treatment; deliberate slight. 2. a snubbing, or checking. ***adj.*** short and turned up, as a nose: also **snub'by** [-BIER, -BIEST]. **—snub'ber,** ***n.*** **—snub'bing·ly,** ***adv.***

**snub-nosed** (snub'nōzd'), ***adj.*** having a snub nose.

**snuff** (snuf), ***n.*** [prob. akin to MHG. *snipfen*, to snip], the charred end of a candlewick. ***v.t.*** 1. to trim off the charred end of (a candlewick). 2. to put out (a candle). **—snuff out,** 1. to put out (a candle, etc.); extinguish. 2. to bring to an end suddenly; destroy. **—snuff'er,** ***n.***

**snuff** (snuf), ***v.t.*** [MD. *snuffen*], 1. to inhale strongly through the nose; sniff. 2. to smell; sniff at. ***v.i.*** 1. to sniff or snort. 2. [Rare], to use snuff. ***n.*** 1. the act or sound of snuffing; sniff. 2. *a*) a preparation of powdered tobacco taken up into the nose by sniffing or applied to the gums. *b*) a pinch of this. **—up to snuff,** [Colloq.], up to the usual standard. **—snuff'y** [-IER, -IEST], ***adj.***

**snuff·box** (snuf'boks'), ***n.*** a small box for snuff.

**snuff·ers** (snuf'ẽrz), ***n.pl.*** an instrument for snuffing a candle: also **pair of snuffers.**

**snuf·fle** (snuf''l), ***v.i.*** [-FLED, -FLING], [freq. of *snuff* (to sniff)], 1. to breathe audibly and with difficulty or by constant sniffing, as a dog in trailing; sniffle. 2. to speak or sing in a nasal tone. ***v.t.*** to utter by snuffling. ***n.*** 1. the act or sound of snuffling. 2. a nasal tone. **—the snuffles,** snuffling caused by mucus in the nostrils, as in a cold. **—snuf'fler,** ***n.***

**snug** (snug), ***adj.*** [SNUGGER, SNUGGEST], [prob. < LG.], 1. protected from the weather; comfortable; cozy. 2. compact and convenient; neat: as, a *snug* cottage. 3. large enough to provide ease: said of an income. 4. tight in fit: as, a *snug* coat. 5. well-built; seaworthy. 6. hidden: as, he kept *snug* behind the door. ***adv.*** so as to be snug. ***v.t.*** [SNUGGED, SNUGGING], to make snug, tight, etc. **—snug'ly,** ***adv.*** **—snug'ness,** ***n.***

**snug·gle** (snug''l), ***v.i.*** [-GLED, -GLING], [freq. of *snug*], to lie closely and comfortably; cuddle, as for warmth, in affection, etc. ***v.t.*** to cuddle.

**so** (sō), ***adv.*** [AS. *swa*], 1. in the way shown, expressed, understood, etc.: as, hold your golf club *so*. 2. *a*) to such an extent: as, why are you *so* late? *b*) very: as, they are *so* happy. *c*) [Colloq.], very much: as, she *so* wants to go. 3. therefore; as a result: as, they were late, and *so* didn't go. 4. more or less; approximately that: as, he won fifty dollars or *so*: in this sense often regarded as a pronoun. 5. also; likewise: as, I'm going and *so* are you: also used colloquially in contradicting a negative, as, I did *so* tell the truth! 6. then: as, *so* you really don't care. ***conj.*** 1. in order that; with the purpose that: usually followed by *that*, as, he died *so* (that) we might live. 2. [Colloq.], with the result that. 3. if only; as long as (often followed by *that*). ***pron.*** that which has been specified or named: as, he is a fool and will remain *so*. ***interj.*** an exclamation of surprise, approval, triumph, etc. **—and so on** (or **forth**), and the rest; et cetera (etc.). **—so as,** with the result or purpose (followed by an infinitive). **—so what?** [Colloq.], even if so, what then?: used to express disregard, challenge, etc.

**so** (sō), ***n.*** in *music*, sol.

**So.,** 1. South. 2. southern.

**soak** (sōk), ***v.t.*** [AS. *socian*], 1. to saturate or make thoroughly wet, as by keeping in liquid. 2. to take in (liquid) by absorbing (usually with *up*). 3. to take in mentally (usually with *up*). 4. [Colloq.], to drink (liquor), especially to excess. 5. [Slang], to punch hard. 6. [Slang], to charge excessively. ***v.i.*** 1. to remain in liquid so as to become thoroughly wet. 2. to penetrate: as, the fact *soaked* into his head. 3. [Colloq.], to drink to excess. ***n.*** 1. a soaking or being soaked. 2. liquid used for soaking. 3. [Slang], a drunkard. 4. [Slang], a hard punch. **—soak'er,** ***n.*** **—soak'ing·ly,** ***adv.***

**so-and-so** (sō''n-sō'), ***n.*** [*pl.* SO-AND-SOS], [Colloq.], some person or thing not specified: often euphemistic for a stronger epithet.

**soap** (sōp), ***n.*** [AS. *sape*], 1. a substance mixed with water to produce suds for washing, usually prepared by the action of an alkali, as potash, on a fat or oil. 2. any metallic salt of a fatty acid. 3. [Slang], bribe money. ***v.t.*** to rub with soap. **—no soap,** [Slang], (it is) not acceptable.

**soap·ber·ry** (sōp'ber'i, -bẽr-i), ***n.*** [*pl.* -RIES], 1. any of various trees with white or yellowish flowers and round fruit containing a soapy material: also **soapberry tree.** 2. the fruit.

**soap·box** (sōp'boks'), ***n.*** 1. a box for soap. 2. any box used as a platform by one making a speech to a street audience. ***adj.*** of such speeches or speakers. ***v.i.*** to speak informally to a street audience.

**soap opera,** [Colloq.], a daytime radio or television serial drama of a melodramatic, sentimental nature: many were sponsored by soap manufacturers.

**soap·stone** (sōp'stōn'), ***n.*** steatite, a soft talc in rock form, used for griddles, bed warmers, etc.

**soap·suds** (sōp'sudz'), ***n.pl.*** soapy water, especially when stirred into a foam.

**soap·y** (sōp'i), ***adj.*** [-IER, -IEST], 1. covered with or containing soap. 2. of or like soap. 3. [Slang], suave; oily. **—soap'i·ly,** ***adv.*** **—soap'i·ness,** ***n.***

**soar** (sôr, sōr), ***v.i.*** [OFr. *essorer* < LL.; ult. < L. *ex-*, out + *aura*, air], 1. to rise or fly high into the air. 2. to sail or glide along high in the air. 3. to rise above the ordinary level. ***n.*** 1. soaring range. 2. the act of soaring. **—soar'er,** ***n.*** **—soar'ing·ly,** ***adv.***

**sob** (sob), ***v.i.*** [SOBBED, SOBBING], [< AS. < base of *supan*, to swallow], 1. to weep aloud with short, gasping breaths. 2. to make a sound like this, as the wind, etc. ***v.t.*** 1. to put (oneself), as to sleep, by sobbing. 2. to utter with sobs. ***n.*** the act or sound of sobbing. **—sob'bing·ly,** ***adv.***

**so·ber** (sō′bẽr), *adj.* [< OFr. < L. *sobrius*], 1. temperate, especially in the use of alcoholic liquor. 2. not drunk. 3. serious, solemn, sedate, etc. 4. quiet; plain: said of color, clothes, etc. 5. not distorted: as, the *sober* truth. 6. characterized by reason, sanity, or self-control. *v.t. & v.i.* to make or or become sober (often with *up* or *down*). —**so′ber·ly,** *adv.* —**so′ber·ness,** *n.*

**so·ber-mind·ed** (sō′bẽr-mīn′did), *adj.* of a sober mind. —**so′ber-mind′ed·ness,** *n.*

**so·bri·e·ty** (sō-brī′ə-ti), *n.* a being sober; specif., *a*) temperance, especially in the use of drink. *b*) seriousness, sedateness, etc.

**so·bri·quet** (sō′bri-kā′), *n.* [Fr.], 1. a nickname. 2. an assumed name. Also **soubriquet.**

**sob story,** a sentimental account or story intended to arouse pity or compassion.

**Soc., soc.,** society.

**so-called** (sō′kôld′), *adj.* known by this term, but usually inaccurately so: as, a *so-called* liberal.

**soc·cer** (sok′ẽr), *n.* [alt. < *association*], a kind of football played with a round ball, moved chiefly by kicking: also called *association football.*

**so·cia·ble** (sō′shə-b′l), *adj.* [see SOCIAL], 1. enjoying the company of others; friendly; affable. 2. characterized by pleasant, informal conversation and companionship. *n.* a social, especially a church social. —**so′cia·bil′i·ty** [*pl.* -TIES], **so′cia·ble·ness,** *n.* —**so′cia·bly,** *adv.*

**so·cial** (sō′shəl), *adj.* [< Fr. < L. *socialis* < *socius*, companion], 1. of or having to do with human beings in their living together and dealings with one another: as, *social* problems. 2. living in this way: as, modern man is *social.* 3. of or having to do with the ranks of society, especially with fashionable society: as, a *social* climber. 4. sociable; getting along well with others. 5. of or for companionship. 6. of or engaged in welfare work: as, a *social* agency. 7. living in groups or communities: as, the ant is a *social* insect. 8. socialist. *n.* an informal gathering for recreation; party. —**so′cial·ly,** *adv.* —**so′cial·ness,** *n.*

**social disease,** venereal disease.

**so·cial·ism** (sō′shəl-iz′m), *n.* 1. the theory of the ownership and operation of the means of production and distribution by society rather than by private individuals, with all members of society sharing in the work and the products. 2. [often S-], *a*) a political movement for establishing such a system. *b*) the doctrines, etc. of the Socialist parties.

**so·cial·ist** (sō′shəl-ist), *n.* 1. an advocate or supporter of socialism. 2. [S-], a member of a Socialist party. *adj.* 1. of or like socialism or socialists. 2. advocating or supporting socialism. —**so′cial·is′tic,** *adj.* —**so′cial·is′ti·cal·ly,** *adv.*

**Socialist Party,** a political party based on the principles of socialism.

**so·cial·ite** (sō′shə-līt′), *n.* [Colloq.], a person who is prominent in fashionable society.

**so·ci·al·i·ty** (sō′shi-al′ə-ti), *n.* 1. sociability. 2. [*pl.* -TIES], the tendency to form social groups.

**so·cial·ize** (sō′shə-līz′), *v.t.* [-IZED, -IZING], 1. to make social, or fit for co-operative group living. 2. to adapt to the common needs of a social group. 3. to put under government ownership. 4. to cause to become socialist. *v.i.* [Colloq.], to take part in social activity. —**so′cial·i·za′tion,** *n.*

**socialized medicine,** complete medical care, made available through public funds, for all the people in a community, nation, etc.

**social register,** a book containing a list of socially prominent people.

**social science,** 1. sociology. 2. any of several studies, as history, economics, civics, etc., dealing with society and the activities of its members.

**social security,** a federal system of old-age, unemployment, or disability insurance, financed jointly by employees, employers, and the government.

**social service,** social work. —**so′cial-serv′ice,** *adj.*

**social work,** any activity designed to promote the welfare of the community and the individual, as through counseling agencies, recreation and rehabilitation centers, etc. —**social worker.**

**so·ci·e·ty** (sə-sī′ə-ti), *n.* [*pl.* -TIES], [Fr. < L. *societas* < *socius*, companion], 1. a group of persons regarded as forming a single community. 2. all people, collectively, as a community of interdependent individuals. 3. a particular system of living together as a community: as, a primitive *society.* 4. companionship. 5. one's friends or associates. 6. an organized group of people with some interest in common: as, a medical *society.* 7. the wealthy, fashionable class. —**so·ci′e·tal,** *adj.*

**Society Islands,** a group of islands belonging to France, in the South Pacific.

**Society of Friends,** a Christian religious sect founded in England in 1650 by George Fox: Friends believe in plainness of dress, manners, and religious worship, and are opposed to military service: see **Quaker.**

**Society of Jesus,** see **Jesuit.**

**so·ci·o-,** [Fr. < L. *socius*, companion], a combining form meaning *society, social.*

**so·ci·ol·o·gy** (sō′si-ol′ə-ji, sō′shi-), *n.* [< Fr.; see SOCIO- & -LOGY], the study of the development, organization, and problems of society and social groups. —**so′ci·o·log′i·cal** (-ə-loj′i-k′l), *adj.* —**so′ci·o·log′i·cal·ly,** *adv.* —**so′ci·ol′o·gist,** *n.*

**sock** (sok), *n.* [< AS. < L. *soccus*, a light, low-heeled shoe], 1. a light shoe worn by comic characters in ancient Greek and Roman drama. 2. comic drama. 3. a short stocking reaching only part way to the knee.

**sock** (sok), *v.t.* [Slang], to hit with force. *n.* [Slang], a blow. *adv.* [Slang], directly; squarely.

**sock·et** (sok′it), *n.* [< Anglo-Fr. < OFr. *soc*, plowshare < Celt.], a hollow part into which something fits: as, an eye *socket*, the *socket* of an electric bulb. *v.t.* to fit into a socket.

**sock·eye** (sok′ī′), *n.* [< Am. Ind. *suk-kegh*], a red salmon of the north Pacific, used for canning.

**Soc·ra·tes** (sok′rə-tēz′), *n.* Athenian idealist philosopher and teacher; 470?–399 B.C. —**So·crat·ic** (sō-krat′ik), *adj. & n.* —**So·crat′i·cal·ly,** *adv.*

**Socratic method,** a method of teaching, as used by Socrates, in which a series of questions leads the answerer to a logical conclusion.

**sod** (sod), *n.* [prob. < MD. *sode*], 1. a surface layer of earth containing grass plants with their matted roots; turf. 2. a piece of this layer. *v.t.* [SODDED, SODDING], to cover with sod or sods.

**so·da** (sō′də), *n.* [ML.], 1. sodium carbonate. 2. sodium bicarbonate. 3. sodium hydroxide. 4. sodium oxide. 5. soda water. 6. a beverage of soda water flavored with sirup, etc., often mixed with ice cream.

**soda ash,** crude sodium carbonate.

**soda cracker,** a light, crisp cracker, made from a dough of flour, water, soda, and cream of tartar.

**soda fountain,** 1. a counter for making and serving soft drinks, sodas, etc. 2. a container for soda water, with faucets by which it is drawn off.

**soda jerk,** [Slang], one who works at a soda fountain.

**so·dal·i·ty** (sō-dal′ə-ti), *n.* [*pl.* -TIES], [< Fr. < L. < *sodalis*, companion], 1. fellowship; companionship. 2. an association or brotherhood. 3. in the *R.C. Church*, a devotional or charitable lay society.

**soda pop,** a soft drink of flavored carbonated water, usually sold in tightly capped bottles.

**soda water,** water charged under pressure with carbon dioxide gas, used in making ice-cream sodas, mixed drinks, etc.

**sod·den** (sod′′n), obs. pp. of **seethe.** *adj.* 1. soaked through. 2. moist from improper cooking; soggy, as bread. 3. dull; stupid, as from fatigue. *v.t. & v.i.* to make or become sodden. —**sod′den·ness,** *n.*

**so·di·um** (sō′di-əm), *n.* [Mod. L. < *soda*], a silver-white, alkaline metallic chemical element, found in nature only in combined form: symbol, Na; at. wt., 22.997; at. no., 11.

**sodium bicarbonate,** a white, crystalline compound, $NaHCO_3$, used in baking powder, as an antacid, etc.: also called *baking soda.*

**sodium carbonate,** 1. the anhydrous sodium salt of carbonic acid, $Na_2CO_3$: also called *soda ash.* 2. any of the hydrated carbonates of sodium; esp., the crystalline compound $Na_2CO_3 \cdot 10H_2O$, commonly called *sal soda* or *washing soda.*

**sodium chloride,** common salt, NaCl.

**sodium cyanide,** a white, highly poisonous salt, NaCN, used in electroplating, as an insecticide, etc.

**sodium fluoride,** a colorless, soluble salt, NaF, used in the fluoridation of water.

**sodium hydroxide,** a white, strongly alkaline substance, NaOH, used in chemistry, etc.: also called *caustic soda, lye, sodium hydrate.*

**sodium hyposulfite,** 1. a clear, crystalline salt, $Na_2S_2O_4$. 2. sodium thiosulfate.

**sodium nitrate,** a clear, crystalline salt, $NaNO_3$, used in manufacturing explosives, fertilizers, etc.: also called *Chile saltpeter.*

**sodium pentothal,** see **pentothal sodium.**

**sodium thiosulfate,** a white, crystalline salt, $Na_2S_2O_3$, used as a fixing agent in photography, etc.: popularly but incorrectly called (*sodium*) *hyposulfite, hypo.*

**Sod·om** (sod′əm), *n.* in the Bible, a city destroyed by fire for its sinfulness: see **Gomorrah.**

**Sod·om·ite** (sod′əm-īt′), *n.* 1. an inhabitant of Sodom. 2. [s-], a person who practices sodomy.

**sod·om·y** (sod′əm-i), *n.* [< OFr. < *Sodom* (Gen. 18-19)], abnormal sexual intercourse, as between persons of the same sex or between a person and an animal.

**so·ev·er** (sō-ev′ẽr), *adv.* 1. in any way; to any extent or degree: as, how dark *soever* it may be. 2. of any kind; at all: as, no rest *soever.*

**-so·ev·er,** a combining form added for emphasis or generalization to *who, what, when, where, how,* etc., and meaning *any* (person, thing, time, place, or manner) *of all those possible.*

**so·fa** (sō′fə), *n.* [Fr. < Ar. *ṣuffah*], an upholstered couch with fixed back and arms.

**So·fi·a** (sō′fi-ə, sō-fē′ə), *n.* the capital of Bulgaria: pop., 437,000.

**S. of Sol.,** Song of Solomon.

**soft** (sôft), *adj.* [AS. *softe*], 1. giving way easily under pressure, as a feather pillow or moist clay. 2. easily cut, worked, etc.: as, a *soft* wood or metal. 3. not as hard as is normal, desirable, etc.: as, *soft* butter. 4. smooth to the touch. 5. bland; not acid, sour, etc. 6. nonalcoholic: said of drinks. 7. having few or none of the mineral salts that interfere with the lathering of soap: said of water. 8. mild or temperate, as a breeze, climate, etc. 9. weak; not strong or vigorous. 10. requiring little effort; easy: as, a *soft* job. 11. *a*) kind or lenient, especially to the point of weakness. *b*) easily impressed, influenced, etc. 12. subdued; not bright: said of color. 13. showing little contrast or distinction: as, a *soft* etching. 14. gentle; low: said of sound. 15. in *phonetics, a*) sibilant: said of *c* and *g*, as in *cent* and *germ. b*) voiced. *adv.* softly; gently; quietly. *n.* something soft; soft part. *interj.* [Archaic], quiet! hush! stop! —**soft′ish,** *adj.* —**soft′ly,** *adv.* —**soft′ness,** *n.*

**soft·ball** (sôft′bôl′), *n.* 1. a kind of baseball played on a smaller diamond and with a ball larger and softer than in ordinary baseball. 2. this ball.

**soft-boiled** (sôft′boild′), *adj.* boiled only a short time so that the yolk is soft: said of eggs.

**soft coal,** bituminous coal.

**soft drink,** a nonalcoholic drink, especially a carbonated drink.

**sof·ten** (sôf′′n), *v.t. & v.i.* to make or become soft or softer. —**sof′ten·er,** *n.*

**soft·heart·ed** (sôft′här′tid), *adj.* full of compassion or tenderness. 2. not strict or severe, as in discipline or authority. —**soft′heart′ed·ly,** *adv.* —**soft′-heart′ed·ness,** *n.*

**soft palate,** the soft, fleshy part at the rear of the roof of the mouth; velum.

**soft-ped·al** (sôft′ped′′l), *v.t.* [-ALED or -ALLED, -ALING or -ALLING], 1. to soften the tone of (a musical instrument) by use of a pedal (**soft pedal**). 2. [Colloq.], to tone down; make less emphatic, less obtrusive, etc.

**soft-shelled crab** (sôft′sheld′), a crab at the stage between the shedding of its old shell and the hardening of the new: also **soft′-shell′,** *n.*

**soft-shoe** (sôft′sho͞o′), *adj.* designating a kind of tap dancing done without metal taps on the shoes.

**soft shoulder,** a soft strip of ground along the edge of a highway.

**soft-soap** (sôft′sōp′), *v.t.* 1. to apply soft soap to. 2. [Colloq.], to flatter. —**soft′-soap′er,** *n.*

**soft soap,** 1. soap in liquid or semifluid form. 2. [Colloq.], flattery.

**soft-spo·ken** (sôft′spō′k′n), *adj.* 1. speaking or spoken with a soft, low voice. 2. smooth; suave. —**soft′-spo′ken·ly,** *adv.* —**soft′-spo′ken·ness,** *n.*

**soft·wood** (sôft′wood′), *n.* 1. any light, easily cut wood. 2. the wood of any tree with true cones. 3. any tree with soft wood.

**soft·y, soft·ie** (sôf′ti), *n.* [*pl.* -IES], [Colloq.], one who is soft or weak in body, resolve, etc.

**sog·gy** (sog′i), *adj.* [-GIER, -GIEST], [prob. < ON. *sog*, lit., a sucking], soft and heavy with moisture; soaked. —**sog′gi·ly,** *adv.* —**sog′gi·ness,** *n.*

**soil** (soil), *n.* [< OFr. < L. *solum*], 1. the surface layer of earth, supporting plant life. 2. figuratively, a place for growth of any kind. 3. land; country: as, foreign *soil.* 4. ground or earth.

**soil** (soil), *v.t.* [< OFr. < LL. < L. *suculus*, dim. of *sus*, pig], 1. to make dirty; smirch; stain. 2. to bring disgrace upon. 3. to corrupt or defile. *v.i.* to become soiled. *n.* 1. a soiled spot; stain. 2. excrement. 3. a soiling or being soiled. —**soil′er,** *n.*

**soi·ree, soi·rée** (swä-rā′), *n.* [< Fr. < *soir*, evening], an evening party or gathering.

**so·journ** (sō′jûrn; *also, for v.*, sō-jûrn′), *v.i.* [< OFr. < L. *sub-*, under + *diurnus*, of a day < *dies*, day], to live somewhere temporarily; stay for a while. *n.* a brief stay; visit. —**so·journ′er,** *n.*

**Sol** (sol), *n.* [L.], 1. the sun. 2. the ancient Roman sun god. 3. in *alchemy*, gold.

**sol** (sōl), *n.* [see GAMUT], in *music*, a syllable representing the fifth tone of the diatonic scale.

**sol·ace** (sol′is), *n.* [< OFr. < L. < *solari*, to comfort], 1. an easing of grief, loneliness, etc. 2. something that eases or relieves; comfort; relief. *v.t.* [-ACED, -ACING], 1. to give solace to; comfort. 2. to lessen (grief, sorrow, etc.). —**sol′ace·ment,** *n.* —**sol′ac·er,** *n.*

**so·lar** (sō′lẽr), *adj.* [L. *solaris* < *sol*, the sun], 1. of or having to do with the sun. 2. produced by or coming from the sun: as, *solar* energy. 3. depending upon the sun's light or energy: as, *solar* heating. 4. measured by the earth's motion with relation to the sun: as, a *solar* day.

**so·lar·i·um** (sō-lâr′i-əm), *n.* [*pl.* -LARIA (-ə)], [L., < *sol*, the sun], a glassed-in room, porch, etc. where people sun themselves, as in treating illness; sunroom.

**solar plexus,** 1. a network of nerves in the abdominal cavity behind the stomach. 2. [Colloq.], the upper middle part of the abdomen.

**solar system,** the sun and all the heavenly bodies that revolve around it.

**sold** (sōld), pt. and pp. of **sell.**

**sol·der** (sod′ẽr), *n.* [< OFr. < L. *solidare*, to make firm], 1. a metal alloy used when melted to join or patch metal parts or surfaces. 2. figuratively, anything that joins or fuses; bond. *v.t. & v.i.* 1. to join (things) with solder. 2. to hold or be held together; unite or become united. —**sol′der·er,** *n.*

**soldering iron,** a pointed metal tool heated for use in melting and applying solder.

**sol·dier** (sōl′jẽr), *n.* [< OFr. < *solde*, pay < L. *solidus*, a coin], 1. a member of an army. 2. an enlisted man, as distinguished from an officer. 3. a man of much military experience. 4. one who works for a specified cause. *v.i.* 1. to serve as a soldier. 2. to shirk one's duty, as by only pretending to work, feigning illness, etc. —**sol′dier·ly,** *adj.* —**sol′dier·li·ness,** *n.* —**sol′dier·ship′,** *n.*

**soldier of fortune,** a military adventurer, serving wherever he can get pay, pleasure, etc.

**sol·dier·y** (sōl′jẽr-i), *n.* [*pl.* -IES], 1. soldiers collectively. 2. military science or skill.

**sole** (sōl), *n.* [< AS. & Fr.; ult. < L. *solum*, a base, bottom], 1. the bottom surface of the foot. 2. the part of a shoe, sock, etc. corresponding to this. 3. the bottom surface of various objects, as a golf club. *v.t.* [SOLED, SOLING], to furnish (a shoe, etc.) with a sole.

**sole** (sōl), *adj.* [< OFr. < L. *solus*], 1. without another; single; one and only. 2. of or having to do with only one (specified) person or group. 3. acting, done, etc. automatically or without help. 4. [Archaic], alone; solitary. —**sole′ness,** *n.*

**sole** (sōl), *n.* [*pl.* SOLE, SOLES; see PLURAL, II, D, 2], [OFr. < Pr. < L. *solea*, sole of a shoe, also a fish (< its shape)], any of certain sea flatfishes highly valued as food.

**sol·e·cism** (sol′ə-siz′m), *n.* [< Fr. < L. < Gr. < *soloikos*, speaking incorrectly < dialect used in *Soloi*, in Asia Minor], 1. a violation of the conventional usage, grammar, etc. of a language (e.g., "I seen him" for "I saw him"). 2. a breach of etiquette or propriety. —**sol′e·cist,** *n.* —**sol′e·cis′tic,** *adj.* —**sol′e·cis′ti·cal·ly,** *adv.*

**sole·ly** (sōl′li), *adv.* 1. alone; without another or others. 2. only, exclusively, merely, or altogether: as, he reads *solely* for pleasure.

**sol·emn** (sol′əm), *adj.* [< OFr. < L. *sollemnis*, yearly < *sollus*, all + *annus*, year], 1. set aside according to ritual, as religious festivals; hence, 2. sacred. 3. according to strict form; formal. 4. serious; deeply earnest. 5. awe-inspiring; very impressive. 6. somber because dark in color. —**sol′emn·ly,** *adv.* —**sol′emn·ness,** *n.*

**so·lem·ni·fy** (sə-lem′nə-fī′), *v.t.* [-FIED, -FYING], to make solemn.

**so·lem·ni·ty** (sə-lem′nə-ti), *n.* [*pl.* -TIES], 1. solemn ceremony, formality, ritual, etc. 2. seriousness; impressiveness; gravity.

**sol·em·nize** (sol′əm-nīz′), *v.t.* [-NIZED, -NIZING], 1. to celebrate formally or according to ritual, as a religious holiday. 2. to perform (a ceremony): as, the marriage was *solemnized.* 3. to make serious or grave. —**sol′em·ni·za′tion,** *n.*

**so·le·noid** (sō′lə-noid′), *n.* [< Fr. < Gr. *sōlēn*, a channel + *eidos*, a form], a coil of wire carrying an electric current and having the properties of a magnet. —**so′le·noi′dal,** *adj.*

**sol-fa** (sōl′fä′), *n.* [It.; *sol* + *fa*, two notes of the gamut], 1. the syllables *do, re, mi, fa, sol, la, ti, do,* used for the tones of a scale, regardless of key. 2. the use of these syllables in vocal exercises. *v.t. & v.i.* [-FAED, -FAING], to sing (a scale, etc.) to these syllables. —**sol′-fa′ist,** *n.*

**sol·feg·gio** (sol-fej′ō, -i-ō′), *n.* [*pl.* -GIOS, -GI (-fej′i)], [It. < *solfa;* see SOL-FA], 1. voice practice in which scales are sung to the sol-fa syllables. 2. the use of these syllables in singing.

**so·lic·it** (sə-lis′it), *v.t.* [< OFr. < L.; see SOLICITOUS], 1. to ask or seek earnestly; beg; entreat: as, we *solicit* your aid. 2. to entice (another) to do wrong. 3. to accost (another) for some immoral purpose, as a prostitute does. *v.i.* to make a plea or request. —**so·lic′i·ta′tion,** *n.*

**so·lic·i·tor** (sə-lis′ə-tēr), *n.* 1. one who solicits; esp., one who seeks trade, contributions, etc. 2. in England, any lawyer other than a barrister. 3. the official law officer for a city, department, etc.

**solicitor general,** [*pl.* SOLICITORS GENERAL, SOLICITOR GENERALS], 1. a law officer of a national government, ranking next below the attorney general. 2. the chief law officer in some States.

**so·lic·i·tous** (sə-lis′ə-təs), *adj.* [L. *sollicitus* < *sollus*, whole + pp. of *ciere*, to set in motion], 1. showing care, attention, or concern: as, *solicitous* for their welfare. 2. showing anxious desire; eager: as, *solicitous* to make friends. 3. full of anxiety or apprehension; troubled. —**so·lic′i·tous·ly,** *adv.*

**so·lic·i·tude** (sə-lis′ə-to͞od′, -tūd′), *n.* the state of being solicitous; care, concern, etc.

**sol·id** (sol′id), *adj.* [< OFr. < L. *solidus*], 1. offering some resistance to pressure; relatively firm or compact; neither liquid nor gaseous. 2. not hollow. 3. in three dimensions; cubic: as, a *solid* yard of earth. 4. substantial; firm; sound: as, a *solid* structure. 5. serious; not trivial. 6. complete: as, *solid* satisfaction. 7. having no breaks or divisions: as, a *solid* word. 8. with no pauses: as, he talked for two *solid* hours. 9. of one or the same color, material, etc. throughout. 10. showing unity; unanimous: as, a *solid* vote. 11. thick or dense, as fog, etc. 12. real; genuine. 13. [Colloq.], firm or dependable in views, sympathy, etc. 14. [Colloq.], having a firmly favorable relationship. 15. [Slang], excellent. 16. in *printing*, having no lead separators between lines of type. *n.* 1. a substance that offers some resistance to pressure and is not easily changed in shape. 2. an object or figure having length, breadth, and thickness. —**sol′id·ly,** *adv.* —**sol′id·ness,** *n.*

**sol·i·dar·i·ty** (sol′ə-dar′ə-ti), *n.* [*pl.* -TIES], agreement of all elements or individuals, as of a group; complete unity.

**solid geometry,** the geometry of solid figures.

**so·lid·i·fy** (sə-lid′ə-fī′), *v.t. & v.i.* [-FIED, -FYING], 1. to make or become solid, firm, hard, etc. 2. to crystallize. —**so·lid′i·fi·ca′tion,** *n.*

**so·lid·i·ty** (sə-lid′ə-ti), *n.* [*pl.* -TIES], a being solid; firmness, soundness, etc.

**sol·id-state** (sol′id-stāt′), *adj.* designating or of electronic devices, circuits, etc. equipped with transistors rather than electron tubes.

**sol·i·dus** (sol′i-dəs), *n.* [*pl.* -DI (-dī′)], [LL.], 1. a gold coin of the Late Roman Empire. 2. the slant line (/) used to separate shillings from pence, as 7/6, or as a dividing line in fractions, dates, etc.

**so·lil·o·quize** (sə-lil′ə-kwīz′), *v.i.* [-QUIZED, -QUIZING], to talk to oneself; deliver a soliloquy. *v.t.* to utter in a soliloquy. —**so·lil′o·quist,** *n.*

**so·lil·o·quy** (sə-lil′ə-kwi), *n.* [*pl.* -QUIES], [< L. < *solus*, alone + *loqui*, to speak], 1. a talking to oneself. 2. lines in a drama in which a character reveals his thoughts by speaking as if to himself.

**sol·i·taire** (sol′ə-târ′, sol′ə-târ′), *n.* [< Fr. < L.; see SOLITARY], 1. a single gem, especially a diamond, set by itself. 2. any of several games, especially card games, played by one person.

**sol·i·tar·y** (sol′ə-ter′i), *adj.* [< OFr. < L. *solitarius* < *solus*, alone], 1. living or being alone. 2. single; only: as, a *solitary* example. 3. characterized by loneliness. 4. lonely; remote: as, a *solitary* place. 5. done in solitude. *n.* [*pl.* -IES], 1. one who lives by himself; esp., a hermit. 2. [Colloq.], solitary confinement. —**sol′i·tar′i·ly,** *adv.* —**sol′i·tar′i·ness,** *n.*

**solitary confinement,** confinement of a prisoner, usually as extra punishment, away from all others.

**sol·i·tude** (sol′ə-to͞od′, -tūd′), *n.* [< OFr. < L. *solitudo* < *solus*, alone], 1. a being solitary, or alone; seclusion. 2. a secluded place.

**sol·ler·et** (sol′ēr-et, sol′ēr-et′), *n.* [OFr. *soleret;* ult. < *sole;* see SOLE (of a shoe)], a kind of shoe worn with a suit of armor: see **armor,** illus.

**sol·mi·za·tion** (sol′mi-zā′shən), *n.* [< Fr. < *sol* + *mi*, two notes of the gamut], the act or practice of singing scales to a system of syllables, especially the sol-fa syllables.

**so·lo** (sō′lō), *n.* [*pl.* -LOS; *rarely* -LI (-lē)], [It. < L. *solus*, alone], 1. a musical piece or passage to be played or sung by one person. 2. an airplane flight made by a pilot alone. 3. any performance by one person alone. 4. any card game in which there are no partners. *adj.* 1. for or by a single voice or instrument. 2. performing a solo. 3. made or done by one person. *v.i.* to make a solo flight, especially one's first. —**so′lo·ist,** *n.*

**Sol·o·mon** (sol′ə-mən), *n.* 1. the son of David and king of Israel in the 10th century B.C.: he was noted for his wisdom. 2. a very wise man.

**Solomon Islands,** a group of British islands in the Pacific, east of New Guinea.

**Sol·o·mon's-seal** (sol′ə-mənz-sēl′), *n.* any of various plants with a scarred rootstock, bell-shaped flowers, and black or blue fruit.

**So·lon** (sō′lən, -lon), *n.* 1. Athenian statesman and lawgiver; 638–559 B.C. 2. [often s-], a wise man, especially a lawmaker.

**so long,** [? < *salaam*], [Colloq.], good-by.

**sol·stice** (sol′stis), *n.* [OFr. < L. *solstitium* < *sol*, the sun + *sistere*, to make stand still < *stare*, to stand], 1. either of two points on the sun's ecliptic at which it is farthest north or farthest south of the equator. 2. the time during the summer (**summer solstice**) or winter (**winter solstice**) when the sun reaches either of these points: in the Northern Hemisphere, June 21 or 22 and December 21 or 22, respectively. —**sol·sti·tial** (sol-stish′əl), *adj.*

**sol·u·ble** (sol′yoo-b'l), *adj.* [OFr. < L. *solubilis* < *solvere;* see SOLVE], 1. that can be dissolved: as, sugar is *soluble* in water. 2. that can be solved. —**sol′u·bil′i·ty** [*pl.* -TIES], *n.* —**sol′u·bly,** *adv.*

**sol·ute** (sol′ūt, sō′lo͞ot), *n.* the substance dissolved in a solution. *adj.* dissolved; in solution.

**so·lu·tion** (sə-lo͞o′shən), *n.* [< OFr. < L. pp. of *solvere;* see SOLVE], 1. the act or process of solving a problem. 2. an explanation, answer, etc.: as, the *solution* of a mystery. 3. the dispersion of one or more substances in another, usually a liquid, so as to form a homogeneous mixture; a dissolving. 4. a being dissolved. 5. the mixture, usually a liquid, so produced: as, a *solution* of sugar and water. 6. a breaking up; dissolution.

**solve** (solv), *v.t.* [SOLVED, SOLVING], [< L. *solvere*, to loosen < *se-*, apart + *luere*, to let go], to find a satisfactory answer for (a problem, mystery, etc.); make clear; explain. —**solv′a·bil′i·ty, solv′a·ble·ness,** *n.* —**solv′a·ble,** *adj.* —**solv′er,** *n.*

**sol·vent** (sol′vənt), *adj.* [< L. ppr. of *solvere;* see SOLVE], 1. able to pay all one's debts. 2. that can dissolve another substance. *n.* 1. a substance used for dissolving another substance. 2. something that solves or explains. —**sol′ven·cy,** *n.*

**Sol·y·man** (sol′i-mən), *n.*, see **Suleiman.**

**So·ma·li** (sō-mä′li, sə-), *n.* [*pl.* -LI, -LIS], 1. a member of a group of Hamitic tribes living in and near Somaliland. 2. their Cushitic language.

**So·ma·li·a** (sō-mä′li-ə, sə-), *n.* a country in E Africa, on the Indian Ocean and the Gulf of Aden: area, 246,201 sq. mi.; pop., 2,250,000; capital, Mogadishu.

**So·ma·li·land** (sō-mä′li-land′, sə-), *n.* a region in E Africa: see **French Somaliland** and **Somalia.**

**so·mat·ic** (sō-mat′ik), *adj.* [< Gr. *sōmatikos* < *sōma*, the body], 1. of the body; corporeal; physical. 2. of the cells (**somatic cells**) of an organism that become differentiated into the tissues, organs, etc. of the body. 3. of the outer walls of the body. —**so·mat′i·cal·ly,** *adv.*

**som·ber, som·bre** (som′bēr), *adj.* [< Fr. *sombre* < LL. < L. *sub*, under + *umbra*, shade], 1. dark and gloomy or dull. 2. mentally depressed or depressing; dismal; melancholy; sad. —**som′ber·ly, som′bre·ly,** *adv.* —**som′ber·ness, som′bre·ness,** *n.*

**som·bre·ro** (som-brâr′ō), *n.* [*pl.* -ROS], [Sp. < *sombra*, shade] a broad-brimmed hat, usually of felt, worn in Spain, Latin America, etc.

**some** (sum), *adj.* [AS. *sum*], 1. being a certain one or ones not specified or known: as, *some* people smoke. 2. being of a certain unspecified quantity, degree, etc.: as, have *some* butter. 3. about: as, *some* twenty of us. 4. [Colloq.], remarkable, striking, etc.: as, that was *some* fight. *pron.* 1. a certain one or ones not specified or known: as, *some* will agree. 2. a certain unspecified quantity, degree, etc.: as, *some* of the time. *adv.* 1. about: as, *some* ten men. 2. [Colloq.], somewhat: as, it is *some* colder. 3. [Colloq.], to or at a great extent, rate, etc.: as, I'll have to go *some* to catch up.

**-some** (səm), [AS. *-sum*], a suffix meaning *like, apt,* or *tending to (be)*, as in *lonesome, tiresome.*

**-some** (səm), [AS. *sum*], a suffix meaning *in* (a specified) *number*: as, in *twosome.*

**-some** (sōm), [< Gr. *sōma*, body], a combining form meaning *body*, as in *chromosome.*

**some·bod·y** (sum'bud'i, -bod'i, -bəd-i), *n.* [*pl.* -IES], a person of importance. *pron.* a person unknown or not named; some person; someone.

**some·day** (sum'dā'), *adv.* at some future time.

**some·how** (sum'hou'), *adv.* in a way or by a method not known, stated, or understood: as, *somehow* they have done it. **—somehow or other,** somehow.

**some·one** (sum'wun', -wən), *pron.* somebody.

**som·er·sault** (sum'ẽr-sôlt'), *n.* [alt. < OFr. *sombresault* < L. *supra*, over + *saltus*, a leap], an acrobatic stunt performed by turning the body one full revolution, heels over head: often used figuratively. *v.i.* to perform a somersault.

**som·er·set** (sum'ẽr-set'), *n. & v.i.* somersault.

**Som·er·ville** (sum'ẽr-vil'), *n.* a city in Massachusetts, near Boston: pop., 102,000.

**some·thing** (sum'thiŋ), *n.* 1. a thing not definitely known, understood, etc.: as, *something* went wrong. 2. some thing or things, definite but unspecified: as, he has *something* for you. 3. an important person or thing. *adv.* somewhat.

**some·time** (sum'tīm'), *adv.* 1. at some time not known or specified. 2. at some unspecified time in the future. 3. [Rare], sometimes. *adj.* former.

**some·times** (sum'tīmz'), *adv.* occasionally.

**some·way** (sum'wā'), *adv.* in some way or manner: also **some way, someways.**

**some·what** (sum'hwät', -wət), *n.* 1. some part, amount, degree, etc. 2. an important person or thing. *adv.* to some extent, degree, etc.; a little; rather: as, he was *somewhat* tardy.

**some·where** (sum'hwâr'), *adv.* 1. in, to, or at some place not known or specified. 2. at some unspecified point in amount, degree, time, etc. (with *about* or *in*): as, *somewhere* in June. *n.* an unspecified or undetermined place.

**some·wheres** (sum'hwârz'), *adv.* [Chiefly Dial.], somewhere: in general use, considered solecistic.

**some·wise** (sum'wīz'), *adv.* [Archaic], in some way or to some degree (usually preceded by *in*).

**Somme** (sum; Fr. sôm), *n.* a river in N France, flowing into the English Channel.

**som·nam·bu·late** (som-nam'byoo-lāt'), *v.i. & v.t.* [-LATED, -LATING], [< L. *somnus*, sleep + pp. of *ambulare*, to walk], to walk in a trancelike state while asleep. **—som·nam'bu·lant,** *adj.* **—som·nam'-bu·la'tion,** *n.* **—som·nam'bu·la'tor** (-lā'tẽr), *n.*

**som·nam·bu·lism** (som-nam'byoo-liz'm), *n.* 1. the habit or act of somnambulating; sleepwalking. 2. the actions of one who somnambulates. **—som-nam'bu·list,** *n.* **—som·nam'bu·lis'tic,** *adj.*

**som·nif·er·ous** (som-nif'ẽr-əs), *adj.* [< L. *somnus*, sleep + *ferre*, to bring], inducing sleep; soporific: also **som·nif'ic. —som·nif'er·ous·ly,** *adv.*

**som·no·lent** (som'nə-lənt), *adj.* [< OFr. < L. *somnolentus* < *somnus*, sleep], 1. sleepy; drowsy. 2. inducing drowsiness. **—som'no·lence, som'no-len·cy,** *n.* **—som'no·lent·ly,** *adv.*

**son** (sun), *n.* [AS. *sunu*], 1. a boy or man in his relationship to either or both parents. 2. a male descendant. 3. a male thought of as if in relation to a parent: as, a *son* of France. 4. anything thought of as like a son in relation to its origin. 5. a familiar form of address to a boy or younger man. **—the Son,** Jesus Christ. **—son'ship,** *n.*

**so·nant** (sō'nənt), *adj.* [< L. ppr. of *sonare*, to sound], 1. of sound. 2. having sound; sounding. 3. in *phonetics*, voiced. *n.* in *linguistics*, 1. a voiced speech sound. 2. a syllabic sound. **—so'nance,** *n.*

**so·nar** (sō'när), *n.* [*so*und *na*vigation *r*anging], an apparatus that transmits high-frequency sound waves in water and registers the vibrations reflected back from an object: used in detecting submarines, finding depths of oceans, etc.

**so·na·ta** (sə-nä'tə), *n.* [It. < L. *sonare*, to sound], a musical composition for solo instrument or instruments, usually in three or four movements having unity of subject but differing in tempo, rhythm, etc.

**song** (sôŋ), *n.* [AS.], 1. the act or art of singing. 2. a piece of music sung or as if for singing. 3. *a)* poetry; verse. *b)* a ballad or lyric set to music. 4. a musical sound like singing: as, the *song* of the lark. **—for a song,** cheaply. **—song'ful,** *adj.* **—song'ful·ly,** *adv.* **—song'less,** *adj.*

**song·bird** (sôŋ'bũrd'), *n.* 1. a bird that makes vocal sounds resembling music. 2. a woman singer.

**Song of Solomon,** a book of the Old Testament consisting of a love poem, dramatic and lyrical in character: also called **Song of Songs, Canticles.**

**song·ster** (sôŋ'stẽr), *n.* [AS. *sangestre*], 1. a singer. 2. a writer of songs or poems. 3. a songbird. **—song'stress,** *n.fem.*

**song thrush,** the mavis, a European songbird.

**son·ic** (son'ik), *adj.* [< L. *sonus*, sound], 1. of or having to do with sound. 2. designating or of a speed equal to the speed of sound (about 738 miles per hour).

**sonic boom,** an explosive sound generated by the accumulation of pressure in a wave preceding an airplane moving at or above the speed of sound.

**son-in-law** (sun''n-lô'), *n.* [*pl.* SONS-IN-LAW], the husband of one's daughter.

**son·net** (son'it), *n.* [Fr. < It. < Pr. dim. of *son*, a song < L. *sonus*, a sound], a poem normally of fourteen lines (usually in iambic pentameter) in any of several fixed verse and rhyme schemes, expressing a single theme: see **Shakespearean sonnet.** *v.t. & v.i.* to write sonnets (about).

**son·net·eer** (son'ə-têr'), *n.* one who writes sonnets. *v.t. & v.i.* to sonnet.

**son·ny** (sun'i), *n.* [*pl.* -NIES], little son: used in addressing any young boy in a familiar way.

**son of a gun,** [Slang], 1. a person or thing regarded angrily, contemptuously, familiarly, etc. 2. an interjection of surprise, annoyance, etc.

**Son of God** (or **Man**), Jesus Christ.

**so·nor·i·ty** (sə-nôr'ə-ti, sə-nor'-), *n.* [*pl.* -TIES], quality or state of being sonorous; resonance.

**so·no·rous** (sə-nôr'əs; *chiefly* Brit. son'ẽr-), *adj.* [< L. < *sonor*, a sound], 1. producing or capable of producing sound; resonant. 2. full, deep, or rich: said of sound. 3. impressive; high-sounding: as, *sonorous* prose. **—so·no'rous·ly,** *adv.*

**Soo·chow** (sōō'chou'; Chin. -jō'), *n.* a city in E China: pop., 500,000.

**soon** (sōōn), *adv.* [AS. *sona*, at once], 1. in a short time; shortly: as, come see us *soon.* 2. promptly; quickly: as, as *soon* as possible. 3. ahead of time; early: as, he left too *soon.* 4. readily; willingly: as, I would as *soon* go as stay. 5. [Obs.], at once. **—had sooner,** would rather. **—sooner or later,** inevitably; eventually.

**soot** (soot, sōōt), *n.* [AS. *sot*], a black substance consisting chiefly of carbon particles formed by the incomplete combustion of burning matter. *v.t.* to cover, soil, etc. with soot.

**sooth** (sōōth), *adj.* [AS. *soth*], 1. [Archaic], true. 2. [Poetic], soothing. *n.* [Archaic], truth. **—in sooth,** [Archaic], in truth. **—sooth'ly,** *adv.*

**soothe** (sōōth), *v.t.* [SOOTHED, SOOTHING], [AS. *sothian* < *soth*, truth], 1. to make calm or composed, as by gentleness, flattery, etc. 2. to relieve, as pain. *v.i.* to have a soothing effect. **—sooth'er,** *n.* **—sooth'ing,** *adj.* **—sooth'ing·ly,** *adv.*

**sooth·say·er** (sōōth'sā'ẽr), *n.* [see SOOTH], one who claims to foretell the future. **—sooth'say'ing,** *n.*

**soot·y** (soot'i, sōōt'i), *adj.* [-IER, -IEST], 1. of or like soot. 2. covered or soiled with soot. 3. dark-brown or black. **—soot'i·ness,** *n.*

**sop** (sop), *n.* [AS. *sopp*], 1. a piece of food, as bread, soaked in milk, gravy, etc. 2. *a)* something given as a reward, appeasement, etc. *b)* a bribe. *v.t.* [SOPPED, SOPPING], 1. to soak, steep, etc. in or with liquid. 2. to take (*up*), as water, by absorption. *v.i.* 1. to soak (with *in*, etc.): said of a liquid. 2. to be or become thoroughly wet.

**SOP, S.O.P.,** standing (or standard) operating procedure.

**sop.,** soprano.

**soph.,** sophomore.

**soph·ism** (sof'iz'm), *n.* [< OFr. < LL. < Gr. < *sophos*, clever], a clever and plausible but fallacious argument; fallacy or sophistry.

**soph·ist** (sof'ist), *n.* [< Fr. < L. < Gr. *sophistēs*, wise man], 1. [often S-], in ancient Greece, any of a group of teachers of rhetoric, philosophy, etc., some of whom were notorious for their clever, specious arguments. 2. a learned person. 3. any person practicing clever, specious reasoning.

**so·phis·ti·cal** (sə-fis'ti-k'l), *adj.* 1. of or characteristic of sophists or sophistry. 2. clever or plausible but misleading. Also **so·phis'tic. —so-phis'ti·cal·ly,** *adv.* **—so·phis'ti·cal·ness,** *n.*

**so·phis·ti·cate** (sə-fis'tə-kāt'; *also, for n.,* -kit), *v.t.* [-CATED, -CATING], [< ML. < L. *sophisticus*, sophistical], 1. to change from a natural, simple, or artless state, etc.; make artificial or worldly-wise. 2. to corrupt or mislead. *v.i.* to use sophistical reasoning. *n.* a sophisticated person.

**so·phis·ti·cat·ed** (sə-fis′tə-kāt′id), *adj.* 1. marked by a lack of simplicity or naturalness; refined to the point of artificiality. 2. worldly-wise; not naive or ingenuous. 3. intellectually perceptive; knowledgeable; subtle. 4. of sophisticates. 5. highly complex or advanced: as, *sophisticated* equipment.

**so·phis·ti·ca·tion** (sə-fis′tə-kā′shən), *n.* 1. sophistry. 2. the act or process of sophisticating. 3. the state or quality of being sophisticated.

**soph·is·try** (sof′is-tri), *n.* [*pl.* -TRIES], 1. unsound or misleading but clever and plausible argument or reasoning. 2. the methods of the Sophists.

**Soph·o·cles** (sof′ə-klēz′), *n.* Greek tragic dramatist; lived 496?–406 B.C.

**soph·o·more** (sof′ə-môr′, -mōr′), *n.* [alt. (after Gr. *sophos*, wise + *mōros*, foolish) < obs. *sophumer*, lit., sophist], 1. a student in the second year of college or high school. 2. a person in his second year of any enterprise. *adj.* of sophomores.

**soph·o·mor·ic** (sof′ə-môr′ik, -mor′-), *adj.* of, like, or characteristic of sophomores, often regarded as self-assured, opinionated, etc., though immature: also **soph′o·mor′i·cal.** —**soph′o·mor′i·cal·ly,** *adv.*

**-so·phy** (sə-fi), [< Gr. *sophia*, skill, wisdom], a suffix meaning *knowledge*, as in *philosophy*.

**so·po·rif·ic** (sop′ə-rif′ik, sō′pə-), *adj.* [< L. *sopor*, sleep; + *-fic*], 1. causing or tending to cause sleep. 2. characterized by sleepiness. Also **so′po·rif′er·ous** (-ēr-əs). *n.* a drug, etc. that causes sleep.

**sop·ping** (sop′iŋ), *adj.* [ppr. of *sop*], thoroughly wet; drenched; soaking.

**sop·py** (sop′i), *adj.* [-PIER, -PIEST], 1. sopping. 2. rainy. 3. [Brit. Slang], too sentimental.

**so·pra·no** (sə-pran′ō, -prä′nō), *n.* [*pl.* -PRANOS, -PRANI (-prä′nē)], [It. < *sopra*, above], 1. the highest singing voice of women and children. 2. a singer with such a range. 3. a part for a soprano. *adj.* of, for, or in the soprano.

**so·ra** (sō′rə), *n.* [? < Am. Ind.], a small, short-billed, wading bird of the rail family: also **sora rail.**

**Sor·bonne** (sôr-bon′; Fr. sôr′bôn′), *n.* the liberal arts college of the University of Paris.

**sor·cer·er** (sôr′sēr-ēr), *n.* a person who practices sorcery; magician; wizard.

**sor·cer·ess** (sôr′sēr-is), *n.* a female sorcerer; witch.

**sor·cer·y** (sôr′sēr-i), *n.* [*pl.* -IES], [< OFr. < *sorcier*, sorcerer < LL. < L. *sors*, lot, fate], the supposed use of an evil supernatural power over people and their affairs; witchcraft. —**sor′cer·ous,** *adj.*

**sor·did** (sôr′did), *adj.* [< Fr. < L. < *sordes*, filth], 1. dirty; filthy. 2. squalid; depressingly wretched. 3. base; ignoble. 4. mercenary, avaricious, etc. —**sor′did·ly,** *adv.* —**sor′did·ness,** *n.*

**sore** (sôr, sōr), *adj.* [AS. *sar*], 1. *a*) giving pain; painful: as, a *sore* tooth. *b*) feeling pain, as from wounds, etc. 2. easily irritated or angered; touchy. 3. filled with sadness, grief, etc.: as, *sore* at heart. 4. causing sadness, misery, etc.: as, a *sore* hardship. 5. provoking irritation. 6. [Colloq.], angry; offended. *n.* 1. a place on the body where tissue is injured, as by a cut, burn, etc. 2. any source of pain, irritation, grief, etc. *adv.* [Archaic], sorely. —**sore′ness,** *n.*

**sore·head** (sôr′hed′, sōr′-), *n.* [Colloq.], one who is angry, resentful, etc., or one easily made so.

**sore·ly** (sôr′li, sōr′-), *adv.* 1. grievously; painfully. 2. urgently; extremely: as, *sorely* needed.

**sor·ghum** (sôr′gəm), *n.* [< It. *sorgo*], 1. any of several cereal grasses with sweet, juicy stalks, grown for grain, fodder, sirup, etc. 2. a sirup made from the juice of some of these grasses.

**so·ror·i·ty** (sə-rôr′ə-ti, -ror′-), *n.* [*pl.* -TIES], [< L. *soror*, sister], 1. a group of women or girls joined together by common interests, etc. 2. a club, etc. of women or girls, as in some colleges.

**sor·rel** (sôr′əl, sor′-), *n.* [< OFr. < OHG. *sur*, sour], 1. any of several plants with sour, fleshy leaves used in salads. 2. any of various similar plants.

**sor·rel** (sôr′əl, sor′-), *n.* [< OFr. < *sor*, a hawk with red plumage], 1. reddish brown. 2. a reddish-brown horse, etc. *adj.* reddish-brown.

**sor·row** (sor′ō, sôr′ō), *n.* [< AS. *sorg*], 1. mental suffering caused by loss, disappointment, etc.; sadness; grief. 2. that which produces such suffering; trouble, etc. 3. the outward expression of such suffering; mourning. *v.i.* to feel sorrow; grieve. —**sor′row·er,** *n.* —**sor′row·ing·ly,** *adv.*

**sor·row·ful** (sor′ō-fəl, sôr′-), *adj.* 1. feeling or expressing sorrow. 2. causing sorrow. —**sor′row·ful·ly,** *adv.* —**sor′row·ful·ness,** *n.*

**sor·ry** (sôr′i, sor′i), *adj.* [-RIER, -RIEST], [< AS. *sarig*, in pain < *sar*, sore], 1. full of sorrow, pity, or regret: as, we were *sorry* to leave. 2. inferior in worth or quality; poor. 3. wretched; dismal; pitiful. —**sor′ri·ly,** *adv.* —**sor′ri·ness,** *n.*

**sort** (sôrt), *n.* [< OFr. < LL. < L. *sors*, a lot], 1. any group of things related by having something in common; kind; class. 2. quality; type: as, it's not your *sort*. 3. [Archaic], manner; fashion; way. 4. *usually in pl.* in *printing*, any of the kinds of characters in a font of type. *v.t.* to arrange according to class or kind. —**of sorts,** 1. of various kinds. 2. of an inferior kind: also **of a sort.** —**out of sorts,** [Colloq.], not in a good humor or health. —**sort of,** [Colloq.], somewhat. —**sort′a·ble,** *adj.* —**sort′er,** *n.*

**sor·tie** (sôr′ti), *n.* [Fr. < *sortir*, to issue], 1. a sudden attack by forces of a besieged place. 2. one mission or attack by a single military plane.

**SOS** (es′ō′es′), 1. the standard signal of distress (· · · — — — · · ·) used internationally in wireless telegraphy, as by ships, etc. 2. [Colloq.], any call or appeal for help.

**so-so** (sō′sō′), *adv.* indifferently; just passably. *adj.* not very good; rather poor. Also **so so.**

**sot** (sot), *n.* [AS. < OFr. < LL. *sottus*, stupid], a habitual drunkard. —**sot′tish,** *adj.* —**sot′tish·ly,** *adv.* —**sot′tish·ness,** *n.*

**sot·to vo·ce** (sot′ō vō′chi), [It., under the voice], in an undertone, so as not to be overheard.

**sou** (so͞o), *n.* [*pl.* SOUS (so͞oz; Fr. so͞o)], [Fr. < L. *solidus*, a coin], a former French coin equal to 1/20 of a franc; 5-centime piece.

**sou·brette** (so͞o-bret′), *n.* [Fr. < Pr. < *soubret*, sly; ult. < L. *superare*, to be above], in the *theater*, 1. a lady's maid, especially one involved in intrigue. 2. any pretty or flirtatious young woman character. 3. an actress who plays such characters.

**sou·bri·quet** (so͞o′bri-kā′), *n.* a sobriquet.

**Sou·dan** (so͞o-dan′), *n.* Sudan: the French spelling.

**souf·flé** (so͞o′flā′, so͞o′flā), *adj.* [Fr., pp. of *souffler*, to blow], in *cooking*, light and puffy: also **souf·fléed** (so͞o′flād′, so͞o′flād). *n.* a baked food made light and puffy by the addition of beaten egg whites before baking.

**sough** (suf, sou), *n.* [< AS. *swogan*, to sound], a soft murmuring, sighing, or rustling sound. *v.i.* to make a sough.

**sought** (sôt), pt. and pp. of **seek.**

**soul** (sōl), *n.* [AS. *sawol*], 1. an entity without material reality, regarded as the spiritual part of the person and as having the functions of thinking and willing. 2. the moral or emotional nature of man. 3. spiritual or emotional warmth, force, etc. 4. vital or essential part, quality, etc. 5. the central or leading figure. 6. embodiment; personification: as, the *soul* of kindness. 7. a person: as, I didn't see a *soul*. 8. the spirit of a dead person, thought of as separate from the body. —**upon my soul!** an exclamation of surprise.

**soul·ful** (sōl′fəl), *adj.* full of or showing deep feeling. —**soul′ful·ly,** *adv.* —**soul′ful·ness,** *n.*

**soul·less** (sōl′lis), *adj.* lacking sensitivity or deep feeling. —**soul′less·ly,** *adv.* —**soul′less·ness,** *n.*

**sound** (sound), *n.* [< OFr. *son* < L. *sonus*], 1. that which is or can be heard, resulting from stimulation of auditory nerves by vibrations carried in the air, etc. 2. such vibrations (*sound waves*). 3. any identifiable noise: as, the *sound* of laughter. 4. any of the individual utterances made by the speech organs; speech sound. 5. the distance within which a sound may be heard; earshot. 6. mental impression; meaning: as, I like the *sound* of his report. 7. mere meaningless noise. *v.i.* 1. to make a sound. 2. to seem or appear through sound: as, she *sounds* troubled. *v.t.* 1. to cause to sound, or to produce the sound of. 2. to express, signal, proclaim, etc.: as, *sound* the alarm, *sound* his praises. 3. to pronounce: as, he doesn't *sound* his r's. 4. to examine, as the chest, by percussion, etc. —**sound off,** 1. to speak in turn, as in counting off. 2. [Slang], to speak in a loud or offensive way. —**sound′er,** *n.*

**sound** (sound), *adj.* [AS. (*ge*)*sund*], 1. free from defect, damage, or decay: as, *sound* timber. 2. normal and healthy: as, a *sound* body and mind. 3. firm; safe; secure: as, a *sound* bank. 4. based on valid reasoning; sensible: as, a *sound* plan. 5. orthodox; conservative. 6. thorough; complete. 7. deep and undisturbed: said of sleep. 8. morally

---

**fat, āpe, bâre, cär;** ten, **ēven, hêre, ovẽr;** is, **bīte;** lot, **gō, hôrn, to͞ol,** look; **oil, out; up, ūse, fũr; get; joy; yet; chin; she; thin, *th*en; zh,** leisure; **ŋ,** ring; **ə** for *a* in *ago*, *e* in *agent*, *i* in *sanity*, *o* in *comply*, *u* in *focus*; ′ in *able* (ā′b'l); **Fr. bål; ë,** Fr. coeur; **ö,** Fr. feu; Fr. mo*n*; **ô,** Fr. coq; **ü,** Fr. duc; **H,** G. ich; **kh,** G. doch. ‡ foreign; < derived from.

strong; honest, loyal, etc. 9. in *law*, valid. ***adv.*** in a sound manner. —**sound′ly, *adv.* —sound′ness, *n.***

**sound** (sound), ***n.*** [< AS. & ON. *sund*], 1. a wide channel linking two large bodies of water or separating an island from the mainland. 2. a long arm of the sea. 3. the air bladder of a fish.

**sound** (sound), ***v.t.*** [< OFr. *sonder* < LL. < L. *sub*, under + *unda*, a wave], 1. to measure the depth of (water), especially with a weighted line (*sounding line*). 2. to examine (the bottom of the sea, etc.) with a line that brings up adhering particles. 3. to try to find out the opinions of (someone) on a given matter (often with *out*). 4. in *medicine*, to examine with a probe. ***v.i.*** 1. to sound water. 2. to move downward through water; dive. 3. to try to find out something. ***n.*** 1. a sounding. 2. in *medicine*, a long probe used in examining body cavities. —**sound′a·ble, *adj.* —sound′er, *n.***

**sound effects,** sounds, as of thunder, animals, etc., often artificially produced, as for radio, TV, etc.

**sound·ing** (soun′diŋ), ***adj.*** 1. giving forth sound. 2. resonant; sonorous. 3. high-sounding; bombastic.

**sound·ing** (soun′diŋ), ***n.*** 1. the act of one who sounds the depth of water. 2. depth so measured. 3. *pl.* a place, usually less than 600 feet in depth, where such measurements can be taken.

**sounding board,** 1. a board, etc. used to reflect sound or increase its resonance. 2. a person on whom one tests one's ideas, opinions, etc.

**sound·less** (sound′lis), ***adj.*** without sound; perfectly quiet; noiseless. —**sound′less·ly, *adv.***

**sound·proof** (sound′proof′), ***adj.*** impervious to sound. ***v.t.*** to make soundproof.

**sound track,** the area along one side of a motion-picture film, carrying the sound record of the film.

**soup** (sōōp), ***n.*** [Fr. *soupe;* of Gmc. origin], 1. a liquid food made by cooking meat, vegetables, etc. in water, milk, etc. 2. [Slang], a heavy overcast, often with rain. —**soup up,** [Slang], to increase in capacity for speed, as an engine, by supercharging, etc. —**soup′y** [-IER, -IEST], ***adj.***

**soup·çon** (sōōp′sōn′), ***n.*** [Fr.], 1. literally, a suspicion. 2. a suggestion or trace, as of a flavor.

**sour** (sour), ***adj.*** [AS. *sur*], 1. having a sharp, acid taste; tart, as lemon juice, vinegar, etc. 2. made acid or spoiled by fermentation: as, *sour* milk. 3. cross; disagreeable: as, failure made him *sour*. 4. not satisfactory; poor: as, his game has gone *sour*. 5. distasteful or unpleasant. 6. excessively acid: said of soil. ***n.*** 1. something sour. 2. an acid drink: as, a whisky *sour*. ***v.t. & v.i.*** to make or become sour. —**sour′ish, *adj.* —sour′ly, *adv.* —sour′ness, *n.***

**source** (sôrs, sōrs), ***n.*** [< OFr. < L. *surgere*, to rise], 1. a spring, etc. from which a stream arises. 2. a place of origin; prime cause. 3. a person, book, etc. from which information is gotten.

**sour·dough** (sour′dō′), ***n.*** 1. fermented dough saved from one baking to the next, for use as leaven. 2. a prospector in the western U.S., Canada, or Alaska: so called from his using sourdough.

**sour grapes,** something scorned only because it cannot be had.

**sour gum,** a kind of tupelo (tree).

**sour·puss** (sour′poos′), ***n.*** [Slang], a morose person.

**Sou·sa, John Philip** (sōō′zə, -sə), 1854–1932; American composer and bandmaster.

**souse** (sous), ***n.*** [< OFr. < OHG. *sulza*, brine], 1. a pickled food, especially the feet, ears, and head of a pig. 2. liquid for pickling; brine. 3. a plunging into a liquid. 4. [Slang], a drunkard. ***v.t. & v.i.*** [SOUSED, SOUSING], 1. to pickle. 2. to plunge or steep in a liquid. 3. to make or become soaking wet. 4. [Slang], to make or become intoxicated.

**sou·tane** (sōō-tän′), ***n.*** [Fr. < It. *sottana*], a cassock worn by Roman Catholic priests.

**south** (south), ***n.*** [AS. *suth*], 1. the direction to the left of a person facing the sunset (180° on the compass, opposite north). 2. a region or district in or toward this direction. 3. [often S-], the southern part of the earth, especially the antarctic regions. ***adj.*** 1. in, of, to, or toward the south. 2. from the south: as, a *south* wind. 3. [S-], designating the southern part of a continent, country, etc. ***adv.*** in or toward the south. —**the South,** that part of the U.S. which is bounded on the north by Pennsylvania, the Ohio River, and N Missouri.

**South Africa,** a country in southernmost Africa: area, 472,359 sq. mi.; pop., 18,733,000; capitals, Cape Town, Pretoria. —**South African.**

**South African Dutch,** 1. the Boers. 2. Afrikaans.

**South America,** the southern continent in the Western Hemisphere: area, 6,814,000 sq. mi.; pop., 169,000,000. —**South American.**

**South·amp·ton** (sou-thamp′tən, south-hamp′-), ***n.*** a seaport in S England: pop., 209,000.

**South Bend,** a city in N Indiana: pop., 132,000.

**South Carolina,** a Southern State of the U.S.: area, 31,055 sq. mi.; pop., 2,383,000; capital, Columbia: abbrev. **S.C.** —**South Carolinian.**

**South China Sea,** an arm of the Pacific, touching Taiwan, the Philippines, Borneo, and SE Asia.

**South Dakota,** a Middle Western State of the U.S.: area, 77,047 sq. mi.; pop., 681,000; capital, Pierre: abbrev. **S.Dak., S.D.** —**South Dakotan.**

**south·east** (south′ēst′; *in nautical usage*, sou-), ***n.*** 1. the direction halfway between south and east (45° east of due south). 2. a region or district in or toward this direction. ***adj.*** 1. in, of, to, or toward the southeast. 2. from the southeast, as a wind. ***adv.*** in, toward, or from the southeast. —**the Southeast,** the southeastern part of the U.S.

**south·east·er** (south′ēs′tēr; *in nautical usage*, sou-), ***n.*** a storm or wind from the southeast.

**south·east·er·ly** (south′ēs′tēr-li; *in nautical usage*, sou-), ***adj. & adv.*** 1. toward the southeast. 2. from the southeast.

**south·east·ern** (south′ēs′tērn; *in nautical usage*, sou-), ***adj.*** 1. in, of, or toward the southeast. 2. from the southeast. 3. [S-], of or characteristic of the Southeast.

**south·east·ward** (south′ēst′wērd; *in nautical usage*, sou-), ***adv. & adj.*** toward the southeast: also **southeastwards, *adv.*** ***n.*** a southeastward direction, point, or region.

**south·east·ward·ly** (south′ēst′wērd-li; *in nautical usage*, sou-), ***adj. & adv.*** 1. toward the southeast. 2. from the southeast, as a wind.

**south·er** (south′ēr), ***n.*** a strong wind from the south.

**south·er·ly** (suth′ēr-li), ***adj. & adv.*** 1. toward the south. 2. from the south. —**south′er·li·ness, *n.***

**south·ern** (suth′ērn), ***adj.*** 1. in, of, or toward the south. 2. from the south. 3. [S-], of or characteristic of the South. —**south′ern·most′, *adj.***

**Southern Cross,** a southern constellation with four bright stars in the form of a cross.

**south·ern·er** (suth′ēr-nēr, -ən-ēr), ***n.*** 1. a native or inhabitant of the south. 2. [S-], a native or inhabitant of a Southern State.

**Southern Hemisphere,** that half of the earth south of the equator.

**southern lights,** the aurora australis.

**Southern Rhodesia,** Rhodesia: the former name.

**Southern Yemen,** a country in S Arabia, including Aden and a group of Arab states: area, c. 110,000 sq. mi.; pop., 1,131,000.

**Sou·they, Robert** (sou′thi, suth′i), 1774–1843; English poet and writer.

**South Gate,** a city in SW California: pop., 54,000.

**South Island,** the larger of the two chief islands of New Zealand.

**south·land** (south′lənd, -land′), ***n.*** the southern region of a country, etc. —**south′land·er, *n.***

**south·paw** (south′pô′), ***n.*** [Slang], in *sports*, a left-handed player. ***adj.*** [Slang], left-handed.

**South Pole,** the southern end of the earth's axis.

**South Sea Islands,** the islands in the South Pacific. —**South Sea Islander.**

**South Seas,** 1. the South Pacific. 2. all the seas located south of the equator.

**south-south·east** (south′south′ēst′; *in nautical usage*, sou′sou-), ***n.*** the direction halfway between due south and southeast (22°30′ east of due south). ***adj. & adv.*** 1. in or toward this direction. 2. from this direction.

**south-south·west** (south′south′west′; *in nautical usage*, sou′sou-), ***n.*** the direction halfway between due south and southwest (22°30′ west of due south). ***adj. & adv.*** 1. in or toward this direction. 2. from this direction.

**south·ward** (south′wērd; *in nautical usage*, suth′-ērd), ***adj. & adv.*** toward the south: also **southwards, *adv.*** ***n.*** a southward direction, point, etc.

**south·ward·ly** (south′wērd-li; *in nautical usage*, suth′ērd-), ***adj. & adv.*** 1. toward the south. 2. from the south.

**south·west** (south′west′; *in nautical usage*, sou-), ***n.*** 1. the direction halfway between south and west (45° west of due south). 2. a district or region in or toward this direction. ***adj.*** 1. in, of, to, or toward the southwest. 2. from the southwest. ***adv.*** in, toward, or from the southwest. —**the Southwest,** the southwestern part of the U.S.

**South West Africa,** a territory in SW Africa: administered by South Africa.

**south·west·er** (south′wes′tēr; *in nautical usage*, sou-), ***n.*** 1. a storm or wind from the southwest. 2. a sailor's waterproof hat, having a broad brim in the back. Also **sou′wester, souwester.**

**south·west·er·ly** (south′wes′tēr-li; *in nautical usage*, sou-), ***adj. & adv.*** 1. toward the southwest. 2. from the southwest.

**south·west·ern** (south'wes'tẽrn; *in nautical usage,* sou-), *adj.* 1. in, of, or toward the southwest. 2. from the southwest. 3. [S-], of or characteristic of the Southwest.
**south·west·ward** (south'west'wẽrd; *in nautical usage,* sou-), *adv. & adj.* toward the southwest: also **southwestwards,** *adv.* *n.* a southwestward direction, point, or region.
**south·west·ward·ly** (south'west'wẽrd-li; *in nautical usage,* sou-), *adj. & adv.* 1. toward the southwest. 2. from the southwest, as a wind.
**sou·ve·nir** (so͞o'və-nêr', so͞o'və-nêr'), *n.* [Fr., orig. an inf., to remember < L. *subvenire,* to come to mind], something kept as a reminder of a place, person, event, etc.; memento.
**sou'·west·er, sou·west·er** (sou-wes'tẽr), *n.* a southwester.
**sov·er·eign** (sov'rin, -ẽr-in, suv'rən), *adj.* [< OFr. *soverain* < LL. < L. *super,* above], 1. above all others; chief; supreme. 2. supreme in power, rank, etc. 3. of or holding the position of ruler; reigning. 4. independent of all others: as, a *sovereign* state. 5. excellent; very effectual, as a remedy. *n.* 1. a person having sovereign authority; monarch; ruler. 2. a British gold coin worth 20 shillings or one pound. —**sov'er·eign·ly,** *adv.*
**sov·er·eign·ty** (sov'rin-ti, -ẽr-in-ti, suv'rən-), *n.* [*pl.* -TIES], 1. a being sovereign. 2. the status, dominion, rule, etc. of a sovereign. 3. supreme and independent political authority.
**so·vi·et** (sō'vi-it, sō'vi-et'), *n.* [Russ., lit., council], 1. a council or body of delegates. 2. in the Soviet Union, any of the various elected governing councils constituting a pyramidal governmental structure with the village and town soviets as its base and the Supreme Soviet as its apex. *adj.* 1. of a soviet or soviets. 2. [S-], of or connected with the Soviet Union. —**so'vi·et·ism,** *n.*
**so·vi·et·ize** (sō'vi-ə-tīz'), *v.t.* [-IZED, -IZING], to change to a soviet form of government. —**so·vi·et·i·za·tion** (sō'vi-it-i-zā'shən), *n.*
**Soviet Russia,** 1. Union of Soviet Socialist Republics. 2. Russian Soviet Federated Socialist Republic.
**Soviet Union,** Union of Soviet Socialist Republics.
**sow** (sou), *n.* [AS. *sugu*], an adult female pig.
**sow** (sō), *v.t.* [SOWED, SOWN (sōn) or SOWED, SOWING], [AS. *sawan*], 1. to scatter or plant (seed) for growing. 2. to plant (a field, etc.) with seed. 3. to spread abroad; disseminate. 4. to implant; inculcate. *v.i.* to sow seed for growing. —**sow'er,** *n.*
**sow·bel·ly** (sou'bel'i), *n.* [Colloq.], salt pork.
**sox** (soks), *n.pl.* socks (hose).
**soy** (soi), *n.* [Japan., colloq. for *shōyū* < Chin. < *chiang,* salted bean + *yu,* oil], 1. an oriental sauce used on fish, meat, etc., made from fermented soybeans. 2. the soybean (plant or seed).
**soy·a** (soi'ə, sō'yə), *n.* [Chiefly Brit.], soy.
**soy·bean** (soi'bēn'), *n.* 1. a plant with white or purple flowers and hairy, brown pods. 2. its seed, which yields flour, oil, and other products.
**Sp.,** 1. Spain. 2. Spaniard. 3. Spanish.
**sp.,** 1. special. 2. [*pl.* SPP.], species. 3. spelling.
**S.P., SP,** Shore Patrol.
**spa** (spä), *n.* [< *Spa,* celebrated watering place in Belgium], 1. a mineral spring. 2. any place, especially a resort, having a mineral spring.
**space** (spās), *n.* [< OFr. < L. *spatium*], 1. the boundless, continuous expanse extending in all directions, within which all material things are contained. 2. distance, area, etc. between, within, or encompassing things; room: as, *space* between shelves. 3. (enough) room for some purpose: as, a parking *space.* 4. reserved accommodations, as on a ship. 5. interval or length of time: as, *space* between wars. 6. the universe outside the earth's atmosphere: in full, **outer space.** 7. in *music,* an open place between the lines of a staff. 8. in *printing,* any blank piece of type metal used to separate words, etc. *v.t.* [SPACED, SPACING], to arrange with spaces between. —**spac'er,** *n.*
**space·craft** (spās'kraft', -kräft'), *n.* a spaceship or satellite designed for travel, exploration, etc. in outer space.
**space fiction,** fiction about space travel.
**space·man** (spās'mən), *n.* [*pl.* -MEN], an astronaut.
**space·ship** (spās'ship'), *n.* a rocket-propelled vehicle for travel in outer space.
**space station** (or **platform**), a structure designed to orbit as a satellite from which to launch other spacecraft, or as an experimentation or observation center.
**space-time** (**continuum**) (spās'tīm'), the continuum involving the three dimensions of space and that of time, in which all things exist.
**spa·cial** (spā'shəl), *adj.* spatial.
**spac·ing** (spās'iŋ), *n.* 1. the arrangement of spaces. 2. space or spaces, as between printed words. 3. the act of a person or thing that spaces.
**spa·cious** (spā'shəs), *adj.* 1. having more than enough space or room; vast; extensive. 2. great; large. —**spa'cious·ly,** *adv.* —**spa'cious·ness,** *n.*
**spade** (spād), *n.* [AS. *spadu*], a heavy, flat-bladed, long-handled digging tool, like a shovel. *v.t. & v.i.* [SPADED, SPADING], to dig or cut with a spade. —**call a spade a spade,** to use plain, blunt words. —**spade'ful',** *n.* —**spad'er,** *n.*
**spade** (spād), *n.* [Sp. *espada,* sword (sign used on Spanish cards) < L. < Gr. *spathē,* flat blade], 1. the black figure (♠) marking one of the four suits of playing cards. 2. *pl.* the suit of cards so marked. 3. a card of this suit.
**spade·work** (spād'wũrk'), *n.* any difficult or tiresome work necessary to make a beginning.
**spa·dix** (spā'diks), *n.* [*pl.* -DIXES, -DICES (spā-dī'sēz)], [L. (< Gr. *spadis*), a palm branch], a fleshy spike of tiny flowers, usually enclosed in a spathe.
**spa·ghet·ti** (spə-get'i), *n.* [It., dim. pl. of *spago,* small cord], a food consisting of long strings of flour paste, cooked by boiling or steaming.
**Spain** (spān), *n.* a country in SW Europe, on the Iberian Peninsula: area, 190,050 sq. mi.; pop., 32,949,000; capital, Madrid.
**spake** (spāk), archaic pt. of **speak.**
**span** (span), *n.* [AS.], 1. a measure of length, equal to nine inches, based on the distance between the tip of the thumb and the tip of the little finger when extended. 2. *a*) the full amount or extent between any two limits. *b*) the distance between ends or supports: as, the *span* of an arch. *c*) a part between two supports: as, a bridge of two *spans.* 3. a short space of time. 4. a team of two animals used together. *v.t.* [SPANNED, SPANNING], 1. to measure, especially by the hand with the thumb and little finger extended. 2. to encircle with the hand or hands as in measuring 3. to extend, reach, or pass over or across: as, a bridge *spans* the river.
**span** (span), archaic pt. of **spin.**
**Span.,** Spanish.
**span·drel** (span'drəl), *n.* [prob. < OFr. *espandre,* to expand], 1. the space between the exterior curve of an arch and a rectangular frame enclosing it. 2. one of the spaces between a series of arches and a straight cornice running above them.
**spang** (spaŋ), *adv.* [Colloq.], abruptly; directly.
**span·gle** (spaŋ'g'l), *n.* [< dim. of AS. *spang,* a clasp], 1. a small piece of bright metal, especially one of many sewed on fabric for decoration. 2. any small, bright object. *v.t.* [-GLED, -GLING], to decorate with spangles. *v.i.* to glitter as with spangles. —**span'gly** [-GLIER, -GLIEST], *adj.*
**Span·iard** (span'yẽrd), *n.* a native or inhabitant of Spain.
**span·iel** (span'yəl), *n.* [< OFr. *espagneul,* Spanish dog < Pr. < It. < *Spagna,* Spain], 1. any of several breeds of dog with a silky coat, large drooping ears, and short legs and tail. 2. a servile person.
**Span·ish** (span'ish), *adj.* of Spain, its people, their language, etc. *n.* 1. the Romance language of Spain and Spanish America. 2. the Spanish people.
**Spanish America,** Mexico and those countries in Central and South America in which chiefly Spanish is spoken.
**Span·ish-A·mer·i·can** (span'ish-ə-mer'ə-kən), *adj.* 1. of both Spain and America. 2. of Spanish America or its people. *n.* a native or inhabitant of Spanish America, especially one of Spanish descent.
**Spanish-American War,** the war between the U.S. and Spain (1898).
**Spanish Armada,** the Armada (sense 2).
**Spanish Inquisition,** the Inquisition in Spain, from 1478 to 1820: notorious for its cruel practices.
**Spanish Main,** 1. formerly, the mainland of America adjacent to the Caribbean Sea. 2. later, the Caribbean Sea.
**Spanish moss,** a mosslike plant growing in long strands from the branches of certain trees, especially in the southern U.S.: also **Florida moss.**
**spank** (spaŋk), *v.t.* [echoic], to strike with something flat, as the open hand, especially on the buttocks, as in punishment. *v.i.* to move along swiftly. *n.* a smart slap given in spanking.
**spank·er** (spaŋ'kẽr), *n.* 1. one that spanks. 2.

[Colloq.], a fast horse. 3. in *nautical usage, a)* a fore-and-aft sail on the aftermast of a square-rigged vessel. *b)* the aftermast and its sail on a schooner-rigged vessel of more than three masts.

**spank·ing** (spaŋ'kiŋ), *n.* an act of one who spanks; beating. *adj.* 1. swiftly moving; rapid. 2. brisk; strong, as a wind, etc. 3. [Colloq.], exceptionally fine, large, strong, etc.

**span·ner** (span'ẽr), *n.* 1. a person or thing that spans. 2. [Brit.], a wrench.

**Spar, SPAR** (spär), *n.* [< *semper paratus* (always prepared), L. motto of the Coast Guard], a member of the U.S. Coast Guard Women's Reserve (SPARS).

**spar** (spär), *n.* [< MD.], any shiny, crystalline mineral that cleaves easily into chips or flakes. **—spar'ry** [-RIER, -RIEST], *adj.*

**spar** (spär), *n.* [< ON. *sparri* or MD. *sparre*], 1. any pole, as a mast, yard, or boom, supporting or extending a sail on a ship. 2. a lengthwise structural member supporting the ribs of an airplane wing. *v.t.* [SPARRED, SPARRING], to equip with spars.

**spar** (spär), *v.i.* [SPARRED, SPARRING], [< OFr. < It. *sparare*, to kick < *parare*, to parry], 1. to fight with the feet and spurs: said of a fighting cock. 2. to box with caution, landing few heavy blows. 3. to wrangle or dispute. *n.* a sparring, boxing match, or dispute.

**spare** (spâr), *v.t.* [SPARED, SPARING], [AS. *sparian*], 1. to save; refrain from killing, injuring, distressing, etc. 2. to save or free (a person) from (something): as, *spare* me the trouble. 3. to omit, avoid using, or use frugally: as, don't *spare* your efforts. 4. to do without; dispense with; give up, as time or money. *v.i.* 1. to be frugal or sparing. 2. to be merciful, as in punishing. *adj.* 1. not in regular use or immediately needed; extra: as, a *spare* room. 2. not taken up by regular duties; free: said of time. 3. meager; scanty: as, *spare* rations. 4. lean; thin; not fleshy. *n.* 1. a spare, or extra, part, thing, etc. 2. in *bowling, a)* the act of knocking down all the pins with two rolls of the ball. *b)* a score so made. **—spare'ly,** *adv.* **—spare'ness,** *n.* **—spar'er,** *n.*

**spare·rib** (spâr'rib'), *n.* [prob. alt. < MLG. *ribbespẽr*], a cut of pork consisting of the thin end of the rib with most of the meat cut away.

**spar·ing** (spâr'iŋ), *adj.* 1. that spares. 2. careful; frugal. 3. scanty; meager. **—spar'ing·ly,** *adv.* **—spar'ing·ness,** *n.*

**spark** (spärk), *n.* [AS. *spearca*], 1. a small, glowing piece of matter, especially one thrown off by a fire. 2. any flash or sparkle of light like this. 3. a particle or trace: as, a *spark* of interest. 4. a trace of life or animation. 5. *a)* the small, brief flash of light accompanying the discharge of an electric current from one point to another. *b)* such a discharge, as in a spark plug. *v.i.* 1. to produce or give off sparks. 2. to come forth as or like sparks. *v.t.* to kindle or fire into activity. **—spark'er,** *n.*

**spark** (spärk), *n.* [< ON. *sparkr*, lively], 1. a dashing young man; gallant. 2. a beau or lover. *v.t. & v.i.* [Colloq.], to court; woo. **—spark'ish,** *adj.*

**spar·kle** (spär'k'l), *v.i.* [-KLED, -KLING], [freq. of *spark*], 1. to give off sparks. 2. to gleam intermittently; glitter, as jewels. 3. to be brilliant and lively. 4. to effervesce. *v.t.* to cause to sparkle. *n.* 1. a spark; glowing particle. 2. a sparkling, or glittering. 3. brilliance; vivacity.

**spar·kler** (spär'klẽr), *n.* a person or thing that sparkles; specif., *a)* a sparkling, pencil-shaped firework. *b) pl.* [Colloq.], bright, clear eyes. *c)* a diamond or other sparkling gem.

**sparkling water,** soda water.

**spark plug,** a piece fitted into a cylinder of an internal-combustion engine to ignite the fuel mixture within: it carries an electric current which sparks.

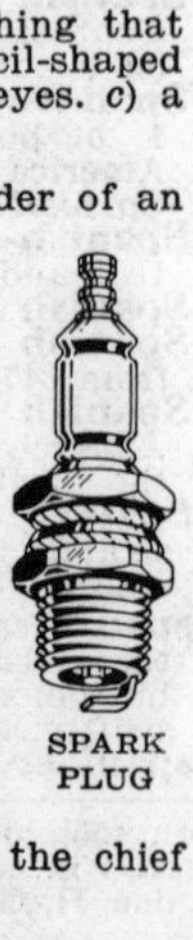

SPARK PLUG

**sparring partner,** any person with whom a prize fighter boxes for practice.

**spar·row** (spar'ō), *n.* [AS. *spearwa*], any of several small finches, especially the common small bird (**house sparrow**) known in America as the *English sparrow*: others are the *song sparrow, chipping sparrow,* etc.

**sparrow hawk,** 1. a small European hawk with short wings. 2. a small American falcon that feeds on insects and small birds and game.

**sparse** (spärs), *adj.* [< L. pp. of *spargere*, to scatter], thinly spread or distributed; not dense; meager. **—sparse'ly,** *adv.* **—spar'si·ty, sparse'ness,** *n.*

**Spar·ta** (spär'tə), *n.* in ancient Greece, the chief city of the Peloponnesus, in Laconia.

**Spar·tan** (spär't'n), *adj.* 1. of ancient Sparta, its people, or their culture. 2. like or characteristic of the Spartans; warlike, hardy, stoical, highly disciplined, etc. *n.* 1. a citizen of Sparta. 2. a person with Spartan traits. **—Spar'tan·ism,** *n.*

**spasm** (spaz'm), *n.* [< OFr. < L. < Gr. *spasma* < *spān*, to pull], 1. a sudden, abnormal, involuntary muscular contraction. 2. any sudden, violent, temporary activity, feeling, etc. **—spas'mic,** *adj.*

**spas·mod·ic** (spaz-mod'ik), *adj.* [< Gr. < *spasmos*, spasm + *eidos*, likeness], 1. of, like, or characterized by a spasm or spasms; fitful; intermittent. 2. characterized by excitability. Also **spas·mod'i·cal. —spas·mod'i·cal·ly,** *adv.*

**spas·tic** (spas'tik), *adj.* [< L. < Gr. *spastikos*, pulling < *spān*, to pull], of or characterized by spasm; specif., designating a form of paralysis in which certain muscles are continuously contracted, causing rigidity of a movable part. *n.* a person with spastic paralysis. **—spas'ti·cal·ly,** *adv.*

**spat** (spat), *n.* [prob. echoic], [Colloq.], 1. a slap. 2. a brief, petty quarrel or dispute. *v.i.* [SPATTED, SPATTING], 1. to slap. 2. to engage in a brief, petty quarrel or dispute. *v.t.* to slap.

**spat** (spat), *n.* [< *spatterdash*], *usually in pl.* a short gaiter covering the instep and ankle.

**spat** (spat), alt. pt. and pp. of **spit.**

**spat** (spat), *n.* [Anglo-Fr.], the spawn of the oyster or other bivalve mollusk. *v.i.* [SPATTED, SPATTING], to spawn: said of oysters.

**spate** (spāt), *n.* [? < OFr. *espoit*], 1. [Brit.], *a)* a flash flood. *b)* a sudden, heavy rain. 2. an unusually large outpouring, as of words.

**spathe** (spāth), *n.* [Fr. < L. < Gr. *spathē*, flat blade], a large, leaflike part or pair of such parts enclosing a flower cluster (especially a spadix).

SPATHE

**spa·tial** (spā'shəl), *adj.* [< L. *spatium*, space], 1. of space. 2. happening or existing in space. Also sp. **spacial. —spa'tial·ly,** *adv.*

**spat·ter** (spat'ẽr), *v.t.* [< LG.], 1. to scatter in drops or small blobs. 2. to splash with such drops or blobs. 3. to injure the reputation of; defame. *v.i.* 1. to spurt out in drops or small blobs, as a boiling liquid. 2. to fall as in a shower, as raindrops. *n.* 1. a spattering. 2. the sound of this. 3. a mark or wet spot caused by spattering. **—spat'ter·ing·ly,** *adv.*

**spat·ter·dash** (spat'ẽr-dash'), *n.* [*spatter* + *dash*], *usually in pl.* a long legging formerly worn to protect the leg from being splashed in wet weather.

**spat·u·la** (spach'oo-lə), *n.* [L., dim. of *spatha* < Gr. *spathē*, flat blade], a knifelike implement with a broad, flexible blade, used for spreading or blending foods, paints, etc. **—spat'u·lar,** *adj.*

**spav·in** (spav'in), *n.* [OFr. *esparvain*], a disease of horses in which a deposit of bone (*bone spavin*) or an infusion of lymph (*bog spavin*) develops in the hock joint, causing lameness. **—spav'ined,** *adj.*

**spawn** (spôn), *v.t. & v.i.* [< Anglo-Fr. < OFr. *espandre*, to shed < L.; see EXPAND], 1. to produce or deposit (spawn). 2. to bring forth (especially something produced prolifically): usually contemptuous. *n.* 1. the mass of eggs emitted by fishes, mollusks, amphibians, etc. 2. something produced, especially in great quantity, or some person or thing regarded as a product or offspring: usually contemptuous. **—spawn'er,** *n.*

**spay** (spā), *v.t.* [< Anglo-Fr. < OFr. < *espee*, sword < L. *spatha*, flat blade], to remove the ovaries of (a living animal); sterilize (a female).

**S.P.C.A.,** Society for Prevention of Cruelty to Animals.

**speak** (spēk), *v.i.* [SPOKE or *archaic* SPAKE, SPOKEN or *archaic* SPOKE, SPEAKING], [AS. *sp(r)ecan*], 1. to utter words with the ordinary voice; talk. 2. to communicate by or as by talking: as, actions *speak* louder than words. 3. to make a speech; discourse. 4. to converse. 5. to give out sound: as, the guns *spoke* sharply. *v.t.* 1. to make known by or as by speaking: as, he *speaks* the truth. 2. to use or be able to use (a given language) in speaking. 3. to utter orally, as words. 4. to speak to; address. **—so to speak,** that is to say. **—speak for,** 1. to speak in behalf of. 2. to ask for; reserve. **—speak of,** to talk about. **—speak out** (or **up**), 1. to speak audibly or clearly. 2. to speak freely, without hesitation. **—to speak of,** worthy of mention. **—speak'a·ble,** *adj.*

**speak-eas·y** (spēk'ēz'i), *n.* [*pl.* -IES], [so named because the orders are given quietly], [Slang], a place where alcoholic drinks are sold illegally.

**speak·er** (spēk'ẽr), *n.* 1. one who speaks; esp., *a*) one who makes a speech in public. *b*) the presiding officer of any of various lawmaking bodies; specif., [S-], the presiding officer of the U.S. House of Representatives: in full, **Speaker of the House.** 2. a loud-speaker. —**speak'er·ship'**, *n.*
**speak·ing** (spēk'iŋ), *adj.* 1. that speaks or seems to speak; expressive; vivid: as, a *speaking* likeness. 2. used in or for speech. 3. allowing or admitting of speech: as, within *speaking* range, on *speaking* terms. *n.* 1. the act or art of one who speaks. 2. utterance; discourse.
**spear** (spêr), *n.* [AS. *spere*], 1. a weapon consisting of a long shaft with a sharp head, for thrusting or throwing. 2. its pointed head. 3. any spearlike, often forked, implement for stabbing fish. 4. a spearman. 5. [var. of *spire* (stem)], a long blade or shoot, as of grass. *v.t.* 1. to pierce or stab as with a spear. 2. to catch, as fish, with a spear. *v.i.* 1. to pierce or shoot like a spear. 2. to sprout into a long stem. —**spear'er**, *n.*
**spear·head** (spêr'hed'), *n.* 1. the point or head of a spear. 2. the leading person, part, or group in an endeavor, especially in a military attack. *v.t.* to serve as the spearhead of (an attack, etc.).
**spear·man** (spêr'mən), *n.* [*pl.* -MEN], a fighting man armed with a spear.
**spear·mint** (spêr'mint'), *n.* [from its flower spikes], a fragrant plant of the mint family, used for flavoring.
**spec.,** 1. special. 2. specially. 3. specification.
**spe·cial** (spesh'əl), *adj.* [< OFr. < L. < *species*, kind], 1. of a kind different from others; distinctive or unique: as, a *special* case. 2. exceptional; extraordinary: as, of *special* merit. 3. especial; chief: as, her *special* friend. 4. of or for a particular occasion, purpose, etc.: as, a *special* edition. 5. not general or regular; specific: as, *special* legislation. 6. specified; definite: as, do you want any *special* kind? *n.* a special person or thing, as a special train. —**spe'cial·ly**, *adv.* —**spe'cial·ness**, *n.*
**special delivery,** the delivery of mail by a special messenger, for an extra fee.
**spe·cial·ist** (spesh'əl-ist), *n.* one who specializes in a particular field of study, work, etc. —**spe'cial·ism,** *n.* —**spe'cial·is'tic**, *adj.*
**spe·ci·al·i·ty** (spesh'i-al'ə-ti), *n.* [*pl.* -TIES], 1. a special or distinctive mark or quality. 2. *pl.* special points or details. 3. a specialty.
**spe·cial·ize** (spesh'ə-līz'), *v.t.* [-IZED, -IZING], 1. to make specific or particular; specify: as, *specialize* your accusation. 2. to direct toward a specific end. 3. to adapt to a special condition, use, or requirement. *v.i.* 1. to concentrate on a special branch of a subject, etc. 2. to become adapted to a special condition, use, etc., as parts of an organism. —**spe'cial·i·za'tion**, *n.*
**spe·cial·ty** (spesh'əl-ti), *n.* [*pl.* -TIES], 1. a special quality, feature, characteristic, etc. 2. a special interest, study, work, etc. 3. a being special. 4. an article or kind of articles having special features superior quality, etc.: as, steaks are our *specialty.*
**spe·cie** (spē'shi), *n.* [abl. of L. *species*: cf. use in phr. below], coin, as distinguished from paper money. —**in specie**, 1. in kind. 2. in coin.
**spe·cies** (spē'shiz), *n.* [*pl.* SPECIES], [L., appearance, shape, kind, etc.], 1. a distinct kind; sort; variety; class. 2. a single, distinct kind of plant or animal, having certain distinguishing characteristics: a biological classification: cf. **genus.** 3. outward form, appearance, etc., as of the elements of the Eucharist. —**the species,** the human race.
**specif.,** specifically.
**spe·cif·ic** (spi-sif'ik), *adj.* [< ML. *specificus;* cf. SPECIFY], 1. specifying or specified; precise; definite; explicit. 2. of a species. 3. peculiar to or characteristic of something, as traits. 4. of a particular sort or kind. 5. *a*) specially indicated as a cure for a particular disease, as a remedy. *b*) produced by a particular microorganism, as a disease. *n.* 1. something specially suited for a given use or purpose. 2. a specific cure or remedy. —**spe·cif'i·cal·ly,** *adv.* —**spec·i·fic·i·ty** (spes'ə-fis'ə-ti), **spe·cif'ic·ness**, *n.*
**spec·i·fi·ca·tion** (spes'ə-fi-kā'shən), *n.* 1. a specifying; detailed mention. 2. *usually pl.* a statement or enumeration of particulars, as to size, quality, terms, etc.: as, *specifications* for a building. 3. something specified; specified item, etc.
**specific gravity,** the ratio of the weight or mass of a given volume of a substance to that of an equal volume of another substance (water for liquids and solids, air or hydrogen for gases) used as a standard.
**spec·i·fy** (spes'ə-fī'), *v.t.* [-FIED, -FYING], [< OFr. < ML. < L. *species*, kind + *facere*, to make], 1. to mention or describe in detail; state definitely or explicitly. 2. to include as an item in a set of specifications. —**spec'i·fi'a·ble**, *adj.* —**spec'i·fi'er**, *n.*
**spec·i·men** (spes'ə-mən), *n.* [L. < *specere*, to see], 1. a part of a whole, or one individual of a group, used as a sample of the rest. 2. [Colloq.], a (specified kind of) individual: as, a fine *specimen.* 3. [Colloq.], a sample of urine for analysis.
**spe·cious** (spē'shəs), *adj.* [< L. *speciosus* < *species*, appearance], seeming to be good, sound, correct, etc. without really being so. —**spe'cious·ly**, *adv.* —**spe'cious·ness**, *n.*
**speck** (spek), *n.* [AS. *specca*], 1. a small spot, mark, or stain. 2. a very small bit; particle. *v.t.* to mark with specks; spot.
**speck·le** (spek''l), *n.* [dim. of *speck*], a small mark; speck. *v.t.* [-LED, -LING], to mark with speckles.
**specs** (speks), *n.pl.* [Colloq.], eyeglasses.
**spec·ta·cle** (spek'tə-k'l), *n.* [< OFr. < L. *spectare*, freq. of *specere*, to see], 1. something to look at, especially some remarkable sight. 2. a public show on a grand scale. 3. *pl.* a pair of eyeglasses worn to aid the vision, shield the eyes, etc.: often **a pair of spectacles.** 4. *usually pl.* something like a pair of spectacles in shape, use, etc. —**spec'ta·cled** (-k'ld), *adj.*
**spec·tac·u·lar** (spek-tak'yoo-lẽr), *adj.* 1. of or like a spectacle, or show. 2. unusual to a striking or wonderful degree. *n.* an elaborate, extended television production, usually in color. —**spec·tac'u·lar'i·ty**, *n.* —**spec·tac'u·lar·ly**, *adv.*
**spec·ta·tor** (spek'tā-tẽr, spek-tā'-), *n.* [L. < *spectare*, to behold], one who watches without taking an active part; onlooker.
**spec·ter** (spek'tẽr), *n.* [< Fr. < L. *spectrum*, apparition < *spectare*, to behold], a ghost; apparition: also, Brit. spelling, **spectre.**
**spec·tra** (spek'trə), alt. pl. of **spectrum.**
**spec·tral** (spek'trəl), *adj.* 1. of or like a specter; ghostly. 2. of or caused by a spectrum. —**spec·tral'i·ty, spec'tral·ness**, *n.* —**spec'tral·ly**, *adv.*
**spec·tro-**, [< *spectrum*], a combining form meaning: 1. *of radiant energy as exhibited in a spectrum.* 2. *of* or *by a spectroscope.*
**spec·tro·scope** (spek'trə-skōp'), *n.* [*spectro-* + *-scope*], an optical instrument used for forming spectra for study. —**spec'tro·scop'ic** (-skop'ik), **spec'tro·scop'i·cal**, *adj.* —**spec'tro·scop'i·cal·ly**, *adv.*
**spec·tros·co·py** (spek-tros'kə-pi, spek'trə-skō'pi), *n.* the study of spectra through the use of the spectroscope. —**spec·tros'co·pist**, *n.*
**spec·trum** (spek'trəm), *n.* [*pl.* -TRA (-trə), -TRUMS], [< L.; see SPECTER], 1. a series of colored bands diffracted and arranged in order of their respective wave lengths, from red (produced by the longest) to violet (produced by the shortest), by the passage of white light through a prism, etc. 2. any of various arrangements of color bands, with invisible components at both ends of the spectrum, similarly formed by various sources of radiant energy. 3. an afterimage. 4. in *radio*, the range of wave lengths of radio waves, from 3 centimeters to 30,000 meters: also **radio spectrum.**

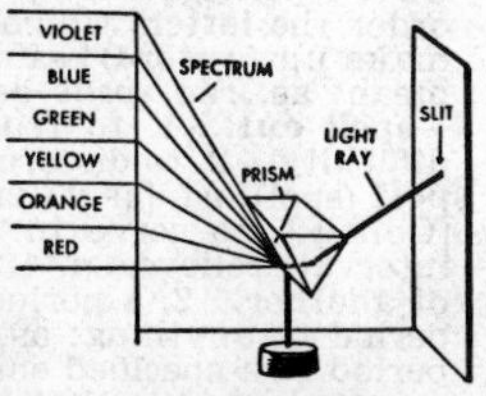

SPECTRUM

**spec·u·late** (spek'yoo-lāt'), *v.i.* [-LATED, -LATING], [< L. pp. < *specula*, watch tower < *specere*, to see], 1. to think about the various aspects of a given subject; ponder; esp., to conjecture. 2. to take part in any risky business venture on the chance of making huge profits. —**spec'u·la'tor**, *n.*
**spec·u·la·tion** (spek'yoo-lā'shən), *n.* 1. a pondering; thought; esp., conjecture. 2. a speculating in stocks, land, etc. 3. a speculative business venture.
**spec·u·la·tive** (spek'yoo-lā'tiv, -lə-tiv), *adj.* 1. of, characterized by, or indulging in speculation. 2. theoretical, not practical. 3. of or characterized by financial speculation. 4. risky. Also **spec'u·la·to'·ry** (-lə-tôr'i, -tō'ri). —**spec'u·la'tive·ly**, *adv.* —**spec'u·la'tive·ness**, *n.*
**spec·u·lum** (spek'yoo-ləm), *n.* [*pl.* -LA (-lə), -LUMS], [L. < *specere*, to look], 1. a mirror, especially one of polished metal used as a reflector in a telescope, etc. 2. in *medicine & surgery*, an instrument for

dilating a passage to facilitate its examination. —**spec′u·lar** (-lẽr), *adj.*
**sped** (sped), alt. pt. and pp. of **speed.**
**speech** (spēch), *n.* [< AS. *sp(r)æc* < base of *sprecan*, to speak], 1. the act of speaking. 2. the power or ability to speak. 3. the manner of speaking. 4. that which is spoken; utterance, remark, etc. 5. a talk given in public. 6. the language of a certain people. 7. the study of oral expression and communication.
**speech·i·fy** (spē′chə-fī′), *v.i.* [-FIED, -FYING], to make a speech or speeches: used humorously or contemptuously. —**speech′i·fi′er,** *n.*
**speech·less** (spēch′lis), *adj.* 1. incapable of speech. 2. silent, as from shock. 3. not expressed or expressible in words: as, *speechless* terror. —**speech′less·ly,** *adv.* —**speech′less·ness,** *n.*
**speed** (spēd), *n.* [AS. *sped*, success], 1. the act or state of moving rapidly; swiftness. 2. rate of movement; velocity: as, what was his *speed?* 3. an arrangement of gears for the drive of an engine: as, a truck with five forward *speeds*. 4. [Archaic], luck; success. *v.i.* [SPED or SPEEDED, SPEEDING], 1. to move rapidly, especially too rapidly. 2. [Archaic], to prosper; succeed. *v.t.* 1. to help to succeed; further; aid. 2. to wish Godspeed to. 3. to cause to go, move, etc. swiftly. 4. to increase the speed of. —**speed up,** to increase in speed.
**speed·boat** (spēd′bōt′), *n.* a motorboat designed for speed.
**speed·er** (spēd′ẽr), *n.* a person or thing that speeds; esp., one who drives a motor vehicle at a higher speed than is safe or legal.
**speed·om·e·ter** (spi-dom′ə-tẽr), *n.* 1. a device attached to an automobile, etc. to indicate speed. 2. loosely, an odometer.
**speed·ster** (spēd′stẽr), *n.* one who speeds.
**speed-up** (spēd′up′), *n.* the act of speeding up; increase in speed, output, etc.
**speed·way** (spēd′wā′), *n.* 1. a track for racing automobiles. 2. a road built for high-speed traffic.
**speed·well** (spēd′wel), *n.* any of various plants with compact clusters of white, blue, or violet flowers.
**speed·y** (spēd′i), *adj.* [-IER, -IEST], 1. rapid; swift. 2. without delay; quick; prompt: as, a *speedy* reply. —**speed′i·ly,** *adv.* —**speed′i·ness,** *n.*
**spe·le·ol·o·gy** (spē′li-ol′ə-ji), *n.* [< L. < Gr. *spelaion*, a cave], the science of exploring caves. —**spe′le·ol′o·gist,** *n.*
**spell** (spel), *n.* [AS. *spel*, a saying], 1. a word or formula supposed to have some magic power. 2. magical power or irresistible influence; charm; fascination. —**cast a spell on,** to enchant. —**under a spell,** enchanted.
**spell** (spel), *v.t.* [SPELLED or SPELT, SPELLING], [< OFr. *espeler* < Gmc.], 1. to name, write, etc. in order the letters which make up (a word). 2. to make up (a word): said of specified letters. 3. to mean: as, red *spells* danger. *v.i.* to spell words. —**spell out,** 1. to read letter by letter or with difficulty. 2. to discern as if by close reading.
**spell** (spel), *v.t.* [SPELLED, SPELLING], [AS. *spelian*], [Colloq.], to serve in place of (another) for an interval; relieve. *n.* 1. a turn of serving in place of another. 2. a period of work, duty, etc. 3. a period of anything: as, a *spell* of brooding. 4. a period of a specified sort of weather. 5. [Colloq.], a period of time that is indefinite, short, etc. 6. [Colloq.], a short distance. 7. [Colloq.], a fit of illness, indisposition, etc.
**spell·bind** (spel′bīnd′), *v.t.* [-BOUND, -BINDING], to cause to be spellbound; to fascinate; enchant. —**spell′bind′er,** *n.*
**spell·bound** (spel′bound′), *adj.* held by or as by a spell; fascinated; enchanted.
**spell·down** (spel′doun′), *n.* a spelling bee.
**spell·er** (spel′ẽr), *n.* 1. a person who spells words. 2. an exercise book used to teach spelling.
**spell·ing** (spel′iŋ), *n.* 1. the act of forming words from letters. 2. the study of this. 3. the way in which a word is spelled.
**spelling bee,** a contest in spelling.
**spelt** (spelt), *n.* alt. pt. and pp. of *spell* (to name the letters of).
**spelt** (spelt), *n.* [AS. < LL. *spelta*], a hard-grained kind of wheat, or any of its varieties.
**spe·lunk·er** (spi-luŋ′kẽr), *n.* [< L. *spelunca*, a cave], a person whose hobby is speleology.
**Spen·cer, Herbert** (spen′sẽr), 1820–1903; English philosopher.
**spend** (spend), *v.t.* [SPENT, SPENDING], [< AS. *spendan* < L. *expendere*, to expend], 1. to use up, exhaust, etc.: as, his fury was *spent*. 2. to pay out (money); disburse. 3. to give or devote, as time, labor, etc., to something. 4. to pass (time): as, he *spent* an hour here. 5. to waste; squander. *v.i.* to pay out or use up money, etc. —**spend′a·ble,** *adj.* —**spend′er,** *n.*
**spend·thrift** (spend′thrift′), *n.* one who spends money carelessly; squanderer. *adj.* wasteful.
**Spen·ser, Edmund** (spen′sẽr), 1552?–1599; English poet.
**spent** (spent), pt. and pp. of **spend.** *adj.* 1. tired out; physically exhausted. 2. used up; worn out.
**sperm** (spũrm), *n.* [< OFr. < LL. < Gr. *sperma*, seed < *speirein*, to sow], 1. the male generative fluid; semen. 2. any of the germ cells in this fluid.
**sperm** (spũrm), *n.* 1. spermaceti. 2. sperm oil. 3. a sperm whale.
**-sperm** (spũrm), [see SPERM (fluid)], a combining form meaning *seed*, as in *gymnosperm*.
**sper·ma·ce·ti** (spũr′mə-set′i, -sē′ti), *n.* [ML. < LL. *sperma*, sperm + L. genit. of *cetus*, a whale], a white, waxlike substance taken from the oil in the head of a sperm whale, dolphin, etc., used in making cosmetics, ointments, candles, etc.
**sper·mat·ic** (spẽr-mat′ik), *adj.* of or having to do with sperm or sperm cells; generative.
**sper·ma·to-,** [< Gr. *sperma*, a seed], a combining form meaning *seed* or *sperm*: also **spermat-, sperm-.**
**sper·ma·to·phyte** (spũr′mə-tə-fīt′), *n.* [< *spermato-* + Gr. *phyton*, a plant], any seed-bearing plant. —**sper′ma·to·phyt′ic** (-fit′ik), *adj.*
**sper·ma·to·zo·on** (spũr′mə-tə-zō′on), *n.* [*pl.* -ZOA (-zō′ə)], [< *spermato-* + Gr. *zōion*, animal], the male germ cell, found in semen, which penetrates the egg of the female to fertilize it. —**sper′ma·to·zo′al, sper′ma·to·zo′an, sper′ma·to·zo′ic,** *adj.*
**sper·mic** (spũr′mik), *adj.* of or having to do with sperm: also **sper′mous** (-məs).
**sperm oil,** a valuable lubricating oil taken from the head of the sperm whale.
**-sper·mous** (spũr′məs), a combining form meaning *having* (a specified number or kind of) *seed*: also **-sper′mal** (-m′l).
**sperm whale,** a large, toothed whale inhabiting the warm seas: a closed cavity in its square head contains spermaceti and sperm oil.
**spew** (spū), *v.t. & v.i.* [AS. *spiwan*], to throw up from or as from the stomach; vomit; eject: also sp. **spue.** *n.* something spewed. —**spew′er,** *n.*
**sp. gr.,** specific gravity.
**sphag·num** (sfag′nəm), *n.* [< Gr. *sphagnos*, kind of moss], 1. any of various grayish mosses found in bogs; peat moss. 2. a mass of such mosses, used to pack and pot plants, to make surgical dressings, etc. —**sphag′nous** (-nəs), *adj.*
**sphal·er·ite** (sfal′ẽr-īt′), *n.* [< Gr. *sphaleros*, deceptive], native zinc sulfide, ZnS, the principal ore of zinc, usually brownish.
**sphe·noid** (sfē′noid), *adj.* [Gr. *sphēn*, a wedge; + *-oid*], in *anatomy*, designating or of the wedge-shaped compound bone at the base of the skull: also **sphe·noi′dal.** *n.* the sphenoid bone.
**sphere** (sfêr), *n.* [< OFr. < L. < Gr. *sphaira*], 1. any round body having the surface equally distant from the center at all points; globe; ball. 2. a star or planet. 3. the visible heavens; sky. 4. the celestial sphere. 5. the place or range of action or existence; field of knowledge, experience, etc. 6. place in society; walk of life. *v.t.* [SPHERED, SPHERING], 1. to put in or as in a sphere. 2. to put among the heavenly spheres. 3. to form into a sphere. —**sphere′less,** *adj.*
**-sphere** (sfêr), a combining form meaning *a sphere* or *like a sphere*, as in *stratosphere*.
**spher·i·cal** (sfer′i-k′l), *adj.* 1. shaped like a sphere; globular. 2. of a sphere or spheres. 3. of the heavenly spheres. Also **spher′ic.** —**spher′i·cal·ly,** *adv.* —**sphe·ric·i·ty** (sfi-ris′ə-ti), **spher·i·cal·i·ty** (sfer′i-kal′ə-ti), **spher′i·cal·ness,** *n.*
**sphe·roid** (sfêr′oid), *n.* a body that is almost but not quite a perfect sphere. —**sphe·roi·dal** (sfi-roi′d′l), *adj.* —**sphe′roi·dic′i·ty** (-oi-dis′ə-ti), **sphe·roi′di·ty,** *n.*
**sphinc·ter** (sfiŋk′tẽr), *n.* [LL. < Gr. *sphinktēr* < *sphingein*, to draw close], in *anatomy*, a ring-shaped muscle that can open or close a natural opening in the body by expanding or contracting. —**sphinc′ter·al,** *adj.*
**sphinx** (sfiŋks), *n.* [*pl.* SPHINXES, SPHINGES (sfin′jēz)], [L. < Gr. *sphinx*, the strangler], 1. any Egyptian statue having a lion's body and the head of a man, ram, or hawk; specif., [S-], such a statue with the head of a man, near Cairo, Egypt. 2. in *Gr. mythology*, a winged monster with a lion's body and the head and breasts of a woman; specif., [S-], such a monster near Thebes, that asked a riddle of every passer-by, strangling all who could not answer. 3. a person whose manner or expression suggests that his character is deep and mysterious. —**sphinx′like′,** *adj.*

**sphyg·mo·ma·nom·e·ter** (sfig′mō-mə-nom′ə-tẽr), *n.* [< Gr. *sphygmos;* + *manometer*], an instrument for measuring arterial blood pressure.

**spi·cate** (spī′kāt), *adj.* [< L. *spicatus*, spiked], in *botany*, 1. spikelike in form. 2. arranged in a spike or spikes. Also **spi′cat·ed.**

**spice** (spīs), *n.* [< OFr. *espice* < L. *species*, sort], 1. *a*) any of several vegetable substances, as clove, nutmeg, pepper, etc., used to season food. *b*) such substances collectively. 2. a spicy fragrance or aroma. 3. that which gives zest or piquancy. 4. a small bit; trace. *v.t.* [SPICED, SPICING], 1. to season or flavor with spice. 2. to add zest or piquancy to. —**spice′like′,** *adj.*

**spice·bush** (spīs′boosh′), *n.* a shrub with small, yellowish flowers and red fruit: also **spice′wood′** (-wood′).

**Spice Islands,** the Molucca Islands.

**spick-and-span** (spik′′n-span′), *adj.* [< *spick*, var. of *spike*, a nail + *span-new* < ON. < *spānn*, a chip + *nȳr*, new], 1. new; fresh. 2. neat and clean; tidy.

**spic·ule** (spik′ūl), *n.* [Fr. < L. dim. of *spica*, a point], 1. a small, hard, sharp-pointed, needlelike piece or process, especially of bony or calcareous material, as in the skeleton of the sponge: also **spic′u·lum** [*pl.* -LA (-lə)]. 2. a small spike of flowers. —**spic′u·late′, spic′u·lar,** *adj.*

**spic·y** (spī′si), *adj.* [-IER, -IEST], 1. containing or full of spices. 2. having the flavor or aroma of spices. 3. piquant; pungent; zestful. 4. risqué; racy. —**spic′i·ly,** *adv.* —**spic′i·ness,** *n.*

**spi·der** (spī′dẽr), *n.* [ME. *spithre* < AS. *spinnan*, to spin], 1. any of various small arachnids with a body composed of a cephalothorax bearing four pairs of legs and an abdomen bearing spinnerets used to spin the silk threads for webs to trap insects. 2. a trivet. 3. a frying pan, originally one with legs. —**spi′der·y,** *adj.*

**spider monkey,** a monkey of South and Central America having long, spidery limbs.

**spi·der·wort** (spī′dẽr-wũrt′), *n.* any of various related plants with grasslike leaves and blue or purplish flowers.

**spiel** (spēl), *n.* [G., play], [Slang], a talk or speech; esp., a harangue, as in selling or promoting something. *v.i.* [Slang], to engage in a spiel. —**spiel′er,** *n.*

**spi·er** (spī′ẽr), *n.* a person who spies; spy.

**spiff·y** (spif′i), *adj.* [-IER, -IEST], [< dial. *spiff*, well-dressed person], [Slang], smart; neat; spruce.

**spig·ot** (spig′ət), *n.* [ME. *spigote*], 1. a plug or peg used to stop the vent in a cask, etc. 2. a faucet.

**spike** (spīk), *n.* [prob. < ON. *spikr*], 1. a sharp-pointed part or projection, as along the top of an iron fence or, in *pl.*, on the soles of shoes used for golf, track, etc. to prevent slipping. 2. a long, heavy nail. *v.t.* [SPIKED, SPIKING], 1. to fasten or fit as with a spike or spikes. 2. to pierce, cut, etc. with a spike or spikes, or impale on a spike. 3. to thwart or block, as a scheme. 4. [Slang], to add alcoholic liquor to (a drink). —**spik′er,** *n.* —**spik′y** [-IER, -IEST], *adj.*

**spike** (spīk), *n.* [L. *spica*], 1. an ear of grain. 2. a long flower cluster with the flowers attached directly to the stalk. —**spike′let,** *n.*

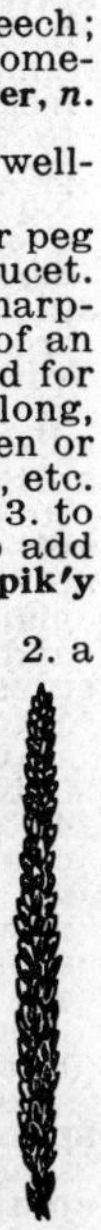
SPIKE

**spike·nard** (spīk′nẽrd, -närd), *n.* [< L. *spica*, ear of grain + *nardus*, nard], 1. a fragrant ointment used by the ancients. 2. the East Indian plant that yielded it.

**spile** (spīl), *n.* [MD., a splinter], 1. a plug or spigot, as for a barrel. 2. a tap driven into a maple tree to draw off sap. 3. a heavy stake driven into the ground as a support. *v.t.* [SPILED, SPILING], 1. to furnish with spiles, or stakes. 2. to set a spile into (a tree, barrel, etc.). 3. to stop up (a hole) with a spile, or plug.

**spill** (spil), *v.t.* [SPILLED or SPILT (spilt), SPILLING], [AS. *spillan*, to destroy], 1. to allow (a fluid substance), especially in an unintentional way, to run, scatter, or flow over from a container. 2. to shed (blood). 3. to empty the wind from (a sail). 4. [Colloq.], to make known (something secret); divulge. 5. [Colloq.], to throw off (a rider, load, etc.). *v.i.* to be spilled from a container; overflow; run out. *n.* 1. a spilling. 2. the amount spilled. 3. a spillway. 4. [Colloq.], a fall, as from a horse, etc. —**spill′er,** *n.*

**spill** (spil), *n.* [var. of *spile*], 1. a splinter. 2. a thin roll of paper, slender stick, etc. to be lighted in a fire and used as a match.

**spill·way** (spil′wā′), *n.* [*spill*, *v.* + *way*], a channel to carry off excess water, as from a reservoir.

**spin** (spin), *v.t.* [SPUN or *archaic* SPAN, SPUN, SPINNING], [AS. *spinnan*], 1. to draw out and twist fibers of (wool, cotton, etc.) into thread. 2. to make (thread, yarn, etc.) by this process. 3. to make (a web, cocoon, etc.) from a viscous fluid that is extruded from the body and hardens on exposure to air: said of spiders, etc. 4. to make in a way suggestive of spinning. 5. to tell (a story, yarn, etc.), especially slowly and with many details: often with *out.* 6. to cause to whirl swiftly: as, to *spin* a top. *v.i.* 1. to spin thread or yarn. 2. to form a thread, web, etc.: said of spiders, etc. 3. to whirl, as a top. 4. to seem to be spinning from dizziness. 5. to move along swiftly and smoothly. *n.* 1. a whirling movement. 2. the act of causing such movement. 3. a moving along swiftly and smoothly. 4. a swift ride in a vehicle. 5. a maneuver in which an airplane comes down nose first along a spiral path.

**spin·ach** (spin′ich, -ij), *n.* [< OFr. < ML. < Sp. *espinaca* < Ar. *isbānah*], 1. a plant of the goosefoot family, with large, dark-green, juicy, edible leaves, usually eaten cooked. 2. its leaves.

**spi·nal** (spī′n'l), *adj.* of the spine or spinal cord. *n.* spinal anesthesia. —**spi′nal·ly,** *adv.*

**spinal anesthesia,** local anesthesia of the lower half of the body by the injection of an anesthetic into the lumbar portion of the spinal cord.

**spinal column,** the series of joined vertebrae forming the axial support for the skeleton; spine.

**spinal cord,** the thick cord of nerve tissue of the central nervous system, in the spinal column.

**spin·dle** (spin′d'l), *n.* [< AS. < *spinnan*, to spin], 1. any of various rods or pins used in hand spinning, on spinning wheels, or in a spinning machine, for twisting, winding, or holding the thread. 2. something with the long, slender shape of a spindle. 3. any rod, pin, or shaft that revolves or serves as an axis for a revolving part. 4. a small axis, axle, mandrel, etc. 5. in a lathe, a shaftlike part that rotates (*live spindle*) or does not rotate (*dead spindle*) while holding the thing to be turned. 6. an easily visible metal rod, pipe, etc. fastened to a rock, shoal, etc. as a warning to vessels. *adj.* of or like a spindle. *v.i.* [-DLED, -DLING], to grow in or into long, slender form. *v.t.* to form into a spindle. —**spin′dle·like′,** *adj.*

**spin·dle·legs** (spin′d'l-legz′), *n.pl.* 1. thin legs. 2. [construed as sing.], [Colloq.], a person with thin legs. Also **spin′dle·shanks′** (-shaŋks′). —**spin′dle-leg′ged** (-leg′id, -legd′), **spin′dle-shanked′,** *adj.*

**spin·dling** (spin′dliŋ), *adj.* slender in proportion to length or height. *n.* a spindling person or thing.

**spin·dly** (spin′dli), *adj.* [-DLIER, -DLIEST], spindling. —**spin′dli·ness,** *n.*

**spin·drift** (spin′drift′), *n.* [alt. < *spoondrift* < earlier *spoom* (? < L. *spuma*, foam) + *drift*], spray blown from a rough sea or surf.

**spine** (spīn), *n.* [< OFr. < L. *spina*, a thorn], 1. any of the short, sharp, woody projections on certain plants, as the cactus. 2. any of the sharp, stiff projections on certain animals, as the quill of a porcupine. 3. anything resembling either of these projections. 4. the spinal column; backbone. 5. anything regarded as resembling a backbone, as the back of a bound book.

**spi·nel** (spi-nel′, spin′′l), *n.* [< Fr. < It. < L. *spina*, spine], a hard, crystalline mineral found in various colors: a red variety (**spinel ruby**) is used as a gem: also sp. **spinelle.**

**spine·less** (spīn′lis), *adj.* 1. having no backbone; invertebrate. 2. having a weak or flexible backbone. 3. lacking moral fiber; without courage or will power. 4. without spines, or thorny processes. —**spine′less·ly,** *adv.* —**spine′less·ness,** *n.*

**spin·et** (spin′it), *n.* [< OFr. < It.; prob. < G. *Spinetti* (c. 1500), It. inventor], 1. an obsolete, small harpsichord. 2. a small upright piano.

**spin·na·ker** (spin′ə-kẽr), *n.* [prob. alt. < *spanker*], a large, triangular sail on racing yachts, set from a boom on the side opposite the main boom and used especially when running before the wind.

**spin·ner** (spin′ẽr), *n.* a person or thing that spins, as, *a*) one who spins yarn, etc. *b*) a shiny fish lure that spins when drawn through the water.

**spin·ner·et** (spin′ẽr-et′), *n.* [dim. of *spinner*], an organ used by spiders, caterpillars, etc. in spinning their threads.

**spin·ning** (spin′iŋ), *n.* the act of making thread or yarn from fibers or filaments. *adj.* that spins.

**spinning jenny,** a spinning machine with a number of spindles, for spinning many threads at a time.
**spinning wheel,** a primitive spinning machine with a single spindle driven by a large wheel.

SPINNING WHEEL

**spin-off** (spin'ôf'), *n.* 1. the distribution to its shareholders by a parent corporation of the stock it holds in a subsidiary corporation. 2. a secondary benefit, product, etc.
**spi·nose** (spī'nōs), *adj.* [< L. < *spina*, spine], covered with spines or thorns: also **spi'nous** (-nəs). —**spi'nose·ly,** *adv.* —**spi·nos'i·ty** (-nos'ə-ti), *n.*
**Spi·no·za, Ba·ruch** or **Benedict** (bä'rookh spi-nō'zə), 1632–1677; Dutch philosopher.
**spin·ster** (spin'stẽr), *n.* [ME. < *spinnen*, to spin; + *-ster*], 1. a woman who spins thread or yarn. 2. an unmarried woman, especially an older one; old maid.—**spin'ster·hood',** *n.* —**spin'ster·ish,** *adj.*
**spin·y** (spīn'i), *adj.* [-IER, -IEST], 1. covered with spines or thorns. 2. full of difficulties; troublesome. 3. spine-shaped. —**spin'i·ness,** *n.*
**spiny anteater,** the echidna.
**spi·ra·cle** (spī'rə-k'l, spir'ə-), *n.* [< L. *spiraculum* < *spirare*, to breathe], an air hole; specif., in *zoology*, an opening for respiration, as the blowhole of a whale or one of the tracheal openings of arthropods. —**spi·rac'u·lar** (-rak'yoo-lẽr), *adj.*
**spi·rae·a, spi·re·a** (spī-rē'ə), *n.* [L. < Gr. < *speira*, a coil], any of various shrubs of the rose family, with clusters of small pink or white flowers.
**spi·ral** (spī'rəl), *adj.* [< ML. < L. *spira*, a coil < Gr. *speira*], 1. circling or coiling continuously around a point or center in curves that constantly increase (or decrease) in size. 2. coiled or coiling in constantly changing planes; helical. *n.* 1. a spiral curve or coil. 2. something having a spiral form. 3. a spiral path or flight. 4. a section of a spiral. 5. a continuous, widening decrease or increase: as, an inflationary *spiral*. *v.i.* & *v.t.* [-RALED or -RALLED, -RALING or -RALLING], to move in or form (into) a spiral. —**spi'ral·ly,** *adv.*

SPIRAL

**spi·rant** (spī'rənt), *n.* & *adj.* [< L. ppr. of *spirare*, to breathe], fricative.
**spire** (spīr), *n.* [AS. *spir*], 1. a sprout, spike, or stalk of a plant, blade of grass, etc. 2. the top part of a pointed, tapering object or structure, as a mountain peak. 3. anything that tapers to a point, as a steeple. *v.i.* [SPIRED, SPIRING], to extend upward, tapering to a point.
**spir·it** (spir'it), *n.* [< OFr. < L. *spiritus*, breath < *spirare*, to breathe], 1. *a)* the life principle, especially in man. *b)* the soul. 2. the thinking, feeling part of man; mind; intelligence. 3. [also S-], life, will, thought, etc., regarded as separate from matter. 4. a supernatural being, as a ghost, angel, demon, fairy, etc. 5. an individual person or personality: as, he is a brave *spirit*. 6. *often pl.* disposition; mood: as, high *spirits*. 7. vivacity, courage, enthusiasm, etc. 8. enthusiastic loyalty: as, school *spirit*. 9. real meaning; true intention: as, to follow the *spirit* if not the letter of the law. 10. a pervading animating principle, essential quality, etc.: as, the *spirit* of the Renaissance. 11. *often pl.* distilled alcoholic liquor. 12. *also pl.* any liquid produced by distillation. 13. an alcoholic solution of a volatile substance: as, *spirits* of camphor. *v.t.* 1. to inspirit, encourage, cheer, etc. 2. to carry (*away* or *off*) secretly and swiftly. *adj.* 1. of spirits or spiritualism. 2. operating by the burning of alcohol: as, a *spirit* lamp. —**out of spirits,** sad; depressed. —**the Spirit,** the Holy Ghost. —**spir'it·less,** *adj.* —**spir'it·less·ly,** *adv.*
**spir·it·ed** (spir'i-tid), *adj.* 1. having a (specified) character, mood, or disposition: as, *evil-spirited*. 2. full of spirit; lively; vigorous; animated. —**spir'it·ed·ly,** *adv.* —**spir'it·ed·ness,** *n.*
**spirit level,** a glass tube held in a frame and containing a liquid, usually alcohol, with a bubble in it: when the frame is on a level surface the bubble moves to the center of the tube.
**spir·it·u·al** (spir'i-chōō-əl, -chool), *adj.* 1. of the spirit or soul, in a religious or moral aspect. 2. of or consisting of spirit; not corporeal. 3. refined in thought and feeling. 4. of religion or the church; sacred, devotional, etc. 5. spiritualistic or supernatural. *n.* 1. a religious folk song of American Negro origin. 2. *pl.* church matters. —**spir'it·u·al'i·ty** (-chōō-al'ə-ti), [*pl.* -TIES], *n.* —**spir'it·u·al·ly,** *adv.*
**spir·it·u·al·ism** (spir'i-chōō-əl-iz'm, -choo-liz'm), *n.* 1. the belief that the dead survive as spirits which can communicate with the living, especially with the help of a medium. 2. the philosophical doctrine that all reality is in essence spiritual. 3. spirituality; spiritual quality, etc. —**spir'it·u·al·ist,** *n.* —**spir'it·u·al·is'tic,** *adj.* —**spir'it·u·al·is'ti·cal·ly,** *adv.*
**spir·it·u·al·ize** (spir'i-chōō-ə-līz', -choo-līz'), *v.t.* [-IZED, -IZING], 1. to make spiritual; deprive of worldliness. 2. to give a spiritual sense or meaning to. —**spir'it·u·al·i·za'tion,** *n.*
‡**spi·ri·tu·el** (spē'rē'tü'el'; Eng. spir'i-chōō-el'), *adj.* [Fr.], 1. having or showing a refined, ethereal nature. 2. having or showing a quick, graceful wit.
**spir·it·u·ous** (spir'i-chōō-əs), *adj.* of, like, or containing alcohol: said of distilled beverages.
**spi·ro-,** [< Gr. *speira*, a coil], a combining form meaning *spiral* or *coil*.
**spi·ro·chete, spi·ro·chaete** (spī'rə-kēt'), *n.* [< Gr. *speira*, a spiral + *chaitē*, hair], any of various spiral-shaped bacteria, some of which cause disease. —**spi'ro·che'tal, spi'ro·chae'tal,** *adj.*
**spirt** (spũrt), *n.*, *v.t.* & *v.i.* spurt.
**spir·y** (spīr'i), *adj.* [-IER, -IEST], 1. of, or having the form of, a spire. 2. having many spires.
**spit** (spit), *n.* [AS. *spitu*], 1. a thin, pointed rod on which meat is impaled and held to be roasted over a fire. 2. a narrow point of land or a long, narrow reef, shoal, etc. extending from the shore. *v.t.* [SPITTED, SPITTING], to impale on or as on a spit. —**spit'ter,** *n.*
**spit** (spit), *v.t.* [SPAT or SPIT, SPITTING], [AS. *spittan*], 1. to eject from the mouth. 2. to eject, emit, or utter explosively: as, to *spit* an oath. *v.i.* 1. to eject saliva from the mouth; expectorate. 2. to make an explosive hissing noise, as a cat. *n.* 1. the act of spitting. 2. saliva. 3. a salivalike, frothy secretion of certain insects. —**spit and image,** [Colloq.], perfect likeness. —**spit on** (or **at**), to express contempt for, hatred of, etc. as by spitting. —**spit'ter,** *n.*
**spit·ball** (spit'bôl'), *n.* 1. a piece of paper chewed up into a wad for throwing. 2. in *baseball*, a pitch, now illegal, made to curve by moistening one side of the ball with saliva.
**spite** (spīt), *n.* [see DESPITE], 1. a mean or evil feeling toward another, characterized by the inclination to hurt, humiliate, etc.; malice. 2. an instance of this; a grudge. *v.t.* [SPITED, SPITING], to vent one's spite upon by hurting, frustrating, etc. —**cut off one's nose to spite one's face,** [Colloq.], to injure oneself in an attempt to injure another. —**in spite of,** regardless of. —**spite'ful,** *adj.* —**spite'ful·ly,** *adv.* —**spite'ful·ness,** *n.*
**spit·fire** (spit'fīr'), *n.* a woman or girl who is easily aroused to violent outbursts of anger.
**Spits·ber·gen** (spits'bũr'gən), *n.* a group of islands in the Arctic Ocean, belonging to Norway.
**spitting image,** [Colloq.], perfect likeness.
**spit·tle** (spit''l), *n.* [alt. < earlier *spattle*, after *spit* (to eject)], spit; saliva.
**spit·toon** (spi-tōōn'), *n.* a container to spit into.
**spitz dog** (spits), [G. < *spitz*, pointed], a Pomeranian dog, usually white, with sharp-pointed muzzle and ears and a long, silky coat: also **spitz.**
**splash** (splash), *v.t.* [intens. extension of *plash*], 1. to cause (a liquid) to fly or scatter. 2. to dash or scatter a liquid, mud, etc. on, so as to wet or soil. 3. to cause to splash a liquid: as, to *splash* the oars. 4. to make (one's way) by splashing. 5. to mark or spot as by splashing: as, *splashed* with sunlight. *v.i.* 1. to cause a liquid to fly or scatter. 2. to move, fall, or strike with a splash. *n.* 1. the act or sound of splashing. 2. a mass of flying water, mud, etc. 3. a spot or mark made as by splashing. —**make a splash,** [Colloq.], to attract great, often brief attention. —**splash'er,** *n.* —**splash'y** [-IER, -IEST], *adj.*
**splash·down** (splash'doun'), *n.* the landing of a spacecraft on water.
**splat** (splat), *n.* [via dial. < base of *split*], a thin, flat piece of wood, especially one forming the central part of a chair back.
**splat·ter** (splat'ẽr), *n.*, *v.t.* & *v.i.* [var. of *spatter*], spatter; splash.
**splay** (splā), *n.* [< *display*], 1. a sloping surface or angle. 2. a spreading; expansion. *adj.* 1. sloping or spreading out. 2. broad and flat. 3. awkward. *v.t.* 1. to spread; expand. 2. to make sloping. *v.i.* to spread out.
**splay·foot** (splā'foot'), *n.* [*pl.* -FEET], a foot that is flat and turned outward. —**splay'foot'ed,** *adj.*
**spleen** (splēn), *n.* [< OFr. or L. < Gr. *splēn*, spleen], 1. a large, vascular, ductless organ in the upper left part of the abdomen: it modifies the blood structure and was formerly regarded as the seat of certain emotions; hence, 2. malice; spite; bad

temper. **—spleen′ful, spleen′ish, spleen′y** [-IER, -IEST], *adj.* **—spleen′ful·ly, spleen′ish·ly,** *adv.*

**splen·did** (splen′did), *adj.* [< L. *splendidus* < *splendere*, to shine], 1. having or showing splendor; specif., *a*) shining; brilliant. *b*) magnificent; gorgeous. 2. worthy of high praise; grand; glorious; illustrious. 3. [Colloq.], very good; excellent; fine. **—splen′did·ly,** *adv.* **—splen′did·ness,** *n.*

**splen·dif·er·ous** (splen-dif′ẽr-əs), *adj.* [Colloq.], gorgeous; splendid: used humorously.

**splen·dor** (splen′dẽr), *n.* [< OFr. < L. < *splendere*, to shine], 1. great luster; brilliance. 2. magnificent richness or glory; pomp; grandeur. Also, Brit. sp., **splendour. —splen′dor·ous, splen′drous,** *adj.*

**sple·net·ic** (spli-net′ik), *adj.* [Fr. < LL. *spleneticus*], 1. of the spleen. 2. irritable; peevish; spiteful. Also **sple·net′i·cal.** *n.* a spleenful person. **—sple·net′i·cal·ly,** *adv.*

**splen·ic** (splen′ik, splē′nik), *adj.* [< Fr. < L. < Gr. *splēnikos*], 1. of or having to do with the spleen. 2. located in or near the spleen.

**splice** (splīs), *v.t.* [SPLICED, SPLICING], [< MD. *splissen*], 1. to join, as ropes or cables, by weaving together the end strands. 2. to join (pieces of wood) by overlapping and binding, especially at the ends. 3. [Slang], to join in marriage. *n.* a joint or joining made by splicing. **—splic′er,** *n.*

SPLICE

**splint** (splint), *n.* [< MD. *splinte*], 1. a thin strip of wood or cane woven together with others to make baskets, chair seats, etc. 2. any device used to hold a broken bone in place or to keep a part of the body in fixed position, as a thin, rigid strip of wood or metal. *v.t.* to fit, support, or hold in place as with a splint or splints.

**splin·ter** (splin′tẽr), *v.t. & v.i.* [MD. < *splinte*, splint], to break or split into thin, sharp pieces. *n.* a thin, sharp piece of wood, bone, etc., made by splitting or breaking. *adj.* designating a group that separates from a main party, church, etc. because of divergent views. **—splin′ter·y,** *adj.*

**split** (split), *v.t. & v.i.* [SPLIT or *obs.* SPLITTED, SPLITTING], [MD. *splitten*], 1. to separate or divide lengthwise into two or more parts. 2. to break or tear apart by force; burst. 3. to divide into shares: as, to *split* the cost of a trip. 4. to separate into factions because of disagreement; disunite. 5. *a*) to break into atoms: said of a molecule. *b*) to produce nuclear fission in or undergo nuclear fission: said of an atom. *n.* 1. the act or result of splitting; specif., *a*) a break; fissure; crack. *b*) a division in a group, between persons, etc. 2. a splinter. 3. a confection made of a split banana or other fruit with ice cream, sauces, nuts, etc. 4. *often pl.* the acrobatic feat of spreading the legs apart until they lie flat on the floor in a straight line. 5. [Colloq.], a bottle of wine, etc., half the usual size. 6. [Slang], a share, as of loot. 7. in *bowling*, an arrangement of pins after the first bowl, so separated as to make a spare very difficult. *adj.* 1. separated along the length or grain. 2. divided; separated. **—split off,** to break off or separate as by splitting. **—split′ter,** *n.*

**split infinitive,** in *grammar*, an infinitive with the verbal and the *to* separated by an adverb. Example: he decided *to gradually change* his style. Despite objections to this construction, many writers use it to avoid ambiguity or awkwardness.

**split-lev·el** (split′lev′əl), *adj.* designating or of a type of house in which the floor levels are staggered so that each level is about a half story above or below the adjacent one.

**split ticket,** a ballot cast for candidates of more than one party.

**split·ting** (split′iŋ), *adj.* 1. that splits. 2. *a*) aching severely: said of the head. *b*) severe or sharp, as a headache.

**splotch** (sploch), *n.* [prob. a fusion of *spot* + *blotch*], a spot, splash, or stain, especially one that is irregular. *v.t.* to mark with a splotch or splotches. **—splotch′y** [-IER, -IEST], *adj.*

**splurge** (splũrj), *n.* [echoic], [Colloq.], any very showy or extravagant display, effort, etc. *v.i.* [SPLURGED, SPLURGING], [Colloq.], to make a splurge. **—splurg′er,** *n.*

**splut·ter** (splut′ẽr), *v.i.* [var. of *sputter*], 1. to make hissing or spitting sounds; sputter. 2. to speak hurriedly and confusedly, as when excited. *v.t.* to utter hurriedly and confusedly; sputter. *n.* a spluttering sound or utterance. **—splut′ter·er,** *n.*

**spoil** (spoil), *v.t.* [SPOILED or SPOILT, SPOILING], [< OFr. < L. *spoliare* < *spolium*, plunder], 1. to damage or injure so as to make useless, valueless, etc.; destroy. 2. to impair the enjoyment, quality, etc. of: as, rain *spoiled* the game. 3. to cause (a person) to demand or expect too much by overindulgence. 4. [Archaic], to rob; plunder; despoil. *v.i.* 1. to be damaged or injured so as to become useless, valueless, etc.; decay, as food. 2. [Colloq.], to be aggressively eager: as, he's *spoiling* for a fight. *n.* 1. *usually pl.* goods, territory, etc. taken by plunder; booty. 2. *usually pl.* public offices to which the successful political party has the power of appointment. 3. an object of plunder; prey. **—spoil′a·ble,** *adj.* **—spoil′er,** *n.*

**spoil·age** (spoil′ij), *n.* 1. a spoiling or being spoiled. 2. something spoiled or the amount spoiled.

**spoils·man** (spoilz′mən), *n.* [*pl.* -MEN], one who aids in a political campaign so as to share in the spoils.

**spoil·sport** (spoil′spôrt′, -spōrt′), *n.* one who acts so as to prevent others from enjoying themselves.

**spoils system,** the practice of treating public offices as the booty of the successful party in an election, to be distributed among party henchmen.

**Spo·kane** (spō-kan′), *n.* a city in E Washington: pop., 182,000.

**spoke** (spōk), *n.* [AS. *spaca*], 1. any of the braces extending from the hub to the rim of a wheel. 2. a ladder rung. 3. a stick, bar, etc. used to prevent a wheel from turning. *v.t.* [SPOKED, SPOKING], 1. to equip with spokes. 2. to thrust a spoke into (a wheel) to prevent movement.

**spoke** (spōk), pt. or archaic pp. of **speak.**

**spo·ken** (spō′kən), pp. of **speak.** *adj.* 1. uttered; oral. 2. characterized by a (specified) kind of voice: used in compounds, as *soft-spoken.*

**spoke·shave** (spōk′shāv′), *n.* a planing tool consisting of a blade with a handle at either end, used for shaping rounded surfaces, as, formerly, spokes.

**spokes·man** (spōks′mən), *n.* [*pl.* -MEN], one who speaks or gives information for another or others.

**spo·li·a·tion** (spō′li-ā′shən), *n.* [< L. pp. of *spoliare*, to spoil], robbery; plundering; esp., the seizure of neutral ships in wartime. **—spo′li·a′tive,** *adj.*

**spon·dee** (spon′dē), *n.* [< Fr. < L. < Gr. < *spondē*, solemn libation (one accompanied by a solemn melody)], a metrical foot consisting of two long or accented syllables. **—spon·da′ic** (-dā′ik), **spon·da′i·cal,** *adj.*

**sponge** (spunj), *n.* [AS. < L. < Gr. *spongia*], 1. a plantlike sea animal having a porous structure and a tough, fibrous skeleton, and growing fixed in large colonies. 2. the skeleton of such animals, light in weight and highly absorbent, used for washing surfaces, in bathing, etc. 3. any substance like this; specif., *a*) a synthetic sponge of rubber, plastic, etc. *b*) an absorbent cotton pad used in surgery. *c*) a light, porous cake or pudding. *d*) bread dough. 4. [Colloq.], a person who lives upon others as a parasite. 5. a sponge bath. *v.t.* [SPONGED, SPONGING], 1. to use a sponge on to dampen or wipe clean. 2. to remove as with a damp sponge (with *off*, *out*, etc.). 3. to absorb with or like a sponge. 4. [Colloq.], to get as by begging, imposition, etc. *v.i.* 1. to take up liquid like a sponge. 2. [Colloq.], to be a sponge (sense 4). **—throw, toss,** etc. **up** (or **in**) **the sponge,** [Colloq.], to admit defeat; give up. **—sponge′like′,** *adj.* **—spong′er,** *n.* **—spon′gy** [-GIER, -GIEST], *adj.* **—spon′gi·ness,** *n.*

**sponge bath,** a bath taken by using a wet sponge or cloth without getting into water.

**sponge·cake** (spunj′kāk′), *n.* a light, porous kind of cake made of flour, beaten eggs, sugar, etc., but no shortening: also **sponge cake.**

**spon·son** (spon′sən), *n.* [? < *expansion*], 1. a structure that projects over the side of a ship or boat, as a gun platform. 2. a winglike piece attached to the hull of a seaplane to give stability in the water.

**spon·sor** (spon′sẽr), *n.* [L. < *spondere*, to promise solemnly], 1. a person who pledges to act as surety for another on a debt, loan, etc. 2. a godparent. 3. a person or agency that endorses, promotes, or vouches for some person or thing. 4. a business firm or other agency that pays the costs of a radio or television program that advertises its products. *v.t.* to act as sponsor for. **—spon·so′ri·al** (-sō′ri-əl, -sôr′i-), *adj.* **—spon′sor·ship′,** *n.*

**spon·ta·ne·i·ty** (spon′tə-nē′ə-ti), *n.* 1. the state or quality of being spontaneous. 2. [*pl.* -TIES], spontaneous behavior, movement, action, etc.

**spon·ta·ne·ous** (spon-tā'ni-əs), *adj.* [< L. < *sponte*, of free will], 1. moved by a natural feeling or impulse, without constraint, effort, or forethought. 2. having no external cause; acting by internal energy, force, etc.; self-acting. 3. growing naturally; indigenous; wild. —**spon·ta'ne·ous·ly,** *adv.* —**spon·ta'ne·ous·ness,** *n.*

**spontaneous combustion,** the process of catching fire and burning as a result of heat generated by internal chemical action.

**spontaneous generation,** the theory that living organisms can originate in nonliving matter independently of other living matter.

**spoof** (spōōf), *n.* [coined, c. 1889], [Slang], a hoax, joke, or deception. *v.t.* & *v.i.* [Slang], to fool; deceive; trick.

**spook** (spōōk), *n.* [D.], [Colloq.], a specter; ghost. —**spook'y** [-IER, -IEST], **spook'ish,** *adj.*

**spool** (spōōl), *n.* [< MD. *spoele*], 1. a cylinder, often hollowed and with a rim at either end, upon which thread, wire, etc. is wound. 2. something like a spool. *v.t.* to wind on a spool.

**spoon** (spōōn), *n.* [< AS. *spon*, a chip], 1. a utensil consisting of a small, shallow bowl with a handle, used for eating or stirring food or drinks. 2. something shaped like a spoon, as a shiny, curved fishing lure (**spoon bait**), usually made of metal. 3. a golf club with a wooden head and more loft than a driver. *v.t.* to take up as with a spoon. *v.i.* [Colloq.], to make love, as by kissing and hugging.

**spoon·bill** (spōōn'bil'), *n.* 1. a wading bird with a broad, flat bill that is spoon-shaped at the tip. 2. any of various birds with a similar bill.

**spoon·drift** (spōōn'drift'), *n.* spindrift.

**spoon·er·ism** (spōōn'ẽr-iz'm), *n.* [after Rev. W. A. *Spooner* (1844–1930), of Oxford Univ.], an unintentional interchange of sounds in two or more words. Example: It is kistomary to cuss the bride.

**spoon·feed** (spōōn'fēd'), *v.t.* [-FED, -FEEDING], 1. to feed with a spoon. 2. to pamper; coddle.

**spoon·ful** (spōōn'fool'), *n.* [*pl.* -FULS], as much as a spoon will hold.

**spoon·y** (spōōn'i), *adj.* [-IER, -IEST], [Colloq.], foolishly sentimental or mawkish: also sp. **spooney.**

**spoor** (spoor, spôr, spōr), *n.* [D.], the track or trail of a wild animal. *v.t.* & *v.i.* to track by a spoor.

**spo·rad·ic** (spô-rad'ik, spō-), *adj.* [< ML. < Gr. *sporadikos* < *sporas*, scattered], 1. happening from time to time; not regular. 2. appearing singly, apart, or in isolated instances: as, a *sporadic* disease. —**spo·rad'i·cal·ly,** *adv.*

**spo·ran·gi·um** (spô-ran'ji-əm, spō-), *n.* [*pl.* -GIA (-ji-ə)], [< Gr. *spora*, a seed + *angeion*, vessel], a spore case, as of a fern. —**spo·ran'gi·al,** *adj.*

**spore** (spôr, spōr), *n.* [< Gr. *spora*, a seed], 1. a small reproductive body, usually a single cell, produced by mosses, ferns, certain protozoans, etc. and capable of giving rise to a new individual. 2. any seed, germ, etc. *v.i.* [SPORED, SPORING], to develop spores.

**spore case,** a case which contains spores.

**spo·ro-,** a combining form meaning *spore*, as in *sporophyte*: also **spor-.**

**spo·ro·go·ni·um** (spôr'ə-gō'ni-əm, spō'rə-), *n.* [*pl.* -NIA (-ni-ə)], [*sporo-* + *-gonium*], the sporophyte in mosses and liverworts, usually a spore-bearing capsule on a stalk.

**spo·ro·phyll, spo·ro·phyl** (spôr'ə-fil, spō'rə-), *n.* [*sporo-* + *-phyll*], a leaf producing spores.

**spo·ro·phyte** (spôr'ə-fīt', spō'rə-), *n.* [*sporo-* + *-phyte*], the asexual-spore-bearing phase of certain plants: cf. *gametophyte*.

**spor·ran** (spor'ən, spôr'-), *n.* [Gael. *sporan* < LL. *bursa*, a purse], a leather pouch, usually fur-covered, worn hanging from the front of the belt in the dress costume of Scottish Highlanders.

**sport** (spôrt, spōrt), *n.* [contr. of *disport*], 1. any recreational activity; diversion. 2. such an activity requiring bodily exertion and carried on according to a set of rules, whether outdoors, as golf, or indoors, as bowling. 3. fun; play. 4. *a*) a thing joked about; laughingstock. *b*) a plaything. 5. [Colloq.], a gambler. 6. [Colloq.], *a*) one who has sportsmanlike characteristics. *b*) one judged according to his ability to take defeat, joking, etc.: as, is he a good *sport?* 7. [Colloq.], a gay, fast, showy person. 8. in *biology*, a plant or animal showing some marked variation from the normal type. *v.t.* [Colloq.], to wear or display: as, to *sport* a loud suit. *v.i.* 1. to play; frolic. 2. *a*) to joke or jest. *b*) to make sport; trifle. *adj.* 1. of or for sports. 2. suitable for informal, casual wear: said of clothes. —**in** (or **for**) **sport,** in joke or jest. —**make sport of,** to mock or ridicule. —**sport'er,** *n.* —**sport'ful,** *adj.* —**sport'ful·ly,** *adv.* —**sport'ful·ness,** *n.*

**sport·ing** (spôr'tiŋ, spōr'-), *adj.* 1. of, interested in, or taking part in sports. 2. sportsmanlike; fair. 3. of or having to do with games, etc. involving gambling or betting. —**sport'ing·ly,** *adv.*

**sporting chance,** [Colloq.], a fair chance, involving loss in case of failure.

**spor·tive** (spôr'tiv, spōr'-), *adj.* 1. fond of sport or merriment; playful. 2. done in fun or playfully. —**spor'tive·ly,** *adv.* —**spor'tive·ness,** *n.*

**sports** (spôrts, spōrts), *adj.* sport: as, *sports* clothes.

**sports·man** (spôrts'mən, spōrts'-), *n.* [*pl.* -MEN], 1. a man who is interested in or takes part in sports, especially fishing, hunting, etc. 2. one who plays fair and can take defeat without complaint or victory without boasting. —**sports'man·like',** **sports'man·ly,** *adj.* —**sports'man·ship',** *n.*

**sports·wear** (spôrts'wâr', spōrts'-), *n.* sport clothes.

**sports·wom·an** (spôrts'woom'ən, spōrts'-), *n.* [*pl.* -WOMEN], a woman who is interested in or takes part in sports.

**sport·y** (spôr'ti, spōr'-), *adj.* [-IER, -IEST], [Colloq.], 1. characteristic of a sport or sporting man. 2. loud, showy, or flashy, as clothes. —**sport'i·ly,** *adv.* —**sport'i·ness,** *n.*

**spor·ule** (spôr'ūl), *n.* a small spore.

**spot** (spot), *n.* [prob. < MD. *spotte*], 1. a small area differing from the surrounding area, as in color. 2. a stain, speck, etc. 3. a flaw, as in character; fault. 4. a locality; place: as, a good fishing *spot.* 5. [Brit. Colloq.], a small quantity: as, a *spot* of lunch. 6. [Slang], a spotlight. *v.t.* [SPOTTED, SPOTTING], 1. to mark with spots. 2. to stain; blemish. 3. to place in or on a given spot or spots; locate. 4. [Colloq.], to see; recognize: as, I *spotted* her in the crowd. 5. [Colloq.], to allow as a handicap: as, I *spotted* him two points. *v.i.* 1. to become marked with spots. 2. to make a stain, as ink, etc. *adj.* 1. *a*) ready; on hand: as, *spot* cash. *b*) involving immediate payment of cash. 2. made at random: as, a *spot* check. 3. inserted between regular radio or television programs: as, a *spot* announcement. —**hit the spot,** [Colloq.], to satisfy a craving. —**in a spot,** [Colloq.], in trouble. —**on the spot,** 1. at the place mentioned. 2. at once. 3. [Slang], in a bad or demanding situation. 4. [Slang], in danger, especially of being murdered. —**spot'less,** *adj.* —**spot'less·ly,** *adv.* —**spot'less·ness,** *n.* —**spot'ta·ble,** *adj.*

**spot·light** (spot'līt'), *n.* 1. a strong beam of light focused on a particular person, thing, etc., as on a stage. 2. a lamp used to project such a light, as on an automobile. 3. public notice.

**spot·ted** (spot'id), *adj.* 1. marked with spots. 2. stained; blemished. —**spot'ted·ness,** *n.*

**spotted fever,** any of various fevers accompanied with skin eruptions.

**spot·ter** (spot'ẽr), *n.* one that spots; specif., *a*) a person hired to watch for dishonesty among employees, as in a bank. *b*) a person whose duty is to keep a lookout for, and report the position of, the enemy: as, an aircraft *spotter.* *c*) a person whose work is removing spots in dry cleaning.

**spot·ty** (spot'i), *adj.* [-TIER, -TIEST], 1. having, occurring in, or marked with spots. 2. not uniform or consistent, as in quality; uneven. —**spot'ti·ly,** *adv.* —**spot'ti·ness,** *n.*

**spous·al** (spou'z'l), *n.* [shortened < *espousal*], *often pl.* [Archaic], a marriage ceremony; nuptials. *adj.* of marriage; nuptial.

**spouse** (spouz, spous), *n.* [< OFr. < L. pp. *sponsus*, betrothed], a partner in marriage. *v.t.* [SPOUSED, SPOUSING], [Archaic], to marry.

**spout** (spout), *n.* [ME. *spute* < MD. *spuiten*, to spout], 1. a projecting pipe or orifice, as on a teapot, pitcher, etc., by which a liquid is poured. 2. a stream, jet, etc. as of a liquid from a spout. 3. a waterspout. *v.t.* 1. to shoot out (liquid, etc.) from a spout. 2. to utter in a loud, pompous manner. *v.i.* 1. to shoot out with force in a jet: said of liquid, etc. 2. to discharge liquid, etc. from a spout. 3. to spout words or speeches. —**spout'er,** *n.* —**spout'less,** *adj.*

**sprad·dle** (sprad''l), *v.t.* & *v.i.* [-DLED, -DLING], [< a merging of *spread* & *straddle*], [Dial. or Colloq.], to spread (the legs) so as to straddle.

**sprain** (sprān), *v.t.* [< OFr. *espreindre*, to strain < L. < *ex*, out + *premere*, to press], to wrench or twist a ligament or muscle of (a joint, as the ankle) without dislocating the bones. *n.* 1. an act of spraining. 2. an injury resulting from this.

**sprang** (spraŋ), alt. pt. of **spring.**

**sprat** (sprat), *n.* [< AS. *sprot*], a small European fish of the herring family.

**sprawl** (sprôl), *v.i.* [AS. *spreawlian*], 1. to spread the limbs in a relaxed or awkward position. 2. to sit or lie in such a position. 3. to crawl awkwardly.

4. to spread awkwardly or without a regular pattern, as handwriting, a line of men, etc. *v.t.* to cause to sprawl. *n.* a sprawling movement or position. —**sprawl′er,** *n.* —**sprawl′y** [-IER, -IEST], *adj.*

**spray** (sprā), *n.* [prob. < LG.], 1. a cloud or mist of fine liquid particles, as of water from breaking waves. 2. a jet of such particles, as from a spray gun. 3. a device for shooting out such a jet. 4. something likened to a spray: as, a *spray* of gunfire. *v.t. & v.i.* 1. to direct a spray (upon). 2. to scatter or shoot out in a spray. —**spray′er,** *n.*

**spray** (sprā), *n.* [ME. *sprai*], 1. a small branch or sprig of a tree or plant, with leaves, berries, flowers, etc. 2. a design or ornament like this.

**spray gun,** a device that shoots out a spray of liquid, as paint or insecticide, by air pressure.

**spread** (spred), *v.t.* [SPREAD, SPREADING], [AS. *sprædan*], 1. to open out or expand so as to cover more space; unfold; unfurl. 2. to stretch out (the fingers, arms, etc.); extend. 3. to distribute over an area; scatter. 4. *a*) to distribute in a thin layer: as, to *spread* butter on toast. *b*) to cover by smearing with a thin layer. 5. to extend over a certain period of time. 6. to cause to be widely or more widely known, felt, existent, etc. 7. to cover or deck with something. 8. *a*) to set (a table) for a meal. *b*) to set (food) on a table. 9. to push apart or farther apart. *v.i.* 1. to extend itself; be expanded. 2. to become distributed. 3. to be made widely or more widely known, felt, etc. 4. to be pushed apart or farther apart. 5. to admit of being smeared, as butter. *n.* 1. the act of spreading; extension. 2. the extent to which something can be spread. 3. an expanse; extent. 4. *a*) two facing pages of a magazine, etc., treated as a single sheet. *b*) printed matter set across a page or several columns of a newspaper, etc. 5. a cloth cover for a table, bed, etc. 6. any soft substance, as jam, used for spreading on bread. 7. [Colloq.], a meal, especially one with a wide variety of food. —**spread oneself,** [Colloq.], 1. to exert oneself in order to make a good impression. 2. to show off. —**spread oneself thin,** to try to do too many things at once. —**spread′er,** *n.*

**spread-ea·gle** (spred′ē′g'l), *adj.* 1. having the figure of an eagle with wings and legs spread. 2. [Colloq.], boastful; bombastic: as, *spread-eagle* patriotism. *v.t.* [-GLED, -GLING], to stretch out in the form of a spread eagle, as for a flogging.

**spree** (sprē), *n.* [18th-c. slang, for earlier *spray*], 1. a lively, noisy frolic. 2. a drinking bout.

**sprig** (sprig), *n.* [ME. *sprigge*], 1. a little twig or spray. 2. a design or ornament like this. 3. a young fellow; stripling. *v.t.* [SPRIGGED, SPRIGGING], to decorate with a design of sprigs. —**sprig′gy** [-GIER, -GIEST], *adj.*

**spright·ly** (sprit′li), *adj.* [-LIER, -LIEST], [var. of *spritely*], gay; lively; brisk; animated. *adv.* in a sprightly manner. —**spright′li·ness,** *n.*

**spring** (spriŋ), *v.i.* [SPRANG or SPRUNG, SPRUNG, SPRINGING], [AS. *springan*], 1. to move suddenly and rapidly; specif., *a*) to leap; bound. *b*) to appear suddenly; dart. *c*) to be resilient or elastic. 2. to arise as from some source; specif., *a*) to grow or develop. *b*) to come as a result: as, disease *springs* from poverty. *c*) to come into existence: as, a town *sprang* up. 3. to become warped, split, etc.: as, the door has *sprung.* 4. to rise up above surrounding objects; tower. Often followed by *up.* *v.t.* 1. to cause to leap forth suddenly. 2. to leap over; vault. 3. to cause to snap shut, as a trap. 4. to cause to warp, bend, split, etc., as by force. 5. to make known suddenly: as, to *spring* a surprise. 6. [Slang], to get (someone) released from jail, as by paying bail. *n.* 1. a springing; specif., *a*) a jump or leap, or the distance so covered. *b*) a sudden darting or flying back. *c*) the ability to do this; resilience; elasticity. 2. a device, as a coil of wire, that returns to its original form after being forced out of shape: used to absorb shock, etc. 3. a flow of water from the ground, the source of a stream. 4. any source or origin. 5. that season of the year in which plants begin to grow after lying dormant all winter. 6. any period of beginning. 7. a bending, crack, warping, etc. *adj.* 1. of, for, appearing in, or planted in the spring. 2. of or like a spring; elastic; resilient. 3. having, or supported on, springs: as, a *spring* mattress. 4. coming from a spring, as water. —**spring a leak,** to begin to leak suddenly.

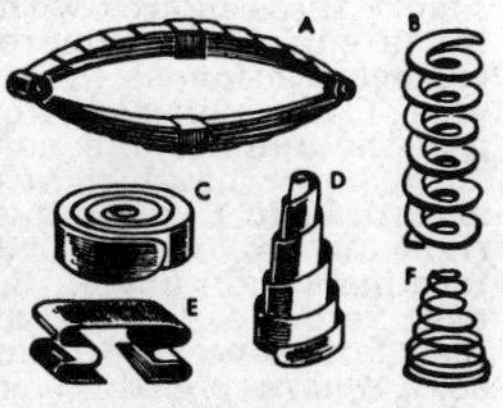

SPRINGS
A, leaf; B, spiral; C, coil; D, volute; E, flat; F, spiral

**spring beauty,** any of various small, spring-blooming plants with white or pinkish flowers.

**spring·board** (spriŋ′bôrd′, -bōrd′), *n.* 1. a flexible, springy board used by acrobats as a take-off in leaping. 2. a diving board.

**spring·bok** (spriŋ′bok′), *n.* [-BOK, -BOKS; see PLURAL, II, D, 2], [D. < *springen*, to spring + *bok*, a buck], a South African gazelle that jumps high into the air when frightened: also **spring′buck′** (-buk′).

**spring chicken,** 1. a young chicken, especially one only a few months old, used for frying. 2. [Slang], a person who is young, naive, etc.

**spring·er** (spriŋ′ēr), *n.* 1. a person or thing that springs. 2. a springer spaniel. 3. a springbok. 4. a spring chicken.

**springer spaniel,** a breed of large field spaniel.

**spring fever,** the listlessness that many people feel during the first warm days of spring.

**Spring·field** (spriŋ′fēld′), *n.* 1. a city in SW Massachusetts: pop., 174,000. 2. the capital of Illinois: pop., 83,000. 3. a city in W Ohio: pop., 83,000. 4. a city in SW Missouri: pop., 96,000.

**spring·halt** (spriŋ′hôlt′), *n.* stringhalt.

**spring lock,** a lock in which the bolt is shot automatically by a spring.

**spring tide,** 1. a tide occurring at the new and the full moon, normally the highest tide of the month. 2. any great flow, rush, or flood.

**spring·time** (spriŋ′tīm′), *n.* the season of spring: also **spring′tide′** (-tīd′).

**spring·y** (spriŋ′i), *adj.* [-IER, -IEST], 1. having spring; flexible; elastic. 2. having many springs of water. —**spring′i·ly,** *adv.* —**spring′i·ness,** *n.*

**sprin·kle** (spriŋ′k'l), *v.t.* [-KLED, -KLING], [< ME. < *sprengen*, to scatter], 1. to scatter in drops or particles, as water or salt. 2. to scatter drops or particles upon. *v.i.* 1. to scatter something in drops or particles. 2. to fall in drops or particles. 3. to rain lightly. *n.* 1. the act of sprinkling. 2. a light rain. —**sprin′kler,** *n.*

**sprin·kling** (spriŋ′kliŋ), *n.* 1. a small number or amount, especially one that is thinly distributed. 2. the act of one that sprinkles.

**sprint** (sprint), *v.i.* [ME. *sprenten*], to run or race at full speed, especially for a short distance. *v.t.* to traverse by sprinting. *n.* 1. the act of sprinting. 2. a short race at full speed. 3. a brief period of intense activity. —**sprint′er,** *n*

**sprit** (sprit), *n.* [AS. *sprēot*], a pole or spar extended diagonally upward from a mast to the topmost corner of a fore-and-aft sail.

**sprite** (sprīt), *n.* [< OFr. *esprit* < L. *spiritus;* see SPIRIT], an elf, pixie, fairy, or goblin.

**sprit·sail** (sprit′sāl′; *in nautical usage,* sprit′s'l), *n.* a sail extended by a sprit.

**sprock·et** (sprok′it), *n.* [prob. < LG.], 1. any of the teeth or points, as on the rim of a wheel, arranged to fit into the links of a chain. 2. a wheel fitted with sprockets: in full, **sprocket wheel.**

SPROCKET WHEEL

**sprout** (sprout), *v.i.* [AS. *sprutan*], 1. to begin to grow or germinate; give off shoots or buds. 2. to grow or develop rapidly. *v.t.* 1. to cause to sprout or grow. 2. to remove sprouts from. *n.* 1. a young growth on a plant, as a stem or branch; shoot. 2. a new growth from a bud, rootstock, etc. 3. any offshoot or scion. 4. *pl.* Brussels sprouts.

**spruce** (sprōōs), *n.* [< ME. *Spruce*, Prussia: ? because first known as from Prussia], 1. any of various evergreen trees with needle-shaped leaves and drooping cones or berrylike fruit. 2. its wood.

**spruce** (sprōōs), *adj.* [SPRUCER, SPRUCEST], [ME. *Spruce*, Prussia, esp. in phr. *Spruce leather*, regarded as fine and elegant], neat; trim; smart; dapper. *v.t. & v.i.* [SPRUCED, SPRUCING], to make or become spruce (usually with *up*). —**spruce′ly,** *adv.* —**spruce′ness,** *n.*

**sprung** (spruŋ), pp. and alt. pt. of **spring.**

**spry** (sprī), *adj.* [SPRIER or SPRYER, SPRIEST or SPRYEST], [< ON.], full of life; active; brisk; agile. —**spry'ly,** *adv.* —**spry'ness,** *n.*

**spud** (spud), *n.* [prob. < ON.], 1. a sharp spade for rooting out weeds. 2. [Colloq.], a potato. *v.t.* [SPUDDED, SPUDDING], to dig up with a spud.

**spue** (spū), *v.t. & v.i.* [SPUED, SPUING], to spew.

**spume** (spūm), *n.* [< OFr. < L. *spuma* < *spuere*, to spit out], foam, froth, or scum. *v.i. & v.t.* [SPUMED, SPUMING], to foam or froth. —**spu'mous, spum'y** [-IER, -IEST], *adj.*

**spu·mo·ni** (spə-mō'ni), *n.* [It.], an Italian frozen dessert made of layers of smooth ice cream, often containing fruits and nuts: also sp. **spumone.**

**spun** (spun), pt. and pp. of **spin.** *adj.* formed by or as if by spinning.

**spunk** (spuŋk), *n.* [< Ir. *sponc* < Gael. < L. *spongia*, sponge], 1. wood or fungus that takes fire easily; punk; tinder. 2. [Brit. Dial.], a spark or small flame. 3. [Colloq.], courage; spirit; pluck.

**spunk·y** (spuŋ'ki), *adj.* [-IER, -IEST], [Colloq.], having spunk; courageous; spirited. —**spunk'i·ly,** *adv.* —**spunk'i·ness,** *n.*

**spur** (spũr), *n.* [AS. *spura*], 1. a pointed device worn on the heel by horsemen, used to urge the horse forward. 2. anything that urges or incites; stimulus. 3. something like a spur; specif., *a*) a spinelike process on the wings or legs of certain birds. *b*) a sharp metal device attached to the leg of a gamecock. *c*) a short branch or shoot of a tree, etc. 4. a ridge projecting from the side of a mountain or mountain range. 5. a short side track (**spur track**) connected with the main track of a railroad. 6. in *botany*, a slender, tubelike structure formed by an extension of one or more petals or sepals, as in larkspur. *v.t.* [SPURRED, SPURRING], 1. to prick with spurs. 2. to urge; incite; stimulate. 3. to provide with a spur or spurs. *v.i.* 1. to spur a horse. 2. to hurry; hasten. —**on the spur of the moment,** abruptly and impulsively. —**win one's spurs,** to gain distinction or honor. —**spur'like',** *adj.* —**spur'rer,** *n.*

HORSEMAN'S SPUR

**spurge** (spũrj), *n.* [< OFr. < *espurger*, to purge < L. *ex-*, out + *purgare*, to cleanse], any of various plants having a milky juice; euphorbia.

**spur gear,** 1. a gearwheel with radial teeth parallel to the axle: also **spur wheel.** 2. gearing having this kind of gearwheel: also **spur gearing.**

**spu·ri·ous** (spyoor'i-əs), *adj.* [L. *spurius*], 1. illegitimate; bastard. 2. false; counterfeit; not genuine. —**spu'ri·ous·ly,** *adv.* —**spu'ri·ous·ness,** *n.*

**spurn** (spũrn), *v.t.* [AS. *spurnan*], 1. to push or drive away as with the foot. 2. to reject with contempt or disdain; scorn. *v.i.* to show contempt or disdain in rejecting something. *n.* 1. a kick. 2. scornful refusal or treatment. —**spurn'er,** *n.*

**spurred** (spũrd), *adj.* having, wearing, or fitted with spurs or spurlike parts.

**spurt** (spũrt), *v.t.* [< AS. *spryttan* < base of *sprutan*, to sprout], to shoot forth suddenly in a stream or gush; squirt; jet. *v.i.* 1. to gush forth in a stream or jet. 2. to show a sudden, brief burst of energy. *n.* 1. a sudden gushing or shooting forth; jet. 2. a sudden, brief burst of energy.

**sput·nik** (spoot'nik), *n.* [Russ.; lit. co-traveler], an artificial satellite of the earth, especially any of those put into orbit by the U.S.S.R. beginning in October, 1957.

**sput·ter** (sput'ẽr), *v.i.* [< *spout* + *-er*, freq.], 1. to spit saliva, bits of food, etc. in an explosive manner; splutter. 2. to speak in a confused, explosive manner. 3. to eject bits or drops of something with sharp sizzling or spitting sounds, as frying fat. *v.t.* 1. to spit out (bits or drops) in an explosive manner. 2. to utter by sputtering. *n.* 1. a sputtering. 2. the noise of sputtering. 3. bits or drops thrown out in sputtering. 4. hasty, confused utterance. —**sput'ter·er,** *n.* —**sput'ter·ing·ly,** *adv.*

**spu·tum** (spū'təm), *n.* [*pl.* -TA (-tə)], [< L. pp. of *spuere*, to spit], 1. saliva; spit. 2. mucus together with saliva, etc., spat out from the mouth.

**spy** (spī), *v.t.* [SPIED, SPYING], [< OFr. < OHG. *spehōn*, to examine], 1. to watch closely and secretly, with unfriendly purpose (usually with *out*). 2. to catch sight of; see. 3. to discover by close examination (with *out*). *v.i.* 1. to watch closely and secretly; act as a spy. 2. to keep watch. *n.* [*pl.* SPIES], 1. one who keeps close and secret watch on another or others. 2. a person employed by a government to get secret information about the affairs, especially military affairs, of another government, as of an enemy in wartime.

**spy·glass** (spī'glas', -gläs'), *n.* a small telescope.

**Sq., sq.,** square.

**squab** (skwäb, skwôb), *n.* [prob. < ON.], 1. a nestling pigeon. 2. a short, stout person. 3. a cushion. 4. a sofa. *adj.* 1. newly hatched. 2. short and stout: also **squab'by** [-BIER, -BIEST].

**squab·ble** (skwäb''l, skwôb'-), *v.i.* [-BLED, -BLING], [< or akin to Scand.], to quarrel noisily over a small matter; wrangle. *v.t.* in *printing*, to disarrange (set type). *n.* a noisy, petty quarrel; wrangle.

**squad** (skwäd, skwôd), *n.* [< Fr. < Sp. *escuadra*, a square < LL.; see SQUARE], 1. a small group of soldiers assembled for drill, duty, etc.: the smallest tactical unit, a subdivision of a platoon. 2. any small group of people acting together: as, a football *squad*. *v.t.* [SQUADDED, SQUADDING], 1. to form into a squad. 2. to assign to a squad.

**squad car,** a police patrol car, now usually equipped with short-wave radiophone.

**squad·ron** (skwäd'rən, skwôd'-), *n.* [< It. < *squadra*, a square], 1. a group of warships assigned to special duty. 2. a unit of cavalry consisting of from two to four troops. 3. a unit of military aviation consisting of two or more flights. 4. any organized body or group.

**squal·id** (skwäl'id, skwôl'-), *adj.* [< L. < *squalere*, to be foul], 1. foul; unclean. 2. wretched; sordid. —**squa·lid'i·ty, squal'id·ness,** *n.* —**squal'id·ly,** *adv.*

**squall** (skwôl), *n.* [prob. < Scand.], 1. a brief, violent windstorm, usually with rain or snow. 2. [Colloq.], trouble or disturbance. *v.i.* to storm briefly. —**squall'y** [-IER, -IEST], *adj.*

**squall** (skwôl), *v.i. & v.t.* [prob. echoic], to cry or scream loudly and harshly. *n.* a harsh, shrill cry or loud scream. —**squall'er,** *n.*

**squal·or** (skwäl'ẽr, skwôl'-), *n.* [L., foulness], a being squalid; filth and wretchedness.

**squa·ma** (skwā'mə), *n.* [*pl.* -MAE (-mē)], [L., a scale], a scale or scalelike part of an animal or plant. —**squa'mate, squa'mous, squa'mose,** *adj.*

**squan·der** (skwän'dẽr, skwôn'-), *v.t.* [prob. < dial. *squander*, to scatter], to spend or use wastefully. *v.i.* to be wasteful. *n.* a squandering.

**square** (skwâr), *n.* [< OFr. < LL. < L. *ex-*, out + *quadare*, to square; ult. < *quattuor*, four], 1. a plane figure having four equal sides and four right angles. 2. anything of or approximating this shape. 3. an area bounded by streets on four sides. 4. the distance along one side of such an area. 5. an open area bounded by several streets, used as a park, memorial, etc. 6. a body of troops formed into a square (sense 1). 7. an instrument having two sides that form a 90° angle, used for making or testing right angles. 8. the product of a number multiplied by itself: as, 9 is the *square* of 3. 9. [Slang], a person who is square (*adj.* 11). *v.t.* [SQUARED, SQUARING], 1. to make into a square (sense 1). 2. to make into a form having straight sides and right angles. 3. to make, or adjust to be, straight, even, etc. 4. to bring to or near to the form of a right angle: as, *square* your shoulders. 5. to settle; adjust: as, to *square* accounts. 6. to adjust the accounts of. 7. to make equal: as, that run *squared* the score. 8. to adapt; regulate: as, *square* these figures with that chart. 9. to mark off (a surface) in squares. 10. to bring into the correct position, as with reference to a line, course, etc. 11. to multiply (a quantity) by itself. 12. to find the number of square units in (an area). *v.i.* 1. to be or fit at right angles. 2. to fit; agree; accord. *adj.* 1. *a*) having four equal sides and four right angles. *b*) more or less cubical, as a box. 2. forming a right angle. 3. correctly adjusted; level, even, etc. 4. leaving no balance; balanced. 5. just; fair; honest. 6. clear; direct; straightforward: as, a *square* refusal. 7. *a*) designating or of a unit of surface measure in the form of a square with sides of a specified length: as, a *square* foot. *b*) given or stated in terms of such measure. 8. having a shape broad for its length or height, with a solid, sturdy appearance: as, a *square* build. 9. designating a number that is the product of another number multiplied by itself. 10. [Colloq.], satisfying; substantial: as, a *square* meal. 11. [Slang], old-fashioned or unsophisticated. *adv.* 1. honestly; fairly. 2. so as to be or form a square; at right angles. 3. directly; exactly. 4. so as to face. 5. firmly; solidly. —**on the square,** 1. at right angles. 2. [Colloq.], honest(ly); fair(ly). —**square away,** 1. to bring a ship's yards around so as to sail before the wind. 2. to square off. —**square off,** to assume a posture of attack or self-defense. —**square oneself,** [Colloq.], to make amends. —**square the circle,** 1. to find a square equal in area to a circle: an insoluble problem. 2. to do or attempt something that seems impossible. —**square up,** to make a settlement, as by payment. —**square'ly,** *adv.* —**square'ness,** *n.* —**squar'er,** *n.* —**squar'ish,** *adj.*

**square dance,** a dance, as a quadrille, in which the couples are grouped in a given form, as a square. **—square dancing.**

**square deal,** [Colloq.], any treatment or dealing that is honest, fair, and just.

**square knot,** a double knot in which the free ends run parallel to the standing parts; reef knot.

**square measure,** a system of measuring area, in which 144 square inches = 1 square foot, 9 square feet = 1 square yard, etc.

**square-rigged** (skwâr′rigd′), *adj.* rigged with square sails as the principal sails. **—square′-rig′ger,** *n.*

**square root,** the quantity which when squared will produce a given quantity: as, the *square root* of 9 is 3.

**square sail,** a four-sided sail rigged on a yard suspended horizontally across the mast.

**square shooter,** [Colloq.], a fair, honest person.

**square-shoul·dered** (skwâr′shōl′dẽrd), *adj.* having an erect posture with the shoulders thrown back.

**squash** (skwäsh, skwôsh), *v.t.* [< OFr. *esquasser* < LL. < L. *ex-*, intens. + pp. of *quatere*, to shake], 1. to beat or press into a soft, flat mass or pulp; crush. 2. to quash; suppress. 3. [Colloq.], to silence (another) in a crushing manner. *v.i.* 1. to be squashed, as by a heavy fall, pressure, etc. 2. to make a sound of squashing. 3. to press; crowd; squeeze. *n.* 1. something easily squashed or crushed. 2. a soft, pulpy mass. 3. a squashing. 4. the sound of squashing. 5. either of two similar games (**squash rackets** or **squash tennis**), played in a walled court with rackets and a rubber ball. *adv.* 1. so as to squash. 2. with a squashing sound. **—squash′er,** *n.* **—squash′ing·ly,** *adv.*

**squash** (skwäsh, skwôsh), *n.* [< Algonquian], 1. the fleshy fruit of various plants of the gourd family, eaten as a vegetable. 2. any such plant.

**squash·y** (skwäsh′i, skwôsh′i), *adj.* [-IER, -IEST], 1. soft and wet; mushy. 2. easily squashed or crushed. **—squash′i·ly,** *adv.* **—squash′i·ness,** *n.*

**squat** (skwät, skwôt), *v.i.* [SQUATTED or SQUAT, SQUATTING], [< OFr. *esquatir;* ult. < L. *ex-*, intens. + *cogere*, to force], 1. to sit on the heels with the knees bent. 2. to crouch with the feet drawn in close to the body. 3. to crouch close to the ground, as an animal. 4. to settle on public or unoccupied land, without right or title. 5. to settle on public land under government regulation in order to get title to it. *v.t.* to cause to squat: usually reflexive. *adj.* 1. seated in a squatting position. 2. short and heavy or thick. *n.* the act or position of squatting. **—squat′ter,** *n.*

**squat·ty** (skwät′i, skwôt′i), *adj.* [-TIER, -TIEST], squat; thickset. **—squat′ti·ness,** *n.*

**squaw** (skwô), *n.* [< Algonquian], 1. an American Indian woman or wife. 2. [Slang], any woman.

**squawk** (skwôk), *v.i.* [echoic], 1. to utter a loud, harsh cry, as a fowl. 2. [Slang], to complain or protest in a loud or raucous voice. *v.t.* to utter in a squawk. *n.* 1. a loud, harsh cry. 2. [Slang], a loud, raucous complaint. **—squawk′er,** *n.*

**squeak** (skwēk), *v.i.* [? fusion of *squeal* & *shriek*], to utter or make a thin, sharp, high-pitched cry or sound. *v.t.* 1. to utter or produce in a squeak. 2. to cause (a door, etc.) to squeak. *n.* 1. a squeaking. 2. a thin, short, sharp cry or sound. **—narrow** (or **close** or **near**) **squeak,** [Colloq.], a narrow escape. **—squeak′er,** *n.* **—squeak′i·ly,** *adv.* **—squeak′i·ness,** *n.* **—squeak′y** [-IER, -IEST], *adj.*

**squeal** (skwēl), *v.i.* [prob. echoic], 1. to utter or make a sharp, high-pitched cry or sound. 2. [Slang], to act as an informer. *v.t.* to utter in a squeal. *n.* 1. a squealing. 2. a sharp, high-pitched cry or sound, somewhat prolonged. **—squeal′er,** *n.*

**squeam·ish** (skwēm′ish), *adj.* [< Anglo-Fr. *escoimous*, orig., shy], 1. easily nauseated; queasy. 2. easily shocked or offended; prudish. 3. excessively fastidious or particular; oversensitive. **—squeam′ish·ly,** *adv.* **—squeam′ish·ness,** *n.*

**squee·gee** (skwē′jē), *n.* [prob. < intens. var. of *squeeze*], a T-shaped tool having the crossbar edged with a strip of rubber, etc., used to scrape water from a flat surface. *v.t.* [-GEED, -GEEING], to scrape, press, etc. with a squeegee.

**squeeze** (skwēz), *v.t.* [SQUEEZED, SQUEEZING], [< AS. *-cwysan*, to crush], 1. to press hard or closely, especially from two or more sides. 2. to get or extract by pressure: as, to *squeeze* juice from a lime. 3. to get or extort by force or unfair means. 4. to force by pressing: as, he *squeezed* his hand into the jar. 5. to oppress with exactions. 6. to embrace closely; hug. 7. [Colloq.], to put pressure, etc. on (someone) to do something. *v.i.* 1. to yield or give way to pressure. 2. to exert pressure. 3. to force one's way by pushing or pressing. *n.* 1. a squeezing or being squeezed. 2. a close embrace; hug. 3. the state of being closely pressed or packed; crush. 4. a small quantity of something extracted by squeezing. 5. [Colloq.], pressure or influence brought to bear, as in extortion. **—squeez′a·ble,** *adj.* **—squeez′er,** *n.*

**squelch** (skwelch), *n.* [< fusion of *quell* & *crush*], 1. the sound of liquid, mud, etc. moving under pressure or suction, as in wet shoes. 2. [Colloq.], a crushing retort, rebuke, etc. *v.t.* 1. to crush or smash as by stamping upon; squash. 2. to suppress or silence completely. *v.i.* 1. to make a squelch (sense 1). 2. to walk heavily, as through mud or slush, making such a sound. **—squelch′a·ble,** *adj.* **—squelch′er,** *n.* **—squelch′ing·ly,** *adv.*

**squib** (skwib), *n.* [prob. echoic], 1. any firework that burns with a hissing noise, ending in an explosion. 2. a broken firecracker that burns with a hissing noise. 3. a short, witty verbal attack; lampoon. *v.t.* & *v.i.* [SQUIBBED, SQUIBBING], 1. to burn or shoot off (a squib). 2. to write or utter a squib or squibs (against).

**squid** (skwid), *n.* [*pl.* SQUIDS, SQUID; see PLURAL, II, D, 1], [prob. < dial. for *squirt*], a long, slender sea mollusk having ten arms, two being much longer than the others.

**squill** (skwil), *n.* [< OFr. < L. < Gr. *skilla*], 1. the dried bulb of a plant of the lily family, used in medicine. 2. the plant: also called *sea onion.*

**squint** (skwint), *v.i.* [< *asquint*], 1. to peer with the eyes partly closed. 2. to look sidewise or askance. 3. to be cross-eyed. 4. *a*) to incline (*toward*). *b*) to deviate. *v.t.* 1. to cause to squint. 2. to keep (the eyes) partly closed in looking at something. *n.* 1. a squinting. 2. an inclination or tendency. 3. a being cross-eyed. 4. [Colloq.], a quick look or sidelong glance. *adj.* 1. squinting; looking obliquely or askance. 2. cross-eyed. **—squint′er,** *n.* **—squint′ing·ly,** *adv.*

**squire** (skwīr), *n.* [contr. of *esquire*], 1. a young man of high birth who attended a knight. 2. in England, a title of respect given to a large rural landowner; country gentleman. 3. a title of respect applied commonly to a justice of the peace, etc. 4. an attendant; esp., a man escorting a woman; gallant. *v.t.* & *v.i.* [SQUIRED, SQUIRING], to act as a squire (to).

**squirm** (skwũrm), *v.i.* [prob. echoic, infl. by *worm*], 1. to twist and turn the body in a snakelike movement; wriggle; writhe. 2. to show or feel distress, as from embarrassment, etc. *n.* a squirming. **—squirm′i·ness,** *n.* **—squirm′y** [-IER, -IEST], *adj.*

**squir·rel** (skwũr′əl, skwũrl), *n.* [*pl.* -RELS, -REL; see PLURAL, II, D, 1], [< OFr. < a LL. dim. < L. *sciurus* < Gr. *skia*, a shadow + *oura*, tail], 1. a small, tree-dwelling rodent with heavy fur and a long, bushy tail: common species are the *gray squirrel*, the *red squirrel*, and the *fox squirrel*. 2. any of various related rodents, as the chipmunk, woodchuck, etc. 3. the fur of some of these animals.

**squirt** (skwũrt), *v.t.* & *v.i.* [< LG. & D. *swirtjen*, to squirt], 1. to spurt; shoot out in a jet or thin stream. 2. to wet with liquid so shot out. *n.* 1. a device for squirting, as a syringe. 2. a squirting. 3. a jet or thin stream. 4. [Colloq.], a small, insignificant, or impudent person. **—squirt′er,** *n.*

**squish** (skwish), *v.t.* & *v.i.*, *n.* [Dial.], squash.

**Sr,** in *chemistry*, strontium.

**Sr.,** 1. Senior. 2. [Sp.], *Señor*. 3. Sir.

**S.R.O.,** standing room only.

**S.S., SS, S/S,** steamship.

**SSE, S.S.E., s.s.e.,** south-southeast.

**S.S.R., SSR,** Soviet Socialist Republic.

**SSW, S.S.W., s.s.w.,** south-southwest.

**St.,** 1. Saint: terms with *St.* are entered in this dictionary as if spelled St-. 2. Strait. 3. Street.

**Sta.,** Station.

**stab** (stab), *v.t.* [STABBED, STABBING], [< ME. *stob*, a stake, a var. of *stub*], 1. to pierce or wound as with a knife, dagger, etc. 2. to thrust (a knife, etc.) into something. 3. to go into in a sharp, thrusting way. *v.i.* 1. to make a thrust or cause a wound as with a knife, etc. 2. to give the sensation of a knife wound: said of pain. *n.* 1. a wound made by stabbing. 2. a thrust, as with a knife, etc. 3. a sudden sensation of anguish or pain. 4. [Colloq.], an attempt; try. **—stab′ber,** *n.*

**sta·bil·i·ty** (stə-bil′ə-ti), *n.* [*pl.* -TIES], 1. a being stable, or fixed; steadiness. 2. firmness of character, purpose, etc. 3. permanence. 4. the capacity of an object to return to its original position after having been displaced.

**sta·bi·lize** (stā′bə-līz′), *v.t.* [-LIZED, -LIZING], 1. to make stable, or firm. 2. to keep from changing, as in price. 3. to equip (an airplane, etc.) with a stabilizer. —**sta′bi·li·za′tion,** *n.*

**sta·bi·liz·er** (stā′bə-līz′ẽr), *n.* a person or thing that stabilizes; specif., any of various devices used to make an airplane steady in flight.

**sta·ble** (stā′b'l), *adj.* [< OFr. < L. *stabilis* < *stare*, to stand], 1. not likely to break down, fall over, or give way; firm; steady. 2. firm in character, purpose, etc. 3. resisting change; permanent. 4. capable of returning to its original position after having been displaced. 5. in *chemistry*, not easily decomposing. —**sta′ble·ness,** *n.* —**sta′bly,** *adv.*

**sta·ble** (stā′b'l), *n.* [< OFr. < L. *stabulum* < *stare*, to stand], 1. a building in which horses or cattle are sheltered and fed. 2. a group of animals kept in such a building. 3. all the race horses belonging to one owner. 4. the people who take care of and train these horses. *v.t. & v.i.* [-BLED, -BLING], to lodge, keep, or be kept in a stable. —**sta′bler,** *n.*

**sta·ble·boy** (stā′b'l-boi′), *n.* a boy who works in a stable.

**stac·ca·to** (stə-kä′tō), *adj.* [It., detached], 1. in *music*, with distinct breaks between successive tones; abrupt; detached. 2. made up of abrupt elements or sounds. *adv.* so as to be staccato. *n.* [*pl.* -TOS], staccato music, speech, etc.

**stack** (stak), *n.* [< ON. *stakkr*], 1. a large, symmetrical pile of straw, hay, etc. for outdoor storage. 2. any somewhat orderly pile. 3. a number of rifles, etc. leaned against one another on end to form a cone. 4. a chimney or smokestack. 5. a set of book shelves. 6. *pl.* the section where the books are kept in a library. 7. [Colloq.], a large number or quantity. *v.t.* 1. to arrange in a stack. 2. to load with stacks of something. —**stack the cards** (or **deck**), 1. to arrange a deck of playing cards secretly so as to control the dealing. 2. to prearrange circumstances unfairly. —**stack′er,** *n.*

**stack·up** (stak′up′), *n.* an arrangement of circling aircraft at various altitudes awaiting their turn to land.

**sta·di·um** (stā′di-əm), *n.* [*pl.* -DIA (-di-ə)], [L. < Gr. *stadion*, stadium (1*b*) < *histanai*, to stand], 1. in ancient Greece, *a*) a track for foot races, with tiers of seats for spectators. *b*) any of several measures of linear distance, based on the length of such tracks. 2. [*pl.* -UMS], a place for outdoor games, meetings, etc., surrounded by tiers of seats.

**staff** (staf, stäf), *n.* [*pl.* STAVES; *also, and for 3, 4, 5 always,* STAFFS], [AS. *stæf*], 1. a stick, rod, or pole used as for support, a weapon, a symbol of authority, a measure, etc. 2. figuratively, a support; sustenance. 3. a group of people assisting a leader. 4. a group of officers serving a military or naval commanding officer in an advisory and administrative capacity. 5. a specific group of workers: as, a teaching *staff*. 6. in *music*, the five horizontal lines and four intermediate spaces on which music is written. *adj.* of or having to do with a staff (senses 3, 4, 5). *v.t.* to provide with a staff, as of workers.

**staff officer,** an officer serving on a staff.

**staff of life,** bread, regarded as the basic food.

**staff sergeant,** 1. in the *U.S. Army*, formerly, the third grade of enlisted man (now *sergeant*). 2. in the *U.S. Marine Corps & Air Force*, an enlisted man ranking just above sergeant.

**stag** (stag), *n.* [*pl.* STAGS, STAG; see PLURAL, II, D, 1], [AS. *stagga*], 1. *a*) a full-grown male deer. *b*) the male of some other animals. 2. a male animal castrated in maturity. 3. *a*) a man who attends a social gathering unaccompanied by a woman. *b*) a social gathering for men only. *adj.* for men only. —**go stag,** [Colloq.], to go as a stag (sense 3*a*).

**stage** (stāj), *n.* [< OFr. *estage* < LL. < L. pp. of *stare*, to stand], 1. a platform or dock. 2. a scaffold. 3. *a*) a raised platform upon which plays, speeches, etc. are presented. *b*) any area in which actors perform. 4. the whole area back of the footlights in a theater. 5. the theater as a profession. 6. the scene of an event or action: as, the *stage* of many wars. 7. a place where a stop is made on a journey, especially a regular stopping point. 8. the distance or part of a route between stopping places. 9. *a*) a stagecoach. *b*) a motor bus. 10. a period or degree in a process of development, growth, etc.: as, the larval *stage* of an insect. 11. one of two or more propulsion systems used in sequence in powering a rocket into outer space: when each is exhausted, it usually separates from the rest. *v.t.* [STAGED, STAGING], 1. to present as on a stage. 2. to plan and carry out: as, to *stage* an attack. *v.i.* to be suitable for presentation on the stage: as, the play *stages* well. —**by easy stages,** 1. traveling only a short distance at a time. 2. working or acting gradually, not hurriedly.

**stage·coach** (stāj′kōch′), *n.* a horse-drawn coach carrying passengers, mail, etc. on scheduled trips over a regular route.

**stage·craft** (stāj′kraft′, -kräft′), *n.* skill in, or the art of, writing or producing plays.

**stage door,** an outside door leading to the backstage of a theater, for the use of actors, etc.

**stage fright,** nervousness felt when appearing before an audience.

**stage·hand** (stāj′hand′), *n.* one who does manual work connected with producing a play, as the preparation of scenery, operation of lights, etc.

**stage-struck** (stāj′struk′), *adj.* having an intense desire to become an actor or actress.

**stage whisper,** 1. a loud whisper by an actor on the stage, intended to be heard by the audience. 2. any similar whisper intended to be overheard.

**stag·ger** (stag′ẽr), *v.i.* [< ON. *stakra*, to cause to stumble], 1. to totter, sway, or reel, as from a blow, fatigue, drunkenness, etc. 2. to lose determination; hesitate. *v.t.* 1. to cause to stagger, as with a blow. 2. to affect strongly, as with grief, etc. 3. to make zigzag in arrangement. 4. to arrange (periods, duties, etc.) so as to eliminate crowding or overconcentration: as, to *stagger* vacations. *n.* 1. a staggering; reeling. 2. a staggered arrangement. 3. *pl.* [construed as sing.], a nervous disease of horses, cattle, etc., causing the animals to stagger or fall. —**stag′ger·er,** *n.* —**stag′ger·ing·ly,** *adv.*

**stag·ing** (stāj′iŋ), *n.* 1. a temporary structure used for support; scaffolding. 2. the business of operating stagecoaches. 3. travel by stagecoach. 4. the act or process of presenting a play on the stage.

**stag·nant** (stag′nənt), *adj.* [< L. ppr. of *stagnare*, to stagnate], 1. without motion; not flowing. 2. foul from lack of movement: said of water, etc. 3. dull; sluggish: as, a *stagnant* mind. —**stag′nan·cy,** *n.* —**stag′nant·ly,** *adv.*

**stag·nate** (stag′nāt), *v.i.* [-NATED, -NATING], [< L. pp. of *stagnare*], to be or become stagnant. *v.t.* to make stagnant. —**stag·na′tion,** *n.*

**stag·y** (stāj′i), *adj.* [-IER, -IEST], 1. of or characteristic of the stage; theatrical. 2. affected; not real or genuine. Also sp. **stagey.** —**stag′i·ly,** *adv.*

**staid** (stād), archaic pt. and pp. of *stay* (to remain). *adj.* sober; sedate; settled and steady. —**staid′ly,** *adv.* —**staid′ness,** *n.*

**stain** (stān), *v.t.* [contr. of *distain* < OFr. < L. *dis-*, from + *tingere*, to color], 1. to spoil the appearance of by discoloring or soiling. 2. to spot (a character, reputation, etc.); corrupt. 3. to change the appearance of (wood, cloth, etc.) by coloring; dye. *v.i.* to impart or take a color or stain. *n.* 1. a color or spot resulting from staining. 2. a moral blemish; dishonor. 3. a dye or pigment for staining wood, cloth, etc. —**stain′a·ble,** *adj.* —**stain′er,** *n.* —**stain′less,** *adj.* —**stain′less·ly,** *adv.* —**stain′less·ness,** *n.*

**stainless steel,** steel alloyed with chromium, etc., virtually immune to rust and corrosion.

**stair** (stâr), *n.* [< AS. *stæger*], 1. *usually pl.* a flight of steps; staircase. 2. one of a series of steps leading from one level to another.

**stair·case** (stâr′kās′), *n.* a flight of stairs with a supporting structure and a handrail.

**stair·way** (stâr′wā′), *n.* a flight of stairs; staircase.

**stake** (stāk), *n.* [AS. *staca*], 1. a length of wood or metal pointed at one end for driving into the ground. 2. the post to which a person is tied for execution by burning. 3. execution by burning: with *the*. 4. *often pl.* money, etc. risked in a wager, game, or contest. 5. *often pl.* a prize given a winner, as in a race. 6. a share or interest, especially a financial one, in property, a person, etc. *v.t.* [STAKED, STAKING], 1. to mark the boundaries of as with stakes: as, to *stake* out a claim. 2. to fasten to or support with a stake or stakes. 3. to risk or gamble. 4. [Colloq.], *a*) to furnish with money or resources, as for a business venture. *b*) to grubstake. —**at stake,** being risked. —**pull up stakes,** [Colloq.], to change one's place of business, residence, etc.

**stake·hold·er** (stāk′hōl′dẽr), *n.* one who holds the stakes in a bet and pays them to the winner.

**stake·out** (stāk′out′), *n.* 1. the stationing of policemen, detectives, etc. in a surveillance of a person or place. 2. a place under such surveillance.

**sta·lac·tite** (stə-lak′tīt, stal′ək-tīt′), *n.* [< Gr. *stalaktos*, dripping < *stalassein*, to drip], an icicle-shaped deposit hanging from the roof or sides of a cave, formed, like stalagmites, by the evaporation of dripping water having a high lime content. —**stal·ac·tit·ic** (stal'ək-tit'ik), **stal'ac·tit'i·cal,** *adj.* —**stal'ac·tit'i·cal·ly,** *adv.*

**sta·lag·mite** (stə-lag'mīt, stal'əg-mīt'), *n.* [< Gr. *stalagmos*, a dropping < *stalassein*, to drip], a cone-shaped deposit on the floor of a cave, often forming beneath a stalactite. —**stal·ag·mit·ic** (stal'əg-mit'-ik), **stal'ag·mit'i·cal,** *adj.* —**stal'ag·mit'i·cal·ly,** *adv.*

**stale** (stāl), *adj.* [ME.], 1. having lost freshness; specif., *a*) flat; tasteless. *b*) hard and dry, as bread, etc. *c*) stagnant, as water or air. *d*) hackneyed; trite, as a joke. 2. out of condition as a result of either too much or too little activity. *v.t. & v.i.* [STALED, STALING], to make or become stale. —**stale'ly,** *adv.* —**stale'ness,** *n.*

**stale·mate** (stāl'māt'), *n.* [< Anglo-Fr. *estale*, fixed location; + *mate* (to checkmate)], 1. in *chess*, any situation in which a player cannot move without placing his king in check: it results in a draw. 2. any situation making further action impossible; deadlock. *v.t.* [-MATED, -MATING], 1. to bring into a stalemate. 2. to bring to a standstill.

**Sta·lin, Joseph** (stä'lin, -lēn), 1879–1953; Soviet dictator and statesman; premier (1941–1953).

**Sta·lin·grad** (stä'lin-grad'), *n.* a city in S European Russia, on the Volga: pop., 663,000. Since 1961, called *Volgograd.*

**stalk** (stôk), *v.i.* [AS. *stealcian*], 1. to walk in a stiff, haughty manner: sometimes used figuratively, as, plague *stalks* across the land. 2. to pursue or approach game, etc. stealthily. *v.t.* 1. to pursue or approach (game, etc.) stealthily. 2. to stalk through: as, terror *stalked* the streets. *n.* 1. a slow, stiff, haughty walk. 2. the act of stalking game, etc. —**stalk'er,** *n.*

**stalk** (stôk), *n.* [< AS. *stæla*], 1. the stem or main axis of a plant. 2. any part resembling this, as in some invertebrate animals. 3. in *botany*, any lengthened support on which an organ grows, as the petiole of a leaf. —**stalk'less,** *adj.* —**stalk'like',** *adj.* —**stalk'y** [-IER, -IEST], *adj.*

**stalk·ing-horse** (stôk'iŋ-hôrs'), *n.* 1. a horse, or a figure of a horse, used as cover by a hunter stalking game. 2. anything used to disguise intentions, schemes, etc.; pretext. 3. in *politics*, a candidate put forth merely as a screen to cover maneuvering during selection.

**stall** (stôl), *n.* [< AS. *steall*], 1. a stable. 2. a compartment for one animal in a stable. 3. a small compartment; specif., *a*) a booth, table, etc., as at a market, at which goods are sold. *b*) a pew, as in the choir of a church. *c*) [Brit.], a seat near the stage in a theater. 4. in *aeronautics*, the condition that is the result of stalling. *v.t.* 1. to put or keep (an animal) in a stall. 2. to cause to stick fast, as in mud. 3. to bring to a standstill, especially unintentionally. 4. to cause (an airplane, motor, etc.) to stall. *v.i.* 1. to be kept in a stall. 2. to stick fast, as in mud. 3. to be brought to a standstill. 4. to stop operating as because of insufficient fuel supply: said of a motor. 5. in *aeronautics*, to lose the amount of forward speed necessary to maintain altitude and be controlled. —**stalled,** *adj.*

**stall** (stôl), *v.i.* [< obs. *stale*, a decoy < Anglo-Fr. *estale*], [Colloq.], to act or speak evasively or hesitantly so as to deceive or delay. *v.t.* [Colloq.], to put off or delay by stalling (usually with *off*). *n.* [Colloq.], any action used in stalling. —**stall'er,** *n.*

**stall-feed** (stôl'fēd'), *v.t.* [-FED, -FEEDING], 1. to feed and keep (an animal) inactive in a stall for fattening. 2. to feed with dry fodder.

**stal·lion** (stal'yən), *n.* [< OFr. < OHG. *stal*, a stall], an uncastrated male horse; studhorse.

**stal·wart** (stôl'wērt), *adj.* [AS. *stælwyrthe* < *stathol*, foundation + *wyrthe*, worth], 1. strong; sturdy. 2. valiant. 3. resolute; firm. *n.* 1. a stalwart person. 2. one who supports a cause with firm partisanship. —**stal'wart·ly,** *adv.* —**stal'wart·ness,** *n.*

**sta·men** (stā'mən), *n.* [*pl.* -MENS, *rare* STAMINA (stam'ə-nə)], [L., warp, thread], a pollen-bearing organ in a flower, made up of a slender stalk (*filament*) and a pollen sac (*anther*).

**Stam·ford** (stam'fērd), *n.* a city in SW Connecticut: pop., 93,000.

**stam·i·na** (stam'ə-nə), *n.* [L., pl. of *stamen;* see STAMEN], resistance to fatigue, illness, hardship, etc.; endurance. —**stam'i·nal,** *adj.*

**stam·i·nate** (stam'ə-nit, -nāt'), *adj.* in *botany*, 1. bearing stamens but no pistils, as male flowers. 2. having or bearing a stamen or stamens.

**stam·mer** (stam'ēr), *v.t. & v.i.* [AS. *stamerian*], to speak or say with involuntary pauses and rapid repetitions of sounds, as from excitement, anxiety, etc. *n.* the act or habit of stammering. —**stam'-mer·er,** *n.* —**stam'mer·ing·ly,** *adv.*

**stamp** (stamp), *v.t.* [ME. *stampen*], 1. to bring (the foot) down forcibly upon something. 2. *a*) to strike down on forcibly with the foot. *b*) to beat, press, crush, etc. as with a downward thrust of the foot: as, *stamp* out a fire. 3. to imprint or cut out by bringing a form forcibly against a material: as, to *stamp* initials in leather. 4. to impress or imprint with a design, characters, etc., as to decorate, show ownership, etc. 5. to impress deeply or indelibly: as, a face *stamped* with grief. 6. to put an official seal or a stamp on (a document, letter, etc.). 7. to characterize or reveal distinctly, as if by imprinting. *v.i.* 1. to bring the foot down forcibly. 2. to walk with loud, heavy steps. *n.* 1. the act of stamping. 2. a machine or tool for stamping or crushing ore, etc. 3. any implement, as a die, brought forcibly against something to mark or shape it. 4. a mark or form so made. 5. a mark, seal, etc. used to show officially that a tax has been paid, authority given, etc. 6. *a*) a small piece of paper, usually a printed gummed label, sold by a government to be put on a letter, document, etc. as evidence that the prescribed fee has been paid. *b*) any similar piece of paper, issued by a firm, organization, etc.: as, a trading *stamp*. 7. any characteristic sign or impression: as, the *stamp* of truth. 8. character; kind; class; type. —**stamp'er,** *n.*

**stam·pede** (stam-pēd'), *n.* [< Am. Sp. < Sp. *estampar*, to stamp], 1. a sudden, headlong running away of a herd of frightened horses, cattle, etc. 2. a confused, headlong rush or flight of a large group of people. 3. any sudden, impulsive mass movement. *v.i.* [-PEDED, -PEDING], to move in a stampede. *v.t.* to cause to stampede. —**stam-ped'er,** *n.*

**stamp·ing ground** (stam'piŋ), [Colloq.], the habitual or favorite gathering place or haunt (of the animals or persons specified).

**stance** (stans), *n.* [< OFr. < LL. < L. *stans*, ppr. of *stare*, to stand], the way a person stands, especially with reference to the position of the feet.

**stanch** (stanch; *also, & for adj. usually,* stänch), *v.t.* [OFr. *estanchier;* ult. < L. *stans*, ppr. of *stare*, to stand], to check the flow of (blood, etc.) from (a cut, etc.). *v.i.* to stop flowing, as blood. *adj.* 1. watertight; seaworthy. 2. trustworthy; loyal: as, a *stanch* supporter. 3. strong; substantial. Also, especially for the *adj.*, **staunch.** —**stanch'ly,** *adv.* —**stanch'ness,** *n.*

**stan·chion** (stan'shən), *n.* [< OFr. < *estance*, a stance; see STANCE], an upright bar or post used as a support. *v.t.* to provide or support with stanchions.

**stand** (stand), *v.i.* [STOOD, STANDING], [AS. *standan*], 1. *a*) to be or remain in an upright position on the feet. *b*) to be or remain in an upright position on its base, bottom, etc.: said of physical objects. *c*) to grow upright: said of plants. 2. to take a standing position. 3. *a*) to take, or be in, a (specified) standing position: as, *stand* back! *b*) to take or maintain a (specified) position or attitude: as, I *stand* opposed to this act. 4. to have a (specified) height when standing: as, he *stands* six feet. 5. to be placed; be situated. 6. to gather and remain, as water. 7. to remain unchanged, intact, etc.: as, my decision *stands*. 8. to be in a (specified) condition, relation, etc.: as, he *stood* in awe. 9. to be at a (specified) rank, degree, etc.: as, he *stands* first on the list. 10. to agree or accord. 11. [Chiefly Brit.], to be a candidate for election. 12. to make resistance, as to hostile action. 13. *a*) to halt. *b*) to be stationary. 14. to show the (specified) relative position of those involved: said of a score, account, etc. 15. in *nautical usage*, to take or hold a certain course at sea. *v.t.* 1. to make stand; place upright. 2. to endure; tolerate. 3. to withstand; resist. 4. to undergo: as, *stand* trial. 5. [Colloq.], to bear the cost of (a meal, etc.), as when treating. *n.* 1. a standing; esp., a halt or stop; specif., *a*) a stopping to counterattack, resist, etc., as in a retreat. *b*) a halt made by a touring theatrical company to give a performance. 2. the place where one stands or is supposed to stand; position. 3. a view, opinion, etc., as on an issue. 4. a structure to stand or sit on; specif., *a*) a raised platform or a set of steplike tiers, as for spectators at an athletic field, etc. *b*) the place where a witness testifies in a courtroom. 5. *a*) a booth, stall, etc. where goods are sold. *b*) a business site or location. 6. a rack, small table, etc. for holding things. 7. a standing growth of trees or plants. —**make a stand,** 1. to take a position for defense or opposition. 2. to support a definite position, opinion, etc. —**stand a chance** (or **show**), to have a chance. —**stand by,** 1. to be near and ready to act as needed. 2. to aid or support. 3. to keep (a promise, etc.). 4. to be present, especially in a passive manner. —**stand for,** 1. to be a symbol for or sign of; represent. 2. [Colloq.], to tolerate or endure. —**stand in,** [Colloq.], to be on good terms; be friendly (usually with *with*). —**stand off,** 1. to keep at a distance. 2. to put off or evade, as an assailant. —**stand on,** 1. to be based or founded upon. 2. to insist upon; demand. —**stand one's ground,** to maintain one's position. —**stand out,** 1. to project. 2. to show up clearly; be distinct. 3. to be prominent, notable, etc. 4. to refuse to give in; be firm. —**stand to,** 1. to keep working at without pause. 2. to be ready. 3. to support; hold to. 4. to keep (a promise, etc.). —**stand up,** 1. to take a standing position. 2. to prove valid, durable, etc. 3. [Slang], to fail to keep an engagement with. —**stand up for,** to support; defend. —**stand up to,** to confront fearlessly. —**stand'er,** *n.*

**stand·ard** (stan'dẽrd), *n.* [< OFr. *estendard;* prob. < Gmc.], 1. a flag, banner, etc. used as an emblem or symbol of a people, military unit, etc. 2. something established as a rule or basis of comparison in measuring or judging capacity, quantity, extent, value, quality, etc. 3. something used by general agreement as a type, model, or pattern; criterion. 4. any upright object used as a support, often a part of the thing it supports; base; stand. 5. a tree or shrub with a tall, erect stem. *adj.* 1. used as, or conforming to, a standard, rule, model, etc. 2. generally recognized as excellent and authoritative. 3. ordinary; typical: as, *standard* design. 4. generally used, and regarded as proper for use, in speaking or writing; not vulgar, solecistic, etc.: as, *standard* English.

**stand·ard-bear·er** (stan'dẽrd-bâr'ẽr), *n.* 1. the man who carries the standard, or flag, of a military unit, etc. 2. the leader or chief representative of a movement, political party, etc.

**standard candle,** a unit of light equal to the light given off by a ⅞-inch sperm candle burning at the rate of 120 grains per hour.

**standard gauge,** 1. a width (between the rails) of 56½ inches. 2. a railroad having such a gauge. —**stand'ard-gauge',** *adj.*

**stand·ard·ize** (stan'dẽr-dīz'), *v.t.* [-IZED, -IZING], 1. to make standard or uniform. 2. to compare with or test by a standard. —**stand'ard·i·za'tion,** *n.* —**stand'ard·iz'er,** *n.*

**standard of living,** a level of subsistence, as of a nation, class, or person, with reference to the adequacy of necessities and comforts in daily life.

**standard time,** the official civil time for any given region; mean solar time, determined by distance east or west of Greenwich, England: the earth is divided into 24 time zones, four of them (*Eastern, Central, Mountain,* and *Pacific*) falling in the U.S. and using the civil times of the 75th, 90th, 105th, and 120th meridians respectively; adjacent time zones are one hour apart.

**stand-by** (stand'bī'), *n.* [*pl.* -BYS], a person or thing that can always be depended upon or used.

**stand·ee** (stan-dē'), *n.* [Colloq.], a person who stands, usually because there are no vacant seats, as at a concert or play.

**stand-in** (stand'in'), *n.* 1. a person who serves as a substitute for a motion-picture actor or actress while lights and camera are being adjusted, etc. 2. any substitute for another. 3. [Slang], a position of favor and influence (*with* someone).

**stand·ing** (stan'diŋ), *n.* 1. the act, state, or position of one that stands. 2. status, rank, or reputation: as, in good *standing.* 3. duration of service, existence, etc.: as, a rule of long *standing.* *adj.* 1. that stands; upright or erect. 2. done from a standing position: as, a *standing* jump. 3. stagnant; not flowing: said of water. 4. permanent or for an unlimited time: as, a *standing* order. 5. not movable. 6. not in operation, use, etc., as a machine.

**standing army,** an army maintained in peace as well as in war, on a permanent organizational basis.

**standing room,** room in which to stand, especially when there are no vacant seats, as in a theater.

**Stan·dish,** Captain **Miles** (stan'dish), 1584?–1656; English military leader of Plymouth Colony.

**stand·off** (stand'ôf'), *n.* 1. a standing off or being stood off. 2. an equalizing effect. 3. a tie or draw in a contest. *adj.* standoffish.

**stand·off·ish** (stand'ôf'ish), *adj.* aloof; reserved. —**stand'off'ish·ly,** *adv.* —**stand'off'ish·ness,** *n.*

**stand·pat** (stand'pat'), *adj.* [Colloq.], of or characterized by a tendency to stand pat, or resist change; conservative. —**stand'pat'ter,** *n.*

**stand·pipe** (stand'pīp'), *n.* a large vertical pipe or tank for storing water to get a uniform pressure.

**stand·point** (stand'point'), *n.* 1. position from which something is viewed. 2. mental position from which things are judged; point of view.

**stand·still** (stand'stil'), *n.* a stop or halt.

**stand-up** (stand'up'), *adj.* 1. standing upright or erect. 2. done or taken while standing.

**stan·hope** (stan'hōp, stan'əp), *n.* [< F. *Stanhope,* 19th-c. Eng. clergyman], a light, open carriage with two or four wheels and, usually, a single seat.

**Stan·i·slav·sky, Kon·stan·tin** (kon'stən-tēn' stan'i-släf'ski), 1863–1938; Russian actor, director, and producer.

**stank** (staŋk), alt. pt. of **stink.**

**stan·nate** (stan'āt), *n.* a salt of stannic acid.

**stan·nic** (stan'ik), *adj.* [< LL. *stannum,* tin], of or containing tin, specifically with a valence of four.

**stan·nous** (stan'əs), *adj.* [< LL. *stannum,* tin], of or containing tin, specifically with a valence of two.

**stan·num** (stan'əm), *n.* [L.], tin: symbol, Sn.

**Stan·ton, Edwin Mc·Mas·ters** (mək-mas'tẽrz stan'tən), 1814–1869; U.S. secretary of war (1862–1867).

**stan·za** (stan'zə), *n.* [It., room; ult. < L. *stare,* to stand], a group of lines of verse forming one of the divisions of a poem: it usually has a regular and recurrent pattern. —**stan·za'ic** (-zā'ik), *adj.* —**stan·za'i·cal·ly,** *adv.*

**sta·pes** (stā'pēz), *n.* [ML., stirrup ? < OHG. *stapf,* a step], a small, stirrup-shaped bone, the innermost of the three bones in the middle ear.

**staph·y·lo·coc·cus** (staf'i-lə-kok'əs), *n.* [*pl.* -COCCI (-kok'sī)], [< Gr. *staphylē,* bunch of grapes; + *-coccus*], any of a group of spherical bacteria that generally occur in irregular clusters and are the cause of pus formation in boils, abscesses, etc. —**staph'y·lo·coc'cic** (-sik), *adj.*

**sta·ple** (stā'p'l), *n.* [< OFr. < MD. *stapel,* mart], 1. the or a chief commodity made, grown, or sold in a particular place, country, etc. 2. a chief item or element in anything. 3. raw material. 4. any common, regularly stocked item of trade, as flour, salt, etc. 5. the fiber of cotton, wool, etc., with reference to length and fineness. 6. [Archaic], a principal market, trading center, etc. *adj.* 1. regularly stocked because of constant demand. 2. produced or consumed regularly and in quantity. 3. most important; principal. *v.t.* [-PLED, -PLING], to sort (cotton, wool, etc.) according to the nature of its staple. —**sta'pler,** *n.*

**sta·ple** (stā'p'l), *n.* [AS. *stapol,* a post], 1. a U-shaped piece of metal with sharp-pointed ends, driven into a surface to hold a hook, wire, etc. 2. a similar piece of thin wire driven through papers, etc. as a binding. *v.t.* [-PLED, -PLING], to fasten with a staple or staples. —**sta'pler,** *n.*

**star** (stär), *n.* [AS. *steorra*], 1. any of the heavenly bodies seen as small, fixed points of light in the night sky. 2. any one of these bodies that is a distant sun: distinguished from *moon, planet, meteor,* etc. 3. a conventionalized flat figure, having five or six projecting points, representing a star. 4. any mark, emblem, etc. resembling such a figure. 5. an asterisk (*). 6. *a*) in *astrology,* a planet, etc. regarded as influencing human fate. *b*) *often pl.* fate; destiny. 7. one who excels in a given activity, especially a sport. 8. a leading actor or actress. *v.t.* [STARRED, STARRING], 1. to mark with stars as a decoration, grade of quality, etc. 2. to mark with an asterisk. 3. to present (an actor or actress) in a leading role. *v.i.* 1. to perform brilliantly; excel. 2. to play a leading role. *adj.* 1. outstanding for skill and talent; leading. 2. of a star or stars. —**star'less,** *adj.* —**star'like',** *adj.*

**star·board** (stär'bẽrd, -bôrd', -bōrd'), *n.* [< AS. < *steoran,* to steer (the old rudder was used on the right side)], the right-hand side of a ship or airplane as one faces forward, toward the bow: opposed to *port.* *adj.* of or on the starboard. *adv.* to or toward the starboard. *v.t.* & *v.i.* to turn (the helm) to the right.

**starch** (stärch), *n.* [< AS. *stercan,* to stiffen < *stearc,* stiff], 1. a white, tasteless, odorless food substance found in potatoes, cereals, peas, etc.: it is a complex carbohydrate $(C_6H_{10}O_5)_n$. 2. a powdered form of this, used in water solution for stiffening cloth fabrics, etc. 3. *pl.* starchy foods. 4. formal, unbending manner; stiffness. 5. [Colloq.], energy; vigor. *v.t.* to stiffen as with starch. —**starch'a·ble,** *adj.* —**starch'less,** *n.*

**Star Chamber,** 1. formerly, an English high court which met in secret, forced confessions, and was arbitrary and severe. 2. [also s- c-], any tribunal, investigating body, etc. using unjust, arbitrary, inquisitorial methods.

**starch·y** (stär′chi), *adj.* [-IER, -IEST], 1. of, like, or containing starch. 2. stiffened with starch. 3. formal; unbending. **—starch′i·ness,** *n.*

**star·dom** (stär′dəm), *n.* 1. the status of a star in the theater, etc. 2. such stars collectively.

**stare** (stâr), *v.i.* [STARED, STARING], [AS. *starian*], 1. to gaze or look steadily and intently, as in fear, wonder, etc. 2. to be glaring or conspicuous: said especially of color. *v.t.* 1. to stare at. 2. to affect in a given way by staring: as, we *stared* her into confusion. *n.* the act of staring; steady, intent look. **—stare down,** to stare back at (another), until he looks away. **—stare one in the face,** to be imminent, pressing, or inescapable. **—star′er,** *n.* **—star′ing·ly,** *adv.*

**star·fish** (stär′fish′), *n.* [*pl.* see FISH], a small sea animal with a hard, spiny covering and five or more arms arranged like the points of a star.

STARFISH (5–6 in. across)

**star·gaze** (stär′gāz′), *v.i.* [-GAZED, -GAZING], 1. to gaze at the stars. 2. to indulge in dreamy, absent-minded thoughts. **—star′gaz′er,** *n.*

**stark** (stärk), *adj.* [AS. *stearc*], 1. stiff; rigid: said of the dead. 2. standing out in sharp outline: as, a tree *stark* in the snow. 3. bleak; desolate. 4. sheer; downright. 5. [Archaic], harsh, severe, etc. *adv.* 1. in a stark manner. 2. utterly; entirely. **—stark′ly,** *adv.* **—stark′ness,** *n.*

**stark-nak·ed** (stärk′nāk′id), *adj.* [alt. < ME. *stertnaked*, lit., tail-naked < AS. *steort*, tail], without any clothing; entirely naked.

**star·let** (stär′lit), *n.* 1. a small star. 2. [Colloq.], a young motion-picture actress being prepared for starring roles.

**star·light** (stär′lit′), *n.* light given by the stars. *adj.* lighted by the stars: also **star′lit′** (-lit′).

**star·ling** (stär′liŋ), *n.* [AS. *stær*], any of various European birds with iridescent plumage: some have been brought into the U.S.

**star-of-Beth·le·hem** (stär′əv-beth′li-əm, -li-hem′), *n.* a plant of the lily family, with white, star-shaped flowers and long, narrow leaves.

**Star of David,** a six-pointed star formed of two equilateral triangles: a symbol of Judaism: as a medieval mystic symbol, called *Solomon's Seal.*

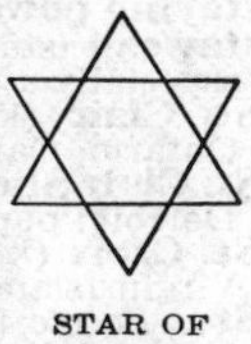
STAR OF DAVID

**starred** (stärd), *adj.* 1. marked or decorated with or as with stars. 2. thought to be affected by the stars. 3. presented as a star actor, etc.

**star·ry** (stär′i), *adj.* [-RIER, -RIEST], 1. set or marked with stars. 2. shining like stars; bright. 3. star-shaped. 4. lighted by or full of stars. 5. of, from, or like stars. **—star′ri·ly,** *adv.* **—star′ri·ness,** *n.*

**Stars and Bars,** the first flag of the Confederacy, with three horizontal bars and a circle of stars.

**Stars and Stripes,** the red, white, and blue flag of the U.S., having 50 stars and 13 stripes.

**star-span·gled** (stär′spaŋ′g'ld), *adj.* studded or spangled with stars.

**Star-Spangled Banner,** 1. the flag of the U.S. 2. the U.S. national anthem: the words were written by Francis Scott Key during the War of 1812.

**start** (stärt), *v.i.* [AS. *styrtan*], 1. to move suddenly, usually involuntarily; jump, jerk, etc. 2. to become loose, displaced, etc. 3. to stick out or seem to stick out, as the eyes in fear. 4. *a*) to begin to do something or go somewhere. *b*) to make or have a beginning; commence. 5. to be among the beginning entrants in a race. 6. to spring into being, activity, etc. *v.t.* 1. to rouse; flush: as, we *started* a bird. 2. to displace, loosen, etc.: as, to *start* a seam. 3. to cause or set into motion or action. 4. to begin using, doing, etc. 5. to introduce (a subject, etc.). 6. to cause to be an entrant in a race, etc. *n.* 1. a sudden, brief shock or fright. 2. a sudden, startled movement; jump, jerk, etc. 3. *pl.* sudden, usually brief bursts of activity: usually in *by fits and starts.* 4. *a*) a part that is loosened, warped, etc. *b*) a break or gap resulting from this. 5. a starting, or beginning; commencement. 6. a place where, or a time when, a beginning is made; starting point. 7. a lead, etc. giving an advantage, as in a race; edge. 8. an opportunity of beginning a career, etc. **—start in,** to begin a task, activity, etc. **—start out,** to start a journey, some course of action or procedure, etc. **—start up,** 1. to come into being suddenly. 2. to cause (a motor, etc.) to begin running.

**start·er** (stärt′ẽr), *n.* one that starts; specif., *a*) the first in a series. *b*) a person or animal that starts in a race. *c*) one who gives the signal to start. *d*) one who supervises the departure of buses, aircraft, etc. *e*) a self-starter.

**star·tle** (stär′t'l), *v.t.* [-TLED, -TLING], [< ME. freq. of *sterten*, to start], 1. to frighten or alarm suddenly; cause to start. 2. to surprise: as, he was *startled* at the damage. *v.i.* to be startled. *n.* a start or shock, as of surprise or fright. **—star′tler,** *n.*

**star·tling** (stär′tliŋ), *adj.* causing a shock of fright or surprise. **—star′tling·ly,** *adv.*

**star·va·tion** (stär-vā′shən), *n.* 1. the act of starving. 2. the state of being starved.

**starve** (stärv), *v.i.* [STARVED, STARVING], [< AS. *steorfan*, to die], 1. to die from lack of food. 2. to suffer or become weak from hunger. 3. to suffer from great poverty. 4. [Colloq.], to be very hungry. *v.t.* 1. to cause to starve. 2. to compel by starvation: as, to be *starved* into submission. **—starve for,** to have a strong desire for.

**starve·ling** (stärv′liŋ), *adj.* 1. starving; weak and hungry. 2. poverty-stricken. *n.* a person or animal that is thin and weak from lack of food.

**stash** (stash), *v.t. & v.i.* [prob. a blend of *store* and *cache*], [Slang], to put or hide away (money, valuables, etc.) in a secret or safe place.

**-stat** (stat), [Gr. *-statēs*], a combining form meaning *stationary, making stationary*, as in *thermostat.*

**state** (stāt), *n.* [< OFr. < L. *status* < *stare*, to stand], 1. a set of circumstances or attributes characterizing a person or thing at a given time; condition: as, mental *state.* 2. a particular mental or emotional condition: as, a *state* of melancholy. 3. condition as regards structure, form, stage of existence, etc. 4. [Obs. or Rare], social status or rank. 5. ceremonious or luxurious display or style of living; pomp. 6. [sometimes S-], *a*) a body of people politically organized under one government within a definite territory. *b*) the authority represented by such a body of people. 7. [usually S-], one of the political units constituting a federal government, as in the United States. 8. the territory of a state (senses 6*a* & 7). 9. civil government; sphere of highest governmental authority: as, matters of *state.* *adj.* 1. of or for occasions of great ceremony; formal; ceremonial. 2. [sometimes S-], of the body politic, government, or state. *v.t.* [STATED, STATING], 1. to set or establish by specifying. 2. to set forth in words in a specific or formal way. **—lie in state,** to be displayed formally to the public before burial. **—the States,** [Colloq.], the United States. **—stat′a·ble,** *adj.* **—state′hood,** *n.* **—state′less,** *adj.*

**state·craft** (stāt′kraft′, -kräft′), *n.* skill in managing state affairs; statesmanship.

**stat·ed** (stāt′id), *adj.* 1. fixed; regular. 2. declared; alleged. 3. formulated. **—stat′ed·ly,** *adv.*

**State·house** (stāt′hous′), *n.* the official meeting place of a State legislature: also **State house.**

**state·ly** (stāt′li), *adj.* [-LIER, -LIEST], 1. imposing; majestic. 2. slow, dignified, and deliberate. *adv.* in a stately manner. **—state′li·ness,** *n.*

**state·ment** (stāt′mənt), *n.* 1. an act of stating, or setting forth in words. 2. something stated; account; declaration. 3. an abstract of a financial account, especially of money due.

**Stat·en Island** (stat′'n), an island between New Jersey and Long Island, forming the Borough of Richmond, New York City.

**state·room** (stāt′rōōm′, -room′), *n.* 1. a cabin on board ship. 2. a private room in a railroad car.

**state's evidence,** in *law*, evidence given by or for the prosecution in a criminal case, especially by a criminal against his associates. **—turn state's evidence,** to give such evidence for the prosecution.

**state·side** (stāt′sīd′), *adj.* [Colloq.], of or characteristic of the U.S.: as, *stateside* newspapers. *adv.* [Colloq.], in, to, or toward the U.S.

**states·man** (stāts′mən), *n.* [*pl.* -MEN], one who is wise and skillful in conducting state affairs and treating public issues, or one experienced in the business of government. **—states′man·like′, states′man·ly,** *adj.* **—states′man·ship′,** *n.* **—states′wom′an** [pl. -WOMEN], *n.fem.*

---

fat, āpe, bâre, cär; ten, ēven, hêre, ovẽr; is, bīte; lot, gō, hôrn, tōōl, look; oil, out; up, ūse, fũr; get; joy; yet; chin; she; thin, *th*en; zh, leisure; ŋ, ring; ə for *a* in *ago*, *e* in *agent*, *i* in *sanity*, *o* in *comply*, *u* in *focus*; ′ in *able* (ā′b'l); Fr. bàl; ë, Fr. coeur; ö, Fr. feu; Fr. moṅ; ô, Fr. coq; ü, Fr. duc; H, G. ich; kh, G. doch. ‡ foreign; < derived from.

**state socialism,** the theory, doctrine, or practice of an economy planned and controlled by the state, based on state-owned utilities, industries, etc.
**States' rights,** all the rights and powers which the Constitution neither grants to the Federal government nor denies to the various State governments: also **State rights.**
**state-wide** (stāt′wīd′), ***adj.*** extending throughout a state.
**stat·ic** (stat′ik), ***adj.*** [< Gr. *statikos,* causing to stand < *histanai,* to cause to stand], 1. acting through weight only: said of pressure exerted by a motionless body. 2. of masses, forces, etc. at rest or in equilibrium: opposed to *dynamic.* 3. at rest; inactive; stationary. 4. in *electricity,* designating, of, or producing stationary electrical charges, as from friction. 5. in *radio,* of or having to do with static. Also **stat′i·cal.** ***n.*** 1. electrical discharges in the atmosphere that interfere with radio reception, etc. 2. interference produced by such discharges. —**stat′i·cal·ly,** ***adv.***
**stat·ics** (stat′iks), ***n.pl.*** [see STATIC], the branch of mechanics dealing with bodies, masses, or forces at rest or in equilibrium.
**sta·tion** (stā′shən), ***n.*** [< OFr. < L. < pp. of *stare,* to stand], 1. the place where one stands or is located; especially, an assigned post, location, etc.: as, a guard's *station,* a police *station.* 2. in Australasia, a sheep or cattle ranch. 3. *a*) a regular stopping place, as on a bus line or railroad. *b*) the building or buildings at such a place. 4. social standing or rank. 5. a place equipped to transmit or receive radio waves; esp., the studios, technical installations, etc. of an establishment for radio or television transmission. ***v.t.*** to assign to a station; place; post.
**station agent,** a person who manages a railroad station: also **sta′tion·mas′ter,** ***n.***
**sta·tion·ar·y** (stā′shən-er′i), ***adj.*** [< L. < *statio;* see STATION], 1. not moving; fixed; at rest. 2. unchanging in condition, value, etc. 3. not migratory or itinerant. ***n.*** [*pl.* -IES], one that is stationary.
**stationary engineer,** a person who takes care of stationary engines and installations, such as steam boilers, ventilating equipment, etc.
**sta·tion·er** (stā′shən-ẽr), ***n.*** [< ML. *stationarius* (L., stationary), a shopkeeper (by contrast with a peddler)], a person who sells paper, ink, pens, etc.
**sta·tion·er·y** (stā′shən-er′i), ***n.*** writing materials; specif., paper and envelopes for writing letters.
**station wagon,** an automobile with folding or removable rear seats and a back end that opens for easy loading of luggage, etc.
**stat·ism** (stāt′iz'm), ***n.*** the doctrine or practice of vesting economic control and planning in a centralized state government. —**stat′ist,** ***n. & adj.***
**sta·tis·tic** (stə-tis′tik), ***adj.*** statistical. ***n.*** a statistical item or element.
**sta·tis·ti·cal** (stə-tis′ti-k'l), ***adj.*** of, having to do with, consisting of, or based on statistics. —**sta·tis′ti·cal·ly,** ***adv.***
**stat·is·ti·cian** (stat′is-tish′ən), ***n.*** a person who compiles and analyzes statistical data.
**sta·tis·tics** (stə-tis′tiks), ***n.pl.*** [< G. < ML. *statisticus* < L. *status;* see STATE], 1. facts or data of a numerical kind, assembled and classified so as to present significant information. 2. [construed as sing.], the science of compiling such facts.
**stat·u·ar·y** (stach′ōō-er′i), ***n.*** [*pl.* -IES], 1. statues collectively. 2. the art of making statues. ***adj.*** of or suitable for statues.
**stat·ue** (stach′ōō, -oo), ***n.*** [< OFr. < L. < *statuere,* to place < *stare,* to stand], the form of a person or animal carved in wood, stone, etc., modeled in clay, etc., or cast in plaster, bronze, etc.
**stat·u·esque** (stach′ōō-esk′), ***adj.*** of or like a statue; specif., *a*) tall and well-proportioned. *b*) stately; graceful; showing poise and dignity. —**stat′u·esque′ly,** ***adv.*** —**stat′u·esque′ness,** ***n.***
**stat·u·ette** (stach′ōō-et′), ***n.*** a small statue.
**stat·ure** (stach′ẽr), ***n.*** [OFr. < L. *statura* < *statuere;* see STATUE], 1. the height of the body in a natural standing position. 2. figuratively, growth or height reached: as, moral *stature.*
**sta·tus** (stā′təs, stat′əs), ***n.*** [*pl.* -TUSES], [L.; see STATE], 1. condition or position with regard to law: as, the *status* of a minor. 2. position; rank; standing: as, his *status* as a scholar. 3. state, or condition, as of affairs.
‡**status quo** (kwō), [L., lit., the state in which], the existing state of affairs: also **status in quo.**
**stat·ute** (stach′oot), ***n.*** [< OFr. < LL. < L. pp. of *statuere;* see STATUE], 1. an established rule or law. 2. *a*) a law passed by a legislative body and set forth in a formal document. *b*) such a document.
**statute law,** law established by a legislative body.
**statute of limitations,** a statute limiting the period within which legal action can be taken in a given matter.
**stat·u·to·ry** (stach′oo-tôr′i, -tō′ri), ***adj.*** 1. of, or having the nature of, a statute. 2. fixed, authorized, or established by statute. 3. declared by statute to be punishable: said of an offense.
**St. Augustine,** a seaport in NE Florida: oldest city in U.S.: pop., 15,000.
**staunch** (stônch, stänch), ***adj., v.t. & v.i.*** stanch. —**staunch′ly,** ***adv.*** —**staunch′ness,** ***n.***
**stave** (stāv), ***n.*** [< *staves,* pl. of *staff*], 1. one of the thin, shaped strips of wood set edge to edge to form the wall of a barrel, bucket, etc. 2. a stick or staff. 3. a rung. 4. a set of lines of a poem or song; stanza. 5. in *music,* a staff. ***v.t.*** [STAVED or STOVE, STAVING], 1. to break or puncture, especially by breaking in staves: as, to *stave* a hole in a boat. 2. to furnish with staves. ***v.i.*** to be or become stove in. —**stave in,** to break a hole in. —**stave off,** to ward, hold, or put off, as by force, guile, etc.
**staves** (stāvz), ***n.*** 1. alt. pl. of **staff.** 2. pl. of **stave.**
**stay** (stā), ***n.*** [AS. *stæg*], a heavy rope or cable, usually of wire, used as a brace, as for the masts of a ship; guy. ***v.t.*** 1. to brace or support with stays. 2. to put (a ship) on the other tack. ***v.i.*** to tack: said of a ship.
**stay** (stā), ***n.*** [< OFr. < base of *stay* (rope)], 1. a support; prop; brace. 2. a strip of stiffening material used in a corset, shirt collar, etc. 3. *pl.* a corset stiffened as with whalebone. ***v.t.*** 1. to support; hold or prop up. 2. to sustain in spirit. 3. to cause to rest (*on, upon,* or *in*). —**stay′er,** ***n.***
**stay** (stā), ***v.i.*** [STAYED or *archaic* STAID, STAYING], [< OFr. *ester* (< L. *stare*), to stand], 1. to continue in the place or condition specified; remain; keep: as, *stay* at home, *stay* well. 2. to live, dwell, or reside. 3. to stop; halt. 4. to pause; wait; delay: as, *stay* a little in your work. 5. [Colloq.], to be able to endure; hold out; last. 6. [Colloq.], to keep up, as with another contestant in a race. 7. [Archaic], to cease. ***v.t.*** 1. to stop, halt, or check. 2. to hinder, impede, or detain. 3. to postpone or delay (legal action). 4. [Rare], to quell or allay (strife, etc.). 5. to satisfy for a time (thirst, appetite, etc.). 6. to remain to the end of: as, *stay* the week (out). ***n.*** 1. *a*) a stopping or being stopped. *b*) a halt, check, or pause. 2. a postponement in legal action: as, a *stay* of execution. 3. the action of remaining, or the time spent, in a place: as, a long *stay* in Spain. —**stay′er,** ***n.***
**staying power,** ability to last; endurance.
**stay·sail** (stā′sāl′; *in nautical usage,* -s'l), ***n.*** a sail, especially a triangular sail, fastened on a stay.
**St. Clair** (klâr), a lake between Michigan and Ontario, Canada.
**St. Clair Shores,** a city in SE Michigan: suburb of Detroit: pop., 77,000.
**St. Croix** (kroi), an island of the U.S. part of the Virgin Islands: also called *Santa Cruz.*
**Ste.,** *Sainte,* [Fr.], Saint (female).
**stead** (sted), ***n.*** [AS. *stede*], the place or position of a person or thing as filled by a substitute or successor: as, he came in my *stead.* —**stand (one) in good stead,** to give (one) good use or service.
**stead·fast** (sted′fast′, -fäst′, -fəst), ***adj.*** [< AS. *stedefæste*], 1. firm, fixed, or established. 2. constant; not changing or fickle. Also sp. **stedfast.** —**stead′fast′ly,** ***adv.*** —**stead′fast′ness,** ***n.***
**stead·y** (sted′i), ***adj.*** [-IER, -IEST], [AS. *stedig* < *stede,* stead], 1. firm; stable; that does not shake, totter, etc. 2. regular, uniform, or continuous; not changing, faltering, etc.: as, a *steady* gaze. 3. constant in behavior, loyalty, etc. 4. not easily excited; calm and controlled: as, *steady* nerves. 5. sober; staid; reliable. 6. keeping almost upright, as in a rough sea: said of a ship. ***interj.*** be steady! keep calm! ***v.t. & v.i.*** [-IED, -YING], to make or become steady. ***n.*** [Slang], one's regular sweetheart. —**go steady,** [Colloq.], to be sweethearts. —**stead′i·ly,** ***adv.*** —**stead′i·ness,** ***n.***
**steak** (stāk), ***n.*** [< base of ON. *steikja,* to roast on a spit], a slice of meat or fish, especially of beef, cut thick for broiling or frying.
**steal** (stēl), ***v.t.*** [STOLE, STOLEN, STEALING], [AS. *stælan*], 1. to take (another's property, etc.) dishonestly, especially in a secret manner. 2. to take slyly, surreptitiously, etc.: as, he *stole* a look. 3. to gain insidiously or artfully: as, he *stole* her heart. 4. to move, put, or convey stealthily. 5. in *baseball,* to gain (a base) safely without the help of a hit or error. ***v.i.*** 1. to practice theft. 2. to move or pass stealthily, quietly, etc. ***n.*** [Colloq.], 1. a stealing. 2. something stolen. 3. something obtained at a ludicrously low cost. —**steal′er,** ***n.***

**stealth** (stelth), *n.* [ME. *stalthe* < *stelen*, to steal], secret or furtive action or behavior. —**stealth′i·ly,** *adv.* —**stealth′i·ness,** *n.* —**stealth′y** [-IER, -IEST], *adj.*

**steam** (stēm), *n.* [AS.], 1. originally, a vapor. 2. water as converted into a vapor or gas by being heated to the boiling point: used for heating, as a source of power, etc. 3. condensed water vapor; mist. 4. steam power. 5. [Colloq.], power; energy. *adj.* 1. using steam; heated, operated, etc. by steam. 2. containing or conducting steam. *v.i.* 1. to give off steam or a vapor. 2. to be given off as steam. 3. to become covered with condensed water vapor. 4. to generate steam. 5. to move by steam power. *v.t.* to expose to the action of steam, as in cooking. —**let** (or **blow**) **off steam,** [Colloq.], to release pent-up emotions.

**steam·boat** (stēm′bōt′), *n.* a steamship.

**steam engine,** an engine using steam under pressure to supply mechanical energy.

**steam·er** (stēm′ēr), *n.* 1. something operated by steam power; specif., *a*) a steamship. *b*) a vehicle driven by steam power. *c*) a steam engine. 2. a container for treating with steam.

**steam fitter,** a mechanic who installs and maintains the boilers, pipes, etc. in steam pressure systems. —**steam fitting.**

**steam heat,** heat given off by steam in a closed system of pipes and radiators.

**steam-roll·er** (stēm′rōl′ēr), *v.t.* to crush, override, or force as if with a steam roller. *v.i.* to move or act with overwhelming, crushing force. *adj.* suggestive of a steam roller.

**steam roller,** 1. a heavy, steam-driven roller used in road building and repair. 2. a power which crushes opposition or forces its way relentlessly.

**steam·ship** (stēm′ship′), *n.* a ship driven by steam power.

**steam shovel,** a large, mechanically operated digger, powered by steam.

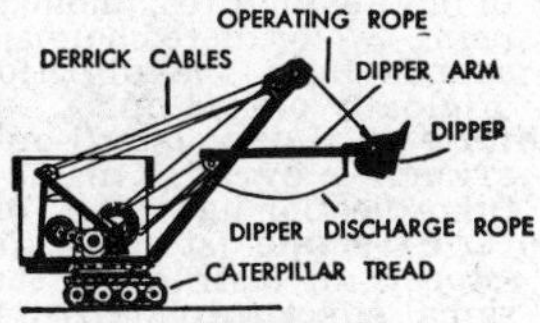

STEAM SHOVEL

**steam table,** a type of table or counter, as in restaurants, having steam-heated compartments in which food may be kept warm.

**steam·y** (stēm′i), *adj.* [-IER, -IEST], 1. of or like steam. 2. filled with steam. 3. giving off steam. —**steam′i·ly,** *adv.* —**steam′i·ness,** *n.*

**ste·ap·sin** (sti-ap′sin), *n.* [G. < *stea*rin + pe*psin*], an enzyme present in the pancreatic juice: it converts fats into glycerol and free acids.

**ste·ar·ic acid** (sti-ar′ik, stêr′-), *adj.* [see STEARIN], a colorless, waxlike fatty acid, $CH_3(CH_2)_{16}COOH$, found in many animal and vegetable fats, and used in making candles, soaps, etc.

**ste·a·rin** (stē′ə-rin, stêr′in), *n.* [< Fr. < Gr. *stear*, tallow], 1. a white, crystalline substance, $(C_{18}H_{35}O_2)_3C_3H_5$, found in the solid portion of most animal and vegetable fats. 2. stearic acid. —**ste·ar·ic** (sti-ar′ik, stêr′-), *adj.*

**ste·a·tite** (stē′ə-tīt′), *n.* [< L. *steatitis* < Gr. *stear*, tallow], talc occurring in the form of a mass; soapstone. —**ste′a·tit′ic** (-tit′ik), *adj.*

**sted·fast** (sted′fast′, -fäst′, -fəst), *adj.* steadfast. —**sted′fast′ly,** *adv.* —**sted′fast′ness,** *n.*

**steed** (stēd), *n.* [AS. *steda*], a horse; esp., a high-spirited riding horse: literary term.

**steel** (stēl), *n.* [see PLURAL, II, D, 3], [AS. *stiele*], 1. a hard, tough metal composed of iron alloyed with a small percentage of carbon: steel may be alloyed with other metals, as nickel, chromium, etc., to increase hardness, etc. 2. something made of steel; specif., [Poetic], a sword or dagger. 3. great strength or hardness: as, sinews of *steel*. *adj.* of or like steel. *v.t.* 1. to cover or edge with steel. 2. to make hard, tough, unfeeling, etc. —**steel′i·ness,** *n.* —**steel′y** [-IER, -IEST], *adj.*

**steel blue,** a metallic blue, as that of tempered steel. —**steel′-blue′,** *adj.*

**Steele,** Sir **Richard** (stēl), 1672–1729; English essayist and playwright.

**steel gray,** a dark, bluish gray. —**steel′-gray′,** *adj.*

**steel mill,** a mill where steel is made, processed, and shaped in various forms: also **steel′works′,** *n.*

**steel wool,** long, hairlike shavings of steel, used for cleaning, smoothing, and polishing.

**steel·work·er** (stēl′wūr′kēr), *n.* a worker in a steel mill.

**steel·yard** (stēl′yärd; *occas.* stil′yērd), *n.* [*steel* + *yard* (in obs. sense of rod)], a scale consisting of a metal arm suspended from above: the object to be weighed is hung from the shorter end and a weight is moved along the graduated longer end until the arm balances.

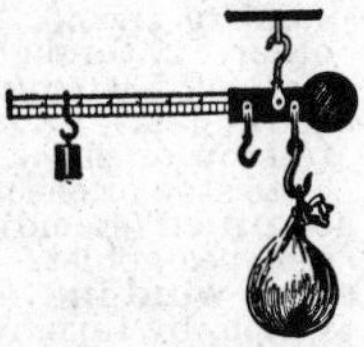
STEELYARD

**steen·bok** (stēn′bok′, stān′-) *n.* [*pl.* -BOK, -BOKS; see PLURAL, II, D, 2], [D. < *steen*, a stone + *bok*, a buck], a small African antelope: also **steinbok.**

**steep** (stēp), *adj.* [AS. *steap*, lofty], 1. having a relatively sharp rise or slope; precipitous. 2. [Colloq.], *a*) unreasonably high or great; excessive: as, a *steep* price. *b*) extreme. *n.* a steep slope. —**steep′ly,** *adv.* —**steep′ness,** *n.*

**steep** (stēp), *v.t.* [< ON. *steypa*], 1. to soak in liquid, as in order to extract the essence of. 2. to immerse, saturate, imbue, etc.: as, *steeped* in folklore. *n.* 1. a steeping or being steeped. 2. liquid in which something is steeped. *v.i.* to be steeped, as tea. —**steep′er,** *n.*

**steep·en** (stēp′'n), *v.t. & v.i.* to make or become steep or steeper.

**stee·ple** (stē′p'l), *n.* [AS. *stypel* < *steap*, lofty], 1. a tower rising above the main structure of a building, especially of a church, usually capped with a spire. 2. a spire. —**stee′pled,** *adj.*

**stee·ple·chase** (stē′p'l-chās′), *n.* [steeples were commonly used as a landmark for the goal], 1. originally, a horse race run across country. 2. a horse race run over a prepared course obstructed with ditches, hedges, etc. —**stee′ple·chas′er,** *n.*

**stee·ple·jack** (stē′p'l-jak′), *n.* a man employed to paint, or make repairs upon, steeples, smokestacks, etc.: also **steeple jack.**

**steer** (stêr), *v.t.* [AS. *stieran*], 1. to guide (a ship or boat) by means of a rudder. 2. to direct the course of (an automobile, etc.). 3. to oversee; direct: as, she *steered* our efforts. 4. to set and follow (a course). *v.i.* 1. to steer a ship, automobile, etc. 2. to be steered: as, the car *steers* easily. 3. to set and follow a course. *n.* [Slang], a suggestion; tip. —**steer clear of,** to avoid. —**steer′a·ble,** *adj.* —**steer′er,** *n.*

**steer** (stêr), *n.* [AS. *steor*], 1. a young castrated ox. 2. any male of beef cattle.

**steer·age** (stêr′ij), *n.* 1. the act of steering. 2. *a*) a ship's reaction to the movement of the helm. *b*) the section of a passenger ship occupied by passengers paying the lowest fare.

**steer·age·way** (stêr′ij-wā′), *n.* the minimum speed needed to make a ship react to the helm.

**steers·man** (stêrz′mən), *n.* [*pl.* -MEN], a person who steers a ship or boat.

**steg·o·my·ia** (steg′ə-mī′ə), *n.* [< Gr. *stegos*, a roof + *myia*, a fly], the yellow-fever mosquito.

**stein** (stīn), *n.* [G.], 1. an earthenware beer mug. 2. popularly, any similar mug, as of glass, etc.

**Stein, Gertrude** (stīn), 1874–1946; American writer in France.

**stein·bok** (stīn′bok′), *n.* [*pl.* -BOK, -BOKS; see PLURAL, II, D, 2], a steenbok.

**Stein·metz, Charles Pro·te·us** (prō′ti-əs stīn′-mets), 1865–1923; American electrical engineer and inventor, born in Germany.

**stel·lar** (stel′ēr), *adj.* [< LL. < L. *stella*, a star], 1. of the stars or a star. 2. like a star, as in shape. 3. by or as by a star performer; excellent. 4. leading; chief: as, the *stellar* role in a play.

**stel·late** (stel′it, -āt), *adj.* [< L. *stellatus*, pp. < *stella*, a star], star-shaped; coming out in rays or points from a center: also **stel′lat·ed** (-ā-tid). —**stel′late·ly,** *adv.*

**St. El·mo's fire** (el′mōz), [< the patron saint of sailors], a flamelike electric discharge sometimes seen on a ship's mast, etc.: also **St. Elmo's light.**

**stem** (stem), *n.* [AS. *stemn*], 1. the main stalk or trunk of a tree, shrub, or other plant, extending above the ground and bearing the leaves, flowers, etc. 2. any stalk supporting leaves, flowers, or fruit. 3. a stemlike part: as, the *stem* of a goblet, a pipe*stem*; specif., *a*) the shaft projecting from a watch, with a knob for winding the spring. *b*) the thick stroke of a letter, as in printing. *c*) the vertical line of a musical note. 4. the prow of a ship; bow. 5. the part of a word to which inflectional endings are added. 6. a branch of a family. *v.t.* [STEMMED, STEMMING], 1. to remove the stem from (a fruit, etc.). 2. to make headway against: as, we could not *stem* the tide. *v.i.* to originate or derive. **—from stem to stern,** 1. from one end of a ship to the other. 2. through the length of anything. **—stem′less,** *adj.* **—stem′mer,** *n.*

**stem** (stem), *v.t.* [STEMMED, STEMMING], [< Scand.], to stop or check; esp., to dam up (a river, etc.), or to stop or check as if by damming up.

**stemmed** (stemd), *adj.* 1. having a stem: as, a thin-*stemmed* goblet. 2. with the stems removed.

**stem-wind·ing** (stem′wīn′diŋ), *adj.* wound, as a watch, by turning a knurled knob at the outer end of the stem. **—stem′-wind′er,** *n.*

**stench** (stench), *n.* [< AS. <*stincan*, to stink], an offensive smell; stink. **—stench′y** [-IER, -IEST], *adj.*

**sten·cil** (sten′s'l), *v.t.* [-CILED or -CILLED, -CILING or -CILLING], [< OFr. *estencele(r)*, spangle; ult. < L. *scintilla*, a spark], to mark or paint with a stencil. *n.* 1. a thin sheet, as of paper or metal, perforated in such a way that when ink, paint, etc. is applied to the sheet, designs, letters, etc. form on the surface beneath the sheet. 2. a design, letters, etc. made by stenciling. **—sten′cil·er, sten′cil·ler,** *n.*

STENCIL

**sten·o-,** [< Gr. *stenos*, narrow], a combining form meaning *small, thin, narrow, abbreviated*, etc.

**ste·nog·ra·pher** (stə-nog′rə-fẽr), *n.* a person skilled in stenography.

**ste·nog·ra·phy** (stə-nog′rə-fi), *n.* [*steno-* + *-graphy*], shorthand writing or, often, the process of taking down dictation in shorthand and later transcribing it in typewriting. **—sten·o·graph·ic** (sten′ə-graf′ik), **sten′o·graph′i·cal,** *adj.* **—sten′o·graph′i·cal·ly,** *adv.*

**sten·o·type** (sten′ə-tīp′), *n.* 1. a symbol or symbols representing a sound, word, etc. in stenotypy. 2. a keyboard machine that prints such symbols: a trade-mark **(Stenotype).**

**sten·o·typ·y** (sten′ə-tīp′i, ste-not′ə-pi), *n.* [< *steno-* + Gr. *typē*, impression], a kind of shorthand using letters as symbols for sounds, words, etc. **—sten′o·typ′ist,** *n.*

**Sten·tor** (sten′tôr), *n.* 1. a Greek herald in the *Iliad* having a very loud voice. 2. [usually s-], a person having a very loud voice.

**sten·to·ri·an** (sten-tôr′i-ən, -tō′ri-), *adj.* [see STENTOR], very loud. **—sten·to′ri·an·ly,** *adv.*

**step** (step), *n.* [AS. *stepe*], 1. the action of moving the foot once and bringing it to rest again, as in walking or running. 2. the distance covered by such a movement. 3. a short distance: as, just a *step* away. 4. a manner of stepping; gait. 5. the sound of stepping; footfall. 6. a mark made by stepping; footprint. 7. a rest for the foot in climbing, as a stair or the rung of a ladder. 8. something resembling a stair step, as a raised frame supporting a mast. 9. a degree; rank; level; stage. 10. any of a series of acts, processes, etc. 11. a sequence of movements in dancing, usually repeated in a set pattern. 12. in *music*, *a*) a degree of the staff or scale. *b*) the interval between two such consecutive degrees. *v.i.* [STEPPED, STEPPING], 1. to move by executing a step. 2. to walk, especially a short distance. 3. to move with measured steps, as in dancing. 4. to move quickly: often with *along.* 5. to come or enter (*into* a situation, etc.). 6. to put or press the foot down (*on* something): as, to *step* on a bug, *step* on the brake. *v.t.* 1. to take (a stride, pace, etc.). 2. to set down (the foot). 3. to execute the steps of (a dance). 4. to measure by taking steps: as, to *step* off ten paces. 5. to provide with steps; specif., *a*) to cut steps in. *b*) to arrange in a series of degrees, etc. **—break step,** to stop marching in cadence. **—in (or out of) step,** 1. (not) conforming to a rhythm in marching, dancing, etc. 2. (not) in conformity or agreement. **—keep step,** to stay in step. **—step by step,** by degrees; gradually. **—step down,** 1. to resign (*from* an office, etc.). 2. to decrease, as in rate. **—step in,** 1. to start to participate. 2. to intervene. **—step on it,** [Colloq.], to go faster; hurry. **—step out,** [Colloq.], to go out for a good time. **—step up,** 1. to approach. 2. to advance. 3. to increase, as in rate. **—take steps,** to adopt certain measures. **—watch one's step,** [Colloq.], to be careful.

**step·broth·er** (step′bruth′ẽr), *n.* one's stepparent's son by a former marriage.

**step·child** (step′chīld′), *n.* [*pl.* -CHILDREN], [AS. *steop-*: orig. applied to the orphaned children (cf. AS. *astypan*, to orphan), but later to those related by remarriage, of a parent], a child of one's husband or wife by a former marriage.

**step·daugh·ter** (step′dô′tẽr), *n.* a female stepchild.

**step-down** (step′doun′), *adj.* that steps down, or decreases, power, speed, etc., as a transformer, gear, etc.

**step·fa·ther** (step′fä′*th*ẽr), *n.* a male stepparent.

**step-ins** (step′inz′), *n.pl.* 1. women's short, loose-fitting underpants. 2. open-heeled slippers.

**step·lad·der** (step′lad′ẽr), *n.* a four-legged ladder having broad, flat steps.

**step·moth·er** (step′mu*th*′ẽr), *n.* a female stepparent.

**step·par·ent** (step′pâr′ənt), *n.* [see STEPCHILD], the person who has married one's parent after the death or divorce of the other parent.

**steppe** (step), *n.* [< Russ. *step'*], 1. one of the great plains of SE Europe and Asia, having few or no trees. 2. any similar plain.

**step·per** (step′ər), *n.* a person or animal that steps (in a specified manner).

**step·ping·stone** (step′iŋ-stōn′), *n.* 1. a stone used to step on, as in crossing a stream, etc. 2. a means for advancement. Also **stepping stone.**

**step·sis·ter** (step′sis′tẽr), *n.* one's stepparent's daughter by a former marriage.

**step·son** (step′sun′), *n.* a male stepchild.

**stept** (stept), poetic pt. and pp. of **step.**

**step-up** (step′up′), *adj.* that steps up, or increases, power, speed, etc., as a transformer, gear, etc.

**-ster** (stẽr), [< AS. *-estre*, orig. a fem. agent suffix], a suffix meaning *a person who is, does,* or *creates* (something specified), as in *oldster, punster,* etc.: often derogatory, as in *rhymester.*

**stere** (stêr), *n.* [< Fr. *stère* < Gr. *stereos*, solid, cubic], a cubic meter.

**ster·e·o** (ster′i-ō′, stêr′i-ō′), *shortened form of* stereophonic, stereoscopic, stereotype, etc.

**ster·e·o-,** [< Gr. *stereos*, hard, firm], a combining form meaning *solid, firm, three-dimensional*, as in *stereoscope:* also **stere-.**

**ster·e·o·phon·ic** (ster′i-ə-fon′ik, stêr′-), *adj.* [*stereo-* + *phonic*], designating or of sound reproduction, as in motion pictures, phonograph recording, or radio, using two or more channels to carry and reproduce sounds from the directions in which they were originally picked up.

**ster·e·op·ti·con** (ster′i-op′ti-kən, stêr′-), *n.* [see STEREO- & OPTIC], a magic lantern having a powerful projection light; esp., one using double pictures.

**ster·e·o·scope** (ster′i-ə-skōp′, stêr′-), *n.* [*stereo-* + *-scope*], an instrument that gives a three-dimensional effect to photographs viewed through it: it has two eyepieces, through which two slightly different views of the same scene are viewed side by side. **—ster′e·o·scop′ic** (-skop′ik), **ster′e·o·scop′i·cal,** *adj.* **—ster′e·o·scop′i·cal·ly,** *adv.*

**ster·e·os·co·py** (ster′i-os′kə-pi, stêr′-), *n.* the science of stereoscopic effects and techniques.

**ster·e·o·type** (ster′i-ə-tīp′, stêr′-), *n.* [< Fr.; see STEREO- & -TYPE], 1. a printing plate cast in type metal from a mold, as of a page of set type. 2. stereotypy. 3. a fixed or conventional expression, notion, mental pattern, etc. *v.t.* [-TYPED, -TYPING], 1. to make a stereotype of. 2. to print from stereotypes. **—ster′e·o·typ′er, ster′e·o·typ′ist,** *n.*

**ster·e·o·typed** (ster′i-ə-tīpt′, stêr′-), *adj.* 1. having the nature of a stereotype; esp., trite; conventional. 2. printed from stereotype plates.

**ster·e·o·typ·y** (ster′i-ə-tīp′i, stêr′-), *n.* the process of making or printing from stereotype plates.

**ster·ile** (ster′'l, -il), *adj.* [L. *sterilis*], 1. incapable of producing others of its kind; barren. 2. producing little or nothing: as, *sterile* soil. 3. lacking in interest or vitality: as, a *sterile* style. 4. free from living microorganisms. **—ster′ile·ly,** *adv.* **—ste·ril·i·ty** (stə-ril′ə-ti), [*pl.* -TIES], *n.*

**ster·i·lize** (ster′ə-līz′), *v.t.* [-LIZED, -LIZING], to make sterile; specif., *a*) to make barren, or incapable of reproduction. *b*) to free from living microorganisms, as by subjecting to great heat. Also sp. **sterilise.** **—ster′i·li·za′tion,** *n.* **—ster′i·liz′er,** *n.*

**ster·ling** (stũr′liŋ), *n.* [< ME. *sterlinge*, Norman coin; prob. < AS. *steorra*, star: from the star stamped on it], 1. sterling silver or articles made of it. 2. the standard of fineness of legal British coinage: since 1920, for silver, 0.500; for gold, 0.91666. 3. British money. *adj.* 1. of standard quality: said of silver that is at least 92.5 per cent pure. 2. of or payable in British money. 3. made of sterling silver. 4. worthy; excellent.

**stern** (stũrn), *adj.* [AS. *styrne*], 1. hard; severe; strict: as, *stern* treatment. 2. grim; forbidding: as, a *stern* face. 3. relentless; firm; inexorable: as, *stern* reality. **—stern′ly,** *adv.* **—stern′ness,** *n.*

**stern** (stũrn), *n.* [prob. < ON. *stjorn*, steering < *styra*, to steer], 1. the rear end of a ship or boat. 2. the rear end of anything.

**Sterne, Laurence** (stũrn), 1713-1768; English novelist and clergyman.

**stern·most** (stûrn′mōst, -məst), *adj.* 1. nearest the stern. 2. farthest astern; rearmost.
**stern·post** (stûrn′pōst′), *n.* the main, upright piece at a vessel's stern, usually supporting the rudder.
**ster·num** (stûr′nəm), *n.* [*pl.* -NA (-nə), -NUMS], [< Gr. *sternon*], a thin, flat structure of bone and cartilage to which most of the ribs are attached in the front of the chest in most vertebrates; breastbone. —**ster′nal** (-n'l), *adj.*
**ster·nu·ta·tion** (stûr′nyoo-tā′shən), *n.* [< L. < freq. of *sternuere*, to sneeze], a sneeze or sneezing. —**ster·nu·ta·to·ry** (stẽr-nū′tə-tôr′i, -tō′ri), **ster·nu′-ta·tive**, *adj.*
**stern·ward** (stûrn′wẽrd), *adv.* toward the stern.
**stern·way** (stûrn′wā′), *n.* backward movement of a ship.
**stern-wheel·er** (stûrn′hwēl′ẽr), *n.* a steamer propelled by a paddle wheel at the stern.
**ster·oid** (ster′oid), *n.* [*ster*ol + *-oid*], any of a group of compounds including the sterols, sex hormones, etc., that are cyclic in structure.
**ster·ol** (ster′ōl, -ol), *n.* [contr. of *cholesterol*], any of a group of solid cyclic alcohols found in plant and animal tissues, as cholesterol.
**ster·to·rous** (stûr′tə-rəs), *adj.* [< L. *stertere*, to snore], characterized by heavy snoring. —**ster′to-rous·ly**, *adv.* —**ster′to·rous·ness**, *n.*
**stet** (stet), [L.], let it stand: a printer's term used to indicate that matter previously struck out is to remain. *v.t.* [STETTED, STETTING], to cancel a correction or deletion previously made by marking with the word *stet.*
**steth·o·scope** (steth′ə-skōp′), *n.* [< Gr. *stethos*, chest; + *-scope*], in *medicine*, a hearing instrument used in auscultation, for examining the heart, lungs, etc. by listening to the sounds they make. —**steth′o·scop′ic** (-skop′ik), **steth′o·scop′i·cal**, *adj.* —**steth′o·scop′i·cal·ly**, *adv.* —**ste·thos·co·py** (ste-thos′kə-pi), *n.*
**Stet·tin** (shte-tēn′), *n.* a seaport in NW Poland: pop., c. 200,000.
**Steu·ben,** Baron **Frederick William von** (von stōō′bin), 1730–1794; German general; served as volunteer in the American Revolutionary Army.
**ste·ve·dore** (stē′və-dôr′, -dōr′), *n.* [< Sp. < *estivar*, to stow < L. *stipare*, to cram], a person employed at loading and unloading ships. *v.t. & v.i.* [-DORED, -DORING], to load or unload the cargo of (a ship).
**Ste·ven·son, Robert Louis** (stē′vən-s'n), 1850–1894; Scottish novelist, poet, and essayist.
**stew** (stōō, stū), *v.t. & v.i.* [< OFr. *estuver* < LL. < L. *ex*, out + Gr. *typhos*, steam], 1. to cook by boiling slowly; simmer. 2. [Colloq.], to worry. *n.* 1. a dish, especially of meat and vegetables, cooked by slow boiling. 2. [Colloq.], a state of worry or anxiety. —**stew in one's own juice,** to suffer, especially from one's own actions.
**stew·ard** (stōō′ẽrd, stū′-), *n.* [< AS. < *sti(g)*, hall + *weard*, a keeper], 1. a person in charge of the affairs of a large estate, who supervises the kitchen and servants, manages the accounts, etc. 2. one who acts as an administrator, as of finances and property, for another. 3. one who buys the provisions, supervises the kitchen and tables, etc. in a club, railroad dining car, etc. 4. a person in charge of arrangements for a ball, race, meeting, etc. 5. one of the staff of servants on a passenger ship. *v.i.* to act as a steward. —**stew′ard·ship′**, *n.*
**stew·ard·ess** (stōō′ẽr-dis, stū′-), *n.* 1. a woman steward. 2. a woman employed to take care of passengers' wants, as on a ship, airplane, etc.
**stewed** (stōōd, stūd), *adj.* 1. cooked by stewing, as food. 2. [Slang], drunk; inebriated.
**stew·pan** (stōō′pan′, stū′-), *n.* a pan for stewing.
**St. He·le·na** (he-lē′nə), a British island in the Atlantic off S Africa: place of Napoleon's exile.
**stib·i·um** (stib′i-əm), *n.* [L. < Gr. *stibi*], antimony: symbol, Sb. —**stib′i·al**, *adj.*
**stick** (stik), *n.* [AS. *sticca*], 1. a twig or small branch broken or cut off, especially a dead and dry one. 2. a long, slender piece of wood, often shaped for a specific purpose, as a wand, staff, club, cane, rod, etc. 3. a stalk, as of celery. 4. something resembling a stick: as, a *stick* of chewing gum. 5. a sticklike playing implement: as, a hockey *stick*. 6. a stab or thrust. 7. the power of adhering or making adhere. 8. a lever for operating the elevators and ailerons of an airplane: also **joy stick.** 9. [Colloq.], a dull, stupid, or spiritless person. *v.t.* [STUCK, STICKING], 1. to pierce or puncture, as with a pointed instrument. 2. to kill by stabbing. 3. to thrust or press (a knife, pin, etc.) so as to pierce. 4. to fasten by piercing through something: as, *stick* a tack in the board. 5. to decorate or set with things so fastened: as, a cushion *stuck* with pins. 6. to thrust or poke: as, *stick* out your hand. 7. to attach as by pinning, gluing, etc.: as, *stick* the poster on the wall. 8. to transfix or impale. 9. to obstruct, detain, delay, etc.: usually in the passive, as, the wheels were *stuck*, I was *stuck* in town. 10. [STICKED, STICKING], to prop (a vine, etc.) with a stick. 11. [Colloq.], to place; put; set. 12. [Colloq.], to make sticky by smearing. 13. [Colloq.], to puzzle; baffle. 14. [Slang], *a*) to make pay exorbitantly; cheat. *b*) to impose a disagreeable task, burden, etc. upon. 15. [Slang], to endure or tolerate: often with *out.* *v.i.* 1. to be fixed by a pointed end, as a nail, etc. 2. to be attached by adhesion; adhere. 3. to remain in the same place; stay: as, they *stick* at home. 4. to cling: as, friends *stick* together. 5. to keep close: as, he *stuck* to the trail. 6. to persevere: as, *stick* at the job. 7. to remain firm and resolute: as, he *stuck* with us. 8. to become fixed, blocked, embedded, jammed, etc.: as, my shoe *stuck* in the mud, the gears *stuck.* 9. to be puzzled. 10. to hesitate; scruple: as, he'll *stick* at nothing. 11. to protrude or extend (with *out*, *up*, etc.). —**stick around,** [Slang], to stay near at hand. —**stick by,** to remain loyal to. —**stick up,** [Slang], to commit armed robbery upon. —**stick up for,** [Colloq.], to uphold; defend. —**the sticks,** [Colloq.], the rural districts. —**stick′like′**, *adj.*
**stick·er** (stik′ẽr), *n.* a person or thing that sticks; specif., *a*) a bur, barb, or thorn. *b*) a gummed label. *c*) [Colloq.], something puzzling.
**stick·ing plaster** (stik′iŋ), court plaster.
**stick·le** (stik′'l), *v.i.* [-LED, -LING], [prob. < ME. *stightlen*, to dispose; ult. < AS. *stihtan*, to arrange], 1. to raise objections, haggle, etc., especially in a stubborn way, usually about trifles. 2. to scruple; demur. —**stick′ler**, *n.*
**stick·le·back** (stik′'l-bak′), *n.* [< AS. *sticel*, a prick], a small, scaleless fish with sharp spines: the male builds a nest for the eggs.
**stick·pin** (stik′pin′), *n.* a pin worn as an ornament in a necktie or cravat.
**stick-to-it·ive·ness** (stik′tōō′it-iv-nis), *n.* [Colloq.], pertinacity.
**stick-up** (stik′up′), *n.* [Slang], a holdup (sense 2).
**stick·y** (stik′i), *adj.* [-IER, -IEST], 1. that sticks; adhesive; clinging. 2. covered with an adhesive substance. 3. [Colloq.], humid: as, *sticky* heat. —**stick′i·ly**, *adv.* —**stick′i·ness**, *n.*
**stiff** (stif), *adj.* [AS. *stif*], 1. hard to bend or stretch; rigid; firm. 2. hard to move or operate: as, the steering gear is *stiff*. 3. stretched tight; taut; tense. 4. sore or limited in movement: said of joints and muscles. 5. having such joints or muscles. 6. not fluid or loose; thick; dense; firm: as, a *stiff* sauce. 7. moving swiftly, as a breeze. 8. containing much alcohol: said of a drink. 9. of high potency: as, a *stiff* dose of medicine. 10. harsh: as, *stiff* punishment. 11. difficult: as, a *stiff* climb. 12. not relaxed or graceful; constrained, or awkward. 13. resolute or stubborn, as a person, fight, etc. 14. [Colloq.], high: said of prices. *n.* [Slang], 1. a corpse. 2. an excessively formal or constrained person. 3. a rough person. —**stiff′ish**, *adj.* —**stiff′ly**, *adv.* —**stiff′ness**, *n.*
**stiff·en** (stif′'n), *v.t. & v.i.* to make or become stiff or stiffer. —**stiff′en·er**, *n.*
**stiff-necked** (stif′nekt′), *adj.* stubborn; obstinate.
**sti·fle** (stī′f'l), *v.t.* [-FLED, -FLING], [< OFr. *estouffer* or < ON. *stīfla*, to stop up], 1. to suffocate; smother. 2. to suppress or check; stop: as, she *stifled* her sobs. *v.i.* 1. to die from lack of air. 2. to suffer from lack of fresh, cool air. —**sti′fler**, *n.* —**sti′fling**, *adj.* —**sti′fling·ly**, *adv.*
**stig·ma** (stig′mə), *n.* [*pl.* -MAS; *also, and for* 4 *and* 6 *usually*, -MATA (-mə-tə)], [L.; Gr., a prick, mark], 1. a brand, as on a criminal. 2. a mark of disgrace or disrepute. 3. a mark, sign, etc. indicating that something is not considered standard. 4. a small mark, scar, or opening, as a pore, on the surface of an animal body. 5. in *botany*, the upper tip of the pistil of a flower, receiving the pollen. 6. in *medicine*, a spot on the skin, especially one that bleeds in certain nervous tensions. —**stig·mat′ic** (-mat′ik), **stig·mat′i·cal**, *adj.*
**stig·ma·tize** (stig′mə-tīz′), *v.t.* [-TIZED, -TIZING], 1. to brand with a stigma. 2. to mark as disgraceful. —**stig′ma·ti·za′tion**, *n.* —**stig′ma·tiz′er**, *n.*
**stile** (stīl), *n.* [AS. *stigel* < *stigan*, to climb], 1. a

step or set of steps used in climbing over a fence or wall. 2. a turnstile.
**sti·let·to** (sti-let′ō), *n.* [*pl.* -TOS, -TOES], [It., dim. of *stilo*, a dagger < L. *stilus;* see STYLE], a small dagger with a slender, tapering blade. *v.t.* [-TOED, -TOING], to stab or kill with a stiletto.
**still** (stil), *adj.* [AS. *stille*], 1. without sound; quiet; silent. 2. hushed, soft, or low in sound. 3. stationary; motionless. 4. tranquil; calm: as, *still* water. 5. not effervescent: said of wine. 6. *a*) designating or of an individual, usually posed photograph. *b*) having to do with a single photograph taken from a motion-picture film. *n.* 1. [Poetic], silence; quiet. 2. a still photograph. *adv.* 1. at or up to the time indicated, whether past, present, or future. 2. even; yet: as, *still* colder. 3. nevertheless; yet: as, he is old and *still* he is able. 4. [Poetic], ever; constantly. *conj.* nevertheless; yet. *v.t.* to make still; specif., *a*) to make silent. *b*) to make motionless. *c*) to calm; relieve. *v.i.* to become still. **—still′er,** *n.* **—still′ness,** *n.*
**still** (stil), *n.* [< obs. *still*, to distill], 1. an apparatus used for distilling liquids, especially alcoholic liquors. 2. a distillery.

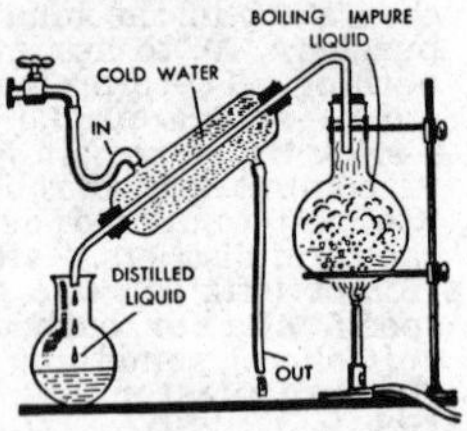

STILL

**still·born** (stil′bôrn′), *adj.* dead when born. **—still′-birth′,** *n.*
**still life,** 1. small inanimate objects, as fruit, flowers, etc., used as subjects for a picture. 2. a picture with such subjects. **—still′-life′,** *adj.*
**Still·son wrench** (stil′s′n), a wrench with a jaw that moves through a collar pivoted to the shaft, used for turning pipes, etc.: pressure applied to the handle tightens the jaw: a trade-mark.
**still·y** (stil′i), *adj.* [-IER, -IEST], [Poetic], still; silent; calm. *adv.* (stil′li), in a still manner.
**stilt** (stilt), *n.* [prob. < LG. or Scand.], 1. either of a pair of poles fitted with a footrest along its length and used for walking, as in play. 2. a long post or pole used to hold something above the ground or out of the water. 3. [*pl.* STILTS, STILT; see PLURAL, II, D, 1], any of several wading birds of the plover family. *v.t.* to set or raise on or as on stilts.
**stilt·ed** (stil′tid), *adj.* 1. raised on or as on stilts. 2. artificially formal or dignified; pompous. **—stilt′-ed·ly,** *adv.* **—stilt′ed·ness,** *n.*
**stim·u·lant** (stim′yoo-lənt), *adj.* stimulating. *n.* anything that stimulates; specif., *a*) an alcoholic drink. *b*) any drug, etc. that temporarily increases the activity of some organ, etc.
**stim·u·late** (stim′yoo-lāt′), *v.t.* [-LATED, -LATING], [< L. *stimulatus*, pp.; ult. < *stimulus*, a goad], 1. to rouse to action, as by goading; excite. 2. to invigorate by an alcoholic drink. 3. in *physiology*, etc., to excite (an organ, etc.) to activity or increased activity. *v.i.* to act as a stimulant or stimulus. **—stim′u·lat′er, stim′u·la′tor,** *n.* **—stim′-u·la′tion,** *n.* **—stim′u·la′tive,** *adj.* **&** *n.*
**stim·u·lus** (stim′yoo-ləs), *n.* [*pl.* -LI (-lī′)], [L., a goad], 1. something that incites to action or increased action; incentive. 2. in *physiology & psychology*, any action or agent that causes or changes an activity in an organism, organ, etc.
**sti·my** (stī′mi), *n.* [*pl.* -MIES], **&** *v.t.* [-MIED, -MYING], stymie.
**sting** (stiŋ), *v.t.* [STUNG or *archaic* STANG, STINGING], [AS. *stingan*], 1. to prick or wound with a sting: said of plants and insects. 2. to cause sharp, sudden, pricking pain to: as, salt will *sting* raw flesh. 3. to cause to suffer mentally: as, his conscience *stung* him. 4. to stimulate suddenly and sharply: as, to *sting* one into action. 5. [Slang], to cheat; dupe: as, he got *stung* on that deal. *v.i.* 1. to use a sting. 2. to cause or feel sharp, smarting pain, either physical or mental. *n.* 1. a stinging. 2. a pain or wound resulting from stinging. 3. a thing that stimulates; goad. 4. the ability to sting. 5. a sharp-pointed organ, as in insects, used to prick, wound, or inject poison. 6. in *botany*, any of the stinging, hollow hairs on some plants, as nettles. **—sting′er,** *n.* **—sting′ing·ly,** *adv.* **—sting′less,** *adj.* **—sting′y,** *adj.*
**sting ray,** a large ray having a whiplike tail with sharp spines capable of inflicting severe wounds: also **sting·a·ree** (stiŋ′ə-rē′), **sting′ray′,** *n.*
**stin·gy** (stin′ji), *adj.* [-GIER, -GIEST], [< *stinge*, dial. form of *sting*], 1. giving or spending grudgingly; miserly. 2. scanty; less than needed or expected. **—stin′gi·ly,** *adv.* **—stin′gi·ness,** *n.*
**stink** (stiŋk), *v.i.* [STANK or STUNK, STUNK, STINKING], [AS. *stincan*], 1. to have a strong, unpleasant smell. 2. to be offensive or hateful. 3. [Slang], to be no good, or of low quality. *v.t.* to cause to stink (usually with *up*). *n.* a strong, unpleasant smell; stench. **—stink out,** to drive out by a strong, unpleasant smell. **—stink′er,** *n.* **—stink′ing,** *adj.* **—stink′ing·ly,** *adv.*
**stink bomb,** a device made to burn or explode and give off an offensive odor.
**stink·bug** (stiŋk′bug′), *n.* any of various foul-smelling bugs.
**stink·weed** (stiŋk′wēd′), *n.* any of several foul-smelling plants, as the Jimson weed.
**stint** (stint), *v.t.* [< AS. *styntan*, to blunt], to restrict to a certain quantity or share, often small. *v.i.* to be sparing in giving or using. *n.* 1. restriction; limit. 2. a limited quantity, share, etc. 3. an assigned task or quantity of work. **—stint′er,** *n.* **—stint′ing·ly,** *adv.* **—stint′less,** *adj.*
**stipe** (stīp), *n.* [Fr. < L. *stipes*, tree trunk], a stalk, as that supporting a pistil, fern frond, etc.
**sti·pend** (stī′pend), *n.* [< OFr. < L. *stipendium* < *stips*, small coin + *pendere*, to weigh out, pay], a regular or fixed payment for services, as a salary, or a periodic payment, as an allowance.
**sti·pen·di·ar·y** (stī-pen′di-er′i), *adj.* 1. receiving, or performing services for, a stipend. 2. paid for by a stipend: said of services. *n.* [*pl.* -ARIES], one who receives a stipend.
**stip·ple** (stip′'l), *v.t.* [-PLED, -PLING], [< D. < *stippel*, a speckle], to paint, draw, or engrave in small dots rather than in lines or solid areas. *n.* 1. the art of painting, drawing, etc. in dots. 2. the effect so produced, or an effect like it. 3. stippled work. Also **stip′pling,** *n.* **—stip′pler,** *n.*
**stip·u·late** (stip′yoo-lāt′), *v.t.* [-LATED, -LATING], [< L. pp. of *stipulari*, to bargain], 1. to arrange definitely, as in a contract. 2. to specify as an essential condition of an agreement. *v.i.* to make a specific demand (*for* something) as a condition of an agreement. **—stip′u·la′tor,** *n.* **—stip′u·la·to′ry** (-lə-tôr′i, -tō′ri), *adj.*
**stip·u·la·tion** (stip′yoo-lā′shən), *n.* 1. act of stipulating. 2. something stipulated, as in a contract.
**stip·ule** (stip′ūl), *n.* [Fr. < L. *stipula*, a stalk], either of two small leaflike parts at the base of some leafstalks, or leaf petioles. **—stip′u·lar** (-yoo-lēr), *adj.* **—stip′u·late** (-lit), **stip′u·lat′ed** (-lāt′id), *adj.*

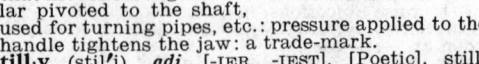

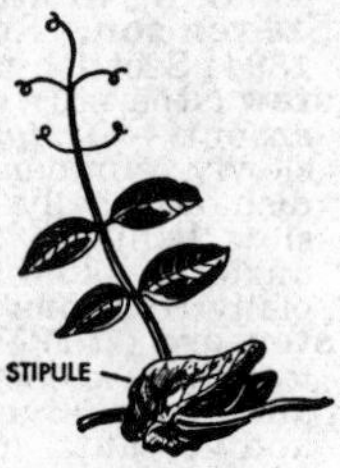

STIPULE (of pea)

**stir** (stũr), *v.t.* [STIRRED, STIRRING], [AS. *styrian*], 1. to move, shake, etc., especially slightly; displace. 2. to rouse from dormancy, lethargy, etc. 3. to put (oneself, one's limbs, etc.) into activity, often briskly. 4. to make (a liquid, etc.) move with an agitated motion, as by passing some implement through it. 5. to excite the feelings of. 6. to incite (often with *up*). *v.i.* 1. to move, especially slightly. 2. to be busy and active. 3. to begin to show signs of activity. 4. to be stirred: as, the paint *stirs* easily. *n.* 1. a stirring, as with a spoon. 2. movement; activity. 3. commotion; tumult. 4. a poke; shove. **—stir′rer,** *n.*
**stir** (stũr), *n.* [Slang], a prison.
**stir·a·bout** (stũr′ə-bout′), *n.* a kind of porridge.
**stir·ring** (stũr′iŋ), *adj.* 1. active; busy. 2. moving; rousing; thrilling: as, *stirring* music. **—stir′ring·ly,** *adv.*
**stir·rup** (stũr′əp, stir′-), *n.* [AS. *stigrap* < *stigan*, to climb + *rap*, a rope], 1. a flat-based ring hung from a saddle and used as a footrest. 2. any of various stirruplike supports, clamps, etc.
**stirrup bone,** in *anatomy*, the stapes.
**stitch** (stich), *n.* [AS. *stice*, a puncture], 1. a single complete in-and-out movement of a threaded needle in sewing, etc. 2. a similar complete movement in knitting, etc. 3. a loop, etc. made by stitching. 4. a particular kind of stitch or stitching. 5. a sudden, sharp pain, as in the side. 6. [Colloq.], a bit: as, I didn't do a *stitch* of work. *v.i.* to make stitches; sew. *v.t.* to fasten, repair, adorn, etc. with or as with stitches; sew. **—stitch′er,** *n.* **—stitch′ing,** *n.*
**sti·ver** (stī′vēr), *n.* [< D. *stuiver*], 1. a Dutch coin equal to 1/20 of a guilder. 2. anything of small value, or a small quantity.
**St. John,** 1. a seaport in New Brunswick, Canada: pop., 51,000. 2. an island of the U.S., part of the Virgin Islands.

**St. John's** (jonz), seaport and capital of Newfoundland: pop., 78,000.
**St.-John's-wort** (sānt-jonz′wũrt′), *n.* any of a number of related plants, as the rose of Sharon, having yellow flowers with many stamens.
**St. Joseph,** a city in NW Missouri, on the Missouri River: pop., 80,000.
**St. Lawrence,** 1. a river flowing from Lake Ontario into the Gulf of St. Lawrence. 2. a gulf off E Canada, at the mouth of this river.
**St. Lawrence Seaway,** an inland waterway, made up of the St. Lawrence River, canals, etc. connecting the Great Lakes with the Atlantic Ocean.
**St. Lou·is** (lōō′is, lōō′i), a port on the Mississippi, in E Missouri: pop., 750,000.
**St. Mo·ritz** (mō′rits), *n.* a town in SE Switzerland: pop., 2,500: mountain resort.
**stoat** (stōt), *n.* [*pl.* STOATS, STOAT; see PLURAL, II, D, 1], [ME. *stote*], an ermine, especially when in its brown summer coat.
**stock** (stok), *n.* [AS. *stocc*], 1. the trunk of a tree. 2. [Archaic], *a*) a tree stump. *b*) a wooden block or log. 3. anything lacking life, motion, or feeling. 4. *a*) a plant stem into which a graft is inserted. *b*) a plant from which cuttings are taken. 5. a rhizome. 6. any of certain plants of the mustard family. 7. *a*) the first of a line of descent. *b*) descent; ancestry. *c*) a strain, race, or other related group of animals or plants. 8. the body or handle of an implement, etc., to which the working parts are attached, as the butt of a whip, the frame of a plow, the part of a rifle holding the barrel, etc. 9. *pl.* a former instrument of punishment consisting of a wooden frame with holes for confining an offender's ankles and, sometimes, his wrists. 10. *pl.* a frame of timbers supporting a ship during construction. 11. raw material: as, paper *stock*. 12. water in which meat, fish, etc. has been boiled, used as a base for soup or gravy. 13. a store or supply; specif., *a*) all the animals, equipment, etc. kept on a farm. *b*) livestock. *c*) the total amount of goods on hand in a store, etc. 14. *a*) the capital used by a business firm in making its transactions. *b*) shares of corporate capital, or the certificates of ownership representing them. *c*) [Colloq.], a part interest in something. 15. *a*) a stock company (sense 2). *b*) its repertoire. 16. a wide, stiff cravat, worn formerly. *v.t.* 1. to attach to a stock, as a plow, etc. 2. to furnish with stock, as a farm or shop. 3. to keep a supply of for sale or for future use. *v.i.* to put in a stock, or supply (often with *up*). *adj.* 1. continually kept in stock: as, *stock* sizes. 2. common, hackneyed, or trite: as, a *stock* joke. 3. that deals with stock. 4. of or relating to a stock company. 5. for breeding: as, a *stock* mare. 6. of, or for the raising of, livestock. —**in** (or **out of**) **stock,** (not) available for sale or use. —**take stock,** 1. to inventory the stock on hand. 2. to estimate, as available resources. —**take stock in,** [Colloq.], to have faith in, regard as important, etc.
**stock·ade** (sto-kād′), *n.* [< Fr. < Pr. *estacado* < *estaca*, a stake], 1. a barrier made of stakes driven into the ground side by side, for defense against attack. 2. any similar enclosure. *v.t.* [-ADED, -ADING], to surround, protect, etc. with a stockade.
**stock·bro·ker** (stok′brō′kẽr), *n.* one who acts as an agent for others in buying and selling stocks and bonds. —**stock′bro′ker·age, stock′bro′king,** *n.*
**stock car,** 1. a railway car for carrying livestock. 2. any standard passenger automobile, but with a supercharged engine, used in certain races.
**stock company,** 1. a company whose capital is divided into shares. 2. a theatrical company established to present a repertoire of plays.
**stock exchange,** 1. a place where stocks and bonds are regularly bought and sold. 2. an association of stockbrokers who meet together for buying and selling stocks and bonds according to fixed rules.
**stock farm,** a farm mainly for raising livestock.
**stock·fish** (stok′fish′), *n.* [*pl.* see FISH], a fish cured by being hung in the open air to dry.
**stock·hold·er** (stok′hōl′dẽr), *n.* a person owning a share or shares of stock in a given company.
**Stock·holm** (stok′hōm′, -hōlm′), *n.* the capital of Sweden, on the Baltic Sea: pop., 805,000.
**stock·i·net** (stok′i-net′), *n.* [prob. for earlier *stocking net*], an elastic, machine-knitted cloth used for making stockings, underwear, etc.
**stock·ing** (stok′iŋ), *n.* [< obs. sense of *stock*], 1. a closefitting covering, usually knitted, for the leg and foot. 2. something like this, as a patch of color on an animal's leg. —**in one's stocking feet,** without one's shoes on but wearing stockings or socks.
**stock·man** (stok′mən), *n.* [*pl.* -MEN], 1. a man who owns or raises livestock. 2. a man who works where goods, etc. are kept, as in a warehouse.
**stock market,** 1. a stock exchange. 2. business carried on at a stock exchange. 3. the prices quoted on stocks and bonds.
**stock·pile** (stok′pīl′), *n.* a reserve supply of goods, raw materials, etc., accumulated for use when needed: also **stock pile.** *v.t. & v.i.* [-PILED, -PILING], to accumulate a stockpile (of).
**stock raising,** the raising of livestock.
**stock·room** (stok′rōōm′, -room′), *n.* a room in which a store of goods, materials, etc. is kept: also **stock room.**
**stock-still** (stok′stil′), *adj.* perfectly motionless.
**Stock·ton** (stok′tən), *n.* a city in central California: pop., 86,000.
**stock·y** (stok′i), *adj.* [-IER, -IEST], heavily built; sturdy; thickset and relatively short. —**stock′i·ly,** *adv.* —**stock′i·ness,** *n.*
**stock·yard** (stok′yärd′), *n.* an enclosure in which cattle, hogs, etc. are kept before being slaughtered.
**stodg·y** (stoj′i), *adj.* [-IER, -IEST], [< dial. *stodge*, heavy food], 1. heavy: said of food. 2. heavily built; bulky. 3. crammed full. 4. dull; uninteresting. —**stodg′i·ly,** *adv.* —**stodg′i·ness,** *n.*
**sto·gie, sto·gy** (stō′gi), *n.* [*pl.* -GIES], [earlier *stoga* < *Conestoga* (wagon)], a long, thin, inexpensive cigar: also sp. **stogey.**
**Sto·ic** (stō′ik), *n.* [< L. < Gr. < *stoa*, colonnade: Zeno taught under a colonnade at Athens], 1. a member of a Greek school of philosophy founded by Zeno about 308 B.C.: the Stoics believed that man should calmly accept divine will and be free from emotions. 2. [s-], a stoical person. *adj.* 1. of the Stoics or their philosophy. 2. [s-], stoical.
**sto·i·cal** (stō′i-k'l), *adj.* 1. showing austere indifference to joy, grief, pain, etc.; impassive. 2. [S-], Stoic. —**sto′i·cal·ly,** *adv.* —**sto′i·cal·ness,** *n.*
**Sto·i·cism** (stō′i-siz'm), *n.* 1. the philosophy of the Stoics. 2. [s-], indifference to pain or pleasure.
**stoke** (stōk), *v.t. & v.i.* [STOKED, STOKING], [< *stoker* < D. < *stoken*, to poke < *stok*, a stick], 1. to stir up and feed fuel to (a fire). 2. to tend (a furnace, boiler, etc.).
**stoke·hold** (stōk′hōld′), *n.* 1. a room containing the boilers on a ship. 2. a stokehole (sense 2).
**stoke·hole** (stōk′hōl′), *n.* 1. the opening in a furnace or boiler through which the fuel is put. 2. a space in front of a furnace or boiler from which the fire is tended, as on a ship.
**stok·er** (stōk′ẽr), *n.* 1. a man who stokes a furnace, especially of a steam boiler, as on a ship, etc. 2. a mechanical device that feeds fuel into a furnace.
**stole** (stōl), *n.* [AS. < L. < Gr. *stolē*, a garment], 1. a long, decorated strip of cloth worn like a scarf by officiating clergymen of various churches. 2. a woman's long scarf of cloth or fur worn with the ends hanging in front.
**stole** (stōl), pt. of **steal.**
**stol·en** (stōl′ən), pp. of **steal.**
**stol·id** (stol′id), *adj.* [< L. *stolidus*, slow], having or showing little or no emotion; unexcitable. —**sto·lid·i·ty** (stə-lid′ə-ti), **stol′id·ness,** *n.* —**stol′id·ly,** *adv.*
**sto·ma** (stō′mə), *n.* [*pl.* STOMATA (-mə-tə, stom′ə-tə)], [< Gr. *stoma*, mouth], 1. a breathing pore in plants. 2. in *zoology*, a mouth or mouthlike opening. —**stom·a·tal** (stom′ə-t'l, stō′mə-), *adj.*
**stom·ach** (stum′ək), *n.* [< Fr. < L. < Gr. *stomachos*, gullet < *stoma*, mouth], 1. the large, saclike organ into which food passes from the esophagus or gullet for storage while undergoing the early processes of digestion. 2. any digestive cavity. 3. the abdomen; belly. 4. appetite. 5. desire or inclination of any kind. *v.t.* 1. to be able to eat or digest. 2. to tolerate; bear.
**stom·ach·er** (stum′ək-ẽr), *n.* an ornamented piece of cloth formerly worn, especially by women, as a covering for the chest and abdomen.
**sto·mach·ic** (stō-mak′ik), *adj.* 1. of or having to do with the stomach. 2. acting as a digestive tonic. Also **sto·mach′i·cal.** *n.* a digestive tonic.
**-stome** (stōm), [< Gr. *stoma*, mouth], a combining form meaning *mouth* or *mouthlike opening*.
**-stomous** (stə-məs), [< Gr. *stoma*, mouth], a combining form meaning *having a* (specified kind of) *mouth*: also **-stomatous.**
**stomp** (stomp), *n., v.t. & v.i.* [Dial.], stamp.
**-stomy** (stə-mi), [< Gr. < *stoma*, mouth], a suffix meaning *a surgical opening into* (a specified part).

fat, āpe, bâre, cär; ten, ēven, hêre, ovẽr; is, bīte; lot, gō, hôrn, tōōl, look; oil, out; up, ūse, fũr; get; joy; yet; chin; she; thin, *th*en; zh, leisure; ŋ, ring; ə for *a* in *ago*, *e* in *agent*, *i* in *sanity*, *o* in *comply*, *u* in *focus*; ' in *able* (ā′b'l); Fr. bal; ë, Fr. coeur; ö, Fr. feu; Fr. mo*n*; ô, Fr. coq; ü, Fr. duc; H, G. ich; kh, G. doch. ‡ foreign; < derived from.

**stone** (stōn), ***n.*** [AS. *stan*], 1. the hard, solid nonmetallic mineral matter of which rock is composed. 2. a small piece of rock. 3. a piece of rock shaped for some purpose; specif., *a*) a building block. *b*) a gravestone. *c*) a milestone. *d*) a grindstone. 4. the stonelike seed of certain fruits. 5. a precious gem. 6. [*pl.* STONE], in Great Britain, 14 pounds avoirdupois. 7. in *medicine*, a small stony mass abnormally formed in the kidney, bladder, etc.; calculus. ***v.t.*** [STONED, STONING], 1. to throw stones at or kill with stones. 2. to furnish, pave, line, etc. with stones. 3. to remove the stone from, as a peach. ***adj.*** of stone or stoneware. **—cast the first stone,** to be the first to censure. **—leave no stone unturned,** to do everything possible.

**stone-,** [< *stone, n.*, with the sense of "like a stone"], a combining form used as an intensive meaning *very, completely*, as in *stone-blind*.

**Stone Age,** the early period in human culture during which stone implements were used.

**stone-blind** (stōn′blīnd′), ***adj.*** completely blind.

**stone-broke** (stōn′brōk′), ***adj.*** [Slang], having no money at all: also **ston′y-broke′.**

**stone·crop** (stōn′krop′), ***n.*** the sedum, a plant commonly used in rock gardens.

**stone·cut·ter** (stōn′kut′ẽr), ***n.*** a person or machine that cuts and dresses stone. **—stone′cut′ting, *n.***

**stoned** (stōnd), ***adj.*** [Slang], 1. drunk; intoxicated. 2. under the influence of a drug.

**stone-deaf** (stōn′def′), ***adj.*** completely deaf.

**Stone·henge** (stōn′henj), ***n.*** a prehistoric stone structure in S England.

**stone·ma·son** (stōn′mā′s′n), ***n.*** a person who cuts stone to shape and uses it in making walls, buildings, etc.: also **stone mason. —stone′ma′son·ry, *n.***

**stone's throw,** a relatively short distance.

**stone·ware** (stōn′wâr′), ***n.*** a coarse, dense, heavily glazed kind of pottery containing much silica.

**stone·work** (stōn′wũrk′), ***n.*** 1. the art or process of working in stone. 2. something made or built in stone. 3. *pl.* a place where masonry stone is cut and dressed. **—stone′work′er, *n.***

**ston·y** (stō′ni), ***adj.*** [-IER, -IEST], 1. covered with or full of stones. 2. of or like stone; specif., *a*) hard. *b*) unfeeling; pitiless. *c*) cold; rigid. 3. petrifying. **—ston′i·ly, *adv.* —ston′i·ness, *n.***

**stood** (stood), pt. and pp. of **stand.**

**stooge** (sto͞oj), ***n.*** [< ?], [Colloq.], 1. an actor who aids a comedian by feeding him lines, being the victim of pranks, etc. 2. anyone who acts as a foil, underling, etc. to another. ***v.i.*** [STOOGED, STOOGING], [Colloq.], to be a stooge (*for* someone).

**stool** (sto͞ol), ***n.*** [AS. *stol*], 1. *a*) a single seat having no back or arms. *b*) a footstool. 2. a toilet; water closet. 3. a bowel movement. 4. feces. 5. a root or tree stump sending out shoots. 6. a cluster of such shoots. ***v.i.*** 1. to put out shoots in the form of a stool. 2. [Colloq.], to act as a stool pigeon.

**stool pigeon,** 1. a pigeon or other bird used as a decoy. 2. [Colloq.], a police spy or informer.

**stoop** (sto͞op), ***v.i.*** [AS. *stupian*], 1. to bend the body forward or in a crouch. 2. to carry the head and shoulders habitually bent forward. 3. to demean oneself; condescend. 4. to swoop down, as a bird of prey. ***v.t.*** to bend forward. ***n.*** 1. the act or position of stooping the body, especially habitually. 2. condescension; lowering of dignity or superiority. 3. a swoop. **—stoop′er, *n.***

**stoop** (sto͞op), ***n.*** [D. *stoep*], a small porch or platform at the entrance of a house.

**stop** (stop), ***v.t.*** [STOPPED or *poetic* STOPT, STOPPING], [< AS. < LL. *stuppare*, to stop up < L. *stuppa*, tow], 1. to close by filling, shutting off, covering, etc. 2. to stanch (a wound, etc.). 3. to block up (a passage, etc.); obstruct. 4. to close (a bottle, etc.) as with a cork. 5. to cause to cease motion, activity, etc. 6. to prevent the passage of (water, light, etc.); block. 7. to halt the progress of (a person, vehicle, etc.). 8. *a*) to check (a blow, stroke, etc. of an opponent); parry; counter. *b*) to defeat (an opponent). 9. to cease; desist from (with a gerund): as, *stop* talking. 10. to cause to end: as, *stop* that racket. 11. to cause (an engine, machine, etc.) to cease operation. 12. to close (a finger hole of a wind instrument) or press down (a violin string, etc.) to produce a desired tone. 13. to keep from beginning, acting, etc.; prevent. 14. to notify one's bank to withhold payment on (one's check). ***v.i.*** 1. to cease moving, walking, etc.; halt. 2. to leave off doing something; desist. 3. to cease operating. 4. to become clogged. 5. to tarry; stay. ***n.*** 1. a stopping or being stopped; check; cessation. 2. a finish; end. 3. a stay or sojourn. 4. a place stopped at, as on a bus route. 5. something that stops; obstruction; specif., *a*) a plug or stopper. *b*) an order to withhold payment on a check. *c*) a mechanical part that stops or regulates motion. *d*) a punctuation mark; esp., a period. 6. *a*) a stopping of a violin string, finger hole, etc. to produce a desired pitch. *b*) a finger hole in a wind instrument. 7. *a*) a tuned set of organ pipes or reeds of the same type and quality. *b*) a pull, lever, or key for putting such a set into or out of operation. 8. in *phonetics*, *a*) a complete stopping of the outgoing breath, as with the velum, lips, or tongue. *b*) a consonant formed in this way, as *k, g, p, b, t,* and *d.* **—put a stop to,** to cause to cease. **—stop off,** to stop for a short stay en route to a place. **—stop over,** 1. to stay for a while. 2. to break a journey, as for rest. **—stop′pa·ble, *adj.***

**stop·cock** (stop′kok′), ***n.*** a valve for controlling the movement of a fluid, as through a pipe.

**stope** (stōp), ***n.*** [akin to *step*], a steplike excavation formed by removing ore from around a mine shaft. ***v.t. & v.i.*** [STOPED, STOPING], to mine in stopes.

**stop·gap** (stop′gap′), ***n.*** a person or thing serving as a temporary substitute. ***adj.*** that is a stopgap.

**stop·o·ver** (stop′ō′vẽr), ***n.*** a brief stop or stay at a place in the course of a journey.

**stop·page** (stop′ij), ***n.*** 1. a stopping or being stopped. 2. an obstructed condition; block.

**stop·per** (stop′ẽr), ***n.*** 1. a person or thing that stops. 2. something inserted to close an opening; plug. ***v.t.*** to close with a stopper.

**stop·ple** (stop′'l), ***n. & v.t.*** [-PLED, -PLING], [< ME. dim. < *stoppen*, to stop], stopper.

**stop street,** a street intersection at which vehicles must come to a complete stop before continuing.

**stop watch,** a watch with a hand that can be started and stopped instantly so as to indicate fractions of seconds, as in timing races, etc.

**stor·age** (stôr′ij, stō′rij), ***n.*** 1. a storing or being stored. 2. a place or space for storing goods. 3. the cost of keeping goods stored.

**storage battery,** a battery of electrochemical cells for generating electric current: the cells can be recharged by passing a current through them in the direction opposite to the discharging current.

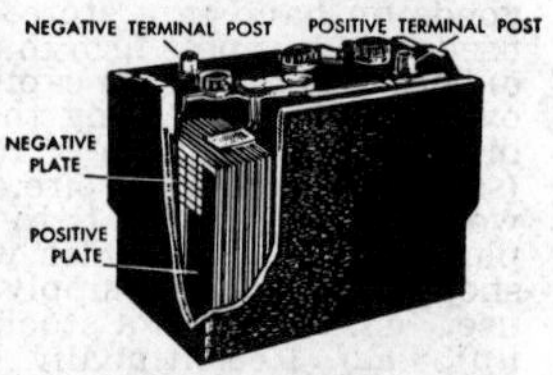


STORAGE BATTERY

**store** (stôr, stōr), ***n.*** [< OFr. < *estorer* (< L. *instaurare*), to restore], 1. a supply (*of* something) for use when needed; reserve. 2. *pl.* supplies, especially of food, clothing, etc. 3. an establishment where goods are offered for sale. 4. a storehouse; warehouse. 5. a great amount; abundance. ***v.t.*** [STORED, STORING], 1. to put aside for use when needed. 2. to furnish with a supply or store. 3. to put in a warehouse, etc. for safekeeping. **—in store,** set aside; in reserve. **—set store by,** to value. **—stor′a·ble, *adj.* —stor′er, *n.***

**store·front** (stôr′frunt′, stōr′-), ***n.*** a room at the ground front of a building, usually with display windows, designed for use as a retail store.

**store·house** (stôr′hous′, stōr′-), ***n.*** a place where things are stored; esp., a warehouse.

**store·keep·er** (stôr′kēp′ẽr, stōr′-), ***n.*** a person in charge of a store or stores.

**store·room** (stôr′ro͞om′, stōr′room′), ***n.*** a room where things are stored.

**sto·rey** (stôr′i, stō′ri), ***n.*** [*pl.* -REYS], [Brit.], a story (of a building).

**sto·ried** (stôr′id, stō′rid), ***adj.*** 1. ornamented with designs showing scenes from history, a story, etc. 2. famous in story or history.

**sto·ried** (stôr′id, stō′rid), ***adj.*** having (a specified number of) stories: as, *three-storied*.

**stork** (stôrk), ***n.*** [*pl.* STORKS, STORK; see PLURAL, II, D, 1], [AS. *storc*], a large, long-legged wading bird with a long neck and bill.

**storm** (stôrm), ***n.*** [AS.], 1. an atmospheric disturbance characterized by a strong wind, usually accompanied by rain, snow, etc. and, often, thunder and lightning. 2. any heavy fall of rain, snow, etc. 3. anything resembling a storm: as, a *storm* of bullets. 4. a strong, emotional outburst: as, a *storm* of criticism. 5. a strong disturbance or upheaval of a political or social nature. 6. a sudden, strong attack on a fortified place. ***v.i.*** 1. to blow violently, rain, snow, etc. 2. to rage; rant. 3. to rush or move violently: as, he *stormed* into the office. ***v.t.*** to attack or assault violently: as, to *storm* a fort, to *storm* with questions. **—storm′er, *n.***

**storm·bound** (stôrm′bound′), ***adj.*** halted, delayed, or cut off by storms.

**storm cellar,** an underground shelter used during hurricanes, tornadoes, etc.
**storm door** (or **window**), an extra door (or window) placed outside of the regular one as added protection against winter weather.
**storm trooper,** a member of the *Sturmabteilung.*
**storm·y** (stôr′mi), *adj.* [-IER, -IEST], 1. of, characteristic of, or affected by storms. 2. having or characterized by storms. 3. violent; raging; passionate. —**storm′i·ly,** *adv.* —**storm′i·ness,** *n.*
**stormy petrel,** 1. any of several small, black-and-white sea birds thought to presage storms. 2. a person thought to presage or bring trouble.
**Stor·ting, Stor·thing** (stôr′tiŋ′, stôr′-), *n.* [Norw. < *stor,* great + *ting,* assembly], the Parliament of Norway.
**sto·ry** (stôr′i, stō′ri), *n.* [*pl.* -RIES], [< OFr. < L. < Gr. *historia;* see HISTORY], 1. the telling of an event or series of events, whether true or fictitious; account; narration. 2. a fictitious literary composition shorter than a novel; narrative; tale. 3. such tales as a form of literature. 4. the plot of a novel, play, etc. 5. a report or rumor. 6. [Colloq.], a falsehood; fib. 7. in *journalism, a*) a news article. *b*) a person or event considered newsworthy. *v.t.* [-RIED, -RYING], to decorate with paintings, etc. of scenes from history or legend.
**sto·ry** (stôr′i, stō′ri), *n.* [*pl.* -RIES], [prob. < prec. entry, referring to "storied" friezes marking the different floors], 1. a horizontal division of a building extending from a floor to the ceiling directly above it: as, ten *stories* high. 2. all the rooms on the same level of a building.
**sto·ry·tell·er** (stôr′i-tel′ẽr, stō′ri-), *n.* 1. one who tells stories. 2. [Colloq.], a fibber; liar. —**sto′ry-tell′ing,** *n. & adj.*
**stoup** (stōōp), *n.* [< ON. *staup*], 1. [Brit. Dial.], a drinking cup; tankard. 2. a basin for holy water in a church. Also sp. **stoop.**
**stout** (stout), *adj.* [< OFr. *estout,* bold; via Gmc.; ult. < L. *stultus,* foolish], 1. courageous; brave. 2. *a*) strong in body; sturdy. *b*) firm; substantial: as, a *stout* wall. 3. powerful; forceful. 4. fat; thickset; corpulent. *n.* 1. a stout person. 2. a garment for a stout person. 3. strong, dark-brown beer. —**stout′ly,** *adv.* —**stout′ness,** *n.*
**stout·heart·ed** (stout′här′tid), *adj.* brave. —**stout′heart′ed·ly,** *adv.* —**stout′heart′ed·ness,** *n.*
**stove** (stōv), *n.* [MD., a heated room], an apparatus using fuel or electricity for heating, cooking, etc.
**stove** (stōv), alt. pt. and pp. of **stave.**
**stove·pipe** (stōv′pīp′), *n.* 1. a metal pipe used to carry off smoke or fumes from a stove. 2. [Colloq.], a man's tall silk hat: in full, **stovepipe hat.**
**stow** (stō), *v.t.* [< AS. *stow,* a place], 1. to pack or store away; esp., to pack in an orderly, compact manner. 2. to fill by packing thus. 3. to hold: said of a container, etc. 4. [Slang], to stop: as, *stow* the chatter. —**stow away,** 1. to put or hide away. 2. to be a stowaway. —**stow′er,** *n.*
**stow·age** (stō′ij), *n.* 1. a stowing or being stowed. 2. place or room for stowing. 3. something stowed. 4. charges for stowing.
**stow·a·way** (stō′ə-wā′), *n.* one who hides aboard a ship, train, etc. so as to obtain free passage or evade port officials, etc.
**Stowe, Harriet Beecher** (stō), 1811–1896; sister of Henry Ward Beecher; U.S. writer.
**St. Paul,** the capital of Minnesota: pop., 313,000.
**St. Pe·ters·burg** (pē′tẽrz-bũrg′), 1. the capital of the former Russian empire: now called *Leningrad.* 2. a city on the W coast of Florida: pop., 181,000.
**stra·bis·mus** (strə-biz′məs), *n.* [< Gr. < *strabizein,* to squint < *strabos,* twisted], a disorder of the eyes, as cross-eye, in which both eyes cannot be focused on the same point at the same time. —**stra·bis′mic, stra·bis′mi·cal, stra·bis′mal,** *adj.*
**strad·dle** (strad′'l), *v.t.* [-DLED, -DLING], [freq. of *stride*], 1. to place oneself with a leg on either side of. 2. to spread (the legs) wide apart. 3. [Colloq.], to appear to take both sides of (an issue); avoid committing oneself on. *v.i.* 1. to sit, stand, or walk with the legs wide apart. 2. [Colloq.], to straddle an issue, etc. *n.* 1. the act or position of straddling. 2. the space between straddled legs. 3. [Colloq.], a refusal to commit oneself definitely. —**strad′dler,** *n.* —**strad′dling·ly,** *adv.*
**Stra·di·va·ri, An·to·ni·o** (än-tô′nyô strä′dē-vä′rē), (Latin name *Antonius Stradivarius*), 1644–1737; Italian violinmaker of Cremona.
**Strad·i·var·i·us** (strad′ə-vâr′i-əs), *n.* a violin, cello, etc. made by Stradivari.
**strafe** (strāf, sträf), *v.t.* [STRAFED, STRAFING], [< G. phr. *Gott strafe England* (God punish England)], 1. to attack with machine-gun fire from low-flying aircraft. 2. to bombard heavily: also used figuratively. —**straf′er,** *n.*
**strag·gle** (strag′'l), *v.i.* [-GLED, -GLING], [prob. < ME. freq. of *straken,* to roam], 1. to stray from the course or wander from the main group. 2. to be scattered over a wide area; ramble. 3. to leave, arrive, etc. at scattered, irregular intervals. —**strag′gler,** *n.* —**strag′gling·ly,** *adv.*
**strag·gly** (strag′li), *adj.* [-GLIER, -GLIEST], spread out in a straggling, irregular way.
**straight** (strāt), *adj.* [< AS. pp. of *streccan,* to stretch], 1. having the same direction throughout its length: as, a *straight* line. 2. not crooked, bent, wavy, etc.: as, *straight* hair. 3. direct; undeviating; continuous: as, a *straight* course. 4. adhering strictly to the principles, candidates, etc. of a political party: as, to vote a *straight* ticket. 5. following a direct course of reasoning, etc.; methodical. 6. in order; properly arranged, etc. 7. *a*) honest; sincere. *b*) [Colloq.], reliable, as information. 8. outspoken; frank. 9. unmixed; undiluted: as, *straight* whisky. 10. unqualified: as, a *straight* answer. 11. at a fixed price regardless of the quantity bought: as, lemons are ten cents *straight.* 12. in *card games,* consisting of cards in sequence. *adv.* 1. in a straight line; unswervingly. 2. upright; erectly. 3. without deviation, detour, etc.; directly. *n.* 1. a being straight. 2. something straight; specif., in *poker,* a series of five cards in sequence. —**straight away** (or **off**), at once; without delay. —**straight′ness,** *n.*
**straight angle,** an angle of 180 degrees.
**straight·a·way** (strāt′ə-wā′), *adj.* extending in a straight line. *n.* a track, or part of a track, that extends in a straight line.
**straight·edge** (strāt′ej′), *n.* a piece of wood, etc. with a straight edge used in drawing straight lines, testing plane surfaces, etc.
**straight·en** (strāt′'n), *v.t. & v.i.* to make or become straight. —**straight′en·er,** *n.*
**straight-faced** (strāt′fāst′), *adj.* showing no amusement or other emotion.
**straight·for·ward** (strāt′fôr′wẽrd), *adj.* 1. moving or leading straight ahead; direct. 2. honest; frank; open. *adv.* in a straightforward manner; directly: also **straight′for′wards.** —**straight′for′ward·ly,** *adv.* —**straight′for′ward·ness,** *n.*
**straight man,** in the *theater,* an actor who serves as a foil for a comedian.
**straight-out** (strāt′out′), *adj.* [Colloq.], 1. unrestrained; outright. 2. thoroughgoing; unqualified.
**straight·way** (strāt′wā′), *adv.* at once.
**strain** (strān), *v.t.* [< OFr. < L. *stringere,* to draw tight], 1. to draw or stretch tight. 2. to exert, use, or tax to the utmost: as, he *strained* every nerve. 3. to injure by exertion; sprain, as a muscle. 4. to injure or weaken by force, pressure, etc.: as, the wind *strained* the roof. 5. to stretch beyond the normal limits: as, he *strained* the rule to his advantage. 6. *a*) to pass through a screen, sieve, etc.; filter. *b*) to remove by filtration, etc. 7. to hug: now only in *to strain to one's bosom. v.i.* 1. to make violent efforts; strive hard. 2. to be or become strained. 3. to be subjected to great stress or pressure. 4. to pull with force. 5. to filter, ooze, etc. *n.* 1. a straining or being strained. 2. great effort, exertion, etc. 3. a sprain or wrench. 4. stress; force. 5. a great or excessive demand on one's emotions, resources, etc. —**strain at,** to use great effort in trying to move (an object). —**strained,** *adj.*
**strain** (strān), *n.* [< AS. *streon,* procreation < base of *strynan,* to produce], 1. ancestry; lineage. 2. the descendants of a common ancestor; race; stock; line. 3. a line of individuals differentiated from its main species or race by certain, generally superior qualities. 4. an inherited character or tendency. 5. a trace; streak. 6. the style or mood of a speech, book, action, etc. 7. *often pl.* a passage of music; tune; air.
**strain·er** (strān′ẽr), *n.* a device for straining, sifting, or filtering; sieve, filter, etc.
**strait** (strāt), *adj.* [< OFr. < L. *strictus,* pp. of *stringere,* to draw tight], 1. [Archaic], *a*) narrow; tight. *b*) strict; rigid. 2. difficult; distressing. *n.* 1. *often in pl.* a narrow waterway connecting two large bodies of water. 2. *often in pl.* difficulty;

distress. 3. [Rare], an isthmus. —**strait′ly,** ***adv.*** —**strait′ness,** ***n.***

**strait·en** (strāt′'n), ***v.t.*** 1. to make strait or narrow; limit. 2. [Rare], to restrict or confine. 3. to bring into difficulties, especially financial hardships: especially in the phrase *in straitened circumstances,* lacking sufficient money.

**strait jacket,** a coatlike device that binds the arms tight against the body: used to restrain violent criminals, mentally deranged persons, etc.

**strait-laced** (strāt′lāst′), ***adj.*** 1. [Archaic], tightly laced, as a corset. 2. narrowly strict or severe in behavior or opinions; prudish.

**Straits Settlements,** a former British colony in the Malay Peninsula.

**strake** (strāk), ***n.*** [ME.], a single line of planking or plating extending along the length of a ship.

**strand** (strand), ***n.*** [AS.], shore, especially ocean shore. ***v.t. & v.i.*** 1. to run or drive aground, as a ship. 2. to put or come into a difficult, helpless position: as, *stranded* in a desert.

**strand** (strand), ***n.*** [< OFr. *estran;* prob. < Gmc.], 1. any of the threads, fibers, wires, etc. that are twisted together to form a string, rope, or cable. 2. any similar ropelike filament: as, a *strand* of beads. ***v.t.*** to break a strand of (a rope, etc.).

**strange** (strānj), ***adj.*** [STRANGER, STRANGEST], [< OFr. < L. *extraneus,* foreign < *extra,* outside], 1. not previously known, seen, heard, etc.; unfamiliar. 2. unusual; extraordinary. 3. peculiar; odd. 4. reserved; distant. 5. unaccustomed; lacking experience: as, *strange* to the job. ***adv.*** in a strange manner. —**strange′ly,** ***adv.*** —**strange′ness,** ***n.***

**stran·ger** (strān′jēr), ***n.*** 1. an outsider; newcomer. 2. a guest or visitor. 3. a person not known or familiar to one. 4. a person unaccustomed (*to* something): as, he is a *stranger* to hate.

**stran·gle** (straŋ′g'l), ***v.t.*** [-GLED, -GLING], [< OFr. < L. *strangulare* < Gr. < *strangalē,* halter], 1. to kill by squeezing the throat so as to shut off the breath; choke. 2. to suffocate in any manner. 3. to suppress; stifle. ***v.i.*** to be strangled; choke. —**stran′gler,** ***n.***

**strangle hold,** 1. a wrestling hold that chokes off an opponent's breath. 2. figuratively, any force that restricts or suppresses freedom.

**stran·gu·late** (straŋ′gyoo-lāt′), ***v.t.*** [-LATED, -LATING], [< L. pp. of *strangulare*], 1. to strangle. 2. in *medicine,* to constrict or obstruct (a tube, duct, etc.) so as to cut off the flow of some fluid. —**stran′gu·la′tion,** ***n.***

**strap** (strap), ***n.*** [dial. form of *strop* < OFr. & AS., both < L. *struppus* < Gr. *strophos,* a band], 1. a narrow strip of leather or other flexible material, often with a buckle at one end, for binding or securing things. 2. any flat, narrow piece used as a fastening. 3. any of several straplike objects, as a shoulder strap. 4. a razor strop. ***v.t.*** [STRAPPED, STRAPPING], 1. to fasten with a strap. 2. to beat with a strap. 3. to strop (a razor). —**strap′less,** ***adj.*** —**strap′like′,** ***adj.*** —**strap′per,** ***n.***

**strap·hang·er** (strap′haŋ′ēr), ***n.*** [Colloq.], a standing passenger, as on a bus, who supports himself by holding onto a suspended strap, etc.

**strap·ping** (strap′iŋ), ***adj.*** [Colloq.], tall and well-built; strong; robust.

**Stras·bourg** (stras′bērg, sträz′-), ***n.*** a city in NE France, on the Rhine: pop., 201,000.

**stra·ta** (strā′tə, strat′ə), ***n.*** alt. pl. of **stratum.**

**strat·a·gem** (strat′ə-jəm), ***n.*** [< Fr. < L. < Gr. *stratēgēma,* act of a general < *stratos,* army + *agein,* to lead], 1. a trick, device, etc. for deceiving an enemy in war. 2. any trick or deception.

**stra·te·gic** (strə-tē′jik), ***adj.*** 1. of or having to do with strategy. 2. sound in strategy; advantageous. 3. essential to effective military strategy. Also **stra·te′gi·cal.** —**stra·te′gi·cal·ly,** ***adv.***

**strat·e·gist** (strat′ə-jist), ***n.*** one skilled in strategy.

**strat·e·gy** (strat′ə-ji), ***n.*** [*pl.* -GIES], [< Fr. < Gr. < *stratēgos,* general], 1. the science of planning and directing large-scale military operations. 2. a plan or action based on this. 3. skill in managing or planning, especially by using stratagem. Also **stra·te·gics** (strə-tē′jiks).

**Strat·ford up·on A·von** (strat′fērd ə-pon′ ā′vən), a town in central England, on the Avon River: Shakespeare's birthplace and burial place: also **Strat′ford-on-A′von.**

**strat·i·fy** (strat′ə-fī′), ***v.t. & v.i.*** [-FIED, -FYING], [< Fr. < ML. < L. *stratum,* layer + *facere,* to make], to form or arrange in layers or strata. —**strat′i·fi·ca′tion** (-fi-kā′shən), ***n.***

**stra·to-cu·mu·lus** (strā′tō-kū′myoo-ləs), ***n.*** [*pl.* -LI (-lī′)], [see STRATUS & CUMULUS], a dark cloud formation having the appearance of mounds piled one on top of the other, usually seen in winter.

**strat·o·sphere** (strat′ə-sfêr′, strā′tə-), ***n.*** [< Fr.; see STRATUM & SPHERE], the upper part of the earth's atmosphere, beginning at an altitude of about seven miles and continuing to the ionosphere: it has an almost constant temperature at all altitudes. —**strat′o·spher′ic** (-sfer′ik), ***adj.***

**stra·tum** (strā′təm, strat′əm), ***n.*** [*pl.* -TA (-tə, -ə), -TUMS], [L. < *stratus,* pp. of *sternere,* to spread], 1. a horizontal layer of matter, especially any of several lying one upon another; specif., in *geology,* a single layer of sedimentary rock. 2. a section or level of society, regarded as like a stratum.

**stra·tus** (strā′təs), ***n.*** [*pl.* -TI (-tī)], [L., a strewing], a cloud formation extending in a long, low layer.

STRATUS CLOUDS

**Strauss, Jo·hann** (yō′hän shtrous; Eng. strous), 1825–1899; Austrian composer of waltzes, etc.

**Strauss, Rich·ard** (riH′ärt), 1864–1949; German composer and conductor.

**Stra·vin·sky, I·gor Fe·do·ro·vich** (ē′gôr fyô′dô-rô′vich strà-vēn′ski; Eng. strə-vin′ski), 1882– ; Russian composer in America.

**straw** (strô), ***n.*** [AS. *streaw*], 1. hollow stalks of grain after threshing: used for fodder, etc. 2. a single one of such stalks. 3. a tube used for sucking beverages. 4. a worthless trifle. ***adj.*** 1. straw-colored; yellowish. 2. made of straw. 3. worthless; meaningless. —**catch** (or **clutch, grasp**) **at a straw,** to try anything that offers even the least hope. —**straw′y** [-IER, -IEST], ***adj.***

**straw·ber·ry** (strô′ber′i, -bēr-i), ***n.*** [*pl.* -RIES], [prob. so called from the small achene on the fruit], 1. the small, red, cone-shaped, fleshy fruit of a vinelike plant of the rose family. 2. this plant.

**strawberry blonde,** reddish blonde.

**strawberry mark,** a small, red birthmark.

**straw boss,** [Colloq.], a person having subordinate authority, as a foreman's assistant.

**straw color,** a pale yellow. —**straw′-col′ored,** ***adj.***

**straw·flow·er** (strô′flou′ēr), ***n.*** a plant with paper-like flowers dried for winter bouquets.

**straw vote,** an unofficial vote or poll taken to determine general group opinion on a given issue.

**stray** (strā), ***v.i.*** [< OFr. *estraier;* prob. < LL. < L. *extra vagare,* to wander outside], 1. to wander from a given place, course, etc.; roam; rove. 2. to be in error; deviate (*from* what is right). 3. to turn aside from the matter at hand: as, their thoughts *strayed.* ***n.*** 1. a person or thing that strays; esp., a domestic animal wandering at large. 2. *usually pl.* in *radio,* static. ***adj.*** 1. having strayed; lost. 2. isolated; occasional: as, a few *stray* words. —**stray′er,** ***n.***

**streak** (strēk), ***n.*** [< AS. *strica*], 1. a line or long, thin mark; stripe or smear. 2. a vein of a mineral. 3. a layer, as of fat in meat. 4. a tendency in behavior, temperament, etc.: as, a nervous *streak.* 5. [Colloq.], a period or spell: as, a *streak* of bad luck. ***v.t.*** to mark with streaks. ***v.i.*** 1. to become streaked. 2. to go fast; hurry. —**like a streak,** [Colloq.], swiftly. —**streak′y** [-IER, -IEST], ***adj.*** —**streak′i·ly,** ***adv.*** —**streak′i·ness,** ***n.***

**stream** (strēm), ***n.*** [AS.], 1. a current or flow of water; specif., a small river. 2. a steady flow of any fluid (a *stream* of cold air) or of rays of energy (a *stream* of light). 3. a continuous series: as, a *stream* of cars. 4. a trend: as, the *stream* of events. ***v.i.*** 1. to flow as in a stream. 2. to flow (*with*): as, eyes *streaming* with tears. 3. to move steadily or swiftly. 4. to float; fly, as a flag in the breeze. ***v.t.*** to cause to stream.

**stream·er** (strēm′ēr), ***n.*** 1. a long, narrow flag. 2. any long, narrow, flowing strip of material. 3. a stream of light extending up from the horizon. 4. a newspaper headline across the full page.

**stream·let** (strēm′lit), ***n.*** a small stream.

**stream·line** (strēm′līn′), ***n.*** 1. the path of a fluid moving past a solid object. 2. a shape with reference to its resistance to air, etc. ***adj.*** designating, of, or having a contour designed to offer the least resistance in moving through air, water, etc.: as, a *streamline* boat. ***v.t.*** [-LINED, -LINING], to give a streamline form to.

**stream·lined** (strēm′līnd′), ***adj.*** 1. having a streamline form. 2. so arranged as to secure the greatest progress and efficiency.

**stream of consciousness,** in *psychology,* individual conscious experience regarded as a continuous series of occurrences.

**stream·y** (strēm′i), ***adj.*** [-IER, -IEST], 1. full of streams or currents. 2. flowing; running.

**street** (strēt), *n.* [AS. *stræt* < LL. < L. *strata via*, paved road], 1. a public road in a city or town; esp., a paved thoroughfare with the sidewalks and buildings along the sides. 2. such a road apart from its sidewalks. 3. the people living, working, etc. in the buildings along a given street.

**street·car** (strēt′kär′), *n.* a large car for public transportation along the streets, usually on rails.

**street urchin** (or **Arab**), a homeless or neglected child left to roam the streets; gamin.

**street·walk·er** (strēt′wôk′ẽr), *n.* a prostitute who seeks trade along the streets.

**strength** (streŋth, streŋkth), *n.* [AS. *strengthu*], 1. the state or quality of being strong; force; vigor. 2. toughness; durability. 3. the power to resist attack. 4. legal, moral, or intellectual force. 5. capacity for producing a reaction; potency, as of drugs, etc. 6. intensity, as of sound, color, etc. 7. force, as measured in numbers: as, an army at full *strength*. 8. a source of strength; support. **—on the strength of,** based or relying on. **—strength′less,** *adj.*

**strength·en** (streŋ′thən, streŋk′-), *v.t.* & *v.i.* to make or become stronger. **—strength′en·er,** *n.*

**stren·u·ous** (stren′ū-əs), *adj.* [L. *strenuus*], 1. requiring or characterized by great effort or energy. 2. ardent, zealous, etc. **—stren′u·ous·ly,** *adv.* **—stren′u·ous·ness, stren′u·os′i·ty** (-os′ə-ti), *n.*

**strep·to·coc·cus** (strep′tə-kok′əs), *n.* [*pl.* -COCCI (-kok′sī)], [< Gr. *streptos*, bent + *kokkos*, a grain], any of a group of spherical bacteria, occurring generally in chains: some species cause serious diseases. **—strep′to·coc′cal** (-kok′əl), **strep′to·coc′cic** (-kok′sik), *adj.*

**strep·to·my·cin** (strep′tə-mī′sin), *n.* [< Gr. *streptos*, twisted + *mykēs*, fungus], an antibiotic drug similar to penicillin, obtained from certain molds and used in treating various diseases.

**stress** (stres), *n.* [< OFr. < LL. < L. *strictus*, strict], 1. strain; pressure; esp., force exerted upon a body, that tends to strain or deform its shape. 2. urgency; importance. 3. tension; strained exertion: as, the *stress* of war. 4. in *music*, accent. 5. *a)* the relative force of utterance given a syllable or word in pronunciation or, according to the meter, in verse. *b)* an accented syllable. *v.t.* 1. to put stress, pressure, or strain on. 2. to give stress or accent to. 3. to emphasize.

**-stress** (stris), [< *-ster* + *-ess*], a feminine suffix corresponding to *-ster*, as in *songstress*.

**stretch** (strech), *v.t.* [AS. *streccan*], 1. to reach out (a hand, etc.). 2. to cause (the body or limbs) to reach out to full length, as in relaxing, etc. 3. to pull or draw out to full extent or to greater size. 4. to cause to extend over a given space or distance. 5. *a)* to extend beyond normal limits; strain: as, they *stretched* the law. *b)* to exaggerate. 6. to make tense with effort; strain (a muscle, etc.). *v.i.* 1. *a)* to spread out to full extent or beyond normal limits. *b)* to extend over a given space or distance. 2. to extend the body or limbs to full length, as in yawning, etc. 3. to become stretched to greater size, as any elastic substance. 4. to lie down at full length (usually with *out*). *n.* 1. a stretching or being stretched. 2. an unbroken period: as, a *stretch* of three months. 3. [Slang], a prison sentence. 4. the extent to which something can be stretched. 5. an unbroken length, tract, etc.: as, a *stretch* of beach. 6. one of the straight sections of a race track, especially the part between the last turn and the finish line. **—stretch′a·ble,** *adj.*

**stretch·er** (strech′ẽr), *n.* 1. one that stretches; specif., any of various devices for stretching or shaping garments, etc. 2. a light frame covered with canvas, etc. and used for carrying the sick, injured, or dead.

**stretch-out** (strech′out′), *n.* [Colloq.], a system of industrial operation in which more work is required with little or no increase in pay.

**stretch·y** (strech′i), *adj.* [-IER, -IEST], 1. that can be stretched; elastic. 2. liable to stretch too far. **—stretch′i·ness,** *n.*

**strew** (strōō), *v.t.* [STREWED, STREWED or STREWN, STREWING], [AS. *streowian*], 1. to scatter; spread here and there as by sprinkling. 2. to cover as by scattering. 3. to be scattered over (a surface).

**stri·a** (strī′ə), *n.* [*pl.* -AE (-ē)], [L.], 1. a narrow groove or channel. 2. a fine streak or line; esp., one of a number of parallel lines.

**stri·ate** (strī′āt; *for adj., usually* strī′it), *v.t.* [-ATED, -ATING], [< L. pp. of *striare*, to groove], to mark with striae. *adj.* striated. **—stri·a′tion,** *n.*

**stri·at·ed** (strī′āt-id), *adj.* marked with striae, as the voluntary muscles.

**strick·en** (strik′ən), occas. pp. of **strike.** *adj.* 1. struck or wounded, as by a missile. 2. afflicted, as by something painful, disagreeable, etc.

**strict** (strikt), *adj.* [< L. pp. of *stringere*, to draw tight], 1. exact; precise. 2. perfect; absolute. 3. *a)* enforcing rules with great care; punctilious. *b)* closely enforced; rigorous. **—strict′ly,** *adv.* **—strict′ness,** *n.*

**stric·ture** (strik′chẽr), *n.* [< L. < *strictus*, pp. of *stringere*, to draw tight], 1. adverse criticism; censure. 2. in *medicine*, an abnormal narrowing of a passage in the body.

**stride** (strīd), *v.i.* & *v.t.* [STRODE, STRIDDEN (strid′'n), STRIDING], [AS. *stridan*], 1. to walk with long steps, in a vigorous or pompous manner. 2. to take a single, long step, as in passing over (something). 3. to straddle. *n.* 1. the act of striding. 2. a long step. 3. a full step in a gait, as of a horse. 4. the distance covered by a stride. 5. *usually pl.* progress; advancement. **—hit one's stride,** to reach one's normal level of efficiency. **—take in one's stride,** to cope with easily and without undue effort. **—strid′er,** *n.*

**stri·dent** (strī′d'nt), *adj.* [< L. ppr. of *stridere*, to rasp], harsh-sounding; shrill; grating. **—stri′dence, stri′den·cy,** *n.* **—stri′dent·ly,** *adv.*

**strid·u·late** (strij′oo-lāt′), *v.i.* [-LATED, -LATING], [< L. < *stridere*, to rasp], to make a shrill grating or chirping sound, as certain insects. **—strid′u·lant, strid′u·lous,** *adj.* **—strid′u·la′tion,** *n.*

**strife** (strīf), *n.* [< OFr. *estrif*], 1. the act of striving; contention. 2. a quarrel; struggle.

**strike** (strīk), *v.t.* [STRUCK, STRUCK or *occas.* STRICKEN, STRIKING], [< AS. *strican*, to go, proceed], 1. *a)* to give a blow to; hit; smite. *b)* to give (a blow, etc.). *c)* to remove as by a blow: as, he *struck* the gun from her hand. 2. to make by stamping, printing, etc.: as, a mint *strikes* coins. 3. to produce (a tone, etc.) by hitting a key as on a piano. 4. to announce (time), as with a bell: said of clocks, etc. 5. *a)* to ignite (a match) by friction. *b)* to produce (a light, etc.) by friction. 6. to come into forceful contact with; collide with: as, the car *struck* the curb. 7. to cause to come into forceful contact: as, he *struck* his head on the door. 8. to wound with the fangs: said of snakes. 9. to attack. 10. to come into contact with; specif., *a)* to fall on; shine on, as light. *b)* to reach (the eye or ear). *c)* to come upon: as, we *struck* the main road. *d)* to notice or find suddenly. *e)* to discover, as after drilling: as, they *struck* oil. 11. to affect as if by contact, a blow, etc.; specif., *a)* to occur to: as, the idea just *struck* me. *b)* to impress (one's fancy, sense of humor, etc.). *c)* to seem to: as, it *strikes* me as silly. *d)* to cause to become suddenly: as, he was *struck* dumb. *e)* to overcome suddenly with strong feeling: as, to be *struck* with amazement. *f)* to arouse: as, it *struck* terror to my heart. 12. *a)* to make and ratify (a bargain, truce, etc.). *b)* to arrive at by figuring, etc.: as, we *struck* a balance. 13. to lower (a sail, flag, etc.). 14. *a)* to dismantle (a stage set). *b)* to turn a stage light down or off. 15. to refuse to continue to work at (a factory, etc.) until certain demands have been met. 16. to level the top of (a measure of grain, etc.) as with a stick. 17. to assume (a pose, etc.). 18. to put forth (roots): said of plants. *v.i.* 1. to deliver or aim a blow; hit (*at*). 2. to attack. 3. *a)* to make sounds by being struck, as a bell. *b)* to be announced as by such striking: as, one o'clock had *struck*. 4. to hit; collide (with *against*, *on*, or *upon*): as, the ball *struck* against the house. 5. to ignite: as, the match won't *strike*. 6. to seize a bait: said of a fish. 7. to dart in an attempt to wound, as a snake. 8. to penetrate; pierce: as, the wind *struck* through the cracks. 9. to come suddenly (with *on* or *upon*): as, we *struck* on an idea. 10. to lower sail. 11. to lower a flag in token of surrender. 12. to refuse to continue to work until certain demands are met. 13. to take root: said of a plant. 14. to proceed: as, they *struck* northward. 15. to move or pass quickly. *n.* 1. a striking; blow. 2. a concerted refusal by employees to go on working in an attempt to gain improved working conditions, as higher wages. 3. a finding of a rich deposit of oil, coal, etc. 4. any sudden success. 5. the seizing of bait by a fish. 6. in *baseball*, a pitched ball which is: *a)* struck at but missed. *b)* fairly delivered but not struck at. *c)* hit as a foul tip caught by the catcher. *d)* hit foul (unless there are already two strikes):

three strikes put the batter out. 7. in *bowling,* *a*) the act of knocking down all the pins on the first bowl. *b*) the score so made. —(**out**) **on strike,** striking (*v.i.* 12). —**strike camp,** to break up a camp by taking down tents, etc. —**strike dumb,** to amaze; astound. —**strike home,** 1. to deliver an effective blow. 2. to have the desired effect. —**strike it rich,** 1. to discover a rich deposit of ore, oil, etc. 2. to become successful suddenly. —**strike off,** 1. to remove as by a blow. 2. to print, stamp, etc. —**strike out,** 1. to remove from a record, etc.; erase. 2. to start out. 3. in *baseball,* *a*) to be put out by three strikes. *b*) to put (a batter) out by pitching three strikes. —**strike up,** 1. to begin playing, singing, etc. 2. to begin (a friendship, etc.).

**strike·break·er** (strīk′brāk′ẽr), *n.* one who tries to break up a workers' strike as by supplying scabs, intimidating workers, etc. —**strike′break′ing,** *n.*

**strik·er** (strīk′ẽr), *n.* 1. one who strikes; specif., a worker who is on strike. 2. a thing that strikes, as the clapper in a bell, etc.

**strik·ing** (strīk′iŋ), *adj.* 1. that strikes or is on strike. 2. extraordinary; remarkable. —**strik′ing·ly,** *adv.* —**strik′ing·ness,** *n.*

**Strind·berg, August** (strind′bẽrg, strin′-), 1849–1912; Swedish novelist and dramatist.

**string** (striŋ), *n.* [AS. *streng*], 1. *a*) a thin line of twisted fiber, or a thin strip of wire, leather, etc., used as for tying or pulling. *b*) a narrow strip of leather or cloth for fastening shoes, clothing, etc. 2. a number of objects on a string: as, a *string* of pearls. 3. a line of things in succession: as, a *string* of houses. 4. a group of athletes arranged according to ability: as, the players of the second *string.* 5. *a*) a slender cord as of gut or wire, stretched on a violin, harp, etc. and bowed, plucked, or struck to make a musical sound. *b*) *pl.* all the stringed instruments of an orchestra, or their players. 6. a strong, slender, stringlike organ, formation, etc.; specif., a fiber of a plant. 7. [Colloq.], a condition or limitation attached to a plan, offer, etc. *v.t.* [STRUNG, STRUNG or *rare* STRINGED, STRINGING], 1. to provide with strings. 2. to thread on a string. 3. to tie, pull, hang, etc. with a string. 4. to adjust or tune the strings of (a musical instrument). 5. to tighten; brace. 6. to make excited or tense. 7. to remove the strings from (beans, etc.). 8. to arrange in a row. 9. to extend: as, to *string* a cable. 10. [Colloq.], to fool; hoax (often with *along*). *v.i.* 1. to form into a string or strings. 2. to stretch out in a line. —**on a string,** helpless; under control. —**pull strings,** 1. to get someone to use influence in one's behalf, often secretly. 2. to influence others, often secretly. —**string up,** [Colloq.], to kill by hanging. —**string′less,** *adj.* —**string′like′,** *adj.*

**string bean,** 1. any of several varieties of bean having thick, meaty pods eaten as a vegetable when unripe. 2. the pod of any of these.

**string·course** (striŋ′kôrs′, -kōrs′), *n.* a decorative, horizontal band set in the wall of a building.

**stringed** (striŋd), rare pp. of **string.** *adj.* having strings, as certain musical instruments.

**strin·gent** (strin′jənt), *adj.* [< L. ppr. of *stringere,* to draw tight], 1. strict; severe. 2. short in loan or investment money: said of a market. 3. compelling; convincing. —**strin′gen·cy** [*pl.* -CIES], **strin′gent·ness,** *n.* —**strin′gent·ly,** *adv.*

**string·er** (striŋ′ẽr), *n.* 1. a person or thing that strings. 2. a long piece of timber used as a support or to connect upright posts in a frame.

**string·halt** (striŋ′hôlt′), *n.* [alt. < *springhalt*], a condition in horses causing the hind legs to jerk spasmodically in walking.

**string·piece** (striŋ′pēs′), *n.* a long, horizontal timber for supporting a framework.

**string quartet,** in *music,* a quartet of or for players on stringed instruments, usually first and second violins, viola, and violoncello.

**string tie,** a narrow necktie tied in a bow.

**string·y** (striŋ′i), *adj.* [-IER, -IEST], 1. like a string or strings; long, thin, wiry, etc. 2. consisting of strings or fibers. 3. having tough fibers, as meat, celery, etc. 4. forming strings; ropy: as, *stringy* molasses. —**string′i·ness,** *n.*

**strip** (strip), *v.t.* [STRIPPED or *rare* STRIPT, STRIPPING], [AS. *strypan* (in comp.)], 1. *a*) to undress (someone); make naked. *b*) to remove (the clothing, covering, etc.) from a person. 2. to dispossess of honors, titles, attributes, etc. 3. to plunder; spoil; rob. 4. to peel or take off (the covering, skin, etc. of something). 5. to make bare or clear by removing fruit, growth, removable parts, etc.: as, to *strip* an attic of rubbish. 6. to dismantle. 7. to break or jam the thread of (a nut, bolt, etc.). 8. to break off the teeth of (a gear). *v.i.* to take off one's clothing; undress. —**strip′per,** *n.*

**strip** (strip), *n.* [alt. < *stripe* by association with *strip, v.*], 1. a long, narrow piece, as of land, tape, etc. 2. a long, narrow runway for the take-off and landing of airplanes: also **landing strip.**

**stripe** (strīp), *n.* [< MD. or MLG.], 1. a long, narrow band, mark, or streak, differing as in color from the surrounding area. 2. a long welt on the skin, as from a whipping. 3. a stroke with a whip, etc. 4. a strip of cloth or braid worn on the sleeve of a uniform to show rank, years served, etc. 5. a distinctive mark or color. 6. type; kind; sort. *v.t.* [STRIPED, STRIPING], to mark with stripes.

**strip·ling** (strip′liŋ), *n.* a grown boy; youth.

**strip mining,** a method of mining, as for coal, by exposing a mineral deposit near the earth's surface.

**stript** (stript), rare pt. and pp. of **strip.**

**strip tease,** an act, as in burlesque shows, in which a woman takes off her clothes piece by piece, usually to the accompaniment of music. —**strip′-tease′,** *adj.* —**strip′-teas′er,** *n.*

**strip·y** (strīp′i), *adj.* [-IER, -IEST], striped.

**strive** (strīv), *v.i.* [STROVE or *less often* STRIVED, STRIVEN (striv′'n), or STRIVED, STRIVING], [< OFr. < *estrif,* effort], 1. to make great efforts; try very hard: as, they *strove* to win. 2. to struggle; contend; fight: as, *strive* against tyranny. —**striv′er,** *n.*

**strobe** (strōb), *n.* 1. [Colloq.], a stroboscope. 2. an electronic tube emitting rapid, brief, and brilliant flashes of light: used in photography, the theater, etc.: also **strobe light.**

**strob·o·scope** (strob′ə-skōp′), *n.* [< Gr. *strobos,* a twisting round; + *-scope*], an instrument for studying motion by illuminating a moving body at frequent, rapid intervals. —**strob′o·scop′ic** (-skop′ik), **strob′o·scop′i·cal,** *adj.*

**strode** (strōd), pt. of **stride.**

**stroke** (strōk), *n.* [< AS. < *strican,* to hit], 1. a striking of one thing against another; impact of an ax, whip, etc. 2. a sudden action resulting as if from a blow: as, a *stroke* of lightning, a *stroke* of luck. 3. a sudden attack, especially of apoplexy or paralysis. 4. *a*) a single strong effort to do or produce something, especially a successful one. *b*) something accomplished by such an effort. 5. *a*) the sound of striking, as of a clock. *b*) the time indicated by this. 6. *a*) a single movement of the arms, hands, etc. or of something held, as a golf club, pen, brush, etc. *b*) any of a series of repeated rhythmic motions made as in swimming, rowing, etc. *c*) a type, manner, or rate of such movement. 7. a mark made by a pen, etc. 8. a beat of the heart. 9. a gentle, caressing motion with the hand. 10. the rower who sits nearest the stern of a shell and sets the rate of rowing. 11. in *mechanics,* any of the continuous, reciprocating movements of a piston, etc. *v.t.* [STROKED, STROKING], 1. to draw one's hand, a tool, etc. gently over the surface of. 2. to set the rate of rowing for (a crew). —**keep stroke,** to make strokes in rhythm. —**strok′er,** *n.*

**stroll** (strōl), *v.i.* [? < G. *strolchen*], 1. to walk in an idle, leisurely manner; saunter. 2. to go idly from place to place; wander. *v.t.* to stroll along or through. *n.* a strolling; leisurely walk.

**stroll·er** (strōl′ẽr), *n.* 1. one who strolls. 2. an itinerant actor. 3. a light, chairlike baby carriage with openings for the legs.

**strong** (strôŋ), *adj.* [AS. *strang*], 1. *a*) physically powerful; having great muscular strength; robust. *b*) healthy; sound; hale. 2. morally or intellectually powerful: as, a *strong* will or mind. 3. having special ability (*in* a specified subject): as, he's *strong* in French. 4. tough; firm; durable; able to resist: as, a *strong* fort. 5. having many resources; powerful in wealth, numbers, supplies, etc. 6. having a specified number: as, a force 6,000 *strong.* 7. having a powerful effect; drastic: as, *strong* measures. 8. having a large amount of its essential quality; not diluted: as, *strong* coffee. 9. affecting the senses powerfully: as, *strong* light, odor, etc. 10. rancid; rank: as, *strong* butter. 11. firm and loud: as, a *strong* voice. 12. intense in degree or quality; specif., *a*) ardent; passionate: as, *strong* affection. *b*) forceful; persuasive. *c*) felt deeply; decided: as, a *strong* opinion. *d*) zealous: as, a *strong* partisan. *e*) vigorous; forthright: as, *strong* language. *f*) distinct; marked: as, a *strong* resemblance. 13. moving rapidly and with force: as, a *strong* wind. 14. characterized by rapidly rising prices: as, a *strong* market. 15. in *grammar,* expressing variation in tense by internal change of vowel rather than by inflectional endings (e.g., *swim, swam, swum*). *adv.* in a strong manner. —**strong′ly,** *adv.*

**strong-arm** (strôŋ′ärm′), *adj.* [Colloq.], using physical force. *v.t.* [Colloq.], to use force upon.

**strong·box** (strôŋ'boks'), ***n.*** a heavily made box or safe for storing valuables.
**strong drink,** drink containing much alcohol.
**strong·hold** (strôŋ'hōld'), ***n.*** a place having strong defenses; fortress; secure refuge.
**strong-mind·ed** (strôŋ'mīn'did), ***adj.*** having a strong, unyielding mind or will; determined. **—strong'-mind'ed·ness, *n.***
**strong-willed** (strôŋ'wild'), ***adj.*** strong-minded.
**stron·ti·um** (stron'shi-əm), ***n.*** [< *Strontian*, Scotland, where first found], a pale-yellow, metallic chemical element resembling calcium in properties and found only in combination: a deadly radioactive isotope of strontium (**strontium 90**) occurs in the fallout of atomic-weapon explosions: symbol, Sr; at. wt., 87.63; at. no., 38. **—stron'tic, *adj.***
**strop** (strop), ***n.*** [AS. < L. *struppus*, band; cf. STRAP], a leather strap; specif., a strap, etc. used for putting a fine edge on razors. ***v.t.*** [STROPPED, STROPPING], to sharpen on a strop. **—strop'per, *n.***
**stro·phe** (strō'fi), ***n.*** [< Gr. < *strephein*, to turn], 1. in the ancient Greek theater, *a*) a turning of the chorus from right to left. *b*) that part of a choric song performed during this. 2. a stanza. **—stroph·ic** (strof'ik, strō'fik), **stroph'i·cal, *adj.***
**strove** (strōv), alt. pt. of **strive.**
**strow** (strō), ***v.t.*** [STROWED, STROWN or STROWED, STROWING], [Archaic], to strew.
**struck** (struk), pt. and alt. pp. of **strike. *adj.*** closed or affected by a labor strike.
**struc·tur·al** (struk'chēr-əl), ***adj.*** 1. of, having, or characterized by structure, or formation. 2. used in construction or building. **—struc'tur·al·ly, *adv.***
**structural steel,** steel prepared and shaped for use in the construction of buildings, bridges, etc.
**struc·ture** (struk'chēr), ***n.*** [< L. < *structus*, pp. of *struere*, to arrange], 1. manner of building, constructing, or organizing. 2. something built or constructed; building, etc. 3. the arrangement of all the parts of a whole: as, the *structure* of the atom. 4. something composed of parts: as, man is a complex *structure*. ***v.t.*** [-TURED, -TURING], to put together systematically; construct; organize.
**stru·del** (stro͞o'd'l; G. shtro͞o'dəl), ***n.*** [G.], a kind of pastry made of a very thin sheet of dough filled with apples, cheese, etc. and rolled.
**strug·gle** (strug''l), ***v.i.*** [-GLED, -GLING], [ME. *strogelen*], 1. to contend or fight violently with an opponent. 2. to make great efforts; strive; labor: as, she *struggled* to learn Latin. 3. to make one's way with difficulty: as, he *struggled* to shore. ***n.*** 1. great effort; exertion. 2. conflict; strife. **—strug'gler, *n.* —strug'gling·ly, *adv.***
**strum** (strum), ***v.t. & v.i.*** [STRUMMED, STRUMMING], [echoic], to play on (a stringed musical instrument) carelessly, idly, or unskillfully. ***n.*** the act or sound of this. **—strum'mer, *n.***
**strum·pet** (strum'pit), ***n.*** [ME.], a prostitute.
**strung** (struŋ), pt. and alt. pp. of **string.**
**strut** (strut), ***v.i.*** [STRUTTED, STRUTTING], [< ME. *struten*, to swell out < AS. *strutian*, to stand rigid], to walk in a vain, swaggering manner. ***v.t.*** to provide with a strut or brace. ***n.*** 1. a vain, swaggering walk. 2. a brace fitted into a framework to resist pressure in the direction of its length. **—strut'ter, *n.* —strut'ting·ly, *adv.***
**strych·nine** (strik'nin, -nēn, -nīn), ***n.*** [Fr. < L. < Gr. *strychnos*, nightshade], a highly poisonous crystalline alkaloid, obtained from nux vomica and related plants: used in small doses as a stimulant: also **strych'nin** (-nin). **—strych'nic** (-nik), ***adj.***
**St. Thomas,** a U.S. island in the Virgin Islands.
**Stu·art** (sto͞o'ērt, stū'-), ***n.*** the royal family of Scotland (1371 to 1603) and of England (1603 to 1714).
**stub** (stub), ***n.*** [AS. *stubb*], 1. a tree stump. 2. a short piece remaining after the main part has been removed or used up: as, a cigar *stub*. 3. any short projection. 4. a pen with a short, blunt point. 5. a short piece of a ticket or of a leaf in a checkbook kept as a record. ***v.t.*** [STUBBED, STUBBING], 1. to root out (weeds, etc.). 2. to clear (land) of stumps. 3. to strike (one's toe, etc.) against something.
**stub·ble** (stub''l), ***n.*** [< OFr. *estouble* < LL. < L. *stipula*, a stalk], 1. the short stumps of grain left standing after the harvest. 2. any growth like this: as, a *stubble* of beard. **—stub'bled, *adj.* —stub'bly** [-BLIER, -BLIEST], ***adj.***
**stub·born** (stub'ērn), ***adj.*** [prob. < AS. *stubb*, a stub], 1. refusing to yield, obey, or comply; determined to have one's way; obstinate. 2. done or carried on in an obstinate or persistent manner: as, a *stubborn* campaign. 3. hard to handle, treat, or deal with: as, a *stubborn* engine. **—stub'born·ly, *adv.* —stub'born·ness, *n.***
**stub·by** (stub'i), ***adj.*** [-BIER, -BIEST], 1. covered with stubs or stubble. 2. short and heavy or dense. 3. short and thickset. **—stub'bi·ness, *n.***
**stuc·co** (stuk'ō), ***n.*** [*pl.* -COES, -COS], [It.; prob. < OHG. *stucchi*, crust], 1. a kind of fine plaster used for surfacing inside or outside walls, etc. 2. work done in stucco: also **stuc'co·work'.** ***v.t.*** [-COED, -COING], to cover with stucco.
**stuck** (stuk), pt. and pp. of **stick.**
**stuck-up** (stuk'up'), ***adj.*** [Colloq.], snobbish; conceited; haughty; arrogant.
**stud** (stud), ***n.*** [AS. *studu*, post], 1. any of a series of small knobs or rounded nailheads used to ornament a surface. 2. a small, buttonlike device used as a collar fastener, shirt-front ornament, etc. 3. an upright piece in the frame of a building, to which horizontal boards are nailed. 4. a metal crossbar bracing a link, as in a chain cable. 5. a projecting pin or peg used as a support, pivot, etc. ***v.t.*** [STUDDED, STUDDING], 1. to set or decorate with studs or studlike objects. 2. to be set thickly on: as, rocks *stud* the hillside. 3. to scatter or cluster (something) thickly. 4. to provide (a building) with studs.
**stud** (stud), ***n.*** [AS. *stod*], 1. a collection of horses kept especially for breeding. 2. the place where such horses are kept. 3. a studhorse. ***adj.*** of or having to do with a stud. **—at stud,** available for breeding: said of male animals.
**stud·book** (stud'book'), ***n.*** a register of pedigreed horses, especially race horses: also **stud book.**
**stud·ding** (stud'iŋ), ***n.*** 1. the studs of a building. 2. the material for these.
**stud·ding·sail** (stud'iŋ-sāl'; *in nautical usage*, stun's'l), ***n.*** [? < D. *stooten*, to push], a light sail set at the edge of a working sail in light weather: also **studding sail.**
**stu·dent** (sto͞o'd'nt, stū'-), ***n.*** [< OFr. < L. ppr. of *studere*, to study], 1. a person who studies something. 2. a person who is enrolled for study at a school, college, etc. **—stu'dent·ship', *n.***
**stud·horse** (stud'hôrs'), ***n.*** a male horse kept for breeding; stallion.
**stud·ied** (stud'id), ***adj.*** 1. prepared by careful study. 2. deliberate; premeditated: as, *studied* indifference. **—stud'ied·ly, *adv.* —stud'ied·ness, *n.***
**stu·di·o** (sto͞o'di-ō', stū'-), ***n.*** [*pl.* -OS], [It., a study], 1. a room, building, etc. in which an artist does his work. 2. a place where motion pictures are produced. 3. a place for producing radio or television programs.
**studio couch,** a kind of sofa that can be opened into a full-sized bed.
**stu·di·ous** (sto͞o'di-əs, stū'-), ***adj.*** 1. fond of study. 2. characterized by careful heed; attentive; zealous. **—stu'di·ous·ly, *adv.* —stu'di·ous·ness, *n.***
**stud poker,** a form of poker in which each player is dealt some cards face down and some face up.
**stud·y** (stud'i), ***n.*** [*pl.* -IES], [< OFr. < L. *studere*, to study], 1. the application of the mind to acquire knowledge, as by reading, investigating, etc. 2. careful and critical examination of a subject, event, etc. 3. a branch of learning. 4. *pl.* education; schooling. 5. an essay, thesis, etc. embodying results of an investigation. 6. a work of literature or art treating a subject in careful detail. 7. a first sketch for a story, picture, etc. 8. an étude. 9. earnest effort or thought. 10. abstracted state of mind; deep thought. 11. a room designed for study, writing, etc. ***v.t.*** [-IED, -YING], 1. to try to learn by reading, thinking, etc. 2. *a*) to investigate carefully: as, I shall *study* your problem. *b*) to look at carefully; scrutinize: as, *study* the map. 3. to read (a book, lesson, etc.) so as to know and understand it. 4. to memorize. 5. to take a course in at a school. 6. to give care and thought to: as, he *studies* to do right. ***v.i.*** 1. to apply the mind in order to acquire knowledge. 2. to be a student. 3. to meditate; ponder.
**stuff** (stuf), ***n.*** [< OFr. *estoffe;* prob. < L. *stuppa*, tow], 1. the material out of which anything is or can be made; raw material. 2. constituent elements; essence; character: as, made of sterner *stuff*. 3. any kind of matter, indefinitely. 4. cloth, especially woolen cloth. 5. *a*) household goods. *b*) personal belongings. *c*) objects; things. 6. worthless objects; junk. 7. foolish or worthless ideas, etc.; nonsense. ***v.t.*** 1. to fill the inside of

(something); pack; specif., *a*) to fill (a cushion, etc.) with padding. *b*) to fill the skin of (a dead animal) in order to mount and preserve it. *c*) to fill (a fowl, etc.) with seasoning, bread crumbs, etc. before roasting. 2. *a*) to fill too full; cram: as, the desk is *stuffed* with papers. *b*) to fill to excess with food. 3. to fill or cram with. 4. to fill with information, ideas, etc. 5. to put fraudulent votes into (a ballot box). 6. *a*) to plug; block. *b*) to choke; stop up, as with phlegm. 7. to force; push: as, she *stuffed* a comb into her purse. ***v.i.*** to eat too much. **—stuff′er, *n.***

**stuffed shirt** (stuft), [Slang], a pompous, pretentious, but actually unimportant person.

**stuff·ing** (stuf′iŋ), ***n.*** 1. the action of one that stuffs. 2. something used to stuff; specif., *a*) soft, springy material used as padding in cushions, etc. *b*) a mixture, as of bread crumbs and seasoning, for stuffing a fowl, etc. before cooking.

**stuff·y** (stuf′i), ***adj.*** [-IER, -IEST], 1. poorly ventilated; having little fresh air; close. 2. having the nasal passages stopped up, as from a cold. 3. [Colloq.], *a*) dull; stodgy; old-fashioned. *b*) prim; strait-laced. *c*) sulky; obstinate. **—stuff′i·ly, *adv.* —stuff′i·ness, *n.***

**stul·ti·fy** (stul′tə-fī′), ***v.t.*** [-FIED, -FYING], [< LL. < L. *stultus*, foolish + *facere*, to make], 1. to cause to appear foolish, stupid, absurd, etc. 2. to make worthless or useless. **—stul′ti·fi·ca′tion** (-fi-kā′shən), ***n.*** **—stul′ti·fi′er, *n.***

**stum·ble** (stum′b'l), ***v.i.*** [-BLED, -BLING], [< ME. *stomblen;* prob. < ON.], 1. to trip in walking, running, etc. 2. to walk unsteadily, as from age. 3. to speak, act, etc. in a confused, blundering manner. 4. to sin or err; do wrong. 5. to come by chance; happen: as, to *stumble* across a clue. ***v.t.*** to cause to stumble. ***n.*** 1. a stumbling. 2. a blunder, error, or sin. **—stum′bler, *n.* —stum′bling·ly, *adv.***

**stumbling block,** an obstacle or difficulty.

**stump** (stump), ***n.*** [prob. < ON. or MLG.], 1. the lower end of a tree or plant left in the ground after most of the stem or trunk has been cut off. 2. *a*) the part of an arm, leg, tooth, etc. left after the rest has been removed. *b*) a butt; stub: as, the *stump* of a pencil. 3. a short, stocky person or animal. 4. the place where a political speech is made. 5. *a*) the sound of a heavy, tramping step. *b*) such a step. 6. *pl.* [Slang], the legs. 7. in *cricket*, any of the three upright sticks of a wicket. ***v.t.*** 1. to reduce to a stump; lop. 2. to remove stumps from (land). 3. to travel over (a district), making political speeches. 4. [Colloq.], to stub (one's toes, etc.). 5. [Colloq.], to puzzle; perplex; baffle. ***v.i.*** 1. to walk heavily or clumsily, as with a wooden leg. 2. to travel about making political speeches. **—stump′er, *n.* —stump′less, *adj.* —stump′like′, *adj.***

**stump·y** (stum′pi), ***adj.*** [-IER, -IEST], 1. covered with stumps. 2. like a stump; short and thickset; stubby. **—stump′i·ness, *n.***

**stun** (stun), ***v.t.*** [STUNNED, STUNNING], [< OFr. *estoner* < L. *ex-*, intens. + *tonare*, to crash], 1. to make senseless or unconscious, as by a blow. 2. to shock deeply; daze; astound. 3. to overpower as by a loud noise or explosion. ***n.*** 1. a being stunned. 2. something that stuns, as a shock or blow.

**stung** (stuŋ), pt. and pp. of **sting.**

**stunk** (stuŋk), pp. and alt. pt. of **stink.**

**stun·ner** (stun′ẽr), ***n.*** one that stuns; specif., [Colloq.], one that is remarkably beautiful, fine, etc.

**stun·ning** (stun′iŋ), ***adj.*** 1. that stuns. 2. [Colloq.], remarkable, especially for beauty, smartness, etc. **—stun′ning·ly, *adv.***

**stun·sail, stun·s'le** (stun′s'l), ***n.*** a studdingsail.

**stunt** (stunt), ***v.t.*** [< AS. *stunt*, stupid], 1. to check the growth or development of; dwarf. 2. to hinder (growth or development). ***n.*** 1. a stunting. 2. a stunted creature or thing.

**stunt** (stunt), ***n.*** [? akin to *stint*], [Colloq.], something done to attract attention, etc.; exhibition of skill or daring. ***v.i.*** [Colloq.], to perform a stunt. ***v.t.*** [Colloq.], to perform stunts in or with (an airplane, etc.). **—stunt′er, *n.***

**stunt man,** in *motion pictures*, a professional acrobat who takes the place of an actor in dangerous scenes involving falls, leaps, etc.

**stu·pe·fac·tion** (stōō′pə-fak′shən, stū′-), ***n.*** 1. a stupefying or being stupefied. 2. great amazement or bewilderment; astonishment.

**stu·pe·fy** (stōō′pə-fī′, stū′-), ***v.t.*** [-FIED, -FYING], [< Fr. < L. < *stupere*, to be stunned + *facere*, to make], 1. to stun; make stupid, dull, or lethargic. 2. to amaze; astonish. **—stu′pe·fi′er, *n.***

**stu·pen·dous** (stōō-pen′dəs, stū-), ***adj.*** [< L. gerundive of *stupere*, to be stunned], overwhelming; astonishingly great; esp., amazingly large; immense. **—stu·pen′dous·ly, *adv.* —stu·pen′dous·ness, *n.***

**stu·pid** (stōō′pid, stū′-), ***adj.*** [< L. *stupidus* < *stupere*, to be stunned], 1. dazed; stunned; stupefied. 2. lacking in understanding; slow-witted; dull. 3. showing or resulting from a lack of intelligence; foolish. 4. dull; boring; as, a *stupid* party. ***n.*** a stupid person. **—stu·pid′i·ty** [*pl.* -TIES], **stu′pid·ness, *n.* —stu′pid·ly, *adv.***

**stu·por** (stōō′pẽr, stū′-), ***n.*** [L.], 1. a state in which the mind and senses are dulled; partial or complete loss of sensibility. 2. mental or moral dullness or apathy. **—stu′por·ous, *adj.***

**stur·dy** (stũr′di), ***adj.*** [-DIER, -DIEST], [< OFr. *estourdi*, stunned], 1. firm; resolute; unyielding: as, *sturdy* defiance. 2. strong; vigorous; hardy. **—stur′di·ly, *adv.* —stur′di·ness, *n.***

**stur·geon** (stũr′jən), ***n.*** [*pl.* -GEONS, -GEON; see PLURAL, II, D, 1], [< OFr. *esturgeon* < Gmc.], any of several large food fishes having rows of spiny plates along the body and a projecting snout: valuable as a source of caviar and isinglass.

‡**Sturm·ab·tei·lung** (shtoorm′äp′tī′looŋ), ***n.*** [G., storm division], the Storm Troopers, a political militia of the Nazi party: also called *Brown Shirts.*

**stut·ter** (stut′ẽr), ***v.t. & v.i.*** [freq. of ME. *stutten*, to stutter], to speak or say with involuntary pauses, spasms, and rapid repetitions of sounds, as because of some psychic disturbance. ***n.*** the act or habit of stuttering. **—stut′ter·er, *n.* —stut′ter·ing·ly, *adv.***

**Stutt·gart** (stut′gärt; G. shtoot′-), ***n.*** a city in S Germany: pop., 498,000.

**Stuy·ve·sant, Peter** (stī′və-s'nt), 1592–1672; Dutch governor of New Netherland (1646–1664).

**St. Vi·tus's dance** (vī′təs-iz), chorea, especially of children: also **St. Vitus' dance.**

**sty** (stī), ***n.*** [*pl.* STIES], [AS. *sti*], 1. a pen for pigs. 2. any filthy or depraved place. ***v.t. & v.i.*** [STIED, STYING], to lodge in or as in a sty.

**sty, stye** (stī), ***n.*** [*pl.* STIES], [< obs. *styany* (taken as *sty on eye*); ult. < AS. *stigend*, ppr. of *stigan*, to rise], a small, inflamed swelling of a sebaceous gland on the rim of the eyelid.

**Styg·i·an** (stij′i-ən), ***adj.*** 1. of or like the river Styx and the infernal regions. 2. [also s-], infernal; dark; gloomy; hellish.

**style** (stīl), ***n.*** [< OFr. < L. *stilus*], 1. a pointed instrument used by the ancients in writing on wax tablets. 2. any device similar in shape or use; specif., *a*) [Obs.], a pen. *b*) an etching needle. *c*) a phonograph needle. *d*) an engraving tool. *e*) the pointer on a dial, chart, etc. *f*) in *botany*, the stalklike part of a pistil between the stigma and the ovary. 3. *a*) manner of expression in writing or speaking. *b*) characteristic manner of expression, execution, or design, in any art, period, etc.: as, Gothic *style.* 4. distinction, originality, etc. in artistic or literary expression: as, this author lacks *style.* 5. fashion or fashionable mode: as, to dress in *style.* 6. elegance of manner and bearing. 7. form of address; title: as, he is entitled to the *style* of mayor. 8. something stylish. 9. sort; kind; type. 10. a way of reckoning time, dates, etc.: see **Old Style, New Style.** 11. in *printing*, any particular manner of dealing with spelling, punctuation, etc. ***v.t.*** [STYLED, STYLING], 1. to name; call: as, Lincoln was *styled* the Great Emancipator. 2. to design the style of. 3. to make conform to a particular style. **—style′less, *adj.***

**style·book** (stīl′book′), ***n.*** a book consisting of examples or rules of style (esp. sense 11).

**styl·ish** (stīl′ish), ***adj.*** conforming to current style in dress, decoration, etc.; smart; fashionable. **—styl′ish·ly, *adv.* —styl′ish·ness, *n.***

**styl·ist** (stīl′ist), ***n.*** 1. a writer, etc. whose work has style (sense 4). 2. a person who designs, or advises on, current styles, as in dress. **—sty·lis·tic** (stī-lis′tik), **sty·lis′ti·cal, *adj.* —sty·lis′ti·cal·ly, *adv.***

**styl·ize** (stīl′īz), ***v.t.*** [-IZED, -IZING], to make conform to a given style rather than to nature; conventionalize. **—styl′i·za′tion, *n.* —styl′iz·er, *n.***

**sty·lus** (stī′ləs), ***n.*** [*pl.* -LUSES, -LI (-lī)], [L., for *stilus*, pointed instrument], 1. a style or other needlelike marking device. 2. *a*) a sharp, pointed device for cutting the grooves of a phonograph record. *b*) a phonograph needle.

**sty·mie** (stī′mi), ***n.*** [prob. < Scot. *stymie*, a person partially blind], in *golf*, 1. the condition that exists on a putting green when an opponent's ball lies in a direct line between the player's ball and the hole. 2. a ball in such a position. ***v.t.*** [-MIED, -MIEING], 1. to obstruct with a stymie. 2. to block; impede.

**sty·my** (stī′mi), *n.* [*pl.* -MIES], *& v.t.* [-MIED, -MYING], stymie.
**styp·tic** (stip′tik), *adj.* [< Fr. < L. < Gr. *styptikos* < *styphein*, to contract], halting bleeding by contracting the tissues or blood vessels; astringent: also **styp′ti·cal.** *n.* any styptic substance. —**styp·tic′i·ty** (-tis′ə-ti), *n.*
**sty·rene** (stī′rēn, stêr′ēn), *n.* [< L. *styrax*, a kind of tree; + *-ene*], a colorless or yellowish, aromatic liquid, $C_6H_5CH{\cdot}CH_2$, used in the manufacture of synthetic rubber and plastics: also **sty·ro·lene** (stī′rə-lēn′).
**Styx** (stiks), *n.* [L.; ult. < Gr. *stygein*, to hate], in *Gr. mythology*, a river encircling the lower world, over which Charon ferried dead souls.
**sua·sion** (swā′zhən), *n.* [< L. pp. of *suadere*, to persuade], persuasion. —**sua′sive,** *adj.* —**sua′sive·ly,** *adv.* —**sua′sive·ness,** *n.*
**suave** (swäv; *occas.* swāv), *adj.* [Fr. < L. *suavis*, sweet], smoothly gracious or polite; polished; urbane. —**suave′ly,** *adv.* —**suav·i·ty** (swav′ə-ti, swä′-və-), [*pl.* -TIES], **suave′ness,** *n.*
**sub** (sub), *n.* [Colloq.], *a contracted form of* submarine, subscription, substitute, and other words beginning with *sub-*. *v.i.* [SUBBED, SUBBING], [Colloq.], to be a substitute (*for* someone).
**sub-,** [< L. *sub*, under], a prefix meaning: 1. *under, beneath*, as in *subsoil*. 2. *lower in rank or position than*, as in *subaltern*. 3. *to a lesser degree than, somewhat*, as in *subtropical*. 4. *by or forming a division into smaller parts*, as in *subsection*. 5. in *chemistry*, *with less than the normal amount of* (specified parts). In words of Latin origin, *sub-* assimilates to *suc-* before *c*, *suf-* before *f*, *sug-* before *g*, *sum-* before *m*, *sup-* before *p*, *sur-* before *r*: *sub-* often changes to *sus-* before *c*, *p*, and *t*.
**sub.,** 1. substitute(s). 2. suburb(an).
**sub·ac·id** (sub-as′id), *adj.* slightly acid. —**sub′a·cid′i·ty** (-ə-sid′ə-ti), *n.*
**sub·al·tern** (səb-ôl′tērn, sub′′l-tūrn′), *adj.* [< Fr. < LL. < L. *sub-*, under + *alternus*, alternate], 1. subordinate. 2. [Chiefly Brit.], holding an army commission below that of captain. *n.* 1. a subordinate. 2. [Chiefly Brit.], a subaltern officer.
**sub·ant·arc·tic** (sub′ant-ärk′tik), *adj.* designating or of the area surrounding the Antarctic Circle.
**sub·arc·tic** (sub-ärk′tik), *adj.* designating or of the area surrounding the Arctic Circle.
**sub·at·om** (sub-at′əm), *n.* a constituent part of an atom. —**sub′a·tom′ic** (-ə-tom′ik), *adj.*
**sub·base·ment** (sub′bās′mənt), *n.* any floor or room below a basement.
**sub·clin·i·cal** (sub-klin′i-k′l), *adj.* without clinical symptoms, as a disease in its early stages.
**sub·com·mit·tee** (sub′kə-mit′i), *n.* a subordinate committee chosen from a main committee.
**sub·con·scious** (sub-kon′shəs), *adj.* 1. occurring with little or no conscious perception on the part of the individual: said of mental processes and reactions. 2. not fully conscious. *n.* that portion of mental activity of which the individual has little or no conscious perception. —**sub·con′scious·ly,** *adv.* —**sub·con′scious·ness,** *n.*
**sub·con·tract** (sub-kon′trakt; *for v.*, sub′kən-trakt′), *n.* a secondary contract undertaking some of the obligations of a primary or previous contract. *v.t. & v.i.* to make a subcontract (for). —**sub′con′trac·tor** (-kon′trak-tēr, -kən-trak′-), *n.*
**sub·cu·ta·ne·ous** (sub′kū-tā′ni-əs), *adj.* being, used, or introduced beneath the skin. —**sub′cu·ta′ne·ous·ly,** *adv.*
**sub·deb** (sub-deb′, sub′-), *n.* [< *sub-* + *debutante*], 1. a girl in the years just preceding her debut into society. 2. any girl of such age. *adj.* of or suitable for a subdeb.
**sub·di·vide** (sub′də-vīd′), *v.t. & v.i.* [-VIDED, -VIDING], 1. to divide further after previous division has been made. 2. to divide (land) into small parcels for ready sale.
**sub·di·vi·sion** (sub′də-vizh′ən, sub′də-vizh′ən), *n.* 1. a subdividing or being subdivided. 2. a piece or part, as of land, resulting from this.
**sub·dom·i·nant** (sub-dom′ə-nənt), *n.* in *music*, the fourth tone of a diatonic scale.
**sub·due** (səb-dōō′, -dū′), *v.t.* [-DUED, -DUING], [< OFr. < L. *subducere*, to remove], 1. to bring into subjection; conquer; vanquish. 2. to overcome, as by persuasion or training; control. 3. to make less intense; diminish; soften. 4. to repress (emotions, passions, etc.). —**sub·du′a·ble,** *adj.* —**sub·du′al,** *n.* —**sub·du′er,** *n.* —**sub·du′ing·ly,** *adv.*
**sub·gum** (sub′gum′), *adj.* [Cantonese, lit., mixed vegetables], designating any of various Chinese or Chinese-American dishes, as chow mein, prepared with water chestnuts, mushrooms, etc.
**sub·head** (sub hed ), *n.* 1. the title of a subdivision of a chapter, article, etc. 2. a subordinate heading or title. Also **sub·head′ing.**
**sub·hu·man** (sub-hū′mən), *adj.* 1. below the human race in development. 2. nearly human.
**sub·in·dex** (sub-in′deks), *n.* [*pl.* -DICES (-də-sēz′)], a subscript.
**subj.,** 1. subject. 2. subjunctive.
**sub·ja·cent** (sub-jā′s′nt), *adj.* [< L. *subjacens*, ppr. < *sub-*, under + *jacere*, to lie], beneath; underlying. —**sub·ja′cen·cy,** *n.* —**sub·ja′cent·ly,** *adv.*
**sub·ject** (sub′jikt; *for v.*, səb-jekt′), *adj.* [< OFr. < L. *subjectus*, pp. < *sub-*, under + *jacere*, to throw], 1. under the authority or control of, or owing allegiance to, another. 2. having a disposition or tendency: as, *subject* to fits of anger. 3. liable to receive: as, *subject* to censure. 4. contingent upon: as, *subject* to my approval. *n.* 1. a person under the authority or control of another; esp., a person who owes allegiance to a ruler, government, etc. 2. someone or something undergoing a treatment, experiment, etc. 3. the self or ego as an individuality in its thinking or feeling. 4. something dealt with in discussion, study, writing, painting, etc.; theme, topic, branch of learning, etc. 5. the main theme of a musical composition or movement. 6. cause; occasion: as, a *subject* for joy. 7. in *grammar*, the word or group of words in a sentence about which something is said. *v.t.* 1. to bring under the authority or control of. 2. to cause to have a disposition or tendency; expose: as, his weakness *subjected* him to disease. 3. to cause to undergo something: as, they *subjected* him to indignities. —**sub·jec′tion,** *n.*
**sub·jec·tive** (səb-jek′tiv), *adj.* 1. of or resulting from the feelings of the subject, or person thinking, rather than the attributes of the object thought of: as, a *subjective* opinion. 2. determined by and emphasizing the ideas, feelings, etc. of the artist, writer, or speaker. 3. in *grammar*, nominative. 4. in *medicine*, designating or of a symptom perceptible only to the patient. —**sub·jec′tive·ly,** *adv.* —**sub·jec′tive·ness,** *n.*
**sub·jec·tiv·i·ty** (sub′jek-tiv′ə-ti), *n.* a subjective quality or state; specif., *a*) the tendency to consider all things only in relation to oneself. *b*) concern with only one's own thoughts and feelings.
**sub·join** (səb-join′), *v.t.* [< OFr. < L.; see SUB- & JOIN], to add (something) at the end; append.
**sub·join·der** (səb-join′dēr), *n.* something subjoined, or said in addition.
**sub·ju·gate** (sub′joo-gāt′), *v.t.* [-GATED, -GATING], [< L. *subjugatus*, pp. < *sub-*, under + *jugum*, a yoke], 1. to bring under control or subjection; conquer. 2. to cause to become subservient; subdue. —**sub′ju·ga′tion,** *n.* —**sub′ju·ga′tor,** *n.*
**sub·junc·tive** (səb-juŋk′tiv), *adj.* [< LL. < L. pp. of *subjungere*, to subjoin], designating or of that mood of a verb used to express supposition, desire, possibility, etc., rather than to state an actual fact. *n.* 1. the subjunctive mood. 2. a subjunctive verb form. —**sub·junc′tive·ly,** *adv.*
**sub·lease** (sub′lēs′; *for v.*, sub-lēs′), *n.* a lease granted by a lessee of all or part of the property. *v.t.* [-LEASED, -LEASING], 1. to grant a sublease of. 2. to hold a sublease of. —**sub′les·see′** (-les-ē′), *n.* —**sub·les·sor** (sub-les′ôr, sub′les-ôr′), *n.*
**sub·let** (sub-let′, sub′let′), *v.t.* [-LET, -LETTING], 1. to lease to another (property leased to oneself). 2. to let out (work) to a subcontractor.
**sub·lieu·ten·ant** (sub′lōō-ten′ənt), *n.* in some armies, an officer ranking next below a lieutenant.
**sub·li·mate** (sub′lə-māt′; *for adj. & n., usually* -mit), *v.t.* [-MATED, -MATING], [< L. *sublimatus*, pp.; see SUBLIME], 1. to sublime (a solid). 2. to purify or refine. 3. to express (certain impulses or biological drives) in constructive, socially acceptable forms. *v.i.* to be sublimed. *adj.* sublimed. *n.* a product of subliming. —**sub′li·ma′tion,** *n.*
**sub·lime** (sə-blīm′), *adj.* [Fr. < L. < *sub-*, up to + *limen*, lintel], 1. noble; exalted; majestic. 2. inspiring awe or admiration through grandeur, beauty, etc. *n.* something sublime (with *the*). *v.t.* [-LIMED, -LIMING], 1. to make sublime. 2. to purify (a solid) by heating directly to a gaseous state and condensing the vapor back into solid form. *v.i.* to go through such a process of purification. —**sub·lime′ly,** *adv.* —**sub·lime′ness,** *n.*
**sub·lim·i·nal** (sub-lim′ə-n′l, -lī′mə-), *adj.* [< *sub-*

+ L. *limen*, threshold], below the threshold of consciousness; subconscious; too slight to be perceived. *n.* the subconscious. **—sub·lim'i·nal·ly,** *adv.*

**sub·lim·i·ty** (sə-blim'ə-ti), *n.* 1. a sublime state or quality. 2. [*pl.* -TIES], something sublime.

**sub·ma·chine gun** (sub'mə-shēn'), a portable, automatic or semiautomatic firearm with a short barrel and a stock, fired from the shoulder or hip.

**sub·mar·gin·al** (sub-mär'ji-n'l), *adj.* 1. considered to be below the standard that yields a satisfactory profit: as, a *submarginal* vein of coal. 2. below the margin. **—sub·mar'gin·al·ly,** *adv.*

**sub·ma·rine** (sub'mə-rēn'; *for n. & v., usually* sub'-mə-rēn'), *adj.* being, living, used, etc. beneath the surface of the sea. *n.* 1. a submarine plant or animal. 2. a kind of warship that can operate under water. *v.t.* [-RINED, -RINING], to attack, especially to torpedo, with a submarine warship.

**sub·max·il·lar·y** (sub-mak'si-ler'i), *adj.* [see SUB- & MAXILLARY], of or below the lower jaw or jawbone; esp., designating or of two salivary glands, one on each side, beneath the lower jaw. *n.* [*pl.* -IES], a submaxillary bone, gland, etc.

**sub·merge** (səb-mũrj'), *v.t.* [-MERGED, -MERGING], [< L. < *sub-*, under + *mergere*, to plunge], 1. to place under or as under water, etc. 2. to cover over; suppress; hide. *v.i.* to sink beneath the surface of water, etc. **—sub·mer'gence,** *n.* **—sub·mer'gi·bil'i·ty,** *n.* **—sub·mer'gi·ble,** *adj.*

**sub·merse** (səb-mũrs'), *v.t.* [-MERSED, -MERSING], [< L. pp. of *submergere*], to submerge. **—sub·mers'i·ble,** *adj.* **—sub·mer'sion** (-mũr'shən, -zhən), *n.*

**sub·mis·sion** (səb-mish'ən), *n.* [OFr. < L. pp. of *submittere*], 1. a submitting, yielding, or surrendering. 2. a submissive quality or state; resignation; obedience. 3. a submitting of something for decision, consideration, etc.

**sub·mis·sive** (səb-mis'iv), *adj.* having or showing a tendency to submit or surrender; docile; yielding. **—sub·mis'sive·ly,** *adv.* **—sub·mis'sive·ness,** *n.*

**sub·mit** (səb-mit'), *v.t.* [-MITTED, -MITTING], [< L. < *sub-*, under + *mittere*, to send], 1. to present to others for decision, consideration, etc. 2. to yield to the control, power, etc. of another; surrender: often used reflexively. 3. to offer as an opinion; propose. *v.i.* 1. to yield to the control, power, etc. of another; surrender. 2. to defer to another's judgment or decision. 3. to be submissive, obedient, etc. **—sub·mit'tal,** *n.* **—sub·mit'ter,** *n.*

**sub·nor·mal** (sub-nôr'm'l), *adj.* below the normal, especially in intelligence. *n.* a subnormal person. **—sub·nor·mal·i·ty** (sub'nôr-mal'ə-ti), *n.* **—sub·nor'mal·ly,** *adv.*

**sub·or·di·nate** (sə-bôr'də-nit; *for v.,* -nāt'), *adj.* [< ML. pp. < L. *sub-*, under + *ordinare*, to order], 1. below another in rank, power, importance, etc.; secondary. 2. under the power or authority of another. 3. subservient or submissive. 4. in *grammar*, introducing a subordinate clause: as, *who, that, if*, etc. are *subordinate* conjunctions. *n.* a subordinate person or thing. *v.t.* [-NATED, -NATING], 1. to place in a subordinate position. 2. to make obedient or subservient (*to*). **—sub·or'di·nate·ly,** *adv.* **—sub·or'di·nate·ness,** *n.*

**subordinate clause,** in *grammar*, a clause that is dependent upon another clause and does not itself constitute a formal sentence.

**sub·or·di·na·tion** (sə-bôr'də-nā'shən), *n.* 1. a subordinating or being subordinate. 2. submission to rank, power, etc. **—sub·or'di·na'tive,** *adj.*

**sub·orn** (sə-bôrn'), *v.t.* [< Fr. < L. < *sub-*, under + *ornare*, to furnish], 1. to get by bribery or other illegal methods. 2. to induce or instigate (another) to do something illegal, especially to commit perjury. **—sub·or·na·tion** (sub'ôr-nā'shən), *n.* **—sub·or'na·tive,** *adj.* **—sub·orn'er,** *n.*

**sub·plot** (sub'plot'), *n.* a secondary or subordinate plot in a play, novel, etc.

**sub·poe·na** (sə-pē'nə, səb-), *n.* [< L. *sub*, under + *poena*, penalty], a written legal order directing a person to appear in court to give testimony, etc. *v.t.* [-NAED, -NAING], to serve or summon with such an order. Also sp. **subpena.**

**sub·ro·gate** (sub'rə-gāt'), *v.t.* [-GATED, -GATING], [< L. pp. < *sub-*, under + *rogare*, to ask], to substitute (one person) for another; esp., to substitute (one creditor) for another. **—sub'ro·ga'tion,** *n.*

‡**sub ro·sa** (sub rō'zə), [L., under the rose, an ancient symbol of secrecy], secretly; privately.

**sub·scribe** (səb-skrīb'), *v.t.* [-SCRIBED, -SCRIBING], [< L. < *sub-*, under + *scribere*, to write], 1. to sign (one's name) at the end of a document, etc. 2. to write one's signature on (a document, etc.) as an indication of consent, etc. 3. to support; consent to. 4. to promise to pay or contribute (money). *v.i.* 1. to sign one's name to a document, etc. 2. to give support or approval: as, he *subscribes* to the measure. 3. to promise to pay or contribute a sum of money. 4. to agree to receive and pay for a periodical, etc. (with *to*). **—sub·scrib'er,** *n.*

**sub·script** (sub'skript), *adj.* [< L. pp.; see SUBSCRIBE], written underneath. *n.* a figure, letter, symbol, etc. that is written underneath, as $_x$ in $3_x$.

**sub·scrip·tion** (səb-skrip'shən), *n.* 1. a subscribing. 2. something subscribed; specif., *a*) a written signature. *b*) a signed document, etc. *c*) consent or sanction, especially in writing. *d*) an amount of money subscribed. *e*) a formal agreement to receive and pay for a periodical, books, theater tickets, etc. **—sub·scrip'tive,** *adj.*

**sub·sec·tion** (sub-sek'shən, sub'sek'-), *n.* a division of a section.

**sub·se·quent** (sub'si-kwənt, -kwent'), *adj.* [< L. ppr. < *sub-*, after + *sequi*, to follow], coming after; following in time, place, or order. **—subsequent to,** after; following. **—sub'se·quence, sub'se·quen·cy, sub'se·quent·ness,** *n.* **—sub'se·quent·ly,** *adv.*

**sub·serve** (səb-sũrv'), *v.t.* [-SERVED, -SERVING], to be useful or helpful to (a cause, etc.); serve; aid.

**sub·ser·vi·ent** (səb-sũr'vi-ənt), *adj.* 1. that is useful or of service, especially in a subordinate capacity. 2. submissive; servile. **—sub·ser'vi·ence, sub·ser'vi·en·cy,** *n.* **—sub·ser'vi·ent·ly,** *adv.*

**sub·side** (səb-sīd'), *v.i.* [-SIDED, -SIDING], [< L. < *sub-*, under + *sidere*, to settle], 1. to sink to the bottom; settle. 2. to sink to a lower level. 3. to become less active, intense, etc.; abate. **—sub·sid·ence** (səb-sīd''ns, sub'si-dəns), *n.*

**sub·sid·i·ar·y** (səb-sid'i-er'i), *adj.* [< L. < *subsidium;* see SUBSIDY], 1. acting as a supplement; giving aid, service, etc.; auxiliary. 2. of, constituting, or maintained by a subsidy or subsidies. *n.* [*pl.* -IES], 1. a person or thing that gives aid, support, etc. 2. a company **(subsidiary company)** controlled by another company which owns most of its shares. **—sub·sid'i·ar'i·ly,** *adv.*

**sub·si·dize** (sub'sə-dīz'), *v.t.* [-DIZED, -DIZING], 1. to support with a subsidy. 2. to buy the aid of with a subsidy. **—sub'si·di·za'tion,** *n.* **—sub'si·diz'er, sub'si·dist,** *n.*

**sub·si·dy** (sub'sə-di), *n.* [*pl.* -DIES], [< Anglo-Fr. < L. *subsidium*, reserve troops], a grant of money; specif., *a*) a grant of money from one government to another. *b*) a government grant to a private enterprise considered of benefit to the public.

**sub·sist** (səb-sist'), *v.i.* [< Fr. < L. < *sub-*, under + *sistere*, to stand], 1. to continue to be; exist; abide. 2. to continue to live (*on* sustenance, *by* specific means, etc.). 3. to inhere (*in*). *v.t.* to maintain with sustenance; support.

**sub·sist·ence** (səb-sis'təns), *n.* 1. a subsisting; existence. 2. the act of providing sustenance. 3. means of support or livelihood. **—sub·sist'ent,** *adj.*

**sub·soil** (sub'soil'), *n.* the layer of soil beneath the surface soil. *v.t.* to turn up the subsoil of.

**sub·stance** (sub'stəns), *n.* [< OFr. < L. < *substare*, to exist], 1. the real or essential part of anything; essence. 2. the physical matter of which a thing consists; material. 3. *a*) solid or substantial quality. *b*) body; consistency. 4. the essential meaning, as of a speech. 5. matter of a particular kind. 6. material possessions; wealth. **—in substance,** 1. essentially. 2. actually; really.

**sub·stand·ard** (sub-stan'dẽrd), *adj.* below standard; specif., *a*) below a legal standard. *b*) deviating from the standard language patterns of cultivated speakers: as, "I seen him" is *substandard*.

**sub·stan·tial** (səb-stan'shəl), *adj.* 1. of or having substance. 2. real; actual; true. 3. strong; solid; firm. 4. ample; large. 5. of considerable value; important. 6. well-to-do. 7. with regard to essential elements. **—sub·stan'ti·al'i·ty** (-shi-al'ə-ti), *n.* **—sub·stan'tial·ly,** *adv.*

**sub·stan·ti·ate** (səb-stan'shi-āt'), *v.t.* [-ATED, -ATING], 1. to give substance to. 2. to give concrete form or body to. 3. to show to be true or real by giving evidence; prove. **—sub·stan'ti·a'tion,** *n.* **—sub·stan'ti·a'tive,** *adj.* **—sub·stan'ti·a'tor,** *n.*

**sub·stan·tive** (sub'stən-tiv), *adj.* [< OFr. < LL. *substantivus;* ult. < L. *substare;* see SUBSTANCE], 1. existing independently. 2. of considerable amount. 3. actual; real. 4. essential. 5. in *grammar*, *a*) showing or expressing existence: as, the *substantive* verb "to be." *b*) of or used as a substantive. *n.* 1. something substantive. 2. in *grammar*, *a*) a noun. *b*) any word or group of words used as an equivalent for a noun. **—sub'stan·ti'val** (-tī'v'l), *adj.* **—sub'stan·ti'val·ly,** *adv.* **—sub'stan·tive·ly,** *adv.*

**sub·sta·tion** (sub'stā'shən), *n.* a branch station.

**sub·sti·tute** (sub′stə-to͞ot′, -tūt′), *n.* [< L. pp.; ult. < *sub-*, under + *statuere*, to put], a person or thing acting or used in place of another. *v.t. & v.i.* [-TUTED, -TUTING], 1. to put, use, or be used in place of another. 2. to serve in place of (another). *adj.* that is a substitute. —**sub′sti·tut′er,** *n.*

**sub·sti·tu·tion** (sub′stə-to͞o′shən, -tū′-), *n.* 1. a substituting or being substituted. 2. a substitute. —**sub′sti·tu′tion·al, sub′sti·tu′tion·ar′y,** *adj.*

**sub·stra·tum** (sub-strā′təm, sub′strat′əm), *n.* [*pl.* -TA (-tə, -ə), -TUMS], [< L.; ult. < *sub-*, under + *sternere*, to strew], 1. a part, substance, etc. which lies beneath and supports another. 2. figuratively, any basis or foundation. 3. subsoil.

**sub·struc·ture** (sub-struk′chẽr), *n.* a part or structure acting as a support; foundation: also **sub·struc′tion.** —**sub·struc′tur·al,** *adj.*

**sub·ten·ant** (sub-ten′ənt), *n.* one who rents from a tenant; tenant of a tenant. —**sub·ten′an·cy,** *n.*

**sub·tend** (səb-tend′), *v.t.* [< L. < *sub-*, under + *tendere*, to stretch], 1. to extend under; be opposite to in position: as, each side of a triangle *subtends* the opposite angle. 2. in *botany*, to enclose in an angle, as between a leaf and its stem.

**sub·ter-,** [< L. *subter*, below, beneath], a prefix meaning *below, under, less than, secretly.*

**sub·ter·fuge** (sub′tẽr-fūj′), *n.* [< Fr. < LL. < L. < *subter-*, below + *fugere*, to flee], any plan or action used to evade something difficult or unpleasant.

**sub·ter·ra·ne·an** (sub′tə-rā′ni-ən), *adj.* [< L. < *sub-*, under + *terra*, earth], 1. lying beneath the earth's surface; underground. 2. secret; hidden. Also **sub′ter·ra′ne·ous.**

**sub·tile** (sut′'l, sub′til), *adj.* subtle. —**sub′tile·ly,** *adv.* —**sub′tile·ness, sub·til·i·ty** (səb-til′ə-ti), *n.*

**sub·til·ize** (sut′'l-īz′, sub′t'l-īz′), *v.t. & v.i.* [-IZED, -IZING], to make or become subtle; esp., to discuss or argue in a subtle way. —**sub′til·i·za′tion,** *n.*

**sub·ti·tle** (sub′tī′t'l), *n.* 1. a secondary or explanatory title, as of a book or play. 2. in *motion pictures*, descriptive titles, translations of original dialogue, etc. thrown on the screen between scenes or superimposed on the film.

**sub·tle** (sut′'l), *adj.* [< OFr. < L. *subtilis*, orig. closely woven < *sub-*, under + *tela*, web], 1. thin; tenuous; not dense. 2. keen; discriminating. 3. delicately skillful; deft. 4. crafty; wily. 5. mysterious; sly: as, a *subtle* wink. 6. hard to solve, detect, etc.; intricate: as, a *subtle* problem. 7. acting in an insidious way: as, a *subtle* poison. Also **subtile.** —**sub′tle·ness,** *n.* —**sub′tly,** *adv.*

**sub·tle·ty** (sut′'l-ti), *n.* 1. a subtle quality or condition. 2. [*pl.* -TIES], something subtle; esp., a fine distinction.

**sub·ton·ic** (sub-ton′ik), *n.* in *music*, the seventh tone of a diatonic scale.

**sub·tract** (səb-trakt′), *v.t. & v.i.* [< L. pp. < *sub-*, under + *trahere*, to draw], to take away or deduct, as a part from a whole or one quantity from another. —**sub·tract′er,** *n.* —**sub·trac′tive,** *adj.*

**sub·trac·tion** (səb-trak′shən), *n.* a subtracting or being subtracted; esp., the mathematical process of finding the difference between two quantities.

**sub·tra·hend** (sub′trə-hend′), *n.* [< L. *subtrahendus*, gerundive; see SUBTRACT], a number or quantity to be subtracted from another.

**sub·treas·ur·y** (sub′trezh′ẽr-i, sub-trezh′-), *n.* [*pl.* -IES], a branch treasury.

**sub·trop·i·cal** (sub-trop′i-k'l), *adj.* designating, of, or characteristic of regions bordering on the tropics; nearly tropical: also **sub·trop′ic.**

**sub·trop·ics** (sub-trop′iks), *n.pl.* subtropical regions.

**sub·urb** (sub′ẽrb), *n.* [< OFr. < L. < *sub-*, under + *urbs*, town], 1. a district on the outskirts of a city: often a separately incorporated city or town. 2. *pl.* outlying parts. —**the suburbs,** the residential areas on the outskirts of a city.

**sub·ur·ban** (sə-bũr′bən), *adj.* 1. of, in, or residing in a suburb or the suburbs. 2. characteristic of the suburbs or suburbanites. *n.* a suburbanite.

**sub·ur·ban·ite** (sə-bũr′bən-īt′), *n.* a person living in a suburb.

**sub·ur·bi·a** (sə-bũr′bi-ə), *n.* the suburbs collectively: usually connoting the values, attitudes, etc. regarded as characteristic of suburban life.

**sub·ven·tion** (səb-ven′shən), *n.* [< OFr. < LL. < L. < *sub-*, under + *venire*, to come], a government subsidy, as in support of a study, institution, etc.

**sub·ver·sion** (səb-vũr′zhən, -shən), *n.* 1. a subverting or being subverted; ruin; overthrow. 2. something that subverts. —**sub·ver′sion·ar′y,** *adj.*

**sub·ver·sive** (səb-vũr′siv), *adj.* tending to subvert, overthrow, or destroy (something established). *n.* a person regarded as subversive. —**sub·ver′sive·ly,** *adv.* —**sub·ver′sive·ness,** *n.*

**sub·vert** (səb-vũrt′), *v.t.* [< OFr. < L. < *sub-*, under + *vertere*, to turn], 1. to overthrow or destroy (something established). 2. to corrupt, as in morals, etc. —**sub·vert′er,** *n.* —**sub·vert′i·ble,** *adj.*

**sub·way** (sub′wā′), *n.* 1. an underground way. 2. an underground, metropolitan electric railway or the tunnel through which this runs.

**suc-,** see **sub-.**

**suc·ceed** (sək-sēd′), *v.i.* [< OFr. < L. < *sub-*, under + *cedere*, to go], 1. to follow another in a series: as, in *succeeding* years. 2. to follow another into office, possession, etc.: as, to *succeed* to a throne. 3. to have success; accomplish something planned or attempted. *v.t.* 1. to take the place left by; follow into office, etc. 2. to come after. —**suc·ceed′er,** *n.*

**suc·cess** (sək-ses′), *n.* [< L. < *succedere;* see SUCCEED], 1. extent of succeeding: as, what *success* did he have? 2. a favorable result. 3. the gaining of wealth, fame, etc. 4. a successful person or thing.

**suc·cess·ful** (sək-ses′fəl), *adj.* 1. having a favorable result. 2. having gained wealth, fame, etc. —**suc·cess′ful·ly,** *adv.* —**suc·cess′ful·ness,** *n.*

**suc·ces·sion** (sək-sesh′ən), *n.* 1. the act of succeeding or coming after another in order or to an office, estate, etc. 2. the right to succeed to an office, etc. 3. a number of persons or things coming one after another; series. 4. *a*) a series of heirs or successors of any kind. *b*) the order of such a series. —**in succession,** one after another. —**suc·ces′sion·al,** *adj.* —**suc·ces′sion·al·ly,** *adv.*

**suc·ces·sive** (sək-ses′iv), *adj.* 1. coming in succession; consecutive. 2. of or involving succession. —**suc·ces′sive·ly,** *adv.* —**suc·ces′sive·ness,** *n.*

**suc·ces·sor** (sək-ses′ẽr), *n.* one that follows; esp., a person who succeeds another, as to an office, estate, etc. —**suc·ces′sor·ship′,** *n.*

**suc·cinct** (sək-siŋkt′), *adj.* [< L. pp. of *succingere*, to tuck up < *sub-*, under + *cingere*, to gird], 1. clearly and briefly stated; terse. 2. characterized by brevity and conciseness of speech. —**suc·cinct′ly,** *adv.* —**suc·cinct′ness,** *n.*

**suc·cor** (suk′ẽr), *v.t.* [< OFr. < L. < *sub-*, under + *currere*, to run], to help in time of need or distress; aid. *n.* 1. aid; relief. 2. one that succors. —**suc′cor·a·ble,** *adj.* —**suc′cor·er,** *n.*

**suc·co·tash** (suk′ə-tash′), *n.* [< Am. Ind.], beans and corn kernels cooked together as a dish.

**suc·cour** (suk′ẽr), *v.t. & n.* succor: Brit. spelling.

**suc·cu·bus** (suk′yoo-bəs), *n.* [*pl.* -BI (-bī′)], [< ML. < L. *sub-*, under + *cubare*, to lie], in *folklore*, a female demon thought to have sexual intercourse with sleeping men.

**suc·cu·lent** (suk′yoo-lənt), *adj.* [< L. *succulentus* < *sucus*, juice], 1. full of juice; juicy. 2. interesting; not dry or dull. 3. in *botany*, having juicy tissues, as a cactus. —**suc′cu·lence, suc′cu·len·cy,** *n.* —**suc′cu·lent·ly,** *adv.*

**suc·cumb** (sə-kum′), *v.i.* [< OFr. < L. < *sub-*, under + *cumbere*, to lie], 1. to give way; yield (often with *to*). 2. to die: as, he *succumbed* to cancer.

**such** (such), *adj.* [< AS. *swylc, swelc*], 1. of this or that kind; similar to something mentioned or implied; specif., *a*) being the same as what was stated before: as, *such* joy was his wish. *b*) being the same in quality or kind: as, bolts, screws, and *such* objects. 2. not named; some; certain: as, on *such* a day as you may go. 3. so extreme, so much, etc.: as, he never expected *such* honor. *As* or *that* is used as a correlative with *such* in a completed comparison (e.g., *such* wit *as* his is rare). An article may occur between *such* and the noun it modifies (e.g., *such* a fellow!). *adv.* [Colloq.], to such a degree: as, he was *such* a good man. *pron.* 1. such a person or thing: as, *such* as live by the sword. 2. that mentioned or implied: as, *such* was his nature. —**as such,** 1. as being what is indicated. 2. in itself: as, a name, *as such*, means nothing. —**such as,** 1. for example. 2. like or similar to.

**such and such,** being a particular one but not specified: as, he went to *such and such* a place.

**such·like** (such′līk′), *adj.* of such a kind; of similar kind. *pron.* persons or things of such a kind.

**suck** (suk), *v.t.* [< AS. *sucan*], 1. to draw (liquid) into the mouth with the lips and tongue. 2. to take as if by sucking; absorb, inhale, etc.: as, he *sucked* air into his lungs. 3. to suck liquid from (fruit, etc.). 4. to dissolve by holding in the mouth or licking, as candy, etc. 5. to hold (the thumb, etc.) in the mouth. *v.i.* 1. to suck something. 2. to suck milk from the breast or udder. 3. to make the sound of sucking. 4. to draw in air instead of water, as a faulty pump. *n.* 1. the act of sucking; suction. 2. the sound of sucking. 3. something drawn in by sucking; esp., [Colloq.], a sip. —**suck in,** [Slang], to fool, swindle, etc.

**suck·er** (suk′ẽr), *n.* 1. one that sucks. 2. a fish of the carp family, with a mouth adapted for sucking. 3. a part used for sucking; specif., *a*) a pipe through which something is sucked. *b*) an organ used by the snail, leech, etc. for sucking or holding fast to a surface. 4. [Slang], a person easily cheated; dupe. 5. [Colloq.], a lollipop. 6. a shoot springing from the roots or stem of a plant. *v.t.* to remove suckers, or shoots, from. *v.i.* to bear suckers, or shoots.

**suck·le** (suk′'l), *v.t.* [-LED, -LING], [freq. of *suck*], 1. to cause to suck at the breast or udder. 2. to bring up; rear; foster. *v.i.* to suck at the breast. —**suck′ler,** *n.*

**suck·ling** (suk′liŋ), *n.* an unweaned child or young animal.

**Su·cre** (so͞o′kre), *n.* the nominal capital of Bolivia, in the south central part: pop., 54,000.

**su·cre** (so͞o′kre), *n.* [after A. de *Sucre,* 19th-c. S.Am. liberator], the monetary unit of Ecuador.

**su·crose** (so͞o′krōs, sū′-), *n.* [< Fr. *sucre,* sugar], a crystalline sugar, $C_{12}H_{22}O_{11}$, found in sugar cane, sugar beets, etc.

**suc·tion** (suk′shən), *n.* [OFr. < L. < pp. of *sugere,* to suck], 1. the act or process of sucking. 2. the production of a vacuum or partial vacuum in a container or over a surface, so that atmospheric pressure forces the surrounding fluid, etc. into the space. 3. the sucking force created by this. *adj.* causing, or operating by means of, suction.

**suction pump,** a pump that draws water up by suction created by pistons fitted with valves.

**suc·to·ri·al** (suk-tôr′i-əl, -tō′ri-), *adj.* [< L. pp. of *sugere,* to suck], 1. of or adapted for sucking or suction. 2. having organs used for sucking.

**Su·dan** (so͞o-dan′), *n.* 1. a country in NE Africa, south of Egypt: area, 967,500 sq. mi.; pop., 11,615,-000; capital, Khartoum. 2. a vast plains region extending across central Africa. —**Su′da·nese′** (-də-nēz′), [*pl.* -NESE], *adj. & n.*

**sud·den** (sud′'n), *adj.* [< OFr. *sodain* < LL. < L. *subitaneus;* ult. < *sub-,* under + *ire,* to go], 1. happening or appearing unexpectedly; not foreseen. 2. done, coming, or taking place quickly or abruptly. —**all of a sudden,** suddenly; unexpectedly. —**sud′den·ly,** *adv.* —**sud′den·ness,** *n.*

**Su·de·ten·land** (so͞o-dā′t'n-land′), *n.* a mountainous region in N Czechoslovakia.

**su·dor·if·ic** (so͞o′də-rif′ik, sū′-), *adj.* [< L. *sudor,* sweat + *facere,* to make], causing or increasing sweating. *n.* a sudorific drug, etc.

**suds** (sudz), *n.pl.* [prob. < MD. *sudse,* marsh water], 1. soapy water. 2. froth or foam, as on soapy water; foam. 3. [Slang], beer. —**suds′y** [-IER, -IEST], *adj.*

**sue** (so͞o, sū), *v.t.* [SUED, SUING], [< OFr. *sevre;* ult. < L. *sequi,* to follow], 1. to appeal to; petition. 2. [Archaic], to act as suitor to; woo. 3. in *law, a*) to petition (a court) for justice or redress through legal action. *b*) to prosecute in a court in seeking redress of wrongs or justice. *v.i.* 1. to make an appeal; petition. 2. [Archaic], to pay suit; woo. 3. to institute legal proceedings in court; bring suit. —**su′er,** *n.*

**suede, suède** (swād), *n.* [Fr. *Suède,* Sweden, in *gants de Suède,* Swedish gloves], 1. tanned leather having the flesh side buffed into a nap. 2. a kind of cloth resembling this: also **suede cloth.**

**su·et** (so͞o′it, sū′-), *n.* [dim. of Anglo-Fr. *sue* < OFr. < L. *sebum,* fat], the hard fat deposited around the kidneys and loins of cattle and sheep: used in cooking and as tallow. —**su′et·y,** *adj.*

**Su·ez** (so͞o-ez′, so͞o′ez), *n.* a seaport in Egypt, on the Suez Canal and the Red Sea: pop., 156,000.

**Suez, Isthmus of,** a strip of land in NE Egypt, connecting Asia and Africa.

**Suez Canal,** a ship canal joining the Mediterranean and Red seas through the Isthmus of Suez.

**suf-,** see **sub-.**

**suf·fer** (suf′ẽr), *v.t.* [< Anglo-Fr. < OFr. *sufrir;* ult. < L. < *sub-,* under + *ferre,* to bear], 1. to undergo (something painful or unpleasant); endure. 2. to undergo (any process, especially change). 3. to permit; tolerate. 4. to bear up under; endure: now only in negative constructions, as, he can't *suffer* criticism. *v.i.* 1. to experience pain, harm, loss, etc. 2. to receive punishment. —**suf′fer·a·ble,** *adj.* —**suf′fer·a·bly,** *adv.* —**suf′fer·er,** *n.*

**suf·fer·ance** (suf′ẽr-əns, -rəns), *n.* 1. the capacity to suffer, or endure, pain, distress, etc. 2. consent, permission, etc. implied by failure to interfere or prohibit. —**on sufferance,** allowed or tolerated but not actually supported.

**suf·fer·ing** (suf′ẽr-iŋ, -riŋ), *n.* 1. the bearing or undergoing of pain, distress, or injury. 2. something suffered. —**suf′fer·ing·ly,** *adv.*

**suf·fice** (sə-fīs′), *v.i.* [-FICED, -FICING], [< OFr. < L. *sufficere* < *sub-,* under + *facere,* to make], 1. to be enough; be adequate. 2. [Obs.], to be competent or able. *v.t.* to be enough for; satisfy. —**suf·fic′er,** *n.* —**suf·fic′ing·ly,** *adv.*

**suf·fi·cien·cy** (sə-fish′ən-si), *n.* 1. sufficient means or resources; an ample amount or quantity (*of* what is needed). 2. the state or quality of being sufficient; adequacy. 3. self-sufficiency.

**suf·fi·cient** (sə-fish′ənt), *adj.* as much as is needed; enough; adequate. —**suf·fi′cient·ly,** *adv.*

**suf·fix** (suf′iks; *for v., usually* sə-fiks′), *n.* [< L. *suffixus,* pp.; ult. < *sub-,* under + *figere,* to fix], a syllable or group of syllables added at the end of a word or word base to alter its meaning or give it grammatical function, as *-ed* in *walked, -ness* in *darkness. v.t.* to add as a suffix. —**suf′fix·al,** *adj.* —**suf·fix′ion,** *n.*

**suf·fo·cate** (suf′ə-kāt′), *v.t.* [-CATED, -CATING], [< L. pp. of *suffocare* < *sub-,* under + *fauces,* throat], 1. to kill by cutting off the supply of oxygen so as to cause asphyxiation. 2. to hinder the free breathing of. 3. to smother, suppress, etc. *v.i.* 1. to die by being suffocated. 2. to be unable to breathe freely; choke; stifle. —**suf′fo·cat′ing·ly,** *adv.* —**suf′fo·ca′tion,** *n.* —**suf′fo·ca′tive,** *adj.*

**Suf·folk** (suf′ək), *n.* a county in E England.

**suf·fra·gan** (suf′rə-gən), *n.* [OFr. < ML. < L. *suffragari,* to support], 1. a bishop appointed to assist another bishop. 2. any bishop in his capacity as a subordinate to his archbishop. *adj.* subordinate; auxiliary. —**suf′fra·gan·ship′,** *n.*

**suf·frage** (suf′rij), *n.* [OFr. < L. *suffragium*], 1. a short prayer of supplication. 2. a vote or voting. 3. the right to vote in political matters; franchise.

**suf·fra·gette** (suf′rə-jet′), *n.* a woman who advocated female suffrage. —**suf′fra·get′tism,** *n.*

**suf·fra·gist** (suf′rə-jist), *n.* one who believes in extending political suffrage, especially to women.

**suf·fuse** (sə-fūz′), *v.t.* [-FUSED, -FUSING], [< L. pp. < *sub-,* under + *fundere,* to pour], to overspread, as with a liquid, light, etc. —**suf·fu′sion,** *n.* —**suf·fu′sive,** *adj.* —**suf·fu′sive·ly,** *adv.*

**sug-,** see **sub-.**

**sug·ar** (shoog′ẽr), *n.* [< OFr. *sucre* < ML. < Ar. < Per. *shakar* < Sans. *ṣarkarā*], 1. a sweet, usually crystalline substance, $C_{12}H_{22}O_{11}$, extracted chiefly from sugar cane and sugar beets and used as a food and for sweetening; sucrose. 2. any of a class of sweet, soluble crystalline carbohydrates, including sucrose, lactose, maltose, glucose, fructose, etc. 3. flattery; honeyed words. 4. [Slang], money. *v.t.* 1. to mix or sprinkle (food) with sugar. 2. to sweeten with sugar. 3. to cause to seem less disagreeable. *v.i.* 1. to form sugar crystals or granules by long, slow boiling (usually with *off*). 2. to make maple sugar. —**sug′ar·less,** *adj.*

**sugar beet,** a variety of beet having a root with white flesh and a high sugar content.

**sugar cane,** a very tall tropical grass with jointed stems, cultivated as the main source of sugar.

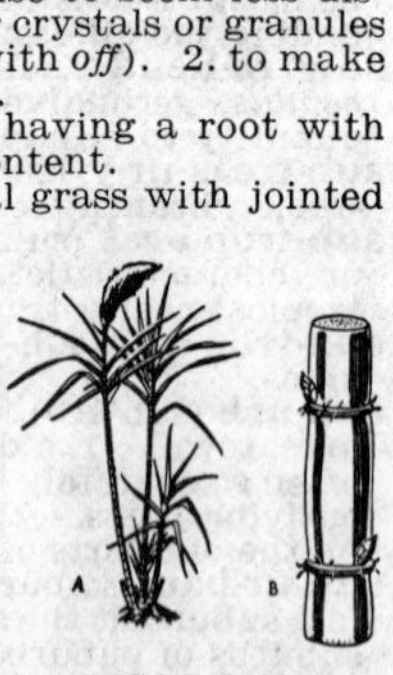

SUGAR CANE
A, plant; B, section of cane

**sug·ar-coat** (shoog′ẽr-kōt′), *v.t.* 1. to cover or coat with sugar. 2. to make seem more pleasant or attractive.

**sug·ar-cured** (shoog′ẽr-kyoord′), *adj.* treated with a pickling preparation containing sugar, as ham.

**sugar loaf,** 1. a conical mass of hard sugar. 2. a hill, etc. shaped like this. —**sug′ar-loaf′,** *adj.*

**sug·ar·plum** (shoog′ẽr-plum′), *n.* a round or oval piece of sugary candy; bonbon.

**sug·ar·y** (shoog′ẽr-i, shoog′ri), *adj.* 1. of or containing sugar. 2. like sugar; specif., *a*) sweet. *b*) granular. 3. sweetly flattering or pleasant; honeyed. —**sug′ar·i·ness,** *n.*

**sug·gest** (səg-jest′; *also, esp. Brit.,* sə-jest′), *v.t.* [< L. pp. < *sub-,* under + *gerere,* to carry], 1. to bring (a thought, etc.) to the mind for consideration. 2. to call to mind through association of ideas. 3. to propose (someone or something) as a possibility. 4. to show indirectly; imply; intimate: as, those clouds *suggest* rain. —**sug·gest′er,** *n.*

**sug·gest·i·ble** (səg-jes′tə-b'l), *adj.* 1. that can be influenced by suggestion. 2. that can be suggested. —**sug·gest′i·bil′i·ty,** *n.* —**sug·gest′i·bly,** *adv.*

**sug·ges·tion** (səg-jes′chən), *n.* 1. a suggesting or being suggested. 2. something suggested. 3. the process by which an idea is brought to mind through its association with another idea. 4. a faint hint; trace: as, a *suggestion* of malice.

**sug·ges·tive** (səg-jes′tiv), *adj.* 1. that suggests or tends to suggest ideas. 2. tending to suggest something considered improper or indecent. —**sug·ges′tive·ly,** *adv.* —**sug·ges′tive·ness,** *n.*

**su·i·cide** (so͞o′i-sīd′, sū′-), *n.* [L. *sui,* of oneself; + *-cide*], 1. the act of killing oneself intentionally. 2. ruin of one's interests through one's own actions, etc. 3. one who commits suicide. *v.i.* [-CIDED, -CIDING], [Colloq.], to commit suicide. —**su′i·cid′al,** *adj.* —**su′i·cid′al·ly,** *adv.*

‡**su·i ge·ne·ris** (sū′i jen′ẽr-is, so͞o′-), [L.], of his (her, or its) own kind; individual; unique.

**suit** (so͞ot, sūt), *n.* [< OFr. *suite;* ult. < L. *se ui,* to follow], 1. a set of clothes to be worn together; especially, a coat and trousers (or skirt), usually of the same material. 2. a set or series of similar things. 3. any of the four sets of playing cards (*spades, clubs, hearts,* and *diamonds*). 4. action to secure justice in a court of law. 5. an act of suing, pleading, etc. 6. a wooing. *v.t.* 1. to meet the requirements of; be suitable for; befit. 2. to make suitable or appropriate; fit; adapt. 3. to please; satisfy: as, nothing *suits* him. 4. [Rare], to furnish with clothes. *v.i.* to be suitable or convenient. —**bring suit,** to institute legal action; sue. —**follow suit,** 1. to play a card of the same suit as the card led. 2. to follow the example set. —**suit oneself,** to act according to one's own wishes.

**suit·a·ble** (so͞ot′ə-b'l, sūt′-), *adj.* that suits a given purpose, occasion, etc.; appropriate. —**suit′a·bil′i·ty, suit′a·ble·ness,** *n.* —**suit′a·bly,** *adv.*

**suit·case** (so͞ot′kās′, sūt′-), *n.* a flat, rectangular traveling bag, or valise.

**suite** (swēt; *also, for* 2*b, occas.* so͞ot, sūt), *n.* [Fr.; see SUIT], 1. a group of attendants or servants; staff. 2. a set of related things; specif., *a*) a group of connected rooms used as a unit. *b*) a number of matched pieces of furniture for a given room. 3. in *music, a*) an early form of composition consisting of a series of dances. *b*) a modern composition in a number of movements.

**suit·ing** (so͞ot′iŋ, sūt′-), *n.* cloth for making suits.

**suit·or** (so͞o′tẽr, sū′-), *n.* 1. one who sues, requests, petitions, etc. 2. one who sues at law. 3. a man who courts a woman.

**su·ki·ya·ki** (so͞o′ki-yä′ki), *n.* [Japan.], a Japanese dish of sliced meat, vegetables, etc. fried together and seasoned with soya sauce, etc.

**Suk·koth** (sook-ōth′, -ōs), *n.pl.* [construed as sing.], a Jewish holiday: see **Jewish holidays.**

**Su·lei·man** (sü′lā-män′), *n.* 1496?–1566; sultan of the Ottoman Empire (1520–1566): also **Solyman.**

**sulf-,** a combining form meaning *of* or *containing sulfur:* also **sulph-.**

**sul·fa** (sul′fə), *adj.* designating or of a family of drugs of the sulfanilamide type, used in combating certain bacterial infections: words beginning with *sulfa-* may also be spelled **sulpha-.**

**sul·fa·di·a·zine** (sul′fə-dī′ə-zēn′, -zin), *n.* [< *sulfa* + *di-* + *azo* + *-ine*], a sulfa drug, $C_{10}H_{10}N_4O_2S$, used in treating pneumonia, streptococcus infections, etc.

**sul·fa·gua·ni·dine** (sul′fə-gwan′ə-dēn′, -gwä′nə-din), *n.* [*sulfa* + *guanidine,* a substance obtained from guano], a sulfa drug, $C_7H_{10}N_4O_2S \cdot H_2O$, used in treating various intestinal infections.

**sulf·a·nil·a·mide** (sul′fə-nil′ə-mīd′), *n.* [*sulfanilic* + *amide*], a white crystalline sulfa drug, $NH_2C_6H_4SO_2NH_2$, used in treating gonorrhea, streptococcus infections, etc.: a synthetic coal-tar product.

**sul·fa·pyr·i·dine** (sul′fə-pêr′ə-dēn′, -din), *n.* [*sulfa* + *pyridine,* a coal-tar compound], a sulfa drug, $C_{11}H_{11}N_3O_2S$, used in treating pneumonia.

**sul·fate** (sul′fāt), *n.* a salt of sulfuric acid. *v.t.* [-FATED, -FATING], 1. to treat with sulfuric acid or a sulfate. 2. to convert into a sulfate. 3. to form a deposit of sulfates on (the plates of a storage battery). *v.i.* to become sulfated.

**sul·fa·thi·a·zole** (sul′fə-thī′ə-zōl′), *n.* [< *sulfa* + *thi-* + *a·o* + *-ole*], a sulfa drug, $C_9H_9N_3O_3S_2$, used in treating pneumonia and certain other infections.

**sul·fide** (sul′fīd), *n.* a compound of sulfur with another element or a radical: also **sul′fid** (-fid).

**sul·fite** (sul′fīt), *n.* a salt of sulfurous acid. —**sul·fit′ic** (-fit′ik), *adj.*

**sul·fo·na·mide** (sul-fon′ə-mīd′, sul′fən-am′id), *n.* any of the sulfa drugs containing the monovalent radical $-SO_2NH_2$, as sulfathiazole.

**sul·fur** (sul′fẽr), *n.* [L. *sulphur, sulfur*], a pale-yellow, nonmetallic chemical element found in crystalline or amorphous form: it burns with a blue flame and a stifling odor: symbol, S; at. wt., 32.06; at. no., 16: see also **sulphur.**

**sul·fu·rate** (sul′fyoo-rit, -fə-; *for v.,* -rāt′), *adj.* of, like, or containing sulfur. *v.t.* [-RATED, -RATING], to combine or treat with sulfur. —**sul′fu·ra′tion,** *n.*

**sulfur dioxide,** a heavy, colorless, suffocating gas, $SO_2$, easily liquefied and used as a bleach, disinfectant, and refrigerant.

**sul·fu·re·ous** (sul-fyoor′i-əs), *adj.* 1. of, like, or containing sulfur. 2. greenish-yellow.

**sul·fu·ret** (sul′fyoo-ret′), *v.t.* [-RETTED or -RETED, -RETTING or -RETING], to combine or impregnate with sulfur or a sulfur compound.

**sul·fu·ric** (sul-fyoor′ik), *adj.* of or containing sulfur, especially sulfur having a valence of six.

**sulfuric acid,** an oily, colorless, corrosive liquid, $H_2SO_4$, used in making explosives, fertilizers, etc.

**sul·fu·rize** (sul′fyoo-rīz′, -fẽr-īz′), *v.t.* [-RIZED, -RIZING], to combine or treat with sulfur or a sulfur compound. —**sul′fu·ri·za′tion,** *n.*

**sul·fu·rous** (sul-fyoor′əs, sul′fẽr-), *adj.* 1. of or containing sulfur, especially sulfur having a valence of four. 2. like burning sulfur in odor, color, etc.: see also **sulphurous.**

**sulfurous acid,** a colorless acid, $H_2SO_3$, known only in the form of its salts or in aqueous solution and used as a chemical reagent, a bleach, etc.

**sul·fur·y** (sul′fẽr-i), *adj.* of or like sulfur.

**sulk** (sulk), *v.i.* [back-formation < *sulky*], to be sulky. *n.* 1. *often pl.* a sulky mood or state. 2. a sulky person: also **sulk′er.**

**sulk·y** (sul′ki), *adj.* [-IER, -IEST], [prob. < AS. *solcen* (in comp.), remiss], showing resentment and ill-humor by sullen, withdrawn behavior. *n.* [*pl.* -IES], a light, two-wheeled carriage for one person. —**sulk′i·ly,** *adv.* —**sulk′i·ness,** *n.*

**sul·len** (sul′ən), *adj.* [< ME. *solein* (< L. *solus*), alone], 1. showing resentment and ill-humor by morose, unsociable withdrawal; sulky; glum. 2. gloomy; dismal; sad. 3. somber; dull. 4. slow-moving; sluggish. 5. baleful; threatening: as, *sullen* clouds. —**sul′len·ly,** *adv.* —**sul′len·ness,** *n.*

**Sul·li·van,** Sir **Arthur Seymour** (sul′i-vən), 1842–1900; English composer; wrote comic operas in collaboration with Sir William S. Gilbert.

**sul·ly** (sul′i), *v.t. & v.i.* [-LIED, -LYING], [prob. < Fr. *souiller;* cf. SOIL, *v.*], to make or become soiled, stained, tarnished, or defiled. *n.* [*pl.* -LIES], a stain or tarnish; defilement. —**sul′li·er,** *n.*

**sulph-,** sulf-: for words beginning **sulph-,** see forms under **sulf-.**

**sul·pha** (sul′fə), *adj.* sulfa.

**sul·phur** (sul′fẽr), *n.* 1. sulfur. 2. any of various small, yellow butterflies. 3. a greenish-yellow color. *adj.* greenish-yellow.

**sul·phur-bot·tom** (sul′fẽr-bot′əm), *n.* the largest of all whales, bluish gray in color.

**sul·phu·rous** (sul′fẽr-əs; *for 1, usually* sul-fyoor′-), *adj.* 1. sulfurous. 2. infernal; hellish. 3. heated; fiery; vehement.

**sul·tan** (sul′t'n), *n.* [Fr. < Ar. *sulṭān*], a Moslem ruler; esp., [S-], formerly, the ruler of Turkey.

**sul·tan·a** (sul-tan′ə, -tä′nə), *n.* 1. the wife, mother, sister, or daughter of a sultan: also **sul′tan·ess.** 2. a small, white, seedless grape used for raisins and in wine-making.

**sul·tan·ate** (sul′t'n-it, -āt′), *n.* 1. the authority, position, or reign of a sultan. 2. the territory or jurisdiction of a sultan. Also **sul′tan·ship′.**

**sul·try** (sul′tri), *adj.* [-TRIER, -TRIEST], [< *swelter*], 1. oppressively hot and moist; close. 2. extremely hot; fiery. 3. inflamed, as with passion or lust. —**sul′tri·ly,** *adv.* —**sul′tri·ness,** *n.*

**Su·lu Archipelago** (so͞o′lo͞o), a group of islands in the Philippines, southwest of Mindanao.

**sum** (sum), *n.* [< OFr. < L. *summa,* fem. of *summus,* highest], 1. an amount of money: as, to pay the agreed *sum.* 2. the whole amount; total result: as, the *sum* of our problems. 3. gist; summary; substance. 4. the result obtained by adding together two or more quantities; total. 5. [Colloq.], a problem in arithmetic. *v.t.* [SUMMED, SUMMING], 1. to determine the sum of by adding. 2. to sum up; summarize. —**sum to,** to total. —**sum up,**

1. to collect into a whole. 2. to summarize or recapitulate.
**sum-**, see **sub-**.
**su·mac, su·mach** (sho͞o′mak, so͞o′-), *n.* [OFr. < ML. < Ar. *summaq*], 1. any of various plants with lance-shaped leaves and cone-shaped clusters of hairy, red fruit. 2. the powdered leaves of some of these plants, used in tanning and dyeing.
**Su·ma·tra** (soo-mä′trə), *n.* a large island of Indonesia, south of Malaya: area, 163,145 sq. mi.; pop., 13,600,000. —**Su·ma′tran,** *adj. & n.*
**Su·mer·i·an, Su·mi·ri·an,** (so͞o-mêr′i-ən, sū-), *adj.* designating or of an ancient people of S Babylonia. *n.* one of the Sumerian people. 2. the language of the Sumerians.
‡**sum·ma cum lau·de** (sum′ə kum lô′di; soom′ə koom lou′de), [L.], with the greatest praise: (graduating) with the highest honors from a college.
**sum·ma·rize** (sum′ə-rīz′), *v.t.* [-RIZED, -RIZING], 1. to make a summary or condensed statement of; state briefly. 2. to be a summary of. —**sum′ma·ri·za′tion,** *n.* —**sum′ma·riz′er, sum′ma·rist,** *n.*
**sum·ma·ry** (sum′ə-ri), *adj.* [< ML. < L. *summa*, a sum], 1. summarizing; concise; condensed. 2. prompt and curt; done without delay or ceremony: as, *summary* procedure. *n.* [*pl.* -RIES], a brief statement covering the substance or main points; digest. —**sum·ma·ri·ly** (sum′ə-rə-li, su-mer′ə-li), *adv.* —**sum′ma·ri·ness,** *n.*
**sum·ma·tion** (sum-ā′shən), *n.* 1. the act or process of finding a total. 2. a total or aggregate. 3. a final summing up of arguments, as in a trial.
**sum·mer** (sum′ẽr), *n.* [AS. *sumor*], 1. the warmest season of the year, following spring. 2. a year as reckoned by this season: as, a boy of ten *summers*. 3. any period regarded, like summer, as a time of growth, fulfillment, etc. *adj.* 1. of or characteristic of summer. 2. done, used, played, etc. during the summer. *v.i.* to pass the summer. *v.t.* to keep, feed, or maintain during the summer. —**sum′mer·y, sum′mer·like′, sum′mer·ly,** *adj.*
**sum·mer·house** (sum′ẽr-hous′), *n.* an open structure in a park, etc., for providing a shady rest.
**summer house,** a house or cottage, as in the country, used during the summer.
**sum·mer·sault** (sum′ẽr-sôlt′), *n. & v.i.* somersault: also **sum′mer·set′** (-set′).
**summer sausage,** dried or smoked, uncooked sausage, that keeps well in warm weather.
**summer solstice,** see **solstice.**
**summer squash,** any of various small squashes grown in summer and eaten before fully ripe.
**sum·mer·time** (sum′ẽr-tīm′), *n.* the summer season.
**sum·mit** (sum′it), *n.* [< OFr.; ult. < L. *summus*, highest], 1. the highest point or part; top; apex. 2. the highest degree or state; acme. 3. the highest level of officialdom; specif., the level involving heads of government: as, a meeting at the *summit.*
**sum·mon** (sum′ən), *v.t.* [< OFr. < L. *summonere*, to give a hint to < *sub-*, secretly + *monere*, to warn], 1. to call together; order to convene. 2. to call or send for with authority. 3. to issue a legal summons against. 4. to call upon to surrender. 5. to call forth; rouse; gather (often with *up*): as, *summon* (*up*) your strength.
**sum·mon·er** (sum′ən-ẽr), *n.* a person who summons; specif., formerly, an official who served court summonses.
**sum·mons** (sum′ənz), *n.* [*pl.* -MONSES], [< Anglo-Fr. *somonse* < OFr.; see SUMMON], a call or order to come, attend, etc.; specif., *a*) in *law*, an official order to appear in court; also, the writ containing such an order. *b*) a call, knock, etc. that summons. *v.t.* [Colloq.], to serve a court summons upon.
‡**sum·mum bo·num** (sum′əm bō′nəm), [L.], highest, or greatest, good.
**sump** (sump), *n.* [< MLG. *sump* or MD. *somp*], a pit or well in which liquids collect, as a cesspool.
**sump·ter** (sump′tẽr), *n.* [< OFr. *sometier*], a pack horse, mule, etc. used for carrying baggage.
**sump·tu·ar·y** (sump′cho͞o-er′i), *adj.* [< L. < *sumptus*, expense], of or regulating the spending of money.
**sump·tu·ous** (sump′cho͞o-əs), *adj.* [< OFr. < L. *sumptus*, expense], 1. involving great expense; costly; lavish. 2. magnificent; splendid. —**sump′tu·ous·ly,** *adv.* —**sump′tu·ous·ness,** *n.*
**sun** (sun), *n.* [AS. *sunne*], 1. the incandescent body of gases about which the earth and other planets revolve and which furnishes light, heat, and energy for the solar system: its distance from the earth is nearly 93,000,000 miles: its diameter is about 865,000 miles. 2. the heat or light of the sun. 3. any similar body that is the center of a system of satellites. 4. something like the sun, as in warmth, brilliance, etc. 5. [Poetic], *a*) a day. *b*) a year. *v.t.* [SUNNED, SUNNING], to warm, dry, bleach, tan, etc. in or as in the sunlight. *v.i.* to sun oneself. —**from sun to sun,** [Archaic], from sunrise to sunset. —**place in the sun,** a prominent or favorable position. —**under the sun,** on earth; in the world.
**Sun.,** Sunday.
**sun bath,** exposure of the body to direct sunlight.
**sun-bathe** (sun′bāth′), *v.i.* [-BATHED, -BATHING], to take a sun bath. —**sun′-bath′er,** *n.*
**sun·beam** (sun′bēm′), *n.* a beam of sunlight.
**sun·bon·net** (sun′bon′it), *n.* a bonnet for women and girls, having a large brim and a flap at the back for shading the face and neck from the sun.
**sun·burn** (sun′bũrn′), *n.* 1. inflammation of the skin from prolonged exposure to the sun's rays. 2. the reddish color of a sunburn. *v.t. & v.i.* [-BURNED or -BURNT, -BURNING], to give or get sunburn.
**sun·burst** (sun′bũrst′), *n.* a jeweled brooch, etc. representing the sun with spreading rays.
**sun-cured** (sun′kyoord′), *adj.* cured, as meat, by drying in the sun.
**sun·dae** (sun′di), *n.* [? < *Sunday*], a serving of ice cream covered with sirup, fruit, nuts, etc.
**Sun·day** (sun′di), *n.* [< AS. *sunnan dæg*, day of the sun], the first day of the week: it is observed as the Sabbath by most Christians.
**Sunday best,** [Colloq.], one's best clothes.
**Sunday school,** 1. a school giving religious instruction on Sunday. 2. its teachers and pupils.
**sun deck,** an open porch for rest in the sun.
**sun·der** (sun′dẽr), *v.t. & v.i.* [< AS. < *sundor*, asunder], to break apart; separate; split. —**in sunder,** into parts or pieces; apart. —**sun′der·ance,** *n.*
**sun·di·al** (sun′dī′əl, -dīl′), *n.* an instrument that shows time by the shadow of a pointer or gnomon cast by the sun on a dial marked in hours.

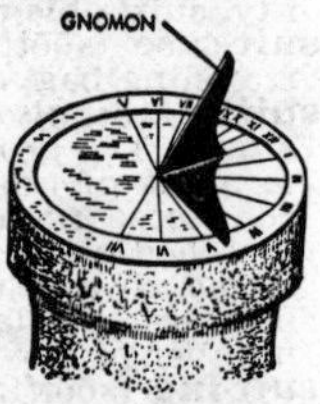

SUNDIAL

**sun·dog** (sun′dôg′), *n.* 1. a parhelion. 2. a small halo or rainbow near the sun.
**sun·down** (sun′doun′), *n.* sunset.
**sun-dried** (sun′drīd′), *adj.* dried by the sun.
**sun·dries** (sun′driz), *n.pl.* sundry items; miscellaneous things of various sorts.
**sun·dry** (sun′dri), *adj.* [AS. *syndrig*, separate < *sunder*, apart], various; miscellaneous; divers: as, *sundry* supplies.
**sun·fish** (sun′fish′), *n.* [*pl.* see FISH], 1. any of various small, fresh-water fishes of North America, as the crappie. 2. a large ocean fish with a short, thick body, a small mouth, and long fins.
**sun·flow·er** (sun′flou′ẽr), *n.* any of various tall plants having yellow, daisylike flowers with disks that contain edible seeds.
**sung** (suŋ), pp. and rare pt. of **sing.**
**sun·glass·es** (sun′glas′iz, -gläs′-), *n.pl.* eyeglasses with special lenses to protect the eyes from the sun's glare.
**sunk** (suŋk), pp. and alt. pt. of **sink.**
**sunk·en** (suŋk′ən), obs. pp. of **sink.** *adj.* 1. sunk in liquid; esp., at the bottom of a body of water: as, a *sunken* ship. 2. beneath the surface of the surrounding medium: as, a *sunken* rock. 3. below the general level: as, a *sunken* room. 4. depressed; hollow: as, *sunken* cheeks. —**sunk′en·ness,** *n.*
**sun lamp,** an electric lamp that radiates ultraviolet rays, used therapeutically, etc.
**sun·less** (sun′lis), *adj.* without sun or sunlight; dark. —**sun′less·ly,** *adv.* —**sun′less·ness,** *n.*
**sun·light** (sun′līt′), *n.* the light of the sun.
**sun·lit** (sun′lit′), *adj.* lighted by the sun.
**sun·ny** (sun′i), *adj.* [-NIER, -NIEST], 1. full of sunshine; bright with sunlight. 2. of, like, or coming from the sun. 3. cheerful; bright: as, a *sunny* smile. —**on the sunny side of,** younger than (a given age). —**sun′ni·ly,** *adv.* —**sun′ni·ness,** *n.*
**sun parlor,** a sitting room with many large windows to admit much sunlight: also **sun′room′,** *n.*
**sun·rise** (sun′rīz′), *n.* 1. the daily appearance of the sun above the eastern horizon. 2. the time of this. 3. the color, etc. of the sky at this time.
**sun·set** (sun′set′), *n.* 1. the daily disappearance of the sun below the western horizon. 2. the time of this. 3. the color, etc. of the sky at this time.
**sun·shade** (sun′shād′), *n.* a parasol, awning, broad hat, etc. for protection against the sun's rays.
**sun·shine** (sun′shīn′), *n.* 1. the shining of the sun. 2. the light and heat given off by the sun. 3. *a*) cheerfulness, happiness, etc. *b*) a source of cheerfulness, etc. —**sun′shin′y,** *adj.*

**sun·spot** (sun′spot'), *n.* any of the dark spots sometimes seen on the surface of the sun.
**sun·stroke** (sun′strōk'), *n.* a form of heatstroke caused by excessive exposure to the sun, characterized by fever, convulsions, etc. —**sun′struck'**, *adj.*
**sun tan,** a darkened condition of the skin resulting from exposure to the sun. —**sun′-tanned'**, *adj.*
**sun·up** (sun′up'), *n.* sunrise.
**Sun Valley,** a resort town in central Idaho.
**sun·ward** (sun′wẽrd), *adj.* facing the sun. *adv.* toward the sun: also **sun′wards.**
**Sun Yat-sen** (soon′ yät′sen′), 1866–1925; Chinese revolutionary leader; president of China (1921–1922).
**sup** (sup), *v.t. & v.i.* [SUPPED, SUPPING], [AS. *supan*], to sip. *n.* a small mouthful of liquid.
**sup** (sup), *v.i.* [SUPPED, SUPPING], [< OFr. *soper*], to eat the evening meal; have supper. *v.t.* to provide with supper.
**sup-,** see **sub-.**
**sup.,** 1. superior. 2. supplement. 3. supplementary. 4. supply. 5. supreme.
**su·per** (so͞o′pẽr, sū′-), *n.* [< *super-*], [Colloq.], 1. a supernumerary. 2. a product of superior grade, extra-large size, etc. 3. a superintendent. *adj.* [Chiefly Colloq.], superfine; of great excellence: often ironical, as, a *super* patriot.
**su·per-,** [L. < *super*, above], a prefix meaning: 1. *over, above, on top of*, as in *superscribe.* 2. *higher in rank than, superior to*, as in *supervisor.* 3. *a*) *surpassing*, as in *superfine. b*) *greater or better than others of its kind*, as in *supermarket.* 4. *to a degree greater than normal*, as in *superheat.* 5. *extra, additional*, as in *supertax.*
**su·per·a·ble** (so͞o′pẽr-ə-b'l, sū′-), *adj.* that can be overcome; surmountable. —**su'per·a·bil′i·ty,** *n.*
**su·per·a·bun·dant** (so͞o'pẽr-ə-bun′dənt, sū'-), *adj.* being more than is usual or needed. —**su'per·a·bun′dance,** *n.* —**su'per·a·bun′dant·ly,** *adv.*
**su·per·an·nu·ate** (so͞o'pẽr-an′ū-āt', sū'-), *v.t.* [-ATED, -ATING], [back-formation < *superannuated*], 1. to retire on a pension because of old age or infirmity. 2. to set aside as old-fashioned or obsolete. —**su'per·an'nu·a′tion,** *n.*
**su·per·an·nu·at·ed** (so͞o'pẽr-an′ū-āt'id, sū'-), *adj.* [< ML. < L. *super annum*, beyond a year], 1. retired on a pension because of old age or infirmity. 2. obsolete; old-fashioned. 3. too old for further work.
**su·perb** (soo-pũrb′, syoo-), *adj.* [< L. *superbus*, haughty < *super*, above], 1. noble; grand; majestic: said of architecture. 2. rich; elegant; luxurious. 3. of the highest quality; excellent. —**su·perb′ly,** *adv.* —**su·perb′ness,** *n.*
**su·per·car·go** (so͞o'pẽr-kär'gō, sū'-), *n.* [*pl.* -GOES, -GOS], [< Sp. *sobrecargo;* see SUPER- & CARGO], an officer on a merchant ship who has charge of the cargo, representing the shipowner.
**su·per·charge** (so͞o′pẽr-chärj', sū′-), *v.t.* [-CHARGED, -CHARGING], to increase the power of (an engine), as by the use of a supercharger.
**su·per·charg·er** (so͞o′pẽr-chär'jẽr, sū′-), *n.* a blower or compressor used to increase the power of an internal-combustion engine by increasing the supply of air to the cylinders.
**su·per·cil·i·ous** (so͞o'pẽr-sil′i-əs, sū'-), *adj.* [< LL. < L. *supercilium*, eyebrow < *super-*, above + *cilium*, eyelid; hence (with reference to raised brows), haughtiness], disdainful or contemptuous; full of or characterized by pride or scorn; haughty. —**su'per·cil′i·ous·ly,** *adv.* —**su'per·cil′i·ous·ness,** *n.*
**su·per·dread·nought** (so͞o'pẽr-dred′nôt, sū'-), *n.* a battleship of the dreadnought class, but larger and with greater firepower.
**su·per·e·go** (so͞o'pẽr-ē′gō, sū'-), *n.* in *psychoanalysis*, that part of the psyche which controls the impulses of the id: cf. *ego.*
**su·per·em·i·nent** (so͞o'pẽr-em′ə-nənt, sū'-), *adj.* eminent beyond others in rank, dignity, etc. —**su'per·em′i·nence,** *n.* —**su'per·em′i·nent·ly,** *adv.*
**su·per·er·o·gate** (so͞o'pẽr-er′ə-gāt', sū'-), *v.i.* [-GATED, -GATING], [< L. pp. < *super-*, above + *erogare*, to pay out], to do more than is required or expected. —**su'per·er'o·ga′tion,** *n.*
**su·per·e·rog·a·to·ry** (so͞o'pẽr-i-rog′ə-tôr'i, sū'-, -tō'-ri), *adj.* 1. done or observed beyond the degree required or expected. 2. superfluous.
**su·per·fi·cial** (so͞o'pẽr-fish′əl, sū'-), *adj.* [< L. < *superficies*, a surface < *super-*, above + *facies*, face], 1. of or being on the surface. 2. concerned with and understanding only the easily apparent and obvious; not profound; shallow. 3. quick and cursory. 4. apparent, but not real; external. —**su'per·fi'ci·al′i·ty** (-i-al′ə-ti), [*pl.* -TIES], **su'per·fi′cial·ness,** *n.* —**su'per·fi′cial·ly,** *adv.*
**su·per·fine** (so͞o'pẽr-fīn′, sū′pẽr-fīn'), *adj.* 1. too subtle, delicate, etc.; overnice. 2. of exceptionally fine quality: said of merchandise, etc.
**su·per·flu·i·ty** (so͞o'pẽr-flo͞o′ə-ti, sū'-), *n.* [*pl.* -TIES], 1. a being superfluous. 2. a quantity beyond what is needed; excess. 3. *usually in pl.* something superfluous.
**su·per·flu·ous** (soo-pũr′flo͞o-əs, syoo-), *adj.* [< L. < *super-*, above + *fluere*, to flow], 1. being more than is needed, useful, or wanted; excessive. 2. not needed; unnecessary. —**su·per′flu·ous·ly,** *adv.* —**su·per′flu·ous·ness,** *n.*
**su·per·heat** (so͞o′pẽr-hēt′, sū′-), *v.t.* 1. to overheat. 2. to heat (a liquid) above its boiling point without vaporization. 3. to heat (steam not in contact with water) beyond its saturation point, so that a drop in temperature will not cause reconversion to water. —**su'per·heat′er,** *n.*
**su·per·het·er·o·dyne** (so͞o'pẽr-het′ẽr-ə-dīn', sū'-), *adj.* [*super*sonic + *heterodyne*], designating or of radio reception in which part of the amplification is carried out at an intermediate supersonic frequency. *n.* a superheterodyne radio set.
**su·per·high·way** (so͞o'pẽr-hī′wā', sū'-), *n.* a divided highway for high-speed traffic, consisting generally of four or more lanes and connecting with crossroads by means of cloverleaves.
**su·per·hu·man** (so͞o'pẽr-hū′mən, sū'-), *adj.* 1. regarded as having a nature above that of man; divine. 2. greater than that of a normal human being. —**su'per·hu′man·ly,** *adv.* —**su'per·hu′man·ness,** *n.*
**su·per·im·pose** (so͞o'pẽr-im-pōz′, sū'-), *v.t.* [-POSED, -POSING], 1. to impose or lay (something) on top of something else. 2. to add. —**su'per·im'po·si′tion** (-im'pə-zish′ən), *n.*
**su·per·in·duce** (so͞o'pẽr-in-do͞os′, sū'pẽr-in-dūs′), *v.t.* [-DUCED, -DUCING], to introduce or bring in as an addition. —**su'per·in·duc′tion** (-duk′shən), *n.*
**su·per·in·tend** (so͞o'pẽr-in-tend′, sū'-), *v.t.* to act as superintendent of; manage; supervise.
**su·per·in·tend·ent** (so͞o'pẽr-in-ten′dənt, sū'-), *n.* [< OFr. < LL. ppr.; see SUPER- & INTEND], a person in charge of a department, institution, etc.; director; manager. *adj.* superintending. —**su'per·in·tend′ence, su'per·in·tend′en·cy,** *n.*
**Su·pe·ri·or** (sə-pêr′i-ẽr, soo-), *n.* the largest of the Great Lakes, between Michigan and Ontario, Canada: usually **Lake Superior.**
**su·pe·ri·or** (sə-pêr′i-ẽr, soo-), *adj.* [OFr. < L. compar. of *superus*, that is above], 1. having greater elevation; higher; upper. 2. printed or written above another figure or letter or the rest of the line: in $n^2$, *2* is *superior.* 3. higher in rank, authority, etc. 4. greater in quality, amount, power, etc. 5. of very high quality, ability, etc.; excellent. 6. showing a feeling that one is better than others; arrogant; haughty. *n.* 1. one who is superior, as in rank, merit, etc. 2. the head of a monastery, convent, etc. —**superior to,** 1. higher than. 2. greater than. 3. unaffected by; not yielding to (something painful, etc.). —**su·pe'ri·or′i·ty** (-ôr′ə-ti, -or′-), *n.* —**su·pe′ri·or·ly,** *adv.*
**superl.,** superlative.
**su·per·la·tive** (soo-pũr′lə-tiv, syoo-), *adj.* [< OFr. < LL. < L. < *super-*, above + *latus*, pp. of *ferre*, to carry], 1. superior to all others; of the highest sort; supreme. 2. excessive. 3. in *grammar*, expressing the extreme degree of comparison of adjectives and adverbs. *n.* 1. the highest degree; acme; height. 2. something superlative. 3. in *grammar, a*) the superlative degree: as, *loveliest* or *most lovely* is the *superlative* of *lovely. b*) an adjective or adverb in this degree. —**su·per′la·tive·ly,** *adv.* —**su·per′la·tive·ness,** *n.*
**su·per·man** (so͞o′pẽr-man', sū′-), *n.* [*pl.* -MEN], 1. in the philosophy of Nietzsche, an idealized superior, dominating man, regarded as an evolutionary goal. 2. an apparently superhuman man.
**su·per·mar·ket** (so͞o′pẽr-mär'kit, sū′-), *n.* a large food store in which shoppers serve themselves and pay at the exit: also **super market.**
**su·per·nal** (so͞o-pũr′n'l, sū-), *adj.* [OFr. < L. *supernus*, upper], 1. high in rank, power, etc.; exalted. 2. celestial; heavenly. —**su·per′nal·ly,** *adv.*
**su·per·nat·u·ral** (so͞o'pẽr-nach′ẽr-əl, sū'-), *adj.* 1.

existing or occurring outside the known forces of nature. 2. attributed to hypothetical forces beyond nature; miraculous; divine. **—the supernatural,** 1. something supernatural. 2. the intervention of supernatural forces. **—su'per·nat'u·ral·ly,** ***adv.***

**su·per·nat·u·ral·ism** (so͞o'pẽr-nach'ẽr-əl-iz'm, sū'-), *n.* 1. a supernatural quality or state. 2. a belief that some supernatural, or divine, force controls nature and the universe. **—su'per·nat'u·ral·ist,** ***n. & adj.*** **—su'per·nat'u·ral·is'tic,** ***adj.***

**su·per·nu·mer·ar·y** (so͞o'pẽr-no͞o'mẽr-er'i; sū'pẽr-nū'-), *adj.* [< LL. < L. *super*, above + *numerus*, number], 1. exceeding the regular or prescribed number; extra. 2. beyond what is needed or desired; superfluous. *n.* [*pl.* -IES], 1. a supernumerary person or thing. 2. in the *theater*, an actor having a small nonspeaking part, as in a mob scene.

**su·per·pose** (so͞o'pẽr-pōz', sū'-), *v.t.* [-POSED, -POSING], [< Fr.; see SUPER- & POSE (to place)], to lay or place on, over, or above something else. **—su'per·pos'a·ble,** ***adj.*** **—su'per·po·si'tion,** ***n.***

**su·per·sat·u·rate** (so͞o'pẽr-sach'oo-rāt', sū'-), *v.t.* [-RATED, -RATING], to saturate beyond the normal point for the given temperature. **—su'per·sat'u·ra'tion,** ***n.***

**su·per·scribe** (so͞o'pẽr-skrīb', sū'-), *v.t.* [-SCRIBED, -SCRIBING], [< L. *super-*, above + *scribere*, to write], 1. to write (something) on the top or outer surface of something. 2. to write a name, address, etc. on the outer cover of (a letter, parcel, etc.). **—su'per·scrip'tion** (-skrip'shən), ***n.***

**su·per·script** (so͞o'pẽr-skript', sū'-), *adj.* written above. *n.* a figure, letter, symbol, etc. that is written above, as 2 in $x^2$.

**su·per·sede** (so͞o'pẽr-sēd', sū'-), *v.t.* [-SEDED, -SEDING], [< OFr. < L. *supersedere*, to preside over < *super-*, above + *sedere*, to sit], 1. to cause to be set aside or discarded as inferior or obsolete; displace. 2. to take the place or office of; succeed. 3. to remove so as to make way for another; supplant. **—su'per·sed'er,** ***n.*** **—su'per·se'dure** (-sē'jẽr), **su'per·sed'ence,** ***n.***

**su·per·sen·si·tive** (so͞o'pẽr-sen'sə-tiv, sū'-), *adj.* sensitive to an abnormal degree. **—su'per·sen'si·tive·ly,** ***adv.*** **—su'per·sen'si·tive·ness,** ***n.***

**su·per·son·ic** (so͞o'pẽr-son'ik, sū'-), *adj.* [< *super* (above) + L. *sonus*, sound], 1. designating or of vibrations with frequencies higher than those audible to the human ear (above about 20,000 per second). 2. designating or of a speed greater than the speed of sound (above 738 miles per hour). 3. traveling at such a speed.

**su·per·son·ics** (so͞o'pẽr-son'iks, sū'-), ***n.pl.*** [construed as sing.], the science dealing with supersonic phenomena.

**su·per·sti·tion** (so͞o'pẽr-stish'ən, sū'-), *n.* [< OFr. < L. *superstitio*; ult. < *super-*, over + *stare*, to stand], 1. any belief that is inconsistent with the known laws of science or with what is considered true and rational; esp., such a belief in omens, the supernatural, etc. 2. any action or practice based on such a belief. 3. such beliefs collectively.

**su·per·sti·tious** (so͞o'pẽr-stish'əs, sū'-), *adj.* of, characterized by, resulting from, or having superstition or superstitions. **—su'per·sti'tious·ly,** ***adv.*** **—su'per·sti'tious·ness,** ***n.***

**su·per·struc·ture** (so͞o'pẽr-struk'chẽr, sū'-), *n.* 1. a structure built on top of another. 2. that part of a building above the foundation. 3. that part of a ship above the main deck.

**su·per·tax** (so͞o'pẽr-taks', sū'-), *n.* an additional tax; esp., a surtax.

**su·per·vene** (so͞o'pẽr-vēn', sū'-), *v.i.* [-VENED, -VENING], [< L. < *super-*, over + *venire*, to come], to come or happen as something additional or unexpected. **—su'per·ven'ient** (-yənt), ***adj.*** **—su'per·ven'tion** (-ven'shən), **su'per·ven'ience** (-yəns), ***n.***

**su·per·vise** (so͞o'pẽr-vīz', sū'-), *v.t. & v.i.* [-VISED, -VISING], [< ML. pp. < L. *super-*, over + *videre*, to see], to oversee or direct (work, workers, a project, etc.); superintend.

**su·per·vi·sion** (so͞o'pẽr-vizh'ən, sū'-), *n.* a supervising or being supervised; direction.

**su·per·vi·sor** (so͞o'pẽr-vī'zẽr, sū'-), *n.* 1. one who supervises; manager; director. 2. in some school systems, an official in charge of the courses and teachers for a particular subject. **—su'per·vi'sor·ship',** ***n.*** **—su'per·vi'so·ry,** ***adj.***

**su·pine** (so͞o-pīn', sū-), *adj.* [L. *supinus*], 1. lying on the back, face upward. 2. mentally or morally inactive; sluggish; listless. **—su·pine'ly,** ***adv.*** **—su·pine'ness,** ***n.***

**supp., suppl.,** 1. supplement. 2. supplementary.

**sup·per** (sup'ẽr), *n.* [< OFr. *soper*, orig. inf., to sup], the last meal of the day, eaten in the evening. **—sup'per·less,** ***adj.***

**sup·plant** (sə-plant', -plänt'), *v.t.* [< Fr. < L. *supplantare*, to trip up < *sub-*, under + *planta*, sole of the foot], 1. to take the place of, especially through force, scheming, etc. 2. to remove in order to replace with something else. **—sup·plan·ta·tion** (sup'lan-tā'shən), **sup·plant'ment,** ***n.*** **—sup·plant'er,** ***n.***

**sup·ple** (sup''l), *adj.* [< OFr. < L. *supplex*, humble < *supplicare*; see SUPPLICATE], 1. easily bent; flexible. 2. lithe; limber: as, a *supple* body. 3. easily changed or influenced; compliant. 4. adaptable; resilient: said of the mind, etc. ***v.t. & v.i.*** [-PLED, -PLING], to make or become supple. **—sup'ple·ly,** ***adv.*** **—sup'ple·ness,** ***n.***

**sup·ple·ment** (sup'lə-mənt; *for v.*, -ment'), *n.* [< L. < *supplere*; see SUPPLY], 1. something added, especially to make up for a lack. 2. a section added to a book, etc., as to give additional information. 3. a separate section containing feature stories, etc., issued with a newspaper. 4. the amount to be added to a given angle or arc to make 180°. ***v.t.*** to provide a supplement to. **—sup'ple·men·ta'tion** (-tā'shən), ***n.*** **—sup'ple·ment'er,** ***n.***

**sup·ple·men·ta·ry** (sup'lə-men'tẽr-i), *adj.* 1. supplying what is lacking; additional. 2. equaling 180° when added together: said of arcs or angles. Also **sup'ple·men'tal.** **—sup'ple·men'ta·ri·ly,** ***adv.***

**sup·pli·ant** (sup'li-ənt), *n.* [< Fr. ppr. < L.; see SUPPLICATE], one who supplicates; petitioner. ***adj.*** 1. supplicating; entreating; beseeching. 2. expressing supplication: as, *suppliant* words. **—sup'pli·ant·ly,** ***adv.*** **—sup'pli·ant·ness,** ***n.***

**sup·pli·cant** (sup'lə-kənt), *adj.* supplicating. *n.* one who supplicates. **—sup'pli·cant·ly,** ***adv.***

**sup·pli·cate** (sup'lə-kāt'), *v.t.* [-CATED, -CATING], [< L. pp. of *supplicare*, to kneel down < *sub-*, under + *plicare*, to fold], 1. to ask for humbly, as by prayer. 2. to make a humble request of. ***v.i.*** to make a humble request, especially in prayer. **—sup'pli·ca'tion,** ***n.*** **—sup'pli·ca'tor,** ***n.*** **—sup'pli·ca·to'ry** (-kə-tôr'i, -tō'ri), ***adj.***

**sup·ply** (sə-plī'), *v.t.* [-PLIED, -PLYING], [< OFr. < L. < *sub-*, under + *plere*, to fill], 1. to give; furnish; provide. 2. to compensate for: as, you must *supply* the deficiency. 3. to meet the needs of: as, we can *supply* you with materials. 4. to act as a substitute in: as, several men have *supplied* his pulpit. ***v.i.*** to serve as a substitute. *n.* [*pl.* -PLIES], 1. the act of supplying. 2. an amount available for use; stock. 3. the amount of a commodity available for purchase. 4. *pl.* materials, provisions, etc. for supplying an army, business, etc. 5. *pl.* an amount of money granted for government expenses. 6. a substitute, as for a minister, etc. ***adj.*** 1. having to do with a supply. 2. serving as a substitute. **—sup·pli'er,** ***n.***

**sup·ply** (sup'li), *adv.* supplely.

**sup·port** (sə-pôrt', -pōrt'), *v.t.* [< Fr. < L.; ult. < *sub-*, under + *portare*, to carry], 1. to carry the weight of; keep steady or in position. 2. to give courage or faith to; help; comfort. 3. to give approval to; advocate; uphold. 4. to maintain (a person, institution, etc.) with money or subsistence. 5. to help prove, vindicate, etc.: as, the evidence *supports* his claim. 6. to bear; endure; tolerate. 7. to keep up; maintain. 8. in the *theater*, *a*) to act (a part). *b*) to have a subordinate role with (a specified star). *n.* 1. a supporting or being supported. 2. a person or thing that supports. 3. a means of support. **—sup·port'a·bil'i·ty,** ***n.*** **—sup·port'a·ble,** ***adj.*** **—sup·port'a·bly,** ***adv.***

**sup·port·er** (sə-pôr'tẽr, -pōr'-), *n.* 1. one who supports; advocate; adherent. 2. a thing that supports; esp., an elastic appliance used to support some part of the body.

**sup·pose** (sə-pōz'), *v.t.* [-POSED, -POSING], [< OFr. < L. *sub*, under + OFr. *poser*; see POSE (to put)], 1. to assume to be true, as for the sake of argument, etc.: as, *suppose* A equals B. 2. to believe to be; imagine; think. 3. to presuppose; assume. 4. to consider as a suggested possibility: as, *suppose* I write him first. 5. to expect: always in the passive, as, I'm *supposed* to visit them. ***v.i.*** to conjecture. **—sup·pos'a·ble,** ***adj.*** **—sup·pos'a·bly,** ***adv.*** **—sup·pos'er,** ***n.***

**sup·posed** (sə-pōzd'), *adj.* 1. regarded as true, possible, etc., without actual knowledge. 2. merely imagined. **—sup·pos'ed·ly,** ***adv.***

**sup·po·si·tion** (sup'ə-zish'ən), *n.* 1. the act of supposing. 2. something supposed; theory. **—sup'po·si'tion·al,** ***adj.*** **—sup'po·si'tion·al·ly,** ***adv.***

**sup·pos·i·to·ry** (sə-poz'ə-tôr'i, -tō'ri), *n.* [*pl.* -RIES], [< LL.; ult. < L. *sub-*, under + *ponere*, to place], a small piece of medicated substance, introduced into the rectum, vagina, etc., where it is melted and diffused by the body temperature.

**sup·press** (sə-pres′), ***v.t.*** [< L. pp. < *sub-*, under + *premere*, to press], 1. to put down by force or authority; quell. 2. to keep back; restrain: as, to *suppress* a laugh. 3. to prevent or prohibit the publication of (a book, etc.). 4. to check the flow or discharge of. 5. in *psychiatry*, to withhold from consciousness. **—sup·press′er, sup·pres′sor, *n.* —sup·press′i·ble, *adj.* —sup·pres′sive, *adj.***

**sup·pres·sion** (sə-presh′ən), ***n.*** 1. a suppressing or being suppressed. 2. the deliberate exclusion of an idea, desire, or feeling from consciousness.

**sup·pu·rate** (sup′yoo-rāt′), ***v.i.*** [-RATED, -RATING], [< L. *suppuratus*, pp.; ult. < *sub-*, under + *pus*, pus], to form or discharge pus; fester. **—sup′pu·ra′tion, *n.* —sup′pu·ra′tive, *adj.***

‡**su·pra** (sōō′prə, sū′-), ***adv.*** [L.], above.

**su·pra-,** [< L. *supra*], a prefix meaning *above, over, beyond.*

**su·pra·re·nal** (sōō′prə-rē′n'l, sū′-), ***adj.*** [*supra-* + *renal*], on or above the kidney; specif., designating or of an adrenal gland. ***n.*** an adrenal gland.

**su·prem·a·cy** (sə-prem′ə-si, syoo-), ***n.*** [*pl.* -CIES], 1. a being supreme. 2. supreme power or authority.

**su·preme** (sə-prēm′, syoo-), ***adj.*** [< Fr. < L. *supremus*, superl. of *superus*, that is above], 1. highest in rank, power, etc. 2. highest in quality, achievement, etc. 3. highest in degree: as, a *supreme* fool. 4. final; ultimate. **—su·preme′ly, *adv.* —su·preme′ness, *n.***

**Supreme Being,** God.

**Supreme Court,** 1. the highest Federal court, consisting of nine judges. 2. the highest court in any of the States.

**supreme sacrifice,** the sacrifice of one's life.

**Supreme Soviet,** the parliament of the Soviet Union: it has two equal chambers, the Council of the Union and the Council of the Nationalities.

**Supt., supt.,** Superintendent.

**sur-,** [< Fr. < OFr. < L. *super*, over, above], a prefix meaning *over, upon, above, beyond.*

**sur-,** see **sub-.**

**Su·ra·ba·ya** (sōō′rä-bä′yä), ***n.*** a seaport in NE Java: pop., 1,311,000.

**su·rah** (soor′ə), ***n.*** [< *Surat*, a seaport in India], a soft, twilled fabric of silk or of silk and rayon.

**sur·cease** (sũr-sēs′), ***v.t. & v.i.*** [-CEASED, -CEASING], [< OFr. *sursis*, pp. of *surseoir*, to pause < L. *supersedere*, to refrain from], [Archaic], to stop; end. ***n.*** [Archaic], end; cessation.

**sur·charge** (sũr-chärj′; *for n., usually* sũr′chärj′), ***v.t.*** [-CHARGED, -CHARGING], 1. to overcharge. 2. to overload. 3. to fill to excess. 4. to mark (a postage stamp) with a surcharge. ***n.*** 1. *a*) an additional charge. *b*) an excessive charge; overcharge. 2. an extra or excessive load. 3. a new valuation overprinted on a postage stamp.

**sur·cin·gle** (sũr′siŋ′g'l), ***n.*** [< OFr. < *sur-*, over + L. *cingulum*, a belt], a strap passed around a horse's body to bind on a saddle, pack, etc.

**sur·coat** (sũr′kōt′), ***n.*** [OFr. *surcote*], an outer coat; esp., a short cloak worn over armor.

**surd** (sũrd), ***adj.*** [< L. *surdus*, deaf, unheard], 1. in *mathematics*, that cannot be expressed in rational numbers. 2. in *phonetics*, voiceless. ***n.*** 1. a surd number or quantity, as $\sqrt{5}$. 2. in *phonetics*, a voiceless sound.

**sure** (shoor), ***adj.*** [< OFr. < L. *securus*], 1. [Rare], secure; safe. 2. that will not fail: as, a *sure* method. 3. that can be relied upon; trustworthy: as, he is my *sure* adviser. 4. that cannot be doubted, questioned, etc.; absolutely true. 5. having no doubt; positive; confident: as, are you *sure* of your facts? 6. bound to be or happen: as, a *sure* defeat. 7. bound to do, experience, etc.: as, he is *sure* to lose. 8. never missing: as, a *sure* aim. ***adv.*** [Colloq.], 1. surely; inevitably. 2. certainly; indeed: an intensive, often used to express affirmation. **—for sure,** certainly; without doubt. **—make sure,** to be or cause to be certain. **—sure enough,** [Colloq.], certainly; without doubt. **—to be sure,** surely; certainly. **—sure′ness, *n.***

**sure-foot·ed** (shoor′foot′id), ***adj.*** not likely to stumble, slip, or fall. **—sure′-foot′ed·ness, *n.***

**sure·ly** (shoor′li), ***adv.*** 1. with confidence; in a sure, unhesitating manner. 2. without a doubt; certainly: as, *surely* you don't believe that!

**sure·ty** (shoor′ti, -ə-ti), ***n.*** [*pl.* -TIES], 1. a being sure; assurance. 2. something sure; certainty. 3. something that makes sure, protects, etc.; security. 4. one who makes himself responsible for another; specif., in *law*, one who makes himself liable for another's debts, etc. **—sure′ty·ship′, *n.***

**surf** (sũrf), ***n.*** [formerly *suffe;* prob. var. of *sough*], 1. the waves of the sea breaking on the shore or a reef. 2. the foam or spray caused by this. **—surf′y** [-IER, -IEST], ***adj.***

**sur·face** (sũr′fis), ***n.*** [< Fr. < *sur-* (see SUB-) + *face*, a face], 1. *a*) the exterior of an object. *b*) any of the faces of a solid. 2. superficial features, as of a personality. 3. in *geometry*, an extent or magnitude having length and breadth, but no thickness. ***adj.*** 1. of, on, or at the surface. 2. exterior; superficial. ***v.t.*** [-FACED, -FACING], 1. to give a specified kind of surface to; esp., to make smooth. 2. to bring (a submarine) to the surface of the water. ***v.i.*** to rise to the surface of the water. **—sur′fac·er, *n.***

**surface tension,** a property of liquids in which the surface tends to contract to the smallest possible area, as in the formation of drops.

**surf·board** (sũrf′bôrd′, -bōrd′), ***n.*** a long, narrow board used in the water sport of surfing.

SURFBOARD

**surf·boat** (sũrf′bōt′), ***n.*** a sturdy, light boat used in heavy surf. **—surf′boat′·man** [*pl.* -MEN], ***n.***

**sur·feit** (sũr′fit), ***n.*** [< OFr. < *surfaire*, to overdo < *sur-*, over + *faire*, to make], 1. too great an amount or supply: as, a *surfeit* of complaints. 2. *a*) overindulgence, especially in food or drink. *b*) discomfort resulting from this. 3. disgust, nausea, etc. resulting from any kind of excess. ***v.t.*** to feed or supply to excess. ***v.i.*** to overindulge.

**surf·ing** (sũrf′iŋ), ***n.*** the sport of riding in toward shore on the crests of waves, especially on a surfboard.

**surg.,** 1. surgeon. 2. surgery. 3. surgical.

**surge** (sũrj), ***n.*** [prob. via Fr. < L. *surgere*, to rise], 1. *a*) a large wave of water; billow. *b*) a swelling or rolling of something like a wave: as, a *surge* of power. 2. a violent rolling or swelling motion: as, the *surge* of the sea. 3. a short, sudden rush of electric current in a circuit. ***v.i.*** [SURGED, SURGING], to move in or as in a surge or surges. **—surg′y** [-IER, -IEST], ***adj.***

**sur·geon** (sũr′jən), ***n.*** a doctor who practices surgery. **—sur′geon·cy** (-si), ***n.***

**sur·ger·y** (sũr′jẽr-i), ***n.*** [*pl.* -IES], [< OFr. *cirurgie;* ult. < Gr. *cheirourgia*, handicraft < *cheir*, the hand + *ergein*, to work], 1. the treatment of disease, injury, etc. by manual or instrumental operations, as the removal of diseased parts by cutting. 2. the branch of medicine dealing with this. 3. the operating room of a surgeon or hospital.

**sur·gi·cal** (sũr′ji-k'l), ***adj.*** 1. of surgeons or surgery. 2. used in or connected with surgery. 3. resulting from surgery. **—sur′gi·cal·ly, *adv.***

**Su·ri·nam** (soor′i-näm′, -nam′), ***n.*** a Dutch colony in N South America, on the Atlantic.

**sur·ly** (sũr′li), ***adj.*** [-LIER, -LIEST], [earlier *sirly*, imperious < *sir*], bad-tempered; uncivil; sullenly rude. **—sur′li·ly, *adv.* —sur′li·ness, *n.***

**sur·mise** (sẽr-mīz′; *also, for n.,* sũr′mīz), ***n.*** [< OFr. pp. < *sur-* (< L. *super*), upon + *mettre* (< L. *mittere*, to send), to put], 1. an idea or opinion formed from inconclusive evidence; conjecture; guess. 2. the act of surmising. ***v.t. & v.i.*** [-MISED, -MISING], to imagine or infer (something) without conclusive evidence; guess. **—sur·mis′er, *n.***

**sur·mount** (sẽr-mount′), ***v.t.*** [< OFr. *surmonter;* see SUR- (over) & MOUNT], 1. to overcome (a difficulty). 2. to be or lie at the top of; be or rise above. 3. to climb up and across (a height, etc.). **—sur·mount′a·ble, *adj.* —sur·mount′er, *n.***

**sur·name** (sũr′nām′; *also, for v.,* sũr′nām′), ***n.*** [altered, after *name* < OFr. < *sur-*, over + *nom*, a name], 1. a family name as distinguished from a given name; last name. 2. an epithet added to a person's given name: e.g., Ivan *the Terrible.* ***v.t.*** [-NAMED, -NAMING], to give a surname to.

**sur·pass** (sẽr-pas′, -päs′), ***v.t.*** [< OFr. < *sur-*, beyond + *passer*, to pass], 1. to excel or be superior to. 2. to exceed in quantity, degree, etc. 3. to go beyond the limit, capacity, range, etc. of. **—sur·pass′a·ble, *adj.* —sur·pass′er, *n.***

**sur·pass·ing** (sẽr-pas′iŋ, -päs′-), ***adj.*** that surpasses the average or usual; exceeding or excelling; unusually excellent. **—sur·pass′ing·ly, *adv.***

**sur·plice** (sũr′plis), ***n.*** [< OFr. < LL. < *super-*, above + *pelliceum*, fur robe], a loose, white, wide-sleeved cloak or gown worn over the cassock by the clergy and choir in some churches. —**sur′pliced,** *adj.*

**sur·plus** (sũr′plus, -pləs), *n.* [OFr. < *sur-*, above + L. *plus*, more], 1. a quantity over and above what is needed or used; excess. 2. the excess of the assets of a business over its liabilities. *adj.* forming a surplus; excess. —**sur′plus·age,** *n.*

**sur·prise** (sẽr-prīz′), *v.t.* [-PRISED, -PRISING], [< OFr. pp. < *sur-* (< L. *super*), above + *prendre* (< L. *prehendere*), to take], 1. to come upon suddenly or unexpectedly; take unawares. 2. to attack or capture without warning. 3. to cause to be amazed because unexpected, unusual, etc.; astonish. 4. *a*) to cause by some sudden or unexpected action to do or say something unintended: often with *into*. *b*) to bring out (something) by such means. *n.* 1. a surprising, or taking unawares. 2. a being surprised; astonishment. 3. something that surprises because unexpected, unusual, etc. —**take by surprise,** 1. to come upon suddenly or without warning. 2. to amaze; astound. —**sur·pris′al,** *n.* —**sur·pris′ed·ly** (-id-li), *adv.* —**sur·pris′er,** *n.*

**sur·pris·ing** (sẽr-prīz′iŋ), *adj.* causing surprise. —**sur·pris′ing·ly,** *adv.* —**sur·pris′ing·ness,** *n.*

**sur·re·al·ism** (sə-rē′əl-iz'm), *n.* [< Fr. < *sur-*, above + *réalisme*, realism], a modern movement in art and literature, in which an attempt is made to portray the workings of the subconscious mind, as by an irrational, noncontextual arrangement of material. —**sur·re′al·ist,** *adj.* & *n.* —**sur·re′al·is′tic,** *adj.* —**sur·re′al·is′ti·cal·ly,** *adv.*

**sur·ren·der** (sə-ren′dẽr), *v.t.* [< OFr. < *sur-*, up + *rendre*, to render], 1. to give up possession of or power over; yield to another on compulsion. 2. to give up or abandon: as, to *surrender* all hope. 3. to yield or resign (oneself) to an emotion, influence, etc. *v.i.* to give oneself up, especially as a prisoner; yield. *n.* the act of surrendering. —**sur·ren′der·er,** *n.*

**sur·rep·ti·tious** (sũr′əp-tish′əs), *adj.* [< L. pp. < *sub-*, under + *rapere*, to seize], 1. done, got, made, etc. in a secret, stealthy way; clandestine. 2. acting in a secret, stealthy way. —**sur′rep·ti′tious·ly,** *adv.* —**sur′rep·ti′tious·ness,** *n.*

**sur·rey** (sũr′i), *n.* [*pl.* -REYS], [< *Surrey*, county in England], a light, four-wheeled carriage with two seats, both facing forward.

SURREY

**sur·ro·gate** (sũr′ə-gāt′; *also, for n.*, -git), *n.* [< L. pp. < *sub-*, in place of + *rogare*, to elect], 1. a deputy or substitute, as for a bishop. 2. in some States, a probate court judge. *v.t.* [-GATED, -GATING], to substitute for another.

**sur·round** (sə-round′), *v.t.* [< OFr.; ult. < L. < *super*, over + *undare*, to rise < *unda*, a wave], 1. to encircle on all or nearly all sides; enclose; encompass. 2. to cut off (a military unit, etc.) from communication or retreat by encircling. —**sur·round′er,** *n.*

**sur·round·ing** (sə-roun′diŋ), *n.* that which surrounds; esp., *pl.*, the things, conditions, circumstances, influences, etc. that surround a given place or person; environment. *adj.* that surrounds.

**sur·tax** (sũr′taks′; *also, for v.*, sũr′taks′), *n.* an extra tax on something already taxed. *v.t.* to levy a surtax on. —**sur′tax′a·ble,** *adj.*

**sur·tout** (sẽr-tōōt′, -tōō′), *n.* [Fr. < *sur*, over + *tout*, all], a man's long, closefitting overcoat.

**sur·veil·lance** (sẽr-vā′ləns, -vāl′yəns), *n.* [Fr. < *sur-* (< L. *super*), over + *veiller* (< L. *vigilare*), to watch], 1. watch kept over a person, especially a suspect. 2. supervision. —**sur·veil′lant,** *n.* & *adj.*

**sur·vey** (sẽr-vā′; *for n., usually* sũr′vā), *v.t.* [< Anglo-Fr. < OFr. < *sur-* (< L. *super*), over + *veoir* (< L. *videre*), to see], 1. to examine, inspect, or consider carefully. 2. to look at or consider, especially in a comprehensive way. 3. to determine the location, form, or boundaries of (a tract of land) by the use of geometry and trigonometry. *v.i.* to survey land. *n.* [*pl.* -VEYS], 1. a general study: as, a *survey* of public opinion. 2. a comprehensive study or examination: as, a *survey* of modern art. 3. the process of surveying an area of land. 4. a plan or written description of the area surveyed. —**sur·vey′a·ble,** *adj.*

**sur·vey·ing** (sẽr-vā′iŋ), *n.* 1. the act of one who surveys. 2. the science of surveying land.

**sur·vey·or** (sẽr-vā′ẽr), *n.* 1. one who surveys land. 2. a customs official who ascertains the amount and value of imported goods. —**sur·vey′or·ship′,** *n.*

**surveyor's measure,** a system of measurement used in surveying, in which 7.92 inches = 1 link; 100 links = 1 chain, or 66 feet; 80 chains = 1 mile; 10 square chains = 1 acre.

**sur·viv·al** (sẽr-vi′v'l), *n.* 1. the act, state, or fact of surviving. 2. something that survives, as an ancient belief, custom, usage, etc.

**survival of the fittest,** see **natural selection.**

**sur·vive** (sẽr-vīv′), *v.t.* [-VIVED, -VIVING], [< OFr. < L. < *super-*, above + *vivere*, to live], 1. to live or exist longer than; outlive. 2. to continue to live after or in spite of: as, we *survived* the fire. *v.i.* to continue living or existing. —**sur·viv′ing,** *adj.* —**sur·vi′vor, sur·viv′er,** *n.*

**sus·cep·ti·bil·i·ty** (sə-sep′tə-bil′ə-ti), *n.* [*pl.* -TIES], 1. a being susceptible; susceptible temperament. 2. *pl.* sensitivities; feelings.

**sus·cep·ti·ble** (sə-sep′tə-b'l), *adj.* [< ML. < L. *suscipere*, to receive < *sus-*, under + *capere*, to take], easily affected emotionally; having sensitive feelings; responsive. —**susceptible of,** admitting; allowing: as, testimony *susceptible of* error. —**susceptible to,** easily influenced by or affected with: as, *susceptible to* disease. —**sus·cep′ti·ble·ness,** *n.* —**sus·cep′ti·bly,** *adv.*

**sus·pect** (sə-spekt′; *for adj. & n., usually* sus′pekt), *v.t.* [< Fr. < L. pp. < *sub-*, under + *spicere*, to look], 1. to believe to be guilty of something specified on little or no evidence. 2. to believe to be bad, wrong, harmful, etc.; distrust. 3. to imagine to be; think likely; suppose. *v.i.* to be suspicious. *adj.* viewed with suspicion; suspected. *n.* one who is suspected, as of a crime, etc. —**sus·pect′er,** *n.*

**sus·pend** (sə-spend′), *v.t.* [< OFr. < L. *sub-*, under + *pendere*, to hang], 1. to exclude from an office, privilege, etc., usually for a specified time, as a penalty. 2. to cause to become inoperative for a time. 3. to keep undecided; hold back (judgment, sentence, etc.). 4. to hang by a support from above. 5. to hold without attachment, as dust in the air. 6. to keep in suspense, wonder, etc. *v.i.* 1. to stop temporarily. 2. to fail to pay debts or obligations. —**sus·pend′i·ble,** *adj.*

**sus·pend·ers** (sə-spen′dẽrz), *n.pl.* 1. a pair of straps or bands passed over the shoulders to support the trousers. 2. [Brit.], garters.

**sus·pense** (sə-spens′), *n.* [< Anglo-Fr. & OFr. < ML. < L. pp. of *suspendere*, to suspend], 1. the state of being undecided. 2. the state of being uncertain, as in awaiting a decision, usually with anxiety. 3. uncertainty; indecisiveness.

**sus·pen·sion** (sə-spen′shən), *n.* 1. a suspending or being suspended; specif., *a*) a barring from office, etc. *b*) a stoppage of payment, etc. *c*) a holding back of a judgment, etc. 2. a supporting device upon or from which something is suspended. 3. the system of springs, etc. supporting a vehicle upon its undercarriage. 4. the condition of a solid whose particles are dispersed through a fluid but not dissolved in it. 5. a substance in this condition. 6. in *music*, *a*) the holding back of one or more tones in a chord while the others progress, so that a temporary dissonance is created. *b*) the tones so held.

**suspension bridge,** a bridge suspended from cables anchored at either end and supported by towers at intervals.

SUSPENSION BRIDGE

**sus·pen·sive** (sə-spen′siv), *adj.* 1. that suspends, defers, or temporarily stops something. 2. tending to suspend judgment; undecided. 3. of, characterized by, or in suspense; apprehensive. —**sus·pen′sive·ly,** *adv.* —**sus·pen′sive·ness,** *n.*

**sus·pen·so·ry** (sə-spen′sə-ri), *adj.* 1. suspending, supporting, etc.: as, a *suspensory* muscle or bandage. 2. suspending or delaying, especially so as to leave something undecided. *n.* [*pl.* -RIES], a suspensory muscle, bandage, etc.: also **sus·pen′sor.**

**sus·pi·cion** (sə-spish′ən), *n.* [< OFr. < LL. < L. < *suspicere*, to suspect], 1. a suspecting or being suspected. 2. the feeling or state of mind of one who suspects. 3. a very small amount or degree; suggestion; trace. *v.t.* [Dial. or Colloq.], to suspect. —**above suspicion,** not to be suspected; honorable. —**on suspicion,** on the basis of suspicion. —**under suspicion,** suspected.

**sus·pi·cious** (sə-spish′əs), *adj.* 1. arousing or likely to arouse suspicion. 2. showing suspicion. 3.

feeling, or inclined to feel, suspicion. —**sus·pi′cious·ly,** *adv.* —**sus·pi′cious·ness,** *n.*

**Sus·que·han·na** (sus′kwi-han′ə), *n.* a river flowing through New York, Pennsylvania, and Maryland into Chesapeake Bay.

**sus·tain** (sə-stān′), *v.t.* [< OFr. < L. < *sub-*, under + *tenere*, to hold], 1. to maintain; keep in existence; prolong: as, *sustained* tones, *sustained* efforts. 2. to keep supplied with necessities; provide for. 3. to support; carry the weight of. 4. to strengthen the spirits, courage, etc. of; comfort. 5. to endure; withstand. 6. to undergo; suffer, as an injury or loss. 7. to uphold the validity of: as, the court *sustained* his claim. 8. to confirm; corroborate. —**sus·tain′a·ble,** *adj.* —**sus·tain′ed·ly,** *adv.* —**sus·tain′er,** *n.* —**sus·tain′ment,** *n.*

**sus·tain·ing program** (sə-stān′iŋ), any radio or television program carried by a station or network without a commercial sponsor.

**sus·te·nance** (sus′ti-nəns), *n.* 1. sustainment. 2. maintenance; support; means of livelihood. 3. that which sustains life; nourishment; food.

**sut·ler** (sut′lẽr), *n.* [< MD. < *soetelen*, to perform menial offices], one who follows an army to sell food, liquor, etc. to its soldiers.

**sut·tee** (su-tē′, sut′ē), *n.* [< Hind. < Sans. *satī*, virtuous wife], 1. formerly, a Hindu widow who threw herself alive, and was cremated, on her husband's funeral pile. 2. such self-cremation. —**sut·tee′ism,** *n.*

**su·ture** (sōō′chẽr, sū′-), *n.* [Fr. < L. pp. of *suere*, to sew], 1. the act of joining together by or as by sewing. 2. the line along which such a joining is made. 3. in *anatomy*, the line of junction of two bones, especially of the skull. 4. in *surgery*, *a*) the stitching together of the two edges of a wound or incision. *b*) any of the stitches of gut, thread, etc. so used. *v.t.* [-TURED, -TURING], to join together as with sutures. —**su′tur·al,** *adj.*

**Su·wan·nee** (sə-wôn′i, swô′nē), *n.* a river in Georgia and Florida, flowing into the Gulf of Mexico: also sp. **Swanee.**

**su·ze·rain** (sōō′zə-rin, sū′zə-rān′), *n.* [Fr. < *sus*, above < L. *su(r)sum*, upward + ending of *souverain*, sovereign], 1. a feudal lord. 2. a state in its relation to another over which it has political control. —**su′ze·rain·ty** [*pl.* -TIES], *n.*

**s.v.,** *sub verbo*, [L.], under the word (specified).

**svelte** (svelt), *adj.* [Fr.], slender and graceful.

**SW, S.W., s.w.,** 1. southwest. 2. southwestern.

**Sw.,** 1. Sweden. 2. Swedish.

**swab** (swäb), *n.* [< *swabber* < D. *zwabber* < *zwabben*, to do dirty work], 1. a mop for cleaning decks, floors, etc. 2. *a*) a small piece of cotton, sponge, etc. used to apply medicine to, or clean discharged matter from, the throat, mouth, etc. *b*) the matter so collected. 3. a brush, etc. for cleaning the barrel of a gun. 4. [Slang], a clumsy, loutish person. *v.t.* [SWABBED, SWABBING], to clean, medicate, etc. with a swab. Also **swob.** —**swab′ber,** *n.*

**swad·dle** (swäd′'l), *n.* [AS. *swæthel* < *swathian*, to swathe], a cloth or bandage used for swaddling. *v.t.* [-DLED, -DLING], 1. to wrap (a newborn baby) in long narrow bands of cloth. 2. to bind in or as in bandages; swathe. —**swad′dler,** *n.*

**swaddling clothes,** 1. formerly, the long, narrow bands of cloth wrapped around a newborn baby. 2. baby clothes. Also **swaddling bands** (or **clouts**).

**swag** (swag), *n.* [prob. < ON.], 1. in Australia, a bundle containing one's personal belongings. 2. [Slang], stolen money or property; loot; plunder.

**swage** (swāj), *n.* [< OFr. < LL. *soca*, a rope], 1. a tool for bending or shaping metal. 2. a die or stamp for shaping metal by hammering. *v.t.* [SWAGED, SWAGING], to shape, etc. with a swage.

**swag·ger** (swag′ẽr), *v.i.* [prob. freq. of *swag*], 1. to walk with a bold or arrogant stride; strut. 2. to boast, brag, or show off in a loud, superior manner. *v.t.* to influence by blustering; bluff. *n.* swaggering walk or manner. —**swag′ger·er,** *n.* —**swag′ger·ing·ly,** *adv.*

**swagger stick,** a short stick or cane as carried by some army officers, etc.

**Swa·hi·li** (swä-hē′li), *n.* 1. [*pl.* -LI], one of a Bantu people inhabiting Zanzibar and the near-by mainland. 2. their Northern Bantu language, used as a lingua franca in E Africa. *adj.* of the Swahili or their language: also **Swa·hi′li·an.**

**swain** (swān), *n.* [< ON. *sveinn*, boy], [Poetic or Archaic], 1. a country youth. 2. a young rustic lover or gallant. 3. a lover.

**swal·low** (swäl′ō), *n.* [AS. *swalewe*], 1. any of a family of small, swift-flying birds with long, pointed wings and forked tails, known for their regular migrations. 2. any of certain swifts resembling swallows. —**swal′low·like′,** *adj.*

**swal·low** (swäl′ō), *v.t.* [AS. *swelgan*], 1. to pass (food, etc.) from the mouth through the esophagus into the stomach. 2. to take in; absorb; engulf: often with *up*. 3. to take back (words said); retract. 4. to put up with; tolerate: as, to *swallow* insults. 5. to refrain from expressing; suppress: as, to *swallow* one's pride. 6. [Colloq.], to accept as true without question or investigation. *v.i.* to perform the muscular actions of swallowing something, especially as in emotion. *n.* 1. the act of swallowing. 2. the amount swallowed at one time. 3. the throat or gullet. —**swal′low·er,** *n.*

**swal·low·tail** (swäl′ō-tāl′), *n.* 1. something having a forked shape like a swallow's tail. 2. a butterfly having taillike points on the lower wings. 3. a swallow-tailed coat. —**swal′low-tailed′,** *adj.*

**swallow-tailed coat,** a man's full-dress coat that tapers down in two long tails at the back.

**swam** (swam), pt. of **swim.**

**swa·mi** (swä′mi), *n.* [*pl.* -MIS], [< Hind. < Sans. *svāmin*, a lord], master: a title of respect for a Hindu religious teacher: also sp. **swa′my** [*pl.* -MIES].

**swamp** (swämp, swômp), *n.* [prob. < D. *zwamp*, marsh], a piece of wet, spongy land; marsh; bog: also **swamp′land′.** *adj.* of or native to a swamp. *v.t.* 1. to plunge in a swamp, deep water, etc. 2. to flood with or as with water. 3. to overwhelm; ruin: as, debts *swamped* them. 4. to sink (a boat) by filling with water. *v.i.* to sink as in a swamp. —**swamp′ish,** *adj.* —**swamp′y** [-IER, -IEST], *adj.*

**swamp fever,** malaria.

**swan** (swän, swôn), *n.* [AS.], 1. [*pl.* SWANS, SWAN; see PLURAL, II, D, 1], a large-bodied, web-footed water bird with a long, graceful neck and, usually, pure white feathers. 2. a poet or singer of great ability: cf. **swan song.** 3. [S-], the constellation Cygnus. —**swan′like′,** *adj.*

**swan dive,** a forward dive in which the legs are held straight and together, the back is curved, and the arms are stretched out to the sides.

**Swa·nee** (swô′nē), *n.* Suwannee.

**swang** (swaŋ), archaic or dial. pt. of **swing.**

**swank** (swaŋk), *n.* [prob. akin to AS. *swancor*, pliant, supple], [Slang], 1. stylish display or ostentation in dress, etc. 2. swaggering, ostentatious behavior, speech, etc. *adj.* [Slang], ostentatiously stylish. *v.i.* [Slang], to show off; swagger.

**swank·y** (swaŋ′ki), *adj.* [-IER, -IEST], [Slang], ostentatiously stylish; swaggering; showy. —**swank′i·ly,** *adv.* —**swank′i·ness,** *n.*

**swan's-down** (swänz′doun′, swônz′-), *n.* 1. the soft, fine underfeathers, or down, of the swan, used for trimming clothes, etc. 2. a soft, thick fabric of wool and silk, rayon, or cotton, used for making baby clothes, etc. Also **swans′down′.**

**swan song,** 1. the song supposed in ancient fable to be sung by a dying swan. 2. the last act, final creative work, etc. of a person.

**swap** (swäp, swôp), *n., v.t. & v.i.* [SWAPPED, SWAPPING], [ME. *swappen*, to strike], [Colloq.], exchange; trade; barter: also sp. **swop.** —**swap′per,** *n.*

**sward** (swôrd), *n.* [< AS. *sweard*, skin], grass-covered soil; turf. *v.t. & v.i.* to cover or become covered with grass or turf. —**sward′y,** *adj.*

**sware** (swâr), archaic pt. of **swear.**

**swarm** (swôrm), *n.* [AS. *swearm*], 1. a large number of bees, led by a queen, leaving a hive to start a new colony. 2. a colony of bees in a hive. 3. a large, moving mass of insects. 4. a moving crowd or throng. *v.i.* 1. to fly off in a swarm: said of bees. 2. to move, collect, etc. in large numbers; throng. 3. to be filled or crowded; teem (usually with *with*). *v.t.* to crowd; throng. —**swarm′er,** *n.*

**swarm** (swôrm), *v.i. & v.t.* [prob. akin to prec. entry], to climb (a tree, mast, etc.); shin.

**swart** (swôrt), *adj.* [AS. *sweart*], [Dial. or Poetic], swarthy. —**swart′ness,** *n.*

**swarth** (swôrth), *n.* [Dial.], sward. *adj.* swarthy.

**swarth·y** (swôr′*th*i, -thi), *adj.* [-IER, -IEST], [< *swart(h)*], having a dark skin; dusky; dark. —**swarth′i·ly,** *adv.* —**swarth′i·ness,** *n.*

**swash** (swäsh, swôsh), *v.i.* [echoic], 1. to dash, strike, wash, etc. with a splashing sound; splash. 2. to swagger. *v.t.* to splash (a liquid), as in a container. *n.* 1. a channel of water cutting through or behind a sandbank. 2. the splashing of water. 3. a swaggering. —**swash′er,** *n.*

**swash·buck·ler** (swäsh′buk′lẽr, swôsh′-), *n.* [*swash* + *buckler*, a shield], a blustering, swaggering fighting man. —**swash′buck′ling, swash′buck′ler·ing,** *n.* & *adj.*

**swas·ti·ka, swas·ti·ca** (swäs′ti-kə, swas′-), *n.* [< Sans. < *svasti*, well-being], 1. a design or ornament of ancient origin in the form of a Greek cross with each arm bent in a right-angle extension. 2. this design with the extensions bent in a clockwise direction: used as the Nazi emblem.

SWASTIKA

**swat** (swät), *v.t.* [SWATTED, SWATTING], [echoic], [Colloq.], to hit with a quick, sharp blow. *n.* [Colloq.], a quick, sharp blow. Also **swot.**—**swat′ter,** *n.*

**swatch** (swäch), *n.* [< N. dial.; orig., a cloth tally], a sample piece of cloth or other material.

**swath** (swäth, swôth), *n.* [AS. *swathu*, a track], 1. the space covered with one cut of a scythe or other mowing device. 2. a line or row of grass, wheat, etc. cut in one course by a scythe, mower, etc. 3. a strip, row, etc. —**cut a wide swath,** to make an ostentatious display; appear important.

**swathe** (swā*th*), *v.t.* [SWATHED, SWATHING], [AS. *swathian*], 1. to wrap or bind up in a bandage. 2. to wrap (a bandage, etc.) around something. 3. to surround; envelop. *n.* a bandage or wrapping.

**swathe** (swā*th*), *n.* a swath.

**sway** (swā), *v.i.* [< ON. *sveigja* & LG. *swājen*], 1. to swing or move from side to side or to and fro; fluctuate. 2. to lean or incline to one side; veer. 3. to incline in judgment or opinion. 4. to have control or influence; rule. *v.t.* 1. to cause to sway (senses 1, 2, & 3). 2. to divert from a given course: as, his threats will not *sway* us. *n.* 1. a swaying or being swayed; a swinging, leaning, etc. 2. influence; force; control: as, the *sway* of passion. 3. rule; dominion. —**sway′a·ble,** *adj.* —**sway′er,** *n.* —**sway′ing·ly,** *adv.*

**sway-back, sway·back** (swā′bak′), *n.* the condition of being sway-backed. *adj.* sway-backed.

**sway-backed** (swā′bakt′), *adj.* having an abnormal inward curve in the spine, as from strain or overwork: said of horses, cattle, etc.: also **swayed.**

**swear** (swâr), *v.i.* [SWORE or *archaic* SWARE, SWORN, SWEARING], [AS. *swerian*], 1. to make a solemn declaration with an appeal to God or to someone or something held sacred for confirmation. 2. to make a solemn pledge or promise; vow. 3. to use profane language; curse. 4. in *law*, to give evidence under oath. *v.t.* 1. to declare solemnly in the name of God or of someone or something held sacred. 2. to pledge or vow on oath. 3. to assert with great emphasis: as, I *swear* the man's a fool. 4. to take (an oath) by swearing. 5. to administer a legal oath to. —**swear by,** 1. to name (a person or thing held sacred) in taking an oath. 2. to have great faith in. —**swear in,** to administer an oath to (a person taking office, a witness, etc.). —**swear off,** to promise to give up, renounce, etc. —**swear out,** to obtain (a warrant for arrest) by making a charge under oath. —**swear′er,** *n.*

**swear·word** (swâr′wûrd′), *n.* a word or phrase used in swearing or cursing; profane word.

**sweat** (swet), *v.i.* [SWEAT or SWEATED, SWEATING], [AS. *swætan* < *swat*, sweat], 1. to give forth a salty moisture through the pores of the skin; perspire. 2. *a*) to give forth moisture in droplets on its surface: as, a ripening cheese *sweats*. *b*) to condense water in droplets on its surface: as, a glass of iced tea *sweats*. 3. to ferment: said of tobacco leaves, etc. 4. to come forth in drops; ooze. 5. [Colloq.], to work so hard as to cause sweating. *v.t.* 1. *a*) to give forth (moisture) through a porous surface. *b*) to condense (moisture) on its surface. 2. to cause to perspire, as by drugs, exercise, etc. 3. to cause to give forth moisture; esp., to ferment. 4. to make wet with perspiration. 5. to try to get rid of by sweating: as, to *sweat* out a cold. 6. to heat (a metal) so as to extract an easily fusible constituent. 7. *a*) to heat (solder) until it melts. *b*) to unite (metal parts) by heating. 8. to cause to work so hard as to sweat. 9. to cause (employees) to work long hours at low wages under poor working conditions. 10. [Colloq.], to question or get information from by severe treatment. *n.* 1. the clear, salty liquid given forth in perspiration. 2. the moisture collected in droplets on the surface of something. 3. a sweating or being sweated. 4. a condition of eagerness, anxiety, etc. regarded as strong enough to cause sweating. 5. hard work; drudgery. —**sweat blood,** [Slang], 1. to work very hard; overwork. 2. to be impatient, anxious, etc. —**sweat (something) out,** [Slang], to wait anxiously or impatiently for (something).

**sweat·band** (swet′band′), *n.* a band of leather, etc. inside a hat to protect it against sweat.

**sweat·er** (swet′ẽr), *n.* 1. a person or thing that sweats. 2. a knitted or crocheted outer garment for the upper part of the body. 3. a sudorific. 4. an employer who sweats his employees.

**sweat gland,** any of the many, tiny tubular glands in the subcutaneous tissue that secrete sweat.

**sweat shirt,** a heavy, long-sleeved cotton jersey, worn to absorb sweat during or after exercise.

**sweat·shop** (swet′shop′), *n.* a shop or plant where employees are forced to work long hours at low wages under poor working conditions.

**sweat·y** (swet′i), *adj.* [-IER, -IEST], 1. sweating. 2. like sweat: as, a *sweaty* odor. 3. causing sweat. —**sweat′i·ly,** *adv.* —**sweat′i·ness,** *n.*

**Swed.,** 1. Sweden. 2. Swedish.

**Swede** (swēd), *n.* a native or inhabitant of Sweden.

**Swe·den** (swē′d'n), *n.* a country in N Europe, on the Scandinavian Peninsula: area, 173,143 sq. mi.; pop., 7,471,000; capital, Stockholm.

**Swe·den·borg, Emmanuel** (swē′d'n-bôrg′), 1688–1772; Swedish theologian and mystic. —**Swe′den·bor′gi·an** (-bôr′ji-ən), *n.* & *adj.* —**Swe′den·bor′gi·an·ism,** *n.*

**Swed·ish** (swē′dish), *adj.* of Sweden, its people, their language, etc. *n.* the North Germanic language of the Swedes. —**the Swedish,** the Swedish people.

**sweep** (swēp), *v.t.* [SWEPT, SWEEPING], [AS. *swapan*], 1. to clear or clean (a room, path, etc.) as by brushing with a broom. 2. to remove or clear away (dirt, debris, etc.) as with a broom or with a brushing movement. 3. to strip, carry away, or destroy with force of movement. 4. to carry along with a sweeping movement: as, he *swept* the cards into a pile. 5. to touch or brush in moving across: as, her dress *sweeps* the ground. 6. to pass swiftly over: as, his eyes *swept* the hills. 7. to drag (*v.t.*, 2). 8. to rake (*v.t.*, 5). 9. [Colloq.], to win overwhelmingly. *v.i.* 1. to clean a surface, room, etc. as with a broom. 2. to move or progress steadily with speed, force, or gracefulness: as, the planes *sweep* across the sky. 3. *a*) to trail one's skirts, etc. in moving. *b*) to trail, as skirts. 4. to extend in a long curve or line: as, the road *sweeps* up the hill. *n.* 1. the act of sweeping, as with a broom. 2. a steady sweeping movement or stroke: as, the *sweep* of a scythe. 3. a trailing, as of skirts. 4. range or scope. 5. a stretch; extent: as, a *sweep* of river. 6. a line, contour, curve, etc. that gives an impression of flow or movement. 7. one whose work is sweeping. 8. *usually pl.* sweepings. 9. complete victory or success. 10. a long oar. 11. a long pole mounted on a pivot, with a bucket at one end: used for raising water. 12. a sweepstakes. —**sweep′er,** *n.*

**sweep·ing** (swēp′iŋ), *adj.* 1. that sweeps. 2. extending over a wide range. 3. extensive; complete; comprehensive. *n.* 1. *pl.* things swept up, as dirt from a floor. 2. the act, work, etc. of one that sweeps. —**sweep′ing·ly,** *adv.* —**sweep′ing·ness,** *n.*

**sweep·stakes** (swēp′stāks′), *n.* [*pl.* -STAKES], 1. a lottery in which each participant puts up a stake of money in a common fund which is given to the winner or winners. 2. a contest, as a horse race, which determines the winner of such a lottery. 3. a prize won in such a lottery. Also **sweep′stake.**

**sweet** (swēt), *adj.* [AS. *swete*], 1. *a*) having a taste of, or like that of, sugar. *b*) containing sugar in some form: as, *sweet* wine. 2. *a*) having an agreeable taste, smell, sound, etc. *b*) gratifying: as, *sweet* praise. *c*) having a friendly, pleasing disposition. *d*) [Slang], good, delightful, etc. 3. not salty or salted. 4. not rancid or spoiled; fresh. 5. good for growing crops: said of soil. 6. in *jazz music*, characterized by rather strict adherence to melody, blandness, moderate tempo, etc. *n.* 1. a being sweet; sweetness. 2. something sweet; specif., *a*) a candy; sweetmeat. *b*) [Brit.], a sweet dessert. 3. a sweetheart; darling. *adv.* sweetly. —**be sweet on,** [Colloq.], to be in love with. —**sweet′ish,** *adj.* —**sweet′ish·ly,** *adv.* —**sweet′ish·ness,** *n.* —**sweet′ly,** *adv.* —**sweet′ness,** *n.*

**sweet alyssum,** a short plant with small spikes of tiny, fragrant, white flowers.

**sweet·bread** (swēt′bred′), *n.* the pancreas (*stomach sweetbread*) or the thymus (*neck*, or *throat, sweetbread*) of a calf, etc., when used as food.

**sweet·bri·er, sweet·bri·ar** (swēt′brī′ẽr), *n.* a rose with pink flowers and prickly stems; eglantine.

**sweet clover,** any of various plants of the pea family, with butterfly-shaped, white or yellow flowers, grown for fodder.

**sweet corn,** a variety of Indian corn, rich in sugar and eaten unripe as a table vegetable.
**sweet·en** (swē′t'n), *v.t.* 1. to make sweet with or as with sugar. 2. to make pleasant or agreeable. 3. to mollify; alleviate. —**sweet′en·er,** *n.*
**sweet·en·ing** (swē′t'n-iŋ, swēt′niŋ), *n.* 1. the act of making sweet. 2. something that sweetens.
**sweet flag,** a marsh plant with long, grasslike leaves and sweet, edible roots.
**sweet gum,** a tall tree with shining, maplelike leaves, spiny balls of fruit, and fragrant juice.
**sweet·heart** (swēt′härt′), *n.* a lover: sometimes used as a term of endearment.
**sweet·meat** (swēt′mēt′), *n.* any sweet food or delicacy, as a cake, preserve, etc.; specif., a candy.
**sweet pea,** a climbing plant with large, variously colored, fragrant flowers.
**sweet pepper,** 1. a kind of pepper plant producing a mild fruit. 2. its fruit.
**sweet potato,** 1. a tropical, trailing plant with purple flowers and a large, fleshy, orange or yellow root used as a vegetable. 2. its root.
**sweet-tem·pered** (swēt′tem′pẽrd), *adj.* having a gentle, amiable disposition; good-natured.
**sweet tooth,** [Colloq.], a craving for sweets.
**sweet William, sweet william,** a plant of the pink family, with dense clusters of small flowers.
**swell** (swel), *v.i.* [SWELLED, SWELLED or SWOLLEN, SWELLING], [AS. *swellan*], 1. to become larger as a result of pressure from within; expand. 2. to curve out; bulge; protrude. 3. to extend above the normal level. 4. to be filled (*with* pride, etc.). 5. to increase within one: as, his anger *swelled.* 6. to increase in size, force, intensity, etc. 7. to increase in loudness. *v.t.* to cause to swell; specif., *a*) to cause to increase in size, volume, etc. *b*) to cause to bulge. *c*) to fill with pride, etc. *d*) to cause to increase in loudness. *n.* 1. a part that swells; bulge; specif., *a*) a large wave that moves steadily without breaking. *b*) a piece of rising ground. 2. a swelling or being swollen. 3. an increase in size, amount, degree, etc. 4. [Colloq.], one who is strikingly stylish, especially in dress. 5. in *music, a*) a crescendo usually followed by a diminuendo. *b*) a sign (< >) indicating this. *c*) a device for controlling the loudness of tones in an organ, etc. *adj.* 1. [Colloq.], stylish; very fashionable. 2. [Slang], excellent.
**swelled head,** [Colloq.], undue self-esteem.
**swell·ing** (swel′iŋ), *n.* 1. an increasing or being increased in size, volume, etc. 2. something swollen; esp., an abnormally swollen part of the body. *adj.* that swells, or curves outward.
**swel·ter** (swel′tẽr), *v.i.* [< AS. *sweltan*, to die], to perspire very much from or feel oppressed with great heat. *v.t.* to cause to swelter. *n.* 1. a sweltering. 2. oppressive heat.
**swel·ter·ing** (swel′tẽr-iŋ), *adj.* 1. that swelters. 2. very hot; sultry. Also **swel′try** (-tri), [-TRIER, -TRIEST]. —**swel′ter·ing·ly,** *adv.*
**swept** (swept), pt. and pp. of **sweep.**
**swerve** (swũrv), *v.i. & v.t.* [SWERVED, SWERVING], [< AS. *sweorfan*, to scour], to turn aside or cause to turn aside from a straight line, course, etc. *n.* the act or degree of swerving. —**swerv′er,** *n.*
**swift** (swift), *adj.* [AS.], 1. moving or capable of moving with great speed; fast. 2. coming, happening, or done quickly. 3. acting or responding quickly. *adv.* in a swift manner. *n.* a brown, swift-flying bird resembling the swallow, as the chimney swift. —**swift′ly,** *adv.* —**swift′ness,** *n.*
**Swift, Jonathan** (swift), 1667–1745; English satirist, born in Ireland.
**swig** (swig), *v.t. & v.i.* [SWIGGED, SWIGGING], [< ?], [Colloq.], to drink in great gulps. *n.* [Colloq.], a deep draft, as of liquor. —**swig′ger,** *n.*
**swill** (swil), *v.t.* [AS. *swilian*], 1. to flood with water so as to wash. 2. to drink greedily. 3. to fill with drink. *v.i.* to drink in large quantities. *n.* 1. garbage, etc. mixed with liquid and fed to pigs, etc. 2. garbage. 3. the act of swilling. 4. a swig.
**swim** (swim), *v.i.* [SWAM or *archaic* or *dial.* SWUM, SWUM, SWIMMING], [AS. *swimman*], 1. to move through water by movements of arms, legs, fins, etc. 2. to move smoothly, as though swimming. 3. to float on the surface of a liquid. 4. to be immersed in a liquid. 5. to overflow: as, eyes *swimming* with tears. *v.t.* 1. to move in or across (a body of water) by swimming. 2. to cause to swim. *n.* 1. the act of swimming. 2. a period of swimming for sport: as, a *swim* before lunch. 3. a distance swum or to be swum. —**in the swim,** active in, or conforming to the ways of, current society, business affairs, etc. —**swim′mer,** *n.*
**swim** (swim), *n.* [AS. *swima*], the condition of being dizzy. *v.i.* [SWAM, SWUM, SWIMMING], 1. to be dizzy. 2. to have a hazy, reeling appearance.
**swimming hole,** a pool or a deep place in a river, creek, etc. used for swimming.
**swim·ming·ly** (swim′iŋ-li), *adv.* easily and with success: as, the play went over *swimmingly.*
**swimming pool,** a pool of water for swimming; esp., an artificially created pool, or tank.
**Swin·burne, Algernon Charles** (swin′bẽrn), 1837–1909; English poet and critic.
**swin·dle** (swin′d'l), *v.t.* [SWINDLED, SWINDLING], [< G. *schwindeln*, to cheat], 1. to get money or property from (another) under false pretenses; cheat. 2. to get by fraud. *v.i.* to engage in swindling others. *n.* an act of swindling. —**swin′dler,** *n.*
**swine** (swīn), *n.* [*pl.* SWINE], [AS. *swin*], 1. a pig or hog: usually used collectively. 2. a vicious, contemptible person.
**swine·herd** (swīn′hũrd′), *n.* one who tends swine.
**swing** (swiŋ), *v.i.* [SWUNG or *archaic* or *dial.* SWANG, SWUNG, SWINGING], [AS. *swingan*], 1. to sway backward and forward, as a freely hanging object. 2. to walk, trot, etc. with freely swaying movements. 3. to turn, as on a hinge or swivel. 4. to hang; specif., to be hanged in execution. 5. to move on a swing (*n.*, 10). 6. [Slang], to be ultra-fashionable, sophisticated, active, etc., esp. in the pursuit of pleasure. *v.t.* 1. *a*) to move (a weapon, bat, etc.) with a sweeping motion; flourish. *b*) to lift with a sweeping motion. 2. to cause (a freely hanging object) to move backward and forward. 3. to cause to turn or pivot, as on a hinge. 4. to cause to hang freely: as, to *swing* a scaffold from the roof. 5. to cause to come about successfully: as, to *swing* an election. 6. to play (music) in the style of swing. *n.* 1. a swinging. 2. the arc through which something swings. 3. the manner or style of swinging, as with a golf club, etc. 4. freedom to do as one wishes. 5. a relaxed motion, as in walking. 6. a sweeping blow or stroke. 7. the course or movement of some activity, etc. 8. the force behind something swung; impetus. 9. rhythm, as of poetry or music. 10. a seat hanging from ropes or chains, on which one can sit and swing. 11. a style of jazz music of the late 1930's, characterized by large bands, contrapuntal improvisation, etc. *adj.* of, in, or playing swing (music). —**in full swing,** in complete and active operation. —**swing′er,** *n.* —**swing′ing·ly,** *adv.*
**swinge** (swinj), *v.t.* [SWINGED, SWINGEING], [< AS. < *swingan*, to swing], [Archaic], to beat; whip.
**swinge·ing** (swin′jiŋ), *adj.* [Colloq.], 1. huge; very large. 2. extremely good; first-rate.
**swing·ing** (swiŋ′iŋ), *adj.* 1. that swings. 2. done with a swing. 3. [Slang], lively, sophisticated, ultra-fashionable, etc.
**swin·gle** (swiŋ′g'l), *v.t.* [-GLED, -GLING], [< MD. < *swinghel*, a swingle], to beat and clean (flax or hemp) with a swingle. *n.* a wooden swordlike tool for beating and cleaning flax or hemp.
**swin·gle·tree** (swiŋ′g'l-trē′), *n.* a singletree.
**swing shift,** [Colloq.], in factories, the evening work shift, from midafternoon to about midnight.
**swin·ish** (swīn′ish), *adj.* of, like, or fit for swine; beastly. —**swin′ish·ly,** *adv.* —**swin′ish·ness,** *n.*
**swipe** (swīp), *n.* [< ON. *svipr*, a stroke], [Colloq.], a hard, sweeping blow. *v.t.* [SWIPED, SWIPING], 1. [Colloq.], to hit with a hard, sweeping blow. 2. [Slang], to steal. *v.i.* [Colloq.], to make a sweeping blow or stroke. —**swip′er,** *n.*
**swirl** (swũrl), *v.i.* [prob. < ON. *svirla*, to whirl], 1. to move with a whirling motion. 2. to be dizzy, as the head. *v.t.* to cause to swirl. *n.* 1. a whirl; eddy. 2. a twist; curl; whirl. —**swirl′y,** *adj.*
**swish** (swish), *v.i.* [echoic], 1. to move with a sharp, hissing sound, as a cane swung through the air. 2. to rustle, as skirts. *v.t.* 1. to cause to swish. 2. to whip. *n.* 1. a hissing or rustling sound. 2. a movement that makes this sound.
**Swiss** (swis), *adj.* of Switzerland, its people, or culture. *n.* [*pl.* SWISS], a native or inhabitant of Switzerland. —**the Swiss,** the Swiss people.
**Swiss chard,** chard.
**Swiss cheese,** a pale-yellow hard cheese with many large holes, originally made in Switzerland.
**Swiss steak,** a thick cut of round or shoulder steak pounded with flour and braised.
**switch** (swich), *n.* [prob. < a LG. source], 1. a thin, flexible twig, stick, etc. used for whipping.

2. the bushy part of the tail of a cow, etc. 3. a tress of detached hair used by women as part of a coiffure. 4. a sharp, lashing movement, as with a whip. 5. a device used to open, close, or divert an electric circuit. 6. a movable section of railroad track used in transferring a train from one track to another. 7. a shift; change; turn. ***v.t.*** 1. to whip as with a switch. 2. to jerk or swing sharply. 3. to shift; change; turn aside. 4. *a*) to operate the switch of (an electric current). *b*) to turn (an electric light, etc.) *on* or *off* in this way. 5. to transfer (a train, etc.) from one track to another. 6. [Colloq.], to change or exchange: as, to *switch* places. ***v.i.*** 1. to move as from one track to another. 2. to shift; transfer. —**switch′er, *n.***

**switch·back** (swich′bak′), ***n.*** 1. a zigzag road up a steep grade. 2. [Brit.], a roller coaster.

**switch·board** (swich′bôrd′, -bōrd′), ***n.*** a panel equipped with apparatus for controlling the operation of a system of electric circuits, as in a telephone exchange.

**switch·man** (swich′mən), ***n.*** [*pl.* -MEN], a railroad employee who operates switches.

**switch·yard** (swich′yärd′), ***n.*** a railroad yard where cars are shifted from one track to another.

**Switz·er** (swit′sẽr), ***n.*** 1. a Swiss. 2. a Swiss mercenary soldier.

**Switz·er·land** (swit′sẽr-lənd), ***n.*** a country in W Europe, in the Alps: area, 15,940 sq. mi.; pop., 5,318,000; capital, Bern.

**swiv·el** (swiv′'l), ***n.*** [< base of AS. *swifan*, to revolve], 1. a fastening that allows free turning of the parts attached to it; specif., *a*) a chain link in two parts, one piece fitting like a collar below the bolthead of the other and turning freely about it. *b*) the platform support for a swivel chair or swivel gun. 2. a swivel gun. ***v.t.*** [-ELED or -ELLED, -ELING or -ELLING], 1. to cause to turn as on a swivel. 2. to fit or support with a swivel. ***v.i.*** to turn as on a swivel. —**swiv′el·like′, *adj.***

SWIVEL
C, chain; S, swivel; H, hook

**swivel chair,** a chair whose seat turns horizontally on a pivot in the base.

**swivel gun,** an artillery piece mounted on a platform in such a way that it can be turned horizontally or vertically for aiming.

**swob** (swob), ***n. & v.t.*** [SWOBBED, SWOBBING], swab.

**swol·len** (swō′lən), alt. pp. of **swell. *adj.*** blown up; distended; bulging.

**swoon** (swōōn), ***v.i.*** [< AS. *geswogen*, unconscious], to faint. ***n.*** a fainting fit. —**swoon′ing·ly, *adv.***

**swoop** (swōōp), ***v.t.*** [< AS. *swapan*, to sweep along], to snatch suddenly: often with *up*, etc. ***v.i.*** to pounce or sweep (*down* or *upon*), as a bird in hunting. ***n.*** the act of swooping. —**swoop′er, *n.***

**swop** (swop, swôp), ***n., v.t. & v.i.*** [SWOPPED, SWOPPING], swap. —**swop′per, *n.***

**sword** (sôrd, sōrd), ***n.*** [AS. *sweord*], 1. a hand weapon having a hilt and a long, sharp, pointed blade. 2. *a*) power; esp., military power. *b*) war. —**at swords' points,** ready to quarrel or fight. —**cross swords,** 1. to fight. 2. to argue. —**put to the sword,** 1. to kill with a sword. 2. to slaughter, especially in war. —**sword′like′, *adj.***

**sword·fish** (sôrd′fish′, sōrd′-), ***n.*** [*pl.* see FISH], a large marine food fish with the upper jawbone extending in a long, swordlike point.

SWORDFISH (7 ft. long)

**sword grass,** any of a number of sedges or grasses with toothed or sword-shaped leaves.

**sword knot,** a loop of leather, ribbon, etc. attached to a sword hilt as an ornament or, originally, for support around the wrist.

**sword·play** (sôrd′plā′, sōrd′-), ***n.*** the act or art of using a sword; fencing. —**sword′play′er, *n.***

**swords·man** (sôrdz′mən, sōrdz′-), ***n.*** [*pl.* -MEN], 1. one who uses a sword in fencing or fighting. 2. one skilled in using a sword. Also **sword′man** [*pl.* -MEN]. —**swords′man·ship′, *n.***

**swore** (swôr, swōr), alt. pt. of **swear.**

**sworn** (swôrn, swōrn), pp. of **swear. *adj.*** bound, pledged, promised, etc. by or as by an oath.

**swot** (swot), ***n. & v.t.*** [SWOTTED, SWOTTING], swat.

**'swounds** (zwoundz, zoundz), ***interj.*** [Archaic], God's wounds: a euphemistic contraction used as an oath: also **zounds.**

**swum** (swum), pp. and archaic or dial. pt. of **swim** (to move through water).

**swum** (swum), pp. of **swim** (to be dizzy).

**swung** (swuŋ), pp. and alt. pt. of **swing.**

**syb·a·rite** (sib′ə-rīt′), ***n.*** [< *Sybarite*, a native of Sybaris, an ancient Greek city in S Italy, famed for its luxury], anyone very fond of luxury and pleasure. —**syb′a·rit′ic** (-rit′ik), **syb′a·rit′i·cal, *adj.*** —**syb′a·rit′i·cal·ly, *adv.***

**syc·a·more** (sik′ə-môr′, -mōr′), ***n.*** [< OFr. < L. < Gr. *sykomoros*], 1. a shade tree of Egypt and Asia Minor, with figlike fruit. 2. a maple shade tree found in Europe and Asia. 3. any of various American plane trees; esp., the buttonwood.

**syc·o·phant** (sik′ə-fənt), ***n.*** [< L. < Gr. *sykophantēs*, informer < *sykon*, a fig + *phainein*, to show], one who seeks favor by flattering people of wealth or influence; toady. —**syc′o·phan·cy** [pl. -CIES], ***n.*** —**syc′o·phan′tic** (-fan′tik), **syc′o·phan′ti·cal, *adj.*** —**syc′o·phan′ti·cal·ly, *adv.***

**Syd·ney** (sid′ni), ***n.*** a seaport in SE Australia: pop., 2,055,000.

**syl-,** see **syn-.**

**syl·la·bar·y** (sil′ə-ber′i), ***n.*** [*pl.* -IES], 1. a table of syllables. 2. a system of written characters representing spoken syllables.

**syl·lab·ic** (si-lab′ik), ***adj.*** 1. of a syllable or syllables. 2. designating a consonant that in itself forms a syllable, as the *l* in *tattle*. 3. pronounced distinctly, syllable by syllable. ***n.*** a syllabic sound. —**syl·lab′i·cal·ly, *adv.***

**syl·lab·i·cate** (si-lab′i-kāt′), ***v.t.*** [-CATED, -CATING], to syllabify. —**syl·lab′i·ca′tion, *n.***

**syl·lab·i·fy** (si-lab′ə-fī′), ***v.t.*** [-FIED, -FYING], [< ML. < L. *syllaba*, syllable + *facere*, to make], to form or divide into syllables. —**syl·lab′i·fi·ca′tion, *n.***

**syl·la·ble** (sil′ə-b'l), ***n.*** [< OFr. < L. < Gr. *syllabē* < *syn-*, together + *lambanein*, to hold], 1. a word (e.g., *sun*) or part of a word (e.g., *per·me·ate*) pronounced with a single, uninterrupted sounding of the voice. 2. one or more letters written to represent, more or less, a spoken syllable. 3. the least bit of expression: as, don't mention a *syllable* of this. ***v.t. & v.i.*** [-BLED, -BLING], to pronounce in or as in syllables.

**syl·la·bus** (sil′ə-bəs), ***n.*** [*pl.* -BUSES, -BI (-bī′)], [< a misprint of pl. of L. *sittyba*, a list < Gr. *syttyba*, parchment label], a summary or outline, especially of a course of study.

**syl·lo·gism** (sil′ə-jiz'm), ***n.*** [< OFr. < L. < Gr. *syn-*, together + *logizesthai*, to reason], 1. a form of reasoning in which two statements or premises are made and a logical conclusion drawn from them. Example: All mammals are warm-blooded (*major premise*); whales are mammals (*minor premise*); therefore, whales are warm-blooded (*conclusion*). 2. reasoning from the general to the particular. —**syl′lo·gis′tic, syl′lo·gis′ti·cal, *adj.*** —**syl′lo·gis′ti·cal·ly, *adv.***

**sylph** (silf), ***n.*** [? < L. *sylvestris*, of a forest + *nympha*, nymph], 1. any of a class of imaginary beings supposed to inhabit the air. 2. a slender, graceful woman or girl. —**sylph′like′, *adj.***

**syl·van** (sil′vən), ***adj.*** [< Fr. *sylvain* or L. *silva*, a wood], 1. of or characteristic of the woods or forest. 2. living, found, or carried on in the woods or forest. 3. wooded. ***n.*** one who lives in the woods. Also sp. **silvan.**

**sym-,** see **syn-.**

**sym.,** 1. symbol. 2. symphony.

**sym·bi·o·sis** (sim′bi-ō′sis, -bī-), ***n.*** [< Gr. *syn-*, together + *bioun*, to live], in *biology*, the living together of two dissimilar organisms in a close association that is advantageous to both: cf. *parasitism*. —**sym′bi·ot′ic** (-ot′ik), **sym′bi·ot′i·cal, *adj.*** —**sym′bi·ot′i·cal·ly, *adv.***

**sym·bol** (sim′b'l), ***n.*** [< Fr. < L. < Gr. *symbolon*, token; ult. < *syn-*, together + *ballein*, to throw], 1. an object used to represent something abstract; emblem: as, the dove is a *symbol* of peace. 2. a mark, letter, abbreviation, etc. standing for an object, quality, process, quantity, etc., as in music, chemistry, mathematics, etc. ***v.t.*** to symbolize.

**sym·bol·ic** (sim-bol′ik), ***adj.*** 1. of or expressed in a symbol; using symbols. 2. that serves as a symbol (*of* something). Also **sym·bol′i·cal.** —**sym·bol′i·cal·ly, *adv.***

**sym·bol·ism** (sim′b'l-iz'm), ***n.*** 1. the representation of things by use of symbols, especially in fine art or literature. 2. a system of symbols. 3. symbolic meaning.

**sym·bol·ist** (sim′b'l-ist), ***n.*** 1. one who uses symbols. 2. one who practices symbolism in representing ideas, etc., especially in art or literature.

**sym·bol·is·tic** (sim′b'l-is′tik), ***adj.*** of symbolism or symbolists. —**sym′bol·is′ti·cal·ly, *adv.***

**sym·bol·ize** (sim′b'l-īz′), ***v.t.*** [-IZED, -IZING], 1. to be a symbol of; typify; stand for. 2. to represent

by a symbol or symbols. 3. to make into a symbol; treat as a symbol. *v.i.* to use symbols. —**sym'bol·i·za'tion,** *n.* —**sym'bol·iz'er,** *n.*
**sym·me·try** (sim'ə-tri), *n.* [*pl.* -TRIES], [< Fr. or L. < Gr. *syn-*, together + *metron*, a measure], 1. similarity of form or arrangement on either side of a dividing line or plane; correspondence of opposite parts in size, shape, and position. 2. excellence of form or balance as a result of such correspondence. —**sym·met·ri·cal** (si-met'ri-k'l), **sym·met'ric,** *adj.* —**sym·met'ri·cal·ly,** *adv.*
**sym·pa·thet·ic** (sim'pə-thet'ik), *adj.* 1. of, resulting from, feeling, or showing sympathy; sympathizing. 2. in agreement with one's tastes, mood, etc.; congenial. 3. [Colloq.], showing favor, approval, etc.: as, he is *sympathetic* to our plan. 4. in *physiology*, *a*) designating or of that part of the autonomic nervous system which acts upon smooth muscles, heart muscle, and glands. *b*) designating pain, etc. in one part of the body that is induced by a similar effect in another part. 5. in *physics*, caused by vibrations transmitted from a near-by vibrating body. —**sym'pa·thet'i·cal·ly,** *adv.*
**sym·pa·thize** (sim'pə-thīz'), *v.i.* [-THIZED, -THIZING], 1. to share or understand the feelings or ideas of another; be in sympathy. 2. to feel or express sympathy, as in pity or compassion; commiserate (*with*). 3. to be in harmony or accord. —**sym'pa·thiz'er,** *n.* —**sym'pa·thiz'ing·ly,** *adv.*
**sym·pa·thy** (sim'pə-thi), *n.* [*pl.* -THIES], [< L. < Gr. < *syn-*, together + *pathos*, feeling], 1. sameness of feeling; affinity between persons. 2. agreement in qualities; harmony; accord. 3. a mutual liking or understanding arising from sameness of feeling. 4. the sharing or ability to share another person's mental state, emotions, etc.; esp., compassion for another's trouble, suffering, etc.
**sympathy** (or **sympathetic**) **strike,** a strike by a group of workers in support of another group of workers who are on strike.
**sym·pho·ny** (sim'fə-ni), *n.* [*pl.* -NIES], [< OFr. < L. < Gr. < *syn-*, together + *phōnē*, sound], 1. harmony of sounds especially of instruments. 2. any harmony, as of color. 3. in *music*, *a*) an extended composition for full orchestra, having several (usually four) movements related in subject, but varying in form and execution. *b*) a large orchestra for playing symphonic works, composed of string, wind, and percussion sections: also **symphony orchestra.** *c*) [Colloq.], a symphony concert. —**symphon·ic** (sim-fon'ik), *adj.* —**sym·phon'i·cal·ly,** *adv.*
**sym·po·si·um** (sim-pō'zi-əm), *n.* [*pl.* -UMS, -A (-ə)], [L. < Gr. < *syn-*, together + *posis*, a drinking], 1. any meeting or social gathering at which ideas are freely exchanged. 2. a conference organized for the discussion of some particular subject. 3. a collection of opinions or essays on a given subject. —**sym·po'si·ac'** (-ak'), *adj.*
**symp·tom** (simp'təm), *n.* [< Gr. *symptōma* < *syn-*, together + *piptein*, to fall], any circumstance, event, or condition that accompanies something and indicates its existence or occurrence; sign; specif., in *medicine*, any condition accompanying a disease and serving as an aid in its diagnosis. —**symp'to·mat'ic** (-tə-mat'ik), **symp'to·mat'i·cal,** *adj.* —**symp'to·mat'i·cal·ly,** *adv.*
**syn-,** [< Gr. *syn*, with], a prefix meaning *with, together with, at the same time, by means of*: *syn-* assimilates to *syl-* before *l*; *sym-* before *m, p, b*; *sys-* before *s* and an aspirate *h*.
**syn.,** 1. synonym. 2. synonymous. 3. synonymy.
**syn·a·gogue** (sin'ə-gôg', -gog'), *n.* [< OFr. < LL. < Gr. *synagōgē*, an assembly < *syn-*, together + *agein*, to bring], 1. an assembly of Jews for worship and religious study. 2. a building or place used for such an assembly. 3. the Jewish religion as organized in such local congregations. —**syn'a·gog'i·cal** (-goj'i-k'l), *adj.*
**syn·apse** (si-naps'), *n.* [< Gr. *synapsis*, a union], the point of contact between adjacent neurons, where nerve impulses are transmitted from one to the other. —**syn·ap'tic** (-nap'tik), *adj.*
**syn·carp** (sin'kärp), *n.* [see SYN- & -CARP], a fruit composed of the ripened pistils of one or more flowers, as a blackberry. —**syn·car'pous,** *adj.*
**syn·chro·mesh** (siŋ'krə-mesh'), *adj.* [*synchro*nized + *mesh*], designating or employing a device by which gears to be meshed are automatically brought to the same speed of rotation before the shift is completed. *n.* a synchromesh gear system.
**syn·chro·nism** (siŋ'krə-niz'm), *n.* 1. the fact or state of being synchronous; simultaneous occurrence. 2. a chronological listing of persons or events in history. —**syn'chro·nis'tic,** *adj.*
**syn·chro·nize** (siŋ'krə-nīz'), *v.i.* [-NIZED, -NIZING], [< Gr. < *synchronos*, contemporary < *syn-*, together + *chronos*, time], to move or occur at the same time or rate; be synchronous. *v.t.* 1. to cause to agree in time or rate of speed; regulate so as to make synchronous. 2. to assign (events, etc.) to the same time or date. —**syn'chro·ni·za'tion,** *n.* —**syn'chro·niz'er,** *n.*
**syn·chro·nous** (siŋ'krə-nəs), *adj.* [see SYNCHRONIZE], 1. happening at the same time; simultaneous. 2. having the same period between movements, occurrences, etc.; having the same rate and phase, as vibrations. Also **syn'chro·nal.** —**syn'chro·nous·ly,** *adv.* —**syn'chro·nous·ness,** *n.*
**syn·cline** (siŋ'klīn), *n.* [< Gr. *syn-*, together + *klinein*, to incline], in *geology*, a fold of stratified rock inclining upward in opposite directions from both sides of its axis: opposed to *anticline*. —**syn·cli'nal** (sin-klī'n'l, siŋ'kli-), *adj.*
**syn·co·pate** (siŋ'kə-pāt'), *v.t.* [-PATED, -PATING], [< LL. pp. of *syncopare*, to swoon < *syncope*; see SYNCOPE], 1. to shorten (a word) by syncope. 2. in *music*, *a*) to begin (a tone) on an unaccented beat and continue it through the next accented beat, or to begin (a tone) on the last half of a beat and continue it through the first half of the following beat. *b*) to use such shifted accents in (a composition, etc.). —**syn'co·pa'tor,** *n.*
**syn·co·pa·tion** (siŋ'kə-pā'shən), *n.* 1. a syncopating or being syncopated. 2. syncopated music. 3. in *grammar*, syncope.

SYNCOPATION

**syn·co·pe** (siŋ'kə-pi, sin'kə-pē'), *n.* [LL. < Gr. *syn-*, together + *koptein*, to cut], 1. the dropping of sounds or letters from the middle of a word, as in *Wooster* for *Worcester*. 2. a fainting caused by an inadequate flow of blood to the brain.
**syn·cre·tize** (siŋ'krə-tīz'), *v.t.* [-TIZED, -TIZING], [< Gr. *synkrētizein*], to combine or reconcile. —**syn'cre·tism,** *n.*
**syn·dic** (sin'dik), *n.* [Fr. < LL. < Gr. *syndikos*, advocate < *syn-*, together + *dikē*, justice], 1. the business manager of a corporation, as a university. 2. a civil magistrate. —**syn'di·cal,** *adj.*
**syn·di·cal·ism** (sin'di-k'l-iz'm), *n.* a theory of trade unionism, originating in France, in which all means of production and distribution would be brought under the control of federations of labor unions by the use of general strikes, etc. —**syn'di·cal·ist,** *n.* & *adj.* —**syn'di·cal·is'tic,** *adj.*
**syn·di·cate** (sin'di-kit; *for v.*, -kāt'), *n.* [< Fr. < ML. < *syndicus*; see SYNDIC], 1. a council of syndics. 2. an association of bankers, corporations, etc. formed to carry out some financial project requiring much capital. 3. an organization that sells articles or features to a number of newspapers for simultaneous publication. *v.t.* [-CATED, -CATING], 1. to manage as or form into a syndicate. 2. to sell (an article, etc.) through a syndicate for publication in many newspapers. *v.i.* to form a syndicate. —**syn'di·ca'tion,** *n.* —**syn'di·ca'tor,** *n.*
**syn·drome** (sin'drōm), *n.* [< Gr. < *syn-*, with + *dramein*, to run], a set of symptoms characterizing a specific disease or condition.
**syne** (sīn), *adv.*, *conj.*, *prep.* [Scot.], since; ago.
**syn·ec·do·che** (si-nek'də-ki), *n.* [L. < Gr. *syn-*, together + *ekdechesthai*, to receive], a figure of speech in which a part or individual is used for a whole or class, or the reverse of this. Example: *bread* for *food*, or *the army* for *a soldier*.
**syn·er·gism** (sin'ẽr-jiz'm), *n.* [< Gr. < *syn-*, together + *ergon*, work], the combined action, as of certain drugs, which is greater in total effect than the sum of their individual effects.
**Synge, John Mil·ling·ton** (mil'iŋ-tən siŋ), 1871–1909; Irish dramatist and poet.
**syn·od** (sin'əd), *n.* [< AS. < L. < Gr. *synodos*, lit., a meeting < *syn-*, together + *hodos*, way], 1. a council of churches or church officials. 2. any assembly or council. —**syn'od·al,** *adj.*
**syn·od·i·cal** (si-nod'i-k'l), *adj.* 1. of a synod. 2. in *astronomy*, of or having to do with conjunction, especially with the interval between two successive conjunctions of the same bodies, as of a planet with the sun. Also **syn·od'ic.** —**syn·od'i·cal·ly,** *adv.*
**syn·o·nym** (sin'ə-nim), *n.* [< Fr. < LL. < Gr. < *syn-*, together + *onyma*, name], 1. a word having

the same or nearly the same meaning as another in the same language. 2. a word used in metonymy. —**syn'o·nym'ic, syn'o·nym'i·cal,** *adj.*

**syn·on·y·mous** (si-non'ə-məs), *adj.* [see SYNONYM], of the same or nearly the same meaning. —**syn-on'y·mous·ly,** *adv.*

**syn·on·y·my** (si-non'ə-mi), *n.* [*pl.* -MIES], 1. the study of synonyms. 2. a list or listing of synonyms. 3. the quality of being synonymous.

**syn·op·sis** (si-nop'sis), *n.* [*pl.* -SES (-sēz)], [LL. < Gr. < *syn-*, together + *opsis*, a sight], a statement giving a brief, general review or condensation; summary, as of a story.

**syn·op·tic** (si-nop'tik), *adj.* 1. of or giving a synopsis. 2. giving an account from the same point of view: said especially [S-] of the first three Gospels. Also **syn·op'ti·cal.** —**syn·op'ti·cal·ly,** *adv.*

**syn·o·vi·a** (si-nō'vi-ə), *n.* [prob. *syn-* + L. *ovum*, egg], the clear, albuminous lubricating fluid secreted by the membranes of joint cavities, tendon sheaths, etc. —**syn·o'vi·al,** *adj.*

**syn·tac·ti·cal** (sin-tak'ti-k'l), *adj.* of, or in accordance with, the rules of syntax: also **syn·tac'tic.** —**syn·tac'ti·cal·ly,** *adv.*

**syn·tax** (sin'taks), *n.* [< Fr. < LL. < Gr. < *syn-*, together + *tassein*, to arrange], 1. the arrangement of words as elements in a sentence to show their relationship; sentence structure. 2. the branch of grammar dealing with this.

**syn·the·sis** (sin'thə-sis), *n.* [*pl.* -SES (-sēz')], [L. < Gr. < *syn-*, together + *tithenai*, to place], 1. the putting together of parts or elements so as to form a whole: cf. *analysis*. 2. a whole formed in this way. 3. the formation of a complex chemical compound by the combining of two or more simpler compounds, elements, etc. —**syn'the·sist,** *n.*

**syn·the·size** (sin'thə-sīz'), *v.t.* [-SIZED, -SIZING], 1. to bring together into a whole by synthesis. 2. to form by bringing together separate parts. 3. to treat in a synthetic manner.

**syn·the·siz·er** (sin'thə-sī'zẽr), *n.* one that synthesizes; specif., an electronic device used to produce sounds unobtainable from ordinary musical instruments.

**syn·thet·ic** (sin-thet'ik), *adj.* 1. of, involving, or using synthesis. 2. produced by synthesis; specif., produced by chemical synthesis, rather than of natural origin. 3. artificial; not real or genuine. Also **syn·thet'i·cal.** *n.* something synthetic. —**syn-thet'i·cal·ly,** *adv.*

**syph·i·lis** (sif'ə-lis), *n.* [< *Syphilus*, hero of a Latin poem (1530)], an infectious venereal disease, caused by a spirochete and usually transmitted by sexual intercourse or acquired congenitally. —**syph'i·lit'ic** (-lit'ik), *adj. & n.*

**sy·phon** (sī'fən), *n., v.i. & v.t.* siphon.

**Syr.,** 1. Syria. 2. Syriac. 3. Syrian.

**Syr·a·cuse** (sêr'ə-kūs', -kūz'), *n.* a city in central New York: pop., 216,000.

**Syr·i·a** (sêr'i-ə), *n.* 1. an ancient country in Asia, along the E coast of the Mediterranean. 2. a country in W Asia, south of Turkey: area, 72,200 sq. mi.; pop., 5,866,000; capital, Damascus.

**Syr·i·ac** (sêr'i-ak'), *adj.* of Syria or its language. *n.* the ancient Aramaic language of Syria.

**Syr·i·an** (sêr'i-ən), *adj.* of Syria, its people, their language, etc. *n.* 1. a member of the Semitic people of Syria. 2. their modern Arabic dialect.

**sy·rin·ga** (sə-riŋ'gə), *n.* [< Gr. *syrinx*, a pipe: from former use as pipestems], 1. any of the lilacs. 2. any of various ornamental shrubs of the saxifrage family, with white flowers; mock orange.

**syr·inge** (sə-rinj', sir'inj), *n.* [< ML. < Gr. < *syrinx*, a tube], a device consisting of a narrow tube fitted at one end with a rubber bulb or piston by means of which a liquid can be drawn in and then ejected in a stream: used to inject fluids into the body, cleanse wounds, etc. *v.t.* [-INGED, -INGING], to cleanse or inject with a syringe.

**syr·inx** (sir'iŋks), *n.* [*pl.* SYRINGES (sə-rin'jēz), -INXES], [Gr., a pipe], 1. the vocal organ of songbirds, located at or near the base of the trachea. 2. a Panpipe. 3. the Eustachian tube.

**syr·up** (sir'əp, sûr'-), *n.* sirup. —**syr'up·like',** *adj.* —**syr'up·y** [-IER, -IEST], *adj.*

**sys·tem** (sis'təm), *n.* [< LL. < Gr. *systēma* < *syn-*, together + *histanai*, to set], 1. a set or arrangement of things so related as to form an organic whole: as, a solar *system*, supply *system*. 2. the world or universe. 3. the body considered as a functioning organism. 4. a set of facts, rules, etc. arranged in an orderly form so as to show a logical plan. 5. a method or plan of classification. 6. a regular, orderly way of doing something; order; method. 7. a number of organs acting together to perform one of the main bodily functions: as, the nervous *system*. 8. an arrangement of rocks formed during a given geological period: as, the Cambrian *system*. —**sys'tem·less,** *adj.*

**sys·tem·at·ic** (sis'tə-mat'ik), *adj.* 1. constituting or based on a system. 2. according to a system, method, or plan; regular; orderly. 3. orderly in method or planning; methodical. 4. of or having to do with classification. Also **sys'tem·at'i·cal.** —**sys'tem·at'i·cal·ly,** *adv.*

**sys·tem·a·tize** (sis'təm-ə-tīz'), *v.t.* [-TIZED, -TIZING], to make into a system; arrange according to a system; make systematic. —**sys'tem·a·ti·za'tion,** *n.* —**sys'tem·a·tiz'er,** *n.*

**sys·tem·ic** (sis-tem'ik), *adj.* of a system; specif., in *physiology*, of or affecting the body as a whole. —**sys·tem'i·cal·ly,** *adv.*

**sys·tem·ize** (sis'təm-iz'), *v.t.* [-IZED, -IZING], to systematize. —**sys'tem·i·za'tion,** *n.* —**sys'tem-iz'er,** *n.*

**sys·to·le** (sis'tə-lē'), *n.* [< Gr. *systolē*; ult. < *syn-*, together + *stellein*, to draw], 1. the usual rhythmic contraction of the heart, especially of the ventricles, during which the blood is driven onward from the chambers. 2. in *Gr. & Latin prosody*, the shortening of a naturally long syllable. Cf. **diastole.** —**sys·tol·ic** (sis-tol'ik), *adj.*

# T

**T, t** (tē), *n.* [*pl.* T's, t's, Ts, ts], 1. the twentieth letter of the English alphabet. 2. the sound of T or t. *adj.* twentieth in a sequence or group.

**T** (tē), *n.* an object shaped like T. *adj.* shaped like T. —**to a T,** to perfection; exactly.

**'t, it**: a contraction, as in *'twas, do't.*

**-t,** a suffix for forming past participles and adjectives derived from them, as *slept*: variant of *-ed.*

**T.,** 1. tablespoon(s). 2. Testament. 3. Tuesday.

**T., t.,** 1. tenor. 2. territory. 3. ton(s).

**t.,** 1. teaspoon(s). 2. temperature. 3. tense. 4. time. 5. town(ship). 6. transitive. 7. troy.

**Ta,** in *chemistry*, tantalum.

**tab** (tab), *n.* [< Eng. dial.], 1. a small, flat loop or strap fastened to something for pulling it, hanging it up, etc. 2. an attached or projecting piece of a card or paper, useful in filing. 3. [Colloq.], a record; reckoning. *v.t.* [TABBED, TABBING], to put a tab or tabs on. —**keep tab (or tabs) on,** [Colloq.], to keep a check on.

**tab·ard** (tab'ẽrd), *n.* [< OFr. *tabart* < L. *tapete*, tapestry], 1. originally, a loose jacket worn out of doors. 2. a short-sleeved, blazoned cloak worn by knights over their armor. 3. a herald's official coat, blazoned with his lord's arms.

**Ta·bas·co** (tə-bas'kō), *n.* [< *Tabasco*, a Mexican State], a very hot sauce made from a kind of pepper: a trade-mark.

**tab·by** (tab'i), *n.* [*pl.* -BIES], [< Fr. < ML. < Ar. *'Attābi*, quarter of Bagdad where it was made], 1. a silk taffeta with wavy markings. 2. a gray or brown cat with dark stripes. 3. any domestic cat, especially a female. 4. a female gossip. *adj.* having dark stripes over gray or brown; brindled.

**tab·er·nac·le** (tab'ẽr-nak''l), *n.* [OFr. < L. *tabernaculum*, a tent, dim. of *taberna*, a hut], 1. a temporary shelter, as a tent. 2. the human body regarded as the dwelling place of the soul. 3. [T-], *a*) the portable sanctuary carried by the Jews in their wanderings from Egypt to Palestine. *b*) later, the Jewish Temple. 4. a shrine, niche, etc. with a canopy. 5. a place of worship with a large seating capacity. 6. an ornamental container for the consecrated Host. *v.i.* [-LED, -LING], to dwell temporarily. *v.t.* to place in a tabernacle. —**tab′er·nac′u·lar** (-nak′yoo-lẽr), *adj.*

**ta·ble** (tā′b'l), *n.* [OFr. < L. *tabula*, a board, tablet], 1. a thin slab of metal, stone, or wood, used for inscriptions; tablet. 2. a piece of furniture consisting of a flat top set horizontally on legs. 3. such a table set with food for a meal. 4. food served at table. 5. the people seated at a table. 6. a compact, systematic list of details, contents, etc. 7. a compact, orderly arrangement of facts, figures, etc., usually in rows and columns: as, the multiplication *table*. 8. a tableland. 9. any flat, horizontal surface, piece, or layer. *v.t.* [-BLED, -BLING], 1. [Rare], to tabulate. 2. to put on a table. 3. to postpone indefinitely the consideration of, as a legislative bill. —**on the table,** postponed: said of a bill, etc. referred to the table of the presiding officer. —**the tables,** laws, as the Ten Commandments, inscribed on flat stone slabs. —**turn the tables,** to reverse a situation completely.

**tab·leau** (tab′lō), *n.* [*pl.* -LEAUX (-lōz), -LEAUS], [Fr., dim. of *table*], 1. a graphic scene; picture. 2. a representation of a scene, picture, etc. by a person or group posed in appropriate costume.

**ta·ble·cloth** (tā′b'l-klôth′), *n.* a cloth for covering a table, especially at meals.

**ta·ble d'hôte** (tä′b'l dōt′), [Fr., lit., table of the host], 1. a common table for guests at a hotel. 2. a complete meal served at a hotel or restaurant for a set price: cf. **à la carte.**

**ta·ble·land** (tā′b'l-land′), *n.* a high, broad, generally level region; plateau.

**table linen,** tablecloths, napkins, etc.

**ta·ble·spoon** (tā′b'l-spōōn′), *n.* 1. a large spoon used for eating soup, for serving, and as a measuring unit in cookery. 2. a tablespoonful.

**ta·ble·spoon·ful** (tā′b'l-spōōn′fool), *n.* [*pl.* -FULS], as much as a tablespoon will hold; 3 teaspoonfuls or ½ fluid ounce.

**tab·let** (tab′lit), *n.* [< OFr. dim. of *table*], 1. a flat, thin piece of stone, metal, etc. with an inscription, used as a memorial wall panel. 2. a smooth, flat leaf of wood, metal, etc., used to write on. 3. a writing pad containing sheets of paper fastened at one edge. 4. a small, flat piece of compressed material, as medicine, soap, etc.

**table tennis,** ping-pong.

**ta·ble·ware** (tā′b'l-wâr′), *n.* dishes, knives, forks, spoons, etc., used at the table for meals.

**tab·loid** (tab′loid), *n.* [< *tablet* + *-oid*], 1. a small, compressed tablet of medicine: a trade-mark (**Tabloid**). 2. a newspaper, usually half the ordinary size, with many pictures and short news stories. *adj.* condensed; short.

**ta·boo** (tə-bōō′, ta-), *n.* [*pl.* -BOOS], [Tongan *tabu*], 1. among primitive tribes, a sacred prohibition which makes certain people or things untouchable, unmentionable, etc. 2. the system of such prohibitions. 3. any social restriction resulting from convention or tradition. *adj.* 1. sacred and prohibited by taboo. 2. restricted by taboo: said of people. 3. prohibited by tradition, etc. *v.t.* [-BOOED, -BOOING], 1. to put under taboo. 2. to prohibit; forbid. Also sp. **tabu.**

**ta·bor, ta·bour** (tā′bẽr), *n.* [< OFr. < Per. *tabīrah*], a small drum, formerly played to accompany a fife or pipe. *v.i.* to drum on or as on a tabor.

**tab·o·ret, tab·ou·ret** (tab′ə-rit, tab′ə-ret′), *n.* [OFr., a stool, dim. of *tabour*, a drum], 1. a small tabor. 2. a stool. 3. a low ornamental stand. 4. an embroidery frame.

**Ta·briz** (tä-brēz′), *n.* a city in NW Iran: pop., 388,000.

**ta·bu** (tə-bōō′, ta-), *n.* [*pl.* -BUS], *adj.*, *v.t.* [-BUED, -BUING], taboo.

**tab·u·lar** (tab′yoo-lẽr), *adj.* [< L. < *tabula*, a table], 1. having a tablelike surface; flat: as, *tabular* rock. 2. *a*) of or arranged in a table or tabulated scheme. *b*) computed from or calculated by such a table or tables. —**tab′u·lar·ly,** *adv.*

**tab·u·late** (tab′yoo-lāt′; *for adj.*, -lit), *v.t.* [-LATED, -LATING], [< L. *tabula*, a table; + *-ate*], 1. to put (facts, statistics, etc.) in a table or tables; list systematically. 2. to give a flat, tablelike surface to. *adj.* having a flat surface. —**tab′u·la′tion,** *n.* —**tab′u·la′tor,** *n.*

**tac·a·ma·hac** (tak′ə-mə-hak′), *n.* [< Sp. < Nahuatl *tecomahca*], 1. a strong-smelling gum resin used in ointments and incenses. 2. any of several trees yielding this resin.

**ta·chom·e·ter** (tə-kom′ə-tẽr), *n.* [< Gr. *tachos*, speed; + *-meter*], a device that measures the revolutions per minute of a revolving shaft. —**ta·chom′e·try,** *n.*

**tac·it** (tas′it), *adj.* [< Fr. < L. pp. of *tacere*, to be silent], 1. making no sound; saying nothing. 2. unspoken; silent. 3. not expressed openly, but implied. —**tac′it·ly,** *adv.* —**tac′it·ness,** *n.*

**tac·i·turn** (tas′ə-tũrn′), *adj.* [< Fr. < L. *tacere;* see TACIT], almost always silent; not liking to talk. —**tac′i·tur′ni·ty,** *n.* —**tac′i·turn′ly,** *adv.*

**Tac·i·tus** (tas′i-təs), *n.* Roman historian; 55?–117? A.D.

**tack** (tak), *n.* [< ONorm.Fr. < OFr. *tache*, a nail < Gmc.], 1. a short nail or pin with a sharp point and, usually, a large, flat head. 2. a long stitch used as for basting. 3. a zigzag course, or movement in such a course. 4. a course of action or policy: as, he's on the wrong *tack*. 5. in *nautical usage*, *a*) a rope for holding securely the forward lower corner of some sails. *b*) the corner thus held. *c*) the direction a ship goes in relation to the position of the sails. *d*) a change of direction made by changing the position of the sails. *e*) a course against the wind. *v.t.* 1. to fasten with tacks. 2. to attach temporarily, as by basting. 3. to attach as a supplement; add: as, *tack* an amendment to the bill. 4. in *nautical usage*, *a*) to change the course of (a ship) by turning her with her head to the wind. *b*) to maneuver (a ship) against the wind by a series of tacks. *v.i.* 1. to go in a zigzag course. 2. to change suddenly one's course of action. 3. in *nautical usage*, *a*) to tack a ship. *b*) to change her course by being tacked: said of a ship. —**on the right** (or **wrong**) **tack,** in the right (or wrong) course. —**tack′er,** *n.*

**tack·le** (tak′'l), *n.* [prob. < LG.], 1. apparatus; equipment: as, fishing *tackle*. 2. a system of ropes and pulleys, used to lower, raise, or move weights. 3. the act of tackling, as in football. 4. in *football*, the player between the guard and the end on either side of the line. 5. the running rigging and pulleys used to operate a ship's sails. *v.t.* [-LED, -LING], 1. to fasten by means of tackle. 2. to harness (a horse). 3. to take hold of; seize. 4. to try to do or solve; undertake: as, he *tackled* the job. 5. in *football*, to stop or throw (an opponent carrying the ball). *v.i.* in *football*, to tackle an opponent. —**tack′ler,** *n.*

**tack·y** (tak′i), *adj.* [-IER, -IEST], [*tack*, in sense of "slight fastening" + *-y*], sticky, as varnish, glue, etc. before completely dry. —**tack′i·ness,** *n.*

**tack·y** (tak′i), *adj.* [-IER, -IEST], [prob. < *tacky* (sticky)], [Colloq.], dowdy; shabby.

**ta·co** (tä′kō), *n.* [Am. Sp. < Sp., light lunch], a Mexican dish consisting of a fried, folded tortilla filled with chopped meat, lettuce, etc.

**Ta·co·ma** (tə-kō′mə), *n.* a seaport in W Washington, on Puget Sound: pop., 148,000.

**tact** (takt), *n.* [Fr. < L. *tactus*, pp. of *tangere*, to touch], delicate perception of the right thing to say or do without offending.

**tact·ful** (takt′fəl), *adj.* having or showing tact. —**tact′ful·ly,** *adv.* —**tact′ful·ness,** *n.*

**tac·ti·cal** (tak′ti-k'l), *adj.* 1. of tactics, especially in military or naval maneuvers. 2. characterized by or showing cleverness and skill in tactics. —**tac′ti·cal·ly,** *adv.*

**tac·ti·cian** (tak-tish′ən), *n.* 1. an expert in tactics. 2. a clever, skillful manager.

**tac·tics** (tak′tiks), *n.pl.* [< Gr. *taktika*, matters of arrangement < *tassein*, to arrange], 1. [construed as sing.], the science of maneuvering military and naval forces in action. 2. actions in accord with this science. 3. skillful methods or procedures.

**tac·tile** (tak′t'l, -til), *adj.* [Fr. < L. *tactilis* < *tangere*, to touch], 1. that can be perceived by the touch; tangible. 2. of or having the sense of touch. —**tac·til′i·ty** (-til′ə-ti), *n.*

**tact·less** (takt′lis), *adj.* not having or showing tact. —**tact′less·ly,** *adv.* —**tact′less·ness,** *n.*

**tad·pole** (tad′pōl′), *n.* [ME. *tade*, toad + *poll*, head; hence, the toad that seems all head], the larva of certain amphibians; as frogs and toads, having gills and a tail and living in water.

**Ta·dzhik Soviet Socialist Republic** (tä-jēk′), a republic of the U.S.S.R. in Central Asia: area, 55,584 sq. mi.

**tael** (tāl), *n.* [Port.; Malay *tahil*, a weight], 1. any of various units of weight of E Asia. 2. a former Chinese unit of money.

**ta'en** (tān), [Poetic], taken.

**taf·fe·ta** (taf′i-tə), *n.* [< OFr.; ult. < Per. < *tāftan*, to weave], 1. a fine, rather stiff, silk cloth with a sheen. 2. loosely, a similar cloth of linen, rayon, etc. *adj.* like or made of taffeta.

**taff·rail** (taf′rāl′), *n.* [< D. *tafereel*, a panel; ult. < L. *tabula*, table], the rail around a ship's stern.

**taf·fy** (taf′i), *n.* [early form of *toffee*], 1. a chewy candy made of sugar or molasses boiled down and pulled: cf. **toffee.** 2. [Colloq.], flattery.

**Taft, William Howard** (taft), 1857–1930; 27th president of the U.S. (1909–1913); chief justice, U.S. Supreme Court (1921–1930).

**tag** (tag), *n.* [prob. < ON.], 1. originally, a hanging end, as on a torn skirt. 2. any hanging part or loosely attached end. 3. a hard-tipped end, as of metal, on a string or lace. 4. a card, paper, etc. attached to something as a label. 5. the sentence or sentences ending a speech, story, play, song, etc. 6. a children's game in which one player, called "it," chases the others until he touches, or tags, one of them, making him "it" in turn. *v.t.* [TAGGED, TAGGING], 1. to provide with a tag. 2. to overtake and touch as in the game of tag. 3. [Colloq.], to follow close behind. *v.i.* [Colloq.], to follow close behind a person or thing (usually with *along, after,* etc.). —**tag′ger,** *n.*

**Ta·ga·log** (tä-gä′log), *n.* 1. a member of a Malayan people of the Philippine Islands. 2. their Indonesian language. Also **Ta·gal** (tä-gäl′).

**Ta·gore,** Sir **Ra·bin·dra·nath** (rə-bēn′drə-nät′ tä′gôr; Eng. tə-gôr′, -gōr′), 1861–1941; Hindu poet.

**Ta·hi·ti** (tä-hē′ti, tī′tē), *n.* one of the Society Islands in the South Pacific. —**Ta·hi·ti·an** (tä-hē′ti-ən, tə-hē′shən), *adj.* & *n.*

**Ta·hoe, Lake** (tä′hō, tā′hō), a lake between California and Nevada: a summer resort.

**Ta·i** (tä′ē, tī), *n.* & *adj.* Thai.

**Tai·ho·ku** (tī-hō′ko͞o), *n.* Taipei: Japanese name.

**tail** (tāl), *n.* [AS. *tægel*], 1. the rear end of an animal's body, especially when extending from the trunk as a distinct appendage. 2. anything like an animal's tail in form or position: as, the *tail* of a shirt. 3. a luminous train behind a comet. 4. the hind, bottom, last, or inferior part of anything. 5. *usually pl.* the side of a coin opposite the side with the head, date, etc. 6. a long tress of hair. 7. a line of people waiting their turn; cue. 8. *pl.* [Colloq.], *a*) a swallow-tailed coat. *b*) full-dress attire for men. 9. a set of stabilizing planes at the rear of an airplane. 10. [Colloq.], a detective, etc. assigned to follow someone stealthily. *v.t.* 1. to provide with a tail. 2. to form the tail or end of, as a procession. 3. to fasten at or by the tail; specif., to fasten one end of (a brick, board, etc.) into a wall, etc. 4. [Slang], to follow stealthily. *v.i.* 1. to become gradually smaller or fainter. 2. to form, or become part of, a line or tail. 3. [Colloq.], to follow close behind. *adj.* 1. at the rear; final. 2. from the rear: as, a *tail* wind. —**turn tail,** to run from danger, difficulty, etc. —**tail′less,** *adj.* —**tail′like′,** *adj.*

**tail** (tāl), *n.* [< OFr. *taille*, a cutting], a limitation on the inheritance of an estate. *adj.* limited in a specified manner as to inheritance.

**tail·board** (tāl′bôrd′, -bōrd′), *n.* the board forming the back of a wagon, truck, etc.: it can be removed or swung down as for loading: also **tail′gate′.**

**tailed** (tāld), *adj.* having a (specified kind of) tail: usually in combination, as *bobtailed.*

**tail·ing** (tāl′iŋ), *n.* 1. *pl.* refuse left in milling, mining, etc. 2. the part of a projecting brick, stone, etc. embedded in a wall.

**tail·light** (tāl′līt′), *n.* a light at the back of a vehicle to warn approaching vehicles of its presence at night: also **tail lamp.**

**tai·lor** (tā′lẽr), *n.* [< OFr. < *taillier* (< LL. *taliare*), to cut], one who makes, repairs, or alters clothes. *v.i.* to work as a tailor. *v.t.* 1. to make (clothes) by tailor's work. 2. to make clothes for. 3. to form, alter, etc. so as to meet certain conditions: as, a novel *tailored* to popular taste. 4. to fashion (women's garments, etc.) with trim, simple lines. —**tai′lor·ing,** *n.*

**tai·lor·bird** (tā′lẽr-bũrd′), *n.* any of several small Asiatic and African birds that stitch leaves together to camouflage and hold their nests.

**tai·lor-made** (tā′lẽr-mād′), *adj.* made by or as by a tailor; specif., *a*) made with trim, simple lines: said of women's clothes. *b*) made to order.

**tail·piece** (tāl′pēs′), *n.* 1. a part forming the end of something. 2. the piece of wood at the lower end of a violin, etc. to which the strings are attached. 3. a short beam with one end fastened in a wall and the other supported by another beam. 4. in *printing,* an ornamental design at the end of a chapter, etc.

**tail·race** (tāl′rās′), *n.* 1. the lower part of a mill-race. 2. the channel through which water flows after going over a water wheel.

**tail·spin** (tāl′spin′), *n.* the descent of an airplane with nose down and tail spinning in circles: often used figuratively: also **(tail) spin.**

**tail wind,** a wind blowing from behind.

**taint** (tānt), *v.t.* [< *attaint*, infl. by Fr. pp. of *teindre* (< L. *tingere*), to wet], 1. to affect with something injurious, unpleasant, etc.; spoil; infect. 2. to make morally corrupt. *v.i.* to become tainted. *n.* 1. a trace of corruption, disgrace, etc. 2. an infectious or contaminating trace.

**Tai·pei, Tai·peh** (tī′pe′), *n.* the capital of Taiwan, in the N part: pop., 759,000.

**Tai·wan** (tī′wän′), *n.* an island province off SE China: area, 13,832 sq. mi.; pop., 9,410,000; capital, Taipei: Portuguese name, *Formosa.*

**Taj Ma·hal** (täj′ mȧ-häl′), a mausoleum at Agra, India, built (1632–1645) by a Mogul Emperor.

**take** (tāk), *v.t.* [TOOK, TAKEN, TAKING], [< AS. < ON. *taka*], 1. to get possession of by force or skill; capture, seize, etc. 2. *a*) to win, as a game, a trick at cards, etc. *b*) to capture (an opponent's chessman, etc.). 3. to get hold of; grasp. 4. to affect; attack: as, *taken* by violent shaking. 5. to capture the fancy of. 6. to obtain, acquire, assume, etc. 7. to get into one's hand or hold. 8. to eat, drink, etc. for bodily nourishment. 9. to enter into a special relationship with: as, he *took* a wife. 10. to rent or lease: as, we *took* a cottage for the summer. 11. to receive regularly: as, we *take* two newspapers. 12. to assume as a responsibility, task, etc.: as, he *took* the job, *take* a vow. 13. to assume (a symbol of duty, office, etc.): as, the president *took* the chair. 14. to join or support (one side) in a contest, quarrel, etc. 15. to assume (something) as if granted: as, he *took* his leave. 16. to get, adopt, etc. by selection or choice. 17. to use: as, he *took* a whip to me. 18. to travel by: as, she *took* a train. 19. to go to for shelter, safety, etc.: as, the birds *took* cover. 20. to consider: as, he *took* the matter gravely. 21. to occupy: as, *take* a chair. 22. to derive, as a name, quality, etc., from. 23. to extract, as for quotation: as, he *took* a verse from the Bible. 24. to obtain by observation, experiment, etc.: as, *take* a poll. 25. to write down: as, *take* notes. 26. to make by photographing: as, *take* his picture. 27. to win, as a prize, etc. 28. to undergo: as, *take* punishment. 29. to occupy oneself or engage in: as, *take* a nap, *take* a walk. 30. to accept (an offer, bet, etc.). 31. to have a specified reaction to: as, he *took* the joke in earnest. 32. to confront and get over, etc.: as, the horse *took* the jump. 33. to be affected by (a disease, etc.). 34. to understand. 35. to suppose: as, I *take* him to be selfish. 36. to have or feel, as an emotion: as, *take* pity. 37. to make as the result of thought, as an objection. 38. to lead: as, this path *takes* you home. 39. to carry: as, to *take* one's lunch. 40. to remove as by stealing: as, the thief *took* the silver. 41. to remove by death. 42. to subtract: as, *take* two from four. 43. to direct (oneself); go. 44. [Colloq.], to require; need: as, it will *take* money. 45. [Colloq.], to aim (a specified action): as, he *took* a shot at me. 46. [Slang], to cheat; trick. 47. in *grammar,* to be used with in construction: as, a transitive verb *takes* an object. *v.i.* 1. to get possession. 2. to take root: said of a plant. 3. to catch: as, the fire *took* rapidly. 4. to gain public favor; be popular. 5. to be effective in action, etc.: as, the vaccination *took.* 6. to detract (with *from*): as, nothing *took* from the scene's beauty. 7. to go: as, *take* to the hills. 8. [Colloq. or Dial.], to become (sick). *n.* 1. the act or process of taking. 2. something taken. 3. the amount taken: as, the day's *take* of fish. 4. [Slang], the money received; receipts. 5. in *motion pictures,* *a*) a scene photographed with an uninterrupted run of the camera. *b*) the process of photographing such a scene. —**take after** to be, act, or look like. —**take amiss,** to become offended at as because of a misunderstanding. —**take at one's word,** to believe. —**take back,** to retract (something said, etc.). —**take down,** 1. to humble (a person). 2. to put in writing; record. —**take for,** 1. to consider to be. 2. to mistake for. —**take in,** 1. to admit; receive. 2. to make smaller. 3. to understand; comprehend. 4. to cheat; trick. 5. to visit: as, we *took in* all the sights. —**take it,** [Slang], to withstand hardship, ridicule, etc. —**take it out on,** [Colloq.], to make (another) suffer for one's own anger, irritation, etc. —**take off,** 1. to leave the ground or water in flight, as an airplane. 2. [Colloq.], to start. 3. [Colloq.], to imitate in a burlesque manner. —**take on,** 1. to acquire; assume. 2. to employ. 3. to begin to do, as a task, etc. 4. to play against;

oppose. 5. [Colloq.], to show violent emotion, especially anger or sorrow. **—take (one's) time,** to be unhurried. **—take out,** [Colloq.], to escort. **—take over,** to begin controlling, managing, etc. **—take to,** to become fond of. **—take up,** 1. to make tighter or shorter. 2. to pay off (a note, etc.). 3. to absorb (a liquid). 4. to accept, as a challenge. 5. to become interested in, as an occupation, study, etc. 6. to occupy (place or time). **—take upon** (or **on) oneself,** 1. to take the responsibility for. 2. to undertake. Also **take upon** (or **on) one.** **—take up with,** [Colloq.], to become an associate or companion of. **—tak′er,** ***n.***

**take-home pay** (tāk′hōm′), wages or salary after deductions for taxes, social security, etc.

**tak·en** (tā′k'n), pp. of **take.** **—taken aback,** suddenly confused or startled.

**take-off** (tāk′ôf′), ***n.*** 1. the act of leaving the ground, as in jumping or flight. 2. the place from which one leaves the ground. 3. [Colloq.], an amusing or mocking imitation; caricature; burlesque.

**tak·ing** (tāk′iŋ), ***adj.*** 1. attractive; winning. 2. [Colloq.], contagious; infectious: said of disease. ***n.*** 1. the act of one that takes. 2. something taken; catch. 3. *pl.* earnings; profits.

**talc** (talk), ***n.*** [Fr. < ML. *talcum* < Ar. *ṭalq* < Per. *talk*], a soft mineral, magnesium silicate, used to make talcum powder, lubricants, etc. ***v.t.*** [TALCKED or TALCED, TALCKING or TALCING], to use talc on.

**tal·cum** (tal′kəm), ***n.*** 1. talc. 2. talcum powder.

**talcum powder,** a powder for the body and face made of purified talc, usually perfumed.

**tale** (tāl), ***n.*** [AS. *talu*], 1. something told or related. 2. a story of true or fictitious events; narrative. 3. idle or malicious gossip. 4. a fiction; lie. 5. a complete tally; total.

**tale·bear·er** (tāl′bâr′ẽr), ***n.*** one who gossips or tells secrets, etc. **—tale′bear′ing, *n. & adj.***

**tal·ent** (tal′ənt), ***n.*** [< OFr. < LL. < L. < Gr. *talanton*, thing weighed], 1. a widely varying unit of weight or money used in ancient Greece, Rome, the Middle East, etc. 2. any natural ability or power. 3. a special, superior ability in an art, etc. 4. people who have talent. **—tal′ent·ed, *adj.***

**ta·ler** (tä′lẽr), ***n.*** [*pl.* TALER], [G.; see DOLLAR], a former German silver coin: also sp. **thaler.**

**ta·les·man** (tālz′mən, tā′liz-), ***n.*** [*pl.* -MEN], [< L. pl. of *talis*, such; + *man*], in *law*, a person summoned to fill a vacancy in a jury when the regular jury panel is deficient in number.

**tale·tell·er** (tāl′tel′ẽr), ***n.*** 1. a storyteller. 2. a talebearer. **—tale′tell′ing, *n. & adj.***

**Ta·li·en·wan** (dä′lyen′wän′), ***n.*** Dairen, a city in NE China: the Chinese name: also **Talien.**

**tal·i·pes** (tal′ə-pēz′), ***n.*** [< L. *talus*, an ankle + *pes*, a foot], clubfoot.

**tal·i·pot** (tal′i-pot′), ***n.*** [< Bengali *tālipāt*, palm leaf < Sans.], a palm tree of the East Indies, with fan-shaped leaves used for fans, umbrellas, writing paper, etc.: also **talipot palm.**

**tal·is·man** (tal′is-mən, -iz-), ***n.*** [*pl.* -MANS], [Fr. < Sp. < Ar. < Gr. *telesma*, religious rite], 1. a ring, stone, etc. bearing engraved figures supposed to bring good luck, avert evil, etc. 2. anything supposed to have magic power; a charm. **—tal′is·man′ic** (-man′ik), **tal′is·man′i·cal, *adj.***

**talk** (tôk), ***v.i.*** [ME. *talken;* prob. freq. based on AS. *talian*, to reckon], 1. to put ideas into, or exchange ideas by, spoken words; speak. 2. to express ideas by speech substitutes: as, *talk* by signs. 3. to speak trivially; chatter. 4. to gossip. 5. to confer; consult. 6. to make noises suggestive of speech. ***v.t.*** 1. to put into spoken words. 2. to use in speaking: as, to *talk* Spanish, to *talk* nonsense. 3. to discuss. 4. to put into a specified condition by talking: as, to *talk* oneself hoarse. ***n.*** 1. *a)* the act of talking. *b)* conversation. 2. a speech. 3. a conference. 4. gossip. 5. the subject of conversation, gossip, etc. 6. empty, frivolous discussion: as, it's just *talk.* 7. [Colloq.], a particular kind of speech; dialect, etc. **—big talk,** [Slang], a bragging. **—talk back,** to answer impertinently. **—talk big,** [Slang], to boast. **—talk down,** to silence by talking louder, longer, or more effectively. **—talk down to,** to patronize by pointedly simple speech. **—talk over,** 1. to discuss. 2. to persuade by talking. **—talk up,** 1. to promote or praise in discussion. 2. [Colloq.], to speak loudly, boldly, etc. **—talk′er, *n.***

**talk·a·tive** (tôk′ə-tiv), ***adj.*** talking, or fond of talking, a great deal; loquacious. **—talk′a·tive·ly, *adv.*** **—talk′a·tive·ness, *n.***

**talk·ie** (tôk′i), ***n.*** [Colloq.], a talking picture.

**talking machine,** a phonograph.

**talking picture,** a motion picture with a synchronized sound track to accompany the action.

**talk·ing-to** (tôk′iŋ-tōō′), ***n.*** [Colloq.], a scolding.

**talk·y** (tôk′i), ***adj.*** 1. talkative. 2. containing too much talk, or dialogue: as, a *talky* novel.

**tall** (tôl), ***adj.*** [< AS. (*ge*)*tæl*, swift], 1. high in stature; higher than the average. 2. having a stated height: as, five feet *tall.* 3. [Colloq.], exaggerated: as, a *tall* tale. 4. [Colloq.], large: as, a *tall* drink. **—tall′ish, *adj.*** **—tall′ness, *n.***

**Tal·la·has·see** (tal′ə-has′i), ***n.*** a city in N Florida: its capital: pop., 48,000.

**Tal·ley·rand-Pé·ri·gord, Charles Mau·rice de** (shärl′ mô′rēs′ də tȧ′lā′rän′pā′rē′gôr′), 1754–1838; French statesman and diplomat: often shortened to **Talleyrand** (Eng. tal′i-rand′).

**Tal·linn** (tȧl′lin), ***n.*** the capital of the Estonian S.S.R., on the Gulf of Finland: pop., 280,000.

**tal·lith** (tal′ith, tä′lis), ***n.*** [< Late Heb. < *tālal*, to cover], in *Judaism*, a fringed shawl worn by men during morning prayer: Deut. 22:12.

**tal·low** (tal′ō), ***n.*** [prob. < MLG. *talg*], the hard, coarse fat in cows, sheep, etc.: it is melted and used to make candles, soap, etc. ***v.t.*** to cover or smear with tallow. **—tal′low·y, *adj.***

**tal·ly** (tal′i), ***n.*** [*pl.* -LIES], [< Anglo-Fr.; ult. < L. *talea*, a stick], 1. originally, a stick with notches representing an amount, as of a debt. 2. anything used as a record for an account. 3. an account; reckoning. 4. either of two corresponding parts; counterpart. 5. agreement; correspondence. 6. a mark made on a tally. 7. an identifying tag or label. ***v.t.*** [-LIED, -LYING], 1. to put on or as on a tally. 2. to count (usually with *up*). 3. to put a label or tag on. 4. to make (two things) agree or correspond. ***v.i.*** 1. to record a score, etc. 2. to agree; correspond. **—tal′li·er, *n.***

**tal·ly·ho** (tal′i-hō′; *for n. & v.*, tal′i-hō′), ***interj.*** [< Fr. *taiaut*], the cry of a hunter on sighting the fox. ***n.*** 1. a cry of "tallyho." 2. a coach drawn by four horses. ***v.t.*** to announce sight of (the fox) by the cry of "tallyho." ***v.i.*** to cry "tallyho."

**Tal·mud** (tal′mud, täl′mood), ***n.*** [< Heb. < *lāmadh*, to learn], the writings constituting the body of early Jewish civil and religious law. **—Tal·mud′ic, Tal·mud′i·cal, *adj.*** **—Tal′mud·ist, *n.***

**tal·on** (tal′ən), ***n.*** [< OFr. < LL. < L. *talus*, an ankle], 1. *usually in pl.* the claw of an animal or bird of prey. 2. *pl.* human fingers or hands like claws in appearance or grasp. **—tal′oned, *adj.***

**ta·lus** (tā′ləs), ***n.*** [*pl.* -LUSES, -LI (-lī)], [L., an ankle], 1. the anklebone. 2. the entire ankle.

**ta·lus** (tā′ləs), ***n.*** [Fr. < OFr. *talu;* said to be < L. *talus*, an ankle], 1. a slope. 2. the sloping face of a wall in a fortification. 3. a sloping pile of rock fragments at the foot of a cliff.

**tam** (tam), ***n.*** a tam-o'-shanter.

**ta·ma·le** (tə-mä′li), ***n.*** [< Mex. Sp. < Nahuatl *tamalli*], a native Mexican food of minced meat and red peppers rolled in corn meal, wrapped in corn husks, and cooked by baking, steaming, etc.

**tam·a·rack** (tam′ə-rak′), ***n.*** [< Am. Ind.], 1. any of a number of related larch trees usually found in swamps. 2. the wood of any of these trees.

**tam·a·rind** (tam′ə-rind′), ***n.*** [< Sp. < Ar. *tamr hindī*, date of India], 1. a tropical tree with yellow flowers and brown pods with an acid pulp. 2. its fruit, used in foods, medicine, etc.

**tam·bour** (tam′boor), ***n.*** [Fr. < It. < Ar. *ṭanbūr*, stringed instrument < Per.; cf. TABOR], 1. a drum. 2. an embroidery frame of two closely fitting hoops that hold the cloth stretched between them. ***v.t. & v.i.*** to embroider on a tambour.

**tam·bou·rine** (tam′bə-rēn′), ***n.*** [< Fr. dim. of *tambour;* see TAMBOUR], a shallow hand drum having one head with jingling metal disks around it: played by shaking, hitting with the knuckles, etc.

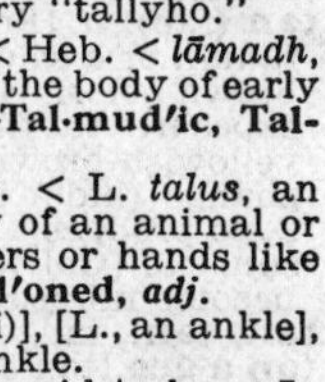

TAMBOURINE

**tame** (tām), ***adj.*** [TAMER, TAMEST], [AS. *tam*], 1. taken from a wild state and trained for man's use. 2. gentle; docile. 3. crushed as by domestication; submissive; servile. 4. without spirit or force; dull. ***v.t.*** [TAMED, TAMING], 1. to make tame, or domestic. 2. to make gentle, docile, or spiritless; subdue. 3. to make less intense; soften; dull. **—tam′a·ble, tame′-**

**a·ble,** *adj.* —**tame'ly,** *adv.* —**tame'ness,** *n.* —**tam'er,** *n.*

**tame·less** (tām'lis), *adj.* 1. not tamed. 2. not tamable. —**tame'less·ly,** *adv.* —**tame'less·ness,** *n.*

**Tam·er·lane** (tam'ẽr-lān'), *n.* (*Timur Lenk*), Mongol warrior whose conquests extended from the Volga River to the Persian Gulf; 1336?–1405.

**Tam·il** (tam'il, tum'-), *n.* 1. any of a Dravidian people of S India and N Ceylon. 2. the Dravidian language of the Tamils, ancient or modern.

**Tam·ma·ny** (tam'ə-ni), *n.* [alt. < *Tamanend,* a 17th-c. Amer. Indian chief], a powerful Democratic political organization of New York City, founded in 1789: also **Tammany Society, Tammany Hall.** *adj.* of Tammany's practices, members, etc.

**Tam·muz** (tä'mooz), *n.* [Heb.], the tenth month of the Jewish year: see **Jewish calendar.**

**tam-o'-shan·ter** (tam'ə-shan'tẽr), *n.* [< main character of Burns's poem "Tam o' Shanter"], a Scottish cap with a round, flat top and, often, a center tassel: also **tam.**

TAM-O'-SHANTER

**tamp** (tamp), *v.t.* [? < *tampion*], 1. in blasting, to pack clay, sand, etc. around the charge in (the drill hole). 2. to pack or pound down by a series of blows or taps. —**tamp'er,** *n.*

**Tam·pa** (tam'pə), *n.* a seaport in W Florida: pop., 275,000.

**tam·per** (tam'pẽr), *v.i.* [var. of *temper*], to plot; scheme. —**tamper with,** 1. to bribe. 2. to interfere with; meddle. 3. to make corrupt, illegal, etc. by meddling. —**tam'per·er,** *n.*

**Tam·pi·co** (tam-pē'kō), *n.* a seaport in E Mexico: pop., 123,000.

**tam·pi·on** (tam'pi-ən), *n.* [< Fr. *tampon* < *tapon,* a bung < Gmc.], 1. a plug or stopper put in the muzzle of a gun when it is not in use. 2. a similar plug for the end of an organ pipe.

**tam·pon** (tam'pon), *n.* [Fr.; see TAMPION], a plug of cotton or other absorbent material put into a wound, cavity, etc. to stop bleeding or absorb secretions. *v.t.* to put a tampon into.

**tan** (tan), *n.* [Fr. < ML. *tannum*], 1. tanbark. 2. tannin or a solution made from it. 3. a yellowish-brown color. 4. such a color given to the skin by exposure to the sun. *adj.* [TANNER, TANNEST], yellowish-brown. *v.t.* [TANNED, TANNING], 1. to change (hide) into leather by soaking in tannin. 2. to produce a tan color in, as by exposure to the sun. 3. [Colloq.], to whip severely; flog. *v.i.* to become tanned. —**tan'ness,** *n.* —**tan'ning,** *n.*

**tan, tan.,** tangent.

**tan·a·ger** (tan'ə-jẽr), *n.* [< Port. < Tupi *tangara*], any of several small American songbirds: the males usually are brilliantly colored.

**tan·bark** (tan'bärk'), *n.* any bark containing tannin, used to tan hides and, after the tannin has been extracted, to cover circus rings, etc.

**tan·dem** (tan'dəm), *adv.* [orig. punning use of L. *tandem,* at length (of time)], one behind another; in single file. *n.* 1. a two-wheeled carriage drawn by horses harnessed tandem. 2. a team, as of horses, harnessed tandem. 3. a bicycle with two seats and two sets of pedals placed tandem. *adj.* having two parts or things placed tandem.

**Ta·ney, Roger Brooke** (tô'ni), 1777–1864; chief justice, U.S. Supreme Court (1836–1864).

**tang** (taŋ), *n.* [< ON. *tangi,* a sting], 1. a projecting point or prong on a chisel, file, etc. to fit into the handle. 2. a strong, penetrating taste or odor. 3. a touch or trace (with *of*). 4. a special or characteristic flavor, quality, etc. *v.t.* to provide (a file, etc.) with a tang.

**Tan·gan·yi·ka** (taŋ'gan-yē'kə), *n.* a former country on the E coast of Africa: see **Tanzania.**

**Tanganyika, Lake,** a lake between the Congo (sense 2) and Tanzania.

**tan·gent** (tan'jənt), *adj.* [< L. ppr. of *tangere,* to touch], 1. touching. 2. in *geometry,* meeting a curved line or surface at one point but not intersecting it: said of a line or surface. *n.* 1. a tangent curve, line, or surface. 2. in *trigonometry,* the ratio of the side opposite the given acute angle in a right-angled triangle to the side opposite the other acute angle. —**go** (or **fly**) **off at** (or **on**) **a tangent,** to change suddenly from one line of action to another. —**tan'gen·cy,** *n.* —**tan'gent·ly,** *adv.*

**tan·gen·tial** (tan-jen'shəl), *adj.* 1. of or like a tangent. 2. drawn as a tangent. 3. turned aside from a straight course; digressing. 4. merely touching on a subject. —**tan·gen'tial·ly,** *adv.*

**tan·ge·rine** (tan'jə-rēn'), *n.* [< Fr. *Tanger,* Tangier], 1. a small, loose-skinned orange with segments that are easily separated and a deep, reddish-yellow color. 2. a deep, reddish-yellow color.

**tan·gi·ble** (tan'jə-b'l), *adj.* [< LL. *tangibilis* < L. *tangere,* to touch], 1. that can be touched or felt by touch; having actual form and substance. 2. that can be appraised for value: as, *tangible* assets. 3. definite; objective. *n. pl.* property that can be appraised for value; material things. —**tan'gi·bil'i·ty, tan'gi·ble·ness,** *n.* —**tan'gi·bly,** *adv.*

**Tan·gier** (tan-jêr'), *n.* a seaport in Morocco, on the Strait of Gibraltar: pop., 170,000.

**tan·gle** (taŋ'g'l), *v.t.* [-GLED, -GLING], [var. of obs. *tagle* < ME. *taglen* < ON.], 1. to hinder, obstruct, or confuse by circling, entwining, etc. 2. to catch as in a net or snare; trap. 3. to make a snarl of; intertwine. *v.i.* to become tangled. *n.* 1. an intertwined, confused mass, as of string, branches, etc.; snarl. 2. a jumbled, confused condition; muddle. 3. a perplexed state. —**tangle with,** [Slang], to become involved with, as in a fight or dispute. —**tan'gly** [-GLIER, -GLIEST], *adj.*

**tan·go** (taŋ'gō), *n.* [*pl.* -GOS], [Am. Sp. < Sp.], 1. a South American dance with long gliding steps and intricate movements. 2. music for this. *v.i.* [-GOED, -GOING], to dance the tango.

**tang·y** (taŋ'i), *adj.* [-IER, -IEST], having a tang, or flavor. —**tang'i·ness,** *n.*

**tank** (taŋk), *n.* [< Port. *tanque* < L. *stagnum,* pond], 1. any large container for liquid or gas: as, an oil *tank,* a swimming *tank.* 2. an armored, self-propelled vehicle carrying guns and moving on caterpillar treads. *v.t.* to put or store in a tank. —**tank'ful** [*pl.* -FULS], *n.*

**tank·age** (taŋk'ij), *n.* 1. the capacity of a tank or tanks. 2. the storage of fluids, gases, etc. in tanks. 3. the charge for such storage. 4. slaughterhouse waste from which the fat has been rendered in tanks.

**tank·ard** (taŋk'ẽrd), *n.* [< OFr. *tanquart*], a large drinking cup with a handle and a hinged lid.

**tank car,** a large tank on wheels, for carrying liquids and gases by rail.

**tank·er** (taŋk'ẽr), *n.* a ship especially equipped to carry large quantities of oil or other liquids.

**tank farming,** hydroponics.

**tank town,** 1. a railroad stop for locomotives to get water. 2. any small or unimportant town.

**tan·ner** (tan'ẽr), *n.* one whose work is making leather by tanning hides.

**tan·ner·y** (tan'ẽr-i), *n.* [*pl.* -IES], a place where leather is made by tanning hides.

**tan·nic** (tan'ik), *adj.* of, like, or obtained from tanbark or tannin.

**tannic acid,** a yellowish, astringent substance, $C_{14}H_{10}O_9$, derived from oak bark, gallnuts, etc. and used in tanning, dyeing, medicine, etc.

**tan·nin** (tan'in), *n.* tannic acid.

**tan·sy** (tan'zi), *n.* [*pl.* -SIES], [< OFr. < ML. < Gr. *athanasia,* immortality], any of various strong-smelling plants with clusters of small, yellow flowers, used in medicine.

**tan·ta·lize** (tan'tə-līz'), *v.t.* [-LIZED, -LIZING], [< *Tantalus*], to promise or show something desirable to (a person) and then remove or withhold it; tease. —**tan'ta·li·za'tion,** *n.* —**tan'ta·liz'er,** *n.* —**tan'ta·liz'ing·ly,** *adv.*

**tan·ta·lum** (tan'tə-ləm), *n.* [< *Tantalus:* from the difficulty in extracting it from its ore], a rare, steel-blue, corrosion-resisting, metallic chemical element used for electric light filaments, surgical instruments, etc.: symbol, Ta; at. wt., 180.88; at. no., 73.

**Tan·ta·lus** (tan'tə-ləs), *n.* in *Gr. mythology,* a king whose punishment in the lower world was to stand in water that always receded when he tried to drink it and under branches of fruit that rose when he reached for them.

**tan·ta·mount** (tan'tə-mount'), *adj.* [< Anglo-Fr. < L. *tantus,* so much + OFr. *amonter* (see AMOUNT)], having equal value, effect, etc.; equivalent.

**tan·trum** (tan'trəm), *n.* [? a pseudo-L. coinage on *tantara,* a fanfare], a violent, willful outburst of annoyance, rage, etc.

**Tan·za·ni·a** (tan-zā'ni-ə, -zan'i-ə), *n.* a country in E Africa, consisting of the former countries of Tanganyika and Zanzibar: a member of the British Commonwealth of Nations: area, 362,820 sq. mi.; pop., 10,046,000; capital, Dar es Salaam.

**Tao·ism** (tou'iz'm, dou'-), *n.* [Chin. *tao,* the way], a Chinese religion and philosophy based on the doctrines of Lao-tse and advocating simplicity, selflessness, etc. —**Tao'ist,** *n.* & *adj.* —**Tao·is'tic,** *adj.*

**tap** (tap), *v.t.* [TAPPED, TAPPING], [< OFr. *taper;* echoic], 1. to strike lightly. 2. to strike something lightly with: as, he *tapped* his cane on the floor. 3. to make or do by tapping: as, to *tap* a message.

4. to repair (a shoe) by adding a tap. ***v.i.*** to strike a light, rapid blow. ***n.*** 1. a light, rapid blow, or the sound made by it. 2. a thickness of leather added in repairing the heel or sole of a shoe. **—tap′per, *n.***

**tap** (tap), ***n.*** [AS. *tæppe*], 1. a device for controlling the flow of liquid in a pipe, barrel, etc.; faucet. 2. a plug, cork, etc. for stopping a hole in a container holding a liquid. 3. liquor of a certain kind, as drawn from a certain tap. 4. a tool used to cut threads in internal screws. 5. a place in an electric circuit where a connection can be made. 6. [Colloq.], a place that serves liquor; bar. ***v.t.*** [TAPPED, TAPPING], 1. to put a tap or spigot on. 2. to put a hole in for drawing off liquid. 3. to pull out the plug from. 4. to draw (liquid) from a container, etc. 5. to drain liquid from (a cavity, abscess, etc.) surgically. 6. to make a connection with: as, to *tap* a water main or telephone lines. 7. to cut the inner threads of (a nut, etc.). **—on tap,** 1. in a tapped cask and ready to be drawn. 2. [Colloq.], ready for consideration or action. **—tap′per, *n.***

**ta·pa** (tä′pä), ***n.*** [< native Polynesian name], an unwoven cloth made in the Pacific Islands from the treated inner bark of a mulberry tree.

**tap dance,** a dance performed with sharp, loud taps of the foot, toe, or heel at each step. **—tap′-dance′** [-DANCED, -DANCING], ***v.i.*** **—tap′-danc′er, *n.***

**tape** (tāp), ***n.*** [AS. *tæppe*, a fillet], 1. a strong, narrow, woven strip of cotton, linen, etc. used for binding, tying, etc. 2. a narrow strip or band of steel, paper, etc. 3. a strip of cloth stretched above the finishing line of a race track. 4. a tape measure. 5. [Colloq.], *a*) adhesive tape. *b*) magnetic tape. *c*) ticker tape. ***v.t.*** [TAPED, TAPING], 1. to put tape on or around, as for binding, tying, etc. 2. to measure by using a tape measure. 3. to record (sound, video material, digital computer data, etc.) on magnetic tape: in full, **tape-record.**

**tape deck,** a simplified, magnetic-tape assembly, without an amplifier or speaker but having tape reels and recording and playback heads.

**tape measure,** a tape marked in inches, feet, etc. for measuring: also **tape·line** (tāp′līn′).

**ta·per** (tā′pẽr), ***n.*** [AS. *tapur*], 1. a slender candle. 2. a long wick coated with wax, used for lighting candles, lamps, etc. 3. any feeble light. 4. *a*) a gradual decrease in width or thickness: as, the *taper* of a pyramid. *b*) a gradual decrease in action, power, etc. ***adj.*** gradually decreased in size to a point. ***v.t. & v.i.*** 1. to decrease gradually in width or thickness. 2. to lessen; diminish. Often with *off*.

**tape recorder,** a device for recording on magnetic tape.

**tap·es·try** (tap′is-tri), ***n.*** [*pl.* -TRIES], [< OFr. < *tapis*, a carpet; ult. < Gr. dim. of *tapēs*, a carpet], a heavy woven cloth with decorative designs and pictures, used as a wall hanging, furniture covering, etc. ***v.t.*** [-TRIED, -TRYING], 1. to decorate as with a tapestry. 2. to depict in a tapestry.

**tape·worm** (tāp′wūrm′), ***n.*** any of various ribbonlike worms that live as parasites in the intestines of man and other animals.

**tap·i·o·ca** (tap′i-ō′kə), ***n.*** [Port. & Sp. < Tupi < *ty*, juice + *pya*, heart + *oc*, to squeeze out], a starchy, granular substance prepared from the root of the cassava plant, used for puddings, etc.

**ta·pir** (tā′pẽr), ***n.*** [*pl.* -PIRS, -PIR; see PLURAL, II, D, 1], [Sp. < Tupi *tapyra*], any of various large, hoglike mammals found mostly in tropical America: tapirs have flexible snouts.

**tap·pet** (tap′it), ***n.*** [< *tap* (to strike)], in a machine, a projection or lever that moves or is moved by intermittent contact with another part.

**tap·room** (tap′rōōm′, -room′), ***n.*** a barroom.

**tap·root** (tap′rōōt′, -root′), ***n.*** [*tap* (faucet) + *root*], a main root, growing almost vertically downward, from which branch roots spread out.

**taps** (taps), ***n.pl.*** [< *tap* (to strike)], a military bugle call or drum signal to put out lights in retiring for the night: also sounded at military burials, etc.

**tap·ster** (tap′stẽr), ***n.*** [see TAP (faucet)], a bartender.

**tar** (tär), ***n.*** [AS. *teru*], a thick, sticky, brown to black liquid obtained by the destructive distillation of wood, coal, etc.: tars are used for protecting and preserving surfaces and are the source of many organic compounds. ***v.t.*** [TARRED, TARRING], to cover or smear with or as with tar. ***adj.*** 1. of or like tar. 2. tarred. **—tar and feather,** to cover (a person) with tar and feathers as a punishment: a practice of mob law.

**tar** (tär), ***n.*** [< *tarpaulin*], [Colloq.], a sailor.

**tar·an·tel·la** (tar′ən-tel′ə), ***n.*** [It., dim. of *Taranto*, Italy], 1. a fast, whirling, southern Italian dance for couples. 2. music for this.

**Ta·ran·to** (tə-ran′tō), ***n.*** a city in SE Italy: pop., 210,000.

**ta·ran·tu·la** (tə-ran′choo-lə), ***n.*** [ML. < *Taranto*, Italy: because found near by], a large, hairy, somewhat poisonous spider of S Europe, the southern U.S., and tropical America.

TARANTULA (1–3 in. long)

**tar·boosh** (tär-bōōsh′), ***n.*** [Ar. *tarbūsh*], a brimless cap of cloth or felt shaped like a truncated cone, worn by Moslem men.

**tar·dy** (tär′di), ***adj.*** [-DIER, -DIEST], [< Fr. < L. *tardus*, slow], 1. slow; slow-moving. 2. late; delayed; dilatory. **—tar′di·ly, *adv.* —tar′di·ness, *n.***

**tare** (târ), ***n.*** [prob. < MD. *tarwe*, wheat], 1. any of various trailing or climbing plants grown for fodder; vetch. 2. in the *Bible*, a noxious weed.

**tare** (târ), ***n.*** [Fr.; ult. < Ar. *ṭaraha*, to reject], the deduction of the weight of a container or wrapper from the total weight to determine the weight of the contents. ***v.t.*** [TARED, TARING], to find out, allow for, or mark the tare of.

**tar·get** (tär′git), ***n.*** [< OFr. dim. of *targe*, a shield < ON.], 1. originally, a small, round shield. 2. a round, flat board, straw coil, etc., marked as with concentric circles, aimed at in archery, rifle practice, etc. 3. any object that is shot at. 4. an object of attack, criticism, or ridicule.

**tar·iff** (tar′if), ***n.*** [< It. < Ar. *ta'rif*, information], 1. a list or system of taxes upon exports or, especially, imports. 2. a tax of this kind, or its rate. 3. any list of prices, charges, etc. ***v.t.*** 1. to set a tariff on. 2. to price according to a tariff.

**tarn** (tärn), ***n.*** [< ON. *tjorn*], a small mountain lake.

**'tar·nal** (tär′n'l), ***adj.*** [Dial.], 1. eternal. 2. confounded; damned. ***adv.*** [Dial.], damned; very.

**tar·na·tion** (tär-nā′shən), ***interj. & n.*** [blend of *'tarnal & damnation*], [Dial.], damnation.

**tar·nish** (tär′nish), ***v.t.*** [< Fr. *ternir*, to make dim < *terne*, dull], 1. to dull the luster of, as a metallic surface by oxidation. 2. to sully (a reputation, etc.). ***v.i.*** 1. to lose luster; discolor, as from oxidation. 2. to become sullied. ***n.*** 1. a being tarnished; dullness. 2. a stain; blemish. 3. a tarnished surface. **—tar′nish·a·ble, *adj.***

**ta·ro** (tä′rō), ***n.*** [*pl.* -ROS], [Tahitian], 1. a tropical plant of the arum family, with a starchy, tuberous root that is edible. 2. the root.

**tar·pau·lin** (tär-pô′lin, tär′pə-), ***n.*** [*tar* + *-paulin* < *pall*, a covering, but infl. by ME. *palyoun*, a canopy], 1. canvas waterproofed with tar, paint, etc., or a sheet of this spread over something as a protection. 2. a hat or coat of tarpaulin.

**tar·pon** (tär′pon), ***n.*** [*pl.* -PONS, -PON; see PLURAL, II, D, 1], [prob. < W.Ind. native name], a large, silvery game fish of the herring group, found in the warmer parts of the W Atlantic.

**Tar·quin** (tär′kwin), ***n.*** (*Lucius Tarquinius Superbus*), last king of early Rome (534–510 B.C.).

**tar·ra·gon** (tar′ə-gon′), ***n.*** [Sp. < Ar. < Gr. *drakōn*, dragon], 1. a plant of the aster family, with fragrant leaves used for seasoning. 2. the leaves.

**tar·ry** (tar′i), ***v.i.*** [-RIED, -RYING], [< AS. *tergan*, to vex, merged with OFr. *targer*, to delay < L. *tardus*, slow], 1. to delay; linger; loiter. 2. to stay for a time, as in a town, etc. 3. to wait. ***v.t.*** [Archaic], to wait for. **—tar′ri·er, *n.***

**tar·ry** (tär′i), ***adj.*** [-RIER, -RIEST], 1. of or like tar. 2. covered with tar. **—tar′ri·ness, *n.***

**tar·sal** (tär′s'l), ***adj.*** of the tarsus. ***n.*** a tarsal bone or plate.

**tar·sus** (tär′səs), ***n.*** [*pl.* -SI (-sī)], [< Gr. *tarsos*, flat of the foot], 1. in *anatomy*, *a*) the ankle. *b*) the seven bones forming the ankle. 2. in *zoology*, *a*) the large bone in the lower part of a bird's leg. *b*) the terminal segment of the leg of insects and certain other arthropods.

**tart** (tärt), ***adj.*** [AS. *teart*], 1. sharp in taste; sour; acid. 2. sharp in meaning; cutting: as, a *tart* answer. **—tart′ly, *adv.* —tart′ness, *n.***

**tart** (tärt), ***n.*** [< OFr. *tarte*], 1. a small shell of pastry filled with jam, jelly, etc. 2. in England, a fruit pie, with a top crust.

**tart** (tärt), ***n.*** [orig., slang for *sweetheart*], a prostitute or any woman of loose morals.

**tar·tan** (tär′t'n), ***n.*** [cf. ME. *tirtaine*, mixed fabric],

1. woolen cloth with a woven plaid pattern, worn especially in the Scottish Highlands, where each clan had its own pattern. 2. any plaid cloth or pattern. *adj.* of or like tartan.

**Tar·tar** (tär′tēr), *n.* [< ML. *Tartarus* < Per. *Tatar*], 1. a Tatar. 2. [usually t-], an irritable, violent, intractable person. *adj.* of Tatary or the Tatars: also **Tar·tar′i·an** (-târ′i-ən). —**catch a tartar,** to attack someone too strong for one.

**tar·tar** (tär′tēr), *n.* [< OFr. < ML. < MGr. *tartaron;* ? < Ar.], 1. a potassium salt of tartaric acid forming a reddish, crustlike deposit in wine casks: in purified form called *cream of tartar.* 2. a hard deposit on the teeth, consisting of saliva proteins and calcium phosphate. —**tar′tar·ous,** *adj.*

**tartar emetic,** a poisonous salt of tartaric acid used in medicine to cause vomiting.

**tar·tare sauce** (tär′tēr), [< Fr.], a sauce, as for fried fish, consisting of mayonnaise with chopped pickles, olives, chives, capers, etc.

**tar·tar·ic** (tär-tar′ik, -tär′-), *adj.* of, containing, or derived from tartar or tartaric acid.

**tartaric acid,** a colorless crystalline acid, $C_4H_6O_6$, found in fruit juices, etc. and obtained from tartar: it is used in cookery, medicine, etc.

**Tar·ta·rus** (tär′tə-rəs), *n.* in *Gr. mythology,* 1. the infernal abyss below Hades. 2. Hades; hell. —**Tar·tar′e·an** (-târ′i-ən), *adj.*

**Tar·ta·ry** (tär′tə-ri), *n.* Tatary.

**Tash·kent, Tash·kend** (täsh-kent′), *n.* the capital of the Uzbek S.S.R., central Asia: pop., 585,000.

**task** (task, täsk), *n.* [< ONorm.Fr.; ult. < L. *taxare,* to rate], 1. a piece of work, especially one assigned to or demanded of a person. 2. any difficult undertaking. *v.t.* 1. to assign a task to. 2. to burden; strain; overtax. —**take to task,** to call to account; scold.

**task force,** a specially trained, self-contained military unit assigned a specific mission or task.

**task·mas·ter** (task′mas′tēr, täsk′mäs′-), *n.* one who assigns tasks to others, especially when severe.

**Tas·ma·ni·a** (taz-mā′ni-ə, -mān′yə), *n.* an island off SE Australia: an Australian state. —**Tas·ma′ni·an,** *adj. & n.*

**Tass** (täs), *n.* [< the initial letters], a Soviet agency for gathering and distributing news.

**tasse** (tas), *n.* [OFr., pouch], *usually in pl.* any of a series of jointed metal plates forming a skirtlike protection of armor: see **armor,** illus.

**tas·sel** (tas′'l), *n.* [OFr., a knob], 1. an ornamental tuft of threads, cords, etc. of equal length, hanging loosely from a knob. 2. something resembling this; specif., the tassellike inflorescence of some plants, as corn. *v.t.* [-SELED or -SELLED, -SELING or -SELLING], 1. to make into tassels. 2. to ornament with tassels. *v.i.* to grow tassels, as corn.

**taste** (tāst), *v.t.* [TASTED, TASTING], [< OFr. *taster,* to touch, taste], 1. to test the flavor of by putting a little in one's mouth. 2. to detect the flavor of by the sense of taste. 3. to eat or drink, especially a small amount of. 4. to experience; have: as, to *taste* defeat. *v.i.* 1. to tell flavors by the sense of taste. 2. to eat or drink a small amount (often with *of*). 3. to have a specific flavor: as, the salad *tastes* of garlic. 4. to have a sensation or limited experience (*of* something). *n.* 1. a tasting. 2. the sense that is stimulated by contact of a substance with the taste buds on the surface of the tongue and is capable of distinguishing between sweet, sour, salt, and bitter. 3. the quality perceived through this sense; flavor; savor. 4. a small amount put into the mouth to test the flavor. 5. a slight experience of something; sample. 6. a bit; trace; touch. 7. the ability to appreciate and judge what is beautiful, appropriate, or excellent, as in art, dress, etc. 8. a liking; inclination. 9. a specific preference: as, a *taste* for red ties. —**in bad, poor,** etc. (or **good, excellent,** etc.) **taste,** in a form, style, or manner showing a bad (or good) sense of beauty, excellence, fitness, etc. —**in taste,** in good taste. —**to one's taste,** 1. pleasing to one. 2. so as to please one.

**taste bud,** any of the clusters of cells at the base of the papillae of the tongue, functioning as the sense organs of taste.

**taste·ful** (tāst′fəl), *adj.* having or showing good taste (sense 7). —**taste′ful·ly,** *adv.* —**taste′ful·ness,** *n.*

**taste·less** (tāst′lis), *adj.* 1. *a*) without taste or flavor; flat; insipid. *b*) dull; uninteresting. 2. lacking good taste. —**taste′less·ly,** *adv.* —**taste′less·ness,** *n.*

**tast·er** (tās′tēr), *n.* a person who tastes; specif., one employed to test the quality of wines, teas, etc. by tasting.

**tast·y** (tās′ti), *adj.* [-IER, -IEST], 1. that tastes good; flavorful. 2. [Colloq.], tasteful: now seldom used. —**tast′i·ly,** *adv.* —**tast′i·ness,** *n.*

**tat** (tat), *v.t.* [TATTED, TATTING], [< *tatting*], to make by tatting. *v.i.* to do tatting.

**Ta·tar** (tä′tēr), *n.* 1. a member of any of the Mongolian and Turkic tribes who invaded W Asia and E Europe in the Middle Ages. 2. any of a Turkic people living in E European Russia, the Crimea, and parts of Asia. 3. any of their Turkic languages. *adj.* of the Tatars. Also **Tartar.** —**Ta·tar·i·an** (-târ′i-ən), **Ta·tar′ic** (-tar′ik), *adj.*

**Ta·ta·ry** (tä′tə-ri), *n.* a vast region of W Siberia and S Russia invaded and inhabited by Tatars.

**'ta·ter** (tā′tēr), *n.* [Dial.], a potato.

**tat·ter** (tat′ēr), *n.* [< ON. *töturr,* rags], 1. a torn and hanging shred or piece, as of a garment. 2. a separate shred; rag. 3. *pl.* torn, ragged clothes. *v.t.* to reduce to tatters; make ragged. *v.i.* to become ragged. —**tat′tered,** *adj.*

**tat·ter·de·mal·ion** (tat′ēr-di-māl′yən, -mal′i-ən), *n.* [*tatter* + extension of *demon*], a ragamuffin.

**tat·ting** (tat′iŋ), *n.* [prob. < Brit. dial. *tat,* to tangle], 1. a kind of lace made by looping and knotting heavy thread that is wound on a hand shuttle. 2. the act or process of making this.

**tat·tle** (tat′'l), *v.i.* [-TLED, -TLING], [< MD. *tatelen;* echoic], 1. to talk idly; chatter. 2. to reveal others' secrets; tell tales. *v.t.* to reveal (a secret) by gossiping. *n.* idle talk; chatter. —**tat′tler,** *n.*

**tat·tle·tale** (tat′'l-tāl′), *n.* a telltale; talebearer.

**tat·too** (ta-tōō′), *v.t.* [-TOOED, -TOOING], [< Tahitian *tatu* < *ta,* a mark], 1. to make permanent marks or designs on (the skin) by puncturing it and inserting indelible colors. 2. to make (designs) on the skin in this way. *n.* [*pl.* -TOOS], a tattooed mark or design. —**tat·too′er,** *n.*

**tat·too** (ta-tōō′), *n.* [*pl.* -TOOS], [< D. *tap toe,* shut the tap: a signal for closing barrooms], 1. a signal on a drum, bugle, etc. summoning soldiers, etc. to their quarters at night. 2. any continuous drumming, rapping, etc.

**tau** (tô, tou), *n.* [Gr.], the nineteenth letter of the Greek alphabet (Τ, τ).

**taught** (tôt), pt. and pp. of **teach.**

**taunt** (tônt, tänt), *v.t.* [? < Fr. *tant pour tant,* tit for tat], 1. to reproach in scornful or sarcastic language; jeer at. 2. to drive or provoke by taunting. *n.* a scornful or jeering remark; gibe. —**taunt′er,** *n.* —**taunt′ing·ly,** *adv.*

**taupe** (tōp), *n.* [Fr. < L. *talpa,* a mole], a dark, brownish gray, the color of moleskin.

**Tau·rus** (tôr′əs), *n.* [L., a bull], 1. a northern constellation supposedly resembling the forequarters of a bull. 2. the second sign of the zodiac (♉), entered by the sun about April 20.

**taut** (tôt), *adj.* [ME. *toght,* tight; prob. < pp. of *togen,* to pull], 1. tightly stretched, as a rope. 2. tense: as, a *taut* smile. 3. neat; trim; tidy. —**taut′ly,** *adv.* —**taut′ness,** *n.*

**tau·to-,** [< Gr. < *to auto,* the same], a combining form meaning *the same,* as in *tautology.*

**tau·tog** (tô-tog′), *n.* [< Algonquian pl. of *tautau,* a blackfish], any of various blackish food fishes found off the Atlantic coast of the U.S.

**tau·tol·o·gy** (tô-tol′ə-ji), *n.* [*pl.* -GIES], [< LL. < Gr.; see TAUTO- & -LOGY], 1. needless repetition of an idea in a different word, phrase, etc.; redundancy. Example: necessary essentials. 2. an example of this. —**tau′to·log′i·cal** (-tə-loj′i-k'l), *adj.* —**tau′to·log′i·cal·ly,** *adv.*

**tav·ern** (tav′ērn), *n.* [< OFr. < L. *taberna*], 1. a place where liquors, beer, etc. are sold to be drunk on the premises; saloon; bar. 2. an inn.

**taw** (tô), *n.* 1. a marble used to shoot with: it is usually large and fancy. 2. a game of marbles. 3. the mark from which players at marbles shoot.

**taw·dry** (tô′dri), *adj.* [-DRIER, -DRIEST], [< *tawdry* (< *St. Audrey*) laces, sold at St. Audrey's fair, Norwich, England], gaudy and cheap; sleazy; showy. —**taw′dri·ly,** *adv.* —**taw′dri·ness,** *n.*

**taw·ny** (tô′ni), *adj.* [-NIER, -NIEST], [< OFr. pp. of *tanner,* to tan], brownish-yellow; tan. *n.* tawny color. Also sp. **tawney.** —**taw′ni·ness,** *n.*

**tax** (taks), *v.t.* [< OFr. < L. *taxare,* to appraise < base of *tangere,* to touch], 1. originally, to determine the value of; assess. 2. to require (a person) to pay a percentage of his income, property value, etc. for the support of the government. 3. to assess a tax on (income, property, purchases, etc.). 4. to impose a burden or strain on: as, the work *taxed* his strength. 5. to accuse; charge: as, *taxed* with negligence. *n.* 1. a compulsory payment of a percentage of income, property value, etc. for the support of a government. 2. a heavy demand; burden; strain. —**tax′a·bil′i·ty,** *n.* —**tax′a·ble,** *adj.* —**tax′er,** *n.*

**tax·a·tion** (tak-sā′shən), *n.* 1. a taxing or being taxed. 2. the principle of levying taxes. 3. a tax or tax levy. 4. revenue from taxes.
**tax-ex·empt** (taks′ig-zempt′), *adj.* exempt from taxation; that may not be taxed.
**tax·i** (tak′si), *n.* [*pl.* -IS], [short for *taxicab*], a taxicab. *v.i.* [-IED, -IING or -YING], 1. to travel by taxi. 2. to move along the ground or water under its own power: said of an airplane. *v.t.* to cause (an airplane) to taxi.
**tax·i·cab** (tak′si-kab′), *n.* [short for *taximeter cab*], an automobile in which passengers are carried for a fare at a rate usually recorded by a taximeter.
**tax·i·der·my** (tak′si-dūr′mi), *n.* [< Gr. *taxis*, arrangement + *derma*, a skin], the art of preparing, stuffing, and mounting the skins of animals to make them appear lifelike. —**tax′i·der′mal, tax′i·der′mic,** *adj.* —**tax′i·der′mist,** *n.*
**tax·i·me·ter** (tak′si-mē′tẽr), *n.* [< Fr. < *taxe*, a tax + *mètre*, meter], an automatic device installed in taxicabs, that registers the fare due.
**tax·on·o·my** (tak-son′ə-mi), *n.* [< Fr. < Gr. *taxis*, arrangement + *nomos*, a law], 1. the science of classification. 2. classification, especially of animals and plants into phyla, species, etc. —**tax′o·nom′ic** (-sə-nom′ik), **tax′o·nom′i·cal,** *adj.* —**tax′o·nom′i·cal·ly,** *adv.* —**tax·on′o·mist,** *n.*
**tax·pay·er** (taks′pā′ẽr), *n.* one who pays a tax.
**Tay·lor, Jeremy** (tā′lẽr), 1613–1667; English bishop and writer.
**Taylor, Zachary,** 1784–1850; U.S. general; 12th president of the U.S. (1849–1850).
**Tb,** in *chemistry*, terbium.
**TB, T.B., tb., t.b.,** tuberculosis.
**Tbi·li·si** (tbi-lē-sē′), *n.* the capital of the Georgian S.S.R.: pop., 519,000.
**T-bone steak** (tē′bōn′), any steak with a T-shaped bone, as a porterhouse.
**tbs., tbsp.,** tablespoon; tablespoons.
**Tc,** in *chemistry*, technetium.
**Tchai·kov·sky, Pëtr Il·ich** (pyô′tr′ il-yēch′ chi-kôf′ski), 1840–1893; Russian composer: also sp. Tschaikowsky, Chaikovsky, etc.
**Tchekhov, Anton Pavlovich,** see **Chekhov.**
**tcher·vo·netz** (cher-vô′nits), *n.* [*pl.* -VONTSI (-vôn′-tsi)], a chervonetz.
**Te,** in *chemistry*, tellurium.
**tea** (tē), *n.* [see PLURAL, II, D, 3], [< D. < Malay <Chin. dial. *t'e*, for Mandarin *ch'a*, teal, 1. a white-flowered evergreen plant grown in China, India, Japan, etc. 2. its dried and prepared leaves, steeped in boiling water to make a beverage. 3. this beverage. 4. a tealike extract made from various other plants or from a meat extract: as, beef *tea*. 5. [Chiefly Brit.], a light meal in the late afternoon at which tea is the usual beverage. 6. a social gathering in the afternoon at which tea, coffee, etc. are served.

TEA SHOOT

**tea bag,** a small, porous bag of cloth or paper, containing tea leaves and used in making an individual cup of tea: also **tea ball.**
**teach** (tēch), *v.t.* [TAUGHT, TEACHING], [AS. *tæcan*], 1. to show how to do something; train: as, he *taught* us to write. 2. to give lessons to (a student, etc.); instruct. 3. to give lessons in (a subject). 4. to provide with knowledge, insight, etc.: as, the accident *taught* him to be careful. *v.i.* to give lessons or instruction; be a teacher. —**teach′a·bil′i·ty, teach′a·ble·ness,** *n.* —**teach′a·ble,** *adj.* —**teach′a·bly,** *adv.*
**teach·er** (tēch′ẽr), *n.* one who teaches, especially as a profession; instructor.
**teach·ing** (tēch′iŋ), *n.* 1. the action of one who teaches; profession of a teacher. 2. *often pl.* something taught; precept, doctrine, or instruction.
**tea·cup** (tē′kup′), *n.* 1. a cup for drinking tea, etc. 2. a teacupful.
**tea·cup·ful** (tē′kup-fool′), *n.* [*pl.* -FULS], as much as a teacup will hold, about four fluid ounces.
**teak** (tēk), *n.* [< Port. < Malayalam *tēkka*], 1. a large East Indian tree with white flowers and hard, yellowish-brown wood used for shipbuilding, carved work, etc. 2. its wood. Also **teak′wood′.**
**tea·ket·tle** (tē′ket′'l), *n.* a covered kettle with a spout and handle, used to heat water for tea, etc.
**teal** (tēl), *n.* [prob. < AS.], 1. [*pl.* TEALS, TEAL; see PLURAL, II, D, 1], any of various small, short-necked, fresh-water ducks. 2. a dark grayish blue: also **teal blue.**
**team** (tēm), *n.* [AS., offspring], 1. two or more horses, oxen, etc. harnessed to the same vehicle or plow. 2. a group of people working or playing together, especially as one side in a contest. *v.t.* 1. to harness together in a team. 2. to haul with a team. *v.i.* 1. to drive a team. 2. to join in co-operative activity (with *up*): as, they *teamed* up on the paper route.
**team·mate** (tēm′māt′), *n.* one on the same team.
**team·ster** (tēm′stẽr), *n.* one who drives a team (now, often, a truck), for hauling loads.
**team·work** (tēm′wūrk′), *n.* 1. joint action by a group of people; co-ordinated effort. 2. work done by or with a team.
**tea party,** a reception at which tea is served.
**tea·pot** (tē′pot′), *n.* a pot with a spout, handle, and lid, for making and pouring tea.
**tear** (târ), *v.t.* [TORE, TORN, TEARING], [AS. *teran*, to rend], 1. to pull apart or separate into pieces by force; rip; rend. 2. to make or cause by tearing: as, to *tear* a hole. 3. to lacerate: as, to *tear* skin. 4. to divide into factions; disrupt; split: as, *torn* by dissension. 5. to divide with doubt, etc.; torment: as, *torn* between duty and desire. 6. to remove as by tearing, pulling, etc. (with *out*, *off*, etc.): as, *tear* off a leaf. *v.i.* 1. to be torn. 2. to move violently or with speed. *n.* 1. a tearing. 2. the result of a tearing; rent. 3. a violent outburst; rage. 4. [Slang], a spree. —**tear at,** to make violent, pulling motions at in an effort to tear or remove. —**tear down,** 1. to dismantle; wreck; demolish. 2. to disprove (an argument, etc.) point by point. —**tear into,** [Colloq.], to attack impetuously. —**tear′er,** *n.*
**tear** (têr), *n.* [AS.], 1. a drop of the salty fluid secreted by the lachrymal gland, which lubricates the eyeball and in weeping flows from the eye. 2. anything like this; tearlike mass. 3. *pl.* sorrow; grief. *v.i.* to shed, or fill with, tears. —**in tears,** weeping. —**tear′less,** *adj.* —**tear′less·ly,** *adv.*
**tear·drop** (têr′drop′), *n.* a tear. *adj.* tear-shaped.
**tear·ful** (têr′fəl), *adj.* 1. in tears; weeping. 2. causing or accompanied by tears; sad. —**tear′ful·ly,** *adv.* —**tear′ful·ness,** *n.*
**tear gas** (têr), a gas causing irritation of the eyes, a flow of tears, and temporary blindness.
**tear·ing** (târ′iŋ), *adj.* violent; impetuous; hasty.
**tear-jerk·er** (têr′jūr′kẽr), *n.* [Slang], a play, motion picture, etc. with a sad or maudlin theme.
**tea·room** (tē′rōōm′, -room′), *n.* a restaurant that serves tea, coffee, light lunches, etc.
**tear·y** (têr′i), *adj.* [-IER, -IEST], 1. tearful; crying. 2. of or like tears. —**tear′i·ness,** *n.*
**tease** (tēz), *v.t.* [TEASED, TEASING], [AS. *tæsan*], 1. to card or comb (flax, wool, etc.). 2. to raise a nap on (cloth) by brushing with teasels. 3. to annoy or harass by persistent, irritating actions or remarks, or by poking fun at. 4. to beg; importune. *v.i.* to indulge in persistent, irritating acts, etc. *n.* 1. a teasing or being teased. 2. one who teases. —**teas′er,** *n.* —**teas′ing·ly,** *adv.*
**tea·sel** (tē′z'l), *n.* [< AS. < base of *tæsan*, to tease], 1. any of various thistlelike plants with bristly flowers. 2. the flower of one species (**fuller's teasel**), used when dried for raising a nap on cloth. 3. any device for doing this. *v.t.* [-SELED or -SELLED, -SELING or -SELLING], to raise a nap on (cloth) by means of teasels. Also sp. **teazel, teazle.** —**tea′sel·er, tea′sel·ler,** *n.*
**tea·spoon** (tē′spōōn′), *n.* 1. a spoon for stirring tea, coffee, etc., for eating some soft foods, and as a measuring unit in cookery. 2. a teaspoonful.
**tea·spoon·ful** (tē′spōōn-fool′), *n.* [*pl.* -FULS], as much as a teaspoon will hold; 1/3 tablespoonful or 1 1/3 fluid drams.
**teat** (tēt), *n.* [< OFr. *tete* < Gmc.], the protuberance on a breast or udder, through which the milk passes in suckling the young; nipple.
**tea·zel** (tē′z'l), *n.* & *v.t.* [-ZELED or -ZELLED, -ZELING or -ZELLING], teasel.
**tea·zle** (tē′z'l), *n.* & *v.t.* [-ZLED, -ZLING], teasel.
**Te·bet, Te·beth** (tā-vāth′, tā′vis), *n.* [Heb.], the fourth month of the Jewish year: see **Jewish calendar.**
**tech.,** 1. technical(ly). 2. technology.
**tech·ne·ti·um** (tek-nē′shi-əm), *n.* [< Gr. *technētos*, artificial], a metallic chemical element obtained as by the irradiation of molybdenum with deuterons: symbol, Tc; at. wt., 99(?); at. no., 43 (formerly designated as *masurium*).

**tech·nic** (tek′nik), *adj.* [< Gr. < *technē*, an art], [Rare], technical. *n.* [Rare], technique.

**tech·ni·cal** (tek′ni-k'l), *adj.* [*technic* + *-al*], 1. dealing with the industrial or mechanical arts or the applied sciences. 2. of, used in, or peculiar to a specific science, art, profession, craft, etc.: as, *technical* terms. 3. of, in, or showing technique: as, *technical* skill. 4. according to the principles of some science, art, etc.: as, a *technical* difference. —**tech′ni·cal·ly,** *adv.*

**tech·ni·cal·i·ty** (tek′ni-kal′ə-ti), *n.* [*pl.* -TIES], 1. the state or quality of being technical. 2. a technical point, detail, term, method, rule, etc. 3. a minute formal point, detail, etc. brought to bear upon a main issue: as, convicted on a *technicality*.

**technical knockout,** in *boxing*, a victory won when the opponent, though not knocked out, is so badly beaten that the referee stops the match.

**technical sergeant,** 1. in the *U.S. Army*, a sergeant first class: the former name. 2. in the *U.S. Air Force*, an enlisted man ranking just above staff sergeant.

**tech·ni·cian** (tek-nish′ən), *n.* a person skilled in the technicalities of some subject or in the technique of some art or science.

**tech·ni·col·or** (tek′ni-kul′ēr), *n.* the process of reproducing colors on a motion-picture film: a trade-mark (**Technicolor**).

**tech·nics** (tek′niks), *n.pl.* [construed as sing.], 1. the study or principles of an art or of the arts, especially the practical arts. 2. technique.

**tech·nique** (tek-nēk′), *n.* [Fr.; see TECHNIC], 1. the method of procedure (as to practical or formal details) in rendering an artistic work or carrying out a scientific or mechanical operation. 2. the degree of expertness in following this.

**tech·no-,** [< Gr. *technē*, an art], a combining form meaning: 1. *art, science, skill*, as in *technocracy*. 2. *technical, technological*.

**tech·noc·ra·cy** (tek-nok′rə-si), *n.* [*techno-* + *-cracy*], government by scientists and engineers. —**tech′no·crat′** (-nə-krat′), *n.* —**tech′no·crat′ic,** *adj.*

**tech·no·log·i·cal** (tek′nə-loj′i-k'l), *adj.* 1. of technology. 2. resulting from technical progress in the use of machinery, etc. Also **tech′no·log′ic.** —**tech′no·log′i·cal·ly,** *adv.*

**tech·nol·o·gy** (tek-nol′ə-ji), *n.* [< Gr. *technologia*, systematic treatment], 1. the science or study of the practical or industrial arts. 2. the terms used in a science, art, etc. 3. applied science. —**tech·nol′o·gist,** *n.*

**ted** (ted), *v.t.* [TEDDED, TEDDING], [prob. < ON. *tethja*, to manure], to spread or scatter (newly cut grass) for drying. —**ted′der,** *n.*

**ted·dy bear** (ted′i), [< *Teddy* (*Theodore*) Roosevelt], a child's toy somewhat like a small stuffed bear.

‡**Te De·um** (tē dē′əm), [L.], 1. an old Christian hymn beginning *Te Deum laudamus* (We praise thee, O God). 2. the music of this hymn.

**te·di·ous** (tē′di-əs, tē′jəs), *adj.* full of tedium; long and wearisome; tiresome; boring. —**te′di·ous·ly,** *adv.* —**te′di·ous·ness,** *n.*

**te·di·um** (tē′di-əm), *n.* [< L. *taedium* < *taedet*, it offends], the condition or quality of being tiresome, wearisome, or monotonous.

**tee** (tē), *n.* [*pl.* TEES], 1. the letter T, t. 2. anything shaped like a T. *adj.* shaped like a T. —**to a tee,** exactly; precisely.

**tee** (tē), *n.* [< *tee* (T): the mark was orig. T-shaped], a mark aimed at in quoits, curling, etc.

**tee** (tē), *n.* [prob. < earlier *teaz*, Scot. dial.], in *golf*, 1. a small, cone-shaped mound of earth, or a small, wooden or plastic holder, on which the ball is placed when a player drives. 2. the place from which a player makes the first stroke on each hole. *v.t. & v.i.* [TEED, TEEING], to place (a golf ball) on a tee. —**tee off,** to play (a golf ball) from a tee.

**teem** (tēm), *v.i.* [AS. *tieman*, to bear < *team*, progeny], to be prolific; abound; swarm: as, the pond *teems* with fish. —**teem′ing,** *adj.*

**teem** (tēm), *v.t.* [< ON. *tæma*], to empty; pour out. *v.i.* to pour: said of rain, water, etc.

**teen-age** (tēn′āj′), *adj.* 1. in one's teens. 2. of, characteristic of, or for persons in their teens. —**teen′-ag′er,** *n.*

**teens** (tēnz), *n.pl.* the numbers, or years of one's age, between thirteen and nineteen inclusive.

**tee·ny** (tē′ni), *adj.* [-NIER, -NIEST], [Colloq.], tiny.

**tee·pee** (tē′pē), *n.* a tepee.

**tee·ter** (tē′tēr), *n., v.i. & v.t.* [dial. *titter* < ON. *titra*, to tremble], seesaw; waver.

**tee·ter-tot·ter** (tē′tēr-tot′ēr, -tô′tēr), *n. & v.i.* seesaw.

**teeth** (tēth), *n.* pl. of **tooth.**

**teethe** (tēth), *v.i.* [TEETHED, TEETHING], to grow teeth; cut one's teeth.

**teeth·ing ring** (tēth′iŋ), a ring of ivory, plastic, etc. for teething babies to bite on.

**tee·to·tal·ism** (tē-tō′t'l-iz'm), *n.* [formed by redupl. of initial letter of *total*], the principle or practice of never drinking alcoholic liquor. —**tee·to′tal·er, tee·to′tal·ler,** *n.*

**tef·lon** (tef′lon), *n.* a tough, insoluble polymer used in making nonsticking coatings, as for cooking utensils, and in gaskets, bearings, etc.: a trade-mark (**Teflon**).

**Te·gu·ci·gal·pa** (te-goo͞′sē-gäl′pä), *n.* the capital of Honduras: pop., 191,000.

**teg·u·ment** (teg′yoo-mənt), *n.* [< L. < *tegere*, to cover], the natural covering of an animal or plant; skin, shell, etc. —**teg′u·men′tal** (-men′t'l), *adj.*

**Te·her·an, Te·hran** (te′ə-rän′, tē′ə-ran′), *n.* the capital of Iran: pop., 2,317,000.

**tel.,** 1. telegram. 2. telegraph(ic). 3. telephone.

**Tel A·viv** (tel′ ä-vēv′, tel′ ə-viv′), a city in Israel, on the Mediterranean: pop., with Jaffa, 393,000.

**tel·e-,** [< Gr. < *tēle*, far off], a combining form meaning: 1. *operating at a distance*, as in *telegraph*. 2. *of, in,* or *by television*. Also **tel-.**

**tel·e·cast** (tel′ə-kast′, -käst′), *v.t. & v.i.* [-CAST or -CASTED, -CASTING], [*tele*vision + broad*cast*], to broadcast by television. *n.* a television broadcast. —**tel′e·cast′er,** *n.*

**tel·e·com·mu·ni·ca·tion** (tel′ə-kə-mū′nə-kā′shən), *n.* 1. communication over a distance by radio, telephone, telegraph, etc. 2. *pl.* all such systems.

**tel·e·gram** (tel′ə-gram′), *n.* a message transmitted by telegraph.

**tel·e·graph** (tel′ə-graf′, -gräf′), *n.* [< Fr.; see TELE- & -GRAPH], 1. originally, any signaling apparatus. 2. an apparatus or system for transmitting messages by signals produced by the closing and opening of an electric circuit by means of a lever, or key.

TELEGRAPH KEY

*v.t.* 1. to send (a message) by or as by telegraph. 2. to send a telegram to. *v.i.* to send a telegram. —**te·leg·ra·pher** (tə-leg′rə-fēr), **te·leg′ra·phist,** *n.*

**tel·e·graph·ic** (tel′ə-graf′ik), *adj.* 1. of or transmitted by telegraph. 2. in the concise style of a telegram. Also **tel′e·graph′i·cal.** —**tel′e·graph′i·cal·ly,** *adv.*

**te·leg·ra·phy** (tə-leg′rə-fi), *n.* the operation of telegraph apparatus or the study of this.

**Te·lem·a·chus** (tə-lem′ə-kəs), *n.* in *Gr. legend*, the son of Odysseus and Penelope, who helped his father slay his mother's suitors.

**tel·e·me·ter** (tel′ə-mē′tēr), *n.* [*tele-* + *-meter*], any electronic device used, as in the study of outer space, to measure pressure, radiation, etc. and transmit the information to a distant receiver. *v.t. & v.i.* to measure or transmit by telemeter.

**tel·e·ol·o·gy** (tel′i-ol′ə-ji, tē′li-), *n.* [< Gr. *telos*, an end; + *-logy*], 1. the study of final causes. 2. the fact of having a purpose or end, as attributed to natural processes. 3. a belief that natural phenomena are determined not only by mechanical causes but by an over-all design in nature. 4. the study of evidence for this belief. —**tel′e·o·log′i·cal** (-ə-loj′i-k'l), *adj.* —**tel′e·ol′o·gist,** *n.*

**te·lep·a·thy** (tə-lep′ə-thi), *n.* [*tele-* + *-pathy*], supposed communication between minds by means other than the normal sensory channels. —**tel·e·path·ic** (tel′ə-path′ik), *adj.* —**tel′e·path′i·cal·ly,** *adv.* —**te·lep′a·thist,** *n.*

**tel·e·phone** (tel′ə-fōn′), *n.* [*tele-* + *-phone*], an instrument or system for conveying speech over distances by converting sound into electric impulses sent through a wire. *v.i.* [-PHONED, -PHONING], to talk over a telephone. *v.t.* 1. to convey (a message) by telephone. 2. to speak to (a person) by telephone. —**tel′e·phon′er,** *n.* —**tel′e·phon′ic** (-fon′ik), *adj.* —**tel′e·phon′i·cal·ly,** *adv.*

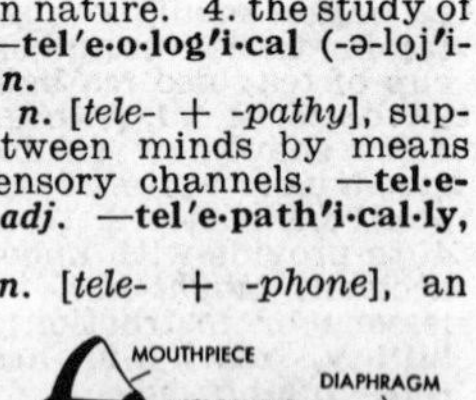

DIAGRAM OF TELEPHONE

**te·leph·o·ny** (tə-lef′ə-ni), *n.* the making or operation of telephones.

**tel·e·pho·to** (tel′ə-fō′tō), *adj.* 1. telephotographic. 2. designating or of a camera lens that produces a large image of a distant object. *n.* a telephotograph.

**tel·e·pho·to·graph** (tel′ə-fō′tə-graf′, -gräf′), *n.* 1. a photograph taken with a telephoto lens. 2. a photograph transmitted by telephotography. *v.t. & v.i.* 1. to take (photographs) with a telephoto lens. 2. to transmit by telephotography.

**tel·e·pho·tog·ra·phy** (tel'ə-fə-tog'rə-fi), *n.* 1. the art or process of photographing distant objects by using a telephoto lens with the camera. 2. the science or process of transmitting photographs over distances by converting light rays into electric signals which are sent over wire or radio channels. —**tel'e·pho'to·graph'ic** (-fō'tə-graf'ik), *adj.*

**Tel·e·promp·ter** (tel'ə-promp'tēr), *n.* an electronic device that unrolls a prepared script, etc. line by line, as a prompting aid: a trade-mark.

**tel·e·ran** (tel'ə-ran'), *n.* [< *tele*vision *r*adar *a*ir *n*avigation], an electronic aid to aerial navigation by which data received by radar, maps, etc. are transmitted to aircraft by television.

**tel·e·scope** (tel'ə-skōp'), *n.* [< It.; ult. < Gr. < *tēle*, far off + *skopein*, to view], an instrument for making distant objects, as stars, appear nearer and larger: it consists of a tube or tubes containing lenses. *adj.* having parts that slide one inside another. *v.i.* [-SCOPED, -SCOPING], to slide or be forced one into another like the tubes of a collapsible telescope. *v.t.* 1. to cause to telescope. 2. to condense; shorten.

**tel·e·scop·ic** (tel'ə-skop'ik), *adj.* 1. of a telescope. 2. seen or obtained by a telescope. 3. visible only through a telescope. 4. farseeing. 5. having sections that slide one inside another. Also **tel'e·scop'i·cal.** —**tel'e·scop'i·cal·ly,** *adv.*

**te·les·co·py** (tə-les'kə-pi), *n.* 1. the art or practice of using a telescope. 2. the science of making telescopes. —**te·les'co·pist,** *n.*

**Tel·e·type** (tel'ə-tīp'), *n.* [often t-], 1. a form of teletypewriter: a trade-mark. 2. communication by means of Teletype. *v.t. & v.i.* [-TYPED, -TYPING], [often t-], to send (messages) by Teletype.

**tel·e·type·writ·er** (tel'ə-tīp'rīt'ēr), *n.* a form of telegraph in which the receiver, by electrical impulses, prints messages typed on the keyboard of the transmitter.

**tel·e·view** (tel'ə-vū'), *v.t. & v.i.* to watch (an event, etc.) by television. —**tel'e·view'er,** *n.*

**tel·e·vise** (tel'ə-vīz'), *v.t.* [-VISED, -VISING], to send or receive by television. —**tel'e·vis'or,** *n.*

**tel·e·vi·sion** (tel'ə-vizh'ən), *n.* 1. the process of transmitting images or scenes by converting light rays into electronic impulses for further conversion into radio waves; the receiving set reconverts the corresponding impulses into electron beams that are projected against a luminescent screen, reproducing the original image. 2. the science of making or operating television apparatus. 3. the field of television broadcasting.

**tell** (tel), *v.t.* [TOLD, TELLING], [< AS. *tellan*, lit., to calculate], 1. to enumerate; reckon: as, *tell* one's beads. 2. to narrate; recount: as, he *told* a story. 3. to express in words; say: as, *tell* the facts. 4. to report; announce. 5. to reveal; disclose: as, her face *told* her joy. 6. to recognize; distinguish: as, I can *tell* the difference. 7. to decide; know: as, I can't *tell* what to do. 8. to let know; inform: as, *tell* me the truth. 9. to request; order: as, I *told* him to be here. 10. to state emphatically: as, I won't go, I *tell* you. *v.i.* 1. to give an account (*of* something). 2. to give evidence (*of* something). 3. to carry tales: as, kiss and *tell*. 4. to produce a result; be effective: as, every hammer blow *told*. —**tell off,** 1. to count (persons, etc.) and separate from the total number. 2. [Colloq.], to criticize severely. —**tell on,** 1. to tire; wear out. 2. [Colloq.], to inform against.

**Tell, William** (tel), in *Swiss legend*, a hero who, ordered by the Austrian governor on pain of death, shot an apple off his son's head with an arrow.

**tell·er** (tel'ēr), *n.* 1. one who tells (a story, etc.). 2. one who counts; specif., *a*) one who counts votes in a legislative body, etc. *b*) a bank clerk who pays out or receives money. —**tell'er·ship',** *n.*

**tell·ing** (tel'iŋ), *adj.* having an effect; forceful; striking: as, a *telling* retort. —**tell'ing·ly,** *adv.*

**tell·tale** (tel'tāl'), *n.* 1. one who carries tales; tattler. 2. an outward indication of something secret. 3. a device for indicating or recording information; indicator. *adj.* that is a telltale.

**tel·lu·ri·um** (te-loor'i-əm, tel-yoor'-), *n.* [< L. *tellus*, the earth], a rare, tin-white, nonmetallic chemical element similar to sulfur and selenium: symbol, Te; at. wt., 127.61; at. no., 52.

**tel·o-,** [< Gr. *telos*, an end], a combining form meaning *end*: also **tel-.**

**tel·pher, tel·fer** (tel'fēr), *n.* [< *tel*(*e*)- + Gr. *pherein*, to bear], an electrically driven car suspended from overhead cables. *v.t.* to transport by telpher. —**tel'pher·age, tel'fer·age,** *n.*

**Tel·u·gu** (tel'oo-gōō'), *n.* 1. a Dravidian language spoken in E India. 2. [*pl.* -GU, -GUS], a member of a Dravidian people living in Hyderabad, India. *adj.* of Telugu or the Telugu.

**tem·blor** (tem-blôr'), *n.* [*pl.* -BLORS, -BLORES (-blô'rās)], [Sp. < *temblar*, to tremble], an earthquake.

**te·mer·i·ty** (tə-mer'ə-ti), *n.* [< L. < *temere*, rashly], foolish boldness; foolhardiness; rashness.

**temp.,** 1. temperature. 2. temporary.

**tem·per** (tem'pēr), *v.t.* [< AS. & OFr. < L. *temperare*, to regulate], 1. to make suitable, desirable, etc. by mingling with something else; moderate: as, *temper* criticism with reason. 2. to bring to the proper consistency, hardness, etc. by treating in some way: as, to *temper* steel by heating and sudden cooling. 3. in *music*, to adjust the pitch of (a note, instrument, etc.) by temperament; tune. *v.i.* to be or become tempered. *n.* 1. a being tempered; specif., the degree of hardness and resiliency of a metal. 2. frame of mind; disposition: as, in a bad *temper*. 3. calmness of mind: only in *lose* (or *keep*) *one's temper*. 4. a tendency to become angry readily: as, she has a *temper*. 5. anger; rage: as, he went into a *temper*. 6. something used to temper a mixture, etc.

**tem·per·a** (tem'pēr-ə), *n.* [It. < *temperare;* see TEMPER], 1. a process of painting in which pigments are mixed with size, casein, or egg to produce a dull finish. 2. the paint used in this process.

**tem·per·a·ment** (tem'prə-mənt, tem'pēr-ə-), *n.* [< L. *temperamentum*, proper mixing < *temperare*, to mingle], 1. frame of mind; disposition; nature: as, an excitable *temperament*. 2. a disposition that rebels at restraints and is often moody or capricious. 3. in *music*, a system of adjusting the intervals between the tones of an instrument of fixed intonation, as to make them suitable for all keys.

**tem·per·a·men·tal** (tem'prə-men't'l, tem'pēr-ə-), *adj.* 1. of or caused by temperament. 2. having a temperament (sense 2). —**tem'per·a·men'tal·ly,** *adv.*

**tem·per·ance** (tem'pēr-əns, -prəns), *n.* 1. a being temperate; self-restraint in conduct, expression, indulgence of the appetites, etc.; moderation. 2. moderation in drinking alcoholic liquors. 3. total abstinence from alcoholic liquors.

**tem·per·ate** (tem'pēr-it, -prit), *adj.* [< L. pp. of *temperare*, to mix in due proportions], 1. moderate in indulging the appetites; abstemious, especially in the use of alcoholic liquors. 2. moderate in one's actions, speech, etc. 3. characterized by moderation, as things, actions, etc. 4. neither very hot nor very cold: said of climate, etc. 5. in *music*, tempered: said of a scale or interval. —**tem'per·ate·ly,** *adv.* —**tem'per·ate·ness,** *n.*

**Temperate Zone,** either of two zones of the earth (*North Temperate Zone* and *South Temperate Zone*) between the tropics and the polar circles.

**tem·per·a·ture** (tem'prə-chēr, tem'pēr-ə-), *n.* [< L. < *temperatus*, temperate], 1. the degree of hotness or coldness of anything, usually as measured on a thermometer. 2. *a*) the degree of heat of a living body. *b*) excess of this over normal (about 98.6°F. or 37°C. in man).

**tem·pered** (tem'pērd), *adj.* 1. having been given the desired temper, hardness, etc.: as, *tempered* steel. 2. modified by other qualities, etc.: as, *tempered* boldness. 3. having a (specified) temper: as, *bad-tempered*. 4. in *music*, adjusted to a temperament. —**tem'pered·ly,** *adv.* —**tem'pered·ness,** *n.*

**tem·pest** (tem'pist), *n.* [< OFr. < L. *tempestas*, portion of time, weather < *tempus*, time], 1. a violent wind, especially one accompanied by rain, snow, etc. 2. any violent commotion or tumult.

**tem·pes·tu·ous** (tem-pes'chōō-əs), *adj.* 1. of or like a tempest; stormy. 2. violent; turbulent. —**tem·pes'tu·ous·ly,** *adv.* —**tem·pes'tu·ous·ness,** *n.*

**Tem·plar** (tem'plēr), *n.* a Knight Templar.

**tem·plate, tem·plet** (tem'plit), *n.* [Fr. < L. *templum*, small timber], 1. a short stone or timber placed under a beam to help distribute the pressure. 2. a beam for supporting joists over a doorway, etc. 3. a pattern, usually a thin plate, for testing accuracy of form in woodworking, etc.

**tem·ple** (tem'p'l), *n.* [< AS. & OFr. < L. *templum*], 1. a building for the worship of God or gods. 2. [T-], any of three buildings for worshiping Jehovah, successively built in Jerusalem. 3. the place of

worship of a Reformed Jewish congregation. 4. a building, usually of imposing size, etc., serving some special purpose: as, a *temple* of art, a Masonic *temple*. —**tem'pled,** *adj.*
**tem·ple** (tem'p'l), *n.* [< OFr. < LL. < L. *tempora*, the temples, pl. of *tempus*, the fatal spot], either of the flat surfaces behind the forehead and in front of the ear.
**tem·po** (tem'pō), *n.* [*pl.* -POS, -PI (-pi)], [It. < L. *tempus*, time], 1. the rate of speed at which a musical composition is, or is supposed to be, played. 2. rate of activity: as, the *tempo* of the age.
**tem·po·ral** (tem'pēr-əl), *adj.* [< OFr. < L. *temporalis* < *tempus*, time], 1. temporary; transitory: cf. *eternal*. 2. of this world; worldly: cf. *spiritual*. 3. civil; secular: cf. *ecclesiastical*. 4. of or limited by time: cf. *spatial*. —**tem'po·ral'i·ty** (-pə-ral'ə-ti), [*pl.* -TIES], *n.* —**tem'po·ral·ly,** *adv.*
**tem·po·ral** (tem'pēr-əl), *adj.* [LL. *temporalis* < L. *tempora*, the temples], of or near the temple or temples (of the head).
**temporal bone,** either of a pair of compound bones forming the sides of the skull.
**tem·po·rar·y** (tem'pə-rer'i), *adj.* [< L. < *tempus*, time], lasting for a time only; not permanent. —**tem'po·rar'i·ly,** *adv.* —**tem'po·rar'i·ness,** *n.*
**tem·po·rize** (tem'pə-rīz'), *v.i.* [-RIZED, -RIZING], [< Fr. *temporiser* < L. *tempus*, time], 1. to suit one's actions to the time or occasion. 2. to give temporary compliance, evade immediate decision, etc., so as to gain time or avoid argument. 3. to effect a compromise (*with* or *between*). —**tem'po·ri·za'tion,** *n.* —**tem'po·riz'er,** *n.* —**tem'po·riz'ing·ly,** *adv.*
**tempt** (tempt), *v.t.* [< OFr. < LL. *temptare* < L. *tentare*, to try the strength of], 1. originally, to test; try. 2. to induce; entice; allure, as to something immoral. 3. to be inviting to; attract: as, that pie *tempts* me. 4. to provoke or risk provoking (fate, etc.). 5. to incline strongly: as, I am *tempted* to go. —**tempt'a·ble,** *adj.* —**tempt'er,** *n.* —**tempt'ress,** *n.fem.*
**temp·ta·tion** (temp-tā'shən), *n.* 1. a tempting or being tempted. 2. something that tempts.
**tempt·ing** (temp'tiŋ), *adj.* that tempts; alluring; attractive. —**tempt'ing·ly,** *adv.* —**tempt'ing·ness,** *n.*
‡**tem·pus fu·git** (tem'pəs fū'jit), [L.], time flies.
**ten** (ten), *adj.* [AS. *ten*], totaling one more than nine. *n.* 1. the cardinal number between nine and eleven; 10; X. 2. something having ten units or members.
**ten·a·ble** (ten'ə-b'l), *adj.* [Fr. < *tenir* (< L. *tenere*), to hold], that can be held, defended, or maintained. —**ten'a·bil'i·ty,** *n.* —**ten'a·bly,** *adv.*
**te·na·cious** (ti-nā'shəs), *adj.* [< L. *tenax* < *tenere*, to hold], 1. holding firmly: as, a *tenacious* grip. 2. that retains well; retentive: as, a *tenacious* memory. 3. that holds together strongly; cohesive: as, a *tenacious* wood. 4. that clings; sticky. 5. persistent; stubborn. —**te·na'cious·ly,** *adv.* —**te·na'cious·ness,** *n.*
**te·nac·i·ty** (ti-nas'ə-ti), *n.* the quality or state of being tenacious.
**ten·an·cy** (ten'ən-si), *n.* [*pl.* -CIES], 1. the condition of being a tenant. 2. property occupied by a tenant. 3. the duration of such an occupancy.
**ten·ant** (ten'ənt), *n.* [< OFr.; orig. ppr. of *tenir* (< L. *tenere*), to hold], 1. one who pays rent to occupy or use land, a building, etc. 2. an occupant; inhabitant. *v.t.* to hold as a tenant; occupy. —**ten'ant·a·ble,** *adj.* —**ten'ant·less,** *adj.*
**tenant farmer,** one who farms the land of another and pays rent in cash or in a share of the crops.
**ten·ant·ry** (ten'ənt-ri), *n.* [*pl.* -RIES], 1. tenants collectively. 2. the condition of being a tenant.
**ten-cent store** (ten'sent'), a dime store.
**Ten Commandments,** in the *Bible*, the ten rules of moral and religious behavior given to Moses by God on Mount Sinai: Ex. 20:2-17; Deut. 5:6-22.
**tend** (tend), *v.t.* [see ATTEND], 1. to take care of; minister to; cultivate: as, to *tend* plants. 2. to be in charge of; manage; operate: as, to *tend* a store. *v.i.* [Colloq.], to pay attention; attend. —**tend on,** to wait upon.
**tend** (tend), *v.i.* [< OFr. < L. *tendere*, to stretch], 1. to proceed; be directed: as, to *tend* east. 2. to have an inclination, disposition, etc. to do something: as, he *tends* to boast. 3. to lead or be directed (*to* or *toward* a specified result).
**tend·en·cy** (ten'dən-si), *n.* [*pl.* -CIES], [< ML. < L. ppr. of *tendere*, to stretch], 1. an inclination to move or act in a particular direction or way; leaning; bias. 2. a course toward some purpose, object, or result; drift. 3. a definite point of view in a literary work: as, *tendency* drama.
**ten·der** (ten'dēr), *adj.* [< OFr. < L. *tener*, soft], 1. easily chewed, broken, cut, etc.; soft, fragile, etc. 2. physically weak; feeble; frail. 3. immature; young: as, the *tender* years. 4. of soft quality or delicate tone; subdued: as, *tender* colors. 5. that requires careful handling; ticklish: as, a *tender* question. 6. light; not rough or heavy: as, a *tender* touch. 7. that has or expresses affection, love, etc.; gentle: as, a *tender* smile. 8. careful; considerate: as, *tender* of another's feelings. 9. acutely sensitive, especially to pain. 10. sensitive to impressions, emotions, etc.: as, *tender* conscience. 11. sensitive to others' feelings; sympathetic: as, a *tender* heart. *v.t.* to make tender. —**ten'der·ly,** *adv.* —**ten'der·ness,** *n.*
**ten·der** (ten'dēr), *v.t.* [< Fr. < L. *tendere*, to stretch], 1. to offer in payment of an obligation. 2. to present for acceptance; offer: as, he *tendered* his resignation. *n.* 1. an offer of money, services, etc. made to satisfy an obligation. 2. a formal offer, as of marriage, a contract, etc. 3. something offered in payment, especially money: cf. *legal tender*. —**ten'der·er,** *n.*
**tend·er** (ten'dēr), *n.* 1. one who tends, or has charge of, something. 2. a small ship for supplying a large one. 3. a boat for carrying passengers, etc. to or from a large ship. 4. a railroad car attached behind, and carrying coal and water for, a steam locomotive.
**ten·der·foot** (ten'dēr-foot'), *n.* [*pl.* -FOOTS, -FEET], 1. a newcomer as to the ranching country of the West, unused to hardships. 2. any newcomer, novice, etc. 3. a beginner in the Boy Scouts.
**ten·der·heart·ed** (ten'dēr-här'tid), *adj.* having a tender heart; easily moved to pity. —**ten'der·heart'ed·ly,** *adv.* —**ten'der·heart'ed·ness,** *n.*
**ten·der·ize** (ten'dēr-īz'), *v.t.* [-IZED, -IZING], to make tender, as meat. —**ten'der·iz'er,** *n.*
**ten·der·loin** (ten'dēr-loin'), *n.* 1. the tenderest part of a loin of beef, pork, etc., located under the short ribs. 2. [usually T-], a district in a city where vice flourishes: so called because regarded as a choice assignment for police grafters.
**ten·don** (ten'dən), *n.* [Fr. < ML. < Gr. < *tenein*, to stretch], any of the inelastic cords of tough, fibrous connective tissue by which muscles are attached to bones or other parts; a sinew. —**ten'di·nous** (-di-nəs), *adj.*
**ten·dril** (ten'dril), *n.* [< Fr. *tendrillon*; prob. < *tendre*, to stretch out, but assoc. with *tendre*, tender], a threadlike part of a climbing plant, serving to support it by clinging to an object.
**ten·e·ment** (ten'ə-mənt), *n.* [< OFr. < ML. < L. *tenere*, to hold], 1. in *law*, land, buildings, etc. held by tenure. 2. a dwelling house. 3. a room or suite tenanted as a separate dwelling. 4. a tenement house. —**ten'e·men'tal** (-men't'l), **ten'e·men'ta·ry,** *adj.*
**tenement house,** a building divided into apartments, especially one that is in the poorer section of a city and is overcrowded, dirty, etc.
**ten·et** (ten'it, tē'nit), *n.* [L., he holds], a principle, doctrine, or opinion maintained, as by an organization or school of thought.
**ten·fold** (ten'fōld'), *adj.* 1. having ten parts. 2. having ten times as much or as many. *adv.* ten times as much or as many.
**ten-gal·lon hat** (ten'gal'ən), a very tall, wide-brimmed felt hat, originally worn by U.S. cowboys.
**Ten·nes·see** (ten'ə-sē'), *n.* 1. a Southern State of the U.S.: area, 42,246 sq. mi.; pop., 3,567,000; capital, Nashville: abbrev. **Tenn.** 2. a river flowing through Tennessee, Alabama, and Kentucky into the Ohio River. —**Ten'nes·se'an,** *adj.* & *n.*
**ten·nis** (ten'is), *n.* [prob. < Anglo-Fr. *tenetz*, hold (imperative)], 1. a game (officially, *lawn tennis*), usually played outdoors, in which players bat a ball back and forth with rackets over a net stretched across a marked court (*tennis court*) of clay, asphalt, etc. 2. an old indoor game (*court tennis*), resembling modern handball and squash.
**tennis shoe,** a light, rubber-soled, heelless shoe of canvas, worn in playing tennis, etc.
**Ten·ny·son, Alfred** (ten'ə-s'n), first Baron Tennyson, 1809–1892; English poet.
**ten·on** (ten'ən), *n.* [< Fr.; ult. < L. *tenere*, to hold], a projecting part cut on the end of a piece of wood for insertion into a mortise to make a joint: see **mortise.** *v.t.* & *v.i.* 1. to make a tenon (on). 2. to joint by mortise and tenon.
**ten·or** (ten'ēr), *n.* [< OFr. < L. < *tenere*, to hold], 1. general course or tendency. 2. general meaning; drift. 3. general character or nature. 4. [because the tenor voice "held" the melody], the highest adult male singing voice. 5. a part for this voice. 6. a person or instrument having a tenor range or part. *adj.* of, in, or for the tenor.

**ten·pins** (ten′pinz′), *n.pl.* 1. [construed as sing.], a game in which ten wooden pins are set up at one end of an alley and bowled at. 2. these pins.

**tense** (tens), *adj.* [TENSER, TENSEST], [< L. pp. of *tendere*, to stretch], 1. stretched tight; strained; taut. 2. undergoing or characterized by mental or nervous strain. 3. in *phonetics*, spoken with tensed muscles, especially of the tongue. *v.t. & v.i.* [TENSED, TENSING], to make or become tense. **—tense′ly,** *adv.* **—tense′ness, ten′si·ty,** *n.*

**tense** (tens), *n.* [< OFr. < L. *tempus*, time], 1. any of the forms of a verb that show the time of its action or state of being: as, past, present, or future *tense*. 2. a set of such forms inflected to show person.

**ten·si·ble** (ten′sə-b'l), *adj.* that can be stretched; tensile. **—ten′si·bil′i·ty,** *n.* **—ten′si·bly,** *adv.*

**ten·sile** (ten′s'l, -sil), *adj.* 1. of, undergoing, or exerting tension. 2. capable of being stretched. **—ten′sile·ly,** *adv.* **—ten·sil′i·ty,** *n.*

**ten·sion** (ten′shən), *n.* 1. a tensing or being tensed. 2. mental or nervous strain, often accompanied by muscular tautness. 3. a state of strained relations due to mutual hostility. 4. a device for making something tense or taut. 5. voltage. 6. the pressure of a gas or vapor. 7. *a*) stress on a material produced by the pull of forces tending to cause extension. *b*) a force exerting such a pull. **—ten′sion·al,** *adj.*

**ten·sor** (ten′sẽr, -sôr), *n.* [< L. pp. of *tendere*, to stretch], any muscle that stretches, or tenses, some part of the body.

**tent** (tent), *n.* [< OFr. < L. pp. of *tendere*, to stretch], 1. a portable shelter consisting of a covering of canvas, etc., stretched over poles and attached to stakes. 2. anything more or less like this, as an oxygen tent. *v.i. & v.t.* to lodge in a tent or tents. **—tent′like′,** *adj.*

**ten·ta·cle** (ten′tə-k'l), *n.* [Mod. L. *tentaculum* < L. *tentare*, to touch], 1. a long, slender, flexible growth about the head or mouth of some invertebrates, used to feel, grasp, propel, etc. 2 in *botany*, a sensitive hair, as on some leaves. **—ten′ta·cled,** *adj.* **—ten·tac′u·lar** (-tak′yoo-lẽr), *adj.*

**ten·ta·tive** (ten′tə-tiv), *adj.* [< ML. *tentativus* < pp. of L. *tentare*, to try], made or done as a trial or provisionally; experimental; provisional. **—ten′ta·tive·ly,** *adv.* **—ten′ta·tive·ness,** *n.*

**tent caterpillar,** a caterpillar that lives in colonies in tentlike webs which it spins in trees.

**ten·ter** (ten′tẽr), *n.* [see TENT], 1. a frame on which cloth is stretched so as to dry evenly without shrinking. 2. a tenterhook. *v.t. & v.i.* to stretch on a tenter.

**ten·ter·hook** (ten′tẽr-hook′), *n.* any of the hooked nails that hold cloth stretched on a tenter. **—on tenterhooks,** in suspense; anxious.

**tenth** (tenth), *adj.* [AS. *teogotha*], 1. preceded by nine others in a series; 10th. 2. designating any of the ten equal parts of something. *n.* 1. the one following the ninth. 2. any of the ten equal parts of something; 1/10. **—tenth′ly,** *adv.*

**tent stitch,** [prob. < *tent* (a shelter)], an embroidery stitch in a series of parallel slanting lines.

**te·nu·i·ty** (ten-ū′ə-ti, ti-nōō′-), *n.* [*pl.* -TIES], the quality or state of being tenuous.

**ten·u·ous** (ten′ū-əs), *adj.* [< L. *tenuis*, thin], 1. physically thin, slender, or fine. 2. rare; not dense, as air at high altitudes. 3. unsubstantial; flimsy. **—ten′u·ous·ly,** *adv.* **—ten′u·ous·ness,** *n.*

**ten·ure** (ten′yẽr), *n.* [< OFr. < *tenir* (< L. *tenere*), to hold], 1. a holding, as of property, office, etc. 2. the right to hold or possess something. 3. the length of time something is held. 4. conditions of possession. 5. permanent possession, as of a position. **—ten·u′ri·al** (-yoor′i-əl), *adj.*

‡**te·nu·to** (te-nōō′tô), *adj.* [It., pp. of *tenere*, to hold], in *music*, held for its full value, as a tone.

**te·pee** (tē′pē), *n.* [< Siouan < *ti*, to dwell + *pi*, used for], a cone-shaped tent used by American Indians: also sp. **teepee.**

**tep·id** (tep′id), *adj.* [< L. < *tepere*, to be slightly warm], moderately warm; lukewarm. **—te·pid·i·ty** (ti-pid′ə-ti), **tep′id·ness,** *n.* **—tep′id·ly,** *adv.*

**te·qui·la** (ti-kē′lä), *n.* [< *Tequila*, a Mexican district], 1. a century plant of Mexico. 2. an alcoholic liquor distilled from the juice of its stem.

**ter.,** 1. terrace. 2. territory.

**ter·a·tism** (ter′ə-tiz'm), *n.* [< Gr. *teras*, a monster], a monstrosity; malformed fetus.

**ter·bi·um** (tũr′bi-əm), *n.* [< *Ytterby*, in Sweden], a metallic chemical element of the rare-earth group: symbol, Tb; at. wt., 159.2; at. no., 65.

**ter·cen·te·nar·y** (tẽr-sen′tə-ner′i, tũr′sen-ten′ə-ri), *n.* [*pl.* -IES], [L. *ter*, three times; + *centenary*], 1. a period of 300 years. 2. a 300th anniversary. *adj.* of a period of 300 years.

**ter·cet** (tũr′sit, tẽr-set′), *n.* [Fr. < It. dim. of *terzo*, a third], 1. a group of three lines that rhyme or are connected by rhyme with an adjacent triplet. 2. in *music*, a triplet.

**Ter·ence** (ter′əns), *n.* (*Publius Terentius Afer*), Roman writer of comedies; 190?–159? B.C.

**ter·gi·ver·sate** (tũr′ji-vẽr-sāt′), *v.i.* [-SATED, -SATING], [< L. pp. < *tergum*, the back + *versari*, to turn], 1. to desert a cause, party, etc.; apostatize. 2. to use evasions or subterfuge; equivocate. **—ter′gi·ver·sa′tor,** *n.* **—ter′gi·ver·sa′tion,** *n.*

**term** (tũrm), *n.* [< OFr. < L. *terminus*, a limit], 1. a date set for payment, termination of tenancy, etc. 2. a period of time having definite limits; duration; specif., *a*) any of the divisions of a school year. *b*) the period stipulated for the holding of an office. 3. *pl.* conditions of a contract, sale, etc. that limit or define its scope. 4. *pl.* mutual relationship between persons: as, on speaking *terms*. 5. a word or phrase having a precise meaning, as in some science, art, etc.: as, a medical *term*. 6. *pl.* language of a specified kind: as, he spoke in derogatory *terms*. 7. in *law*, *a*) the period during which a court is in session. *b*) the length of time for which an estate is granted. *c*) the estate itself. 8. in *logic*, the subject or predicate of a proposition. 9. in *mathematics*, *a*) either of the two quantities of a fraction or a ratio. *b*) each of the quantities in a series or in an algebraic expression. *v.t.* to call by a term; name. **—bring to terms,** to force to agree. **—come to** (or **make**) **terms,** to arrive at an agreement. **—term′less,** *adj.*

**ter·ma·gant** (tũr′mə-gənt), *n.* [< OFr. *Tervagant*, imaginary Moslem deity], a boisterous, quarrelsome, scolding woman; shrew; virago. *adj.* of the nature of a termagant; quarrelsome; scolding. **—ter′ma·gan·cy,** *n.* **—ter′ma·gant·ly,** *adv.*

**term·er** (tũr′mẽr), *n.* a person serving a term, as in prison: usually compounded, as, *third-termer*.

**ter·mi·na·ble** (tũr′mi-nə-b'l), *adj.* 1. that can be terminated. 2. that terminates after a specified time, as a contract. **—ter′mi·na·bil′i·ty, ter′mi·na·ble·ness,** *n.* **—ter′mi·na·bly,** *adv.*

**ter·mi·nal** (tũr′mə-n'l), *adj.* [< L. *terminalis*], 1. of, at, or forming the end or extremity of something. 2. occurring at the end of a series; concluding; final. 3. having to do with a term, or period of time. 4. connected with, charged at, etc. the end of a railroad line. 5. in *botany*, growing at the end of a stem or branch. *n.* 1. a terminating part; end; extremity. 2. either end of an electric circuit or a connection at either end. 3. either end of a transportation line, as a railroad, including station, yards, etc. 4. a station or city at such a terminus or at an important junction in such a line. **—ter′mi·nal·ly,** *adv.*

**ter·mi·nate** (tũr′mə-nāt′), *v.t.* [-NATED, -NATING], [< L. pp. < *terminus*, a limit], 1. to form the end or conclusion of; limit, bound, or conclude. 2. to put an end to; stop; cease. *v.i.* 1. to come to an end. 2. to have its end (*in* something): as, the road *terminates* in woods. **—ter′mi·na′tive, ter′mi·na·to′ry** (-mi-nə-tôr′i, -tō′ri), *adj.* **—ter′mi·na′tor,** *n.*

**ter·mi·na·tion** (tũr′mə-nā′shən), *n.* 1. a terminating or being terminated. 2. the end, limit, or conclusion. 3. the end of a word; final sound, morpheme, or syllable. **—ter′mi·na′tion·al,** *adj.*

**ter·mi·nol·o·gy** (tũr′mə-nol′ə-ji), *n.* [*pl.* -GIES], the terms used in a specific field of art, science, etc. **—ter′mi·no·log′i·cal** (-mi-nə-loj′i-k'l), *adj.*

**ter·mi·nus** (tũr′mə-nəs), *n.* [*pl.* -NI (-nī′), -NUSES], [L., a limit], 1. a boundary stone or marker. 2. an end; extremity or goal. 3. either end of a railroad, bus, or air line. 4. [Chiefly Brit.], the station or city at the end of such a line.

**ter·mite** (tũr′mīt), *n.* [L. *termes*, wood-boring worm], any of various pale-colored social insects that are very destructive to wooden structures: also called *white ant*.

**tern** (tũrn), *n.* [< ON. *therna*], any of several sea birds related to the gulls, but smaller, with a more slender body and beak, and a deeply forked tail.

**ter·na·ry** (tũr′nẽr-i), *adj.* [< L. < *terni*, three each], 1. made up of three parts; threefold. 2. third. *n.* [*pl.* -RIES], [Rare], a set of three.

**ter·nate** (tũr′nāt), *adj.* [< L. *terni*, three each],

1. consisting of three. 2. arranged in threes, as some leaves. —**ter′nate·ly,** *adv.*
**ter·pene** (tũr′pēn), *n.* [< obs. var. of *turpentine*], any of a series of isomeric hydrocarbons of the general formula $C_{10}H_{16}$, found in resins, etc.
**Terp·sich·o·re** (tũrp-sik′ə-rē′), *n.* in *Gr. mythology,* the Muse of dancing.
**terp·si·cho·re·an** (tũrp′si-kə-rē′ən), *adj.* 1. [T-], of Terpsichore. 2. having to do with dancing. *n.* a dancer: literary or humorous usage.
**ter·race** (ter′is), *n.* [< Fr. < L. *terra,* earth], 1. a raised, flat mound of earth with sloping sides. 2. any of a series of flat platforms of earth with sloping sides, rising one above the other, as on a hillside. 3. a geological formation of this kind. 4. an unroofed, paved area immediately adjacent to a house and overlooking a lawn or garden. 5. a flat roof, especially of a house of Spanish or Oriental architecture. 6. a row of houses on ground raised from the street. 7. a street in front of such houses. *v.t.* [-RACED, -RACING], to form into or surround with a terrace or terraces.
**ter·ra cot·ta** (ter′ə kot′ə), [It., lit., baked earth], 1. a hard, brown-red, usually unglazed earthenware used for pottery, ornamental facing, etc. 2. its brown-red color. —**ter′ra-cot′ta,** *adj.*
**terra fir·ma** (fũr′mə), [L.], firm or solid ground.
**ter·rain** (tə-rān′, ter′ān), *n.* [Fr. < L. < *terra,* earth], ground or a tract of ground, especially with regard to its features or fitness for some use.
**ter·ra·my·cin** (ter′ə-mī′sin), *n.* [< L. *terra,* earth + Gr. *mykēs,* fungus], an antibiotic drug derived from an earth, effective against certain viruses, bacteria, rickettsiae, etc.
**ter·ra·pin** (ter′ə-pin), *n.* [< Algonquian], 1. any of various American fresh-water or tidewater turtles; esp., the diamondback. 2. its flesh used as food.
**ter·rar·i·um** (te-râr′i-əm), *n.* [*pl.* -IUMS, -IA (-i-ə)], [< L. *terra,* earth + *-arium* as in *aquarium*], an enclosure for keeping small animals.
**Ter·re Haute** (ter′ə hōt′), a city in W Indiana, on the Wabash River: pop., 73,000.
**ter·res·tri·al** (tə-res′tri-əl), *adj.* [< L. *terrestris* < *terra,* earth], 1. of this world; worldly; mundane. 2. of or constituting the earth. 3. consisting of land as distinguished from water. 4. living on land: cf. *aquatic, arboreal, aerial.* 5. growing in the ground. *n.* an inhabitant of the earth. —**ter·res′tri·al·ly,** *adv.*
**ter·ret** (ter′it), *n.* [< OFr. *toret,* dim. of *tour,* a turn], any of the rings on a harness, through which the reins pass.
**ter·ri·ble** (ter′ə-b'l), *adj.* [OFr. < L. *terribilis* < *terrere,* to frighten], 1. causing terror; fearful; dreadful. 2. extreme; intense; severe. 3. [Colloq.], very bad, unpleasant, or disagreeable. —**ter′ri·ble·ness,** *n.* —**ter′ri·bly,** *adv.*
**ter·ri·er** (ter′i-ēr), *n.* [< Fr. (*chien*) *terrier,* hunting (dog) < *terrier,* hillock; ult. < L. *terra,* earth], any of several breeds of active, typically small dog, formerly used to burrow after small game: they include the schnauzer, fox terrier, Scottish terrier, etc.
**ter·rif·ic** (tə-rif′ik), *adj.* [< L. < *terrere,* to frighten + *facere,* to make], 1. causing great fear; terrifying; dreadful. 2. [Colloq.], unusually great, intense, etc.; extraordinary. —**ter·rif′i·cal·ly, ter·rif′ic·ly,** *adv.*
**ter·ri·fy** (ter′ə-fī′), *v.t.* [-FIED, -FYING], [see TERRIFIC], to fill with terror; frighten greatly; alarm. —**ter′ri·fi′er,** *n.* —**ter′ri·fy′ing·ly,** *adv.*
**ter·ri·to·ri·al** (ter′ə-tôr′i-əl, -tō′ri-), *adj.* 1. of territory or land. 2. of or limited to a specific territory or district. 3. [T-], of a Territory or Territories. 4. [often T-], organized primarily for home defense. *n.* [T-], [Chiefly Brit.], a member of a Territorial force. —**ter′ri·to′ri·al′i·ty** (-al′ə-ti), *n.* —**ter′ri·to′ri·al·ly,** *adv.*
**ter·ri·to·ry** (ter′ə-tôr′i, -tō′ri), *n.* [*pl.* -RIES], [< L. *territorium* < *terra,* earth], 1. the land and waters under the jurisdiction of a nation, state, ruler, etc. 2. a part of a country or empire without the full status of a principal division; specif., *a*) [T-], formerly, a part of the U.S. without the status of a State and having an appointed governor: Hawaii was the last U.S. Territory. *b*) [T-], a similar region in Canada or Australia. 3. any large tract of land; region. 4. an assigned area, as of a traveling salesman. 5. a sphere of action, existence, etc.
**ter·ror** (ter′ēr), *n.* [< OFr. < L. < *terrere,* to frighten], 1. intense fear. 2. *a*) one that causes intense fear. *b*) the quality of causing dread; terribleness. 3. [Colloq.], a very annoying or difficult person.
**ter·ror·ism** (ter′ēr-iz'm), *n.* 1. the use of terror and violence to intimidate, subjugate, etc., especially as a political policy. 2. a state of intimidation, etc. produced by terror. —**ter′ror·ist,** *n.* —**ter′ror·is′tic,** *adj.*
**ter·ror·ize** (ter′ə-rīz′), *v.t.* [-IZED, -IZING], 1. to fill with terror; terrify. 2. to coerce, maintain power, etc. by inducing terror. —**ter′ror·i·za′tion,** *n.* —**ter′ror·iz′er,** *n.*
**ter·ror-strick·en** (ter′ēr-strik′'n), *adj.* stricken with terror; terrified.
**ter·ry** (ter′i), *n.* [*pl.* -RIES], [prob. < Fr. pp. of *tirer,* to draw], a cloth having a pile in which the loops are left uncut: also **terry cloth.**
**terse** (tũrs), *adj.* [TERSER, TERSEST], [< L. pp. of *tergere,* to wipe], free of superfluous words; concise; succinct. —**terse′ly,** *adv.* —**terse′ness,** *n.*
**ter·tial** (tũr′shəl), *adj.* [< L. *tertius,* third], designating or of the third row of flight feathers on a bird's wing. *n.* a tertial feather.
**ter·tian** (tũr′shən), *adj.* [< L. < *tertius,* third], occurring every other day. *n.* a tertian fever, etc.
**ter·ti·ar·y** (tũr′shi-er′i, -shə-ri), *adj.* [< L. < *tertius,* third], 1. of the third rank, order, formation, etc.; third. 2. [T-], in *geology,* designating or of the first period of the Cenozoic Era: see **geology,** chart. 3. tertial. *n.* [*pl.* -IES], 1. [T-], the Tertiary Period. 2. a tertial feather.
**tes·sel·late** (tes′ə-lāt′), *v.t.* [-LATED, -LATING], [< L. < *tessella,* little square stone], to lay out or pave in a mosaic pattern of small, square blocks. *adj.* (-lit), tessellated. —**tes′sel·la′tion,** *n.*
**test** (test), *n.* [OFr., cup used in assaying < L. *testum,* earthen vessel], 1. *a*) an examination or trial, as to prove the value or ascertain the nature of something. *b*) the method or process, or a standard or criterion, used in this. 2. an event, situation, etc. that tries a person's qualities. 3. a set of questions, problems, etc. for determining a person's knowledge, abilities, etc.; examination. 4. in *chemistry, a*) a trial or reaction for identifying a substance. *b*) the reagent used in the procedure. *c*) a positive indication obtained by it. *v.t.* to subject to, or examine by, a test; try. —**test′a·ble,** *adj.* —**test′er,** *n.*
**Test.,** Testament.
**tes·ta** (tes′tə), *n.* [*pl.* -TAE (-tē)], [L., a shell], in *botany,* the hard outer covering of a seed.
**tes·ta·ment** (tes′tə-mənt), *n.* [Fr. < L.; ult. < *testis,* a witness], 1. in the *Bible,* a covenant. 2. [T-], either of the two parts of the Bible, the *Old Testament* and the *New Testament*: so called because considered covenants between God and man. 3. [T-], [Colloq.], the New Testament. 4. in *law,* a will: usually in *last will and testament.*
**tes·ta·men·ta·ry** (tes′tə-men′tə-ri), *adj.* 1. of a testament, or will, or its administration. 2. bequeathed by, or contained in, a will. 3. done in accordance with a will. —**tes′ta·men′ta·ri·ly,** *adv.*
**tes·tate** (tes′tāt), *adj.* [L. *testatus,* pp. of *testari,* to testify], having made and left a legally valid will. *n.* a person who has died testate.
**tes·ta·tor** (tes′tā-tēr, tes-tā′-), *n.* one who has made a will or has died testate. —**tes·ta′trix** [*pl.* -TRICES (-tri-sēz′)], *n.fem.*
**tes·ti·cle** (tes′ti-k'l), *n.* [< L. dim. of *testis,* testicle], the male sex gland; either of two oval structures in the scrotum, that secrete spermatozoa. —**tes·tic′u·lar** (-tik′yoo-lēr), *adj.*
**tes·ti·fy** (tes′tə-fī′), *v.i.* [-FIED, -FYING], [< OFr. < L. < *testis,* a witness + *facere,* to make], 1. to bear witness; give evidence, especially under oath in court. 2. to be evidence; serve as an indication: as, his words *testify* to his rage. *v.t.* 1. to bear witness to; affirm; give as evidence, especially under oath in court. 2. to be evidence of; indicate. 3. to profess publicly, as one's belief. —**tes′ti·fi·ca′tion,** *n.* —**tes′ti·fi′er,** *n.*
**tes·ti·mo·ni·al** (tes′tə-mō′ni-əl), *n.* 1. a written statement testifying as to a person's abilities, character, etc. or to the value of some product, etc. 2. something given as an expression of gratitude or as a tribute. *adj.* given as a testimonial.
**tes·ti·mo·ny** (tes′tə-mō′ni), *n.* [*pl.* -NIES], [< L. < *testis,* a witness], 1. a statement made to establish a fact, especially one made under oath in court. 2. any affirmation or declaration. 3. any form of evidence; indication: as, his smile was *testimony* of his joy. 4. public avowal, as of faith.
**tes·tis** (tes′tis), *n.* [*pl.* -TES (-tēz)], [L.], a testicle.
**tes·tos·ter·one** (tes-tos′tə-rōn′), *n.* [< *testes* + *sterol* + *-one*], a male sex hormone, $C_{19}H_{28}O_2$, a crystalline steroid obtained from animal testes or synthesized.
**test pilot,** a pilot who tests new airplanes in flight to prove their fitness for use.
**test tube,** a tube of thin, clear glass closed at one end, used in chemical experiments, etc.

**tes·tu·do** (tes-tōō′dō, -tū′-), *n.* [*pl.* -DINES (-də-nēz′)], [L., tortoise (shell)], in ancient Rome, 1. a movable, roofed shelter for protection, as during a siege. 2. a protection formed by a body of soldiers by overlapping their shields over their heads.
**tes·ty** (tes′ti), *adj.* [-TIER, -TIEST], [< OFr. < L. *testa*, skull], irritable; touchy; peevish. **—tes′ti·ly,** *adv.* **—tes′ti·ness,** *n.*
**tet·a·nus** (tet′ə-nəs), *n.* [L. < Gr. *tetanos*, spasm, lit., stretched], an acute infectious disease, often fatal, caused by the toxins of a bacillus which usually enters the body through wounds: characterized by spasmodic contractions and rigidity of muscles: cf. **lockjaw. —te·tan·ic** (ti-tan′ik), *adj.*
**tetched** (techt), *adj.* [Dial. or Humorous], touched; slightly demented.
**tetch·y** (tech′i), *adj.* [-IER, -IEST], [< OFr. *tache*, a quality], touchy; irritable; peevish. **—tetch′i·ly,** *adv.* **—tetch′i·ness,** *n.*
**tête-à-tête** (tāt′ə-tāt′), *n.* [Fr., head-to-head], 1. a private conversation between two people. 2. an S-shaped seat on which two people can sit facing each other. *adj.* for or of two people in private. *adv.* together privately: as, to speak *tête-à-tête.*
**teth·er** (teth′ẽr), *n.* [< ON. *tiōthr*], 1. a rope or chain fastened to an animal so as to keep it within certain bounds. 2. the range of one's abilities, resources, etc. *v.t.* to fasten with a tether. **—at the end of one's tether,** at the end of one's endurance, resources, etc.
**tet·ra-,** [Gr. < base of *tettares*, four], a combining form meaning *four*: also **tetr-.**
**tet·ra·chlo·ride** (tet′rə-klôr′īd, -klō′rid), *n.* [*tetra-* + *chloride*], any chemical compound with four chlorine atoms to the molecule.
**tet·ra·chord** (tet′rə-kôrd′), *n.* [< Gr.; see TETRA- & CHORD], in *music*, a series of four tones comprising an interval of a fourth. **—tet′ra·chor′dal,** *adj.*
**tet·rad** (tet′rad), *n.* [< Gr. *tetras*, four], 1. the number four. 2. a group or set of four.
**tet·ra·eth·yl lead** (tet′rə-eth′əl), see **ethyl.**
**tet·ra·he·dron** (tet′rə-hē′drən), *n.* [*pl.* -DRONS, -DRA (-drə)], [< LGr.; see TETRA- & -HEDRON], a solid figure with four triangular surfaces. **—tet′ra·he′dral,** *adj.*

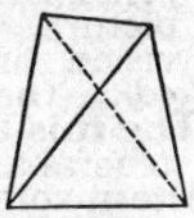
TETRAHEDRON

**te·tral·o·gy** (te-tral′ə-ji), *n.* [*pl.* -GIES], [see TETRA- & -LOGY], any series of four related dramatic, operatic, or literary compositions.
**te·tram·e·ter** (te-tram′ə-tẽr), *n.* [< LL. < Gr.; see TETRA- & -METER (rhythm)], 1. a line of verse containing four metrical feet. 2. verse consisting of tetrameters. *adj.* having four metrical feet.
**te·trarch** (tet′rärk, tē′trärk), *n.* [< LL. < L. < Gr. < *tetra-*, four + *archos*, ruler], 1. in the ancient Roman Empire, the ruler of part (originally a fourth part) of a province. 2. a subordinate prince, governor, etc. **—te·trar′chic** (-trär′kik), *adj.*
**te·trarch·y** (tet′rär-ki, tē′trär-), *n.* [*pl.* -IES], the rule or territory of a tetrarch.
**tet·ra·va·lent** (tet′rə-vā′lənt, te-trav′ə-), *adj.* 1. having a valence of four. 2. having four valences. Also, esp. for 2, **quadrivalent. —tet′ra·va′lence, tet′ra·va′len·cy,** *n.*
**te·trox·ide** (te-trok′sīd, -sid), *n.* any oxide with four atoms of oxygen in each molecule: also **te-trox′id** (-sid).
**tet·ter** (tet′ẽr), *n.* [AS. *teter*], any of various skin diseases, as eczema, characterized by itching.
**Teut.,** 1. Teuton. 2. Teutonic.
**Teu·ton** (tōō′t'n, tū′-), *n.* 1. a member of the Teutones. 2. a member of any Teutonic people; esp., a German.
**Teu·to·nes** (tōō′tə-nēz′, tū′-), *n.pl.* an ancient tribe, either Teutonic or Celtic, that lived in Jutland.
**Teu·ton·ic** (tōō-ton′ik, tū-), *adj.* 1. of the ancient Teutons. 2. German. 3. designating or of a group of north European peoples including the German, Scandinavian, Dutch, English, etc. 4. [Now Rare], in *linguistics*, Germanic.
**Tex·as** (tek′səs), *n.* a Southern State of the U.S.: area, 267,339 sq. mi.; pop., 9,580,000; capital, Austin: abbrev. **Tex. —Tex′an,** *adj.* & *n.*
**Texas fever,** an infectious disease of cattle.
**Texas leaguer,** [Slang], in *baseball*, a safely hit fly ball falling between the infield and outfield.
**text** (tekst), *n.* [< OFr. < L. *textus*, fabric, pp. of *texere*, to weave], 1. the actual or original words of an author, as distinguished from notes, paraphrase, etc. 2. *a*) the version set forth by a particular editor as most nearly representing the author's original work. *b*) any form in which a writing exists: as, a corrupt *text.* 3. the principal matter on a printed page, as distinguished from notes, pictures, etc. 4. a Biblical passage used as the topic of a sermon, etc. 5. a topic; subject. 6. a textbook.
**text·book** (tekst′book′), *n.* a book giving instruction in the principles of a subject of study.
**tex·tile** (teks′t'l, -til, -tīl), *adj.* [< L. *textilis* < *textus*; see TEXT], 1. having to do with weaving or woven fabrics. 2. woven. 3. that can be woven. *n.* 1. a woven fabric; cloth. 2. raw material suitable for weaving, as cotton, flax, wool, etc.
**tex·tu·al** (teks′chōō-əl), *adj.* of, contained in, or based on a text. **—tex′tu·al·ly,** *adv.*
**tex·ture** (teks′chẽr), *n.* [< L. < *texere*, to weave], 1. the character of a fabric, determined by the arrangement, size, etc. of its threads: as, a coarse, or ribbed, *texture.* 2. the arrangement of the constituent parts of anything, as wood, a food, etc.; structure; composition. **—tex′tur·al,** *adj.* **—tex′tur·al·ly,** *adv.* **—tex′tured,** *adj.*
**-th,** [< AS.], a suffix meaning: 1. *the action of -ing*, as in *stealth.* 2. *the state* or *quality of being* or *having*, as in *wealth.*
**-th,** [< AS.], a suffix used in forming ordinal numerals, as *fourth*: also **-eth.**
**-th,** archaic inflectional verbal ending: see **-eth.**
**Th,** in *chemistry*, thorium.
**Th.,** Thursday.
**T.H.,** (former) Territory of Hawaii.
**Thack·er·ay, William Make·peace** (māk′pēs′ thak′ẽr-i), 1811–1863; English novelist.
**Tha·i** (tä′ē, tī), *n.* 1. a branch of the Sino-Tibetan languages, including Siamese. 2. a member of a group of Thai-speaking peoples in Indochina. 3. a native of Thailand. *adj.* 1. of these people or their language. 2. of Thailand.
**Thai·land** (tī′lənd), *n.* a country in SE Asia: area, 200,234 sq. mi.; pop., 25 520,000; capital, Bangkok: former name, *Siam.*
**thal·a·mus** (thal′ə-məs), *n.* [*pl.* -MI (-mī′)], [L. < Gr. *thalamos*, inner room], 1. in *anatomy*, a large, ovoid mass of gray matter at the base of the brain, involved in the transmission of certain sensations: also **optic thalamus.** 2. in *botany*, the receptacle of a flower. **—tha·lam·ic** (thə-lam′ik), *adj.*
**tha·ler** (tä′lẽr), *n.* [*pl.* THALER], a taler.
**Tha·li·a** (thə-lī′ə, thāl′yə), *n.* in *Gr. mythology*, 1. the Muse of comedy and pastoral poetry. 2. one of the three Graces.
**thal·li·um** (thal′i-əm), *n.* [< Gr. *thallos*, green shoot: from its green spectrum line], a rare, bluish-white, soft, metallic chemical element: symbol, Tl; at. wt., 204.39; at. no., 81.
**thal·lo·phyte** (thal′ə-fīt′), *n.* [see THALLUS & -PHYTE], any of a primary division of plants including the bacteria, algae, fungi, and lichens: cf. **thallus. —thal′lo·phyt′ic** (-fit′ik), *adj.*
**thal·lus** (thal′əs), *n.* [*pl.* -LI (-ī), -LUSES], [< Gr. *thallos*, young shoot], the plant body of a thallophyte, showing no clear distinction of roots, stem, or leaves. **—thal′loid** (-oid), *adj.*
**Thames** (temz), *n.* a river in S England, flowing eastward through London to the North Sea.
**than** (*th*an, *th*en; *unstressed th*ən), *conj.* [< AS. *thenne*, orig., then], a particle used: 1. to introduce the second element in a comparison: as, I am taller *than* Bill. 2. to express exception: as, it was none other *than* Sam. *prep.* compared to: only in the phrases *than whom, than which*, as, a writer *than whom* there is none finer.
**than·a·top·sis** (than′ə-top′sis), *n.* [< Gr. *thanatos*, death; + *-opsis*], a musing upon death.
**thane** (thān), *n.* [< AS. *thegen*], 1. in early England, one of a class of freemen who held land of the king or a lord in return for military services. 2. in early Scotland, a person of rank who held land of the king. Also sp. **thegn.**
**thank** (thaŋk), *v.t.* [< AS. *thancian*], 1. to give one's thanks to. 2. to hold responsible; blame: an ironic use, as, he can be *thanked* for our failure. **—have oneself to thank,** to be oneself the cause of (something unpleasant). **—thank′er,** *n.*
**thank·ful** (thaŋk′fəl), *adj.* feeling or expressing thanks. **—thank′ful·ly,** *adv.* **—thank′ful·ness,** *n.*
**thank·less** (thaŋk′lis), *adj.* 1. not feeling or expressing thanks; ungrateful. 2. that receives or deserves no thanks; unappreciated. **—thank′-less·ly,** *adv.* **—thank′less·ness,** *n.*
**thanks** (thaŋks), *n.pl.* an expression of gratitude. *interj.* I thank you. **—thanks to,** 1. thanks be given to. 2. on account of.

**thanks·giv·ing** (thaŋks′giv′iŋ, thaŋks′giv′-), *n.* 1. a giving of thanks. 2. an expression of this. 3. a formal public expression of thanks to God. 4. [T-], an annual U.S. holiday, usually the fourth Thursday of November, instituted by the Pilgrims to give thanks to God for their survival: in full, **Thanksgiving Day.**

**Thant, U** (o͞o thônt), 1909– ; Burmese statesman; secretary-general of the United Nations (1961– ).

**that** (*that*; *unstressed* thət), *pron.* [*pl.* THOSE], [AS. *thæt*], *as a demonstrative pronoun*: 1. the person or thing mentioned or understood: as, *that* is John. 2. the thing farther away: as, I can see this more clearly than *that*. 3. something being contrasted: as, this is better than *that*. *as a relative pronoun*: 1. who, whom, or which: generally in restrictive clauses (e.g., the road *that* we took). 2. where; at which: as, the place *that* I saw him. 3. when; in which: as, the year *that* he died. *adj.* 1. designating the one mentioned or understood: as, *that* man is John. 2. designating the thing farther away: as, this house is newer than *that* one across the street. 3. designating something being contrasted: as, this car is better than *that* one. 4. designating a person or thing that is not described but that is well known: as, *that* certain feeling. *conj.* *that* is used: 1. to introduce a noun clause: as, *that* he's gone is obvious. 2. to introduce a clause expressing purpose: as, they died *that* we might live. 3. to introduce a clause expressing result: as, he ran so fast *that* I lost him. 4. to introduce a clause expressing cause: as, I'm sorry *that* I won. 5. to introduce an ellipitical sentence expressing surprise, desire, etc.: as, oh, *that* he were here! *adv.* to that extent; so: as, I can't see *that* far: also used colloquially before an adjective modified by a clause of result, as, I'm *that* tired I could drop. **—at that,** [Colloq.], 1. at that point. 2. all things considered; even so. **—in that,** because. **—that's that** that is settled!

**thatch** (thach), *n.* [< AS. *thæc*], 1. a roof or roofing of straw, rushes, palm leaves, etc. 2. material for such a roof: also **thatch′ing.** 3. any of various palms whose leaves are used for thatch: also **thatch palm.** *v.t.* to cover with or as with thatch. **—thatch′y** [-IER, -IEST], *adj.*

**thau·ma·tur·gy** (thô′mə-tũr′ji), *n.* [< Gr. < *thauma*, a wonder + *ergon*, work], the supposed working of miracles; magic. **—thau′ma·tur′gic, thau′ma·tur′gi·cal,** *adj.*

**thaw** (thô), *v.i.* [< AS. *thawian*], 1. to melt, as ice, snow, etc. 2. to have its contents melt: as, our water pipe *thawed*. 3. to rise above freezing, so that snow, etc. melts: with *it*, said of weather, as, it will *thaw* tomorrow. 4. to lose one's coldness or reserve of manner. *v.t.* to cause to thaw. *n.* 1. a thawing. 2. a spell of weather warm enough to allow a thawing. 3. a becoming less reserved. **—thaw′er,** *n.*

**Th. B.,** *Theologiae Baccalaureus*, [L.], Bachelor of Theology.

**Th. D.,** *Theologiae Doctor*, [L.], Doctor of Theology.

**the** (*thə*; *before vowels*, *thi*), *adj.*, *definite article* [< AS. *se, the*], 1. *the* (as opposed to *a, an*) refers to a particular person or thing, as: *a*) that (one) being spoken of: as, *the* story ended. *b*) that (one) which is present, close, etc.: as, *the* day is hot. *c*) that (one) designated, as by a title: as, *the* Ohio (River). *d*) that (one) considered outstanding, etc.: as, that's *the* hotel in town: usually given special emphasis. *e*) that (one) belonging to a person previously mentioned: as, take me by *the* hand. *f*) that (one) considered as a unit of purchase, etc.: as, ten cents *the* dozen. *g*) [Colloq.], that (one) in a specified relationship to one: as, *the* wife. 2. *the* is used to refer to that one of a number of persons or things which is identified by a modifier, as by an attributive adjective, relative clause, prepositional phrase, etc. 3. *the* is used to refer to a person or thing considered generically, as: *a*) one taken as the representative of the entire genus or type: as, *the* cow is a domestic animal. *b*) an adjective used substantively: as, *the* good, *the* true. *adv.* 1. that much; to that extent: as, *the* better to see you with. 2. by how much. . . by that much; to what extent. . . to that extent: used in a correlative construction expressing comparison, as, *the* sooner *the* better.

**the·a·ter, the·a·tre** (thē′ə-tẽr; *now dial.*, thē-ā′tẽr), *n.* [< OFr. < L. < Gr. *theatron* < base of *theasthai*, to view], 1. a place or building where plays, motion pictures, etc. are presented. 2. any place like a theater, especially one having ascending rows of seats, as a surgical clinic. 3. any scene of events: as, the Pacific *theater* of war. 4. *a*) the dramatic art; drama. *b*) the theatrical world.

**the·at·ri·cal** (thi-at′ri-k'l), *adj.* 1. having to do with the theater. 2. characteristic of the theater; dramatic; histrionic; esp. (in disparagement), melodramatic; affected. Also **the·at′ric. —the·at′ri·cal·ism, the·at′ri·cal′i·ty** (-kal′ə-ti), **the·at′ri·cal·ness,** *n.* **—the·at′ri·cal·ly,** *adv.*

**the·at·ri·cals** (thi-at′ri-k'lz), *n.pl.* performances of stage plays, especially by amateurs.

**Thebes** (thēbz), *n.* 1. an ancient city in Egypt on the Nile. 2. an ancient city of Greece in Boeotia. **—The·ban** (thē′bən), *adj.* & *n.*

**the·ca** (thē′kə), *n.* [*pl.* -CAE (-sē)], [L. < Gr. *thēkē*, a case], 1. in botany, a spore case, sac, or capsule. 2. in *zoology*, any sac enclosing an organ or a whole organism, as the covering of an insect pupa. **—the′cal,** *adj.* **—the′cate** (-kit), *adj.*

**thee** (*thē*), *pron.* [AS. *the*], the objective case of **thou**: also used in place of **thou** by Friends (Quakers): as, *thee* speaks well.

**theft** (theft), *n.* [AS. *thiefth*], the act or an instance of stealing; larceny.

**thegn** (thān), *n.* a thane.

**the·ine** (thē′in, -ēn), *n.* [< Fr. < *thé*, tea], caffeine, especially as found in tea: also **the′in** (-in).

**their** (thâr), *pron.* [< ON. *theirra*], possessive form of **they.** *possessive pronominal adj.* of, belonging to, or done by them: as, *their* work.

**theirs** (*th*ârz), *pron.* that or those belonging to them: as, that book is *theirs*, *theirs* are better: often after *of*, as, a friend of *theirs*.

**the·ism** (thē′iz'm), *n.* [< Gr. *theos*, god], 1. belief in a god or gods. 2. belief in one God who is creator and ruler of the universe. **—the′ist,** *n.* & *adj.* **—the·is′tic, the·is′ti·cal,** *adj.* **—the·is′ti·cal·ly,** *adv.*

**them** (*them*; *unstressed* thəm), *pron.* [< ON. *theim*], the objective case of **they**: also used colloquially as a predicate complement with a linking verb (e.g., that's *them*).

**theme** (thēm), *n.* [< OFr. < L. < Gr. *thema* < base of *tithenai*, to put], 1. a topic, as of a lecture, essay, etc. 2. a short essay, especially one written as a school assignment. 3. a short melody constituting the subject of a musical composition or a phrase upon which variations are developed. 4. the principal tune or song of a musical play or motion picture, or the signature music of a radio or television program: also **theme song. —the·mat′ic,** *adj.* **—the·mat′i·cal·ly,** *adv.*

**The·mis·to·cles** (thə-mis′tə-klēz′), *n.* Athenian general and statesman; 527?–460? B.C.

**them·selves** (*th*əm-selvz′), *pron.* a form of the third person plural pronoun, used: 1. as an intensive: as, they went *themselves*. 2. as a reflexive: as, they hurt *themselves*.

**then** (*th*en), *adv.* [see THAN], 1. at that time: as, I did it *then*. 2. soon afterward; next in time: as, he ate and *then* slept. 3. next in order: as, yours is first, *then* mine. 4. in that case; accordingly: as, if he read it, *then* he knows. 5. besides; moreover: as, I like to walk, and *then* it's cheaper. 6. at another time: as, now she's sullen, *then* gay. *adj.* being such at that time: as, the *then* director. *n.* that time: as, by *then*, they were gone. **—but then,** but on the other hand. **—then and there,** at that time and in that place; at once. **—what then?** what would happen in that case?

**thence** (*th*ens, thens), *adv.* [< AS. *thanan*], 1. from that place; therefrom. 2. from that time; thenceforth. 3. on that account; therefore.

**thence·forth** (thens′fôrth′, thens′fōrth′), *adv.* from that time onward; thereafter: also **thence′for′ward, thence′for′wards.**

**the·o-,** [< Gr. *theos*, god], a combining form meaning *a god* or *God*: also **the-.**

**the·oc·ra·cy** (thē-ok′rə-si), *n.* [*pl.* -CIES], [< Gr. < *theos*, god + *kratein*, to rule], 1. literally, the rule of a state by God or a god. 2. government by priests claiming to rule with divine authority. 3. a country so governed. **—the·o·crat** (thē′ə-krat′), *n.* **—the′o·crat′ic, the′o·crat′i·cal,** *adj.* **—the′o·crat′i·cal·ly,** *adv.*

**the·od·o·lite** (thē-od′ə-līt′), *n.* [prob. coined, c. 1571], a surveying instrument used to measure vertical and horizontal angles.

**theol.,** 1. theologian. 2. theology.

**the·o·lo·gi·an** (thē′ə-lō′jən, -ji-ən), *n.* a student of or authority on theology.

**the·o·log·i·cal** (thē′ə-loj′i-k'l), *adj.* 1. of the word of God; scriptural. 2. of theology. Also **the′o·log′ic. —the′o·log′i·cal·ly,** *adv.*

**the·ol·o·gize** (thē-ol′ə-jīz′), *v.t.* [-GIZED, -GIZING], to put into theological terms. *v.i.* to speculate in a theological manner.

**the·ol·o·gy** (thē-ol′ə-ji), *n.* [*pl.* -GIES], [< OFr. < L. < Gr. < *theos*, god + *logos*, discourse], 1. the study of God and of religious doctrines and matters of divinity. 2. a specific system of this study.

**the·o·rem** (thē′ə-rəm), *n.* [< Fr. < L. < Gr.

*theōrēma* < *theōrein*, to view], 1. a proposition that is not self-evident but that can be proved from accepted premises and so is established as a law or principle. 2. an expression of relations in an equation or formula. 3. in *mathematics & physics*, a proposition embodying something to be proved. **—the′o·re·mat′ic** (-rə-mat′ik), *adj.*

**the·o·ret·i·cal** (thē′ə-ret′i-k'l), *adj.* 1. of or constituting theory. 2. limited to or based on theory; hypothetical; ideal. 3. tending to theorize; speculative. Also **the′o·ret′ic.**

**the·o·ret·i·cal·ly** (thē′ə-ret′i-k'l-i, -ik-li), *adv.* in theory; according to theory.

**the·o·re·ti·cian** (thē′ə-rə-tish′ən), *n.* a student of or authority on the theory of an art, science, etc.

**the·o·rist** (thē′ə-rist), *n.* one who theorizes; esp., a specialist in the theory of an art, science, etc.

**the·o·rize** (thē′ə-rīz′), *v.i.* [-RIZED, -RIZING], to form a theory or theories; speculate. **—the′o·riz′er,** *n.* **—the′o·ri·za′tion,** *n.*

**the·o·ry** (thē′ə-ri), *n.* [*pl.* -RIES], [< Fr. < LL. < Gr. < *theōrein*, to view], 1. an idea or plan of the way to do something. 2. a systematic statement of principles involved. 3. a formulation of apparent relationships or underlying principles of certain observed phenomena which has been verified to some degree. 4. that branch of an art or science consisting in a knowledge of its principles and methods rather than in its practice. 5. popularly, a mere conjecture, guess, etc.

**the·os·o·phy** (thē-os′ə-fi), *n.* [< ML. < LGr.; ult. < Gr. *theos*, god + *sophos*, wise], 1. any of various philosophies or religions that propose to establish direct contact with divine principle through contemplation, revelation, etc. 2. [often T-], the doctrines of a modern sect of this nature, incorporating elements of Buddhism and Brahmanism. **—the′o·soph′ic** (-ə-sof′ik), **the′o·soph′i·cal,** *adj.* **—the′o·soph′i·cal·ly,** *adv.* **—the·os′o·phist,** *n.*

**ther·a·peu·tic** (ther′ə-pū′tik), *adj.* [< Gr. < *therapeuein*, to nurse], 1. serving to cure or heal; curative. 2. of therapeutics. Also **ther′a·peu′ti·cal.** **—ther′a·peu′ti·cal·ly,** *adv.*

**ther·a·peu·tics** (ther′ə-pū′tiks), *n.pl.* [construed as sing.], the branch of medicine that deals with the treatment and cure of diseases; therapy.

**ther·a·py** (ther′ə-pi), *n.* [*pl.* -PIES], [< Gr. < *therapeuein*, to nurse], 1. therapeutics: often used in compounds, as *hydrotherapy*. 2. therapeutic nature or power. **—ther′a·pist,** *n.*

**there** (thâr), *adv.* [AS. *ther*], 1. at or in that place: often used as an intensive, as, John *there* is a good boy. 2. toward, to, or into that place: as, go *there.* 3. at that point in action, speech, etc. 4. in that matter, respect, etc.: as, *there* you are wrong. 5. right now: as, *there* goes the whistle. *There* is also used: *a*) in interjectional phrases of approval, etc. (e.g., *there's* a fine fellow!). *b*) in impersonal constructions in which the real subject follows the verb (e.g., *there* are three men here). *n.* that place: as, we left *there* at six. *interj.* *there* is used as an exclamation expressing defiance, dismay, satisfaction, sympathy, etc. (e.g., *there, there!* don't worry). **—not all there,** [Colloq.], insane or feebleminded.

**there·a·bouts** (*th*âr′ə-bouts′), *adv.* 1. near that place. 2. near that time. 3. near that number, amount, degree, etc. Also **there′a·bout′.**

**there·aft·er** (*th*âr-af′tẽr, -äf′-), *adv.* 1. after that; subsequently. 2. [Rare], accordingly.

**there·at** (*th*âr-at′), *adv.* 1. at that place; there. 2. at that time. 3. at that; for that reason.

**there·by** (*th*âr-bī′, *th*âr′bī′), *adv.* 1. by that means; by or through that. 2. connected with that: as, *thereby* hangs a tale. 3. thereabouts.

**there·for** (*th*âr-fôr′), *adv.* for this or that; for it.

**there·fore** (*th*âr′fôr′, -fōr′), *adv. & conj.* for this or that reason; consequently; hence.

**there·from** (*th*âr-frum′, -from′), *adv.* from this or that; from it.

**there·in** (*th*âr-in′), *adv.* 1. in there; in or into that place or thing. 2. in that matter, detail, etc.

**there·in·to** (*th*âr-in′tōō, *th*âr′in-tōō′), *adv.* 1. into that place or thing. 2. into that matter.

**there·of** (*th*âr-uv′, -ov′), *adv.* 1. of that; of it. 2. from that as a cause, reason, etc.

**there·on** (*th*âr-on′, -ôn′), *adv.* 1. on that. 2. immediately following that; thereupon.

**there's** (*th*ârz), there is.

**there·to** (*th*âr-tōō′), *adv.* 1. to that place, thing, etc. 2. [Archaic or Poetic], in addition to that.

**there·to·fore** (*th*âr′tə-fôr′, -fōr′), *adv.* up to that time; until then; before that.

**there·un·der** (*th*âr-un′dẽr), *adv.* 1. under that; under it. 2. by that authority.

**there·un·to** (*th*âr′ən-tōō′, *th*âr-un′tōō), *adv.* thereto (sense 1).

**there·up·on** (*th*âr′ə-pon′, *th*âr′ə-pôn′), *adv.* 1. immediately following that. 2. as a consequence of that. 3. concerning that subject, etc.

**there·with** (*th*âr-*with*′, -with′), *adv.* 1. with that or this; with it. 2. in addition to that. 3. immediately thereafter; thereupon.

**there·with·al** (*th*âr′*with*-ôl′), *adv.* 1. in addition; besides. 2. [Obs.], with that or this.

**ther·mal** (thũr′m'l), *adj.* [Fr. < Gr. *thermē*, heat], 1. having to do with heat, hot springs, etc. 2. warm or hot. **—ther′mal·ly,** *adv.*

**ther·mic** (thũr′mik), *adj.* of or caused by heat. **—ther′mi·cal·ly,** *adv.*

**ther·mo-,** [< Gr. *thermē*, heat], a combining form meaning: *heat*, as in *thermodynamics*: also **therm-.**

**ther·mo·dy·nam·ic** (thũr′mō-dī-nam′ik), *adj.* 1. having to do with thermodynamics. 2. operated by heat converted into motive power. Also **ther′mo·dy·nam′i·cal.**

**ther·mo·dy·nam·ics** (thũr′mō-dī-nam′iks), *n.pl.* [construed as sing.], the science that deals with the relationship of heat and mechanical energy and the conversion of one into the other.

**thermoelectric couple,** a junction of two bars, wires, etc. of dissimilar metals which produces thermoelectric current when heated, used in temperature measurements, etc.: also **thermoelectric pair.**

**ther·mo·e·lec·tric·i·ty** (thũr′mō-i-lek′tris′ə-ti), *n* electricity produced by heat. **—ther′mo·e·lec′tric, ther′mo·e·lec′tri·cal,** *adj.* **—ther′mo·e·lec′tri·cal·ly,** *adv.*

**ther·mom·e·ter** (thẽr-mom′ə-tẽr), *n.* [*thermo-* + *-meter*], an instrument for measuring temperatures, as one consisting of a graduated glass tube with a capillary bore in which mercury, etc. rises or falls as it expands or contracts from changes in temperature: see **centigrade, Fahrenheit.** **—ther·mo·met·ric** (thũr′mə-met′rik), **ther′mo·met′ri·cal,** *adj.*

**ther·mo·nu·cle·ar** (thũr′mō-nōō′kli-ẽr, -nū′-), *adj.* designating, of, or employing the heat energy released in nuclear fission.

**ther·mo·pile** (thũr′mə-pīl′), *n.* [*thermo-* + *pile* (a heap)], an instrument for measuring minute changes in temperature or for generating thermoelectric current.

**ther·mo·plas·tic** (thũr′mə-plas′tik), *adj.* soft and moldable when subjected to heat: said of certain plastics. *n.* a thermoplastic substance.

**Ther·mop·y·lae** (thẽr-mop′ə-li), *n.* a mountain pass in E Greece: scene of a battle (480 B.C.) in which the Spartans were overcome after holding off the Persian army.

**ther·mos bottle** (or **flask, jug**) (thũr′məs), [Gr. *thermos*, hot], a bottle, flask, or jug for keeping liquids at almost their original temperature for several hours: a trade-mark (**Thermos**).

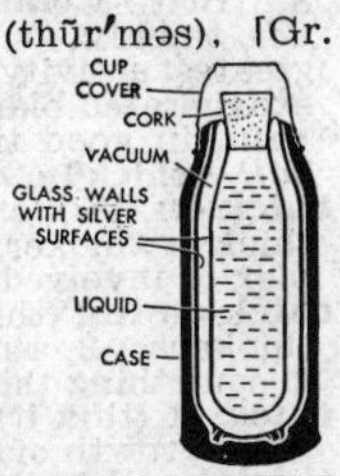

THERMOS BOTTLE

**ther·mo·set·ting** (thũr′mō-set′-iŋ), *adj.* becoming permanently hard and unmoldable when once subjected to heat: said of certain plastics.

**ther·mo·stat** (thũr′mə-stat′), *n.* [*thermo-* + *-stat*], 1. an apparatus for regulating temperature, especially one that automatically controls a heating unit. 2. a device that sets off a sprinkler, etc. at a certain heat. **—ther′mo·stat′ic,** *adj.* **—ther′mo·stat′i·cal·ly,** *adv.*

**ther·mot·ro·pism** (thẽr-mot′rə-piz′m), *n.* [*thermo-* + *-tropism*], the tendency of a plant to grow toward or away from a source of heat. **—ther′mo·trop′ic** (-mə-trop′ik), *adj.* **—ther′mo·trop′i·cal·ly,** *adv.*

**-ther·my** (thũr′mi), [< Gr. *thermē*, heat], a combining form meaning *heat* or *the production of heat.*

**the·sau·rus** (thi-sô′rəs), *n.* [*pl.* -RI (-rī), -RUSES], [L. < Gr. *thēsauros*, a treasure], 1. a treasury or storehouse. 2. a book containing a store of words, as a dictionary, book of synonyms, etc.

**these** (*th*ēz), *pron. & adj.* pl. of **this.**

**The·seus** (thē′sōōs, -sūs, -si-əs), *n.* in *Gr. legend*, the principal hero of Attica, king of Athens: he is famed for many exploits, especially for his killing of the Minotaur.

**the·sis** (thē′sis), *n.* [*pl.* -SES (-sēz)], [L. < Gr. *thesis*, a placing < base of *tithenai*, to put], 1. a proposition to be defended in argument. 2. an essay presented by a candidate for an academic degree as evidence of individual research in a subject. 3. in *logic*, an unproved statement assumed as a premise.

**Thes·pi·an** (thes′pi-ən), *adj.* [after *Thespis*, Greek poet of 6th c. B.C.], having to do with the drama, especially with tragedy. *n.* an actor; esp., a tragedian: humorous or pretentious usage.

**Thes·sa·lo·ni·ans** (thes′ə-lō′ni-ənz), *n.pl.* [construed as sing.], either of two books of the New Testament, messages from the Apostle Paul to the Christians of Thessalonica: abbrev. **Thess.**

**Thes·sa·lon·ic·a** (thes′ə-lon′i-kə), *n.* Salonika, a city in Greece: an ancient name. —**Thes′sa·lo′ni·an** (-lō′ni-ən), *adj. & n.*

**Thes·sa·ly** (thes′ə-li), *n.* an ancient region in NE Greece. —**Thes·sa·li·an** (the-sā′li-ən), *adj. & n.*

**the·ta** (thā′tə, thē′-), *n.* [Gr.], the eighth letter of the Greek alphabet (Θ, θ, ϑ).

**The·tis** (thē′tis), *n.* in *Gr. mythology*, Achilles' mother, one of the Nereids.

**thews** (thūz, thōōz), *n.pl.* [*sing.* THEW], [< AS. *theaw*, custom, habit], 1. muscular power; bodily strength. 2. *rarely in sing.* muscles or sinews. —**thew′y** [-IER, -IEST], *adj.*

**they** (*th*ā), *pron.* [for *sing.* see HE, SHE, IT], [< ON. *their*], 1. the persons, animals, or things previously mentioned: *they* is the nominative, *them* the objective, *their* and *theirs* the possessive, and *themselves* the intensive and reflexive, of the third personal plural pronoun. 2. people generally or indefinitely: as, *they* say it will rain.

**they'd** (*th*ād), 1. they had. 2. they would.

**they'll** (*th*āl), 1. they will. 2. they shall.

**they're** (*th*âr), they are.

**they've** (*th*āv), they have.

**thi-**, thio-.

**thi·a·mine** (thī′ə-mēn′, -min), *n.* [*thi-* + *amine*], a white, crystalline compound, $C_{12}H_{17}ON_4SCl \cdot HCl$, found in cereal grains, egg yolk, liver, etc., or prepared synthetically; vitamin $B_1$: a deficiency of this vitamin results in beriberi and certain nervous disorders: also **thi′a·min** (-min).

**Thi·bet** (ti-bet′), *n.* Tibet. —**Thi·bet′an**, *adj. & n.*

**thick** (thik), *adj.* [AS. *thicce*], 1. of relatively great depth or extent from side to side: as, a *thick* board. 2. having large diameter in relation to length: as, a *thick* rod. 3. measured between opposite surfaces: as, three inches *thick*. 4. dense; compact; specif., *a*) filled or covered completely; luxuriant: as, a *thick* woods. *b*) great in number; abundant: as, a *thick* crowd. *c*) not very fluid; viscous; heavy: as, *thick* soup. *d*) not clear; muddy; foggy: as, air *thick* with fumes. 5. not clear; husky: as, a *thick* voice. 6. stupid; dull. 7. [Colloq.], very friendly. 8. [Brit. Colloq.], too much to be tolerated. *adv.* thickly. *n.* the thickest part or the period of greatest activity. —**lay it on thick,** [Colloq.], to give exaggerated blame or praise. —**through thick and thin,** in good times and hard times. —**thick′ish,** *adj.* —**thick′ly,** *adv.* —**thick′ness,** *n.*

**thick·en** (thik′ən), *v.t. & v.i.* 1. to make or become thick or thicker. 2. to make or become more complex or involved. —**thick′en·er,** *n.*

**thick·en·ing** (thik′ən-iŋ), *n.* 1. the act of one that thickens. 2. a material used to thicken soup, etc. 3. something thickened or the thickened part.

**thick·et** (thik′it), *n.* [AS. *thiccet* < *thicce*, thick], a thick growth of shrubs, underbrush, or small trees.

**thick·head** (thik′hed′), *n.* a stupid person. —**thick′-head′ed,** *adj.* —**thick′head′ed·ness,** *n.*

**thick·set** (thik′set′), *adj.* 1. planted thickly or closely. 2. thick in body; stout. *n.* a thicket.

**thick-skinned** (thik′skind′), *adj.* 1. having a thick skin. 2. insensitive to criticism, insult, etc.

**thick-wit·ted** (thik′wit′id), *adj.* thickheaded.

**thief** (thēf), *n.* [*pl.* THIEVES (thēvz)], [< AS. *theof*], one who steals, especially secretly.

**thieve** (thēv), *v.t. & v.i.* [THIEVED, THIEVING], [< AS. < *theof*, thief], to steal. —**thiev′ish,** *adj.* —**thiev′-ish·ly,** *adv.* —**thiev′ish·ness,** *n.*

**thiev·er·y** (thēv′ēr-i), *n.* [*pl.* -IES], the act or practice of stealing or an instance of this.

**thigh** (thī), *n.* [AS. *theoh*], 1. the part of the human leg between the knee and the hip. 2. a corresponding part in other vertebrates.

**thigh·bone** (thī′bōn′), *n.* the bone of the thigh, articulating with the tibia and the pelvis; femur: also **thigh bone.**

**thill** (thil), *n.* [< AS. *thille*, a stake, pole], either of the two long pieces between which a horse is hitched to a wagon; shaft.

**thim·ble** (thim′b'l), *n.* [< AS. *thymel* < *thuma*, a thumb], 1. a small, pitted cap of metal, plastic, etc. worn on the finger in sewing to protect it in pushing the needle. 2. something resembling this; esp., a grooved, metal ring inserted in a loop of rope, etc. to prevent wear.

**thim·ble·ful** (thim′b'l-fool′), *n.* [*pl.* -FULS], 1. as much as a thimble will hold. 2. a very small quantity.

**thim·ble·rig** (thim′b'l-rig′), *n.* the shell game. *v.t.* [-RIGGED, -RIGGING], to swindle, as by this game.

**thin** (thin), *adj.* [THINNER, THINNEST], [AS. *thynne*], 1. of relatively little depth or extent from side to side: as, a *thin* board. 2. having small diameter in relation to length: as, *thin* thread. 3. lean; gaunt; slender. 4. not dense or compact; sparse; specif., *a*) scant in number; scattered: as, the audience was *thin*. *b*) very fluid; rare; tenuous: as, *thin* milk, *thin* air. *c*) of little body, richness, etc.: as, *thin* soup. 5. of little intensity; dim: as, *thin* colors. 6. high-pitched and weak: as, a *thin* voice. 7. transparent; flimsy: as, a *thin* fabric. 8. easily seen through: as, a *thin* excuse. 9. unsubstantial; inadequate: as, a *thin* plot. 10. in *photography*, lacking contrast of light and shade: said of a negative or print. *adv.* thinly. *v.t. & v.i.* [THINNED, THINNING], to make or become thin or thinner: with *out*, *down*, etc. —**thin′ly,** *adv.* —**thin′ner,** *n.* —**thin′ness,** *n.* —**thin′-nish,** *adj.*

**thine** (*th*īn), *pron.* [AS. *thin*], the possessive case of **thou.** *possessive pronominal adj.* thy: used especially before a vowel or unaspirated *h.*

**thing** (thiŋ), *n.* [AS., orig., a council], 1. any matter, affair, or concern. 2. a happening, act, deed, incident, etc.: as, what a *thing* to do. 3. an end to be achieved, a step in a process, etc.: as, the next *thing* is to mix thoroughly. 4. that which exists or is conceived of as existing as an individual, distinguishable entity; specif., *a*) a tangible object, as distinguished from a concept, quality, etc. *b*) an inanimate object. *c*) an item, detail, etc.: as, not a *thing* was ignored. 5. *pl. a*) personal belongings. *b*) clothes. 6. [Colloq.], a person or creature: as, poor *thing!* 7. [Colloq.], something mentioned but unnamed: as, it's that other *thing* I want. 8. [Colloq.], a complex, often neurotic liking, fear, etc.: as, to have a *thing* about flying. —**do one's (own) thing,** [Colloq.], to express one's personality by doing what one wants to do or is adept at. —**make a good thing of,** [Colloq.], to profit by or from. —**see things,** [Colloq.], to have hallucinations. —**the thing,** 1. that which is wise, essential, etc. 2. that which is the height of fashion.

‡**thing** (thiŋ, tiŋ), *n.* [ON., assembly], a Scandinavian legislative body; also **ting.**

**thing·um·bob** (thiŋ′əm-bob′), *n.* [Colloq.], any device or gadget: humorous substitute for a name not known or temporarily forgotten: also **thing′-um·a·jig′** (-ə-jig′).

**think** (thiŋk), *v.t.* [THOUGHT, THINKING], [AS. *thencan*], 1. to form or have in the mind: as, to *think* bad thoughts. 2. to judge; consider: as, I *think* her charming. 3. to believe; surmise; expect: as, they *think* they can come. 4. to determine, work out, etc. by reasoning: as, to *think* a problem through. 5. to purpose; intend: as, he *thinks* to deceive me. 6. to put, bring, etc. by mental concentration: as, she *thought* herself into this predicament. 7. to recollect: as, *think* how we were once friends. *v.i.* 1. to use the mind; reflect; reason: as, learn to *think*. 2. to have an opinion, belief, etc.: as, I just *think* so. 3. to weigh something mentally: as, *think* before you act. —**think aloud,** to speak one's thoughts as they occur: also **think out loud.** —**think better of,** 1. to form a new, more favorable opinion of. 2. to make a more sensible decision after reconsidering. —**think nothing of,** 1. to attach no importance to. 2. to regard as easy to do. —**think of,** 1. to remember. 2. to have an opinion of. 3. to invent; conceive of. 4. to consider. —**think out,** 1. to think about to a conclusion: also **think through.** 2. to work out by thinking. —**think over,** to give thought to; ponder. —**think twice,** to reconsider. —**think up,** to invent, contrive, etc. by thinking. —**think′a·ble,** *adj.* —**think′er,** *n.*

**think** (thiŋk), *v.i.* [THOUGHT, THINKING], [AS. *thyncan*], to seem; appear: used now only in the compounds *methinks* and *methought.*

**think·ing** (thiŋk′iŋ), *adj.* 1. that thinks or can think; rational. 2. thoughtful or reflective. *n.* thought. —**think′ing·ly,** *adv.*

**thin-skinned** (thin′skind′), *adj.* 1. having a thin skin. 2. sensitive to insult, etc.; easily hurt.

**thi·o-**, [< Gr. *theion*, brimstone], a combining form meaning *sulfur*, used to indicate the replacement of oxygen by sulfur: also **thi-.**

**thi·o·sul·fate** (thī′ə-sul′fāt), *n.* a salt of thiosulfuric acid; esp., sodium thiosulfate.

**thi·o·sul·fu·ric acid** (thī′ō-sul-fyoor′ik), [*thio-* + *sulfuric*], an unstable acid, $H_2S_2O_3$, whose salts are used in photography, bleaching, etc.

**third** (thûrd), *adj.* [< AS. *thridda* < base of *thrie*, three], 1. preceded by two others in a series; 3(r)d. 2. designating any of the three equal parts of something. *n.* 1. the one following the second. 2. any of three equal parts of something; 1/3. 3. in *music*, *a*) the tone three degrees above a given tone in a diatonic scale. *b*) the interval between, or a combination of, these tones. —**third′ly,** *adv.*

**third-class** (thûrd′klas′, -kläs′), *adj.* of the class, rank, excellence, etc. next below the second; specif., *a*) designating or of travel accommodations next below the second. *b*) designating or of a class of mail consisting of books, circulars, etc. *adv.* 1. with third-class travel accommodations. 2. as or by third-class mail.

**third degree,** severe treatment or torture by police, etc. to force a confession or information.

**third person,** that form of a pronoun or verb which refers to the person or thing spoken of: in *he does*, *he* and *does* are in the third person.

**third rail,** a center rail used in some electric railroads for supplying power.

**third-rate** (thûrd′rāt′), *adj.* 1. third in quality or other rating; third-class. 2. very poor.

**third world,** [often T- W-], the underdeveloped or emergent countries of the world, especially of Africa and Asia.

**thirst** (thûrst), *n.* [AS. *thurst*], 1. the discomfort or distress caused by a desire or need for water or other drink, characterized generally by dryness in the mouth and throat. 2. [Colloq.], a craving for alcoholic liquor. 3. a strong desire; craving. *v.i.* 1. to be thirsty. 2. to have a strong desire.

**thirst·y** (thûrs′ti), *adj.* [-IER, -IEST], 1. feeling thirst. 2. lacking water or moisture; dry: as, *thirsty* fields. 3. [Colloq.], causing thirst: as, *thirsty* work. 4. having strong desire; craving. —**thirst′i·ly,** *adv.* —**thirst′i·ness,** *n.*

**thir·teen** (thûr′tēn′), *adj.* [AS. *threotyne*], three more than ten. *n.* the cardinal number between twelve and fourteen; 13; XIII.

**thir·teenth** (thûr′tēnth′), *adj.* 1. preceded by twelve others in a series; 13th. 2. designating any of the thirteen equal parts of something. *n.* 1. the one following the twelfth. 2. any of the thirteen equal parts of something; 1/13.

**thir·ti·eth** (thûr′ti-ith), *adj.* 1. preceded by twenty-nine others in a series; 30th. 2. designating any of the thirty equal parts of something. *n.* 1. the one following the twenty-ninth. 2. any of the thirty equal parts of something; 1/30.

**thir·ty** (thûr′ti), *adj.* [AS. *thritig* < *thri*, three], three times ten. *n.* [*pl.* -TIES], the cardinal number between twenty-nine and thirty-one; 30; XXX. —**the thirties,** the years from thirty through thirty-nine (of a century or a person's age).

**thir·ty-sec·ond note** (thûr′ti-sek′ənd), in *music*, a note (𝅘𝅥𝅰) having 1/32 the duration of a whole note.

**this** (*th*is), *pron.* [*pl.* THESE], [< AS. *thes*, masc., *this*, neut.], 1. the person or thing mentioned or understood: as, *this* is John. 2. the thing that is nearer: as, I can see *this* more clearly than that. 3. something being contrasted: as, *this* is better than that. 4. the fact, idea, etc. that is about to be stated: as, now hear *this*. *adj.* 1. designating the one mentioned or understood: as, *this* man is John. 2. designating the thing that is nearer: as, *this* house is newer than that one across the street. 3. designating something being contrasted: as, *this* car is better than that one. 4. designating something about to be stated: as, *this* claim I make: I was his friend. *adv.* to this extent; so: as, it was *this* big.

**this·tle** (this′'l), *n.* [AS. *thistel*], any of various plants with prickly leaves and heads of white, purple, etc. flowers. —**this′tly** [-TLIER, -TLIEST], *adj.*

THISTLE

**this·tle·down** (this′'l-doun′), *n.* the down attached to the flower head of a thistle.

**thith·er** (thi*th*′ēr, thi*th*′-), *adv.* [AS. *thider*], to or toward that place or direction. *adj.* on that (more distant) side.

**thith·er·to** (thi*th*′ēr-tōō′, thi*th*′-ēr-tōō′), *adv.* until that time; up to then.

**thith·er·ward** (thi*th*′ēr-wērd, thi*th*′-), *adv.* thither: also **thith′er·wards.**

**tho, tho′** (*th*ō), *conj.* & *adv.* though.

**thole** (thōl), *n.* [AS. *thol*], a pin or either of a pair of pins set vertically in the gunwale of a boat as a fulcrum for an oar: also **thole′pin′.**

**Thom·as** (tom′əs), *n.* one of the twelve apostles, who doubted at first the resurrection of Jesus: John 20:24-29.

**Thomas, Norman Mat·toon** (mə-tōōn′), 1884–1968; U.S. Socialist leader.

**Thomas à Beck·et,** Saint (ə bek′it), 1118?–1170; archbishop of Canterbury.

**Thomas à Kem·pis** (ə kem′pis), (*Thomas Hamerken von Kempen*), 1380–1471; German monk and scholar.

**Thomp·son, Francis** (tomp′s'n, tom′-), 1859–1907; English poet.

**Thompson submachine gun,** a type of submachine gun: a trade-mark: see **submachine gun.**

**thong** (thôŋ), *n.* [AS. *thwang*], 1. a narrow strip of leather, etc. used as a lace, strap, etc. 2. a whiplash, as of plaited strips of hide.

**Thor** (thôr), *n.* in *Norse mythology*, the god of thunder, war, and strength, and the son of Odin.

**tho·ra·co-,** (thôr′ə-kō, thō-rā′kō), a prefix meaning *the thorax (and)*: also **thorac-.**

**tho·rax** (thôr′aks, thō′raks), *n.* [*pl.* -RAXES, -RACES (-ə-sēz′)], [L. < Gr. *thorax*], 1. in man and the higher vertebrates, the part of the body between the neck and the abdomen; chest. 2. the middle one of the three segments of an insect's body. —**tho·rac·ic** (thô-ras′ik, thō-), *adj.*

**Thor·eau, Henry David** (thôr′ō, thə-rō′), 1817–1862; U.S. naturalist, philosopher, and writer.

**tho·ri·um** (thôr′i-əm, thō′ri-), *n.* [< *Thor*], a rare, grayish, radioactive chemical element: symbol, Th; at. wt., 232.12; at. no., 90. —**thor′ic,** *adj.*

**thorn** (thôrn), *n.* [AS.], 1. a very short, hard, leafless branch or stem with a sharp point. 2. any small tree or shrub bearing thorns. 3. any tenacious cause of hurt, irritation, worry, etc. 4. in Old English, the runic character (þ), corresponding to either sound of English *th*, as in *thin* or *then*. —**thorn in the flesh** (or **side**), thorn (sense 3). —**thorn′less,** *adj.* —**thorn′like′,** *adj.*

**thorn apple,** 1. a hawthorn or its applelike fruit; haw. 2. a Jimson weed.

**thorn·y** (thôr′ni), *adj.* [-IER, -IEST], 1. full of thorns; prickly. 2. difficult or full of obstacles, vexations, pain, etc. —**thorn′i·ly,** *adv.* —**thorn′i·ness,** *n.*

**thor·o** (thûr′ō, -ə), *adj.*, *prep.*, *adv.* thorough.

**tho·ron** (thôr′on, thō′ron), *n.* [< *thorium*], a radioactive isotope of radon, resulting from the disintegration of thorium: symbol, Tn.

**thor·ough** (thûr′ō), *prep.* & *adv.* [ME. *thoruh*: a var. of *through*], [Obs.], through. *adj.* 1. done or proceeding through to the end; complete. 2. that is completely (as described); absolute: as, a *thorough* rascal. 3. very exact, accurate, or painstaking, especially about details. —**thor′ough·ly,** *adv.* —**thor′ough·ness,** *n.*

**thor·ough·bred** (thûr′ə-bred′), *adj.* 1. of pure stock or official pedigree: said of horses, dogs, etc. 2. thoroughly trained, cultured, etc.; well-bred. *n.* 1. a thoroughbred animal; specif., [T-], any of a breed of race horses. 2. a cultured, well-bred person.

**thor·ough·fare** (thûr′ə-fâr′), *n.* a public, unobstructed street open at both ends, especially a main road or highway.

**thor·ough·go·ing** (thûr′ə-gō′iŋ), *adj.* very thorough.

**those** (*th*ōz), *adj.* & *pron.* [AS. *thas*], pl. of **that.**

**thou** (*th*ou), *pron.* [AS. *thu*], the nom. 2d pers. sing. of the personal pronoun: formerly used in familiar address but now replaced by *you* except in poetic, religious, and some dialectal use, and in the speech of Friends (Quakers): *thee* is the objective case form, *thy* or *thine* the possessive, and *thyself* the intensive and reflexive.

**though** (*th*ō), *conj.* [< AS. *theah*, infl. by ON. *tho*], 1. in spite of the fact that; notwithstanding that: as, *though* it rained, he went. 2. all the same; yet; still: as, she was pretty, *though* not as striking as her sister. 3. even if; supposing that: as, *though* he may fail, he will have tried. *adv.* however; nevertheless: used as a conjunctive adverb. Also sp. **tho, tho′.** —**as though,** as it (or I, you, he, etc.) would if.

**thought** (thôt), *n.* [< AS. *thoht*], 1. the act or process of thinking; reflection; meditation. 2. the

power of reasoning; intellect; imagination. 3. a result of thinking; idea, concept, etc. 4. the ideas, opinions, etc. prevalent at a given time or place, or among a given people: as, modern *thought* in education. 5. attention; consideration. 6. mental engrossment; concentration. 7. intention or expectation. 8. a little; trifle: as, be a *thought* more careful.
**thought** (thôt), pt. and pp. of **think.**
**thought·ful** (thôt′fəl), *adj.* 1. full of thought; meditative. 2. characterized by thought; serious. 3. heedful, careful, etc.; esp., considerate of others. **—thought′ful·ly,** *adv.* **—thought′ful·ness,** *n.*
**thought·less** (thôt′lis), *adj.* 1. not stopping to think; careless. 2. not given thought; rash. 3 inconsiderate; remiss. 4. stupid; dull-witted **—thought′less·ly,** *adv.* **—thought′less·ness,** *n.*
**thou·sand** (thou′z′nd), *adj. & n.* [AS. *thusendl*, ten hundred; 1,000; M.
**thou·sand·fold** (thou′z′nd-fōld′), *adj.* 1. having a thousand parts. 2. having a thousand times as much or as many. *adv.* a thousand times as much or as many.
**Thousand Island dressing,** a salad dressing of mayonnaise with minced pickles, catsup, etc.
**Thousand Islands,** a group of islands in the upper St. Lawrence River, belonging to New York State and Ontario, Canada.
**thou·sandth** (thou′z′ndth), *adj.* 1. coming last in a series of a thousand. 2. designating any of the thousand equal parts of something. *n.* 1. the thousandth one of a series. 2. any of the thousand equal parts of something.
**Thrace** (thrās), *n.* an ancient region in the E Balkan Peninsula. **—Thra·cian** (thrā′shən), *adj. & n.*
**thrall** (thrôl), *n.* [< AS. < ON. *thræll*], 1. originally, a slave or bondman. 2. a person in moral or psychological bondage. 3. thralldom.
**thrall·dom, thral·dom** (thrôl′dəm), *n.* the condition of being a thrall; servitude; slavery.
**thrash** (thrash), *v.t.* [AS. *threscan*], 1. to thresh. 2. to beat, as with a flail. *v.i.* 1. to thresh. 2. to move or toss about violently. *n.* a thrashing. **—thrash out,** to discuss thoroughly and conclusively. **—thrash′ing·ly,** *adv.*
**thrash·er** (thrash′ẽr), *n.* 1. a person or thing that thrashes. 2. a thresher (sense 3).
**thrash·er** (thrash′ẽr), *n.* [Eng. dial. *thresher*], any of various American thrushlike songbirds having a long, stiff tail and a long bill.
**thread** (thred), *n.* [AS. *thræd*], 1. a very fine cord composed of strands of spun silk, cotton, etc., used in sewing. 2. a fine, threadlike filament, as of metal, glass, plastic, etc. 3. a thin line, stratum, vein, ray, etc. of something. 4. something like a thread in its length, sequence, etc.: as, the *thread* of a story. 5. the spiral or helical ridge of a screw, bolt, nut, etc. *v.t.* 1. to put a thread through the eye of (a needle, etc.). 2. to string (beads, etc.) on a thread. 3. *a)* to weave in and out of like a thread: as, he *threaded* the streets. *b)* to make (one's way) in a threadlike, winding fashion. 4. to fashion a thread (sense 5) on or in (a screw, pipe, etc.). *v.i.* 1. to wind one's or its way in a threadlike fashion. 2. to form a thread when dropped from a spoon: said of boiling sirup, etc. of a certain consistency. **—thread′er,** *n.* **—thread′like′,** *adj.*
**thread·bare** (thred′bâr′), *adj.* 1. worn down so that the threads show; having the nap worn off. 2. wearing worn clothes; shabby. 3. that has lost freshness; stale; trite. **—thread′bare′ness,** *n.*
**thread·y** (thred′i), *adj.* [-IER, -IEST], 1. of or like a thread; stringy; fibrous. 2. forming threads; viscid: said of liquids. 3. like a thread in thinness or feebleness: as, a *thready* voice. **—thread′i·ness,** *n.*
**threat** (thret), *n.* [< AS. *threat*, press, throng], 1. an expression of intention to hurt, destroy, punish, etc., as in intimidation. 2. an indication of imminent danger: as, the *threat* of war.
**threat·en** (thret′'n), *v.t.* [AS. *threatnian*], 1. to make threats against. 2. to indicate (something dangerous, etc.): as, those clouds *threaten* snow. 3. to be a source of danger, harm, etc. to. 4. to express intention to inflict (injury, retaliation, etc.). *v.i.* 1. to make threats. 2. to give an indication of danger, etc. **—threat′en·er,** *n.* **—threat′en·ing·ly,** *adv.*
**three** (thrē), *adj.* [AS. *threo, thrie*], totaling one more than two. *n.* 1. the cardinal number between two and four; 3; III. 2. a domino, die, card, etc. with three spots.
**three-base hit** (thrē′bās′), in *baseball*, a triple.
**3-D** (thrē′dē′), three dimensions or three-dimensional: used of a motion-picture system in which a stereoscopic picture is projected on a flat screen and viewed through polaroid glasses.
**three-deck·er** (thrē′dek′ẽr), *n.* 1. a ship with three decks. 2. anything having three levels, layers, etc.
**three·fold** (thrē′fōld′), *adj.* 1. having three parts. 2. having three times as much or as many. *adv.* three times as much or as many.
**three-mile limit** (thrē′mīl′), the outer limit of a zone of water extending three miles offshore, regarded under international law as the extent of the jurisdiction of the adjacent country.
**three·pence** (thrip′'ns, threp′-), *n.* 1. the sum of three pence; three British pennies. 2. a British silver coin of this value. Also **thrippence.**
**three·pen·ny** (thrē′pen′i, thrip′ə-ni), *adj.* 1. worth three pence. 2. of little value; cheap.
**three-ply** (thrē′plī′), *adj.* having three layers, strands, etc.
**three-quar·ter** (thrē′kwôr′tẽr), *adj.* of or involving three fourths of something.
**three·score** (thrē′skôr′, -skōr′), *adj.* sixty.
**three·some** (thrē′səm), *adj.* of or engaged in by three. *n.* 1. a group of three persons. 2. a game played by three persons.
**thren·o·dy** (thren′ə-di), *n.* [*pl.* -DIES], [< Gr. < *thrēnos*, lamentation + *ōdē*, song], a song of lamentation; dirge. **—thre·nod·ic** (thri-nod′ik), **thre·no′di·al** (-nō′di-əl), *adj.* **—thren′o·dist,** *n.*
**thresh** (thresh), *v.t.* [AS. *threscan*], 1. to beat out (grain) from its husk, as with a flail. 2. to beat grain out of (husks). *v.i.* 1. to thresh grain. 2. to toss about; thrash. **—thresh out,** to discuss thoroughly and conclusively.
**thresh·er** (thresh′ẽr), *n.* 1. one who threshes. 2. a large, power-driven farm machine for threshing: also **threshing machine.** 3. a large, long-tailed shark: also **thresher shark.**
**thresh·old** (thresh′ōld, -hōld), *n.* [AS. *thersc(w)old* < *therscan*, to tread down], 1. a piece of wood, stone, etc. placed beneath a door; doorsill. 2. the entrance or beginning point of something. 3. in *physiology & psychology*, the point at which a stimulus is just strong enough to be perceived or produce a response: as, the *threshold* of pain.
**threw** (thrōō), pt. of **throw.**
**thrice** (thrīs), *adv.* [ME. *thries*], 1. three times. 2. threefold. 3. very; greatly.
**thrift** (thrift), *n.* [ON. < *thrifa;* see THRIVE], 1. [Rare], a thriving. 2. economical management; economy; frugality. **—thrift′less,** *adj.* **—thrift′less·ly,** *adv.* **—thrift′less·ness,** *n.*
**thrift·y** (thrif′ti), *adj.* [-IER, -IEST], 1. practicing thrift; economical. 2. thriving; prospering. **—thrift′i·ly,** *adv.* **—thrift′i·ness,** *n.*
**thrill** (thril), *v.i. & v.t.* [< AS. *thyr(e)lian*, to pierce < *thyrel*, hole < *thurh*, through], 1. to feel or cause to feel emotional excitement; tingle with excitement. 2. to quiver or cause to quiver; tremble; vibrate. *n.* 1. a thrilling or being thrilled; tremor of excitement. 2. the quality of thrilling, or ability to thrill. 3. a vibration; tremor; quiver. **—thrill′er,** *n.* **—thrill′ing,** *adj.* **—thrill′ing·ly,** *adv.* **—thrill′ing·ness,** *n.*
**thrip·pence** (thrip′'ns), *n.* threepence.
**thrive** (thrīv), *v.i.* [THROVE or THRIVED, THRIVED or THRIVEN, THRIVING], [< ON. *thrīfask*, to have oneself in hand < *thrifa*, to grasp], 1. to prosper; be successful, especially by practicing thrift. 2. to grow luxuriantly. **—thriv′er,** *n.* **—thriv′ing·ly,** *adv.*
**thro′, thro** (thrōō), *prep., adv., adj.* through.
**throat** (thrōt), *n.* [AS. *throte*], 1. the front part of the neck. 2. the upper passage from the mouth and nose to the stomach and lungs, including the pharynx, upper larynx, trachea, and esophagus. 3. any narrow, throatlike passage. **—jump down one's throat,** [Colloq.], to attack or criticize one suddenly and violently. **—lump in the throat,** a feeling of constriction in the throat, as from restrained emotion. **—stick in one's throat,** to be hard to say, as from reluctance.
**-throat·ed** (thrōt′id), a combining form meaning *having a* (specified kind of) *throat*, as in *ruby-throated.*
**throat·y** (thrōt′i), *adj.* [-IER, -IEST], produced in the throat, as some speech sounds or tones, or characterized by such sounds, as the voice; husky. **—throat′i·ly,** *adv.* **—throat′i·ness,** *n.*
**throb** (throb), *v.i.* [THROBBED, THROBBING], [ME. *throbben*], 1. to beat, pulsate, vibrate, etc. 2. to beat strongly or fast; palpitate, as the heart under exertion. 3. to feel or show emotional excitement, as by quivering. *n.* the act of throbbing; beat or pulsation, especially a strong one. **—throb′ber,** *n.* **—throb′bing·ly,** *adv.*
**throe** (thrō), *n.* [prob. < AS. *thrawu*, pain, infl. by *thrawen*, to twist], 1. a spasm or pang of pain. 2. *pl.* pangs of childbirth; labor pains. 3. *pl.* desperate or agonizing struggle; agony.

**throm·bin** (throm′bin), *n.* [< Gr. *thrombos*, a clot], the enzyme of the blood that causes clotting by forming fibrin.

**throm·bo·sis** (throm-bō′sis), *n.* [< Gr. < *thrombos*, a clot], coagulation of the blood in some part of the circulatory system, forming a clot that obstructs circulation. —**throm·bot′ic** (-bot′ik), *adj.*

**throne** (thrōn), *n.* [< OFr. < L. < Gr. *thronos*, a seat], 1. the chair on which a king, cardinal, etc. sits on formal occasions. 2. the power or rank of a king, etc.; sovereignty. 3. a sovereign, ruler, etc.: as, orders from the *throne.* ***v.t.*** [THRONED, THRONING], to enthrone. —**throne′less,** *adj.*

**throng** (thrôŋ), *n.* [AS. (*ge*)*thrang* < *thringan*, to crowd], 1. a great number of people gathered together; crowd. 2. any great number of things considered together; multitude. ***v.i.*** to gather together, move, or press in a throng; crowd. ***v.t.*** to crowd into; fill with a multitude.

**thros·tle** (thros′'l), *n.* [AS.], [Scot.], a thrush, as the European song thrush.

**throt·tle** (throt′'l), *n.* [dim. of *throat*], 1. [Rare], the throat or windpipe. 2. the valve in an internal-combustion engine that regulates the amount of fuel vapor entering the cylinders. 3. the lever or pedal that controls this valve. ***v.t.*** [-TLED, -TLING], 1. to choke; strangle. 2. to stop the utterance of; suppress. 3. to reduce the flow of (fuel vapor) by means of a throttle. 4. to slow (*down*) by this or similar means. ***v.i.*** to choke or suffocate. —**throt′tler,** *n.*

**through** (thrōō), *prep.* [AS. *thurh*], 1. in one side and out the other side of; from end to end of. 2. in the midst of; among. 3. by way of. 4. over the entire extent of. 5. to various places in; around: as, he toured *through* France. 6. from beginning to end of; throughout. 7. by means of. 8. as a result of; because of. ***adv.*** 1. in one side and out the other; from end to end. 2. from the beginning to the end. 3. completely to the end: as, see it *through.* 4. thoroughly; completely: as, soaked *through* (often, *through and through*). ***adj.*** 1. extending from one place to another: as, a *through* street. 2. traveling to the destination without stops: as, a *through* train. 3. arrived at the end; finished. 4. at the end of one's usefulness, resources, etc.: as, he's *through* in politics. 5. having no further dealings, etc.: as, I'm *through* with them. Also **thro′, thro, thru.**

**through·out** (thrōō-out′), *prep.* all the way through; in or during every part of. ***adv.*** in or during every part; everywhere; the whole time.

**throve** (thrōv), alt. pt. of **thrive.**

**throw** (thrō), *v.t.* [THREW, THROWN, THROWING], [AS. *thrawan*, to twist], 1. to twist strands of (silk, etc.) into thread. 2. to send through the air by releasing from the hand at the end of a rapid motion of the arm, a catapult, etc.; cast; hurl. 3. to cause to fall; upset: as, he *threw* the wrestler. 4. to move or send rapidly: as, they *threw* troops into the battle. 5. to put suddenly and forcibly into a specified place, condition, or situation: as, *thrown* into confusion. 6. to make (a specified cast) at dice: as, I *threw* a five. 7. to cast off; shed: as, snakes *throw* their skins. 8. to move (the lever of a switch, clutch, etc.) or connect, disconnect, etc. by so doing. 9. to direct, cast, turn, etc. (with *at, on, upon,* etc.): as, to *throw* a glance, shadow, light, etc. 10. to put (blame *on*, obstacles *before*, etc.). 11. [Colloq.], to lose (a game, race, etc.) deliberately. 12. [Slang], to give (a party, dance, etc.). 13. in *ceramics*, to shape on a potter's wheel. ***v.i.*** to cast or hurl something. ***n.*** 1. the act of one who throws; a cast. 2. the distance something is or can be thrown: as, a stone's *throw.* 3. *a*) a spread for draping over a bed, etc. *b*) a scarf, etc. for the shoulders. 4. *a*) the motion of a moving part, as a cam, eccentric, etc. *b*) the extent of such a motion. —**throw away,** 1. to rid oneself of; discard. 2. to waste. 3. to fail to make use of. —**throw a (monkey) wrench into,** to obstruct by direct interference; sabotage. —**throw back,** to revert to the type of an ancestor. —**throw cold water on,** to discourage by indifference or disparagement. —**throw in,** 1. to engage (a clutch). 2. to add extra or free. 3. to add to others. —**throw off,** 1. to rid oneself of. 2. to expel, emit, etc. —**throw on,** to put on (a garment) hastily. —**throw oneself at,** to try very hard to win the friendship, love, etc. of. —**throw oneself into,** to engage in with great vigor. —**throw oneself upon** (or **on**), to rely on for support or aid. —**throw open,** 1. to open completely and suddenly. 2. to remove all restrictions from. —**throw out,** 1. to discard. 2. to reject. 3. to disengage (a clutch). 4. in *baseball*, to throw the ball to a baseman so as to put out (a runner). —**throw over,** 1. to give up; abandon. 2. to jilt. —**throw together,** to make or assemble hurriedly. —**throw up,** 1. to give up; abandon. 2. to vomit. 3. to construct rapidly. 4. to mention (something) repeatedly (*to* someone), as in reproach. —**throw′er,** *n.*

**throw·back** (thrō′bak′), *n.* 1. a throwing back; check. 2. reversion to an ancestral type, or an instance of this.

**thru** (thrōō), *prep., adv., adj.* through.

**thrum** (thrum), *n.* [AS., a ligament], 1. *pl.* the row of warp thread ends left on a loom when the web is cut off. 2. any of these ends. 3. any shortened thread or fringe.

**thrum** (thrum), *v.t. & v.i.* [THRUMMED, THRUMMING], [echoic], 1. to strum (a stringed instrument). 2. to drum (on) with the fingers. ***n.*** the act or sound of thrumming. —**thrum′mer,** *n.*

**thrush** (thrush), *n.* [AS. *thrysce*], any of a large group of songbirds, often plain-colored, including the robin, bluebird, wood thrush, blackbird, etc.

**thrush** (thrush), *n.* [cf. Dan. *troske*], a disease, especially of children, caused by a fungus and characterized by the formation of milky-white lesions on the mouth, lips, and throat.

**thrust** (thrust), *v.t.* [THRUST, THRUSTING], [< ON. *thrysta*], 1. to push with sudden force; shove. 2. to pierce; stab. 3. to put (a person) in some situation against his wishes or the wishes of others. ***v.i.*** 1. to push or shove against something. 2. to stab. 3. to force one's way: with *into, through,* etc. 4. to extend, as in growth. ***n.*** 1. a thrusting; specif., *a*) a sudden, forceful push. *b*) a stab, as with a weapon. 2. continuous pressure of one part against another, as of a rafter against a wall. 3. *a*) the driving force of a propeller in the line of its shaft. *b*) the forward force produced by the escaping gases in jet propulsion. —**thrust′er,** *n.* —**thrust′ing·ly,** *adv.*

**Thu·cyd·i·des** (thōō-sid′ə-dēz′, thū-), *n.* Athenian historian; 471?–400? B.C.

**thud** (thud), *n.* [prob. ult. < AS. *thyddan*, to strike], 1. a blow. 2. a dull sound, as of a heavy object dropping on a soft, solid surface. ***v.i.*** [THUDDED, THUDDING], to hit or fall with a thud. —**thud′ding·ly,** *adv.*

**thug** (thug), *n.* [< Hind. *ṭhag* < Sans. *sthaga*, a rogue], 1. [also T-], a member of a former religious organization of India who murdered and robbed. 2. any assassin, cutthroat, or ruffian.

**Thu·le** (thōō′li, thū′lē), *n.* [L.], among the ancients, the northernmost region of the world.

**thu·li·um** (thōō′li-əm, thū′-), *n.* [< *Thule*], a metallic chemical element of the rare-earth group: symbol, Tm; at. wt., 169.4; at. no., 69.

**thumb** (thum), *n.* [AS. *thuma*], 1. the short, thick inner digit of the human hand, apposable to the other fingers. 2. a corresponding part in other animals. 3. that part of a glove, etc. which covers the thumb. ***v.t.*** 1. to handle, turn, soil, etc. as with the thumb: as, to *thumb* the pages of a book. 2. [Colloq.], to solicit (a ride) in a passing automobile by signaling with one's thumb. —**all thumbs,** clumsy; fumbling. —**thumb one's nose,** to raise one's thumb to the nose in a coarse gesture of defiance or insult. —**thumbs down,** a signal of disapproval. —**thumbs up,** a signal of approval. —**under one's thumb,** under one's influence.

**thumb index,** a reference index for books, consisting of a series of rounded notches cut in the front edge of a book with a letter or title tab at the base of each notch. —**thumb′-in′dex,** *v.t.*

**thumb·nail** (thum′nāl′), *n.* 1. the nail of the thumb. 2. something as small as a thumbnail. ***adj.*** very small or brief: as, a *thumbnail* sketch.

**thumb·screw** (thum′skrōō′), *n.* 1. a screw with a head flattened in such a way that it may be turned with the thumb and fingers. 2. a former instrument of torture for squeezing the thumbs.

**thumb·tack** (thum′tak′), *n.* a kind of tack with a wide, flat head, that can be pressed into a board, etc. with the thumb.

**thump** (thump), *n.* [echoic], 1. a blow with something heavy and blunt. 2. the dull sound made by such a blow. ***v.t.*** 1. to strike with a thump or thumps. 2. to thrash; beat severely. ***v.i.*** 1. to hit or fall with a thump. 2. to make a dull, heavy sound; pound; throb. —**thump′er,** *n.*

**thun·der** (thun'dẽr), *n.* [AS. *thunor*], 1. the sound that follows a flash of lightning, caused by the sudden disturbance of air by electrical discharge. 2. any sound resembling this. 3. a vehement threat or denunciation. *v.i.* 1. to produce thunder: as, it is *thundering*. 2. to make a sound like thunder. 3. to make vehement denunciations, etc. *v.t.* to utter, effect, etc. with a thundering sound. —**steal one's thunder,** to lessen the effectiveness of another's statement or action by anticipating him in this. —**thun'der·er,** *n.*

**thun·der·bolt** (thun'dẽr-bōlt'), *n.* 1. a flash of lightning and the accompanying thunder. 2. something that stuns or acts with sudden violence.

**thun·der·clap** (thun'dẽr-klap'), *n.* 1. a clap, or loud crash, of thunder. 2. anything resembling this in being sudden, startling, violent, etc.

**thun·der·cloud** (thun'dẽr-kloud'), *n.* a storm cloud charged with electricity and producing lightning and thunder.

**thun·der·head** (thun'dẽr-hed'), *n.* a round mass of cumulus clouds coming before a thunderstorm.

**thun·der·ous** (thun'dẽr-əs), *adj.* 1. full of or making thunder. 2. making a noise like thunder. —**thun'der·ous·ly,** *adv.*

**thun·der·show·er** (thun'dẽr-shou'ẽr), *n.* a shower accompanied by thunder and lightning.

**thun·der·squall** (thun'dẽr-skwôl'), *n.* a squall accompanied by thunder and lightning.

**thun·der·storm** (thun'dẽr-stôrm'), *n.* a storm accompanied by thunder and lightning.

**thun·der·struck** (thun'dẽr-struk'), *adj.* struck with amazement, terror, etc.; astonished; astounded: also **thun'der·strick'en** (-strik''n).

**thun·der·y** (thun'dẽr-i), *adj.* 1. that sounds like thunder. 2. full of or betokening thunder.

**Thur., Thurs.,** Thursday.

**thu·ri·ble** (thoor'ə-b'l, thyoor'-), *n.* [< L. *thus*, incense < Gr. *thyos*, sacrifice], a censer.

**Thurs·day** (thũrz'di), *n.* [< AS. < ON. *Thorsdagr*, Thor's day], the fifth day of the week.

**thus** (*th*us), *adv.* [AS.], 1. in this or that manner; in the way just stated or in the following manner. 2. to this or that degree or extent; so. 3. consequently; therefore; hence.

**thwack** (thwak), *v.t.* [prob < AS. *thaccian*, to clap; echoic], to strike with something flat; whack. *n.* a heavy blow; whack. —**thwack'er,** *n.*

**thwart** (thwôrt), *adj.* [< ON. *thvert*, transverse], lying across something else; transverse. *adv. & prep.* [Archaic], athwart. *n.* 1. a rower's seat extending across a boat. 2. a brace extending across a canoe. *v.t.* to obstruct, frustrate, or defeat (a person, plans, etc.). —**thwart'er,** *n.*

**thy** (*th*ī), *possessive pronominal adj.* [ME. *thi*, contr. < *thin*, thy], of, belonging to, or done by thee: archaic or dial. variant of *your*: see **thine.**

**thyme** (tīm), *n.* [< OFr. < L. < Gr. *thymon* < *thyein*, to offer sacrifice], any of various plants of the mint family, with white, pink, or red flowers and fragrant leaves used for seasoning. —**thym'ic,** *adj.* —**thym'y,** *adj.*

**thy·mol** (thī'mōl, -mol), *n.* [< *thyme* + *-ol*], a colorless compound, extracted from thyme or made synthetically, and used as an antiseptic.

**thy·mus** (thī'məs), *n.* [Gr. *thymos*], a ductless, glandlike body, of undetermined function, situated near the throat: the thymus of an animal, when used as food, is called *sweetbread:* also **thymus gland.** —**thy'mic,** *adj.*

**thy·roid** (thī'roid), *adj.* [< Gr. < *thyreos*, shield + *-eidēs*, form], 1. designating or of a large ductless gland near the trachea, secreting the hormone thyroxine, which regulates growth: malfunctioning of this gland can cause goiter. 2. designating or of the principal cartilage of the larynx, forming the Adam's apple. *n.* 1. the thyroid gland. 2. the thyroid cartilage. 3. a preparation of the thyroid gland of certain animals, used in treating goiter, etc.: also **thyroid extract.** —**thy·roi'dal,** *adj.*

**thy·rox·ine** (thī-rok'sēn, -sin), *n.* [< *thyroid* + *oxy-* + *-ine*], a colorless, crystalline compound, the active hormone of the thyroid gland, used in treating goiter, etc.: also **thy·rox'in** (-sin).

**thyr·sus** (thũr'səs), *n.* [*pl.* -SI (-sī)], [L. < Gr. *thyrsos*], a staff tipped with a pine cone and sometimes entwined with ivy, which Dionysus, the satyrs, etc. were represented as carrying.

**thy·self** (*th*ī-self'), *pron.* the reflexive or emphatic form of **thou**: an archaic variant of *yourself.*

**ti** (tē), *n.* [alt. < *si*], in *music*, a syllable representing the seventh tone of the diatonic scale.

**Ti,** in *chemistry*, titanium.

**ti·ar·a** (tī-âr'ə, ti-ä'rə), *n.* [L. < Gr. *tiara*], 1. an ancient Persian headdress. 2. the Pope's triple crown. 3. a woman's crownlike headdress of jewels, flowers, etc.; coronet.

**Ti·ber** (tī'bẽr), *n.* a river in central Italy, flowing through Rome to the Mediterranean.

**Ti·bet** (ti-bet'), *n.* an autonomous part of China in central Asia: area, 469,194 sq. mi.; pop., 3,000,000 capital, Lhasa: also sp. **Thibet.**

**Ti·bet·an** (ti-bet''n), *adj.* of Tibet, its people, their language, etc. *n.* 1. a member of the Mongolic people of Tibet. 2. the Sino-Tibetan language of Tibet. Also sp. **Thibetan.**

**tib·i·a** (tib'i-ə), *n.* [*pl.* -AE (-ē'), -AS], [L.], the inner and thicker of the two bones of the leg below the knee; shinbone. —**tib'i·al,** *adj.*

**tic** (tik), *n.* [Fr.; ult. < Gmc.], any involuntary, regularly repeated, spasmodic contraction of a muscle, generally of neurotic origin.

**tick** (tik), *n.* [prob. echoic], 1. a light clicking or tapping sound, as that made by a watch or clock. 2. a mark made to check off items; check mark (√, /, etc.). 3. [Colloq.], the time between two ticks of a clock; moment; instant. *v.i.* to make a tick or ticks. *v.t.* 1. to record or count by a tick or ticks. 2. to check off (an item in a list, etc.) with a tick.

**tick** (tik), *n.* [AS. *ticia*], 1. any of various wingless, blood-sucking insects or mites that infest man, cattle, sheep, etc. 2. any of various degenerate, two-winged, parasitic insects.

**tick** (tik), *n.* [< L. < Gr. *thēkē*, a case], 1. the cloth case that is filled with cotton, feathers, etc. to form a mattress or pillow. 2. [Colloq.], ticking.

**tick** (tik), *n.* [contr. of *ticket*], [Chiefly Brit. Colloq.], credit; trust: as, I bought it on *tick.*

**tick·er** (tik'ẽr), *n.* 1. a person or thing that ticks. 2. a telegraphic device that records stock market quotations, etc. on paper tape (**ticker tape**). 3. [Slang], *a*) a watch or clock. *b*) the heart.

**tick·et** (tik'it), *n.* [< Fr. *étiquette* < OFr. < *estiquer*, to stick], 1. a printed card or piece of paper that gives one a specified right, as to attend a theater, ride a bus, etc. 2. a license or certificate, as of a ship's captain. 3. a card or piece of paper or cloth fastened to goods to tell the size, price, etc.; label; tag. 4. the list of candidates nominated by a political party in an election. 5. [Colloq.], a summons to court for a traffic violation. *v.t.* 1. to put a ticket on; label; tag. 2. to give a ticket to.

**ticket of leave,** [Brit.], formerly, a permit allowing a convict to be at liberty, with certain restrictions, before his sentence had expired: equivalent to *parole.* —**tick'et-of-leave',** *adj.*

**tick·ing** (tik'iŋ), *n.* strong, heavy cotton or linen cloth of which bed ticks, etc. are made.

**tick·le** (tik''l), *v.t.* [-LED, -LING], [ME. *tikelen*], 1. to please; gratify: as, pie that *tickles* the palate. 2. to amuse; delight. 3. to excite the surface nerves of by touching or stroking lightly so as to cause involuntary twitching, laughter, etc. 4. to rouse, move, get, etc. by or as by tickling. *v.i.* 1. to have a tingling sensation. 2. to be ticklish. *n.* 1. a tickling or being tickled. 2. a tickling sensation. —**tickle one pink,** [Slang], to please one greatly.

**tick·ler** (tik'lẽr), *n.* 1. one that tickles. 2. a memorandum pad, file, etc. for aiding the memory.

**tick·lish** (tik'lish), *adj.* 1. sensitive to tickling. 2. easily upset; unstable or touchy. 3. needing careful handling; delicate. —**tick'lish·ly,** *adv.* —**tick'lish·ness,** *n.*

**tick-tack-toe** (tik'tak-tō', ti'ta-tō'), *n.* a game in which two players take turns marking either crosses or circles in a block of nine squares, the object being to complete a line of three of one's mark first: also **tit-tat-toe.**

**tick·tock** (tik'tok'), *n.* the sound made by a clock or watch. *v.i.* to make this sound.

**Ti·con·der·o·ga, Fort** (tī'kon-də-rō'gə, tī-kon'-), an old fort in New York State, on Lake Champlain.

**tid·al** (tī'd'l), *adj.* of, having, caused by, determined by, or dependent on a tide or tides.

**tidal wave,** 1. an unusually great, destructive wave sent inshore by an earthquake or a very strong wind. 2. any great or widespread movement, expression of prevalent feeling, etc.

**tid·bit** (tid'bit'), *n.* [dial. *tid*, small object + *bit*], a choice bit of food, gossip, etc.: also **titbit.**

**tid·dly·winks** (tid'li-wiŋks'), *n.* a game in which the players try to snap little colored disks into a cup by pressing their edges with larger disks: also **tid'dle·dy·winks'** (tid''l-di-).

**tide** (tīd), *n.* [AS. *tid*, time], 1. a period of time: now only in combination, as in *Eastertide.* 2. the alternate rise and fall of the surface of oceans, seas, etc., caused by the attraction of the moon and sun, and occurring twice in each period of 24 hours and

51 minutes. 3. something that rises and falls like the tide. 4. a stream, current, etc.: as, the *tide* of public opinion. 5. [Archaic], an opportune time. *adj.* tidal. *v.i.* [TIDED, TIDING], to surge like a tide. *v.t.* to carry as with the tide. —**tide over,** to help along temporarily, as through a period of difficulty. —**turn the tide,** to reverse a condition.

**tide·land** (tīd′land′), *n.* land covered by flood tide.

**tide·mark** (tīd′märk′), *n.* the high-water mark or, sometimes, the low-water mark of the tide.

**tide·wa·ter** (tīd′wô′tēr, -wä′-), *n.* 1. water that is affected by the tide. 2. an area in which water is affected by the tide. *adj.* of or along a tidewater.

**ti·dings** (tī′diŋz), *n.pl.* [sometimes construed as sing.], [AS. *tidung*], news; information.

**ti·dy** (tī′di), *adj.* [-DIER, -DIEST], [< AS. *tid*, time], 1. neat in personal appearance, ways, etc.; orderly. 2. neat in arrangement; in order; trim. 3. [Colloq.], *a*) fairly good; satisfactory. *b*) rather large; considerable: as, a *tidy* sum. *v.t. & v.i.* [-DIED, -DYING], to make (things) tidy: often with *up*. *n.* [*pl.* -DIES], an antimacassar. —**ti′di·ness,** *n.*

**tie** (tī), *v.t.* [TIED, TYING], [AS. *tigan* < base of *teag*, a rope], 1. to fasten or bind together by entwining with string, rope, etc., which is then knotted. 2. to tighten and knot the laces, strings, etc. of: as, to *tie* one's shoes. 3. to make (a knot). 4. to make a knot in. 5. to fasten or join in any way. 6. to confine; restrict. 7. to equal (the score) of (an opponent) in a contest. 8. in *music*, to connect with a tie. *v.i.* 1. to make a tie. 2. to make the same score in a contest. *n.* 1. a string, cord, etc. used to tie things. 2. something that connects, binds, etc.; bond. 3. something that confines or restricts: as, legal *ties*. 4. a necktie, or cravat. 5. a beam, rod, etc. that holds together and strengthens parts of a building. 6. any of the parallel crossbeams to which the rails of a railroad are fastened. 7. an equality of scores in a contest. 8. a contest in which there is such an equality. 9. in *music*, a curved line joining two notes of the same pitch, indicating that the tone is to be held unbroken. —**tie down,** to confine; restrain; restrict. —**ties,** low, laced shoes. —**tie up,** 1. to tie securely. 2. to wrap up and tie with string, etc. 3. to moor to a dock. 4. to obstruct; hinder. 5. to cause to be already in use, committed, etc. —**ti′er,** *n.*

**tie·back** (tī′bak′), *n.* a sash, ribbon, tape, etc. used to tie curtains or draperies to one side.

**tie beam,** a beam serving as a tie in a roof, etc.

**tie-dye** (tī′dī′), *n.* 1. a method of dyeing designs on cloth by tying bunches of it with waxed thread so that the dye affects only exposed parts. 2. cloth so decorated.

**tie-in** (tī′in′), *adj.* designating or of a sale in which something scarce or desirable can be bought only in combination with some other, undesired item. *n.* 1. such a sale. 2. an article so sold.

**Tien·tsin** (tin′tsin′), *n.* a city and port in NE China: pop., 3,278,000.

**tie·pin** (tī′pin′), *n.* a decorative pin for fastening a necktie.

**tier** (têr), *n.* [< OFr. *tire*, order; or < Fr. *tir*, a shooting], any of a series of rows, as of seats, arranged one above or behind another. *v.t. & v.i.* to arrange or be arranged in tiers. —**tiered,** *adj.*

**tierce** (têrs), *n.* [< OFr. < L. *tertia*, fem. of *tertius*, third], 1. originally, a third. 2. the third of the seven canonical hours.

**Tier·ra del Fue·go** (ti-er′ə del′ fū-ā′gō), 1. a group of islands belonging to Chile and Argentina, south of the Strait of Magellan. 2. the chief island in the group.

**tie-up** (tī′up′), *n.* 1. a temporary interruption or stoppage of production, traffic, etc. 2. [Colloq.], connection; relation.

**tiff** (tif), *n.* [? echoic], 1. a slight fit of anger. 2. a slight quarrel. *v.i.* to be in or have a tiff.

**tif·fin** (tif′in), *n., v.i. & v.t.* [Anglo-Ind. for *tiffing*, drinking], [Brit.], lunch.

**ti·ger** (tī′gēr), *n.* [*pl.* -GERS, -GER; see PLURAL, II, D, 1], [< OFr. < L. < Gr. *tigris*], 1. a large, flesh-eating animal of the cat family, native to Asia, having a tawny coat striped with black. 2. a cruel or aggressive person. —**ti′ger·ish,** *adj.*

**tiger beetle,** any of various beetles with larvae that burrow in soil and feed on other insects.

**ti·ger·eye** (tī′gēr-ī′), *n.* a semiprecious, yellow-brown stone: also **ti′ger's-eye′** (-gērz-).

**tiger lily,** a variety of lily having orange flowers with purplish-black spots.

**tiger moth,** any of a group of stout-bodied moths with brightly striped or spotted wings.

**tight** (tīt), *adj.* [< AS. *thiht* (in comp.), strong], 1. so compact in structure that water, air, etc. cannot pass through: as, the boat is *tight*. 2. drawn, packed, etc. closely together: as, a *tight* weave. 3. [Dial.], snug; trim; neat; shapely. 4. fixed securely; firm: as, a *tight* joint. 5. fully stretched; taut. 6. fitting so closely as to be uncomfortable. 7. strict: as, to keep *tight* control. 8. difficult to manage: especially in *a tight corner, squeeze*, etc., a difficult situation. 9. showing strain: as, a *tight* smile. 10. almost even or tied: as, a *tight* race. 11. *a*) difficult to get; scarce. *b*) characterized by such scarcity: as, a *tight* market. 12. concise: said of language. 13. [Colloq.], stingy. 14. [Slang], drunk. *adv.* tightly. —**sit tight,** to maintain one's opinion or position. —**tight′ly,** *adv.* —**tight′ness,** *n.*

**-tight,** [< *tight*], a combining form meaning *impervious to*, as in *watertight, airtight*.

**tight·en** (tīt′'n), *v.t. & v.i.* to make or become tight or tighter. —**tight′en·er,** *n.*

**tight·fist·ed** (tīt′fis′tid), *adj.* stingy.

**tight-lipped** (tīt′lipt′), *adj.* 1. having the lips closed tightly. 2. not saying much; secretive.

**tight·rope** (tīt′rōp′), *n.* a tightly stretched rope on which acrobats perform balancing acts.

**tights** (tīts), *n.pl.* a tightly fitting garment for the lower half of the body and legs, worn by acrobats, dancers, etc.

**tight·wad** (tīt′wäd′, -wôd′), *n.* [*tight* + *wad* (roll of money)], [Slang], a stingy person; miser.

**ti·gress** (tī′gris), *n.* a female tiger.

**Ti·gris** (tī′gris), *n.* a river in SE Turkey and Iraq, joining with the Euphrates to flow into the Persian Gulf.

**tike** (tīk), *n.* a tyke.

**til·bur·y** (til′bēr-i), *n.* [*pl.* -IES], [< *Tilbury*, a London coach builder], a light, two-wheeled carriage for two persons.

**til·de** (til′də), *n.* [Sp. < L. *titulus*, title], a diacritical mark (~) used in various ways; esp., in Spanish, over an *n* to indicate a palatal nasal sound (ny), as in *señor*.

**tile** (tīl), *n.* [< AS. < L. *tegula*], 1. a thin piece of glazed or unglazed, fired clay, stone, etc., used for roofing, flooring, decorative borders, bathroom walls, etc. 2. a similar piece of plastic, etc., used in the same way. 3. tiles collectively. 4. a drain of tiles or earthenware pipe. 5. any of the pieces in mah-jongg. 6. [Colloq.], a high, stiff hat. *v.t.* [TILED, TILING], to cover with tiles. —**til′er,** *n.*

**til·ing** (tīl′iŋ), *n.* 1. the action of one who tiles. 2. tiles collectively. 3. a covering of tiles.

**till** (til), *prep. & conj.* [< AS. *til*], until.

**till** (til), *v.t. & v.i.* [AS. *tilian*, lit., to strive for], to prepare (land) for raising crops, as by plowing, fertilizing, etc.; cultivate. —**till′a·ble,** *adj.* —**till′er,** *n.*

**till** (til), *n.* [prob. < ME. *tyllen*, to draw], 1. a drawer or tray, as in a store counter, etc., for keeping money. 2. ready cash.

**till·age** (til′ij), *n.* 1. the tilling of land. 2. the state of being tilled; cultivation. 3. land that is tilled. 4. the crops on such land.

**till·er** (til′ēr), *n.* [< OFr. < ML. *telarium*, weaver's beam < L. *tela*, a web], a bar or handle for turning a boat's rudder.

**tilt** (tilt), *v.t.* [< AS. *tealt*, shaky], 1. to cause to slope; tip. 2. to poise or thrust (a lance) in a tilt. 3. to rush at (one's opponent) in a tilt. *v.i.* 1. to slope; incline. 2. to poise or thrust one's lance (*at* one's opponent) in a tilt. 3. to engage in a tilt or joust. 4. to dispute; argue. *n.* 1. a medieval contest in which two horsemen thrust with lances in an attempt to unseat each other. 2. any spirited contest between two persons. 3. a tilting or being tilted (sense 1). 4. a slope. —(**at**) **full tilt,** at full speed; with the greatest force. —**tilt at windmills,** to attack imaginary opponents. —**tilt′er,** *n.*

**tilth** (tilth), *n.* [AS. < *tilian*, to work for], 1. a tilling or being tilled. 2. tilled land.

**Tim.,** Timothy.

**tim·bal** (tim′b'l), *n.* [Fr. *timbale;* ult. < Ar. < *al*, the + *tabl*, drum], a kettledrum.

**tim·bale** (tim′b'l), *n.* [Fr.; see TIMBAL], 1. a highly flavored dish made of chicken, lobster, fish, etc. baked in a small, drum-shaped mold. 2. a type of fried pastry shell, filled with a cooked food: also **timbal case.**

**tim·ber** (tim′bēr), *n.* [AS.], 1. wood suitable for

building houses, ships, etc. 2. a large, heavy, dressed piece of wood used in building; beam. 3. [Brit.], lumber. 4. trees collectively. 5. timberland. 6. personal quality or character: as, a man of his *timber*. 7. a wooden rib of a ship. ***v.t.*** to provide, build, or prop up with timbers. ***adj.*** of or for timber. **—tim′bered, *adj.* —tim′ber·ing, *n.***

**timber hitch,** in *nautical usage*, a knot used for tying a rope to a spar.

**tim·ber·land** (tim′bẽr-land′), ***n.*** land with trees suitable for timber; wooded land.

**timber line,** the imaginary line on mountains and in polar regions beyond which trees do not grow because of cold. **—tim′ber-line′, *adj.***

**timber wolf,** a large, gray wolf of North America.

**tim·bre** (tim′bẽr, tam′-), ***n.*** [Fr. < OFr.; see TIMBREL], the characteristic quality of sound that distinguishes one voice or musical instrument from another: distinguished from *intensity, pitch.*

**tim·brel** (tim′brəl), ***n.*** [< OFr. *timbre*, small bell < L.; see TYMPANUM], an ancient type of tambourine.

**Tim·buk·tu** (tim-buk′tōō, tim′buk-tōō′), ***n.*** a town in French West Africa: pop., 7,000.

**time** (tīm), ***n.*** [AS. *tima*], 1. the period between two events or during which something exists, happens, etc. 2. *often pl.* a period of history; age, epoch, era, etc.: as, medieval *times*, in Lincoln's *time*. 3. *usually pl.* prevailing conditions: as, *times* are bad. 4. a period characterized by a prevailing condition: as, a *time* of sorrow. 5. a period with reference to one's personal reaction to it: as, I had a good *time*. 6. a set period or term, as a lifetime, the period of pregnancy, a term of imprisonment, etc. 7. a period necessary, available, measured, etc. for an action: as, *time* for recreation, baking *time*, 20 minutes. 8. *a*) the period worked or to be worked by an employee. *b*) the pay due for this. 9. rate of speed in marching, driving, etc. 10. in *music*, a) the grouping of rhythmic beats into measures of equal length. *b*) the characteristic rhythm of a composition in terms of this grouping. *c*) the rate of speed at which a composition is played; tempo. *d*) the duration of a note or rest. 11. a precise instant, minute, hour, day, year, etc.: as, the *time* of the accident was 5:46 P.M. 12. the point at which something happens; occasion: as, at the *time* they arrived, I was away. 13. the usual or appointed moment for something to happen, begin, or end: as, *time* to get up. 14. the suitable or proper moment: as, now is the *time* to act. 15. any one of a series of moments at which the same or nearly the same thing recurs: as, this is the fifth *time* I've told you. 16. indefinite, unlimited duration; every moment there has ever been or ever will be. 17. a system of measuring duration: as, solar *time*, standard *time*, etc. ***interj.*** in *sports*, etc., a signal that a period of play or activity is ended or that play is temporarily suspended. ***v.t.*** [TIMED, TIMING], 1. to arrange the time of so as to be acceptable, suitable, opportune, etc. 2. to adjust, set, etc. so as to coincide in time: as, *time* your watch with mine. 3. to set the duration of (a syllable or note) as a unit of rhythm. 4. to record the pace, speed, etc. of: as, the horse was *timed* at 3:02. ***adj.*** 1. having to do with time. 2. set to explode, open, etc. at a given time: as, a *time* bomb. 3. payable later: as, a *time* loan. 4. having to do with purchases paid for over a period of time: as, a *time* payment. **—abreast of the times,** 1. up-to-date. 2. informed about current matters. **—against time,** trying to finish in a given time. **—ahead of time,** sooner than due; early. **—at one time,** 1. simultaneously. 2. formerly. **—at the same time,** nonetheless; however. **—at times,** occasionally; sometimes. **—behind the times,** out-of-date; old-fashioned. **—behind time,** late. **—for the time being,** for the present; temporarily. **—from time to time,** at intervals; now and then. **—in good time,** 1. at the proper time. 2. in a creditably short time. **—in no time,** very quickly. **—in time,** 1. eventually. 2. before it is too late. 3. keeping the set tempo, pace, etc. **—make time,** to travel, work, etc. at a fast rate of speed. **—many a time,** often; frequently. **—on time,** 1. at the appointed time; punctual(ly). 2. to be paid for in installments over a period of time. **—pass the time of day,** to exchange a few words of greeting, etc. **—time after time,** again and again; continually: also **time and again. —time of one's life,** [Colloq.], an experience of unusual pleasure for one. **—times,** multiplied by: symbol, ×.

**time·card** (tīm′kärd′), ***n.*** a card for showing the number of hours an employee has worked.

**time clock,** a clock with a mechanism for recording on a timecard the time an employee begins and ends a work period.

**time exposure,** 1. a relatively long exposure of photographic film, generally for more than half a second. 2. a photograph taken in this way.

**time-hon·ored** (tīm′on′ẽrd), ***adj.*** honored because in existence or usage for a long time.

**time·keep·er** (tīm′kēp′ẽr), ***n.*** 1. a timepiece. 2. one who keeps time; specif., *a*) one who keeps account of the hours worked by employees. *b*) one who keeps account of the elapsed time in races, etc.

**time·less** (tīm′lis), ***adj.*** 1. unending; eternal. 2. restricted to no specific time; dateless. **—time′less·ly, *adv.* —time′less·ness, *n.***

**time limit,** a fixed period of time during which something must be done or ended.

**time loan,** a loan to be paid by a specified time.

**time·ly** (tīm′li), ***adj.*** [-LIER, -LIEST], happening, done, said, etc. at a suitable time; well-timed; opportune. **—time′li·ness, *n.***

**time out,** in *sports*, etc., any temporary suspension of play, as to discuss strategy, etc.

**time·piece** (tīm′pēs′), ***n.*** any apparatus for measuring and recording time; esp., a clock or watch.

**tim·er** (tīm′ẽr), ***n.*** 1. a timekeeper. 2. a timepiece. 3. in internal-combustion engines, a mechanism for causing the spark to be produced in the cylinder at the required instant.

**time·serv·er** (tīm′sũr′vẽr), ***n.*** one who for his own advantage acts in conformity with the opinions prevailing at the time or sanctioned by those in authority. **—time′serv′ing, *n. & adj.***

**time signature,** in *music*, a sign, after the key signature, indicating the time, or tempo.

**time study,** study of operational or production procedures and the time consumed by them.

**time·ta·ble** (tīm′tā′b'l), ***n.*** a schedule of the times certain things are to happen, especially of the times of arrival and departure of trains, etc.

**time-test·ed** (tīm′tes′tid), ***adj.*** having value proved by long use or experience.

**time·worn** (tīm′wôrn′), ***adj.*** worn or deteriorated by long use or existence.

**time zone,** see **standard time.**

**tim·id** (tim′id), ***adj.*** [< L. < *timere*, to fear], 1. easily frightened; shy. 2. showing lack of self-confidence. **—tim′id·ly, *adv.* —tim′id·ness, *n.***

**ti·mid·i·ty** (ti-mid′ə-ti), ***n.*** the condition or quality of being timid.

**tim·ing** (tīm′iŋ), ***n.*** the regulation of the speed with which something is performed so as to produce the most effective results.

**Ti·mor** (tē′môr, ti-môr′), ***n.*** an island of the East Indies, partly in Indonesia and partly a Portuguese colony: area, 13,700 sq. mi.

**tim·or·ous** (tim′ẽr-əs), ***adj.*** [< OFr. < ML. < L. *timor*, fear], 1. full of or subject to fear; timid. 2. showing or caused by timidity. **—tim′or·ous·ly, *adv.* —tim′or·ous·ness, *n.***

**Tim·o·thy** (tim′ə-thi), ***n.*** in the *Bible*, 1. a disciple of the Apostle Paul. 2. either of two books of the New Testament, messages from the Apostle Paul to Timothy.

**tim·o·thy** (tim′ə-thi), ***n.*** [< *Timothy* Hanson, who took the seed to the Carolinas, c. 1720], a grass with long, narrow leaves and bearded spikes of flowers, used for fodder: also **timothy grass.**

**tim·pa·ni** (tim′pə-ni), ***n.pl.*** [*sing.* -NO (-nō′)], [It.; see TYMPANUM], kettledrums; esp., a set of kettledrums of different pitches played by one performer in an orchestra. **—tim′pa·nist, *n.***

**tin** (tin), ***n.*** [AS.], 1. a soft, silver-white, metallic chemical element, malleable at ordinary temperatures: symbol, Sn; at. wt., 118.70; at. no., 50. 2. tin plate. 3. *a*) a pan, pot, box, etc. made of tin plate. *b*) [Brit.], a can (sense 2). ***adj.*** of tin or tin plate. ***v.t.*** [TINNED, TINNING], 1. to plate with tin. 2. [Brit.], to preserve in tins; can.

**tin·a·mou** (tin′ə-mōō′), ***n.*** [Fr. < Carib name, *tinamu*], a South American bird resembling the partridge and quail, but related to the ostrich.

**tinc·ture** (tiŋk′chẽr), ***n.*** [< L. *tinctura* < pp. of *tingere*, to dye], 1. a dye. 2. a light color; tint; tinge. 3. a slight trace, shade, vestige, etc. 4. a medicinal substance in solution, especially in alcohol: as, *tincture* of iodine. ***v.t.*** [-TURED, -TURING], 1. to color lightly; tint; tinge. 2. to imbue with a trace, taste, etc.

**tin·der** (tin′dẽr), ***n.*** [AS. *tynder*], any dry, easily inflammable material, especially that formerly used for starting a fire by catching a spark from flint and steel struck together.

**tin·der·box** (tin′dẽr-boks′), ***n.*** 1. a metal box for holding tinder, flint, and steel. 2. any highly inflammable object, excitable person, etc.

**tine** (tīn), ***n.*** [AS. *tind*], a sharp, projecting point; prong: as, the *tines* of a fork. **—tined, *adj.***

**tin foil,** a very thin sheet or sheets of tin or an alloy of tin and lead, used to wrap candy, cigarettes, etc. —**tin′-foil′,** *adj.*

**ting** (tiŋ), *n.* [echoic], a single, light, ringing sound, as of a small bell being struck. *v.t. & v.i.* to make or cause to make a ting.

‡**ting** (tiŋ), *n.* a thing (assembly).

**ting-a-ling** (tiŋ′ə-liŋ′), *n.* the sound of a small bell ringing.

**tinge** (tinj), *v.t.* [TINGED, TINGEING or TINGING], [< L. *tingere*, to dye], 1. to color slightly; give a tint to. 2. to give a trace, slight flavor or odor, shade, etc. to: as, a memory *tinged* with sorrow. *n.* 1. a slight coloring; tint. 2. a slight trace, flavor, odor, etc. —**tin′gi·ble,** *adj.*

**tin·gle** (tiŋ′g'l), *v.i.* [-GLED, -GLING], [var. of *tinkle*], 1. to have a prickling, slightly stinging feeling, as from cold, excitement, etc. 2. to cause this feeling. *v.t.* to cause to have this feeling. *n.* this feeling. —**tin′gler,** *n.* —**tin′gling·ly,** *adv.* —**tin′gly** [-GLIER, -GLIEST], *adj.*

**tin·horn** (tin′hôrn′), *adj.* [Slang], flashy and cheap, petty, etc.: as, a *tinhorn* gambler.

**tink·er** (tiŋ′kẽr), *n.* [prob. ult. echoic], 1. one who mends pots, pans, etc., usually traveling at his trade. 2. one who can make all kinds of minor repairs. 3. a clumsy or unskillful worker; bungler. 4. the action of such a person. *v.i.* 1. to work as a tinker. 2. to make clumsy attempts to mend something. 3. to putter aimlessly or uselessly. *v.t.* to mend as a tinker; patch up. —**tink′er·er,** *n.*

**tinker's damn** (or **dam**), [< *tinker* + *damn*: with reference to the lowly status and profane speech of tinkers], something of no value: especially in *not worth a tinker's damn.*

**tin·kle** (tiŋ′k'l), *v.i.* [-KLED, -KLING], [echoic], to make a series of light, clinking sounds like those of a very small bell. *v.t.* 1. to cause to tinkle. 2. to indicate, signal, etc. by tinkling. *n.* 1. the act of tinkling. 2. a tinkling sound. —**tin′kler,** *n.* —**tin′kly** [-KLIER, -KLIEST], *adj.*

**tin·ner** (tin′ẽr), *n.* 1. a tin miner. 2. a tinsmith. 3. [Brit.], a canner.

**tin·ny** (tin′i), *adj.* [-NIER, -NIEST], 1. of or yielding tin. 2. like tin; bright but cheap; not durable. 3. of or like the sound made in striking a tin object. —**tin′ni·ly,** *adv.* —**tin′ni·ness,** *n.*

**tin-pan alley** (tin′pan′), 1. a district, especially of New York, where there are many song writers, music publishers, etc. 2. the publishers, writers, and promoters of popular music.

**tin plate,** thin sheets of iron or steel plated with tin. —**tin′-plate′** [-PLATED, -PLATING], *v.t.*

**tin·sel** (tin′s'l), *n.* [< Fr. *étincelle* < OFr. < L. *scintilla*, a flash], 1. formerly, a cloth interwoven with glittering threads of gold, silver, etc. 2. thin sheets, strips, or threads of tin, metal foil, etc., used for inexpensive decoration. 3. something that glitters like precious metal but has little worth. *adj.* 1. of or decorated with tinsel. 2. showy; gaudy. *v.t.* [-SELED or -SELLED, -SELING or -SELLING], 1. to make glitter as with tinsel. 2. to give a false appearance of splendor to. —**tin′sel·ly,** *adj.*

**tin·smith** (tin′smith′), *n.* one who works in tin or tin plate; maker of tinware: also **tin′man** [*pl.* -MEN], **tins′man** [*pl.* -MEN].

**tint** (tint), *n.* [< L. *tinctus*, pp. of *tingere*, to dye], 1. a delicate color or hue; tinge. 2. a color; esp., a gradation of a color with reference to its mixture with white. 3. in *engraving*, an even shading produced by fine parallel lines. *v.t.* to give a tint to. —**tint′er,** *n.*

**tin·tin·nab·u·la·tion** (tin′ti-nab′yoo-lā′shən), *n.* [< L. *tintinnabulum*, little bell], the ringing sound of bells.

**Tin·to·ret·to Il** (ēl tin′tə-ret′ō), (*Jacopo Robusti*), 1518–1594; Venetian painter.

**tin·type** (tin′tīp′), *n.* a photograph taken directly on a sensitized plate of enameled tin or iron.

**tin·ware** (tin′wâr′), *n.* pots, pans, kettles, etc. made of tin plate.

**ti·ny** (tī′ni), *adj.* [-NIER, -NIEST], [< ME. *tine*, a little], very small; diminutive; minute. —**ti′ni·ly,** *adv.* —**ti′ni·ness,** *n.*

**-tion** (shən), [< Fr. < OFr. < L. *-tio, -tionis*], a suffix used to form nouns from verbs, meaning: 1. *a —ing* or *being —ed*, as in *relation.* 2. *something —ed*, as in *creation.*

**-tious** (shəs), [< Fr. < L. *-tiosus*], a suffix used in forming adjectives corresponding to nouns in *-tion*, as *cautious.*

**tip** (tip), *n.* [ME. *tippe*], 1. the pointed or rounded end or top of something. 2. something attached to the end, as a cap, ferrule, etc. 3. a top or apex, as of a mountain. *v.t.* [TIPPED, TIPPING], 1. to make a tip on. 2. to cover the tip or tips of (*with* something). 3. to serve as the tip of.

**tip** (tip), *v.t.* [TIPPED, TIPPING], [prob. akin to prec. entry], 1. to strike lightly and sharply; tap. 2. to hit, as a baseball, a glancing blow. 3. to give a small present of money to (a waiter, porter, etc.) for some service. 4. [Colloq.], to give secret information to: often with *off.* *v.i.* to give a tip or tips. *n.* 1. a light, sharp blow; tap. 2. a piece of information given confidentially: as, a *tip* on a race. 3. a suggestion, hint, warning, etc. 4. a small present of money given to a waiter, porter, etc. for services; gratuity. —**tip′per,** *n.*

**tip** (tip), *v.t.* [TIPPED, TIPPING], [prob. < ON.], 1. to overturn or upset: often with *over.* 2. to cause to tilt or slant. 3. to raise (one's hat) slightly in salutation. *v.i.* 1. to tilt or slant. 2. to overturn or topple: often with *over.* *n.* a tipping or being tipped; tilt; slant. —**tip′per,** *n.*

**tip-off** (tip′ôf′), *n.* a tip; confidential disclosure, hint, or warning.

**Tip·per·ar·y** (tip′ə-râr′i), *n.* 1. a county in S Ireland. 2. a town in this county.

**tip·pet** (tip′it), *n.* [prob. dim. of *tip*, a point], 1. formerly, a long, hanging part of a hood, cape, or sleeve. 2. a long scarf, as of fur, for the neck and shoulders, hanging down in front.

**tip·ple** (tip′'l), *v.i. & v.t.* [TIPPLED, TIPPLING], [prob. freq. of *tip* (to overturn)], to drink (alcoholic liquor) habitually. *n.* alcoholic liquor. —**tip′pler,** *n.*

**tip·ster** (tip′stẽr), *n.* [Colloq.], one who sells tips, as on horse races, for stock speculation, etc.

**tip·sy** (tip′si), *adj.* [-SIER, -SIEST], 1. that tips easily; not steady. 2. crooked; awry. 3. somewhat drunk. —**tip′si·ly,** *adv.* —**tip′si·ness,** *n.*

**tip·toe** (tip′tō′), *n.* the tip of a toe or the tips of the toes. *v.i.* [-TOED, -TOEING], to walk stealthily or cautiously on one's tiptoes. *adj.* 1. standing on one's tiptoes. 2. *a*) lifted up; exalted. *b*) eager; alert. *c*) stealthy; cautious. *adv.* on tiptoe. —**on tiptoe,** 1. on one's tiptoes. 2. eager or eagerly. 3. silently; stealthily.

**tip·top** (tip′top′), *n.* [*tip* (end) + *top*], 1. the highest point; very top. 2. [Colloq.], the highest in quality or excellence; best. *adj. & adv.* 1. at the highest point, or top. 2. [Colloq.], at the highest point of excellence, health, etc.

**ti·rade** (tī′rād, ti-rād′), *n.* [Fr. < It. *tirata*, a volley < pp. of *tirare*, to fire], a long, vehement speech or denunciation; harangue.

**Ti·ra·na, Ti·ra·në** (tē-rä′nə), *n.* the capital of Albania: pop., 31,000.

**tire** (tīr), *v.t. & v.i.* [TIRED, TIRING], [AS. *tiorian*], 1. to make or become weary or fatigued, as by exertion. 2. to make or become bored or impatient, as by dull talk. —**tire of,** to become bored by. —**tire out,** to tire completely; exhaust. —**tir′ing·ly,** *adv.*

**tire** (tīr), *n.* [< ME. contr. of *attire*, equipment], a hoop of iron or rubber, or a rubber tube filled with air, fixed around the wheel of a vehicle to form the tread. *v.t.* [TIRED, TIRING], to furnish with a tire.

**tired** (tīrd), *adj.* fatigued; weary. —**tired′ly,** *adv.* —**tired′ness,** *n.*

**tire·less** (tīr′lis), *adj.* that does not become tired. —**tire′less·ly,** *adv.* —**tire′less·ness,** *n.*

**tire·some** (tīr′səm), *adj.* tiring; boring; wearisome. —**tire′some·ly,** *adv.* —**tire′some·ness,** *n.*

**ti·ro** (tī′rō), *n.* [*pl.* -ROS], a tyro.

**Tir·ol** (tir′ol, ti-rōl′), *n.* Tyrol. —**Tir·o·lese** (tir′ə-lēz′), *adj. & n.*

**'tis** (tiz), it is.

**Tish·ah b'Ab** (tish′ä bôv′), see **Jewish holidays.**

**Tish·ri** (tish′ri), *n.* the first month of the Jewish year: see **Jewish calendar.**

**tis·sue** (tish′oo, -oo), *n.* [< OFr. *tissu*, pp. of *tistre* (< L. *texere*), to weave], 1. cloth; esp., light, thin cloth, as gauze. 2. an interwoven mass or series; mesh; network; web: as, a *tissue* of lies. 3. tissue paper. 4. in *biology*, *a*) the substance of an organic body or organ, consisting of cells and intercellular material. *b*) any of the distinct structural materials of an organism, having a particular function: as, epithelial *tissue.*

**tissue paper,** very thin, unsized, nearly transparent paper for wrapping gifts, for toilet use, etc.

**tit** (tit), *n.* [< *titmouse*], a titmouse, titlark, etc.
**tit** (tit), *n.* [AS. *titt*], a teat; nipple.
**Tit.,** Titus.
**Ti·tan** (tī′t'n), *n.* 1. in *Gr. mythology*, any of a race of giant deities who were overthrown and succeeded by the Olympian gods. 2. Helios, the sun god. 3. [t-], any person or thing of great size or power. *adj.* [also t-], Titanic. —**Ti′tan·ess,** *n.fem.*
**Ti·ta·ni·a** (ti-tā′ni-ə, tī-), *n.* in *early folklore*, the queen of fairyland and wife of Oberon.
**Ti·tan·ic** (tī-tan′ik), *adj.* 1. of or like the Titans. 2. [t-], of great size, strength, or power.
**ti·ta·ni·um** (tī-tā′ni-əm, ti-), *n.* [< L. < Gr. pl. of *Titan*, a Titan], a dark-gray, lustrous, metallic chemical element found in various minerals and used as a deoxidizing agent in molten steel, etc.: symbol, Ti; at. wt., 47.90; at. no., 22.
**tit·bit** (tit′bit′), *n.* a tidbit.
**tit for tat,** [earlier *tip for tap* < *tip*, to strike + *tap*, a blow], blow for blow; retaliation in kind.
**tithe** (tīth), *n.* [AS. *teothe*, a tenth], 1. one tenth of one's annual income or of the produce of one's land, etc., paid as a tax to support the church or the clergy. 2. a tenth part or any small part. 3. any tax or levy. *v.t. & v.i.* [TITHED, TITHING], 1. to pay a tithe of (one's income, produce, etc.). 2. to levy a tithe on (someone). —**tith′a·ble,** *adj.* —**tith′er,** *n.*
**Ti·tian** (tish′ən), *n.* (*Tiziano Vecellio*), Venetian painter; 1477–1576.
**ti·tian** (tish′ən, -i-ən), *n. & adj.* reddish yellow; auburn: Titian often painted hair this shade.
**tit·il·late** (tit′'l-āt′), *v.t.* [-LATED, -LATING], [< L. pp. of *titillare*, to tickle], 1. to tickle. 2. to excite or stimulate pleasurably. —**tit′il·lat′er,** *n.* —**tit′il·la′tion,** *n.* —**tit′il·la′tive,** *adj.*
**tit·i·vate, tit·ti·vate** (tit′ə-vāt′), *v.t. & v.i.* [-VATED, -VATING], [prob. < *tidy*, with quasi-Latin suffix], [Colloq.], to dress up; spruce up. —**tit′i·va′tion, tit′ti·va′tion,** *n.* —**tit′i·va′tor, tit′ti·va′tor,** *n.*
**tit·lark** (tit′lärk′), *n.* [*tit* (small bird, etc.) + *lark*], a pipit, a larklike bird.
**ti·tle** (tī′t'l), *n.* [OFr. < L. *titulus*], 1. the name of a poem, chapter, book, picture, piece of music, etc. 2. a title page. 3. a descriptive name or appellation; epithet. 4. an appellation given to a person or family as a sign of privilege, distinction, or profession: as, the *title* of lord. 5. a claim or right. 6. in *law*, *a*) a right to ownership, especially of real estate. *b*) evidence of such right. *c*) a document stating such a right; deed. 7. in *sports*, etc., a championship. *v.t.* [TITLED, TITLING], to give a title to; name; entitle. —**ti′tled,** *adj.*
**title page,** the page in the front of a book that gives the title, author, publisher, etc.
**title role** (or **part**), the character in a play, opera, etc. whose name is used as (or in) the title.
**tit·mouse** (tit′mous′), *n.* [*pl.* -MICE], [ME. *titemose*; prob. < *tit-*, little + AS. *mase*, titmouse], any of various small birds with dull-colored feathers, including the chickadee.
**Ti·to** (tē′tō), Marshal (*Josip Broz*), 1891– ; Communist leader of Yugoslavia; premier (1945– ).
**ti·trate** (tī′trāt, tit′rāt), *v.t. & v.i.* [-TRATED, -TRATING], [< Fr. *titrer* (< *titre*, a standard)], to test by or be subjected to titration.
**ti·tra·tion** (tī-trā′shən, ti-), *n.* in *chemistry*, etc., the process of finding out how much of a certain substance is contained in a solution by measuring how much of another substance it is necessary to add to produce a given reaction.
**tit-tat-toe** (ti′ta-tō′), *n.* tick-tack-toe.
**tit·ter** (tit′ẽr), *v.i.* [echoic], to laugh in a half-suppressed way, suggestive of foolishness, nervousness, etc.; giggle. *n.* a tittering; giggle. —**tit′ter·er,** *n.* —**tit′ter·ing·ly,** *adv.*
**tit·tle** (tit′'l), *n.* [ME. *titel*, orig. same word as *title*], 1. a dot or other small mark used as a diacritic. 2. a very small particle; iota; jot.
**tit·tle-tat·tle** (tit′'l-tat′'l), *n. & v.i.* [-TLED, -TLING], [redupl. of *tattle*], gossip; chatter.
**tit·u·lar** (tich′oo-lẽr, tit′yoo-), *adj.* [< L. *titulus*, title], 1. of, or having the nature of, a title. 2. having a title. 3. existing only in title; in name only: as, a *titular* leader. 4. from whose name the title is taken: as, a *titular* character of a novel. Also **tit′u·lar·y.** —**tit′u·lar·ly,** *adv.*
**Ti·tus** (tī′təs), *n.* 1. a disciple of the Apostle Paul. 2. a book of the New Testament which was a message from the Apostle Paul to Titus.
**tiz·zy** (tiz′i), *n.* [*pl.* -ZIES], [< ?], [Slang], a state of frenzied excitement or distraction, especially over a triviality.
**T.K.O., TKO,** in *boxing*, a technical knockout.
**Tl,** in *chemistry*, thallium.
**T.L.,** trade-last.
**Tm,** in *chemistry*, thulium.
**Tn,** in *chemistry*, thoron.
**tn.,** ton; tons.
**TNT, T.N.T.,** trinitrotoluene.
**to** (to͞o; *unstressed* too, tə), *prep.* [AS.], 1. *a*) in the direction of; toward: as, turn *to* the left. *b*) in the direction of and reaching: as, he went *to* Boston. 2. as far as: as, wet *to* the skin. 3. into a condition of: as, a rise *to* fame. 4. on, onto, against, at, next, etc.: as, tie it *to* the post. 5. [Dial.], at or in: as, he's *to* home. 6. until: as, from noon *to* night. 7. for the purpose of: as, come *to* my aid. 8. as concerns; in respect of: as, open *to* attack. 9. producing or resulting in: as, torn *to* pieces. 10. with; along with: as, add this *to* the rest. 11. belonging with; of: as, the coat *to* this suit. 12. compared with; as against: as, a score of 7 *to* 0. 13. in agreement or correspondence with: as, not *to* my taste. 14. constituting; in: as, ten *to* the peck. 15. with (a specified person or thing) as the recipient, or indirect object, of the action: as, give it *to* me. 16. in honor of: as, a toast *to* victory. *To* is also used as a sign of the infinitive (e.g., I want *to* stay). *adv.* 1. forward: as, his hat is on wrong side *to*. 2. in the normal or desired position or condition; esp., shut or closed: as, the door was blown *to*. 3. to the matter at hand: as, let's all fall *to*. 4. at hand: as, we were close *to* when it fell. —**to and fro,** back and forth.
**toad** (tōd), *n.* [AS. *tade*], 1. any of various small, froglike animals that eat insects and live on land rather than in water, except during breeding. 2. a person regarded as loathsome, contemptible, etc.
**toad·fish** (tōd′fish′), *n.* [*pl.* see FISH], any of various scaleless fishes with broad heads, found in shallows off the Atlantic coast of America.
**toad·stool** (tōd′sto͞ol′), *n.* a mushroom; esp., in popular usage, any poisonous mushroom.
**toad·y** (tōd′i), *n.* [*pl.* -IES], [short for *toadeater*, quack doctor's assistant who pretended to eat toads to show the efficacy of quack medicines], a servile flatterer; sycophant: also **toad′eat′er.** *v.t. & v.i.* [-IED, -YING], to be a toady (to); flatter. —**toad′y·ism,** *n.*
**to-and-fro** (to͞o′ən-frō′, -ənd-), *adj.* moving forward and backward; back-and-forth.
**toast** (tōst), *v.t.* [< OFr. < L. *tostus*, pp. of *torrere*, to parch], 1. to brown the surface of (bread, etc.) by heating. 2. to warm thoroughly: as, *toast* yourself by the fire. *v.i.* to become toasted. *n.* sliced bread browned by heat. —**toast′er,** *n.*
**toast** (tōst), *n.* [< the toasted spiced bread formerly put in the wine], 1. a person, institution, sentiment, etc. in honor of which glasses are raised and drunk. 2. a proposal to drink to some person, etc. 3. a drink in honor of a person, etc. *v.t. & v.i.* to propose or drink a toast (to). —**toast′er,** *n.*
**toast·mas·ter** (tōst′mas′tẽr, -mäs′-), *n.* the person at a banquet who proposes toasts, introduces after-dinner speakers, etc.
**Tob.,** Tobit.
**to·bac·co** (tə-bak′ō), *n.* [*pl.* -COS], [< Sp. < Carib *tabaco*, pipe in which the Indians smoked the plant], 1. any of various plants of the nightshade family, with white or pink flowers and large, lance-shaped leaves. 2. the leaves of any of these plants, prepared for smoking, chewing, or snuffing. 3. cigars, cigarettes, snuff, etc.

TOBACCO PLANT

**to·bac·co·nist** (tə-bak′ə-nist), *n.* [Chiefly Brit.], a dealer in tobacco and other smoking supplies.
**To·ba·go** (tō-bā′gō), *n.* an island in the West Indies: see **Trinidad and Tobago.**
**To·bit** (tō′bit), *n.* a book of the Old Testament Apocrypha: also called **To·bi′as** (-bī′əs).
**to·bog·gan** (tə-bog′ən), *n.* [Canad. Fr. *tabagan* < Algonquian], 1. a long, narrow, flat sled without runners, curved back at the front end: now used for coasting downhill. 2. a similar sled with very low runners. *v.i.* [-GANED, -GANING], 1. to coast, travel, etc. on a toboggan. 2. to decline rapidly. —**to·bog′gan·er, to·bog′gan·ist,** *n.*

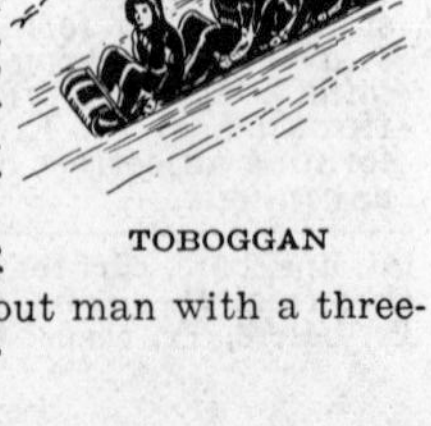
TOBOGGAN

**To·by** (tō′bi), *n.* [*pl.* -BIES], [< *Tobias*], a jug or mug for beer or ale, shaped like a stout man with a three-cornered hat: also **Toby jug.**

**toc·ca·ta** (tə-kä′tə), *n.* [It. < pp. of *toccare*, to touch], a composition in free style for the organ, piano, etc., often used as the prelude of a fugue.

**to·coph·er·ol** (tō-kof′ēr-ōl′, -ol), *n.* [< Gr. *tokos*, childbirth + *pherein*, to bear; + *-ol*], any of a group of alcohols having the properties of vitamin E.

**toc·sin** (tok′sin), *n.* [Fr. < Pr. < *toc*, a stroke + *senh*, a bell < L. *signum*, a sign], 1. an alarm bell. 2. its sound. 3. any alarm.

**to·day, to-day** (tə-dā′), *adv.* [AS. *to dæg*], 1. on or during the present day. 2. in the present time or age; nowadays. *n.* 1. the present day; this day. 2. the present time, period, or age.

**tod·dle** (tod′'l), *v.i.* [-DLED, -DLING], [? freq. of *totter*], to walk with short, uncertain steps, as a child. *n.* a toddling. **—tod′dler,** *n.*

**tod·dy** (tod′i), *n.* [*pl.* -DIES], [< Hind. *tārī* < *tār*, palm tree], 1. the sweet or fermented sap of various East Indian palms, used as a beverage. 2. a drink of brandy, whisky, etc. mixed with hot water, sugar, etc.: also **hot toddy.**

**to-do** (tə-do͞o′), *n.* [Colloq.], a commotion; fuss.

**toe** (tō), *n.* [AS. *ta*], 1. any of the digits of the foot. 2. the fore part of the foot: distinguished from *heel*. 3. that part of a shoe, sock, etc. which covers the toes. 4. anything like a toe in location, shape, or function. *v.t.* [TOED, TOEING], 1. to provide with a toe or toes. 2. to touch, kick, etc. with the toes. 3. *a*) to drive (a nail) slantingly. *b*) to fasten with nails so driven; toenail. *v.i.* to stand, walk, or be formed so that the toes are in a specified position: as, he *toes* in. **—on one's toes,** [Colloq.], mentally or physically alert. **—toe the line** (or **mark**), to follow orders, rules, etc. strictly. **—toe′like′,** *adj.*

**toed** (tōd), *adj.* having (a specified kind or number of) toes: usually in compounds, as, *pigeon-toed*.

**toe dance,** a dance performed on the tips of the toes, as in ballet. **—toe′-dance′** [-DANCED, -DANCING], *v.i.* **—toe′-danc′er,** *n.*

**toe hold,** 1. a small space or ledge for supporting the toe of the foot in climbing, etc. 2. any means of surmounting obstacles, gaining entry, etc. 3. a slight footing.

**toe·less** (tō′lis), *adj.* 1. having no toe or toes. 2. having the toe open: as, *toeless* shoes.

**toe·nail** (tō′nāl′), *n.* 1. the nail of a toe. 2. in *carpentry*, a nail driven obliquely. *v.t.* in *carpentry*, to fasten with a toenail.

**tof·fee, tof·fy** (tôf′i, tof′i), *n.* [? connected with *tafia*, a rum distilled from molasses; cf. TAFFY], a hard, chewy candy made with brown sugar or molasses, often with nuts; kind of taffy.

**tog** (tog, tôg), *n.* [prob. ult. < L. *toga*, toga], *pl.* [Colloq.], clothes. *v.t. & v.i.* [TOGGED, TOGGING], [Colloq.], to dress (often with *up* or *out*).

**to·ga** (tō′gə), *n.* [*pl.* -GAS, -GAE (-jē)], [L. < *tegere*, to cover], 1. in ancient Rome, a loose, one-piece outer garment worn in public by citizens. 2. a robe of office. **—to′gaed** (-gəd), *adj.*

ROMAN TOGA

**to·geth·er** (tə-geth′ēr), *adv.* [AS. < *to* (see TO) + *gædre*, together < base of *gaderian*, to gather], 1. in or into one gathering, group, or place: as, the family ate *together*. 2. in or into contact, collision, union, etc.: as, the cars skidded *together*. 3. considered collectively: as, he's lost more than all of us *together*. 4. with one another; in association: as, the books were compared *together*. 5. at the same time: as, the shots were fired *together*. 6. in succession; continuously: as, he worked for two days *together*. 7. in or into agreement, co-operation, etc.: as, let's get *together*. *Together* is also used colloquially as an intensive after *add*, *join*, etc.

**to·geth·er·ness** (tə-geth′ēr-nis), *n.* the spending of much time together, as in social activities by the members of a family.

**tog·ger·y** (tog′ēr-i, tôg′-), *n.* [Colloq.], 1. clothes; togs. 2. [*pl.* -IES], a clothing store.

**tog·gle** (tog′'l), *n.* [prob. < dial. *tuggle*, freq. of *tug*], 1. a rod, pin, or bolt for inserting through a loop of a rope, a link of a chain, etc. to make an attachment, prevent slipping, etc. 2. a toggle joint or a device having one. *v.t.* [-GLED, -GLING], to provide or fasten with a toggle.

**toggle joint,** a knee-shaped joint consisting of two bars pivoted together at one end: pressure put on the joint to straighten it transmits opposite, outward pressure to the open ends.

**toggle switch,** a switch consisting of a projecting lever moved back and forth through a small arc to open or close an electric circuit.

**To·go** (tō′gō), *n.* a country in W Africa, on the Atlantic: area, 22,000 sq. mi.; pop., 1,815,000.

**To·go·land** (tō′gō-land′), *n.* a former British trust territory in NW Africa: see **Gold Coast.**

**toil** (toil), *v.i.* [< Anglo-Fr. < OFr. < L. *tudiculare*, to stir about; ult. < *tudes*, mallet], 1. to work hard and continuously. 2. to proceed laboriously: as, to *toil* up a hill. *v.t.* to make with great effort: as, to *toil* one's way. *n.* 1. hard, exhausting work or effort. 2. a task performed by such effort. **—toil′er,** *n.* **—toil′ful,** *adj.*

**toil** (toil), *n.pl.* [< OFr. *toile* < L. *tela*, a web], any snare or trap suggestive of a net.

**toi·let** (toi′lit), *n.* [Fr. *toilette* < *toile*, cloth < L. *tela*, a web], 1. a dressing table. 2. the act of dressing or grooming oneself. 3. dress; attire. 4. *a*) a room equipped with a washbowl, water closet, etc. *b*) a water closet. *adj.* of or for the toilet. **—make one's toilet,** to bathe, dress, etc.

**toi·let·ry** (toi′lit-ri), *n.* [*pl.* -RIES], soap, powder, cologne, etc. used in making one's toilet.

**toi·lette** (toi-let′, twä-), *n.* [Fr.; see TOILET], 1. the process of grooming oneself, including bathing, dressing, hairdressing, etc.: said of women. 2. dress or manner of dress; attire.

**toilet water,** a perfumed liquid, as cologne, applied to the skin in making one's toilet.

**toil·some** (toil′səm), *adj.* requiring toil; laborious.

**toil·worn** (toil′wôrn′), *adj.* worn out by toil.

**To·kay** (tō-kā′), *n.* 1. a sweet, rich wine made in Tokay, Hungary. 2. any wine like this. 3. a large, sweet grape used for the wine.

**to·ken** (tō′kən), *n.* [AS. *tacn*], 1. a sign, indication, etc.: as, this gift is a *token* of my affection. 2. something serving as a sign of authority, identity, etc. 3. a distinguishing mark or feature. 4. a keepsake. 5. a metal disk with a face value higher than its real value, issued as a substitute for currency. 6. any similar device of metal, paper, etc. used as for transportation fares, etc. *adj.* 1. by way of a token, symbol, etc. 2. merely simulated; slight: as, *token* resistance. **—by this** (or **the same**) **token,** following from this; furthermore. **—in token of,** as evidence of.

**to·ken·ism** (tō′kən-iz′m), *n.* the making of small, merely formal concessions to a demand, principle, etc.; specif., token integration of Negroes, as in schools, jobs, etc.

**To·ky·o** (tō′ki-ō′), *n.* the capital of Japan, on Honshu Island: pop., 8,991,000 (with suburbs, 11,027,000).

**told** (tōld), pt. and pp. of **tell. —all told,** all (being) counted: as, there were ten *all told*.

**To·le·do** (tə-lē′dō), *n.* 1. a port in NW Ohio, on Lake Erie: pop., 318,000. 2. a city in central Spain: pop., 35,000. 3. [*pl.* -DOS], a fine-tempered sword or sword blade made in Toledo, Spain.

**tol·er·a·ble** (tol′ēr-ə-b'l), *adj.* 1. that can be tolerated; endurable. 2. fairly good; passable. **—tol′er·a·bly,** *adv.* **—tol′er·a·ble·ness,** *n.*

**tol·er·ance** (tol′ēr-əns), *n.* 1. a being tolerant of others' beliefs, practices, etc. 2. the amount of variation allowed from a standard, accuracy, etc.; specif., the difference between the allowable maximum and minimum sizes of some mechanical part. 3. in *medicine*, the ability to endure, or resist the effects of, a drug, poison, etc.

**tol·er·ant** (tol′ēr-ənt), *adj.* 1. inclined to tolerate others' beliefs, practices, etc. 2. in *medicine*, of or having tolerance. **—tol′er·ant·ly,** *adv.*

**tol·er·ate** (tol′ə-rāt′), *v.t.* [-ATED, -ATING], [< L. pp. of *tolerare*, to bear], 1. to allow; permit. 2. to recognize and respect (others' beliefs, practices, etc.) without necessarily agreeing. 3. to put up with; bear. 4. in *medicine*, to have tolerance for (a drug, etc.). **—tol′er·a′tive,** *adj.* **—tol′er·a′tor,** *n.*

**tol·er·a·tion** (tol′ə-rā′shən), *n.* tolerance; esp., freedom to hold religious views that differ from the established ones. **—tol′er·a′tion·ist,** *n.*

**toll** (tōl), *n.* [AS.; prob. ult. < Gr. *telos*, tax], 1. a tax or charge for a privilege, especially for permission to use a bridge, highway, etc. 2. the right to demand toll. 3. a charge for some service, as for a long-distance telephone call. 4. the number lost, taken, etc.: as, the storm took a heavy *toll* of lives.

**toll** (tōl), *v.t.* [prob. akin to AS. *-tillan*, to touch], 1. to ring (a church bell, etc.) with slow, regular strokes, as for announcing a death. 2. to announce, summon, etc. by this. *v.i.* to sound or ring slowly: said of a bell. *n.* 1. the act or sound of tolling a bell. 2. a single stroke of the bell. **—toll′er,** *n.*

**toll bar,** a bar, gate, etc. for stopping travel at a point where toll is taken.
**toll bridge,** a bridge at which a toll is paid.
**toll call,** a long-distance telephone call, for which there is a charge beyond the local rate.
**toll·gate** (tōl′gāt′), *n.* a gate for stopping travel at a point where toll is taken.
**toll·keep·er** (tōl′kēp′ēr), *n.* a person who takes toll at a tollgate.
**Tol·stoy,** Count **Lev** (Eng. **Leo**) **Ni·ko·la·ye·vich** (lyev nē′kô-lä′ye-vich tôl-stoi′), 1828–1910; Russian novelist and social reformer: also sp. **Tolstoi.**
**Tol·tec** (tol′tek), *n.* any of a group of Nahuatl Indians who lived in Mexico before the Aztecs. *adj.* of the Toltecs or their culture: also **Tol′tec·an.**
**to·lu** (tō-lo͞o′), *n.* [< Santiago de *Tolú*, seaport in Colombia], the balsam from a large South American tree (**tolu tree**), used in medicine, etc.
**tol·u·ene** (tol′ū-ēn′), *n.* [*tolu* (from which orig. derived) + benz*ene*], a liquid hydrocarbon, $C_6H_5 CH_3$, used in making dyes, explosives, etc.: also **tol′u·ol′, tol′u·ole′** (-ū-ōl′).
**tom** (tom), *n.* [< *Tom*, dim. of *Thomas*], the male of some animals, especially of the cat. *adj.* male.
**tom·a·hawk** (tom′ə-hôk′), *n.* [< Algonquian], a light ax with a head of stone, bone, etc., used by North American Indians as a tool and a weapon. *v.t.* to hit, cut, or kill with a tomahawk.
**Tom and Jerry** (jer′i), a hot drink made of rum, beaten eggs, sugar, water or milk, and nutmeg.
**to·ma·to** (tə-mā′tō, -mä′-), *n.* [*pl.* -TOES], [< Sp. < Nahuatl *tomatl*], 1. a red or yellowish, round fruit, with a juicy pulp, used as a vegetable: botanically it is a berry. 2. the plant that it grows on. 3. [Slang], a woman or girl.
**tomb** (to͞om), *n.* [< Anglo-Fr. < LL. < Gr. *tymbos*], 1. a vault or grave for the dead. 2. a tombstone or burial monument. *v.t.* [Rare], to entomb. **—the tomb,** death. **—tomb′less,** *adj.* **—tomb′like′,** *adj.*
**tom·boy** (tom′boi′), *n.* a girl who behaves like a boisterous boy; hoyden. **—tom′boy′ish,** *adj.*
**tomb·stone** (to͞om′stōn′), *n.* a stone, usually with an inscription, marking a tomb or grave.
**tom·cat** (tom′kat′), *n.* a male cat.
**Tom Collins,** see **Collins.**
**Tom, Dick, and Harry,** everyone; anyone: usually preceded by *every* and used disparagingly.
**tome** (tōm), *n.* [Fr. < L. < Gr. *tomos*, piece cut off], 1. originally, any volume of a work of several volumes. 2. a book, especially a large one.
**tom·fool** (tom′fo͞ol′), *n.* a foolish, stupid, or silly person. *adj.* foolish, stupid, or silly.
**tom·fool·er·y** (tom′fo͞ol′ēr-i), *n.* [*pl.* -IES], foolish behavior; silliness; nonsense.
**Tom·my, tom·my** (tom′i), *n.* [*pl.* -MIES], a Tommy Atkins; British soldier: a nickname.
**Tommy At·kins** (at′kinz), [fictitious name used in Brit. Army sample forms], a British soldier: a nickname.
**Tommy gun,** [Colloq.], 1. a Thompson submachine gun. 2. loosely, any submachine gun.
**tom·my·rot** (tom′i-rot′), *n.* [Slang], nonsense; foolishness; rubbish.
**to·mor·row, to-mor·row** (tə-mor′ō, -môr′ō), *adv.* [AS. *to morgen*], on the day after today. *n.* 1. the day after today. 2. an indefinite future time.
**Tomsk** (tômsk), *n.* a city in Siberian U.S.S.R.: pop., 311,000.
**Tom Thumb,** 1. a tiny hero of many English folk tales. 2. any dwarf or small person.
**tom·tit** (tom′tit′), *n.* 1. [Brit.], a titmouse. 2. any of various small birds, as a wren.
**tom-tom** (tom′tom′), *n.* [Hind. *tam-tam*], any of various primitive drums, played with the hands or with sticks. *v.i.* to play on or beat a tom-tom.
**-to·my,** (tə-mi), [< Gr. < *temnein*, to cut], a combining form meaning: 1. *a cutting, dividing*, as in *dichotomy*. 2. *a surgical operation*, as in *appendectomy*.
**ton** (tun), *n.* [AS. *tunne;* var. of *tun*], 1. a unit of weight equal to 2,240 pounds avoirdupois, commonly used in Great Britain: in full, **long ton.** 2. a unit of weight equal to 2,000 pounds avoirdupois, commonly used in the U.S., Canada, South Africa, etc.: in full, **short ton.** 3. a metric ton. 4. a unit of internal capacity of ships, equal to 100 cubic feet. 5. a unit of carrying capacity of ships, usually equal to 40 cubic feet: in full, **measurement ton, freight ton.** 6. a unit for measuring displacement of ships, equal to 35 cubic feet: it is nearly equal to the volume of a long ton of sea water: in full, **displacement ton.** 7. [Colloq.], a very large amount or number.
**ton·al** (tō′n'l), *adj.* of a tone or tones. **—ton′al·ly,** *adv.*
**to·nal·i·ty** (tō-nal′ə-ti), *n.* [*pl.* -TIES], 1. quality of tone. 2. in *art*, the color scheme in a painting. 3. in *music*, *a*) a key. *b*) the tonal character of (a) composition, as determined by the relationship of the tones to the keynote.
**tone** (tōn), *n.* [< OFr. < L. < Gr. *tonos* < *teinein*, to stretch], 1. *a*) a vocal or musical sound. *b*) its quality as to pitch, intensity, modulation, etc. 2. an intonation of the voice that expresses a particular feeling: as, a *tone* of contempt. 3. a manner of speaking or writing that shows a certain attitude: as, the letter had a friendly *tone*. 4. normal resiliency: as, this wood has lost its *tone*. 5. *a*) the prevailing style, character, etc. of a place or period: as, her house has a conservative *tone*. *b*) distinctive style; elegance. 6. *a*) a quality of color; shade. *b*) a slight modification of a particular color; hue. 7. in *music*, *a*) a sound of distinct pitch that may be put into harmonic relation with other such sounds: distinguished from *noise*. *b*) the simple tone of a musical sound as distinguished from its overtones. *c*) any one of the full intervals of a diatonic scale: also **whole tone.** 8. in *painting*, the effect produced by the combination of light, shade, and color. 9. in *physiology*, normal, healthy condition of an organism, organ, muscle, etc. *v.t.* [TONED, TONING], 1. [Rare], to intone. 2. to give a tone to. 3. to change the tone of. *v.i.* to assume a tone. **—tone down,** 1. to give a less intense tone to. 2. to become softened. **—tone in with,** to harmonize with. **—tone up,** 1. to give a more intense tone to. 2. to become strengthened or heightened. **—tone′less,** *adj.* **—tone′less·ly,** *adv.* **—tone′less·ness,** *n.* **—ton′er,** *n.*
**tone color,** timbre.
**tone-deaf** (tōn′def′), *adj.* not able to distinguish accurately differences in musical pitch.
**tone poem,** an orchestral composition, usually in one movement, based upon some nonmusical theme: also called *symphonic poem*.
**tong** (tôŋ, toŋ), *v.t.* to seize, collect, handle, or hold with tongs. *v.i.* to use tongs.
**tong** (tôŋ, toŋ), *n.* [Chin. *t'ang*, a meeting place], 1. a Chinese association or political party. 2. in the U.S., a private or secret Chinese society.
**Ton·ga** (toŋ′gə), *n.* an independent island kingdom in the South Pacific, east of the Fiji Islands: a member of the British Commonwealth of Nations: area, 270 sq. mi.; pop., 80,000.
**Ton·gan** (toŋ′gən), *n.* 1. a native of Tonga. 2. the Polynesian language of the Tongans.
**tongs** (tôŋz, toŋz), *n.pl.* [sometimes construed as sing.], [AS. *tange*], a device for seizing, lifting, or moving objects, generally consisting of two long arms pivoted or hinged together.
**tongue** (tuŋ), *n.* [AS. *tunge*], 1. the movable muscular structure attached to the floor of the mouth: it is used in eating, tasting, and (in man) speaking. 2. an animal's tongue used as food. 3. talk; speech. 4. the act or power of speaking. 5. a manner of speaking in regard to tone, meaning, etc. 6. a language or dialect. 7. something like a tongue in shape, position, use, etc.; specif., *a*) the flap under the laces of a shoe. *b*) the clapper of a bell. *c*) the pole of a wagon, etc. *d*) the projecting tenon of a tongue-and-groove joint. *e*) the vibrating end of the reed in a wind instrument. *f*) a narrow strip of land extending into a sea, river, etc. *g*) a long, narrow flame. *v.t.* [TONGUED, TONGUING], 1. [Archaic], to speak. 2. to touch, etc. with the tongue. 3. in *music*, to play by tonguing: see **tonguing.** *v.i.* 1. to project like a tongue. 2. in *music*, to use tonguing. **—find one's tongue,** to recover the ability to talk after shock, etc. **—hold one's tongue,** to refrain from speaking. **—on every-one's tongue,** prevailing as common gossip. **—on the tip of one's** (or **the**) **tongue,** 1. almost said. 2. about to be said: especially of something forgotten but almost recalled. **—tongue′less,** *adj.*
**tongue-and-groove joint** (tuŋ′'n-gro͞ov′), a kind of joint in which a tongue or rib on one board fits exactly into a groove in another.
**tongued** (tuŋd), *adj.* having a specified kind of tongue: usually in compounds, as *loose-tongued*.
**tongue-tie** (tuŋ′tī′), *n.* limited motion of the tongue, caused by shortness of the membrane underneath. *v.t.* [-TIED, -TYING], to make tongue-tied.
**tongue-tied** (tuŋ′tīd′), *adj.* 1. having a condition of tongue-tie. 2. speechless from amazement, etc.
**tongue twister,** a phrase or sentence hard to speak fast. Example: the sheik's sixth sheep.
**tongu·ing** (tuŋ′iŋ), *n.* the use of the tongue to produce a rapidly staccato effect on a musical wind instrument or to modify the intonation.
**ton·ic** (ton′ik), *adj.* [< Gr. < *tonos;* see TONE], 1. of or producing good muscular tone. 2. mentally or morally invigorating. 3. in *music*, designating or

based on a keynote. 4. in *phonetics*, accented. 5. in *medicine*, *a*) of or characterized by tone. *b*) of or characterized by continuous muscular contraction: as, a *tonic* spasm. ***n.*** 1. anything that invigorates or stimulates; specif., a tonic medicine. 2. in *music*, the basic tone of a diatonic scale; keynote. 3. in *phonetics*, an accented syllable. **—ton′i·cal·ly, *adv.***

**to·nic·i·ty** (tō-nis′ə-ti), ***n.*** the quality or condition of being tonic; esp., in *physiology*, the normal tension of a muscle at rest.

**to·night, to-night** (tə-nīt′, too-), ***adv.*** [AS. *to niht*], on or during the present or coming night. ***n.*** the present or the coming night.

**ton·ite** (tōn′īt), ***n.*** a high explosive made of guncotton and barium nitrate.

**ton·nage** (tun′ij), ***n.*** 1. a duty or tax on ships, based on tons carried. 2. the total amount of shipping of a country or port, calculated in tons. 3. the carrying capacity of a ship, calculated in tons. 4. weight in tons. Also sp. **tunnage.**

**ton·neau** (tu-nō′), ***n.*** [*pl.* -NEAUS, -NEAUX (-nōz′)], [Fr., lit., a cask], an enclosed rear compartment for passengers in an early type of automobile.

**ton·sil** (ton′s'l, -sil), ***n.*** [L. *tonsillae*, *pl.*], either of a pair of oval masses of lymphoid tissue, one on each side at the back of the mouth. **—ton′sil·lar, ton′sil·ar, *adj.***

**ton·sil·lec·to·my** (ton′s'l-ek′tə-mi, -si-lek′-), ***n.*** [*pl.* -MIES], the surgical removal of the tonsils.

**ton·sil·li·tis** (ton′s'l-ī′tis, -si-lī′-), ***n.*** inflammation of the tonsils. **—ton′sil·lit′ic** (-it′ik), ***adj.***

**ton·so·ri·al** (ton-sôr′i-əl, -sō′ri-), ***adj.*** [< L. < *tonsor*, clipper < pp. of *tondere*, to clip], of a barber or his work: usually used humorously.

**ton·sure** (ton′shẽr), ***n.*** [< OFr. < L. *tonsura* < *tondere*, to clip], 1. the act of shaving the head or, especially, the crown of a person entering the priesthood or a monastic order. 2. the state of being so shaven. 3. the part of the head left bare by so shaving. ***v.t.*** [-SURED, -SURING], to shave the head or crown of. **—ton′sured, *adj.***

**ton·tine** (ton′tēn, ton-tēn′), ***n.*** [< L. *Tonti*, 17th-c. banker of Naples], an annuity shared among a group of persons: as each beneficiary dies, his share is divided among the survivors until the entire amount accrues to the last survivor.

**ton·y** (tō′ni), ***adj.*** [-IER, -IEST], [Slang], high-toned; luxurious; stylish: often ironic.

**too** (to͞o), ***adv.*** [< *to*, *prep.*], 1. in addition; besides; also. 2. more than enough: as, the hat is *too* big. 3. to a regrettable extent: as, that's *too* bad! 4. very: as, it's just *too* delicious! *Too* is often used as a mere emphatic, as, I will *too* go!

**took** (took), pt. of **take.**

**tool** (to͞ol), ***n.*** [AS. *tol*], 1. any implement, instrument, etc. held in the hand and used for some work: knives, saws, shovels, etc. are tools. 2. *a*) any similar instrument that is part of a power-driven machine, as a drill, etc. *b*) the whole machine. 3. anything that serves as a means: as, books are a scholar's *tools*. 4. a person used by another to accomplish his purposes; stooge. ***v.t.*** 1. to shape or work with a tool. 2. to provide tools or machinery for (a factory, etc.). 3. to impress designs, etc. as on leather with a tool. ***v.i.*** to use a tool or tools. **—tool′er, *n.* —tool′ing, *n.***

**tool·mak·er** (to͞ol′māk′ẽr), ***n.*** a machinist who makes, maintains, and repairs machine tools.

**toot** (to͞ot), ***v.i.*** [< D. or LG. *tuten*; echoic], 1. to blow a horn, whistle, etc., especially in short blasts. 2. to sound in short blasts: said of a horn, etc. ***v.t.*** 1. to cause to sound in short blasts. 2. to sound (tones, etc.), as on a horn. ***n.*** a short blast of a horn, etc. **—toot′er, *n.***

**tooth** (to͞oth), ***n.*** [*pl.* TEETH (tēth)], [AS. *toth*], 1. *a*) any of a set of hard, bonelike structures in the jaws of most vertebrates, used for biting, tearing, and chewing. *b*) any of various analogous processes in invertebrates. 2. a toothlike part, as on a saw, comb, gearwheel, plant leaf, etc. 3. appetite for something: as, a sweet *tooth*. 4. something that bites or gnaws like a tooth: as, the *teeth* of the storm. ***v.t.*** 1. to provide with teeth. 2. to make jagged; indent. ***v.i.*** to become interlocked, as gears. **—armed to the teeth,** fully armed. **—in the teeth of,** 1. directly against. 2. defying. **—put teeth in** (a law, etc.), to make the enforcement of (a law, etc.) effective. **—tooth and nail,** with all one's strength or resources. **—tooth′less, *adj.***

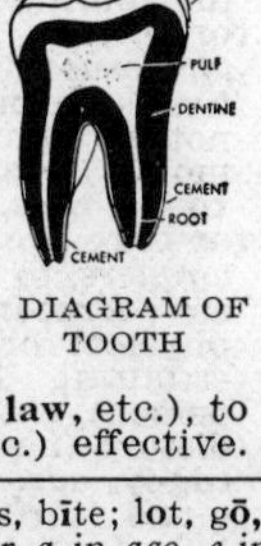

DIAGRAM OF TOOTH

**tooth·ache** (to͞oth′āk′), ***n.*** an ache in a tooth.

**tooth·brush** (to͞oth′brush′), ***n.*** a small brush for cleaning the teeth.

**toothed** (to͞otht, to͞othd), ***adj.*** 1. having (a specified number or kind of) teeth: as, buck-*toothed*. 2. notched; indented.

**tooth paste,** a paste for brushing the teeth.

**tooth·pick** (to͞oth′pik′), ***n.*** a slender, pointed instrument, as a sliver of wood, etc., for dislodging food particles from between the teeth.

**tooth powder,** a powder for brushing the teeth.

**tooth·some** (to͞oth′səm), ***adj.*** pleasing to the taste; tasty. **—tooth′some·ly, *adv.* —tooth′some·ness, *n.***

**too·tle** (to͞o′t'l), ***v.i.*** [-TLED, -TLING], to toot softly and more or less continuously on a horn, whistle, etc. ***n.*** the act or sound of tootling.

**toot·sy** (toot′si), ***n.*** [*pl.* -SIES], [child's term], [Slang], 1. a child's or woman's small foot. 2. darling; dear: playful term of address: also **toots.**

**top** (top), ***n.*** [AS.], 1. the head or crown. 2. the highest part, point, or surface of anything. 3. the part of a plant growing above ground: as, beet *tops*. 4. the uppermost part or covering of something else; specif., *a*) a lid, cover, cap, etc. *b*) the folding roof of a convertible automobile. *c*) the platform around the head of each lower mast of a sailing ship. 5. one that is first in order, excellence, etc.; specif., *a*) the highest degree or pitch; acme: as, at the *top* of his voice. *b*) the highest rank, position, etc.: as, at the *top* of the class. *c*) a person in this rank, etc.; head. *d*) the choicest part; pick: as, the *top* of the crop. 6. in *sports*, *a*) a stroke that hits the ball near its top. *b*) the forward spin given the ball by such a stroke. ***adj.*** of, at, or being the top; uppermost; highest: as, *top* honors. ***v.t.*** [TOPPED, TOPPING], 1. to take off the top of (a plant, etc.). 2. to provide with a top. 3. to be a top for. 4. to reach the top of. 5. to exceed in amount, height, etc.: as, the fish *topped* 75 pounds. 6. to surpass; outdo: as, he *tops* them all at golf. 7. to go over the top of (a rise of ground, etc.). 8. to be at the top of; head; lead. 9. in *sports*, to hit (a ball) near its top, giving it a forward spin. ***v.i.*** to top someone or something. **—blow one's top,** [Slang], to lose one's temper. **—on top,** at the top; successful. **—on top of,** 1. resting upon. 2. in addition to; besides. **—over the top,** 1. over the front of the trench, as in attacking. 2. exceeding the quota or goal. **—(the) tops,** [Slang], the very best. **—top off,** to complete by adding a finishing touch.

**top** (top), ***n.*** [AS.], a child's cone-shaped toy with a point at its apex upon which it is spun. **—sleep like a top,** to sleep soundly.

**to·paz** (tō′paz), ***n.*** [< OFr. < L. < Gr. *topazos*], 1. a native aluminum silicate, $Al_2SiO_4F_2$, occurring in various pale-colored crystals: the yellow variety is used as a gem. 2. any of various similar gems, as a yellow variety of sapphire.

**top boot,** any of several high boots reaching to just below the knee and usually having its upper part of a different material.

**top·coat** (top′kōt′), ***n.*** a lightweight overcoat.

**top-drawer** (top′drôr′), ***adj.*** of first importance, rank, privilege, etc.

**top·dress·ing** (top′dres′iŋ), ***n.*** 1. material applied to a surface, as fertilizer on land. 2. the applying of such material. **—top′-dress′, *v.t.***

**tope** (tōp), ***v.t.* & *v.i.*** [TOPED, TOPING], to drink (alcoholic liquor) to the point of intoxication. **—top′er, *n.***

**To·pe·ka** (tə-pē′kə), ***n.*** the capital of Kansas, on the Kansas River: pop., 119,000.

**top-flight** (top′flīt′), ***adj.*** [Colloq.], best; first-rate.

**top·gal·lant** (tə-gal′ənt, top′-), ***adj.*** situated next above the topmast on a sailing ship. ***n.*** a topgallant mast, sail, spar, etc.

**top hat,** a tall, black, cylindrical hat, usually of silk, worn by men in formal dress.

**top-heav·y** (top′hev′i), ***adj.*** too heavy at the top, so as to be unstable: also used figuratively. **—top′-heav′i·ly, *adv.* —top′-heav′i·ness, *n.***

**top·ic** (top′ik), ***n.*** [< L. < Gr. *ta topika*, title of work by Aristotle; ult. < *topos*, a place], 1. the subject of an essay, speech, etc. 2. a subject for discussion. 3. a heading in an outline.

**top·i·cal** (top′i-k'l), ***adj.*** 1. of a particular place; local. 2. of or using topics. 3. having to do with topics of the day; of current or local interest. 4. of or for a particular part of the body: as, a *topical* remedy. **—top′i·cal·ly, *adv.***

**top kick,** [Military Slang], a first sergeant.
**top·knot** (top'not'), *n.* 1. a knot of feathers, ribbons, etc. worn as a headdress. 2. a tuft of hair or feathers on the crown of the head.
**top·loft·y** (top'lôf'ti), *adj.* [Colloq.], lofty in manner; haughty; pompous; supercilious. **—top'loft'i·ly,** *adv.* **—top'loft'i·ness,** *n.*
**top·mast** (top'məst, -mast', -mäst'), *n.* the second mast above the deck of a sailing ship.
**top·most** (top'mōst', -məst), *adj.* of the very top; uppermost; highest.
**top-notch** (top'noch'), *adj.* [Colloq.], first-rate.
**to·pog·ra·pher** (tə-pog'rə-fẽr), *n.* 1. an expert in topography. 2. a person who describes or maps the topography of a place or region.
**to·pog·ra·phy** (tə-pog'rə-fi, tō-), *n.* [*pl.* -PHIES], [< LL. < Gr. < *topos*, a place + *graphein*, to write], 1. the science of representing, as on maps and charts, the surface features of a region, as hills, rivers, roads, cities, etc. 2. these surface features. 3. surveying done in this way. **—top·o·graph·i·cal** (top'ə-graf'i-k'l), **top'o·graph'ic,** *adj.* **—top'o·graph'i·cal·ly,** *adv.*
**top·per** (top'ẽr), *n.* 1. one who tops. 2. [Slang], *a)* a top-notch person or thing. *b)* a top hat. *c)* a topcoat.
**top·ping** (top'iŋ), *n.* something put on top of something else. *adj.* [Brit. Colloq.], excellent.
**top·ple** (top''l), *v.i.* [-PLED, -PLING], [< *top*, *v.* + freq. *-le*], 1. to fall top forward; fall over from top-heaviness, etc. (often with *over*). 2. to lean forward as if on the point of falling; overhang; totter. *v.t.* to cause to topple; overturn.
**top·sail** (top's'l, -sāl'), *n.* 1. in a square-rigged vessel, the square sail next above the lowest sail on a mast. 2. in a fore-and-aft-rigged vessel, the small sail set above the gaff.
**top-se·cret** (top'sē'krit), *adj.* designating or of information of the greatest secrecy.
**top sergeant,** [Colloq.], a first sergeant.
**top·side** (top'sīd'), *n.* *usually in pl.* the part of a ship's side above the water line. *adv.* on or to the upper side of a ship; on deck.
**top·soil** (top'soil'), *n.* the upper layer of soil, usually darker and richer than the subsoil.
**top·sy-tur·vy** (top'si-tũr'vi), *adv.* & *adj.* [prob. < *top*, highest part + ME. *terven*, to roll], 1. upside down; in a reversed condition. 2. in confusion or disorder. *n.* 1. a topsy-turvy condition; inverted state. 2. a state of confusion. **—top'sy-tur'vi·ly,** *adv.* **—top'sy-tur'vi·ness,** *n.*
**toque** (tōk), *n.* [Fr.], a woman's small, round hat, with little or no brim.
**to·rah, to·ra** (tō'rə, -rô), *n.* [*pl.* -ROTH (-rōth, -rōs)], [Heb.], in *Judaism*, 1. *a)* learning, law, instruction, etc. *b)* the whole body of Jewish religious literature, including the Scripture, the Talmud, etc. 2. [usually T-], *a)* the Pentateuch. *b)* a parchment scroll containing the Pentateuch.
**torch** (tôrch), *n.* [< OFr. *torche* < L. *torquere*, to twist], 1. a portable light consisting of a long piece of resinous wood, etc. flaming at one end. 2. anything considered as a source of enlightenment, inspiration, etc.: as, the *torch* of science. 3. any of various devices for producing a very hot flame, used in welding, burning off paint, etc. 4. [Brit.], a flashlight. **—carry a (or the) torch for,** [Slang], to be in love with.
**torch·bear·er** (tôrch'bâr'ẽr), *n.* 1. one who carries a torch. 2. one who brings inspiration, truth, etc.
**torch·ier, torch·iere** (tôr-chêr', -shêr'), *n.* [< Fr. < OFr. *torche;* see TORCH], a floor lamp with a reflector bowl and no shade, for casting light upward so as to give indirect illumination.
**torch·light** (tôrch'lit'), *n.* the light of a torch or torches. *adj.* done or carried on by torchlight.
**torch song,** [< *carry a torch for*], a sentimental song, especially of unrequited love.
**tore** (tôr, tōr), pt. of **tear** (to pull apart).
**tor·e·a·dor** (tôr'i-ə-dôr'), *n.* [Sp. < *torear*, to fight bulls; ult. < L. *taurus*, a bull], a bullfighter: term no longer used in bullfighting.
**to·ri·i** (tō'ri-ē'), *n.* [*pl.* -RII], [Japan.], a gateway at the entrance to a Shinto temple, consisting of two uprights supporting a curved lintel and a straight crosspiece.

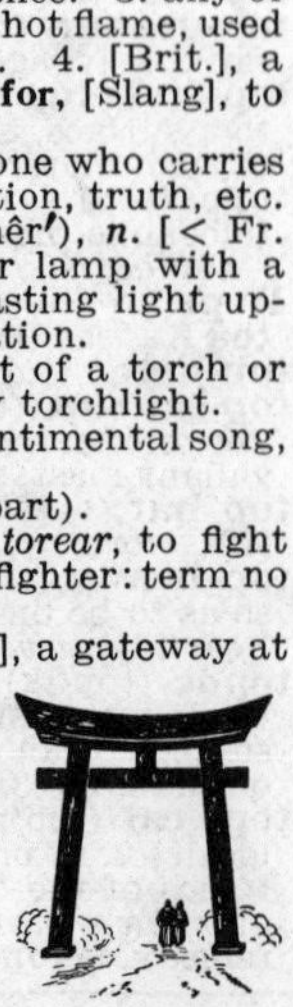
TORII

**tor·ment** (tôr'ment; *for v.,* tôr-ment'), *n.* [< OFr. < L. *tormentum*, a rack, torture < *torquere*, to twist], 1. great pain or anguish, physical or mental; agony. 2. a source of pain, anxiety, or annoyance. *v.t.* 1. to cause great physical pain or mental anguish in. 2. to annoy; harass; tease. **—tor·ment'ing·ly,** *adv.* **—tor·men'tor, tor·ment'er,** *n.*
**torn** (tôrn, tōrn), pp. of **tear** (to pull apart).
**tor·na·do** (tôr-nā'dō), *n.* [*pl.* -DOES, -DOS], [< Sp. *tronada*, thunder < L. *tonare*, to thunder], 1. a violent, destructive wind, especially in the central U.S., accompanied by a whirling, funnel-shaped cloud that moves in a narrow path. 2. any whirlwind or hurricane. **—tor·nad'ic** (-nad'ik), *adj.*
**To·ron·to** (tə-ron'tō), *n.* the capital of Ontario, Canada, on Lake Ontario: pop., 646,000 (metropolitan area, 1,412,000).
**tor·pe·do** (tôr-pē'dō), *n.* [*pl.* -DOES], [L., numbness < *torpere*, to be stiff], 1. an electric ray (kind of fish). 2. a large, cigar-shaped, self-propelled, underwater projectile containing explosives, launched against enemy ships from a submarine, etc. 3. any of various explosive devices used as underwater mines, in oil-well drilling, etc. *v.t.* [-DOED, -DOING], to attack, destroy, etc. as with a torpedo.
**torpedo boat,** a small, fast, maneuverable warship for attacking with torpedoes.
**tor·pid** (tôr'pid), *adj.* [< L. *torpere*, to be numb], 1. having lost temporarily all or part of the power of sensation or motion, as a hibernating animal; dormant. 2. dull; sluggish; apathetic. **—tor·pid'i·ty, tor'pid·ness,** *n.* **—tor'pid·ly,** *adv.*
**tor·por** (tôr'pẽr), *n.* 1. a torpid or dormant state. 2. sluggishness; apathy. **—tor'por·if'ic,** *adj.*
**torque** (tôrk), *n.* [< L. *torques*, a twisted metal necklace], in *physics*, *a)* a force or combination of forces that produces a twisting or rotating motion. *b)* the tendency to produce this motion.
**Tor·rance** (tôr'əns, tor'-), *n.* a city in SW California: suburb of Los Angeles: pop., 101,000.
**tor·rent** (tôr'ənt, tor'-), *n.* [Fr. < L. *torrens*, burning, rushing, ppr. of *torrere*, to parch], 1. a swift, violent stream, as of water. 2. a rapid or violent flow, as of words, mail, etc. 3. a heavy fall of rain.
**tor·ren·tial** (tô-ren'shəl, to-), *adj.* 1. of or like a torrent; overwhelming. 2. caused by a torrent. **—tor·ren'tial·ly,** *adv.*
**Tor·ri·cel·li E·van·ge·lis·ta** (ē-vän'je-lēs'tä tôr'rē-chel'lē), 1608–1647; Italian physicist; discovered principle of the barometer.
**tor·rid** (tôr'id, tor'-), *adj.* [< L. pp. of *torrere*, to parch], 1. dried by or subjected to intense heat, especially of the sun; scorched; parched; arid. 2. so hot as to be parching; scorching. 3. highly passionate, ardent, etc. **—tor·rid·i·ty** (tô-rid'ə-ti), **tor'rid·ness,** *n.* **—tor'rid·ly,** *adv.*
**Torrid Zone,** the area of the earth between the Tropic of Cancer and the Tropic of Capricorn and divided by the equator: see **tropic.**
**tor·sion** (tôr'shən), *n.* [< OFr. < pp. of L. *torquere*, to twist], 1. a twisting or being twisted; specif., the twisting of a body by holding one end firm and turning the other along the longitudinal axis. 2. in *mechanics*, the tendency of a twisted wire, bar, etc. to return to its untwisted condition. **—tor'sion·al,** *adj.* **—tor'sion·al·ly,** *adv.*
**tor·so** (tôr'sō), *n.* [*pl.* -SOS, -SI (-sē)], [It. < L. < Gr. *thyrsos*, a stem], 1. the trunk of a statue of the nude human figure lacking the head and limbs. 2. the trunk of the human body.
**tort** (tôrt), *n.* [< OFr. < L. *tortus*, pp. of *torquere*, to twist], in *law*, a wrongful act, injury, or damage (not involving a breach of contract), for which a civil action can be brought.
**torte** (tôrt), *n.* [G.], a rich cake, variously made, as of eggs, chopped nuts, and crumbs.
**tor·til·la** (tôr-tē'yä), *n.* [Sp., dim. of *torta*, a cake; ult. < LL. pp. of *torquere*, to twist], a flat, unleavened corn cake baked on an iron or stone plate: used in Mexico as the equivalent of bread.
**tor·toise** (tôr'təs), *n.* [*pl.* -TOISES, -TOISE; see PLURAL, II, D, 1], [prob. ult. < Gr. *tartaruchos*, demon], a turtle, especially one that lives on land.
**tortoise shell,** the hard, mottled, yellow-and-brown shells of some turtles, used in inlaying and in making combs, etc. **—tor'toise-shell',** *adj.*
**tor·tu·ous** (tôr'chōō-əs), *adj.* [Anglo-Fr. < L. *tortuosus* < pp. of *torquere*, to twist], 1. full of twists, turns, curves, etc.; winding; crooked. 2. not straightforward; devious. 3. deceitful; immoral. **—tor'tu·os'i·ty** (-os'ə-ti), [*pl.* -TIES], **tor'tu·ous·ness,** *n.* **—tor'tu·ous·ly,** *adv.*
**tor·ture** (tôr'chẽr), *n.* [Fr. < LL. *tortura* < pp. of L. *torquere*, to twist], 1. the inflicting of severe pain, as to force information or confession. 2. any severe physical or mental pain; agony. *v.t.* [-TURED, -TURING], 1. to subject to torture. 2. to cause (a person) extreme pain; agonize. 3. to twist or distort (meaning, etc.). **—tor'tur·er,** *n.* **—tor'tur·ing·ly,** *adv.* **—tor'tur·ous,** *adj.*
**to·rus** (tôr'əs, tō'rəs), *n.* [*pl.* -RI (-ī, -rī)], [L., a bulge], 1. a large convex molding used at the base of columns, etc. 2. in *botany*, the receptacle.

**To·ry** (tôr′i, tō′ri), *n.* [*pl.* -RIES], [< Ir. *tōruidhe*, robber < *tōir*, to pursue], 1. formerly, a member of one of the two major political parties of England: opposed to *Whig*, and, later, to *Liberal*, *Radical*, *Laborite;* changed officially (c. 1830) to *Conservative*. 2. in the American Revolution, a person who favored continued allegiance to Great Britain. 3. [often t-], any extreme conservative. *adj.* [also t-], of, being, or having the principles of a Tory. —**To′ry·ism,** *n.*

**Tos·ca·ni·ni, Ar·tu·ro** (är-tōō′rô tôs′kä-nē′nē), 1867–1957; Italian orchestral conductor in America.

**toss** (tôs, tos), *v.t.* [TOSSED or *obs.* or *poetic* TOST, TOSSING], [prob. < ON.], 1. to throw about; fling about; buffet: as, the waves *tossed* the boat. 2. to disturb; agitate. 3. to throw lightly and easily from the hand. 4. to lift quickly; jerk upward: as, to *toss* one's head. 5. to toss up with (someone *for* something): see phrase below. *v.i.* 1. to be thrown about. 2. to fling oneself about in sleep, etc.: as, I *tossed* all night. 3. to move or go impatiently, angrily, etc.: as, she *tossed* out of the room. 4. to toss up: see phrase below. *n.* 1. a tossing or being tossed. 2. the distance that something is or can be tossed. —**toss off,** 1. to make, do, etc. quickly and without effort. 2. to drink up in one draft. —**toss up,** to toss a coin for deciding something according to which side lands uppermost.

**toss·up** (tôs′up′, tos′-), *n.* 1. the act of tossing a coin, etc. to decide something according to which side lands uppermost. 2. an even chance.

**tot** (tot), *n.* [prob. < ON. *tuttr*, dwarf], 1. a very small amount or thing. 2. a young child.

**tot** (tot), *v.t.* [TOTTED, TOTTING], [contr. of *total*], [Brit. Colloq.], to add up; total (with *up*).

**to·tal** (tō′t'l), *adj.* [OFr. < LL. < L. *totus*, all], 1. constituting the (or a) whole; entire. 2. complete; utter: as, a *total* loss. *n.* the whole amount or number; sum. *v.t.* [-TALED or -TALLED, -TALING or -TALLING], 1. to find the total of; add. 2. to equal a total of; add up to. *v.i.* to amount (*to*) as a whole. —**to′tal·ly,** *adv.*

**to·tal·i·tar·i·an** (tō-tal′ə-târ′i-ən, tō′tal-), *adj.* [< *totality* + *-arian*], designating, of, or characteristic of a government or state in which one political group maintains complete control and illegalizes all others. *n.* one who favors such a government. —**to·tal′i·tar′i·an·ism,** *n.*

**to·tal·i·ty** (tō-tal′ə-ti), *n.* 1. the fact or condition of being total. 2. the total amount or sum.

**to·tal·i·za·tor** (tō′t'l-ə-zā′tẽr), *n.* a machine for computing and showing the total number and amount of bets, as at a horse race; pari-mutuel: also **to′tal·i·sa′tor** (-zā′tẽr), **to′tal·iz′er** (-īz′ẽr).

**tote** (tōt), *v.t.* [TOTED, TOTING], [? < early Fr. *tauter*, to remove on rollers], [Colloq.], to carry or haul. *n.* [Colloq.], 1. a toting. 2. something toted; load; haul. —**tot′er,** *n.*

**tote board** (tōt), [Colloq.], a totalizator.

**to·tem** (tō′təm), *n.* [< Algonquian], 1. among primitive peoples, an animal or natural object considered as being related by blood to a given family or clan and taken as its symbol. 2. an image of this. —**to·tem′ic** (-tem′ik), *adj.* —**to′tem·ism,** *n.* —**to′tem·ist,** *n.* —**to′tem·is′tic,** *adj.*

**totem pole,** a pole or post carved and painted with totems, often erected in front of their dwellings by Indian tribes of NW North America.

**toth·er, t'oth·er, 'toth·er** (tu*th*′ẽr), *adj. & pron.* [Chiefly Dial.], that (or the) other.

**tot·ter** (tot′ẽr), *v.i.* [prob. < ON.], 1. to rock or shake as if about to fall. 2. to be unsteady on one's feet; stagger; toddle. *n.* a tottering. —**tot′ter·er,** *n.* —**tot′ter·ing·ly,** *adv.* —**tot′ter·y,** *adj.*

**tou·can** (tōō′kan, too-kän′, tōō′kən), *n.* [Fr. < Port. < Tupi *tucano*], a brightly colored, fruit-eating bird of tropical America, with a very large, downcurved beak.

**touch** (tuch), *v.t.* [< OFr. *tochier*], 1. to put the hand, finger, etc. on, so as to feel. 2. to bring (something) into contact with (something else): as, he *touched* the match to his cigar. 3. to be or come into contact with. 4. to adjoin; border on. 5. to strike lightly. 6. to affect through contact: as, water won't *touch* these grease spots. 7. to injure slightly: as, frost *touched* the plants. 8. to give a light tint, aspect, etc. to: as, clouds *touched* with pink. 9. to stop at in passing, as a ship. 10. to lay hands on; handle; use. 11. to mishandle; molest. 12. to partake of: as, he didn't *touch* his supper. 13. to come up to; reach. 14. to compare with; equal: as, my cooking can't *touch* yours. 15. to deal with; mention, especially in passing. 16. to affect; concern: as, a subject that *touches* our welfare. 17. to cause to be slightly ill mentally: usually in *touched in the head*, somewhat demented. 18. to arouse an emotion, especially sympathy, gratitude, etc., in. 19. to provoke; irritate: as, *touched* to the quick. 20. [Slang], to ask for, or get by asking, a loan or gift of money from. 21. in *geometry*, to be tangent to. *v.i.* 1. to touch a person or thing. 2. to be or come in contact. 3. in *geometry*, to be tangent. *n.* 1. a touching or being touched; specif., a light tap, stroke, etc. 2. the sense by which physical objects are felt. 3. a sensation caused by this; feel. 4. a mental or emotional response roused as if by touching. 5. a mental capacity analogous to the sense of touch; moral sensitivity. 6. an effect of being touched; specif., *a*) a mark, impression, etc. left by touching. *b*) a subtle change or addition in a painting, story, etc. 7. a very small amount, degree, etc.; specif., *a*) a trace, tinge, etc.: as, a *touch* of humor. *b*) a slight attack: as, a *touch* of the flu. 8. a touchstone. 9. any test or criterion. 10. [Slang], the act of asking for, or getting in this way, a gift or loan of money. 11. in *music*, *a*) the manner of striking the keys of a piano, etc.: as, a delicate *touch*. *b*) the response of a piano, etc. to the fingers: as, a piano with a heavy *touch*. —**in** (or **out of**) **touch with,** in (or no longer in) communication or contact with. —**touch down,** to land: said of a spacecraft, etc. —**touch off,** 1. to represent accurately or aptly. 2. to make explode; fire. 3. to motivate or initiate. —**touch on** (or **upon**), 1. to come near to; verge on. 2. to pertain to. 3. to merely mention. —**touch up,** to improve or finish (a painting, story, etc.) by minor changes or additions. —**touch′a·ble,** *adj.* —**touch′er,** *n.*

**touch and go,** an uncertain or dangerous situation. —**touch′-and-go′,** *adj.*

**touch·back** (tuch′bak′), *n.* in *football*, a play in which a player grounds the ball behind his own goal line when the ball was caused to pass the goal line by an opponent: cf. *safety*.

**touch·down** (tuch′doun′), *n.* 1. the moment at which an aircraft or spacecraft lands. 2. in *football*, *a*) a scoring play in which a player grounds the ball on or past the opponent's goal line. *b*) a score of six points so made.

‡**tou·ché** (tōō′shā′), *adj.* [Fr.], in *fencing*, touched: said of a point scored by a touch. *interj.* good point!: an exclamation acknowledging a successful point in debate or a witty retort.

**touched** (tucht), *adj.* 1. emotionally affected. 2. slightly demented or mentally unbalanced.

**touch·hole** (tuch′hōl′), *n.* in early firearms, the hole in the breech through which the charge was ignited.

**touch·ing** (tuch′iŋ), *adj.* arousing tender emotion; moving. *prep.* [Archaic], concerning; with regard to. —**touch′ing·ly,** *adv.* —**touch′ing·ness,** *n.*

**touch-me-not** (tuch′mi-not′), *n.* any of various plants whose ripe seed pods burst at the touch.

**touch·stone** (tuch′stōn′), *n.* 1. a black stone formerly used to test the purity of gold or silver by the streak left on it when it was rubbed with the metal. 2. any test of genuineness or value.

**touch·wood** (tuch′wood′), *n.* dried, decayed wood or dried fungus used as tinder; punk.

**touch·y** (tuch′i), *adj.* [-IER, -IEST], [alt. (after *touch*) < *te(t)chy* < OFr. *tache*, a mark, spot], 1. easily offended; oversensitive; irritable. 2. very risky or precarious: as, a *touchy* situation. —**touch′i·ly,** *adv.* —**touch′i·ness,** *n.*

**tough** (tuf), *adj.* [AS. *toh*], 1. strong but pliant; that will bend, twist, etc. without tearing or breaking. 2. that will not cut or chew easily: as, *tough* steak. 3. glutinous; viscous; sticky: as, *tough* putty. 4. strong; robust; hardy. 5. hard to influence; stubborn. 6. overly aggressive; brutal; rough. 7. very difficult; toilsome. 8. violent; severe: as, a *tough* fight. *n.* a tough person; thug. —**tough′ly,** *adv.* —**tough′ness,** *n.*

**tough·en** (tuf′'n), *v.t. & v.i.* to make or become tough or tougher. —**tough′en·er,** *n.*

**Tou·lon** (tōō-lon′), *n.* a seaport in S France, on the Mediterranean: pop., 162,000.

**Tou·louse** (tōō′lōōz′), *n.* a city in S France: pop., 324,000.

**Tou·louse-Lau·trec, Hen·ri Ma·rie Ray·mond de** (än′rē′ mȧ′rē′ re′mōn′ də tōō′lōōz′lō′trek′), 1864–1901; French painter and lithographer.

**tou·pee** (to͞o-pā′, -pē′), *n.* [< Fr. < OFr. *toup,* tuft of hair], a small wig for covering a bald spot.
**tour** (toor), *n.* [OFr. < *to(u)rner,* to turn], 1. a turn, spell, or shift, as of work; esp., a period of military duty at a single place. 2. a long trip, as for sightseeing. 3. any trip, as for inspection; round; circuit; specif., a trip by a theatrical company to give performances at a number of cities. ***v.i.*** to go on a tour. ***v.t.*** 1. to take a tour through. 2. to take (a play, etc.) on a tour. —**on tour,** touring.
**tour de force** (toor′ də fôrs′), [Fr.], a feat of strength, skill, or ingenuity, often one that is merely clever or spectacular.
**touring car,** an early type of open automobile, seating five or more passengers.
**tour·ism** (toor′iz'm), *n.* tourist travel, especially when regarded as a source of income for a country, business, etc.
**tour·ist** (toor′ist), *n.* 1. one who makes a tour, especially for pleasure. 2. tourist class. ***adj.*** 1. of or for tourists. 2. designating or of the lowest-priced accommodations, as on a ship. ***adv.*** in or by means of tourist class.
**tour·ma·line** (toor′mə-lin, -lēn′), *n.* [Fr.; ult. < Singh. *tōramalli,* a carnelian], a red, green, yellow, black, or colorless semiprecious mineral, a silicate, used as a gem.
**tour·na·ment** (toor′nə-mənt, tũr′-), *n.* [< OFr. < *torneier;* see TOURNEY], 1. in the Middle Ages, a sport consisting of an encounter between knights on horseback who tried to unseat one another with lances. 2. a series of contests in some sport, game, etc., usually a competition for championship.
**tour·ney** (toor′ni, tũr′-), *n.* [*pl.* -NEYS], [< OFr. *torneier* < base of *tourner;* see TURN], a tournament. ***v.i.*** [-NEYED, -NEYING], to take part in a tournament; joust.
**tour·ni·quet** (toor′ni-ket′, tũr′ni-kā′), *n.* [Fr. < *tourner,* to turn], any device for compressing a blood vessel to stop bleeding, as a bandage twisted about a limb or a pad pressed down by a screw.
**tou·sle** (tou′z'l), ***v.t.*** [-SLED, -SLING], [freq. of ME. *tusen,* to pull], to disorder, dishevel, muss, etc. ***n.*** a tousled condition, mass of hair, etc.
**Tous·saint L'Ou·ver·ture, Pierre Do·mi·nique** (pyâr dô′mē′nēk′ to͞o′san′ lo͞o′vâr′tür′), 1743–1803; Haitian Negro liberator and general.
**tout** (tout), ***v.i.* & *v.t.*** [< AS. *totian,* to peep], 1. [Colloq.], to solicit (customers, patrons, votes, etc.). 2. [Colloq.], to praise or recommend (a person or thing) highly. 3. [Slang], *a)* [Chiefly Brit.], to spy on (race horses, their trainers, etc.) in order to secure tips for betting. *b)* to give betting tips on (race horses). ***n.*** one who touts (esp. in sense 3). —**tout′er,** ***n.***
‡**tout à fait** (to͞o′tà′fe′), [Fr.], entirely; quite.
‡**tout de suite** (to͞ot′swēt′), [Fr.], immediately.
‡**tout en·sem·ble** (to͞o′tän′sän′bl′), [Fr.], the general effect, as of a work of art or a costume.
**tou·zle** (tou′z'l), ***n.* & *v.t.*** [-ZLED, -ZLING], tousle.
**tow** (tō), ***v.t.*** [AS. *togian*], to pull as by a rope or chain. ***n.*** 1. a towing or being towed. 2. something towed. 3. a towline. —**in tow,** 1. being towed. 2. in one's company or retinue. 3. under one's influence or charge. —**tow′er,** ***n.***
**tow** (tō), *n.* [AS. *tow-,* for spinning], the coarse and broken fibers of hemp, flax, etc. before spinning.
**tow·age** (tō′ij), *n.* 1. a towing or being towed. 2. the charge for this.
**to·ward** (tôrd, tō′ẽrd; *also, for prep.,* tə-wôrd′), ***prep.*** [AS. *toweard;* see TO & WARD], 1. in the direction of. 2. facing. 3. along a course likely to result in: as, efforts *toward* peace. 4. concerning; regarding; about: as, his attitude *toward* me. 5. just before: as, they left *toward* noon. 6. in anticipation of; for: as, I'm saving *toward* a car. ***adj.*** [Archaic or Rare], 1. apt; docile. 2. imminent or in progress.
**to·wards** (tôrdz, tō′ẽrdz, tə-wôrdz′), ***prep.*** toward.
**tow·boat** (tō′bōt′), *n.* a tugboat.
**tow·el** (tou′'l, toul), *n.* [< OFr. *toaille* < Gmc.], a piece of cloth or absorbent paper for wiping or drying things. ***v.t.*** [-ELED or -ELLED, -ELING or -ELLING], to wipe or dry with a towel.
**tow·el·ing, tow·el·ling** (toul′iŋ, tou′'l-), *n.* material for making towels.
**tow·er** (tou′ẽr), *n.* [< OFr. < L. *turris*], 1. a relatively high structure, either a separate building or part of another. 2. such a structure used as a fortress or prison. 3. a person or thing that resembles a tower in height, strength, etc. ***v.i.*** to rise high like a tower. —**tow′ered,** ***adj.***
**tow·er·ing** (tou′ẽr-iŋ), ***adj.*** 1. that towers; very high. 2. very intense. —**tow′er·ing·ly,** ***adv.***
**tow·head** (tō′hed′), *n.* 1. a head of pale-yellow hair. 2. a person with such hair. —**tow′head′ed,** ***adj.***
**tow·hee** (tou′hē, tō′-), *n.* [echoic], any of various small North American finches related to the sparrows; esp., the chewink: also **towhee bunting.**
**tow·line** (tō′līn′), *n.* a rope, chain, etc. for towing.
**town** (toun), *n.* [AS. *tun*], 1. [Dial.], a hamlet; village. 2. a concentration of houses and buildings, larger than a village but smaller than a city. 3. *a)* in most of the U.S., a township. *b)* in New England, a rural or urban unit of local government smaller than a city, having its sovereignty vested in a town meeting. 4. the business center of a city: as, I'm going into *town.* 5. the town or city being spoken of or understood: as, they just left *town.* 6. the people of a town. ***adj.*** of, for, or characteristic of a town. —**go to town,** [Slang], 1. to go on a spree. 2. to act fast and efficiently. 3. to be eminently successful. —**on the town,** [Slang], out for a good time. —**paint the town red,** [Slang], to carouse.
**town clerk,** an official in charge of the records, legal business, etc. of a town.
**town crier,** formerly, one who cried public announcements through the streets of a town.
**town hall,** a building in a town, housing the offices of officials, the council chamber, etc.
**town house,** the city residence of a person who also owns a country residence.
**town meeting,** 1. a meeting of the people of a town. 2. a meeting of the qualified voters of a town, as in New England, to act on town business.
**town·ship** (toun′ship), *n.* 1. originally, in England, a parish or division of a parish. 2. in most of the U.S., a division of a county, constituting a unit of local government. 3. in New England, a town. 4. a unit of territory in the U.S. land survey, generally six miles square. 5. in Canada, a subdivision of a province.
**towns·man** (tounz′mən), *n.* [*pl.* -MEN], 1. a person who lives in, or has been reared in, a town. 2. a person who lives in one's own or the same town.
**towns·peo·ple** (tounz′pē′p'l), ***n.pl.*** 1. the people of a town. 2. people brought up in a town or city. Also **towns′folk′** (-fōk′).
**tow·path** (tō′path′, -päth′), *n.* a path alongside a canal, used by men or animals towing canalboats.
**tow·rope** (tō′rōp′), *n.* a rope used in towing.
**tox·e·mi·a, tox·ae·mi·a** (tok-sē′mi-ə), *n.* [< L. *toxicum* (see TOXIC) + Gr. *haima,* blood], any condition of blood poisoning, especially that caused by bacterial toxins. —**tox·e′mic, tox·ae′mic,** ***adj.***
**tox·ic** (tok′sik), ***adj.*** [< ML. < L. *toxicum,* a poison < Gr. *toxikon,* orig., poison for arrows < *toxon,* a bow], 1. of, affected by, or caused by a toxin, or poison. 2. poisonous. —**tox′i·cal·ly,** ***adv.*** —**tox·ic′i·ty** (-sis′ə-ti), [*pl.* -TIES], ***n.***
**tox·i·co-,** [< Gr. *toxikon;* see TOXIC], a combining form meaning *poison:* also **toxic-.**
**tox·i·col·o·gy** (tok′si-kol′ə-ji), *n.* [< Fr.; see TOXIC & -LOGY], the science of poisons, their effects, antidotes, etc. —**tox′i·co·log′i·cal** (-kə-loj′i-k'l), ***adj.*** —**tox′i·co·log′i·cal·ly,** ***adv.*** —**tox′i·col′o·gist,** ***n.***
**tox·in** (tok′sin), *n.* [< *toxic* + *-in*], 1. any of various poisonous compounds produced by some microorganisms and causing certain diseases. 2. any of various poisons secreted by plants and animals.
**tox·oid** (tok′soid), *n.* a toxin that has been chemically treated to eliminate the toxic qualities while retaining the properties of an antigen.
**toy** (toi), *n.* [< D. *tuig,* tools], 1. a thing of little value or importance. 2. a bauble; trinket. 3. a plaything for children. 4. anything small; specif., a small breed of dog, etc.: as, a *toy* terrier. ***adj.*** 1. like a plaything in size, use, etc. 2. made as a toy; esp., being a miniature imitation: as, a *toy* stove. ***v.i.*** to play or trifle (*with* food, an idea, etc.).
**to·yon** (tō′yən), *n.* [Sp.], an evergreen shrub with white flowers and red berries.
**tp.,** township.
**tr.,** 1. transitive. 2. translated. 3. translation. 4. translator. 5. transpose. 6. treasurer.
**trace** (trās), *n.* [< OFr. < LL. < L. pp. of *trahere,* to draw], 1. a mark, footprint, etc. left by the passage of a person, animal, or thing. 2. a beaten path or trail. 3. a visible mark left by something in the past; sign; evidence: as, the war left its *traces.* 4. a barely observable amount: as, a *trace* of anger. 5. a drawn or traced mark. 6. the traced record of a recording instrument. ***v.t.*** [TRACED, TRACING], 1. to move along or follow (a path, route, etc.). 2. to follow the trail of; track. 3. to follow the development or history of. 4. to determine (an origin, source, etc.) by this procedure. 5. to ascertain by investigating traces of (something prehistoric, etc.). 6. to draw, outline, etc. 7. to ornament with tracery. 8. to copy (a drawing etc.) by following its lines on a superimposed

transparent sheet. 9. to record by means of a broken or wavy line, as in a seismograph. *v.i.* to follow a path, route, etc. —**trace'a·ble,** *adj.* —**trace'a·ble·ness, trace'a·bil'i·ty,** *n.* —**trace'a·bly,** *adv.* —**trace'less,** *adj.*

**trace** (trās), *n.* [< OFr. pl. of *trait;* see TRAIT], either of two straps, chains, etc. connecting a draft animal's harness to the vehicle. —**kick over the traces,** to shake off control.

**trac·er** (trās'ẽr), *n.* 1. one that traces; specif., *a*) one whose work is tracing missing articles. *b*) an instrument for tracing designs on cloth, etc. 2. an inquiry sent out for a letter, etc. that is missing in transport. 3. the chemical added to a tracer bullet or shell to leave a trail of smoke or fire.

**tracer bullet** (or **shell**), a bullet or shell that traces its own course with a trail of smoke or fire, so as to facilitate adjustment of the aim.

**trac·er·y** (trās'ẽr-i), *n.* [*pl.* -IES], [< *trace, v.* + *-ery*], ornamental work of interlacing or branching lines, as in a Gothic window, etc.

**tra·che·a** (trā'ki-ə, trə-kē'-), *n.* [*pl.* -AE (-ē')], [< LL. < Gr. *tracheia* (*arteria*), rough (windpipe)], 1. in the respiratory tract of vertebrates, that part which conveys air from the larynx to the bronchi; windpipe. 2. in the respiratory system of insects and other invertebrates, any of the small tubules for conveying air. —**tra'che·al,** *adj.*

**tra·che·o-,** a combining form meaning: 1. *of the trachea.* 2. *the trachea and:* also **trache-.**

**tra·che·ot·o·my** (trā'ki-ot'ə-mi), *n.* [*pl.* -MIES], [see -TOMY], surgical incision of the trachea.

**tra·cho·ma** (trə-kō'mə), *n.* [< Gr. < *trachys*, rough], a contagious form of conjunctivitis, characterized by inflammatory granulations on the inner eyelid. —**tra·chom'a·tous** (-kom'ə-təs, -kō'mə-), *adj.*

**trac·ing** (trās'iŋ), *n.* 1. the action of one that traces. 2. something traced; specif., *a*) a copy of a drawing, etc. made by tracing the lines on a superimposed, transparent sheet. *b*) the record of a recording instrument.

**tracing paper,** thin, strong, transparent paper on which tracings may be made.

**track** (trak), *n.* [< OFr. *trac*, a track], 1. a mark or marks left by a person, animal, or thing, as a footprint, wheel rut, etc. 2. a trace or vestige. 3. a beaten path or trail. 4. a course of motion or action; route; way. 5. a sequence of ideas, events, etc. 6. a path or circuit laid out for running, horse racing, etc. 7. a pair of parallel metal rails on which trains, etc. run. 8. *a*) athletic sports performed on a track, as running, hurdling, etc. *b*) these sports along with those held in the field (see *field*, 11*b*). *v.t.* 1. to follow the track of: as, to *track* game. 2. to trace by means of vestiges, evidence, etc. 3. to travel; traverse. 4. to leave tracks on (often with *up*). 5. to leave in the form of tracks: as, to *track* dirt over the floor. *adj.* 1. having to do with a railroad track. 2. of or performed on an athletic track. —**in one's tracks,** where one is at the moment. —**keep track of,** to stay informed about. —**lose track of,** to fail to keep informed about. —**make tracks,** [Colloq.], to proceed or depart hurriedly. —**off the track,** straying from the subject; in error. —**on the track,** keeping to the subject; correct. —**track down,** 1. to pursue until caught, as by following tracks. 2. to investigate or search for until found. —**track'er,** *n.* —**track'less,** *adj.* —**track'less·ly,** *adv.*

**track·age** (trak'ij), *n.* 1. all the tracks of a railroad. 2. permission for a railroad to use the tracks of another. 3. a charge for this.

**trackless trolley,** a trolley bus.

**track man,** one who competes in track events.

**tract** (trakt), *n.* [< L. pp. of *trahere*, to draw], 1. [Poetic], *a*) duration of time. *b*) a period of time. 2. a continuous expanse of land, etc. 3. in *anatomy & zoology*, a system of organs having some special function: as, the digestive *tract.*

**tract** (trakt), *n.* [< L. *tractatus*, a treatise; pp. of *tractare;* see TRACTABLE], a pamphlet or leaflet, especially one on a religious subject.

**trac·ta·ble** (trak'tə-b'l), *adj.* [< L. < *tractare*, to drag, freq. of *trahere*, to draw], 1. easily managed, taught, etc.; docile; compliant. 2. easily worked; malleable. —**trac'ta·bil'i·ty, trac'ta·ble·ness,** *n.* —**trac'ta·bly,** *adv.*

**trac·tile** (trak't'l, -til), *adj.* [< L. *tractus* (see TRACTION); + *-ile*], that can be drawn out in length; ductile. —**trac·til'i·ty** (-til'ə-ti), *adj.*

**trac·tion** (trak'shən), *n.* [< ML. < L. *tractus*, pp. of *trahere*, to draw], 1. *a*) a pulling or drawing, as of a load over a track. *b*) a being pulled or drawn. 2. the pulling power of a locomotive, etc. 3. adhesive friction: as, the car had no *traction* on the ice. —**trac'tion·al,** *adj.* —**trac'tive,** *adj.*

**traction engine,** a steam locomotive for pulling heavy wagons, plows, etc. on roads or in fields.

**trac·tor** (trak'tẽr), *n.* [< L.; see TRACTION], 1. a small, powerful, motor-driven vehicle for pulling farm machinery, hauling loads, etc. 2. a kind of truck with a driver's cab and no body, for hauling large vans, etc. 3. an airplane with the propeller or propellers in front of the wings.

**trade** (trād), *n.* [MLG., a track], 1. work or occupation; esp., skilled labor. 2. buying and selling; commerce. 3. all the persons in a particular line of business. 4. customers; clientele. 5. a purchase or sale; deal. 6. an exchange; swap. 7. *pl.* the trade winds. *v.i.* [TRADED, TRADING], 1. to carry on a business. 2. to have business dealings (*with* someone). 3. to make an exchange (*with* someone). 4. [Colloq.], to be a customer (*at* a specified store). *v.t.* to exchange; swap. —**trade in,** to give (one's used automobile, etc.) as part of the purchase price of a new one. —**trade on** (or **upon**), to take advantage of.

**trade-in** (trād'in'), *n.* 1. something given or taken as payment or part payment for something else. 2. an exchange involving a trade-in.

**trade journal,** a magazine devoted to the interests of a specific trade, business, or industry.

**trade-last** (trād'last', -läst'), *n.* [Colloq.], a flattering remark that one has overheard and offers to report to the person so complimented if he will report a similar compliment about oneself.

**trade-mark, trade·mark** (trād'märk'), *n.* a symbol, word, etc. used by a manufacturer or dealer to distinguish his products from those of competitors: usually registered and protected by law. *v.t.* 1. to put a trade-mark on (a product). 2. to register (a symbol, etc.) as a trade-mark.

**trade name,** 1. the name by which a commodity is commonly known in trade. 2. a name used as a trade-mark. 3. the name under which a company carries on business.

**trad·er** (trād'ẽr), *n.* 1. a person who trades; merchant. 2. a ship used in trade.

**trade school,** a school where trades are taught.

**trades·man** (trādz'mən), *n.* [*pl.* -MEN], a person engaged in trade; esp., a storekeeper. —**trades'-wom'an** [*pl.* -WOMEN], *n.fem.*

**trades·peo·ple** (trādz'pē'p'l), *n.pl.* people engaged in trade, as storekeepers: also **trades'folk'** (-fōk').

**trades union,** [Chiefly Brit.], a trade union.

**trade union,** an association of workers to promote and protect the interests, rights, etc. of its members; labor union: also **trade-union.** —**trade-union,** *adj.* —**trade unionism, trade-unionism,** *n.* —**trade unionist, trade-unionist,** *n.*

**trade wind,** a wind that blows toward the equator from the northeast on the north side of the equator and from the southeast on the south side.

**trad·ing** (trād'iŋ), *adj.* that trades; commercial. *n.* buying and selling; commerce.

**trading post,** a store in an outpost, settlement, etc. where trading is done, as with natives.

**trading stamp,** a stamp given by some merchants as a premium, redeemable in merchandise.

**tra·di·tion** (trə-dish'ən), *n.* [< OFr. < L. pp. of *tradere*, to deliver], 1. the handing down orally of customs, beliefs, etc. from generation to generation. 2. a story, belief, etc. handed down this way. 3. a long-established custom that has the effect of an unwritten law. 4. *a*) among Jews, the unwritten religious code regarded as handed down from Moses. *b*) among Christians, the unwritten teachings regarded as handed down from Jesus.

**tra·di·tion·al** (trə-dish'ən-'l), *adj.* of, handed down by, or conforming to tradition; conventional: also **tra·di'tion·ar'y.** —**tra·di'tion·al·ist, tra·di'tion·ist,** *n.* —**tra·di'tion·al·is'tic,** *adj.* —**tra·di'tion·al·ly,** *adv.*

**tra·duce** (trə-dōōs', -dūs'), *v.t.* [-DUCED, -DUCING], [< L. *traducere*, to disgrace < *trans*, across + *ducere*, to lead], to defame; slander. —**tra·duce'ment,** *n.* —**tra·duc'er,** *n.* —**tra·duc'ing·ly,** *adv.*

**Tra·fal·gar** (trə-fal'gẽr), *n.* a cape at the entrance of the Strait of Gibraltar, SW Spain: site of a naval battle (1805) in which Napoleon's fleet was defeated by the British fleet.

**traf·fic** (traf'ik), *n.* [< Fr. < It. < *trafficare*, to trade < L. *trans*, across + It. *ficcare*, to bring], 1. buying and selling; trade; commerce. 2. corrupt or illegal trade. 3. dealings or business (*with* someone). 4. *a*) the movement or number of automobiles along a street, pedestrians along a sidewalk, etc. *b*) the automobiles, pedestrians, etc. 5. the business done by a transportation company, measured by the number of passengers, quantity of freight, etc. carried. 6. the business done by a communications company, measured by the telegrams, calls, etc. transmitted. *adj.* of, for, or regulating traffic. *v.i.* [-FICKED, -FICKING], 1. to carry on traffic (*in* a commodity). 2. to have traffic or dealings (*with* someone). —**traf'fick·er,** *n.*

**traffic light,** a set of signal lights placed at intersections of streets to regulate traffic.

**tra·ge·di·an** (trə-jē'di-ən), *n.* 1. a writer of tragedies. 2. an actor of tragedy.

**tra·ge·di·enne, tra·gé·di·enne** (trə-jē'di-en'), *n.* an actress of tragedy.

**trag·e·dy** (traj'ə-di), *n.* [*pl.* -DIES], [< OFr. < L. < Gr. *tragōidia;* ult. < *tragos,* goat + *ōidē,* song; ? < a goat offered as a prize], 1. a literary work, especially a serious play, having an unhappy or disastrous ending brought about ultimately by fate, moral weakness in a character, social pressures, etc. 2. the branch of drama consisting of such plays. 3. the writing or acting of such plays. 4. the tragic element in literature or life. 5. a very sad or tragic event.

**trag·ic** (traj'ik), *adj.* 1. of, or having the nature of, tragedy. 2. very sad, disastrous, etc. 3. appropriate to tragedy: as, a *tragic* voice. Also **trag'i·cal.** —**trag'i·cal·ly,** *adv.* —**trag'i·cal·ness,** *n.*

**trag·i·com·e·dy** (traj'i-kom'ə-di), *n.* [*pl.* -DIES], 1. a play, novel, etc. combining tragic and comic elements. 2. a real situation like this. —**trag'i·com'ic, trag'i·com'i·cal,** *adj.* —**trag'i·com'i·cal·ly,** *adv.*

**trail** (trāl), *v.t.* [< OFr. < LL. < *tragula,* sledge < L. *trahere,* to drag], 1. *a*) to drag or let drag behind one. *b*) to bring along behind: as, he *trailed* dirt into the house. 2. *a*) to make (a path, etc.), as by treading down. *b*) to make a path in (grass, etc.). 3. to follow the tracks of. 4. to hunt by tracking. 5. to follow behind. 6. in *military usage,* to carry (a rifle, etc.) with the muzzle slightly forward and the butt near the ground. *v.i.* 1. to drag along on the ground, etc. 2. to grow so long as to extend along the ground, etc.: said of some plants. 3. to extend in an irregular line; straggle. 4. to flow behind in a long, thin stream, wisp, etc., as smoke. 5. to follow or lag behind. 6. to diminish or dwindle, as a sound. 7. to track game: said of hounds. *n.* 1. something that trails behind. 2. a mark, scent, etc. left by a person, animal, or thing that has passed. 3. a path made as by continual passing. 4. a part of a gun carriage, which may be lowered to the ground to form a rear brace. —**trail'ing·ly,** *adv.*

**trail blazer,** 1. a person who blazes a trail; hence, 2. a pioneer in any field.

**trail·er** (trāl'ēr), *n.* 1. a person, animal, or thing that trails another. 2. a cart, wagon, or large van designed to be pulled by an automobile, truck, or tractor. 3. a closed vehicle designed to be pulled by an automobile and equipped as a place to live in. 4. scenes on film from a motion picture to be shown later, used for advertising.

**trailer camp,** a number of parked trailers serving as a housing project for workers, tourists, etc.

**trailing arbutus** (trāl'iŋ), a trailing, evergreen plant with pink flowers; Mayflower.

**train** (trān), *n.* [< OFr. < *trainer,* to draw on < L. *trahere,* to pull], 1. something that drags along behind, as a part of a dress, etc. that trails. 2. a group of followers or attendants in a procession; retinue. 3. a group of persons, animals, vehicles, etc. moving in a line; procession; caravan. 4. the persons, vehicles, etc. carrying the supplies, ammunition, etc. of an army. 5. a series of events that follow some happening: as, the war brought famine in its *train.* 6. any connected sequence; series: as, a *train* of thought. 7. a series of connected parts for transmitting motion: as, a gear *train.* 8. a line of connected railroad cars pulled or pushed by a locomotive. 9. a line of gunpowder used to set off an explosive charge. *v.t.* 1. to guide the growth of (a plant) by tying, pruning, etc. 2. to guide the mental, moral, etc. development of; bring up; rear. 3. to instruct so as to make proficient. 4. to discipline (animals) to perform tricks. 5. to make fit for an athletic contest, etc. 6. to aim (a gun, etc.) at something (usually with *on*). *v.i.* to administer or undergo training. —**train'a·ble,** *adj.* —**train'er,** *n.*

**train·ee** (trān-ē'), *n.* one receiving training; esp., a recruit undergoing military training.

**train·ing** (trān'iŋ), *n.* 1. the action of one that trains. 2. a being trained or undergoing training. *adj.* of or used in training.

**train·man** (trān'mən), *n.* [*pl.* -MEN], one who works on a railroad train; esp., a brakeman.

**traipse** (trāps), *v.i.* [TRAIPSED, TRAIPSING], [prob. < OFr. *trapasser,* to pass beyond], [Dial. or Colloq.], 1. to walk or wander idly; gad; trudge. 2. to trail untidily. *v.t.* [Dial.], to tramp; trample.

**trait** (trāt), *n.* [Fr. < L. pp. of *trahere,* to draw], a distinguishing quality or characteristic.

**trai·tor** (trā'tēr), *n.* [< OFr. < L. < *tradere,* to betray], one who betrays his country, cause, friends, etc.; one guilty of treason. —**trai'tress,** *n.fem.*

**trai·tor·ous** (trā'tēr-əs), *adj.* 1. of or like a traitor; treacherous. 2. of or involving treason. —**trai'tor·ous·ly,** *adv.* —**trai'tor·ous·ness,** *n.*

**tra·jec·to·ry** (trə-jek'tēr-i), *n.* [*pl.* -RIES], [< L. *trajectus,* pp. < *trans,* across + *jacere,* to throw], the curved path of something hurtling through space, especially that of a projectile.

**tram** (tram), *n.* [prob. < LG. *traam,* a beam], 1. an open railway car used in mines. 2. [Brit.], *a*) a streetcar: also called **tram'car'.** *b*) a streetcar line: also called **tram'line', tram'way'.**

**tram·mel** (tram''l), *n.* [< OFr. < LL. *tramacula* < L. *tres,* three + *macula,* a mesh], 1. a three-ply fishing net: also **trammel net.** 2. a shackle for a horse, especially one to teach ambling. 3. *often pl.* something that confines, restrains, etc. 4. a pothook. 5. an instrument for drawing ellipses. *v.t.* [-MELED or -MELLED, -MELING or -MELLING], 1. to entangle, as in a trammel. 2. to confine, restrain, or shackle. —**tram'mel·er, tram'mel·ler,** *n.*

**tramp** (tramp), *v.i.* [ME. *trampen* < LG.], 1. to walk firmly and heavily. 2. to travel about on foot, especially as a vagrant. *v.t.* 1. to step on heavily; trample. 2. to walk or ramble through. *n.* 1. one who travels about on foot doing odd jobs or begging; hobo; vagrant. 2. the sound of heavy steps. 3. a journey on foot; hike. 4. a freight ship that picks up cargo and passengers wherever it may be. —**tramp'er,** *n.* —**tramp'ing·ly,** *adv.*

**tram·ple** (tram'p'l), *v.i.* [-PLED, -PLING], [< freq. of ME. *trampen,* to tramp], to tread heavily; tramp. *v.t.* to crush, destroy, etc. as by treading heavily on. *n.* the sound of trampling. —**trample under foot,** 1. to hurt by trampling. 2. to treat harshly. Also **trample on** (or **upon**). —**tram'pler,** *n.*

**tram·po·line, tram·po·lin** (tram'pə-lin), *n.* [< It. *trampoli,* stilts], a net of strong canvas stretched tightly on a frame, used by acrobats.

**trance** (trans, träns), *n.* [< OFr. < L. *transire,* to die < *trans,* across + *ire,* to go], 1. a state resembling sleep, in which consciousness may remain, as in hypnosis. 2. a daze; stupor. 3. a condition of great mental abstraction, as that of a religious mystic. 4. a condition in which a spiritualist medium allegedly communicates with the dead. *v.t.* [TRANCED, TRANCING], to put into a trance.

**tran·quil** (traŋ'kwil, tran'-), *adj.* [-QUILER or -QUILLER, -QUILEST or -QUILLEST], [< Fr. < L. < *trans-,* beyond + *quies,* rest], 1. free from emotional disturbance or agitation; calm; serene. 2. quiet or motionless: as, *tranquil* waters. —**tranquil'li·ty, tran·quil'i·ty,** *n.* —**tran'quil·ly,** *adv.*

**tran·quil·ize, tran·quil·lize** (traŋ'kwə-līz', tran'-), *v.t. & v.i.* [-IZED, -IZING; -LIZED, -LIZING], to make or become tranquil; quiet; calm. —**tran'quil·i·za'tion, tran'quil·li·za'tion,** *n.*

**tran·quil·iz·er, tran·quil·liz·er** (traŋ'kwə-līz'ēr, tran'-), *n.* any of certain drugs used as a depressant in relieving and controlling various emotional disturbances, certain neuroses, etc.

**trans-,** [L. < *trans,* across], a prefix meaning: 1. *on* or *to the other side of, over, across,* as in *transatlantic.* 2. *so as to change thoroughly,* as in *transliterate.* 3. *above and beyond, transcending.*

**trans.,** 1. transactions. 2. transitive. 3. translated. 4. translation. 5. transportation.

**trans·act** (tran-sakt', -zakt'), *v.t.* [< L. *transactus,* pp. < *trans-* + *agere,* to drive], to carry on, conduct, or complete (business, etc.). *v.i.* [Rare.], to do business; negotiate. —**trans·ac'tor,** *n.*

**trans·ac·tion** (tran-sak'shən, -zak'-), *n.* 1. a transacting or being transacted. 2. something transacted; specif., *a*) a piece of business; deal. *b*) *pl.* a record of the proceedings of a society, convention, etc. —**trans·ac'tion·al,** *adj.*

**trans·al·pine** (trans-al'pin, tranz-al'pīn), *adj.* on that (the northern) side of the Alps, from Rome.

**trans·at·lan·tic** (trans'ət-lan'tik, tranz'-), *adj.* 1. crossing or spanning the Atlantic. 2. on the other side of the Atlantic.

**Trans·cau·ca·sia** (trans'kô-kā'zhə, -shə), *n.* the region south of the Caucasus Mountains, U.S.S.R., containing the republics of Georgia, Armenia, and Azerbaijan. —**Trans'cau·ca'sian,** *adj. & n.*

**tran·scend** (tran-send′), *v.t.* [< L. < *trans-*, over + *scandere*, to climb], 1. to go beyond the limits of; exceed. 2. to be superior to; surpass; excel. *v.i.* [Archaic], to be transcendent; excel.

**tran·scend·ent** (tran-sen′dənt), *adj.* 1. transcending; surpassing; excelling. 2. in *theology*, that exists apart from the material universe: said of God, divine spirit, etc. —**tran·scend′ence, tran·scend′en·cy,** *n.* —**tran·scend′ent·ly,** *adv.*

**tran·scen·den·tal** (tran′sen-den′t'l), *adj.* 1. transcendent. 2. supernatural. 3. abstract; metaphysical. 4. of transcendentalism. —**tran′scen·den′tal·ly,** *adv.*

**tran·scen·den·tal·ism** (tran′sen-den′t'l-iz'm), *n.* 1. any of various philosophies that propose to discover the nature of reality by investigating the process of thought rather than the objects of sense experience. 2. the philosophical ideas of Emerson and some other 19th-century New Englanders, based on a search for reality through spiritual intuition. 3. any obscure, visionary, or idealistic thought. —**tran′scen·den′tal·ist,** *n.*

**trans·con·ti·nen·tal** (trans′kon-tə-nen′t'l), *adj.* 1. that crosses a (or the) continent. 2. on the other side of a (or the) continent.

**tran·scribe** (tran-skrīb′), *v.t.* [-SCRIBED, -SCRIBING], [< L. < *trans-*, over + *scribere*, to write], 1. to make a written or typewritten copy of (shorthand notes, a speech, etc.). 2. in *music* *radio*, to make a transcription of. See **transcription,** 3, 4*a*. —**tran·scrib′er,** *n.*

**tran·script** (tran′skript′), *n.* 1. something made by transcribing; a written or typewritten copy. 2. any copy or reproduction.

**tran·scrip·tion** (tran-skrip′shən), *n.* 1. the act or process of transcribing. 2. a transcript; copy. 3. an arrangement of a piece of music for an instrument, voice, etc. other than that for which it was originally written. 4. *a*) a recording of a program, etc. made for radio broadcasting. *b*) the act or practice of using such recordings.

**tran·sect** (tran-sekt′), *v.t.* [*trans-* + L. *sectus*, pp. of *secare*, to cut], to cut across or divide by cutting across. —**tran·sec′tion,** *n.*

**tran·sept** (tran′sept), *n.* [< ML. < L. < *transversus*, transverse + *septum*, enclosure], 1. the part of a cross-shaped church at right angles to the long, main section, or nave. 2. either arm of this part, outside the nave. —**tran·sep′tal,** *adj.*

**trans·fer** (trans-fũr′; *also, and for n. always,* trans′fẽr), *v.t.* [-FERRED, -FERRING], [< L. < *trans-*, across + *ferre*, to bear], 1. to convey, carry, send, etc. from one person or place to another. 2. to make over the legal title or ownership of to another. 3. to convey (a picture, design, etc.) from one surface to another. *v.i.* 1. to transfer oneself. 2. to be transferred. 3. to change from one bus, streetcar, etc. to another, as by presenting a transfer (sense 3). *n.* 1. a transferring or being transferred. 2. one that is transferred; specif., a picture or design transferred or to be transferred from one surface to another. 3. a ticket entitling the bearer to change from one bus, streetcar, etc. to another. 4. a document effecting a transfer. —**trans·fer′a·ble,** *adj.* —**trans·fer′ence,** *n.* —**trans·fer′rer;** in *law*, **trans·fer′or** (-ẽr), *n.*

**trans·fig·u·ra·tion** (trans-fig′yoo-rā′shən, trans′-fig-), *n.* 1. a transfiguring or being transfigured. 2. [T-], *a*) the change in the appearance of Jesus on the mountain: Matt. 17; Mark 9. *b*) a church festival, on August 6, commemorating this.

**trans·fig·ure** (trans-fig′yoor), *v.t.* [-URED, -URING], [< OFr. < L. < *trans-*, across + *figura*; see FIGURE], 1. to change the figure, form, or appearance of; transform. 2. to transform so as to exalt or glorify. —**trans·fig′ur·er,** *n.*

**trans·fix** (tran-fiks′), *v.t.* [< L. pp. < *trans-*, through + *figere*, to fix], 1. to pierce through as with something pointed. 2. to fasten in this manner; impale. 3. to make motionless, as if impaled: as, *transfixed* with horror. —**trans·fix′ion,** *n.*

**trans·form** (trans-fôrm′), *v.t.* [< OFr.; ult. < L. *trans-*, over + *forma*, a shape], 1. to change the form or appearance of. 2. to change the condition, character, or function of. 3. in *electricity*, to change (a current) in potential or type. 4. in *mathematics*, to change (an expression, figure, etc.) in form but not in value. 5. in *physics*, to change (one form of energy) into another. *v.i.* [Rare], to be or become transformed. —**trans·form′a·ble,** *adj.* —**trans′for·ma′tion,** *n.* —**trans·form′a·tive,** *adj.*

**trans·form·er** (trans-fôr′mẽr), *n.* 1. one that transforms. 2. an apparatus for transforming the voltage of an electric current.

**trans·fuse** (trans-fūz′), *v.t.* [-FUSED, -FUSING], [< L. pp. < *trans-*, across + *fundere*, to pour], 1. to pour from one container into another. 2. to instill; imbue; infuse. 3. in *medicine*, *a*) to transfer (blood) from one individual into a blood vessel of another. *b*) to inject (a saline solution, etc.) directly into a blood vessel. —**trans·fus′er,** *n.* —**trans·fus′i·ble,** *adj.* —**trans·fu′sive,** *adj.*

**trans·fu·sion** (trans-fū′zhən), *n.* a transfusing, especially of blood.

**trans·gress** (trans-gres′, tranz-), *v.t.* [< Fr. < L. pp. < *trans-*, over + *gradi*, to step], 1. to overstep or break (a law, commandment, etc.). 2. to go beyond (a limit, boundary, etc.). *v.i.* to break a law, commandment, etc.; sin. —**trans·gres′sor,** *n.*

**trans·gres·sion** (trans-gresh′ən, tranz-), *n.* a transgressing; violation; sin.

**tran·ship** (tran-ship′), *v.t.* [-SHIPPED, -SHIPPING], to transship. —**tran·ship′ment,** *n.*

**tran·sient** (tran′shənt), *adj.* [< L. *transiens*, ppr. < *trans-*, over + *ire*, to go], 1. *a*) passing away with time; temporary; transitory. *b*) passing quickly; fleeting; ephemeral. 2. staying only for a short time: as, a *transient* lodger. *n.* a transient person or thing; esp., a temporary lodger, etc. —**tran′sience, tran′sien·cy,** *n.* —**tran′sient·ly,** *adv.*

**tran·sis·tor** (tran-zis′tẽr, -sis′-), *n.* [< *transfer* + *resistor*], a minute electronic device, used like an electronic tube, which controls current flow by means of the conductive properties of germanium.

**tran·sis·tor·ized** (tran-zis′tẽr-īzd′, -sis′-), *adj.* equipped with a transistor or transistors.

**trans·it** (tran′sit, -zit), *n.* [< L. *transitus*, pp. < *trans-*, over + *ire*, to go], 1. *a*) passage through or across. *b*) a transition; change. 2. a carrying or being carried through or across; conveyance. 3. a surveying instrument for measuring horizontal angles: in full, **transit theodolite.** 4. in *astronomy*, *a*) the apparent passage of a heavenly body across a given meridian or through the field of a telescope. *b*) the apparent passage of a smaller heavenly body across the disk of a larger one. *v.t. & v.i.* to make a transit through or across.

**tran·si·tion** (tran-zish′ən, -sish′-), *n.* 1. a passing from one condition, place, activity, etc. to another. 2. the period of this. 3. a word, phrase, sentence, etc. that relates a topic with a succeeding one. 4. in *music*, a modulation. —**tran·si′tion·al,** *adj.* —**tran·si′tion·al·ly,** *adv.*

**tran·si·tive** (tran′sə-tiv), *adj.* 1. [Rare], transitional. 2. taking a direct object to complete the meaning: said of certain verbs. *n.* a transitive verb. —**tran′si·tive·ly,** *adv.* —**tran′si·tive·ness,** *n.*

**tran·si·to·ry** (tran′sə-tôr′i, -zə-tō′ri), *adj.* of a passing nature; not enduring; temporary; fleeting. —**tran′si·to′ri·ly,** *adv.* —**tran′si·to′ri·ness,** *n.*

**Trans-Jor·dan** (trans-jôr′d'n, tranz-), *n.* Jordan: former name: also, formerly, **Trans′jor·da′ni·a** (-dā′ni-ə, -dān′yə).

**trans·late** (trans-lāt′, tranz′lāt), *v.t.* [-LATED, -LATING], [< L. *translatus*, used as pp. of *transferre*, to transfer], 1. to change from one place, position, etc. to another; transfer. 2. to change from one language into another. 3. to change into another medium or form: as, *translate* ideas into action. 4. to put into different words; interpret. *v.i.* 1. to make translations (into other languages). 2. to be capable of being translated. —**trans·lat′a·ble,** *adj.* —**trans·lat′a·ble·ness,** *n.* —**trans·la′tor,** *n.*

**trans·la·tion** (trans-lā′shən, tranz-), *n.* 1. a translating or being translated. 2. a translated version of a literary work. —**trans·la′tion·al,** *adj.*

**trans·lit·er·ate** (trans-lit′ə-rāt′, tranz-), *v.t.* [-ATED, -ATING], [< *trans-* + L. *litera*, letter], to write or spell (words, etc.) in the characters of another alphabet that represent the same sounds. —**trans·lit′er·a′tion,** *n.* —**trans·lit′er·a′tor,** *n.*

**trans·lu·cent** (trans-lōō′s'nt, tranz-), *adj.* [< L. ppr. < *trans-*, through + *lucere*, to shine], 1. originally, shining through. 2. letting light pass but diffusing it so that objects on the other side cannot be distinguished, as frosted glass. —**trans·lu′cence, trans·lu′cen·cy,** *n.* —**trans·lu′cent·ly,** *adv.*

**trans·mi·grate** (trans-mī′grāt, tranz-), *v.i.* [-GRATED, -GRATING], [< L.; see TRANS- & MIGRATE], 1. to move from one habitation, country, etc. to another. 2. in some religions, to pass into another body at death: said of the soul. —**trans′mi·gra′tion,** *n.* —**trans·mi′gra·tor,** *n.* —**trans·mi′gra·to′ry** (-grə-tôr′i, -tō′ri), *adj.*

**trans·mis·si·ble** (trans-mis′ə-b'l, tranz-), *adj.* capable of being transmitted. —**trans·mis′si·bil′i·ty,** *n.*

**trans·mis·sion** (trans-mish′ən, tranz-), *n.* 1. a transmitting or being transmitted. 2. something transmitted. 3. the part of an automobile, etc. that transmits motive force from the engine to the wheels, as by gears. 4. the passage of radio waves through space between the transmitting station and the receiving station. —**trans·mis′sion·al,** *adj.* —**trans·mis′sive,** *adj.*

**trans·mit** (trans-mit′, tranz-), *v.t.* [-MITTED, -MITTING], [< L. < *trans-*, over + *mittere*, to send], 1. to send or cause to go from one person or place to another; transfer; convey. 2. to hand down to others by heredity, inheritance, etc. 3. to communicate. 4. to cause (light, heat, etc.) to pass through some medium. 5. to conduct: as, water *transmits* sound. 6. to convey (force, movement, etc.) from one mechanical part to another. 7. to send out (radio or television signals) by electromagnetic waves. —**trans·mit′tal, trans·mit′tance,** *n.* —**trans·mit′ti·ble,** *adj.*

**trans·mit·ter** (trans-mit′ẽr, tranz-), *n.* one that transmits; specif., *a*) the part of a telegraphic instrument by which messages are sent. *b*) the part of a telephone, behind the mouthpiece, that converts sound into electric impulses for transmission. *c*) the apparatus that generates, modulates, and sends out radio waves: also **transmitting set.**

**trans·mu·ta·tion** (trans′mū-tā′shən, tranz′-) *n.* 1. a transmuting or being transmuted. 2. the conversion of one element into another, as sought in alchemy or as occurring in nuclear fission, etc.

**trans·mute** (trans-mūt′, tranz-), *v.t.* [-MUTED, -MUTING], [< L. < *trans-*, over + *mutare*, to change], to change from one form, nature, substance, etc. into another; transform. —**trans·mut′a·bil′i·ty,** *n.* —**trans·mut′a·ble,** *adj.* —**trans·mut′a·bly,** *adv.* —**trans·mut′a·tive,** *adj.* —**trans·mut′er,** *n.*

**trans·o·ce·an·ic** (trans′ō-shi-an′ik, tranz′-), *adj.* 1. crossing or spanning the ocean. 2. on the other side of the ocean.

**tran·som** (tran′səm), *n.* [prob. < L. *transtrum*, crossbeam], 1. a horizontal crossbar across the top or middle of a window or the top of a door. 2. a small window directly over a door or window, usually hinged to the transom. 3. any crosspiece, as the horizontal beam of a gallows.

**trans·pa·cif·ic** (trans′pə-sif′ik), *adj.* 1. crossing the Pacific. 2. on the other side of the Pacific.

**trans·par·en·cy** (trans-pâr′ən-si), *n.* 1. a transparent state or quality: also **trans·par′ence.** 2. [*pl.* -CIES], something transparent; specif., a piece of material having a picture, etc. that is visible when light shines through it.

**trans·par·ent** (trans-pâr′ənt), *adj.* [< Fr. < ML. ppr. < L. *trans-*, through + *parere*, to appear], 1. transmitting light rays so that objects on the other side may be distinctly seen, as window glass. 2. so fine in texture or open in mesh as to be seen through; sheer; gauzy. 3. easily understood, recognized, or detected; obvious. 4. open; frank. 5. [Poetic], luminous. —**trans·par′ent·ly,** *adv.*

**tran·spire** (tran-spīr′), *v.t.* [-SPIRED, -SPIRING], [< Fr. < L. *trans*, through + *spirare*, to breathe], to cause (vapor, moisture, etc.) to pass through tissue or other permeable substances, especially through the pores of the skin or the surface of plant leaves. *v.i.* 1. to give off vapor, moisture, etc., as through pores. 2. to be given off in this way. 3. to leak out; become known. 4. to come to pass; happen: regarded by some as a loose usage. —**tran′spi·ra′tion** (-spə-rā′shən), *n.* —**tran·spir′a·to′ry** (-ə-tôr′i, -tō′ri), *adj.*

**trans·plant** (trans-plant′, -plänt′; *for n.*, trans′plant, -plänt), *v.t.* [< LL.; see TRANS- & PLANT], 1. to remove from one place and plant in another. 2. to remove (people) from one place and resettle in another. 3. in *surgery*, to transfer (tissue or an organ) from one individual or part of the body to another; graft. *v.i.* to be capable of being transplanted. *n.* something transplanted, as a seedling or body tissue. —**trans·plant′a·ble,** *adj.* —**trans′plan·ta′tion,** *n.* —**trans·plant′er,** *n.*

**trans·port** (trans-pôrt′, -pōrt′; *for n.*, trans′pôrt, -pōrt), *v.t.* [< OFr. < L. *trans-*, over + *portare*, to carry], 1. to carry from one place to another, especially over long distances. 2. to carry away with emotion; enrapture. 3. to banish or deport to a penal colony, etc. 4. [Obs.], to kill. *n.* 1. a transporting; transportation. 2. strong emotion; rapture. 3. a ship used for transporting soldiers, supplies, etc. 4. a large airplane for carrying passengers, freight, etc. 5. a transported convict. —**trans·port′a·ble,** *adj.* —**trans·port′a·bil′i·ty, trans·port′a·ble·ness,** *n.* —**trans·port′er,** *n.*

**trans·por·ta·tion** (trans′pẽr-tā′shən), *n.* 1. a transporting or being transported. 2. a means of conveyance. 3. fare; a ticket for transport. 4. banishment for crime, as to a penal colony.

**trans·pose** (trans-pōz′), *v.t.* [-POSED, -POSING], [< OFr. *transposer;* see TRANS- & POSE (to put)], 1. to change the usual, relative, or respective order or position of; interchange. 2. to transfer (an algebraic term) from one side of an equation to the other, reversing the plus or minus value. 3. to write or play (a musical composition) in a different key. *v.i.* 1. to write or play music in a different key. 2. to be capable of being transposed. —**trans·pos′a·ble,** *adj.* —**trans·pos′a·bil′i·ty, trans·pos′a·ble·ness,** *n.* —**trans·pos′er,** *n.* —**trans′po·si′tion** (-pə-zish′ən), **trans·pos′al,** *n.*

**trans·ship** (trans-ship′, tran-), *v.t.* [-SHIPPED, -SHIPPING], to transfer from one ship, train, etc. to another for reshipment. —**trans·ship′ment,** *n.*

**trans·son·ic** (trans-son′ik, tran-), *adj.* [< *trans-* + L. *sonus*, sound], of, designating, or traveling at speeds approximating the speed of sound in air (c. 738 miles per hour): the limits range from 550 to 900 miles per hour.

**tran·sub·stan·ti·ate** (tran′səb-stan′shi-āt′), *v.t.* [-ATED, -ATING], [ <ML. pp. < L. *trans-*, over + *substantia*, substance], 1. to change one substance into another. 2. to bring about transubstantiation (sense 2) in (bread and wine).

**tran·sub·stan·ti·a·tion** (tran′səb-stan′shi-ā′shən), *n.* 1. a transubstantiating. 2. in *Roman Catholic & Orthodox Eastern doctrine*, the changing, in the Eucharist, of the whole substance of the bread and wine into the body and blood of Christ, only the accidents of bread and wine remaining.

**trans·u·ran·ic** (trans′yoo-ran′ik), *adj.* designating or of the elements, as plutonium, having atomic numbers higher than that of uranium.

**Trans·vaal** (trans-väl′, tranz-), *n.* a province of the Union of South Africa, in the NE part.

**trans·ver·sal** (trans-vũr′s'l, tranz-), *adj.* transverse. *n.* a line that intersects two or more other lines. —**trans·ver′sal·ly,** *adv.*

**trans·verse** (trans-vũrs′, tranz-), *adj.* [< L. pp. < *trans-*, across + *vertere*, to turn], 1. lying, situated, placed, etc. across; crosswise. 2. in *geometry*, designating the axis that passes through the foci of a conic section. *n.* 1. a transverse part, beam, etc. 2. in *geometry*, a transverse axis. —**trans·verse′ly,** *adv.*

**Tran·syl·va·ni·a** (tran′sil-vā′ni-ə, -s'l-vān′yə), *n.* a province in Romania. —**Tran′syl·va′ni·an,** *adj. & n.*

**trap** (trap), *n.* [< AS. *træppe*], 1. any device for catching animals; gin; snare. 2. any stratagem, ambush, etc. designed to catch or trick unsuspecting persons. 3. any of various devices for preventing the escape of gas, offensive odors, etc., as a U-shaped part in a drainpipe. 4. an apparatus for throwing the targets into the air in trapshooting. 5. a light, two-wheeled carriage with springs. 6. a rattletrap. 7. a trap door. 8. *pl.* the drums, cymbals, etc. in an orchestra or band. 9. [Slang], the mouth. 10. in *golf*, any of various hazards: as, a sand *trap*. *v.t.* [TRAPPED or *occas.* TRAPT, TRAPPING], 1. to catch as in a trap; entrap. 2. to hold back or seal off by a trap (also with *out*). 3. to furnish with a trap or traps. *v.i.* to set traps to catch animals, especially for their furs.

**trap** (trap), *n.* [< Sw. *trappa*, stair], any of various dark-colored igneous rocks found in other rock in steplike formations: also **trap′rock′.**

**trap** (trap), *v.t.* [TRAPPED, TRAPPING], [prob. < OFr. *drap*, cloth], to cover with trappings; caparison. *n.* 1. [Obs.], trappings for a horse, etc. 2. *pl.* [Colloq.], personal belongings; luggage.

**trap door,** a hinged or sliding door in a roof, or floor.

**tra·peze** (tra-pēz′, tra-), *n.* [Fr. < L. *trapezium*: from its shape], 1. a short horizontal bar, hung at a height by two ropes, on which gymnasts, acrobats, etc. swing. 2. a trapezium (senses 1 & 2).

**tra·pe·zi·um** (trə-pē′zi-əm), *n.* [*pl.* -ZIUMS, -ZIA (-zi-ə)], [< Gr. dim. of *trapeza*, table < *tetra*, four + *peza*, a foot], 1. a plane figure with four sides no two of which are parallel. 2. [Brit.], a trapezoid (sense 1). 3. a small bone of the wrist near the base of the thumb.

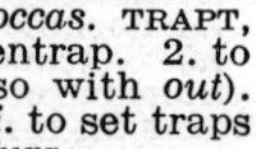

TRAPEZIUM

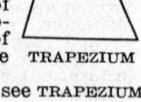

**trap·e·zoid** (trap′ə-zoid′), *n.* [< Gr.; see TRAPEZIUM & -OID], 1. a plane figure with four sides two of which are parallel. 2. [Brit.], a trapezium (sense 1). 3. in *anatomy*, a small bone of the wrist near the base of the index finger. *adj.* shaped like a trapezoid: also **trap′e·zoi′dal.**

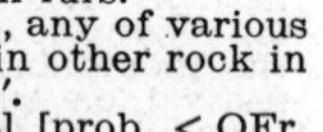

TRAPEZOID

**trap·per** (trap′ẽr), *n.* a person who traps; esp., one who traps fur-bearing animals for their skins.
**trap·pings** (trap′iŋz), *n.pl.* [see TRAP (to caparison)], 1. an ornamental covering for a horse. 2. ornamental dress; adornments.
**Trap·pist** (trap′ist), *n.* [< Fr. < La *Trappe*, abbey in Normandy], a monk of a branch of the Cistercian order, known for austerity and perpetual silence. *adj.* of or having to do with the Trappists.
**trap·rock** (trap′rok′), *n.* trap (rock).
**trap·shoot·ing** (trap′shōōt′iŋ), *n.* the sport of shooting at clay pigeons, glass balls, etc. sprung into the air from traps. **—trap′shoot′er,** *n.*
**trash** (trash), *n.* [cf. Norw. dial. *trask*], 1. parts that have been broken off, stripped off, etc., especially leaves, twigs, etc. 2. worthless things; rubbish. 3. worthless ideas, talk, or writing; nonsense. 4. a disreputable person or people.
**trash·y** (trash′i), *adj.* [-IER, -IEST], containing, consisting of, or like trash; worthless. **—trash′i·ly,** *adv.* **—trash′i·ness,** *n.*
**trau·ma** (trô′mə, trou′-), *n.* [*pl.* -MATA (-mə-tə), -MAS], [Gr.], 1. in *medicine, a*) an injury violently produced. *b*) the condition or neurosis resulting from this. 2. in *psychiatry*, an emotional shock which has a lasting psychic effect.
**trau·mat·ic** (trô-mat′ik), *adj.* 1. of, having the nature of, or resulting from a trauma. 2. used in the treatment of wounds. **—trau·mat′i·cal·ly,** *adv.*
**trau·ma·tize** (trô′mə-tīz′), *v.t.* [-TIZED, -TIZING], to subject to a trauma.
**trav·ail** (trav′āl, -′l), *n.* [OFr. < LL. < *tria*, three + *palus*, a stake: orig. referring to a torture device], 1. very hard work. 2. the pains of childbirth. 3. intense pain; agony. *v.i.* 1. to toil. 2. to suffer the pains of childbirth.
**trav·el** (trav′'l), *v.i.* [-VELED or -VELLED, -VELING or -VELLING], [var. of *travail*], 1. to go from one place to another; make a journey. 2. to go from place to place as a traveling salesman. 3. to walk or run. 4. to move, pass, or be transmitted. 5. to move in a given course: said of mechanical parts, etc. 6. [Colloq.], to move with speed. *v.t.* to make a journey over or through. *n.* 1. the act or process of traveling. 2. *pl.* trips, journeys, tours, etc. 3. movement of any kind. 4. *a*) mechanical motion, especially reciprocating motion. *b*) the distance of a mechanical stroke, etc. **—trav′el·er, trav′el·ler,** *n.*
**trav·eled, trav·elled** (trav′'ld), *adj.* 1. that has traveled much. 2. much used by those who travel.
**traveler's check,** any of a set of checks of a specific denomination issued by a bank, etc. and sold to a traveler who signs them and can cash them by having the payer witness his endorsement.
**traveling salesman,** a salesman who travels for a business firm, soliciting orders.
**trav·e·logue, trav·e·log** (trav′ə-lôg′, -log′), *n.* 1. a lecture on travels, accompanied by the showing of pictures. 2. a motion picture of travels.
**tra·verse** (trav′ẽrs, trə-vũrs′), *v.t.* [-VERSED, -VERSING], [< OFr. < LL. < L. pp. < *trans-*, over + *vertere*, to turn], 1. *a*) to pass over, across, or through. *b*) to go back and forth over or along. 2. to go counter to; oppose. 3. to examine carefully. 4. to turn (a gun, etc.) laterally. 5. in *law*, to deny formally (an allegation, etc.). *v.i.* 1. to cross over. 2. to move back and forth over a place, etc. 3. to pivot or swivel. *n.* 1. something that traverses or crosses; specif., *a*) a crossbar, crossbeam, etc. *b*) a screen, curtain, etc. placed crosswise. *c*) a gallery, loft, etc. crossing a building. 2. something that opposes; obstacle. 3. a traversing or a passing across: also **trav′er·sal.** 4. a device that causes a traversing movement. 5. a way across. 6. a zigzag course taken by a vessel. *adj.* 1. extending across. 2. designating or of drapes hung in pairs so that they can be drawn by pulling cords at the side. *adv.* [Obs.], across; crosswise. **—trav′ers·a·ble,** *adj.* **—trav′ers·er,** *n.*
**trav·es·ty** (trav′is-ti), *n.* [*pl.* -TIES], [< Fr. pp. of *travestir*, to disguise < It. < L. *trans*, over + *vestire*, to dress], 1. a grotesque or farcical imitation for purposes of ridicule; burlesque. 2. a crude and ridiculous representation. *v.t.* [-TIED, -TYING], to make a travesty of.
**trawl** (trôl), *n.* [prob. var. of *trail*], 1. a large, baglike net dragged along the bottom of a fishing bank. 2. a long line supported by buoys, from which short, baited fishing lines are hung: also **trawl line.** *v.t. & v.i.* to fish or catch with a trawl.
**trawl·er** (trôl′ẽr), *n.* 1. a person who trawls. 2. a boat used in trawling.
**tray** (trā), *n.* [< AS. *treg*, wooden board], 1. a flat receptacle with low sides, for holding or carrying articles. 2. a tray with its contents: as, a *tray* of food. 3. a shallow, removable compartment of a trunk, cabinet, etc.
**treach·er·ous** (trech′ẽr-əs), *adj.* 1. characterized by treachery; traitorous. 2. untrustworthy; unreliable: as, *treacherous* rocks. **—treach′er·ous·ly,** *adv.* **—treach′er·ous·ness,** *n.*
**treach·er·y** (trech′ẽr-i), *n.* [*pl.* -IES], [< OFr. < *trichier*, to trick, cheat], 1. betrayal of trust or faith; deceit; perfidy. 2. treason.
**trea·cle** (trē′k'l), *n.* [< OFr. < L. < Gr. *thēriakē*, remedy for venomous bites < *thērion*, dim. of *thēr*, beast], [Brit.], molasses. **—trea′cly** (-kli), [-CLIER, -CLIEST], *adj.*
**tread** (tred), *v.t.* [TROD or *archaic* TRODE (trōd), TRODDEN or TROD, TREADING], [AS. *tredan*], 1. to walk on, in, along, over, etc. 2. to do or follow by walking, dancing, etc.: as, to *tread* the measures gaily. 3. to trample; press or beat with the feet. 4. to subdue or oppress. 5. to copulate with: said of male birds. *v.i.* 1. to move on foot; walk. 2. to set one's foot (with *on* or *upon*). 3. to trample (with *on* or *upon*). 4. to copulate: said of birds. *n.* 1. a treading. 2. manner or sound of treading. 3. something on which a person or thing treads, as the part of a shoe sole, wheel, etc. that makes contact, the upper surface of a stair, etc. 4. the distance between the points of contact (with the ground) of paired wheels. **—tread on air,** to be gay or happy. **—tread on one's toes,** to offend one. **—tread the boards,** to act in plays. **—tread water,** [pt. usually TREADED], in *swimming*, to keep the body upright and the head above water by moving the legs up and down. **—tread′er,** *n.*
**trea·dle** (tred′'l), *n.* [AS. *tredel* < *tredan*, to tread], a lever moved by the foot to operate a sewing machine, etc. *v.i.* [-DLED, -DLING], to work a treadle.
**tread·mill** (tred′mil′), *n.* 1. a mill wheel turned by persons treading steps around its circumference, or by an animal treading an endless belt. 2. any monotonous round of duties, work, etc.
**treas.,** 1. treasurer. 2. treasury.
**trea·son** (trē′z'n), *n.* [< OFr. < L. < pp. of *tradere*, to deliver up < *trans*, over + *dare*, to give], 1. [Rare], betrayal of trust or faith. 2. betrayal of one's country to an enemy.
**trea·son·a·ble** (trē′z'n-ə-b'l), *adj.* of or involving treason; traitorous: also **trea′son·ous.** **—trea′son·a·bly,** *adv.* **—trea′son·a·ble·ness,** *n.*
**treas·ure** (trezh′ẽr), *n.* [< OFr. < L. < Gr. *thēsauros*], 1. accumulated wealth, as money, gold, jewels, etc. 2. any person or thing considered valuable. *v.t.* [-URED, -URING], 1. to save up (money, etc.) for future use. 2. to value greatly.
**treas·ur·er** (trezh′ẽr-ẽr), *n.* a person in charge of a treasure or treasury; specif., an officer in charge of the funds of a government, corporation, society, etc. **—treas′ur·er·ship′,** *n.*
**treas·ure-trove** (trezh′ẽr-trōv′), *n.* [< Anglo-Fr. *tresor*, treasure + OFr. *trové*, pp. of *trover*, to find], 1. treasure found hidden, the original owner of which is unknown. 2. any valuable discovery.
**treas·ur·y** (trezh′ẽr-i), *n.* [*pl.* -IES], 1. a place where treasure is kept. 2. a place where public or private funds are kept, recorded, etc. 3. the funds or revenues of a state, corporation, etc. 4. [T-], the governmental department in charge of revenue, taxation, etc. 5. a collection of treasures in art, literature, etc.
**treasury note,** a note or bill issued by the U.S. Treasury Department, serving as legal tender.
**treat** (trēt), *v.i.* [< OFr. *traitier* < L. *tractare*, freq. of *trahere*, to draw], 1. to carry on business or discuss terms (*with* a person). 2. to pay for another's entertainment. *v.t.* 1. to deal with (a subject) in writing, music, etc. in a certain manner. 2. to act toward (someone or something) in a specified manner. 3. to regard in a specified way: as, he *treated* it as a joke. 4. to pay for the food, drink, etc. of (another). 5. to subject to some process; specif., *a*) to give medical or surgical care to. *b*) to cover with some preparation for protection, appearance, etc. *n.* 1. a meal, drink, etc. paid for by someone else. 2. anything that gives great pleasure. 3. the act of treating or entertaining. **—treat of,** to deal with in speaking or writing. **—treat′a·ble,** *adj.* **—treat′er,** *n.*
**trea·tise** (trē′tis), *n.* [< Anglo-Fr. < OFr. < *traitier;* see TREAT], a formal, systematic essay or book on some subject.

**treat·ment** (trēt′mənt), *n.* 1. act, manner, method, etc. of treating. 2. medical or surgical care.
**trea·ty** (trē′ti), *n.* [*pl.* -TIES], [< Anglo-Fr. < OFr. *traité;* ult. < pp. of L. *tractare*, to manage], a formal agreement between two or more nations, relating to peace, alliance, trade, etc.
**tre·ble** (treb′′l), *adj.* [< OFr. < L. *triplus*, triple], 1. threefold; triple. 2. of, for, or performing the treble. 3. high-pitched; shrill. *n.* 1. the highest part in musical harmony; soprano. 2. a singer or instrument that takes this part. 3. a high-pitched voice or sound. *v.t. & v.i.* [-BLED, -BLING], to make or become threefold. **—tre′bly** [-BLIER, -BLIEST], *adj.*
**treble clef,** in *music*, a sign on a staff (𝄞) indicating that the notes on the staff are above middle C.
**tree** (trē), *n.* [AS. *treow*], 1. a large, woody perennial plant with one main trunk which develops many branches. 2. a treelike bush or shrub. 3. a wooden beam, bar, post, etc. 4. anything resembling a tree; specif., a diagram of family descent (*family tree*). 5. shortened form of **clothes tree, shoe tree,** etc. *v.t.* [TREED, TREEING], 1. to chase up a tree. 2. to stretch on a shoe tree. **—up a tree,** [Colloq.], in a situation without escape; cornered. **—tree′less,** *adj.* **—tree′like′,** *adj.*
**tree fern,** any treelike fern with a woody trunk.
**tree frog,** 1. any of various frogs that live in trees. 2. a tree toad.
**tree lawn,** the unpaved strip of ground between a city street and its parallel sidewalk: lawns and trees are often planted here.
**tree·nail** (trē′nāl′, tren′′l), *n.* [< ME. *tre*, wood], a wooden peg used to join timbers: it swells from moisture and is therefore used in shipbuilding, etc.: also sp. **trenail.**
**tree of heaven,** the ailanthus.
**tree surgery,** treatment of damaged trees as by filling cavities, pruning, etc. **—tree surgeon.**
**tree toad,** any of many tree-dwelling, toadlike amphibians with adhesive pads on the toes.
**tree·top** (trē′top′), *n.* the top branches of a tree.
**tre·foil** (trē′foil), *n.* [< Anglo-Fr. < L. < *tri-*, three + *folium*, leaf], 1. a plant with leaves divided into three leaflets, as the clover. 2. any ornament, etc. resembling a threefold leaf. **—tre′foiled,** *adj.*
**trek** (trek), *v.i.* [TREKKED, TREKKING], [S.Afr.D. < D. *trekken*, to draw], 1. in South Africa, to travel by ox wagon. 2. to travel slowly or laboriously. *v.t.* in South Africa, to draw (a wagon): said of an ox. *n.* 1. in South Africa, a journey made by ox wagon. 2. a journey or leg of a journey. 3. a migration. **—trek′ker,** *n.*
**trel·lis** (trel′is), *n.* [< OFr. < L. *trilix*, triple-twilled < *tri-*, three + *licium*, a thread], an openwork structure of thin, crossed, wooden or metal strips on which vines are trained; lattice. *v.t.* 1. to furnish with a trellis. 2. to train upon a trellis. 3. to cross like a trellis.
**trem·a·tode** (trem′ə-tōd′, trē′mə-), *n.* [< Gr. < *trēma*, a hole + *eidos*, form], any of various parasitic flatworms, including the flukes. *adj.* of a trematode.
**trem·ble** (trem′b′l), *v.i.* [-BLED, -BLING], [< OFr. < LL. < L. < *tremere*], 1. to shake involuntarily from cold, fear, excitement, etc.; shiver. 2. to feel great fear or anxiety. 3. to quiver, totter, vibrate, etc. *n.* 1. a trembling. 2. *sometimes pl.* a fit or state of trembling. **—trem′bler,** *n.* **—trem′bling,** *adj.* **—trem′bling·ly,** *adv.*
**trem·bly** (trem′bli), *adj.* [-BLIER, -BLIEST], trembling; tremulous.
**tre·men·dous** (tri-men′dəs), *adj.* [< L. *tremendus* < *tremere*, to tremble], 1. such as to make one tremble; terrifying. 2. [Colloq.], *a*) very large; great. *b*) wonderful, amazing, etc. **—tre·men′dous·ly,** *adv.* **—tre·men′dous·ness,** *n.*
**trem·o·lo** (trem′ə-lō′), *n.* [*pl.* -LOS], [It. < L.; see TREMULOUS], 1. a tremulous effect produced by the rapid reiteration of the same tone. 2. a device, as in an organ, for producing such a tone.
**trem·or** (trem′ēr, trē′mēr), *n.* [< OFr. < L. < *tremere*, to tremble], 1. a trembling, shaking, etc. 2. a vibratory motion. 3. a nervous thrill; trembling sensation. 4. a trembling sound.
**trem·u·lous** (trem′yoo-ləs), *adj.* [< L. *tremulus* < *tremere*, to tremble], 1. trembling; quivering. 2. fearful; timid. 3. marked by or showing trembling or quivering. Also **trem′u·lant, trem′u·lent** (-lənt). **—trem′u·lous·ly,** *adv.* **—trem′u·lous·ness,** *n.*
**tre·nail** (trē′nāl, tren′′l), *n.* a treenail.
**trench** (trench), *v.t.* [< OFr. < L. *truncare*, to cut off], 1. to cut or make by cutting. 2. to slice; slash. 3. to dig a ditch or ditches in. 4. to surround or fortify with trenches. *v.i.* 1. to cut or make a cutting. 2. to dig a ditch or ditches. *n.* 1. a deep furrow. 2. a long, narrow ditch with earth banked in front as a parapet, used in battle for cover, etc. **—trench on** (or **upon**), 1. to infringe upon (another's rights, land, etc.). 2. to come close to in meaning, etc. **—trench′er,** *n.*
**trench·ant** (tren′chənt), *adj.* [< OFr.; see TRENCH], 1. originally, cutting; sharp. 2. keen; penetrating; incisive: as, *trenchant* words. 3. forceful; vigorous: as, a *trenchant* argument. 4. clear-cut; distinct: as, a *trenchant* pattern. **—trench′an·cy, trench′ant·ness,** *n.* **—trench′ant·ly,** *adv.*
**trench coat,** a belted raincoat in a military style.
**trench·er** (tren′chēr), *n.* [< OFr.; see TRENCH], 1. formerly, a wooden platter for carving and serving meat. 2. any platter.
**trench·er·man** (tren′chēr-mən), *n.* [*pl.* -MEN], an eater; esp., a heavy eater.
**trench fever,** an infectious disease, as of troops in trenches, transmitted by body lice and characterized by a remittent fever, muscular pains, etc.
**trench foot,** a diseased condition of the feet resulting from prolonged exposure to wet and cold, as of soldiers in trenches.
**trench mortar** (or **gun**), any of various portable mortars or guns for shooting projectiles at a high trajectory, used in trench warfare.
**trench mouth,** an infectious disease of the mucous membranes of the mouth and throat.
**trend** (trend), *v.i.* [AS. *trendan*], 1. to extend, turn, bend, etc. in a specific direction. 2. to have a general tendency: said of events, opinions, etc. *n.* 1. the general direction of a river, road, etc. 2. the general tendency or course, as of events, public opinion, etc.; drift.
**Trent, Council of,** the council of the Roman Catholic Church held intermittently at Trent, Italy, 1545–1563, to counteract the Reformation.
**Tren·ton** (tren′tən), *n.* the capital of New Jersey, on the Delaware River: pop., 114,000.
**tre·pan** (tri-pan′), *n.* [< ML. < Gr. < *trypan*, to bore], 1. an obsolete form of the trephine. 2. a heavy boring tool. *v.t.* [-PANNED, -PANNING], to trephine. **—trep·a·na·tion** (trep′ə-nā′shən), *n.*
**tre·pang** (tri-paŋ′), *n.* [< Malay], a sea cucumber found in the Malay Archipelago, etc., used in China for making soup.
**tre·phine** (tri-fīn′, -fēn′), *n.* [formed (after *trepan*) < L. *tres*, three + *fines*, ends], a type of small crown saw used in surgery to remove circular disks of bone from the skull. *v.t.* [-PHINED, -PHINING], to operate on with a trephine.
**trep·i·da·tion** (trep′ə-dā′shən), *n.* [< L. < pp. of *tripidare*, to tremble < *trepidus*, disturbed], 1. tremulous or trembling movement. 2. fear; dread.
**tres·pass** (tres′pəs, -pas′), *v.i.* [< OFr. < L. *trans-*, across + *passare*, to pass], 1. to go beyond the limits of what is considered right or moral; transgress; sin. 2. to enter another's property unlawfully. 3. to intrude; encroach. 4. in *law*, to commit a trespass. *n.* a trespassing; specif., *a*) an offense; sin. *b*) an encroachment; intrusion. *c*) in *law*, an illegal, violent act against another's person, rights, or property. **—tres′pass·er,** *n.*
**tress** (tres), *n.* [< OFr. < LL. *tricia*], 1. originally, a braid of hair. 2. a lock or curl of hair. 3. *pl.* a woman's or girl's hair. **—tressed,** *adj.*
**-tress** (tris), see **-ess.**
**tres·tle** (tres′′l), *n.* [< OFr. *trestel* < LL.; ult. < L. *transtrum*, a beam], 1. a frame consisting of a horizontal beam fastened to two pairs of spreading legs, used to support planks to form a table, etc. 2. a framework of uprights and crosspieces, supporting a bridge, etc.

TRESTLE (frame)

**tres·tle·work** (tres′′l-wũrk′), *n.* a system of trestles for supporting a bridge, etc.
**trey** (trā), *n.* [< OFr. < L. *tres*, three], 1. a throw or play of three at dice, dominoes, or cards. 2. a die, domino, or playing card with three spots.
**tri-,** [< Fr., L., or Gr.], a combining form meaning: 1. *of three, having three parts*, etc., as in *triangle.* 2. *three times, into three*, as in *trisect.* 3. *every third*, as in *triannual.* 4. in *chemistry, having three atoms, groups*, or *equivalents of* (the thing specified), as in *trioxide.*
**tri·a·ble** (trī′ə-b′l), *adj.* 1. that can be tried or tested. 2. subject to trial in a law court.
**tri·ad** (trī′ad), *n.* [< Fr. < L. < Gr. *treis*, three], 1. a group of three persons, things, etc. 2. a musical chord of three tones, especially one consisting of a root tone and its third and fifth: a triad with a major third and perfect fifth is called a *major triad;* a triad with a minor third and perfect fifth is called a *minor triad.*

**tri·al** (trī′əl, trīl), ***n.*** [Anglo-Fr. < *trier,* to try], 1. *a*) the act or process of trying, testing, etc.; test. *b*) a testing of qualifications, attainments, etc.; probation. *c*) an experiment. 2. a being tried by suffering, temptation, etc. 3. a hardship, pain, etc. 4. a source of annoyance or irritation. 5. a formal examination of the facts of a case by a court of law to decide the validity of a charge or claim. 6. an attempt; effort. ***adj.*** 1. of a trial or trials. 2. done or used for the purpose of trying, testing, etc.

**trial and error,** the process of making repeated trials, tests, etc. to find a desired result.

**trial balance,** a statement of the debit and credit balances of all open accounts in a double-entry bookkeeping ledger to test their equality.

**trial balloon,** any action, statement, etc. intended to test public opinion on an issue.

**trial jury,** a jury of twelve persons impaneled to decide a court case: cf. *grand jury.*

**tri·an·gle** (trī′aŋ′g'l), ***n.*** [OFr. < L.; see TRI- & ANGLE], 1. a geometrical figure having three angles and three sides. 2. any three-sided or three-cornered figure, area, object, etc. 3. a group of three involved in some situation: as, a love *triangle.* 4. a musical percussion instrument consisting of a steel rod bent in a triangle: it produces a high-pitched tingling sound.

**tri·an·gu·lar** (trī-aŋ′gyoo-lẽr), ***adj.*** 1. of or shaped like a triangle; three-cornered. 2. of or involving three persons, factions, things, etc. —**tri′an·gu·lar′i·ty** (-lar′ə-ti), ***n.*** —**tri·an′gu·lar·ly,** ***adv.***

**tri·an·gu·late** (trī-aŋ′gyoo-lāt′; *for adj., usually* -lit), ***v.t.*** [-LATED, -LATING], 1. to divide into triangles. 2. to survey (a region) by dividing into triangles and measuring their angles. 3. to make triangular. 4. to measure by trigonometry. ***adj.*** triangular. —**tri·an′gu·la′tion,** ***n.***

**Tri·as·sic** (trī-as′ik), ***adj.*** designating or of the first period of the Mesozoic Era: see **geology,** chart. ***n.*** the Triassic Period.

**trib·al·ism** (trī′b'l-iz'm), ***n.*** tribal organization, culture, loyalty, etc.

**tribe** (trīb), ***n.*** [< L. *tribus,* any of the divisions (orig., three) of the ancient Romans], 1. a group of persons, families, or clans descended from a common ancestor and forming a community, as any of the twelve divisions of the ancient Israelites. 2. any primitive or nomadic group of people of generally common ancestry, possessing common leadership. 3. any group of people with interests in common: chiefly derogatory, as, the *tribe* of hacks. 4. any group, class, or kind of animals, plants, etc. —**trib′al,** ***adj.*** —**trib′al·ly,** ***adv.***

**tribes·man** (trībz′mən), ***n.*** [*pl.* -MEN], a member of a tribe.

**trib·u·la·tion** (trib′yoo-lā′shən), ***n.*** [< OFr. < LL. < pp. of L. *tribulare,* to thrash < *tribulum,* threshing sledge], 1. great misery or distress, as from oppression; deep sorrow. 2. something that causes distress; an affliction.

**tri·bu·nal** (tri-bū′n'l, trī-), ***n.*** [see TRIBUNE], 1. a seat or bench upon which a judge or judges sit in a court. 2. a court of justice. 3. any real or imagined seat of judgment.

**trib·une** (trib′ūn, tri-būn′), ***n.*** [< L. *tribunus* < *tribus,* tribe], 1. in ancient Rome, a magistrate appointed to protect the interests and rights of plebeians against violation by patricians. 2. a champion of the people. —**trib′une·ship′,** ***n.*** —**trib′u·ni′tial, trib′u·ni′cial** (-yoo-nish′əl), ***adj.***

**trib·une** (trib′ūn), ***n.*** [Fr. < It. < L.; see TRIBUNAL, sense 1], a raised platform for speakers.

**trib·u·tar·y** (trib′yoo-ter′i), ***adj.*** 1. paying tribute. 2. subject: as, a *tributary* nation. 3. owed or paid as tribute. 4. making additions; contributory: as, *tributary* streams. ***n.*** [*pl.* -IES], 1. a tributary nation. 2. a stream or river that flows into a larger one. —**trib′u·tar′i·ly,** ***adv.***

**trib·ute** (trib′ūt), ***n.*** [< OFr. < L. pp. of *tribuere,* to allot, pay < *tribus,* tribe], 1. money paid regularly by one ruler or nation to another as acknowledgment of subjugation, for protection, etc. 2. a tax levied for this. 3. any forced payment or levy. 4. a gift, statement, testimonial, etc. that shows gratitude, respect, or honor. 5. praise.

**trice** (trīs), ***v.t.*** [TRICED, TRICING], [< MD. *trisen,* to pull < *trise,* windlass], to haul up (a sail, etc.) and secure with a small line (usually with *up*). ***n.*** [< *at a trice,* with one pull], an instant; moment: now only in *in a trice.*

**tri·cen·ten·ni·al** (trī′sen-ten′i-əl), ***adj. & n.*** tercentenary.

**tri·ceps** (trī′seps), ***n.*** [*pl.* -CEPSES (-sep-siz)], [< L. < *tri-,* three + *caput,* a head], a muscle having three points of origin; esp., the large muscle at the back of the upper arm that extends the forearm.

**tri·chi·na** (tri-kī′nə), ***n.*** [*pl.* -NAE (-nē)], [< Gr. *trichinos,* hairy < *thrix,* hair], a very small worm whose larvae infest the intestines and voluntary muscles of man, causing trichinosis.

**trich·i·no·sis** (trik′ə-nō′sis), ***n.*** a disease caused by the presence of trichinae in the intestines and muscle tissues and usually acquired from eating insufficiently cooked pork from an infected hog: it is characterized by fever, nausea, etc. —**trich′i·nous, trich′i·nosed′** (-nōzd′), ***adj.***

**trick** (trik), ***n.*** [ONorm.Fr. *trique* < OFr. *trichier,* *v.*], 1. something designed to deceive, swindle, etc.; ruse; stratagem. 2. a practical joke; prank. 3. a freakish or foolish act. 4. *a*) a clever or difficult act intended to amuse; esp., an act of jugglery, legerdemain, etc. *b*) any feat requiring skill. 5. the art or process of doing something successfully, quickly, etc.; knack: as, the *trick* of making good pies. 6. an expedient or convention of an art or craft: as, the *tricks* of the trade. 7. a personal mannerism: as, a *trick* of winking. 8. a round of duty; shift. 9. [Colloq.], a child or girl. 10. in *card games,* the cards played in a single round. ***v.t.*** to deceive or cheat. ***adj.*** 1. having to do with a trick or tricks. 2. that tricks. —**do** (or **turn**) **the trick,** to produce the desired result. —**trick out** (or **up**), to dress up; adorn.

**trick·er·y** (trik′ẽr-i), ***n.*** [*pl.* -IES], the act or practice of tricking; deception; fraud.

**trick·le** (trik′'l), ***v.i.*** [-LED, -LING], [prob. < freq. of ME. *striken,* to strike], 1. to flow slowly in a thin stream or fall in drops. 2. to move, enter, etc. little by little: as, the crowd *trickled* away. ***v.t.*** to cause to trickle. ***n.*** 1. a trickling. 2. a slow flow or drip. —**trick′ling·ly,** ***adv.***

**trick·ster** (trik′stẽr), ***n.*** one who tricks; cheat.

**trick·sy** (trik′si), ***adj.*** [-SIER, -SIEST], 1. playful; mischievous. 2. tricky. —**trick′si·ly,** ***adv.*** —**trick′si·ness,** ***n.***

**trick·y** (trik′i), ***adj.*** [-IER, -IEST], 1. given to or characterized by trickery; deceitful. 2. like a trick in deceptiveness; intricate; catchy. —**trick′i·ly,** ***adv.*** —**trick′i·ness,** ***n.***

**tri·col·or** (trī′kul′ẽr), ***n.*** a flag having three colors in large areas; esp., the flag of France. ***adj.*** having three colors. Also, Brit., **tri′col′our.** —**tri′col′ored, tri′col′oured,** ***adj.***

**tri·corn** (trī′kôrn), ***adj.*** [< Fr. < L. < *tri-,* three + *cornu,* horn], having three horns or corners, as a hat. ***n.*** a tricorn hat.

**tri·cot** (trē′kō), ***n.*** [Fr. < *tricoter,* to knit; ult. < LG.], 1. any of various cloth materials, knitted, or woven so as to resemble knitting. 2. a type of ribbed cloth for dresses.

**tric·o·tine** (trik′ə-tēn′), ***n.*** [Fr.; see TRICOT & -INE], a woolen cloth resembling twill.

**tri·cus·pid** (tri-kus′pid), ***adj.*** [< L. < *tri-,* three + *cuspis,* a point], 1. having three cusps, or points, as some teeth: also **tri·cus′pi·date′.** 2. designating a valve with three flaps, between the right auricle and right ventricle of the heart. ***n.*** 1. a tricuspid tooth. 2. the tricuspid valve.

**tri·cy·cle** (trī′si-k'l), ***n.*** [Fr.], a light, three-wheeled vehicle operated by pedals; esp., one for children.

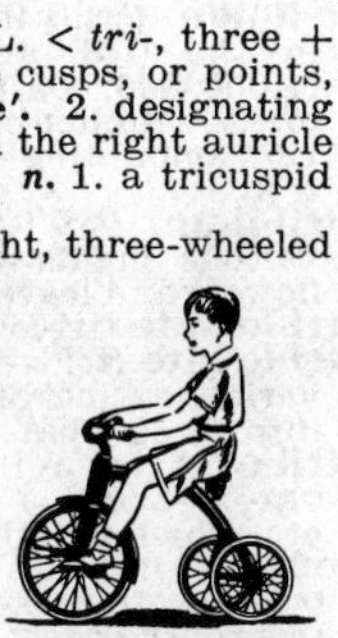

TRICYCLE

**tri·dent** (trī′d'nt), ***n.*** [< L. *tri-,* three + *dens,* a tooth], a three-pronged spear. ***adj.*** three-pronged.

**tri·den·tate** (trī-den′tāt), ***adj.*** having three teeth, prongs, or points: also **tri·den′tat·ed.**

**tried** (trīd), pt. and pp. of **try.** ***adj.*** 1. tested; proved. 2. trustworthy; faithful.

**tri·en·ni·al** (trī-en′i-əl), ***adj.*** [< L. *tri-,* three + *annus,* a year], 1. happening every three years. 2. lasting three years. ***n.*** 1. an event that takes place every three years. 2. a third anniversary. —**tri·en′ni·al·ly,** ***adv.***

**tri·er** (trī′ẽr), ***n.*** a person or thing that tries.

**Tri·este** (tri-est′), ***n.*** a city on the Adriatic in NE Italy: pop., 271,000: an area (**Free Territory of Trieste**) including this city was administered by the UN (1947–1954) until its division between Italy and Yugoslavia, the city going to Italy.

**tri·fid** (trī′fid), ***adj.*** [< L. *tri-,* three + *findere,* to divide], divided into three parts; tridentate.

**tri·fle** (trī'f'l), *n.* [< OFr. dim. of *truffe*, mockery], 1. something of little value or importance. 2. a small sum of money. 3. a small amount; a little. 4. a dessert of spongecake soaked in wine and covered with whipped cream, nuts, etc. *v.i.* [-FLED, -FLING], 1. to talk or act jokingly or with levity. 2. to play or toy (*with* something). *v.t.* to spend idly; waste: as, he *trifles* time away. —**tri'fler,** *n.*

**tri·fling** (trī'fliŋ), *adj.* 1. that trifles; frivolous; shallow; fickle. 2. having little value; trivial.

**tri·fo·cal** (trī-fō'k'l, trī'fō'-), *adj.* adjusted to three different focal lengths. *n.* a lens like a bifocal but with an additional area ground to adjust the eye for intermediate focus (about 30 inches).

**tri·fo·li·ate** (trī-fō'li-it, -āt'), *adj.* [< *tri-* + L. *folium*, a leaf], having three leaves or leaflets.

**tri·fo·li·o·late** (trī-fō'li-ə-lāt'), *adj.* [< *tri-* + dim. of L. *folium*, a leaf], divided into three leaflets, as the leaf of a clover.

**tri·fo·ri·um** (trī-fôr'i-əm, -fō'ri-), *n.* [*pl.* -RIA (-ə)], [< ML. < L. *tri-*, three + *foris*, door], a gallery in the wall above the arches of the nave, choir, or transept of a church.

**trig** (trig), *adj.* [< ON. *tryggr*, true], 1. trim; neat. 2. in good condition; sound. *v.t.* [TRIGGED, TRIGGING], [Dial.], to make trig (often with *out* or *up*).

**trig., trigon.,** 1. trigonometric. 2. trigonometry.

**tri·gem·i·nal** (trī-jem'ə-n'l), *adj.* [< L. < *tri-*, three + *geminus*, twin], designating or of either of the pair of three-branched nerves supplying the face. *n.* a trigeminal nerve. Also **tri·fa'cial.**

**trig·ger** (trig'ēr), *n.* [< D. < *trekken*, to pull], a lever which when pulled or pressed releases a catch, spring, etc.; esp., the small lever in a firearm which releases the firing hammer. *v.t.* [Colloq.], to initiate (an action); set off. —**quick on the trigger,** [Colloq.], 1. quick to fire a gun. 2. quick to act.

**trig·o·nom·e·try** (trig'ə-nom'ə-tri), *n.* [< Gr. *trigōnon*, triangle + *-metria*, measurement], the branch of mathematics that deals with the ratios between the sides of a right triangle with reference to either acute angle (*trigonometric functions*), the relations between these ratios, and the application of these facts in finding the unknown sides or angles of any triangle. —**trig'o·no·met'ric** (-nə-met'rik), **trig'o·no·met'ri·cal,** *adj.*

**tri·he·dron** (trī-hē'drən), *n.* [*pl.* -DRONS, -DRA (-drə)], [see TRI- & -HEDRON], a solid figure with three plane surfaces meeting in a point. —**tri·he'dral,** *adj.*

**tri·lat·er·al** (trī-lat'ēr-əl), *adj.* [< L. < *tri-*, three + *latus*, side], having three sides. —**tri·lat'er·al·ly,** *adv.*

**trill** (tril), *n.* [< Fr. < It. *trillare;* echoic], 1. a rapid alternation of two musical tones a degree or half degree apart. 2. a warble, as of birds. 3. a rapid vibration of the tongue or uvula, as in pronouncing *r* in some languages. 4. a consonant so pronounced. *v.t. & v.i.* to sound, speak, sing, or play with a trill. —**trill'er,** *n.*

**tril·lion** (tril'yən), *n.* [Fr.; *tri-* + mil*lion*], 1. in the U.S. and France, a thousand billions (1,000,000,000,000). 2. in Great Britain and Germany, a million billions (1,000,000,000,000,000,000). *adj.* amounting to one trillion. —**tril'lionth,** *adj. & n.*

**tril·li·um** (tril'i-əm), *n.* [< L. *tri-*, three], any of various plants with white, pinkish, or greenish flowers and leaves in groups of three.

**tri·lo·bate** (trī-lō'bāt), *adj.* having three lobes.

**tri·lo·bite** (trī'lə-bīt'), *n.* [see TRI- & LOBE], any of various extinct arthropods having the body divided into three lobes. —**tri'lo·bit'ic** (-bit'ik), *adj.*

**tril·o·gy** (tril'ə-ji), *n.* [*pl.* -GIES], [< Gr. *trilogia;* see TRI- & -LOGY], a set of three related plays, novels, etc. which together form a larger work.

**trim** (trim), *v.t.* [TRIMMED, TRIMMING], [< AS. *trymian*, to make firm < *trum*, strong], 1. to put in proper order; make neat or tidy, especially by clipping, etc.: as, to *trim* hair. 2. to clip, lop, cut, etc. (often with *off*): as, to *trim* dead branches. 3. to dress (lumber). 4. to decorate, as a Christmas tree. 5. *a*) to balance (a ship) by shifting cargo, etc. *b*) to put (sails) in order for sailing. 6. [Colloq.], *a*) to scold. *b*) to beat, punish, etc. *c*) to defeat. *d*) to cheat. *v.i.* to alter one's viewpoint so as to satisfy opposing factions, etc.; compromise. *n.* 1. order; arrangement: as, in proper *trim.* 2. good condition or order: as, he got into *trim.* 3. equipment; dress. 4. a trimming by clipping, cutting, etc. 5. the decorative woodwork of a building, especially around windows and doors. 6. any ornamental trimming. 7. *a*) the condition of being trimmed or ready to sail: said of ships. *b*) the position of a ship in the water. *c*) the adjustment of the sails or yards in managing a vessel. *adj.* [TRIMMER, TRIMMEST], 1. orderly; neat. 2. well-proportioned; smartly designed. 3. in good condition. *adv.* in a trim manner. —**trim'ly,** *adv.* —**trim'mer,** *n.* —**trim'ness,** *n.*

**tri·mes·ter** (trī-mes'tēr, trī'mes-), *n.* [< Fr. < L. *tri-*, three + *mensis*, month], in some colleges and universities, any of the three periods into which the academic year is divided.

**trim·e·ter** (trim'ə-tēr), *n.* [< L. < Gr.; see TRI- & METER (rhythm)], 1. a line of verse containing three metrical feet. 2. verse consisting of trimeters. *adj.* having three metrical feet.

**trim·ming** (trim'iŋ), *n.* 1. the act of one who trims; specif., [Colloq.], *a*) a scolding. *b*) a beating. *c*) a defeat. *d*) a cheating. 2. something used to trim; specif., *a*) decoration; ornament. *b*) *pl.* the side dishes of a meal: as, turkey with all the *trimmings.* 3. *pl.* parts trimmed off.

**tri·month·ly** (trī-munth'li), *adj.* happening or appearing every three months.

**tri·nal** (trī'n'l), *adj.* [< LL. < L. *trinus*, triple < *tres*, three], threefold; triple: also **tri'na·ry** (-nēr-i), **trine** (trīn).

**Trin·i·dad** (trin'ə-dad'), *n.* an island in the West Indies, off the coast of Venezuela.

**Trinidad and Tobago,** a country on the islands of Trinidad and Tobago, north of Venezuela, in the British Commonwealth of Nations: area, 1,976 sq. mi.; pop., 1,021,000; capital, Port of Spain.

**Trin·i·tar·i·an** (trin'ə-târ'i-ən), *adj.* 1. [also t-], *a*) of the Trinity or the doctrine of the Trinity. *b*) believing in this doctrine. 2. [t-], forming a trinity. *n.* one who believes in the doctrine of the Trinity.

**tri·ni·tro·tol·u·ene** (trī-nī'trō-tol'ū-ēn'), *n.* [*tri-* + *nitro-* + *toluene*], a high explosive, any of several derivatives, $C_7H_5O_6N_3$, of toluene, used for blasting, in artillery shells, etc.: also **tri·ni'tro·tol'u·ol** (-ōl, -ol): abbrev. **TNT, T.N.T.**

**trin·i·ty** (trin'ə-ti), *n.* [*pl.* -TIES], [< OFr. < L. *trinus*, triple], 1. a set of three persons or things that form a unit. 2. [T-], in *Christian theology*, the union of the three divine persons (Father, Son, and Holy Ghost) in one Godhead.

**Trinity Sunday,** the Sunday next after Whitsunday or Pentecost, dedicated to the Trinity.

**trink·et** (triŋ'kit), *n.* [< ME. *trenket*, ornamental toy knife carried by ladies], 1. a small ornament, piece of jewelry, etc. 2. a trifle or toy.

**tri·no·mi·al** (trī-nō'mi-əl), *adj.* [*tri-* + bi*nomial*], consisting of three terms. *n.* a mathematical expression consisting of three terms connected by plus or minus signs. —**tri·no'mi·al·ly,** *adv.*

**tri·o** (trē'ō), *n.* [*pl.* -OS], [Fr. < It. < L. *tres*, three], 1. a musical composition for three voices or three instruments. 2. the three performers of such a composition. 3. the middle section of a minuet, scherzo, etc. 4. a set of three persons or things.

**tri·ox·ide** (trī-ok'sīd, -sid), *n.* an oxide having three oxygen atoms to the molecule: also **tri·ox'id** (-sid).

**trip** (trip), *v.i.* [TRIPPED or *occas.* TRIPT, TRIPPING], [< OFr.; prob. < MD. *trippen*], 1. to walk, run, or dance with light, rapid steps; skip; caper. 2. to stumble. 3. to make a mistake; err. 4. to run past the pallet of the escapement: said of a tooth of an escape wheel. 5. to tilt; tip. *v.t.* 1. to perform (a dance) lightly and nimbly. 2. to make stumble, as by catching the foot (often with *up*). 3. to cause to make a mistake. 4. to catch (a person) in a lie, error, etc. (also with *up*). 5. *a*) to release (a spring, wheel, etc.), as by the action of a detent. *b*) to start or operate by this. 6. to tilt; tip up. *n.* 1. a light, quick tread. 2. a journey, excursion, voyage, jaunt, etc. 3. a stumble or slip. 4. a mistake. 5. a tripping of someone, as by catching his foot. 6. *a*) any mechanical contrivance for tripping a part, as a pawl. *b*) its action. 7. [Slang], the sensations experienced under the influence of a psychedelic drug.

**tri·par·tite** (trī-pär'tīt), *adj.* [< L. < *tri-*, three + pp. of *partiri*, to divide], 1. divided into three parts. 2. having three parts. 3. made or existing between three parties, as an agreement.

**tripe** (trīp), *n.* [< OFr. < Ar. *tharb*, entrails], 1. part of the stomach of an ox, etc. used as food. 2. [Slang], anything worthless, offensive, etc.

**trip·ham·mer** (trip'ham'ēr), *n.* a heavy, power-driven hammer, alternately raised and allowed to fall by a tripping device: also **trip hammer.**

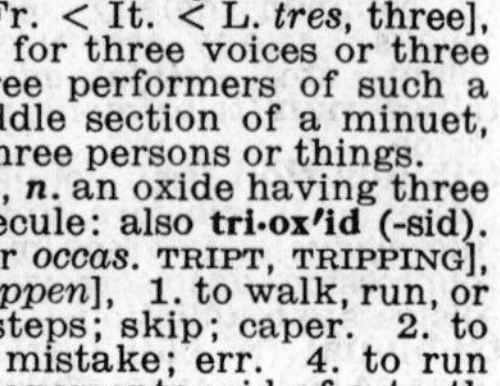

TRIPHAMMER

**tri·ple** (trip''l), *adj.* [< OFr. < L. < *tri-*, three + *-plus*, -fold], 1. consisting of three; threefold. 2. three times as much or as many. *n.* 1. an amount three times as much or as many. 2. a group of

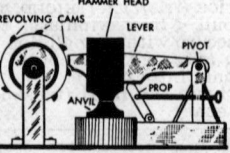

three. 3. in *baseball*, a hit by which the batter reaches third base. *v.t.* [-PLED, -PLING], to make three times as much or as many. *v.i.* 1. to be tripled. 2. in *baseball*, to hit a triple. —**trip′ly,** *adv.*

**triple play,** in *baseball*, a play by which three players are put out.

**tri·plet** (trip′lit), *n.* [< *triple*], 1. a group of three of one kind. 2. a group of three musical notes to be played in the time of two of the same value. 3. one of three offspring born at a single birth.

**triple time,** musical time or rhythm having three beats to the measure, with the first beat accented: also **triple measure.**

**trip·li·cate** (trip′lə-kit; *also, and for the v. always,* -kāt′), *adj.* [< L. pp. of *triplicare*, to treble < *triplex*, threefold], 1. made in or forming three identical copies. 2. threefold; triple. *n.* one of three identical copies or things. *v.t.* [-CATED, -CATING], 1. to make three copies of. 2. to increase threefold; treble. —**in triplicate,** in three identical copies. —**trip′li·ca′tion,** *n.*

**tri·pod** (trī′pod), *n.* [< L. < Gr. *tri-*, three + *pous*, a foot], 1. a three-legged caldron, stool, etc. 2. a three-legged support for a camera, etc. —**trip·o·dal** (trip′ə-d'l), **tri·pod·ic** (trī-pod′ic), *adj.*

**Trip·o·li** (trip′ə-li), *n.* 1. a former Barbary State, now a part of Libya. 2. the capital of Libya, on the Mediterranean Sea: pop., 140,000. —**Tri·pol·i·tan** (tri-pol′ə-t'n), *adj. & n.*

**trip·per** (trip′ẽr), *n.* a person or thing that trips; specif., *a*) a mechanism, as a cam, pawl, etc., for tripping. *b*) [Brit. Colloq.], a tourist.

**trip·ping** (trip′iŋ), *adj.* stepping lightly and quickly; nimble. —**trip′ping·ly,** *adv.*

**tript** (tript), occas. pt. and pp. of **trip.**

**trip·tych** (trip′tik), *n.* [< Gr. *triptychos*, threefold < *tri-*, three + *ptyx*, a fold], 1. an ancient writing tablet of three leaves hinged together. 2. a set of three panels with pictures, carvings, etc., often hinged: it is used as an altarpiece.

**tri·reme** (trī′rēm), *n.* [Fr. < L. < *tri-*, three + *remus*, an oar], an ancient Greek or Roman warship with three banks of oars on each side.

**tri·sect** (trī-sekt′), *v.t.* [< *tri-* + L. pp. of *secare*, to cut], 1. to cut or divide into three parts. 2. in *geometry*, to divide into three equal parts. —**tri·sec′tion,** *n.* —**tri·sec′tor,** *n.*

‡**triste** (trēst), *adj.* [Fr.], sad; sorrowful.

**Tris·tram** (tris′trəm), *n.* in *medieval legend*, a knight who is involved in a tragic romance with the princess Isolde: also called **Tris′tam** (-təm), **Tris′tan** (-tən).

**tri·syl·la·ble** (trī-sil′ə-b'l, tri-), *n.* a word of three syllables. —**tri′syl·lab′ic** (-si-lab′ik), *adj.* —**tri′syl·lab′i·cal·ly,** *adv.*

**trite** (trīt), *adj.* [TRITER, TRITEST], [< L. *tritus*, pp. of *terere*, to wear out], worn out by constant use; no longer having freshness, originality, etc.; stale. —**trite′ly,** *adv.* —**trite′ness,** *n.*

**trit·i·um** (trit′i-əm, trish′-), *n.* [< Gr. *tritos*, third + L. *-ium*, *n.* suffix], an isotope of hydrogen having an atomic weight of 3: symbol, T or $H^3$.

**Tri·ton** (trī′t'n), *n.* 1. in *Gr. mythology*, a sea god pictured as having the head and upper body of a man and the tail of a fish. 2. [t-], *a*) a kind of sea snail with a long, spiral shell. *b*) its shell.

**trit·u·rate** (trich′ə-rāt′), *v.t.* [-RATED, -RATING], [< LL. pp. of *triturare*, to grind < L. < *terere*, to rub], to rub, crush, or grind into a very fine powder; pulverize. *n.* a triturated substance. —**trit′u·ra·ble** (-ẽr-ə-b'l), *adj.* —**trit′u·ra′tion,** *n.* —**trit′u·ra′tor,** *n.*

**tri·umph** (trī′əmf), *n.* [< OFr. < L. *triumphus* < Gr. *thriambos*, hymn to Bacchus], 1. in ancient Rome, a procession celebrating a victorious general. 2. a victory; success. 3. exultation or joy for a victory, etc. *v.i.* 1. to gain victory or success; win mastery. 2. to rejoice or exalt over victory, achievement, etc. —**tri·um′phal** (-um′f'l), *adj.* —**tri′umph·er,** *n.*

**tri·um·phant** (trī-um′fənt), *adj.* 1. successful; victorious. 2. rejoicing for victory; elated. —**tri·um′phant·ly,** *adv.*

**tri·um·vir** (trī-um′vẽr), *n.* [*pl.* -VIRS, -VIRI (-vi-rī′)], [< L. < *trium virorum*, of three men], in ancient Rome, any of three administrators sharing authority equally. —**tri·um′vi·ral,** *adj.*

**tri·um·vi·rate** (trī-um′vẽr-it), *n.* 1. the office, functions, or term of a triumvir. 2. government by a group of three men. 3. any association of three in authority. 4. any group or set of three.

**tri·une** (trī′ūn, trī-ūn′), *adj.* [< *tri-* + L. *unus*, one], being three in one: as, a *triune* God. *n.* 1. a triad. 2. [T-], the Trinity. —**tri·u′ni·ty** (-ū′nə-ti), *n.*

**tri·va·lent** (trī-vā′lənt, triv′ə-), *adj.* [*tri-* + *-valent*], 1. having a valence of three. 2. having three valences. —**tri·va′lence, tri·va′len·cy,** *n.*

**triv·et** (triv′it), *n.* [AS. *trefet* < L. *tripes*, tripod], 1. a three-legged stand for holding pots, kettles, etc. over or near a fire. 2. a short-legged metal plate for holding hot dishes on a table.

**triv·i·a** (triv′i-ə), *n.pl.* [see TRIVIAL], unimportant matters; trivialities; trifles.

**triv·i·al** (triv′i-əl) *adj.* [< L. *trivialis*, of the crossroads, commonplace < *tri-*, three + *via*, a road], 1. unimportant; insignificant; trifling; petty. 2. [Archaic], commonplace. —**triv′i·al·ly,** *adv.*

**triv·i·al·i·ty** (triv′i-al′ə-ti), *n.* 1. a being trivial. 2. [*pl.* -TIES], a trivial thing, idea, etc.; trifle.

**tri·week·ly** (trī-wēk′li), *adj. & adv.* (occurring or appearing) every three weeks or three times a week. *n.* [*pl.* -LIES], a triweekly publication.

**-trix** (triks), [*pl.* -TRIXES, -TRICES (tri-sēz′, trī′sēz)], [L.], an ending of some feminine nouns of agent, corresponding to masculine *-(t)or*, as in *aviatrix.*

**tro·cha·ic** (trō-kā′ik), *adj.* of or made up of trochees. *n.* 1. a trochaic verse. 2. a trochee.

**tro·che** (trō′ki), *n.* [< Fr. < L. *trochiscus*, a pill < Gr. < *trochos*, a wheel], a small, usually round, medicinal lozenge.

**tro·chee** (trō′kē), *n.* [< L. < Gr. *trochaios*, running < *trechein*, to run], a metrical foot consisting of a long syllable followed by a short one, or an accented syllable followed by an unaccented one. Example: "Pétẽr, | Pétẽr, | púmpkin | éatẽr."

**trod** (trod), pt. and alt. pp. of **tread.**

**trod·den** (trod′'n), alt. pp. of **tread.**

**trode** (trōd), archaic pt. of **tread.**

**trog·lo·dyte** (trog′lə-dīt′), *n.* [< L. < Gr. < *trōglē*, a cave + *dyein*, to enter], 1. a cave man. 2. a hermit. 3. one who lives in a primitive or crude fashion. —**trog′lo·dyt′ic** (-dit′ik), **trog′lo·dyt′i·cal,** *adj.*

**tro·gon** (trō′gon), *n.* [< Gr. ppr. of *trōgein*, to gnaw], any of a large group of brightly colored tropical birds.

**Tro·i·lus** (trō′i-ləs, troi′-), *n.* in *Gr. legend*, a son of King Priam: in Chaucer and Shakespeare, Troilus was the lover of the faithless Cressida.

**Tro·jan** (trō′jən), *adj.* of ancient Troy, its people, etc. *n.* 1. a native or inhabitant of ancient Troy. 2. a person of energy and determination.

**Trojan horse,** in *Gr. legend*, a huge, hollow wooden horse filled with Greek soldiers and left at the gates of Troy: it was brought inside the gates, thus leading to the destruction of the city: also called *wooden horse.*

**Trojan War,** in *Gr. legend*, the war waged against Troy by the Greeks in order to get back Helen, who had been abducted by Paris.

**troll** (trōl), *v.t. & v.i.* [< OFr. < MHG. *trollen*, to take short steps], 1. to roll; revolve. 2. to sing the parts of (a round, etc.) in succession. 3. to sing lustily or in a full, rolling voice. 4. to fish (for or in) with a moving line, especially one with a revolving lure. *n.* 1. a going or moving round. 2. a song having parts sung in succession; round; catch. 3. *a*) the method of trolling in fishing. *b*) a lure or lure and line used in trolling. —**troll′er,** *n.*

**troll** (trōl), *n.* [ON. & Sw., lit., wanderer < base of *troll, v.*], in *Scandinavian folklore*, any of a race of supernatural beings, as giants, dwarfs, etc., living underground or in caves.

**trol·ley** (trol′i), *n.* [*pl.* -LEYS], [< *troll, v.*], 1. a wheeled carriage, basket, etc. that runs suspended from an overhead track. 2. an apparatus for transmitting electric current from an overhead wire to a motor of a streetcar, etc.: the *bow trolley* has a bow-shaped contact on a flexible frame, and the *wheel trolley* has a wheel contact at the end of a pole. 3. a trolley car; streetcar. *v.t. & v.i.* to carry or ride on a trolley car.

**trolley bus,** an electric bus that gets its motive power from overhead wires by means of a trolley, but does not run on tracks.

**trolley car,** an electric streetcar powered from an overhead wire by means of a trolley.

**trol·lop** (trol′əp), *n.* [Scot. < ME. *trollen*, to troll; prob. infl. by *trull*], 1. an untidy or dirty woman; slattern. 2. a prostitute.

**Trol·lope, Anthony** (trol′əp), 1815–1882; English novelist.

**trol·ly** (trol′i), *n.* [*pl.* -LIES], a trolley. *v.t. & v.i.* [-LIED, -LYING], to trolley.

**trom·bone** (trom′bōn, trom-bōn′), *n.* [It. < *tromba*, a trumpet < Gmc.], a large, brass-wind instrument consisting of a long tube bent parallel to itself twice and ending in a bell mouth: different tones are produced by moving the slide, or movable section of the tube, in or out: also called **slide trombone. —trom′bon·ist,** *n.*

TROMBONE

**troop** (tro͞op), *n.* [< Fr. < LL. *troppus*, a flock], 1. a group of persons or animals; herd, flock, etc. 2. loosely, a great number; lot. 3. *usually pl.* a body of soldiers. 4. a subdivision of a cavalry regiment, corresponding to an infantry company. 5. a unit of boy scouts or girl scouts. *v.i.* 1. to gather or go as in troops: as, the crowd *trooped* out of the gate. 2. to walk, go, etc.: as, to *troop* up the road. *v.t.* to form into troops.

**troop·er** (tro͞op′ẽr), *n.* [*troop* + *-er*], 1. a cavalryman. 2. a cavalry horse. 3. a mounted policeman. 4. [Colloq.], a State policeman.

**troop·ship** (tro͞op′ship′), *n.* a ship used for carrying troops; transport.

**trope** (trōp), *n.* [< Fr. < L. < Gr. *tropos*, a turning < *trepein*, to turn], 1. the use of a word or phrase in a figurative sense. 2. a figure of speech. 3. figurative language in general.

**tro·phy** (trō′fi), *n.* [*pl.* -PHIES], [< Fr. < L. < Gr. *tropaion*, token of defeat; ult. < *trepein*, to turn], 1. arms, etc. captured from the enemy and kept as a memorial of victory. 2. an animal's skin, head, etc. displayed as evidence of hunting prowess. 3. a prize awarded for achievement, as in an athletic contest. 4. any memorial or memento. **—tro′phied,** *adj.*

**tro·pic** (trop′ik), *n.* [< LL. < Gr. *tropikos*, of a turn (of the sun at the solstices) < *tropē*, a turn], 1. either of two circles of the celestial sphere parallel to the equator, one, the **Tropic of Cancer,** 23°27′ north, and the other, the **Tropic of Capricorn,** 23°27′ south: they are the limits of the apparent north-and-south journey of the sun. 2. either of two lines of latitude on the earth that correspond to these. 3. [also T-], *pl.* the region between these latitudes. *adj.* of the tropics; tropical.

**-trop·ic** (trop′ik), [< Gr. < *trepein*, to turn], a combining form meaning *turning, responding to a* (specified kind of) *stimulus*, as in *phototropic*.

**trop·i·cal** (trop′i-k'l), *adj.* 1. of, in, or characteristic of the tropics. 2. very hot; sultry; torrid. 3. of, or having the nature of, a trope; figurative. **—trop′i·cal·ly,** *adv.*

**tropic bird,** any of various tropical sea birds characterized by white plumage with black markings and webbed toes.

**tro·pism** (trō′piz'm), *n.* [< Gr. *tropē*, a turn], the tendency of a plant or animal to move or turn in response to an external stimulus, as light, either by attraction (*positive tropism*) or repulsion (*negative tropism*). **—tro·pis′tic** (-pis′tik), *adj.*

**-tropism,** a combining form meaning *tropism*, as in *heliotropism*: also **-tropy.**

**trop·o·sphere** (trop′ə-sfêr′), *n.* [< Fr.; see TROPE & SPHERE], the atmosphere below the stratosphere: in this stratum clouds form and the temperature decreases as the altitude increases.

‡**trop·po** (trôp′pô; Eng. trop′ō), *adv.* [It.], in *music*, too; too much so (e.g., *adagio ma non troppo*, slowly but not too much so).

**trot** (trot), *v.i.* [TROTTED, TROTTING], [< OFr. < OHG. *trottōn*, to tread], 1. to move, ride, go, etc. at a trot. 2. to hurry; run. *v.t.* to cause to go at a trot. *n.* 1. a gait of a horse, etc. in which the legs are lifted in alternating diagonal pairs. 2. a jogging gait of a person. 3. the sound of a trotting horse. 4. [Slang], a pony (sense 4). **—trot out,** [Colloq.], to bring out for others to see or admire.

**troth** (trôth, trōth), *n.* [AS. *treowth*], [Archaic], 1. faithfulness; loyalty. 2. truth. 3. betrothal. *v.t.* [Archaic], to pledge; betroth.

**trot·line** (trot′līn′), *n.* a strong fishing line with short, baited lines hung from it.

**Trot·sky, Leon** (trot′ski), (born *Lev Davidovich Bronstein*), 1877–1940; Russian revolutionist and writer; exiled (1929).

**Trot·sky·ism** (trot′ski-iz'm), *n.* the doctrines, methods, and practices of Leon Trotsky and his followers. **—Trot′sky·ite, Trot′sky·ist,** *n.*

**trot·ter** (trot′ẽr), *n.* 1. an animal that trots; esp., a horse bred and trained for trotting races. 2. the foot of a sheep or pig used as food.

**trou·ba·dour** (tro͞o′bə-dôr′, -dōr′, -door′), *n.* [Fr. < Pr. < *trobar*, to compose in verse], 1. any of a class of lyric poets who lived in S France and N Italy from the 11th to the 13th centuries and wrote poems of love and chivalry. 2. loosely, any minstrel.

**trou·ble** (trub′'l), *v.t.* [-BLED, -BLING], [< OFr. < LL. < L. *turbula*, dim. of *turba*, tumult, crowd], 1. to disturb or agitate: as, the waters were *troubled*. 2. to worry; harass; perturb. 3. to cause pain and discomfort to: as, his wound *troubles* him. 4. to cause (a person) inconvenience: as, may I *trouble* you to move? 5. to pester, annoy, etc. *v.i.* 1. to take pains; bother: as, don't *trouble* about a reply. 2. to be distressed; worry. *n.* 1. a state of mental distress; worry. 2. a misfortune; calamity. 3. a person, event, situation, etc. that causes annoyance, distress, difficulty, etc. 4. public disturbance. 5 effort; pains: as, he took the *trouble* to listen. 6. an illness. **—trou′bler,** *n.* **—trou′bling·ly,** *adv.*

**trou·ble·mak·er** (trub′'l-māk′ẽr), *n.* one who habitually makes trouble for others.

**trou·ble-shoot·er** (trub′'l-sho͞ot′ẽr), *n.* a person charged with locating and eliminating sources of trouble in any flow of work: also **trouble shooter.**

**trou·ble·some** (trub′'l-səm), *adj.* characterized by or causing trouble. **—trou′ble·some·ly,** *adv.* **—trou′ble·some·ness,** *n.*

**trou·blous** (trub′ləs), *adj.* 1. troubled; agitated. 2. that causes trouble; troublesome.

**trough** (trôf; *occas.* trôth), *n.* [AS. *trog*], 1. a long, narrow, open container for holding water or food for animals. 2. any similarly shaped vessel, as one for washing something. 3. a gutter under the eaves of a building, for carrying off rain water. 4. a long, narrow hollow, as between waves.

**trounce** (trouns), *v.t.* [TROUNCED, TROUNCING], [< ?], 1. to beat; flog. 2. [Colloq.], to defeat.

**troupe** (tro͞op), *n.* [Fr.], a troop; company; group, especially of actors, singers, etc. *v.i.* [TROUPED, TROUPING], to travel as a member of a company of actors, etc.

**troup·er** (tro͞op′ẽr), *n.* 1. a member of a troupe. 2. any actor of long experience.

**trou·sers** (trou′zẽrz), *n.pl.* [< obs. *trouse* < Ir. *triubhas*], an outer garment, especially for men and boys, reaching from the waist to the ankles and divided into separate coverings for the legs: also called *pants*.

**trous·seau** (tro͞o-sō′, tro͞o′sō), *n.* [*pl.* -SEAUX, -SEAUS (-sōz′, -sōz)], [< Fr., small bundle], a bride's outfit of clothes, linen, jewelry, etc.

**trout** (trout), *n.* [*pl.* TROUT, TROUTS; see PLURAL, II, D, 2], [AS. *truht* < LL. < Gr. *trōktēs*, kind of fish < *trōgein*, to gnaw], any of various kinds of food and game fishes of the salmon family, found chiefly in fresh water, as the brook (or speckled) trout, rainbow trout etc.

**trow** (trō, trou), *v.i. & v.t.* [AS. *treowian* < *treowa*, faith], 1. [Obs.], to believe. 2. [Archaic], to think; suppose

**trow·el** (trou′əl), *n.* [< OFr. < LL. < L. *trulla* < *trua*, ladle], 1. a flat, rectangular tool for smoothing plaster. 2. a flat, pointed tool for applying and shaping mortar, as in bricklaying. 3. a pointed, scooplike tool for loosening soil, digging holes, etc. *v.t.* [-ELED or -ELLED, -ELING or -ELLING], to spread, smooth, shape, dig, etc. with a trowel. **—trow′el·er, trow′el·ler,** *n.*

TROWELS
A, brick trowel; B, garden trowel; C, cement trowel

**Troy** (troi), *n.* 1. an ancient city in NW Asia Minor: also called *Ilium*. 2. a city in E New York, on the Hudson River: pop., 67,000.

**troy** (troi), *adj.* by troy weight. *n.* troy weight.

**troy weight,** [< *Troyes*, a city in France], a system of weights for gold, silver, gems, etc., in which 24 grains = 1 pennyweight, 20 pennyweights = 1 ounce, and 12 ounces = 1 pound.

**tru·ant** (tro͞o′ənt), *n.* [OFr., a beggar < Celtic], 1. a pupil who stays away from school without permission. 2. one who shirks his duties. *adj.* 1. that is a truant. 2. idle; shiftless. 3. errant; straying: as, a *truant* impulse. *v.i.* to play truant. **—tru′an·cy** [*pl.* -CIES], *n.* **—tru′ant·ly,** *adv.*

**truant officer,** a school official who deals with truants.

**truce** (tro͞os), *n.* [< AS. *treowa*, faith], 1. a temporary cessation of warfare by agreement between the belligerents. 2. any respite, especially from trouble, pain, etc. **—truce′less,** *adj.*

**truck** (truk), *n.* [prob. < L. < Gr. *trochos*, a wheel < *trechein*, to run], 1. a small, solid wheel, as for a gun carriage. 2. a small, wooden disk with holes for halyards, as at the top of a flagpole or mast. 3. any of various vehicles for carrying heavy articles, as an open frame with a pair of wheels at one end, a low platform on wheels, etc. 4. an automotive vehicle for hauling loads along highways, etc. 5. a swiveling frame, with two or more pairs of wheels, under each end of a railroad car, streetcar, etc. *v.t.* to carry on a truck. *v.i.* 1. to engage in trucking. 2. to drive a truck.
**truck** (truk), *v.t. & v.i.* [Fr. *troquer*], to exchange; barter. *n.* 1. barter. 2. payment of wages in goods instead of money. 3. small commercial articles. 4. small articles of little value. 5. vegetables raised for sale in markets. 6. [Colloq.], dealings. 7. [Colloq.], trash; rubbish.
**truck·age** (truk'ij), *n.* 1. transportation of goods by truck. 2. the charge for this.
**truck·er** (truk'ẽr), *n.* 1. a person who drives a truck. 2. a person or company engaged in trucking. Also **truck'man** [*pl.* -MEN].
**truck farm,** a farm where vegetables are grown to be marketed. —**truck farmer.**
**truck·ing** (truk'iŋ), *n.* the business or process of transporting goods by truck.
**truck·le** (truk''l), *n.* [< OFr. < L. *trochlea*, a pulley < Gr. < *trochos*, a wheel], 1. originally, a small wheel. 2. a truckle bed. *v.i.* [-LED, -LING], 1. to move on small wheels. 2. to be servile; submit; toady (with *to*). *v.t.* to move (something) on small wheels. —**truck'ler,** *n.* —**truck'ling·ly,** *adv.*
**truckle bed,** a low bed on small wheels, that can be rolled under another bed when not in use.
**truc·u·lent** (truk'yoo-lənt, tro͞o'kyoo-), *adj.* [< L. < *trux*], fierce; savage; cruel. —**truc'u·lence, truc'u·len·cy,** *n.* —**truc'u·lent·ly,** *adv.*
**trudge** (truj), *v.i.* [TRUDGED, TRUDGING], [earlier *tredge*; prob. < AS.], to walk, especially wearily or laboriously. *n.* a walk, especially a wearying, tedious one. —**trudg'er,** *n.*
**trudg·en stroke** (truj'ən), [after J. *Trudgen*, 19th-c. Eng. swimmer], a swimming stroke in which a double overarm motion and a scissors kick are used: also **trudgen.**
**true** (tro͞o), *adj.* [TRUER, TRUEST], [AS. *treowe*], 1. faithful; loyal. 2. reliable; certain. 3. in accordance with fact; not false. 4. truthful. 5. conforming to an original, standard, etc.; exact; accurate. 6. rightful; lawful: as, the *true* heirs. 7. accurately fitted, shaped, directed, etc.: as, the board is not *true*. 8. *a*) real; genuine: as, a *true* diamond. *b*) conforming to the ideal character of such: as, a *true* scholar. 9. [Archaic], honest; virtuous. *adv.* truly. *v.t.* [TRUED, TRUING or TRUEING], to make true; esp., to fit, place, or shape accurately. *n.* that which is true (with *the*). —**come true,** to happen as predicted or expected —**in** (or **out of**) **true,** (not) properly set, adjusted, etc. —**true'ness,** *n.*
**true bill,** a bill of indictment endorsed by a grand jury as supported by evidence sufficient to warrant a hearing of the case.
**true-blue** (tro͞o'blo͞o'), *adj.* very loyal; stanch.
**true·bred** (tro͞o'bred'), *adj.* well-bred.
**true·love** (tro͞o'luv'), *n.* a sweetheart; loved one.
**truelove knot,** a bowknot that is hard to untie: a symbol of lasting love: also **true'-lov'er's knot.**
**truf·fle** (truf''l, tro͞o'f'l), *n.* [< Fr. < OIt. *truffa*; ult. < L. *tuber*, a knob], any of various fleshy, edible fungi that grow underground.
**tru·ism** (tro͞o'iz'm), *n.* a statement the truth of which is obvious and well known; platitude.
**trull** (trul), *n.* [G. *trolle*], a prostitute.
**tru·ly** (tro͞o'li), *adv.* 1. in a true manner; accurately, genuinely, etc. 2. in fact; really.
**Tru·man, Harry S.** (tro͞o'mən), 1884– ; 33d president of the U.S. (1945–1953).
**trump** (trump), *n.* [alt. < *triumph*], 1. any playing card of a suit that for the duration of a particular hand is ranked higher than any other suit, as through a winning bid. 2. *sometimes pl.* a suit of trumps. 3. [Colloq.], a fine person. *v.t.* 1. to take (a trick, card, etc.) by playing a trump. 2. to surpass; beat. *v.i.* to play a trump. —**trump up,** to devise deceitfully or fraudulently.
**trump** (trump), *n., v.t. & v.i.* [OFr. *trompe*], [Archaic or Poetic], trumpet.
**trump·er·y** (trum'pẽr-i), *n.* [*pl.* -IES], [< Fr. < *tromper*, to deceive], 1. something showy but worthless. 2. nonsense. *adj.* showy but worthless.
**trum·pet** (trum'pit), *n.* [< OFr. dim. of *trompe*, trumpet], 1. a brass-wind instrument with a powerful tone, consisting of a tube in an oblong loop, with a flared bell at one end. 2. something shaped like a trumpet; esp., an ear trumpet. 3. a sound like that of a trumpet. *v.i.* 1. to blow a trumpet. 2. to make a sound like a trumpet. *v.t.* 1. to sound on or as on a trumpet. 2. to proclaim loudly.

TRUMPET

**trumpet creeper,** a woody vine with red, trumpet-shaped flowers: also **trumpet vine.**
**trum·pet·er** (trum'pit-ẽr), *n.* 1. one who plays or sounds a trumpet. 2. one who proclaims or heralds something. 3. a long-legged, long-necked South American bird having a loud cry. 4. a trumpeter swan. 5. a crested pigeon with feathered feet.
**trumpeter swan,** a North American wild swan with a loud, resonant cry.
**trun·cate** (truŋ'kāt), *v.t.* [-CATED, -CATING], [< L. pp. of *truncare*, to cut off < *truncus*, a stem], to cut off a part of; lop. *adj.* 1. truncated. 2. in *botany & zoology*, having a square or broad end. —**trun'cate·ly,** *adv.* —**trun·ca'tion,** *n.*
**trun·cat·ed** (truŋ'kāt-id), *adj.* 1. cut short or appearing as if cut short. 2. having the vertex cut off by a plane.
**trun·cheon** (trun'chən), *n.* [< OFr. < LL. < L. *truncus*, a stem], 1. a short, thick staff; club; esp., a policeman's baton. 2. any staff or baton of authority. *v.t.* to beat with a truncheon.
**trun·dle** (trun'd'l), *n.* [AS. *trendel*, a circle < *trendan*, to roll], 1. a small wheel or caster. 2. a small cart with low wheels. 3. a trundle bed. 4. *a*) a rolling motion. *b*) its sound. *v.t. & v.i.* [-DLED, -DLING], 1. to roll along. 2. to rotate. —**trun'dler,** *n.*
**trundle bed,** a low bed on casters; truckle bed.
**trunk** (truŋk), *n.* [< OFr. < L. *truncus*, trunk, orig., mutilated], 1. the main stem of a tree. 2. the body of a human being or animal, not including the head and limbs. 3. the main body of a nerve, blood vessel, etc. 4. a long snout, as of an elephant. 5. a large, reinforced box for carrying clothing, etc. in travel. 6. a large, boxlike pipe, etc. for conveying air, water, etc. 7. *pl.* tight-fitting, very short breeches worn by men for athletics, etc. 8. a trunk line. 9. the shaft of a column. 10. a compartment in an automobile, usually in the rear, for holding a spare tire, luggage, etc. *adj.* designating or of a main line, as of a railroad.
**trunk·fish** (truŋk'fish'), *n.* [*pl.* see FISH], a tropical fish covered with fused, bony plates.
**trunk hose,** full, baglike breeches halfway to the knee, worn by men in the 16th and 17th centuries.
**trunk line,** a main line of a railroad, canal, telephone system, etc.
**trun·nion** (trun'yən), *n.* [< Fr. *trognon*, a stump], either of two projecting journals on each side of a cannon, etc., on which it pivots.
**truss** (trus), *v.t.* [< OFr. *trousser*], 1. originally, to tie into a bundle. 2. to tie, fasten, or tighten. 3. to bind the wings, etc. of (a fowl) before cooking. 4. to support or strengthen with a constructional truss. *n.* 1. a bundle or pack. 2. a bundle of hay (usually 56–60 lbs.) or of straw (usually 36 lbs.). 3. an iron band around a mast, for securing a yard. 4. a framework for supporting a roof, bridge, etc. 5. an appliance for giving support in cases of rupture or hernia, usually a pad on a special belt.
**truss bridge,** a bridge supported by trusses.
**trust** (trust), *n.* [< ON. *traust*], 1. firm belief in the honesty, reliability, etc. of some person or thing; faith. 2. the one trusted. 3. confident expectation, hope, etc.: as, have *trust* in the future. 4. *a*) the fact of having confidence placed in one. *b*) responsibility resulting from this. 5. care; custody. 6. something entrusted to a person; charge, duty, etc. 7. confidence in a purchaser's intention or future ability to pay for goods, etc.; credit. 8. *a*) a combination of corporations, constituting a monopoly, in which the stockholders turn over their stock to a board of trustees, who issue trust certificates to them and pay them dividends. *b*) any association of industrialists, business firms, etc. for establishing a monopoly by price fixing, ownership of controlling stock, etc. 9. in *law*, *a*) confidence reposed in a

person by giving him nominal ownership of property, which he is to keep, use, or administer for another's benefit. *b*) the property involved. ***v.i.*** 1. to have trust or faith; be confident. 2. to hope (with *for*). 3. to give business credit. ***v.t.*** 1. to have confidence in; rely on. 2. to commit (*to* a person's care). 3. to put something confidently in the charge of (a person): as, I *trusted* him with my car. 4. to allow to do something without fear of the outcome. 5. to believe. 6. to hope; expect. 7. to give business credit to. ***adj.*** 1. relating to a trust or trusts. 2. held in trust. 3. acting as trustee. **—in trust,** in the condition of being entrusted to another's care. **—trust to,** to rely on. **—trust′a·ble,** ***adj.*** **—trust′er,** ***n.***

**trus·tee** (trus-tē′), ***n.*** 1. a person to whom another's property or the management of another's property is entrusted. 2. any of a group of persons appointed to manage the affairs of a college, hospital, etc. ***v.t.*** [-TEED, -TEEING], to commit (property or management) to a trustee or trustees.

**trus·tee·ship** (trus-tē′ship), ***n.*** 1. the position or function of a trustee. 2. *a*) a commission from the United Nations to a country to administer some region, colony, etc. (called a *trust territory*). *b*) the state or fact of being a trust territory.

**trust·ful** (trust′fəl), ***adj.*** full of trust; ready to confide. **—trust′ful·ly,** ***adv.*** **—trust′ful·ness,** ***n.***

**trust fund,** money, stock, etc. held in trust.

**trust·ing** (trus′tiŋ), ***adj.*** that trusts; trustful. **—trust′ing·ly,** ***adv.*** **—trust′ing·ness,** ***n.***

**trust·less** (trust′lis), ***adj.*** 1. not to be trusted; unreliable; treacherous. 2. distrustful.

**trust territory,** see **trusteeship.**

**trust·wor·thy** (trust′wūr′*th*i), ***adj.*** worthy of trust; dependable; reliable. **—trust′wor′thi·ly,** ***adv.*** **—trust′wor′thi·ness,** ***n.***

**trust·y** (trus′ti), ***adj.*** [-IER, -IEST], that can be relied upon; dependable. ***n.*** [*pl.* -IES], 1. a trusted person. 2. a convict granted special privileges because of good behavior. **—trust′i·ly,** ***adv.*** **—trust′i·ness,** ***n.***

**truth** (trōōth), ***n.*** [*pl.* TRUTHS (trōō*th*z, trōōths)], [AS. *treowth*], 1. the quality or state of being true; specif., *a*) formerly, loyalty. *b*) sincerity; honesty. *c*) conformity with fact. *d*) reality; actual existence. *e*) agreement with a standard, rule, etc.; correctness. 2. that which is true. 3. an established or verified fact, etc. **—in truth,** truly; in fact. **—of a truth,** certainly.

**truth·ful** (trōōth′fəl), ***adj.*** 1. telling the truth; honest. 2. corresponding with fact or reality. **—truth′ful·ly,** ***adv.*** **—truth′ful·ness,** ***n.***

**try** (trī), ***v.t.*** [TRIED, TRYING], [OFr. *trier*], 1. to melt out or render, as fat. 2. *a*) to examine and decide (a case) in a law court. *b*) to determine legally the guilt or innocence of (a person). 3. to put to the proof; test. 4. to subject to trials, etc.; afflict: as, he was sorely *tried.* 5. to subject to a severe test or strain. 6. to experiment with; make a trial of: as, *try* this recipe. 7. to attempt; endeavor. ***v.i.*** 1. to make an effort, attempt, etc. 2. to experiment. ***n.*** [*pl.* TRIES], an attempt; effort; trial. **—try on,** to test the fit, etc. of (a garment) by putting it on. **—try out,** 1. to experiment with. 2. to test one's ability to qualify in a competition, for a job, etc.

**try·ing** (trī′iŋ), ***adj.*** that tries; annoying; irksome. **—try′ing·ly,** ***adv.*** **—try′ing·ness,** ***n.***

**try·out** (trī′out′), ***n.*** [Colloq.], a test to determine fitness or qualifications, as for competition in sports, a role in a play, etc.

**tryp·sin** (trip′sin), ***n.*** [G. < Gr. < *tribein*, to rub; + pep*sin*], a digestive enzyme in the pancreatic juice. it changes proteins into peptones. **—tryp′tic** (-tik), ***adj.***

**try·sail** (trī′s′l, -sāl′), ***n.*** [< naut. phr. *a try*, position of lying to in a storm], a small, stout, fore-and-aft sail used for keeping a vessel's head to the wind in a storm.

**try square,** an instrument for testing the accuracy of square work and for marking off right angles.

**tryst** (trist, trīst), ***n.*** [< OFr. *tristre*, hunting station], 1. an appointment to meet at a specified time and place, as one made by lovers. 2. a meeting held by appointment. 3. an appointed meeting place, as of lovers: also **trysting place.**

**tsar** (tsär), ***n.*** a czar. **—tsar′dom,** ***n.*** **—tsar′ism,** ***n.*** **—tsar′ist,** ***adj.*** **&** ***n.***

**tsar·e·vitch** (tsär′ə-vich′), ***n.*** a czarevitch.

**tsa·rev·na** (tsä-rev′nə), ***n.*** a czarevna.

**tsa·ri·na** (tsä-rē′nə), ***n.*** a czarina.

**tsa·rit·za** (tsä-rēt′sä), ***n.*** a czarina.

**Tschaikowsky,** see **Tchaikovsky.**

**tset·se** (tset′si), ***n.*** [S.Afr.D. < the Bantu name], any of several small flies of central and S Africa, one of which is a carrier of sleeping sickness: also **tsetse fly.**

**T-shirt** (tē′shūrt′), ***n.*** [so named because T-shaped], a collarless pull-over shirt with very short sleeves.

**Tsing·ta·o** (tsiŋ′tou′), ***n.*** a seaport in NE China, on the Yellow Sea: pop., 788,000.

**tsp.,** teaspoon; teaspoons.

**T square,** a T-shaped ruler for drawing parallel lines.

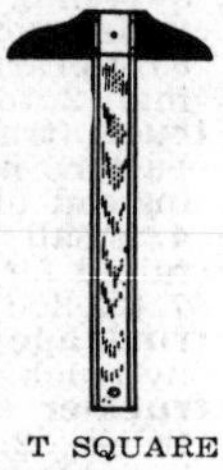

T SQUARE

**Tu,** in *chemistry*, thulium.

**Tu.,** Tuesday.

**tub** (tub), ***n.*** [< MD. *tubbe*], 1. a round, open, wooden container, usually formed of staves and hoops fastened around a flat bottom. 2. any large, open container of metal, etc., as for washing. 3. the contents of a tub. 4. a bathtub. 5. [Brit. Colloq.], a bath in a tub. 6. [Colloq.], a slow-moving, clumsy ship or boat. ***v.t. & v.i.*** [TUBBED, TUBBING], [Colloq.], to wash or bathe in a tub. **—tub′ber,** ***n.*** **—tub′like′,** ***adj.***

**tu·ba** (tōō′bə, tū′-), ***n.*** [*pl.* -BAS, -BAE (-bē)], [L., a trumpet], a large brass-wind instrument of the saxhorn group.

TUBA

**tub·by** (tub′i), ***adj.*** [-BIER, -BIEST], 1. shaped like a tub. 2. short and fat. **—tub′bi·ly,** ***adv.*** **—tub′bi·ness,** ***n.***

**tube** (tōōb, tūb), ***n.*** [Fr. < L. *tubus*, a pipe], 1. a slender, hollow cylinder or pipe of metal, glass, rubber, etc., used for conveying fluids. 2. an enclosed, hollow cylinder of thin, soft metal, fitted at one end with a screw cap and used for holding toothpaste, glue, etc. 3. an instrument, part, organ, etc. resembling a tube: as, a bronchial *tube.* 4. an electron tube. 5. *a*) an underground tunnel for an electric railroad. *b*) [Colloq.], the railroad itself. ***v.t.*** [TUBED, TUBING], 1. to provide with, place in, or pass through a tube or tubes. 2. to make tubular. **—tub′al,** ***adj.*** **—tu′bate,** ***adj.*** **—tube′like′,** ***adj.***

**tu·ber** (tōō′bẽr, tū′-), ***n.*** [L., lit., a swelling], 1. a short, thickened, fleshy part of an underground stem, as a potato. 2. a tubercle; swelling.

**tu·ber·cle** (tōō′bẽr-k′l, tū′-), ***n.*** [< L. *tuberculum*, dim. of *tuber;* see TUBER], 1. a small, rounded projection, as on a bone or on the roots of some plants. 2. any abnormal hard nodule or swelling; esp., the typical nodular lesion of tuberculosis.

**tubercle bacillus,** the bacillus of tuberculosis.

**tu·ber·cu·lar** (tōō-būr′kyoo-lẽr, tū-, tə-), ***adj.*** 1. of, like, or having tubercles. 2. tuberculous. ***n.*** a tuberculous person. **—tu·ber′cu·lar·ly,** ***adv.***

**tu·ber·cu·lin** (tōō-būr′kyoo-lin, tū-, tə-), ***n.*** a sterile solution prepared from a tubercle bacillus culture and injected into the skin as a test for tuberculosis: also **tu·ber′cu·line** (-lin, -lēn′).

**tu·ber·cu·lo·sis** (tōō-būr′kyoo-lō′sis, tū-, tə-), ***n.*** [see TUBERCLE + -OSIS], an infectious disease caused by the tubercle bacillus and characterized by the formation of tubercles in body tissues; esp., tuberculosis of the lungs; consumption.

**tu·ber·cu·lous** (tōō-būr′kyoo-ləs, tū-, tə-), ***adj.*** 1. having tuberculosis. 2. tubercular.

**tube·rose** (tōōb′rōz′, tūb′-), ***n.*** [see TUBEROUS], a plant with a bulblike root and sweet, white, funnel-shaped flowers.

**tu·ber·ous** (tōō′bẽr-əs, tū′-), ***adj.*** [< Fr. < L. *tuberosus* < *tuber;* see TUBER], 1. covered with rounded, wartlike swellings; knobby. 2. of, like, or having a tuber or tubers: also **tu′ber·ose′** (-ōs′). **—tu′ber·os′i·ty** (-bə-ros′ə-ti), [*pl.* -TIES], ***n.***

**tub·ful** (tub′fool′), ***n.*** [*pl.* -FULS], as much as a tub can hold.

**tub·ing** (tōōb′iŋ, tūb′-), ***n.*** 1. a series or system of tubes. 2. tubes collectively. 3. material in the form of a tube. 4. a piece of a tube.

**tu·bu·lar** (tōō′byoo-lẽr, tū′-), ***adj.*** [< L. dim. of *tubus*, a pipe], 1. of or shaped like a tube or tubes. 2. made with tubes. Also **tu′bu·late′** (-lāt′, -lit), **tu′bu·lat′ed.** **—tu′bu·lar·ly,** ***adv.***

**tuck** (tuk), ***v.t.*** [< MD. *tucken*, to tuck & AS. *tucian*, to tug], 1. to pull up or gather up in a fold or folds, as to make shorter (usually with *up*). 2. *a*) to thrust the edges of (a sheet, napkin, etc.) under or in, in order to make secure (usually with *up, in,* etc.). *b*) to cover or wrap snugly: as, *tuck* the baby in bed. 3. to put or press snugly into a small space; cram: as, to *tuck* shoes in a suitcase. 4. to make a tuck or tucks in (a garment). ***v.i.*** 1. to draw together; pucker. 2. to make tucks. ***n.*** a sewed fold in a garment.

**tuck·er** (tuk'ẽr), *n.* 1. a person who makes tucks. 2. a sewing machine attachment for making tucks. 3. a neck and shoulder covering formerly worn with a low-cut bodice by women.

**tuck·er** (tuk'ẽr), *v.t.* [prob. related to *tuck*], [Colloq.], to tire; weary (usually with *out*).

**Tuc·son** (tōō'son, tōō-son'), *n.* a city in S Arizona: pop., 213,000.

**-tude** (tōōd, tūd), [Fr. < L. *-tudo*], a noun-forming suffix corresponding to *-ness*, as in *certitude*.

**Tu·dor** (tōō'dẽr, tū'-), *adj.* 1. of or belonging to a ruling family of England (1485–1603) that ended with Elizabeth I. 2. of this period in English history. *n.* a sovereign of the Tudor line.

**Tues·day** (tōōz'di, tūz'-), *n.* [AS. *Tiwes dæg*, lit., day of the god of war *Tiw*], the third day of the week: abbrev. **T., Tu., Tues.**

**tu·fa** (tōō'fə, tū'-), *n.* [It. *tufo* < L. *tofus*], 1. a porous limestone formed by deposits from springs, etc. 2. tuff. —**tu·fa'ceous** (-fā'shəs), *adj.*

**tuff** (tuf), *n.* [< Fr. < It. *tufo;* see TUFA], a porous rock formed by consolidation of volcanic ashes, dust, etc.

**tuft** (tuft), *n.* [< OFr. *tuffe;* prob. < Gmc.], 1. a bunch of hairs, feathers, grass, etc. growing or tied closely together. 2. any similar cluster, as a clump of trees. *v.t.* 1. to provide or decorate with a tuft or tufts. 2. to secure the padding of (a quilt, mattress, etc.) by regularly spaced tufts of thread. *v.i.* to grow in or form into tufts. —**tuft'ed,** *adj.*

**tuft·y** (tuf'ti), *adj.* [-IER, -IEST], 1. full of or covered with tufts. 2. growing in tufts.

**tug** (tug), *v.i.* [TUGGED, TUGGING], [prob. < ON. *toga*, to draw], 1. to labor; toil. 2. to exert great effort in pulling (often with *at*). *v.t.* 1. to pull with great force; drag; haul. 2. to tow with a tugboat. *n.* 1. a hard pull. 2. a great effort or strenuous contest. 3. a trace of a harness. 4. a tugboat. —**tug'ger,** *n.* —**tug'ging·ly,** *adv.*

**tug·boat** (tug'bōt'), *n.* a small, sturdily built boat designed for towing or pushing ships, etc.

**tug of war,** 1. a contest in which two teams pull at opposite ends of a rope, each trying to drag the other across a central line. 2. any hard struggle.

**tu·i·tion** (tōō-ish'ən, tū-), *n.* [< Anglo-Fr. < L. pp. of *tueri*, to protect], 1. teaching; instruction. 2. the charge for instruction. —**tu·i'tion·al, tu·i'tion·ar'y,** *adj.*

**tu·la·re·mi·a, tu·la·rae·mi·a** (tōō'lə-rē'mi-ə), *n.* [< *Tulare* County, California + *-emia*], an infectious disease of rodents, especially rabbits, sometimes transmitted to man: also called *rabbit fever.*

**tu·lip** (tōō'lip, tū'ləp), *n.* [< Fr. < It. < Turk. *dülbend*, turban: the flower resembles a turban], 1. any of various bulb plants, mostly spring-blooming, with long, broad, pointed leaves and a large, cup-shaped flower. 2. the flower. 3. the bulb.

**tulip tree,** a tree of the magnolia family, with bluish-green leaves, tulip-shaped, greenish-yellow flowers, and long, conelike fruit.

**tu·lip·wood** (tōō'lip-wood', tū'ləp-), *n.* 1. the light, soft wood of the tulip tree, used in cabinetwork, etc. 2. any tree having such wood.

**tulle** (tōōl; Fr. tül), *n.* [< *Tulle*, city in France], a thin, fine netting of silk, rayon, or nylon, used for veils, scarfs, etc.

**Tul·sa** (tul'sə), *n.* a city in NE Oklahoma: pop., 262,000.

**tum·ble** (tum'b'l), *v.i.* [-BLED, -BLING], [< ME. freq. < AS. *tumbian*, to jump, dance], 1. to do somersaults, handsprings, or other acrobatic feats. 2. to fall suddenly or helplessly. 3. to stumble; trip. 4. to toss or roll about. 5. to move in a hasty, disorderly manner. 6. [Slang], to understand suddenly (with *to*). *v.t.* 1. to cause to tumble. 2. to put into disorder as by tossing here and there; disarrange. *n.* 1. a tumbling; specif., *a)* a somersault, handspring, etc. *b)* a fall or stumble. 2. *a)* confusion. *b)* a confused heap.

**tum·ble·bug** (tum'b'l-bug'), *n.* any of various beetles that roll balls of dung, in which they deposit their larvae: also **tum'ble·dung'** (-duŋ').

**tum·ble-down** (tum'b'l-doun'), *adj.* ready to tumble down; dilapidated.

**tum·bler** (tum'blẽr), *n.* 1. one who does somersaults, handsprings, etc.; acrobat. 2. a kind of pigeon that does somersaults in flight. 3. an ordinary drinking glass, with no foot or stem. 4. its contents. 5. a part of a lock whose position must be changed by a key in order to release the bolt.

**tum·ble·weed** (tum'b'l-wēd'), *n.* any of various plants which break off near the ground in autumn and are blown about by the wind.

**tum·brel, tum·bril** (tum'brəl), *n.* [< OFr. < *tomber*, to fall], 1. a farmer's cart, especially one that may be tilted for emptying. 2. any of the carts used to carry the condemned to the guillotine during the French Revolution. 3. a two-wheeled military cart for carrying ammunition, etc.

**tu·me·fy** (tōō'mə-fī', tū'-), *v.t. & v.i.* [-FIED, -FYING], [< Fr. < L. < *tumere*, to swell + *facere*, to make], to swell. —**tu'me·fac'tion** (-fak'shən), *n.*

**tu·mes·cent** (tōō-mes''nt, tū-), *adj.* [< L. ppr. of *tumescere*, to swell up], swelling; becoming swollen. —**tu·mes'cence,** *n.* —**tu·mes'cent·ly,** *adv.*

**tu·mid** (tōō'mid, tū'-), *adj.* [< L. < *tumere*, to swell], 1. swollen; bulging. 2. inflated; pompous. —**tu·mid'i·ty, tu'mid·ness,** *n.* —**tu'mid·ly,** *adv.*

**tum·my** (tum'i), *n.* [*pl.* -MIES], stomach: a child's word.

**tu·mor** (tōō'mẽr, tū'-), *n.* [L. < *tumere*, to swell], a swelling on some part of the body; esp., a mass of new tissue growth independent of its surrounding structures, having no physiological function: Brit. spelling **tumour.** —**tu'mor·ous,** *adj.*

**tu·mult** (tōō'mult, tū'-), *n.* [< OFr. < L. *tumultus* < *tumere*, to swell], 1. noisy commotion, as of a crowd; uproar. 2. confusion; agitation; disturbance. 3. great emotional disturbance.

**tu·mul·tu·ous** (tōō-mul'chōō-əs, tū-), *adj.* 1. full of or characterized by tumult; noisy and violent. 2. making a tumult. 3. greatly disturbed. —**tu·mul'tu·ous·ly,** *adv.* —**tu·mul'tu·ous·ness,** *n.*

**tun** (tun), *n.* [AS. *tunne*], 1. a large cask. 2. a varying measure of capacity for liquids, formerly 252 wine gallons. *v.t.* [TUNNED, TUNNING], to store in a tun or tuns.

**tu·na** (tōō'nə), *n.* [*pl.* -NA, -NAS; see PLURAL, II, D, 2], [Am. Sp.; cf. TUNNY], a tunny, a large food fish of the mackerel group: also **tuna fish.**

**tun·a·ble** (tōō'nə-b'l, tū'-), *adj.* 1. capable of being tuned. 2. in tune. 3. tuneful. Also sp. **tuneable.** —**tun'a·ble·ness,** *n.* —**tun'a·bly,** *adv.*

**tun·dra** (tun'drə, toon'-), *n.* [Russ.], any of the vast, nearly level, treeless plains of the arctic.

**tune** (tōōn, tūn), *n.* [< OFr. *ton*, tone; see TONE], 1. a rhythmical succession of musical tones; melody; air. 2. *a)* the condition of being in proper musical pitch or of agreeing in pitch. *b)* agreement; concord. Now chiefly in phrases *in tune, out of tune.* *v.t.* [TUNED, TUNING], 1. to adjust (a musical instrument) to some standard of pitch. 2. to adapt (music, the voice, etc.) to some pitch or tone. 3. to adapt to some condition, mood, etc.; adjust. *v.i.* to be in tune; harmonize. —**change one's tune,** to change one's attitude or manner: also **sing a different tune.** —**to the tune of,** [Colloq.], to the sum of. —**tune in (on),** to adjust a radio receiver to a given frequency so as to receive (a station, program, etc.). —**tune out,** to adjust a radio receiver so as to eliminate (interference, etc.). —**tune up,** 1. to adjust (musical instruments) to the same pitch. 2. to adjust to the proper condition, as a motor. —**tun'er,** *n.*

**tune·ful** (tōōn'fəl, tūn'-), *adj.* 1. full of music or melody; melodious. 2. producing musical sounds. —**tune'ful·ly,** *adv.* —**tune'ful·ness,** *n.*

**tune·less** (tōōn'lis, tūn'-), *adj.* 1. not musical or melodious; untuneful. 2. not producing music; silent. —**tune'less·ly,** *adv.* —**tune'less·ness,** *n.*

**tune-up** (tōōn'up'), *n.* an adjusting, as of a motor, to the proper condition.

**tung oil** (tuŋ), [< Chin. *yu-t'ung* < *yu*, oil + *t'ung*, name of the tree], an oil from the nut of an Asiatic tree, used in paints, linoleum, etc.

**tung·sten** (tuŋ'stən), *n.* [Sw. < *tung*, heavy + *sten*, stone], a hard, heavy, gray-white, metallic chemical element, used in steel, electric lamp filaments, etc.: symbol, W; at. wt., 183.92; at. no., 74: also called *wolfram.*

**tu·nic** (tōō'nik, tū'-), *n.* [< L. *tunica*], 1. a loose, gownlike garment worn by men and women in ancient Greece and Rome. 2. a blouselike garment extending to the hips or lower, usually belted. 3. [Chiefly Brit.], a short coat forming part of the uniform of soldiers, policemen, etc. 4. a natural covering of a plant, animal, organ, etc.

**tu·ni·cate** (tōō'ni-kāt', tū'-), *adj.* [< L. pp. of *tunicare*, to put on a tunic], in *botany & zoology*, covered with or having a tunic or tunics: also **tu'ni·cat'ed.** *n.* any of several primitive sea vertebrates enclosed by a thick tunic.

**tuning fork,** a small steel instrument with two prongs, which when struck sounds a certain fixed tone: it is used as a guide in tuning instruments.

TUNING FORK

**Tu·nis** (to͞o'nis, tū'-), *n.* 1. the capital of Tunisia, on the Mediterranean: pop., 410,000. 2. a former Barbary State in N Africa, now Tunisia.

**Tu·ni·si·a** (to͞o-nish'i-ə, tū-nish'ə, -nē'zhə), *n.* a country in N Africa, on the Mediterranean: area, 48,300 sq. mi.; pop., 3,965,000; capital, Tunis. —**Tu·ni'si·an,** *adj. & n.*

**tun·nage** (tun'ij), *n.* tonnage.

**tun·nel** (tun''l), *n.* [< Fr. *tonnelle,* vault & OFr. dim. of *tonne,* a tun], 1. an underground or underwater passageway, as for autos, trains, etc. 2. an animal's burrow. 3. any tunnellike passage, as in a mine. *v.t.* [-NELED or -NELLED, -NELING or -NELLING], 1. to make a tunnel or tunnellike passage through or under. 2. to make (one's way or a way) by digging a tunnel. *v.i.* to make a tunnel. —**tun'nel·er, tun'nel·ler,** *n.*

**tun·ny** (tun'i), *n.* [*pl.* -NIES, -NY; see PLURAL, II, D, 1], [< Fr. < Pr. < L. < Gr. *thynnos*], any of several large, edible sea fishes of the mackerel group, with coarse, somewhat oily flesh; a tuna.

**tup** (tup), *n.* [prob. < ON.], a male sheep; ram. *v.t.* [TUPPED, TUPPING], to copulate with (a ewe): said of a ram. —**tup'per,** *n.*

**tu·pe·lo** (to͞o'pi-lō'), *n.* [*pl.* -LOS], [of Muskhogean origin], 1. any of various trees with small, greenish flowers and blue or purple fruit; black, sour, or cotton gum tree. 2. the tough wood of any of these trees. Also **tupelo gum.**

**Tu·pi** (to͞o-pē'), *n.* 1. [*pl.* -PIS, -PI], a member of a group of South American Indian tribes living chiefly along the lower Amazon. 2. their language, especially the northern dialect: Guarani is the southern dialect. —**Tu·pi'an,** *adj.*

**tup·pence** (tup''ns), *n.* twopence.

**tuque** (to͝ok, tūk), *n.* [Canad. Fr. < Fr. *toque,* a cap], a kind of knitted winter cap.

**Tu·ra·ni·an** (too-rā'ni-ən, tyoo-), *n.* 1. the Ural-Altaic family of languages. 2. a member of any of the peoples who speak them. *adj.* designating or of these languages or peoples.

**tur·ban** (tũr'bən), *n.* [< Fr. < Port. < Turk. dial. of *dülbend* < Ar. & Per. < *dul,* a turn + *band,* a band], 1. a headdress of Moslem origin, consisting of a cap with a scarf wound round it. 2. a similar headdress consisting of a scarf wound round the head. 3. a hat having no brim or a very short brim turned up closely. —**tur'baned,** *adj.*

**tur·bid** (tũr'bid), *adj.* [< L. < *turbare,* to trouble < *turba,* a crowd], 1. having the sediment stirred up; muddy; cloudy. 2. thick, dense, or dark, as clouds or smoke. 3. confused; perplexed. —**tur'bid·ly,** *adv.* —**tur·bid'i·ty, tur'bid·ness,** *n.*

**tur·bine** (tũr'bin, -bīn), *n.* [Fr. < L. *turbo,* whirl], an engine driven by the pressure of steam, water, or air against the curved vanes of a wheel.

**tur·bo-,** [< L. *turbo,* thing that spins], a combining form meaning: 1. *consisting of a turbine.* 2. *driven by a turbine.*

**tur·bo·gen·er·a·tor** (tũr'bō-jen'ẽr-ā'tẽr), *n.* a generator driven by and directly coupled to a turbine.

**tur·bo·jet (engine)** (tũr'bō-jet'), in *aeronautics,* a jet engine in which the energy of the jet operates a turbine which in turn operates the air compressor.

**tur·bo·prop (engine)** (tũr'bō-prop'), [*turbo-* + *propeller*], in *aeronautics,* a jet engine in which the energy of the jet operates a turbine which in turn drives the propeller.

**tur·bot** (tũr'bət), *n.* [*pl.* -BOT, -BOTS; see PLURAL, II, D, 2], [< OFr. *tourbout;* prob. < OSw. *törn,* a thorn + *but,* butt], 1. a large European flatfish, highly regarded as food. 2. any of various similar flatfishes.

**tur·bu·lent** (tũr'byoo-lənt), *adj.* [Fr. < L.; see TURBID], 1. causing disturbance; disorderly; unruly. 2. disturbed; agitated; tumultuous. —**tur'bu·lence, tur'bu·len·cy,** *n.* —**tur'bu·lent·ly,** *adv.*

**tu·reen** (too-rēn'), *n.* [< Fr. *terrine,* earthen vessel < L. < *terra,* earth], a large, deep dish with a lid, for serving soup, etc.

**turf** (tũrf), *n.* [*pl.* TURFS, *archaic* TURVES], [AS.], 1. a surface layer of earth containing grass plants with their matted roots; sod. 2. a piece of this. 3. peat. 4. *a*) a track for horse racing. *b*) horse racing. Usually with *the* (in sense 4). *v.t.* to cover with turf. —**turf'y** [-IER, -IEST], *adj.*

**turf·man** (tũrf'mən), *n.* [*pl.* -MEN], a person interested in horse racing.

**Tur·ge·nev, I·van Ser·ge·ye·vich** (ē-vän' syer-gyā'ye-vich toor-gā'nyef), 1818–1883; Russian novelist: also sp. **Turgenieff, Turgeniev.**

**tur·ges·cent** (tũr-jes''nt), *adj.* [< L. ppr. of *turgescere,* to swell up], becoming turgid or swollen. —**tur·ges'cence, tur·ges'cen·cy,** *n.*

**tur·gid** (tũr'jid), *adj.* [< L. *turgidus* < *turgere,* to swell], 1. swollen; distended; bloated; inflated. 2. bombastic; pompous; grandiloquent. —**tur·gid'i·ty, tur'gid·ness,** *n.* —**tur'gid·ly,** *adv.*

**Tu·rin** (toor'in, tyoor'-, tyoo-rin'), *n.* a city in NW Italy: pop., 722,000.

**Turk** (tũrk), *n.* 1. a native or inhabitant of Turkey; esp., a member of the Moslem people of Turkey or, formerly, of the Ottoman Empire. 2. a member of any of the Turki peoples.

**Turk.,** 1. Turkey. 2. Turkish.

**Tur·ke·stan, Tur·ki·stan** (tũr'ki-stan', -stän'), *n.* a region in central Asia, including parts of the U.S.S.R., Sinkiang, and Afghanistan.

**Tur·key** (tũr'ki), *n.* a republic occupying Asia Minor and part of the Balkan Peninsula: area, 296,380 sq. mi.; pop., 26,881,000; capital, Ankara.

**tur·key** (tũr'ki), *n.* [*pl.* -KEYS, -KEY; see PLURAL, II, D, 1], [orig. erroneously identified with the guinea fowl, which bore name because formerly imported through Turkey], 1. a large North American bird, wild or domesticated, with a small head and spreading tail, bred as poultry. 2. its flesh, prized as food. 3. [Slang], a failure: said of a play, musical comedy, etc. —**talk turkey,** to talk candidly and bluntly.

**turkey buzzard,** a dark-colored vulture of the Southwest and South America, having a naked head.

**Tur·ki** (toor'kē), *adj.* 1. designating or of the Southern branch of the Turkic languages, including Turkish, Osmanli, etc. 2. designating or of the peoples who speak them. *n.* the Turki languages.

**Tur·kic** (tũr'kik), *adj.* 1. designating or of a subfamily of Altaic languages, including Turki. 2. designating or of the peoples who speak any of these languages.

**Turk·ish** (tũr'kish), *adj.* of Turkey, the Turks, etc. *n.* Osmanli, the language of Turkey.

**Turkish bath,** a bath in which the bather, after a period of heavy perspiration in a room of hot air or steam, is washed and massaged.

**Turkish Empire,** the Ottoman Empire.

**Turkish towel, turkish towel,** a thick cotton towel with a rough nap of uncut loops.

**Turk·men Soviet Socialist Republic** (tũrk'men), a republic of the U.S.S.R., in central Asia: capital, Ashkhabad: also **Turk'men·i·stan'** (-i-stan', -stän'), **Tur·ko·men** (tũrk'ə-men').

**Tur·ko-** (tũr'kō, -kə), a prefix meaning *Turkish, of Turkey* or *the Turks:* also **Turco-.**

**tur·mer·ic** (tũr'mẽr-ik), *n.* [< Fr. < ML. *terra merita,* lit., deserving earth], 1. an East Indian plant whose root in powdered form is used as a yellow dye, seasoning, and medicine. 2. its root.

**tur·moil** (tũr'moil), *n.* [? a blend of OFr. *trumel,* tumult & Eng. *moil*], tumult; commotion; confusion.

**turn** (tũrn), *v.t.* [< AS. *turnian* & OFr. *tourner,* both < L. *tornare,* to turn in a lathe; ult. < Gr. *tornos,* a lathe], 1. to rotate (a wheel, etc.). 2. to move around or partly around: as, *turn* the key. 3. to do by a revolving motion: as, he *turned* a somersault. 4. to give circular or rounded shape to, as in a lathe. 5. to give a graceful form to: as, to *turn* a phrase. 6. to change the position or direction of: as, *turn* your chair around. 7. to revolve in the mind; ponder (often with *over*). 8. to bend, fold, etc.: as, *turn* the sheet back. 9. to change so that the underside is on top and vice versa; reverse; invert: as, to *turn* pages, a collar, the soil, etc. 10. to make topsy-turvy. 11. to upset (the stomach). 12. to divert; avert: as, to *turn* a blow. 13. to convert; persuade; prejudice: as, he *turned* her against us. 14. to go around (a corner, etc.). 15. to pass (a certain age, amount, etc.). 16. to reverse the course of; make recoil; repel, as an attack. 17. to drive, set, let go, etc. in some way: as, to *turn* loose. 18. to direct, point, aim, etc.: as, eyes *turned* ahead, thoughts *turned* to the past. 19. to employ; apply: as, he *turned* his hand to writing. 20. to change; convert: as, to *turn* cream into butter. 21. to exchange for: as, she *turns* her eggs into cash. 22. to subject: as, she *turned* his remarks to ridicule. 23. to translate or paraphrase. 24. to derange, distract, or infatuate. 25. to make sour. 26. to affect (a person) in some way: as, it *turns* her sick. 27. to change the color of. *v.i.* 1. to rotate; revolve; pivot. 2. to move around or partly around. 3. to reel; whirl: as, my head is *turning.* 4. to be shaped on a lathe. 5. to become curved or bent. 6. to become reversed or inverted. 7. to become upset, as the stomach. 8. to change or reverse one's or its course, movement, or direction: as, the tide *turned*. 9. to direct or shift one's attention, abilities, etc.: as, he *turned* to music. 10. to reverse one's feelings, allegiance, etc.: as, he *turned* against his father. 11. to become: as, the milk *turned* sour. 12. to change into another form: as, the rain *turned* to sleet. 13. to become rancid, sour, etc. 14. to change color, as leaves. ***n.*** 1. a turning around; rotation, as of a wheel; revolution. 2. a single twist, coil, winding, etc. 3. a musical figure of four tones, the second and fourth being the same, the first a degree above, and the third a degree below. 4. a change or reversal of course or direction. 5. a short walk, ride, tour, etc., as for exercise or inspection. 6. the place where a change in direction occurs; bend; curve. 7. a change in trend, events, health, etc. 8. the time of a chronological change: as, the *turn* of the century. 9. a turning point. 10. an action or deed: as, a good *turn*. 11. a bout; spell; try. 12. an attack of illness, dizziness, etc. 13. the right or duty to do something, usually in regular order: as, it's my *turn* to go. 14. an act in a variety show. 15. a distinctive form, manner, detail, etc.: as, a quaint *turn* to her speech. 16. natural inclination: as, a curious *turn* of mind. 17. [Colloq.], a momentary shock, as from fright. —**at every turn,** in every instance; constantly. —**by turns,** one after another; alternately: also **turn and turn about.** —**in turn,** in proper sequence or order. —**out of turn,** 1. not in proper sequence or order. 2. [Colloq.], rashly. —**take turns,** to speak, do, etc. one after another in regular order. —**to a turn,** perfectly. —**turn down,** to reject (the request, etc. of someone). —**turn in,** 1. to make a turn into; enter. 2. to deliver; hand in. 3. to give back. 4. [Colloq.], to go to bed. —**turn off,** 1. to branch off, as a road. 2. to shut off. 3. to put out (a light). —**turn on,** 1. to start the flow of; open. 2. to cause (a light) to go on. 3. to attack or oppose suddenly. 4. to depend on. —**turn out,** 1. to shut off. 2. to put out (a light). 3. to put outside. 4. to dismiss. 5. to come or go out: as, to *turn out* for a picnic. 6. to produce. 7. to result. 8. to prove to be. 9. to become. 10. to equip, dress, etc. 11. [Colloq.], to get out of bed. —**turn over,** 1. to change or reverse the position of. 2. to shift one's position. 3. to consider; ponder. 4. to hand over; relinquish. 5. to convert. 6. to sell and replenish (a stock of goods). 7. to do business to the amount of. —**turn to,** 1. to refer to. 2. to go to for help; rely on. 3. to get to work. —**turn up,** 1. to fold back or over upon itself. 2. to lift up or turn over, as to see the other side. 3. to increase the speed, loudness, etc. of, as by turning a knob. 4. to make a turn onto or into (a street, etc.). 5. to have an upward direction. 6. to happen. 7. to arrive. 8. to be found. —**turn upon,** to turn on (senses 3 & 4). —**turn'er,** ***n.***

**turn·a·bout** (tũrn'ə-bout'), ***n.*** 1. a turning about, as to face the other way. 2. a shift or reversal of allegiance, opinion, etc.; about-face.

**turn·buck·le** (tũrn'buk''l), ***n.*** a coupling for use between lengths of rod or wire, consisting of a metal loop with opposite internal threads at each end or with a swivel at one end.

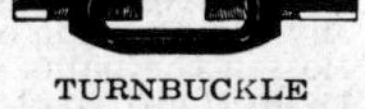

TURNBUCKLE

**turn·coat** (tũrn'kōt'), ***n.*** one who goes over to the opposite side or party; renegade; apostate.

**turn·down** (tũrn'doun'), ***adj.*** 1. that can be turned down. 2. having the upper part folded down: as a *turndown* collar.

**Tur·ner, Joseph Mal·lord William** (mal'ẽrd tũr'nẽr), 1775–1851; English painter.

**turn·ing** (tũr'niŋ), ***n.*** 1. a revolving, winding, twisting, inverting, etc. 2. the art or process of shaping things on a lathe. 3. a fashioning, as of a phrase. 4. a place where a road, etc. turns.

**turning point,** 1. a point at which something turns or changes direction. 2. a point in time at which a decisive change occurs; crisis.

**tur·nip** (tũr'nip), ***n.*** [prob. < *turn* or < Fr. *tour*, in sense of "round" + ME. *nepe* < AS. < L. *napus*, a turnip], 1. either of two plants of the mustard family (the *white turnip* and the *Swedish turnip*, or *rutabaga*), with hairy leaves and a roundish, light-colored root used as a vegetable. 2. the root.

**turn·key** (tũrn'kē'), ***n.*** [*pl.* -KEYS], a person in charge of the keys of a prison; warden; jailer.

**turn·out, turn-out** (tũrn'out'), ***n.*** 1. a turning out. 2. a gathering of people, as at a meeting. 3. output. 4. a railroad siding. 5. a carriage with its horse or horses. 6. equipment; outfit.

**turn·o·ver** (tũrn'ō'vẽr), ***n.*** 1. a turning over; specif., *a*) an upset. *b*) a change from one side, opinion, etc. to another. 2. a small pie made by folding one half of the crust back over the other. 3. *a*) the selling out and replenishing of a stock of goods. *b*) the amount of business done during a given period in terms of the money used in buying and selling. 4. *a*) the number of workers hired as replacements during a given period. *b*) the ratio of this to the average number of workers employed. ***adj.*** that turns over.

**turn·pike** (tũrn'pīk'), ***n.*** [ME. *turnpyke*, a spiked barrier across a road; see TURN & PIKE], 1. a tollgate. 2. a road having tollgates; toll road. 3. loosely, any highway.

**turn·stile** (tũrn'stīl'), ***n.*** a device, as a post supporting two revolving crossed bars, placed in an entrance to allow the passage of persons one at a time: often coin-operated.

TURNSTILE

**turn·stone** (tũrn'stōn'), ***n.*** a small, ploverlike shore bird that turns over pebbles to seek food.

**turn·ta·ble** (tũrn'tā'b'l), ***n.*** 1. a circular revolving platform with a track, as in a railroad roundhouse. 2. any of various revolving platforms: as, a phonograph *turntable*.

**turn·up** (tũrn'up'), ***n.*** something turned up. ***adj.*** that turns up or is turned up.

‡**Turn·ver·ein** (toorn'fer-īn'), ***n.*** [G. < *turnen*, to exercise + *verein*, a club], a club of gymnasts.

**tur·pen·tine** (tũr'pən-tīn'), ***n.*** [< OFr. < L. < Gr. *terebinthos*, a tree yielding turpentine], 1. any of the various oleoresins obtained from pines and other coniferous trees. 2. a light-colored, volatile oil distilled from such oleoresins, used in paints, in medicine, etc.: in full, **oil** (or **spirits**) **of turpentine.** ***v.t.*** [-TINED, -TINING], to apply turpentine to.

**tur·pi·tude** (tũr'pə-tōōd', -tūd'), ***n.*** [Fr. < L. < *turpis*, vile], baseness; vileness; depravity.

**tur·quoise** (tũr'koiz, -kwoiz), ***n.*** [< OFr. fem. of *turqueis*, Turkish: because brought to W Europe through Turkey], 1. a greenish-blue semiprecious stone, a hydrous phosphate of aluminum containing a small amount of copper. 2. a greenish blue: also **turquoise blue.** ***adj.*** greenish-blue.

**tur·ret** (tũr'it), ***n.*** [< OFr. dim. of *tour*; see TOWER], 1. a small tower projecting from a building, usually at a corner. 2. *a*) a low, armored, usually revolving, towerlike structure for guns and their crew, as on a warship, tank, etc. *b*) a transparent hemisphere of plexiglass, etc., for a gun and gunner, as on a bomber. 3. an attachment for a lathe, drill, etc. consisting of a block holding several cutting tools, which may be rotated to present any of the tools to the work: also **tur'ret-head'.** —**tur'ret·ed,** ***adj.***

**turret lathe,** a lathe with a turret (sense 3).

**tur·tle** (tũr't'l), ***n.*** [*pl.* -TLES, -TLE; see PLURAL, II, D, 1], [alt. after *turtledove* < Fr. *tortue* or Sp. *tortuga*, tortoise], 1. any of various land and water reptiles having a toothless beak and a soft body encased in a hard shell into which, in most species, the head, tail, and four legs may be withdrawn: land species are usually called *tortoise*. 2. the flesh of some turtles, used as food. 3. [Archaic], a turtledove. ***v.i.*** [-TLED, -TLING], to hunt for turtles. —**turn turtle,** to turn upside down.

**tur·tle·back** (tũr't'l-bak'), ***n.*** an arched structure over the bow or stern of a ship as a protection against heavy seas: also **turtle deck.**

**tur·tle·dove** (tũr't'l-duv'), ***n.*** [AS. *turtle* < L. *turtur*; of echoic origin], any of several wild doves noted for their plaintive cooing and the devotion that the mates show toward each other.

**turtle neck,** a high, turned-down collar that fits snugly about the neck, as on some pull-over sweaters. —**tur'tle-neck',** ***adj.***

**Tus·ca·loo·sa** (tus'kə-lōō'sə), ***n.*** a city in west central Alabama: pop., 63,000.

**Tus·ca·ny** (tus'kə-ni), ***n.*** a department of W Italy: chief city, Florence. —**Tus'can,** ***adj.*** **& *n.***

**Tus·ca·ror·a** (tus'kə-rôr'ə, -rō'rə), ***n.*** [*pl.* -RORA, -RORAS], a member of a tribe of Iroquoian Indians at one time living in North Carolina, but later in New York and Ontario.

**tusk** (tusk), ***n.*** [AS. *tucs*], 1. a long, pointed tooth

projecting outside the mouth, as in elephants, wild boars, etc. 2. any tusklike tooth or part. *v.t.* to dig, gore, etc. with a tusk or tusks. —**tusked,** *adj.* —**tusk'like',** *adj.*
**tus·sah** (tus'ə), *n.* [< Hind. < Sans. *tasara,* a shuttle], 1. an Asiatic silkworm that produces a coarse, tough silk. 2. this silk: also **tussah silk.** Also **tusseh, tussa, tussar, tusser,** etc.
**tus·sle** (tus''l), *n. & v.i.* [-SLED, -SLING], [< ME. *tusen* (in comp.), to pull], struggle; wrestle; scuffle.
**tus·sock** (tus'ək), *n.* [prob. < earlier *tusk,* tuft of hair, after words in *-ock*], a thick tuft or clump of grass, twigs, etc. —**tus'sock·y,** *adj.*
**tut** (tut), *interj.* an exclamation of impatience, annoyance, contempt, etc.
**Tut·ankh·a·men** (to͞ot'äŋk-ä'mən), *n.* Egyptian king; 14th century B.C.
**tu·te·lage** (to͞o't'l-ij, tū'-), *n.* [< L. *tutela,* protection], 1. guardianship; care, protection, etc. 2. teaching; instruction. 3. the condition of being under a guardian or tutor.
**tu·te·lar·y** (to͞o't'l-er'i, tū'-), *adj.* [< L. < *tutela,* protection], 1. protecting; watching over; guardian. 2. of or serving as a guardian. *n.* [*pl.* -IES], a tutelary god, spirit, etc. Also **tu'te·lar.**
**tu·tor** (to͞o'tẽr, tū'-), *n.* [OFr. < L. < *tuitus,* pp. of *tueri,* to guard], 1. a private teacher. 2. a legal guardian of a minor. 3. in English universities, an official in charge of the studies of an undergraduate. 4. in some U.S. colleges, a teaching assistant. *v.t.* 1. to act as a tutor to. 2. to teach; instruct. 3. to discipline; admonish. *v.i.* 1. to act as a tutor. 2. [Colloq.], to be tutored. —**tu'tor·age,** *n.* —**tu·to'ri·al** (-tôr'i-əl, -tō'ri-), *adj.* —**tu'tor·ship',** *n.*
**tut·ti** (to͞o'ti), *adj.* [It. < L. *totus,* all], in *music,* for all instruments or voices. *n.* [*pl.* -TIS], 1. a passage played or sung by all performers. 2. a tonal effect produced in this way.
**tut·ti-frut·ti** (to͞o'ti-fro͞o'ti), *n.* [It., all fruits], a preserve, candy, or ice cream made with a mixture of fruits or fruit flavorings. *adj.* made or flavored with a mixture of fruits.
**tu·tu** (to͞o'to͞o), *n.* [Fr.], a very short, full, projecting skirt worn by ballet dancers.
**Tu·tu·i·la** (to͞o'to͞o-ē'lä), *n.* an island of U.S. Samoa, in the South Pacific: chief city, Pago Pago.
**tux** (tuks), *n.* [Colloq.], a tuxedo.
**tux·e·do** (tuk-sē'dō), *n.* [*pl.* -DOS], [< the name of a country club near *Tuxedo* Lake, N.Y.], 1. a man's tailless jacket for semi-formal evening wear, usually black. 2. a suit with such a jacket.
**TV,** television.
**TVA, T.V.A.,** Tennessee Valley Authority.
**twa** (twä), *adj. & n.* [AS.], [Scot.], two.
**twad·dle** (twäd''l), *n.* [akin to *tattle*], foolish, empty talk or writing; nonsense. *v.t. & v.i.* [-DLED, -DLING], to talk or write in a foolish or senseless manner; prattle. —**twad'dler,** *n.*
**twain** (twān), *n. & adj.* [AS. *twegen,* two], [Archaic or Poetic], two.
**Twain, Mark** (twān), (pseudonym of *Samuel Langhorne Clemens*), 1835–1910; U.S. novelist and humorist.
**twang** (twaŋ), *n.* [echoic], 1. a quick, sharp, vibrating sound, as of a plucked string. 2. a sharp, nasal speech sound. 3. a way of speaking characterized by such sounds. *v.i. & v.t.* 1. to make or cause to make a twang, as a bowstring, banjo, etc. 2. to speak or say with a twang. 3. to shoot or be released with a twang, as an arrow. —**twang'y** [-IER, -IEST], *adj.*
**'twas** (twuz, twäz; *unstressed* twəz), it was.
**twat·tle** (twät''l), *n., v.i. & v.t.* [-TLED, -TLING], [< *tattle*] twaddle.
**tweak** (twēk), *v.t.* [AS. *twiccan,* to twitch], to seize and pull (the nose, ear, etc.) with a sudden jerk. *n.* a sudden, twisting pinch. —**tweak'er,** *n.*
**tweed** (twēd), *n.* [< misreading of *tweel,* Scot. form of *twill;* later assoc. with the *Tweed,* river in Scotland], 1. a wool fabric with a rough surface, in a weave of two or more colors. 2. a jacket, suit, etc. of this. 3. *pl.* clothes of tweed.
**twee·dle** (twē'd'l), *v.i.* [-DLED, -DLING], [echoic], to play a series of shrill tones. *v.t.* to play carelessly or casually on (a musical instrument). *n.* a sound produced by tweedling.
**twee·dle·dum and twee·dle·dee** (twē'd'l-dum' 'n twē'd'l-dē'), [< *tweedle*], two persons or things so much alike as to be almost indistinguishable.
**'tween** (twēn), *prep.* [Poetic], between.
**tweet** (twēt), *n. & interj.* [echoic], the chirping sound of a small bird. *v.i.* to utter this sound.
**tweeze** (twēz), *v.t.* [TWEEZED, TWEEZING], [back-formation < *tweezers*], [Colloq.], to pluck, remove, handle, etc. with or as with tweezers.
**tweez·ers** (twēz'ẽrz), *n.pl.* [< obs. *tweeze,* a set of instruments < Fr. pl. of *étui,* a case], small pincers for plucking out hairs, handling little objects, etc.: often **pair of tweezers** also **tweez'er.**

TWEEZERS

**twelfth** (twelfth), *adj.* [AS. *twelfta*], 1. preceded by eleven others in a series; 12th. 2. designating any of the twelve equal parts of something. *n.* 1. the one following the eleventh. 2. any of the twelve equal parts of something; 1/12.
**Twelfth-day** (twelfth'dā'), *n.* January 6, the twelfth day after Christmas, on which the Epiphany is celebrated: formerly observed as the official end of the Christmas season.
**Twelfth-night** (twelfth'nīt'), *n.* the eve or evening of Twelfth-day.
**twelve** (twelv), *adj.* [< AS. *twelf*], two more than ten. *n.* 1. the cardinal number between eleven and thirteen; 12; XII. 2. a group of twelve persons or things. —**the Twelve,** the Twelve Apostles.
**Twelve Apostles,** the twelve disciples chosen by Jesus to go forth to teach the gospel.
**twelve·fold** (twelv'fōld'), *adj.* 1. having twelve parts. 2. having twelve times as much or as many. *adv.* twelve times as much or as many.
**twelve·mo** (twelv'mō), *adj. & n.* [*pl.* -MOS], duodecimo.
**twelve·month** (twelv'munth'), *n.* a year.
**twelve-tone** (twelv'tōn'), *adj.* in *music,* designating or of a system of composition in which the twelve tones of the chromatic scale are used without a key, but in an arbitrary, fixed order.
**twen·ti·eth** (twen'ti-ith), *adj.* 1. preceded by nineteen others in a series; 20th. 2. designating any of the twenty equal parts of something. *n.* 1. the one following the nineteenth. 2. any of the twenty equal parts of something; 1/20.
**twen·ty** (twen'ti), *adj.* [AS. *twentig*], two times ten. *n.* [*pl.* -TIES], the cardinal number between nineteen and twenty-one; 20; XX. —**the twenties,** the years from twenty through twenty-nine (of a century or a person's age).
**twen·ty·fold** (twen'ti-fōld'), *adj.* 1. having twenty parts. 2. having twenty times as much or as many. *adv.* twenty times as much or as many.
**twen·ty-one** (twen'ti-wun'), *n.* blackjack, a gambling game at cards.
**'twere** (twũr), it were.
**twice** (twīs), *adv.* [AS. *twiga*], 1. on two occasions or in two instances. 2. two times. 3. in twofold amount or degree: as, *twice* the money.
**twid·dle** (twid''l), *v.t.* [-DLED, -DLING], [prob. < ON. *tvidla,* to stir], to twirl or play with lightly. *v.i.* 1. to toy with some object. 2. to be busy about trifles. *n.* a twirling motion, as with the fingers. —**twiddle one's thumbs,** 1. to twirl one's thumbs idly around one another. 2. to be idle. —**twid'dler,** *n.*
**twig** (twig), *n.* [AS. *twigge*], a small branch or shoot of a tree or shrub. —**twigged,** *adj.* —**twig'gy** [-GIER, -GIEST], *adj.*
**twi·light** (twī'līt'), *n.* [ME. < *twi-,* two + *light*], 1. the subdued light just after sunset or, sometimes, just before sunrise. 2. the period from sunset to dark. 3. any faint light. 4. any condition or period suggestive of twilight. *adj.* of or characteristic of twilight.
**twilight sleep,** a state of partial anesthesia induced by the injection of morphine and scopolamine, as to lessen the pains of childbirth.
**twill** (twil), *n.* [AS. *twili* < *twi-,* two; cf. DRILL (cloth)], 1. a cloth woven so as to have parallel diagonal lines or ribs. 2. the pattern of this weave. *v.t.* to weave with a twill. —**twilled,** *adj.*
**'twill** (twil), it will.
**twin** (twin), *adj.* [AS. *twinn* & ON. *tvinnr,* double], 1. consisting of, or being one of a pair of, two separate but similar or closely related things; paired. 2. being two, or either of two, that have been born at the same birth: as, *twin* girls, a *twin* sister. *n.* 1. either of two born at the same birth. 2. either of two persons or things very much alike in appearance, shape, etc. 3. [T-], *pl.* Gemini. *v.i.* [TWINNED, TWINNING], 1. to give birth to twins. 2. to be paired (with another). *v.t.* 1. to give birth to as twins. 2. to pair or couple.
**twine** (twīn), *n.* [AS. *twin* < base of *twi-,* two], 1. strong thread, string, or cord of two or more strands twisted together. 2. a twining or being twined. 3. a twined thing or part; twist. *v.t.* [TWINED, TWINING], 1. *a*) to twist together; intertwine. *b*) to form in this way. 2. to wreathe or wind (one thing) around or with another. 3. to encircle, enfold, etc.: as, the wreath *twined* his brow. *v.i.* 1. to twist, interlace, etc. 2. to twist and turn; wind about. —**twin'er,** *n.* —**twin'ing·ly,** *adv.*

**twinge** (twinj), ***v.t. & v.i.*** [TWINGED, TWINGING], [AS. *twengan*, to squeeze], to have or cause to have a sudden, sharp pain, qualm, etc. ***n.*** 1. a sudden, sharp pain. 2. a qualm, as of conscience.
**twin·kle** (twiŋ'k'l), ***v.i.*** [-KLED, -KLING], [AS. *twinclian*], 1. to shine in rapid, intermittent gleams, as some stars; sparkle. 2. to light up, as with amusement: said of the eyes. 3. to move rapidly to and fro, as dancers' feet; flutter. ***v.t.*** 1. to cause to twinkle. 2. to emit (light) in rapid, intermittent gleams. ***n.*** 1. a wink of the eye. 2. a glint, as of amusement, in the eye. 3. an intermittent gleam; sparkle. 4. the time occupied by a wink; a twinkling. —**twin'kler,** ***n.***
**twin·kling** (twiŋ'kliŋ), ***n.*** 1. the action of a thing that twinkles. 2. a rapid gleam or little flash; twinkle. 3. the time occupied by a wink; instant. —**twin'kling·ly,** ***adv.***
**twirl** (twûrl), ***v.t. & v.i.*** [alt. < ME. *tirlen* < *trillen*, to turn], 1. to rotate rapidly; spin. 2. to whirl in a circle. 3. in *baseball*, to pitch. ***n.*** 1. a twirling or being twirled. 2. something twirled; specif., a twist, coil, flourish, etc. —**twirl'er,** ***n.***
**twist** (twist), ***v.t.*** [ME. *twisten* < AS. *twist*, a rope], 1. to entwine or wind, as threads or strands, around one another. 2. to wreathe; twine. 3. to wind (thread, rope, etc.) around something. 4. to give spiral shape to. 5. to subject to torsion. 6. to wrench; sprain. 7. to contort or distort (the face, etc.). 8. to wring; torment; harass. 9. to confuse. 10. to break off by turning the end (with *off*). 11. to distort or pervert the meaning of. 12. to revolve or rotate. 13. to make (a ball) go in a curve by giving it a spinning motion. ***v.i.*** 1. to undergo twisting. 2. to spiral, coil, twine, etc. (*around* or *about* something). 3. to revolve or rotate. 4. to turn to one side. 5. to meander; wind, as a path. 6. to twist something. 7. to squirm; writhe. 8. to move in a curved path, as a ball. ***n.*** 1. a thread or cord of twisted strands of hemp, cotton, silk, etc. 2. a twisted roll of tobacco. 3. a loaf of bread or roll made of twisted pieces of dough. 4. a knot, etc. made by twisting. 5. a twisting or being twisted. 6. a spin given to a ball in throwing it; twirl. 7. torsional stress or the angle of torsion. 8. a contortion, as of the face. 9. a wrench or sprain. 10. a turning aside; turn; bend. 11. a personal tendency; eccentricity or bias. 12. a distorting of meaning. —**twist'ed·ly,** ***adv.*** —**twist'ing·ly,** ***adv.***
**twist·er** (twis'tẽr), ***n.*** 1. a person or thing that twists; specif., a thrown or batted ball that has been given a twist. 2. a tornado or cyclone.
**twit** (twit), ***v.t.*** [TWITTED, TWITTING], [< AS. *ætwitan; æt*, at + *witan*, to accuse], to reproach, upbraid, taunt, etc., especially by reminding of a fault or mistake. ***n.*** a reproach or taunt.
**twitch** (twich), ***v.t. & v.i.*** [< AS. *twiccian*, to pluck], 1. to pull (at) with a sudden jerk; pluck. 2. to move with a quick, sudden motion or convulsively. ***n.*** 1. a sudden, quick pull. 2. a sudden, quick motion, especially a convulsive or spasmodic one. —**twitch'er,** ***n.*** —**twitch'ing·ly,** ***adv.***
**twit·ter** (twit'ẽr), ***v.i.*** [ME. *twiteren*], 1. to make a series of light, sharp vocal sounds; chirp: said of birds. 2. to talk in a rapid or agitated manner; chatter. 3. to tremble with excitement. 4. to titter. ***v.t.*** to say by twittering. ***n.*** 1. a chirping. 2. a condition of tremulous excitement; flutter. —**twit'ter·er,** ***n.*** —**twit'ter·ing·ly,** ***adv.***
**'twixt** (twikst), ***prep.*** [Poetic or Dial.], betwixt.
**two** (to͞o), ***adj.*** [AS. *twa*], totaling one more than one. ***n.*** 1. the cardinal number between one and three; 2; II. 2. a domino, die, card, etc. with two spots. —**in two,** in two parts. —**put two and two together,** to reach an obvious conclusion by considering several facts together.
**two-base hit** (to͞o'bās'), in *baseball*, a double.
**two-bit** (to͞o'bit'), ***adj.*** [Slang], 1. worth twenty-five cents. 2. cheap; worthless.
**two bits,** [Slang], twenty-five cents.
**two-by-four** (to͞o'bə-fôr', -bī-fôr'), ***adj.*** 1. that measures two inches (or feet, etc.) by four inches (or feet, etc.). 2. [Colloq.], small, narrow, cramped, etc. ***n.*** a piece of lumber two inches thick, four inches wide, and of varying length.
**two-edged** (to͞o'ejd'), ***adj.*** 1. that has two edges, usually on opposite sides. 2. that can have a double meaning, as a dubious compliment.
**two-faced** (to͞o'fāst'), ***adj.*** 1. having two faces. 2. deceitful; hypocritical. —**two'-fac'ed·ly** (-fās'id-li, -fāst'li), ***adv.*** —**two'-fac'ed·ness,** ***n.***
**two-fist·ed** (to͞o'fis'tid), ***adj.*** [Colloq.], 1. able to use both fists; hence, 2. vigorous; virile.
**two·fold** (to͞o'fōld'), ***adj.*** 1. having two parts. 2. having twice as much or as many. ***adv.*** twice as much or as many.
**two-hand·ed** (to͞o'han'did), ***adj.*** 1. that needs to be used or wielded with both hands. 2. worked by two people: as, a *two-handed* saw. 3. engaged in by two people, as a card game. 4. having two hands. 5. using both hands equally well.
**two-leg·ged** (to͞o'leg'id), ***adj.*** having two legs.
**two-part time** (to͞o'pärt'), musical time with two beats or multiples of two beats to a measure.
**two·pence** (tup''ns), ***n.*** 1. two pence; two British pennies. 2. a British coin of this value: now coined only as alms money for Maundy Thursday.
**two·pen·ny** (tup'ən-i), ***adj.*** 1. worth or costing twopence. 2. cheap; worthless.
**two-piece** (to͞o'pēs'), ***adj.*** consisting of two separate parts: as, a *two-piece* bathing suit.
**two-ply** (to͞o'plī'), ***adj.*** 1. having two thicknesses, layers, strands, etc. 2. woven double.
**two-sid·ed** (to͞o'sīd'id), ***adj.*** 1. having two sides. 2. having two aspects: as, a *two-sided* question.
**two·some** (to͞o'səm), ***n.*** 1. two people; couple. 2. a game for or played by two people. 3. these people. ***adj.*** consisting of or engaged in by two.
**two-spot** (to͞o'spot'), ***n.*** 1. a playing card, domino, etc. with two spots, or pips; deuce. 2. [Colloq.], *a*) a two-dollar bill. *b*) two dollars.
**two-step** (to͞o'step'), ***n.*** 1. a ballroom dance in 2/4 time. 2. a piece of music for this dance.
**two-time** (to͞o'tīm'), ***v.t.*** [-TIMED, -TIMING], [Slang], to be unfaithful or deceitful to. —**two'-tim'er,** ***n.***
**'twould** (twood), it would.
**two-way** (to͞o'wā'), ***adj.*** 1. having two ways, lanes, etc.; allowing passage in either direction. 2. that connects a pipe, wire, etc. to two others.
**-ty** (ti), [< OFr. *-té* < L. *-tas*], a suffix meaning *quality of, condition of*, as in *paucity*.
**-ty** (ti), [AS. *-tig*], a suffix meaning *tens, times ten*, as in *twenty, thirty*, etc.
**ty·coon** (tī-ko͞on'), ***n.*** [< Japan. < Chin. *ta*, great + *kiun*, prince], 1. a title applied by foreigners to the former shogun of Japan. 2. [Colloq.], a wealthy and powerful industrialist, financier, etc.
**ty·ing** (tī'iŋ), ppr. of **tie.**
**tyke** (tīk), ***n.*** [< ON. *tik*, a bitch], 1. a dog; esp., a mongrel or cur. 2. [Colloq.], a small child: term of endearment. Also sp. **tike.**
**Ty·ler, John** (tī'lẽr), 1790–1862; tenth president of the U.S. (1841–1845).
**tym·pa·ni** (tim'pə-ni), ***n.pl.*** [*sing.* -NO (-nō')], timpani.
**tym·pan·ic membrane** (tim-pan'ik), the eardrum.
**tym·pa·nist** (tim'pə-nist), ***n.*** a member of an orchestra who plays drums and other percussion instruments.
**tym·pa·num** (tim'pə-nəm), ***n.*** [*pl.* -NUMS, -NA (-nə)], [L., a drum < Gr. *tympanon*], 1. the middle ear, a cavity separated from the external ear by the eardrum. 2. the eardrum. 3. a drum or drumlike instrument. 4. in *architecture*, *a*) the recessed space, usually triangular, enclosed by the slanting cornices of a pediment. *b*) the space enclosed by an arch and the top of the door or window below it. —**tym·pan'ic** (-pan'ik), ***adj.***
**Tyn·dale, William** (tin'd'l), 1492?–1536; English theologian; translator of the Bible; executed: also sp. **Tindal, Tindale.**
**typ·al** (tīp''l), ***adj.*** of or serving as a type.
**type** (tīp), ***n.*** [Fr. < L. < Gr. *typos*, a mark < *typtein*, to strike], 1. a person, thing, or event that represents another, especially another that is to come; symbol; token; sign. 2. the characteristic form, plan, style, etc. of a particular class or group. 3. a class, group, etc. having characteristics in common: as, a new *type* of airplane (colloquially, *of* is often omitted). 4. a person, animal, or thing that is representative or characteristic of a class or group. 5. *a*) a perfect example; model; pattern. *b*) in *biology*, a genus (**type genus**) or species (**type species**) that best exemplifies a larger group and often gives its name to it. 6. *a*) a rectangular piece of metal or, sometimes, wood with

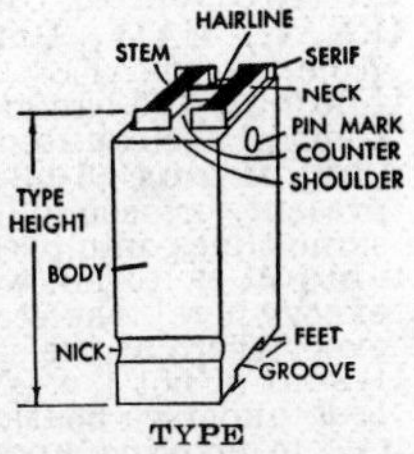

TYPE

a raised letter, figure, etc. in reverse on its upper end, used in printing. *b*) such pieces collectively. 7. a printed character or characters. *v.t.* [TYPED, TYPING], 1. to prefigure. 2. to typify; represent. 3. to classify according to type: as, to *type* a blood sample. 4. to typewrite. *v.i.* to typewrite.

**-type,** [< Gr. *typos;* see TYPE], a combining form meaning: 1. *type, example,* as in *prototype.* 2. *stamp, print, printing type,* etc., as in *monotype.*

**type metal,** an alloy of tin, lead, and antimony used for making type, etc.

**type·set·ter** (tīp'set'ẽr), *n.* 1. a person who sets type; compositor. 2. a machine for setting type. **—type'set'ting,** *n. & adj.*

**type·write** (tīp'rīt'), *v.t. & v.i.* [-WROTE, -WRITTEN, -WRITING], to write with a typewriter: now usually shortened to *type.* **—type'writ'ing,** *n.* **—type'-writ'ten** (-rit''n), *adj.*

**type·writ·er** (tīp'rīt'ẽr), *n.* 1. a writing machine with a keyboard for reproducing letters, figures, etc. that resemble printed ones. 2. a typist.

**ty·phoid** (tī'foid), *adj.* [< Gr. *typhos,* a fever + *-oid*], 1. originally, of or like typhus. 2. designating or of an infectious disease (**typhoid fever**) caused by a bacillus (**typhoid bacillus**) and acquired by drinking infected milk, water, etc.: it is characterized by fever, intestinal disorders, etc. *n.* typhoid fever. **—ty·phoi'dal,** *adj.*

**ty·phoon** (tī-fo͞on'), *n.* [< Chin. dial. *tai-fung,* lit., great wind], a violent cyclonic storm, especially one in the China Sea and adjacent regions; hurricane. **—ty·phon'ic** (-fon'ik), *adj.*

**ty·phus** (tī'fəs), *n.* [< Gr. *typhos,* a fever], an acute infectious disease caused by a rickettsia transmitted to man by fleas, lice, etc. and characterized by fever, red spots on the skin, etc.: also **typhus fever.** **—ty'phous** (-fəs), *adj.*

**typ·i·cal** (tip'i-k'l), *adj.* 1. serving as a type; symbolic. 2. having the distinguishing characteristics, qualities, etc. of a class, group, etc.; representative. 3. belonging to a type; characteristic. Also **typ'ic.** **—typ'i·cal·ly,** *adv.* **—typ'i·cal·ness,** *n.*

**typ·i·fy** (tip'ə-fī'), *v.t.* [-FIED, -FYING], [< L. *typus,* a type; + *-fy*], 1. to be a type or emblem of; symbolize. 2. to have or show the distinctive characteristics of; exemplify. **—typ'i·fi·ca'tion** (-fi-kā'shən), *n.* **—typ'i·fi'er,** *n.*

**typ·ist** (tīp'ist), *n.* a person who operates a typewriter; esp., one whose work is typewriting.

**ty·po** (tī'pō), *n.* [*pl.* -POS], [Colloq.], a typographical error.

**ty·po-,** [< Gr. *typos;* see TYPE], a combining form meaning *type.*

**ty·pog·ra·pher** (tī-pog'rə-fẽr), *n.* a person skilled in typography; printer.

**ty·po·graph·i·cal** (tī'pə-graf'i-k'l), *adj.* 1. of typography. 2. in print; printed. Also **ty'po·graph'ic.** **—ty'po·graph'i·cal·ly,** *adv.*

**ty·pog·ra·phy** (tī-pog'rə-fi), *n.* [< Fr. < ML.; see TYPO- & -GRAPHY], 1. the art of printing with type. 2. the setting and arranging of types and printing from them. 3. the arrangement, style, or appearance of matter printed from type.

**Tyr** (têr), *n.* in *Norse mythology,* the god of war and son of Odin.

**ty·ran·ni·cal** (ti-ran'i-k'l, tī-), *adj.* 1. of or suited to a tyrant; arbitrary; despotic. 2. harsh, cruel, unjust, etc. Also **ty·ran'nic.** **—ty·ran'ni·cal·ly,** *adv.* **—ty·ran'ni·cal·ness,** *n.*

**ty·ran·ni·cide** (ti-ran'ə-sīd', tī-), *n.* 1. the act of killing a tyrant. 2. one who kills a tyrant.

**tyr·an·nize** (tir'ə-nīz'), *v.i.* [-NIZED, -NIZING], 1. to govern as a tyrant. 2. to rule with cruelty, injustice, etc. 3. to use power or authority harshly. *v.t.* to treat tyrannically. **—tyr'an·niz'er,** *n.* **—tyr'-an·niz'ing·ly,** *adv.*

**tyr·an·nous** (tir'ə-nəs), *adj.* 1. tyrannical; despotic. 2. involving tyranny; cruel, oppressive, unjust, severe, etc. **—tyr'an·nous·ly,** *adv.*

**tyr·an·ny** (tir'ə-ni), *n.* [*pl.* -NIES], 1. the office, authority, government, etc. of a tyrant. 2. oppressive and unjust government; despotism. 3. very cruel and unjust use of power or authority. 4. harshness; severity. 5. a tyrannical act.

**ty·rant** (tī'rənt), *n.* [< OFr. < L. < Gr. *tyrannos,* lord], 1. an absolute ruler. 2. a cruel, oppressive ruler; despot. 3. any person who exercises his authority in an oppressive manner.

**Tyre** (tīr), *n.* an important seaport in ancient Phoenicia. **—Tyr·i·an** (tir'i-ən), *adj. & n.*

**tyre** (tīr), *n.* a tire: Brit. spelling.

**Tyrian purple** (or **dye**), 1. a purple or crimson dye used by the ancient Romans and Greeks: it was made from certain mollusks. 2. bluish red.

**ty·ro** (tī'rō), *n.* [*pl.* -ROS], [ML. < L. *tiro,* recruit], a beginner in learning something; novice: also sp. **tiro.**

**Tyr·ol** (tir'ol, tē-rōl'), *n.* a region in the Alps of W Austria and N Italy: also sp. **Tirol.**

**Tyr·o·lese** (tir'ə-lēz'), *adj.* of the Tyrol or its people. *n.* [*pl.* -LESE], a native of the Tyrol. Also **Ty·ro·le·an** (ti-rō'li-ən).

**tzar** (tsär), *n.* a czar. **—tzar'dom,** *n.* **—tzar'ism,** *n.* **—tzar'ist,** *adj. & n.*

**tzar·e·vitch** (tsär'ə-vich), *n.* a czarevitch.

**tza·rev·na** (tsä-rev'nə), *n.* a czarevna.

**tza·ri·na** (tsä-rē'nə), *n.* a czarina.

**tza·rit·za** (tsä-rēt'sä), *n.* a czarina.

**tzet·ze** (tset'si), *n.* a tsetse.

**‡tzi·gane** (tsē'gàn'), *n.* [Fr. < Hung.], a gypsy.

# U

**U, u** (ū), *n.* [*pl.* U's, u's, Us, us], 1. the twenty-first letter of the English alphabet. 2. a sound of U or u. *adj.* twenty-first in a sequence or group.

**U** (ū), *n.* 1. an object shaped like U. 2. in *chemistry, the symbol for* uranium. *adj.* shaped like U.

**U.,** 1. Union. 2. University.

**U.A.W., UAW,** United Automobile Workers of America: an AFL-CIO labor union.

**U·ban·gi** (o͞o-bäŋ'gi), *n.* a river between the Central African Republic and the Congo (sense 2).

**u·biq·ui·tous** (ū-bik'wə-təs), *adj.* [see UBIQUITY], present, or seemingly present, everywhere at the same time; omnipresent. **—u·biq'ui·tous·ly,** *adv.*

**u·biq·ui·ty** (ū-bik'wə-ti), *n.* [< Fr. < L. *ubique,* everywhere], the state, fact, or capacity of being everywhere at the same time; omnipresence.

**U-boat** (ū'bōt'), *n.* [< G. *U-boot,* abbrev. of *Unterseeboot,* undersea boat], a German submarine.

**u.c.,** in *printing,* upper case.

**ud·der** (ud'ẽr), *n.* [AS. *udr*], a mammary gland, especially one with two or more teats, as in cows.

**U.E.W., UEW,** United Electrical, Radio, and Machine Workers of America: a labor union.

**UFO,** unidentified flying object.

**U·gan·da** (ū-gan'də, o͞o-gän'dä), *n.* a country in east central Africa, in the British Commonwealth of Nations: area, 93,981 sq. mi.; pop., 7,740,000; capital, Kampala.

**ugh** (ookh, uH, oo, ug, *etc.*), *interj.* [echoic], an exclamation of annoyance, disgust, horror, etc.

**ug·li·fy** (ug'lə-fī'), *v.t.* [-FIED, -FYING], to make ugly. **—ug'li·fi·ca'tion** (-fi-kā'shən), *n.*

**ug·ly** (ug'li), *adj.* [-LIER, -LIEST], [< ON. *uggligr,* fearful < *uggr,* fear], 1. very unpleasant to the sight; unsightly. 2. bad; vile; repulsive; offensive. 3. ominous; dangerous. 4. [Colloq.], cross; quarrelsome. **—ug'li·ly,** *adv.* **—ug'li·ness,** *n.*

**ugly duckling,** [from a story by H. C. Andersen], one whose lack of beauty, charm, promise, etc. in youth turns out to be only temporary.

**U·gri·an** (o͞o'gri-ən, ū'-), *adj.* 1. designating or of a group of Finno-Ugric peoples of W Siberia and Hungary. 2. Ugric. *n.* 1. a member of any of the Ugrian peoples. 2. Ugric.

**U·gric** (o͞o'grik, ū'-), *adj.* 1. designating or of a branch of the Finno-Ugric family of languages including Hungarian (Magyar). 2. Ugrian. *n.* the Ugric languages.

**UHF,** ultrahigh frequency.

**uh·lan, u·lan** (o͞o'län, ū'lən, o͞o-län'), *n.* [G. < Pol. < Turk. *oghlān,* a youth], formerly, in Germany and Poland, a mounted soldier armed with a lance.

**‡uit·land·er** (üt'län'dẽr; Eng. īt'lan'-), *n.* [S.Afr.D. < *uit,* out + *land,* land], [sometimes U-], in South Africa, a foreigner; outlander.

**U.K.,** United Kingdom.

**u·kase** (ū'kās, ū-kāz'), *n.* [Russ. *ukaz*, edict], 1. in Czarist Russia, an imperial order or decree. 2. any official decree or proclamation.
**U·kraine** (ū'krān, ū-krān', ū-krīn'), *n.* the Ukrainian S.S.R.: abbrev. **Ukr.**
**U·krain·i·an** (ū-krā'ni-ən, -krī'-), *adj.* of the Ukraine, its people, their language, etc. *n.* 1. a native or inhabitant of the Ukraine. 2. the East Slavic language of the Ukrainians.
**Ukrainian Soviet Socialist Republic,** a republic of the U.S.S.R., in the SW European part: area, 202,540 sq. mi.; pop., 42,273,000; capital, Kiev.
**u·ku·le·le** (ū'kə-lā'li), *n.* [Haw., lit., flea], a small, four-stringed musical instrument of the guitar family: also [Colloq.], **uke** (ūk).
**ul·cer** (ul'sẽr), *n.* [< L. *ulcus*], 1. an open sore on the skin or some mucous membrane, discharging pus. 2. any corrupting condition or influence.
**ul·cer·ate** (ul'sə-rāt'), *v.t. & v.i.* [-ATED, -ATING], [< L. pp. of *ulcerare*], to make or become ulcerous. **—ul'cer·a'tion,** *n.* **—ul'cer·a'tive,** *adj.*
**ul·cer·ous** (ul'sẽr-əs), *adj.* 1. having an ulcer or ulcers. 2. of an ulcer or ulcers. **—ul'cer·ous·ly,** *adv.* **—ul'cer·ous·ness,** *n.*
**-ule** (ūl), [< Fr. < L. *-ulus, -ula, -ulum*], a suffix used to form diminutives, as in *sporule.*
**-u·lent** (yoo-lənt), [< Fr. < L. *-ulentus*], a suffix meaning *full of, abounding in,* as in *fraudulent.*
**ul·na** (ul'nə), *n.* [*pl.* -NAE (-nē), -NAS], [L., the elbow], the larger of the two bones of the forearm, on the side opposite the thumb. **—ul'nar** (-nẽr), *adj.*
**-u·lose** (yoo-lōs'), [< L. *-ulosus*], a suffix meaning *characterized by, marked by,* as in *granulose.*
**-u·lous** (yoo-ləs), [< L. *-ulosus*], a suffix meaning *tending to, characterized by,* as in *populous.*
**Ul·ster** (ul'stẽr), *n.* 1. a former province in N Ireland, now divided between Northern Ireland and the Republic of Ireland. 2. a N province of the Republic of Ireland. 3. [Colloq.], Northern Ireland. 4. [u-], [orig. made in *Ulster*], a long, loose, heavy overcoat.
**ult.,** 1. ultimate. 2. ultimately. 3. ultimo.
**ul·te·ri·or** (ul-tẽr'i-ẽr), *adj.* [L., compar. of *ulter*, beyond], 1. lying beyond or on the farther side. 2. later, subsequent, or future. 3. beyond what is expressed or implied; undisclosed: as, an *ulterior* motive. **—ul·te'ri·or·ly,** *adv.*
**ul·ti·ma** (ul'tə-mə), *n.* [L., fem. of *ultimus*, last], the last syllable of a word.
**ul·ti·mate** (ul'tə-mit), *adj.* [< LL. pp. of *ultimare*, to come to an end < L. *ultimus*, last], 1. beyond which it is impossible to go; farthest. 2. final; concluding. 3. beyond further analysis, etc.; fundamental; primary. 4. greatest possible; maximum. *n.* something ultimate; final point or result. **—ul'ti·mate·ly,** *adv.* **—ul'ti·mate·ness,** *n.*
**ul·ti·ma Thu·le** (ul'tə-mə thōō'li, thū'-), [L.], 1. in *ancient geography*, the northernmost region of the world. 2. any far-off, unknown region.
**ul·ti·ma·tum** (ul'tə-mā'təm), *n.* [*pl.* -TUMS, -TA (-tə)], [< LL., neut. pp.; see ULTIMATE], a final offer or proposal; esp., the final statement of terms by either of the parties in diplomatic negotiations.
**ul·ti·mo** (ul'tə-mō'), *adv.* [L. *ultimo* (*mense*), (in the) last (month)], in the last (month); in the preceding month.
**ul·tra** (ul'trə), *adj.* [L., beyond], going beyond the usual limit; extreme, especially in opinions. *n.* one having extreme opinions, etc.; extremist.
**ul·tra-,** [L.], a prefix meaning: 1. *beyond*, as in *ultraviolet.* 2. (something) *excessive*, as in *ultramodern.* 3. *beyond the range of*, as in *ultramicroscopic.*
**ul·tra·con·serv·a·tive** (ul'trə-kən-sũr'və-tiv), *adj.* conservative to an extreme degree. **—ul'tra·con·serv'a·tive·ly,** *adv.* **—ul'tra·con·serv'a·tism,** *n.*
**ul·tra·high frequency** (ul'trə-hī'), in *radio & television*, any frequency of 300 megacycles or higher.
**ul·tra·ism** (ul'trə-iz'm), *n.* 1. the opinions, principles, etc. of those who are extreme. 2. an instance of this. **—ul'tra·ist,** *n. & adj.*
**ul·tra·ma·rine** (ul'trə-mə-rēn'), *adj.* [< ML.; see ULTRA- & MARINE], 1. beyond the sea. 2. deep-blue. *n.* 1. a blue pigment made from powdered lapis lazuli. 2. any similar pigment prepared from other substances. 3. deep blue.
**ul·tra·mi·crom·e·ter** (ul'trə-mī-krom'ə-tẽr), *n.* a very sensitive micrometer.
**ul·tra·mi·cro·scope** (ul'trə-mī'krə-skōp'), *n.* an instrument for making visible, by dispersed light, objects too small to be seen with an ordinary microscope. **—ul'tra·mi'cro·scop'ic** (-skop'ik), **ul'tra·mi'cro·scop'i·cal,** *adj.* **—ul'tra·mi·cros'co·py** (-kros'kə-pi), *n.*
**ul·tra·mod·ern** (ul'trə-mod'ẽrn), *adj.* modern to an extreme degree.
**ul·tra·na·tion·al·ism** (ul'trə-nash'ən-'l-iz'm), *n.* nationalism that is excessive or extreme. **—ul'tra·na'tion·al·ist, ul'tra·na'tion·al·is'tic,** *adj.*
**ul·tra·son·ic** (ul'trə-son'ik), *adj.* supersonic.
**ul·tra·vi·o·let** (ul'trə-vī'ə-lit), *adj.* lying just beyond the violet end of the visible spectrum: said of certain light rays of extremely short wave length: cf. **infrared.**
**ul·u·late** (ūl'yoo-lāt', ul'-), *v.i.* [-LATED, -LATING], [< L. pp. of *ululare*, to howl; echoic], 1. to howl or hoot. 2. to wail or lament loudly. **—ul'u·lant** (-lənt), *adj.* **—ul'u·la'tion,** *n.*
**U·lys·ses** (yoo-lis'ēz), *n.* [L.], Odysseus.
**um·bel** (um'b'l), *n.* [< L. *umbella;* see UMBRELLA], a cluster of flowers with stalks of nearly equal length which spring from about the same point. **—um'bel·late** (-it, -āt'), **um'bel·lat'ed, um'bel·lar** (-ẽr), *adj.*

UMBEL (of wild carrot)

**um·ber** (um'bẽr), *n.* [< Fr. < It. (*terra d'*)*ombra*, lit., (earth of) shade; prob. < L. *umbra*, a shade], 1. a kind of earth containing oxides of manganese and iron, used as a pigment: *raw umber* is yellowish-brown; *burnt*, or *calcined, umber* is reddish-brown. 2. a yellowish-brown or reddish-brown color. *adj.* of the color of raw umber or burnt umber. *v.t.* to color with or as with umber.
**um·bil·i·cal** (um-bil'i-k'l), *adj.* 1. of or like an umbilicus. 2. designating or of a cordlike structure (**umbilical cord**) connecting a fetus with the placenta of the mother and serving to convey food to, and remove waste from, the fetus.
**um·bil·i·cus** (um-bil'i-kəs, um'bi-lī'-), *n.* [*pl.* -CI (-sī', -sī)], [L.], 1. the navel. 2. a navellike depression, as the hilum of a seed.
**um·bra** (um'brə), *n.* [*pl.* -BRAE (-brē)], [L., a shade], 1. shade; shadow. 2. the dark cone of shadow projecting from a planet or satellite on the side opposite the sun.
**um·brage** (um'brij), *n.* [OFr. < L. < *umbra*, a shade], 1. [Obs.], shade. 2. foliage, considered as shade-giving. 3. offense; resentment and displeasure. **—um·bra'geous** (-brā'jəs), *adj.*
**um·brel·la** (um-brel'ə), *n.* [< It. < LL. < L. *umbella*, dim. of *umbra*, shade], 1. a shade or screen, usually of cloth on a folding radial frame, carried for protection against the rain or sun. 2. something like or suggestive of this, as a force of aircraft sent up to protect ground or naval forces.
**umbrella tree,** a variety of magnolia with clusters of long leaves at the ends of the branches, bad-smelling white flowers, and reddish fruit.
**u·mi·ak, u·mi·ack** (ōō'mi-ak'), *n.* [Esk.], a large open boat made of skins stretched on a wooden frame, used by Eskimos: also sp. **oomiac, oomiak.**
**um·laut** (oom'lout), *n.* [G. < *um*, about + *laut*, a sound], in *linguistics*, 1. a change in sound of a vowel, caused by its assimilation to another vowel or semivowel originally in the next syllable but now generally lost. 2. a vowel resulting from such assimilation. 3. the diacritical mark (¨) placed over such a vowel, especially in German: cf. **dieresis.** *v.t.* to sound or write with an umlaut.
**um·pire** (um'pīr), *n.* [loss of initial *n* through faulty separation of *a numpire* (ult. < OFr. *non*, not + *per*, even)], a person chosen to render a decision in a dispute; arbiter; esp., an official who administers the rules in certain sports, as baseball. *v.t. & v.i.* [-PIRED, -PIRING], to act as umpire (in or of). **—um'pir·age,** *n.*
**ump·steen** (ump'stēn'), *adj.* [Slang], a great number of; very many: also **ump'teen'.** (-tēn').
**UMT,** Universal Military Training.
**UMW, U.M.W.,** United Mine Workers of America: a labor union.
**un-,** either of two prefixes, meaning: 1. [AS. *un-*], *not, lack of, the opposite of*, as in *unhappy, untruth.* 2. [AS. *un-, on-, and-*], *back*: added to verbs to indicate a reversal of action, as in *unfasten*, and to nouns to indicate a removal or release from the state expressed by the noun, as in *unbosom;* sometimes merely intensive, as in *unloosen.* The list at

the bottom of the following pages includes the more common compounds formed with *un-* (either prefix) that do not have special meanings.
**UN, U.N.,** United Nations.
**un·ac·count·a·ble** (un′ə-koun′tə-b'l), *adj.* 1. that cannot be explained or accounted for; strange. 2. not accountable; not responsible. —**un′ac·count′a·ble·ness,** *n.* —**un′ac·count′a·bly,** *adv.*
**un·ac·cus·tomed** (un′ə-kus′təmd), *adj.* 1. not accustomed (*to*). 2. uncommon; strange.
**un·ad·vised** (un′əd-vīzd′), *adj.* 1. without counsel or advice. 2. indiscreet; thoughtlessly hasty. —**un′ad·vis′ed·ly,** *adv.* —**un′ad·vis′ed·ness,** *n.*
**un·af·fect·ed** (un′ə-fek′tid), *adj.* 1. not affected, or influenced. 2. without affectation; sincere. —**un′af·fect′ed·ly,** *adv.* —**un′af·fect′ed·ness,** *n.*
**un-A·mer·i·can** (un′ə-mer′ə-kən), *adj.* not American; regarded as not characteristically or properly American; esp., regarded as opposed or dangerous to the U.S., its institutions, etc.
**u·nan·i·mous** (yoo-nan′ə-məs), *adj.* [< L. < *unus*, one + *animus*, the mind], 1. agreeing completely; united in opinion. 2. showing, or based on, complete agreement. —**u·na·nim·i·ty** (ū′nə-nim′ə-ti), **u·nan′i·mous·ness,** *n.* —**u·nan′i·mous·ly,** *adv.*
**un·ap·proach·a·ble** (un′ə-prōch′ə-b'l), *adj.* 1. not to be approached; inaccessible; aloof. 2. having no rival or equal; unmatched. —**un′ap·proach′a·ble·ness,** *n.* —**un′ap·proach′a·bly,** *adv.*
**un·arm** (un-ärm′), *v.t.* to disarm. —**un·armed′,** *adj.*
**un·as·sail·a·ble** (un′ə-sāl′ə-b'l), *adj.* not assailable; specif., *a*) that cannot be successfully attacked. *b*) that cannot be successfully denied. —**un′as·sail′a·ble·ness,** *n.* —**un′as·sail′a·bly,** *adv.*
**un·as·sum·ing** (un′ə-sōōm′iŋ, -sūm′-), *adj.* not assuming, pretending, or forward; modest. —**un′as·sum′ing·ly,** *adv.* —**un′as·sum′ing·ness,** *n.*
**un·at·tached** (un′ə-tacht′), *adj.* 1. not attached or fastened. 2. not connected with any group, institution, etc. 3. not engaged or married.
**un·a·vail·ing** (un′ə-vāl′iŋ), *adj.* not availing; futile; ineffectual. —**un′a·vail′ing·ly,** *adv.*
**un·a·void·a·ble** (un′ə-void′ə-b'l), *adj.* that cannot be avoided; inevitable. —**un′a·void′a·ble·ness,** *n.* —**un′a·void′a·bly,** *adv.*
**un·a·ware** (un′ə-wâr′), *adj.* 1. not aware or conscious. 2. unwary; heedless. *adv.* unawares.
**un·a·wares** (un′ə-wârz′), *adv.* 1. without knowing or being aware; unintentionally. 2. unexpectedly; by surprise: as, we took him *unawares*.
**un·bal·ance** (un-bal′əns), *v.t.* [-ANCED, -ANCING], 1. to disturb the balance or equilibrium of. 2. to disturb the functioning of; derange (the mind). *n.* the condition of being unbalanced.
**un·bal·anced** (un-bal′ənst), *adj.* 1. not in balance or equilibrium. 2. not equal as to debit and credit. 3. *a*) deranged; mentally ill; insane. *b*) not stable, steady, etc. in character or judgment.
**un·bar** (un-bär′), *v.t. & v.i.* [-BARRED, -BARRING], to unlock; unbolt; open.
**un·be·com·ing** (un′bi-kum′iŋ), *adj.* 1. not becoming; not appropriate. 2. not proper or decent. —**un′be·com′ing·ly,** *adv.* —**un′be·com′ing·ness,** *n.*
**un·be·known** (un′bi-nōn′), *adj.* not known.
**un·be·lief** (un′bə-lēf′), *n.* a withholding or lack of belief, especially in religion.
**un·be·liev·er** (un′bə-lēv′ēr), *n.* 1. one who does not believe; doubter. 2. one who does not accept the doctrines of a given religion.
**un·be·liev·ing** (un′bə-lēv′iŋ), *adj.* doubting; skeptical; incredulous. —**un′be·liev′ing·ly,** *adv.*
**un·bend** (un-bend′), *v.t. & v.i.* [-BENT or -BENDED, -BENDING], 1. to release or be released, as a bow, from tension. 2. to relax, as from mental strain or formality. 3. to make or become straight.
**un·bend·ing** (un-ben′diŋ), *adj.* 1. rigid; stiff; inflexible. 2. firm; unyielding; resolute. *n.* relaxation of restraint, severity, etc. —**un·bend′ing·ly,** *adv.* —**un·bend′ing·ness,** *n.*
**un·bid·den** (un-bid′'n), *adj.* 1. not commanded. 2. uninvited.
**un·bind** (un-bīnd′), *v.t.* [-BOUND, -BINDING], 1. to untie; unfasten. 2. to release from restraint.
**un·blessed, un·blest** (un-blest′), *adj.* 1. not hallowed. 2. not blessed. 3. accursed. 4. unhappy.
**un·blush·ing** (un-blush′iŋ), *adj.* 1. not blushing. 2. shameless. —**un·blush′ing·ly,** *adv.*
**un·bolt** (un-bōlt′), *v.t. & v.i.* to withdraw the bolt or bolts of (a door, etc.); unbar; open.
**un·bolt·ed** (un-bōl′tid), *adj.* not fastened with a bolt, as a door.
**un·bolt·ed** (un-bōl′tid), *adj.* not sifted.
**un·born** (un-bôrn′), *adj.* 1. not born. 2. not yet born; yet to come or be; future.
**un·bos·om** (un-booz′əm, -bōō′zəm), *v.t. & v.i.* to tell or reveal (feelings, secrets, etc.). —**unbosom oneself,** to tell or reveal one's feelings, etc.
**un·bowed** (un-boud′), *adj.* 1. not bowed or bent. 2. not yielding or giving in; unsubdued.
**un·brace** (un-brās′), *v.t.* [-BRACED, -BRACING], 1. to free from braces. 2. to relax or make slack.
**un·bri·dled** (un-brī′d'ld), *adj.* 1. having no bridle on, as a horse. 2. unrestrained; uncontrolled.
**un·bro·ken** (un-brō′k'n), *adj.* 1. whole; intact. 2. not tamed or subdued. 3. continuous; uninterrupted. —**un·bro′ken·ly,** *adv.* —**un·bro′ken·ness,** *n.*
**un·buck·le** (un-buk′'l), *v.t.* [-LED, -LING], to unfasten the buckle or buckles of.
**un·bur·den** (un-būr′d'n), *v.t.* 1. to free from a burden. 2. to relieve, as one's soul, mind, etc., by disclosing something hard to bear, as guilt. 3. to get rid of the burden of, as guilt, in this way.
**un·cage** (un-kāj′), *v.t.* [-CAGED, -CAGING], to free, as from a cage.
**un·called-for** (un-kôld′fôr′), *adj.* 1. not required. 2. unnecessary and out of place; impertinent.
**un·can·ny** (un-kan′i), *adj.* 1. mysterious in an eerie way; weird. 2. so good, acute, etc. as to seem preternatural: as, *uncanny* vision. —**un·can′ni·ly,** *adv.* —**un·can′ni·ness,** *n.*
**un·cap** (un-kap′), *v.t.* [-CAPPED, -CAPPING], 1. to remove the cap from the head of (a person). 2. to remove the cap from (a bottle, etc.). *v.i.* to remove one's cap from the head, as in respect.
**un·cer·e·mo·ni·ous** (un′ser-ə-mō′ni-əs), *adj.* 1. less ceremonious than is expected; informal. 2. curt; abrupt; lacking courtesy. —**un′cer·e·mo′ni·ous·ly,** *adv.* —**un′cer·e·mo′ni·ous·ness,** *n.*
**un·cer·tain** (un-sūr′t'n), *adj.* 1. not surely or certainly known; questionable. 2. not sure or certain in knowledge; doubtful. 3. vague; not definite. 4. liable to change; not dependable or reliable. 5. not steady or constant; varying. —**un·cer′tain·ly,** *adv.* —**un·cer′tain·ness,** *n.*

---

**unabashed**
**unabated**
**unabbreviated**
**unabetted**
**unable**
**unabridged**
**unabsolved**
**unacademic**
**unaccented**
**unacceptable**
**unacclimated**
**unaccommodating**
**unaccompanied**
**unaccomplished**
**unaccounted-for**
**unaccredited**
**unacknowledged**
**unacquainted**
**unadaptable**
**unaddressed**
**unadjustable**
**unadorned**
**unadulterated**
**unadvisable**
**unaffiliated**
**unafraid**
**unaided**
**unaimed**
**unallied**
**unallowable**
**unalloyed**
**unalterable**
**unaltered**
**unambiguous**
**unambitious**
**unamusing**
**unannounced**
**unanswerable**
**unanswered**
**unapparent**
**unappeasable**
**unappeased**
**unappetizing**
**unappreciated**
**unappreciative**
**unapproached**
**unapt**
**unarmored**
**unarrested**
**unartistic**
**unashamed**
**unasked**
**unaspiring**
**unassailed**
**unassigned**
**unassisted**
**unattainable**
**unattained**
**unattempted**
**unattended**
**unattested**
**unattired**
**unattractive**
**unauthentic**
**unauthenticated**
**unauthorized**
**unavailable**
**unavenged**
**unbacked**
**unbaked**
**unbandaged**
**unbaptized**
**unbearable**
**unbeaten**
**unbefitting**
**unbelievable**
**unbetrothed**
**unbiased**
**unbiassed**
**unblamable**
**unblamed**
**unbleached**
**unblemished**
**unboned**
**unbought**
**unbound**
**unbounded**
**unbraid**
**unbranched**
**unbranded**
**unbreakable**
**unbreeched**
**unbridgeable**
**unbridged**
**unbrotherly**
**unbruised**
**unbrushed**
**unbuilt**
**unburied**
**unburned**
**unburnt**
**unbusinesslike**
**unbutton**
**uncanceled**
**uncancelled**
**uncared-for**
**uncarpeted**
**uncaught**
**unceasing**
**uncelebrated**
**uncensored**
**uncensured**

**un·cer·tain·ty** (un-sũr′t'n-ti), *n.* 1. lack of certainty; doubt. 2. [*pl.* -TIES], something uncertain.
**un·char·i·ta·ble** (un-char′ə-tə-b'l), *adj.* harsh or severe, as in opinion; unforgiving; ungenerous. —**un·char′i·ta·ble·ness,** *n.* —**un·char′i·ta·bly,** *adv.*
**un·chris·tian** (un-kris′chən), *adj.* 1. not Christian; non-Christian. 2. unworthy of a Christian or any decent, civilized person. —**un·chris′tian·like′,** *adj.* —**un·chris′tian·ly,** *adj. & adv.*
**un·church** (un-chũrch′), *v.t.* 1. to deprive of membership in a given church. 2. to deprive (a congregation) of its rights as a church.
**un·ci·al** (un′shi-əl, -shəl), *adj.* [< L. < *uncia,* an inch], designating or of a kind of writing with large, rounded letters, used in manuscripts between 300 and 900 A.D. *n.* 1. an uncial letter. 2. uncial script. —**un′ci·al·ly,** *adv.*
**un·cir·cum·cised** (un-sũr′kəm-sīzd′), *adj.* 1. not circumcised. 2. Gentile. 3. heathen.
**un·civ·il** (un-siv′'l), *adj.* 1. uncivilized; barbarous. 2. not civil or courteous; ill-mannered. —**un·civ′il·ly,** *adv.* —**un·civ′il·ness,** *n.*
**un·civ·i·lized** (un-siv′'l-īzd′), *adj.* not civilized; barbarous; savage.
**un·clad** (un-klad′), *adj.* wearing no clothes; naked.
**un·clasp** (un-klasp′, -kläsp′), *v.t.* 1. to loosen the clasp of. 2. to release from a clasp. *v.i.* 1. to become unfastened; open. 2. to relax the clasp.
**un·cle** (uŋ′k'l), *n.* [OFr. < L. *avunculus,* one's mother's brother < *avus,* grandfather], 1. the brother of one's father or mother. 2. the husband of one's aunt. 3. [Colloq.], elderly man: term of address.
**un·clean** (un-klēn′), *adj.* 1. dirty; filthy; foul. 2. ceremonially impure. 3. morally impure; unchaste; obscene. —**un·clean′ly,** *adv.* —**un·clean′ness,** *n.*
**un·clean·ly** (un-klen′li), *adj.* unclean; dirty. —**un·clean′li·ness,** *n.*
**Uncle Sam,** [< abbrev. U.S.], [Colloq.], the United States (government or people), personified as a tall, spare man with chin whiskers.
**un·cloak** (un-klōk′), *v.t. & v.i.* 1. to remove a cloak, etc. (from). 2. to reveal; expose.
**un·close** (un-klōz′), *v.t. & v.i.* [-CLOSED, -CLOSING], 1. to open. 2. to disclose or reveal.
**un·clothe** (un-klōth′), *v.t.* [-CLOTHED or -CLAD, -CLOTHING], to strip of or as of clothes; undress, uncover, or divest.
**un·coil** (un-koil′), *v.t. & v.i.* to unwind.
**un·com·fort·a·ble** (un-kum′fẽr-tə-b'l, -kumf′tẽr-b'l), *adj.* 1. feeling discomfort. 2. causing discomfort. 3. ill at ease. —**un·com′fort·a·ble·ness,** *n.* —**un·com′fort·a·bly,** *adv.*
**un·com·mon** (un-kom′ən), *adj.* 1. rare; not usual. 2. strange; remarkable; extraordinary. —**un·com′mon·ly,** *adv.* —**un·com′mon·ness,** *n.*
**un·com·mu·ni·ca·tive** (un′kə-mū′nə-kā′tiv, -kə-tiv), *adj.* not communicative; reserved; silent; taciturn. —**un′com·mu′ni·ca′tive·ly,** *adv.* —**un′com·mu′ni·ca′tive·ness,** *n.*
**un·com·pro·mis·ing** (un-kom′prə-mīz′iŋ), *adj.* not yielding; firm; inflexible. —**un·com′pro·mis′ing·ly,** *adv.*
**un·con·cern** (un′kən-sũrn′), *n.* 1. lack of interest; indifference. 2. lack of concern; freedom from solicitude or anxiety.
**un·con·cerned** (un′kən-sũrnd′), *adj.* not solicitous or anxious; indifferent. —**un′con·cern′ed·ly** (-sũr′nid-li), *adv.* —**un′con·cern′ed·ness,** *n.*
**un·con·di·tion·al** (un′kən-dish′ən-'l), *adj.* without conditions or reservations; absolute. —**un′con·di′tion·al·ly,** *adv.*
**un·con·di·tioned** (un′kən-dish′ənd), *adj.* 1. unconditional. 2. in *psychology,* natural; not learned: as, an *unconditioned* reflex.
**un·con·scion·a·ble** (un-kon′shən-ə-b'l), *adj.* 1. not guided or restrained by conscience; unscrupulous. 2. unreasonable, excessive, etc. —**un·con′scion·a·ble·ness,** *n.* —**un·con′scion·a·bly,** *adv.*
**un·con·scious** (un-kon′shəs), *adj.* 1. deprived of consciousness. 2. not aware (*of*). 3. not realized or intended by the person himself: as, an *unconscious* act. —**the unconscious,** in *psychoanalysis,* the sum of all thoughts, impulses, desires, etc. of which the individual is not conscious but which influence his behavior. —**un·con′scious·ly,** *adv.* —**un·con′scious·ness,** *n.*
**un·con·sti·tu·tion·al** (un′kon-stə-tōō′shən-'l, -tū′-), *adj.* not in accordance with the principles of the constitution. —**un′con·sti·tu′tion·al′i·ty** (-al′ə-ti), *n.* —**un′con·sti·tu′tion·al·ly,** *adv.*
**un·con·ven·tion·al** (un′kən-ven′shən-'l), *adj.* not conforming to the usual rules, customs, or patterns. —**un′con·ven′tion·al′i·ty** (-al′ə-ti), [*pl.* -TIES], *n.* —**un′con·ven′tion·al·ly,** *adv.*
**un·cork** (un-kôrk′), *v.t.* to pull the cork out of.
**un·count·ed** (un-koun′tid), *adj.* 1. not counted. 2. inconceivably numerous; innumerable.
**un·cou·ple** (un-kup′'l), *v.t.* [-PLED, -PLING], to disconnect; unfasten (something coupled).
**un·couth** (un-kōōth′), *adj.* [AS. *uncuth,* unknown < *un-,* not + *cuth,* pp. of *cunnan,* to know], 1. awkward; clumsy; ungainly. 2. uncultured; crude; boorish. —**un·couth′ly,** *adv.* —**un·couth′ness,** *n.*
**un·cov·er** (un-kuv′ẽr), *v.t.* 1. to make known; disclose. 2. to lay bare by removing a covering. 3. to remove the cover or protection from. 4. to remove the hat, cap, etc. from (the head), as in respect. *v.i.* to bare the head, as in respect.
**unc·tion** (uŋk′shən), *n.* [< L. *unctio* < *ungere,* to anoint], 1. the act of anointing, as in medical treatment or a religious ceremony. 2. the oil, ointment, etc. used for this. 3. anything that soothes or comforts. 4. utterance that is fervent and earnest; esp., utterance characterized by a mere pretense or affectation of fervor, etc.
**unc·tu·ous** (uŋk′chōō-əs), *adj.* [< ML. < L. *unctum,* ointment < *ungere,* to anoint], 1. having the nature or quality of an ointment; oily or greasy. 2. like oil, soap, or grease to the touch. 3. characterized by a smug, smooth pretense of fervor or earnestness; too suave, bland, or oily. —**unc′tu·os′i·ty** (-os′ə-ti), **unc′tu·ous·ness,** *n.* —**unc′tu·ous·ly,** *adv.*
**un·cut** (un-kut′), *adj.* not cut; specif., *a*) having untrimmed margins: said of the pages of a book. *b*) not ground to shape: said of a gem.

**uncertified**
**unchain**
**unchallenged**
**unchangeable**
**unchanged**
**unchanging**
**unchaperoned**
**uncharged**
**uncharted**
**unchartered**
**unchaste**
**unchastened**
**unchastised**
**unchecked**
**uncherished**
**unchewed**
**unchilled**
**unchivalrous**
**unchosen**
**unchristened**
**unclaimed**
**unclarified**
**unclassed**
**unclassifiable**
**unclassified**
**uncleaned**
**uncleared**
**unclipped**
**unclog**
**unclothed**
**unclouded**
**uncloyed**
**uncoated**
**uncocked**
**uncoerced**
**uncollectable**
**uncollected**
**uncollectible**
**uncolonized**
**uncolored**
**uncombed**
**uncombinable**
**uncombined**
**uncomely**
**uncomforted**
**uncommissioned**
**uncommitted**
**uncompanionable**
**uncomplaining**
**uncompleted**
**uncomplicated**
**uncomplimentary**
**uncomplying**
**uncompounded**
**uncomprehending**
**uncompressed**
**uncomputed**
**unconcealed**
**unconceded**
**unconceited**
**unconcluded**
**uncondemned**
**uncondensed**
**unconfined**
**unconfirmed**
**unconfused**
**uncongenial**
**unconnected**
**unconquerable**
**unconquered**
**unconscientious**
**unconsecrated**
**unconsidered**
**unconsoled**
**unconsolidated**
**unconstrained**
**unconstricted**
**unconsumed**
**uncontaminated**
**uncontemplated**
**uncontested**
**uncontradictable**
**uncontradicted**
**uncontrollable**
**uncontrolled**
**unconverted**
**unconvinced**
**unconvincing**
**uncooked**
**un-co-operative**
**un-co-ordinated**
**uncorked**
**uncorrected**
**uncorroborated**
**uncorrupted**
**uncountable**
**uncourteous**
**uncredited**
**uncritical**
**uncross**
**uncrowded**
**uncrowned**
**uncrystallized**
**uncultivated**
**uncultured**
**uncurbed**
**uncured**
**uncurl**

**un·daunt·ed** (un-dôn′tid, -dän′-), *adj.* not daunted; not hesitating because of fear or discouragement. —**un·daunt′ed·ly,** *adv.* —**un·daunt′ed·ness,** *n.*

**un·de·ceive** (un′di-sēv′), *v.t.* [-CEIVED, -CEIVING], to free from deception, mistake, error, etc.

**un·de·cid·ed** (un′di-sīd′id), *adj.* 1. that is not decided. 2. not having come to a decision. —**un′de·cid′ed·ly,** *adv.* —**un′de·cid′ed·ness,** *n.*

**un·de·ni·a·ble** (un′di-nī′ə-b'l), *adj.* 1. that cannot be denied. 2. unquestionably good or excellent. —**un′de·ni′a·ble·ness,** *n.* —**un′de·ni′a·bly,** *adv.*

**un·der** (un′dẽr), *prep.* [AS.], 1. in, at, or to a position down from; below. 2. covered or concealed by: as, he has a gun *under* his coat. 3. beneath the surface of: as, *under* the sod. 4. *a*) lower in authority, position, etc. than. *b*) lower in value, amount, etc. than; less than. *c*) lower than the required degree of: as, *under* age. 5. below and to the other side of: as, we drove *under* the bridge. 6. subject to the control, government, direction, influence, etc. of. 7. bound by: as, *under* oath. 8. subjected to; undergoing: as, *under* repair. 9. with the character, disguise, etc. of: as, he goes *under* an alias. 10. in (the designated category): as, whales are classified *under* mammals. 11. in the time of: as, France *under* Louis XV. 12. being the subject of: as, the question *under* discussion. 13. because of: as, *under* the circumstances. 14. with the authorization of: as, *under* her signature. *adv.* 1. in or to a lower position; beneath. 2. in or to an inferior or subordinate state. 3. so as to be covered, concealed, etc. 4. less than the required amount, etc. *adj.* lower in position, authority, rank, amount, degree, etc. —**go under,** to fail, as in business.

**un·der-,** a prefix meaning: 1. *in, on, to,* or *from a lower place* or *side; beneath* or *below,* as in *undershirt.* 2. *in an inferior* or *subordinate position* or *rank,* as in *undergraduate.* 3. *to a degree* or *extent below standard,* as in *underdevelop.*

**un·der·a·chieve** (un′dẽr-ə-chēv′), *v.i.* [-CHIEVED, -CHIEVING], to fail to do as well in school as might be expected from intelligence tests.

**un·der·act** (un′dẽr-akt′), *v.t. & v.i.* to act (a theatrical role) with too great restraint; underplay.

**un·der·age** (un′dẽr-āj′), *adj.* 1. not of full or mature age. 2. below the usual or required age.

**un·der·arm** (un′dẽr-ärm′), *adj.* 1. under the arm; in the armpit. 2. underhand (sense 1). *adv.* with an underarm, or underhand, delivery or motion.

**un·der·bid** (un′dẽr-bid′), *v.t.* [-BID, -BIDDING], to offer a lower price than; bid lower than.

**un·der·brush** (un′dẽr-brush′), *n.* small trees, shrubs, etc. that grow beneath large trees in woods or forests; undergrowth.

**un·der·buy** (un′dẽr-bī′), *v.t.* [-BOUGHT, -BUYING], 1. to buy at less than the real value. 2. to buy more cheaply than (another or others).

**un·der·car·riage** (un′dẽr-kar′ij), *n.* 1. a supporting frame or structure, as of an automobile. 2. the landing gear of an airplane.

**un·der·charge** (un′dẽr-chärj′; *for n.,* un′dẽr-chärj′), *v.t.* [-CHARGED, -CHARGING], 1. to charge less than is usual or correct (for). 2. to load with an insufficient charge. *n.* an insufficient charge.

**un·der·class·man** (un′dẽr-klas′mən, -kläs′-), *n.* [*pl.* -MEN], a freshman or sophomore.

**un·der·clothes** (un′dẽr-klōz′, -klōthz′), *n.pl.* underwear: also **un′der·cloth′ing** (-klōth′iŋ).

**un·der·coat** (un′dẽr-kōt′), *n.* 1. a coat worn under another. 2. a tarlike coating applied to the undersurface of an automobile to prevent rust, etc. *v.t.* to apply an undercoat (sense 2) to.

**un·der·cov·er** (un′dẽr-kuv′ẽr), *adj.* acting or carried out in secret.

**un·der·cur·rent** (un′dẽr-kũr′ənt), *n.* 1. a current flowing below another or beneath the surface. 2. a hidden or underlying tendency, opinion, etc., usually at variance with a more obvious one.

**un·der·cut** (un′dẽr-kut′; *for v.,* un′dẽr-kut′), *n.* 1. a cut made underneath another so as to leave an overhang. 2. in *sports, a*) backspin, as in golf. *b*) a cut, slice, or chop made with an underhand motion, as in tennis. *adj.* that is undercut. *v.t.* [-CUT, -CUTTING], 1. to make a cut below or under. 2. to undersell or work for lower wages than. 3. in *sports,* to give an undercut to (a ball). *v.i.* to undercut something or someone.

**un·der·de·vel·op** (un′dẽr-di-vel′əp), *v.t. & v.i.* to develop to a point below what is needed.

**un·der·do** (un′dẽr-dōō′), *v.i. & v.t.* [-DID, -DONE, -DOING], to do less than is usual, needed, etc.

**un·der·dog** (un′dẽr-dôg′), *n.* the one that is losing, as in a contest; one that is handicapped, underprivileged, unfavored, etc.

**un·der·done** (un′dẽr-dun′), *adj.* not thoroughly cooked: said of food, especially beef.

**un·der·es·ti·mate** (un′dẽr-es′tə-māt′; *for n., usually* -mit), *v.t. & v.i.* [-MATED, -MATING], to estimate below the actual value, amount, etc. *n.* an estimate that is too low. —**un′der·es′ti·ma′tion,** *n.*

**un·der·ex·pose** (un′dẽr-ik-spōz′), *v.t.* [-POSED, -POSING], to expose (a photographic plate or film, etc.) for too short a time. —**un′der·ex·po′sure** (-spō′zhẽr), *n.*

**un·der·feed** (un′dẽr-fēd′), *v.t.* [-FED, -FEEDING], to feed less than is needed.

**un·der·fired** (un′dẽr-fīrd′), *adj.* fired, or heated, from beneath.

**un·der·foot** (un′dẽr-foot′), *adv. & adj.* 1. under the foot or feet; hence, 2. in the way.

**un·der·gar·ment** (un′dẽr-gär′mənt), *n.* a garment worn beneath a suit, dress, etc., especially next to the skin.

**un·der·go** (un′dẽr-gō′), *v.t.* [-WENT, -GONE, -GOING], to experience; endure; be subjected to.

**un·der·grad·u·ate** (un′dẽr-graj′ōō-it), *n.* a student at a university or college who has not yet received the bachelor's degree.

**un·der·ground** (un′dẽr-ground′; *also, for adj. & adv.,* -ground′), *adj.* 1. occurring, working, etc. beneath the surface of the earth. 2. secret; undercover. *adv.* 1. beneath the surface of the earth. 2. in or into secrecy or hiding. *n.* 1. the entire region beneath the surface of the earth. 2. a secret movement organized to oppose the government in power or enemy forces of occupation. 3. [Brit.], an underground railway; subway.

**underground railroad,** 1. a railroad running through tunnels under the ground; esp., a subway: also **underground railway.** 2. in the U.S. before 1861, a system set up by abolitionists to help fugitive slaves escape from the South.

**un·der·growth** (un′dẽr-grōth′), *n.* underbrush.

**un·der·hand** (un′dẽr-hand′), *adj.* 1. done with the hand below the level of the elbow or shoulder. 2. secret; sly; deceitful. *adv.* 1. with an underhand motion. 2. slyly; secretly; unfairly.

**un·der·hand·ed** (un′dẽr-han′did), *adj.* 1. underhand; secret, sly, etc. 2. lacking the required number of hands, or workers, etc.; short-handed. —**un′der·hand′ed·ly,** *adv.* —**un′der·hand′ed·ness,** *n.*

**un·der·lay** (un′dẽr-lā′; *for v.,* un′dẽr-lā′), *n.* something laid underneath; esp., a thickness of paper, etc. laid under type to raise it. *v.t.* [-LAID, -LAYING], 1. to cover the bottom of. 2. to raise or support with something laid underneath.

**un·der·lie** (un′dẽr-lī′), *v.t.* [-LAY, -LAIN, -LYING], 1. to lie or be placed under; be beneath. 2. to support; form the basis or foundation of.

**un·der·line** (un′dẽr-līn′), *v.t.* [-LINED, -LINING], 1. to draw a line beneath; underscore. 2. to stress or emphasize.

**un·der·ling** (un′dẽr-liŋ), *n.* [AS.; see UNDER & -LING, dim. suffix], a person who has little rank or authority; subordinate: usually contemptuous.

**un·der·ly·ing** (un′dẽr-lī′iŋ), *adj.* 1. lying under; placed beneath. 2. fundamental; basic.

**un·der·mine** (un′dẽr-mīn′), *v.t.* [-MINED, -MINING], 1. to dig beneath, so as to form a tunnel or mine. 2. to wear away at the foundation. 3. to injure, weaken, or impair, especially by subtle or stealthy means. —**un′der·min′er,** *n.*

**un·der·most** (un′dẽr-mōst′), *adj. & adv.* lowest in place, position, rank, etc.

**un·der·neath** (un′dẽr-nēth′), *adv.* 1. under; below; beneath. 2. at a lower level. *prep.* 1. under; below; beneath. 2. under the form, guise, or authority of. *adj.* under; lower. *n.* the under part.

**un·der·nour·ish** (un′dẽr-nũr′ish), *v.t.* to give insufficient nourishment to. —**un′der·nour′ished,** *adj.*

**un·der·pass** (un′dẽr-pas′, -päs′), *n.* a passage under something; esp., a road under a railway or highway.

---

**undamaged**
**undamped**
**undated**
**undazzled**
**undebatable**
**undecayed**
**undecipherable**
**undeclared**
**undeclinable**
**undecorated**
**undefeatable**
**undefeated**
**undefended**
**undefiled**
**undefinable**
**undefined**
**undelayed**
**undelivered**
**undemocratic**
**undemonstrable**
**undemonstrative**
**undenied**
**undenominational**
**undependable**
**undeplored**
**undeposed**
**undepraved**
**undepreciated**

**un·der·pay** (un'dẽr-pā'), *v.t.* [-PAID, -PAYING], to pay less than is right; pay insufficiently.
**un·der·pin·ning** (un'dẽr-pin'iŋ), *n.* 1. a supporting structure, especially one placed beneath a wall. 2. a support. 3. *pl.* [Colloq.], the legs.
**un·der·play** (un'dẽr-plā'), *v.t. & v.i.* to act (a role in a play) in an intentionally restrained manner or with too great restraint; underact.
**un·der·priv·i·leged** (un'dẽr-priv'ə-lijd), *adj.* deprived of fundamental social rights, or privileges, through poverty, discrimination, etc. **—the underprivileged,** those who are underprivileged.
**un·der·rate** (un'dẽr-rāt'), *v.t.* [-RATED, -RATING], to rate too low; undervalue; underestimate.
**un·der·score** (un'dẽr-skôr', -skōr'), *v.t.* [-SCORED, -SCORING], to underline. *n.* a line underneath a printed or written word, etc.
**un·der·sea** (un'dẽr-sē'), *adj. & adv.* beneath the surface of the sea: also **un'der·seas',** *adv.*
**un·der·sec·re·tar·y** (un'dẽr-sek'rə-ter'i), *n.* [*pl.* -IES], an assistant secretary.
**un·der·sell** (un'dẽr-sel'), *v.t.* [-SOLD, -SELLING], to sell at a lower price than.
**un·der·shirt** (un'dẽr-shũrt'), *n.* a piece of underclothing worn under an outer shirt.
**un·der·shot** (un'dẽr-shot'), *adj.* 1. having the lower front teeth protruding beyond the upper teeth when the mouth is closed, so that the lower jaw protrudes. 2. turned by water passing beneath: said of a water wheel.

UNDERSHOT WHEEL

**un·der·side** (un'dẽr-sīd'), *n.* the side or surface that is underneath.
**un·der·sign** (un'dẽr-sīn'), *v.t.* to sign one's name at the end of (a letter, document, etc.). **—the undersigned,** the person or persons undersigning.
**un·der·sized** (un'dẽr-sīzd'), *adj.* smaller in size than is usual, standard, etc.: also **un'der·size'.**
**un·der·slung** (un'dẽr-sluŋ'), *adj.* 1. attached to the underside of the axles: said of an automobile frame. 2. having an underslung frame.
**un·der·staffed** (un'dẽr-staft', -stäft'), *adj.* having too small a staff; having insufficient personnel.
**un·der·stand** (un'dẽr-stand'), *v.t.* [-STOOD (-stood'), -STANDING], [AS. *understandan*, lit., to stand under], 1. to get or perceive the meaning of. 2. to take or interpret as the meaning; infer; assume. 3. to take as meant or meaning; interpret. 4. to take as a fact; accept as a condition. 5. to supply mentally (an idea, word, etc.). 6. to learn. 7. to know clearly or fully the nature, character, etc. of. *v.i.* 1. to have understanding, comprehension, etc., either in general or with reference to something specific. 2. to be informed; believe; assume. **—un'der·stand'a·ble,** *adj.* **—un'der·stand'a·bly,** *adv.*
**un·der·stand·ing** (un'dẽr-stan'diŋ), *n.* 1. the quality, act, or state of one who understands; comprehension; knowledge. 2. the power to think and learn; intelligence; judgment; sense. 3. a specific interpretation: as, this is my *understanding* of the case. 4. mutual agreement, especially one that settles differences. 5. mutual comprehension, as of ideas, intentions, etc. *adj.* that understands; characterized by comprehension, sympathy, etc. **—un'der·stand'ing·ly,** *adv.*
**un·der·state** (un'dẽr-stāt'), *v.t. & v.i.* [-STATED, -STATING], to make a weaker statement (of) than is warranted by truth, accuracy, or importance. **—un'der·state'ment,** *n.*
**un·der·stud·y** (un'dẽr-stud'i), *n.* [*pl.* -IES], an actor who studies the part of another actor so that he can serve as a substitute when necessary. *v.t. & v.i.* [-IED, -YING], 1. to act as an understudy (to). 2. to learn (a part) as an understudy.
**un·der·sur·face** (un'dẽr-sũr'fis), *n.* the underside.
**un·der·take** (un'dẽr-tāk'), *v.t.* [-TOOK, -TAKEN, -TAKING], 1. to take upon oneself (a task, etc.); agree to do. 2. to give a promise or pledge that; contract. 3. to promise; guarantee.
**un·der·tak·er** (un'dẽr-tāk'ẽr; *for 2,* un'dẽr-tāk'ẽr), *n.* 1. a person who undertakes something. 2. a person whose business is to prepare the dead for burial and manage funerals.
**un·der·tak·ing** (un'dẽr-tāk'iŋ; *for 3,* un'dẽr-tāk'-), *n.* 1. something undertaken; task; enterprise. 2. a promise; guarantee. 3. the business of an undertaker (sense 2). 4. the act of one who undertakes some task, etc.
**un·der·tone** (un'dẽr-tōn'), *n.* 1. a low tone as of voice. 2. something said in an undertone. 3. a subdued color. 4. an underlying quality, factor, element, etc.: as, an *undertone* of horror.
**un·der·tow** (un'dẽr-tō'), *n.* a current of water moving beneath the surface water and in a different direction, as seaward under the surf.
**un·der·val·ue** (un'dẽr-val'ū), *v.t.* [-UED, -UING], 1. to value too low, or below the real worth. 2. to esteem too lightly. **—un'der·val'u·a'tion,** *n.*
**un·der·wa·ter** (un'dẽr-wô'tẽr, -wät'ẽr), *adj.* 1. being, placed, done, etc. beneath the surface of the water. 2. used or for use under water.
**un·der·wear** (un'dẽr-wâr'), *n.* clothes worn next to the skin beneath outer clothing; underclothes.
**un·der·weight** (un'dẽr-wāt'), *adj.* weighing too little; deficient in weight. *n.* weight below what is normal, required, etc.
**un·der·went** (un'dẽr-went'), pt. of **undergo.**
**un·der·wood** (un'dẽr-wood'), *n.* underbrush.
**un·der·world** (un'dẽr-wũrld'), *n.* 1. the supposed world of the dead; Hades. 2. the criminal members of society; people living by vice or crime.
**un·der·write** (un'dẽr-rīt'), *v.t.* [-WROTE, -WRITTEN, -WRITING], 1. to write under something; subscribe. 2. to agree to buy (an issue of stocks, bonds, etc.) on a given date and at a fixed price, or to agree to buy (the unsubscribed stocks or bonds of an issue available to the public). 3. to agree to finance (an undertaking, etc.). 4. to sign one's name to (an insurance policy), thus assuming liability. 5. to insure. **—un'der·writ'er,** *n.*
**un·de·sir·a·ble** (un'di-zīr'ə-b'l), *adj.* not desirable; objectionable. *n.* an undesirable person. **—un'de·sir'a·bil'i·ty,** *n.* **—un'de·sir'a·bly,** *adv.*
**un·dies** (un'diz), *n.pl.* [dim. euphemistic abbrev.], [Colloq.], (women's or children's) underwear.
**un·do** (un-dōō'), *v.t.* [-DID, -DONE, -DOING], 1. to open, release, or untie (a fastening). 2. to open (a parcel, door, etc.) thus. 3. to reverse the doing of (something accomplished); annul. 4. to bring to ruin or downfall. **—un·do'er,** *n.*
**un·do·ing** (un-dōō'iŋ), *n.* 1. a reversal; canceling or annulling. 2. the act of bringing to ruin or destruction. 3. the cause of ruin or destruction.
**un·done** (un-dun'), pp. of **undo.** *adj.* ruined.
**un·done** (un-dun'), *adj.* not done; not performed, accomplished, completed, etc.
**un·doubt·ed** (un-dout'id), *adj.* not doubted or called in question; accepted. **—un·doubt'ed·ly,** *adv.*
**un·draw** (un-drô'), *v.t. & v.i.* [-DREW, -DRAWN, -DRAWING], to draw back or away, as curtains.
**un·dress** (un-dres'; *for n., usually* un'dres'), *v.t.* 1. to take off the clothing of; strip. 2. to remove the dressing from (a wound). *v.i.* to take off one's clothing; strip. *n.* 1. loose, informal dress. 2.

---

**undeserved**
**undeserving**
**undesignated**
**undesigned**
**undesigning**
**undesired**
**undesirous**
**undespairing**
**undestroyed**
**undetachable**
**undetached**
**undetected**
**undetermined**
**undeterred**
**undeveloped**
**undeviating**
**undevoured**
**undevout**
**undifferentiated**
**undiffused**
**undigested**
**undigestible**
**undignified**
**undiluted**
**undiminished**
**undimmed**
**undiplomatic**
**undirected**
**undiscerned**
**undiscerning**
**undischarged**
**undisciplined**
**undisclosed**
**undiscouraged**
**undiscovered**
**undiscredited**
**undiscriminating**
**undiscussed**
**undisguised**
**undisillusioned**
**undismayed**
**undismissed**
**undispatched**
**undispelled**
**undispensed**
**undisputed**
**undissected**
**undisseminated**
**undissolved**
**undistilled**
**undistinguished**
**undistracted**
**undistressed**
**undistributed**
**undisturbed**
**undiversified**
**undiverted**
**undivested**
**undivided**
**undivorced**
**undivulged**
**undomestic**
**undomesticated**
**undoubting**
**undrained**
**undramatic**
**undraped**
**undreamed**

---

ordinary clothing, as opposed to a uniform, etc. *adj.* of undress.
**un·due** (un-dōō′, -dū′), *adj.* 1. not yet owing or payable. 2. improper; not appropriate. 3. not just, legal, etc. 4. excessive; unreasonable.
**un·du·lant** (un′joo-lənt, -doo-), *adj.* undulating.
**undulant fever,** a persistent, infectious disease transmitted to man in the milk of infected cows and characterized by an undulating, or recurrent, fever, pains in the joints, etc.
**un·du·late** (un′joo-lāt′, -doo-; *for adj., usually* -lit), *v.t.* [-LATED, -LATING], [< L. *undulatus*, undulated < *unda*, a wave], 1. to cause to move in waves. 2. to give a wavy form, surface, etc. to. *v.i.* 1. to move in waves. 2. to have a wavy form, surface, etc. *adj.* having a wavy form, margin, or surface: also **un′du·lat′ed.** —**un′du·la′tive, un′du·la·to′ry** (-lə-tôr′i, -tō′ri), *adj.*
**un·du·la·tion** (un joo-lā′shən, -doo-), *n.* 1. an undulating or undulating motion. 2. a wavy, curving form or outline. 3. pulsation. 4. in *physics*, wave motion, as of light or sound, or a vibration.
**un·du·ly** (un-dōō′li, -dū′-), *adv.* 1. improperly; unjustly. 2. beyond a due degree; excessively.
**un·dy·ing** (un-dī′iŋ), *adj.* not dying or ending; immortal or eternal.
**un·earth** (un-ũrth′), *v.t.* 1. to dig up from out of the earth. 2. to bring to light; disclose.
**un·earth·ly** (un-ũrth′li), *adj.* 1. not of this world; supernatural. 2. weird; mysterious. 3. [Colloq.], fantastic; outlandish. —**un·earth′li·ness,** *n.*
**un·eas·y** (un-ē′zi), *adj.* [-IER, -IEST], 1. having, showing, or allowing no ease of body or mind; uncomfortable. 2. awkward; constrained. 3. disturbed by anxiety or apprehension; restless; perturbed. —**un·eas′i·ly,** *adv.* —**un·eas′i·ness,** *n.*
**un·em·ploy·a·ble** (un′im-ploi′ə-b'l), *adj.* not employable, as because of age, physical handicap, etc. *n.* an unemployable person.
**un·em·ployed** (un′im-ploid′), *adj.* 1. not employed; without work. 2. not being used; idle. —**the unemployed,** people who are out of work.
**un·em·ploy·ment** (un′im-ploi′mənt), *n.* the state of being unemployed; lack of employment.
**unemployment compensation,** payment, as by a State government, of a certain amount of money to the unemployed, during a fixed period.
**un·e·qual** (un-ē′kwəl), *adj.* 1. not of the same size, strength, ability, value, rank, amount, etc. 2. not balanced or symmetrical. 3. not even, regular, etc.; variable. 4. not equal or adequate: as, *unequal* to the job. 5. not equitable; unjust. —**un·e′qual·ly,** *adv.* —**un·e′qual·ness,** *n.*
**un·e·qualed, un·e·qualled** (un-ē′kwəld), *adj.* not equaled; unmatched; unrivaled; supreme.
**un·e·quiv·o·cal** (un′i-kwiv′ə-k'l), *adj.* not equivocal; straightforward; clear. —**un′e·quiv′o·cal·ly,** *adv.* —**un′e·quiv′o·cal·ness,** *n.*
**un·err·ing** (un-ũr′iŋ, -er′-), *adj.* 1. free from error. 2. not missing or failing; sure; exact. —**un·err′ing·ly,** *adv.* —**un·err′ing·ness,** *n.*
**UNESCO** (yoo-nes′kō), *n.* the United Nations Educational, Scientific, and Cultural Organization.
**un·e·ven** (un-ē′vən), *adj.* 1. not even; not level, smooth, or flat; rough; irregular. 2. unequal. 3. in *mathematics*, odd; not evenly divisible by two. —**un·e′ven·ly,** *adv.* —**un·e′ven·ness,** *n.*
**un·ex·am·pled** (un′ig-zam′p'ld, -zäm′-), *adj.* having no parallel or precedent; unprecedented.
**un·ex·cep·tion·a·ble** (un′ik-sep′shən-ə-b'l), *adj.* not exceptionable; not warranting even the slightest criticism. —**un′ex·cep′tion·a·bly,** *adv.*
**un·ex·cep·tion·al** (un′ik-sep′shən-'l), *adj.* 1. not uncommon or unusual; ordinary. 2. not admitting of any exception. —**un′ex·cep′tion·al·ly,** *adv.*
**un·ex·pect·ed** (un′ik-spek′tid), *adj.* not expected; sudden. —**un′ex·pect′ed·ly,** *adv.* —**un′ex·pect′ed·ness,** *n.*
**un·fail·ing** (un-fāl′iŋ), *adj.* 1. not failing. 2. never ceasing or falling short; inexhaustible. 3. always reliable; certain. —**un·fail′ing·ly,** *adv.*
**un·fair** (un-fâr′), *adj.* 1. not just or impartial; biased; inequitable. 2. unethical in business dealings. —**un·fair′ly,** *adv.* —**un·fair′ness,** *n.*
**un·faith·ful** (un-fāth′fəl), *adj.* 1. failing to observe an allegiance or the terms of a vow, promise, etc.; faithless. 2. lacking faith; dishonest. 3. not true, accurate, etc.; untrustworthy. 4. adulterous. —**un·faith′ful·ly,** *adv.* —**un·faith′ful·ness,** *n.*
**un·fa·mil·iar** (un′fə-mil′yẽr), *adj.* 1. not well known; strange. 2. having no acquaintance (*with*). —**un′fa·mil′i·ar′i·ty** (-i-ar′ə-ti), *n.* —**un′fa·mil′iar·ly,** *adv.*
**un·fa·vor·a·ble** (un-fā′vẽr-ə-b'l), *adj.* not propitious; adverse, contrary, or disadvantageous. —**un·fa′vor·a· ly,** *adv.*
**un·feel·ing** (un-fēl′iŋ), *adj.* 1. incapable of feeling; insensate or insensible. 2. hardhearted; cruel. —**un·feel′ing·ly,** *adv.* —**un·feel′ing·ness,** *n.*
**un·feigned** (un-fānd′), *adj.* genuine; real; sincere. —**un·feign′ed·ly** (-fān′id-li), *adv.*
**un·fin·ished** (un-fin′isht), *adj.* 1. not finished; incomplete; not perfected. 2. having no finish, or final coat, as of paint.
**un·fit** (un-fit′), *adj.* 1. not meeting requirements; not suitable. 2. not physically fit. 3. not adapted. *v.t.* [-FITTED, -FITTING], to make unfit; incapacitate. —**un·fit′ly,** *adv.* —**un·fit′ness,** *n.*
**un·fix** (un-fiks′), *v.t.* to unfasten; loosen.
**un·fledged** (un-flejd′), *adj.* not feathered, as a young bird. 2. immature; undeveloped.
**un·flinch·ing** (un-flin′chiŋ), *adj.* steadfast; resolute; firm. —**un·flinch′ing·ly,** *adv.*
**un·fold** (un-fōld′), *v.t.* 1. to open the folds of; open and spread out. 2. to lay open to view; reveal, disclose, display, or explain. 3. to develop. *v.i.* to become unfolded. —**un·fold′er,** *n.*
**un·for·tu·nate** (un-fôr′chə-nit), *adj.* characterized by bad fortune; unsuccessful, unhappy, or unlucky. *n.* an unfortunate person. —**un·for′tu·nate·ly,** *adv.* —**un·for′tu·nate·ness,** *n.*
**un·found·ed** (un-foun′did), *adj.* 1. not founded on fact or truth; baseless. 2. not established. —**un·found′ed·ly,** *adv.* —**un·found′ed·ness,** *n.*
**un·friend·ly** (un-frend′li), *adj.* 1. not friendly or kind; hostile. 2. not favorable or propitious. *adv.* in an unfriendly manner. —**un·friend′li·ness,** *n.*

---

**undried**
**undrilled**
**undrinkable**
**undutiful**
**undyed**
**unearned**
**uneatable**
**uneaten**
**uneclipsed**
**uneconomical**
**unedifying**
**uneducated**
**uneliminated**
**unemancipated**
**unembarrassed**
**unembellished**
**unemotional**
**unemphatic**
**unemptied**
**unenclosed**
**unencumbered**
**unending**
**unendorsed**
**unendowed**
**unendurable**
**unenforceable**
**unenforced**
**unengaged**
**unenjoyable**
**unenlightened**
**unenriched**
**unenrolled**
**unenslaved**
**unentangled**
**unenterprising**
**unentertaining**
**unenthusiastic**
**unentitled**
**unenviable**
**unenvied**
**unequipped**
**unessential**
**unestablished**
**unestimated**
**unethical**
**uneventful**
**unexacting**
**unexaggerated**
**unexamined**
**unexcelled**
**unexchangeable**
**unexciting**
**unexcused**
**unexecuted**
**unexercised**
**unexhausted**
**unexpended**
**unexpired**
**unexplainable**
**unexplained**
**unexploded**
**unexploited**
**unexplored**
**unexposed**
**unexpressed**
**unexpurgated**
**unextended**
**unextinguished**
**unfaded**
**unfading**
**unfaltering**
**unfashionable**
**unfasten**
**unfathomable**
**unfathomed**
**unfavored**
**unfeared**
**unfearing**
**unfeasible**
**unfed**
**unfederated**
**unfelt**
**unfeminine**
**unfenced**
**unfermented**
**unfertilized**
**unfettered**
**unfilial**
**unfilled**
**unfilmed**
**unfiltered**
**unfitting**
**unfixed**
**unflagging**
**unflattering**
**unflavored**
**unfleshly**
**unflickering**
**unforbearing**
**unforbidden**
**unforced**
**unforeboding**
**unforeseeable**
**unforeseen**
**unforested**
**unforfeited**
**unforged**
**unforgetful**
**unforgettable**
**unforgivable**
**unforgiven**
**unforgiving**
**unforgotten**
**unformed**
**unformulated**
**unforsaken**
**unfortified**
**unfought**
**unframed**
**unfranchised**
**unfraternal**
**unfree**
**unfreezable**
**unfrequented**

**un·frock** (un-frok′), *v.t.* 1. to remove a frock from. 2. to deprive of the rank of priest or minister.

**un·furl** (un-fũrl′), *v.t. & v.i.* to open or spread out from a furled state; unfold.

**un·gain·ly** (un-gān′li), *adj.* awkward; clumsy. *adv.* in an ungainly manner. —**un·gain′li·ness,** *n.*

**un·god·ly** (un-god′li), *adj.* 1. not godly or religious; impious. 2. sinful; wicked. 3. [Colloq.], outrageous; dreadful. —**un·god′li·ness,** *n.*

**un·gov·ern·a·ble** (un-guv′ẽrn-ə-b'l), *adj.* that cannot be governed or restrained; unruly. —**un·gov′ern·a·ble·ness,** *n.* —**un·gov′ern·a·bly,** *adv.*

**un·gra·cious** (un-grā′shəs), *adj.* 1. unacceptable; unpleasant. 2. rude; discourteous; impolite. —**un·gra′cious·ly,** *adv.* —**un·gra′cious·ness,** *n.*

**un·guard·ed** (un-gär′id), *adj.* 1. unprotected. 2. careless; imprudent. —**un·guard′ed·ly,** *adv.*

**un·guent** (uŋ′gwənt), *n.* [< L. < *unguere,* to anoint], a salve or ointment. —**un′guen·tar′y,** *adj.*

**un·gu·la** (uŋ′gyoo-lə), *n.* [*pl.* -LAE (-lē′)], [L. < *unguis*], 1. a hoof. 2. a nail or claw. —**un′gu·lar,** *adj.*

**un·gu·late** (uŋ′gyoo-lit, -lāt′), *adj.* having hoofs; of or belonging to the group of mammals having hoofs. *n.* a mammal having hoofs.

**un·hal·lowed** (un-hal′ōd), *adj.* 1. not hallowed or consecrated; unholy. 2. wicked; profane.

**un·hand** (un-hand′), *v.t.* to loose or release from the hand or hands; let go of.

**un·hap·py** (un-hap′i), *adj.* [-PIER, -PIEST], 1. unfortunate. 2. sad; wretched; sorrowful. 3. not suitable. —**un·hap′pi·ly,** *adv.* —**un·hap′pi·ness,** *n.*

**un·health·y** (un-hel′thi), *adj.* [-IER, -IEST], 1. having or showing poor health; sickly; not well. 2. harmful to health; unwholesome. 3. harmful to morals. —**un·health′i·ly,** *adv.* —**un·health′i·ness,** *n.*

**un·heard** (un-hũrd′), *adj.* 1. not perceived by the ear. 2. not given a hearing. 3. unheard-of.

**un·heard-of** (un-hũrd′uv′, -ov′), *adj.* not heard of before; unprecedented or unknown.

**un·hinge** (un-hinj′), *v.t.* [-HINGED, -HINGING], 1. to remove from the hinges. 2. to remove the hinges from. 3. to dislodge or detach. 4. to throw (the mind, etc.) into confusion; unbalance or upset.

**un·hitch** (un-hich′), *v.t.* 1. to free from a hitch. 2. to unfasten; release; detach.

**un·ho·ly** (un-hō′li), *adj.* [-LIER, -LIEST], 1. not sacred, hallowed, or consecrated. 2. wicked; profane; impious. 3. [Colloq.], frightful; dreadful. —**un·ho′li·ly,** *adv.* —**un·ho′li·ness,** *n.*

**un·hook** (un-hook′), *v.t.* 1. to remove or loosen from a hook. 2. to undo or unfasten the hook or hooks of. *v.i.* to become unhooked.

**un·horse** (un-hôrs′), *v.t.* [-HORSED, -HORSING], 1. to throw (a rider) from a horse. 2. to overthrow.

**un·hu·man** (un-hū′mən), *adj.* 1. [Rare], inhuman. 2. superhuman. 3. nonhuman. —**un·hu′man·ly,** *adv.* —**un·hu′man·ness,** *n.*

**u·ni-,** [< L. *unus,* one], a combining form meaning *having* or *consisting of one only.*

**U·ni·at** (ū′ni-at′), *n.* [< Russ. *uniyat;* ult. < L. *unus,* one: from "union" with the Roman Church], a member of any Eastern Christian Church that recognizes the Pope as primate but keeps to its own liturgy, rites, etc. *adj.* of such a church.

**U·ni·ate** (ū′ni-it, -āt′), *n. & adj.* Uniat.

**u·ni·cam·er·al** (ū′ni-kam′ẽr-əl), *adj.* [< *uni-* + LL. *camera,* a chamber], of or having a single legislative chamber.

**u·ni·cel·lu·lar** (ū′ni-sel′yoo-lẽr), *adj.* having or consisting of a single cell.

**u·ni·corn** (ū′nə-kôrn′), *n.* [< OFr. < L. < *unus,* one + *cornu,* a horn], a mythical horselike animal having a single horn in the center of its forehead.

UNICORN

**u·ni·cy·cle** (ū′ni-sī′k'l), *n.* any vehicle having a single wheel.

**u·ni·fi·ca·tion** (ū′nə-fi-kā′shən), *n.* 1. a unifying or being unified. 2. an instance of this.

**u·ni·form** (ū′nə-fôrm′), *adj.* [< Fr. < L. < *unus,* one + *forma,* a form], 1. always the same; not varying in form, rate, degree, manner, etc. 2. not varying among themselves; all alike. *n.* the official or distinctive clothes worn by the members of a particular group, as policemen or soldiers. *v.t.* to clothe or supply with a uniform. —**uniform with,** having the same form, appearance, etc. as. —**u′ni·form′ly,** *adv.* —**u′ni·form′ness,** *n.*

**u·ni·form·i·ty** (ū′nə-fôr′mə-ti), *n.* [*pl.* -TIES], state, quality, or instance of being uniform.

**u·ni·fy** (ū′nə-fī′), *v.t.* [-FIED, -FYING], [< Fr. or ML.; ult. < L. *unus,* one + *facere,* to make], to make into a unit; cause to become one; consolidate; unite. —**u′ni·fi′a·ble,** *adj.* —**u′ni·fi′er,** *n.*

**u·ni·lat·er·al** (ū′ni-lat′ẽr-əl), *adj.* 1. of, occurring on, or affecting one side only. 2. involving one only of several parties; not reciprocal: as, a *unilateral* contract. 3. taking into account one side only of a matter; one-sided. 4. turned to, or having its parts on, one side. —**u′ni·lat′er·al·ism,** *n.* —**u′ni·lat′er·al·ly,** *adv.*

**un·im·peach·a·ble** (un′im-pēch′ə-b'l), *adj.* that cannot be doubted, questioned, or discredited; blameless; irreproachable. —**un′im·peach′a·ble·ness,** *n.* —**un′im·peach′a·bly,** *adv.*

**un·im·proved** (un′im-pro͞ovd′), *adj.* 1. not improved, as by building, etc.: as, *unimproved* land. 2. not turned to advantage. 3. not better in health.

**un·ion** (ūn′yən), *n.* [OFr. < L. < *unus,* one], 1. a uniting or being united; combination; junction. 2. an alliance for mutual benefit. 3. the unity produced by this. 4. a grouping together of nations, political groups, etc. for some specific purpose. 5. marriage. 6. something united; a whole made up of united parts. 7. a device symbolizing political union, used in a flag or ensign, as the white stars on a blue field in the U.S. flag. 8. a trade union; labor union. 9. a device for joining together parts; esp., a coupling for linking the ends of pipes. —**the Union,** the United States of America.

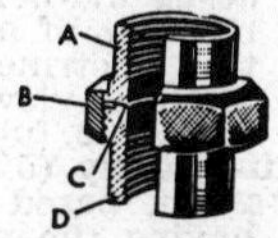

UNION (of pipe) A, D, sections of pipe; B, nut; C, fitted seat

**unfrozen**
**unfruitful**
**unfulfilled**
**unfurnished**
**unfurrowed**
**ungallant**
**ungarnished**
**ungathered**
**ungenerous**
**ungenial**
**ungentle**
**ungentlemanly**
**ungifted**
**ungird**
**unglazed**
**ungloved**
**unglued**
**ungoverned**
**ungraceful**
**ungraded**
**ungrained**
**ungrammatical**
**ungrateful**
**ungratified**
**ungrounded**
**ungrudging**
**unguided**
**unhampered**
**unhandicapped**
**unhandled**
**unhandsome**
**unhandy**
**unhanged**
**unharassed**
**unhardened**
**unharmed**
**unharmful**
**unharmonious**
**unharness**
**unharrowed**
**unharvested**
**unhatched**
**unhealed**
**unhealthful**
**unheated**
**unheeded**
**unheeding**
**unhelped**
**unhelpful**
**unheralded**
**unheroic**
**unhesitating**
**unhindered**
**unhired**
**unhistoric**
**unhonored**
**unhoped-for**
**unhoused**
**unhung**
**unhurried**
**unhurt**
**unhygienic**
**unhyphenated**
**unidentified**
**unidiomatic**
**unilluminated**
**unillustrated**
**unimaginable**
**unimaginative**
**unimagined**
**unimbued**
**unimitated**
**unimpaired**
**unimpassioned**
**unimpeded**
**unimportance**
**unimportant**
**unimposing**
**unimpressed**
**unimpressible**
**unimpressive**
**unincorporated**
**unindexed**
**unindicated**
**uninfected**
**uninfested**
**uninflammable**
**uninflected**
**uninfluenced**
**uninformed**
**uninhabitable**
**uninhabited**
**uninhibited**
**uninitiated**
**uninjured**
**uninspired**
**uninstructed**
**uninsurable**
**uninsured**
**unintelligent**
**unintelligible**
**unintended**
**unintentional**
**uninterested**
**uninteresting**
**uninterrupted**
**unintimidated**
**uninventive**
**uninvested**
**uninvited**
**uninviting**
**uninvolved**

**Union City,** a city in New Jersey: pop, 52,000.
**un·ion·ism** (ūn'yən-iz'm), *n.* 1. the principle of union. 2. support of this principle or of a specified union. 3. the system or principles of labor unions. 4. [U-], loyalty to the federal union of the U. S., especially during the Civil War. **—un'ion·ist, Un'ion·ist,** *n. & adj.* **—un'ion·is'tic,** *adj.*
**un·ion·ize** (ūn'yən-īz'), *v.t.* [-IZED, -IZING], 1. to organize (a group of workers) into a labor union. 2. to bring into conformity with the rules, standards, etc. of a labor union. *v.i.* to join or organize a labor union. **—un'ion·i·za'tion,** *n.*
**union jack,** 1. a jack or flag, especially a national flag, consisting only of a union. 2. [U- J-], the national flag of the United Kingdom.
**Union of South Africa,** South Africa: the former name.
**Union of Soviet Socialist Republics,** a federation of 15 republics of E Europe and N Asia: area, 8,518,000 sq. mi.; pop., 234,401,000; capital, Moscow: also called *Soviet Union.*
**union shop,** a shop, business, etc. operating under a contract with a labor union, which requires that new workers join the union after being hired.
**union suit,** a suit of men's underwear uniting shirt and drawers in a single garment.
**u·nique** (ū-nēk'), *adj.* [Fr. < L. *unicus*, single], 1. one and only; sole. 2. different from all others; having no like or equal. 3. singular; unusual; rare. **—u·nique'ly,** *adv.* **—u·nique'ness,** *n.*
**u·ni·sex·u·al** (ū'ni-sek'shōō-əl), *adj.* of only one sex; not hermaphroditic.
**u·ni·son** (ū'nə-s'n, -z'n), *n.* [OFr. < ML. < L. *unus*, one + *sonus*, a sound], 1. identity of musical pitch, as of two or more voices or tones. 2. agreement; concord; harmony. **—in unison,** 1. sounding the same note at the same time. 2. with all the voices or instruments performing the same part.
**u·nit** (ū'nit), *n.* [< *unity*], 1. the smallest whole number; one. 2. any fixed quantity, measure, etc. used as a standard; specif., in *medicine*, etc., the amount of a drug, vaccine, etc. needed to produce a given result. 3. a single person or group, especially as distinguished from others or as a part of a whole. 4. a single, distinct part, especially as used for a specific purpose: as, the lens *unit* of a camera.
**U·ni·tar·i·an** (ū'nə-târ'i-ən), *n.* 1. one who denies the doctrine of the Trinity, rejecting the divinity of Jesus and holding that God is a single being. 2. a member of a Protestant denomination based on this doctrine and characterized by tolerance of differing views. *adj.* 1. of Unitarians or their doctrines. 2. [u-], unitary. **—U'ni·tar'i·an·ism,** *n.*
**u·ni·tar·y** (ū'nə-ter'i), *adj.* 1. of a unit or units. 2. of, based on, or characterized by unity. 3. having the nature of or used as a unit.
**u·nite** (yoo-nīt'), *v.t. & v.i.* [UNITED, UNITING], [< L. pp. of *unire*, to unite < *unus*, one], 1. to put or join together so as to make one; combine; consolidate; merge. 2. to bring or come together in common cause, interest, action, etc.; join through fellowship, legal bonds, etc. **—u·nit'er,** *n.*
**u·nit·ed** (yoo-nīt'id), *adj.* 1. combined; joined. 2. of or resulting from joint action or association. 3. in agreement. **—u·nit'ed·ly,** *adv.* **—u·nit'ed·ness,** *n.*
**United Arab Republic,** Egypt: the official name.
**United Kingdom,** Great Britain and Northern Ireland: area, 94,279 sq. mi.; pop., 54,744,000; capital, London: official name, **United Kingdom of Great Britain and Northern Ireland.**
**United Nations,** an international organization for promoting world peace and security under a charter signed in 1945 by 51 nations, based on an organization formed in 1942 by the 26 nations opposed to the fascist coalition of Germany, Japan, Italy, etc.: 72 additional members had been admitted by 1968: the headquarters are in New York City.
**United Provinces,** Uttar Pradesh: former name.
**United States of America,** a country mostly in North America, made up of 50 States and the District of Columbia: its possessions include the Panama Canal Zone, Guam, etc.: (of the U.S. proper) area, 3,615,211 sq. mi.; pop., 179,323,000; capital, Washington, D.C.: also called *United States, America, the States.*
**u·ni·tive** (ū'nə-tiv), *adj.* 1. having unity. 2. tending to unite.
**u·ni·tize** (ū'nə-tīz'), *v.t.* [-TIZED, -TIZING], to form, construct, or organize into a single unit.

**u·ni·ty** (ū'nə-ti), *n.* [*pl.* -TIES], [< OFr. < L. *unitas* < *unus*, one], 1. the state of being one; a being united; oneness. 2. a single, separate thing. 3. harmony; agreement; concord. 4. unification. 5. a group or body formed by this. 6. a complex that is a union of related parts. 7. an arrangement of parts that will produce a single, harmonious effect in an artistic or literary production. 8. an effect so produced. 9. constancy or continuity of purpose, action, etc. 10. in *mathematics*, any quantity, magnitude, etc. identified as a unit or 1.
**Univ.,** 1. Universalist. 2. University.
**u·ni·va·lent** (ū'nə-vā'lənt, yoo-niv'ə-), *adj.* in *chemistry, a)* having one valence. *b)* having a valence of one. Also, esp. for *b*, **monovalent. —u'ni·va'lence, u'ni·va'len·cy,** *n.*
**u·ni·valve** (ū'nə-valv'), *n.* 1. a mollusk having a one-piece shell, as a snail. 2. such a one-piece shell. *adj.* having one valve, or shell, only: also **u'ni-valved', u'ni·val'vu·lar** (-val'vyoo-lẽr).
**u·ni·ver·sal** (ū'nə-vũr's'l), *adj.* [see UNIVERSE], 1. of, for, or including all or the whole; not limited. 2. of the universe; present or occurring everywhere. 3. whole; entire. 4. broad in knowledge, interests, etc. 5. that can be used for all kinds, forms, sizes, etc. 6. used, intended to be used, or understood by all. 7. in *logic*, predicating something of every member of a class; generic. *n.* in *logic*, a universal proposition. **—u'ni·ver'sal·ness,** *n.*
**U·ni·ver·sal·ism** (ū nə-vũr's'l-iz'm), *n.* the theological doctrine that all souls will eventually find salvation. **—U'ni·ver'sal·ist,** *adj. & n.*
**u·ni·ver·sal·i·ty** (ū'nə-vẽr-sal'ə-ti), *n.* [*pl.* -TIES], 1. quality, state, or instance of being universal. 2. universal range, as of knowledge, interests, etc.
**u·ni·ver·sal·ize** (ū'nə-vũr's'l-īz'), *v.t.* [-IZED, -IZING], to make universal.
**universal joint** (or **coupling**), a joint or coupling that permits a swing of limited angle in any direction, especially one used to transmit rotary motion from one shaft to another not in line with it, as in an automobile.

UNIVERSAL JOINT A, single; B, double

**u·ni·ver·sal·ly** (ū'nə-vũr's'l-i), *adv.* 1. in every instance. 2. in every part or place.
**universal suffrage,** suffrage for all adult citizens of either sex.
**u·ni·verse** (ū'nə-vũrs'), *n.* [< Fr. < L. *unus*, one + pp. of *vertere*, to turn], 1. the totality of all the things that exist; the cosmos. 2. the world.
**u·ni·ver·si·ty** (ū'nə-vũr'sə-ti), *n.* [*pl.* -TIES], [< OFr. < L. *universitas*, the whole, a society; see UNIVERSE], an educational institution of the highest level, typically having one or more undergraduate colleges and graduate and professional schools.
**un·joint** (un-joint'), *v.t.* 1. to separate (a joint). 2. to separate the joints of.
**un·just** (un-just'), *adj.* not just or right; unfair. **—un·just'ly,** *adv.* **—un·just'ness,** *n.*
**un·kempt** (un-kempt'), *adj.* [*un-* + *kempt*, pp. of dial. *kemben*, to comb], 1. not combed. 2. untidy; messy. **—un·kempt'ly,** *adv.* **—un·kempt'ness,** *n.*
**un·kind** (un-kīnd'), *adj.* not kind, sympathetic, or considerate of the feelings of others; harsh; cruel. **—un·kind'ly,** *adv.* **—un·kind'ness,** *n.*
**un·known** (un-nōn'), *adj.* 1. not known; not in one's knowledge, recognition, etc.; unfamiliar. 2. not discovered, identified, etc.: as, an *unknown* island. *n.* an unknown person or thing.
**un·lace** (un-lās'), *v.t.* [-LACED, -LACING], to undo the laces of; unfasten (something laced).
**un·lade** (un-lād'), *v.t. & v.i.* [-LADED, -LADEN or -LADED, -LADING], 1. to unload (a ship, etc.). 2. to discharge (a cargo, etc.).
**un·latch** (un-lach'), *v.t.* to open by releasing a latch. *v.i.* to become unfastened at the latch.
**un·law·ful** (un-lô'fəl), *adj.* 1. against the law; illegal. 2. illegitimate. **—un·law'ful·ly,** *adv.*
**un·lay** (un-lā'), *v.t. & v.i.* [-LAID, -LAYING], in *nautical usage*, to untwist, as a rope.
**un·learn** (un-lũrn'), *v.t.* [-LEARNED or -LEARNT, -LEARNING], 1. to forget (something learned). 2. to teach the contrary of (something learned).
**un·learn·ed** (un-lũr'nid; *for* 3, -lũrnd'), *adj.* 1. not learned or educated; ignorant. 2. showing a lack

---

**unissued**
**unjoined**
**unjudged**
**unjudicial**
**unjustifiable**
**unkept**
**unkindled**
**unkingly**
**unkissed**
**unknit**
**unknot**
**unknowable**
**unknowing**
**unlabeled**
**unlabelled**
**unlabored**
**unlaboured**
**unladylike**
**unlamented**
**unlaundered**

of learning or education. 3. known or possessed, as knowledge, without being learned. —**un·learn′ed·ly,** *adv.* —**un·learn′ed·ness,** *n.*

**un·leash** (un-lēsh′), *v.t.* to release as from a leash.

**un·less** (ən-les′), *conj.* [earlier *on lesse that,* at less than], if not; in any case other than; except that. *prep.* except (with a verb implied): as, *unless* disaster, nothing will result.

**un·let·tered** (un-let′ẽrd), *adj.* 1. not lettered; ignorant; uneducated. 2. illiterate.

**un·like** (un-līk′), *adj.* not alike; different; dissimilar. *prep.* different from; not like: as, it is *unlike* him to cry. —**un·like′ness,** *n.*

**un·like·ly** (un-līk′li), *adj.* 1. not likely; improbable. 2. not likely to succeed; unpromising. *adv.* improbably. —**un·like′li·hood′, un·like′li·ness,** *n.*

**un·lim·ber** (un-lim′bẽr), *v.t. & v.i.* 1. to prepare (a field gun) for use by detaching the limber. 2. to get ready for use or action.

**un·lim·it·ed** (un-lim′it-id), *adj.* 1. without limits or restrictions. 2. vast; illimitable. 3. not defined; indefinite. —**un·lim′it·ed·ly,** *adv.* —**un·lim′it·ed·ness,** *n.*

**un·load** (un-lōd′), *v.t.* 1. to remove (a load, cargo, etc.). 2. to relieve of something that troubles, burdens, etc. 3. to take a load or cargo from. 4. to remove the charge from (a gun). 5. to get rid of. *v.i.* to discharge or get rid of something.

**un·lock** (un-lok′), *v.t.* 1. to open or unfasten (something locked). 2. to open, release, or unfasten by or as by undoing a lock. 3. to bring to light; reveal. *v.i.* to become unlocked.

**un·looked-for** (un-lookt′fôr′), *adj.* not looked for; not expected or foreseen.

**un·loose** (un-lo͞os′), *v.t.* [-LOOSED, -LOOSING], to loose; set free, release, undo, or unfasten.

**un·loos·en** (un-lo͞os′'n), *v.t.* to loosen; unloose.

**un·luck·y** (un-luk′i), *adj.* [-IER, -IEST], having, bringing, or involving bad luck; unfortunate, ill-fated, or ill-omened. —**un·luck′i·ly,** *adv.* —**un·luck′i·ness,** *n.*

**un·make** (un-māk′), *v.t.* [-MADE, -MAKING], 1. to cause to be as before being made; undo. 2. to ruin; destroy. 3. to depose from a position, rank, etc.

**un·man** (un-man′), *v.t.* [-MANNED, -MANNING], to deprive of the qualities considered manly; make weak, nervous, timid, etc.; unnerve.

**un·man·ner·ly** (un-man′ẽr-li), *adj.* having or showing poor manners; rude. *adv.* in an unmannerly way; rudely. —**un·man′ner·li·ness,** *n.*

**un·mask** (un-mask′, -mäsk′), *v.t. & v.i.* 1. to remove a mask or disguise (from). 2. to disclose the true nature of or appear in true character.

**un·mean·ing** (un-mēn′iŋ), *adj.* 1. lacking in meaning or sense. 2. showing no sense; expressionless. —**un·mean′ing·ly,** *adv.* —**un·mean′ing·ness,** *n.*

**un·meet** (un-mēt′), *adj.* not meet, fit, or proper; unseemly; unbecoming.

**un·men·tion·a·ble** (un-men′shən-ə-b'l), *adj.* considered improper for polite conversation; not fit to be mentioned. *n. pl.* things regarded as unfit for mention; specif., undergarments. —**un·men′tion·a·bly,** *adv.* —**un·men′tion·a·ble·ness,** *n.*

**un·mer·ci·ful** (un-mũr′si-fəl), *adj.* having or showing no mercy; cruel; pitiless. —**un·mer′ci·ful·ly,** *adv.* —**un·mer′ci·ful·ness,** *n.*

**un·mis·tak·a·ble** (un′mis-tāk′ə-b'l), *adj.* that cannot be mistaken or misinterpreted; clear. —**un′mis·tak′a·ble·ness,** *n.* —**un′mis·tak′a·bly,** *adv.*

**un·mit·i·gat·ed** (un-mit′ə-gāt′id), *adj.* 1. not lessened or eased: as, *unmitigated* suffering. 2. clear-cut; absolute: as, an *unmitigated* villain.

**un·mor·al** (un-môr′əl, -mor′-), *adj.* 1. neither moral nor immoral; nonmoral. 2. unable to distinguish right from wrong. —**un·mo·ral·i·ty** (un′mô-ral′ə-ti, un′mə-), *n.* —**un·mor′al·ly,** *adv.*

**un·muz·zle** (un-muz′'l), *v.t.* [-ZLED, -ZLING], 1. to free (a dog, etc.) from a muzzle. 2. to free from restraint or censorship.

**un·nat·u·ral** (un-nach′ẽr-əl), *adj.* 1. contrary to, or at variance with, nature; abnormal. 2. artificial or affected. 3. abnormally evil or cruel. —**un·nat′u·ral·ly,** *adv.* —**un·nat′u·ral·ness,** *n.*

**un·nec·es·sar·y** (un-nes′ə-ser′i), *adj.* not necessary or required; needless. —**un·nec′es·sar′i·ly,** *adv.*

**un·nerve** (un-nũrv′), *v.t.* [-NERVED, -NERVING], to deprive of nerve, courage, self-confidence, etc.

**un·num·bered** (un-num′bẽrd), *adj.* 1. countless; innumerable. 2. not numbered. 3. not counted.

**un·oc·cu·pied** (un-ok′yoo-pīd′), *adj.* not occupied; specif., *a)* vacant; empty. *b)* at leisure; idle.

**un·or·gan·ized** (un-ôr′gə-nīzd′), *adj.* 1. having no organic structure. 2. having no regular order, system, etc. 3. not belonging to a labor union.

**un·pack** (un-pak′), *v.t.* 1. to open and remove the contents of. 2. to take out of a package, trunk, etc. *v.i.* to unpack a packed trunk, etc.

**un·paged** (un-pājd′), *adj.* having the pages not numbered: said of a book, etc.

**un·par·al·leled** (un-par′ə-leld′), *adj.* that has no parallel, equal, or counterpart; unmatched.

**un·par·lia·men·ta·ry** (un′pär-lə-men′tə-ri, -men′tri), *adj.* contrary to parliamentary law or usage. —**un′par·lia·men′ta·ri·ly,** *adv.*

**un·peg** (un-peg′), *v.t.* [-PEGGED, -PEGGING], to unfasten by removing a peg or pegs.

**un·peo·ple** (un-pē′p'l), *v.t.* [-PLED, -PLING], to remove people from; depopulate. —**un·peo′pled,** *adj.*

---

**unleased**
**unleavened**
**unlevied**
**unlicensed**
**unlifelike**
**unlighted**
**unlikable**
**unlikeable**
**unlined**
**unlisted**
**unlit**
**unlively**
**unlocated**
**unlovable**
**unloved**
**unlovely**
**unlubricated**
**unmagnified**
**unmaidenly**
**unmailable**
**unmalleable**
**unmanageable**
**unmanly**
**unmannered**
**unmanufactured**
**unmarked**
**unmarketable**
**unmarred**
**unmarried**
**unmastered**
**unmatched**
**unmated**
**unmatted**
**unmatured**
**unmeant**
**unmeasurable**
**unmeasured**
**unmechanical**
**unmedicated**
**unmelodious**
**unmelted**
**unmended**
**unmentioned**
**unmerited**
**unmethodical**
**unmilitary**
**unmilled**
**unmindful**
**unmingled**
**unmistaken**
**unmitigable**
**unmixed**
**unmodified**
**unmoistened**
**unmold**
**unmolested**
**unmollified**
**unmoor**
**unmortgaged**
**unmotivated**
**unmounted**
**unmourned**
**unmovable**
**unmoved**
**unmoving**
**unmown**
**unmuffle**
**unmurmuring**
**unmusical**
**unmystified**
**unnail**
**unnamable**
**unnameable**
**unnamed**
**unnaturalized**
**unnavigable**
**unnavigated**
**unneeded**
**unneedful**
**unnegotiable**
**unneighborly**
**unnoted**
**unnoticeable**
**unnoticed**
**unnurtured**
**unobjectionable**
**unobliged**
**unobliging**
**unobscured**
**unobservant**
**unobserved**
**unobserving**
**unobstructed**
**unobtainable**
**unobtrusive**
**unoccasioned**
**unoffending**
**unoffensive**
**unoffered**
**unofficial**
**unofficious**
**unoiled**
**unopen**
**unopened**
**unopposed**
**unoppressed**
**unordained**
**unoriginal**
**unornamental**
**unorthodox**
**unostentatious**
**unowned**
**unoxidized**
**unpacified**
**unpaid**
**unpaid-for**
**unpainful**
**unpaired**
**unpalatable**
**unpardonable**
**unpardoned**
**unparted**
**unpartisan**
**unpasteurized**
**unpatched**
**unpatented**
**unpatriotic**
**unpaved**
**unpeaceful**
**unpen**
**unpenetrated**
**unpensioned**
**unperceived**
**unperceiving**
**unperfected**
**unperformed**
**unperplexed**
**unpersuadable**
**unpersuaded**
**unpersuasive**
**unperturbed**
**unperused**
**unphilosophic**
**unphilosophical**
**unphonetic**
**unpicked**
**unpierced**
**unpile**

---

fat, āpe, bâre, cär; ten, ēven, hêre, ovẽr; is, bīte; lot, gō, hôrn, to͞ol, look; oil, out; up, ūse, fũr; get; joy; yet; chin; she; thin, *th*en; zh, leisure; ŋ, ring; ə for *a* in *ago*, *e* in *agent*, *i* in *sanity*, *o* in *comply*, *u* in *focus*; ′ in *able* (ā′b'l); Fr. bål; ë, Fr. coeur; ö, Fr. feu; Fr. mo*n*; ô, Fr. coq; ü, Fr. duc; H, G. ich; kh, G. doch. ‡ foreign; < derived from.

**un·pin** (un-pin′), *v.t.* [-PINNED, -PINNING], to unfasten by removing a pin or pins from.
**un·pleas·ant** (un-plez′'nt), ***adj.*** not pleasant; offensive; disagreeable. **—un·pleas′ant·ly, *adv.* —un·pleas′ant·ness, *n.***
**un·plumbed** (un-plumd′), ***adj.*** 1. not fathomed or measured; unknown. 2. having no plumbing.
**un·polled** (un-pōld′), ***adj.*** 1. not having voted. 2. not cast or entered: said of a vote.
**un·pop·u·lar** (un-pop′yoo-lẽr), ***adj.*** not liked or approved of by the public or by the majority. **—un·pop·u·lar·i·ty** (un′pop-yoo-lar′ə-ti), ***n.*** **—un·pop′u·lar·ly, *adv.***
**un·prac·ticed, un·prac·tised** (un-prak′tist), ***adj.*** 1. not habitually or repeatedly done, performed, etc. 2. not skilled or experienced; inexpert.
**un·prec·e·dent·ed** (un-pres′ə-den′tid), ***adj.*** having no precedent or parallel; unheard-of; novel; unexampled. **—un·prec′e·dent′ed·ly, *adv.***
**un·prej·u·diced** (un-prej′oo-dist), ***adj.*** 1. without prejudice or bias; impartial. 2. not impaired.
**un·priced** (un-prist′), ***adj.*** having no fixed price.
**un·prin·ci·pled** (un-prin′sə-p'ld), ***adj.*** lacking moral principles; unscrupulous. **—unprincipled in,** uninstructed in the principles of.
**un·print·a·ble** (un-print′ə-b'l), ***adj.*** not fit to be printed, as because of obscenity.
**un·pro·fes·sion·al** (un′prə-fesh′ən-'l), ***adj.*** 1. violating the ethical code of a given profession. 2. not of, characteristic of, or belonging to a profession. **—un′pro·fes′sion·al·ly, *adv.***
**un·qual·i·fied** (un-kwäl′ə-fīd′), ***adj.*** 1. lacking the necessary qualifications. 2. not modified or limited: as, an *unqualified* endorsement. 3. absolute; thoroughgoing: as, an *unqualified* success. **—un·qual′i·fied′ly, *adv.* —un·qual′i·fied′ness, *n.***
**un·ques·tion·a·ble** (un-kwes′chən-ə-b'l), ***adj.*** 1. not to be questioned, doubted, or disputed; certain. 2. unexceptionable. **—un·ques′tion·a·ble·ness, *n.* —un·ques′tion·a·bly, *adv.***
**un·qui·et** (un-kwī′ət), ***adj.*** 1. not quiet; restless; disturbed. 2. anxious; uneasy. 3. disturbing. **—un·qui′et·ly, *adv.* —un·qui′et·ness, *n.***
**un·quote** (un-kwōt′), *v.t. & v.i.* [-QUOTED, -QUOTING], to end (a quotation): generally used absolutely.
**un·rav·el** (un-rav′'l), *v.t.* [-ELED or -ELLED, -ELING or -ELLING], 1. to undo (something woven, tangled, etc.); separate the threads of. 2. to make clear; solve. ***v.i.*** to become unraveled.
**un·read** (un-red′), ***adj.*** 1. not having been read, as a book, etc. 2. having read little or nothing.
**un·read·y** (un-red′i), ***adj.*** 1. not ready; not prepared, as for action. 2. not prompt or alert; slow. **—un·read′i·ly, *adv.* —un·read′i·ness, *n.***
**un·re·al** (un-rē′əl, -rēl′), ***adj.*** not real or actual; fantastic; imaginary; fanciful. **—un·re·al·i·ty** (un′ri-al′ə-ti), **un·re′al·ness, *n.***
**un·rea·son·a·ble** (un-rē′z'n-ə-b'l), ***adj.*** 1. not reasonable or rational. 2. excessive; immoderate. **—un·rea′son·a·ble·ness, *n.* —un·rea′son·a·bly, *adv.***
**un·rea·son·ing** (un-rē′z'n-iŋ), ***adj.*** not reasoning; thoughtless; irrational. **—un·rea′son·ing·ly, *adv.***
**un·re·con·struct·ed** (un′rē-kən-struk′tid), ***adj.*** opposed to the Reconstruction or unwilling to accept the results of the Civil War.
**un·reel** (un-rēl′), *v.t. & v.i.* to unwind as from a reel.
**un·re·gen·er·ate** (un′ri-jen′ẽr-it), ***adj.*** 1. not spiritually reborn or converted. 2. wicked; sinful. Also **un′re·gen′er·at′ed** (-āt′id). **—un′re·gen′er·ate·ly, *adv.* —un′re·gen′er·ate·ness, *n.***
**un·re·lent·ing** (un′ri-len′tiŋ), ***adj.*** 1. refusing to yield or relent. 2. without mercy; cruel. 3. not relaxing in effort, speed, etc. **—un′re·lent′ing·ly, *adv.* —un′re·lent′ing·ness, *n.***
**un·re·li·gious** (un′ri-lij′əs), ***adj.*** 1. irreligious. 2. neither religious nor irreligious; nonreligious. **—un′re·li′gious·ly, *adv.* —un′re·li′gious·ness, *n.***
**un·re·mit·ting** (un′ri-mit′iŋ), ***adj.*** not stopping, relaxing, etc.; incessant; persistent. **—un′re·mit′ting·ly, *adv.* —un′re·mit′ting·ness, *n.***
**un·re·served** (un′ri-zũrvd′), ***adj.*** 1. not reserved in speech or behavior; frank. 2. not restricted or qualified. **—un′re·serv′ed·ly** (-zũr′vid-li), ***adv.***
**un·rest** (un-rest′), ***n.*** 1. a troubled or disturbed state; restlessness; disquiet. 2. angry discontent verging on revolt.
**un·rid·dle** (un-rid′'l), *v.t.* [-DLED, -DLING], to solve or explain (a riddle, mystery, etc.).
**un·right·eous** (un-rī′chəs), ***adj.*** 1. wicked; sinful. 2. not right; unjust; unfair. **—un·right′eous·ly, *adv.* —un·right′eous·ness, *n.***
**un·ripe** (un-rīp′), ***adj.*** not ripe or mature; green. **—un·ripe′ness, *n.***
**un·ri·valed, un·ri·valled** (un-rī′v'ld), ***adj.*** having no rival, equal, or competitor; matchless.
**un·roll** (un-rōl′), *v.t.* 1. to open or extend (something rolled up). 2. to present to view; display. ***v.i.*** to become unrolled.
**un·ruf·fled** (un-ruf′'ld), ***adj.*** not ruffled or disturbed; calm; smooth; serene.
**un·rul·y** (un-rōō′li), ***adj.*** [-IER, -IEST], hard to control, restrain, or keep in order; disobedient; unmanageable; disorderly. **—un·rul′i·ness, *n.***
**un·sad·dle** (un-sad′'l), *v.t.* [-DLED, -DLING], 1. to take the saddle off (a horse, etc.). 2. to throw

---

**unpitied**
**unpitying**
**unplaced**
**unplait**
**unplanned**
**unplanted**
**unplayed**
**unpleasing**
**unpledged**
**unpliable**
**unploughed**
**unplowed**
**unplucked**
**unplug**
**unpoetic**
**unpoetical**
**unpointed**
**unpoised**
**unpolished**
**unpolitical**
**unpolluted**
**unpopulated**
**unposted**
**unpredictable**
**unpremeditated**
**unprepared**
**unprepossessing**
**unprescribed**
**unpresentable**
**unpressed**
**unpretending**
**unpretentious**
**unpreventable**
**unprinted**
**unprivileged**
**unprocessed**
**unprocurable**
**unproductive**
**unprofaned**
**unprofitable**
**unprogressive**
**unpromising**
**unprompted**
**unpronounceable**
**unpronounced**
**unpropitious**
**unproportionate**
**unprosperous**
**unprotected**
**unproved**
**unproven**
**unprovided**
**unprovoked**
**unpruned**
**unpublished**
**unpunctual**
**unpunished**
**unpurchasable**
**unpurged**
**unpurified**
**unpursuing**
**unquailing**
**unqualifying**
**unquenchable**
**unquestioned**
**unquestioning**
**unquotable**
**unraised**
**unransomed**
**unrated**
**unratified**
**unreachable**
**unreadable**
**unrealized**
**unreasoned**
**unrebuked**
**unreceipted**
**unreceived**
**unreceptive**
**unreclaimed**
**unrecognizable**
**unrecognized**
**unrecommended**
**unrecompensed**
**unreconcilable**
**unreconciled**
**unrecorded**
**unrecruited**
**unredeemed**
**unrefined**
**unreflected**
**unreflecting**
**unreformed**
**unrefreshed**
**unregarded**
**unregistered**
**unregulated**
**unrehearsed**
**unrelated**
**unrelaxed**
**unreliable**
**unrelieved**
**unremedied**
**unremembered**
**unremovable**
**unremoved**
**unremunerated**
**unremunerative**
**unrendered**
**unrenowned**
**unrented**
**unrepaid**
**unrepairable**
**unrepaired**
**unrepealed**
**unrepentant**
**unrepenting**
**unreplaced**
**unreplenished**
**unreported**
**unrepresentative**
**unrepresented**
**unrepressed**
**unreproved**
**unrequested**
**unrequited**
**unresented**
**unresentful**
**unresigned**
**unresisted**
**unresisting**
**unresolved**
**unrespectable**
**unresponsive**
**unrested**
**unrestrainable**
**unrestraint**
**unrestricted**
**unretarded**
**unretentive**
**unretracted**
**unretrieved**
**unreturned**
**unrevealed**
**unrevenged**
**unreversed**
**unrevised**
**unrevoked**
**unrewarded**
**unrhetorical**
**unrhymed**
**unrhythmic**
**unrhythmical**
**unrig**
**unrighted**
**unrightful**
**unroasted**
**unromantic**
**unrounded**
**unruled**
**unsafe**
**unsaid**
**unsaintly**
**unsalable**
**unsalaried**
**unsaleable**
**unsalted**
**unsanctified**

from the saddle; unhorse. ***v.i.*** to take the saddle off a horse, etc.

**un·sa·vor·y** (un-sā′vẽr-i), ***adj.*** 1. tasteless. 2. unpleasant to taste or smell. 3. offensive or unpleasant, especially morally. Also, Brit. sp., **unsavoury.** —**un·sa′vor·i·ly, un·sa′vour·i·ly,** ***adv.*** —**un·sa′vor·i·ness, un·sa′vour·i·ness,** ***n.***

**un·say** (un-sā′), ***v.t.*** [-SAID, -SAYING], to take back or retract (what has been said).

**un·scathed** (un-skā*th*d′), ***adj.*** uninjured.

**un·scram·ble** (un-skram′b'l), ***v.t.*** [-BLED, -BLING], [Colloq.], to cause to be no longer scrambled, disordered, or mixed up.

**un·screw** (un-skrōō′), ***v.t.*** 1. to remove a screw or screws from. 2. to remove or loosen by doing this or by turning. ***v.i.*** to be unscrewed.

**un·scru·pu·lous** (un-skrōō′pyoo-ləs), ***adj.*** having no moral principles or scruples; unprincipled. —**un·scru′pu·lous·ly,** ***adv.*** —**un·scru′pu·lous·ness,** ***n.***

**un·seal** (un-sēl′), ***v.t.*** to break the seal of; open.

**un·search·a·ble** (un-sũrch′ə-b'l), ***adj.*** that cannot be searched into; mysterious; inscrutable. —**un·search′a·ble·ness,** ***n.*** —**un·search′a·bly,** ***adv.***

**un·sea·son·a·ble** (un-sē′z'n-ə-b'l), ***adj.*** 1. not usual for the season. 2. untimely; inopportune. —**un·sea′son·a·ble·ness,** ***n.*** —**un·sea′son·a·bly,** ***adv.***

**un·seat** (un-sēt′), ***v.t.*** 1. to throw or dislodge from a seat. 2. to remove from office, deprive of rank, etc. 3. to unhorse.

**un·seem·ly** (un-sēm′li), ***adj.*** not seemly, decent, or becoming; improper; indecorous. ***adv.*** in an unseemly manner. —**un·seem′li·ness,** ***n.***

**un·set·tle** (un-set′'l), ***v.t. & v.i.*** [-TLED, -TLING], to make or become unstable; disturb, displace, or disorder.

**un·sex** (un-seks′), ***v.t.*** to deprive of the qualities considered characteristic of one's sex.

**un·shack·le** (un-shak′'l), ***v.t.*** [-LED, -LING], 1. to loosen or remove the shackles from. 2. to free.

**un·sheathe** (un-shē*th*′), ***v.t.*** [-SHEATHED, -SHEATHING], to remove (a sword, etc.) from a sheath.

**un·ship** (un-ship′), ***v.t.*** [-SHIPPED, -SHIPPING], 1. to unload from a ship. 2. to remove (an oar, etc.) from the proper position for use.

**un·sight·ly** (un-sīt′li), ***adj.*** not sightly; not pleasant to look at; ugly. —**un·sight′li·ness,** ***n.***

**un·skilled** (un-skild′), ***adj.*** having or requiring no special skill or training: as, *unskilled* labor.

**un·skill·ful, un·skil·ful** (un-skil′fəl), ***adj.*** having little or no skill; awkward; clumsy. —**un·skill′ful·ly, un·skil′ful·ly,** ***adv.*** —**un·skill′ful·ness, un·skil′ful·ness,** ***n.***

**un·snap** (un-snap′), ***v.t.*** [-SNAPPED, -SNAPPING], to detach by undoing the snap or snaps of.

**un·snarl** (un-snärl′), ***v.t.*** to untangle; free of snarls or entanglement.

**un·so·cia·ble** (un-sō′shə-b'l), ***adj.*** 1. avoiding association with others; not sociable. 2. not conducive to sociability. —**un′so·cia·bil′i·ty, un·so′cia·ble·ness,** ***n.*** —**un·so′cia·bly,** ***adv.***

**un·sol·der** (un-sod′ẽr), ***v.t.*** 1. to take apart (things soldered together). 2. to disunite.

**un·so·phis·ti·cat·ed** (un′sə-fis′tə-kāt′id), ***adj.*** 1. not sophisticated; artless; simple. 2. genuine or pure. —**un′so·phis′ti·cat′ed·ly,** ***adv.*** —**un′so·phis′ti·ca′tion,** ***n.***

**un·sound** (un-sound′), ***adj.*** 1. not sound, whole, or perfect. 2. false; ill-founded. 3. not safe, firm, etc.; insecure. 4. not deep; light: said of sleep. —**un·sound′ly,** ***adv.*** —**un·sound′ness,** ***n.***

**un·spar·ing** (un-spâr′iŋ), ***adj.*** 1. not sparing or stinting; lavish. 2. not merciful; severe. —**un·spar′ing·ly,** ***adv.*** —**un·spar′ing·ness,** ***n.***

**un·speak·a·ble** (un-spēk′ə-b'l), ***adj.*** 1. that cannot be spoken. 2. unutterable; ineffable. 3. inexpressibly bad, evil, or objectionable. —**un·speak′a·bly,** ***adv.*** —**un·speak′a·ble·ness,** ***n.***

**un·sta·ble** (un-stā′b'l), ***adj.*** 1. not stable; easily upset, shifted, or unbalanced. 2. changeable; variable. 3. unreliable; fickle. 4. in *chemistry,* tending to decompose or change into other compounds. —**un·sta′ble·ness,** ***n.*** —**un·sta′bly,** ***adv.***

**un·stead·y** (un-sted′i), ***adj.*** 1. not steady or firm; shaky. 2. changeable; inconstant. 3. erratic in habits, purpose, etc. —**un·stead′i·ly,** ***adv.*** —**un·stead′i·ness,** ***n.***

**un·stop** (un-stop′), ***v.t.*** [-STOPPED, -STOPPING], 1. to remove the stopper from. 2. to clear (a pipe, etc.) of an obstruction; open.

**un·strap** (un-strap′), ***v.t.*** [-STRAPPED, -STRAPPING], to loosen or remove the strap or straps of.

**un·string** (un-striŋ′), ***v.t.*** [-STRUNG, -STRINGING], 1. to loosen or remove the string or strings of. 2. to remove from a string. 3. to weaken or disorder; make unstrung (usually in the passive).

**un·strung** (un-struŋ′), ***adj.*** 1. weak; nervous; upset. 2. having the strings loosened or detached.

**un·stud·ied** (un-stud′id), ***adj.*** 1. not got by study or conscious effort. 2. spontaneous; natural; unforced. 3. not having studied; unlearned.

**un·sub·stan·tial** (un′səb-stan′shəl), ***adj.*** 1. having no material substance. 2. not solid; flimsy. 3. unreal; visionary. —**un′sub·stan′ti·al′i·ty** (-shi-al′ə-ti), ***n.*** —**un′sub·stan′tial·ly,** ***adv.***

**un·suit·a·ble** (un-sōōt′ə-b'l, -sūt′-), ***adj.*** not suitable; unbecoming. —**un·suit′a·bil′i·ty, un·suit′a·ble·ness,** ***n.*** —**un·suit′a·bly,** ***adv.***

**un·sung** (un-suŋ′), ***adj.*** 1. not sung. 2. not honored or celebrated as in song or poetry.

---

**unsanctioned**
**unsanitary**
**unsated**
**unsatiable**
**unsatiated**
**unsatisfactory**
**unsatisfied**
**unsatisfying**
**unsaturated**
**unsaved**
**unsawn**
**unsayable**
**unscaled**
**unscanned**
**unscarred**
**unscented**
**unscheduled**
**unscholarly**
**unschooled**
**unscientific**
**unscorched**
**unscorned**
**unscoured**
**unscourged**
**unscraped**
**unscratched**
**unscreened**
**unscriptural**
**unsculptured**
**unseam**
**unseasoned**
**unseaworthy**
**unseconded**
**unsectarian**
**unsecured**
**unseeded**
**unseeing**
**unseen**
**unsegmented**
**unseized**
**unselected**
**unselfish**
**unsent**
**unsentimental**
**unserved**
**unserviceable**
**unset**
**unsevered**
**unsew**
**unshaded**
**unshadowed**
**unshakable**
**unshakeable**
**unshaken**
**unshamed**
**unshaped**
**unshapely**
**unshared**
**unshaved**
**unshaven**
**unshed**
**unshell**
**unsheltered**
**unshod**
**unshorn**
**unshrinkable**
**unshrinking**
**unshriven**
**unshrunk**
**unshut**
**unsifted**
**unsighted**
**unsigned**
**unsilenced**
**unsimilar**
**unsingable**
**unsinkable**
**unsisterly**
**unsized**
**unslacked**
**unslaked**
**unsleeping**
**unsmiling**
**unsmoked**
**unsoaked**
**unsocial**
**unsoftened**
**unsoiled**
**unsold**
**unsoldierly**
**unsolicited**
**unsoluble**
**unsolvable**
**unsolved**
**unsorted**
**unsought**
**unsounded**
**unsowed**
**unsown**
**unspecified**
**unspent**
**unspilled**
**unspiritual**
**unspoiled**
**unspoilt**
**unspoken**
**unsportsmanlike**
**unsprinkled**
**unsprung**
**unsquandered**
**unstained**
**unstamped**
**unstandardized**
**unstarched**
**unstated**
**unstatesmanlike**
**unstemmed**
**unsterilized**
**unstinted**
**unstitched**
**unstrained**
**unstratified**
**unstressed**
**unstriated**
**unstuck**
**unstuffed**
**unsubdued**
**unsubmissive**
**unsubscribed**
**unsubsidized**
**unsubstantiated**
**unsuccessful**
**unsuggestive**
**unsuited**
**unsullied**
**unsupportable**
**unsupported**
**unsure**
**unsurmountable**
**unsurpassable**
**unsurpassed**
**unsusceptible**
**unsuspected**
**unsuspecting**

---

fat, āpe, bâre, cär; ten, ēven, hêre, ovẽr; is, bīte; lot, gō, hôrn, tōōl, look; oil, out; up, ūse, fũr; get; joy; yet; chin; she; thin, *th*en; zh, leisure; ŋ, ring; ə for *a* in *ago, e* in *agent, i* in *sanity, o* in *comply, u* in *focus;* ′ in *able* (ā′b'l); Fr. bål; ë, Fr. coeur; ö, Fr. feu; Fr. mo*n*; ô, Fr. coq; ü, Fr. duc; H, G. ich; kh, G. doch. ‡ foreign; < derived from.

**un·tan·gle** (un-taŋ′g'l), *v.t.* [-GLED, -GLING], 1. to free from a snarl or tangle; disentangle. 2. to put in order; straighten out.
**un·taught** (un-tôt′), *adj.* 1. not taught; uneducated. 2. got without teaching; natural.
**un·thank·ful** (un-thaŋk′fəl), *adj.* 1. ungrateful. 2. thankless; unappreciated. **—un·thank′ful·ly,** *adv.* **—un·thank′ful·ness,** *n.*
**un·think·a·ble** (un-thiŋk′ə-b'l), *adj.* that cannot be thought, conceived, or considered. **—un·think′a·ble·ness,** *n.* **—un·think′a·bly,** *adv.*
**un·think·ing** (un-thiŋk′iŋ), *adj.* thoughtless; heedless; inconsiderate. **—un·think′ing·ly,** *adv.* **—un·think′ing·ness,** *n.*
**un·thread** (un-thred′), *v.t.* 1. to draw the thread from. 2. to unravel. 3. to find one's way through.
**un·ti·dy** (un-tī′di), *adj.* not tidy; slovenly; careless. **—un·ti′di·ly,** *adv.* **—un·ti′di·ness,** *n.*
**un·tie** (un-tī′), *v.t.* [-TIED, -TYING or -TIEING], 1. to unfasten (something tied or knotted). 2. to free, as from restraint. *v.i.* to become untied.
**un·til** (un-til′, ən-), *prep.* [ME. *untill* < *un-* (see UNTO) + *till*, till], 1. up to the time of; till: as, *until* your departure. 2. before (a time specified): as, don't come *until* nine o'clock. *conj.* 1. up to the time when or that. 2. to the point, degree, etc. that: as, he ate *until* he was full. 3. before: as, don't leave *until* he does.
**un·time·ly** (un-tīm′li), *adj.* 1. before the proper time; premature: as, an *untimely* death. 2. at the wrong time; inopportune. *adv.* 1. inopportunely. 2. prematurely. **—un·time′li·ness,** *n.*
**un·to** (un′to͞o, -too), *prep.* [ME. *un-* (< ON. *und*, unto) + *to*], [Archaic or Poetic], 1. to. 2. until.
**un·told** (un-tōld′), *adj.* 1. not told or revealed. 2. too many to be counted; incalculable; vast.
**un·touch·a·ble** (un-tuch′ə-b'l), *adj.* 1. out of reach. 2. not to be touched, as because of a taboo. *n.* in India, formerly, a member of the lowest caste, whose touch was regarded as defiling to Hindus of high caste. **—un′touch·a·bil′i·ty,** *n.*
**un·to·ward** (un-tôrd′, -tō′ẽrd), *adj.* 1. hard to manage; perverse; stubborn. 2. inconvenient; unfortunate; unfavorable. 3. unseemly. 4. [Obs.], awkward. **—un·to·ward′ly,** *adv.* **—un·to·ward′ness,** *n.*
**un·true** (un-tro͞o′), *adj.* 1. incorrect; false. 2. not conforming to a standard or rule. 3. not faithful or loyal. **—un·tru′ly,** *adv.*
**un·truth** (un-tro͞oth′), *n.* 1. falsity; lack of veracity. 2. a falsehood; lie.
**un·truth·ful** (un-tro͞oth′fəl), *adj.* 1. not in accordance with the truth. 2. telling lies often. **—un·truth′ful·ly,** *adv.* **—un·truth′ful·ness,** *n.*
**un·tu·tored** (un-to͞o′tẽrd, -tū′-), *adj.* 1. uneducated; untaught. 2. naive; unsophisticated.
**un·twine** (un-twīn′), *v.t.* [-TWINED, -TWINING], to undo (something twined or twisted); disentangle. *v.i.* to become untwined.
**un·twist** (un-twist′), *v.t.* & *v.i.* to untwine.
**un·used** (un-ūzd′), *adj.* 1. not in use. 2. unaccustomed. 3. that has never been used.
**un·u·su·al** (un-ū′zho͞o-əl), *adj.* not usual or common; rare. **—un·u′su·al·ly,** *adv.* **—un·u′su·al·ness,** *n.*
**un·ut·ter·a·ble** (un-ut′ẽr-ə-b'l), *adj.* 1. that cannot be pronounced. 2. that cannot be expressed or described. **—un·ut′ter·a·bly,** *adv.*
**un·var·nished** (un-vär′nisht), *adj.* 1. not varnished. 2. plain; simple; unadorned.
**un·veil** (un-vāl′), *v.t.* to remove a veil from; disclose. *v.i.* to take off a veil; reveal oneself.
**un·war·y** (un-wâr′i), *adj.* not watchful or cautious; unguarded. **—un·war′i·ly,** *adv.* **—un·war′i·ness,** *n.*
**un·well** (un-wel′), *adj.* not well; ill; sick.
**un·wept** (un-wept′), *adj.* 1. not shed: said of tears. 2. not wept for; unmourned.
**un·whole·some** (un-hōl′səm), *adj.* 1. harmful to body or mind. 2. of unsound health, or of unhealthy appearance. 3. morally harmful or corrupt. **—un·whole′some·ly,** *adv.* **—un·whole′some·ness,** *n.*
**un·wield·y** (un-wēl′di), *adj.* [-IER, -IEST], 1. hard to wield, manage, handle, etc., as because of large size, awkward form, etc. 2. awkward; clumsy. **—un·wield′i·ly,** *adv.* **—un·wield′i·ness,** *n.*
**un·will·ing** (un-wil′iŋ), *adj.* 1. not willing or inclined; reluctant. 2. done, said, etc. reluctantly. **—un·will′ing·ly,** *adv.* **—un·will′ing·ness,** *n.*
**un·wind** (un-wīnd′), *v.t.* [-WOUND, -WINDING], 1. to wind off or undo (something wound). 2. to untangle (something involved). *v.i.* to become unwound.
**un·wise** (un-wīz′), *adj.* having or showing a lack of wisdom or sound judgment. **—un·wise′ly,** *adv.*
**un·wit·ting** (un-wit′iŋ), *adj.* 1. not knowing or aware; unconscious. 2. unintentional. **—un·wit′ting·ly,** *adv.* **—un·wit′ting·ness,** *n.*
**un·wont·ed** (un-wun′tid), *adj.* 1. not accustomed, familiar, etc. (usually with *to*). 2. uncommon; rare. **—un·wont′ed·ly,** *adv.* **—un·wont′ed·ness,** *n.*
**un·wor·thy** (un-wũr′*th*i), *adj.* [-THIER, -THIEST], 1. without merit or value; worthless. 2. not deserving (usually with *of*). 3. not fit, becoming, etc. (usually with *of*). 4. shameful; despicable. **—un·wor′thi·ly,** *adv.* **—un·wor′thi·ness,** *n.*
**un·wrap** (un-rap′), *v.t.* [-WRAPPED, -WRAPPING], to take off the wrapping of; open (something wrapped). *v.i.* to become unwrapped.
**un·writ·ten** (un-rit′'n), *adj.* 1. not in writing. 2. operating only through custom or tradition: said of laws, etc. 3. not written on; blank.
**unwritten law,** 1. common law. 2. any rule or principle rigidly observed although it is not law. 3. the assumed right of a person to avenge his family's honor, especially in cases of seduction, adultery, or rape, as by criminally harming the person regarded as guilty.
**un·yoke** (un-yōk′), *v.t.* [-YOKED, -YOKING], 1. to release from a yoke. 2. to separate or disconnect.
**up** (up), *adv.* [AS.], 1. from a lower to a higher place. 2. in or on a higher position or level. 3. in a direction or place thought of as higher. 4. above the horizon. 5. from an earlier to a later period or person: as, from childhood *up*. 6. from a lower

---

**unsuspicious**
**unsustained**
**unswayed**
**unsweetened**
**unswept**
**unswerving**
**unsymmetrical**
**unsympathetic**
**unsympathizing**
**unsystematic**
**untactful**
**untainted**
**untalented**
**untamable**
**untameable**
**untamed**
**untanned**
**untapped**
**untarnished**
**untasted**
**untaxable**
**untaxed**
**unteachable**
**untempered**
**untenable**
**untenanted**
**untended**
**unterrified**
**untested**
**untether**
**unthanked**
**unthatched**
**untheatrical**
**unthoughtful**
**unthought-of**
**unthrifty**
**untillable**
**untilled**
**untinged**
**untired**
**untiring**
**untitled**
**untouched**
**untraceable**
**untraced**
**untracked**
**untractable**
**untrained**
**untrammeled**
**untrammelled**
**untransferable**
**untransferred**
**untranslatable**
**untranslated**
**untransmitted**
**untrapped**
**untraveled**
**untravelled**
**untraversable**
**untraversed**
**untreasured**
**untried**
**untrimmed**
**untroubled**
**untruss**
**untrustworthy**
**untufted**
**untunable**
**untuned**
**untuneful**
**unturned**
**untwilled**
**untypical**
**unusable**
**unutilized**
**unuttered**
**unvaccinated**
**unvacillating**
**unvalued**
**unvanquished**
**unvaried**
**unvarying**
**unventilated**
**unverifiable**
**unverified**
**unversed**
**unvexed**
**unvisited**
**unvoiced**
**unvulcanized**
**unwakened**
**unwalled**
**unwanted**
**unwarlike**
**unwarmed**
**unwarned**
**unwarranted**
**unwashed**
**unwasted**
**unwatched**
**unwavering**
**unweakened**
**unweaned**
**unwearable**
**unwearied**
**unweary**
**unwearying**
**unweathered**
**unweave**
**unwed**
**unwedded**
**unweeded**
**unwelded**
**unwifely**
**unwilled**
**unwincing**
**unwinking**
**unwithered**
**unwitnessed**
**unwomanly**
**unwooded**
**unwooed**
**unworkable**
**unworked**
**unworkmanlike**
**unworldly**
**unworn**
**unworshiped**
**unworshipped**
**unwounded**
**unwoven**
**unwrinkle**
**unwrought**
**unyielding**
**unyouthful**
**unzealous**

to a higher condition or station. 7. to a higher amount, degree, etc.: as, prices are going *up*. 8. *a*) in or into a standing position. *b*) out of bed. 9. in or into action, view, consideration, etc.: as, bring it *up* at the next meeting. 10. into an excited or troubled state: as, wrought *up* by the news. 11. aside; away; by: as, to lay *up* grain. 12. so as to be even with in time, degree, etc.: as, to keep *up* with the times. 13. in or into a close space: as, fold *up* the sheets. 14. completely; entirely; thoroughly. 15. in *baseball*, to one's turn at batting. 16. in *nautical usage*, to the windward point: as, put *up* the helm. 17. in *sports*, ahead of an opponent by a specified number of points, goals, etc. The adverb *up* is used idiomatically: *a*) to form a verb-adverb combination which changes the meaning of the verb (e.g., look *up* this word). *b*) as an intensive with verbs (e.g., dress *up*). *c*) [Colloq.], as a meaningless element added to a verb (e.g., light *up* a cigarette). ***prep.*** 1. to, toward, or at a higher place, condition, or station on or in. 2. to, toward, or at a point farther along. 3. toward the source of (a river, etc.). 4. in or toward the interior of (a country, territory, etc.). ***adj.*** 1. directed toward a higher position. 2. in a higher position, condition, or station. 3. *a*) above the ground. *b*) above the horizon. 4. advanced in amount, degree, etc.: as, rents are *up*. 5. *a*) in a standing position. *b*) out of bed. 6. in an active or excited state: as, her anger was *up*. 7. even with in time, degree, etc. 8. living or located in the inner part of a country, territory, etc. 9. at an end; over: as, time's *up*. 10. [Colloq.], going on; happening: as, what's *up?* 11. in *baseball*, at bat. ***n.*** *usually pl.* a person or thing that is up; specif., *a*) an upward slope. *b*) an upward movement or course. ***v.i.*** [UPPED, UPPING], [Colloq.], to get up; rise. ***v.t.*** [Colloq.], 1. to put up, lift up, or take up. 2. to increase, or cause to rise: as, to *up* prices. **—on the up and up,** [Slang], honest. **—up against,** [Colloq.], confronted with. **—up and doing,** busy; active. **—up for,** 1. presented or considered for (an elective office, a vote, etc.). 2. before a court for (trial). **—up on** (or **in**), [Colloq.], well informed concerning. **—ups and downs,** changes in fortune. **—up to,** [Colloq.], 1. occupied with; doing; scheming. 2. equal to; capable of (doing, etc.). 3. dependent upon the decision or action of. 4. incumbent upon.

**up** (up), ***adv.*** [phonetic respelling of *ap*iece], apiece; each: as, the score is seven *up*.

**up-,** a combining form meaning *up*, as in *uphill*.

**up-and-com·ing** (up'n-kum'iŋ), ***adj.*** [Colloq.], enterprising, alert, and promising.

**up-and-down** (up'n-doun'), ***adj.*** 1. going alternately up and down, to and fro, etc. 2. variable.

**u·pas** (ū'pəs), ***n.*** [< Malay *pohon upas*, tree of poison], 1. a tall Javanese tree whose whitish bark yields a poisonous milky juice. 2. this juice.

**up·beat** (up'bēt'), ***n.*** in *music*, an unaccented beat, especially when on the last note of a bar.

**up·borne** (up-bôrn', -bōrn'), ***adj.*** borne up; lifted or carried aloft; elevated.

**up·braid** (up-brād'), ***v.t.*** [< AS. < *up-*, up + *bregdan*, to pull, shake], to scold or chide for some wrongdoing, offense, etc.; reprove; reproach. ***v.i.*** to speak with reproach. **—up·braid'er,** ***n.***

**up·braid·ing** (up-brād'iŋ), ***n.*** the act or utterance of one who upbraids; reproof. ***adj.*** reproachful.

**up·bring·ing** (up'briŋ'iŋ), ***n.*** the training and education received during childhood; rearing.

**up·coun·try** (up'kun'tri), ***adj.*** in the interior of a country; inland. ***n.*** the interior of a country. ***adv.*** in or toward the interior of a country.

**up·date** (up-dāt'), ***v.t.*** [-DATED, -DATING], to bring up to date; make current.

**up·end** (up-end'), ***v.t. & v.i.*** to set or stand on end.

**up·grade** (up'grād'), ***n.*** an upward slope. ***adj. & adv.*** uphill. ***v.t.*** [-GRADED, -GRADING], to raise to a higher grade, rate of pay, etc. **—on the upgrade,** 1. rising. 2. progressing; improving.

**up·heav·al** (up-hē'v'l), ***n.*** 1. a heaving up or being heaved up. 2. a sudden, violent change.

**up·heave** (up-hēv'), ***v.t.*** [-HEAVED or -HOVE, -HEAVING], to heave or lift up. ***v.i.*** to rise as if forced up.

**up·hill** (up'hil'), ***adj.*** 1. going or sloping up. 2. tiring; difficult. 3. located on higher ground. ***n.*** a sloping rise. ***adv.*** upward as on a hillside.

**up·hold** (up-hōld'), ***v.t.*** [-HELD, -HOLDING], 1. to hold up; raise. 2. to keep from falling; support. 3. to give moral support to. 4. to decide in favor of; confirm; sustain. **—up·hold'er,** ***n.***

**up·hol·ster** (up-hōl'stēr), ***v.t.*** [ult. < ME. *upholder*, tradesman], to fit out (furniture) with coverings, springs, padding, etc. **—up·hol'stered,** ***adj.*** **—up·hol'ster·er,** ***n.***

**up·hol·ster·y** (up-hōl'stēr-i, -stri), ***n.*** [*pl.* -IES], 1. the fittings and material used in upholstering. 2. the business or work of an upholsterer.

**UPI,** United Press International: formed (1958) by a merger of **UP** (United Press) and **INS.**

**up·keep** (up'kēp'), ***n.*** 1. maintenance. 2. state of repair. 3. the cost of maintenance.

**up·land** (up'lənd, -land'), ***n.*** land elevated above other land. ***adj.*** of or situated in upland.

**up·lift** (up-lift'; *for n.*, up'lift'), ***v.t.*** 1. to lift up; elevate. 2. to raise to a higher moral, social, or spiritual level. ***n.*** 1. a lifting up; elevation. 2. a raising to a higher moral, social, or spiritual level. 3. a movement for moral, social, etc. betterment. 4. a type of brassiere designed to lift and support the breasts: in full, **uplift brassiere. —up·lift'er,** ***n.***

**up·on** (ə-pon', -pôn'), ***prep.*** on or up and on: used interchangeably with *on* depending on rhythm, etc. ***adv.*** on: used only to complete the idea of a verb, as, the canvas has not been painted *upon*.

**up·per** (up'ēr), ***adj.*** 1. higher in place. 2. farther inland. 3. higher in rank; superior. 4. worn outside others: said of clothes. 5. [U-], in *geology*, more recent in a period: as, *Upper* Cambrian. ***n.*** 1. the part of a shoe or boot above the sole. 2. [Colloq.], an upper berth. **—on one's uppers,** [Colloq.], 1. wearing worn-out shoes. 2. poor; shabby.

**up·per-case** (up'ēr-kās'), ***adj.*** designating, of, or in capital letters. ***v.t.*** [-CASED, -CASING], to set in, or change to, capital letters.

**upper case,** capital-letter type used in printing as distinguished from small letters (*lower case*).

**up·per-class** (up'ēr-klas', -kläs'), ***adj.*** 1. of or characteristic of the aristocracy or very wealthy class. 2. of or characteristic of the junior and senior classes in a school, college, etc.

**up·per·class·man** (up'ēr-klas'mən, -kläs'-), ***n.*** [*pl.* -MEN], a junior or senior in a college, etc.

**up·per·cut** (up'ēr-kut'), ***n.*** in *boxing*, a short, swinging blow directed upward. ***v.t. & v.i.*** [-CUT, -CUTTING], to hit with an uppercut.

**upper hand,** the position of advantage or control.

**Upper House,** [often u- h-], that branch of a bicameral legislature which is usually smaller and less representative, as the Senate in Congress.

**up·per·most** (up'ər-mōst'), ***adj.*** highest in place, power, authority, etc.; topmost; foremost. ***adv.*** in the highest place, rank, etc.; first.

**Upper Vol·ta** (vol'tə), a country in W Africa, north of Ghana: a member of the French Community: area, 105,800 sq. mi.; pop., 3,567,000; capital, Ouagadougou.

**up·pish** (up'ish), ***adj.*** [Colloq.], haughty, arrogant, snobbish, etc. **—up'pish·ly,** ***adv.*** **—up'pish·ness,** ***n.***

**up·pi·ty** (up'ə-ti), ***adj.*** [Colloq.], uppish.

**up·raise** (up-rāz'), ***v.t.*** [-RAISED, -RAISING], to raise up; lift; elevate.

**up·rear** (up-rêr'), ***v.t.*** 1. to rear up; raise. 2. to exalt. 3. to bring up. ***v.i.*** to rise up.

**up·right** (up'rīt'; *also, for adv.*, up-rīt'), ***adj.*** 1. standing, pointing, or directed straight up; erect. 2. honest; just. ***adv.*** in an upright position or direction. ***n.*** 1. the state of being upright or vertical. 2. something having an upright position. 3. an upright piano. 4. *pl.* in *football*, the goal posts. **—up'right'ly,** ***adv.*** **—up'right'ness,** ***n.***

**upright piano,** a piano with a rectangular body mounted vertically.

**up·ris·ing** (up'rīz'iŋ, up-rīz'-), ***n.*** 1. a rising up. 2. an upward slope. 3. a revolt.

**up·roar** (up'rôr', -rōr'), ***n.*** [D. *oproer*, a stirring up], 1. a violent disturbance or commotion; tumult. 2. loud, confused noise; din.

**up·roar·i·ous** (up-rôr'i-əs, -rō'ri-), ***adj.*** 1. making, or full of, an uproar. 2. loud and boisterous, as laughter. 3. provoking such laughter. **—up·roar'i·ous·ly,** ***adv.*** **—up·roar'i·ous·ness,** ***n.***

**up·root** (up-rōōt', -root'), ***v.t.*** 1. to tear up by the roots. 2. to destroy or remove utterly.

**up·set** (up-set'; *for n., and occas. adj.*, up'set'), ***v.t.*** [-SET, -SETTING], 1. to tip over; overturn. 2. to disturb the functioning or course of: as, the delay *upset* our schedule, the food *upset* his stomach. 3. to defeat, especially unexpectedly. 4. to perturb; discompose. ***v.i.*** to become overturned or upset. ***n.*** 1. an upsetting or being upset. 2. a disturbance; disorder. 3. an unexpected defeat. ***adj.*** 1. tipped over; overturned. 2. disturbed; disordered. 3. perturbed; distressed. **—up·set'ter,** ***n.***

**up·shot** (up′shot′), *n.* [orig., the final shot in an archery match], the conclusion; result; outcome.
**up·side** (up′sīd′), *n.* the upper side or part.
**upside down,** 1. with the upper part underneath. 2. in disorder; topsy-turvy. —**up′side′-down′,** *adj.*
**up·si·lon** (ūp′sə-lon′, -lən), *n.* [Gr.], the twentieth letter of the Greek alphabet (Υ, υ).
**up·stage** (up′stāj′), *adv.* toward or at the rear of the stage. *adj.* 1. of or having to do with the rear of the stage. 2. [Colloq.], haughtily aloof, conceited, etc. *v.t.* [-STAGED, -STAGING], to treat in a haughty manner.
**up·stairs** (up′stârz′), *adv.* 1. up the stairs. 2. in, on, or toward an upper floor. *adj.* of or on an upper floor. *n.* an upper story or stories.
**up·stand·ing** (up-stan′diŋ), *adj.* 1. erect. 2. having good posture. 3. honorable; straightforward.
**up·start** (up′stärt′), *n.* one who has recently come into wealth, power, etc.; esp., such a person who is pushing, presumptuous, etc. —**up′start′,** *adj.*
**up·start** (up-stärt′), *v.i. & v.t.* to start up or cause to start up.
**up·state** (up′stāt′), *adj.* designating, of, or from the more northerly or inland part of a State. *n.* such a part of a State, especially of New York. *adv.* in or toward such a part of a State. —**up′stat′er,** *n.*
**up·stream** (up′strēm′), *adv.* against the current of a stream. *adj.* 1. of or situated at the upper part of a stream. 2. moving against the current.
**up·surge** (up-sũrj′; *for n.,* up′sũrj′), *v.i.* [-SURGED, -SURGING], to surge up. *n.* a surge upward.
**up·sweep** (up′swēp′), *n.* 1. a sweep or curve upward. 2. a hair-do in which the hair is combed up and piled on the top of the head. *v.t. & v.i.* [-SWEPT, -SWEEPING], to sweep or curve upward.
**up·swing** (up′swiŋ′), *n.* 1. a swing, trend, or movement upward. 2. an advance or improvement.
**up·take** (up′tāk′), *n.* 1. the act of lifting or taking up. 2. the act of or capacity for understanding or comprehending: as, quick on the *uptake.*
**up·thrust** (up′thrust′), *n.* 1. an upward push. 2. an upheaval of a part of the earth's crust.
**up-tight, up·tight** (up′tīt′), *adj.* [Slang], 1. very tense, nervous, etc. 2. overly conventional in attitudes. 3. in a bad way or state.
**up-to-date** (up′tə-dāt′), *adj.* 1. extending to the present time. 2. keeping up with what is most recent, modern, etc. —**up′-to-date′ness,** *n.*
**up·town** (up′toun′), *adj. & adv.* of, in, or toward the upper part of a city or town. *n.* the upper part of a city or town.
**up·turn** (up-tũrn′; *for n.,* up′tũrn′), *v.t. & v.i.* to turn up or over. *n.* an upward turn, curve, or trend. —**up·turned′,** *adj.*
**up·ward** (up′wẽrd), *adv.* 1. to or toward a higher place, position, or part. 2. to or toward the source, center, etc. 3. toward a higher degree, rank, price, etc. 4. on into future years or later life. 5. more; above. *adj.* directed or moving toward, or situated in, a higher position. —**upward of,** more than. —**up′ward·ly,** *adv.* —**up′ward·ness,** *n.*
**up·wards** (up′wẽrdz), *adv.* upward.
**U·ral** (yoor′əl), *n.* 1. *in pl.* a mountain range in the U.S.S.R., between Europe and Asia. 2. a river flowing from the Urals into the Caspian. *adj.* designating or of these mountains or this river.
**U·ral-Al·ta·ic** (yoor′əl-al-tā′ik), *adj.* 1. of the region of the Ural and Altai mountains. 2. designating or of a group of languages which includes the Uralic and Altaic families. 3. of the peoples using these languages. *n.* this group of languages.
**U·ra·li·an** (yoo-rā′li-ən), *adj. & n.* Uralic.
**U·ra·lic** (yoo-rā′lik), *adj.* designating or of a family of languages including the Finno-Ugric subfamilies. *n.* this family of languages.
**U·ra·ni·a** (yoo-rā′ni-ə), *n.* in *Gr. mythology,* the Muse of astronomy.
**u·ra·ni·um** (yoo-rā′ni-əm), *n.* [< *Uranus,* the planet], a very hard, heavy, radioactive metallic chemical element: it is found only in combination, and its isotopes are important in work on atomic energy: symbol, U; at. wt., 238.07; at. no., 92.
**U·ra·nus** (yoor′ə-nəs), *n.* 1. in *Gr. mythology,* the heavens personified, a god regarded as the father of the Titans, Furies, and Cyclopes: he was overthrown by his son Cronus (Saturn). 2. a planet of the solar system: diameter, c. 31,000 mi.
**ur·ban** (ũr′bən), *adj.* [< L. < *urbs,* a city], 1. of, in, or constituting a city or town. 2. characteristic of the city as distinguished from the country.
**ur·bane** (ũr-bān′), *adj.* [< Fr. < L.; see URBAN], polite and suave; smooth and polished in manner. —**ur·bane′ly,** *adv.* —**ur·bane′ness,** *n.*
**ur·ban·i·ty** (ũr-ban′ə-ti), *n.* [*pl.* -TIES], 1. the quality of being urbane; suave politeness. 2. *pl.* civilities, courtesies, or amenities.
**ur·ban·ize** (ũr′bən-īz′), *v.t.* [-IZED, -IZING], to change from rural to urban. —**ur′ban·i·za′tion,** *n.*
**ur·chin** (ũr′chin), *n.* [< OFr. < L. *ericius,* a hedgehog < *er,* hedgehog], 1. a sea urchin. 2. a small boy, or any youngster, especially one who is mischievous.
**Ur·du** (oor′do͞o, oor-do͞o′, ũr-), *n.* 1. a language used by Moslems in India: it developed from Hindustani but with Arabic characters. 2. Hindustani.
**-ure** (ẽr), [Fr. < L. *-ura*], a suffix meaning *act* or *result of an action, agent* or *instrument of action, state of being,* etc., as in *exposure.*
**u·re·a** (yoo-rē′ə, yoor′i-ə), *n.* [< Fr. < Gr. *ouron,* urine], a soluble, crystalline solid, $CO(NH_2)_2$, found in the urine of mammals and produced synthetically: it is used in the manufacture of plastics, adhesives, etc. —**u·re′al,** *adj.*
**u·re·mi·a** (yoo-rē′mi-ə, -rēm′yə), *n.* [< Gr. *ouron,* urine + *haima,* blood], a toxic condition caused by the presence in the blood of waste products normally eliminated in the urine: also sp. **uraemia.** —**u·re′mic,** *adj.*
**u·re·ter** (yoo-rē′tẽr), *n.* [< Gr. < *ourein,* to urinate], a duct or tube that carries urine from a kidney to the bladder or cloaca. —**u·re′ter·al, u·re·ter·ic** (yoor′ə-ter′ik), *adj.*
**u·re·thra** (yoo-rē′thrə), *n.* [*pl.* -THRAE (-thrē), -THRAS], [< LL. < Gr. < *ouron,* urine], the canal through which urine is discharged from the bladder in most mammals: in the male, sperm is also discharged through the urethra. —**u·re′thral,** *adj.*
**urge** (ũrj), *v.t.* [URGED, URGING], [< L. *urgere,* to press hard], 1. to press upon the attention; advocate earnestly and repeatedly. 2. to drive or force onward. 3. to entreat or plead with; ask, persuade, etc. 4. to force; incite; impel. *v.i.* 1. to make an earnest presentation of arguments, claims, charges, etc. 2. to exert a force that drives, as to action. *n.* 1. the act of urging. 2. an impulse to do a certain thing. —**urg′er,** *n.*
**ur·gen·cy** (ũr′jən-si), *n.* [*pl.* -CIES], 1. an urgent quality or state; need for action, haste, etc. 2. insistence. 3. something urgent.
**ur·gent** (ũr′jənt), *adj.* [Fr. < L. ppr. of *urgere,* to urge], 1. calling for haste, immediate action, etc.; pressing. 2. insistent. —**ur′gent·ly,** *adv.*
**-ur·gy** (ũr′ji), [< Gr. < *-ourgos,* worker], a combining form meaning *a fabricating* or *working of* (a specified material), as in *zymurgy.*
**u·ric** (yoor′ik), *adj.* of, contained in, or derived from urine.
**uric acid,** a white, odorless, crystalline substance, $C_5H_4N_4O_3$, found in urine.
**u·ri·nal** (yoor′ə-n'l), *n.* 1. a receptacle for urine. 2. a place for urinating.
**u·ri·nal·y·sis** (yoor′ə-nal′ə-sis), *n.* [*pl.* -SES (-sēz′)], chemical analysis of the urine: also sp. **uranalysis.** Also **urine analysis.**
**u·ri·nar·y** (yoor′ə-ner′i), *adj.* 1. of urine. 2. of the organs concerned in the secretion and discharge of urine. *n.* [*pl.* -IES], a urinal.
**u·ri·nate** (yoor′ə-nāt′), *v.i.* [-NATED, -NATING], to discharge urine from the body. —**u′ri·na′tion,** *n.* —**u′ri·na′tive,** *adj.*
**u·rine** (yoor′in), *n.* [< OFr. < L. *urina*], in mammals, the yellowish fluid containing urea and other waste products, secreted from the blood by the kidneys, passed to the bladder, and periodically discharged through the urethra.
**u·ri·no-,** [< L. *urina,* urine], a combining form meaning *urine, urinary tract:* also **urin-.**
**u·ri·no·gen·i·tal** (yoor′ə-nō-jen′ə-t'l), *adj.* designating or of the urinary and genital organs.
**urn** (ũrn), *n.* [L. *urna*], 1. a vase in any of various forms, usually with a pedestal; esp., one used to hold the ashes of the dead after cremation. 2. the grave. 3. a metal container with a faucet, used for making or serving coffee, etc.
**u·ro-,** [< Gr. *ouron,* urine], a combining form meaning *urine, urinary tract,* etc.: also **ur-.**
**u·ro·gen·i·tal** (yoor′ō-jen′ə-t'l), *adj.* urinogenital.
**u·rol·o·gy** (yoo-rol′ə-ji), *n.* the branch of medicine dealing with the urinogenital system and its diseases. —**u′ro·log′i·cal,** (yoor′ə-loj′i-k'l), **u·ro·log·ic** *adj.* —**u·rol′o·gist,** *n.*
**u·ros·co·py** (yoo-ros′kə-pi), *n.* examination of the urine, as for the diagnosis of disease. —**u·ro·scop·ic** (yoor′ə-skop′ik), *adj.*
**Ur·sa Major** (ũr′sə), [L., lit., Great Bear], the most conspicuous of the constellations in the N sky: it is near the pole and contains the stars which form the Big Dipper: also called *Great Bear.*
**Ursa Minor,** [L., lit., Little Bear], the northernmost constellation: it contains Polaris, the North Star: also called *Little Bear.*

**ur·sine** (ūr′sīn, -sin), *adj.* [< L. < *ursus,* a bear], of or like a bear or the bear family.
**Ur·su·line** (ūr′syoo-lin, -sə-līn′), *n.* [< Saint *Ursula* (c. 300 A.D.), their patron], in the *R.C. Church,* a member of an order of nuns founded c. 1537 to carry on the work of teaching and nursing. *adj.* of or having to do with this order.
**ur·ti·ca·ri·a** (ūr′tə-kâr′i-ə), *n.* [< L. *urtica,* a nettle], hives.
**U·ru·guay** (yoor′ə-gwā′, -gwī′), *n.* 1. a country in S South America, on the Atlantic: area, 72,153 sq. mi.; pop., 2,914,000; capital, Montevideo. 2. a river in S South America, flowing into the Plata River. —**U′ru·guay′an,** *adj.* & *n.*
**us** (us), *pron.* [AS.], the objective case of **we**: also used colloquially as a predicate complement (e.g., that's *us*).
**U.S., US,** United States.
**U.S.A., USA,** 1. United States of America. 2. United States Army.
**us·a·ble, use·a·ble** (ūz′ə-b'l), *adj.* that can be used; fit or available for use. —**us′a·bil′i·ty, use′a·bil′i·ty, us′a·ble·ness, use′a·ble·ness,** *n.*
**U.S.A.F., USAF,** United States Air Force.
**us·age** (ūs′ij, ūz′-), *n.* 1. the act or way of using; treatment. 2. long-continued or established practice; custom; habit. 3. the way in which a word, phrase, etc. is used to express a particular idea.
**U.S.C.G., USCG,** United States Coast Guard.
**use** (ūz; *for n.,* ūs), *v.t.* [USED, USING], [< OFr. < LL. < L. *usus,* pp. of *uti,* to use], 1. to put or bring into action or service. 2. to practice; exercise: as, *use* your judgment. 3. to deal with; treat: as, she *used* her friends badly. 4. to consume, expend, etc. by use: as, to *use* up one's energy. 5. to smoke or chew (tobacco). 6. to accustom (used in the passive): as, they were *used* to the old ways. 7. [Colloq.], to exploit, as a person. *v.i.* to be accustomed (only in the past tense): as, he *used* to play golf. *n.* 1. a using or being used; usage. 2. the ability to use: as, he lost the *use* of his hand. 3. the right or permission to use. 4. the need or opportunity to use: as, we have no *use* for his services. 5. way of using. 6. usefulness; utility. 7. the object or purpose for which something is used. 8. function; service. 9. custom; habit; practice. 10. in *law, a)* the enjoyment of property, as from occupying or employing it. *b)* profit or benefit, especially that of property held in trust by another. —**have no use for,** 1. to have no need of. 2. to dislike strongly. —**in use,** being used. —**make use of,** to use; have occasion to use. —**put to use,** to use. —**us′er,** *n.*
**use·ful** (ūs′fəl), *adj.* that can be used; serviceable; helpful. —**use′ful·ly,** *adv.* —**use′ful·ness,** *n.*
**use·less** (ūs′lis), *adj.* having or of no use; worthless. —**use′less·ly,** *adv.* —**use′less·ness,** *n.*
**USES, U.S.E.S.,** United States Employment Service.
**U-shaped** (ū′shāpt′), *adj.* having the shape of a U.
**ush·er** (ush′ēr), *n.* [< OFr. < *huis* (< L. *ostium*), door], 1. an official doorkeeper. 2. one whose duty it is to show people to their seats in a church, theater, etc. 3. any of the bridegroom's attendants at a wedding. 4. [Brit.], formerly, an assistant teacher. *v.t.* 1. to escort or conduct (others) to seats, etc. 2. to be a forerunner of.
**ush·er·ette** (ush′ēr-et′), *n.* a woman or girl usher, as in a theater.
**USIA, U.S.I.A.,** United States Information Agency.
**U.S.M.,** 1. United States Mail. 2. United States Marines.
**U.S.M.A.,** United States Military Academy.
**USMC, U.S.M.C.,** United States Marine Corps.
**U.S.N., USN,** United States Navy.
**U.S.N.A.,** United States Naval Academy.
**U.S.N.G., USNG,** United States National Guard.
**U.S.N.R., USNR,** United States Naval Reserve.
**USO, U.S.O.,** United Service Organizations.
**U.S.P., U.S.Pharm.,** United States Pharmacopoeia.
**U.S.S.,** 1. United States Senate. 2. United States Ship. 3. United States Steamer *or* Steamship.
**U.S.S.R., USSR,** Union of Soviet Socialist Republics.
**u·su·al** (ū′zhōō-əl, -zhool), *adj.* [< OFr. < LL. *usualis* < L. *usus;* see USE], such as is in common or ordinary use; such as ordinarily happens; customary; habitual. —**as usual,** in the usual way. —**u′su·al·ly,** *adv.* —**u′su·al·ness,** *n.*
**u·su·fruct** (ū′zyoo-frukt′, -syoo-), *n.* [< LL. < L. *usus,* a use + *fructus,* a fruit], in *law,* the right to use and enjoy the advantages and profits of the property of another without altering or damaging the substance. —**u′su·fruc′tu·ar′y** (-fruk′chōō-er′i). *n.* [*pl.* -IES], & *adj.*
**u·su·rer** (ū′zhoo-rēr), *n.* one who engages in usury.
**u·su·ri·ous** (ū-zhoor′i-əs), *adj.* 1. practicing usury. 2. of or constituting usury. —**u·su′ri·ous·ly,** *adv.* —**u·su′ri·ous·ness,** *n.*
**u·surp** (ū-zūrp′, -sūrp′), *v.t.* & *v.i.* [< OFr. < L. < *usus,* a use + *rapere,* to seize], to take or assume and hold (power, position, rights, etc.) by force or without right. —**u·surp′er,** *n.* —**u·surp′ing·ly,** *adv.*
**u·sur·pa·tion** (ū′zēr-pā′shən, -sēr-), *n.* unlawful or violent seizure of a throne, power, rights, etc.
**u·su·ry** (ū′zhoo-ri), *n.* [*pl.* -RIES], [< OFr. < L. *usura* < *usus;* see USE], 1. the lending of money at an excessive or unlawfully high rate of interest. 2. an excessive or unlawfully high interest.
**U·tah** (ū′tô, ū′tä), *n.* a Western State of the United States: area, 84,916 sq. mi.; pop., 891,000; capital, Salt Lake City: abbrev. **Ut.** —**U′tah·an,** *adj.* & *n.*
**Ute** (ūt, ū′ti), *n.* [*pl.* UTE, UTES (ūts, ū′tiz)], 1. a member of a tribe of nomadic Shoshonean Indians that lived in Colorado, Utah, New Mexico, and Arizona. 2. their Uto-Aztecan language.
**u·ten·sil** (ū-ten′s'l), *n.* [< OFr. < L. *utensilis,* fit for use < *uti,* to use], 1. any implement or container ordinarily used in a kitchen, dairy, etc. 2. any implement or tool.
**u·ter·ine** (ū′tēr-in, -īn′), *adj.* 1. of the uterus. 2. having the same mother but a different father.
**u·ter·us** (ū′tēr-əs), *n.* [*pl.* -TERI (-tēr-ī′)], [L.], a hollow, muscular organ of female mammals in which the ovum is deposited and the embryo and fetus are developed and protected; womb.
**U·ti·ca** (ū′ti-kə), *n.* a city in central New York: pop., 100,000.
**u·ti·lise** (ū′t'l-īz′), *v.t.* [-LISED, -LISING], to utilize: Brit. spelling. —**u′ti·li·sa′tion,** *n.*
**u·til·i·tar·i·an** (ū-til′ə-târ′i-ən), *adj.* 1. of or having to do with utility. 2. stressing utility over beauty, decorativeness, etc. 3. of or believing in utilitarianism. *n.* one who believes in utilitarianism.
**u·til·i·tar·i·an·ism** (ū-til′ə-târ′i-ən-iz'm), *n.* 1. the doctrine that the value of anything is determined by its utility. 2. the doctrine that the purpose of all action should be to bring about the greatest happiness of the greatest number.
**u·til·i·ty** (ū-til′ə-ti), *n.* [*pl.* -TIES], [< Fr. < L. < *utilis,* useful < *uti,* to use], 1. usefulness. 2. the greatest happiness of the greatest number. 3. something useful. 4. something useful to the public, as the service of gas, water, etc. 5. a company providing such a service. 6. in *economics,* the power to satisfy the wants of humanity.
**u·ti·lize** (ū′t'l-īz′), *v.t.* [-LIZED, -LIZING], to put to profitable use; make use of. —**u′ti·liz′a·ble,** *adj.* —**u′ti·li·za′tion,** *n.* —**u′ti·liz′er,** *n.*
**ut·most** (ut′mōst′, -məst), *adj.* [< AS. *utemest,* double superl. of *ut,* out], 1. most extreme or distant; farthest. 2. of or to the greatest degree, amount, etc.; greatest. *n.* the most that is possible.
**U·to-Az·tec·an** (ū′tō-az′tek-ən), *adj.* designating or of a large American Indian linguistic family of the W United States, Mexico, and Central America. *n.* the Uto-Aztecan languages.
**U·to·pi·a** (ū-tō′pi-ə), *n.* [< Gr. *ou,* not + *topos,* a place], 1. an imaginary island described as having a perfect political and social system: subject of Sir Thomas More's *Utopia* (1516). 2. [often u-], any place, state, etc. of ideal perfection. 3. [often u-], any visionary scheme or system for an ideally perfect social order.
**U·to·pi·an** (ū-tō′pi-ən), *adj.* 1. of or like Utopia. 2. [often u-], idealistic; visionary. *n.* 1. an inhabitant of Utopia. 2. [often u-], one who believes in a utopia, especially of a social or political nature; idealist. —**u·to′pi·an·ism,** *n.*
**U·trecht** (ū′trekt), *n.* a city in the central part of the Netherlands: pop., 268,000.
**u·tri·cle** (ū′tri-k'l), *n.* [< Fr. < L. dim. of *uter,* leather bag], a small sac, vesicle, or baglike part. —**u·tric′u·lar,** *adj.*
**Ut·tar Pra·desh** (ut′ēr prä′desh), a state of N India: area, 113,409 sq. mi.; pop., 73,746,000; capital, Lucknow.
**ut·ter** (ut′ēr), *adj.* [< AS. *utor,* compar. of *ut,* out], 1. complete; total. 2. unqualified; absolute. —**ut′ter·ly,** *adv.*

**ut·ter** (ut′ẽr), ***v.t.*** [< ME. < *utter*, outward < *ut*, out], 1. to pass (counterfeit money, forgeries, etc.). 2. to speak or express audibly, as words, thoughts, etc. 3. to express in any way. 4. to make known; divulge. —**ut′ter·a·ble,** ***adj.*** —**ut′ter·er,** ***n.***
**ut·ter·ance** (ut′ẽr-əns, ut′rəns), ***n.*** 1. the act of uttering. 2. the power or style of speaking. 3. that which is uttered.
**ut·ter·most** (ut′ẽr-mōst′), ***adj. & n.*** utmost.
**u·vu·la** (ū′vyoo-lə), ***n.*** [*pl.* -LAS, -LAE (-lē′)], [ML. < dim. of L. *uva*, a grape], the small, fleshy process hanging down from the middle of the soft palate above the back of the tongue.
**u·vu·lar** (ū′vyoo-lẽr), ***adj.*** 1. of or having to do with the uvula. 2. in *phonetics*, pronounced with a vibration of the uvula, or with the back of the tongue near the uvula. ***n.*** a uvular sound.
**ux·o·ri·ous** (uk-sôr′i-əs, ug-zō′ri-), ***adj.*** [< L. < *uxor*, wife], irrationally fond of or submissive to one's wife. —**ux·o′ri·ous·ly,** ***adv.*** —**ux·o′ri·ous·ness,** ***n.***
**Uz·beg** (uz′beg), ***n. & adj.*** Uzbek.
**Uz·bek** (uz′bek; Russ. ooz′bek), ***n.*** 1. a member of a Turkic people living in the region of the Uzbek S.S.R. 2. their Central Turkic language. ***adj.*** of the Uzbek S.S.R., its people, their language, etc.
**Uz·bek Soviet Socialist Republic** (ooz-bek′), a republic of the U.S.S.R., in central Asia: area, 146,000 sq. mi.; pop., 6,282,000; capital, Tashkent.

# V

**V, v** (vē), ***n.*** [*pl.* V's, v's, Vs, vs], 1. the twenty-second letter of the English alphabet. 2. the sound of V or v. ***adj.*** twenty-second in a sequence or group.
**V** (vē), ***n.*** 1. an object shaped like V. 2. a Roman numeral for 5. 3. *a symbol for* victory of the United Nations in World War II. 4. in *chemistry, the symbol for* vanadium. ***adj.*** shaped like V.
**V, v,** 1. velocity. 2. volt(s). 3. vector.
**v.,** 1. verb. 2. verse. 3. version. 4. versus. 5. *vide*, [L.], see. 6. violin. 7. voice. 8. voltage. 9. volume. 10. *von*, [G.], of.
**VA, V.A.,** Veterans' Administration.
**Va.,** Virginia.
**va·can·cy** (vā′kən-si), ***n.*** [*pl.* -CIES], 1. the state of being vacant; emptiness. 2. *a*) empty space. *b*) a vacant space. 3. lack of intelligence, interest, or thought. 4. *a*) a vacating or being vacant, or unoccupied: of a position or office. *b*) an unoccupied position or office. 5. untenanted quarters, as in a motel.
**va·cant** (vā′kənt), ***adj.*** [< OFr. < L. ppr. of *vacare*, to be empty], 1. having nothing in it, as a space; empty. 2. not held, filled, or occupied, as a position, a seat, a house, etc. 3. free from work; leisure. 4. lacking in intelligence, thought, etc. —**va′cant·ly,** ***adv.*** —**va′cant·ness,** ***n.***
**va·cate** (vā′kāt), ***v.t.*** [-CATED, -CATING], [< L. pp. of *vacare*, to be empty], 1. to make vacant, as an office, position, etc. or a house, room, etc. 2. to make void; annul. ***v.i.*** 1. to make an office, place, etc. vacant. 2. [Colloq.], to leave.
**va·ca·tion** (və-kā′shən, vā-), ***n.*** [< OFr. < L. *vacatio*], 1. freedom from any activity; rest; esp., a specific interval of rest from work, study, etc.: as, two weeks' *vacation*. ***v.i.*** to take one's vacation. —**va·ca′tion·ist, va·ca′tion·er,** ***n.***
**vac·ci·nate** (vak′sə-nāt′), ***v.t.*** [-NATED, -NATING], to inoculate with a specific vaccine in order to prevent or lessen the effect of some disease; specif., to inoculate with cowpox vaccine in order to immunize against smallpox. ***v.i.*** to perform vaccination. —**vac′ci·na′tor,** ***n.***
**vac·ci·na·tion** (vak′sə-nā′shən), ***n.*** 1. the act or practice of vaccinating. 2. the scar on the skin where the vaccine has been applied.
**vac·cine** (vak′sēn, -sin), ***adj.*** [< L. *vaccinus*, of cows < *vacca*, a cow], of vaccination. ***n.*** 1. a substance containing the causative virus of cowpox, used in vaccination against smallpox. 2. any preparation of dead bacteria, etc. introduced into the body to produce immunity to a specific disease. —**vac′ci·nal,** ***adj.***
**vac·cin·i·a** (vak-sin′i-ə), ***n.*** cowpox.
**vac·il·late** (vas′ə-lāt′), ***v.i.*** [-LATED, -LATING], [< L. pp. of *vacillare*], 1. to sway to and fro; waver; totter. 2. to fluctuate. 3. to waver in mind; show indecision. —**vac′il·lat′ing,** ***adj.*** —**vac′il·lat′ing·ly,** ***adv.*** —**vac′il·la′tion,** ***n.*** —**vac′il·la·to′ry** (-lə-tôr′i, -tō′ri), ***adj.***
**va·cu·i·ty** (va-kū′ə-ti), ***n.*** [*pl.* -TIES], [< L. < *vacuus*, empty], 1. a being empty; emptiness. 2. an empty space; void; vacuum. 3. lack of intelligence, thought, etc. 4. something foolish. 5. inanity.
**vac·u·ole** (vak′ū-ōl′), ***n.*** [Fr. < L. *vacuus*, empty], in *biology*, 1. a bubblelike cavity in the protoplasm of a cell, containing air, water, or partially digested fluid. 2. a small cavity in the tissues of an organism.
**vac·u·ous** (vak′ū-əs), ***adj.*** [L. *vacuus*], 1. empty. 2. stupid; senseless; inane. 3. lacking purpose; idle. —**vac′u·ous·ly,** ***adv.*** —**vac′u·ous·ness,** ***n.***
**vac·u·um** (vak′ū-əm; *also, esp. for adj.*, vak′yoom), ***n.*** [*pl.* -UMS, -A (-ə)], [L., neut. of *vacuus*, empty], 1. a space with nothing at all in it. 2. a space, as that inside a vacuum tube, out of which most of the air or gas has been taken, as by pumping. 3. a space left empty as by the removal of something; void: often figurative. ***adj.*** 1. of a vacuum. 2. used to make a vacuum. 3. having a vacuum. 4. working by the creation of a partial vacuum. ***v.t.*** [Colloq.], to clean with a vacuum cleaner.
**vacuum bottle,** a bottlelike container used to keep liquids hot or cold by means of a vacuum between its inner and outer walls.
**vacuum cleaner,** a machine for cleaning carpets, floors, upholstery, etc. by suction.
**vacuum pump,** a pump used to draw air or gas out of sealed space.
**vacuum tube,** a sealed glass or metal tube containing highly rarefied air or gas and a cathode (or filament), an anode (or plate), and a grid for controlling the flow of electrons from one to the other: used in radio, television, etc. as a rectifier, detector, etc.

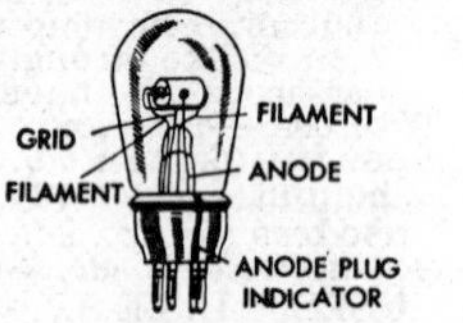

VACUUM TUBE

**va·de me·cum** (vā′di mē′kəm), [L., lit., go with me], something carried about by a person for constant use, reference, etc.; specif., a handbook.
**vag·a·bond** (vag′ə-bond′), ***adj.*** [< OFr. < L. *vagabundus*, strolling about < *vagari*, to wander], 1. moving from place to place; wandering. 2. of, characteristic of, or living an unsettled or irresponsible life; vagrant; shiftless. 3. aimlessly following an irregular course; drifting. ***n.*** 1. a person who wanders from place to place, having no fixed abode. 2. a tramp. 3. an idle, disreputable, or shiftless person. —**vag′a·bond′age, vag′a·bond·ism,** ***n.***
**va·gar·y** (və-gâr′i), ***n.*** [*pl.* -IES], [< L. *vagari*, to wander], 1. an odd or eccentric action or conduct. 2. a whimsical or freakish idea or notion; caprice. —**va·gar′i·ous,** ***adj.*** —**va·gar′i·ous·ly,** ***adv.***
**va·gi·na** (və-ji′nə), ***n.*** [*pl.* -NAS, -NAE (-nē)], [L., a sheath], a sheath or sheathlike structure; specif., in female mammals, the canal leading from the vulva to the uterus. —**vag·i·nal** (vaj′ə-n'l, və-ji′-), ***adj.***
**vag·i·nate** (vaj′ə-nit, -nāt′), ***adj.*** 1. having a vagina or sheath; sheathed. 2. like a sheath.
**va·gran·cy** (vā′grən-si), ***n.*** [*pl.* -CIES], [< *vagrant*], 1. a wandering in thought or talk. 2. a wandering from place to place. 3. shiftless or idle wandering without money or work.
**va·grant** (vā′grənt), ***n.*** [prob. < OFr. ppr. of *wa(u)crer*, to wander about; infl. by L. *vagari*, to wander], a person who wanders from place to place; esp., one without a regular job, supporting himself by begging, etc.; vagabond; tramp. ***adj.*** 1. wandering from place to place; roaming; nomadic. 2. of, characteristic of, or living the life of a vagrant. 3. following no fixed direction or course; wayward: said of things. —**va′grant·ly,** ***adv.***

**vague** (vāg), *adj.* [Fr. < L. *vagus,* wandering], 1. not clearly or precisely expressed or stated. 2. indefinite in shape or form. 3. not sharp, certain, or precise in thought or expression: said of persons, the mind, etc. —**vague′ly,** *adv.* —**vague′ness,** *n.*

**va·gus** (vā′gəs), *n.* [*pl.* -GI (-jī)], [L., wandering], either of a pair of cranial nerves acting upon the larynx, lungs, heart, esophagus, and most of the abdominal organs: also **vagus nerve.**

**vain** (vān), *adj.* [< OFr. < L. *vanus,* empty], 1. having no real value or significance; worthless, empty, etc.: as, *vain* pomp. 2. without force or effect; futile, fruitless, etc.: as, a *vain* endeavor. 3. having or showing an excessively high regard for one's self, looks, ability, etc.; conceited. —**in vain,** 1. fruitlessly; unsuccessfully. 2. lightly; profanely. —**vain′ly,** *adv.* —**vain′ness,** *n.*

**vain·glo·ri·ous** (vān′glôr′i-əs, -glō′ri-), *adj.* [< *vainglory*], 1. boastfully vain and proud of oneself. 2. characterized by boastful vanity. —**vain′glo′ri·ous·ly,** *adv.* —**vain′glo′ri·ous·ness,** *n.*

**vain·glo·ry** (vān′glôr′i, -glō′ri), *n.* [< OFr. < ML. *vana gloria;* see VAIN & GLORY], extreme self-pride and boastfulness; excessive vanity.

**val·ance** (val′əns), *n.* [prob. < OFr. ppr. of *avaler,* to hang], 1. a short drapery or curtain hanging from the edge of a bed, shelf, etc., often to the floor. 2. a short drapery across the top of a window. —**val′anced,** *adj.*

**vale** (vāl), *n.* [< OFr. < L. *vallis*], [Poetic], a valley.

‡**va·le** (vā′li), *interj. & n.* [L.], farewell.

**val·e·dic·tion** (val′ə-dik′shən), *n.* [< L. *valedictus,* pp. < *vale,* farewell (imper. of *valere,* to be well) + *dicere,* to say], 1. a bidding farewell. 2. a farewell utterance.

**val·e·dic·to·ri·an** (val′ə-dik-tôr′i-ən, -tō′ri-), *n.* in schools and colleges, the student, usually the one ranking highest in scholarship, who delivers the valedictory at graduation.

**val·e·dic·to·ry** (val′ə-dik′tə-ri), *adj.* said or done at parting, by way of farewell; uttered as a valediction. *n.* [*pl.* -RIES], a farewell speech, especially one delivered at a graduation.

**va·lence** (vā′ləns), *n.* [< L. ppr. of *valere,* to be strong], in *chemistry,* the combining capacity of an element or radical, as measured by the number of hydrogen atoms which one radical or one atom of the element will combine with or replace. Also **va′len·cy** [*pl.* -CIES].

**Va·len·ci·a** (və-len′shi-ə, -shə), *n.* a city in E Spain, on the Mediterranean: pop., 522,000.

**-va·lent,** in *chemistry,* a suffix meaning: 1. *having a specified valence.* 2. *having a specified number of valences.*

**val·en·tine** (val′ən-tīn′), *n.* 1. a sweetheart chosen or complimented on Saint Valentine's Day. 2. a greeting card or gift sent on this day.

**Valentine,** Saint, 3d-century Christian martyr.

**va·le·ri·an** (və-lêr′i-ən), *n.* [< Fr. < ML.; as if < the personal name *Valerius*], 1. any of various plants with clusters or spikes of white, pink, red, or purplish flowers. 2. a drug made from the roots of some of these plants and used as a sedative.

**val·et** (val′it, -ā; Fr. và′lā′), *n.* [Fr. < OFr. *valet, varlet*], 1. a personal manservant who takes care of one's clothes, helps one in dressing, etc. 2. a hotel employee who cleans or presses clothes, etc. *v.t. & v.i.* to serve as a valet.

**val·e·tu·di·nar·i·an** (val′ə-tōō′də-nâr′i-ən, -tū′-), *n.* [< L. < *valetudo,* state of health < *valere,* to be strong], 1. a person in poor health; invalid. 2. a person who worries constantly about his health. *adj.* 1. sickly; invalid. 2. anxiously concerned about one's health. Also **val′e·tu′di·nar′y.**

**Val·hal·la** (val-hal′ə), *n.* in *Norse mythology,* the great hall where Odin receives and feasts the souls of heroes who have fallen in battle.

**val·ian·cy** (val′yən-si), *n.* [< *valiant*], 1. bravery; courage. 2. [*pl.* -CIES], a brave deed.

**val·iant** (val′yənt), *adj.* [< OFr. ppr. of *valoir* < L. *valere,* to be strong], brave; courageous. —**val′iant·ly,** *adv.* —**val′iant·ness,** *n.*

**val·id** (val′id), *adj.* [< Fr. < L. *validus,* strong < *valere,* to have power], 1. having legal force. 2. sound; well grounded on principles or evidence, as an argument. 3. effective, cogent, etc. —**val′id·ly,** *adv.* —**val′id·ness,** *n.*

**val·i·date** (val′ə-dāt′), *v.t.* [-DATED, -DATING], [< ML. pp. of *validare*], 1. to give legal force to; declare legally valid. 2. to prove to be valid. —**val′i·da′tion,** *n.*

**va·lid·i·ty** (və-lid′ə-ti), *n.* [*pl.* -TIES], the state, quality, or fact of being valid; (legal) soundness.

**va·lise** (və-lēs′), *n.* [Fr. < It. *valigia;* ? < Ar.], a traveling bag; suitcase.

**Val·kyr·ie** (val-kêr′i, -kī′ri, val′ki-ri), *n.* in *Norse mythology,* any of the maidens of Odin who conduct the souls of heroes slain in battle to Valhalla: also **Val′kyr** (-kêr). —**Val·kyr′i·an,** *adj.*

**Val·le·jo** (va-lā′hō), *n.* a city in California, just north of Oakland: pop., 61,000.

**val·ley** (val′i), *n.* [*pl.* -LEYS], [< OFr. < L. *vallis,* a vale], 1. a stretch of low land lying between hills or mountains. 2. the land drained or watered by a great river system: as, the Nile *valley.* 3. any dip or hollow like a valley.

**Valley Forge,** a village in SE Pennsylvania, where Washington and his troops encamped in the winter of 1777–1778.

**val·or** (val′ẽr), *n.* [< OFr. < LL. < L. *valere,* to be strong], courage; fearlessness: also, Brit. spelling, **valour.** —**val′or·ous,** *adj.* —**val′or·ous·ly,** *adv.* —**val′or·ous·ness,** *n.*

**val·or·i·za·tion** (val′ẽr-i-zā′shən), *n.* [< Port. *valorização;* ult. < L. *valor,* valor], a fixing of prices, usually by government action, as by buying up a commodity at the fixed price, etc. —**val′or·ize** [-IZED, -IZING], *v.t. & v.i.*

**Val·pa·rai·so** (val′pə-rā′zō, -rī′sō), *n.* a seaport in central Chile: pop., 222,000.

‡**valse** (vàls), *n.* [Fr.], a waltz.

**val·u·a·ble** (val′yoo-b'l, -ū-ə-b'l), *adj.* 1. having material value. 2. having great value in terms of money. 3. highly thought of; prized. *n. usually in pl.* an article of value, as a piece of jewelry. —**val′u·a·ble·ness,** *n.* —**val′u·a·bly,** *adv.*

**val·u·a·tion** (val′ū-ā′shən), *n.* 1. the act of determining the value of anything; evaluation. 2. determined or estimated value. 3. estimation of the worth, merit, etc. of anything.

**val·ue** (val′ū), *n.* [< OFr. pp. of *valoir* (< L. *valere*), to be worth], 1. a fair equivalent in money, etc. for something sold or exchanged. 2. the worth of a thing in money or goods at a certain time. 3. estimated or appraised worth. 4. purchasing power. 5. that quality of a thing according to which it is thought of as being more or less desirable, useful, etc. 6. precise meaning, as of a word. 7. in *art,* the relative lightness or darkness of a color, or the tonal quality of a painting. 8. in *mathematics,* the quantity for which a symbol stands. 9. in *music,* the relative duration of a note, tone, or rest. 10. in *phonetics,* the quality of sound of a letter or diphthong. 11. *pl.* in *sociology,* acts, customs, etc. regarded in a particular, especially favorable, way by a people, etc. *v.t.* [-UED, -UING], 1. to estimate the value of; appraise. 2. to place a certain estimate of worth on in a scale of values: as, I *value* health above wealth. 3. to think highly of; prize: as, I *value* your friendship. —**val′u·er,** *n.* —**val′ue·less,** *adj.* —**val′ue·less·ness,** *n.*

**val·ued** (val′ūd), *adj.* 1. estimated; appraised. 2. highly thought of; esteemed.

**val·vate** (val′vāt), *adj.* [L. *valvatus,* having folding doors], in *botany,* 1. meeting without overlapping, as petals, etc. 2. opening by valves. 3. having a valve or valves.

**valve** (valv), *n.* [< L. *valva,* leaf of a folding door], 1. a sluice gate. 2. in *anatomy,* a membranous structure which permits body fluids to flow in one direction only, or opens and closes a tube, etc. 3. in *botany,* one of the segments into which a seed capsule separates. 4. in *mechanics, a*) any device in a pipe, etc. that permits a flow in one direction only, or regulates or stops the flow by means of a flap, lid, plug, etc. *b*) this flap, plug, etc. 5. in *music,* a device, as in the trumpet, that opens an auxiliary to the main tube, lengthening the air column and lowering the pitch. 6. in *zoology,* one of the parts making up the shell of a mollusk, clam, etc. *v.t. & v.i.* [VALVED, VALVING], 1. to fit with a valve or valves. 2. to regulate the flow of (a fluid) by means of a valve. —**valv′al,** *adj.* —**valve′less,** *adj.* —**valve′-like′,** *adj.*

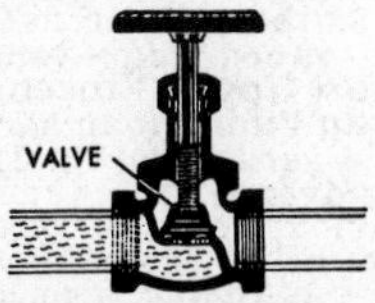

GLOBE VALVE

**val·vu·lar** (val′vyoo-lẽr), *adj.* 1. having the form of a valve. 2. having a valve or valves. 3. of a valve or valves; esp., of the valves of the heart.

fat, āpe, bâre, cär; ten, ēven, hêre, ovẽr; is, bīte; lot, gō, hôrn, tōōl, look; oil, out; up, ūse, fũr; get; joy; yet; chin; she; thin, *th*en; zh, leisure; ŋ, ring; ə for *a* in *ago, e* in *agent, i* in *sanity, o* in *comply, u* in *focus;* ' in *able* (ā′b'l); Fr. bàl; ë, Fr. coeur; ö, Fr. feu; Fr. mon; ô, Fr. coq; ü, Fr. duc; H, G. ich; kh, G. doch. ‡ foreign; < derived from.

**va·moose** (va-mo͞os′), *v.i. & v.t.* [-MOOSED, -MOOSING], [Sp. *vamos*, let us go], [Slang], to leave quickly; go away or depart (from) hurriedly: also **va·mose′** (-mōs′), [-MOSED, -MOSING].

**vamp** (vamp), *n.* [< OFr. *avampié* < *avant*, before + *pié*, a foot], 1. the part of a boot or shoe covering the instep and toe. 2. something patched up to seem new. 3. in *music*, a simple accompaniment improvised to fit a song. *v.t.* 1. to put a vamp on (a shoe, etc.). 2. to patch (*up*); repair. 3. to make over (something old). 4. in *music*, to improvise (a vamp). *v.i.* in *music*, to improvise a vamp. —**vamp′er,** *n.*

**vamp** (vamp), *n.* [Slang], a vampire (sense 3). *v.t. & v.i.* [Slang], to flirt with or beguile (a man).

**vam·pire** (vam′pīr), *n.* [Fr. < G. *vampir;* of Slav. origin], 1. in *folklore*, a corpse that becomes reanimated at night and sucks the blood of sleeping persons. 2. an unscrupulous person who preys ruthlessly on others. 3. a beautiful but unscrupulous woman who seduces men, etc. 4. a vampire bat. —**vam′pir·ism,** *n.*

**vampire bat,** 1. a tropical American bat that lives on the blood of animals. 2. any of various other bats mistakenly believed to be bloodsuckers.

**van** (van), *n.* [abbrev. < *vanguard*], 1. the front of an army or fleet when advancing. 2. the foremost in a line, movement, endeavor, etc.

**van** (van), *n.* [< *caravan*], 1. a large closed truck or wagon for carrying furniture, etc. 2. [Brit.], a closed railway car for baggage, etc.

**va·na·di·um** (və-nā′di-əm), *n.* [< ON. *Vanadis*, a name of Freya, goddess of love], a ductile metallic chemical element: cf. *vanadium steel:* symbol, V; at. wt., 50.95; at. no., 23.

**vanadium steel,** a steel alloy containing vanadium to harden and toughen it.

**Van Allen (radiation) belt** (van al′ən), [after J. A. *Van Allen* (1914– ), Am. physicist], either of two zones of intense, natural radiation encircling the earth in the upper atmosphere.

**Van Bu·ren, Martin** (van byoor′ən), 1782–1862; eighth president of the U.S. (1837–1841).

**Van·cou·ver** (van-ko͞o′vẽr), *n.* 1. a seaport in SW British Columbia, Canada: pop., 385,000. 2. an island of British Columbia, off the SW coast.

**Van·dal** (van′d'l), *n.* 1. a member of an East Germanic tribe that ravaged Gaul, Spain, etc. and sacked Rome (455 A.D.). 2. [v-], a person who, out of malice or ignorance, destroys or spoils works of art, public property, etc. *adj.* 1. of the Vandals. 2. [v-], like or characteristic of a vandal.

**van·dal·ism** (van′d'l-iz'm), *n.* malicious or ignorant destruction of works of art, property, etc.

**van·dal·ize** (van′də-līz′), *v.t.* [-IZED, -IZING], to destroy or damage (property) maliciously.

**Van Dyck,** Sir **Anthony** (van dīk′), 1599–1641; Flemish painter in England: also sp. **Vandyke.**

**Van·dyke (beard)** (van-dīk′), a closely trimmed, pointed beard, as seen in portraits by Van Dyck.

VANDYKE BEARD

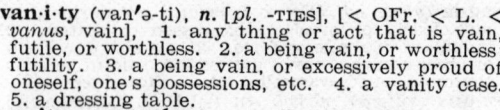

**vane** (vān), *n.* [< AS. *fana*, a flag], 1. a shaped, free-swinging piece of metal, etc. set up high to show which way the wind is blowing; weathervane. 2. any of several flat or curved pieces set around an axle, forming a wheel to be rotated by, or to rotate, air, water, etc.: as, the *vane* of a windmill, propeller, etc. 3. the web or flat part of a feather. —**vaned,** *adj.* —**vane′less,** *adj.*

**van Gogh, Vincent,** see **Gogh, Vincent van.**

**van·guard** (van′gärd′), *n.* [< OFr. < *avant*, before + *garde*, guard], 1. the front part of an army in an advance; the van. 2. the leading position in a movement. 3. those leading a movement.

**va·nil·la** (və-nil′ə), *n.* [< Sp. dim. of *vaina*, a pod < L. *vagina*, a sheath], 1. any of various climbing orchids with fragrant flowers. 2. the podlike capsule (**vanilla bean**) of some of these plants. 3. a flavoring made from these capsules. —**va·nil′lic** (-ik), *adj.*

VANILLA (branch with fruit 6-10 in. long)

**van·il·lin** (van′ə-lin, və-nil′in), *n.* a fragrant substance, $C_8H_8O_3$, produced from the vanilla bean or made synthetically, and used for flavoring.

**van·ish** (van′ish), *v.i.* [< OFr. < LL. < L. *evanescere;* see EVANESCE], 1. to disappear; pass suddenly from sight. 2. to pass gradually out of existence. 3. to cease to exist. —**van′ish·er,** *n.*

**van·ish·ing point** (van′ish-iŋ), in *perspective*, the point where parallel lines receding from the observer seem to come together.

**van·i·ty** (van′ə-ti), *n.* [*pl.* -TIES], [< OFr. < L. < *vanus*, vain], 1. any thing or act that is vain, futile, or worthless. 2. a being vain, or worthless; futility. 3. a being vain, or excessively proud of oneself, one's possessions, etc. 4. a vanity case. 5. a dressing table.

**vanity case** (or **box**), a small case containing powder, rouge, a mirror, etc., carried by women.

**van·quish** (vaŋ′kwish), *v.t.* [< OFr. < L. *vincere*, to conquer], 1. to conquer or defeat in battle. 2. *a)* to defeat in any conflict. *b)* to overcome (a feeling, condition, etc.); suppress. —**van′quish·a·ble,** *adj.* —**van′quish·er,** *n.* —**van′quish·ment,** *n.*

**van·tage** (van′tij), *n.* [see ADVANTAGE], advantage; favorable position against one's opponent: as, point of *vantage.*

**vantage ground,** a favorable or advantageous situation; good position for defense or attack.

**van·ward** (van′wẽrd), *adj.* in or toward the van, or front, as of an army.

**Van·zet·ti, Bar·to·lo·me·o** (bär′tō-lō-mā′ō van-zet′i), 1888–1927: see **Sacco, Nicola.**

**vap·id** (vap′id), *adj.* [L. *vapidus*], 1. tasteless; flavorless. 2. lifeless; dull; unexciting. —**va·pid·i·ty** (və-pid′ə-ti), **vap′id·ness,** *n.* —**vap′id·ly,** *adv.*

**va·por** (vā′pẽr), *n.* [< Anglo-Fr. < OFr. < L. *vapor*], 1. *a)* visible particles of moisture floating in the air; fog; mist; steam. *b)* any cloudy exhalation, as smoke, fumes, etc. 2. the gaseous form of any substance which is usually a liquid or a solid. 3. anything insubstantial. 4. *pl.* [Archaic], depressed spirits (often with *the*). *v.i.* 1. to rise or pass off as vapor; evaporate. 2. to give off vapor. 3. to brag or bluster. *v.t.* to vaporize. —**va′por·er,** *n.* —**va′por·ish,** *adj.* —**va′por·less,** *adj.*

**va·por·es·cent** (vā′pẽr-es′'nt), *adj.* forming, or tending to form, vapor. —**va′por·es′cence,** *n.*

**va·por·ing** (vā′pẽr-iŋ), *adj.* 1. that vapors. 2. boastful, ostentatious, etc. *n.* boastful talk or behavior. —**va′por·ing·ly,** *adv.*

**va·por·ize** (vā′pẽr-īz′), *v.t. & v.i.* [-IZED, -IZING], to change into vapor, as by heating or spraying. —**va′por·iz′a·ble,** *adj.* —**va′por·i·za′tion,** *n.* —**va′por·iz′er,** *n.*

**va·por·ous** (vā′pẽr-əs), *adj.* 1. giving off or forming vapor. 2. full of vapor; foggy. 3. like vapor. 4. *a)* fleeting, fanciful, etc.: said of things, ideas, etc. *b)* given to such ideas or talk. Also **va′por·y.** —**va′por·ous·ly,** *adv.* —**va′por·os′i·ty** (-os′ə-ti), *n.*

**va·pour** (vā′pẽr), *n., v.i. & v.t.* vapor: Brit. spelling. —**va′pour·ish,** *adj.* —**va′pour·ize,** *v.t. & v.i.* —**va′pour·less,** *adj.* —**va′pour·ous, va′pour·y,** *adj.*

**va·que·ro** (vä-kâr′ō), *n.* [*pl.* -os], [Sp. < *vaca* (L. *vacca*), a cow], in Spanish America and the Southwest, a cowboy.

**var.,** 1. [*pl.* VARS.], variant. 2. variety. 3. various.

**var·i·a·ble** (vâr′i-ə-b'l), *adj.* 1. apt to change or vary; changeable, inconstant, etc. 2. that can be changed or varied. 3. in *biology*, tending to deviate in some way from the fixed type. 4. in *mathematics*, having no fixed value. *n.* 1. anything changeable; thing that varies. 2. in *mathematics*, *a)* a quantity that may have a number of different values. *b)* a symbol for such a quantity. 3. in *nautical usage*, a shifting wind. —**the variables,** a region of shifting winds. —**var′i·a·bil′i·ty,** *n.* —**var′i·a·bly,** *adv.*

**Variable Zone,** Temperate Zone.

**var·i·ance** (vâr′i-əns), *n.* 1. a varying or being variant. 2. degree of change or difference; discrepancy. 3. a quarrel; dispute. —**at variance,** 1. disagreeing; quarreling: said of persons. 2. differing; conflicting: said of things.

**var·i·ant** (vâr′i-ənt), *adj.* 1. varying; different; esp., different in some way from others of the same kind. 2. variable; changeable. *n.* anything that is variant, as a different spelling of the same word, etc.

**var·i·a·tion** (vâr′i-ā′shən), *n.* 1. the act, fact, or process of varying; change in form, condition, extent, etc. 2. the degree of such change: as, a *variation* of ten feet. 3. a thing which is somewhat different from another of the same kind. 4. in *biology*, a deviation from the usual or parental type in structure or form. 5. in *music*, the repetition of a melody or theme with changes in harmony, rhythm, key, etc. —**var′i·a′tion·al,** *adj.*

**var·i·col·ored** (vâr′i-kul′ẽrd), *adj.* 1. of several or many colors. 2. varied; diversified.

**var·i·cose** (var′ə-kōs ), *adj.* [< L. *varicosus* < *varix*, enlarged vein], 1. abnormally and irregularly swollen: as, *varicose* veins. 2. of or having varicose veins. —**var′i·cosed′,** *adj.* —**var′i·cos′i·ty** (-kos′ə-ti), **var′i·cose′ness,** *n.*

**var·ied** (vâr′id), *adj.* 1. of different kinds; various. 2. variegated. 3. changed; altered. —**var′ied·ly,** *adv.* —**var′ied·ness,** *n.*

**var·i·e·gate** (vâr′i-ə-gāt′, vâr′i-gāt ), *v.t.* [-GATED, -GATING], [< LL. pp. of *variegare* < L. *varius*, various], 1. to make varied in appearance by differences, as in color. 2. to make varied; diversify. —**var′i·e·ga′tion,** *n.*

**var·i·e·gat·ed** (vâr′i-ə-gāt′id, vâr′i-gāt′-), *adj.* 1. of different colors in spots, streaks, etc. 2. varied.

**va·ri·e·ty** (və-rī′ə-ti), *n.* [*pl.* -TIES], 1. a being various or varied; absence of sameness. 2. a different form of some thing, condition, etc.; sort; kind: as, *varieties* of cloth. 3. a number of different things thought of together: as, a *variety* of foods. 4. difference; variation. 5. in *biology*, a group having characteristics of its own within a species. 6. vaudeville: also **variety show.**

**va·ri·o·la** (və-rī′ə-lə), *n.* [ML. < L. *varius*, various], smallpox. —**va·ri′o·lous, va·ri′o·lar,** *adj.*

**var·i·om·e·ter** (vâr′i-om′ə-tēr), *n.* an instrument for varying inductance in an electric circuit, consisting of a movable coil within a fixed coil, the two connected in series: used in radio tuning.

**var·i·o·rum** (vâr′i-ôr′əm, vā′ri-ō′rəm), *n.* [L., of various (scholars)], an edition of a literary work containing variant readings of the text, or notes, by various editors. *adj.* of such an edition.

**var·i·ous** (vâr′i-əs), *adj.* [L. *varius*, diverse], 1. differing one from another; of several kinds. 2. several; many. 3. many-sided; versatile. 4. varied in nature or appearance. 5. [Rare], changeable. —**var′i·ous·ly,** *adv.* —**var′i·ous·ness,** *n.*

**var·let** (vär′lit), *n.* [OFr., a valet; var. of *vaslet*], [Archaic], 1. an attendant. 2. a rascal; scoundrel. —**var′let·ry,** *n.*

**var·mint, var·ment** (vär′mənt), *n.* [Dial. or Colloq.], vermin; esp., a person or animal regarded as objectionable.

**var·nish** (vär′nish), *n.* [< OFr. < ML. *veronix*, a resin; ? ult. < Gr. *Berenikē*, ancient city], 1. a preparation made of resinous substances dissolved in oil **(oil varnish)** or in alcohol, turpentine, etc. **(spirit varnish),** and used to give a glossy surface to wood, metal, etc. 2. the smooth, hard, glossy surface of this after it has dried. 3. a surface gloss or smoothness, as of manner; outward, deceptive attractiveness. *v.t.* 1. to cover with varnish. 2. to give a varnished appearance or superficial attractiveness to. —**var′nish·er,** *n.*

**var·si·ty** (vär′sə-ti), *n.* [*pl.* -TIES], [contr. < *university*], a team representing a university, college, or school in some competition. *adj.* designating or of a university, college, or school team.

**var·y** (vâr′i), *v.t.* [-IED, -YING], [< OFr. < L. < *varius*, various], 1. to change in form, appearance, nature, etc.; alter. 2. to make different from one another. 3. to give variety to: as, *vary* your reading. 4. in *music*, to repeat (a melody or theme) with changes in harmony, rhythm, key, etc. *v.i.* 1. to undergo change in any way. 2. to be different; differ. 3. to deviate or depart (*from*). 4. to alternate. 5. in *biology*, to show variation. —**var′i·er,** *n.* —**var′y·ing·ly,** *adv.*

‡**vas** (vas), *n.* [*pl.* VASA (vā′sə)], [L., a vessel], in *anatomy & biology*, a vessel or duct. —**va′sal,** *adj.*

**vas·cu·lar** (vas′kyoo-lēr), *adj.* [< L. *vasculum*, dim. of *vas*, a vessel], of or having vessels or ducts; specif., *a*) in *anatomy & zoology*, designating or of the vessels for conveying blood or lymph. *b*) in *botany*, designating or of the ducts for conveying sap. —**vas′cu·lar′i·ty** (-lar′ə-ti), *n.* —**vas′cu·lar·ly,** *adv.*

‡**vas de·fe·rens** (def′ə-renz′), [*pl.* VASA DEFERENTIA (def′ə-ren′shi-ə)], [< L. *vas*, a vessel + *deferens*, carrying down], the convoluted duct that conveys sperm from the testicle to the ejaculatory duct of the penis.

**vase** (vās, vāz; Brit. väz), *n.* [< Fr. < L. *vas*, a vessel], an open container of metal, glass, etc., used for decoration, displaying flowers, etc.

**vas·e·line** (vas′ə-lēn′, -′l-in), *n.* [< G. *wasser*, water + Gr. *elaion*, oil], a petroleum jelly, used as a lubricant or ointment: a trade-mark (**Vaseline).**

**vas·o-,** [< L. *vas*, a vessel], a combining form meaning: 1. *the blood vessels*, as in *vasomotor*. 2. *vasomotor*. Also **vas-.**

**vas·o·mo·tor** (vas′ō-mō′tēr), *adj.* [*vaso-* + *motor*], in *physiology*, regulating the size (i.e., caliber) of blood vessels: said of a nerve, drug, etc.

**vas·sal** (vas′′l), *n.* [OFr. < ML. *vassalus* < *vassus*, servant < Celt.], 1. in the Middle Ages, a person who held land under the feudal system, pledging fealty to an overlord, and performing various duties in return for his protection. 2. a subordinate, dependent, etc. 3. *a*) a servant. *b*) a slave. *adj.* of or like a vassal; dependent, subject, servile, etc.

**vas·sal·age** (vas′′l-ij), *n.* 1. the state of being a vassal. 2. the homage, loyalty, and service required of a vassal. 3. dependence; servitude. 4. lands held by a vassal. 5. a body of vassals.

**vast** (vast, väst), *adj.* [L. *vastus*], 1. of very great size; huge; enormous; immense. 2. of very great extent; far-reaching. 3. very great in number, amount, or quantity. 4. very great in degree, intensity, etc. —**vast′ly,** *adv.* —**vast′ness,** *n.*

**vast·y** (vas′ti, väs′-), *adj.* [-IER, -IEST], vast; huge.

**vat** (vat), *n.* [< AS. *fæt*, a cask], a large tank, tub, or cask for holding liquids to be used in a manufacturing process or to be stored for fermenting. *v.t.* [VATTED, VATTING], to store in a vat.

**Vat·i·can** (vat′i-kən), *n.* 1. the papal palace, consisting of a group of buildings in Vatican City. 2. the papal government.

**Vatican City,** the papal state within Rome, established in 1929: it includes the Vatican and St. Peter's Church: area, 1/6 sq. mi.

**vaude·ville** (vōd′vil, vô′də-vil), *n.* [Fr. < *Vau-de-Vire*, a valley in Normandy, famous for light, convivial songs], 1. a stage show consisting of various acts of songs, dances, skits, etc.; variety show. 2. such entertainment generally.

**vault** (vôlt), *n.* [< OFr. < LL. < L. *volutus*, pp. of *volvere*, to roll], 1. an arched roof, ceiling, etc. of masonry. 2. an arched chamber or space, especially when underground. 3. a cellar room used for storage. 4. a burial chamber. 5. a room for the safekeeping of valuables or money, as in a bank. 6. the sky as a vault-like canopy. *v.t.* 1. to cover with a vault. 2. to build as a vault. *v.i.* to curve like a vault. —**vault′ed,** *adj.* —**vault′like′,** *adj.*

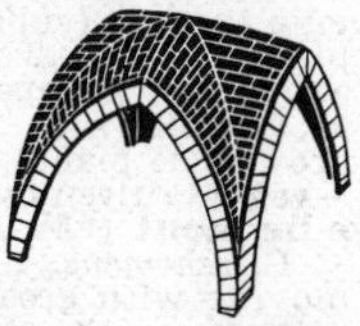
GROINED VAULT

**vault** (vôlt), *v.i.* [< OFr. *volter;* akin to prec. entry], to jump, leap, or spring; esp., to leap over a barrier, etc. with the help of the hands supported on the barrier, or holding a long pole. *v.t.* to vault over. *n.* a vaulting. —**vault′er,** *n.*

**vault·ing** (vôl′tiŋ), *n.* 1. the arched work forming a vault. 2. a vault, or vaults collectively.

**vault·ing** (vôl′tiŋ), *adj.* [ppr. of *vault* (to leap)], 1. leaping; leaping over. 2. overreaching; unduly confident: as, *vaulting* ambition.

**vaunt** (vônt, vänt), *v.i. & v.t.* [< OFr. < LL. *vanitare* < L. *vanus*, vain], to boast or brag (of). *n.* a boast; brag. —**vaunt′er,** *n.* —**vaunt′ing·ly,** *adv.*

**v. aux.,** auxiliary verb.

**vb.,** 1. verb. 2. verbal.

**V.C.,** 1. Vice-Chairman. 2. Vice-Chancellor. 3. Victoria Cross.

**Vd,** in *chemistry*, vanadium.

**V.D., VD,** venereal disease.

**V-Day** (vē′dā′), *n.* Victory Day: see **V-E Day, V-J Day.**

**′ve,** have: a contraction.

**Ve·a·dar** (vē′ə-där′, vā-ô′där), *n.* [Heb.], an extra month of the Jewish year: see **Jewish calendar.**

**veal** (vēl), *n.* [< OFr. *veël* < L. dim. of *vitulus*, a calf], the flesh of a calf used as food.

**Veb·len, Thor·stein** (thôr′stīn veb′lən), 1857–1929; U.S. political economist and author.

**vec·tor** (vek′tēr), *n.* [L., a carrier < pp. of *vehere*, to carry], in *mathematics*, *a*) a quantity, such as a force or velocity, having direction and magnitude. *b*) a line representing such a quantity. —**vec·to′ri·al** (-tôr′i-əl, -tō′ri-), *adj.*

**Ve·da** (vā′də, vē′-), *n.* [Sans. *veda*, knowledge], *often in pl.* the ancient sacred literature of Hinduism, consisting of four collections of psalms, chants, sacred formulas, etc. —**Ve·da·ic** (vi-dā′ik), **Ve′dic,** *adj.* —**Ve′da·ism,** *n.*

**V-E Day** (vē′ē′), May 8, 1945, the day on which Germany surrendered, ending the European phase of World War II.

**veer** (vêr), *v.i.* [alt. < Fr. *virer*, to turn around], 1. to change direction; shift; turn. 2. to change sides; shift, as from one opinion or attitude to another. *v.t.* to turn or swing; change the course of. *n.* a change of direction. —**veer′ing·ly,** *adv.*

**veer·y** (vêr′i), *n.* [*pl.* -IES], [prob. echoic], a brown thrush of the eastern U.S.

**Ve·ga** (vē′gə), *n.* a blue-white star of the first magnitude in the constellation Lyra.

**Ve·ga, Lo·pe de** (lô′pe *the* ve′gä), (*Lope Félix de Vega Carpio*), 1562–1635; Spanish dramatist and poet.

**veg·e·ta·ble** (vej′tə-b'l, vej′i-tə-), *n.* [Fr. < LL. *vegetabilis*, animating < L. *vegetare;* see VEGETATE], 1. broadly, any plant, as distinguished from animal or inorganic matter. 2. *a*) specifically, any plant that is eaten whole or in part, raw or cooked, generally in a salad or with an entree, as the tomato, potato, lettuce, pea, etc. *b*) the edible part of such a plant. *adj.* 1. of, like, made from, or produced by edible vegetables. 2. of plants in general: as, the *vegetable* kingdom.

**veg·e·tal** (vej′ə-t'l), *adj.* of, or having the nature of, plants or vegetables.

**veg·e·tar·i·an** (vej′ə-târ′i-ən), *n.* one who eats no meat; one who advocates a strict vegetable diet as proper for all people. *adj.* 1. of vegetarians or vegetarianism. 2. advocating vegetarianism. 3. consisting only of vegetables.

**veg·e·tar·i·an·ism** (vej′ə-târ′i-ən-iz'm), *n.* the principles or practices of vegetarians.

**veg·e·tate** (vej′ə-tāt′), *v.i.* [-TATED, -TATING], [< L. pp. of *vegetare*, to enliven < *vegetus*, lively < *vegere*, to quicken], 1. to grow as plants. 2. to lead a very inactive life.

**veg·e·ta·tion** (vej′ə-tā′shən), *n.* 1. the act or process of vegetating. 2. plant life in general. 3. dull, passive existence. **—veg′e·ta′tion·al,** *adj.*

**veg·e·ta·tive** (vej′ə-tā′tiv), *adj.* 1. of plants or plant growth. 2. growing, or capable of growing, as plants. 3. capable of causing growth in plants: as, *vegetative* soil. 4. involuntary or passive like the growth of plants; inactive. **—veg′e·ta′tive·ly,** *adv.* **—veg′e·ta′tive·ness,** *n.*

**ve·he·ment** (vē′ə-mənt; *occas.* vē′hi-), *adj.* [< Fr. < L. *vehemens* < *vehere*, to carry], 1. acting or moving with great force; violent; impetuous. 2. having or showing intense feeling; passionate. **—ve′he·mence, ve′he·men·cy,** *n.* **—ve′he·ment·ly,** *adv.*

**ve·hi·cle** (vē′ə-k'l; *occas.* vē′hi-), *n.* [< Fr. < L. *vehiculum*, carriage < *vehere*, to carry], 1. any device on wheels or runners for conveying persons or objects, as a cart, sled, automobile, etc. 2. any means of carrying, conveying, or communicating. 3. a means by which ideas are expressed. 4. in *painting*, a liquid, as water or oil, with which pigments are mixed for use. 5. in *pharmacy*, a substance, as sirup, in which medicines are given. 6. in the *theater*, a play thought of as a means of presenting a certain idea, actor, or company. **—ve·hic·u·lar** (vē-hik′yoo-lẽr), *adj.*

**veil** (vāl), *n.* [< ONorm.Fr. < L. *vela*, pl. of *velum*, cloth], 1. a piece of light fabric, as of net or gauze, worn, especially by women, over the face or head to conceal, protect, or enhance the face. 2. any piece of cloth used as a concealing or separating curtain. 3. anything that covers or conceals: as, a *veil* of mist, a *veil* of silence. 4. a part of a nun's headdress, draped along the face and over the shoulders. 5. the state or life of a nun: especially in *take the veil*, to become a nun. *v.t.* 1. to cover with a veil. 2. to conceal; hide or disguise. **—veiled,** *adj.* **—veil′like′,** *adj.*

**veiled** (vāld), *adj.* 1. wearing a veil. 2. covered with a veil. 3. concealed; hidden. 4. not openly expressed: as, a *veiled* threat.

**veil·ing** (vāl′iŋ), *n.* 1. the act of covering with or as with a veil. 2. a veil; curtain. 3. thin, transparent fabric used for veils.

**vein** (vān), *n.* [< OFr. < L. *vena;* ? < base of *vehere*, to carry], 1. any blood vessel that carries blood from some part of the body back to the heart. 2. any of the ribs strengthening the membranous wings of an insect. 3. any of the bundles of vascular tissue forming the framework of a leaf blade. 4. *a*) a fissure or crack in rock, filled with a mineral. *b*) a deposit of such mineral. 5. a stratum or bed of coal, etc. 6. a streak or marking of a different color or substance from the surrounding material, as in marble or wood. 7. any distinctive quality regarded as running through one's character, speech, etc.: as, a *vein* of humor. 8. a temporary state of mind; mood: as, a serious *vein*. *v.t.* 1. to mark with or as with veins. 2. to branch out through in the manner of veins. **—veined,** *adj.* **—vein′like′,** *adj.*

**vein·ing** (vān′iŋ), *n.* the formation or arrangement of veins or veinlike markings.

**vein·let** (vān′lit), *n.* a small vein: also **vein′ule** (-ūl).

**vein·y** (vān′i), *adj.* [-IER, -IEST], 1. having or showing veins. 2. full of veins, as marble.

**ve·lar** (vē′lẽr), *adj.* 1. of a velum; esp., of the soft palate. 2. in *phonetics*, pronounced with the back of the tongue touching or near the soft palate, as the sound of *k* when followed by a back vowel, such as *ô*. *n.* a velar sound.

**Ve·láz·quez, Die·go Ro·drí·gues de Sil·va y** (dye′gô rô-*th*rē′geth *the* sēl′vä ē ve-läth′keth; Eng. və-las′kwiz), 1599–1660; Spanish painter: also **Ve·lás′quez.**

**veld, veldt** (velt, felt), *n.* [D. *veld*, a field], in South Africa, open grassy country, with few bushes and almost no trees; grassland.

**vel·lum** (vel′əm), *n.* [< OFr. *velin* < *vel;* see VEAL], 1. a fine parchment prepared from calfskin, lambskin, etc., used for writing on or for binding books. 2. a manuscript written on vellum. 3. paper made to resemble vellum. *adj.* of or like vellum.

**ve·loc·i·pede** (və-los′ə-pēd′), *n.* [< Fr. < L. *velox*, swift + *pes*, a foot], 1. any of various early bicycles or tricycles. 2. a child's tricycle.

**ve·loc·i·ty** (və-los′ə-ti), *n.* [*pl.* -TIES], [< Fr. < L. < *velox*, swift], 1. quickness of motion or action; speed. 2. *a*) rate of change of position, in relation to time. *b*) rate of motion in a particular direction, in relation to time.

**ve·lours** (və-loor′), *n.* [*pl.* -LOURS], [Fr.; see VELURE], a fabric with a nap like velvet, made of wool, silk, linen, or cotton, and used for upholstery, draperies, clothing, etc.: also sp. **velour.**

**ve·lum** (vē′ləm), *n.* [*pl.* -LA (-lə)], [L., a veil], in *biology*, any of various veillike membranous partitions or coverings; specif., the soft palate.

**ve·lure** (və-loor′), *n.* [Fr. *velours* < OFr. < LL. *villosus*, shaggy < *villus*, shaggy hair], 1. velvet or a fabric like velvet, used for draperies, etc. 2. a plush pad used for brushing silk hats. *v.t.* [-LURED, -LURING], to brush with a velure.

**vel·vet** (vel′vit), *n.* [< ML. *velvetum;* ult. < L. *villus*, shaggy hair], 1. a rich fabric of silk, silk and cotton, rayon, etc. with a soft, thick pile. 2. anything with a surface like that of velvet. 3. the soft, furry skin on a deer's growing antlers. 4. [Slang], clear profit; winnings. *adj.* 1. made of velvet. 2. smooth or soft like velvet. **—vel′vet·y** [-IER, -IEST], *adj.*

**vel·vet·een** (vel′və-tēn′), *n.* 1. a cotton cloth with a short, thick pile, resembling velvet. 2. *pl.* clothes, especially trousers, made of this.

**ve·na ca·va** (vē′nə kā′və), *n.* [*pl.* -NAE -VAE (-nē -vē)], [< L. *vena*, vein + *cava*, fem. of *cavus*, hollow], in *anatomy*, either of two large veins conveying blood to the right atrium of the heart.

**ve·nal** (vē′n'l), *adj.* [< L. *venalis*, salable < *venum*, sale], 1. that can readily be bribed or corrupted; mercenary. 2. open to, or characterized by, corruption or bribery. **—ve·nal′i·ty** (-nal′ə-ti), [*pl.* -TIES], *n.* **—ve′nal·ly,** *adv.*

**ve·na·tion** (vē-nā′shən), *n.* [< L. *vena*, a vein], 1. the arrangement of veins, as in an insect's wing or a leaf. 2. such veins collectively.

**vend** (vend), *v.t. & v.i.* [< Fr. < L. *vendere*, contr. < *venum dare*, to offer for sale], to sell.

**vend·ee** (ven-dē′), *n.* the person to whom a thing is sold; buyer.

**ven·det·ta** (ven-det′ə), *n.* [*pl.* -TAS], [It. < L. *vindicta*, vengeance], a blood feud in which the relatives of a murdered person try to kill the murderer or members of his family. **—ven·det′tist,** *n.*

**vend·i·ble** (ven′də-b'l), *adj.* [see VEND], capable of being sold. *n.* something vendible. **—vend′i·bil′i·ty, vend′i·ble·ness,** *n.* **—vend′i·bly,** *adv.*

**vending machine,** a coin slot machine for selling merchandise.

**ven·dor, vend·er** (ven′dẽr), *n.* 1. one who vends, or sells; seller. 2. a vending machine.

**ve·neer** (və-nêr′), *v.t.* [G. *furniren* < Fr. *fournir*, to furnish], 1. to cover with a thin layer of fine material; esp., to cover (wood) with wood of finer quality. 2. to cover (anything) with a material having an attractive or superior surface. *n.* 1. a thin surface layer, usually of wood, laid over a base of common material. 2. any attractive but superficial appearance or display: as, a *veneer* of culture.

**ve·neer·ing** (və-nêr′iŋ), *n.* 1. the act of one who veneers. 2. veneer (sense 1).

**ven·er·a·ble** (ven′ẽr-ə-b'l, ven′rə-), *adj.* [see VENERATE], 1. worthy of respect or reverence by reason of age, dignity, etc. 2. in the *Anglican Church*, a title given to an archdeacon. 3. in the *R.C. Church*, a title given to persons who have attained the lowest degree of sanctity. **—ven′er·a·bil′i·ty, ven′er·a·ble·ness,** *n.* **—ven′er·a·bly,** *adv.*

**ven·er·ate** (ven′ə-rāt′), *v.t.* [-ATED, -ATING], [< L. pp. of *venerari*, to worship], to look upon with feelings of deep respect; revere. **—ven′er·a′tor,** *n.*

**ven·er·a·tion** (ven′ə-rā′shən), *n.* 1. a venerating or being venerated. 2. deep respect and reverence. 3. an act showing this.

**ve·ne·re·al** (və-nêr′i-əl), *adj.* [< L. *venereus* < *Venus*, Venus, love], 1. having to do with sexual love or intercourse. 2. transmitted by sexual intercourse with an infected person, as a disease. 3. infected with a venereal disease. 4. for the cure of such a disease. —**ve·ne′re·al·ly,** *adv.*

**ven·er·y** (ven′ēr-i), *n.* [< L. *Venus*, Venus, love], [Archaic], indulgence of sexual desire.

**ven·er·y** (ven′ēr-i), *n.* [< OFr. < *vener* (< L. *venari*), to hunt], hunting, as an art or sport.

**Ve·ne·tian** (və-nē′shən), *adj.* of Venice, its people, etc. *n.* a native or inhabitant of Venice.

**Venetian blind,** a window blind made of a number of thin wooden or metal slats that can be set at any angle to regulate the light and air.

**Ven·e·zue·la** (ven′ə-zwē′lə, -i-zwā′-), *n.* a country in N South America, on the Caribbean: area, 352,051 sq. mi.; pop. 6,709,000; capital, Caracas: abbrev. **Venez.** —**Ven′e·zue′lan,** *adj.* & *n.*

**venge·ance** (ven′jəns), *n.* [OFr. < *venger* (< L. *vindicare*), to avenge], the return of an injury for an injury, in punishment or retribution; an avenging; revenge. —**with a vengeance,** 1. with great force or fury. 2. extremely. 3. excessively.

**venge·ful** (venj′fəl), *adj.* 1. desiring revenge; seeking vengeance; vindictive. 2. showing a desire for vengeance: said of actions or feelings. —**venge′ful·ly,** *adv.* —**venge′ful·ness,** *n.*

**ve·ni·al** (vē′ni-əl, vēn′yəl), *adj.* [OFr. < LL. *venialis* < L. *venia*, grace], 1. that may be forgiven; pardonable: as, a *venial* sin. 2. excusable: as, a *venial* fault. —**ve′ni·al′i·ty** (-al′ə-ti), **ve′ni·al·ness,** *n.* —**ve′ni·al·ly,** *adv.*

**Ven·ice** (ven′is), *n.* a seaport in NE Italy, built on more than a hundred small islands in an inlet of the Gulf of Venice: pop., 322,000.

**Venice, Gulf of,** the N end of the Adriatic.

**ve·ni·re fa·ci·as** (vi-nī′rē fā′shi-as′), [L., cause to come], in *law*, a writ or order summoning persons to serve as jurors: also **venire.**

**ve·ni·re·man** (vi-nī′ri-mən), *n.* [*pl.* -MEN], a person called to jury service on a writ of venire.

**ven·i·son** (ven′i-z'n), *n.* [< OFr. < L. < pp. of *venari*, to hunt], the flesh of deer, used as food.

‡**ve·ni, vi·di, vi·ci** (vē′nī vī′dī vī′sī, wā′nē wē′dē wē′kē), [L.], I came, I saw, I conquered: Caesar's report to the Roman Senate of a victory.

**ven·om** (ven′əm), *n.* [< OFr. < L. *venenum*, a poison], 1. the poison secreted by some snakes, spiders, insects, etc., introduced into the body of the victim by bite or sting. 2. spite; malice.

**ven·om·ous** (ven′əm-əs), *adj.* 1. full of venom; poisonous. 2. malignant; spiteful; malicious. 3. in *zoology*, able to inflict a poisonous bite or sting. —**ven′om·ous·ly,** *adv.* —**ven′om·ous·ness,** *n.*

**ve·nous** (vē′nəs), *adj.* [L. *venosus*], 1. of a vein or veins. 2. having veins. 3. designating blood being carried in the veins back to the heart and lungs. —**ve′nous·ness, ve·nos·i·ty** (vi-nos′ə-ti), *n.* —**ve′nous·ly,** *adv.*

**vent** (vent), *n.* [alt. (after Fr. *vent*, a wind) < OFr. *fente*, a rift < L. *findere*, to split], 1. the action or a means of escaping; issue; outlet; passage. 2. expression; release: as, giving *vent* to emotion. 3. a small opening to permit passage or escape, as of a gas. 4. a slit in a garment, as at the back of a coat. 5. in *zoology*, the excretory opening of animals. *v.t.* 1. to make a vent in. 2. to let out at an opening. 3. to give release or expression to. 4. to publish or utter. —**vent′less,** *adj.*

**ven·ti·late** (ven′t'l-āt′), *v.t.* [-LATED, -LATING], [< L. pp. of *ventilare*, to fan < *ventus*, a wind], 1. *a*) to circulate fresh air in (a room, etc.). *b*) to circulate in (a room, etc.): said of fresh air. 2. to provide with an opening for the escape of foul air, gas, etc. 3. to examine and discuss openly, as a grievance. 4. to aerate (blood); oxygenate. —**ven′ti·la′tion,** *n.* —**ven′ti·la′tive,** *adj.*

**ven·ti·la·tor** (ven′t'l-ā′tēr), *n.* a thing that ventilates; esp., any opening or device used to bring in fresh air and drive out foul air.

**ven·tral** (ven′trəl), *adj.* [Fr. < L. *ventralis* < *venter*, belly], of, near, on, or toward the belly. —**ven′tral·ly,** *adv.*

**ven·tri·cle** (ven′tri-k'l), *n.* [< Fr. < L. dim. of *venter*, belly], in *anatomy & zoology*, a cavity; specif., either of the two lower chambers of the heart which receive blood from the auricles and pump it into the arteries. —**ven·tric′u·lar** (-trik′yoo-lēr), *adj.*

**ven·tril·o·quism** (ven-tril′ə-kwiz'm), *n.* [< L. < *venter*, belly + *loqui*, to speak], the art or practice of speaking in such a way that the voice seems to come from some source other than the speaker: also **ven·tril′o·quy** (-kwi). —**ven·tril′o·quist,** *n.* —**ven·tril′o·quis′tic,** *adj.* —**ven·tril′o·quize′** (-kwīz′), [-QUIZED, -QUIZING], *v.i.* & *v.t.*

**ven·ture** (ven′chēr), *n.* [< ME. *aventure;* see ADVENTURE], 1. a risky undertaking; esp., a business enterprise in which there is danger of loss as well as chance for profit. 2. something on which a risk is taken. 3. chance; fortune: now only in *at a venture*, by mere chance. *v.t.* [-TURED, -TURING], 1. to expose to danger: as, he *ventured* his life. 2. to expose to chance of loss, as money, etc. 3. to take the risk of; brave. 4. to express at the risk of criticism, etc.: as, to *venture* an opinion. *v.i.* to do or go at some risk; dare. —**ven′tur·er,** *n.*

**ven·ture·some** (ven′chēr-səm), *adj.* 1. inclined to venture; daring. 2. venturous; risky; hazardous. —**ven′ture·some·ly,** *adv.* —**ven′ture·some·ness,** *n.*

**ven·tur·ous** (ven′chēr-əs), *adj.* 1. inclined to venture; bold. 2. risky; hazardous. —**ven′tur·ous·ly,** *adv.* —**ven′tur·ous·ness,** *n.*

**ven·ue** (ven′ū, -ōō), *n.* [OFr., arrival < *venir*, to come], in *law*, 1. the county or locality in which a cause of action or a crime occurs. 2. the county or locality in which a jury is drawn and a case tried. —**change of venue,** in *law*, the substitution of another place of trial, as when the jury is likely to be prejudiced.

**Ve·nus** (vē′nəs), *n.* 1. the Roman goddess of love and beauty: identified with the Greek Aphrodite. 2. a statue or image of Venus. 3. a very beautiful woman. 4. the most brilliant planet in the solar system: diameter, 7,600 mi.

**Ve·nus's-fly·trap** (vē′nəs-iz-flī′trap′), *n.* a swamp plant of the Carolinas, having leaves with two hinged blades which close upon insects.

**ve·ra·cious** (və-rā′shəs), *adj.* [< L. < *verus*, true], 1. habitually truthful; honest. 2. true; accurate. —**ve·ra′cious·ly,** *adv.* —**ve·ra′cious·ness,** *n.*

**ve·rac·i·ty** (və-ras′ə-ti), *n.* [*pl.* -TIES], [< Fr. < ML. < L. *verus*, true], 1. habitual truthfulness; honesty. 2. accuracy of statement. 3. accuracy or precision, as of perception. 4. truth.

**Ver·a·cruz** (ver′ə-krōōz′), *n.* a city on the E coast of Mexico: pop., 138,000: formerly **Vera Cruz.**

**ve·ran·da, ve·ran·dah** (və-ran′də), *n.* [Port. *varanda*, a balcony < Hind.], an open porch, usually roofed, along the outside of a building; piazza.

**verb** (vūrb), *n.* [< OFr. < L. *verbum*, a word], in *grammar*, 1. any of a class of words expressing action, existence, or occurrence: as, *take* and *be* are *verbs*. 2. any construction used as a verb. *adj.* of, or having the function of, a verb.

**ver·bal** (vūr′b'l), *adj.* 1. of, in, or by means of words. 2. concerned merely with words, as distinguished from ideas. 3. in speech; oral, not written. 4. word for word; literal: as, a *verbal* translation. 5. in *grammar*, *a*) of, having the nature of, or derived from a verb: as, a *verbal* noun. *b*) used to form verbs: as, *-ate* is a *verbal* suffix. *n.* a verbal noun or other word derived from a verb: in English, gerunds, infinitives, and participles are verbals. —**ver′bal·ly,** *adv.*

**ver·bal·ism** (vūr′b'l-iz'm), *n.* 1. expression in words; a word or phrase. 2. words only, without any real meaning; mere verbiage. 3. any virtually meaningless phrase or form of words.

**ver·bal·ist** (vūr′b'l-ist), *n.* 1. a person who uses words well. 2. a person who fixes his attention on mere words, rather than facts or ideas.

**ver·bal·ize** (vūr′b'l-īz′), *v.i.* [-IZED, -IZING], to be wordy, or verbose. *v.t.* 1. to express in words. 2. to change (a noun, etc.) into a verb. —**ver′bal·i·za′tion,** *n.* —**ver′bal·iz′er,** *n.*

**verbal noun,** in *grammar*, a noun derived from a verb and acting in some respects like a verb: in English, it is either a gerund or an infinitive, as, *swimming* is fun, *to err* is human.

**ver·ba·tim** (vēr-bā′tim), *adv.* [ML. < L. *verbum*, a word], word for word; in exactly the same words. *adj.* following the original word for word.

**ver·be·na** (vēr-bē′nə), *n.* [L., foliage], any of various plants with spikes or clusters of red, white, or purplish flowers.

**ver·bi·age** (vūr′bi-ij), *n.* [Fr. < OFr. < L. *verbum*, a word], an excess of words beyond those needed to express concisely what is meant; wordiness.

**ver·bose** (vēr-bōs′), *adj.* [L. *verbosus*, full of words < *verbum*, a word], using or containing too many words; wordy; long-winded. —**ver·bose′ly,** *adv.* —**ver·bos′i·ty** (-bos′ə-ti), **ver·bose′ness,** *n.*

‡**ver·bo·ten** (fer-bō'tən), *adj.* [G.], forbidden.
**ver·dant** (vũr'd'nt), *adj.* [prob. < *verdure* + *-ant*], 1. green. 2. covered with green vegetation. 3. inexperienced; immature; innocent: as, *verdant* youth. —**ver'dan·cy,** *n.* —**ver'dant·ly,** *adv.*
**Verde, Cape** (vũrd), the westernmost point of Africa, at Dakar, Senegal.
**Ver·di, Gui·sep·pe** (jōō-zep'pe ver'dē), 1813–1901; Italian operatic composer.
**ver·dict** (vũr'dikt), *n.* [< Anglo-Fr. < ML. < L. *vere*, truly + *dictum*, a thing said < *dicere*, to say], 1. in *law*, the formal and unanimous finding of a jury. 2. a decision; judgment.
**ver·di·gris** (vũr'di-grēs', -gris), *n.* [< OFr. < *verd*, green + *de*, of + *Grece*, Greece], a green or greenish-blue coating that forms like rust on brass, bronze, or copper.
**Ver·dun** (vâr-dun'), *n.* a city in NE France, on the Meuse River; scene of a battle in World War I.
**ver·dure** (vũr'jẽr), *n.* [OFr. < *verd*, green], 1. the fresh green color of growing things; greenness. 2. green vegetation. —**ver'dur·ous,** *adj.*
‡**Ver·ein** (fer-īn'), *n.* [G.], a society; association.
**verge** (vũrj), *n.* [< OFr. < L. *virga*, rod], 1. a rod or staff symbolic of an office. 2. an enclosing line or border; boundary, especially of something circular. 3. the edge, brink, or margin (*of* something): as, the *verge* of a forest, the *verge* of hysteria. *v.i.* [VERGED, VERGING], to be on the verge, edge, brink, or border (usually with *on* or *upon*).
**verge** (vũrj), *v.i.* [VERGED, VERGING], [L. *vergere*], 1. to tend; incline (*to* or *toward*). 2. to come close to in gradation; approach (with *into* or *on*): as, humor *verging* on slapstick.
**Ver·gil** (vũr'jil), *n.* Virgil. —**Ver·gil'i·an,** *adj.*
**ver·i·fi·a·ble** (ver'ə-fī'ə-b'l), *adj.* that can be proved to be true by examination or investigation. —**ver'i-fi'a·bil'i·ty, ver'i·fi'a·ble·ness,** *n.* —**ver'i·fi'a·bly,** *adv.*
**ver·i·fi·ca·tion** (ver'ə-fi-kā'shən), *n.* 1. a verifying or being verified. 2. the confirmation of the truth of a fact, theory, etc. —**ver'i·fi·ca'tive,** *adj.*
**ver·i·fy** (ver'ə-fī'), *v.t.* [-FIED, -FYING], [< OFr. < L. *verus*, true + *facere*, to make], 1. to prove to be true by evidence, testimony, etc.; confirm. 2. to test the accuracy of, as by investigation. 3. in *law*, to affirm formally or upon oath. —**ver'i·fi'er,** *n.*
**ver·i·ly** (ver'ə-li), *adv.* [Archaic], in fact; really.
**ver·i·sim·i·lar** (ver'ə-sim'ə-lẽr), *adj.* [< L. *verus*, true + *similis*, like], probable.
**ver·i·si·mil·i·tude** (ver'ə-si-mil'ə-tōōd', -tūd'), *n.* [< L. < *verus*, true + *similis*, like], 1. the appearance of being true or real. 2. something that has the mere appearance of being true or real.
**ver·i·ta·ble** (ver'i-tə-b'l), *adj.* [OFr. < L. *veritas*, truth], true; real; actual; genuine: as, a *veritable* tyrant. —**ver'i·ta·ble·ness,** *n.* —**ver'i·ta·bly,** *adv.*
**ver·i·ty** (ver'i-ti), *n.* [*pl.* -TIES], [< OFr. < L. *veritas*, truth < *verus*, true], 1. truth; reality. 2. a principle, belief, etc. taken to be fundamentally and permanently true; a truth.
**ver·juice** (vũr'jōōs'), *n.* [< OFr. < *vert*, green + *jus*, juice], 1. the sour, acid juice of green or unripe fruit. 2. sourness of temper, looks, etc.
**Ver·meer, Jan** (yän vẽr-mâr'; Eng. vẽr-mêr'), 1632–1675; Dutch painter.
**ver·mi-,** [< L. *vermis*], a combining form meaning *worm*, as in *vermicide*.
**ver·mi·cel·li** (vũr'mə-sel'i, -chel'i), *n.* [It., little worms < L. dim. of *vermis*, a worm], a food made of a wheat flour paste dried in long threads, thinner than spaghetti.
**ver·mi·cide** (vũr'mə-sīd'), *n.* [*vermi-* + *-cide*], in *medicine*, a drug used to kill worms, especially intestinal worms. —**ver'mi·cid'al,** *adj.*
**ver·mic·u·lar** (vẽr-mik'yoo-lẽr), *adj.* [< L. dim. of *vermis*, a worm], 1. of or like a worm in appearance or movement. 2. worm-eaten.
**ver·mi·form** (vũr'mə-fôrm'), *adj.* [*vermi-* + *-form*], shaped like a worm.
**vermiform appendix,** a small, saclike appendage of the large intestine.
**ver·mi·fuge** (vũr'mə-fūj'), *adj.* [< L.; see VERMI- & -FUGE], serving to expel worms and other parasites from the intestinal tract. *n.* a vermifuge drug.
**ver·mil·ion** (vẽr-mil'yən), *n.* [< OFr. < *vermeil*, bright-red < L. dim. of *vermis*, a worm], 1. any of several bright-red pigments. 2. bright yellowish red. *adj.* of the color vermilion.
**ver·min** (vũr'min), *n.* [*pl.* -MIN], [< OFr. < L. *vermis*, a worm], 1. any of various small, destructive or troublesome animals, as flies, lice, rats, weasels, etc. 2. [Brit.], any bird or animal that kills game. 3. a vile or offensive person. —**ver'min·ous,** *adj.*
**Ver·mont** (vẽr-mont'), *n.* a New England State of the U.S.: area, 9,609 sq. mi.; pop., 390,000; capital, Montpelier: abbrev. **Vt.** —**Ver·mont'er,** *n.*
**ver·mouth** (vẽr-mōōth', vũr'mōōth), *n.* [Fr. < G. *wermuth*, wormwood], a fortified white wine flavored with aromatic herbs: it may be sweet or dry, and is used chiefly in cocktails.
**ver·nac·u·lar** (vẽr-nak'yoo-lẽr), *adj.* [< L. *vernaculus*, native < *verna*, a homeborn slave], 1. using the native language of a place, as a writer. 2. commonly spoken by the people of a particular country or place. 3. of or in the native language. 4. native to a country. *n.* 1. the native language or dialect of a country or place. 2. the common everyday language of the people in a particular locality. 3. the shoptalk of a profession or trade. 4. a vernacular word or term. —**ver·nac'u·lar·ly,** *adv.*
**ver·nal** (vũr'n'l), *adj.* [< L. *vernalis* < *vernus* < *ver*, spring], 1. of, or occurring in, the spring. 2. springlike. 3. youthful. —**ver'nal·ly,** *adv.*
**vernal equinox,** the equinox that is reached about March 21.
**ver·nal·ize** (vũr'n'l-īz'), *v.t.* [-IZED, -IZING], to stimulate the growth of (a plant) by artificially hastening the dormant period. —**ver'nal·i·za'tion,** *n.*
**ver·na·tion** (vẽr-nā'shən), *n.* [< L. *vernare*, to flourish], in *botany*, the arrangement of leaves in a leaf bud.
**Verne, Jules** (jōōlz vũrn), 1828–1905; French novelist.
**ver·ni·er** (vũr'ni-ẽr, -nêr), *n.* [< P. *Vernier*], a short graduated scale that slides along a longer graduated instrument and is used to indicate fractional parts of divisions: also **vernier scale.**
**Ver·nier, Pierre** (pyâr vâr'nyā'; Eng. vũr'ni-ẽr), 1580–1637; French mathematician.
**Ve·ro·na** (və-rō'nə), *n.* a city in NE Italy: pop., 187,000. —**Ver'o·nese'** (ver'ə-nēz'), *adj. & n.* [*pl.* -NESE].
**ver·o·nal** (ver'ə-n'l), *n.* [G. < L. *ver*, spring], barbital: a trade-mark (**Veronal**).
**Ve·ro·ne·se, Pa·o·lo** (pä'ô-lô' ve'rô-ne'se; Eng. ver'ə-nēz'), 1528–1588; Venetian painter born in Verona.
**ve·ron·i·ca** (və-ron'i-kə), *n.* [Mod. L.], any of a group of plants of the figwort family; esp., the speedwell.
**Ver·sailles** (vẽr-sālz', vẽr-sī'), *n.* a city in France, near Paris: pop., 84,000: scene of signing of a treaty (1919) between the Allies and Germany following World War I.
**ver·sa·tile** (vũr'sə-til), *adj.* [Fr. < L. pp. of *versare*, freq. of *vertere*, to turn], 1. competent in many things; able to turn easily from one subject or occupation to another. 2. in *botany*, turning about freely on the filament to which it is attached. 3. in *zoology*, moving forward or backward, as the toes of a bird. —**ver'sa·tile·ly,** *adv.* —**ver'sa·til'i·ty** (-til'ə-ti), **ver'sa·tile·ness,** *n.*
**verse** (vũrs), *n.* [< AS. & OFr. < L. *versus*, a turning, row, pp. of *vertere*, to turn], 1. a single line of poetry. 2. *a*) poetry in general; esp., poetry without much serious content. *b*) a particular form of poetry: as, blank *verse*. 3. a poem. 4. a stanza of a poem. 5. in the *Bible*, any of the short divisions of a chapter. *v.t. & v.i.* [VERSED, VERSING], [Now Rare], to versify.
**versed** (vũrst), *adj.* [< L. pp. of *versari*, to be busy], acquainted by experience and study; skilled; learned.
**ver·si·cle** (vũr'si-k'l), *n.* [< L. *versiculus*, dim. of *versus*, verse], a short verse or sentence said or sung in a church service by a minister and followed by the response of the congregation.
**ver·si·fi·ca·tion** (vũr'sə-fi-kā'shən), *n.* 1. the act of versifying. 2. the art, practice, or theory of poetic composition. 3. metrical structure.
**ver·si·fy** (vũr'sə-fī'), *v.i.* [-FIED, -FYING], [< OFr. < L. < *versus*, verse + *facere*, to make], to compose verses. *v.t.* 1. to tell in verse. 2. to rewrite (prose) in verse form. —**ver'si·fi'er,** *n.*
**ver·sion** (vũr'zhən, -shən), *n.* [Fr. < ML. < L. *versus*; see VERSE], 1. *a*) a translation. *b*) [often V-], a translation of the Bible: as, the King James *version*. 2. an account showing one point of view: as, his *version* agreed with ours. 3. a particular form of something. —**ver'sion·al,** *adj.*
**vers li·bre** (vâr' lē'br'), [Fr.], free verse. —**vers li'brist** (-brist).
**ver·so** (vũr'sō), *n.* [*pl.* -SOS], [L., abl. of *versus*; see VERSE], 1. in *printing*, any left-hand page of a book. 2. the back of a coin or medal.
**verst** (vũrst, verst), *n.* [< Russ. *versta*], a Russian unit of linear measure, equal to c. 3,500 ft.
**ver·sus** (vũr'səs), *prep.* [L., toward < *vertere*, to turn], 1. in *law & sports*, against. 2. contrasted with: as, the open shop *versus* the closed shop.

**ver·te·bra** (vũr′tə-brə), ***n.*** [*pl.* -BRAE (-brē′), -BRAS], [L., a joint < *vertere*, to turn], any of the single bones of the spinal column. —**ver′te·bral,** ***adj.*** —**ver′te·bral·ly,** ***adv.***

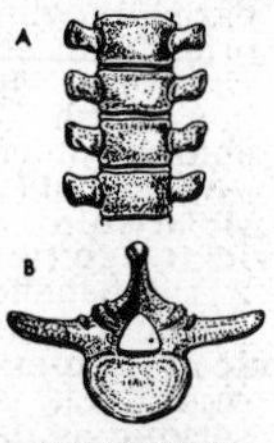

VERTEBRA A, four vertebrae joined together; B, top view of vertebra

**ver·te·brate** (vũr′tə-brāt′, -brit), ***adj.*** [< L.; see VERTEBRA], 1. having a backbone, or spinal column. 2. of or belonging to the vertebrates. ***n.*** any of a large division of animals that have a spinal column, or backbone. —**ver′te·brat′ed,** ***adj.***

**ver·tex** (vũr′teks), ***n.*** [*pl.* -TEXES, -TICES (-tə-sēz′)], [L., the top < *vertere*, to turn], 1. the highest point; top. 2. in *astronomy*, the point in the sky directly overhead. 3. in *geometry*, the point opposite to the base and furthest from it.

**ver·ti·cal** (vũr′ti-k'l), ***adj.*** 1. of or at the vertex, or highest point; directly overhead. 2. perpendicular to the plane of the horizon; upright. 3. in *economics*, of or controlling businesses concerned with all the processes in the manufacture of a particular product. ***n.*** 1. a vertical line, plane, etc. 2. a vertical member in a truss. —**ver′ti·cal′i·ty** (-kal′ə-ti), **ver′ti·cal·ness,** ***n.*** —**ver′ti·cal·ly,** ***adv.***

**vertical union,** a labor union whose members all work in the same industry but not necessarily at the same trade; industrial union.

**ver·ti·cil** (vũr′ti-sil), ***n.*** [< L. *verticillus*, a whirl, dim. of *vertex;* see VERTEX], in *botany*, a whorl.

**ver·tic·il·late** (vẽr-tis′'l-it, -āt′, vũr′tə-sil′āt), ***adj.*** in *botany*, 1. arranged in verticils. 2. having leaves, flowers, etc. so arranged. Also **ver·tic′il·lat′ed.** —**ver·tic′il·la′tion,** ***n.***

**ver·tig·i·nous** (vẽr-tij′ə-nəs), ***adj.*** 1. rotating; whirling. 2. of or having vertigo; dizzy. 3. tending to cause vertigo. 4. unstable; inconstant. —**ver·tig′i·nous·ly,** ***adv.*** —**ver·tig′i·nous·ness,** ***n.***

**ver·ti·go** (vũr′ti-gō′), ***n.*** [*pl.* -GOES, VERTIGINES (vẽr-tij′ə-nēz′)], [L. < *vertere*, to turn], in *medicine*, a sensation of dizziness or giddiness.

**ver·tu** (vẽr-to͞o′, vũr′to͞o), ***n.*** virtu.

**ver·vain** (vũr′vān), ***n.*** [< OFr. < L. *verbena*, a shoot], any of various plants of the verbena family, with red, white, or purplish flowers.

**verve** (vũrv), ***n.*** [Fr.; prob. < L. *verbum*, a word], 1. vigor of ideas. 2. energy; enthusiasm.

**ver·y** (ver′i), ***adj.*** [-IER, -IEST], [< OFr. < LL. < L. *verus*, true], 1. in the fullest sense; complete: as, the *very* reverse of the truth. 2. the same: as, that is the *very* hat I lost. 3. even: used as an intensive, as, the *very* rafters shook. 4. actual: as, caught in the *very* act. ***adv.*** 1. in a high degree; extremely. 2. truly; really: used as an intensive, as, the *very* same man.

**very high frequency,** in *radio & television*, any frequency of between 30 and 300 megacycles.

**Ver·y signal** (or **light**) (ver′i, vêr′i), [after E. W. *Very*, the inventor], a colored signal flare fired from a special pistol (the **Very pistol**) at night.

**ves·i·cant** (ves′i-kənt), ***adj.*** [< L. *vesica*, a blister], causing blisters. ***n.*** a vesicant substance.

**ves·i·cate** (ves′i-kāt′), ***v.t. & v.i.*** [-CATED, -CATING], [< L. *vesica*, a bladder, blister], to blister. —**ves′i·ca′tion,** ***n.***

**ves·i·ca·to·ry** (ves′i-kə-tôr′i, və-sik′ə-tō′ri), ***adj.*** causing blisters. ***n.*** [*pl.* -RIES], a vesicatory agent.

**ves·i·cle** (ves′i-k'l), ***n.*** [< Fr. < L. dim. of *vesica*, bladder], a small membranous cavity, sac, or cyst; specif., a blister. —**ve·sic·u·lar** (və-sik′yoo-lẽr), **ve·sic′u·late** (-lit), ***adj.*** —**ve·sic′u·lar·ly,** ***adv.***

**Ves·pa·si·an** (ves-pā′zhi-ən, -zhən), ***n.*** Roman emperor (69–79 A.D.); lived 9–79 A.D.

**ves·per** (ves′pẽr), ***n.*** [L.], 1. evening; eventide. 2. an evening prayer, service, etc. 3. [V-], the evening star, Venus. ***adj.*** 1. of evening. 2. of vespers.

**ves·pers** (ves′pẽrz), ***n.pl.*** 1. *a*) a church service held in the late afternoon or evening. *b*) a prayer or song for this service. 2. in the *R.C. Church*, the sixth of the seven canonical hours. Also **Vespers.**

**Ves·puc·ci, A·me·ri·go** (ä′me-rē′gô ves-po͞ot′chē), (L. name *Americus Vespucius*), 1451–1512; Italian navigator after whom America is named.

**ves·sel** (ves′'l), ***n.*** [< OFr. < L. dim. of *vas*, a vessel], 1. a utensil for holding something, as a bowl, kettle, tub, etc. 2. a ship or boat, especially one larger than a rowboat. 3. an airship. 4. in *zoology*, a tube circulating a body fluid: as, a blood *vessel*.

**vest** (vest), ***n.*** [< Fr. & It. < L. *vestis*, a garment], 1. a short, sleeveless garment worn under a suit coat by men; waistcoat. 2. an undershirt. 3. an insert worn under the bodice by women, simulating the front of a man's vest. ***v.t.*** 1. to dress, as in church vestments. 2. to place (authority, etc.) in the control of a person or group (with *in*). 3. to put (a person) in possession or control of, as power, etc.; invest (*with* something). ***v.i.*** 1. to put on garments or vestments. 2. to become vested in a person, as property (with *in*). —**vest′less,** ***adj.***

**Ves·ta** (ves′tə), ***n.*** [L.], in *Rom. mythology*, the goddess of the hearth and the hearth fire.

**ves·tal** (ves′t'l), ***adj.*** 1. of or sacred to Vesta. 2. of the vestal virgins. 3. chaste; pure. ***n.*** 1. a vestal virgin. 2. a virgin. 3. a nun.

**vestal virgin,** in ancient Rome, any of six virgins, priestesses of Vesta, who tended the sacred fire in her temple.

**vest·ed** (ves′tid), ***adj.*** 1. clothed, especially in church vestments. 2. in *law*, fixed; settled; absolute: as, a *vested* interest.

**vest·ee** (ves-tē′), ***n.*** [dim. of *vest*], a vest (sense 3).

**ves·ti·bule** (ves′tə-būl′), ***n.*** [L. *vestibulum*, entrance hall], 1. a small entrance hall, either to a building or to a room. 2. the enclosed passage between passenger cars of a train. 3. in *anatomy & zoology*, any cavity serving as an entrance to another cavity: as, the *vestibule* of the inner ear. ***v.t.*** [-BULED, -BULING], to furnish with a vestibule. —**ves·tib′u·lar** (-tib′yoo-lẽr), ***adj.***

**ves·tige** (ves′tij), ***n.*** [Fr. < L. *vestigium*, a footprint], 1. a trace, mark, or sign, especially of something which has disappeared or passed away. 2. in *biology*, a degenerate organ or part, more functional or fully developed in an earlier stage of the individual or of the species. —**ves·tig′i·al** (-tij′i-əl), ***adj.*** —**ves·tig′i·al·ly,** ***adv.***

**ves·tig·i·um** (ves-tij′i-əm), ***n.*** [*pl.* -IA (-i-ə)], in *biology*, a vestige; vestigial organ or part.

**vest·ment** (vest′mənt), ***n.*** [< OFr. < L. *vestimentum* < *vestire*, to clothe], 1. a garment; robe. 2. any of the garments worn by clergymen during certain services. —**vest′men·tal,** ***adj.***

**vest-pock·et** (vest′pok′it), ***adj.*** 1. made to fit into a vest pocket. 2. relatively small.

**ves·try** (ves′tri), ***n.*** [*pl.* -TRIES], [< OFr. < ML. *vestiarium*, a wardrobe < L. *vestis*, a garment], 1. a room in a church, where vestments and sacred vessels are kept. 2. a room in a church where prayer meetings, etc. are held. 3. in the *Anglican & Episcopal churches*, a group of church members who manage the temporal affairs of the church.

**ves·try·man** (ves′tri-mən), ***n.*** [*pl.* -MEN], a member of a vestry.

**ves·ture** (ves′chẽr), ***n.*** [< OFr. < LL. < L. *vestire*, to clothe], [Rare or Archaic], 1. clothing; apparel. 2. a covering. ***v.t.*** [-TURED, -TURING], [Rare or Archaic], to cover; clothe. —**ves′tur·al,** ***adj.***

**Ve·su·vi·us** (və-so͞o′vi-əs, -sū′-), ***n.*** an active volcano near Naples, Italy: an eruption in 79 A.D. destroyed Pompeii. —**Ve·su′vi·an,** ***adj.***

**vet** (vet), ***n.*** [Colloq.], a veterinarian. ***v.t.*** [VETTED, VETTING], [Colloq.], to treat as a veterinarian does. ***v.i.*** [Colloq.], to be a veterinarian.

**vet** (vet), ***n.*** [Colloq.], a veteran.

**vet.,** 1. veteran. 2. veterinarian. 3. veterinary.

**vetch** (vech), ***n.*** [< OFr. < L. *vicia*, vetch], any of a number of climbing or trailing plants of the pea family, grown chiefly for fodder.

**vet·er·an** (vet′ẽr-ən, vet′rən), ***adj.*** [< L. *veteranus* < *vetus*, old], 1. old and experienced; long-practiced, especially in war or military service. 2. of veterans. ***n.*** 1. a person of long experience in some service or position. 2. a person who has served in the armed forces of a country.

**Veterans' Day,** Armistice Day: so called since 1955.

**vet·er·i·nar·i·an** (vet′ẽr-ə-nâr′i-ən, vet′rə-), ***n.*** one who practices veterinary medicine or surgery.

**vet·er·i·nar·y** (vet′ẽr-ə-ner′i, vet′rə-), ***adj.*** [< L. < *veterina*, beasts of burden], designating or of the branch of medicine dealing with the treatment of diseases in animals. ***n.*** [*pl.* -IES], a veterinarian.

**ve·to** (vē′tō), ***n.*** [*pl.* -TOES], [L., I forbid < *vetare*, to forbid], 1. an order prohibiting some proposed act; prohibition. 2. the power to prevent action by such prohibition. 3. the right or power of a ruler or legislature to reject bills passed by another branch of the government; specif., in the U.S., *a*) the power of the President to refuse to sign a bill passed by Congress. *b*) a similar power held by the governors of States. *c*) the exercise of this power. 4. a document giving the reasons of the executive for rejecting a bill: also **veto message.** ***v.t.*** [-TOED, -TOING], 1. to prevent (a bill) from becoming law by a veto. 2. to forbid; prohibit. —**ve′to·er,** ***n.***

**vex** (veks), ***v.t.*** [< OFr. < L. *vexare*, to agitate < *vehere*, to carry], 1. to disturb; annoy, especially in little things. 2. to trouble seriously; torment. 3. to discuss at length: as, a *vexed* point. 4. [Obs.], to shake; agitate. —**vexed,** ***adj.*** —**vex·ed·ly** (vek′-sid-li), ***adv.*** —**vex′ed·ness,** ***n.*** —**vex′er,** ***n.***

**vex·a·tion** (vek-sā′shən), ***n.*** 1. a vexing or being vexed. 2. something that vexes.

**vex·a·tious** (vek-sā′shəs), ***adj.*** 1. causing vexation; annoying. 2. characterized by vexation. —**vex-a′tious·ly,** ***adv.*** —**vex·a′tious·ness,** ***n.***

**V.F.W., VFW,** Veterans of Foreign Wars.

**VHF,** very high frequency.

**Vi,** in *chemistry*, virginium.

**V.I.,** Virgin Islands.

**v.i.,** intransitive verb.

**vi·a** (vī′ə; *occas.* vē′ə), ***prep.*** [L., abl. sing. of *via*, a way], by way of; passing through.

**vi·a·ble** (vī′ə-b′l), ***adj.*** [< Fr. < *vie* (< L. *vita*), life], able to live; specif., at that stage of development that will permit it to live outside of the uterus: said of a fetus or prematurely born infant. —**vi′a·bil′i·ty,** ***n.***

**vi·a·duct** (vī′ə-dukt′), ***n.*** [(after *aqueduct*) < L. *via*, a way], a bridge consisting of a series of short spans supported on piers or towers, usually to carry a road or railroad over a gorge, etc.

VIADUCT

**vi·al** (vī′əl), ***n.*** [< OFr. < L. < Gr. *phialē*, shallow cup], a small vessel, usually of glass, for containing medicines or other liquids. ***v.t.*** [-ALED or -ALLED, -ALING or -ALLING], to put in or as in a vial.

**vi·a me·di·a** (vī′ə mē′di-ə), [L.], a middle way; course between two extremes.

**vi·and** (vī′ənd), ***n.*** [< OFr. < LL. < L. *vivenda*, neut. pl. gerundive of *vivere*, to live], 1. an article of food. 2. *pl.* food; esp., choice dishes.

**vi·at·i·cum** (vī-at′i-kəm), ***n.*** [*pl.* -CA (-kə), -CUMS], [L. < *viaticus*, of a way < *via*, way], 1. money or supplies for a journey. 2. the Eucharist as given to a person dying or in danger of death.

**vi·brant** (vī′brənt), ***adj.*** 1. quivering; vibrating. 2. produced by vibration; resonant: said of sound. 3. giving the impression of much energetic activity: as, a *vibrant* city street. 4. vigorous; energetic. 5. in *phonetics*, voiced. ***n.*** a voiced sound. —**vi′bran·cy,** ***n.*** —**vi′brant·ly,** ***adv.***

**vi·bra·phone** (vī′brə-fōn′), ***n.*** [< *vibrate* + *-phone*], a kind of marimba with electrically operated valves in the resonators, that produce a vibrato.

**vi·brate** (vī′brāt), ***v.t.*** [-BRATED, -BRATING], [< L. pp. of *vibrare*, to vibrate], 1. to give off (light or sound) by vibration. 2. to set in to-and-fro motion. ***v.i.*** 1. to swing back and forth, as a pendulum. 2. to move rapidly back and forth; quiver. 3. to resound: said of sounds. 4. to be emotionally stirred; thrill.

**vi·bra·tile** (vī′brə-til, -tīl′), ***adj.*** 1. of or characterized by vibration. 2. capable of vibrating or being vibrated. 3. having a vibratory motion. —**vi′bra·til′i·ty** (-til′ə-ti), ***n.***

**vi·bra·tion** (vī-brā′shən), ***n.*** 1. a vibrating; specif., *a*) oscillation. *b*) rapid motion back and forth; quiver. 2. in *physics*, *a*) rapid rhythmic motion back and forth across a position of equilibrium of the particles of a fluid or an elastic solid, as in transmitting sound. *b*) the vibrating motion of a string, etc. in producing sound. *c*) a single, complete vibrating motion. —**vi·bra′tion·al,** ***adj.*** —**vi·bra′tion·less,** ***adj.***

**vi·bra·to** (vi-brä′tō), ***n.*** [It.], in *music*, a tremulous effect obtained by rapidly alternating the original tone with a slight variation in the pitch.

**vi·bra·tor** (vī′brā-tēr), ***n.*** something that vibrates, as the hammer of an electric bell, etc.

**vi·bra·to·ry** (vī′brə-tôr′i, -tō′ri), ***adj.*** 1. of, having the nature of, or consisting of vibration. 2. causing vibration. 3. vibrating or capable of vibrating. Also **vi′bra·tive.**

**vi·bur·num** (vī-būr′nəm), ***n.*** [L., the wayfaring tree], 1. any of various shrubs or small trees of the honeysuckle family. 2. the bark of several species, used in medicine to relieve spasm.

**Vic.,** Victoria.

**vic·ar** (vik′ēr), ***n.*** [< OFr. < L. *vicarius* < *vicis*, a change], 1. a person who acts in place of another; deputy. 2. in the *Anglican Church*, the priest of a parish in which the tithes go to a layman, etc., the priest himself receiving only a salary. 3. in the *Episcopal Church*, a minister in charge of one chapel in a parish. 4. in the *R.C.Church*, a priest or other church officer acting as deputy of a bishop. —**vi·car·i·al** (vī-kâr′i-əl), ***adj.*** —**vi·car′i·ate** (-it, -āt′), **vic′ar·ship′,** ***n.*** —**vic′ar·ly,** ***adv.***

**vic·ar·age** (vik′ēr-ij), ***n.*** 1. the residence of a vicar. 2. the benefice or salary of a vicar. 3. [Rare], the position or duties of a vicar.

**vic·ar-gen·er·al** (vik′ēr-jen′ēr-əl), ***n.*** [*pl.* VICARS-GENERAL], 1. in the *Anglican Church*, a layman serving as deputy to an archbishop or bishop. 2. in the *R.C. Church*, a priest, etc. acting as deputy to a bishop in administering his diocese.

**vi·car·i·ous** (vī-kâr′i-əs, vi-), ***adj.*** [< L. *vicarius*, substituted < *vicis*, a change], 1. taking the place of another. 2. endured or performed by one person in place of another. 3. delegated: as, *vicarious* power. 4. felt by imagined participation in another's experience: as, a *vicarious* thrill. —**vi·car′i·ous·ly,** ***adv.*** —**vi·car′i·ous·ness,** ***n.***

**vice** (vīs), ***n.*** [< OFr. < L. *vitium*], 1. a serious fault of character. 2. evil conduct; corruption; depravity. 3. an immoral or degrading habit. 4. a fault, defect, or blemish. —**vice′less,** ***adj.***

**vi·ce** (vī′si), ***prep.*** [L., abl. of *vicis*, a change, turn], in the place of; instead of.

**vice** (vīs), ***n. & v.t.*** [VICED, VICING], vise.

**vice-,** [< L. *vice;* see VICE, *prep.*], a prefix meaning *subordinate, deputy*, as in *vice-president*.

**vice-ad·mi·ral** (vīs′ad′mə-rəl), ***n.*** a naval officer ranking just below an admiral. —**vice′-ad′mi·ral·ty,** ***n.***

**vice-con·sul** (vīs′kon′s′l), ***n.*** an officer who is subordinate to or a substitute for a consul. —**vice′-con′su·lar,** ***adj.*** —**vice′-con′su·late** (-it), **vice′-con′sul·ship′,** ***n.***

**vice·ge·ren·cy** (vīs′jêr′ən-si), ***n.*** 1. the office of a vicegerent. 2. a district ruled by a vicegerent.

**vice·ge·rent** (vīs′jêr′ənt), ***n.*** [< ML. < L. < *vice* (see VICE, *prep.*) + *gerere*, to direct], a person appointed by another to exercise the latter's power; deputy. ***adj.*** 1. wielding the power of another. 2. characterized by delegated power. —**vice′ge′ral,** ***adj.***

**vice-pres·i·dent** (vīs′prez′ə-dənt), ***n.*** 1. an executive assistant to a president, acting in his place during his absence. 2. [V- P-], the elected officer of this rank in the U.S. government: he succeeds to the Presidency if the President dies or otherwise leaves office. Also **vice president.** —**vice′-pres′i·den·cy,** ***n.*** —**vice′-pres′i·den′tial** (-den′shəl), ***adj.***

**vice·re·gal** (vīs′rē′g′l), ***adj.*** of a viceroy. —**vice′re′gal·ly,** ***adv.***

**vice-re·gent** (vīs′rē′jənt), ***n.*** one who acts in place of a regent. ***adj.*** of, or holding the office of, vice-regent. —**vice′-re′gen·cy,** ***n.***

**vice·roy** (vīs′roi), ***n.*** [< Fr. < *vice-* (see VICE-) + *roi* (< L. *rex*), a king], a person ruling a country, province, etc. as the deputy of a sovereign. —**vice′roy′al·ty** [*pl.* -TIES], **vice′roy·ship′,** ***n.***

**vice squad,** the division of a police force charged with the suppression or control of prostitution, gambling, and other vices.

**vi·ce ver·sa** (vī′si vūr′sə; *now often* vīs′ vūr′sə), [L.], the order or relation being reversed.

**Vi·chy** (vish′i, vē′shi), ***n.*** a city in central France: pop., 29,000: capital of unoccupied France (1940–1944).

**Vi·chy·ssoise** (vē′shē′swâz′), ***n.*** [Fr.], a thick cream soup of potatoes, etc., usually served cold.

**Vichy water,** 1. a mineral water found at Vichy. 2. a natural or manufactured water like this.

**vic·i·nage** (vis′'n-ij), ***n.*** [< OFr. < L. *vicinus*, near], neighborhood; vicinity.

**vi·cin·i·ty** (və-sin′ə-ti), ***n.*** [*pl.* -TIES], [< L. < *vicinus*, near], 1. a being near or close by; nearness: as, two theaters in close *vicinity*. 2. a near-by or surrounding region; neighborhood.

**vi·cious** (vish′əs), ***adj.*** [< OFr. < L. < *vitium*, a vice], 1. characterized by vice or evil; depraved; immoral. 2. having a vice, flaw, etc.; faulty: as, a *vicious* argument. 3. having bad habits; unruly: as, a *vicious* horse. 4. malicious; spiteful: as, a *vicious* rumor. 5. debasing; corrupting. 6. [Colloq.], very intense, sharp, etc. —**vi′cious·ly,** ***adv.*** —**vi′cious·ness,** ***n.***

**vicious circle,** 1. a situation in which the solution of one problem gives rise to another, but the solution of this brings back the first, etc. 2. in *logic*, an argument which is invalid because its conclusion rests on a premise which itself depends on the conclusion.

**vi·cis·si·tude** (vi-sis′ə-tōōd′, -tūd′), *n.* [Fr. < L. *vicissitudo* < *vicis*, a turn], 1. *usually pl.* changes occurring irregularly in the course of something; esp., change of circumstances in life; hazards of fortune. 2. change or alternation. —**vi·cis′si·tu′di·nar′y, vi·cis′si·tu′di·nous,** *adj.*
**Vicks·burg** (viks′bũrg), *n.* a city in Mississippi, on the Mississippi River: pop., 29,000: besieged (1863) in the Civil War by Grant.
**vic·tim** (vik′tim), *n.* [L. *victima*], 1. a person or animal killed as a sacrifice to a god. 2. someone or something killed, destroyed, etc.: as, *victims* of war, a *victim* of his own greed. 3. one who suffers some loss, especially by being swindled.
**vic·tim·ize** (vik′tim-īz′), *v.t.* [-IZED, -IZING], to make a victim of. —**vic′tim·iz′a·ble,** *adj.* —**vic′tim·i·za′tion,** *n.* —**vic′tim·iz′er,** *n.*
**vic·tor** (vik′tẽr), *n.* [L. < *vincere*, to conquer], the winner in a battle, contest, etc.; conqueror.
**Vic·to·ri·a** (vik-tôr′i-ə, -tōr′yə), *n.* 1. 1819–1901; queen of England (1837–1901). 2. a state of the commonwealth of Australia. 3. the capital of Hong Kong colony: pop., c. 1,000,000. 4. the capital of British Columbia, Canada: pop., 55,000.
**Vic·to·ri·a** (vik-tôr′i-ə, -tōr′yə), *n.* [after Queen *Victoria*], 1. a low four-wheeled carriage for two passengers, with a folding top and a high seat for the coachman. 2. a South American water lily with large leaves and flowers which turn from white to pink.

VICTORIA

**Victoria, Lake,** a lake in east central Africa.
**Victoria Cross,** the highest British military decoration, given for deeds of exceptional valor.
**Vic·to·ri·an** (vik-tôr′i-ən, -tōr′yən), *adj.* 1. of or characteristic of the time when Victoria was queen of England. 2. showing the middle-class respectability, prudery, etc. attributed to the Victorians. *n.* a person, especially a writer, of the time of Queen Victoria. —**Vic·to′ri·an·ism,** *n.*
**vic·to·ri·ous** (vik-tôr′i-əs, -tōr′yəs), *adj.* 1. having won a victory; conquering. 2. of or bringing about victory. —**vic·to′ri·ous·ly,** *adv.*
**vic·to·ry** (vik′tə-ri, -tri), *n.* [*pl.* -RIES], [< OFr. < L. *victoria*; ult. < *vincere*, to conquer], 1. final supremacy in battle or war. 2. an instance of this. 3. success in any struggle involving the defeat of an opponent, etc.
**vict·ual** (vit′'l), *n.* [< OFr. < LL. < L. *victualis*, of food < *victus*, food], 1. [Archaic or Dial.], food or other provisions. 2. *pl.* [Dial. or Colloq.], articles of food. *v.t.* [-UALED or -UALLED, -UALING or -UALLING], to supply with victuals. *v.i.* to take on a supply of food. —**vict′ual·less,** *adj.*
**vict·ual·er, vict·ual·ler** (vit′'l-ẽr, vit′lẽr), *n.* 1. one who supplies victuals, as to an army, etc.; sutler. 2. [Brit.], an innkeeper. 3. a supply ship.
**vi·cu·ña** (vi-kōōn′yə, -kū′nə), *n.* [*pl.* -NAS, -NA; see PLURAL, II, D, 1], [Sp.; of Quechuan origin], 1. an animal of South America, related to the alpaca and llama, and domesticated for its soft, shaggy wool. 2. a soft fabric made from this wool or from a substitute for it: also **vicuña cloth.**
‡**vi·de** (vī′di), [L.], see: used to direct attention to a particular page, etc.: abbrev. **v., vid.**
‡**vi·de an·te** (vī′di an′ti), [L.], see before (in the book, etc.): abbrev. **v.a.**
‡**vi·de in·fra** (vī′di in′frə), [L.], see below; see further on (in the book, etc.): abbrev. **v.i.**
‡**vi·de·li·cet** (vi-del′ə-sit), *adv.* [L. < *videre licet*, it is permitted to see], namely; to wit: abbrev. **viz.**
**vid·e·o** (vid′i-ō′), *adj.* [L., I see], 1. of or used in television. 2. designating or of the picture phase of a television broadcast: cf. *audio.* *n.* television.
**video tape,** a magnetic tape on which the electronic impulses of the video and audio portions of a television program can be recorded for later broadcasting.
‡**vi·de su·pra** (vī′di sōō′prə, sū′-), [L.], see above (in the book, etc.): abbrev. **v.s.**
**vie** (vī), *v.i.* [VIED, VYING], [< OFr. < L. *invitare*, to invite], to struggle for superiority (*with* someone); compete. —**vi′er,** *n.*
**Vi·en·na** (vi-en′ə), *n.* the capital of Austria, on the Danube: pop., 1,628,000. —**Vi·en·nese** (vē′ə-nēz′), *adj.* & *n.* [*pl.* -NESE].
**Vien·tiane** (vyan′tyän′), *n.* the capital of Laos, on the Mekong River: pop., 125,000.
**Vi·et Cong** (vē′ət koŋ′), [< Vietnamese *Viet Nam Cong San*, Vietnamese Communist], 1. collectively, the native military force of the National Liberation Front of Vietnam, a revolutionary political party working for national independence. 2. a member of this force. Also **Vi′et·cong′,** *n.*
**Vi·et·nam, Vi·et-Nam** (vē′ət-näm′, vēt′-), *n.* a country in SE Asia: since 1954 divided into two republics: *a*) South Vietnam, area, 65,958 sq. mi.; pop., 17,414,000; capital, Saigon, and *b*) North Vietnam, area, 60,156 sq. mi.; pop., 16,400,000; capital, Hanoi. Also **Viet Nam.** —**Vi·et·nam·ese, Vi·et-Nam·ese** (vēt′nə-mēz′), *adj.* & *n.* [*pl.* -ESE].
**view** (vū), *n.* [< OFr. < *veoir* (< L. *videre*), to see], 1. a seeing or looking, as in inspection. 2. sight or vision; esp., range of vision. 3. mental examination or survey: as, a correct *view* of the situation. 4. *a*) a scene or prospect, as of a landscape. *b*) a picture of such a scene. 5. visual appearance of something. 6. manner of regarding something; opinion. 7. an object; aim; goal: as, with a *view* to helping. 8. expectation: as, we had no *view* of failure. *v.t.* 1. to inspect; look at closely. 2. to see; behold. 3. to survey mentally; consider. —**in view,** 1. in sight. 2. under consideration. 3. as an object aimed at. 4. in expectation; as a hope. —**in view of,** because of. —**on view,** displayed publicly. —**point of view,** viewpoint. —**with a view to,** 1. with the purpose of. 2. with a hope of; looking forward to. —**view′er,** *n.*
**view finder,** a finder (sense 2).
**view·less** (vū′lis), *adj.* 1. offering no view, or prospect. 2. having or expressing no opinions.
**view·point** (vū′point′), *n.* 1. place of observation. 2. mental attitude. Also **point of view.**
**vi·ges·i·mal** (vī-jes′ə-m'l), *adj.* [< L.; ult. < *viginti*, twenty], 1. twentieth. 2. of or based on twenty.
**vig·il** (vij′əl), *n.* [< OFr. < L. < *vigil*, awake < *vigere*, to be lively], 1. a watchful staying awake during the usual hours of sleep. 2. a watch kept. 3. in *ecclesiastical usage*, *a*) the eve of a festival. *b*) a devotional watch kept on such an eve. *c*) *pl.* devotional services held on such an eve.
**vig·i·lance** (vij′ə-ləns), *n.* 1. a being vigilant; watchfulness; alertness to danger. 2. sleeplessness.
**vigilance committee,** a group of persons organized without legal authorization professedly to keep order and punish crime.
**vig·i·lant** (vij′ə-lənt), *adj.* [Fr. < L. ppr. of *vigilare*, to watch < *vigil*, awake], staying watchful and alert to danger or trouble. —**vig′i·lant·ly,** *adv.*
**vig·i·lan·te** (vij′ə-lan′ti), *n.* [Sp., vigilant], a member of a vigilance committee.
**vi·gnette** (vin-yet′), *n.* [Fr., dim. < *vigne*, a vine], 1. an ornamental design used as a border, inset, headpiece, or tailpiece on a page. 2. a picture, photograph, etc. shading off gradually at the edges. 3. a short literary composition characterized by compactness, delicacy, etc. *v.t.* [-GNETTED, -GNETTING], to make a vignette of.
**vig·or** (vig′ẽr), *n.* [< OFr. < L. < *vigere*, to be strong], 1. active physical or mental force; vitality. 2. active or healthy growth. 3. intensity, force, or energy. 4. effective legal force; validity. Also, Brit. spelling, **vigour.**
**vig·or·ous** (vig′ẽr-əs), *adj.* 1. strong; robust. 2. of, characterized by, or requiring vigor. 3. forceful; powerful; strong; energetic. —**vig′or·ous·ly,** *adv.* —**vig′or·ous·ness,** *n.*
**vik·ing** (vī′kiŋ), *n.* [< ON. *vikingr*], any of the Scandinavian pirates who ravaged the coasts of Europe during the 8th, 9th, and 10th centuries.
**vile** (vīl), *adj.* [< OFr. < L. *vilis*, cheap, base], 1. morally base or evil; wicked. 2. repulsive; disgusting. 3. degrading; lowly: said of conditions, etc. 4. of poor quality; very inferior; bad: as, *vile* weather. —**vile′ly,** *adv.* —**vile′ness,** *n.*
**vil·i·fy** (vil′ə-fī′), *v.t.* [-FIED, -FYING], [< LL. < L. *vilis*, base + *facere*, to make], to use abusive or slanderous language about or of; revile; defame. —**vil′i·fi·ca′tion,** *n.* —**vil′i·fi′er,** *n.*
**vil·la** (vil′ə), *n.* [It. < L.], 1. originally, a country house. 2. a rural or suburban residence, especially a large and pretentious one.
**Vil·la, Fran·cis·co** (frän-sēs′kô vē′yä), 1877–1923; Mexican revolutionary leader: called *Pancho Villa.*
**vil·lage** (vil′ij), *n.* [< OFr. < L. < *villa*, a country house], 1. a group of houses in the country, larger than a hamlet and smaller than a town. 2. such a community incorporated as a municipality. 3. the people of a village, collectively. *adj.* of a village.
**vil·lag·er** (vil′ij-ẽr), *n.* one who lives in a village.

**vil·lain** (vil′ən), *n.* [< OFr. < LL. *villanus*, a farm servant < *villa*, a country seat], 1. a person guilty of evil deeds; scoundrel. 2. a wicked character in a novel, play, etc. who opposes the hero. 3. a villein. —**vil′lain·ess,** *n.fem.*
**vil·lain·ous** (vil′ən-əs), *adj.* 1. of or like a villain; depraved; evil. 2. very bad: as, *villainous* weather. —**vil′lain·ous·ly,** *adv.* —**vil′lain·ous·ness,** *n.*
**vil·lain·y** (vil′ən-i), *n.* [*pl.* -IES], 1. the fact or state of being villainous. 2. villainous conduct; great wickedness. 3. a villainous act.
**vil·lein** (vil′ən), *n.* [see VILLAIN], in feudal England, any member of a class of serfs who by the 13th century had become freemen in their legal relations to all others except their lord. —**vil′lein·age, vil′len·age, vil′lan·age,** *n.*
**Vil·lon, Fran·çois** (frän′swȧ′ vē′yôn′), 1431–?; French lyric poet; banished from Paris (1463).
**vil·lus** (vil′əs), *n.* [*pl.* -LI (-ī)], [L., shaggy hair], 1. in *anatomy*, any of numerous hairlike processes on certain mucous membranes of the body, as of the small intestine, serving to secrete mucus and absorb fats, etc. 2. in *botany*, any of the long, soft hairs on certain plants. —**vil′lous,** *adj.*
**Vil·na** (vil′nə; Russ. vēl′nȧ), *n.* Vilnius.
**Vil·ni·us** (vil′ni-oos′), *n.* the capital of the Lithuanian S.S.R.: pop., 209,000: Russian name, **Vilna;** Polish name, **Wilno.**
**vim** (vim), *n.* [L., acc. of *vis*, strength], energy; vigor.
‡**vin** (van), *n.* [Fr.], wine.
**vi·na·ceous** (vī-nā′shəs), *adj.* [< L. < *vinum*, wine], 1. of or like wine or grapes. 2. red.
**vin·ai·grette** (vin′i-gret′), *n.* [Fr. < *vinaigre*, vinegar], 1. a small ornamental box or bottle for holding aromatic vinegar, smelling salts, etc. 2. vinaigrette sauce.
**vinaigrette sauce,** a savory sauce of vinegar, oil, herbs, etc., used on cold meats.
‡**vin blanc** (van′ blänk′), [Fr.], white wine.
**Vin·cent's angina** (or **infection**) (vin′s′nts), [after Jean H. *Vincent* (1862–1950), Fr. physician], trench mouth.
**Vin·ci, Le·o·nar·do da** (le′ô-när′dô dä vēn′chē; Eng. də vin′chi), 1452–1519; Italian painter, sculptor, architect, scientist, etc.
**vin·ci·ble** (vin′sə-b′l), *adj.* [< L. < *vincere*, to overcome], that can be overcome or defeated. —**vin′ci·bil′i·ty, vin′ci·ble·ness,** *n.*
**vin·di·ca·ble** (vin′di-kə-b′l), *adj.* that can be vindicated; justifiable. —**vin′di·ca·bil′i·ty,** *n.*
**vin·di·cate** (vin′də-kāt′), *v.t.* [-CATED, -CATING], [< L. pp. of *vindicare*, to claim < *vim*, acc. of *vis*, force + *dicere*, to say], 1. to clear from criticism, suspicion, blame, etc. 2. to defend (a cause, etc.) against opposition. 3. to justify: as, he *vindicated* their belief in him. —**vin′di·ca′tive** (-kā′tiv, vin-dik′ə-tiv), **vin′di·ca·to′ry** (-kə-tôr′i, -tō′ri), *adj.* —**vin′di·ca′tor,** *n.*
**vin·di·ca·tion** (vin′də-kā′shən), *n.* 1. a vindicating or being vindicated. 2. a fact or circumstance that vindicates.
**vin·dic·tive** (vin-dik′tiv), *adj.* [< *vindicative* (associated with L. *vindicta*, a revenge); see VINDICATE], 1. revengeful in spirit. 2. said or done in revenge: as, *vindictive* punishment. —**vin·dic′tive·ly,** *adv.* —**vin·dic′tive·ness,** *n.*
**vine** (vīn), *n.* [< OFr. < L. < *vinum*, wine], 1. any plant with a long stem that grows along the ground or climbs a wall or other support by means of tendrils, etc. 2. the stem of such a plant. 3. a grapevine. —**vine′less,** *adj.* —**vine′like′,** *adj.*
**vin·e·gar** (vin′i-gēr), *n.* [< OFr. < *vin*, wine + *aigre* (< L. *acer*), sour], 1. a sour liquid containing acetic acid, made by fermenting cider, wine, malt, etc.: it is used as a condiment and preservative. 2. ill-tempered speech, character, etc. —**vin′e·gar·y, vin′e·gar·ish,** *adj.*
**vin·er·y** (vīn′ēr-i), *n.* [*pl.* -IES], 1. a greenhouse in which grapevines are grown. 2. vines collectively.
**vine·yard** (vin′yērd), *n.* land devoted to cultivating grapevines.
‡**vingt et un** (van′ tā′ ēn′), [Fr., lit., twenty-one], blackjack, a card game.
**vin·i-,** [< L. *vinum*, wine], a combining form meaning *wine grapes* or *wine*, as in *viniculture*.
**vin·i·cul·ture** (vin′i-kul′chēr), *n.* the cultivation of wine grapes. —**vin′i·cul′tur·al,** *adj.*
**vi·nous** (vī′nəs), *adj.* [< L. < *vinum*, wine], 1. of, having the nature of, or characteristic of wine. 2. *a)* addicted to drinking wine. *b)* resulting from such addiction. —**vi·nos′i·ty** (-nos′ə-ti), *n.*
**Vin·son, Frederick Moore** (vin′sən), 1890–1953; chief justice of the United States (1946–1953).
**vin·tage** (vin′tij), *n.* [< OFr. < L. *vindemia* < *vinum*, wine + *demere*, to remove], 1. the crop of grapes or the resultant wine of a vineyard or grape-growing region in a single season. 2. the wine of a particular region in a specified year. 3. the act or season of gathering grapes or of making wine. 4. the type or model of some earlier time: as, a car of ancient *vintage*. *adj.* of choice vintage: as, *vintage* wine.
**vint·ner** (vint′nēr), *n.* [< OFr. < *vinot*, dim. of *vin*, wine], [Chiefly Brit.], a wine merchant.
**vin·y** (vīn′i), *adj.* [-IER, -IEST], 1. of, or having the nature of, vines. 2. abounding in vines.
**vi·nyl** (vī′nil, vin′il), *n.* [< L. *vinum*, wine; + *-yl*], the monovalent radical $CH_2CH$, derived from ethylene: various vinyl compounds are polymerized to form resins and plastics.
**vi·ol** (vī′əl), *n.* [< earlier *vielle* < OFr. < ML. < L. *vitula*], 1. any of an early family of stringed instruments, forerunner of the violin family. 2. any instrument of the violin family.
**vi·o·la** (vi-ō′lə, vī-), *n.* [It. ], a stringed instrument of the violin family, slightly larger than a violin and tuned a fifth lower.
**vi·o·la·ble** (vī′ə-lə-b′l), *adj.* that can be violated; easily violated. —**vi′o·la·bil′i·ty, vi′o·la·ble·ness,** *n.* —**vi′o·la·bly,** *adv.*
‡**vi·o·la da gam·ba** (vyô′lä dä gäm′bä), [It., lit., viol for the leg], an early instrument of the viol family, a forerunner of the cello.
**vi·o·late** (vī′ə-lāt′), *v.t.* [-LATED, -LATING], [< L. pp. of *violare*], 1. to break (a law, rule, promise, etc.); fail to observe. 2. to infringe on. 3. to rape (a girl or woman). 4. to desecrate or profane, as a sacred place. 5. to break in on; disturb: as, to *violate* one's privacy. 6. to offend, insult, etc., as one's sense of decency. —**vi′o·la′tive,** *adj.* —**vi′o·la′tor,** *n.*
**vi·o·la·tion** (vī′ə-lā′shən), *n.* a violating or being violated; specif., *a)* infringement or breach, as of a law, etc. *b)* rape. *c)* desecration of something sacred. *d)* interruption; disturbance.
**vi·o·lence** (vī′ə-ləns), *n.* [< OFr. < L. < *violentus*, violent], 1. physical force used so as to injure or damage. 2. a use of force in this way; rough, injurious act. 3. intensity; severity: as, the *violence* of the storm. 4. unjust use of force or power. 5. great force of feeling, conduct, etc.; passion. 6. desecration.
**vi·o·lent** (vī′ə-lənt), *adj.* 1. acting with or characterized by great physical force, so as to injure, etc. 2. acting with or characterized by unlawful force. 3. caused by violence. 4. passionate; immoderate: as, *violent* language. 5. extreme; intense: as, a *violent* storm. —**vi′o·lent·ly,** *adv.*
**vi·o·let** (vī′ə-lit), *n.* [< OFr. < L. *viola*, a violet], 1. any of a number of related short plants with fragrant white, blue, purple, or yellow flowers. 2. the flower of any of these plants. 3. a bluish-purple color. *adj.* of a violet color.
**violet ray,** 1. the shortest ray of the visible spectrum. 2. loosely, the ultraviolet ray.
**vi·o·lin** (vī′ə-lin′), *n.* [< It. dim. of *viola*, a viol], 1. any instrument of the modern family of stringed instruments played with a bow and having four strings and no frets; specif., the smallest and highest pitched instrument of this family, held horizontally under the chin. 2. a violinist, as in an orchestra.
**vi·o·lin·ist** (vī′ə-lin′ist), *n.* a player on the violin.
**vi·ol·ist** (vī′əl-ist; *for* 2, vi-ō′-list), *n.* 1. a player on the viol. 2. a player on the viola.
**vi·o·lon·cel·lo** (vē′ə-lon-chel′ō, vī′ə-lən-), *n.* [*pl.* -LOS], [It., dim. of *violone*, bass viol < *viola*, viol], a cello. —**vi′o·lon·cel′list,** *n.*

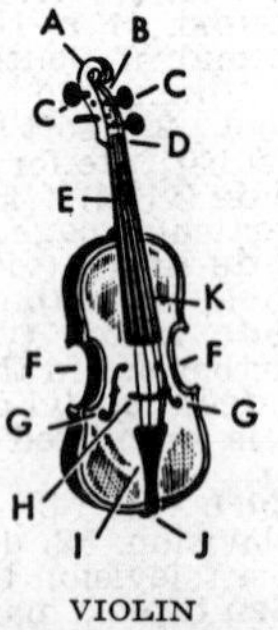

VIOLIN
A, scroll; B, pegbox; C, pegs; D, nut; E, neck; F, waist; G, sound holes; H, bridge; I, tailpiece; J, button; K, finger board

**V.I.P., VIP,** [Slang], very important person.
**vi·per** (vī′pēr), *n.* [< OFr. < L. *vipera*; prob. < *vivus*, living + *parere*, to bear], 1. a snake belonging to either of two groups of venomous snakes: the **true vipers,** of Europe, Africa, and Asia, include the common horned vipers, puff adders, etc., and the **pit vipers,** of Asia and America, include the copperhead, rattlesnake, etc. 2. a malicious or treacherous person. —**vi′per·ine,** *adj.*
**vi·per·ous** (vī′pēr-əs), *adj.* of, having the nature of, or like a viper; esp., spiteful or venomous: also **vi′per·ish.** —**vi′per·ous·ly,** *adv.* —**vi′per·ous·ness,** *n.*

**vi·ra·go** (vi-rā′gō, vī-), *n.* [*pl.* -GOES, -GOS], [AS. < L. < *vir*, a man], a bold, shrewish woman; scold.
**vi·ral** (vī′rəl), *adj.* of, pertaining to, or caused by a virus.
**vir·e·o** (vir′i-ō′), *n.* [*pl.* -OS], [L., a type of finch], any of a number of small, insect-eating North American songbirds, with olive-green or gray plumage.
**vi·res·cent** (vī-res′'nt), *adj.* [< L. *virescens;* ult. < *virere*, to be green], 1. turning or becoming green. 2. greenish. —**vi·res′cence,** *n.*
**Vir·gil** (vũr′jil), *n.* (*Publius Vergilius Maro*), Roman poet; 70–19 B.C.; author of *The Aeneid*, etc.: also sp. **Vergil.** —**Vir·gil′i·an,** *adj.*
**vir·gin** (vũr′jin), *n.* [< OFr. < L. *virgo*, a maiden], 1. *a*) a person, especially a woman, who has not had sexual intercourse. *b*) a girl or unmarried woman. 2. [V-], the constellation Virgo. 3. [V-], Mary, the mother of Jesus: usually with *the.* *adj.* 1. being a virgin. 2. proper to a virgin; chaste; modest. 3. untouched, clean, etc.: as, *virgin* snow. 4. as yet unused, untrod, etc. by man: as, a *virgin* forest. 5. with no experience (*of*).
**vir·gin·al** (vũr′ji-n'l), *adj.* 1. of or like a virgin; maidenly. 2. pure; fresh; unsullied. —**vir′gin·al·ly,** *adv.* —**vir′gin·al·ness,** *n.*
**vir·gin·al** (vũr′ji-n'l), *n.* [< Fr.; ? because played by virgins, or young girls; ? < L. *virga*, a jack], a harpsichord; esp., a small, rectangular harpsichord of the 16th century, placed on a table or in the lap to be played: also **pair of virginals.**
**virgin birth,** in *Christian theology*, the doctrine that Jesus was born to Mary, a virgin, and that she was his only human parent.
**Vir·gin·ia** (vẽr-jin′yə), *n.* a Southern State of the U.S.: area, 40,815 sq. mi.; pop., 3,967,000; capital, Richmond: abbrev. **Va.** —**Vir·gin′ian,** *adj. & n.*
**Virginia cowslip** (or **bluebell**), a plant with clusters of blue or purple bell-shaped flowers.
**Virginia creeper,** a climbing vine having leaflets in groups of five and bluish-black berries: also called *American ivy, woodbine.*
**Virginia deer,** an American white-tailed deer having a white-spotted red coat in summer and a diffuse gray-brown coat in winter.
**Virginia reel,** 1. the American variety of the reel, danced by couples facing each other in two parallel lines. 2. music for this dance.
**Virgin Islands,** a group of islands in the West Indies. —**British Virgin Islands,** those of the Virgin Islands that are a part of the Leeward Islands colony of Great Britain. —**Virgin Islands of the United States,** those of the Virgin Islands that the U.S. bought from Denmark in 1917: formerly called **Danish West Indies.**
**vir·gin·i·ty** (vẽr-jin′ə-ti), *n.* 1. the state or fact of being a virgin; maidenhood, chastity, etc. 2. the state of being virgin, pure, clean, etc.
**vir·gin·i·um** (vẽr-jin′i-əm), *n.* [< *Virginia* (the State)], francium: former name.
**Virgin Mary,** Mary, the mother of Jesus.
**Virgin Queen,** Queen Elizabeth I of England.
**vir·gin's-bow·er** (vũr′jinz-bou′ẽr), *n.* a white-flowered, rambling variety of clematis.
**virgin wool,** new wool not previously processed.
**Vir·go** (vũr′gō), *n.* [L., lit., virgin], 1. a constellation between Leo and Libra, supposedly outlining a woman. 2. the sixth sign of the zodiac (♍), which the sun enters about August 22.
**vir·gule** (vũr′gūl), *n.* [Fr. < L. dim. of *virga*, a twig], a short diagonal line (/) placed between two words to indicate that either word can be used. Example: and/or; i.e., either "and" or "or."
**vir·i·des·cent** (vir′ə-des′'nt), *adj.* [< LL.; ult. < *viridis*, green], greenish. —**vir′i·des′cence,** *n.*
**vir·ile** (vir′əl; *rarely*, vī′rəl), *adj.* [< Fr. < L. < *vir*, a man], 1. of or characteristic of an adult man; masculine; male. 2. having manly strength or vigor. 3. of or capable of procreation. —**vir′ile·ly,** *adv.* —**vi·ril·i·ty** (vi-ril′ə-ti), *n.*
**vi·ro·sis** (vī-rō′sis), *n.* [*pl.* -SES (-sēz)], any disease caused by a virus.
**vir·tu** (vẽr-to͞o′, vũr′to͞o), *n.* [It. < L. *virtus*, virtue], 1. a knowledge of, or taste for, artistic objects. 2. the quality of being so artistic, beautiful, rare, etc. as to interest a collector. 3. such art objects, collectively. Also sp. **vertu.**
**vir·tu·al** (vũr′cho͞o-əl), *adj.* being so in effect or essence, although not in actual fact or name: as, a *virtual* king. —**vir′tu·al′i·ty** (-al′ə-ti), *n.*
**vir·tu·al·ly** (vũr′cho͞o-əl-i), *adv.* in effect although not in fact; for all practical purposes.
**vir·tue** (vũr′cho͞o), *n.* [< OFr. < L. *virtus*, manliness, worth], 1. general moral excellence; goodness of character. 2. a specific moral quality regarded as good. 3. chastity. 4. *a*) excellence in general; merit. *b*) a specific excellence; good quality. 5. efficacy, as of a medicine. —**by** (or **in**) **virtue of,** because of; on the grounds of. —**make a virtue of necessity,** to do what one has to do as if from inclination. —**vir′tue·less,** *adj.*
**vir·tu·os·i·ty** (vũr′cho͞o-os′ə-ti), *n.* [*pl.* -TIES], [< *virtuoso*], great technical skill in some fine art, especially in the performance of music.
**vir·tu·o·so** (vũr′cho͞o-ō′sō), *n.* [*pl.* -SOS, -SI (-si)], [It., skilled], 1. a person with great interest and sensitive taste in the fine arts. 2. a person having great technical skill in some fine art, especially in the performance of music.
**vir·tu·ous** (vũr′cho͞o-əs), *adj.* 1. having, or characterized by, moral virtue. 2. chaste: said of a woman. —**vir′tu·ous·ly,** *adv.* —**vir′tu·ous·ness,** *n.*
**vir·u·lent** (vir′yoo-lənt, -oo-), *adj.* [< L. *virulentus* < *virus*, a poison], 1. poisonous; extremely injurious; deadly. 2. bitterly hostile; full of hate and enmity. 3. in *medicine*, *a*) violent and rapid in its course: said of a disease. *b*) highly infectious: said of a microorganism. —**vir′u·lence, vir′u·len·cy,** *n.* —**vir′u·lent·ly,** *adv.*
**vi·rus** (vī′rəs), *n.* [L., a poison], 1. venom, as of a snake. 2. any of a group of ultramicroscopic infective agents that cause various diseases, as smallpox; specif., a filtrable virus. 3. an evil or harmful influence.
‡**vis** (vis), *n.* [*pl.* VIRES (vī′rēz)], [L.], force.
**Vis., Visc.,** 1. Viscount. 2. Viscountess.
**vi·sa** (vē′zə), *n.* [Fr. < L. *visus*, pp. of *videre*, to see], an endorsement on a passport, showing that it has been examined by the proper officials of a country and granting entry into that country. *v.t.* [-SAED, -SAING], 1. to put a visa on (a passport). 2. to give a visa to (someone).
**vis·age** (viz′ij), *n.* [< OFr. < L. *visus*, a look < *videre*, to see], 1. the face; countenance. 2. appearance; aspect. —**vis′aged,** *adj.*
**vis-à-vis** (vē′zə-vē′), *adj. & adv.* [Fr.], face to face; opposite. *prep.* 1. face to face with; opposite to. 2. in relation to.
**vis·cer·a** (vis′ẽr-ə), *n.pl.* [*sing.* (rare) VISCUS (-kəs)], [L.], 1. the internal organs of the body, as the heart, lungs, liver, intestines, etc. 2. popularly, the intestines. —**vis′cer·al,** *adj.*
**vis·cid** (vis′id), *adj.* [< LL. < L. *viscum*, birdlime], thick, sirupy, and sticky. —**vis·cid·i·ty** (vi-sid′ə-ti), **vis′cid·ness,** *n.* —**vis′cid·ly,** *adv.*
**vis·cose** (vis′kōs), *adj.* 1. viscous. 2. of viscose. *n.* a siruplike solution made by treating cellulose with potassium hydroxide and carbon disulfide: used in making rayon, cellophane, etc.
**vis·cos·i·ty** (vis-kos′ə-ti), *n.* [*pl.* -TIES], 1. a viscous quality or state. 2. in *physics*, the internal fluid resistance of a substance, caused by molecular attraction.
**vis·count** (vī′kount), *n.* [< OFr. < ML. < L. *vice*, in place of + *comes*, a count], a nobleman next below an earl or count and above a baron. —**vis′count·cy, vis′count·y, vis′count·ship′,** *n.*
**vis·count·ess** (vī′koun-tis), *n.* 1. the wife of a viscount. 2. a woman holding a corresponding rank in her own right.
**vis·cous** (vis′kəs), *adj.* [< LL. < L. *viscum*, birdlime], 1. thick, sirupy, and sticky; viscid. 2. in *physics*, having the property of viscosity. —**vis′cous·ly,** *adv.* —**vis′cous·ness,** *n.*
**vise** (vīs), *n.* [< OFr. < L. *vitis*, a vine, lit., that which winds], a device consisting of two jaws opened and closed by a screw, lever, etc., used for holding firmly an object being worked on. *v.t.* [VISED, VISING], to hold or squeeze as with a vise. Also sp. **vice.** —**vise′like′,** *adj.*

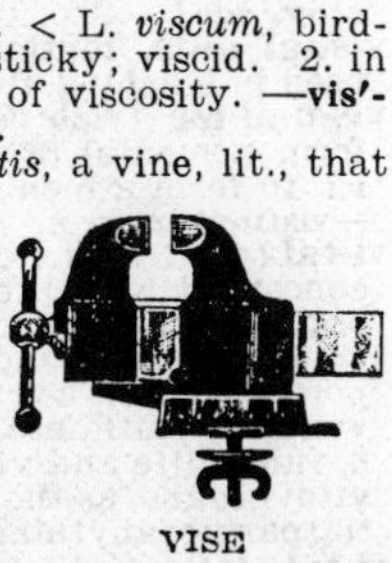
VISE

**vi·sé** (vē′zā, vē-zā′), *n. & v.t.* [-SÉED, -SÉING], [Fr.], visa.
**Vish·nu** (vish′no͞o), *n.* in *Hindu theology*, the second member of the trinity (Brahma, Vishnu, and Siva), called "the Preserver."
**vis·i·bil·i·ty** (viz′ə-bil′ə-ti), *n.* [*pl.* -TIES], 1. a being visible. 2. *a*) the relative possibility of being seen under prevailing conditions of distance, light, and atmosphere: as, low *visibility.* *b*) range of vision.

**vis·i·ble** (viz′ə-b'l), *adj.* [< L. *visibilis* < *videre*, to see], 1. that can be seen. 2. that can be perceived with the mind; evident. 3. on hand: as, *visible* supply. **—vis′i·ble·ness,** *n.* **—vis′i·bly,** *adv.*

**Vis·i·goth** (viz′i-goth′, -gôth′), *n.* any of the West Goths who overran the Roman Empire late in the 4th century A.D. and set up a kingdom in France and Spain. **—Vis′i·goth′ic,** *adj.*

**vi·sion** (vizh′ən), *n.* [< OFr. < L. *visio* < pp. of *videre*, to see], 1. the act or power of seeing. 2. something supposedly seen by other than normal sight, as in a dream, trance, etc. 3. a mental image: as, *visions* of power. 4. the ability to foresee or perceive something not actually visible, as through mental acuteness. 5. force or power of the imagination: as, a writer of great *vision*. 6. something or someone of extraordinary beauty. *v.t.* to see as in a vision. **—vi′sion·al,** *adj.* **—vi′sion·al·ly,** *adv.*

**vi·sion·ar·y** (vizh′ən-er′i), *adj.* 1. seeing, or habitually seeing, visions. 2. of, having the nature of, or seen in a vision. 3. *a*) imaginary. *b*) merely speculative and impractical, as an idea, etc. *n.* [*pl.* -IES], 1. a person who sees visions. 2. a person who has impractical ideas.

**vis·it** (viz′it), *v.t.* [< OFr. < L. < *visere*, to go to see < pp. of *videre*, to see], 1. to go or come to see (someone) out of friendship, in a professional capacity, etc. 2. to stay with as a guest. 3. to go or come to (a place) as in order to inspect. 4. to come upon or afflict: as, a drought *visited* the valley. 5. to inflict (punishment, suffering, etc.) upon (someone). *v.i.* to visit someone or something; specif., *a*) to make a social call (often with *with*). *b*) [Colloq.], to converse, as during a visit. *n.* a visiting; specif., *a*) a social call. *b*) a stay as a guest. *c*) an official call, as of a doctor, inspector, etc. *d*) [Colloq.], a friendly chat. **—vis′it·a·ble,** *adj.*

**vis·it·ant** (viz′ə-tənt), *n.* 1. a visitor. 2. a migratory bird in any of its temporary resting places.

**vis·it·a·tion** (viz′ə-tā′shən), *n.* 1. a visiting; esp., an official visit as to inspect. 2. a visiting of reward or punishment, as by God. 3. [V-], in the *R.C. Church*, *a*) the visit of the Virgin Mary to Elisabeth: Luke 1:39-56. *b*) a church feast (July 2) commemorating this. **—vis′it·a′tion·al,** *adj.* **—vis′it·a·to′ri·al** (tə-tôr′i-əl, -tō′ri-), *adj.*

**visiting card** (viz′it-iŋ), a calling card.

**vis·i·tor** (viz′ə-tẽr), *n.* a person making a visit.

**vi·sor** (vī′zẽr, viz′ẽr), *n.* [< Anglo-Fr. < OFr. < *vis*, a face], 1. in armor, the movable part of a helmet, covering the face. 2. a mask. 3. the projecting brim of a cap, for shading the eyes. 4. a device over the windshield of a car for shading the eyes. Also sp. **vizor. —vi′sored,** *adj.* **—vi′sor·less,** *adj.*

**VIS·TA** (vis′tə), [*V*olunteers *i*n *S*ervice *t*o *A*merica], a U.S. government program providing volunteers to work at improving the living conditions of persons in impoverished areas of the U.S.

**vis·ta** (vis′tə), *n.* [< It. < L. *visus*, pp. of *videre*, to see], 1. a view, especially one seen through a long passage, as between rows of houses, trees, etc. 2. the trees, etc. framing such a view. 3. a comprehensive mental view of a series of events.

**Vis·tu·la** (vis′choo-lə), *n.* a river in Poland, flowing into the Baltic Sea.

**vis·u·al** (vizh′ōō-əl), *adj.* [< LL. < L. *visus*, a sight < *videre*, to see], 1. of, connected with, or used in seeing. 2. that is or can be seen; visible. **—vis′u·al·ly,** *adv.*

**visual aids,** motion pictures, slides, charts, etc. used in teaching, illustrating lectures, etc.

**vis·u·al·ize** (vizh′ōō-əl-īz′), *v.t.* [-IZED, -IZING], to form a mental image of (something not visible). *v.i.* to form a mental image. **—vis′u·al·i·za′tion,** *n.* **—vis′u·al·iz′er,** *n.*

**vi·tal** (vī′t'l), *adj.* [< OFr. < L. < *vita*, life], 1. of or concerned with life. 2. essential to life: as, *vital* organs. 3. destroying life; fatal: as, *vital* wounds. 4. *a*) essential; indispensable. *b*) of greatest importance: as, a *vital* matter. 5. affecting the validity, truth, etc. of something: as, a *vital* error. 6. full of life and vigor; energetic. *n.* [*pl.*], 1. the vital organs, as the heart, brain, etc. 2. the essential parts of anything. **—vi′tal·ly,** *adv.* **—vi′tal·ness,** *n.*

**vi·tal·ism** (vī′t'l-iz'm), *n.* the doctrine that the life in living organisms is caused and sustained by a basic force (**vital principle** or **force**) that is distinct from all physical and chemical forces. **—vi′tal·ist,** *n.* **—vi′tal·is′tic,** *adj.*

**vi·tal·i·ty** (vī-tal′ə-ti), *n.* [*pl.* -TIES], 1. power to live or go on living. 2. power to endure or survive. 3. mental or physical vigor; energy.

**vi·tal·ize** (vī′t'l-īz′), *v.t.* [-IZED, -IZING], 1. to make vital; give life to. 2. to give vigor or animation to. **—vi′tal·i·za′tion,** *n.*

**vi·tal·li·um** (vī-tal′i-əm), *n.* an alloy of cobalt, chromium, and molybdenum, used in bone surgery, etc.: a trade-mark (**Vitallium**).

**vital statistics,** data about births, deaths, marriages, etc.

**vi·ta·min** (vī′tə-min), *n.* [< L. *vita*, life; + *amine*], any of a number of complex organic substances found variously in foods and essential for the normal functioning of the body: the principal known vitamins include:

- **vitamin A,** a fat-soluble alcohol found in fish-liver oil, egg yolk, butter, carrots and other vegetables, etc.: a deficiency of this vitamin results in night blindness: it occurs in two forms, **vitamin $A_1$,** and **vitamin $A_2$.**
- **vitamin B (complex),** a group of unrelated water-soluble substances including: *a*) **vitamin $B_1$,** thiamine. *b*) **vitamin $B_2$,** riboflavin. *c*) **vitamin $B_6$,** pyridoxine. *d*) nicotinic acid. *e*) biotin: also called **vitamin H.** *f*) folic acid.
- **vitamin C,** an organic compound, $C_6H_8O_6$, occurring in citrus fruits, tomatoes, etc.: a deficiency of this vitamin tends to produce scurvy: also called *ascorbic acid, cevitamic acid.*
- **vitamin D,** any of several related vitamins occurring in fish-liver oil, milk, egg yolk, etc.: a deficiency of this vitamin tends to produce rickets: this group includes **vitamin $D_1$, vitamin $D_2$,** and **vitamin $D_3$.**
- **vitamin E,** a substance consisting of tocopherols, occurring in wheat-germ oil, lettuce, etc., believed to restore fertility to sterile mammals.
- **vitamin G,** vitamin $B_2$.
- **vitamin K,** a substance occurring in alfalfa leaves, etc. (**vitamin $K_1$**), and fish meal, etc. (**vitamin $K_2$**), and used to promote blood clotting.
- **vitamin P,** citrin: a deficiency of this vitamin increases susceptibility to hemorrhage.

**vi·ta·mine** (vī′tə-mēn′, -min′, -min), *n.* [Rare], a vitamin.

**vi·ta·min·ic** (vī′tə-min′ik), *adj.* of vitamins.

**vi·ti·ate** (vish′i-āt′), *v.t.* [-ATED, -ATING], [< L. pp. of *vitiare* < *vitium*, a vice], 1. to make imperfect or faulty; spoil. 2. to weaken morally; debase. 3. to make legally ineffective. **—vi′ti·a·ble,** *adj.* **—vi′ti·at′ed,** *adj.* **—vi′ti·a′tion,** *n.* **—vi′ti·a′tor,** *n.*

**vit·i·cul·ture** (vit′i-kul′chẽr), *n.* [< L. *vitis*, a vine; + *culture*], the cultivation of the grapevine. **—vit′i·cul′tur·al,** *adj.* **—vit′i·cul′tur·ist,** *n.*

**vit·re·ous** (vit′ri-əs), *adj.* [< L. < *vitrum*, glass], 1. of or like glass; glassy. 2. derived from or made of glass. 3. of the vitreous humor. **—vit′re·ous·ly,** *adv.* **—vit′re·ous·ness,** *n.*

**vitreous humor** (or **body**), the transparent, colorless, jellylike substance that fills the eyeball between the retina and lens.

**vit·ri·fy** (vit′rə-fī′), *v.t. & v.i.* [-FIED, -FYING], [< Fr. < L. *vitrum*, glass + *facere*, to make], to change into glass or a glasslike substance by fusion due to heat. **—vit′ri·fi′a·ble,** *adj.* **—vit′ri·fi′a·bil′i·ty,** *n.* **—vit′ri·fi·ca′tion, vit′ri·fac′tion** (-fak′shən), *n.*

**vit·ri·ol** (vit′ri-əl), *n.* [< OFr. < ML. *vitriolum* < L. *vitreus*, glassy], 1. any of several sulfates of metals, as of copper (*blue vitriol*), of iron (*green vitriol*), of zinc (*white vitriol*), etc. 2. sulfuric acid. 3. anything sharp or caustic.

**vit·ri·ol·ic** (vit′ri-ol′ik), *adj.* 1. of, like, or derived from a vitriol. 2. extremely biting or caustic: as, *vitriolic* talk.

**vit·ri·ol·ize** (vit′ri-əl-īz′), *v.t.* [-IZED, -IZING], 1. to convert into vitriol. 2. to subject to the action of vitriol. **—vit′ri·ol·i·za′tion,** *n.*

**vit·tle** (vit′'l), *n.* [Dial.], victual.

**vi·tu·per·ate** (vī-tōō′pə-rāt′, vi-tū′-), *v.t.* [-ATED, -ATING], [< L. pp. < *vitium*, a fault + *parare*, to make ready], to speak abusively to or about; berate. **—vi·tu′per·a′tion,** *n.* **—vi·tu′per·a′tive,** *adj.* **—vi·tu′per·a′tive·ly,** *adv.* **—vi·tu′per·a′tor,** *n.*

‡**vi·va** (vē′vä), *interj.* [It.], literally, (long) live (someone specified)!: an exclamation of acclaim.

‡**vi·va·ce** (vē-vä′che), *adj.* [It.], in *music*, lively; spirited: abbrev. **viv.**

**vi·va·cious** (vi-vā′shəs, vī-), *adj.* [< L. *vivax* < *vivere*, to live], full of animation; spirited; lively. **—vi·va′cious·ly,** *adv.* **—vi·va′cious·ness,** *n.*

**vi·vac·i·ty** (vi-vas′ə-ti, vī-), *n.* 1. the quality or state of being vivacious; liveliness. 2. [*pl.* -TIES], a vivacious act or expression.

**vi·var·i·um** (vī-vâr′i-əm), *n.* [*pl.* -IUMS, -IA (-i-ə)], [L.; ult. < *vivere*, to live], an enclosed place for raising plants or animals under conditions very much like those of their natural environment.

**vi·va vo·ce** (vī′və vō′si), [L., with living voice], by word of mouth; orally. **—vi′va-vo′ce,** *adj.*

‡**vive** (vēv), *interj.* [Fr.], (long) live (someone specified)!: an exclamation of acclaim.

**viv·id** (viv′id), *adj.* [< L. < *vivere*, to live], 1. full of life; vigorous. 2. bright; intense: said of colors, light, etc. 3. forming or suggesting clear or striking mental images: as, a *vivid* imagination, *vivid* description. 4. clearly perceived, as a recollection. —**viv′id·ly,** *adv.* —**viv′id·ness,** *n.*

**viv·i·fy** (viv′ə-fī′), *v.t.* [-FIED, -FYING], [< Fr. < LL. < L. *vivus*, alive + *facere*, to make], 1. to give life to; animate. 2. to make more lively, active, striking, etc. —**viv′i·fi·ca′tion** (-fi-kā′shən), *n.* —**viv′i·fi′er,** *n.*

**vi·vip·a·rous** (vī-vip′ə-rəs), *adj.* [< L. < *vivus*, alive + *parere*, to produce], bearing living young (as most mammals) instead of laying eggs. —**viv·i·par·i·ty** (viv′i-par′ə-ti), **vi·vip′a·rous·ness,** *n.* —**vi·vip′a·rous·ly,** *adv.*

**viv·i·sect** (viv′ə-sekt′, viv′ə-sekt′), *v.t.* to perform vivisection on. *v.i.* to practice vivisection.

**viv·i·sec·tion** (viv′ə-sek′shən), *n.* [< L. *vivus*, alive; + *section*], 1. a surgical operation performed on a living animal to study the living organs and to investigate the effects of diseases, etc. 2. experimental research involving such operation. —**viv′i·sec′tion·al,** *adj.* —**viv′i·sec′tion·ist, viv′i·sec′tor,** *n.*

**vix·en** (vik′s′n), *n.* [dial. form of ME. *fixen* < AS. < base of *fox*], 1. a female fox. 2. an ill-tempered, shrewish woman. —**vix′en·ish,** *adj.*

**viz.** (viz; *often read* "namely"), [alt. < contr. for L. *videlicet*], videlicet; that is; namely.

**viz·ard** (viz′ẽrd), *n.* [alt. < *visar*, var. of *visor*], 1. a visor. 2. a mask. Also sp. **visard.**

**vi·zier, vi·zir** (vi-zêr′), *n.* [< Turk. < Ar. *wazīr*, lit., a porter < *wazara*, to bear a burden], in Moslem countries, a high officer in the government; esp., a minister of state. —**vi·zier′ate, vi·zir′ate** (-it, -āt′), **vi·zier′ship, vi·zir′ship,** *n.* —**vi·zier′i·al, vi·zir′i·al,** *adj.*

**viz·or** (vī′zẽr, viz′ẽr), *n.* a visor.

**V-J Day** (vē′jā′), the day on which the fighting with Japan officially ended in World War II (August 14, 1945) or the day of formal surrender (September 2, 1945).

**VL,** Vulgar Latin.

**Vla·di·vos·tok** (vlad′i-vos′tok; Russ. vlä′di-vôs-tôk′), *n.* a seaport in Siberia, U.S.S.R., on the Pacific: pop., 206,000.

**V-mail** (vē′māl′), *n.* a mail service of World War II, by which letters to or from the armed forces were reduced to microfilm to save shipping space.

**voc.,** vocative.

**vocab.,** vocabulary.

**vo·ca·ble** (vō′kə-b′l), *n.* [< Fr. < L. *vocabulum* < *vocare*, to call], a word; esp., a word regarded as a unit of sounds or letters rather than as a unit of meaning.

**vo·cab·u·lar·y** (vō-kab′yoo-ler′i), *n.* [*pl.* -IES], [< ML. < L. *vocabulum;* see VOCABLE], 1. a list of words, usually arranged in alphabetical order and defined; dictionary, glossary, etc. 2. all the words of a language, or all those used by a particular person, class, etc.

**vo·cal** (vō′k′l), *adj.* [< L. *vocalis* < *vox*, a voice], 1. uttered or performed by the voice: as, *vocal* music. 2. having a voice; capable of speaking, etc. 3. of, used in, connected with, or belonging to the voice: as, *vocal* organs. 4. full of voices. 5. speaking freely or vociferously. —**vo·cal′i·ty** (-kal′ə-ti), **vo′cal·ness,** *n.* —**vo′cal·ly,** *adv.*

**vocal cords,** either of two pairs of membranous cords or folds in the larynx, consisting of an upper pair (*false vocal cords*) and a lower pair (*true vocal cords*): voice is produced when air from the lungs causes the lower (true) cords to vibrate.

**vo·cal·ic** (vō-kal′ik), *adj.* 1. having many vowels. 2. of, or having the nature of, a vowel.

**vo·cal·ist** (vō′k′l-ist), *n.* a singer.

**vo·cal·ize** (vō′k′l-īz′), *v.t.* [-IZED, -IZING], 1. to make vocal; utter with the voice. 2. to give a voice to. 3. in *phonetics*, *a*) to change into or use as a vowel: as, a *vocalized w.* *b*) to voice. *v.i.* to utter sounds; speak or sing. —**vo′cal·i·za′tion,** *n.* —**vo′cal·iz′er,** *n.*

**vo·ca·tion** (vō-kā′shən), *n.* [< L. < *vocare*, to call], 1. a call or impulsion to enter a certain career. 2. the career toward which one believes himself to be called. 3. any trade, profession, or occupation. —**vo·ca′tion·al,** *adj.* —**vo·ca′tion·al·ly,** *adv.*

**vocational guidance,** the work of testing and interviewing persons in order to guide them toward the choice of a suitable vocation.

**voc·a·tive** (vok′ə-tiv), *adj.* [< OFr. < L. < *vocare*, to call < *vox*, the voice], in *grammar*, in certain languages, designating or of the case indicating the person or thing addressed. *n.* 1. the vocative case. 2. a word in this case. —**voc′a·tive·ly,** *adv.*

**vo·cif·er·ant** (vō-sif′ẽr-ənt), *adj.* vociferating. *n.* a vociferous person. —**vo·cif′er·ance,** *n.*

**vo·cif·er·ate** (vō-sif′ẽr-āt′), *v.t.* & *v.i.* [-ATED, -ATING], [< L. pp. of *vociferari* < *vox*, voice + *ferre*, to bear], to cry out loudly; shout; clamor. —**vo·cif′er·a′tion,** *n.* —**vo·cif′er·a′tor,** *n.*

**vo·cif·er·ous** (vō-sif′ẽr-əs), *adj.* 1. shouting noisily; clamorous. 2. characterized by clamor. —**vo·cif′er·ous·ly,** *adv.* —**vo·cif′er·ous·ness,** *n.*

**vod·ka** (vod′kə), *n.* [Russ., dim. of *voda*, water], a Russian alcoholic liquor distilled from wheat, rye, potatoes, etc.

**vogue** (vōg), *n.* [Fr., a fashion, lit., a rowing < *voguer*, to row < MHG.], 1. the current accepted fashion; mode: often with *the.* 2. popularity; general acceptance.

**voice** (vois), *n.* [< OFr. < L. *vox*], 1. sound made through the mouth, especially by human beings in talking, singing, etc. 2. the ability to make such sounds. 3. any sound, influence, etc. regarded as like vocal utterance: as, the *voice* of the sea, the *voice* of his conscience. 4. expressed wish, choice, opinion, etc. 5. the right to express one's wish, opinion, etc.; vote. 6. expression: as, give *voice* to your opinion. 7. the means by which something is expressed: as, this newspaper is the *voice* of the administration. 8. in *grammar*, a form of a verb showing the connection between the subject and the verb, either as performing (**active voice**) or receiving (**passive voice**) the action. 9. in *music*, *a*) the quality of a particular person's singing: as, a good *voice.* *b*) a singer. *c*) any of the parts of a musical composition in harmony. *d*) ability to sing: as, he has no *voice.* 10 in *phonetics*, sound made by vibrating the vocal cords with air from the lungs, as in pronouncing vowels and such consonants as *b, d, g,* etc. *v.t.* [VOICED, VOICING], 1. to give utterance to (an opinion, etc.). 2. in *music*, to regulate the tone of (organ pipes, etc.). 3. in *phonetics*, to utter with voice. —**in voice,** with the voice in good condition, as for singing. —**with one voice,** unanimously. —**voic′er,** *n.*

**voiced** (voist), *adj.* 1. having a voice. 2. having (a specified kind of) voice: as, *deep-voiced.* 3. expressed by the voice. 4. in *phonetics*, made with voice: said of certain consonants.

**voice·less** (vois′lis), *adj.* 1. having no voice; esp., mute. 2. not speaking or spoken. 3. in *phonetics*, uttered without voice: as, *k, p, t,* etc. are *voiceless* consonants. —**voice′less·ly,** *adv.* —**voice′less·ness,** *n.*

**void** (void), *adj.* [< OFr. < LL. < *vocuus*, for L. *vacuus*, empty], 1. not occupied; vacant: said of offices, etc. 2. containing nothing; empty. 3. lacking: as, *void* of judgment. 4. ineffective; useless. 5. in *law*, not binding; invalid; of no legal force. *n.* 1. an empty space. 2. a feeling of emptiness or loss. *v.t.* 1. to make empty. 2. to empty (the contents); evacuate. 3. to make void; annul. —**void′a·ble,** *adj.* —**void′a·ble·ness,** *n.* —**void′er,** *n.* —**void′ly,** *adv.* —**void′ness,** *n.*

‡**voi·là** (vwà′là′), [Fr., see there], behold; there it is: often used as an interjection.

**voile** (voil), *n.* [Fr., a veil], a thin, sheer fabric of cotton, silk, wool, rayon, etc.

**vol.,** 1. volcano. 2. [*pl.* VOLS.], volume.

**vo·lant** (vō′lənt), *adj.* [< Fr. < L. ppr. of *volare*, to fly], 1. flying or capable of flying. 2. nimble; agile. 3. in *heraldry*, represented as flying.

**vol·a·tile** (vol′ə-t′l), *adj.* [< L. *volatilis* < *volare*, to fly], 1. changing readily to vapor; quickly evaporating. 2. changeable; fickle; transient. —**vol′a·til′i·ty** (-til′ə-ti), **vol′a·tile·ness,** *n.*

**vol·a·til·ize** (vol′ə-t′l-īz′), *v.t.* & *v.i.* [-IZED, -IZING], to make or become volatile; evaporate. —**vol′a·til·iz′a·ble,** *adj.* —**vol′a·til·i·za′tion,** *n.* —**vol′a·til·iz′er,** *n.*

**vol·can·ic** (vol-kan′ik), *adj.* 1. of, caused by, or characteristic of a volcano. 2. having volcanoes. 3. like a volcano; violently explosive. —**vol·can′i·cal·ly,** *adv.* —**vol′can·ic′i·ty** (-kə-nis′ə-ti), *n.*

**vol·can·ism** (vol′kə-niz′m), *n.* volcanic action or phenomena.

**vol·ca·no** (vol-kā′nō), *n.* [*pl.* -NOES, -NOS], [It. < L. *Volcanus*, Vulcan, the god of fire], 1. a vent in the earth's crust through which rocks, ash, molten rock, etc. are ejected. 2. a cone-shaped hill or mountain, chiefly of volcanic materials, built up around the vent.

**vole** (vōl), *n.* [< *vole mouse; vole*, a field < ON.

*võllr*], any of several burrowing rodents, including the North American meadow mouse.

**Vol·ga** (vol′gə), *n.* a river in the European U.S.S.R., flowing into the Caspian Sea.

**vo·li·tion** (vō-lish′ən), *n.* [Fr. < ML. < L.; ult. < *velle*, to will], 1. act or power of willing. 2. settlement of deliberation by a decision. —**vo·li′tion·al, vo·li′tion·ar′y,** *adj.* —**vo·li′tion·al·ly,** *adv.*

**vol·i·tive** (vol′ə-tiv), *adj.* 1. of the will. 2. in *grammar*, expressing a wish, as a verb, etc.

‡**Volk** (fôlk), *n.* [G.], a folk; people; nation.

**vol·ley** (vol′i), *n.* [*pl.* -LEYS], [< Fr. < *voler* (< L. *volare*), to fly], 1. the simultaneous discharge of a number of weapons. 2. the missiles so discharged. 3. a rapid outpouring: as, a *volley* of curses. 4. in *sports*, *a*) the flight of a ball before it touches the ground. *b*) a return of a ball before it touches the ground. *v.t.* & *v.i.* [-LEYED, -LEYING], 1. to discharge or be discharged as in a volley. 2. in *sports*, to return (a ball) before it touches the ground. —**vol′ley·er,** *n.*

**vol·ley·ball** (vol′i-bôl′), *n.* 1. a game played by two teams who hit a large ball back and forth over a high net with the hands, trying to return the ball before it touches the ground. 2. the ball.

**vol·plane** (vol′plān′), *v.i.* [-PLANED, -PLANING], [Fr. *vol plané*; ult. < *voler* (< L. *volare*), to fly + *planer*, to glide < L. *planus*, level surface], to glide down in an airplane with the engine cut off. *n.* such a glide. —**vol′plan′er,** *n.*

**Vol·sun·ga Saga** (vol′soo̅ŋ-gə), an Icelandic saga relating the same legend as the Nibelungenlied.

**volt** (vōlt), *n.* [< Fr. < It. < L. pp. of *volvere*, to turn about], 1. a turning movement of a horse. 2. in *fencing*, a leap to avoid a thrust.

**volt** (vōlt), *n.* [after Count *Volta*], the unit of electromotive force, being that force which will cause a current of one ampere to flow through a conductor whose resistance is one ohm.

**Vol·ta, Count A·les·san·dro** (ä′le-sän′drô vôl′tä), 1745–1827; Italian physicist.

**volt·age** (vōl′tij), *n.* in *electricity*, electromotive force, expressed in volts.

**vol·ta·ic** (vol-tā′ik), *adj.* 1. *a*) designating or of electricity produced by chemical action. *b*) used in producing such electricity. 2. designating or of electricity that moves in a current, as distinguished from static electricity.

**voltaic battery,** in *electricity*, 1. a battery composed of voltaic cells. 2. a voltaic cell.

**voltaic cell,** a device for producing an electric current by the action of two plates of different metals in an electrolyte.

**Vol·taire** (vol-târ′), *n.* (born *François Marie Arouet*), French satirist and philosopher: lived 1694–1778.

**vol·tam·e·ter** (vol-tam′ə-tẽr), *n.* an instrument used to measure the amount of electricity passing through a conductor by the amount of electrolysis produced. —**vol′ta·met′ric** (-tə-met′rik), *adj.*

**volt·am·me·ter** (vōlt′am′mē′tẽr), *n.* an instrument for measuring voltage and amperage.

**volt-am·pere** (vōlt′am′pêr), *n.* a unit of electrical measurement equal to the product of one volt and one ampere.

**volt·me·ter** (vōlt′mē′tẽr), *n.* an instrument for measuring an electromotive force, or a difference in electrical potential, by volts.

**vol·u·ble** (vol′yoo-b'l), *adj.* [Fr. < L. *volubilis* < *volvere*, to roll], characterized by a great flow of words; talkative, glib, etc. —**vol′u·bil′i·ty, vol′u·ble·ness,** *n.* —**vol′u·bly,** *adv.*

**vol·ume** (vol′yoom), *n.* [OFr. < L. *volumen*, a scroll < *volvere*, to roll], 1. *a*) a collection of written or printed sheets bound together; book. *b*) one of the books of a set. 2. the amount of space occupied in three dimensions; cubic contents. 3. a quantity, bulk, or amount. 4. a large quantity. 5. the strength or loudness of sound. 6. in *music*, fullness of tone. —**speak volumes,** to be very meaningful. —**vol′umed,** *adj.*

**vol·u·met·ric** (vol′yoo-met′rik), *adj.* of or based on the measurement of volume: also **vol′u·met′ri·cal.** —**vol′u·met′ri·cal·ly,** *adv.* —**vo·lu·me·try** (və-loo̅′mə-tri), *n.*

**vo·lu·mi·nous** (və-loo̅′mə-nəs), *adj.* 1. writing, producing, or consisting of enough to fill volumes. 2. of great volume; large; bulky; full. —**vo·lu′mi·nos′i·ty** (-nos′ə-ti), **vo·lu′mi·nous·ness,** *n.* —**vo·lu′mi·nous·ly,** *adv.*

**vol·un·tar·y** (vol′ən-ter′i), *adj.* [< L. < *voluntas*, free will; ult. < *velle*, to will], 1. brought about by one's own free choice; given or done of one's own free will. 2. acting of one's own accord: as, a *voluntary* guide. 3. intentional: as, *voluntary* manslaughter. 4. controlled by the will: as, *voluntary* muscles. 5. having the power of free decision: as, man is a *voluntary* agent. *n.* [*pl.* -IES], 1. a voluntary act or piece of work. 2. an organ solo played in a church service. —**vol′un·tar′i·ly,** *adv.* —**vol′un·tar′i·ness,** *n.*

**vol·un·teer** (vol′ən-têr′), *n.* [< Fr. *volontaire*, a voluntary], 1. one who offers to enter into any service of his own free will. 2. one who enters military service of his own free will. *adj.* 1. of or composed of volunteers. 2. serving as a volunteer. 3. voluntary. *v.t.* to offer or give of one's own free will. *v.i.* to enter or offer to enter into any service of one's own free will.

**vo·lup·tu·ar·y** (və-lup′choo̅-er′i), *n.* [*pl.* -IES], [< L. < *voluptas*, pleasure], one devoted to luxurious living and sensual pleasures. *adj.* of or characterized by luxury and sensual pleasures.

**vo·lup·tu·ous** (və-lup′choo̅-əs), *adj.* [< OFr. < L. < *voluptas*, pleasure], 1. full of, producing, or characterized by sensual pleasures. 2. fond of luxury, the pleasures of the senses, etc. 3. suggesting, or arising from, sensual pleasure. —**vo·lup′tu·ous·ly,** *adv.* —**vo·lup′tu·ous·ness,** *n.*

**vo·lute** (və-loo̅t′), *n.* [Fr. < It. < L.; ult. < *volvere*, to roll], 1. in *architecture*, a spiral scroll, as of an Ionic capital. 2. a spiral or twisting form; whorl. 3. in *zoology*, any of the whorls of a spiral shell. *adj.* spiraled: also **vo·lut′ed,** *adj.* —**vo·lu′tion,** *n.*

**vom·it** (vom′it), *n.* [< L. < pp. of *vomere*], 1. the ejecting of the contents of the stomach through the mouth. 2. matter so ejected. *v.i.* 1. to eject the contents of the stomach through the mouth; throw up. 2. to be thrown up or out with force. *v.t.* 1. to throw up, as food. 2. to discharge with force; belch forth. —**vom′it·er,** *n.*

**vom·i·tive** (vom′i-tiv), *adj.* of or causing vomiting; emetic. *n.* an emetic.

‡**von** (fôn; Eng. von), *prep.* [G.], of; from: a prefix occurring in many names of German and Austrian families, especially of the nobility.

**voo·doo** (voo̅′doo̅), *n.* [*pl.* -DOOS], [Creole Fr. < a W. Afr. word], 1. a body of primitive rites and practices, based on a belief in sorcery, fetishism, etc. and of African origin, found among West Indian natives and in the southern U.S. 2. one who practices these rites. 3. a voodoo charm, fetish, etc. *adj.* of voodoos or their beliefs, practices, etc. *v.t.* to affect by voodoo magic. —**voo′doo·ism,** *n.* —**voo′doo·ist,** *n.* —**voo′doo·is′tic,** *adj.*

**vo·ra·cious** (vô-rā′shəs, vō-), *adj.* [< L. *vorax* < *vorare*, to devour], 1. greedy in eating; ravenous. 2. very greedy or eager in some desire or pursuit: as, a *voracious* reader. —**vo·ra′cious·ly,** *adv.* —**vo·rac′i·ty** (-ras′ə-ti), **vo·ra′cious·ness,** *n.*

**-vo·rous** (vẽr-əs), [< L. < *vorare*, to devour], a combining form meaning *feeding on*, as in *carnivorous*.

**vor·tex** (vôr′teks), *n.* [*pl.* -TEXES, -TICES (-tə-sēz′)], [L. < *vertere*, to whirl], 1. a whirling mass of water forming a vacuum at its center, into which anything caught in the motion is drawn; whirlpool. 2. a whirl of air; whirlwind. 3. any activity, situation, etc. that resembles a whirl in its rush, irresistible and catastrophic power, etc. —**vor′ti·cal,** *adj.* —**vor′ti·cal·ly,** *adv.*

**Vosges Mountains** (vōzh), a range in NE France, west of the Rhine.

**vo·ta·ress** (vō′tə-ris), *n.* a girl or woman votary: also **vo′tress** (-tris).

**vo·ta·ry** (vō′tə-ri), *n.* [*pl.* -RIES], [< L. pp. of *vovere*, to vow], 1. one bound by a vow, especially by religious vows, as a monk. 2. a devoted supporter or one who is devoted to a religion, cause, study, etc. Also **vo′ta·rist.** *adj.* 1. consecrated by a vow. 2. of, or having the nature of, a vow.

**vote** (vōt), *n.* [L. *votum*, a vow], 1. a decision on a proposal, etc., or a choice between candidates for office. 2. *a*) the expression of such a decision or choice. *b*) the ballot, voice, etc. by which it is expressed. 3. the right to exercise such a decision, etc.; suffrage. 4. votes collectively. 5. [Obs.], a voter. *v.i.* [VOTED, VOTING], to express preference in a matter by ballot, etc. *v.t.* 1. *a*) to decide, enact, or authorize by vote. *b*) to confer by vote. *c*) to support (a specified party) in voting. 2. to declare by general opinion. 3. [Colloq.], to suggest. —**vote down,** to defeat by voting. —**vote in,** to elect. —**vote out,** to defeat an incumbent in an election. —**vot′a·ble, vote′a·ble,** *adj.* —**vote′less,** *adj.*

**vot·er** (vōt′ẽr), *n.* 1. a person who has a right to vote; elector. 2. a person who votes.

**voting machine,** a machine on which the votes in an election are cast, registered, and counted.

**vo·tive** (vō′tiv), *adj.* [L. *votivus* < *votum*; see VOTE], given, done, etc. in fulfillment of a vow. —**vo′tive·ly,** *adv.* —**vo′tive·ness,** *n.*

**vouch** (vouch), *v.t.* [< OFr. < L. *vocare*, to call < *vox*, a voice], 1. to attest; affirm or guarantee: as, *vouch* a statement. 2. to cite (authority, books, etc.) in support of one's views, etc. 3. to uphold by demonstration. *v.i.* 1. to give assurance, a guarantee, etc. (with *for*): as, we *vouch* for his honesty. 2. to serve as evidence or assurance (with *for*).
**vouch·er** (vouch'ēr), *n.* 1. one who vouches, as for the truth of a statement. 2. a paper attesting or serving as evidence; specif., a statement serving as evidence of payment of a debt, etc.
**vouch·safe** (vouch-sāf'), *v.t.* [-SAFED, -SAFING], [< ME. *vouchen safe*, to vouch as safe], to condescend to grant, do, etc.: as, *vouchsafe* a reply. *v.i.* to condescend; deign. **—vouch·safe'ment,** *n.*
**vous·soir** (vōō-swär'), *n.* [< OFr. < LL. < L. pp. of *volvere*, to roll], in *architecture*, any of the wedge-shaped sections of which an arch is built.
**vow** (vou), *n.* [< OFr. < L. *votum*], 1. a solemn promise; esp., one made to God or a god. 2. a promise of fidelity and love: as, marriage *vows*. 3. a solemn affirmation. *v.t.* 1. to promise solemnly. 2. to make a solemn resolution to do, get, etc. 3. to declare emphatically, earnestly, etc. *v.i.* to make a vow. **—take vows,** to enter a religious order. **—vow'er,** *n.* **—vow'less,** *adj.*
**vow·el** (vou'əl), *n.* [< OFr. < L. *vocalis* (*littera*), vocal (letter) < *vox*, a voice], 1. a voiced speech sound characterized by generalized friction of the air passing in a continuous stream through the pharynx and opened mouth. 2. a letter, as *a*, *e*, *i*, *o*, and *u*, representing such a sound. *adj.* of a vowel or vowels. **—vow'el·less,** *adj.*
**‡vox** (voks), *n.* [*pl.* VOCES (vō'sēz)], [L.], voice.
**‡vox po·pu·li** (voks pop'yoo-lī'), [L.], the voice of the people: abbrev. **vox pop.**
**‡vox populi, vox De·i** (dē'ī), [L.], the voice of the people (is) the voice of God.
**voy·age** (voi'ij), *n.* [< OFr. < L. *viaticum*, provision for a journey < *via*, way], 1. a relatively long journey by water, or, formerly, by land. 2. a journey by aircraft. *v.i.* [-AGED, -AGING], to travel by sea, water, or air. *v.t.* to sail or travel over or on. **—voy'age·a·ble,** *adj.* **—voy'ag·er,** *n.*
**‡vo·ya·geur** (vwȧ'yȧ'zhër'), *n.* [*pl.* -GEURS (-zhër')], [Fr.], 1. a traveler. 2. in Canada, *a*) a person who transports goods and men for the fur companies. *b*) any woodsman or boatsman of the wilds.
**vo·yeur** (vwä-yūr'), *n.* [Fr. < *voir*, to see], one who obtains sexual gratification by looking at sexual objects or scenes; a peeping Tom. **—vo·yeur'ism,** *n.*
**V.P., VP,** Vice-President.
**V. Rev.,** Very Reverend.
**Vries, Hu·go de** (hü'gō də vrēs'), 1848–1935; Dutch botanist.
**vs.,** versus.
**V.S.,** Veterinary Surgeon.
**v.s.,** *vide supra*, [L.], see above.
**V-shaped** (vē'shāpt'), *adj.* shaped like the letter V.
**Vt.,** Vermont.
**v.t.,** transitive verb.
**V-type engine** (vē'tīp'), an engine in which the cylinders are set at an angle forming a V.
**Vul·can** (vul'kən), *n.* in *Rom. mythology*, the god of fire and of metalworking. **—Vul·ca'ni·an** (-kā'ni-ən), *adj.*
**vul·can·ite** (vul'kən-īt'), *n.* [*Vulcan* + *-ite*], a hard rubber made by treating crude rubber with a large amount of sulfur and subjecting it to intense heat; ebonite: used in combs, etc.
**vul·can·ize** (vul'kən-īz'), *v.t.* & *v.i.* [-IZED, -IZING], to treat (crude rubber) with sulfur and subject it to heat in order to increase its strength and elasticity. **—vul'can·i·za'tion,** *n.* **—vul'can·iz'er,** *n.*
**vul·gar** (vul'gēr), *adj.* [< L. *vulgaris* < *vulgus*, the common people], 1. of the great mass of people in general; common; popular: as, a *vulgar* superstition. 2. of or in the vernacular. 3. characterized by a lack of culture, refinement, taste, etc.; crude; boorish. **—vul'gar·ly,** *adv.* **—vul'gar·ness,** *n.*
**vul·gar·i·an** (vul-gâr'i-ən), *n.* a vulgar person; esp., a rich person with coarse, showy tastes.
**vul·gar·ism** (vul'gēr-iz'm), *n.* 1. a word, phrase, etc. occurring only in common colloquial usage or, especially, in coarse speech. 2. vulgar behavior, quality, etc.; vulgarity.
**vul·gar·i·ty** (vul-gar'ə-ti), *n.* 1. the state or quality of being vulgar, crude, etc. 2. [*pl.* -TIES], a vulgar act, habit, usage in language, etc.
**vul·gar·ize** (vul'gēr-īz'), *v.t.* [-IZED, -IZING], to make vulgar. **—vul'gar·i·za'tion,** *n.* **—vul'gar·iz'er,** *n.*
**Vulgar Latin,** the everyday speech of the Roman people, from which the Romance languages developed.
**Vul·gate** (vul'gāt, -git), *n.* [< ML. *vulgata* (*editio*), popular (edition)], a Latin version of the Bible prepared in the 4th century, serving as the authorized version of the Roman Catholic Church. *adj.* 1. of or in the Vulgate. 2. [v-], popular; vernacular: as, *vulgate* English.
**vul·ner·a·ble** (vul'nēr-ə-b'l), *adj.* [< LL. < L. *vulnerare*, to wound < *vulnus*, a wound], 1. that can be wounded or physically injured. 2. open to, or liable to be hurt by, criticism or attack. 3. open to attack by armed forces. 4. in *contract bridge*, liable to an increased penalty or an increased bonus: said of a team which has won a game. **—vul'ner·a·bil'i·ty, vul'ner·a·ble·ness,** *n.* **—vul'ner·a·bly,** *adv.*
**vul·pine** (vul'pīn, -pin), *adj.* [< L. < *vulpes*, a fox], of or like a fox or foxes; clever; cunning.
**vul·ture** (vul'chēr), *n.* [< OFr. < L. *vultur*], 1. a large bird of prey with a naked head, related to the eagles and hawks: vultures live on carrion. 2. a greedy, ruthless person who preys on others. **—vul'ture·like',** *adj.* **—vul'tur·ous,** *adj.*
**vul·va** (vul'və), *n.* [L., womb], the external genital organs of the female. **—vul'val, vul'var,** *adj.* **—vul'vi·form',** *adj.*
**vv.,** 1. verses. 2. violins.
**v.v.,** vice versa.
**vy·ing** (vī'iŋ), *adj.* that vies; that competes. **—vy'ing·ly,** *adv.*

VULTURE (2½ ft. long)

# W

**W, w** (dub''l-yoo), *n.* [*pl.* W's, w's, Ws, ws], 1. the twenty-third letter of the English alphabet. 2. the sound of W or w. *adj.* twenty-third in a sequence or group.
**W,** 1. watt; watts. 2. west. 3. western. 4. in *chemistry, the symbol for* tungsten (wolfram).
**W.,** 1. Wales. 2. Wednesday. 3. Welsh. 4. Western. 5. West.
**W., w.,** 1. watt; watts. 2. weight. 3. west. 4. western. 5. width.
**w.,** 1. week; weeks. 2. wide. 3. wife. 4. with.
**WAAC, W.A.A.C.,** 1. Women's Auxiliary Army Corps: replaced by WAC. 2. [Brit.], Women's Army Auxiliary Corps.
**Wa·bash** (wô'bash), *n.* a river flowing through Ohio, Indiana, and Illinois into the Ohio River.
**wab·ble** (wäb''l), *n.*, *v.i.* & *v.t.* [-BLED, -BLING], wobble. **—wab'bler,** *n.* **—wab'bling,** *adj.* **—wab'bly** [-BLIER, -BLIEST], *adj.*
**Wac** (wak), *n.* a member of the WAC.
**WAC, W.A.C.,** the Women's Army Corps.
**wack·y** (wak'i), *adj.* [-IER, -IEST], [? < *whack* (a blow) + *-y*], [Slang], erratic, eccentric, or irrational: also **whacky.**
**Wa·co** (wā'kō), *n.* a city in central Texas: pop., 98,000.
**wad** (wäd, wôd), *n.* [akin to Sw. *vadd*], 1. a small, soft mass, as a handful of cotton, crumpled paper,

etc. 2. a lump or small, compact mass: as, a *wad* of chewing tobacco. 3. a mass of soft material used for padding, packing, etc. 4. a plug stuffed against a charge to keep it firmly in place, as in a muzzle-loading gun. 5. [Colloq.], a roll of paper money. 6. [Slang], a supply of money. ***v.t.*** [WADDED, WADDING], 1. to compress, or roll up, into a wad. 2. to plug or stuff with a wad. 3. to pad with wadding. 4. to hold (a charge) in place by a wad, as in a gun, etc. —**wad′der,** ***n.***

**wad·ding** (wäd′iŋ, wôd′-), ***n.*** any soft material for use in padding, packing, stuffing, etc.; esp., cotton made up into loose, fluffy sheets.

**wad·dle** (wäd′'l, wôd′-), ***v.i.*** [-DLED, -DLING] [freq. of *wade*], 1. to walk with short steps and a swaying motion from side to side, as a duck. 2. to move clumsily like this, as a baby. ***n.*** 1. the act of waddling. 2. a waddling gait. —**wad′dler,** ***n.***

**wade** (wād), ***v.i.*** [WADED, WADING], [< AS. *waden*, to go], 1. to walk through any substance, as water, mud, tall grass, etc., that offers resistance. 2. to go forward with difficulty: as, *wade* through a dull book. ***v.t.*** to go across or through by wading. ***n.*** an act of wading. —**wade in** (or **into**), [Colloq.], to begin energetically or with vigor.

**wad·er** (wād′ēr), ***n.*** 1. a person or thing that wades. 2. any of several long-legged shore birds that wade the shallows for food, as the crane, heron, snipe, etc. 3. *pl.* high waterproof boots.

**wa·di** (wä′di), ***n.*** [*pl.* -DIS, -DIES], [Ar. *wādī*], in Arabia, N Africa, etc., 1. a valley, ravine, etc. that is dry except during the rainy season. 2. the rush of water that flows through it. Also sp. **wady** [*pl.* -DIES].

**wa·fer** (wā′fēr), ***n.*** [< OFr. < D. *wafel*], 1. a thin, flat, crisp cracker or cake. 2. anything resembling this. 3. a thin cake of unleavened bread used in the Eucharist. 4. a small adhesive disk, as of dried paste, used as a seal on letters, documents, etc. 5. a thin, flat piece of candy. —**wa′fer-like′,** ***adj.*** —**wa′fer·y,** ***adj.***

**waf·fle** (wäf′'l, wôf′'l), ***n.*** a batter cake cooked in a waffle iron: it is crisper than a pancake.

**waffle iron,** a utensil for cooking waffles, having two flat, studded plates pressed together so that the waffle bakes between them.

**waft** (waft, wäft), ***v.t.*** [< obs. *wafter*, a convoy < D. *wachter*, lit., a watcher], 1. to carry or propel lightly over water or through the air, as sounds, odors, etc. 2. to transport as if in this manner. ***v.i.*** to float, as on the wind. ***n.*** 1. the act of floating lightly along. 2. an odor, sound, etc. carried through the air. 3. a gust of wind. 4. a wafting movement. —**waft′er,** ***n.***

**wag** (wag), ***v.t.*** [WAGGED, WAGGING], [prob. < ON.], 1. to cause to move rapidly back and forth, up and down, etc.: as, the dog *wagged* his tail. 2. to move (the tongue) in talking, especially in idle gossip. ***v.i.*** 1. to move rapidly back and forth, up and down, etc. 2. to keep moving in talk: said of the tongue. ***n.*** the act or an instance of wagging. —**wag′ger,** ***n.***

**wag** (wag), ***n.*** [< *wag*, *v.*], a comical or humorous person; joker; wit.

**wage** (wāj), ***v.t.*** [WAGED, WAGING], [< ONorm.Fr. *wagier* < *wage* (< OFr. *gage*), a pledge < Gmc.], to engage in; carry on: as, to *wage* war. ***n.*** 1. *usually pl.* money paid to an employee for work done, usually on an hourly, daily, or piecework basis. 2. *usually pl.* what is given in return; reward: formerly construed as singular, as, "The *wages* of sin is death." —**wage′less,** ***adj.***

**wage earner,** a person who works for wages.

**wag·er** (wā′jēr), ***n.*** [< ONorm.Fr.; see WAGE], a bet (senses 1, 2). ***v.t.* & *v.i.*** to bet (all senses). —**wager of battle,** a challenge by a defendant to prove his innocence by personal combat. —**wag′er·er,** ***n.***

**wage·work·er** (wāj′wũr′kēr), ***n.*** a person who works for wages. —**wage′work′ing,** ***adj.* & *n.***

**wag·ger·y** (wag′ēr-i), ***n.*** [*pl.* -IES], 1. roguish jocularity. 2. a joke; esp., a practical joke.

**wag·gish** (wag′ish), ***adj.*** 1. of or like a wag; roguishly merry. 2. playful; jesting, as a remark. —**wag′gish·ly,** ***adv.*** —**wag′gish·ness,** ***n.***

**wag·gle** (wag′'l), ***v.t.* & *v.i.*** [-GLED, -GLING], to wag, especially with short, abrupt movements. ***n.*** the act or an instance of waggling. —**wag′gling·ly,** ***adv.*** —**wag′gly,** ***adj.***

**wag·gon** (wag′ən), ***n.* & *v.t.*** wagon: Brit. spelling.

**Wag·ner, Rich·ard** (riH′ärt väg′nēr), (*Wilhelm Richard Wagner*), 1813–1883; German composer.

**Wag·ne·ri·an** (väg-nêr′i-ən), ***adj.*** of or like Richard Wagner or his music, theories, etc. ***n.*** an admirer or follower of Wagner's music, etc.

**wag·on** (wag′ən), ***n.*** [< D. *wagen*], 1. a four-wheeled vehicle, especially one for hauling heavy loads. 2. [Brit.], a railroad freight car. 3. [Colloq.], an enclosed vehicle used by the police for carrying arrested people: usually **the wagon**: in full, **police** (or **patrol**) **wagon.** ***v.t.*** to carry in a wagon. —**hitch one's wagon to a star,** to set oneself an ambitious goal. —**on the (water) wagon,** [Slang], no longer drinking alcoholic liquors.

**wag·on·er** (wag′ən-ēr), ***n.*** a person who drives a wagon: also, Brit. spelling, **wag′gon·er.**

**wag·on·load** (wag′ən-lōd′), ***n.*** the load that a wagon carries: also, Brit. spelling, **wag′gon·load′.**

**wagon train,** a line of wagons traveling together, especially one carrying military supplies.

**wag·tail** (wag′tāl′), ***n.*** 1. a small bird related to the pipit, characterized by a long tail that wags up and down. 2. any of various similar birds.

**Wa·ha·bi, Wa·ha·bee, Wah·ha·bi** (wä-hä′bē), ***n.*** [Ar. *Wahhābī*], a member of a puristic sect of Moslems.

**wa·hoo** (wä-hōō′, wä′hōō), ***n.*** [Am. Ind.], a large shrub or tree having purple fruit with red seeds.

**waif** (wāf), ***n.*** [ONorm.Fr. (OFr. *gaif*); ? < ON.], 1. anything found that is without an owner. 2. a person without home or friends; esp., a homeless child. 3. a strayed animal.

**Wai·ki·ki** (wī′kē-kē′, wī′kē-kē′), ***n.*** a famous bathing resort in Honolulu, Hawaii.

**wail** (wāl), ***v.i.*** [< ON. *væla* < *væ*, woe], 1. to express grief or pain by long, loud cries. 2. to make a sad, crying sound: as, the wind *wails*. ***v.t.*** 1. to lament; mourn. 2. to cry out in mourning, etc. ***n.*** 1. a long cry of grief or pain. 2. a sound like this. 3. a wailing. —**wail′er,** ***n.*** —**wail′ful,** ***adj.*** —**wail′ful·ly,** ***adv.*** —**wail′ing·ly,** ***adv.***

**wain** (wān), ***n.*** [< AS. *wægn*], [Archaic], a wagon.

**wain·scot** (wān′skət, -skot′), ***n.*** [< MLG. or MD.; cf. D. *wagenschot*], 1. a lining or paneling of wood, etc. on the walls of a room, often on the lower part only. 2. the lower part of a wall of a room when it is finished differently from the upper. ***v.t.*** [-SCOTED or -SCOTTED, -SCOTING or -SCOTTING], to line (a wall or room) with wainscoting.

**wain·scot·ing, wain·scot·ting** (wān′skət-iŋ, -skot′-), ***n.*** 1. wainscot. 2. material used for wainscots.

**wain·wright** (wān′rīt′), ***n.*** [*wain* (a wagon) + *wright*], a person who builds or repairs wagons.

**waist** (wāst), ***n.*** [< base of AS. *weaxan*, to grow], 1. the part of the body between the ribs and the hips. 2. *a*) the part of a garment that covers the waist. *b*) the narrow part of a woman's dress, etc.; waistline. *c*) the part of a garment covering the body from the shoulders to the waistline. *d*) a blouse. 3. the narrow part of any object which is wider at the ends. —**waist′less,** ***adj.***

**waist·band** (wāst′band′), ***n.*** a band encircling the waist, as at the top of a skirt, trousers, etc.

**waist·coat** (wāst′kōt′, wes′kət), ***n.*** [Brit.], a man's vest. —**waist′coat′ed,** ***adj.***

**waist·line** (wāst′līn′), ***n.*** 1. the line of the waist between the ribs and the hips. 2. the narrow part of a woman's dress, etc., worn at the waist or above or below it as styles change.

**wait** (wāt), ***v.i.*** [< ONorm.Fr. *waitier* < OHG. < *wahta*, a guard], 1. to stay in a place or remain inactive until something expected takes place (often with *for*, *until*, etc.): as, *wait* for the signal. 2. to be ready: as, dinner is *waiting* for us. 3. to remain temporarily undone: as, it will have to *wait*. 4. to serve food (with *at* or *on*): as, she will *wait* at table. ***v.t.*** 1. to be, remain, or delay in expectation of: as, *wait* orders. 2. to serve food at: as, he *waits* table. 3. [Colloq.], to put off serving: as, *wait* dinner. ***n.*** 1. act or duration of waiting: as, a four-hour *wait*. 2. an ambush; trap: usually in *lie in wait*. —**wait on** (or **upon**), 1. to act as a servant to. 2. to visit (a superior) in order to pay one's respects, ask a favor, etc. 3. to be a consequence of. 4. to serve (a customer), as a clerk, etc. —**wait up (for)**, [Colloq.], to put off going to bed until the arrival of (someone expected).

**wait·er** (wāt′ēr), ***n.*** 1. a person who waits or awaits. 2. a man who waits on table, as in a restaurant. 3. a tray for carrying dishes.

**wait·ing** (wāt′iŋ), ***adj.*** 1. that waits. 2. of or for a wait. ***n.*** 1. the act of one that waits. 2. a period of waiting. —**in waiting,** in attendance (on a king or other royal person).

**waiting room,** a room in which people wait, as in a railroad station, a dentist's office, etc.

**wait·ress** (wāt′ris), ***n.*** a woman or girl who waits on table, as in a restaurant.

**waive** (wāv), ***v.t.*** [WAIVED, WAIVING], [< Anglo-Fr. *waiver*, to renounce; prob. < ON. *veifa*, to fluctuate], 1. to give up or forego, as a right, claim, etc. 2. to refrain from insisting on or taking advantage of. 3. to postpone; defer.

**waiv·er** (wāv′ẽr), ***n.*** in *law*, 1. a waiving, or relinquishing voluntarily, a right, claim, etc. 2. a written statement of such relinquishment.

**wake** (wāk), ***v.i.*** [WAKED or WOKE, WAKED or *rarely* WOKEN, WAKING], [< AS. *wacian*, to be awake & *wacan*, to arise], 1. to come out of sleep or a state like sleep; awake (often with *up*). 2. to stay awake. 3. to become active again. 4. to become alert (*to* a realization, etc.). 5. [Dial.], to hold a wake (sense 2). ***v.t.*** 1. to cause to wake (senses 1, 3, 4): often with *up*. 2. to arouse or excite, as passions. 3. to keep watch over (a corpse). ***n.*** 1. [Poetic], the state of being awake. 2. a watch kept at night; esp., an all-night vigil over a corpse before burial, formerly often with festivities.

**wake** (wāk), ***n.*** [D. *wak;* prob. < ON. *vök*, a hole], 1. the track left in the water by a moving ship. 2. the track of anything that has gone before. **—in the wake of,** following close behind.

**wake·ful** (wāk′fəl), ***adj.*** 1. keeping awake. 2. alert; watchful. 3. unable to sleep. 4. sleepless. **—wake′ful·ly,** ***adv.*** **—wake′ful·ness,** ***n.***

**Wake Island** (wāk), a small U.S. island in the N Pacific between Midway and Guam: naval air base.

**wak·en** (wāk′'n), ***v.i. & v.t.*** [AS. *wacnian*], to wake. **—wak′en·er,** ***n.***

**wake-rob·in** (wāk′rob′in), ***n.*** 1. the trillium. 2. the jack-in-the-pulpit.

**Wal·dorf salad** (wôl′dôrf), [after a former hotel in New York City], a salad made of diced apples, celery, and walnuts, with mayonnaise.

**wale** (wāl), ***n.*** [AS. *walu*, a rod], 1. a raised line made on the skin by the slash of a whip, etc.; welt. 2. *a)* a ridge on the surface of cloth, as corduroy. *b)* texture of cloth. 3. *pl.* heavy planks fastened to the outside of the hull of a wooden ship. ***v.t.*** [WALED, WALING], 1. to mark (the skin) with wales. 2. to make, as cloth, with wales.

**Wales** (wālz), ***n.*** a division of Great Britain, bounded on the east by England: area, 7,466 sq. mi.; pop., 2,597,000.

**walk** (wôk), ***v.i.*** [AS. *wealcan*, to roll], 1. to move along on foot at a moderate pace by placing one foot (or, with quadrupeds, two feet) on the ground before lifting the other (or others). 2. to appear after death as a ghost. 3. to follow a certain course of life: as, let us *walk* in peace. 4. in *baseball*, to be advanced to first base as a result of being pitched four balls: cf. **ball.** ***v.t.*** 1. to go along, over, etc. at a moderate pace on foot: as, to *walk* the deck. 2. to traverse on foot in order to inspect or repair, as a fence, etc. 3. to cause (a horse, dog, etc.) to move at a walk, as for exercise. 4. to accompany (a person) on a walk: as, I'll *walk* you home. 5. to bring to a specified state by walking: as, they *walked* me to exhaustion. 6. in *baseball*, to advance (a batter) to first base by pitching four balls. ***n.*** 1. the act of walking. 2. a stroll or hike. 3. a route traversed by walking. 4. a distance walked: as, an hour's *walk*. 5. the pace of one who walks. 6. a manner of walking: as, I knew her by her *walk*. 7. a sphere of activity, mode of living, etc.: as, people from all *walks* of life. 8. a path set apart for walking. 9. an enclosure for grazing animals. 10. in *baseball*, an advancing to first base on four balls. **—walk off,** 1. to go away, especially abruptly. 2. to get rid of by walking, as excess fat. **—walk off with,** 1. to steal. 2. to win or gain. **—walk out,** [Colloq.], to go on strike. **—walk out on,** [Colloq.], to leave; desert. **—walk′er,** ***n.***

**walk·a·way** (wôk′ə-wā′), ***n.*** an easily won victory.

**walk·ie-talk·ie** (wôk′i-tôk′i), ***n.*** a compact radio transmitter and receiver that can be carried by one person: also **walk′y-talk′y.**

**walking papers,** [Colloq.], dismissal from a position or job.

**walking stick,** 1. a cane. 2. an insect resembling a twig.

**walk-on** (wôk′on′), ***n.*** a minor role in which the actor has no speaking lines.

**walk·out** (wôk′out′), ***n.*** [Colloq.], a labor strike.

**walk·o·ver** (wôk′ō′vẽr), ***n.*** [Colloq.], an easily won victory.

**walk-up** (wôk′up′), ***n.*** [Colloq.], an apartment house without an elevator. ***adj.*** [Colloq.], of or in such a building: as, a *walk-up* apartment.

**wall** (wôl), ***n.*** [AS. *weall* < L. *vallum*, a rampart < *vallus*, a stake], 1. an upright structure of wood, stone, etc., serving to enclose, divide, support, or protect: as, the *walls* of a room, building, garden, etc. 2. *usually in pl.* a fortification. 3. something resembling a wall in appearance or function. ***adj.*** of, on, or for a wall. ***v.t.*** 1. to furnish, enclose, divide, etc. with or as with a wall (often with *off*). 2. to close (an opening) with a wall (often with *up*). **—drive** (or **push**) **to the wall,** to place in a desperate position. **—go to the wall,** 1. to yield; suffer defeat. 2. to fail in business. **—walled,** ***adj.*** **—wall′-less,** ***adj.*** **—wall′-like′,** ***adj.***

**wal·la·by** (wäl′ə-bi), ***n.*** [*pl.* -BIES, -BY; see PLURAL, II, D, 1], [< Australian name], a small kangaroo, sometimes as small as a rabbit.

**wall·board** (wôl′bôrd′, -bōrd′), ***n.*** fibrous material made up into thin slabs for use in making or covering walls, etc., in place of plaster, etc.

**wal·let** (wäl′it, wôl′-), ***n.*** [ME. *walet*], 1. [Now Rare], a bag for carrying provisions on a journey. 2. a flat pocketbook, usually of leather, for carrying cards, paper money, etc.; billfold.

**wall·eye** (wôl′ī′), ***n.*** [< *walleyed*], 1. an eye, as of a horse, with a whitish iris. 2. an eye that turns outward, showing more white than is normal. 3. any of several fishes with large, staring eyes.

**wall·eyed** (wôl′īd′), ***adj.*** [< ON. < *vagl*, a film on the eye + *eygr*, having eyes], 1. having a walleye or walleyes. 2. having large, staring eyes, as some fishes.

**walleyed pike** (or **perch**), any of several North American fresh-water food fishes of the perch family, with large, staring eyes.

**wall·flow·er** (wôl′flou′ẽr), ***n.*** 1. any of a number of plants with lance-shaped leaves and clusters of fragrant yellow, red, orange, etc. flowers. 2. [Colloq.], a person who sits by the wall, or only looks on, at a dance, as from shyness, etc.

**Wal·loon** (wä-lo͞on′), ***n.*** [Fr. *Wallon*], 1. a member of a people living chiefly in S and SE Belgium and near-by parts of France. 2. the French dialect of the Walloons. ***adj.*** of the Walloons or Walloon.

**wal·lop** (wäl′əp, wôl′-), ***v.i.*** [< ONorm.Fr. *waloper* (OFr. *galoper*), to gallop], [Dial. or Colloq.], to gallop. ***v.t.*** [Colloq.], 1. to beat soundly. 2. to strike hard. 3. to defeat crushingly. ***n.*** 1. [Dial. or Colloq.], a gallop. 2. [Colloq.], *a)* a hard blow. *b)* the power to strike a hard blow.

**wal·lop·er** (wäl′əp-ẽr, wôl′-), ***n.*** [Colloq.], 1. one that wallops. 2. something huge.

**wal·lop·ing** (wäl′əp-iŋ, wôl′-), ***adj.*** [Colloq.], enormous; very large. ***n.*** [Colloq.], 1. a thrashing; beating. 2. a crushing defeat.

**wal·low** (wäl′ō, wôl′ō), ***v.i.*** [< AS. *wealwian*, to roll around], 1. to roll about, as in mud, dust, etc.: as, pigs *wallow* in filth. 2. to roll and pitch, as a ship. 3. to indulge oneself fully with animal pleasure (*in* a specified thing, etc.): as, to *wallow* in riches, *wallow* in vice. ***n.*** 1. an act of wallowing. 2. a place where animals wallow. 3. a pit made by animals' wallowing. **—wal′low·er,** ***n.***

**wall·pa·per** (wôl′pā′pẽr), ***n.*** paper for covering the walls or ceiling of a room. ***v.t.*** to hang or apply wallpaper on or in.

**Wall Street,** 1. a street in lower Manhattan, New York City: main financial center of the U.S. 2. American financiers and their power, influence, policies, etc., or the American money market.

**wal·nut** (wôl′nut′, -nət), ***n.*** [< AS. < *wealh*, foreign + *hnutu*, a nut], 1. a roundish, edible nut with a two-lobed seed. 2. any of a number of related trees bearing such a nut, as the *English walnut*. 3. the wood of any of these trees, used in furniture, etc. 4. a shagbark tree or its nut. 5. the brown color of the heartwood of the black walnut.

**Wal·pur·gis Night** (väl-poor′gis), 1. April 30, the eve of May Day, when witches were supposed to gather and revel. 2. a witches' sabbath.

**wal·rus** (wôl′rəs, wäl′-), ***n.*** [*pl.* -RUSES, -RUS; see PLURAL, II, D, 1], Dan. *hvalros;* prob. < ON. *hrosshvalr*, lit., horse whale], a massive sea animal of the seal family, having two tusks protruding from the upper jaw, a thick mustache, a thick hide, and a heavy layer of blubber. ***adj.*** like that of a walrus: as, a *walrus* mustache.

WALRUS (10–11 ft. long)

**Wal·ton, I·zaak** (ī′zək wôl′t'n), 1593–1683; English writer and celebrated fisherman.

**waltz** (wôlts; *esp.* Brit. wôls), ***n.*** [< G. < *walzen*, to roll, dance about], 1. a ballroom dance for couples, in 3/4 time. 2. music for this dance or in its characteristic rhythm. ***adj.*** of, for, or charac-

teristic of a waltz. *v.i.* 1. to dance a waltz. 2. to move lightly and nimbly. *v.t.* to cause to waltz. —**waltz′er,** *n.* —**waltz′like′,** *adj.*
**wam·pum** (wäm′pəm, wôm′-), *n.* [< Algonquian], 1. small beads made of shells and used by North American Indians as money, for ornament, etc. 2. [Slang], money.
**wan** (wän, wôn), *adj.* [WANNER, WANNEST], [AS. *wann,* dark], 1. sickly pale; pallid: as, a *wan* complexion. 2. suggestive of a sickly condition or great weariness; feeble: as, a *wan* smile. *v.t. & v.i.* [WANNED, WANNING], to make or become sickly pale. —**wan′ly,** *adv.* —**wan′ness,** *n.*
**wand** (wänd, wônd), *n.* [ON. *vöndr*], 1. a slender, supple switch, as of a young tree. 2. a slender rod, as a musician's baton. 3. a rod carried as a symbol of authority; scepter. 4. any rod of supposed magic power. —**wand′like′,** *adj.*
**wan·der** (wän′dẽr, wôn′-), *v.i.* [AS. *wandrian*], 1. to move or go aimlessly about; ramble; roam. 2. to move idly from one point to another. 3. *a*) to stray (*from* a path, course, etc.). *b*) to stray from home, friends, etc. (often with *off*). 4. to go astray in mind or purpose; specif., *a*) to drift away from a subject, as in discussion. *b*) to be disjointed, incoherent, etc. 5. to meander, as a river. *v.t.* [Poetic], to roam through, in, or over. —**wan′der·er,** *n.* —**wan′der·ing,** *adj. & n.* —**wan′der·ing·ly,** *adv.*
**wan·der·lust** (wän′dẽr-lust′, wôn′-), *n.* [G.], an impulse, longing, or urge to wander or travel.
**wane** (wān), *v.i.* [WANED, WANING], [AS. *wanian* < base of *wana,* lacking], 1. to grow gradually less in extent: said of the moon after it has become full. 2. to grow dim or faint: said of light, etc. 3. to decline in power, importance, etc. 4. to approach the end: as, the day *wanes.* *n.* 1. a waning. 2. a period of waning. —**on the wane,** declining, decreasing, etc.
**wan·gle** (waŋ′g'l), *v.t.* [-GLED, -GLING], [prob. a slang formation on *angle*], [Colloq.], to get, make, or bring about by persuasion, influence, manipulation, etc. *v.i.* [Colloq.], 1. to make use of tricky and indirect methods to achieve one's aims. *n.* [Colloq.], a wangling. —**wan′gler,** *n.*
**wan·nish** (wän′ish, wôn′-), *adj.* somewhat wan.
**want** (wänt, wônt), *v.t.* [< ON. *vanta*], 1. to lack; be deficient in. 2. to be short by (a specified amount): as, it *wants* two minutes of noon. 3. to feel the need of; crave: as, he *wants* love. 4. to desire (followed by the infinitive): as, he *wants* to go home. 5. *a*) to wish to see or speak with: as, mother *wants* you. *b*) to wish to apprehend, as for arrest: as, *wanted* by the police. 6. [Chiefly Brit.], to require; need. *Want* is also used colloquially as an auxiliary meaning *ought* or *should*: as, you *want* to eat before you go. *v.i.* 1. to have a need or lack (usually with *for*). 2. to be destitute or impoverished. *n.* 1. a lack; shortage; scarcity. 2. poverty; destitution. 3. a wish for something; craving. 4. something needed; need. —**want′er,** *n.* —**want′less,** *adj.*
**want ad,** [Colloq.], an advertisement, as in a newspaper, announcing that one wants a job, an apartment, employee, etc.
**want·ing** (wän′tiŋ, wôn′-), *adj.* 1. absent; lacking: as, a coat with buttons *wanting.* 2. not up to a standard or need: as, weighed and found *wanting.* *prep.* 1. lacking (something); without. 2. minus. —**wanting in,** deficient in (some quality, etc.).
**wan·ton** (wän′tən, wôn′-), *adj.* [< AS. < *wan,* lacking + *togen,* pp. of *teon,* to bring up], 1. originally, undisciplined: as, *wanton* boys. 2. unchaste; lewd. 3. [Poetic], *a*) frisky; playful. *b*) unrestrained in play. 4. senseless, unprovoked, or deliberately malicious: as, *wanton* cruelty. 5. recklessly disregardful of justice, decency, etc. 6. lavish, luxurious, unrestrained, etc. *n.* a wanton person or thing; esp., an immoral woman. *v.i.* to be wanton. —**wan′ton·ly,** *adv.* —**wan′ton·ness,** *n.*
**wap·i·ti** (wäp′ə-ti), *n.* [*pl.* -TIS, -TI; see PLURAL, II, D, 1], [< Algonquian], a North American deer with large, branching antlers; American elk.
**war** (wôr), *n.* [< ONorm.Fr. < OHG. *werra,* strife], 1. open armed conflict between countries or between factions within the same country. 2. any active hostility; conflict; strife: as, the *war* between the sexes. 3. military operations as a science. *adj.* of, used in, or resulting from war. *v.i.* [WARRED, WARRING], 1. to carry on war. 2. to contend; strive. —**at war,** engaged in war. —**declare war (on),** 1. to make a formal declaration of being at war (with). 2. to announce one's hostility (to). —**go to war,** 1. to enter into a war. 2. to become a soldier, etc. during a war. —**war′less,** *adj.*
**War between the States,** the American Civil War (1861–1865): so called generally in the South.
**war·ble** (wôr′b'l), *v.t.* [-BLED, -BLING], [< ONorm. Fr. *werbler* < Gmc.], 1. to sing with trills, quavers, runs, etc., as a bird. 2. to tell in song or verse. *v.i.* 1. to sing with trills, runs, etc. 2. to make a musical sound; babble, as a stream. 3. to yodel. *n.* 1. a song or carol. 2. an act of warbling. 3. a warbling sound; trill.
**war·bler** (wôr′blẽr), *n.* 1. a bird or person that warbles. 2. any of a family of small, insect-eating New World birds, many of which are brightly colored. 3. any of a family of small songbirds, found chiefly in the Old World.
**war bonnet,** a ceremonial headdress worn by some tribes of North American Indians.
**war cry,** 1. a name, phrase, etc. shouted in a charge or battle. 2. a phrase or slogan adopted by a party in any conflict, contest, election, etc.
**ward** (wôrd), *v.t.* [< AS. *weardian,* to keep, watch], 1. to turn aside; fend off: as, to *ward* off a blow. 2. [Archaic], to guard. *n.* 1. a guarding: now only in *watch and ward.* 2. a being under guard. 3. *a*) guardianship, as of a child or incompetent person. *b*) a person under the care of a guardian or court. *c*) a person under another's care. 4. each of the divisions of a jail, etc. 5. a division of a hospital, etc.: as, a maternity *ward.* 6. a division of a city or town, for purposes of administration, voting, etc. 7. a means of defense. 8. a defensive posture, as in fencing.
**-ward** (wẽrd), [< AS. *-weard, -weardes*], a suffix meaning *in a* (specified) *direction* or *course,* as in *backward*: also, in adverbial variants, **-wards.**
**Ward, Ar·te·mus** (är′ti-məs wôrd), (pseudonym of *Charles F. Browne*), 1834–1867; U.S. humorist.
**war dance,** a ceremonial dance performed by primitive tribes before battle or after victory.
**Ward·en** (wôr′d'n), *n.* [prob. < ONorm.Fr. *warder,* to keep], a type of winter pear: also **warden.**
**ward·en** (wôr′d'n), *n.* [< ONorm.Fr. <OFr. *gardein*], 1. a person who guards, or has charge of, something; keeper: as, a game *warden.* 2. the top administrative official of a prison. 3. in England, a governing officer in certain colleges, hospitals, etc. 4. in Connecticut, the chief executive of a borough. 5. in the *Episcopal Church,* etc., a churchwarden. 6. [Rare], a watchman. —**ward′en·ry** [*pl.* -RIES], **ward′en·ship′,** *n.*
**ward·er** (wôr′dẽr), *n.* 1. a watchman. 2. one who guards an entrance. 3. [Chiefly Brit.], a jail official in charge of prisoners. —**ward′er·ship′,** *n.*
**ward heeler,** a hanger-on of a politician, etc.; ward worker who solicits votes and performs small tasks for his party bosses: contemptuous term.
**ward·robe** (wôrd′rōb′), *n.* 1. a closet or cabinet for holding clothes. 2. a room where clothes are kept, as the costume room of a theater. 3. one's supply of clothes.
**ward·room** (wôrd′rōōm′, -room′), *n.* in a warship, living or eating quarters for all officers above ensign in rank, except the commanding officer.
**ward·ship** (wôrd′ship′), *n.* 1. guardianship; custody, as of a minor. 2. the condition of being a ward.
**ware** (wâr), *n.* [AS. *waru*], 1. anything made to sell. 2. *pl.* things for sale: also used collectively in the singular in compounds, as *hardware.* 3. pottery.
**ware·house** (wâr′hous′; *for v., usually* -houz′), *n.* 1. a building where wares, or goods, are stored; storehouse. 2. [Chiefly Brit.], a wholesale store or, sometimes, a large retail store. *v.t.* [-HOUSED, -HOUSING], to place or store in a warehouse.
**ware·house·man** (wâr′hous′mən), *n.* [*pl.* -MEN], a man who owns, manages, or works in a warehouse.
**war·fare** (wôr′fâr′), *n.* 1. the action of waging war; armed conflict. 2. conflict of any kind.
**war game,** 1. military tactical exercises in which maps, pins, etc. are used to represent terrain, troops, etc. 2. *pl.* practice maneuvers.
**war head,** the forward section of a torpedo, rocket bomb, etc., containing the explosive charge.
**war horse,** 1. a horse used in battle. 2. [Colloq.], a person who has engaged in many struggles.
**war·i·ly** (wâr′ə-li), *adv.* in a wary manner.
**war·i·ness** (wâr′i-nis), *n.* a being wary; caution.
**war·like** (wôr′līk′), *adj.* 1. fit for, fond of, or ready for war. 2. of or belonging to war. 3. threatening war.
**war·lock** (wôr′lok′), *n.* [AS. *wærloga,* a traitor, liar], [Scot. & Archaic], a sorcerer; wizard.
**warm** (wôrm), *adj.* [AS. *wearm*], 1. *a*) having or feeling a moderate degree of heat: as, *warm* weather, try to get *warm.* *b*) giving off heat: as, a *warm* fire. 2. *a*) overheated, as with exercise. *b*) such as to make one heated: as, *warm* work. 3. made of material which keeps body heat in: as, *warm* clothing. 4. characterized by lively disagree-

ment, as an argument. 5. ardent; enthusiastic: as, *warm* encouragement. 6. lively, vigorous, etc. 7. fiery; quick to anger. 8. *a*) genial; cordial; sincere: as, a *warm* welcome. *b*) sympathetic or loving. 9. suggesting warmth: yellow, orange, and red are *warm* colors. 10. newly made; fresh, as a scent or trail. 11. [Colloq.], close to discovering something. 12. [Colloq.], disagreeable: as, we'll make things *warm* for him. ***adv.*** so as to be warm. ***v.t. & v.i.*** 1. to make or become warm. 2. to make or become excited, ardent, lively, etc. 3. to make or become friendly, affectionate, etc.: as, *warmed* by the sight. ***n.*** [Colloq.], a warming or being warmed. **—warm up,** 1. to make or become warm. 2. to heat again, after cooling: said of food: also **warm over.** 3. in *sports,* to practice or exercise a while before going into a game, etc. **—warm′er,** ***n.*** **—warm′ish,** ***adj.*** **—warm′ly,** ***adv.*** **—warm′ness,** ***n.***

**warm-blood·ed** (wôrm′blud′id), ***adj.*** 1. having warm blood and a constant natural body heat: said of mammals and birds. 2. ardent; fervent; impetuous. **—warm′-blood′ed·ly,** ***adv.*** **—warm′-blood′ed·ness,** ***n.***

**warm·heart·ed** (wôrm′här′tid), ***adj.*** 1. kind; sympathetic; friendly. 2. loving; ardent. **—warm′-heart′ed·ly,** ***adv.*** **—warm′heart′ed·ness,** ***n.***

**warming pan,** a long-handled, covered pan for holding live coals: formerly used to warm beds.

**war·mon·ger** (wôr′muŋ′gẽr), ***n.*** a person or agency that advocates war or tries to bring about war. **—war′mon′ger·ing,** ***n. & adj.***

**Warm Springs,** a town in W Georgia: site of a foundation for treatment of poliomyelitis.

**warmth** (wôrmth), ***n.*** 1. the state or quality of being warm. 2. the natural heat of a living body. 3. mild heat. 4. excitement or vigor of feeling; ardor. 5. slight anger. 6. a warm effect obtained by using red, yellow, or orange.

**warm-up** (wôrm′up′), ***n.*** the act of practicing or exercising before going into a game, etc.

**warn** (wôrn), ***v.t.*** [AS. *wearnian*], 1. to tell (a person) of a danger, coming evil, etc. 2. to advise to be wary or cautious. 3. to notify in advance. 4. to give notice to (a person), as that he must stay (*off,* etc.). ***v.i.*** to give warning. **—warn′er,** ***n.***

**warn·ing** (wôr′niŋ), ***n.*** 1. the act of one that warns, or the state of being warned. 2. something that warns. ***adj.*** that warns. **—warn′ing·ly,** ***adv.***

**War of 1812,** a war (1812–1815) between the U.S. and Great Britain.

**War of (American) Independence,** the American Revolution.

**warp** (wôrp), ***n.*** [AS. *wearp* < *weorpan,* to throw], 1. *a*) a distortion, as a twist or bend, in wood. *b*) any like distortion. 2. a mental twist, quirk, bias, etc. 3. a rope run from a ship to a dock, etc., used to move the ship into position. 4. in *weaving,* the threads running lengthwise in the loom and crossed by the weft or woof. ***v.t.*** 1. to bend or twist out of shape. 2. to distort, pervert, bias, etc.: as, a *warped* mind. 3. to move, as a ship, by hauling on a line fastened to a dock, etc. ***v.i.*** 1. to become bent or twisted out of shape. 2. to turn aside from the natural or right course.**—warp′er,** ***n.***

**war paint,** 1. paint applied to the face and body by primitive tribes before going to war. 2. [Slang], *a*) ceremonial dress. *b*) women's cosmetics.

**war·path** (wôr′path′, -päth′), ***n.*** the path taken by North American Indians on a warlike expedition. **—on the warpath,** 1. at war, ready for war, etc. 2. actively angry; ready to fight.

**war·plane** (wôr′plān′), ***n.*** any airplane designed or built for use in war.

**war·rant** (wôr′ənt, wär′-), ***n.*** [< ONorm.Fr. < OFr. *garant* < OHG. *weren,* a warranty], 1. *a*) authorization, as by the law. *b*) justification for some act, belief, etc. 2. something that serves as a guarantee of some event or result. 3. a written authorization or certification for something; specif., *a*) authorization for the payment or receipt of money. *b*) in *law,* a writ authorizing an officer to make an arrest, seizure, search, etc. *c*) in *military usage,* the certificate of appointment to the grade of warrant officer. ***v.t.*** 1. *a*) to give (someone) authorization to do something. *b*) to authorize (the doing of something). 2. to serve as justification for (an act, belief, etc.). 3. *a*) to guarantee the quality, quantity, etc. of (goods) to (a purchaser). *b*) to guarantee to (the purchaser) that goods sold are as represented. 4. [Colloq.], to state with confidence: as, I *warrant* he'll be late. **—war′rant·a·ble,** ***adj.*** **—war′rant·a·ble·ness,** ***n.*** **—war′rant·a·bly,** ***adv.***

**war·ran·tee** (wôr′ən-tē′, wär′-), ***n.*** in *law,* a person to whom a warranty is given.

**war·rant·er** (wôr′ən-tẽr, wär′-), ***n.*** a person who warrants.

**warrant officer,** in the *U.S. armed forces,* an officer ranking above an enlisted man but below a second lieutenant or ensign, generally holding his office on a warrant instead of a commission.

**war·ran·tor** (wôr′ən-tôr′, wär′-), ***n.*** in *law,* a person who gives warranty.

**war·ran·ty** (wôr′ən-ti, wär′-), ***n.*** [*pl.* -TIES], [see WARRANT], 1. official authorization. 2. justification, as for an opinion or action. 3. in *law,* a guarantee; specif., a covenant by which the seller of real estate gives assurances of, and binds himself to defend, the security of the title.

**War·ren** (wôr′ən, wär′-), ***n.*** 1. a city in NE Ohio: pop., 60,000. 2. a city in SE Michigan: pop., 89,000.

**war·ren** (wôr′ən, wär′-), ***n.*** [< ONorm.Fr. < OFr. *warir,* to preserve < Gmc.], 1. an area in which rabbits breed or are raised. 2. any building or buildings crowded like a rabbit warren.

**Warren, Earl,** 1891– ; chief justice of the United States (1953– ).

**war·ri·or** (wôr′i-ẽr, wär′yẽr), ***n.*** [< ONorm.Fr. < *werrier,* to make war < *werre,* war], a fighting man; veteran soldier. **—war′ri·or·like′,** ***adj.***

**War·saw** (wôr′sô), ***n.*** the capital of Poland, on the Vistula River: pop., 1,095,000.

**war·ship** (wôr′ship′), ***n.*** any ship for combat use, as a battleship, destroyer, etc.

**wart** (wôrt), ***n.*** [AS. *wearte*], 1. a small, usually hard, tumorous growth on the skin. 2. a small protuberance on a plant. **—wart′y** [-IER, -IEST], ***adj.***

**wart hog,** a wild African hog with large incurved tusks, and a number of warts below the eyes.

**war·time** (wôr′tīm′), ***n.*** any period of war.

**war whoop,** a loud shout uttered, as by North American Indians, on going into battle, etc.

**War·wick** (wôr′wik), ***n.*** a city in E Rhode Island: pop., 69,000.

**war·y** (wâr′i), ***adj.*** [-IER, -IEST], [< archaic adj. *ware,* watchful + *-y*], 1. cautious; on one's guard. 2. characterized by caution. **—wary of,** careful of.

**was** (wuz, wäz, wəz), [AS. *wæs*], 1st and 3d pers. sing., pt., of **be.**

**wash** (wôsh, wäsh), ***v.t.*** [AS. *wæscan*], 1. to clean by means of water or other liquid, often with soap, etc. 2. to make clean in a religious or moral sense; purify. 3. to wet; moisten. 4. to flow over, past, or against: as, the sea *washed* the shore. 5. *a*) to soak out and carry (*off, out,* or *away*), as dirt, a dye, etc., with or as with water. *b*) to pick up and carry away: as, the *waves* washed the stick away. 6. *a*) to make by flowing over and wearing away substance: as, the rain *washed* gullies in the bank. *b*) to erode (with *out* or *away*): as, the flood *washed* out the road. 7. to be a cleansing agent for: as, that soap will *wash* silks. 8. to cover with a thin coating of paint or metal. 9. in *chemistry,* to pass (a gas) over or through a liquid in order to remove soluble matter. 10. in *mining,* to pass water through or over (earth, etc.) in order to separate (ore, precious stones, etc.). ***v.i.*** 1. to wash oneself or one's hands, face, etc.: often with *up.* 2. to wash clothes. 3. to undergo washing, especially without fading, etc. 4. to be removed by washing: as, the stain *washed* out. 5. to be worn or carried away by the action of water: as, the bridge had *washed* out. 6. [Brit. Colloq.], to withstand a test: as, his story won't *wash.* ***n.*** 1. the act or process of washing. 2. a quantity of clothes, etc. washed, or to be washed. 3. refuse liquid food; hogwash. 4. *a*) the rush or surge of water or waves. *b*) the sound of this. *c*) the eddy of water caused by a propeller, oars, etc. *d*) a slip stream. 5. erosion caused by the action of water. 6. silt, mud, etc. carried and dropped by running water. 7. earth from which ores, metals, etc. may be washed. 8. *a*) low ground which is flooded part of the time and partly dry the rest. *b*) a bog; marsh. 9. a thin coating of paint or metal. 10. any of various liquids for cosmetic or toilet use: as, a mouth *wash.* 11. weak liquor or liquid food. 12. [Colloq.], water, beer, etc. drunk after strong liquor; chaser. ***adj.*** that can be washed without damage: as, a *wash* dress. **—come out in the wash,** [Slang], to be revealed sooner or later. **—wash down,** 1. to clean by washing. 2. to follow (a bite of food, a meal, etc.) with a drink, as of water. **—wash one's hands of,** to disclaim any further responsibility for or interest in.

**Wash.,** Washington (State).

**wash·a·ble** (wôsh′ə-b'l, wäsh′-), *adj.* that can be washed without damage: said of fabric, dyes, etc.

**wash·board** (wôsh′bôrd′, wäsh′-), *n.* a board or frame with a ridged surface of metal, glass, etc., used for scrubbing dirt out of clothes.

**wash·bowl** (wôsh′bōl′, wäsh′-), *n.* a bowl or basin for use in washing one's hands and face, etc.: also **wash′ba′sin** (-bā′s'n).

**wash·cloth** (wôsh′klôth′, wäsh′-), *n.* a small cloth used in washing the body.

**wash·day** (wôsh′dā′, wäsh′-), *n.* a day when the clothes of a household are washed.

**washed-out** (wôsht′out′, wäsht′-), *adj.* 1. faded; having little color. 2. [Colloq.], tired; spiritless. 3. [Colloq.], tired-looking; pale and wan.

**washed-up** (wôsht′up′, wäsht′-), *adj.* 1. cleaned up. 2. [Colloq.], tired; exhausted. 3. [Slang], finished; discarded or dismissed as a failure.

**wash·er** (wôsh′ẽr, wäsh′-), *n.* 1. a person who washes. 2. a flat disk or ring of metal, rubber, etc., used to make a seat for the head of a bolt or for a nut, to lock a nut in place, to provide packing, etc. 3. a machine for washing something.

**wash·er·wom·an** (wôsh′ẽr-woom′ən, wäsh′-), *n.* [*pl.* -WOMEN], a woman whose work is washing clothes, etc. —**wash′er·man** [*pl.* -MEN], *n.masc.*

**wash goods,** washable fabrics or garments.

**wash·ing** (wôsh′iŋ, wäsh′-), *n.* 1. the act or process of a person or thing that washes. 2. *also pl.* *a*) liquid which has been used to wash something. *b*) matter removed by washing. 3. *a*) the process of carrying away matter by the flow of water. *b*) matter carried away by this action. 4. clothes, etc. washed or to be washed, especially in one batch. *adj.* of, for, or used in washing.

**washing machine,** a machine for washing clothes, etc., by moving or tumbling them through suds.

**washing soda,** a crystalline form of sodium carbonate, used in washing.

**Wash·ing·ton** (wôsh′iŋ-tən, wäsh′-), *n.* 1. a Northwestern State of the U.S.: area, 68,192 sq. mi.; pop., 2,853,000; capital, Olympia: abbrev. **Wash., W.** 2. the capital of the U.S., coextensive with the District of Columbia: pop., 764,000 (metropolitan area, 2,002,000): also **Washington, D.C.** —**Wash′ing·to′ni·an** (-tō′ni-ən), *adj. & n.*

**Wash·ing·ton, Book·er Tal·ia·ferro** (book′ẽr täl′ə-vẽr wôsh′iŋ-tən, wäsh′-), 1856–1915; American Negro educator and author.

**Washington, George,** 1732–1799; first president of the U.S. (1789–1797); commander in chief of the colonial armies in the American Revolution.

**wash·out** (wôsh′out′, wäsh′-), *n.* 1. the washing away of soil, rocks, etc. by a strong flow of water. 2. a hole made by such washing away, as in a road. 3. [Slang], a complete failure.

**wash·rag** (wôsh′rag′, wäsh′-), *n.* a washcloth.

**wash·room** (wôsh′rōōm′, wäsh′room′), *n.* 1. a room for washing. 2. a rest-room.

**wash·stand** (wôsh′stand′, wäsh′-), *n.* 1. a table holding a bowl and pitcher, etc., for washing the face and hands. 2. a plumbing fixture consisting of a washbowl with water faucets and a drain.

**wash·tub** (wôsh′tub′, wäsh′-), *n.* a tub for washing clothes, etc.: often, a stationary metal tub fitted with water faucets and a drain.

**wash·wom·an** (wôsh′woom′ən, wäsh′-), *n.* [*pl.* -WOMEN], a washerwoman.

**wash·y** (wôsh′i, wäsh′i), *adj.* [-IER, -IEST], 1. watery; diluted. 2. insipid; feeble.

**was·n't** (wuz′'nt, wäz′-), was not.

**WASP, Wasp** (wäsp, wôsp), *n.* a white Anglo-Saxon Protestant.

**wasp** (wäsp, wôsp), *n.* [AS. *wæsp*], 1. a winged insect with a slender body, biting mouth parts, and, in the females and workers, a vicious sting. 2. a waspish person. —**wasp′like′,** **wasp′y** [-IER, -IEST], *adj.*

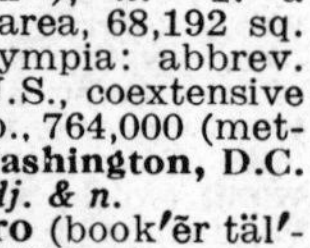

WASP (cicada killer, 1 1/5 in. long)

**wasp·ish** (wäsp′ish, wôsp′-), *adj.* 1. of or like a wasp. 2. having a slender waist. 3. bad-tempered; snappish. —**wasp′ish·ly,** *adv.* —**wasp′ish·ness,** *n.*

**wasp waist,** a very slender or pinched-in waist. —**wasp′-waist′ed,** *adj.*

**was·sail** (wäs′'l, was′'l, wäs′āl), *n.* [< ON. *ves heill*, lit., be hearty], 1. a former toast in drinking healths. 2. the spiced ale, etc. with which such healths were drunk. 3. a festivity with much drinking. *v.i. & v.t.* to drink a wassail (to).

**Was·ser·mann test** (or **reaction**) (wäs′ẽr-mən), [< A. von *Wassermann* (1866–1925), G. physician], a test for syphilis by determining the presence of syphilitic antibodies in the blood serum.

**wast** (wäst; *unstressed* wəst), archaic 2d pers. sing., past indic. of **be**: used with *thou*.

**wast·age** (wās′tij), *n.* 1. loss by use, decay, etc. 2. the process of wasting. 3. what is wasted.

**waste** (wāst), *v.t.* [WASTED, WASTING], [< ONorm.Fr. *waster* < L. *vastare*, to lay waste], 1. to destroy; devastate, as land. 2. to wear away; use up. 3. to make weak or emaciated: said especially of disease, age, etc. 4. to use up or spend without need, profit, etc.; squander. 5. to fail to take advantage of: as, to *waste* an opportunity. *v.i.* 1. to lose strength, health, flesh, etc., as by disease (often with *away*). 2. to be used up or worn down gradually. 3. to be wasted, or not put to full or proper use. *adj.* 1. uncultivated or uninhabited, as a desert; wild; barren; desolate. 2. left over; superfluous: as, *waste* paper. 3. excreted from the body, as urine. 4. used to carry off or hold waste: as, a *waste* pipe. *n.* 1. uncultivated or uninhabited land, as a desert. 2. a desolate or devastated area. 3. a wasting or being wasted; specif., *a*) a squandering, as of money, time, etc. *b*) a failure to take advantage (*of* something). *c*) a gradual loss or decrease by use, wear, decay, etc. 4. useless matter or discarded material, as ashes, garbage, etc. 5. matter excreted from the body, as urine, etc. 6. refuse cotton fiber or yarn, used for wiping machinery, etc. —**go to waste,** to be or become wasted. —**lay waste,** to destroy; devastate. —**wast′er,** *n.*

**waste·bas·ket** (wāst′bas′kit, -bäs′-), *n.* a basket or container for waste paper or other discarded material: also **wastepaper basket.**

**waste·ful** (wāst′fəl), *adj.* 1. characterized by waste. 2. using more than is needed; extravagant. —**waste′ful·ly,** *adv.* —**waste′ful·ness,** *n.*

**waste·land** (wāst′land′), *n.* land that is uncultivated or barren: also **waste land.**

**waste·pa·per** (wāst′pā′pẽr), *n.* paper thrown away after use or as useless: also **waste paper.**

**waste pipe,** a pipe for carrying off waste water, sink drainage, excess steam, etc.

**wast·ing** (wās′tiŋ), *adj.* 1. desolating; destructive. 2. causing waste. 3. destructive to health.

**wast·rel** (wās′trəl), *n.* 1. one who wastes; esp., a spendthrift. 2. a good-for-nothing.

**watch** (wäch, wôch), *n.* [AS. *wæcce* < base of *wacian*, to wake], 1. the act or fact of keeping awake, especially in order to protect or guard. 2. *a*) close observation for a time, as to find out something. *b*) vigilant, careful guarding. 3. a person or group on duty to protect or guard. 4. the period of duty of a guard. 5. a small spring-driven timepiece carried in the pocket, worn on the wrist, etc. 6. in *nautical usage*, *a*) any of the periods of duty (usually four hours) into which the day is divided on shipboard. *b*) the part of the crew on duty during such a period. *v.i.* 1. to stay awake at night; keep vigil. 2. to be on the alert; keep guard. 3. to look; observe: as, most people just *watched*. 4. to be looking or waiting attentively: as, *watch* for your chance. *v.t.* 1. to guard. 2. to observe carefully and constantly. 3. to keep informed about. 4. to wait for and look for: as, *watch* your chance. 5. to keep watch over; tend. —**on the watch,** watching; on the lookout. —**watch out,** to be alert and on one's guard. —**watch′er,** *n.*

**watch·case** (wäch′kās′, wôch′-), *n.* the metal case, or outer covering, of a watch.

**watch·dog** (wäch′dôg′, wôch′-), *n.* 1. a dog kept to guard property. 2. any watchful guardian.

**watch fire,** a fire kept burning at night as a signal or for the use of those on guard.

**watch·ful** (wäch′fəl, wôch′-), *adj.* 1. alert; attentive. 2. characterized by vigilance. —**watch′ful·ly,** *adv.* —**watch′ful·ness,** *n.*

**watch·mak·er** (wäch′māk′ẽr, wôch′-), *n.* one who makes or repairs watches. —**watch′mak′ing,** *n.*

**watch·man** (wäch′mən, wôch′-), *n.* [*pl.* -MEN], a person hired to watch or guard, especially at night.

**watch meeting,** a religious service held on New Year's Eve: also **watch night.**

**watch pocket,** a small pocket, usually in a vest or trousers, for carrying a watch.

**watch·tow·er** (wäch′tou′ẽr, wôch′-), *n.* a high tower from which watch is kept, as for forest fires.

**watch·word** (wäch′wũrd′, wôch′-), *n.* 1. a password. 2. a slogan; motto.

**wa·ter** (wô′tẽr, wät′ẽr), *n.* [AS. *wæter*], 1. the colorless, transparent liquid occurring on earth as rivers, lakes, oceans, etc., and falling as rain: chemically a compound of hydrogen and oxygen, $H_2O$, it freezes at 32°F. (0°C.) and boils at 212°F. (100°C.). 2. *often pl.* a large body of water, as a river, lake, sea, etc. 3. water with reference to its depth, its surface, or its level: as, ten feet of *water*, above *water*, high *water*. 4. *pl.* the water of a mineral spring, etc. 5. any body fluid or secretion, as urine, saliva, tears, etc. 6. a solution of any substance, often a gas, in water: as, ammonia *water.* 7. *a*) the degree of transparence and luster of a precious stone: as, a diamond of the first *water.* *b*) degree of quality or conformity to type: as, an artist of the first *water.* 8. a wavy, lustrous finish given to linen, silk, etc., or to a metal surface. 9. in *finance*, an issue of capital stock which brings the face value of all the stock issued by a business to a figure higher than the actual value of its assets. ***v.t.*** 1. to give (an animal) water to drink. 2. to supply (soil, crops, etc.) with water, as by sprinkling, irrigating, etc. 3. to moisten, soak, or wash down with water. 4. to dilute with water. 5. to give a wavy luster to the surface of (silk, etc.). 6. in *finance*, to add to the total face value of (stock) without increasing assets to justify this valuation. ***v.i.*** 1. to fill with tears: said of the eyes. 2. to secrete or fill with saliva: as, his mouth *watered.* 3. to take on a supply of water. 4. to drink water: said of animals. ***adj.*** 1. of or for water. 2. in or on water: as, *water* sports. 3. growing in or living on or near water: as, *water* plants, *water* birds. 4. derived from, or operated by, water: as, a *water* wheel, *water* power. **—above water,** free from debt, worry, etc. **—by water,** by ship or boat. **—hold water,** to remain or prove sound, logical, etc.: as, the argument won't *hold water.* **—like water,** lavishly; freely: said of money spent, etc. **—make one's mouth water,** to create a desire or appetite in one. **—make (or pass) water,** to urinate. **—wa′tered,** ***adj.*** **—wa′ter·er,** ***n.*** **—wa′ter·less,** ***adj.***

**Water Bearer,** in *astronomy*, Aquarius.

**wa·ter-borne** (wô′tẽr-bôrn′, wät′ẽr-bōrn′), ***adj.*** 1. floating on water. 2. carried in a ship, etc.

**wa·ter·buck** (wô′tẽr-buk′, wät′ẽr-), ***n.*** [*pl.* -BUCK, -BUCKS; see PLURAL, II, D, 2], [< D. *waterbok*], an African antelope having lyre-shaped horns, that frequents streams or rivers.

**water buffalo,** any of several slow, powerful, oxlike draft animals native to Asia, Malaya, Africa, and the Philippine Islands.

**Wa·ter·bur·y** (wô′tẽr-ber′i, wät′ẽr-), ***n.*** a city in Connecticut: pop., 107,000.

**water chestnut,** 1. a water plant with small white flowers and nutlike fruit. 2. its fruit.

**water clock,** a mechanism for measuring time by the fall or flow of water; clepsydra.

**water closet,** 1. a small room with a bowl-shaped fixture in which to defecate or urinate, fitted with a device for flushing with water. 2. the bowl-shaped fixture.

**water color,** 1. a paint composed of a pigment mixed with water instead of oil. 2. (a) painting done with water colors. **—wa′ter-col′or,** ***adj.*** **—wa′ter-col′or·ist,** ***n.***

**wa·ter-cool** (wô′tẽr-kōōl′, wät′ẽr-), ***v.t.*** to keep (an engine, etc.) from overheating by circulating water around it, as in pipes or a jacket. **—wa′ter-cooled′,** ***adj.***

**water cooler,** a device for cooling water by passing it in a coil through ice or other refrigerant.

**wa·ter·course** (wô′tẽr-kôrs′, wät′ẽr-kōrs′), ***n.*** 1. a stream of water; river, brook, etc. 2. a channel for water, as a canal or stream bed.

**wa·ter·craft** (wô′tẽr-kraft′, wät′ẽr-kräft′), ***n.*** 1. skill in water sports, boating, etc. 2. a boat, ship, etc. 3. ships or boats collectively.

**water cress,** a plant of the mustard family, whose leaves are used in salads, etc.: it grows in water or wet soil. **—wa′ter-cress′,** ***adj.***

**water cure,** hydropathy or hydrotherapy.

**wa·ter·fall** (wô′tẽr-fôl′, wät′ẽr-), ***n.*** a steep fall of water, as of a stream, from a height.

**wa·ter·fowl** (wô′tẽr-foul′, wät′ẽr-), ***n.*** [*pl.* -FOWLS, -FOWL; see PLURAL, II, D, 1], a water bird, especially one that swims.

**water front,** 1. land at the edge of a stream, harbor, etc. 2. the part of a city or town on such land; wharf or dock area. **—wa′ter-front′,** ***adj.***

**water gap,** a break in a mountain ridge, with a stream flowing through it.

**water gas,** a poisonous mixture of hydrogen and carbon monoxide, made by forcing steam over hot carbon fuel, as coke, and used as a fuel gas, etc.

**water gate,** a floodgate.

**water gauge,** 1. a gauge for measuring the level or flow of water in a stream, etc. 2. a device, as a glass tube, that shows the water level in a tank, etc.

**water glass,** 1. a drinking glass; tumbler. 2. a glass water gauge. 3. sodium silicate or, sometimes, potassium silicate, usually dissolved in water to form a sirupy liquid used as an adhesive, as a preservative for eggs, etc. Also **wa′ter·glass′,** ***n.***

**water hole,** a dip or hole in the surface of the ground, in which water collects; pond; pool.

**water ice,** [Brit.], sherbet.

**wa·ter·ing** (wô′tẽr-iŋ, wät′ẽr-), ***n.*** the act of a person or thing that waters. ***adj.*** 1. that waters. 2. having water, as for animals. 3. [Chiefly Brit.], of or having mineral springs or resort facilities for bathing, boating, etc.: as, a *watering* place.

**watering pot,** a can with a spout, often having a perforated nozzle, for watering plants, etc.

**water jacket,** a casing holding circulating water, placed around something to be cooled or kept at a constant temperature; esp., such a casing around the cylinders of an internal-combustion engine.

**water jump,** a pond, ditch, etc. that a horse has to jump over, as in a steeplechase.

**water level,** 1. *a*) the surface of still water. *b*) the height of this. 2. water line (sense 1).

**water lily,** 1. any of various water plants having large, flat, floating leaves and showy flowers in many colors. 2. the flower of such a plant.

**water line,** 1. the line to which the surface of the water comes on the side of a ship or boat. 2. any of several lines parallel with this, indicating the degrees of submergence when the ship is fully or partly loaded, or unloaded. Also **wa′ter·line′,** ***n.***

**wa·ter-logged** (wô′tẽr-lôgd′, wät′ẽr-logd′), ***adj.*** 1. soaked or filled with water so as to be heavy and sluggish in movement: said of boats or floating objects. 2. soaked with water; swampy.

**Wa·ter·loo** (wô′tẽr-lōō′; *now often* wô′tẽr-lōō′), ***n.*** 1. a village in Belgium: scene of Napoleon's final defeat (1815). 2. any disastrous or decisive defeat. 3. a city in E Iowa: pop., 72,000.

**water main,** a main pipe in a system of pipes which carry water.

**wa·ter·man** (wô′tẽr-mən, wät′ẽr-), ***n.*** [*pl.* -MEN], 1. a person who works on or handles boats. 2. an oarsman. **—wa′ter·man·ship′,** ***n.***

**wa·ter·mark** (wô′tẽr-märk′, wät′ẽr-), ***n.*** 1. a mark showing the limit to which water has risen. 2. in *papermaking*, a mark in paper, produced by pressure of a projecting design, as in the mold. ***v.t.*** 1. to mark (paper) with a watermark. 2. to impress (a design) as a watermark.

**wa·ter·mel·on** (wô′tẽr-mel′ən, wät′ẽr-), ***n.*** 1. a large, seedy fruit with a green rind and juicy, pink or red pulp. 2. the vine on which it grows.

**water mill,** a mill whose machinery is run by water.

**water moccasin,** 1. a large, poisonous, olive-brown viper found along rivers and swamps of the southern U.S.: also called *cottonmouth.* 2. any of several harmless water snakes resembling this.

**water nymph,** in *Gr. & Rom. mythology*, a goddess having the form of a lovely young girl, supposed to dwell in a stream, pool, lake, etc.

**water of crystallization,** water that occurs in crystalline substances and can be removed by heat: the loss of water usually results in the loss of crystalline structure.

**water ouzel,** any of a group of water birds with thick plumage, related to the thrushes.

**water ox,** the water buffalo.

**water pipe,** a pipe for carrying water.

**water plant,** any plant living entirely below water or sending up stems to or above the surface.

**water polo,** a water game played with a round, partly inflated ball by two teams of swimmers.

**water power,** 1. the power of running or falling water, used to drive machinery, etc. 2. a fall of water that can be so used.

**wa·ter·proof** (wô′tẽr-prōōf′, wät′ẽr-), ***adj.*** that keeps out water; esp., treated with rubber, plastic, etc. so that water will not penetrate: said of fabric, a garment, etc. ***n.*** 1. waterproof material. 2. [Chiefly Brit.], a raincoat, etc. of waterproof material. ***v.t.*** to make waterproof.

**water rat,** 1. any of several European voles that live on the banks of streams, etc. 2. an American muskrat. 3. [Slang], a water-front thief.

**wa·ter·shed** (wô′tẽr-shed′, wät′ẽr-), ***n.*** 1. a ridge dividing the areas drained by different river systems. 2. the area drained by a river system.

**wa·ter·side** (wô′tẽr-sīd′, wät′ẽr-), ***n.*** land at the edge of a body of water. ***adj.*** of, located on, or living along the waterside.

**wa·ter-ski** (wô′tẽr-skē′, wät′ẽr-), ***v.i.*** [-SKIED, -SKIING], in water sports, to be towed on skilike boards by a line attached to a speedboat.

**water snake,** any of various nonpoisonous snakes living in fresh-water streams and rivers.
**wa·ter-soak** (wô′tẽr-sōk′, wät′ẽr-), *v.t.* to soak with water; saturate. —**wa′ter-soaked′,** *adj.*
**water spaniel,** either of two breeds of spaniel especially suited to retrieving game shot over water.
**wa·ter·spout** (wô′tẽr-spout′, wät′ẽr-), *n.* 1. a pipe or spout from which water runs. 2. a rotating, tubelike column of air full of moisture, extending downward from a storm cloud to a body of water.
**water sprite,** a spirit, nymph, etc. dwelling in or haunting the water.
**water table,** the level below which the ground is saturated with water.
**wa·ter·tight** (wô′tẽr-tīt′, wät′ẽr-), *adj.* 1. so snugly put together that no water can get in or through. 2. that cannot be misconstrued, defeated, nullified, etc., as an argument, plan, etc.
**water tower,** 1. an elevated tank used for water storage and for equalizing water pressure. 2. a firefighting apparatus that can be used to lift high-pressure hose, etc. to great heights.
**water vapor,** water in the form of a more or less diffused mist, especially when below the boiling point, as in the air: distinguished from *steam.*
**water wave,** a wave made in hair by moistening and setting it with a comb, and drying it with heat. —**wa′ter-wave′** [-WAVED, -WAVING], *v.t.*
**wa·ter·way** (wô′tẽr-wā′, wät′ẽr-), *n.* 1. a channel through or along which water runs. 2. any body of water on which boats, ships, etc. can travel.
**water wheel,** 1. a wheel turned by running water, as for power. 2. a wheel for lifting water.
**water wings,** a device, inflated with air, used to keep one afloat while learning to swim.
**wa·ter·works** (wô′tẽr-wũrks′, wät′ẽr-), *n.pl.* [often construed as sing.], 1. a system of reservoirs, pumps, etc. used to bring a water supply to a city, etc. 2. a pumping station in such a system.
**wa·ter·worn** (wô′tẽr-wôrn′, wät′ẽr-wōrn′), *adj.* worn or smoothed by the action of running water.
**wa·ter·y** (wô′tẽr-i, wät′ẽr-i), *adj.* 1. of or connected with water. 2. containing or full of water. 3. like water. 4. diluted; thin, weak, insipid, etc. 5. tearful. 6. in or consisting of water: as, a *watery* grave. 7. soft or soggy. —**wa′ter·i·ness,** *n.*
**watt** (wät, wôt), *n.* [after James *Watt*], a unit of electric power, equal to a current of one ampere under one volt of pressure.
**Watt, James** (wät, wôt), 1736–1819; Scottish inventor.
**watt·age** (wät′ij, wôt′-), *n.* amount of electric power (as needed to operate an appliance, etc.), expressed in watts, and arrived at by multiplying amperage by voltage.
**Wat·teau, Jean An·toine** (zhän än′twån′ vȧ′tō′; Eng. wä-tō′), 1684–1721; French painter.
**watt-hour** (wät′our′, wôt′-), *n.* a unit of electrical energy or work, equal to one watt acting for one hour: abbrev. **watt-hr.** (*sing. & pl.*).
**wat·tle** (wät′'l, wôt′'l), *n.* [AS. *watel*], 1. a woven work of sticks intertwined with twigs or branches, used for walls, roofs, etc. 2. [Brit. Dial.], a stick, twig, etc. 3. in Australia, any of various acacias. 4. a fleshy, often brightly colored flap of skin hanging from the throat of a cock, turkey, etc. *adj.* made of or roofed with wattle. *v.t.* [-TLED, -TLING], 1. to intertwine (sticks, twigs, etc.) so as to form an interwoven structure. 2. to construct, as a fence, by intertwining twigs, etc. 3. to build of wattle. —**wat′tled,** *adj.*
**watt·me·ter** (wät′mē′tẽr, wôt′-), *n.* an instrument for measuring in watts the power in an electric circuit.
**waul** (wôl), *v.i. & n.* wail, squall, or howl: also sp. **wawl.**
**Wave, WAVE** (wāv), *n.* [< *W*omen *A*ppointed for *V*oluntary *E*mergency *S*ervice], a member of the Women's Reserve of the U.S. Naval Reserve (**WAVES**).
**wave** (wāv), *v.i.* [WAVED, WAVING], [AS. *wafian*], 1. to move up and down or back and forth in a curving motion; sway to and fro: as, the flag *waves.* 2. to signal by moving a hand, arm, etc. to and fro. 3. to have the form of a series of curves: as, her hair *waves* nicely. *v.t.* 1. to cause to wave, as a flag. 2. to brandish, as a weapon. 3. *a*) to move or swing (something) as a signal. *b*) to signal (something) by doing this: as, we *waved* farewell. *c*) to signal to (someone) by doing this: as, he *waved* me back. 4. to give an undulating form to (hair, etc.). *n.* 1. a curving swell moving along the surface of the ocean, etc. 2. [Poetic], water; esp., the sea, etc. 3. *a*) an undulation or series of undulations in or on a surface. *b*) a curve or series of curves, as in the hair, etc. 4. a motion to and fro or up and down, as that made by the hand in signaling. 5. something like a wave in action or effect; specif., an upsurge: as, a crime *wave.* 6. a periodic variation of an electric current or voltage. 7. in *physics,* any of the series of advancing impulses set up by a vibration, etc., as in the transmission of heat, light, sound, etc. —**wav′a·ble,** *adj.* —**wave′less,** *adj.* —**wave′like′,** *adj.* —**wav′er,** *n.*
**wave length,** in *physics,* the distance, measured in the direction of progression of a wave, from any given point to the next point characterized by the same phase.
**wave·let** (wāv′lit), *n.* a little wave; ripple.
**wa·ver** (wā′vẽr), *v.i.* [< ME. < *waven,* to wave], 1. to sway to and fro; flutter. 2. to show indecision; vacillate. 3. to become unsteady; falter. 4. to tremble: said of the voice, etc. 5. to flicker: said of light. *n.* a wavering. —**wa′ver·er,** *n.* —**wa′ver·ing·ly,** *adv.* —**wa′ver·y,** *adj.*
**wav·y** (wāv′i), *adj.* [-IER, -IEST], 1. having waves. 2. moving in a wavelike motion. 3. having curves; sinuous. 4. like or characteristic of waves. 5. wavering. —**wav′i·ly,** *adv.* —**wav′i·ness,** *n.*
**wax** (waks), *n.* [< AS. *weax*], 1. a plastic, dull-yellow substance secreted by bees for building cells; beeswax: it is used for candles, modeling, etc. 2. any plastic substance like this; specif., *a*) paraffin. *b*) earwax. *c*) sealing wax. *v.t.* to rub, polish, cover, or treat with wax. *adj.* made of wax. —**wax′er,** *n.* —**wax′like′,** *adj.*
**wax** (waks), *v.i.* [WAXED, WAXED or *poetic* WAXEN, WAXING], [< AS. *weaxan,* to grow], 1. to increase in strength, size, etc. 2. to become gradually full: said of the moon. 3. to become: as, *wax* old.
**wax bean,** a variety of string bean with long, edible, yellow pods: also called *butter bean.*
**wax·ber·ry** (waks′ber′i), *n.* [*pl.* -RIES], 1. a shrub with showy white berries. 2. the bayberry.
**wax·en** (wak′s'n), *adj.* 1. made of, or covered with, wax. 2. like wax, as in being white, soft, plastic, impressionable, etc.
**wax myrtle,** any of various shrubs or trees having grayish berries coated with a waxy substance used for candles; bayberry.
**wax palm,** either of two South American palm trees yielding a wax used in making candles.
**wax paper,** a kind of paper made moistureproof by a wax, or paraffin, coating: also **waxed paper.**
**wax·weed** (waks′wēd′), *n.* a small plant with sticky, hairy stems and purple flowers.
**wax·wing** (waks′wiŋ′), *n.* any of a group of birds with silky-brown plumage, a showy crest, and scarlet spines, suggesting sealing wax, at the ends of the secondary quill feathers.
**wax·work** (waks′wũrk′), *n.* work, as a figure or figures, made of wax. —**wax′work′er,** *n.*
**wax·works** (waks′wũrks′), *n.pl.* [construed as sing.], an exhibition of wax figures.
**wax·y** (wak′si), *adj.* [-IER, -IEST], 1. full of, covered with, or made of wax. 2. like wax in nature or appearance. —**wax′i·ness,** *n.*
**way** (wā), *n.* [< AS. *weg*], 1. a road, street, path, etc. 2. *a*) room for passing; an opening, as in a crowd. *b*) freedom of action or opportunity. 3. a route from one place to another. 4. movement along a certain route, etc.: as, lead the *way.* 5. course or habits of life: as, fall into evil *ways.* 6. a method of doing something. 7. a customary or characteristic manner of living, acting, etc.: as, I have learned their *ways.* 8. manner; style. 9. progress; movement, as of a boat: as, under *way*: also sp. **weigh.** 10. distance: as, a long *way* off: also [Colloq.], **ways.** 11. direction of movement, etc.: as, go this *way.* 12. respect; particular: as, in some *ways* you are right. 13. wish; will: as, to have one's *way.* 14. range, as of experience: as, that never came my *way.* 15. *pl.* a timber framework on which a ship is built and from which it slides in launching. 16. [Colloq.], a state or condition: as, he is in a bad *way.* 17. [Colloq.], a district; locality: as, out our *way.* *adv.* [Colloq.], away; far: as, *way* behind. —**by the way,** 1. incidentally. 2. on or beside the way. —**by way of,** 1. passing through; via. 2. as a way, method, etc. of. —**come one's way,** to come to one. —**give way,** 1. to withdraw; yield. 2. to break down. —**give way to,** yield to. —**go out of the** (or one's) **way,** to inconvenience oneself. —**in the way,** in such a position as to obstruct, hinder, etc. —**make one's way,** 1. to proceed. 2. to advance in life. —**make way,** to clear a passage. —**out of the way,** 1. in a position so as not to hinder, etc. 2. disposed of. 3. (put) to death. 4. not on the right or usual route. 5. *a*) improper; amiss. *b*) unusual. —**pave the way for,** to prepare for. —**take one's way,** to go. —**under way,** 1. moving; advancing. 2. in

*nautical usage,* making headway: said of a boat: also **under weigh.**
**way·bill** (wā′bil′), *n.* a list of goods and shipping instructions, sent with goods in transit.
**way·far·er** (wā′fâr′ẽr), *n.* a person who travels by road, especially on foot; traveler.
**way·far·ing** (wā′fâr′iŋ), *adj. & n.* traveling, especially on foot.
**way·lay** (wā′lā′), *v.t.* [-LAID (-lād′), -LAYING], 1. to lie in wait for and attack; ambush. 2. to wait for and accost by surprise. —**way′lay′er,** *n.*
**Wayne, Anthony** (wān), 1745–1796; American Revolutionary general: called *Mad Anthony Wayne.*
**-ways** (wāz), [*way* + adv. genit. *-s*], a suffix used to form adverbs, meaning *in a* (specified) *direction, position,* or *manner,* as in *endways.*
**ways and means,** 1. methods and resources at the disposal of a person, company, etc. 2. methods of raising money, as for government.
**way·side** (wā′sīd′), *n.* the edge of a road. *adj.* on, near, or along the side of a road.
**way station,** a small railroad station between more important ones.
**way train,** a train that stops at all stations on the line; local.
**way·ward** (wā′wẽrd), *adj.* [see AWAY & -WARD], 1. insistent upon having one's own way; willful, disobedient, perverse, etc. 2. unpredictable; erratic. —**way′ward·ly,** *adv.* —**way′ward·ness,** *n.*
**way·worn** (wā′wôrn′, -wōrn′), *adj.* tired from traveling.
**W.C.T.U.,** Woman's Christian Temperance Union.
**we** (wē; *unstressed* wi), *pron.* [for *sing.* see I], [AS.], the persons speaking or writing: sometimes used by a person in referring to several persons including himself, or by a king, author, editor, etc. in referring to himself. *We* is the nominative case form, *us* the objective, *our* and *ours* the possessive, and *ourselves* the intensive and reflexive, of the first personal plural pronoun.
**weak** (wēk), *adj.* [< ON. *veikr*], 1. lacking in physical strength or soundness; frail, feeble, etc.: as, *weak* from illness, *weak* muscles. 2. not strong in competition: as, a *weak* team. 3. lacking in moral strength or firmness of character. 4. lacking in mental power. 5. lacking force, power, effectiveness, or authority: as, *weak* discipline. 6. lacking in strength of material; easily torn, broken, etc.: as, a *weak* rail. 7. suggesting moral or physical weakness: as, *weak* features. 8. lacking in volume, intensity, etc.: as, a *weak* voice. 9. lacking in the proper strength of some ingredient: as, *weak* tea. 10. poor or deficient in something specified: as, *weak* in grammar. 11. *a*) unconvincing: as, a *weak* argument. *b*) faulty: as, *weak* logic. 12. in *grammar,* inflected by the addition of a suffix such as *-ed* or *-d* rather than by an internal vowel change: said of regular verbs. 13. in *phonetics,* unstressed or lightly stressed. 14. in *prosody,* designating or of a verse ending in which the stress falls on a word or syllable that is normally unstressed.
**weak·en** (wē′kən), *v.t. & v.i.* to make or become weak or weaker. —**weak′en·er,** *n.*
**weak·fish** (wēk′fish′), *n.* [*pl.* see FISH], [< obs. D. < *week,* soft + *visch,* a fish], any of several ocean fishes used for food, especially a species common off the Atlantic coast of the U.S.
**weak-kneed** (wēk′nēd′), *adj.* 1. having weak knees. 2. lacking in courage, firmness, etc.; timid.
**weak·ling** (wēk′liŋ), *n.* 1. a person or animal low in physical strength. 2. a person of weak character or intellect. *adj.* weak; feeble.
**weak·ly** (wēk′li), *adj.* [-LIER, -LIEST], sickly; feeble. *adv.* in a weak manner. —**weak′li·ness,** *n.*
**weak-mind·ed** (wēk′min′did), *adj.* 1. not firm of mind; indecisive. 2. feeble-minded. —**weak′-mind′ed·ly,** *adv.* —**weak′-mind′ed·ness,** *n.*
**weak·ness** (wēk′nis), *n.* 1. a being weak. 2. a weak point; fault. 3. an unreasonable fondness (*for* something). 4. something of which one is unreasonably fond.
**weal** (wēl), *n.* [form of *wale* (a ridge)], a mark or ridge raised on the skin, as by a blow; welt.
**weal** (wēl), *n.* [AS. *wela*], [Archaic], a sound or prosperous state; well-being; welfare.
**weald** (wēld), *n.* [AS.], [Poetic], 1. a wooded area; forest. 2. wild open country.
**wealth** (welth), *n.* [< ME.; cf. WEAL (welfare) & -TH], 1. much money or property; riches. 2. a large amount; abundance: as, a *wealth* of ideas. 3. valuable products, contents, etc.: as, the *wealth* of the oceans. 4. in *economics, a*) everything having economic value measurable in price. *b*) any useful material thing capable of being bought and sold.
**wealth·y** (wel′thi), *adj.* [-IER, -IEST], 1. having wealth; rich. 2. of or suggestive of wealth. 3. abundant: as, a home *wealthy* in love. —**wealth′i·ly,** *adv.* —**wealth′i·ness,** *n.*
**wean** (wēn), *v.t.* [AS. *wenian*], 1. to accustom (a child or young animal) gradually to take food other than by suckling. 2. to withdraw (a person) by degrees (*from* a habit, object of affection, etc.), as by substituting some other interest. —**wean′er,** *n.*
**wean·ling** (wēn′liŋ), *n.* a child or young animal that has just been weaned. *adj.* recently weaned.
**weap·on** (wep′ən), *n.* [AS. *wæpen*], 1. an instrument of any kind used for fighting. 2. any organ (of an animal or plant) so used. 3. any means of attack or defense: as, his best *weapon* was silence. —**weap′oned,** *adj.* —**weap′on·less,** *adj.*
**weap·on·ry** (wep′ən-ri), *n.* 1. the design and production of weapons. 2. weapons collectively; esp., a nation's stockpile of weapons of war.
**wear** (wâr), *v.t.* [WORE, WORN, WEARING], [AS. *werian*], 1. to carry on the person for covering, ornament, defense, etc., as a hat, a ring, a pistol, etc. 2. to have or show in one's appearance, etc.: as, she *wore* a smile. 3. to impair, diminish, etc. by constant use, friction, etc. (often with *away*). 4. to bring by use to a specified state: as, he *wore* his coat to rags. 5. to make by the friction of rubbing, flowing, etc.: as, to *wear* a hole in the rug. 6. to tire or exhaust. *v.i.* 1. to become impaired, diminished, etc. by constant use, friction, etc. 2. to hold up in use; last: as, that suit *wears* well. 3. to gradually reach a specified state: as, my courage *wore* thin. 4. to pass away gradually: said of time, as, the year *wore* on. *n.* 1. a wearing or being worn, as on the person. 2. things worn, or for wearing, on the body: as, men's *wear.* 3. the gradual impairment, loss, etc. from use, friction, etc. 4. the ability to resist such loss: as, there's much *wear* left in that coat. —**wear down,** 1. to decrease in thickness or height by use, friction, etc. 2. to tire or exhaust. 3. to overcome the resistance of by persistence. —**wear off,** to pass away or diminish by degrees. —**wear out,** 1. to make or become useless from continued use. 2. to tire out. —**wear′a·ble,** *adj.* —**wear′a·bil′i·ty,** *n.* —**wear′er,** *n.*
**wear** (wâr), *v.t.* [WORE, WORN, WEARING], [alt. < *veer* (to let out)], to turn (a ship) about by swinging its bow away from the wind. *v.i.* to turn about by having the bow swung away from the wind.
**wear and tear,** loss and damage caused by use.
**wear·ing** (wâr′iŋ), *adj.* 1. of or intended for wear. 2. causing wear or loss. 3. wearying.
**wearing apparel,** garments; clothing.
**wea·ri·some** (wêr′i-səm), *adj.* causing weariness; tiresome; tedious. —**wea′ri·some·ly,** *adv.*
**wea·ry** (wêr′i), *adj.* [-RIER, -RIEST], [AS. *werig*], 1. tired; worn out. 2. without further patience, tolerance, zeal, etc.: as, *weary* of singing. 3. tiring: as, *weary* work. 4. irksome; tedious. *v.t. & v.i.* [-RIED, -RYING], to make or become weary. —**wea′ri·less,** *adj.* —**wea′ri·ly,** *adv.* —**wea′ri·ness,** *n.*
**wea·sand** (wē′z′nd), *n.* [AS. *wæsand*], [Archaic], 1. the trachea, or windpipe. 2. the throat.
**wea·sel** (wē′z′l), *n.* [*pl.* -SELS, -SEL; see PLURAL, II, D, 1], [AS. *wesle*], 1. a cunning, agile, flesh-eating mammal related to the martens, with a long, slender body, short legs, and a long, bushy tail: they feed on rats, mice, birds, etc. 2. a cunning, sneaky person.

WEASEL (15 in. long including tail)

**weasel words,** equivocal or ambiguous remarks.
**weath·er** (we*th*′ẽr), *n.* [AS. *weder*], 1. the general condition of the atmosphere with regard to temperature, moisture, etc. 2. storm, rain, tempest, etc. *v.t.* 1. to expose to the action of weather, as for airing, drying, etc. 2. to wear away, discolor, etc. by exposure to the atmosphere. 3. to pass through safely: as, to *weather* a storm. 4. in *nautical usage,* to pass to the windward of (a cape, etc.). *v.i.* 1. to become discolored, worn, etc. by exposure to the weather. 2. to endure such exposure in a specified manner: as, it *weathers* well. *adj.* designating or of the side of a ship, etc. facing the wind. —**keep one's weather eye open,** [Colloq.], to be on the alert. —**under the weather,** [Colloq.], not feeling well; ill. —**weather through,** to pass safely through a storm, peril, etc. —**weath′ered,** *adj.*

**weath·er-beat·en** (we*th*ʹẽr-bēʹt'n), ***adj.*** showing the effect of weather, as by being stained, damaged, etc. or sunburned, roughened, etc.
**weath·er·board** (we*th*ʹẽr-bôrdʹ, -bōrdʹ), ***n.*** a clapboard. ***v.t.*** to nail weatherboards on (a roof or wall).
**weath·er-bound** (we*th*ʹẽr-boundʹ), ***adj.*** delayed or halted by bad weather, as a ship, airplane, etc.
**Weather Bureau,** a division of the Department of Commerce that compiles data on weather conditions over the U.S., on the basis of which weather forecasts are made.
**weath·er·cock** (we*th*ʹẽr-kokʹ), ***n.*** 1. a vane in the form of a cock, which swings to point the direction of the wind. 2. a fickle person.
**weath·er·glass** (we*th*ʹẽr-glasʹ, -gläsʹ), ***n.*** an instrument used to forecast the weather by showing changes in atmospheric pressure, as a barometer.
**weath·er·ing** (we*th*ʹẽr-iŋ), ***n.*** the erosive effects of the forces of weather on the surface of the earth, forming soil, sand, etc.
**weath·er·man** (we*th*ʹẽr-manʹ), ***n.*** [*pl.* -MEN], [Colloq.], a person who forecasts the weather.
**weather map,** a map showing weather conditions in a certain area at a given time by indicating barometric pressures, temperatures, etc.
**weath·er·proof** (we*th*ʹẽr-pro͞ofʹ), ***adj.*** that can withstand exposure to wind, rain, snow, etc. without being damaged. ***v.t.*** to make weatherproof.
**weather station,** a place where weather conditions are recorded and studied and forecasts are made.
**weath·er-strip** (we*th*ʹẽr-stripʹ), ***v.t.*** [-STRIPPED, -STRIPPING], to fit with weather strips.
**weather strip,** a strip of metal, felt, etc. used to cover the joint between a door or window and the casing, so as to keep out drafts, rain, etc.
**weather stripping,** 1. a weather strip. 2. weather strips collectively.
**weather vane,** a vane for showing in what direction the wind is blowing; weathercock.
**weath·er-wise** (we*th*ʹẽr-wīzʹ), ***adj.*** 1. skilled in predicting the weather. 2. skilled in predicting shifts of opinion, feeling, etc.
**weath·er·worn** (we*th*ʹẽr-wôrnʹ, -wōrnʹ), ***adj.*** weather-beaten.
**weave** (wēv), ***v.t.*** [WOVE or *rarely* WEAVED, WOVEN or WOVE, WEAVING], [AS. *wefan*], 1. *a*) to make (a fabric) by interlacing threads or yarns, as on a loom. *b*) to form (threads) into a fabric. 2. *a*) to construct in the mind. *b*) to form (incidents, etc.) into a story, poem, etc. 3. *a*) to interlace (twigs, reeds, etc.) so as to form something. *b*) to make in this way. 4. to twist (something) into or through: as, to *weave* flowers into one's hair. 5. to spin (a web): said of spiders, etc. ***v.i.*** 1. to do weaving. 2. to become interlaced. 3. to move from side to side or in and out. ***n.*** a method or pattern of weaving. **—weave one's way,** to go by turning and twisting from side to side.

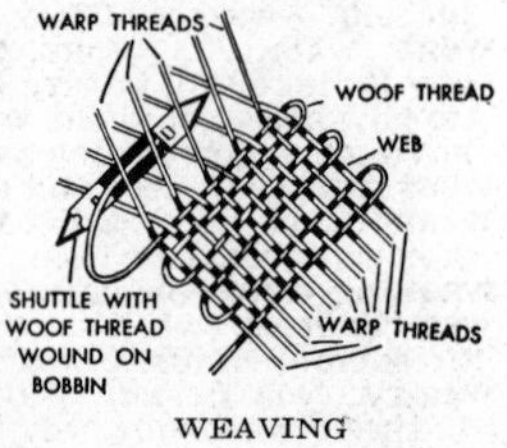

WEAVING

**weav·er** (wēvʹẽr), ***n.*** 1. a person who weaves; esp., one whose work is weaving. 2. a weaverbird.
**weav·er·bird** (wēvʹẽr-bũrdʹ), ***n.*** any of various finchlike Asian and African birds that weave elaborate nests of sticks, grass, etc.
**web** (web), ***n.*** [AS. *webb*], 1. any woven fabric; esp., a length of cloth on a loom or just taken off one. 2. the network spun by a spider or by the larvae of certain insects. 3. a carefully woven trap. 4. a complicated work of the mind, etc.: as, a *web* of lies. 5. anything like a web; network. 6. in *anatomy*, a tissue or membrane. 7. in *mechanics*, a thin plate between stiffeners, ribs, or other heavy structures. 8. in *zoology*, *a*) the vane of a feather. *b*) a membrane joining the toes of various water birds, water animals, etc. ***v.t.*** [WEBBED, WEBBING], 1. to join by a web. 2. to cover as with a web. **—webbed,** ***adj.*** **—webʹlikeʹ,** ***adj.***
**web·bing** (webʹiŋ), ***n.*** 1. a strong fabric woven in strips and used for belts, in upholstery, etc. 2. a strong edging strip woven into rugs, etc. 3. a membrane uniting the toes, as of a duck or frog.
**web·by** (webʹi), ***adj.*** [-BIER, -BIEST], of, having the nature of, or like a web.
**We·ber, Karl Ma·ri·a von** (kärl mä-rēʹä fôn vāʹbẽr), Baron, 1786–1826; German composer.
**web·foot** (webʹfootʹ), ***n.*** [*pl.* -FEET], 1. a foot with two or more toes webbed. 2. a person, animal, or bird with webbed feet. **—webʹ-footʹed,** ***adj.***
**web·ster** (webʹstẽr), ***n.*** [< AS.], [Obs.], a weaver.
**Web·ster, Daniel** (webʹstẽr), 1782–1852; U.S. statesman and orator.
**Webster, Noah,** 1758–1843; U.S. lexicographer.
**Web·ste·ri·an** (web-stêrʹi-ən), ***adj.*** of Daniel or Noah Webster.
**web-toed** (webʹtōdʹ), ***adj.*** web-footed.
**wed** (wed), ***v.t.*** [WEDDED, WEDDED or WED, WEDDING], [AS. *weddian*], 1. to marry; specif., *a*) to take for one's husband or wife. *b*) to conduct the marriage ceremony for. 2. to unite: as, the project *weds* science and art. ***v.i.*** to become married.
**we'd** (wēd), 1. we had. 2. we should. 3. we would.
**Wed.,** Wednesday.
**wed·ded** (wedʹid), ***adj.*** 1. married. 2. of or arising from marriage: as, *wedded* bliss. 3. devoted: as, *wedded* to one's work. 4. united.
**wed·ding** (wedʹiŋ), ***n.*** [AS. *weddung*], 1. *a*) the act of becoming married. *b*) the marriage ceremony with its attendant festivities. 2. an anniversary of a marriage or the celebration of this.
**wedge** (wej), ***n.*** [AS. *wecg*], 1. a piece of wood, metal, etc. tapering to a thin edge that can be driven into a narrow opening: used to split wood, lift weights, etc. 2. anything shaped like a wedge: as, a *wedge* of pie. 3. any act that serves to open the way for a gradual change, intrusion, etc. ***v.t.*** [WEDGED, WEDGING], 1. to force apart as with a wedge. 2. to fix solidly in place by driving a wedge under, etc. 3. to crowd together or pack in (often with *in*). ***v.i.*** to push or be forced as or like a wedge. **—wedgeʹlikeʹ,** ***adj.*** **—wedgʹy,** ***adj.***
**wedg·ie** (wejʹi), ***n.*** [Colloq.], a style of women's shoe having a wedge-shaped piece under the heel and forming a solid sole, flat from heel to toe.
**Wedg·wood (ware)** (wejʹwoodʹ), [< J. *Wedgwood*, 18th-c. English potter], a fine English pottery, with delicate figures which are applied in a white, cameolike relief on a tinted background.
**wed·lock** (wedʹlok), ***n.*** [< AS. < *wed*, a pledge + *-lac*, n. suffix], the state of being married; matrimony.
**Wednes·day** (wenzʹdi), ***n.*** [< AS. *Wodnes dæg*, Woden's day], the fourth day of the week.
**wee** (wē), ***adj.*** [WEER (wēʹẽr), WEEST (wēʹist)], [< AS. *wege*], very small; tiny. ***n.*** [Scot. & Eng. Dial.], a little; esp., a short time: as, bide a *wee*.
**weed** (wēd), ***n.*** [AS. *weod*], 1. any undesired, uncultivated plant that grows in profusion so as to crowd out a desired crop, etc. 2. [Colloq.], *a*) tobacco: with *the*. *b*) a cigar. 3. something useless. ***v.t.*** 1. to remove the weeds from, as a garden. 2. to remove as useless, harmful, etc.: often with *out*. 3. to rid of useless or harmful elements. ***v.i.*** to remove weeds, etc. **—weedʹer, *n.*** **—weedʹless, *adj.*** **—weedʹlikeʹ, *adj.***
**weed** (wēd), ***n.*** [<AS. *wæde*, a garment], *pl.* black mourning clothes, as those worn by a widow.
**weed·y** (wēdʹi), ***adj.*** [-IER, -IEST], 1. full of weeds. 2. of or like a weed, as in rapid growth. 3. lean, lanky, ungainly, etc. **—weedʹi·ness, *n.***
**week** (wēk), ***n.*** [AS. *wicu*], 1. a period of seven days, especially one beginning with Sunday and ending with Saturday. 2. the hours or days of work in a seven-day period: as, to work a 40-hour *week*. **—week after week,** every week. **—week by week,** each week. **—week in, week out,** every week.
**week·day** (wēkʹdāʹ), ***n.*** 1. any day of the week except Sunday (or, in *Judaism*, Saturday). 2. any day not in the weekend.
**week·end, week-end** (wēkʹendʹ), ***n.*** 1. the period from Friday night or Saturday to Monday morning. 2. a house party held over this period. Also **week end.** ***adj.*** of or on a weekend. ***v.i.*** to spend the weekend (*at* or *in* a specified place).
**week·ly** (wēkʹli), ***adj.*** 1. of, for, or lasting a week. 2. done, happening, payable, etc. once every week. ***adv.*** once a week; every week. ***n.*** [*pl.* -LIES], a periodical published once a week.
**ween** (wēn), ***v.i.* & *v.t.*** [AS. *wenan*], [Archaic], to think; suppose; imagine.
**wee·nie, wee·ny** (wēʹni), ***n.*** [*pl.* -NIES], [Colloq.], a wiener.
**weep** (wēp), ***v.i.*** [WEPT, WEEPING], [AS. *wepan* < *wop*, outcry], 1. to shed tears, as in grief; cry; wail. 2. to lament or mourn (with *for*). 3. to drip or exude water or other liquid. ***v.t.*** 1. to weep for; lament: as, she *wept* her fate. 2. to shed (tears, etc.). ***n.*** *often pl.* a fit of weeping. **—weepʹer, *n.*** **—weepʹy, *adj.***
**weep·ing** (wēpʹiŋ), ***n.*** the act of one who or that which weeps. ***adj.*** 1. that weeps; tearful. 2. having graceful, drooping branches. **—weepʹing·ly, *adv.***
**wee·vil** (wēʹv'l), ***n.*** [AS. *wifel*], any of a large number of beetles whose larvae are very destructive to many crops, the various species attacking cotton,

fruits, grain, and nuts, and destroying plants and trees by boring. —**wee'vil·y, wee'vil·ly,** *adj.*

**weft** (weft), *n.* [<AS. *weft* < *wefan*, to weave], 1. in weaving, the woof. 2. something woven.

**weigh** (wā), *v.t.* [< AS. *wegan*, to carry], 1. to determine the weight of by means of a scale or balance. 2. to measure out, or apportion, by or as by weight. 3. *a*) to consider and choose carefully: as, *weigh* one's words. *b*) to ponder in the mind: as, *weigh* one plan against another. 4. to burden; bear down heavily upon (with *down*). 5. in *nautical usage*, to hoist, or lift (an anchor). *v.i.* 1. to have weight; esp., to have a specified weight: as, it *weighs* ten pounds. 2. to have significance, importance, etc. 3. to be a burden: as, the theft *weighs* on his mind. 4. to hoist anchor. —**weigh in,** 1. to weigh (a boxer, jockey, etc.) before or after a contest in order to verify his declared weight. 2. to be so weighed. —**weigh'a·ble,** *adj.*

**weigh** (wā), *n.* way: a popular variant in the phrase *under way*, progressing.

**weight** (wāt), *n.* [AS. (*ge*)*wiht*], 1. a quantity weighing a definite amount: as, a ten-pound *weight* of lead. 2. heaviness; attraction of a material body by gravitational pull toward the center of the earth. 3. amount of heaviness: as, the *weight* of an egg. 4. *a*) any unit of heaviness. *b*) any system of such units: as, troy *weight*. *c*) a piece of metal, wood, etc. of a specific standard heaviness, used on a scale, etc. in weighing. 5. any block or mass used for its heaviness; specif., *a*) one used to hold light things down: as, a paper *weight*. *b*) one of a particular heaviness, lifted as an athletic exercise. 6. a burden, as of responsibility or sorrow. 7. importance or consequence: as, a matter of great *weight*. 8. influence, power, etc.: as, he threw his *weight* against us. 9. the relative heaviness of a garment: as, a suit of summer *weight*. 10. any of the classifications into which boxers and wrestlers are placed according to how much they weigh. *v.t.* 1. to add weight to. 2. to burden; oppress. —**by weight,** as determined by weighing. —**carry weight,** to be important, influential, etc. —**pull one's weight,** to do one's share.

**weight·less** (wāt'lis), *adj.* having little or no apparent weight; specif., lacking acceleration of gravity, as a satellite in earth orbit when the gravitational pull of the earth is counterbalanced by the centrifugal force imparted by the initial rocket blast. —**weight'less·ness,** *n.*

**weight·y** (wāt'i), *adj.* [-IER, -IEST], 1. very heavy. 2. burdensome; oppressive. 3. of great significance; serious. 4. of great influence or importance. —**weight'i·ly,** *adv.* —**weight'i·ness,** *n.*

**weir** (wêr), *n.* [AS. *wer*], 1. a low dam built in a river to back up or divert water, as for a mill. 2. a brushwood or stake fence built in a stream, channel, etc., for catching fish.

**weird** (wêrd), *adj.* [ult. < AS. *wyrd*, fate], 1. suggestive of ghosts, or other supernatural things; eerie. 2. [Colloq.], queer; unusual. 3. [Archaic], of fate or destiny. —**weird'ly,** *adv.* —**weird'ness,** *n.*

**Welch** (welch, welsh), *adj.* & *n.* Welsh.

**welch** (welch, welsh), *v.t.* & *v.i.* [Slang], to welsh.

**wel·come** (wel'kəm), *adj.* [< AS. *wilcuma*, a welcome guest < *wil-*, pleasure + *cuma*, a comer], 1. gladly received: as, a *welcome* guest. 2. agreeable or gratifying: as, *welcome* news. 3. freely permitted or invited (to use): as, you are *welcome* to (use) my car. 4. under no obligation: in *you're welcome*, a conventional response to thanks. *n.* an act or expression of welcoming: as, a hearty *welcome*. *interj.* you are welcome: an expression of cordial greeting. *v.t.* [-COMED, -COMING], 1. to greet with pleasure, etc. 2. to receive with pleasure, etc.: as, to *welcome* criticism. —**bid welcome,** to receive with expressions of hospitality. —**wear out one's welcome,** to come so often or stay so long that one is no longer welcome. —**wel'come·ly,** *adv.* —**wel'come·ness,** *n.* —**wel'com·er,** *n.*

**weld** (weld), *v.t.* [< *well* (to boil)], 1. to unite (pieces of metal) by heating until fused or until soft enough to hammer or press together. 2. to bring into close union. *v.i.* to be welded or capable of being welded. *n.* 1. a welding. 2. the joint formed by welding. —**weld'a·ble,** *adj.* —**weld'er,** *n.*

**wel·fare** (wel'fâr'), *n.* [< ME. *wel*, well + *fare* < AS. < *faran*, to fare], 1. condition of health, happiness, and prosperity; well-being. 2. welfare work. 3. those government agencies which grant aid to the poor, the unemployed, etc. —**on welfare,** receiving government aid because of poverty, etc.

**welfare state,** a state, or nation, in which the welfare of its citizens is promoted largely by the government rather than by private institutions.

**welfare work,** the organized effort of a community or group to improve the living conditions and standards of its members. —**welfare worker.**

**wel·kin** (wel'kin), *n.* [< AS. *wolcen*], [Archaic or Poetic], the curved vault of the sky.

**well** (wel), *n.* [< AS. *wella* < base of *weallan*, to boil up], 1. a natural spring and pool. 2. a deep hole sunk into the earth to get water, gas, oil, etc. 3. a source of abundant supply: as, a *well* of information. 4. a shaft, etc. resembling a well; specif., *a*) an open shaft in a building for a staircase. *b*) an elevator shaft. *c*) in *nautical usage*, an enclosure for the pumps in the hold of a ship. 5. any of various containers, etc. for holding liquid, as an inkwell. *v.i.* to flow or spring as from a well; gush (often with *up*, *forth*, etc.). *v.t.* to pour forth; gush.

**well** (wel), *adv.* [BETTER, BEST], [AS. *wel*], 1. in a desirable or satisfactory manner: as, the affair ended *well*. 2. in a proper or friendly manner: as, treat him *well*. 3. skillfully; expertly: as, she sings *well*. 4. in an appropriate manner: as, spoken *well*. 5. prosperously: as, they lived *well*. 6. with good reason: as, you may *well* ask. 7. to a considerable degree: as, *well* advanced. 8. thoroughly: as, stir it *well*. 9. with certainty: as, you know perfectly *well* that he did it. 10. familiarly; closely: as, I know him *well*. 11. with good grace: as, he took the news *well*. *Well* is used in hyphenated compounds to mean *properly*, *thoroughly*, etc., as in *well-defined*, *well-worn*. *adj.* 1. suitable; proper: as, it is *well* that you came. 2. in good health. 3. favorable; comfortable: as, things are *well* with us. *interj.* an exclamation used to express surprise, agreement, resignation, etc., or merely to preface one's remarks. —**as well,** 1. in addition. 2. equally. —**as well as,** 1. just as much or as good as. 2. in addition to. —**well'ness,** *n.*

**we'll** (wēl, wil), 1. we shall. 2. we will.

**Wel·land Canal** (wel'ənd), a canal in Ontario, Canada, between Lake Erie and Lake Ontario.

**well-ap·point·ed** (wel'ə-poin'tid), *adj.* excellently furnished: as, a *well-appointed* office.

**well·a·way** (wel'ə-wā'), *interj.* [ME. *wei la wei*, lit., woe! lo! woe!], [Archaic], alas!: an exclamation of sorrow, etc.: also **well'a·day'** (-dā').

**well-bal·anced** (wel'bal'ənst), *adj.* 1. nicely balanced, adjusted, etc.; evenly proportioned: as, a *well-balanced* formula. 2. sane, sensible, etc.

**well-be·haved** (wel'bi-hāvd'), *adj.* behaving well; displaying good manners.

**well-be·ing** (wel'bē'iŋ), *n.* the state of being well, happy, or prosperous; welfare.

**well·born** (wel'bôrn'), *adj.* born of good family.

**well-bred** (wel'bred'), *adj.* showing good breeding; courteous and considerate.

**well-chos·en** (wel'chō'z'n), *adj.* chosen with care and judgment; proper; appropriate.

**well-con·tent** (wel'kən-tent'), *adj.* thoroughly pleased or satisfied.

**well-dis·posed** (wel'dis-pōzd'), *adj.* 1. suitably placed or arranged. 2. inclined to be friendly (*toward* a person) or receptive (*to* an idea, etc.).

**well·do·ing** (wel'dōō'iŋ), *n.* good or benevolent action or conduct. —**well'-do'er,** *n.*

**well-done** (wel'dun'), *adj.* 1. performed with skill. 2. thoroughly cooked: said of meat. *interj.* an exclamation of approval of another's action.

**well-fa·vored** (wel'fā'vērd), *adj.* handsome; pretty.

**well-fed** (wel'fed'), *adj.* plump; fat.

**well-found** (wel'found'), *adj.* properly and adequately equipped: as, a *well-found* ship.

**well-found·ed** (wel'foun'did), *adj.* based on facts, good evidence, or sound judgment.

**well-groomed** (wel'grōōmd'), *adj.* 1. carefully cared for, as a horse. 2. clean and neat.

**well-ground·ed** (wel'groun'did), *adj.* 1. having a thorough basic knowledge of a subject. 2. based on good reasons.

**well-heeled** (wel'hēld'), *adj.* [Slang], rich; wealthy.

**well-in·formed** (wel'in-fôrmd'), *adj.* 1. having thorough knowledge of a subject. 2. having considerable knowledge of many subjects.

**Wel·ling·ton** (wel'iŋ-tən), *n.* capital of New Zealand, on North Island: pop., 223,000.

**Wel·ling·ton** (wel'iŋ-tən), first Duke of, (*Arthur Wellesley*), 1769–1852; British general and statesman; defeated Napoleon at Waterloo (1815).

**well-in·ten·tioned** (wel'in-ten'shənd), *adj.* having or showing good or kindly intentions.

**well-known** (wel′nōn′), *adj.* 1. widely or generally known; famous. 2. thoroughly known.
**well-made** (wel′mād′), *adj.* 1. skillfully and soundly put together. 2. having a skillfully contrived plot: as, a *well-made* play.
**well-man·nered** (wel′man′ẽrd), *adj.* having or showing good manners; polite; courteous.
**well-mean·ing** (wel′mēn′iŋ), *adj.* having or showing good or kindly intentions.
**well-meant** (wel′ment′), *adj.* said or done with good intention.
**well-nigh** (wel′nī′), *adv.* very nearly; almost.
**well-off** (wel′ôf′), *adj.* 1. in a fortunate condition or circumstance. 2. prosperous. Also **well off.**
**well-pre·served** (wel′pri-zũrvd′), *adj.* in good condition or of good appearance, in spite of age.
**well-read** (wel′red′), *adj.* 1. having read much. 2. having a wide knowledge of books.
**Wells, H. G.** (welz), (*Herbert George Wells*), 1866–1946; English novelist and historian.
**well-spo·ken** (wel′spō′kən), *adj.* 1. speaking easily or graciously. 2. aptly spoken.
**well·spring** (wel′spriŋ′), *n.* 1. the source of a stream or spring. 2. a source of abundant supply.
**well-thought-of** (wel′thôt′uv′), *adj.* having a good reputation; of good repute.
**well-timed** (wel′tīmd′), *adj.* timely.
**well-to-do** (wel′tə-dōō′), *adj.* prosperous; well-off.
**well-wish·er** (wel′wish′ẽr), *n.* one who wishes well to another, or to a cause, movement, etc.
**well-worn** (wel′wôrn′, -wōrn′), *adj.* 1. much worn: much used. 2. overused; trite.
**Welsh** (welsh, welch), *adj.* of Wales, its people, their language, etc. *n.* the (Brythonic) Celtic language spoken in Wales. —**the Welsh,** the people of Wales.
**welsh** (welsh), *v.t.* & *v.i.* [Slang], 1. to cheat by failing to pay a bet or debt. 2. to evade (an obligation). Often with *on.* Also **welch.** —**welsh′er,** *n.*
**Welsh·man** (welsh′mən, welch′-), *n.* [*pl.* -MEN], a native of Wales.
**Welsh rabbit,** [prob., orig., a humorous usage], a dish of melted cheese, often mixed with ale or beer, served on crackers or toast: also, through faulty etymologizing, **Welsh rarebit.**
**welt** (welt), *n.* [ME. *welte*], 1. a strip of leather in the seam between the sole and upper of a shoe to strengthen the joining. 2. a strip of material at the edge of a garment to reinforce or trim it. 3. *a*) a ridge raised on the skin by a slash or blow. *b*) such a slash or blow. *v.t.* 1. to furnish with a welt. 2. [Colloq.], to beat severely.
**wel·ter** (wel′tẽr), *v.i.* [< MD. *welteren*], 1. to roll about or wallow. 2. to be soaked, stained, etc.: as, to *welter* in blood. *n.* 1. a tossing and tumbling. 2. a confusion; turmoil.
**wel·ter·weight** (wel′tẽr-wāt′), *n.* [prob. < *welt,* to thrash], a boxer or wrestler who weighs between 136 and 147 pounds. *adj.* of welterweights.
**Welt·schmerz** (velt′shmerts′), *n.* [G., world pain], a melancholy weariness of life.
**wen** (wen), *n.* [AS. *wenn*], a benign skin tumor, especially of the scalp.
**wench** (wench), *n.* [< ME. *wenchel,* child < AS. *wencel*], 1. a girl or young woman: derogatory or facetious term. 2. [Archaic], *a*) a female servant. *b*) a prostitute or loose woman.
**wend** (wend), *v.i.* [< AS. *wendan,* to turn], [Archaic], to go; journey. *v.t.* [Chiefly Poetic], to direct one's steps on; go: as, *wend* one's way.
**went** (went), pt. of **go.**
**wept** (wept), pt. and pp. of **weep.**
**were** (wũr; *unstressed* wẽr), [AS. *wæron*], the pl. and 2d pers. sing., past indicative, and the past subjunctive, of **be.**
**we're** (wêr), we are.
**were·n't** (wũrnt), were not.
**were·wolf** (wêr′woolf′, wũr′-), *n.* [*pl.* -WOLVES], [< AS. *wer,* a man + *wulf,* a wolf], in *folklore,* a person changed into a wolf, or one who can assume the form of a wolf at will: also sp. **werwolf.**
**wert** (wũrt, wẽrt), archaic 2d pers. sing., past indicative and subjunctive, of **be**: used with *thou.*
**Wes·ley, John** (wes′li, wez′-), 1703–1791; English clergyman; founder of Methodism.
**Wes·ley·an** (wes′li-ən, wez′-), *adj.* of John Wesley or the Methodist Church. *n.* a follower of John Wesley; Methodist. —**Wes′ley·an·ism,** *n.*
**Wes·sex** (wes′iks), *n.* 1. a former Anglo-Saxon kingdom in S England. 2. a corresponding section in modern England.
**west** (west), *n.* [AS.], 1. the direction to the left of a person facing north; direction in which sunset occurs (270° on the compass, opposite east). 2. a region or district in or toward this direction. 3. [W-], the Western Hemisphere or the Western Hemisphere and Europe; the Occident. 4. [W-], the Western Roman Empire. *adj.* 1. in, of, to, or toward the west. 2. from the west: as, a *west* wind. 3. [W-], designating the western part of a continent, country, etc. *adv.* in or toward the west. —**the West,** the western part of the U.S.; specif., the part west of the Mississippi.
**West Al·lis** (al′is), a city in Wisconsin, near Milwaukee: pop., 68,000.
**west·er·ly** (wes′tẽr-li), *adj.* & *adv.* 1. toward the west. 2. from the west. —**west′er·li·ness,** *n.*
**west·ern** (wes′tẽrn), *adj.* 1. in, of, or toward the west. 2. from the west. 3. [W-], of or characteristic of the West. *n.* a story, motion picture, etc. on the life of cowboys or frontiersmen in the western U.S. —**west′ern·most′,** *adj.*
**Western Church,** that part of the Catholic Church which recognizes the Pope as patriarch as well as pontiff and which follows the Latin Rite.
**west·ern·er** (wes′tẽr-nẽr), *n.* 1. a native or inhabitant of the west. 2. [W-], a native or inhabitant of the W part of the U.S.
**Western Hemisphere,** that half of the earth which includes North and South America.
**west·ern·ize** (wes′tẽrn-īz′), *v.t.* [-IZED, -IZING], to make western in character, habits, ideas, etc.
**Western (Roman) Empire,** the western part of the Roman Empire after its division (395 A.D.).
**Western Samoa,** a country in the South Pacific, consisting of two large islands and several small ones: area, 1,130 sq. mi.; pop., 141,000; capital, Apia.
**West Indies,** a large group of islands between the U.S. and South America: it is divided into the Bahamas, Greater Antilles, and Lesser Antilles. —**West Indian.**
**West·ing·house, George** (wes′tiŋ-hous′), 1846–1914; U.S. inventor and manufacturer.
**West Ir·i·an** (ir′i-ən), the W half of New Guinea, a province of Indonesia: a former territory (*Netherlands New Guinea*) of the Netherlands: area, 160,000 sq. mi.; pop., 896,000; capital, Kotabaru.
**West·min·ster Abbey** (west′min′stẽr), a Gothic church in London where English monarchs are crowned: burial place of many famous persons.
**west-north·west** (west′nôrth′west′; *nautical,* -nôr-), *n.* the direction halfway between due west and northwest (22°30′ north of due west). *adj.* & *adv.* 1. in or toward this direction. 2. from this direction.
**West Point,** a military post in SE New York, on the Hudson: site of the U.S. Military Academy.
**west-south·west** (west′south′west′), *n.* the direction halfway between due west and southwest (22°30′ south of due west). *adj.* & *adv.* 1. in or toward this direction. 2. from this direction.
**West Virginia,** an Eastern State of the U.S.: area, 24,181 sq. mi.; pop., 1,860, 000; capital, Charleston: abbrev. **W. Va.** —**West Virginian.**
**west·ward** (west′wẽrd), *adj.* & *adv.* toward the west: also **west′wards,** *adv.* *n.* a westward direction, point, or region.
**west·ward·ly** (west′wẽrd-li), *adj.* & *adv.* 1. toward the west. 2. from the west: as, a *westwardly* wind.
**wet** (wet), *adj.* [WETTER, WETTEST], [AS. *wæt*], 1. covered or saturated with water or other liquid. 2. rainy; misty: as, a *wet* day. 3. not yet dry: as, *wet* paint. 4. with or in water or other liquid: as, *wet* sanding. 5. permitting or favoring the manufacture or sale of alcoholic liquor. *n.* 1. that which makes wet; water or other liquid. 2. rain or rainy weather. 3. one who favors the manufacture or sale of alcoholic liquor. *v.t.* & *v.i.* [WET or WETTED, WETTING], to make or become wet (often with *through* or *down*). —**all wet,** [Slang], wrong; mistaken. —**wet′ness,** *n.* —**wet′ter,** *n.* —**wet′tish,** *adj.*
**wet·back** (wet′bak), *n.* [from the fact that many enter by swimming or wading the Rio Grande], [Colloq.], a Mexican agricultural laborer who illegally enters the U.S. to work.
**wet blanket,** a person or thing that dampens, or discourages, activity, enthusiasm, or pleasure.
**weth·er** (weth′ẽr), *n.* [AS.], a castrated male sheep.
**wet nurse,** a woman hired to suckle another's child. —**wet′-nurse′** [-NURSED, -NURSING], *v.t.*
**wet pack,** a type of bath, as for reducing a fever, in which the patient is wrapped in wet sheets.
**wet suit,** a closefitting, usually one-piece suit of rubber, especially of foam neoprene, worn by skin divers for warmth.
**we've** (wēv), we have.
**W. Gmc., W. Ger.,** West Germanic.
**whack** (hwak), *v.t.* & *v.i.* [echoic], [Colloq.], to strike

or slap with a sharp, resounding blow. *n.* 1. [Colloq.], *a*) a sharp, resounding blow. *b*) the sound of this. 2. [Slang], a share. 3. [Slang], an attempt; trial. 4. [Slang], proper condition or adjustment: as, out of *whack.* —**whack'er,** *n.*

**whack·ing** (hwak'iŋ), *adj.* [Colloq.], very large.

**whack·y** (hwak'i), *adj.* [-IER, -IEST], [Slang], wacky.

**whale** (hwāl), *n.* [*pl.* WHALES, WHALE; see PLURAL, II, D, 1], [AS. *hwæl*], a large, warm-blooded, fishlike sea mammal that breathes air and bears live young. *v.i.* [WHALED, WHALING], to hunt for whales. —**a whale of a,** [Colloq.], an exceptionally large, fine, etc. example of a (class of things).

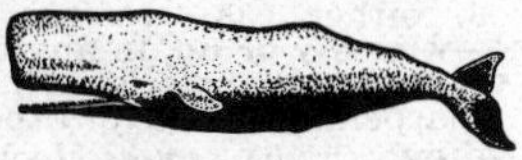

SPERM WHALE (63 ft. long)

**whale** (hwāl), *v.t.* [WHALED, WHALING], [var. of *wale* (to ridge)], [Colloq.], to beat; thrash.

**whale·back** (hwāl'bak'), *n.* something rounded on top like a whale's back; specif., a freight steamer with the bow and upper deck rounded.

**whale·boat** (hwāl'bōt'), *n.* a long rowboat, pointed at both ends to increase maneuverability.

**whale·bone** (hwāl'bōn'), *n.* 1. the horny elastic material that hangs in fringed sheets from the upper jaw of certain whales; baleen. 2. something made of whalebone, as a corset stay.

**whal·er** (hwāl'ẽr), *n.* 1. a whaling ship. 2. a man whose work is whaling: also **whale'man** [*pl.* -MEN].

**whal·ing** (hwāl'iŋ), *n.* the hunting and killing of whales for their blubber, whalebone, etc.

**wham·my** (hwam'i), *n.* [*pl.* -MIES], [Slang], a jinx; evil eye: usually in *put a* (or *the*) *whammy on.*

**whang** (hwaŋ), *v.t.* [echoic], to strike with a resounding blow; whack. *v.i.* to make a whanging noise. *n.* a whack.

**whap** (hwop), *v.i.* [WHAPPED, WHAPPING], [Dial. or Archaic], to whop.

**wharf** (hwôrf), *n.* [*pl.* WHARVES (hwôrvz), WHARFS], [AS. *hwerf,* a dam < base of *hweorfan,* to turn], a structure built at the shore of a harbor, river, etc. for ships to lie alongside, as during loading or unloading; pier; dock. *v.t.* 1. to bring to a wharf. 2. to unload or store on a wharf.

**wharf·age** (hwôr'fij), *n.* 1. the use of a wharf as for loading, unloading, or storing goods. 2. the charge for this. 3. wharves collectively.

**wharf·in·ger** (hwôr'fin-jẽr), *n.* [< earlier *wharfager* < *wharfage*], one who owns or manages a wharf.

**wharf rat,** a large brown rat found near wharves.

**Whar·ton, Edith** (hwôr't'n), (born *Edith Newbold Jones*), 1862–1937; U.S. novelist.

**what** (hwut, hwät; *unstressed* hwət), *pron.* [AS. *hwæt,* neut. of *hwa,* who], 1. which thing, event, etc.: used interrogatively as in asking about the nature of a thing (*what* is that object?) or in asking for a repetition of something said (you told him *what?*). 2. that or those which: used as a relative pronoun; specif., *a*) anything that: as, do *what* you will. *b*) the exact person or thing that: as, I'm not *what* I used to be. Also used elliptically for *what it is, what to do,* etc. (I'll tell you *what*). *adj.* 1. which or which kind of: used interrogatively or relatively: as, *what* man told you that? I know *what* books you want. 2. as much, or as many, as: as, take *what* men you need. 3. how great, surprising, etc.: in exclamations, as, *what* nonsense! *adv.* 1. to what degree? how? as, *what* does it help to complain? 2. partly: as, *what* with singing and joking, the time passed quickly. 3. how greatly, surprisingly, etc.: in exclamations, as, *what* tragic news! *conj.* that: in *but what,* but that, as, never doubt *but what* he loves you. *interj.* as exclamation of surprise, anger, etc.: as, *what!* no dinner? —**and what not,** and other things of all sorts. —**what for,** why? —**what have you,** [Colloq.], any similar thing: as, games, toys, or *what have you.* —**what if,** what would happen if; suppose. —**what's what,** [Colloq.], the true state of affairs.

**what·e'er** (hwət-er'), *pron.* & *adj.* [Poetic], whatever.

**what·ev·er** (hwət-ev'ẽr), *pron.* what: an emphatic variant; specif., *a*) which thing, event, etc.: used interrogatively, as, *whatever* can it be? *b*) anything that: as, tell her *whatever* you like. *c*) no matter what: as, *whatever* you do, don't hurry. *adj.* 1. of no matter what type, degree, etc.: as, make *whatever* repairs are needed, I have no plans *whatever.* 2. being who it may be: as, *whatever* man told you that, it isn't true.

**what·not** (hwut'not', hwät'-), *n.* a set of open shelves used for bric-a-brac, books, etc.

**what's** (hwuts, hwäts; *unstressed* hwəts), what is.

**what·so·e'er** (hwut'sō-er', hwät'-), *pron.* & *adj.* [Poetic], whatsoever.

**what·so·ev·er** (hwut'sō-ev'ẽr, hwät'-), *pron.* & *adj.* whatever: an emphatic form.

**wheal** (hwēl), *n.* [akin to AS *hwelian,* to suppurate], 1. a pustule; pimple. 2. a small, itching elevation of the skin, as from an insect's bite.

**wheal** (hwēl), *n.* [< *weal,* a wale; infl. by *wheal,* a pimple], a raised stripe on the skin; wale.

**wheat** (hwēt), *n.* [see PLURAL, II, D, 3], [AS. *hwæte*], 1. any of various cereal grasses having spikes filled with seeds: some have spikes with awns (*bearded wheat*) and others do not (*beardless,* or *bald, wheat*). 2. the seed of any of these grasses, used for making flour, cereals, etc.

**wheat·en** (hwēt''n), *adj.* 1. made of wheat or wheat flour. 2. of the pale-yellow color of wheat.

**whee·dle** (hwē'd'l), *v.t.* & *v.i.* [-DLED, -DLING], [prob. < G. *wedeln,* to wag the tail, hence to flatter], 1. to influence or persuade by flattery, begging, etc.; coax. 2. to get by wheedling. —**whee'dler,** *n.*

**wheel** (hwēl), *n.* [AS. *hweol*], 1. a solid disk, or a circular frame connected by spokes to a central hub, capable of turning on a central axis. 2. anything like a wheel in shape, movement, etc. 3. a device of which the principal element is a wheel or wheels; specif., *a*) a medieval, wheel-shaped instrument of torture. *b*) the steering wheel, as of a motor vehicle. *c*) [Colloq.], a bicycle. 4. *usually pl.* the moving, propelling, or controlling forces or machinery: as, the *wheels* of progress. 5. a turning movement. *v.t.* & *v.i.* 1. to move or roll on wheels or in a vehicle with wheels. 2. to turn, revolve, or rotate. 3. to turn in or as in a circular movement so as to change direction or course: often with *about.* —**at the wheel,** 1. steering a ship or motor vehicle. 2. directing activities. —**wheel of fortune,** the changes or vicissitudes of life. —**wheeled,** *adj.*

**wheel·bar·row** (hwēl'bar'ō), *n.* a shallow, open box for moving small loads, having a single wheel in front, two legs in back, and two shafts with handles for raising the vehicle off its legs and pushing it. *v.t.* to move in a wheelbarrow.

**wheel·base** (hwēl'bās'), *n.* in a motor vehicle, the distance in inches from the front axle to the rear axle: also **wheel base.**

**wheel chair,** a mobile chair for invalids, mounted on large wheels.

**wheel·er** (hwēl'ẽr), *n.* 1. a person or thing that wheels. 2. a wheel horse (sense 1). 3. something having a wheel or wheels: usually in hyphenated compounds, as, *side-wheeler.*

**wheel horse,** 1. the horse, or one of the horses, nearest the front wheels of a vehicle. 2. a person who works especially hard and effectively.

**wheel·house** (hwēl'hous'), *n.* a pilothouse.

**Wheel·ing** (hwēl'iŋ), *n.* a port in N West Virginia, on the Ohio River: pop., 53,000.

**wheel·wright** (hwēl'rīt'), *n.* a person who makes and repairs wheels and wheeled vehicles.

**wheeze** (hwēz), *v.i.* [WHEEZED, WHEEZING], [< ON. *hvaesa,* to hiss], 1. to breathe hard with a whistling, breathy sound, as in asthma. 2. to make a similar sound: as, the old organ *wheezed.* *v.t.* to utter with a sound of wheezing. *n.* 1. an act or sound of wheezing. 2. [Slang], a trite remark, joke, or gag. —**wheez'er,** *n.* —**wheez'ing·ly,** *adv.*

**wheez·y** (hwēz'i), *adj.* [-IER, -IEST], wheezing. —**wheez'i·ly,** *adv.* —**wheez'i·ness,** *n.*

**whelk** (hwelk), *n.* [AS. *wiloc*], any of various large marine snails with spiral shells, especially those used in Europe for food.

**whelk** (hwelk), *n.* [AS. *hwylca*], a pimple or pustule.

**whelm** (hwelm), *v.t.* [prob. a merging of AS. *-hwelfan,* to overwhelm, with *helmian,* to cover], 1. to submerge, cover, etc. 2. to overwhelm.

**whelp** (hwelp), *n.* [AS. *hwelp*], 1. the young of a dog or other flesh-eating animal, as of a lion, tiger, bear, wolf, etc. 2. a youth or child: a contemptuous usage. *v.t.* & *v.i.* to bring forth (young): said of animals and, contemptuously, of a woman.

**when** (hwen; *unstressed,* hwən), *adv.* [AS. *hwænne*], at what time?: used interrogatively and in indirect questions, as, *when* did it start? he asked *when* he should go. *conj.* 1. at what time: as, he told us *when* to eat. 2. at which time: as, he came at six, *when* the sun rose. 3. at which: as, now is the time *when* we must fight. 4. at the time that: as, *when* we were young. 5. as soon as: as, we will eat *when* he comes. 6. whenever: as, she cries *when* you scold her. 7. although: as, he's reading *when* he might be playing. 8. if: as, how can we finish, *when* you won't help? *pron.* what or which time: as, until *when* will you stay? *n.* the time or moment (*of* an event): as, the *when* and where of his arrest.

**when·as** (hwen-az′), *conj.* [Archaic], 1. when. 2. inasmuch as. 3. whereas.

**whence** (hwens), *adv.* [AS. *hwanan*], from what place, source, cause, etc.; from where: as, *whence* do you come? *whence* does he get his speed?

**whence·so·ev·er** (hwens′sō-ev′ẽr), *adv. & conj.* from whatever place, source, or cause.

**when·e'er** (hwen-er′, hwən-), *adv. & conj.* [Poetic], whenever.

**when·ev·er** (hwen-ev′ẽr, hwən-), *adv.* [Colloq.], when: an emphatic variant, as, *whenever* will you learn? *conj.* at whatever time; on whatever occasion: as, visit us *whenever* you can.

**when·so·ev·er** (hwen′sō-ev′ẽr), *adv. & conj.* whenever: an emphatic variant.

**where** (hwâr), *adv.* [AS. *hwær*], 1. in or at what place?: as, *where* is my hat? 2. to or toward what place?: as, *where* did he go? 3. in what situation?: as, *where* will we be if we lose? 4. in what respect?: as, *where* do I come into the matter? 5. from what place or source?: as, *where* did you find out? *conj.* 1. in or at what place: as, I know *where* they are. 2. in or at which place: as, we came home, *where* we had dinner. 3. in or at the place or situation in which: as, I am *where* I should be. 4. in whatever place, situation, or respect in which: as, there is never peace *where* men are greedy. 5. *a*) to or toward the place to which: as, we'll go *where* you go. *b*) to a place in which: as, I never go *where* I'm not wanted. 6. to or toward whatever place: as, I don't care *where* you go. *pron.* 1. the place or situation in, at, or to which: as, it is a mile from *where* you live. 2. what or which place: as, *where* are you from? *n.* the place (*of* an event): as, I know the *where* of the outbreak.

**where·a·bouts** (hwâr′ə-bouts′), *adv.* near or at what place? where? *n.* the place where a person or thing is: as, do you know his *whereabouts?*

**where·as** (hwâr-az′), *conj.* 1. in view of the fact that: used in the preamble to a formal document. 2. while on the contrary: as, she is slender, *whereas* he is stout. *n.* [*pl.* -ASES], a statement beginning with "whereas."

**where·at** (hwâr-at′), *adv.* [Archaic], at what?: as, *whereat* was he angry? *conj.* at which; upon which: as, he turned to go, *whereat* she began to weep.

**where·by** (hwâr-bī′), *adv.* 1. by which: as, a device *whereby* to make money. 2. by what? how?

**where·e'er** (hwâr-er′), *adv. & conj.* [Poetic], wherever.

**where·fore** (hwâr′fôr′, -fōr′), *adv.* 1. for what reason or purpose? why?: as, *wherefore* did you go? 2. for which: as, the reason *wherefore* we have met. *conj.* because of which; therefore: as, we had fewer men, *wherefore* we lost. *n.* the reason; cause.

**where·from** (hwâr-frum′, -from′), *adv.* whence.

**where·in** (hwâr-in′), *adv.* 1. in what?: as, *wherein* was I wrong? 2. in which: as, the bed *wherein* he lay.

**where·of** (hwâr-uv′, -ov′), *adv.* of what, which, or whom.

**where·on** (hwâr-on′), *adv.* 1. on what? 2. on which: as, the hill *whereon* we stand.

**where·so·e'er** (hwâr′sō-er′), *adv. & conj.* [Poetic], wheresoever.

**where·so·ev·er** (hwâr′sō-ev′ẽr), *adv. & conj.* wherever: an emphatic variant.

**where·to** (hwâr-too′), *adv.* 1. to what? toward what place, direction, or end? 2. to which.

**where·up·on** (hwâr′ə-pon′), *adv.* upon what or upon which? whereon? *conj.* at which; upon which: as, I told the story, *whereupon* they laughed.

**wher·ev·er** (hwâr-ev′ẽr), *adv.* [Colloq.], where: an emphatic variant, as, *wherever* did you hear that? *conj.* in, at, or to whatever place or situation: as, he thinks of us *wherever* he is.

**where·with** (hwâr-with′, -with′), *adv.* with which: as, I have not the money *wherewith* to pay him. *pron.* that with which: as, they shall have *wherewith* to build. *n.* [Rare], wherewithal.

**where·with·al** (hwâr′with-ôl′), *n.* that with which something can be done; necessary means, especially money: as, I haven't the *wherewithal* to buy it. *adv.* (hwâr′with-ôl′), [Archaic], wherewith.

**wher·ry** (hwer′i), *n.* [*pl.* -RIES], [? < *whir*, with idea of fast movement], 1. a light rowboat used on rivers. 2. a racing scull for one person. 3. [Brit.], a large, broad, but light barge. *v.t.* [-RIED, -RYING], to transport in a wherry.

**whet** (hwet), *v.t.* [WHETTED, WHETTING], [< AS. < *hwæt*, keen], 1. to sharpen by rubbing or grinding, as the edge of a knife or tool; hone. 2. to stimulate: as, to *whet* the appetite. *n.* 1. an act of whetting. 2. something that whets. —**whet′ter,** *n.*

**wheth·er** (hweth′ẽr), *conj.* [AS. *hwæther*], 1. if it be the case or fact that: as, he asked *whether* I would help. 2. in case; in either case that: used to introduce alternatives: as, *whether* it rains or snows. 3. either: as, *whether* by accident or design. —**whether or no,** in any case.

**whet·stone** (hwet′stōn′), *n.* an abrasive stone for sharpening knives or other edged tools.

**whew** (hwū), *interj.* [echoic], an exclamation of relief, surprise, dismay, etc.

**whey** (hwā), *n.* [AS. *hwæg*], the thin, watery part of milk which separates from the thicker part (curds) after coagulation. —**whey′ey** (-i), *adj.*

**whey·face** (hwā′fās′), *n.* 1. a pale or pallid face. 2. one having such a face. —**whey′faced′,** *adj.*

**which** (hwich), *pron.* [< AS. *hwylc*], 1. what one (or ones) of the persons, things, or events mentioned or implied?: as, *which* do you want? 2. the one (or ones) that: as, I know *which* you want. 3. that: used as a relative referring to the thing or event specified in the antecedent word, phrase, or clause: as, my hat, *which* is blue; the boat *which* sank. 4. any that; whichever: as, take *which* you like. 5. a thing or fact that: as, you are late—*which* reminds me, where is Alan? *adj.* 1. what one or ones (of the number mentioned or implied): as, *which* man (or men) came? 2. whatever: as, try *which* plan you like. 3. being the one just mentioned: as, he is old, *which* fact is important.

**which·ev·er** (hwich-ev′ẽr), *pron. & adj.* 1. any one (of two or more): as, he may choose *whichever* (desk) he likes. 2. no matter which: as, *whichever* (desk) he chooses, they won't be pleased.

**which·so·ev·er** (hwich′sō-ev′ẽr), *pron. & adj.* whichever: an emphatic variant.

**whiff** (hwif), *n.* [echoic], 1. a light puff or gust of air or wind; breath. 2. a slight gust of odor: as, a *whiff* of garlic. 3. an inhaling or exhaling of tobacco smoke. *v.t.* 1. to blow with a puff or gust; waft. 2. to smoke (a pipe, etc.). *v.i.* 1. to blow or move in puffs. 2. to inhale or exhale whiffs, as in smoking. —**whiff′er,** *n.*

**whif·fet** (hwif′it), *n.* [dim. of *whiff*], 1. a small dog. 2. [Colloq.], an insignificant person.

**whif·fle** (hwif′'l), *v.i.* [-FLED, -FLING], [freq. of *whiff*], 1. to blow in gusts: said of the wind. 2. to shift; veer; vacillate. *v.t.* to blow or scatter with or as with a puff of wind. —**whif′fler,** *n.*

**whif·fle·tree** (hwif′'l-trē′), *n.* a whippletree.

**Whig** (hwig), *n.* [< *whiggamore* (applied to Scot. Presbyterians who marched on Edinburgh in 1648) < W. Scot. < *whig*, a cry to urge on horses + *mare*, a horse], 1. in England, a political party (1697–c. 1832) which championed popular rights: it later became the Liberal Party: opposed to *Tory*. 2. in the American Revolution, a person who supported the struggle against England. 3. an American political party (c. 1836–1856) opposing the Democratic Party. *adj.* 1. that is a Whig. 2. composed of Whigs. 3. adhering to, or characteristic of, the principles of the Whigs. —**Whig′ger·y, Whig′gism,** *n.* —**Whig′gish,** *adj.*

**while** (hwīl), *n.* [AS. *hwil*], a period of time: as, a short *while*. *conj.* 1. during or throughout the time that: as, we talked *while* we ate. 2. *a*) at the same time that; although: as, *while* he was not poor, he had no ready cash. *b*) [Colloq.], whereas; and: as, the walls are green, *while* the ceiling is white. *v.t.* [WHILED, WHILING], to spend (time) in a pleasant way; occupy: as, we *whiled* away the hours. —**between whiles,** at intervals. —**the while,** during the same time. —**worth one's while,** worth one's time; profitable.

**whiles** (hwīlz), *adv.* [Archaic or Dial.], sometimes. *conj.* [Archaic], while.

**whi·lom** (hwī′ləm), *adv.* [AS. *hwilum*, dat. pl. of *hwil*, while], [Archaic], at one time; formerly. *adj.* [Archaic], former: as, their *whilom* friends.

**whilst** (hwīlst), *conj.* [Chiefly Brit.], while.

**whim** (hwim), *n.* [short for *whim-wham;* a redupl. ? based on ON. *hvima*, to wander with the eyes], a sudden fancy; idle and passing notion; caprice.

**whim·per** (hwim′pẽr), *v.i.* [? freq. < base of *whine*], to cry with low, whining, broken sounds. *v.t.* to utter with a whimper. *n.* a whimpering sound or cry. —**whim′per·er,** *n.* —**whim′per·ing·ly,** *adv.*

**whim·si·cal** (hwim′zi-k'l), *adj.* 1. full of or characterized by whims or whimsy. 2. oddly out of the ordinary; freakish. —**whim′si·cal′i·ty** (-kal′ə-ti), [*pl.* -TIES], ***n.*** —**whim′si·cal·ly,** ***adv.***

**whim·sy** (hwim′zi), ***n.*** [*pl.* -SIES], [prob. < *whim*], 1. an odd fancy; idle notion; whim. 2. quaint or fanciful humor. Also **whim′sey** [*pl.* -SEYS].

**whin** (hwin), ***n.*** [prob. < ON.], furze.

**whin·chat** (hwin′chat′), ***n.*** [*whin* (furze) + *chat,* a warbler: so named from frequenting furze], any of a group of migrating songbirds of Europe and W Asia with brown plumage and white markings.

**whine** (hwīn), ***v.i.*** [WHINED, WHINING], [AS. *hwinan*], 1. to utter a low, plaintive cry, as in complaint, fear, etc. 2. to complain in a childish, undignified way. ***v.t.*** to utter with a whine. ***n.*** 1. an act or sound of whining. 2. a complaint uttered in a whining tone. —**whin′er,** ***n.*** —**whin′ing·ly,** ***adv.*** —**whin′y** [-IER, -IEST], ***adj.***

**whin·ny** (hwin′i), ***v.i.*** [-NIED, -NYING], [< *whine*], to neigh in a low and gentle way: said of a horse. ***v.t.*** to express with a whinny. ***n.*** [*pl.* -NIES], the whinnying of a horse, or a similar sound.

**whip** (hwip), ***v.t.*** [WHIPPED or WHIPT, WHIPPING], [< MD. *wippen,* to swing], 1. to move, pull, throw, etc. suddenly and quickly (usually with *out, off,* etc.): as, he *whipped* out a knife. 2. to strike, as with a strap, rod, etc.; lash; beat. 3. to drive, urge, etc. by or as by whipping. 4. to strike as a whip does: as, the rain *whipped* her face. 5. *a*) to wind (cord or thread) around something, as a rope, to prevent fraying. *b*) to cover (a rope, etc.) in this manner. 6. to fish (a stream, etc.) by making repeated casts. 7. to beat (eggs, cream, etc.) into a froth. 8. to sew (a seam, etc.) with a loose overcasting or overhand stitch. 9. [Colloq.], to defeat or outdo. ***v.i.*** 1. to move, go, etc. quickly and suddenly: as, he *whipped* out the door. 2. to flap about in a whiplike manner: as, flags *whip* in high wind. ***n.*** 1. an instrument for striking or flogging, consisting of a rod with a lash attached to one end. 2. a blow, cut, etc. made with or as with a whip. 3. a person who uses a whip, as a coachman. 4. an officer of a political party in Congress, Parliament, etc. who enforces party discipline, attendance, etc.: also **party whip.** 5. a whipping motion. 6. a dessert made of fruit, sugar, and whipped cream or stiffly beaten egg whites. 7. something resembling a whip in its action. —**whip up,** 1. to rouse; excite. 2. [Colloq.], to cook or prepare quickly and easily. —**whip′like′,** ***adj.*** —**whip′per,** ***n.***

**whip·cord** (hwip′kôrd′), ***n.*** 1. a hard, twisted or braided cord used for whiplashes, etc. 2. a strong worsted cloth with a diagonally ribbed surface.

**whip hand,** 1. the hand in which a driver holds his whip. 2. the position of advantage or control.

**whip·lash** (hwip′lash′), ***n.*** the lash of a whip.

**whip·per·snap·per** (hwip′ẽr-snap′ẽr), ***n.*** [< *whip-snapper,* one who snaps whips], an insignificant person who appears impertinent or presumptuous.

**whip·pet** (hwip′it), ***n.*** [dim. < *whip*], a swift dog resembling a small greyhound, used in racing.

**whip·ping** (hwip′iŋ), ***n.*** 1. a flogging or beating, as in punishment. 2. cord, twine, etc. used to whip, or bind.

**whipping boy,** a scapegoat (sense 2).

**whipping post,** a post to which offenders are tied to be publicly whipped as a punishment.

**whip·ple·tree** (hwip′'l-trē′), ***n.*** [< *whip*], the pivoted crossbar at the front of a wagon or carriage, to which the traces of the harness are attached.

**whip·poor·will** (hwip′ẽr-wil′), ***n.*** [*pl.* -WILLS, -WILL; see PLURAL, II, D, 1], [echoic], a North American bird related to the goatsucker and active at night.

**whip·saw** (hwip′sô′), ***n.*** a long, narrow, tapering ripsaw with its ends held in a wooden frame: used by one or two persons. ***v.t.*** to cut with a whipsaw.

**whip·stitch** (hwip′stich′), ***v.t.*** & ***v.i.*** in *sewing,* to overcast or whip. ***n.*** a stitch made in this way.

**whip·stock** (hwip′stok′), ***n.*** the handle of a whip.

**whir** (hwũr), ***v.i.*** & ***v.t.*** [WHIRRED, WHIRRING], [? < *whirl*], to fly, revolve, vibrate, etc. with a whizzing or buzzing sound. ***n.*** 1. such a sound, as that from a revolving propeller. 2. hurry; bustle.

**whirl** (hwũrl), ***v.i.*** [< ON. *hvirfla*], 1. to move rapidly in a circular manner or as in an orbit. 2. to rotate or spin fast; gyrate. 3. to move, go, etc. swiftly. 4. to seem to spin; reel: as, my head is *whirling.* ***v.t.*** 1. to cause to rotate, revolve, etc. rapidly. 2. to move, carry, etc. with a rotating motion: as, the wind *whirled* the leaves. ***n.*** 1. the act of whirling. 2. a whirling motion. 3. something whirling or being whirled. 4. a fast round of parties, etc. 5. a tumult; uproar; stir. 6. a confused or giddy condition: as, my head is in a *whirl.* —**whirl′er,** ***n.*** —**whirl′ing·ly,** ***adv.***

**whirl·i·gig** (hwũr′li-gig′), ***n.*** 1. a child's toy that whirls or spins. 2. a merry-go-round. 3. a whirling motion.

**whirl·pool** (hwũrl′po͞ol′), ***n.*** 1. water in rapid, violent, whirling motion tending to form a vacuum at the center of the circle into which floating objects are drawn; eddy of water. 2. anything resembling a whirlpool, as in violent motion.

**whirl·wind** (hwũrl′wind′), ***n.*** 1. a current of air whirling violently in spiral form and having a forward motion. 2. anything resembling a whirlwind, as in violent or destructive action, etc.

**whirr** (hwũr), ***v.i.*** & ***v.t.,*** ***n.*** whir.

**whish** (hwish), ***v.i.*** [echoic], to move with a soft rushing sound; whiz; swish. ***n.*** a sound so made.

**whisk** (hwisk), ***v.t.*** [< MScot. & prob. < ON.], 1. to move, pull, brush, etc. with a quick, sweeping motion (usually with *away, off, out,* etc.). 2. [Chiefly Brit.], to beat (eggs, cream, etc.) into a froth; whip. ***v.i.*** to move quickly, nimbly, etc. ***n.*** 1. the act of whisking. 2. a quick, light, sweeping motion. 3. a whisk broom. 4. [Chiefly Brit.], a utensil consisting of looped wires fixed in a handle, for whipping eggs, etc.

**whisk broom,** a small, short-handled broom for brushing clothes, etc.

**whisk·er** (hwis′kẽr), ***n.*** 1. *pl.* the hair growing on a man's face; esp., the beard on the cheeks. 2. *a*) a single hair of a man's beard. *b*) any of the long bristly hairs growing on the upper lip of a cat, rat, etc. —**whisk′ered,** ***adj.***

**whis·key** (hwis′ki), ***n.*** [*pl.* -KEYS] & ***adj.*** whisky.

**whis·ky** (hwis′ki), ***n.*** [*pl.* -KIES], [short for *usquebaugh* < Ir. *uisge,* water + *beatha,* life, lit., water of life], 1. a strong alcoholic liquor distilled from the fermented mash of various grains, especially of rye, wheat, corn, or barley. 2. a drink of whisky. ***adj.*** of or made with whisky.

**whis·per** (hwis′pẽr), ***v.i.*** [AS. *hwisprian*], 1. to speak very softly, especially without vibration of the vocal chords. 2. to talk quietly or furtively, as in gossiping or plotting. 3. to make a soft, rustling sound. ***v.t.*** 1. to say very softly, especially without vibration of the vocal chords. 2. to tell as a secret. 3. [Rare], to speak to in a whisper. ***n.*** 1. a whispering; soft, low speech produced with breath but, usually, without voice. 2. something whispered; a secret, hint, rumor, etc. 3. a soft rustling sound. —**whis′per·er,** ***n.*** —**whis′per·ing,** ***adj.*** —**whis′per·ing·ly,** ***adv.***

**whispering campaign,** a campaign to defame a person, group, etc. by spreading rumors privately.

**whist** (hwist), ***interj.*** [echoic], hush! ***adj.*** still; silent. ***v.t.*** to silence. ***v.i.*** to be silent. ***n.*** silence. Now archaic or dial.

**whist** (hwist), ***n.*** [< earlier *whisk*], a card game usually played by two pairs of players, similar to, and the forerunner of, bridge.

**whis·tle** (hwis′'l), ***v.i.*** [-TLED, -TLING], [AS. *hwistlian*], 1. to make a clear, shrill sound by forcing breath between the teeth or through the contracted lips. 2. to make a clear, shrill cry: said of some birds and animals. 3. to move with a high shrill sound: as, the wind *whistled* past. 4. *a*) to blow a whistle. *b*) to have its whistle blown, as a train. ***v.t.*** 1. to produce (a tune, etc.) by whistling. 2. to summon, signal, etc. by whistling. 3. to cause to move with a whistling sound. ***n.*** 1. an instrument for making whistling sounds. 2. the act or sound of whistling. —**wet one's whistle,** to take a drink. —**whistle for,** to seek or expect in vain. —**whis′tler,** ***n.*** —**whis′tling,** ***adj.*** —**whis′tling·ly,** ***adv.***

**Whis·tler, James Ab·bott Mc·Neill** (ab′ət mək-nēl′ hwis′lẽr), 1834–1903; U.S. painter and etcher in England. —**Whis·tle′ri·an** (-lêr′i-ən), ***adj.***

**whistle stop,** a small town, originally one at which a train stopped only upon signal.

**whit** (hwit), ***n.*** [resp. of AS. *wiht,* a wight], the least bit; jot; iota: used in negative constructions, as, not a *whit* concerned.

**white** (hwīt), ***adj.*** [AS. *hwit*], 1. having the color of pure snow or milk; of the color of reflected light containing all of the visible rays of the spectrum: opposite to black. 2. of a light or pale color; specif., *a*) gray; silvery. *b*) very blond. *c*) pale; wan: as, a face *white* with terror. *d*) light-yellow or amber: as, *white* wine. *e*) blank, as a space unmarked by printing. *f*) snowy. 3. clothed in white:

as, a *White* Friar. 4. pure; innocent. 5. free from evil intent; harmless: as, *white* magic. 6. *a*) having a light-colored skin; Caucasian. *b*) of or controlled by the white race: as, *white* supremacy. 7. [Slang], honest; fair. ***n.*** 1. the color of pure snow or milk. 2. the state of being white; specif., *a*) fairness of complexion. *b*) purity; innocence. 3. a white or light-colored part or thing, as the albumen of an egg, the white part of the eyeball, the light-colored part of meat, wood, etc., a white garment, white wine, white pigment, etc. 4. a person with a light-colored skin; Caucasian. ***v.t.*** [WHITED, WHITING], to make white; whiten. **—bleed white,** to drain (a person) completely of money, resources, etc. **—white′ly,** ***adv.*** **—white′ness,** ***n.***

**white ant,** a termite.

**white·bait** (hwīt′bāt′), ***n.*** [*pl.* -BAIT], 1. the young of the herring and sprat, eaten as a delicacy. 2. any of various small fishes used as food.

**white bear,** a polar bear.

**white birch,** the North American birch with white or ash-colored paperlike bark.

**white bread,** bread of a light color made from finely sifted wheat flour.

**white·cap** (hwīt′kap′), ***n.*** a wave with its crest broken into white foam.

**white cedar,** 1. a variety of cedar growing in swampy land. 2. its soft, light-colored wood.

**white clover,** a creeping variety of clover with small, round, white flowers.

**white coal,** water as a source of power.

**white-col·lar** (hwīt′kol′ẽr), ***adj.*** [from customary business dress], designating or of clerical or professional workers or the like.

**whited sepulcher,** a hypocrite: Matt. 23:27.

**white elephant,** 1. a rare, pale-gray variety of elephant, regarded as sacred in SE Asia. 2. a thing from which little profit or use is derived, usually acquired and maintained at much expense.

**white-el·e·phant sale** (hwīt′el′ə-fənt), a sale of discarded clothing, bric-a-brac, etc., to raise money for charity, a club, etc.

**white feather,** [from belief that a white feather in a gamecock's tail shows bad breeding, hence cowardice], a symbol of cowardice. **—show the white feather,** to behave like a coward.

**white·fish** (hwīt′fish′), ***n.*** [*pl.* see FISH], 1. any of various white or silvery food fishes of the salmon family, found in lakes of the northeastern U.S. 2. any of various other whitish fishes.

**white flag,** a white banner or cloth hoisted as a signal of truce or surrender.

**White Friar,** a Carmelite friar: so called from the white habit of the order.

**white gold,** gold alloyed with platinum, palladium, nickel, etc. to give it a white, platinumlike appearance for use in jewelry.

**White·hall** (hwīt′hôl′), ***n.*** 1. a street in London where several government offices are located. 2. the British government.

**white heat,** 1. the degree of intense heat at which metal, etc. becomes glowing white. 2. a state of intense emotion, excitement, etc.

**White·horse** (hwīt′hôrs′), ***n.*** the capital of the Yukon Territory, Canada, in the S part: pop., 3,000.

**white-hot** (hwīt′hot′), ***adj.*** 1. glowing white with heat. 2. extremely angry, excited, etc.

**White House, the,** 1. the official residence of the President of the U.S. in Washington, D.C.: officially called *Executive Mansion.* 2. the executive branch of the U.S. government.

**white lead,** 1. a poisonous, heavy, white powder, basic lead carbonate, $2PbCO_3 \cdot Pb(OH)_2$, used in making paint. 2. native lead carbonate.

**white lie,** a lie about a trivial matter, told out of politeness and without harmful intent.

**white-liv·ered** (hwīt′liv′ẽrd), ***adj.*** 1. pale and sickly. 2. cowardly.

**white matter,** whitish nerve tissue of the brain and spinal cord, consisting chiefly of nerve fibers.

**white meat,** any light-colored meat, as the breast of chicken or turkey, veal, etc.

**White Mountains,** a mountain range of the Appalachian system, in N New Hampshire.

**whit·en** (hwīt′'n), ***v.t. & v.i.*** to make or become white or whiter. **—whit′en·er,** ***n.*** **—whit′en·ing,** ***n.***

**white oak,** 1. any of various oaks having whitish or grayish bark and hard wood. 2. the wood of any of these trees, used in furniture, etc.

**white pepper,** pepper ground from the husked dried seeds of the pepper berry.

**white pine,** 1. a pine of E North America, with hanging brown cones and soft, light wood. 2. this wood. 3. any of various closely related pines.

**white plague,** tuberculosis, especially of the lungs.

**white poplar,** 1. any of various poplar trees having lobed leaves with white or gray down on the undersides. 2. the wood of the tulip tree.

**white potato,** the common potato; Irish potato: see **potato** (sense 1).

**white primary,** in some southern States of the U.S., a direct primary election from which Negroes are excluded from voting.

**white race,** loosely, the Caucasian division of mankind.

**White Russia,** Byelorussia.

**White Russian,** 1. Byelorussian. 2. a Russian member of, or sympathizer with, a faction which fought the Bolsheviks in the Russian civil war.

**White Russian Soviet Socialist Republic,** the Byelorussian S.S.R.

**white sauce,** a sauce for meat, fish, etc., made of butter, flour, milk, etc. cooked together.

**White Sea,** an arm of the Arctic Ocean extending into the European U.S.S.R.

**white slave,** a woman forced into prostitution for the profit of others. **—white′-slave′,** ***adj.*** **—white slaver. —white slavery.**

**white-tailed deer** (hwīt′tāld′), Virginia deer: also **white′tail′,** ***n.***

**white tie,** 1. a white bow tie, properly worn with a swallow-tailed coat. 2. a swallow-tailed coat and the proper accessories. Distinguished from *black tie.*

**white·wash** (hwīt′wôsh′, -wäsh′), ***n.*** 1. a mixture of lime, whiting, size, water, etc., for whitening walls, etc. 2. *a*) a concealing of faults or defects as in an effort to exonerate. *b*) something said or done for this purpose. 3. [Colloq.], in *sports,* a defeat in which the loser scores no points. ***v.t.*** 1. to cover with whitewash. 2. to conceal the faults or defects of. 3. [Colloq.], in *sports,* to defeat (an opponent) without permitting him to score. **—white′wash′er,** ***n.*** **—white′wash′ing,** ***n.***

**white whale,** the beluga.

**whith·er** (hwi*th*′ẽr), ***adv.*** [< AS. *hwider*], to what place, condition, etc.? where? ***conj.*** 1. to which place, condition, etc. 2. wherever. Chiefly in poetical or rhetorical usage.

**whith·er·so·ev·er** (hwi*th*′ẽr-sō-ev′ẽr), ***conj.*** to whatever place; wherever: an emphatic variant.

**whit·ing** (hwīt′iŋ), ***n.*** [*pl.* -INGS, -ING; see PLURAL, II, D, 1], [< MD. *wijting* < *wit,* white], 1. a European sea fish of the cod family. 2. any of various spiny-finned North American fishes, as the weakfish. 3. the silver hake.

**whit·ing** (hwīt′iŋ), ***n.*** [< *white, v.* + *-ing*], powdered chalk used in whitewash, silver polish, etc.

**whit·ish** (hwīt′ish), ***adj.*** somewhat white. **—whit′ish·ness,** ***n.***

**whit·low** (hwit′lō), ***n.*** [ME. *whitflawe;* of disputed origin], a pus-producing inflammation at the end of a finger or toe, near or under the nail.

**Whit·man, Walt** (wôlt hwit′mən), (*Walter Whitman*), 1819–1892; U.S. poet.

**Whit·ney, Eli** (hwit′ni), 1765–1825; U.S. inventor of the cotton gin.

**Whit·ney, Mount** (hwit′ni), a mountain in E California: height, 14,501 ft.: highest in the U.S.

**Whit·sun** (hwit′s'n), ***adj.*** of or observed on Whitsunday or at Whitsuntide.

**Whit·sun·day** (hwit′sun′di, -s'n-dā′), ***n.*** [AS. *Hwita Sunnandæg,* white Sunday], the seventh Sunday (fiftieth day) after Easter; Pentecost.

**Whit·sun·tide** (hwit′s'n-tīd′), ***n.*** the week beginning with Whitsunday, especially the first three days of that week: also **Whitsun Tide.**

**Whit·ti·er, John Green·leaf** (grēn′lēf hwit′i-ẽr), 1807–1892; U.S. poet.

**whit·tle** (hwit′'l), ***v.t.*** [-TLED, -TLING], [< AS. *thwitan,* to cut], 1. *a*) to cut thin shavings from (wood) with a knife. *b*) to carve (an object) in this manner: as, he *whittled* a boat. 2. to reduce, destroy, etc. gradually, as if by whittling: usually with *down, away,* etc., as, to *whittle* down costs. ***v.i.*** to whittle wood. **—whit′tler,** ***n.***

**whit·y** (hwīt′i), ***adj.*** [-IER, -IEST], whitish.

**whiz, whizz** (hwiz), ***v.i.*** [WHIZZED, WHIZZING], [echoic], 1. to make the whirring or hissing sound of something rushing through the air. 2. to speed by with this sound: as, the bus *whizzed* past him. ***v.t.*** to cause to whiz. ***n.*** 1. the whirring or hissing sound of something rushing through the air. 2. [Slang], a person who is very quick, adroit, or skilled at something: as, he's a *whiz* at history. **—whiz′zer,** ***n.*** **—whiz′zing·ly,** ***adv.***

**who** (ho͞o), *pron.* [*obj.* WHOM, *poss.* WHOSE], [AS. *hwa*], 1. what person or persons: used interrogatively, as, *who* came? 2. which person or persons: as, I don't know *who* came. 3. *a*) (the, or a, person or persons) that: used to introduce a relative clause, as, the man *who* came to dinner. *b*) any person or persons that: used as an indefinite relative, as, "*who* steals my purse steals trash." —**who's who,** who the important people are.

**whoa** (hwō), *interj.* [for *ho, interj.*], stop!: used especially in directing a horse to stand still.

**who·dun·it** (ho͞o-dun'it), *n.* [Slang], a novel, play, etc. in which a crime is solved at the end by means of clues scattered throughout the story.

**who·ev·er** (ho͞o-ev'ẽr), *pron.* 1. any person at all that; whatever person. 2. no matter what person: as, *whoever* did it, I didn't. 3. what person? who?: an emphatic variant, as, *whoever* did that?

**whole** (hōl), *adj.* [AS. *hal*], 1. healthy; not diseased or injured. 2. not broken, damaged, defective, etc.; intact. 3. containing all of its elements or parts; complete. 4. not divided up; in a single unit. 5. constituting the entire amount, extent, etc.: as, one *whole* week. 6. having both parents in common: as, a *whole* brother. 7. in *arithmetic*, not a fraction: as, 25 is a *whole* number. *n.* 1. the entire amount, etc. of something; totality. 2. a complete organization of parts; unity, entirety, etc. —**as a whole,** as a complete unit; altogether. —**made out of whole cloth,** completely fictitious or false. —**on the whole,** all things considered; in general. —**whole'ness,** *n.*

**whole·heart·ed** (hōl'här'tid), *adj.* doing or done with all one's energy, enthusiasm, etc.; sincere. —**whole'heart'ed·ly,** *adv.* —**whole'heart'ed·ness,** *n.*

**whole note,** in *music*, a note (𝅝) having four times the duration of a quarter note; semibreve.

**whole number,** a number that is not a fraction or a mixed number; integer.

**whole·sale** (hōl'sāl'), *n.* the sale of goods in relatively large quantities, especially to retailers who then sell them to the consumer: cf. *retail*. *adj.* 1. of or engaged in selling at wholesale. 2. sold in relatively large quantities, usually at a lower cost per item. 3. extensive and general: as, *wholesale* destruction. *adv.* in relatively large quantities. *v.i.* [-SALED, -SALING], 1. to be engaged in wholesale selling. 2. to be sold at wholesale. *v.t.* to sell (goods) at wholesale. —**whole'sal'er,** *n.*

**whole·some** (hōl'səm), *adj.* [< ON. *heilsamr*], 1. promoting or conducive to good health or well-being; healthful. 2. tending to improve the mind or morals. 3. characterized by health and vigor. 4. suggesting health: as, a *wholesome* smile. —**whole'some·ly,** *adv.* —**whole'some·ness,** *n.*

**whole step,** in *music*, an interval consisting of two adjacent half steps: also **whole tone.**

**whole-wheat** (hōl'hwēt'), *adj.* 1. made of the entire grain of wheat: as, *whole-wheat* flour. 2. made of whole-wheat flour: as, *whole-wheat* bread.

**who'll** (ho͞ol), 1. who shall. 2. who will.

**whol·ly** (hō'li), *adv.* to the whole quantity or extent; completely, entirely, exclusively, etc.

**whom** (ho͞om), *pron.* the obj. case of **who**: in colloquial usage, now often replaced by *who*.

**whom·ev·er** (ho͞om-ev'ẽr), *pron.* the objective case of **whoever.**

**whom·so·ev·er** (ho͞om'sō-ev'ẽr), *pron.* the objective case of **whosoever.**

**whoop** (ho͞op, hwo͞op), *n.* [< OFr. *houper*, to cry out], 1. a loud shout, cry, etc., as of excitement, joy, etc. 2. a hoot, as of an owl. 3. the deep-sounding, convulsive intake of air immediately following a fit of coughing in whooping cough. *v.i. & v.t.* to utter, or utter with, a whoop or whoops. *interj.* an exclamation of excitement, joy, etc. —**not worth a whoop,** [Colloq.], worth nothing at all. —**whoop it** (or **things**) **up,** [Slang], 1. to create a noisy disturbance, as in celebrating. 2. to create enthusiasm (*for*). —**whoop'er,** *n.*

**whoop·ee** (hwo͞o'pē, hwoop'ē), *interj.* [< *whoop*], an exclamation expressing great enjoyment, gay abandonment, etc. *n.* a shout of "whoopee!" —**make whoopee,** [Slang], to have a gay, noisy time.

**whooping cough,** an acute infectious disease, usually affecting children, characterized by repeated attacks of coughing that end in a whoop.

**whoops** (hwo͞ops, hwoops), *interj.* an exclamation uttered as in regaining one's balance after stumbling or one's composure after a slip of the tongue.

**whop** (hwop), *v.t. & v.i.* [WHOPPED, WHOPPING], [prob. echoic], [Dial. or Archaic], to beat, strike, etc. *n.* [Dial. or Archaic], 1. a blow, stroke, etc. 2. the noise made by a whop. Also sp. **whap.**

**whop·per** (hwop'ẽr), *n.* [< *whop*], [Colloq.], anything extraordinarily large; esp., a great lie.

**whop·ping** (hwop'iŋ), *adj.* [< *whop*], [Colloq.], extraordinarily large or great.

**whore** (hôr, hōr), *n.* [AS. *hore* < ON. *hara*], a promiscuous woman; esp., a prostitute. *v.i.* [WHORED, WHORING], 1. to be a whore. 2. to fornicate with whores. —**whor'ish,** *adj.*

**whore·mon·ger** (hôr'muŋ'gẽr, hōr'-), *n.* a pimp; pander: also **whore'mas'ter.**

**whorl** (hwũrl, hwôrl), *n.* [< dial. var. of *whirl*], anything that whirls or appears to whirl; specif., *a*) any of the circular ridges that form the design of a fingerprint. *b*) in *botany*, an arrangement of leaves, petals, etc. about the same point on a stem. *c*) in *zoology*, any of the turns in a spiral shell. —**whorled,** *adj.*

**whor·tle·ber·ry** (hwũr't'l-ber'i), *n.* [*pl.* -RIES], [< AS. *horta*, a bilberry], 1. *a*) a small European shrub with pink flowers and blue or blackish edible berries. *b*) any of these berries. 2. the huckleberry.

**who's** (ho͞oz), who is.

**whose** (ho͞oz), *pron.* [AS. *hwæs*], the poss. case of **who,** and now, usually, of **which.**

**who·so** (ho͞o'sō), *pron.* [< AS. *hwa swa*], [Archaic], whoever; whosoever.

**who·so·ev·er** (ho͞o'sō-ev'ẽr), *pron.* whoever: an emphatic variant.

**why** (hwī), *adv.* [AS. *hwi*, instrumental case of *hwa*, who], 1. for what reason, cause, or purpose: as, *why* did he go? I know *why* he went. 2. because of which: as, there is no reason *why* you should go. 3. the reason for which: as, this is *why* he went. *n.* [*pl.* WHYS], the reason, cause, etc.: as, never mind the *why* and wherefore. *interj.* an exclamation of surprise, impatience, hesitation, etc.

**W.I.,** 1. West Indies. 2. West Indian.

**Wich·i·ta** (wich'ə-tô'), *n.* a city in S Kansas, on the Arkansas River: pop., 255,000.

**Wichita Falls,** a city in N Texas: pop., 102,000.

**wick** (wik), *n.* [AS. *weoca*], a piece of cord or tape, or a thin bundle of threads, in a candle, oil lamp, cigarette lighter, etc., that absorbs the fuel and, when lighted, burns.

**wick·ed** (wik'id), *adj.* [ME. < *wikke*, evil; akin to AS. *wicca*, witch], 1. having or resulting from bad moral character; evil; depraved. 2. generally bad, unpleasant, painful, etc.: as, a *wicked* blow on the head. 3. naughty; mischievous. —**wick'ed·ly,** *adv.* —**wick'ed·ness,** *n.*

**wick·er** (wik'ẽr), *n.* [prob. < ON.], 1. a thin, flexible twig; withe. 2. wickerwork. *adj.* made of or covered with wicker.

**wick·er·work** (wik'ẽr-wũrk'), *n.* 1. thin, flexible twigs woven together; wicker. 2. baskets, furniture, etc. made of such interwoven twigs.

**wick·et** (wik'it), *n.* [Anglo-Fr. *wiket*], 1. a small door or gate, especially one set in or near a larger one. 2. a small window or opening, as in a box office. 3. a small gate for regulating the flow of water as to a water wheel. 4. in *cricket*, *a*) either of two sets of three stumps each, with two bails resting on top of them. *b*) the playing space between the two wickets. *c*) a player's turn at bat. 5. in *croquet*, any of the small wire arches through which the balls must be hit.

**wick·et·keep·er** (wik'it-kēp'ẽr), *n.* in *cricket*, the fielder stationed immediately behind the wicket.

**wick·ing** (wik'iŋ), *n.* cord, yarn, etc. for wicks.

**Wickliffe,** or **Wiclif, John,** see **Wycliffe, John.**

**wide** (wīd), *adj.* [AS. *wid*], 1. extending over a large area; esp., extending over a larger area from side to side than is usual. 2. of a specified extent from side to side: as, two feet *wide*. 3. of great extent, range, etc.: as, a *wide* variety. 4. roomy; ample; full: as, a *wide* blouse. 5. open to full width: as, eyes *wide* with fear. 6. far from the point, issue, etc. aimed at: as, *wide* of the mark. 7. in *phonetics*, pronounced with the tongue, etc. in relaxed position. *adv.* 1. over a relatively large area; widely. 2. to a large or full extent; fully: as, *wide* open. 3. so as to miss the point, issue, etc. aimed at; astray: as, his shot went *wide*. *n.* 1. [Rare], a wide area. 2. in *cricket*, a ball bowled out of the batsman's reach. —**wide'ly,** *adv.* —**wide'ness,** *n.*

**wide-an·gle** (wīd'aŋ'g'l), *adj.* 1. designating or of a kind of camera lens covering a wide angle of view. 2. designating or of any of several motion-picture systems (trade-marked as **CinemaScope, Cinerama,** etc.) employing one or more cameras (and projectors) and an especially wide, curved screen to simulate normal panoramic vision.

**wide-a·wake** (wīd'ə-wāk'), *adj.* 1. completely awake; hence, 2. alert. —**wide'-a·wake'ness,** *n.*

**wide-eyed** (wīd'īd'), *adj.* with the eyes wide open.

**wid·en** (wīd''n), *v.t. & v.i.* to make or become wide or wider. —**wid'en·er,** *n.*

**wide-o·pen** (wīd'ō'p'n), *adj.* 1. opened wide. 2. lax in enforcing laws regulating prostitution, gambling, etc.: as, a *wide-open* city.

**wide·spread** (wīd'spred'), *adj.* spread widely; esp., occurring over a wide area or extent.

**widg·eon** (wij'ən), *n.* [*pl.* -EONS, -EON; see PLURAL, II, D, 1], [< OFr. *vigeon;* prob. < L. *vipio,* small crane], any of various kinds of wild, fresh-water ducks: also sp. **wigeon.**

**wid·ow** (wid'ō), *n.* [< AS. *widewe*], 1. a woman whose husband has died; esp., such a woman who has not remarried. 2. in certain card games, an extra hand dealt to the table. *v.t.* to cause to become a widow. —**wid'ow·hood',** *n.*

**wid·ow·er** (wid'ō-ēr), *n.* a man whose wife has died and who has not remarried.

**widow's mite,** a small sum freely given by one who can scarcely afford it: Mark 12:41-44.

**widow's peak,** a point formed by hair growing down at the middle of a forehead.

**width** (width), *n.* [< *wide,* by analogy with *length*], 1. a being wide; wideness. 2. the distance from side to side. 3. a piece of something having a specified width: as, a *width* of cloth.

**wield** (wēld), *v.t.* [AS. *wealdan, wyldan*], 1. to handle and use (a tool or weapon), especially with skill and control. 2. to exercise (power, control, influence, etc.). —**wield'er,** *n.*

**wield·y** (wēl'di), *adj.* [-IER, -IEST], that can be wielded easily; manageable: also **wield'a·ble.**

**Wien** (vēn), *n.* Vienna, Austria: the German name.

**wie·ner** (wē'nēr), *n.* [short for G. *Wiener wurst,* Vienna sausage], a smoked link sausage of beef or beef and pork, usually enclosed in a membranous casing; frankfurter: also **wie'ner·wurst'** (-wũrst').

**wife** (wīf), *n.* [*pl.* WIVES], [AS. *wif*], 1. a woman: now only in compounds, as, *housewife.* 2. a married woman. —**take to wife,** to marry (a woman). —**wife'hood,** *n.* —**wife'less,** *adj.* —**wife'like',** *adj.*

**wife·ly** (wīf'li), *adj.* [-LIER, -LIEST], of, like, or suitable to a wife.

**wig** (wig), *n.* [shortened < *periwig*], an artificial covering of hair for the head, worn as part of a costume, to conceal baldness, etc. *v.t.* [WIGGED, WIGGING], 1. to furnish with a wig or wigs. 2. [Brit. Colloq.], to scold, censure, etc. —**wigged,** *adj.* —**wig'less,** *adj.* —**wig'like',** *adj.*

**wi·geon** (wij'ən), *n.* [*pl.* -GEONS, -GEON; see PLURAL, II, D, 1], a widgeon.

**wig·gle** (wig''l), *v.t. & v.i.* [-GLED, -GLING], [prob. < MD. & MLG. freq. of *wiggen,* to move from side to side], to move or cause to move with short, jerky motions from side to side. *n.* the act or an instance of wiggling.

**wig·gler** (wig'lēr), *n.* 1. a person or thing that wiggles. 2. the larva of a mosquito; wriggler.

**wig·gly** (wig'li), *adj.* [-GLIER, -GLIEST], 1. that wiggles; wiggling. 2. having a form that suggests wiggling; wavy: as, a *wiggly* line.

**wight** (wīt), *n.* [AS. *wiht*], [Archaic], a human being; person: now sometimes used humorously.

**Wight, Isle of** (wīt), an English island in the English Channel.

**wig·wag** (wig'wag'), *v.t. & v.i.* [-WAGGED, -WAGGING], [? short for *wiggle-waggle,* redupl. of *wiggle*], 1. to move back and forth; wag. 2. to send (a message) by waving flags, lights, etc. back and forth in accordance with a code. *n.* 1. the act or practice of sending messages in this way. 2. a message so sent. —**wig'wag'ger,** *n.*

**wig·wam** (wig'wäm, -wôm), *n.* [< Algonquian], a more or less conical shelter made by North American Indians, consisting of a framework of poles covered with bark, hides, etc.

WIGWAM

**Wil·ber·force, William** (wil'bēr-fôrs', -fōrs'), 1759–1833; English statesman and vigorous opponent of the slave trade.

**wild** (wīld), *adj.* [AS. *wilde*], 1. living or growing in its original, natural state; not domesticated or cultivated: as, *wild* flowers or *wild* animals. 2. not lived in or cultivated; desolate: as, *wild* land. 3. not civilized; savage: as, a *wild* tribe. 4. not easily restrained or regulated: as, *wild* children. 5. dissipated, licentious, promiscuous, etc.: as, *wild* youth. 6. unbridled, unrepressed, boisterous, etc.: as, a *wild* time. 7. turbulent; stormy: as, *wild* seas. 8. eager or enthusiastic: as, *wild* with delight. 9. angered, vexed, crazed, etc.: as, *wild* with grief. 10. in a state of disorder, confusion, etc.: as, *wild* hair. 11. fantastically impractical: as, a *wild* scheme. 12. reckless: as, a *wild* chance. 13. missing the target: as, a *wild* pitch. 14. in certain card games, having any value desired by the holder: said of a card. *adv.* in a wild manner: as, to fire *wild.* *n. usually pl.* wilderness, waste, desert, etc. —**run wild,** to grow or exist without control or regulation. —**wild'ly,** *adv.* —**wild'ness,** *n.*

**wild boar,** a variety of hog living wild in Europe and Asia.

**wild carrot,** a weed with white, lacelike flowers.

**wild·cat** (wīld'kat'), *n.* [*pl.* -CATS, -CAT; see PLURAL, II, D, 1], 1. any of various fierce, medium-sized, undomesticated animals of the cat family, as the bobcat. 2. a fierce, aggressive person. 3. an unsound or risky business scheme. 4. a productive oil well drilled in an area not previously known to have oil. 5. a locomotive and tender without cars. Also **wild cat.** *adj.* 1. unsound or financially risky. 2. illegal or unethical: said of a business, etc. 3. running without authorization or on an irregular schedule: said of a train, etc. *v.t. & v.i.* [-CATTED, -CATTING], to drill for oil in (an area previously considered unproductive). —**wild'cat'ter,** *n.* —**wild'-cat'ting,** *n.*

**wildcat strike,** a labor strike without the authorization of the proper union officials.

**Wilde, Oscar** (wīld), 1854–1900; British poet, novelist, and dramatist, born in Ireland.

**wil·de·beest** (wil'də-bēst'), *n.* [*pl.* -BEESTS, -BEEST; see PLURAL, II, D, 1], [S.Afr.D. < D. *wild,* wild + *beeste,* beast], a gnu.

**wil·der·ness** (wil'dēr-nis), *n.* [< ME. *wilderne* < AS. < *wilde,* wild + *deor,* animal], 1. an uncultivated, uninhabited region; waste; wild. 2. any barren, empty, or open area, as of ocean. 3. a large, confused mass or tangle of persons or things.

**wild-eyed** (wīld'īd'), *adj.* staring in a wild or distracted manner, as from fear.

**wild·fire** (wīld'fīr'), *n.* a highly inflammable substance, difficult to extinguish, formerly used in warfare: now mainly in phrase *spread like wildfire,* to be disseminated widely and rapidly.

**wild flower,** 1. any plant growing without cultivation in fields, etc. 2. its flower. Also **wild'flow'er.**

**wild fowl,** wild birds; esp., game birds, as wild ducks or geese, quail, etc.: also **wild'fowl'.**

**wild-goose chase** (wīld'gōōs'), a futile attempt or enterprise; esp., a useless search or pursuit.

**wild oat** (or **oats**), a tall, oatlike grass used for fodder. —**sow one's wild oats,** to be promiscuous or dissolute in youth: usually said of a man.

**wild pansy,** an uncultivated pansy with small flowers of purple mixed with white and yellow.

**Wild West, wild West,** the western U.S. in its early frontier period of lawlessness.

**wild·wood** (wīld'wood'), *n.* a natural woodland or forest, especially when unfrequented.

**wile** (wīl), *n.* [AS. *wil;* prob. ult. < ON. *vēl,* a trick], 1. a sly trick; stratagem. 2. a beguiling or coquettish trick. 3. trickery; deceit. *v.t.* [WILED, WILING], to beguile; lure. —**wile away,** to while away (time, etc.): by confusion with *while.*

**wil·ful** (wil'fəl), *adj.* willful. —**wil'ful·ly,** *adv.*—**wil'-ful·ness,** *n.*

**Wil·helm II** (vil'helm), William II: German name.

**Wil·hel·mi·na** (wil'hel-mē'nə), *n.* 1880–1962; queen of the Netherlands (1890–1948).

**Wilkes-Bar·re** (wilks'bar'i), *n.* a city in NE Pennsylvania: pop., 64,000.

**will** (wil), *n.* [< AS. *willa*], 1. wish or desire; inclination. 2. something wished, especially by one with power or authority; specif., *a)* a request. *b)* a command; decree. 3. strong purpose or determination: as, where there's a *will* there's a way. 4. energy or enthusiasm: as, to work with a *will.* 5. the power of self-direction or self-control. 6. the power of conscious and deliberate action or choice: as, freedom of the *will.* 7. attitude toward others: as, ill *will.* 8. *a)* the statement of a person's wishes concerning the disposal of his property after death. *b)* the legal document containing this. *v.t.* 1. to decide upon; make a choice of. 2. to resolve firmly: as, he *willed* to survive. 3. to decree; ordain. 4. to influence or control as by hypnotic power. 5. to bequeath by a will. —**at will,** when one wishes. —**do the will of,** to obey the wish or command of. —**will'a·ble,** *adj.* —**will'er,** *n.* —**will'-less,** *adj.*

**will** (wil), *v.* [pt. WOULD], [AS. *willan*], an auxiliary used: 1. to express futurity, usually with implications of intention, determination, compulsion, obligation, etc. 2. in formal speech, *a*) to express determination, obligation, etc. in the first person, and futurity in the second and third persons. *b*) in a question expecting *will* in the answer. See note following **shall.** 3. to express willingness: as, *will* you go? 4. to express ability or capacity: as, it *will* hold a pint. 5. to express habit or customary practice: as, she *will* talk for hours on end. ***v.t.* & *v.i.*** to wish; desire: as, do as you *will*.

**will-call** (wil′kôl′), *adj.* designating or of that department in a store at which a deposit may be made on an item to be held until paid for in full.

**willed** (wild), *adj.* having a (specified kind of) will: as, *strong-willed*.

**will·ful** (wil′fəl), *adj.* 1. done or said deliberately or intentionally. 2. obstinate; stubborn. Also sp. **wilful. —will′ful·ly,** ***adv.*** **—will′ful·ness,** ***n.***

**Wil·liam I** (wil′yəm), (*William the Conqueror*), 1027–1087; Norman duke who conquered England at Battle of Hastings (1066); king of England (1066–1087).

**William II,** 1859–1941; last German emperor (1888–1918); abdicated.

**William III,** Prince of Orange, (*William of Nassau*), 1650–1702; king of England (1689–1702); reigned jointly with his wife, Mary II, until 1694.

**Williams, Roger,** 1603?–1683; English colonist in America; founder of Rhode Island.

**Wil·liams·burg** (wil′yəmz-bũrg′), *n.* a town in SE Virginia: the early capital of Virginia, restored in part to its colonial appearance.

**wil·lies** (wil′iz), *n.pl.* [? < *willy-nilly*], [Slang], nervousness; jitters (with *the*).

**will·ing** (wil′iŋ), *adj.* 1. favorably disposed or consenting: as, *willing* to play. 2. acting, giving, etc. readily and cheerfully: as, a *willing* assistant. 3. done, given, etc. readily or gladly; voluntary. **—will′ing·ly,** ***adv.*** **—will′ing·ness,** ***n.***

**will-o'-the-wisp** (wil′ə-*th*ə-wisp′), *n.* [earlier *Will* (personal name) *with the wisp*], 1. ignis fatuus. 2. anything deceptive, elusive, or misleading.

**wil·low** (wil′ō), *n.* [AS. *wilig*], 1. any of various trees with narrow leaves, tassellike spikes of flowers, and, usually, flexible twigs used in weaving baskets, etc. 2. the wood of any of these trees. 3. [Colloq.], something made of willow wood. ***adj.*** 1. of willows. 2. made of willow wood. **—wil′low·ish, wil′low·like′,** ***adj.***

**wil·low·y** (wil′ō-i, -ə-wi), *adj.* 1. covered or shaded with willows. 2. like a willow; slender, graceful, lithe, etc.

**will power,** strength of will, mind, or determination; self-control.

**wil·ly-nil·ly** (wil′i-nil′i), *adv.* [contr. < *will I, nill I; nill* < AS. *ne*, not + *wille*, to will], whether one wishes it or not; willingly or unwillingly. ***adj.*** 1. happening whether one wishes it or not. 2. indecisive; vacillating.

**Wil·ming·ton** (wil′miŋ-tən), *n.* a port in N Delaware, on the Delaware River: pop., 110,000.

**Wil·no** (vil′nō), *n.* Vilnius: Polish name.

**Wil·son, Mount** (wil′s'n), a mountain in SW California: site of a famous observatory.

**Wilson, Woodrow,** (*Thomas Woodrow Wilson*), 1856–1924; 28th president of the U.S. (1913–1921).

**wilt** (wilt), *v.i.* [var. of obs. *welk*, to wither], 1. to become limp, as from heat or lack of water; wither; droop: said of plants. 2. to become weak or faint; lose strength. 3. to lose courage; quail. ***v.t.*** to cause to wilt. ***n.*** a wilting. **—wilt′ing·ly,** ***adv.***

**wilt** (wilt), archaic 2d pers. sing., pres. indic., of **will.**

**Wil·ton** (wil′t'n), *n.* [< *Wilton*, England, where first made], a kind of carpet with a velvety pile of cut loops: also **Wilton carpet, Wilton rug.**

**wi·ly** (wī′li), *adj.* [-LIER, -LIEST], full of wiles; crafty; sly. **—wi′li·ly,** ***adv.*** **—wi′li·ness,** ***n.***

**wim·ble** (wim′b'l), *n.* [< OFr. < MD. *wimmel*, an auger], any of various boring tools, as a gimlet, auger, etc. ***v.t.*** [-BLED, -BLING], to bore with a wimble.

**Wim·ble·don** (wim′b'l-dən), *n.* a city in SE England: pop., 58,000: scene of international tennis matches.

**wim·ple** (wim′p'l), *n.* [AS. *wimpel*], a woman's head covering consisting of a cloth so arranged as to leave only the face exposed: worn by certain orders of nuns. ***v.t.*** [-PLED, -PLING], 1. to clothe with a wimple. 2. to lay in folds. 3. to cause to ripple. ***v.i.*** 1. to lie in folds. 2. to ripple.

**win** (win), *v.i.* [WON or *obs.* WAN, WON, WINNING], [< AS. *winnan*, to fight], 1. to gain a victory; succeed (sometimes with *out*). 2. to reach a specified state or condition; get (with a preposition or certain adverbs): as, he *won* loose from the crowd. ***v.t.*** 1. to get by labor, struggle, etc.; specif., *a*) to acquire: as, he *won* distinctions. *b*) to make, achieve, etc.: as, you've *won* your point. *c*) to gain in competition, as a prize. *d*) to earn (a livelihood, etc.). 2. to be victorious in (a contest, dispute, etc.). 3. to get to, usually with effort: as, they *won* the camp by noon. 4. to influence; persuade (also with *over*): as, I *won* him over to my side. 5. *a*) to gain the sympathy, favor, etc. of: as, he *won* a supporter. *b*) to gain (one's sympathy, love, etc.). 6. to persuade to marry one. ***n.*** [Colloq.], an act of winning; victory, as in a contest.

**wince** (wins), *v.i.* [WINCED, WINCING], [< Anglo-Fr. < MHG. *wenken*], to shrink or draw back suddenly; flinch. ***n.*** a wincing. **—winc′er,** ***n.***

**winch** (winch), *n.* [AS. *wince*], 1. a crank with a handle for transmitting motion. 2. any of various devices operated by turning a crank; specif., a type of windlass for hoisting or hauling.

WINCH

**Win·ches·ter (rifle)** (win′ches′tẽr, -chis-tẽr), [after O.F. *Winchester*, the manufacturer], a type of repeating rifle: a trade-mark.

**wind** (wīnd), *v.t.* [WOUND or *rarely* WINDED, WINDING], [AS. *windan*], 1. to turn: as, *wind* the crank. 2. to coil into a ball or around something else; twine: as, *wind* the rope around the pole. 3. to cover by encircling with something; entwine: as, *wind* the spool with thread. 4. to make (one's way) in an indirect course. 5. to cause to move in a twisting course. 6. to introduce deviously: as, he *wound* his criticism into his argument. 7. to hoist or haul as with a winch (often with *up*). 8. to tighten the spring of (a clock, etc.) as by turning a stem. ***v.i.*** 1. to move, go, or extend in a curving or sinuous manner. 2. to take a devious or subtle course in behavior, argument, etc. 3. to coil or spiral (*about* or *around* something). 4. to undergo winding: as, this clock *winds* easily. ***n.*** a turn; twist; curve. **—wind up,** 1. to wind into a ball, etc. 2. to conclude; end; settle. 3. to excite greatly. 4. in *baseball*, to swing the arm preparatory to pitching. **—wind′a·ble,** ***adj.*** **—wind′er,** ***n.*** **—wind′ing·ly,** ***adv.***

**wind** (wind; *for n., also poetic* wīnd), *n.* [AS.], 1. air in motion; esp., any noticeable natural movement of air. 2. a strong, fast-moving current of air; gale. 3. air regarded as a bearer of scents, as in hunting: as, the dogs are keeping the *wind*. 4. figuratively, air regarded as bearing information, trends, etc.; hint: as, to get *wind* of something. 5. breath or the power of breathing: as, he got the *wind* knocked out of him. 6. *a*) idle or empty talk. *b*) bragging; pomposity. 7. gas in the stomach or intestines. 8. *pl.* the wind instruments of an orchestra. ***v.t.*** 1. to expose to the wind, as for drying. 2. to get or follow the scent of. 3. to cause to be out of breath. 4. to rest (a horse, etc.) so as to allow recovery of breath. **—break wind,** to expel gas from the bowels. **—get (or have) wind of,** to receive (or have) information concerning. **—how the wind blows (or lies),** what the trend of affairs, public opinion, etc. is. **—in the teeth of the wind,** straight against the wind: also **in the wind's eye. —in the wind,** happening or about to happen. **—into the wind,** in the direction from which the wind is blowing. **—take the wind out of one's sails,** to remove one's advantage, nullify one's argument, etc. suddenly. **—wind′less,** ***adj.***

**wind** (wīnd, wind), *v.t.* [WOUND or *rarely* WINDED, WINDING], [< *wind, n.*], 1. to blow (a horn, etc.). 2. to sound (a signal, etc.), as on a horn.

**wind·age** (win′dij), *n.* 1. the disturbance of air around a moving projectile. 2. deflection of a projectile by the wind, or the degree of this.

**wind·bag** (wind′bag′), *n.* [Colloq.], a person who talks much but says little of importance.

**wind-blown** (wind′blōn′), *adj.* 1. blown by the wind. 2. designating or of a woman's coiffure in which the hair is bobbed and brushed forward.

**wind-borne** (wind′bôrn′, -bōrn′), *adj.* transported by the wind, as certain pollen.

**wind·break** (wind′brāk′), *n.* a hedge, fence, or row of trees that serves as a protection from wind.
**wind·break·er** (wind′brāk′ēr), *n.* a sports jacket of leather, etc., having a closefitting elastic waistband and cuffs: a trade-mark (**Windbreaker**).
**wind-bro·ken** (wind′brō′k'n), *adj.* having the heaves: said of a horse.
**wind·ed** (win′did), *adj.* out of breath. **—wind′ed·ly,** *adv.* **—wind′ed·ness,** *n.*
**wind·fall** (wind′fôl′), *n.* 1. something blown down by the wind, as fruit from a tree. 2. an unexpected stroke of luck or financial gain.
**wind·flaw** (wind′flô′), *n.* a gust of wind; flaw
**wind·flow·er** (wind′flou′ēr), *n.* anemone (the flower).
**wind gauge,** an instrument for measuring wind velocity; anemometer.
**wind·hov·er** (wind′huv′ēr), *n.* a kestrel.
**wind·ing** (wīn′diŋ), *n.* 1. the action or effect of a person or thing that winds; a coiling, twining, turn, bend, etc. 2. something that winds or is wound around an object. *adj.* that winds, turns, coils, etc. **—wind′ing·ly,** *adv.*
**winding sheet,** a shroud.
**wind instrument** (wind), a musical instrument played by blowing air, especially breath, through it, as a *wood wind* (flute, oboe, clarinet, etc.) or a *brass wind* (trumpet, trombone, tuba, etc.).
**wind·jam·mer** (wind′jam′ēr), *n.* in *nautical usage,* a sailing ship or one of its crew.
**wind·lass** (wind′ləs), *n.* [< ON. *vindass* < *vinda,* to wind + *ass,* a beam], an apparatus for hauling or hoisting, consisting of a cylinder upon which is wound the rope, cable, etc. which is attached to the object to be lifted. *v.t. & v.i.* to hoist or haul with a windlass.
**wind·mill** (wind′mil′), *n.* a mill operated by the wind's rotation of large vanes radiating from a shaft: it is used for pumping water, etc. **—fight** (or **tilt at**) **windmills,** to fight imaginary opponents: from Don Quixote's mistaking windmills for giants.

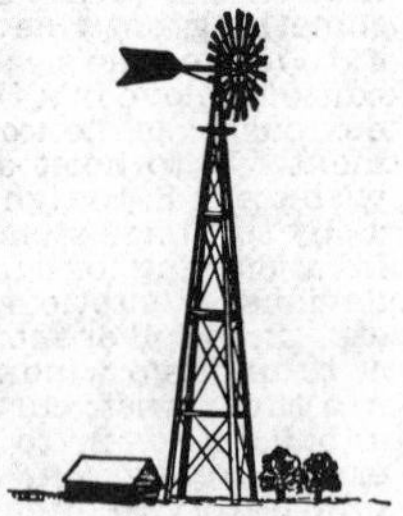
WINDMILL

**win·dow** (win′dō), *n.* [< ON. < *vindr,* wind + *auga,* an eye], 1. an opening in a building, vehicle, etc. for admitting light and air, usually having a pane or panes of glass, etc. set in a movable frame. 2. a windowpane. 3. a window with its sash (or casement) and frame. 4. any opening resembling a window. *v.t.* to provide with windows. **—win′dowed,** *adj.* **—win′dow·less,** *adj.* **—win′dow·like′,** *adj.*
**window box,** a long, narrow box on or outside a window ledge, for growing plants.
**window dressing,** 1. the display of goods and trimmings in a store window to attract customers. 2. statements or actions to give a misleadingly favorable impression.
**window envelope,** an envelope with a transparent part through which the address can be seen.
**win·dow·pane** (win′dō-pān′), *n.* a pane of glass in a window.
**window seat,** a seat built in beneath a window or windows and usually containing storage space.
**window shade,** a shade for a window, especially one of heavy paper or cloth on a spring roller.
**win·dow-shop** (win′dō-shop′), *v.i.* [-SHOPPED, -SHOPPING], to look at displays of goods in store windows without entering the stores to buy. **—win′dow-shop′per,** *n.* **—win′dow-shop′ping,** *adj. & n.*
**wind·pipe** (wind′pīp′), *n.* the trachea.
**wind·row** (wind′rō′, win′rō′), *n.* 1. a row of hay raked together to dry before being made into heaps. 2. any similar row, as of grain. 3. a row of dry leaves, dust, etc. swept together by the wind. *v.t.* to rake, sweep, etc. into windrows.
**wind·shield** (wind′shēld′), *n.* in motor vehicles, etc., a transparent screen in front, as of glass, that protects the occupants from wind, etc.
**wind sock** (or **sleeve, cone**), a long, cone-shaped cloth bag attached to the top of a mast, as at an airfield, to show the direction of the wind.
**Wind·sor** (win′zēr), *n.* 1. a city in S England: pop., 29,000: site of Windsor Castle. 2. a city in Ontario, Canada, opposite Detroit: pop., 126,000.
**Wind·sor** (win′zēr), *n.* the name of the ruling family of England since 1917.
**Windsor Castle,** a residence of English sovereigns since the time of William the Conqueror.
**Windsor chair,** a style of wooden chair, especially popular in the 18th century, with a spindle back, spreading legs, and a saddle seat.

WINDSOR CHAIR

**Windsor tie,** a wide necktie of soft silk cut on the bias, tied in a double bow.
**wind·storm** (wind′stôrm′), *n.* a storm with a strong wind but little or no rain.
**wind-swept** (wind′swept′), *adj.* swept by winds.
**wind tunnel,** a tunnellike chamber through which air is forced for testing scale models of airplanes, etc. against the effects of wind pressure.
**wind·up** (wīnd′up′), *n.* 1. a winding up; close; end. 2. in *baseball,* the loosening movements of the arm preparatory to pitching the ball.
**wind·ward** (wind′wērd; *nautical,* win′dērd), *n.* the direction from which the wind blows: opposed to *leeward.* *adv.* toward the wind. *adj.* 1. moving windward. 2. on the side from which the wind blows.
**Windward Islands,** 1. the southern group of islands in the Lesser Antilles, in the West Indies. 2. a British possession made up of some of these islands and one of the Leeward Islands.
**wind·y** (win′di), *adj.* [-IER, -IEST], 1. characterized by wind: as, a *windy* day. 2. exposed to wind: as, a *windy* city. 3. like wind; stormy, gusty, etc. 4. airy; intangible. 5. verbose; garrulous. 6. boastful; pompous. 7. *a*) causing gas in the stomach or intestines. *b*) caused by flatulence. **—wind′i·ly,** *adv.* **—wind′i·ness,** *n.*
**wine** (wīn), *n.* [AS. *win* < L. *vinum*], 1. the fermented juice of grapes, used as an alcoholic beverage, and in cooking, etc. 2. the fermented juice of other fruits or plants: as, dandelion *wine.* 3. intoxication. 4. a dark, purplish red, the color of some wines. *v.t.* [WINED, WINING], to entertain with wine. *v.i.* to drink wine.
**wine·bib·ber** (wīn′bib′ēr), *n.* one who drinks a great deal of wine. **—wine′bib′ing,** *adj. & n.*
**wine cellar,** 1. a cellar where wine is stored. 2. a stock of wine.
**wine-col·ored** (wīn′kul′ērd), *adj.* having the color of red wine; dark purplish-red.
**wine gallon,** an old English gallon of 231 cu. in., now the standard gallon in the U.S.
**wine·glass** (wīn′glas′, -gläs′), *n.* a small glass for drinking wine. **—wine′glass·ful′** [*pl.* -FULS], *n.*
**wine·grow·er** (wīn′grō′ēr), *n.* one who grows grapes and makes wine from them. **—wine′grow′ing,** *n.*
**wine press,** a vat in which grapes are trodden, or a machine for pressing them, in order to extract the juice for making wine.
**win·er·y** (wīn′ēr-i), *n.* [*pl.* -IES], an establishment where wine is made.
**Wine·sap** (wīn′sap′), *n.* a dark-red, medium-sized variety of winter apple grown in the U.S.
**wine·skin** (wīn′skin′), *n.* in Eastern countries, a bag for holding wine, made of an animal's skin.
**wing** (wiŋ), *n.* [< ON. pl. of *vaengr*], 1. either of the two forelimbs of a bird, developed in most species for flying. 2. either of the paired organs of flight of a bat, or of insects. 3. either of a pair of similar structures attributed to angels, demons, etc. 4. any of various winglike structures, as of the flying fish. 5. something used like a wing; specif., one of the main supporting structures of an airplane. 6. something like a wing in position or in relation to the main part; specif., *a*) a part of a building subordinate to the main part. *b*) in *botany,* a winglike extension on some stems and leafstalks. *c*) in the *theater,* either side of the stage out of sight of the audience. 7. a group of persons or things having a winglike relation to another; specif., *a*) the right or left section of an army, fleet, etc. *b*) a political faction or group representing some specified shade of opinion: as, a right *wing.* *c*) a position or player on a team to the right or left of the center. 8. *a*) a means of flying. *b*) a flying or manner of flying. 9. anything represented as flying or soaring: as, on *wings* of song. 10. [Colloq.], an arm of a human being: a humorous usage. 11. in the *U.S. Air Force,* *a*) a unit of aircraft and their personnel, larger than a group. *b*) *pl.* the insignia worn by pilots and crew members. *v.t.* 1. to fly across, through, etc. 2. to provide with wings. 3. to enable to fly or hasten; speed: as, he *winged* his words. 4. to do, make, etc. by means of wings. 5. to transport by or as by flight. 6. to wound (a bird) in the wing or (a person) in the arm, shoulder, etc. *v.i.* to fly. **—on the wing,** in flight; continually moving about. **—take wing,** to fly away. **—under the wing of,** under the protection, etc. of. **—wing′less,** *adj.* **—wing′like′,** *adj.*

**wing chair,** an upholstered armchair with a high back from which high sides, or wings, are extended.
**winged** (wiŋd; *for 2 & 3, often poetic* wiŋ′id), *adj.* 1. having wings or winglike parts. 2. moving on or as if on wings. 3. *a*) lofty; sublime. *b*) swift; rapid. 4. *a*) wounded in the wing. *b*) [Colloq.], wounded in an arm, shoulder, etc.
**wing·spread** (wiŋ′spred′), *n.* the distance between the tips of a pair of wings when spread.
**wink** (wiŋk), *v.i.* [AS. *wincian*], 1. to close the eyelids and open them again quickly. 2. to close one eyelid and open it again quickly, as a signal, etc. 3. to twinkle. *v.t.* 1. to make (the eyes or an eye) wink. 2. to move, remove, etc. by winking: as, he *winked* back his tears. 3. to signal, etc. by winking. *n.* 1. a winking. 2. an instant. 3. a nap: now only in *not a wink.* 4. a signal given by winking. 5. a twinkle. **—forty winks,** [Colloq.], a short nap. **—wink at,** to pretend not to see, as in connivance.
**wink·er** (wiŋk′ẽr), *n.* 1. a person or thing that winks. 2. a horse's blinder. 3. [Colloq.], an eyelash.
**win·kle** (wiŋ′k'l), *n.* [< *periwinkle*], any of various edible sea snails; periwinkle.
**win·ner** (win′ẽr), *n.* a person or thing that wins.
**win·ning** (win′iŋ), *adj.* 1. that wins; victorious. 2. attractive; charming. *n.* 1. a victory. 2. *pl.* something won, especially money. **—win′ning·ly,** *adv.*
**Win·ni·peg** (win′ə-peg′), *n.* 1. the capital of Manitoba, Canada: pop., 255,000. 2. a large lake in S Manitoba.
**win·now** (win′ō), *v.t.* [AS. *windwian* < *wind,* wind], 1. *a*) to blow the chaff from (grain). *b*) to blow off (chaff). 2. to blow away; scatter. 3. to sift or sort out. 4. to eliminate or select by sifting. 5. *a*) to fan with the wings. *b*) to flap (the wings). *v.i.* to winnow grain. *n.* 1. a winnowing. 2. an apparatus for winnowing. **—win′now·er,** *n.*
**win·o** (wī′nō), *n.* [*pl.* -os], [Slang], an alcoholic who drinks cheap wine.
**win·some** (win′səm), *adj.* [AS. *wynsum,* pleasant], attractive; charming. **—win′some·ly,** *adv.*
**Win·ston-Sa·lem** (win′st'n-sā′ləm), *n.* a city in north central North Carolina: pop., 111,000.
**win·ter** (win′tẽr), *n.* [AS.], 1. the coldest season of the year, following autumn. 2. a year as reckoned by this season: as, a man of eighty *winters.* 3. any period regarded, like winter, as a time of decline, distress, etc. *adj.* 1. of or characteristic of the winter. 2. done, used, played, etc. during the winter. 3. that will keep in the winter: as, *winter* apples. 4. planted in the fall to be harvested in the spring: as, *winter* wheat. *v.i.* to pass the winter. *v.t.* to keep, feed, or maintain during the winter. **—win′ter·er,** *n.*
**win·ter·green** (win′tẽr-grēn′), *n.* 1. an evergreen plant with white flowers and red berries; checkerberry. 2. an oil (**oil of wintergreen**) made from the leaves of this plant and used as a flavor and in medicine. 3. its flavor.
**win·ter·ize** (win′tẽr-īz′), *v.t.* [-IZED, -IZING], to put into condition for winter, as a motor vehicle.
**win·ter·kill** (win′tẽr-kil′), *v.t. & v.i.* to kill or die by exposure to winter cold: said of plants.
**winter solstice,** see **solstice.**
**win·ter·time** (win′tẽr-tīm′), *n.* the season of winter.
**Win·throp, John** (win′thrəp), 1588–1649; first governor of Massachusetts Bay colony.
**win·try** (win′tri), *adj.* [-TRIER, -TRIEST], of or like winter; cold, bleak, etc.: as, a *wintry* day, a *wintry* stare: also **win′ter·ly** (-tẽr-li), **win′ter·y.** **—win′tri·ly,** *adv.* **—win′tri·ness,** *n.*
**win·y** (win′i), *adj.* [-IER, -IEST], like wine in taste, smell, color, etc.
**wipe** (wīp), *v.t.* [WIPED, WIPING], [AS. *wipian*], 1. to rub with a cloth, etc., as for cleaning or drying. 2. to clean or dry in this manner. 3. to rub or pass (a cloth, etc.) over something. 4. to apply by wiping. 5. to remove as by wiping (with *away, off,* etc.). *n.* 1. a wiping. 2. a blow; swipe. 3. [Slang], a handkerchief. **—wipe out,** 1. to remove; erase. 2. to kill off. 3. to destroy. 4. [Slang], to be capsized by a wave in surfing. **—wip′er,** *n.*
**wire** (wīr), *n.* [AS. *wir*], 1. metal that has been drawn into a long thread. 2. a length of this, used for conducting electric current, etc. 3. wirework. 4. anything made of wire or wirework, as a telephone cable, a snare, etc. 5. telegraph: as, reply by *wire.* 6. [Colloq.], a telegram. 7. in *horse racing,* a wire above the finish line of a race. *adj.* made of wire or wirework. *v.t.* [WIRED, WIRING], 1. to furnish, connect, bind, etc. with wire. 2. to snare with a wire or wires. 3. to install a system of wires for electric current. 4. [Colloq.], to telegraph. *v.i.* [Colloq.], to telegraph. **—get under the wire,** to enter or achieve barely on time. **—pull wires,** to use private influence to achieve a purpose. **—wired,** *adj.* **—wire′like′,** *adj.* **—wir′er,** *n.*
**wire cutter,** a scissorlike tool for cutting wire.
**wire·draw** (wīr′drô′), *v.t.* [-DREW, -DRAWN, -DRAWING], 1. to draw out, as metal into wire. 2. to overrefine, as points in an argument.
**wire gauge,** a device for measuring the diameter of wire, thickness of sheet metal, etc.: usually a disk with notches of graduated sizes along its edge.
**wire·hair** (wīr′hâr′), *n.* a fox terrier with a wiry coat: also **wire-haired terrier.**
**wire-haired** (wīr′hârd′), *adj.* having stiff and coarse, or wiry, hair.
**wire·less** (wīr′lis), *adj.* 1. without wire or wires; specif., operating with electromagnetic waves and not with conducting wire. 2. [Chiefly Brit.], radio. *n.* 1. wireless telegraphy or telephony. 2. [Chiefly Brit.], radio. 3. a message sent by wireless. *v.t. & v.i.* to communicate (with) by wireless.
**wireless telegraphy,** telegraphy by radio-transmitted signals: also **wireless telegraph.**
**wireless telephony,** telephony by radio-transmitted signals.
**wire·pho·to** (wīr′fō′tō), *n.* 1. a system of reproducing photographs at a distance by means of electric impulses transmitted by wire. 2. a photograph so reproduced. A trade-mark (**Wirephoto**).
**wire·pull·er** (wīr′pool′ẽr), *n.* one who uses private influence to gain his ends. **—wire′pull′ing,** *n.*
**wire recorder,** a machine for recording sound electromagnetically on a thin wire running between two spools: replaced by the tape recorder.
**wire·tap** (wīr′tap′), *v.i. & v.t.* [-TAPPED, -TAPPING], to tap (a telephone wire, etc.) to get information secretly. *n.* 1. the act or an instance of wiretapping. 2. a device used in wiretapping.
**wire·work** (wīr′wũrk′), *n.* netting, grilled work, etc. made of wire.
**wir·ing** (wīr′iŋ), *n.* 1. the action of one that wires. 2. a system of wires, as for carrying electricity. *adj.* 1. that wires. 2. used in wiring.
**wir·y** (wīr′i), *adj.* [-IER, -IEST], 1. of wire. 2. like wire; stiff: as, *wiry* hair. 3. lean, sinewy, and strong. 4. produced as if by a vibrating wire: as, a *wiry* sound. **—wir′i·ly,** *adv.* **—wir′i·ness,** *n.*
**wis** (wis), *v.t.* [< *iwis,* erroneously understood as "I know"], [Archaic], to suppose; imagine.
**Wis·con·sin** (wis-kon′s'n), *n.* a Middle Western State of the U.S.: area, 56,154 sq. mi.; pop., 3,952,000; capital, Madison: abbrev. **Wis., Wisc.** **—Wis·con′sin·ite′** (-īt′), *n.*
**wis·dom** (wiz′dəm), *n.* [AS. < *wis,* wise + *-dom* (see -DOM)], 1. the quality of being wise; good judgment, based on knowledge, etc.; discretion; sagacity. 2. learning; knowledge; erudition. 3. wise teaching. 4. [Rare], a wise saying, action, etc.
**Wisdom of Solomon,** a book of the Old Testament Apocrypha: called *Wisdom* in the Douay Bible.
**wisdom tooth,** the back tooth on each side of each jaw in human beings, appearing usually between the ages of 17 and 25. **—cut one's wisdom teeth,** to arrive at the age of discretion.
**wise** (wīz), *adj.* [< AS. *wis*], 1. having or showing good judgment; sagacious. 2. judicious; sound: as, a *wise* saying. 3. informed: as, none the *wiser.* 4. learned; erudite. 5. shrewd; cunning. 6. [Slang], *a*) annoyingly self-assured, etc.: as, a *wise* guy. *b*) impudent; fresh. **—be (or get) wise to,** [Slang], to be (or become) aware of. **—put wise (to),** [Slang], to give (a person) information, etc. (about). **—wise up,** [Slang], to make or become informed. **—wise′ly,** *adv.* **—wise′ness,** *n.*
**wise** (wīz), *n.* [AS.], way; manner: used chiefly in the phrases *in no wise, in this wise,* etc.
**-wise** (wīz), [< *wise, n.*], a suffix meaning: 1. *in a* (specified) *direction, position,* or *manner,* as in *sidewise.* 2. *in a manner characteristic of* (something specified), as in *clockwise.* 3. *with regard to; in connection with,* as in *weatherwise, budgetwise.*
**wise·a·cre** (wīz′ā′kẽr), *n.* [< D. < OHG. *wizzago,* a prophet], one who thinks he knows everything.
**wise·crack** (wīz′krak′), *n.* [Slang], a flippant or facetious remark, often a retort. *v.i.* [Slang], to make wisecracks: also **crack wise.** *v.t.* [Slang], to say as a wisecrack. **—wise′crack′er,** *n.*
**wish** (wish), *v.t.* [AS. *wyscan*], 1. to have a longing

for; want; desire. 2. to have or express a desire concerning: as, I *wish* the week were over, I *wish* you good luck. 3. to bid: as, she *wished* me good morning. 4. to request: as, I *wish* you to leave. 5. to impose (with *on*): as, another duty *wished* on him. ***v.i.*** 1. to long; yearn. 2. to make a wish. ***n.*** 1. a wishing; desire for something. 2. something wished for: as, he got his *wish*. 3. a request: as, it is her *wish* that you enter. 4. *pl.* expressed desire for a person's health, etc.: as, they send their *wishes*. **—wish′er, *n.***

**wish·bone** (wish′bōn′), ***n.*** the forked bone in front of the breastbone of most birds.

**wish·ful** (wish′fəl), ***adj.*** having or showing a wish; desirous; longing. **—wish′ful·ly, *adv.* —wish′ful·ness, *n.***

**wishful thinking,** thinking in which one interprets facts in terms of what he wants to believe.

**wish·y-wash·y** (wish′i-wôsh′i, -wäsh′i), ***adj.*** [redupl. of *washy*], 1. watery; insipid; thin. 2. weak; feeble.

**wisp** (wisp), ***n.*** [prob. < ON.], 1. a small bundle or bunch, as of straw. 2. a thin, slight, or filmy piece, strand, etc.: as, a *wisp* of smoke. 3. anything slight, frail, etc.: as, a *wisp* of a girl. 4. a will-o'-the-wisp. 5. a whisk broom. **—wisp′y** [-IER, -IEST], **wisp′ish, wisp′like′, *adj.***

**wist** (wist), pt. and pp. of **wit** (to know).

**wis·te·ri·a** (wis-têr′i-ə), ***n.*** [after C. *Wistar*, Am. anatomist], a twining shrub of the pea family, with showy clusters of bluish, white, or purplish flowers: also **wis·ta′ri·a** (-târ′-).

**wist·ful** (wist′fəl), ***adj.*** [alt. (after *wishful*) < earlier *wistly*, intently], showing or expressing vague yearnings; longing pensively. **—wist′ful·ly, *adv.* —wist′ful·ness, *n.***

**wit** (wit), ***n.*** [AS.], 1. *pl.* *a*) powers of thinking and reasoning. *b*) mental faculties, especially in their normal condition of sanity. 2. [Rare], good sense; wisdom. 3. the ability to make clever remarks, usually by perceiving the incongruous and expressing it in a surprising or ironic way. 4. a person having this ability. **—at one's wits' end,** at a loss as to what to do. **—keep (or have) one's wits about one,** to remain mentally alert. **—live by one's wits,** to live by trickery or craftiness.

**wit** (wit), ***v.t. & v.i.*** [WIST, WITTING], [AS. *witan*], [Archaic], to know or learn. *Wit* was conjugated, in the present indicative: (I) *wot*, (thou) *wost* or *wot(t)est*, (he, she, it) *wot* or *wot(t)eth*, (we, ye, they) *wite*. **—to wit,** that is to say; namely.

**witch** (wich), ***n.*** [AS. *wicce*, fem. of *wicca*, sorcerer], 1. a woman supposedly having supernatural power by a compact with evil spirits. 2. an ugly and ill-tempered old woman. 3. [Colloq.], a bewitching or fascinating woman or girl. ***adj.*** of a witch. ***v.t.*** 1. to put a magic spell on. 2. to charm; fascinate. **—witch′like′, *adj.***

**witch·craft** (wich′kraft′, -kräft′), ***n.*** 1. the power or practices of witches; sorcery. 2. an instance of this. 3. bewitching attraction or charm.

**witch doctor,** among primitive tribes, a person who professes to counteract the effects of witchcraft.

**witch·er·y** (wich′ēr-i), ***n.*** [*pl.* -IES], 1. witchcraft; sorcery. 2. bewitching charm; fascination.

**witch hazel,** [AS. *wice*], 1. a shrub with yellow flowers and woody fruit. 2. an alcoholic lotion of an extract from the bark and leaves of this plant.

**witch hunt,** an investigation usually conducted with much publicity, supposedly to uncover subversion, disloyalty, etc., but really to harass and weaken political opposition.

**witch·ing** (wich′iŋ), ***adj.*** that witches; bewitching or enchanting. **—witch′ing·ly, *adv.***

**with** (wi*th*, with), ***prep.*** [AS., orig., against], 1. in opposition to: as, he argued *with* his wife. 2. *a*) alongside of; near to. *b*) in the company of. *c*) into; among: as, mix blue *with* yellow. 3. as an associate of, in conversation, games, etc.: as, he talked *with* me. 4. as a member of: as, he sings *with* a quartet. 5. *a*) in terms of relationship to: as, friendly *with* strangers. *b*) in regard to: as, pleased *with* her gift. 6. in the same terms as; compared to: as, having equal standing *with* the others. 7. as well as: as, he can jump *with* the best. 8. of the same opinions as: as, I'm *with* you. 9. on the side of: as, he voted *with* the Tories. 10. *a*) in the region, sphere, circumstances, etc. of. *b*) in the opinion of: as, it's all right *with* me. 11. as a result of: as, faint *with* hunger. 12. *a*) by means of: as, stir *with* a spoon. *b*) by: as, filled *with* air. 13. having received: as, *with* your permission, I'll go. 14. having as a possession, attribute, etc.: as, the man *with* brown hair. 15. exhibiting: as, he plays *with* skill. 16. in the keeping, care, etc. of: as, leave the children *with* Bill. 17. and: as, the woman, *with* her son, arrived. 18. in spite of: as, *with* all his boasting, he is a coward. 19. *a*) at the same time as: as, to rise *with* the chickens. *b*) in the same direction as: as, travel *with* the sun. *c*) in proportion to: as, grow wise *with* age. 20. to; onto: as, join this end *with* that one. 21. from: as, to part *with* one's gains. **—in with,** associated with. **—with that,** after that.

**with-,** [AS.], a combining form meaning: 1. *away, back*, as in *withdraw*. 2. *against, from*, as in *withhold*.

**with·al** (wi*th*-ôl′, with-), ***adv.*** [Archaic], 1. besides. 2. thereby. 3. thereupon. 4. still. ***prep.*** [Archaic], with: used at the end of a clause, etc.

**with·draw** (wi*th*-drô′, with-), ***v.t.*** [-DREW, -DRAWN, -DRAWING], 1. to take back; remove. 2. to retract or recall (a statement, etc.). ***v.i.*** to move back; go away; retire; retreat. **—with·draw′al, with·draw′ment, *n.* —with·draw′er, *n.***

**with·drawn** (wi*th*-drôn′, with-), ***adj.*** withdrawing within oneself; shy, reserved, abstracted, etc.

**withe** (with, wi*th*, wī*th*), ***n.*** [AS. *withthe*], a tough, flexible twig of willow, etc., used for binding things. ***v.t.*** [WITHED, WITHING], to bind with withes.

**with·er** (wi*th*′ēr), ***v.i.*** [< ME. var. of *wederen*, lit., to weather], 1. to dry up; shrivel; wilt: said of plants. 2. to become wasted or decayed. 3. to languish: as, her affections *withered*. ***v.t.*** 1. to cause to wither. 2. to cause to feel abashed, as by a scornful glance. **—with′er·ing·ly, *adv.***

**with·ers** (wi*th*′ērz), ***n.pl.*** [< ME. *wither*, resistance < AS. < *wither*, against], the highest part of the back of a horse, etc. between the shoulder blades.

**with·hold** (with-hōld′, wi*th*-), ***v.t.*** [-HELD, -HOLDING], 1. to hold back; restrain. 2. to refrain from granting, etc.; refuse. ***v.i.*** to refrain; forbear. **—with·hold′er, *n.* —with·hold′ment, *n.***

**withholding tax,** the amount of income tax withheld from employees' wages or salaries.

**with·in** (wi*th*-in′, with-), ***adv.*** [AS. *withinnan*], 1. on or to the inside; internally. 2. indoors. 3. inside the body, mind, etc. ***prep.*** 1. in the inner part of. 2. not beyond in time, distance, degree, etc.: as, *within* a mile. 3. inside the limits of.

**with·out** (wi*th*-out′, with-), ***adv.*** [AS. *withutan*], 1. on or to the outside; externally. 2. out of doors. ***prep.*** 1. at, on, or to the outside of. 2. beyond: as, *without* his reach. 3. not with; lacking. 4. free from: as, *without* fear. 5. with avoidance of: as, he passed *without* speaking. 6. lacking (something understood): as, we'll do *without*. ***conj.*** [Dial.], unless: as, I can't go, *without* I get some money.

**with·stand** (with-stand′, wi*th*-), ***v.t. & v.i.*** [-STOOD, -STANDING], to oppose, resist, or endure.

**with·y** (wi*th*′i, with′i), ***n.*** [*pl.* -IES], [AS. *withig*], a tough, flexible twig of willow, etc.; withe.

**wit·less** (wit′lis), ***adj.*** lacking wit or intelligence; stupid. **—wit′less·ly, *adv.* —wit′less·ness, *n.***

**wit·ling** (wit′liŋ), ***n.*** a would-be wit.

**wit·ness** (wit′nis), ***n.*** [< AS. *gewitnes*, knowledge, testimony], 1. evidence; testimony. 2. a person who saw, or can give a firsthand account of, something. 3. one who testifies in court. 4. one who observes a transaction, signing, etc. so that he may testify concerning its occurrence. 5. something serving as evidence. ***v.t.*** 1. to testify to. 2. to serve as evidence of. 3. to act as witness of. 4. to be present at; see personally. 5. to be the scene of: as, this field has *witnessed* many battles. ***v.i.*** to serve as evidence; testify. **—bear witness,** to be or give evidence. **—wit′ness·er, *n.***

**witness stand,** the place from which a witness gives his testimony in a law court.

**wit·ted** (wit′id), ***adj.*** having a (specified kind of) wit: as, *slow-witted*.

**wit·ti·cism** (wit′ə-siz′m), ***n.*** [< *witty*, after *criticism*, etc.], a witty remark.

**wit·ting** (wit′iŋ), ***adj.*** [ME. *wything*], deliberate; intentional. **—wit′ting·ly, *adv.***

**wit·ty** (wit′i), ***adj.*** [-TIER, -TIEST], [AS. *wittig*], having or showing wit; cleverly amusing. **—wit′ti·ly, *adv.* —wit′ti·ness, *n.***

**wive** (wīv), ***v.i. & v.t.*** [WIVED, WIVING], [AS. *wifian*], to marry (a woman).

**wives** (wīvz), ***n.*** pl. of **wife.**

**wiz** (wiz), ***n.*** [< *wizard;* but cf. WHIZ], [Slang], one regarded as exceptionally clever or gifted.

**wiz·ard** (wiz′ērd), ***n.*** [< OFr. < ON. *viskr*, clever], 1. a magician; conjurer. 2. [Colloq.], a very skillful or clever person. ***adj.*** of wizards or wizardry. **—wiz′ard·like′, *adj.* —wiz′ard·ly, *adj.***

**wiz·ard·ry** (wiz′ērd-ri), ***n.*** magic; sorcery.

**wiz·en** (wiz′'n; *dial.* wē′z'n), ***v.t. & v.i.*** [< AS. *wisnian*], to dry up; wither. ***adj.*** wizened.

**wiz·ened** (wiz′'nd; *dial.* wē′z'nd), *adj.* [pp. of *wizen*], dried up; shriveled; withered; shrunken.
**wk.,** [*pl.* WKS.], 1. week. 2. work.
**w.l.,** wave length.
**WNW, W.N.W., w.n.w.,** west-northwest.
**W.O.,** Warrant Officer.
**woad** (wōd), *n.* [AS. *wad*], 1. a plant of the mustard family. 2. a blue dye made from its leaves.
**wob·ble** (wob′'l), *v.i.* [-BLED, -BLING], [? < LG. *wabbeln*], 1. to move unsteadily from side to side; shake. 2. to vacillate. *v.t.* [Colloq.], to cause to wobble. *n.* wobbling motion. Also **wabble.** —**wob′bler,** *n.* —**wob′bling,** *adj.* —**wob′bling·ly,** *adv.* —**wob′bly** [-BLIER, -BLIEST], *adj.*
**Wo·den, Wo·dan** (wō′d'n), *n.* the chief Germanic god, identified with the Norse Odin.
**woe, wo** (wō), *n.* [AS. *wa*], 1. great sorrow; grief. 2. trouble. *interj.* alas!
**woe·be·gone, wo·be·gone** (wō′bi-gôn′, -gon′), *adj.* of woeful appearance; looking mournful.
**woe·ful, wo·ful** (wō′fəl), *adj.* 1. full of woe; mournful. 2. of, causing, or involving woe. 3. pitiful; wretched. —**woe′ful·ly, wo′ful·ly,** *adv.* —**woe′fulness, wo′ful·ness,** *n.*
**woke** (wōk), alt. pt. of **wake.**
**wok·en** (wō′kən), rare pp. of **wake.**
**wold** (wōld), *n.* [AS. *wald*], a treeless, rolling plain, especially a high one.
**wolf** (woolf), *n.* [*pl.* WOLVES], [AS. *wulf*], 1. any of a group of wild, flesh-eating, doglike mammals widely distributed throughout the Northern Hemisphere. 2. *a*) a fierce, cruel, or greedy person. *b*) [Slang], a man who flirts aggressively with many women. *v.t.* to eat ravenously. —**cry wolf,** to give a false alarm. —**keep the wolf from the door,** to provide the necessities of life. —**wolf′ish,** *adj.* —**wolf′ish·ly,** *adv.* —**wolf′ish·ness,** *n.*
**wolf·ber·ry** (woolf′ber′i), *n.* [*pl.* -RIES], a shrub with spikelike clusters of white berries.
**Wolfe, James** (woolf), 1727–1759; British general; defeated Montcalm at Quebec (1759).
**Wolfe, Thomas Clay·ton** (klā′t'n), 1900–1938; U.S. novelist.
**wolf·hound** (woolf′hound′), *n.* a large dog of any of several breeds once used for hunting wolves.
**wolf·ram** (wool′frəm), *n.* [G., apparently < *wolf* + MHG. *ram*], 1. tungsten. 2. wolframite.
**wolf·ram·ite** (wool′frəm-īt′), *n.* a brownish or blackish mineral, a compound of tungsten (wolfram), iron, and manganese.
**wolfs·bane** (woolfs′bān′), *n.* any of various poisonous plants having large, blue, white, or yellow hoodlike flowers; aconite: also sp. **wolf's-bane.**
**Wol·sey, Thomas** (wool′zi), Cardinal, 1475?–1530; English statesman and prelate.
**wol·ver·ine** (wool′və-rēn′, wool′və-rēn′), *n.* [*pl.* -INES, -INE; see PLURAL, II, D, 1], [dim. < *wolf*], a stocky, flesh-eating mammal with thick fur, found in the northern U.S. and Canada: the European variety is called *glutton*: also sp. **wolverene.**

WOLVERINE (3 ft. long)

**wolves** (woolvz), *n.* pl. of **wolf.**
**wom·an** (woom′ən), *n.* [*pl.* WOMEN], [< AS. *wifmann* < *wif*, a female + *mann*, a human being], 1. the female human being, or women collectively. 2. an adult female human being. 3. a female servant. 4. *a*) a wife. *b*) a sweetheart or a mistress. 5. womanly qualities: as, it's the *woman* in her. *adj.* 1. feminine. 2. female.
**wom·an·hood** (woom′ən-hood′), *n.* 1. the state of being a woman. 2. womanly qualities. 3. womankind.
**wom·an·ish** (woom′ən-ish), *adj.* like, characteristic of, or suitable to a woman; feminine. —**wom′anish·ly,** *adv.* —**wom′an·ish·ness,** *n.*
**wom·an·ize** (woom′ən-īz′), *v.t.* [-IZED, -IZING], to make effeminate.
**wom·an·kind** (woom′ən-kīnd′), *n.* women in general.
**wom·an·like** (woom′ən-līk′), *adj.* womanly.
**wom·an·ly** (woom′ən-li), *adj.* 1. like a woman; womanish. 2. characteristic of a woman. 3. suitable to a woman. —**wom′an·li·ness,** *n.*
**woman suffrage,** the right of women to vote in governmental elections. —**wom′an-suf′frage,** *adj.* —**wom′an-suf′fra·gist,** *n.*
**womb** (wōōm), *n.* [AS. *wamb*], 1. the uterus. 2. any place or part that holds, generates, etc.
**wom·bat** (wom′bat), *n.* [< Australian native name *womback*], a burrowing marsupial resembling a small bear, found in Australia.
**wom·en** (wim′in), *n.* pl. of **woman.**
**wom·en·folk** (wim′in-fōk′), *n.pl.* women; womankind: also **wom′en·folks′.**
**women's** (or **woman's**) **rights,** the rights claimed by and for women, equal to those of men.
**won** (wun), pt. and pp. of **win.**
**won·der** (wun′dẽr), *n.* [AS. *wundor*], 1. a person, thing, or event that causes astonishment and admiration; marvel. 2. the feeling aroused by something strange, unexpected, etc.; surprise. 3. a miracle. *v.i.* 1. to be filled with wonder; marvel. 2. to have doubt mingled with curiosity. *v.t.* to have doubt and curiosity about; want to know: as, I *wonder* why he came. —**won′der·er,** *n.* —**won′der·ing,** *adj.* —**won′der·ing·ly,** *adv.*
**won·der·ful** (wun′dẽr-fəl), *adj.* 1. that causes wonder; marvelous. 2. [Colloq.], very good; excellent. —**won′der·ful·ly,** *adv.* —**won′der·ful·ness,** *n.*
**won·der·land** (wun′dẽr-land′), *n.* 1. an imaginary land full of wonders. 2. any place of beauty, etc.
**won·der·ment** (wun′dẽr-mənt), *n.* 1. a state or expression of wonder. 2. something causing wonder.
**won·der-strick·en** (wun′dẽr-strik′'n), *adj.* struck with wonder; feeling surprise, admiration, etc.: also **won′der-struck′.**
**won·der·work** (wun′dẽr-wũrk′), *n.* 1. a wonderful work; wonder. 2. a miraculous act; miracle. —**won′der-work′er,** *n.* —**won′der-work′ing,** *adj.*
**won·drous** (wun′drəs), *adj.* wonderful. *adv.* extraordinarily; surprisingly. Now a literary usage. —**won′drous·ly,** *adv.* —**won′drous·ness,** *n.*
**wont** (wunt, wōnt, wônt), *adj.* [< pp. of AS. *wunian*, to be used to], accustomed: as, he was *wont* to rise early. *n.* usual practice; habit.
**won't** (wōnt), [< ME. *wol not*], will not.
**wont·ed** (wun′tid, wōn′-, wôn′-), *adj.* customary; accustomed. —**wont′ed·ly,** *adv.* —**wont′ed·ness,** *n.*
**woo** (wōō), *v.t.* [AS. *wogian*], 1. to make love to, usually with the intention of proposing marriage; court. 2. to try to get; seek: as, she *wooed* fame. 3. to entreat; coax; urge. *v.i.* to woo a person. —**woo′er,** *n.* —**woo′ing·ly,** *adv.*
**wood** (wood), *n.* [AS. *wudu*], 1. *often pl.* a thick growth of trees; forest; grove. 2. the hard, fibrous substance beneath the bark of trees and shrubs. 3. lumber or timber. 4. firewood. 5. something made of wood. 6. a wooden cask: as, liquor aged in *wood.* 7. a wooden wind instrument, or wood winds collectively. *adj.* 1. made of wood; wooden. 2. for cutting or holding wood. 3. growing or living in woods. *v.t.* 1. to plant trees thickly over. 2. to furnish with wood, especially firewood. *v.i.* to get a supply of wood. —**out of the woods,** [Colloq.], out of difficulty, danger, etc. —**wood′ed,** *adj.* —**wood′less,** *adj.* —**wood′like′,** *adj.*
**wood alcohol,** methyl alcohol; methanol.
**wood·bine** (wood′bīn′), *n.* [*wood* + *bine*], 1. a European variety of climbing honeysuckle. 2. the Virginia creeper. Also **wood′bind′** (-bīnd′).
**wood block,** 1. a block of wood. 2. a printing die cut on wood. 3. a woodcut. —**wood′-block′,** *adj.*
**wood·chuck** (wood′chuk′), *n.* [folk-etymologized < Algonquian *wejack*], a North American burrowing and hibernating marmot with coarse, red-brown fur: also called *ground hog.*

WOODCHUCK (20 in. long)

**wood·cock** (wood′kok′), *n.* [*pl.* -COCKS, -COCK; see PLURAL, II, D, 1], 1. a small, European, migratory game bird with short legs and a long bill. 2. a similar, related North American bird.
**wood·craft** (wood′kraft′, -kräft′), *n.* 1. matters relating to the woods, as camping, hunting, trapping, etc. 2. woodworking. 3. skill in either of these. —**wood′crafts′man** [*pl.* -MEN], *n.*
**wood·cut** (wood′kut′), *n.* 1. a wooden block engraved with a picture, etc. 2. a print made from it.
**wood·cut·ter** (wood′kut′ẽr), *n.* a person who fells trees, cuts wood, etc. —**wood′cut′ting,** *n.*
**wood·en** (wood′'n), *adj.* 1. made of wood. 2. stiff, lifeless, expressionless, etc. 3. dull or insensitive. —**wood′en·ly,** *adv.* —**wood′en·ness,** *n.*
**wood engraving,** 1. the art or process of engraving on wood. 2. a woodcut. —**wood engraver.**

**wood·en·head·ed** (wood′'n-hed′id), *n.* [Colloq.], stupid; dull. —**wood′en·head′ed·ness,** *n.*
**wooden horse,** Trojan horse.
**wood·en·ware** (wood′'n-wâr′), *n.* bowls, tubs, dishes, etc. made of wood.
**wood·land** (wood′land′; *also, and for adj. always,* -lənd), *n.* land covered with woods or trees. *adj.* of, in, or relating to the woods. —**wood′land·er,** *n.*
**wood louse,** any of various crustaceans with flattened, oval, segmented bodies, found in damp soil, under decaying wood, etc.
**wood·man** (wood′mən), *n.* [*pl.* -MEN], 1. a woodcutter. 2. a person who lives in the woods.
**wood-note** (wood′nōt′), *n.* a sound of a forest bird or animal.
**wood nymph,** a nymph living in the woods; dryad.
**wood·peck·er** (wood′pek′ẽr), *n.* any of various climbing birds distinguished by a strong, pointed bill used to peck holes in bark to get insects.
**wood·pile** (wood′pīl′), *n.* a pile of wood, especially of firewood.
**wood pulp,** pulp made from wood fiber, used in paper manufacture.
**wood·shed** (wood′shed′), *n.* a shed for firewood.
**woods·man** (woodz′mən), *n.* [*pl.* -MEN], 1. one who lives or works in the woods, as a hunter, trapper, etc. 2. one who is skilled in woodcraft.
**wood sorrel,** any of a group of plants with variously colored, five-petaled flowers.
**wood·sy** (wood′zi), *adj.* [-SIER, -SIEST], of or like the woods. —**wood′si·ness,** *n.*
**wood tar,** a dark, sticky, siruplike substance obtained by the dry distillation of wood.
**wood thrush,** a large, rusty-brown thrush of E North America, having a strong, clear song.
**wood turning,** the art of turning, or shaping, wood on a lathe. —**wood′-turn′ing,** *adj.* —**wood turner.**
**wood wind,** 1. *pl.* the wind instruments of an orchestra made, especially originally, of wood; flutes, clarinets, oboes, English horns, and bassoons. 2. any of these instruments. —**wood′-wind′,** *adj.*
**wood·work** (wood′wũrk′), *n.* 1. work done in wood. 2. things made of wood, especially the interior moldings, doors, stairs, etc. of a house.
**wood·work·ing** (wood′wũr′kiŋ), *n.* the art or process of making things out of wood. *adj.* of woodworking. —**wood′work′er,** *n.*
**wood·worm** (wood′wũrm′), *n.* any of various insect larvae that live on and burrow in wood.
**wood·y** (wood′i), *adj.* [-IER, -IEST], 1. covered with trees; wooded. 2. consisting of or forming wood; ligneous. 3. like wood. —**wood′i·ness,** *n.*
**woof** (wōōf), *n.* [alt. (after *weave*) < ME. *oof* < AS. *o-*, prefix + *wefan*, to weave], 1. the threads woven back and forth across the fixed threads of the warp in a loom; weft. 2. cloth; texture; fabric.
**wool** (wool), *n.* [see PLURAL, II, D, 3], [AS. *wull*], 1. the soft, curly hair of sheep. 2. the hair of some other animals, as the goat, llama, etc. 3. woolen yarn or cloth, clothing, etc. made of wool. 4. anything with the texture of wool. *adj.* of wool or woolen goods. —**all wool and a yard wide,** genuine. —**pull the wool over one's eyes,** to deceive or trick one. —**wool′like′,** *adj.*
**wool·en, wool·len** (wool′ən), *adj.* 1. made of wool. 2. of or relating to wool or woolen cloth. *n. pl.* woolen goods or clothing.
**wool·gath·er·ing** (wool′gath′ẽr-iŋ), *n.* absent-mindedness or daydreaming. *adj.* absent-minded or indulging in fancies. —**wool′gath′er·er,** *n.*
**wool·grow·er** (wool′grō′ẽr), *n.* a person who raises sheep for wool. —**wool′grow′ing,** *n.*
**wool·ly** (wool′i), *adj.* [-LIER, -LIEST], 1. of or like wool. 2. bearing wool. 3. covered with wool or something like wool in texture. 4. rough and uncivilized: chiefly in *wild and woolly*. *n.* [*pl.* -LIES], 1. in the western U.S., a sheep. 2. a woolen garment. Also sp. **wooly.** —**wool′li·ness,** *n.*
**wool·sack** (wool′sak′), *n.* 1. a sack of wool. 2. a cushion stuffed with wool, on which the British Lord Chancellor sits in the House of Lords.
**wool·y** (wool′i), *adj.* [-IER, -IEST], *& n.* [*pl.* -IES], woolly. —**wool′i·ness,** *n.*
**Woon·sock·et** (wōōn-sok′it), *n.* a city in N Rhode Island: pop., 47,000.
**wooz·y** (wōō′zi, wooz′i), *adj.* [-IER, -IEST], [Slang], befuddled, as with liquor; muddled. —**wooz′i·ly,** *adv.* —**wooz′i·ness,** *n.*
**Worces·ter** (woos′tẽr), *n.* a city in central Massachusetts: pop., 187,000.
**Worces·ter·shire sauce** (woos′tẽr-shir′), [orig. made in *Worcester*, England], a spicy sauce for meats, poultry, etc., containing soy, vinegar, etc.
**word** (wũrd), *n.* [AS.], 1. a brief expression; remark: as, a *word* of advice. 2. a promise: as, he gave his *word*. 3. news; information: as, no *word* from home. 4. *a*) a password; signal: as, give the *word*. *b*) a command; order. 5. *usually pl. a*) talk; speech. *b*) lyrics; text; libretto. 6. *pl.* a quarrel; dispute. 7. a speech sound or series of sounds having meaning and used as a unit of language. 8. a letter or group of letters, written or printed, representing such a unit of language. *v.t.* to express in words; phrase. —**by word of mouth,** by speech; orally. —**eat one's words,** to retract a statement. —**have a word with,** to have a brief conversation with. —**have no words for,** to be incapable of describing. —**in a word,** in short, briefly. —**in so many words,** precisely; succinctly. —**man of his word,** one who keeps his promises. —**of many** (or **few**) **words,** talkative (or untalkative). —**take the words out of one's mouth,** to say what one was about to say oneself. —**the Word,** 1. the Bible: also **Word of God.** 2. Jesus as the second person of the Trinity: John 1. —**(upon) my word,** indeed! really! —**word for word,** in precisely the same words. —**word′less,** *adj.*
**word·age** (wũr′dij), *n.* words collectively, or the number of words (*of* a story, novel, etc.).
**word·book** (wũrd′book′), *n.* 1. a dictionary or vocabulary. 2. a libretto. 3. a book of song lyrics.
**word·ing** (wũr′diŋ), *n.* choice and arrangement of words; phrasing.
**word of honor,** pledged word; solemn promise.
**word order,** the arrangement of words in a phrase, clause, or sentence.
**word square,** a square made of letters so arranged that they spell the same words in the same order horizontally and vertically.

| | | | |
|---|---|---|---|
| D | A | T | E |
| A | C | I | D |
| T | I | N | G |
| E | D | G | E |

**Words·worth, William** (wũrdz′wẽrth), 1770–1850; English poet.
**word·y** (wũr′di), *adj.* [-IER, -IEST], containing or using many or too many words; verbose. —**word′i·ly,** *adv.* —**word′i·ness,** *n.*
**wore** (wôr, wōr), pt. of **wear.**
**work** (wũrk), *n.* [AS. *we(o)rc*], 1. bodily or mental effort exerted to do or make something; labor; toil. 2. employment: as, out of *work*. 3. occupation; business; trade; profession: as, his *work* is selling. 4. *a*) something one is making, doing, or acting upon; task: as, he laid out his *work*. *b*) the amount of this: as, a day's *work*. 5. something that has been made or done; specif., *a*) *usually pl.* an act; deed: as, good *works*. *b*) *pl.* collected writings. *c*) *pl.* engineering structures, as bridges, dams, etc. *d*) a fortification. *e*) needlework; embroidery. *f*) a work of art. 6. *pl.* [construed as sing.], a place where work is done, as a factory. 7. *pl.* the working parts of a watch, etc.; mechanism. 8. workmanship. 9. in *mechanics*, transference of force from one body or system to another, measured by the product of the force and the amount of displacement in the line of force. *adj.* of, for, or used in work. *v.i.* [WORKED or WROUGHT, WORKING], 1. to do work; labor; toil. 2. to be employed. 3. to perform its function; operate; act. 4. to ferment. 5. to operate effectively: as, the makeshift *works*. 6. to produce results or exert an influence: as, let it *work* in his mind. 7. to be manipulated, kneaded, etc.: as, putty *works* easily. 8. to move, proceed, etc. slowly and with or as with difficulty. 9. to move, twitch, etc. as from agitation: as, her face *worked* with emotion. 10. to become, as by repeated movement: as, the door *worked* loose. 11. to make a passage: as, her elbow had *worked* through her sleeve. *v.t.* 1. to cause; bring about: as, his idea *worked* wonders. 2. to mold; shape: as, to *work* clay. 3. to weave, knit, etc.: as, she *worked* the rug. 4. to solve (a mathematical problem). 5. to manipulate; knead: as, *work* the butter well. 6. to bring into a specified condition: as, they *worked* it loose. 7. to cultivate (soil). 8. to cause to function; operate; use. 9. to cause to ferment. 10. to cause to work: as, he *works* his men hard. 11. to influence; persuade: as, *work* him to your ideas. 12. to make (one's way, etc.) by work or effort. 13. to provoke; rouse: as, she *worked* herself into a rage. 14. to carry on activity; operate in: as, a salesman *working* Ohio. 15. [Colloq.], to make use of by artful contriving to gain some advantage: as, *work* your connections. —**at work,** working. —**get** (or **give one**) **the works,** [Slang], to be (or cause one to be) the victim of an ordeal. —**make short** (or **quick**) **work of,** to do or dispose of quickly. —**out of work,** unemployed. —**shoot the works,** [Slang], 1. to risk everything on one chance. 2. to make a supreme effort. —**the works,** [Slang], everything. —**work in,** to insert or be inserted. —**work off,** to get rid of, as by exertion. —**work on** (or **upon**), 1. to influence. 2. to try to persuade. —**work out,** 1. to make its way out,

as from being embedded. 2. to exhaust (a mine, etc.). 3. to pay off (an obligation) by work. 4. to accomplish. 5. to solve. 6. to result in some way. 7. to develop; elaborate. 8. [Colloq.], to engage in a workout. —**work up,** 1. to advance; rise. 2. to develop; elaborate. 3. to arouse; excite. —**work′less,** *adj.*

**work·a·ble** (wũr′kə-b'l), *adj.* 1. that can be worked. 2. practicable; feasible. —**work′a·bil′i·ty,** *n.*

**work·a·day** (wũr′kə-dā′), *adj.* 1. of working days; everyday. 2. commonplace; ordinary.

**work·bench** (wũrk′bench′), *n.* a table at which work is done, as by a mechanic.

**work·book** (wũrk′book′), *n.* 1. a book containing questions and exercises to be worked by students. 2. a book of operating instructions. 3. a book containing a record of work planned or done.

**work·day** (wũrk′dā′), *n.* 1. a day on which work is done; working day. 2. the part of a day during which work is done, specifically the number of hours regularly scheduled. *adj.* workaday.

**work·er** (wũr′kẽr), *n.* a person, animal, or thing that works; specif., *a*) a person who works for a living. *b*) any of various sterile ants, bees, etc. that do work for the colony.

**work·house** (wũrk′hous′), *n.* 1. in England, a poorhouse. 2. a kind of prison, where petty offenders are confined and made to work.

**work·ing** (wũr′kiŋ), *adj.* 1. that works. 2. of, for, or used in work. 3. sufficient to get work done: as, a *working* majority. 4. on which further work may be based: as, a *working* hypothesis. *n.* 1. the act or process of a person or thing that works (in various senses). 2. *usually pl.* a part of a mine, quarry, etc. where work is or has been done.

**working capital,** the part of a company's capital that remains readily convertible into cash.

**working class,** workers as a class; esp., industrial workers as a class. —**work′ing-class′,** *adj.*

**working day,** 1. a day on which work is ordinarily done, as distinguished from a Sunday, holiday, etc. 2. a workday. —**work′ing-day′,** *adj.*

**work·ing·man** (wũr′kiŋ-man′), *n.* [*pl.* -MEN], a worker; esp., an industrial or manual worker; laborer. —**work′ing·wom′an** [*pl.* -WOMEN], *n.fem.*

**work·man** (wũrk′mən), *n.* [*pl.* -MEN], 1. a worker; laborer. 2. a person with reference to the quality of his work: as, a careful *workman.* —**work′wom′an** [*pl.* -WOMEN], *n.fem.*

**work·man·like** (wũrk′mən-līk′), *adj.* characteristic of a good workman; skillful. *adv.* in a workmanlike manner: also **work′man·ly.**

**work·man·ship** (wũrk′mən-ship′), *n.* 1. skill as a workman; craftsmanship. 2. evidence of such skill: as, it has high *workmanship.* 3. something produced.

**work of art,** 1. something produced in one of the fine arts, as a painting, sculpture, etc. 2. anything beautifully made, played, sung, etc.

**work·out** (wũrk′out′), *n.* [Colloq.], 1. a test, practice, etc. 2. any strenuous exercise, work, etc.

**work·peo·ple** (wũrk′pē′p'l), *n.pl.* workers; esp., industrial or manual workers.

**work·room** (wũrk′rōōm′, -room′), *n.* a room in which work is done.

**work·shop** (wũrk′shop′), *n.* 1. a room or building where work is done. 2. a group of people who meet for a period of intensive study, work, etc. in some field.

**work·ta·ble** (wũrk′tā′b'l), *n.* a table at which work is done; esp., a small table with drawers, for needlework.

**work·week** (wũrk′wēk′), *n.* the total number of hours worked in a week.

**world** (wũrld), *n.* [AS. *weoruld*], 1. the earth. 2. the universe. 3. the earth and its inhabitants. 4. *a*) mankind. *b*) people generally; the public. 5. *a*) [also W-], some part of the earth: as, the Old *World. b*) some period of history, its society, etc.: as, the ancient *world. c*) any sphere or domain: as, the dog *world. d*) any sphere of human activity: as, the *world* of music. 6. individual experience, outlook, etc.: as, his *world* is narrow. 7. secular life and interests, as distinguished from the religious or spiritual, or people primarily concerned with these. 8. *often pl.* a large amount; great deal: as, to do a *world* (or *worlds*) of good. 9. a star or planet. —**bring into the world,** to give birth to. —**come into the world,** to be born. —**for all the world,** 1. for any reason or consideration at all. 2. in every respect; exactly.

**World Court,** a court (*Permanent Court of International Justice*) set up by the League of Nations to settle disputes between nations.

**world·ling** (wũrld′liŋ), *n.* a worldly person.

**world·ly** (wũrld′li), *adj.* [-LIER, -LIEST], 1. of this world; temporal or secular: opposed to *heavenly, spiritual,* etc. 2. devoted to or concerned with the affairs, pleasures, etc. of this world. 3. worldly-wise. —**world′li·ness,** *n.*

**world·ly-mind·ed** (wũrld′li-mīn′did), *adj.* worldly (sense 2). —**world′ly-mind′ed·ness,** *n.*

**world·ly-wise** (wũrld′li-wīz′), *adj.* wise in the ways or affairs of the world; sophisticated.

**world power,** a nation large or powerful enough to have a world-wide influence.

**world series,** an annual series of games played in the autumn between the winning teams of the two major American baseball leagues to decide the championship: also **world's series.**

**World War I,** the war (1914–1918) between the Allies (Great Britain, France, Russia, the United States, Italy, Japan, etc.) and the Central Powers (Germany, Austria-Hungary, etc.).

**World War II,** the war (1939–1945) between the United Nations (Great Britain, France, the Soviet Union, the United States, etc.) and the Axis (Germany, Italy, Japan, etc.).

**world-wea·ry** (wũrld′wêr′i), *adj.* weary of the world or of living.

**world-wide** (wũrld′wīd′), *adj.* extending throughout the world.

**worm** (wũrm), *n.* [< AS. *wyrm,* serpent], 1. any of many long, slender, soft-bodied, creeping animals, as the earthworm. 2. popularly, an insect larva, as a grub. 3. an abject or contemptible person. 4. something wormlike or spiral in shape, etc., as the thread of a screw. 5. *pl.* any disease caused by parasitic worms in the intestines, etc. *v.i.* to move, proceed, etc. like a worm, in a winding, creeping, or devious manner. *v.t.* 1. to bring about, make, etc. in a winding, creeping, or devious manner. 2. to purge of intestinal worms. —**worm′er,** *n.* —**worm′less,** *adj.* —**worm′like′,** *adj.*

**worm-eat·en** (wũrm′ēt′'n), *adj.* 1. eaten into by worms, termites, etc. 2. worn-out, decrepit, etc.

**worm gear,** 1. a worm wheel. 2. a gear consisting of a rotating screw meshed with a worm wheel.

WORM GEAR

**worm·hole** (wũrm′hōl′), *n.* a hole made by a worm, termite, etc. —**worm′holed′,** *adj.*

**Worms** (vôrmz; Eng. wũrmz), *n.* a city in W Germany, on the Rhine: pop., 50,000: at a meeting (**Diet of Worms**) held there in 1521, Martin Luther was condemned as a heretic.

**worm wheel,** a toothed wheel designed to gear with the thread of a rotating screw.

**worm·wood** (wũrm′wood′), *n.* [alt. by folk etym. < AS. *wermod*], 1. any of various strong-smelling plants; specif., a species that yields a bitter-tasting, dark-green oil used in making absinthe. 2. any bitter, unpleasant experience; bitterness.

**worm·y** (wũr′mi), *adj.* [-IER, -IEST], 1. containing a worm or worms. 2. infested with worms. 3. like a worm. —**worm′i·ness,** *n.*

**worn** (wôrn, wōrn), pp. of **wear.** *adj.* 1. showing the effects of wear. 2. damaged by use or wear. 3. showing the effects of worry. 4. exhausted; spent.

**worn-out** (wôrn′out′, wōrn′-), *adj.* 1. used until no longer effective, usable, etc. 2. tired out.

**wor·ri·ment** (wũr′i-mənt), *n.* 1. a worrying or being worried; anxiety. 2. a cause of worry.

**wor·ri·some** (wũr′i-səm), *adj.* 1. causing worry or anxiety. 2. having a tendency to worry.

**wor·ry** (wũr′i), *v.t.* [-RIED, -RYING], [< AS. *wyrgan,* to strangle], 1. to treat roughly as with continual biting, etc.: as, the dog *worried* a shoe. 2. to annoy; bother. 3. to cause to feel troubled or uneasy. *v.i.* 1. to bite or tear (*at* an object) with the teeth. 2. to be anxious, troubled, etc. 3. to manage to get (*along* or *through*) in the face of difficulties. *n.* [*pl.* -RIES], 1. an act of worrying. 2. a troubled state of mind; anxiety. 3. something that causes this. —**wor′ri·er,** *n.* —**wor′ry·ing·ly,** *adv.*

**worse** (wũrs), *adj.* [compar. of *bad* & *ill*], [AS. *wiersa*], 1. bad, evil, harmful, etc. in a greater degree. 2. in poorer health; more ill. 3. in a more unsatisfactory situation. *adv.* [compar. of *badly* & *ill*], in a worse manner; to a worse extent. *n.* that which is worse.

**wors·en** (wũr′s'n), ***v.t. & v.i.*** [orig., a dial. word < *worse* + *-en*], to make or become worse.

**wor·ship** (wũr′ship), ***n.*** [< AS. < *weorth*, worthy + *-scipe*, -ship], 1. a prayer, church service, or other rite showing reverence for a deity. 2. intense love or admiration of any kind. 3. something worshiped. 4. [Chiefly Brit.], a title of honor, used in addressing magistrates, etc. ***v.t.*** [-SHIPED or -SHIPPED, -SHIPING or -SHIPPING], 1. to show religious reverence for. 2. to have intense love or admiration for. ***v.i.*** to engage in worship. —**wor′ship′er, wor′ship′per,** ***n.***

**wor·ship·ful** (wũr′ship-fəl), ***adj.*** 1. honorable; respected: used as a title of respect. 2. feeling or offering great devotion or respect. —**wor′ship·ful·ly,** ***adv.*** —**wor′ship·ful·ness,** ***n.***

**worst** (wũrst), ***adj.*** [superl. of *bad* & *ill*], [AS. *wyrsta*], bad, evil, harmful, etc. in the highest degree. ***adv.*** [superl. of *badly* & *ill*], in the worst manner; to the worst extent. ***n.*** that which is worst. ***v.t.*** to defeat. —**at worst,** under the worst circumstances. —**if worst comes to worst,** if the worst possible thing happens. —**(in) the worst way,** [Slang], very much; greatly. —**make the worst of,** to be pessimistic about.

**wor·sted** (woos′tid; woor′stid *is a sp. pronun.*), ***n.*** [after *Worsted*, now *Worstead*, England, where first made], 1. a smooth, hard-twisted thread or yarn made from long-staple wool. 2. fabric made from this. ***adj.*** made of worsted.

**wort** (wũrt), ***n.*** [AS. *wyrt-*], a liquid prepared with malt which, after fermenting, becomes beer, ale, etc.

**wort** (wũrt), ***n.*** [AS. *wyrt*, a root], a plant or herb: now usually in compounds, as *liverwort.*

**worth** (wũrth), ***n.*** [AS. *weorth*], 1. material value, especially as expressed in terms of money. 2. the esteem in which a person or thing is held; importance, value, etc. 3. the quantity of something that may be had for a given sum: as, a dime's *worth* of nuts. 4. wealth; possessions. ***adj.*** 1. deserving or worthy of; meriting. 2. equal in value to (something specified). 3. having wealth amounting to. —**for all one is worth,** to the utmost. —**put in one's two cents' worth,** to give one's opinion.

**worth·less** (wũrth′lis), ***adj.*** without worth or merit; useless, valueless, etc. —**worth′less·ly,** ***adv.*** —**worth′less·ness,** ***n.***

**worth-while** (wũrth′hwil′), ***adj.*** important or valuable enough to repay time or effort spent; of true value, merit, etc. —**worth′-while′ness,** ***n.***

**wor·thy** (wũr′*thi*), ***adj.*** [-THIER, -THIEST], 1. having worth, value, or merit. 2. deserving; meriting (often with *of* or an infinitive). ***n.*** [*pl.* -THIES], a person of outstanding worth or importance: often used humorously. —**wor′thi·ly,** ***adv.*** —**wor′thi·ness,** ***n.***

**wot** (wot), [Archaic], 1st and 3d pers. sing., pres. indic., of **wit** (to know).

**would** (wood), [AS. *wolde*, pt. of *willan*, to will], pt. of **will.** *Would* is also used: 1. to express condition, as, I *would* write if you *would.* 2. in indirect discourse to express futurity, as, he said he *would* come. 3. to express a wish, as, *would* that she were here. 4. to soften a request, as, *would* you do this for me?

**would-be** (wood′bē′), ***adj.*** 1. that would be; wishing or pretending to be. 2. intended to be.

**would·n't** (wood′'nt), would not.

**wouldst** (woodst), archaic 2d pers. sing. of **would:** also **would·est** (wood′ist).

**wound** (wōōnd; *archaic* wound), ***n.*** [AS. *wund*], 1. an injury in which the skin or other tissue is broken, cut, torn, etc. 2. a scar resulting from this. 3. any hurt to the feelings, honor, etc. ***v.t. & v.i.*** to inflict a wound (on or upon); injure. —**wound′er,** ***n.***

**wound** (wound), 1. pt. and pp. of **wind** (to twist). 2. pt. and pp. of **wind** (to blow).

**wove** (wōv), pt. and alt. pp. of **weave.**

**wo·ven** (wōv′'n), alt. pp. of **weave.**

**wow** (wou), ***interj.*** an expression of surprise, pleasure, pain, etc. ***n.*** [Slang], 1. something very amusing. 2. a great success. ***v.t.*** [Slang], to be a great success with.

**WPA, W.P.A.,** Work Projects Administration.

**wrack** (rak), ***n.*** [MD. *wrak*, a wreck], 1. ruin; destruction: now chiefly in phrase *wrack and ruin.* 2. seaweed, etc. cast up on shore.

**wraith** (rāth), ***n.*** [Scot.; ult. < ON. *vörthr*, guardian < *vartha*, to guard], a ghost; specif., the spectral figure of a person supposedly seen just before or after his death. —**wraith′like′,** ***adj.***

**wran·gle** (raŋ′g'l), ***v.i.*** [-GLED, -GLING], [< ME. freq. of *wringen*, to wring; prob. < LG.], 1. to dispute or quarrel angrily and noisily. 2. to argue. ***v.t.*** 1. to argue (with *into, out of*, etc.). 2. to herd or round up (livestock). ***n.*** an angry, noisy dispute or quarrel. —**wran′gler,** ***n.***

**wrap** (rap), ***v.t.*** [WRAPPED or WRAPT, WRAPPING], [< ME. *wrappen*], 1. to wind or fold (a covering) around something. 2. to cover by this means. 3. to conceal; envelop; hide: as, *wrapped* in darkness. 4. to enclose and fasten in a wrapper of paper, etc. 5. to wind or fold: as, she *wrapped* her arms around him. ***v.i.*** to twine, extend, coil, etc. (usually with *over, around*, etc.). ***n.*** 1. an outer covering, especially a garment worn by being wrapped around the body. 2. a blanket. —**wrapped up in,** 1. devoted to; absorbed in (work, etc.). 2. involved in.

**wrap·per** (rap′ẽr), ***n.*** 1. a person or thing that wraps. 2. that in which something is wrapped; covering; cover. 3. a woman's dressing gown.

**wrap·ping** (rap′iŋ), ***n.*** *usually pl.* the material, as paper, in which something is wrapped.

**wrasse** (ras), ***n.*** [Corn. *wrach*], any of various sea food fishes with spiny fins and bright coloring.

**wrath** (rath, räth; Brit. rôth), ***n.*** [AS. *wræththo* < *wrath*, wroth], 1. intense anger; rage; fury. 2. any action carried out in great anger, especially for punishment or vengeance. —**wrath′less,** ***adj.***

**wrath·ful** (rath′fəl, räth′-), ***adj.*** 1. full of wrath. 2. resulting from or expressing wrath. —**wrath′ful·ly,** ***adv.*** —**wrath′ful·ness,** ***n.***

**wrath·y** (rath′i, räth′i), ***adj.*** [-IER, -IEST], [Colloq.], wrathful. —**wrath′i·ly,** ***adv.*** —**wrath′i·ness,** ***n.***

**wreak** (rēk), ***v.t.*** [AS. *wrecan*, to revenge], 1. to give vent or free play to (anger, malice, etc.). 2. to inflict (vengeance, etc.). —**wreak′er,** ***n.***

**wreath** (rēth), ***n.*** [*pl.* WREATHS (rē*th*z)], [AS. *wræth*], 1. a twisted band or ring of leaves, flowers, etc. 2. something suggesting this in shape: as, *wreaths* of smoke. —**wreath′like′,** ***adj.***

**wreathe** (rē*th*), ***v.t.*** [WREATHED, WREATHING], 1. to coil, twist, or entwine so as to form a wreath. 2. to coil, twist, or entwine around; encircle: as, clouds *wreathed* the hills. 3. to decorate with wreaths. 4. to cover or envelop: as, *wreathed* with wrinkles. ***v.i.*** 1. to have a twisting or coiling movement. 2. to form a wreath.

**wreck** (rek), ***n.*** [< Anglo-N. *wrek*], 1. goods or wreckage cast ashore after a shipwreck. 2. *a*) the disabling or destruction of a ship by any disaster of navigation; shipwreck. *b*) a ship thus broken or destroyed. 3. the remains of anything that has been destroyed or badly damaged. 4. a person in very poor health. 5. a wrecking or being wrecked; ruin. ***v.t.*** 1. to destroy or damage badly. 2. to tear down (a building, etc.). 3. to overthrow; thwart. 4. to destroy the health of. ***v.i.*** 1. to be wrecked. 2. to be a wrecker.

**wreck·age** (rek′ij), ***n.*** 1. a wrecking or being wrecked. 2. the remains of something wrecked.

**wreck·er** (rek′ẽr), ***n.*** 1. a person or thing that wrecks. 2. a person who causes ruin, obstruction, etc. 3. a person, car, train, etc. that salvages or clears away wrecks. 4. a person who tears down and salvages old buildings, etc.

**wreck·ing** (rek′iŋ), ***n.*** the act or work of a wrecker. ***adj.*** engaged or used in dismantling or salvaging wrecks: as, a *wrecking* crew.

**wren** (ren), ***n.*** [AS. *wrenna*], any of various small songbirds having a long bill, rounded wings, and a stubby, erect tail.

**Wren, Sir Christopher** (ren), 1632–1723; English architect.

**wrench** (rench), ***n.*** [AS. *wrenc*, a trick < *wrencan*, to twist], 1. a sudden, violent twist or pull. 2. an injury caused by a twist or jerk, as to the back. 3. a sudden feeling of anguish, grief, etc., as from separation. 4. any of various tools used for holding and turning nuts, bolts, pipes, etc. ***v.t.*** 1. to twist, pull, or jerk violently. 2. to injure (a part of the body) with a twist or wrench. 3. to distort (a meaning, statement, etc.). —**wrench′like′,** ***adj.***

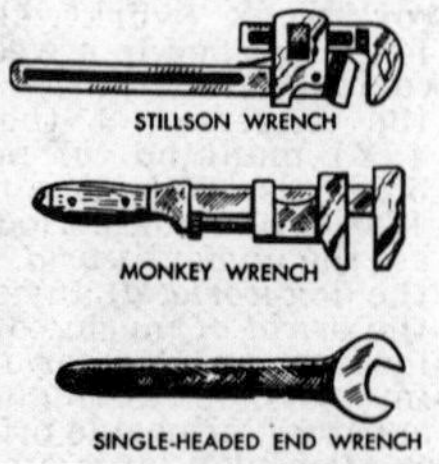


WRENCHES

**wrest** (rest), ***v.t.*** [AS. *wræstan*], 1. to pull or force away violently with a twisting motion. 2. to take by force; usurp. 3. to distort or change the true meaning, purpose, etc. of. ***n.*** 1. the act of wresting; a twist; wrench. 2. a wrenchlike key used for tuning pianos, harps, etc. by turning the pins (**wrest pins**) holding the strings.

**wres·tle** (res′'l), ***v.i. & v.t.*** [-TLED, -TLING], [< AS.

freq. of *wræstan*, to twist], 1. to struggle hand to hand with (an opponent) in an attempt to throw or force him to the ground without striking blows. 2. to struggle (with) in opposition; strive; contend. *n.* 1. a wrestling; wrestling bout. 2. a struggle or contest. —**wres′tler,** *n.*

**wres·tling** (res′liŋ), *n.* a form of sport in which the opponents wrestle, or struggle hand to hand.

**wretch** (rech), *n.* [AS. *wrecca*, an outcast], 1. a miserable or unhappy person. 2. one who is despised, scorned, etc.

**wretch·ed** (rech′id), *adj.* 1. very unhappy; miserable; unfortunate. 2. distressing; depressing. 3. very inferior; unsatisfactory. 4. despicable; mean. —**wretch′ed·ly,** *adv.* —**wretch′ed·ness,** *n.*

**wrig·gle** (rig′'l), *v.i.* [-GLED, -GLING], [MLG. *wriggeln*], 1. to twist and turn to and fro; squirm. 2. to move along with a twisting, writhing motion. 3. to make one's way by subtle or shifty means; dodge. *v.t.* 1. to cause to wriggle. 2. to bring into a specified condition by wriggling. *n.* a wriggling. —**wrig′gly** [-GLIER, -GLIEST], *adj.*

**wrig·gler** (rig′lẽr), *n.* 1. a person or thing that wriggles. 2. the larva of a mosquito.

**wright** (rīt), *n.* [AS. *wyrhta* < *wyrcan*, to work], one who makes or constructs: used chiefly in compounds, as, *shipwright.*

**Wright, Frank Lloyd** (rīt), 1869–1959; U.S. architect.

**Wright, Or·ville** (ôr′vil), 1871–1948; U.S. airplane inventor with his brother *Wilbur* (1867–1912).

**wring** (riŋ), *v.t.* [WRUNG or *rare* WRINGED, WRINGING], [AS. *wringan*], 1. to squeeze, press, or twist, especially so as to force out water or other liquid. 2. to force out (water, etc.) by this means (usually with *out*). 3. to wrench or twist forcibly. 4. to extract by force, threats, persistence, etc. 5. to afflict with anguish, pity, etc.: as, the story *wrung* her heart. *v.i.* to squirm or twist with force or great effort. *n.* a wringing.

**wring·er** (riŋ′ẽr), *n.* 1. a person or thing that wrings. 2. a machine fitted with opposed rollers which squeeze water from wet clothes.

**wrin·kle** (riŋ′k'l), *n.* [AS. *wrincle* < base of *wringan*, to press], 1. a small ridge or furrow in a normally smooth surface. 2. a crease or pucker in the skin. *v.t.* [-KLED, -KLING], to make wrinkles in. *v.i.* to be or become wrinkled; form wrinkles. —**wrin′kly** [-KLIER, -KLIEST], *adj.*

**wrin·kle** (riŋ′k'l), *n.* [prob. dim. ult. < AS. *wrenc*, a trick], [Colloq.], a clever trick, idea, etc.

**wrist** (rist), *n.* [AS.], 1. the joint or part of the arm between the hand and forearm; carpus. 2. the corresponding part in an animal.

**wrist·band** (rist′band′, riz′bənd), *n.* the band at the wrist end of a full-length sleeve; cuff.

**wrist·let** (rist′lit), *n.* 1. a band or strap worn around the wrist, as for warmth. 2. a bracelet.

**wrist pin,** the stud or pin by which a connecting rod is attached to a wheel, crank, etc.

**wrist watch,** a watch worn on a strap or band that fits around the wrist.

**writ** (rit), *n.* [AS. < *writan*, to write], 1. [Rare], something written. 2. a formal legal document ordering or prohibiting some action.

**write** (rīt), *v.t.* [WROTE, WRITTEN, WRITING; *archaic* pt. & pp. WRIT], [AS. *writan*, to scratch, hence write], 1. to form (words, letters, etc.) on a surface, especially with a pen or pencil. 2. to form the words, letters, etc. of: as, *write* your name. 3. to produce (a literary or musical composition); compose. 4. to fill in (a check, printed form, etc.) with necessary writing. 5. to cover with writing: as, he *wrote* 10 pages. 6. to communicate in writing: as, he *wrote* that he was ill. 7. to communicate with in writing: as, *write* me every day. 8. to leave signs or evidence of: as, greed was *written* on his face. *v.i.* 1. to form words, letters, etc. on a surface, especially with a pen or pencil. 2. to write books or other literary matter. 3. to write a letter. 4. to produce writing of a specified kind: as, the pen *writes* scratchily. —**write down,** 1. to put into written form. 2. to depreciate by writing. —**write off,** to cancel or remove from accounts: said of bad debts, claims, etc. —**write out,** 1. to put into writing. 2. to write in full. —**write up,** 1. to write an account of. 2. to praise in writing.

**writ·er** (rīt′ẽr), *n.* one who writes, especially as a business or occupation; author, journalist, etc.

**write-up** (rīt′up′), *n.* [Colloq.], a written report, especially one that praises the subject written about.

**writhe** (rīth), *v.t.* [WRITHED, WRITHED or *archaic* or *poetic* WRITHEN (rith′'n), WRITHING], [< AS. *writhan*, to twist], to cause to twist or turn; contort. *v.i.* 1. to make twisting or turning movements; squirm. 2. to suffer great emotional distress. *n.* a writhing movement. —**writh′er,** *n.* —**writh′ing·ly,** *adv.*

**writ·ing** (rīt′iŋ), *n.* 1. the act of one who writes. 2. something written, as a letter, document, etc. 3. written form. 4. handwriting. 5. a literary work. 6. the profession or occupation of a writer. 7. the art, style, etc. of literary composition. *adj.* 1. that writes. 2. used in writing.

**writ·ten** (rit′'n), pp. of **write.**

**Wroc·law** (vrôts′läf), *n.* Breslau: Polish name.

**wrong** (rôŋ), *adj.* [AS. *wrang* < ON. *rangr*, twisted], 1. not morally right or just; sinful; wicked. 2. not in accordance with an established standard, etc.: as, the *wrong* method. 3. not suitable or appropriate: as, the *wrong* thing to say. 4. *a*) contrary to truth, fact, etc.; incorrect. *b*) acting, believing, etc. incorrectly; mistaken. 5. in an unsatisfactory condition. 6. not functioning properly: as, what's *wrong* with the light? 7. designed to be placed inward or under and not displayed: as, the *wrong* side of a fabric. *adv.* in a wrong manner, direction, etc.; incorrectly. *n.* 1. something wrong, especially a wicked or unjust act. 2. in *law*, a violation of a legal right. *v.t.* 1. to treat badly or unjustly; injure. 2. to think badly of without real justification. —**go wrong,** 1. to turn out badly. 2. to change from good behavior to bad. —**in the wrong,** wrong. —**wrong′er,** *n.* —**wrong′ly,** *adv.* —**wrong′ness,** *n.*

**wrong·do·ing** (rôŋ′do͞o′iŋ), *n.* any act or behavior that is wrong; transgression. —**wrong′do′er,** *n.*

**wrong·ful** (rôŋ′fəl), *adj.* 1. full of wrong; unjust, unfair, or injurious. 2. unlawful. —**wrong′ful·ly,** *adv.* —**wrong′ful·ness,** *n.*

**wrong·head·ed** (rôŋ′hed′id), *adj.* stubbornly refusing to yield, agree, etc. even when wrong. —**wrong′head′ed·ly,** *adv.* —**wrong′head′ed·ness,** *n.*

**wrote** (rōt), pt. of **write.**

**wroth** (rôth; Brit. rōth), *adj.* [AS. *wrath*], angry; wrathful; incensed.

**wrought** (rôt), alt. pt. and pp. of **work.** *adj.* 1. formed; fashioned; made. 2. shaped by hammering or beating: said of metals. 3. made with great care; elaborated. 4. decorated; ornamented.

**wrought iron,** a kind of iron that contains some slag and very little carbon: it is tough and hard to break but malleable. —**wrought′-i′ron,** *adj.*

**wrought-up** (rôt′up′), *adj.* disturbed; excited.

**wrung** (ruŋ), pt. and pp. of **wring.**

**wry** (rī), *v.t. & v.i.* [WRIED, WRYING], [AS. *wrigian*, to turn], to writhe or twist. *adj.* [WRIER, WRIEST], 1. turned or bent to one side; twisted; distorted. 2. made by twisting or distorting the features: as, a *wry* face. —**wry′ly,** *adv.* —**wry′ness,** *n.*

**wry·neck** (rī′nek′), *n.* 1. a condition in which the neck is twisted by a muscle spasm. 2. a bird related to the woodpecker, having the habit of stretching and twisting its neck.

**WSW, W.S.W., w.s.w.,** west-southwest.

**wt.,** weight.

**Wu·han** (wo͞o′hän′), *n.* three cities in E China, forming one metropolitan area: pop., 1,800,000.

**Wup·per·tal** (voop′ẽr-täl′), *n.* a city in W Germany: pop., 416,000.

**Würt·tem·berg** (wũr′təm-bẽrg; G. vür′təm-berkh′), *n.* a former division of SW Germany; earlier, a kingdom.

**W. Va.,** West Virginia.

**Wy·an·dotte** (wī′ən-dot′), *n.* any of a breed of American domestic fowls.

**wych-elm** (wich′elm′), *n.* [< *witch*, as in *witch hazel*], 1. a small variety of elm found in Europe and N Asia. 2. its wood. Also sp. **witch-elm.**

**Wych·er·ley, William** (wich′ẽr-li), 1640?–1716; English dramatist.

**Wyc·liffe** or **Wyc·lif, John** (wik′lif), 1320?–1384; English religious reformer; first translator of the Bible into English: also sp. **Wiclif, Wickliffe.**

**Wy·o·ming** (wī-ō′miŋ), *n.* a Western State of the U.S.: area, 97,914 sq. mi.; pop., 330,000; capital, Cheyenne: abbrev. **Wyo., Wy.** —**Wy·o′ming·ite′,** *n.*

# X

**X, x** (eks), *n.* [*pl.* X's, x's, Xs, xs], 1. the twenty-fourth letter of the English alphabet. 2. the sound of X or x. *adj.* twenty-fourth in a sequence or group.
**X** (eks), *n.* 1. an object or mark shaped like X. 2. the Roman numeral for 10. 3. a person or thing unknown or unrevealed. *adj.* shaped like X.
**x,** in *mathematics,* 1. an unknown quantity. 2. a sign of multiplication: as, 3 x 3 = 9.
**xan·the·in** (zan′thi-in), *n.* [< *xantho-* + *-in*], the water-soluble part of the pigment of yellow flowers.
**xan·thic** (zan′thik), *adj.* [< Fr.; see XANTHO- & -IC], 1. yellow. 2. of or containing xanthine.
**xan·thine** (zan′thēn, -thin), *n.* [*xanth(o)-* + *-ine*], a white crystalline nitrogenous compound present in blood, urine, and some plants.
**Xan·thip·pe, Xan·tip·pe** (zan-tip′i), *n.* wife of Socrates: the prototype of the nagging wife.
**xan·tho-,** [< Gr. *xanthos,* yellow], a combining form meaning *yellow:* also **xanth-.**
**xan·thous** (zan′thəs), *adj.* [Gr. *xanthos*], yellow.
**Xa·vi·er,** Saint **Francis** (zā′vi-ēr, zav′i-), 1506–1552; Spanish Jesuit missionary.
**X chromosome,** a sex chromosome: fertilized eggs containing two X chromosomes (one from each parent germ cell) develop into females, those containing one X and one Y chromosome (male germ cells carry either) develop into males.
**Xe,** in *chemistry,* xenon.
**xe·bec** (zē′bek), *n.* [< Fr. *chébec* < Sp. < Ar. *shabbak*], a small, three-masted ship with overhanging bow and stern: once common in the Mediterranean.
**xen·o-,** [< Gr. *xenos*], a combining form meaning *stranger, foreigner,* as in *xenophobia.*
**xe·non** (zē′non, zen′on), *n.* [Gr., strange], a heavy, colorless, inert, gaseous chemical element present in the air in minute quantities: symbol, Xe; at. wt., 131.3; at. no., 54.
**xen·o·pho·bi·a** (zen′ə-fō′bi-ə), *n.* [*xeno-* + *-phobia*], fear or hatred of strangers or foreigners.
**Xen·o·phon** (zen′ə-fən), *n.* Greek general and historian; lived 434?–355? B.C.
**xe·rog·ra·phy** (zi-rog′rə-fi), *n.* [< *Xerox* + *-graphy*], a process for copying printed material, pictures, etc. by the transfer of dry ink particles to an electrically charged surface.
**xe·roph·i·lous** (zi-rof′ə-ləs), *adj.* [< Gr. *xēros,* dry; + *-philous*], thriving in a hot, dry climate.
**xe·ro·phyte** (zêr′ə-fīt′), *n.* [< Gr. *xēros,* dry; + *-phyte*], a xerophilous plant.
**Xe·rox** (zir′oks), *n.* a process of xerography: a trade-mark. *v.t. & v.i.* to reproduce by this process.
**Xer·xes I** (zũrk′sēz), 519?–465 B.C.; king of Persia (486–465 B.C.): called *the Great.*
**xi** (zī, sī; Gr. ksē), *n.* [Gr.], the fourteenth letter of the Greek alphabet (Ξ, ξ).
**Xmas** (kris′məs; *popularly* eks′məs), *n.* Christmas.
**X-ray** (eks′rā′), *adj.* of, by, or relating to X rays. *v.t.* to examine, treat, or photograph with X rays.
**X ray,** 1. an electromagnetic ray or radiation of extremely short wave length produced by the bombardment of a metal by a stream of electrons, as in a vacuum tube. X rays can penetrate solid substances and are widely used in medicine to study internal body structures and to diagnose and treat various disorders. 2. a photograph made by means of X rays.
**xy·lem** (zī′lem), *n.* [G. < Gr. *xylon,* wood], the woody tissue of a plant, especially, in higher forms, the firm part that conducts moisture.
**xy·lo-,** [< Gr. *xylon*], a combining form meaning *wood,* as in *xylophone:* also **xyl-.**
**xy·lo·phone** (zī′lə-fōn′, zil′ə-), *n.* [*xylo-* + *-phone*], a musical percussion instrument consisting of a series of wooden bars graduated in length so as to sound the notes of the scale when struck with small wooden hammers. —**xy·lo·phon·ist** (zī′lə-fō′nist, zī-lof′ə-nist), *n.*

XYLOPHONE

# Y

**Y, y** (wī), *n.* [*pl.* Y's, y's, Ys, ys], 1. the twenty-fifth letter of the English alphabet. 2. the sound of Y or y. *adj.* twenty-fifth in a sequence or group.
**Y** (wī), *n.* 1. an object shaped like Y. 2. in *chemistry, the symbol for* yttrium. *adj.* shaped like Y.
**y,** in *mathematics,* the second of a set of unknown quantities, *x* usually being the first.
**-y** (i; *occas.* ē), [ME. *-y, -i, -ie*], a suffix used in forming diminutives, nicknames, and terms of endearment, as in *kitty, Billy:* often sp. **-ie.**
**-y** (i; *occas.* ē), [AS. *-ig*], a suffix meaning: 1. *having, full of,* or *characterized by,* as in *dirty.* 2. *somewhat,* as in *dusky.* 3. *inclined to,* as in *sticky.* 4. *suggestive of, somewhat like,* as in *wavy.*
**-y** (i; *occas.* ē), [< Fr. *-ie* < L. *-ia* or Gr. *-ia*], a suffix meaning *quality* or *condition of (being),* as in *jealousy.*
**-y** (i; *occas.* ē), [Anglo-Fr. *-ie* < L. *-ium*], a suffix meaning *action of,* as in *inquiry.*
**y.,** 1. yard(s). 2. year(s).
**yacht** (yät), *n.* [< D. *jacht* (ult. < *jagen,* to hunt), short for *jaghtschip,* lit. hunting ship (against pirates)], any of various relatively small ships for pleasure cruises, racing, etc. —**yacht′ing,** *n.*
**yachts·man** (yäts′mən), *n.* [*pl.* -MEN], a person who owns or sails a yacht. —**yachts′man·ship′,** *n.*
**yah** (yä, ya, *etc.*), *interj.* an exclamation of derision, defiance, or disgust.
**Ya·hoo** (yä′hōō, yā′-, ya-hōō′), *n.* 1. in Swift's *Gulliver's Travels,* any of a race of brutish, degraded creatures having the form and vices of man. 2. [y-], a crude or ill-mannered person.
**Yah·weh, Yah·we** (yä′we), *n.* Jehovah: a modern transliteration: also **Yah′ve, Yah′veh** (-ve).
**yak** (yak), *n.* [*pl.* YAKS, YAK; see PLURAL, II, D, 1], [Tibet. *gyak*], the long-haired wild ox of central Asia, often used as a beast of burden.
**Yal·ta** (yäl′tə), *n.* a town in the Crimea, U.S.S.R., on the Black Sea.
**Ya·lu** (yä′lü′), *n.* a river flowing between Manchuria and Korea into the Yellow Sea.
**yam** (yam), *n.* [< Port. *inhame* < W.Afr.], 1. the edible, starchy, tuberous root of any of various tropical climbing plants. 2. any of these plants. 3. [Dial.], the sweet potato.
**Yang·tze** (yaŋ′sē′; Chin. yäŋ′tse′), *n.* a river in China flowing from Tibet to the East China Sea.
**Yank** (yaŋk), *n.* [Slang], a Yankee; esp., a U.S. soldier. *adj.* of or like a Yank or Yanks.
**yank** (yaŋk), *n.* [< New England Dial.], [Colloq.], a jerk. *v.t. & v.i.* [Colloq.], to jerk.
**Yan·kee** (yaŋ′ki), *n.* [prob. < D. *Jan Kees* (taken as pl.); *Jan,* John + *Kees,* dial. form of *kaas,* cheese: a disparaging nickname as applied by Dutch colonists in America], 1. a native or inhabitant of New England. 2. *a)* a native or inhabitant of a Northern State; Northerner. *b)* a

Union Soldier in the Civil War. 3. a native or inhabitant of the U.S. *adj.* of, like, or characteristic of Yankees. **—Yan′kee·dom,** *n.* **—Yan′kee·ism,** *n.*

**Yankee Doo·dle** (do͞o′d'l), an early American song, popular during the Revolutionary War.

**yap** (yap), *v.i.* [YAPPED, YAPPING], [echoic], 1. to make a sharp, shrill bark or yelp. 2. [Slang], to talk noisily and stupidly. *n.* 1. a sharp, shrill bark or yelp. 2. [Slang], *a*) noisy, stupid talk. *b*) a crude, noisy person. *c*) the mouth.

**yard** (yärd), *n.* [AS. *gyrd*, a rod], 1. a measure of length, equal to 3 feet, or 36 inches. 2. in *nautical usage*, a slender rod or spar fastened across a mast to support a sail.

**yard** (yärd), *n.* [AS. *geard*, enclosure], 1. the space or grounds surrounding or surrounded by a building or group of buildings. 2. an enclosed place used for a particular purpose or business: as, a lumber *yard.* 3. a railroad center where trains are made up, serviced, switched, etc. *v.t.* to put or enclose in a yard (often with *up*).

**yard·age** (yär′dij), *n.* 1. measurement in yards. 2. the extent of something so measured.

**yard·arm** (yärd′ärm′), *n.* in *nautical usage*, either end of a yard supporting a square sail.

**yard·man** (yärd′mən), *n.* [*pl.* -MEN], a man who works in a yard, especially a railroad yard.

**yard·mas·ter** (yärd′mas′tẽr, -mäs′-), *n.* a man in charge of a railroad yard.

**yard·stick** (yärd′stik′), *n.* 1. a graduated stick or rod one yard in length, used in measuring. 2. any standard used in measuring, judging, etc.

**yarn** (yärn), *n.* [AS. *gearn*], 1. any fiber, as wool, silk, flax, cotton, nylon, etc., spun into strands for weaving, knitting, or making thread. 2. [Colloq.], a tale or story, especially an exaggerated one. *v.i.* [Colloq.], to tell yarns. **—spin a yarn,** [Colloq.], to tell a yarn.

**yar·row** (yar′ō), *n.* [AS. *gæruwe*], a common herb having a strong smell, finely divided leaves, and clusters of pink or white flowers.

**yat·a·ghan, yat·a·gan** (yat′ə-gan, -gən), *n.* [Turk. *yātāghan*], a type of Turkish short saber with a double-curved blade and a handle without a guard.

**yaw** (yô), *v.i.* [< ON. *jaga*, to sway], 1. to turn unintentionally from the intended heading: said of a ship. 2. to swing on the vertical axis to the right or left: said of an aircraft, etc. *v.t.* to cause to yaw. *n.* an act of yawing.

**yawl** (yôl), *n.* [< MLG. *jolle* or D. *jol*], 1. a ship's boat. 2. a small sailboat rigged fore and aft, with a short mizzenmast astern of the rudder post.

**yawn** (yôn), *v.i.* [< merging of AS. *ginian* & *ganian*, to gape], 1. to open the mouth wide, especially involuntarily, and with a deep inhalation, as a result of fatigue, drowsiness, etc. 2. to open wide; gape: as, a *yawning* chasm. *v.t.* to express with a yawn. *n.* 1. an act of yawning. 2. a chasm. **—yawn′er,** *n.* **—yawn′ing·ly,** *adv.* **—yawn′y,** *adj.*

YAWL

**yawp** (yôp, yäp), *v.i.* [ME. *yolpen*], to utter a loud, harsh call or cry. *n.* the act or sound of yawping. Also sp. **yaup.**

**yaws** (yôz), *n.pl.* [prob. of W.Ind. origin], a tropical infectious disease caused by a spirochete and characterized by raspberrylike skin eruptions followed by destructive lesions (with *the*).

**Yb,** in *chemistry*, ytterbium.

**Y chromosome,** a sex chromosome: see **X chromosome.**

**y·clept, y-clept** (i-klept′), *pp.* [AS. *geclypod*, pp. of *clipian*, to call], [Archaic], called; named: also sp. **ycleped, y-cleped.**

**yd.,** 1. yard. 2. yards: also **yds.**

**ye** (*th*ē, *th*ə, *th*i; yē *is incorrect*), *adj.* [Archaic], the: *Y* was mistakenly substituted for an Old and Middle English character representing the sound *th.*

**ye** (yē; *unstressed* yi), *pron.* [AS. *ge*], [Archaic], you.

**yea** (yā), *adv.* [AS. *gea*], 1. yes: used to express affirmation. 2. indeed; truly: used to introduce a question or statement. *n.* 1. an affirmative statement or vote. 2. a voter in the affirmative.

**yeah** (ye, ya, *etc.*), *adv.* [Colloq.], yes.

**yean** (yēn), *v.t.* & *v.i.* [< AS. hyp. *ge-eanian*], to bring forth (young): said of a sheep or goat.

**yean·ling** (yēn′liŋ), *n.* a lamb or kid. *adj.* newborn.

**year** (yêr), *n.* [AS. *gear*], 1. a period of 365 days (in leap year, 366 days) divided into 12 months and beginning January 1. 2. the period of time, 365 days, 5 hours, 48 minutes, and 45.51 seconds, spent by the earth in making one complete revolution around the sun: also **astronomical** or **solar year.** 3. the period of time, 365 days, 6 hours, 9 minutes, and 9 seconds, spent by the sun in its apparent passage from a fixed star and back to the same position: also **sidereal year.** 4. the period of time in which any planet makes its revolution around the sun. 5. a period of 12 calendar months reckoned from any date: as, six *years* old. 6. a particular annual period of less than 365 days: as, a school *year.* 7. *pl.* *a*) age: as, old for his *years.* *b*) time; esp., a long time: as, *years* ago. **—year after year,** every year. **—year by year,** each year. **—year in, year out,** every year.

**year·book** (yêr′book′), *n.* an annual book; esp., one giving statistics, etc. of the preceding year.

**year·ling** (yêr′liŋ, yũr′-), *n.* an animal one year old or in its second year.

**year·long** (yêr′lôŋ), *adj.* lasting for a full year.

**year·ly** (yêr′li), *adj.* 1. lasting a year. 2. done, happening, etc. once a year, or every year. 3. of a year, or each year. *adv.* annually; every year.

**yearn** (yũrn), *v.i.* [AS. *gyrnan* < *georn*, eager], 1. to be filled with longing or desire. 2. to be deeply moved, especially with pity or sympathy. **—yearn′ing,** *n.* & *adj.* **—yearn′ing·ly,** *adv.*

**yeast** (yēst), *n.* [AS. *gist*], 1. a yellow, frothy substance consisting of minute fungi which multiply in the presence of starch or sugar and form alcohol and carbon dioxide during a process of fermentation induced by an enzyme: used in making beer and as a leavening agent in baking. 2. any of the fungi that form yeast: also **yeast plant.** 3. yeast mixed with flour or meal, made up in small cakes: also **yeast cake.** 4. foam; froth. 5. *a*) something that causes ferment; leaven. *b*) ferment; agitation. **—yeast′like′,** *adj.*

**yeast·y** (yēs′ti), *adj.* [-IER, -IEST], 1. of, like, or containing yeast. 2. frothy; foamy. 3. light; frivolous. 4. in a ferment; unsettled; restless. **—yeast′i·ly,** *adv.* **—yeast′i·ness,** *n.*

**Yeats, William Butler** (yāts), 1865–1939; Irish essayist, poet, and dramatist.

**yegg** (yeg), *n.* [Slang], a criminal; esp., a safecracker or burglar: also **yegg′man** [*pl.* -MEN].

**yell** (yel), *v.i.* [AS. *gellan*], to cry out loudly; scream. *v.t.* to utter by yelling. *n.* 1. a loud outcry or shout; scream. 2. a rhythmic cheer given in unison, as by students at a football game.

**yel·low** (yel′ō), *adj.* [AS. *geolo*], 1. of the color of gold, butter, or ripe lemons. 2. having a yellowish skin, as the Mongolians. 3. jealous. 4. [Colloq.], cowardly. 5. sensational: said of certain newspapers. *n.* 1. a yellow color; color between red and green in the spectrum. 2. a yellow pigment or dye. 3. the yolk of an egg. *v.t.* & *v.i.* to make or become yellow. **—yel′low·ish,** *adj.* **—yel′low·ly,** *adv.* **—yel′low·ness,** *n.*

**yel·low·bird** (yel′ō-bũrd′), *n.* 1. the American goldfinch. 2. the yellow warbler.

**yel·low-dog contract** (yel′ō-dôg′), a contract, now illegal, by which a new employee is made to agree that he will join no labor union.

**yellow fever,** an acute infectious tropical disease caused by a virus transmitted by the bite of certain mosquitoes, and marked by fever, jaundice, etc.

**yel·low·ham·mer** (yel′ō-ham′ẽr), *n.* [< yellow + AS. *amore*, kind of bird], 1. a European finch having a yellow head, neck, and breast. 2. the golden-winged woodpecker, or flicker, of North America.

**yellow jack,** 1. yellow fever. 2. a yellow flag used as a signal of quarantine.

**yellow jacket,** any of several social wasps and hornets having bright-yellow markings.

**yellow journalism,** [< use of yellow ink, to attract readers], the use of cheaply sensational or unscrupulous methods in newspapers, etc.

**yellow metal,** 1. gold. 2. brass that is 60 parts copper and 40 parts zinc.

**yellow peril,** the alleged danger to the world supremacy of the white, or Caucasian, peoples created by the vast numbers and potential political power of the yellow, or Mongolian, peoples.

**yellow pine,** 1. any of several American pines

having yellowish wood. 2. the wood of any of these.

**yellow race,** loosely, the Mongolian division of mankind.

**Yellow River,** Hwang Ho, a river in China.

**Yellow Sea,** an arm of the Pacific, between China and Korea.

**Yel·low·stone** (yel'ō-stōn'), *n.* a river in Wyoming and Montana, flowing into the Missouri.

**Yellowstone National Park,** a national park mainly in NW Wyoming, containing geysers, boiling springs, etc.

**yellow streak,** a tendency to be cowardly.

**yellow warbler,** a small, bright-yellow North American warbler.

**yel·low·wood** (yel'ō-wood'), *n.* 1. a smooth-barked, white-flowering tree of the southern U.S., having yellow wood. 2. this wood.

**yel·low·y** (yel'ō-i), *adj.* [-IER, -IEST], somewhat yellow.

**yelp** (yelp), *v.i.* [AS. *gilpan*, to boast], 1. to utter a short, sharp cry or bark, as a dog. 2. to cry out sharply, as in pain. *v.t.* to express by yelping. *n.* a short, sharp cry or bark. —**yelp'er,** *n.*

**Yem·en** (yem'ən, yā'mən), *n.* an independent Arab kingdom in SW Arabia, on the Red Sea: area, 75,000 sq. mi.; pop., 5,000,000; capital, San'a. —**Yem'en·ite'** (-it'), **Yem'en·i** (-i), *n.* & *adj.*

**yen** (yen), *n.* [*pl.* YEN], [Japan. < Chin. *yüan*, round], the monetary unit of Japan.

**yen** (yen), *n.* [Chin., opium], [Colloq.], a deep longing or desire. *v.i.* [YENNED, YENNING], [Colloq.], to have a yen (*for*); long; yearn.

**yeo·man** (yō'mən), *n.* [*pl.* -MEN], [ME. *yeman;* prob. contr. < *yung man*, young man], 1. originally, *a*) an attendant or manservant in a royal or noble household. *b*) a freeholder of a class below the gentry. 2. [Brit.], *a*) a yeoman of the guard. *b*) a member of the yeomanry (sense 2). 3. in the *U.S. Navy*, a petty officer assigned to clerical duty.

**yeo·man·ly** (yō'mən-li), *adj.* 1. of, characteristic of, or befitting a yeoman. 2. brave; sturdy; faithful. *adv.* in a yeomanly manner; bravely.

**yeoman of the (royal) guard,** any of the 100 men forming a ceremonial guard for English royalty.

**yeo·man·ry** (yō'mən-ri), *n.* 1. yeomen collectively. 2. a British voluntary cavalry force, originally a home guard, now part of the Territorial Army.

**yeoman's service,** exceptionally good or loyal service or assistance: also **yeoman service.**

**yep** (yep), *adv.* [Slang], yes: an affirmative reply.

**-yer** (yēr), -ier: usually after *w*, as in *lawyer.*

**yes** (yes), *adv.* [AS. *gese;* prob. < *gea*, yea + *si*, be it so], 1. aye; yea; it is so: used to express agreement, consent, affirmation, etc. 2. not only that, but more; moreover: as, I am ready, *yes*, eager to help you. *Yes* is sometimes used alone in inquiry to signify "What is it?", or in conversation by a listener as a polite expression of interest. *n.* [*pl.* YESES], 1. the act of saying *yes.* 2. an affirmative reply, vote, voter, etc. *v.t.* & *v.i.* [YESSED, YESSING], to say *yes* (to).

**yes man,** [Slang], one who indicates indiscriminate approval of every idea offered by his superior.

**yes·ter** (yes'tēr), *adj.* [< *yesterday*], [Archaic or Poetic], of yesterday: usually in combination, as, *yestereve(ning), yestermorn(ing).*

**yes·ter·day** (yes'tēr-di, -dā'), *n.* [< AS. < *geostran*, yesterday + *dæg*, day], 1. the day before today. 2. a recent day or time. *adv.* 1. on the day before today. 2. recently. *adj.* of yesterday.

**yes·ter·year** (yes'tēr-yêr'), *n.* & *adv.* [Archaic or Poetic], last year.

**yet** (yet), *adv.* [AS. *giet*], 1. up to now or to the time specified; thus far: as, he has not *yet* come. 2. at the present time; now: as, we can't leave just *yet.* 3. still; even now: as, there is *yet* a chance for peace. 4. now or at a particular time, as continuing from a preceding time: as, I could hear him *yet.* 5. in addition; even: as, he was *yet* more kind. 6. as much as; even: as, he did not come, nor *yet* write. 7. now, after all the time that has elapsed: as, hasn't he finished *yet?* 8. nevertheless: as, she was lovely, *yet* stupid. *conj.* nevertheless; however: as, she seems happy, *yet* she is troubled. —**as yet,** up to now.

**yew** (ū), *n.* [AS. *iw*], 1. a cone-bearing evergreen tree of Europe and Asia, having fine-grained, elastic wood and dark-green leaves. 2. its wood.

**Yid·dish** (yid'ish), *n.* [G. *jüdisch* < *Jude* (< L. *Judaeus*), a Jew], a language spoken by many European Jews and their descendants on other continents: it is a dialect of High German written in characters of the Hebrew alphabet and containing elements of Hebrew, Russian, Polish, etc. *adj.* 1. of or in this language. 2. [Slang], Jewish.

**yield** (yēld), *v.t.* [AS. *gieldan*, to pay], 1. to produce; specif., *a*) to give or furnish as a natural process: as, the orchard *yielded* a good crop. *b*) to give in return; produce as a result, profit, interest, etc. 2. to give up under pressure; surrender. 3. to concede; grant. *v.i.* 1. to produce or bear. 2. to give up; surrender. 3. to give way to physical force. 4. to give place; lose precedence, leadership, etc. (often with *to*). *n.* the amount yielded or produced. —**yield'er,** *n.*

**yield·ing** (yēl'diŋ), *adj.* that yields; submissive; obedient. —**yield'ing·ly,** *adv.* —**yield'ing·ness,** *n.*

**yip** (yip), *n.* [echoic], [Colloq.], a yelp. *v.i.* [YIPPED YIPPING], [Colloq.], to yelp, as a dog.

**yipe** (yip), *interj.* an exclamation of pain, alarm, etc.

**yip·pie** (yip'i), *n.* [< *Y*outh *I*nternational *P*arty (a nonexistent group) + hip*pie*], [Slang], any of a group of young persons in the U.S. loosely organized for radical political action.

**-yl** (il; *rarely* ēl), [< Gr. *hylē*, wood], a combining form used in chemistry to form the names of radicals, as in *amyl.*

**Y.M.C.A.,** Young Men's Christian Association.

**Y.M.H.A.,** Young Men's Hebrew Association.

**yo·del** (yō'd'l), *v.t.* & *v.i.* [-DELED or -DELLED, -DELING or -DELLING], [G. *jodeln*], to sing with abrupt alternating changes between the normal chest voice and the falsetto. *n.* the act or sound of yodeling. —**yo'del·er, yo'del·ler,** *n.*

**yo·ga** (yō'gə), *n.* [Sans., union], in *Hindu philosophy*, a practice involving complete concentration upon something, especially the deity, in order to establish identity of consciousness with it.

**yo·gi** (yō'gi), *n.* [*pl.* -GIS], 1. one who practices yoga: also **yo'gin** (-gin). 2. loosely, yoga.

**yo·gurt, yo·ghurt** (yō'goort), *n.* [Turk. *yoghurt*], a thick, semisolid food made from milk fermented by a bacterium: also **yoh'ourt** (-oort).

**yo-heave-ho** (yō'hēv'hō'), *interj.* a chant formerly used by sailors while pulling or lifting together.

**yoicks** (yoiks), *interj.* [Brit.], a cry used for urging on the hounds in fox hunting.

**yoke** (yōk), *n.* [AS. *geoc*], 1. a wooden frame with bows at either end, used for harnessing together a pair of oxen, etc. 2. a pair of animals harnessed together. 3. bondage; servitude. 4. something that binds, unites, etc. 5. something like a yoke, as a frame fitting over the shoulders for carrying pails, etc. 6. a part of a garment fitted closely to the shoulders or hips as a support for the gathered parts below. *v.t.* [YOKED, YOKING], 1. to put a yoke on. 2. to harness (an animal) to (a plow, etc.). 3. to join together. 4. to marry. *v.i.* to be joined together.

YOKE (on pair of oxen)

**yoke·fel·low** (yōk'fel'ō), *n.* 1. a companion, partner, or associate. 2. a husband or wife.

**yo·kel** (yō'k'l), *n.* a person living in a rural area; country bumpkin: used contemptuously.

**Yo·ko·ha·ma** (yō'kə-hä'mə), *n.* a seaport in Honshu, Japan: pop., 1,789,000.

**yolk** (yōk; *rarely* yōlk), *n.* [AS. *geolca*], 1. the yellow, principal substance of an egg. 2. the oily secretion in sheep's wool. —**yolked,** *adj.* —**yolk'less,** *adj.* —**yolk'y** [-IER, -IEST], *adj.*

**Yom Kip·pur** (yom' kip'ēr; Heb. yōm' ki-po͞or'), a Jewish holiday and day of fasting, the Day of Atonement: Lev. 16:29–34: see **Jewish holidays.**

**yon** (yon), *adj.* & *adv.* [AS. *geon*], [Archaic or Dial.], yonder: also **yond** (yond). *pron.* [Archaic or Dial.], that or those at a distance.

**yon·der** (yon'dēr), *adj.* [ME.], 1. farther; more distant (with *the*). 2. being at a distance, but within, or as within, sight. *adv.* at or in that (specified or relatively distant) place; over there.

**Yon·kers** (yoŋ'kērz), *n.* a city in SE New York, on the Hudson: pop., 191,000.

**yore** (yôr, yōr), *adv.* [AS. *geara*], [Obs.], long ago. *n.* time long ago: now only in *of yore*, formerly.

**York** (yôrk), *n.* 1. Yorkshire, England. 2. a city in SE Pennsylvania: pop., 55,000.

**York** (yôrk), *n.* the ruling family of England (1461–1485). —**York'ist,** *n.* & *adj.*

**York·shire** (yôrk'shir), *n.* the largest county of England, on the NE coast: pop., 4,723,000.

**Yorkshire pudding,** a batter pudding baked in the drippings of roasting meat.

**Yorkshire terrier,** a small, long-haired terrier of a breed originating in Yorkshire, England.

**Yo·sem·i·te** (yō-sem'ə-ti), *n.* a valley in central California: part of Yosemite National Park.

**Yosemite National Park,** a national park in east central California, containing high waterfalls (**Yosemite Falls**), cliffs, and redwood trees.
**you** (ū; *unstressed* yoo, yə), *pron.* [< AS. *eow*, dat. & acc. pl. of *ge*, ye], 1. the person or persons to whom one is speaking or writing: *you* is the nominative and objective form (sing. & pl.), *your* and *yours* the possessive (sing. & pl.), and *yourself* (sing.) and *yourselves* (pl.) the intensive and reflexive, of the second personal pronoun. 2. a person or people generally: as, *you* can never tell!
**you'd** (ūd, yood, yəd), 1. you had. 2. you would.
**you'll** (ūl, yool, yəl), 1. you will. 2. you shall.
**young** (yuŋ), *adj.* [AS. *geong*], 1. being in an early period of life or growth. 2. characteristic of youth in quality, appearance, etc.; fresh; vigorous. 3. representing or embodying a new tendency, social movement, etc. 4. of youth or early life. 5. lately begun; in an early stage. 6. lacking experience or practice; immature; green. 7. younger than another of the same name or family. *n.* offspring; esp., young offspring, collectively: as, a bear and her *young*. **—the young,** young people. **—with young,** pregnant. **—young'ish,** *adj.* **—young'ness,** *n.*
**Young, Brig·ham** (brig'əm yuŋ), 1801–1877; U.S. head of the Mormon Church (1847–1877).
**young·ber·ry** (yuŋ'ber'i), *n.* [*pl.* -RIES], [< B. M. *Young*, Am. horticulturist], a sweet, dark-red berry, a cross between a blackberry and a dewberry.
**young blood,** 1. young people. 2. youthful strength, vigor, ideas, etc.
**young·ling** (yuŋ'liŋ), *n.* 1. a young person; youth. 2. a young animal or plant. 3. an inexperienced person; novice. *adj.* young.
**young·ster** (yuŋ'stẽr), *n.* 1. a child. 2. a youth. 3. a young animal.
**Youngs·town** (yuŋz'toun'), *n.* a city in NE Ohio: pop., 168,000.
**youn·ker** (yuŋ'kẽr), *n.* [< D. < *jong*, young + *heer*, lord], [Now Rare], a youngster.
**your** (yoor; *unstressed* yẽr), *pron.* [AS. *eower*], possessive form of **you** (sing. & pl.). *poss. pronominal adj.* of, belonging to, or done by you: also used before some titles, as *your* Honor.
**you're** (yoor, ūr, yẽr), you are.
**yours** (yoorz), *pron.* that or those belonging to you: as, a friend of *yours*, *yours* are better.
**your·self** (yoor-self', yẽr-), *pron.* [*pl.* -SELVES], a form of the 2d pers. sing. pronoun, used: *a*) as an intensive: as, you *yourself* went. *b*) as a reflexive: as, you hurt *yourself*. *c*) as a quasi-noun meaning "your true self" (e.g., you're not *yourself* today).
**yours truly,** 1. a phrase used before the signature in ending a letter. 2. [Colloq.], I or me.
**youth** (ūth), *n.* [*pl.* YOUTHS (ūths, ūthz)], [AS. *geoguthe*], 1. the state or quality of being young. 2. the period of life coming between childhood and maturity; adolescence. 3. an early stage of growth or existence. 4. young people collectively. 5. a young person; esp., a young man.
**youth·ful** (ūth'fəl), *adj.* 1. young; possessing youth. 2. of, characteristic of, or suitable for youth. 3. fresh; vigorous. 4. new; early; in an early stage. **—youth'ful·ly,** *adv.* **—youth'ful·ness,** *n.*
**you've** (ūv, yoov, yəv), you have.
**yow** (you), *interj.* an exclamation of pain, surprise, alarm, etc.
**yowl** (youl), *v.i.* [< ON. *gaula*], to utter a long, mournful cry; howl; wail. *n.* a howl; wail.
**yo-yo** (yō'yō'), *n.* [arbitrary formation], a spoollike toy attached to one end of a string upon which it may be made to spin up and down: a trade-mark (**Yo-Yo**).
**Y·pres** (ē'pr'), *n.* a town in NW Belgium: center of hostilities, World War I.
**yr.,** 1. [*pl.* YRS.], year. 2. younger. 3. your.
**yrs.,** 1. years. 2. yours.
**Yt,** in *chemistry*, yttrium.
**yt·ter·bi·um** (i-tũr'bi-əm), *n.* [< *Ytterby*, Sweden], a rare, metallic chemical element of the rare-earth group: symbol, Yb; at. wt., 173.04; at. no., 70. **—yt·ter'bic,** *adj.*
**yt·tri·um** (it'ri-əm), *n.* [< *Ytterby*, Sweden], a rare, metallic chemical element: symbols, Y, Yt; at. wt., 88.92; at. no., 39. **—yt'tric,** *adj.*
**Yu·ca·tan, Yu·ca·tán** (ū'kä-tän'; Eng. ū'kə-tan'), *n.* a peninsula of S North America extending into the Gulf of Mexico.
**yuc·ca** (yuk'ə), *n.* [< Sp. *yuca*], 1. a plant of the lily family with stiff, sword-shaped leaves and white flowers. 2. its flower.
**Yu·go·slav** (ū'gō-släv', ū'gə-slav'), *adj.* of Yugoslavia or its people. *n.* a native or inhabitant of Yugoslavia. Also sp. **Jugoslav. —Yu'go·slav'ic,** *adj.*
**Yu·go·sla·vi·a** (ū'gō-slä'vi-ə, ū'gə-släv'yə), *n.* a republic on the Balkan Peninsula, bordering the Adriatic: area, 95,576 sq. mi.; pop., 19,958,000; capital, Belgrade: also sp. **Jugoslavia. —Yu'go·sla'vi·an,** *adj.* **&** *n.*
**Yu·kon** (ū'kon), *n.* 1. a territory of NW Canada: pop., 16,000; capital, Whitehorse. 2. a river flowing through Yukon and Alaska into the Bering Sea.
**yule** (ūl), *n.* [AS. *geol*], Christmas or the Christmas season.
**yule log,** a large log formerly used as the foundation for the ceremonial Christmas-Eve fire.
**yule·tide** (ūl'tīd'), *n.* Christmas time.
**yum·my** (yum'i), *adj.* [-MIER, -MIEST], [Colloq.], very tasty; delectable.
**Y.W.C.A.,** Young Women's Christian Association.
**Y.W.H.A.,** Young Women's Hebrew Association.

# Z

**Z, z** (zē; Brit. zed), *n.* [*pl.* Z's, z's, Zs, zs], 1. the twenty-sixth and last letter of the English alphabet. 2. the sound of Z or z. *adj.* twenty-sixth in a sequence or group.
**Z** (zē; Brit. zed), *n.* an object shaped like Z. *adj.* shaped like Z.
**Z.,** in *astronomy*, zenith distance.
**Z., z.,** zone.
**z,** in *mathematics*, an unknown quantity.
**Zach·a·ri·as** (zak'ə-rī'əs), *n.* Zechariah.
**Za·greb** (zä'greb), *n.* a city in NW Yugoslavia: pop., 457,000.
**zai·ba·tsu** (zī'bät-sōō'), *n.* [*pl.* -TSU], [Japan. *zai*, property + *batsu*, family], the few families that own and control most of the industry in Japan.
**Zam·be·zi** (zam-bē'zi, zàm-bā'-), *n.* a river in S Africa, flowing into the Indian Ocean.
**Zam·bi·a** (zam'bi-ə), *n.* a country in S Africa: a member of the British Commonwealth of Nations: area, 290,323 sq. mi.; pop., 3,894,000; capital, Lusaka: formerly, *Northern Rhodesia*.
**za·ny** (zā'ni), *n.* [*pl.* -NIES], [< Fr. < It. *zanni*, orig., an abbrev. pronun. of *Giovanni*, John], 1. a clown or buffoon. 2. a fool; dolt; simpleton. *adj.* [-NIER, -NIEST], of or characteristic of a zany; extravagantly foolish or comical. **—za'ni·ness,** *n.*
**Zan·zi·bar** (zan'zə-bär', zan'zə-bär'), *n.* 1. a former country on two islands off the E coast of Africa: see **Tanzania.** 2. the larger of these islands.
**Zar·a·thus·tra** (zar'ə-thōōs'trə), *n.* Zoroaster. **—Zar'a·thus'tri·an** (-tri-ən), *adj.* **&** *n.*
**zeal** (zēl), *n.* [< OFr. < LL. *zelus* < Gr. *zēlos*], eager interest and enthusiasm; ardent endeavor; fervor.
**Zea·land** (zē'lənd), *n.* an island of Denmark to the west of Sweden: chief city, Copenhagen.
**zeal·ot** (zel'ət), *n.* [< LL. < Gr. < *zēlos*, zeal], one who is zealous, especially to an extreme or excessive degree; fanatic. **—zeal'ot·ry,** *n.*

**zeal·ous** (zel′əs), *adj.* full of, characterized by, or showing zeal; fervent; enthusiastic. **—zeal′ous·ly,** *adv.* **—zeal′ous·ness,** *n.*

ZEBRA (4½ ft. high at shoulder)

**ze·bec, ze·beck** (zē′bek), *n.* a xebec.

**ze·bra** (zē′brə), *n.* [*pl.* -BRAS, -BRA; see PLURAL, II, D, 1], [Port. < native name in Congo], an African animal related to and resembling the horse and the ass: it has dark stripes on a light body.

**ze·bu** (zē′bū), *n.* [*pl.* -BUS, -BU; see PLURAL, II, D, 1], [Fr. *zébu;* of Tibet. origin], an oxlike domestic animal of Asia and Africa: it has a large hump and short, curving horns.

ZEBU (4½ ft. at shoulder)

**Zech·a·ri·ah** (zek′ə-rī′ə), *n.* 1. a Hebrew prophet of the 6th century B.C. 2. a book of the Old Testament containing his prophecies: abbrev. **Zech.**

**zed** (zed), *n.* [< OFr. < L. < Gr. *zēta*], the British name for the letter Z, z.

**zee** (zē), *n.* [*pl.* ZEES], the letter Z, z.

**‡Zeit·geist** (tsīt′gīst′), *n.* [G., time spirit], the trend of thought and feeling in a period.

**Zen** (zen), *n.* [Jap. < Chin.; ult. < Sans. *dhyāna*], 1. an anti-rational Buddhist sect widespread in Japan: it seeks the truth through introspection and intuition rather than in Pali scripture. 2. the doctrines of this sect.

**Zend** (zend), *n.* [Per., interpretation], 1. the Middle Persian translation of and commentary on the Zoroastrian Avesta. 2. the ancient Persian or Iranian language of the Avesta. **—Zend′ic,** *adj.*

**Zend-Av·es·ta** (zen′də-ves′tə), *n.* the sacred writings of the Zoroastrians.

**ze·nith** (zē′nith; Brit. zen′ith), *n.* [< OFr. < ML. *cenith* < Ar. *semt*, road (as in *semt-ar-ras*, lit., way of the head) < L. *semita*, path], 1. the point in the sky directly overhead: cf. *nadir*. 2. the highest point; culmination; peak. **—ze′nith·al,** *adj.*

**Ze·no** (zē′nō), *n.* Greek philosopher; 336?–264? B.C.; founder of Stoicism.

**Zeph·a·ni·ah** (zef′ə-nī′ə), *n.* 1. a Hebrew prophet of the 7th century B.C. 2. a book of the Old Testament with his prophecies: abbrev. **Zeph.**

**zeph·yr** (zef′ẽr), *n.* [< L. < Gr. *zephyros*], 1. the west wind. 2. a soft, gentle breeze. 3. a fine, soft, lightweight yarn, cloth, or garment.

**zep·pe·lin** (zep′ə-lin, zep′lin), *n.* [after F. von *Zeppelin* (1838–1917), G. inventor], [often Z-], a type of rigid dirigible airship.

**ze·ro** (zêr′ō), *n.* [*pl.* -ROS, -ROES], [Fr. *zéro* < It. < Ar. *sifr*, a cipher], 1. the symbol or numeral 0; cipher; naught. 2. the point, marked 0, from which positive or negative quantities are reckoned on a graduated scale, as on thermometers. 3. a temperature that causes a thermometer to register zero. 4. nothing. 5. the lowest point: as, his chances sank to *zero*. *adj.* of or at zero. **—zero in,** to adjust the sight settings of (a rifle, etc.) by calibrated firing on a standard range.

**zero hour,** 1. the time set for the beginning of an attack or other military operation. 2. any crucial or decisive moment; critical point.

**zest** (zest), *n.* [Fr. *zeste*, orange peel used to give piquancy], 1. something that gives flavor or relish. 2. stimulating or exciting quality; piquancy. 3. keen enjoyment; gusto (often with *for*): as, a *zest* for life. *v.t.* to give zest to. **—zest′ful,** *adj.* **—zest′ful·ly,** *adv.* **—zest′ful·ness,** *n.*

**ze·ta** (zā′tə, zē′-), *n.* [Gr.], the sixth letter of the Greek alphabet (Z, ζ).

**Zeus** (zōōs, zūs), *n.* the supreme deity of the ancient Greeks, son of Cronus and Rhea and husband of Hera: identified with the Roman Jupiter.

**zig·zag** (zig′zag′), *n.* [Fr.], 1. any of a series of short, sharp angles or turns in alternate directions, as in a line or course. 2. something characterized by such a series, as a design. *adj.* having the form of a zigzag. *adv.* in a zigzag course. *v.t. & v.i.* [-ZAGGED, -ZAGGING], to move or form in a zigzag.

**zil·lion** (zil′yən), *n.* [arbitrary coinage, after *million*, etc.], [Colloq.], an indefinitely large number.

**zinc** (ziŋk), *n.* [G. *zink*], a bluish-white, metallic chemical element, used in electric batteries and in various alloys, as a protective coating for iron, and, in the form of salts, in medicines: symbol, Zn; at. wt., 65.38; at. no., 30. *v.t.* [ZINCKED or ZINCED, ZINCKING or ZINCING], to coat or treat with zinc. **—zinc′ic, zinck′y, zin′cous, zink′y,** *adj.*

**zinc ointment,** a salve containing zinc oxide.

**zinc oxide,** a white powder, ZnO, used as a pigment and in making glass, paints, ointments, etc.

**zinc white,** zinc oxide used as a white pigment.

**zing** (ziŋ), *n.* [echoic], [Slang], 1. vitality; zest. 2. a shrill, high-pitched sound, as of something moving at high speed. *v.i.* [Slang], to make such a sound.

**zin·ni·a** (zin′i-ə, zin′yə), *n.* [< J. G. *Zinn*, 18th-c. G. botanist], any of several plants of the aster family, having colorful, composite flowers.

**Zi·on** (zī′ən), *n.* 1. a hill in Jerusalem, site of the Temple and of the royal palace of David and his successors: a symbol of the center of Jewish national life. 2. the Jewish people. 3. heaven; the heavenly city. 4. the theocracy of God.

**Zi·on·ism** (zī′ən-iz′m), *n.* a movement formerly for re-establishing, now for supporting, the Jewish national state of Israel. **—Zi′on·ist,** *n. & adj.*

**zip** (zip), *n.* [echoic], 1. a short, sharp hissing sound, as of a passing bullet. 2. [Colloq.], energy; vim. *v.i.* [ZIPPED, ZIPPING], 1. to make, or move with, a zip. 2. [Colloq.], to move with speed or energy. *v.t.* to fasten with a slide fastener.

**ZIP code,** [*z*one *i*mprovement *p*lan], a system devised to speed mail deliveries, under which a code number is assigned to individual areas and places.

**zip·per** (zip′ẽr), *n.* 1. a boot or overshoe fitted with a slide fastener: a trade-mark (**Zipper**). 2. popularly, a slide fastener.

**zip·py** (zip′i), *adj.* [-PIER, -PIEST], [< *zip* + *-y*], [Colloq.], full of vim and energy; brisk; gay; snappy.

**zir·con** (zũr′kon), *n.* [Fr. < Ar. < Per. *zargūn*, gold-colored < *zar*, gold], a crystalline silicate of zirconium, $ZrSiO_4$, colored yellow, brown, red, etc.: transparent varieties are used as gems.

**zir·co·ni·um** (zẽr-kō′ni-əm), *n.* [see ZIRCON], a gray or black metallic chemical element used in alloys and in heat-resistant materials: symbol, Zr; at. wt., 91.22; at. no., 40. **—zir·con′ic** (-kon′ik), *adj.*

**zith·er** (zith′ẽr, zith′-), *n.* [G. < L. < Gr. *kithara*, a lute], a musical instrument having from thirty to forty strings stretched across a flat soundboard and played with a plectrum: also **zith′ern** (-ẽrn).

**zlo·ty** (zlô′ti), *n.* [*pl.* -TYS], the monetary unit of Poland.

**Zn,** in *chemistry*, zinc.

**zo·di·ac** (zō′di-ak′), *n.* [< OFr. < L. < Gr. *zōdiakos* (*kyklos*), lit., (circle) of animals < dim. of *zōion*, animal], 1. an imaginary belt in the heavens extending on either side of the apparent path of the sun and including the paths of the moon and the principal planets: it is divided into twelve equal parts, or signs, each named for a different constellation. 2. a diagram representing the zodiac and its signs: used in astrology. 3. [Rare], a circle or circuit. **—zo·di′a·cal** (-dī′ə-k′l), *adj.*

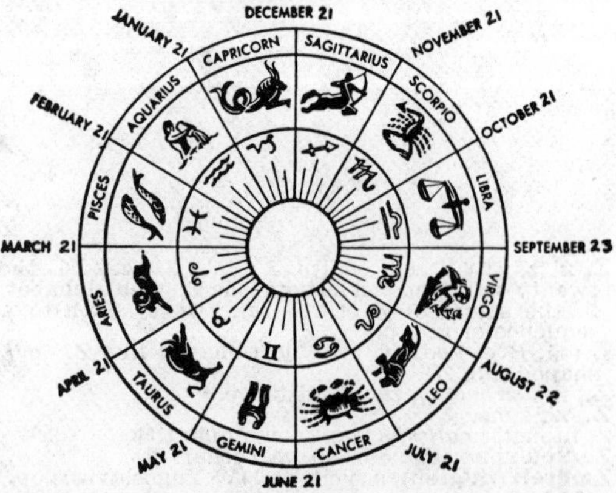


ZODIAC

**Zo·la, É·mile** (ā′mēl′ zô′lä′; Eng. zō′lə), 1840–1902; French novelist and critic.

**zom·bi** (zom′bi), *n.* [*pl.* -BIS], [of Afr. origin], 1. in West Indian superstition, a supernatural power through which a corpse may be brought to a state of trancelike animation. 2. a corpse so animated. 3. [Slang], a dull, stupid, unattractive person. 4. a cocktail made of various rums, fruit juices, etc. Also sp. **zom′bie** [*pl.* -BIES].

**zone** (zōn), *n.* [Fr. < L. < Gr. *zōnē* < *zōnnynai*, to gird], 1. [Poetic], a belt or girdle. 2. an encircling band, course, etc. distinct from the surrounding medium. 3. any of the five great latitudinal divisions of the earth's surface (the *torrid zone*, two *temperate zones*, and two *frigid zones*). 4. any region considered with reference to its particular use, crops, geological features, etc.: as, a canal *zone*, cotton *zone*. 5. any section of a city restricted by law for a particular use, as for homes, businesses, etc. 6. *a*) any of the numbered sections into which a metropolitan area is divided to facilitate postal delivery. *b*) any of a series of concentric areas about a given point, each having a different postage rate for goods shipped from that point. *v.t.* [ZONED, ZONING], 1. to mark off into zones; specif., to divide (a city, etc.) into areas determined by specific restrictions. 2. to encircle. —**zon'al, zon'a·ry,** *adj.*

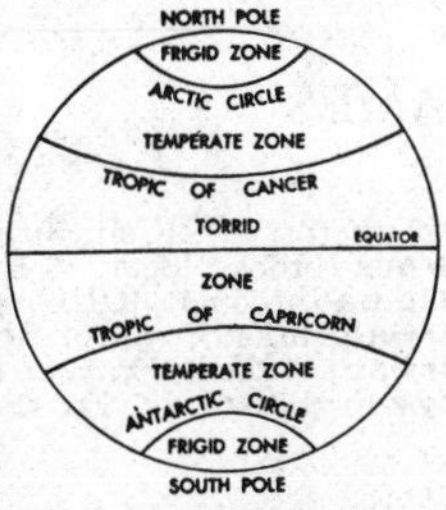

ZONES

**zonked** (zoŋkt), *adj.* [pp. of *zonk*, to strike; echoic term, intens. of *conk*], [Slang], highly intoxicated or under the influence of a drug.

**zoo** (zōō), *n.* [abbrev. < *zoological garden*], a place where a collection of wild animals is kept for public showing; menagerie.

**zo·o-**, [< Gr. *zōion*, an animal], a combining form meaning: 1. *animal, animals*, etc., as in *zoology*. 2. *zoology and*, as in *zoogeography*. Words beginning with *zoo-* are also written **zoö-**. Also **zo-**.

**zo·o·ge·og·ra·phy** (zō'ə-ji-og'rə-fi), *n.* [*zoo-* + *geography*], the science dealing with the geographical distribution of animals. —**zo'o·ge·og'ra·pher,** *n.* —**zo'o·ge'o·graph'ic** (-jē'ə-graf'ik), **zo'o·ge'o·graph'i·cal,** *adj.* —**zo'o·ge'o·graph'i·cal·ly,** *adv.*

**zo·og·ra·phy** (zō-og'rə-fi), *n.* [*zoo-* + *-graphy*], the branch of zoology concerned with the description of animals, their habits, etc. —**zo·og'ra·pher,** *n.* —**zo'o·graph'ic** (-ə-graf'ik), **zo'o·graph'i·cal,** *adj.* —**zo'o·graph'i·cal·ly,** *adv.*

**zo·oid** (zō'oid), *n.* [*zo-* + *-oid*], in *biology*, 1. an independent animal organism produced by nonsexual methods, as by fission, gemination, etc. 2. any of the distinct individuals of a compound organism, as the coral. —**zo·oi'dal** (-oi'd'l), *adj.*

**zoological garden,** a zoo.

**zo·ol·o·gy** (zō-ol'ə-ji), *n.* [*zoo-* + *-logy*], 1. the branch of biology dealing with the classification of animals and the study of animal life. 2. the animals collectively (*of* a particular region). —**zo'o·log'i·cal** (-ə-loj'i-k'l), **zo'o·log'ic,** *adj.* —**zo'o·log'i·cal·ly,** *adv.* —**zo·ol'o·gist,** *n.*

**zoom** (zōōm), *v.i.* [echoic], 1. to make a loud, low-pitched, buzzing or humming sound. 2. to climb suddenly and sharply: said of an airplane. 3. to rise rapidly: as, prices *zoomed*. 4. to focus a camera by using a zoom lens. *v.t.* to cause to zoom. *n.* the act of zooming.

**zoom lens,** a system of lenses, as in a motion-picture camera, that can be rapidly adjusted for close-up shots or distance views while keeping the image in focus.

**zo·o·phyte** (zō'ə-fīt'), *n.* [< Gr. < *zōion*, an animal + *phyton*, a plant], any animal, as a coral, sponge, etc., that looks and grows somewhat like a plant. —**zo'o·phyt'ic** (-fit'ik), **zo'o·phyt'i·cal,** *adj.*

**zo·o·spore** (zō'ə-spôr', -spōr'), *n.* an asexual spore, as of certain fungi or algae, capable of independent motion usually by means of cilia.

**Zo·ro·as·ter** (zō'rō-as'tēr), *n.* Persian founder of Zoroastrianism; fl. 6th or 7th century B.C. —**Zo'ro·as'tri·an** (-tri-ən), *adj. & n.*

**Zo·ro·as·tri·an·ism** (zō'rō-as'tri-ən-iz'm), *n.* the religious system of the ancient Persians, teaching the eventual triumph of the spirit of good over the spirit of evil.

**Zou·ave** (zōō-äv', zwäv), *n.* [Fr. < Ar. *Zouaoua*, an Algerian tribe], 1. a member of a former infantry unit in the French army, noted for their colorful oriental uniform. 2. a member of any military group having a similar uniform.

**zounds** (zoundz), *interj.* [alt. < oath *God's-wounds*], [Archaic], a mild oath of surprise or anger.

**Zr,** in *chemistry*, zirconium.

**zuc·chet·to** (tsōō-ket'ō), *n.* [*pl.* -TOS], [< It. < *zucca*, a gourd], in the *R. C. Church*, a skullcap worn by ecclesiastics, black for priests, purple for bishops, red for cardinals, and white for the Pope.

**zuc·chi·ni** (zōō-kē'ni), *n.* [It., pl. of *zucchino*, dim. of *zucca*, a squash], a kind of green-skinned summer squash, shaped somewhat like a cucumber.

**Zui·der Zee, Zuy·der Zee** (zī'dēr zē'), an arm of the North Sea extending into the Netherlands: it is shut off by dikes and partly reclaimed.

**Zu·lu** (zōō'lōō), *n.* [*pl.* -LUS, -LU], 1. a member of a great Bantu nation of SE Africa. 2. their language. *adj.* of the Zulus, their language, etc.

**Zu·lu·land** (zōō'lōō-land'), *n.* a region in Natal province, South Africa.

**Zu·ñi** (zōō'nyi, sōō'-), *n.* [*pl.* -ÑI, -ÑIS], [Sp. < Am. Ind.], 1. a member of a pueblo-dwelling tribe of Indians living in New Mexico. 2. their language. *adj.* of this tribe, their language, etc. Also **Zu'ñi·an.**

**Zur·ich, Zür·ich** (zoor'ik; G. tsü'riH), *n.* a city in N Switzerland: pop., 444,000.

**zwie·back** (tswē'bäk', zwē'-, swī'bak; G. tsvē'-bäk'), *n.* [G. < *zwie-*, twice + *backen*, to bake], a kind of rusk or biscuit that is sliced and toasted after baking.

**Zwing·li, Ul·rich** (ool'riH tsviŋ'lē; Eng. zwiŋ'gli), 1484–1531; Swiss patriot and Protestant reformer. —**Zwing'li·an,** *adj. & n.*

**zy·gote** (zī'gōt, zig'ōt), *n.* [< Gr. *zygōtos*, yoked < *zygon*, a yoke], any cell formed by the union of two gametes.

**zy·mase** (zī'mās), *n.* [Fr.: see ZYME & -ASE], an enzyme, present in yeast, which causes fermentation by breaking down glucose and some other carbohydrates into alcohol and carbon dioxide or into lactic acid.

**zyme** (zīm), *n.* [Gr. *zymē*, a leaven], 1. a ferment or enzyme. 2. the principle regarded as the specific cause of an infectious disease.

**zy·mo-**, (zī'mō, -mə), [< Gr. *zymē*, a leaven], a combining form meaning *fermentation*: also **zym-**.

**zy·mol·o·gy** (zī-mol'ə-ji), *n.* [*zymo-* + *-logy*], the science dealing with fermentation. —**zy'mo·log'ic** (-mə-loj'ik), *adj.*

**zy·mur·gy** (zī'mēr-ji), *n.* [*zym-* + *-urgy*], the chemistry of fermentation, as applied in brewing, etc.

# COMMON GIVEN NAMES

## MEN'S NAMES

**Aar·on** (âr'ən, ar'-), [LL. < Gr. < Heb. *aharōn*, the exalted one].
**A·bel** (ā'b'l), [L. < Gr. < Heb. *hebel*, breath].
**Ab·ner** (ab'nēr), [L. < Heb. *'abnēr*, the father is a light].
**A·bra·ham** (ā'brə-ham'), [Heb., father of many], also *Abram.*
**A·bram** (ā'brəm), [Heb., father is exalted], var. of **Abraham.**
**Ad·am** (ad'əm), [Heb. < *ādām*, a human being].
**Ad·el·bert** (ə-del'bērt, ad''l-), var. of **Albert.**
**Ad·olph** (ad'olf, ā'dôlf, ə-dolf'), [< L. < OHG. *adal*, nobility + *wolf*, wolf].
**A·dri·an** (ā'dri ən), [< L. < *Adria*, name of an Italian city], fem., *Adrienne.*
**Al·an** (al'ən), [ML. *Alanus*, of Breton origin], also *Allan, Allen.*
**Al·bert** (al'bērt), [Fr. < OHG. *Adalbrecht*, bright through nobility], also *Adelbert, Elbert;* fem., *Alberta, Albertine.*
**Al·ex·an·der** (al'ig-zan'dēr), [L. < Gr. *alexein*, to defend + *anēr, andros*, man], fem., *Alexandra.*
**Al·fon·so** (al-fon'zō, -sō), var. of **Alphonso.**
**Al·fred** (al'frid), [< AS. *Ælfred*, lit., wise counselor < *ælf*, wise + *ræd*, counsel], fem., *Alfreda.*
**Al·ger·non** (al'jēr-nən), [prob. < OFr. *al grenon*, with a mustache].
**Al·lan, Al·len** (al'ən), var. of **Alan.**
**A·lon·so, A·lon·zo** (ə-lon'zō), var. of **Alphonso.**
**Al·o·ys·i·us** (al'ō-ish'əs, -is'i-əs), [< ML.; prob. < OFr. *Loeis*; see LOUIS].
**Al·phon·so** (al-fon'zō, -sō), [< Sp. < OHG. *adal*, nobility + *funs*, ready], also *Alfonso, Alonso, Alonzo.*
**Al·vah, Al·va** (al'və), [Heb. *'alvāh, 'alvān;* often assoc. with L. *albus*, white], also *Alvan.*
**Al·van** (al'vən), var. of **Alvah.**
**Al·vin** (al'vin), [< G. < OHG. *adal*, nobility + *wini*, friend], also *Alwin.*
**Al·win** (al'win), var. of **Alvin.**
**Am·brose** (am'brōz), [< L. < Gr. *ambrotos*, immortal].
**A·mos** (ā'məs), [Heb. *'āmōs*, borne (by God?)].
**An·drew** (an'drōō), [< OFr. < L. < Gr. *Andreas*, lit., manly < *anēr, andros*, man], fem., *Andrea.*
**An·gus** (aŋ'gəs), [< Gael. & Ir. *aon*, one].
**An·sel** (an's'l), var. of **Anselm.**
**An·selm** (an'selm), [< L.; ? < Gmc. hyp. *Anshelm*, lit., God's defender], also *Ansel;* fem. *Selma.*
**An·tho·ny** (an'thə-ni, -tə-), [L. *Antonius*, name of a Roman gens], also *Antony, Tony;* fem., *Antoinette, Antonia.*
**An·to·ny** (am'tə-ni), var. of **Anthony.**
**Ar·chi·bald** (är'chi-bôld'), [< OHG. *Erchaubald*, prob. nobly bold].
**Ar·nold** (är'nəld), [G. < OHG. < Gmc. bases *aran*, eagle + *wald*, power].
**Ar·thur** (är'thēr), [ML. *Arthurus;*? < W. *ardd*, height].
**A·sa** (ā'sə), [Heb. *āsā*, healer].
**Au·brey** (ô'bri), [< Fr. < G. < OHG. *alb*, elf + *rihhi*, ruler], also *Avery.*
**Au·gust** (ô'gəst), [G.], var. of **Augustus.**
**Au·gus·tin** (ô-gus'tin), [< L. dim. of *Augustus;* see AUGUSTUS], also *Augustine, Austin.*
**Au·gus·tine** (ô'gəs-tēn', ô-gus'tin), var. of **Augustin.**
**Au·gus·tus** (ô-gus'təs), [L. < *augere*, to increase], also *August;* fem., *Augusta.*
**Aus·tin** (ôs'tin, -tən), var. of **Augustin.**
**A·ver·y** (ā'və-ri), var of **Aubrey.**

**Bald·win** (bôld'win), [< OFr. < MHG. < OHG. *bald*, bold + *wini*, friend].
**Bar·nard** (bär'nērd), var. of **Bernard.**
**Bar·ney** (bär'ni), var. of **Bernard.**
**Bar·ry** (bar'i), [ ? Ir.].
**Bar·thol·o·mew** (bär-thol'ə-mū'), [< OFr. < L. < Gr. *Bartholomaios* < Aram., lit., son of Talmai].
**Bas·il** (baz''l, bā'z'l), [< L. < Gr. *Basileios*, lit., kingly < *basileus*, king].
**Ben·e·dict** (ben'ə-dikt'), [< L. *Benedictus*, lit., blessed], also *Bennet, Bennett.*
**Ben·ja·min** (ben'jə-mən), [Heb. *binyāmīn*, son of the right hand, hence favorite son].
**Ben·net, Ben·nett** (ben'it), var. of **Benedict.**
**Ber·nard** (būr'nērd, bēr-närd'), [Fr. < G. < OHG. *bero*, bear + *hart*, bold], also *Barnard, Barney.*
**Ber·tram** (būr'trəm), [G. < OHG. < *beraht*. bright + *hraban, hramn*, raven], also *Bertrand.*
**Ber·trand** (būr'trənd), var. of **Bertram.**
**Bob** (bob), dim. of **Robert.**
**Bor·is** (bôr'is, bō'ris), [Russ., lit., fight].
**Bri·an** (brī'ən), [Celt., lit., strong], also *Bryan, Bryant.*
**Bruce** (brōōs), [Scot. < Fr. *Brieux*, place in France].
**Bru·no** (brōō'nō), [OHG. < *brun*, brown].
**Bry·an** (brī'ən), var. of **Brian.**
**Bry·ant** (brī'ənt), var. of **Brian.**
**By·ron** (bī'rən), [< Fr. < *Biron*, district in France].

**Ca·leb** (kā'ləb), [Heb. *kālēb*, dog, hence faithful].
**Cal·vin** (kal'vin), [< Fr.; prob. < L. *calvus*, bald].
**Car·ey, Car·y** (kâr'i), [? < *Car(e)y*, Brit. river name].
**Carl** (kärl), var. of **Charles**; also *Karl.*
**Car·ol** (kar'əl), var. of **Charles.**
**Cas·par, Cas·per** (kas'pēr), var. of **Jasper.**
**Ce·cil** (sē's'l, ses''l), [< L.; prob. < *caecus*, blind], fem., *Cecile, Cecilia, Cecily, Cicely.*
**Ced·ric** (sed'rik, sē'drik), [? < Celt. base meaning "war chief"].
**Charles** (chärlz), [Fr.; ult. < OHG. *Karl*, full-grown], also *Carl, Carol;* fem., *Caroline, Charlotte.*
**Ches·ter** (ches'tēr), [< AS. *ceaster*, walled town < L. *castra*, a camp].
**Chris·tian** (kris'chən), [< AS. < L. < Gr. < *Christos*, lit., the Anointed], fem., *Christiana.*
**Chris·to·pher** (kris'tə-fēr), [< L. < Gr. *Christophoros*, lit., bearing Christ < *Christos* lit., the Anointed + *pherein*, to bear].
**Clair, Clare** (klâr), var. of **Clarence.**
**Clar·ence** (klar'əns), [< *Clare*, English town; as if < *clarens*, pp. < *clarus*, clear, illustrious], also *Clair, Clare.*
**Clark** (klärk), [< AS. & OFr. *clerc*, clerk < LL. *clericus* < Gr. *klērikos*, priest].
**Claude, Claud** (klôd), [Fr. < L. *Claudius;* prob. < *claudus*, lame], fem., *Claudia.*
**Clem·ent** (klem'ənt), [< L. < *clemens*, mild, gentle], fem., *Clementine.*
**Clif·ford** (klif'ērd), [< *cliff* + *ford;* hence, ford at the cliff].
**Clif·ton** (klif'tən), [< *cliff* + *-ton* (town); hence, town at a cliff].
**Clin·ton** (klin'tən), [? < Anglo-N. *klint*, hill + AS. *tun*, town].
**Clive** (klīv), [< *cliff*].
**Clyde** (klīd), [? < Scot. river name].
**Col·in** (kol'in, kō'lin), [prob. < L. *columba*, a dove].
**Con·rad** (kon'rad), [< G. or Fr. < OHG. < *kuon*, bold, wise + *rat* counsel < *ratan*, to advise].
**Con·stant** (kon'stənt), [Fr. < L. *constans*, constant, faithful], fem., *Constance.*
**Cor·nel·ius** (kôr-nēl'yəs), [L., name of a Roman gens], fem., *Cornelia.*
**Craig** (krāg), [< Celt.; prob. < W. *craig*, a crag].
**Cur·tis** (kūr'tis), [< OFr. *corteis*, courteous].
**Cyr·il** (sir'əl), [< LL. < Gr. < *kyrios*, a lord].
**Cy·rus** (sī'rəs), [L. < Gr. *Kyros* < OPer. *Kūrush*].

**Dale** (dāl), [prob. < AS. *dæl*, a small valley].
**Dan·iel** (dan'yəl), [Heb. *dānī'ēl*, God is my judge].
**Da·vid** (dā'vid), [Heb. *dāvīd*, beloved], fem., *Vida.*
**Dean, Deane** (dēn), [? < AS. *denu*, valley or < LL. *decanus*, one who is head of ten < L. *decem*, ten].
**Den·is, Den·nis** (den'is), [< Fr. < L. *Dionysius* < Gr. *Dionysos*, god of wine], fem., *Denise.*
**Dex·ter** (dek'stēr), [< L. *dexter*, right, skillful].
**Dick** (dik), dim. of **Richard.**
**Dom·in·ic, Dom·i·nick** (dom'ə-nik), [< L. *Dominicus*, belonging to a lord < *dominus*, a master, lord].
**Don·ald** (don''ld), [Ir. *Donghal*, lit., brown stranger; or Gael. *Domhnall*, lit., world ruler].
**Doug·las** (dug'ləs), [< Celt., dark, gray].
**Drew** (drōō), [prob. < OFr. *dru, dru*, strong].
**Dud·ley** (dud'li), [< Celt., fair field].
**Dun·can** (duŋ'kən), [Gael. *Donnchadh*, lit., brown warrior].
**Dwight** (dwīt), [Gmc., wise person].

**Earl, Earle** (ūrl), [< AS. *eorl*, warrior].
**Ear·nest** (ūr'nist), var. of **Ernest.**
**Eb·en·e·zer** (eb'ə-nē'zēr), [Heb. *eben-ha-'ēzer*, stone of help].
**Ed·gar** (ed'gēr), [< AS. *ead*, riches + *gar*, a spear].
**Ed·mond, Ed·mund** (ed'mənd), [< AS. *ead*, riches + *mund*, protection; hence, wealthy protector].
**Ed·ward** (ed'wērd), [< AS. < *ead*, riches + *weard*, guardian hence, wealthy guardian], also *Ned.*
**Ed·win** (ed'win), [< AS. < *ead*, riches + *wine*, friend hence, wealthy friend], fem., *Edwina.*

**Eg·bert** (eg'bērt), [< AS. < *ecg*, edge + *beorht*, bright; hence, bright sword].
**El·bert** (el'bērt), var. of **Albert.**
**El·dred** (el'drid), [< AS. < *eald*, old + *ræd*, counsel].
**E·li** (ē'lī), [Heb. *'ēlī*, high].
**E·li·jah** (i-lī'jə, ə-lī'-), [Heb. *'ēlīyāhu*, Jehovah is God].
**El·i·ot, El·li·ot, El·li·ott** (el'i-ət), [< *Ellis*].
**E·li·sha** (i-lī'shə, ə-lī'-), [Heb. *elīshā'*, God is salvation], also *Ellis.*
**El·lis** (el'is), var. of **Elisha.**
**El·mer** (el'mēr), [? < AS. < *æthel*, noble or *egil-* (< *ege*, awe) + *mære*, famous].
**Em·er·y, Em·mer·y, Em·or·y** (em'ēr-i), [prob. < OFr. < OHG. *Amalrich*, lit., work ruler].
**E·mil** (ā'm'l, ē'-, ēm''l), [G. < Fr. < L. *aemulus*, trying to excel], also *Émile;* fem., Emily.
**É·mile** (ā-mēl'), var. of **Emil.**
**Em·man·u·el, E·man·u·el** (i-man'ū-əl), [< Gr. < Heb. *'immānūēl*, God with us], also *Immanuel, Manuel.*
**E·noch** (ē'nək), [< Gr. < Heb. *ḥānōkh*, dedicated].
**E·ras·tus** (i-ras'təs), [L. < Gr. *Erastos*, lit., beloved].
**Er·ic** (er'ik), [Scand. < ON. *Eirīkr*, lit., honorable ruler < Gmc.].
**Er·nest** (ũr'nist), [< G. < OHG. *Ernust*, lit., resolute fighter < *ernust*, seriousness], also *Earnest;* fem., *Ernestine.*
**Er·win** (ũr'win), [G. < OHG. *heri*, host, army + *wini*, friend; hence, friend of hosts], also *Irwin.*
**E·than** (ē'thən), [L. < Heb. *ēthān*, strength].
**Eth·el·bert** (eth'əl-bērt), [< AS. < *æthele*, noble + *beorht*, bright]
**Eu·gene** (yoo-jēn', ū'jēn), [< Fr. < L. < Gr. < *eugenēs*, well-born], also *Gene;* fem., *Eugenia.*
**Eus·tace** (ūs'tis), [OFr. < L. < Gr. *Eustachios* < *eustachys*, rich in corn, fruitful].
**Ev·an** (ev'ən), [< Celt. *Eoghan*, young man].
**Ev·e·lyn** (ev'ə-lin, ēv'lin), [< Celt., pleasant], fem., *Evelina, Eveline, Evelyn.*
**Ev·er·ard** (ev'ēr-ärd'), [< OFr. <OHG. *Eberhard* < *eber*, wild boar + *hard*, strong].
**Ev·er·ett** (ev'ēr-it, ev'rit), [< D. *Everhart;* see EVERARD].
**E·zek·i·el** (i-zē'ki-əl, -kyəl), [< LL. < Gr. < Heb. *yeḥezq'ēl*, God strengthens].
**Ez·ra** (ez'rə), [LL. < Heb. *ezrā*, help].

**Fe·lix** (fē'liks), [L., lit., happy], fem., *Felicia.*
**Fer·di·nand** (fũr'd'n-and'), [Fr.; prob. < Gmc. bases meaning "bold in peace"].
**Floyd** (floid), var. of **Lloyd.**
**Fran·cis** (fran'sis, frän'-), [< OFr. < LL. *Franciscus* < OHG. *Franco*, a Frank], fem., *Frances.*
**Frank·lin** (fraŋk'lin), [< Anglo-Fr. < ML. < *Francus*, a Frank, hence free man].
**Fred·er·ick, Fred·er·ic** (fred'ēr-ik, fred'rik), [< Fr. < G. OHG. *Fridurih*, "peaceful ruler"], also *Fredric, Fredrick;* fem., *Frederica.*
**Fred·rick, Fred·ric** (fred'rik), var. of **Frederick.**

**Ga·bri·el** (gā'bri-əl), [Heb. *gabhrī'ēl*, God is (my) strength], fem., *Gabrielle.*
**Ga·ma·li·el** (gə-mā'li-əl, -māl'yəl), [L. < Gr. < Heb. *gamlī'ēl*, reward of God].
**Gar·rett, Gar·ret** (gar'it), [< AS. < *gar*, spear + *rathe*, quick; hence, swift spear; cf. GERARD].
**Gene** (jēn), var. of **Eugene.**
**Geof·frey** (jef'ri), [< Fr. < OFr. < ML. *Gaufridus* < OHG. *Godafrid;* see GODFREY], also *Jeffrey.*
**George** (jôrj), [< Fr. < LL. < Gr. < *geōrgos*, husbandmen < *gaia, gē*, earth + base of *ergon*, work], fem., *Georgia, Georgiana, Georgina.*
**Ger·ald** (jer'əld), [< OFr. < OHG. < *ger*, spear + base of *waldan*, to rule], fem., *Geraldine.*
**Ger·ard** (ji-rärd'), [< OFr. < OHG. < *ger*, spear + *hart*, hard; hence, hard spear].
**Gid·e·on** (gid'i-ən), [Heb. *gid'ōn*, hewer].
**Gil·bert** (gil'bērt), [< OFr. < OHG. < *willo*, will, wish + *beraht*, bright].
**Giles** (jīlz), [< OFr. < L. *aegis*, shield < Gr. *aigis*, goatskin < *aix*, goat].
**Glen, Glenn** (glen), [Celt., lit., valley].
**God·frey** (god'fri), [< OFr. < OHG. *Godafrid* < *god*, God + *fridu*, peace; hence, peace (of) God].
**God·win** (god'win), [< AS. *Godewine*, lit., friend (of) God].
**Gor·don** (gôr'd'n), [Scot. < surname *Gordon*].
**Gra·ham** (grā'əm), [< ?].
**Grant** (grant), [< ?].
**Greg·or** (greg'ēr), var. of **Gregory.**
**Greg·o·ry** (greg'ēr-i), [< LL. < Gr. *Grēgorios*, lit., vigilant, hence watchman], also *Gregor.*
**Grif·fith** (grif'ith), [W. *Gruffydd* < L. *Rufus;* see RUFUS].
**Gus·ta·vus** (gus-tā'vəs, -tä'-), [< G. *Gustav* or Sw. *Gustaf*, prob. staff of the Goths].
**Guy** (gī), [Fr. *Gui, Guy*, lit., leader].

**Hans** (hans, hanz), [G. abbrev. of *Johannes* < same origin as *John;* see JOHN].
**Har·old** (har'əld), [AS. < ON. *Haraldr*, lit., leader].
**Har·ry** (har'i), var. of **Henry;** fem., *Harriet.*
**Har·vey** (här'vi), [< Fr. < G. *Herwig*, lit., army battle].
**Hec·tor** (hek'tēr), [L. < Gr. *Hēktor*, lit., holding fast < *echein*, to hold].
**Hen·ry** (hen'ri), [< OFr. < G. < OHG. *Haganrih*, lit., ruler of an enclosure & *Heimerich*, lit., home ruler], also *Harry;* fem., *Henrietta.*
**Her·bert** (hũr'bērt), [AS. *Herebeorht*, lit., bright army].
**Her·man** (hũr'mən), [< G. < OHG. *Hariman* < *heri*, army + *man*, man].
**Hi·ram** (hī'rəm), [Heb. *ḥīrām*, prob. < *'aḥīrām*, exalted brother].
**Ho·mer** (hō'mēr), [< L. < Gr. *Homēros;* identical with *homēros*, a pledge, but said to mean "blind"].
**Hor·ace** (hôr'is, hor'-), var. of **Horatio.**
**Ho·ra·ti·o** (hə-rā'shō, hō-rā'shi-ō), [< L. *Horatius*, name of a Roman gens], also *Horace.*
**How·ard** (hou'ērd), [< the surname *Howard*].
**Hu·bert** (hū'bērt), [Fr. < OHG. < *hugu*, mind, spirit + *beraht*, bright].
**Hugh** (hū), [< OFr. < OHG. *Hugo*, prob. < *hugu*, the mind], also *Hugo.*
**Hu·go** (hū'gō), var. of **Hugh.**
**Hum·phrey, Hum·phry** (hum'fri), [< AS. *Hunfrith*, lit., strength in peace].

**I·an** (ē'ən, ī'-, ē'än), var. of **John.**
**Ig·na·ti·us** (ig-nā'shəs, -shi-əs), [L. < Gr. *Ignatios;* ? akin to L. *ignis*, a fire].
**Im·man·u·el** (i-man'ū-əl), var. of **Emmanuel.**
**I·ra** (ī'rə), [Heb. *'īrā*, watchful].
**Ir·vin** (ũr'vin), var. of **Irving.**
**Ir·ving** (ũr'viŋ), [north Brit. surname; prob. orig. a place name], also *Irvin.*
**Ir·win** (ũr'win), var. of **Erwin.**
**I·saac** (ī'zək), [< LL. < Heb. *yitsḥāq*, laughter].
**Is·i·dore, Is·i·dor, Is·a·dore, Is·a·dor** (iz'ə-dôr', -dōr'), [< G. < Fr. < L. < Gr. < *Isis*, Isis + *dōron*, gift; hence, gift of Isis], fem., *Isadora.*
**Is·ra·el** (iz'ri-əl), [L. < Gr. < Heb. *yisrā'ēl*, contender with God < *sārāh*, to wrestle + *ēl*, God].
**I·van** (ī'vən), [Russ. < Gr. *Iōannēs;* see JOHN].
**I·vor** (ē'vēr, ī'-), [< ?].

**Jack** (jak), [< OFr. *Jaques;* ult. < Heb.; see JACOB], var. of **John.**
**Ja·cob** (jā'kəb), [< LL. < Gr. < Heb. *ya'aqob*, seizing by the heel, hence supplanter], also *James.*
**James** (jāmz), var. of **Jacob.**
**Jar·ed** (jâr'id), [L. < Gr. < Heb. *yeredh*, descent].
**Jar·vis** (jär'vis), [< Fr. < LL. *Gervasius*, name of an early Christian saint], also *Jervis.*
**Ja·son** (jā's'n), [< L. < Gr. *Iāson*, lit., healer].
**Jas·per** (jas'pēr), [< OFr.; ? < Per. base meaning "lord of the treasure"], also *Caspar, Casper.*
**Jay** (jā), [< OFr. < LL. *gaius*, a jay, infl. by Latin name *Gaius*].
**Jean** (jēn), var. of **John.**
**Jeff·rey** (jef'ri), var. of **Geoffrey.**
**Jer·e·mi·ah** (jer'ə-mī'ə), [< LL. < Heb. *yirmeyāhu*, the Lord loosens (i.e., from the womb)], also *Jeremy.*
**Jer·e·my** (jer'ə-mi), var. of **Jeremiah.**
**Je·rome** (jə-rōm'; *chiefly* Brit. jer'əm), [< Fr. < L. < Gr. < *hieros*, holy + *onyma*, name].
**Jer·vis** (jũr'vis; Brit. jär'-), var. of **Jarvis.**
**Jes·se** (jes'i), [L. < Gr. < Heb. *yīshay;* meaning ?].
**Job** (jōb), [L. < Gr. < Heb. *iyyōbh*, prob., afflicted].
**Jo·el** (jō'əl), [L. < Gr. < Heb. *yō'ēl*, the Lord is God].
**John** (jon), [< ML. < Gr. *Iōannēs* < Heb. contr. of *yehōḥānān*, the Lord is gracious], also *Hans, Ian, Ivan, Jack, Jean;* fem., *Jane, Jean, Jeanne, Joan, Joanna, Johanna.*
**Jo·nah** (jō'nə), [< L. < Gr. < Heb. *yōnāh*, a dove], also *Jonas.*
**Jo·nas** (jō'nəs), var. of **Jonah.**
**Jon·a·than** (jon'ə-thən), [< Heb. contr. < *yehōnāthān*, the Lord has given].
**Jo·seph** (jō'zəf), [L. < Gr. < Heb. *yōsēph*, may he add], fem., *Josephine.*
**Josh·u·a** (josh'oo-ə), [Heb. *yehōshū'a*, help of Jehovah].
**Jo·si·ah** (jō-sī'ə), [Heb. *yōshiyāh*, the Lord supports], also *Josias.*
**Jo·si·as** (jō-sī'əs), var. of **Josiah.**
**Ju·dah** (jōō'də), [Heb. *yehūdhāh*, praised (by the Lord)], also *Judas;* fem., *Judith.*
**Ju·das** (jōō'dəs), var. of **Judah.**
**Jules** (jōōlz), var. of **Julius.**
**Jul·ian** (jōōl'yən), [< L. *Julius;* see JULIUS], fem., *Juliana.*
**Jul·ius** (jōōl'yəs), [L., name of a Roman gens], also *Jules;* fem., *Julia, Juliet.*
**Jun·ius** (jōōn'yəs, jōō'ni-əs), [L., name of a Roman gens], fem., *June.*
**Jus·tin** (jus'tin), [< L. *justus*, proper < *jus*, right, law], also *Justus;* fem., *Justina, Justine.*

**Jus·tus** (jus′təs), var. of **Justin.**

**Karl** (kärl), var. of **Carl.**
**Keith** (kēth), [Scot. < Gael. base meaning "the wind"].
**Kel·vin** (kel′vin), [< Eng. surname *Kelvin*].
**Ken·neth** (ken′ith), [Scot. < Gael. *Caioneach*, lit., handsome].
**Kent** (kent), [? < W. *cant*, border country].
**Kev·in** (kev′in), [< Ir. < OIr. *Coemgen*, lit., comely birth].

**Lance** (lans, läns), var. of **Lancelot.**
**Lan·ce·lot, Laun·ce·lot** (lan′sə-lot′, län′sə-lət), [< Fr. < OHG. *Lanzo* < *lant*, land], also *Lance.*
**Lau·rence, Law·rence** (lôr′əns, lär′-), [< L. *Laurentius;* prob. < *laurus*, laurel], also *Lorenzo;* fem., *Laura.*
**Lee** (lē), var. of **Leigh.**
**Leigh** (lē), [< AS. *leah*, meadow], also *Lee.*
**Leo** (lē′ō), [< L. < Gr. *leōn*, lion], also *Leon, Lionel;* fem., *Leona.*
**Le·on** (lē′on), var. of **Leo.**
**Leon·ard** (len′ẽrd), [< Fr. < OFr. < OHG. < *lewo*, lion + *hart*, strong; hence, strong as a lion].
**Le·o·pold** (lē′ə-pōld′), [G. < OHG. < *liut*, people (orig., prob., free man) + *balt*, bold, strong].
**Le·roy** (lə-roi′, lē′roi), [< Fr. *le roi*, the king].
**Les·lie** (les′li, lez′-), [said to be < *less lee* (*lea*), i.e., smaller meadow].
**Les·ter** (les′tẽr), [< *Leicester*, Eng. city].
**Lew·is** (lōō′is, lū′-), var. of **Louis.**
**Lin·coln** (liŋ′kən), [prob. < *Lincoln*, Eng. city].
**Li·nus** (lī′nəs), [L. < Gr. *Linos*, lit., flaxen-haired].
**Li·o·nel** (lī′ə-n′l, -nel′), [Fr., dim. of *lion*, lion], var. of **Leon.**
**Lisle** (līl), var. of **Lyle.**
**Llew·el·lyn** (lōō-el′in), [W. *Llewelyn*, lit., prob., lionlike].
**Lloyd** (loid), [W. *Llwyd*, lit., gray], also *Floyd.*
**Lo·ren·zo** (lô-ren′zō, lə-), var. of **Laurence.**
**Lou·is** (lōō′is, -i), [Fr. < OFr. *Loeis;* prob. via ML. <OHG. *Hluodowig* < Gmc. bases meaning "famous in war"], also *Lewis;* fem., *Louise.*
**Lov·ell** (luv″l), var. of **Lowell.**
**Low·ell** (lō′əl), [< ?], also *Lovell.*
**Lu·cian** (lōō′shən), [L. *Lucianus*, of Lucius].
**Lu·cius** (lōō′shəs), [L. < *lux*, light], fem., *Lucia.*
**Luke** (look), [< L. < Gr. *Loukas;* prob. contr. of *Loukanos*].
**Lu·ther** (lōō′thẽr), [G. < OHG. *Chlothar* < Gmc. bases meaning "famous fighter"].
**Lyle** (līl), [< Brit. place name & surname], also *Lisle.*
**Lynn** (lin), [prob. < W. *llyn*, a lake].

**Mal·colm** (mal′kəm), [Celt. *Maolcolm*, lit., servant of (St.) Columba].
**Man·u·el** (man′ū-əl, -el′), var. of **Emmanuel.**
**Marc** (märk), var. of **Mark.**
**Mar·cel** (mär-sel′), var. of **Marcellus.**
**Mar·cel·lus** (mär-cel′əs), [L., dim. of *Marcus*], also *Marcel;* fem., *Marcella.*
**Mar·cus** (mär′kəs), [L. < *Mars*, the god of war], also *Mark;* fem., *Marcia.*
**Mar·i·on** (mâr′i-ən), [Fr.; prob. ult. < dim. of *Marie*].
**Mark** (märk), var. of **Marcus,** also *Marc.*
**Mar·shal, Mar·shall** (mär′shəl), [< OFr. < OHG. < *marah*, horse + *scalh*, servant].
**Mar·tin** (mär′t'n), [Fr. < L. *Martinus*, lit., warlike < *Mars*, god of War].
**Mar·vin** (mär′v'n), [prob. ult. < Gmc. bases meaning "sea" & "friend"], also *Mervin, Mervyn, Merwyn.*
**Mat·thew** (math′ū), [< OFr. < LL. < Gr. contr. < Heb. *mattithyāh*, gift of God], also *Matthias.*
**Mat·thi·as** (mə-thī′əs), var. of **Matthew.**
**Mau·rice** (môr′is, mär′-, mô-rēs′), [Fr. < LL. *Maurus*, a Moor], also *Morris.*
**Max** (maks), dim. of **Maximilian;** fem., *Maxine.*
**Max·i·mil·ian** (mak′sə-mil′yən, -i-ən), [said to be from two Roman names, *Maximus* & *Aemilianus*], also *Max.*
**May·er** (mā′ẽr), var. of **Meyer.**
**May·nard** (mā′nẽrd, -närd), [< Anglo-Fr. < OHG. < *magan*, power + *hart*, strong].
**Mel·vin** (mel′vin), [ult. prob. < AS. *mæl*, council + *wine*, friend].
**Mer·e·dith** (mer′ə-dith), [W., sea protector].
**Merle** (mũrl), [Fr.; prob. < L. *merula*, blackbird].
**Mer·lin** (mũr′lin), [< ML. < W. *Merddin*, sea-fort].
**Mer·ton** (mũr′t'n), [prob. < AS. *Mere-tun*, town by a lake].
**Mer·vin, Mer·vyn** (mũr′vin), var. of **Marvin.**
**Mer·wyn** (mũr′win), var. of **Marvin.**
**Mey·er** (mī′ẽr), [< ?], also *Mayer.*
**Mi·cah** (mī′kə), [Heb. *mākhā(yah)*, who is like (God)].
**Mi·chael** (mī′k'l), [LL. < Gr. < Heb. *mīkhā'ēl*, who is like God], also *Mitchell.*
**Miles** (mīlz), [OFr. < OHG. *Milo*], also *Myles.*
**Mi·lo** (mī′lō), [Gmc. & Gr. name].
**Mil·ton** (mil′t'n), [< AS. *Middle-tun*, Middletown or *Mylen-tun*, Mill town].
**Mitch·ell** (mich″l), var. of **Michael.**
**Mon·roe** (mən-rō′), [< ?].
**Mon·ta·gue** (mon′tə-gū′), [? < Fr. place name meaning "pointed hill"].
**Mor·gan** (môr′gən), [W., sea dweller].
**Mor·ris** (môr′is, mor′-), var. of **Maurice.**
**Mor·ti·mer** (môr′tə-mẽr), [< Norm. surname].
**Mor·ton** (môr′t'n), [< AS. < *mor*, moor + *tun*, town].
**Mo·ses** (mō′ziz, -zəz), [L. < Gr. < Heb.; prob. < Egypt. *mes, messu*, child], also *Moss.*
**Moss** (môs), var. of **Moses.**
**Mur·ray** (mũr′i), [? < Celt.; cf. W. *mor*, the sea].
**Myles** (mīlz), var. of **Miles.**
**My·ron** (mī′rən), [? < Gr. *myron*, an ointment].

**Na·than** (nā′thən), [Heb. *nāthān*, gift].
**Na·than·a·el, Na·than·i·el** (nə-than′yəl, -i-əl), [LL. < Gr. <Heb. *nĕthan'ēl*, gift of God].
**Neal, Neil** (nēl), [prob. < Ir. < *niadh*, a champion].
**Ned** (ned), [by faulty division of *mine Ed*], var. of **Edgar, Edmond, Edward.**
**Nel·son** (nel′s'n), [< surname *Nelson*, Neal's son].
**Nev·il, Nev·ile, Nev·ill, Nev·ille** (nev″l, -il), [< Norman surname *Nevil* < *Neuville*, town in Normandy (lit., new city)].
**New·ton** (nōō′t'n, nū′-), [< Eng. place name < AS. *neowa tun*, new town].
**Nich·o·las, Nic·o·las** (nik″l-əs), [< OFr. < L. < Gr. *Nikolaos* < *nikē*, victory + *laos*, the people].
**Ni·gel** (nī′jəl), [? < same base as *Neal*].
**No·ah** (nō′ə), [Heb. *nōaḥ*, rest, comfort].
**No·el** (nō′əl), [< OFr. *No(u)el*, lit., natal; see NATALIE], also *Nowell.*
**Nor·bert** (nôr′bẽrt), [< ?].
**Nor·man** (nôr′mən), [< AS. < OHG. *Nordemann*, Northman].
**Now·ell** (nō′əl), var. of **Noel.**

**O·ba·di·ah** (ō′bə-dī′ə), [LL. < Heb. *'ōbadhyah*, servant of the Lord].
**Oc·ta·vi·us** (ok-tā′vi-əs), [L. < *octavus*, eighth], fem., *Octavia.*
**O·laf** (ō′ləf, ō′läf), [? Scand.].
**Ol·i·ver** (ol′ə-vẽr), [< Fr. *Olivier;* prob. < MLG. < *alf*, elf + *hari*, an army].
**O·mar** (ō′mẽr, ō′mär), [Heb. *'omar*, name of a chief].
**Or·lan·do** (ôr-lan′dō), var. of **Roland.**
**Or·son** (ôr′s'n), [< Fr. dim. of *ours* (L. *ursus*), a bear].
**Os·bert** (oz′bẽrt), [? < AS. < *os*, a god + *beorht*, bright].
**Os·car** (os′kẽr), [< AS. < *os*, a god + *gar*, a spear].
**Os·wald, Os·wold** (oz′wəld, -wôld), [< AS. < *os*, a god + *weald*, power].
**Ot·to** (ot′ō), [< OHG. *Otho, Odo* < *auda*, rich].
**Ow·en** (ō′in, ō′wən), [W. < Celt.; cf. EUGENE].

**Pat·rick** (pat′rik), [L. *patricius*, a patrician], fem., *Patricia.*
**Paul** (pôl), [L. *Paulus*, a Roman surname, prob. < *paulus*, small], fem., *Paula, Pauline.*
**Per·ci·val, Per·ce·val** (pũr′sə-v'l), [< OFr.; prob. < *perce val*, pierce valley].
**Per·ry** (per′i), [< AS. *pirige*, pear tree].
**Pe·ter** (pē′tẽr), [< LL. < Gr. *petra*, a rock].
**Phil·ip, Phil·lip** (fil′əp), [< L. < Gr. < *philos*, loving + *hippos*, a horse], fem., *Philippa.*
**Phin·e·as** (fin′i-əs), [< LL. < Gr. < Heb. *pīnĕḥās*, mouth of brass].

**Quen·tin** (kwen′tin), var. of **Quintin.**
**Quin·cy** (kwin′si, -zi), [< ?].
**Quin·tin** (kwin′tin), [< Fr. < L. *Quintinus* < *quintus*, the fifth], also *Quentin.*

**Ralph** (ralf, rälf; Brit. rāf), [< ON. < *rath*, counsel + *ulfr*, a wolf].
**Ran·dal, Ran·dall** (ran′d'l), [< AS. *Randwulf* < *rand*, a shield + *wulf*, a wolf].
**Ran·dolph** (ran′dolf, -dôlf), [< ML. < AS. *Randwulf;* see RANDAL].
**Raph·a·el** (rā′fi-əl, raf′i-), [LL. < Gr. < Heb. *rephā'ēl*, God hath healed].
**Ray·mond, Ray·mund** (rā′mənd), [< ONorm.Fr. < Frank. *Raginmund*, lit., wise protection].
**Reg·i·nald** (rej′i-nəld), [< ML. < OG. *Raganald* < Gmc. bases meaning "strong ruler"], also *Reynold.*
**Reu·ben** (rōō′bin), [Heb. *rĕ'ūbēn*, behold, a son].
**Rex** (reks), [L., a king].
**Reyn·old** (ren′əld), var. of **Reginald.**
**Rich·ard** (rich′ẽrd), [< OFr. < OHG. *Richart* < Gmc. bases meaning "strong king"], also *Dick.*
**Rob·ert** (rob′ẽrt), [Fr. < OHG. < *hruod-*, fame + *beraht*, bright], also *Bob, Robin, Rupert;* fem., *Roberta.*
**Rob·in** (rob′in), dim. of **Robert.**

**Rod·er·ic, Rod·er·ick** (rod'ə-rik, rod'rik), [< ML. < OHG. < *hruod-*, fame + Gmc. base meaning "king"].
**Rod·ney** (rod'ni), [< Eng. place name *Rodney Stoke*].
**Ro·dolph** (rō'dolf), var. of **Rudolph.**
**Rog·er** (roj'ẽr), [< AS. *Hrothgar* & OHG. bases meaning "famous with the spear"].
**Ro·land** (rō'lənd), [Fr. < OHG. < *hruod-*, fame + *land*, land], also *Orlando, Rowland.*
**Rolf** (rolf), var. of **Rudolph.**
**Rol·lo** (rol'ō), var. of **Rudolph.**
**Ron·ald** (ron''ld), [Scot. < ON. *Rögnvaldr;* cf. REGINALD].
**Ros·coe** (ros'kō), [? <Celt. place name].
**Ross** (rôs), [prob. < W. *rhos,* hill, promontory, moor, etc].
**Row·land** (rō'lənd), var. of **Roland.**
**Roy** (roi), [as if < OFr. *roy,* a king; but prob. < Gael. *rhu,* red].
**Ru·dolph, Ru·dolf** (ro͞o'dolf, -dôlf), [< G. < OHG. < *hruod-*, fame + *wolf,* a wolf], also *Rodolph, Rolf, Rollo.*
**Ru·fus** (ro͞o'fəs), [L., red, red-haired].
**Ru·pert** (ro͞o'pẽrt), var. of **Robert.**
**Rus·sel, Rus·sell** (rus''l), [< surname *Russell,* orig. dim. of Fr. *roux,* red].

**Samp·son** (sam's'n, samp'-), var. of **Samson.**
**Sam·son** (sam's'n), [LL. < Gr. < Heb. < *shemesh,* sun; interpretation of name uncertain], also *Sampson.*
**Sam·u·el** (sam'ū-əl, -yool), [LL. < Gr. < Heb. *shĕmūēl,* name of God].
**San·ford** (san'fẽrd), [Eng. place name, "sandy ford"].
**Saul** (sôl), [LL. < Gr. < Heb. *shā'ūl,* asked (i.e., of God)].
**Scott** (skot), [< AS. < LL. *Scotus,* orig., an Irishman, later, a Scotsman].
**Se·bas·tian** (si-bas'chən), [< L.; ult. < Gr. < *sebastos,* venerable, august].
**Seth** (seth), [LL. < Gr. < Heb. *shēth,* appointed].
**Sey·mour** (sē'môr -mōr), [< Eng. surname; prob. < AS. *sæ,* sea, lake + *mor,* a hill].
**Shel·don** (shel'd'n), [< AS. *scylf,* crag, ledge, etc. + *denu,* valley, or *dun,* hill].
**Sid·ney** (sid'ni), [prob. < *St. Denis;* see DENIS], also *Sydney.*
**Si·las** (sī'ləs), [LL. < Gr. *Silas;* prob. of Sem. origin].
**Sil·van** (sil'vən), [< L. *silvanus* < *silva, sylva,* a wood], also *Sylvan.*
**Sil·ves·ter** (sil-ves'tẽr), [< L. *silvester, silvestris,* of a wood < *silva,* a wood], also *Sylvester.*
**Sim·e·on** (sim'i-ən), [LL. < Gr. < Heb. *shim'ōn,* heard].
**Si·mon** (sī'mən), [L. < Gr. < Heb. *shim'ōn,* heard].
**Sol·o·mon** (sol'ə-mən), [LL. < Gr. < Heb. *shĕlōmōh,* peaceful < *shālōm,* peace].
**Stan·ley** (stan'li), [< AS. *stan leah,* stone lea].
**Ste·phen** (stē'vən), [< L. < Gr. *stephanos,* a crown], also *Steven;* fem., *Stephana, Stephanie.*
**Ster·ling** (stũr'liŋ), [prob. < AS. hyp. *steorling,* small star].
**Ste·ven** (stē'vən), var. of **Stephen.**
**Stu·art, Stew·art** (sto͞o'ert, stū'-), [? < AS. *stigweard,* chamberlain].
**Syd·ney** (sid'ni), var. of **Sidney.**
**Syl·van** (sil'vən), var. of **Silvan.**
**Syl·ves·ter** (sil-ves'tẽr), var. of **Silvester.**

**Ter·ence** (ter'əns), [L. *Terentius,* name of a Roman gens].
**Thad·de·us, Thad·e·us** (thad'i-əs), [< LL. < Gr. *Thaddaios*].
**The·o·dore** (thē'ə-dôr', -dōr'), [< L. < Gr. < *theos,* god + *dōron,* gift], fem., *Theodora.*
**The·o·do·si·us** (thē'ə-dō'shi-əs), [LL. < Gr. < *theos,* god + *dosis,* a giving], fem., *Theodosia.*
**Thom·as** (tom'əs), [LL. < Gr. < Ar. *tĕ'ōma,* a twin].
**Tim·o·thy** (tim'ə-thi), [< Fr. < L. < Gr. < *timē,* honor + *theos,* God].
**To·bi·as** (tō-bī'əs, tə-), [LL. < Gr. < Heb. *tōbhīyāh,* the lord is good], also *Toby.*
**To·by** (tō'bi), dim. of **Tobias.**
**To·ny** (tō'ni), var. of **Anthony.**

**U·lys·ses** (yoo-lis'ēz), [L., var. of *Ulixes* (for Gr. *Odysseus,* but prob. < Etruscan *Uluxe*)].
**U·ri·ah** (yoo-rī'ə), [Heb. *ūrīyāh,* God is light].

**Val·en·tine** (val'ən-tīn'), [< L. < *Valens* < *valens,* ppr. of *valere,* to be strong or healthy].
**Van** (van), [D., of, from: used in Dutch family names to indicate place of origin].
**Vaughan, Vaughn** (vôn), [<?].
**Ver·gil** (vũr'jil), var. of **Virgil.**
**Ver·non** (vũr'nən), [< surname *Vernon;* prob. < *Vernon,* a town in France], fem., *Verna.*
**Vic·tor** (vik'tẽr), [L. < *vincere,* to conquer]. fem., *Victoria.*
**Vin·cent** (vin's'nt), [< LL. < *vincens,* ppr. of *vincere,* to conquer].
**Vir·gil** (vũr'jil), [< L. *Vergilius,* name of a Roman gens], also *Vergil.*

**Wal·do** (wôl'dō, wäl'-), [Frank. or OHG. < *waldan,* to rule].
**Wal·lace** (wôl'is, wäl'-), [prob. < ME. *Walisc,* Welsh, foreign].
**Wal·ter** (wôl'tẽr), [< ONorm.Fr. < Frank. < *waldan,* to rule + *heri,* army; also < G. *Walther* < OHG.].
**Ward** (wôrd), [prob. < AS. *weardian,* to watch].
**War·ren** (wôr'ən, wär'-), [< ONorm.Fr.; prob. < Gmc. *Warin,* the Varini, a people mentioned by Tacitus].
**Wayne** (wān), [< surname *Wayne*].
**Wes·ley** (wes'li, wez'-), [< surname *Wesley*].
**Wil·bert** (wil'bẽrt), [< G. < OHG. *willeo,* a will, wish + *beraht,* bright].
**Wil·bur, Wil·ber** (wil'bẽr), [< AS. *Wilburh;* prob. a place name meaning "willow town"].
**Wil·fred, Wil·frid** (wil'frid), [< AS. < *will,* a will, wish + *frith,* peace].
**Will** (wil), dim. of **William.**
**Wil·lard** (wil'ẽrd), [< surname *Willard*].
**Wil·liam** (wil'yəm), [< ONorm.Fr. < OHG. < *willeo,* a will, wish + *helm,* protection], also *Will.*
**Wil·lis** (wil'is), [prob. < *Willson, Wilson* (<*Will's son*)].
**Win·ston** (win'stən), [prob. < Eng. place name].
**Wood·row** (wood'rō), [? < AS. *wudu,* wood + *raw,* row].

**Xa·vi·er** (zā'vi-ẽr, zav'i-), [< ?].

**Yale** (yāl), [< ?].

**Zach·a·ri·ah** (zak'ə-rī'ə), [< LL. < Gr. < Heb. *zĕharyah,* God remembers], also *Zacharias, Zachary, Zechariah.*
**Zach·a·ri·as** (zak'ə-rī'əs), var. of **Zachariah.**
**Zach·a·ry** (zak'ẽr-i), var. of **Zachariah.**
**Zech·a·ri·ah** (zek'ə-rī'ə), var. of **Zachariah.**

## WOMEN'S NAMES

**Ab·i·gail** (ab'i-gāl', -g'l), [Heb. *abīgayil,* father is rejoicing], also *Gail.*
**A·da, A·dah** (ā'də), [Heb. *'ādāh,* beauty].
**Ad·a·line** (ad'ə-līn'), var. of **Adeline.**
**Ad·e·la** (ad''l-ə), var. of **Adelaide;** also *Adele, Adelia, Della.*
**Ad·e·laide** (ad''l-ād'), [< Fr. < G. < OHG. *Adalheit,* lit., nobility], also *Adela, Adeline.*
**A·dele** (ə-del'), var. of **Adela.**
**A·de·li·a** (ə-dē'li-ə, ə-dēl'yə), var. of **Adela.**
**Ad·e·li·na** (ad''l-ī'nə, -ē'nə), var. of **Adeline.**
**Ad·e·line** (ad''l-īn', -ēn'), var. of **Adelaide;** also *Adaline, Adelina, Aline.*
**A·dri·enne** (ā'dri-en'), fem. of **Adrian.**
**Ag·a·tha** (ag'ə-thə), [< Gr. fem. of *agathos,* good].
**Ag·nes** (ag'nis), [< Fr. < L. < Gr. *hagnē,* fem. of *hagnos,* chaste].
**Ai·leen** (ī-lēn', ā-lēn'), [Ir.], var. of **Helen.**
**Al·ber·ta** (al-bũr'tə), fem. of **Albert;** also *Albertina, Albertine.*
**Al·ber·ti·na** (al'bẽr-tē'nə), var. of **Alberta.**
**Al·ber·tine** (al'bẽr-tēn'), var. of **Alberta.**
**Al·ex·an·dra** (al'ig-zan'drə), fem. of **Alexander;** also *Sandra.*
**Al·fre·da** (al-frē'də), fem. of **Alfred.**
**Al·ice** (al'is), [< L. < Gr. *alētheia,* truth], also *Alicia, Elsie.*
**A·li·ci·a** (ə-lish'i-ə), var. of **Alice.**
**A·line** (ə-lēn'), var. of **Adeline.**
**Al·ma** (al'mə), [L., fem. of *almus,* nourishing].
**Al·the·a** (al-thē'ə), [< L. < Gr. *Althaia,* healer < *althainein,* to heal].
**A·man·da** (ə-man'də), [L., worthy to be loved < *amare,* to love].
**A·me·li·a** (ə-mē'li-ə, ə-mēl'yə), [of Gmc. origin; prob., diligent < base of *amal,* work].
**A·my** (ā'mi), [Fr. *Aimée,* lit., beloved < fem. pp. of *aimer,* to love].
**An·as·ta·sia** (an'ə-stā'shə, -zhə), [< LL. < Gr. *Anastasios,* lit., of the resurrection].
**An·dre·a** (an'dri-ə), fem. of **Andrew.**
**An·ge·la** (an'jə-lə), [< ML. < L. *angelicus,* angelic], also *Angelica, Angelina, Angeline.*
**An·gel·i·ca** (an-jel'i-kə), var. of **Angela.**
**An·ge·li·na** (an'jə-lē'nə, -lī'-), var. of **Angela.**

**An·ge·line** (an′jə-līn′), var. of **Angela.**
**A·ni·ta** (ə-nē′tə), [Sp. dim. of *Ana*].
**Ann, Anne** (an), var. of **Anna.**
**An·na** (an′ə), [< Fr. < L. < Gr. *Anna* < Heb. *hannāh*, grace], also *Ann, Anne, Annette, Nannette, Nina.*
**An·na·bel, An·na·belle** (an′ə-bel′), [prob. < *Anna* + L. *bella*, fem. of *bellus*, pretty].
**An·nette** (an-et′, ə-net′), [Fr.], var. of **Anna.**
**An·toi·nette** (an′twə-net′, -tə-), var. of **Antonia;** also *Nettie.*
**An·to·ni·a** (an-tō′ni-ə), fem. of **Anthony;** also *Antoinette.*
**Ar·lene, Ar·line** (är-lēn′), [? formed < *Aline*].
**Au·drey** (ô′dri), [OFr. < Gmc.; akin to AS. *æthelthryth*, noble might].
**Au·gus·ta** (ô-gus′tə), fem. of **Augustus.**

**Bar·ba·ra** (bär′bə-rə, bär′brə), [< L. < Gr. *barbaros*, foreign, strange].
**Be·a·trice** (bē′ə-tris), [It. < L. *beatrix*, she who makes happy < *beatus*, happy], also *Beatrix.*
**Be·a·trix** (bē′ə-triks), var. of **Beatrice.**
**Be·lin·da** (bə-lin′də), [L., graceful], also *Linda.*
**Bel·la** (bel′ə), dim. of **Isabella.**
**Belle** (bel), dim. of **Isabelle.**
**Ber·e·ni·ce** (bēr-nēs′, bũr′nis, ber′ə-nī′si), [L. < Gr. *Berenikē*, lit., victory-bringing], also *Bernice.*
**Ber·nice** (bēr-nēs′, bũr′nis), var. of **Berenice.**
**Ber·tha** (bũr′thə), [G. < OHG. < *beraht*, bright].
**Bess** (bes), dim. of **Elizabeth.**
**Beth** (beth), dim. of **Elizabeth.**
**Bet·sy** (bet′si), dim. of **Elizabeth.**
**Bet·ty** (bet′i), dim. of **Elizabeth.**
**Beu·lah** (bū′lə), [Heb. *be'ūlāh*, married].
**Bev·er·ley, Bev·er·ly** (bev′ẽr-li), [< ME. *bever*, beaver + *ley*, lea].
**Blanche, Blanch** (blanch), [Fr. < OFr. < OHG. *blanch*, white].
**Bon·nie, Bon·ny** (bon′i), [< Fr. < OFr. < L. *bonus*, fem. *bona*, good].
**Bren·da** (bren′də), [prob. < G. *brand* or ON. *brandr*, a sword].
**Bridg·et** (brij′it), [Ir. *Brighid*, lit., strong, lofty].

**Ca·mil·la** (kə-mil′ə), var. of **Camille.**
**Ca·mille** (kə-mēl′), [Fr. < L. *camilla*, virgin of unblemished character], also *Camilla.*
**Can·da·ce** (kan′də-sē′, kən-dā′si, kan′dis), [L. < Gr. *Kandakē*, an ancient Ethiopian title].
**Can·di·da** (kan′di-də), [? < L. *candidus*, white, pure].
**Car·lot·ta** (kär-lot′ə), var. of **Charlotte.**
**Car·ol** (kar′əl), var. of **Caroline.**
**Car·o·line** (kar′ə-līn′, -lin), fem. of **Charles;** also *Carol, Carolyn, Carrie.*
**Car·o·lyn** (kar′ə-lin), var. of **Caroline.**
**Car·rie** (kar′i), dim. of **Caroline.**
**Cath·er·ine, Cath·a·rine** (kath′rin, -ẽr-in), [< Fr. < L. *Catharina;* infl. by Gr. *katharos*, pure], also *Karen, Katharine, Katherine, Kathleen.*
**Ce·cile** (sə-sēl′, ses′'l), var. of **Cecilia.**
**Ce·cil·ia** (si-sil′yə, -sēl′-), fem. of **Cecil;** also *Cecile, Cecily, Cicely, Sheila.*
**Cec·i·ly** (ses′'l-i), var. of **Cecilia.**
**Ce·leste** (sə-lest′), [< Fr. < L. *caelestis*, celestial < *caelum*, heaven], also *Celestine, Celia.*
**Ce·les·tine** (sə-les′tēn, -tin), var. of **Celeste.**
**Cel·ia** (sēl′yə, sē′li-ə), var. of **Celeste.**
**Char·lotte** (shär′lət), fem. of **Charles;** also *Carlotta, Lottie*
**Chlo·e, Chlo·ë** (klō′i), [L. < Gr. *Chloē*, blooming].
**Chris·ti·an·a** (kris′ti-an′ə), fem. of **Christian;** also *Christina, Christine.*
**Chris·ti·na** (kris-tē′nə), var. of **Christiana.**
**Chris·tine** (kris-tēn′), var. of **Christiana.**
**Cic·e·ly** (sis′'l-i), var. of **Cecily.**
**Claire, Clare** (klâr), var. of **Clara.**
**Clar·a** (klâr′ə), [< L. fem. of *clarus*, clear, bright], also *Claire, Clare, Clarice, Clarissa.*
**Clar·ice** (klâr′is, klə-rēs′), var. of **Clara.**
**Cla·ris·sa** (klə-ris′ə), [It.], var. of **Clara.**
**Clau·di·a** (klô′di-ə), [L.], fem. of **Claude.**
**Clem·en·ti·na** (klem′ən-tē′nə), var. of **Clementine.**
**Clem·en·tine** (klem′ən-tēn′, -tīn′), fem. of **Clement;** also *Clementina.*
**Col·leen** (kol′ēn, kə-lēn′), [< Ir. dim. of *caile*, girl].
**Con·stance** (kon′stəns), fem. of **Constant.**
**Con·suel·o** (kən-swel′ō), [? < Sp., consolation, comfort].
**Cor·a** (kôr′ə, kō′re), [L. < Gr. *Korē*, lit., maiden], also *Corinne.*
**Cor·del·ia** (kôr-dēl′yə), [said to be < Celt. *Creiryddlydd*, lit., daughter of the sea].
**Co·rinne** (kə-rin′, kô-rēn′), [Fr.], var. of **Cora.**
**Cor·nel·ia** (kôr-nēl′yə), fem. of **Cornelius.**
**Cyn·thi·a** (sin′thi-ə), [L. < Gr. *Kynthia*, epithet of Artemis, goddess of the moon].

**Dag·mar** (dag′mär), [Dan. < Gmc. *dag-*, day + *-mar;* akin to AS. *mære* splendid].
**Dai·sy** (dā′zi), [< name of the flower].
**Daph·ne** (daf′ni), [L. < Gr. < *daphnē*, the bay tree].
**Dawn** (dôn), [AS. *dagian*, to dawn < *dæg*, day].
**Deb·o·rah** (deb′ə-rə), [Heb. *debōrāh*, a bee].
**Del·ia** (dēl′yə), [L., fem. of *Delius*, of Delos, an island of the Cyclades].
**De·li·lah** (di-lī′lə), [Heb. *delīlāh*, delicate].
**Del·la** (del′ə), dim. of **Adela.**
**De·nise** (də-nēz′), fem. of **Denis.**
**Di·an·a** (dī-an′ə), [L. < *divus*, divine, godly], also *Diane.*
**Di·ane** (dī-an′), var. of **Diana.**
**Di·nah** (dī′nə), [Heb. *dīnāh*, judged].
**Dol·ly** (dol′i), dim. of **Dorothea.**
**Do·lor·es** (də-lôr′is, -lō′ris, -lō′rēz), [Sp. < *María de los Dolores*, Mary of the sorrows].
**Don·na** (don′ə), [It. < L. fem. of *dominius*, a lord].
**Dor·a** (dôr′ə, dō′rə), dim. of **Dorothea** and **Theodora.**
**Dor·is** (dôr′is, dor′-), [L. < Gr. *Dōris*, an ancient region of Greece].
**Dor·o·the·a** (dôr′ə-thē′ə, dor′-), [L. < Gr. *Dōrothea*, gift of God, < *dōron*, gift + *theos*, God], also *Dolly, Dora, Dorothy.*
**Dor·o·thy** (dôr′ə-thi, dor′-, dôr′thi), var. of **Dorothea.**
**Dul·cie, Dul·ce** (dul′si), [< L. *dulcis*, charming].

**E·dith** (ē′dith), [< AS. < *ead*, riches + *guth*, battle].
**Ed·na** (ed′nə), [< Gr. < Heb. *'ēdnāh*, rejuvenation].
**Ed·win·a** (ed-wē′nə, -win′ə), fem. of **Edwin.**
**Ei·leen** (ī-lēn′, ī′lēn′, ā-lēn′), [Ir.], var. of **Helen.**
**E·laine** (i-lān′), [Fr.], var. of **Helen.**
**El·ea·nor** (el′ə-nẽr, -i-nôr′), var. of **Helen;** also *Elinor, Ella, Leonora, Nell, Nellie, Nora.*
**El·e·na** (el′ə-nə), [It. & Sp.], var. of **Helen.**
**El·i·nor** (el′ə-nẽr, -i-nôr′), var. of **Eleanor.**
**E·li·za** (i-lī′zə), var. of **Elizabeth.**
**E·liz·a·beth, E·lis·a·beth** (i-liz′ə-bəth, ə-), [< L. < Heb. *elīsheba'*, God is (my) oath], also *Bess, Beth, Betsy, Betty, Eliza, Elsie, Libby.*
**El·la** (el′ə), dim. of **Eleanor.**
**El·len** (el′ən), var. of **Helen.**
**El·o·ise** (el′ō-ēz′, -ə-wēz′, el′e-wēz′), var. of **Louise.**
**El·sa** (el′sə), [G.; apparently orig. name of a certain water sprite].
**El·sie** (el′si), dim. of **Alice** and **Elizabeth.**
**El·vi·ra** (el-vī′rə, -vẽr′ə), [Sp.; prob. < Goth. < Gmc. *ala*, complete + *wer-*, cover].
**Em·e·line** (em′ə-līn′, -lēn′), var. of **Emily.**
**E·mil·i·a** (i-mil′i-ə, -yə), var. of **Emily.**
**Em·i·ly** (em′'l-i), fem. of **Emil;** also *Emiline, Emilia, Emmeline.*
**Em·ma** (em′ə), [G. < *Erma*, contr. < names beginning with *Erm-;* see IRMA].
**Em·me·line** (em′ə-līn′, -lēn′), var. of **Emily.**
**E·nid** (ē′nid), [Celt., spotless purity].
**Er·nes·tine** (ũr′nəs-tēn′), fem. of **Ernest.**
**Es·tel·la** (e-stel′ə), [Sp. < L. *stella*, star], also *Estelle, Stella.*
**Es·telle** (es-tel′), [Fr.], var. of **Estella.**
**Es·ther** (es′tẽr), [L. < Heb. *estēr;* prob. < Bab. *Ishtar*, goddess of love], also *Hester.*
**Eth·el** (eth′əl), [< AS. *æthel*, noble].
**Et·ta** (et′ə), dim. of **Henrietta.**
**Eu·ge·ni·a** (yoo-jē′ni-ə), fem. of **Eugene.**
**Eu·nice** (ū′nis), [L. < Gr. *Eunikē*, good victory].
**E·va** (ē′və, ev′ə), var. of **Eve.**
**E·van·ge·line** (i-van′jə-lin, -līn′, -lēn′), [< Fr. < LL. *evangelium*, gospel].
**Eve** (ēv), [< AS. < LL. < Heb. *hawwāh*, ? life], also *Eva.*
**Ev·e·li·na** (ev-ə-lī′nə), var. of **Eveline.**
**Ev·e·line** (ev′ə-līn′, -lin), [< Celt., pleasant], also *Evelina, Evelyn.*
**Ev·e·lyn** (ev′ə-lin, ēv′lin), var. of **Eveline.**

**Faith** (fāth), [< OFr. < L. < *fidere*, to trust].
**Fan·nie, Fan·ny** (fan′i), dim. of **Frances.**
**Fay, Faye** (fā), [< OFr. *fei* < L. *fidere*, to trust].
**Fe·li·ci·a** (fə-lish′i-ə, -lish′ə), fem. of **Felix.**
**Flo·ra** (flôr′ə, flō′rə), [L. < *flos, floris*, a flower].
**Flor·ence** (flôr′əns, flor′-), [Fr. < L. *Florentia*, lit., a blooming].
**Fran·ces** (fran′sis, frän′-), fem. of **Francis;** also *Fannie, Fanny.*
**Fre·da** (frē′də), var. of **Frieda.**
**Fred·er·i·ca** (fred′ə-rē′kə), fem. of **Frederick.**
**Frie·da** (frē′də), [G. < OHG. *fridu*, peace], also *Freda.*

**Ga·bri·elle** (gā′bri-el′, gab′ri-), [Fr.], fem. of **Gabriel.**
**Gail** (gāl), dim. of **Abigail.**
**Gen·e·vieve** (jen′ə-vēv′, jen′ə-vēv′), [Fr. < LL. *Genovefa;* ? < Celt.].
**Geor·gia** (jôr′jə), fem. of **George.**
**Geor·gi·an·a** (jôr-jan′ə, jôr′ji-an′ə), fem. of **George.**
**Geor·gi·na** (jôr-jē′nə), fem. of **George.**
**Ger·al·dine** (jer′əl-dēn′, -din), [Fr.], fem. of **Gerald.**
**Ger·trude** (gũr′trood), [< Fr. & G. < OHG. *ger*, spear + *trut*, dear, beloved], also *Trudy.*

**Glad·ys** (glad′is), [W. *Gwladys;* prob. < L. *Claudia*].
**Glo·ri·a** (glôr′i-ə, glō′ri-ə), [L., glory].
**Gold·ie, Gold·y** (gōl′di), [< *gold*].
**Grace** (grās), [< OFr. < L. *gratia,* grace < *gratus,* pleasing.
**Gret·a** (gret′ə, grē′tə), dim. of **Margaret.**
**Gretch·en** (grech″n), [G.], var. of **Margaret.**
**Gwen·do·len, Gwen·do·line, Gwen·do·lyn** (gwen′də-lin), [< Celt.; cf. W. *gwen,* white].

**Han·nah, Han·na** (han′ə), [Heb. *hannāh,* grace].
**Har·ri·et, Har·ri·ot, Har·ri·ott** (har′i-ət), fem. of **Harry;** also *Hatty, Hattie.*
**Hat·ty, Hat·tie** (hat′i), var. of **Harriet.**
**Ha·zel** (hā′z'l), [Heb. *ḥazā'ēl,* God sees].
**Heath·er** (heth′ẽr), [< name of the plant].
**Hed·da** (hed′ə), [< ?].
**Hel·en** (hel′ən), [< Fr. < L. < Gr. *Helenē,* lit., torch], also *Aileen, Eileen, Elaine, Eleanor, Elena, Ellen, Helena, Nell, Nellie.*
**Hel·e·na** (hel′i-nə, he-lē′nə), var. of **Helen;** also *Lena.*
**Hel·ga** (hel′gə), [? < N. *Helga,* holy].
**Hen·ri·et·ta** (hen′ri-et′ə), [< Fr.], fem. of **Henry;** also *Etta, Nettie.*
**Hes·ter, Hes·ther** (hes′tẽr), var. of **Esther.**
**Hil·da** (hil′də), [G. < Gmc. hyp. *hild-,* war].
**Hil·de·gard** (hil′də-gärd′), [G. < Gmc. bases meaning "battle protector"].
**Hope** (hōp), [< AS. *hopa,* hope].
**Hor·tense** (hôr-tens′, hôr′tens), [Fr. < L. < *hortensius,* of a garden < *hortus,* a garden].

**I·da** (ī′də), [? < ON. *Ithunn,* goddess of youth].
**Im·o·gen** (im′ə-jən), [< ?], also *Imogene.*
**Im·o·gene** (im′ə-jēn′), var. of **Imogen.**
**I·nez** (ī′niz, ī′nez′), [Sp. *Iñez;* ult. < L.; see AGNES].
**Ing·rid** (iŋ′grid), [< Scand.; ult. < ON. *Ingvi,* name of a Gmc. god + *rida,* ride].
**I·rene** (ī-rēn′), [< Fr. < L. < Gr. *Eirēnē,* lit., peace].
**I·ris** (ī′ris), [L. < Gr. *iris,* rainbow].
**Ir·ma** (ũr′mə), [G., orig. contr. of names beginning with *Irm-* < OHG. *Irmin,* name of a Gmc. god of war].
**Is·a·bel, Is·o·bel** (iz′ə-bel′, -b'l), [Sp.; ? alt. from *Elizabeth*], also *Isabelle, Isabella.*
**Is·a·bel·la** (iz′ə-bel′ə), [It.], var. of **Isabel;** also *Bella.*
**Is·a·belle** (iz′ə-bel′, -b'l), [Fr.], var. of **Isabel;** also *Belle.*
**Is·a·dor·a** (iz′ə-dôr′ə, -dō′rə), fem. of **Isidore.**

**Jac·que·line** (jak′wə-lin), [Fr., fem. of *Jacques;* see JACK].
**Jane** (jān), var. of **Joanna;** also *Janet, Jenny.*
**Jan·et** (jan′it, jə-net′), dim. of **Jane.**
**Jan·ice** (jan′is), [< *Jane, Janet*].
**Jean** (jēn), var. of **Joanna;** also *Jeanne.*
**Jeanne** (jēn), [Fr.], var. of **Jean;** also *Jeannette.*
**Jean·nette** (jə-net′), dim. of **Jeanne;** also *Nettie.*
**Jen·ni·fer** (jen′i-fẽr), [adaptation of *Winifred*].
**Jen·ny** (jen′i), dim. of **Jane.**
**Jes·si·ca** (jes′i-kə), [see JESSE], also *Jessie.*
**Jes·sie** (jes′i), var. of **Jessica.**
**Jill** (jil), [< proper name *Gillian* < L. *Juliana*].
**Joan** (jōn, jō′ən, jō-an′), var. of **Joanna.**
**Jo·an·na** (jō-an′ə), fem. of **John;** also *Jane, Jean, Joan, Johanna.*
**Joc·e·lin, Joc·e·line, Joc·e·lyn** (jos′ə-lin, jos′lin), [prob. ult. < L. *jocus,* a jest].
**Jo·han·na** (jō-han′ə), [G.], var. of **Joanna.**
**Jo·se·phine** (jō′zə-fēn′), [Fr.], fem. of **Joseph.**
**Joy** (joy), [< OFr. < L. *gaudium,* joy].
**Joyce** (jois), [< L. fem. of *jocosus,* merry].
**Jua·ni·ta** (wä-nē′tə), [< Sp. dim. of *Juana,* Joan].
**Ju·dith** (jōō′dith), fem. of **Judah.**
**Jul·ia** (jōōl′yə), fem. of **Julius;** also *Juliet.*
**Ju·li·an·a** (jōō′li-an′ə), fem. of **Julian.**
**Ju·li·et** (jōōl′yət, jōō′li-ət), dim. of **Julia.**
**June** (jōōn), fem. of **Junius.**
**Jus·ti·na** (jus-tī′nə), fem. of **Justin;** also *Justine.*
**Jus·tine** (jus-tēn′), var. of **Justina.**

**Kar·en** (kar′ən), [Scand.], var. of **Catherine.**
**Kate** (kāt), dim. of **Katherine.**
**Kath·a·rine, Kath·er·ine** (kath′ẽr-in, kath′rin), var. of **Catherine;** also *Kate, Kathryn, Kitty.*
**Kath·leen** (kath′lēn, kath-lēn′), [Ir.], var. of **Catherine.**
**Kath·ryn** (kath′rin), var. of **Katharine.**
**Kit·ty** (kit′i), dim. of **Katharine.**

**Lau·ra** (lô′rə), [It.], fem. of **Laurence;** also *Laurinda, Loretta, Lorinda.*
**Lau·rin·da** (lô-rin′də), var. of **Laura.**
**La·verne** (lə-vũrn′), [< ?].
**La·vin·i·a** (lə-vin′i-ə, -vin′yə), [L.].
**Le·ah** (lē′ə), [Heb. *lē'āh,* gazelle, wild cow].
**Lei·la, Lei·lah** (lē′lə), [Ar. *layla,* darkness].
**Le·na** (lē′nə), dim. of **Helena.**
**Le·o·na** (lē-ō′nə), fem. of **Leo.**
**Le·nore** (lə-nôr′, -nōr′), var. of **Leonora.**
**Le·o·no·ra** (lē′ə-nôr′ə, -nō′rə), var. of **Eleanor;** also *Lenore, Leonore, Nora.*
**Le·o·nore** (lē′ə-nôr′, -nōr′), var. of **Leonora.**
**Les·lie** (les′li, lez′-), [said to be < *less lee (lea),* i.e., smaller meadow].
**Le·ti·ti·a** (li-tish′i-ə, -tish′ə), [< L. *laetitia,* gladness < *laetus,* gay].
**Lib·by** (lib′i), dim. of **Elizabeth.**
**Lil·i·an, Lil·li·an** (lil′i-ən), [prob. < L. *lilium,* lily], also *Lily, Lilly.*
**Lil·y, Lil·ly** (lil′i), dim. of **Lilian, Lillian.**
**Lin·da** (lin′də), dim. of **Belinda.**
**Lo·is** (lō′is), [L. < Gr. *Lōis*].
**Lo·la** (lō′lə), [Sp., dim. of *Dolores*].
**Lo·ret·ta** (lô-ret′ə, lə-), dim. of **Laura.**
**Lo·rin·da** (lô-rin′də, lə-), var. of **Laura.**
**Lor·na** (lôr′nə), [prob. < AS.; akin to Eng. *lorn*].
**Lor·raine** (lô-rān′, lō-), [Fr.; ? < *Lorraine,* a former province in France].
**Lot·tie, Lot·ty** (lot′i), dim. of **Charlotte.**
**Lou·i·sa** (loo-wē′zə), var. of **Louise.**
**Lou·ise** (loo-wēz′), fem. of **Louis;** also *Eloise, Louisa, Lulu.*
**Lu·cia** (lōō′shə), var. of **Lucy;** fem. of **Lucius.**
**Lu·cile, Lu·cille** (lōō-sēl′), var. of **Lucy.**
**Lu·cin·da** (lōō-sin′də), var. of **Lucy.**
**Lu·cy** (lōō′si), [prob. via Fr. < L. *Lucia,* fem. of *Lucius;* see LUCIUS], also *Lucia, Lucile, Lucinda.*
**Lu·lu** (lōō′lōō), dim. of **Louise.**
**Lyd·i·a** (lid′i-ə), [L. < Gr., fem. of *Lydios,* Lydian].
**Lynn** (lin), [prob. < W. *llyn,* a lake].

**Ma·bel** (mā′b'l), [< L. *Amabel* < *amabilis,* lovable].
**Mad·e·line** (mad′ə-lin, -'l-in), var. of **Magdalene.**
**Madge** (maj), dim. of **Margaret.**
**Mae** (mā), var. of **May.**
**Mag·da·len** (mag′də-lin, -lən), var. of **Magdalene.**
**Mag·da·lene** (mag′də-lēn′), [< Gr. < *Magdala,* a town on the Sea of Galilee], also *Madeline, Magdalen.*
**Mag·gie** (mag′i), dim. of **Margaret.**
**Mai·sie** (mā′zi), dim. of **Margaret.**
**Ma·mie** (mā′mi), dim. of **Mary.**
**Mar·cel·la** (mär-sel′ə), fem. of **Marcellus.**
**Mar·cia** (mär′shə), fem. of **Marcus.**
**Mar·ga·ret** (mär′grit, -gə rit), [< OFr. < L. *margarita,* a pearl], also *Greta, Madge, Maggie, Maisie, Margery, Margot, Marguerite, Marjorie, Peggy.*
**Mar·ger·y** (mär′jẽr-i), var. of **Margaret;** also *Marjorie, Marjory.*
**Mar·got** (mär′gō, mär′gət), [Fr.], var. of **Margaret.**
**Mar·gue·rite** (mär′gə-rēt′), [Fr.], var. of **Margaret.**
**Ma·ri·a** (mə-rī′ə, -rē′ə), var. of **Mary.**
**Mar·i·an** (mâr′i-ən), var. of **Marion;** also *Marianna, Marianne.*
**Mar·i·an·na** (mâr′i-an′ə), var. of **Marian.**
**Mar·i·anne** (mâr′i-an′), var. of **Marian.**
**Ma·rie** (mə-rē′), var. of **Mary.**
**Mar·i·et·ta** (mâr′i-et′ə), dim. of **Mary.**
**Mar·i·lyn** (mar′ə-lin), var. of **Mary.**
**Mar·i·on** (mâr′i-ən), var. of **Mary;** also *Marian.*
**Mar·jo·rie, Mar·jo·ry** (mär′jẽr-i), var. of **Margaret;** also *Margery.*
**Mar·tha** (mär′thə), [LL. < Gr. < Aram. *Mārthā,* lit., lady].
**Mar·y** (mâr′i), [< L. *Maria* < Gr. < Heb. *Miryām* or Aram. *Maryam,* lit., rebellion], also *Mamie, Maria, Marie, Marietta, Marilyn, Marion, Maureen, May, Miriam, Molly.*
**Ma·til·da, Ma·thil·da** (mə-til′də), [< ML. < OHG. < *maht,* power + *hiltia,* battle; hence, powerful (in) battle], also *Maud, Tillie.*
**Maud, Maude** (môd), dim. of **Matilda.**
**Mau·reen** (mô-rēn′), [Ir.], var. of **Mary.**
**Max·ine** (mak-sēn′), fem. of **Max.**
**May** (mā), dim. of **Mary;** also *Mae.*
**Mel·i·cent** (mel′ə-s'nt), var. of **Millicent.**
**Me·lis·sa** (mə-lis′ə), [Gr. *Melissa,* lit., a bee].
**Mer·ce·des** (mẽr-sē′dēz, -sā′-), [Sp. < *María de las Mercedes,* Mary of the mercies, graces, etc.].
**Mil·dred** (mil′drid), [< AS. < *milde,* mild + *thryth,* power].
**Mil·li·cent, Mil·i·cent** (mil′ə-s'nt), [<OFr. <OHG. < *amal,* work + hyp. *swind,* strong], also *Melicent.*
**Mi·mi** (mē′mē′), [Fr.].
**Mi·ner·va** (mi-nũr′və), [L.; said to be < base of *mens, mentis,* mind].
**Min·nie** (min′i), [dim. of *Mary* or var. of G. *Minne* < MHG. *minne,* love, orig. memory].
**Mi·ran·da** (mə-ran′də), [L., fem. of *mirandus,* strange, wonderful].
**Mir·i·am** (mir′i-əm), var. of **Mary.**
**Molly** (mol′i), dim. of **Mary;** also *Polly.*
**Mon·i·ca** (mon′i-kə), [LL.; ? < L. *monere,* to warn].
**Mu·ri·el** (myoor′i-əl), [prob. < Celt.; cf. Ir. *Muirgheal* < *muir,* the sea + *geal,* bright].
**My·ra** (mī′rə), [? < Ir. *Moira, Moyra* < L. *Maria,* Mary].
**Myr·tle** (mũr′t'l), [< name of the shrub].

**Na·dine** (nə-dēn′, nā-), [Fr. < Russ. *nadezhda,* hope].

**Nan·cy** (nan′si), [prob. by faulty division of *mine* + *Ancy*, dim. of ME. *Annis*, Agnes].
**Nan·nette** (nan-et′), [Fr.], var. of **Anna.**
**Na·o·mi** (nā-ō′mi, na-, nā′ə-mī′), [Heb. *nā'omī*, my delight].
**Nat·a·lie** (nat″l-i), [Fr. < LL. < L. *natalis* (*dies*), natal (day), name given to children born on Christmas Day].
**Nell** (nel), dim. of **Eleanor** and **Helen.**
**Nel·lie, Nel·ly** (nel′i), dim. of **Eleanor** and **Helen.**
**Net·tie, Net·ty** (net′i), dim. of **Antoinette, Henrietta,** and **Jeannette.**
**Ni·na** (nī′nə, nē′-), dim. of **Anna.**
**No·el** (nō′əl), [< OFr. *No(u)el*, lit., natal; see NATALIE].
**No·ra** (nôr′ə, nō′rə), dim. of **Eleanor** and **Leonora.**
**Nor·ma** (nôr′mə), [< L. *norma*, carpenter's square].

**Oc·ta·vi·a** (ok-tā′vi-ə), fem. of **Octavius.**
**Ol·ga** (ol′gə, ôl′-), [Russ.; ? < *Oleg*, holy, or < N. *Helga*, holy].
**Ol·ive** (ol′iv), [OFr. < It. < L. *oliva*, an olive], also *Olivia.*
**O·liv·i·a** (ō-liv′i-ə, ə-liv′yə), var. of **Olive.**
**O·pal** (ō′p′l), [prob. < name of the mineral].
**O·phe·lia** (ō-fēl′yə, ə-), [prob. < Gr. *ōphelia*, a help].

**Pam·e·la** (pam′ə-lə), [apparently coined by Sir Philip Sidney for a character in his *Arcadia*].
**Pan·sy** (pan′zi), [prob. < name of the flower].
**Pa·tri·cia** (pə-trish′ə), fem. of **Patrick.**
**Pau·la** (pô′lə), fem. of **Paul.**
**Pau·line** (pô-lēn′), fem. of **Paul.**
**Pearl** (pũrl), [< name of the gem].
**Peg·gy** (peg′i), dim. of **Margaret.**
**Pe·nel·o·pe** (pə-nel′ə-pi), [L. < Gr. *Pēnelopē*, lit., a weaver], also *Penny.*
**Pen·ny** (pen′i), var. of **Penelope.**
**Phoe·be, Phe·be** (fē′bi), [L. < Gr. fem. of *Phoibos*, lit., bright one <*phoibos*, bright].
**Phyl·lis, Phil·lis** (fil′is), [L. < Gr. *Phyllis*, lit., green leaf].
**Pol·ly** (pol′i), var. of **Molly.**
**Por·ti·a** (pôr′shə, pōr′shi-ə), [< L. fem. of *Porcius*, name of a Roman gens; prob. < *porcus*, a hog].
**Pris·cil·la** (pri-sil′ə), [< L. fem. of *Priscus*, a Roman surname < *priscus*, ancient].
**Pru·dence** (proo͞′d'ns), [< LL. < L. *prudentia*, prudence, discretion].

**Ra·chel** (rā′chəl), [LL. < Gr. < Heb. *rāḥēl*, ewe].
**Re·bec·ca** (ri-bek′ə), [LL. < Gr. < Heb. *ribbqāh*, noose].
**Re·gi·na** (ri-jī′nə, -jē′-), [L., queen].
**Re·née** (rə-nā′, rā′ni, rē′ni), [Fr.].
**Rho·da** (rō′də), [L. *Rhode* < Gr. < *rhodon*, a rose].
**Ri·ta** (rē′tə), [It. < *Margherita*, Margaret].
**Ro·ber·ta** (rə-bũr′tə, rō-), fem. of **Robert.**
**Ro·sa** (rō′zə), [It. & Sp.], var. of **Rose.**
**Ros·a·lie** (roz′ə-lē′, rō′zə-), [Fr.; prob. ult. < L. *rosa*, rose].
**Ros·a·lind** (roz′ə-lind, -līnd′), [Sp. *Rosalinda*, as if from *rosa linda*, pretty rose].
**Ros·a·mond** (roz′ə-mənd, rō′zə-), [< OFr. < LL. *Rosamunda*, as if from *rosa munda*, clean rose].
**Rose** (rōz), [< name of the flower], also *Rosa, Rosita.*
**Rose·mar·y** (rōz′mâr′i, -mẽr-i), [< name of the shrub].
**Ro·si·ta** (rō-zē′tə), var. of **Rose.**
**Ro·we·na** (rō-ē′nə), [? < AS. < *hroth*, fame + *wina*, a friend].
**Ru·by** (roo͞′bi), [< name of the gem].
**Ruth** (roo͞th), [LL. < Heb. *rūth*, prob. contr. < *rē'uth*, companion].

**Sa·die** (sā′di), dim. of **Sarah.**
**Sal·ly** (sal′i), dim. of **Sarah.**
**San·dra** (san′drə), dim. of **Alexandra.**
**Sar·ah, Sar·a** (sâr′ə), [Heb. *sārāh*, princess], also *Sadie, Sally.*
**Sel·ma** (sel′mə), [? < Gr. *selma*, a ship].
**Shar·on** (shâr′ən), [< *Sharon* (a plain in Palestine); ? contr. of *rose of Sharon*].
**Shei·la** (shē′lə), [Ir.], var. of **Cecilia.**
**Shir·ley** (shũr′li), [< AS. *scir*, shire + *leah*, lea, hence lea where the shire moot (sheriff's court) was held].
**Sib·yl, Syb·il** (sib″l), [< L. *sibylla*, prophetess].
**Sid·ney** (sid′ni), [prob. < *St. Denis;* see DENNIS].
**Sil·vi·a** (sil′vi-ə), var. of **Sylvia.**
**So·nia, So·nya** (sōn′yə), var. of **Sophia.**
**So·phi·a** (sō-fī′ə, sō′fi-ə), [< Gr. *sophia*, wisdom < *sophos*, wise], also *Sonia, Sophie.*
**So·phie, So·phy** (sō′fi), var. of **Sophia.**
**Stel·la** (stel′ə), var. of **Estella.**
**Steph·a·na** (stef′ə-nə), fem. of **Stephen.**
**Steph·a·nie** (stef′ə-ni), fem. of **Stephen.**
**Su·san** (soo͞′z'n, sū′-), var. of **Susanna.**
**Su·san·na, Su·san·nah** (soo͞-zan′ə, sū-), [< LL. *Susanna* < Gr. < Heb. *shōshannāh*, lily], also *Susan.*
**Su·zanne** (soo͞-zan′, sū-), [Fr.], var. of **Susan.**
**Syl·vi·a** (sil′vi-ə), [< L. *Silvia* < *silva*, a wood], also *Silvia.*

**Tab·i·tha** (tab′ə-thə), [LL. < Gr. *Tabitha* < Aram. *ṭabhītha*, roe, gazelle].
**Te·re·sa** (tə-rē′sə, -zə), var. of **Theresa.**
**Ter·ry** (ter′i), dim. of **Theresa.**
**Tess** (tes), dim. of **Theresa.**
**Thel·ma** (thel′mə), [said to be Gr., nurseling].
**The·o·dor·a** (thē′ə-dôr′ə, -dō′rə), fem. of **Theodore**: also *Dora.*
**The·o·do·si·a** (thē′ə-dō′shi-ə), fem. of **Theodosius.**
**The·re·sa** (tə-rē′sə, -zə), [< Fr. or Port. < L. *Therasia;* ? < Gr. *therizein*, to reap], also *Teresa, Terry, Tess.*
**Til·lie, Til·ly** (til′i), var. of **Matilda.**
**Tru·dy** (troo͞′di), dim. of **Gertrude.**

**Ul·ri·ca** (ul′ri-kə), [G. < OHG. < *Uodalrich* < *udal*, home + *rikhi*, rich].
**U·na** (ū′nə), [Ir. *Una;* also < L. *una*, one].
**Ur·su·la** (ũr′syoo-lə, -sə-), [ML., dim. of L. *ursa*, she-bear].

**Va·le·ri·a** (və-lêr′i-ə), [< L. name of a Roman gens; prob. < *valere*, to be strong], also *Valerie.*
**Val·er·ie** (val′ẽr-i), var. of **Valeria.**
**Ver·a** (vêr′ə), [Russ. *Vjera*, faith; also < L. fem. of *verus*, true].
**Ver·na** (vũr′nə), fem. of **Vernon.**
**Ve·ron·i·ca** (və-ron′i-kə), [ML. < LL. < L. *verus*, true + *iconicus*, of an image].
**Vic·tor·i·a** (vik-tôr′i-ə, -tōr′yə), fem. of **Victor.**
**Vi·da** (vē′də, vī′-), [W.], fem. of **David.**
**Vi·o·la** (vī-ō′lə, vi-), [< L. *viola*, a violet].
**Vi·o·let** (vī′ə-lit), [< name of the flower].
**Vir·gin·i·a** (vẽr-jin′yə, -jin′i-ə), [L., fem. of *Virginius*, name of a Roman gens].
**Viv·i·an, Viv·i·en** (viv′i-ən, viv′yən), [L. *Vivianus* < *vivus*, alive].

**Wan·da** (wôn′də), [< ?].
**Wen·dy** (wen′di), [? dim. of *Gwendolen*].
**Wil·hel·mi·na** (wil′hel-mē′nə), [< G. fem. of *Wilhelm*, William].
**Wil·ma** (wil′mə), [G., var. of *Wilmot* < fem. of *Wilhelm*, William].
**Win·i·fred** (win′ə-frid), [alt. < W. *Gwenfrewi*, lit., white wave].

**Yo·lan·da, Yo·lan·de** (yō-lan′də), [? OFr.].
**Y·vonne** (i-von′), [Fr.].

**Zel·da** (zel′də), [< ?].
**Zo·e** (zō′ē), [Gr. *Zōē*, lit., life].
**Zor·a** (zôr′ə), [< ?].

# TABLES OF WEIGHTS AND MEASURES

### Linear Measure

| | | | |
|---|---|---|---|
| 1 inch | | = | 2.54 centimeters |
| 12 inches | = 1 foot | = | 0.3048 meter |
| 3 feet | = 1 yard | = | 0.9144 meter |
| 5½ yards or 16½ feet | = 1 rod (or pole or perch) | = | 5.029 meters |
| 40 rods | = 1 furlong | = | 201.17 meters |
| 8 furlongs or 1,760 yards or 5,280 feet | = 1 (statute) mile | = | 1,609.3 meters |
| 3 miles | = 1 (land) league | = | 4.83 kilometers |

### Square Measure

| | | | |
|---|---|---|---|
| 1 square inch | | = | 6.452 square centimeters |
| 144 square inches | = 1 square foot | = | 929 square centimeters |
| 9 square feet | = 1 square yard | = | 0.8361 square meter |
| 30¼ square yards | = 1 square rod (or square pole or square perch) | = | 25.29 square meters |
| 160 square rods or 4,840 square yards or 43,560 square feet | = 1 acre | = | 0.4047 hectare |
| 640 acres | = 1 square mile | = | 259 hectares or 2.59 square kilometers |

### Cubic Measure

| | | |
|---|---|---|
| 1 cubic inch | | = 16.387 cubic centimeters |
| 1,728 cubic inches | = 1 cubic foot | = 0.0283 cubic meter |
| 27 cubic feet | = 1 cubic yard | = 0.7646 cubic meter |
| | (in units for cordwood, etc.) | |
| 16 cubic feet | = 1 cord foot | |
| 8 cord feet | = 1 cord | = 3.625 cubic meters |

### Nautical Measure

| | | |
|---|---|---|
| 6 feet | = 1 fathom | = 1.829 meters |
| 100 fathoms | = 1 cable's length (ordinary) (In the U.S. Navy 120 fathoms or 720 feet = 1 cable's length; in the British Navy, 608 feet = 1 cable's length.) | |
| 10 cables' lengths | = 1 nautical mile (6,076.10333 feet, by international agreement in 1954) | = 1.852 kilometers |
| 1 nautical mile (Also called geographical, sea, or air mile, and, in Great Britain, Admiralty mile.) | = 1.1508 statute miles (the length of a minute of longitude at the equator) | |
| 3 nautical miles | = 1 marine league (3.45 statute miles) | = 5.56 kilometers |
| 60 nautical miles | = 1 degree of a great circle of the earth | |

### Dry Measure

| | | | |
|---|---|---|---|
| 1 pint | | = 33.60 cubic inches | = 0.5505 liter |
| 2 pints | = 1 quart | = 67.20 cubic inches | = 1.1012 liters |
| 8 quarts | = 1 peck | = 537.61 cubic inches | = 8.8096 liters |
| 4 pecks | = 1 bushel | = 2,150.42 cubic inches | = 35.2383 liters |

1 British dry quart = 1.032 U.S. dry quarts.

According to United States government standards, the following are the weights avoirdupois for single bushels of the specified grains: for wheat, 60 pounds; for barley, 48 pounds; for oats, 32 pounds; for rye, 56 pounds; for corn, 56 pounds. Some States have specifications varying from these.

### Liquid Measure

| | | | |
|---|---|---|---|
| 1 gill | = 4 fluid ounces (see next table) | = 7.219 cubic inches | = 0.1183 liter |
| 4 gills | = 1 pint | = 28.875 cubic inches | = 0.4732 liter |
| 2 pints | = 1 quart | = 57.75 cubic inches | = 0.9463 liter |
| 4 quarts | = 1 gallon | = 231 cubic inches | = 3.7853 liters |

The British imperial gallon (4 imperial quarts) = 277.42 cubic inches = 4.546 liters. The barrel in Great Britain equals 36 imperial gallons, in the United States, usually 31½ gallons.

### Apothecaries' Fluid Measure

| | | | |
|---|---|---|---|
| 1 minim | | = 0.0038 cubic inch | = 0.0616 milliliter |
| 60 minims | = 1 fluid dram | = 0.2256 cubic inch | = 3.6966 milliliters |
| 8 fluid drams | = 1 fluid ounce | = 1.8047 cubic inches | = 0.0296 liter |
| 16 fluid ounces | = 1 pint | = 28.875 cubic inches | = 0.4732 liter |

See table immediately preceding for quart and gallon equivalents.
The British pint = 20 fluid ounces.

### Circular (or Angular) Measure

| | |
|---|---|
| 60 seconds (″) | = 1 minute (′) |
| 60 minutes | = 1 degree (°) |
| 90 degrees | = 1 quadrant or 1 right angle |
| 4 quadrants or 360 degrees | = 1 circle |

### Avoirdupois Weight

(The grain, equal to 0.0648 gram, is the same in all three tables of weight)

| | | |
|---|---|---|
| 1 dram or 27.34 grains | | = 1.772 grams |
| 16 drams or 437.5 grains | = 1 ounce | = 28.3495 grams |
| 16 ounces or 7,000 grains | = 1 pound | = 453.59 grams |
| 100 pounds | = 1 hundredweight | = 45.36 kilograms |
| 2,000 pounds | = 1 ton | = 907.18 kilograms |

In Great Britain, 14 pounds (6.35 kilograms) = 1 stone, 112 pounds (50.80 kilograms) = 1 hundredweight, and 2,240 pounds (1,016.05 kilograms) = 1 long ton.

# Tables of Weights and Measures

### Troy Weight

(The grain, equal to 0.0648 gram, is the same in all three tables of weight)

| | | | | | | |
|---|---|---|---|---|---|---|
| 3.086 grains | = | 1 carat | = | 200 | milligrams |
| 24 grains | = | 1 pennyweight | = | 1.5552 | grams |
| 20 pennyweights or 480 grains | = | 1 ounce | = | 31.1035 | grams |
| 12 ounces or 5,760 grains | = | 1 pound | = | 373.24 | grams |

### Apothecaries' Weight

(The grain, equal to 0.0648 gram, is the same in all three tables of weight)

| | | | | | |
|---|---|---|---|---|---|
| 20 grains | = | 1 scruple | = | 1.296 | grams |
| 3 scruples | = | 1 dram | = | 3.888 | grams |
| 8 drams or 480 grains | = | 1 ounce | = | 31.1035 | grams |
| 12 ounces or 5,760 grains | = | 1 pound | = | 373.24 | grams |

## THE METRIC SYSTEM

### Linear Measure

| | | | | | |
|---|---|---|---|---|---|
| 10 millimeters | = | 1 centimeter | = | 0.3937 | inch |
| 10 centimeters | = | 1 decimeter | = | 3.937 | inches |
| 10 decimeters | = | 1 meter | = | 39.37 | inches or 3.28 feet |
| 10 meters | = | 1 decameter | = | 393.7 | inches |
| 10 decameters | = | 1 hectometer | = | 328 feet 1 inch | |
| 10 hectometers | = | 1 kilometer | = | 0.621 | mile |
| 10 kilometers | = | 1 myriameter | = | 6.21 | miles |

### Square Measure

| | | | | | |
|---|---|---|---|---|---|
| 100 square millimeters | = | 1 square centimeter | = | 0.15499 | square inch |
| 100 square centimeters | = | 1 square decimeter | = | 15.499 | square inches |
| 100 square decimeters | = | 1 square meter | = | 1,549.9 | square inches or 1.196 square yards |
| 100 square meters | = | 1 square decameter | = | 119.6 | square yards |
| 100 square decameters | = | 1 square hectometer | = | 2.471 | acres |
| 100 square hectometers | = | 1 square kilometer | = | 0.386 | square mile |

### Land Measure

| | | | | | |
|---|---|---|---|---|---|
| 1 square meter | = | 1 centiare | = | 1,549.9 | square inches |
| 100 centiares | = | 1 are | = | 119.6 | square yards |
| 100 ares | = | 1 hectare | = | 2.471 | acres |
| 100 hectares | = | 1 square kilometer | = | 0.386 | square mile |

### Volume Measure

| | | | | | |
|---|---|---|---|---|---|
| 1,000 cubic millimeters | = | 1 cubic centimeter | = | .06102 | cubic inch |
| 1,000 cubic centimeters | = | 1 cubic decimeter | = | 61.02 | cubic inches |
| 1,000 cubic decimeters | = | 1 cubic meter (the unit is called a *stere* in measuring firewood) | = | 35.314 | cubic feet |

### Capacity Measure

| | | | | | |
|---|---|---|---|---|---|
| 10 milliliters | = | 1 centiliter | = | .338 | fluid ounce |
| 10 centiliters | = | 1 deciliter | = | 3.38 | fluid ounces |
| 10 deciliters | = | 1 liter | = | 1.0567 | liquid quarts or 0.9081 dry quart |
| 10 liters | = | 1 decaliter | = | 2.64 | gallons or 0.284 bushel |
| 10 decaliters | = | 1 hectoliter | = | 26.418 | gallons or 2.838 bushels |
| 10 hectoliters | = | 1 kiloliter | = | 264.18 | gallons or 35.315 cubic feet |

### Weights

| | | | | | |
|---|---|---|---|---|---|
| 10 milligrams | = | 1 centigram | = | 0.1543 | grain |
| 10 centigrams | = | 1 decigram | = | 1.5432 | grains |
| 10 decigrams | = | 1 gram | = | 15.432 | grains |
| 10 grams | = | 1 decagram | = | 0.3527 | ounce |
| 10 decagrams | = | 1 hectogram | = | 3.5274 | ounces |
| 10 hectograms | = | 1 kilogram | = | 2.2046 | pounds |
| 10 kilograms | = | 1 myriagram | = | 22.046 | pounds |
| 10 myriagrams | = | 1 quintal | = | 220.46 | pounds |
| 10 quintals | = | 1 metric ton | = | 2,204.6 | pounds |

# SPECIAL SIGNS AND SYMBOLS

## ASTRONOMY

### 1. SUN, MOON, PLANETS, ETC.

⊙ (1) The Sun. (2) Sunday.

☾ *or* ☽ (1) The Moon. (2) Monday.

● New Moon.

☽, ◐, *or* ◗ First Quarter.

○ Full Moon.

☾, ◑, *or* ◖ Last Quarter.

⁎ *or* ✳ Fixed Star.

☿ (1) Mercury. (2) Wednesday.

♀ (1) Venus. (2) Friday.

⊕, ⊖, *or* ♁ The Earth.

♂ (1) Mars. (2) Tuesday.

♃ (1) Jupiter. (2) Thursday.

♄ (1) Saturn. (2) Saturday.

♅ *or* ♅ Uranus.

♆ Neptune.

P Pluto.

☄ Comet.

①, ②, ③, *etc.* Asteroids in the order of their discovery.

α, β, γ, *etc.* The stars (of a constellation) in the order of their brightness; the Greek letter is followed by the Latin genitive of the name of the constellation.

### 2. SIGNS OF THE ZODIAC

*Spring Signs*

1. ♈ Aries (the Ram).
2. ♉ Taurus (the Bull).
3. ♊ *or* Π Gemini (the Twins).

*Summer Signs*

4. ♋ *or* ♋ Cancer (the Crab).
5. ♌ Leo (the Lion).
6. ♍ Virgo (the Virgin).

*Autumn Signs*

7. ♎ Libra (the Balance).
8. ♏ Scorpio (the Scorpion).
9. ♐ Sagittarius (the Archer).

*Winter Signs*

10. ♑ *or* ♑ Capricorn (the Goat).
11. ♒ Aquarius (the Water Bearer).
12. ♓ Pisces (the Fish).

### 3. ASPECTS AND NODES

☌ Conjunction;—with reference to bodies having the same longitude, or right ascension.

⚹ Sextile;—being 60° apart in longitude, or right ascension.

□ Quadrature;—being 90° apart in longitude, or right ascension.

△ Trine;—being 120° apart in longitude, or right ascension.

☍ Opposition;—being 180° apart in longitude, or right ascension.

☊ Ascending Node.

☋ Descending Node.

### 4. SIGNS AND ABBREVIATIONS USED IN ASTRONOMICAL NOTATION

*a.* Mean distance.

A.R. Right ascension.

β Celestial latitude.

D. Diameter.

δ Declination.

△ Distance.

E. East.

*e* Eccentricity.

h. *or* $^h$ Hours: as, 5h. or $5^h$.

*i* Inclination to the ecliptic.

L, l, *or* ϵ Mean longitude in orbit.

λ Longitude.

M. Mass.

m. *or* $^m$ Minutes of time: as, 5m. or $5^m$.

μ *or n* Mean daily motion.

+ *or* N. North.

N. P. D. North polar distance.

ν, ☊, *or* L. Longitude of ascending node.

π *or* ω Longitude of perihelion.

q. Perihelion distance.

ρ *or* R. Radius or radius vector.

— *or* S. South.

s. *or* $^s$ Seconds of time: as, 16s. or $16^s$.

T. Periodic time.

W. West.

φ Angle of eccentricity; also, geographical latitude.

° Degrees of arc.

′ Minutes of arc.

″ Seconds of arc.

## BIOLOGY

○, ⊙, ① Annual plant.

②, ⊙⊙, ♂ Biennial plant.

♃ Perennial herb.

△ Evergreen plant.

⊙ Monocarpic plant, that bears fruit but once.

5 Shrub.

5 Treelike shrub.

5 Tree.

Climbing plant.

♂, ♁ (1) Male organism or cell. (2) Staminate plant or flower.

♀ (1) Female organism or cell. (2) Pistillate plant or flower.

☿ Perfect, or hermaphroditic, plant or flower.

○ Individual, especially female, organism.

□ Individual, especially male, organism.

♁ ♀ Unisexual; having male and female flowers separate.

♁—♀ Monoecious; having male and female flowers on the same plant.

♁ : ♀ Dioecious; having male and female flowers on different plants.

♀ ♁ ♀ Polygamous; having hermaphroditic and unisexual flowers on the same or different plants.

∞ Indefinite number, as of stamens when there are more than twenty.

0 Lacking or absent, as a part.

) Turning or winding to the left.

( Turning or winding to the right.

× Crossed with: used of a hybrid.

P Parental (generation).

F Filial (generation); offspring.

$F_1$, $F_2$, $F_3$, *etc.* Offspring of the first, second, third, etc. filial generation.

+ Possessing a (specified) characteristic.

— Lacking a (specified) characteristic.

⁎ Northern hemisphere.

⁎ Southern hemisphere.

✳ Old World.

✳ New World.

°, ′, ″ Feet, inches, lines.

′, ″, ‴ Feet, inches, lines (in European usage).

## COMMERCE AND FINANCE

$ Dollar or dollars: as, $100.

¢ Cent or cents: as, 13¢.

£ Pound or pounds sterling: as, £100.

/ Shilling or shillings: as, 2/6, two shillings and sixpence.

℔ Pound (in weight).

@ (1) At: as, 200 @ $1 each. (2) To: as, shoes per pr. $10 @ $15.

℘ Per.

% (1) Per cent: as, 5%. (2) Order of.

*a/c* Account.

B/L Bill of lading.

B/S Bill of sale.

c/d, C/D Carried down (in bookkeeping).

c/f, C/F Carried forward (in bookkeeping).

*c/o* (1) Care of. (2) Carried over (in bookkeeping).

d/a Days after acceptance.

d/s Days after sight.

L/C Letter of credit.

# (1) Number (before a figure): as, #5 can. (2) Pounds (after a figure): as, 25#.

## MATHEMATICS

### 1. NUMERATION

| *Arabic* | *Greek* | *Roman* |
|---|---|---|
| 0 | ... | ... |
| 1 | α | I |
| 2 | β | II |
| 3 | γ | III |
| 4 | δ | IV *or* IIII |
| 5 | ε | V |
| 6 | ς | VI |
| 7 | ζ | VII |
| 8 | η | VIII *or* IIX |
| 9 | θ | IX *or* VIIII |
| 10 | ι | X |
| 11 | ια | XI |
| 12 | ιβ | XII |
| 13 | ιγ | XIII *or* XIIV |
| 14 | ιδ | XIV *or* XIIII |
| 15 | ιε | XV |
| 16 | ις | XVI |
| 17 | ιζ | XVII |
| 18 | ιη | XVIII *or* XIIX |
| 19 | ιθ | XIX *or* XVIIII |
| 20 | κ | XX |
| 30 | λ | XXX |
| 40 | μ | XL *or* XXXX |
| 50 | ν | L |
| 60 | ξ | LX |
| 70 | ο | LXX |
| 80 | π | LXXX *or* XXC |
| 90 | ϙ | XC *or* LXXXX |
| 100 | ρ | C |
| 200 | σ | CC |
| 300 | τ | CCC |
| 400 | υ | CD *or* CCCC |
| 500 | φ | D *or* IↃ |
| 600 | χ | DC *or* IↃC |
| 700 | ψ | DCC *or* IↃCC |
| 800 | ω | DCCC *or* IↃCCC |
| 900 | ... | CM, DCCCC, *or* IↃCCCC |
| 1,000 | ... | M *or* CIↃ |
| 2,000 | ... | MM *or* CIↃCIↃ |

Capital letters were sometimes used for the Greek numerals, and lower-case letters are often used for the Roman. In the Roman notation, the value of a character to the right of a larger numeral is added to that of the numeral: as, VI = V + I = 6. I, X, and sometimes C, are also placed to the left of larger numerals and when so situated their value is subtracted from that of such numerals: as, IV, that is, V − I = 4. After the sign IↃ for D, when the character Ↄ was repeated, each repetition had the effect of multiplying IↃ by ten: as, IↃↃ, 5,000; IↃↃↃ, 50,000; and the like. In writing numbers twice as great as these, C was placed as many times before the stroke I as the Ↄ was written after it. Sometimes a line was drawn over a numeral to indicate thousands: as, $\overline{C}$ = 100,000.

### 2. CALCULATION

+ (1) Plus, the sign of addition; used also to indicate that figures are only approximately exact, some figures being omitted at the end: as, 2.1557+. (2) Positive.

− (1) Minus, the sign of subtraction; used also to indicate that figures have been left off from the end of a number, and that the last figure has been increased by one: as, 2.9378 = 2.94−. (2) Negative.

± *or* ∓ Plus or minus; indicating that either of the signs + or − may properly be used; also used to introduce the probable error after a figure obtained by experimentation, etc.

× Multiplied by: 5 × 4 = 20; multiplication is also indicated by a centered dot (5 · 4 = 20) or by placing the factors in immediate juxtaposition ($2ab = 2 \times a \times b$).

÷ Divided by; division is also indicated by the sign: ($x \div y = x : y$), by a straight line between the dividend and the divisor $\left(\frac{x}{y}\right)$, or by an oblique line ($x/y$).

= Is equal to; equals.

≠ Is not equal to.

> Is greater than: as, $x > y$; that is, $x$ is greater than $y$.

< Is less than: as, $x < y$; that is, $x$ is less than $y$.

≮, ≧, *or* ≥ Is not less than; is equal to or greater than.

≯, ≦, *or* ≤ Is not greater than; is equal to or less than.

≎ Is equivalent to; applied to magnitudes or quantities that are equal in area or volume, but are not of the same form.

≡ Is identical with.

≅ Is congruent to.

∼ The difference between; used to designate the difference between two quantities without indicating which is the greater; as, $x \sim z$ = the difference between $x$ and $z$.

∝ Varies as; is directly proportional to: as, $x \propto y$; that is, $x$ varies as $y$.

∻ Geometric proportion: as, ∻ $x : y :: a : b$; that is, the geometric proportion, $x$ is to $y$ as $a$ is to $b$.

: Is to; the ratio of.

: : As; equals: used between ratios.

∞ Indefinitely great: the symbol for infinity.

! *or* ⌊ The factorial of, or the continued product of numbers from one upward: as, 5! = 5 × 4 × 3 × 2 × 1.

∴ Therefore.

∵ Since; because.

. . . And so on.

∠ Angle: as, ∠XYZ.

∟ Right angle.

⊥ The perpendicular; is perpendicular to: as, EF ⊥ MN = EF is perpendicular to MN.

|| Parallel; is parallel to: as, EF || DG.

○ Circle; circumference; 360°.

⌒ Arc of a circle.

△ Triangle.

□ Square.

▭ Rectangle.

▱ Parallelogram.

√‾ *or* √ Radical sign; root, indicating, when used without a figure placed above it, the square root: as, $\sqrt{9} = 3$. When any other than the square root is meant, a figure (called the *index*) expressing the degree of the required root, is placed above the sign: as, $\sqrt[3]{27} = 3$.

$^1, ^2, ^3$, *etc.* Exponents, placed above and to the right of a quantity to indicate that it is raised to the first, second, third, etc. power: as, $a^2$, $(a + b)^3$.

′, ″, ‴, *etc.* Prime, double (or second) prime, triple (or third) prime, etc., used to distinguish between different values of the same variable: as, $x'$, $x''$, $x'''$, etc.

‾ Vinculum: as, $\overline{x + y}$

( ) Parentheses: as, $2(x + y)$

[ ] Brackets: as, $a[2(x + y)]$

{ } Braces: as, $b + \{2 - a[2(x + y)]\}$

These signs indicate that the quantities connected or enclosed by them are to be taken together, as a single quantity.

*f or* F Function; function of: as, $f(a)$, a function of $a$.

*d* Differential of: as, $da$.

δ Variation of: as, $\delta a$.

△ Finite difference, or increment.

D Differential coefficient, or derivative.

∫ Integral; integral of, indicating that the expression following it is to be integrated: as, $\int f(x)dx$ indicates the indefinite integral of $f(x)$ with respect to $x$.

$\int_a^b$ Definite integral, indicating the limits of integration: as, $\int_a^b f(x)dx$ indicates the integral of $f(x)$ with respect to $x$, between the limits $a$ and $b$.

Σ Sum; algebraic sum; when used to indicate the summation of finite differences, it has a sense similar to that of the symbol ∫.

Π The continued product of all terms such as (those indicated).

π Pi, the number 3.14159265+; the ratio of the circumference of a circle to its diameter, of a semicircle to its radius, and of the area of a circle to the square of its radius.

*e* or ε The number 2.7182818+; the base of the Napierian system of logarithms; also, the eccentricity of a conic section.

M The modulus of a system of logarithms, especially of the common system of logarithms, where it is equal to 0.4342944819+.

*g* The acceleration of gravity.

° Degrees: as, 90°.

′ (1) Minutes of arc. (2) Feet.

″ (1) Seconds of arc. (2) Inches.

*h* Hours.

*m* Minutes of time.

*s* Seconds of time.

### MEDICINE AND PHARMACY

ĀĀ, Ā, *or* āā [Gr. *ana*], of each.

a. c. [L. *ante cibum*], before meals.

ad [L.], up to; so as to make: as, *ad*ʒij, so as to make two drams.

ad. [L. *adde*], let there be added; add.

ad lib. [L. *ad libitum*], at pleasure; as needed or desired.

aq. [L. *aqua*], water.

b. (i.) d. [L. *bis* (*in*) *die*], twice daily.

C. [L. *congius*], a gallon.

coch. [L. *cochleare*], a spoonful.

D. [L. *dosis*], a dose.

dil. [L. *dilue*], dilute or dissolve.

ess. [L. *essentia*], essence.

ft. mist. [L. *fiat mistura*], let a mixture be made.

ft. pulv. [L. *fiat pulvis*], let a powder be made.

gr. [L. *granum*], a grain.

gtt. [L. *guttae*], drops.

guttatim [L.], drop by drop.

haust. [L. *haustus*], a draft.

hor. decub. [L. *hora decubitus*], at bedtime.

lot. [L. *lotio*], a lotion.

M. [L. *misce*], mix.

mac. [L. *macera*], macerate.

O. *or* o. [L. *octarius*], a pint.

p.c. [L. *post cibum*], after meals.

pil. [L. *pilula(e)*], pill(s).

p.r.n. [L. *pro re nata*], as circumstances may require.

pulv. [L. *pulvis*], powder.

q. (i.) d. [L. *quater* (*in*) *die*], four times daily.

q.l. [L. *quantum libet*], as much as you please.

q. s. [L. *quantum sufficit*], as much as will suffice.

q.v. [L. *quantum vis*], as much as you like.

℞ [L. *recipe*], take: used at the beginning of a prescription.

S *or* Sig. [L. *signa*], write: used in prescriptions to indicate the directions to be placed on the label of the medicine.

t. (i.) d. [L. *ter* (*in*) *die*], three times daily.

℥ ounce; ℥i = one ounce; ℥ij = two ounces; ℥ss = half an ounce; ℥iss = one ounce and a half, etc.; *f*℥ = a fluid ounce.

ʒ dram; ʒi = one dram; ʒij = two drams; ʒss = half a dram; ʒiss = one dram and a half, etc.; *f*ʒ = a fluid dram.

℈ scruple; ℈i = one scruple; ℈ij = two scruples; ℈ss = half a scruple; ℈iss = one scruple and a half, etc.

♏ *or* ♍ minim.

### MISCELLANEOUS

& *or* & (the ampersand) and: as A. B. Smith & Co.

&c. [L. *et cetera*], and others; and so forth.

© copyrighted.

℟ response: in religious services, used to mark the part to be uttered by the congregation in answer to the officiant.

* in Roman Catholic service books, a mark used to divide each verse of a psalm into two parts, indicating where the response begins.

℣, V', *or* V, versicle: in religious services, used to mark the part to be uttered by the officiant.

✠ (1) a sign of the cross used by the pope, by archbishops, and by bishops, before their names. (2) in religious services, used to mark the places where the sign of the cross is to be made.

† died: used in genealogies, etc.

× (1) by: used in dimensions, as paper 8 × 11 inches. (2) a mark representing a signature, as on a legal document, made by someone unable to write; the name is added by someone else; e.g.

*his*<br>
*John* × *Doe*<br>
*mark*

# TABLE OF ALPHABETS

*The sounds of the letters in Arabic, Hebrew, Greek, Russian, and German are shown in parentheses*

| ENGLISH Upper and Lower Case | ARABIC | | HEBREW | | GREEK Print and Script | | RUSSIAN Upper and Lower Case | | GERMAN Upper and Lower Case | |
|---|---|---|---|---|---|---|---|---|---|---|
| A a | ا | Alif *1* | א | Aleph *4* | Α α | Alpha (ä) | А а | (ä) | 𝔄 𝔞 | (ä) |
| B b | ب ـبـ بـ | Be (b) | בּ | Beth (b) | Β β | Beta (b) | Б б | (b) | 𝔄̈ 𝔞̈ | (e) *5* |
| C c | ت ـتـ تـ | Te (t) | ב | Veth (v) *5* | Γ γ | Gamma (g) | В в | (v) | 𝔅 𝔟 | (b) |
| D d | ث ـثـ ثـ | Se (th) | ג | Gimel (g) | Δ δ | Delta (d) | Г г | (g) | ℭ 𝔠 | (k, ts, s) |
| E e | ج ـجـ جـ | Jim (j) *2* | ד | Daleth (d) | Ε ϵ | Epsilon (e) | Д д | (d) | ℭ𝔥 𝔠𝔥 | (H, kh) |
| F f | ح ـحـ حـ | He (h) *2* | ה | Heh (h) | Ζ ζ | Zeta (z) | Е е | (ye) | 𝔇 𝔡 | (d) |
| G g | خ ـخـ خـ | Khe (kh) *2* | ו | Vav (v) | Η η | Eta (ā) | Ж ж | (zh) | 𝔈 𝔢 | (e, ā) |
| H h | د | Dal (d) | ז | Zayin (z) | Θ θ | Theta (th) | З з | (z) | 𝔉 𝔣 | (f) |
| I i | ذ | Zal (*th*) | ח | Kheth (kh) | Ι ι | Iota (ē) | И и | (i, ē) | 𝔊 𝔤 | (g, kh) |
| J j | ر | Re (r) | ט | Teth (t) | Κ κ | Kappa (k) | Й й | (ē) *7* | ℌ 𝔥 | (h) |
| K k | ز | Ze (z) | י | Yod (y) | Λ λ | Lambda (l) | К к | (k) | ℑ 𝔦 | (i, ē) |
| L l | س ـسـ سـ | Sin (s) *2* | כּ ךּ | Kaph (k) *6* | Μ μ | Mu (m) | Л л | (l) | 𝔍 𝔧 | (y) |
| M m | ش ـشـ شـ | Shin (sh) *2* | כ ך | Khaph (kh) *5, 6* | Ν ν | Nu (n) | М м | (m) | 𝔎 𝔨 | (k) |
| N n | ص ـصـ صـ | Sad (s) *2* | ל | Lamedh (l) | Ξ ξ | Xi (ks) | Н н | (n) | 𝔏 𝔩 | (l) |
| O o | ض ـضـ ضـ | Dad (*th*) *2* | מ ם | Mem (m) *6* | Ο ο | Omicron (o) | О о | (ô, o) | 𝔐 𝔪 | (m) |
| P p | ط | Ta (t) | נ ן | Nun (n) *6* | Π π | Pi (p) | П п | (p) | 𝔑 𝔫 | (n) |
| Q q | ظ | Za (z) | ס | Samekh (s) | Ρ ρ | Rho (r) | Р р | (r) | 𝔒 𝔬 | (ō, ô) |
| R r | ع ـعـ عـ | Ain *2, 3* | ע | Ayin *4* | Σ σ ς | Sigma (s) *6* | С с | (s) | 𝔒̈ 𝔬̈ | (ö) *5* |
| S s | غ ـغـ غـ | Ghain (kh) *2* | פּ | Peh (p) | Τ τ | Tau (t) | Т т | (t) | 𝔓 𝔭 | (p) |
| T t | ف ـفـ فـ | Fe (f) *2* | פ ף | Feh (f) *5,6* | Υ υ | Upsilon (ü, ōō) | У у | (ōō) | 𝔔(𝔲) 𝔮(𝔲) | (kv) |
| U u | ق ـقـ قـ | Qaf (kä) *2* | צ ץ | Tsadi (ts) *6* | Φ φ | Phi (f) | Ф ф | (f) | ℜ 𝔯 | (r) |
| V v | ك ـكـ كـ | Kef (k) *2* | ק | Koph (k) | Χ χ | Chi (H) | Х х | (kh) | 𝔖 ſ 𝔰 | (s, z) *6* |
| W w | ل ـلـ لـ | Lam (l) *2* | ר | Resh (r) | Ψ ψ | Psi (ps) | Ц ц | (ts) | 𝔖𝔠𝔥 ſ𝔠𝔥 | (sh) |
| X x | م ـمـ مـ | Mim (m) *2* | שׁ | Shin (sh) | Ω ω | Omega (ō) | Ч ч | (ch) | 𝔗 𝔱 | (t) |
| Y y | ن ـنـ نـ | Nun (n) *2* | שׂ | Sin (s) *5* | | | Ш ш | (sh) | 𝔘 𝔲 | (ōō) |
| Z z | ه | He (h) | תּ | Tav (t) | | | Щ щ | (shch) | 𝔘̈ 𝔲̈ | (ü) *5* |
| | و | Waw (w) | ת | Thav (th, s) *5* | | | Ъ ъ | *8* | 𝔙 𝔳 | (f) |
| | ي ـيـ | Ye (y) *6* | | | | | Ы ы | (ē) | 𝔚 𝔴 | (v) |
| | | | | | | | Ь ь | *9* | 𝔛 𝔵 | (ks) |
| | | | | | | | Э э | (e) | 𝔜 𝔶 | (ē, ü) |
| | | | | | | | Ю ю | (ū) | ℨ 𝔷 | (ts) |
| | | | | | | | Я я | (yä) | | |

*Diacritical Marks used with Hebrew Characters*

| | | | | | |
|---|---|---|---|---|---|
| ָ | (ŏ, ô) | ֵ | (ā) | ְ | (silent) |
| ַ | (ä) | ֶ | (e) | ֻ | (ōō) |
| | | ִ | (i, ē) | | |

## NOTES

1. *A neutral letter, silent in the middle of words, but represented by ('), indicating the glottal stop, when used at the beginning of a word.*
2. *The first form is used at the beginning of a word; the second, in the middle; the third, at the end.*
3. *A neutral letter represented by ('), indicating rough breathing, when used at the beginning of a word.*
4. *A neutral letter, either silent or sounded according to the accompanying diacritical mark.*
5. *A variant of the preceding character, not counted in the alphabet.*
6. *The final form is used only as the last letter of a word and (in German) of some syllables.*
7. *Used only as the second vowel in a diphthong.*
8. *Indicates nonpalatalization of a preceding consonant.*
9. *Indicates palatalization of a preceding consonant.*

# THE INDO-EUROPEAN FAMILY OF LANGUAGES

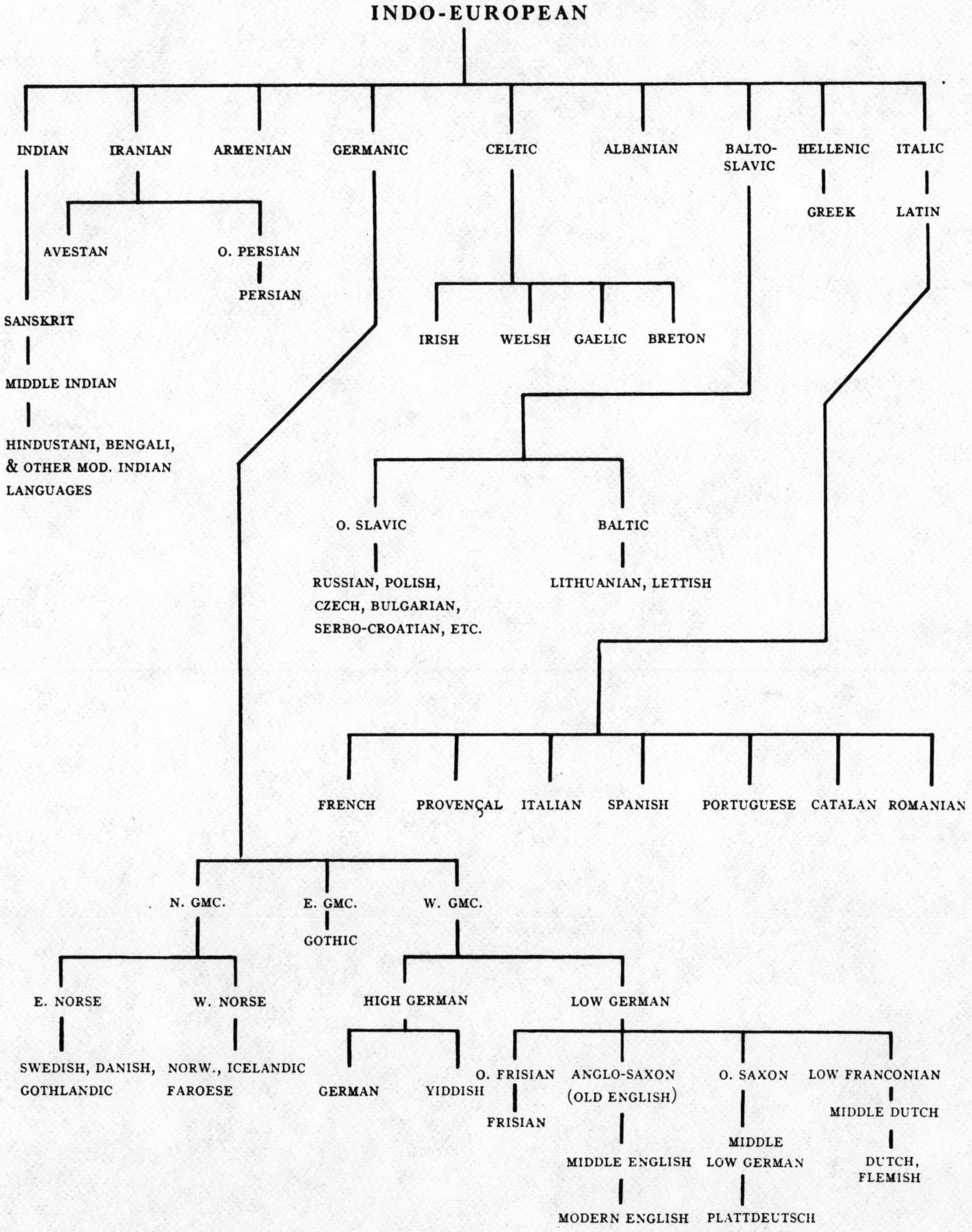

# *Student*
# HANDBOOK

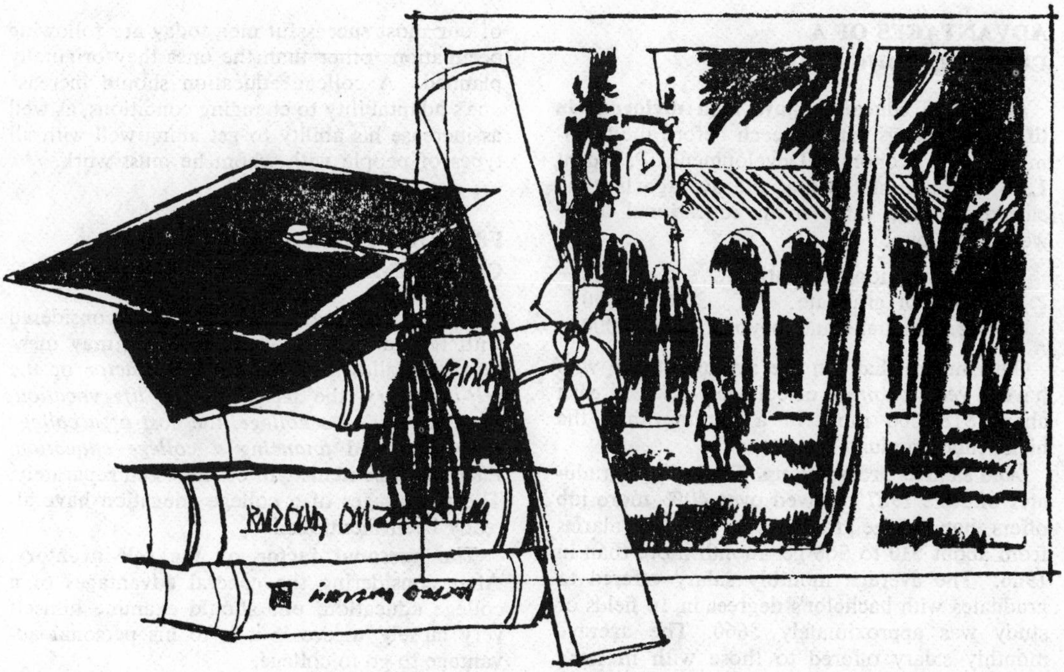

# Education

**W**HAT IS EDUCATION? In one sense, the term *education* is used to designate the number of years of formal training that one has completed in a school situation. For example, a *grammar school education* is equal to *8 years* of completed school work, a *high school graduate* has completed *12 years* of school work, and a *college graduate* will have completed *16 or more years* of school work, depending on whether he has completed four or more years of college work. In this article we shall usually use the term education in this sense. In a broader sense, however, *true education* involves much more than the number of years successfully completed in the school room. Someone has defined true education as "learning to do, gracefully and well, the thing that ought to be done at the time it ought to be done, whether one wants to do it or not." Someone else may define true education as "learning to change the things in one's environment that should be and can be changed, and learning to adapt himself to the things in his environment that should not or cannot be changed, all to the ultimate good of himself and his fellowman." In this broad sense, true education involves not only the *acquisition of knowledge* in the classroom, or elsewhere, but the *wise use of this knowledge*.

**How much education should one have?** Generally speaking, one should have as much education as his ability and opportunity will allow. To say that everyone should have the same amount of education is not true. There are one-talent, two-talent, and five-talent individuals, and each should get as much education as is profitable to him under the circumstances that he must live. Some individuals who have the natural ability to take a college education may find it impossible to do so because of dependents whom they must rightfully support. The amount of education that each individual should get depends on many factors of a personal nature, some of which will be discussed in this article.

ROBERT OWENS BEAUCHAMP, B.S., M.A., Ph.D., *Associate Professor of Science Education, Emeritus,* George Peabody College for Teachers, Nashville, Tennessee; Associate Professor of Chemistry and Physics, Middle Tennessee State University, Murfreesboro, Tennessee.

## ADVANTAGES OF A COLLEGE EDUCATION

**A college education pays high dividends in lifetime earnings.** In a speech before the Committee for Economic Development, President L. B. Johnson stated that the average lifetime earnings at the three main educational levels were as follows:

| | |
|---|---|
| Grammar school education | $152,000 |
| High school graduate | $272,000 |
| College graduate and beyond | $452,000 |

This means that, on the average, those who have *4 years or more* of college work will earn about $180,000 more in a lifetime than the high school graduate.

**And salaries are going up.** The college graduates of June 1967 received over 40% more job offers than did the graduates of 1966, at salaries from about $30 to $66 per month more than in 1966. The average monthly salary offered to graduates with bachelor's degrees in 14 fields of study was approximately $660. The average monthly salary offered to those with master's degrees and some experience was about $800. Average offers to those with doctor's degrees were from $1,087 per month in chemistry to $1,277 in electrical engineering.

**Other dividends of a college education.** Besides the monetary gains of a college education, it pays many other dividends that are quite worth while. The personal satisfaction of "knowing" is a dividend that cannot be measured in dollars and cents. We might say that *"knowledge" brings its own reward.* It enables one to render a greater service to himself, his family, and his fellowman. It also enables one to appreciate more the fields of music, art, and literature. It broadens his knowledge of government, economics, and international relations. It helps him to understand better the part that politics, industry, and technology play in the life of his community, the nation, and the world. Thus it should enable him to vote more intelligently and to be a better citizen.

**This is the day of specialization.** A specialist has been defined as "one who learns more and more about less and less". In the complex life of the world today, only the highly trained man can hope to fill the best positions. The *best education for a specialist,* however, *is one with a broad foundation, sharpened to a point.* A college education should not only make one highly trained in a particular field, but should give him such a broad foundation that he will be more or less familiar with other fields closely related to his own. It should enable him to do more than just the one thing in which he is most highly trained; so that if it becomes necessary to change from his primary field of specialization, he will be able to do so with the least difficulty. Many of our most successful men today are following occupations other than the ones they originally planned. A college education should increase one's adaptability to changing conditions, as well as increase his ability to get along well with all types of people with whom he must work.

## FACTORS TO BE CONSIDERED CONCERNING A COLLEGE EDUCATION

Among the many factors to be considered with regard to going to college, we may mention the following: the *personal factor* or the *self-inventory,* the *selection of a life vocation,* the *selection of a college,* the *cost of a college education,* and *financing a college education.* Each of these items will be discussed separately. The advantages of a college education have already been mentioned.

**The personal factor or the self-inventory.** After considering the general advantages of a college education, one should examine himself very closely to see if it is to his personal advantage to go to college.

*First,* does he really *enjoy studying and learning? Does he have a genuine thirst for knowledge?* If so, he has one trait that is essential to success on the college level.

*Second,* does he have the *native ability* to do college work? He should have a conference with his principal or advisor and find out how he ranks with his class, and with the nation as a whole, on standardized tests. Scores on the American College Testing Program, or on the College Entrance Examination Board's Scholastic Aptitude Tests, or Achievement Tests, should give an indication of his ability to do college work. They also should indicate the type of college that it would be expedient for him to attend.

*Third,* is it possible for him to go to college; or are there certain conditions that make it necessary for him to go to work on graduation from high school? If he *must* go to work to earn a living, or to support others who might be dependent on him, then he may consider college at a later date; or he may attend college night classes, if they are available.

All of these are important personal factors to be considered.

**Selection of a Vocation.** Anyone who goes to college should have in mind a definite goal. If possible, he should have some idea of what he would like to make his life's work. *First,* he should *select a vocation that he really wants to follow for the rest of his life. Second,* he should have a conference with his principal, or counselor, to see if he has the special aptitudes that would make success probable, or possible, in his chosen field. *Third,* he should see if he has taken the proper high school subjects to fit him for college work in his chosen field. For example, he should not choose engineering if he has had insufficient mathematics in high school, or if his grades in mathematics are too low for an engineering course in college. *Fourth,* he should *keep an open mind,* and be willing to change his field of study at the end of his freshman or sophomore year in college, if he finds that his abilities and desires lie in some field other than the one he has chosen. Many college students do not really decide what field they want to specialize in until the close of their sophomore year.

**Selection of a college.** The *main factor* one should consider in choosing a college is the strength of the department (or departments) in which he desires to specialize. Other factors to be considered are:

a. Location of college — at home or away from home; and if away from home, the part of the country preferred.
b. Size of city or community in which college is located.
c. Size of the college — large, medium, or small.
d. Type of college — liberal arts or specialized.
e. Co-educational or not.
f. Total cost per year — tuition, room, board, books, etc.

**Sources of information about colleges.** In order to choose a college wisely, one should obtain pertinent information about the colleges under consideration. The chief sources of information are:

a. The high school principal or counselor.
b. The college catalogues of the particular colleges under consideration; these may be obtained on request by writing the Director of Admissions of each of the colleges being *definitely considered.* Some college catalogues may already be in the counselor's office or in the school library.
c. Some of the books listed under *"References"* at the close of this article. Some of these certainly should be in either the counselor's office or in the school library.
d. College representatives who may visit his school.
e. Alumni of the college, or students already enrolled in the college.
f. A visit to the Director of Admissions of any college being definitely considered, if this is feasible. This is desirable, but not necessary.

**Making application to a college.** When one has selected the college (or colleges) to which he wishes to apply, he should write to the Director of Admissions and request an application form. This should be filled out carefully and promptly and returned to the Director of Admissions, together with any fee that is required. If he is applying to a college that has "early admissions", he should place his application in the second half of his junior year; otherwise, he should place his application in the first half of his senior year. If letters of recommendation from teachers or other friends are required, he should see that these are sent in promptly. He also should request his principal to have his high school transcript sent in promptly.

**How colleges evaluate applicants.** College admissions officers consider many factors in evaluating their applicants. Some of the most important are:

a. *A good, strong academic high school record.* This shows an applicant's *actual performance record* for a period of four years, which is one of the most important factors to be considered. The more hard academic subjects taken in high school, the better. Easy courses taken to accumulate good marks are not necessarily an asset; they could be considered with disfavor.
b. *Scores on standardized tests.* These may include the scores on such tests as the following: intelligence tests, the National Educational Development Tests, the National Merit Scholarship Qualifying Test, the College Entrance Examination Board's Scholastic Aptitude Test and Achievement Tests, and the American College Tests. High scores on any of these help, but one who scores high on tests and has a poor academic record is looked on with disfavor, because it indicates that he is a "loafer". On the other hand, one whose test scores may not be so high, but who has a good academic record, is looked on with favor, because it shows that he is a "worker"; and *actual performance may count for more than mere native ability.*
c. *Rank in class* is considered an important factor because it shows whether a person stands high or low with his competitors. However, a high rank with easy subjects may not be considered as good as a somewhat lower rank with hard subjects. Admission officers know how to evaluate this.
d. *Recommendations from principal, counselor, teachers* (or others, if requested). These recommendations should be *in line with his high school record and test scores,* however, or they may be discounted, unless there are some particular extenuating circumstances that should be explained and considered. A student might have some particular talent or qualities of leadership that do not show on his record, and these may be brought out in the letters of recommendation.

e. *The ability to write.* Some colleges require the Writing Sample of the College Entrance Examination Board. This is in the student's own handwriting, and carbon copies are sent to those colleges that require it. Other colleges require a student to write an essay on some assigned subject which may be autobiographical in nature, or telling why he has selected that particular college.

f. *The type of high school from which one graduates.* A high ranking student from a strong high school would, in all probability, be better prepared for a selective college than one with an equally high rank from a poor school with low academic standards.

## COST OF A COLLEGE EDUCATION

**College costs are rising.** The cost of a college education is rising so rapidly that any exact data given as of today would probably be out-of-date one year from now. For this reason, the data given in the following paragraphs are reasonable approximations of the cost of a college education in various types of schools, at the date of this article. These costs may rise 5% or even more in one year's time.

**Approximate average cost for room and board only per academic year in:**

Public junior colleges..............$540
Public 4-year colleges............$720

Tuition and fees for in-state residents vary widely from about $100 in some municipal colleges to $200 or more in some of the state colleges and universities. Out-of-state residents pay more for tuition and fees.

Added to the above costs must be the "extras", such as: books and supplies, laundry and dry cleaning, clothes, and traveling expenses.

**Approximate average cost for tuition, fees, room, and board in:**

Private junior colleges............$1,500
Private 4-year colleges............$2,000

The cost in highly selective private colleges is much more and varies from about $2,200 to over $3,000. The "extras" mentioned above must be added to these amounts.

**Just what does an average 4-year college education cost?** It has been reasonably estimated that the *average* 4-year college education costs about $6,000. Granting that this is true, if the life-time earnings are increased $180,000 (see page 868) there is a $30 return for each dollar invested, which is 3,000%. Not bad.

Of course in the highly selective private colleges the cost may run as high as $12,000 to $15,000 (or even more, counting the "extras") for four years of college work. However, if one can live at home and attend a public college in his own city, the cost of tuition, fees, books, and supplies may cost less than $1,000 for the four years. If there is no public college or university close enough for him to live at home, he could attend a state college or university *in his own state,* and probably reduce the total cost (tuition, fees, room and board, books, supplies, and "extras") to about $1,000 per year. He might have to practice frugal economy, but this would be good for him. He could secure summer employment and thus make part of his expenses. He might also secure part-time employment during the school year and help pay his way. If he needs additional help to attend college, he may find many helpful suggestions in the next section of this article on *Financing a College Education.* He also may find helpful suggestions in some of the *"References"* at the close of this article.

## FINANCING A COLLEGE EDUCATION

College is expensive, and many worthy students require financial aid in order to attend college. If this is the case, he should ask for the financial aid bulletin when he writes for the college catalogue. Most of the scholarships and other financial aids are handled through the colleges, so that specific information concerning any required financial aid should be obtained directly from the college that the student plans to enter. There was never a time when so much help was available to the worthy student who is in need of financial aid and who really wants to go to college. For additional sources of information, see the *"References"* at the close of this article.

SCHOLARSHIPS are outright gifts, usually awarded to students of high scholastic standing. Nearly 250,000 are awarded annually. The amount of a scholarship is frequently adjusted to the student's needs. There are about 2,200 four-year National Merit Scholarships awarded annually. The amounts vary from an honorarium of $100 to as much as $1,500 per year.

GRANTS-IN-AID are similar to scholarships except that the recipient may be required to perform some service for the college. Students who have some particular talent in music, art, athletics, debating, etc., may be eligible for these grants-in-aid, even though their scholastic standing would not merit an outright scholarship.

WORKSHIPS are similar to grants-in-aid. The recipients may be assigned to various teachers on the faculty to help grade papers, type, etc.

The RESERVE OFFICERS TRAINING CORPS (ROTC) program pays all tuition, fees, some travel, and a monthly subsistence to future officers of the Army, Navy, and Air Force. A competitive examination is required to enter this program. Specific information may be obtained from the college one plans to enter, if it has such a program.

The VETERANS ADMINISTRATION has a program for orphans of veterans or children of disabled veterans. A copy of their booklet "War Orphan Education" may be obtained from the Veterans Administration, Washington, D.C.

## FOUR FEDERAL PROGRAMS OF ASSISTANCE IN FINANCING A COLLEGE EDUCATION

The United States Office of Education has four major financial aid programs intended for students in any course of study above the high school level. Specific information concerning these programs may be obtained from the *Financial Aid Officer* of the college or school in which one is enrolled, or in which he has been accepted or plans to enroll. The following is merely a brief description of these four programs.

NATIONAL DEFENSE STUDENT LOANS — a program of borrowing. High school graduates who have been accepted for enrollment by colleges and universities, or college students enrolled in full-time, or at least half-time courses, and who *need* financial help for educational expenses, are eligible for these loans. An undergraduate may borrow as much as $1,000 each academic year to a total of $5,000. A graduate student may borrow up to $2,500 a year up to a total of $10,000. The repayment period and interest start 9 months after the student ends his studies. If he goes into the teaching profession, part of the debt is forgiven. The colleges and universities approve and make the loans and are responsible for collections.

GUARANTEED LOANS — a program of borrowing. Under this program a student may borrow from a bank or other financial institution to attend an *eligible college, business college,* or *technical or vocational school.* An undergraduate may borrow as much as $1,000 a year and a graduate student may borrow as much as $1,500 a year. *The main objective of this program is to make loan insurance available to any eligible student who wants to borrow.*

EDUCATIONAL OPPORTUNITY GRANTS — a program of direct awards. Under this program, colleges and universities will make *Educational Opportunity Grants* available to a limited number of *undergraduate* students with *exceptional financial need* who require these grants to attend college. Grants range from $200 to $800 a year and can be no more than one-half of the total assistance given the student. An additional award of $200, *if needed,* will be given to those students who were in the upper half of their college class during the preceding academic year.

COLLEGE WORK-STUDY — a program of employment. Students, particularly from low-income families, who need a job to help pay for college expenses are potentially eligible for employment by their colleges under the federally supported Work-Study Programs. Students may work up to 15 hours a week while attending classes full time. During the summer or other vacation periods when they do not have classes, students may work 40 hours a week under this program. The basic pay is $1.25 an hour, although up to $3.00 an hour may be paid for highly specialized work. On-campus jobs may include work in libraries, laboratories, dining halls, and maintenance. Off-campus jobs are assigned in public or non-profit organizations and include work in health, welfare, and recreation programs.

**Education is big business.** In July of 1966 the *total population* of the United States was estimated at 196,800,000. In October of 1966, the *total enrollment of full-time and part-time students in school* was 55,070,000, or about 28% of the total population. The following table gives the total enrollment of full-time and part-time students enrolled at the various educational levels in October of 1966.

| *Educational level* | *Total enrollment* |
|---|---|
| Kindergarten and elementary school | 35,624,000 |
| High school | 13,364,000 |
| College and professional school | 6,085,000 |
| Total | 55,070,000 |

*Source:* Bureau of the Census. The parts do not add exactly to the total, due to rounding off.

The increase in total school enrollment from October 1960 to October 1966 was 8,800,000, or 19% over the 46,300,000 enrolled in 1960. During this six year period the kindergarten and elementary schools increased 10%, the high schools increased 30%, and the colleges increased 70%. It is estimated that by 1970, the total enrollment in all schools will increase 5% over the 1966 figure; but it is estimated that the enrollment in colleges and professional schools will increase 12% over the 1966 figure, for the same 4-year period. This shows the greater emphasis that is being placed on higher education.

There are approximately 2,200 accredited colleges and universities in the United States. Since 1955, about 200 new 4-year colleges have been established, and the junior colleges are growing in number at the rate of about 50 each year.

Education seems to be the largest and fastest growing industry in the United States, but the most rapid growth is at the college and university level where it is expected that more than $18,000,000,000 will be spent during the school year of 1967-68.

The United States has twice as many students enrolled on the college level as all the countries of Western Europe combined. For each 1,000 of the total population, the United States has 31 enrolled on the college level; France has 10; Belgium and Sweden 9 each; Britain and Italy 8 each; Austria 7; Netherlands and Switzerland 6 each; and West Germany 5.

For each 1,000 total population of all Europe there are 7 enrolled on the college level. For each 1,000 negroes in the United States, there are 15 enrolled on the college level. This shows that the average negro in the United States has more than double the chance of going to college than does the average of all European countries combined. This is certainly the land of opportunity.

**If you can't go to college, you may still succeed.** If feasible, one should go to college; but in any event, he should get all the education that circumstances allow. College is not for everyone, however, and the annals of history are filled with the names of men and women who have attained remarkable success in their various fields without the advantage of being a college graduate. Among these we may mention: Thomas A. Edison, Henry Ford, W. K. Kellogg, Henry Kaiser, David Sarnoff, Harry S. Truman, Lewis Strauss, Eleanor Roosevelt, Ernest Hemingway, Noel Coward, William Faulkner, and Frank Sparkes who became president of Wabash College. *All* of these were (or are) *highly educated,* however, in the broadest sense of the term, even though they did not graduate from college.

The one thing that is common to all successful individuals is an *untiring "drive" and determination to succeed.* So regardless of the level of education that you may be able to achieve, GIVE LIFE ALL THAT YOU HAVE, AND TRUE SUCCESS WILL BE YOURS.

## REFERENCES


Angel, J. L. *National Register of Scholarships and Fellowships,* Vol. I: *Scholarships and Loans.* Regents Pub. Co., New York.

Bowles, F. H. *How to Get into College.* E. P. Dutton and Co., New York.

Brown, Judy, and Donald Grossfield. *I Wish I'd Known That before I Went to College.* Essanders Special Editions, a division of Simon and Schuster, Inc., New York. $1.00 paper.

Brownstein, S. C., and Mitchel Weiner. *Barron's How to Prepare for College Entrance Examinations.* Barron's Educational Series, Inc., Woodbury, N. Y.

Brownstein, S. C. *College Bound.* Barron's Educational Series, Inc., Woodbury, N. Y. $1.98 paper.

Brownstein, S. C., and Mitchel Weiner. *You Can Win a Scholarship.* Barron's Educational Series, Inc., Woodbury, N. Y.

Burckel, C. E., ed. *College Blue Book.* Universal Lithographers, Baltimore.

Cartter, Allan, ed. *American Universities and Colleges.* American Council on Education, Washington, D.C.

Cass, James, and M. Birnbaum. *Comparative Guide to American Colleges.* Harper and Row, New York.

College Entrance Examination Board, Princeton, N. J. *The College Handbook.* Published annually.

Cox, Claire. *How to Beat the High Cost of College.* Bernard Geis Associates, New York.

Craig, W. B. *How to Finance a College Education.* Henry Holt and Co., New York.

Educational Research Corporation, Cambridge, Mass. *College Admissions Data.* Published annually.

Einstein, Bernice W. *College Entrance Guide.* Grosset and Dunlap, New York. Published annually.

Eskow, Seymour. *Barron's Guide to the Two-Year Colleges.* Barron's Educational Series, Inc., Woodbury, N. Y. $2.98 paper.

Feingold, S. N. *Scholarships, Fellowships, and Loans.* Bellman Publishing Co., Cambridge, Mass.

Fine, Benjamin. *Barron's Profiles of American Colleges.* Barron's Educational Series, Inc., Woodbury, N. Y.

Fine, Benjamin. *How to be Accepted by the College of Your Choice.* Meredith Press, Des Moines, Iowa.

Fine, Benjamin, and S. A. Eisenberg. *How to Get Money for College.* Doubleday and Co., Inc., Garden City, N. Y.

Gleazer, E. J., Jr. *American Junior Colleges.* American Council on Education, Washington, D.C.

Hawes, G. R. *The New American Guide to Colleges.* Columbia University Press, New York.

Keeslar, O. *A National Catalog of Scholarships and Other Financial Aids for Students Entering College.* William C. Brown Co., Dubuque, Iowa.

Lass, Abraham H. *How to Prepare for College.* David White Co., New York. Also in paperback by Pocket Books, New York.

Lovejoy, C. E. *College Scholarship Guide.* Simon and Schuster, New York. Published bi-annually.

Lovejoy, C. E. *Lovejoy's Complete Guide to American Colleges and Universities.* Simon and Schuster, New York.

R. L. Polk Co., Nashville. "What about College". An excellent 32-page bulletin.

Sabo, Alex., ed. *College Facts and Financial Aid.* Chronical Guidance Publications. Moravia, N. Y.

Sulkin, Sidney. (Education Editor for *Changing Times*). *Complete Planning for College.* McGraw-Hill Co., New York.

United States Office of Education. *Financial Aid for College Students: Undergraduate.* Government Printing Office, Washington, D.C. Published annually.

Weigand, George. *How to Succeed in High School and Score High on College Entrance Examinations.* Barron's Educational Series, Inc., Woodbury, N. Y.

Wilson, J. W., and E. H. Lyons. *Work-Study College Programs.* Harper and Row, New York.


NOTE: Many of these references may be found in the counselor's office or in the school library. It is important, however, to use the latest editions of all of these publications.

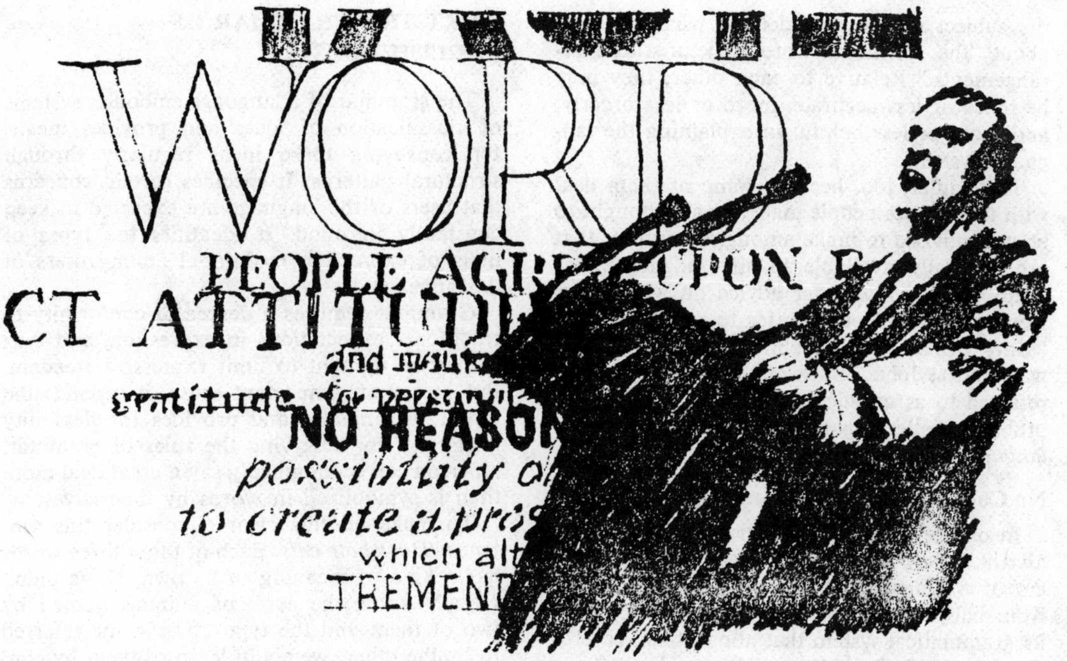


# English

## Outline of English Grammar

### INTRODUCTION

#### Words Alone Do Not Make a Language

No human language is just a collection of words. In English, words themselves are often built from smaller meaningful units, and we observe certain rules in building them. If we speak of more than one map, we say *maps,* and the sound we have added to *map* must be put at the end, nowhere else — *smap* or *masp* would not do. The order of words is also governed by rules.

We recognize "The boy is reading the book" as a normal English sentence; we would have an entirely different judgement on "Boy book the reading is the." Such rules as have just been illustrated are a small part of the *grammar* of English, an indispensable part of our language.

#### The Various Meanings of "Grammar"

One dictionary definition of *grammar* is "The system of word structures and arrangements of a given language at a given time." The grammar of a particular language could be said to be the whole set of rules that specify the structural patterns speakers of the language must or may follow if they are to be understood as using the language normally. Of course, a language that has been reduced to writing has a grammar of its written form, too.

The term *grammar* is also used to name "that part of the study of language which deals with the forms of words (*morphology*) and with their arrangements in sentences (*syntax*)." Naturally, a book or briefer piece of writing that carries on such a study is called "a grammar."

Grammar books and shorter treatments of

---

WILLIAM J. GRIFFIN, Ph.D., University of Iowa. *Professor of English,* George Peabody College for Teachers.

the subject may vary widely in what they say about "the system of word structures and arrangements." Relative to each other, they may be more or less accurate, more or less orderly, and more or less helpful in explaining the language system.

They differ, too, because some of them deal with the choices people make, or are thought to be well advised to make among the options that are normally available in the language. For example, they may offer advice on whether or when a person should prefer to say (or write) "Mary was angry with John" rather than "Mary was mad at John." Such matters are sometimes referred to as questions of grammar. They are probably better regarded as matters of *usage, language etiquette*, or *style*.

### No Complete Account of Grammar Exists

In one respect, however, grammar books are all alike; they are all incomplete. Native speakers of a language (those who have spoken it from babyhood) have a kind of knowledge of its grammatical system that allows them to produce and understand an endless number of sentences, very few of which are exactly alike. People are not usually, however, consciously aware of the principles that guide them in this remarkable accomplishment. Grammarians undertake to explain and account for those principles, but thus far they have been only partially successful in doing so.

A language system is so complicated and is so deeply embedded in human minds that a thoroughly comprehensive grammar book may never be written.

It is important to understand, too, that there are *dialects* within languages, and dialects may have special features in their grammatical systems as well as in vocabulary and patterns of pronunciation. Grammar books usually try to explain only the structural system of standard dialects, which are those that (for economic, political, social, or other cultural reasons) are regarded as particularly admirable.

Discussions of grammar often, indeed, concentrate on the literary language characteristically used by scholars and other well educated writers. They are likely to say a great deal about the customs established in writing and printing. We ought to recognize, however, that such matters as spelling, punctuation, and capitalization are not elements of the grammar of the language itself. They are important, of course, and our customs in handling them are generally related to the structural system of the language. They provide means of visually representing meaningful uses of the language.

In the brief explanation of grammar offered here, the focus will be on Standard English and the conventions observed in its literary use.

## WHAT THE GRAMMAR OF ENGLISH DOES

The grammar of a language embodies systems of classification of ideas and provides means for conveying those ideas regularly through structural patterns. It specifies certain concerns that users of the language are expected to keep constantly in mind. It identifies the types of units of expression traditional among users of the language.

Grammar requires a degree of conformity to traditional expectations in expression, and thus it may be thought to limit expressive freedom. But in a more important sense, it expands the power of language and provides for flexibility in its use. By observing the rules of grammar, a person can economically say a great deal more than is symbolized in words by themselves.

To make all this clearer, consider this sentence: *Dogs hate cats.* Each of those three words has a kind of meaning of its own. If we didn't already know the sorts of animals named by two of them and the type of behavior referred to by the other, we could learn of them by consulting a dictionary. There we could find the "dictionary meaning" of the words, which is often spoken of as "lexical meaning."

But notice how many other meanings are expressed in the grammatical combination, *Dogs hate cats.* First, we know this is a statement, not a command or a question. Then, we know that more than one dog and more than one cat are being talked about. We understand, too, that the dogs do the hating and the cats are being hated. The sentence tells us that the hating was not finished and over with when the statement was made (for the form of the second word is not *hated*). And it also tells us (since the second word is *hate* and not *hates*) that more than one dog does the hating. (English grammar often insists on the repetition of certain kinds of information.)

The kinds of meaning expressed just by use of the system of grammar may be called "grammatical meaning." They are also often referred to as "structural meaning."

## FIVE WAYS TO SIGNAL GRAMMATICAL MEANING

Every language has characteristic ways of conveying grammatical meanings. English makes systematic use of five kinds of signals.

### Grammatical Inflection

Like many (but not all) languages, English changes the forms of some kinds of words to express grammatical meanings without basically affecting their classifications as parts of speech. What is called *grammatical inflection* (or simply *inflection*) is seen in the form *dogs*, in which the idea "more than one" is added to the noun *dog*. Another example is found in the grammatical contrasts in the verb forms *hate*, *hates*, *hated*.

Inflection produces small sets of related word forms, among which one is regarded as the *base form* that the others are built upon. In English, inflection usually consists of addition of a suffix to a base form; sometimes, however, it involves change inside the word (*broke* is the finite past tense form related to the base *break*). Occasionally (for historical reasons not always clear to us now), the inflected set of related forms (called a *paradigm*) has a member drawn from an entirely different inflectional group. Examples can be seen in the verb series *go*, *went*, *gone*, and the adjective series *good*, *better*, *best*.

As it is used in this discussion, the term *inflection* has nothing to do with the popular employment of the term to mean the raising or lowering of the pitch of one's voice.

### Derivational Contrasts

We do not think of inflection as producing new words, but just different forms of the base. But English has regular ways of making (or, as we say, deriving) different words from a base. From the verb *govern*, for example, we have derived *governor*, *governess*, *government*, *governable*, *ungovernable*, and *misgovern*. Notice that three of these words are nouns, two are adjectives, and only the last is a verb like the base from which it was derived.

#### DIFFERENCES BETWEEN DERIVATION AND INFLECTION

*Misgovern* illustrates the fact that we can derive words by using prefixes as well as suffixes. Similarly, we can make the verb *enlarge* out of the adjective *large* or the adverb *away* from the noun *way*. The term *affix* is used to cover both prefixes and suffixes, and we can say that either kind of affix may be used to derive a new word from a base in English. By contrast, prefixes never produce inflectional forms.

Other facts also distinguish derivation from inflection. Whereas inflections can be applied to very large classes of words (most nouns can be pluralized, and almost all verbs have a form ending in *s* and another ending in *-ing*, for example), no particular derivational affix has such a general privilege. There are many derivational affixes, and each may be used with only a relatively small group of words. The most regularly applicable derivational affix in English is the suffix *-ly*, which can turn most (but by no means all) adjectives into adverbs.

Furthermore, we are often able to add several derivational affixes to a stem, one after the other. (A "stem" is simply whatever an affix is added to.) From the adjective *large* we can make the verb *enlarge*, and then the noun *enlargement*. Or we can begin with *organ* and add first *-ize*, then *-ation*, then *-al*, then *-ly*. With each addition of a suffix we would have a new word; the last would be the adverb *organizationally*. But we cannot operate with inflectional suffixes this way; they end words to which they are attached. If to *organ* we had added the plural noun inflection *-s*, we couldn't have added any more suffixes; or if to *organize* we had added the past tense verb inflection *-d*, we would have been stopped right there.

#### GRAMMATICAL IMPORTANCE OF DERIVATIONAL CONTRASTS

One of the important functions of derivational affixes is to identify the form it produces as belonging to a particular part of speech. Note that we immediately recognize *enlarge* as a verb and *enlargement* as a noun, though both are derived from the adjective *large*. Observe, too, that out of *organ* we first made a verb, then a noun, then an adjective, then an adverb. Of course, most of our derivational affixes carry some measure of lexical meaning, too; but it is because they operate as signals of the traditional classifications of words that they have special importance in our system of grammar. We can speak of what they do in this respect as providing derivational contrasts.

### Word Order

The sequential arrangement of words is a third (and extremely important) way of signaling grammatical meanings. Since the operation of word order signals is so obvious, the sort of thing referred to here can be readily made clear. The details of how word order works, of course, could be explained only in a very big book.

We have already illustrated one kind of message carried by word order in the sentence, "Dogs hate cats." If we reversed the positions of the two nouns, we would be saying that cats do the hating and that dogs are hated by them. In more complicated sentences, various other kinds of relations between words may be marked simply by word order. It makes a good deal of difference, for example, whether we say, "Mr. Smith gave his secretary an assistant," or "Mr. Smith gave an assistant his secretary."

Word order can make a great difference in the meaning of briefer units, too. For instance, compare "red light" and "light red," noting that the position of *light* tells us whether the word is a noun or an adjective. Or compare the meanings of "high shoulder" and "shoulder high."

Sometimes, of course, alternative patterns available to us make little difference in the essential meaning but only in the style of speech or writing. It is just a bit more informal, perhaps, to say, "I called my friend up on the telephone" than to say, "I called up my friend on the telephone." Sometimes, differences in word order simply allow differences in emphasis. Instead of "He works there every night," we could call special attention to *there* by saying, "There he works every night."

Very often, however, there are no grammatically allowable alternative order patterns. If we want to speak of something as being *in the park* we must use those three words in exactly that order and no other. Sometimes, it is true, people choose deliberately to violate the English rules of word order (and other rules of grammar, too) for special effects. Poets often depart from the rules; deviations are especially prominent in the verse of E. E. Cummings, who writes, for instance, of "an only moon the with star."

**Function Words**

Another very important means of conveying grammatical meanings in English is the use of a fairly small number of words whose main job is to perform that function, and hence are called *function words*. These are words like *a, the, and, but, in, on, why, who,* and the verbal auxiliaries (*must, do, have, be,* etc.). Such words will be later classified in this Outline. Here it is appropriate only to make general observations about their characteristics. It has already been said that, relative to the whole English vocabulary, the number of function words is quite small. Since their uses group them into several classes, the members of each class are very limited indeed. Speakers of the language do not feel free to develop new function words as they do feel free to make new nouns, verbs, adjectives, and adverbs of the ordinary kind. Nor do we often lose such words from our vocabulary. One characteristic of function words is their stability in the language.

Another is the frequency of their use. Though there are few of them, we use them over and over again. They are absolutely indispensable, whatever other particular words we could get along without.

Most of them are "little words," that is, words of one syllable. Very few of them can be inflected. (The function words we call prepositions express grammatical meanings that in various other languages are regularly carried by inflections.) They usually do not take derivational affixes, either. Some of them, however, can be combined (that is, compounded) and yet retain their grammatical status. That is how we got such forms as *into, without,* and *also*.

Though function words vary a great deal in the amount of lexical meaning they may carry, ordinary dictionary definitions can only partially explain any of them. They can be fully accounted for only by explanation of the ways they are used in language structures. At least one of them appears to have absolutely no lexical meaning. The *to* which identifies certain uses of the base forms of verbs (as in *to have* and *to hold*) is simply "the sign of the infinitive."

**Intonation Patterns; Punctuation**

The fifth kind of signal systematically used to identify grammatical meanings in English speech is what will be called here *intonation patterns*. In this context, *intonation* will be used to refer to features of stress, pitch, and juncture.

GRAMMATICAL USES OF STRESS

One way variations in stress signal grammatical meanings can be heard in the sentences, "I suspect he will be late" and "The police arrested the suspect" or "His actions were suspect." When *suspect* has the heavier stress on the second syllable, it can be used as a verb; when the heavier stress is on the first syllable, it may be a noun or adjective. English has a number of words that show similar contrasts by stress placement.

More important, however, is the operation of contrasting stress patterns in marking different kinds of phrases. Thus, we can meaningfully say, "Blackberries are not always black berries," for the heavy stress on the first adjective (*black*) shows it to be part of the kind of phrase we call a compound noun. Note that the second adjective (*black*) has a secondary stress, while the noun that follows it takes the heaviest stress. Numerous stress patterns differentiate various phrase types.

In English, there are four structurally contrastive degrees of stress: primary (the heaviest), secondary, tertiary, and weak (the lightest).

GRAMMATICAL FUNCTIONS OF PITCH

There are four contrastive pitch levels, too. A speaker, under any particular circumstances, establishes his fundamental pitch level that (for the time being, at least) is recognized as normal for him. But at certain points, his pitch will drop enough lower so that a listener will notice the contrast; at others it is likely to rise enough above the normal tone to provide a different contrast. On some occasions, it may rise still higher to express certain special kinds of meaning. The significant pitch levels in speech are usually referred to by number, from 1 (the lowest) to 4 (the highest). The speaker's normal tone at any particular time, then, is Level 2. The levels can also be described as low, normal, high, and extra-high.

To recognize a few of the many ways variations in pitch level convey grammatical meanings, consider some possible expressions relating to a boy named Johnny. If his mother said, "Johnny came home early today," she might maintain her normal tone until the word *early,* when her pitch would probably rise to Level 3. Dropping back to the normal level for a moment, she would then let her voice fall toward Level 1 at the end of *today* — unless she wanted to emphasize the contrast between his behavior today and on other days, in which case her pitch would go up to Level 3 on the first part of *-day* and drop back to Level 2 at the end of the sentence.

But if Johnny's mother said to him, "Johnny, come home early today," her pitch would certainly go up to Level 3 at some point in saying *Johnny,* for that is part of our way of signaling the name of someone we are addressing. If, however, Johnny did something his mother heartily disapproved, she might address him in another fashion, striking Level 4 at the beginning of his name — perhaps dropping clear down to Level 1 at the end.

#### TYPES AND USES OF JUNCTURE

Pitch, stress, and timing all enter into another type of intonation signal we call juncture. The term *juncture* is related to the more familiar word *junction,* and it refers to our ways of joining units to each other.

##### *Internal Juncture*

There are two different types of juncture. What is called *internal juncture* often signals the end of one word which is to be followed by another in the same phrase. It is the feature of speech that, for example, distinguishes "an aim" from "a name." Or compare the pronunciations of "star dancers" and "starred answers." Observe that in the first phrase the *r* of *star* is prolonged a bit, is given a special kind of voice fade-away, and is followed by a little sliver of silence. In the second phrase, the *r* of *starred* is not so prominent; the *d* in the same word gets a pronunciation different from what it has at the beginning of the next word, and it is followed by a sliver of silence. In writing, the spaces between the words often (but not always) represent the internal junctures of speech.

##### *Terminal Junctures*

The second type of juncture is called *terminal juncture,* because it usually marks the end of a phrase, clause, or sentence. Terminal junctures are characterized by a somewhat clearer holding and fading of the final sounds, by contrasting treatments of pitch, and by relatively longer silence before the beginning of another speech unit.

There are three different kinds of terminal juncture. The first is called *level pitch juncture,* because the holding and fading at the end of the unit being concluded are produced on a single pitch. An example of this kind of terminal juncture can be heard in the sentence, "This is my book, I think." A level pitch juncture occurs here at the end of *book.*

Now, compare that sentence with these: "That is my book. I think it is very interesting." Here, the pitch goes downward at the end of *book;* the same kind of drop in pitch occurs at the end of *interesting. Falling pitch juncture* often marks the ends of sentences that are statements, though that is not its only use.

Finally, consider the question, "This is my book?" (equivalent to "Is this my book?"). Here the pitch at the end of *book* goes up, so we speak of the *rising pitch juncture* that closes this sentence. Questions that are not marked as such by other grammatical devices normally end with a rising pitch juncture. There are, of course, other uses of the rising pitch juncture.

### Punctuation Often Reflects the Junctures of Speech

In writing, punctuation marks often (but not always) are used where terminal junctures would occur in speech. This fact is illustrated in the examples given in the last three paragraphs. But notice that the correspondence between punctuation and speech junctures is not a simple and consistent one. The question mark does not always stand for rising pitch juncture. Falling pitch juncture may be marked by a semicolon as well as by a period. An exclamation mark often suggests special stress and pitch patterns earlier in the utterance as well as the appropriate terminal juncture.

It is also important to recognize that our conventions of writing allow the omission of juncture marks at many points, while at the same time they require punctuation of certain kinds that do not reflect anything heard in speech. If, for example, one writes the facts about his birth, he is expected to use such a form as the following: "I was born in Denver, Colorado, in May, 1952." But in speaking that sentence, he may not in fact use any terminal juncture between *Denver* and *Colorado* or between *May* and *1952.* Our writing system provides a very imperfect means of representing the intonation patterns of speech. Grammatical meanings are often less clearly signaled in writing; that is one reason why written expression needs to be more carefully controlled.

## THE PARTS OF SPEECH

The grammar of English allows us to use many different words in structurally similar ways. In explaining our grammar, or in just talking about it, we need to classify words on the bases of similarities in form and shared privileges of occurrence. We apply the term *parts of speech* to the most inclusive word classes we find it convenient to identify.

It has been traditional to speak of eight parts of speech: nouns, pronouns, adjectives, verbs, adverbs, prepositions, conjunctions, and interjections. The traditional classification will be generally followed here, but additional observations will be introduced. Function classes and interjections will be treated last.

It should be understood that we may use larger units (phrases and clauses) to perform many of the same jobs single words may perform. Another important fact is that our language often allows a particular word to belong to more than one class.

**Nouns**

Nouns are words having such forms and uses as may be exemplified by *man, girl, shyness,* and *Chicago.* With pronouns they share ability to be subjects, objects, and complements of verbs, as well as that of being the second elements in prepositional phrases. Many (but not all) nouns can be recognized because they can be modified by a special type of function words called noun determiners, such as *the, a* or *an, any, some, my, this* and *that.*

Some nouns (such as *shyness*) have distinctive derivational suffixes. Much more important in identifying nouns, however, is inflection for *number* and *case.*

NUMBER

Grammatical number in English simply distinguishes between one (the *singular*) and more than one (the *plural*). Regular noun plurals are formed by adding to the singular base one of the sounds represented in spelling by *-s* or that represented by *-es.* Compare *cups, dogs,* and *dishes.*

Regular plurals are usually spelled by adding *-s* to the singular form unless *-es* is required because the form ends in the spellings *-s* or *-ss, -x, -z, -sh, -ch,* or *-tch* (*glasses, axes, matches,* etc.). A few nouns ending in *-o* also take plurals in *-es* (*Negroes, heroes,* for example), but most do not. A few others ending in the sound of *f* drop the *-f* or *-fe* of the singular spelling and add *-ves* (*half* becomes *halves, knife* becomes *knives*). When the singular noun is spelled with a final *-y* preceded by a consonant letter or by *-qu-,* we change the *-y* to *i* and add *-es* (*flies, soliloquies,* but *monkeys*). Plurals of numbers, letters, graphic signs, and words cited as things rather than used for their meanings are represented by an apostrophe and *-s* (as *6's, M's, $'s, why's*).

Some nouns (such as *sheep, deer*) are unchanged in form even when they are used with plural verbs. We also have three kinds of quite irregular plural forms. (1) The plural of *ox* is *oxen.* (2) *Child* has the plural *children,* and *brother* has both the plural *brethren* and the more common *brothers.* (3) Seven nouns form their plurals by altering the internal vowels. These words are *man—men, woman—women, tooth—teeth, goose—geese, mouse—mice,* and *louse—lice.*

Nouns taken from other languages sometimes retain their foreign plurals; *phenomenon —phenomena* (from Greek), *basis—bases* and *alumnus—alumni* (from Latin), and *cherub—cherubim* (from Hebrew) are examples. Many such words are also given regular English plurals (as *cherubs*).

CASE

The singular and plural forms that have been exemplified here are said to be in the *subjective-objective case,* because they are typically used as subjects and objects of verbs. Most nouns can take another inflection to mark use in what is called the *possessive case.* An example can be seen in *a child's toy.* But this phrase may refer to a toy designed for a child (it may be somebody else's property). The possessive case can carry various meanings. The forms can be used as modifiers of other nouns.

In speech, singular nouns are made possessive by addition of exactly the same sounds as would be expected in the formation of regular plurals; in writing, the singular possessives are uniformly identified by an apostrophe and the letter *s.* An occasional exception is made for a proper noun that already ends in an *s* sound: we may speak and write of *Keats' poems.*

In speech, plural nouns that already end in an *s* or *z* sound are given no distinctive possessive form, but when they are used in possessive functions they are marked in writing by a final apostrophe (example: *a ladies' maid*). Irregular plurals, however, are made possessive, in both speech and writing, in the same ways singular nouns are.

DECLENSION

The whole set of inflectional forms a noun may be given is called its *declension.* Declensions of four nouns are tabulated here.

| | | | | |
|---|---|---|---|---|
| | | SINGULAR | | |
| *Subj.-obj.* | man | girl | family | wife |
| *Possessive* | man's | girl's | family's | wife's |
| | | PLURAL | | |
| *Subj.-obj.* | men | girls | families | wives |
| *Possessive* | men's | girls' | families' | wives' |

PROPER NOUNS

The names of particular persons, places, or things (*Plato, Chicago, the Eiffel Tower*) are called *proper nouns.* They can be given possessive inflection, but since a particular person, place, or thing is singular, they cannot be pluralized. Nor can they be modified by such words as *a, any,* or *two.* If we speak of "a Plato of the modern age," *Plato* ceases to be a proper noun.

In writing, we capitalize proper nouns as

well as (usually) words made out of them: *Platonic, Chicagoans*.

#### COMMON NOUNS

Common nouns are all those not proper nouns. An unmodified common noun can refer only to a class or some kind of category.

*Count Nouns*

Common nouns readily modified by numbers or words like *few* and *many* are count nouns. They can usually be given both plural and possessive inflections.

*Mass Nouns*

Contrasting with count nouns, mass nouns designate abstract qualities or substances that have extent or bulk but are not associated with numbers. We speak of *a little music* or *much shyness*, but not of *two musics* or *many shynesses*. Mass nouns are not pluralized, though most of them can take possessive inflection. A word is sometimes a mass noun in one of its senses and a count noun in another.

*Collective Nouns*

Count nouns that name groups we think of as collections of individuals are called *collective nouns*. Their special privilege is that their singular forms can be subjects of either singular or plural verbs, depending on whether attention is focused on the group unit or on the individuals in it. Examples: *The family often goes picnicking. The family were going their separate ways.*

#### GENDER

In English, what we call gender of nouns is wholly dependent on our system of referring to them by use of *he* (masculine), *she* (feminine), or *it* (neuter). English gender is mainly concerned with whether what is referred to is male or female in sex, or is not an animal possessing sex. But we often speak of animals—and babies—whose sex is unidentified (by us, at least), and so we use the reference word *it*: *The bird fluttered its wings.* We also often personify inanimate objects and refer to them with *he*, or *she*.

### Adjectives

Adjectives may modify nouns or pronouns, but so do several other kinds of words. Adjectives are such words as can be used in both the positions occupied by *happy* in the sentence, *The happy man is very happy*. Other sentences like this but with a different noun and different qualifiers (such as *quite* or *more*) will suggest many of our adjectives. Inflected forms of adjectives, however, do not normally follow *very* or any other qualifier.

Adjectives of one syllable and many of those with two can be inflected by addition of the sounds we represent in spelling by *-er* and *-est*. The uninflected form (for example, *red*) shows the *positive degree;* inflection with *-er* (*redder*) shows the *comparative degree;* inflection with *-est* (*reddest*) shows the *superlative degree.*

#### COMPARISON OF ADJECTIVES

Inflection of the kind just described is called *comparison*. The comparison of some adjectives is irregular. *Good*, for example, is inflected as *better* and *best*. Both *bad* and *ill* (in the sense "not in good health") have the comparative and superlative forms *worse* and *worst*. *Well* (meaning "not ill") has the comparative *better*, but no superlative. *Old* may be inflected either as *elder, eldest* or *older, oldest*.

Most adjectives of more than two syllables are uninflected but are used with the qualifiers *more* and *most*, which express the comparative and superlative notions. Sometimes we have a choice between inflection and use of these words (*lovelier* or *more lovely, loveliest* or *most lovely*).

### Verbs

Verbs are typically used to make assertions or ask questions about subjects of clauses or sentences. They operate as do *seems, lived*, and *want* in the following sentences: *Betty seems happy. Indians lived here. The boys want a job.*

Verbs are said to be inflected for *person, number, mood*, and *tense*. Two types of forms called *participles* indicate special kinds of syntactic uses to which they may be assigned.

#### INFLECTION FOR PERSON AND NUMBER

Most verbs in the present tense of the indicative mood are given an inflection to produce forms which must be used with the subjects *he, she, it*, or any other subjects these words can refer to. Such subjects are described as third person singulars.

The inflection of verbs for the third person singular of the present indicative is almost completely regular. It simply adds to the base form (such as *walk, play, watch*) one of the three sounds we represent in spelling by *-s* or *-es* (*walks, plays, watches*) according to the same rules as apply to normal noun plurals. Such forms as *does, says*, and *has* are exceptional.

The irregular verb *be* has five different forms that mark contrasts in person and number. See the tabular illustration of conjugation later given here.

#### MOOD

Earlier English made elaborate inflectional distinctions between *indicative* uses of verbs (to express independent statements or questions assumed to be factual), *subjunctive* uses (expressing wishes, suppositions, possibilities, and related notions), and *imperative* uses (expressing requests and commands). Verbs, then, were said to have three *moods* (or *modes*).

In present-day English, imperative notions

are expressed in syntactic patterns that uniformly use the verb form we call the infinitive (or "name form"). Examples: *Be a good girl. Come here.*

We now have only three inflective contrasts in verb forms to mark subjunctive uses. One not frequently used is *be* in the present tense, as in *Be it ever so humble, there's no place like home.* The second is a past tense subjunctive that employs *were* where otherwise we would expect *was.* Example: *If I were a king. . . .* Much more frequent is a third type of subjunctive form, the base or "name form" of the verb used in positions that normally require the third person singular. This subjunctive often follows main verbs such as *ask, demand, suggest.* Example: *The principal suggested that Tom come early.*

#### TENSE

We have only two inflected tenses in English, the *present* and the *past.* There are, of course, numerous ways of referring to past, present, or future time. A present tense verb may refer to the future, as in *We play Howard High next Friday.* Present tense forms may refer to past time continuing into the present, as in *John studies hard.* We also make various types of reference to time in verb phrases such as *has walked, had been studying, am working, may go, will come.*

Present tense verb forms are all those that are not marked as belonging to the past tense. Past tense *finite* forms (those that can make independent assertions when associated with grammatical subjects) show inflection in regular and irregular ways. The regular inflection adds the sounds of *t, d,* or *ed* to the base forms of verbs. If the base ends in the sound of *t* or *d,* we add the full syllable (*-ed*). If the base ends in the sound of *k, f, p, s, sh, tch,* or *th* as in *path,* we add the sound of *t.* To all other bases of regular verbs we add the sound of *d.*

In writing, we spell the past tense finite forms of regular verbs by adding *-ed* to the base forms of all of them — unless the base already ends in *e,* in which case we simply add *-d.* Some bases ending in a single consonant letter double the consonant before taking the inflectional suffix. See rules of spelling outlined later.

##### *Irregular Past Tense Forms*

More than a hundred verbs in common use have irregular finite past tense forms. Some eighteen (like *cut* and *put*) do not change forms for past tense uses. Some add the sound and spelling *-t* and also show internal changes (*creep — crept, teach — taught,* for example). Some whose bases end in *-d* simply change that sound and letter to *-t* (*bend — bent, build — built*). Others (called *strong verbs*) mark past tense forms only by changes in internal vowels (examples: *come — came, run — ran, write — wrote*). The most irregular of all is *be,* which has two past tense forms.

#### NONFINITE FORMS

Three types of verb forms cannot make independent assertions about grammatical subjects. They are called *nonfinite* because they are not limited in application to a particular grammatical person or number.

##### *The Infinitive*

The only inflectionally distinct infinitive in present-day English is *be.* Some characteristic uses are illustrated in *Fred may be here* and *Fred wants to be here.* Note that *be* is often, but not always, associated with *to,* which in this use is called the *infinitive marker.* Forms of other verbs are infinitives when used as *be* and *to be* typically are.

##### *Present Participles*

Present participles all have the distinctive inflectional suffix we spell as *-ing.* See the rules of spelling outlined later about doubling of final consonants in some bases to which this suffix is added. When the spelling of the base ends in a silent *-e,* we normally drop it before adding *-ing.* If the base ends in *-ie,* we usually substitute *y* for those two letters (*die — dying*); such substitution sometimes leads us to break the rule about dropping the silent *-e,* to prevent confusion (*dye — dyeing*).

Present participles typically combine with other verb forms to make up verb phrases (as in *Tom is working, was working, had been working, and will be working*).

##### *Past Participles*

The verb forms *been, broken,* and *done* are *past participles.* They typically operate as parts of verb phrases (as in *had been working*). Verb forms that function in ways characteristic of these examples are past participles, even if they do not have distinctive inflections.

None of our regular verbs have past participial forms distinct from past tense finite forms. Verbs having special forms produce them in four different ways. They may add the sound of *n* or *en* (sometimes spelled *-ne*) to the base form (examples: *seen, taken, gone*). They may add the same suffix to the finite past tense form (*forgotten, stolen*). They may add the suffix to forms with vowel sounds different from those of either the base or the finite past tense (*ridden, written*). Or they may have past participles distinct from the base and the finite past tense only because of difference in internal vowels (as in *begun, rung*).

#### CONJUGATION OF VERBS

The full set of forms a verb may have is called its *conjugation.* Four verbs will be conjugated here. The imperative mood will not be represented, for the forms said to be imperative are always the same as the infinitives.

NONFINITE FORMS

| | | | | |
|---|---|---|---|---|
| Infinitive: | be | ride | pull | cut |
| Participles | | | | |
| Present: | being | riding | pulling | cutting |
| Past: | been | ridden | pulled | cut |

FINITE FORMS OF *be*

Indicative —

| | Present Tense: *Singular* | *Plural* | Past Tense: *Singular* | *Plural* |
|---|---|---|---|---|
| 1. | I am | We are | I was | We were |
| 2. | You are | You are | You were | You were |
| 3. | He, She, It is | They are | He, She, It was | They were |

Subjunctive —

| Present Tense | Past Tense |
|---|---|
| All persons and numbers: *be* | All persons and numbers: *were* |

FINITE FORMS OF *ride*

Indicative —

| | Present Tense: *Singular* | *Plural* | Past Tense: *Singular* | *Plural* |
|---|---|---|---|---|
| 1. | I ride | We ride | I rode | We rode |
| 2. | You ride | You ride | You rode | You rode |
| 3. | He, She, It rides | They ride | He, She, It rode | They rode |

Subjunctive — contrasting form only in 3rd person singular of present tense: *ride*

FINITE FORMS OF *pull*

Indicative —

| | Present Tense: *Singular* | *Plural* | Past Tense: *Singular* | *Plural* |
|---|---|---|---|---|
| 1. | I pull | We pull | I pulled | We pulled |
| 2. | You pull | You pull | You pulled | You pulled |
| 3. | He, She, It pulls | They pull | He, She, It pulled | They pulled |

Subjunctive — contrasting form only in 3rd person singular of present tense: *pull*

FINITE FORMS OF *cut*

Indicative —

| | Present Tense: *Singular* | *Plural* | Past Tense: *Singular* | *Plural* |
|---|---|---|---|---|
| 1. | I cut | We cut | I cut | We cut |
| 2. | You cut | You cut | You cut | You cut |
| 3. | He, She, It cuts | They cut | He, She, It cut | They cut |

Subjunctive — contrasting form only in 3rd person singular of present tense: *cut*

### SUBCLASSES OF VERBS

Many features of English syntax relate to differences in the subclasses of verbs.

#### *Transitive Verbs*

Fully transitive verbs can take objects that are privileged to become subjects of the same verbs in what we call *passive constructions.* Thus, the same idea can be expressed in either *Pete hit Jerry* (active) or *Jerry was hit by Pete* (passive).

*Middle verbs.* Some verbs can take objects that cannot become their subjects in passive constructions. We can say, "The football cost ten dollars," but cannot comfortably say, "Ten dollars was cost by the football." Verbs of this sort (other examples: *weigh* and *have*) are called *middle verbs.*

*Factitive verbs.* A few transitive verbs (such as *elect, make, call, consider*) have the privilege of being followed by both a direct object and an object complement — that is, a word or phrase describing, or identifying what is named by the object, or indicating a changed status for it. Such verbs are called *factitive verbs.* An example is seen in *Let's elect Mary secretary,* where *secretary* is the object complement.

#### *Intransitive Verbs*

Intransitive verbs are simply verbs that do not have objects. *Lived* is transitive in *Cicero lived a dangerous life,* but it is intransitive in *Cicero lived dangerously.* Some verbs (like *be* and *seem*) are always intransitive; others are intransitive in only some of their senses.

#### *Linking Verbs*

Linking verbs (sometimes called *copulatives*) are not followed by objects but by words or phrases that identify, classify, or describe their subjects. *Became* and *felt* are linking verbs in *Ted became a hero* and *Joan felt happy.* In those sentences, the noun *hero* and the adjective *happy* are called *subjective complements.* The linking verb *be* has the unique privilege of being followed by adverbs of location that operate much as subjective complements do.

#### *Two-Part Verbs*

English makes use of a good many word combinations that operate as single verbal units. These units have two parts, the first being a verb form, the second being a word (or sometimes more than one word) that is commonly used as a preposition or adverb. An example of such a two-part verb is *look up* in the sentence, *Look up that word in the dictionary.* Notice the difference in meaning when *look* is followed by an ordinary prepositional phrase, as in *Look up the street.*

There are two types of two-part verbs. One type is always used transitively. It is characterized by the fact that its second part is a preposition that immediately follows the verb form and cannot be separated from it. Examples are *speak to* (*The Senator will speak to the issue*), *think about* (*We thought about the problem*), *seek after* (*Man should seek after righteousness*), and *look at* (*He looked at the situation carefully*). Observe that if the sample sentences are made passive, the prepositions are kept with the verbs: *Righteousness should be sought after. The situation was looked at carefully.*

A second type may be called *separable two-part verbs.* These units are composed of verb forms and prepositions or adverbs (often called *particles*) that may immediately follow the verb or may be placed after an intervening nominal. An example of this type has already been given in the expression *look up*. Notice that instead of the sentence that was offered to illustrate its use, we could as easily say, *Look that word up in the dictionary*. Similarly, we can say either *Bring in the laundry* or *Bring the laundry in.* A special rule, however, requires us always to place the particle after a pronoun that is the object of the verb. We may say, *I wore out my coat* or *I wore my coat out;* but *I wore it out* is the only possibility if we use the pronoun. The separable two-part verbs are generally used as transitives, but they can be used intransitively, too. Examples of intransitive uses: *The coat wore out. He fought hard, but he finally gave up.*

*Verbal Auxiliaries*

A few very special verbs operate systematically as nonfinal elements in verb phrases such as *is going, does go, may have gone*. Such verbs, which help define the grammatical meaning of other verbs are our verbal auxiliaries (sometimes called *helping verbs*). They all share the exclusive privilege of combining with *not* in such contractions as *isn't, won't,* and *oughtn't.* Auxiliaries are one type of function words.

*Modal auxiliaries.* A subgroup of verbal auxiliaries cannot carry notions of person and number. Members of this subgroup are called *modal auxiliaries,* because they express kinds of ideas long ago marked by inflection for the subjunctive mood (or mode). Two of them (*must* and *ought*) have no contrasting forms relating to tense. The present and past tense forms of others that are most common are *can — could, may — might, will — would, shall — should.* Modal auxiliaries have no infinitives or participles.

**Adverbs**

Adverbs are modifiers that answer such questions as Where? When? How? but not such questions as Who? and What? Adverbs are sometimes called *movables,* because most of them can be readily shifted from one position in a sentence to another. Yet a typical position for them is the stressed one immediately following an object of a transitive verb. Finishing with single words such sentences as "John drove his car___________" will suggest many of our adverbs (*away, out, slow* or *slowly, fast, home, carefully, sometimes,* etc.).

The suffix *-ly* regularly makes adverbs out of adjectives, but it is not attached to adjectives that already (like *manly*) end in *-ly*. Some other affixes characteristic of adverbs are *-ward(s)* (*backwards, homeward*), *-wise* (*lengthwise, crabwise*), and *a-* (*aloud, afar*).

COMPARISON OF ADVERBS

Most adverbs take no inflection, but a few are inflected to show comparative and superlative degrees. The regular inflection is like that of adjectives (*often — oftener — oftenest*). A few adverbs have quite irregular inflectional series. The other forms of the adverb *well* are *better* and *best.* Both *badly* and the adverb *ill* have *worse* as the comparative, *worst* as the superlative.

Adverbs that are not inflected can often be compared by associating them with the qualifiers *more* and *most.* Other qualifiers (like *less, least, very*) may also modify them. But some common adverbs (such as *perhaps, still, then, there, thus*) cannot be qualified.

Of the several ways of classifying adverbs, the most useful divides them into those of location (replaceable by *there*), of time (replaceable by *then*), and of manner (replaceable by *thus*). To these subclasses, we must add a miscellaneous group including such words as *perhaps.* Some words traditionally called adverbs are here treated as members of function classes.

**Pronouns**

Pronouns are a special set of words systematically used to refer to or take the place of nouns, noun phrases, or noun clauses. Pronouns cannot be modified by such words as *a* or *an, the,* or *five. He* is a noun in *The cat is a he.* Although some kinds of pronouns are highly inflected, they constitute a class of function words.

SUBCLASSES OF PRONOUNS

Grammar books differ in their identification of subclasses of pronouns. Certain words sometimes called pronouns are here assigned to other function classes.

*Personal Pronouns*

A major subclass is that called *personal pronouns* because its members have different forms to refer to the person speaking (called *first person*) the person spoken to (called *second person*), and whatever is spoken about (called *third person*). There are distinctive singular and plural forms for each person except the second. (The older second person singular forms — *thou, thee, thy, thine* — are seldom used.) In the third person, distinct forms show whether what is referred to is male, female, or without sex (at least that is identified).

Personal pronouns have two unique inflectional features: (1) all except *you* and *it* have objective forms (typically used as objects of verbs and in prepositional phrases); (2) all except *he* and *it* have two possessive forms, the first used to precede nouns that they modify, the second used independently (as in *That book is ours*).

*Declension of personal pronouns.* Personal pronouns are declined as follows:

SINGULAR

| | *Subj.* | *Obj.* | *1st poss.* | *2nd poss.* |
|---|---|---|---|---|
| 1st pers. | I | me | my | mine |
| 2nd pers. | you | you | your | yours |
| 3rd pers. | | | | |
| Masc. | he | him | his | his |
| Fem. | she | her | her | hers |
| Neut. | it | it | its | — |

PLURAL

| | | | | |
|---|---|---|---|---|
| 1st pers. | we | us | our | ours |
| 2nd pers. | you | you | your | yours |
| 3rd pers. | they | them | their | theirs |

In writing, we are expected to capitalize *I*. Note, too, that writing conventions *never* employ an apostrophe in the spelling of possessive forms of personal pronouns.

*Reflexives and Intensives*

The words *myself, yourself, himself, herself, itself, ourselves, yourselves,* and *themselves* are reflexive pronouns in such sentences as *John cut himself;* they are intensives when used in such constructions as *John himself cut the watermelon.*

*Relative Pronouns*

The simple relative pronouns are *who, which, that,* and *what* (in the sense of "that or those which"). *Who,* a word confined to reference to human beings or beings regarded as having personality, has the objective form *whom. Whose* is used as the possessive form of *who, which,* or *that.*

Relative pronouns introduce dependent clauses and link them with another element in the sentence, while at the same time they operate as subjects or objects (or, in the case of *whose,* sometimes as modifiers) within the clauses they introduce. Examples: *Here is the man who won the election. Tom knew what he wanted. We bought a house whose roof leaked.*

In the first of those examples, *the man* is said to be the *antecedent* of the relative *who,* for it is what the pronoun refers to. Relative pronouns are said to be *definite* if they have expressed antecedents or if *whose* modifies an expressed noun. *What* is an *indefinite relative* because its antecedent is not expressed. Other indefinite relatives have been produced by compounding *who, which,* and *what* with *-ever* and *-soever.*

*Indefinite Pronouns*

When *one* has the sense of "a person" (as in *One hardly knows what to think*) it may be regarded as an indefinite pronoun. We can put *none* in the same subclass. Some grammarians also include such phrasal compounds as *everybody, anybody, anyone,* and *nothing.*

*Reciprocal Pronouns*

For convenience, we can refer to the phrases *each other* and *one another* as *reciprocal pronouns.* They are used as objects of some verbs that have plural subjects, as in *The boys helped each other.*

**Prepositions**

Words used as *with* is in *He wants to go with me* are called *prepositions.* They typically introduce phrases which they link in modifying relations with other words or word groups. A preposition may relate a clause to some other part of the sentence, and when it does, it may be placed either at the beginning or the end. Instead of *It was a gift for which I longed,* we may say more informally either *It was a gift which* (or *that*) *I longed for* or *It was a gift I longed for.*

When personal pronouns are the second element in a prepositional phrase, they *must* have the objective form (as in *for him, to me*). By far the most common prepositions are *at, by, on, in, to, from, of, for,* and *with.* In other uses, some of these words are adverbs.

**Conjunctions**

Relative pronouns and prepositions share connective functions with words called *conjunctions.* But unlike relative pronouns, conjunctions cannot operate as subjects, objects, or modifiers in clauses with which they are associated. Unlike prepositions, they do not require personal pronouns following them to be in the objective case, and they never appear as the last word in a well-formed clause or sentence.

COORDINATING CONJUNCTIONS

A coordinating conjunction connects two grammatically equivalent units and is always placed between the units it joins. *And* is always a coordinating conjunction; other words frequently so used are *but, for, so.*

To illustrate the limitations on use of coordinating conjunctions, note first that one is not expected to say, "We went fishing and to hunt," for a participial form and an infinitive are not grammatically equivalent. One may say, "We went hunting and fishing," but not "We went and fishing hunting," for a coordinating conjunction must come *between* the units it joins.

#### CORRELATIVE CONJUNCTIONS

Certain pairs of words whose second members operate like coordinating conjunctions are called *correlatives.* Examples are *both . . . and, not . . . but, either . . . or, neither . . . nor.* The first member of the pair precedes the first of the two grammatically equivalent units to be joined, as in *Neither Jack nor his parents were happy.* When the units joined are subjects of a verb, the grammatical number of the verb usually agrees with that of the last unit.

#### SUBORDINATING CONJUNCTIONS

Subordinating conjunctions introduce dependent clauses that function in a sentence as nouns or adverbs do. Unlike coordinating conjunctions, they and the clauses they introduce may usually either precede the other units to which they are joined (as in *If the weather is nice, I will go*), or follow them (as in *I will go if the weather is nice*).

Subordinating conjunctions introducing noun clauses are words such as *that* (as in *That it will snow is certain*), *whether, when, why, how.* Those that introduce adverbial clauses are exemplified by *when, because, although, if, so,* and *where.* Comparison is expressed by *than* after adjectives or adverbs in the comparative degree, *as* after an earlier *as,* and *that* after a preceding *such* or *so.*

### Other Function Classes

By emphasizing some features of their form, function, or meaning, almost all our words could be squeezed into the seven major categories that have already been discussed. But because several sets of words operate in very special ways, they will be dealt with separately.

#### NOUN DETERMINERS

Some words always appear to say, "A noun is coming." *The, a* or *an, my, your, our,* and *their* are never normally used without being followed by nouns that we understand to be associated with them. They can, therefore, be called *noun determiners.* Other words that often operate as determiners are *any, every, each, some, no, this* and *that* (and their plurals), as well as most possessive forms. Note that only a single determiner can stand before a noun (we cannot say *The any mother*), though ordinary adjectives can be readily piled up in front of it (as in *a kind, gentle, thoughtful mother*).

Among determiners, *the* is known as the *definite article* because it carries the sense of pointing to something particular — often, to what has been mentioned. *A* and *an* are forms of what we call the *indefinite article* because it only indicates that the noun it is associated with applies to one of several members in a class named.

#### PREDETERMINERS AND POSTDETERMINERS

Only words of a special set have the privilege of immediately preceding noun determiners. Such words, called *predeterminers,* are exemplified by *all, both,* and *just.* We can say, "All the kind mothers. . . ." We cannot say, "Kind the mothers. . . ."

Another special set of words has the privilege of immediately following determiners or of taking their place (as predeterminers can also). These words, called *postdeterminers* consist of the ordinal numerals (together with *next, last,* and *final*), cardinal numerals, and the words *several, many, few, more, most, fewer, fewest, less,* and *least.* Like some of the predeterminers, postdeterminers can be piled up if they are arranged in proper order. We may say, "All the last five least kind mothers. . . ."

#### QUALIFIERS

Just as determiners announce the coming of a noun, so our word *very* almost always tells that an adjective or adverb should be expected at some not too distant point in the sentence. Words that operate as *very* does in *I am very happy* or *John drives very carefully* are called *qualifiers.* Other words of this type are *rather, quite, somewhat, more, most, less,* and *least.* Some qualifiers, such as *really, surely, fairly,* have the common adverbial suffix.

#### QUESTION WORDS

Questions that cannot be answered with *yes* or *no* are typically introduced by words such as *who, which, what, how, why, when, where,* etc. Since the function they all perform in introducing questions is so distinct, it seems useful to class them as *question words.* The question word *who* has the possessive form *whose* (*Whose is the red car?*) and the objective form *whom* (*Whom should we elect?*).

#### EXPLETIVES

Sometimes speakers wish to withhold for a moment the subject of a verb, shifting it from the normal position preceding the verb to one following it. When the verb is appropriate, it is possible to do that by placing the empty word *there* in the position usually occupied by the subject. *Four boys are here* may become *There are four boys here.* Obviously, the *there* in that last sentence is a mere spacefiller; it is therefore called an *expletive.*

The word *it* can also be used as an expletive in such a sentence as *It is true that I was tardy.*

The equivalent sentence in normal order would be *That I was tardy is true.*

SENTENCE-CONNECTORS

Words like *therefore, moreover, nevertheless, however,* and *thus* have the typical function of linking sentences or independent clauses while expressing notions quite different from those of coordinating conjunctions. They can be called *sentence-connectors,* though they have also been labeled *conjunctive adverbs.* Unlike subordinating conjunctions, they must appear in the second of the two syntactic units they join. Unlike coordinating conjunctions, they have the privilege of occupying various positions in the clause they appear in. Thus, we may say, "Mary was ill. Nevertheless, she went to school," or "She nevertheless went to school," or "She went to school, nevertheless."

AFFIRMERS AND DENIERS

*Yes* and *no* as they are used at the beginnings of sentences (or by themselves in responses) are often regarded as special adverbs, but they can be usefully classed as affirmers and deniers. Other expressions that would go in the same class are the *yeah* of speech (seldom used in writing), *okay, all right,* and the *nope* of speech.

THE NEGATOR: *not*

Though it shares some of the uses of adjectives and adverbs, *not* is quite different from them in its privileges. We cannot say, "John drove his car not," or "The men were fat, happy, and not." This word in most of its uses can conveniently be called *the negator.*

THE INFINITIVE-MARKER: *to*

The "sign of the infinitive," *to,* can be called *the infinitive-marker.*

ATTENTION-CLAIMERS

Greetings such as "Hi!" or "Hello" and empty words like *oh* and *well* that sometimes open sentences in speech may, as a group, be called *attention-claimers.* When *well* (like *uh*) is merely a sound to fill time while the speaker organizes his ideas, it might be called a *hesitator.*

**Interjections**

The class of words called *interjections* is not parallel with other "parts of speech." Like attention-claimers, interjections actually are syntactically isolated from sentences (though they may be loosely attached to them). They are generally described as expressions loaded with emotion of one kind or another. Any word, then, can be an interjection if it is so loaded. A very limited number of words are characteristically interjections. Among them are such expressions as *ouch, phooey,* and *alas,* as well as "swear words" and their disguised forms like *cripes, gosh,* and *golly.* Phrases such as *gee whiz* and *for crying out loud* also act as interjections in speech. It hardly need be said that most of the examples given here are seldom found in literary English, except when very informal speech is being represented. There are, of course, interjections (like *alas*) that are often seen in writing but seldom heard, and some (like *ah* or *aha*) that fit comfortably into both speech and writing.

## SYNTAX

Facts about syntax were constantly involved in classifying words as parts of speech. Here a brief account will be given of ways words may be arranged to construct phrases, clauses, and sentences.

**Phrases**

Current discussions of grammar often refer to one-word phrases, but traditionally, a phrase has been defined as a group of words making up a syntactic unit that is not a subject-predicate structure. *Babies grow* is a clause, not a phrase. *Babies the* is not a phrase, for these words in this order cannot work as a unit in any syntactic structure. *All the babies* is a phrase, for these words could, for instance, replace *Babies* in the clause, *Babies grow.*

A phrase may be part of another phrase or other structural unit. *The babies* is a phrase within *all the babies.* Phrases used as nouns can be called *noun* (or *nominal*) *phrases.* We also have *verb* (or *verbal*) *phrases, adjective* (or *adjectival*) *phrases,* and *adverb* (or *adverbial*) *phrases.* Some kinds of phrases take names from particular types of words in them, as *prepositional* (*with me*), *infinitive* or *infinitival* (*to go, to have been*), and *participial* (*going home* or *beaten biscuits*). Infinitive and participial phrases may be either nominal, adjectival, or adverbial; prepositional phrases are normally adjectival or adverbial.

AUXILIARY VERB PHRASES

Verb phrases of a particularly important kind have a principal verb preceded by auxiliaries in rigidly controlled patterns.

*Basic Active Auxiliary Verb Phrases*

Auxiliary verb phrases in the active voice that do not employ the auxiliary *do* may be called *basic.* Auxiliaries used in them are the modals (which require a following infinitive form), forms of *have* (which require an immediately following past participle), and forms of *be* (which require an immediately following present participle).

The range of possibilities is shown in the following table, where the common descriptive label is applied to each construction. Note that the idea of tense is carried in the first member of each phrase.

| | |
|---|---|
| will go | : FUTURE |
| has gone | : PRESENT PERFECT |
| had gone | : PAST PERFECT |
| will have gone | : FUTURE PERFECT |
| is going | : PRESENT PROGRESSIVE |
| was going | : PAST PROGRESSIVE |
| will be going | : FUTURE PROGRESSIVE |
| has been going | : PRES. PERF. PROGRESSIVE |
| had been going | : PAST PERF. PROGRESSIVE |
| will have been going | : FUT. PERF. PROGRESSIVE |

Passive verb phrases and those using forms of *do* will be identified later.

**Clauses**

When a grammatical subject is properly tied (by form and position) to a finite verbal expression to form a subject-predicate structure, we have what we call a *clause. Babies grow* is a clause; so is *Some of the gardeners grow flowers.* If, as in these examples, the clause is not a subordinate unit in a larger syntactic structure, it is said to be *independent.*

DEPENDENT CLAUSES

If we say *when babies grow,* the clause has been subordinated by *when;* we would expect it to be normally attached to some other element in a sentence, as in *Mothers are pleased when babies grow.* Such a subordinated clause is called *dependent.*

Dependent clauses may be adverbial, as in the example above, or they may be adjectival (as in *We made the statement that babies grow*), or they may be nominal (as in *We observe that babies grow,* where the dependent clause is the direct object of *observe*).

**What Is a Sentence?**

The term *sentence* has been used in so many different ways that it is impossible to provide a definition of it that is both brief and adequate. There is not much point in saying a sentence is an arrangement of words that expresses a complete thought until someone is willing (and able) to define "a complete thought." Grammarians who attempt to define this latter term turn out to be saying, not very helpfully, that a complete thought is what a sentence expresses.

It is true, however, that a notion of *grammatical* completeness is involved in our identification of sentences. That kind of completeness is often signaled in speech by at least momentary silence immediately preceding a sentence and a rising pitch or falling pitch juncture at the end of it. Such boundaries are usually marked in writing by a capital letter at the beginning and a period, question mark, or exclamation point at the end. But boundary signals of these kinds can also be given to expressions that are not sentences or that (if we wish to use such a label) are badly-formed sentences.

One kind of definition describes a complete and correct English sentence as consisting of *a well-formed independent clause, which may have attached to it (in proper grammatical fashion) one or more other well-formed independent clauses, any of the independent clauses being capable of having well-formed subordinate clauses attached to them in grammatically acceptable ways.* Though cumbersome, this description is useful, for it gives an account of the kind of expression that conforms to a fundamental concept held by normal users of English. We could limit our use of the term *sentence* to apply only to expressions covered by this definition. But if we do, we shall have to find some other term to apply to perfectly acceptable expressions such as "Come here," "Good morning," or "Because he was late" as an answer to such a question as "Why didn't Johnny understand the assignment?" We can say, of course, that these are sentence fragments, and that they are acceptable fragments when they operate in communication just as a standard sentence would.

Another shortcoming in the definition is that it doesn't tell us what "well-formed" clauses are, and it doesn't throw any light on "grammatically acceptable ways." In an importance sense, any definition of *sentences* must depend on a comprehensive account of the grammar of the language. It will be most useful here to identify and try to explain some of the common English sentence types and the structures that may appear in them.

**Sentences: Basic Patterns**

A sentence may consist of a single independent clause; that would be called a *simple sentence.* A sentence that makes a statement is called *declarative.* Many more complicated structures may possibly be best explained on the basis of patterns in a small set of simple declarative sentences that will here, for convenience, be called *kernels.*

The three basic types of kernel sentences to be identified here are active (not passive) and affirmative. Ordinary adjectives appear only in predicates of one of the types, but nouns may be directly modified by determiners, predeterminers, and postdeterminers. Adjectives and adverbs in them may be modified only by qualifiers.

There are two major positions in the kernels, the first occupied by a subject, the second by a predicate. Within the predicate, there are three positions, the first of which is always occupied by a finite verbal expression. The verbal expression controls what fits into the second predicate position. The third position need not be filled, but it may be occupied by one or more adverbs or adverbial phrases.

The positions in kernels are represented in the following diagram, where major slots are marked by Roman numerals and predicate positions are labeled with Arabic numbers. The parentheses mark a position that may or may not be filled.

| I | II | | |
|---|---|---|---|
| | 1 | 2 | (3) |
| Subject | Predicate | | |

TYPE I KERNEL: INTRANSITIVE VERBS

In a Type I kernel the first predicate position is filled by an intransitive verb that is *not* a linking verb. The second predicate position is not filled. Examples, with position units labeled:

| *Babies* | *grow.* |
|---|---|
| I | II-1 |

| *Babies* | *grow* | *rapidly in the first few days.* |
|---|---|---|
| I | II-1 | II-3 |

TYPE II KERNEL: LINKING VERBS

Linking verbs fill the first predicate position in Type II kernels. The second predicate position must be filled by nouns or adjectives — with one exception. If the verb is a form of *be,* the second predicate position may be occupied by an adverb (or adverbial phrase) of location. Examples:

| *Babies* | *become* | *adults.* |
|---|---|---|
| I | II-1 | II-2 |

| *All the girls* | *may have been* | *happy* | *here.* |
|---|---|---|---|
| I | II-1 | II-2 | II-3 |

| *Ted* | *will be* | *at home* | *later.* |
|---|---|---|---|
| I | II-1 | II-2 | II-3 |

TYPE III KERNELS: TRANSITIVE VERBS

Transitive verbs are used in Type III kernels; they must be followed in the second predicate position by direct-object nominals. Examples:

| *The boy* | *lost* | *a dollar.* |
|---|---|---|
| I | II-1 | II-2 |

| *Father* | *will buy* | *a bicycle* | *for Joe.* |
|---|---|---|---|
| I | II-1 | II-2 | II-3 |

## Sentences: Simple Derived Constructions

Many other constructions can be derived from kernel patterns. The last Type III sentence above, for example, could be rewritten as *Father will buy Joe a bicycle.* Here, *Joe* is what we call an *indirect object.*

PASSIVE CONSTRUCTIONS

We can make passive phrases out of most (but not all) verbs that fit into Type III kernels by using a past participial form of the principal verb and preceding it with a proper form of *be* as an auxiliary. The most elaborated passive possible is illustrated by *will have been being bought.*

To form a passive clause from a Type III kernel, we may shift the direct object to the subject position, either suppressing the original subject or placing it at the end, in a phrase introduced with the preposition *by.* Thus, we may say *A dollar was lost* or *A dollar was lost by the boy.* Or, retaining a direct object in its normal position, we may make an indirect object the subject: *Joe will be bought a bicycle by Father.*

VERB PHRASES WITH "DO" AS AUXILIARY

A special kind of derived verb phrase is that in which *do, does,* or *did* precedes the infinitive form of any principal verb except *be* (example: *does go*). In some uses, such a phrase is called *emphatic.*

NEGATIVE STATEMENTS

We can make statements negative by putting the word *not* after a single form of *be* when it is a principal verb: *He is not here.* But usually, we put *not* right after the first auxiliary in a verb phrase, as in *He is not sleeping.* To negate a sentence such as *He sleeps,* we must replace the single verb with a *do* phrase and put the negator after the auxiliary: *He does not sleep.*

The negative expressions *never, neither, nor* are derived forms (from *not ever,* etc.). They have the special privilege of preceding a single verb or a verb phrase: *He never sleeps.*

INTERROGATIVE SENTENCES

Interrogative sentences (those that ask questions) are of two types. Those that can be answered with *yes* or *no* are formed in three ways. (a) In speech, we can make a statement into a question simply by giving it a final rising-pitch juncture; in writing, the juncture is represented by a question mark. (b) We can turn a declarative clause into a question by putting the subject after a single form of *be* or *have* which is a principal verb: *Was Mary happy? Have you any wool?* (c) Usually, we have to put the subject after the first auxiliary in a verb phrase, as in *May Jack come now?* If the clause has only a single verb that is not a form of *be* or *have,* we must substitute a phrase with *do,* so the subject can follow it: *Does he sleep?*

Interrogatives not answerable with *yes* or *no* are introduced by question words such as *who, where, when, why, how,* and phrases like *how much.* These words may be followed by inversion of subject and verb if the principal verb is a form of *be* or *have: Why are the men here?* More often, the subject must follow the first auxiliary in a verb phrase, as in *When does he sleep? Who, which,* and *what,* however, may take the place of subjects, as in *Who lost a dollar? What, which,* and phrases like *how much* may simply precede a whole clause: *How many boys rike bikes?* Still another form of question can be made from a Type III kernel by transposing the direct object to a position immediately following the question word: *What dollar did the boy lose?*

NEGATIVE QUESTIONS

Three types of negative questions are illustrated by *Are the girls not happy?* (where *not* follows an inverted subject), *Does he not sleep?* (where *not* follows the first auxiliary in a verb phrase), and *Who is not happy?* (where *not* follows a single form of a linking verb). Another type of negative question attaches the contraction *-n't* to auxiliaries, as in *Isn't he happy?*

TAG QUESTIONS

Some statements have tag questions attached at the end. The tags can be either negative or affirmative: *Today is Tuesday, isn't it? Today isn't Tuesday, is it?* The negative tag always follows an affirmative statement, and it anticipates the answer "Yes" (*Yes, this is Tuesday*). The affirmative tag always follows a negative statement, and it anticipates a negative answer (*No, this is not Tuesday*).

The first word in the tag question can be a form of *be, do,* or *have* that has appeared in the statement as a principal verb; otherwise it is the first auxiliary in the verb phrase or a form of *do* which must be supplied: *He did the job, didn't he? Tom will not go, will he? Tom went, didn't he?* The negative contraction is always attached to the verb form it follows in a tag question. If *not* is used, it is placed after the pronoun that is required to follow the verb: *Tom went, did he not?* (Use of *not* in a tag question is a mark of quite formal style.)

THE EXPLETIVE PATTERN WITH "THERE"

Some kernels of Types I and II can have their subjects shifted to follow the verbs, while positions vacated by the subjects are filled by the expletive *there.* Examples: *There are some men here. There lived three bears in the forest.*

IMPERATIVE EXPRESSIONS

Imperative expressions (those that give commands — either mild or emphatic) are best understood by relating them to clauses in which the subject is *you* and the verb is a phrase with *will* as the single auxiliary. To produce an imperative from *You will come home early,* we simply delete the pronoun and auxiliary: *Come home early.* The *you will* reappears in the tag questions so often attached to imperatives: *Come home early, will you* (or *won't you*)? To negate an imperative, we must supply a verb phrase with a form of *do,* so the negator can follow the auxiliary. Thus, applying the whole set of rules identified in this paragraph, *You will be silly* can be turned into *Don't be silly.*

*Shifting Positions for Emphasis*

For stylistic reasons, including that of achieving special emphasis, we may make various kinds of rearrangements of units that fill the kernel sentence positions. Adverbs that fill the third predicate position are particularly easy to move about. Instead of *The General came next,* we may want to say, *Next came the General.*

**Sentences: Patterns Derived from Two or More Kernels**

Many structures in elaborated sentences are describable as deriving from rule-governed combinations of two or more kernel patterns. Only the frequent types of such transformations will be identified here.

COORDINATED STRUCTURES

Two or more independent clauses may be coordinated simply by placing them side by side (with appropriate junctures in speech and punctuation in writing) or by joining them with coordinating conjunctions. The results are what we call *compound sentences.* The statements *My grandmother is eighty years old* and *She is still very lively,* for instance, can be incorporated into the compound sentence, *My grandmother is eighty years old, but she is still very lively.*

When clauses that may be coordinated all have the same subject, we may form a single clause with a coordinated predicate. Instead of *I came, I saw, I conquered,* we could say *I came, saw, and conquered.* From structures with common elements we derive all the varied kinds of coordinations our language allows. *Dogs bark* and *Seals bark* could be combined in a sentence with a coordinated subject: *Dogs and seals bark.* As another example, we may get coordinated adjectives (here, in a coordinated subjective complement) by combining *Helen is happy* and *Helen is friendly* to produce *Helen is happy and friendly.*

SUBORDINATED STRUCTURES:
COMPLEX SENTENCES

Subordinating conjunctions or relative expressions can make a clause dependent on another clause or some element in it. Sentences that contain a dependent clause are called *complex sentences.* If they have two or more independent clauses and at least one dependent clause, they are called *compound-complex.*

Relative (adjectival) clauses require special attention. Their derivation can be seen in the combination of *These men work hard* and *These men are strong* as *These men, who are strong, work hard.* Sometimes, the relative pronoun that normally introduces an adjective clause may be suppressed; instead of *Here is a fish that I caught,* we can say *Here is a fish I caught.*

MODIFIERS DERIVED FROM RELATIVE CLAUSES

Type II kernels that have adjectives in the second predicate position may be incorporated into other sentences as relative clauses. Thus *I caught a fish* and *The fish was very large* may be turned into *I caught a fish that was very large.* But we can delete both the relative and the verb *was,* and shift what is left of the relative clause to a position in front of the noun: *I caught a very large fish.* Thus, adjectives that appear only in predicates of Type II kernels can come to modify nouns and pronouns directly.

Type II kernels whose verbs are forms of *be* may have adverbial expressions in the second predicate position. These, too, may become parts of relative clauses. *These men work hard* and *These men are in the barn* may give us *These men who are in the barn work hard;* but if we delete *who are,* we have left *These men in the barn work hard.* The adverbial phrase here modifies *men* because it stands for an underlying adjective clause.

*Appositives and Noun Adjuncts*

If the Type III kernel *This material costs a lot* absorbs the Type II *This material is stone,* we may get *This material, which is stone, costs a lot.* But if we delete *which is,* the noun *stone* becomes (in *This material, stone, costs a lot*) the kind of modifier we call an *appositive.* If, now, we place *stone* before the noun it modifies (*This stone material costs a lot*), it is what is called a *noun adjunct.*

VERB FORMS USED AS OTHER PARTS OF SPEECH

Infinitives and participles that are used as nominals, adjectivals, or adverbials are derived from underlying kernels. For example, the present participle in the verb phrase of *John was fishing* can replace the indefinite direct object in a sentence like *John enjoyed something,* with this result: *John enjoyed fishing.* When a present participle is used as a noun, as it is here, it is often called a *gerund.*

Use of past participles as adjectives derives from Type III kernels that have been turned into passives. *The pig lived in a house* can incorporate a passive verb phrase such as that in *The house was built with straw.* In *The pig lived in a house built with straw,* the participial phrase is an adjectival modifier.

An infinitive transformation can be seen in a combination of *Something is unusual for me* and *I will work hard.* The result may be *For me to work hard is unusual.*

*The Expletive Structure with "It"*

*For me to work hard is unusual* can undergo another transformation: we can make the whole subject follow the adjective if we fill the position it had occupied with the expletive *it: It is unusual for me to work hard.*

THE OBJECTIVE COMPLEMENT STRUCTURE

A Type III sentence such as *We elected Sarah* can be combined with a Type II sentence like *Sarah became the treasurer.* In *We elected Sarah treasurer,* the word *treasurer* is what is called an *objective complement.* An objective complement may also be an adjective. *The experience scared Sam* and *Sam was silly* may be transformed into *The experience scared Sam silly.*

ELLIPSIS

The omission of words that would appear in fully complete syntactic structures is called *ellipsis.* Ellipses of a normal kind are enclosed in parentheses in this sentence: *I like Hardy's novels, but* (I do) *not* (like) *Galsworthy's* (novels). Responses to questions are often elliptical. Answers to the query, "Will you go to the party?" may be either *"No* (I will not go to the party)" or *"No, I won't* (go to the party)."

Ellipses can cause trouble. *I like Mary better than John* could mean either . . . *better than* (I like) *John* or . . . *better than John* (likes Mary). Principles controlling ellipsis should be those of avoiding both useless repetition and possible misinterpretation.

SYSTEMATIC SUBSTITUTION

We avoid repetitions not only by ellipses but also by systematic substitutions.

The common pronouns provide the most regularly used substitutes for nominals (that is, nouns, noun phrases, and noun clauses). Another type of nominal substitution derives from noun determiners. Thus, instead of repeating *boy's* three times, we can say, *One boy's speech was short, the other's was long, but neither's was effective.*

Forms of the verb *do* are systematically employed as substitutes for other verbs and verb phrases. *In Jack started to school later than I did,* the substitute for *started* is *did.* We could well call such a substitute a *proverb,* on analogy with *pronoun.*

**Principles of Selection and Agreement**

Rules of selection and agreement have to do with which inflected forms may be used in various circumstances. Naturally, they do not apply where contrasting inflectional forms are not available. They will be listed here without extensive notes on exceptions.

1. A grammatical subject selects a verb form that agrees with it in number and person. Compound subjects are usually (but not always) regarded as plural. For verb agreement with cor-

relative subjects and collective nouns, see those topics in the outline of "Parts of Speech."

2. Every verb except *be* selects an objective form of a following pronoun. The pronoun complement following *be* is often (but not always) a subjective form (as in *It was she who was here*).

3. A preposition selects an objective form of a following pronoun.

4. According to its own number, a nominal selects the singular or plural form of *this* and *that*.

5. An antecedent selects a reference pronoun of the same number, person, and gender. When the sex of what is referred to by such indefinites as *everybody* and *everyone* is unknown or known to be both male and female, formal usage requires reference to them by *he* (or *he or she*); informal usage allows the genderless *they*.

6. In indirect discourse and in constructions where noun clauses are objects of verbs like *know, think,* or *believe,* a past tense verb in the main clause has traditionally selected a past tense verb in the object clause. Example: *George remarked that he was bored.* But where misunderstanding of the time reference might result from such agreement, tense selection by the main verb may be denied. Example: *The students reported that they are willing to come early.*

# Outline of Conventions in Writing

CUSTOMARY HABITS in representing language visually are called *writing conventions.* Our conventions are fairly well standardized, though at many points they allow alternative choices.

## SPELLING

No set of general rules will account for all details of English spelling. Consonant sounds are spelled quite regularly, but vowels in many different ways.

Three types of positions in words must be distinguished: initial, medial, and final. The usefulness of such distinctions is seen in these observations:

1. At beginnings of words, the first sound of *just* is often spelled with *j*; initially or medially, it may be spelled *ge* or *gi* (*gentle, engine*); at ends of words, it is regularly *ge* or *dge* (*age, judge*).

2. The sound of *k* is often spelled by that letter alone in initial or medial positions; at the end of a word, *k* is almost always preceded by *c* or followed by *e* (*black, like*).

3. The sound of *k* is often spelled initially or medially by *c* followed by *a, o,* or *u* (*can, curd, abscond*). The letter *c* normally never appears finally unless preceded by a consonant (*zinc*) or *i* as in *panic, picnic.*

4. At ends of words, the so-called "long a" sound is almost always spelled *-ay* (*say, dismay*).

5. At ends of words, *v* is regularly followed by a "silent e" (*give, above*).

6. No words end in *qu,* but several end in *que* (*brusque, torque*).

7. Only one *l* appears at ends of words whose last syllable is the suffix carried by *cupful* and *hopeful.*

### A Systematic Use of the "Silent e"

The "silent e" quite regularly marks what are often called "long vowels." It may immediately follow the vowel it identifies, as in *doe* (compare *do*), *die, sue;* more often, it follows a single consonant but indicates the sound of the vowel that precedes it. Thus it contrasts *mat* and *mate, sit* and *site, mop* and *mope.* It makes a different distinction between *on* and *one.*

### The Order of "i" and "e"

When *i* and *e* are combined to represent the sound of "ee" following a *c,* their order is almost always *ei: receive, deceit,* etc.; exceptions are *species* and *financier.* Standing for the same sound, they are combined in the same way before or after *s* (*leisure, seize*) and in *either, neither,* and *weird.* In other words where they may be pronounced as "ee" they are combined as *ie: relieve, chief, field, priest,* etc.

When they appear in words in which they cannot be pronounced as "ee," they are regularly combined as *ei: neighbor, weigh, heir, their, freight,* etc.

### Spelling of Words with Prefixes

Attaching a prefix to a stem usually requires no change in spelling of either the prefix or the stem. Some Latin prefixes, however, adjust their sound and spelling to the first sound in the stem. Thus, *ad-* takes such different forms as those in *admire, affect, accent; in-* (meaning "not") lies behind *innocent, illegal, immediate, irreverent; ob-* has produced *occur* as well as *obscure.*

### Spelling Words with Suffixes

Special spelling rules applying to plurals of nouns, possessive forms of nouns and pronouns, and inflected forms of verbs are detailed at appropriate points in the outline of "Parts of Speech." Here, only general rules relating to suffixes will be listed.

1. A "silent e" at the end of a word is usually dropped before addition of a suffix beginning with a vowel, unless it is needed to prevent possible mispronunciation (*likable*, but *peaceable*). When a suffix begins with a consonant, the "silent e" is usually retained (*likeness;* but note *truly* and *duly*).

2. A final *y* preceded by a consonant usually is changed to *i* before suffixes that do not begin with *i* (*reliance,* but *denying*). When final *y* follows a vowel, it is usually retained, as in *played;* but note exceptions such as *daily, said, laid.*

3. Words ending in *c* usually add *k* before an *e, i,* or *y* (*panicky, picnicking*); but this is not true if the sound of *c* becomes that usually represented by *s* (*musician, criticism*) or if the *c* is preceded by a consonant, as in *disced.*

4. One-syllable words or those in which heaviest stress falls on a final syllable double a single final consonant preceded by a single vowel letter before adding a suffix that begins with a vowel. Compare *matted* with *mated, stopper* with *steeper, referred* with *reference.*

## PUNCTUATION

Except for such devices as capitalization and underlining, our ordinary system of punctuation involves uses of an even dozen marks. The apostrophe (') and the hyphen (-) are associated with individual words. The period (.), the question mark (?), and the exclamation point (!) are generally sentence-end marks, though they have a few other uses. The comma (,), the semicolon (;), the colon (:), and the dash (—) are used internally in sentences. The other marks are used in pairs; they are the quotation marks (" " or ' '), parentheses (illustrated repeatedly in this paragraph), and square brackets ( [ ] ).

### The Apostrophe

For uses of the apostrophe in marking possessive forms of nouns and the plurals of letters, numbers, signs, and cited words, see the discussion of noun inflections in the outline of "Parts of Speech."

The apostrophe is also used as a mark of omission in contractions such as *can't, sec'y* (for *secretary*) or *'67* (for a date such as *1967*).

### The Hyphen

Hyphens are used to (a) link words in compounds (*self-starter*), (b) separate an affix from a stem to prevent misreading (*re-cover*—meaning "cover again"), (c) mark a form as an affix (*a-, -ing*), (d) link a part of a word broken off (at a syllable boundary) at the end of a line with the rest of the word on the next line, and (e) show omission of letters (as in *e - - - t*).

### The Period

Periods most often mark the ends of declarative sentences and mild imperatives, or of elliptical expressions functioning as those units do. In addition, they may indicate omissions of two kinds: (a) They are put at the ends of abbreviations, as in *Mr. J. V. Jones* or *Vt.* (for *Vermont*). (b) A series of three periods indicates omission of a word or several words, usually (but not always) in quoted material.

### The Question Mark

The question mark (or interrogation point) is typically used to mark the end of a direct question; but inside a sentence, it may indicate a writer's doubt or uncertainty, as in *Greene's dates are 1560?—1592.*

### The Exclamation Mark

The exclamation mark separates an exclamatory word, phrase or sentence from a following expression, as in *But alas! he didn't come,* or *Listen! It's raining.* It also marks the end of any exclamatory expression.

### The Comma

Since the comma dissociates units, it is never used between essential parts of the sentence, such as subject and verb or the verb and an object or complement. The following are its proper separating uses:

1. It separates coordinate words or phrases in a series, as in *Bob, Mary, and Jim packed a lunch, got their bikes, and went on a picnic.* It is never incorrect to use a comma before a conjunction that joins the last two items in a series (unless in official names), and such usage often prevents misinterpretation.

2. It is placed before a conjunction that joins two coordinate clauses, unless the clauses are quite short and very closely related in meaning: *It rained, so we canceled the game,* but *It rained and it poured.*

3. It is used to set off elements loosely related to the rest of the sentence—a vocative, an absolute, or a sentence-connector. Examples: *"I didn't see you, John." The sun having set, we went home. I came; however, I didn't stay.*

4. It sets off introductory adverbial modifiers, unless they are very closely associated in meaning with what follows: *Mornings, we usually go to school* but *Sometimes we have fun.*

5. It is used to set off various kinds of modifiers or other expressions when they are not in their normal word-order position. Example: *It was an old stove, sooty and rusted.*

6. It is placed between an independent clause and a dependent clause that is not a close modifier: *I will go, though I don't know why.*

7. It is placed after the introduction to a direct quotation, or after the quotation followed by an explanatory tag: *He said, "I won't go"* or *"I won't go," he said.*

8. It is used to separate adjectives that modify a nominal in coordinate fashion; hence, we can contrast *a bright, red coat* with *a bright red coat.*

9. It is used to separate items in addresses (*Provo, Utah*), dates (*Oct. 1, 1967*), large numbers (*5,280*), and bibliographical entries.

10. In letters, it separates the complimentary close from the signature, and it may set off an informal salutation.

Paired commas are used to enclose three types of expressions occurring within sentences: (a) nonidentifying appositives (*Jefferson, a native of Virginia, was our third President*), (b) nonrestrictive clauses (*Jefferson, who was a native of Virginia, was our third President*), and (c) interpolated clauses or other units, including sentence-connectors (*Jefferson, I repeat, was our third President* or *Jefferson, moreover, was our third President*).

Occasionally, commas link very closely related parallel clauses in a series, as in *I came, I saw, I conquered.* A comma may also be used to indicate omission of words, as in *The infant becomes a child; the child, an adolescent.*

**The Semicolon**

The semicolon typically links independent clauses not joined by conjunctions, as in *The soldiers fought with courage; they died with honor.* It links clauses, even if the second is introduced by a sentence-connector: *He worked hard; nevertheless, he failed.*

A semicolon separates units that might be expected to be separated by a comma, when the units have commas within them and a heavier mark of separation is needed. Example: *They visited Albia, Iowa; Topeka, Kansas; and Ada, Oklahoma.*

**The Colon**

The colon draws attention to what follows it. It promises explanation, specification, or qualification of what has already been said. For this reason, it is used after a formal salutation in a letter, after an introduction to a long direct quotation (*He spoke as follows:*), between numbers of hours and minutes (*12:15 p.m.*), between Bible chapter and verse numbers (*Exodus 3:5*), and between volume and issue numbers of serial publications or volume and page numbers of a set of books (*Encyclopedia Americana* 6:87).

Typical use of the colon is illustrated in the order, *Please send me these items: a wrench, a hammer, and a saw.*

**The Dash**

The single dash has several different uses. (a) It directs attention backward when it is used to link units of expression; what follows it is subsidiary to what has gone before, often an unexpected addition. Example: *She was very nervous — fidgety and talkative.* (b) It may mark the breaking off of an expression before it is completed. (c) It may be put before the name of an author or a book that has been quoted (*"Great men are not always wise." — Job 32:9*). (d) It may mark omission of letters (*Mr. B —*) or numbers (*one day in 18—*). (e) It sometimes stands for *to* or *through,* as in *pages 71 — 76.*

Paired dashes enclose parenthetical expressions less closely related to the main thought of the sentence than those enclosed by commas. They can set off expressions within which commas are used: *Whatever happens — come rain, hail, or hurricane — the mail must go through.*

**Parentheses**

Parentheses are enclosures still more emphatic than the paired dashes. They set off loosely related expressions within sentences or whole sentences within a text.

Figures or letters marking items in a series may be enclosed in parentheses, as they often have been in this outline.

**Square Brackets**

Square brackets are even heavier marks of enclosure than are parentheses. In a quotation, they set off comments or corrections made by the person doing the quoting. They sometimes isolate interpolations within matter already enclosed in parentheses.

**Quotation Marks**

In America, the custom is to use single quotation marks only to enclose a quotation within a quotation that is identified by the double marks.

Quotation marks are used not only to enclose direct quotations but (a) in definitions, to identify the common equivalent of the term explained (*Inverted* means "reversed in order"); (b) to set off expressions regarded as technical, slangy, ironical, or not quite proper; (c) to enclose titles of paintings, essays, poems, or stories (but not full volumes).

When a quotation mark comes at the end of a punctuated syntactic unit, it is normally placed outside the period, the question mark, the exclamation point, and the comma; it is usually placed inside the semicolon, the colon, and the dash.

**Italics**

Italics in print have their counterpart in underlining in longhand and typing. Italics generally serve four purposes: (a) to indicate foreign words that have not attained common use in English; (b) to mark names of ships and titles of books, magazines, newspapers and operas; (c) to call attention to something regarded as particularly important; (d) to mark words, letters, numbers, and signs cited as things in themselves, not used for their meanings.

**Capitalization**

A capital letter is used for:

1. The pronoun *I* and the interjection *O*.

2. The first letter in a sentence or line of verse.

3. The first letter in a quotation falling within a sentence, if the quotation itself could be a sentence: *Tom shouted, "Come away from there."*

4. The first letter in a proper noun or a word made from a proper noun, unless the word has become very common: *Spain, Spanish*; but *italics* and *roman type*. Months of the year are capitalized, and names of seasons take capitals when they are particularized, as in *the Spring, 1956, issue of Midwest Journal*.

5. The first letter of each main word in titles of books, magazines, chapter headings, poems, plays, etc.

6. The first letter in each main word in titles of honor or office: *His Eminence the Cardinal Archbishop of New York*.

7. The first letter of a word naming the Deity, and of a pronoun referring to it: *God sends His rain. . . .* (The practice relating to such pronouns is not uniform).

8. The first letter of a name registered as a trademark of a product: *Jello, Spam*. When such names become common designations, they may cease to be capitalized, as has *frigidaire*.

9. The first letter in salutations and complimentary closes in letters.

10. Each letter in an expression to which very special attention is to be called.

11. The first letter in fragments of sentences arranged in outline form.

Conventions of capitalization are not always simple and consistent. Details of practice are best identified by observing usage in reputable publications.

# *Style and Accuracy in Usage*

THE STYLE of a speaker or writer is his particular manner of using the language. It reflects his choices among possible expressions — and there are always choices to make, though an individual may be unaware of the full range available.

## GENERAL ASPECTS OF STYLE

Only one directive relating to style is always applicable and always right: style should be appropriate. Appropriate to what? Appropriateness depends on such factors as the subject dealt with, the situation, the purpose of the speaker or writer, and the kinds of listeners or readers involved — their backgrounds, understandings, and interests. It may also depend on the character of the speaker or writer, the role he is playing at the moment, and his relations with those with whom he wishes to communicate.

**Functional Varieties of Language Use**

Language performs many functions. For example, it may establish or reinforce a sense of association and good will among people. Our greetings to each other do that, and the particular kind of association may be marked by the difference between "Good morning, Sir," "Morning!" (perhaps to a member of the family), and "Hi, there!" This kind of use of language is as legitimate as is deliberative discussion, a sermon on Sunday, or a book on causes of the first World War. The different kinds of language appropriate to different circumstances, purposes, and relations between people who are communicating are called *functional varieties*. It is a mistake to think we ought to "talk like a book" or always to write as if we were composing the Constitution of the United States.

**The Informality-Formality Scale**

In word choice, syntactic structures, pronunciation in speech, and larger matters of elaboration and organization, we need to honor the demands of degrees of informality or formality. It is useful to distinguish styles on a five-point scale: (a) the intimate, (b) the casual, (c) the consultative (which is normal in conversations that explore problems or identify opinions), (d) the formal, and (e) the very formal (represented in the Constitution). Writing is always more formal than speech. Kinds of expression much more often heard in easy conversation than seen in writing are called *colloquial*. The label does not imply that they ought not to be used in writing, only that they are quite informal.

**Limited Dialects of English**

The kind of English that has very wide prestige is called *Standard*. (It has various functional varieties.) More limited dialects are either regional or social. Social groups, even as small as families, may have their special words and patterns of expression. To identify an expression as characteristic of a limited dialect does not mean that it must not be used in our speech and writing; it may, though, call attention to the problem of appropriateness.

**Correctness and Style**

A person's style may be correct (grammatically and so far as conventions of usage go) but relatively ineffective. It *may* also be effective and yet marked by incorrectness and unconventionality. Some people achieve just the communication they want by flouting conventions and the rules of grammar. Such success is unlikely, however, unless a person knows what is accurate and deliberately chooses, for good reason, to disregard custom. Efficient use of language most frequently exploits patterns of expression provided by tradition.

**Figures of Speech**

In some kinds of discourse words are properly confined to literal, denotative meanings. But many of our uses of language draw on the connotations of words and effectively suggest what they do not literally say. (See *connote, denote* in the section below.) To expand expressiveness, we may use numerous stylistic devices such as alliteration, assonance, onomatopoeia, or antithesis (see dictionary entries under these terms); we also employ *figures of speech* intended to imply meanings distinctly different from those the words would normally carry.

Imaginative comparison produces figures of speech we call *similes* and *metaphors.* A simile is an explicit comparison that makes use of words such as *like, as,* or *seems*: Wordsworth said of Milton, "Thy soul was like a Star. . . . " This is an *open simile,* for it does not specify the respect in which the things compared are thought of as being alike. Wordsworth used a *closed simile,* however, in the line, "I wandered lonely as a cloud," for there he indicated the particular way he felt himself to be like a cloud. Similes should not be confused with literal comparisons such as "John is as tall as Tom is."

A metaphor implies comparison, but it does not use such words as *like*; it boldly states something to be that which it literally is not. Shakespeare's Romeo says, "Juliet is the sun"; Isaiah remarks that "All flesh is grass." To interpret metaphors we must understand the significance of the comparisons suggested. A particular kind of metaphor is *personification,* which attributes human characteristics to nonhuman things or abstract ideas. We say that Justice is blind. We personify a ship or an automobile when we refer to it as "she."

Associational figures are very common. We employ what is called *metonymy* when we refer to something indirectly by naming something else commonly associated with it, as when we speak of "the British Crown" and mean either the monarch or the monarchy, or when we talk about "Wall Street" when referring to the Stock Exchange. *Synecdoche* is the figure that substitutes a part for the whole, as when we refer to farm laborers as "hired hands" or to an automobile as a "motor." *Synesthesia* is exemplified in our speaking of "hot music" or "blue notes," where we transfer terms normally used to refer to one kind of sense experience to description of another that somehow seems related.

Some other nonliteral uses of language are *overstatement, understatement,* and *irony.* The first (technically called *hyperbole*) would be exemplified in speaking of a heavy rain if we said, "The skies opened and let loose a Noah's flood." Understatement (sometimes called *litotes*) would be a reference to the same rain as "a little dampness." Irony implies meanings contradictory (sometimes exactly the opposite) to what literally appears to be said. Job, for example, ironically indicated he thought his "comforters" to be foolish when he said "No doubt but . . . wisdom shall die with you." When irony is harsh and quite obvious, we label it *sarcasm.*

## COMMON PROBLEMS IN ENGLISH USAGE

The alphabetical arrangement of items in this section is mainly based on words that present problems to a good many users of English. It also, however, includes some topics entered under capitalized descriptive titles. Though the discussions are generally concerned with matters of style and usage, they do not always exclude remarks on obligatory features of grammar and the English writing system.

### A

**a, an.** *A* and *an* are forms of the indefinite article (a noun determiner). They are used to indicate reference to one person, place, abstraction or other "thing" within a class named by a following noun — they do not indicate *which* one. Since the forms carry the notion of "one," they are used only before singular count nouns.

The form *an* is used before any word beginning with a vowel sound, and sometimes before a word beginning with an *h* sound, if the first syllable of that word is not stressed. The form *a* (usually pronounced ə — see the dictionary pronunciation key) is used before words beginning with a consonant sound, with the possible exception already noted. Some words spelled with an initial vowel letter, of course, are pronounced with a beginning consonant sound. Examples: *a universe, a history, a historian, a green apple; an apple, an early riser, an historian, an honor.*

It is considered to be more formal and more literary to say *this kind of book* or *that sort of egg* rather than *this kind of a book* or *that sort of an egg.* The indefinite article after *kind of* and *sort of* is not uncommon in colloquial use.

**Abbreviations.** Courtesy dictates that abbreviations should not be used unless they are explained or are likely to be understood without explanation. Technical writing and discussion may make use of numerous abbreviations established within the specialty; many abbreviations (such as *Mr., a.m.* and *p.m.*) are so common that avoiding them would be thought eccentric. Excessive use of abbreviations, however, is generally unpleasant, especially when they are slangy. Except for items such as have already been referred to, abbreviations are regarded as more informal than full forms. Such term as *prof, exam, math* (produced by "clipping" words) are characteristic of student jargon generally appropriate only in very informal use among students themselves.

**about, almost.** *About* in the sense of "almost" is quite informal usage when it appears in such phrases as *about done, about through, about dead.*

**absolute(ly), positive(ly).** The indiscriminate colloquial use of these words as intensives is common. Careful speakers and writers, being aware of the traditional meanings of the terms, usually confine them to expressions in which they may be taken literally, such as *I am absolutely certain; I heard his positive denial.*

**accept, except.** These words in speech are usually distinguished by the pronunciation of their first syllables; in correct writing, they are always distinguished by spelling. *Accept* means to take willingly what is offered, to agree to (a proposal), or to believe (an explanation or a doctrine). *Except* is either a verb or a preposition. As verb, it means to exclude (*I except him from my generalization*), to omit, or to object (a lawyer may *except to a witness*). As a preposition, *except* means "leaving out" (*John is kind to everybody except himself*).

**accidentally, incidentally.** Note that the present-day spelling of these words adds *-ly* to the adjective forms *accidental* and *incidental.*

**across.** The pronunciation *acrost* (with a final *t* sound) is not Standard English. The expression *over across* is sometimes heard in colloquial use; it is avoided (*across* being used by itself) in formal speech and writing.

**adapt, adopt.** *Adapt* means to change something to make it suitable for a new use. One may adapt himself to different circumstances. A novel may be adapted for the stage. *Adopt* means to decide upon (a plan), to choose to treat someone as a close relation, or to vote to accept a motion or resolution.

**advice, advise.** An adviser gives advice. *Advice* is a noun; *advise* is a verb, from which an agentive noun, *adviser* (sometimes spelled *advisor*) is formed.

**affect, effect.** Though these words are often pronounced alike, they *can* be differentiated in speech. They *must* be distinguished in spelling if writing is to be correct. *Affect* is usually a verb meaning to like, to pretend, or to influence or change something in some way. Less commonly, it is a noun meaning "a feeling or emotion."

*Effect* is a verb meaning to accomplish (something), or it is a noun meaning "result" or "what is accomplished." Examples: *The principal effected changes in the school, but I didn't like the effects.*

**aggravate.** The original meaning of *aggravate* was "to add weight to." Colloquially, it is often used to mean "irritate," as in "His way of speaking aggravated me." In speech or writing that is in any degree formal, *aggravate* is used only to mean "to make worse," as in "The difficulty was aggravated by misunderstanding."

**Agreement in inflected forms of words.** *See* SELECTION AND AGREEMENT in the "Outline of English Grammar."

**ain't.** *Ain't* was originally a contraction of *am not* (compare *can't,* which in some regions is pronounced *cain't*). Well over a hundred years ago, it came to be widely used also as a contraction for *are not* and even for *is not* and *have* or *has not.* Perhaps because of the indiscriminate use, *ain't* fell into disfavor among many careful speakers. It is now not used in published writing, except in representation of speech. The expression is pretty generally regarded by educated people (even by some who use it) as nonstandard, uncultivated speech.

**all ready, already.** *All ready* means "completely ready" (*I was all ready for the picnic*) or it means that all of what has been referred to is ready (*The boys were all ready to shout*). *Already* is an adverbial expression meaning "by or before a particular time": *The sun was already up when I awoke.* Though often pronounced alike, these expressions should not be confused in writing.

**all right.** Although there would be logical justification for a spelling form *alright,* it is not firmly established among our conventions of writing. It sometimes appears in advertising and in very informal writing, but never in the sense "completely right" or "everyone right."

**all the farther, as far as.** In the sense of "as far as," *all the farther* (*That's all the farther he can walk*) is a regional expression, though in regions where it is current, it may be used by educated people. It is *not* characteristic of literary English.

**all together, altogether.** This is another pair of expressions often pronounced alike but kept distinct in spelling. *Altogether* means "entirely," as in "Harry was altogether too late." The two separate words can have other words put between them: *The family were all together,* or *All the family were together.*

**allude, elude.** To allude to something is to refer to it; usually, the verb carries the idea of indirectness in referring: *The poet subtly alluded to King Arthur.* Note that the verb *allude* is regularly followed by the particle *to.*

To elude something or somebody is to evade or escape: *The suspect eluded the police.*

**allusion, illusion, delusion.** These three nouns have quite different meanings. An allusion is a reference, either direct or implied: *The poet made an allusion to King Arthur.* An illusion is a mistaken notion, either serious or harmless: *What you thought you saw the magician do was an illusion.* A delusion (from the verb *delude*) is a serious deception: *Hitler's fatal delusion was that he was infallible.*

**almost, most.** In speech, *almost* is often shortened to *most,* and the shortened form is sometimes written with an initial apostrophe: *They had done 'most everything necessary.* But *almost* is still the standard form in written English. *See also* ABOUT.

**already.** *See* ALL READY.

**alright.** *See* ALL RIGHT.

**although, though.** As subordinating conjunctions, these two words are equivalent. It is not good practice to spell the shorter form with an initial apostrophe. *Although* is generally felt to be a little more formal than *though. Altho* and *tho* as simplified spellings have some uses, but they are seldom allowed in formal writing.

The colloquial use of *though* in place of the sentence-connector *however* (*I thought, though, that he would never get here*) is not generally considered suitable for writing.

**altogether.** *See* ALL TOGETHER.

**aluminum, aluminium.** Both these two forms of the same word are established. The first is most common in the United States, the second in the British Commonwealth.

**among, between.** *Among* is used when referring to more than two persons or things: *The prize money was distributed among three winners. Between* is historically related to the word *twain,* which in turn comes from *two.* Some people prefer to confine use of *between* to references to only two persons or things, but many excellent speakers and writers do not observe any such rule.

**amongst.** This is a legitimate variant of *among,* but it is not in very common use in the United States. Elsewhere, it is frequent.

**amount, number.** Measurement of what is named by a mass noun or abstract noun is reported as an amount; number refers to the counting of units: *a certain amount of courage, a large amount of money, a large number of pennies.*

**an.** *See* A.

**and.** Like other coordinating and correlative conjunctions, *and* is sometimes used by good writers (and speakers) as the first word in a sentence felt to be coordinate with the sentence immediately preceding it. It is usually unwise, stylistically, to repeat such coordination very often in a particular discourse. Use of *and* to produce compound sentences is a practice it is wise to control carefully, too.

Such an expression as "Come and visit us" is generally considered more informal than "Come to visit us."

**and/or.** Useful as this expression might be, most cultivated speakers and writers feel that it should usually be confined to use in legal or commercial writing. It is regarded as accurate but awkward.

**and so.** The connective idea carried by this pair of words can usually be carried by either one of them alone. Frequent use of *and so* (as in *It rained, and so we came home*) is generally avoided by adults.

**antenna.** In scientific discourse about bugs, the plural of *antenna* is usually *antennae.* In reference to radio and television, it is regularly *antennas.*

**anticlimactic.** Note the spelling of this adjective, which means "characterized by arrangement that does not culminate in a climax." It has nothing to do with *climate.*

**anyway.** In Standard English, this adverb never takes a final *-s. Anyways* is heard only in dialects that have not generally been turned to literary use.

**anywhere, everywhere, nowhere, somewhere.** None of these words takes a final *-s* in Standard English. These words are widely felt to be more appropriate in writing than are the related colloquial terms, *anyplace, everyplace, noplace, someplace.*

**appraise, apprise, apprize.** *Appraise* means to judge or to estimate the value of something. *Apprize* (whether spelled this way or with an *s*) means to notify or inform about. Examples: *We apprised him of his duty to appraise the property.*

**apt, liable, likely.** These words are sometimes treated colloquially as equivalents, the first two being given the sense of "likely." The basic meaning of *apt* is "fitted" or "naturally suited" for something or to do something. The basic meaning of *liable* is "legally bound" or "responsible" for something. Meanings from these basic ones have brought the uses of *apt* and *liable* nearer to that of *likely,* but many writers carefully avoid interchanging the three words.

**aren't I?** Some people have the curious notion that this is an elegant expression to be used in avoiding *ain't I?* Many other people find *aren't I?* particularly distasteful. The cumbersome alternative to both locutions, of course, is *am I not?*

**around, 'round.** *Around* in the senses of "about" or "nearby" is colloquial rather than literary. Examples of colloquial use: *Let's start around ten o'clock. The book is around here someplace.* The preposition or adverb *around* is often shortened in speech by suppression of the first syllable. When such shortening is represented in writing, an apostrophe should be used to indicate the omitted syllable: *'round,* as in *the other way 'round.*

**as.** The use of *as* in the sense of "because" or "since" is very often ambiguous; it is generally a mark of immaturity in speaking or writing. *We were bored, because we knew what he would say* is better than *We were bored, as we knew what he would say.*

**assay, essay.** As verbs, these words mean, respectively, to test or evaluate and to attempt. As nouns, *assay* means "the result of testing or evaluation," and *essay* means "the result of an attempt." A specialized meaning of essay is "a piece of writing resulting from a person's attempting to express his observations and ideas on a particular subject."

**astronomy, astrology.** Nowadays, the distinction between these two words involves the distinction between a science of celestial bodies (astronomy) and a pseudo science that purports to deal with the influence of the stars (astrology). Long ago, astrology was widely regarded as a science.

**at.** The use of *at* in such expressions as *Where are we at?* is colloquial in some regions. It is not characteristic of literary English.

**athlete, athletics.** In cultivated circles, a pronunciation of these words that puts a vowel sound after *ath-* calls attention to itself and is usually disapproved.

**avocation, vocation.** One's avocation is what he does (because he likes to) in addition to his vocation (which is his main occupation). A special (older) meaning of *vocation* suggests a supernatural calling to a way of life.

**awful(ly).** These expressions (adjective and adverb) have lost their original force through overuse in speech and informal writing. If one intends to identify something as producing awe, he will usually need to select different terms. *See* COUNTER WORDS.

**awhile, a while.** *Awhile* is an adverb. After a preposition, *a while* should be used: *Help me for a while.* Similarly, we use the noun and article in *The lesson will take a while.* The original meaning of *while* is "time."

## B

**back.** Since the prefix in words like *return* or *replace* means "again" or "back," it sometimes seems like unnecessary repetition to say such things as *returned back.*

**back of, in back of.** Many people feel it is more elegant to say, for example, *The tree is behind the school* rather than . . . *back of the school. In back of* is colloquial; it is avoided (in favor of *behind*) in writing that is not very informal.

**backward(s), forward(s), inward(s), outward(s), onward(s), toward(s).** As adverbs, these words may or may not have a final *s,* though the forms without *s* are more common in this country. As adjectives, they never have a final *s. The backward boy walked forward,* or . . . *forwards.*

**bad, badly.** *Bad* is the adjective, *badly* the adverb. There is no rational justification for saying *The flower smells sweetly* or *I feel badly* (when the meaning is that you feel either sick or sorry). The first of these examples would be taken by most cultivated people as a sign of grammatical ignorance, but expressions like the second are quite often used by people who ought to know better. The adverb form is required only to qualify the nonlinking senses of verbs of feeling, taste, and smell.

**barely.** *See* DOUBLE NEGATIVE.

**because.** *See* DUE TO and REASON IS BECAUSE.

**began, begun.** These are, respectively, the standard past tense and past participial forms of the verb *begin.* Right now, *I begin;* yesterday *I began; I have begun. Begin* or *begun* as simple past tense forms are localisms.

**beside(s).** As a preposition in the sense of "at the side of" or "next to," we normally use *beside* (without the final *s*): *I walked beside him.* As an adverb or a preposition carrying other senses, the forms with or without the final *s* are interchangeable.

**better, best.** *See* HAD BETTER, BEST.

**between.** *Between* as a preposition takes objective forms of personal pronouns as objects to follow it, no matter what words intervene. Correct: *between him and me, between the repulsive old man and me. See* AMONG.

**biannual, biennial, bimonthly, biweekly.** The only one of these words that is always unequivocally understood is *biennial,* which means "every two years." The prefix *bi-* has reference, of course, to *two.* Do *biannual, bimonthly,* and *biweekly* mean "once every two years, months, or weeks" or "twice every year, month, or week?" Since they have been used in both senses, concern for clarity suggests avoiding them in use unless the context explains the intended meaning.

**borrow, lend.** One borrows *from* someone and lends *to* someone: *John borrowed from Jane the book he had asked me to lend him.*

**boughten.** The Standard English form of the past participle of *buy* is *bought.* In some regional dialects, the form *boughten* has developed on analogy with past participles like *broken.*

**bunch.** *Bunch* is in general use applied to things like radishes; when applied to things for which we have other established group names, *bunch* is usually confined to informal speech. We say *group of girls, flock of sheep,* etc.

**burst, bust.** The verb *bust* originated as a dialect form of *burst. Bust* (with its past tense and past participial form *busted*) was long felt to be slang, and it still is in the sense of "hit hard" (*Ed busted Jed on the nose*). The past participal is colloquial when it is made to mean "moneyless." Several other uses of the verb *bust* are in quite general use.

**but.** For use of *but* as the first word in a sentence, *see* AND.

## C

**calculate, reckon.** In general Standard English, both these words mean "to compute" or "to arrive at a conclusion after careful consideration." In regional dialects they came to be indiscriminately used for such verbs as *think, suppose, expect.* They are not so used in literary English.

**Calvary, cavalry.** *Calvary* is a proper noun — the name of the place where Christ was crucified. *Cavalry* refers to soldiers on horseback. Note the difference in pronunciation.

**came.** The past tense form of *come* in Standard English is *came: He came yesterday.*

**can, may.** In quite formal writing, a careful distinction is usually made between the modal auxiliaries *can* and *may. Can* is not allowed to refer to permission to do something, or to the mere possibility of an act or occurrence. The special use of *may* to refer to permission (*May I have a cookie?*) is a convenient one, and is widely admired. But since the power to act is often dependent on permission to act, *can* is often used informally to express both ability and permission to act (*Can I take the car tonight, Father?*).

**cannot (can't) hardly, barely.** *See* DOUBLE NEGATIVE.

**can't** *See* CONTRACTIONS.

**capital, capitol.** The form spelled with *-ol* refers only to the temple of Jupiter in Rome or to a building set apart as the seat of government. For all other uses, the spelling requires *-al.*

**case.** *See* CIRCUMLOCUTION.

**catchup, catsup, ketchup.** All these forms refer to the same thing (a table sauce). They are all established in standard use.

**catalog, catalogue.** Both these spellings are established. Perhaps it is a good rule to prefer the simplest spelling of a word that is allowable.

**censor, censure, censer.** Though these words all sound somewhat alike, only the first two are related. A censor is a person who undertakes to control public morals (nowadays, usually by prohibiting certain kinds of expression in literature and visual art). *Censure* is "blame" or "condemnation." *To censure* someone is to blame or condemn him.

A *censer* is a vessel in which incense is burned; it is used in certain religious rituals.

**Circumlocution.** Being concise is usually a virtue in speaking and writing. The opposite of conciseness is circumlocution, talking around a subject before getting to the point. Some words seem to invite circumlocution; one such is *case.* "In case I can't come . . ." is less direct than "If I can't come. . . ." "In all except a few cases, our winters are mild" could well be replaced by the more concise "Our winters are almost always mild."

**cite, site, sight.** *Cite* is a verb, meaning to mention specifically as an example, illustration or authority (*He cited the Constitution to support his argument*). *Site* is a noun meaning "a location" (*We live on the site of an ancient Indian village*). *Sight* may be a noun meaning "a view," "the capacity for seeing," or "an aiming device on a gun"; it may also be a verb with such meanings as "to observe" or "to take aim."

**climactic, climatic.** These are both adjectives, but the first is related to *climax,* the second to *climate. See* ANTICLIMACTIC.

**comprehensible, comprehensive.** *Comprehensible* means "capable of being understood" (*The explanation was comprehensible*). *Comprehensive* means "complete" (*The explanation was comprehensive*).

**connote, denote.** Each of these words has been given special meanings by philosophers, but in ordinary discourse, the distinction between them is simple. To denote means to express a specific, literal meaning. To connote is to suggest meanings that are incidental, dependent on associations, often ones that touch the emotions. Words that denote the same thing may connote quite different meanings. To use a standard example, your house is your home, but *home* suggests a set of associations that *house* does not. It is also true that a word which has the same denotation for different people may have quite varied connotations. We can suppose that *snow* has different connotations for people in Newfoundland from those it has for people in Florida. It should be added that the mere sound of a word may affect its connotation.

**consensus.** Note the spelling of this word; it is not related to *census.* A consensus is a general agreement: *Though a few members still disapproved, the convention reached a consensus in favor of the proposed action.*

**continual(ly), continuous(ly).** A traditional distinction between these words applies *continual* and *continually* to a succession of repeated events (such as continual showers), while it applies *continuous* and *continuously* to what is unbroken or uninterrupted (as in *continuous traffic*).

**Contractions.** Contractions of verbal auxiliaries and of the negator *not* are thoroughly established in English. Examples: *can't, I'm, he's, we've, she'd.* It is true that they tend to be avoided in very formal writing, but even there forms such as *can't, won't,* and *couldn't* are often appropriate. *Could've, would've, should've,* though common in speech, normally appear only in informal writing.

**could of, would of, should of.** These spellings are usually taken to be signs of ignorance or carelessness. For correct spelling *see* CONTRACTIONS.

**council, counsel.** The first of these forms is a noun meaning "a deliberative assembly" (*The Boy Scouts held a Council*); the second is either a noun meaning "advice" or a verb meaning "to advise." Neither word should be confused with *consul,* which refers to a particular kind of official who represents his government in a foreign country.

**Counter words.** Words that have been so long used indiscriminately to express approval or disapproval that they now carry only general, not specific, meanings are called *counter words.* The label calls attention to the ease with which we pick up words like *awful, cute, lovely, lousy, marvelous, nice, terrible, terrific,* and use them without bothering to preserve distinctions they were once capable of making. Such words have lost their denotations, and even their connotations may be vague. Though useful in informal speech, counter words are avoided in careful expression.

**cute.** *See* COUNTER WORDS.

**credible, credulous, creditable.** A statement is credible if it is believable. A person is credulous if he tends to believe what he is told, even though it is nonsense. We say something is creditable when it is worthy of being praised — that is, of being given credit.

**criterion, criteria.** *Criterion* (meaning "a standard or test for judging something") is a Greek word whose Greek plural is *criteria.* We may also give it the English plural *criterions.* To use *criteria* as if it were a singular noun is to display pretentious ignorance — or so it seems to many cultivated people.

**curriculum, curricula.** The Latin plural of the noun *curriculum* is *curricula. Curriculums* is a perfectly respectable English plural of the same word.

## D

**dairy, diary.** A dairy has to do with milk or the cows that produce it. A diary is a daily record of some kind. Confusion of the spellings of these words is guaranteed to produce at least a smile.

**Dangling modifier.** A modifier is said to be "dangling" when no word that it can properly modify is supplied. Such dangling modifiers usually appear at the beginnings of sentences. The prepositional phrase dangles in *At the age of three, John's father died.* Of course, we know that a father did not die at the age of three, but for a moment we are aware that the syntax of the sentence suggests just that — and so we smile. Naturally, dangling modifiers that are likely to elicit such a reaction ought to be avoided.

Most frequently, dangling modifiers are participial or gerund phrases that open sentences. Example: *Coming into the room, my eyes fell upon the dresser.* That sentence is also momentarily humorous, but not all dangling modifiers invite misinterpretation. If we say, "On looking farther into the subject, the problems seem more and more complex," nobody is likely to be misled. The rule should be to avoid dangling modifiers that call attention to themselves or that might really be misunderstood.

**darling.** *See* COUNTER WORDS.

**datum, data.** *Data* is the Latin plural of *datum.* In technical writing, it always takes a plural verb as well as the modifier *these.* In common speech and in much informal writing, however, it is treated as a singular collective noun. *Datum* is rarely used in any kind of expression.

**defence, defense.** Take your choice of spellings; both are correct. *Defence* is more common in the United States.

**definite(ly).** This adjective and adverb seem to be well on their way to becoming counter words used simply to gain emphasis. *See* COUNTER WORDS. Note the correct spellings, too.

**delusion.** *See* ALLUSION.

**denote.** *See* CONNOTE.

**dialog, dialogue.** Either spelling is correct; *dialogue* is probably more common.

**diary.** *See* DAIRY.

**did, done.** The standard past tense finite form of *do* is *did: He did it yesterday. Done* is the past participle: *He has done it many times.*

**different from, than, to.** *Different than* is common in speech and informal writing: *The work today is different than it was yesterday.* In formal writing, many people carefully choose to use *from* after *different: The work is different from what it was yesterday. Different to* is an established British usage.

**disinterested, uninterested.** Careful speakers and writers are likely to use *disinterested* only to mean "impartial" or "unbiased." *Uninterested,* of course, means "indifferent" or "without interest." The useful distinction is not always preserved, even by good writers.

**dived, dove.** Both these past tense forms of *dive* are current; the regular inflection (*dived*) has more prestige as the finite past, and it is the only standard form of the past participle: *He has dived.*

**doesn't, don't.** *Don't* is plural. Say *He doesn't; they don't.*

**Double genitive.** *A friend of John's* illustrates, with its preposition *of* and its inflected possessive, what is called a double genitive. This is a usage that is thoroughly established and indispensable.

**Double negative.** Speakers of English use at least three types of double negatives. If one says "It is not unlikely that John will come," the double negative will certainly be understood as a qualified affirmative: there is at least some likelihood that John will come. This type of double negative is in standard use; indeed, it has a kind of literary flavor.

If one says "I don't have no money," anyone who knows English will understand that he has made an emphatic statement about his finances. Two such negatives do *not* make a positive, no matter what happens in mathematical multiplication. But, though such double negatives were in standard use 600 years ago, they have long been banished from literary English. In speech, they are used only in nonstandard dialects.

A third type of double negative is that in which a negator is associated with such weakly negative adverbs as *hardly, barely,* or *scarcely,* as in *I can't hardly hear you.* These also are banned from literary English, though they are more widely heard in speech than are those identified in the last paragraph. Avoid these double negatives to avoid possibility of criticism.

**downtown, uptown.** These expressions often have no obvious relation to higher or lower; sometimes, but certainly not always, they are related to the directions north (up) and south (down). Use the terms as they are customarily applied in the locality to which they refer.

**dreamed, dreamt.** Both these forms are established as the past tense of *dream.*

**drink, drank, drunk.** These are the principal parts of the verb in general Standard English, although there is a great deal of regional variation in speech. The form *drunken* is standard as the past participle when it comes before the noun it modifies (as in *a drunken sailor*).

**drowned.** This is the correct form of the finite past tense and the past participle of the verb *drown.* Don't say or write *drownded.*

**due to.** Many people (even some who do not follow their own prescription) insist that *due to* should always be used in the sense of "attributable to," never in the sense of "because of" or "as a result of." The traditional rule would allow "His weariness was due to iron-poor blood." but not "He was tired, due to iron-poor blood." The tradition is weakening, but it is by no means obsolete.

## E

**each and every.** This phrase has a special use in legal documents, and it once was an emphatic expression. It has been so overworked that it is in general use now simply a cliché. *See* COUNTER WORDS.

**easy.** There are some established expressions in colloquial English in which *easy* is an adverb: *take it easy, easy come, easy go.* Elsewhere, the correct adverbial form is *easily: We can say that easily.*

**economic, economical.** Both these forms are adjectives, but one applies to general matters of finance and livelihood (*economic aid, economic planning*), the other to specific instances of thrift (*economical shopping*). The adverb related to both the adjectives is *economically.*

**effect.** *See* AFFECT.

**egoism, egotism.** *Egoism* is a term applied to self-centeredness or to the conviction that one's own personal interests ought always to be served. Though *egotism* is sometimes made to mean the same thing, it usually connotes boasting and much talk about oneself.

**elegy, eulogy.** An elegy is a formal composition (usually in words or music) mourning the death of someone or the passing away of things or conditions that have been admired. A eulogy is formal praise of somebody or something.

**else's.** *Anybody else's, everyone else's,* and similar "group genitives" are current in present-day English. *Anybody's else* is a kind of expression once thought to be elegant; such constructions now seem stiff and old fashioned.

**emigrant, immigrant.** These words can be readily distinguished if one recognizes the first is formed with the Latin prefix *ex-* meaning "from" or "out of" while the second carries the prefix *in-,* meaning "in" or "into." One emigrates from a country and immigrates into another. The same person, of course, does the emigrating and the immigrating; the difference is in the point of reference.

**enthuse.** Many people object to making a verb *enthuse* out of the adjective *enthusiastic.*

**epic, epoch.** An epic is a particular kind of long poem about a hero (or heroes); as an adjective, *epic* refers to a quality thought to be like one found in an epic. The noun, of course, is also loosely applied to what people want to represent as extraordinary, as in advertisements announcing "an epic" when a store is initiating a sale. An epoch, on the other hand is an historical period of time — an important one having distinct and special characteristics.

**epilog, epilogue.** Both spellings are established; the second is the more common.

**especial(ly), special(ly).** In some contexts, these words are interchangeable. In others, careful writers are likely to use *especially* when the meaning is "principally," "particularly," or "most importantly," but *specially* when the meaning is "uniquely." Examples: *The car was specially built as a racer. Jack was especially fond of fried chicken.*

**etc.** This abbreviation stands for the Latin *et cetera,* meaning "and others." It is a sign of ignorance to write "and etc." or to say "and *et cetera.*" Use of the abbreviation is often justified, but its availability is a temptation to be vague or unspecific.

**evolve, evolution.** *Evolution* is the noun related to the verb *evolve.* There is no established verb *to evolute.*

**except.** *See* ACCEPT.

**expect.** In literary English, *expect* means "to look forward to" or to assume something as proper or likely. As a synonym for *think, suppose,* or *guess,* the use of *expect* is colloquial only.

## F

**fact that.** This expression is often used to no good purpose. *It is a fact that he overslept* may be more directly stated, *He overslept,* or *I know he overslept. Due to the fact that . . .* is characteristically weaker than *because. See* CIRCUMLOCUTION.

**famous, infamous.** Whereas *famous* means literally "widely known," it may suggest an admirable reason for the fame. *Infamous* means "widely known for something considered reprehensible." *Al Capone is infamous.*

**farther, further.** Some people carefully confine *farther* to reference to physical distance, using *further* to refer to additional ideas, thoughts, and other immaterial things. The distinction, however, is not required in good usage. There is no *fartherer* in Standard English. *See also* ALL THE FARTHER.

**faze.** This verb, which means "to disturb" or "to disconcert," is more common in speech than in writing. It should not be confused with *phase,* which has a completely different meaning.

**feel.** *See* BAD, BADLY.

**fewer, less.** *Fewer* is applied to count nouns, *less* to mass nouns. *Fewer people were present, and they spent less time in discussion.*

**fine.** *See* COUNTER WORDS.

**fix.** This word in various contexts can mean so many things that objections to what seems its overuse have often been voiced. More formal synonyms are available to express most of its meanings. In the sense of "getting ready," as in "She's fixing to go shopping," the verb is regional. The noun meaning "a predicament," as in "He was in a fix," is colloquial only.

**flammable, inflammable.** There is a very serious reason to understand that both these words mean "easy to set afire." The negative of *flammable* is *nonflammable.*

**flaunt, flout.** The long-established meaning of *flaunt* is "to display boldly what some people may disapprove." To flout someone or something is to treat him or it with contempt. The distinction between these two words is a clear and useful one.

**fly, flee.** Birds fly; criminals flee. But figuratively, fugitives are also said to fly from their pursuers. *Flew* and *flown,* the finite past and the past participle of *fly,* however, are seldom applied to fugitives. The verb flee has only one past tense form, *fled.*

**folk, folks.** Both these forms are plural. *Folk* usually refers to culturally associated common people in the aggregate, as in *mountain folk* or *folk song.*

**formally, formerly.** The first of these forms is the adverb built on *formal;* the second is the adverb built on *former.* They should not be confused in pronunciation or spelling.

**former, latter.** These terms apply properly to a pair of items. When there are more than two items in a series, we can use *first* and *last.*

**formulae, formulas.** These are, respectively, the Latin plural and the English plural of *formula.* The former is usually found in technical writing. *Formulas* is a thoroughly respectable form.

**forward(s).** *See* BACKWARD(S).

**funny.** Since this word can mean either simply "odd" or, in fact, "humorous," it can raise a problem of interpretation. Besides, it is overworked in informal speech. *See* COUNTER WORD. In literary English it is seldom used in the sense of "peculiar."

**further.** *See* FARTHER.

## G

**Genitive.** *See* DOUBLE GENITIVE.

**get.** *Get* (with its other forms, *got* and *gotten*) has acquired dozens of meanings. Often, a more specific verb is more forceful. Both *got* and *gotten* are used as the past participle.

**go, went, gone.** These are the principal parts of the verb *go.* In Standard English, *went* is never used as the past participle.

**good, well.** *Well* may be either an adjective (meaning "in good health") or an adverb describing how something is done (*She sang well*). In Standard English, *good* is usually an adjective. One says something sounds, smells, or tastes *good. I feel good* usually indicates that the person speaking is happy or in good spirits, while *I feel well* implies that he is not ill. *See* BAD, BADLY.

**got, gotten.** *Got* is usually preferred to *gotten* as the past participle. *See* GET.

**grand.** *See* COUNTER WORDS.

**guess.** As a synonym for *suppose* or *assume,* this verb is colloquial only. *See* EXPECT.

## H

**had better (best), had rather.** These expressions have long been established in English and are perfectly appropriate in both speech and writing. Examples: *You had better come early. I had rather give than receive.*

**had of, had've.** Neither of these expressions is used in Standard English; the first is doubly inept, for it is a misspelling of the second. Say "I wish I had worked harder," not "I wish I had've worked harder."

**had ought.** Neither this expression nor its negative (*hadn't ought*) is Standard English.

**hanged, hung.** The second of these forms is more widely used as both finite past tense form and past participle of the verb *hang*. Some people carefully avoid use of *hung* in reference to death by hanging; other equally reputable speakers and writers do not.

**hardly.** *See* DOUBLE NEGATIVE.

**have got.** Use of this expression (as in *We've got to go* or *They had got the debt paid off*) is certainly more common in informal speech than in writing. When not overused, the construction is perfectly respectable.

**healthful, healthy.** Some writers make a useful distinction between these two adjectives, assigning to *healthful* the meaning "health giving" and to *healthy* the meaning "in good health."

**height.** This standard spelling suggests the standard pronunciation. In older English, a pronunciation and spelling ending in *-th* was fairly frequent.

## I

**if, whether.** It is a little less formal to say, "I don't know if he intends to come" than to say, "I don't know whether he intends to come or not." Both constructions are well established. For subjunctive verb forms used after *if, see* VERBS in the "Outline of English Grammar."

**illusion.** *See* ALLUSION.

**imply, infer.** A useful distinction is made by careful speakers and writers who employ *imply* only to mean "suggest" or "state indirectly" and *infer* to mean "draw a conclusion from evidence." The evidence for an inference can be either verbal or of some other sort. It is possible to say, "The speaker did not imply what the hearers inferred."

**ingenious, ingenuous.** *Ingenious* means "skilful, clever, inventive." *Ingenuous* means "innocent, guileless, or unsophisticated."

**in back of.** *See* BACK OF.

**in regard to.** *See* REGARD.

**incidentally.** *See* ACCIDENTALLY.

**incredible, incredulous.** *See* CREDIBLE.

**infer.** *See* IMPLY.

**inflammable.** *See* FLAMMABLE.

**inside, inside of.** Since both these expressions mean the same thing, the former is more economical. It is the one much more frequently used in writing.

**interesting.** This word is overused, with the result that it has lost specific meaning. *See* COUNTER WORDS.

**invitation, invite.** In Standard English, *invite* is a verb only. Its use as an equivalent for the noun *invitation* originated as slang.

**inward(s).** *See* BACKWARD(S).

**irregardless.** *Regardless* has a negative suffix and does not need a negative prefix. One sometimes hears *irregardless* in speech, but it is generally felt to be nonstandard.

**it is me, it's me.** *See* SELECTION and AGREEMENT in the "Outline of English Grammar."

**it says.** Such an expression as "It says in the paper . . ." is colloquial. The more formal and literary expression would be "The paper says. . . ."

**its, it's.** The possessive forms of personal pronouns are *never* properly spelled with an apostrophe. *It's* is a contraction of *it is.*

## J

**judicial, judicious.** *Judicial* is properly used to describe behavior or procedure related to or befitting a judge or court of law. *Judicious* is an adjective applied to carefully considered and wise conduct that has required a decision.

**judgment, judgement.** Both these spellings are established. The first is the more common in the United States.

## K

**kind of, sort of.** These phrases are often postdeterminers preceded by *this* or *that, these* or *those.* A problem of grammatical agreement arises when the phrases are followed by a plural noun. In easy conversation, speakers have long said such things as "These kind of machines." Careful speakers, on the other hand, have generally made a virtue of saying "This kind (or sort) of machines" or "These kinds (or sorts) of machines." In formal writing, the demonstrative always agrees in number with the grammatical number of *kind* or *sort.*

## L

**laboratory.** Note the correct spelling of this word, which does not necessarily reflect its pronunciation.

**latter.** *See* FORMER.

**lay.** *See* LIE.

**lead.** This may be a verb whose past tense form is *led*. It may also be a noun referring to a kind of metal.

**learn, teach.** We learn many things that nobody specifically teaches us. These verbs should not be confused. The past tense form of *learn* (*learned*) has two pronunciations. It is usually given one syllable, but when it is made to describe a person extraordinarily well educated (*a learned person*), it has the older pronunciation in which the *-ed* is made a separate second syllable.

**leave, let.** In Standard English, *leave* never has the meaning "allow." The verb that carries such a meaning is *let: Let us go. Leave,* of course, is also a noun (as in *a soldier's leave*). An older meaning of *let* was "to hinder," or (as a noun) "prevention." These older meanings are preserved in the expression "without let or hindrance" and in the tennis term, "a let ball."

**lend, loan.** It may be useful to confine *loan* to use as a noun referring to what is (or might be) lent. In England, the distinction between *lend* as a verb and *loan* as a noun is preserved among educated speakers; in the United States it is not.

**less, lesser.** These are both comparative forms of *little. Lesser* is less commonly used, and it is generally confined to comparisons involving judgment of importance (as in *the lesser of two evils*). *See also* FEWER.

**let.** *See* LEAVE.

**liable.** *See* APT.

**lie, lay.** As a verb meaning "to be untruthful," *lie* has the past tense form *lied.* When *lie* means "to recline," its finite past tense form is *lay* and its past participle is *lain.* These are the forms careful speakers and writers use as intransitives. The transitive verb *lay,* meaning "to place" something or "to cause to lie," has the past tense form *laid.* It is possible, of course, to say, "The hens laid well," for this expression is derived from "The hens laid eggs. . . ."

**lief.** This archaic word is seldom seen in literary writing nowadays, but in speech it may be heard in such expressions as "I would (or had) as lief come as not."

**like, as (if).** *Like* is rarely used as a conjunction in formal writing, and it almost never appears in a position where *as if* would fit. In speech and informal writing, however, it is not uncommon in the meaning of either "as" or "as if." This usage is disliked by many educated people who insist that *like,* when not a verb, should be confined to use as a preposition, as in *The marines fought like tigers.* Unfortunately, consciousness of objections to use of *like* in such a sentence as "Do like I do" has misled some speakers into avoiding the word and producing such ridiculous statements as "The marines fought as tigers." Here the meaning could be "in the form of tigers."

**likely.** *See* APT.

**loan.** *See* LEND.

**look bad.** *See* BAD.

**lovely, lousy.** *See* COUNTER WORDS.

**lying.** This is the present participle of *lie* in both its meanings. *See* LIE.

## M

**mad.** The basic meaning of *mad* is "insane" or "mentally deranged." Use of *mad* as an equivalent of *angry* or *annoyed* is colloquial.

**majority, plurality.** When applied to votes, *majority* means "more than half." In the same context, *plurality* means "the largest number cast for a particular candidate." If more than two candidates run for an office, it is obvious that one may win a plurality of the votes without winning a majority of them. In other contexts, *majority* is often a pretentious word that could be replaced by *most. Majority,* of course, has other meanings that are explained in the dictionary entry.

**may.** *See* CAN.

**me, I.** *See* SELECTION AND AGREEMENT in the "Outline of English Grammar."

**median.** This word should not be confused with *medium,* though the two words are related in origin and meaning. *Median* means "middle." It may refer, for example, to the strip that separates the traffic on an expressway, or it may refer to the middle number in a series. The plural of *median* is *medians.*

**medium.** This word has several quite distinct meanings; see the dictionary entry. As applied to numerical calculations, it refers to an average (sometimes called a *mean*). It is often applied to that which makes something else possible, as in *Television is a medium of communication.* The Latin plural of *medium* is *media;* the established English plural is *mediums.* People who mistake *media* for a singular form are likely to invent *medias* as a new plural.

**mighty.** The use of *mighty* as an adjective qualifier (*He is mighty good at golf*) is colloquial.

**moral, morale.** *Morale* is a noun only, and it refers to the way people feel (whether in good spirits or not). *Moral* may be either an adjective or a noun, but it is concerned with what is right or wrong (ethically). It is possible for people to have high morale and low morals.

**most.** *See* ALMOST.

**myself.** Sometimes, speakers feel that it is less self-assertive to use *myself* rather than *I* or *me.* There is no good reason for such expressions as "They asked John and myself to come," or "My mother and myself were given the responsibility."

## N

**native, citizen.** One is a native of the place where he was born; he is a citizen of the country or political subdivision where he has legal rights and duties of citizenship.

**never, not.** The indiscriminate use of *never* to mean simply *not* is colloquial. *Never* means, literally, "not at any time." Colloquial: "I was late this morning, because Mother never woke me up."

**nice.** *See* COUNTER WORDS.

**none is, none are.** Although *none* is a compound made from *no* and *one,* the word long ago ceased being only a singular. The grammatical number of the verb used with it depends, as it does with collective nouns, on the meaning ascribed to it.

**noplace.** *See* ANYPLACE.

**not un-.** *See* DOUBLE NEGATIVE.

**notable, notorious.** *Notable* is an adjective that is at least neutral; *notorious* describes something or somebody well known for qualities that are unpleasant or are disapproved. *See* FAMOUS.

**nowheres.** *See* ANYWHERE.

**number.** *See* AMOUNT.

**Numbers.** It is customary to use figures for numbers in addresses, dates, page references, and official names such as *Public School 31.* Naturally, figures are used in lists of numbers, statistics, and mathematics texts. In ordinary writing that is at all formal, numbers are spelled out at the beginning of a sentence, and consistency in practice elsewhere is maintained. Many writers make a practice of spelling out any numbers that take only two words (*ninety-nine,* but *101*). Small numbers are generally spelled out, but some writers use figures for all beyond ten.

## O

**O, oh.** The form *O,* when used as part of a vocative expression, is always capitalized and is not separated by punctuation from the name of what is called on ("Where is thy sting, O Death?"). *Oh* is capitalized only at the beginning of a sentence, and it is often followed by a comma or exclamation point ("Oh, Harry! Come here, won't you?"). *Oh* is not confined to use in vocatives; it is often simply an attention-claimer.

**of.** *See* COULD OF and INSIDE.

**off from, off of.** *Off* and *of* were originally simply the stressed and unstressed forms of the same word; as adverbs, they could carry the meaning of "away from." Many people still feel *off from* and *off of* are uneconomical (unnecessarily redundant) expressions. In formal writing *from* or *off* are used by themselves.

**oh.** *See* O.

**O.K., OK, okay, okeh.** This expression is America's contribution to international communication! Known and used almost everywhere in the world as an indication of approval or correctness, it is still felt to be colloquial; it is not generally used in formal writing. When it is represented in writing, any of the forms noted here may be used, and some others as well. Variants such as *okeydoke* are clearly slang.

**on, onto, on to.** The prepositions *on* and *onto* sometimes mean the same thing: *She got on* (or *onto*) *the streetcar.* But in some contexts, *onto* indicates direction of movement, whereas *on* does not: *He stood on* (not *onto*) *the desk and then climbed onto the bookcase. Onto* should not be confused in spelling with the adverb *on* plus the preposition *to* as in *Go on to the next lesson.*

**on, upon.** These prepositions usually have the same meaning, but *upon* often seems a little more formal.

**on account of.** It is slangy to use *on account of* as a substitute for *because,* as in "He broke the date with Jane on account of she annoyed him." In some localities this usage may have become a colloquialism.

**one.** Use of *one* as an indefinite pronoun meaning "a person" is not characteristic of easy speech or informal writing, where the same notion is often expressed by the indefinite *you.* When *one* is used in the sense described here, custom in the United States allows reference to it by means of *he* and *himself: One finds it difficult to understand himself.* Some writers of formal English, however, make a virtue of referring to it only with *one, one's* and *oneself: When one loses one's temper, one has only oneself to blame.* This kind of writing seems unbearably stiff and artificial to many readers.

**only.** Intonation in speech almost always indicates clearly what *only* should be taken to modify. In writing, it is important to place *only* in a position where it is not likely to be misinterpreted. A sign, THIS ELEVATOR ONLY FOR DELIVERIES could mean that only one elevator was available for deliveries, or that "this elevator" was to be used only for deliveries, nothing else. Normally, putting *only* just before the word it modifies prevents ambiguity: *Only I gave her flowers. I gave her only flowers* (or . . . *flowers only*).

**onto.** *See* ON.

**onward(s).** *See* BACKWARD(S).

**ought.** *See* HAD OUGHT.

**ourn, yourn.** *Like theirn, hisn,* and *hern,* these forms were invented on analogy with *mine* and *thine,* but only *mine* and *thine* are Standard English. The other forms are found in some regional dialects.

**outside of.** *See* INSIDE.

**outward(s).** *See* BACKWARD(S).

**over across.** In most contexts this expression is unnecessarily redundant; one of the words can usually be omitted with good effect.

## P

**Participle.** *See* DANGLING MODIFIER.

**pass.** The spelling of the finite past tense and the past participle of this verb is *passed.* Though the noun, adverb, adjective, and preposition *past* is pronounced in exactly the same way, a distinction in spelling is expected. Example: *The* *past president passed past the house, thinking of days gone past.*

**pay.** The past tense form of *pay* is *paid,* except in nautical contexts where a line may be described as being *payed out.*

**peeve.** This is a colloquial term used either as a noun or verb.

**per, percent, percentage.** *Per* is an established preposition (as in *per diem, per year,* and *per student*), but it has a technical or statistical connotation. What it says usually can be said more simply (*a day,* etc.). But the term *percent* (note the spelling) is indispensable. This word is represented by the graphic symbol % only when it follows a specific figure (as in *40%*) — and even in such a position it is often spelled out. *Percentage* is the term often (but not always) used when a figure is not specified (as in *an impressive percentage*).

**perfect, perfectly.** *See* COUNTER WORDS.

**persecute, prosecute.** To persecute someone is to harass him and cause him to suffer unjustly. To prosecute someone is to take legal action against him, presumably for the purpose of securing justice. If a person carries on a course of action, he can also be said to be prosecuting it; a nation is said to prosecute a war.

**personal, personnel.** These words should not be confused in spelling; they are, of course, also pronounced differently. The second is used only to refer impersonally to employees or people on the staff of an organization of some kind.

**perspective, prospective.** Perspective has to do with ways of seeing things or ways of understanding something: *A school seems very different from the perspective of a student than from the perspective of a teacher. Prospective* is usually an adjective meaning "possible in the future": *Ted is a prospective member of the literary society.*

**phase.** *See* FAZE.

**phenomenon.** This is a singular form. The Greek plural is *phenomena;* there is also an established English plural: *phenomenons. Phenomena* is not properly used as a singular form. Compare *criterion, criteria.*

**playwright.** This word (note the spelling) means literally "play maker," just as *wheelwright* means "wheel maker." It is possible to speak or write of a play writer, but it is never correct to write *playwrite.*

**plenty.** It is colloquial to use *plenty* as a qualifier of an adjective (as in *He was plenty good*). The omission of the preposition *of* in such expressions as *plenty of time* is widely regarded as nonstandard.

**plurality.** *See* MAJORITY.

**politics.** Like many other nouns that end in *-ics, politics* was originally a plural form but may now also be used as a singular.

**positive(ly).** *See* ABSOLUTE(LY).

**Possessive with gerund.** In formal speech and writing, a possessive form often precedes a gerund, particularly if the word related to the gerund is a pronoun. Thus, in formal English we are more likely to find *The government disapproved his going to Cuba* than . . . *disapproved him going to Cuba.* The usage preferred in formal writing is appropriate in other kinds of expression as well, but it is not necessarily a mark of good English. There is a subtle distinction, too, that can be made between *I liked his dancing that way* and *I liked him dancing that way.* In the latter example, *dancing* will be taken as a participle modifying *him.*

**practicable, practical, practically.** A plan is practicable if it is capable of being put into practice. It is practical if it is sensible, if it works, or if it seems likely to work advantageously. *Practically* is, of course, the adverb made from *practical,* and it usually carries its original meaning in formal speech and writing. In informal speech and writing, it is often made to mean "almost" or "nearly": *He was practically a moron.* Some people object to this use.

**practice, practise.** The first of these established spellings is more common in the United States.

**precede, proceed, procedure.** Note the conventional spelling of the second syllable in these words.

**precedence, precedents.** The first of these words may be pronounced with the heaviest stress on either the first or the second syllable. It means "priority in rank or order." *Precedents* is the plural of *precedent;* both forms take the heaviest stress on the first syllable. A precedent is an action or event that has already occurred.

**predominant, predominate.** Beware of confusing the adjective *predominant* with the verb *predominate.*

**Preposition at the end of a clause.** Despite false rules to the contrary, prepositions often appear quite naturally at the ends of clauses and sentences in Standard English. To put them there frequently may give an unwanted flavor of the colloquial or very informal. But to torture a sentence in order to avoid such placement of a preposition can produce a ridiculous construction, as Winston Churchill pointed out when he remarked, "This is the kind of arrant nonsense up with which I will not put."

**prescribe, proscribe.** To prescribe is to require or strongly advise; a doctor prescribes medicine or a course of action. To proscribe something is to prohibit it, and when a governmental authority banishes or condemns a person to drastic penalties, it may be said to have proscribed him.

**pretty.** Though *pretty* was originally simply an adjective, in colloquial English it is now often (perhaps too often) used as a qualifier of adjectives and adverbs. In formal writing, of course, we are not likely to find such expressions as, "The book is pretty good, and I read it pretty carefully."

**principal, principle.** The basic meaning of *principal* is that of an adjective meaning "most important"; but like its synonym *chief*, it has also become a noun through omission of words that it might modify. We now speak of the principal of a school, or of a sum of money as principal (in contrast to the interest it may draw). *Principle* is always a noun; some people find it useful to note that in spelling it, we give it the same last two letters used in its synonym *rule*.

**procedure, proceed.** *See* PRECEDE.

**prolog, prologue.** Both these spellings are established; the second is more common.

**prophecy, prophesy.** If a person *prophesies*, he produces a *prophecy*. The *s* marks the verb; the *c* marks the noun.

**proposition.** As a noun, the basic meaning of this word is "something set forth for consideration." It is often overused colloquially as a synonym for *deal, transaction, situation, scheme*. As a verb, *to proposition* generally connotes the making of a disreputable or illegal proposal.

**proved, proven.** Both these forms are used as the past participle of the verb *prove*. The form ending in *n* is less frequent, except when it precedes a noun which it modifies: *a proven evil.*

## Q

**quantity.** Uncountable things such as milk, sand, and lumber are measured as quantities; countable things should not be referred to as quantities. We say, "There are many people here," but not "There is a large quantity of people here."

**quick(ly).** *See* SLOW(LY).

**quite.** The basic meaning of *quite* was "completely" or "wholly." It still carries that meaning in some contexts, particularly in more formal speech and writing: *Are you quite sure?* Used colloquially, however, the word has become also a synonym for *very: He came quite near me.*

**quote, quotation.** A quotation is something that is actually quoted. It is illogical to say that a piece of literature contains many quotations, when the meaning is that people have drawn many quotations from it. *Quote* has traditionally been a verb; its use as a shortening of the noun *quotation* is colloquial, and is not appropriate in writing that has any degree of formality.

## R

**raise, rise, rear.** *Rise* is an intransitive verb; in many contexts, an equivalent is *arise*. The finite past tense forms of these verbs are *rose* and *arose;* the past participles are *risen* and *arisen*. *Raise* is the transitive verb, meaning "to cause to rise"; its past tense form is *raised*. Some people insist that we should speak of raising such things as flowers or chickens, but of rearing children. This distinction is not regularly honored, even in formal writing. In the United States, an increase in wages is usually spoken of as "a raise."

**rarely ever, seldom ever.** These are colloquial expressions. In more formal (and economical) use, *ever* is omitted.

**rather.** *See* HAD BETTER.

**real(ly).** Only in colloquial use is *real* a qualifier of adjectives and adverbs. Speakers are sometimes advised to substitute *really* in such an expression as "The teacher was real helpful." But since the adverb *really* more often carries an affirmation of genuineness than an indication of extent, that advice may not seem really helpful. An unobjectionable substitute for *real* as a qualifier is *very*.

**reason is because.** Instead of using this expression, it is more logical to say *the reason is that* . . . . Often, it is more direct to say that something happened because . . . , rather than *The reason it happened is that* . . . *See* CIRCUMLOCUTION.

**reckon.** *See* CALCULATE.

**regard.** *As regards, in regard to,* and *with regard to* are established expressions in Standard English; *in regards to* or *with regards to* are not.

**remember of.** The preposition in this expression is unnecessarily redundant.

**respectfully, respectively.** *Respectfully* describes courteous behavior. *Respectively* means "considering each of two or more items or persons individually and in the order named." Correct: *John respectfully apologized to his father, his mother, and his teacher, respectively.*

**revenge.** *See* AVENGE.

**Rev., Reverend.** Many people consider it disrespectful to refer to a clergyman as *Reverend* or *the Reverend* without using his name. Still others regard it as proper only to use *Reverend* (or in writing, the abbreviation *Rev.*) with a following *Mr.* or with a given name: *Rev. Mr. Smith* or *the Rev. John Smith.*

**rhyme, rime, rhythm.** The spellings *rhyme* and *rime* are equally well established. There is only one conventional spelling of *rhythm*.

**rise.** *See* RAISE.

**'round.** *See* AROUND.

**run.** The standard finite past tense form of this verb is *ran: The rabbit ran away*. The past participle is *run: The rabbit has run away.*

## S

**sacrilegious.** This adjective is associated with the noun *sacrilege* rather than with *religious*. Note the spelling carefully.

**said, same.** These words, when used in legal papers, may mean "exactly the person or thing that has been identified earlier." Except in legal contexts, use of these words in such a sense is generally frowned on.

**scarcely.** *See* DOUBLE NEGATIVE.

**see, saw, seen.** These are the standard principal parts of the verb *see*. Correct: *I see today; I saw yesterday; I have seen.*

**seldom ever.** *See* RARELY EVER.

**-self.** *See* MYSELF.

**set, sit.** *Sit* is usually an intransitive verb. Its past tense form is *sat. Set* originally meant "to cause to sit," and in many of its uses that is still what it means. This usually transitive verb is *set* in both the present and the past tense. Its occasional intransitive uses are illustrated by *The sun sets in the west* and *A hen sets on eggs.*

**shall, will.** The distinction between these words when referring to the future is usually only that *shall* is more formal (and less frequently used). In questions involving a first person pronoun as subject, however, *shall* is meaningfully used where there is a choice to be made, *will* where no choice is in question. *Shall we go through Atlanta on the way to Miami?* implies that we might go to Miami by at least two routes. *Will we go through Atlanta?* merely asks whether the route decided on will take us through Atlanta.

**should, would.** Historically, *should* is the past tense form of *shall* and *would* is the past tense form of *will. Should* has more regularly than *shall* retained the sense of expressing obligation; it also expresses probability (*We should be able to finish the job by noon*). *Would* expresses habitual past action and polite requests (*He would often ask, "Would you please close the door?"*). Both *should* and *would* are used in conditional clauses; in them, *should* often connotes greater uncertainty (compare *If she should come, I could leave* and *If she would come, I could leave*). Where the two words are interchangeable, *should* seems the more formal. *See also* WOULD HAVE.

**should of.** *See* COULD OF.

**sight.** *See* CITE.

**sing.** In formal English, *sang* is the finite past tense form of *sing,* while *sung* is its past participle only. Colloquially, sometimes, and occasionally in informal writing, *sung* may be used as the finite past tense form. Such an expression as *She has sang* is never used in Standard English.

**sink.** Both *sank* and *sunk* are used as the finite past tense form of this verb. The past participle is *sunk,* unless the form *sunken* is used to precede a noun that it modifies (*a sunken ship*).

**sit.** *See* SET.

**site.** *See* CITE.

**slow(ly).** Both *slow* and *slowly* are adverbs in good standing. There are, of course, some positions where only *slowly* would normally be used. We would not say, "He slow climbed the hill." *Slow,* it hardly need be said, is also an adjective.

**so.** In informal speech and writing *so* is sometimes used as a qualifier approximately equivalent to *very.* Such usage can easily become tiresome; it is regularly avoided in writing that is at all formal.

**someplace.** *See* ANYPLACE.

**somewhere.** *See* ANYWHERE.

**sort of.** *See* KIND OF.

**special(ly).** *See* ESPECIAL(LY).

**specie, species.** *Specie* means "money in the form of coins"; the word has no plural form. *Species,* a term meaning "a distinct kind" of something, is used without change as either a singular or plural noun.

**Split infinitive.** To split an infinitive (as in *He failed to fully understand the problem*) is in itself neither a virtue nor a vice. Accuracy and clarity in expression of meaning, or rhythm appropriate to style are the considerations that do or do not justify placing an adverbial modifier between *to* (the sign of the infinitive) and the verb form it introduces.

**splendid.** *See* COUNTER WORDS.

**stanza, verse.** Technically, a verse (the term originally meant "a turning") is a single line of poetry, while a stanza is a patterned unit made up of verses. Popular usage, however, has applied *verse* to poetry in general (*Sandburg wrote verse*) and to what is more accurately called a stanza.

**stationary, stationery.** The first of these words is an adjective that means "unchanging" or "not moving." The second is a noun referring to writing materials. Note the spellings.

**statistics.** In Standard English, the normal form of this word usually has a final *s. Statistics* is always treated as a plural except when the word names a branch of study: *Statistics is a kind of applied mathematics.*

**stratum.** The Latin plural of this word is *strata;* the English plural is *stratums.* Both forms are established in English.

**such.** Use of *such* as a mere qualifier (as in *I had such a good time!*) is colloquial.

**sure(ly).** Use of *sure* as an adverb ("Are you going?" "Sure.") is colloquial only.

**swell.** *Swell* as a term of approval or as a noun referring to someone thought to be pretentious *(He was a swell)* has the odor of slang. *See* COUNTER WORDS.

**swim.** The finite past tense form of this verb is *swam*; the past participle is *swum.* In some regional dialects, *swum* may be heard as the finite past tense.

## T

**teach.** *See* LEARN.

**terrible, terrific.** *See* COUNTER WORDS.

**that, who, which.** *See* ADJECTIVE (RELATIVE) CLAUSES in the "Outline of English Grammar.")

**that there.** *See* THIS (THESE) HERE.

**the fact that.** *See* FACT THAT.

**theirn.** *See* OURN.

**theirselves.** *Themselves,* not theirselves, is the standard form.

**them kinds, them there.** These are nonstandard expressions. The standard substitute for the first is *those kinds,* for the second, simply *those.*

**there is, there are.** In colloquial usage, the expletive *there* is often followed by the singular verb even when the true subject of the sentence is plural. In expression with any degree of formality, agreement of verb and true subject is generally expected: *There are lots of things to do.* An exception, however, is made when the subject is a compound in which the first element is singular: *There is ham and eggs for breakfast.*

**this (these) here, that (those) there.** These expressions are nonstandard when used as unitary modifiers of nouns. Such expressions as *this car here* are, of course, standard.

**though (tho).** *See* ALTHOUGH.

**those (these) kind.** *See* KIND OF.

**thru.** This simplified spelling of *through* is almost never used in formal writing.

**thusly.** Nowadays, this form is not generally used. *Thus* is the common form of the adverb.

**till, until.** These words may be used interchangeably. There is no need to write *'til.* Note that *till* has two *l's, until* only one.

**to.** *See* SPLIT INFINITIVE.

**toward(s).** *See* BACKWARD(S).

**transpire.** The original meaning of *transpire* was "to exhale." Many people feel that using it to mean "to happen" is distastefully pretentious.

**try and, try to.** *See* AND.

## U

**uninterested.** *See* DISINTERESTED.

**United States.** The name of our nation is nowadays normally made the subject of singular verbs, although political orators still sometimes speak of *these United States.*

**unless.** To substitute *without* for *unless* is nonstandard usage.

**until.** *See* TILL.

**used.** Be careful in spelling not to drop the *d* in this past tense form of *use.*

## V

**venal, venial.** The first of these adjectives describes corruption or corruptibility as a result of greed for money or other material gain. *Venial* means "forgivable." A venial sin is not so serious as a deadly sin.

**verse.** *See* STANZA.

**very.** Like other qualifiers of adjectives and adverbs, *very* has lost much of its force through overuse. Sometimes the omission of the qualifier produces a stronger expression than does its use.

**virtue, virtuosity.** *Virtue* refers to merit of any sort. *Virtuosity* refers to an artist's technical skill.

**vocation.** *See* AVOCATION.

## W

**wait for, wait on.** With the meaning "to serve," *wait on* is in general English use (*She was hired to wait on tables*). In the sense of "wait for" (*We haven't time to wait on Fred*) *wait on* is colloquial in certain regions.

**'way, away.** In informal speech, *away* is often shortened by omission of the first syllable. Such usage is not common in writing, but when it occurs, it should be represented by *'way* (*We saw him 'way down the road*).

**ways.** In speech, we often hear such expressions as *a little ways farther.* In writing, it is generally considered good practice to use *way* following a singular determiner.

**well.** *See* GOOD. In speech, *well* is often overused as an attention-claimer or mere time-filler (*Well . . . well, I don't know*).

**went.** *See* GO.

**whether.** *See* IF.

**which.** *See* ADJECTIVE (RELATIVE) CLAUSES in the "Outline of English Grammar."

**while.** *See* AWHILE.

**whilst.** In England, but not in the U. S., *whilst* is common as an alternative to the conjunction *while.*

**who, whom.** *See* ADJECTIVE (RELATIVE) CLAUSES in the "Outline of English Grammar."

**whose, who's.** *Whose* is the possessive form of *who, which,* or *that.* It should not be confused with *who's,* the contraction of *who is.*

**will.** *See* SHALL.

**with regard.** *See* REGARD.

**without.** *See* UNLESS.

**would.** *See* SHOULD. *See also* COULD OF.

**would rather.** This is an established expression, equivalent, to *had rather. See* HAD RATHER.

## Y

**you.** *See* ONE.

**you all.** As a plural of *you,* this is a regional colloquialism.

**you and I.** The second person personal pronoun has no distinctive forms for subjective and objective uses. Perhaps that is the reason some people have difficulty in choosing the correct form of other personal pronouns that may be coordinated with it. *You and I* (*he*) (*she*) may be correctly used only in subjective positions (*You and I can do the job*). As an object of the verb (*He called you and me*) or as an object of a preposition (*We will choose between you and him*), only an objective form can be properly coordinated with *you.*

**your, you're.** In writing, the possessive *your* should not be confused with *you're,* which is a contraction of *you are.*

**yourn.** This is a nonstandard possessive form of *you.*

**youse.** This is a plural of *you* that has never been admitted to standard use.

# SYNONYMS AND ANTONYMS

## Words of Similar and Opposite Meaning

A synonym is a word having the same or nearly the same meaning in one or more senses as another in the same language. Thus, after the entry word *beautiful* in the following list, these words are shown as synonyms: fine, handsome, pretty, bewitching, attractive, comely. The synonyms share one characteristic: they all, in one or more senses, have the meaning or nearly the meaning of *beautiful*. Antonyms (opposite meanings) follow in parentheses.

### A

**abandon,** leave, forsake, desert, renounce, surrender, relinquish, quit, forgo, waive. (Keep, hold, maintain, cherish.)

**abandoned,** deserted, forsaken, wicked, reprobate, dissolute, profligate, flagitious, corrupt, depraved, vicious. (Virtuous.)

**abandonment,** leaving, desertion, dereliction, renunciation, defection.

**abasement,** degradation, fall, degeneracy, humiliation, adjection, debasement, servility. (Honor.)

**abash,** embarrass, humiliate, mortify, bewilder, disconcert, discompose, confound, confuse, shame. (Encourage, cheer, embolden.)

**abate,** decrease, ebb, dwindle, subside, moderate, reduce, lessen. (Increase, revive, enlarge, aggravate, enhance.)

**abbreviate,** shorten, abridge, curtail, contract, condense, reduce. (Extend.)

**abdicate,** give up, resign, renounce, abandon, forsake, relinquish, quit, forgo.

**abet,** sanction, support, uphold, help, encourage, instigate, incite, stimulate, aid, assist. (Deter, dissuade, hinder, impede.)

**abettor,** assistant, accessory, accomplice, promoter, instigator, particeps criminis, coadjutor, associate, companion, co-operator. (Opponent.)

**abhor,** despise, dislike, hate, detest, abominate, loathe, nauseate. (Love, admire, esteem, approve.)

**abide,** endure, tolerate, bear, continue, wait. (Avoid, resist, abandon, shun.)

**ability,** capability, talent, faculty, capacity, qualification, aptitude, aptness, expertness, skill, efficiency, accomplishment, attainment. (Incompetency.)

**abject,** groveling, low, mean, base, ignoble, worthless, despicable, servile, vile, contemptible. (Noble.)

**abjure,** recant, forswear, disclaim, recall, revoke, retract, renounce. (Maintain.)

**able,** strong, powerful, muscular, stalwart, vigorous, athletic, robust, brawny, skillful, adroit, competent, efficient, capable, clever, self-qualified, telling, fitted. (Weak.)

**abode,** residence, habitation, dwelling, domicile, home, quarters, lodging.

**abolish,** quash, destroy, revoke, abrogate, annul, cancel, annihilate, extinguish, vitiate, invalidate, nullify, end, remove, repeal. (Establish, continue, support, sustain, enforce.)

**abominable,** hateful, detestable, odious, vile, execrable. (Lovable.)

**abortive,** fruitless, ineffectual, idle, inoperative, vain, futile. (Effectual.)

**about,** concerning, regarding, relative to, with regard to, as to, respecting, referring to, around, nearly, approximately.

**abscond,** run off, steal away, decamp, bolt, depart, disappear.

**absent,** inattentive, abstracted, not present, away, dreamy. (Present.)

**absolute,** entire, complete, unconditional, unqualified, unrestricted, despotic, arbitrary, tyrannous, imperative, authoritative, imperious, autocratic, positive, unequivocal. (Limited, conditional, accountable.)

**absorb,** engross, swallow up, engulf, imbibe, consume, merge. (Eject, exude, emit, disgorge.)

**absurd,** silly, foolish, preposterous, ridiculous, irrational, unreasonable, nonsensical, inconsistent, ludicrous. (Wise, solemn, logical, sensible.)

**abuse,** *v.*, asperse, revile, vilify, reproach, calumniate, defame, slander, scandalize, malign, traduce, disparage, depreciate, ill-use, defile, desecrate. (Praise, protect, eulogize, laud, extol.)

**abuse,** *n.*, scurrility, ribaldry, contumely, obloquy, opprobrium, foul invective, vituperation, ill-usage. (Praise, protection.)

**accede,** assent, consent, acquiesce, comply, agree, coincide, concur, approve. (Protest.)

**accelerate,** hasten, hurry, expedite, forward, quicken, dispatch. (Retard.)

**accept,** receive, take, admit. (Refuse.)

**acceptable,** agreeable, pleasing, gratifying, pleasurable, welcome. (Displeasing.)

**accident,** casualty, incident, contingency, mishap, adventure, chance.

**accommodate,** serve, oblige, adapt, adjust, fit, suit. (Disoblige, impede.)

**accomplice,** confederate, accessory, abettor, coadjutor, assistant, ally, associate, particeps criminis. (Adversary.)

**accomplish,** do, effect, finish, execute, achieve, complete, perfect, consummate. (Fail.)

**accomplishment,** attainment, qualification, acquirement. (Defect.)

**accord,** grant, allow, admit, concede. (Deny.)

**accost,** salute, address, speak to, stop, greet.

**account,** narrative, description, narration, relation, detail, recital, reckoning, bill, charge.

**accountable,** punishable, answerable, amenable, responsible, liable.

**accumulate,** bring together, amass, collect, gather. (Scatter, dissipate.)

**accumulation,** collection, store, mass, congeries, concentration.

**accurate,** correct, exact, precise, nice, truthful. (Erroneous, careless.)

**achieve,** do, accomplish, effect, fulfill, execute, gain, win.

**achievement,** feat, exploit, accomplishment, attainment, performance, acquirement, gain. (Failure.)

**acknowledge,** admit, confess, own, avow, grant, recognize, allow, concede. (Deny.)

**acquaint,** inform, enlighten, apprise, make aware, make known, notify, communicate. (Deceive.)

**acquaintance,** familiarity, intimacy, cognizance, fellowship, companionship, friendship, knowledge. (Unfamiliarity.)

**acquiesce,** agree, accede, assent, comply, consent, give way, coincide, concur. (Protest.)

**acquit,** pardon, forgive, discharge, set free, clear, absolve. (Condemn, convict.)

**acrimony,** harshness, severity, unkindness, asperity, bitterness, malignity, virulence. (Gentleness, amiability, kindness, mildness, courtesy, sweetness.)

**act,** do, operate, make, perform, play, enact.

**action,** deed, achievement, feat, exploit, accomplishment, battle, engagement, agency, instrumentality.

**active,** lively, sprightly, alert, agile, nimble, brisk, quick, supple, prompt, vigilant, bustling, energetic, busy, laborious, industrious. (Lazy, idle, inactive, slow, sluggish, indolent, passive.)

**actual,** real, positive, genuine, certain. (Fictitious.)

**acumen,** keenness, insight, discernment, acuteness, shrewdness, sagacity, sharpness. (Dullness, stupidity, obtuseness, bluntness.)

**acute,** shrewd, intelligent, penetrating, piercing, keen. (Dull.)

**adapt,** accommodate, suit, fit, conform.

**addicted,** devoted, wedded, attached, accustomed, habituated, given up to, boring, beside, close, nigh. (Distant, dedicated. (Averse, unaccustomed.)

**addition,** increase, accession, augmentation, reinforcement. (Subtraction, separation.)

**address,** *n.*, speech, discourse, appeal, oration, tact, skill, ability, dexterity, deportment, demeanor.

**address,** *v.*, greet, accost, salute, hail. (Shun, pass, avoid, ignore.)

**adequate,** fit, equal, capable, able, suited, qualified, competent. (Inferior, unfit, unequal, inadequate, incompetent.)

**adhesion,** adherence, attachment, fidelity, devotion. (Aloofness.)

**adjacent,** near to, adjoining, contiguous, conterminous, bordering, neigh- remote.)

**adjourn,** defer, prorogue, postpone.

**adjunct,** appendage, appurtenance, appendency, dependency.

**adjust,** set right, fit, accommodate, adapt, arrange, settle, regulate, organize. (Confuse.)

**admirable,** striking, surprising, wonderful, astonishing. (Detestable.)

**admire,** esteem, love, extol, respect, venerate, honor, adore, approve, enjoy, applaud. (Abhor, detest, scorn, execrate, dislike, despite, abominate.)

**admit,** allow, permit, suffer, tolerate. (Deny.)

**advantageous,** beneficial. (Hurtful.)

**adverse,** opposed, unfavorable, inimical, antagonistic, contrary, hostile. (Helpful, favorable, aiding, assisting, co-operative.)

**affection,** love. (Aversion.)

**affectionate,** fond, kind. (Harsh.)

**affront,** insult, offend, irritate, exasperate, vex, provoke, annoy, displease, aggravate. (Gratify, please, concilate.)

**afraid,** apprehensive, scared, fearful, timid, alarmed, cautious, anxious. (Audacious, brave, confident, bold, gallant, heroic, intrepid, valiant, daring, courageous.)

**agree,** accord, acquiesce, concur, harmonize, assent, coincide. (Contradict, differ, oppose, disagree, dissent.)

**agreeable,** pleasant, pleasing, charming. (Disagreeable.)

**alacrity,** briskness, swiftness, promptness, speed, celerity, alertness, activity. (Apathy, laziness, sluggishness, slowness, indolence, aversion, repugnance.)

**alarm,** fright, panic, terror, fear, dread, dismay, affront. (Confidence, assurance, calmness, security.)

**alert,** nimble, active, prompt, brisk, lively. (Dull, inactive, slow, sluggish.)

**allay,** pacify, quiet, soothe, still, compose, calm, alleviate, mollify, appease. (Excite, rouse, stir, provoke, agitate, arouse.)

**altercation,** dispute, discord, contention, argument, row, quarrel, scrap, disturbance, brawl. (Harmony, unanimity, agreement, union.)

**alternating,** intermittent. (Continual.)

**amazement,** surprise, awe, wonder, bewilderment, confusion, astonishment. (Indifference, steadiness, coolness, stoicism, calmness, composure.)

**ambassador,** envoy, plenipotentiary, minister.

**amend,** improve, correct, better, mend, rectify, repair. (Impair, harm, spoil, injure.)

**anger,** ire, wrath, indignation, resentment, animosity, displeasure, rage. (Good nature, amiability.)

**antipathy,** dislike, hatred, hostility, aversion, detestation, abhorrence, antagonism. (Regard, harmony, sympathy, agreement, congeniality.)

**appropriate,** assume, ascribe, arrogate, usurp.

**argue,** debate, dispute, reason upon.

**arise,** flow, emanate, spring, proceed, rise, issue.

**artful,** disingenuous, sly, tricky, insincere. (Candid.)

**artifice,** trick, stratagem, finesse.

**association,** combination, company, partnership, society. (Isolation, solitude, separation.)

**attack,** assail, assault, encounter. (Defend.)

**attain,** gain, master, accomplish, achieve, win, reach, get, acquire. (Forfeit, abandon, lose.)

**audacity,** boldness, effrontery, hardihood, temerity. (Meekness.)

**austere,** rigid, rigorous, severe, stern. (Dissolute.)

**avaricious,** niggardly, miserly, parsimonious. (Generous.)

**aversion,** antipathy, dislike, hatred, repugnance. (Affection.)

**awe,** dread, fear, reverence. (Familiarity.)

**awkward,** clumsy, uncouth, ungainly. (Graceful, adroit.)

**axiom,** adage, aphorism, apothegm, byword, maxim, proverb, saying, saw.

## B

**babble,** chatter, prattle, prate, murmur, cackle.

**bad,** wicked, evil. (Good.)

**baffle,** confound, defeat, disconcert. (Aid, abet.)

**barbarous,** cruel, merciless, pitiless, atrocious, brutal, inhuman, savage, uncivilized. (Humane, polite, civilized, cultured, refined, urbane.)

**base,** vile, mean. (Noble.)

**battle,** action, combat, engagement.

**bear,** carry, convey, transport.

**bear,** endure, suffer, support.

**beastly,** brutal, sensual, bestial.

**beat,** defeat, overpower, overthrow, rout.

**beautiful,** fine, handsome, pretty, bewitching, attractive, comely. (Homely, ugly, hideous, horrid, unattractive.)

**becoming,** decent, fit, seemly, suitable, befitting, graceful. (Unbecoming, unsuitable, unfitting, misplaced.)

**beg,** beseech, crave, entreat, implore, solicit, supplicate. (Give.)

**behavior,** carriage, conduct, deportment, bearing, manner, demeanor.

**belief,** credit, faith, trust. (Doubt.)

**beneficent,** bountiful, generous, liberal, munificent. (Covetous, miserly.)

**benefit,** favor, advantage, kindness, civility. (Injury.)

**benevolence,** beneficence, benignity, humanity, kindness, tenderness, generosity, liberality, unselfishness. (Malevolence, selfishness, unkindness.)

**blame,** censure, condemn, reprove, reproach, upbraid. (Praise.)

**bleak,** cheerless, bare, dismal, blank, desolate, waste, unsheltered, dreary. (Cheery, balmy, sunny, warm, mild.)

**blemish,** defect, disfigurement, imperfection, flaw, speck, spot, stain. (Ornament.)

**blind,** sightless, heedless. (Farsighted.)

**blot,** cancel, efface, expunge, erase, obliterate.

**bold,** brave, daring, fearless, intrepid, undaunted. (Timid.)

**border,** brim, brink, edge, margin, rim, verge, boundary, confine, frontier.

**bound,** circumscribe, confine, limit, restrict.

**brave,** daring, bold, courageous, adventurous, heroic, intrepid, fearless, valiant, dauntless. (Afraid, timid, cowardly, fearful.)

**bravery,** courage, valor. (Cowardice.)

**break,** crack, split, smash, bruise, crush, pound, squeeze.

**breeze,** blast, gale, gust, hurricane, storm, tempest.

**bright,** brilliant, luminous, resplendent, clear, radiant, shining. (Dull.)

**brittle,** fragile, breakable. (Solid.)

**burial,** interment, sepulture. (Resurrection.)

**business,** avocation, employment, engagement, occupation, art, profession, trade.

**bustle,** stir, tumult, fuss. (Quiet.)

## C

**calamity,** disaster, misfortune, mischance, mishap. (Good fortune.)

**calm,** cool, mild, quiet, peaceful, still, tranquil, collected, composed, placid, serene. (Stormy, disturbed, agitated, excited, ruffled, violent, unsettled.)

**cancel,** nullify, abolish, annul, rescind, quash, revoke, repeal. (Maintain, establish, sustain, uphold, approve.)

**candid,** sincere, honest, truthful, frank, fair, impartial, unbiased. (Cunning, adroit, crafty, sly, shrewd, tricky, wily, subtle, deceitful, artful.)

**capable,** able, competent. (Incompetent.)

**captious,** fretful, cross, peevish, petulant. (Good-natured.)

**care,** anxiety, concern, solicitude, heed, attention. (Heedlessness, negligence.)

**caress,** fondle, pet, kiss, embrace. (Spurn, buffet.)

**carnage,** butchery, massacre, slaughter.

**catch,** grasp, grip, capture, clutch, clasp, seize, snatch, secure, take. (Miss, lose, restore, release.)

**cause,** motive, reason. (Effect, consequence.)

**cavity,** hollow, indentation, hole, opening, bore, perforation, fissure. (Lump, hill, mound, knoll, elevation.)

**cease,** finish, quit, stop, terminate, discontinue, leave off, end. (Continue, begin, inaugurate, start.)

**censure,** animadvert, criticise. (Praise.)

**certain,** secure, sure. (Doubtful.)

**cessation,** intermission, rest, stop. (Continuance.)

**chance,** fate, fortune. (Design.)

**change,** barter, exchange, substitute.

**changeable,** fickle, inconstant, mutable, variable. (Unchangeable.)

**character,** reputation, repute, standing.

**charm,** captivate, enchant, enrapture, fascinate.

**chastity,** purity, continence, virtue. (Lewdness.)

**cheap,** inexpensive, inferior, common. (Dear.)
**cheerful,** gay, merry, sprightly. (Mournful.)
**chief,** chieftain, head, leader. (Subordinate, attendant, follower.)
**circumstance,** fact, incident.
**class,** degree, order, rank.
**clear,** bright, lucid, vivid. (Opaque, ambiguous, dim, obscure, vague.)
**clever,** adroit, dexterous, expert, skillful. (Stupid, awkward, bungling.)
**clothed,** clad, dressed. (Naked.)
**coarse,** rude, rough, unpolished. (Fine.)
**coax,** cajole, fawn, wheedle.
**cold,** cool, frigid, wintry, unfeeling, stoical. (Warm.)
**color,** dye, stain, tinge.
**colorable,** ostensible, plausible, specious.
**combination,** cabal, conspiracy, plot.
**command,** injunction, order, precept.
**commodity,** goods, merchandise, ware.
**common,** mean, ordinary, vulgar. (Uncommon, extraordinary.)
**compassion,** sympathy, pity, clemency. (Cruelty, severity.)
**compel,** force, oblige, necessitate, make, coerce. (Coax, lead.)
**compensation,** amends, recompense, remuneration, requital, reward.
**compendium,** compend, abridgment. (Enlargement.)
**complain,** lament, murmur, regret, repine. (Rejoice.)
**comply,** accede, conform, submit, yield. (Refuse.)
**compound,** complex. (Simple.)
**comprehend,** comprise, include, embrace, grasp, understand, perceive. (Exclude, mistake.)
**comprise,** comprehend, contain, embrace, include.
**conceal,** hide, secrete. (Uncover.)
**conceive,** comprehend, understand.
**conclusion,** inference, deduction.
**condemn,** censure, blame, disapprove, reprove. (Justify, exonerate, acquit, approve.)
**conduct,** direct, guide, lead, govern, regulate, manage.
**confirm,** corroborate, approve, attest. (Contradict.)
**conflict,** combat, contest, contention, struggle. (Peace, quiet.)
**confute,** disprove, refute, oppugn. (Approve.)
**conquer,** master, beat, overcome, subdue, surmount, vanquish. (Defeat, lose, capitulate.)
**consequence,** effect, event, issue, result. (Cause.)
**consider,** reflect, ponder, weigh.
**consistent,** constant, compatible. (Inconsistent.)
**console,** comfort, solace. (Harrow, worry.)
**constancy,** firmness, stalibity, steadiness. (Fickleness.)
**contaminate,** corrupt, defile, pollute, taint.
**contemn,** despise, disdain, scorn. (Esteem.)
**contemplate,** meditate, muse.
**contemptible,** despicable, paltry, pitiful, vile, mean. (Noble.)
**contend,** contest, dispute, strive, struggle, combat.
**continual,** constant, continuous, perpetual, incessant. (Intermittent.)
**continuance,** continuation, duration. (Cessation.)
**continue,** persist, persevere, pursue, prosecute. (Cease.)
**contradict,** deny, gainsay, oppose. (Confirm.)
**contrast,** compare, discriminate, differentiate.
**convey,** transfer, shift, move, change, carry, transport, transmit, give. (Keep, hold, possess, retain.)
**cool,** cold, frigid. (Hot.)
**correct,** rectify, reform.
**cost,** charge, expense, price.
**covetousness,** avarice, cupidity. (Beneficence.)
**cowardice,** fear, timidity, pusillanimity. (Courage.)
**crime,** sin, vice, misdemeanor. (Virtue.)
**criminal,** convict, culprit, felon, malefactor.
**crooked,** bent, curved, oblique. (Straight.)
**cruel,** barbarous, brutal, inhuman, savage. (Kind.)
**cultivation,** culture, refinement.
**cursory,** desultory, hasty, slight. (Thorough.)
**custom,** fashion, manner, practice.

## D

**danger,** hazard, peril. (Safety.)
**dark,** sombre, gloomy, dismal, opaque, obscure, dim. (Light, bright, clear, radiant.)
**deadly,** fatal, destructive, mortal.
**dear,** beloved, precious, costly, expensive. (Despised, cheap.)
**death,** departure, decease, demise. (Life.)
**decay,** decline, consumption. (Growth.)
**deceive,** delude, impose upon, overreach, gull, dupe, cheat.
**deceit,** cheat, imposition, trick, delusion, guile, beguilement, treachery, sham. (Truthfulness.)
**decide,** determine, settle, adjudicate, terminate, resolve.
**decipher,** read, spell, interpret, solve.
**decision,** determination, conclusion, resolution, firmness. (Vacillation.)
**declamation,** oratory, elocution, harangue, effusion, debate.
**declaration,** avowal, manifestation, statement, profession.
**decrease,** diminish, lessen, wane, decline, retrench, curtail, reduce. (Growth.)
**dedicate,** devote, consecrate, offer, set, apportion.
**deed,** act, action, commission, achievement, instrument, document.
**deem,** judge, estimate, consider, think, suppose, conceive.
**deep,** profound, subterranean, submerged, designing, abstruse, learned. (Shallow.)
**deface,** mar, spoil, injure, disfigure. (Beautify.)
**default,** lapse, forfeit, omission, absence, want, failure.
**defect,** imperfection, flaw, fault, blemish. (Beauty, improvement.)
**defend,** guard, protect, justify.
**defense,** excuse, plea, vindication, bulwark, rampart.
**defer,** delay, postpone, put off, prorogue, adjourn. (Force, expedite.)
**deficient,** short, wanting, inadequate, scanty, incomplete. (Complete.)
**defile,** *v.*, pollute, corrupt, sully, befoul, contaminate, spoil. (Beautify, clean, purify.)
**define,** fix, settle, determine, limit.
**defray,** meet, liquidate, pay, discharge.
**degree,** grade, extent, measure.
**deliberate,** *v.*, consider, meditate, consult, ponder, debate.
**deliberate,** *a.*, purposed, intentional, designed, determined. (Hasty.)
**delicacy,** nicety, daintiness, refinement, tact, softness, modesty. (Boorishness, indelicacy.)
**delicate,** tender, fragile, dainty, refined. (Coarse.)
**delicious,** sweet, palatable, luscious, savory. (Nauseous, bitter, unpalatable.)
**deight,** enjoyment, pleasure, happiness, transport, ecstasy, gladness, rapture, bliss. (Annoyance.)
**deliver,** liberate, free, rescue, pronounce, give, hand over. (Retain.)
**demonstrate,** prove, show, exhibit, illustrate.
**depart,** leave, quit, decamp, retire, withdraw, vanish. (Remain.)
**deprive,** strip, bereave, despoil, rob, divest.
**despute,** appoint, commission, charge, intrust, delegate, authorize, accredit.
**derision,** scorn, contempt, contumely, disrespect.
**derivation,** origin, source, beginning, cause, etymology, root.
**describe,** delineate, portray, explain, illustrate, define, picture.
**desecrate,** profane, secularize, misuse, abuse, pollute. (Keep holy.)
**deserve,** merit, earn, justify, win.
**design,** *n.*, delineation, sketch, drawing, cunning, artfulness, contrivance.
**desirable,** expedient, advisable, valuable, acceptable, proper, judicious, beneficial, profitable, good.
**desire,** *n.*, longing, affection, craving, coveting, wish.
**desist,** cease, stop, discontinue, drop, abstain, forbear. (Continue, persevere.)
**desolate,** bereaved, forlorn, forsaken, deserted, wild, waste, bare, bleak, lonely. (Pleasant, happy.)
**desperate,** wild, daring, audacious, determined, reckless.
**despised,** degraded, worthless. (Admired.)
**destiny,** fate, decree, doom, end.
**destructive,** detrimental, hurtful, noxious, injurious, deleterious, baleful, baneful, subversive. (Creative.)
**desuetude,** disuse, discontinuance. (Maintenance.)
**desultory,** rambling, discursive, loose, unmethodical, superficial, unsettled, erratic, fitful. (Thorough.)
**detail,** *n.*, particular, specification, minutiæ.
**detail,** *v.*, particularize, enumerate, specify. (Generalize.)
**deter,** warn, stop, dissuade, terrify, scare. (Encourage.)

**detriment,** loss, harm, injury, deterioration. (Benefit.)
**develop,** unfold, amplify, expand, enlarge.
**device,** artifice, expedient, contrivance.
**devoid,** void, wanting, destitute, unendowed, unprovided. (Full, complete.)
**devoted,** attached, fond, absorbed, dedicated.
**dictate,** prompt, suggest, enjoin, order, command.
**dictatorial,** imperative, imperious, domineering, arbitrary, tyrannical, overbearing. (Submissive.)
**die,** perish, decease, expire, depart, decline, languish, wane, sink, fade, decay.
**diet,** foods, victuals, nourishment, nutriment, sustenance, fare.
**difference,** variation, contrast, disparity, separation, disagreement, discord, dissent, estrangement, variety.
**different,** various, manifold, diverse, unlike, separate, distinct. (Similar.)
**difficult,** severe, arduous, laborious, trying, hard, intricate, involved, perplexing, obscure, unmanageable. (Easy.)
**diffuse,** discursive, prolix, diluted, copious.
**dignify,** aggrandize, elevate, invest, exalt, advance, promote, honor. (Degrade.)
**dilate,** stretch, widen, expand, swell, distend, enlarge, descant, expatiate.
**dilatory,** tardy, procrastinating, behindhand, lagging, dawdling. (Prompt.)
**diligence,** care, assiduity, attention, heed, industry. (Negligence.)
**diminish,** lessen, reduce, contract, curtail, retrench. (Increase.)
**disability,** unfitness, incapacity.
**discern,** behold, descry, observe, recognize, see, discriminate, separate, perceive.
**discipline,** order, strictness, training, coercion, punishment, organization. (Confusion, demoralization.)
**discover,** disclose, detect, make known, find, invent, contrive, expose, reveal.
**discreditable,** shameful, disgraceful, scandalous, disreputable. (Creditable.)
**discreet,** cautious, prudent, wary, judicious. (Indiscreet.)
**discrepancy,** disagreement, difference, variance. (Agreement.)
**discrimination,** acuteness, discernment, judgment, caution.
**disease,** illness, unhealthiness, complaint, malady, disorder, ailment, sickness.
**disgrace,** *n.*, disrepute, reproach, dishonor, shame, odium. (Honor.)
**disgrace,** *v.*, debase, degrade, defame, discredit. (Exalt.)
**disgust,** dislike, distaste, loathing, abomination, abhorrence. (Admiration.)
**dishonest,** unjust, fraudulent, unfair, deceitful, cheating, deceptive, wrongful. (Honest.)
**dismay,** *v.*, terrify, frighten, scare, daunt, appal, dishearten. (Encourage.)
**dismay,** *n.*, terror, dread, fear, fright. (Assurance.)
**dismiss,** send off, discharge, discard, banish. (Retain.)
**dispel,** scatter, drive away, disperse, dissipate. (Collect.)
**display,** show, spread out, exhibit, expose. (Hide.)
**dispose,** arrange, place, order, give, bestow.
**dispute,** *v.*, argue, contest, contend, question, impugn. (Assent.)
**dispute,** *n.*, argument, debate, controversy, quarrel, disagreement. (Harmony.)
**dissent,** disagree, differ, vary. (Assent.)
**distinct,** clear, plain, obvious, different, separate. (Obscure, indistinct.)
**distinguish,** perceive, discern, mark out, divide, discriminate.
**distinguished,** famous, glorious, farfamed, noted, illustrious, eminent, celebrated. (Obscure, unknown, ordinary.)
**distract,** perplex, bewilder. (Calm, concentrate.)
**distribute,** allot, share, dispense, apportion, deal. (Collect.)
**disturb,** derange, discompose, agitate, rouse, interrupt, confuse, trouble, annoy, vex, worry. (Pacify, quiet.)
**disuse,** discontinuance, abolition, desuetude. (Use.)
**divide,** part, separate, distribute, deal out, sever, sunder.
**divine,** godlike, holy, heavenly, sacred, a parson, clergyman, minister.
**do,** effect, make, perform, accomplish, finish, transact, achieve, complete, realize, perpetrate, execute.
**docile,** tractable, teachable, compliant, tame. (Stubborn, determined, inflexible, firm, resolute.)
**doctrine,** tenet, article of belief, creed, dogma, teaching.
**doleful,** dolorous, woebegone, rueful, dismal, piteous. (Joyous.)
**doom,** *n.*, sentence, verdict, judgment, fate, lot, destiny.
**doubt,** *n.*, uncertainty, suspense, hesitation, scruple, ambiguity. (Certainty.)
**draw,** pull, haul, drag, attract, inhale, sketch, describe.
**dread,** *n.*, fear, horror, terror, alarm, dismay, awe. (Boldness, assurance.)
**dreadful,** fearful, frightful, shocking, awful, horrible, horrid, terrific.
**dress,** *n.*, clothing, attire, apparel, garments, costume, garb, livery, raiment.
**drift,** purpose, meaning, scope, aim, tendency, direction.
**droll,** funny, laughable, comic, whimsical, queer, amusing. (Solemn.)
**drown,** inundate, swamp, submerge, overwhelm, engulf.
**dry,** *a.*, arid, parched, lifeless, dull, tedious, uninteresting, meagre. (Moist, interesting, succulent.)
**due,** owing to, attributable to, just, fair, proper, debt, right.
**dull,** stupid, gloomy, sad, dismal, commonplace. (Bright.)
**dunce,** simpleton, fool, ninny, idiot. (Sage.)
**duplicate,** facsimile, replica, likeness, imitation copy, counterpart, reproduction. (Model, original, pattern, prototype.)
**durable,** lasting, permanent, abiding, continuing. (Ephemeral, perishable.)
**dwell,** stay, stop, abide, sojourn, linger, tarry.
**dwindle,** pine, waste, diminish, decrease, fall off. (Grow.)

## E

**eager,** fervent, desirous, hot, ardent, impassioned, forward, impatient. (Diffident, apathetic, indifferent, unconcerned.)
**earn,** acquire, obtain, win, gain, achieve.
**earnest,** *a.*, ardent, serious, grave, solemn, warm. (Trifling.)
**earnest,** *n.*, pledge, pawn.
**ease,** *n.*, comfort, rest. (Worry.)
**ease,** *v.*, calm, alleviate, allay, mitigate, appease, assuage, pacify, disburden, rid. (Annoy, worry.)
**easy,** light, comfortable, unconstrained. (Difficult, hard.)
**eccentric,** irregular, anomalous, singular, odd, abnormal, wayward, particular, strange. (Regular, ordinary.)
**economical,** sparing, saving, provident, thrifty, frugal, careful, niggardly. (Wasteful.)
**edge,** border, brink, rim, brim, margin, verge.
**education,** instruction, knowledge, schooling, tuition, learning, teaching, training, study.
**efface,** blot out, expunge, obliterate, wipe out, cancel, erase.
**effect,** *n.*, consequence, result, issue, event, execution, operation.
**effect,** *v.*, accomplish, fulfill, realize, achieve, execute, operate, complete.
**effective,** efficient, operative, serviceable. (Vain, ineffectual.)
**efficacy,** efficiency, energy, agency, instrumentality.
**efficient,** effectual, effective, competent, capable, able, fitted.
**eliminate,** drive out, expel, thrust out, eject, cast out, oust, dislodge, banish, proscribe.
**eloquence,** oratory, rhetoric, declamation.
**elucidate,** make plain, explain, clear up, illustrate.
**elude,** evade, escape, avoid, shun.
**embarrass,** perplex, entangle, distress, trouble. (Assist.)
**embellish,** adorn, decorate, bedeck, beautify, deck. (Disfigure.)
**embolden,** inspirit, animate, encourage, cheer, urge, impel, stimulate. (Discourage.)
**eminent,** distinguished, signal, conspicuous, noted, prominent, elevated, renowned, famous, glorious, illustrious. (Obscure, unknown.)
**emit,** give out, throw out, exhale, discharge, vent.
**emotion,** perturbation, agitation, trepidation, tremor, mental conflict.
**employ,** occupy, busy, take up with, engross.
**employment,** business, avocation, engagement, office, function, trade, profession, occupation, calling, vocation.

**encompass,** *v.*, encircle, surround, gird, beset.
**encounter,** attack, conflict, combat, assault, onset, engagement, battle, action.
**encourage,** countenance, sanction, support, foster, cherish, inspirit, embolden, animate, cheer, incite, urge, impel, stimulate. (Deter.)
**end,** *n.*, aim, object, purpose, result, conclusion, upshot, close, expiration, termination, extremity, sequel.
**endeavor,** attempt, try, essay, strive, aim.
**endurance,** continuation, duration, fortitude, patience, resignation.
**endure,** *v.*, last, continue, support, bear, sustain, suffer, brook, submit to, undergo, tolerate. (Perish, succumb, yield.)
**enemy,** foe, antagonist, adversary, opponent. (Friend.)
**energetic,** industrious, effectual, efficacious, powerful, binding, stringent, forcible, nervous. (Lazy.)
**engage,** employ, busy, occupy, attract, invite, allure, entertain, engross, take up, enlist.
**engross,** absorb, take up, busy, occupy, engage, mobilize.
**engulf,** swallow up, absorb, imbibe, drown, submerge, bury, entomb, overwhelm.
**enjoin,** order, ordain, appoint, prescribe.
**enjoyment,** pleasure, gratification. (Grief, sorrow, sadness.)
**enlarge,** increase, extend, augment, broaden, swell. (Diminish.)
**enlighten,** illumine, illuminate, instruct, inform. (Befog, becloud.)
**enliven,** cheer, vivify, stir up, animate, inspire, exhilarate. (Sadden, quiet.)
**enmity,** animosity, hostility, ill will, maliciousness. (Friendship.)
**enormous,** gigantic, colossal, huge, vast, immense, prodigious. (Insignificant.)
**enough,** sufficient, plenty, abundance. (Want.)
**enraged,** infuriated, raging, wrathful. (Pacified.)
**enrapture,** enchant, fascinate, charm, captivate, bewitch. (Repel.)
**enroll,** enlist, list, register, record.
**enterprise,** undertaking, endeavor, venture, energy.
**entertain,** beguile, amuse, cheer, divert, interest, please. (Annoy, disturb, tire, bore, weary, distract.)
**enthusiasm,** fervor, warmth, intensity, earnest, devotion, zeal, ardor. (Ennui, timidity, wariness, lukewarmness.)
**enthusiast,** fanatic, visionary.
**entrance,** ingress, access, door, approach, inlet, entry, gate, opening, portal. (Ejection, refusal, expulsion exit, egress, withdrawal.)
**equal,** equable, even, like, alike, uniform. (Unequal.)
**eradicate,** root out, extirpate, exterminate.
**erroneous,** incorrect, inaccurate, inexact. (Exact.)
**error,** blunder, mistake. (Truth.)
**especially,** chiefly, particularly, principally. (Generally.)
**essay,** dissertation, tract, treatise.
**establish,** build up, confirm. (Overthrow.)
**esteem,** regard, respect. (Contempt.)
**estimate,** appraise, appreciate, esteem, compute, rate.
**estrangement,** abstraction, alienation.
**eternal,** imperishable, perpetual, undying, timeless, unceasing, endless, everlasting. (Finite.)
**evade,** equivocate, prevaricate.
**even,** level, plain, smooth. (Uneven.)
**event,** accident, adventure, incident, occurrence.
**evil,** ill, harm, mischief, misfortune. (Good.)
**exact,** nice, particular, punctual. (Inexact.)
**exalt,** ennoble, dignify, raise. (Humble.)
**examination,** investigation, inquiry, research, search, scrutiny.
**exceed,** excel, outdo, surpass, transcend. (Fall short.)
**exceptional,** uncommon, rare, extraordinary. (Common.)
**excess,** profusion, surplus, superfluity, waste, lavishness, luxuriance, dissipation, extravagance. (Poverty, want, need, lack, scantiness, frugality, economy, dearth, destitution.)
**excite,** awaken, provoke, rouse, stir up. (Lull.)
**excursion,** jaunt, ramble, tour, trip.
**execute,** fulfill, perform.
**exempt,** free, cleared. (Subject.)
**exercise,** practice.
**exhaustive,** thorough, complete. (Cursory.)
**exigency,** emergency.
**experiment,** proof, trial, test.
**explain,** expound, interpret, illustrate, elucidate.
**express,** declare, signify, utter, tell.
**extend,** reach, stretch. (Abridge.)
**exterminate,** expel, banish, destroy, remove, annihilate, eradicate. (Beget, develop, breed, increase, replenish, populate, propagate, augment.)
**extravagant,** lavish, profuse, prodigal. (Parsimonious.)

## F

**fable,** apologue, novel, romance, tale.
**face,** visage, countenance.
**facetious,** pleasant, jocular, jocose. (Serious.)
**factor,** agent.
**fail,** to fall short, be deficient. (Accomplish.)
**faint,** weak, irresolute, faltering, feeble, languid. (Forcible, fresh, hearty, resolute.)
**fair,** clear. (Stormy.)
**fair,** equitable, honest, reasonable. (Unfair.)
**faith,** creed. (Unbelief, infidelity.)
**faithful,** stanch, devoted, trusty, true. loyal, constant. (Faithless, false, untrue.)
**faithless,** perfidious, treacherous. (Faithful.)
**fall,** drop, droop, sink, tumble. (Rise.)
**fame,** renown, reputation, distinction, eminence.
**famous,** celebrated, renowned, illustrious. (Obscure.)
**fanciful,** capricious, fantastical, whimsical.
**fancy,** imagination.
**fast,** rapid, quick, fleet, expeditious. (Slow.)
**fatigue,** weariness, lassitude. (Vigor.)
**fear,** timidity, timorousness, fright, apprehension, trepidation. (Bravery.)
**feeling,** sensation, sense.
**feeling,** sensibility, susceptibility. (Insensibility.)
**ferocious,** fierce, savage, wild, barbarous. (Mild.)
**fertile,** fruitful, prolific, plenteous, productive. (Sterile.)
**feud,** bitterness, contest, affray, animosity, brawl, dispute, fray, enmity, riot, quarrel, strife, row, controversy, dissension.
**fickle,** fluctuate, changeable, inconstant, restless, irresolute, uncertain, unreliable, versatile, wavering, vacillating. (Constant, firm, fixed, determined, resolute, stable, sure, steady, uniform, decided, unchanging.)
**fiction,** falsehood, fabrication. (Fact.)
**figure,** allegory, emblem, metaphor, symbol, picture, type.
**find,** descry, discover, espy. (Lose, overlook.)
**fine,** *a.*, delicate, nice, admirable, splendid. (Coarse, clumsy, huge.)
**fine,** *n.*, forfeit, forfeiture, mulct, penalty.
**fire,** glow, warmth, heat.
**firm,** constant, solid, steadfast, fixed, stable. (Weak.)
**first,** foremost, chief, earliest. (Last.)
**fit,** accommodate, adapt, adjust, suit.
**fix,** determine, establish, settle, limit, decide.
**flame,** blaze, flare, flash, glare.
**flat,** level, even.
**flexible,** pliant, pliable, ductile, supple. (Inflexible.)
**flourish,** prosper, thrive. (Decay.)
**fluctuating,** wavering, hesitating, oscillating, vacillating, change. (Firm, steadfast, decided.)
**fluent,** flowing, glib, voluble, unembarrassed, ready. (Hesitating.)
**folks,** persons, people, individuals.
**follow,** succeed, ensue, imitate, copy, pursue.
**follower,** partisan, disciple, adherent, retainer, pursuer, successor.
**folly,** silliness, foolishness, imbecility, weakness. (Wisdom.)
**fond,** enamored, attached, affectionate. (Distant.)
**fondness,** affection, attachment, kindness, love. (Aversion.)
**foolhardy,** venturesome, incautious, hasty, adventurous, rash. (Cautious.)
**foolish,** simple, silly, irrational, brainless, imbecile, crazy, absurd, preposterous, ridiculous, nonsensical. (Discreet, wise.)
**fop,** dandy, dude, beau, coxcomb, puppy, jackanapes. (Gentleman.)
**forbear,** abstain, refrain, withhold.
**force,** *n.*, strength, vigor, dint, might, energy, power, violence, army, host.
**force,** *v.*, compel. (Persuade.)
**forecast,** forethought, foresight, premeditation, prognostication.
**forego,** quit, relinquish, let go, waive.
**foregoing,** antecedent, anterior, preceding, previous, prior, former.

**forerunner,** herald, harbinger, precursor, omen.
**foresight,** forethought, forecast, premeditation.
**forge,** coin, invent, frame, feign, fabricate, counterfeit.
**forgive,** pardon, remit, absolve, acquit, excuse, except.
**forlorn,** forsaken, abandoned, deserted, desolate, lone, lonesome.
**form,** *n.*, ceremony, solemnity, observance, rite, figure, shape, conformation, fashion, appearance, representation, resemblance.
**form,** *v.*, make, create, produce, constitute, arrange, fashion, mould.
**formal,** ceremonious, precise, exact, stiff, methodical, affected. (Informal, natural.)
**former,** antecedent, anterior, previous, prior, preceding, foregoing.
**forsaken,** abandoned, forlorn, deserted, desolate, lone, lonesome.
**forthwith,** immediately, directly, instantly, instantaneously. (Anon.)
**fortitude,** endurance, resolution, fearlessness, dauntlessness. (Weakness.)
**fortunate,** lucky, happy, auspicious, prosperous, successful. (Unfortunate.)
**fortune,** chance, fate, luck, doom, destiny, property, possession, riches.
**foster,** cherish, nurse, tend, harbor, nurture. (Neglect.)
**foul,** impure, nasty, filthy, dirty, unclean, defiled. (Pure, clean.)
**fractious,** cross, captious, petulant, touchy, testy, peevish, fretful, splenetic. (Tractable.)
**fragile,** brittle, frail, delicate, feeble. (Strong.)
**fragments,** pieces, scraps, leavings, chips, remains, remnants.
**frailty,** weakness, failing, foible, imperfection, fault, blemish. (Strength.)
**frame,** *v.*, construct, invent, coin, fabricate, forge, mold, feign, make, compose.
**franchise,** right, exemption, immunity, privilege, freedom, suffrage.
**frank,** artless, candid, sincere, free, easy, familiar, open, ingenuous, plain. (Tricky, insincere.)
**frantic,** distracted, mad, furious, raving, frenzied. (Quiet, subdued.)
**fraud,** deceit, deception, duplicity, guile, cheat, imposition. (Honesty.)
**freak,** fancy, humor, vagary, whim, caprice, crotchet. (Purpose, resolution.)
**free,** *adj.*, liberal, generous, bountiful, bounteous, munificent, frank, artless, candid, familiar, open, independent, unconfined, unreserved, unrestricted, exempt, clear, loose, easy, careless. (Slavish, stingy, artful, costly.)
**free,** *v.*, release, set free, deliver, rescue, liberate, enfranchise, affranchise, emancipate, exempt. (Enslave, bind.)
**freedom,** liberty, independence, unrestraint, familiarity, license, franchise, exemption, privilege. (Slavery.)
**frequent,** often, common, usual, general. (Rare.)
**fret,** gall, chafe, agitate, irritate, vex.
**friendly,** cordial, fond, companionable, affable, amicable, genial, kind, hearty, neighborly, sociable, social. (Antagonistic, belligerent, cold, alienated, frigid, hostile, distant, unfriendly, unkind, indifferent.)
**frightful,** fearful, dreadful, dire, direful, terrific, awful, horrible, horrid.
**frivolous,** trifling, trivial, petty. (Serious, earnest.)
**frugal,** provident, economical, saving. (Wasteful, extravagant.)
**frugality,** parsimony, prudence, economy, miserliness, scrimping, saving, thrift, sparing. (Luxury, riches, waste, wealth, opulence, liberality, bounty, abundance, affluence, extravagance.)
**fruitful,** fertile, prolific, productive, abundant, plentiful, plenteous. (Barren, sterile.)
**fruitless,** vain, useless, idle, abortive, bootless, unavailing, without avail.
**frustrate,** defeat, foil, balk, disappoint.
**fulfill,** accomplish, effect, complete
**fully,** completely, abundantly, perfectly.
**fulsome,** coarse, gross, sickening, offensive, rank. (Moderate.)
**furious,** violent, boisterous, vehement, dashing, sweeping, rolling, impetuous, frantic, distracted, stormy, angry, raging, fierce. (Calm.)
**futile,** trifling, trivial, frivolous, useless. (Effective.)

## G

**gain,** *n.*, profit, emolument, advantage, benefit, winnings, earnings. (Loss.)
**gain,** *v.*, get, acquire, obtain, attain, procure, earn, win, achieve, reap, realize, reach. (Lose.)
**gallant,** brave, bold, courageous, gay, fine, showy, intrepid, heroic, fearless.
**galling,** chafing, irritating, vexing. (Soothing.)
**game,** play, pastime, diversion, sport, amusement.
**gang,** band, horde, company, troop, crew.
**gap,** breach, chasm, hollow, cavity, cleft, crevice, rift, chink.
**garnish,** embellish, adorn, beautify, deck, decorate.
**gather,** pick, cull, assemble, muster, infer, collect. (Scatter.)
**gaudy,** showy, flashy, tawdry, gay, glittering, bespangled. (Somber.)
**gaunt,** emaciated, scraggy, skinny, meagre, lank, attenuated, spare, lean, thin. (Well-fed.)
**gay,** cheerful, merry, lively, jolly, sprightly, blithe. (Solemn.)
**generate,** form, make, beget, produce.
**generation,** formation, race, breed, stock, kind, age, era.
**generous,** beneficent, noble, honorable, bountiful, liberal, free, magnanimous. (Niggardly, greedy, miserly, stingy, parsimonious.)
**genial,** cordial, hearty, festive, joyous. (Distant, cold.)
**genius,** intellect, invention, talent, nature, character, adept. (Stupidity, dullness.)
**genteel,** refined, polished, fashionable, polite, well-bred. (Boorish.)
**gentle,** placid, bland, mild, meek, tame, docile. (Rough, uncouth.)
**genuine,** real, true, unaffected, sincere. (False.)
**gesture,** attitude, action, posture.
**get,** obtain, earn, gain, attain, procure, achieve, acquire.
**ghastly,** pallid, wan, hideous, grim, shocking.
**ghost,** specter, sprite, apparition, shade, phantom.
**gibe,** scoff, sneer, flout, jeer, mock, taunt, deride.
**giddy,** unsteady, flighty, thoughtless. (Steady.)
**gift,** donation, benefaction, grant, alms, bequest, present, gratuity, boon, faculty, talent.
**gigantic,** colossal, huge, enormous, vast, prodigious, immense. (Diminutive.)
**give,** cede, deliver, grant, bestow, confer, yield, impart.
**glad,** pleased, cheerful, joyful, gladsome, gratified, cheering. (Sad.)
**gleam,** glimmer, glance, glitter, shine, flash.
**glee,** gaiety, merriment, mirth, joviality, joy, hilarity. (Sorrow.)
**glide,** slip, slide, run, roll on.
**glimmer,** gleam, flicker, glitter.
**glimpse,** glance, look, glint.
**glitter,** gleam, shine, glisten, glister, radiate.
**gloom,** cloud, darkness, dimness, blackness, dullness, sadness. (Light, brightness, joy.)
**gloomy,** lowering, lurid, dim, dusky, sad, glum. (Bright, clear.)
**glorify,** magnify, celebrate, adore, exalt.
**glorious,** famous, renowned, distinguished, noble, exalted. (Infamous.)
**glory,** honor, fame, renown, splendor, grandeur. (Infamy.)
**glut,** gorge, stuff, cram, cloy, satiate, block up.
**go,** depart, proceed, move, budge, stir.
**God,** Creator, Lord, Almighty, Jehovah, Omnipotence, Providence.
**godly,** righteous, devout, holy, pious, religious.
**good,** *n.*, benefit, weal, advantage, profit, boon. (Evil.)
**good,** *a.*, virtuous, righteous, upright, just, true. (Wicked, bad.)
**gorge,** glut, fill, cram, stuff, satiate.
**gorgeous,** superb, grand, magnificent, splendid. (Plain, simple.)
**govern,** control, rule, direct, manage, command.
**government,** rule, state, control, sway.
**graceful,** becoming, comely, elegant, beautiful. (Awkward.)
**gracious,** merciful, kindly, beneficent.
**gradual,** slow, progressive. (Sudden.)
**grand,** majestic, stately, dignified, lofty, elevated, exalted, splendid, gorgeous, superb, magnificent, sublime, pompous. (Shabby.)
**grant,** *v.*, bestow, impart, give, yield, cede, allow, confer, invest.
**grant,** *n.*, gift, boon, donation.
**graphic,** forcible, telling, picturesque, vivid, pictorial.
**grasp,** catch, seize, gripe, clasp, grapple.
**grateful,** agreeable, pleasing, welcome, thankful. (Harsh.)
**gratification,** enjoyment, pleasure, delight, reward. (Disappointment.)

**grave,** *a.*, serious, sedate, solemn, sober, pressing, heavy. (Giddy.)
**grave,** *n.*, tomb, sepulcher, vault.
**great,** big, huge, large, majestic, vast, grand, noble, august. (Small.)
**greediness,** avidity, eagerness, voracity. (Generosity.)
**grief,** affliction, sorrow, trial, woe, tribulation, sadness, melancholy. (Joy.)
**grieve,** mourn, lament, sorrow, pain, hurt, wound, bewail. (Rejoice.)
**grievous,** painful, afflicting, heavy, baleful, unhappy.
**grind,** crush, oppress, grate, harass, afflict.
**grisly,** terrible, hideous, grim, ghastly, dreadful. (Pleasing.)
**gross,** coarse, outrageous, unseemly, shameful, indelicate. (Delicate.)
**group,** assembly, cluster, collection, clump, order, class.
**grovel,** crawl, cringe, fawn, sneak.
**grow,** increase, vegetate, expand, advance. (Decay, diminish.)
**growl,** grumble, snarl, murmur, complain.
**grudge,** malice, rancor, spite, pique, hatred, aversion.
**gruff,** rough, rugged, blunt, rude, harsh, surly, bearish. (Pleasant.)
**guile,** deceit, fraud. (Candor.)
**guiltless,** harmless, innocent.
**guilty,** culpable, sinful, criminal.

## H

**habit,** custom, practice, fashion, routine, system.
**hail,** accost, address, greet, salute, welcome.
**happiness,** beatitude, blessedness, bliss, felicity, contentment, joy, merriment, rapture, pleasure, enjoyment. (Unhappiness.)
**harbor,** haven, port.
**hard,** firm, solid, arduous, difficult. (Soft, easy.)
**harm,** injury, hurt, wrong, infliction. (Benefit.)
**harmless,** safe, innocuous, innocent. (Hurtful.)
**harmony,** accord, amity, agreement, unison, unity, consistency, symmetry, conformity. (Conflict, contention, dissension, hostility, variance, discord, difference, controversy.)
**harsh,** rough, rigorous, severe, gruff, morose. (Gentle.)
**harvest,** crop, fruit, growth, result, return, yield, proceeds, product, increase.
**hasten,** accelerate, dispatch, expedite, speed. (Delay.)
**hasty,** hurried, ill-advised. (Deliberate.)
**hateful,** odious, detestable. (Lovable.)
**hatred,** enmity, ill will, rancor, animosity, hostility, revenge, spite, hate. (Friendship.)
**haughtiness,** arrogance, pride. (Modesty.)
**haughty,** arrogant, disdainful, supercilious, proud.
**hazard,** peril, chance, risk, venture.
**healthy,** hale, vigorous, well, salubrious, salutary, wholesome. (Unhealthy, diseased, fragile, ill, sick.)
**heap,** accumulate, amass, pile.
**hearty,** cordial, sincere, warm. (Insincere.)
**heavy,** burdensome, ponderous, weighty. (Light.)
**heed,** care, attention.
**heighten,** enhance, exalt, elevate, raise.
**heinous,** atrocious, flagitious, flagrant, (Venial.)
**help,** abet, encourage, aid, assist, relieve, succor. (Hinder, oppose, thwart, discourage.)
**heretic,** pervert, renegade, traitor, sectary, sectarian, schismatic, dissenter, nonconformist.
**hesitate,** falter, stammer, stutter.
**hide,** cover, disguise, cloak, conceal, bury, veil, suppress, screen, entomb, secrete. (Betray, confess, admit, avow, exhibit, divulge, expose, show, reveal, publish, advertise, tell, uncover.)
**hideous,** grim, ghastly, grisly. (Beautiful.)
**high,** exalted, steep, towering, lofty, tall, elevated. (Deep.)
**hinder,** retard, hamper, delay, deter, check, balk, impede, obstruct, prevent. (Help.)
**hint,** allude, refer, suggest, intimate, insinuate.
**hold,** detain, keep, retain.
**holiness,** sanctity, piety, sacredness.
**holy,** devout, pious, religious.
**home,** habitation, dwelling, fireside, hearth, house, residence, domicile, abode.
**homely,** plain, ugly, coarse. (Beautiful.)
**honesty,** integrity, probity, uprightness. (Dishonesty.)
**honor,** respect, reverence, esteem. (Dishonor.)
**hope,** confidence, expectation, trust.
**hopeless,** desperate.
**hot,** ardent, burning, fiery. (Cold.)
**however,** nevertheless, notwithstanding, yet.
**humane,** kind, merciful, human, tender, gentle, gracious, sympathetic, forgiving, charitable, benevolent, benignant, pitying.
**humble,** *a.*, modest, submissive, plain, unostentatious, simple. (Haughty.)
**humble,** *v.*, degrade, humiliate, mortify, abase. (Exalt.)
**humor,** mood, temper.
**hunt,** pursuit, search, seek, chase.
**hurtful,** noxious, pernicious. (Beneficial.)
**husbandry,** cultivation, tillage.
**hypocrite,** cheat, deceiver, dissembler, impostor.
**hypothesis,** theory, supposition.

## I

**idea, thought, imagination.**
**ideal,** imaginary, fancied. (Actual.)
**idle,** indolent, lazy. (Industrious.)
**ignominious,** shameful, scandalous, infamous. (Honorable.)
**ignominy,** shame, disgrace, obloquy, infamy, reproach.
**ignorant,** unlearned, illiterate, uninformed, uneducated. (Knowing.)
**ill,** *n.*, evil, wickedness, misfortune, mischief, harm. (Good.)
**ill,** *a.*, sick, indisposed, unwell, diseased. (Well.)
**ill-tempered,** crabbed, sour, surly, acrimonious. (Good-natured.)
**ill will,** enmity, hatred, antipathy. (Good will.)
**illegal,** unlawful, illicit, contraband, illegitimate. (Legal.)
**illimitable,** boundless, immeasurable, unlimited, infinite.
**illiterate,** unlettered, unlearned, untaught, uninstructed. (Learned, educated.)
**illusion,** fallacy, deception, phantasm.
**illusory,** imaginary, chimerical, visionary. (Real.)
**illustrate,** explain, elucidate, clear.
**illustrious,** celebrated, noble, eminent, famous, renowned. (Obscure.)
**image,** likeness, picture, representation, effigy.
**imaginary,** ideal, fanciful, illusory. (Real.)
**imagine,** conceive, fancy, apprehend, think, presume.
**imbecility,** silliness, senility, dotage.
**imitate,** copy, ape, mimic, mock, counterfeit.
**immaculate,** unspotted, spotless, unsullied. (Soiled.)
**immediate,** pressing, instant, next, proximate.
**immediately,** instantly, forthwith, directly, presently.
**immense,** vast, enormous, huge, prodigious, monstrous.
**immunity,** privilege, prerogative, exemption.
**impair,** injure, diminish, decrease.
**impart,** reveal, divulge, disclose, discover, bestow, afford.
**impartial,** just, equitable, unbiased. (Partial.)
**impassioned,** glowing, burning, fiery, vehement, intense.
**impeach,** accuse, charge, arraign, censure.
**impede,** hinder, retard, obstruct, prevent. (Help.)
**impediment,** obstruction, hindrance, obstacle, barrier, bar, clog, encumbrance. (Aid, assistance, benefit, help.)
**impel,** animate, induce, incite, instigate, embolden. (Retard.)
**impending,** imminent, threatening.
**imperative,** commanding, despotic, authoritative.
**imperfection,** fault, blemish, defect, vice.
**imperil,** endanger, hazard, jeopardize.
**imperious,** commanding, lordly, dictatorial, authoritative, imperative, domineering, overbearing.
**impertinent,** intrusive, meddling, officious, rude, saucy, impudent, insolent.
**impetuous,** violent, boisterous, furious, vehement. (Calm.)
**impious,** profane, irreligious, godless, (Reverent.)
**implicate,** involve, entangle, embarrass, compromise.
**imply,** involve, comprise, infold, import, denote, signify.
**importance,** signification, significance,

avail, consequence, weight, gravity, moment.
**imposing,** impressive, striking, majestic, august, noble, grand. (Insignificant.)
**impotence,** weakness, incapacity, infirmity, frailty, feebleness. (Power.)
**impotent,** weak, feeble, helpless, enfeebled, nerveless, infirm. (Strong.)
**impressive,** stirring, forcible, exciting, affecting, moving.
**imprison,** incarcerate, shut up, immure, confine. (Liberate.)
**imprisonment,** captivity, durance.
**improve,** amend, better, mend, reform, rectify, ameliorate, apply, use, employ. (Deteriorate.)
**improvident,** careless, incautious, imprudent, prodigal, wasteful, reckless, rash. (Thrifty.)
**impudence,** forwardness, boldness, effrontery, assurance, impertinence, confidence, insolence, rudeness.
**impudent,** saucy, brazen, bold, impertinent, forward, rude, insolent, immodest, shameless.
**impulse,** incentive, incitement, motive, instigation.
**impulsive,** rash, hasty, forcible, violent. (Deliberate.)
**imputation,** blame, censure, reproach, charge, accusation.
**inadvertency,** error, oversight, blunder, inattention, carelessness, negligence.
**incentive,** motive, inducement, impulse.
**incite,** instigate, excite, provoke, stimulate, encourage, urge, impel.
**inclination,** leaning, slope, disposition, tendency, bent, bias, affection, attachment, wish, liking, desire. (Aversion.)
**incline,** *v.*, slope, lean, slant, tend, bend, turn, bias, dispose.
**inclose,** surround, shut in, fence in, cover, wrap.
**include,** comprehend, comprise, contain, embrace, take in.
**incommode,** annoy, plague, molest, disturb, inconvenience, trouble. (Accommodate.)
**incompetent,** incapable, unable, inadequate, insufficient. (Competent.)
**incongruous,** contrary, discrepant, conflicting, absurd, inconsistent, mismated, incoherent, irreconcilable, incompatible. (Consistent, harmonious, suitable, accordant, compatible.)
**increase,** *v.*, extend, enlarge, augment, dilate, expand, amplify, raise, enhance, aggravate, magnify, grow. (Diminish.)
**increase,** *n.*, augmentation, accession, addition, enlargement, extension. (Decrease.)
**incumbent,** obligatory.
**indefinite,** vague, uncertain, unsettled, loose, lax. (Definite.)
**indicate,** point out, show, mark.
**indifference,** apathy, carelessness, listlessness, insensibility. (Application, assiduity.)
**indigence,** want, neediness, penury, poverty, destitution, privation. (Affluence.)
**indignation,** anger, wrath, ire, resentment.
**indignity,** insult, affront, outrage, obloquy, opprobriumr reproach, ignominy. (Honor.)
**indiscriminate,** pomiscuous, indistinct, chance, confused. (Select, chosen.)
**indispensable,** essential, necessary, requisite, expedient. (Unnecessary, supernumerary.)
**indisputable,** undeniable, undoubted, incontestable, indubitable, unquestionable, sure, infallible.
**indorse,** ratify, confirm, superscribe.
**indulge,** foster, cherish, fondle. (Deny.)
**ineffectual,** vain, useless, unavailing, fruitless, abortive, inoperative. (Effective.)
**inequality,** disparity, disproportion, dissimilarity, unevenness. (Equality )
**inevitable,** unavoidable, not to be avoided, certain.
**infamous,** scandalous, shameful, ignominious, opprobrious, disgraceful. (Honorable.)
**inference,** deduction, corollary, conclusion, consequence.
**infernal,** diabolical, fiendish, devilish, hellish.
**infest,** annoy, plague, harass, disturb.
**infinite,** eternal, absolute, boundless, countless, limitless, unbounded, numberless, unlimited, unfathomable. (Brief, bounded, restricted, small, moderate, limited, little, measurable.)
**infirm,** weak, feeble, enfeebled. (Robust.)
**inflame,** anger, irritate, enrage, chafe, incense, nettle, aggravate, embitter, exasperate. (Allay, soothe.)
**influence,** *v.*, bias, sway, prejudice, prepossess, induce, stir, persuade.
**influence,** *n.*, credit, favor, reputation, character, weight, authority, sway, ascendency.
**infringe,** invade, intrude, contravene, break, transgress, violate.
**ingenuous,** artless, candid, generous, open, frank, plain, sincere. (Crafty.)
**inherent,** ingrained, inbred, inborn, native, natural, intrinsic. (Casual, accidental, incidental, superfluous, subsidiary, supplemental.)
**inhuman,** cruel, brutal, savage, barbarous, ruthless, merciless, ferocious. (Humane.)
**iniquity,** injustice, wrong, grievance.
**injure,** damage, hurt, deteriorate, wrong, aggrieve, harm, spoil, mar, sully. (Benefit.)
**injurious,** hurtful, baneful, pernicious, deleterious, noxious, prejudicial, wrongful, damaging. (Beneficial.)
**injustice,** wrong, iniquity, grievance, unfairness. (Right.)
**innocent,** guiltless, sinless, harmless, inoffensive, innoxious, exemplary, stainless, virtuous. (Guilty.)
**innocuous,** harmless, safe, innocent. (Hurtful.)
**inordinate,** intemperate, irregular, disorderly, excessive, immoderate. (Moderate.)
**inquiry,** investigation, examination, research, scrutiny, disquisition, question, query, interrogation.
**inquisitive,** prying, peeping, curious, peering, searching.
**insane,** mad, deranged, delirious, demented. (Sane.)
**insanity,** madness, mental aberration, lunacy, delirium, craziness, derangement, hallucination. (Sanity.)
**insinuate,** hint, intimate, suggest, infuse, introduce, ingratiate.
**insipid,** dull, flat, mawkish, tasteless, vapid, inanimate, lifeless. (Bright, sparkling.)
**insolent,** rude, saucy, pert, impertinent, abusive, scurrilous, opprobrious, insulting, offensive.
**inspire,** animate, exhilarate, enliven, cheer, breathe, inhale.
**instability,** mutability, fickleness, mutableness, wavering. (Stability, firmness.)
**instigate,** stir up, persuade, animate, incite, urge, stimulate, encourage.
**instill,** implant, inculcate, infuse, insinuate.
**instruct,** inform, teach, educate, enlighten, initiate.
**instrumental,** conducive, assistant, helping, ministerial.
**insufficiency,** inadequacy, incompetency, incapability, deficiency, lack.
**insult,** affront, outrage, indignity, blasphemy. (Honor.)
**insulting,** insolent, rude, saucy, impertinent, abusive.
**integrity,** uprightness, honesty, probity, entirety, entireness, completeness, rectitude, purity. (Dishonesty.)
**intellect,** understanding, sense, brains, mind, intelligence, ability, talent, genius. (Body.)
**intellectual,** mental, ideal, metaphysical. (Brutal.)
**intelligible,** clear, obvious, plain, distinct. (Abstruse.)
**intemperate,** immoderate, excessive, drunken, nimious, inordinate. (Temperate.)
**intense,** ardent, earnest, glowing, fervid, burning, vehement.
**intent,** design, purpose, intention, drift, view, aim, purport, meaning.
**intercourse,** commerce, connection, intimacy, acquaintance.
**interdict,** forbid, prohibit, inhibit, proscribe, debar, restrain from. (Allow.)
**interfere,** meddle, intermeddle, interpose.
**interminable,** endless, interminate, infinite, unlimited, illimitable, boundless, limitless. (Brief, concise.)
**interpose,** intercede, arbitrate, meditate, interfere, meddle.
**interpret,** explain, expound, elucidate, unfold, decipher.
**intimate,** hint, suggest, insinuate, express, signify, impart, tell.
**intimidate,** dishearten, alarm, frighten, scare, appall, daunt, cow, browbeat. (Encourage.)
**intolerable,** insufferable, unbearable, insupportable, unendurable.
**intrepid,** bold, brave, daring, fearless, dauntless, undaunted, courageous, valorous, valiant, heroic, gallant, chivalrous, doughty. (Cowardly, faint-hearted.)
**intrigue,** plot, cabal conspiracy, combination, artifice, ruse, amour.
**intrinsic,** real, true, genuine, sterling, native, natural. (Extrinsic.)
**invalidate,** quash, cancel, overthrow, vacate, nullify, annul.

**invasion,** incursion, irruption, inroad, aggression, raid, fray.

**invective,** abuse, reproach, railing, censure, sarcasm, satire.

**invent,** devise, contrive, frame, find out, discover, design.

**investigation,** examination, search, inquiry, research, scrutiny.

**inveterate,** confirmed, chronic, malignant. (Inchoate.)

**invidious,** envious, hateful, odious, malignant.

**invigorate,** brace, harden, nerve, strengthen, fortify. (Enervate.)

**invincible,** unconquerable, impregnable, insurmountable.

**invisible,** unseen, imperceptible, impalpable, unperceivable.

**invite,** ask, call, bid, request, allure, attract, solicit.

**invoke,** invocate, call upon, appeal, refer, implore, beseech.

**involve,** implicate, entangle, compromise, envelop.

**irksome,** wearisome, tiresome, tedious, annoying. (Pleasant.)

**irony,** sarcasm, satire, ridicule, raillery.

**irrational,** foolish, silly, imbecile, brutish, absurd, ridiculous. (Rational.)

**irregular,** eccentric, anomalous, inordinate, intemperate. (Regular.)

**irreligious,** profane, godless, impious, sacrilegious, desecrating.

**irreproachable,** blameless, spotless, irreprovable.

**irresistible,** resistless, irrepressible.

**irresolute,** wavering, undetermined, undecided, vacillating. (Determined.)

**irritable,** excitable, irascible, susceptible, sensitive. (Calm.)

**irritate,** aggravate, worry, embitter, madden, exasperate.

**issue,** *v.*, emerge, rise, proceed, flow, spring, emanate.

**issue,** *n.*, end, upshot, effect, result, offspring, progeny.

## J

**jade,** harass, weary, tire, worry.

**jangle,** wrangle, conflict, disagree.

**jarring,** conflicting, discordant, inconsonant, inconsistent.

**jaunt,** ramble, excursion, trip.

**jealousy,** suspicion, envy.

**jeopard,** hazard, peril, endanger.

**jest,** joke, sport, divert, make game of.

**journey,** travel, tour, passage, excursion, voyage, trip.

**joy,** gladness, mirth, delight. (Grief.)

**joyful,** glad, rejoicing, exultant. (Mournful.)

**judge,** justice, referee, arbitrator, arbiter.

**judgment,** discernment, discrimination, understanding.

**justice,** equity, right. Justice is right as established by law; equity according to the circumstances of each particular case. (Injustice.)

**justness,** accuracy, correctness.

## K

**keep,** preserve, save. (Abandon.)

**kill,** execute, massacre, assassinate, murder, slay.

**kindred,** affinity, consanguinity, relationship.

**knowledge,** intelligence, wisdom, comprehension, erudition, learning, science. (Ignorance, illiteracy, unfamiliarity.)

## L

**labor,** toil, work, effort, drudgery. (Idleness.)

**lack,** need, deficiency, scarcity, insufficiency. (Plenty.)

**lament,** mourn, grieve, weep. (Rejoice.)

**language,** dialect, idiom, speech, tongue, vocabulary.

**large,** ample, big, capacious, abundant, coarse, colossal, commodious, enormous, vast, huge, gigantic, great, massive, spacious. (Little, petty, paltry, scanty, small, tiny, trivial, brief, diminutive, insignificant.)

**lascivious,** loose, unchaste, lustful, lewd, lecherous. (Chaste.)

**last,** final, latest, ultimate. (First.)

**laudable,** commendable, praiseworthy. (Blamable.)

**laughable,** comical, droll, ludicrous. (Serious.)

**lawful,** legal, legitimate, licit. (Illegal.)

**lead,** conduct, guide. (Follow.)

**lean,** meager. (Fat.)

**learned,** erudite, scholarly. (Ignorant.)

**leave,** *v.*, quit, relinquish.

**leave,** *n.*, liberty, permission, license. (Prohibition.)

**life,** existence, animation, spirit, vivacity. (Death.)

**lifeless,** dead, inanimate.

**lift,** erect, elevate, exalt, raise. (Lower.)

**light,** clear, bright. (Dark.)

**lightness,** flightiness, giddiness, levity, volatility. (Seriousness.)

**likeness,** resemblance, similarity. (Unlikeness.)

**linger,** lag, loiter, tarry, saunter. (Hasten.)

**little,** diminutive, small. (Great.)

**livelihood,** living, maintenance, subsistence, support.

**lively,** jocund, sprightly, vivacious, merry, sportive. (Slow, languid, sluggish.)

**long,** extended, extensive. (Short.)

**look,** appear, seem.

**look,** gaze, discern, behold, glance, see, stare, view, watch, scan, inspect.

**lose,** miss, forfeit. (Gain.)

**loss,** detriment, damage, deprivation. (Gain.)

**loud,** clamorous, high-sounding, noisy. (Low, quiet.)

**love,** fondness, attachment, devotion, affection. (Hatred.)

**low,** abject, mean. (Noble.)

**lunacy,** derangement, insanity, mania, madness. (Sanity.)

**luster,** brightness, brilliancy, splendor.

**luxuriant,** exuberant. (Sparse.)

## M

**machination,** plot, intrigue, cabal, conspiracy. (Artlessness.)

**mad,** crazy, insane, delirious, rabid, violent, frantic. (Sane, rational, quiet.)

**madness,** insanity, fury, rage, frenzy.

**magisterial,** august, dignified, majestic, pompous, stately.

**make,** form, create, produce, build, construct. (Destroy.)

**malediction,** anathema, curse, imprecation, execration.

**malevolent,** malicious, virulent, malignant. (Benevolent.)

**malice,** spite, rancor, ill feeling, ill will, grudge, animosity. (Benignity.)

**malicious.** See malevolent.

**manacle,** *v.*, shackle, fetter, chain. (Free.)

**manage,** contrive, concert, direct.

**management,** direction, superintendence, care, economy.

**mangle,** tear, lacerate, mutilate, cripple, maim.

**mania,** madness, insanity, lunacy.

**manifest,** *a.*, clear, plain, evident, open, apparent, visible. (Hidden, occult.)

**manifold,** several, sundry, various, divers, numerous.

**manly,** masculine, vigorous, courageous, brave, heroic. (Effeminate.)

**manner,** habit, custom, way, air, look, appearance.

**manners,** morals, habits, behavior, carriage.

**mar,** spoil, ruin, disfigure. (Improve.)

**march,** tramp, tread, walk, step, space.

**margin,** edge, rim, border, brink, verge.

**mark,** *n.*, sign, note, symptom, token, indication, trace, vestige, track, badge, brand.

**mark,** *v.*, impress, print, stamp, engrave, note, designate.

**marriage,** wedding, nuptials, matrimony, wedlock.

**martial,** military, warlike, soldierlike.

**marvel,** wonderful, miracle, prodigy.

**marvelous,** wondrous, wonderful, amazing, miraculous.

**masculine,** manly, mannish, virile, male, manful, manlike.

**massive,** bulky, heavy, weighty, ponderous, solid, substantial. (Flimsy.)

**mastery,** dominion, rule, sway, ascendency, supremacy.

**matchless,** unrivaled, unequaled, unparalleled, peerless, incomparable, inimitable, surpassing. (Common, ordinary.)

**material,** *a.*, corporeal, bodily, physical, temporal, momentous, important. (Spiritual, immaterial.)

**maxim,** adage, apothegm, proverb, saying, by-word, saw.

**meager,** poor, lank, emaciated, barren, dry, uninteresting. (Rich.)

**mean,** *a.*, stingy, niggardly, low, abject, vile, ignoble, degraded, contemptible, vulgar, despicable. (Generous.)

**mean,** *v.*, design, purpose, intent, contemplate, signify, denote, indicate.

**meaning,** signification, import, acceptation, sense, purport.

**medium,** organ, channel, instrument, means.
**medley,** mixture, variety, diversity, miscellany.
**meek,** unassuming, mild, gentle, soft, demure, humble. (Proud, arrogant, bold, haughty, impudent, presumptuous.)
**melancholy,** low-spirited, dispirited, dreamy, sad. (Jolly, buoyant.)
**mellow,** ripe, mature, soft. (Immature.)
**melodious,** tuneful, musical, silver, dulcet, sweet. (Discordant.)
**memorable,** signal, distinguished, marked.
**memorial,** monument, memento, commemoration.
**memory,** reminiscence, remembrance, recollection.
**menace,** *n.*, threat.
**mend,** repair, amend, correct, better, ameliorate, improve, rectify.
**mention,** tell, name, communicate, impart, divulge, reveal, disclose, inform, acquaint.
**merciful,** compassionate, lenient, clement, tender, gracious, kind. (Cruel.)
**merciless,** hard-hearted, cruel, unmerciful, pitiless, remorseless, unrelenting. (Kind.)
**mercy,** favor, grace, kindness, leniency, pardon, tenderness, pity, compassion, benevolence, clemency, benignity, blessing. (Revenge, cruelty, harshness, severity, sternness, punishment, implacability, hardness.)
**merriment,** mirth, joviality, jollity, hilarity. (Sorrow.)
**merry,** cheerful, mirthful, joyous, gay, lively, sprightly, hilarious, jovial, blithe, blithesome, sportive, jolly. (Sad.)
**metaphorical,** figurative, allegorical, symbolical.
**method,** way, manner, mode, process, order, rule, regularity, system.
**mien,** air, look, manner, aspect, appearance.
**migratory,** roving, strolling, wandering, vagrant. (Settled, sedate, permanent.)
**mimic,** imitate, ape, mock.
**mind,** intellect, brain, instinct, reason, sense, soul, thought, understanding, intelligence.
**mindful,** observant, attentive, heedful, thoughtful. (Heedless.)
**miscellaneous,** promiscuous, indiscriminate, mixed.
**mischief,** injury, harm, damage, evil, hurt, ill. (Benefit.)
**miscreant,** caitiff, villain, ruffian.
**miserable,** unhappy, wretched, distressed, afflicted. (Happy.)
**miserly,** stingy, niggardly, avaricious, gripping.
**misery,** wretchedness, woe, destitution, penury, privation, beggary. (Happiness.)
**misfortune,** trouble, tribulation, affliction, failure, sorrow, calamity, disaster, mishap, catastrophe. (Good luck, happiness, joy.)
**miss,** omit, lose, fail, miscarry.
**mitigate,** alleviate, relieve, diminish, abate. (Aggravate.)
**mix,** blend, combine, amalgamate, associate, fuse, join, unite, mingle, compound. (Divide, sift, part, segregate, sort, unravel, disjoin, classify, assort, analyze.)
**moderate,** temperate, abstemious, sober, abstinent. (Immoderate.)
**modest,** chaste, virtuous, bashful, reserved. (Immodest.)
**moist,** wet, damp, dank, humid. (Dry.)
**monotonous,** unvaried, dull, undiversified, tiresome. (Varied.)
**monstrous,** shocking, dreadful, horrible, huge, immense.
**monument,** memorial, record, remembrancer, cenotaph.
**mood,** humor, disposition, vein, temper.
**morbid,** sick, ailing, sickly, diseased, corrupted. (Normal, sound.)
**morose,** gloomy, sullen, surly, fretful, crabbed, crusty, sour, sulky. (Joyous, pleasant, friendly, amiable.)
**mortal,** deadly, fatal, human.
**motion,** proposition, proposal, movement.
**motionless,** still, stationary, torpid, stagnant. (Active, moving.)
**mount,** arise, rise, ascend, soar, tower, climb, scale.
**mournful,** sad, sorrowful, lugubrious, grievous, doleful, heavy. (Happy.)
**move,** actuate, impel, induce, prompt, instigate, persuade, stir, agitate, propel, push.
**multitude,** crowd, throng, host, mob, swarm.
**murder,** *v.*, kill, assassinate, slay, massacre, dispatch.
**muse,** *v.*, meditate, contemplate, reflect, think, cogitate, ponder.
**music,** harmony, melody, symphony.
**musical,** tuneful, melodious, harmonious, dulcet, sweet.
**musty,** stale, sour, fetid. (Fresh, sweet.)
**mute,** dumb, silent, speechless.
**mutilate,** maim, cripple, disable, disfigure.
**mutinous,** insurgent, seditious, tumultuous, turbulent, riotous. (Obedient, orderly.)
**mutual,** reciprocal, interchanged, correlative. (Sole, solitary.)
**mysterious,** dark, obscure, hidden, secret, dim, mystic, enigmatical, unaccountable, inexplicable, abstruse. (Open, clear.)
**mystify,** confuse, perplex, puzzle. (Clear, explain.)

## N

**naked,** nude, bare, uncovered, rude, unclothed, rough, simple. (Covered, clad.)
**name,** *v.*, denominate, entitle, style, designate, term, call, christen.
**name,** *n.*, appellation, designation, denomination, title, cognomen, reputation, character, fame, credit, repute.
**narrate,** tell, relate, detail, recount, describe, enumerate, rehearse, recite.
**nasty,** filthy, foul, dirty, unclean, indecent, impure, gross, vile.
**nation,** people, community, realm, state.
**native,** indigenous, inborn, vernacular.
**natural,** original, regular, normal, bastard. (Unnatural, forced.)
**near,** nigh, neighboring, close, adjacent, contiguous, intimate. (Distant.)
**neat,** natty, nice, orderly, clean, dapper, tidy, trim, prim, spruce. (Dirty, rough, disorderly, unkempt, soiled, untidy, negligent.)
**necessary,** needful, expedient, essential, requisite, indispensable. (Useless.)
**necessitate,** compel, force, oblige.
**necessity,** need, occasion, exigency, emergency, urgency, requisite.
**need,** *n.*, necessity, distress, poverty, indigence, want, penury.
**need,** *v.*, require, want, lack.
**neglect,** *v.*, disregard, slight, omit, overlook.
**neglect,** *n.*, omission, failure, default, negligence, remissness, carelessness, slight.
**neighborhood,** environs, vicinity, adjacency, nearness, proximity.
**nervous,** timid, timorous, shaky.
**new,** modern, late, young, fresh, recent, novel. (Old.)
**news,** tidings, intelligence, information.
**nice,** exact, accurate, good, particular, precise, fine, delicate. (Careless, coarse, unpleasant.)
**nimble,** spry, active, brisk, lively, alert, quick, agile, prompt. (Awkward, slow, clumsy.)
**nobility,** aristocracy, greatness, grandeur, peerage.
**noble,** exalted, elevated, illustrious, great, grand, lofty. (Low.)
**noise,** cry, outcry, row, clamor, din, uproar, tumult. (Silence.)
**nonsensical,** irrational, absurd, silly, foolish. (Sensible.)
**notable,** plain, evident, remarkable, signal, striking, rare. (Obscure.)
**note,** *n.*, token, symbol, mark, sign, indication, remark, comment.
**noted,** distinguished, remarkable, renowned, eminent. (Obscure.)
**notice,** *n.*, advice, notification, intelligence, information.
**notice,** *v.*, mark, note, observe, attend to, regard, heed.
**notify,** *v.*, publish, acquaint, apprise, inform, declare.
**notion,** conception, idea, belief, opinion, sentiment.
**notorious,** conspicuous, open, obvious, ill-famed. (Unknown.)
**nourish,** nurture, cherish, foster, supply. (Starve, famish.)
**nourishment,** food, diet, sustenance, nutrition.
**novel,** modern, new, fresh, recent, unused, strange, rare. (Old.)
**noxious,** hurtful, deadly, poisonous, deleterious, baneful. (Beneficial.)
**nullify,** annul, vacate, invalidate, repeal, quash, cancel. (Affirm.)
**nutrition,** food, diet, nutriment, nourishment.

## O

**obdurate,** hard, callous, hardened, unfeeling, insensible. (Tractable, yielding.)
**obedient,** compliant, submissive, dutiful, respectful. (Obstinate.)

**obese,** corpulent, fat, adipose, fleshy. (Attenuated.)
**obey,** *v.*, conform, comply, submit. (Rebel, disobey.)
**object,** *n.*, aim, end, purpose, design, mark, butt.
**object,** *v.*, oppose, except to, contravene, impeach, deprecate. (Assent.)
**obnoxious,** offensive. (Agreeable.)
**obscure,** dense, deep, profound, undistinguished, unknown. (Distinguished.)
**obsolete,** old, rare, obsolescent, ancient, disused, antiquated, archaic.
**obstinate,** contumacious, headstrong, stubborn, obdurate. (Yielding.)
**obstruct,** block, hinder, clog, bar, arrest, retard, stay, barricade, impede, oppose, interrupt. (Aid, clear, promote, facilitate, free, advance, accelerate.)
**occasion,** opportunity.
**offense,** affront, misdeed, misdemeanor, transgression, trespass.
**offensive,** insolent, abusive, obnoxious. (Inoffensive.)
**office,** charge, function, place.
**offspring,** issue, progeny.
**old,** aged, superannuated, ancient, antique, antiquated, obsolete, old-fashioned, senile, elderly, venerable. (Young, new.)
**omen,** presage, prognostic.
**opaque,** dark. (Bright, transparent.)
**open,** candid, unreserved, clear, fair. (Hidden, dark.)
**opinion,** notion, view, judgment, belief, sentiment.
**opinionated,** conceited, egotistical. (Modest.)
**oppose,** resist, withstand, thwart. (Give way.)
**option,** choice.
**order,** method, rule, system, regularity. (Disorder.)
**origin,** cause, occasion, source, beginning. (End.)
**ostentation,** pageant, parade, pomp, show, vaunt, display, boast, flourish, brag. (Modesty, shrinking, timidity, reserve, diffidence, quietness, retirement.)
**outlive,** survive.
**outward,** external, outside, exterior. (Inner.)
**over,** above. (Under.)
**overbalance,** outweigh, preponderate.
**overbear,** bear down, overwhelm, overpower, subdue.
**overbearing,** haughty, proud, arrogant. (Gentle.)
**overflow,** inundation, deluge.
**overrule,** supersede, suppress.
**overspread,** overrun, ravage.
**overturn,** invert, overthrow, reverse, subvert. (Establish, fortify.)
**overwhelm,** crush, defeat, vanquish.

## P

**pain,** suffering, qualm, pang, agony, anguish, torment, ache, torture. (Pleasure, delight, rapture.)
**pallid,** pale, wan. (Florid.)
**part,** division, portion, share, fraction. (Whole.)
**particular,** exact, distinct, singular, odd, strange. (General.)
**patient,** passive, submissive, meek. (Obdurate.)
**peace,** calm, quiet, tranquility. (War, riot, trouble, turbulence.)
**peaceable,** pacific, peaceful, quiet. (Troublesome, riotous.)
**penetrate,** bore, pierce, perforate.
**penetration,** acuteness, sagacity. (Dulness.)
**people,** nation, persons, folks.
**perceive,** note, observe, discern, distinguish, comprehend, understand.
**perception,** conception, notion, idea.
**perfect,** ideal, sinless, spotless, stainless, holy, complete, immaculate, unblemished, consummate, correct, faultless. (Bad, defaced, corrupt, blemished, spoiled, worthless, perverted, inferior, marred, defective, faulty, deficient, imperfect.)
**peril,** danger, pitfall, snare. (Safety.)
**permanent,** fixed, constant, lasting, perpetual, stable, steadfast, unchanging, imperishable, durable, enduring, changeless.
**permission,** constant, liberty, leave, permit, license, allowance, authority. (Denial, objection, refusal, prevention.)
**permit,** allow, tolerate. (Forbid.)
**pernicious,** evil, foul, pestiferous, bad, ruinous, detrimental, injurious, harmful, destructive, unhealthful, unwholesome, pestilential. (Good, healthful, helpful, salutary, wholesome, beneficent, advantageous, beneficial, invigorating.)
**perplexity,** confusion, doubt, distraction, amazement, astonishment, bewilderment.
**persuade,** coax, convince, urge, allure, entice, prevail upon.
**pertness,** sauciness, smartness, boldness, briskness, flippancy, impudence, liveliness. (Modesty, diffidence, shyness, demureness, bashfulness.)
**physical,** corporeal, bodily, material. (Mental.)
**picture,** engraving, print, representation, illustration, image.
**piteous,** doleful, woeful, rueful. (Joyful.)
**pitiful,** mournful, pathetic, pitiable, woeful, sorrowful, abject, lamentable, mean, miserable, wretched. (Glorious, great, grand, mighty, lofty, noble, superb, exalted, commanding, august, superior.)
**pitiless.** See **merciless.**
**pity,** mercy, condolence, compassion, sympathy. (Cruelty, brutality, harshness, severity, sternness.)
**place,** *n.*, spot, site, position, post, situation, station.
**place,** *v.*, order, dispose.
**plain,** open, manifest, evident. (Secret.)
**play,** game, sport, amusement. (Work.)
**plead,** beseech, ask, beg, entreat, implore, urge, solicit, argue, advocate.
**please,** gratify, pacify. (Displease.)
**pleasure,** charm, delight, joy. (Pain.)
**plentiful,** abundant, ample, copious, plenteous, rich, teeming, luxuriant, full, bountiful, affluent. (Scarce, deficient, impoverished, scant.)
**poise,** balance.
**polite,** cultured, courtly, elegant, genteel, civil, urbane, gracious, obliging, courteous, accomplished. (Awkward, coarse, boorish, raw, rude, uncivil, insulting, uncouth, impolite, impudent.)
**positive,** absolute, peremptory, decided, certain. (Negative.)
**possessor,** owner, proprietor.
**possible,** practical, practicable. (Impossible.)
**poverty,** penury, indigence, need, want. (Wealth.)
**power,** authority, force, strength, dominion.
**powerful,** mighty, potent. (Weak.)
**praise,** acclaim, approbation, commendation, eulogy, plaudit, commend, extol, laud. (Blame.)
**prayer,** entreaty, petition, request, suit.
**precarious,** perilous, risky, uncertain, hazardous, dubious, doubtful. (Firm, assured, infallible, sure, undeniable.)
**pretense,** *n.*, pretext, subterfuge.
**prevailing,** predominant, prevalent, general. (Isolated, sporadic.)
**prevent,** obviate, preclude.
**previous,** antecedent, introductory, preparatory, preliminary. (Subsequent.)
**pride,** haughtiness, vainglory, arrogance, vanity, conceit. (Humility.)
**principally,** chiefly, mainly, essentially.
**principle,** ground, reason, motive, impulse, maxim, rule, rectitude, integrity.
**privilege,** immunity, advantage, favor, prerogative, exemption, right, claim.
**probity,** rectitude, uprightness, honesty, integrity, sincerity, soundness. (Dishonesty.)
**problematical,** uncertain, doubtful, dubious, questionable, disputable, suspicious. (Certain.)
**prodigious,** huge, enormous, vast, amazing, astonishing, remarkable, astounding, surprising, wonderful. (Insignificant.)
**profession,** business, trade, occupation, vocation, office, employment, engagement, avowal.
**proffer,** volunteer, offer, propose, tender.
**profligate,** abandoned, dissolute, depraved, vicious, degenerate, corrupt, demoralized. (Virtuous.)
**profound,** deep, fathomless, penetrating, solemn, abstruse, recondite. (Shallow.)
**profuse,** extravagant, prodigal, lavish, improvident, excessive, copious, plentiful. (Succinct.)
**prohibit,** forbid, hinder, prevent, debar, disallow, interdict. (Permit, license, sanction, allow, tolerate, authorize.)
**prolific,** productive, generative, fertile, fruitful, teeming. (Barren.)
**prolix,** diffuse, long, prolonged, tedious, tiresome, wordy, verbose, prosaic. (Concise, brief.)
**prominent,** eminent, marked, important, conspicuous, leading. (Obscure.)
**promiscuous,** mixed, unarranged, indiscriminate, mingled. (Select.)
**prompt.** See **punctual**

**prop,** *v.*, maintain, sustain, support, stay.
**propagate,** spread, circulate, diffuse, disseminate, extend, breed, increase. (Suppress.)
**proper,** legitimate, right, just, fair, equitable, honest, suitable, fit, decent, meet, becoming, benefitting, adapted, pertinent, appropriate. (Wrong.)
**prosper,** flourish, succeed, grow rich, thrive, advance. (Fail.)
**prosperity,** well-being, weal, welfare, happiness, good luck. (Poverty.)
**proxy,** agent, representative, substitute, delegate, deputy.
**prudence,** carefulness, judgment, discretion, wisdom. (Indiscretion.)
**prurient,** itching, craving, hankering, longing.
**puerile,** youthful, juvenile, boyish, childish, infantile, trifling, weak, silly. (Mature.)
**punctilious,** nice, particular, formal, precise. (Negligent.)
**punctual,** exact, precise, nice, particular, prompt, timely. (Dilatory.)
**putrefy,** rot, decompose, corrupt, decay.
**puzzle,** *v.*, perplex, confound, embarrass, bewilder, confuse, pose, mystify. (Enlighten.)

## Q

**quack,** imposter, pretender, charlatan, empiric, mountebank. (Savant.)
**quaint,** artful, curious, far-fetched, fanciful, odd, singular.
**qualified,** competent, fitted, adapted. (Incompetent.)
**quality,** attribute, rank, distinction.
**queer,** odd, peculiar, singular, quaint, unique, strange, unusual, ridiculous, preposterous, bizarre, curious, eccentric, ludicrous, fantastic, funny. (Common, natural, usual, normal, ordinary, regular.)
**querulous,** doubting, complaining, repining, fretting. (Patient.)
**question,** query, inquiry, interrogatory.
**quibble,** cavil, evade, equivocate, prevaricate, shuffle.
**quick,** lively, brisk, expeditious, impetuous, adroit, fleet, rapid, swift, sweeping, dashing, clever, sharp, ready, prompt, alert, nimble, agile, active. (Slow.)
**quote,** note, repeat, cite, adduce.

## R

**rabid,** mad, furious, raging, frantic. (Rational.)
**race,** course, match, pursuit, career, family, clan, house, ancestry, lineage, pedigree.
**rack,** agonize, wring, torture, excruciate, distress, harass. (Soothe.)
**racy,** spicy, pungent, smart, spirited, lively, vivacious. (Dull, insipid.)
**radiance,** splendor, brightness, brilliance, brilliancy, lustre, glare. (Dulness.)
**radical,** organic, innate, fundamental, original, constitutional, inherent, entire, complete. (Superficial. In a political sense, uncompromising; antonym, moderate.)
**rancid,** fetid, rank, stinking, sour, tainted, reasty. (Fresh, sweet.)
**rancor,** malignity, hatred, hostility, antipathy, animosity, enmity, ill will, spite. (Forgiveness.)
**rank,** order, degree, dignity, nobility, consideration.
**ransack,** rummage, pillage, overhaul, explore, plunder.
**ransom,** emancipate, free, unfetter.
**rant,** bombast, fustian, cant.
**rapacious,** ravenous, greedy, voracious, grasping. (Generous.)
**rapt,** ecstatic, transported, ravished, entranced, charmed. (Distracted.)
**rapture,** ecstasy, transport, delight, bliss. (Dejection.)
**rare,** curious, unique, unusual, strange, peculiar, odd, extraordinary, scarce, singular, uncommon.
**rascal,** scoundrel, rogue, knave, vagabond, scamp.
**rash,** hasty, precipitate, foolhardy, adventurous, heedless, reckless, careless. (Deliberate.)
**rate,** value, compute, appraise, estimate, chide, abuse.
**ratify,** confirm, establish, substantiate, sanction. (Protest, oppose.)
**rational,** reasonable, sagacious, judicious, wise, sensible, sound. (Unreasonable.)
**ravage,** overrun, overspread, desolate, despoil, destroy.
**ravish,** enrapture, enchant, charm, delight, abuse.
**raze,** demolish, destroy, overthrow, ruin, dismantle. (Build up.)
**reach,** touch, stretch, attain, gain, arrive at.
**ready,** prepared, ripe, apt, prompt, adroit, handy. (Slow, dilatory.)
**real,** authentic, actual, literal, practical, positive, certain, genuine, true. (Unreal.)
**realize,** accomplish, achieve, effect, gain, get, acquire, comprehend.
**reap,** gain, get, acquire, obtain.
**reason,** *n.*, motive, design, end, proof, cause, ground, purpose.
**reason,** *v.*, deduce, draw from, trace, infer, conclude.
**reasonable,** rational, wise, honest, fair, right, just. (Unreasonable.)
**rebellion,** insurrection, revolt.
**rebellious,** mutinous, seditious, refractory, disobedient, ungovernable, insubordinate, contumacious. (Docile, obedient, yielding, tractable, subservient, compliant, gentle.)
**recant,** recall, abjure, retract, revoke.
**recede,** retire, retreat, withdraw, ebb.
**receive,** accept, take, admit, entertain.
**reception,** receiving, levee, receipt, admission.
**recess,** retreat, depth, niche, vacation, intermission.
**recreation,** sport, pastime, amusement, play, game, fun.
**redeem,** ransom, recover, rescue, deliver, save, free.
**redress,** remedy, repair, remission, abatement, relief.
**reduce,** abate, lessen, decrease, lower, shorten, conquer.
**refined,** polite, courtly, polished, cultured, genteel, purified. (Boorish.)
**reflect,** consider, cogitate, think, ponder, muse, censure.
**reform,** amend, correct, better, restore, improve. (Corrupt.)
**reformation,** improvement, reform, amendment. (Corruption.)
**refuge,** asylum, protection, harbor, shelter, retreat.
**refuse,** *v.*, deny, reject, repudiate, decline, withhold. (Accept.)
**refuse,** *n.*, dregs, dross, scum, rubbish, leavings, remains.
**refute,** disprove, falsify, negative. (Affirm.)
**regard,** *v.*, mind, heed, notice, behold, view, consider, respect.
**regret,** *n.*, grief, sorrow, lamentation, repentance, remorse.
**regular,** orderly, uniform, customary, ordinary, stated. (Irregular.)
**regulate,** methodize, arrange, adjust, organize, govern, rule. (Disorder.)
**reimburse,** refund, repay, satisfy, indemnify.
**relevant,** fit, proper, suitable, appropriate, pertinent, apt. (Irrelevant.)
**reliance,** trust, hope, dependence, confidence. (Suspicion.)
**relief,** succor, aid, help, redress, alleviation.
**relinquish,** give up, forsake, resign, surrender, quit, leave, forego, (Retain.)
**remedy,** help, relief, redress, cure, specific, reparation.
**remorseless,** pitiless, relentless, merciless, cruel, ruthless, barbarous. (Merciful, humane.)
**remote,** distant, far, secluded, indirect. (Near.)
**renounce,** disown, recant, refute, reject, retract, revoke, repudiate, recall, discard, deny, abandon, disclaim, disavow. (Assert, avow, advocate, acknowledge, cherish, claim, uphold, defend, vindicate, proclaim, retain.)
**report,** record, rumor, story, tale, statement, narrative, account, description, recital.
**reproduce,** propagate, imitate, represent, copy.
**repudiate,** disown, discard, disavow, renounce, disclaim. (Acknowledge.)
**repugnant,** antagonistic, distasteful. (Agreeable.)
**repulsive,** forbidding, odious, ugly, disagreeable, revolting. (Attractive.)
**respite,** reprieve, interval, stop.
**restive,** frisky, balky, fractious, fidgety, unruly, restless, impatient. (Obedient, docile, quiet, submissive, peaceable, gentle.)
**revenge,** vengeance, retaliation, requittal, retribution. (Forgiveness.)
**revenue,** produce, income, proceeds, fruits, wealth.
**reverence,** *n.*, honor, respect, awe, veneration, deference, homage, worship. (Execration.)
**revise,** review, reconsider.
**revive,** refresh, renew, renovate, animate, resuscitate, vivify, cheer, comfort.
**rich,** wealthy, affluent, opulent, copious, ample, abundant, exuberant,

plentiful, fertile, fruitful, superb, gorgeous. (Poor.)
**rival,** *n.*, antagonist, opponent, competitor.
**road,** way, highway, route, course, path, pathway, anchorage.
**roam,** ramble, rove, stray, wander, stroll.
**robber,** footpad, bandit, brigand, burglar, pirate, thief, raider, plunderer, pillager, marauder, forager, buccaneer.
**robust,** strong, lusty, vigorous, sinewy, stout, sturdy, stalwart, able-bodied. (Puny.)
**rout,** *v.*, discomfit, beat, defeat, overthrow, scatter.
**route,** road, course, march, way, path, journey, direction.
**rude,** rugged, rough, uncouth, unpolished, harsh, gruff, impertinent, impudent, saucy, flippant, insolent, churlish. (Polished, polite.)
**rule,** sway, method, system, law, maxim, precept, guide, formula, regulation government, standard, test.
**rumor,** hearsay, talk, fame, report, bruit.
**rustic,** awkward, clownish, plain, pastoral, verdant, uncouth, country, coarse, artless.
**ruthless,** cruel, savage, barbarous, inhuman, merciless, remorseless, relentless, unrelenting. (Considerate.)

## S

**sacred,** holy, hallowed, divine, consecrated, dedicated, devoted. (Profane.)
**safe,** secure, harmless, trustworthy, reliable. (Perilous, dangerous.)
**sagacious,** keen, judicious, intelligent, acute, apt, able, discerning, sage, sharp, shrewd, wise, sensible. (Absurd, foolish, dull, silly, simple, stupid, ignorant, obtuse, senseless.)
**sanction,** confirm, countenance, encourage, support, ratify, authorize. (Disapprove.)
**sane,** sober, lucid, sound, rational. (Crazy.)
**saucy,** impertinent, rude, impudent, insolent, flippant, forward. (Modest.)
**scandalize,** shock, disgust, offend, calumniate, vilify, revile, malign, traduce, defame, slander.
**scanty,** bare, pinched, insufficient, slender, meager. (Ample.)
**scatter,** strew, spread, disseminate, disperse, dissipate, dispel. (Collect.)
**secret,** clandestine, concealed, hidden, sly, underhand, latent, private. (Open.)
**seduce,** allure, attract, decoy, entice, abduct, inveigle, deprave.
**send,** fling, hurl, emit, drive, despatch, cast, delegate, throw, launch, project. (Get, bring, carry, convey, hand, keep, receive, retain, hold.)
**sense,** discernment, appreciation, perception, view, opinion, feeling, sensibility, susceptibility, thought, signification, judgment, import, significance, meaning, purport, wisdom.
**sensible,** wise, intelligent, reasonable, sober, sound, conscious, aware. (Foolish.)
**settle,** arrange, adjust, regulate, conclude, determine.
**several,** sundry, divers, many, various.
**severe,** austere, inexorable, strict, harsh, stern, stringent, unmitigated, rough, unyielding. (Lenient, affable, easy, indulgent.)
**shake,** tremble, shudder, shiver, quiver, quake.
**shallow,** superficial, flimsy, slight. (Deep, thorough.)
**shame,** disgrace, dishonor. (Honor.)
**shameful,** degrading, scandalous, disgraceful, outrageous. (Honorable.)
**shameless,** immodest, impudent, indecent, indelicate, brazen.
**shape,** form, fashion, mold, model.
**share,** portion, lot, division, quantity, quota, contingent.
**sharp,** acute, keen. (Dull.)
**shine,** glare, glitter, radiate, sparkle.
**short,** brief, concise, succinct, summary. (Long.)
**show,** *v.*, indicate, mark, point out, exhibit, display.
**show,** *n.*, appearance, exhibition, pretence, profession, sight, spectacle.
**sick,** diseased, sickly, unhealthy, morbid. (Healthy.)
**sickness,** illness, indisposition, disease, disorder. (Health.)
**significant,** *a.*, expressive, material, important. (Insignificant.)
**signification,** import, sense, meaning.
**silence,** speechlessness, dumbness. (Noise.)
**silent,** dumb, mute, speechless. (Talkative.)
**simile,** comparison, similitude.
**simple,** single, uncompounded, plain, artless. (Complex, compound.)
**simulate,** dissimulate, dissemble, pretend.
**sincere,** candid, hearty, honest, pure, genuine, real. (Insincere.)
**situation,** condition, plight, predicament, state, position.
**size,** bulk, greatness, magnitude, dimension.
**skeptic,** deist, agnostic, atheist, doubter, infidel, freethinker, unbeliever. (Believer, Christian.)
**slander,** defame, detract, revile, vilify, traduce, libel, malign, disparage, asperse, decry, calumniate. (Defend, extol, laud, praise, eulogize.)
**slavery,** servitude, enthrallment, thralldom. (Freedom.)
**sleep,** doze, drowse, nap, slumber.
**sleepy,** somnolent. (Wakeful.)
**slow,** dilatory, tardy, lingering, sluggish. (Fast.)
**smell,** fragrance, odor, scent, perfume.
**smooth,** even, level, mild. (Rough.)
**soak,** drench, imbrue, steep.
**social,** sociable, friendly, communicative. (Unsocial.)
**soft,** gentle, meek, mild. (Hard.)
**solicit,** importune, urge.
**solitary,** sole, only, single.
**sorry,** grieved, poor, paltry, insignificant. (Glad, respectable.)
**soul,** mind, spirit. (Soul is opposed to body, mind to matter.)
**sound,** *a.*, healthy, sane. (Unsound.)
**sound,** *n.*, tone, noise, silence.
**space,** room.
**sparse,** scanty, thin. (Luxuriant.)
**speak,** converse, talk, say, tell, confer, articulate, express, utter.
**special,** particular, specific. (General.)
**spend,** expend, exhaust, consume, dissipate, waste, squander. (Save.)
**sporadic,** isolated, rare. (General, prevalent.)
**spread,** disperse, diffuse, expand, disseminate, scatter.
**spring,** fountain, source.
**staff,** prop, support, stay.
**stagger,** reel, totter.
**stain,** soil, discolor, spot, sully, tarnish, color, blot.
**state,** commonwealth, realm.
**sterile,** barren, unfruitful. (Fertile.)
**stifle,** choke, suffocate, smother.
**stormy,** rough, boisterous, tempestuous. (Calm.)
**straight,** direct, right. (Crooked.)
**strait,** *a.*, narrow, confined.
**stranger,** alien, foreigner. (Friend.)
**strengthen,** fortify, invigorate, encourage. (Weaken.)
**strong,** robust, sturdy, powerful. (Weak.)
**stupid,** dull, foolish, obtuse, witless. (Clever.)
**stupor,** swoon, torpor, unconsciousness, syncope, lethargy, coma, fainting, apathy, asphyxia.
**subject,** exposed to, liable, obnoxious. (Exempt.)
**subject,** inferior, subordinate. (Superior to, above.)
**subsequent,** succeeding, following. (Previous.)
**substantial,** solid, durable. (Unsubstantial.)
**suit,** accord, agree. (Disagree.)
**superficial,** flimsy, shallow, untrustworthy. (Thorough.)
**superfluous,** unnecessary, excessive. (Necessary.)
**surrender,** cede, give, yield, sacrifice, relinquish, abandon, capitulate, alienate.
**surround,** encircle, encompass, environ.
**sustain,** maintain, support.
**symmetry,** proportion.
**sympathy,** commiseration, compassion, condolence.
**synonymous,** alike, corresponding, equivalent, like, same, identical, similar, synonymic.
**system,** rule, manner, method, plan, order.
**systematic,** orderly, regular, methodical. (Chaotic.)

## T

**taciturn,** silent, reticent, mute, reserved, close, dumb, speechless, uncommunicative. (Talkative, unreserved, loquacious, garrulous, free, communicative.)
**take,** accept, receive. (Give.)
**talkative,** garrulous, communicative, loquacious. (Silent.)
**taste,** flavor, relish, savor. (Tastelessness.)
**tax,** custom, duty, impost, excise, toll.
**tax,** assessment, rate.
**tease,** taunt, tantalize, torment, vex.
**temerity,** rashness, presumption, recklessness, audacity, hastiness, fool-

hardiness, heedlessness, precipitation. (Care, caution, timidity, wariness, hesitation, cowardice, circumspection.)
**temporary,** *a.*, fleeting, transient, transitory. (Permanent.)
**tenacious,** pertinaceous, retentive.
**tendency,** aim, drift, scope.
**tenet,** position, view, conviction, belief.
**term,** boundary, limit, period, time.
**territory,** dominion.
**thankful,** grateful, obliged. (Thankless.)
**thankless,** ungracious, profitless, ungrateful, unthankful.
**thaw,** melt, dissolve, liquefy. (Freeze.)
**theatrical,** dramatic, showy, ceremonious, meretricious.
**theft,** robbery, depredation, spoliation.
**theme,** subject, topic, text, essay.
**theory,** speculation, scheme, plea, hypothesis, conjecture.
**therefore,** accordingly, consequently, hence.
**thick,** dense, close, compact, solid, coagulated, muddy, turbid, misty, foggy, vaporous. (Thin.)
**thin,** slim, slender, slight, flimsy, attenuated, lean, scraggy.
**think,** cogitate, consider, reflect, ponder, contemplate, meditate, muse, conceive, fancy, imagine, apprehend, hold, esteem, reckon, consider, regard, deem, believe, opine.
**thorough,** accurate, correct, trustworthy, reliable, complete. (Superficial.)
**thought,** idea, conception, imagination, fancy, conceit, notion, supposition, care, provision, consideration, opinion, view, sentiment, reflection, deliberation.
**thoughtful,** considerate, careful, reflective, cautious, heedful, contemplative, provident, pensive, dreamy. (Thoughtless.)
**thoughtless,** inconsiderate, rash, improvident, precipitate, heedless.
**tie,** *v.*, bind, restrain, restrict, oblige, secure, unite, join. (Loose.)
**tie,** *n.*, band, ligament, ligature.
**time,** duration, season, period, era, age, date, span, spell.
**tolerate,** allow, admit, receive, suffer, permit, let, endure, abide. (Oppose.)
**top,** summit, apex, head, crown, surface. (Bottom, base.)
**torrid,** burning, hot, parching, scorching, sultry.
**tortuous,** twisted, winding, crooked, indirect.
**torture,** torment, anguish, agony.
**touching,** tender, affecting, moving, pathetic.
**tractable,** docile, manageable, amenable.
**trade,** traffic, commerce, dealing, occupation, employment, office.
**traditional,** oral, uncertain, transmitted.
**traffic,** trade, exchange, commerce, intercourse.
**trammel,** *n.*, fetter, shatter, clog, bond, chain, impediment, hindrance.
**tranquil,** still, unruffled, peaceful, quiet, hushed. (Noisy, boisterous.)
**transaction,** negotiation, occurrence, proceeding, affair.
**trash,** nonsense, twaddle, trifles.
**travel,** trip, ramble, peregrination, excursion, journey, tour, voyage.
**treacherous,** traitorous, treasonable, disloyal, faithless, false-hearted, perfidious, sly, false. (Trustworthy, faithful.)
**trite,** stale, old, ordinary, commonplace, hackneyed. (Novel.)
**triumph,** achievement, ovation, victory, conquest, jubilation. (Failure, defeat.)
**trivial,** trifling, petty, small, frivolous, unimportant, insignificant. (Important.)
**true,** genuine, actual, sincere, truehearted, unaffected, honest, upright, veritable, real, veracious, authentic, exact, accurate, correct.
**tumultuous,** turbulent, riotous, disorderly, disturbed, confused, unruly. (Orderly.)
**tune,** tone, air, melody, strain.
**turbid,** foul, thick, muddy, impure, unsettled.
**type,** emblem, symbol, figure, sign, letter, sort, kind.
**tyro,** novice, beginner, learner.

## U

**ugly,** unsightly, plain, homely, ill-favored, hideous. (Beautiful.)
**umbrage,** offense, dissatisfaction, displeasure, resentment.
**umpire,** referee, arbitrator, judge, arbiter.
**unanimity,** accord, agreement, unity, concord. (Discord.)
**unanimous,** agreeing, like-minded.
**unbridled,** wanton, licentious, dissolute, loose, lax.
**uncertain,** doubtful, dubious, questionable, fitful, equivocal, ambiguous, indistinct, variable, fluctuating.
**uncivil,** discourteous, disrespectful, disobliging, rude. (Civil.)
**unclean,** dirty, filthy, sullied. (Clean.)
**uncommon,** rare, strange, scarce, singular, choice. (Common, ordinary.)
**unconcerned,** careless, indifferent, apathetic. (Anxious.)
**uncouth,** strange, odd, clumsy, ungainly. (Graceful.)
**uncover,** reveal, strip, expose, lay bare, invest. (Hide.)
**under,** below, underneath, beneath, subordinate, lower, inferior. (Above.)
**understanding,** knowledge, intellect, intelligence, faculty, comprehension, mind, reason, brains.
**undertake,** engage in, embark in, agree, promise.
**undo,** annul, frustrate, unfasten, destroy.
**uneasy,** restless, disturbed, unquiet, stiff, awkward. (Quiet.)
**unequal,** uneven, not alike, irregular, insufficient. (Even.)
**unequaled,** matchless, unique, novel, new, unheard of.
**unfair,** wrongful, dishonest, unjust. (Fair.)
**unfit,** *a.*, improper, unsuitable, inconsistent, untimely, incompetent. (Fit.)
**unfit,** *v.*, disable, disqualify, incapacitate. (Fit.)
**unfortunate,** calamitous, ill-fated, unlucky, wretched, unhappy, miserable. (Fortunate.)
**ungainly,** clumsy, awkward, lumbering, uncouth. (Pretty.)
**unhappy,** miserable, wretched, distressed, afflicted, painful, disastrous, drear, dismal. (Happy.)
**uniform,** regular, symmetrical, even, equal, alike, unvaried. (Irregular.)
**uninterrupted,** continuous, perpetual, unceasing, incessant, endless. (Intermittent.)
**union,** junction, combination, alliance, confederacy, league, coalition, agreement, concert. (Disunion, separation.)
**unique,** unequal, uncommon, rare, choice, matchless. (Common, ordinary.)
**unite,** join, conjoin, combine, concert, add, attach, incorporate, embody, clench, merge. (Separate, disrupt, sunder.)
**universal,** general, all, entire, total, catholic. (Sectional.)
**unlimited,** absolute, boundless, undefined, infinite. (Limited.)
**unreasonable,** foolish, silly, absurd.
**unrivaled,** unequaled, unique, unexampled, incomparable, matchless. (Mediocre.)
**unroll,** unfold, open, discover.
**unruly,** ungovernable, unmanageable, refractory. (Tractable, docile.)
**unusual,** rare, unwonted, singular, uncommon, remarkable, strange, extraordinary. (Common.)
**uphold,** maintain, defend, sustain, support, vindicate. (Desert, abandon.)
**upright,** vertical, perpendicular, just, erect, equitable, fair, pure, honorable. (Prone, horizontal.)
**uprightness,** honesty, integrity, fairness, goodness, probity, honor, virtue. (Dishonesty.)
**urge,** incite, impel, push, drive, instigate, stimulate, press, solicit, induce.
**urgent,** pressing, important, imperative, immediate, serious, wanted. (Unimportant.)
**usage,** custom, fashion, practice, prescription.
**use,** *n.*, usage, practice, habit, custom, avail, advantage, utility, benefit, application. (Disuse, desuetude.)
**use,** *v.*, employ, exercise, occupy, accustom, practice, inure. (Abuse.)
**useful,** advantageous, serviceable, available, helpful, beneficial, good. (Useless.)
**useless,** unserviceable, fruitless, idle, profitless. (Useful.)
**usual,** ordinary, common, accustomed, habitual, wonted, customary, general, prevalent, regular. (Unusual, exceptional, rare, singular, strange.)
**usurp,** arrogate, seize, appropriate, assume.
**utmost,** farthest, remotest, uttermost, greatest.
**utter,** *a.*, extreme, excessive, sheer, mere, pure.
**utter,** *v.*, speak, articulate, express, pronounce, issue.

**utterly,** totally, completely, wholly, quite, altogether, entirely.

V

**vacant,** empty, unfilled, unoccupied, thoughtless, unthinking, void, vacuous. (Occupied, crowded, full, jammed, packed.)
**vagrant,** *n.*, wanderer, beggar, tramp, vagabond, rogue.
**vague,** unsettled, undetermined, uncertain, pointless, indefinite. (Definite.)
**vain,** useless, fruitless, empty, worthless, inflated, proud, conceited, unreal, unavailing, frivolous. (Effectual, humble, real.)
**valiant,** brave, bold, valorous, courageous, gallant. (Cowardly.)
**valid,** weighty, strong, powerful, efficient, sound, binding. (Invalid.)
**volar,** courage, gallantry, boldness, bravery, heroism. (Cowardice.)
**value,** *v.*, appraise, assess, reckon, appreciate, estimate, prize, treasure, esteem. (Despise, condemn.)
**vanish,** disappear, fade, melt, dissolve.
**vanity,** emptiness, conceit, self-conceit, effectedness.
**vapid,** dull, flat, insipid, stale, tame. (Sparkling.)
**vapor,** fume, smoke, mist, fog, steam.
**variable,** changeable, unsteady, shifting, inconstant, wavering, fickle, fitful,restless. (Constant.)
**variety,** difference, diversity, change, diversification, mixture, medley, miscellany. (Sameness, monotony.)
**vast,** spacious, boundless, mighty, immense, enormous, colossal, gigantic, huge, prodigious. (Confined.)
**vaunt,** boast, brag, puff, hawk, advertise, flourish, parade.
**venerable,** grave, sage, wise, old, revcrend.
**venial,** pardonable, excusable, justifiable. (Grave, serious.)
**venom,** poison, virus, spite, malice, malignity.
**venture** *n.*, speculation, chance, peril, stake.
**venture,** *v.*, dare, adventure, risk, hazard, jeopardize.
**veracity,** truth, truthfulness, credibility, accuracy, candor, verity, honesty. (Falsehood, deception, fabrication, lie, untruth.)
**verbal,** oral, spoken, literal, parole, unwritten.
**verdict,** judgment, finding, decision, answer.
**vexation,**chagrin,mortification. (Pleasure.)
**vibrate,** oscillate, swing, sway, wave, undulate, thrill.
**vice,** vileness, corruption, depravity, pollution, immorality, wickedness, guilt, iniquity, crime. (Virtue.)
**vicious,** corrupt, depraved, debased, bad, contrary, unruly, demoralized, profligate, faulty. (Virtuous, gentle.)
**victim,** sacrifice, food, prey, sufferer, dupe, gull.
**victuals,** viands, bread, meat, repast, provisions, fare, food.
**view,** prospect, survey.
**violent,** boisterous, furious, impetuous, vehement. (Gentle.)
**virtue,** honesty, morality, honor, truth, worth, uprightness, virtuousness, probity, purity, integrity, chastity, goodness, duty, rectitude, faithfulness. (Vice, viciousness, evil, wrong, wickedness.)
**virtuous,** upright, honest, moral. (Profligate.)
**vision,** apparition, ghost, phantom, specter.
**voluptuary,** epicure, sensualist.
**vote,** suffrage, voice.
**vouch,** affirm, asseverate, aver, assure.

W

**wait,** await, expect, look for, wait for.
**wakeful,** vigilant, watchful. (Sleepy.)
**wander,** range, ramble, roam, rove, stroll, stray, deviate.
**want,** lack, need. (Abundance.)
**wary,** circumspect, cautious. (Foolhardy.)
**wash,** clean, rinse, wet, moisten, tint, stain.
**waste,** *v.*, squander, dissipate, lavish, destroy, decay, dwindle, wither.
**wasteful,** extravagant, profligate. (Economical.)
**wave,** breaker, billow, surge.
**way,** method, plan, system, means, manner, mode, form, fashion, course, process, road, route, track, path, habit, practice.
**weak,** feeble, infirm. (Strong.)
**weaken,** debilitate, enfeeble, enervate, invalidate. (Strengthen.)
**wealth,** money, pelf, plenty, opulence, means, riches, prosperity, lucre, luxury, assets, abundance, affluence, property. (Need, destitution, lack, beggary, misery, poverty, privation, want, scarcity, mendicancy, pauperism, impecuniosity.)
**wearisome,** tedious, tiresome. (Interesting, entertaining.)
**weary,** harass, jade, tire, fatigue. (Refresh.)
**weight,** gravity, heaviness, burden, load. (Lightness.)
**well-being,** happiness, prosperity, welfare.
**whole,** entire, complete, total, integral. (Part.)
**wicked,** iniquitous, nefarious. (Virtuous.)
**will,** wish, desire.
**willingly,** spontaneously, voluntarily. (Unwillingly.)
**win,** get, obtain, gain, procure, effect, realize, accomplish, achieve. (Lose.)
**winning,** attractive, charming, fascinating, bewitching, enchanting, dazzling, brilliant. (Repulsive.)
**wisdom,** prudence, foresight, sagacity, far-sightedness, judiciousness, sense. (Foolishness, absurdity, idiocy, silliness, stupidity, nonsense.)
**wit,** humor, satire, fun, raillery.
**wonder,** *v.*, admire, amaze, astonish, surprise.
**wonder,** *n.*, marvel, miracle, prodigy.
**word,** *n.*, expression, term.
**work,** labor, task, toil, occupation, business, employment, exertion. (Play.)
**worthless,** valueless. (Valuable.)
**writer,** author, penman.
**wrong,** injustice, injury. (Right.)

Y

**yawn,** gape, open wide.
**yearn,** hanker after, long for, desire, crave.
**yell,** bellow, cry out, scream.
**yellow,** golden, saffronlike.
**yelp,** bark, sharp cry, howl.
**yet,** besides, nevertheless, however, ultimately, notwithstanding, still, at last, so far, thus far.
**yield,** bear, give, afford, impart, communicate, confer, bestow, abdicate, resign, cede, surrender, relinquish, relax, quit, forego, giveup, let go, waive, comply, accede, assent, acquiesce, succumb, submit. (Withdraw, withhold, retain, deny, refuse, vindicate, assert, claim, disallow, resist, dissent, protest, struggle, strive.)
**yielding,** conceding, producing, surrendering, supple, pliant, submissive, accommodating, unresisting. (Firm, defiant, hard, unyielding, resisting, unfruitful.)
**yoke,** *v.*, couple, link, connect, conjoin, enslave, subjugate. (Dissever, divorce, disconnect, liberate, release, manumit, enfranchise.)
**yore,** long ago, long since. (Recently, today, now.)
**youth,** boy, lad, minority, adolescence, juvenility. (Old, ancient, antiquated, elderly, senile, patriarchal, primeval, time-honored, olden.)
**youthful,** young, juvenile, boyish, girlish, puerile, immature, adolescent. (Aged, senile, mature, decrepit, decayed, venerable, antiquated, superannuated.)

Z

**zeal,** energy, fervor, ardor, earnestness, enthusiasm, eagerness. (Indifference, apathy, torpor, coldness, carelessness, sluggishness.)
**zealot,** partisan, bigot, fanatic, devotee, visionary, enthusiast. (Traitor, deserter, renegade.)
**zealous,** warm, ardent, fervent, enthusiastic, anxious, eager, earnest, steadfast. (Bold, indifferent, dispassioned, apathetic, passionless, phlegmatic, platonic.)
**zenith,** height, highest point, pinnacle, summit, culmination, maximum. (Depth, lowest point, minimum.)
**zephyr,** mild breeze, west wind, gentle wind. (Gale, furious wind.)
**zero,** nothing, naught, cipher. (Something.)
**zest,** flavor, appetizer, gusto, pleasure, enjoyment, relish, sharpener, enhancement. (Distaste, disgust, disrelish, detriment.)

# HOMONYMS

Homonyms are two or more words with essentially the same pronunciation, but with a different meaning, origin, and, usually, spelling. Here is a representative list of homonyms:

**ad,** an advertisement
**add,** to increase; join to

**adieu,** good-by
**ado,** fuss, excitement

**affect,** to influence; concern
**effect,** bring about, accomplish

**air,** atmosphere; a melody
**e'er,** ever
**ere,** before
**heir,** one who inherits

**aisle,** passageway in theaters, churches
**isle,** an island

**all,** the whole of; everyone of
**awl,** tool for making holes

**aloud,** audibly
**allowed,** permitted, granted

**altar,** raised platform in a place of worship
**alter,** to change, vary

**ant,** a small insect
**aunt,** father's or mother's sister

**ante-,** before
**anti-,** against

**arc,** part of circle
**ark,** flat-bottomed boat; refuge

**ascent,** movement upward
**assent,** to concur

**ate,** past tense of *eat*
**eight,** two times four

**aught,** anything
**ought,** should

**aye, ay,** yes
**eye,** organ of sight
**I,** the person speaking

**bad,** wicked
**bade,** past tense of *bid*

**bail,** money deposited with a court
**bale,** large bundle (of goods)

**bait,** to torment; lure
**bate,** to abate, reduce

**bald,** without hair
**bawled,** shouted loudly

**ball,** a sphere; dance
**bawl,** to shout loudly

**band,** a binding strip; orchestra
**banned,** prohibited

**bard,** a poet
**barred,** obstructed

**bare,** naked
**bear,** a large mammal; to carry

**base,** foundation; vile
**bass,** lowest part in musical composition

**be,** to exist
**bee,** honey-producing insect

**beat,** to strike
**beet,** edible plant

**been,** past participle of *be*
**bin,** enclosed storage space

**beer,** a drink made with malt
**bier,** platform for a coffin

**bell,** a metal object that rings
**belle,** a pretty woman

**berry,** a small, juicy fruit
**bury,** to inter; sink

**berth,** a sleeping place on trains
**birth,** origin; being born

**blew,** past tense of *blow*
**blue,** color of the clear sky

**board,** flat piece of wood
**bored,** wearied by dullness

**bold,** daring; impudent
**bowled,** rolled a ball

**bole,** a tree trunk
**boll,** cotton or flax pod
**bowl,** round, deep dish

**born,** brought forth
**borne,** carried
**bourn, bourne,** a stream

**bough,** branch of a tree
**bow,** to nod in greeting

**bow,** knot; device for shooting arrows
**beau,** a lover; man of fashion

**boy,** a male child
**buoy,** floating guide for ships

**brake,** device for stopping a vehicle
**break,** to shatter

**bred,** raised
**bread,** baked food of grain

**breech,** under or back part
**breach,** a gap

**brews,** begins to form
**bruise,** injury

**bridal,** a wedding
**bridle,** horse's head harness

**broach,** to bring up
**brooch,** ornamental pin

**brows,** the eyebrows
**browse,** to graze; read leisurely

**build,** to construct
**billed,** solicited for payment due

**burrow,** hole in the ground, tunnel
**borough,** district; corporate town
**burro,** donkey

**but,** however; except
**butt,** a thick end; to bump

**buy,** to purchase
**bi-,** a prefix meaning two
**by,** near
**bye,** incidental; secondary

**calendar,** an almanac
**calender,** a machine for glazing paper

**call,** to summon
**caul,** a membrane

**canon,** a decree; law
**cannon,** large gun

**can't,** cannot
**cant,** jargon

**canvas,** a coarse cloth
**canvass,** to solicit votes

**capital,** chief city
**capitol,** legislative building

**cast,** to throw; form in mold
**caste,** a social class

**caster,** furniture roller
**castor,** an oil from the beaver

**cede,** to grant; yield
**seed,** to plant seed, sow

**ceiling,** overhead surface of room
**sealing,** closing securely

**cell,** a room for confinement
**sell,** to vend; betray

**cellar,** room below ground
**seller,** one who sells

**cent,** a penny
**scent,** perfume
**sent,** past tense of *send*

**cereal,** edible grain
**serial,** story in installments

**cession,** a giving up
**session,** a meeting

**chased,** followed
**chaste,** virtuous

**chews,** masticates
**choose,** to pick out

**choir,** church singers
**quire,** a set of sheets of paper

**chord,** a musical term
**cord,** string

**cite,** to summon; mention
**sight,** power of seeing
**site,** a location

**clause,** part of a sentence
**claws,** nails of animals or birds

**climb,** to ascend
**clime,** a region, climate

**coal,** a mineral fuel
**cole,** cabbage

**coarse,** rough; vulgar
**course,** route; part of meal

**complement,** complete number
**compliment,** praise

**core,** central part
**corps,** a body of troops

**correspondence,** communication
**correspondents,** letter writers

**council,** an assembly
**counsel,** advice

**cousin,** child of one's uncle or aunt
**cozen,** to cheat

**coward,** one who lacks courage
**cowered,** crouched in fear

**creak,** to squeak
**creek,** a small stream

**crews,** personnel for ships
**cruise,** a voyage
**cruse,** a small container

**currant,** a sour berry
**current,** flow of stream

**Dane,** a native of Denmark
**deign,** to condescend

**dear,** beloved; costly
**deer,** animal

**dew,** moisture of condensing air
**do,** to perform
**due,** owed; expected

**die,** to stop living
**dye,** coloring matter

**discreet,** prudent
**discrete,** separate

**doe,** a female deer
**do,** first and last tone of diatonic scale
**dough,** a soft mixture for baking

**done,** finished, completed
**dun,** to insist on payment

**dual,** of two
**duel,** a fight

**earn,** receive as salary or wages
**urn,** vase

**exercise,** to practice, train
**exorcise,** to drive out

**fain,** glad
**fane,** a temple
**feign,** to pretend

**faint,** to lose consciousness
**feint,** a pretense

**fair,** impartial; a carnival
**fare,** charge for transportation

**faker,** a fraud
**fakir,** a beggar

**faun,** a rural deity
**fawn,** young deer; to flatter

**felloe,** rim of wheel
**fellow,** a man or boy; associate

**find,** to discover
**fined,** punished

**flea,** bloodsucking insect
**flee,** to escape

**flour,** finely ground grain
**flower,** blossom of plant

**flue,** shaft of chimney
**flew,** past tense of *fly*

**for,** because; in place of
**fore,** at the front
**four,** two times two

**fourth,** ordinal of four
**forth,** out; onward

**foul,** stinking; unfair
**fowl,** poultry

**franc,** a French coin
**frank,** outspoken

**freeze,** harden into ice
**frieze,** heavy wool cloth

**gate,** entrance; barrier
**gait,** manner of walking or running

**gild,** overlay with gold
**guild,** an association

**gilt,** a thin layer of gold
**guilt,** responsibility for crime

**great,** large; eminent
**grate,** to grind; irritate

**grieves,** feels sorrow
**greaves,** armor for the legs

**groan,** moan from pain
**grown,** mature, full-sized

**guessed,** surmised
**guest,** visitor

**hail,** to greet
**hale,** vigorous

**hair,** threadlike growth from the skin
**hare,** a rabbit

**hall,** corridor
**haul,** to pull

**handsome,** good-looking; proper
**hansom,** a kind of carriage

**hart,** male red deer
**heart,** muscular organ

**hay,** cut and dried grass
**hey,** an exclamation

**heal,** to cure
**heel,** back part of the foot
**he'll,** he will

**hear,** to become aware of sound
**here,** in this place

**heard,** past tense of *hear*
**herd,** number of cattle

**hew,** to cut with an ax
**hue,** color

**hide,** skin of animal; to conceal
**hied,** went in haste

**high,** tall
**hie,** to hasten

**ho,** an exclamation of surprise
**hoe,** a garden tool

**hoard,** to store away
**horde,** a swarm; wandering tribe

**hoes,** works with a hoe
**hose,** a flexible pipe; stockings

**holy,** deserving of worship
**wholly,** completely

**hymn,** religious song of praise
**him,** objective case of *he*

**idle,** unemployed
**idol,** image of a god

**indict,** to charge with a crime
**indite,** to compose

**kernel,** seed
**colonel,** army officer

**knot,** an interlacement as of cords
**not,** no

**knows,** possesses knowledge
**noes,** plural of *no*
**nose,** the organ of smell

**lade,** to load
**laid,** past tense of *lay*

**lane,** a narrow road
**lain,** past participle of *lie*

**lea,** a meadow
**lee,** side sheltered from the wind

**leaf,** part of plant or book
**lief,** gladly

**leased,** given by a lease
**least,** the smallest

**led,** past tense of *lead* (to guide)
**lead,** a chemical element

**liar,** one who tells lies
**lyre,** musical instrument

**lie,** a falsehood; to be situated
**lye,** a strong alkali

**load,** a burden
**lode,** a mineral vein

**loan,** something lent
**lone,** solitary

**made,** constructed
**maid,** a girl; female servant

**mail,** letters; armor
**male,** of men

**main,** principal
**mane,** hair on horse's neck

**manner,** behavior; habit
**manor,** estate

**mantel,** shelf over fireplace
**mantle,** a sleeveless cloak

**marshal,** an official
**martial,** military

**massed,** gathered into a mass
**mast,** spar of ship

**maze,** labyrinth
**maize,** Indian corn

**mead,** liquour made of fermented honey
**meed,** reward

**mean,** poor; to denote
**mien,** manner, air

**meat,** animal flesh
**meet,** to come upon
**mete,** to allot; a boundary

**merry,** gay; festive
**marry,** join in wedlock

**might,** strength
**mite,** very small object

**mind,** intellect
**mined,** excavated

**miner,** a worker in a mine
**minor,** not of age

**missed,** failed to get
**mist,** water vapor in atmosphere

**moan,** a low, mournful sound
**mown,** cut down

**mussel,** edible salt-water bivalve
**muscle,** organ of fibrous tissue

**mustard,** a plant with yellow flowers
**mustered,** assembled

**nave,** main body of church
**knave,** a rogue

**nay,** no
**neigh,** to whinny

**need,** a necessity
**knead,** work dough into a mass

**new,** recent; fresh
**gnu,** Africa antelope
**knew,** past tense of *know*

**night,** opposite of day
**knight,** a military attendant

**no,** expression of refusal
**know,** to perceive

**oar,** pole used to row
**o'er,** over
**or,** a conjunction
**ore,** a natural metal

**ode,** a lyric poem
**owed,** past tense of *owe*

**oh,** exclamation of surprise
**owe,** to be indebted

**our,** possessive form of *we*
**hour,** sixty minutes

**pail,** a bucket
**pale,** lacking color

**pain,** suffering
**pane,** section of window glass

**pair,** two similar things
**pare,** to peel
**pear,** a fruit

**passed,** past tense of *pass*
**past,** gone by

**pause,** hesitation
**paws,** feet of a four-footed animal

**peace,** freedom from war
**piece,** a section of a whole

**peal,** ringing of bells
**peel,** to cut away, pare

**pedal,** a foot lever
**peddle,** to sell

**peer,** an equal; to look closely
**pier,** dock for ships

**plain,** simple; unfigured
**plane,** a flat surface

**plait,** a braid
**plate,** a table dish

**please,** to satisfy
**please,** appeals

**plum,** a fruit
**plumb,** weight for testing the vertical

**pore,** tiny skin opening
**pour,** to cause to flow in a stream

**pray,** to say prayers to God
**prey,** a victim

**prays,** beseeches
**praise,** to express approval
**preys,** plunders

**pride,** self-respect
**pried,** opened with a lever

**prier,** one who pries
**prior,** earlier

**principal,** a chief; governing officer
**principle,** rule; law

**quarts,** plural of *quart*
**quartz,** a mineral

**quoin,** wedge-shaped stone
**coin,** metal money

**rabbet,** joint of boards
**rabbit,** a burrowing rodent

**rain,** water falling in drops from the atmosphere
**reign,** to rule
**rein,** strap to control a horse

**raise,** to lift
**rays,** beams of light
**raze,** to demolish

**rap,** a quick, sharp knock
**wrap,** an outer garment

**rapped,** knocked on (a door)
**rapt,** enraptured
**wrapped,** covered

**read,** to peruse
**reed,** a kind of grass

**read,** past tense of *read*
**red,** a color

**real,** genuine
**reel,** to stagger

**rest,** sleep
**wrest,** take by force

**right,** correct
**rite,** solemn ceremony
**wright,** one who makes
**write,** to compose

**rime,** hoarfrost
**rhyme,** poetry

**ringing,** sound of bells
**wringing,** twisting

**road,** way for travel
**rode,** past tense of *ride*
**rowed,** past tense of *row*

**roe,** fish eggs
**row,** to propel (with oars)

**role,** part in a play
**roll,** to move by turning over

**rood,** quarter of an acre
**rude,** impolite
**rued,** regretted

**rote,** routine
**wrote,** past tense of *write*

**rough,** harsh; uneven
**ruff,** a high, frilled, starched collar

**rung,** step of a ladder
**wrung,** past tense of *wring*

**rye,** a cereal grass
**wry,** distorted

**sac,** pouchlike part
**sack,** bag of coarse cloth

**sail,** to travel on water
**sale,** act of selling

**scene,** view; part of a play
**seen,** past participle of *see*

**sea,** body of salt water
**see,** to look at

**seem,** appear
**seam,** line formed by joining two edges

**sees,** looks at
**seize,** to capture

**seine,** large fishing net
**sane,** mentally healthy

**sew,** to fasten with stitches
**so,** therefore
**sow,** to scatter seed

**shoe,** foot covering
**shoo,** to drive away

**sign,** an indication
**syne,** since (Scottish term)

**skull,** the cranium
**scull,** a boat; an oar

**slay,** to kill
**sleigh,** a snow vehicle

**sleight,** trick; dexterity
**slight,** slender; frail

**slew,** killed
**slough,** a swamp
**slue,** to swing around a point

**sloe,** a fruit
**slow,** not fast

**soared,** flew high
**sword,** a weapon

**sold,** past tense of *sell*
**soled,** furnished with a sole

**sole,** only; bottom of the foot
**soul,** spiritual part of a person

**some,** an unspecified quantity
**sum,** total

**son,** a male child
**sun,** heavenly body

**staid,** steady, sedate
**stayed,** remained

**stair,** one of a series of steps
**stare,** to gaze intently

**stake,** a pointed piece of wood
**steak,** a slice of meat

**stationary,** fixed; permanent
**stationery,** writing materials

**steal,** to take dishonestly
**steel,** iron alloyed with carbon

**stile,** turnstile
**style,** fashion

**straight,** not curved; direct
**strait,** narrow waterway

**sucker,** shoot of a plant
**succor,** to help, assist

**suite,** a musical composition
**sweet,** tasting like sugar

**sutler,** one who sells goods at an army camp
**subtler,** more crafty or skillful

**tail,** the rear end of an animal
**tale,** a story

**taper,** a candle
**tapir,** hoglike animal

**tare,** a plant; a weed
**tear,** to rip

**tea,** a beverage
**tee,** small mound in golf

**tear,** salty fluid from the eyes
**tier,** a row

**teem,** to swarm
**team,** a group working together

**tern,** sea bird
**turn,** to rotate

**their,** possessive pronoun
**there,** in that place

**threw,** past tense of *throw*
**through,** finished

**throe,** spasm of pain
**throw,** to hurl

**tide,** rise and fall of the sea
**tied,** fastened

**timber,** building wood
**timbre,** quality of sound

**time,** period between events
**thyme,** plant with fragrant leaves

**tire,** to become fatigued
**Tyre,** city of ancient Phoenicia

**toe,** digit of the foot
**tow,** to pull

**told,** past tense of *tell*
**tolled,** past tense of *toll*

**too,** also
**to,** toward
**two,** one more than one

**tract,** a pamphlet
**tracked,** followed

**travail,** hard work
**travel,** to make a journey

**use,** to put into action
**ewes,** female sheep (pl.)
**yews,** evergreen trees

**vain,** conceited
**vane,** weathervane
**vale,** valley
**veil,** a light fabric worn as a face covering

**wade,** to walk through water
**weighed,** past tense of *weigh*

**wail,** a long cry of grief or pain
**wale,** a welt

**wait,** to remain until something expected happens
**weight,** heaviness

**ware,** things for sale
**wear,** to be clothed in

**waste,** useless matter
**waist,** body between the ribs and the hips

**wave,** moving swell of water
**waive,** to give up a claim

**way,** manner; road
**weigh,** to determine the weight of

**weak,** feeble
**week,** a period of seven days

**weather,** atmospheric condition
**whether,** if

**wheal,** pustule
**wheel,** circular frame

**whole,** intact; complete
**hole,** cavity

**with,** among
**withe,** a twig

**wood,** lumber
**would,** past tense of *will*

**yew,** an evergreen tree
**you,** second personal pronoun

# Some Processes of Composition

## THE WRITING OF THEMES

If you've ever taken particular pains to write a good letter to someone you wanted to impress, and then read it and felt that exhilarated feeling that comes from having done something well, you have some idea how enjoyable writing can be.

No matter what kind of theme you're asked to write, you can experience that same exhilaration — if you know what you're going to write about, and how to go about writing it. The steps you take in these writing assignments, whether the theme be argumentative, descriptive, expository or narrative, are relatively the same. Follow them and you'll be trodding the paths of many authors.

**General Planning**

Select a subject that interests you, one you know something about. A bored and ignorant writer seldom pens stimulating lines. Once having selected a subject, write about it frankly and sincerely. There is only one of you on this earth and to exploit this you should comment freely and truthfully. French novelist Gustave Flaubert once said on the subject: "Fear of bad taste engulfs us like a fog (a foul December fog that suddenly appears, freezes your guts, stinks, and stings your eyes), and not daring to advance, we stand still."

Your reason for writing is "to advance."

To make certain you'll have something to write about, as you go about your day keep a list of those things that make an impression upon you.

Perhaps it will be an overheard conversation. That girl who smiles across a coffee cup at her male escort — for the benefit of the boy at the next table. Or that facial expression of that boy swinging a sledge-hammer at a '53 Dodge on a college campus for a fraternity benefit.

Chances are these lively sparks have fallen upon unorganized feelings and memories. Keep those sparks smouldering in a notebook someplace, or in the back of your mind. Breathe on them from time to time by thinking about them. Develop related ideas and thoughts and expand these by more incidents, illustrations and examples and possible conclusions. A topic selected at the last minute, with little thought, is not apt to catch fire in an essay.

E. R. Hutchison, B.S., B.J., A.M., Ph.D., *Associate Professor,* English Department, Peabody College, Nashville, Tennessee.

**Titles**

Once you've decided on a topic, start turning possible titles over in your mind. A good title can provide you with the impetus needed to sit down and actually write the essay. It can inspire. Open the well-springs of creativity. Good titles promote good writing and, what's more, they're fun to create.

The primary function of the title is to attract the reader. Who could resist reading what comes after these titles: "The House of the Dead," "Rocks in the Road," "Streams that Nobody Fords," or "The Dream of the Red Chamber"? A title also summarizes or suggests exactly the subject of the theme. And it serves as a focus and guide while writing, as well as set the tone of the theme.

**The Essay Interest Line**

Before writing the theme you should outline what you're going to write. And that outline should reflect this *Essay Interest Line:*

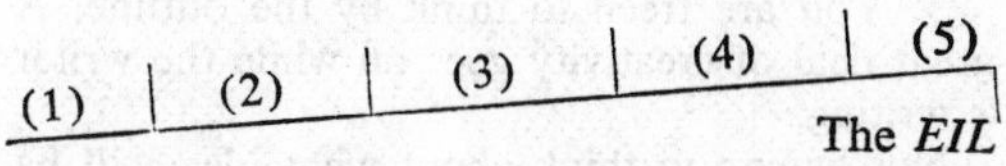


Arrange the things you're going to say with this graphic representation in mind. Reader interest begins with (1) the Title. It is kept and intensified with (2) A Good Beginning. After the opening paragraph there may be a slight drop in reader interest not indicated by that ascending line, while (3) The Developing Paragraph.

Once fully caught up by these paragraphs, however, reader interest mounts through the succeeding (4) Generating Paragraphs — the meat of the theme — to the (5) Climactic Paragraph which is either the final paragraph or that paragraph immediately before the final paragraph. If the latter is the case, the last paragraph is indicated by the slight dip in the *EIL*.

**In the Beginning — The Outline**

When it finally comes time for you to write, indulge yourself. Do whatever it takes to increase that desire to write. Find a clean, well-lighted place, or a quiet, secluded nook. And then, outline what you're going to write.

Many students do not so much learn *how* to write in high school or college as they do to organize materials and thoughts for presentation. Outlining aids this organizational process in the following ways —

*Before writing:*

1. Forces you to think about your subject matter, and then to know and organize that knowledge.

2. Forces you into a more exhaustive survey of the materials available. If there are not enough, the outline will expose that fault. And you will not find yourself stranded in the middle of an essay and perhaps "pad" or hand in an undeveloped essay.

3. You gain a sense of proportion of the various theme ideas present through outlining. Is one idea more important than another? Then that should be reflected by its position in the essay and the amount of space devoted to it.

4. Outlining gives you a sense of relationship of one idea to another so that coherence is aided at this early moment of writing. Many times good paragraph transitions come to mind while outlining.

*While writing, outlining:*

1. Gives you confidence. After outlining your theme, you know what you're going to say, and how you're going to go about saying it.

2. The outline forces you to focus on the task at hand and, concomitantly, provides a highway for the mind to follow.

3. You are freed to think by the outline. A great deal of creativity goes on while the writer is writing.

Not having to think about what idea will be taken up next — it's on the outline — the writer is free to develop new and related ideas, incidents or illustrations to amplify the idea at hand.

4. An outline frees you to write. There is enough to do in "putting proper words in proper places" without having to worry about how to further develop paragraphs and ideas.

What is the best word? The best figure of speech? The best image? The best phrase? The best sentence?

The writer, however, should *master* the outline — not follow it slavishly.

Outlining is so important to beginning writers that teachers would do well to refuse themes unless they are accompanied by outlines. (For a sample outline see the section on Research Paper Writing.)

**The Opening Paragraph**

The critical point in a theme is the opening paragraph. Attracted by the title, the reader may be repelled by an uninteresting, colorless beginning. A good theme opening would entice the reader into the body of the essay by identifying the topic to be discussed and giving a brief preview of the plan of discussion. The scope and tone of the theme should also be indicated.

**The Body**

If a theme is properly outlined the body of the theme writes itself — almost. Write, without stopping, until the theme is completed. The words, phrases, clauses, sentences, paragraphs should be as poetic as the subject matter and audience can bear.

**The Concluding Paragraphs**

A poor concluding paragraph can ruin a good theme in much the same way an improperly delivered punch line can ruin a good joke. Nothing is worse than anti-climaxes — revelations that you have nothing more to say.

Some ways of avoiding that let-down reader feeling are:

(1) Summarize, in different words, the theme idea. (2) Leave the reader with a provocative statement. (3) If problems have been aired, suggest ways of solving them. (4) Try to rouse the reader to action.

**Revision**

If you never discover how to revise, you (and the world) will never discover how good a writer you may be. For there's no such thing as good writing, it's all good revision.

In your revision your writing should be as poetic as possible. Since poetry is the highest form of writing, it's only natural to strive for it in all writing. Poetic writing, however, does not mean ornate writing. In revising you should strive for clear, concise prose which may be more plain and yet more attractive than what you've written before.

A writer always writes something two times. First, for himself, and secondly, for his reader. (Writing starts in the subjective and ends in the objective.

This "second writing" is called revision, and is the hardest of all writing steps, simply because it is the most important. Irwin Shaw, one of our great short story writers, revised his first story twenty-three (23!) times before he sold it. If this many revisions are necessary for a professional writer, think of how many revisions you, the amateur writer, should go through.

In the *first* writing of the theme you trip and sprawl all over the paper and contaminate it. Contaminate it in the sense that it would take another person *just like you* to read the theme to get what you wrote into it. Since you are unique, you must rewrite the theme so that someone else besides you can understand what you're trying to say. In this way, by making your writing less personal, you communicate more.

But to do this, you must be able to view your

work with a cold objective eye, the eye of your reader. Like a sculptor, you must be able to step back and survey your work, so that you can chip away at that unwieldy sentence, and shape that paragraph to still finer form. So that you can add lines of beauty to your creation.

Once you're able to develop this self-discipline, then, and only then, will you write well. What you will have done is toughen the mind and the eye, and that enables you to whisk away that obscuring subjective cloud so you can see *not* what you *hoped* you had written, but what in actuality you have *indeed* written.

The best way to help develop that critical eye is to allow a lapse of time between the first writing and the first revision. We all tend to think, at the time of writing (and immediately afterwards), that what we've written is good. (If we didn't, we'd probably be so discouraged over our sloppy writing that we'd never finish the theme.) The passing of time erodes that rosy glow.

Once you've allowed the time lapse and have sat down to revise, say something like this about the theme, to yourself: "I know you're no good the way you are — but with this revision I'm going to make you worth reading."

Read the theme through and then ask yourself these questions: Does the title reflect the idea and hook the reader? Is the central idea of the theme stated or implied in an interesting opening paragraph? Is there enough substance to the theme? Is it arranged effectively and logically along the Essay Interest Line? Is the theme unified? Does the concluding paragraph cinch this unity?

After determining if there are adequate transitions between sentences and paragraphs and that the theme is grammatically correct and clear, follow these suggestions: Shun the trite expressions — leave them for Batman. Avoid such passive verbs as "to be" and "to have." Use instead vivid action verbs and words. Abstain from the abstract. Be concrete and vivid. Don't say "dog." Say "a miniature brown and white shepherd." Use specific incidents, illustrations and details to flesh out the theme and make it vivid. Subordinate unimportant ideas and details. Do not shift verb tenses, or point of view in a theme needlessly. Strive for concise writing. Delete such phrases as "as a matter of fact" and pronoun referents such as "that is" and "which is."

Prime sentences and paragraphs for proper emphasis. Here is a graphic representation of a sentence and paragraph:

(2) / (3) / (1)

The least important part of a sentence or paragraph is the middle. Bury those unimportant details and transitions (however, etc.) in the middle. Save beginnings and endings of sentences and paragraphs for more important things. Use periodic sentences. For those things you want to emphasize, use the last part of the sentence and paragraph — build up to them and then spring them like a punch line on the reader.

Above all, seek rhythm, flow and proper stress in your writing. *Wed* the *sense* of what you're writing to the *sound*. And, "Pursue the prize."

# THE RESEARCH PAPER

ONE OF the most enjoyable experiences a student can have in English courses comes with the research paper assignment. But once again, as in theme writing, you must know where you're going and how you're going to get there.

With the research paper comes the opportunity to learn about that subject which has piqued your interest. Whatever that might be — the nuclear submarine Thresher tragedy, a flying saucer sighting, crime and comic books, or the apprenticeship of Nathaniel Hawthorne — here is your chance to sleuth at your independent leisure.

Your chance to do independent research, to analyze and evaluate your facts and write up your findings.

The steps you follow in doing this research assignment are generally the steps followed by scholarly researchers.

**Selecting a Topic**

If you do not choose a topic for a research paper that interests you, you run the risk of forcing yourself into sheer drudgery. In this selection process, make certain you're capable of investigating the topic. Make certain the materials necessary for research are available in the school and public libraries or other community facilities. If the scope of the topic is too large, e.g., "The Influences on Hawthorne's Writings" — limit it: "The Early Influence on Hawthorne's Writing." Since a research paper runs from ten to twenty pages, a limited topic is essential.

**The Tentative Outline**

After selecting a topic, go to a source that will give you a brief account of your topic. If you're investigating someone like Hawthorne, then a biographical dictionary will give you an account of his life and works.

Perhaps you will have time to read a critical study of him. (Research paper topics from rock and roll and submarines, to expressionistic painting and lacrosse are briefly covered in most encyclopedias.) From this account you will be able to construct a tentative outline for your research paper.

Unlike the theme outline or the later, more detailed, research paper outline, the tentative outline serves you in notetaking. With it you will be able to know what material is important for your paper, and take notes accordingly. This outline guides you and gives your paper a focus in these early stages.

Here is an outline for a paper now more enticingly entitled, "That Lonely Hawthorne Chamber":

I. Introduction
II. Puritan Ancestry
III. Early Childhood
IV. School Days
V. College
VI. Conclusion

Simple as it is, it is an invaluable tool for the researcher. As he reads his materials, he selects from them according to this outline.

**The Bibliography**

Once the outline is completed start gathering your bibliography. The library card catalog will reveal what books related to your topic are available in the library. To find articles about your topic, go to the indexes: The *Essay and General Literature Index*, the *Readers' Guide to Periodical Literature*, the *International Index*, the *Art Index*, the *Biography Index*, the *Applied Science and Technology Index*, etc. Your librarian will be more than willing to direct you to still other indexes (or still other more specialized reference books) such as the *PMLA* annual bibliographies.

Bibliography cards should be made out for every book and article which appear to have some interest for you in your investigation. Use a 3 x 5 card (or paper cut to this size) for each book or article investigated. Here is the form to use for a book:

```
Plimpton, George. ed. Writ-
ers at Work. New York: The
Viking Press, 1963.
                       PN
                       453
                       .P3
                        2
```

Notice the call number in the lower right corner.

For an article, use this form:

```
Barbara Hofer "Prude and
  the Lewd." Nation, CLXXXI
  (Nov. 5, 1955), 382-84.

            In periodical Rm.
```

Once again, where the magazine may be found is indicated in the lower right corner. Also noted on the card are the *inclusive* pages of the article. The call numbers can save valuable time if you should want to go back to these sources. All other entries on your cards are used in footnoting and/or in the final research paper bibliography. Individual cards for each bibliography item are necessary because they can then be shuffled into alphabetical order saving valuable minutes when footnoting and bibliography time comes. Some twenty bibliographical entries, equally divided between books and articles, are adequate for a research paper. Teachers generally look with jaundiced eye on any bibliography with less than twenty entries.

Go to the books and articles that look most promising first and read thoroughly two or three books and from four to six articles. To speed up reading, insert slips of paper between pages where you intend to take notes. Once the book is read, then go back and take the necessary notes. With this solid base of information from your initial readings in your mind, you can afford to skim as many other books and articles as you have time for. (As many as thirty or forty.

Scan tables of contents, chapter headings and indexes for clues on where your topic information may be found.

For notetaking use 4 x 6 cards or comparably sized pieces of paper. For *each* bit of information or idea use a separate notecard. Do *not* ignore this advice. Once again you'll save invaluable time when writing. You'll be able to shuffle the information into place according to your detailed outline and then write, without interruption or frustration. If you don't use separate note cards, you'll be flipping pages back and forth, back and forth, trying to find that note you put on some page with all those other notes. USE SEPARATE NOTE CARDS FOR DISPARATE IDEAS AND INFORMATION. All scholars use this time-saving technique.

Here is a typical notecard:

```
(puritan ancestry)
   Hawthorne's first Ameri-
can ancestor, William, per-
secuted Quakers. Another,
John,  presided  over  the
Salem witchcraft trials.
                Pattee, p. 61
```

All of these items should be on every notecard: In the upper left corner, your notecard is keyed to your tentative outline. The information on the card is about Hawthorne's puritan ancestors. Whenever possible, paraphrase (put into your own words) the information you've discovered. This paraphrasing once again will save you time, not only in notetaking, but later on when you start writing. When you do use the author's words, be sure to place quotation marks around them to indicate that it is a direct quote. In the right lower corner simply put the author's last name and the page number where you got your information. There is no need to put more than this here, because all the information you'll later need for footnoting is on your bibliography card.

Reread your note and compare it with the source you took it from. Is it fact or opinion? Is it copied correctly? Is it paraphrased accurately? Note the context in which it appears — is it an idea the author's propounding or refuting?

**The Detailed Outlines**

Once you've read a couple of books and articles about your research topic you'll probably find the tentative outline inadequate for your notetaking. Other major categories in your topic emerge from your reading. At this time, revise the tentative outline, making it as detailed and complete as possible. As you do your research, and find it necessary, add still other categories and sub-categories to facilitate your notetaking. This emendation of the outline, by the way, is why you *never* use outline numerals, such as "III. A." to key your notecards. The outline changes (and consequently the numerals, if you're using them) as you investigate. Key words such as "early childhood" rarely need changing even though they may float from place to place in the revised outline. So use outline words on your notecards.

It's difficult enough just writing a good paper without having to play the "musical numbers game" while you're at it.

Once you're through investigating, go quickly over your notes and construct the *final* detailed outline. It may look something like this:

"That Lonely Hawthorne Chamber"

I. Introduction
II. Early Childhood
  A. The early years
  B. Death of father
    1. Effect on Hawthorne
    2. Consequent self-imposed isolation of Hawthorne's mother.
    3. Life with relatives
III. New England School Days.
  A. Education
  B. Foot injury and subsequent two-year isolation.
  C. Life in Maine
IV. Bowdoin College Days
  A. Education
  B. Companions
  C. Decision on writing career.
V. The Lonely Chamber—Gestation period
  A. Twelve years of isolation
    1. Critics: pro and con
    2. An apprenticeship
  B. The Puritan Ancestry ferments in Hawthorne's mind here?
  C. The emergence from the chrysalis
VI. Themes in Hawthorne's works indicative of early influences.
  A. Isolation of mankind
  B. Evils of Puritanism
VII. Conclusion

Your final outline should be even more detailed than this. *See* the benefits to be derived from the outline in the preceding section treating "Theme Writing."

**The First Draft**

Once you've written your final outline, arrange your notecards in the order in which the information will be used according to that final outline: All cards relating to the "Introduction" in one group; those relating to Hawthorne's "Early Childhood" in another group; and so on. Then, within each group, arrange the notecards as you believe the material will appear in your actual writing, from the first sentence to the last. If you've done your research thoroughly, you should have notes on all sections of your outline. Otherwise, now is the time to do more investigation. You should have to discard as many as one-third of your notecards. Some may be repetitious. Some information or ideas may not "fit" into the outline or the research paper. Once you've done all this, and arranged your bibliography alphabetically, you're ready to write.

Arrange the Introduction notecards so that you can read them all at once. Make your introduction interesting — put your reader in a good frame of mind. State the purpose of your paper and suggest the outline of it in lively prose. Here is one merely adequate introduction.

"Much has been written about that 'lonely chamber' of Hawthorne's and how it affected his writing. This paper will treat the early influences working on Hawthorne and how that lonely chamber may have merely served as a place for gestation of those influences."

Now you simply write what you've found out in your research, gracefully weaving the material together with transitions, remembering always to copy accurately the information you've gathered and to properly document it. Conclude by summarizing the strong points of the case you've been building (in this particular instance) and restating, in different words, what you've suggested in your introduction.

*Don't* footnote this first draft. At the end of the material you intend to footnote simply put that information that is in the lower right corner of the notecard. And place parentheses around it. Like this: (Pattee, p. 201) Or this: (Bleicher, p. 97) This procedure is important because if you find in revising that you want to change paragraphs around, you won't have to bother changing footnote numbers throughout your entire paper.

Once you've finished the first draft, follow the revision suggestions given in the theme writing section of this encyclopedia.

When you're sure your paper is saying what you want it to say, you can write your final draft, putting your footnote citations in at this time.

**Footnoting**

Every direct quotation or original idea that is not your own, you must footnote (or document), including paraphrasing of original ideas. (General information or knowledge, such as schooling and places of employment, need not be documented.) At the last word of such material in the text place a footnote number. Like this.[1] Or this.[2] Then at the bottom of the page leave a double space and draw a twelve-space line. Then put your footnote citations. Like this:

---

[1] Fred Lewis Pattee, The Development of the American Short Story (New York: Harper & Brothers Publishers, 1923), p. 201.

[2] William Morse, "Hawthorne and the Crucible," Harper's Magazine, XXIII (August, 1954), 62. [no abbreviation for "page."]

Notice the elevated footnotes and the single spaced footnotes with double spaces between. The information for these footnotes, of course, comes from your bibliography cards.

If you cite Pattee and his book again in your paper, it is not necessary to use the full footnote citation. Simply do this:

---

[3] Pattee, p. 324.

And if you cite the same work twice in succession all you do is this:

---

[4] Bleicher, p. 445.
[5] Ibid., p. 325.

You've indicated to your reader that you quoted from the same place by using *ibid.* (from the Latin *ibidem,* "in the same place").

Modern scholarship requires only this in footnoting.

**The Bibliography**

Finished with the final draft, you still have one step left — the bibliography. Make certain all your bibliography cards are in alphabetical order and then simply list them. Like this:

BIBLIOGRAPHY

Bleicher, Susan. We Are People. Philadelphia: Artesian Press, 1967. [No page numbers needed.]

Morse, William. "Hawthorne and the Crucible." Harper's Magazine, XXIII (August, 1954), 59-69. [Notice no abbreviation for "page."]

Pattee, Fred Lewis. The Development of the American Short Story. New York: Harper & Brothers Publishers, 1923.

For a more complete description of footnoting and the writing of bibliographies as well as other information concerning documentation, go to the *MLA Style Sheet* printed by the Modern Language Association of America.

Precede your paper with a title page:

THAT LONELY HAWTHORNE CHAMBER

by

David Gillis Clark

On another page write your detailed outline. These two items, along with your paper and bibliography, complete the research paper.

Go over it carefully for last minute errors, and hand it in.

# PREPARING AND MAKING SPEECHES

In some ways, the process of preparing to make a speech is like that of planning and writing a theme. It involves selecting an appropriate subject, narrowing the subject down to a topic that can be well handled in the time limit allowed, organizing a plan of development, and filling out that plan in the most suitable ways that can be devised.

**Demands of the Speech Situation**

In important ways, however, speaking to an audience is different from writing for a reader. A speech is not just a theme that is read aloud. A skilful speaker doesn't memorize something he has written and merely "spout" it, either — though he may make use of some preplanned phrases or sentences. He may write out much of what he thinks it would be appropriate to say, but he does that mainly as an exercise in organizing his ideas; he realizes that in the speech situation he may express himself somewhat differently.

The speech situation is always a particular occasion, with attendant circumstances of time and place, when a speaker is expected to communicate with a special audience whose interest must be quickly engaged and continuously held. The listening audience, unlike a reader, is not able to go back over something it has misunderstood or to pick up details it has lost through inattention. The audience, of course, normally uses its eyes as well as its ears, but what it sees is not handwriting or print on a page; it sees the speaker as it hears him talk. Preparation to make a speech ought to take account of all these facts — and more.

**Advantages of the Speech Situation**

Some of the additional facts that ought to be kept in mind are those that point up the advantages a speaker has over a writer. For one thing, a speaker is engaging in an activity he has been already prepared for by long experience in conversation. To speak before a group, of course, requires a little more formality and a good deal more planning, but it is very much like talking to people without being interrupted by them. As in conversation, the speaker can reinforce his meanings by his tone of voice and gestures. And though the audience does not usually enter into the conversation vocally, it does respond in various ways (by attention, by looking puzzled, by smiles, or by looking out the window, for example). The wise speaker is prepared to make use of such cues in adapting what he is saying.

A speaker also has the great advantage of being able to use visual aids (not only pictures and maps but three dimensional objects as well). He can, when appropriate, give certain kinds of demonstrations. These are only some examples of numerous ways the speaker can capitalize on the physical presence of the people with whom he is communicating.

**General Purposes of Speeches**

It is customary to say that there are three legitimate purposes of public speeches: to inform, to persuade, or to entertain. Such an analysis is not meant to suggest that persuasive speeches may not also be informative, or that an audience may not be entertained while it is being informed. An effective speaker, however, knows which of these purposes is dominant in his planning of what he will say. Whatever he does or says should contribute ultimately to achievement of the dominant purpose.

A further analysis of what we call *persuasion* is needed, for it means at least three different things. A speaker whose purpose is to persuade may intend to convince his audience, leading them to a belief they had not held or had not been certain of. But, on the other hand, his intention may be to confirm them in a belief they already hold, perhaps to inspire them to cherish more dearly certain values or ideas he and they are agreed upon. Often, of course, some people in the audience may be persuaded to accept for the first time a speaker's view while others, who already share it with him, are stimulated to value it more highly.

A third possibility is that the speaker whose purpose is to persuade may intend to move his audience to take some sort of action — to vote in a certain way, for example, or to contribute to some cause. Naturally, convincing the listeners and inspiring them will contribute to the achievement of this purpose.

**Choosing a Subject and Narrowing It Down**

If a speaker has the opportunity to choose his own subject, it stands to reason that he ought to select one he is genuinely interested in. He is likely to do best if he already has a stock of information and experience relating to the subject he expects to talk about, though learning more about it will usually be a part of the preparation of the speech.

A suitable subject is one that is also appropriate to the particular audience and fitting to the occasion on which the speech is to be given. The interests, experience, and expectations of the audience need to be considered. These fac-

William J. Griffin, Ph.D., University of Iowa, *Professor of English,* George Peabody College for Teachers.

tors are most crucially important, however, when a general subject is being narrowed down to a specific, limited topic the speech will be concerned with. Within the range of most big subjects, some aspect fitting for treatment in the speech situation can usually be found.

The narrowing down of a general subject, of course, is necessary. A speaker has to operate within time limits; just as importantly, he has to deal with the natural limitations of audience attention and interest. Experience consistently shows that successful speakers are those who concentrate their efforts, not those who spread themselves thin.

Ordinarily, it will not be possible to make a wise decision about narrowing down a general subject until a serious exploration of the possibilities it offers has been made. The exploration may involve setting down notes about what you already know of the subject, investigating some of the published material relating to it, and talking informally to other people who know something about it. Suppose, for example, that you have chosen "Highway Safety" as an appropriate general subject for an eight-minute talk before a high school English class. Very likely, you will have accumulated some broad ideas on the subject — but so have most other people. The appropriate subject will be turned into a promising topic only when you discover that it can be broken down into parts that can be given such titles as "Traffic Hazards in the Horse-and-Buggy Days," "Danger Spots on Local Streets and Highways," "Planning Highways for Safety," "Defensive Driving," "Ralph Nader's Contributions to Highway Safety," "Pedestrian Responsibilities," etc.

The process of narrowing down requires an explicit decision about the dominant purpose of the speech, whether it is mainly to inform, to entertain, or to persuade. When the specific topic and purpose have been chosen, material to develop the speech can be efficiently collected and organized. The speaker will have a sound basis for selecting ideas and information that will be useful, and for ordering the content of his speech to achieve the desired effect.

## The Content of Speeches

To collect material for the speech, we can go to one or more of the same sources already named in suggestions made about the preliminary exploration of a subject: our own experience and observations, public sources (which may include films and recordings as well as printed matter), or individuals who may have useful information or ideas. Our own first-hand knowledge is often particularly important. Sometimes, we can extend it purposefully in the course of preparing the speech. A person planning to speak on "Local Traffic Hazards" would do well to inspect a number of them himself.

In looking for material in printed sources, a person can save himself a great deal of time if he properly uses the library reference aids available — card files, *Reader's Guide to Periodical Literature, Education Index,* encyclopedias and yearbooks. Encyclopedias, of course, generally summarize subjects very briefly; they are likely to be most useful in directing readers to fuller discussions elsewhere.

A responsible speaker will be careful in taking notes on what he reads or what he is told by someone else. Whatever he uses when he makes his speech ought to be accurately reported. Honesty as well as the interest of the audience also requires that he identify the sources of information or ideas he has acquired from other people. The honest speaker will also refuse to make use of statements that he knows or suspects to be false or misleading, even though they have appeared in print.

The material for a speech, of course, may include not only facts and interpretations of them but also examples and dramatic illustrations, contrasts and comparisons, and perhaps appropriate anecdotes. As the speaker collects his material he may also find that some of it can best be presented in visual displays.

## The Basic Four-part Structure of Speeches

Speeches appropriate to different purposes and occasions may take many different forms. For over two thousand years, however, men have observed that the most commonly effective form is one that has four parts. The parts have been given various sets of names, but here they will be called *introduction, focusing, development,* and *conclusion.*

### THE INTRODUCTION

The introduction of a speech has three main purposes: to capture the attention of the audience, to establish a feeling of good will between the audience and the speaker, and to lead into the subject that is to be discussed. To achieve these purposes, the speaker may make reference to common interests that he and the audience share; he may tell a dramatic story illustrating the topic he will discuss or his point of view relating to it; he may tell an appropriate humorous anecdote that relates to the subject or the situation in which it is being discussed; he may begin with a startling statement or with a pertinent literary quotation; he may suggest reasons why he is qualified to deal with the topic; or he may ask a question that leads the audience to think along lines he wishes them to follow. Naturally, the speaker may use a combination of these devices, or he may invent others. But the introduction should not be too long drawn out. On some occasions, when attention and good will are assured, it may be reduced to a single sentence — or it may be omitted altogether.

#### THE FOCUSING

The second part of the speech focuses the attention of the audience on what the speaker intends to do in the rest of his time. It may consist of a concise statement of the speaker's purpose; it may outline the procedure he plans to follow; it may raise a series of questions he expects to explore. Sometimes the focusing is achieved by a generalization that everything he intends to say will support; such a generalization is called a *thesis*.

The kind of focusing a speaker chooses to employ will depend largely on the purpose of the speech. Statement of a thesis is particularly appropriate to informative or inspirational speeches; it is often not wise in a persuasive speech to announce beforehand the conviction a speaker wishes to induce. In a speech intended mainly to entertain, the focusing may identify the thread (however slight) that will hold the speech together, it may assure the audience that it should not look for seriousness, or it may display the grain of seriousness that is mixed with the chaff of humor.

#### THE DEVELOPMENT

The greatest amount of time, of course, will be given to the development of the speech, which is often called its *body*. Here, careful outlining is important. The parts of the discussion, identified by analysis, ought to be clearly differentiated. What those parts are and how they are organized will depend on the topic and the purpose of the speech. They may consist of description of a situation and then an explanation of causes and proposals for reform; they may account for different views of a problem; they may be a chronological arrangement of explanations that describe stages in a process; they may be a topical organization of different aspects of a situation; in a humorous speech, the parts are sometimes loosely related to each other by various types of association. It is often wise to arrange the parts of the body in climactic order, building up to a final point that is the most impressive.

A speaker is well advised to limit the main headings to a number he can develop well in the time allowed him, realizing that the normal rate of speech is about 130 words a minute.

Subtopics can be developed in many ways, including use of examples, extended illustrations, comparisons and contrasts, quotations and citations of testimony of authorities, statistics, and logical reasoning. Selection of developmental material should be controlled by concern with the general effect the speech is intended to achieve. Each subtopic should be rounded out clearly, and transitions from one to another should be provided. Transitions, however, need not always be carried by expressions such as "in the second place," "next," or "then too." There are many ways of passing gracefully but clearly from one point to another. Speakers sometimes indicate a transition by an appropriate movement of the body.

#### THE CONCLUSION

The conclusion may be relatively brief, but it is very important. The effectiveness of a speaker is reduced by a weak conclusion; a good conclusion can leave a lasting impression.

The conclusion may restate the thesis (perhaps in different words); it may also review the steps by which the thesis was supported. Or it may consist of a little story that points up what the whole speech was about. Or it may make an application to the special interests of the audience. In some persuasive speeches, the conclusion is a rousing appeal to action. In any event, it should round out the speech in a lively way.

### Delivering the Speech

When a speech is carefully prepared, it is easy to put on cards or a sheet of paper an outline and brief notes to jog your memory and keep you on the planned track as you talk to the audience. Practice speaking from your notes, imagining the audience before you; the practice may show where changes ought to be made, and it may indicate where your notes should be filled out further. The notes, of course, should include any direct quotations or other matter that should be exactly reported.

Facing an actual audience naturally produces some nervous tension. Every normal person feels that, but the tension *can* have the good effect of enlivening the speaker and making him more sensitive to the demands of the speech situation. Control of one's nervous energy is best achieved by taking one's place confidently before the audience and establishing immediate contact with it. Look directly at individuals in the audience, shifting the eye-contact naturally from one part of the room to another. Remember that you are engaged in a kind of conversation in which you have the advantage of not being interrupted. As in a conversation, you will want to speak distinctly enough to be easily heard.

As in a conversation, too, you should feel free to associate facial expression and bodily movement with what you are saying. From ordinary experience, you know, too, that the tempo of speaking varies with what is being said, and that pauses can give emphasis to important points. As you acquire ease and confidence before an audience, you will be able to interpret the audience responses and adjust your speaking to them.

Preparing and making speeches becomes progressively easier with repeated experience.

# Literature

## INTRODUCTION

### I

**A Student's Guide to Literary Appreciation**
**Great Authors and Their Major Works**
(*See page 938*)

This section is not intended to furnish the student with a summary of plots but to serve as a key to the *understanding* and *appreciation* of great literature, and hopefully to whet the student's appetite for reading. Thus the brief introductions to writers from Homer to Hemingway present the style, themes, and other distinguishing characteristics of each author, with one work usually singled out for special study. Enough is said of these writings to give the student a general idea of what to expect without having the story spelled out and ruined for him. Equally as dangerous, however, is the idea that the story alone suffices for the entire composition, and in some cases a bare outline is supplied to aid in a fuller appreciation of other elements of the work. The method for treating poets is perforce a little different from the novelists, but in most cases a single selection is given special attention. All major writings mentioned in this section appear in the "Outline of Western World Literature"; and since the "Outline" supplies the dates, this section follows an alphabetical arrangement by writer for easy reference.

For those students who find the vocabulary a little advanced, the *Webster's New World Dictionary,* of which this handbook is a part, will be especially valuable and educational.

To choose from among all the great books of the Western world a few for special analysis is not to claim that these are *the* most important, but rather that they all are among the world's significant works. The authors included

Introduction and Parts I and II written by EDWIN S. GLEAVES, Ph.D., *Director,* Library School, George Peabody College for Teachers.

Part III written by WALTER K. THIGPEN, M.A., Ed.S., George Peabody College for Teachers.

are representative of those whom students are likely to encounter in their high school and college careers.

## II

### An Outline of Western World Literature

(*See page 950*)

This outline is divided into three main parts. *Part A* is a parallel outline of the literatures of Greece and Rome, including works of philosophy, religion, history, and biography which are now considered classics. Dates are given when possible, though often as approximations.

*Part B* is a running outline of the literature of the Middle Ages and the Renaissance. Except for the anonymous sagas and epics, dates are a little more nearly exact than in the ancient period. As in Part A, very brief notations follow the names of the authors.

*Part C* is considerably more detailed than the others, and purports to offer more than a mere literary chronology. In addition to the authors, their outstanding works, and the dates of both, this outline includes (1) brief annotations which characterize each author, (2) nationalities of Continental writers, and (3) divisions by literary periods which, though very generalized, afford the rare opportunity to compare the modern development of the literatures of England and America with other Western literatures. A glance at the comparative dates in the three parallel columns suggests the universality of the great literary movements — so often thought of in purely local or national terms. Even so, the classification by periods, e.g., Neo-Classical, should be thought of less in terms of specific dates than in the lives and works of the writers through whom the principles of the movement are best exemplified. Thus one notes that the "Romantic Period," usually dated in England from 1798 to as late as 1870, is anticipated by the *Sturm und Drang* movement in Germany in the 1770's, is given special impetus in France by Chateaubriand's *Atala* (1801) and *René* (1802), but then does not cross the ocean to America until the late 1820's or 1830's. Even though the early writings on the American continent can hardly be said to be part of the Neo-Classical "movement," most of the publications during that time partake of the characteristics of their English counterparts. Once the seeds are in the wind, literary ideas blow far and wide, and are rarely confined to national boundaries, taking root at different places at different times.

Nevertheless, literary periods and labels should never be thought of as absolutes, for some writers defy categorization. To speak of Dickens as either "romantic" or "realistic" is inadequate, and since the character of his works changed as his career progressed, he is listec in two periods in the outline.

As a matter of convenience, most foreign titles in this outline appear in English translation. A few non-literary works, which nonetheless are usually considered a part of a nation's literary history (e.g., The Declaration of Independence), are included. Some titles are slightly abbreviated or updated in spelling. Writers are represented by published works, not individual poems or stories. Some dates, especially those of composition, are approximations.

## III

### The Plays of William Shakespeare

(*See page 956*)

This section differs markedly from Part I. See the special introduction for brief biographical information on Shakespeare and an explanation of how to use the section.

#### SPECIAL NOTE

This guide to literature should not be thought of as restrictive or final. Let it be a doorway to broader reading and deeper appreciation of great literature — "What oft was thought, but ne'er so well expressed." And remember that no amount of reading about a book will substitute for reading the book itself.

Everyone, student or not, would do well to set for himself a reading plan to assure a balanced and nourishing reading diet. Those interested in furthering their knowledge and in realizing more fully the rewards of reading would profit from the following books, all available in inexpensive paperback editions:

ALM, RICHARD S., ed. *Books for You: A Reading List for Senior High Students.* New York: Washington Square Press, 1964.

Committee on College Reading. *Good Reading.* New York: New American Library (latest edition).

National Council of Teachers of English. Committee on College and Adult Reading List. *The College and Adult Reading List of Books in Literature and the Fine Arts.* New York: Washington Square Press, 1962.

STEFFERUD, ALFRED, ed. *The Wonderful World of Books.* New York: New American Library, 1956.

In addition, the American Library Association compiles various reading lists for college-bound students which can be obtained from a public library or the Young Adult Services Division, American Library Association, Chicago, Illinois 60611.

#### ABBREVIATIONS

| | | | |
|---|---|---|---|
| ca. | —circa, about approximately | Ger. | —German |
| comp. | —date of composition | It. | —Italian |
| C. | —century | pub. | —date of publication |
| d. | —died | Rus. | —Russian |
| Fr. | —French | Sp. | —Spanish |

# I

# A Student's Guide to Literary Appreciation

## GREAT AUTHORS AND THEIR MAJOR WORKS

**Brontë, Charlotte and Emily** (*Jane Eyre* and *Wuthering Heights*). No explanation can account fully for *Jane Eyre* and *Wuthering Heights.* That two spinsters, daughters of a parson at that, who lived on the remote Yorkshire moors, could create two such tempestuous novels remains one of the great mysteries of literature. Their sister, Anne, was also a competent novelist, and writing under the names of Currer, Ellis, and Acton Bell, the three published their most important novels (*Jane Eyre, Wuthering Heights,* and *Agnes Grey*) all in one year, 1847. *Jane Eyre* was well received, *Wuthering Heights* was scorned, and *Agnes Grey* was mildly acclaimed. Emily and Anne, who also wrote poetry, died at the ages of 30 and 29 respectively; Charlotte lived to be almost 39.

Both *Jane Eyre* and *Wuthering Heights* are imbued with passion and imagination more akin to poetry than fiction; both are set in Gothic gloom and in strange old houses (Thornfield Hall and Wuthering Heights); both depict strong male characters (Rochester and Heathcliff) whose behaviors are unaccountable to normal people; and though the two novels are far from identical, they both stand apart from the main tradition of the English novel as monuments to two original geniuses.

Of the two, *Jane Eyre* suffers more from melodrama, but the love between the orphaned Jane Eyre and the mysterious Mr. Rochester, whose great secret is revealed just as he and Jane are about to be married, is not easily forgotten. The intense emotions of these two, however, pale before the Catherine-Heathcliff relationship in *Wuthering Heights* — a passionate, mystical love that lives beyond Catherine's death and eventually drives Heathcliff to his own death. *Wuthering Heights* frames two generations of the Linton-Earnshaw families, whose history revolves around Heathcliff's love for Catherine Earnshaw and his satanic desire for revenge against the Earnshaw family.

The Gothic setting heightens the wild nature of the main characters, who contrast sharply with the more "normal" Lockwood and Ellen Dean, through whom the story is told. Though not perfectly done, the novel begins near the end of the story and picks up its threads as they are discovered by the curious and patient Lockwood.

Charlotte Bronte said of her sister's masterpiece: "It is moorish, and wild, and knotty as the root of heath, . . . hewn in a wild workshop." Consider the artist and marvel.

**Bunyan, John** (*Pilgrim's Progress*). Both the virtues and the shortcomings of oversimplification are found in *The Pilgrim's Progress from This World to That Which Is to Come.* Widely read and translated, this simple allegory is a description of Christian's journey from the City of Destruction to the Celestial City, a journey fraught with hazards which have since become bywords among religious and non-religious people alike: the Slough of Despond, the Valley of Humiliation, Vanity Fair.

Certain allegorical characters (personified abstractions) accompany him: Faithful, Hopeful, Giant Despair, and others. His climactic triumph over death is stirring in its unassuming and majestic beauty.

In our age of subtlety and relativism, *Pilgrim's Progress* is definite and absolute in its views of good and evil, and thus hardly harmonious with modern theology. But as a vision of the clash of the great ideas and ideals of the world, as a testimony to one man's faith in the ultimate triumph of Good over Evil, as proof that simplicity can endure beyond the full acceptance of its ideas, *Pilgrim's Progress* lives on.

**Camus, Albert** (*The Stranger*). Modern writers have, by and large, rejected abstract values (Hemingway, in *A Farewell to Arms,* called them "obscene") but often have held fast to more concrete ones, such as individual human relationships. Camus, winner of the Nobel Prize for Literature in 1957, rejects them all, for life itself, he says, is absurd. This absurdity is reflected in *The Stranger,* one of the most significant novels of the century.

Meursault, its hero (or anti-hero), is sure of little and cares about less. "Mother died today. Or, maybe, yesterday; I can't be sure." Thus begins the story as he tells it, and this attitude reflected through his point of view is the key — and perhaps the theme — of the novel. Meursault's only purpose in life is for life to leave him alone.

Love and marriage, God and religion — all have lost meaning for him. When his girl friend asks if he loves her, he says her question means nothing or next to nothing, although he "doesn't mind getting married." But the world closes in on him until he commits a meaningless murder which he does not care to defend, and he is finally judged, not by the murder itself, but by his apathy, his refusal to embrace any conventional values. From this experience he can only reflect on the "benign indifference of the universe."

Camus' "philosophy" is not rebellion, but rejection; he does not offer another side of the coin of traditional Christianity, but a new currency altogether, absurd in that, by normal standards, it is blank.

**Cervantes Saavedra, Miguel de** (*Don Quixote de la Mancha*). The life of Cervantes, unlike that of Shakespeare, his English contemporary, has never been shrouded in mystery; also unlike Shakespeare, his real fame rests on one great work, *Don Quixote,* sometimes called the "Bible of Humanity." Cervantes' interest in adventure tales and character types, as seen in his *Exemplary Novels,* is given full expression in this first, and perhaps the most penetrating, of modern novels. Ostensibly an attack on the books of chivalry of the time, *Don Quixote* has become the greatest of chivalry books, and in some ways the most profound commentary on the place of idealism in a mundane and unimaginative universe.

Part I describes the would-be exploits of a gentleman-farmer turned knight-errant who takes the name Don Quixote and sallies forth to make the world safe for fair damsels. Though constantly corrected by his lowly side-kick, Sancho Panza, he sees windmills as giants, sheep as advancing armies, cheap inns as castles, and slatternly hags as beautiful young maidens. The object of his affections, whom he calls Dulcinea del Toboso, is in reality a rugged farm girl hardly worthy of any knightly gestures, but Don Quixote is determined to live with his impossible dream. Throughout Part I and the more serious Part II the rollicking humor of Don Quixote's misadventures becomes increasingly pathetic and eventually tragic, with the line between illusion and reality less distinct—even for the reader.

Though often hailed as polar personalities, representing high idealism and stubborn realism, Don Quixote and Sancho interact progressively throughout the novel, so that, in a supreme touch of irony, Sancho finally becomes the idealist, urging on a broken and disillusioned Don Quixote.

Superlatives abound in descriptions of this great book, and none higher than the Spanish philosopher's reference to "Our Lord and Savior Don Quixote." Whatever you call him, read about him in a modern translation.

**Chaucer, Geoffrey** (*The Canterbury Tales*). Chaucer, the first notable English poet, has always ranked among the greatest, and his supreme achievement is *The Canterbury Tales.*

Chaucer's thirty or so story-telling pilgrims are traveling to the shrine of Thomas à Becket in the Canterbury Cathedral. On the journey, they were to tell four stories apiece, two going and two returning, but Chaucer completed only twenty of the tales. The Prologue presents the cast of characters: the Knight, the Miller, the Wife of Bath, the Merchant, the Pardoner, the Prioress, and others — a cross-section of the population of fourteenth-century England. Their stories illustrate several kinds of tales popular at the time, including the beast fable (Nun's Priest's Tale), sermon (Parson), chivalric romance (Knight), literary legend (Clerk), and the fabliau (Miller). Chaucer makes the character rather than the tale engage our attention, and each of the stories illuminates the personalities of both teller and listener.

It is all poetry, written in rhymed couplets. Students deterred by the antiquated language should enjoy the *Tales* in a modern prose or verse rendering. But reading Chaucer in his own Middle English can be a very satisfying experience.

**Dante Alighieri** (*The Divine Comedy*). Dante's *Divine Comedy* is the literary embodiment of the medieval religious mind. Catholic theology, as propounded by Thomas Aquinas, finds its greatest exemplar in Dante's masterpiece.

It is called a "Comedy" (the "Divine" was added by later scholars) only in the sense that it describes a physical journey (and allegorically, a spiritual one) from Hell through Purgatory to Paradise, which ends triumphantly. It is intricately structured, with heavy use of such symbolic numbers as 3, 7, 9, and 10; three main books are composed of 33 cantos each, and one introductory canto makes an even 100. Moreover, the whole poem is written in terza rima (aba, bcb, cdc, and so forth), thus saturating the work with the concept of 3's. The symmetry of this long poem almost surpasses belief.

As is true with many masterpieces, *The Divine Comedy* can be read on several levels (Dante himself spoke of four levels of meaning), but it *is* readable, even exciting, despite its many contemporary allusions, esoteric theology, and complex symbolism. T. S. Eliot advises the novice to charge ahead and disregard such complications, but thorough notes can deepen one's appreciation of this great religious Odyssey. One soon becomes aware that Dante's journey through Hell and Purgatory, guided by Vergil, and through Paradise, guided by the beautiful Beatrice, corresponds to a journey of the Soul of Everyman; the moral implications, through allegory and analogy, of this other-worldly saga make *The Divine Comedy* relevant to all ages.

**Charles Dickens** (*Great Expectations*). The sheer inventiveness of Dickens is unparalleled in English literature. "The Dickens World," as his creation has been called, is populated by an unforgettable gallery of characters: Sam Weller (*Pickwick Papers*), Little Nell (*Old Curiosity Shop*), Pecksniff (*Martin Chuzzlewit*), Ebenezer Scrooge and Tiny Tim (*A Christmas Carol*), the Murdstones and the Micawbers (*David Copperfield*), Thomas Gradgrind and Josiah Bounderby (*Hard Times*). By his choice of names alone, Dickens' method is essentially comic, often indulging in caricature and melodrama at the expense of depth of character and credibility of plot. But as some of the social problems of Victorian England, which he treated as early as *Oliver Twist,* weighed more heavily upon him, his books developed an increasing seriousness with a corresponding complexity of characterization, so that by his writing of *Hard Times* and his last complete novel, *Our Mutual Friend,* the light-hearted Dickens of *Pickwick Papers* seems far away indeed.

Of his many novels, *Great Expectations* is perhaps the most satisfying blend of the early and the later Dickens. Without losing completely his gift for caricature, he still creates three-dimensional characters; and without sacrificing a plot of high suspense, his story is credible and the novel artistically structured.

The great expectations of Philip Pirrip (Pip) are that he will inherit money, but its actual source comes as a surprise to Pip and the reader alike. In the process, Pip learns the meaning of gratitude through his harsh treatment of the devoted but unpolished Joe Gargery, and only the true origin of the money brings him to his senses.

The story of Pip's education is peopled with the usual variety of Dickensian characters: the mysterious Miss Havisham; the fawning Pumblechook; the crude and stupid Bently Drummle; the faithful Herbert Pocket, the clever and enterprising Jaggers; and his clerk, Wemmick, perhaps the first suburban dweller in English literature.

**Dostoevsky, Fyodor** (*Crime and Punishment*). The agony that Dostoevsky experienced as he faced a firing squad on December 22, 1849 (a reprieve from the Czar arriving at the last minute), pervades all of his novels. His own bitter experiences in childhood and in his first marriage helped mold the artist who pioneered in the writing of "psychological" novels.

If one views Tolstoy as a physician who examines man as a fairly normal physical being, he would have to see Dostoevsky as a kind of spiritual psychiatrist who delves relentlessly into the human mind. But whereas Dostoevsky's own epilepsy is reflected in the Christ-like Prince Mishkin of *The Idiot,* one should not draw a similar parallel between the author and Raskolnikov of *Crime and Punishment.* The crime of the novel is Raskolnikov's murder of an old hag in his attempt to prove to himself that he is above the laws that bind ordinary people; but in the self-imposed mental torture that he undergoes after the murder he finds that (1) he is not a "superior" person, and (2) the murder was wrong in any case.

In this novel, however, nothing is "wrong" or "right" by our usual standards, as is evidenced by the angelic prostitute Sonia, who is primarily responsible for Raskolnikov's moral redemption.

Read simply as a detective story, *Crime and Punishment* is a gripping tale of a crime committed and detected; read as a record of one man's "dark night of the soul," it is an unnerving glimpse into the nether regions of the psyche. From this novel, the ambitious reader may proceed to *The Brothers Karamazov.*

**Eliot, George** (*Middlemarch*). To the student whose only exposure to George Eliot (Mary Ann Evans) has been an early reading of *Silas Marner,* her great power as a writer of realistic fiction comes as a surprise. Though an intellectual and scholar herself, she never lost her sympathetic respect for the humble rural people that she knew so well, and her earlier novels, such as *Adam Bede* and *The Mill on the Floss,* have rustic settings that portray the people of rural England. Since George Eliot takes seriously her role as a novelist, however, she is rarely content to present experience as it is without commenting on it, invariably toward some moral purpose. But her preaching becomes less noticeable, and her ability to construct a complex plot more artistic, in her long masterpiece, *Middlemarch.*

This sweeping novel is nothing less than the story of a whole community ("A Study of Provincial Life," she calls it), of high aspirations and ruined hopes, of genuine integrity and rationalized hypocrisy. Three or four plots intertwine throughout the novel and eventually dovetail at the end. Both the heroine, Dorothea Brooke, and the hero, Dr. Lydgate, become unhappy in their marriages (not to each other), and Eliot stubbornly refuses to tag on a romantic, unrealistic solution to these or any other problems in the novel. Even the hypocrisy of Bulstrode lacks the caricature of Moliere's Tartuffe, and the pedant Casaubon evokes a certain pity as he claims to work on his "Key to All Mythologies." To the complex and interrelated problems of human lives, George Eliot says there are no simple solutions, and by the time she has analyzed all the motivations of her three-dimensional characters, the reader is usually convinced.

For some reason, *Middlemarch* was slow in attaining its present recognition as George Eliot's masterpiece. A careful reading of this great novel makes the delay even more puzzling.

**Eliot, T. S.** (*The Waste Land*). Eliot brought a new language to poetry — a foreign language, it seems, upon first reading. A closer look reveals that the difficulty is not so much the language itself as (1) the unusual figures of speech and (2) the many obscure allusions.

An excellent introduction to Eliot is "The Love Song of J. Alfred Prufrock," the ironically titled portrait of a modern man incapable of living fully and meaningfully: he does not know how to love a woman, and he continually debates with himself over whether or not to eat a peach, to climb a stair, or to part his hair behind. "I have measured out my life in coffee spoons," he says. (Other images are just as startling: "the evening spread out against the sky / Like a patient etherized upon a table"; streets that "follow like a tedious argument / Of insidious intent"; the "yellow fog that rubs its back upon the windowpanes.")

Prufrock decides that he should have been "a pair of ragged claws / Scuttling across the floors of silent seas" — anything to avoid the responsibilities and tensions of life.

The aridity of the modern age, the pictures of the dirty London fog, the emptiness and triviality of daily life — all recur in *The Waste Land*. Symbols of fertility (rain, the Fisher King, "The Burial of the Dead") and sterility (the dry bones, the "rats' alley," abortion, the rocks in the desert) pervade the poem, reinforcing the idea of the modern "waste land." Many of the symbols derive from ancient fertility cults (as seen in Bulfinch's *Mythology* and Frazer's *The Golden Bough*) and become meaningful through Eliot's own notes accompanying the poem, though additional footnotes are often necessary to fuller understanding.

*The Waste Land* is a veritable repository of classical quotations, many of them obscure, usually so placed in the poem as to furnish ironic contrast between the nobility of the past and the degeneracy of the present. Thus when the bored and listless secretary yields to the advances of the carbuncular clerk, Eliot invokes Goldsmith's "When lovely woman stoops to folly." The sudden shifts, the patchwork of quotations, and the rush of changing images, though bewildering at first, begin to present a meaningful mosaic of modern times.

All of Eliot's poetry gains by being read aloud, and no one does it better than the poet himself (several recordings are available).

In addition to poetry, Eliot has written some excellent plays (including *Murder in the Cathedral*) and some of the most perceptive and influential literary criticism of the century. He received the Nobel Prize for Literature in 1948.

**Emerson, Ralph Waldo.** Emerson's reputation is almost extra-literary. He never wrote a short story, novel, or play; his poetic output was relatively small; and many of his essays are on nonliterary subjects. Still, his influence on American letters was enormous, and even if today his optimism is out of fashion, he cannot be ignored.

Though more a philosopher than a poet, Emerson is remembered for his direct, pithy, epigrammatic prose style, and his rather rough "un-poetic" meter in poetry. His prose, which usually took the form of addresses and essays, is especially memorable, as the highly quotable "Self-Reliance": "Trust thyself: every heart vibrates to that iron string." "Nothing is sacred but the integrity of your own mind." "A foolish consistency is the hobgoblin of little minds." "To be great is to be misunderstood." "An institution is the lengthened shadow of one man."

Emerson's subjects are diverse. In *Nature* (1836) he lays a philosophical foundation for the Romantic idea of nature as teacher. In "The American Scholar" he proclaims what is sometimes called America's Intellectual Declaration of Independence, urging American writers to disregard foreign patterns and ideas and to trust themselves implicitly. In "The Divinity School Address," he urges the students of Harvard to trust their intuition rather than written revelation; the formal church, he says, is an outworn institution, and divinity is no more than the best of which man is capable: "Yourself a newborn bard of the Holy Ghost, cast behind you all conformity, and acquaint men at first hand with Deity." Other famous essays include "Friendship," "Compensation," and "The Over-Soul," the latter expressing most clearly Emerson's concept of Transcendentalism.

Emerson's poems, such as "Each and All" and "Brahma," express in unconventional meters and images his philosophical notions.

Never simple, always challenging, Emerson is the epitome of the thinking man.

**Faulkner, William** (*The Bear*). To know the writings of William Faulkner is to know the South — and the world as well. His novels and stories, limited as most of them are in geographical scope, reach back in time to the Indians and cover a range of characters rare in all literature — from the decadent aristocracy to the poor white man to the enduring Negro. Carefully considered, Faulkner's works comprise an extensive, though not always exact, genealogy of the folk of his mythical Yoknapatawpha County (based on his native Lafayette County, Mississippi), and can be read as perhaps the greatest of American sagas.

The technical brilliance of *The Sound and the Fury* and *As I Lay Dying,* rewarding but difficult novels, has overawed some readers, but Faulkner at his best can also be seen in *The Bear,* a novelette in the collection *Go Down, Moses.* Here are combined the lucid style of *Light in August* and the stream of consciousness of *Absalom, Absalom!;* the concern with the vanishing wilderness and the haunting problems of race relations; the simple story of a bear hunt and the epic grandeur of a symbolic conquest of nature; the acquisitiveness of the white man and the "communal anonymity of brotherhood" of the American Indian; a boy (Ike McCaslin) learning the ways of the woods and a young man (Ike) becoming aware of the truth behind his tainted heritage — a heritage which he finally rejects. Specific events merge into symbols as the Old Indian guide, Sam Fathers, dies just as the great bear is slain, and the reader senses that more has changed than meets the eye. In short, *The Bear* chronicles the passing of the American wilderness, and relates the process to the white man's burden of guilt.

The long fourth chapter which records a conversation between Ike and his older cousin McCaslin Edmonds, as filtered through Ike's consciousness, is indispensable to a full appreciation of the novel, though this section has been cut from some abbreviated versions of *The Bear*.

Faulkner was awarded the Nobel Prize for Literature in 1949.

**Flaubert, Gustave** (*Madame Bovary*). Whereas *War and Peace* is often considered the world's greatest novel, *Madame Bovary* vies for recognition as the most nearly perfect. Moreover, its reputation as the finest of French realistic novels, and as a forerunner of French naturalism, makes it one of the most influential writings of the nineteenth century.

Part of its influence stems from its actual writing — a well-known long and arduous process of stripping away romantic excesses in an attempt to produce an honest, unadorned, impersonal, realistic view of life — a difficult task for a writer schooled under the influence of Chateaubriand and Hugo. Disregarding polite literary conventions, Flaubert described life as he saw it — ordinary people in ordinary surroundings, too often, as in Emma Bovary's case, deluded by their own romantic notions. Although Flaubert is careful to withhold his own judgments on Emma's gradual degradation and ultimate tragedy, his clinical analysis of her motivations and his ironic juxtaposition of scenes leaves little doubt of his contempt and pity for the bourgeoisie. (Both are even more apparent in his short story "A Simple Heart," but here there is less contempt than pity.) Still, the novel is rigidly controlled by the author's search for *le mot juste* (the right word), his precise handling of each scene, and his emotional detachment from his characters. *Madame Bovary* is a "slice of life" given artistic form and thematic significance.

Nearly every modern novelist owes something to Flaubert. The character of Emma alone has been the model for countless modern tragic heroines. But it is one of the ironies of literary history that upon the publication of *Madame Bovary* Flaubert was taken to court and charged by the government with "outrage of public morals and religion." He was acquitted, and modern literary history has confirmed that judgement.

**Frost, Robert.** For generations to come, Robert Frost will live as a symbol of the birch-lined roads and trails of New England, a fairly conventional and simple poet who had "a lover's quarrel with the world" but who always remained essentially positive in his outlook. Though not without some truth, these stereotyped images do not do justice to one of America's most versatile and enigmatic poets. He is not merely regional; he is often inventive in poetic forms, often ambiguous and elusive, and sometimes skeptical and downright negative.

Brief but tantalizing poems such as "Fire and Ice" and "Dust of Snow" do not easily yield a "meaning." "Design" and "The Rabbit Hunter" suggest through sinister images that all is not well in nature. "Acquainted With the Night" and "Out, Out —" stress the darker side of life — and death. "Birches" and "Stopping by Woods on a Snowy Evening," Frost's most popular poems, express a certain weariness with the ways of the world which can be relieved only by escape, through a temporary near-mystical experience. Dramatic dialogue is rarely more forcefully written than in Frost's "The Death of the Hired Man" and "Home Burial," neither a very cheerful poem. Read in its context, the statement "Good fences make good neighbors" takes on an ironic significance that makes "Mending Wall" a powerful indictment of ignorance that lives through blind and meaningless tradition.

Behind the traditional image of Robert Frost lies a hard core of realism surprising to many readers. Never a simple poet, Frost is the master of "saying one thing and meaning another."

Frost was awarded the Pulitzer Prize four times.

**Goethe, Johann Wolfgang von** (*Faust*). Goethe is the Shakespeare of the German language, the Olympian of German literature. As a young man in the 1770's, he was a leader of the *Sturm und Drang* (Storm and Stress) movement in literature, from which sprang his influential romantic novel, *The Sorrows of Young Werther*. Although a prolific writer (nearly 150 volumes), and no stranger to any area of knowledge, Goethe's lifework is intimately tied to his poetic masterpiece, *Faust,* which he began as early as 1771, publishing Part I in 1808, and Part II in 1832, the year of his death.

The frustrating difficulty of *Faust* is evident in the infinite number of interpretations of its "meaning," ranging from the search for the meaning of life to the retention of man's moral sense against the forces of evil. One can say with certainty that the dispute between Man (Faust) and Satan (Mephistophales) springs from the duality of Man ("Two souls, alas, cohabit in my breast," says Faust) — his worldly and his spiritual natures. The famous wager, in which Satan binds himself to Faust's service in exchange, he hopes, for his soul, hinges on Faust's ability to resist complacency, to refuse to say to the passing moment, "Linger a while! Thou art so fair." As the angels say in Part II, "Should a man strive with all his heart/ Heaven can foil the devil."

Part I is a series of loosely connected incidents dramatizing Faust's struggle with earthly experience, and especially human love, symbolized by Gretchen. Part II reviews in sweeping episodes his thirst for more intellectual beauty, personified by Helen of Troy. At the end of the play, Faust *almost* becomes satisfied with his accomplishments, but not sufficiently for the Devil to claim him.

The Faust story is not original with Goethe, dating to the "real" Johannes Faustus of the 15th and 16th centuries, and appearing in such works as Marlowe's *Doctor Faustus* and Calderón's *The Prodigious Magician.*

**Hardy, Thomas** (*Tess of the D'Urbervilles*). The intense pessimism of Hardy's novels does not arise from any contempt for his characters but from the conviction that these people live in a world that is arranged to thwart their every aspiration, a world of chance, of "crass casualty," which takes no account of man's needs.

The powerful beginning of *The Return of the Native,* through its description of ominous Egdon Heath, is a key to understanding Hardy's view of the world — as are the many poems that he composed after he ceased writing novels. "The Immanent Will and its designs," taken largely from the pessimism of Schopenhauer, is the philosophical basis of much of Hardy's fiction.

Philosophy aside, his stories are really about the people who live in this blind and capricious universe, but who are more victims than villains — victims of a changing society, of their own sensitive natures, of coincidence and chance. In *The Return of the Native,* Eustacia Vye finds herself incompatible with her humble surroundings, but it is by ironic chance that she causes the death of Clym Yeobright's mother, and her death near the end of the story is accidental. Henchard, in *The Mayor of Casterbridge,* comes nearer to being responsible for his own doom, but outside forces and occasional coincidence help drive him to his inevitable ruin. Jude Fawley of *Jude the Obscure* never has a chance; Hardy marshalls all the forces imaginable against this young man's attempt to rise from the lower class to an Oxford scholar. The bitterness of this novel supposedly raised such an outcry at the time that Hardy wrote only poetry for the rest of his life.

Nowhere is Hardy's sympathy for people more obvious than in his portrait of Tess of the D'Urbervilles. "A Pure Woman," he calls her; a surface look at her life would indicate otherwise: she is twice seduced by one man (Alec D'Urberville) and ends with his blood on her hands. But her essential goodness in the face of Alec's insistence and Angel Claire's idealism is unmistakable. Even with Tess, though, coincidence determines the outcome of crucial episodes — as when a letter intended for Angel Claire does not reach its destination simply because of a rug.

More than a story of frustrated love, *Tess of the D'Urbervilles* is a profound challenge to Victorian morality and an inside account of the passing of rural England in the nineteenth century. As always, Hardy sees beyond individual human experience to its universal significance; and upon the death of Tess, he says with his usual grim irony: " 'Justice' was done, and the President of the Immortals . . . had ended his sport with Tess."

**Hawthorne, Nathaniel** (*The Scarlet Letter*). Hawthorne's novels and tales are all cut from the same cloth, and the student, once having learned the composition of the material, can approach any of his works knowledgeably. Perhaps the best one pattern is the preface to *The House of the Seven Gables,* in which he distinguishes between a Romance and a Novel; the Romance, he says, does not "aim at a very minute fidelity," but it "sins unpardonably so far as it may swerve aside from the truth of the human heart."

*The Scarlet Letter* is also a Romance, and aims at the "truth of the human heart." Set in Puritan New England, *The Scarlet Letter* explores the consciences of sinners, but Hawthorne is more the psychologist than the theologian. The adulteress, Hester Prynne, is actually the most admirable person in the story, and the scarlet "A" (for Adultery) with which she is branded takes on a rich symbolic significance (Angel?), and comes to be "looked upon with awe, yet with reverence too." Arthur Dimmesdale, the young minister who tries to hide his sin, languishes as the guilt burns into his heart and finally kills him; Hawthorne *suggests* that the same "A" appeared on Dimmesdale's chest just before he dies. But the great sinner is the calculating, intellectual physician, Roger Chillingworth, who violates in cold blood the "sanctity of a human heart" by pursuing Dimmesdale relentlessly. *His* is the unpardonable sin which, says Hawthorne, puts the head above the heart, revenge above forgiveness, law above mercy. The same human values run through many of his stories and tales, such as "The Minister's Black Veil," "Young Goodman Brown," and "Ethan Brand."

The special beauty of *The Scarlet Letter* lies in its near-perfect structure, its infinitely suggestive symbolism, and its calm and unhurried style. It bears rereading often.

**Hemingway, Ernest** (*For Whom the Bell Tolls*). Hemingway is one of the molders of modern fiction. His famous style — lean, spare, reserved, grammatically unconventional — has been the model for hosts of lesser imitators, none of whom has been able to wed his style so closely to the emotions and events conveyed. This is the style mentioned by the critics upon awarding the Nobel Prize for Literature in 1954 to Hemingway, citing especially *The Old Man and the Sea.* It is the style of the opening scene of *A Farewell to Arms* which almost catches the cadence of the moving armies, while reflecting the non-casual thinking of its narrator, Frederick Henry, a more cynical version of whom is found in Jake Barnes of *The Sun Also Rises.*

Stylistically and thematically, the latter two novels are triumphs of restraint, *The Sun Also Rises* capturing in few words the mood of the "Lost Generation" in post-war Europe, *A Farewell to Arms* understating the absurdity and futility of war, from which human love is the only refuge. Thus devoid of the claptrap of much fiction, these novels are often adjudged Hemingway's best.

A more faulty but more ambitious work is *For Whom the Bell Tolls,* one of the greatest war novels ever penned. Though more verbose and didactic than in much of his writing, Hemingway is more profound in *For Whom the Bell Tolls: this* war *does* have meaning for its hero, Robert Jordan, and romantic love takes on an almost mystical significance under the cloud of war and imminent death. In fact, Hemingway seems to be saying that *only* in the face of death can life take on the intensity realized by Robert Jordan. Covering only three days of the Spanish Civil War, the author gives a staggering richness to this novel, and moves back and forth in time deftly enough to add a surprising depth of dimension to time. Such characters as Pilar and Anselmo are truly unforgettable, though Maria, Jordan's girl friend, has been accused of being Hemingway's Hollywood pipe-dream. Ripe with adventure, humor, love, and profanity, *For Whom the Bell Tolls* is Hemingway's most full-blown novel, and perhaps his supreme achievement.

**Homer** (*The Iliad* and *The Odyssey*). Although the exact identity of Homer has never been established, modern scholarship favors the theory that there *was* a Homer and that *The Iliad* and *The Odyssey* were probably written by one man who lived about the seventh century B.C. Epic poetry begins with Homer; these two works are the foundation stones of Western literature, and still retain much of their amazing vitality.

The *Iliad,* meaning Tale of Troy, is generally recognized as the world's greatest epic of war, but it is less an account of the ten-year seige of Troy than a dramatization of the wrath of Achilles, the greatest warrior of the Greeks. Insulted by Agamennon and aware of his own approaching death at the hands of the Trojans, Achilles refuses to fight. At the death of Patroclus, he storms back into battle, finally slaying the noble Hector with savage abuse, only to be killed by Paris's arrow, which strikes him in his one vunerable spot — his heel. Played against the spectacle of armies clashing, of brutality and nobility, of searing hate and tender love, the wrath of Achilles makes *The Iliad* the first internal and external view of the glory and the tragedy of war.

The *Odyssey* is a more single-minded adventure story, centering on the exploits and perils of Odysseus, King of Ithaca, who had fought in the Trojan War and is now on his ten-year voyage home. The picture switches occasionally to his wife Penelope, repelling suitors, firm in her belief that her husband will eventually return, and to their son Telemachus, searching to find his father and to preserve his honor. Odysseus' adventures are familiar to all: the island of Calypso, the Lotus-eaters, the Cyclops, the Sirens, the twin perils of Scylla and Charybdis — Western folklores and languages abound with allusions to *The Odyssey*. Less grim than *The Iliad,* this great tale maintains the impersonal tone, the extended ("Homeric") similes, the thematic unity, and the high seriousness of its companion piece, and together they comprise the greatest poems of the ancient world.

Both may be read in modern translations, of which there are many.

**James, Henry** (*Portrait of a Lady*). Someone has said that James can evoke more drama from the way a person holds a teacup than most writers can extract from a major war. The action in James's stories and novels *is* an internal, subjective action, and thus he is known as one of the masters of the psychological novel. Indeed, the main difficulty that readers sometimes find with James is that the action is *too* subtle (some would say trivial) to create excitement, that the principles of some of his characters are not universal enough to draw a response from many readers.

Still, few writers have seen deeper into the psychology of motivation; few have treated more intelligently European-American relations; few have developed a more sensitive and refined style; and few have been more conscious of their art. In fact, this consciousness led James from a fluent and lucid style (*The American, The Europeans*) to the complex and convoluted writing in his later novels (*The Ambassadors, The Golden Bowl.*) Though he never sacrificed the realism and near-naturalism of his early and middle productions, action in his later novels becomes more psychological, and his characters further removed from the mainstream of life.

For brevity alone, the student may want to begin with *Daisy Miller,* the captivating story of a naive American girl in the complex European society, or *The Turn of the Screw,* a tale of the supernatural and the psychological, heavy with Freudian overtones. For sheer beauty of achievement, *The Portrait of a Lady* presents one of the novelist's most memorable and admirable characters. Isabel Archer, a proud American girl, goes to England to find herself beseiged by suitors. When she makes an unfortunate choice, she has the strength and the moral courage to accept the situation. Not as difficult as some of James's later novels, *The Portrait of a Lady* incorporates most of the elements that made James a master of realistic fiction.

**Joyce, James** (*Ulysses*). The immense talent of Joyce is sometimes as bewildering as it is enlightening. *Dubliners,* a collection of stories (epiphanies he called them), unveils the various lives of Dubliners in a moment of subtle revelation. The semi-autobiographical *Portrait of the Artist as a Young Man* foreshadows the stream-of-consciousness technique of *Ulysses,* and is a comfortable beginning point for those planning to read the greater work, though *Portrait* is an excellent novel itself.

With *Ulysses,* modern literature reaches a mountain peak of achievement. Seven years in the writing, it at first appears insurmountable, but little by little it becomes intelligible to those who persist in their reading. *Ulysses* is the record of one day (June 16, 1904) in the life of Leopold Bloom (Joyce's modern, unheroic counterpart of Odysseus — Ulysses — of *The Odyssey*), his wife Molly (Penelope) and Stephen Dedalus (Telemachus). The novel is intricately structured to present a modern version of the travels of Odysseus, and a detailed analysis of the novel points up numerous parallels, though often not clear, with characters and events of *The Odyssey*. The confusion, however, stems from the stream-of-consciousness technique through which we follow the wandering minds of Stephen, then Leopold Bloom, then Molly. With an almost magical facility for coining new words and giving new twists to old ones, Joyce can wring the fullest meaning from the least significant event — and 768 pages from a single day. Joyce penetrates the minds of his characters while sweeping across Dublin with a panoramic pen. Subtle symbolism and occasional parody, as well as numerous other literary devices, increase the richness of this great work. Though not impossible to scale, this Olympian novel is best conquered with an experienced guidebook, of which several are in print.

If *Ulysses* seems to be the ultimate in difficulty and complexity, *Finnegans Wake,* seventeen years in the making, pushes the imagination to its outer limits where it blends with the world of sound and feeling. It too requires aids to understanding.

**Melville, Herman** (*Moby Dick*). The literary reputation of *Moby Dick* came very late, and Melville's last novel, *Billy Budd,* was not even published until thirty-three years after the author's death. Why? Could it be that Melville's affirmation of evil was not palatable to his own generation? Whatever the reasons, his time has come, and *Moby Dick* is now considered one of the most profound (and sometimes bewildering) masterpieces of world literature.

The student reads *Moby Dick* with the frustrating feeling that "some certain significance lurks in all things." The inexplicable viciousness of the sharks, the baptism of the harpoon in the name of the devil, the biblical names of the characters (Ahab, Ishmael, Bildad, Peleg), the names of the ships (*Delight, Rachel*), the monkey-rope binding the seamen together, the whiteness of the whale — all seem to carry a symbolic significance that resists simple equations, but which gives the book an infinite range of possible "meanings."

The narrator, Ishmael, is the port-hole through which we first view the coming calamitous conflict between Captain Ahab and the great white whale, Moby Dick; but Ishmael's point of view fades into omniscient narration through the greater part of the novel. Ahab, having lost his leg to Moby Dick, pursues the whale with unrelenting fury, and the surface story of this pursuit is a thrilling tale in itself. But Ahab's obsession to destroy Moby Dick surpasses normality (insanity, Ishmael calls it), and one can quite easily read Man for Ahab and Evil for Moby Dick to recognize that the theme of this novel is that of Man throwing himself against all the forces of Evil, or trying to resolve the mystery of Evil, or attempting to understand the essence of Evil — all at the risk of his soul.

*Moby Dick* is only one of about a dozen works of fiction by Melville, some of which, like *Typee*, and *Billy Budd*, now enjoy a literary reputation of their own.

**Milton, John** (*Paradise Lost*). "The grand manner" best describes the writings of Milton. In such poems as "L'Allegro" and "Il Penseroso," and the great pastoral elegy "Lycidas," Milton composed, in his younger years, some immortal poetry. But his greatest work was done after he retired from public life as his eyesight was fading into total blindness.

Always politically minded, and ever a defender of freedom (his prose work *Areopagitica* is a classic in the defense of freedom of the press), Milton toyed with the idea of writing an epic based on the legends of King Arthur, glorifying England much as Vergil had Rome in *The Aeneid.* But becoming disillusioned with the republican cause, and sensing the limitations of a chivalric romance, he turned to a Christian subject: the Fall of Man. In treating a religious theme, in attempting to "assert Eternal Providence, / And justify the ways of God to Men," Milton is not abandoning his obsession with liberty and freedom, but expanding it to cosmic proportions. In tracing Man's Fall from Grace, Milton is less concerned with theological and philosophical problems, like the reasons for suffering and the nature of divine love, than with ethical problems, such as individual freedom and responsibility. These he explores through Adam, Eve, and the fascinating Satan, whose moral responsibility becomes one of the great issues of the work.

As the theme is of epic proportions, so is the structure and style in the grand manner of Homer and Vergil: twelve books, each with an "argument" describing its contents, Homeric similes, literary and biblical allusions. Perhaps most striking is the elevated, heroic style, amazing in its power to convey actions of titanic proportions: "Him the Almighty Power / Hurled headlong flaming from the ethereal sky, / With hideous ruin and combustion, down / To bottomless perdition, there to dwell / In adamantine chains and penal fire / Who durst defy the Omnipotent to arms." In one sweeping sentence, Milton thus describes the great event upon which the whole epic is based.

*Paradise Regained,* its sequel, is considered an inferior work, but the classical poetic tragedy *Samson Agonistes* is a drama of highest order.

**Poe, Edgar Allan** ("The Fall of the House of Usher"). The dark and morbid romanticism of Poe is unique in American literature. He has had many imitators, and he had few predecessors. Although his work is uneven and limited in scope, Poe stands today as (1) our first great literary critic; (2) the formulator of the modern idea of the short story, including science fiction and the detective tale; (3) the progenitor of the symbolist movement in France through his poetry, which he describes as the rhythmical creation of beauty. Always conscious of his artistic method, Poe describes in "The Philosophy of Composition" the step-by-step process by which he wrote his famous poem "The Raven." Though one may doubt the absolute veracity of this account, one never doubts Poe's seriousness as a writer.

The magic ingredients of love, death, and beauty pervade his poetry. Scorning the long poem (a contradiction in terms, he called it), and rejecting any didactic intention, Poe writes primarily for the ear. Such onomatopoetic poems as "The Bells" and "Annabel Lee" prompted Emerson to call him the "jingle man," but in poems such as "The Raven," "The City in the Sea" and "Ulalume," his ability to evoke a mood through sonorous sounds and haunting meter emerges most clearly. "To Helen" reveals an image-making facility ("The Raven" is almost devoid of figurative language) and a restraint rarely seen in Poe.

Poe's interest in abnormal behavior, in the cult of Gothicism, in the twilight zones of credibility, carries into many of his short stories. His detective stories (tales of ratiocination) include "The Purloined Letter" and "The Gold Bug"; his tales of murder and revenge, "The Tell-Tale Heart" and "The Cask of Amontillado"; of calculated horror, "The Pit and the Pendulum" and "The Masque of the Red Death." None, though, is more carefully contrived to produce the unified effect which Poe made the aim of all his art than "The Fall of the House of Usher." Every element in this story — the weather, the landscape, the dreary nights, the eerie house and its even stranger occupants, and the mysterious maladies that plague them both — builds to the feeling of horror at seeing the dissolution of the House of Usher, and thus the brilliant but diseased mind of Roderick Usher. The allegorical poem "The Haunted Palace" ingeniously pulls these two themes together. Though a noteworthy poem apart from the story, it plays an integral part in the exposition of theme; nothing is superfluous in the tales of Poe.

**Swift, Jonathan** (*Gulliver's Travels*). Swift hated people. Or at least some of his writings gives that impression. No one has depicted man as a more despicable creature than the Yahoos of Book IV of *Gulliver's Travels,* or has indulged in more bitter irony than *A Modest Proposal* — a satirical proposition that the English eat the children of the Irish and thereby solve the problems of poverty and overpopulation. Is this Jonathan Swift, the author of *Gulliver's Travels,* so beloved by children for over two hundred years?

It is. Perhaps this picture is overdrawn, however, for the most savage satire can be used toward constructive ends, and the harshest criticism of man's foibles can reveal an underlying desire to improve him. Moreover, the adult satire of *Gulliver's Travels* is partially obscured by the meticulousness with which he envisions his imaginary worlds, especially diminuative Lilliput and gigantic Brobdingnag. He scrupulously adheres to the scale of measurements he sets up, and one can easily become lost in the marvel of it all — although the triviality of the Lilliputians (who at one point quarrel over which end of an egg to crack) is hard to miss. Satire in Parts III and IV is more obvious: the hairbrained ideas of the scientists and educators on the island of Laputa have sounded uncomfortably familiar to generations of scholars; and the comparison of the gentle and reasonable horses with the filthy and revolting Yahoos (men?) in Part IV leaves the impression that Swift is completely disenchanted with the human race. By the end of his adventures, Gulliver is so disgusted with humanity that he cannot even eat at the same table with his family. But surely this is excessive, even to Swift, a warning, perhaps, to man to be aware of his animality while striving to use his reason and good sense to its fullest advantage. The Brobdingnagians, one recalls, present both sides of the picture, a more realistic view of human virtues and vices. *Gulliver's Travels,* a devastating satire, is not without hope.

**Thackeray, William Makepeace (*Vanity Fair*).** Whereas Dickens' popularity has always been high, that of Thackeray, his eminent contemporary, has waned and has been revived only partially by the recent upsurge of interest in Victorian literature. The reason for the difference is not hard to understand: although they both were prolific writers, scarcely ever writing a short novel, Dickens' energy was expended on action and a vigorous, fast-moving style, with almost no personal commentary; Thackeray was more concerned with motivation and effects than action, and his leisurely though clever style fits his penchant to comment, to preach, and to chat with the reader at every opportunity. This last characteristic has affected his reputation with modern critics, who object to any authorial intrusion into a novel.

Yet Thackeray, often accused in his day of being a cynic, is a satirist and a creator of character of the first order. Few characters of Dickens have the depth and the complexity of Becky Sharp in *Vanity Fair,* or Henry Esmond in the novel of that title. *Vanity Fair,* "A Novel Without a Hero" as it is sub-titled, exemplifies all of Thackeray's greatness as well as his faults. Masterful story-telling and wasteful though entertaining chattiness reveal the lives of the scheming but fascinating Becky Sharp and the sweet but insipid Amelia Sedley. Scorning the romantic, and relegating sensational events such as the Battle of Waterloo to the background, Thackeray follows for many years the everyday lives of Becky and Amelia, their loves and fortunes. Romantic notions are exploded by Amelia's blind devotion to the memory of a husband who had betrayed her. And to the displeasure of many readers of the day, the sinful Becky, who remains the stronger character, never learns her lesson. Thackeray's aim is truth about people. If he did become over-anxious to *tell* us the truth, he *showed* it as the puppet-master of *Vanity Fair.*

**Thoreau, Henry David (*Walden*).** "Whoso would be a man, must be a nonconformist," Emerson intoned, and Henry Thoreau was that man. Almost unnoticed in his time, Thoreau has become recognized as one of the most influential writers of the last century. The paradox is a natural one: Thoreau was almost a century ahead of his time.

Determined to live by his dictum to "simplify, simplify," Thoreau retired to Walden Pond in the summer of 1845, where he built his own house for about $28, and lived frugally but intensely for two years. The story of time spent there, and the philosophy of life that took him there, is related in *Walden.*

In strong, vivid, inimitable prose, Thoreau describes the foibles and the ills of men as he saw them, and he was seeing far into the twentieth century: "The mass of men lead lives of quiet desperation." "How vigilant we are! determined not to live by faith if we can avoid it." "Most of the luxuries, and many of the so-called comforts of life, are not only not indispensable, but positive hindrances to the elevation of mankind." "Men have become the tools of their tools." "Our inventions are wont to be pretty toys, which distract our attention from serious things. They are but improved means to an unimproved end." "Our life is frittered away by detail." "We do not ride on the railroad; it rides upon us." "We have the Saint Vitus' dance, and cannot possibly keep our heads still." Where, among modern writings on sociology and group behavior, can one find a more accurate or honest diagnosis of the social ills that beset us today?

Thoreau's bold experiment at Walden was his answer to the complexity of life that he saw encroaching upon man's freedom and dignity. The simple life that he enjoyed is the actual subject of most of Walden — and his nature writing that has never been excelled. The chapters "Sounds" and "Spring" are especially memorable.

Much of Thoreau's philosophy of life can also be found in his essay "Walking." In the political realm, *Civil Disobedience* has had profound repercussions through twentieth-century India and America.

**Twain, Mark** (*Adventures of Huckleberry Finn*). *Huckleberry Finn* is proof of the need to reread great literature. Whereas *Tom Sawyer* remains forever a boy's book, and *Huckleberry Finn* appears to children no more than its exciting sequel, to the adult reader *Huckleberry Finn* soars above the juvenile to some of the most mature and incisive views of human nature in literature.

Samuel Langhorne Clemens took the name "Mark Twain" from an expression of the rivermen which indicated the sounding of two fathoms. Many of his books grew out of his experience on and along the Mississippi; and the setting, the history, and the folklore of such books as *Life on the Mississippi* and *Tom Sawyer* come to greatest fruition in *Huckleberry Finn*. The pervading image of the great river, the ugliness of the frontier towns, the adventures and the authentic language of a frontier boy — all contribute to the book's appeal as one of the most vivid accounts of nineteenth-century frontier life along the Mississippi. But the greatness of *Huckleberry Finn* lies primarily in the fine *irony* between what Huck says and what he does, between what he has been taught to accept by slave-state standards and how he must act when confronted by a personal moral choice. In refusing to expose the runaway slave Jim, he still persists in the belief that he is doing wrong ("All right, then, I'll go to hell!" is probably the climax of the book), but his very ignorance of his own integrity accentuates the hypocrisy of the adults who surround him, though Huck is still quick to distinguish between the phoneys and the sincere adults whom he meets. Among the phoneys, none is more memorable or disgusting than the "Duke" and the "Dauphin," the rogues who victimize the gullible folk of the river towns.

Mark Twain's influence on modern American literature has been great. Hemingway has said that "All modern American literature comes from a book by Mark Twain called *Huckleberry Finn* . . . It's the best book we've had." However exaggerated this tribute, *Huckleberry Finn* is one of the significant novels to come from nineteenth-century America.

For Twain himself, *Huckleberry Finn* is often considered a watershed between his lighter, more humorous books and his more somber ones.

The implied pessimism of *Huckleberry Finn* becomes almost vicious in *The Man that Corrupted Hadleyburg* and dismally cynical in his posthumous *The Mysterious Stranger*.

**Tolstoy, Leo** (*War and Peace*). Superlatives are dangerous in discussing works of literature, but Tolstoy's reputation as one of the world's great novelists, and *War and Peace* as one of the very greatest novels, are well founded.

It is all too easy to confuse Tolstoy the man with Tolstoy the artist. Before his "transformation" or "conversion" to a kind of religious humanism, Count Leo Tolstoy produced two great masterpieces of fiction, *War and Peace* and *Anna Karenina;* afterwards he dedicated himself to more didactic writing (the most powerful of which is *The Resurrection*), while condemning his own earlier work.

In *War and Peace,* Tolstoy the man explains in long passages his theory of history, which, in short, is that history controls man rather than, as Carlyle would say, that man controls history. Even the mighty Napoleon cannot conquer Russia, despite the fact that the Russian general Kutuzof is more a dreamer than a commander-in-chief.

Tolstoy the artist expresses himself in perhaps the richest congregation of characters ever assembled in a novel. The list is long and confusing, but persistent reading unravels the relationships of these people and their stories with great cumulative power. Indeed, though an immense and sprawling novel, *War and Peace* is not planless or formless. Ultimately it gives the impression of a complete *world* such as few writers have ever created. Owing to its great length, this novel often appears in abridged editions.

**Vergil** (*The Aeneid*). As *The Odyssey* is the story of Odysseus, so *The Aeneid* is the story of Aeneas. Both epics are mythological accounts of events occurring after the Trojan War, the latter ending in the founding of Rome by the Trojans. In fact, *The Aeneid* became the epitome of the glory and the ideals of Augustan Rome as well as the most influential Latin poem ever written; to speak of the "classics" has always included Vergil.

Relying upon Homer as literary example and the legends of the Greeks and the Romans for the stories themselves, Vergil traces the adventures of Aeneas from the conquered Troy to the ends of the earth: in Carthage he confronts the passionate Queen Dido; from Cumae, he descends into Hades and finds his father, who tells him of the glory of Rome that is to come; finally on the coast of Italy he slays his challenger Turnus and establishes the Trojan people on Roman soil, laying the foundation for Imperial Rome. Some of the story is told, not in strict chronological order, but by means of the flashback method borrowed from *The Odyssey*.

Like such great writers as Homer, Boccaccio, Chaucer, and Shakespeare, Vergil borrows heavily from other sources, but like them he gives form and meaning to the diverse materials of mythology and folk legend. More literary and philosophical than Homer, Vergil creates from similar legends the first great national epic.

**Voltaire** (*Candide*). "The Age of Voltaire," Will Durant, in his series "The Story of Civilization," calls the eighteenth century. Voltaire's name is synonymous with the Enlightenment; the French people paid him this tribute: "Poet, philosopher, historian, he gave wings to the human intelligence; he prepared us for freedom." But of the one hundred or so volumes that he wrote, he is best remembered for the slim little tale entitled *Candide,* written after he was sixty.

Subtitled *Optimism,* the book is primarily an attack on the reigning philosophy of the day, best summarized in Alexander Pope's dictum, "Whatever is, is right," and in the philosopher Leibnitz's theory of "the best of all possible worlds." Voltaire destroys it all in this convincing satire. He subjects the hero, Candide ("naive") to a horrible series of adventures, all well calculated to destroy his faith, not in God, but in the optimistic views as preached by his tutor Pangloss. Candide learns from experience slowly, but by the time he has survived the Lisbon earthquake, several wars, the Inquisition, has seen his friends hanged and abused, and has observed his beautiful Cunegonde become wretched and ugly, he senses the flaw in the scheme of things and finally admits that it is only left for men "to cultivate our gardens" in quiet solitude.

Though brief, *Candide* is panoramic, and, through an exciting series of episodes, exposes the greediness, brutality, and irrationality of man. Its form is the romantic travel story so popular in Voltaire's time; but after a suspicious number of recognition scenes in which dead people reappear and the lost are found, the reader catches the spirit of the piece and reads *Candide* for what it is — a satire *par excellence.*

**Whitman, Walt** (*Leaves of Grass*). Of the readers of the first edition of *Leaves of Grass,* Emerson and Thoreau were among the few who dared to compliment it, and later Emerson partially retracted his judgement. Small wonder: poetry without rhyme and apparently without meter, the constant presence of the authorial "I," the frank treatment of sex, the boasting and the swaggering — these were hardly likely to win him an immediate audience. Yet Whitman may well have been the greatest of American poets.

On his way to becoming the nearest we have to a national poet, Whitman revolutionized the poetic line. What seemed to be a lack of meter ("free verse") was actually a reclamation of a poetic form as old as the biblical Psalms, a kind of "thought rhythm" in which each line contains a thought which is complemented, paralleled, or contrasted by the next line, and the comma becomes the catch-all form of punctuation. Long "catalogs" of peoples and scenes afford Whitman the expansiveness he needs, but his poems can range from as few lines as "Calvary Crossing to Ford" to "Crossing Brooklyn Ferry." His brief portraits, or vignettes, can freeze in art the essence of a scene in the poet's mind.

Though he claims to glory in himself ("Song of Myself"), Whitman's subject is Everyman, especially the American Man. He shouts the promise of this country ("Pioneers! O Pioneers") and mourns its tragedies ("O Captain! My Captain"); he sees the loneliness of man allegorized in the small things of nature ("A Noiseless Patient Spider") and sings of the ("Open Road"); he rejoices in the recurrent miracle of birth ("Out of the Cradle Endlessly Rocking") and poignantly understates the grim tragedy of a death in the family ("Come Up From the Fields, Father").

In his sharpest and most tightly controlled poetry, Whitman was capable of sustaining a mood and an image (or a set of images) that give these poems an impact impossible in his looser pieces. Such is "When Lilacs Last in the Dooryard Bloom'd," a tribute to Lincoln, perhaps the most sublime elegy in American literature.

**Wolfe, Thomas** (*Look Homeward, Angel*). Sometimes accused of being perpetually adolescent, Thomas Wolfe left an eloquent testimony to his lust for life, a hunger for experience that sometimes borders on the profound, sometimes, indeed, reeks of the immature. At his best, as in *Look Homeward, Angel* (heavily edited from his mammoth manuscript), Wolfe is unequalled in the recreation of a life (*his* life, as in all his books) searching for experience and the meaning of that experience.

In *Look Homeward, Angel,* a stone, a leaf, and a door — modern equivalents of Thoreau's hound, bay-horse, and turtle-dove — symbolize young Eugene Gant's search for "the lost lane-end into heaven" in the oppressively mundane environment of a North Carolina mountain town (Asheville, called Altamont in the novel). A drunkard father, a miserly mother, and a set of brothers and sisters all challenge the younger Eugene's quest for identity. Though minor events are often blown out of proportion, the slow and agonizing death of his brother Ben is the book's best claim to tragedy and Eugene's most traumatic, though meaningful, experience.

*Look Homeward, Angel* traces the lightly disguised life of its author from birth through college, and then points him toward Harvard and more long autobiographical fiction, which continues through *Of Time and the River, The Web and the Rock* and *You Can't Go Home Again.*

# II
# Outline of Western World Literature

## THE ANCIENT WORLD
### 850 B.C. – A.D. 500

### GREECE

**Literature:** Epics, dramas, satires, fables, odes.

HOMER (ca. 850-ca. 750 B.C.): Epic poetry
*The Iliad* *The Odyssey*

AESOP (6th Cent. B.C.)
*Fables*

AESCHYLUS (525-456 B.C.): Tragedies
*The Persians* (472 B.C.)
*The Seven Against Thebes* (467 B.C.)
*The Orestaia* (458 B.C.)
*Agamemnon*, *Choephoroc*, *Eumenides* — Trilogy

PINDAR (522-443 B.C.): Odes
*Victory Odes*

SOPHOCLES (496-406 B.C.): Tragedies
*Ajax* (445-440 B.C.) *Antigone* (441 B.C.)
*Oedipus the King* (430 B.C.)
*Electra* (410 B.C.)

EURIPEDES (ca. 480-ca. 406 B.C.): Tragedies
*Alcestis* (438 B.C.) *Medea* (431 B.C.)
*Hippolytus* (428 B.C.)
*Trojan Woman* (415 B.C.)

ARISTOPHANES (ca. 450-ca. 385 B.C.): Comedies
*Lysistrata* (411 B.C.) *The Clouds* (423 B.C.)
*The Frogs* (405 B.C.) *The Birds* (414 B.C.)

**Philosophy and Religion**

PLATO (ca. 428-347 B.C.): Dialogues
*Republic* *Phaedo*
*Apology* *Symposium*

ARISTOTLE (384-322 B.C.)
*Nicomachean Ethics* *Metaphysics*
*Politics* *Poetics*
Philosophy on almost every major area of knowledge

**History and Biography**

HERODOTUS (ca. 484-ca. 428 B.C.)
*History of the Persian Wars*

THUCYDIDES (ca. 470-ca. 400 B.C.)
*History of the Peloponnesian Wars* (ca. 424-404 B.C.)

XENOPHON (ca. 430-ca. 354 B.C.)
*Anabasis* (*March Up Country*)
*Hellenica* (*History of Greece*)

PLUTARCH (ca. A.D. 45-ca. 125)
*Parallel Lives* (Lives of the noble Greeks and Romans)

### ROME

**Literature:** Epics, dramas, satires, poetry, prose fiction

PLAUTUS (ca. 251-184 B.C.): Comedies
*The Pot of Gold*
*The Braggart Soldier*
*The Prisoners*

TERENCE (ca. 195-159 B.C.): Comedies
*The Woman of Andros* (166 B.C.)
*The Eunuch* (161 B.C.)
*The Brothers* (160 B.C.)

HORACE (65-8 B.C.): Poetry and criticism
*Satires* *Odes*
*The Art of Poetry*

VERGIL (70-19 B.C.): Epic poetry
*Eclogues* *Georgics*
*The Aeneid* (17 B.C.)

OVID (43 B.C.-A.D. 17): Poetry
*The Art of Love*
*Metamorphoses*

JUVENAL (ca. A.D. 60-ca. 140): Satires
*Satires* (ca. A.D. 100-ca. 128)

APULIUS (ca. A.D. 125): Prose fiction
*The Golden Ass*

**Philosophy and Religion**

CICERO (106-43 B.C.): Oratory and essays
*Catilinarian Orations*
*On the Nature of the Gods*
Various other orations and essays

LUCRETIUS (ca. 94-55 B.C.): Philosophical poetry
*On the Nature of Things*

AURELIUS, Marcus (A.D. 121-180): Stoic philosophy
*Meditations*

AUGUSTINE, Saint (A.D. 354-430): Christian philosophy
*Confessions* (ca. 397)
*The City of God* (ca. 413)

BOETHIUS (A.D. 480-524): Philosophy
*The Consolation of Philosophy*

**History and Biography**

LIVY (59 B.C.-A.D. 17)
*Annals of the Roman People* (History of Rome)

CAESAR, Julius (100-44 B.C.): History
*Commentaries on the Gallic War*
*The Civil War*

# THE MIDDLE AGES AND THE RENAISSANCE

## A.D. 500-1650

**Anonymous Sagas and Epics**

*Beowulf* (8th C.): Anglo-Saxon epic
*Song of Roland* (11th C.): Old French *Chanson de geste* (song of great deeds)
*The Story of Burnt Njal* (12th C.): Icelandic Saga
*Tristan and Iseult* (12th C.): Medieval love story; many versions
*The Nibelungenlied* (12th C.): Middle High German epic poem
*The Volsung Saga* (13th C.): Scandinavian prose epic version of *The Nibelungenlied*
*The Romance of the Rose* (13th C.): French Allegory and satire in verse
*Aucassin and Nicolette* (13th C.): French tale in prose and verse
*The Kalevala* [Land of Heroes]: Finnish folk epic poem, immortalized by Elias Lönnrot (1802-1884)
*Sir Gawain and the Green Knight* (14th C.): Arthurian romance attributed to the "Pearl Poet"

**Religious Literature**

FRANCIS OF ASSISI, Saint (1182-1226): Gentleness and love for all
*The Sermon to the Birds*
*The Little Flowers*

THOMAS AQUINAS, Saint (1225-74): Roman Catholic theology
*Summa Theologica*

DANTE ALIGHIERI (1265-1321): Greatest religious poetry of the age
*The Divine Comedy* (comp. ca. 1310-21)
"Inferno" "Purgatory" "Paradise"

**Poetry**

PETRARCH (1304-74): Birth of the Italian sonnet
Poetry to "Laura" (366 poems)
*Ode to Italy*

LANGLAND, William (ca. 1330-ca. 1400): Middle English allegory in alliterative verse
*Piers Plowman*

CHAUCER, Geoffrey (1340-1400): Lusty tales in Middle English verse
*Troilus and Criseyde* (ca. 1385)
*The Legend of Good Women* (1380-86)
*The Canterbury Tales* (comp. ca. 1386-90)

SPENSER, Edmund (ca. 1552-99): Medieval allegory in modern poetry
*The Epithalamion* (1595)
*The Prothalamion* (1596)
*The Shepherd's Calendar* (1579)
*The Faerie Queen* (1590, 1596, incomplete)

DONNE, John (1573-1631): Bold metaphors of love and religion
*Devotions* (1624)
*Anniversaries* (1611, 1612)
Various songs and sonnets

**Drama**

*Everyman* (late 15th C.): Outstanding English morality play

VEGA, Lope de (1562-1635): Prolific founder of Spanish drama
Over 2000 plays, about 500 extant

MARLOWE, Christopher (1564-93): New power for English poetic drama
*Tamburlaine* (comp. 1587-88)
*The Tragical History of Dr. Faustus* (comp. ca. 1589-92)
*The Jew of Malta* (comp. ca. 1588-90)

SHAKESPEARE, William (1564-1616): The best of Western world literature
See Part III, "The Plays of William Shakespeare"

CALDERÓN DE LA BARCA, Pedro (1600-81): Philosophical and religious drama
*Life is a Dream* (1635)
*The Prodigious Magician* (1637)

**Various Prose Works**

BOCCACCIO, Giovanni (1313-75): Modern tales of love and adventure
*The Decameron* (ca. 1353)
Other works, poetry and prose

MALORY, Sir Thomas (ca. 1394-1471): Unity and form to the Arthurian legend
*Le Morte d'Arthur* (1471)

ERASMUS, Desiderius (ca. 1466-1536): Dutch satire and scholarship
*In Praise of Folly* (1509)
Greek text of the New Testament

MACHIAVELLI, Niccolò (1469-1527): Early political realism
*The Prince* (1513)

MORE, Sir Thomas (1478-1535): A scholarly humanist's visionary world
*Utopia* (1516) [in Latin]

RABELAIS, François (ca. 1494-1553): Erudite and earthy burlesque
*Gargantua and Pantagruel* (1532-64)

MONTAIGNE, Michel de (1533-92): Personal, witty, and urbane skepticism
*Essays* (1580-88)

CERVANTES SAAVEDRA, Miguel de (1547-1616): Satire, comedy, and tragedy in the first great modern novel
*Don Quixote de la Mancha* (1605, 1615)
*Exemplary Novels* (1613)

BUNYAN, John (1628-88): Timeless Puritan allegory
*The Pilgrim's Progress* (1678)

# MODERN WESTERN WORLD LITERATURE
# A COMPARATIVE CHRONOLOGY

## NEO-CLASSICISM — 1650-1800

### ENGLAND

PEPYS, Samuel (1633-1703)
Intimate view of Restoration England
*Diary* (comp. 1660-69)
MILTON, John (1608-74)
Epic Christian poetry
*Paradise Lost* (1667)
*Paradise Regained* (1671)
*Samson Agonistes* (1671)
DRYDEN, John (1631-1700)
Didactic poetry and satire
*All for Love* (1678)
*Mac Flecknoe* (1682)
*Alexander's Feast* (1697)
ADDISON, Joseph (1672-1719) and STEELE, Richard (1672-1729)
The periodical essay
*The Spectator* (1711-12)
POPE, Alexander (1688-1744)
Epitome of Neo-Classical poetry
*Essay on Criticism* (1711)
*The Rape of the Lock* (1712, 1714)
*Essay on Man* (1733)
*Epistle to Dr. Arbuthnot* (1735)
DEFOE, Daniel (ca. 1660-1731)
Fiction and journalism
*Robinson Crusoe* (1719)
*Moll Flanders* (1722)
*Journal of the Plague Year* (1722)
SWIFT, Jonathan (1667-1745)
Bitter, timeless satire on man
*Gulliver's Travels* (1726)
*A Modest Proposal* (1729)
THOMSON, James (1700-48)
Restrained nature poetry
*The Seasons* (1726-30)
GRAY, Thomas (1716-71)
"Graveyard poetry" and signs of Romanticism
*Elegy Written in a Country Churchyard* (1751)
JOHNSON, Samuel (1709-84)
Early lexicography and Neo-Classical didacticism
*Dictionary* (1755)
*Rasselas* (1759)
GOLDSMITH, Oliver (1728-74)
Versatility and sentimentality
*The Vicar of Wakefield* (1766)
*The Deserted Village* (1770)
*She Stoops to Conquer* (1773)

### AMERICA

BRADFORD, William (1590-1657)
Beginnings in American history
*History of Plymouth Plantation* (comp. 1630-51)
First American Book
*Bay Psalm Book* (1640)
WILLIAMS, Roger (ca. 1603-83)
Movement toward religious freedom
*Bloody Tenant of Persecution* (1644)
BRADSTREET, Anne (ca. 1612-72)
Beginnings in poetry
*The Tenth Muse, Lately Sprung Up in America* (1650)
WIGGLESWORTH, Michael (1631-1705)
Popular theology in ballad form
*The Day of Doom* (1662)
SEWALL, Samuel (1652-1730)
The American Pepys
*Diary* (comp. 1674-1729)
MATHER, Cotton (1663-1728)
Puritan views of New England
*Magnalia Christi Americani* (1702)
*Essays to Do Good* (1710)
BYRD, William (1674-1744)
Exploration of the South
*History of the Dividing Line* (comp. 1729)
FRANKLIN, Benjamin (1706-90)
Yankee frugality and inventiveness
*Poor Richard's Almanac* (1732-57)
*Autobiography* (comp. ca. 1771-?)
EDWARDS, Jonathan (1703-58)
Great Puritan theology
*Sinners in the Hands of an Angry God* (1741)
*Freedom of the Will* (1754)
*The Great Christian Doctrine of Original Sin Defended* (1758)
PAINE, Thomas (1737-1809)
Stirrings of freedom
*Common Sense* (1776)
*The American Crisis* (1776-83)
*The Age of Reason* (1792)
JEFFERSON, Thomas (1743-1826)
The American Magna Carta
*The Declaration of Independence* (1776)
Toward national unity
*Articles of Confederation* (1777)

### CONTINENTAL EUROPE

CORNEILLE, Pierre [Fr.] (1606-84)
Classical drama
*The Cid* (1636)
*Horace* (1640)
*Cinna* (1640)
MOLIÈRE [Fr.] (1622-73)
Satirical drama
*Tartuffe* (1664)
*The Misanthrope* (1666)
*The Miser* (1668)
LA ROCHEFOUCAULD [Fr.] (1613-80)
Witty cynicism
*Maxims* (1665)
RACINE, Jean [Fr.] (1639-99)
Classical tragedy
*Andromache* (1667)
*Phaedra* (1677)
LA FONTAINE, Jean de [Fr.] (1621-95)
The French Aesop
*Fables* (1668-94)
PASCAL, Blaise [Fr.] (1623-62)
Christian rationalism
*Thoughts* (comp. ca. 1670)
BOILEAU, Nicolas [Fr.] (1636-1711)
Literary rationalism defined
*The Art of Poetry* (1674)
VOLTAIRE [Fr.] (1694-1778)
Satirical romance
*Candide* (1759)
Many other works
DIDEROT, Denis [Fr.] (1713-84)
Scholarly culmination of the Enlightenment
*The Encyclopedia* (1751-80)
*Rameau's Nephew* (comp. ca. 1765-70)

## ROMANTICISM — 1800-1860

### ENGLAND

WALPOLE, Horace (1717-97)
Early Gothic novel
*Castle of Otranto* (1764)
BLAKE, William (1757-1827)
Mystical symbolism, pre-Romanticism
*Songs of Innocence* (1789)
*Songs of Experience* (1794)
WORDSWORTH and COLERIDGE
Romantic declaration of independence
*Lyrical Ballads* (1798)

### AMERICA

BROWN, Charles Brockden (1771-1810)
Early Gothic novel in America
*Wieland* (1798)
IRVING, Washington (1783-1859)
Burlesque, folk tales and travels
*The Knickerbocker History of New York* (1809)
*The Sketch Book* (1820)
*The Alhambra* (1832)

### CONTINENTAL EUROPE

ROUSSEAU, Jean Jacques [Fr.] (1712-78)
Praise for natural man
*The Social Contract* (1762)
*Émile* (1762)
*Confessions* (1781-88)
GOETHE, Johann W. von [Ger.] (1749-1832)
*Sturm und Drang* in immortal legend
*The Sorrows of Young Werther* (1774)
*Wilhelm Meister* (1795-96)
*Faust* (Part I: 1808; Part II: 1833)

## ENGLAND

**WORDSWORTH**, William (1770-1850)
Nature poetry with humanitarian bent
*The Prelude* (comp. 1798-1805, pub. 1850)

**BYRON**, George Gordon, Lord (1788-1824)
The epic Romantic hero
*Childe Harold* (1812, 1816, 1817)
*Don Juan* (1819-24)

**AUSTEN**, Jane (1775-1817)
Delicate novels of manners
*Pride and Prejudice* (1813)
*Emma* (1816)

**SCOTT**, Walter (1771-1832)
Romantic historical novels
*Waverly* (1814)
*Heart of Midlothian* (1818)
*Ivanhoe* (1820)

**KEATS**, John (1795-1821)
Truth and beauty in sensuous poetry
*Endymion* (1818)
*Lamia, Isabella, The Eve of St. Agnes and other Poems* (1820)

**SHELLEY**, Percy Bysshe (1792-1822)
High idealism, high lyric poetry
*Prometheus Unbound* (1820)
*Adonais* (1821)

**COLERIDGE**, Samuel Taylor (1772-1834)
The great critic
*Biographia Literaria* (1817)

**CARLYLE**, Thomas (1795-1881)
Explosive criticism of the age
*Sartor Resartus* (1833-34)
*Heroes and Hero-Worship* (1841)

**DICKENS**, Charles (1812-70)
Humor and caricature of the early years
*Pickwick Papers* (1836)
*Oliver Twist* (1837-38)
*David Copperfield* (1849-50)

**TENNYSON**, Alfred, Lord (1809-92)
Earnest poet of faith and doubt
*Poems, Chiefly Lyrical* (1830)
*In Memoriam* (1850)

**BROWNING**, Robert (1812-89)
Psychological perception through the dramatic monologue
*Bells and Pomgranates* (1841-46)
*The Ring and the Book* (1868)

**THACKERAY**, William Makepeace (1811-63)
Satirical panorama of Victorian England
*Vanity Fair* (1846)
*Henry Esmond* (1852)

**THE BRONTËS**
Gloom and passions of the moors
Anne (1820-49), *Agnes Grey* (1847)
Charlotte (1816-55), *Jane Eyre* (1847)
Emily (1818-48), *Wuthering Heights* (1848)

**FITZGERALD**, Edward (1809-83)
Oriental mysticism in translation
*The Rubáiyát of Omar Khayyám* (1859)

**ARNOLD**, Matthew (1822-88)
Poet and critic of Victorian Society
*Essays in Criticism* (1865)
*Thyrsis* (1866)
*Culture and Anarchy* (1869)

**SWINBURNE**, Algernon Charles (1837-1909)
Shocking challenge to Victorian goodness
*Atalanta in Calydon* (1865)
*Poems and Ballads* (1866)

## AMERICA

**BRYANT**, William Cullen (1794-1878)
Nature and death in early American Romanticism
*Thanatopsis* (1817)
*Poems* (1821, 1832)

**COOPER**, James Fenimore (1789-1851)
Leatherstocking and other frontier tales
*The Pioneers* (1823)
*The Last of the Mohicans* (1826)
*The Prairie* (1827)
*The Deerslayer* (1841)

**POE**, Edgar Allan (1809-49)
Love, death and beauty in a new philosophy of composition
*Poems* (1831)
*Tales of the Grotesque and Arabesque* (1840)
*The Raven and Other Poems* (1845)
*Tales* (1845)

**EMERSON**, Ralph Waldo (1803-1882)
Transcendental philosophy in essay and poetry
*Nature* (1836)
*The American Scholar* (1837)
*Essays* (1841)

**WHITTIER**, John Greenleaf (1807-92)
Idyllic and humanitarian Romanticism
*Voices of Freedom* (1846)
*Snowbound* (1866)

**MELVILLE**, Herman (1819-91)
High adventure and struggle with Good and Evil
*Typee* (1846)
*Moby Dick* (1851)
*Billy Budd* (comp. 1888-91, pub. 1924)

**LOWELL**, James Russell (1819-1891)
Literary criticism and Yankee humor
*A Fable for Critics* (1848)
*Biglow Papers* (1846-48, 1967)

**HAWTHORNE**, Nathaniel (1804-64)
Allegory and symbolism, the "power of blackness"
*Mosses from an Old Manse* (1846)
*The Scarlet Letter* (1850)
*The House of the Seven Gables* (1851)

**THOREAU**, Henry David (1817-62)
A voice of independence in the wilderness
*A Week on the Concord and Merrimac Rivers* (1849)
*Civil Disobedience* (1849)
*Walden* (1854)

**LONGFELLOW**, Henry Wadsworth (1807-82)
German Romanticism in American legend
*Song of Hiawatha* (1855)
*The Courtship of Miles Standish* (1858)
*Tales of a Wayside Inn* (1863)

**WHITMAN**, Walt (1819-92)
Free verse and the Romantic dream of a nation
*Leaves of Grass* (1855-92 — 9 editions)

**HOLMES**, Oliver Wendell (1809-94)
Unitarian enlightenment *vs.* the old Puritanism
*The Autocrat of the Breakfast-Table* (1858)
*Elsie Venner* (1861)

## CONTINENTAL EUROPE

**HöLDERLIN**, Friedrich [Ger.] (1770-1843)
Hellenic Romanticism
*Hyperion* (1799)

**NOVALIS** [Ger.] (1772-1801)
Mystical Romantic symbolism
*Hymns to the Night* (1800)

**CHATEAUBRIAND**, François René de [Fr.] (1768-1848)
The Christian Romantic hero
*Atala* (1801)
*René* (1802)

**SCHILLER**, Friedrich von [Ger.] (1759-1805)
Great German drama and legend
*Don Carlos* (1787)
*Wallenstein* (1800)
*William Tell* (1805)

**HOFFMAN**, E.T.A. [Ger.] (1776-1822)
"Black" Romanticism
*The Devil's Elixir* (1815)
*Kater Murr* (1820-22)

**LAMARTINE**, Alphonse de [Fr.] (1790-1869)
New freedom for poetry
*Poetic Meditations* (1820)
*Poetic and Religious Harmonies* (1830)

**LEOPARDI**, Conte Giacomo [It.] (1798-1837)
Romantic pessimism in classical forms
*Versi* (1826)
*Canti* (1831)

**STENDHAL** [Fr.] (1783-1842)
Early psychological novel
*The Red and the Black* (1830)
*The Charterhouse of Parma* (1839)

**HEINE**, Heinrich [Ger.] (1797-1856)
Romantic folk poetry
*Book of Songs* (1827)

**PUSHKIN**, Alexander [Rus.] (1799-1837)
Byronic novel in verse
*Eugene Onegin* (1831)

**HUGO**, Victor [Fr.] (1802-1885)
Humanitarian and melodramatic Romanticism
*Hernandi* (1830)
*Notre Dame de Paris* (1831)
*Songs of Twilight* (1835)
*Les Misérables* (1862)

## REALISM AND NATURALISM — 1860-1900

### ENGLAND

**DICKENS, Charles (1812-70)**
A more serious view of Victorian England, the later novels
*Bleak House* (1852-53)
*Hard Times* (1854)
*Great Expectations* (1860-61)
*Our Mutual Friend* (1864-65)

**ELIOT, George (1819-80)**
Morality and moralisms in realistic fiction
*Adam Bede* (1859)
*The Mill on the Floss* (1860)
*Silas Marner* (1861)
*Middlemarch* (1872)
*Daniel Deronda* (1876)

**MEREDITH, George (1829-1909)**
Sophisticated psychology and social realism
*The Ordeal of Richard Feverel* (1859)
*Modern Love* (1862)
*The Egoist* (1879)

**CARROLL, Lewis (1832-98)**
Signs of surrealism
*Alice's Adventures in Wonderland* (1865)
*Through the Looking-Glass* (1871)

**BUTLER, Samuel (1835-1902)**
Sharpest critic of Victorian smugness
*Erewhon* (1872)
*The Way of All Flesh* (1903)

**HARDY, Thomas (1840-1928)**
Bleak realism in a malevolent universe
*The Return of the Native* (1878)
*The Mayor of Casterbridge* (1886)
*Tess of the D'Urbervilles* (1891)
*Jude the Obscure* (1896)
*Wessex Poems* (1898)
*The Dynasts* (1903, 1906, 1908)

**STEVENSON, Robert Louis (1850-94)**
Romance, adventure and psychological insight
*Treasure Island* (1883)
*Kidnapped* (1886)
*Dr. Jekyll and Mr. Hyde* (1886)
*The Master of Ballantree* (1889)
*Weir of Hermiston* (uncompleted at death)

**KIPLING, Rudyard (1865-1936)**
The voice of English imperialism
*The Light that Failed* (1890)
*Barrack-Room Ballads* (1892)
*The Jungle Books* (1894, 1895)
*Kim* (1901)

**GISSING, George (1857-1903)**
The realism of poverty
*New Grub Street* (1891)
*The Private Papers of Henry Ryecroft* (1903)

**WILDE, Oscar (1854-1900)**
Versatile eccentric and wit of the Decadents
*The Picture of Dorian Gray* (1891)
*The Importance of Being Earnest* (1895)
*The Ballad of Reading Gaol* (1898)
*De Profundis* (1905)

**MOORE, George (1852-1933)**
French naturalism in England
*Esther Waters* (1894)
*Evelyn Innes* (1898)

### AMERICA

**TWAIN, Mark (1835-1910)**
Adventure, humor and tragedy on the American frontier
*Roughing It* (1872)
*Tom Sawyer* (1876)
*Life on the Mississippi* (1882)
*Huckleberry Finn* (1884)
*The Man that Corrupted Hadleyburg* (1900)
*The Mysterious Stranger* (1916)

**JAMES, Henry (1843-1916)**
Subtle master of style and characterization
*The American* (1877)
*The Europeans* (1878)
*Daisy Miller* (1879)
*The Portrait of a Lady* (1881)
*The Turn of the Screw* (1898)
*The Ambassadors* (1903)
*The Golden Bowl* (1904)

**HOWELLS, William Dean (1837-1920)**
Realism in theory and practice
*A Modern Instance* (1882)
*The Rise of Silas Lapham* (1885)
*A Hazard of New Fortunes* (1890)
*My Literary Passions* (1895)

**DICKINSON, Emily (1830-86)**
Poetess of paradox, metaphor and melody
Several collections of her poetry published posthumously

**BELLAMY, Edward (1850-98)**
Socialist Utopian dream for America
*Looking Backward* (1888)

**GARLAND, Hamlin (1860-1940)**
Hard life on the prairies
*Main-Travelled Roads* (1891)
*A Son of the Middle Border* (1917)

**CRANE, Stephen (1871-1900)**
The irony of war and nature
*Maggie: A Girl of the Streets* (1893)
*The Red Badge of Courage* (1895)
*The Open Boat* (1898)
*War is Kind* (1899)

**NORRIS, Frank (1870-1902)**
Naturalism of social realities
*McTeague* (1899)
*The Octopus* (1901)
*The Pit* (1903)

**DREISER, Theodore (1871-1945)**
Relentless social and physiological naturalism
*Sister Carrie* (1900)
*Jennie Gerhardt* (1911)
*The Financier* (1912)
*An American Tragedy* (1925)

**SINCLAIR, Upton (1878- )**
Muckraking and Socialism in fiction
*The Jungle* (1916)

**LONDON, Jack (1876-1916)**
Primitive violence and prophetic Socialism
*The Call of the Wild* (1903)
*The Sea-Wolf* (1904)
*The War of the Classes* (1905)
*Martin Eden* (1909)

### CONTINENTAL EUROPE

**BALZAC, Honoré de [Fr.] (1799-1850)**
Lifelong view of the "Human Comedy"
*Eugénie Grandet* (1833)
*Old Goriot* (1834)

**TURGENEV, Ivan [Rus.] (1818-83)**
Russian realism attuned to the times
*A Sportsman's Sketches* (1852)
*Fathers and Sons* (1861)

**FLAUBERT, Gustave [Fr.] (1821-80)**
Objective focus on ordinary life
*Madame Bovary* (1857)
*Sentimental Education* (1869)

**DOSTOEVSKY, Fyodor [Rus.] (1821-81)**
Supreme psychoanalysis of the human soul
*Notes from Underground* (1864)
*Crime and Punishment* (1866)
*The Idiot* (1868)
*The Possessed* (1871-72)
*The Brothers Karamazov* (1880)

**TOLSTOY, Leo [Rus.] (1828-1910)**
Panorama of epic proportions
*War and Peace* (1865-69)
*Anna Karenina* (1875-77)
*The Resurrection* (1899)

**DAUDET, Alphonse [Fr.] (1840-97)**
Sympathetic naturalism
*Tartarin of Tarascon* (1872)
*The Nabob* (1877)

**ALARCÓN, Pedro Antonio [Sp.] (1833-91)**
Spanish local color
*The Three-Cornered Hat* (1874)

**PÉREZ GALDÓS, Benito [Sp.] (1843-1920)**
Romance and realism in historical fiction
*Doña Perfecta* (1876)
*Fortunata y Jacinta* (1886-87)

**ZOLA, Émile [Fr.] (1840-1902)**
Grim and pioneering naturalism
*L'Assommoir* (1877)
*Nana* (1880)
*The Experimental Novel* (1880)
*Germinal* (1885)

**MAUPASSANT, Guy de [Fr.] (1850-93)**
Realistic irony in short fiction
*A Life* (1883)
Numerous short stories

**IBSEN, Henrik [Norway] (1828-1906)**
Social realism in conventional drama
*A Doll's House* (1879)
*Ghosts* (1881)
*An Enemy of the People* (1882)
*The Wild Duck* (1884)
*Hedda Gabler* (1890)

**FRANCE, Anatole [Fr.] (1844-1924)**
The world through wit, irony and fantasy
*The Crime of Sylvestre Bonnart* (1881)
*Penguin Island* (1908)

**STRINDBERG, Johann August [Sweden] (1849-1912)**
Nietzschian pessimism in drama
*The Father* (1887)

**CHEKHOV, Anton [Rus.] (1860-1904)**
Russia in transition through stories and plays
*Uncle Vanya* (1899)
*Three Sisters* (1901)
*The Cherry Orchard* (1904)

## SYMBOLISTIC AND CONTEMPORARY LITERATURE — 1900-PRESENT

### ENGLAND

**HOPKINS, Gerard Manley (1844-89)**
God's grandeur in striking new poetry
Various poems, none published in his lifetime

**YEATS, William Butler (1865-1939)**
From the *Celtic Twilight* (1893) to the beauty of Byzantium
*The Land of Heart's Desire* (1894)
*The Wild Swans of Coole* (1919)
*The Tower* (1928)

**HOUSMAN, A. E. (1859-1936)**
Poignant lyrics of the English countryside
*A Shropshire Lad* (1896)

**CONRAD, Joseph (1857-1924)**
Inner man and the open sea
*The Nigger of the "Narcissus"* (1898)
*Lord Jim* (1900)
*Nostromo* (1904)
*Victory* (1915)

**SHAW, George Bernard (1856-1950)**
Intellectual iconoclast of the theatre
*Man and Superman* (1903)
*Major Barbara* (1905)
*Pygmalion* (1912)
*Androcles and the Lion* (1913)

**FORSTER, E. M. (1879- )**
Urbane comedy of human relations
*Howard's End* (1910)
*Passage to India* (1924)

**LAWRENCE, D. H. (1885-1930)**
Sexuality in a sterile century
*Sons and Lovers* (1913)
*The Rainbow* (1915)
*Lady Chatterly's Lover* (1928)

**JOYCE, James (1882-1941)**
Artistry with language and "stream of consciousness"
*Dubliners* (1914)
*A Portrait of the Artist as a Young Man* (1916)
*Ulysses* (1922)
*Finnegan's Wake* (1939)

**MAUGHAM, W. Somerset (1874- )**
Modern classic autobiography
*Of Human Bondage* (1915)

**ELIOT, T. S. (1888-1965)**
Modern metaphor and ancient symbol
*The Sacred Wood* (1920)
*The Waste Land* (1922)
*Murder in the Cathedral* (1935)
*Four Quartets* (1944)
*The Cocktail Party* (1950)

**WOOLF, Virginia (1882-1941)**
The elusiveness of reality
*To the Lighthouse* (1927)
*Orlando* (1929)

**HUXLEY, Aldous (1894-1963)**
Frightful Utopia of the future
*Point Counter Point* (1928)
*Brave New World* (1932)

**THOMAS, Dylan (1914-53)**
Poetry for the ear, prose for the imagination
*Map of Love* (1939)
*The World I Breathe* (1939)
*Adventures in the Skin Trade* (1955)

**ORWELL, George (1903-50)**
Political allegory and satire
*Animal Farm* (1945)
*Nineteen Eighty-Four* (1949)
*Shooting an Elephant* (1950)

### AMERICA

**ROBINSON, Edward Arlington (1869-1935)**
Poignant portraits of personalities
*The Children of the Night* (1897)
*The Man Against the Sky* (1916)

**FROST, Robert (1874-1963)**
Restrained New England realism
*A Boy's Will* (1913)
*North of Boston* (1914)
*New Hampshire* (1923)
*A Further Range* (1936)

**SANDBURG, Carl (1878-1967)**
Songs and symbols of the American people
*Chicago Poems* (1916)
*Cornhuskers* (1918)
*The People, Yes* (1936)

**CATHER, Willa (1873-1947)**
Sympathetic portraits of the pioneer, the artist, and the man of God
*My Antonia* (1918)
*The Professor's House* (1925)
*Death Comes for the Archbishop* (1927)

**LEWIS, Sinclair (1885-1951)**
Satire of the American *Main Street* (1920)
*Babbitt* (1922) *Arrowsmith* (1925)

**O'NEILL, Eugene (1888-1953)**
Modern expressionism and Greek high tragedy
*The Hairy Ape* (1922)
*Strange Interlude* (1928)
*Mourning Becomes Electra* (1931)
*The Iceman Cometh* (1946)
*Long Day's Journey Into Night* (1956)

**FITZGERALD, F. Scott (1896-1940)**
Tragedy and cynicism of the "Jazz Age"
*The Great Gatsby* (1925)
*Tender Is the Night* (1934)

**HEMINGWAY, Ernest (1898-1961)**
Love and courage *vs.* war and violence
*The Sun Also Rises* (1926)
*A Farewell to Arms* (1929)
*For Whom the Bell Tolls* (1940)
*The Old Man and the Sea* (1952)

**FAULKNER, William (1897-1962)**
Universal saga of the American South
*The Sound and the Fury* (1929)
*As I Lay Dying* (1930)
*Light in August* (1932)
*Absalom, Absalom!* (1936)
*Go Down, Moses* (1942)

**WOLFE, Thomas (1900-1938)**
Intense and lyrical autobiographical romanticism
*Look Homeward, Angel* (1929)
*Of Time and the River* (1935)
*The Web and the Rock* (1936)
*You Can't Go Home Again* (1940)

**STEINBECK, John (1902- )**
Realism touched with sociology, symbol, and sentiment
*Tortilla Flat* (1935)
*In Dubious Battle* (1936)
*Of Mice and Men* (1937)
*The Grapes of Wrath* (1939)

**WILLIAMS, Tennessee (1914- )**
Sordid symbols of frustration
*The Glass Menagerie* (1945)
*A Streetcar Named Desire* (1947)
*Cat on a Hot Tin Roof* (1955)

### CONTINENTAL EUROPE

**BAUDELAIRE, Charles [Fr.] (1821-67)**
Forests of symbols in poetry
*Flowers of Evil* (1857)

**RIMBAUD, Arthur [Fr.] (1854-91)**
Brilliant kaleidoscope of metaphors
*A Season in Hell* (1883)
*Les Illuminations* (1886)

**MALLARMÉ, Stéphane [Fr.] (1842-98)**
The fruits of Poe in France
Collections of poems — 1887, 1899
*A Throw of the Dice* (1914)

**MAETERLINCK, Maurice (1862-1949)**
Belgian master of psychological symbolism
*Pelléas and Mélisande* (1892)
*The Life of the Bee* (1901)
*The Blue Bird* (1909)

**MANN, Thomas [Ger.] (1875-1955)**
Philosophical view of man in the modern world
*Buddenbrooks* (1901)
*Death in Venice* (1911)
*The Magic Mountain* (1924)

**GIDE, André [Fr.] (1869-1951)**
Literary life-long self-examination
*The Immoralist* (1902)
*The Pastoral Symphony* (1919)
*The Counterfeiters* (1925)

**RILKE, Ranier Maria [Ger.] (1875-1926)**
Mystical love of daily life
*Requium* (1909)
*Sonnets to Orphens* (1923)
*Diuno Elegies* (1923)

**PROUST, Marcel [Fr.] (1871-1922)**
The search for the meaning of time
*Remembrance of Things Past* (1913-27)

**KAFKA, Franz [Ger.] (1833-1924)**
Mystical view of the improbable and the bureaucratic
*The Trial* (1924)
*The Castle* (1926)
*America* (1927)
*The Metamorphosis* (1937)

**GARCIA LORCA, Federico [Sp.] (1899-1936)**
Literary soul of Spanish life
*Gipsy Ballads* (1928)
*Blood Wedding* (1935)
*The House of Bernarda Alba* (1935)
*Yerma* (1937)

**SARTRE, Jean Paul [Fr.] (1905- )**
Literary and philosophical purveyor of existentialism
*Nausea* (1938)
*The Wall* (1939)
*Being and Nothingness* (1943)
*No Exit* (1944)

**BRECHT, Bertold [Ger.] (1898-1956)**
Revolutionary dramatist and poet
*The Good Woman of Sezuan* (1938-40)
*The Caucasian Chalk Circle* (1943-45)

**CAMUS, Albert [Fr.] (1913-60)**
Literary philosopher of the absurd
*The Stranger* (1942)
*The Myth of Sisyphus* (1942)
*The Fall* (1957)
*The Plague* (1948)

# III
# *The Plays of William Shakespeare*

WILLIAM SHAKESPEARE (1564-1616) was born in Stratford-on-Avon where his father was a tanner and a councilman, where he went to grammar school, and where he married Anne Hathaway (1582) and had fathered three children.

He apprenticed, served, and invested in London's Globe and Blackfriars theaters until retirement to Stratford in 1612 and his subsequent death in 1616. The famous First Folio of his plays appeared in 1623.

Below appear, in summary form, all of the thirty-six plays of the First Folio (controversial *Pericles,* omitted then, is omitted here) with approximate dates of composition. Plays which appeared before the First Folio are indicated with an asterisk (*), and significant characters not named in the summaries themselves are added in parentheses, and are followed by the probable sources of the plays. A brief bibliography is included at the end of this section for further study.

## A. COMEDIES

**Comedy of Errors** (1591) — Two brothers named Antipholus, "the one so like the other as could not be distinguished," and their servants named Dromio, "male twins, both alike," are separated in infancy by a shipwreck. Bachelors Antipholus and Dromio of Syracus search for their brothers for five years before they enter Ephesus and meet two women who claim to be their wives and ask them home to food and bed. The ensuing "comedy of errors" has merchants, wives, and servants mistaking the brothers Antipholus until the confusion is cleared up and all are happily reunited. (Pinch) PLAUTUS.

**Two Gentlemen of Verona** (1591) — "He after honor hunts; I after love," says fickle Proteus about his constant friend Valentine. While Proteus woos Julia in Verona, Valentine serves in the Duke's court in Milan where he falls in love with the Duke's daughter Silvia. Soon Proteus too is ordered to Milan, and, after pledging eternal love to Julia, proceeds to the court where he also falls for Silvia, and subsequently reveals Valentine's elopement plans to the Duke. With Valentine banished from court and leading a group of outlaws in a nearby forest, Proteus bids openly for Silvia's hand with the help of a page named Sebastian, really Julia in disguise. Desperate, Silvia flees in search of Valentine but is caught by Proteus who tries to force his affections upon her. Caught by Valentine, Proteus begs forgiveness and receives it easily. The Duke's change of heart allows Valentine and Silvia to be reunited as Julia, her true identity disclosed, is joined with Proteus. (Speed, Launce, Crab, Lucetta) MONTEMAYOR.

**Love's Labour's Lost*** (1593) — "Our court shall be a little Academe," states Ferdinand, King of Navarre, as he pledges himself and his lords to three years' study and seclusion from the outside world. However, after the arrival of the Princess of France and her beautiful ladies, the courtly gentlemen attempt to woo secretly and provide comedy with their misguided love letters and poems. At the moment that love seems victorious, the ladies hastily depart to mourn the death of the King of France and thus suspend the fates of the lovesick courtiers for a year and a day. (Costard, Holofernes, Dull) UNKNOWN.

**A Midsummer Night's Dream*** (1594) — "The course of true love never did run smooth," sighs Lysander to his beloved Hermia after her father Egeus promises her to another, Demetrius. Athenian Duke Theseus supports Egeus' ruling, and Hermia and Lysander plan to meet secretly in the woods to elope. Helena tries to regain Demetrius' love by revealing Hermia's plans to him, but Demetrius sets out in search of the lovers instead. In honor of the Duke's marriage to Amazon queen Hippolyta, various tradesmen rehearse in the woods a play of which Peter Quince is the director and vain Nick Bottom is the star. In the woods, enchanted by fairies come from India to bless the royal wedding, fairy king Oberon and his mischievous Puck have "unsmooth love" join the fairy queen Titania and Bottom as well as Lysander and Demetrius to Helena. Once corrected, "The Lamentable Comedy of Pyramus and Thisby" is presented, and the fairy kingdom watches over the Duke's house until morning when all couples. including Hermia and Lysander, will be happily married. (Pease Hossoun, Flute, Snug, Starveling) OVID, CHAUCER, PLUTARCH.

**The Merchant of Venice*** (1594) — "A pound of flesh," demands Jewish moneylender Shylock of his Christian enemy Antonio if he fails to repay within three months a loan made for friend Bassanio. While Bassanio is at Belmont winning Portia by choosing from three chests the right one, Shylock's daughter Jessica flees Venice with her father's money and her Christian lover Lorenzo. Antonio's message about his ships' failures causes Bassanio to rush to court where Shylock refuses late payment of the money, ignores pleas of mercy, and demands flesh from around the heart. Portia, disguising herself as a lawyer, feigns to grant his request but then charges him with threatening the life of a Venetian citizen and orders him to give up his money to Jessica and become a Christian. (Nerissa, Launcelot, Gobbo) FIORENTINO, VARIOUS.

**The Taming of the Shrew** (1595) — "I am he born to tame you, Kate," vows Petruchio to the tempestuous older daughter of Baptista, rich merchant of Padua. When Petruchio agrees to wed Katharina, Baptista allows younger Bianca to receive suitors Gremio, Hortensio, and Lucentio who compete for Bianca before Lucentio wins out. On his wedding day, Petruchio arrives late at church dressed like a madman, swears throughout the service, and leaves town immediately with his wife without attending the reception. In Verona Petruchio tames Kate by torturing her with "kindness": her food is not good enough to eat, nor her bed to sleep in, nor her clothes to wear. For the sake of peace, Kate gives in completely. Back in Padua Kate amazes the henpecked husband of "gentle" Bianca by lecturing on the duties of a wife to her husband. (Grumio, Sly) ANON., *The Taming of a Shrew*.

**The Merry Wives of Windsor*** (1597) — "Briefly, I do mean to make love to Ford's wife," announces Sir John Falstaff as he writes identical love letters to the wives of Windsor gentlemen Ford and Page. The honest wives pretend encouragement, but plan revenge on the knight. Meanwhile, the Pages' daughter Anne is courted by Dr. Caius, Slender, and the well-favored Fenton. Falstaff's first visit to Mistress Ford ends in humiliation when the basket of dirty clothes in which he hides from Ford is dumped into a muddy ditch. The second time, he hides in the disguise of a woman whom Ford hates and is then beaten. The last humiliation, planned by both wives and husbands, results in Falstaff's being pinched and burned by "fairies" while Anne Page elopes with Fenton. (Quickly, Robin, Pistol, Shallow) UNKNOWN.

**Much Ado About Nothing*** (1599) — "In mine eye she is the sweetest lady that ever I look'd on," declares Claudio about Hero, daughter of the Duke of Messina. With his own wedding date set, Claudio successfully arranges for his friend Benedick and Hero's cousin Beatrice to fall in love. Don John seeks revenge on his brother Don Pedro, Prince of Arragon, by wrecking the marriage of Pedro's favorite, Claudio. After witnessing a clandestine meeting between Hero's maid and one of Don John's men, Claudio thinks Hero unfaithful and subsequently disgraces her at church. Hero's supporters hide her and report her death, which provokes Benedick to challenge Claudio to a duel. The crisis ends when Hero's presumed lover confesses the ruse, and Claudio agrees to marry one of Hero's cousins in order to gain forgiveness. Finally, Claudio and Hero are united in marriage, as are Benedick and Beatrice. (Dogberry, Verges) BANDELLO.

**As You Like It** (1600) — "Get you from our court," Rosalind is told by her uncle Frederick, usurper of her father's throne. Disguised as rural lad Ganymede and accompanied by her friend and cousin Celia, Rosalind travels to the Forest of Arden where her secret love Orlando has joined the followers of her exiled father, Duke Senior. Ganymede pretends to help Orlando purge himself of his foolish infatuation by having him make love to her as though she were Rosalind. Orlando is en route to such a meeting when he kills a lion and saves the life of his wicked brother Oliver who has actually come to kill Orlando. Remorseful, Oliver asks Ganymede's forgiveness for the delay and falls in love with Celia. The couples are married as Duke Senior regains his lands from the penitent Frederick. (Jaques, Audrey, Touchstone) LODGE.

**Twelfth Night; or, What You Will** (1600) — "Disguise, I see thou art a wickedness," moans the fair maiden Viola who, disguised as a lad and employed in Illyria by Duke Orsino as a messenger in his courtship of beautiful Olivia, finds herself in love with the Duke. Melancholic Malvolio, Olivia's steward, continually rails against the sloth of Olivia's uncle, Sir Toby Belch, and his hanger-on, Sir Andrew Aguecheek, until the knights trick the steward into humiliating circumstances and lock him up as mad. Viola's twin brother, Sebastian, presumed drowned in a shipwreck, appears in Illyria where he is mistaken for the King's page and married by Olivia. Confused and furious at first, the Duke readily marries Viola after she sheds her disguise and professes her love. (Maria, Feste) BANDELLO.

**All's Well That Ends Well** (1602) — "Our remedies oft in ourselves do lie, / Which we ascribe to heaven," muses Helena, secret admirer of young count Bertram. When Bertram departs for the King's court, Helena follows administering to the sick King a cure inherited from her father. Once well, the King gives Helena a ring and grants her Bertram for a husband. Bertram sends low-born Helena to his mother, flees to Florence, and promises to be "husband" when she can get his ring and bear his child, both improbable. Seeing a remedy, Helena travels to Florence, changes places with a local maiden in Bertram's bed, and switches rings. Believing Helena dead, Bertram returns home where the King sees Helena's ring and demands an explanation. Helena appears, confesses the plot, and, by her devotion, gains Bertram as a true husband. (Parolles) BOCCACCIO.

**Measure for Measure** (1604) — "Lord Angelo is precise," says the Duke of Vienna of the man ruling in his absence. To observe Angelo's justice, the Duke disguises himself as Friar Ludovick and returns among his people just as Angelo revives capital punishment for fornication. Unable to marry his beloved, young Claudio is unjustly seized and sentenced to immediate execution. His sister Isabella leaves her nunnery to plead for mercy from Angelo who offers her "brother" for "honor." Indignant, Isabella refuses but, at Ludovick's direction, consents and is replaced by Mariana, once betrothed to Angelo. Afterwards, Angelo orders Claudio's head and, unknown to him, receives another's. On the Duke's "return," Angelo is forced to honor his marriage with Mariana, Claudio appears and marries his Juliet, and the Duke gains Isabella. (Lucio, Overdone, Elbow, Froth) WHETSTONE, CINTHIO.

**Cymbeline** (1610) — "I dare you to this match. Here's my ring," boasts British Posthumus, exiled in Italy and angered into betting on the constancy of his wife Imogen, daughter of British King Cymbeline. After Italian Iachimo returns from Britain, repelled by Imogen, he tricks Posthumus into believing the worst and gains the ring. Posthumus orders his wife killed, but, disguised as a boy, Fidele, she retreats to a wood where her "lost" brothers, hostages of the banished Belarius, are reared, and is forced to be page of Roman general Lucius as his army advances. Belarius and Posthumus join to free captive Cymbeline and defeat the Romans; after which the King favors Fidele and supports her question about enemy Iachimo's ring. Iachimo's answer provokes Posthumus to repent, Imogen to reveal her identity, and Belarius to return Cymbeline's sons. Cymbeline pardons everyone, and all are united in peace. (Cloten) HOLINSHED, BOCCACCIO.

**The Winter's Tale** (1611) — "To mingle friendship far, is mingling bloods," muses Leontes, King of Sicilia, jealous of his boyhood friend Polixenes, King of Bohemia, whom he wrongly suspects of seducing his wife Hermione. Leontes sends a servant to poison Polixenes (who aids his escape instead), imprisons Hermione, and, after her death is reported, sends her new babe to a foreign land. At sixteen, "Perdita," raised by a shepherd, elopes with her high-born lover while his father, Polixenes, follows them to Sicilia and ultimate reunion with Leontes, still in mourning for his wife. The marriage is sanctioned, and a statue of Hermione is given Leontes which reveals Hermione alive, hiding while awaiting Perdita's return. (Camillo) GREENE.

**The Tempest** (1612) — "Your reason for raising this sea-storm?" asks fair Miranda of her magician father Prospero who, with his sprite Ariel, has produced a tempest and caused a shipwreck. Prospero reveals the cause of their being exiled twelve years on an island deserted except for bestial Caliban, now a slave. Aided by the weak-willed King of Naples, Alonso, Antonio usurped the dukedom of his brother Prospero who, along with his daughter Miranda, was set adrift in an aged vessel. Now that Fate has brought Prospero the means of revenge, he makes a match between his daughter and Ferdinand, Alonso's son, while he scatters the rest of the survivors around the island. Ariel foils an attempt on Alonso's life, and Prospero intercepts Caliban's drunken advances against his own life, after which Antonio restores the Duke's rights. Ariel is then given his freedom, and all voyagers are reconciled for their trip home. (Sebastian, Gonzalo, Trinculo, Stephano) UNCERTAIN, MONTAIGNE.

## B. HISTORIES

**Henry VI, Part 1** (1592) — "The Dauphine crowned king," reports a messenger from France as Henry V is buried. Complicating defense of French possessions is the quarreling between Gloucester and Winchester, between the Lancaster "Red Rose" and York "White Rose" factions. Joan of Arc takes and loses Orleans, regains Burgundy's force, but dies at the stake betrayed by her own people. Richard Plantagenet presses his claim to the throne after dying Mortimer reveals his father no traitor and is named Duke of York. Childlike Henry VI goes to France for coronation and elevates brave Talbot, victor over Joan at Rouen but victim of Burgundy at Bordeaux, inadequately supplied by the English factions. After Henry accepts a truce and promises to marry Armagnac's daughter, he is persuaded by crafty Suffolk of Lancaster to marry Margaret of Anjou instead. (Beaufort, Dauphine) HOLINSHED, HALLE.

**Henry VI, Part 2** (1592) — "We'll quickly hoise Duke Humphrey from his seat," resolve the enemies of the Lord Protector, Humphrey of Gloucester, critic of territorial concessions made to the French by Henry VI's marriage treaty. A conspiracy involving militantly ambitious Queen Margaret results in the exile of the Duchess of Gloucester while her husband, after resigning his office to follow her, is imprisoned and murdered. To appease Commons, the Queen's favorite Suffolk is exiled, later killed, to fulfill a prophecy. Having urged Jack Cade to agitate in London, York leads troops against an Irish rebellion and, subsequently, threatens rebellion in England unless Somerset is jailed. Later, forces of Lancaster fight and lose to those of York with the Duke's deformed son Richard killing Somerset. As the King and Queen flee to Parliament, York hastens in pursuit. (Beaufort, Eleanor, Richard) HOLINSHED.

**Henry VI, Part 3** (1592) — "Thou preferr'st thy life before thine honor," says Queen Margaret, the "she-wolf of France," to her weak husband, Henry VI, after he has agreed to will the throne to the Duke of York instead of his own son. An ensuing battle between the forces of York and Margaret ends in the Duke's death. Warwick deserts Henry and joins Edward and Richard, sons of York, to defeat the Queen and put Edward on the throne. While the deposed Henry is imprisoned in the Tower, King Edward marries the Lady Elizabeth Grey instead of the Lady Bona of France, causing Warwick and the French to join Margaret in restoring Henry to the throne temporarily. But the ineffectual Henry is soon in the Tower again while Margaret's forces are defeated by Edward at Tewkesbury, and her son slain. King Edward's brother, Richard, Duke of Gloucester, his eye on the throne, kills Henry in the Tower. Edward and Elizabeth reign while Richard, meaning "all harm," falsely pledges his loyalty. (Edward, Prince of Wales) *True Tragedy of Richard, Duke of York.*

**Richard III*** (1593)—"I am determined to prove a villain," declares the deformed Richard, Duke of Gloucester, as he suggests his plot to secure the throne. By manipulating his brother, the sickly King Edward IV, Richard causes the death of his other, the Duke of Clarence. Edward IV dies; Richard cleverly sends the Crown Prince and his brother to the Tower to await coronation, while he dispatches an aide to persuade the people that he should be king. As King, Richard murders the young princes and plans to kill his wife in order to marry his niece Elizabeth, sought by the Lancastrian Earl of Richmond. When Richmond's forces march on London, Richard is slain, Richmond accepts the crown, plans to wed Elizabeth and to join forever the houses of Lancaster and York. HOLINSHED.

**Richard II*** (1595) — "You pluck a thousand dangers on your head," the Duke of York warns as heedless King Richard confiscates the lands of dying John of Gaunt and departs for Ireland. Gaunt's son and heir Henry Bolingbroke, exiled for a quarrel with the Duke of Norfolk, seeks redress by invading England, and, on the King's return, seizing Richard at Flint, forcing abdication of his crown, and ordering him imprisoned in Pomfret Castle while his Queen is ordered to France. Loyal York foils his son Aumerle's plot against Henry IV, and Sir Pierce, hoping to please his King, murders Richard and is banished by Henry who pledges a Holy Land pilgrimage to gain forgiveness. (Mowbray, Hotspur) HOLINSHED.

**King John** (1596) — "I am not worth this coil that's made for me," protests young Arthur, pretender to the English throne, as the French and English fight over his claim. The armies battle to a stand-off and conclude peace with the marriage of the French Dauphine Philip to King John's niece Blanch, but fighting is renewed when Rome orders France to support its spurned appointee to Canterbury. John yields and Rome forgives, but Philip continues to march on, this time claiming the English throne for himself. When Arthur is captured and accidentally killed, English nobles accuse John of murder and join the French armies; however, learning they are but pawns, the rebels return as John dies of poison, the Dauphine retreats, and Prince Henry prepares to ascend the throne. (Bastard Philip Faulconbridge, Elinor, Constance, Pandulph, Hubert) An earlier *King John.*

**Henry V*** (1599) — "We will in France play a set," vows Henry after receiving tennis balls from the Dauphine as an insulting reply to England's claim, by hereditary right from Edward III, to certain French dukedoms. A French assassination plot is uncovered, and, through irony, Hal has the traitorous lords pass their own execution sentences. Falstaff dies in London, and his comrades join the battles in France during which Nym and Bardolph, who "steal anything," are hanged, and frightened Pistol decides to return to England. The French town of Harfleur falls to the English, and Hal, after going disguised among his weary but valiant men, leads his troops to fight the larger French armies at Agincourt, a well-led and decisive

English victory. The defeated French king gives his daughter Katherine to Hal and the union yields Henry VI, king of France and England. HOLINSHED.

**Henry IV, Part 2*** (1598) — "Uneasy lies the head that wears a crown," sighs sleepless Henry IV as Mowbray, Hastings, and the Archbishop of York combine armies against the throne. Pressed with debts and charged with recruiting soldiers, Falstaff examines the men that Justices Shallow and Silence present and picks the ones who fail to bribe him. On the battlefield, Prince John deceives the rebel leaders into dismissing their troops and surrendering and, contrary to his promise, orders them executed. Prince Hal visits the dying king, dreads the anxiety a crown entails, and promises his father to mend his ways. During the coronation, Falstaff's familiar greetings incense Henry V who orders his old friends banished. (Pistol, Poins, Quickly) HOLINSHED.

**Henry IV, Part 1*** (1598) — "I will not send them," replies Henry Percy, called Hotspur, to the King's demand for prisoners gained in recent wars. The ensuing battle aligns Percy, Douglas, and others against Henry's forces, including recreant Prince Hal, the Prince of Wales, and his epicurean friend Falstaff with whom Hal has been carousing and accosting travelers on the king's highway. Although killed by Hal, Hotspur is claimed by coward Falstaff as Henry pursues the remaining rebel forces. (Quickly, Glendower, Archibald) HOLINSHED.

**Henry VIII** (1613) — "I have been to you a true and humble wife, / At all times to your will conformable," says Queen Katherine to King Henry when she is brought to a public divorce trial. Cardinal Wolsey, the conniving churchman fresh from his false accusation and subsequent execution of the noble Duke of Buckingham, tries the faithful Katherine, once the widow of the King's brother, but then opposes the King's marriage to Anne Bullen (Boleyn), a Protestant. Wolsey's power wanes as the King discovers his great wealth, and he dies while under the sentence of treason. The King's marriage to Anne Bullen precedes the death of the rejected Katherine, whose marriage to Henry has been annulled by Archbishop Cranmer. Though accused as a heretic, Cranmer is defended by King Henry, and then made godfather of the newborn Princess Elizabeth. (Cromwell, porter and his man) HOLINSHED.

## C. TRAGEDIES

**Titus Andronicus*** (1593) — "Andronicus, stain not thy tomb with blood," warns Tamora, captive Queen of the defeated Goths, as Roman general Titus sacrifices her eldest son in honor of his own dead. After Titus' daughter Lavinia marries Bassianus instead of the Emperor Saturninus, Tamora becomes Empress and is empowered to gain revenge. Through the designs of Tamora and her lover Aaron, the Moor who fathers the child she later bears, Bassianus is killed, Lavinia is raped and mutilated, two of Titus' sons are executed, and Titus himself is duped into cutting off a hand. Titus feigns madness while his last son Lucius raises in exile an army which, upon advance, prompts Saturninus and Tamora to seek a parley at Titus' house. Titus kills Tamora's sons, serves them as a dish for the royal couple, kills Lavinia to end her shame, and stabs Tamora. Saturninus kills Titus, but is killed by Lucius who then becomes Emperor and executes Aaron. LEGENDARY.

**Romeo and Juliet*** (1596) — "For never was a story of more woe/ Than this of Juliet and her Romeo," fateful lovers from the warring houses of Montague and Capulet. Romeo Montague meets Juliet Capulet at a ball and falls in love at once. After professing love in Juliet's garden, they decide to marry, going the next morning to Friar Laurence for the ceremony. Soon, new fighting occurs and Romeo's friend Mercutio is killed by Juliet's cousin Tybalt who is then killed by Romeo, subsequently banished for his crime. Juliet, desperate for help, plans at the Friar's insistence to take a potion which will cause a death-like state from which Romeo can rescue her. Romeo fails to receive word of the plan, and, hearing of Juliet's death, he visits the tomb and kills himself. Juliet awakens, sees Romeo dead, and kills herself. Racked with remorse, the families reconcile through their common grief. (Nurse) BROOKE, *Tragical History*.

**Julius Caesar** (1599) — "He doth bestride the narrow world like a Colossus," says envious Cassius to noble Brutus about Roman hero Julius Caesar. During the victory celebration, Caesar refuses the crown three times prior to falling into a fit. Caesar belittles his wife's fears and a soothsayer's warnings before going to the capital on the "Ides of March" where Brutus, won to the "good" of Rome, joins Caesar's assassins. "Et tu, Brute?" asks dying Caesar, to whose later funeral, held by the murderers to defend their motives, Mark Antony speaks ironically of the "honorable" conspirators and plies the crowd with tears and teases them with Caesar's "will." In the ensuing civil war, Cassius mistakes Brutus' capture and commits suicide, victor Brutus is overwhelmed and kills himself, and is proclaimed by Antony as "the noblest Roman of them all." (Calphurnia, Portia, Octavius) PLUTARCH.

**Hamlet*** (1600) — "Revenge this foul and unnatural death," Prince Hamlet is ordered by the ghost of his father, the slain Danish king whose murderous brother Claudius marries his widow and takes his throne. Feigning madness while awaiting his opportunity, Hamlet misleads crafty courtesan Polonius into mistaking love for his daughter Ophelia as the cause of the Prince's frenzy. Hamlet enlists the services of itinerant actors to recreate the poisoning scene and, with friend Horatio, notes Claudius' reaction to the portrayal. Queen Gertrude calls Hamlet to her room where he rashly stabs eavesdropper Polonious and subsequently causes Ophelia, mad from grief, to drown herself. Claudius' attempts to remove Hamlet to England fail, and he plots with Polonius' son Laertes to fence with Hamlet and wound him with a poisoned foil. In the fray, Hamlet is mortally wounded, Laertes and Claudius are killed, and Gertrude dies drinking a cup of poison intended for her son. (Rosencrantz, Guildenstern) *Historica Danica*, KYD'S *Hamlet* (?)

**Troilus and Cressida*** (1602) — "Men prize the thing ungained more than it is," says young Cressida who pretends indifference to her uncle Pandarus' proposal to match her with Troilus, youngest son of King Priam of Troy. Outside the city walls, Greek Ulysses complains to his generals of a lack of unified effort in sustaining their eight-year seige to regain Greek Helena from her abductor Paris. When the Trojan champion Hector challenges to single combat the best Greek, Ulysses tries to arouse lazy, vain Achilles to arms by choosing Ajax. The plan fails, and, Hector, surprised by the choice of Ajax, calls a truce. Deep in love, Cressida promises eternal fidelity to Troilus before being sent to the Greek camp where she joins her father and takes a new lover, Diomedes. In a final battle, Achilles' best friend is killed by Hector who, while unarmed, is killed by Achilles, his body being dragged away by Achilles' horse. Troilus leaves the stage cursing Pandarus who then delivers an epilogue. (Agamemnon, Menelaus, Thersites, Andromache, Cassandra, Aeneas) CHAUCER, LYDGATE.

**Othello*** (1604) — "My life upon her faith," replies Venetian moor and general Othello to the charge of "deceit" made by Brabantio, irate father of his bride Desdemona. After swearing her elopement was not an abduction, Desdemona is entrusted to the care of "honest Iago" while Othello rushes to defend Cyprus from a Turk invasion which is soon ended by a storm. Iago, insulted by Othello's preference of Cassio for top lieutenant, plots revenge and enlists the aid of foolish Roderigo in disgracing Cassio and making Othello jealous. Roderigo's brawl with Cassio gains the first objective, and Desdemona's handkerchief, got by unsuspecting Emilia and placed by her husband Iago in Cassio's possession, gains the second. Obsessed by "the green-eyed monster," Othello kills his wife, murders himself, and leaves Iago, murderer of his own wife, to be punished for his treachery. (Bianca) CINTHIO.

**King Lear*** (1606) — "Thy truth, then, be thy dower," decrees King Lear to his loving daughter Cordelia who refuses to follow her sisters in improvidently flattering their father. The Earl of Kent is banished for defending Cordelia, and the King of France accepts the disinherited for his wife as Lear leaves his kingdom divided between his "true" daughters Goneril and Regan. Suddenly stripped of his remaining rights, Lear goes mad from the knowledge of his error and wanders out in a storm accompanied by his fool where he rails against the ingratitude of children. Aided by Goneril and Regan, Edmund causes his father, the Earl of Gloucester, to be blinded for aiding Lear. Kent sends Lear to Cordelia's care in Dover while Gloucester's true son Edgar tends his father. Victorious over the invading French, Edmund executes Cordelia and causes Lear to die of grief. With Gloucester dead, Regan killed by Goneril who commits suicide, and Edmund executed; Edgar and faithful Kent rebuild England. (Oswald) GEOFFREY OF MONMOUTH, HOLINSHED.

**Macbeth** (1606) — "Fair is foul, and foul is fair," chant the witches who greet King Duncan's victorious generals Banquo and Macbeth. Amazed by the prophecies that he is to be "thane of Cawdor" and "king hereafter," Macbeth travels to Duncan and finds the first prophecy come true. Lady Macbeth presses her husband to make the second true by killing Duncan during his imminent visit, but she finds Macbeth reluctant ("too full o' the milk of human kindness"). But after he murders Duncan, Banquo, and the wife and child of Macduff, Macbeth fills well the role of tyrant while Lady Macbeth goes mad from the sins of too much blood. Another visit to the witches assures Macbeth "none of woman born" shall harm him, and he returns home satisfied he is safe. After Lady Macbeth's suicide, Macbeth resolutely faces Macduff, "born" by Caesarian, and meets his death. Duncan's son Malcolm succeeds as King of Scotland. (Hecate, porter, Fleance, Siward) HOLINSHED.

**Timon of Athens** (1607) — "I wonder men dare

trust themselves with men," remarks misanthrope Apemantus as flattering opportunists surround wealthy, gullible Timon of Athens and divide his dwindling fortunes. Once bankrupt, Timon confidently but futilely requests loans from his "friends" whom he subsequently invites to one last feast and serves water to the ingrates. Cursing all men, particularly Athenians, Timon retreats to a cave where he accidentally finds gold which he gives to thieves to further their profession and to a dissident general to destroy Athens. The resulting attack frightens Athenian senators who, seeking Timon's military leadership, are told to hang themselves. The general is appeased as Timon dies cursing mankind with his epitaph. (Flavius, Alcibiades) PLUTARCH.

**Antony and Cleopatra** (1607) — "I see men's judgments are a parcel of their fortunes," says Enobarbus about his friend and general Antony who, torn between reason and passion for Cleopatra, realizes he is losing respect and position in Rome. Antony effects a reconciliation with his fellow rulers Lepidus and Octavius and marries the latter's sister to stabilize the situation. Cleopatra is enraged but, assured of the unattractiveness of Antony's wife, knows he will return. The situation degenerates into battle between Antony and Octavius at Actium. Losing this battle and another in Egypt, Antony returns to Rome, and Cleopatra attempts to lure him back with word that she is dead. In grief, Antony slays himself. Facing imprisonment or capitulation to Octavius, Cleopatra also dies by her own design. Even Octavius recognizes the essential nobility of the two as he eulogizes, "No grave on earth shall clip in it a pair so famous." (Dolabella, Pompey, Octavia) PLUTARCH.

**Coriolanus** (1608) — "Was ever man so proud as this Marcius," complain jealous Roman tribunes Sicinius and Junius Brutus about the general commanding troops against the city of Corioli and its warrior Aufidius. Corioli is taken, Aufidius is routed, and modest Marcius is hailed "Coriolanus" for his bravery. In Rome Coriolanus is elected Consul, but Sicinius and Brutus arouse the plebeians to protest the election and thus enable Coriolanus' outspoken contempt for the rabble to earn him banishment. Merging with his archenemy Aufidius, Marcius subdues Rome, grants the mercy begged by his family, and returns to Corioli where Aufidius accuses Marcius of treason and plots his assassination. Marcius' pride offends many who recall his invasion, and the Roman is killed. Aufidius, repentant, mourns the noble soldier and helps bear away the body. (Menenius) PLUTARCH.

**SELECTED BIBLIOGRAPHY**

BRADLEY, A. C. *Shakespearian Tragedy*. New York: Macmillan, 1904.

CHAMBERS, EDMUND K. *William Shakespeare*. 2 vols. London: Oxford, 1930 (abridgement by Charles Williams, 1933).

CHARLTON, H. B. *Shakespearian Comedy*. New York: Macmillan, 1938.

GRANVILLE-BARKER, HARLEY, and G. B. HARRISON, eds. *A Companion to Shakespeare Studies*. New York: Macmillan, 1934.

ONIONS, C. T., ed. *A Shakespeare Glossary*. London: Oxford, 1919.

TILLYARD, E. M. W. *Shakespeare's History Plays*. New York: Macmillan, 1946.

WILSON, J. DOVER. *The Essential Shakespeare*. Cambridge: The University, 1930.

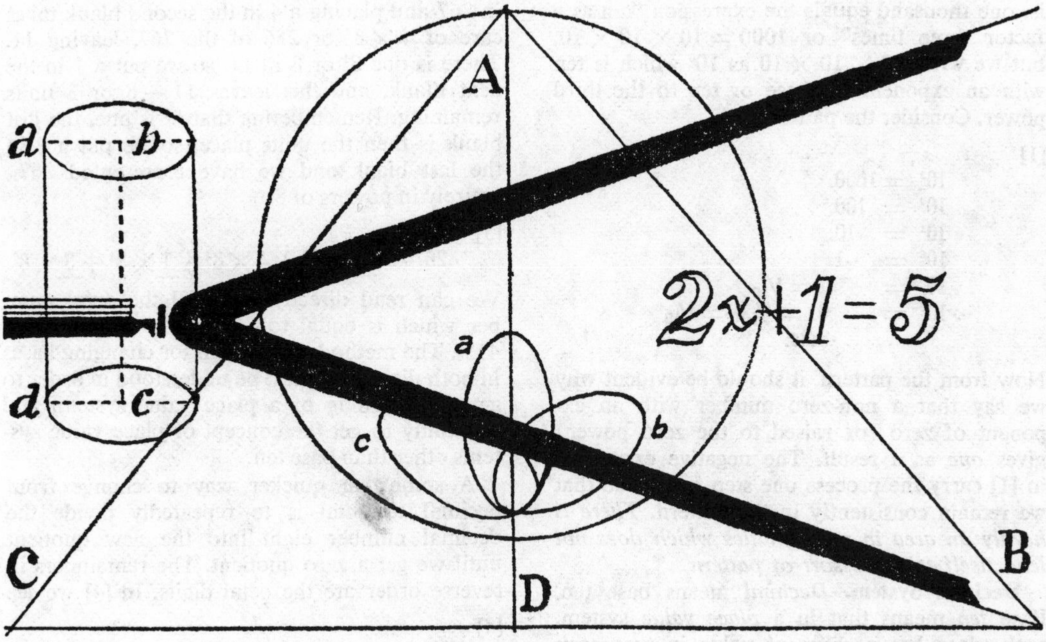


# Mathematics

## *Arithmetic*

### INTEGERS

**Numbers, Numerals.** A *number* is an idea. As such, it cannot be defined, seen, written, or otherwise sensed. The group of stars that form the Big Dipper and the group of days that form a week have nothing more in common than the *idea* of the *number* seven.

A *numeral* is that which represents or symbolizes a number. The number seven can be symbolized by either of these numerals: 7, VII, seven, and of course many others. In application, we manipulate these numerals in order to solve problems in arithmetic.

A *whole number* is a counting number, or natural number, and may be zero. Thus the whole numbers are: 0, 1, 2, 3, . . . , where the ". . ." means "continued in the same pattern indefinitely."

An *integer* is a whole number or its negative. In symbols, the integers can be represented as . . . — 3, — 2, — 1, 0, 1, 2, 3, . . . . The integers one and negative one are called *units.*

**Factors, Primes, Composites.** *Factors* of a number are numbers whose product gives the number. Six and five are factors of thirty. A number is *prime* if its *only* positive factors are itself and one. Two, three, and five are the *prime factors* of thirty. The prime factors of a number are important in many applications. A *composite* number is an integer which is not zero, not a unit, and not a prime number or its negative. Thus all integers can be classified into one of the four categories: units, zero, primes, or composites.

**Exponents, Powers.** An *exponent* of a number is a number which tells how many times the number is used as a factor in an expression. That

JOE MACK THWEATT, *Assistant Professor of Mathematics,* Middle Tennessee State University; B. A. David Lipscomb; M. A. Middle Tennessee.

is, one thousand equals the expression "ten as a factor three times" or $1000 = 10 \times 10 \times 10$, but we write $10 \times 10 \times 10$ as $10^3$ which is ten with an exponent of three or ten to the third power. Consider the pattern:

[1]

$$\begin{aligned} 10^3 &= 1000. \\ 10^2 &= 100. \\ 10^1 &= 10. \\ 10^0 &= 1. \\ 10^{-1} &= .1 = 1/10 \\ 10^{-2} &= .01 = 1/100 = 1/10^2 \\ &\text{etc.} \end{aligned}$$

Now from the pattern, it should be evident why we say that a non-zero number with an exponent of zero (or raised to the zero power) gives *one* as a result. The negative exponents in [1] carry the process one step further so that we remain consistently in the pattern. *There is hardly an area in mathematics which does not lend itself to some sort of pattern.*

**Decimal System.** *Decimal* means base ten. Base *ten* means that in a *place value* system, each place has a different value in that each represents a multiplier (or coefficient) of some different exponent or power of ten. The power of ten increases by one for each place value reading from right to left. In the number 264, the 2, 6, and 4 are coefficients of: ten to the second power, ten to the first power and ten to the zero power, respectively. That is:

$$264 = 200 + 60 + 4 = 2 \times 10^2 + 6 \times 10^1 + 4 \times 10^0.$$

**Octal System.** The *octal system* means base eight. So here we deal in powers of *eight* instead of ten. The base of a number is usually indicated by appropriate small characters in the lower right corner. The base ten number 139 can be represented as $139_{10}$. Furthermore, $139_{10}$ will be shown to be the same as the base eight number $213_8$. To show this, expand the $213_8$ by using the meaning of place value in the *octal system.* That is:

$$213_8 = 2 \times 8^2 + 1 \times 8^1 + 3 \times 8^0 = 2 \times 64 + 1 \times 8 + 3 \times 1 = 128 + 8 + 3 = 139 = 139_{10}.$$

To change from octal to decimal then, we expand the octal number in powers of eight and add the results. From decimal to octal, the change is in the opposite sense. We look for multipliers of powers of eight which when added give us the decimal number. Consider the problem of changing $267_{10}$ to octal. It is a matter of filling in the blanks in [2].

[2]

$$267_{10} = \_ \times 8^3 + \_ \times 8^2 + \_ \times 8^1 + \_ \times 8^0.$$

Begin at the left and work to the right. There are how many $8^3$'s or 512's in 267? Of course there are none, so we place a 0 in the first blank. Then we see there are four $8^2$'s or 64's in 267 and placing a 4 in the second blank takes care of $4 \times 8^2$ or 256 of the 267, leaving 11. There is one $8^1$ or 8 in 11, so we put a 1 in the next blank, and this leaves $11 - 8$ or 3 units remaining. Remembering that $8^0$ is one, the last blank is then the units place, so we put a 3 in the last blank and we have represented $267_{10}$ entirely in powers of 8.

[3]

$$267_{10} = \underline{0} \times 8^3 + \underline{4} \times 8^2 + \underline{1} \times 8^1 + \underline{3} \times 8^0.$$

We can read directly from [3] the octal number which is equal to $267_{10}$; it is $0413_8$ or just $413_8$. The methods here given for changing bases in both directions must be understood in order to get the meaning of a place value system, and especially to get the concept of place value systems other than base ten.

A somewhat quicker way to change from decimal to octal is to repeatedly divide the decimal number eight into the new quotient until we get a zero quotient. The remainders in reverse order are the octal digits. In [4] we see

[4]

$$\begin{array}{r} 33 \\ 8\overline{)267} \\ \underline{24} \\ 27 \\ \underline{24} \\ 3 \end{array} \qquad \begin{array}{r} 4 \\ 8\overline{)33} \\ \underline{32} \\ 1 \end{array} \qquad \begin{array}{r} 0 \\ 8\overline{)4} \\ \underline{0} \\ 4 \end{array}$$

$267_{10}$ again being changed to octal to get $413_8$.

**Binary System, Conversion between Systems.** The *binary system* is the base two system. It is just like the octal only a 2 is used in place of 8. Then the base two number $1001_2$ in [5] should be $9_{10}$ in base ten.

[5]

$$1001_2 = 1 \times 2^3 + 0 \times 2^2 + 0 \times 2^1 + 1 \times 2^0 = 1 \times 8 + 0 \times 4 + 0 \times 2 + 1 \times 1 = 8 + 0 + 0 + 1 = 9_{10}$$

We change from base two to base ten in the same fashion as from octal to decimal.

RULE: *To change from another base to base ten, expand the other base number in powers of its base and add the results.*

RULE: *To change a decimal whole number to any other base, divide the new base repeatedly into the quotients and write the remainders in reverse order.*

(If fractions are involved, see *Decimal, Octal, Binary Fractions.*)

Counting to nine in base two would go: $1_2$, $10_2$, $11_2$, $100_2$, $101_2$, $110_2$, $111_2$, $1000_2$, $1001_2$. Note that there is no *digit* for 2 in base two; it is written "$10_2$". Similarly, in octal counting to nine we get: $1_8$, $2_8$, $3_8$, $4_8$, $5_8$, $6_8$, $7_8$, $10_8$, $11_8$. We have to use the 1 and 0 again to write $10_{10}$ for a ten in base ten. We write $10_8$ for an eight. *There is no single digit for ten in base ten.*

There is an interesting and very applicable relationship between octal and binary. (See

Computer Arithmetic.) Consider again the octal number $413_8$ which is the decimal number $267_{10}$. Changing $267_{10}$ to binary will get $100001011_2$. Notice that if we break $100001011_2$ into 100 001 011, we can read each octal digit directly from the corresponding group. $100_2$ is a $4_8$, $001_2$ is a $1_8$, and $011_2$ is a $3_8$. We can then bypass the decimal form if we change from octal to binary or vice versa.

RULE: *To change octal into binary, take each octal digit and write it as three binary digits.*

RULE: *To change binary into octal, break up the binary number in groups of three starting at the right and adding zeros on the left if necessary to complete the groups. Then convert each group of three binary digits into a single octal digit.* It is important to remember that we are dealing only with integers here.

The construction of the memory and circuitry of most computers makes the binary system indispensible. The memory cells, or cores, have two "states". In simplified terms, they are either on or off. As each binary digit is either a one or a zero, numbers are represented by a series of cores either on or off in the computer. In particular, this concept is illustrated by the series of lights in [6]. The lights are black if on and white if off. The *binary* number represented then is $10010_2$ which is $18_{10}$.

[6]

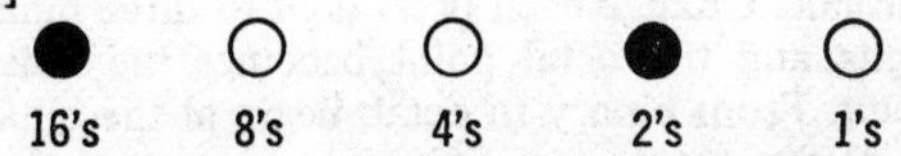


It takes 5 lights or cells to represent the number $18_{10}$ and thus a considerable amount of computer memory space must be devoted for storage of relatively small numbers. This inconvenience is greatly overcome by the sheer speed of the *computer operations on binary numbers* and by other means such as the *floating point.* (See *Computer Arithmetic, Scientific and Floating Notation.*)

Because it is easier even in computer circuits to change from octal to binary, numbers are often input to and output from the computer in octal rather than decimal.

## FRACTIONS

**Types of Fractions.** A *fraction* may be thought of as indicated division. Restricting ourselves momentarily to nonnegative numbers, we have four main types of fractions. A *proper fraction* is the quotient of two integers where the divisor, or denominator, is larger than the dividend, or numerator. The denominator must not be zero. An *improper fraction* can be represented as the quotient of two integers where the numerator is equal to or greater than the denominator. A *mixed number* is a type of fraction that can be represented as a whole number and (added to) a proper fraction. A *complex fraction* is generally the quotient of two fractions or a fraction made up of fractions. *Complicated* fractions could perhaps be a better name for *complex* fractions in that *complex* numbers (see *Sets of Numbers*) are not ordinarily involved.

**Fundamental Theorem of Arithmetic.** The fundamental theorem of arithmetic states in essence that every composite number can be expressed as a product of prime factors and that this collection of prime factors without regard to order is *unique*.

**Greatest Common Divisor.** The *greatest common divisor,* G.C.D., or *highest common factor,* H.C.F., of a collection of positive integers is the *largest* integer that will divide into *each* of the integers of the collection without remainder. It may be found by breaking each of the numbers in the collection into its prime factors. The G.C.D. is then the *product* of all *common factors* among the collection. If there is no common prime factor, then the G.C.D. is 1 and the numbers in the collection are said to be relatively prime. The number one is always a *common divisor,* but a larger number may be the G.C.D. (See [7].)

**Least Common Multiple.** The *least common multiple,* L.C.M., of a collection of positive integers is the *smallest* integer that *each element* of the collection will divide into without remainder. To find the L.C.M. we again factor the elements of the collection into prime factors as when finding the G.C.D., only here we put together the *product* of factors in which is found *all* the factors of *each* of the integers of the collection. The product of all the elements of the collection is certainly a *common multiple,* but it may not be the smallest number that will suffice. (See [7].)

[7]

| | | |
|---|---|---|
| COLLECTIONS: | 12, 18, 78 | 5, 14, 9 |
| FACTORS: | 2•2•3,2•3•3,2•3•13 | 5,2•7,3•3 |
| G.C.D.: | 2•3 = 6 | 1 |
| L.C.M.: | 2•2•3•3•13 = 468 | 5•2•7•3•3 = 630 |

**Equivalent Fractions.** Fractions are *equivalent* if they can be expressed so that they indicate the same quotient. We can re-express fractions by *multiplying* or *dividing* the numerators *and* denominators by the *same* non-zero number. Thus 2/3 is equivalent to 4/6 for we can multiply the 2 and the 3 each by 2 to get 4/6. We could have shown equivalence by dividing the 4 and 6 each by 2 to get 2/3.

A fraction is said to be *reduced to lowest terms* if we divide numerator and denominator by the G.C.D. of the numerator and denominator. Fractions are *equivalent* if they *reduce* to the same fraction. 18/24 and 12/16 are equivalent as they both reduce to 3/4.

A type of problem often given is to express 5/6 as an equivalent fraction with a denominator of 24. The solution is found by noticing that if we multiply the 6 by 4, we get 24; so to get an equivalent fraction, we must also multiply the 5 by 4 and we get 20/24.

To change a *mixed fraction* like 2 3/4 to an *improper fraction,* we multiply the 4 by the 2, then add the 3 to get 11. Putting the 11 over the 4 gives us the equivalent fraction, 11/4.

**Addition, Subtraction.** If two or more proper or improper fractions are to be added, we find the *L.C.M.* of their denominators and express each fraction as an *equivalent* fraction with the L.C.M. as the *new denominator.* Then we *add* the numerators and put the sum over the L.C.M. denominator. It is good practice to reduce this fraction to lowest terms.

To subtract one proper or improper fraction from another, we first, as in addition, find equivalent fractions with the L.C.M. denominators; then we subtract the numerators and try to reduce the resulting fraction.

Now if the fractions to be added or subtracted are mixed fractions, first express them as improper fractions; then proceed as before.

**Multiplication.** To *multiply fractions,* we simply multiply their *numerators* to get the *numerator* of the answer and *multiply denominators* to get the *denominator* of the answer. This answer should be simplified if possible.

**Division.** *To divide fractions,* we *multiply* the *reciprocal* of the *divisor* by the *dividend.* The reciprocal of X is Y if X•Y = 1. The division problem, $3/4 \div 7/12$, will be written as the multiplication problem, $3/4 \times 12/7$, using 12/7, the reciprocal of 7/12. The product is 36/28 which simplifies to 9/7. Some simplification could have been done prior to the multiplication by division of common factors. (See [8].)

[8]

$$\frac{3}{4} \div \frac{7}{12} = \frac{3}{\cancel{4}_{1}} \times \frac{\cancel{12}^{3}}{7} = \frac{9}{7}$$

**Decimal, Octal, Binary Fractions.** The number $129.67_{10}$ in expanded form is

$$1X100 + 2X10 + 9X1 + 6X.1 + 7X.01$$

which is also

$$1X10^2 + 2X10^1 + 9X10^0 + 6X10^{-1} + 7X10^{-2}$$

Note the use of negative exponents to handle the fractional parts of the decimal number. In the same manner, an octal number like $476.053_8$ in expanded form is

$$4X8^2 + 7X8^1 + 6X8^0 + 0X8^{-1} + 5X8^{-2} + 3X8^{-3}$$

which equals

$$4X64 + 7X8 + 6X1 + 0X^1/_8 + 5X^1/_{64} + 3X^1/_{512}$$

and when combined gives 318 $^{43}/_{512}$ as the base ten equivalent. The binary system is expanded in the same way with, of course, 2's in place of 8's in the expression.

RULE: *To change a proper fraction in decimal form to another base, multiply the fractional part by the new base to get a product. Multiply the fractional part of this product by the new base to get a new product, etc. The digits, zero or otherwise, that appear to the left of the decimal point are the digits of the fraction in the new base from left to right.*

Consider the examples: $.265625_{10}$ and $.99_{10}$ to be changed to octal. We repeatedly multiply by 8, as in [9], and in the solution

[9]

$$\begin{array}{r} .265625 \\ \times\ 8 \\ \hline 2.125000 \\ \times\ 8 \\ \hline 1.000000 \end{array} \qquad \begin{array}{r} .99 \\ \times\ 8 \\ \hline 7.92 \\ \times\ 8 \\ \hline 7.36 \end{array} \qquad \begin{array}{r} .36 \\ \times\ 8 \\ \hline 2.88 \\ \times\ 8 \\ \hline 7.04 \end{array}$$

we find .265625 in decimal equals .21 in octal. The zero fractional part indicates the conversion was complete and exact, i.e. without remainder. The decimal .99 is shown in [9] to be multiplied four times to get .7727 in octal. However, this is not exact because the .04 could still be multiplied by 8 to carry on the process and thus add more digits to .7727.

The change from octal to binary on the fractional side is the same as with the whole number side. Change each octal digit to three binary digits and the octal point becomes the binary point. From binary to octal, begin at the binary point separating the digits into groups of three adding zeros on each end if necessary. Change each group of three binary digits to one octal digit preserving the binary point for the octal point. For example, the octal number $2.703_8$ becomes $10.111000011_2$. The binary number $1101.11001_2$ will be separated to

001 101.110 010

and changed to octal as $15.62_8$.

**Computer Arithmetic.** The relationship just noted between octal and binary is utilized in most kinds of computers. Very often the instructions given by the programmer are coded in octal and the computer converts them to binary for storage. The computer later reads these instructions from storage and executes them.

Many computer instructions, or operations, are arithmetic in nature. The following binary *addition* operation is straightforward in that it closely resembles ordinary decimal addition. The computer's arithmetic unit basically adds only two numbers at a time, place by place, and so only one of the four cases in [10] will happen as each place or column is added. The last case

[10]

$$\begin{array}{r} 0 \\ +0 \\ \hline 0 \end{array} \qquad \begin{array}{r} 0 \\ +1 \\ \hline 1 \end{array} \qquad \begin{array}{r} 1 \\ +0 \\ \hline 1 \end{array} \qquad \begin{array}{r} 1 \\ +1 \\ \hline 10 \end{array}$$

presents the only problem in that a 1 must be carried or added to the left column. However, this problem is handled very easily in the arithmetic unit circuits.

The form of computer subtraction that is discussed here uses the one's *complement.* The six place one's complement of a binary number is the six place number made by exchanging ones for zeroes and vice versa. [11] shows the six place one's complement below three binary numbers.

| [11] | | | |
|---|---|---|---|
| | 101001 | 111000 | 11 |
| | 010110 | 000111 | 111100 |

Binary *subtraction* by use of one's complement in a six place system is as follows:

**1.** Make sure that the two numbers to be subtracted each have *six* places by adding zeroes if necessary.

**2.** Take one's complement of the lower number.

**3.** *Add* the one's complement binarily to the upper number.

**4.** If the sum carries a 1 into the *seventh* place on the left, go to step 5. Otherwise, go to step 6.

**5.** Drop the 1 from the seventh place and add 1 to the first place on the right. The result is the *answer* which is a *positive* binary number. (End of problem.)

**6.** Take one's complement of the six place sum and the result is the *answer* and it is a *negative* binary number. (End of problem.)

*Multiplication* of binary numbers can be done by repeated addition in the computer. Binary *division* is done usually by some form of repeated subtraction. *The two basic computer operations then are addition and complementation. All* of the *arithmetic operations* are derived from these.

## MEASUREMENT

**Definition, Error, Precision, Accuracy.** A *measurement* is a comparison with a standard. There are many kinds of standards to use, depending on how an item is to be measured. We have standards of length, weight, volume, and many others. However these standards are established by man and therefore are only relatively fixed and subject to change.

When measuring, as when measuring the length of an item with a ruler, we can be correct only to the smallest unit division on the ruler. For example, if the ruler is marked in *eighths* of an inch, then our result will be correct to the *nearest eighth* of an inch. We have to then *round* the answer we get to the nearest eighth of an inch. Thus we lose the exactness of the result by rounding. Now any comparison with any standard will call for rounding even if it appears to be exact, and the rounding causes an error. Therefore *no measurement is exact.* All measurements involve some kind of error. There are errors other than the roundoff error such as misreading the measuring instrument, using a faulty standard and many more.

Consider the roundoff error in particular. This one is necessary; the others are not. *The smallest unit of measure is called the precision.* That is, on a ruler which is marked in eighths of an inch, the precision is 1/8 inch. The roundoff error will be at *most* 1/16 of an inch. Thus *the greatest possible error (G.P.E.) is one-half of the precision of the measuring device.*

A greatest possible error of 1/16 inch in measuring a diamond would make more difference to a jeweler than a G.P.E. of 1/16 inch would make to a road builder constructing ten miles of highway. Thus we have the term *relative error,* which *is the G.P.E. divided by the measurement.* For example, if a measurement is made of a table length by a ruler marked in eighths of an inch and the result is $29\frac{3}{8}$ inches, then the relative error of the measurement is $\frac{1}{16} \div 29\frac{3}{8}$ or $\frac{1}{470}$. If we measure the diameter of a dime with the same ruler we would get 5/8 inch, to the nearest eighth. The relative error of this measurement is $\frac{1}{16} \div \frac{5}{8}$ or $\frac{1}{10}$ and is therefore greater than the table measurement. *The measurement with the least relative error is, by definition, the most accurate measurement.*

**Rounding Off, Significant Digits.** When a measurement is made and the result is to be recorded or when a number is to be rounded to a certain place, then the following rule applies: *To round off a number, consider the amount to be dropped. If it is greater than half, round up or increase the digit to be kept by one. If the amount to be dropped is less than half, leave the digit as is. If the amount to be dropped is exactly half, make the digit to be kept an even digit.*

In [12], the top row of numbers are rounded to the hundredths place and the results are placed beneath the numbers.

| [12] | | | | |
|---|---|---|---|---|
| 10.679 | 3.074 | 21.045 | 16.075 | 1 345001 |
| 10.68 | 3.07 | 21.04 | 16.08 | 1.35 |

In explanation, the results are: 10.68, the 9 is over half; 3.07, the 4 is less than half; 21.04 and 16.08, make the digit even if exactly halfway; 1.35, the 1 in 5001 makes it greater than a half.

Notice that the "make it even" rule rounds up half the time and down half the time. Thus in general, after many roundoffs, the accumulated error is approximately zero.

If a certain lot measured 120 feet to the nearest ten feet, it would be written just 120 feet. If it was 120 feet to the nearest foot, then it should be written $12\underline{0}$ feet. A 120 foot measurement to the nearest tenth of a foot should be written 120.0 feet. To show that a zero to the left of the decimal point is part of the actual measurement and not a result of rounding off, underline the zero. Note that in any case, at most one zero will be underlined. Also, as in the 120.0 foot measurement, none of the zeros are underlined because of the fact that a zero is written to the right of the decimal indicating the measurement was carried to the tenths place and happened to be a zero.

*Digits of a measurement are significant if they are necessary to tell how many of the smallest unit of measure there are.* In [13], the significant digits of the first row measurements are *italicized* in the bottom row.

[13]

| | | | | | |
|---|---|---|---|---|---|
| 0.049 | 0.0490 | 20.049 | 120 | 2000 | 2000.0 |
| 0.0*49* | 0.0*490* | *20.049* | *120* | *2000* | *2000.0* |

**Scientific and Floating Notation.** A number is in *scientific notation* if it is expressed as a product of a number between one and ten (the mantissa), and a number which is a power of ten (the characteristic or exponent). This certainly simplifies the notation for very small numbers like .00000000123 and very large numbers like 456,700,000,000,000 which are written $1.23 \times 10^{-9}$ and $4.567 \times 10^{14}$ respectively in scientific notation. Note that the mantissa contains only the significant digits of the number.

The Fortran scientific computer language has two basic kinds of numbers: integer and real. The integer numbers are handled and stored more or less as discussed in the *Computer Arithmetic* section. An integer number will be represented as a binary number. The real numbers are also called floating numbers because they are handled and stored in such a way that the decimal point "floats". Actually, floating notation is very similar to scientific notation, in that $1.23 \times 10^{-9}$ might be written $+.123E-8$ and $-4.567 \times 10^{14}$ might be $-.4567E+15$ where the E indicates the exponent of ten. A real or floating number will be stored and manipulated separately by mantissa and by characteristic, partly because it facilitates multiplication and division.

To *multiply* two numbers in scientific notation together, *multiply* their *mantissas, add* their *characteristics,* and the results give the mantissa and characteristic of the answer in scientific notation after possibly an adjustment of decimal point and characteristic. The answer *should* contain no more significant digits than the multiplier with the least number of significant digits, thus calling frequently for rounding off the mantissa to the correct number of digits. This rounding, according to significance, is practical in scientific (slide rule) applications; however, the computer using Fortran generally does not adjust for significant digits. *Division* of two numbers in scientific notation is performed by *dividing* the *mantissas* and *subtracting* the *exponents.* The number of significant digits in the resulting mantissa should not exceed the number in either the divisor or the dividend. For example, $2.31 \times 10^{4}$ times $6.4 \times 10^{-3}$ should be rounded to $1.5 \times 10^{2}$ for scientific notation, but left as $1.536E+2$ on the computer. $9.287 \times 10^{-4}$ divided by $9.25 \times 10^{6}$ becomes $1.00 \times 10^{-10}$ in scientific notation and $1.004E-10$ on the computer.

**Length, Distance.** Measuring the *length* of an object, or the *distance* from one object to another, requires finding the number obtained by counting how many times some standard can be applied to successive positions on or between the objects. This includes reading the fractional part of the divisions marked on the standard, which is the *precision.*

**Angle.** An angle may be considered to be an

[14]

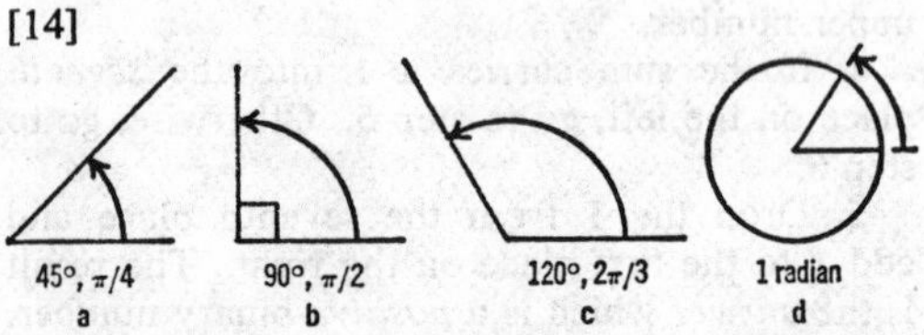


amount of rotation. The first angle in [14a] shows the rotation from the *initial* side to the *terminal* side.

A complete rotation or revolution is defined to be 360 degrees (°). The angle in [14a] is 1/8 of a complete revolution which is 1/8 of 360° or 45°. Two other angles are similarly labeled in terms of degrees. The second angle, [14b], is also called a right angle.

Another procedure for measuring angles uses the term radian. A *radian* is the angle formed by two radii of a circle (See *Circles*) fixed so that the distance around the circle from the endpoint of one radius to the endpoint of the other is one radius. (See [14d].) A radian is approximately 57.2°. Radian measure is often expressed in terms of $\pi$ as in [14] where $45° = \pi/4$ radians, $90° = \pi/2$ radians, etc. (See *Trigonometry, Measures.*)

**Area, Volume, Capacity.** The area of an object is described as the amount of surface enclosed by the object. Mostly we consider areas as being on a level surface or plane. We measure area by counting how many standard units of area there are in the object. Some of the most common standards of area are square inch, square foot, and square mile. A square inch is just a way of referring to a square (see *Formulas and Applications, Polygons*) which has one inch sides, or an inch square.

Measurement of length involves measurement along one line and is called one dimensional measure. Measure in the plane is called two dimensional measure where measurement is in square *units* and the *unit* is one dimensional. An example of two dimensional area is given in [15a]. Assume the little square on the left of [15a] is the standard unit of area. We want to find the area of [15a] by finding how many of the standard units will fit into [15a]. As [15a] has been sectioned already into little squares the same size as the standard unit square to the left, we just count the number of these shown and we get 32 square units as the area.

If the figure is irregularly shaped like [15b] then the problem of finding the area is toughened to the extent that fitting square units inside of [15b] will probably still leave some area uncovered. If we use smaller units, we should cover some more of the area but still not all of it. It is therefore necessary sometimes, in the case of irregular shaped figures, to approximate the area for application.

Corresponding to area in two dimensions, we

[15]

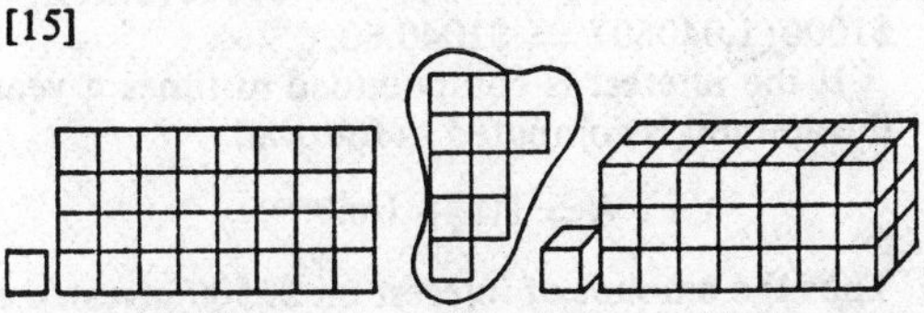

(a) (b) (c)

have volume in three dimensions. Here we talk about the number of standard unit cubes or cubic units (see *Formulas and Applications, Solids*) of an object. Some common standard units are cubic inches, cubic feet, cubic yards, etc. To find the volume of [15c], we evaluate how many of the unit cubes on the left of [15c] are in [15c], and the sectioning shows a volume of 42 cubic units.

To find the volume of an irregularly shaped object, we will probably have to approximate as with irregular area. With few exceptions, however, the volume of almost any shaped object in three dimensions will be measured in cubic *units* where the basic *unit* is one dimensional. Thus we can measure volume in cubic *inches,* area in square *inches,* and length in just *inches.*

Capacity is the term used for the measurement of the containment of an object. We have cups, quarts, liters, bushels, and other standard measures of capacity. The *volume* of a basket is practically fixed, but the capacity of a basket could be a bushel if measuring corn, but zero if measuring water as it will not *contain* water. When the capacity and volume of an object are the same amount, then conversion can be made between the systems. For example, one liter is approximately .264 gallons and about .0353 cubic feet.

**Weight, Time.** To *weigh* an object usually means to balance the object equally by some means with a standard weight or combination of such weights. The pound, gram, and ton are some of the basic standards of weight. The process of measuring weight is fundamentally the same as measuring length in that we can question the equality of the weights of two objects by simultaneous comparison.

*Time* occurs only once and is gone from grasp. Thus, of course, we cannot simultaneously compare two intervals of time. We measure time usually in terms of so many cycles, or parts thereof. We have seconds, days, years, etc., and some physical applications require milli-(thousandth), micro-(millionth), even nano-(billionth) second measurement of time.

**Temperature.** The Fahrenheit temperature scale measures 32° at the freezing point of water and 212° at the boiling point. The original intent it seems was to have 100° be the normal human body temperature. The Centigrade scale is based on 0° freezing of water and 100° boiling thus making the size of a degree different for each scale. (See *Formulas and Applications, Centigrade, Fahrenheit.*)

## FORMULAS AND APPLICATIONS

**Ratio, Proportion.** A *ratio* is a comparison of two numbers. It is often expressed as a fraction and can be reduced or simplified as such. However, we cannot add ratios as we can add fractions. As long as it is a ratio, it is two numbers and our usual operands are single numbers.

A *proportion* is two or more equal ratios. An example is: one compares to two as three compares to six. This can be written as $1:2 = 3:6$ or $1/2 = 3/6$.

To *solve a proportion* like $2:3 = X:9$, we find the product of the extremes, $2 \cdot 9 = 18$, and the product of the means, $3 \cdot X = 3X$, and set them equal. That is: $3X = 18$. We then divide both sides by the multiplier of X so the left side is $3X/3$ which is just X (three of something divided by three is just the something), and the right side is $18/3$ or 6. Then X on the left equals 6 on the right and we have solved the proportion by finding $X = 6$, so the proportion is $2:3 = 6:9$.

EXAMPLE: Solve the proportion $4\frac{1}{2}:21 = \frac{6}{5}:X$.

Product of means and extremes, $4\frac{1}{2}X = 21 \cdot \frac{6}{5}$

Simplify, $\frac{9}{2}X = \frac{21 \cdot 6}{5}$

Divide by $\frac{9}{2}$, $X = \left(\frac{21 \cdot 6}{5}\right) \div \left(\frac{9}{2}\right) = \left(\frac{21 \cdot 6}{5}\right) \cdot \left(\frac{2}{9}\right)$

Simplify, $X = \frac{21 \cdot 6 \cdot 2}{5 \cdot 9} = \frac{28}{5}$

**Percent.** *Percent* (%) means per hundreds. An event which would occur 75 times out of 100 trials would occur 75 per 100 or 75 percent

(75%) of the time. 75 per 100 is also .75 and we can change percents in application to decimal fractions by dividing by 100.

One type of problem in percents finds a certain percentage of a number. For example, what is 36% of 150? The result is found by changing 36% to .36 and multiplying it by 150. So we have $.36 \times 150 = 54$.

To change a decimal to a percent, we multiply by 100 and insert the % sign. So 1.75 becomes 175%. A mixed decimal like 1.4 $^1/_3$ must first be thought of as $1.4 + {}^1/_3$ of $^1/_{10}$ which is the same as 1.43 $^1/_3$ and changing to percent, we get 143 $^1/_3$%.

Another percent problem involves the question: X is what percent of Y? This is like: 21 is what percent of 60? We divide 60 into 21 to get the decimal equivalent, then change to percent. That is: $21/60 = .35 = 35\%$.

Finally, the problem might be stated in this form: X% of what number is Y? A typical one is: Find a number such that 18% of it is 423. To find it, we divide 423 by .18, which gives 2350.

**Interest, Rate, Time, Principal.** When an amount of money is invested at a certain simple interest rate (expressed as a percent) over a length of time, it gathers more money called interest. *Interest* is the product of the amount of money (*principal*) and the interest *rate* and the length of *time* in years ($I = PxRxT$). Thus 700 dollars (P) invested at 5% (R) for 9 months (T) will amount to $I = PxRxT = \$700x.05x.75 = \$26.25$. Note that .75 is used for 9 months which is .75 of a year.

If the problem is to find P, R, or T if given the other three, including I, we may use the methods of *Algebraic Equations, Linear* in the algebra section. We can also employ the formulas below directly.

$$I = P{\cdot}R{\cdot}T,\ P = I/(R{\cdot}T),\ R = I/(P{\cdot}T),\ T = I/(P{\cdot}R)$$

For example, to find the rate of interest if the interest is 50 dollars, the principal is 1000 dollars and the length of time is 11 months. We use $R = I/(P{\cdot}T) = 55/(1000{\cdot}11/12) = 660/11000 = .06$ or 6%. The other formulas are applied in a similar manner.

An interesting short cut in computation is called the 60 day 6% method. Realizing that 6% on P dollars for 60 days gives $I = P{\cdot}R{\cdot}T = P{\cdot}(6/100) \cdot (1/6)$, in which the 6's divide out, we have $I = P/100$. So if money is invested at 6% for 60 days, the amount of interest will be the amount invested divided by 100 which is the same as moving the decimal point two places to the left. Then 6% for 60 days on \$547.00 is \$5.47. In addition to this, we can find multiples of either the days or the interest and broaden the application of the method. For example, to find 3% of 200 dollars for 8 months (240 days), we work with ½ the interest rate (3% is ½ of 6%) for 4 times the 60 days. We take \$200 and mark off two places to get \$2, then take ½ of it because it's 3% instead of 6%; finally we multiply by 4 for $4 \times 60$ days and we get $\$2 \times ½ \times 4 = \$4$ interest.

**Compound Interest.** If an interest rate is applied periodically to a sum of money and the amounts of interest are left in order to accumulate, then the interest is compounded. That is, we will apply the interest rate at the end of a period of time to the principal, plus the interest from the previous period of time. If the interest is computed or compounded annually, the formula is

$$A = P(1 + i)^n,$$

where A is the amount (principal + interest), P is the principal, i is the interest rate per year, and n is the number of years. Then the amount on \$1000 invested at 1% for 4 years is $A = \$1000(1 + .01)^4 = \$1000(1.01)^4 = \$1000(1.04060) = \$1040.60$.

If the interest is compounded m times a year, the amount is computed as follows:

$$A = P(1 + i/m)^{nxm}.$$

Thus the amount of interest on \$2500 invested at 2% for 9 months compounded quarterly (every 3 months) is found by $A = \$2500(1+.02/4)^{.75x4} = \$2500(1.005)^3 = \$2500(1.15075) = \$2537.69$. To help with some of the arithmetic involved in problems like these, and also to be able to manipulate the formulas so as to find other quantities, like P, i, m, or n, see *Algebraic Equations.*

**Distance, Rate, Time.** *Rate* is usually expressed as a ratio of amount of *distance* covered per unit of *time.* Sixty miles per hour is a rate meaning every hour the distance covered is sixty miles. Two hours means one hundred twenty miles are covered and a half hour means thirty miles are covered. The three formulas involved here are:

$$R = D/T, \quad D = R{\cdot}T, \quad T = D/R$$

where R = Rate, D = Distance, and T = Time.

A train traveling at the rate of 60 miles per hour for 5 hours will cover a distance ($D = R{\cdot}T$) of (60 miles/hour)$\cdot$(5 hours) = 300 miles. Note that the units (miles/hour, hours) in the problem were indicated and the hour in the denominator of 60 miles/hour cancelled with the hours in 5 hours leaving miles as the unit for the resulting distance.

A satellite encircles the earth at a rate of 2/3 of an orbit per hour. How much time will it take for 50 orbits? We compute the time ($T = D/R$) as follows: (50 orbits) $\div$ (2/3 orbits/hour) = (50 orbits) $\times$ (3/2 hours/orbits) = 75 hours. For other examples of distance, rate, time problems, see *Algebraic Equations* and *Applications* in the algebra section.

**Centigrade, Fahrenheit.** The formulas relating the *Fahrenheit* scale (F) to the *Centigrade* scale (C) are:

$$F = \tfrac{9}{5}(C) + 32 \qquad C = \tfrac{5}{9}(F - 32)$$

Thus to change 75°C to Fahrenheit, we put the value of C in $\tfrac{9}{5}C + 32$ to get $\tfrac{9}{5}(75) + 32 = 9(15) + 32 = 135 + 32 = 167$. 75°C = 167°F. Now to change 99°F to Centigrade, we have F = 99 in $\tfrac{5}{9}(F - 32) = \tfrac{5}{9}(99 - 32) = \tfrac{5}{9}(67) = 37\tfrac{2}{9}$. 99°F = $37\tfrac{2}{9}$°C.

**Square Root.** Finding the *square root* of a number called N means to find some number which multiplied by itself will equal N. For example, the square root of 9 is 3 because 3 times 3 equals 9. The symbol for the square root of a number is $\sqrt{\ }$, so the $\sqrt{9} = 3$. There are others that may be found by inspection, like $\sqrt{4} = 2$, $\sqrt{25} = 5$, $\sqrt{1} = 1$, etc. However, the $\sqrt{3}$ cannot be written in decimal form exactly. We usually approximate $\sqrt{3}$ and others like it by representing it in decimal form correct to as many places as are actually needed in application. A number is a *square* if it is equal to some whole number squared, 1, 4, 9, 16, etc. are squares.

To find the square root of a decimal number, study the example of the $\sqrt{164}$ given in [16].

[16]

```
           1  2 . 8  0  6  2  4  8          (3)
       √ 01'64.00'00'00'00'00'00            (1)
         01                                 (2)
      20 |0064                              (4)
      22 |  44                              (5)
      240|2000                              (6)
      248|1984                              (7)
      2560  |1600
      2560  |  00
      25600 |160000
      25606 |153636
      256120  |636400
      256122  |512244
      2561140 |12415600
      2561144 |10244576
      25612480|217102400
      25612488|204899904
                12202496
```

Note the steps indicated on the right which regulate the basic procedure.

**Steps**

**(1)** Divide the digits of the number into pairs from the decimal point in both directions adding zeros if necessary. The zeros on the right are added to give finer precision to the answer. Put a decimal point above the line over the existing decimal point.

**(2)** Consider the first pair of digits on the left and write down under them the largest square equal to or less than the number represented by the first two digits.

**(3)** Write the square root of this square above the line over the two digits. This becomes the first digit of the answer above the line. In this case, we have a 1.

**(4)** Subtract the square (01) from the two digit number above (01) and put the result below (00). Bring down on this line the next two digits to the right (64). Without regard to the decimal point, multiply the answer so far obtained (1) by 20 and write the result (20) to the left on the same line. We are now ready to compare the number on the left (20) with the number on the right (0064).

**(5)** Roughly divide the left number into the right to get the trial quotient. Add the trial quotient (which the first time is a 2) to the left number and put the result called the trial divisor (22 first time) on the next line to the left. Now multiply the trial quotient by the trial divisor and put this product (44 first time) to the right and subtract it from above. Now we must get the product as close to the upper number (64 first time) as we can without exceeding it. Thus, in practice, it may take several different trial divisors before the product is just below the upper number in value. When we find the correct trial divisor, we write the trial quotient above the top line as the next digit to our answer (the "2" in 12 the first time).

**(6)** Next we subtract the lower number from the upper and write the result on the next line. We bring down two more digits and place them beside the result of subtraction to form another number which we will call the new upper number. Multiply the answer computed thus far by 20 and write the result to the left of the new upper number.

**(7)** We now repeat steps (5) and (6) to compute the other decimal places of the answer.

**Polygons.** A *simple polygon* is a plane closed figure bounded by straight lines (see *Geometry, Basic Terms Defined*). By this, we mean that the lines that form the polygon lie in the same plane and the polygon itself divides the whole plane into three distinct collections of points: those inside the polygon, on the polygon, and outside the polygon. The straight lines of the polygon are called sides; the points of intersection of the sides are called vertices.

A three-sided polygon is called a triangle; a four-sided polygon is a quadrilateral, and as the number of sides increase, we have pentagon (5), hexagon (6), septagon (7), octagon (8), nonogon (9), decagon (10), undecagon (11), and dodecagon (12).

*Triangles* are classified as acute, obtuse, and right triangles. An *acute* triangle has all angles less than 90°. An *obtuse* triangle has one angle greater than 90°. A *right* triangle has one right (90°) angle. The sum of the interior angles of a triangle is 180°. Thus if we know two angles of a triangle, we can find the third by subtracting the sum of the known angles from 180°.

A triangle with two equal sides is called isosceles. With three equal sides, it is called equilateral, and in this case, it is also equalangular (equal angles).

The area of a triangle may be found if the three sides, a, b, and c, are known by the formulas:

$$s = (a + b + c)/2 \qquad \text{area} = \sqrt{s(s-a)(s-b)(s-c)}$$

The sides which form the 90° angle of a right triangle are called the legs. The side opposite the right angle is called the hypotenuse. The area of a right triangle is one-half the product of the two legs.

The *Pythagorean Theorem* states that the square of the hypotenuse of a right triangle is equal to the sum of the squares of the other two legs. A particular right triangle with legs of length 3 and 4 would have a hypotenuse equal to

$$\sqrt{3^2 + 4^2} = \sqrt{9 + 16} = \sqrt{25} = 5.$$

*Pythagorean triples* are whole numbers which can be the lengths of the sides of a right triangle. Thus, 3, 4, and 5 are Pythagorean triples as $3^2 + 4^2 = 5^2$. There are many others; in fact, we may use the following formulas to derive any number of such triples. Let a, b, and c be the sides of a right triangle such that $a^2 + b^2 = c^2$, then

$$a = 2 \cdot X \cdot Y \cdot Z \text{ or } a = 2XYZ,$$
$$b = X(Y^2 - Z^2),$$
$$c = X(Y^2 + Z^2),$$

with these restrictions: X is any positive integer, either Y or Z is divisible by 2, and Y and Z are relatively prime.

Some of the triples found by this formula are: 5, 12, 13; 7, 24, 25; 9, 40, 41; 11, 60, 61; and 13, 42, 85.

A right triangle with a 45° angle will have two 45° angles and the legs will each be equal to the hypothenuse divided by the $\sqrt{2}$. A right triangle with a 30° angle will also have a 60° angle and the side opposite the 30° angle will be one-half the hypotenuse. The other leg will be half the hypothenuse multiplied by the $\sqrt{3}$.

**Quadrilaterals.** Adjacent vertices of a quadrilateral are on the same side. The line joining non-adjacent vertices is called a diagonal. The sum of the interior angles of a quadrilateral is 360°. There are five special kinds of quadrilaterals: trapezoids, parallelograms, rhombuses, rectangles, and squares.

*Trapezoids* are quadrilaterals with one pair of opposite sides parallel. An isosceles trapezoid has the nonparallel sides equal. The area of a trapezoid is given by

$$\text{area} = h(a + b)/2$$

where a and b are the lengths of the parallel sides and h is the distance between them.

*Parallelograms* are quadrilaterals with both sets of opposite sides parallel. Also, the opposite sides and opposite angles are equal. The area of a parallelogram equals the length of a side times the distance from it to the opposite side. Area equals base times height.

*Rhombuses* are parallelograms which have all four sides equal. The diagonals of a rhombus form right angles (perpendicular). The area of a rhombus is base times height.

*Rectangles* are parallelograms with a right interior angle. This means that all the other interior angles are right angles. The area of a rectangle is base times height.

*Squares* can be considered as rhombuses with right angles or as rectangles with equal sides. The diagonals are perpendicular and are equal. The area of a square is the square of one of its sides.

**Circles.** A *circle* is a closed curve in a plane such that every point of it is equidistant (equal in distance) from a fixed point called the center. A line segment from the center of a circle to the curve is called a radius. A line passing through the center of a circle will intersect the circle at two points. The line segment joining these two points is a diameter of the circle. Thus the diameter is twice the radius.

The circumference of a circle is the distance around the circle. The ratio of the circumference to the diameter of a circle is always a constant, no matter which circle is considered. The circumference divided by the diameter is called $\pi$ and is approximately given by:

$$\pi = 3.141592654$$

and $\pi$ may be computed to more decimal places by using this formula:

$$\pi = 4(1 - 1/3 + 1/5 - 1/7 + \ldots).$$

The formula for the circumference is

$$\text{circumference} = 2\pi R = \pi D$$

where R is the radius and D is the diameter of the circle. The area of a circle is given by

$$\text{area} = \pi R^2 = \pi D^2/4$$

When measurement is used to find R or D for these formulas, then remember to use as many decimal places for $\pi$ as are used for R or D. This will give the result as many significant digits as possible.

**Solids.** A *solid* figure or object will lie in more than one plane. A *closed* solid figure will divide the whole space into three collections of points: the points inside the figure, the points on the figure or the ones that comprise the figure itself, and the points outside the figure.

A *polyhedron* is a closed solid which has sides or faces which are polygons. A polyhedron must have at least four faces.

[17]

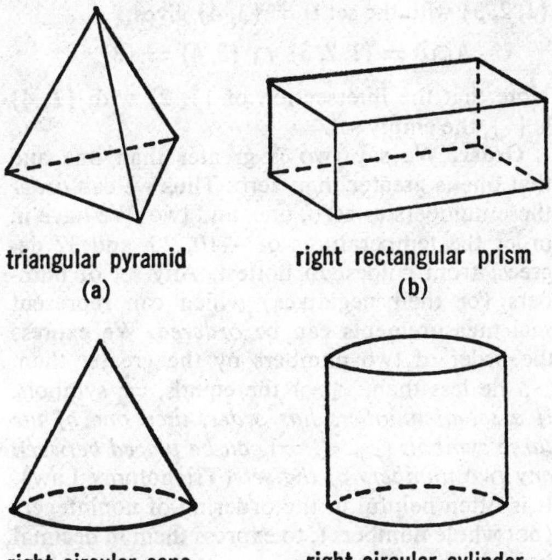

triangular pyramid (a) right rectangular prism (b)

right circular cone (c) right circular cylinder (d)

The intersection of two faces of a polyhedron is called an edge.

The simplest *pyramid* [17a] has four triangular faces, but a pyramid can have any number of faces as long as all but one face (the base) have a common vertex. The distance from this vertex to the base is the height of the pyramid. The volume of a pyramid is

$$\text{volume} = BH/3,$$

where B is the area of the base and H is the height. The shape of the base of a pyramid classifies the pyramid as triangular, square, etc.

A *prism* [17b] is a polyhedron which has two congruent (same size and shape) polygon faces, called bases, which are parallel and have corresponding vertices joined by parallel lines. These lines are the edges of parallelogram faces and are called lateral edges. Prisms are classified by the shape of their bases, and are also classified as right prisms if their lateral edges are perpendicular to the bases; otherwise, they are oblique prisms.

If B is the area of a base and H is the height or distance between bases of a prism, then the volume of a prism is

$$\text{volume} = BH$$

A special right prism is the *cube* which has squares as bases and all edges are equal in length to the sides of the bases. The volume of a cube is

$$\text{volume} = S^3,$$

where S is the length of an edge.

A circular *cone* [17c] is determined by a circle (base), a point (vertex) not in the plane of the base, and the collection of all lines that connect a point on the circle to the vertex. The surface formed by these lines is called the lateral area. The volume of a circular cone is

$$\text{volume} = \pi R^2H/3,$$

where R is the radius of the base and H is the distance from the vertex to the base.

A circular *cylinder* [17d] is a solid figure determined by two congruent circles (bases) in parallel planes and the collection of all lines connecting the points on the circles in such a way that any two distinct lines are parallel. A right circular cylinder has each of these lines perpendicular to the bases.

The volume of a circular cylinder is

$$\text{volume} = \pi R^2H,$$

where R is the radius of the base and H is the distance between bases.

It is worth noting that the "pointed" figures, the pyramids and the cones, have the same general formula for volume; volume equals one-third the area of the base times the height. Similarly, the prisms and cylinders have the common volume formula; volume equals area of base times height.

The *sphere* is a solid figure defined to be the collection in space of all points equidistant from a fixed point called the center. The distance from a point on the sphere to the center is a radius. A diameter of a sphere is defined similarly to the diameter of a circle. The surface area of a sphere is

$$\text{area} = 4\pi R^2,$$

and the volume of a sphere is

$$\text{volume} = 4\pi R^3/3,$$

where R is the radius of the sphere.

# Modern Algebra

## TERMINOLOGY

**Undefined Terms.** In mathematics, *undefined terms* are concepts which are usually intuitively obvious, yet cannot be flawlessly defined. Clearly we want as few undefined terms as possible.

**Points.** A *point* is an undefined term which represents a location only. It may be described as being infinitely thin or without thickness. The concept of point is used in one, two, three, and even higher dimensional space.

**Sets, Subsets.** A *set* is an undefined term that refers to a collection along with some rule which gives a means of determining whether or not some certain element is in the collection. The collection of whole numbers from 1 to 5 is a set because we have a definite means of determining whether or not a given number is in the set. This set can be written as {1, 2, 3, 4, 5}, where the brackets indicate that a *set* is enclosed. It could also be written as {1, 2, 3, . . . 5}, where the ". . ." means to continue in the pattern. A set can be named or labeled, like X = {1, 2, 3}.

A set, S, is a subset of a set, T, if there are no elements in S which are not also in T. The set, T, is a subset of itself.

The *empty set,* or *null set,* { }, is the set which contains no elements. By definition then, the empty set is a subset of any set, even itself.

**Lines.** A straight *line* is the idea of the set of all points between two points and the extension thereof in both directions. (See *Geometry.*) Thus a line is infinite in length in each direction. A *line segment* is finite in length and can be determined by its two endpoints.

**Variables.** In mathematics, a *variable* is a symbol that represents some element of a set. In certain situations, a variable may take on the value of *several,* even an *infinite* number of elements from a set. Such a set is called the *replacement set.* Variables are usually represented by letters like X, Y, etc., and are called *unknowns.*

**Union.** *The union (∪) of two sets is the set made up of the elements that are in one or the other of the two sets or in both sets simultaneously.* The union of three or more sets can be found by taking the union of any two of the sets, then union this set with any of the others, etc., until all have been taken. The union of the set A = {1, 2, 3} with the set B = {3, 4} gives

$$A \cup B = \{1, 2, 3\} \cup \{3, 4\} = \{1, 2, 3, 4\}.$$

**Intersection.** *The intersection (∩) of two sets is the set made up only of the elements that are in both sets simultaneously.* The intersection of three or more sets is found by taking the intersection of any two of the sets then intersect this set with any of the others, etc., until all have been taken. The intersection of the set A = {1, 2, 3} with the set B = {3, 4} gives

$$A \cap B = \{1, 2, 3\} \cap \{3, 4\} = \{3\}.$$

Note that the intersection of {1, 2} with {3, 4} is { }, the empty set.

**Order.** We say two is greater than one and that one is greater than zero. Thus we can *order* these numbers as zero, one, and two. We have in order the temperatures of −10, 20, and 32 degrees, from coldest to hottest. Any set of numbers (or their negatives) which can represent real measurements can be *ordered.* We express the order of two numbers by the greater than, >, the less than, <, or the equals, =, symbols. *If a set of numbers has order, then one of the three symbols (>, <, =) can be placed between any two numbers of the set* (Trichotomy Law). It is often helpful in the ordering of nonintegers (not whole numbers), to express them in decimal form for comparison.

For example, to order the numbers $\sqrt{22}$ and 14/3, we change each to decimal form: $\sqrt{22} =$ 4.69; 14/3 = 4.66; and as 4.69 > 4.66, we have $\sqrt{22} > 14/3$.

**Statements, Open Sentences.** 2 + 3 = 5 is a true *statement.* 2 + 2 = 5 is a statement, but it is false. The sentence X + 3 = 5 is neither true nor false. It is an *open sentence* because the value of X must be known before it becomes a statement. In mathematics, we usually say that sentences like X + 3 = 5 are equations. We mean by this that if a correct value is assigned to X from the replacement set, then we have *equated* both sides. That is, in X + 3 = 5, let the replacement set be all real numbers (see *Sets of Numbers*), then assign the value 2 to X and both sides of the equation will be equal, 2 + 3 = 5. The open sentence, X + 3 > 5, is called an *inequality.* This sentence is more than just a presentation of unequalness, however, for it tells which way the unequalness is applied, in that X + 3 *is greater than* 5. To make a true statement of the inequality open sentence, we could replace X by 4, so that 4 + 3 > 5, or by 10, giving 10 + 3 > 5 and, of course, many others.

**Solution Sets.** A *solution set* is the set of all values in the replacement set which, when substituted for the unknown (variable) in an open sentence, make a true statement. In X + 3 = 5, the solution set is {2}. X + 3 > 5 has, as a solution set, the set of all real numbers greater than 2. When we say that we solve an equation or inequality, we mean that we find the solution set.

## SETS OF NUMBERS

**Integers.** An *integer* is a whole number, positive, negative, or zero. In set notation, the set of integers is {. . . —2, —1, 0, 1, 2, . . .}. Here the ". . ." means continued in the same pattern (without end) and thus the set of integers is infinite. Thus the integers are the natural (counting) numbers, their negatives and zero.

**Countable Sets.** A set is *countable* if it can be placed into a one-to-one correspondence with the natural numbers or with a subset of the natural numbers.

For example, the set of positive even numbers can be placed into a one-to-one correspondence with the natural numbers,

| 1 | 2 | 3 | 4 | 5 | 6 | . . . |
|---|---|---|---|---|---|---|
| ↕ | ↕ | ↕ | ↕ | ↕ | ↕ | |
| 2 | 4 | 6 | 8 | 10 | 12 | . . . |

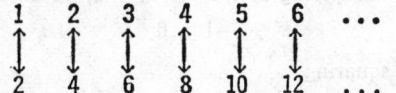

because for each natural number, there is a positive even integer, and for each positive even integer there is a natural number.

**Rational Numbers.** A number is *rational* if it can be expressed as the quotient of two integers, a/b, b not 0. In decimal form, a rational number will terminate or repeat in a pattern. The numbers, ½, 6, 0, .4, 7½, .333 . . . , are all rational because respectively, they are equal to $^1/_2$, $^6/_1$, $^0/_1$, $^4/_{10}$, $^{15}/_2$, and $^1/_3$ where each is the quotient of two integers. We say .333 . . . = $^1/_3$, because .333 . . . is actually an infinite series (see *Sequences and Series*) and $^1/_3$ is the sum or limit of this infinite series.

We can show that the *rationals are countable* by considering [18]. Notice that the row number is also the numerator of the fractions in that row and the column number gives us the denominator of the fractions in that column. Thus any rational number will be found in the array because all possible combinations of integer numerators and denominators are given. There are some numbers repeated ($^1/_1 = {}^2/_2$, $^1/_2 = {}^2/_4$, etc.), so the rule is to match the rational number with the corresponding fraction in the array which is in lowest terms. *We have now shown that the rationals are in a one-to-one correspondence with a subset of the set of numbers in the array. The array itself can be counted* by following the arrows moving diagonally back and forth, beginning at the upper left. ■ (■ means end of proof.)

[18]

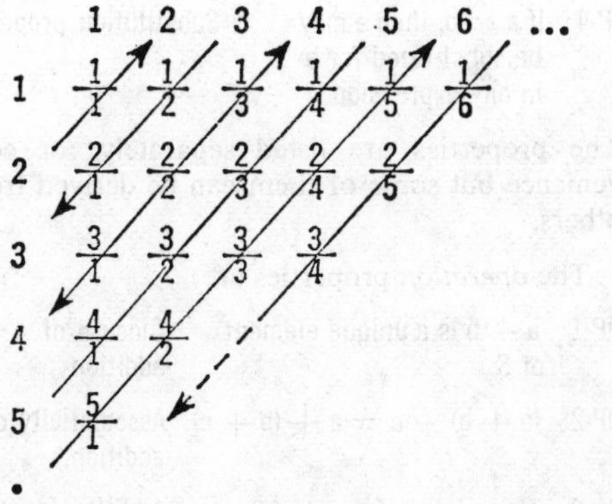

The rational numbers are dense in that between any two rationals, there is another rational.

**Irrational Numbers.** A number is *irrational* if in decimal form it does not terminate or repeat in a pattern. An irrational number cannot be expressed as the quotient of two integers. Among the irrationals are such numbers as $\sqrt{2}$, $\pi$, and $-\sqrt{11}$.

To prove that $\sqrt{2}$ is irrational, we can show that it cannot be expressed as the quotient of two integers. Euclid proved the irrationality of $\sqrt{2}$ by assuming it was rational, then showing that this reached a contradiction. So let's assume $\sqrt{2} = a/b$, where a and b are *relatively prime integers*. Squaring both sides, we have

$$2 = a^2/b^2,$$

and solving for $a^2$,

$$2b^2 = a^2.$$

Obviously, if $a^2 = 2b^2$, then as b is an integer, $b^2$ is an integer, and $2b^2$ is an even integer. Thus $a^2$ is even and therefore *a is even.* Let a = 2c, where c is an integer. Then $a^2 = 4c^2$, and substituting gives

$$2b^2 = 4c^2,$$

$$b^2 = 2c^2,$$

which means *b is even.* But we assumed that a and b *existed* as *relatively prime* integers (no common factors), so a and b must not exist. Note, if two numbers existed, a and b, which would do the job, $a/b = \sqrt{2}$, then we could make them relatively prime in the beginning. The proof, however, shows that *if they exist,* no matter how many times we might reduce the fraction, a/b, there would always be a common factor of 2. Therefore, the a and b do not exist. ■

*The irrationals are uncountable.* We prove this by showing that the numbers between 0 and 1 are uncountable. Assume that they *all are* countable and it can be shown that at least one was *not* counted. If they were countable, then we could arrange them, in decimal form, in a *list,* [19], so that there is a first element of the list, a second element, and so on. Let the *first* irrational number be

$$.a_{11}a_{12}a_{13}a_{14}\ldots$$

where the a's are the digits (0 through 9) of the decimal number which is less than one. Note that the "..." does not here necessarily mean a pattern, but it represents the part of the number that was not printed. Let the *second* irrational number in the list be

$$.a_{21}a_{22}a_{23}a_{24}\ldots,$$

so that, for example, $a_{23}$ means the *third* digit of the *second* irrational number in the list. Then [19] shows "all" the numbers between 0 and 1

[19]
$$\begin{array}{l} .a_{11}a_{12}a_{13}a_{14}a_{15}\ldots \\ .a_{21}a_{22}a_{23}a_{24}a_{25}\ldots \\ .a_{31}a_{32}a_{33}a_{34}a_{35}\ldots \\ .a_{41}a_{42}a_{43}a_{44}a_{45}\ldots \\ \quad\vdots \end{array}$$

so as to count them. They are *not* all there because one that was left out was a decimal made up of 0's and 1's. It is found by writing a 0 for the *first* digit if the *first* number in the list had anything but a 0 in the *first* place. Otherwise, put a 1. The *second* digit is a 0 if the *second* number in the list had anything but a 0 in the *second* place. Otherwise, put a 1. We do the same for all the digits and this number differs from the first number in the list in the first place, it differs from the second number in the list in the second place, and so on throughout the list, so this number is not anywhere in the list.

Thus the numbers from 0 to 1 are uncountable, but the rationals from 0 to 1 are countable, therefore the numbers that remain, the irrationals, are uncountable. ■

The irrationals are also *dense,* for between any two irrationals, there is an irrational. Furthermore, between any two irrationals, there is a rational and vice versa.

**Real Numbers.** The *real numbers* are the set of all rational and irrational numbers, or the rationals union the irrationals. The reals are a dense and uncountable set since they contain the irrationals as a subset.

**Imaginary Numbers.** An *imaginary number* is a number that can be expressed in the form, bi, where b is a real number and $i = \sqrt{-1}$, meaning $i^2 = -1$. An imaginary number is not a real number since in the section *Algebraic Expressions, multiplication rule,* a real number squared is not negative.

**Complex Numbers.** A *complex number* is a number that can be expressed in the form, a + bi, where a and b are real and $i = \sqrt{-1}$. If $b = 0$, then a + bi is also a *real* number; if $a = 0$ and $b \neq 0$, then a + bi is also a *pure imaginary* number. *Thus any number (integer, rational, irrational, or imaginary) can be expressed as a complex number.*

*Order (greater than; less than) does not exist in the pure imaginary or in the complexes with non-zero imaginary parts.* The proof of this is by contradiction. If the numbers, i and 0, can be ordered, then either $i > 0$, $i = 0$, or $i < 0$. Obviously, $i \neq 0$ (i does not equal 0) and this leaves $i > 0$ or $i < 0$. If

$$i > 0,$$

then both are non-negative, so squaring both sides gives

$$-1 > 0 \ \otimes$$

which is a contradiction (indicated by $\otimes$). So we let

$$i < 0,$$

and multiplying both sides by $-1$, we have

$$-i > 0$$

then squaring

$$\begin{array}{c} (-i)^2 > 0 \\ +i^2 > 0 \\ -1 > 0 \ \otimes \end{array}$$

which is again a contradiction. So by a specific example we have shown that the imaginaries cannot be ordered in the usual sense. ■

**Field Properties.** In order to lay a foundation for further study, we make basic assumptions in the form of equality and operation properties that we want a set, S, to have in order to be a *field.* It is assumed that a, b, and c are elements of S.

The *equality* properties are:

| | | |
|---|---|---|
| EP-1 | $a = a$. | Reflexive property. |
| EP-2 | If $a = b$, then $b = a$. | Symmetric property. |
| EP-3 | If $a = b$ and $b = c$, then $a = c$. | Transitive property. |
| EP-4 | If $a = b$, then a may be substituted for b in any expression. | Substitution property. |

The properties are listed separately for convenience but some of them can be derived from others.

The *operation* properties are:

| | | |
|---|---|---|
| OP-1 | $a + b$ is a unique element of S. | Closure of addition |
| OP-2 | $(a + b) + c = a + (b + c)$. | Associativity of addition. |
| OP-3 | There is an element of S, called 0, such that $a + 0 = a$. | Additive identity element. |
| OP-4 | For each a in S, there is an element, $-a$ (the negative of a), such that $a + (-a) = 0$. | Additive inverse. |

| | | |
|---|---|---|
| OP-5 | $a + b = b + a$. | Commutativity of addition. |
| OP-6 | $a \cdot b$ is a unique element of S. | Closure of multiplication. |
| OP-7 | $(a \cdot b) \cdot c = a \cdot (b \cdot c)$. | Associativity of multiplication. |
| OP-8 | There is an element of S, called 1, such that $a \cdot 1 = a$. | Multiplicative identity element. |
| OP-9 | For each $a \neq 0$ in S there is an element, $a^{-1}$ (the reciprocal of a), such that $a \cdot (a^{-1}) = 1$. | Multiplicative inverse or Reciprocal. |
| OP-10 | $a \cdot b = b \cdot a$. | Commutativity of multiplication. |
| OP-11 | $a \cdot (b + c) = a \cdot b + a \cdot c$, or $a(b + c) = ab + ac$. | Distributive property. |

A set which has the four equality and the eleven operation properties under operations of + and • is called a field. Thus the set of rationals, reals, and complex numbers each constitute a field. A set with OP-1 through OP-4 is a *group.*

With these field properties, we can establish some very important concepts in algebra and mathematics. As we make a statement in the proof, the justification for this step is shown on the right.

*Equals added to (or subtracted from) equals are equal.* If $a = b$, then $a + c = b + c$. Proof:

[20]

| | |
|---|---|
| $a + c = a + c$ | EP-1 |
| $a = b$ | Given |
| $a + c = b + c$ | EP-4 |

We know that equals subtracted from equals are equal, for in the proof we could use $(-c)$ instead of $(c)$ (see *Algebraic Expressions, Subtraction Rule).* ■

*Equals multiplied (or divided) by equals are equal* (except division by zero). If $a = b$, then $a \cdot c = b \cdot c$. Proof:

[21]

| | |
|---|---|
| $a \cdot c = a \cdot c$ | EP-1 |
| $a = b$ | Given |
| $a \cdot c = b \cdot c$ | EP-4 |

For the division part of the proof, we use $(c^{-1})$ instead of c (see *Algebraic Expressions, Division Rule).* ■

*Zero multiplied by any number is zero.* $a \cdot 0 = 0$. Proof:

[22]

| | |
|---|---|
| $a + 0 = a$ | OP-3 |
| $a \cdot (a + 0) = a \cdot a$ | [21] |
| $a \cdot a + a \cdot 0 = a \cdot a$ | OP-11 |
| $-(a \cdot a) = -(a \cdot a)$ | EP-1 |
| $a \cdot 0 = 0$ | [20] ■ |

*If the product of two numbers is zero, then one or the other or both numbers are zero.* If $a \cdot b = 0$, either $a = 0$, $b = 0$, or $a = b = 0$. Proof: Assume $a \neq 0$, then

[23]

| | |
|---|---|
| $a \cdot b = 0$ | Given |
| $(a^{-1}) = (a^{-1})$ | EP-1 |
| $(a^{-1}) \cdot a \cdot b = (a^{-1}) \cdot 0$ | [21] |
| $(1) \cdot b = 0$ | OP-9, [22] |
| $b = 0$ | OP-8 |

Similarly, if $b \neq 0$, then $a = 0$. ■

## SET EQUATIONS AND INEQUALITIES

**Set Notation. The expression, a is an element of S, is symbolized by $a \in S$. Thus, $3 \in \{3, 4\}$. A subset is designated by $\subset$, so that $\{3\} \subset \{3, 4\}$. A slash, /, denotes negation, so that $3 \notin \{1, 2\}$ and $\{1\} \not\subset \{2, 3\}$. Note that $3 \not\subset \{3, 4\}$ because a subset should be enclosed by { }. A** vertical line, |, means *such that.* Let I represent the set of all integers, then the expression,

$$\{X \mid X \in I,\ X > 0\},$$

means the set of all X such that X is an integer *and* X is greater than zero. This is called *set builder* notation, and the set built here is the set of positive integers. *If the set of real numbers is represented by R,* then the set of real numbers greater than 1 and less than 3 would be

$$\{X \mid X \in R,\ 1 < X < 3\}.$$

The symbol, $\geq$, means greater than or equal to; $\leq$ means less than or equal to. Then the set of real numbers greater than $-3$ and less than or equal to 2 is given by

$$\{X \mid X \in R,\ -3 < X \leq 2\}.$$

**Number Line Graphs.** The real number line (below) is a graph constructed so that for each

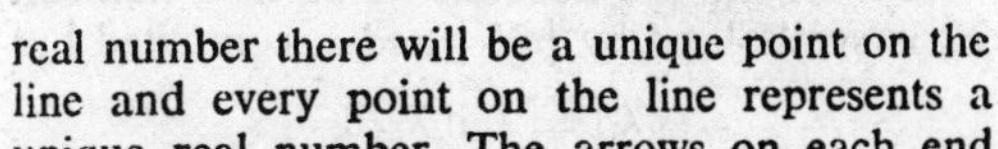

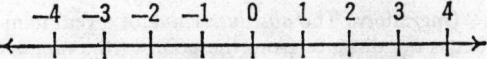


real number there will be a unique point on the line and every point on the line represents a unique real number. The arrows on each end mean that the line goes on indefinitely in each direction. Some of the points are labeled for reference.

Below are some sets given by set builder notation and shown on the number line. The heavy portion "covers" the set of values which X can have.

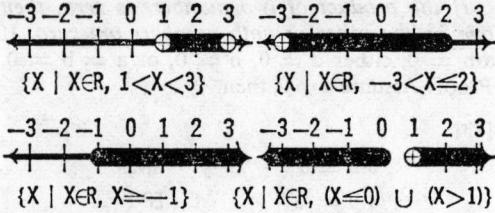

$\{X \mid X \in R, 1 < X < 3\}$ $\{X \mid X \in R, -3 < X \leq 2\}$

$\{X \mid X \in R, X \geq -1\}$ $\{X \mid X \in R, (X \leq 0) \cup (X > 1)\}$

**Ordered Pairs.** The idea of a set of *ordered pairs* of numbers is a basic concept in algebra and higher mathematics (see *Functions*). The set of ordered pairs, $\{(3,1), (3,2), (3,3), (4,1), (4,2), (4,3),\}$ is the same as $\{(X, Y) \mid X, Y \in I, 3 \leq X \leq 4, 1 \leq Y \leq 3\}$, where $X, Y \in I$ means $X \in I$ and $Y \in I$. We indicate by (X, Y) that the names of the variables are X and Y, and they are ordered so that X is given first. We could write such an ordered pair, (X, Y), as $\{\{X\}, \{X, Y\}\}$ or $\{\{X, Y\}, \{X\}\}$, all meaning the same thing. The number line is not designed for number pairs so we construct two number lines in such a way that number pairs can be employed. In [24a], the number lines are set at right angles at the zero (origin) point of each. Number pairs are indicated by points in this plane formed by the number lines (axes). The points shown in [24a] are labeled according to the units marked on each number line (axis). That is, the first number of the pair is called the X coordinate, and is read from the horizontal X axis. The second number is the Y coordinate and is read from the vertical Y axis.

[24]

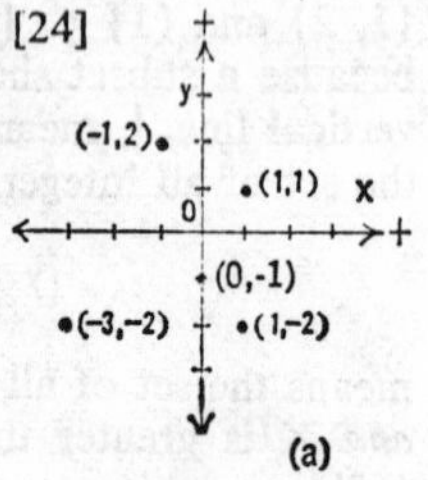


(a)

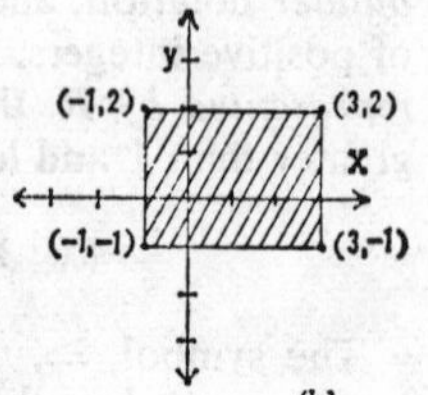


(b)

The set of ordered pairs, $\{(X, Y) \mid X, Y \in R, 3 \leq X \leq 4, 1 \leq Y \leq 3\}$, cannot be listed but is shown on the graph in [24b] as the shaded area.

## ALGEBRAIC EXPRESSIONS

**Operations.** The *absolute value* of a real number is the distance from the point of the number to the origin. The absolute value of a number, X, is symbolized by $|X|$ and is computed by:

$$|X| = X, \text{ if } X \geq 0;$$

$$|X| = -X, \text{ if } X < 0.$$

Thus, $|4| = 4$, $|-3| = 3$, and $|0| = 0$.

ADDITION RULE — To add two signed numbers with *like* signs, add their absolute values and insert their common sign. If their signs are *unlike*, then *subtract* their absolute values and insert the sign of the number with the larger absolute value.

The addition of positive and negative numbers is like rises and falls in temperature. If we begin at 80° and rise 20°, then fall 30°, we can compute the present temperature as $80° + 20° - 30° = 100° - 30° = 70°$.

Subtraction is performed by subtracting the *subtrahend* from the *minuend*. Thus, in $6 - 4$, the subtrahend is the 4 and the 6 is the minuend.

SUBTRACTION RULE — To subtract one signed number (subtrahend) from another (minuend), change the sign of the subtrahend, then *add* the two numbers by the addition rule.

To change the sign of a number is the same as using the additive inverse of the number. Then to subtract $-10$ from $-8$, we compute: $+10$ added to $-8$ and we get $+2$.

Subtraction of real numbers is the *directed distance* from the subtrahend to the minuend on the number line. So the directed distance from $-3$ to $+5$ is $(+5) - (-3) = (+5) + (+3) = +8$.

Multiplication of signed numbers is performed as in ordinary multiplication, only the sign of the product is given for non-zero numbers as follows:

MULTIPLICATION RULE — If the two signed numbers that form the product have *like* signs, then the product is *positive*. If they have *unlike* signs, the product is *negative*.

To show that the multiplication rule is consistent, consider the following patterns:

$$(+2)(+2) = +4 \qquad (-1)(2) = -2$$

$$(+2)(+1) = +2 \qquad (-1)(1) = -1$$

$$(+2)(+0) = +0 \qquad (-1)(0) = 0$$

$$(+2)(-1) = -2 \qquad (-1)(-1) = +1$$

To prove that a positive times a negative is negative, we again use the field properties. $(a)\cdot(-a) = -(a\cdot a)$. Proof:

[25]

| | |
|---|---|
| $a + (-a) = 0$ | OP-4 |
| $(a)\cdot(a + (-a)) = a\cdot 0$ | [21] |
| $(a)\cdot(a) + (a)\cdot(-a) = 0$ | OP-11, [23] |
| $a\cdot a + (a)\cdot(-a) = a\cdot a + (-(a\cdot a))$ | OP-4 |
| $(a)\cdot(-a) = -(a\cdot a)$ | [20] ■ |

A negative times a negative is a positive. $(-a)\cdot(-a) = +a\cdot a$. Proof:

[26]

| | |
|---|---|
| $a + (-a) = 0$ | OP-4 |
| $(-a)\cdot(a + (-a)) = (-a)\,0$ | [21] |
| $(-a)\cdot(a) + (-a)\cdot(-a) = 0$ | OP-11, [22] |
| $-a\cdot a + (-a)\cdot(-a) = -a\cdot a + a\cdot a$ | OP-4 |
| $(-a)\cdot(-a) = +a\cdot a$ | [20] ■ |

The division operation on signed numbers is

the inverse of multiplication. The rule of signs is the same as multiplication.

DIVISION RULE — The quotient of two signed numbers is found by multiplying the dividend by the reciprocal of the non-zero divisor with a positive sign attached if the signs of the numbers are the same; otherwise, the quotient is negative.

The proofs of the division rule of signs are essentially the same as the multiplication proofs, using $(a^{-1})$ for (a) in the second line of each proof, and also the commutative property.

*Division by zero is a concept which is undefined in mathematics.* A point is also an undefined concept, but we have an intuitive notion about what a point is. Intuition seems to fail on all approaches to division by zero. Therefore, we carefully avoid division by zero.

Dividing zero by zero is called *indeterminant* (see *College Preparatory Mathematics, Derivatives*).

**Algebraic Terms.** An algebraic term is made up of constant and variable *factors.* A constant, like a 2 or a —10, is sometimes written as an a or b or other letters of the first of the alphabet. Variables are usually denoted by letters nearer the end of the alphabet; x, y, etc. The following are algebraic terms: 2, —10, $x^2$, $ax^2$, $-3y^2$, $-xy/z$. $x + 3$ is not a term.

**Coefficients, Exponents.** The term, $2x^3$, means x is raised to the third power and then doubled. The 2 is the constant *coefficient* of $x^3$; the 3 is the *exponent* of x; x is the *base* of the 3.

$$(x^3)(x^2) = (x{\cdot}x{\cdot}x)(x{\cdot}x) = x{\cdot}x{\cdot}x{\cdot}x{\cdot}x = x^5$$

RULE — To *multiply* two terms involving like bases, add the like bases' exponents.

$$(x^5) \div (x^2) = (x{\cdot}x{\cdot}x{\cdot}x{\cdot}x) \div (x{\cdot}x)$$

$$\frac{x{\cdot}x{\cdot}x{\cdot}x{\cdot}x}{x{\cdot}x} = x{\cdot}x{\cdot}x = x^3$$

RULE — To *divide* two terms involving like bases, *subtract* the exponent of the divisor from the exponent of the like base in the dividend.

EXAMPLES:

$$(2x^2y^3)(3xy^4) = 6x^3y^7,$$

$$\frac{8x^3y}{4xy^2} = 2x^2y^{-1} = \frac{2x^2}{y}, \quad \frac{x^2}{x^2} = x^0 = 1.$$

RULE — To *raise* an algebraic term *to a power,* multiply the exponents of the variable and constant factors of the term by the power.

EXAMPLE:

$$(2x^3)^2(3y^{-1})^3 = (4x^6)(27y^{-3}) = 108x^6y^{-3}.$$

**Fractional Exponents, Radicals.** We indicate by the term, $x^{1/b}$, that x is the *base* and b is the root being taken of x. This is also written $\sqrt[b]{x}$, where the $\sqrt{\ }$ is called a radical. The root b of x means the number N such that $N^b = x$. Thus, $8^{1/3} = \sqrt[3]{8} = 2$, because $2^3 = 8$. The fractional exponent term, $x^{a/b}$, is the same as $\sqrt[b]{x^a}$. $27^{2/3} = \sqrt[3]{27^2} = 9$.

To simplify an nth root radical, $\sqrt[n]{\ }$, of a term, we re-express it by removing the factors, which are nth powers of whole terms, and placing their nth root in front of the radical and multiplying. Then the $\sqrt{72} = \sqrt{36{\cdot}2} = 6\sqrt{2}$. Here we had the *square* root, so we found a *square* factor and removed it. The $\sqrt{20x^2y^3} = \sqrt{4{\cdot}5{\cdot}x^2{\cdot}y^2{\cdot}y} = 2xy\sqrt{5y}$ in simplified form. On a radical like $\sqrt{2x^2-x^3}$, we use the distributive property, $\sqrt{2x^2-x^3} = \sqrt{x^2(2-x)}$ and simplify it to $x\sqrt{2-x}$.

To simplify a radical with a denominator, we work with it until the denominator is one. The $\sqrt{3}$ is simplified; the $\sqrt{1/3}$ is not. We simplify it as follows:

$$\sqrt{\frac{1}{3}} = \sqrt{\frac{1}{3}\cdot\frac{3}{3}} = \sqrt{\frac{3}{9}} = \frac{1}{3}\sqrt{\frac{3}{1}} = \frac{\sqrt{3}}{3}.$$

Also:

$$\sqrt{\frac{xy^2}{2x^2z}} = \frac{y}{x}\sqrt{\frac{x}{2z}\cdot\frac{2z}{2z}} = \frac{y}{x}\sqrt{\frac{2xz}{4z^2}} = \frac{y}{2xz}\sqrt{2xz}.$$

**Products, Factors.** An algebraic term is also called a *monomial.* The sum of two terms is a *binomial,* and the sum of three terms is a *trinomial.* A *polynomial* has *any number of terms,* but the usual sense is a sum of terms involving the same variable raised to different integer powers, and with constant coefficients. For example, $x^3 + 4x^2 - 3x + 10$ is called a third degree polynomial in x.

To find the *products* of various polynomials, we employ the distributive property and simplify.

EXAMPLES:

$$2x^2(3xy^2 - yz) = 6x^3y^2 - 2x^2yz.$$

$$(2x+y)(x-y) = 2x(x-y) + y(x-y) = 2x^2 - 2xy + xy - y^2 = 2x^2 - xy - y^2.$$

$$(x-2)(x^2-3x+6) = x(x^2-3x+6) - 2(x^2-3x+6) = x^3 - 3x^2 + 6x - 2x^2 + 6x - 12 = x^3 - 5x^2 + 12x - 12.$$

To *factor* a polynomial, we look for lesser degree polynomials which will multiply to get the polynomial. In practice, we try to remove, by the distributive property, first monomials, then binomials if possible.

EXAMPLES:

$$x^3 + 2x^2 - 6x = x(x^2+2x-6).$$

$$x^3yz^4 - x^2yz^3 + 2xy^2z^2 = xyz^2(x^2z^2-xz+2y).$$

$$x^2 - 5x + 6 = (x-2)(x-3).$$

In explanation of the last example, to factor a trinomial into binomials:

**1.** Remove common monomial factors.

**2.** Arrange the trinomial in the descending

order of a variable. That is, put the highest power on the left, etc., to lowest power on the right. (Ascending order will work also.) Place two sets of parentheses on the right.

3. Place some *trial* factors of the first term in the left side of the parentheses. Place trial factors of the last term in the right side of the parentheses.
4. Find the product under these *trial* conditions to see if the middle term of the product agrees with the middle term of the trinomial. If yes, we have factored the trinomial. If no, go back to step 3 if there are some unused factors. If all have been tried, we say the trinomial cannot be factored with whole number factors.

EXAMPLES:

$$x^2 + 5x + 6 = (x+2)(x+3),$$
$$x^2 - x - 6 = (x-3)(x+2),$$
$$2x^2 - 15x + 18 = (2x-3)(x-6).$$

Some special cases of factoring are:
Differences of two squares;

$$x^2 - y^2 = (x+y)(x-y).$$

Sum of two squares;

$x^2 + y^2$ is *not* factorable with whole numbers, but can be factored with imaginary numbers so that

$$x^2 + y^2 = (x+yi)(x-yi), \text{ where } i = \sqrt{-1}.$$

Difference of two cubes;

$$x^3 - y^3 = (x-y)(x^2+xy+y^2).$$

Sum of two cubes;

$$x^3 + y^3 = (x+y)(x^2-xy+y^2).$$

We may use radicals if necessary to factor some expressions. For example:

$$3x^2 - 2y^2 = (\sqrt{3}x + \sqrt{2}y)(\sqrt{3}x - \sqrt{2}y).$$

These techniques of factoring are used for many purposes in mathematics; however, we will apply them here for simplification purposes. To simplify fractions, sums, products, and quotients of polynomials (in particular trinomials), factor and divide through by common factors.

EXAMPLES:

$$\frac{x^2+x-6}{x^2-4x-21} = \frac{(x-2)(x+3)}{(x+3)(x-7)} = \frac{x-2}{x-7}.$$

$$\frac{6x}{x^2+x-2} + \frac{1}{x+2} - \frac{2}{x-1} = \frac{6x+1(x-1)-2(x+2)}{(x-1)(x+2)} =$$

$$\frac{6x+x-1-2x-4}{(x-1)(x+2)} = \frac{5x-5}{(x-1)(x-2)} = \frac{5(x-1)}{(x-1)(x-2)} =$$

$$\frac{5}{x-2}.$$

$$\left(\frac{x+1}{x-1}\right)\left(\frac{x^2-2x+1}{x^2-1}\right) = \frac{(x+1)(x-1)(x-1)}{(x-1)(x+1)(x-1)} = 1.$$

$$\frac{x^2-x-2}{x^2-4x-5} \div \frac{x^2+x-6}{x^2-3x-18} = \frac{x^2-x-2}{x^2-4x-5}\,\frac{x^2-3x-18}{x^2+x-6} =$$

$$\frac{(x-2)(x+1)(x-6)(x+3)}{(x-5)(x+1)(x+3)(x-2)} = \frac{x-6}{x-5}.$$

The radical expression,

$$\frac{1+\sqrt{x}}{1-\sqrt{x}},$$

is simplified by using the radical *conjugate* as follows:

$$\frac{1+\sqrt{x}}{1-\sqrt{x}} = \left(\frac{1+\sqrt{x}}{1-\sqrt{x}}\right)\left(\frac{1+\sqrt{x}}{1+\sqrt{x}}\right) =$$

$$\frac{1+2\sqrt{x}+x}{1-x}.$$

**Logarithms.** *A logarithm is an exponent.* If $a^b = c$, then we can also write $\log_a c = b$, which means the logarithm to the base of *a* of *c* is *b*. Thus, $3^2 = 9$ and $\log_3 9 = 2$. Also $10^{1.2304} = 17$, so $\log_{10} 17 = 1.2304$. The *characteristic* is 1 and the *mantissa* is .2304 of the base 10 log of 17. Ten is the *common* logarithm base.

To find the common logarithm of a number, we put the number into scientific notation. We find the mantissa of the logarithm by looking in the log table on page 1023 for the log which corresponds to the part of the number in scientific notation between 1 and 10. We insert the characteristic of the logarithm by adding the exponent of the number in scientific notation.

In particular, the log of 351 is computed as follows: $351 = 3.51 \times 10^2$. The 3.51 is found in the log table to correspond to .5453. We add the characteristic, 2, to .5453 so that log 351 = 2.5453. We compute log .906 by $.906 = 9.06 \times 10^{-1}$; looking up 9.06, we get .9571. We then add the —1 and write the sum as .9571—1 or 9.9571—10.

If the logarithm of a number is given, we can find the number or *antilog* by the reverse process. We find the number that is associated with the mantissa in the log table and multiply it by 10 raised to the characteristic power.

For example, if $\log_{10} 4 = 0.6021$, then 4 is the antilog of 0.6021. The antilog of 8.7938—10 is found by looking up .7938 in the log table. The corresponding number is 6.22, so we multiply 6.22 by 10 to the power represented by 8.—10 or —2 which gives $6.22 \times 10^{-2} = .0622$.

We use *interpolation* when we want the log of an N or more place number from an N-1 place table. For example, on page 1023 we have a three place table so we must interpolate to find the log of a four place number. We also *interpolate* when we want the antilog of a logarithm which is found between two logarithms in the table. Examples of these are:

(1) The log of 2.876 is found by noting that 2.876 is between 2.870 and 2.880, therefore, its logarithm will be between the logs of these numbers, .4579 and .4594, respectively. We set up a proportion relating distances between numbers and distances between logarithms. Thus .006: .010 = x: .0015, and solving the proportion we get x = .0009, so we add the .0009 to the .4579 and get .4588 as the desired logarithm.

(2) The antilog of .9530 is found by setting up a similar proportion. We have .9530 between .9528 and .9533, which have corresponding numbers of 8.97 and 8.98. We solve the proportion, x: .010 = .002: .0005, and have x = .004 which makes our desired number .004 + 8.97 = 8.974.

Logarithms may be applied to multiplication, division, raising to powers, and extracting roots.

RULE — *To multiply two numbers, add their logs then the antilog of the sum is the product of the numbers.*

RULE — *To divide two numbers, subtract the log of the divisor from the log of the dividend then the antilog of the difference is the quotient of the numbers.*

RULE — *To raise a number to a power, multiply its logarithm by the power, then the antilog of the product is the number raised to the power.*

RULE — *To extract a root of a number, divide its logarithm by the root, then the antilog of the quotient is the extracted root of the number.*

EXAMPLE: To find

$$\frac{(1.2)\,(6.7)^2}{\sqrt[4]{.35}} = \log\frac{(1.2)\,(6.7)^2}{\sqrt[4]{.35}}$$

$= \log(1.2) + 2\log(6.7) - \frac{1}{4}\log .35$
$= .0792 + 2\,(.8261) - \frac{1}{4}(7.5441 - 8) = .0792 + 1.6522 - 1.8860 + 2 = 1.8454$, Antilog (1.8454) = 7.01, approximately.

**Functions.** *A function is a set of ordered pairs of elements such that no two pairs have the same first elements and different second elements.* Thus several different first elements may be paired with the same second element.

The set of first elements is called the *domain* of the function. The set of second values is called the *range*. A function is said to *map* the domain into the range.

If Y is the range and X is the domain of a function, we often symbolize this as: y= f(x), meaning that to get an element of the range, y, the function, f, maps an element, x, from the domain. For example, if the function is defined by $y = f(x) = x^2 - 2$, then a *subset* of the set of function values is {(0, —2), (1, —1), (2, 2)}.

*If a function, f, is such that no two ordered pairs with different first elements have the same second element, then the inverse function, $f^{-1}$, exists and is the set of ordered pairs formed by interchanging first and second elements of the ordered pairs of f.* For example,

if f = { (1,2), (4,5), (—1,3) }, then $f^{-1}$ = {(2,1), (5,4), (3,—1)}.

## ALGEBRAIC EQUATIONS

**Linear Equations.** A polynomial equation is termed *linear* if it is of the form

$$ax + b = 0,$$

where a and b are real numbers and $a \neq 0$. It is called a *first degree* equation in x as the highest power of x is 1. The solution is $x = -b/a$.

The equation, $w = 2x^2 + 7y - 1$, is not a linear equation, but w is a *linear combination* of $x^2$ and y. Let y be a linear combination of x, like y = 2x — 2 in [27a]. Then in the x, y plane, if the set of number pairs which satisfy the equation are plotted as points on the graph, they form a straight line. Thus, y is a *linear function* of x.

**Slope.** The *slope* is the amount of steepness of a line. It is measured as the rise over the run or the change of y divided by the change in x by going from one point to another on the line in the x, y plane. If a line goes through the points,

[27]

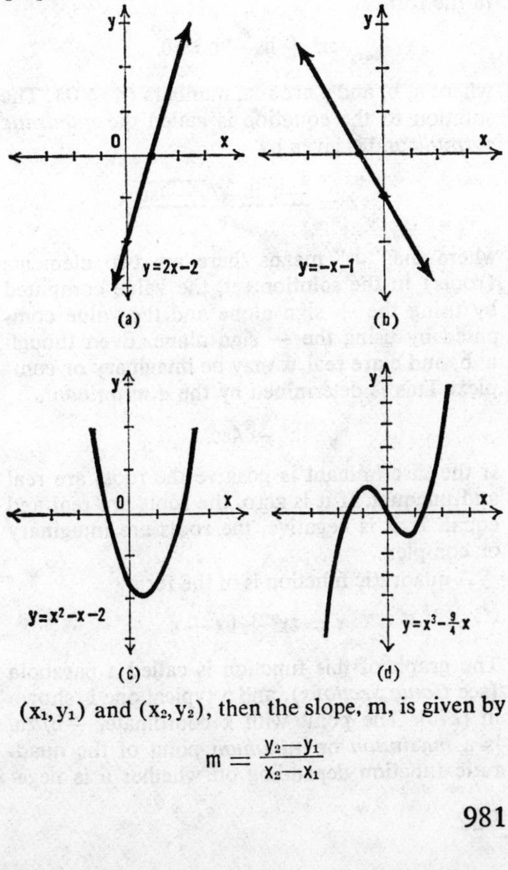


$(x_1, y_1)$ and $(x_2, y_2)$, then the slope, m, is given by

$$m = \frac{y_2 - y_1}{x_2 - x_1}$$

In [27a], two points on the line are (0, —2) and (1, 0) and the slope is

$$m = \frac{0 - (-2)}{1 - (0)} = \frac{2}{1} = 2.$$

Using the same formula, we find the slope of the line in [27b], passing through (—1, 0) and (0, —1), to be —1. [27b] is also considered as a linear equation in x and y.

In general, the equation of a straight line in the x, y plane is

$$(y - y_1) = m(x - x_1),$$

where $(x_1, y_1)$ is a point on the line and m is the slope.

The *intercepts* of a line are the values of x and y where the line crosses the x and y axes respectively. Thus, in [27a] the x-intercept is 1 and the y-intercept is —2. Then

$$y = mx + b$$

is the equation of a line of slope m and y-intercept b.

**Distance Between Points.** The distance between two points in the x, y plane which have coordinates, $(x_1, y_1)$ and $(x_2, y_2)$ is

$$d = \sqrt{(x_1 - x_2)^2 + (y_1 - y_2)^2}.$$

**Quadratic Equations.** A *quadratic* or *second degree* polynomial equation in x can be written in the form

$$ax^2 + bx + c = 0,$$

where a, b, and c are real numbers ($a \neq 0$). The solution to the equation is called the *quadratic formula* and is given by

$$x = \frac{-b \pm \sqrt{b^2 - 4ac}}{2a},$$

where the "±" means there are two elements (roots) in the solution set, the value computed by using the + sign alone and the value computed by using the — sign alone. Even though a, b, and c are real, x may be imaginary or complex. This is determined by the *discriminant,*

$$b^2 - 4ac.$$

If the discriminant is positive the roots are real and unequal. If it is zero, the roots are real and equal. If it is negative, the roots are imaginary or complex.

A quadratic function is of the form

$$y = ax^2 + bx + c.$$

The graph of this function is called a parabola (see *Conic Sections*), and a typical one is shown in [27c]. The point with x coordinate, $-b/2a$, is a *maximum* or *minimum* point of the quadratic function depending on whether a is negative or positive. See *Applications, Quadratic Max-Min Problem.*

**Polynomial Equations.** A polynomial equation of the third degree is called a *cubic equation.* The general form is

$$ax^3 + bx^2 + cx + d = 0.$$

At least one of the three roots is real. A cubic function is shown in [27d].

The general *nth degree polynomial equation* is of the form

$$a_n x^n + a_{n-1} x^{n-1} + \ldots + a_1 x + a_0 = 0,$$

where $a_n$, $a_{n-1}$, etc., are real constants. There is no general formula for finding the roots of an nth degree equation. Often the closest we can come to computing the roots is by approximation procedures. See *Derivative, Newton's Method* in the college math section.

**The Fundamental Theorem of Algebra.** We are assured by the fundamental theorem of algebra that *a polynomial equation of degree n will have n real or complex roots.* If the degree of the equation is odd, then there is at least one real root.

**Exponential Equations.** If an equation has constant bases, and exponents which are variables, then we say it is an exponential equation. A frequently applied exponential equation is the compound interest equation,

$$A = P(1+r)^n,$$

when we are given A, P, and r, thus to solve for n. If A = 500, P = 120, and r = .04, the equation becomes

$$500 = 120(1.04)^n$$

and we can solve for n by taking the log of both sides.

$$\log 500 = \log (120(1.04)^n) = \log 120 + n \log 1.04$$
$$2.6990 = 2.0792 + n(.0170)$$

$$n = \frac{2.6990 - 2.0792}{.0170} = \frac{.6198}{.0170} = 36.5.$$

This means 37 years in actuality.

An exponential function is shown in [28a]. The x-axis (y = 0) is called an asymptote, meaning that the function approaches this line as a limit (here as x approaches negative infinity, y approaches zero).

**Logarithmic Equations.** An equation involving logarithms is a logarithmic equation. For example, $\log_{10} x = 3$ has x = 1000 as the solution. $y = \log_{10} x$ is a logarithmic function. See [28b] for the graph. Note that $y = \log_{10} x$ can be stated as $x = 10^y$, but is still different from $y = 10^x$, which is an exponential function. In [28b] the y-axis (x = 0) is an asymptote. The growth rate of most animals is a form of the logarithmic curve shown in [28b].

[28]

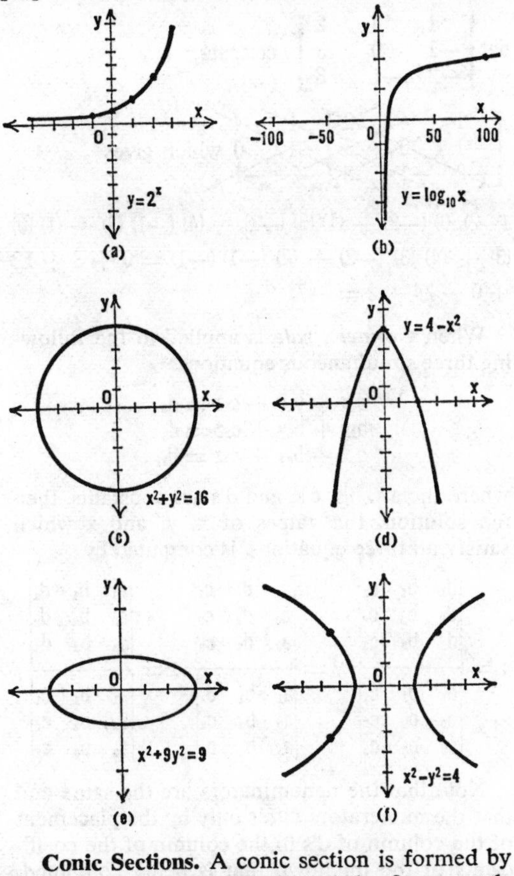


**Conic Sections.** A conic section is formed by the intersection of a plane and the figure made by two identical cones which share only the vertex and line of symmetry. The point and line are special cases of conic sections. The circle and parabola have been mentioned earlier; however, we now study them as well as the ellipse and hyperbola in regard to conic sections.

The *circle* with center at (h, k) and radius of c has a general equation of

$$(x-h)^2 + (y-k)^2 = c^2.$$

See [28c].

The *parabola* has a general equation of

$$(y-k) = c(x-h)^2$$

where (h, k) is the vertex and is the minimum point if $c>0$ and a maximum point if $c<0$. See [28d].

The *ellipse* is generally given by the equation

$$\frac{(x-h)^2}{a^2} + \frac{(y-k)^2}{b^2} = 1$$

where (h, k) is the center of the ellipse, with 2a and 2b the lengths of the axes of symetry. See [28e].

The *hyperbola,* which is centered about the point, (h, k), and has asymptotes, $y = \pm(b/a)(x-h) + k$, is shown in [28f] and given by the equation

$$\frac{(x-h)^2}{a^2} - \frac{(y-k)^2}{b^2} = 1.$$

The theory behind conic sections is applied all the way from the minute orbits of electrons about the nucleus of an atom, to the giant movements of the heavenly bodies of outer space. In particular, circles, ellipses and hyperbolas are employed in the lunar and interplanetary space travel program.

## SIMULTANEOUS EQUATIONS

**Dependence, Consistence.** Two equations are said to be *dependent* if the information of one of them can be derived from the other. For example, $x + y = 3$ and $2x + 2y = 6$ are dependent equations, for we can multiply both sides of the first one by 2 to get the second one. They represent the same set of points (number pairs) and if they are graphed, they are the same line.

Equations like $x + y = 4$ and $x + z = 6$ are called *independent* as we cannot derive one equation from the other. The equations $x + y = 4$ and $2x - y = 5$, are independent, but they are also *consistent* in that if these two equations are graphed simultaneously, they share the point, (3,1). The locating of number pairs (or triples, etc.) which consistent equations share is called the solution of the simultaneous equations.

If no solution exists, as in $x + y = 3$ and $x + y = 4$, then the equations are called *inconsistent*. Graphically speaking, this means the lines or curves do not intersect. These particular lines are parallel.

**Graphical Solution.** To find the solution of two equations and two unknowns, we graph both equations on the same coordinate axes; the point(s) of intersection is the solution. For example, to solve

[29]

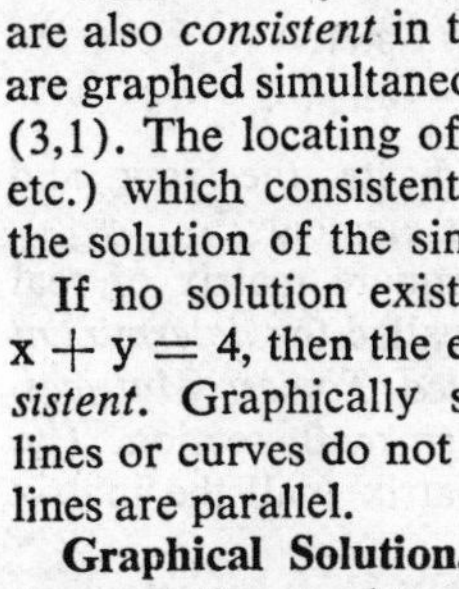

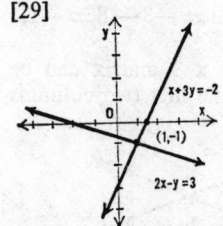


$$\begin{cases} x + 3y = -2 \\ 2x - y = 3 \end{cases}$$

We plot the graphs in [29] and get the point of intersection to be (1, −1).

**Algebraic Solutions.** We may solve simultaneous systems of two or more equations by means of *algebraic* manipulation if the solution is non-empty. The two most common approaches are *addition* and *substitution.*

We can employ the *addition* method to the equations in [29] by multiplying both sides of $x + 3y = -2$ by $-2$.

$$\begin{cases} -2x - 6y = 4 \\ 2x - y = 3. \end{cases}$$

We now add equals to equals and the x terms drop out leaving $-7y = 7$, and thus $y = -1$. Knowing that $y = -1$, we insert a $-1$ for y in $x + 3y = -2$, and get $x + 3(-1) = -2$; from this we know that $x - 3 = -2$, so $x = -2 + 3 = +1$.

The same problem may be solved by *substitution.* Noting that $x + 3y = -2$ can be stated as $x = -2 - 3y$, we substitute the $-2 - 3y$ for x in the other equation getting an equation involving y only which we can solve.

$$\begin{aligned} 2(-2-3y) - y &= 3 \\ -4 - 6y - y &= 3 \\ -7y &= 7 \\ y &= -1 \end{aligned}$$

So again as $x = -2 - 3y$, $y = -1$ means that $x = -2 - 3(-1) = -2 + 3 = 1$.

**Cramer's Rule.** A *matrix* is a rectangular array of numbers. We use subscripts to denote the elements of a matrix. That is, the matrix is arranged in rows and columns as below,

$$\begin{bmatrix} 5 & 7 & 0 \\ 3 & -2 & 4 \end{bmatrix}$$

so that the first row first column element is 5, the first row second column element is 7 and so on. We represent a 2 x 3, (2 by 3), matrix by

$$\begin{bmatrix} a_{11} & a_{12} & a_{13} \\ a_{21} & a_{22} & a_{23} \end{bmatrix},$$

where the subscripts indicate the row and column, respectively, of the elements.

Associated with every square matrix of real numbers is a real number called the *determinant* of the matrix. See *Selected Topics; Matrices, Determinants* in the college math section. The determinant of a 2 x 2 matrix (call the matrix M) is symbolized as

$$\det (M) \text{ or } \det \begin{bmatrix} a_{11} & a_{12} \\ a_{21} & a_{22} \end{bmatrix} \text{ or } \begin{vmatrix} a_{11} & a_{12} \\ a_{21} & a_{22} \end{vmatrix}$$

and is equal to $a_{11}a_{22} - a_{12}a_{21}$. Thus we compute

$$\det \begin{bmatrix} 1 & 2 \\ 4 & -3 \end{bmatrix} = 1(-3) - 2(4) = -3 - 8 = -11.$$

The determinant of a 3 x 3 matrix can be found as follows: Repeat the first two columns and draw

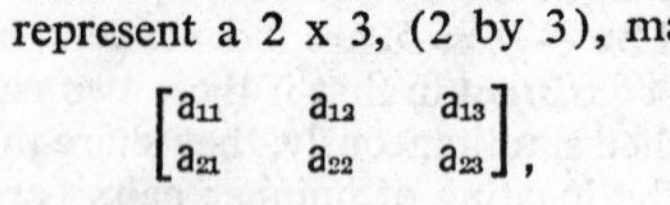

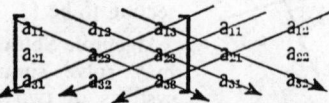

arrows as shown; form the six products of the numbers crossed by each arrow; the products indicated by the three arrows pointing to the right are added to the negatives of the remaining three products to get the value of the determinant.

EXAMPLE: To find

$$\det \begin{bmatrix} 1 & 4 & 2 \\ -1 & 0 & 3 \\ -2 & -1 & 3 \end{bmatrix}, \text{ compute}$$

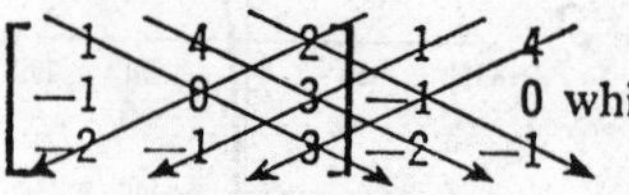

which gives

$(-2)(0)(-2) - (1)(3)(-1) - (4)(-1)(3) + (1)(0)(3) + (4)(3)(-2) + (2)(-1)(-1) = 0 + 3 + 12 + 0 - 24 + 2 = -7.$

When *Cramer's rule* is applied to the following three simultaneous equations:

$$\begin{aligned} a_1x + b_1y + c_1z &= d_1 \\ a_2x + b_2y + c_2z &= d_2 \\ a_3x + b_3y + c_3z &= d_3, \end{aligned}$$

where the a's, b's, c's, and d's are constants, then the solution, the values of x, y, and z which satisfy all three equations, is computed by

$$x = \frac{\begin{vmatrix} d_1 & b_1 & c_1 \\ d_2 & b_2 & c_2 \\ d_3 & b_3 & c_3 \end{vmatrix}}{\begin{vmatrix} a_1 & b_1 & c_1 \\ a_2 & b_2 & c_2 \\ a_3 & b_3 & c_3 \end{vmatrix}},\ y = \frac{\begin{vmatrix} a_1 & d_1 & c_1 \\ a_2 & d_2 & c_2 \\ a_3 & d_3 & c_3 \end{vmatrix}}{\begin{vmatrix} a_1 & b_1 & c_1 \\ a_2 & b_2 & c_2 \\ a_3 & b_3 & c_3 \end{vmatrix}},\ z = \frac{\begin{vmatrix} a_1 & b_1 & d_1 \\ a_2 & b_2 & d_2 \\ a_3 & b_3 & d_3 \end{vmatrix}}{\begin{vmatrix} a_1 & b_1 & c_1 \\ a_2 & b_2 & c_2 \\ a_3 & b_3 & c_3 \end{vmatrix}}.$$

Note that the denominators are the same and that the numerators differ only by the placement of the column of d's in the column of the coefficients of the unknown that is being computed. Thus, there are only four determinants to evaluate and perhaps even fewer if we, for example, substitute the computed values of x and y in an equation and solve for z.

EXAMPLE: Solve $\begin{cases} x + y + z = 2 \\ 2x - y = 3 \\ x - 2y - 3z = -3 \end{cases}$

SOLUTION:

$$x = \frac{\begin{vmatrix} 2 & 1 & 1 \\ 3 & -1 & 0 \\ -3 & -2 & -3 \end{vmatrix}}{\begin{vmatrix} 1 & 1 & 1 \\ 2 & -1 & 0 \\ 1 & -2 & -3 \end{vmatrix}} = \frac{6}{6} = 1,$$

$$y = \frac{\begin{vmatrix} 1 & 2 & 1 \\ 2 & 3 & 0 \\ 1 & -3 & -3 \end{vmatrix}}{6} = \frac{-6}{6} = -1$$

and from the first equation, $z = 2 - x - y = 2 - (1) - (-1) = 2$.

Cramer's rule can be applied to two simultaneous equations in two unknowns as well as to three equations as shown.

For four equations in four unknowns and higher, see *Selected Topics, Cramer's Rule* in the college math section.

## SEQUENCES AND SERIES

**Sequence.** *A sequence is a set of numbers that are arranged in a one-to-one correspondence with a subset of the natural numbers.* There is a first number, a second, etc., throughout the set. For example, 1, 3, 5, 7 is a sequence and so is —2, 0, 2, 4, 6, . . . , where the dots mean continued in the same pattern, indicating that the set has an infinite number of elements or *terms.* If all of the terms of a sequence are not given then there must be a *pattern,* or *rule,* given to identify a particular sequence.

**Arithmetic Sequence.** An *arithmetic sequence* is a sequence of terms such that the *difference* between any two consecutive terms is a constant. The first term of an arithmetic sequence is called *a,* and the difference is called *d.* Thus, the terms of an arithmetic sequence are given by

$$a, a + d, a + 2d, a + 3d, \ldots,$$

and the *n*th term of the sequence is denoted by

$$t_n = a + (n-1)d.$$

For example, to find the 20th term of —3, 1, 5, . . . , we have $a = -3$, $d = 4$, $n = 20$, so that

$$t_{20} = -3 + (20-1)4 = -3 + 19(4) = 73.$$

**Series.** *A series is the indicated sum of a sequence.* Thus, $-2 + 0 + 2 + 4 + 6$ is a series and the sum is 10. The series $10 + 20 + 30 + \ldots$ is an *infinite series.*

**Arithmetic Series.** The sum of the terms of an arithmetic sequence is an *arithmetic series.* The sum of n terms of an arithmetic series is computed by the formula

$$s_n = \frac{n}{2}(a+t_n) = \frac{n}{2}(a+a+(n-1)d) =$$

$$\frac{n}{2}(2a+(n-1)d).$$

So to find the sum of 15 terms of the series $\frac{1}{2} + \frac{3}{2} + \frac{5}{2} + \ldots$, we have $a = \frac{1}{2}$, $d = 1$, $n = 15$, and then

$$s_{15} = \tfrac{15}{2}(1+(15-1)1) = \tfrac{15}{2}(15) = \tfrac{225}{2}.$$

**Geometric Sequence.** A *geometric sequence* is a sequence of terms such that if a certain constant (called r the ratio) is multiplied by any term of the sequence, the product is the following term. The first term of a geometric sequence is called *a.* For example, the series $\frac{1}{3}$, 1, 3, 9, 27, . . . is a geometric sequence with $a = \frac{1}{3}$ and $r = 3$.

The terms of a geometric sequence are then

$$a, ar, ar^2, ar^3, \ldots,$$

and the *n*th term is given by

$$t_n = ar^{n-1}.$$

So to find the 7th term of the sequence 10, 5, 2.5, . . . , we have $a = 10$, $r = \frac{1}{2}$, $n = 7$, and

$$t_7 = 10(\tfrac{1}{2})^6 = 10(\tfrac{1}{64}) = \tfrac{10}{64}.$$

**Geometric Series.** The sum of a geometric sequence is a *geometric series.* The sum of n terms of a geometric series is

$$s_n = \frac{a-ar^n}{1-r} = \frac{a(1-r^n)}{1-r}, \text{ where } r \neq 1.$$

Thus r can be positive, negative, or zero, but not one. If $r = 1$, the series is arithmetic. As an example, to find the sum of 7 terms of $\frac{3}{4} - \frac{3}{8} + \frac{3}{16} - \frac{3}{32} + \ldots$, we note that $\frac{3}{4}(-\frac{1}{2}) = -\frac{3}{8}$, and $(-\frac{3}{8})(-\frac{1}{2}) = \frac{3}{16}$, so $r = -\frac{1}{2}$, $a = \frac{3}{4}$, and $n = 7$.

$$s_n = \frac{\frac{3}{4}(1-(-\frac{1}{2})^7)}{1-(-\frac{1}{2})} = \frac{\frac{3}{4}(1-(-\frac{1}{128}))}{\frac{3}{2}} =$$

$$\tfrac{1}{2}(\tfrac{129}{128}) = \tfrac{129}{256}.$$

If $|r| < 1$ in an infinite geometric series, then we can find the limit of the infinite series (called the *sum of the infinite series* and symbolized by $S_\infty$) by noting that

$$S_n = \frac{a-ar^n}{1-r} = \frac{a}{1-r} - \frac{ar^n}{1-r}$$

and that $r^n$ in the second term approaches 0 as n gets larger with $|r| < 1$ (see *Limits* in the college math section). Therefore the sum of an infinite series with $|r| < 1$ is

$$S_\infty = \frac{a}{1-r}.$$

To find the sum of the infinite series $1 + \frac{1}{2} + \frac{1}{4} + \ldots$, we use $a = 1$, $r = \frac{1}{2}$ and get

$$S_\infty = \frac{1}{1-\frac{1}{2}} = \frac{1}{\frac{1}{2}} = 2.$$

See *Applications, The Hare and Tortoise,* for another example.

**Σ, !, Π, Notations.** We often represent a series with the aid of the Σ symbol. The series $1 + 2 + 3 + \ldots + 10$ would be symbolized as in [30a]. In [30b] we have the

[30]

$$\sum_{i=1}^{10} i \qquad \sum_{i=1}^{n} x_i \qquad \sum_{i=1}^{n}(m-x_i)^2$$

(a) (b) (c)

summation of the n terms $x_1 + x_2 + x_3 + \ldots + x_n$. To symbolize the statistical series $(m-x_1)^2 + (m-x_2)^2 + \ldots + (m-x_n)^2$ we use [30c].

If c is a constant, then we have the formulas

$$\sum_{i=1}^{n} c = nc, \quad \sum_{i=1}^{n} cx_i = c\sum_{i=1}^{n} x_i, \quad \sum_{i=1}^{n}(x_i+y_i) = \sum_{i=1}^{n} x_i + \sum_{i=1}^{n} y_i$$

If n is a positive integer then n! (read n factoral) is the product of n and all positive integers less than n. Thus $3! = 3 \cdot 2 \cdot 1 = 6$, $5! = 5 \cdot 4 \cdot 3 \cdot 2 \cdot 1 = 120$ and in general $n! = n(n-1)(n-2) \ldots 3 \cdot 2 \cdot 1$.

The symbol $\Pi$ indicates the product of the elements of a given set. If the dimensions of a rectangular solid are Length $= x_1$, width $= x_2$, and height $= x_3$, then the volume is given in [31a]. For n! we use $\Pi$ as in [31b].

[31]

$$V = \prod_{i=1}^{3} x_i \qquad\qquad n! = \prod_{i=1}^{n} i$$

(a) (b)

**Mathematical Induction.** Many times we may think, perhaps intuitively, that a certain formula holds for all values of n. We may have arrived at the formula by accident and we may have tried a few (or a million) cases and it worked every time. However, we may have still not actually proved the formula. If we are able to prove the formula by mathematical induction, then it is proved for all cases. Mathematical induction is a method of proof which is widely applied. It is similar to proving that one can climb a ladder. If we can get on the first step of the ladder, and if being on any step means that we can climb to the next step, then we can climb the ladder.

First, we *prove* that the formula holds for $n = 1$. Second, we *assume* that the formula holds for $n = k$. Third, we *prove* the formula holds for $n = k+1$. When these three steps are accomplished, then we have proved the formula by mathematical induction.

In explanation, to prove that $n(n+1)$ is the correct formula for the sum of n positive even integers, that is

$$2 + 4 + 6 + \ldots + 2n = n(n+1),$$

then we verify it by mathematical induction.

(1) $n = 1, 2 = 1(1+1) = 2$, is proved.
(2) $n = k, 2 + 4 + 6 + \ldots + 2k = k(k+1)$, is assumed.

We now have to prove the formula for $n = k+1$ which is

(3) $2 + 4 + 6 + \ldots + 2(k+1) = (k+1)((k+1)+1)$.

We must prove this formula by working with the left and right sides separately until we show they are the same. The formula in (4) is the same as (3)

(4) $2 + 4 + 6 + \ldots + 2k + 2(k+1) = (k+1)(k+2)$

because we merely indicate in (4) that the 2k was in the left series. We assumed in step (2) that $2 + 4 + 6 + \ldots + 2k$ was equal to $k(k+1)$, so we replace the $2 + 4 + 6 + \ldots + 2k$ in step (4) by $k(k+1)$ and get (5).

(5) $k(k+1) + 2(k+1) = k^2 + 3k + 2$
(6) $k^2 + k + 2k + 2 = k^2 + 3k + 2$
(7) $k^2 + 3k + 2 = k^2 + 3k + 2$

Steps (5), (6), and (7) show that the left side equals the right and this completes the proof. ■

EXAMPLE: Prove that $(a^n - b^n)$ is divisible by $(a-b)$, for *n* a positive integer.

PROOF: We can prove it for $n = 1$ as $a-b$ is divisible by $a-b$. We now let $n = k$ and assume $a^k - b^k$ is divisible by $a-b$. Then we must prove that $a^{k+1} - b^{k+1}$ is divisible by $a-b$. Write $a^{k+1} - b^{k+1}$ as $a^{k+1} - ab^k + ab^k - b^{k+1}$. We factor this to get $a(a^k - b^k) + b^k(a-b)$. The first term of this expression is divisible by $a-b$ by our assumption, and the second term is also divisible by $a-b$. ■

## APPLICATIONS

*In the next few sections, selected application problems are discussed and solved by using algebra.*

**Work Problem.** Suppose Fred can complete a project in 6 days, Jack can complete the same project in 5 days, and David takes 4 days, then how many days will it take if all three work together?

Consider the condition of the project after one day. Fred will have completed 1/6 of the project, Jack will have done 1/5, and David will have finished 1/4 of the project. We also know that if we let x be the number of days required to do the project together then 1/x of the project will be done after one day, 2/x of the project will be finished after two days, and so on until x days elapse and the whole $(x/x = 1)$ project is done. Individually, x/6 of the project will be completed by Fred after x days, x/5 will be done by Jack, and x/4 by David. The sum of their work is *one* project, therefore, w can write

$$\frac{x}{6} + \frac{x}{5} + \frac{x}{4} = 1,$$

as the equation that we wish to solve. Multiplying both sides by the least common denominator, 60, gives

$$10x + 12x + 15x = 60$$
$$37x = 60$$
$$x = 60/37 = 1\ 23/37 \text{ (days)}$$

**Mixture Problems.** Assume that candy selling for 29¢ a pound is to be mixed with candy which sells for 39¢ a pound. If we want five pounds of the mixture to sell for 36¢ a pound, then how many pounds of each kind of candy should be mixed?

Let x and y be the number of pounds of the 29¢ and the 39¢ candy, respectively, that go into the mixture. Then the value of the candies put in will be .29x for the 29¢ and .39y for the 39¢ candy. We write first the equation based on *weight,* and second the equation based on *value.*

$$x + y = 5$$
$$.29x + .39y = .36(5)$$

These simultaneous equations can be solved for x and y to give: x = 1½ (pounds), y = 3½ (pounds).

In another application, suppose a radiator system is full of 3 gallons of a mixture of 30% antifreeze in water. How much should be drained and replaced by an 80% antifreeze solution to bring the antifreeze content of the 3 gallon system to 60%?

Let x be the number of gallons drained and replaced in the radiator. If we write an equation based on amounts of antifreeze, we get

$$.30(3-x) + .80x = .60(3),$$

which interpreted is: .30(3—x) means we have 30% antifreeze of what is left after taking out x gallons; to this we have added some antifreeze which is 80% of the x gallons replaced, and all of this adds to make 60% antifreeze of the 3 gallon radiator. Completing the solution we have

$$.90 - .30x + .80x = 1.80$$
$$.50x = 1.80 - .90 = .90$$
$$x = .90/.50 = 1.8 \text{ (gallons)}.$$

**Apportionment Problem.** If a $12,000 inheritance is to be divided among three heirs in the apportion of $1/2$, $3/4$, and $5/6$, then how much does each receive?

We notice that the fractions do not add to one, so we get a common denominator of 24 and express each fraction with this denominator.

$$1/2 = 12/24,\ 3/4 = 18/24,\ 5/6 = 20/24.$$

We then add the numerators, 12 + 18 + 20 = 50, and 50 becomes the new denominator. We divide the inheritance into parts of:

$$12/50,\ 18/50,\ 20/50.$$

Multiplying $12,000 by each of these fractions yields $2880, $4320, and $4800, respectively.

**Distance, Rate, Time Problem.** Two trains traveled towards each other from points 200 miles apart. If one train is traveling at 50 m.p.h. and the other at 60 m.p.h., when and where will they meet if they begin at the same time?

We set up our equation on the basis of the equal *times* that the trains traveled. We know D = RT and so T = D/R. Letting D be the distance traveled by the 50 m.p.h. train and 200 — D be the distance of the other train, the equal time equation with solution is given.

$$\frac{D}{50} = \frac{200-D}{60}$$
$$60D = 50(200-D)$$
$$60D + 50D = 10000$$
$$D = \frac{10000}{110} = 91$$

Thus the trains meet 91 miles from the starting point of the 50 m.p.h. train. The length of time is

$$T = D/R = 91/50 = 1.8 \text{ (hours)}.$$

**Consecutive Integer Problem.** Find two consecutive odd integers such that their product is 143.

Let the first integer be x, then the second integer is x + 2. The equation is

$$x(x+2) = 143,$$

and the solution is found by grouping and applying the quadratic formula.

$$x^2 + 2x - 143 = 0$$
$$x = \frac{-2 \pm \sqrt{4-4(-143)}}{2} = \frac{-2 \pm \sqrt{576}}{2} = \frac{-2 \pm 24}{2}$$
$$x = 22/2 = 11,\ x = -26/2 = -13.$$

The solution is 11 and 13, and also —13, —11.

**Quadratic Max-Min Problems.** A farmer's field borders a straight river bank. He wants to enclose three sides of a rectangular field with 400 feet of fencing and let the fourth side be the river bank. If he wants maximum area, what should be the dimensions?

Let x be the length of the side bordering the river bank. The opposite side then has length x, and the other two sides are each equal to ½(400—x). The area (length times width) is given by

$$A = x(\tfrac{1}{2})(400-x) = -\tfrac{1}{2}x^2 + 200x.$$

The graph of this quadratic function has a maximum point and no minimum point. We want to find the maximum of this function. The x value for maximum A is —b/(2a), where a = —½, and b = 200. Therefore, the x value wanted is

$$x = \frac{-b}{2a} = \frac{-(200)}{(2)(-\tfrac{1}{2})} = \frac{-200}{-1} = 200.$$

The dimensions of the field are: length = 200 (feet), and width = ½(400—x) = ½(400—200) = 100 (feet).

**The Hare and Tortoise.** A hare and a tortoise engaged in a race. The hare, being 10 times faster, agreed to give the tortoise a head start of 100 feet. Will the hare ever catch the tortoise and if so, where?

Someone might conjecture the opinion that the hare will never catch the tortoise. They could say that when the hare covers the first 100 feet, the tortoise has moved ahead by 10 feet. When the hare covers this 10 feet, the tortoise stays ahead by 1 foot, and so on, the tortoise always slowly staying just ahead, and the hare feverishly closing the gap but always in second place.

From the mathematical point of view, the hare and tortoise situation is an infinite geometric series with $r = 1/10$ and $a = 100$. The sum of this series is

$$\frac{a}{1-r} = \frac{100}{1-1/10} = \frac{100}{.90} = 111\ 1/9.$$

Thus we know that the hare *did* catch the tortoise at the distance of 111 1/9 feet.

# Geometry

## TERMINOLOGY

**Undefined Terms.** We will have the same undefined terms in geometry as we did in algebra. The foundation can be laid in other ways under different approaches. This means a term which is undefined under one approach may be defined by another approach. For geometry in particular the *undefined* terms are *point, length, betweenness,* and *congruence.*

The notions of point and length should be intuitively obvious. If an object is not strictly and precisely between two objects then it will not have the characteristic of betweenness. Two objects have congruence in geometry if they have the same size and shape.

**Basic Terms Defined.** We can *define* a *line segment* with endpoints p and q as the set of points *between* p and q *union* p and q.

A line is defined as a line segment *union* the set of *all* points, l, such that l and a point on the line segment (not an endpoint) have an endpoint *between* them.

If two lines, a and b, share one and only one point, p, then they determine a plane. A *plane* is the set of all *lines* that share point p and are *between* lines a and b.

The whole *space* can be defined as the union of *all* lines (each a set of points) containing a point, p.

Two lines are said to *coincide* if they share two different points. If two lines coincide then they share *all* points. Two planes coincide if they share three different points, and then they share all points.

**Angle.** A *ray* is the part of a line which is made up of the union of a point, p, called the endpoint, and all points on one side of p. An *angle* can be defined as the figure formed by two rays, called sides, with a common endpoint p, called the vertex. If one ray of an angle is rotated about p it will eventually coincide with the other ray. The amount of rotation is the measure of the angle.

If two rays coincide and one is rotated in a counterclockwise fashion until they coincide again the amount of the angle (complete rotation) formed is called 360°. (Also see *Trigonometry, Terminology, Measures*). One-fourth of such a rotation is thus 90°. A 90° angle is called a *right* angle and the lines which form a 90° angle are said to be *perpendicular*. The shortest distance from a point, p, to a line, l, is along the perpendicular to the line, l, through point p.

The angle between two planes which intersect is the same as the angle formed by two rays, one in each plane, which are each perpendicular to the line of intersection of the planes at the same point. A line and a plane are perpendicular at point p, if the line is perpendicular to each of two distinct lines in the plane which contain p.

When two lines intersect, there are four angles formed by the four rays from the point of intersection. Opposite or nonadjacent (do not share a side) angles of these four are called *vertical* angles. The smallest angle of the four is generally called the angle between the lines.

A *straight* angle has rays which extend oppositely about the vertex to form a line. A straight angle has a measure of 180°.

An *acute* angle has measure greater than 0° and less than 90°. An *obtuse* angle is greater than 90° and less than 180°.

The sum of the measures of two right angles is a straight angle.

*Complementary* angles are two angles the sum of whose measures is 90°. *Supplementary* angles are two angles with total measure 180°. If two angles are complementary or supplementary, then each angle is called the complement or supplement, respectively, of the other.

Two angles are *equal* if they have the same measure. Thus we say that all right angles are equal, etc. Complements of equal angles are equal, and the same for supplements.

In [32a] we have a 30° angle indicating a rotation from initial side to terminal side of 1/12 of 360°. The angle in [32b] can be referred to by any of the following: ∠ A (which means angle A), ∠ BAC, ∠ CAB, ∠ 1.

[32]

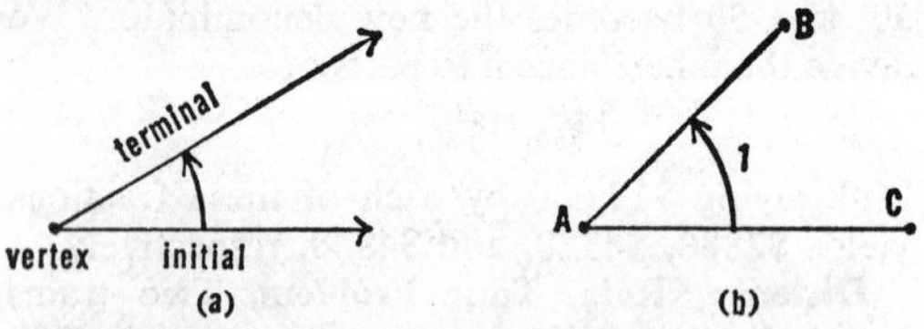


**Parallel.** If two lines in a plane are each perpendicular to the same line then the lines are *parallel*. In *Euclidean* geometry, through a point, p, not on a line, l, one and only one line can be passed which is parallel to l. Other (*non-Euclidean*) geometries are: *Hyperbolic* Geometry, where more than one line can be passed through point p parallel to line l; *Elliptic* geometry, where all lines in a plane meet in at least one point.

If two distinct planes are each perpendicular to the same line, then the planes are parallel. Planes perpendicular to the same plane are not necessarily parallel. For example, two adjacent walls of a room may each be perpendicular to the floor, yet not parallel to each other.

**Incommensurable Segments.** Two line segments are said to be *commensurable* if the quotient of their measures equals a rational number. If their quotient is irrational then the line segments are *incommensurable.*

## EQUALITY AND PROOF

**Equality.** The following properties constitute an equivalent relation:

*reflexive,* $a = a$.
*symmetric,* If $a = b$, then $b = a$.
*transitive,* If $a = b$ and $b = c$, then $a = c$.

Two line segments are *equal* if they have the same length. If a, b, and c are line segments, the above properties are true.

**Proof.** The nature of proof in geometry is *reason by precise deduction.* Deductive reasoning is usually made in the form of "if-then" statements. For example, *if* the numbers we are adding are 2 and 3, *then* the sum will be 5. *If* same size and shape, *then* congruent. In general,

*if hypothesis, then conclusion*

is the pattern we want to follow. A proof is considered correct, and therefore the conclusion is true, if (1) by previous agreements (definitions, other proofs, etc.) we know that if the hypothesis is met then the conclusion is true, and (2) we know that the terms or conditions of our hypothesis are satisfied by what we have established.

If A and B are statements, then the statement, "If A, then B.", is also given as "A implies B" and is often symbolized as $A \Rightarrow B$. The statement $A \Rightarrow B$ is called a *theorem.* A theorem can be true or false. In geometry we are mainly interested in true theorems.

If $A \Rightarrow B$ is the theorem, then the *converse* is $B \Rightarrow A$ and is read "B implies A." If the theorem is, "If the figure is a square then, it is a rectangle.", then the converse is, "If the figure is a rectangle, then it is a square.". We know this theorem is true but the converse is false.

Let $A'$ mean not A, then the *opposite* of the theorem $A \Rightarrow B$ is $A' \Rightarrow B'$. The converse and the opposite are *always* either both true or both false. The opposite of the preceding theorem is, "If the figure is not a square, then it is not a rectangle.", which is false.

$B' \Rightarrow A'$ is called the *contrapositive* and is true or false exactly as the theorem is true or false. Thus the contrapositive of the given theorem is, "If the figure is not a rectangle, then it is not a square.", which is true.

If the theorem and its converse are true then the opposite and contrapositive are true. Thus we have in this case $A \Rightarrow B$, $B \Rightarrow A$, $A' \Rightarrow B'$, and $B' \Rightarrow A'$, all of which can be symbolized by $A \Leftrightarrow B$. Also, there are other equivalent word expressions for $A \Leftrightarrow B$ so that all of the following have the same effect:

A implies B and B implies A.

A if and only if B (A iff B).

A is necessary and sufficient for B.

If we prove that the contrapositive is true, then this makes the theorem true. It is often easier to prove (true) the contrapositive than the theorem. Hereafter, *proving* a statement will be the same as proving a statement to be true.

## BASIC CONSTRUCTIONS

**Bisecting Line Segment.** To bisect the line segment AB in [33a], we set the point of the compass at point A and, with radius greater than one-half AB, we draw a small arc above and below AB. With the same radius, we draw two arcs with point at B so that each of the first arcs are crossed. We then join the two points of intersection of the arcs, C and D, with a straight line and where this line CD crosses the line AB is the point E which bisects AB. Note that CD is actually perpendicular to AB, thus it is called the perpendicular bisector of AB. Notice also that we could have made both sets of arcs above the line to get points C and F from which the line CF will also bisect AB at E.

[33]

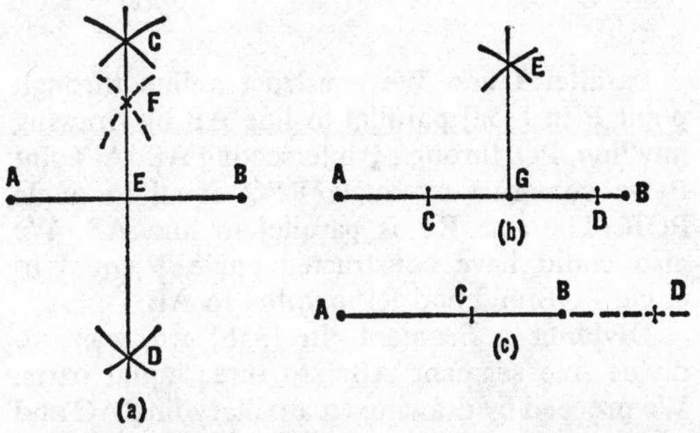


**Perpendicular.** If we want to construct a perpendicular to the line AB at a point G in [33b], we set the point of the compass at G and draw equal arcs at C and D on AB. With a larger radius, set the point at C and draw an arc above AB, then with the same radius, draw an arc with point at D crossing the other arc locating point E. Connect E and G and EG is perpendicular to AB at G. If we want a perpendicular to AB at point B, then we extend AB as shown by the dotted segment in [33c]. We now set the compass point at B, strike arcs at C and D, and then proceed as in [33b].

**Equal Angles.** To construct an angle equal to a given angle A in [34a], we draw a base line XY in [34b], set the compass point at X and draw an arc through Z. We strike the same arc with point at A to intersect at B

[34]

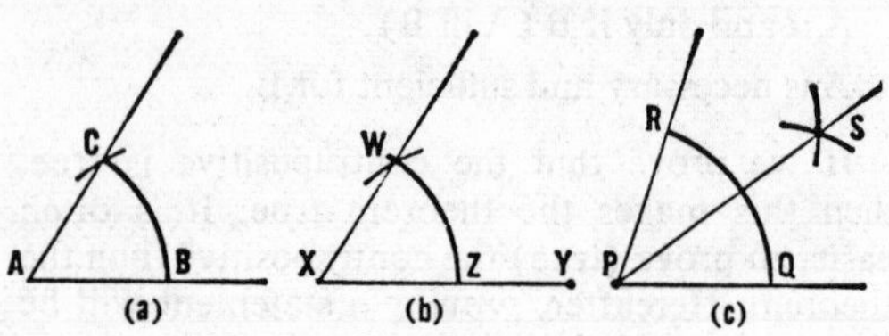


and C in [34a]. We set the point at B and draw arc through C and use this same arc with point at Z to locate point W. Drawing the line XW completes angle X equal to angle A.

**Bisecting Angle.** In [34c] we bisect angle P by drawing an arc with point at P to get points Q and R. With a sufficiently large radius we set the point at Q and strike an arc then set the point at R and with the same radius intersect the other arc to get point S. The line PS is the bisector of angle P.

[35]

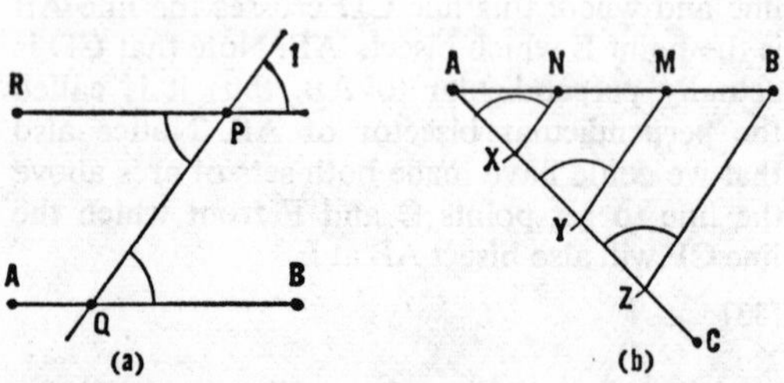


**Parallel Lines.** We construct a line through point P in [35a] parallel to line AB by drawing any line, PQ, through P intersecting AB. At point P we construct an angle RPQ equal to angle PQB. The line RP is parallel to line AB. We also could have constructed angle 1 equal to angle PQB and had RP parallel to AB.

**Dividing a Segment.** In [35b] we want to divide line segment AB into three equal parts. We proceed by drawing an auxiliary line AC and with point at A, we mark point X. With the same radius we set point at X and mark point Y, and similarly we get point Z. Drawing line ZB we form angle AZB. We now construct angles at Y and at X each equal to angle AZB. The new lines drawn at X and Y strike the line AB at N and M so that AN = NM = MB. Note that we could have divided AB into any number of (say n) equal parts by making n marks on AC (extending AC if necessary) and proceeding as before.

**Internal, External Division.** We divide the line segment AB *internally* in [36a] in the ratio p:q by: drawing the line AC and locating point D so that AD = p; from D we locate point E so that DE = q; we draw EB and duplicate angle DEB at point D to get line DF; then F is the point which divides AB internally in the ratio p:q. Thus AF:FB = p:q.

[36]

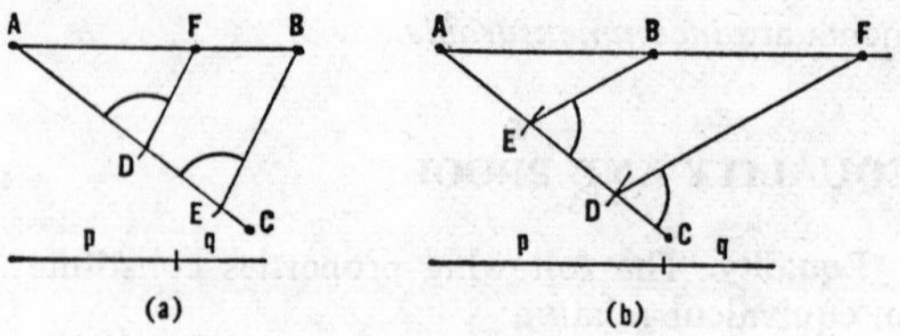


We may divide *externally* the line AB in [36b] in the ratio p:q by: drawing the line AC and locating the points D and E so that p = AD and q = DE; we then draw EB and duplicate angle DEB at point D to get line DF which intersects the extended line AB at F. Point F divides AB externally so that AF:BF = p:q.

**Fourth Proportional.** Given three line segments, a, b, and c, if we wish to find a fourth segment, d, so that a:b = c:d, then using [36a]: we let a = AD, b = DE, and c = AF; after drawing DF, we construct a line parallel to DF through E which intersects the extended line AF at point B. The line segment FB has the length d which is the fourth proportional.

**Mean Proportional.** If we are given two line segments, a and b, and we wish to find the mean proportional segment, m, such that p:m = m:q, then in [37a] we do the following: we form the line segment ABC so that AB = p and BC = q;

[37]

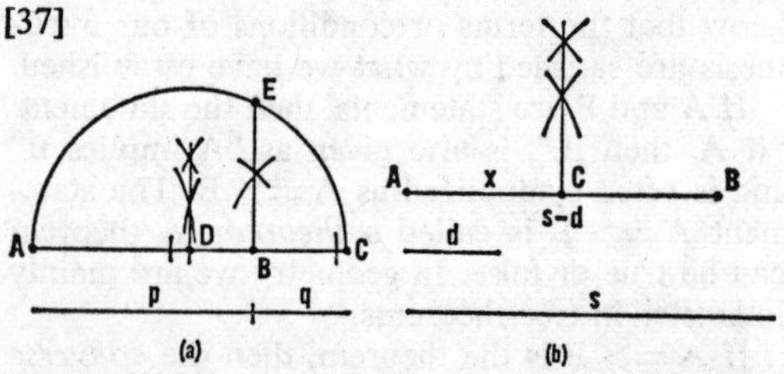


bisecting AC at point D, we draw a semicircle with center at D and radius AD = DC; we erect a perpendicular to AC at B which meets the semicircle at E. Segment BE is the desired mean proportional m of p and q (See *Circle Theorems*). Here we have p:m = m:q or $m^2 = p \cdot q$ which indicates the method of constructing a square, of side m, equal in area to a rectangle of length p and width q.

**Sum, Difference.** Knowing the sum, s, and difference, d, of two line segments in [37b], we can find the unknown segments, x and y, by: drawing segment AB equal to s-d; bisecting AB at C which gives AC = CB = x which is the smaller of the segments we are seeking; adding d to x gives us y, the larger segment.

## BASIC THEOREMS

*The following theorems are stated without proof as the proofs should be found in any reasonable geometry text.*

**Angles.** If two angles are equal then their *sup-*

*plements* and their *complements* are equal and *conversely* if we know either the complements or the supplements or both are equal then the angles are equal. *Vertical* angles are equal.

**Parallels.** Lines are *parallel* if, when cut by a transversal, the alternate interior angles are equal and *conversely* (see *Equality and Proof*). Lines are *parallel* if the angles on the same side of the transversal are supplementary and *conversely*. Lines parallel to the same line are *parallel* to each other.

**Perpendiculars.** Through a point, p, not on a line, 1, one and only one line can be passed through p *perpendicular* to 1. If a point lies on the *perpendicular bisector* of a line segment, then the point is equidistant from the ends of the line segment and *conversely*. Two planes are *perpendicular* if one plane contains a line which is perpendicular to the other plane.

## TRIANGLES

**Definitions.** For some basic definitions about the triangle see *Formulas and Applications* in the arithmetic section. Two triangles are *congruent* if corresponding sides and corresponding angles are equal. The *altitude* of a side of a triangle is the perpendicular segment from the side to the opposite vertex. The three *altitudes* of a triangle meet at a point called the *orthocenter*. The *median* of a triangle is the segment drawn from a vertex to the midpoint of the opposite side. The three medians of a triangle meet at a point called the *centroid*. The perpendicular bisectors of the sides of a triangle meet in a point called the *circumcenter*. The bisectors of the angles of a triangle meet in a point called the *incenter*.

*The next few paragraphs illustrate basic constructions relating to triangles.*

**Three Sides.** To construct a triangle given the three sides, a, b, and c, in [38a]: we draw side c and with the radius of the compass equal to side b we make an arc with point at A; we then set the radius of the compass to the length of a and made an arc with point at B which intersects the first arc at point C. Drawing AC and CB gives us the required triangle.

[38]

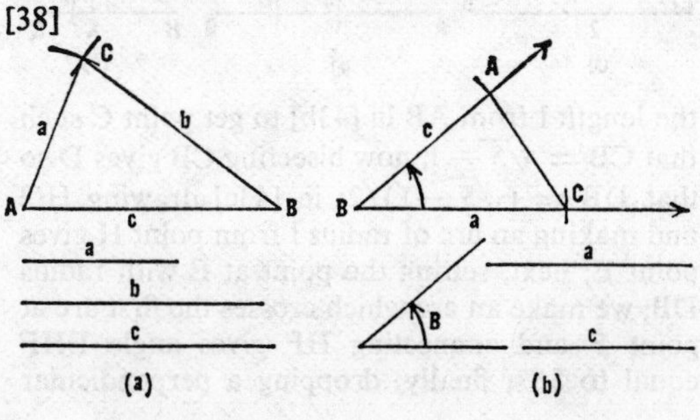


**Two Sides, Angle.** If we know two sides and the included angle of a triangle in [38b] we may construct the triangle by drawing the angle B and marking off the lengths of a and c on the sides of B to locate points A and C, respectively. We then draw segment AC to complete the required triangle.

**Two Angles, Side.** To construct a triangle given two angles, A and B, and the included side, c, we can draw the side c horizontally and construct the two angles on opposite ends of c so that the sides of the angles intersect above side c to locate point C. We then have the required triangle.

**Hypotenuse, Leg.** Knowing the hypotenuse, c, and a leg, b, we can in [39a] construct the triangle by: drawing the leg b thus locating points A and C; constructing a perpendicular at C; setting the compass point at A with radius of c and making an arc on the perpendicular to locate point B. We then draw AB to complete the required triangle.

[39]

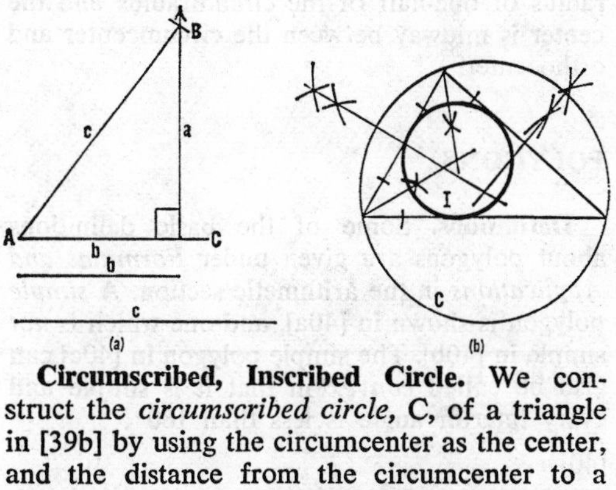


**Circumscribed, Inscribed Circle.** We construct the *circumscribed circle*, C, of a triangle in [39b] by using the circumcenter as the center, and the distance from the circumcenter to a vertex as the radius (*circumradius*). This circle intersects *all* vertices of the triangle.

The *inscribed circle*, I, in [39b] is drawn by using the incenter as the center, and the perpendicular distance from the incenter to a side as the radius. This circle lies within the triangle and is tangent (see *Circles*) to each side.

**Triangle Theorems.** Two triangles are congruent if any of the following conditions are true:

S.S.S., three corresponding sides are equal;

S.A.S., two corresponding sides and included angle are equal;

A.S.A., two corresponding angles and included side are equal;

Hyp.L., they are right triangles and corresponding hypotenuse and leg are equal.

The *converses* of S.S.S., S.A.S., and A.S.A. are true. The converse of Hyp.L. would state that if two *right* triangles are congruent, then corresponding hypotenuse and leg are equal.

If a triangle has two equal sides, then the angles opposite these sides are equal and conversely. A triangle with three equal sides has three equal angles and conversely. If two angles of a triangle are correspondingly equal to two angles of another triangle, then the third angles are equal.

A line segment joining the midpoints of two sides of a triangle is parallel to the third side and one-half the length of the third side. Also a line which is parallel to one side of a triangle, and bisects a second side will bisect the third side. If a side of a triangle is extended, then the exterior angle formed will be equal to the sum of the two opposite interior angles.

The distance of the centroid from a vertex is two-thirds of the median drawn to that vertex. The *centroid* is also the *center of gravity* of a triangle. The *centroid, circumcenter,* and *orthocenter* of a triangle are *collinear* (fall in a line).

**Nine Point Circle.** An *Euler point* is the midpoint of the line segment joining the orthocenter of a triangle to its vertex. In a triangle the Euler points, the midpoints of the sides, and the feet of the altitudes all lie on the same circle. This circle is called the *nine point circle* and it has a radius of one-half of the circumradius and the center is midway between the circumcenter and orthocenter.

## POLYGONS

**Definitions.** Some of the basic definitions about polygons are given under *Formulas and Applications* in the arithmetic section. A *simple* polygon is shown in [40a], and one which is *not* simple in [40b]. The simple polygon in [40c] can also be called *convex* in that it is simple and every interior angle is less than 180°.

[40]

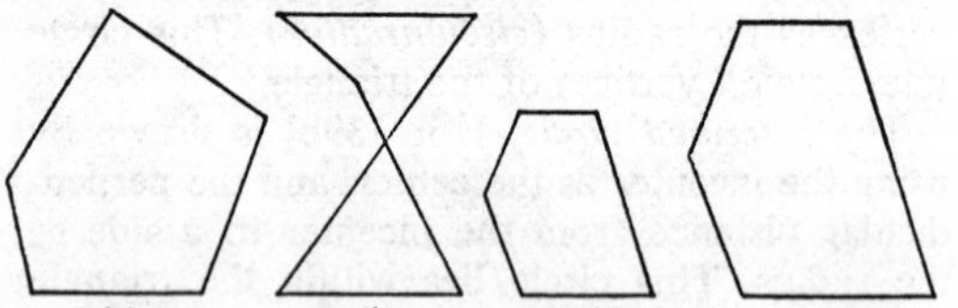


Polygons are *similar* if they have corresponding angles equal and corresponding sides proportional. See [40c,d]. A polygon is regular if it has all sides and angles equal, thus it is both equilateral and equiangular (see [41a]).

*The following are basic polygonal constructions.*

**Parallelograms.** We construct a parallelogram when given two sides and an angle in [41b] by the following: we draw the given angle B and lay off one given side, BA, to locate point A; at A we construct a line parallel to the other side of angle B; we then locate C on this parallel line by making the distance from A to C equal to the given line AC; we lay off the same distance on the parallel side of angle B to get point D. Drawing CD then completes the required parallelogram.

[41]

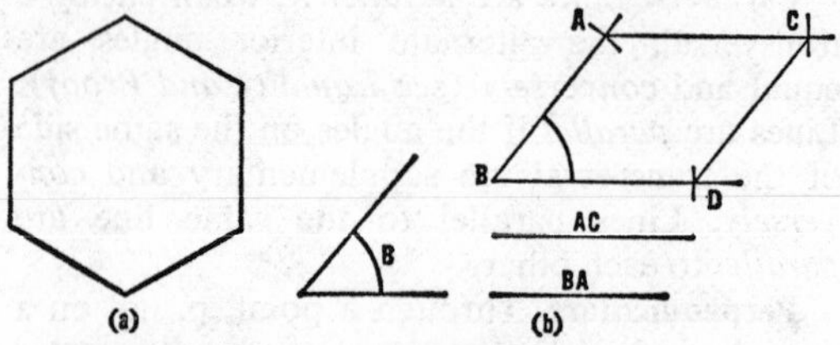


**Square Equal to Triangle.** To construct a square equal in area to a given triangle, we proceed as follows: we determine the altitude, h, to the base, b, realizing that a rectangle of base b and height ½h will have the same area as the triangle; we construct the mean proportional of b and ½h to get the length, m. The square of side m is the desired square.

**Square Equal to Sum of Squares.** If given three squares, of sides a, b, and c, respectively, and we want to construct a square equal in area to the sums of the three areas of the given squares, then in [42] we: on the left, construct a right triangle with legs a and b, and get d, the hypotenuse; in the middle, construct a right triangle with legs c and d and get the hypotenuse e. The square on the right with side e is the desired square. This process can be repeated to add more than three squares.

[42]

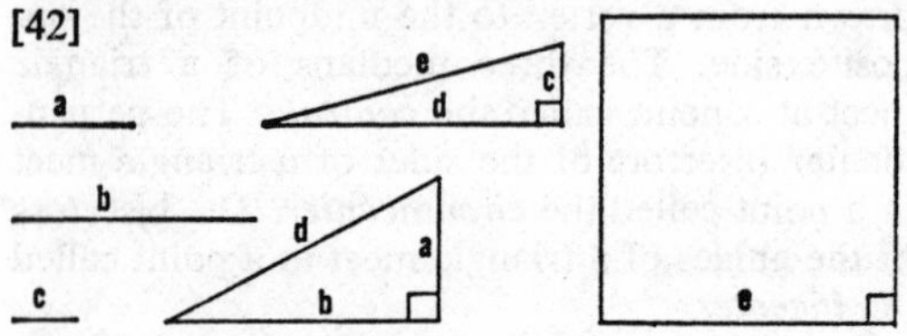


**Regular Pentagon.** The construction of a regular pentagon, with sides of length x, first involves the construction of a 54° angle. We do this in [43] by: first obtaining the length $\sqrt{5}$ units as the hypotenuse, AB, of a triangle with legs of 1 and 2 units in [43a]; then subtracting

[43]

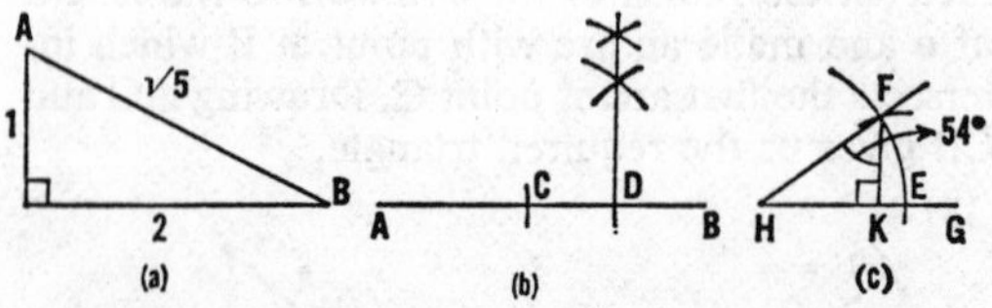


the length 1 from AB in [43b] to get point C such that $CB = \sqrt{5} - 1$; now bisecting CB gives D so that $DB = (\sqrt{5} - 1)/2$; in [43c] drawing HG and making an arc of radius 1 from point H gives point E; next, setting the point at E with radius DB, we make an arc which crosses the first arc at point F and connecting HF gives angle EHF equal to 36°; finally, dropping a perpendicular from F to get point K, we have a 54° angle at KFH.

[44]

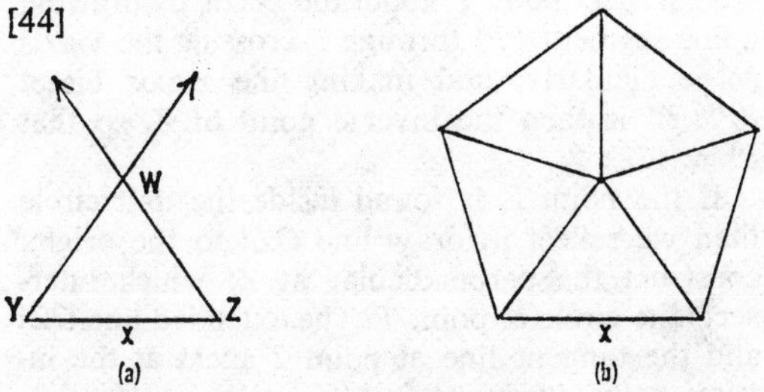


We utilize the 54° angle in [44a] by drawing line x = YZ, and constructing 54° angles at Y and Z locating point W. The triangle YZW has W = 72°, one-fifth of 360°, so we can construct four more such triangles in [44b] to complete the required pentagon.

**Polygon Construction.** We can construct any regular polygon of n sides by using a protractor and the formula,

$$A = \frac{n-2}{n}\,(180°),$$

where A is the size of an interior angle. If each side is to have a length of x, then we draw a segment of length x and construct an angle on one end using a protractor to establish the angle computed by the formula. Marking off the length on the side of the angle gives a new side to the polygon. We continue until the polygon is complete.

Perhaps the easiest way to draw a regular polygon of n sides is to inscribe it in a given circle. We simply divide 360° by n to get the central angle (see *Circles*) which cuts off an arc whose chord is the length of a side. The compass can then be used to duplicate this chord around the circle completing the required inscribed polygon.

*Quadrilaterals, Trapezoids, Polyhedrons, etc., are discussed under Formulas and Applications in the arithmetic section.*

**Polygon Theorems.** The sum of the interior angles of a polygon of n sides is (n—2)180°. If one side of each angle of a polygon is extended, *the sum of these exterior angles* is 360°.

A quadrilateral is a parallelogram if any of the following is true:

O.S.E., *opposite sides* are *equal;*

O.A.E., *opposite angles* are *equal;*

D.B., *diagonals bisect* each other;

P.E.P., one *pair* of opposite sides are *equal* and *parallel.*

## CIRCLES

**Definitions.** A *secant* of a circle is a line passing through the circle. A *chord* is a line segment with endpoints on the circle. An *arc* is the portion of the circle intercepted (cut off) by a chord. A *tangent* is a line which contains only one point of a circle and is perpendicular to the

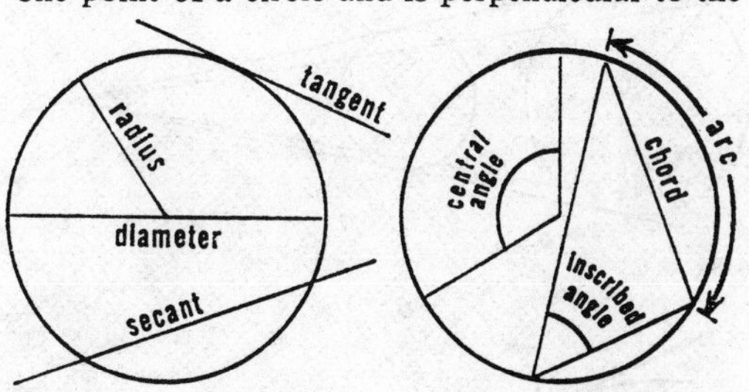


radius at that point. A *central angle* has its vertex at the center of the circle. An *inscribed angle* has a vertex on the circle and intersects the circle at two other points. A *semicircle* is half a circle. One-fourth of a circle is a *quadrant.*

**Circle, Given Three Points.** If we are given three points, A, B, and C, and we want to construct the circle containing these points, then we draw the perpendicular bisector of two lines connecting the points, say AB and BC. Then the point of intersection of the bisectors is the center, O, of the circle and the radius is the distance from O to A.

**Tangent From Point.** To construct the tangents to a circle from a point, P, outside the circle, in [45a] we execute the following: we connect the center of the circle, O, to point P and bisect OP getting point M; with point at M and radius MO we draw an arc intersecting the circle at T and T'. The lines PT and PT' are the required tangents.

[45]

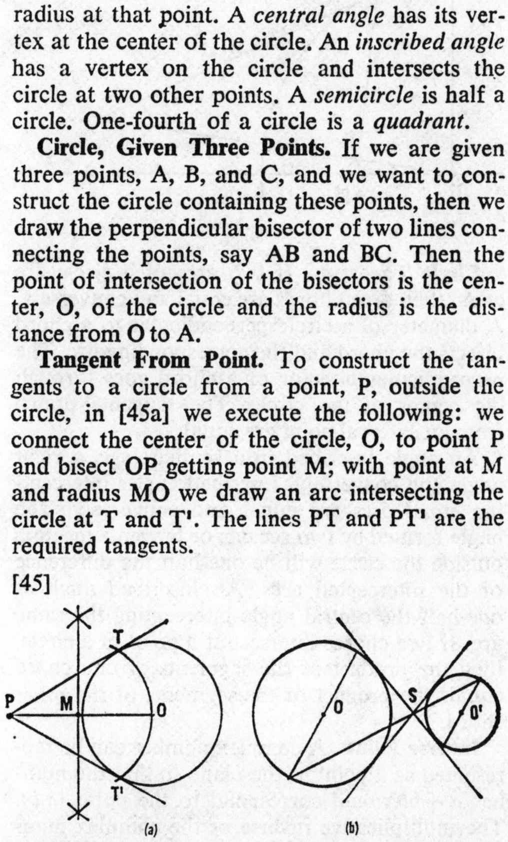


**Internal Tangents.** We construct the internal (common) tangents to two given circles as follows: in [45b], we draw a diameter in circle O and a parallel diameter in circle O'; we then connect opposite ends of the diameters locating point S, the *internal center* of *similitude;* the internal tangents to both circles pass through S, therefore we construct the tangents to circle O through S and these lines will be tangent to O'.

**External Tangents.** The external tangents to two given circles can be formed in [46a], by connecting the corresponding ends of parallel diameters to locate point S, the *external center* of *similitude.* Then as with internal tangents, we construct tangents to one circle through S and they will also be tangent to the other circle.

[46]

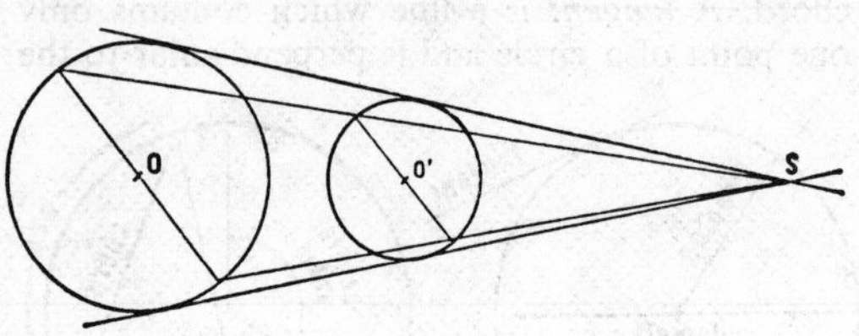


(a)

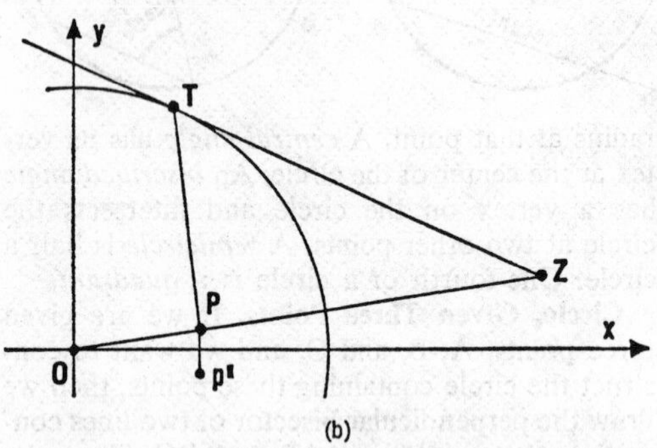


(b)

**Circle Theorems.** If two arcs of a circle are equal then their chords are equal and conversely. A diameter of a circle perpendicular to a chord bisects the chord and the corresponding arc. The perpendicular bisector of a chord goes through the center of the circle. The tangents drawn from an external point are equal.

An angle inscribed in a semicircle is a right angle and conversely. Inscribed angles intercepting equal arcs are equal and conversely. The angle formed by two secants or tangents meeting outside the circle will be one-half the difference of the intercepted arcs. An inscribed angle is one-half the central angle intercepting the same arc. If two chords intersect at a point in a circle, then the product of the segments of one chord equals the product of the segments of the other chord.

**Inverse Points.** A complex number can be represented as a point in the plane so that the number $a+bi$ would correspond to the point $(a,b)$. The multiplicative inverse of the complex number $a+bi$ is the number $c+di$ if and only if

$$(a+bi)\,(c+di) = 1 + 0i = 1.$$

We may find the multiplicative inverse of a complex number $Z = a + bi$ by representing it in the plane then constructing its *inverse point* geometrically. The procedure for computing the inverse point of the complex number $Z$ is shown in [46b] and described as follows:

1. Draw a line from the origin, $O$, to the point $Z$, and draw a circle about the origin of radius 1 unit.
2. Construct a tangent line from $Z$ to the circle and locate point $T$.
3. Drop a perpendicular from $T$ to the line $OZ$ getting point $P$.
4. Reflect point $P$ about the $x$-axis by drawing a line segment $PP'$ through $P$ crossing the $x$-axis perpendicularly, and making the $x$-axis bisect $PP'$. $P'$ is then the inverse point of $Z$, so that $P' = 1/Z$.

If the point $Z$ is found inside the unit circle then we reflect it, draw line $OZ'$ to the origin, construct the perpendicular at $Z'$ which intersects the circle at point $T$. The extended line $OZ'$ and the tangent line at point $T$ meet at the inverse point, $P'$, which is $1/Z$.

## SPHERICAL GEOMETRY

**Definitions.** Some definitions concerning the sphere are found under *Formulas and Applications* in the arithmetic section. A *great circle* of a sphere is the intersection of a sphere and a plane passing through the center of the sphere. Two points on a great circle, which are not ends of the same diameter, intercept two arcs which according to length are the *major* and *minor* arcs. The *distance* between two points on a sphere is the length of the minor arc of their common great circle.

A *spherical angle* is the figure formed by intersecting great circles. Their point of intersection is the *vertex* and the *measure* of the spherical angle is the same as the measure of the angle between tangent lines to the great circles at the vertex. If three distinct arcs of great circles share endpoints and form a figure in such a way that the sphere is divided into three distinct regions (inside the figure, on the figure, and outside the figure), then the figure is called a *spherical triangle. Spherical polygons* are similarly defined.

A *spherical degree* is the area of a spherical triangle with two right angles and a 1° angle. Each of the four areas formed by two great circles (which always intersect) on a sphere are called *lines*. When parallel planes intersect a sphere the portion of the sphere between the planes is called a *zone*. The *spherical excess* of a triangle is the amount that the sum of the angles of a spherical triangle exceeds 180°.

**Spherical Theorems.** A *line* of x degrees has an area of $\pi r^2 x/90$, where r is the radius. The *sum of the angles* of a spherical triangle exceeds 180°. The *area of a spherical triangle* is the number of degrees in the spherical excess. The *area* in spherical degrees of a *spherical polygon* of n sides with the sum of its angles, S, is given by $(S-(n-2)180°)r^2$, where r is the radius of the sphere. The *area of a zone* of height h, radius of sphere, r, is $2\pi rh$. The volume of *a zone* with units as above is $\pi h^2(3r-h)/3$.

# Trigonometry

## TERMINOLOGY

**Angles.** An angle is said to be represented in *standard position* in the *xy* coordinate system if its vertex is at the origin and its initial side is on the positive *x*-axis. If the terminal side of the angle is measured as a counterclockwise rotation from the initial side, then the angle is *positive*. If measured clockwise, the angle is *negative* (see [47a]). If the terminal side coincides with an axis then the angle is called a *quadrantal* angle.

[47]

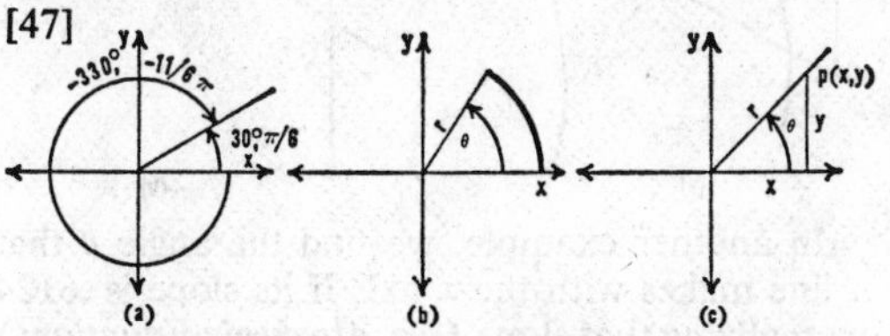


**Measures.** Angles are measured in degrees, radians, and mils. A *degree* is the measure of the central angle which subtends an arc equal to 1/360 of the circumference of the circle. A *radian* is the measure of a central angle which subtends an arc equal to the radius of the circle. A *mil* is the measure of the central angle subtending an arc of 1/6400 of the circumference of the circle. Thus $360° = 2\pi$ radians $= 6400$ mils and

$$1 \text{ degree} = \frac{\pi}{180} \text{ radians} = .01745 \text{ radians} = 17.778 \text{ mils},$$

$$1 \text{ radian} = \frac{180}{\pi} \text{ degrees} = 57.29578 \text{ degrees} = 1018.6 \text{ mils},$$

$$1 \text{ mil} = \frac{1}{1000} \text{ radian} = .00098 \text{ radians} = .05625 \text{ degrees approximately.}$$

There are 60 minutes (') in a degree and 60 seconds ('') in a minute. This nearly makes 1 radian $= 57°17'45''$.

The *length of arc* of a circle is given by

$$s = r\theta$$

where *r* is the radius and $\theta$ is the central angle in radians (see [47b]). So on a circle of radius 10 inches the length of arc subtended by a central angle of 2 radians is $10(2) = 20$ (inches). On a 5 inch circle, a central angle of 30° subtends an arc of length:

$$5(30)\left(\frac{\pi}{180}\right) = \frac{5}{6}\pi \text{ (inches).}$$

**Trigonometric Functions.** If $\theta$ is an angle in standard position, see [47c], and *p* is a distinct point on the terminal side with coordinates *x* (ordinate) and *y* (abscissa), and *r* is the positive distance between point *p* and the origin, then the six *trigonometric functions* of angle $\theta$ are defined as follows:

$$\text{sine } \theta = \frac{y}{r},$$

$$\text{cosine } \theta = \frac{x}{r},$$

$$\text{tangent } \theta = \frac{y}{x},$$

$$\text{cotangent } \theta = \frac{x}{y},$$

$$\text{secant } \theta = \frac{r}{x},$$

$$\text{cosecant } \theta = \frac{r}{y}.$$

These functions are abbreviated respectively as $\sin\theta$, $\cos\theta$, $\tan\theta$, $\cot\theta$, $\sec\theta$, and $\csc\theta$.

The four quadrants and typical angles are shown in [48a]. In [48b] the six trigonometric functions are given with regard to their sign in a particular quadrant.

[48]

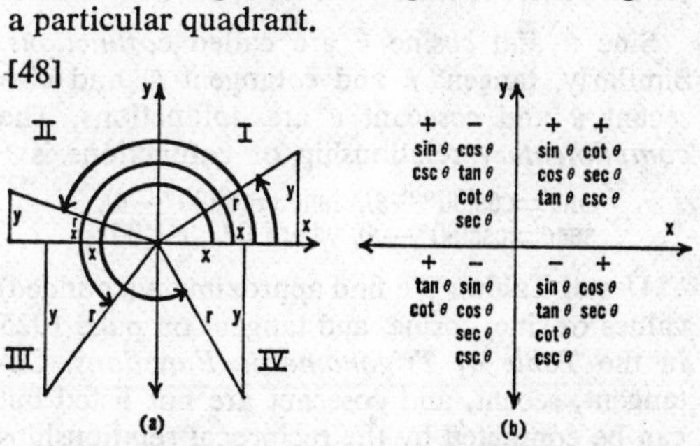


For example, in [49a], the angle in standard position has $\sin\theta = 3/5$, $\cos\theta = 4/5$, $\tan\theta = 3/4$, $\cot\theta = 4/3$, $\sec\theta = 5/4$, and $\csc\theta = 5/3$. In [49b] $\sin\theta = -5/13$, $\cos\theta = -12/13$, $\tan\theta = 5/12$, $\cot\theta = 12/5$, $\sec\theta = 13/(-12)$, and $\csc\theta = 13/(-5)$.

Note that any point, except the origin, on the terminal side of an angle can be used to determine the six functions. Thus in [49a], the point $p = (8, 6)$ is on line *op* extended and we would get the same function values by using the 6, 8, and hypotenuse of 10 as we would with 3, 4, and 5.

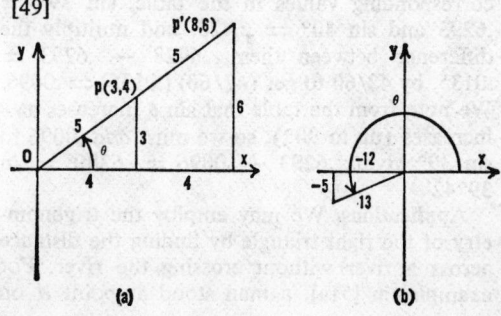

[49]

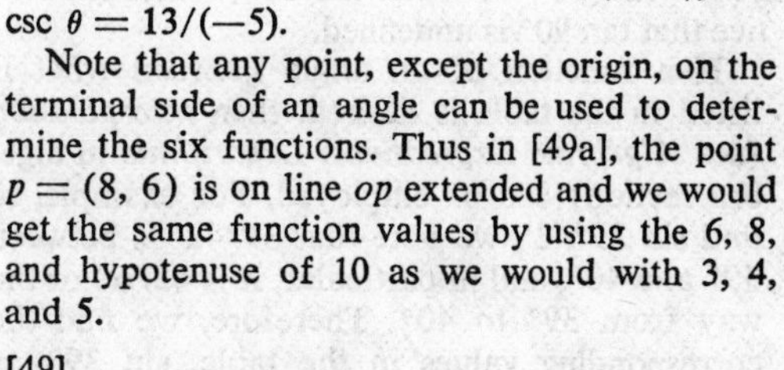

**Special Angles.** We find in [50] some special angles often encountered in application. The length of the hypotenuse is understood to be one. We utilize the fact that the side opposite the 30° angle in a right triangle is ½ the hypotenuse and the side opposite the 60° angle is $\sqrt{3}/2$ times the hypotenuse. We also use the fact that the side opposite the 45° angle in a right triangle is $\sqrt{2}/2$ times the hypotenuse. A dash means the function is undefined for that angle (division by zero).

[50]

| ANGLE | SIN | COS | TAN | COT | SEC | CSC |
|---|---|---|---|---|---|---|
| 0° | 0 | 1 | 0 | — | 1 | — |
| 30° | $1/2$ | $\sqrt{3}/2$ | $\sqrt{3}/3$ | $\sqrt{3}$ | $2\sqrt{3}/3$ | 2 |
| 45° | $\sqrt{2}/2$ | $\sqrt{2}/2$ | 1 | 1 | $\sqrt{2}$ | $\sqrt{2}$ |
| 60° | $\sqrt{3}/2$ | $1/2$ | $\sqrt{3}$ | $\sqrt{3}/3$ | 2 | $2\sqrt{3}/3$ |
| 90° | 1 | 0 | — | 0 | — | 1 |
| 180° | 0 | —1 | 0 | — | —1 | — |
| 270° | —1 | 0 | — | 0 | — | —1 |

The reciprocal relationships among the functions are:

$\sin\theta = 1/\csc\theta$, $\cos\theta = 1/\sec\theta$, $\tan\theta = 1/\cot\theta$.

Sine $\theta$ and *co*sine $\theta$ are called *cofunctions.* Similarly, tangent $\theta$ and *co*tangent $\theta$, and also secant $\theta$ and *co*secant $\theta$ are cofunctions. The *complimentary* relationship of cofunctions is:

$$\sin\theta=\cos(90°-\theta),\ \tan\theta=\cot(90°-\theta),$$
$$\sec\theta=\csc(90°-\theta),\ \text{where } 0°<\theta<90°.$$

**Use of Tables.** We find approximate (rounded) values of sine, cosine, and tangent on page 1025 in the *Table of Trigonometric Functions.* Cotangent, secant, and cosecant are not listed but can be computed by the reciprocal relationships of the trigonometric functions. The cotangent can also be found by the complement relationship with tangent. So, from the table, sin 84° = .9945, cos 50° = .6428, tan 6° = .1051, and cot 10° = tan(90°—10°) = tan 80° = 5.6713. Notice that tan 90° is undefined.

If a function of an angle *between* what is listed in the table is desired, then *interpolation* (see *Algebraic Expressions, Logarithms* in algebra section) can be employed. For example, to find sin 39°42', we note that 39°42' is between 39° and 40°, and in particular, it is 42/60 of the way from 39° to 40°. Therefore, we find the corresponding values in the table, sin 39° = .6293 and sin 40° = .6428, and multiply the difference between them, .6428 — .6293 = .0135, by 42/60 to get (42/60) (.0135) = .0096. We note from the table that sin $\theta$ increases as $\theta$ increases (up to 90°), so we must *add* .0096 to sin 39° giving .6293 + .0096 = .6389 = sin 39°42'.

**Applications.** We may employ the trigonometry of the right triangle by finding the distance across a river without crossing the river. For example, in [51a], a man stood at point $A$ on one side of a river and noted a small tree, point $B$, across the river. He turned 90° to the right, walked 100 meters to point $C$, and then found the angle of the line of sight of the tree and his line of walk to be 63°. The distance $AB$ can now be found from the right triangle $ABC$ knowing $\tan C = AB/AC$; but $C = 63°$ and $AC = 100$ so that tan 63° = $AB/100$. We find tan 63° in the table to be 1.9626, making the equation read 1.9626 = $AB/100$, which has the solution $AB = 196$ (meters).

[51]

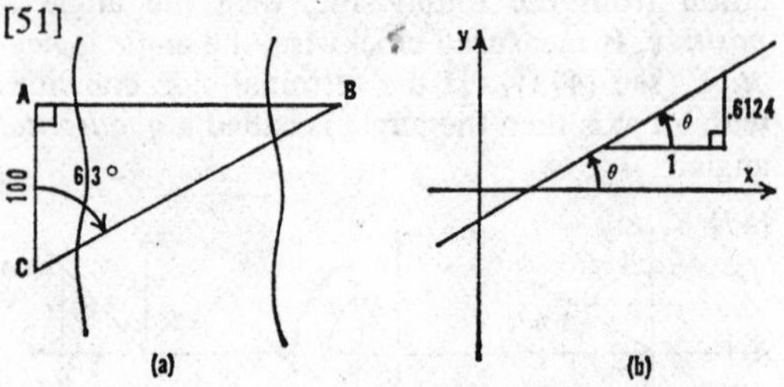


In another example, we find the angle $\theta$ that a line makes with the $x$ axis if its slope is .6124 by realizing that slope (see *Algebraic Equations*) is the $y$ distance over the $x$ distance or the tangent of the angle. Thus in [51b] slope = tan $\theta$ = .6124, which means the angle is between 31° and 32° according to the table. We interpolate by observing that tan 31° = .6009 and tan 32° = .6249, and their difference is .0240. Now the difference in tan $\theta$ = .6124 and tan 31° = .6009 is .0115, so the angle desired is .0115/.0240 of the way from 31° to 32°. We multiply, (115/240)(60) = 28.75, and get for our answer $\theta$ = 31°29'. Note that we should not make our answer read 31°28'45", because we used a four place table which should be interpolated only to the nearest minute.

**Period.** If $n$ is an integer, positive, negative, or zero, then we have:

| | |
|---|---|
| $\sin(\theta+n360°) = \sin\theta$ | $\cot(\theta+n360°) = \cot\theta$ |
| $\cos(\theta+n360°) = \cos\theta$ | $\sec(\theta+n360°) = \sec\theta$ |
| $\tan(\theta+n360°) = \tan\theta$ | $\csc(\theta+n360°) = \csc\theta$ |

which shows that all trigonometric functions are periodic and repeat functional values at least every 360°. We also have

$$\tan(\theta+n180°) = \tan\theta \qquad \cot(\theta+n180°) = \cot\theta$$

revealing that tangent and cotangent repeat functional values every 180°. The distance between repeated functional values is the *period* of the function. Thus the period of the sine, cosine, secant, and cosecant functions is 360° or $2\pi$ radians. The period of the tangent and cotangent functions is 180° or $\pi$ radians.

**Amplitude.** As noted in [50], all trigonometric functions except sine and cosine are undefined from some $\theta$. So we discuss *amplitude,* meaning peak or maximum $y$ value, only for sine and cosine functions. The functions $y = \sin x$ and $y = \cos x$ have amplitudes of 1.

*In general,* **y = a** *sin* **bx** *and* **y = a** *cos* **bx** *have period* $2\pi/\mathbf{b}$ *and amplitude* **a**, *where* **a** *and* **b** *are positive.*

**Negative Angle.** The functions of the negative angles are

$$\sin(-\theta) = -\sin\theta \qquad \cot(-\theta) = -\cot\theta$$
$$\cos(-\theta) = \cos\theta \qquad \sec(-\theta) = \sec\theta$$
$$\tan(-\theta) = -\tan\theta \qquad \csc(-\theta) = -\csc\theta$$

so that $\sin(-30°) = -\sin 30° = -\frac{1}{2}$, and $\cos(-30°) = \cos 30° = \sqrt{3}/2$. See *General Functions* in the college preparatory mathematics section.

## GRAPHS

**Circular Functions.** In [52] we have $\theta$ an acute angle in standard position. A circle of radius one unit, centered at the origin, intersects the terminal side of $\theta$ at P. PQ is perpendicular to the $x$ axis. ST and S'T' are tangents to the circle and intersect line OP at S and S' respectively. We note that triangle OPQ is similar to triangle OST, and angle $\theta$ = angle T'S'O.

[52]

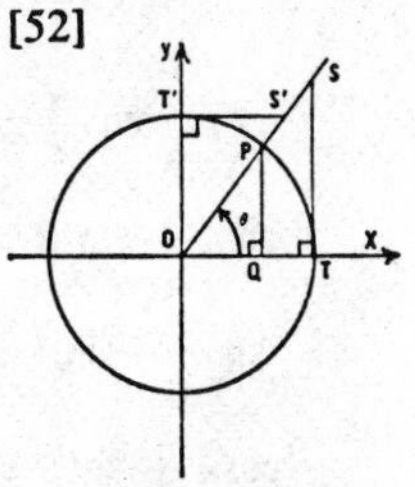


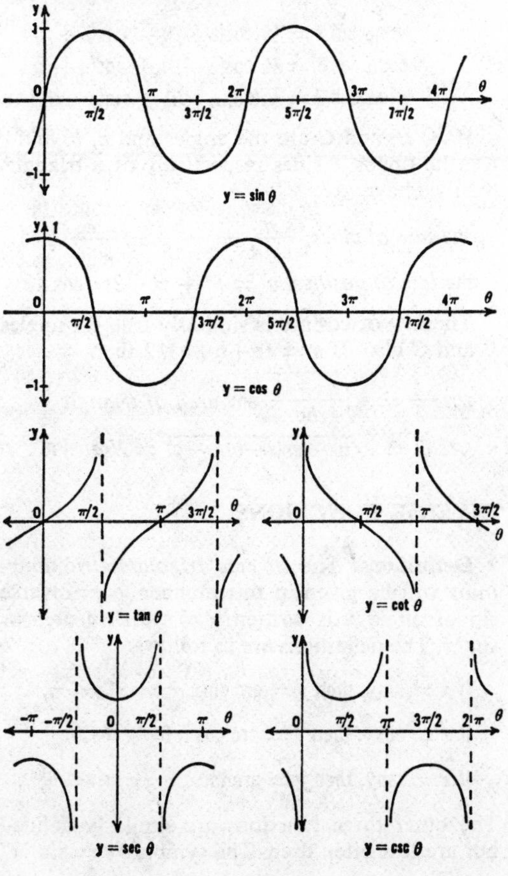


We can now determine the six trigonometric functions of $\theta$ as lengths of line segments in relationship to the circle.

| | |
|---|---|
| $\sin\theta = QP/OP = QP$ | $\cot\theta = S'T'/OT' = S'T'$ |
| $\cos\theta = OQ/OP = OQ$ | $\csc\theta = OS'/OT' = OS'$ |
| $\tan\theta = ST/OT = ST$ | $\sec\theta = OS/OT = OS$ |

**Trigonometric Functions.** By plotting angle values in radians with the corresponding function values we get the graphs of the trigonometric functions. The vertical dotted lines are the asymptotes (see *Exponential Equations* in algebra section) of the given functions.

**Special Graphs.** In [53] we have $y = \frac{3}{4}\sin 2\theta$, with a period of $\pi$ and amplitude of $\frac{3}{4}$, shown as the solid line. The dotted line is $y = \frac{1}{3}\sin\theta/2$, with period $4\pi$ and amplitude $\frac{1}{3}$.

[53]

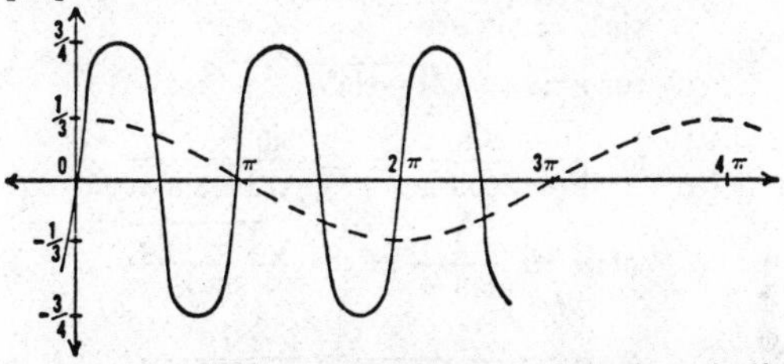

The sum of two trigonometric functions is illustrated in [54a]. The resulting graphs can be sketched by drawing each of the curves on the same set of axes, then "adding" corresponding $y$ values. The sine and cosine waves are the dotted curves and their sum is the solid curve.

[54]

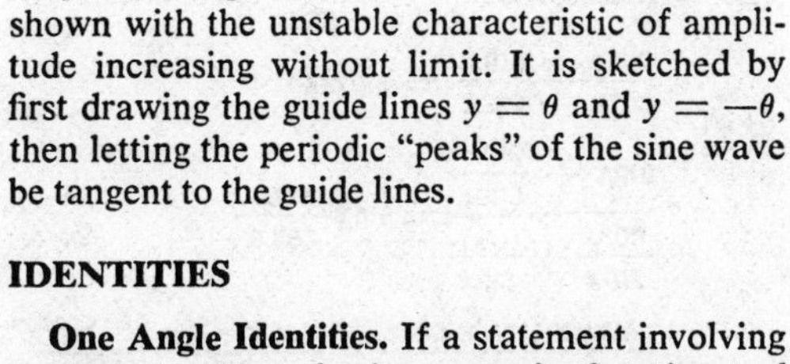

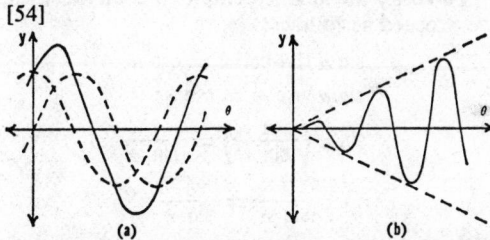


In [54b] the product function, $y = \theta\sin\theta$, is shown with the unstable characteristic of amplitude increasing without limit. It is sketched by first drawing the guide lines $y = \theta$ and $y = -\theta$, then letting the periodic "peaks" of the sine wave be tangent to the guide lines.

## IDENTITIES

**One Angle Identities.** If a statement involving the relationship of trigonometric functions of the same angle is true for *all* values of that angle then the statement is called an *identity*. The *fundamental identities* are:

$$\sin\alpha = 1/\csc\alpha,\ \csc\alpha = 1/\sin\alpha$$
$$\cos\alpha = 1/\sec\alpha,\ \sec\alpha = 1/\cos\alpha$$
$$\tan\alpha = 1/\cot\alpha = \sin\alpha/\cos\alpha,\ \tan\alpha\cos\alpha = \sin\alpha$$
$$\cot\alpha = 1/\tan\alpha = \cos\alpha/\sin\alpha,\ \cot\alpha\sin\alpha = \cos\alpha$$
$$\sin^2\alpha + \cos^2\alpha = 1,\ 1-\sin^2\alpha = \cos^2\alpha$$
$$\sec^2\alpha - \tan^2\alpha = 1,\ 1+\tan^2\alpha = \sec^2\alpha$$
$$\csc^2\alpha - \cot^2\alpha = 1,\ 1+\cot^2\alpha = \csc^2\alpha$$

The notation $\sin^2\alpha$ means $(\sin\alpha)^2$.

The verification of an identity, sometimes called proving an identity, is the process of verifying that a statement is true for all values of an angle by using algebraic *factoring* and *simplification,* and *substitution* of the given *fundamental identities.* We thus transform one side of the identity into the other by these processes. We can not *operate* on both sides of an identity simultaneously (like multiplying both sides by $\sin\alpha$) because this means that we are proving a *different identity.* We usually then work with the more complicated side first.

It may be helpful to change *both* sides to sines and cosines before attempting the transformation. A good exercise is the changing of every trigonometric function into terms of $\sin\alpha$.

$$\sin\alpha = \sin\alpha$$

$$\cos\alpha = \pm\sqrt{1-\sin^2\alpha}$$

$$\tan\alpha = \frac{\sin\alpha}{\cos\alpha} = \pm\frac{\sin\alpha}{\sqrt{1-\sin^2\alpha}}$$

$$\cot\alpha = \frac{1}{\tan\alpha} = \pm\frac{\sqrt{1-\sin^2\alpha}}{\sin\alpha}$$

$$\sec\alpha = \frac{1}{\cos\alpha} = \pm\frac{1}{\sqrt{1-\sin^2\alpha}}$$

$$\csc\alpha = \frac{1}{\sin\alpha}$$

The appropriate $\pm$ sign is used according to the quadrant of the angle.

To verify the identity, $\sin\alpha\,(1+\cot^2\alpha) = \csc\alpha$, we proceed as follows:

$$\sin\alpha\,(1+\cot^2\alpha) = \csc\alpha$$

$$\sin\alpha\,(\csc^2\alpha) = \csc\alpha$$

$$\sin\alpha\left(\frac{1}{\sin^2\alpha}\right) = \frac{1}{\sin\alpha}$$

$$\frac{1}{\sin\alpha} = \frac{1}{\sin\alpha}$$

The verification of $\dfrac{\sin x + \tan x}{\cot x + \csc x} = \sin x \tan x$ is:

$$\frac{\sin x + \tan x}{\cot x + \csc x} = \sin x \tan x$$

$$\frac{\sin x + \dfrac{\sin x}{\cos x}}{\dfrac{\cos x}{\sin x} + \dfrac{1}{\sin x}} = \sin x \frac{\sin x}{\cos x}$$

$$\frac{\sin x\cos x + \sin x}{\cos x} \div \frac{\cos x + 1}{\sin x} = \frac{\sin^2 x}{\cos x}$$

$$\frac{\sin x(\cos x + 1)}{\cos x} \cdot \frac{\sin x}{\cos x + 1} = \frac{\sin^2 x}{\cos x}$$

$$\frac{\sin^2 x}{\cos x} = \frac{\sin^2 x}{\cos x}$$

**Multiple Angle Identities.** If $\alpha$ and $\beta$ are two given angles, then we have:

$$\sin(\alpha+\beta) = \sin\alpha\cos\beta + \cos\alpha\sin\beta$$

$$\cos(\alpha+\beta) = \cos\alpha\cos\beta - \sin\alpha\sin\beta$$

$$\tan(\alpha+\beta) = \frac{\tan\alpha+\tan\beta}{1-\tan\alpha\tan\beta}$$

$$\sin(\alpha-\beta) = \sin\alpha\cos\beta - \cos\alpha\sin\beta$$

$$\cos(\alpha-\beta) = \cos\alpha\cos\beta + \sin\alpha\sin\beta$$

$$\tan(\alpha-\beta) = \frac{\tan\alpha-\tan\beta}{1+\tan\alpha\tan\beta}$$

$$\sin 2\alpha = 2\sin\alpha\cos\alpha$$

$$\cos 2\alpha = \cos^2\alpha - \sin^2\alpha$$

$$\tan 2\alpha = \frac{2\tan\alpha}{1-\tan^2\alpha}$$

$$\sin 3\alpha = 3\sin\alpha - 4\sin^3\alpha$$

$$\cos 3\alpha = 4\cos^3\alpha - 3\cos\alpha$$

$$\sin\frac{\alpha}{2} = \pm\sqrt{\frac{1-\cos\alpha}{2}}$$

$$\cos\frac{\alpha}{2} = \pm\sqrt{\frac{1+\cos\alpha}{2}}$$

$$\tan\frac{\alpha}{2} = \pm\sqrt{\frac{1-\cos\alpha}{1+\cos\alpha}}$$

$$\sin\alpha + \sin\beta = 2\sin\frac{\alpha+\beta}{2}\cos\frac{\alpha-\beta}{2}$$

$$\sin\alpha - \sin\beta = 2\sin\frac{\alpha-\beta}{2}\cos\frac{\alpha+\beta}{2}$$

$$\cos\alpha + \cos\beta = 2\cos\frac{\alpha-\beta}{2}\cos\frac{\alpha+\beta}{2}$$

$$\cos\alpha - \cos\beta = -2\sin\frac{\alpha+\beta}{2}\sin\frac{\alpha-\beta}{2}$$

$$\sin\alpha\sin\beta = \tfrac{1}{2}(\cos(\alpha-\beta) - \cos(\alpha+\beta))$$

$$\cos\alpha\cos\beta = \tfrac{1}{2}(\cos(\alpha-\beta) + \cos(\alpha+\beta))$$

$$\sin\alpha\cos\beta = \tfrac{1}{2}(\sin(\alpha+\beta) + \sin(\alpha-\beta))$$

If $A$, $B$, and $C$ are the angles and $a$, $b$, and $c$ are the opposite sides respectively of a triangle, then we have:

the *law of sines,* $\dfrac{a}{\sin A} = \dfrac{b}{\sin B} = \dfrac{c}{\sin C}$, and

the *law of cosines,* $a^2 = b^2 + c^2 - 2bc\cos A$.

The law of cosines is similarly true for angles $B$ and $C$ also. If $s = (a+b+c)/2$ then

$\cos\dfrac{A}{2} = \sqrt{\dfrac{s(s-a)}{bc}}$, and *area of triangle*

$ABC = \sqrt{s(s-a)(s-b)(s-c)} = \tfrac{1}{2}ab\sin C.$

## INVERSE FUNCTIONS

**Definitions.** The *inverse trigonometric functions* will be given in this manner: $y =$ inverse sin of angle $x$ is written $y = \text{arc}\sin x$ or $y = \sin^{-1}x$. The definitions are as follows:

If $x = \sin y$, then $y = \text{arc}\sin x$, $\dfrac{-\pi}{2} \leq y \leq \dfrac{\pi}{2}$.

If $x = \cos y$, then $y = \text{arc}\cos x$, $0 \leq y \leq \pi$.

If $x = \tan y$, then $y = \text{arc}\tan x$, $\dfrac{-\pi}{2} \leq y \leq \dfrac{\pi}{2}$.

The other three functions are similarly defined but are less often used. The symbol "$y = \sin^{-1}x$"

means "$y$ is the angle whose sine is $x$," and therefore $\sin^{-1}x$ does not equal $1/\sin x$ or $(\sin x)^{-1}$. The restrictions on angle $y$ keep its range in *principal values*. That is, $y = \text{arc}\sin x$ has $\frac{-\pi}{2} \leq y \leq \frac{\pi}{2}$ so the principal values of $y$ go from $\frac{-\pi}{2}$ to $\frac{\pi}{2}$, making $y$ a (single-valued) function of $x$. We know then that $\sin(\sin^{-1}x) = x$.

For example, $y = \sin^{-1} .5$ means the angle whose sine is .5. Thus $y = \frac{\pi}{6}$ or 30°. $\text{Tan}(\cos^{-1}4/5)$ can be found by realizing that if $\cos\theta = 4/5$ then the right triangle containing $\theta$ must have sides of 4, 5, and $\sqrt{5^2 - 4^2}$ or 3. $\text{Tan}(\cos^{-1}4/5) = 3/4$. We may compute $\pi$ by the formula $\pi = 4\tan^{-1}1$.

**Graphs.** The principal values of arc sin$x$, arc cos$x$ and arc tan$x$ are graphed in [55].

[55]

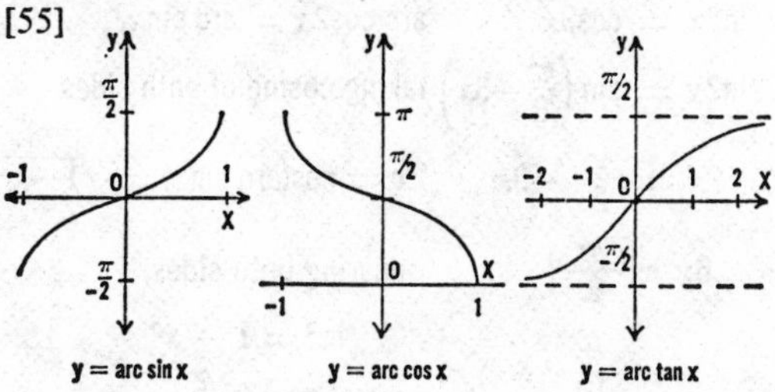


## APPLICATIONS

**Identity.** If $A$, $B$, and $C$ are the angles of a triangle, prove that $\tan A + \tan B + \tan C = \tan A \tan B \tan C$. We know that $C = 180° - (A+B)$ and also tangent is periodic so that $\tan x = \tan(x - 180°)$. But $\tan(-x) = -\tan x$ so we have $\tan(180° - x) = -\tan x$. Thus $\tan C = \tan(180° - (A+B)) = -\tan(A+B)$. We proceed as follows:

$$\tan A + \tan B + \tan C = \tan A + \tan B - \tan(A+B) =$$
$$\tan A + \tan B - \frac{\tan A + \tan B}{1 - \tan A \tan B} =$$
$$(\tan A + \tan B)\left(1 - \frac{1}{1 - \tan A \tan B}\right) =$$
$$(\tan A + \tan B)\left(\frac{1 - \tan A \tan B - 1}{1 - \tan A \tan B}\right) =$$
$$\tan A \tan B \left(-\frac{\tan A + \tan B}{1 - \tan A \tan B}\right) =$$
$$\tan A \tan B(-\tan(A+B)) = \tan A \tan B \tan C.$$

**Oblique Triangles.** An *oblique triangle* does not contain a right angle. We may apply trigonometry to oblique triangles as follows:

In [56a], two observation posts, $A$ and $B$, spot the flash of an enemy gun, $G$, at angles of 40° and 76° respectively. It is required to find the distance, $BG$, to the gun from post $B$ if $A$ and $B$ are three kilometers apart. We note that angle $AGB$ must be 64°, and we use the law of sines to get

$$\frac{BG}{\sin 40°} = \frac{3}{\sin 64°} \text{ or } BG = 3(\sin 40°)/\sin 64°,$$

which gives $BG = 3(.6428)/(.8988) = 2.16$ (kilometers).

[56]

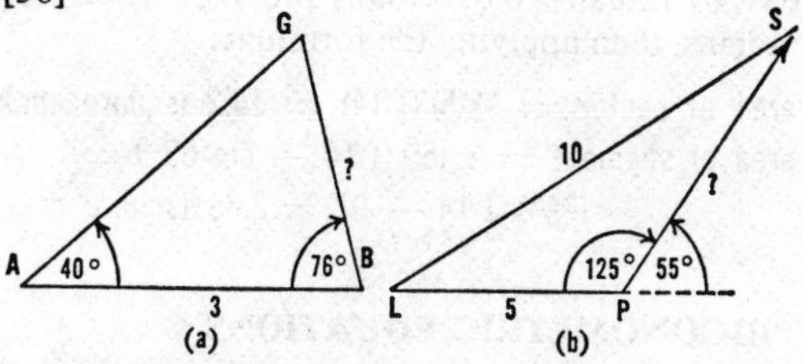


A ship sails from port, $P$ in [56b], on a bearing of N35°E at a rate of 12 miles per hour. In what length of time will the ship be 10 miles from a lighthouse which is 5 miles due west from the port? The answer is computed by using the following facts: angle $P$ is 125° and $\cos 125° = -\cos 55° = -.5736$; the law of cosines should be employed as one angle and two sides are involved. We have then,

$$LS^2 = LP^2 + PS^2 - 2(LP)(PS)\cos P,$$
$$10^2 = 5^2 + PS^2 - 2(5)(PS)(-.5736),$$

and $PS^2 + 5.736\,PS - 75 = 0$. Using the quadratic formula we get $PS = 6.2$ and $PS = -11.9$. We reject the negative, so $PS = 6.2$. This means at 12 miles per hour, the ship will take $6.2/12 = .52$ (hours) to reach the designated location.

**Area of Triangle.** To find the area of a triangle $ABC$ given $a = 20''$, $b = 15''$, and $C = 37°$, we use area $= \frac{1}{2}ab\sin C$ to get

$$\text{area} = \tfrac{1}{2}(20)(15)\sin 37° = \tfrac{1}{2}(20)(15)(.6018) = 90 \text{ (square inches)}$$

**Inverse Function.** We show that $\text{arc}\sin 1/\sqrt{10} + \text{arc}\sin 3/\sqrt{10} = \pi/2$ by the following: let $\alpha = \text{arc}\sin 1/\sqrt{10}$ and $\beta = \text{arc}\sin 3/\sqrt{10}$ so that the left member is just $\alpha + \beta$. Now $\alpha + \beta = \text{arc}\sin(\sin(\alpha+\beta)) = \text{arc}\sin(\sin\alpha\cos\beta + \cos\alpha\sin\beta) =$

$$\text{arc}\sin\left(\frac{1}{\sqrt{10}}\frac{1}{\sqrt{10}} + \frac{3}{\sqrt{10}}\frac{3}{\sqrt{10}}\right) = \text{arc}\sin\left(\frac{1}{10} + \frac{9}{10}\right) = \text{arc}\sin(1) = \frac{\pi}{2}.$$

**Sector, Segment.** A *circular sector* is the set of points covered by a radius of a circle which is rotated by some angle $\alpha$. The figure formed is intuitively shaped like a piece of pie. A sector has an area given by

$$\text{area of sector} = \tfrac{1}{2}r^2\alpha,$$

where $\alpha$ is in radians and $r$ is the radius. A *circular segment* is the part of the sector left when the triangle, formed by the two radii on each side of the sector and the chord connecting the endpoints of the radii, is removed. The area of a segment subtended by a central angle of $\alpha$ in radians, with a radius of $r$ is:

$$\text{area of segment} = \tfrac{1}{2}r^2(\alpha - \sin\alpha).$$

For example, we compute the area of the circular sector and segment of a central angle of 65° in a circle of radius 5 cm. by first changing 65° to radians, $65° = 65\pi/180$ radians $= 1.14$ radians, then applying the formulas:

$$\text{area of sector} = \tfrac{1}{2}(5)^2(1.14) = 14.2 \text{ (square cm.)},$$

$$\text{area of segment} = \tfrac{1}{2}(5^2)(1.14 - \sin 65°) = (25/2)(1.14 - .91) = 2.88 \text{ (square cm.)}.$$

## TRIGONOMETRIC EQUATIONS

**Linear.** A linear trigonometric equation is of the form $aT(x) + b = 0$, $a \neq 0$, where $T(x)$ is a trigonometric function of $x$. The following examples with solutions use principal values.

| | |
|---|---|
| $2\sin x - 1 = 0$ | $\sin x\cos x - \cos x = 0$ |
| $2\sin x = 1$ | $\cos x(\sin x - 1) = 0$ |
| $\sin x = \tfrac{1}{2}$ | $\cos x = 0$ |
| $x = \pi/6$ | $\sin x - 1 = 0$ |
| | $\sin x = 1$ |
| | $x = \pi/2$ |

The equation $\cos x = 2$ has no solution as $-1 \leq \cos x \leq 1$ for all real $x$.

**Quadratic.** A quadratic trigonometric equation is of the form $aT(x)^2 + bT(x) + c = 0$, $a \neq 0$. We obtain solutions by factoring or using the quadratic formula. Examples:

| | |
|---|---|
| $\sin^2 x + \sin x + 2 = 0$ | $\cos^2 x + 3\cos x - 3 = 0$ |
| Factoring: | By the formula: |
| $(\sin x + 2)(\sin x + 1) = 0$ | $\cos x = \dfrac{-3 \pm \sqrt{9+12}}{2}$ |
| $\sin x + 2 = 0$ | |
| $\sin x = -2$ No solution | $\cos x = -3.8$ and $.8$ |
| $\sin x + 1 = 0$ | the only solution is |
| $\sin x = -1$ | $\cos x = .8$ |
| $x = -\pi/2$ | $x = 36.5° = .64$ radians |

**Special.** Some special equations and their solutions will now be given. As the sine of the angle and the cosine of twice the angle must be equal in the second example, the first quadrant angle is the only solution.

| | |
|---|---|
| $\sin 2x = \cos 3x$ | $\arccos 2x = \arcsin x$, |
| $\sin 2x = \sin\left(\frac{\pi}{2} - 3x\right)$ | taking cosine of both sides |
| $2x = \frac{\pi}{2} - 3x$ | $2x = \cos(\arcsin x) = \sqrt{1 - x^2}$, |
| $5x = \frac{\pi}{2}$ | squaring both sides, |
| | $4x^2 = 1 - x^2$, |
| $x = \frac{\pi}{10}$ | $x = 1/\sqrt{5}$ |

# *College Preparatory Mathematics*

## PRELIMINARY TOPICS

**General Functions.** If a variable $x \in$ (is an element of) a set $X$ and a variable $y \in$ a set $Y$, then *$y$ is a function of $x$*, written $y = f(x)$, if there is a rule associating each value of $x$ with one value of $y$. The set $X$ is called the *domain* and $Y$ the *range*. The variable $y$ is called the *dependent* variable and $x$ is the *independent* variable. The function just defined is more precisely a *single-valued* function of $x$. A *multi-valued* function assigns two or more values of $y$ to each value of $x$. Unless otherwise stated, functions will be single-valued functions.

On the real number line, an *interval* is the set of points between two given points. A *closed interval* contains its endpoints. An *open interval* does not contain its endpoints. We can say a number is *finite* if there is an integer $m$ such that $|m| \geqq |n|$. A *finite interval* is an interval with finite endpoints. An *infinite interval* is an interval which is not finite.

A function is *defined* on an interval if it is defined at each point of the interval. If $a$ is a constant in the domain of $f$ then we assign to $f(a)$ the value $f(x)$ when $x = a$. The $a$ is called the *argument* of the function and $f(a)$ is called the *image* of $a$.

The symbol $f(x,y)$ means $f$ is a function of two variables $x$ and $y$. For example, $f(x,y) = x^2 + 2xy + y^2$ is a function of two independent variables, $x$ and $y$, which are also called arguments. Two functions, $f$ and $g$, are equal if they have the same domain $X$ and $f(x) = g(x)$ for each $x \in X$.

A function is sometimes called a *mapping* or *transformation*. We can symbolize the mapping $y = f(x)$ in each of the following ways:

$$f: x \rightarrow y, \qquad x \xrightarrow{f} y, \qquad f: X \rightarrow Y.$$

A function $f$ maps the domain $X$ *onto* the range $Y$ if for every $y \in Y$, $y = f(x)$ for some *element* $x \in X$. If distinct elements of $X$ have distinct images in $Y$ then $f$ is called *one-to-one*.

The function, $f(x) = 3$, is constant since for all values of $x$ the image is a constant 3. The *identity* function is given by $f(x) = x$, making the image and the argument equal. An *even* function has the characteristic that $f(-x) = f(x)$. An *odd* function has $f(-x) = -f(x)$. If the domain is the set of real numbers then the graph of an even function is symmetric about the

$y$ axis and the graph of an odd function is symmetric about the origin. A function does not have to be either odd or even.

A function is said to be *bounded* if there is a constant $M>0$ such that $|f(x)|<M$ for all $x$ in the domain.

See *Algebraic Equations* in the algebra section for a discussion of *polynomial, exponential,* and *logarithmic* functions.

**Rational Functions.** If $f(x)$ and $g(x)$ are two polynomial functions then the quotient $f(x)/g(x)$ is called a *rational function.* It is defined and it is smooth for all $x$ such that $g(x) \neq 0$ (see *Continuity*). This makes the graph of a rational function have a *vertical asymptote* at a zero (a point $a$ where $g(a) = 0$) of the denominator if the numerator is not zero. Thus $g(x)$ approaches zero near such a point.

A rational function of the form

$$\frac{(a_0p^n+a_1p^{n-1}+ \ldots +a_{n-1}p+a_n)}{(b_0q^m+b_1q^{m-1}+\ldots+b_{m-1}q+b_m)}$$

has a *horizontal asymptote:*

at $y = 0$, if $m>n$;

at $y = a_0/b_0$, if $m = n$;

nowhere, if $m<n$.

If $m = n - 1$, then we can divide the denominator into the numerator and get a quotient, $cx + d + R$, where $R$ is the remainder of the two terms. The line $y = cx + d$ is the *oblique asymptote* of the rational function.

**Partial Fractions.** The rational function $(4x-5)/(x^2-x-2)$ when expressed as partial fractions is

$$\frac{1}{x-2}+\frac{3}{x+1}.$$

This process is the opposite of adding fractions. The degree of the numerator must be less than the degree of the denominator; if not, the rational function is not in proper form. If such be the case then we divide the denominator into the numerator and then the *remainder,* which is a rational function, will be in proper form and can be changed to partial fractions.

The procedure for changing a given rational function, in proper form, to partial fractions is as follows:

1. We factor the denominator, $g(x)$, into *real* linear and quadratic factors. This may prove to be difficult but it is necessary. Also, in some applications, complex linear factors are required.
2. Suppose that $x - r$ is a factor and that we have $m$ of them, then $(x-r)^m$ is a factor of $g(x)$. For this factor we will have $m$ partial fractions of the form:

$$\frac{a_1}{x-r}+\frac{a_2}{(x-r)^2}+\frac{a_3}{(x-r)^3}+\ldots+\frac{a_m}{(x-r)^m},$$

where the $a_1, a_2, \ldots, a_m$ are constant coefficients which are to be determined. We do this for all such linear factors.

3. If $x^2 + sx + t$ is a quadratic factor and we have $n$ of them, then $(x^2+sx+t)^n$ is a factor of $g(x)$. We have corresponding to this factor $n$ partial fractions of the form:

$$\frac{b_1x+c_1}{x^2+sx+t}+\frac{b_2x+c_2}{(x^2+sx+t)^2}+\ldots+\frac{b_nx+c_n}{(x^2+sx+t)^n},$$

where again we have the undetermined coefficients, $b_1, b_2, \ldots, b_n$ and $c_1, c_2, \ldots, c_n$.

4. We now set the given rational function equal to the sum of these partial fractions with the undetermined coefficients. We multiply both sides by $g(x)$ in order to clear the fractions.
5. Next we set equal the coefficients of like powers of $x$, and the resulting equations can be solved for the undetermined coefficients.

For example, to express $\dfrac{4x^3+5x-3}{x^4+2x^3+3x^2+4x+2}$ in partial fractions, we factor the denominator,

$$\frac{4x^3+5x-3}{(x^2+2)\ (x+1)^2},$$

then set the rational function equal to the appropriate partial fractions with undetermined coefficients. So we have

$$\frac{4x^3+5x-3}{(x^2+2)\ (x+1)^2}=\frac{ax+b}{x^2+2}+\frac{c}{x+1}+\frac{d}{(x+1)^2}.$$

We now multiply both sides by $(x^2+2)(x+1)^2$ to get

$$4x^3 + 5x - 3 = (ax+b)\ (x+1)^2 + c(x^2+2)\ (x+1) + d(x^2+2)$$

$$4x^3 + 5x - 3 = ax^3 + 2ax^2 + ax + bx^2 + 2bx + b + cx^3 + cx^2 + 2cx + 2c + dx^2 + 2d$$

$$4x^3 + 5x - 3 = (a+c)x^3 + (2a+b+c+d)x^2 + (a+2b+2c)x + (b+2c+2d)$$

Equating like coefficients of the above *identity* gives us four simultaneous equations in four unknowns. See *Simultaneous Equations* in algebra section for methods of solution.

$$4 = a + c$$
$$0 = 2a + b + c + d$$
$$5 = a + 2b + 2c$$
$$-3 = b + 2c + 2d$$

The solution is $a = 1$, $b= -1$, $c = 3$, $d = -4$, therefore we have

$$\frac{4x^3+5x-3}{x^4+2x^3+3x^2+4x+2}=\frac{x-1}{x^2+2}+\frac{3}{x+1}-\frac{4}{(x+1)^2}.$$

*There are two basic plane and three basic three space coordinate systems. The next four topics involve these systems.*

**Polar coordinates.** The coordinate system so far discussed has been the *Cartesian* system with the points located by their $x$— and $y$— coordinates. We also have the *polar* coordinate system which locates a point, $p$, by the coordinates $r$, $\theta$, where $r$ is the directed distance from the origin to $p$ along the terminal side of an angle $\theta$ in standard position. In [57a], the point $p$ is named by both Cartesian and polar coordinates.

[57]

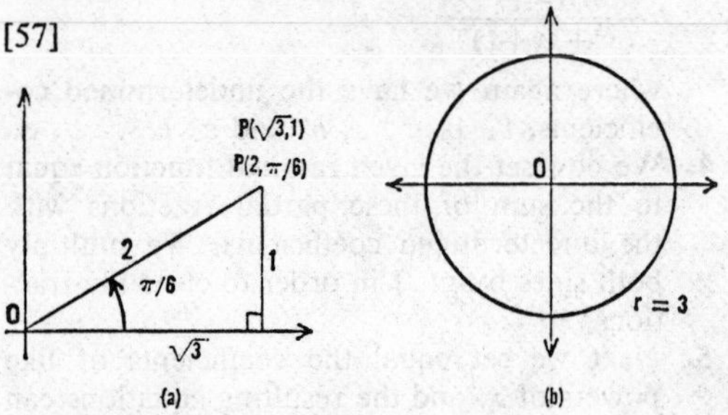


(a) (b)

The point $p$ in [57a] could also have polar coordinate representations of $(2,-11\pi/6)$, $(-2,7\pi/6)$, $(-2,-5\pi/6)$, and in general $(2,\pi/6+2\pi n)$ when $n$ is an integer. There are still others but these will suffice.

The relationship between polar and Cartesian is

$$x = r\cos\theta, \quad y = r\sin\theta,$$

and also

$$r = \sqrt{x^2+y^2}, \quad \theta = \tan^{-1}y/x.$$

The equation of the circle of radius 3 centered at the origin is $x^2+y^2=9$. In polar coordinates we have $r^2=9$ or $r=3$ (See [57b]).

In [58a] we have the graph of $r = 1 - \cos\theta$ which is called a *cardioid*. The graph of $r^2 = 2\cos 2\theta$ in [58b] is called a *lemniscate*.

[58]

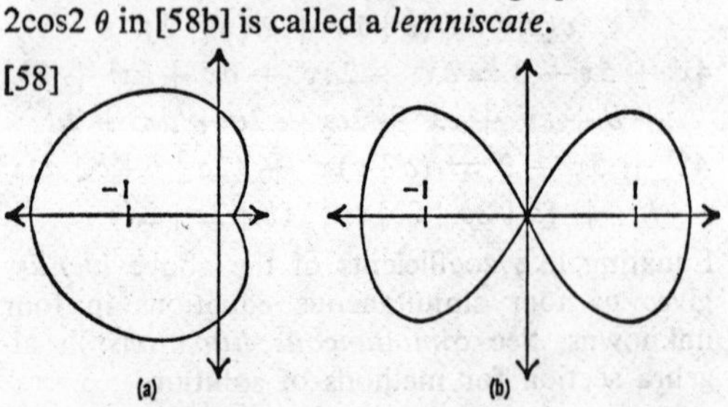


(a) (b)

**Cartesian Three Space.** To locate a point $p$ in three (dimensional) space we can use $x$, $y$, and $z$ as in [59a], with the $z$-axis perpendicular to the plane of the $x$ and $y$ axes at the common origin. This is called the three dimensional *Cartesian* system.

[59]

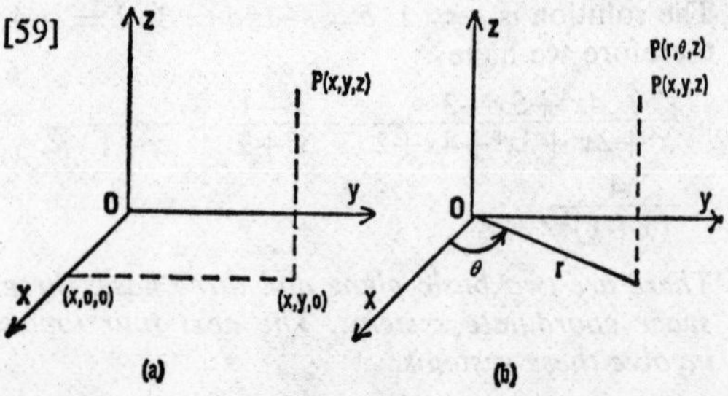


(a) (b)

**Cylindrical System.** When using cylindrical coordinates to locate a three dimensional point $p$, we change the $x$— and $y$— coordinates to polar and use the same $z$ coordinate (See [59b]). That is, if $p$ has Cartesian coordinates $(x,y,z)$, then the cylindrical coordinates $(r,\theta,z)$ are given by

$$r = \sqrt{x^2+y^2}, \quad \theta = \tan^{-1}y/x, \quad z = z,$$

and we convert from cylindrical to Cartesian by

$$x = r\cos\theta, \quad y = r\sin\theta, \quad z = z.$$

For example, the Cartesian equation of a cylinder of radius 4, centered at the origin is $x^2+y^2=16$. The equivalent equation in cylindrical coordinates is $r=4$.

**Spherical System.** In [60] we note that a point in three space can be located by: $\rho$, the distance from the origin to the point; $\phi$, the angle the line $OP$ makes with the positive $z$-axis; and $\theta$, the angle that the projection of $OP$ on the $xy$ plane, $OQ$, makes with the positive $x$-axis. For conversion between spherical and Cartesian we have:

[60]

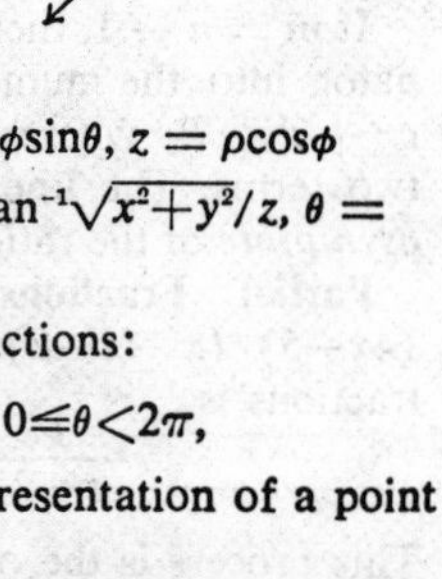

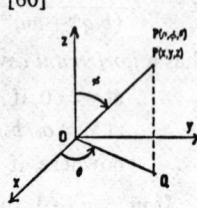


$$x = \rho\sin\phi\cos\theta,\ y = \rho\sin\phi\sin\theta,\ z = \rho\cos\phi$$

$$\rho = \sqrt{x^2+y^2+z^2},\ \phi = \tan^{-1}\sqrt{x^2+y^2}/z,\ \theta = \tan^{-1}y/x.$$

With the following restrictions:

$$\rho \geqq 0,\ 0 \leqq \phi \leqq \pi,\ 0 \leqq \theta < 2\pi,$$

we make the spherical representation of a point unique.

The Cartesian equation of a sphere of radius 5 centered at the origin is $x^2+y^2+z^2=25$. The same spherical equation is $\rho=5$.

In *general* the *Cartesian* system is most useful. However, when the graph of the object under consideration has a line or *axis of symmetry* it may be advantageous to use *cylindrical* coordinates. If there is a *point* of symmetry then *spherical* coordinates may possibly simplify computation.

**Trigonometric Substitutions.** It is helpful in some applications to make a trigonometric substitution for a given expression. For example, we can restate the expression $1/(x^2+1)$ by noting the right triangle in [61a]. Here $1/(x^2+1) = \sin^2\theta$.

[61]

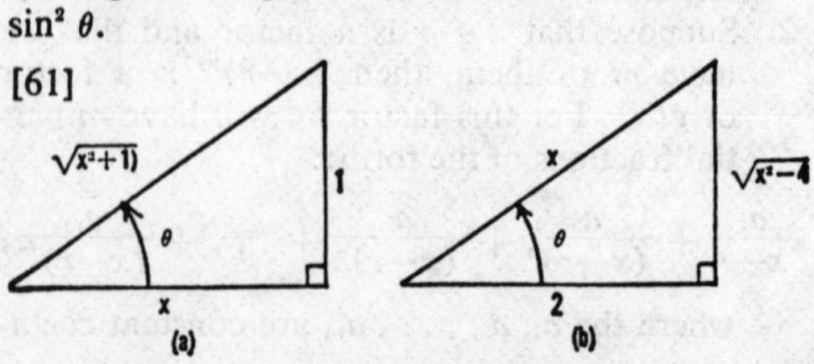


(a) (b)

Again consider the expression $x/\sqrt{x^2-4}$. In [61b] we find that $x/\sqrt{x^2-4} = \csc\theta$.

**Parametric Equations.** If $x = f(t)$ and $y = g(t)$ then these equations are called *parametric equations* and the parameter is the variable $t$. Then as $t$ takes on values we can obtain corresponding values for $x$ and $y$. For example, if $x = t-1$ and $y = t^2$, then these parametric equations are equivalent to $y = x^2 + 2x + 1$ if the domain at $t$ is the set of real numbers.

**Equations, Inequalities.** We will use the following basic equations and inequalities in further calculations. Here $a$, $b$, and $c$ are real numbers.

1. If $a>b$ and $b>c$ then $a>c$.
2. If $a>b$ then $1/a<1/b$.
3. $|a+b| \leq |a| + |b|$.
4. $|a| - |b| \leq |a-b| = |b-a| \geq |b| - |a|$.
5. $|a|\,|b| = |a \cdot b|$.

The first inequality is often given as an axiom. The second is proved by multiplying both sides of $a>b$ by $1/ab$, with either $a>b>0$ or $0>a>b$. If $a>0>b$ the proof is trivial. ■

The proof of the third is as follows: as $-|a| \leq a \leq |a|$, and $-|b| \leq b \leq |b|$ then by addition we have

$$-|a| - |b| \leq a + b \leq |a| + |b|$$
$$-(|a| + |b|) \leq a + b \leq (|a| + |b|).$$

Now if $a + b \geq 0$, then $a + b = |a + b| \leq |a| + |b|$. If $a + b < 0$, then $|a + b| = -(a+b)$ but multiplying both sides of $-(|a| + |b|) \leq a + b$ by $-1$ gives $-(a+b) \leq |a| + |b|$. ■

The results given by the fourth inequality can be shown by substitution into the third inequality. The fifth one can easily be proved by taking cases like $a>b>0$, $a>0>b$, $0>a>b$, etc.

## LIMITS

**Sequences.** *A sequence,* $\mathbf{x}_1, \mathbf{x}_2, \mathbf{x}_3, \ldots$ *is said to converge to a limit* $\mathbf{L}$ *if and only if for each* $\epsilon>0$ *there is an integer* $\mathbf{m}>0$*, such that if* $\mathbf{n}>\mathbf{m}$ *then* $|\mathbf{L}-\mathbf{x}_n|<\epsilon$. *A sequence which does not converge is said to diverge.*

The sequence 0, 7/8, 26/27, . . . , converges to 1 as we shall prove, because for each $\epsilon$ there is an $m$ that will fit the definition. We know that the $n$th term of the given sequence is $(n^3-1)/n^3 = 1 - 1/n^3$.

Thus $|L-x_n| = |1-1+1/n^3| = 1/n^3$.

We are trying to prove then that $1/n^3$ will be less than any given positive number $\epsilon$ if $n$ is large enough. This will be true if $n>m$ and $1/m^3 = \epsilon$, which makes $m = 1/\sqrt[3]{\epsilon}$. Therefore given an $\epsilon>0$ there is an $m = 1/\sqrt[3]{\epsilon}$ such that when $n>m$ then $|L-x_n| = |1/n^3| < 1/m^3 = \epsilon$. ■

As an illustration, suppose someone gives us an $\epsilon$ of .001 and we must find the required $m$. We then let $m = 1/\sqrt[3]{\epsilon} = 1/\sqrt[3]{.001} = 1/.1 = 10$ and we find that any term after the tenth term will be closer to the limit 1 than an $\epsilon$ of .001. In particular, the eleventh term is $(11^3-1)/11^3 = 1330/1331$ and the difference between 1330/1331 and the limit 1 is 1/1331 which is less than .001.

It is noteworthy that the sequence just mentioned will never reach its limit. It is correct to say that if a sequence, $x_1, x_2, \ldots$, has a limit $L$ then the $n$th term, $x_n$, *approaches* $L$. This is written $x_n \to L$. Note also that we used the definitions of the limit of a sequence to prove that a number $L$ was the limit, and not to actually find the limit $L$.

**Series.** A series $x_1 + x_2 + \ldots$ can be thought of as a sequence of partial sums like:

$$s_1 = x_1$$
$$s_2 = x_1 + x_2$$
$$s_3 = x_1 + x_2 + x_3$$
$$\vdots$$
$$s_n = x_1 + x_2 + \ldots + x_n$$
$$\vdots$$

where the number of partial sums is infinite. *A series is said to converge to a limit* **L** *if and only if the corresponding sequence of partial sums converges to* **L**. *If a series does not converge then it diverges.* See *Selected Topics, Convergence, Divergence.*

The series ½ + ¼ + ⅛ + . . . converges to 1. This can be proved by noting that the sequence of partial sums is ½, ¾, ⅞, . . . , which converges to the limit 1.

**Functions.** *A function* $\mathbf{f(x)}$ *has a limit* $\mathbf{L}$ *as* $\mathbf{x}$ *approaches* $\mathbf{a}$ $(\mathbf{x} \to \mathbf{a})$ *if and only if for each* $\epsilon>0$ *there exists a* $\delta>0$ *such that if* $|\mathbf{x}-\mathbf{a}|<\delta$ *then* $|\mathbf{L}-\mathbf{f(x)}|<\epsilon$. The idea in the definition is that as $x$ gets close to but does not actually take on the value of $a$ then the function $f(x)$ will get close to $L$ without necessarily taking on the value $L$. Note that we must determine the limit ourselves since the definition does not tell us how to find the $L$ that will be the limit of the function at the point $a$. The limit of a function $f(x)$ as $x$ approaches $a$ is written:

$$\lim_{x \to a} f(x).$$

As an example, prove that $\lim_{x \to 2} (x^2-3x+3) = 1$.

Given an $\epsilon>0$, we must find a $\delta$ such that when $|x-2|<\delta$ then $|(x^2-3x+3) - 1|<\epsilon$. In this case we write $|(x^2-3x+3) - 1|$ in terms of $x-2$ and get $|(x-2)^2 + (x-2)|$. Thus

$$|(x-2)^2 + (x-2)| \leq |x-2|^2 + |x-2|.$$

Now if we choose $\delta<1$ then $|x-2|<\delta$ means

$$|x-2|^2 + |x-2| < 2|x-2| < 2\delta.$$

Then let $\delta = 1$ or $\epsilon/2$, whichever is smaller. ■

Now the value of $f(x) = x^2 - 3x + 3$ at $x = 2$ is 1 which is the same as the limit. This is not always true, however, for when we consider

$$f(x) = \frac{x^2-4}{x-2},$$

we find the value of the function at $x=2$ is indeterminant (0/0). However, the limit exists and is found by

$$\lim_{x\to 2}\frac{x^2-4}{x-2} = \lim_{x\to 2}\frac{(x+2)(x-2)}{(x-2)} =$$

$$\lim_{x\to 2}(x+2) = 4,$$

and can be verified by letting $\delta = \epsilon$. When we consider the limit of the function as $x\to 2$ then $x$ does not take on the value 2. This means that $(x-2)$ is not zero and we can divide through by $x-2$ thus simplifying the function to $x+2$.

*If* $\mathbf{f(x)} = \mathbf{c}$ *where* $\mathbf{c}$ *is a constant, then* $\lim_{x\to a}\mathbf{f(x)} = \mathbf{c}$ *for all* $\mathbf{a}$, $-\infty \leq \mathbf{a} \leq \infty$.

*We say* $\lim_{x\to a}\mathbf{f(x)} \to \infty$ *if for each positive number* $\mathbf{M}$, *however large, there exists a* $\delta>0$ *such that if* $|\mathbf{x}-\mathbf{a}|<\delta$ *then* $\mathbf{f(x)}>\mathbf{M}$. In the above definition if $f(x)>\mathbf{M}$ is replaced by $f(x)<-\mathbf{M}$ then $\lim_{x\to a} f(x)\to -\infty$. In each of these cases we say that the functions increase (or decrease) without limit or that no limit exists.

*We define* $\lim_{x\to\infty}\mathbf{f(x)} = \mathbf{L}$ *if for each* $\epsilon>0$, *however small, there exists a positive number* $\mathbf{M}$ *such that if* $|\mathbf{x}|>\mathbf{M}$ *then* $|\mathbf{f(x)}-\mathbf{L}|<\epsilon$.

For some examples using these definitions, we will prove:

**1.** $\lim_{x\to 2}\frac{x^2-4}{(x-2)^2}\to\infty$ and **2.** $\lim_{x\to\infty}\frac{x^2-4}{(x-2)^2} = 1$.

**1.** Given an $M>0$,

$$\lim_{x\to 2}\frac{x^2-4}{(x-2)^2} = \lim_{x\to 2}\frac{(x+2)(x-2)}{(x-2)(x-2)} =$$

$$\lim_{x\to 2}\frac{x+2}{x-2}.$$

Let $x-2<\delta<1$, so that $\frac{x+2}{x-2} > \frac{x+2}{\delta} > \frac{1}{\delta}$, and if we let $\delta$ be $1/M$ or 1 whichever is smaller, then

$$\frac{x+2}{x-2} > \frac{1}{\delta} > M \text{ and } \lim_{x\to 2}\frac{x^2-4}{(x-2)^2}\to\infty \quad ■$$

**2.** Given an $\epsilon>0$, we know that

$$\lim_{x\to\infty}\frac{x^2-4}{(x-2)^2} = \lim_{x\to\infty}\frac{x+2}{x-2} = \lim_{x\to\infty}\frac{\frac{x}{x}+\frac{2}{x}}{\frac{x}{x}-\frac{2}{x}}$$

$$= \lim_{x\to\infty}\frac{1+\frac{2}{x}}{1-\frac{2}{x}} = 1,$$

and that eventually the function will be less than $\epsilon$ away from 1. In a case such as this we can forego some of the formalism and note that the trick of dividing each term by $x$ gave us the obvious limit of the function. ■

The following very useful theorems on limits are given for completeness. After each one, either the proof or a leading hint will be given. Let $\lim_{x\to a} f(x) = A$, and $\lim_{x\to a} g(x) = B$; this means that for each $\epsilon>0$ there exists a $\delta_1$ and a $\delta_2$ such that if $|x-a|<\delta_1$, then $|f(x)-A|<\epsilon/2$ and if $|x-a|<\delta_2$ then $|g(x)-B|<\epsilon/2$. If we let $\delta$ be the smaller of $\delta_1$ and $\delta_2$, then if $|x-a|<\delta$, we have $|f(x)-A|<\epsilon/2$ and $|g(x)-B|<\epsilon/2$.

**1.** $\lim_{x\to a} cf(x) = c\lim_{x\to a} f(x) = cA$. The proof can be completed after noting that if given an $\epsilon>0$, such that $|x-a|<\delta$ makes $|f(x)-A|<\epsilon$, then $|cf(x)-cA| = |c(f(x)-A)| = |c|\,|f(x)-A|$. Now let $\delta_3$ be the smaller of $\delta$ or the $\delta_4$ necessary to make $|f(x)-A|<\epsilon/|c|$ and we have $|x-a|<\delta_3$ makes $|cf(x)-cA|<\epsilon$. ■

**2.** $\lim_{x\to a}(f(x)+g(x)) = A+B$. Given an $\epsilon>0$, we have $|f(x)+g(x) - (A+B)| = |f(x)-A+g(x)-B| \leq |f(x)-A| + |g(x)-B|$. Now when $|x-a|<\delta$ we have $|f(x)+g(x) - (A+B)|<\epsilon/2+\epsilon/2=\epsilon$. ■

**3.** $\lim_{x\to a}(f(x)\cdot g(x)) = A\cdot B$. Let $\epsilon>0$ be given. We know that $|(f(x)\cdot g(x)) - (A\cdot B)| = |f(x)(g(x)-B) + B(f(x)-A)| \leq |f(x)|\,|g(x)-B| + |B|\,|f(x)-A|$. For this $\epsilon$ we will have $f(x)$ bounded by some positive constant $N$ which is greater than $|A|$ and greater than $|B|$. For this $N$, $|f(x)|\,|g(x)-B| + |B|\,|f(x)-A| \leq N|g(x)-B| + N|f(x)-A| = N(|g(x)-B| + |f(x)-A|)$. Choosing $\delta_3$ as the smaller of $\delta$ or the $\delta_4$ which would make $|g(x)-B| + |f(x)-A|<\epsilon/N$, allows $|x-a|<\delta_3$ to mean $|(f(x)\cdot g(x)) - A\cdot B|<\epsilon$. ■

**4.** $\lim_{x\to a}(f(x)/g(x)) = A/B$, $B\neq 0$. Let $\epsilon>0$ be given. We can write $|f(x)/g(x) - A/B| =$

$$\left|\frac{Bf(x)-Ag(x)}{g(x)\cdot B}\right| = \left|\frac{Bf(x)-AB+AB-Ag(x)}{g(x)\cdot B}\right|$$

$$\leq \frac{|B|\,|f(x)-A|+|A|\,|g(x)-B|}{|g(x)|\cdot|B|} =$$

$$\frac{1}{|g(x)|}|f(x)-A| + \frac{|A|}{|g(x)|\cdot|B|}|g(x)-B|.$$

As $B\neq 0$, the $\epsilon$ given, or a smaller one, will bound $g(x)$ away from zero, so that both $1/|g(x)|$ and $|A|/(|g(x)|\cdot|B|)$ are bounded (each less than some constant $N>0$) by a suitable $\epsilon_1\leq\epsilon$. Let $\delta_3$ be the smaller of $\delta$ or the $\delta_4$ which would make $|f(x)-A| + |g(x)-B|<\epsilon/N$. We then have $|x-a|<\delta_3$ implies that

$$\frac{1}{|g(x)|}|f(x)-A| + \frac{|A|}{|g(x)|\cdot|B|}|g(x)-B| \leq N(|f(x)-A| + |g(x)-B|) \leq \epsilon_1 \leq \epsilon. \quad ■$$

**5.** $\lim_{x\to a} 1/g(x) = 1/B$, $B\neq 0$. Given an $\epsilon>0$, we can let $f(x) = 1$, a constant function, and we have $\lim_{x\to a} 1/g(x) = \lim_{x\to a} f(x)/g(x)$. Then we can finish the proof by using theorem **4.** ■

*The next two limits are important in later applications.*

$$\lim_{n\to 0} \frac{(x+n)^2-x^2}{n} = 2x.$$

$$\lim_{n\to 0} \frac{x^2+2nx+n^2-x^2}{n} = \lim_{n\to 0} \frac{2nx+n^2}{n} =$$

$\lim_{n\to 0} (2x+n) = 2x.$ ■ As $x$ is not involved in the limit process, it can be treated as a constant. This kind of limit is an essential concept of differential calculus. See *Derivatives.*

$$\lim_{\theta\to 0} \frac{\sin\theta}{\theta} = 1.$$

[62]

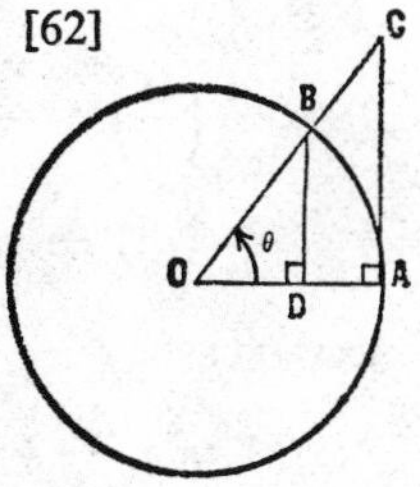


We shall prove this by the geometric consideration in [62]. Let $\theta$ in radians be less than $\pi/4$ as a central angle in a unit circle. By inspection of [62] and recalling [52] we have $\sin\theta = BD$, $\tan\theta = CA$.

We also know that $BD <$ arc $BA < CA$. This gives us

$$\sin\theta < \theta < \tan\theta,$$

and we can divide by $\sin\theta \neq 0$ to get

$$1 < \frac{\theta}{\sin\theta} < \frac{\tan\theta}{\sin\theta} = \sec\theta.$$

Knowing that if $A > B$ then $1/A < 1/B$, we take reciprocals and

$$1 > \frac{\sin\theta}{\theta} > \cos\theta.$$

Now as $\theta\to 0$, $\cos\theta\to 1$ and $(\sin\theta)/\theta$ is wedged to the limit 1. ■

## CONTINUITY

**Definition.** *A function* **f(x)** *is said to be continuous at a point* **a** *if* $\lim_{x\to a}$ **f(x)** *exists and equals* **f(a)**. *A function is discontinuous at* **a** *if the limit fails to exist at* **a** *or if the limit is not* **f(a)**. A function is continuous on an interval if it is continuous at each point of the interval. Intuitively speaking, a function is continuous, if, when graphed, there are no "breaks" in the curve.

**Discontinuites.** The function, $f(x) = (x^2-4)/(x-2)$ has a *removable* discontinuity at $x = 2$. By this we mean that we can *redefine* the function so that $f(2) = 4$, and $f(x) = (x^2-4)/(x-2)$ for $x\neq 2$, and thus make the function continuous everywhere (for each real number $x$).

The function $f(x) = [x]$ is called the greatest integer function and its value for any $x$ is the greatest integer less than or equal to $x$. In [63] we note that at each integer value of $x$ there is a *jump discontinuity* in the curve. Thus the function is discontinuous at the integers. As $x\to 2$ from above (written $x\to 2^+$), that is as $x$ takes on values less than 3 approaching 2, then the functional values are always 2. At $x = 2$, $f(x) = 2$, so looking at the limit from the right ($\lim_{x\to 2^+} f(x)$) it appears to be continuous. On the other hand, the left limit ($\lim_{x\to 2^-} f(x)$) is 1 and the right and left limits are not the same. This is another way of saying that the limit does not exist because there is no $\delta$ that will work for an $\epsilon$ less than the difference of the right and left limits.

[63]

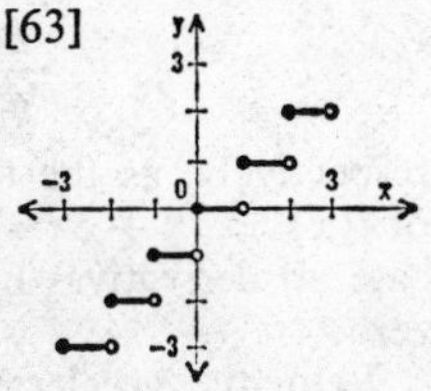


The function $f(x) = 2/(x-1)$ has an *infinite discontinuity* at $x = 1$.

**Properties.** The sum, difference, product, or quotient (denominator $\neq 0$) of continuous functions is a continuous function. These properties can be proved separately using the methods of the section on limits of sums, products and quotients.

If $f(x)$ is continuous on $a\leq x\leq b$ and $f(a)\neq f(b)$, then for any value $t$ between $f(a)$ and $f(b)$ there will be a number $c$ between $a$ and $b$ such that $f(c) = t$ (*Intermediate Value Theorem*).

**Uniform Continuity.** *A function* **f(x)** *is uniformly continuous on an interval if for each* $\epsilon > 0$ *there exists a* $\delta > 0$ *such that* $|\mathbf{f(a)} - \mathbf{f(b)}| < \epsilon$ *whenever* $|\mathbf{a}-\mathbf{b}| < \delta$ *where* **a** *and* **b** *are any two points in the interval.* Here $\delta$ depends only upon $\epsilon$ and not upon the choice of points $a$ and $b$.

A function which is continuous on a closed interval is uniformly continuous on that interval.

## DERIVATIVES

**Definition.** Let $P(x_0, y_0)$ be a *fixed* point on a curve, $y = f(x)$, in [64]. Let $Q(x_0+\Delta x, y_0+\Delta y)$ be any other point on the curve. Here $\Delta x$ and $\Delta y$ suggest increments or changes in coordinates. For example, if $P = (2,1)$ and $Q = (4,5)$ then $\Delta x = 3$ and $\Delta y = 4$. Now the slope of the secant line $PQ$ is

[64]

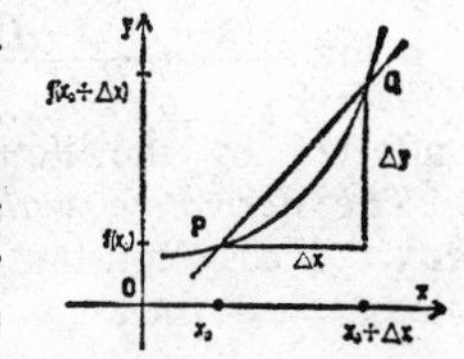


$$\frac{\Delta y}{\Delta x} = \frac{f(x_0+\Delta x)-f(x_0)}{\Delta x}.$$

If we let $\Delta x$ get smaller then the secant line $PQ$ approaches the tangent line at point $P$. If the slope of the secant line approaches a constant value $s$ as $\Delta x\to 0$ then $s$ is defined to be the slope of the tangent to the curve at point $P$. Thus we have

$$s = \lim_{\Delta x\to 0} \frac{\Delta y}{\Delta x} = \lim_{\Delta x\to 0} \frac{f(x_0+\Delta x)-f(x_0)}{\Delta x}.$$

This number $s$ is symbolized by $f'(x_0)$ and is called the *derivative* of $f(x)$ at $x_0$. In general, we usually write

$$f'(x) = \lim_{\Delta x \to 0} \frac{f(x+\Delta x)-f(x)}{\Delta x},$$

and realize that $x$ is really held constant during the limiting process.

For example, if $f(x) = x^2 - 3x + 7$, then $f'(x)$ and $f'(2)$ are found as follows:

$$f(x) = x^2-3x+7$$
$$f(x+\Delta x) = (x+\Delta x)^2-3(x+\Delta x)+7$$
$$f(x+\Delta x) = x^2+2x\Delta x+\Delta x^2-3x-3\Delta x+7$$
$$f(x+\Delta x) - f(x) = 2x\Delta x+\Delta x^2-3\Delta x$$
$$\frac{f(x+\Delta x) - f(x)}{\Delta x} = \frac{2x\Delta x+\Delta x^2-3\Delta x}{\Delta x}$$
$$\frac{f(x+\Delta x)-f(x)}{\Delta x} = 2x-3+\Delta x$$
$$f'(x) = \lim_{\Delta x \to 0} \frac{f(x+\Delta x)-f(x)}{\Delta x} = 2x-3$$
$$f'(2) = 2(2)-3 = 1$$

Because the limit is taken on $\Delta x$ in computing $f'(x)$ we say $f'(x)$ is the derivative with respect to $x$. If $y = f(x)$ then $f'(x)$ is the derivative of $y$ with respect to $x$ and is symbolized by

$$\frac{dy}{dx}, \frac{d}{dx}(y), y', \text{ and } D_x y.$$

A function is *differentiable,* at a point, if the derivative exists at the point, and it is differentiable on an interval if it is differentiable at each point of the interval.

**Polynomials.** *The derivative of a constant is zero.* $y = f(x) = c$, thus $f(x+\Delta x) = f(x)$ for all $x$ and

$$f'(x) = \lim_{\Delta x \to 0} \frac{f(x+\Delta x)-f(x)}{\Delta x} = 0 \quad ■$$

*The derivative with respect to* **x** *of* **cf(x)** *is* **cf'(x),** if $f(x)$ is differentiable and $c$ is a constant. We have

$$\lim_{\Delta x \to 0} \frac{cf(x+\Delta x)-cf(x)}{\Delta x} =$$

$$c \lim_{\Delta x \to 0} \frac{f(x+\Delta x)-f(x)}{\Delta x} = cf'(x), \text{ as } c \text{ is not}$$

affected by the limit process. ■

*The derivative with respect to* **x** of **cx$^n$** *is* **cnx$^{n-1}$**, if $c$ is a constant and $n$ is a positive integer. Let $y = cx^n$, then

$$\frac{dy}{dx} = c\frac{d}{dx}(x^n) = c\left(\lim_{\Delta x \to 0} \frac{(x+\Delta x)^n-x^n}{\Delta x}\right).$$

By the binomial theorem (see *Selected Topics*) we have $(x+\Delta x)^n = x^n + nx^{n-1}\Delta x +$ terms involving $\Delta x$ to the second or higher powers. So $(x+\Delta x)^n-x^n = nx^{n-1}\Delta x +$ terms involving $\Delta x$ to the second or higher powers. When we divide by $\Delta x$ we get $nx^{n-1} +$ terms involving $\Delta x$ to the first or higher powers. Now as $\Delta x \to 0$ we just have $nx^{n-1}$. Therefore

$$\frac{dy}{dx} = c\left(\lim_{\Delta x \to 0} \frac{(x+\Delta x)^n-x^n}{\Delta x}\right) = cnx^{n-1}. \quad ■$$

*The derivative of a sum of differentiable functions is equal to the sum of the derivatives.* This is evident from the fact that the limit of a sum is the sum of the limits.

In application, let us find the slope of the tangent line to the curve, $y = f(x) = x^4 - x^3 + 2x^2 + 4$, when $x = 1$. We compute the slope in general as $dy/dx = 4x^3 - 3x^2 + 4x$, and when $x = 1$, the slope $4(1)^3 - 3(1)^2 + 4(1) = 5$.

**Derivative Formulas.** The following formulas are given without proof for $u$ and $v$ differentiable functions of $x$ with $c$ and $n$ constants, **$n \neq 0$.**

$$\frac{d}{dx}(uv) = u\frac{dv}{dx} + v\frac{du}{dx}$$

$$\frac{d}{dx}\left(\frac{u}{v}\right) = \frac{v\frac{du}{dx} - u\frac{dv}{dx}}{v^2}, \quad v \neq 0$$

$$\frac{d}{dx}(u^n) = nu^{n-1}\frac{du}{dx}$$

EXAMPLES:

$$\frac{d}{dx}(x \cdot y) = x\frac{dy}{dx} + y\frac{dx}{dx} = xy' + y$$

$$\frac{d}{dx}\left(\frac{2x}{x-1}\right) = \frac{(x-1)(2)-2x(1)}{(x-1)^2} = \frac{-2}{(x-1)^2}$$

$$\frac{d}{dx}\left(\frac{1}{\sqrt{3-x}}\right) = \frac{d}{dx}\left((3-x)^{-1/2}\right) =$$

$$-\frac{1}{2}(3-x)^{-3/2}\frac{d}{dx}(3-x) = \tfrac{1}{2}(3-x)^{-3/2}.$$

**Higher Derivatives.** The derivative of $y$ with respect to $x$, $dy/dx$, is also the *first* derivative of $y$ with respect to $x$. The first derivative of $dy/dx$ which is called the *second* derivative of $y$ with respect to $x$ is given by any of the following forms:

$$\frac{d}{dx}\left(\frac{dy}{dx}\right), \frac{d^2y}{dx^2}, y'', \text{ and } D_x^2 y \text{ among others.}$$

For example, given $y = f(x) = x^3 + 5x^2 - 7x + 10$, find $d^2y/dx^2$. We take successive derivatives to get

$$\frac{dy}{dx} = 3x^2 + 10x - 7,$$
$$\frac{d^2y}{dx^2} = 6x + 10.$$

In general we can find higher derivatives than the second (as long as the successive derivatives are themselves differentiable) by repeated differentiation. We have then

$$\frac{d^3y}{dx^3} = 6,$$
$$\frac{d^4y}{dx^4} = 0,$$

respectively, as the third and fourth derivatives of $f(x) = x^3 + 5x^2 - 7x + 10$. Note that in this case all derivatives higher than the third will be zero.

**Velocity, Acceleration.** If $s = f(t)$ is a function relating the position of a body at a time $t$, then

$$\text{the velocity is } v = \frac{ds}{dt} \text{ and}$$

$$\text{the acceleration is } a = \frac{d^2s}{dt^2},$$

of the body at a given time $t$.

EXAMPLE: A projectile fired vertically upward at a speed of 100 ft/sec will reach an elevation of $s = 100t - 16t^2$ after $t$ seconds. The maximum height occurs when $v = 0$, therefore we find

$$v = \frac{ds}{dt} = 100 - 32t$$

and set $v = 0$ to get $100 - 32t = 0$ and $t = 100/32$. Now the height when $t = 100/32$ is $100(100/32) - 16(100/32)^2 = 156$ (ft.). The acceleration is

$$a = \frac{d^2s}{dt^2} = -32,$$

and this is constant for all $t$ at $-32$ ft/sec$^2$.

**Maximum, Minimum, Inflection.** When the tangent line to a curve $y = f(x)$ at a point $p$ is parallel to the $x$-axis, its slope is zero and the curve has a relative maximum or minimum at $p$. A relative maximum (minimum) at $p$ means that there are no other points in the vicinity of $p$ which have greater (smaller) $y$-coordinates than $p$.

A point of inflection, $q$, is a point where the acceleration is zero. The slope at $q$ is at a relative maximum or minimum. In [65a] we have shown the maximum, minimum, and inflection points of the curve $y = x^3 - 2x^2 + 1$.

To find the maximum and minimum points of a curve, $y = f(x)$, we set the first derivative function equal to zero and solve for all values of $x$. Once a value of $x$ is obtained, we may then substitute it into the second derivative function and if the result is *positive* then the $x$ value is the $x$-coordinate of a minimum point. If the result is *negative*, the point is a *maximum*. [65b] helps us to remember that if $d^2y/dx^2$ is positive (yes, the curve holds water) we have a minimum point, and if $d^2y/dx^2$ is negative (no, it won't hold water) then we have a maximum point. Once we have the $x$-coordinate of the point, the $y$-coordinate is found by substitution into the original function.

[65]

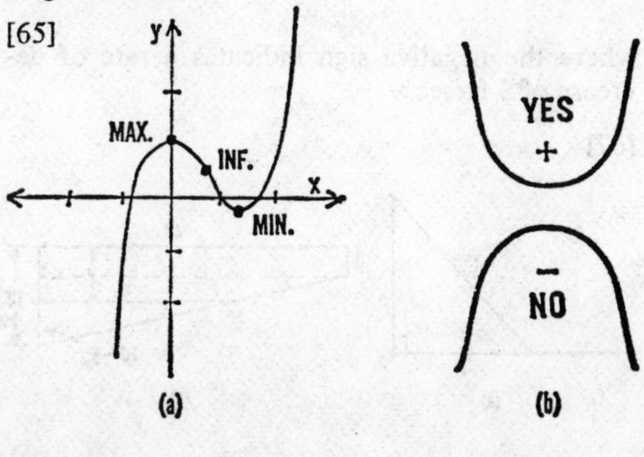


(a) (b)

A *point of inflection* is found by setting the second derivative function equal to zero and solving for all $x$ values then going to the original function for the corresponding $y$ values.

Given an ordinary function we can compute and plot these *critical* points and draw a pretty good sketch of the graph of the function. The idea of maximum, minimum, and inflection points can be useful in many other ways also.

EXAMPLE: Find a rectangle whose area is 20 and the sum of whose sides is a minimum. The solution is found by observing that the function to be minimized is $s = 2l + 2w$, and as $lw = 20$, $s = 2l + 2(20/l)$, from which we get $ds/dl = 2 - 40/l^2$. Then we set $ds/dl = 0$ and we have

$$2 - 40/l^2 = 0$$

$$\frac{2l^2 - 40}{l^2} = 0$$

and so $2l^2 - 40 = 0$ making $l^2 = 20$ and $l = \sqrt{20}$. We have $d^2s/dl^2 = 80l^{-3}$

which is positive at $l = \sqrt{20}$ which is then a minimum point.

$$w = 20/l = 20/\sqrt{20} = \sqrt{20}$$

and the required rectangle is a square.

**Implicit Derivatives.** The variable(s) $y$ is said to be defined as one or more *implicit functions* of $x$ by $f(x,y) = 0$, if a substituted value of $x$ yields one or more values of $y$. For example, $f(x,y) = x^2 + y^2 - 1 = 0$ defines $y = \sqrt{1-x^2}$ and $y = -\sqrt{1-x^2}$, where it is understood that the domain of $x$ is restricted to keep $y$ a real number.

We may not always be able to express $y$ as an implicit function of $x$, but in application we can usually find $dy/dx$ of $f(x,y) = 0$. The procedure is this: we differentiate both sides with respect to $x$ and solve for $dy/dx$.

In particular, we find $dy/dx$ if $x^2 + 2xy - y^2 = 9$, by:

$$\frac{d}{dx}(x^2) + \frac{d}{dx}(2xy) - \frac{d}{dx}(y^2) = \frac{d}{dx}(9)$$

$$2x + 2x\frac{dy}{dx} + 2y - 2y\frac{dy}{dx} = 0$$

$$\frac{dy}{dx}(2x - 2y) = -(2x + 2y)$$

$$\frac{dy}{dx} = \frac{y+x}{y-x}.$$

As another example, if we are given a circle of radius 2 centered at the origin, and we want the slope of the tangent line at the point $(1,\sqrt{3})$, then we differentiate

$$x^2 + y^2 = 4$$

$$\text{to get } 2x + 2y\frac{dy}{dx} = 0 \text{ and } \frac{dy}{dx} = \frac{-x}{y}$$

which at $(1,\sqrt{3})$ gives slope $= -1/\sqrt{3} = -\sqrt{3}/3$.

Working with the same circle equation we can find

$$\frac{d^2y}{dx^2} = \frac{d}{dx}\left(\frac{-x}{y}\right) = \frac{y(-1)-(-x)\frac{dy}{dx}}{y^2} =$$

$$\frac{-y+x\left(\frac{-x}{y}\right)}{y^2} = \frac{-y^2-x^2}{y^3} = \frac{-4}{y^3}$$

**Normals.** A line is *normal* to a curve at a point $p$ if it contains $p$ and is perpendicular to the tangent line to the curve at $p$. Let $\theta$ be the angle that the tangent lines make with the positive $x$-axis, then the normal will make an angle of $\theta + \pi/2$ and the slope will be $-1/m$, where $m = \tan\theta$, the slope of the tangent line. As proof we take points $p_1$ $(x_1, y_1)$ and $p_2$ $(x_2, y_2)$ on the sides of a right angle with vertex at $p(x,y)$. We want to show that (slope $p_1p$) $=$ $-1/$(slope $p_2p$). We know: $\overline{p_1p}^2 = (x-x_1)^2 + (y-y_1)^2 = x^2-2x_1x+x_1^2+y^2-2y_1y + y_1^2$, $\overline{p_2p}^2 = x^2 - 2x_2x + x_2^2 + y^2 - 2y_2y + y_2^2$, and $\overline{p_1p_2}^2 = x_1^2 - 2x_1x_2 + x_2^2 + y_1^2 - 2y_1y_2 + y_2^2$. As $\overline{p_1p}^2 + \overline{p_2p}^2 = \overline{p_1p_2}^2$, we substitute the above information and simplify to get

[66]

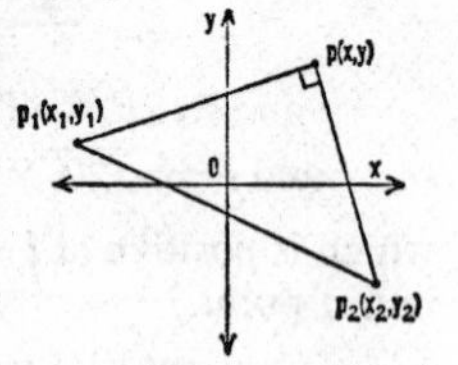


$$x^2-x_1x+y^2-y_1y-x_2x-y_2y = -x_1x_2-y_1y_2,$$

$$y_1y_2-y_1y-y_2y+y^2 = -(x_1x_2-x_1x-x_2x+x^2),$$

$$\frac{(y_1-y)}{(x_1-x)}\frac{(y_2-y)}{(x_2-x)} = -1,$$

which makes the slope of one line the negative recriprocal of the slope of the other line. ■

EXAMPLE: Find the equations of the lines that are tangent and normal to $x^2y = 36$ at (3,4). We find the slope of the tangent line,

$$2xy + x^2\frac{dy}{dx} = 0$$

$$\frac{dy}{dx} = \frac{-2xy}{x^2} = \frac{-2y}{x},$$

which at (3,4) is $m = \frac{-2(4)}{3} = \frac{-8}{3}$.

We now use the general equation of a line, $y-y_1 = m(x-x_1)$, to get the equation of the tangent line

$$y-4 = (-8/3)\,(x-3).$$

The slope of the normal line is $-1/m = -1/(-8/3) = 3/8$, and

$$y-4 = (3/8)\,(x-3)$$

is the equation of the normal line.

**Chain Rule.** If $f$ is a differentiable function of $g$ and $g$ is a differentiable function of $x$ then $f$ is a differentiable function of $x$ and we write

$$\frac{df}{dx} = \frac{df}{dg}\frac{dg}{dx}$$

which is the chain rule for derivatives.

Suppose that $y = \sqrt{x^2-1}$ and $x = t^2$, and we want to find $dy/dt$. We find

$$\frac{dy}{dx} = 1/2(x^2-1)^{-1/2}(2x) = x(x^2-1)^{-1/2} =$$

$$t^2(t^4-1)^{-1/2} \text{ and } \frac{dx}{dt} = 2t$$

then use the chain rule $\frac{dy}{dt} = \frac{dy}{dx}\frac{dx}{dt}$ and get

$$\frac{dy}{dt} = t^2(t^4-1)^{-1/2}(2t) = 2t^3(t^4-1)^{-1/2}.$$

If we have parametric equations giving

$$y = t^2 + 2t + 2$$
$$x = 3t^2 - 1$$

then we can find $dy/dx$ by computing

$$\frac{dy}{dt} = 2t + 2, \frac{dx}{dt} = 6t,$$

and using the chain rule so that

$$\frac{dy}{dt}\Big/\frac{dx}{dt} = \frac{dy}{dx} = \frac{2t+2}{6t} = \frac{t+1}{3t}.$$

**Applications.** A 20 foot ladder is leaning against a wall. The foot begins to slide away from the wall at 3 feet/sec. How fast is the top of the ladder moving down the wall when the foot is 10 feet from the wall?

In [67a] we know that if $h$ is the height of the top of the ladder from the ground and $g$ is the distance of the foot of the ladder from the wall at any time $t$, then $h^2 + g^2 = 20$. The rates of change are related in the differential equation formed by differentiating both sides of $h^2 + g^2 = 20$ with respect to $t$.

$$2h\frac{dh}{dt} + 2g\frac{dg}{dt} = 0.$$

We can substitute what is known: $g = 10$, $dg/dt = 3$, $h = \sqrt{20^2-10^2} = \sqrt{300} = 10\sqrt{3}$, and have

$$10\sqrt{3}\frac{dh}{dt} + 10(3) = 0$$

$$\frac{dh}{dt} = \frac{-30}{10\sqrt{3}} = \frac{-3}{\sqrt{3}} = -\sqrt{3}\text{ (ft/sec)}$$

where the negative sign indicates a rate of decrease of 3 ft/sec.

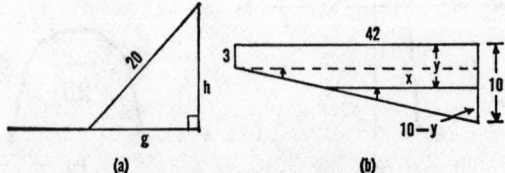

[67]

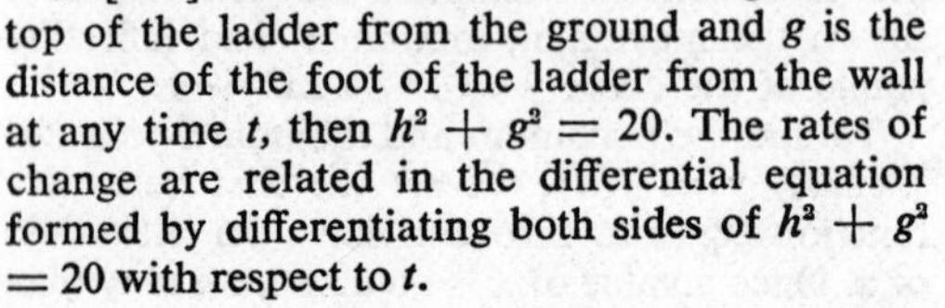


(a) (b)

A swimming pool has a width 20 feet, a length 42 feet, and a depth tapering from 3 feet at the shallow end to 10 feet at the deep end. If water fills the pool at a rate of 3 cubic feet a minute, then how fast is the water level rising when the level is 4 feet from the top?

In [67b] we see that the volume of water for any depth up to 3 feet from the top is $v = 20(x/2)\,(10-y) = 10x(10-y)$. Differentiating gives

$$\frac{dv}{dt} = 100\frac{dx}{dt} - 10y\frac{dx}{dt} - 10x\frac{dy}{dt}.$$

By similar triangles we know that $x/42 = (10-y)/7$, so that $x = 6(10-y) = 60 - 6y$. This gives $dx/dt = -6dy/dt$. When $y = 4$, $x = 36$. We can substitute what is known to get:

$$3 = 100\left(-6\frac{dy}{dt}\right) - 40\left(-6\frac{dy}{dt}\right) - 360\frac{dy}{dt}$$

so that $\frac{dy}{dt} = 3/(-600+240-360) =$

$-1/240$ (ft/min).

The $-1/240$ ft/min indicates of course that $y$ is decreasing with time.

**Newton's Method.** We may use *Newton's method* for approximating a real root of $f(x) = 0$. It is an iterative process by which we continue to compute until the answer has the desired precision. We first make a rough *approximation* about where the root might be. In [68] our first estimate is at $x = x_1$. The functional value is $f(x_1) \neq 0$, so we compute where the tangent line through $(x_1, f(x_1))$ meets the $x$-axis and get $x_2$. The idea is that $x_2$ should be closer to the root $a$ than was $x_1$. We call $x_2$ the new approximation and compute where the tangent line through $(x_2, f(x_2))$ meets the $x$-axis, which is at $x = x_3$. Now $x_3$ replaces $x_2$ as the new approximation, and so on. We stop when our approximation satisfies the equation to within the desired precision.

[68]

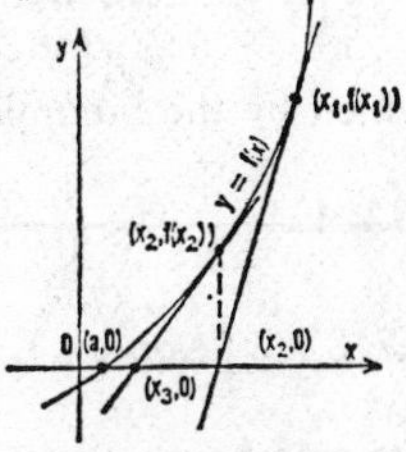


We first approximate an $x_1$ and then compute $f(x_1)$. If it is zero or undefined we pick a value near $x_1$ to replace $x_1$. The equation of the tangent line through $(x_1, f(x_1))$ is

$$y - f(x_1) = f'(x_1)\,(x - x_1),$$

and it crosses the $x$-axis $(y=0)$ at $x_2$ in

$$0 - f(x_1) = f'(x_1)\,(x_2 - x_1)$$

$$\text{so that } x_2 = x_1 - \frac{f(x_1)}{f'(x_1)}$$

We call the last equation Newton's equation and use it as the key to further approximations. That is we compute $x_2$ by Newton's equation then let $x_2$ replace $x_1$ in the same equation to get $x_3$, etc.

For example, we can compute the square root of 3 to six decimal places by solving the equation $f(x) = x^2 - 3 = 0$. Let our first approximation be $x_1 = 2$. Then

$$x_2 = 2 - \frac{f(2)}{f'(2)} = 2 - \frac{(2)^2-3}{2(2)} = 2 - \frac{1}{4}$$

$= 1.75$,

$$x_3 = 1.75 - \frac{(1.75)^2-3}{2(1.75)} = 1.75 - .0179 =$$

1.7321,

$$x_4 = 1.7321 - \frac{(1.7321)^2-3}{2(1.7321)} = 1.7321 -$$

$.000049 = 1.732051$

which is correct to six places, that is 1.732051 satisfies $x^2 - 3 = 0$ better than either 1.73204 or 1.73206.

**Trigonometric Functions.** Let $y = \sin x$; we can calculate the *derivative of* $\sin x$ with respect to $x$,

$$\frac{dy}{dx} = \frac{d}{dx}(\sin x),$$

by the following procedure: we have

$$y + \Delta y = \sin(x+\Delta x),$$

$$\Delta y = \sin(x+\Delta x) - y,$$

$$\Delta y = \sin(x+\Delta x) - \sin x,$$

and by the trigonometric formula

$$\sin\alpha - \sin\beta = 2\sin\frac{\alpha-\beta}{2}\cos\frac{\alpha+\beta}{2},$$

we let $\alpha = x + \Delta x$ and $\beta = x$ and get

$$\Delta y = 2\sin\frac{x+\Delta x - x}{2}\cos\frac{2x+\Delta x}{2}$$

$$\Delta y = 2\sin\frac{\Delta x}{2}\cos\left(x+\frac{\Delta x}{2}\right),$$

$$\frac{\Delta y}{\Delta x} = \left(\frac{\sin\frac{\Delta x}{2}}{\frac{\Delta x}{2}}\right)\cos\left(x+\frac{\Delta x}{2}\right),$$

$$\lim_{\Delta x\to 0}\frac{\Delta y}{\Delta x} = (1)\,(\cos x) = \cos x.$$

Thus we have

$$\frac{d}{dx}(\sin x) = \cos x.$$

If $u$ is a differentiable function of $x$, and $y = \sin u$, then the chain rule gives us

$$\frac{d}{dx}(\sin u) = \frac{dy}{dx} = \frac{dy}{du}\frac{du}{dx} = \frac{d(\sin u)}{du}\frac{du}{dx} =$$

$$\cos u\,\frac{du}{dx}.$$

The *derivative of* $\cos x$ with respect to $x$ is

$$\frac{d}{dx}(\cos x) = \frac{d}{dx}\sin(\pi/2-x) =$$

$$\cos(\pi/2-x)\frac{d}{dx}(\pi/2-x) = -\sin x.$$

The chain rule gives us for $u$ a differentiable function of $x$:

$$\frac{d}{dx}(\cos u) = -\sin u\frac{du}{dx}.$$

We find the *derivative of* $y = \sin^{-1}x$, for $y$ in the range of principal values, as follows:

$$y = \sin^{-1}x,$$

$$x = \sin y.$$

Differentiating both sides with respect to $x$ gives

$$1 = \cos y\frac{dy}{dx}.$$

But $dy/dx$ is the desired derivative so

$$\frac{dy}{dx} = \frac{1}{\cos y} = \frac{1}{\sqrt{1-\sin^2 y}} = \frac{1}{\sqrt{1-x^2}}.$$

If $u$ is a differentiable function of $x$ then the chain rule gives

$$\frac{d}{dx}(\sin^{-1}u) = \frac{1}{\sqrt{1-u^2}}\frac{dy}{dx}$$

For completeness, we give the following formulas which can be easily verified:

$$\frac{d}{dx}\sin u = \cos u\frac{du}{dx}$$

$$\frac{d}{dx}\cos u = -\sin u\frac{du}{dx}$$

$$\frac{d}{dx}\tan u = \sec^2 u\frac{du}{dx}$$

$$\frac{d}{dx}\cot u = -\csc^2 u\frac{du}{dx}$$

$$\frac{d}{dx}\sec u = \tan u\sec u\frac{du}{dx}$$

$$\frac{d}{dx}\csc u = -\cot u\csc u\frac{du}{dx}$$

$$\frac{d}{dx}\sin^{-1}u = \frac{1}{\sqrt{1-u^2}}\frac{du}{dx}$$

$$\frac{d}{dx}\cos^{-1}u = \frac{-1}{\sqrt{1-u^2}}\frac{du}{dx}$$

$$\frac{d}{dx}\tan^{-1}u = \frac{1}{1+u^2}\frac{du}{dx}$$

$$\frac{d}{dx}\cot^{-1}u = \frac{-1}{1+u^2}\frac{du}{dx}$$

$$\frac{d}{dx}\sec^{-1}u = \frac{1}{u\sqrt{u^2-1}}\frac{du}{dx}$$

$$\frac{d}{dx}\csc^{-1}u = \frac{-1}{u\sqrt{u^2-1}}\frac{du}{dx}$$

EXAMPLE: Find $dy/dx$ if $y = \sin 2x + x\cos x + 3x^2$.

$$\frac{dy}{dx} = \cos 2x\frac{d}{dx}(2x) + x\frac{d}{dx}(\cos x) +$$

$$\cos x\frac{d}{dx}(x) + 6x = 2\cos 2x + x\sin x + \cos x + 6x$$

EXAMPLE: Find $dy/dx$ implicitly if $y\sin x = \cos(x+y)$. We differentiate both sides with respect to $x$ getting

$$\frac{dy}{dx}\sin x + y\cos x = \frac{d}{dx}(\cos x\cos y - \sin x\sin y)$$

$$\sin x\frac{dy}{dx} + y\cos x = -\cos x\sin y\frac{dy}{dx} - \cos y\sin x$$

$$-\sin x\cos y\frac{dy}{dx} - \sin y\cos x$$

$$(\sin x+\cos x\sin y+\sin x\cos y)\frac{dy}{dx} =$$

$$-\cos y\sin x-\sin y\cos x-y\cos x$$

$$\frac{dy}{dx} = -\frac{\cos y\sin x+\sin y\cos x+y\cos x}{\sin x+\cos x\sin y+\sin x\cos y}$$

**Logarithmic, Exponential Functions.** The number $e$ is defined by the limit

$$e = \lim_{a\to+\infty}\left(1+\frac{1}{a}\right)^a,$$

which by the binomial expansion is

$$1+1+\frac{1}{2!}+\frac{1}{3!}+\ldots+\frac{1}{n!}+\ldots=$$

2.718282 (Approx.).

We also have

$$e^x = 1 + x + \frac{x^2}{2!} + \frac{x^3}{3!} + \ldots + \frac{x^n}{n!} + \ldots.$$

We will employ this important limit in the *differentiation of the logarithmic function*, $y = \log_a x$.

$$y + \Delta y = \log_a(x+\Delta x)$$

$$\Delta y = \log_a(x+\Delta x) - \log_a x$$

$$\Delta y = \log_a\frac{x+\Delta x}{x} = \log_a\left(1+\frac{\Delta x}{x}\right)$$

$$\frac{\Delta y}{\Delta x} = \frac{1}{\Delta x}\log_a\left(1+\frac{\Delta x}{x}\right) =$$

$$\frac{1}{x}\log_a\left(1+\frac{\Delta x}{x}\right)^{x/\Delta x}$$

$$\lim_{\Delta x\to 0}\frac{\Delta y}{\Delta x} = \frac{1}{x}\log_a\left(\lim_{\Delta x\to 0}\left(1+\frac{\Delta x}{x}\right)^{x/\Delta x}\right)$$

$$= \frac{1}{x}\log_a e.$$

If $u$ is a differentiable function of $x$, the chain rule gives

$$\frac{d}{dx}(\log_a u) = \frac{1}{u}\log_a e\,\frac{du}{dx}.$$

In particular, this means that if $y = \log_e x$ then

$$\frac{dy}{dx} = \frac{d}{dx}(\log_e x) = \frac{1}{x}$$

The expression $\log_e x$ is symbolized as $\ln x$ and is called the natural logarithm of $x$.

The *derivative of the exponential function,* $y = a^x$, is found implicitly by taking the natural log of both sides getting

$$\ln y = x \ln a.$$

Differentiation gives

$$\frac{1}{y}\frac{dy}{dx} = \ln a,$$

$$\frac{dy}{dx} = y\ln a = a^x \ln a.$$

Now if $a = e$ then

$$\frac{d}{dx}(e^x) = e^x \ln e = e^x.$$

EXAMPLE: Find $dy/dx$ if $y = e^{-x}\sin x + e^{\cos x}$

$$\frac{dy}{dx} = e^{-x}\cos x - e^{-x}\sin x - e^{\cos x}\sin x$$

EXAMPLE: Show that $y = e^{2x} + e^{-x}$ satisfies $y''' - 2y'' = -3e^{-x}$.

$$y' = \frac{dy}{dx} = 2e^{2x} - e^{-x}$$

$$y'' = 4e^{2x} + e^{-x}$$

$$y''' = 8e^{2x} - e^{-x}$$

$$y''' - 2y'' = 8e^{2x} - e^{-x} - 2(4e^{2x} + e^{-x}) =$$

$$8e^{2x} - e^{-x} - 8e^{2x} - 2e^{-x} = -3e^{-x}.$$

**Hyperbolic Functions.** The hyperbolic sine, sinh, and cosine, cosh, are defined by

$$\sinh x = \frac{e^x - e^{-x}}{2}, \quad \cosh x = \frac{e^x + e^{-x}}{2}$$

and their *derivatives* are

$$\frac{d}{dx}(\sinh x) = \cosh x, \quad \frac{d}{dx}(\cosh x) = \sinh x.$$

**Indeterminate Forms.** If $f(a) = g(a) = 0$ or if $f(x)$ and $g(x)$ each $\to \infty$ as $x \to a$, then l'Hôpital's rule gives

$$\lim_{x\to a}\frac{f(a)}{g(a)} = \lim_{x\to a}\frac{f'(a)}{g'(a)}$$

if the limit on the right exists.

EXAMPLE:

$$\lim_{x\to 0}\frac{2x}{3x} = \lim_{x\to 0}\frac{\frac{d}{dx}(2x)}{\frac{d}{dx}(3x)} = \lim_{x\to 0}\frac{2}{3} = \frac{2}{3}$$

EXAMPLE:

$$\lim_{x\to\infty}\frac{x^2-2x-7}{4x^2-5x+6} = \lim_{x\to\infty}\frac{2x-2}{8x-5} = \lim_{x\to\infty}\frac{2}{8} = \frac{1}{4}$$

We say then that $0/0$ and $\infty/\infty$ are *indeterminate forms.* There are other forms which may possibly be treated by algebraic manipulation until they are in one of the above indeterminate forms. These are

$$\infty - \infty,\ 0 \cdot \infty,\ 0^0,\ 1^\infty, \text{ and } \infty^0.$$

For example, the $\lim_{x\to 1}\left(\frac{1}{x-1} - \frac{2}{x^2-1}\right) = \lim_{x\to 1}\frac{(x+1)-2}{(x+1)(x-1)} = \lim_{x\to 1}\frac{x-1}{x^2-1} = \lim_{x\to 1}\frac{1}{2x} = \frac{1}{2}$. Consider also $\lim_{x\to 0} x\cot x = \lim_{x\to 0}\frac{x}{\tan x} = \lim_{x\to 0}\frac{1}{\sec^2 x} = \frac{1}{1} = 1.$

**Differentials.** We define the *differentials* $dx$ and $dy$ of $y = f(x)$ as follows:

$$dx = \triangle x$$

$$dy = \left(\lim_{\triangle x\to 0}\frac{\triangle y}{\triangle x}\right)dx = f'(x)dx.$$

This definition makes the quotient ($dx \neq 0$) of $dy$ and $dx$

$$\frac{dy}{dx} = f'(x)$$

For example, if $y = x^3$, then $dy = 3x^2dx$, and $dy/dx = 3x^2$. Now we find $dy/dx$ in $x^2 + xy + y^2 = 0$ by

$$d(x^2) + d(xy) + d(y^2) = 0$$

$$2xdx + xdy + ydx + 2ydy = 0$$

$$(2x+y)dx + (x+2y)dy = 0$$

$$\frac{dy}{dx} = \frac{-(2x+y)}{x+2y}$$

## AREA UNDER CURVE, INTEGRATION

**Trapezoidal Rule.** We may approximate the area under the curve (area bounded by the curve, the $x$-axis, $x = a$, and $x = b$), $y = f(x)$, by the formula:

$$A = \frac{d}{2}[f(a)+f(a+d)] + \frac{d}{2}[f(a+d)+f(a+2d)] + \ldots \frac{d}{2}[f(a+(n-1)d)+f(b)] = \frac{d}{2}[f(a)+2f(a+d)+2f(a+2d)+\ldots+2f(a+(n-1)d)+f(b)]. \qquad [69]$$

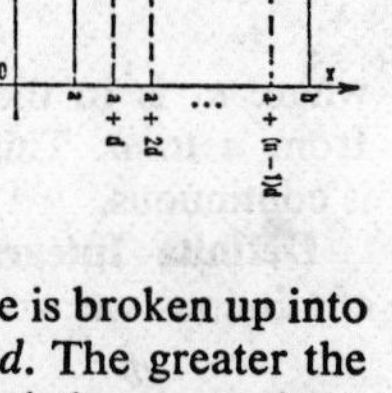


In [69] the area under the curve is broken up into $n$ trapezoids each with a side $d$. The greater the value of $n$ the better in general the approximation will be to the true area.

EXAMPLE: Use the trapezoidal rule with $n = 4$ to approximate the area under $y = x^3$ from

$x = 1$ to $x = 3$. We have $d = (3-1)/4 = .5$. We use the formula to get

$A = (.5/2)\ [f(1)+2f(1.5)+2f(2)+2f(2.5)+f(3)] = (1/4)\ [1+2(27/8)+2(8)+2(125/8)+27] = 82/4 = 20.5.$

**Simpson's Rule.** Simpson's rule is applied by the approximation formula below for the area under the curve $y = f(x)$ between $x = a$ and $x = b$ where the segment $ab$ is broken into $2n$ parts each equal to $d$.

$$A = \frac{d}{3}[f(a)+4f(a+d)+2f(a+2d)+4f(a+3d)+\ldots+2f(a+(2n-2)d)+4f(a+(2n)d)+f(b)].$$

In application, we compute a Simpson approximation to the area under $y = x^3$ from $x = 1$ to 3 by letting $n = 2$, making $2n = 4$ parts. Then with $d = 2/4 = .5$, we get

$A = (.5/3)\ [f(1)+4f(1.5)+2f(2)+4f(2.5)+f(3)] = 1/6\ [1+4(27/8)+2(8)+4(125/8)+27] = 119/6 = 19.83.$

See *Fundamental Theorem of Integral Calculus.*

Note that from the trapezoidal and Simpson's rule formulas, the part of the curve which dips below the $x$-axis will give a negative answer for the area. Then the negative part below the $x$-axis adds algebraically to the positive part above the $x$-axis to give the total area under the curve. For example, the area under $y = \sin x$ from $x = 0$ to $2\pi$ is 0.

**Area Under Curve.** We define the area under a curve, $y = f(x)$, from $a$ to $b$ as the limit of the sum of the areas of rectangles, which have width $\Delta x$ and are inscribed between the curve, and the $x$-axis from $a$ to $b$, as the number of such rectangles increases without limit. We have then, that $f(c_i)$ is the length of the $i$th rectangle so that $f(c_i)\Delta x$ is the area of the $i$th rectangle. The area under the curve from $a$ to $b$ is given by

[70]

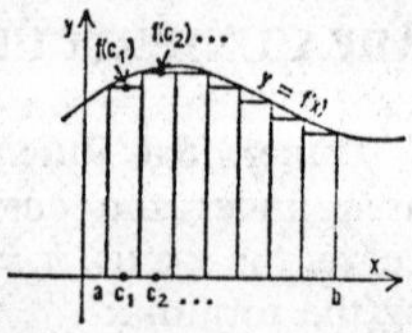


$$A = \lim_{n\to\infty} \sum_{i=1}^{n} f(c_i)\Delta x,$$

where $c_i$ is in the $i$th interval (of length $\Delta x$) from $a$ to $b$. This limit will exist if $y = f(x)$ is continuous.

**Definite Integral.** By definition, if $f(x)$ is continuous we write

$$\int_a^b f(x)dx = \lim_{n\to\infty} \sum_{i=1}^{n} f(c_i)\Delta x$$

where the left member is called the *definite integral* of $f(x)$, with respect to $x$, from $x = a$ to $b$. The right member is the limit of the summation of rectangles inscribed between the curve $y = f(x)$ and the $x$-axis, from $x = a$ to $b$.

From the definition, it can be shown that

$$\int_c^a f(x)dx = 0,$$

$$\int_a^b f(x)dx = \int_a^c f(x)dx + \int_c^b f(x)dx,\ a<c<b,$$

$$\int_a^b cf(x)dx = c\int_a^b f(x)dx,\ c \text{ a constant},$$

$$\int_a^b f(x)dx = -\int_b^a f(x)dx,$$

$$\int_a^b (f(x)+g(x))dx = \int_a^b f(x)dx + \int_a^b g(x)dx,$$

for $f(x)$ and $g(x)$ continuous for $a \leq x \leq b$.

**Indefinite Integral.** If $F(x)$ is a function such that

$$\frac{d}{dx}(F(x)) = f(x) \text{ or } d(F(x)) = f(x)dx,$$

then $F(x)$ is called an indefinite integral of $f(x)$ with respect to $x$. In particular, if $f(x) = x + 3$, then $F(x)$ could be $x^2/2 + 3x$ or $x^2/2 + 3x + 10$ or $x^2/2 + 3x - 20$ or of course many others. This leads us to say that in general the *indefinite integral* or *anti-derivative* of $f(x)$ with respect to $x$ is $F(x) + C$ where $C$ is called the *constant of integration.* We use the following notation:

$$F(x) + C = \int f(x)dx$$

Here $f(x)$ is called the *integrand* and $F(x)$ is called the *integral* of $f(x)$.

Given that $f(x)dx = d(F(x))$, we can *integrate* both sides and get

$$\int f(x)dx = \int d(F(x)) = F(x) + C.$$

As we have $d(x^{n+1}) = (n+1)x^n$, then

$$\int x^n dx = \frac{x^{n+1}}{n+1} + C.$$

The integral (indefinite integral) of a finite sum is the sum of the integrals. The integral of a constant times a variable is equal to the constant times the integral of the variable.

Suppose that we have the *differential equation* (an equation involving derivatives) given as follows:

$$\frac{dy}{dx} = x^2 - 3x,$$

where we also know the *initial condition* that when $x = 0$ then $y = 2$, and we are required to find $y$ (a function of $x$) which will satisfy the given equation.

This value of $y$ is called the *solution* to the differential equation, and it can be found by integrating

$$dy = (x^2-3x)dx,$$
$$\int dy = \int (x^2-3x)dx,$$
$$y = x^3/3 - 3x^2/2 + C,$$

and substituting the initial condition

$$2 = 0 - 0 + C,$$
$$C = 2,$$

so that the solution is

$$y = x^3/3 - 3x^2/2 + 2.$$

**Fundamental Theorem of Integral Calculus.** The idea of the slope or tangent to a curve, the *derivative,* the idea of the limit of the sum, the *definite integral,* and the idea of the *anti-derivative* or *indefinite integral* are connected by the *fundamental theorem of integral calculus* which is in essence:

*If* **y = f(x)** *is continuous over the domain* **a≤x≤b** *and* **dF(x) = f(x)dx** *over the same domain, then the area under the curve is*

$$A = \int_a^b f(x)dx = F(b) - F(a).$$

Notice that there is no constant, $C$, in this *definite* integration.

We may now find the *exact* area under the curve $y = x^3$ from $x = 1$ to 3 by

$$A = \int_1^3 x^3 dx = \Big[\, x^4/4 \,\Big]_1^3 = 3^4/4 - 1^4/4 = (81-1)/4 = 20.$$

In application then, it is a matter of evaluating the *anti-derivative* of the function and substituting in the upper and lower limits ($a$ and $b$) to evaluate the definite integral. To do this we may use "in reverse" any derivative formula that we have discovered already. For example,

$$\int_0^{\pi/2}(\sin x+e^x+1/(x+1)dx = \int_0^{\pi/2}\sin x dx + \int_0^{\pi/2} e^x dx + \int_0^{\pi/2}\frac{1}{x+1}dx = \Big[-\cos x\Big]_0^{\pi/2} + \Big[e^x\Big]_0^{\pi/2} + \Big[\ln(x+1)\Big]_0^{\pi/2}$$
$$= -\cos\pi/2 + \cos 0 + e^{\pi/2} - e^0 + \ln(\pi/2+1) - \ln(0+1) = 0 + 1 + e^{\pi/2} - 1 + \ln(\pi/2+1) - 0 = e^{\pi/2} + \ln(\pi/2+1)$$

**Formulas.** For completeness we give the following formulas which may be applied to definite or indefinite integration. If definite then the upper and lower limits should be evaluated, and if indefinite, a constant of integration should be supplied.

$\int dx = x.$

$\int cf(x)dx = c\int f(x)dx.$

$\int (u+v)dx = \int udx + \int vdx$, $u$ and $v$ are functions of $x$.

$$\int x^n dx = \frac{x^{n+1}}{n+1},\ n \neq -1$$

$$\int \frac{dx}{x} = \ln|x|$$

$\int e^x dx = e^x$

$\int \ln x dx = x\ln x - x$

$\int \sin x dx = -\cos x$

$\int \cos x dx = \sin x$

$\int \tan x dx = -\ln|\cos x|$

$\int \cot x dx = \ln|\sin x|$

$\int \sec x dx = \ln|\sec x + \tan x|$

$\int \csc x dx = -\ln|\csc x + \cot x|$

$\int \sin^n x dx = (-1/n)(\sin^{n-1}x\cos x + (n-1)\int \sin^{n-2}x dx)$

$\int \cos^n x dx = (1/n)(\cos^{n-1}x\sin x + (n-1)\int \cos^{n-2}x dx)$

## INTEGRATION PROCEDURES

*The next few sections illustrate by example various important integration processes.*

**$u^n du$.** If we can express the integrand in the form $u^n du$, then the integral will be $(u^{n+1})/(n+1)$. In order to evaluate

$$\sqrt{1-2x}dx$$

we let $u = 1 - 2x$, therefore $du$ is $(-2)dx$. If we put $-2$ times the $dx$, then $(1-2x)^{1/2}(-2)dx$ would be of the form $u^n du$ with $n = 1/2$. We obtain this form by writing

$$\int \sqrt{1-2x}\,dx = \frac{1}{-2}\int (1-2x)^{1/2}(-2)dx,$$

and as $\int u^n du = \dfrac{u^{n+1}}{n+1}$, $n \neq -1$, then

$$\frac{1}{-2}\int (1-2x)^{1/2}(-2)dx = -\left(\frac{1}{2}\right)\frac{(1-2x)^{3/2}}{3/2} + C = \frac{-(1-2x)^{3/2}}{3} + C.$$

Note that when we supply a constant number in the integrand that we must divide by the same number on the outside.

EXAMPLE: $\int \sin^5 x\cos^3 x dx$.

We may first write $\int \sin^5 x \cos^3 x dx =$
$\sin^5 x(1-\sin^2 x)\cos x dx = \int \sin^5 x\cos x dx - \int \sin^7 x\cos x dx,$

where both integrals are of the form $u^n du$. The result is

$$\int \sin^5 x\cos^3 x dx = \frac{\sin^6 x}{6} - \frac{\sin^8 x}{8} + C.$$

EXAMPLE: $\int \csc x dx$

We multiply numerator and denominator by $\csc x + \cot x$:

$$\int \csc x dx = \int \frac{\csc x(\csc x+\cot x)}{\cot x + \csc x}dx = -\int \frac{-\csc^2 x - \cot x\csc x}{\cot x + \csc x}dx,$$

but the numerator is the derivative of the denominator so we have the form $u^n du$ with $n = -1$. $\int u^{-1}du = \ln|u|$ so we get

$$\int \csc x dx = -\ln|\cot x + \csc x|.$$

**Integration by Parts.** We know that $d(uv) = udv + vdu$ if $u$ and $v$ are differentiable functions of $x$. Therefore

$$udv = d(uv) - vdu,$$
$$\int udv = uv - \int vdu,$$

and we have broken up $\int udv$ into two parts. The method works best when $v$ is easily integrable.

EXAMPLE: $\int x \sin x dx$

We must choose $u$ and $dv$ from what is given, so let $u = x$, $du = dx$, $dv = \sin x dx$, then $v = -\cos x$. Substituting gives

$$\int x \sin x dx = -x\cos x - \int (-\cos x) dx = -x\cos x + \sin x + C$$

EXAMPLE: $\int e^{2x} \sin 3x dx$

Let $u = e^{2x}$ then $du = 2e^{2x}dx$; let $dv = \sin 3x dx$ then $v = (-1/3)\cos 3x$.

$$\int e^{2x}\sin 3x dx = -\frac{1}{3}e^{2x}\cos 3x + \frac{2}{3}\int e^{2x}\cos 3x dx$$

Using the method again on the right integral, let $u = e^{2x}$ then $du = 2e^{2x}dx$; let $dv = \cos 3x dx$ then $v = \frac{1}{3}\sin 3x$.

$$\int e^{2x}\sin 3x dx = -\frac{1}{3}e^{2x}\cos 3x + \frac{2}{3}\left[\frac{1}{3}e^{2x}\sin 3x - \frac{2}{3}\int e^{2x}\sin 3x dx\right] = -\frac{1}{3}e^{2x}\cos 3x + \frac{2}{9}e^{2x}\sin 3x - \frac{4}{9}\int e^{2x}\sin 3x dx.$$

We now transpose the right term and add

$$\int e^{2x}\sin 3x dx + \frac{4}{9}\int e^{2x}\sin 3x dx = -\frac{1}{3}e^{2x}\cos 3x + \frac{2}{9}e^{2x}\sin 3x, \frac{13}{9}\int e^{2x}\sin 3x dx = -\frac{1}{3}e^{2x}\cos 3x + \frac{2}{9}e^{2x}\sin 3x,$$ to get $$\int e^{2x}\sin 3x dx = -\frac{3}{13}e^{2x}\cos 3x + \frac{2}{13}e^{2x}\sin 3x + C.$$

**Trigonometric Substitution.** The idea of trigonometric substitution is discussed under *Preliminary Topics*. We employ it in the following examples.

EXAMPLE: $\int \frac{dx}{x^2\sqrt{x^2+1}}$

From [61a] we have $x^2 = \cot^2\theta$, $\sqrt{x^2+1} = \csc\theta$ and $x = \cot\theta$ so that $dx = -\csc^2\theta\, d\theta$.

$$\int \frac{dx}{x^2\sqrt{x^2+1}} = -\int \frac{\csc^2\theta\, d\theta}{\cot^2\theta \csc\theta} = \int \frac{(-\sin\theta)d\theta}{\cos^2\theta} = \frac{-1}{\cos\theta} + C = -\sec\theta + C$$

Now we substitute back referring to [61a] then

$$\int \frac{dx}{x^2\sqrt{x^2+1}} = -\sec\theta + C = -\frac{\sqrt{x^2+1}}{x} + C.$$

EXAMPLE: $\int_2^4 \frac{dx}{\sqrt{x^2+2x-3}}$

We complete the square

$$\int_2^4 \frac{dx}{\sqrt{x^2+2x-3}} = \int_2^4 \frac{dx}{\sqrt{(x+1)^2-4}}$$

then in [71] we note that $2\tan\theta = \sqrt{(x+1)^2-4}$, [71] $2\sec\theta = x+1$, $x = 2\sec\theta - 1$ and thus $dx = 2\tan\theta\sec\theta\, d\theta$. The new limits can be computed from $\sec\theta = (x+1)/2$ giving that when $x = 2$, $\theta = 0$, and when $x = 4$, $\theta = \pi/3$.

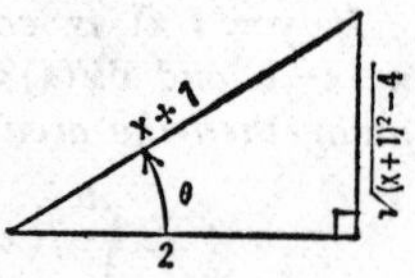


$$\int_2^4 \frac{dx}{\sqrt{(x+1)^2-4}} = \int_0^{\pi/3} \frac{2\tan\theta\sec\theta\, d\theta}{2\tan\theta} =$$

$$\int_0^{\pi/3} \sec\theta\, d\theta = \Big[\ln|\sec\theta + \tan\theta|\Big]_0^{\pi/3} =$$

$$\ln|\sec\pi/3 + \tan\pi/3| - \ln|\sec 0 + \tan 0| =$$

$$\ln\frac{2+\sqrt{3}}{1+0} = \ln(2+\sqrt{3}).$$

**Partial Fractions.** We use the method of partial fractions, which is discussed in *Preliminary Topics,* to aid in evaluating certain integrals.

EXAMPLE: $\int \frac{(5x+1)dx}{x^3-x^2-x+1}$

We factor the denominator and find that

$$\frac{5x+1}{x^3-x^2-x+1} = \frac{(5x+1)}{(x+1)(x-1)^2} = \frac{A}{x-1} + \frac{B}{(x-1)^2} + \frac{C}{x+1},$$

where $A$, $B$, and $C$ are constants to be computed. We multiply by the common denominator and have $5x+1 = A(x-1)(x+1) + B(x+1) + C(x-1)(x-1)$ and we simplify and equate like coefficients to get

$$5x+1 = Ax^2 - A + Bx + B + Cx^2 - 2Cx + C$$

$0 = A + C$, (coefficients of $x^2$)
$5 = B - 2C$, (coefficients of $x$)
$1 = -A + B + C$, (constant coefficients).

These three simultaneous equations in three unknowns can be solved for $A$, $B$, and $C$, to get

$$A = 1, B = 3, \text{and } C = -1.$$

Therefore we substitute and have

$$\frac{5x+1}{x^3-x^2-x+1}=\frac{1}{x-1}+\frac{3}{(x-1)^2}-\frac{1}{x+1},$$

which means

$$\int\frac{(5x+1)dx}{x^3-x^2-x+1}=\int\frac{dx}{x-1}+\int\frac{3dx}{(x-1)^2}-$$

$$\int\frac{dx}{x+1}=\ln|x-1|-3(x-1)^{-1}-\ln|x+1|+$$

$$C=\ln\frac{|x-1|}{|x+1|}-\frac{3}{x-1}+C$$

## APPLICATIONS OF INTEGRATION

**Families of Curves.** If we know the equation of the slope of a function, for example $dy/dx = x^2+x$, then we can find the equation of the family by integrating.

$dy/dx = x^2+x$, $dy = (x^2+x)dx$, $\int dy = \int(x^2+x)dx$, and $y = x^3/3 + x^2/2 + C$

is the equation of the family of curves. The members of the family differ by the choice of the constant $C$.

**Orthogonal Trajectories.** The orthogonal trajectories of a given family of curves is another family of curves each of which cuts the given curves at right angles. For example, we can find the orthogonal trajectories of $x^2+2y^2 = C_0$ by finding $dy/dx$,

$$2x+4y\frac{dy}{dx}=0$$

$$\frac{dy}{dx}=\frac{-x}{2y},$$

then solving the negative reciprocal derivative:

$$\frac{dy}{dx}=\frac{2y}{x}$$

$$\frac{dy}{2y}=\frac{dx}{x}$$

$$\tfrac{1}{2}\ln|y| = \ln|x| + \ln C$$

$$\ln|y|^{1/2} - \ln|x| = \ln C$$

$$\ln\frac{\sqrt{|y|}}{|x|} = \ln C$$

$$y = Cx^2$$

**Motion Equations.** A projectile is fired upward at an initial velocity of $V_0$ from a position $S_0$ above the ground. Find the equations of distance and velocity if the acceleration of gravity is $-32$ ft/sec².

We know that the only force acting on the projectile after the initial thrust is that of gravity. The acceleration is then

$$a=\frac{d^2s}{dt^2}=\frac{d}{dt}\left(\frac{ds}{dt}\right)=-32$$

integrating both sides with respect to $t$ we get

$$d\left(\frac{ds}{dt}\right)=-32dt,$$

$$\int d\left(\frac{ds}{dt}\right)=\int -32dt,$$

$$\frac{ds}{dt}=-32t+C_1.$$

We know when $t=0$, the velocity, $ds/dt$, is $V_0$, so

$$V_0 = -32(0) + C_1,$$

$$C_1 = V_0,$$

$$V=\frac{ds}{dt}=-32t+V_0. \text{ (velocity equation)}$$

We integrate with respect to $t$ again to get

$$ds = (-32t+V_0)dt$$

$$\int ds = \int(-32t+V_0)dt$$

$$s = -16t^2 + V_0t + C_2$$

We now use the other initial condition, $s = S_0$ when $t = 0$, and

$$S_0 = -16(0) + V_0(0) + C_2,$$

$$C_2 = S_0,$$

$$s = 16t^2 + V_0t + S_0. \text{ (distance equation)}$$

**Areas.** We can often find the area *between* two curves as in [72a] by considering the representative rectangle of width $\Delta x$ and of length

[72]

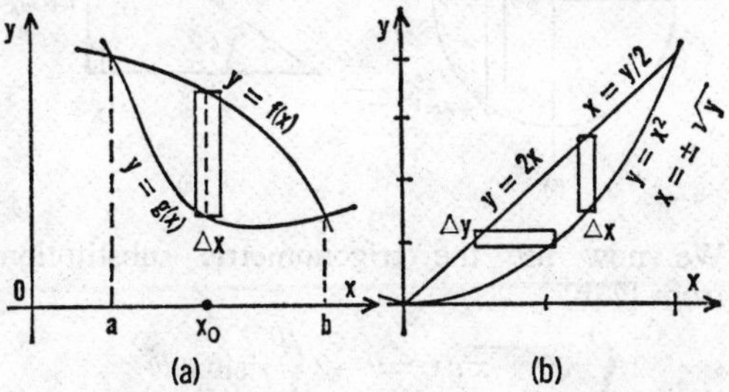


(a) (b)

$f(x_0) - g(x_0)$. This vertical rectangle has its length determined by the distance between horizontal sides which have midpoints on the curves. This resembles an abbreviated way of showing one of the rectangles used in an approximation to the area. We are not going to approximate, however, but we are going to take the limit of the sum of all such rectangles as $\Delta x \to 0$. This is of course just the definite integral, but the representative rectangle is commonly used as an aid in expressing the integrand and in determining the limits of integration with respect to $x$.

Also we often may use horizontal representative rectangles with width $\Delta y$ and integrate with respect to $y$.

For example, we shall solve for the area between $y = x^2$ and $y = 2x$ in [72b] by each method.

By using the vertical strips, we have as integrand the length of the vertical strip, which is $2x-x^2$, and we have as limits of the definite integral, $x = 0$ to $x = 2$. Then

$$\text{Area} = \int_0^2 (2x-x^2)dx = \Big[x^2-x^3/3\Big]_0^2 = 4/3.$$

By using horizontal strips, we have as integrand the length of the horizontal strip, $\sqrt{y} - y/2$, and as limits of integration we have $y = 0$ to $y = 4$. Then

$$\text{Area} = \int_0^4 (\sqrt{y} - y/2)\,dy = \Big[(2/3)y^{3/2} - y^2/4\Big]_0^4 =$$

4/3.

EXAMPLE: Find the area of a circle of radius $r$. We could find the area of one fourth of the circle and then multiply it by four. However, we will apply the method of this section with vertical strips for illustration. The integrand will be the value of $y$ on the upper semi-circle minus the value on the lower which in [73a] is

$$\sqrt{r^2-x^2} - (-\sqrt{r^2-x^2}) = 2\sqrt{r^2-x^2},$$

and the limits on $x$ go from $-r$ to $r$. Thus

$$\text{Area} = \int_{-r}^{r} 2\sqrt{r^2-x^2}\,dx.$$

[73]

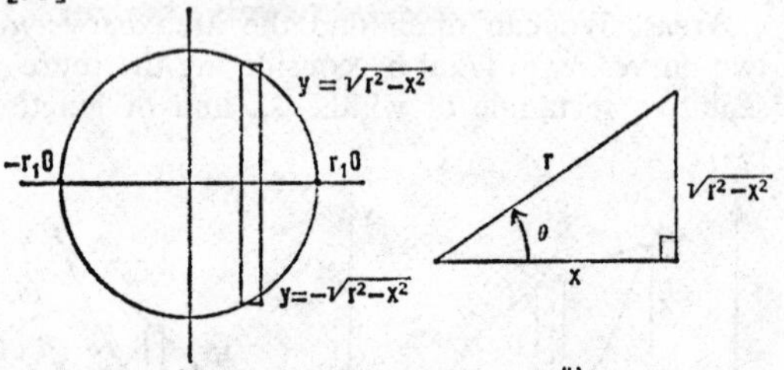


(a) (b)

We now use the trigonometric substitution from [73b]

$$2\int_{-r}^{r}\sqrt{r^2-x^2}\,dx = -2\int_{\pi}^{0} r^2\sin^2\theta\,d\theta =$$

$$-2r^2\int_{\pi}^{0}\left(\frac{1-\cos 2\theta}{2}\right)d\theta =$$

$$-2r^2\left[\int_{\pi}^{0}\frac{d\theta}{2} - \frac{1}{4}\int_{\pi}^{0}\cos 2\theta(2)\,d\theta\right] =$$

$$-2r^2\left[\frac{\theta}{2}\right]_{\pi}^{0} + \frac{r^2}{2}\Big[\sin\theta\Big]_{\pi}^{0} =$$

$$-2r^2(-\pi/2) + 0 = \pi r^2$$

**Volumes.** If we rotate a bounded area about one of the axes, we generate a solid of revolution. In particular, if the given area is rotated about the $x$-axis, then the representative vertical strip becomes a washer (flat disc with a hole in it). The volume of this washer is the volume of the solid disc minus the volume of the hole which is

$$\pi R^2\Delta x - \pi r^2\Delta x.$$

For example, we will find the volume of the figure formed by rotating the area bounded by $y = x^2$ and $y = 2x$ around the $x$-axis.

The representative washer has volume $(\pi(2x)^2 - \pi(x^2)^2)\Delta x$, and we set up an integral from $x = 0$ to $x = 2$ to get

$$\text{volume} = \pi\int_0^2 (4x^2 - x^4)\,dx =$$

$$\pi\Big[(4x^3/3 - x^5/5)\Big]_0^2 = 64\pi/15.$$

EXAMPLE: Find the volume of a sphere of radius $r$. We rotate a circle of radius $r$ about the $x$-axis. The representative washer is really a disc. Its volume is given by $\pi(\sqrt{r^2-x^2})^2\Delta x$ which means the sphere has

$$\text{volume} = \int_{-r}^{r}\pi(r^2-x^2)\,dx = \pi\Big[(xr^2 - x^3/3)\Big]_{-r}^{r} =$$

$$\pi(2r^3 - 2r^3/3),$$

$$\text{volume} = 4\pi r^3/3.$$

**Center of Gravity.** The center of gravity of a given area is the balance point or geometric center. The coordinates of this point are usually designated by $(\bar{x}, \bar{y})$ where

$$\bar{x} = M_y/A,\ \bar{y} = M_x/A.$$

Here $A$ is the area given by $\int_L f(x)\,dx$ (where the $L$ designates the proper limits) and $M_y$ and $M_x$ are the *moments* about the $y$- and $x$-axes respectively. They are computed by

$$M_y = \int_L \mathbf{x}f(x)\,dx,\ M_x = \int_L \mathbf{y}f(x)\,dx,$$

where $\mathbf{x}$ is the distance from the $y$-axis to the center of the representative rectangle, and $\mathbf{y}$ is the distance from the $x$-axis to the center of the representative rectangle.

As an illustration, we find the center of gravity of the area bounded by $y = x^2$ and $y = 2x$ in [72b] by first computing the area getting

$$\text{Area} = \int_0^2 (2x - x^2)\,dx = 4/3,$$

then the moments. The distance to the representative rectangle from the $y$-axis is $x$. The distance from the $x$-axis is $(2x+x^2)/2$. Therefore $\mathbf{x} = x$ and $\mathbf{y} = (2x+x^2)/2$ and

$$M_y = \int_0^2 x(2x-x^2)\,dx = \int_0^2 (2x^2-x^3)\,dx =$$

$$\Big[2x^3/3 - x^4/4\Big]_0^2 = 4/3$$

$$M_x = \frac{1}{2}\int_0^2 (2x+x^2)(2x-x^2)\,dx =$$

$$\frac{1}{2}\int_0^2 (4x^2-x^4)\,dx = \frac{1}{2}\Big[4x^3/3 - x^5/5\Big]_0^2 =$$

$$\frac{1}{2}(32/3 - 32/5) = 32/15$$

therefore $\bar{x} = M_y/A = (4/3)/(4/3) = 1$,

$$\bar{y} = M_x/A = (32/15)/(4/3) = 8/5,$$

and the center of gravity is the point $(1, 8/5)$.

**Length of Arc.** We find the length of the continuous plane curve, $y = f(x)$, $a \leq x \leq b$, by

$$\text{Length} = \int_a^b \sqrt{1+\left(\frac{dy}{dx}\right)^2}\, dx.$$

When we are given a function $y = f(x)$, we determine $dy/dx$, and then we substitute and integrate for the arc length.

EXAMPLE: Find the length of the curve $x^2 = y^4$, from (1,1) to (4,2).

We determine $dy/dx$ as follows:

$$x^2 = y^4$$
$$2x = 4y^3 \frac{dy}{dx}$$
$$\frac{dy}{dx} = \frac{x}{2y^3}$$

Then as $x^2 = y^4$, $y = \sqrt{x}$, so that

$$\text{length} = \int_1^4 \sqrt{1+\frac{x^2}{4y^6}}\, dx = \int_1^4 \sqrt{1+\frac{x^2}{4x^3}}\, dx =$$
$$\int_1^4 \sqrt{1+\frac{1}{4x}}\, dx = \int_1^4 \sqrt{\frac{4x+1}{4x}}\, dx.$$

Let $z = 2\sqrt{x}$, then $4x = z^2$ and $dx = \frac{1}{2} z dz$, so we have

$$\int_1^4 \sqrt{\frac{4x+1}{4x}}\, dx = \int_2^4 \sqrt{\frac{z^2+1}{z^2}}\, (\tfrac{1}{2} z) dz =$$
$$\tfrac{1}{2}\int_2^4 \sqrt{z^2+1}\, dz.$$

We use a trigonometric substitution where $z = \tan\theta$, $dz = \sec^2\theta d\theta$ and $\sqrt{z^2+1} = \sec\theta$, but we will convert back before substituting the new limits so this is indicated by limits of "$L$."

$$\tfrac{1}{2}\int_1^2 \sqrt{z^2+1}dz = \tfrac{1}{2}\int_L \sec^3\theta d\theta = \tfrac{1}{2}\int_L \sec\theta\sec^2\theta d\theta.$$

We now use integration by parts, with $u = \sec\theta$, $dv = \sec^2\theta d\theta$, and then $du = \sec\theta\tan\theta d\theta$, $v = \tan\theta$.

$$\tfrac{1}{2}\int_L \sec\theta\sec^2\theta d\theta = \tfrac{1}{2}\sec\theta\tan\theta - \tfrac{1}{2}\int_L \tan^2\theta\sec\theta d\theta =$$
$$\tfrac{1}{2}\sec\theta\tan\theta - \tfrac{1}{2}\int_L \frac{\sin^2\theta}{\cos^3\theta} d\theta.$$

$$\tfrac{1}{2}\int_L \sec^3\theta d\theta = \tfrac{1}{2}\sec\theta\tan\theta - \tfrac{1}{2}\int_L \frac{d\theta}{\cos^3\theta} +$$
$$\tfrac{1}{2}\int_L \frac{\cos^2\theta}{\cos^3\theta} d\theta.$$

We now simplify and transpose the middle term on the right:

$$\int_L \sec^3\theta d\theta + \int_L \sec^3\theta d\theta = \sec\theta\tan\theta + \int_L \sec\theta d\theta,$$
$$2\int_L \sec^3\theta d\theta = \Big[\sec\theta\tan\theta + \ln|\sec\theta+\tan\theta|\Big]_L.$$

The left member is now changed to terms of $z$ with the proper limits.

$$\text{length} = \tfrac{1}{4}\left[z\sqrt{z^2+1} + \ln|\sqrt{z^2+1}+z|\right]_2^4 =$$
$$\tfrac{1}{4}\Big[4\sqrt{17} + \ln(\sqrt{5}+2) - 2\sqrt{5} -$$
$$\ln(\sqrt{5}+2)\Big] = 3.168$$

Note that this problem could be solved in an easier way. However, as presented, it illustrates many methods of integration.

## DIFFERENTIAL EQUATIONS

**Introduction.** *A differential equation is essentially an equation containing differentials or derivatives.* For example:

$$\frac{dy}{dx} = x^2 + 2x,\ \frac{d^2y}{dx^2} - \frac{dy}{dx} + y^2 = \sin x,$$
$$dy = 2xdx,\ y'' + (y')^2 - y = e^x,$$

are differential equations.

We say $y = f(x)$ is a *solution* of a differential equation if when $f(x)$ and its derivatives are substituted into the differential equation for $y$ and its derivatives, then the result is an identity in terms of $x$.

EXAMPLE: Prove that $y = \sin x$ is a solution to the differential equation $y'' + y' + y = \cos x$.

We compute the derivatives

$$y = \sin x,\ y' = \cos x,\ y'' = -\sin x,$$

then substitute

$$-\sin x + \cos x + \sin x = \cos x,$$
$$\cos x = \cos x.$$

The *order* of a differential equation is the order of the highest derivative in the differential equation. The *degree* of a differential equation is the exponent of the derivative with the highest order.

In general, we solve a differential equation by first classifying it as to form, then applying the known solution procedure for that form of differential equation. There are relatively few types to choose from and if a given differential equation does not fit into one of them, then we may not be able to find the solution. The next few paragraphs discuss some of the more prevalent forms of *first order* differential equations and their solutions.

**Variables Separable.** A first order differential equation is in variables separable form if we can write it as:

$$f(x)dx + g(y)dy = 0.$$

That is the coefficients of $dx$ and $dy$ are respectively functions of $x$ and $y$ alone. The solution is then found by integration.

EXAMPLE: Solve $x^2dx - 2ydy = 0$.

We integrate to get

$$x^3/3 - y = C_1$$
$$x^3 - 3y = C,$$

where $C$ is an arbitrary constant and in this case

we have $C = 3C_1$. Solutions which contain arbitrary constants are called *general* solutions.

EXAMPLE: Solve $x^2y + y^2\frac{dy}{dx} = 0$.

We can change the given equation into variables separable form by multiplying by $dx$ and dividing by $y$ and get

$$x^2dx + \frac{y^2dy}{y} = 0$$
$$x^2dx + ydy = 0$$
$$x^3/3 + y^2/2 = C_1$$
$$2x^3 + 3y^2 = C$$

EXAMPLE: Solve $xydy + dx = 0$.

$$ydy + \frac{dx}{x} = 0$$
$$y^2/2 + \ln|x| = C_1$$
$$y^2 + \ln|x|^2 = C$$

**Homogeneous.** An expression $f(x,y)$ is said to be homogeneous if when $tx$ and $ty$ are substituted for $x$ and $y$ respectively, then $f(x,y)$ becomes $t^nf(x,y)$ where $n$ is the degree of the homogeneous expression. A differential equation

$$f(x,y)dx + g(x,y)dy = 0$$

is homogeneous if $f(x,y)$ and $g(x,y)$ are homogeneous in the same degree.

If a differential equation is homogeneous then we substitute $y = zx$ or $x = zy$ and reduce the equation to the variables separable form.

EXAMPLE: Solve $(x^2+y^2)dx + (2xy)dy = 0$. We note that $(tx)^2 + (ty)^2 = t^2(x^2+y^2)$ and $2(tx)(ty) = t^2(2xy)$ and the equation is homogeneous. We substitute $x = zy$, $dx = zdy + ydz$, to get

$$(z^2y^2+y^2)(zdy+ydz) + 2zy^2dy = 0$$
$$y^2(z^2+1)zdy + y^2(z^2+1)ydz + 2y^2zdy = 0$$
$$(z^3+3z)dy + y(z^2+1)dz = 0$$
$$\frac{dy}{y} + \frac{z^2+1}{z^3+3z}dz = 0$$
$$\int y^{-1}dy + (1/3)\int(z^3+3z)^{-1}d(z^3+3z) = 0$$
$$\ln|y| + \ln|z^3+3z|^{1/3}| = \ln C_1$$
$$\ln|(y)(z^3+3z)^{1/3}| = \ln C_1$$
$$y\left(\frac{x^3}{y^3} + 3\frac{x}{y}\right)^{1/3} = C_1$$
$$(x^3+3xy^2)^{1/3} = C_1$$
$$x^3 + 3xy^2 = C$$

**Exact.** An exact differential equation is one that can be written such that the right member is zero and the left member is the differential of a function $f(x,y)$.

We now discuss *partial derivatives* as they will be needed to find solutions to exact differential equations. *The partial derivative of* **f(x,y)** *with respect to* **x** *is the result of differentiating with respect to* **x** *while holding* **y** *constant*. Similarly, we find the partial derivative with respect to $y$ by holding $x$ constant.

The partial derivative of $f$ with respect to $x$ is symbolized by

$$\frac{\partial}{\partial x}(f) \text{ or } \frac{\partial f}{\partial x},$$

and similarly for $y$.

A differential equation of the form

$$Mdx + Ndy = 0,$$

is exact if $\frac{\partial M}{\partial y} = \frac{\partial N}{\partial x}$ where

$$M = \frac{\partial f}{\partial x},\ N = \frac{\partial f}{\partial y}.$$

The following example illustrates a method for finding the solution $f(x,y) = 0$ for an exact differential equation.

EXAMPLE:

Solve $(2xy+y+1)dx + (x^2+x)dy = 0$

We have $M = 2xy + y + 1$, $N = x^2 + x$, and

$$\frac{\partial M}{\partial y} = 2x + 1 = \frac{\partial N}{\partial x},$$

and the equation is exact. We know $\partial f/\partial x = M$, so

$$\frac{\partial f}{\partial x} = 2xy + y + 1,$$

and we integrate, holding $y$ constant, to get

$$\int\partial f = \int(2xy+y+1)\partial x,$$
$$f(x,y) = x^2y + xy + x + g(y).$$

Holding $y$ constant while integrating means that the constant term $g(y)$ is a function of $y$. We use $N = \partial f/\partial y$, thus

$$x^2 + x = \frac{\partial}{\partial y}(x^2y+xy+x+g(y)) =$$
$$x^2 + x + g'(y),$$

and $g'(y) = 0$, making $g(y) = C$. The solution is

$$f(x,y) = x^2y + xy + x + C = 0.$$

**First Order, Linear.** A first order linear differential equation can always be put in the form

$$\frac{dy}{dx} + P(x)y = Q(x).$$

If $Q(x) = 0$, then it can be put in variables separable form. We obtain the *general* solution of a first order linear differential equation by multiplying both sides by

$$e^{\int Pdx},$$

and then integrating. The general solution is the sum of a particular solution of $dy/dx + P(x)y = Q(x)$, where $Q(x) \neq 0$, and a nonzero particular solution of $dy/dx + P(x)y = 0$. This nonzero particular solution is often found by inspection.

EXAMPLE: Find the general solution of

$$\frac{dy}{dx} + xy = x^3.$$

Here $P = x$, $\int Pdx = \int xdx = x^2/2$, so we multiply by $e^{x^2/2}$.

$$e^{x^2/2}\left[\frac{dy}{dx}+xy\right] = e^{x^2/2}x^3$$

$$e^{x^2/2}dy + xye^{x^2/2}dx = e^{x^2/2}x^3dx$$

$$\int d(ye^{x^2/2}) = \int x^2 \cdot e^{x^2/2}(x)dx$$

$$ye^{x^2/2} = x^2e^{x^2/2} - 2e^{x^2/2} + C$$

$$y = x^2 - 2 + Ce^{-x^2/2}$$

EXAMPLE: Find the general solution of

$$\frac{dy}{dx} + y = 2.$$

By inspection we see that $y = 2$ is a solution. The reduced equation

$$\frac{dy}{dx} + y = 0$$

has the solution $y = Ce^{-x}$. The general solution is

$$y = Ce^{-x} + 2.$$

**Undetermined Coefficients.** If the first order linear differential equation has constant coefficients of $y$ and $y'$ then the method of undetermined coefficients is often used. We illustrate the method by solving

$$3y' - 6y = x^3 + 2x^2 - 1.$$

Let $y = ax^3 + bx^2 + cx + d$. Then $y' = 3ax^2 + 2bx + c$, and we substitute into the equation,

$$3(3ax^2+2bx+c) - 6(ax^3+bx^2+cx+d) = x^3 + 2x^2 - 1$$

$$9ax^2 + 6bx + 3c - 6ax^3 - 6bx^2 - 6cx - 6d = x^3 + 2x^2 - 1.$$

We equate like coefficients

$$-6a = 1,$$
$$9a - 6b = 2,$$
$$6b - 6c = 0,$$
$$3c - 6d = -1,$$

to get $a = -1/6$, $b = -7/12$, $c = -7/12$, and $d = -1/8$. Thus a particular solution is

$$y = -x^3/6 - 7x^2/12 - 7x/12 - 1/8.$$

We now need a solution to $3y' - 6y = 0$ or $y' - 3y = 0$, and by inspection we get

$$y = Ce^{3x}$$

therefore the general solution is

$$y = Ce^{3x} - x^3/6 - 7x^2/12 - 7x/12 - 1/8.$$

Note that this method could be applied to linear equations of higher order with constant coefficients.

## SELECTED TOPICS

**Vectors.** A quantity which represents magnitude only is called a *scaler.* A *vector* represents magnitude and direction. [74]

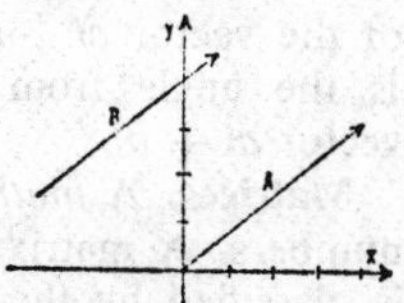

Two vectors in a plane are equal if they have the same magnitude and direction. Vectors $A$ and $B$ in [74] are equal. We represent either of these vectors by the same pair of numbers (4,3). The vector with tail at the origin has the characteristic that the coordinate pair at its tip will represent all vectors which have the same magnitude and direction. A parallel displacement then will not change the value of a vector.

The vector (1,0) is called the *unit* vector $i$, and (0,1) is called the *unit* vector $j$. We mean by $3i$ a vector with the same direction as $i$ but 3 units long. By $-2j$ we mean a vector with exactly opposite direction to $j$ and 2 units long. Vector $A$ in [74] is equal to $4i + 3j$. That is, if we move from the origin $4i$ then $3j$ we will be at the same point as if we had moved along vector $A$.

The length of any vector $ai + bj$ is written $ai+bj$ and is computed by

$$|ai + bj| = \sqrt{a^2+b^2}.$$

The *sum* of two vectors is

$$(ai+bj) + (ci+dj) = (a+c)i + (b+d)j,$$

and the difference is

$$(ai+bj) - (ci+dj) = (a-c)i + (b-d)j.$$

The *product* of a *scaler*, $c$, and a *vector*, $A = a_1i + a_2j$, is

$$c(a_1i+a_2j) = ca_1i + ca_2j.$$

The *scaler* or *dot product* of *two vectors*, $A = a_1i + a_2j$ and $B = b_1i + b_2j$ is

$$A \cdot B = a_1b_1 + a_2b_2,$$

and is a scaler quantity.

The *vector* or *cross product* of *two vectors*, $A$ and $B$, is

$$A \times B = V|A|\,|B|\sin\theta,\ 0 \leqq \theta \leqq \pi,$$

where $\theta$ the angle between $A$ and $B$ and $V$ is a unit vector with direction perpendicular to the plane of vectors $A$ and $B$, so that it points in the direction that a right-threaded screw would move if it is rotated through angle $\theta$ from vector $A$ to vector $B$.

**Complex Arithmetic.** Complex numbers of the form $a + bi$ can be treated as vectors when *adding* or *subtracting*. When *multiplying* two complex numbers we get

$$(a+bi)(c+di) = (ac-bd) + (ad+bc)i.$$

The quotient of two complex numbers is given by

$$\frac{a+bi}{c+di} = \frac{ac+bd}{c^2+d^2} + \frac{bc-ad}{c^2+d^2}i$$

The reciprocal of a complex number is discussed under *Inverse Points* in the geometry section.

The *modulus* of a complex number, $a + bi$, is written $|a+bi|$ and is the same as the length of the vector $ai + bj$. The *amplitude* of $a + bi$ is the angle from the positive $x$-axis to the vector $ai + bj$.

**Matrices.** A *matrix* is a rectangular array of numbers. A matrix has rows and columns and is classified by the number of each. A matrix with only one row (or column) is also a vector. Two matrices can be added (or subtracted) if they are *equivalent* (they have the same number of rows and the same number of columns). This is performed by adding (or subtracting) their corresponding elements. A *scaler times a matrix* is equal to the scaler times each element of the matrix.

We can find the *product of two matrices A* and *B* if the number of columns of *A* equals the number of rows of *B*. The resulting matrix will have the number of rows of *A* and the number of columns of *B*. We multiply the elements of the *i*th row of *A* by the corresponding elements in the *j*th column of *B*, add these products, and the sum is the *i*th row and *j*th column element in the product matrix. For example,

$$\begin{bmatrix} 1 & 0 & -1 \\ 4 & 2 & 1 \end{bmatrix} \times \begin{bmatrix} 2 \\ -1 \\ 1 \end{bmatrix} = \begin{bmatrix} (2+0-1) \\ (8-2+1) \end{bmatrix} = \begin{bmatrix} 1 \\ 7 \end{bmatrix},$$

where of course the matrices are enclosed in brackets.

**Determinants.** The determinant of a square matrix with $n$ rows and columns is found by summing the $n!$ possible products of $n$ elements (where no two elements in the product are from the same row or column) with each product multiplied by $(-1)^M$ where $M = 1$ if the number of elements in the product, which have the sum of their row and column numbers odd, is odd; if not then $M = 2$. For an example, see *Simultaneous Equations* in the algebra section.

We may use the following theorems to simplify the work of evaluating a determinant. A constant multiplied by any row or column of a determinant, multiplies the value of the determinant by that constant. If two rows (or columns) are interchanged, then the value of the determinant is opposite in sign. If the rows and columns are interchanged then the value of the determinant remains the same. If any row (or column) of a determinant is zero then the value of the determinant is zero. Any row (or column) may be multiplied by any constant and added to any other row (or column) and the value of the determinant is the same. If a determinant has one row (or column) proportional to another row (or column) then the value of the determinant is zero.

**Cramer's Rule.** Cramer's Rule can be applied in general to solve $n$ equations in $n$ unknowns by evaluating $n+1$ determinants. We find the determinant of the matrix of coefficients of the unknowns and call its value $D$. We then augment the matrix just used by substituting the constant coefficients in place of the coefficients of the unknown desired. This unknown is now found to be the determinant of the augmented matrix divided by $D$. We may do the same for any and all of the $n$ unknowns.

**Permutations, Combinations.** *A permutation is a distinct arrangement of a finite set of elements.* Thus $(A, B, C)$ and $(A, C, B)$ are two *distinct* permutations although they are the same set of elements. The number of permutations of $n$ elements taken $n$ at a time is $n!$ *The number of permutations of* **n** *elements taken* **r** *at a time is*

$$\frac{n!}{(n-r)!}$$

*If a set of elements is considered without regard to order or arrangement then it is called a combination.* Thus $(A, B, C)$ and $(A, C, B)$ are the *same* combination. *The number of combinations of* **n** *things taken* **r** *at a time is*

$$\frac{n!}{(n-r)!r!}$$

**Binomial Theorem.** The binomial theorem states that if $n$ is a positive integer then

$$(x+y)^n = x^n + nx^{n-1}y + \frac{n(n-1)}{2!}x^{n-2}y^2 + \ldots + \frac{\mathbf{n(n-1)\ldots(n-r+2)}}{\mathbf{(r-1)!}}\mathbf{x^{n-r+1}y^{r-1}} + \ldots + nxy^{n-1} + y^n.$$

Note the general or *r*th term of the binomial expansion is shown in bold print.

**Convergence, Divergence.** In *Sequences, Series* we said that an infinite series converges if the sequence of partial sums converges. If a series does not converge then it diverges. The following statements are theorems about convergence and divergence of positive series.

The *comparison test* states that a series *converges* if each of its terms is less than or equal to the corresponding term in a *known* convergent series. Also if each term is greater than or equal to the corresponding term of a known divergent series then the series diverges. The *p-series* given by

$$\frac{1}{1^p} + \frac{1}{2^p} + \frac{1}{3^p} + \ldots + \frac{1}{n^p} + \ldots$$

converges if $p>1$ and diverges if $p \leq 1$. This is an excellent series for the comparison test.

The *ratio test* applies to an infinite series of positive terms and states that if $a_n$ is the general term of the series and the ratio $r$ is defined by

$$\lim_{n\to\infty} \frac{a_n+1}{a_n} = r$$

then the series converges if $|r|<1$, it diverges if $|r|>1$, and the test fails if $r = 1$.

The *integral test* is applied to a decreasing

series of terms. It states that if we insert $x$, a continuous variable, in the $n$th term formula for $n$, an integer variable, and get $f(x)$ for the "$n$th" term, then the infinite series converges or diverges as does the improper integral,

$$\int_1^\infty f(x)dx = \lim_{k\to\infty}\int_1^k f(x)dx.$$

**Maclaurin's Series.** If $x$ is near zero then the following Maclaurin's series converges to $f(x)$.

$$f(x) = f(0)+f'(0)x+\frac{f''(0)}{2!}x^2+\ldots+\frac{f^{(n)}(0)}{n!}x^n+\ldots$$

From this series we can evaluate the following:

$$e^x = 1+x+\frac{x^2}{2!}+\frac{x^3}{3!}+\ldots,$$

$$\sin x = x-\frac{x^3}{3!}+\frac{x^5}{5!}-\frac{x^7}{7!}+\ldots,$$

$$\cos x = 1-\frac{x^2}{2!}+\frac{x^4}{4!}-\frac{x^6}{6!}+\ldots,$$

$$e^{ix} = 1+ix-\frac{x^2}{2!}-i\frac{x^3}{3!}+\frac{x^4}{4!}+i\frac{x^5}{5!}-\ldots$$

$$=(1-\frac{x^2}{2!}+\frac{x^4}{4!}-\ldots)+i(x-\frac{x^3}{3!}+\frac{x^5}{5!}-\ldots).$$

Therefore we have $e^{ix} = \cos x + i\sin x$, and if we let $x=\pi$, then

$$e^{i\pi} = \cos\pi + i\sin\pi = -1+0,$$

$$e^{i\pi}+1=0$$

and the *five great numbers* of mathematics, $e$, $i$, $\pi$, unity, and zero are related in one equation.

# COMPUTER PROGRAMMING: FORTRAN

## INTRODUCTION

**Computers.** *A computer is a device that is able to receive, store, and execute sets of instructions which require input, processing, and output of data.* This set of instructions usually is received and stored in some coded *binary* form called the *machine language program.* This is the only language that the computer basically "understands." For various reasons, however, machine language programs called *compilers* were developed which when executed by the computer would read in a set of more *humanly understandable* instructions, called the *source* program, and translate these instructions into another set of machine language instructions called the *object* program.

**Programming.** The programmer first acquaints himself with the problem to be executed on the computer and then draws a logical diagram of the sequence of operations, called the *flow chart.* Then he writes the source program on paper which is then punched on cards or tape, or put into some form which can be handled by an input device of the computer. Under control of the compiler program, the computer then reads the source program, compiles it, and generates the object program which at that time can be executed or put on cards or tape, etc., and be executed later.

## ELEMENTS OF FORTRAN IV

**Fortran Compiler.** *Fortran* means *for*mula *tran*slation. It is a compiler language which is oriented mostly toward scientific applications.

**Constants.** In *Fortran* we have two kinds of *constants: integer* and *real.* Real numbers inside the computer are mathematically rational and are represented in *floating point* form (see *Scientific and Floating Notation* in the algebra section). A real number must have a decimal point, and an integer must not have a decimal point. If we follow a real number by an E and a one or two digit integer $N$ then the number is understood to be multiplied by ten raised to the $N$th power. For example, 1.24E—2 would be the same as .0124.

**Variables.** *Fortran variables* are either *integer* or *real* as they represent one of these two kinds of numbers. Unlike in algebra, a variable can have as many as *six* letters. The first letter of an integer variable must begin with *I,J,K,L,M,* or *N.* A real variable must begin with any other *alphabetic* letter. The other characters of any variable can be letters or digits.

**Operations.** The *operations* of *Fortran* are *addition* +, *subtraction* —, *multiplication* *, *division* /, and *exponentiation* **. We relate variables with these operations to form *expressions.* The constants and variables that make up an expression must *all* be integer or *all* be real with two exceptions: the exponents of real variables *can* be integers, and the subscripts of a subscripted variable *must* be integers. For example, $b^2—4ac$ in algebra would be B**2—4.*A*C in *Fortran.*

**Supplied Functions.** Some of the supplied functions are: absolute value ABS, square root SQRT, sine (in radians) SIN, cosine (in radians) COS, exponential EXP, natural logarithms ALOG. We apply these functions by writing the function name then an expression in parenthesis. For example, the square root of $1—\sin^2\theta$ could be written SQRT(1.—SIN(THETA) ).

**Replacement Equations.** By X = Y+Z in *Fortran* we mean *replace* the value of X by the sum of the values of Y and Z. Thus we can say N = N+1 in *Fortran* means **let** N be replaced by one more than the old value of N. On the left must be a single variable name (real or integer) and on the right must be some expression (real or integer). Note that X = M+1 is acceptable and makes the *integers* value of M+1 to be stored as a *real* number in a place called X. Also, M = X+1. will convert *real* to *integer* and *truncate to the greatest integer* in X+1. Therefore if X is 2.9 then M = X+1. makes M have the value 3.

**Subscripted Variables.** A subscripted variable is an element of an array of numbers. The first letter of the name of the array must agree with the kind of numbers in the array. The array can be one-, two-, or three-dimensional. Before a subscripted variable can be used in a program, the compiler must know its name, dimensions, and maximum size. This can be accomplished by a DIMENSION statement. DIMENSION I(10) sets aside 10 integer numbers in an array called I, DIMENSION XMATRX(10,20) sets aside 200 real numbers in an array called XMATRX.

**Use of Tab Cards.** A tab card has 80 columns. We punch the *source* program *one statement per card* into the first 72 columns. A C in column 1 indicates a comment line with no required compilation. Columns 1 to 5 ordinarily contain statement numbers. Statements do not have to be numbered and if they are then there is no order required. A 1 in column 6 means this line is a continuation of the preceding line. *Fortran* statements begin in column 7. When a tab card is used for *data,* then any column 1-80 may be punched.

**Sample Program.** The following program reads one number each from a variable number, N, of cards by the card reader into an array called WEIGHT and finds the weighted average of the array. That is, the average of: 1 times the first number, 2 times the second, etc., down to N times the Nth number. It then outputs the sum and the average of the new array. An explanation in parentheses follows each *Fortran* statement.

**THIS IS A WEIGHTED AVERAGE PROGRAM**

`DIMENSION DATA (150)`
*(Sets aside 150 real numbers in a place called* DATA)

`30 READ (2,1) N` *(Statement number "30", reads "2", which is the card reader, according to "1", which is the format statement number; "N" is the variable name of the number read on the card)*

`1 FORMAT (I3)` *(Describes the number* N *as an integer which will be found punched in the first 3 columns of the card)*

`IF (N.EQ.0) STOP` *(If* N *equals* O *on the card just read, then stop the program, otherwise proceed to next statement; in other programs we can use* .NE. (≠), .LT. (<), .LE. (≤), .GT. (>), .GE. (≥), *in place of* .EQ. *and we can use* .AND., .OR., *and* .NOT. *as in* IF(A.LE.5..OR..NOT.X.GT. SUM) GO TO 4. *We may use any executable statement except an* IF *statement in place of* STOP.

`SUM=0.0` *(Sets sum cell initially to* 0.0)

`DO 2 I = 1,N` *(Sets up a* DO *loop which will execute all statements down to statement number* 2, *while* I = 1, *then it will go back and execute the same statements again, this time with* I = 2, *etc., until it executes the same statements the* Nth *time with* I = N; *after this it proceeds with the next statement following statement* 2.

`READ (2,101) DATA (I)`
*(Reads card reader according to* FORMAT 101 *and receives value of* DATA (I) *on the card; as this statement is within the* DO *loop, it will be executed* N *times with* I = 1,2, . . . ,N, *therefore we will read* DATA (1), DATA (2), . . . , DATA (N) )

`101 FORMAT (F10.0)` *(Reads a real number from the first* 10 *columns)*

```
2 SUM = SUM + DATA (I)
  1* FLOAT (I)
```
(SUM *is a sum cell which keeps a running total of the weighted numbers; in this statement alone,* FLOAT (I) *makes a real number out of* I *so that the right side is a real expression; this is statement number* 2, *the end of the* DO *loop)*

`AVG = SUM/FLOAT (N)`
*(Replaces* AVG *by the quotient of* SUM *and* N, *where* N *is made temporarily a real number)*

`WRITE (3,10) SUM,AVG`
*(Writes "3", which means* SUM *and* AVG *are to be printed according to* FORMAT 10)

```
10 FORMAT (4H0SUM,7X,8H
1 AVERAGE/2F10.3)
```
(FORMAT *statement* 10, *the "H" means that there are Hollerith characters to be printed, the "4" tells how many characters; as this is the first* H *on the line then the digit after the* H *is a carriage control character meaning skip two lines if* O, *skip one line if a space, skip no lines if a* + *and skip to head of form if a* 1; *now there are* 3 *characters left,* SUM, *out of the* 4 *and these are to be printed;* 7X *means leave the next* 7 *spaces blank;* 8H AVERAGE *means print all* 8 *characters, " AVERAGE"; "/" means go to next line for printing; in a* READ *statement a "/" would mean to go to next card for reading; "2F10.3" means there are* 2 *real numbers to be printed in* 10 *spaces each, with* 3 *of the* 10 *places devoted to the*

*right of the decimal point, and the decimal point itself counts as one of the* 10; *the effect of this* WRITE *and* FORMAT *statement combination is that* SUM *and* AVERAGE *will be printed on one line and immediately under them their values will be printed)*

GO TO 30 *(Transfers control to statement* 30 *which will read another card)*

END *(Ends the compilation of this program)*

Note that this program was written to illustrate as many elements of *Fortran* as possible in the allowable space. There are numerous elements of *Fortran IV* which were regretfully left out. Also note that on a particular computer, there may be slight modifications to be made (such as a number other that 2 for the card reader) before the program will run successfully.

**Comments on Fortran.** Since the main bulk of programming concerns the *input, output,* and *manipulation* of data, we now conclude by discussing these further to give an indication of the applicability of *Fortran.*

A read statement may read several cards and/or several numbers per card. For example, "READ(2,5)I,X,J,K,Y,L" with format statement "5 FORMAT (I3,F10.0,I4)" reads I,X, and J on one card by formats I3, F10.0, I4 respectively, then reads K, Y, and L on the next card by the *same* formats. This procedure can also be used with a write statement, like "WRITE(2,5)I,X,J,K,Y,L", and the result would be I,X, and J printed on one line and K, Y, and L printed on the next line with the same formats.

We may have DO loops (nested) within DO loops. For example, DO 101 I=1,5 followed by DO 101 J=1,6 and 101 READ(2,102)X(I,J) will read in the matrix X which has 5 rows and 6 columns, by letting the J subscript vary most rapidly. That is, the order of reading would be X(1,1),X(1,2), etc. The (implied DO) statement: READ(2,102) ( (V(I,J),J=1,6),I=1,5), does exactly the same thing. Implied DO statements may also be used with write statements. Nested DO loops may be used anywhere in the program.

There are other supplied functions available to the programmer such as arctan, ATAN, maximum of a set of real numbers, AMAX1, and minimum of a set, AMIN1, and many others.

The STOP statement may be used independently anywhere in the program where we want to stop the *object* program. This will not stop the *source* program.

## TABLE OF LOGARITHMS

| No. | 0 | 1 | 2 | 3 | 4 | 5 | 6 | 7 | 8 | 9 |
|---|---|---|---|---|---|---|---|---|---|---|
| **1.0** | 0000 | 0043 | 0086 | 0128 | 0170 | 0212 | 0253 | 0294 | 0334 | 0374 |
| **1.1** | 0414 | 0453 | 0492 | 0531 | 0569 | 0607 | 0645 | 0682 | 0719 | 0755 |
| **1.2** | 0792 | 0828 | 0864 | 0899 | 0934 | 0969 | 1004 | 1038 | 1072 | 1106 |
| **1.3** | 1139 | 1173 | 1206 | 1239 | 1271 | 1303 | 1335 | 1367 | 1399 | 1430 |
| **1.4** | 1461 | 1492 | 1523 | 1553 | 1584 | 1614 | 1644 | 1673 | 1703 | 1732 |
| **1.5** | 1761 | 1790 | 1818 | 1847 | 1875 | 1903 | 1931 | 1959 | 1987 | 2014 |
| **1.6** | 2041 | 2068 | 2095 | 2122 | 2148 | 2175 | 2201 | 2227 | 2253 | 2279 |
| **1.7** | 2304 | 2330 | 2355 | 2380 | 2405 | 2430 | 2455 | 2480 | 2504 | 2529 |
| **1.8** | 2553 | 2577 | 2601 | 2625 | 2648 | 2672 | 2695 | 2718 | 2742 | 2765 |
| **1.9** | 2788 | 2810 | 2833 | 2856 | 2878 | 2900 | 2923 | 2945 | 2967 | 2989 |
| **2.0** | 3010 | 3032 | 3054 | 3075 | 3096 | 3118 | 3139 | 3160 | 3181 | 3201 |
| **2.1** | 3222 | 3243 | 3263 | 3284 | 3304 | 3324 | 3345 | 3365 | 3385 | 3404 |
| **2.2** | 3424 | 3444 | 3464 | 3483 | 3502 | 3522 | 3541 | 3560 | 3579 | 3598 |
| **2.3** | 3617 | 3636 | 3655 | 3674 | 3692 | 3711 | 3729 | 3747 | 3766 | 3784 |
| **2.4** | 3802 | 3820 | 3838 | 3856 | 3874 | 3892 | 3909 | 3927 | 3945 | 3962 |
| **2.5** | 3979 | 3997 | 4014 | 4031 | 4048 | 4065 | 4082 | 4099 | 4116 | 4133 |
| **2.6** | 4150 | 4166 | 4183 | 4200 | 4216 | 4232 | 4249 | 4265 | 4281 | 4298 |
| **2.7** | 4314 | 4330 | 4346 | 4362 | 4378 | 4393 | 4409 | 4425 | 4440 | 4456 |
| **2.8** | 4472 | 4487 | 4502 | 4518 | 4533 | 4548 | 4564 | 4579 | 4594 | 4609 |
| **2.9** | 4624 | 4639 | 4654 | 4669 | 4683 | 4698 | 4713 | 4728 | 4742 | 4757 |
| **3.0** | 4771 | 4786 | 4800 | 4814 | 4829 | 4843 | 4857 | 4871 | 4886 | 4900 |
| **3.1** | 4914 | 4928 | 4942 | 4955 | 4969 | 4983 | 4997 | 5011 | 5024 | 5038 |
| **3.2** | 5051 | 5065 | 5079 | 5092 | 5105 | 5119 | 5132 | 5145 | 5159 | 5172 |
| **3.3** | 5185 | 5198 | 5211 | 5224 | 5237 | 5250 | 5263 | 5276 | 5289 | 5302 |
| **3.4** | 5315 | 5328 | 5340 | 5353 | 5366 | 5378 | 5391 | 5403 | 5416 | 5428 |
| **3.5** | 5441 | 5453 | 5465 | 5478 | 5490 | 5502 | 5514 | 5527 | 5539 | 5551 |
| **3.6** | 5563 | 5575 | 5587 | 5599 | 5611 | 5623 | 5635 | 5647 | 5658 | 5670 |
| **3.7** | 5682 | 5694 | 5705 | 5717 | 5729 | 5740 | 5752 | 5763 | 5775 | 5786 |
| **3.8** | 5798 | 5809 | 5821 | 5832 | 5843 | 5855 | 5866 | 5877 | 5888 | 5899 |
| **3.9** | 5911 | 5922 | 5933 | 5944 | 5955 | 5966 | 5977 | 5988 | 5999 | 6010 |

**TABLE OF LOGARITHMS, continued**

| No. | 0 | 1 | 2 | 3 | 4 | 5 | 6 | 7 | 8 | 9 |
|---|---|---|---|---|---|---|---|---|---|---|
| **4.0** | 6021 | 6031 | 6042 | 6053 | 6064 | 6075 | 6085 | 6096 | 6107 | 6117 |
| **4.1** | 6128 | 6138 | 6149 | 6160 | 6170 | 6180 | 6191 | 6201 | 6212 | 6222 |
| **4.2** | 6232 | 6243 | 6253 | 6263 | 6274 | 6284 | 6294 | 6304 | 6314 | 6325 |
| **4.3** | 6335 | 6345 | 6355 | 6365 | 6375 | 6385 | 6395 | 6405 | 6415 | 6425 |
| **4.4** | 6435 | 6444 | 6454 | 6464 | 6474 | 6484 | 6493 | 6503 | 6513 | 6522 |
| **4.5** | 6532 | 6542 | 6551 | 6561 | 6571 | 6580 | 6590 | 6599 | 6609 | 6618 |
| **4.6** | 6628 | 6637 | 6646 | 6656 | 6665 | 6675 | 6684 | 6693 | 6702 | 6712 |
| **4.7** | 6721 | 6730 | 6739 | 6749 | 6758 | 6767 | 6776 | 6785 | 6794 | 6803 |
| **4.8** | 6812 | 6821 | 6830 | 6839 | 6848 | 6857 | 6866 | 6875 | 6884 | 6893 |
| **4.9** | 6902 | 6911 | 6920 | 6928 | 6937 | 6946 | 6955 | 6964 | 6972 | 6981 |
| **5.0** | 6990 | 6998 | 7007 | 7016 | 7024 | 7033 | 7042 | 7050 | 7059 | 7067 |
| **5.1** | 7076 | 7084 | 7093 | 7101 | 7110 | 7118 | 7126 | 7135 | 7143 | 7152 |
| **5.2** | 7160 | 7168 | 7177 | 7185 | 7193 | 7202 | 7210 | 7218 | 7226 | 7235 |
| **5.3** | 7243 | 7251 | 7259 | 7267 | 7275 | 7284 | 7292 | 7300 | 7308 | 7316 |
| **5.4** | 7324 | 7332 | 7340 | 7348 | 7356 | 7364 | 7372 | 7380 | 7388 | 7396 |
| **5.5** | 7404 | 7412 | 7419 | 7427 | 7435 | 7443 | 7451 | 7459 | 7466 | 7474 |
| **5.6** | 7482 | 7490 | 7497 | 7505 | 7513 | 7520 | 7528 | 7536 | 7543 | 7551 |
| **5.7** | 7559 | 7566 | 7574 | 7582 | 7589 | 7597 | 7604 | 7612 | 7619 | 7627 |
| **5.8** | 7634 | 7642 | 7649 | 7657 | 7664 | 7672 | 7679 | 7686 | 7694 | 7701 |
| **5.9** | 7709 | 7716 | 7723 | 7731 | 7738 | 7745 | 7752 | 7760 | 7767 | 7774 |
| **6.0** | 7782 | 7789 | 7796 | 7803 | 7810 | 7818 | 7825 | 7832 | 7839 | 7846 |
| **6.1** | 7853 | 7860 | 7868 | 7875 | 7882 | 7889 | 7896 | 7903 | 7910 | 7917 |
| **6.2** | 7924 | 7931 | 7938 | 7945 | 7952 | 7959 | 7966 | 7973 | 7980 | 7987 |
| **6.3** | 7993 | 8000 | 8007 | 8014 | 8021 | 8028 | 8035 | 8041 | 8048 | 8055 |
| **6.4** | 8062 | 8069 | 8075 | 8082 | 8089 | 8096 | 8102 | 8109 | 8116 | 8122 |
| **6.5** | 8129 | 8136 | 8142 | 8149 | 8156 | 8162 | 8169 | 8176 | 8182 | 8189 |
| **6.6** | 8195 | 8202 | 8209 | 8215 | 8222 | 8228 | 8235 | 8241 | 8248 | 8254 |
| **6.7** | 8261 | 8267 | 8274 | 8280 | 8287 | 8293 | 8299 | 8306 | 8312 | 8319 |
| **6.8** | 8325 | 8331 | 8338 | 8344 | 8351 | 8357 | 8363 | 8370 | 8376 | 8382 |
| **6.9** | 8388 | 8395 | 8401 | 8407 | 8414 | 8420 | 8426 | 8432 | 8439 | 8445 |
| **7.0** | 8451 | 8457 | 8463 | 8470 | 8476 | 8482 | 8488 | 8494 | 8500 | 8506 |
| **7.1** | 8513 | 8519 | 8525 | 8531 | 8537 | 8543 | 8549 | 8555 | 8561 | 8567 |
| **7.2** | 8573 | 8579 | 8585 | 8591 | 8597 | 8603 | 8609 | 8615 | 8621 | 8627 |
| **7.3** | 8633 | 8639 | 8645 | 8651 | 8657 | 8663 | 8669 | 8675 | 8681 | 8686 |
| **7.4** | 8692 | 8698 | 8704 | 8710 | 8716 | 8722 | 8727 | 8733 | 8739 | 8745 |
| **7.5** | 8751 | 8756 | 8762 | 8768 | 8774 | 8779 | 8785 | 8791 | 8797 | 8802 |
| **7.6** | 8808 | 8814 | 8820 | 8825 | 8831 | 8837 | 8842 | 8848 | 8854 | 8859 |
| **7.7** | 8865 | 8871 | 8876 | 8882 | 8887 | 8893 | 8899 | 8904 | 8910 | 8915 |
| **7.8** | 8921 | 8927 | 8932 | 8938 | 8943 | 8949 | 8954 | 8960 | 8965 | 8971 |
| **7.9** | 8976 | 8982 | 8987 | 8993 | 8998 | 9004 | 9009 | 9015 | 9020 | 9025 |
| **8.0** | 9031 | 9036 | 9042 | 9047 | 9053 | 9058 | 9063 | 9069 | 9074 | 9079 |
| **8.1** | 9085 | 9090 | 9096 | 9101 | 9106 | 9112 | 9117 | 9122 | 9128 | 9133 |
| **8.2** | 9138 | 9143 | 9149 | 9154 | 9159 | 9165 | 9170 | 9175 | 9180 | 9186 |
| **8.3** | 9191 | 9196 | 9201 | 9206 | 9212 | 9217 | 9222 | 9227 | 9232 | 9238 |
| **8.4** | 9243 | 9248 | 9253 | 9258 | 9263 | 9269 | 9274 | 9279 | 9284 | 9289 |
| **8.5** | 9294 | 9299 | 9304 | 9309 | 9315 | 9320 | 9325 | 9330 | 9335 | 9340 |
| **8.6** | 9345 | 9350 | 9355 | 9360 | 9365 | 9370 | 9375 | 9380 | 9385 | 9390 |
| **8.7** | 9395 | 9400 | 9405 | 9410 | 9415 | 9420 | 9425 | 9430 | 9435 | 9440 |
| **8.8** | 9445 | 9450 | 9455 | 9460 | 9465 | 9469 | 9474 | 9479 | 9484 | 9489 |
| **8.9** | 9494 | 9499 | 9504 | 9509 | 9513 | 9518 | 9523 | 9528 | 9533 | 9538 |
| **9.0** | 9542 | 9547 | 9552 | 9557 | 9562 | 9566 | 9571 | 9576 | 9581 | 9586 |
| **9.1** | 9590 | 9595 | 9600 | 9605 | 9609 | 9614 | 9619 | 9624 | 9628 | 9633 |
| **9.2** | 9638 | 9643 | 9647 | 9652 | 9657 | 9661 | 9666 | 9671 | 9675 | 9680 |
| **9.3** | 9685 | 9689 | 9694 | 9699 | 9703 | 9708 | 9713 | 9717 | 9722 | 9727 |
| **9.4** | 9731 | 9736 | 9741 | 9745 | 9750 | 9754 | 9759 | 9763 | 9768 | 9773 |
| **9.5** | 9777 | 9782 | 9786 | 9791 | 9795 | 9800 | 9805 | 9809 | 9814 | 9818 |
| **9.6** | 9823 | 9827 | 9832 | 9836 | 9841 | 9845 | 9850 | 9854 | 9859 | 9863 |
| **9.7** | 9868 | 9872 | 9877 | 9881 | 9886 | 9890 | 9894 | 9899 | 9903 | 9908 |
| **9.8** | 9912 | 9917 | 9921 | 9926 | 9930 | 9934 | 9939 | 9943 | 9948 | 9952 |
| **9.9** | 9956 | 9961 | 9965 | 9969 | 9974 | 9978 | 9983 | 9987 | 9991 | 9996 |

## TABLE OF TRIGONOMETRIC FUNCTIONS

| Deg | Sin | Cos | Tan | Deg | Sin | Cos | Tan |
|---|---|---|---|---|---|---|---|
| 0 | 0.0000 | 1.0000 | 0.0000 | 46 | 0.7193 | 0.6947 | 1.0355 |
| 1 | 0.0175 | 0.9998 | 0.0175 | 47 | 0.7314 | 0.6820 | 1.0724 |
| 2 | 0.0349 | 0.9994 | 0.0349 | 48 | 0.7431 | 0.6691 | 1.1106 |
| 3 | 0.0523 | 0.9986 | 0.0524 | 49 | 0.7547 | 0.6561 | 1.1504 |
| 4 | 0.0698 | 0.9976 | 0.0699 | 50 | 0.7660 | 0.6428 | 1.1918 |
| 5 | 0.0872 | 0.9962 | 0.0875 | 51 | 0.7771 | 0.6293 | 1.2349 |
| 6 | 0.1045 | 0.9945 | 0.1051 | 52 | 0.7880 | 0.6157 | 1.2799 |
| 7 | 0.1219 | 0.9925 | 0.1228 | 53 | 0.7986 | 0.6018 | 1.3270 |
| 8 | 0.1392 | 0.9903 | 0.1405 | 54 | 0.8090 | 0.5878 | 1.3764 |
| 9 | 0.1564 | 0.9877 | 0.1584 | 55 | 0.8192 | 0.5736 | 1.4281 |
| 10 | 0.1736 | 0.9848 | 0.1763 | 56 | 0.8290 | 0.5592 | 1.4826 |
| 11 | 0.1908 | 0.9816 | 0.1944 | 57 | 0.8387 | 0.5446 | 1.5399 |
| 12 | 0.2079 | 0.9781 | 0.2126 | 58 | 0.8480 | 0.5299 | 1.6003 |
| 13 | 0.2250 | 0.9744 | 0.2309 | 59 | 0.8572 | 0.5150 | 1.6643 |
| 14 | 0.2419 | 0.9703 | 0.2493 | 60 | 0.8660 | 0.5000 | 1.7321 |
| 15 | 0.2588 | 0.9659 | 0.2679 | 61 | 0.8746 | 0.4848 | 1.8040 |
| 16 | 0.2756 | 0.9613 | 0.2867 | 62 | 0.8829 | 0.4695 | 1.8807 |
| 17 | 0.2924 | 0.9563 | 0.3057 | 63 | 0.8910 | 0.4540 | 1.9626 |
| 18 | 0.3090 | 0.9511 | 0.3249 | 64 | 0.8988 | 0.4384 | 2.0503 |
| 19 | 0.3256 | 0.9455 | 0.3443 | 65 | 0.9063 | 0.4226 | 2.1445 |
| 20 | 0.3420 | 0.9397 | 0.3640 | 66 | 0.9135 | 0.4067 | 2.2460 |
| 21 | 0.3584 | 0.9336 | 0.3839 | 67 | 0.9205 | 0.3907 | 2.3559 |
| 22 | 0.3746 | 0.9272 | 0.4040 | 68 | 0.9272 | 0.3746 | 2.4751 |
| 23 | 0.3907 | 0.9205 | 0.4245 | 69 | 0.9336 | 0.3584 | 2.6051 |
| 24 | 0.4067 | 0.9135 | 0.4452 | 70 | 0.9397 | 0.3420 | 2.7475 |
| 25 | 0.4226 | 0.9063 | 0.4663 | 71 | 0.9455 | 0.3256 | 2.9042 |
| 26 | 0.4384 | 0.8988 | 0.4877 | 72 | 0.9511 | 0.3090 | 3.0777 |
| 27 | 0.4540 | 0.8910 | 0.5095 | 73 | 0.9563 | 0.2924 | 3.2709 |
| 28 | 0.4695 | 0.8829 | 0.5317 | 74 | 0.9613 | 0.2756 | 3.4874 |
| 29 | 0.4848 | 0.8746 | 0.5543 | 75 | 0.9659 | 0.2588 | 3.7321 |
| 30 | 0.5000 | 0.8660 | 0.5774 | 76 | 0.9703 | 0.2419 | 4.0108 |
| 31 | 0.5150 | 0.8572 | 0.6009 | 77 | 0.9744 | 0.2250 | 4.3315 |
| 32 | 0.5299 | 0.8480 | 0.6249 | 78 | 0.9781 | 0.2079 | 4.7046 |
| 33 | 0.5446 | 0.8387 | 0.6494 | 79 | 0.9816 | 0.1908 | 5.1446 |
| 34 | 0.5592 | 0.8290 | 0.6745 | 80 | 0.9848 | 0.1736 | 5.6713 |
| 35 | 0.5736 | 0.8192 | 0.7002 | 81 | 0.9877 | 0.1564 | 6.3138 |
| 36 | 0.5878 | 0.8090 | 0.7265 | 82 | 0.9903 | 0.1392 | 7.1154 |
| 37 | 0.6018 | 0.7986 | 0.7536 | 83 | 0.9925 | 0.1219 | 8.1443 |
| 38 | 0.6157 | 0.7880 | 0.7813 | 84 | 0.9945 | 0.1045 | 9.5144 |
| 39 | 0.6293 | 0.7771 | 0.8098 | 85 | 0.9962 | 0.0872 | 11.430 |
| 40 | 0.6428 | 0.7660 | 0.8391 | 86 | 0.9976 | 0.0698 | 14.301 |
| 41 | 0.6561 | 0.7547 | 0.8693 | 87 | 0.9986 | 0.0523 | 19.081 |
| 42 | 0.6691 | 0.7431 | 0.9004 | 88 | 0.9994 | 0.0349 | 28.636 |
| 43 | 0.6820 | 0.7314 | 0.9325 | 89 | 0.9998 | 0.0175 | 57.290 |
| 44 | 0.6947 | 0.7193 | 0.9657 | 90 | 1.0000 | 0.0000 | — |
| 45 | 0.7071 | 0.7071 | 1.0000 | | | | |

# Reference Manual for Business Office

## *Business Letters*

THE BUSINESS LETTER is one of the basic means of communication in the world of business. Thousands of business transactions take place daily by means of incoming and outgoing business letters.

A large part of the activities of the average secretary is centered around the business letter. In various studies conducted to analyze the specific duties of secretaries, the handling of incoming and outgoing mail and the taking, writing, and transcribing of letters rank high in frequency of activities performed.

### WRITING THE BUSINESS LETTER

Business letters are written to communicate ideas. The preliminary steps in writing a business letter are to determine the purpose of the letter and to obtain all the facts necessary for writing. The writer should plan what needs to be said and then organize the material in a logical manner.

No definite set of rules can be made to follow for the correct writing of a business letter, but each effective business letter possesses certain recognized qualities.

The following check list is valuable to summarize the various qualities every letter should possess.

1. IS THE LETTER CLEAR? Letters should be written in a natural, direct manner. Simple words and short sentences are the most effective way to communicate ideas; letters are written to express, not to impress. The reader needs to be able to understand easily what has been written.

Trite, worn-out expressions and phrases are to be avoided.

2. IS THE LETTER COURTEOUS? Sincerity and

JOHN H. RICH, A.B., M.A., Ed.D., and JOAN S. RICH, A.B., M.A., George Peabody College for Teachers, Nashville, Tennessee.

respect are a basic part of all good letters. Even though a letter may be one of refusal, tact can be used in presenting the contents.

The individual to whom the letter is written should be kept in mind so that the letter is personal.

3. IS THE LETTER CONSIDERATE? Consideration for the reader is of utmost importance in business-letter writing. Letters written from the reader's point of view, using the "you-attitude" rather than the "I-attitude," are most effective. The positive side should always be emphasized in writing.

4. IS THE LETTER CORRECT? The information contained in a letter needs to be verified for its correctness. The writer must be truthful and honest in presenting the information if a letter is to communicate well.

Correct grammar and correct punctuation are also very basic qualities necessary for every business letter.

5. IS THE LETTER CONCRETE? The meaning of the letter should be exact and definite. Words must be chosen to convey specific meanings.

6. IS THE LETTER COMPLETE? All necessary points need to be covered in order that the reader will not be left with any unanswered questions.

7. IS THE LETTER CONCISE? Letters in business should be brief and to the point. The reader is interested in the needed facts and no more. Flattery and exaggeration are to be avoided, and all unnecessary elements should be eliminated.

8. IS THE LETTER COHERENT? The facts should be presented in a logical and effective order. The letter needs to be organized for easy comprehension.

## APPEARANCE OF THE LETTER

A neat, attractive appearance is essential if a letter is to create a favorable impression. Most letters are typed on 8½ by 11-inch stationery which has the name and address of the firm imprinted upon it. The letter should be typed on high-quality paper and placed on the page so that a "picture-frame" appearance is created. This means that to give a balanced appearance the side margins are equal to each other with the bottom margin slightly larger than the side margins. Any erasures should be unnoticeable. A dark typewriter ribbon and even stroking help to produce an attractive letter. At least one carbon copy is made of all business correspondence.

### Letter-Placement Guide

The length of a letter will determine the side margins and the vertical placement of the letter. The following guide may be used as an aid to letter placement until judgment placement becomes natural. The guide must not be used unconditionally because such factors as paragraphing, enumerations, and size of the paper will affect the placement of the letter.

| *Words in Body of Letter* | *Length of Line* | | *Lines Between Date and Inside Address* |
|---|---|---|---|
| | *Pica Spaces* | *Elite Spaces* | |
| Up to 100 | 50 | 50 | 8-10 |
| 100-200 | 60 | 60 | 6-8 |
| Over 200 | 60 | 70 | 3-6 |

### Letter Styles

Three basic letter styles are used most frequently in typing business letters: (1) modified-block style with either blocked or indented paragraphs, (2) block style, and (3) the simplified letter. Basic styles may be changed and unusual styles are sometimes used for special effects, but here the three basic styles will be discussed. The indented style is considered out of date in the modern business office and as with most unusual styles is often considered to be too time consuming to be practical.

MODIFIED-BLOCK STYLE. This letter style has the date line and the closing lines typed near the horizontal center point of the letter (*see Figure 1*). The date may be centered, started at the center, started under the address in the letterhead, or typed to end at the right margin. The most efficient method, however, is to set a tabulator stop at the center point and begin both the date and the closing lines at that point. Para-

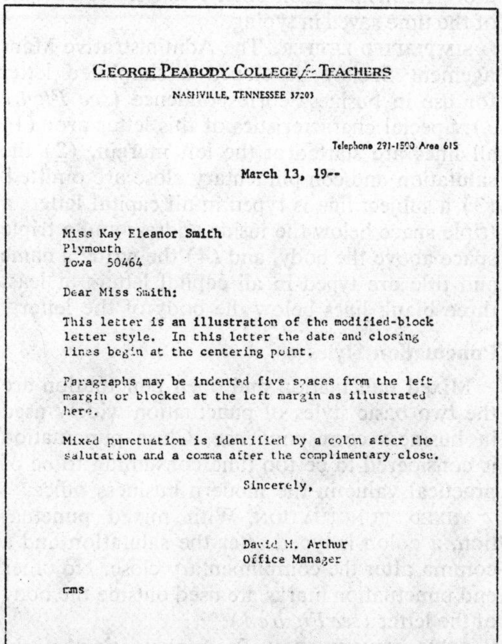
GEORGE PEABODY COLLEGE for TEACHERS

NASHVILLE, TENNESSEE 37203

Telephone 291-1500 Area 615

March 13, 19--

Miss Kay Eleanor Smith
Plymouth
Iowa 50464

Dear Miss Smith:

This letter is an illustration of the modified-block letter style. In this letter the date and closing lines begin at the centering point.

Paragraphs may be indented five spaces from the left margin or blocked at the left margin as illustrated here.

Mixed punctuation is identified by a colon after the salutation and a comma after the complimentary close.

Sincerely,

David M. Arthur
Office Manager

cms

**Fig. 1.** *Modified-Block Style with Blocked Paragraphs and Mixed Punctuation.*

GEORGE PEABODY COLLEGE *for* TEACHERS
NASHVILLE, TENNESSEE 37203

Telephone 291-1500 Area 615

December 23, 19--

Mr. Jay Strand Rich
2305 Oxford Road
Nashville, Tennessee 37215

Dear Mr. Rich

The block-style letter is typed with all lines beginning at the left margin. Open punctuation requires no end punctuation outside the body of the letter.

The letter is quick and easy to type and is gaining increased use in the business world.

The word "Enclosure" below the identification notation shows that an additional paper is enclosed in the envelope.

Sincerely yours

Charles V. Carson

jar

Enclosure

**Fig. 2.** *Block Style and Open Punctuation.*

GEORGE PEABODY COLLEGE *for* TEACHERS
NASHVILLE, TENNESSEE 37203

Telephone 291-1500 Area 615

January 28, 19--

Dr. Oswald Charles Smith
2319 Wedgewood Boulevard
Elkhart, Indiana 46514

THE SIMPLIFIED LETTER

This letter style has been recommended by the Administrative Management Society (formerly NOMA). The time-saving style helps to reduce letter-writing costs.

If enumerated items are included in a letter of this style, the numbered items are typed at the left margin; unnumbered lists are indented five spaces.

MARK VAN HOGAN - PRESIDENT

jss

**Fig. 3.** *The Simplified Letter.*

graphs may be typed at either the left margin or indented five spaces.

BLOCK STYLE. The block style is typed with all the letter parts beginning at the left margin (*see Figure 2*). This letter style is being used more frequently than other letter styles because of the time saved in typing.

SIMPLIFIED LETTER. The Administrative Management Society developed a simplified letter for use in business correspondence (*see Figure 3*). Special characteristics of this letter are: (1) all lines are started at the left margin, (2) the salutation and complimentary close are omitted, (3) a subject line is typed in all capital letters a triple space below the inside address and a triple space above the body, and (4) the writer's name and title are typed in all capital letters at least three blank lines below the body of the letter.

### Punctuation Styles

Mixed punctuation and open punctuation are the two basic styles of punctuation widely used in business correspondence. Close punctuation is considered to be too time consuming to be of practical value in the modern business office.

MIXED PUNCTUATION. With mixed punctuation, a colon is typed after the salutation and a comma after the complimentary close. No other end punctuation marks are used outside the body of the letter (*see Figure 1*).

OPEN PUNCTUATION. No punctuation marks are used at the end of any line outside the body of the letter when typing a letter with open punctuation (*see Figure 2*).

## PARTS OF THE LETTER

A knowledge of the correct placement and form of the various letter parts is essential to the writing of any business letter.

### Basic Letter Parts

The heading, date, inside address, salutation, body, complimentary close, and signature block are included in nearly all business letters and are considered to be basic letter parts.

HEADING. Most business correspondence is written on printed letterhead paper which has the firm name and address and perhaps other information printed on it. If plain paper is used, the return address of the sender is typed on the tenth or eleventh line from the top of the paper. In the modified-block style the return address is typed near the horizontal center; in the block style the return address is typed at left margin.

DATE LINE. When letterhead paper is used, the date line is typed a double space below the last line of the printed letterhead. If plain paper is used, the date is placed directly below the return address. The horizontal placement is determined by the letter style being used. The name of the month precedes the day and should not be abbreviated. Figures are used for the day of the month and the year and are separated with a comma.

```
1104 North Federal Avenue
Great Falls, Montana  59401
February 21, 19--
```

INSIDE ADDRESS. The number of lines left between the date and inside address varies according to the length of the letter (*see Letter-Placement Guide*). The address is typed at the left margin usually three to ten lines below the date line and a double space above the salutation. The addressee is always given a personal title such as *Mr., Mrs.,* or *Miss.* If a woman's title is unknown, the title *Miss* or *Ms.* may be used.

The lines of an address should be kept as nearly equal in length as possible. A business title may be typed on the line with the name of the addressee or on the line with the firm name, whichever is shorter. A title which is unusually long is placed on a separate line.

The address should consist of at least three lines. If no street address is necessary, the city and state are typed on separate lines. The ZIP code is typed a double space after the state with no intervening punctuation. The names of states are usually spelled out in full, and such words as *Street* or *Avenue* are not abbreviated. A personal name should not be abbreviated unless the owner himself abbreviates it.

Miss Carol Lynn Raye
Assistant Librarian
West End High School
Eugene, Oregon  97405

Dr. Bruce W. Miller, Head
Department of Business
Central State University
Boulder, Colorado  80302

Mr. O. Leroy Samuelson
Manager, Fargo Company
1324 East 37 Avenue
Paterson, New Jersey  07510

Miss Juanita Carson
Williamsburg
Virginia  23185

SALUTATION. The salutation is typed at the left margin with a double space both above and below it. The first word, all titles, and all proper names are capitalized. The salutation should correspond with the addressee as given in the first line of the inside address. For letters sent to a group or firm, *Gentlemen* is the preferred salutation. For groups composed entirely of women, *Ladies* is used. Personal salutations such as *Dear Mr. Carter* or *Dear Miss Thane* are generally used in letters addressed to individuals. The punctuation style being used determines whether or not a colon follows the salutation. The salutation is omitted in the simplified letter.

BODY. The body of a letter is usually single spaced with double spacing between paragraphs. In the modified-block style letter paragraphs may be indented. The body may be double spaced for extremely short letters; when the body is double spaced, paragraphs must be indented. Enumerated items and quoted or tabulated material are generally indented from both the left and right margins.

COMPLIMENTARY CLOSE. The complimentary close is typed a double space below the body of the letter; the horizontal placement is determined by the letter style being used. When mixed punctuation is used, the complimentary close is followed by a comma; with open punctuation no punctuation follows the complimentary close. Only the first word of the complimentary close is capitalized. Typical closings being used in business letters today are:

Sincerely
Sincerely yours
Cordially
Cordially yours

The simplified letter omits the closing line.

SIGNATURE BLOCK. If the firm name is used in the signature block, the firm name is typed in all capital letters a double space below and directly under the complimentary close. The trend today is to omit typing the firm name because of its identification in the letterhead. Three blank lines are left (below the firm name or below the complimentary close if the firm name is omitted) before typing the signature. Sometimes only the name is typed, and sometimes only the title is typed. If both the name and title are used in the signature, the title is placed on the line with the name when both are short. If either the name or title is long, two lines are used. A man never uses a personal title in the signature line. Women usually precede their typed name with either *Miss* or *Mrs.* enclosed in parentheses. The following are correct forms for the signature block:

---

Sincerely

*Paul W. Hawkins*

Purchasing Agent

---

Sincerely yours

*Pamela Anderson*

(Miss) Pamela Anderson
Office Manager

---

Cordially

NATIONAL MACHINE COMPANY

*Austin K. Smith*

Austin K. Smith

---

Cordially yours

*Joseph O. Rich*

Joseph O. Rich, President

**Miscellaneous Letter Parts**

**In addition to the basic letter parts several miscellaneous parts are often found in business letters.**

**MAILING NOTATION. If a mailing notation such as *Special Delivery* or *Airmail* is included in a letter, the notation is typed halfway between the date and inside address at the left margin. The notation is typed in all capital letters. Sometimes this notation is typed only on the carbon copy for use as reference as to how the letter was sent.**

March 10, 19--<br>
AIRMAIL<br>
Miss Pegi Dee Smith<br>
32 Laurel Drive<br>
San Marcos, Texas 78666

**ATTENTION LINE. When a letter is to be directed to a special department within a firm, an attention line may be used. The current tendency is to address the letter to an individual or department and omit the attention line. When used, the attention line is typed a double space below the inside address and a double space above the salutation at the left margin. The word *Attention* may be typed in all capital letters or with only the first letter capitalized and may or may not be followed by a colon. The attention line does not alter the salutation.**

Lincoln Manufacturing Company<br>
2900 East 56 Avenue<br>
St. Petersburg, Florida 33714

Attention Credit Manager

Gentlemen

SUBJECT LINE. The subject line is used in some letters to let the writer know what the letter is about. The subject line is typed a double space below the salutation and a double space above the body of the letter. In block or simplified letters the line is started at the left margin; in the modified-block style the subject line may begin at the paragraph point or be centered horizontally. The word *Subject* is typed in either all capitals or with only the first letter capitalized and is followed by a colon. In the simplified letter the word *Subject* is omitted entirely.

Gentlemen

SUBJECT: Business Letters<br>
Letters

The body of the letter would be typed in this position.

**REFERENCE LINE. When the writer wants a reader to refer to previous correspondence, a reference line may be used. The reply reference notation is typed in the same manner as the subject line.**

Gentlemen

Reference: Invoice #238

In the modified-block letter the body would begin in this position.

**SECOND-PAGE HEADING. If a letter is too long for one page, a plain sheet of paper, never a letterhead, is used for the second page. At least three lines of the body must be carried over to the second page and at least two lines of a started paragraph must be left on the first page. The second-page heading includes the name of the addressee, the page number, and the date. This information is typed in either the block or the horizontal form. The horizontal form has the page number centered and the date ending at the right margin. The heading is started on the seventh line from the top edge of the paper; three blank lines follow the heading before beginning the continued letter.**

Miss Roxie Smith<br>
Page 2<br>
June 30, 19--

or

Miss Roxie Smith 2 June 1, 19--

**IDENTIFICATION NOTATION. The typist of a letter is identified by the identification notation or reference initials. The initials of the typist are typed in lower-case letters at the left margin a double space below the last line of the signature block. The initials of the dictator typed in all capital letters and followed by a colon or a diagonal often precede the initials of the typist. If the name of the dictator is not typed in the signature block, his name should be typed as part of the identification notation.**

sms<br>
OBS/sms<br>
OBStrand:sms<br>
O. B. Strand/sms

ENCLOSURE NOTATION. When a letter contains enclosures, the word *Enclosure* is typed at the left margin a double space below the identification notation. An attached sheet is considered to be an enclosure. Several acceptable forms are:

Enclosure
Enclosures 2
Enclosure: Lease

CARBON COPY NOTATION. When a carbon copy is sent to another person, the fact is indicated at the left margin a double space below the identification or enclosure notation.

sms

cc Mr. Dean Philips

POSTSCRIPT. A postscript is typed a double space below the last typed line. The letters *P. S.* or *PS* may or may not be used. The postscript is blocked or indented to agree with the letter style being used.

## THE ENVELOPE

A large envelope (No. 10 — 4⅛ by 9½ inches) is used for letters of more than one page and for letters with enclosures. A small envelope (No. 6¾ — 3⅝ by 6½ inches) is used for one-page letters with no enclosures. Current practice often uses the large envelope for all business correspondence.

### Addressing the Envelope

An envelope address must consist of at least three lines. All three-line addresses are double spaced; addresses of four or more lines are single spaced. The address is blocked and typed with no end punctuation. The addressee must always be given a personal title. The ZIP-code number is typed on the line with the state with at least two spaces intervening. An envelope address is typed exactly the same as the inside address except for the vertical spacing of a three-line envelope address.

On the large envelope the address starts about 13 lines down from the top edge of the envelope and 5 spaces to the left of the horizontal center.

On the small envelope the address starts about 12 lines down from the top edge of the envelope and 5 to 8 spaces left of the horizontal center.

NOTATION TO POST OFFICE. Special notations to the post office such as *Airmail* or *Special Delivery* are typed in all capital letters directly below the space required for the stamp.

NOTATION TO ADDRESSEE. Instructions for the addressee such as *Personal, Please Forward,* or an attention line are typed in the lower-left corner of the envelope. The first letter of each principal word is capitalized.

RETURN ADDRESS. If the name and address of the sender are not printed in the upper-left corner of the envelope, this information must be typed beginning two lines down from the top and three spaces from the left.

### Folding and Inserting the Letter

The rules for folding and inserting letters are made for ease and convenience in removing the letter.

For the large envelope with the letter face up (1) slightly less than a third of the letter is folded from the bottom to the top, (2) the top third is folded down to within ½ inch of the bottom crease, and (3) the letter is inserted into the envelope with the last crease toward the bottom of the envelope and the open edge of the letter against the back of the envelope.

For the small envelope with the letter face up (1) the bottom half is folded up to within ½ inch of the top, (2) the right third is folded to the left, (3) the left third is folded over to within ½ inch of the last crease, and (4) the letter is inserted into the envelope with the last crease toward the bottom of the envelope and the open edge of the letter against the back of the envelope.

# *Secretarial Methods and Etiquette*

LONG LISTS may be made showing the duties performed by secretaries. The activities of an individual secretary will vary according to the size and type of business organization and the desires of the employer. In addition to activities related to business letters, a secretary may handle telephone calls, meet callers, make appointments, perform filing duties, write and type business reports, operate duplicating and calculating machines, keep financial records, prepare itineraries, and perform personal tasks for an employer.

The duties of a secretary may be summarized by saying that she does everything she can to assist her employer in his work by relieving him of details and performing each task he assigns.

## SECRETARIAL METHODS

Rules applying to many of the functions a secretary may be called upon to perform are helpful for reference. Rules will vary from one business firm to another, and the rules of a particular firm or employer must take precedence over any others. Some standard is important, however, in order to keep the work consistent and uniform.

**Business Reports or Manuscripts**

Business reports are typed on plain 8½ by 11-inch paper with at least one carbon copy. Only one side of the paper is used.

1. A title page covers the report and includes the title of the report, the name of the author, and the date.

2. All business reports are double spaced with paragraphs indented five spaces.

3. The report is typed with 1-inch top, bottom, and side margins except (a) the first page should have a 2-inch top margin, (b) an extra ½-inch margin is allowed at the top of all pages for a top-bound manuscript, or (c) an extra ½-inch margin is allowed at the left for a left-bound manuscript and the center point is adjusted accordingly.

4. A title is centered horizontally on the first page and typed in all capital letters and followed by a triple space.

5. All pages are numbered except the first. Page numbers for unbound or left-bound reports are typed in the upper-right corner even with the right margin and ½-inch from the top of the page. Page numbers for top-bound reports are centered ½-inch from the bottom of the page.

6. Quoted material of four or more lines is single spaced and indented five spaces from the left and right margins with quotation marks omitted. Shorter quotations are enclosed in quotation marks in the regular body of the report.

7. All words italicized in print are underscored.

8. Footnote references are identified by superior numbers a half line space above the line of writing. Footnotes may be numbered consecutively throughout the report or numbered starting anew on each page.

9. An underline 1½-inches long is typed a single space below the last line of the body on a page to divide the footnote from the body. This line is followed by a double space.

10. Footnotes are single spaced with a double space between footnotes.

11. Each footnote should be preceded by the superior number identifying it in the body. Footnotes must be on the page on which reference is made to the footnote. The first line of each footnote is indented five spaces.

12. Side headings are typed at the left margin, underscored, preceded by a triple space, and followed by a double space.

13. Paragraph headings are indented on the first line beginning a paragraph, underscored, and followed by a period.

**Filing**

Filing is the process of systematically classifying, arranging, and storing business papers so that the papers are readily available when needed. Filing may be done according to an alphabetical, numerical, geographical, or decimal system. The vast majority of all filing is based on the alphabetical system, however, and several rules for this system will be discussed here. The two steps in filing are indexing and alphabetizing.

INDEXING. Indexing is the arrangement of names for filing purposes. Each part of a name is an indexing unit. When indexing, some names remain as they appear and others need to be rearranged.

1. For indexing names of individuals, the surname (last name) is considered as the first unit, the first name or initial as the second unit, and the middle name or initial as the third unit.

| | *Index Units* | | |
|---|---|---|---|
| *Names* | *Unit 1* | *Unit 2* | *Unit 3* |
| Dixie E. Adams | Adams | Dixie | E. |
| L. Donald Braden | Braden | L. | Donald |
| William Mason Clay | Clay | William | Mason |

2. When firm names are made up of names of individuals, the order is the same as for individual names; otherwise, each word of a firm name is considered as it appears. Articles and prepositions appear in parentheses but are disregarded in indexing.

| | | | |
|---|---|---|---|
| The Jones Company | Jones | Company | (The) |
| Ralph Jones Co. | Jones | Ralph | Company |
| Jones & Jones | Jones (&) | Jones | |

ALPHABETIZING. Alphabetizing is the arranging of indexed units in alphabetical order.

1. The first unit of each name is considered first. Only when the first units are identical are the second units considered.

| | | |
|---|---|---|
| Gray | Allen | R. |
| Gray | Bryan | Frank |
| Gray | Bryan | Will |

2. When two or more names are of unequal length but contain the same letters up to a certain point, the shorter name comes first.

| | | |
|---|---|---|
| Sander | Ross | M. |
| Sanders | Dorothy | L. |
| Sanderson | Aaron | John |
| Smith | M. | May |
| Smith | Marilyn | M. |
| Smith | Marilyn | May |

3. A surname prefix is considered to be a part of the first indexing unit.

| | | |
|---|---|---|
| McArthur | Paul | S. |
| O'Dell | Robert | |
| von Hagen | Dale | Kelly |

4. Abbreviations are alphabetized as if they were spelled in full. For example, the names *St. James Church, Wm. Spar,* and *Willis Spar* are alphabetized as follows:

| | | |
|---|---|---|
| Saint | James | Church |
| Spar | William | |
| Spar | Willis | |

5. Titles are usually placed in parentheses at the end of a name and are not considered in filing. When a title is followed by a given name only, the title is considered as the first indexing unit.

| | | |
|---|---|---|
| Martin | J. | J. (Dr.) |
| Princess | Mary | |
| Sister | Mary | Martha |

6. Letters used as words are considered as words in alphabetizing. The firms *A A Store, B & B Co.*, and *OK Drug* are alphabetized as follows:

| | | |
|---|---|---|
| A | A | Store |
| B (&) | B | Company |
| O | K | Drug |

7. Hyphenated words are treated as one word. When a hyphen is used to join two individual names in a firm name, each name is considered an indexing unit.

| | | |
|---|---|---|
| Cole (-) | Clark | Company |
| Co-operative | Store (The) | |

8. Names of married women are alphabetized according to the married surname and then the given name. The husband's name is in parentheses below the name.

| | | |
|---|---|---|
| Ross | Shirley | D. (Mrs.) |
| (Mrs. Charles N. Ross) | | |

9. Numbers in names are alphabetized as though the numbers were spelled out in words. To illustrate, *A-1 Credit Co. and 12th Street Drug* are alphabetized as follows:

| | | |
|---|---|---|
| A (-) | One | Credit |
| Twelfth | Street | Drug |

**Numbers**

Many numbers are used in business writing, and a uniform guide for expressing numbers is important. In general, exact numbers are written in figures; but this rule has several modifications. Figures and symbols are always used in statistical or tabular work.

1. Numbers ten and under are spelled out in words; exact numbers over ten are written in figures. If numbers under and over ten are used together, the numbers must be kept uniform.

five boxes
12 cartons
15 boxes, 5 cartons, 40 crates

2. Approximate numbers are spelled out.

about fifty cars

3. Numbers beginning a sentence must be expressed in words even though there are other numbers in the sentence. Sometimes the sentence is more effective if revised so that the number will not come at the beginning.

Fifty-two men attended the meeting.
The meeting was attended by 52 men.

4. The shorter of two numbers forming one item is spelled out.

12 six-cent stamps
twelve 50-gallon drums

5. A comma is used to separate two unrelated groups of numbers coming together.

in 1967, 49 houses
on page 64, 36 items

6. Measures, weights, dimensions, and distances are always expressed in figures.

3 feet; 55 pounds; 7 miles

7. A number preceded by a noun is usually expressed in figures.

page 52; Volume 3

8. Isolated fractions are spelled out but a series of fractions is expressed in figures. Fractions on the typewriter must be kept uniform. In mixed numbers a space is left between a whole number and a *made* fraction.

one-half of the class
1/2, 3/4, 7/8
½, ¼
3 5/8

9. Compound numbers from 21 to 99 are hyphenated when expressed as words.

thirty-two; sixty-seven

10. Figures are used to express percentages. In business correspondence exact percentages are expressed with the % sign. With approximate percentages, the word *per cent* is spelled out.

12%; about 10 per cent

11. When the word *number* is followed by a figure in business correspondence, the abbreviation *No.* and a figure are used.

No. 6; No. 78

12. Numbers of four or more digits are divided with commas every third digit left of the decimal point. No comma is used in serial, invoice, policy, house, or ZIP-code numbers.

21,068
3,955,421
Policy No. 3740528

13. Plurals of most numbers are made by adding an *'s.*

ten's; 15's

ADDRESSES. Small numbered avenues and streets (ten and under) are spelled out. House numbers except house number *One* are expressed in figures. The use of *st, d,* or *th* following a street name is sometimes omitted.

One 87th Avenue
3048 23 Street
1230 East Second Avenue

DATES. When the month precedes the day, *st, d,* and *th* are not used. When the day is used alone or precedes the month, *st, d,* and *th* are used.

June 7; 4th of September; the 10th

MONEY. Money is expressed in figures. For even dollars the decimal is not used. The word *cents* is written out in ordinary work.

$352; 12 cents; $1.24

TIME. The hour is spelled out with *o'clock* and figures are used with *a.m.* or *p.m.*

ten o'clock; 10:30 a.m.; 7 p.m.; 12 noon

**Word Division**

Basic rules have been set up as a guide to word division. The use of a dictionary is often necessary to determine syllable identification; dictionaries, however, show all syllables and not the preferred division to be used in typing.

1. Words are divided between syllables only. Words of one syllable are not to be divided.

con-tain; knowl-edge; through; worked

2. Words of less than six letters should not be divided.

into

3. A one-letter syllable is not to be left alone at the beginning of a word.

*a*mount

4. A one- or two-letter syllable is not to be left alone at the end of a word.

teach*er*

5. A syllable without a vowel is not to be divided from the remainder of the word.

could*n't*

6. When a one-letter syllable comes within a word, the word is divided after the one-letter syllable unless it forms part of a word ending such as *able, ible,* or *ical*.

congrat*u*-late; feas-*i*ble

7. When two one-letter syllables come together within a word, the word is divided between the one-letter syllables.

grad*u*-*a*tion

8. Hyphenated words should not be divided except at the hyphen.

self-control

9. The division of proper names, abbreviations, and numbers should be avoided.

10. Words should not be divided at the end of two or more lines in succession, and a word at the end of a page is never divided.

## ETIQUETTE

Employers are quick to recognize that two major factors are related to the success of any secretary. These factors are: (1) the performance of her secretarial functions and (2) her relationships with those around her. No secretary can expect to succeed unless she is highly skilled in performing her secretarial duties and is pleasing in personality and appearance to those she meets.

The following check lists have been constructed both positively and negatively to serve as a self-analysis guide for any acting or prospective secretary.

**Qualities to Develop**

From the positive viewpoint, the secretary should ask herself, "Do I have these qualities?"

PERFORMANCE QUALITIES

1. Highly developed skill in the secretarial functions.
2. A good knowledge of the functions of business.
3. Attentiveness to listen to orders, to grasp them, and to follow through.
4. Accuracy in performing all tasks.
5. Intelligence and common sense.
6. Good judgment and logic.
7. Alertness to see what needs to be done.
8. Ambition to put in a full day of work.
9. Initiative in going ahead with any assigned task and in making plans or changes.
10. Dependability and reliability to do a job and to do it well.
11. Efficiency in planning and performing tasks.
12. Willingness to learn a new skill or to do a new job.
13. Orderliness and a systematic way of doing the work.
14. Trustworthiness; ability to keep information confidential.
15. Resourcefulness to find the correct answer or the correct way to perform a task.
16. Perseverance in accomplishing a task and in meeting the demands of an employer.
17. Determination to please an employer.
18. Impersonal attitude; an understanding of the wishes of an employer rather than one's own.
19. Confidence in the work performed.
20. Acceptance of criticism.

HUMAN-RELATIONS QUALITIES

1. Femininity.
2. Dignity.
3. Poise.
4. Cleanliness in body and dress.
5. Conservative dress; neat and quiet apparel, hair, make-up, and jewelry.
6. Ability to keep personal problems carefully in the background.
7. Good manners.
8. Good posture.
9. Well-modulated voice.
10. Understanding of people.
11. Friendliness.
12. Tact.
13. Self-control.
14. Calmness.
15. Confidence.
16. Courtesy.
17. Patience.
18. Cheerfulness.
19. Sense of humor.
20. Sincerity.
21. Integrity.
22. Honesty.
23. Discretion.
24. Promptness.
25. Consideration of others.
26. Respect for others.
27. Co-operative attitude.
28. Loyalty to employer and his business.
29. Ability to accept personal criticism.
30. Objectivity.

**Qualities to Avoid**

The negative approach also may be used in a self-analytical check list. The following list has been constructed to include some of the things to be avoided by any secretary. The secretary should ask herself, "Am I guilty of any of these qualities or actions?"

1. Brusqueness or unwomanliness.
2. Over-femininity or coyness.
3. Coming to work frilly, over-dressed, or highly perfumed.
4. Habitual lateness.
5. Dashing out when the bell rings.
6. Performing personal chores such as reading, writing letters, or making telephone calls while on the job.
7. Accepting personal telephone calls or personal callers at the office.
8. Grooming at the desk.
9. Eating at the desk.
10. Chewing gum.
11. Moodiness.
12. Blaming other workers.
13. Being rude to telephone callers.
14. Being rude to personal callers.
15. Telling too much to callers.
16. Talking much of the time.
17. Bringing personal problems to the office.
18. Bearing sad tales to the office.
19. Gossiping or telling rumors; being a troublemaker.
20. Using poor grammar.
21. Talking shop off the job.
22. Snooping in the affairs or desk of another; eavesdropping; reading over the shoulder of another.
23. Borrowing from fellow workers.
24. Whistling, humming, or singing.
25. Crying or giggling.

# FORMS OF ADDRESS

| Person Being Addressed | Envelope Address | Salutation | | In Speaking |
|---|---|---|---|---|
| | | *Formal* | *Less Formal* | |
| **Ambassador (American)** | The Honorable (full name), American Ambassador, (city and country) | Sir (*or* Madam): | My dear Mr. (*or* Madam) Ambassador: | Your Excellency *or* Mr. Ambassador (*or* Madam Ambassador) |
| **Ambassador (Foreign)** | His (*or* Her) Excellency (full name), Ambassador of (country), Washington, D.C. (Zip Code.) | Sir (*or* Madam): *or* Your Excellency: | My dear Mr. (*or* Madam) Ambassador: | Your Excellence *or* Mr. Ambassador (*or* Madam Ambassador) |
| **Archbishop (Roman Catholic)** | The Most Reverend (full name), Archbishop of (city), (city, State, and Zip Code.) | Your Excellency: *or* Most Reverend Sir: | Most Reverend and dear Sir: | Your Excellency |
| **Bishop (Methodist)** | Bishop (full name), (city, State, and Zip Code.) | Dear Bishop (surname): | | Bishop (surname) |
| **Bishop (Protestant Episcopal)** | The Right Reverend (full name), Bishop of (diocese), (city, State, and Zip Code.) | Right Reverend and dear Sir: | Dear Bishop (surname): | Bishop (surname) |
| **Bishop (Roman Catholic)** | The Most Reverend (full name), Bishop of (diocese), (city, State, and Zip Code.) | Your Excellency: or Most Reverend Sir: | Dear Bishop (surname): | Bishop (surname) |
| **Cabinet Officer of the U.S.** | The Honorable (full name), (title), Washington, D.C. (Zip Code.) | Sir (*or* Madam): | My dear Mr. (*or* Madam) Secretary: | Mr. (*or* Madam) Secretary |
| **State** | 20520 | | | |
| **Treasury** | 20220 | | | |
| **Defense** | 20301 | | | |
| **Justice** | 20530 | | | |
| **Post Office** | 20260 | | | |
| **Interior** | 20240 | | | |
| **Agriculture** | 20250 | | | |
| **Commerce** | 20230 | | | |
| **Labor** | 20210 | | | |
| **Health, Education, and Welfare** | 20201 | | | |
| **Housing and Urban Affairs** | 20410 | | | |
| **Transportation** | 20590 | | | |
| **Cardinal (Roman Catholic)** | His Eminence (given name) Cardinal (surname), Archbishop of (city), (city, State, and Zip Code.) | Your Eminence: | | Your Eminence |
| **Common Form (Man)** | Mr. (full name) | My dear Mr. (surname): *or* My dear Sir: *in plural,* Gentlemen: | Dear Mr. (surname): *or* Dear Sir: | |
| **Common Form (Woman)** | Mrs. (*or* Miss) (full name) | My dear Mrs. (*or* Miss) (surname): *or* My dear Madam: *in plural,* Ladies: *or* Mesdames: | Dear Mrs. (*or* Miss) (surname): *or* Dear Madam: | |
| **Congressman** | The Honorable (full name), House of Representatives, Washington, D.C. 20515 | Sir (*or* Madam): | My dear Mr. (*or* Mrs. *or* Miss) (surname): | Mr. (*or* Mrs. *or* Miss) (surname) |
| **Consul (American or other)** | (full name), Esq., American (*or* other) Consul, (city and country, or State and Zip Code.) | Sir: *or* My dear Sir: | My dear Mr. Consul: | Mr. (surname) |

| *Person Being Addressed* | *Envelope Address* | *Salutation* | | *In Speaking* |
|---|---|---|---|---|
| | | *Formal* | *Less Formal* | |
| **Doctor (of Philosophy, Medicine, Divinity, etc.)** | (full name), Ph.D., M.D., D.D., etc. *or* Dr. (full name) | My dear Dr. (surname): *or* My dear Sir: | | Dr. (surname) |
| **Governor (of a State)** | The Honorable (full name), Governor of (State), (capital city, State, and Zip Code.) | Sir: | My dear Governor (surname): | Governor (surname) |
| **Judge (see also Supreme Court)** | The Honorable (full name), (name of court), (city, State, and Zip Code.) | Sir (*or* Madam): | My dear Judge (surname): | Judge (surname) |
| **Mayor** | The Honorable (full name), Mayor of (city), (city, State, and Zip Code.) | Sir (*or* Madam): | My dear Mr. (*or* Madam) Mayor: *or* My dear Mayor (surname): | Mr. (*or* Madam) Mayor |
| **Minister (Protestant)** | The Reverend (full name) (address, city, State, and Zip Code.) | My dear Mr. (*or* Dr., *if a D.D.*) (surname): | | Mr. (*or* Dr. *or, if a Lutheran,* Pastor) (surname) |
| **Monsignor (Roman Catholic)** | The Right Reverend Monsignor (full name), (city, State, and Zip Code.) | Right Reverend Monsignor (surname): | | Monsignor (surname) |
| **Nun** | Sister (religious name), (initials of her order) | My dear Sister: | Dear Sister (religious name): | Sister (religious name) |
| **President (of the United States)** | The President, The White House, Washington, D.C. 20500 | Sir: | My dear Mr. President: | Mr. President |
| **Priest (Roman Catholic)** | The Reverend (full name) (address, city, State, and Zip Code.) | Reverend and dear Sir: | My dear Father (surname): | Father (surname) |
| **Rabbi** | Rabbi (full name), (address, city, State, and Zip Code.) | My dear Rabbi (*or* Dr., *if the holder of a doctor's degree*) (surname): | | Rabbi (*or* Dr.) (surname) |
| **Representative (of a State legislature)** | The Honorable (full name), Member of Assembly (or other name of the legislature), (capital city, State, and Zip Code.) | Sir (*or* Madam): | My dear Mr. (*or* Mrs. *or* Miss) (surname): | Mr. (*or* Mrs. *or* Miss) (surname) |
| **Senator (of the United States)** | The Honorable (full name), United States Senate, Washington, D.C. 20510 | Sir (*or* Madam): | My dear Senator (surname): | Senator (surname) *or* Mr. (*or* Madam) Senator |
| **Senator (of a State)** | The Honorable (full name), (State) Senate, (capital city and State) | Sir (*or* Madam): | My dear Senator (surname): | Senator (surname) |
| **Supreme Court (Associate Justice)** | The Honorable (full name), Associate Justice of the United States Supreme Court, Washington, D.C. 20543 | Sir: | My dear Mr. Justice: | Mr. Justice |
| **Supreme Court (Chief Justice)** | The Honorable (full name), Chief Justice of the United States, Washington, D.C. 20543 | Sir: | My dear Mr. Chief Justice: | Mr. Chief Justice |
| **Vice President (of the United States)** | The Vice President, Washington, D.C. 20501 | Sir: | My dear Mr. Vice President: | Mr. Vice President |

# DICTIONARY OF BUSINESS TERMS

THE PURPOSE of this Dictionary is to supplement the word list of the main Dictionary for the specific objective of aiding those who are interested in business. Due to limitations of space some terms are omitted; however, the Dictionary contains many of the most frequently used and encountered business terms. Information pertaining to pronunciation of these words may be located in the word list of the main Dictionary.

## A

**abandon:** to terminate employment; give up possession of personal property with intent to disown title.

**abate:** to take possession without right because the estate of the testator is inadequate to make payment in full.

**abeyance:** a state of suspension; as settlement of an estate is held in abeyance pending certain developments, such as proof of ownership.

**abstract of title:** a set of notes showing the history of transfers of ownership of real estate.

**acceptance:** **1.** endorsement of a bill of exchange by the person on whom it is drawn committing him to payment when due; the endorsement is written on the face of the bill with the word "accepted" accompanying the signature; the acceptor becomes responsible for payment; in event of his failure to pay, the original maker of the bill is responsible; thus, the acceptance is a transaction between these two parties. **2.** an acknowledgement of receipt, as of goods, by a buyer. **3.** an acknowledgement of agreement, as to a contract, thus binding the purchaser. *See also* bank acceptance; trade acceptance.

**acceptor:** a person who signs a promise to pay a draft or bill of exchange; also accepter.

**accessory after the fact:** one who is not present but knows of the commission of a felony and contributes as an assistant to the felon.

**accessory before the fact:** one who aids and abets in the commission of a crime but is not present when the crime is committed.

**accommodation party:** a person who endorses commercial paper to assist another in securing credit.

**accord and satisfaction:** a new contract permitting the substituting of a performance different from that which is called for in the original contract and the performance of such.

**account:** **1.** an itemized record of transactions, showing credits and debits. **2.** a business relation, especially one in which credit is used; charge account.

**accounting:** the method of classifying, recording, and summarizing business transactions in terms of money and reporting the results.

**account payable:** liability to a creditor, usually an open account, may be limited to unpaid amounts for goods and services purchased.

**accrued dividend:** loosely, any unpaid dividend; strictly, a dividend not due until specifically declared.

**accrued expense:** charge incurred but not yet paid, as wages and other overhead for any period.

**accrued income:** income that has been earned but has not yet been received.

**accrued interest:** interest figured at a given time between the regular dates for payment; when a security is sold at a stated price "plus accrued interest," the buyer has to pay that price and the interest from the last interest date to the date of delivery; he is recompensed by receiving interest for the full term.

**acid-test:** ratio of the total of cash, trade receivables, and marketable securities to the current liabilities of a business firm.

**action:** legal proceeding to enforce a right.

**Act of God:** the forces of nature which lead to a property loss, the loss could not be prevented by reasonable care; e.g., flood, lightning, earthquake.

**addendum:** something added or to be added.

**adjudicate:** **1.** to submit (a contested matter) to judicial settlement. **2.** to settle (such a matter).

**administered price:** a per unit price established or strongly influenced by a controlling agent; e.g., government administered ceiling price and support price.

**administrator:** the person appointed by the court to administer the estate of a deceased person.

**ADP:** Automatic Data Processing. *See* processing, automatic data.

**advisory opinion:** an opinion given by the courts in some States when no actual controversy exists before the court.

**affidavit:** a statement made under oath and in writing.

**AFL-CIO:** American Federation of Labor and Congress of Industrial Organizations, merged in 1955.

**agency:** a relationship whereby one person (the principal) delegates the authority to another person (the agent) to make a contract for the principal with a third person.

**agent:** one who is authorized to represent the principal in an agency relationship.

**allocate:** to charge an item or group of items of income or expense to an activity, or operation, in accordance with some measure of apportionment.

**amortization:** the gradual using up of an amount over a period of time; e.g., the periodic writedown of an unexpired insurance premium.

**analyst:** a person skilled in the definition and development of techniques for the solving of problems with a computer.

**annexation:** the attaching of personal property to real property in such a manner as to cause the personal property to become real property.

**annual interest:** interest due yearly, rather than at more or less frequent intervals.

**annuity:** an agreement whereby money or other property is paid to the insurer, and the insured or other designated person is to receive fixed payments at a later time.

**antitrust acts:** statutes prohibiting contracts in restraint of trade; e.g., the Sherman Antitrust Act of 1890.

**appeal:** a request to transfer a case to a reviewing court to determine the correctness of the decision of the lower court or administrative agency.

**appraisal:** an estimate of the value of property or assets.

**appraise:** to examine and make an estimate of value.

**appreciation:** increase in value.

**appropriation:** an authorized expenditure which has limitations as to amount, period, and purpose; a formal approval in advance of the appropriation.

**appurtenance:** something added to a more important thing, may be an easement permitting the right of way over one piece of land to pass with another piece of land.

**arbitration:** the settlement of matters of difference between contending parties by one or more arbitrators by whose decision the parties agree to be bound.

**array:** the placing of a group of numbers in order; may be increasing or decreasing in size.

**arrears:** sums due but not paid; as an overdue account is in arrears; a delinquent customer is in arrears.

**arson:** the malicious burning of another's buildings or property, or of one's own so as to collect insurance.

**ask (ed or ing) price:** the price at which the owner formally offers to sell or exchange.

**assessed valuation:** value placed upon property by an official assessor, as for determination of tax; it is commonly less than the true or market value.

**asset:** any owned physical object or right having monetary value.

**assignee:** the person to whom any asset, as a contract, right, or security, has been made over.

**assignment:** the making over to another of ownership or interest in any property or right; it may be made to an individual person, a corporation, or one's creditors in general; if acceptable to the creditors, in shares proportioned to the claims of each, it saves the cost of bankruptcy proceedings; but if it is not satisfactory to all the creditors, any of them may override the assignment by instituting bankruptcy action.

**assume:** to take over, as bonds of one company by another, as in case of a merger or a transfer of control.

**at a premium:** at a price above par; said of the price of a security.

**at par:** a price or quotation which

is identical with the face amount of the security.
**attachment:** 1. seizure of property or person by legal writ. 2. the writ authorizing such seizure.
**auction:** a public sale of property to the highest bidder, usually after a notice has been given to the general public.
**auctioneer:** one who conducts the public sale of property at auctions.
**audit:** the examination of records the objective of which is substantiating their accuracy.
**auditor:** one who audits records kept by others.
**audit trail:** a system of tracing a machine report back to the original source of data; a step by step procedure is necessary.
**automatic data processing equipment:** a machine, or series of interconnected machines, which uses electronic circuitry to the main computing element to perform arithmetic and/or logical operations by means of internally stored or externally controlled programmed instruction and does the operations automatically.
**automation:** the use of automatic processes; the development and application of processes to work in an automatic manner.
**available assets:** unencumbered resources, especially those that can be converted into money through sale or can serve as security for a new obligation.

## B

**bad check laws:** statutes making it unlawful to issue a bad check with the intent to defraud.
**bad debt:** a receivable determined to be uncollectible in part or in whole.
**bailment:** goods delivered in trust against an obligation and to be returned when that obligation is ended.
**balance of trade:** excess of a country's exports over its imports (favorable balance) or of imports over exports (unfavorable balance); the terms favorable and unfavorable are based upon the flow of gold into or out of a country.
**balance sheet:** a statement showing the financial position of a firm or unit at a given time by disclosing assets, liabilities, and the equity of owners.
**bank acceptance:** acceptance of a bill of exchange by a bank or other credit-loaning institution.
**bank balance:** the amount to a depositor's credit in a bank; the amount to which a bank or trust company is obligated to the depositor and must hold subject to his order.
**bank discount:** interest deducted by a bank from a loan when the loan is made; it is equal to the normal interest from the date of the loan to the date of the final payment.
**bank draft:** an order by one bank for payment by another.
**bank note:** a bank's promise to pay bearer on demand, at face value; these notes circulate as money; in 1935 the privilege of issuing such notes was greatly restricted.
**bank of deposit:** any bank, and in most of the States any trust company, which accepts deposits of money subject to order by check.
**bank paper:** bank notes or commercial paper which can be handled by banks, as notes subject to discount.
**bank statement:** 1. a bank's public report of its condition. 2. a detailed report of financial condition given to a bank by an applicant for a loan. 3. popularly, a bank's summary of activity in a depositor's account for a certain period.
**bearer:** the person in possession of commercial paper which is payable to bearer or an instrument of title which directs delivery to bearer.
**bear market:** a period of sustained downward tendency in prices on stock or commodity exchanges.
**bench warrant:** order by a court that a certain person be brought before it.
**beneficiary:** one to whom the proceeds of an insurance policy are payable; one who enjoys the property which is held in trust, or who is given property by a will.
**bid:** an offer by a prospective purchaser to pay a definite price for property.
**billing terms:** conditions, as of time and rate of discount, on which an order is accepted.
**bill of lading:** a document for the carriage and delivery of goods.
**bill of sale:** a legally formal paper attesting transfer of title to goods or chattels and safeguarding the buyer in his ownership thereof.
**binary:** a situation in which there are only two alternatives; e.g., the binary number system, conventionally using zero (0) and one (1).
**BIT:** an abbreviation for binary digit; the unit of information capacity of a storage device.
**blank endorsement:** endorsement of a check or other commercial paper with signature only, making the paper payable to bearer, not to a named individual or his order.
**blue-sky law:** any law protecting the investing public against exploitation by promoters to whom "the sky's the limit."
**board of directors:** individuals elected by the stockholders and responsible under corporation law for supervising the operation and affairs of a corporation.
**bond:** 1. in commerce, *a)* an agreement by an agency holding taxable goods that taxes on them will be paid before they are sold. *b)* the condition of such goods. *c)* an insurance contract by which a bonding agency guarantees payment of a specified sum to an employer, etc., in the event of a financial loss caused him by the act of a specified employee or by some contingency over which the payee has no control. 2. in finance, an interest-bearing certificate issued by a government or business, promising to pay the holder a specified sum on a specified date; it is a common means of raising capital. 3. in law, *a)* a written obligation under seal to pay specified sums, or to do or not do specified things. *b)* a person acting as surety for another's action; payer of bail. *c)* an amount paid as surety or bail.
**bond expense (and discount):** the interest or service charge usually expressed as a percentage of principal; the excess of the face amount of a bond over the net sales receipt. Bond issue cost is usually absorbed as an expense in the period in which it is incurred.
**bond premium:** the net amount received in excess of face value.
**bookkeeper:** the business worker who keeps the records and may make the financial reports which reflect conditions of the business.
**book of account:** any ledger, register, or journal that forms a part of a system of accounts.
**book of final entry:** a book of record into which money amounts are posted or transferred; generally referred to as a ledger.
**book of original entry:** the source book for postings or transfers to the ledger; business transactions are recorded first in the book of original entry.
**books closed:** 1. designating a period when the books of a corporation are closed, to provide a period of adjustment during which the list of stockholders is checked to determine who is entitled to vote in a stockholder's meeting, after which the books are opened again to record transfers of shares. 2. designating a period when the books are closed because an issue of shares has been fully subscribed and no more orders can be taken.
**book value:** 1. the worth of stock or any asset as shown in the financial records of the company that issues or owns it, as distinguished from par value or market value; it reflects the amount of capital invested per share of the stock. 2. the value of a company's assets as carried on its books.
**breakpoint:** a checkpoint in a computer program that permits print out, visual check, or other analyzing generally used in the debugging process.
**broker:** one who buys and sells for others on commission.
**budget period:** the time period covered by a budget; may be a month, quarter, or year.
**bug:** a malfunction; mistake in the design of the routine or computer.
**bull market:** a condition of sustained activity and rising prices in a stock market.
**buyer's market:** a state of the market in which the buyer is at an advantage, because the supply is greater than demand. *See* seller's market.
**buyer's option:** a buyer's privilege, when so stipulated in an agreement, to postpone completion of an order over a certain period but to demand delivery, should he so desire, on stated notice at any time within that period.
**buy on margin:** to buy (stocks, etc.) on credit established by a deposit

with a broker who advances the rest.

**by-laws:** rules adopted by shareholders establishing the general method for carrying out corporate functions. By-laws must agree with State statutes and the articles of incorporation.

## C

**call: 1.** demand for payment. **2.** privilege of demanding fulfillment of an order at a given price within a stated period of time. **3.** to redeem, as an issue of bonds, before maturity.

**capital:** money available for investment; wealth used to finance production.

**capital goods:** goods used productively, as raw materials, machinery, buildings, etc.; producer's goods distinguished from consumer's goods.

**capitalize: 1.** to calculate the present value of (a periodical payment, annuity, income, etc.); convert (an income, etc.) into one payment or a sum the equivalent to the computed present value. **2.** to convert (floating debt) into stock or shares.

**capital stock:** the monetary value assigned to the outstanding stock of a corporation. Also the account utilized for par or stated value.

**card control:** a card that contains input data for specific application in a general routine.

**card, eighty column:** a punch card having columns capable of representing 80 characters.

**card, programmed:** the potential ability of being programmed by punch cards.

**card, punch:** heavy paper of constant shape and size which is suitable for punching in a pattern that has meaning and may be handled mechanically.

**carrying charge:** a percentage paid by a customer making deferred payments on his debt, to cover interest on the seller's money, costs of service, etc., as in purchase of stock on margin or of goods on the installment plan.

**carte blanche:** a signed paper, as an order or other authorization, to be filled in as the holder may please.

**cash basis:** a basis for keeping accounting records where income and expense are recorded on the books when received and paid without regard to the period to which they apply.

**cashier's check:** a check drawn by a bank against itself and carrying the signature of the cashier.

**cash sale:** sale of goods for immediate payment, or payment in full within a certain short period of time.

**cash surrender value:** the amount recoverable by the insured if he cancels his insurance policy.

**certificate of deposit:** a paper given by a bank acknowledging receipt of money to be held for the customer, subject to his demand, but not to be treated as a checking account; the holder of the certificate is not regarded as a depositor.

**certified check:** a check by a depositor on which the bank by endorsement guarantees payment.

**charter:** a written instrument from the government authorizing the existence of a corporation.

**chattel mortgage:** a lien on personal property, taken to secure a loan or to enable seizure and sale of property bought on the installment plan should the buyer default.

**check:** a bill of exchange drawn on a bank and payable on demand.

**checkpoint:** a point in a machine run at which a temporary halt is made in order to make a magnetic tape record of what has occurred up to that point. Checkpoints are utilized in connection with a restart routine to minimize reprocessing time.

**close corporation:** a corporation whose stock is owned and controlled by only a few persons, as a family group.

**closed shop:** a firm in which only union members are employed.

**COBAL:** Common Business Oriented Language; a specific language having a standard form by which data processing procedures may be described.

**coder:** a person who prepares instructional sequences from flow charts which have been prepared by someone else.

**coinsurance:** insurance on commercial property in which two or more insurers (coinsurers) carry the risk in proportion to the coverage of the full property value which each has insured; sometimes the insured stands as a coinsurer in assuming part of the risk.

**collateral:** property, such as securities, pledged by a borrower to protect a lender.

**collator:** equipment used to collate decks of cards or other units into a sequence.

**collective bargaining:** a process by which employment terms are worked out through negotiations with employer and the bargaining representative of the employee.

**commercial paper:** negotiable instruments, such as drafts and notes, issued by business houses.

**commission broker:** one who buys or sells on commission.

**commission house:** a firm that handles transactions, as purchase or sale of securities or goods, for others, on a percentage basis.

**commission merchant:** a person who buys or sells goods for others and is paid a commission by them.

**common carrier:** a person or company engaged in the business of transporting passengers or goods, or both; railroads, ships, ferries, streetcar lines and bus lines, airlines, and trucking systems are common carriers; each State regulates their operation within its own boundaries, and the Federal Interstate Commerce Commission fixes rates and rules for operation across State lines; this supervision is exercised in the interest both of the carriers and of the public.

**common law:** the unwritten law based on established custom; it is now largely regularized by legislative definition.

**common stock:** stock which does not carry the privileges granted to holders of preferred issues, and which shares in the profits of a business only after the claims of the preferred have been satisfied; income on preferred stock is usually a fixed percentage of par or face value; that on common stock is proportionate to earnings and may be very high or nothing at all.

**computer:** a piece of equipment possessing the ability to accept data, apply prescribed processes, and supply results based upon the processes used.

**consideration:** that which is given or promised by the parties to a contract; it may be money or another thing of value, or an action of some kind.

**consignee:** the person to whom a shipment of goods is addressed.

**consignment: 1.** an order of goods shipped. **2.** commitment of goods, especially to an agent or distributor, for sale.

**consignor:** one who ships goods, as to an agent or distributor; the maker of a consignment.

**consolidation:** the joining of two or more business houses under one management; technically distinguished from a merger in the details of financing and reorganizing.

**contract:** an agreement between two or more people to do something; a contract follows an offer and acceptance and implies a legal means and purpose, as well as a sufficient consideration.

**convertible bond:** bond subject to surrender in exchange for stock, either by act of the issuing company or of the holder, or as required under stated conditions.

**copyright:** the exclusive legal right of an author to publish and sell his literary work for a period of 28 years, with a renewal right for 28 additional years.

**corporation:** a group of persons legally empowered to act as a single personality in business.

**co-signor:** a person who signs a promissory note in addition to the maker, thus becoming responsible for the obligation if the maker should default; also called co-maker.

**cost plus:** a method of establishing purchase price by providing that the buyer pay the seller his cost plus a stated percentage of cost as profit.

**court of equity:** a court having a chancery or equity jurisdiction; it is not limited by the common law.

**CPU:** Central Processing Unit; consists of arithmetic units, special register groups, and main storage unit.

**credit instrument:** a paper (aside from paper currency) acknowledging obligation to pay, as a check or draft, a note, a bond coupon, etc.

**cumulative preferred stock:** a stock on which successive unpaid dividends accrue and have to be paid before any dividend can be paid on the common stock.

**cumulative voting:** a method of voting for the election of the board of directors of a corporation whereby the stockholder is allowed as many votes for each share of stock as there are directors on the board.
**current asset:** a resource that can be converted into cash quickly and easily.
**current expense:** a day to day cost of doing business.
**current liability:** an obligation attendant upon the day to day conduct of business, such as wages.

### D

**deed:** a paper in legal form conveying ownership in real estate.
**deferred dividend:** a dividend, as on cumulative preferred stock, not paid when due but permitted to accrue.
**demand deposit:** a deposit in a bank subject to withdrawal at any time; the usual form of checking account.
**demurrage:** a charge made by the carrier for excessive unloading time by the consignor or consignee.
**depletion:** the using up of a natural resource; e.g., stone, timber.
**deposit slip:** the printed form supplied by a bank on which the depositor makes an itemized statement of each deposit.
**depreciation:** expired usefulness; caused by wear and tear, inadequacy, and obsolescence.
**discount rate:** percentage at which commercial paper is discounted by the banks.
**dishonor:** the refusal to pay a bill at maturity or the refusal to accept a bill of exchange.
**disposable income:** (governmental accounting) personal income less income and other taxes paid by a person; the balance is disposable income and is available as consumption or savings.
**double taxation:** taxation of one person or property by two governments, as State and Federal, or by two States, as where a man lives in one State on income derived from property in another State.
**draft:** a written order by which one person directs another to pay a certain sum to a third person, charging it to the maker of the draft; a check is a form of draft.
**drawee:** the person who is requested to pay the amount of money stated on a draft.
**drawer:** the person drawing or issuing the bill of exchange.
**drawing account:** an account showing money paid for expenses or as advances on salary, commissions, etc., as to a salesman; the privilege of such an account.
**drop shipment:** an order for which the goods go to the retailer directly from the factory but the bill comes to him from the distributor or wholesale agent from whom he would normally receive the goods.
**drum, magnetic:** a magnetic cylinder which stores binary data on or near its surface.
**due bill:** a paper given to a customer who returns ordered goods, granting him credit for the amount against a future purchase.
**duress:** illegal conduct which deprives one from his own free will.

### E

**easement:** a right to certain uses of another's land, as of passage over it to a highway.
**EDP:** Electronic Data Processing; the processing of data primarily by electronic equipment.
**eleemosynary corporation:** a charitable or benevolent corporation.
**eminent domain:** the power of certain kinds of corporations and the government to take private property against the objection of the owner.
**encumbrance:** a lien against property held by a third person.
**endorse:** to place a signature on the back of a paper, as a check or note, in order to cash it or to assume responsibility for its payment.
**endorsee:** one to whom a note or check is made over through endorsement by its holder.
**endorsement:** the act of writing on the back of a check, note, etc., or that which is written, as the signature of a payee, by which money or property is made over to someone. *See* blank endorsement; qualified endorsement.
**endorser:** the person who owns commercial paper and transfers such to another by placing his signature on the back of the paper in order to assume responsibility for its payment.
**entry:** **1.** an item of record in an account. **2.** the officially recognized and recorded arrival of a ship or goods at a port.
**equipment, tabulating:** machines using punched cards; frequently called tabulator equipment or Punch Card Machine (PCM).
**equity:** **1.** a body of laws supplementary to statute law, designed to correct injustices due to legal technicality. **2.** a participation in ownership, as the share of a part owner.
**escrow:** a fund or deposit delivered to an escrow holder who makes final delivery when a specified condition has been satisfied.
**estate:** the interest one has in property.
**estoppel:** the prevention of a person from asserting a fact or doing an act inconsistent with previous acts or declarations.
**exchange:** **1.** to make an exchange; barter; trade. **2.** in finance, to pass in exchange; as, the currency of this country exchanges at par. **3.** the checks, drafts, etc., presented for exchange and settlement between banks in a clearinghouse. **4.** in law, a contract by which parties agree to exchange one thing for another.
**excise tax:** a government tax on goods made and sold within its domain, as the Federal taxes on domestic liquors, automobiles, cigarettes, etc.; differentiated from customs duties or tariffs on imported goods.
**exports:** the goods or merchandise exported; especially, all of the goods sent from one country to another or others.
**ex post facto:** acting backward; retrospective; an ex post facto law is one that can be applied to offenses charged as occurring before the law's enactment.

### F

**factor:** an agent to whom goods are consigned for sale.
**fair market value:** value determined by honest bargaining between buyers and sellers.
**featherbedding:** the demanding of money for services not performed and not to be performed.
**Federal Deposit Insurance Corporation:** a government corporation set up to protect bank depositors; all deposits are insured against loss, theft, etc., up to a limit of $15,000 for each account.
**Federal Reserve Bank:** any of the twelve district banks of the Federal Reserve System.
**Federal Reserve Board:** a board composed of seven (originally eight) members which directs the Federal Reserve System; in 1935, the name was changed to Board of Governors of the Federal Reserve System.
**Federal Reserve System:** a centralized banking system in the U.S. consisting of twelve Federal Reserve Banks, each acting as the central bank for its district, and over 10,000 affiliated banks; it was established by the Federal Reserve Act of 1913 to develop a currency which would fluctuate with business demands and to regulate the member banks of each district.
**Federal Securities Act:** a law that has the purpose of protecting the public from fraudulent securities.
**Federal Securities Exchange Act:** a law which prohibits improper practices on the part of security exchanges.
**Federal Trade Commission Act:** a law which prohibits unfair methods of competition in interstate commerce.
**fee simple:** absolute ownership; ownership of property without limitations of heirs to whom it must descend.
**felony:** a term used to describe a crime as being more serious than a misdemeanor.
**fiduciary:** **1.** a trustee of an estate or director of a corporation. **2.** a person engaged in a confidential financial capacity, as an agent.
**fiscal year:** the year by which accounts are settled or balanced; for most individuals their fiscal year ends on December 31; for the Federal government, on June 30.
**fixed asset:** a tangible asset held for use in the production of other goods and/or services; any capital asset.
**fixture:** personal property which has been attached to real property in such a manner that it has become a part of the real property.
**f.o.b.:** free on board; used to indicate that the seller provides transportation from the factory to steamship or railroad cars, after which the buyer pays all carriage charges.

**foreclosure:** legal action for sale of mortgaged property to enable the mortgagee to recover his loaned money in case of default by the mortgagor; if the sale realizes more than the claim, the surplus goes to the holders of secondary liens; if there are none, it is paid to the mortgagor; foreclosure sales may also be held on pledged property other than real estate, and by a government, local, State, or Federal, for unpaid taxes on land and building.

**foreign corporation:** a corporation that is incorporated under the laws of another State.

**FORTRAN:** a computer programming language created for problems which can be expressed in algebraic notation.

**franchise: 1.** right to operate a business in public service, granted by a government; as a bus franchise. **2.** the right to market a product, often exclusive in a specified area, as granted by the manufacturer.

**fraud:** the making of a deceitful statement with the intent to cause another to rely upon the statement and be injured.

**funded debt:** indebtedness in the form of long-term obligations; debt is frequently funded by transforming a number of short-term issues into long-term, interest-bearing bonds.

**fungible: 1.** in law, designating goods, as grain, coffee, etc., any unit or part of which can replace another unit, as in discharging a debt; capable of being used in place of another. **2.** a fungible thing.

**futures:** securities or commodities bought and sold for delayed delivery; frequently done as speculation, selling of futures is a factor of business stability, enabling manufacturers to price their products with due regard to future cost of raw materials.

## G

**going concern:** a basic concept in accounting, the firm is considered to be of a continuing nature as opposed to the termination and winding-up of business affairs.

**goods in process:** (work in process) a partly finished unit of production; raw material on which some labor has been utilized in the course of converting or assembling the output.

**goodwill:** favorable attitude of the buying public toward a business constituting an intangible asset in valuing the business; sometimes written good will.

**gross income:** total receipts, without deductions; distinguished from net income.

**gross profit:** the amount by which receipts on sales exceed the cost of the goods, without deduction of costs of running the business.

**guaranty:** an undertaking to pay the debt of another or perform some duty, in case the primary debtor fails to pay or perform.

## H

**hardware:** the equipment forming a computer.

**hedge:** to buy or sell, in order to balance threatened loss in other transactions.

**heir:** the person who succeeds by statutes to receive the estate of a decedent when no will exists.

**heuristic:** relating to trial and error methods of problem solution.

**holder in due course:** one to whom a check, note, or other bill of exchange has come through earlier endorsements without protest or notice of defect.

**holding company:** a company organized to control subsidiary companies through possession of their stock issues.

## I

**IDP:** Integrated Data Processing; a system which treats all data processing requirements to accomplish a sequence of data as a whole.

**implied contract:** a contract where intention is not expressly mainfested by direct words but is gathered or implied from the facts.

**imports:** goods brought into one country from another or into one region from another.

**income and expense account** (profit and loss account): a summary ledger account to which the balances are periodically transferred from income and expenses. The balance in this account represents net income or net loss for the period.

**indenture: 1.** a formal legal agreement, of which identical copies are held by each party; originally, the two copies had correspondingly notched edges. **2.** an official, authenticated list, inventory, etc.

**indictment:** the formal written accusation of a crime as stated by a grand jury.

**indirect cost:** cost not directly incurred or identified with the production of certain goods or services, but is a necessary part of the production process.

**industrial union:** a labor union composed of members of an industry, regardless of specialized occupation; also called vertical union.

**input:** data to be transferred into the internal storage of a computer.

**insolvency:** the inability to pay one's liabilities.

**insurable interest:** a sufficient personal concern in the object of insurance to establish a reason for assuming responsibility for premium payment; for example, the insurable interest a company may have in the life of its chief executives.

**investment banking:** the business of buying all or part of new stock issues for sale to the buying public.

**IOU:** an informal instrument giving evidence of a cash debt.

## J

**job analysis:** a study of a specific job, as in industry, with respect to operations and hazards involved, qualifications required of the worker, etc.

**job-order costing:** a cost accounting method where cost is compiled for a specific item that moves through the production process as a continuous unit.

**joint and several note:** a note with two or more signers; any or all signers can be held liable for performance of the pledge.

**joint tenancy:** tenure of property by two or more persons under which the holdings of any who die are held jointly by the survivors.

**judgment note:** a promissory note by the terms of which the holder is authorized, upon default, to take out and execute a judgment of ex parte; it is illegal in some States. Also called cognovit note.

## K

**keypunch:** special equipment for punching holes in cards or tapes.

**key-verify:** the use of a punch card machine with a keyboard to make sure the information on a punch card has been correctly punched.

**kiting:** the drawing and cashing of a check on one bank, followed very shortly thereafter by a deposit adequate to cover the check on another bank which will in turn be covered by a check drawn on still another bank.

**knocked down:** in commerce, not assembled; said of furniture, etc.

## L

**language:** a system for representing and communicating data between people and machines, or people. A language system must consist of definite characters and rules for combining the characters.

**lease:** a contract between a tenant and a property owner by which the tenant gains possession of the property in consideration of payment of rent.

**ledger:** any record or book of final entry.

**legacy:** a gift of personal property by last will and testament.

**lessee:** one to whom a lease is made.

**lessor:** one who grants a lease.

**liability:** an amount owed by one person to another; may be payable in services, property, or money.

**lien:** a claim upon property for the satisfaction of some debt until such claim is satisfied; the claim or lien against the property provides greater security than would otherwise exist.

**limited partnership:** a partnership in which some but not all of the partners have limited liability to creditors of the firm.

**line of credit:** amount of credit to which a customer is entitled.

**liquidation:** conversion, either voluntary or forced, of assets into cash, either to take profits or to close out a business.

**log:** a record of relevant data pertaining to a machine run.

**long-term bond:** a bond of slow maturity, running over a longer-than-average period.

**long-term capital gain:** a capital gain taxed at one-half the regular rate because the asset on whose sale it was realized had been held for over six months.

M

**machine, data processing:** a name for any machine that can store and process alphabetic and numeric data.
**machine, electrical accounting:** a set of conventional punch card equipment consisting of tabulators, collators, and sorters.
**management:** the direction, supervision, control, and coordination of all activities of a business.
**markdown:** a reduction from the original retail selling price.
**market price:** the price of a commodity which a buyer is willing to pay and a seller is willing to sell, assuming both the buyer and seller have adequate knowledge of the market.
**markup:** an increase added to the original retail selling price.
**mean:** the midpoint in an array of numbers.
**mechanic's lien:** a lien against property filled by one who has been engaged in its construction or repair and has not been paid for work done or materials supplied; to safeguard against double liability, the owner may require the contractor to give a bond pledging himself to satisfy those who work for him, thus confining the matter to the two principals, the owner and the contractor.
**median:** the central item or value at which an equal number of items fall above and below.
**memory:** *see* storage.
**merger:** a unification of business houses by concentration of their properties under the name of the corporation taking over the business of all.
**mode:** the item which occurs most frequently in a frequency distribution.
**mortgage:** a security interest on land, equipment, buildings, and other fixed or movable property given by a borrower to a lender; also called a deed of trust.
**municipal bond:** a bond issued by a municipality, as for schools, improvements, and other needs of town or city government.
**mutual fund:** a type of investment company formed by the pooling together of funds contributed by a number of investors; profits from the investment of this money are shared mutually by all concerned.
**mutual savings bank:** a savings bank in which the profits are distributed among the depositors; it has no capital.

N

**negotiable instrument:** commercial paper of such nature that the total amount of money, title, and the right to sue therefor may be transferred to another.
**net income:** the balance left for the owners of a business after all operating expenses and income deductions have been made from gross income.
**net profit:** the excess or remaining balance in income after deducting pertinent costs; may be computed with or without income tax liability.
**number, binary:** *see* binary.
**number, check:** a number used to detect malfunctions in equipment that occur during information transfer.

O

**obsolescence:** the gradual reduction in usefulness of an asset.
**odd lot:** in the sale of securities and commodities, a lot of less than one hundred shares of stock, or less than ten thousand dollars' worth of bonds, figuring in a sale. *See* round lot.
**open account: 1.** an account that has not yet been balanced. **2.** an account with credit privileges.
**OR:** Operations Research; the use of analytical methods and procedures adapted from mathematics for solving operational problems.
**output:** the data transferred from internal computer storage to some external computer storage device.
**over-and-under:** (over-and-short) an account in which the differences in actual receipts and expenses and the supporting documents is recorded. The account should be closed as an income or expense account.
**overhead:** cost of conducting a business; costs which do not come under particular expenses but belong to the whole business, as rent, taxes, insurance, depreciation of plant, etc.
**overpunch:** the adding of holes to a punch card column which already has one or more holes.

P

**paid-in capital:** sum of cash, property, and services contributed to a corporation by the shareholders.
**par:** the established or face value of a security.
**partnership:** a legal relationship based upon an agreement between two or more persons who share in profits and losses and also may participate in the management of a business.
**patent:** a monopoly right granted by the Federal government to an inventor for a period of 17 years.
**PCM:** Punched Card Machine.
**personal property:** property which is temporary or movable including intangible property; chattels.
**personal-service firm:** a firm deriving its revenue from the rendering of personal services.
**planned economy:** organization of the economy of a country by which all phases of production are planned as an interdependent whole by some central authority, usually the State; in most modern countries, the phrase may be applied to some parts of the economy.
**pool:** in the stock market, a combination of traders seeking market control; in commodity trading, a group posing as rivals but actually cooperating in an endeavor to control supply and prices.
**post:** a section of the floor of a trading room where trade in one stock is carried on.
**posting:** the transfer from a daybook or journal to the ledger.
**power of attorney:** the written authorization granted by the principal to his agent.
**preferred stock:** stock on which dividends must be paid before any are paid on the common stock, and whose holders have precedence when the assets of a dissolved corporation are distributed.
**prepaid expense:** a disbursement for a benefit which is to be received at a later time.
**price fixing:** artificial regulation of prices, as by a combination of sellers.
**price index:** a table of prices of commodities compiled as an indicator of the purchasing power of the dollar.
**price maintenance:** control, by manufacturer, of price to be charged by retailers; fair-trade agreement or control.
**processing, automatic data:** a system of electronic or electrical machines used in performing data processing.
**profit and loss account:** a ledger showing profits, losses, and expenses, with favorable or unfavorable balance; also called income statement.
**program:** the complete plan for problem solution; specifically the sequence of machine instructions and routines utilized in problem solution.
**program, internally stored:** instructions stored in the computer with other computer data.
**programming, linear:** an operations research and mathematics theory using many variables where a best value or best set of values is to be found.
**property:** the ownership interests and rights one has in property; a legal right.
**prorate:** to divide in proportion to respective claims.
**protest: 1.** a formal declaration in writing made by a notary public in behalf of the holder of a bill or note, protesting against all parties liable for any loss or damage by nonpayment; a declaration and service of notice of dishonor. **2.** declaration by a shipmaster that damage to ship or cargo was due to no fault of ship, officers, or crew.
**proxy:** authority in writing which gives a certain person the right to vote for the holder of shares or to act for him in the transaction of business.

Q

**qualified endorsement:** an endorsing signature, with the note "without recourse" or some other qualification.
**quick asset:** current asset; goods or other resource which can readily be converted into cash.
**quitclaim deed:** a deed of release of title, interest, or claim in property.
**quota:** a proportional part; as a foreign nation's quota of immigration.

**R**

**rate of exchange:** the ratio between currency of one country and that of another country; it fluctuates as conditions change, and is regulated through stabilization funds by governments having managed currencies, as Great Britain and the United States.

**rating:** the credit standing of a person or firm, as set by mercantile agencies.

**reader, character:** a device capable of converting type or script into machine language.

**real property:** real estate; land, buildings, etc.

**receiver:** a person appointed by a court to manage the property and affairs of a person or business house while legal processes affecting the property or business are under way.

**record: 1.** placing data into a storage device. **2.** a listing of data.

**registered bond:** a bond with principal and interest payable only to a listed owner or on his order.

**resale price maintenance agreement:** an agreement that the buyer will not sell a trademark or brand name item below a certain stated price.

**restart:** to return to a definite planned point in a routine for the purpose of rerunning a part of a routine that has an error.

**risk: 1.** hazard of a new undertaking; as a good risk; a poor risk. **2.** degree of credit standing of an applicant for credit.

**round lot:** in the sale of securities and commodities, a lot of shares in a normal trading unit, as 100 shares. *See* odd lot.

**royalty:** a percentage fee paid the holder of a patent or copyright for the right to make or sell, etc., the article in question.

**run:** the performance of a single routine or several routines if linked together on a computer.

**S**

**sale or return:** a sale on which title passes to the buyer at the time of purchase, however, the buyer has the option of returning goods and title to original owner.

**salvage:** compensation given those who rescue a ship or cargo from loss.

**scrap value:** the potential selling price of used fixed assets.

**second mortgage:** a real estate mortgage that already has a first mortgage.

**secured transaction (conditional sale):** a credit sale in which possession and risk pass to the buyer but the seller retains a security interest and may retain title until the goods are paid for.

**self-insurance:** insurance of oneself or one's property, usually by providing a fund out of current income.

**self-liquidating:** providing profit in a short time; converting itself into cash in the normal course of business.

**seller's market:** a state of the market in which the seller is at an advantage because demand exceeds supply. *See* buyer's market.

**sell short: 1.** to sell securities not owned, but borrowed in expectation of a favorable change in the market. **2.** to sell a commodity, as wheat, for future delivery, in expectation of a drop in prices.

**shade:** to make a concession in the price of a commodity or security.

**share:** one of the unit parts of securities issued by a company.

**sight draft:** a draft that is due to be paid when presented.

**sinking fund:** assets set aside to retire a debt; also any income earned from the assets.

**social security acts:** laws providing assistance for certain classes of people; e.g., blind and unemployed.

**sole proprietor:** an individual who owns a business.

**sort:** the classification of items of data into a particular order.

**speculation:** buying and selling for immediate profit rather than for investment.

**split commission:** a commission shared, as with a customer.

**standard cost:** a forecast of anticipated costs subject to certain conditions; used as a basis for cost control and as a measure of efficiency when compared to actual cost.

**Statute of Frauds:** a statute designed to prevent certain types of fraud by requiring that certain transactions be in writing to be enforceable.

**Statute of Limitations:** a statute setting forth time limitations within which legal action may be brought.

**stockbroker:** one who trades in or buys and sells securities.

**stock certificate:** a paper evidencing ownership of shares; also certificate of stock.

**stock in trade:** goods kept on hand, ready for sale.

**stop payment:** order by a bank's customer to refuse payment on a check or draft that has been issued.

**storage:** a data processing term used in lieu of memory.

**subrogation:** putting one thing in place of another; substituting one creditor for another.

**syndicate:** a group of bankers or capitalists acting together for an agreed purpose, such as underwriting a new issue of securities.

**T**

**tabulator:** a machine that sorts and selects data from tapes and cards and prints out tables, lists, and totals.

**tangible asset:** resource consisting of real estate or chattels.

**tape:** a narrow strip of material capable of accepting data input, output, or storage.

**tare: 1.** an allowance for the weight of a container. **2.** the difference between gross and net weight of a shipment.

**taxable income:** income which is subject to a tax levy by some governmental agency.

**time deposit:** a deposit not to be withdrawn until a certain period has elapsed or a specified number of days' notice of intention to withdraw has been given.

**time draft:** a draft payable at a future date specified on the draft.

**title:** a document that establishes title to property.

**trade acceptance:** a bill of exchange in payment for goods, marked as accepted by the purchaser; when properly executed, it constitutes an acceptance of obligation to pay.

**trade discount:** percentage off from list prices allowed a dealer as his profit on reselling the goods.

**transmitting:** the reproducing of data in a new location replacing that which was stored.

**treasury stock:** reacquired stock of a corporation from its own stockholders either by purchase or gift.

**trial balance:** a list of the total debits and total credits in a ledger.

**trust deed: 1.** a deed by which power is given to a group of creditors to foreclose mortgages upon default. **2.** a deed to property, serving as collateral for a bond issue, and held by a trustee.

**U**

**ultra vires:** beyond (legal) power; beyond authority (of a court, corporation, etc.).

**underwriter: 1.** a person who guarantees against losses or who guarantees loans, stock or bond issues, etc. **2.** a person or agent who underwrites insurance.

**undue influence:** such influence exerted over another person that he is dominated and therefore prevented from exercising his own will.

**union shop:** a business where a nonunion employee may be employed for a trial period of not more than 30 days and after that the nonunion employee must join the union or be discharged.

**V**

**variable cost:** operating cost which varies according to production, use, or some measure of activity.

**verifier:** a device used to check the accuracy of a previous recording of information.

**voucher: 1.** a receipt for a payment. **2.** a check that has been paid and returned to its maker by the bank. **3.** a document proving a transaction.

**W**

**warehouse receipt:** a receipt for goods deposited in a warehouse; sometimes it is made negotiable and traded in as representing ownership of the merchandise.

**will:** a written document, in the form required by law, by which an individual makes a disposition of his property.

**without recourse:** without liability on the part of an endorser of a promissory note to pay the amount of the note if the maker or any following endorser fails to do so.

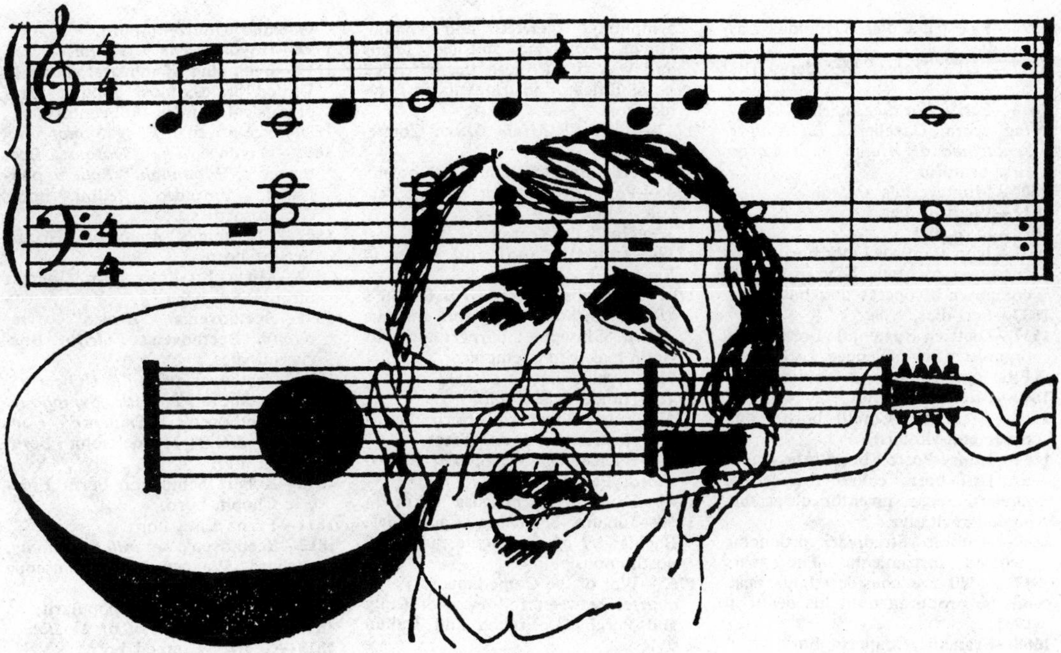

# Music

## *Music History Highlights*

Music begins with most primitive man. Stone Age drawings in European caves show dancers, indicating at least rhythmic beat. Pictures from earlier civilizations depict musical instruments, in wall painting at Thebes, Egypt from the fifteenth century B.C. showing lute and harp. Such stringed instruments were preceded by drums (sticks beaten together, beating on logs, skin drums) and wind instruments (reeds, hollow animal horns, notched twigs of pithy plants).

**Second Century B.C.**—Earliest complete pieces of Greek music still extant.

**Fourth Century A.D.**—Ambrosian chant, early antiphonal church music.

**Sixth Century**—Gregorian chant.

**Ninth Century**—Earliest true harmonic music.

**Eleventh Century**—Guido d'Arezzo (c. 995-1050) or (c. 995-c. 1050), inventor of staff and tonic sol-fa solmization (ut, re, mi, fa, sol, la).

**Twelfth and Thirteenth Century**—Minnesingers in Germany, trouvères and troubadours in France.

**Late Thirteenth Century**—"Sumer is icumin in," earliest known English canon.

**1364**—Guillaume de Machaut's Mass, first complete Mass by one composer, sung at coronation of Charles V of France.

**1476**—First printed music in Europe, Ulrich Hahn's *Missale.*

**1526**—Giovanni Palestrina born, greatest polyphonic composer.

**1530**—Orlandus Lassus born.

**1540**—Tomás Victoria born, Spanish polyphonic composer.

**1542**—William Byrd born, English contrapuntist.

**1561**—Jacopo Peri born, early operatic composer.

**1562**—Complete English Psalter of Sternhold and Hopkins published.

**1564**—Congregation of Oratorians founded in Rome by Philip Neri: beginnings of the oratorio at their services.

**1567**—Claudio Monteverdi born, innovator in vocal and instrumental music.

**1575**—Andrea Amati flourishes at Cremona. The Amati family, noted for their stringed instruments, reached the peak of their work in Nicola Amati (1596-1684). The modern violin took shape in the work of Andrea Amati, Gasparo di Bertolotti (1540-1609) and Giovanni Maggini (1580-1630).

**1576**—Hans Sachs, greatest Meistersinger, dies.

**1581**—*La Ballet Comique de la Reine Louise* produced at Versailles, said to be the first modern ballet.

**1594**—Palestrina dies. Orlandus Lassus dies.
**1597**—Peri's *Dafne,* considered first opera.
**1600**—Peri's *Euridice,* earliest surviving opera. Cavalieri's *La Rappresentazione di Anima e di Corpo,* first oratorio.
**1607**—Monteverdi's *Orfeo.*
**1611**—Victoria dies.
**1623**—Byrd dies.
**1632**—Jean Baptiste Lully born, court composer to Louis XIV of France, composer of operas and ballets.
**1633**—Peri dies.
**1637**—Dietrich Buxtehude born, noted organist who influenced J. S. Bach. First opera house, at Venice.
**1643**—Monteverdi dies.
**1653**—Arcangelo Corelli born, composer and violinist.
**1659**—Henry Purcell born. Alessandro Scarlatti born, called founder of modern opera, inventor of accompanied recitative.
**1669**—Antonio Stradivari producing stringed instruments. The years 1700-1720 are considered his best, but he produced until his death in 1737.
**1668**—François Couperin born.
**1673**—Antonio Vivaldi born.
**1683**—Jean Philippe Rameau born, theorist in harmony. Domenico Scarlatti born, innovator in harpsichord playing who is considered founder of modern piano technique.
**1685**—George Frederick Handel born, greatest of oratorio composers. Johann Sebastian Bach born, often considered greatest composer. One of six generations of musicians, of whom 37 held notable musical posts. An organist, Bach wrote mostly vocal music for the Church.
**1687**—Lully dies.
**1689**—Purcell's *Dido and Aeneas.*
**1690**—Clarinet devised by J. C. Denner.
**1695**—Purcell dies.
**1705**—Handel's first operas, *Almira* and *Nero.*
**1707**—Buxtehude dies.
**1708**—Bach becomes organist at Weimar.
**1709**—Handel and Domenico Scarlatti meet in contest at Rome for harpsichord and organ mastery.
**1710**—Thomas Arne born. Giovanni Battista Pergolesi born.
**1711**—Bartolommeo Cristofori invents pianoforte hammer action.
**1713**—Corelli dies.
**1714**—Christoph Willibald Gluck born. Karl Philipp Emanuel Bach born.
**1721**—Griselda, Alessandro Scarlatti's 114th opera, produced. Bach's *Brandenburg Concertos.*
**1722**—Rameau's *Traité de l'Harmonie* published. First part of Bach's *Well-Tempered Clavichord.*
**1723**—Bach's *St. John Passion.*
**1725**—Alessandro Scarlatti dies.
**1728**—Bach's *St. Matthew Passion. The Beggar's Opera* produced in England, words set to traditional tunes by John Gay, arrangements by Johann Pepusch.
**1732**—Franz Joseph Haydn born. Often called the founder of the symphony, quartet, and sonata, Haydn expanded musical forms and was first to use the extended possibilities of instruments in combination.
**1733**—Bach's *B Minor Mass.* Couperin dies.
**1735**—Johann Christian Bach born.
**1736**—Pergolesi's *Stabat Mater.* Pergolesi dies.
**1737**—Handel's *Xerxes.*
**1739**—Handel's *Saul* and *Israel in Egypt.*
**1740**—Handel's *Concerti Grossi.* Arne's "Rule Britannia" in the masque *Alfred.* Giuseppe Guarneri active as violin maker in Cremona.
**1741**—Vivaldi dies.
**1742**—Handel's *Messiah.*
**1743**—Luigi Boccherini born, cellist and instrumental composer.
**1744**—Bach's *Well-Tempered Clavichord,* Part 2.
**1749**—Domenico Cimarosa born.
**1750**—Johann Sebastian Bach dies. Bach's *Art of the Fugue* published posthumously.
**1752**—War of the Comedians in Paris, quarrel between followers of Lully and Pergolesi, French and Italian styles.
**1755**—Haydn's first string quartet.
**1756**—Wolfgang Amadeus Mozart born, great innovator in symphony, piano concerto, opera.
**1757**—Domenico Scarlatti dies.
**1759**—Handel dies.
**1760**—Maria Luigi Cherubini born.
**1762**—Gluck's *Orfeo ed Euridice.*
**1764**—Rameau dies. Mozart composes his first symphonies.
**1770**—Ludwig van Beethoven born. Beethoven is often considered the world's greatest composer, Johann Sebastian Bach alone rivaling him. His works, especially his nine symphonies, mark the transition to the subjective music of the nineteenth century and are especially important for their influence on other composers.
**1777**—Gluck's *Armide* precipitates argument in Paris between his followers and those of Niccolò Piccinni.
**1778**—Arne dies.
**1780**—Waltz becomes popular dance.
**1782**—J. C. Bach dies. Nicolò Paganini born, called greatest violin virtuoso.
**1786**—Mozart's *Marriage of Figaro.* Karl Maria von Weber born.
**1787**—Mozart's *Don Giovanni.* Gluck dies.
**1788**—Mozart's *Eine Kleine Nachtmusik.* Mozart composes *39th, 40th,* and *41st Symphonies.* K. P. E. Bach dies.
**1789**—Mozart's *Clarinet Quintet.*
**1791**—Giacomo Meyerbeer born. Paganini plays first public concert at age of nine, Mozart's *Magic Flute.* Mozart dies.
**1792**—Cimarosa's *Secret Marriage.* Beethoven studies with Haydn. Gioacchino Rossini born.
**1795**—Beethoven's *First Piano Concerto.*
**1797**—Franz Peter Schubert born. Gaetano Donizetti born.
**1798**—Haydn's *The Creation.*
**1799**—Beginning of minstrel shows in United States, most popular form of musical show in 19th century.
**1800**—Beethoven's *First Symphony.*
**1801**—Haydn's *The Seasons.* Beethoven's *"Moonlight" Sonata* published. Vincenzo Bellini born. Cimarosa dies.
**1803**—Cherubini's *Anacreon.* Hector Berlioz born.
**1804**—Michael Glinka born. Johann Strauss, Sr., born.
**1805**—Beethoven's *"Eroica" Symphony.* Beethoven's *Fidelio.* Boccherini dies.
**1806**—Beethoven's *Violin Concerto.*
**1808**—Beethoven's *Fifth Symphony.*
**1809**—Beethoven's *"Emperor" Concerto.* Felix Mendelssohn born. Haydn dies.
**1810**—Robert Schumann born. Frédéric Chopin born.
**1811**—Franz Liszt born.
**1813**—Beethoven's *Seventh Symphony.* Richard Wagner born. Giuseppe Verdi born.
**1815**—Quadrille attains popularity.
**1816**—Rossini's *Barber of Seville.*
**1818**—Charles Gounod born.
**1819**—Weber's *Invitation to the Dance.* Jacques Offenbach born. Franz von Suppé born.
**1820**—Beethoven almost completely deaf.
**1821**—Weber's *Freischütz.*
**1822**—Schubert's *Unfinished Symphony* (first performed 1865). César Franck born.
**1823**—Schubert's *Schöne Müllerin* written.
**1824**—Bedrich Smetana born. Anton Bruckner born. Beethoven's *Ninth Symphony.*
**1825**—Johann Strauss, Jr., born.
**1826**—Beethoven's *B Flat Major Quartet.* Weber's *Oberon.* Weber dies. Stephen Collins Foster born.
**1827**—Beethoven dies. Mendelssohn composes overture to *A Midsummer Night's Dream.* Schubert's *Winterreise* written.
**1828**—Schubert composes *Symphony in C Minor.* Schubert dies.
**1829**—Rossini writes the last of his 39 operas, *William Tell.* Anton Rubinstein born.
**1830**—Mendelssohn's first *Songs Without Words.* Berlioz' *Fantastic Symphony.* Chopin's *First* and *Second Piano Concertos.* "Jim Crow," minstrel song.
**1831**—Bellini's *Norma* and *La Sonnambula.* Rossini's *Stabat Mater* (finished in 1841 and performed in 1842).
**1832**—Donizetti's *Elisir d'Amore.*
**1833**—Mendelssohn's *Italian Symphony.* Johannes Brahms born.
**1834**—Berlioz' *Harold in Italy.* Alexander Borodin born.
**1835**—Bellini's *The Puritans.* Donizetti's *Lucia di Lammermoor.* Bellini dies. Camille Saint-Saëns born. Johann Strauss, Sr., becomes conductor at Vienna court balls.
**1836**—Meyerbeer's *Les Huguenots.* Glinka's *A Life for the Czar,* be-

ginning inspiration of Russian nationalist school of music. John Stafford Smith, probable composer of music used for "The Star-Spangled Banner," dies.

**1838**—Berlioz' *Benvenuto Cellini*. Georges Bizet born.

**1839**—Verdi's first opera, *Oberto*. Berlioz' *Romeo and Juliet*. Modeste Mussorgsky born.

**1840**—Donizetti's *The Daughter of the Regiment*. Paganini dies. Pëtr Ilich Tchaikovsky born.

**1841**—Schumann's *Spring Symphony*. Anton Dvorák born.

**1842**—Schumann's *Piano Quintet*. Glinka's *Russlan and Ludmilla*. Cherubini dies. Arthur Sullivan born. Jules Massenet born.

**1843**—Donizetti's *Don Pasquale*. Wagner's *Flying Dutchman*. Michael Balfe's *The Bohemian Girl*. Edvard Grieg born.

**1844**—Mendelssohn's *Violin Concerto* written. Berlioz' *Roman Carnival Overture*. Nikolai Rimski-Korsakov born.

**1845**—Wagner's *Tannhäuser*.

**1846**—Schumann's *Piano Concerto*. Berlioz' *Damnation of Faust*. Mendelssohn's *Elijah*.

**1847**—Verdi's *Macbeth*. Mendelssohn dies.

**1848**—Donizetti dies. Foster's "O Susanna."

**1849**—Meyerbee's *The Prophet*. Chopin dies. Johann Strauss, Sr., dies.

**1850**—Wagner's *Lohengrin*.

**1851**—Schumann's *Rhenish Symphony*. Verdi's *Rigoletto*. Foster's "Old Folks at Home."

**1853**—Verdi's *Il Trovatore* and *La Traviata*. Foster's "My Old Kentucky Home."

**1854**—Liszt's *Les Préludes*. Leos Janácek born. John Philip Sousa born.

**1855**—Liszt's *First Piano Concerto*.

**1856**—Schumann dies.

**1857**—Glinka dies. Edward Elgar born.

**1858**—Offenbach's *Orpheus in Hades*. Giacomo Puccini born.

**1859**—Gounod's *Faust*. Brahms' *First Piano Concerto*. Verdi's *Masked Ball*.

**1860**—Gustav Mahler born. Hugo Wolf born. Ignace Jan Paderewski born, piano virtuoso. Foster's "Old Black Joe."

**1861**—Edward MacDowell born. Rise of Russian nationalist school: The Five—Mily Balakirev, César Cui, Modeste Mussorgsky, Nikolai Rimski-Korsakov, Alexander Borodin.

**1862**—Claude Debussy born. Frederick Delius born.

**1863**—Liszt's *Second Piano Concerto*. Bizet's *The Pearl Fishers*.

**1864**—Offenbach's *La Belle Hélène*. Meyerbeer dies. Foster dies. Richard Strauss born.

**1865**—Wagner's *Tristan und Isolde*. Alexander Glazunov born. Jean Sibelius born.

**1866**—Smetana's *The Bartered Bride*. Ambroise Thomas' *Mignon*.

**1867**—Verdi's *Don Carlos*. Johann Strauss, Jr.'s *Blue Danube* waltz. Arturo Toscanini born.

**1868**—Wagner's *Die Meistersinger von Nürnberg*. Brahms' *German Requiem*. Bruckner's *First Symphony*. Rossini dies.

**1869**—Berlioz dies.

**1870**—Grieg's *Piano Concerto*. Tchaikovsky's *Romeo and Juliet* overture. Franz Lehar born. Oskar Straus born.

**1871**—Verdi's *Aïda*.

**1872**—Bizet's *L'Arlésienne*. Sullivan's "Onward Christian Soldiers." Alexander Scriabin born. Ralph Vaughan Williams born.

**1873**—Brahms' *Variations on a Theme by Haydn*. Sergei Rachmaninoff born. Enrico Caruso born.

**1874**—Verdi's *Manzoni Requiem*. Mussorgsky's *Boris Godunov* and *Pictures at an Exhibition*. Johann Strauss, Jr.'s *Die Fledermaus*. Charles Ives born. Arnold Schönberg born. Gustav Holst born.

**1875**—Bizet's *Carmen*. Tchaikovsky's *First Piano Concerto*. Saint-Saëns' *Danse Macabre*. *Trial by Jury* (Gilbert and Sullivan's first success). Bizet dies. Maurice Ravel born.

**1876**—Wagner's *Der Ring des Nibelungen* cycle in first complete performance at Bayreuth. Brahms' *First Symphony*. Grieg's *Peer Gynt*. Manuel de Falla born.

**1877**—Saint-Saëns' *Samson and Delilah*. Borodin's *Second Symphony*. Sullivan's "The Lost Chord."

**1879**—Brahms' *Violin Concerto*. Smetana's cycle *My Country* finished. Ottorino Respighi born.

**1880**—Tchaikovsky's *Violin Concerto*. Borodin's *In the Steppes of Central Asia*. Offenbach dies. Ernest Bloch born.

**1881**—Bruckner's *Fourth Symphony*. Offenbach's *Tales of Hoffmann* produced posthumously. Mussorgsky dies. Béla Bartók born. Heitor Villa-Lobos born.

**1882**—Wagner's *Parsifal*. MacDowell's *First Piano Concerto*. Igor Stravinsky born.

**1883**—Wagner dies. Anton von Webern born.

**1884**—Massenet's *Manon*. Puccini's first opera, *Le Villi*. Smetana dies.

**1885**—Brahms' *Fourth Symphony*. Franck's *Symphonic Variations*. Johann Strauss, Jr.'s *Gypsy Baron*. Alban Berg born. Deems Taylor born. Jerome Kern born.

**1886**—Liszt dies. Toscanini makes debut as conductor in Rio de Janeiro.

**1887**—Verdi's *Otello*. Rimski-Korsakov's *Capriccio Espagnol*. Borodin dies. Sigmund Romberg born.

**1888**—Tchaikovsky's *Fifth Symphony*.

**1889**—Franck's *Symphony in D Minor*. Rimski-Korsakov's *Schéhérazade*. Strauss' *Don Juan*. Gilbert and Sullivan's *The Gondoliers*.

**1890-1895**—Genesis of jazz from New Orleans marching-band music.

**1890**—Tchaikovsky's *Sleeping Beauty*. Mascagni's *Cavalleria Rusticana*. Borodin's *Prince Igor* (completed by Rimski-Korsakov and Glazunov). Strauss' *Death and Transfiguration*. Franck dies.

**1891**—Brahms' *Clarinet Quintet*. Rachmaninoff's *First Piano Concerto*. Sergei Prokofiev born.

**1892**—Tchaikovsky's *Nutcracker*. Sibelius' *En Saga*. Ruggiero Leoncavallo's *I Pagliacci*. Darius Milhaud born. Sousa leaves U. S. Marine Band to organize his own band.

**1893**—Dvorák's *New World Symphony*. Tchaikovsky's *Pathétique Symphony*. Debussy's *String Quartet*. Verdi's *Falstaff*. Puccini's *Manon Lescaut*. Tchaikovsky dies. Gounod dies. Douglas Moore born.

**1894**—Debussy's *The Afternoon of a Faun*. Rubinstein dies.

**1895**—Von Suppé dies. Paul Hindemith born.

**1896**—Puccini's *La Bohème*. MacDowell's *Woodland Sketches*. Bruckner dies. Virgil Thompson born.

**1897**—Brahms dies. Henry Cowell born.

**1898**—Strauss' *Don Quixote*. George Gershwin born. Toscanini becomes artistic director of La Scala, Milan.

**1899**—Elgar's *Enigma Variations*. Schönberg's *Transfigured Night*. Sibelius' *Finlandia*. Johann Strauss, Jr., dies. Carlos Chavez born.

**1900**—Puccini's *Tosca*. Sibelius' *First Symphony*. Sullivan dies. Aaron Copland born. Kurt Weill born.

**1901**—Rachmaninoff's *Second Piano Concerto*. Verdi dies.

**1902**—Debussy's *Pelléas et Mélisande*. Elgar's *Pomp and Circumstance* marches. William Walton born. Richard Rodgers born.

**1903**—Bruckner's *Ninth Symphony*. Ravel's *String Quartet*. Sibelius' *Valse Triste*. Wolf dies. Aram Khatchaturian born.

**1904**—Puccini's *Madame Butterfly*. Delius' *Appalachia*. Dvorak dies.

**1905**—Debussy's *La Mer*. Strauss' *Salome*. Lehar's *The Merry Widow*.

**1906**—Dmitri Shostakovich born.

**1907**—Straus' *A Waltz Dream*. Grieg dies.

**1908**—Scriabin's *Poem of Ecstasy*. Rachmaninoff's *Second Symphony*. Straus' *The Chocolate Soldier*. Rimski-Korsakov dies. MacDowell dies.

**1909**—Strauss' *Elektra*.

**1910**—Stravinsky's *Firebird*. Elgar's *Violin Concerto*. Ravel's *Mother Goose Suite*. Vaughan Williams' *Sea Symphony*. Popularity of ragtime at peak.

**1911**—Mahler's *Das Lied von der Erde*. Strauss' *Der Rosenkavalier*. Stravinsky's *Petrushka*. Mahler dies. Gian-Carlo Menotti born. Alan Hovhaness born.

**1912**—Ravel's *Daphnis and Chloé*. Mahler's *Ninth Symphony*, Schönberg's *Pierrot Lunaire*. Massenet dies.

**1913**—Stravinsky's *Rite of Spring*. Falla's *La Vida Breve*. Benjamin Britten born. Morton Gould born.

**1914**—Vaughan Williams' *London Symphony*. Popularity of the blues.

**1915**—Falla's *El Amor Brujo*. Bloch's *Schelomo Rhapsody*. Scriabin dies.

**1916**—Falla's *Nights in the Gardens of Spain*.

**1918**—Prokofiev's *Classical Symphony*. Stravinsky's *L'Histoire du Sol-*

*dat.* Holst's *The Planets.* Puccini's "triptych" of one-act operas: *Il Tabarro, Sour Angelica,* and *Gianni Schicchi.* Debussy dies. Leonard Bernstein born.

**1919**—Falla's *Three-Cornered Hat.* Delius' *Eventyr.*

**1920**—Ravel's *La Valse.*

**1921**—Prokofiev's *The Love for Three Oranges.* Saint-Saëns dies. Caruso dies.

**1922**—Taylor's *Through the Looking-Glass.*

**1923**—Stravinsky's *Octet for Wind Instruments.*

**1924**—Respighi's *The Pines of Rome.* Gershwin's *Rhapsody in Blue.* Puccini dies.

**1925**—Sibelius' *Seventh Symphony.* Berg's *Wozzeck.* Copland's *Music for the Theatre.* Gershwin's *Piano Concerto in F.*

**1926**—Puccini's *Turandot.* Shostakovich's *First Symphony.* Walton's *Façade.*

**1927**—Taylor's *The King's Henchman.* Kern's *Show Boat.*

**1928**—Ravel's *Bolero.* Gershwin's *An American in Paris.* Janácek dies.

**1929**—Villa-Lobos' *Amazonas.*

**1930**—Stravinsky's *Symphony of Psalms.*

**1931**—Taylor's *Peter Ibbetson.* First opera broadcast from Metropolitan Opera House, New York (*Hansel and Gretel* by Humperdinck).

**1932-1935**—Beginning of swing era in jazz.

**1932**—Sousa dies.

**1934**—Khatchaturian's *First Symphony.* Thomson's *Four Saints in Three Acts.* Shostakovich's *Lady Macbeth of Mzensk.* Rachmaninoff's *Rhapsody on a Theme by Paganini.* Elgar dies. Delius dies. Holst dies.

**1935**—Gershwin's *Porgy and Bess.* Berg dies. Berkshire Music Festivals inaugurated.

**1936**—Prokofiev's *Romeo and Juliet* and *Peter and the Wolf.* Glazunov dies. Respighi dies.

**1937**—Shostakovich's *Fifth Symphony.* Copland's *El Salón Mexico.* Menotti's *Amelia Goes to the Ball.* Blitzstein's *The Cradle Will Rock.* BBC performs *Faust* in first performance of opera on television. Ravel dies. Gershwin dies.

**1938**—Hindemith's *Mathis der Mahler.* Bloch's *Violin Concerto.* Barber's *Adagio for Strings.*

**1939**—Menotti's *The Old Maid and the Thief.*

**1941**—Paderewski dies.

**1943**—Rodgers' *Oklahoma.* Rachmaninoff dies.

**1944**—Barber's *Capricorn Concerto.* Bernstein's *Fancy Free.*

**1945-1950**—Bop and cool jazz attain popularity.

**1945**—Britten's *Peter Grimes.* Bartók's *Concerto for Orchestra.* Copland's *Appalachian Spring.* Bartók dies. Webern dies. Kern dies.

**1946**—Khatchaturian's *Concerto for Violoncello and Orchestra.* Ives' *Third Symphony.* Britten's *The Rape of Lucretia.* Falla dies.

**1947**—Weill's *Street Scene.*

**1948**—Stravinsky's *Orpheus.* Lehar dies.

**1949**—Rodgers' *South Pacific.* Shostakovich's *Song of the Forest.* Richard Strauss dies.

**1950**—Menotti's *The Consul.* Weill dies.

**1951**—Stravinsky's *The Rake's Progress.* Menotti's *Amahl and the Night Visitors,* first opera written for television. Honegger's *Fifth Symphony.* Romberg dies. Schönberg dies.

**1952**—Hovhaness' *Saint Vartan Symphony.*

**1953**—Shostakovich's *Tenth Symphony.* Prokofiev dies.

**1954**—Oskar Straus dies. Ives dies.

**1955**—Britten's *The Turn of the Screw.* Menotti's *The Saint of Bleecker Street.* Milhaud's *David.* Walton's *Troilus and Cressida.*

**1956**—Vaughan Williams' *Eighth Symphony.*

**1957**—Stravinsky's *Agon.* Toscanini dies. Sibelius dies.

**1958**—Barber's *Vanessa.* Vaughan Williams dies.

**1959**—Villa-Lobos dies.

**1960**—Carter's *String Quartet No. 2.* Copland's *Nonet for Strings.* Frank Martin's *Mystère de la Nativite.* Berio's *Circles.*

**1961**—Carter's *Double Concerto.* Robert Ward's *The Crucible.*

**1962**—Britten's *War Requiem.* Brown's *Available Forms I.*

**1963**—Foss' *Echoi.* Stockhausen's *Microphonic I.*

**1964**—Stravinskii's *Elegy for JFK.* Shifrin's *Satires of Circumstance.* Maderna's *Hyperion.* The Beatles.

**1965**—Stravinskii's *Variations "In Memory of Aldous Huxley."* Finney's *Three Studies in Fours* and *Concerto for Percussion and Orchestra.* Henry Cowell dies.

**1966**—Rochberg's *Nach Bach.* Barber's *Anthony and Cleopatra.*

**1967**—Carter's *Piano Concerto.* Schuller's *The Visitation.*

# DICTIONARY OF MUSIC TERMS

***Many musical terms not found in this list can be found in the main body of the Dictionary.***

## A

**A** (ā), *n.* 1. the sixth tone in the scale of C major. 2. the scale having A as the key-note. 3. upon string instruments, the name of the string which, with the open tone, gives the sixth of the natural scale; in tuning, this string is usually first brought to the requisite pitch and from it the others are then regulated; it is the first string of the violoncello, the second of the violin, etc.

**a ballata** (ä bäl-lä′tä), [It.], in ballad style.

**abandon** (ə-ban′dən), *n.* freedom from restraint; ease.

**a battuta** (ä bät-to͞o′tä), [It.], as beaten; strictly in time.

**abbadare** (äb-bä-dä′re), *v.i.* [It.], take care; pay attention.

**abbandonatamente** (äb-bän-dô-nä-tä-men′te), *adv.* [It.], vehemently; violently.

**abbassamento di voce** (äb-bäs-sä-men′tô dē vô′che), [It.], diminishing or lowering of the voice.

**abbellire** (ä-bel-lē′re), *v.t.* [It.], to embellish with ornaments.

**abendlied** (ä′bent-lēt), *n.* [G.], evening song or hymn.

**a beneplacito** (ä bā′nā-plä′chē-tô), [It.], at pleasure: the time may be retarded or ornaments introduced.

**abgestossen** (äp′gē-shtō-sen), *adj.* [G.], detached; struck off; staccato.

**abrupt modulation,** a sudden modulation into keys not closely related to the original key.

**a cappella** (ä′ kä-pel′lä), [It.], in the church or chapel style; unaccompanied: said of choral singing.

**a capriccio** (ä′ kä-prēt′chô), [It.], at pleasure; at whatever tempo and with whatever expression the performer likes.

**accelerando** (ak-sel′ēr-an′dō; It. ät-che′le-rän′dô), *adv. & adj.* [It.], with gradually quickening tempo.

**acceleratamente** (ät-chä-lä-rä-tä-men′te), *adv.* [It.], speedily.

**accent** (ak′sent), *n.* a stress or emphasis upon a certain note or chord to mark its position in the bar, or its relative importance in regard to the composition.

**accentuation** (ak-sen′choo-ā′shən), *n.* 1. the act of accenting or placing accents. 2. the giving to the several notes of a piece their proper emphasis or expression.

**acciaccare** (ät-chäk-kä′re), *n.* [It.], a broken and unexpected way of striking a chord.

**acciaccatura** (ät-chäk′kä-to͞o′rä), *n.* [It.], a short grace note sounded very quickly just before a principal note: it has a small line through the stem, and is shown as smaller.

**accidental** (ak′sə-den′t'l), *n.* a sign used to show a change of pitch in the note before which it is placed.

**accolade** (ak′ə-läd′), *n.* [Fr.], a vertical line joining two or more staves.

**accompagnamento ad libitum** (ä-kôm-pän-yä-men′tô ad lib′i-təm), [It.], an accompaniment that may be either played or dispensed with.

**accompagnamento obbligato** (ob′li-gä′tō), [It.], an accompaniment that must be played, being indispensable to the proper performance of a piece.

**accompaniment** (ə-kum′pə-ni-mənt), *n.* a part, usually instrumental, played together with the main part, as with a vocal solo.

**accorciare** (äk-kôr-chä′re), *v.t.* [It.], to contract; to abridge.

**accordion** (ə-kôr′di-ən), *n.* a keyed musical instrument with a bellows, which is pressed together between the hands of the player to force air through reeds and thus produce tones.

**adagio** (ə-dä′jō), *adv.* [It.], slowly and leisurely.

**adagio assai** (äs-sä′ē), [It.], very slow and with much expression.

**adagio cantabile e sostenuto** (kän-tä′bi-lä′ ā sôs′te-no͞o′tô), [It.], slow; in a singing style and sustained.

**adagio con gravita** (kôn grä-vē′tä), [It.], slow; with gravity and majesty.

**adagio molto** (môl′tô), [It.], very slow and expressive.

**adagio non troppo** (nôn trôp′pô), [It.], slow, but not too slow.

**adagio patetico** (pä-tä′tē-kô), [It.], slowly and pathetically.

**adagio pesante** (pe-sän′te), [It.], slowly and heavily.

**adagio poi allegro** (pō′ē ə-lā′grō), [It.], slow, then quick.

**adagio quasi una fantasia** (kwä′si ū′nə fan-tä′zi-ə), [It.], an adagio similar to a fantasia.

**ad libitum** (ad lib′i-təm), [L.], at will; at pleasure; changing the tempo, interpretation, etc. of a particular passage at the discretion of the performer.

**agitato** (ä′jē-tä′tô), *adj. & adv.* [It.], fast and with excitement.

**air à boire** (âr à bwär), [Fr.], a drinking song.

**air détaché** (dā-tà-shā′), [Fr.], a single air or melody extracted from an opera or larger work.

**al fine** (äl fē′ne), [It.], to the end.

**al fine, e poi la coda** (ā pō′ē lä kō′də), [It.], after playing to where the *fine* is marked, go on to the coda.

**à livre ouvert** (à lē′vr′ o͞o-vâr′), [Fr.], at the opening of the book; to play a piece at first sight.

**alla camera** (äl′lä kä′me-rä), [It.], in the style of chamber music.

**allegretto** (al′ə-gret′ō), *adj. & adv.* [It.], moderately fast; faster than andante but slower than allegro.

**allegro** (ə-lā′grō, ə-leg′rō), *adj. & adv.* [It.], quick; fast; faster than allegretto but not so fast as presto.

**allegro agitato** (ä′jē-tä′tô), [It.], quick; with anxiety and agitation.

**allegro appassionato** (äp-päs-syô-nä′tô), [It.], passionately joyful.

**allegro assai** (äs-sä′ē), [It.], very quick.

**allegro brillante** (brēl-län′tä), [It.], requiring a brilliant style of execution.

**allegro comodo** (kô′mô-dô), [It.], with a convenient degree of quickness.

**allegro con brio** (kôn brē′ô), [It.], quick; with brilliancy.

**allegro con fuoco** (fwô′kô), [It.], quick; with fire and animation.

**allegro con moto** (mô′tô), [It.], quick; with more than the usual degree of movement.

**allegro di molto** (dē môl′tô), [It.], exceedingly quick and animated.

**allegro furioso** (fo͞o-rē-ô′sô), [It.], quick; with fury and impetuosity.

**allegro ma grazioso** (mä grä-tsyô′sô), [It.], quick, but gracefully.

**allegro ma non troppo** (nôn trôp′pô), [It.], quickly and lively, but not too fast.

**allegro moderato** (mod′ə-rä′tō), [It.], moderately quick.

**allegro molto** (môl′tô), [It.], very quick and animated.

**allegro vivace** (vē-vä′che), [It.], with vivacity; very rapidly.

**allentando** (äl-len-tän′dô), *adj.* [It.], decreasing the time until the close.

**al rigore di tempo** (äl rē-gô′rä dē tem′pô), [It.], in very rigorous and strict time.

**al segno** (äl sä′nyô), [It.], to the sign: the performer must return to the sign *S* in a previous part of the piece and play from that place to the word *fine,* or a mark over a double bar.

**alto** (al′tō), *n.* [It.], 1. the range of the lowest female voice or the highest male voice. 2. a voice or singer with such a range. 3. a part for a voice or instrument with such a range.

**Amati** (ä-mä′ti), *n.* [It.], a violin made by Nicolo Amati or his family, in Italy, in the seventeenth century: it is smaller than the ordinary violin, and distinguished for its sweetness of tone.

**amoroso** (am′ä-rô′sô), *adv.* [It.], lovingly; tenderly.

**andante** (än-dän′tä), *adj. & adv.* [It.], moderately slow; slower than allegretto but faster than larghetto.

**andante con moto** (kôn mô′tô), [It.], moving easily, with motion or agitation; rather lively.

**andante largo** (lär′gō), [It.], slow, distinct and exact.

**andante maestoso** (mä′es-tô′sô), [It.], moving rather slowly and in a majestic and dignified style.

**andante quasi allegretto** (kwä′si al′e-gret′ô), [It.], an andante nearly as rapid as allegretto.

**andantino** (än-dän-tē′nô), *adj. & adv.* [It.], slightly faster than andante: *according to some composers,* a little slower than andante.

**andare a tempo** (än-dä′re ä tem′pô), [It.], to play or sing in time.

**apertus** (a-pūr′tus), *adj.* [L.], open; as, open diapason, open canon, etc.

**a poco a poco** (ä pô′kô ä pô′kô), [It.], by little and little.

**appoggiatura** (ə-poj′ə-to͞o′rə), *n.* [It.], an ornamental tone preceding another tone; grace note.

**a prima vista** (ä prē′mä vēs′tä), [It.], at first sight.

**a punta d'arco** (ä po͞on′tä där′kô), [It.], at, or with, the point of the bow.

**à quatre mains** (à kà′tr′ man), [Fr.], for four hands, as a pianoforte duet.

**aria** (ä′ri-ə, âr′i-ə), *n.* [It.], an air or melody in an opera, cantata, or oratorio, especially for solo voice with accompaniment.

**aria buffa** (ä′ri-ə bo͞of′fä), [It.], a comic or humorous air.

**aria cantabile** (kän-tä′bi-lā′), [It.], an air in a graceful, flowing style.

**aria di bravura** (dē brä-vo͞o′rä), [It.], a florid air in bold, marked style and permitting great freedom of execution.

**aria parlante** (pär-län′te), [It.], an air in the declamatory style; a recitative *a tempo.*

**a rigore del tempo** (ä rē-gô′rä del tem′pô), [It.], in strict time.

**arpa** (är′pä), *n.* [It.], the harp.

**arpeggio** (är-pej′ō), *n.* 1. the playing of the notes of a chord quickly one after another instead of simultaneously. 2. a chord so played.

**arrangement** (ə-rānj′mənt), *n.* 1. the adaptation of a composition or parts of a composition to instruments for which it was not originally designed, or for some other use for which it was not at first written. 2. the composition as thus arranged.

**assez** (á-sā′), *adv.* [Fr.], enough; sufficiently.

**a tempo** (ä tem′pō), [It.], in regular time.

**a tempo rubato** (rōō-bä′tō), [It.], irregular time; deviation in time so as to give more expression, but so that the time of each bar is not altered on the whole.

**a tre mani** (ä trā mä′ni), [It.], for three hands.

**a tre voci** (vō′chi), [It.], for three voices.

**attacca subito** (ät-täk′kä sōō′bi-tō), [It.], attack or commence the next movement immediately.

**aubade** (ō′bād′), *n.* a piece of music suitable for performance at sunrise, or in the morning: the counterpart of *serenata,* or of *nocturne.*

**ausdruck** (ous′drook), *n.* [G.], expression.

**authentic keys,** among the ancient Greeks, those keys whose tones extend from the tonic to the fifth and octave above.

## B

**B** (bē), *n.* 1. the seventh tone in the scale of C major. 2. the scale having B as the keynote: it is called in France and Italy *si* and by the Germans *h:* the Germans use the letter *B* to indicate *B flat.*

**bagatelle** (bag′ə-tel′), *n.* [Fr.], a short musical composition, especially for the piano.

**bagpipe** (bag′pīp′), *n.* a shrill-toned musical instrument having a leather bag which receives the air by a tube stopped by a valve, and three or four sounding pipes into which the air is pressed; the pipe known as the *chanter,* gives the melody; the other pipes, known as the *drones,* produce continuous bass tones: the *bagpipe* is chiefly used in Scotland.

**balalaika** (bal′ə-lī′kə), *n.* [Russ.], a musical instrument having a triangular-shaped wooden body and from two to four strings: the *balalaika* is used especially in Russia.

**ballad** (bal′əd), *n.* a short simple song, often a folk song, usually in the narrative or descriptive form: it also has a wider meaning and is applied to music set to romantic or sentimental poems, and also to a light kind of music used both in singing and dancing; the word *ballad* means, now, any unvaried, simple song, each verse being sung to the same melody.

**ballet** (bal-ā′), *n.* [Fr.], an intricate group dance using pantomime and conventionalized movements to tell a story, accompanied with music.

**banjo** (ban′jō), *n.* a stringed musical instrument of the guitar class, consisting usually of five strings which are plucked with a plectrum or with the fingers.

**bar** (bär), *n.* 1. a vertical line drawn across the staff dividing it into measures. 2. a measure.

**bari-basso** (bä′ri-bäs′sō), *n.* [It.], a deep baritone voice.

**baritone** (bar′i-tōn), *n.* [Fr.], 1. a male voice with a range between tenor and bass. 2. a man with such a voice. 3. a musical part for a baritone.

**bass** (bās), *n.* 1. the lowest male singing voice. 2. the lowest part in vocal or instrumental music. 3. a singer or instrument having a very low range; specif., a bass viol.

**bass alberti** (bās äl-ber′ti), a bass formed by taking the notes of chords in arpeggios.

**basso buffo** (bäs′sō bōōf′fō), [It.], the principal bass singer in the comic opera.

**basso cantante** (kän-tän′te), [It.], the vocal bass part; also, the principal bass singer in an opera.

**bassoon** (ba-sōōn′), *n.* a double-reed bass musical instrument of the wood-wind class: it has a long curved mouthpiece and a double wooden tube with holes, which are stopped by the fingers and by the keys.

**bass viol** (bās vī′əl), the largest and deepest-toned musical instrument of the violin family, resembling a huge violin: also called *double bass, contrabass.*

**bel canto** (bel kän′tō), [It.], beautiful song; singing in a style characterized by beauty of sound.

**beneplacito** (bā′ne-plä′chi-tō), *adv.* [It.], at will; at pleasure; at liberty to retard the time and ornament the passage.

**ben marcato** (ben mär-kä′tō), [It.], well marked; in a distinct and strongly accented manner.

**bis** (bis), *adv.* [L.], twice; indicating that the passage marked is to be repeated.

**bourrée** (bōō′rā′), *n.* [Fr.], 1. a lively French or Spanish dance similar to a gavotte. 2. music for this dance or in a similar rapid tempo.

**brace** (brās), *n.* either of the signs [ ], used to connect or enclose words, lines, or staves of music.

**brasses** (bras′iz), *n.pl.* brass-wind musical instruments.

**brass winds** (windz), musical instruments made of coiled metal tubes, through which tones are made by blowing into a cup-shaped mouthpiece.

**bravo** (brä′vō), *interj.* [It.], an exclamation of approval often used in theaters; excellent; very good.

**bravura** (brə-vyoor′ə; It. brä-vōō′rä), *n.* [It.], spirit; skill; great dexterity and skill in performance.

**breve** (brēv), *n.* [It.], formerly, the *breve* was the shortest note; the notes then used were the large, the long and the *breve;* the *breve* is now the longest note; it is equal to two whole notes; a double note.

**breve alla** (äl′lä), [It.], a term to indicate a tempo so fast that a bar which seems to have four beats really has only two.

**brillante** (brēl-län′te), *adj.* [It.], bright; sparkling.

**brio** (brē′ō), *n.* [It.], vigor; animation; spirit.

**broken chords,** chords whose notes are not taken simultaneously, but in a broken and interrupted manner.

**buffa, opera** (ō′pä-rä bōōf′fä), [It.], a comic opera.

## C

**C** (sē), *n.* 1. the first tone in the scale of C major. 2. the scale having C as the keynote: the major scale of C is called the natural scale, because it has no flats and sharps.

**cabaletta** (kä-bä-let′tä), *n.* [It.], 1. a simple melody of a pleasing and attractive character. 2. a cavatina.

**cadence** (kā′d'ns), *n.* the harmonic ending, final trill, etc. of a phrase or movement.

**cadence, authentic,** a perfect or final cadence; the harmony of the dominant followed by that of the tonic or the progression of the dominant to the tonic.

**cadence, complete,** a full cadence, when the final sound of a verse in a chant is on the keynote.

**cadence, deceptive,** a cadence formed when the dominant chord resolves into another harmony instead of the tonic.

**cadence, false,** an imperfect or interrupted cadence.

**cadence, imperfect,** a cadence formed when the dominant harmony is preceded by the common chord of the tonic.

**cadence, interrupted,** similar to the perfect cadence except that in place of the final tonic harmony some other chord is introduced.

**cadence marks,** short lines placed vertically to indicate the cadence notes in chanting.

**cadence, perlée** (pēr-lā′), [Fr.], a brilliant cadence.

**cadence, plagal** (plā′gal), a cadence formed when tonic harmony is preceded by subdominant.

**cadence, suspended,** where the cadence passes through several modulations from the dominant to the tonic chord.

**cadenza** (kə-den′zə; It. kä-dent′sä), *n.* [It.], 1. an elaborate, often improvised musical passage played by the solo instrument in a concerto, usually near the end of the first movement. 2. any brilliant flourish in an aria or solo passage.

**cadenza fiorita** (fyôr-ē′tä), [It.], an ornate, florid cadenza with graces and embellishments.

**camera musica** (kä′me-rä mū′zi-kə), [It.], chamber music.

**canon** (kan′ən), *n.* a round; a composition in which there are exact repetitions of a preceding part in the same or related keys.

**cantabile** (kän-tä′bi-lā′), *adj.* [It.], that can be sung; in an easy, flowing manner; songlike.

**cantabile con molto portamento** (kôn môl′tô pôr-tä-men′tô), [It.], in a singing, melodious style, with embellishments at pleasure, but few and well chosen.

**cantante ariose** (kän-tän′te ar′i-ōs), [It.], a kind of melody which, by its frequent changes of measure and conversational style, first served to mark the distinction between the air and the recitative.

**cantare a aria** (kän-tä′re ä ä′ri-ə), [It.], to sing without confining oneself strictly to the music as written.

**cantata** (kən-tä′tə, kan-tä′tə), *n.* [It.], a choral composition consisting of choruses, solos, interludes, and recitatives, used as a setting for a story to be sung but not acted.

**cantatrice** (kän-tä-trē′che), *n.* [It.], a female singer.

**cantilena** (kän-ti-lā′nä), *n.* [It.], the melody, air, or principal part in any composition; generally, the highest vocal part.

**canto** (kan′tō), *n.* [It.], song; air; melody; the highest vocal part in choral music.

**canto fermo** (fer′mô), [It.], 1. a chant or melody; choral singing in unison on a plain melody. 2. any subject consisting of a few long plain notes given as a theme for counterpoint.

**canto figurato** (fē-gōō-rä′tô), [It.], a figured melody embellishing a plain song.

**canto fioritto** (fyôr-ē′tô), [It.], a song in which many ornaments are introduced.

**Canto Gregariano** (grē-gôr-ē-än′ô), [It.], the Gregorian chant.

**canto primo** (prē′mô), [It.], the first treble or soprano.

**canzonet** (kan-zō-net′), *n.* a short song in one, two, or three parts.

**capo** (kä′pô), *n.* [It.], the head or beginning; the top.

**capo d'opera** (dô′pä-rä), [It.], the masterpiece of a composer.

**capo d'orchestra** (dôr′kes-trä), [It.], the leader of the orchestra.

**capella** (kä-pel′lä), *n.* [It.], 1. a chapel or church. 2. a band of musicians that sing or play in a church.

**capriccio** (kə-prē′chi-ō; It. kä-prēt′chô), *n.* [It.], a lively musical composition of irregular form, usually whimsical in spirit.

**capriccioso** (kə-prē′chi-ō′sō; It. kä-prēt-chô′sô), *adj. & adv.* [It.], in a light, free, whimsical style.

**castanets** (kas′tə-nets′, kas′tə-nets′), *n. pl.* small, hollowed pieces of hard wood or ivory, used in pairs to beat time to music, especially in Spanish dances: they are held in the hand by a connecting cord or ribbon over the thumb, and clapped against each other by the fingers.

**cavatina** (kä-vä-tē′nä), *n.* [It.], an air of one strain only, of dramatic style sometimes preceded by a recitative.

**celesta** (sə-les′tə), *n.* [Fr.], a small keyboard instrument in which hammers strike plates of steel suspended over wooden resonance boxes with pianolike action; the tone of the celesta is of exquisite purity.

**cello, 'cello** (chel′ō), *n.* [It.], an instrument of the violin family, between the viola and the double bass in size and pitch; violoncello.

**chaconne** (shȧ′kôn′), *n.* [Fr.], a graceful, slow Spanish movement, in 3/4 time, and composed upon a ground bass; it is always in the major key and the first and third beats of each bar are strongly accented.

**chamber music,** instrumental or vocal music intended for performance in a chamber or small music hall, as trios, quartets, and quintets.

**chanson** (shäṉ′sôṉ′; Eng. shan′sən), *n.* [Fr.], a song.

**chant** (chant, chänt), *n.* a simple melody, generally harmonized in four parts, to which lyrical portions of the Scriptures are set, part of the words being recited ad libitum, and part sung in strict time. *v. t.* to recite musically; to sing.

**chant, Ambrosian** (am-brō′zi-ən, am-brō′-zhən), the chant introduced by St. Ambrose into the church at Milan, in the fourth century.

**chanteuse** (shäṉ′töz′), *n.* [Fr.], a woman singer.

**chant, plain,** a single chant, seldom extending beyond the limits of an octave, or through more than one verse.

**chef d'orchestre** (shef dôr-kes′tr′), [Fr.], the leader of an orchestra.

**chimes** (chīmz), *n.pl.* a set of bells tuned to the musical scale.

**Chinese musical scale,** a scale consisting of five notes without semitones, the music being written on five lines in perpendicular columns, and the elevation and depression of tones indicated by distinctive names.

**choragus** (kō-rā′gəs), *n.* [L.], the leader of a chorus, choir, or band.

**chord, fundamental,** a chord consisting of the fundamental tone with its third and fifth and its inversions.

**chord, inverted,** a chord whose lowest tone is not the fundamental but the third, fifth or seventh from the lowest or bass note.

**chords, diminished,** chords with less than perfect intervals.

**clarinet** (klar′ə-net′), *n.* a single-reed, woodwind instrument: it consists of a mouthpiece furnished with a single reed, and a cylindrical tube which is pierced with side holes, ending in a flaring bell.

**clavichord** (klav′ə-kôrd′), *n.* a stringed musical instrument with a keyboard like the spinet, and the forerunner of the piano: the tone of the clavichord was agreeable and impressive but not strong.

**clavier** (klav′i-ẽr, klə-vêr′), *n.* [Fr.], the keys or keyboard of a pianoforte, organ, etc.; also, any stringed instrument that has a keyboard; now, usually, a piano.

**clef, mezzo-soprano** (met′sō-sə-pran′ō klef), the C clef placed on the second line of the staff.

**clef, soprano** (sə-pran′ō), the C clef placed on the first line.

**clef, tenor** (ten′ẽr), the C clef placed on the fourth line.

**clef, treble** (treb′′l), the G clef; soprano clef.

**coda** (kō′də), *n.* [It.], a final passage, closing a composition or movement.

**coda brillante** (brēl-län′te), [It.], a brilliant final passage.

**codetta** (kô-det′tä), *n.* [It.], a short coda or passage added to a piece, or serving to connect one movement with another.

**colla destra** (kôl′lä des′trä), [It.], with the right hand.

**colla sinistra** (sē-nē′strä), [It.], with the left hand.

**comma** (kom′ə), *n.* [It.], the smallest of all the perceptible intervals of tone, and used in treating or analyzing musical sounds; an illustration of a *comma* is the difference between D sharp and E flat as played upon the violin by the best performers; a tone is divided into nine almost imperceptible intervals, called *commas,* five of which constitute the major semitone, and four the minor semitone.

**common chord,** a chord consisting of a bass note with its third and fifth, to which its octave is usually added.

**compensating piano,** an English piano with heavy strings by means of which full power is obtained from a small or cottage piano.

**con amore** (kôn′ ä-mô′rə), [It.], tenderly; with love.

**con anima** (ä′nē-mä), [It.], with animation.

**con brio** (brē′ô), [It.], with spirit.

**con calore** (kä-lō′re), [It.], with warmth; with fire.

**con carita** (kä-rē′tä), [It.], with tenderness.

**con celerita** (chel-ā-rē′tä), [It.], with celerity; with rapidity.

**concertina** (kon′sẽr-tē′nə), *n.* a small musical instrument of the accordion type, having a keyboard at each end, with expansible bellows between the two; the pressure of air from the bellows on free metallic reeds produces the sound; it is occasionally used in orchestras for special effects.

**concertino** (kôn′cher-tē′nô), *n.* [It.], a brief concerto.

**concertmaster** (kon′sẽrt-mas′tẽr), *n.* the leader of the first violin section of a symphony orchestra, often an assistant to the conductor: also **concertmeister** (-mīs′-).

**concerto** (kən-cher′tō), *n.* [It.], a composition in sonata form for one or more solo instruments and an orchestra: it usually has three movements.

**concerto a solo** (ä sō′lō), [It.], a concerto written for the purpose of displaying the powers of a particular instrument, without accompaniment.

**concerto doppio** (dôp′pyô), [It.], a concerto for two or more instruments.

**concerto grosso** (grō′sō), [It.], a concerto for a small group of solo instruments and a full orchestra.

**concert pitch,** a pitch, slightly higher than the usual pitch, to which concert instruments are tuned in order to compensate acoustically for the relatively high room temperature of crowded concert halls.

**con dolore** (kôn′ dô-lô′re), [It.], mournfully; with grief and pathos.

**conductor** (kən-duk′tẽr), *n.* the director of an orchestra or other musical group.

**confretta** (kôn-fret′tä), *adv.* [It.], hurriedly; with an increase of time.

**con fuoco** (kôn fwô′kô), [It.], with fire; impetuously.

**con gusto** (gūs′tô), [It.], with taste.

**con moto** (mô′tô), [It.], with animated movement; not dragging.

**consecutive octaves,** two parts moving in unison or octaves with each other.

**conservatoire** (kən-sũr′və-twär′), *n.* [Fr.], a school or academy of music, in which every branch of musical art is taught.

**con spirito** (kôn spē′rē-tô), [It.], with spirit; with animation.

**contrabass** (kon′trə-bās′), *n.* an instrument or voice having the lowest bass tone; specif., the largest and deepest-toned instrument of the violin family; bass viol.

**contrabassist** (kon′trə-bā′sist), *n.* a person who plays the contrabass.

**contrabasso** (kon′trə-bäs′ō), n. a contrabass.

**contrabassoon** (kon′trə-bə-so͞on′), *n.* the double bassoon, which is larger than the regular bassoon and an octave lower in pitch.

**contralto** (kən-tral′tō), *n.* [It.], 1. the part sung by the lowest female voice. 2. a female voice of the lowest range. 3. a woman or girl who sings in this range.

**contrary motion,** motion in an opposite direction to some other part, one rising as the other falls.

**contretemps** (kôṉ′trə-täṉ′), *n.* [Fr.], syncopation; shifted accent; notes tied and accented contrary to the natural rhythmic flow of the measure.

**con vigore** (kôn vi-gô′re), [It.], with vigor, sprightliness, and strength.

**cor anglais** (kôr äṉ-gle′), [Fr.], 1. English horn. 2. the tenor oboe. 3. a reed stop in an organ.

**corchea** (kôr-chā′ä), *n.* [Sp.], a crotchet.

**cornet stop,** an organ stop, consisting of five pipes to each note.

**corps de ballet** (kôr′ də bȧ′le′; Eng. kôr′ də bal-ā′), [Fr.], a troupe or company of ballet dancers.

**counterpoint** (koun′tẽr-point′), *n.* 1. a melody accompanying another melody note for note. 2. the art of adding related but independent melodies to a basic melody, in accordance with the fixed rules of harmony. 3. this kind of composition.

**counterpoint, double,** counterpoint in which the upper and lower parts may change place.

**counterpoint, fugued,** counterpoint consisting of four, five, six, or seven parts; the only counterpoint in use before the eighteenth century.

**counterpoint, quadruple,** counterpoint in four parts.

**counterpoint, triple,** a counterpoint in three parts, all of which may be inverted.

**courante** (ko͞o-ränt′), *n.* [Fr.], 1. an old, lively French dance. 2. the music for this dance.

**cres. al forte** (kres äl fôr′tä), [It.], increasing as loud as possible.

**cres. al fortissimo** (fôr-tis′ə-mō′), [It.], increasing to very loud.

**crescendo** (krə-shen′dō, -sen′-), *adj. & adv.* gradually increasing in loudness or intensity.

**crescendo e diminuendo** [It.], gradually increasing and then diminishing in loudness or intensity.

**crescendo poco a poco** (pō′kō ä pō′kō), [It.], increasing the tone little by little.

**cymbal** (sim′b'l), *n.* either of a pair of slightly concave plates of brass having a leather strap through the center of each plate by which they are held by the performer, one in each hand; when struck together they produce a sharp, ringing sound.

## D

**D** (dē), n. 1. the second tone in the scale of C major. 2. the scale having D as the keynote.

**da capo** (dä kä′pô), [It.], from the beginning; an expression placed at the end of a passage to indicate that the performer is to repeat it.

**da capo al fine** (äl fē′ne), [It.], return to the beginning and conclude with the word *fine.*

**dal segno** (däl se′nyô), [It.], from the sign: a direction to return and repeat from the sign.

**damper pedal,** that pedal in a pianoforte which raises the dampers from the strings and allows them to vibrate freely: its use is indicated by the abbreviation *ped.*

**decrescendo** (dē′krə-shen′dō), *adj. & adv.* [It.], with a gradual decrease in loudness.

**descant** (des′kant), *n.* 1. a varied song or melody. 2. in medieval music, a counterpoint sung above the main melody. 3. the art of composing part music. 4. a piece of part music.

**design** (di-zīn′), *n.* the general sketch or idea and arrangement of a musical composition.

**diapason** (dī′ə-pā′z′n, -s′n), *n.* 1. the entire range of a musical instrument or voice. 2. either of two principal stops of an organ (*open diapason* and *stopped diapason*), covering the entire range: when either is used, any note played is sounded in two or more octaves.

**diatonic scale,** any standard major or minor scale of eight tones without the chromatic intervals.

**di grado** (dē grä′dô), [It.], by degrees; step by step: opposed to *di salto*.

**diminished chords,** chords that are composed of diminished intervals.

**diminished interval,** an interval that has been lessened by a semitone.

**diminuendo** (də-min′ū-en′dō), *adj.* [It.], lessening the tone from loud to soft; decrescendo.

**di molto** (dē môl′tô), [It.], very; much.

**di salto** (säl′tô), [It.], by leaps or by skips: opposed to *di grado*.

**discantus** (dis-kan′təs), *n.* [L.], descant; singing in parts; a piece of music in parts.

**divertimento** (di-ver′ti-men′tō), *n.* [It.], any of various light, melodic instrumental compositions in several movements.

**divertissement** (dē′ver′tēs′män), *n.* [Fr.], 1. a series of airs and dances resembling a short ballet introduced between the acts or at the conclusion of an opera. 2. a divertimento.

**dolce** (dôl′che), *adj.* [It.], sweet and soft; smooth in performance.

**dolce e cantabile** (e kän-tä′bi-le), [It.], sweet; soft; in singing style.

**dolce ma marcato** (mä mär-kä′tô), [It.], soft and delicate but marked and accented.

**dolore** (dô-lô′re), *n.* [It.], grief; sorrow.

**doloroso** (dô′lô-rô′sô), *adj. & adv.* [It.], with sorrow or plaintive quality.

**dominant** (dom′ə-nənt), *adj.* of or based upon the fifth tone of a diatonic scale. *n.* the fifth tone of a diatonic scale.

**dot** (dot), *n.* a mark which, when placed after a note or rest, increases its duration one half; when the dot is placed over a note it signifies that the note is to be played staccato.

**double bass,** the bass viol.

**double bassoon,** the contrabassoon.

**duple** (doo′p′l, dū′-), *adj.* containing an even number of beats to the measure: as, *duple* time.

**dur** (door), *adj.* [G.], major, in speaking of keys and modes: as, C *dur*.

**dynamics** (dī-nam′iks), *n. pl.* [construed as sing.], that aspect of musical expression which deals with degrees of loudness and softness in performance.

## E

**E** (ē), *n.* 1. the third tone in the scale of C major. 2. the scale having E as the keynote.

**eighth note,** a note (♪) having one eighth the duration of a whole note.

**eingang** (īn′gäŋ), *n.* [G.], introduction; preface; prelude.

**einleitung** (īn′lī-tooŋ), *n.* [G.], introduction; prelude.

**élégante** (ā-lā-gänt′), *adj.* [Fr.], elegant; graceful.

**embouchure** (om′boo-shoor′), *n.* [Fr.], 1. the mouthpiece of a flute, oboe, or other wind instrument. 2. the way of applying the lips and tongue to the mouthpiece of a wind instrument.

**enharmonic** (en′här-mon′ik), *adj.* 1. designating or of an interval less than a half step. 2. relating to tones nearly identical in pitch, as E♭ and D♯.

**episode** (ep′ə-sōd′), *n.* any incidental passage between repetitions of the main theme, especially in a fugue or rondo.

**espressivo** (es-pres-sē′vô), *adj.* [It.], expressive; to be played or sung with expression.

**extension pedal,** the loud pedal of a piano.

## F

**F** (ef), *n.* 1. the fourth tone in the scale of C major. 2. the scale having F as the keynote.

**false intonation,** incorrect intonation; intonation where the voice does not express the intended or correct intervals.

**fanfare** (fan′fâr′), *n.* a loud blast or flourish of trumpets.

**fantasia** (fan-tä′zi-ə, -zhə, fan′tə-zē′ə), *n.* 1. a musical composition of no fixed form, with a structure determined by the composer's fancy. 2. a medley of familiar tunes.

**figured bass,** a bass with figures placed over or under the notes to indicate the harmony.

**figured harmony,** harmony in which one or more of the parts of a composition move during the continuance of a chord, through certain notes which do not form any of the constituent parts of that chord.

**fine** (fē′ne), *n.* [It.], the end: a direction marking the close of a repeated passage.

**fingering, American,** the use of the sign (x) to indicate the thumb in piano playing, in distinction from the German or foreign fingering, in which the thumb is called the first finger.

**fioco** (fyô′kô), *adj.* [It.], hoarse; faint; feeble.

**fioretta** (fyô-ret′tä), *n.* [It.], little graces or ornaments, in vocal music.

**fioriture** (fyô-ri-tū′re), *n.* [It.], literally, little flowers; graces and embellishments in singing.

**first inversion,** a term applied to a chord when the bass takes the third.

**first-movement form,** sonata form.

**flat** (flat), *n.* 1. a note or tone one half step below another. 2. the symbol (♭) for such a note.

**flute** (floot), *n.* a high-pitched wind instrument having a long, slender tube with holes along its length, which are stopped by the fingers or by keys opened by the fingers.

**fluted** (floot′id), *adj.* a term applied to the upper notes of a soprano voice, when they are of a thin and flutelike tone.

**forte** (fôr′tā), *adj.* [It.], loud; strong.

**fortiss.** (fôr′tis), *adj.* an abbreviation of fortissimo.

**fortissimo quanto possibile** (fôr-tis′ə-mō′ kwän′tô pôs-sē′bi-le), [It.], as loud as possible.

**forza** (fôr′tsä), *n.* [It.], force; strength; power.

**forzando** (fôr-tsän′dō), *adj.* [It.], with force; with stress.

**forzato** (fôr-tsä′tô), *adj.* [It.], forced; laying a stress upon one note or chord.

**four-part song,** a song arranged for four parts.

**fox trot,** a ballroom dance in 4/4 time; it consists of slow walking steps, trotting steps, etc.

**frei** (frī), *adj.* [G.], free and unrestrained as to style.

**frivolo** (fri-vô′lô), *adj.* [It.], frivolous; trifling; trashy.

**fugue** (fūg), *n.* a musical composition in the strict style, in which a theme is taken up and developed by the various instruments and voices in succession, according to the laws of counterpoint.

**full orchestra,** an orchestra in which all the string, wood-wind, brass, and percussion sections are employed.

**full score,** a complete score of all the parts of a composition, vocal or instrumental, or both combined, written on separate staves placed under each other.

**furioso** (foo-ri-ô′sô), *adj.* [It.], furious; vehement; mad.

## G

**G** (jē), *n.* 1. the fifth tone in the scale of C major. 2. the scale having G as the keynote.

**gamut** (gam′ət), *n.* 1. the entire series of recognized notes in modern music. 2. any complete musical scale, especially the major scale.

**gavotte, gavot** (gə-vot′), *n.* 1. a 17th-century dance like the minuet, but livelier. 2. the music for this dance, in 4/4 time.

**gigue** (zhēg), *n.* [Fr.], a jig.

**grand opera,** opera, generally on a serious theme, in which the whole text is set to music: distinguished from *operetta, comic opera*.

**grand piano,** a large piano with strings set horizontally in a harp-shaped case.

**grand sonata,** an extended sonata, consisting generally of four movements.

**grazioso** (grä-tsyô′sô), *adj.* [It.], graceful; smooth; elegant.

**Gregorian chant,** the ritual plain song of the Roman Catholic Church, introduced by Pope Gregory I: it is unaccompanied and without meter.

**guitar** (gi-tär′), *n.* a stringed musical instrument of the lute family consisting of a long fretted neck and six strings which are plucked with the fingers or a plectrum.

## H

**H** (äch), *n.* the German name for the note B natural.

**half note,** a note (𝅗𝅥) having one half the duration of a whole note.

**half step,** the difference in pitch between two adjacent keys on the piano: also called *half tone*.

**harmonica** (här-mon′i-kə), *n.* a small wind instrument played by the mouth; the tones are produced by a series of graduated metal reeds that vibrate when air is blown or sucked across them: also called *mouth organ*.

**harmonics** (här-mon′iks), *n. pl.* overtones, especially those produced by lightly stopping a vibrating string at some specified point.

**harmonium** (här-mō′ni-əm), *n.* a small keyboard organ in which the tones are produced by forcing air through metal reeds by means of a bellows operated by pedals.

**harmony** (här′mə-ni), *n.* 1. the pleasing combination of two or more tones in a chord. 2. musical structure in terms of the arrangement, progression, etc. of chords. 3. the study of this structure.

**harp** (härp), *n.* a triangular-shaped musical instrument having strings set in an open frame and plucked with the fingers.

**harpsichord** (härp′si-kôrd′), *n.* a stringed musical instrument with a keyboard, forerunner of the piano; the strings are plucked by points rather than struck by hammers, as in the piano: it resembles the grand piano and has sometimes two rows of keys, but it is very inferior to that instrument in capacity for power and expression; the various shades of loud or soft can only be obtained by changing from one set of keys to the other, or by moving certain stops as in the organ; the range is about four octaves.

**hautboy** (hō′boi), *n.* an oboe.

**head tones,** tones produced by the upper register of the voice.

**helicon** (hel′i-kon′, -kən), *n.* a brass-wind instrument similar to a bass tuba, consisting of a long tube bent into a circle so that it can be carried over the shoulder.

**heptachord** (hep′tə-kôrd′), *n.* 1. the interval of a major seventh. 2. a diatonic scale of seven tones. 3. a musical instrument, especially a lyre, with seven strings.
**heptaphonos** (hep′tə-fō′nəs), *n.* [Gr.], the name given to each of the ten musical notes used during the middle ages.
**hexachord** (hek′sə-kôrd′), *n.* a diatonic scale of six tones, with a semitone between the third and the fourth.
**high bass,** a voice between bass and tenor; a baritone.
**high soprano,** the first soprano.
**high tenor,** the highest male voice.
**homophony** (hō-mof′ə-ni), *n.* 1. music in which a single voice carries the melody, often with an accompaniment in chords. 2. formerly, music written, sung, or played in unison.
**horn, English,** a wood-wind instrument of the double-reed kind similar to the oboe but larger and a fifth lower in pitch.
**horn, French,** 1. a brass-wind instrument, consisting of a long tube twisted into several circular folds, and gradually increasing in diameter from the mouthpiece to the end, which is a wide, flaring bell. 2. an eight-foot organ stop of a smooth full tone.

## I

**il doppio movimento** (ēl dôp′pyô mô-vē-men′tô), [It.], double movement; double speed.
**imitation** (im′ə-tā′shən), *n.* a kind of fugue, in which the parts imitate each other, though not in the same intervals, or according to the strict laws of a fugue or canon.
**impresario** (im′pri-sä′ri-ō′), *n.* [It.], the organizer, manager, or director of an opera or ballet company, concert series, etc.
**improvvisatore** (ēm′prô-vē′zä-tô′re), *n.* [It.], a performer who improvises songs or poems.
**inconsolato** (in-kôn-sô-lä′tô), *adv.* [It.], in a mournful style.
**in disparte** (in dis-pär′te), [It.], a term used in operatic music, signifying that the part is to be addressed to some one aside, or not taking part in the performance.
**infinite canon,** a canon which is so constructed that the end leads to the beginning, and the performance may be indefinitely repeated: also called *circular* or *endless canon.*
**intermezzo** (in′tēr-met′sō, -med′zō), *n.* [It.], 1. a short, light dramatic, musical, or ballet entertainment between the acts of a play or opera. 2. a short movement connecting the main parts of a composition. 3. any of certain short instrumental pieces similar to this.
**interval** (in′tēr-v'l), *n.* the difference in pitch between two tones.
**interval, augmented,** an interval which is a semitone, or half step, greater than the corresponding major interval.
**interval, diminished,** an interval less than a perfect interval by a half step or semitone.
**intonation** (in′tō-nā′shən), *n.* 1. the manner of producing or uttering tones with regard to rise and fall in pitch. 2. the opening phrase of a Gregorian chant.
**invention** (in-ven′shən), *n.* a short piano composition developing a single theme in two-part counterpoint; especially, any of a group of these by Bach.
**inversion** (in-vũr′zhən, -shən), *n.* the reversal of the position of the tones in an interval, chord, etc., as by raising the lower tone by an octave, etc.

## K

**kammermusik** (käm′ər-moo-zēk′), *n.* [G.], chamber music.
**Kapellmeister** (kä-pel′mīs-tēr), *n.* [G.], the conductor of a choir or orchestra.
**kettledrum** (ket′'l-drum′), *n.* a drum consisting of a hollow hemisphere of copper or brass and a parchment top that can be tightened or loosened to change the pitch.
**key** (kē), *n.* 1. any of a set of levers, or the disks, buttons, etc. connected to them, pressed down in operating a piano, organ, accordion, clarinet, oboe, etc. 2. a system of related notes or tones based on and named after a certain note (*keynote*) and forming a given scale; the main tonality of a composition.

## L

**l,** left hand; notes to be played with the left hand or foot are sometimes written with an *l* over them.
**la destra** (lä des′trä), [It.], the right hand.
**larghetto** (lär-get′ō), *adj. & adv.* [It.], relatively slow, but not quite so slow as largo.
**largo** (lär′gō), *adj. & adv.* [It.], slow and stately.
**largo di molto** (dē môl′tô), [It.], very slow.
**largo ma non troppo** (mä nôn trôp′pô), [It.], slow, but not too much so.
**laut** (lout), *adj.* [G.], loud.
**ledger lines,** the short extra, or additional lines drawn above or below the staff, for such notes as are too high or too low to be placed on or within the staff.
**legatissimo** (lā-gä-tis′i-mô), *adj.* [It.], exceedingly smooth and connected.
**legato** (li-gä′tō), *adj. & adv.* [It.], in a smooth, even style, with no noticeable interruption between the notes.
**legato assai** (äs-sä′ē), [It.], very close and connected.
**leggermente** (lā-jer-men′tā), *adv.* [It.], with a light and easy movement.
**lento** (len′tō), *adj. & adv.* [It.], slow; slowly.
**libretto** (li-bret′ō), *n.* [It.], the text of an opera or other extended piece of music.
**lied** (lēd; G. lēt), *n.* [G.], a German song or lyric.
**lieder** (lē′dēr), *n. pl.* [G.], German songs or lyrics.
**lied ohne worte** (ō′ne vôr′te), [G.], a song without words.
**loco** (lō′kō), *adj.* [It.], a word used in opposition to *8va-alta,* signifying that the notes over which it is placed are not to be played an octave higher, but just as they are written.
**long appoggiatura,** an appoggiatura consisting of a single note forming a part of the melody; it borrows half the length of the next note and is accented.
**lo stretto** (lô stret′tô), [It.], that part of a composition designed to be played in a quicker time than the rest.
**lugubre** (lū-gū′brā), *adj.* [It.], lugubrious; sad; mournful.
**lunga pausa** (loon′gä pou′sä), [It.], a long pause or rest.
**lustig** (loos′tik), *adv.* [G.], merrily; cheerfully; gaily.

## M

**m,** an abbreviation of mezzo, and of other words, as metronome, mano, main, and also in connection with other letters: as, m. f. for mezzo forte.
**madrigal** (mad′ri-g'l), *n.* a contrapuntal song with parts for several voices, sung without accompaniment, popular in the 15th, 16th, and 17th centuries.
**maestoso** (mä′es-tô′sô), *adj. & adv.* with majesty or dignity.
**maestro** (mīs′trō, mä-es′trō), *n.* [It.], 1. a great composer, conductor, or teacher of music. 2. a master in any art.
**maestro di camera** (dē kä′mä-rä), [It.], the leader or conductor of chamber music.
**maestro di canto** (dē kän′tô), [It.], a singing teacher.
**maestro di capella** (dē käp-pel′lä), [It.], choirmaster; composer; director of the musical performances in a church or chapel.
**mandolin** (man′d'l-in′, man′də-lin′), *n.* a musical instrument with eight, ten, or twelve metal strings, usually paired, stretched over a deep, rounded sound box: it is played with a plectrum, which is moved rapidly back and forth to give a tremolo effect.
**mandolute** (man′də-lūt), *n.* an instrument very similar to the mandolin.
**mandore** (man-dōr′), *n.* a small lute having four strings.
**mano** (mä′nô), *n.* [It.], the hand.
**mano destra** (des′trä), [It.], the right hand.
**mano sinistra** (sē-nēs′trä), [It.], the left hand.
**marcando** (mär-kän′dô), *adj.* [It.], marked; accented; well-pronounced.
**marcato il pollice** (mär-kä′tô ēl pô′lē-che), [It.], mark or accent strongly the note played by the thumb.
**marimba** (mə-rim′bə), *n.* a musical instrument somewhat like a xylophone, consisting of a series of hard wooden bars, usually with resonators beneath, played by being struck with small hammers.
**mässig geschwind** (mā′sik ge-shvint′), [G.], moderately playful; moderately fast.
**mazurka, mazourka** (mə-zūr′kə, -zoor′-), *n.* 1. a lively Polish dance like the polka. 2. music for this, generally in 3/4 or 3/8 time.
**measure** (mezh′ēr), *n.* 1. the notes or rests, or both, contained between two vertical lines on the staff, subdividing a part of a composition into equal groups of beats; bar. 2. musical time or rhythm.
**mediant** (mē′di-ənt), *n.* [Lat.], the third tone of a musical scale, halfway between the tonic and the dominant.
**melody** (mel′ə-di), *n.* 1. a sequence of single tones, usually in the same key or mode, to produce a rhythmic whole; often, a tune, air, or song. 2. the element of form having to do with the arrangement of single tones in sequence. 3. the leading part, or voice, in a harmonic composition; the air.
**meno** (mā′nô), *adv.* [It.], less.
**messa di voce** (mās′sä dē vô′chā), [It.], the gradual swelling and diminishing of the voice.
**metronome** (met′rə-nōm′), *n.* a clockwork device with an inverted pendulum that beats time at a rate determined by the position of a sliding weight on the pendulum: it is used especially to help a person maintain regular tempo in practicing on the piano, etc.
**mezza voce** (med′zä vô′che), [It.], half the power of the voice; with moderate strength of tone.
**mezzo** (met′sō, med′zō, mez′ō), *adj.* medium; moderate; half. *adv.* moderately; somewhat.
**mezzo forte,** [It.], moderately loud.
**mezzo piano,** [It.], rather soft.
**mezzo-soprano** (met′sō-sə-pran′ō, med′zō-sə-prä′nō, mez′ō-), *n.* 1. a voice or part between soprano and contralto. 2. a singer with such a voice.
**minuet** (min′ū-et′), *n.* 1. a slow, stately dance for groups of couples, introduced in France in the 17th century. 2. the music for this, in 3/4 time: often a movement of certain musical compositions.
**mit** (mit), *prep.* [G.], with; by.
**mit begleitung** (be-glī′tooŋ), [G.], with an accompaniment.
**mit bewegung** (be-vā′gooŋ), [G.], with movement; spiritedly.
**moll** (môl), *adj.* [G.], minor.
**molto** (môl′tô), *adv.* [It.], much; very much; extremely; a great deal.
**molto adagio** (ə-dä′jō), [It.], very slowly.
**molto allegro** (ə-lā′grō), [It.], very fast.
**molto staccato con grazia** (stə-kä′tō kôn

grä′tsyä), [It.], in staccato style and with grace.

**mordent** (môr′d'nt), *n.* a trill made by a rapid alternation of a principal tone with a supplementary tone a half step below it: in a *single* (or *short*) *mordent,* the supplementary tone occurs once; in a *double* (or *long*) *mordent,* more than once; in an *inverted mordent,* the supplementary tone is a half step above the principal tone.

**mordente** (môr-den′tā), *n.* [It.], a mordent.

**morendo** (mô-ren′dô), *adj.* [It.], dying.

**motif** (mō-tēf′), *n.* [F.], a main theme or subject for development.

**motive** (mō′tiv), *n.* a motif.

**movement** (mo͞ov′mənt), *n.* 1. tempo or rhythm. 2. any of the principal divisions of a symphony, sonata, or other extended composition.

**musik stunde** (mū′zik shtoon′de), [G.], a music lesson.

## N

**natural** (nach′ēr-əl), *adj.* having neither flats nor sharps; neither sharped nor flatted.

**naturalmente** (nä-to͞o-räl-men′tä), *adv.* [It.], naturally.

**nocturne** (nok′tẽrn, nok-tũrn′), *n.* a composition of a romantic or dreamy character thought appropriate to night: also spelled *nocturn.*

**non troppo presto** (nôn trôp′pô pres′tô), [It.], not too fast.

**nota di piacere** (nō′tä dē pyä-chā′rā), [It.], an optional grace note.

**nota sostenuta** (nō′tä sôs′te-no͞o′tä), [It.], a sustained note.

## O

**obbligato** (ob′li-gä′tō), *adj.* [It.], indispensable; necessary. *n.* a part or accompaniment which cannot be omitted, being indispensably necessary to a proper performance.

**oboe** (ō′bō, ō′boi), *n.* 1. a double-reed wood-wind instrument having a range of nearly three octaves and a high, penetrating, melancholy tone. 2. an organ stop producing an oboelike tone.

**ocarina** (ok′ə-rē′nə), *n.* [It.], a small, simple wind instrument shaped like a sweet potato and usually made of terra cotta, with finger holes and a mouthpiece: it produces soft, hollow tones.

**octave** (ok′tāv, ok′tiv), *n.* 1. the eighth full tone above or below a given tone. 2. the interval of eight diatonic degrees between a tone and either of its octaves. 3. the series of tones (a full scale) within this interval, or the keys of an instrument producing such a series. 4. a tone and either of its octaves sounded together.

**opera** (op′ẽr-ə), *n.* 1. a play having all or most of its text set to music, with arias, recitatives, choruses, duets, trios, etc. sung to orchestral accompaniment, usually characterized by elaborate costuming, scenery, and choreography. 2. the branch of art represented by such plays. 3. the score, libretto, or performance of such a play. 4. a theater in which operas are given.

**opera buffa** (ô′pā-rä bo͞of′fä), [It.], comic opera.

**opéra bouffe** (ô′pā′rà′ bo͞of′; Eng. op′ẽr-ə bo͞of′), [Fr.], comic opera, especially if farcical.

**operetta** (op′ə-ret′ə), *n.* [It.], a short, amusing musical play.

**oratorio** (ôr′ə-tôr′i-ō′, or′ə-tō′ri-), *n.* a long, dramatic musical work, usually on a religious theme, consisting of arias, recitatives, duets, trios, choruses, etc. sung to orchestral accompaniment: it is presented without stage action, scenery, or costumes.

**organ** (ôr′gən), *n.* any of several musical instruments, especially one consisting of various sets of pipes which, as they are opened by their corresponding keys on the keyboard, allow passage to a column of compressed air that causes sound by vibration.

**organ point,** a long pedal note, or stationary bass, upon which is formed a series of chords, or harmonic progressions.

**organ stop,** 1. a tuned set of organ pipes or reeds of the same specific type and tone quality. 2. a pull, lever, or key for putting such a set or sets into or out of operation.

**organum** (ôr′gə-nəm), *n.* an early type of two-part harmony in which the voices are separated by an interval of a fourth or fifth.

**ostinato** (ôs′tē-nä′tô), *n.* [It.], a short melodic phrase constantly repeated by the same voice or instrument and in the same pitch.

**ottava bassa** (ôt-tä′vä bäs′sä), [It.], the octave below, marked thus: 8va bassa.

**overtone** (ō′vẽr-tōn′), *n.* any of the higher tones which faintly accompany the fundamental tone produced by a musical instrument, created by the vibration of small sections of the string or air column; upper partial; harmonic.

## P

**Panpipe** (pan′pīp′), *n.* a primitive musical instrument made of a row of reeds or tubes of graduated lengths, played by blowing across the open ends: also called *Panpipes, Pan's pipes, syrinx.*

**passacaglia** (pas′ə-käl′yə, It. päs′sä-käl′yä), *n.* [It.], 1. formerly, a slow, stately Italian dance similar to the chaconne. 2. the music for this dance. 3. a musical form based on this dance, characterized by 3/4 meter and a continuous ground bass.

**pedal** (ped′'l), *n.* a lever operated by foot, used in changing the tone or volume of a musical instrument, as an organ, harp, or piano.

**pedal point,** a single continuous tone, usually in the bass, held against the changing figures or harmonies of the other parts.

**percussion instrument,** a musical instrument in which the tone is produced when some part is struck, as the drums, cymbals, tambourine, triangle, bells, xylophone, etc., and, broadly, the piano.

**petits morceaux** (pə-tē′ môr-sō′), [Fr.], short pieces.

**philharmonic** (fil′här-mon′ik, fil′ẽr-), *adj.* [Gr.], music-loving.

**phrase** (frāz), *n.* a short, distinct passage, usually of two, four, or eight measures.

**pianissimo** (pē′ə-nis′ə-mō′), *adj. & adv.* [It.], very soft.

**piano** (pi-an′ō, pyan′-), *n.* [It.], a large stringed, percussion instrument played from a keyboard, each key of which operates a small, felt-covered hammer that strikes and vibrates a corresponding steel wire: the wires produce tones ranging over seven octaves.

**piano** (pi-ä′nō, pyä′nō), *adj. & adv.* [It.], soft.

**piano assai** (äs-sä′ē), [It.], as soft as possible.

**pianoforte** (pi-an′ə-fôrt′, pyan′ə-fōr′ti), *n.* [It.], a piano.

**pianoforte score,** a score in which every part has been so arranged that it may be played on a piano.

**piccolo** (pik′ə-lō′), *n.* a small flute with its pitch an octave higher than the ordinary flute.

**pipe organ,** a musical instrument with a keyboard that controls the flow of compressed air through one or more sets of pipes of varying length.

**più** (pū), *adv.* [It.], more.

**più allegro,** [It.], more quickly.

**più che lento** (kā len′tô), [It.], slower than lento.

**più mosso, più moto** (môs′sô, pū mô′tô), [It.], more motion; quicker.

**più piano** (pyä′nō), [It.], softer.

**più più,** [It.], somewhat more.

**più presto** (pres′tō), [It.], quicker; more rapidly.

**pizzicato** (pit′sə-kä′tō; It. pēt′tsē-kä′tô), *adj.* plucked: a direction to the performers of stringed instruments to pluck the strings with the fingers instead of running the bow across them.

**plagal** (plā′g'l), *adj.* 1. with its keynote in the middle of the compass, as a mode. 2. designating a cadence with the subdominant chord immediately preceding the tonic chord.

**plain song,** early Christian church music, still used in Roman Catholic and Anglican services, in free rhythm and the limited Gregorian scale, sung in unison without accompaniment: also **plain chant.**

**plectrum** (plek′trəm), *n.* a small, thin piece of metal, bone, plastic, etc., used for plucking the strings of a guitar, mandolin, etc.

**poco** (pô′kô; Eng. pō′kō), *adj.* [It.], somewhat.

**poco adagio** (ə-dä′jō), [It.], somewhat slower.

**poco allegro** (ə-lā′grō), [It.], somewhat faster.

**poco animato** (ä-nē-mä′tô), [It.], somewhat more animated.

**poco a poco** (pô′kô ä pô′kô), [It.], little by little; by degrees; gradually.

**poco a poco crescendo** (krə-shen′dō), [It.], gradually louder and louder.

**poco a poco diminuendo** (də-min′ū-en′dō), [It.], gradually diminishing.

**poco a poco, più lento** (len′tō), [It.], gradually slower and slower.

**poco a poco, più moto** (mô′tô), [It.], gradually increasing the time.

**poco a poco, rallentando** (räl-en-tän′dô), [It.], gradually diminishing.

**poco presto** (pres′tō), [It.], rather quick.

**poi a poi** (pō′ē ä pō′ē), [It.], by degrees.

**polacca** (pō-lak′ə), n. [It.], the polonaise.

**polka** (pōl′kə), *n.* 1. a fast dance for couples, developed in Bohemia in the early 19th century. 2. music for this dance, in fast duple time.

**polonaise** (pol′ə-nāz′, pō′lə-), *n.* [Fr.], 1. a stately Polish dance in triple time. 2. music for this dance.

**portamento** (pôr′tə-men′tō; It. pôr′tä-men′tô), *n.* [It.], a continuous gliding from one note to another, sounding all intervening tones; glide.

**portando la voce** (pôr-tän′dô lä vô′chā), [It.], carrying the voice; holding it firmly on the notes.

**potpourri** (pō′poo-rē′, pot-poor′i), *n.* [Fr.], a medley; capriccio or fantasia in which favorite airs and fragments of musical pieces are strung together and contrasted.

**preciso** (prā-chē′sô), *adj.* [It.], precise; exact.

**prelude** (prel′ūd, prē′lo͞od), n. 1. an introductory section or movement of a suite, fugue, etc. 2. since the 19th century, any short romantic composition.

**preparation** (prep′ə-rā′shən), *n.* 1. the preparing for a dissonant chord by using the dissonant tone as a consonant tone in the immediately preceding chord. 2. a tone so used.

**prestissimo** (pres-tis′ə-mō′), *adj. & adv.* [It.], very fast; as fast as possible.

**presto** (pres′tō), *adj. & adv.* [It.], fast; in fast tempo.

**presto assai** (äs-sä′ē), [It.], very quick; with the utmost rapidity.

**prima donna** (prē′mə don′ə), [It.], the principal woman singer in an opera or concert.

**prima donna assoluta** (äs-sō-lōō'tä), [It.], the first woman singer in an opera company: the only one who can claim that title.

**profane music,** all music not adapted to church service; secular music.

**progression** (prə-gresh'ən), *n.* 1. the movement forward from one tone or chord to another. 2. a succession of tones or chords.

**psalmody** (säm'ə-di, sal'mə-), *n.* the practice or art of singing psalms; a style or collection of music designed for church service.

Q

**quadruple time** (or **measure**), 1. a measure having four beats, of which the first and third are accented. 2. the rhythm resulting from this.

**quarter note,** a note (♩) having one fourth the duration of a whole note: also called *crotchet.*

**quarter step** (or **tone**), an interval of one quarter of a whole tone.

**quartet, quartette** (kwôr-tet'), *n.* 1. a composition for four voices or four instruments. 2. the four performers of such a composition.

**quaver** (kwā'vẽr), *v.* to sing or play with a trill or trills. *n.* an eighth note; half of a crotchet.

**quintet, quintette** (kwin-tet'), *n.* 1. a composition for five voices or five instruments, as for string quartet and piano. 2. the five performers of such a composition.

R

**r,** the right hand in piano playing.

**racleur** (rȧ-klẽr'), *n.* [Fr.], a poor player.

**rallentamento** (räl-en-tä-men'tô), *n.* [It.], the time gradually slower and the sound gradually softer.

**rebec, rebeck** (rē'bek), *n.* a stringed musical instrument played with a bow, a kind of violin used during the Middle Ages.

**recapitulation** (rē'kə-pich'oo-lā'shən), *n.* reprise.

**recitative** (res'ə-tə-tēv'), *n.* 1. a type of declamatory singing, free in rhythm and tempo, used in the prose parts and dialogue of operas and oratorios. 2. a work or passage in this style. 3. music for such passages.

**recitativo instromentato** (res-i-tä-tē'vô in-strô-men-tä'tô), [It.], accompanied recitative.

**recitativo parlante** (pär-län'tä), [It.], unaccompanied recitative; also, when accompanied only by the cello and double bass, or the piano or organ.

**recorder** (ri-kôr'dẽr), *n.* an early form of flute, with eight finger holes and a fipple, held straight up and down when played.

**redowa** (red'ə-wə, -və), *n.* [Fr. & G.], 1. either of two ballroom dances of the 19th century, one like a polka, the other like a waltz. 2. music for these.

**reed** (rēd), *n.* 1. in certain wind instruments, as the clarinet, a thin strip of some flexible substance, placed against the opening of the mouthpiece so as to leave a narrow opening: when vibrated by the breath, it produces a musical tone. 2. an instrument with a reed or reeds. 3. in an organ, a similar contrivance that vibrates in a current of air.

**reed instrument,** any instrument whose sound is produced by the vibration of a reed, or thin strip of flexible substance: reed instruments include the oboe, clarinet, saxophone, English horn, and bassoon.

**reed organ,** an organ with a free set of metal reeds instead of pipes to produce the tones.

**reed pipe,** an organ pipe in which the tone is produced by a current of air striking a vibrating reed in an opening in the pipe.

**reed stop,** 1. a set of reed pipes (in an organ) operated by one knob. 2. the knob.

**refrain** (ri-frān'), *n.* 1. a phrase or verse repeated at intervals in a song. 2. music for this.

**register** (rej'is-tẽr), *n.* a musical range or compass, or a particular portion of the compass of an instrument or voice, of which all the tones are produced in the same manner or are similar in quality.

**related** (ri-lāt'id), *adj.* closely connected melodically or harmonically: said of tones, chords, etc.

**relative major,** the major key whose tonic is the third degree of a specified minor key.

**relative minor,** the minor key whose tonic is the sixth degree of a specified major key.

**repeat** (ri-pēt'), *n.* 1. a passage repeated in playing. 2. the symbol for this (:||), placed after, and often before, (||:), a passage to be repeated.

**reprise** (rə-prēz', ri-prīz'), *n.* repetition: now usually restricted to the repetition of or return to the first subject, or theme, of a sonata movement, after the development: also called *recapitulation.*

**resolution** (rez'ə-lōō'shən), *n.* 1. the passing of a dissonant tone (in a chord), as an appoggiatura, to a consonant tone. 2. the passing of a dissonant chord to a consonant chord or, sometimes, to another dissonant chord. 3. a tone or chord to which such passing occurs.

**rest** (rest), *n.* 1. an interval of silence between tones. 2. any of various symbols indicating the length of such an interval.

**retard** (ri-tärd'), *n.* [Fr.], a slowing down.

**rhapsody** (rap'sə-di), *n.* an instrumental composition of free, irregular form, suggesting improvisation.

**rhythm** (rith''m, -əm), *n.* 1. regular (or, occasionally, somewhat irregular) recurrence of grouped strong and weak beats, or heavily and lightly accented tones, in alternation. 2. arrangement of successive tones, usually in measures, according to their relative accentuation and duration. 3. form or pattern of this.

**ricercato** (rē-cher-cä'tô), *adj.* [It.], sought after; this term was applied, from the 16th to the 18th centuries, to an instrumental composition using highly elaborate counterpoint.

**ripieno** (rē-pyā'nô), *n.* [It.], all the performers, as distinguished from a solo performer or the group of solo performers, as in a concerto grosso.

**riposta** (rē-pôs'tä), *n.* [It.], repeat.

**risoluto** (rē-zô-lōō'tô), *adj.* [It.], resolved; resolute; bold.

**ritardando** (rē'tär-dän'dō), *adj.* [It.], becoming gradually slower.

**ritardo** (rē-tär'dô), *n.* [It.], retardation; gradual delay; in harmony, the prolonging of some note of a previous chord into the succeeding one.

**ritmo** (rēt'mô), *n.* [It.], rhythm; cadence; measure.

**ritournelle** (ri-tōōr-nel'), *n.* [Fr.], 1. a short symphony or an introduction to an air. 2. a tutti passage in a concerto. 3. an instrumental interlude between the parts of an opera.

**romance** (rō-mans'), *n.* [Fr.], a short, lyrical, usually sentimental piece, suggesting a love song.

**rondeau** (ron'dō, ron-dō'), *n.* [Fr.], a rondo.

**rondo** (ron'dō, ron-dō'), *n.* a composition or movement, often the last movement of a sonata, having its principal theme stated three or more times in the same key, interposed with subordinate themes.

**root** (rōōt, root), *n.* the basic tone of a chord, on which the chord is constructed.

**roulade** (rōō-läd'), *n.* [Fr.], a musical ornament consisting of a rapid succession of tones sung to only one syllable.

**rubato** (rōō-bä'tō), *adj.* having some notes arbitrarily lengthened (or shortened) in performance and, often, others correspondingly changed in length; intentionally and temporarily deviating from a strict tempo. *n.* 1. rubato modification or execution. 2. a rubato passage, phrase, etc. *adv.* with rubato; in a rubato manner.

**rumba** (rum'bə; Sp. rōōm'bä), *n.* 1. a dance of Cuban Negro origin and complex rhythm. 2. a modern ballroom adaptation of this. 3. music for, or in the rhythm of, this dance. Also spelled **rhumba.**

S

**saltarello** (sal'tə-rel'ō), *n.* [It.], 1. a lively Italian dance with a hopping, skipping step. 2. music for this dance.

**salto** (säl'tô), *n.* [It.], a leap, or skip, from one note to a distant one; also, a dance.

**sans frapper** (sän' frȧ'pā'), [Fr.], without striking; playing the notes without striking them hard or forcibly.

**sans pedales** (sän' pā'däl'), [Fr.], without using the pedals.

**saraband** (sar'ə-band'), *n.* [Fr.], 1. a graceful, stately, slow Spanish dance in triple time, developed from an earlier lively dance. 2. music for, or in the tempo of, this dance, with decided emphasis on the second beat of the measure, often constituting one of the movements of the classical suite.

**saxhorn** (saks'hôrn'), *n.* any of a group of valved brass-wind instruments, with a full, even tone and a wide range.

**saxophone** (sak'sə-fōn'), *n.* any of a group of single-reed, keyed wind instruments somewhat like the clarinet but having a curved metal body and a deeper, mellower tone.

**saxtuba** (saks'tōō'bə, -tū'-), *n.* a large, deep-toned saxhorn.

**scale** (skāl), *n.* [It. or L. *scala,* a ladder], a series of tones arranged in a sequence of rising or falling pitches in accordance with any of various systems of intervals; especially, all of such a series contained in one octave.

**scale of nature,** the scale from which our modern scales arise; it is a gradual succession of fixed sounds, which naturally comes from a string when divided into equal parts; the three grand divisions are the diatonic, the chromatic, and the enharmonic scales.

**scenario** (si-nâr'i-ō', -nä'ri-), *n.* [It.], an outline or synopsis of the plot of a drama, opera, etc., indicating scenes, characters, etc.

**scherzando** (sker-tsän'dō, -tsan'-), *adj.* [It.], playful; sportive. *adv.* playfully; sportively.

**scherzo** (sker'tsō), *n.* [It.], a lively, playful movement in 3/4 time, usually following a slow one, and often constituting the third section of a sonata, symphony, or quartet.

**schnell** (shnel), *adv.* [G.], quickly; rapidly.

**schottische, schottish** (shot'ish), *n.* [G.], 1. a form of round dance in 2/4 time, similar to the polka, but with a slower tempo. 2. music for this dance.

**score, full,** a complete score of all the parts of a composition, either vocal or instrumental, or both.

**sdegnante** (zdā-nän'tä), *adj.* [It.], angry; passionate.

**sdrucciolando** (zdrōōt-chô-län'dô), *adj.* [It.], sliding; slipping.

**sdrueciolare** (zdrōō-ā-chô-lä'rä), *v.t.* [It.], to slide the hand, by turning the fingernails toward the keys of the piano, and drawing the hand lightly, and rapidly, up or down.

**sec** (sek), *adj.* [Fr.], dry; unornamented: coldly; the note, or chord, to be struck plainly without ornament or arpeggio.

**second** (sek'ənd), *adj.* 1. lower in pitch. 2. playing or singing a part that is lower in pitch. *n.* 1. the interval between consecutive diatonic tones. 2. a tone separated from another by this interval. 3. the combination of two such tones in harmony. 4. the second part in a harmonized composition, as the alto. 5. an instrument or voice taking this part.

**section** (sek'shən), *n.* a complete, but not an independent musical idea; a part of a musical period, composed of one or more phrases.

**segno** (se'nyô), *n.* a sign, especially the one (𝄋 or :S:) at the beginning or end of a repeat.

**segue** (sā'gwā), [It.], continue without break into the next section, piece, etc.

**seguidilla** (se'gē-dē'lyä), *n.* [Sp.], 1. a fast Spanish dance, danced with castanets. 2. music for this dance.

**semibreve** (sem'ə-brēv'), *n.* [It.], a whole note (𝅝), equal to four quarter notes.

**semitone** (sem'ə-tōn'), *n.* 1. a tone at an interval of a half step from another in a diatonic scale; half tone. 2. such an interval.

**sempre** (sem'prā), *adv.* [It.], always; throughout.

**septet, septette** (sep-tet'), *n.* 1. a composition for seven voices or seven instruments. 2. the seven performers of such a composition.

**serenata** (sā-rā-nä'tä), *n.* [It.], 1. night music; an evening concert in the open air and under the window of the person to be entertained. 2. a musical composition on an amorous subject. 3. any light, pleasing instrumental composition comprising several movements.

**sextet, sextette** (seks-tet'), *n.* 1. a composition for six voices or six instruments. 2. the six performers of such a composition.

**sextuple** (seks'too-p'l, seks-tū'-), *adj.* having six beats to the measure.

**sforzando** (sfôr-tsän'dô), *adj. & adv.* [It.], with force or emphasis.

**sforzato** (sfôr-tsä'tô), *adj. & adv.* [It.], sforzando.

**sharp** (shärp), *n.* 1. a note or tone one half step above another. 2. the symbol (♯) for such a note.

**sight reading,** the act or skill of playing or singing readily upon sight written music unfamiliar to one.

**signature** (sig'nə-chēr), *n.* a sign or signs placed at the beginning of a staff to show key or time.

**sinfonia** (sēn'fô-nē'ä), *n.* [It.], a symphony.

**sistrum** (sis'trum), *n.* [L.], an instrument of percussion of very great antiquity, supposed to have been invented by the Egyptians, and much used by their priests of Isis and Osiris in sacrifice; it consisted of a metal handle and a frame with an oval or oblong shape, or square at two corners and curved at the others, and fitted with loosely held rods or with a number of movable rings, so that, when shaken, or struck with another rod of iron, it jingled.

**sixteenth note,** a note (𝅘𝅥𝅯) having one sixteenth the duration of a whole note.

**sixth** (siksth), *adj.* 1. an interval of six degrees in a diatonic scale. 2. a tone six degrees above or below a given tone. 3. the combination of two tones separated by this interval. 4. the sixth tone of a diatonic scale.

**sixth chord,** an inverted triad, as e-g-c.

**slur** (slūr), *n.* 1. a combination of slurred notes, played by gliding from one to another without a break. 2. a mark (‿) or (⁀) connecting such notes.

**sol-fa** (sōl'fä'), *n.* [It.], 1. the syllables *do, re, mi, fa, sol, la, ti, do,* used to represent the tones of a scale, regardless of its key. 2. the use of these syllables, as in vocal exercises.

**solfeggio** (sol-fej'ō, -i-ō'), *n.* 1. voice practice in which the scales are sung to the sol-fa syllables; solmization. 2. the use of these syllables in singing, especially in sight reading.

**solmization** (sol'mi-zā'shən), *n.* [Fr.], the act or practice of using a system of syllables, especially the sol-fa syllables, in singing the tones of a scale.

**solo** (sō'lō), *n.* a musical piece or passage to be played or sung by one person, with or without accompaniment.

**sonata** (sə-nä'tə), *n.* [It.], an extended instrumental composition for piano or for some other solo instrument or instruments, often with piano accompaniment; it is usually in three or four movements having a unity of subject and style but differing in tempo, rhythm, and melody: the movements are as follows: an allegro, sometimes preceded by a slow introduction; an andante, adagio, or largo movement, often in song or variation form; the minuet and trio, or scherzo; lastly, the finale, frequently in rondo form.

**sonata form,** a complex form of musical composition, typically used for the first movement of a sonata, symphony, concerto, etc.; the *sonata form* consists of the following: the *exposition,* giving out the main theme in the tonic key, and the secondary theme in the dominant key; the *development,* giving a full working out of one or both themes; the *recapitulation,* repeating both themes in the original key, and ending with a coda.

**sonatina** (son'ə-tē'nə, sō'nə-), *n.* [It.], a short or simplified sonata.

**soprano** (sə-pran'ō, -prä'nō), *n.* 1. the highest singing voice, of women and boys, usually ranging two octaves or more up from middle C. 2. a singer with such a range. 3. a part for such a voice. *adj.* of, for, or having the range of, a soprano.

**sostenuto** (sos'tə-nōō'tō; It. sôs'te-nōō'tô), *adj.* held for the full indicated time value, or somewhat prolonged in the time value of the tones.

**sotto voce** (sot'ō vō'chi; It. sôt'tô vô'che), [It.], softly; in a low voice; in an undertone, so as not to be overheard.

**stop** (stop), *n.* 1. an organ stop. 2. a stopping of a violin string, finger hole, etc. to produce a desired pitch. 3. a finger hole in a wind instrument.

**string** (striŋ), *n.* 1. a slender cord of wire, gut, nylon, etc. stretched on a musical instrument, as a violin, harp, piano, etc., and bowed, plucked, or struck to make a musical sound. 2. *pl.* all the stringed instruments of an orchestra, especially those played with a bow. 3. *pl.* the players of such instruments.

**stringed** (striŋd), *adj.* 1. having strings, as certain musical instruments. 2. produced by strings: as, *stringed* music.

**stringendo** (strēn-jen'dô), *adj.* [It.], accelerating the tempo, as toward a climax.

**string quartet,** 1. a quartet of players on stringed instruments, usually comprising first and second violins, a viola, and a cello. 2. a composition to be performed by such a group.

**subdominant** (sub-dom'ə-nənt), *n.* the fourth tone of a diatonic scale; tone next below the dominant.

**suite** (swēt), *n.* 1. an early form of instrumental composition consisting of a series of dances in the same or related keys. 2. a modern instrumental composition consisting of several movements.

**suspension** (sə-spen'shən), *n.* 1. the holding back of one or more tones in a chord while the others progress, so that a temporary dissonance is created. 2. the tone or tones so held.

**symphony** (sim'fə-ni), *n.* 1. an extended composition in sonata form for full orchestra, having several (usually four) movements related in subject, but varying in form and execution; also, a symphony orchestra. 2. an instrumental passage in a composition that is largely vocal or choral.

**symphony concert,** a concert given by a symphony orchestra.

**symphony orchestra,** a large orchestra, composed of string, wind, and percussion sections, which performs symphonic works.

**syncopate** (siŋ'kə-pāt'), *v.* 1. to begin (a tone) on an unaccented beat and continue it through the next accented beat, or to begin (a tone) on the last half of a beat and continue it through the first half of the following beat. 2. to use such shifted accents in (a musical composition, passage, etc.).

**syncopation** (siŋ'kə-pā'shən), *n.* 1. a syncopating or being syncopated. 2. syncopated music.

## T

**tarantella** (tar'ən-tel'ə), *n.* [It.], 1. a swift, delirious sort of Italian dance in 6/8 time. 2. the music for this.

**temperament** (tem'prə-mənt, tem'pēr-ə-), *n.* a system of adjustment of the intervals between the tones of an instrument of fixed intonation: it may be *pure temperament,* in which the intervals are set exactly according to theory, or *equal temperament* (as in a piano), in which the pitch of the tones is slightly adjusted to make them suitable for all keys.

**tempered** (tem'pērd), *adj.* adjusted to a temperament, especially equal temperament.

**tempo** (tem'pō), *n.* [It.], time; the rate of speed at which a musical composition is, or is supposed to be, played.

**tempo di marcia** (dē mär'chä), [It.], in the time of a march.

**tempo di menuetto** (dē men-ū-et'tô), [It.], in minuet rhythm.

**tempo di valse** (vâls), [It.], in waltz time.

**tenuto** (te-nōō'tô), *adj.* [It.], held for its full value; sustained: said of a tone or chord.

**timbre** (tim'bēr, tam'-), *n.* [Fr.], the characteristic quality of sound that distinguishes one voice or musical instrument from another: it is determined by the harmonics of the sound, not the intensity or pitch.

**toccata** (tə-kä'tə), *n.* [It.], a composition in free style for the organ, piano, etc., generally characterized by the use of full chords and running passages and often used as the prelude of a fugue: it was originally designed to display the technique of the performer.

**timpani** (tim'pə-ni), *n. pl.* [It.], kettledrums; especially, a set of kettledrums of different pitches played by one performer in an orchestra.

**tom-tom** (tom'tom'), *n.* any of various drums of primitive origin, played with the hands or with sticks.

**tone** (tōn), *n.* 1. a sound that is distinct and identifiable by its regularity of vibration, or constant pitch, and that may be put into harmonic relation with other such sounds. 2. the simple or fundamental tone of a musical sound as distinguished from its overtones. 3. any one of the full intervals of a diatonic scale; step; whole tone. 4. any of the nine psalm tunes in plain song.

**tone color,** timbre.

**tone poem,** an elaborate, orchestral composition, usually in one movement, having no fixed form and based upon some nonmusical poetic or descriptive theme: also called *symphonic poem.*

**tonic** (ton′ik), *n.* the first, or basic, tone of a diatonic scale; keynote.

**tonic sol-fa,** a system of writing and teaching music based on the relationship between the tones of a key, using the syllables of solmization (*do, re, mi,* etc.), instead of the usual staff symbols; in this system *do* is always applied to the tonic.

**touch** (tuch), *n.* the manner of striking or pressing the keys of an organ, piano, or similar instrument; the resistance made to the fingers by the keys of any instrument, as, when the keys are put down with difficulty, an instrument is said to have a hard or heavy *touch;* when there is little resistance the *touch* is said to be soft or light.

**transition** (tran-zish′ən, -sish′-), *n.* an abrupt change out of one key into another, without preparation for, or hinting at another key, or without making use of chords common to both keys: sometimes *transition* means *modulation,* or a change that does make use of such chords.

**transpose** (trans-pōz′), *v.t.* to perform or write a composition in a different key.

**treble** (treb′'l), *n.* 1. the highest part in musical harmony; soprano. 2. a singer or instrument that takes this part.

**trio** (trē′ō), *n.* [It.], 1. a composition for three instruments or three voices. 2. the performers of such a composition. 3. the middle section of a minuet, scherzo, etc.

**triple time,** musical time or rhythm having three beats to the measure, with the first beat accented.

**trombone** (trom′bōn), *n.* a brass-wind instrument consisting of a long cylindrical tube bent twice upon itself and ending in a bell; its mouthpiece is cup-shaped; the *trombone* is of two types, the *slide trombone,* in which different tones are produced by moving the movable section of the tube in and out, and the *valve trombone,* played, like the trumpet, with valves.

**trumpet** (trum′pit), *n.* a brass-wind instrument with a powerful tone, consisting of a tube in an oblong loop, with a flared bell at one end, a cupped mouthpiece at the other, three valves for producing changes in tone, and small, secondary, looped tubes.

**tuba** (tōō′bə, tū′-), *n.* a large brass-wind instrument of the saxhorn group.

**tutti** (tōō′ti; It. tōōt′tē), *adj.* [It.], all; for all instruments or voices; in a solo or concerto, indicating that the full orchestra takes part.

**twelve-tone** (twelv′tōn′), *adj.* designating or of a system or technique of composition, developed by Arnold Schönberg, in which the twelve tones of the chromatic scale are used without reference to a specific tonal center, or key, but in an arbitrary, fixed order.

**tympani** (tim′pə-ni), *n. pl.* timpani.

## U

**un poco ritenuto** (ōōn pô′kô rē-tā-nōō′tô), [It.], a little slower.

**upright piano,** a piano with a rectangular body mounted vertically.

## V

**variation** (vâr′i-ā′shən), *n.* the repetition of a melody or theme with changes or embellishments in harmony, rhythm, key, etc., especially one of a series of such repetitions.

**velata** (vā-lä′tä), *adj.* [It.], veiled: said of a voice that sounds hoarse or husky, as if it were heard through a veil.

**velocemente** (vā-lô-chā-men′tā), *adv.* [It.], swiftly; quickly; in a rapid time.

**vibrato** (vi-brä′tō; It. vē-brä′tô), *n.* [It.], a tremulous effect obtained by rapidly alternating the original tone with a slightly perceptible variation in the pitch, as by the rapid pulsation of the finger on the string of a violin: in singing, sometimes interchangeable with *tremolo.*

**viol** (vī′əl), *n.* any of an early family of stringed instruments, characterized generally by six strings, frets, a flat back, and C-shaped sound holes: the *bass viol* in the modern orchestra developed from one of the larger viols of this family.

**viola** (vi-ō′lə, vī-), *n.* a stringed instrument of the violin family similar in tone and formation to the violin, but larger in size and tuned a fifth lower.

**viola da gamba** (vyô′lä dä gäm′bä), [It.], a large viol, the forerunner of the cello.

**violin** (vī′ə-lin′), *n.* any instrument of the modern family of stringed instruments played with a bow and characterized by four strings, a lack of frets, a somewhat rounded back, and *f*-shaped sound holes; specifically, the smallest and highest pitched instrument of this family, held horizontally under the chin.

**violoncello** (vē′ə-lon-chel′ō, vī′ə-lən-), *n.* a cello.

**virginal** (vūr′ji-n'l), *n.* a harpsichord; especially, a small, rectangular harpsichord of the 16th century, placed on a table or in the lap to be played.

**virtuoso** (vūr′chōō-ō′sō), *n.* [It.], a very skillful performer upon some musical instrument.

**vivace** (ve-vä′che), *adj.* [It.], lively; vivacious; spirited.

**voluntary** (vol′ən-ter′i), *n.* a piece or solo, often an improvisation, played on the organ before, during, or after a church service.

## W

**waltz** (wôlts; esp. Brit. wôls), *n.* 1. a ballroom dance for couples, in moderate 3/4 time with marked accent on the first beat of the measure. 2. music for this dance or in its characteristic rhythm.

**wenig** (vā′nik), *adv.* [G.], little; *ein wenig stark,* a little strong; rather loud.

**whole note,** a note (○) having four times the duration of a quarter note: also called *semibreve.*

**whole step,** an interval consisting of two adjacent half steps: also called *whole tone.*

**wiederholung** (vē′der-hōl′ooŋ), *n.* [G.], repeating; repetition.

**wind instrument** (wind), a musical instrument played by blowing air, especially breath, through it, as a *wood wind* (flute, oboe, clarinet, etc.) or a *brass wind* (trumpet, trombone, tuba, etc.).

**wood winds** (windz), the wind instruments of an orchestra made, especially originally, of wood: the principal modern wood winds are the clarinet, oboe, bassoon, flute, and English horn.

**wrest pin,** either of two metal pins between which a single string of a piano, harp, etc. is stretched; by turning these *wrest pins* the instrument can be tuned.

## X

**xylophone** (zī′lə-fōn′, zil′ə-), *n.* a percussion instrument composed of a series of graduated wooden bars which, when struck with small wooden hammers, sound the notes of the scale; the bars rest on strips of felt and are usually arranged in two rows containing a total of from thirty to fifty-five bars.

# Social Sciences

## *Geography*

### FACTS AND FIGURES ABOUT THE EARTH

**THE OCEANS**

(*Approximate Square Miles*)

| | |
|---|---|
| Pacific | 63,750,000 |
| Atlantic | 31,830,000 |
| Indian | 28,357,000 |
| Antarctic | 7,500,000 |
| Arctic | 5,440,000 |

**THE PRINCIPAL SEAS**

| | |
|---|---|
| Mediterranean Sea | 1,145,000 |
| South China Sea | 895,000 |
| Bering Sea | 876,000 |
| Caribbean Sea | 750,000 |
| Okhotsk, Sea of | 590,000 |
| Yellow Sea | 480,000 |
| East China Sea | 480,000 |
| Japan, Sea of | 389,000 |
| Andaman Sea | 300,000 |
| North Sea | 222,000 |
| Red Sea | 169,000 |
| Caspian Sea | 169,000 |
| Black Sea | 164,000 |
| Baltic Sea | 163,000 |
| Dead Sea | 370 |

**WORLD DIMENSIONS**

| | |
|---|---|
| Diameter at the Equator | 7,926.68 miles |
| Diameter at the Poles | 7,899.99 miles |
| Mean diameter | 7,918.00 miles |
| Circumference at the Equator | 24,902.32 miles |
| Total surface area | 196,940,400 square miles |
| Water area | 141,055,400 square miles |
| Land area | 55,885,000 square miles |

**THE GREAT LAKES**

| *Lake* | *Length miles* | *Breadth miles* | *Depth feet* | *Total Area sq. mi.* | *Area (Canada) sq. mi.* |
|---|---|---|---|---|---|
| Superior | 350 | 160 | 1,290 | 31,810 | 11,200 |
| Huron | 206 | 183 | 750 | 23,010 | 13,675 |
| Michigan | 307 | 118 | 923 | 22,400 | —— |
| Erie | 240 | 57 | 210 | 9,940 | 5,094 |
| Ontario | 193 | 53 | 778 | 7,540 | 3,725 |

### OTHER IMPORTANT LAKES OF THE WORLD
*(in Square Miles)*

| | |
|---|---|
| **Victoria**, Africa | 26,200 |
| **Aral**, U.S.S.R. | 24,400 |
| **Nyasa**, Africa | 14,000 |
| **Baikal**, U.S.S.R. | 13,300 |
| **Tanganyika**, Africa | 12,700 |
| **Great Bear**, Canada | 11,800 |
| **Great Slave**, Canada | 11,172 |
| **Winnipeg**, Canada | 8,555 |
| **Balkhash**, U.S.S.R. | 7,200 |
| **Ladoga**, U.S.S.R. | 7,000 |
| **Chad**, Africa | 6,500 |
| **Eyre**, Australia | 4,000 |
| **Onega**, U.S.S.R. | 3,764 |
| **Rudolf**, Africa | 3,475 |
| **Titicaca**, South America | 3,200 |
| **Nicaragua**, Nicaragua | 3,089 |
| **Athabaska**, Canada | 3,085 |
| **Reindeer**, Canada | 2,435 |
| **Torrens**, Australia | 2,400 |
| **Great Salt Lake**, United States | 2,360 |
| **Issyk-Kul**, U.S.S.R. | 2,230 |
| **Koko Nor**, China | 2,200 |

### THE WORLD'S PRINCIPAL RIVERS
*(in Miles)*

| | |
|---|---|
| **Mississippi-Missouri**, U. S. | 4,240 |
| **Nile**, Africa | 4,000 |
| **Amazon**, South America | 3,900 |
| **Ob**, Siberia | 3,200 |
| **Yangtze**, China | 3,100 |
| **Congo**, Africa | 3,000 |
| **Amur**, Asia | 2,900 |
| **Yenisei**, U.S.S.R. | 2,800 |
| **Lena**, U.S.S.R. | 2,800 |
| **Hwang Ho**, China | 2,700 |
| **Mekong**, China & Thailand | 2,600 |
| **Niger**, Africa | 2,600 |
| **Mississippi**, United States | 2,560 |
| **Mackenzie**, Canada | 2,500 |
| **Missouri**, United States | 2,475 |
| **Paraná**, Brazil & Argentina | 2,450 |
| **Murray**, Australia | 2,310 |
| **Yukon**, Canada & U. S. | 2,300 |
| **Volga**, U.S.S.R. | 2,300 |
| **Irtish**, U.S.S.R. | 2,250 |
| **St. Lawrence**, Canada | 2,100 |
| **Madeira**, Brazil | 2,000 |
| **Indus**, India | 2,000 |
| **Purus**, Brazil | 1,850 |
| **Rio Grande**, U. S. & Mexico | 1,800 |
| **São Francisco**, Brazil | 1,800 |
| **Salween**, Tibet & Burma | 1,750 |
| **Danube**, Germany | 1,725 |
| **Brahmaputra**, Tibet & India | 1,700 |
| **Euphrates**, Asia | 1,700 |
| **Tocantins**, Brazil | 1,700 |
| **Orinoco**, Venezuela | 1,600 |
| **Zambezi**, Africa | 1,600 |
| **Ganges**, India | 1,550 |
| **Amu Darya**, U.S.S.R. | 1,500 |
| **Paraguay**, Brazil & Paraguay | 1,500 |
| **Arkansas**, United States | 1,460 |
| **Ural**, U.S.S.R. | 1,400 |
| **Dnepr**, U.S.S.R. | 1,400 |
| **Negro**, Brazil | 1,400 |

### THE WORLD'S GREAT RIVER BASINS
*(in approx. Square Miles)*

| | |
|---|---|
| **Amazon**, South America | 2,700,000 |
| **La Plata**, South America | 1,500,000 |
| **Congo**, Africa | 1,450,000 |
| **Mississippi-Missouri**, U. S. | 1,244,000 |
| **Ob**, U.S.S.R. | 1,125,000 |
| **Nile**, Africa | 1,100,000 |
| **Yenisei**, U.S.S.R. | 1,042,000 |
| **Lena**, U.S.S.R. | 1,000,000 |
| **Amur**, U.S.S.R. | 709,000 |
| **Yangtze**, China | 700,000 |
| **Mackenzie-Peace**, Canada | 699,000 |
| **Niger**, Africa | 584,000 |
| **St. Lawrence**, Canada | 565,000 |
| **Volga**, U.S.S.R. | 563,000 |

### IMPORTANT ACTIVE VOLCANOES
*(in Feet)*

| | |
|---|---|
| **Lascar**, Chile | 19,652 |
| **Popocatepetl**, Mexico | 17,887 |
| **Cotacachi**, Ecuador | 16,197 |
| **Purace**, Colombia | 15,604 |
| **Wrangell**, Alaska | 14,005 |
| **Mauna Loa**, Hawaii | 13,680 |
| **Rindjani**, Indonesia | 12,225 |
| **Slamat**, Java | 11,247 |
| **Spurr**, Alaska | 11,070 |
| **Etna**, Sicily | 10,705 |
| **Torbert**, Alaska | 10,600 |
| **Llaima**, Chile | 10,249 |
| **Nyamlagira**, Congo | 10,123 |
| **Merapi**, Java | 9,551 |
| **Fogo**, Cape Verde Islands | 9,281 |
| **Ruapehu**, New Zealand | 9,175 |
| **Big Ben**, Heard Island | 9,000 |
| **Asama**, Japan | 8,340 |
| **Pavlof**, Alaska | 8,215 |
| **Vesuvius**, Italy | 3,891 |
| **Stromboli**, Italy | 3,038 |
| **Krakatau**, Indonesia | 2,667 |

### THE WORLD'S PRINCIPAL MOUNTAINS
*(in Feet)*

| | |
|---|---|
| **Everest**, Tibet & Nepal | 29,002 |
| **Godwin Austen** *or* **K2**, India | 28,250 |
| **Kanchenjunga**, Nepal & India | 28,146 |
| **Makalu**, Nepal | 27,790 |
| **Dhaulagiri**, Nepal | 26,795 |
| **Nanga Parbat**, India | 26,620 |
| **Gosainthan**, Tibet | 26,291 |
| **Nanda Devi**, India | 25,645 |
| **Kamet**, India | 25,447 |
| **Namcha Barwa**, Tibet | 25,445 |
| **Gurla Mandhata**, Tibet | 25,355 |
| **Tirach Mir**, Pakistan | 25,263 |
| **Kula Kangri**, Tibet | 24,740 |
| **Muztagh-Ata**, China | 24,388 |
| **Minya Kanka**, China | 24,000 |
| **Chomo Lhari**, Bhutan & Tibet | 23,930 |
| **Api**, Nepal | 23,899 |
| **Tengri Khan**, U.S.S.R. | 23,622 |
| **Aconcagua**, Argentina | 23,080 |
| **Ojos del Salado**, Argentina | 22,572 |
| **Mercedario**, Argentina | 22,211 |
| **Huascaran**, Peru | 22,180 |
| **Llullaillaco**, Chile | 22,057 |
| **Kailas**, Tibet | 22,000 |
| **Tupungato**, Argentina & Chile | 21,810 |
| **Incahuasi**, Argentina | 21,719 |
| **Sajama**, Bolivia | 21,491 |
| **Illampu**, Bolivia | 21,489 |
| **Nanadas de Cachi**, Argentina | 21,325 |
| **Illimani**, Bolivia | 21,280 |
| **Antofalla**, Argentina | 21,129 |
| **Chimborazo**, Ecuador | 20,702 |
| **McKinley**, Alaska | 20,300 |
| **Logan**, Yukon (Canada) | 19,850 |
| **Cotopaxi**, Ecuador | 19,498 |
| **Kilimanjaro**, Tanganyika | 19,321 |
| **Misti**, Peru | 19,200 |
| **Cayambe**, Ecuador | 19,170 |
| **Orizaba**, Mexico | 18,701 |
| **Demavend**, Iran | 18,603 |
| **Elbruz**, U.S.S.R. | 18,468 |
| **Tolima**, Colombia | 18,438 |
| **St. Elias**, Alaska & Canada | 18,008 |
| **Popocatepetl**, Mexico | 17,887 |
| **Maipo**, Argentina & Chile | 17,388 |
| **Lucania**, Yukon (Canada) | 17,147 |
| **Dykh Tau**, U.S.S.R. | 17,085 |
| **Kenya**, Kenya | 17,040 |
| **Foraker**, Alaska | 17,000 |
| **Ixtacihuatl**, Mexico | 16,960 |
| **Ararat**, Turkey | 16,915 |
| **Kazbek**, U.S.S.R. | 16,547 |
| **Carstensz**, New Guinea | 16,404 |
| **Sanford**, Alaska | 16,206 |
| **Blackburn**, Alaska | 16,140 |
| **Klyuchevskaya**, U.S.S.R. | 15,912 |
| **Mont Blanc**, France & Italy | 15,781 |
| **Vancouver**, Alaska & Yukon (Canada) | 15,696 |

# FACTS ABOUT THE STATES

### THE NAMES OF STATES AND THEIR MEANINGS

**Alabama:** Choctaw Indian, "I open or clear the thicket."

**Alaska:** possibly from Eskimo, "great country."

**Arizona:** Papago Indian (an Indian of the Pimian tribe), "place of the few or little springs."

**Arkansas:** meaning unknown: Name of tribe of Indians who lived near mouth of Ark. River.

**California:** from a 16th century Spanish romance whose heroine, Calafiá, ruled an island called California. The name was first applied to Lower California by its Spanish discoverer.

**Colorado:** Spanish, "red": first applied to the River and later to the State.

**Connecticut:** Mohican Indian, "at the long tidal river."

**Delaware:** after Thomas West, Lord de la Warr, governor of Virginia.

**District of Columbia:** named after Columbus.
**Florida:** Spanish "flowery": so named by Ponce de. León because he landed there during the *Feast of the Flowers* in the spring of 1513.
**Georgia:** in honor of King George II of England.
**Hawaii:** English spelling of *Owhyhee.*
**Idaho:** probably from Shoshonean Indian, "Behold the sun coming down the mountains," or "It is sunup."
**Illinois:** a tribe of Algonquian Indians called themselves *Illini* (the native word for men).
**Indiana:** probably from "Indian" and "-a."
**Iowa:** Dakota Indian, "sleepy ones." It was applied to the Iowa Indians in ridicule.
**Kansas:** the plural of Kansa, a member of a Sioux tribe living in this region.
**Kentucky:** possibly from Iroquois Indian, "tomorrow" or "land of tomorrow."
**Louisiana:** named for King Louis XIV of France.
**Maine:** name given to distinguish the mainland from the islands. It was once called the *Main Land of New England.*
**Maryland:** named in 1632 by King Charles I of England in honor of his queen, Henrietta Maria.
**Massachusetts:** Algonquian Indian, "at or about the great hill."
**Michigan:** probably from Chippewa Indian, "expansive waste"; applied first to Lake Michigan since there were few or no islands in the lake.
**Minnesota:** probably from Dakota Indian, "sky-blue water."
**Mississippi:** Choctaw Indian, "beyond age" or Illinois Indian, "great water." The name was first applied to the river.
**Missouri:** Indian, "people of the big canoes." Name was first applied to French by Indians who lived at mouth of Missouri River.
**Montana:** Spanish, "mountainous region."
**Nebraska:** Indian, "river in the flatness." The name was first applied to the Platte River that flows through this region.
**Nevada:** Spanish, "snow-covered": first applied to the Sierra Nevada Mountains.
**New Hampshire:** from Hampshire County, England.
**New Jersey:** named after the island of Jersey.
**New Mexico:** so called because the early Spanish explorers considered it a hoped-for scene of wealth like the Mexico of Cortez.
**New York:** named after the Duke of York who was granted this region by Charles II of England.
**North Carolina:** this region and that of South Carolina were originally called Carolina, after King Charles I of England. *Carolus* is the Latin name for Charles.
**North Dakota:** after a tribe of Sioux Indians called Dakota or "allies."
**Ohio:** probably from Iroquois Indian, "beautiful."
**Oklahoma:** Choctaw Indian, "red people."
**Oregon:** name of uncertain origin; it was first applied to the river now known as the Columbia.
**Pennsylvania:** after William Penn who proposed to name this territory Sylvania or "woodland," but King Charles II added his name, Penn, to it.
**Rhode Island:** from the island of Rhodes in the Mediterranean.
**South Carolina:** *see* NORTH CAROLINA.
**South Dakota:** *see* NORTH DAKOTA.
**Tennessee:** Indian word, but the meaning is obscure; probably a mispronunciation of a mispronunciation of a Creek Indian name.
**Texas:** American Spanish word used by some Indians to mean "friends" or "allies."
**Utah:** possibly from Ute Indians, meaning "person" or "people."
**Vermont:** probably from French *Les Monts Verts,* "the Green Mountains."
**Virginia:** in honor of Elizabeth, the "Virgin Queen."
**Washington:** named after George Washington.
**West Virginia:** *see* VIRGINIA.
**Wisconsin:** probably from Ojibway Indian, "place of the beaver or muskrat hole."
**Wyoming:** possibly Indian, "at the big plains."

## THE NICKNAMES OF THE STATES

**Alabama:** "The Cotton State," or "The Yellowhammer State."
**Alaska:** "The Eldorado of the North."
**Arizona:** "The Grand Canyon State."
**Arkansas:** "The Wonder State," or "The Land of Opportunity."
**California:** "The Golden State."
**Colorado:** "The Centennial State."
**Connecticut:** "The Constitution State," or "The Nutmeg State."
**Delaware:** "The First State," or "The Diamond State."
**Florida:** "The Sunshine State."
**Georgia:** "The Empire State of the South."
**Hawaii:** "Paradise of the Pacific."
**Idaho:** "The Gem State."
**Illinois:** "The Prairie State."
**Indiana:** "The Hoosier State."
**Iowa:** "The Hawkeye State."
**Kansas:** "The Sunflower State."
**Kentucky:** "The Bluegrass State."
**Louisiana:** "The Pelican State."
**Maine:** "The Pine Tree State."
**Maryland:** "The Old Line State," or "The Free State."
**Massachusetts:** "The Bay State," or "The Old Colony State."
**Michigan:** "The Wolverine State."
**Minnesota:** "The North Star State," or "The Gopher State."
**Mississippi:** "The Magnolia State."
**Missouri:** "The Show Me State."
**Montana:** "The Treasure State."
**Nebraska:** "The Beef State," or "The Cornhusker State."
**Nevada:** "The Sagebrush State," or "The Silver State."
**New Hampshire:** "The Granite State."
**New Jersey:** "The Garden State."
**New Mexico:** "The Land of Enchantment."
**New York:** "The Empire State."
**North Carolina:** "The Tar Heel State," or "The Old North State."
**North Dakota:** "The Sioux State," or "The Flickertail State."
**Ohio:** "The Buckeye State."
**Oklahoma:** "The Sooner State."
**Oregon:** "The Beaver State."
**Pennsylvania:** "The Keystone State."
**Rhode Island:** "Little Rhody."
**South Carolina:** "The Palmetto State."

**South Dakota:** "The Coyote State," or "The Sunshine State."
**Tennessee:** "The Volunteer State."
**Texas:** "The Lone-Star State."
**Utah:** "The Beehive State."
**Vermont:** "The Green Mountain State."
**Virginia:** "Old Dominion."
**Washington:** "The Evergreen State."
**West Virginia:** "The Mountain State."
**Wisconsin:** "The Badger State."
**Wyoming:** "The Equality State."

## MOTTOES OF THE STATES

**Alabama:** We Dare Defend Our Rights.
**Alaska:** No Motto.
**Arizona:** *Didat Deus.* God Enriches.
**Arkansas:** *Regnat Populus.* Let The People Rule.
**California:** *Eureka.* I Have Found It.
**Colorado:** *Nil Sine Numine.* Nothing Without God.
**Connecticut:** *Qui Transtulit Sustinet.* He Who Transplanted Sustains.
**Delaware:** Liberty and Independence.
**District of Columbia:** *Justitia Omnibus.* Justice to All.
**Florida:** In God We Trust.
**Georgia:** Wisdom, Justice, Moderation.
**Hawaii:** Righteousness Perpetuates the Life of the Land.
**Idaho:** *Esto Perpetua.* Exist Forever.
**Illinois:** State Sovereignty, National Union.
**Indiana:** The Crossroads of America.
**Iowa:** Our Liberties We Prize and Our Rights We Will Maintain.
**Kansas:** *Ad Astra per Aspera.* To the Stars Through Difficulties.
**Kentucky:** United We Stand, Divided We Fall.
**Louisiana:** Union, Justice, Confidence.
**Maine:** *Dirigo.* I Guide.
**Maryland:** *Fatti Maschili, Parole Femine.* Manly Deeds, Womanly Words.
**Massachusetts:** *Ense Petit Placidam sub Libertate Quietem.* By the Sword She Seeks Peace, but Peace Only Under Liberty.
**Michigan:** *Si Quaeris Peninsulam Amoenam Circumspice.* If You Seek a Pleasant Peninsula, Look About You.
**Minnesota:** *L'Etoile du Nord.* The Star of the North.
**Mississippi:** *Virtute et Armis.* By Valor and Arms.
**Missouri:** *Salus Populi Suprema Lex Esto.* Welfare of the People Shall Be the Supreme Law.
**Montana:** *Oro y Plata.* Gold and Silver.
**Nebraska:** Equality Before the Law.
**Nevada:** All for Our Country.
**New Hampshire:** Live Free or Die.
**New Jersey:** Liberty and Prosperity.
**New Mexico:** *Crescit Eundo.* It Grows as It Goes.
**New York:** *Excelsior.* Higher, Always Upward.
**North Carolina:** *Esse Quam Videri.* To Be, Rather Than to Seem.
**North Dakota:** Liberty and Union, Now and Forever, One and Inseparable.
**Ohio:** With God All Things Are Possible.
**Oklahoma:** *Labor Omnia Vincit.* Labor Conquers All Things.
**Oregon:** The Union.
**Pennsylvania:** Virtue, Liberty and Independence.
**Rhode Island:** Hope.
**South Carolina:** *Dum Spiro Spero.* While I Breathe, I Hope.
**South Dakota:** Under God, the People Rule.
**Tennessee:** Agriculture, Commerce.
**Texas:** Friendship.
**Utah:** Industry.
**Vermont:** Freedom and Unity.
**Virginia:** *Sic Semper Tyrannis.* Thus Always to Tyrants.
**Washington:** *Ai-Ki.* By and By.
**West Virginia:** *Montani Semper Liberi.* Mountaineers Always Free.
**Wisconsin:** Forward.
**Wyoming:** *Cedant Arma Togae.* Let Arms Yield to the Gown.

## STATE FLOWERS

**Alabama:** Camelia
**Alaska:** Forget-Me-Not
**Arizona:** Saguaro
**Arkansas:** Apple Blossom
**California:** Golden Poppy
**Colorado:** Columbine
**Connecticut:** Mountain Laurel
**Delaware:** Peach Blossom
**District of Columbia:** American Beauty Rose
**Florida:** Orange Blossom
**Georgia:** Cherokee Rose
**Hawaii:** Red Hibiscus
**Idaho:** Syringa
**Illinois:** Butterfly Violet
**Indiana:** Peony
**Iowa:** Carolina Rose
**Kansas:** Sunflower
**Kentucky:** Goldenrod
**Louisiana:** Magnolia Grandiflora
**Maine:** Pine Cone
**Maryland:** Black-Eyed Susan
**Massachusetts:** Trailing Arbutus
**Michigan:** Apple Blossom
**Minnesota:** Showy Lady-slipper
**Mississippi:** Magnolia
**Missouri:** Hawthorn
**Montana:** Bitterroot
**Nebraska:** Goldenrod
**Nevada:** Sagebrush
**New Hampshire:** Purple Lilac
**New Jersey:** Bogbice Violet
**New Mexico:** Yucca
**New York:** Rose
**North Carolina:** Dogwood
**North Dakota:** Arkansas Rose
**Ohio:** Scarlet Carnation
**Oklahoma:** Mistletoe
**Oregon:** Oregon Grape
**Pennsylvania:** Mountain Laurel
**Rhode Island:** Violet
**South Carolina:** Yellow Jessamine
**South Dakota:** Pasque
**Tennessee:** Iris
**Texas:** Bluebonnet
**Utah:** Sego Lily
**Vermont:** Red Clover
**Virginia:** American Dogwood
**Washington:** Rhododendron
**West Virginia:** Rosebay Rhododendron
**Wisconsin:** Butterfly Violet
**Wyoming:** Painted Cup

# STATES

Capitals, Settled, and Date Entry Into Union

| *State* | *Capital* | *Settled* | *Entered Union* |
|---|---|---|---|
| **Alabama** | Montgomery | 1702 | 1819, December 14 |
| **Alaska** | Juneau | 1784 | 1959, January 3 |
| **Arizona** | Phoenix | 1848 | 1912, February 14 |
| **Arkansas** | Little Rock | 1785 | 1836, June 15 |
| **California** | Sacramento | 1769 | 1850, September 9 |
| **Colorado** | Denver | 1858 | 1876, August 1 |
| **Connecticut** | Hartford | 1635 | 1788, January 9 |
| **Delaware** | Dover | 1638 | 1787, December 7 |
| **Florida** | Tallahassee | 1565 | 1845, March 3 |
| **Georgia** | Atlanta | 1733 | 1788, January 2 |
| **Hawaii** | Honolulu | 500 | 1960, July 4 |
| **Idaho** | Boise | 1842 | 1890, July 3 |
| **Illinois** | Springfield | 1720 | 1818, December 3 |
| **Indiana** | Indianapolis | 1733 | 1816, December 11 |
| **Iowa** | Des Moines | 1788 | 1846, December 28 |
| **Kansas** | Topeka | 1727 | 1861, January 29 |
| **Kentucky** | Frankfort | 1774 | 1792, June 1 |
| **Louisiana** | Baton Rouge | 1699 | 1812, April 30 |
| **Maine** | Augusta | 1624 | 1820, March 15 |
| **Maryland** | Annapolis | 1634 | 1788, April 28 |
| **Massachusetts** | Boston | 1620 | 1788, February 6 |
| **Michigan** | Lansing | 1668 | 1837, January 26 |
| **Minnesota** | St. Paul | 1805 | 1858, May 11 |
| **Mississippi** | Jackson | 1699 | 1817, December 10 |
| **Missouri** | Jefferson City | 1764 | 1821, August 10 |
| **Montana** | Helena | 1809 | 1889, November 8 |
| **Nebraska** | Lincoln | 1847 | 1867, March 1 |
| **Nevada** | Carson City | 1850 | 1864, October 31 |
| **New Hampshire** | Concord | 1623 | 1788, June 21 |
| **New Jersey** | Trenton | 1664 | 1787, December 18 |
| **New Mexico** | Santa Fe | 1605 | 1912, January 6 |
| **New York** | Albany | 1614 | 1788, July 26 |
| **North Carolina** | Raleigh | 1650 | 1789, November 21 |
| **North Dakota** | Bismarck | 1766 | 1889, November 2 |
| **Ohio** | Columbus | 1788 | 1803, March 1 |
| **Oklahoma** | Oklahoma City | 1889 | 1907, November 16 |
| **Oregon** | Salem | 1811 | 1859, February 14 |
| **Pennsylvania** | Harrisburg | 1682 | 1787, December 12 |
| **Rhode Island** | Providence | 1636 | 1790, May 29 |
| **South Carolina** | Columbia | 1670 | 1788, May 23 |
| **South Dakota** | Pierre | 1856 | 1889, November 2 |
| **Tennessee** | Nashville | 1757 | 1796, June 1 |
| **Texas** | Austin | 1691 | 1845, December 29 |
| **Utah** | Salt Lake City | 1847 | 1896, January 4 |
| **Vermont** | Montpelier | 1724 | 1791, March 4 |
| **Virginia** | Richmond | 1607 | 1788, June 26 |
| **Washington** | Olympia | 1811 | 1889, November 11 |
| **West Virginia** | Charleston | 1727 | 1863, June 20 |
| **Wisconsin** | Madison | 1766 | 1848, May 29 |
| **Wyoming** | Cheyenne | 1834 | 1890, July 10 |

## NATIONAL PARKS OF THE UNITED STATES, THEIR LOCATION, AREA, AND CHARACTERISTICS

| Name | Location | When Established | Area (Acres) | Special Characteristics |
|---|---|---|---|---|
| Acadia | Southern Maine | 1919 | 30,865 | Mostly on Mount Desert Island, a mountainous, wooded island bridged to the mainland; part of the park is also on the tip of a peninsula that sticks out into the Atlantic opposite this island. |
| Big Bend | Western Texas | 1944 | 694,225 | On a big bend of the Rio Grande forming the Mexican border at this point; region of deserts, mountain ranges, and canyons; remains of prehistoric Indian civilization. |
| Bryce Canyon | Southwestern Utah | 1928 | 36,010 | Brightly colored area of wide canyons and many towering domes, spires, and pinnacles; Bryce Canyon is 1,000 feet deep, 3 miles long, and 2 miles wide. |
| Carlsbad Caverns | Southeastern New Mexico | 1930 | 45,847 | Many large and beautiful caves; a network of subterranean chambers formed by erosion of limestone; many caverns are still unexplored. |
| Crater Lake | Southwestern Oregon | 1902 | 160,290 | Lake with a deep-blue color lies in the crater of an extinct volcano; lake has no inlet or outlet, but level is kept constant by rainfall and snowfall; 500- to 2,000-foot cliffs encircle lake. |
| Everglades | Southern Florida | 1947 | 1,258,670 | Swampy, subtropical region with water prairies, mangrove forests, and sandy beaches; abundant bird life and variety of plants and animals; includes a Seminole Indian reservation. |
| Glacier | Northwestern Montana | 1910 | 999,567 | Scenic glacier-carved region on the Canadian border; includes some of the highest peaks of the Rockies, over 60 glaciers, over 200 lakes; numerous streams and waterfalls, extensive forests. |
| Grand Canyon | North central Arizona | 1919 | 673,108 | Includes 105 miles of the Grand Canyon gorge; canyon cut by Colorado River is 1 mile deep; reveals varicolored rock strata by erosion begun in Archaeozoic era. |
| Grand Teton | Northwestern Wyoming | 1929 | 299,326 | Glacier-carved region in Teton range of Rockies; includes 2 glaciers, many streams, and coniferous forests; abundant wildlife, such as moose, elk, etc. |
| Great Smoky Mountains | North Carolina and Tennessee | 1930 | 507,542 | Crest of highest section of Great Smokies runs through the park; almost unbroken forest land, 40% of it virgin growth; includes Cherokee Indian reservation. |
| Hawaii | Hawaii and Maui, islands of Hawaii | 1916 | 176,951 | Volcanoes Mauna Loa and Kilauea are on the island of Hawaii; the inactive volcano Haleakala with the largest inactive crater in the world is on Maui. |
| Hot Springs | Central Arkansas | 1921 | 986 | Health resort containing 47 mineral hot springs thought to have therapeutic value; numerous bathhouses under government supervision. |
| Isle Royale | Northern Michigan | 1940 | 539,339 | Wilderness area on Isle Royale and 200 surrounding islets; Isle Royale is the largest island in Lake Superior. |
| Kings Canyon | East central California | 1940 | 453,718 | Mountainous area with many peaks, chasms, and glacial formations; contains stands of giant sequoias including the General Grant tree (267 feet high, 3,500 years old); this park adjoins Sequoia National Park. |
| Lassen Volcanic | Northern California | 1916 | 104,241 | Mount Lassen (10,453 feet high), active volcano until 1921; spectacular lava formations, hot sulfur springs, and other remnants of volcanic action. |
| Mammoth Cave | Southwestern Kentucky | 1936 | 50,696 | A series of huge subterranean chambers formed by the dissolving of limestone; caves are on 5 levels, over 150 miles of them have been explored; a hilly and forested park surrounds the area |
| Mesa Verde | Southwestern Colorado | 1906 | 51,018 | Ruins of over 300 Pueblo Indian dwellings on top and in the canyons of a high mesa; pueblos, pit houses, and cliff dwellings represent stages of cultural progress over a period of 1,200 years, until abandoned about 1300 A.D. |
| Mount McKinley | South central Alaska | 1917 | 1,939,319 | Mount McKinley (20,300 feet high), highest peak in North America; several other high peaks and extensive glaciers. |
| Mount Rainier | West central Washington | 1899 | 241,571 | Mount Rainier (14,408 feet high), a volcanic peak supporting a large glacier system; heavily forested, with many lakes and meadows, much wildlife, and alpine wildflowers. |
| Olympic | Northwestern Washington | 1938 | 888,558 | A wild, rainy mountainous area including Mount Olympus (7,954 feet high); 7 glaciers; large virgin forests and much wildlife, especially Roosevelt Elk. |
| Platt | Southern Oklahoma | 1906 | 912 | Wooded, hilly area; numerous sulfur, bromide, and fresh-water springs. |
| Rocky Mountain | North central Colorado | 1915 | 255,706 | Heart of the Rockies with many high peaks, including more than 65 over 10,000 feet high; numerous glaciers, waterfalls, canyons, lakes, and streams; forests and meadows; a wildlife sanctuary. |
| Sequoia | East central California | 1890 | 385,258 | Giant sequoia groves, deep canyons, and lofty peaks including Mount Whitney (14,495 feet high), one of the highest peaks in the U.S.; General Sherman, a sequoia, 272 feet high, 30 feet in diameter, and about 3,500 years old. |
| Shenandoah | Northern Virginia | 1935 | 193,473 | Crest of Blue Ridge Mountains, a portion of the Appalachians, extends through the park, about 75 miles; heavily wooded with abundance of wildlife and wild flowers; Skyline Drive runs through the length of the park. |
| Wind Cave | Southwestern South Dakota | 1903 | 27,893 | In the Black Hills; includes a cavern (Wind Cave) which contains ornamental calcite and limestone formations; a game preserve of buffalo, antelope, and deer. |
| Yellowstone | Northwestern Wyoming, Southwestern Montana, and Northeastern Idaho | 1872 | 2,213,207 | A broad volcanic plateau surrounded by mountains rising 2,000 to 4,000 feet; about 3,000 geysers and hot springs; mud volcanoes; petrified forests; many large lakes, streams, and waterfalls; extensive forests; sanctuary for many kinds of wild animals and over 200 species of birds. |
| Yosemite | East central California | 1890 | 757,827 | Yosemite Valley (7 miles long & 1 mile wide) was formed by glacier and stream erosion; mountainous region with many lofty peaks and cliffs, high waterfalls, lakes and meadows, and enormous trees including 3 groves of sequoias. |
| Zion | Southwestern Utah | 1919 | 94,241 | Area of deep canyons, high cliffs and mesas; Zion Canyon, running the length of the park, is about 15 miles long and ½ mile deep; it has brightly colored rock formations, mostly of red and yellowish-red. |

# LARGEST CITIES OF THE UNITED STATES

## POPULATION OF 100,000 OR MORE — FINAL 1970 CENSUS

| | |
|---|---|
| New York, N.Y. | 7,867,760 |
| Chicago, Ill. | 3,366,957 |
| Los Angeles, Calif. | 2,816,061 |
| Philadelphia, Pa. | 1,948,609 |
| Detroit, Mich. | 1,511,482 |
| Houston, Texas | 1,232,802 |
| Baltimore, Md. | 905,759 |
| Dallas, Texas | 844,401 |
| Washington, D.C. | 756,510 |
| Cleveland, Ohio | 750,903 |
| Indianapolis, Ind. | 744,624 |
| Milwaukee, Wisc. | 717,099 |
| San Francisco, Calif. | 715,674 |
| San Diego, Calif. | 696,769 |
| San Antonio, Texas | 654,153 |
| Boston, Mass. | 641,071 |
| Memphis, Tenn. | 623,530 |
| St. Louis, Mo. | 622,236 |
| New Orleans, La. | 593,471 |
| Phoenix, Ariz. | 581,562 |
| Columbus, Ohio | 539,677 |
| Seattle, Wash. | 530,831 |
| Jacksonville, Fla. | 528,865 |
| Pittsburgh, Pa. | 520,117 |
| Denver, Colo. | 514,678 |
| Kansas City, Mo. | 507,087 |
| Atlanta, Ga. | 496,973 |
| Buffalo, N.Y. | 462,768 |
| Cincinnati, Ohio | 452,524 |
| Nashville, Tenn. | 447,877 |
| San Jose, Calif. | 445,779 |
| Minneapolis, Minn. | 434,400 |
| Fort Worth, Texas | 393,476 |
| Toledo, Ohio | 383,818 |
| Portland, Ore. | 382,619 |
| Newark, N.J. | 382,417 |
| Oklahoma City, Okla. | 366,481 |
| Oakland, Calif. | 361,561 |
| Louisville, Ky. | 361,472 |
| Long Beach, Calif. | 358,633 |
| Omaha, Neb. | 347,328 |
| Miami, Fla. | 334,859 |
| Tulsa, Okla. | 331,638 |
| Honolulu, Hawaii | 324,871 |
| El Paso, Texas | 322,261 |
| St. Paul, Minn. | 309,980 |
| Norfolk, Va. | 307,951 |
| Birmingham, Ala. | 300,910 |
| Rochester, N.Y. | 296,233 |
| Tampa, Fla. | 277,767 |
| Wichita, Kans. | 276,554 |
| Akron, Ohio | 275,425 |
| Tucson, Ariz. | 262,933 |
| Jersey City, N.J. | 260,545 |
| Sacramento, Calif. | 254,413 |
| Austin, Texas | 251,808 |
| Richmond, Va. | 249,621 |
| Albuquerque, N.M. | 243,751 |
| Dayton, Ohio | 243,601 |
| Charlotte, N.C. | 241,178 |
| St. Petersburg, Fla. | 216,232 |
| Corpus Christi, Texas | 204,525 |
| Yonkers, N.Y. | 204,370 |
| Des Moines, Iowa | 200,587 |
| Grand Rapids, Mich. | 197,649 |
| Syracuse, N.Y. | 197,208 |
| Flint, Mich. | 193,317 |
| Mobile, Ala. | 190,026 |
| Shreveport, La. | 182,064 |
| Warren, Mich. | 179,260 |
| Providence, R.I. | 179,213 |
| Ft. Wayne, Ind. | 177,671 |
| Worcester, Mass. | 176,572 |
| Salt Lake City, Utah | 175,885 |
| Gary, Ind. | 175,415 |
| Knoxville, Tenn. | 174,587 |
| Arlington, Va. | 174,284 |
| Madison, Wisc. | 173,258 |
| Virginia Beach, Va. | 172,106 |
| Spokane, Wash. | 170,516 |
| Kansas City, Mo. | 168,213 |
| Anaheim, Calif. | 166,701 |
| Fresno, Calif. | 165,972 |
| Baton Rouge, La. | 165,963 |
| Springfield, Mass. | 163,905 |
| Hartford, Conn. | 158,017 |
| Santa Ana, Calif. | 156,601 |
| Bridgeport, Conn. | 156,542 |
| Tacoma, Wash. | 154,581 |
| Columbus, Ga. | 154,168 |
| Jackson, Miss. | 153,968 |
| Lincoln, Neb. | 149,518 |
| Lubbock, Texas | 149,101 |
| Rockford, Ill. | 147,370 |
| Paterson, N.J. | 144,824 |
| Greensboro, N.C. | 144,076 |
| Riverside, Calif. | 140,089 |
| Youngstown, Ohio | 139,788 |
| Ft. Lauderdale, Fla. | 139,590 |
| Evansville, Ind. | 138,764 |
| Newport News, Va. | 138,177 |
| Huntsville, Ala. | 137,802 |
| New Haven, Conn. | 137,707 |
| Metairie, La. | 135,816 |
| Colorado Spgs., Colo. | 135,060 |
| Torrance, Calif. | 134,584 |
| Montgomery, Ala. | 133,386 |
| Winston-Salem, N.C. | 132,913 |
| Glendale, Calif. | 132,752 |
| Little Rock, Ark. | 132,483 |
| Lansing, Mich. | 131,546 |
| Erie, Pa. | 129,231 |
| Amarillo, Texas | 127,010 |
| Peoria, Ill. | 126,963 |
| Las Vegas, Nev. | 125,787 |
| South Bend, Ind. | 125,580 |
| Topeka, Kans. | 125,011 |
| Garden Grove, Calif. | 122,524 |
| Macon, Ga. | 122,423 |
| Raleigh, N.C. | 121,577 |
| Hampton, Va. | 120,779 |
| Springfield, Mo. | 120,096 |
| Chattanooga, Tenn. | 119,082 |
| Savannah, Ga. | 118,349 |
| Berkeley, Calif. | 116,716 |
| Huntington Beach., Calif. | 115,960 |
| Beaumont, Texas | 115,919 |
| Albany, N.Y. | 114,873 |
| Columbia, S.C. | 113,542 |
| Pasadena, Calif. | 113,327 |
| Elizabeth, N.J. | 112,654 |
| Independence, Mo. | 111,662 |
| Portsmouth, Va. | 110,963 |
| Alexandria, Va. | 110,938 |
| Cedar Rapids, Iowa | 110,642 |
| Livonia, Mich. | 110,109 |
| Canton, Ohio | 110,053 |
| Allentown, Pa. | 109,527 |
| Stamford, Conn. | 108,798 |
| Lexington, Ky. | 108,137 |
| Waterbury, Conn. | 108,033 |
| Hammond, Ind. | 107,790 |
| Stockton, Calif. | 107,644 |
| Hollywood, Fla. | 106,873 |
| Trenton, N.J. | 104,638 |
| San Bernard'o, Calif. | 104,251 |
| Dearborn, Mich. | 104,199 |
| Scranton, Pa. | 103,564 |
| Camden, N.J. | 102,551 |
| Hialeah, Fla. | 102,297 |
| New Bedford, Mass. | 101,777 |
| Fremont, Calif. | 100,869 |
| Duluth, Minn. | 100,578 |
| Cambridge, Mass. | 100,361 |
| Parma, Ohio | 100,216 |

# PRINCIPAL CITIES OF THE UNITED STATES

## FINAL 1970 CENSUS

### ALABAMA

| | |
|---|---|
| Albertville | 9,963 |
| Alexander City | 12,358 |
| Andalusia | 10,092 |
| Anniston | 31,533 |
| Arab | 4,399 |
| Athens | 14,360 |
| Atmore | 8,293 |
| Attalla | 7,510 |
| Auburn | 22,767 |
| Bay Minette | 6,727 |
| Bessemer | 33,428 |
| Birmingham | 300,910 |
| Bluff Park | 12,372 |
| Boaz | 5,621 |
| Brewton | 6,747 |
| Center Point | 15,675 |
| Chickasaw | 8,447 |
| Childersburg | 4,831 |
| Clanton | 5,868 |
| Cullman | 12,601 |
| Daleville | 5,182 |
| Decatur | 38,044 |
| Demopolis | 7,651 |
| Dothan | 36,733 |
| Elba | 4,634 |
| Enterprise | 15,591 |
| Eufaula | 9,102 |
| Evergreen | 3,924 |
| Fairfield | 14,369 |
| Fairhope | 5,720 |
| Fayette | 4,568 |
| Florence | 34,031 |
| Foley | 3,368 |
| Forestdale | 6,091 |
| Fort McClellan | 5,334 |
| Fort Payne | 8,435 |
| Fort Rucker | 14,242 |
| Fultondale | 5,163 |
| Gadsden | 53,928 |
| Gardendale | 6,502 |
| Geneva | 4,398 |
| Greensboro | 3,371 |
| Greenville | 8,033 |
| Guntersville | 6,491 |
| Haleyville | 4,134 |
| Hartselle | 7,355 |
| Homewood | 21,245 |
| Hueytown | 7,095 |
| Huntsville | 137,802 |
| Jackson | 5,957 |
| Jacksonville | 7,715 |
| Jasper | 10,798 |
| Lafayette | 3,530 |
| Lanett | 6,908 |
| Leeds | 6,991 |
| Lipscomb | 3,225 |
| Marion | 4,289 |
| Midfield | 6,399 |
| Mobile | 190,026 |
| Monroeville | 4,846 |
| Montevallo | 3,719 |
| Montgomery | 133,386 |
| Mountain Brook | 19,474 |
| Muscle Shoals | 6,907 |
| Northport | 9,435 |
| Oneonta | 4,390 |
| Opelika | 19,027 |
| Opp | 6,493 |
| Oxford | 4,361 |
| Ozark | 13,555 |
| Pell City | 5,381 |
| Phenix City | 25,281 |
| Piedmont | 5,063 |
| Pleasant Grove | 5,090 |
| Prattville | 13,116 |
| Prichard | 41,578 |
| Roanoke | 5,251 |
| Roosevelt | 3,663 |
| Russellville | 7,814 |

### ALABAMA—Continued

| | |
|---|---|
| Saraland | 7,840 |
| Scottsboro | 9,324 |
| Selma | 27,379 |
| Sheffield | 13,115 |
| Sylacauga | 12,255 |
| Talladega | 17,662 |
| Tallassee | 4,809 |
| Tarrant City | 6,835 |
| Thomasville | 3,769 |
| Troy | 11,482 |
| Tuscaloosa | 65,773 |
| Tuscumbia | 8,828 |
| Tuskegee | 11,028 |
| Union Springs | 4,324 |
| Vestavia Hills | 8,311 |
| West End-Cobb | 5,515 |
| Wetumpka | 3,786 |
| Winfield | 3,292 |

### ALASKA

| | |
|---|---|
| Anchorage | 48,029 |
| College | 3,434 |
| Eielson | 6,149 |
| Elmendorf | 6,018 |
| Fairbanks | 14,771 |
| Fort Richardson | 8,960 |
| Fort Wainwright | 9,097 |
| Juneau | 6,050 |
| Kenai | 3,533 |
| Ketchikan | 6,994 |
| Kodiak | 3,798 |
| Sand Lake | 4,168 |
| Sitka | 3,370 |
| Spenard | 18,089 |

### ARIZONA

| | |
|---|---|
| Ajo | 5,881 |
| Avondale | 6,304 |
| Bisbee | 8,328 |
| Casa Grande | 10,536 |
| Chandler | 13,763 |
| Clifton | 5,087 |
| Coolidge | 4,651 |
| Douglas | 12,462 |
| El Mirage | 3,258 |
| Eloy | 5,381 |
| Flagstaff | 26,117 |
| Fort Huachuca | 6,659 |
| Glendale | 36,228 |
| Globe | 7,333 |
| Holbrook | 4,759 |
| Kingman | 7,312 |
| Luke | 5,047 |
| Mesa | 62,853 |
| Miami | 3,394 |
| Nogales | 8,946 |
| Paradise Valley | 7,155 |
| Peoria | 4,792 |
| Phoenix | 581,562 |
| Prescott | 13,030 |
| Safford | 5,333 |
| San Manuel | 4,332 |
| Scottsdale | 67,823 |
| Sierra Vista | 6,689 |
| Sun | 13,670 |
| Superior | 4,975 |
| Tempe | 62,907 |
| Tolleson | 3,881 |
| Tucson | 262,933 |
| Williams | 3,443 |
| Winslow | 8,066 |
| Yuma | 29,007 |

### ARKANSAS

| | |
|---|---|
| Arkadelphia | 9,841 |
| Ashdown | 3,522 |
| Batesville | 7,209 |
| Benton | 16,499 |
| Bentonville | 5,508 |
| Blytheville | 24,752 |
| Booneville | 3,239 |
| Brinkley | 5,275 |

### ARKANSAS—Continued

| | |
|---|---|
| Camden | 15,147 |
| Clarksville | 4,616 |
| Conway | 15,510 |
| Crossett | 6,191 |
| Dardanelle | 3,297 |
| De Queen | 3,863 |
| Dermott | 4,250 |
| De Witt | 3,728 |
| Dumas | 4,600 |
| El Dorado | 25,283 |
| Eudora | 3,687 |
| Fayetteville | 30,729 |
| Fordyce | 4,837 |
| Forrest City | 12,521 |
| Fort Smith | 62,802 |
| Harrison | 7,239 |
| Helena | 10,415 |
| Hope | 8,810 |
| Hot Springs | 35,631 |
| Jacksonville | 19,832 |
| Jonesboro | 27,050 |
| Lake Village | 3,310 |
| Little Rock | 132,483 |
| McGehee | 4,683 |
| Magnolia | 11,303 |
| Malvern | 8,739 |
| Marianna | 6,196 |
| Marked Tree | 3,208 |
| Mena | 4,530 |
| Monticello | 5,085 |
| Morrilton | 6,814 |
| Mountain Home | 3,936 |
| Nashville | 4,016 |
| Newport | 7,725 |
| North Little Rock | 60,040 |
| Osceola | 7,204 |
| Paragould | 10,639 |
| Paris | 3,646 |
| Pine Bluff | 57,389 |
| Pocahontas | 4,544 |
| Prescott | 3,921 |
| Rogers | 11,050 |
| Russellville | 11,750 |
| Searcy | 9,040 |
| Siloam Springs | 6,009 |
| Springdale | 16,783 |
| Stuttgart | 10,477 |
| Texarkana | 21,682 |
| Trumann | 5,938 |
| Van Buren | 8,373 |
| Walnut Ridge | 3,800 |
| Warren | 6,433 |
| West Helena | 11,007 |
| West Memphis | 25,892 |
| Wynne | 6,696 |

### CALIFORNIA

| | |
|---|---|
| Alameda | 70,968 |
| Alamo-Danville | 14,059 |
| Albany | 14,674 |
| Alhambra | 62,125 |
| Alondra Park | 12,193 |
| Altadena | 42,380 |
| Alum Rock | 18,355 |
| Anaheim | 166,701 |
| Anderson | 5,492 |
| Antioch | 28,060 |
| Apple Valley | 6,702 |
| Aptos | 8,704 |
| Arcadia | 42,868 |
| Arcata | 8,985 |
| Arden-Arcade | 82,492 |
| Arroyo Grande | 7,454 |
| Artesia | 14,757 |
| Arvin | 5,090 |
| Ashland | 14,810 |
| Atascadero | 10,290 |
| Atherton | 8,085 |
| Atwater | 11,640 |
| Auburn | 6,570 |

### CALIFORNIA—Continued

| | |
|---|---|
| August School | 6,293 |
| Avocado Heights | 9,810 |
| Azusa | 25,217 |
| Bakersfield | 69,515 |
| Baldwin Park | 47,285 |
| Banning | 12,034 |
| Barstow | 17,442 |
| Baywood-Los Osos | 3,487 |
| Beale East | 7,029 |
| Beaumont | 5,484 |
| Bell | 21,836 |
| Bellflower | 51,454 |
| Bell Gardens | 29,308 |
| Belmont | 23,667 |
| Benicia | 8,783 |
| Berkeley | 116,716 |
| Beverly Hills | 33,416 |
| Big Bear | 5,268 |
| Bishop | 3,498 |
| Bloomington | 11,957 |
| Blythe | 7,047 |
| Bonnyview | 4,882 |
| Boyes Hot Springs | 3,558 |
| Brawley | 13,746 |
| Brea | 18,447 |
| Broderick-Bryte | 12,782 |
| Buena Park | 63,646 |
| Burbank | 88,871 |
| Burlingame | 27,320 |
| Calexico | 10,625 |
| Calwa | 5,191 |
| Camarillo | 19,219 |
| Camarillo Heights | 5,892 |
| Cambrian Park | 5,316 |
| Campbell | 24,770 |
| Capistrano Beach | 4,149 |
| Capitola | 5,080 |
| Cardiff-By-The-Sea | 5,724 |
| Carlsbad | 14,944 |
| Carmel-By-The-Sea | 4,525 |
| Carmichael | 37,625 |
| Carpinteria | 6,982 |
| Carson | 71,150 |
| Castro Valley | 44,760 |
| Castroville | 3,235 |
| Cathedral | 3,640 |
| Ceres | 6,029 |
| Cerritos | 15,856 |
| Cherryland | 9,969 |
| Chico | 19,580 |
| China Lake | 11,105 |
| Chino | 20,411 |
| Chowchilla | 4,349 |
| Chula Vista | 67,901 |
| Citrus Heights | 21,760 |
| Claremont | 23,464 |
| Cloverdale | 3,251 |
| Clovis | 13,856 |
| Coachella | 8,353 |
| Coalinga | 6,161 |
| Colton | 19,974 |
| Colusa | 3,842 |
| Commerce | 10,536 |
| Compton | 78,611 |
| Concord | 85,164 |
| Corcoran | 5,249 |
| Corning | 3,573 |
| Corona | 27,519 |
| Coronado | 20,910 |
| Corte Madera | 8,464 |
| Costa Mesa | 72,660 |
| Covina | 30,380 |
| Crest Forest | 3,509 |
| Cucamonga | 5,796 |
| Cudahy | 16,998 |
| Culver City | 31,035 |
| Cupertino | 18,216 |
| Cypress | 31,026 |
| Daly City | 66,922 |

**CALIFORNIA—Continued**

| | |
|---|---|
| Dana Point | 4,745 |
| Davis | 23,488 |
| Del Aire | 11,930 |
| Delano | 14,559 |
| Del Mar | 3,956 |
| Diamond Bar | 12,234 |
| Dinuba | 7,917 |
| Dixon | 4,432 |
| Dominguez | 5,980 |
| Downey | 88,445 |
| Duarte | 14,981 |
| Dublin | 13,641 |
| East La Mirada | 12,339 |
| Edwards | 10,331 |
| El Cajon | 52,273 |
| El Centro | 19,272 |
| El Cerrito | 25,190 |
| El Encanto Heights | 6,225 |
| Elk Grove | 3,721 |
| El Monte | 69,837 |
| El Paso De Robles | 7,168 |
| El Rio | 6,173 |
| El Segundo | 15,620 |
| Elsinore | 3,530 |
| El Toro | 8,654 |
| Encinitas | 5,375 |
| Enterprise | 11,486 |
| Escondido | 36,792 |
| Eureka | 24,337 |
| Exeter | 4,475 |
| Fairfax | 7,661 |
| Fairfield | 44,146 |
| Fair Oaks | 11,256 |
| Fallbrook | 6,945 |
| Farmersville | 3,456 |
| Fillmore | 6,285 |
| Florence-Graham | 42,895 |
| Florin | 9,646 |
| Folsom | 5,810 |
| Fontana | 20,673 |
| Ford | 3,503 |
| Fort Bragg | 4,455 |
| Fortuna | 4,203 |
| Foster | 9,327 |
| Fountain Valley | 31,826 |
| Freedom | 5,563 |
| Fremont | 100,869 |
| Fresno | 165,972 |
| Fullerton | 85,826 |
| Galt | 3,200 |
| Gardena | 41,021 |
| Garden Acres | 7,870 |
| Garden Grove | 122,524 |
| George | 7,404 |
| Gilroy | 12,665 |
| Glen Avon | 5,759 |
| Glendale | 132,752 |
| Glendora | 31,349 |
| Grand Terrace | 5,901 |
| Grass Valley | 5,149 |
| Gridley | 3,534 |
| Grossmont-Mt. Helix | 8,723 |
| Grover City | 5,939 |
| Hacienda Heights | 35,969 |
| Half Moon Bay | 4,023 |
| Hanford | 15,179 |
| Hawaiian Gardens | 8,811 |
| Hawthorne | 53,304 |
| Hayward | 93,058 |
| Healdsburg | 5,438 |
| Hemet | 12,252 |
| Hermosa Beach | 17,412 |
| Hesperia | 4,592 |
| Highland | 12,669 |
| Hillsborough | 8,753 |
| Hollister | 7,663 |
| Holtville | 3,496 |
| Home Gardens | 5,116 |
| Huntington Beach | 115,960 |
| Huntington Park | 33,744 |
| Imperial Beach | 20,244 |
| Indio | 14,459 |
| Inglewood | 89,985 |
| Isla Vista | 13,441 |
| Kensington | 5,823 |
| King City | 3,717 |
| Kingsburg | 3,843 |
| La Canada-Flintridge | 20,652 |
| La Crescenta-Montrose | 19,594 |
| Ladera Heights | 6,079 |
| Lafayette | 20,484 |
| Laguna Beach | 14,550 |
| Laguna Hills | 13,676 |
| Laguna Niguel | 4,644 |
| La Habra | 41,350 |
| Lakeside | 11,991 |
| Lakewood | 82,973 |
| La Mesa | 39,178 |
| La Mirada | 30,808 |
| Lamont | 7,007 |
| Lancaster | 30,948 |
| La Palma | 9,687 |
| La Puente | 31,092 |
| Larkspur | 10,487 |
| La Verne | 12,965 |
| Lawndale | 24,825 |
| Lemon Grove | 19,690 |
| Lemoore Station | 8,512 |
| Lennox | 16,121 |
| Lenwood | 3,834 |
| Lincoln | 6,722 |
| Linda | 7,731 |
| Lindsay | 5,206 |
| Live Oak | 6,443 |
| Livermore | 37,703 |
| Lodi | 28,691 |
| Loma Linda | 9,797 |
| Lomita | 19,784 |
| Lompoc | 25,284 |
| Long Beach | 358,633 |
| Los Alamitos | 11,346 |
| Los Altos | 24,956 |
| Los Altos Hills | 6,865 |
| Los Angeles | 2,816,061 |
| Los Banos | 9,188 |
| Los Gatos | 23,735 |
| Lynwood | 43,353 |
| McFarland | 4,177 |
| Madera | 16,044 |
| Manhattan Beach | 35,352 |
| Manteca | 13,845 |

**CALIFORNIA—Continued**

| | |
|---|---|
| Marina | 8,343 |
| Martinez | 16,506 |
| Marysville | 9,353 |
| Mather | 7,027 |
| Maywood | 16,996 |
| Meiners Oaks-Mira Monte | 7,025 |
| Menlo Park | 26,734 |
| Merced | 22,670 |
| Millbrae | 20,781 |
| Mill Valley | 12,942 |
| Milpitas | 27,149 |
| Mira Loma | 8,482 |
| Mission Viejo | 11,933 |
| Modesto | 61,712 |
| Monrovia | 30,015 |
| Montclair | 22,546 |
| Montebello | 42,807 |
| Monterey | 26,302 |
| Monterey Park | 49,166 |
| Moorpark | 3,380 |
| Moraga | 14,205 |
| Morgan Hill | 6,485 |
| Morro Bay | 7,109 |
| Mountain View | 51,092 |
| Muscoy | 7,091 |
| Napa | 35,978 |
| National City | 43,184 |
| Needles | 4,051 |
| Newark | 27,153 |
| Newhall | 9,651 |
| Newport Beach | 49,422 |
| Nipomo | 3,642 |
| Norco | 14,511 |
| North Highlands | 31,854 |
| North Island | 6,002 |
| Norwalk | 91,827 |
| Novato | 31,006 |
| Oakdale | 6,594 |
| Oakland | 361,561 |
| Oak View | 4,872 |
| Oceanside | 40,494 |
| Oildale | 20,879 |
| Ojai | 5,591 |
| Olivehurst | 8,100 |
| Ontario | 64,118 |
| Opal Cliffs | 5,425 |
| Orange | 77,374 |
| Orange Cove | 3,392 |
| Orangevale | 16,493 |
| Orcutt | 8,500 |
| Orinda | 6,790 |
| Oroville | 7,536 |
| Otay-Castle Park | 15,445 |
| Oxnard | 71,225 |
| Pacifica | 36,020 |
| Pacific Grove | 13,505 |
| Palmdale | 8,511 |
| Palm Desert | 6,171 |
| Palm Springs | 20,936 |
| Palo Alto | 35,966 |
| Palos Verdes Estates | 13,641 |
| Palos Verdes Peninsula | 39,616 |
| Paradise | 14,539 |
| Paramount | 34,734 |
| Parkway-Sacramento South | 28,574 |
| Pasadena | 113,327 |
| Pendleton North | 11,803 |
| Pendleton South | 13,692 |
| Perris | 4,228 |
| Petaluma | 24,870 |
| Pico Rivera | 54,170 |
| Piedmont | 10,917 |
| Pinole | 15,850 |
| Pismo Beach | 4,043 |
| Pittsburg | 20,651 |
| Placentia | 21,948 |
| Placerville | 5,416 |
| Pleasant Hill | 24,610 |
| Pleasanton | 18,328 |
| Point Mugu | 3,351 |
| Pomona | 87,384 |
| Porterville | 12,602 |
| Port Hueneme | 14,295 |
| Portola Valley | 4,999 |
| Poway | 9,422 |
| Quartz Hill | 4,935 |
| Quincy | 3,343 |
| Ramona | 3,554 |
| Rancho Cordova | 30,451 |
| Rancho Rinconada | 5,149 |
| Rancho Santa Clarita | 4,860 |
| Red Bluff | 7,676 |
| Redding | 16,659 |
| Redlands | 36,355 |
| Redondo Beach | 56,075 |
| Redwood City | 55,686 |
| Reedley | 8,131 |
| Rialto | 28,370 |
| Richmond | 79,043 |
| Ridgecrest | 7,629 |
| Rio Linda | 7,524 |
| Riverbank | 3,949 |
| Riverside | 140,089 |
| Rodeo | 5,356 |
| Rohnert Park | 6,133 |
| Rolling Hills Estates | 6,027 |
| Roseland | 5,105 |
| Rosemead | 40,972 |
| Roseville | 17,895 |
| Rossmoor | 12,922 |
| Rowland Heights | 16,881 |
| Rubidoux | 13,969 |
| Ryans Slough | 3,922 |
| Sacramento | 254,413 |
| Salinas | 58,896 |
| San Anselmo | 13,031 |
| San Bernardino | 104,251 |
| San Bruno | 36,254 |
| San Carlos | 25,924 |
| San Clemente | 17,063 |
| San Diego | 696,769 |
| San Dimas | 15,692 |
| San Fernando | 16,571 |
| San Francisco | 715,674 |
| San Gabriel | 29,176 |
| Sanger | 10,088 |
| San Jacinto | 4,385 |

**CALIFORNIA—Continued**

| | |
|---|---|
| San Jose | 445,779 |
| San Juan Capistrano | 3,781 |
| San Leandro | 68,698 |
| San Lorenzo | 24,633 |
| San Luis Obispo | 28,036 |
| San Marcos | 3,896 |
| San Marino | 14,177 |
| San Mateo | 78,991 |
| San Pablo | 21,461 |
| San Rafael | 38,977 |
| San Ramon | 4,084 |
| Santa Ana | 156,601 |
| Santa Barbara | 70,215 |
| Santa Clara | 87,717 |
| Santa Cruz | 32,076 |
| Santa Fe Springs | 14,750 |
| Santa Maria | 32,749 |
| Santa Monica | 88,289 |
| Santa Paula | 18,001 |
| Santa Rosa | 50,006 |
| Santee | 21,107 |
| Saratoga | 27,110 |
| Sausalito | 6,158 |
| Scotts Valley | 3,621 |
| Seal Beach | 24,441 |
| Searles Valley | 3,828 |
| Seaside | 35,935 |
| Sebastopol | 3,993 |
| Selma | 7,459 |
| Shafter | 5,327 |
| Sierra Madre | 12,140 |
| Signal Hill | 5,582 |
| Simi Valley | 56,464 |
| Solana Beach | 5,023 |
| Soledad | 6,843 |
| Sonoma | 4,112 |
| Soquel | 5,795 |
| South El Monte | 13,443 |
| South Gate | 56,909 |
| South Lake Tahoe | 12,921 |
| South Pasadena | 22,979 |
| South San Francisco | 46,646 |
| South San Jose Hills | 12,386 |
| Spring Valley | 29,742 |
| Stanford | 8,691 |
| Stanton | 17,947 |
| Stockton | 107,644 |
| Sun | 5,519 |
| Sunnymead | 6,708 |
| Sunnyvale | 95,408 |
| Susanville | 6,608 |
| Taft | 4,285 |
| Tehachapi | 4,211 |
| Temple City | 29,673 |
| Thermalito | 4,217 |
| Thousand Oaks | 36,334 |
| Tiburon | 6,209 |
| Torrance | 134,584 |
| Tracy | 14,724 |
| Tulare | 16,235 |
| Turlock | 13,992 |
| Tustin | 21,178 |
| Tustin-Foothills | 26,598 |
| Twentynine Palms | 5,667 |
| Ukiah | 10,095 |
| Union City | 14,724 |
| Upland | 32,551 |
| Vacaville | 21,690 |
| Valencia | 4,243 |
| Valinda | 18,837 |
| Vallejo | 66,733 |
| Vandenburg | 13,193 |
| Ventura | 55,797 |
| Victorville | 10,845 |
| View Park-Windsor Hills | 12,268 |
| Visalia | 27,268 |
| Vista | 24,688 |
| Walnut | 5,992 |
| Walnut Creek | 39,844 |
| Walnut Park | 8,925 |
| Wasco | 8,269 |
| Watsonville | 14,569 |
| West Athens | 13,286 |
| West Covina | 68,034 |
| West Hollywood | 29,448 |
| Westminster | 59,865 |
| Westmont | 29,310 |
| West Puente Valley | 20,733 |
| West Sacramento | 12,002 |
| West Whittier-Los Nietos | 20,845 |
| Whittier | 72,863 |
| Willowbrook | 28,705 |
| Willows | 4,085 |
| Winton | 3,393 |
| Woodlake | 3,371 |
| Woodland | 20,677 |
| Woodside | 4,731 |
| Yorba Linda | 11,856 |
| Yreka City | 5,394 |
| Yuba City | 13,986 |
| Yucaipa | 19,284 |
| Yucca Valley | 3,893 |

**COLORADO**

| | |
|---|---|
| Alamosa | 6,985 |
| Applewood | 8,214 |
| Arvada | 46,814 |
| Aurora | 74,974 |
| Boulder | 66,870 |
| Brighton | 8,309 |
| Broomfield | 7,261 |
| Brush | 3,377 |
| Canon City | 9,206 |
| Cherry Hills Village | 4,605 |
| Colorado Springs | 135,060 |
| Commerce City | 17,407 |
| Cortez | 6,032 |
| Craig | 4,205 |
| Delta | 3,694 |
| Denver | 514,678 |
| Derby | 10,206 |
| Durango | 10,333 |
| Edgewater | 4,866 |
| Englewood | 33,695 |
| Fort Carson | 19,399 |
| Fort Collins | 43,337 |
| Fort Morgan | 7,594 |
| Fountain | 3,515 |
| Glenwood Springs | 4,106 |
| Golden | 9,817 |

**COLORADO—Continued**

| | |
|---|---|
| Grand Junction | 20,170 |
| Greeley | 38,902 |
| Gunnison | 4,613 |
| Lafayette | 3,498 |
| La Junta | 7,938 |
| Lakewood | 92,787 |
| Lamar | 7,797 |
| Leadville | 4,314 |
| Littleton | 26,466 |
| Longmont | 23,209 |
| Loveland | 16,220 |
| Manitou Springs | 4,278 |
| Monte Vista | 3,909 |
| Montrose | 6,496 |
| North Glenn | 27,937 |
| Orchard Mesa | 5,824 |
| Pueblo | 97,453 |
| Rocky Ford | 4,859 |
| Salida | 4,355 |
| Security-Widefield | 15,297 |
| Sheridan | 4,787 |
| Sherrelwood | 18,868 |
| Sterling | 10,636 |
| Stratton Meadows | 6,223 |
| Thornton | 13,326 |
| Trinidad | 9,901 |
| Walsenburg | 4,329 |
| Welby | 6,875 |
| Westminster | 19,432 |
| Wheat Ridge | 29,795 |

**CONNECTICUT**

| | |
|---|---|
| Ansonia | 21,160 |
| Avon | 8,352 |
| Beacon Falls | 3,546 |
| Berlin | 14,149 |
| Bethany | 3,857 |
| Bethel | 10,945 |
| Bloomfield | 18,301 |
| Bolton | 3,691 |
| Branford | 20,444 |
| Bridgeport | 156,542 |
| Bristol | 55,487 |
| Brookfield | 9,688 |
| Brooklyn | 4,965 |
| Burlington | 4,070 |
| Canton | 6,868 |
| Cheshire | 19,051 |
| Clinton | 10,267 |
| Colchester | 6,603 |
| Conning Towers-Nautilus Park | 9,791 |
| Coventry | 8,140 |
| Cromwell | 7,400 |
| Danbury | 50,781 |
| Danielson | 4,580 |
| Darien | 20,411 |
| Deep River | 3,690 |
| Derby | 12,599 |
| Durham | 4,489 |
| East Granby | 3,532 |
| East Haddam | 4,474 |
| East Hampton | 7,078 |
| East Hartford | 57,583 |
| East Haven | 25,120 |
| East Lyme | 11,399 |
| Easton | 4,885 |
| East Windsor | 8,513 |
| Ellington | 7,707 |
| Enfield | 46,189 |
| Essex | 4,911 |
| Fairfield | 56,487 |
| Farmington | 14,390 |
| Glastonbury | 20,651 |
| Granby | 6,150 |
| Greenwich | 59,755 |
| Griswold | 7,763 |
| Groton | 38,523 |
| Guilford | 12,033 |
| Haddam | 4,934 |
| Hamden | 49,357 |
| Hartford | 158,017 |
| Harwinton | 4,318 |
| Hebron | 3,815 |
| Jewett City | 3,372 |
| Killingly | 13,573 |
| Lebanon | 3,804 |
| Ledyard | 14,558 |
| Litchfield | 7,399 |
| Madison | 9,768 |
| Manchester | 47,994 |
| Mansfield | 19,994 |
| Meriden | 55,959 |
| Middlebury | 5,542 |
| Middlefield | 4,132 |
| Middletown | 36,924 |
| Milford | 50,858 |
| Monroe | 12,047 |
| Montville | 15,662 |
| Moosup | 3,376 |
| Morningside Park | 3,458 |
| Naugatuck | 23,034 |
| New Britain | 83,441 |
| New Canaan | 17,455 |
| New Fairfield | 6,991 |
| New Hartford | 3,970 |
| New Haven | 137,707 |
| Newington | 26,037 |
| New London | 31,630 |
| New Milford | 14,601 |
| Newtown | 16,942 |
| Niantic | 3,422 |
| North Branford | 10,778 |
| North Haven | 22,194 |
| North Stonington | 3,748 |
| Norwalk | 79,113 |
| Norwich | 41,433 |
| Old Lyme | 4,964 |
| Old Saybrook | 8,468 |
| Orange | 13,524 |
| Oxford | 4,480 |
| Pawcatuck | 5,255 |
| Plainfield | 11,957 |
| Plainville | 16,733 |
| Plymouth | 10,321 |
| Portland | 8,812 |
| Preston | 3,593 |
| Prospect | 6,543 |
| Putnam | 8,598 |
| Redding | 5,590 |
| Ridgefield | 18,188 |
| Rocky Hill | 11,103 |

**CONNECTICUT—Continued**

| | |
|---|---|
| Salisbury | 3,573 |
| Seymour | 12,776 |
| Shelton | 27,165 |
| Simsbury | 17,475 |
| Somers | 6,893 |
| Southbury | 7,852 |
| Southington | 30,946 |
| South Windsor | 15,553 |
| Stafford Springs | 3,339 |
| Stafford | 8,680 |
| Stamford | 108,798 |
| Stonington | 15,940 |
| Storrs | 10,691 |
| Stratford | 49,775 |
| Suffield | 8,634 |
| Thomaston | 6,233 |
| Thompson | 7,580 |
| Tolland | 7,857 |
| Torrington | 31,952 |
| Trumbull | 31,394 |
| Vernon | 27,237 |
| Wallingford | 35,714 |
| Waterbury | 108,033 |
| Waterford | 17,227 |
| Watertown | 18,610 |
| Westbrook | 3,820 |
| West Hartford | 68,031 |
| West Haven | 52,851 |
| Weston | 7,417 |
| Westport | 27,414 |
| Wethersfield | 26,662 |
| Willimantic | 14,402 |
| Willington | 3,755 |
| Wilton | 13,572 |
| Winchester | 11,106 |
| Windham | 19,626 |
| Windsor Locks | 15,080 |
| Windsor | 22,502 |
| Winsted | 8,954 |
| Wolcott | 12,495 |
| Woodbridge | 7,673 |
| Woodbury | 5,869 |
| Woodstock | 4,311 |

**DELAWARE**

| | |
|---|---|
| Brookside Park | 7,856 |
| Claymont | 6,584 |
| Dover | 17,488 |
| Dover Base | 8,106 |
| Elsmere | 8,415 |
| Milford | 5,314 |
| Newark | 20,757 |
| New Castle | 4,814 |
| Seaford | 5,537 |
| Smyrna | 4,243 |
| Wilmington | 80,386 |
| Wilmington Manor-Chelsea-Leedom | 10,134 |

**DISTRICT OF COLUMBIA**

| | |
|---|---|
| Washington | 756,510 |

**FLORIDA**

| | |
|---|---|
| Altamonte Springs | 4,391 |
| Apopka | 4,045 |
| Arcadia | 5,658 |
| Auburndale | 5,386 |
| Avon Park | 6,712 |
| Azalea Park | 7,367 |
| Bartow | 12,891 |
| Bay Harbor Islands | 4,619 |
| Bayshore Gardens | 9,255 |
| Belle Glade | 15,949 |
| Boca Raton | 28,506 |
| Boynton Beach | 18,115 |
| Bradenton | 21,040 |
| Brandon | 12,749 |
| Broadview Park-Rock Hill | 6,049 |
| Brooksville | 4,060 |
| Browardale | 17,444 |
| Browns | 23,442 |
| Buena Vista | 3,407 |
| Bunche Park | 5,773 |
| Callaway | 3,240 |
| Cantonment | 3,241 |
| Cape Canaveral | 4,258 |
| Cape Coral | 10,193 |
| Carol | 27,361 |
| Carver Ranch Estates | 5,515 |
| Casselberry | 9,438 |
| Cedar Hammock-Bradenton South | 10,820 |
| Chattahoochee | 7,944 |
| Chipley | 3,347 |
| Clearwater | 52,074 |
| Clermont | 3,661 |
| Clewiston | 3,896 |
| Cocoa Beach | 9,952 |
| Cocoa | 16,110 |
| Collier Manor-Cresthaven | 7,202 |
| Combee | 4,963 |
| Conway | 8,642 |
| Coral Gables | 42,494 |
| Crestview | 7,952 |
| Cutler Ridge | 17,441 |
| Cypress Gardens | 3,757 |
| Dade City | 4,241 |
| Dania | 9,013 |
| Daytona Beach | 45,327 |
| Deerfield Beach | 17,130 |
| De Funiak Springs | 4,966 |
| De Land | 11,641 |
| Delray Beach | 19,366 |
| Deltona | 4,868 |
| Dunedin | 17,639 |
| East Lake-Orient Park | 5,697 |
| Edgewater | 3,348 |
| Eglin | 7,769 |
| Egypt Lake | 7,556 |
| Englewood | 5,182 |
| Eustis | 6,722 |
| Fernandina Beach | 6,955 |
| Florida City | 5,133 |
| Fort Lauderdale | 139,590 |
| Fort Meade | 4,374 |
| Fort Myers | 27,351 |
| Fort Pierce | 29,721 |
| Fort Walton Beach | 19,994 |
| Gainesville | 64,510 |
| Gifford | 5,772 |
| Goulds | 6,690 |

**FLORIDA—Continued**

| | |
|---|---|
| Green Cove Springs | 3,857 |
| Gulf Breeze | 4,190 |
| Gulf Gate Estates | 5,874 |
| Gulfport | 9,730 |
| Haines City | 8,956 |
| Hallandale | 23,849 |
| Hialeah | 102,297 |
| Hiland Park | 3,691 |
| Holden Heights | 6,206 |
| Holly Hill | 8,191 |
| Hollywood | 106,873 |
| Homestead | 13,674 |
| Immokalee | 3,764 |
| Indian Harbour Beach | 5,371 |
| Jacksonville | 528,865 |
| Kendall | 35,497 |
| Kenneth City | 3,862 |
| Key West | 27,563 |
| Kissimmee | 7,119 |
| Lake Carroll | 5,577 |
| Lake City | 10,575 |
| Lake Forest | 5,216 |
| Lake Holloway | 6,227 |
| Lakeland | 41,550 |
| Lake Magdalene | 9,266 |
| Lake Park | 6,993 |
| Lake Wales | 8,240 |
| Lake Worth | 23,714 |
| Lantana | 7,126 |
| Largo | 22,031 |
| Lauderdale Lakes | 10,577 |
| Lauderhill | 8,465 |
| Leesburg | 11,869 |
| Lehigh Acres | 4,394 |
| Leto | 8,458 |
| Lighthouse Point | 9,071 |
| Live Oak | 6,830 |
| Lockhart | 5,809 |
| Longwood | 3,203 |
| Lynn Haven | 4,044 |
| Madeira Beach | 4,158 |
| Madison | 3,737 |
| Maitland | 7,157 |
| Marathon | 4,397 |
| Margate | 8,867 |
| Marianna | 6,741 |
| Melbourne | 40,236 |
| Melrose Park | 6,111 |
| Memphis | 3,207 |
| Merritt Island | 29,233 |
| Miami Beach | 87,072 |
| Miami | 334,859 |
| Miami Shores | 9,425 |
| Miami Springs | 13,279 |
| Milton | 5,360 |
| Mims | 8,309 |
| Miramar | 23,973 |
| Mount Dora | 4,543 |
| Myrtle Grove | 16,186 |
| Naples | 12,042 |
| New Port Richey | 6,098 |
| New Smyrna Beach | 10,580 |
| Niceville | 4,024 |
| Nokomis-Laurel | 3,328 |
| North Andrews Terrace | 7,082 |
| North Bay | 4,831 |
| North Miami | 34,767 |
| North Palm Beach | 9,035 |
| Norwood | 14,973 |
| Oakland Park | 16,261 |
| Ocala | 22,583 |
| Ocean | 5,267 |
| Ocoee | 3,937 |
| Okeechobee | 3,715 |
| Oneco | 3,246 |
| Opa-Locka | 11,902 |
| Orange Park | 7,619 |
| Orlando | 99,006 |
| Ormond Beach | 14,063 |
| Ormond By-The-Sea | 6,002 |
| Pahokee | 5,663 |
| Palatka | 9,310 |
| Palm Bay | 6,927 |
| Palm Beach Gardens | 6,102 |
| Palm Beach | 9,086 |
| Palmetto | 7,422 |
| Palm River-Clair Mel | 8,536 |
| Palm Springs | 4,340 |
| Panama City | 32,096 |
| Parker | 4,212 |
| Pembroke Pines | 15,520 |
| Pensacola | 59,507 |
| Perrine | 10,257 |
| Perry | 7,701 |
| Pine Hills | 13,882 |
| Pinellas Park | 22,287 |
| Plantation | 23,523 |
| Plant City | 15,451 |
| Pompano Beach | 37,724 |
| Port Charlotte | 10,769 |
| Port Orange | 3,781 |
| Port St. Joe | 4,401 |
| Punta Gorda | 3,879 |
| Quincy | 8,334 |
| Richmond Heights | 6,663 |
| Riverland Village-Lauderdale Isles | 5,512 |
| Riviera Beach | 21,401 |
| Rockledge | 10,523 |
| St. Augustine | 12,352 |
| St. Cloud | 5,041 |
| St. Petersburg Beach | 8,024 |
| St. Petersburg | 216,232 |
| Samoset | 4,070 |
| Sanford | 17,393 |
| Sarasota | 40,237 |
| Satellite Beach | 6,558 |
| Sebring | 7,223 |
| Siesta Key | 4,460 |
| South Daytona | 4,979 |
| South Miami | 19,571 |
| South Miami Heights | 10,395 |
| South Patrick Shores | 10,313 |
| South Peninsula | 3,302 |
| Springfield | 5,949 |
| Starke | 4,848 |
| Stuart | 4,820 |
| Sunrise Golf Village | 7,403 |
| Surfside | 3,614 |
| Sweetwater | 3,357 |

**FLORIDA—Continued**

| | |
|---|---|
| Sweetwater Creek | 19,453 |
| Tallahassee | 71,897 |
| Tamarac | 5,078 |
| Tampa | 277,767 |
| Tarpon Springs | 7,118 |
| Tavares | 3,261 |
| Temple Terrace | 7,347 |
| Tice | 7,254 |
| Titusville | 30,515 |
| Treasure Island | 6,120 |
| Tyndall | 4,248 |
| University | 10,039 |
| Valparaiso | 6,504 |
| Venice | 6,648 |
| Vero Beach | 11,908 |
| Warrington | 15,848 |
| Watertown | 3,624 |
| West End | 5,289 |
| West Miami | 5,494 |
| West Palm Beach | 57,375 |
| Westwood Lakes | 12,811 |
| Whiting Field | 3,439 |
| Wilton Manors | 10,948 |
| Winston | 4,505 |
| Winter Garden | 5,153 |
| Winter Haven | 16,136 |
| Winter Park | 21,895 |
| Zephyrhills | 3,369 |

**GEORGIA**

| | |
|---|---|
| Acworth | 3,929 |
| Adel | 4,972 |
| Albany | 72,623 |
| Alma | 3,756 |
| Americus | 16,091 |
| Ashburn | 4,209 |
| Athens | 44,342 |
| Atlanta | 496,973 |
| Augusta | 59,864 |
| Bainbridge | 10,887 |
| Barnesville | 4,935 |
| Baxley | 3,503 |
| Blakely | 5,267 |
| Bremen | 3,484 |
| Brunswick | 19,585 |
| Buford | 4,640 |
| Cairo | 8,061 |
| Calhoun | 4,748 |
| Camilla | 4,987 |
| Canton | 3,654 |
| Carrollton | 13,520 |
| Cartersville | 9,929 |
| Cedartown | 9,253 |
| Chamblee | 9,127 |
| Cochran | 5,161 |
| College Park | 18,203 |
| Columbus | 154,168 |
| Commerce | 3,702 |
| Conyers | 4,890 |
| Cordele | 10,733 |
| Covington | 10,267 |
| Cuthbert | 3,972 |
| Dalton | 18,872 |
| Dawson | 5,383 |
| Decatur | 21,943 |
| Dock Junction | 6,009 |
| Doraville | 9,039 |
| Douglas | 10,195 |
| Douglasville | 5,472 |
| Dublin | 15,143 |
| Eastman | 5,416 |
| East Point | 39,315 |
| Eatonton | 4,125 |
| Elberton | 6,438 |
| Fitzgerald | 8,015 |
| Forest Park | 19,994 |
| Forsyth | 3,736 |
| Fort Benning | 27,495 |
| Fort Gordon | 15,589 |
| Fort Oglethorpe | 3,869 |
| Fort Stewart | 4,467 |
| Fort Valley | 9,251 |
| Gainesville | 15,459 |
| Garden City | 5,741 |
| Griffin | 22,734 |
| Hapeville | 9,567 |
| Hartwell | 4,865 |
| Hawkinsville | 4,077 |
| Hazlehurst | 4,065 |
| Hinesville | 4,115 |
| Jackson | 3,778 |
| Jesup | 9,091 |
| Jonesboro | 4,105 |
| Kennesaw | 3,548 |
| La Fayette | 6,044 |
| La Grange | 23,301 |
| Lawrenceville | 5,115 |
| Lyons | 3,739 |
| Macon | 122,423 |
| Manchester | 4,779 |
| Marietta | 27,216 |
| Midway-Hardwick | 14,047 |
| Milledgeville | 11,601 |
| Millen | 3,713 |
| Monroe | 8,071 |
| Montezuma | 4,125 |
| Morrow | 3,708 |
| Moultrie | 14,302 |
| Nashville | 4,323 |
| Newnan | 11,205 |
| Pelham | 4,539 |
| Perry | 7,771 |
| Port Wentworth | 3,905 |
| Quitman | 4,818 |
| Rockmart | 3,857 |
| Rome | 30,759 |
| Rossville | 3,869 |
| Roswell | 5,430 |
| St. Marys | 3,408 |
| St. Simons | 5,346 |
| Sandersville | 5,546 |
| Savannah | 118,349 |
| Smyrna | 19,157 |
| Statesboro | 14,616 |
| Summerville | 5,043 |
| Swainsboro | 7,325 |
| Sylvester | 4,226 |
| Thomaston | 10,024 |
| Thomasville | 18,155 |
| Thomson | 6,503 |
| Tifton | 12,179 |
| Toccoa | 6,971 |

**GEORGIA—Continued**

| | |
|---|---|
| Valdosta | 32,303 |
| Vidalia | 9,507 |
| Villa Rica | 3,922 |
| Warner Robins | 33,491 |
| Washington | 4,094 |
| Waycross | 18,996 |
| Waynesboro | 5,530 |
| West Point | 4,232 |
| Wilmington Island | 3,284 |
| Winder | 6,605 |
| Windsor Forest | 7,288 |

**HAWAII**

| | |
|---|---|
| Aiea | 12,560 |
| Ewa Beach | 7,765 |
| Foster Village | 3,755 |
| Halawa Heights | 5,809 |
| Hickam | 7,352 |
| Hilo | 26,353 |
| Honolulu | 324,871 |
| Iroquois Point | 4,572 |
| Kahului | 8,280 |
| Kailua | 33,783 |
| Kaneohe | 29,903 |
| Kapaa | 3,794 |
| Lahaina | 3,718 |
| Maili | 4,397 |
| Makaha | 4,644 |
| Makakilo City | 3,499 |
| Maunawili | 5,303 |
| Mokapu | 7,860 |
| Nanakuli | 6,506 |
| Pacific Palisades | 7,846 |
| Pearl City | 19,552 |
| Schofield Barracks | 13,516 |
| Wahlawa | 17,598 |
| Waialua | 4,047 |
| Waianae | 3,302 |
| Wailuku | 7,979 |
| Waipahu | 22,798 |

**IDAHO**

| | |
|---|---|
| Blackfoot | 8,716 |
| Boise City | 74,990 |
| Burley | 8,279 |
| Caldwell | 14,219 |
| Coeur D'Alene | 16,228 |
| Emmett | 3,945 |
| Grangeville | 3,636 |
| Idaho Falls | 35,776 |
| Jerome | 4,183 |
| Kellogg | 3,811 |
| Lewiston | 26,068 |
| Moscow | 14,146 |
| Mountain Home | 6,451 |
| Nampa | 20,768 |
| Orofino | 3,883 |
| Payette | 4,521 |
| Pocatello | 40,036 |
| Preston | 3,310 |
| Rexburg | 8,272 |
| Rupert | 4,563 |
| Sandpoint | 4,144 |
| Twin Falls | 21,914 |
| Weiser | 4,108 |

**ILLINOIS**

| | |
|---|---|
| Abingdon | 3,936 |
| Addison | 24,482 |
| Aledo | 3,325 |
| Algonquin | 3,515 |
| Alorton | 3,573 |
| Alsip | 11,141 |
| Alton | 39,700 |
| Anna | 4,766 |
| Arlington Heights | 64,884 |
| Aurora | 74,182 |
| Barrington | 7,701 |
| Bartlett | 3,501 |
| Bartonville | 7,221 |
| Batavia | 8,994 |
| Beardstown | 6,222 |
| Belleville | 41,699 |
| Bellwood | 22,096 |
| Belvidere | 14,061 |
| Bensenville | 12,833 |
| Benton | 6,833 |
| Berkeley | 6,152 |
| Berwyn | 52,502 |
| Bethalto | 7,074 |
| Bloomington | 39,992 |
| Blue Island | 22,958 |
| Bolingbrook | 7,275 |
| Bourbonnais | 5,909 |
| Bradley | 9,881 |
| Bridge View | 12,522 |
| Broadview | 9,307 |
| Brookfield | 20,284 |
| Buffalo Grove | 11,799 |
| Burnham | 3,634 |
| Bushnell | 3,703 |
| Cahokia | 20,649 |
| Cairo | 6,277 |
| Calumet City | 32,956 |
| Calumet Park | 10,069 |
| Canton | 14,217 |
| Carbondale | 22,816 |
| Carlinville | 5,675 |
| Carmi | 6,033 |
| Carol Stream | 4,434 |
| Carpentersville | 24,059 |
| Carthage | 3,350 |
| Cary | 4,358 |
| Caseyville | 3,411 |
| Centralia | 15,217 |
| Centreville | 11,378 |
| Champaign | 56,532 |
| Charleston | 16,421 |
| Chester | 5,310 |
| Chicago | 3,366,957 |
| Chicago Heights | 40,900 |
| Chicago Ridge | 9,187 |
| Glendale Heights | 11,406 |
| Glen Ellyn | 21,909 |
| Glenview | 24,880 |
| Glenwood | 7,416 |
| Granite City | 40,440 |
| Grayslake | 4,907 |
| Greenville | 4,631 |
| Hanover Park | 11,916 |
| Harrisburg | 9,535 |
| Harvard | 5,177 |
| Harvey | 34,636 |
| Harwood Heights | 9,060 |

### ILLINOIS—Continued

| | |
|---|---|
| Havana | 4,376 |
| Hazel Crest | 10,329 |
| Herrin | 9,623 |
| Hickory Hills | 13,176 |
| Highland | 5,981 |
| Highland Park | 32,263 |
| Highwood | 4,973 |
| Hillsboro | 4,267 |
| Hillside | 8,888 |
| Hinsdale | 15,918 |
| Hoffman Estates | 22,238 |
| Hometown | 6,729 |
| Homewood | 18,871 |
| Hoopeston | 6,461 |
| Itasca | 4,638 |
| Jacksonville | 20,553 |
| Jerseyville | 7,446 |
| Johnston City | 3,928 |
| Joliet | 80,378 |
| Justice | 9,473 |
| Kankakee | 30,944 |
| Ken Rock | 5,945 |
| Kewanee | 15,762 |
| La Grange Highlands | 6,920 |
| La Grange Park | 15,626 |
| La Grange | 16,773 |
| Lake Bluff | 4,979 |
| Lake Forest | 15,642 |
| Lake In The Hills | 3,240 |
| Lake Zurich | 4,082 |
| Lansing | 25,805 |
| La Salle | 10,736 |
| Lawrenceville | 5,863 |
| Lebanon | 3,564 |
| Lemont | 5,080 |
| Libertyville | 11,684 |
| Lincoln | 17,582 |
| Lincolnwood | 12,929 |
| Lisle | 5,329 |
| Litchfield | 7,190 |
| Lockport | 9,985 |
| Lombard | 35,977 |
| Loves Park | 12,390 |
| Lyons | 11,124 |
| McHenry | 6,772 |
| Macomb | 19,643 |
| Madison | 7,042 |
| Marengo | 4,235 |
| Marion | 11,724 |
| Markham | 15,987 |
| Marseilles | 4,320 |
| Marshall | 3,468 |
| Mascoutah | 5,045 |
| Matteson | 4,741 |
| Mattoon | 19,681 |
| Maywood | 30,036 |
| Melrose Park | 22,706 |
| Mendota | 6,902 |
| Metropolis | 6,940 |
| Midlothian | 15,939 |
| Milan | 4,873 |
| Moline | 46,237 |
| Monmouth | 11,022 |
| Montgomery | 3,278 |
| Monticello | 4,130 |
| Morris | 8,194 |
| Morrison | 4,387 |
| Morton Grove | 26,369 |
| Morton | 10,419 |
| Mount Carmel | 8,096 |
| Mount Prospect | 34,995 |
| Mount Vernon | 15,980 |
| Mundelein | 16,128 |
| Murphysboro | 10,013 |
| Naperville | 23,885 |
| Niles | 31,432 |
| Normal | 26,396 |
| Norridge | 16,880 |
| North Aurora | 4,833 |
| Northbrook | 27,297 |
| North Chicago | 47,275 |
| Northfield | 5,010 |
| Northlake | 14,212 |
| North Park | 15,679 |
| North Riverside | 8,097 |
| Oak Brook | 4,118 |
| Oak Forest | 17,870 |
| Oak Lawn | 60,305 |
| Oak Park | 62,511 |
| Oakwood Heights | 3,229 |
| O'Fallon | 7,268 |
| Oglesby | 4,175 |
| Olney | 8,974 |
| Olympia Fields | 3,478 |
| Oregon | 3,539 |
| Orland Park | 6,391 |
| Ottawa | 18,716 |
| Palatine | 25,904 |
| Palos Heights | 9,915 |
| Palos Hills | 6,629 |
| Palos Park | 3,297 |
| Pana | 6,326 |
| Paris | 9,971 |
| Park Forest | 30,638 |
| Park Ridge | 42,466 |
| Paxton | 4,373 |
| Pekin | 31,375 |
| Peoria | 126,963 |
| Peoria Heights | 7,943 |
| Peru | 11,772 |
| Phoenix | 3,596 |
| Pinckneyville | 3,377 |
| Pittsfield | 4,244 |
| Plano | 4,664 |
| Pontiac | 9,031 |
| Posen | 5,498 |
| Princeton | 6,959 |
| Prospect Heights | 13,333 |
| Quincy | 45,288 |
| Rantoul | 25,562 |
| Riverdale | 15,806 |
| River Forest | 13,402 |
| River Grove | 11,465 |
| Riverside | 10,432 |
| Robbins | 9,641 |
| Robinson | 7,178 |
| Rochelle | 8,594 |
| Rock Falls | 10,287 |
| Rockford | 147,370 |
| Rock Island | 50,166 |
| Rolling Meadows | 19,178 |
| Romeoville | 12,674 |
| Roselle | 4,583 |
| Rosemont | 4,360 |
| Rosewood Heights | 3,391 |
| Round Lake Beach | 5,717 |
| Rushville | 3,300 |
| St. Charles | 12,928 |
| Salem | 6,187 |
| Sandwich | 5,056 |
| Sauk | 7,479 |
| Savanna | 4,942 |
| Schaumburg | 18,730 |
| Schiller Park | 12,712 |
| Scott | 7,871 |
| Shelbyville | 4,597 |
| Silvis | 5,907 |
| Skokie | 68,627 |
| South Beloit | 3,804 |
| South Chicago Heights | 4,923 |
| South Elgin | 4,289 |
| South Holland | 23,931 |
| Sparta | 4,307 |
| Springfield | 91,753 |
| Spring Valley | 5,605 |
| Staunton | 4,396 |
| Steger | 8,104 |
| Sterling | 16,113 |
| Stickney | 6,601 |
| Stone Park | 4,451 |
| Streamwood | 18,176 |
| Streator | 15,600 |
| Sullivan | 4,112 |
| Summit | 11,569 |
| Swansea | 5,432 |
| Sycamore | 7,843 |
| Taylorville | 10,644 |
| Thornton | 3,714 |
| Tinley Park | 12,382 |
| Tuscola | 3,917 |
| Urbana | 32,800 |
| Vandalia | 5,160 |
| Venice | 4,680 |
| Villa Park | 25,891 |
| Virden | 3,504 |
| Warrenville | 3,854 |
| Washington | 6,790 |
| Washington Park | 9,524 |
| Waterloo | 4,546 |
| Watseka | 5,294 |
| Wauconda | 5,460 |
| Waukegan | 65,269 |
| Westchester | 20,033 |
| West Chicago | 10,111 |
| West Dundee | 3,295 |
| West End | 7,554 |
| Western Springs | 12,147 |
| West Frankfort | 8,836 |
| Westmont | 8,482 |
| West Peoria | 6,873 |
| Westville | 3,655 |
| Wheaton | 31,138 |
| Wheeling | 14,746 |
| Willow Springs | 3,318 |
| Wilmette | 32,134 |
| Wilmington | 4,335 |
| Winfield | 4,285 |
| Winnetka | 14,131 |
| Winthrop Harbor | 4,794 |
| Wonder Lake | 4,806 |
| Wood Dale | 8,831 |
| Woodridge | 11,028 |
| Wood River | 13,186 |
| Woodstock | 10,226 |
| Worth | 11,999 |
| Zion | 17,268 |

### INDIANA

| | |
|---|---|
| Alexandria | 5,097 |
| Anderson | 70,787 |
| Angola | 5,117 |
| Attica | 4,262 |
| Auburn | 7,337 |
| Aurora | 4,293 |
| Austin | 4,902 |
| Batesville | 3,799 |
| Bedford | 13,087 |
| Beech Grove | 13,468 |
| Bicknell | 3,717 |
| Black Oak | 9,624 |
| Bloomington | 42,890 |
| Bluffton | 8,297 |
| Boonville | 5,736 |
| Brazil | 8,163 |
| Bremen | 3,487 |
| Brownsburg | 5,186 |
| Carmel | 6,568 |
| Cedar Lake | 7,589 |
| Charlestown | 5,890 |
| Chesterton | 6,177 |
| Clarksville | 13,806 |
| Clinton | 5,340 |
| Columbia City | 4,911 |
| Columbus | 27,141 |
| Connersville | 17,604 |
| Crawfordsville | 13,842 |
| Crown Point | 10,931 |
| Danville | 3,771 |
| Decatur | 8,445 |
| Dunkirk | 3,465 |
| Dyer | 4,906 |
| East Chicago | 46,982 |
| East Gary | 9,858 |
| Edinburg | 4,906 |
| Elkhart | 43,152 |
| Elwood | 11,196 |
| Evansville | 138,764 |
| Fairmount | 3,427 |
| Fort Wayne | 177,671 |
| Frankfoit | 14,956 |
| Franklin | 11,477 |
| Garrett | 4,715 |
| Gary | 175,415 |
| Gas City | 5,742 |
| Goshen | 17,171 |
| Greencastle | 8,852 |
| Greendale | 3,783 |
| Greenfield | 9,986 |
| Greensburg | 8,620 |
| Greenwood | 11,408 |
| Griffith | 18,168 |
| Grissom | 4,963 |
| Hammond | 107,790 |
| Hartford City | 8,207 |
| Highland | 24,947 |
| Hobart | 21,485 |
| Huntingburg | 4,794 |
| Huntington | 16,217 |
| Indianapolis | 744,624 |
| Jasper | 8,641 |
| Jeffersonville | 20,008 |
| Kendallville | 6,838 |
| Knox | 3,519 |
| Kokomo | 44,042 |
| Lafayette | 44,955 |
| La Porte | 22,140 |
| Lawrence | 16,646 |
| Lawrenceburg | 4,636 |
| Lebanon | 9,766 |
| Linton | 5,450 |
| Logansport | 19,255 |
| Lowell | 3,839 |
| Madison | 13,081 |
| Marion | 39,607 |
| Martinsville | 9,723 |
| Merrillville-Lottaville-Rexville | 15,918 |
| Michigan City | 39,369 |
| Mishawaka | 35,517 |
| Mitchell | 4,092 |
| Monticello | 4,869 |
| Mooresville | 5,800 |
| Mount Vernon | 6,770 |
| Muncie | 69,080 |
| Munster | 16,514 |
| Nappanee | 4,159 |
| New Albany | 38,402 |
| New Castle | 21,215 |
| New Haven | 5,728 |
| New Whiteland | 4,200 |
| Noblesville | 7,548 |
| North Manchester | 5,791 |
| North Vernon | 4,582 |
| Oakland City | 3,289 |
| Paoli | 3,281 |
| Peru | 14,139 |
| Plainfield | 8,211 |
| Plymouth | 7,661 |
| Portage | 19,127 |
| Portland | 7,115 |
| Princeton | 7,431 |
| Rensselaer | 4,688 |
| Richmond | 43,999 |
| Rochester | 4,631 |
| Rushville | 6,686 |
| Salem | 5,041 |
| Schererville | 3,663 |
| Scottsburg | 4,791 |
| Seymour | 13,352 |
| Shelbyville | 15,094 |
| South Bend | 125,580 |
| Speedway | 15,056 |
| Sullivan | 4,683 |
| Tell City | 7,933 |
| Terre Haute | 70,286 |
| Tipton | 5,176 |
| Union City | 3,995 |
| Upland | 3,202 |
| Valparaiso | 20,020 |
| Vincennes | 19,867 |
| Wabash | 13,379 |
| Warsaw | 7,506 |
| Washington | 11,358 |
| West Glen Park | 6,602 |
| West Lafayette | 19,157 |
| Whiting | 7,247 |
| Winchester | 5,493 |

### IOWA

| | |
|---|---|
| Albia | 4,151 |
| Algona | 6,032 |
| Ames | 39,505 |
| Anamosa | 4,389 |
| Ankeny | 9,151 |
| Atlantic | 7,306 |
| Bettendorf | 22,126 |
| Boone | 12,468 |
| Burlington | 32,366 |
| Camanche | 3,470 |
| Carroll | 8,716 |
| Carter Lake | 3,268 |
| Cedar Falls | 29,597 |
| Cedar Rapids | 110,642 |
| Centerville | 6,531 |
| Chariton | 5,009 |
| Charles City | 9,268 |
| Cherokee | 7,272 |
| Clarinda | 5,420 |
| Clear Lake City | 6,430 |
| Clinton | 34,719 |
| Coralville | 6,130 |
| Council Bluffs | 60,348 |
| Cresco | 3,927 |
| Creston | 8,234 |
| Davenport | 98,469 |
| Decorah | 7,458 |
| Denison | 5,882 |
| Des Moines | 200,587 |
| De Witt | 3,647 |
| Dubuque | 62,309 |
| Dyersville | 3,437 |
| Eagle Grove | 4,489 |
| Eldora | 3,223 |
| Emmetsburg | 4,150 |
| Estherville | 8,108 |
| Evansdale | 5,038 |
| Fairfield | 8,715 |
| Forest City | 3,841 |
| Fort Dodge | 31,263 |
| Fort Madison | 13,996 |
| Glenwood | 4,195 |
| Grinnell | 8,402 |
| Hampton | 4,376 |
| Harlan | 5,049 |
| Humboldt | 4,665 |
| Independence | 5,910 |
| Indianola | 8,852 |
| Iowa City | 46,850 |
| Iowa Falls | 6,454 |
| Jefferson | 4,735 |
| Keokuk | 14,631 |
| Knoxville | 7,755 |
| Le Mars | 8,159 |
| Manchester | 4,642 |
| Maquoketa | 5,677 |
| Marion | 18,028 |
| Marshalltown | 26,219 |
| Mason City | 30,491 |
| Missouri Valley | 3,519 |
| Monticello | 3,509 |
| Mount Pleasant | 7,007 |
| Muscatine | 22,405 |
| Nevada | 4,952 |
| New Hampton | 3,621 |
| Newton | 15,619 |
| Oelwein | 7,735 |
| Orange City | 3,572 |
| Osage | 3,815 |
| Oskaloosa | 11,224 |
| Ottumwa | 29,610 |
| Pella | 6,668 |
| Perry | 6,906 |
| Red Oak | 6,210 |
| Sac City | 3,268 |
| Sheldon | 4,535 |
| Shenandoah | 5,968 |
| Sioux Center | 3,450 |
| Sioux City | 85,925 |
| Spencer | 10,278 |
| Storm Lake | 8,591 |
| Urbandale | 14,434 |
| Vinton | 4,845 |
| Washington | 6,317 |
| Waterloo | 75,533 |
| Waukon | 3,883 |
| Waverly | 7,205 |
| Webster City | 8,488 |
| West Des Moines | 16,441 |
| Windsor Heights | 6,303 |
| Winterset | 3,654 |

### KANSAS

| | |
|---|---|
| Abilene | 6,661 |
| Arkansas City | 13,216 |
| Atchison | 12,565 |
| Augusta | 5,977 |
| Baxter Springs | 4,489 |
| Beloit | 4,121 |
| Bonner Springs | 3,662 |
| Camp Forsyth | 3,290 |
| Camp Funston | 4,147 |
| Chanute | 10,341 |
| Clay Center | 4,963 |
| Coffeyville | 15,116 |
| Colby | 4,658 |
| Columbus | 3,356 |
| Concordia | 7,221 |
| Derby | 7,947 |
| Dodge City | 14,127 |
| El Dorado | 12,308 |
| Emporia | 23,327 |
| Eureka | 3,576 |
| Fairway | 5,133 |
| Fort Leavenworth | 8,060 |
| Fort Scott | 8,967 |
| Galena | 3,712 |
| Garden City | 14,708 |
| Goodland | 5,510 |
| Great Bend | 16,133 |
| Hays | 15,396 |
| Haysville | 6,483 |
| Hiawatha | 3,365 |
| Hoisington | 3,710 |
| Hutchinson | 36,885 |
| Independence | 10,347 |
| Iola | 6,493 |
| Junction City | 19,018 |
| Kansas City | 168,213 |
| Kingman | 3,622 |
| Lansing | 3,797 |
| Larned | 4,567 |
| Lawrence | 45,698 |
| Leavenworth | 25,147 |
| Leawood | 10,349 |
| Lenexa | 5,242 |
| Liberal | 13,471 |
| Lyons | 4,355 |
| McPherson | 10,851 |
| Manhattan | 27,575 |
| Marysville | 3,588 |
| Merriam | 10,851 |
| Mission | 8,376 |
| Mission Hills | 4,177 |
| Neodesha | 3,295 |
| Newton | 15,439 |
| North Fort Riley | 12,469 |
| Norton | 3,627 |
| Olathe | 17,917 |
| Osawatomie | 4,294 |
| Ottawa | 11,036 |
| Overland Park | 76,623 |
| Paola | 4,622 |
| Parsons | 13,015 |
| Phillipsburg | 3,241 |
| Pittsburg | 20,171 |
| Prairie Village | 28,138 |
| Pratt | 6,736 |
| Roeland Park | 9,974 |
| Russell | 5,371 |
| Salina | 37,714 |
| Scott City | 4,001 |
| Shawnee | 20,482 |
| Topeka | 125,011 |
| Ulysses | 3,779 |
| Wellington | 8,072 |
| Wichita | 276,554 |
| Winfield | 11,405 |

## KENTUCKY

| | |
|---|---|
| Alexandria | 3,844 |
| Ashland | 29,245 |
| Barbourville | 3,549 |
| Bardstown | 5,816 |
| Bellevue | 8,847 |
| Benton | 3,652 |
| Berea | 6,956 |
| Bowling Green | 36,253 |
| Buechel | 5,359 |
| Campbellsville | 7,598 |
| Carrollton | 3,884 |
| Catlettsburg | 3,420 |
| Central City | 3,455 |
| Cold Spring | 5,348 |
| Columbia | 3,234 |
| Corbin | 7,317 |
| Covington | 52,535 |
| Cumberland | 3,317 |
| Cynthiana | 6,356 |
| Danville | 11,542 |
| Dayton | 8,691 |
| Edgewood | 4,139 |
| Elizabethtown | 11,748 |
| Elsmere | 5,161 |
| Erlanger | 12,676 |
| Flatwoods | 7,380 |
| Florence | 11,457 |
| Fort Campbell North | 13,616 |
| Fort Knox | 37,608 |
| Fort Mitchell | 6,982 |
| Fort Thomas | 16,338 |
| Fort Wright-Lookout Heights | 4,819 |
| Frankfort | 21,356 |
| Franklin | 6,553 |
| Fulton | 3,250 |
| Georgetown | 8,629 |
| Glasgow | 11,301 |
| Greenville | 3,875 |
| Harlan | 3,318 |
| Harrodsburg | 6,741 |
| Hazard | 5,459 |
| Henderson | 22,976 |
| Hopkinsville | 21,250 |
| Jeffersontown | 9,701 |
| Lancaster | 3,230 |
| Lawrenceburg | 3,579 |
| Lebanon | 5,528 |
| Lexington | 108,137 |
| London | 4,337 |
| Lone Oak | 3,759 |
| Louisville | 361,472 |
| Ludlow | 5,815 |
| Madisonville | 15,332 |
| Mayfield | 10,724 |
| Maysville | 7,411 |
| Middlesborough | 11,844 |
| Monticello | 3,618 |
| Morehead | 7,191 |
| Morganfield | 3,563 |
| Mount Sterling | 5,083 |
| Murray | 13,537 |
| Newport | 25,998 |
| Nicholasville | 5,829 |
| Okolona | 17,643 |
| Owensboro | 50,329 |
| Paducah | 31,627 |
| Paintsville | 3,868 |
| Paris | 7,823 |
| Park Hills | 3,999 |
| Pikeville | 4,576 |
| Pleasure Ridge Park | 28,566 |
| Prestonsburg | 3,422 |
| Princeton | 6,292 |
| Providence | 4,270 |
| Radcliff | 7,881 |
| Richmond | 16,861 |
| Russellville | 6,456 |
| St. Matthews | 13,152 |
| Scottsville | 3,584 |
| Shelbyville | 4,182 |
| Shively | 19,223 |
| Somerset | 10,436 |
| Southgate | 3,212 |
| Taylor Mill | 3,253 |
| Valley Station | 24,471 |
| Versailles | 5,679 |
| Williamsburg | 3,687 |
| Wilmore | 3,466 |
| Winchester | 13,402 |

## LOUISIANA

| | |
|---|---|
| Abbeville | 10,996 |
| Alexandria | 41,557 |
| Amite City | 3,593 |
| Baker | 8,281 |
| Bastrop | 14,713 |
| Baton Rouge | 165,963 |
| Bayou Cane | 9,077 |
| Bayou Vista | 5,121 |
| Berwick | 4,168 |
| Bogalusa | 18,412 |
| Bossier City | 41,595 |
| Breaux Bridge | 4,942 |
| Bunkie | 5,395 |
| Buras-Triumph | 4,113 |
| Church Point | 3,865 |
| Cooper Road | 9,034 |
| Covington | 7,170 |
| Crowley | 16,104 |

## LOUISIANA—Continued

| | |
|---|---|
| Denham Springs | 6,752 |
| De Quincy | 3,448 |
| De Ridder | 8,030 |
| Donaldsonville | 7,367 |
| England | 3,715 |
| Eunice | 11,390 |
| Farmerville | 3,416 |
| Ferriday | 5,239 |
| Franklin | 9,325 |
| Franklinton | 3,562 |
| Gonzales | 4,512 |
| Grambling | 4,407 |
| Gretna | 24,875 |
| Hammond | 12,487 |
| Harahan | 13,037 |
| Harvey | 6,347 |
| Homer | 4,483 |
| Houma | 30,922 |
| Jackson | 4,697 |
| Jeanerette | 6,322 |
| Jefferson Heights | 16,489 |
| Jennings | 11,783 |
| Jonesboro | 5,072 |
| Kaplan | 5,540 |
| Kenner | 29,858 |
| Lafayette | 68,908 |
| Lake Arthur | 3,551 |
| Lake Charles | 77,998 |
| Lake Providence | 6,183 |
| Laplace | 5,953 |
| Larose | 4,267 |
| Leesville | 8,928 |
| Little Farms | 15,713 |
| Luling | 3,255 |
| Lutcher | 3,911 |
| Mamou | 3,275 |
| Mansfield | 6,432 |
| Marksville | 4,519 |
| Marrero | 29,015 |
| Metairie | 135,816 |
| Minden | 13,996 |
| Monroe | 56,374 |
| Morgan City | 16,586 |
| Natchitoches | 15,974 |
| New Iberia | 30,147 |
| New Orleans | 593,471 |
| New Roads | 3,945 |
| Norco | 4,773 |
| North Fort Polk | 7,955 |
| Oakdale | 7,301 |
| Opelousas | 20,121 |
| Patterson | 4,409 |
| Pineville | 8,951 |
| Plaquemine | 7,739 |
| Ponchatoula | 4,545 |
| Port Allen | 5,728 |
| Raceland | 4,880 |
| Rayne | 9,510 |
| Rayville | 3,962 |
| Reserve | 6,381 |
| Ruston | 17,365 |
| St. Martinville | 7,153 |
| Samtown | 4,210 |
| Scotlandville | 22,557 |
| Shreveport | 182,064 |
| Slidell | 16,101 |
| South Fort Polk | 15,600 |
| Springhill | 6,496 |
| Sulphur | 13,551 |
| Tallulah | 9,643 |
| Terry | 13,832 |
| Thibodaux | 14,925 |
| Vidalia | 5,538 |
| Ville Platte | 9,692 |
| Vinton | 3,454 |
| Vivian | 4,046 |
| Welsh | 3,203 |
| Westlake | 4,082 |
| West Monroe | 14,868 |
| Westwego | 11,402 |
| Winnfield | 7,142 |
| Winnsboro | 5,349 |
| Zachary | 4,964 |

## MAINE

| | |
|---|---|
| Auburn | 24,151 |
| Augusta | 21,945 |
| Bangor | 33,168 |
| Bar Harbor | 3,716 |
| Bath | 9,679 |
| Belfast | 5,957 |
| Biddeford | 19,983 |
| Brewer | 9,300 |
| Brunswick | 16,195 |
| Bucksport | 3,756 |
| Calais | 4,044 |
| Camden | 4,115 |
| Cape Elizabeth | 7,873 |
| Caribou | 10,419 |
| Cumberland | 4,096 |
| Dexter | 3,725 |
| Dover-Foxcroft | 4,178 |
| Eliot | 3,497 |
| Ellsworth | 4,603 |
| Fairfield | 5,684 |
| Falmouth | 6,291 |
| Farmington | 5,657 |
| Fort Fairfield | 4,859 |
| Fort Kent | 4,575 |
| Freeport | 4,781 |

## MAINE—Continued

| | |
|---|---|
| Gardiner | 6,685 |
| Gorham | 7,839 |
| Hampden | 4,693 |
| Houlton | 8,111 |
| Jay | 3,954 |
| Kennebunk | 5,646 |
| Kittery | 11,028 |
| Lewiston | 41,779 |
| Limestone | 8,745 |
| Lincoln | 4,759 |
| Lisbon | 6,544 |
| Livermore Falls | 3,450 |
| Loring | 6,266 |
| Madawaska | 5,585 |
| Madison | 4,278 |
| Mexico | 4,309 |
| Millinocket | 7,742 |
| Norway | 3,595 |
| Oakland | 3,535 |
| Old Orchard Beach | 5,404 |
| Old Town | 9,057 |
| Orono | 9,989 |
| Paris | 3,739 |
| Pittsfield | 4,274 |
| Portland | 65,116 |
| Presque Isle | 11,452 |
| Rockland | 8,505 |
| Rumford | 9,363 |
| Saco | 11,678 |
| Sanford | 15,812 |
| Scarborough | 7,845 |
| Skowhegan | 7,601 |
| South Berwick | 3,488 |
| South Portland | 23,267 |
| Topsham | 5,022 |
| Van Buren | 3,971 |
| Waterville | 18,192 |
| Wells | 4,448 |
| Westbrook | 14,444 |
| Wilton | 3,802 |
| Windham | 6,593 |
| Winslow | 7,299 |
| Winthrop | 4,335 |
| Yarmouth | 4,854 |
| York | 5,690 |

## MARYLAND

| | |
|---|---|
| Aberdeen | 12,375 |
| Andrews | 6,418 |
| Annapolis | 29,592 |
| Arbutus | 22,745 |
| Aspen Hill | 16,799 |
| Avenel-Hillandale | 19,520 |
| Bainbridge Center | 5,257 |
| Baltimore | 905,759 |
| Bel Air | 6,307 |
| Beltsville | 8,912 |
| Berwyn Heights | 3,934 |
| Bethesda | 71,621 |
| Birchwood | 9,558 |
| Bladensburg | 7,488 |
| Bowie | 35,028 |
| Brentwood | 3,426 |
| Brooklyn | 13,896 |
| Brunswick | 3,566 |
| Calverton | 6,543 |
| Cambridge | 11,595 |
| Camp Springs | 22,776 |
| Carmody Hills-Pepper Mill | 6,245 |
| Catonsville | 54,812 |
| Chapel Oaks-Cedar Heights | 6,049 |
| Chestertown | 3,476 |
| Cheverly | 6,696 |
| Chevy Chase | 16,424 |
| Chillum | 35,656 |
| Colesville | 9,455 |
| College Park | 26,156 |
| Columbia | 8,815 |
| Coral Hills | 7,105 |
| Crofton | 4,478 |
| Cumberland | 29,724 |
| Defense Heights | 6,775 |
| District Heights | 8,424 |
| Dundalk | 85,377 |
| Easton | 6,809 |
| Edgemere | 10,352 |
| Edgewood | 8,551 |
| Elkton | 5,362 |
| Ellicott | 9,506 |
| Essex | 38,193 |
| Ferndale | 9,929 |
| Forest Heights | 3,600 |
| Forestville | 16,152 |
| Fort Meade | 16,699 |
| Frederick | 23,641 |
| Frostburg | 7,327 |
| Gaithersburg | 8,344 |
| Glenarden | 4,502 |
| Glen Burnie | 38,608 |
| Good Luck | 10,584 |
| Greenbelt | 18,199 |
| Hagerstown | 35,862 |
| Halfway | 6,106 |
| Halpine | 5,912 |
| Havre De Grace | 9,791 |
| Hillcrest Heights | 24,037 |
| Hyattsville | 14,998 |

## MARYLAND—Continued

| | |
|---|---|
| Joppatowne | 9,092 |
| Kemp Mill | 10,037 |
| Kentland | 9,649 |
| Landover | 5,597 |
| Langley Park | 11,564 |
| Lanham-Seabrook | 13,244 |
| Lansdowne-Baltimore Highlands | 16,976 |
| Laurel | 10,525 |
| La Vale-Narrows Park | 3,971 |
| Lexington Park-Patuxent River | 9,136 |
| Linthicum | 9,830 |
| Londontowne | 3,864 |
| Lutherville-Timonium | 24,055 |
| Maryland | 7,102 |
| Middle River | 19,935 |
| Montrose | 6,140 |
| Mount Rainier | 8,180 |
| New Carrollton | 13,395 |
| Odenton | 5,989 |
| Overlea | 13,086 |
| Owings Mills | 7,360 |
| Oxon Hill | 11,974 |
| Palmer Park | 8,172 |
| Parkville | 33,897 |
| Perry Hall | 5,446 |
| Pikesville | 25,395 |
| Pocomoke City | 3,573 |
| Potomac Valley | 5,094 |
| Pumphrey | 6,370 |
| Randallstown | 33,683 |
| Randolph | 13,233 |
| Reisterstown | 14,037 |
| Riverdale Heights-East Pines | 8,941 |
| Riverdale | 5,724 |
| Riviera Beach | 7,464 |
| Rockville | 41,564 |
| Rosedale | 19,417 |
| Salisbury | 15,252 |
| Seat Pleasant | 7,217 |
| Severna Park | 16,358 |
| Silver Spring | 77,496 |
| South Gate | 9,356 |
| Suitland-Silver Hill | 30,355 |
| Takoma Park | 18,455 |
| Towson | 77,809 |
| Waldorf | 7,368 |
| Walker Mill | 6,322 |
| Westminster | 7,207 |
| Wheaton | 66,247 |
| White Oak | 19,769 |
| Woodlawn-Woodmoor | 28,811 |

## MASSACHUSETTS

| | |
|---|---|
| Abington | 12,334 |
| Acton | 14,770 |
| Acushnet | 7,767 |
| Adams | 11,772 |
| Agawam | 21,717 |
| Amesbury | 11,388 |
| Amherst | 26,331 |
| Andover | 23,695 |
| Arlington | 53,524 |
| Ashburnham | 3,484 |
| Ashland | 8,882 |
| Athol | 11,185 |
| Attleboro | 32,907 |
| Auburn | 15,347 |
| Avon | 5,295 |
| Ayer | 7,393 |
| Barnstable | 19,842 |
| Barre | 3,825 |
| Bedford | 13,513 |
| Belchertown | 5,936 |
| Bellingham | 13,967 |
| Belmont | 28,285 |
| Beverly | 38,348 |
| Billerica | 31,648 |
| Blackstone | 6,566 |
| Boston | 641,071 |
| Bourne | 12,636 |
| Boxford | 4,032 |
| Braintree | 35,050 |
| Bridgewater | 11,829 |
| Brockton | 89,040 |
| Brookline | 58,886 |
| Burlington | 21,980 |
| Cambridge | 100,361 |
| Canton | 17,100 |
| Charlton | 4,654 |
| Chatham | 4,554 |
| Chelmsford | 31,432 |
| Chelsea | 30,625 |
| Chicopee | 66,676 |
| Clinton | 13,383 |
| Cohasset | 6,954 |
| Concord | 16,148 |
| Dalton | 7,505 |
| Danvers | 26,151 |
| Dartmouth | 18,800 |
| Dedham | 26,938 |
| Deerfield | 3,850 |
| Dennis | 6,454 |
| Dighton | 4,667 |
| Dover | 4,529 |
| Dracut | 18,214 |

**MASSACHUSETTS—Continued**

| | |
|---|---|
| Dudley | 8,087 |
| Duxbury | 7,636 |
| East Bridgewater | 8,347 |
| Easthampton | 13,012 |
| East Longmeadow | 13,029 |
| Easton | 12,157 |
| Everett | 42,485 |
| Fairhaven | 16,332 |
| Fall River | 96,898 |
| Falmouth | 15,942 |
| Fitchburg | 43,343 |
| Fort Devens | 12,951 |
| Foxborough | 14,218 |
| Framingham | 64,048 |
| Franklin | 17,830 |
| Freetown | 4,270 |
| Gardner | 19,748 |
| Georgetown | 5,290 |
| Gloucester | 27,941 |
| Grafton | 11,659 |
| Granby | 5,473 |
| Great Barrington | 7,537 |
| Greenfield | 18,116 |
| Groton | 5,109 |
| Groveland | 5,382 |
| Hadley | 3,750 |
| Halifax | 3,537 |
| Hamilton | 6,373 |
| Hampden | 4,572 |
| Hanover | 10,107 |
| Hanson | 7,148 |
| Harvard | 13,426 |
| Harwich | 5,892 |
| Haverhill | 46,120 |
| Hingham | 18,845 |
| Holbrook | 11,775 |
| Holden | 12,564 |
| Holliston | 12,069 |
| Holyoke | 50,112 |
| Hopedale | 4,292 |
| Hopkinton | 5,981 |
| Hudson | 16,084 |
| Hull | 9,961 |
| Hyannis | 6,847 |
| Ipswich | 10,750 |
| Kingston | 5,999 |
| Lakeville | 4,376 |
| Lancaster | 6,095 |
| Lawrence | 66,915 |
| Lee | 6,426 |
| Leicester | 9,140 |
| Lenox | 5,804 |
| Leominster | 32,939 |
| Lexington | 31,886 |
| Lincoln | 7,567 |
| Littleton | 6,380 |
| Longmeadow | 15,630 |
| Lowell | 94,239 |
| Ludlow | 17,580 |
| Lunenburg | 7,419 |
| Lynn | 90,294 |
| Lynnfield | 10,826 |
| Malden | 56,127 |
| Manchester | 5,151 |
| Mansfield | 9,939 |
| Marblehead | 21,295 |
| Marion | 3,466 |
| Marlborough | 27,936 |
| Marshfield | 15,223 |
| Mattapoisett | 4,500 |
| Maynard | 9,710 |
| Medfield | 9,821 |
| Medford | 64,397 |
| Medway | 7,938 |
| Melrose | 33,180 |
| Merino | 3,470 |
| Merrimac | 4,245 |
| Methuen | 35,456 |
| Middleborough | 13,607 |
| Middleton | 4,044 |
| Milford | 19,352 |
| Millbury | 11,987 |
| Millis-Clicquot | 3,217 |
| Millis | 5,686 |
| Milton | 27,190 |
| Monson | 7,355 |
| Montague | 8,451 |
| Nahant | 4,119 |
| Nantucket | 3,774 |
| Natick | 31,057 |
| Needham | 29,748 |
| New Bedford | 101,777 |
| Newburyport | 15,807 |
| Newbury | 3,804 |
| Newton | 91,066 |
| Norfolk | 4,656 |
| North Adams | 19,195 |
| Northampton | 29,664 |
| North Andover | 16,284 |
| North Attleborough | 18,665 |
| Northborough | 9,218 |
| Northbridge | 11,795 |
| North Brookfield | 3,967 |
| North Reading | 11,264 |
| Norton | 9,487 |
| Norwell | 7,796 |
| Norwood | 30,815 |
| Orange | 6,104 |
| Otis | 5,596 |
| Oxford | 10,345 |
| Palmer | 11,680 |
| Paxton | 3,731 |
| Peabody | 48,080 |
| Pembroke | 11,193 |
| Pepperell | 5,887 |
| Pinehurst | 5,681 |
| Pittsfield | 57,020 |
| Plainville | 4,953 |
| Plymouth | 18,606 |
| Quincy | 87,966 |
| Randolph | 27,035 |
| Raynham | 6,705 |
| Reading | 22,539 |
| Rehoboth | 6,512 |
| Revere | 43,159 |
| Rockland | 15,674 |
| Rockport | 5,636 |
| Salem | 40,556 |
| Salisbury | 4,179 |
| Sandwich | 5,239 |
| Saugus | 25,110 |
| Scituate | 16,973 |
| Seekonk | 11,116 |
| Sharon | 12,367 |
| Sherborn | 3,309 |
| Shirley | 4,909 |
| Shrewsbury | 19,196 |
| Somerset | 18,088 |
| Somerville | 88,779 |
| Southborough | 5,798 |
| Southbridge | 17,057 |
| South Hadley | 17,033 |
| Southwick | 6,330 |
| Spencer | 8,779 |
| Springfield | 163,905 |
| Sterling | 4,247 |
| Stoneham | 20,725 |
| Stoughton | 23,459 |
| Stow | 3,984 |
| Sturbridge | 4,878 |
| Sudbury | 13,506 |
| Sutton | 4,590 |
| Swampscott | 13,578 |
| Swansea | 12,640 |
| Taunton | 43,756 |
| Templeton | 5,863 |
| Tewksbury | 22,755 |
| Three Rivers | 3,366 |
| Topsfield | 5,225 |
| Townsend | 4,281 |
| Turners Falls | 5,168 |
| Tyngsborough | 4,204 |
| Upton | 3,484 |
| Uxbridge | 8,253 |
| Wakefield | 25,402 |
| Walpole | 18,149 |
| Waltham | 61,582 |
| Ware | 8,187 |
| Wareham | 11,492 |
| Warren | 3,633 |
| Watertown | 39,307 |
| Wayland | 13,461 |
| Webster | 14,917 |
| Wellesley | 28,051 |
| Wenham | 3,849 |
| Westborough | 12,594 |
| West Boylston | 6,369 |
| West Bridgewater | 7,152 |
| Westfield | 31,433 |
| Westford | 10,368 |
| Westminster | 4,273 |
| Weston | 10,870 |
| Westport | 9,791 |
| West Springfield | 28,461 |
| Westwood | 12,750 |
| Weymouth | 54,610 |
| Whitinsville | 5,210 |
| Whitman | 13,059 |
| Wilbraham | 11,984 |
| Williamstown | 8,454 |
| Wilmington | 17,102 |
| Winchendon | 6,635 |
| Winchester | 22,269 |
| Winthrop | 20,335 |
| Woburn | 37,406 |
| Worcester | 176,572 |
| Wrentham | 7,315 |
| Yarmouth | 12,033 |

**MICHIGAN**

| | |
|---|---|
| Adrian | 20,382 |
| Albion | 12,112 |
| Algonac | 3,684 |
| Allegan | 4,516 |
| Allen Park | 40,747 |
| Alma | 9,790 |
| Alpena | 13,805 |
| Ann Arbor | 99,797 |
| Battle Creek | 38,931 |
| Bay City | 49,449 |
| Belding | 5,121 |
| Benton Harbor | 16,481 |
| Berkley | 22,618 |
| Beverly Hills | 13,598 |
| Big Rapids | 11,995 |
| Birmingham | 26,170 |
| Bloomfield Hills | 3,672 |
| Buchanan | 4,645 |
| Caledonia | 9,990 |
| Caro | 3,701 |
| Carrollton | 7,300 |

**MICHIGAN—Continued**

| | |
|---|---|
| Center Line | 10,379 |
| Charlevoix | 3,519 |
| Charlotte | 8,244 |
| Cheboygan | 5,553 |
| Chelsea | 3,858 |
| Clawson | 17,617 |
| Coldwater | 9,099 |
| Comstock | 5,003 |
| Comstock Park | 5,766 |
| Cutlerville | 6,267 |
| Davison | 5,259 |
| Dearborn | 104,199 |
| Dearborn Heights | 80,069 |
| Detroit | 1,511,482 |
| Dowagiac | 6,583 |
| Drayton Plains | 16,462 |
| Durand | 3,678 |
| East Detroit | 45,920 |
| East Grand Rapids | 12,565 |
| East Lansing | 47,540 |
| Eastwood | 9,682 |
| Eaton Rapids | 4,494 |
| Ecorse | 17,515 |
| Escanaba | 15,368 |
| Essexville | 4,990 |
| Fair Plain | 3,680 |
| Farmington | 13,337 |
| Fenton | 8,284 |
| Ferndale | 30,850 |
| Flat Rock | 5,643 |
| Flint | 193,317 |
| Flushing | 7,190 |
| Franklin | 3,344 |
| Fraser | 11,868 |
| Fremont | 3,465 |
| Garden City | 41,864 |
| Gibraltar | 3,325 |
| Gladstone | 5,237 |
| Grand Blanc | 5,132 |
| Grand Haven | 11,844 |
| Grand Ledge | 6,032 |
| Grand Rapids | 197,649 |
| Grandville | 10,764 |
| Greenville | 7,493 |
| Grosse Ile | 7,799 |
| Grosse Pointe | 6,637 |
| Grosse Pointe Farms | 11,701 |
| Grosse Pointe Park | 15,585 |
| Grosse Pointe Woods | 21,878 |
| Hamtramck | 27,245 |
| Hancock | 4,820 |
| Harper Woods | 20,186 |
| Hastings | 6,501 |
| Hazel Park | 23,784 |
| Highland Park | 35,444 |
| Hillsdale | 7,728 |
| Holland | 26,337 |
| Holly | 4,355 |
| Holt | 6,980 |
| Houghton | 6,067 |
| Howell | 5,224 |
| Hudsonville | 3,523 |
| Huntington Woods | 8,536 |
| Inkster | 38,595 |
| Ionia | 6,361 |
| Iron Mountain | 8,702 |
| Ironwood | 8,711 |
| Ishpeming | 8,245 |
| Jackson | 45,484 |
| Jenison | 11,266 |
| Kalamazoo | 85,555 |
| Kentwood | 20,310 |
| Kincheloe | 6,331 |
| Kingsford | 5,276 |
| K I Sawyer | 6,679 |
| Lakeview | 11,391 |
| Lambertville | 5,721 |
| Lansing | 131,546 |
| Lapeer | 6,270 |
| Lapeer Heights | 7,130 |
| Lincoln Park | 52,984 |
| Livonia | 110,109 |
| Ludington | 9,021 |
| Madison Heights | 38,599 |
| Manistee | 7,723 |
| Manistique | 4,324 |
| Marine City | 4,567 |
| Marquette | 21,967 |
| Marshall | 7,253 |
| Marysville | 5,610 |
| Mason | 5,468 |
| Melvindale | 13,862 |
| Menominee | 10,748 |
| Midland | 35,176 |
| Milan | 4,533 |
| Milford | 4,699 |
| Monroe | 23,894 |
| Mount Clemens | 20,476 |
| Mount Morris | 3,778 |
| Mount Pleasant | 20,504 |
| Munising | 3,677 |
| Muskegon | 44,631 |
| Muskegon Heights | 17,304 |
| Negaunee | 5,248 |
| New Baltimore | 4,132 |
| Niles | 12,988 |
| North Muskegon | 4,243 |
| Northville | 5,400 |
| Norton Shores | 22,271 |
| Novi | 9,668 |
| Oak Park | 36,762 |
| Okemos | 7,770 |
| Oscoda-Au Sable | 3,475 |
| Otsego | 3,957 |
| Owosso | 17,179 |
| Paw Paw Lake | 3,726 |
| Petoskey | 6,342 |
| Pleasant Ridge | 3,989 |
| Plymouth | 11,758 |
| Pontiac | 85,279 |
| Portage | 33,590 |
| Port Huron | 35,794 |
| Portland | 3,817 |
| Quakertown North | 7,101 |
| Richmond | 3,234 |
| River Rouge | 15,947 |
| Riverview | 11,342 |
| Rochester | 7,054 |
| Rogers City | 4,275 |
| Romeo | 4,012 |
| Roosevelt Park | 4,176 |
| Roseville | 60,529 |
| Royal Oak | 85,499 |
| Saginaw | 91,849 |
| St. Clair | 4,770 |
| St. Clair Shores | 88,093 |
| St. Johns | 6,672 |
| St. Joseph | 11,042 |
| St. Louis | 4,101 |
| Saline | 4,811 |
| Sault Ste Marie | 15,136 |
| Southfield | 69,285 |
| Southgate | 33,909 |
| South Haven | 6,471 |
| Springfield | 3,994 |
| Sterling Heights | 61,365 |
| Sturgis | 9,295 |
| Swartz Creek | 4,928 |
| Taylor | 70,020 |
| Tecumseh | 7,120 |
| Three Rivers | 7,355 |
| Traverse City | 18,048 |
| Trenton | 24,127 |
| Troy | 39,419 |
| Utica | 3,504 |
| Walker | 11,492 |
| Walled Lake | 3,759 |
| Warren | 179,260 |
| Wayne | 21,054 |
| Westland | 86,749 |
| Westwood | 9,143 |
| White Lake-Seven Harbors | 4,504 |
| Wolverine Lake | 4,301 |
| Woodhaven | 3,330 |
| Wurtsmith | 6,932 |
| Wyandotte | 41,061 |
| Wyoming | 56,560 |
| Ypsilanti | 29,538 |
| Zeeland | 4,734 |

**MINNESOTA**

| | |
|---|---|
| Albert Lea | 19,418 |
| Alexandria | 6,973 |
| Anoka | 13,489 |
| Apple Valley | 8,502 |
| Arden Hills | 5,628 |
| Austin | 25,074 |
| Bemidji | 11,490 |
| Benson | 3,484 |
| Blaine | 20,640 |
| Bloomington | 81,970 |
| Blue Earth | 3,965 |
| Brainerd | 11,667 |
| Breckenridge | 4,200 |
| Brooklyn Center | 35,173 |
| Brooklyn Park | 26,230 |
| Buffalo | 3,275 |
| Burnsville | 19,940 |
| Cambridge | 3,467 |
| Chanhassen | 4,879 |
| Chaska | 4,352 |
| Chisholm | 5,913 |
| Circle Pines | 3,918 |
| Cloquet | 8,699 |
| Columbia Heights | 23,997 |
| Coon Rapids | 30,505 |
| Cottage Grove | 13,419 |
| Crookston | 8,312 |
| Crystal | 30,925 |
| Deephaven | 3,853 |
| Detroit Lakes | 5,797 |
| Duluth | 100,578 |
| East Grand Forks | 7,607 |
| Eden Prairie | 6,938 |
| Edina | 44,046 |
| Ely | 4,904 |
| Eveleth | 4,721 |
| Fairmont | 10,751 |
| Falcon Heights | 5,507 |
| Faribault | 16,595 |
| Fergus Falls | 12,443 |
| Forest Lake | 3,207 |
| Fridley | 29,233 |
| Glencoe | 4,217 |
| Golden Valley | 24,246 |
| Grand Rapids | 7,247 |
| Granite Falls | 3,225 |
| Hastings | 12,195 |
| Hibbing | 16,104 |
| Hopkins | 13,428 |
| Hoyt Lakes | 3,634 |

**MINNESOTA—Continued**

| | |
|---|---|
| Hutchinson | 8,031 |
| International Falls | 6,439 |
| Inver Grove Heights | 12,148 |
| Jackson | 3,550 |
| Lake City | 3,594 |
| Lake Elmo | 4,032 |
| Lakeville | 7,556 |
| Le Sueur | 3,745 |
| Lino Lakes | 3,692 |
| Litchfield | 5,262 |
| Little Canada | 3,481 |
| Little Falls | 7,467 |
| Luverne | 4,703 |
| Mankato | 30,895 |
| Maple Grove | 6,275 |
| Maplewood | 25,222 |
| Marshall | 9,886 |
| Mendota Heights | 6,165 |
| Minneapolis | 434,400 |
| Minnetonka | 35,776 |
| Montevideo | 5,661 |
| Moorhead | 29,687 |
| Morris | 5,366 |
| Mounds View | 9,988 |
| Mound | 7,572 |
| New Brighton | 19,507 |
| New Hope | 23,180 |
| New Ulm | 13,051 |
| Northfield | 10,235 |
| North Mankato | 7,347 |
| North St. Paul | 11,950 |
| Oakdale | 7,304 |
| Orono | 6,787 |
| Owatonna | 15,341 |
| Pipestone | 5,328 |
| Plymouth | 17,593 |
| Red Wing | 10,441 |
| Redwood Falls | 4,774 |
| Richfield | 47,231 |
| Robbinsdale | 16,845 |
| Rochester | 53,766 |
| Roseville | 34,518 |
| St. Anthony | 9,239 |
| St. Cloud | 39,691 |
| St. James | 4,027 |
| St. Louis Park | 48,883 |
| St. Paul | 309,980 |
| St. Paul Park | 5,587 |
| St. Peter | 8,339 |
| Sauk Centre | 3,750 |
| Sauk Rapids | 5,051 |
| Savage | 3,611 |
| Shakopee | 6,876 |
| Shoreview | 11,034 |
| Shorewood | 4,223 |
| Silver Bay | 3,504 |
| Sleepy Eye | 3,461 |
| South St. Paul | 25,016 |
| Spring Lake Park | 6,417 |
| Stillwater | 10,191 |
| Thief River Falls | 8,618 |
| Two Harbors | 4,437 |
| Vadnais Heights | 3,391 |
| Virginia | 12,450 |
| Wadena | 4,640 |
| Waseca | 6,789 |
| Wayzata | 3,700 |
| West St. Paul | 18,799 |
| White Bear Lake | 23,313 |
| Willmar | 12,869 |
| Windom | 3,952 |
| Winona | 26,438 |
| Woodbury | 6,184 |
| Worthington | 9,825 |

**MISSISSIPPI**

| | |
|---|---|
| Aberdeen | 6,157 |
| Amory | 7,236 |
| Batesville | 3,796 |
| Bay St. Louis | 6,752 |
| Biloxi | 48,486 |
| Booneville | 5,895 |
| Brookhaven | 10,700 |
| Canton | 10,503 |
| Clarksdale | 21,673 |
| Cleveland | 13,327 |
| Clinton | 7,246 |
| Columbia | 7,587 |
| Columbus | 25,795 |
| Corinth | 11,581 |
| Crystal Springs | 4,180 |
| D'Iberville | 7,288 |
| Ellisville | 4,643 |
| Forest City | 4,085 |
| Greenville | 39,648 |
| Greenwood | 22,400 |
| Grenada | 9,944 |
| Gulfport | 40,791 |
| Hattiesburg | 38,277 |
| Hazlehurst | 4,577 |
| Hollandale | 3,260 |
| Holly Springs | 5,728 |
| Indianola | 8,947 |
| Jackson | 153,968 |
| Kosciusko | 7,266 |
| Laurel | 24,145 |
| Leland | 6,000 |
| Long Beach | 6,170 |
| Louisville | 6,626 |
| McComb | 11,969 |
| Meridian | 45,083 |
| Moss Point | 19,321 |

**MISSISSIPPI—Continued**

| | |
|---|---|
| Natchez | 19,704 |
| New Albany | 6,426 |
| Newton | 3,556 |
| Ocean Springs | 9,580 |
| Oxford | 13,846 |
| Pascagoula | 27,264 |
| Pearl | 9,623 |
| Petal | 6,986 |
| Philadelphia | 6,274 |
| Picayune | 10,467 |
| Pontotoc | 3,453 |
| Ripley | 3,482 |
| Senatobia | 4,247 |
| Southaven | 8,931 |
| Starkville | 11,369 |
| State College | 4,595 |
| Tupelo | 20,471 |
| Vicksburg | 25,478 |
| Water Valley | 3,285 |
| Waynesboro | 4,368 |
| West Point | 8,714 |
| Winona | 5,521 |
| Yazoo City | 10,796 |

**MISSOURI**

| | |
|---|---|
| Afton | 24,067 |
| Aurora | 5,359 |
| Ballwin | 10,656 |
| Bellefontaine Neighbors | 13,987 |
| Bel-Ridge | 5,561 |
| Belton | 9,783 |
| Berkeley | 19,743 |
| Blue Springs | 6,779 |
| Bolivar | 4,769 |
| Bonne Terre | 3,622 |
| Boonville | 7,514 |
| Breckenridge Hills | 7,011 |
| Brentwood | 11,248 |
| Bridgeton | 19,992 |
| Brookfield | 5,491 |
| Butler | 3,984 |
| Cameron | 3,960 |
| Cape Girardeau | 31,282 |
| Carrollton | 4,847 |
| Carthage | 11,035 |
| Caruthersville | 7,350 |
| Centralia | 3,618 |
| Charleston | 5,131 |
| Chillicothe | 9,519 |
| Clayton | 16,222 |
| Clinton | 7,504 |
| Columbia | 58,804 |
| Concord | 21,217 |
| Crestwood | 15,398 |
| Creve Coeur | 8,967 |
| Crystal City | 3,898 |
| Dellwood | 7,137 |
| De Soto | 5,984 |
| Des Peres | 5,333 |
| Dexter | 6,024 |
| East Prairie | 3,275 |
| Eldon | 3,520 |
| Eldorado Springs | 3,300 |
| Ellisville | 4,681 |
| Excelsior Springs | 9,411 |
| Farmington | 6,590 |
| Fayette | 3,520 |
| Ferguson | 28,915 |
| Festus | 7,530 |
| Flat River | 4,550 |
| Florissant | 65,908 |
| Fort Leonard Wood | 33,799 |
| Fredericktown | 3,799 |
| Frontenac | 3,920 |
| Fulton | 12,148 |
| Gladstone | 23,128 |
| Glendale | 6,891 |
| Grandview | 17,456 |
| Hannibal | 18,609 |
| Harrisonville | 4,928 |
| Hayti | 3,841 |
| Hazlewood | 14,082 |
| Higginsville | 4,318 |
| Independence | 111,662 |
| Jackson | 5,896 |
| Jefferson City | 32,407 |
| Jennings | 19,379 |
| Joplin | 39,256 |
| Kansas City | 507,087 |
| Kennett | 9,852 |
| Kinloch | 5,629 |
| Kirksville | 15,560 |
| Kirkwood | 31,890 |
| Ladue | 10,491 |
| Lamar | 3,760 |
| Lebanon | 8,616 |
| Lee's Summit | 16,230 |
| Lemay | 40,115 |
| Lexington | 5,388 |
| Liberty | 13,679 |
| Louisiana | 4,533 |
| Macon | 5,301 |
| Malden | 5,374 |
| Manchester | 5,031 |
| Maplewood | 12,785 |
| Marshall | 11,847 |
| Maryland Heights | 8,805 |
| Maryville | 9,970 |
| Mexico | 11,807 |
| Moberly | 12,988 |

**MISSOURI—Continued**

| | |
|---|---|
| Moline Acres | 3,722 |
| Monett | 5,937 |
| Mountain Grove | 3,377 |
| Neosho | 7,517 |
| Nevada | 9,736 |
| Normandy | 6,306 |
| North Kansas City | 5,183 |
| Northwoods | 4,611 |
| O'Fallon | 7,018 |
| Olivette | 9,341 |
| Overland | 24,949 |
| Pacific | 3,247 |
| Pagedale | 5,571 |
| Perryville | 5,149 |
| Pine Lawn | 5,773 |
| Pleasant Hill | 3,396 |
| Poplar Bluff | 16,653 |
| Raytown | 33,632 |
| Richmond | 4,948 |
| Richmond Heights | 13,802 |
| Riverview | 3,741 |
| Rock Hill | 7,275 |
| Rolla | 13,245 |
| St. Ann | 18,215 |
| St. Charles | 31,834 |
| Ste. Genevieve | 4,468 |
| St. John | 8,960 |
| St. Joseph | 72,691 |
| St. Louis | 622,236 |
| Salem | 4,363 |
| Sappington | 10,603 |
| Savannah | 3,324 |
| Sedalia | 22,847 |
| Shrewsbury | 5,896 |
| Sikeston | 14,699 |
| Spanish Lake | 15,647 |
| Springfield | 120,096 |
| Sugar Creek | 4,755 |
| Sullivan | 5,100 |
| Sunset Hills | 3,728 |
| Trenton | 6,063 |
| Union | 5,183 |
| University City | 46,309 |
| Valley Park | 3,662 |
| Vinita Park | 3,684 |
| Warrensburg | 13,125 |
| Washington | 8,499 |
| Waynesville | 3,375 |
| Webb City | 6,811 |
| Webster Groves | 26,995 |
| Wellston | 7,050 |
| Wentzville | 3,223 |
| West Plains | 6,893 |
| Whiteman | 5,040 |
| Woodson Terrace | 5,936 |

**MONTANA**

| | |
|---|---|
| Anaconda | 9,771 |
| Billings | 61,581 |
| Bozeman | 18,670 |
| Butte | 23,368 |
| Cut Bank | 4,004 |
| Deer Lodge | 4,306 |
| Dillon | 4,548 |
| Floral Park | 5,113 |
| Glasgow | 4,700 |
| Glendive | 6,305 |
| Great Falls | 60,091 |
| Havre | 10,558 |
| Helena | 22,730 |
| Kalispell | 10,526 |
| Laurel | 4,454 |
| Lewistown | 6,437 |
| Libby | 3,286 |
| Livingston | 6,883 |
| Malmstrom | 8,374 |
| Miles City | 9,023 |
| Missoula | 29,497 |
| Sidney | 4,543 |
| Silver Bow Park | 5,524 |
| Whitefish | 3,349 |

**NEBRASKA**

| | |
|---|---|
| Alliance | 6,862 |
| Auburn | 3,650 |
| Beatrice | 12,389 |
| Bellevue | 19,449 |
| Blair | 6,106 |
| Broken Bow | 3,734 |
| Chadron | 5,853 |
| Columbus | 15,471 |
| Cozad | 4,219 |
| Crete | 4,444 |
| Fairbury | 5,265 |
| Falls City | 5,444 |
| Fremont | 22,962 |
| Gering | 5,639 |
| Grand Island | 31,269 |
| Hastings | 23,580 |
| Holdrege | 5,635 |
| Kearney | 19,181 |
| Kimball | 3,680 |
| La Vista | 4,807 |
| Lexington | 5,618 |
| Lincoln | 149,518 |
| McCook | 8,285 |
| Millard | 7,460 |
| Nebraska City | 7,441 |
| Norfolk | 16,607 |
| North Platte | 19,447 |
| Offutt East | 5,195 |

**NEBRASKA—Continued**

| | |
|---|---|
| Offutt West | 8,445 |
| Ogallala | 4,976 |
| Omaha | 347,328 |
| O'Neill | 3,753 |
| Papillion | 5,606 |
| Plattsmouth | 6,371 |
| Ralston | 4,265 |
| Schuyler | 3,597 |
| Scottsbluff | 14,507 |
| Seward | 5,294 |
| Sidney | 6,403 |
| South Sioux City | 7,920 |
| Wahoo | 3,835 |
| Wayne | 5,379 |
| West Point | 3,385 |

**NEVADA**

| | |
|---|---|
| Boulder City | 5,223 |
| Carson City | 15,468 |
| Elko | 7,621 |
| Ely | 4,176 |
| Hawthorne | 3,539 |
| Henderson | 16,395 |
| Las Vegas | 125,787 |
| Nellis | 6,449 |
| North Las Vegas | 36,216 |
| Paradise | 24,477 |
| Reno | 72,863 |
| Sparks | 24,187 |
| Sunrise Manor | 10,886 |
| Vegas Creek | 8,970 |
| Winchester | 13,981 |
| Winnemucca | 3,587 |

**NEW HAMPSHIRE**

| | |
|---|---|
| Amherst | 4,605 |
| Bedford | 5,859 |
| Berlin | 15,256 |
| Charlestown | 3,274 |
| Claremont | 14,221 |
| Concord | 30,022 |
| Conway | 4,865 |
| Derry | 11,712 |
| Dover | 20,850 |
| Durham | 8,869 |
| Exeter | 8,892 |
| Farmington | 3,588 |
| Franklin | 7,292 |
| Gilford | 3,219 |
| Goffstown | 9,284 |
| Hampton | 8,011 |
| Hanover | 8,494 |
| Hinsdale | 3,276 |
| Hooksett | 5,564 |
| Hudson | 10,638 |
| Jaffrey | 3,353 |
| Keene | 20,467 |
| Laconia | 14,888 |
| Lebanon | 9,725 |
| Littleton | 5,290 |
| Londonderry | 5,346 |
| Manchester | 87,754 |
| Merrimack | 8,595 |
| Milford | 6,622 |
| Nashua | 55,820 |
| Newmarket | 3,361 |
| Newport | 5,899 |
| North Hampton | 3,259 |
| Pelham | 5,408 |
| Pembroke | 4,261 |
| Peterborough | 3,807 |
| Plaistow | 4,712 |
| Plymouth | 4,225 |
| Portsmouth | 25,717 |
| Rochester | 17,938 |
| Rye | 4,083 |
| Salem | 20,142 |
| Somersworth | 9,026 |
| Suncook | 4,280 |
| Swanzey | 4,254 |

**NEW JERSEY**

| | |
|---|---|
| Absecon | 6,094 |
| Allendale | 6,240 |
| Asbury Park | 16,533 |
| Atlantic City | 47,859 |
| Atlantic Highlands | 5,102 |
| Audubon | 10,802 |
| Barrington | 8,409 |
| Bayonne | 72,743 |
| Beachwood | 4,390 |
| Belleville | 34,643 |
| Bellmawr | 15,618 |
| Belmar | 5,782 |
| Bergenfield | 33,131 |
| Berlin | 4,997 |
| Bernardsville | 6,652 |
| Bloomfield | 52,029 |
| Bloomingdale | 7,797 |
| Bogota | 8,125 |
| Boonton | 9,261 |
| Bordentown | 4,490 |
| Bound Brook | 10,450 |
| Bradley Beach | 4,163 |
| Bridgeton | 20,435 |
| Brielle | 3,594 |
| Brigantine | 6,741 |
| Browns Mills | 7,144 |
| Buena | 3,283 |
| Burlington | 11,991 |
| Butler | 7,051 |
| Caldwell | 8,719 |

## NEW JERSEY—Continued

| | |
|---|---|
| Camden | 102,551 |
| Candlewood | 5,629 |
| Cape May | 4,392 |
| Carlstadt | 7,947 |
| Carteret | 23,137 |
| Chatham | 9,566 |
| Clayton | 5,193 |
| Clementon | 4,492 |
| Cliffside Park | 14,387 |
| Cliffwood-Cliffwood Beach | 7,056 |
| Clifton | 82,437 |
| Closter | 8,604 |
| Collingswood | 17,422 |
| Cresskill | 7,164 |
| Demarest | 6,262 |
| Dover | 15,039 |
| Dumont | 17,534 |
| Dunellen | 7,072 |
| East Orange | 75,471 |
| East Paterson | 22,749 |
| East Rutherford | 8,536 |
| Eatontown | 14,619 |
| Edgewater | 4,849 |
| Egg Harbor City | 4,304 |
| Elizabeth | 112,654 |
| Emerson | 8,428 |
| Englewood | 24,985 |
| Englewood Cliffs | 5,938 |
| Fairfield | 6,731 |
| Fair Haven | 6,142 |
| Fair Lawn | 37,975 |
| Fairview | 10,698 |
| Fanwood | 8,920 |
| Flemington | 3,917 |
| Florence-Roebling | 7,551 |
| Florham Park | 8,094 |
| Fort Dix | 26,290 |
| Fort Lee | 30,631 |
| Franklin | 4,236 |
| Franklin Lakes | 7,550 |
| Freehold | 10,545 |
| Garfield | 30,722 |
| Garwood | 5,260 |
| Gilford Park | 4,007 |
| Glassboro | 12,938 |
| Glen Ridge | 8,518 |
| Glen Rock | 13,011 |
| Gloucester City | 14,707 |
| Guttenberg | 5,754 |
| Hackensack | 35,911 |
| Hackettstown | 9,472 |
| Haddonfield | 13,118 |
| Haddon Heights | 9,365 |
| Haledon | 6,767 |
| Hammonton | 11,464 |
| Harrington Park | 4,841 |
| Harrison | 11,811 |
| Hasbrouck Heights | 13,651 |
| Haworth | 3,760 |
| Hawthorne | 19,173 |
| Highland Park | 14,385 |
| Highlands | 3,916 |
| Hightstown | 5,431 |
| Hillsdale | 11,768 |
| Hoboken | 45,380 |
| Hohokus | 4,348 |
| Hopatcong | 9,052 |
| Irvington | 59,743 |
| Jamesburg | 4,584 |
| Jersey City | 260,545 |
| Keansburg | 9,720 |
| Kearny | 37,585 |
| Kendall Park | 7,412 |
| Kenilworth | 9,165 |
| Keyport | 7,205 |
| Kinnelon | 7,600 |
| Lake Hiawatha | 11,389 |
| Lake Mohawk | 6,262 |
| Lake Parsippany | 7,488 |
| Lakewood | 17,874 |
| Lambertville | 4,359 |
| Laurence Harbor | 6,715 |
| Leonia | 8,847 |
| Lincoln Park | 9,034 |
| Linden City | 41,409 |
| Lindenwold | 12,199 |
| Linwood | 6,159 |
| Little Ferry | 9,042 |
| Little Silver | 6,010 |
| Lodi | 25,213 |
| Long Branch | 31,774 |
| McGuire | 10,933 |
| Madison | 16,710 |
| Magnolia | 5,893 |
| Manasquan | 4,971 |
| Manville | 13,029 |
| Margate City | 10,576 |
| Marlton | 10,180 |
| Matawan | 9,136 |
| Maywood | 11,087 |
| Medford Lakes | 4,792 |
| Mendham | 3,729 |
| Mercerville-Hamilton Sq. | 24,465 |
| Merchantville | 4,425 |
| Metuchen | 16,031 |
| Middlesex | 15,038 |
| Midland Park | 8,159 |

## NEW JERSEY—Continued

| | |
|---|---|
| Milltown | 6,470 |
| Millville | 21,366 |
| Montclair | 44,043 |
| Montvale | 7,327 |
| Moorestown-Lenola | 14,179 |
| Morris Plains | 5,540 |
| Morristown | 17,662 |
| Mountain Lakes | 4,739 |
| Mountainside | 7,520 |
| Mount Arlington | 3,590 |
| Mount Ephraim | 5,625 |
| National Park | 3,730 |
| Neptune City | 5,502 |
| Newark | 382,417 |
| New Brunswick | 41,885 |
| New Milford | 20,201 |
| New Providence | 13,796 |
| New Shrewsbury | 5,925 |
| Newton | 7,297 |
| North Arlington | 18,096 |
| North Caldwell | 6,425 |
| North Cape May | 3,812 |
| Northfield | 8,875 |
| North Haledon | 7,614 |
| North Plainfield | 21,796 |
| Northvale | 5,177 |
| North Wildwood | 3,914 |
| Norwood | 4,398 |
| Nutley | 32,099 |
| Oakhurst | 5,558 |
| Oakland | 14,420 |
| Oaklyn | 4,626 |
| Ocean City | 10,575 |
| Oceanport | 7,503 |
| Old Bridge | 25,176 |
| Old Tappan | 3,917 |
| Oradell | 8,903 |
| Orange | 32,566 |
| Palisades Park | 13,351 |
| Palmyra | 6,969 |
| Paramus | 29,495 |
| Park Ridge | 8,709 |
| Passaic | 55,124 |
| Paterson | 144,824 |
| Paulsboro | 8,084 |
| Penns Grove | 5,727 |
| Pennsville | 11,014 |
| Perth Amboy | 38,798 |
| Phillipsburg | 17,849 |
| Pine Hill | 5,132 |
| Pitman | 10,257 |
| Plainfield | 46,862 |
| Pleasantville | 13,778 |
| Point Pleasant Beach | 4,882 |
| Point Pleasant | 15,968 |
| Pompton Lakes | 11,397 |
| Princeton | 12,311 |
| Prospect Park | 5,176 |
| Rahway | 29,114 |
| Ramblewood | 5,556 |
| Ramsey | 12,571 |
| Raritan | 6,691 |
| Red Bank | 12,847 |
| Ridgefield | 11,308 |
| Ridgefield Park | 14,453 |
| Ridgewood | 27,547 |
| Ringwood | 10,393 |
| River Edge | 12,850 |
| Riverton | 3,412 |
| Rockaway | 6,383 |
| Roseland | 4,453 |
| Roselle | 22,585 |
| Roselle Park | 14,277 |
| Rumson | 7,421 |
| Runnemede | 10,475 |
| Rutherford | 20,802 |
| Salem | 7,648 |
| Sayreville | 32,508 |
| Secaucus | 13,228 |
| Shrewsbury | 3,315 |
| Somerdale | 6,510 |
| Somers Point | 7,919 |
| Somerville | 13,652 |
| South Amboy | 9,338 |
| South Bound Brook | 4,525 |
| South Orange | 16,971 |
| South Plainfield | 21,142 |
| South River | 15,428 |
| South Toms River | 3,981 |
| Spotswood | 7,891 |
| Spring Lake | 3,896 |
| Spring Lake Heights | 4,602 |
| Stratford | 9,801 |
| Strathmore | 7,674 |
| Summit | 23,620 |
| Tenafly | 14,827 |
| Toms River | 7,303 |
| Totowa | 11,580 |
| Trenton | 104,638 |
| Union Beach | 6,472 |
| Union City | 58,537 |
| Upper Saddle River | 7,949 |
| Ventnor City | 10,385 |
| Verona | 15,067 |
| Vineland | 47,399 |
| Waldwick | 12,313 |
| Wallington | 10,284 |
| Wanaque | 8,636 |
| Washington | 5,943 |

## NEW JERSEY—Continued

| | |
|---|---|
| Watchung | 4,750 |
| West Caldwell | 11,887 |
| Westfield | 33,720 |
| West Long Branch | 6,845 |
| West New York | 40,627 |
| West Orange | 43,715 |
| West Paterson | 11,692 |
| Westville | 5,170 |
| Westwood | 11,105 |
| Wharton | 5,535 |
| White Horse-Yardville | 18,680 |
| White Meadow Lake | 8,499 |
| Wildwood | 4,110 |
| Wildwood Crest | 3,483 |
| Williamstown | 4,075 |
| Woodbury | 12,408 |
| Woodbury Heights | 3,621 |
| Woodcliff Lake | 5,506 |
| Wood-Ridge | 8,311 |

## NEW MEXICO

| | |
|---|---|
| Alamogordo | 23,035 |
| Albuquerque | 243,751 |
| Artesia | 10,315 |
| Aztec | 3,354 |
| Belen | 4,823 |
| Cannon | 5,461 |
| Carlsbad | 21,297 |
| Clovis | 28,495 |
| Deming | 8,343 |
| Espanola | 4,136 |
| Farmington | 21,979 |
| Gallup | 13,779 |
| Grants | 8,768 |
| Hobbs | 26,025 |
| Las Cruces | 37,857 |
| Las Vegas | 7,528 |
| Lordsburg | 3,429 |
| Los Alamos | 11,310 |
| Lovington | 8,915 |
| North Valley | 10,366 |
| Portales | 10,554 |
| Raton | 6,962 |
| Roswell | 33,908 |
| Sandia | 6,867 |
| Santa Fe | 41,167 |
| Silver City | 7,751 |
| Socorro | 4,687 |
| South Valley | 29,389 |
| Truth or Consequences | 4,656 |
| Tucumcari | 7,189 |
| University Park-Tortugas | 4,165 |
| White Rock | 3,861 |
| White Sands | 4,167 |
| Zuni Pueblo | 3,958 |

## NEW YORK

| | |
|---|---|
| Albany | 114,873 |
| Albertson | 6,792 |
| Albion | 5,122 |
| Alfred | 3,804 |
| Amityville | 9,857 |
| Amsterdam | 25,524 |
| Ardsley | 4,470 |
| Arlington | 11,203 |
| Auburn | 34,599 |
| Avon | 3,260 |
| Babylon | 12,588 |
| Baldwin | 34,525 |
| Baldwinsville | 6,298 |
| Ballston Spa | 4,968 |
| Balmville | 3,214 |
| Batavia | 17,338 |
| Bath | 6,053 |
| Bayport | 7,995 |
| Bay Shore | 11,119 |
| Bayville | 6,147 |
| Beacon | 13,255 |
| Bellmore | 18,431 |
| Bethpage | 18,555 |
| Binghamton | 64,123 |
| Blasdell | 3,910 |
| Blauvelt | 5,426 |
| Bohemia | 8,718 |
| Brentwood | 27,868 |
| Briarcliff Manor | 6,521 |
| Brightwaters | 3,808 |
| Brockport | 7,878 |
| Bronxville | 6,674 |
| Brookville | 3,212 |
| Buffalo | 462,768 |
| Canandaigua | 10,488 |
| Canastota | 5,033 |
| Canton | 6,398 |
| Carle Place | 6,326 |
| Carmel | 3,395 |
| Carthage | 3,889 |
| Catskill | 5,317 |
| Cedarhurst | 6,941 |
| Centereach | 9,427 |
| Center Moriches | 3,802 |
| Central Islip | 36,369 |
| Chittenango | 3,605 |
| Clifton Knolls | 5,771 |
| Cobleskill | 4,368 |
| Cohoes | 18,613 |
| Cold Spring Harbor | 5,498 |
| Colonie | 8,701 |
| Commack | 22,507 |

## NEW YORK—Continued

| | |
|---|---|
| Congers | 5,928 |
| Copiague | 19,578 |
| Corinth | 3,267 |
| Corning | 15,792 |
| Cortland | 19,621 |
| Croton-on-Hudson | 7,523 |
| Dannemora | 3,735 |
| Dansville | 5,436 |
| Deer Park | 31,120 |
| Depew | 22,158 |
| DeWitt | 10,032 |
| Dix Hills | 9,840 |
| Dobbs Ferry | 10,353 |
| Dunkirk | 16,855 |
| East Aurora | 7,033 |
| Eastchester | 21,330 |
| East Glenville | 5,898 |
| East Half Hollow Hills | 9,691 |
| East Hills | 8,675 |
| East Meadow | 46,252 |
| East Neck | 5,144 |
| East Rochester | 8,347 |
| East Rockaway | 10,323 |
| East Syracuse | 4,333 |
| Ellenville | 4,482 |
| Elmira | 39,945 |
| Elmira Heights | 4,906 |
| Elmont | 29,363 |
| Elmsford | 3,911 |
| Elwood | 15,031 |
| Endicott | 16,556 |
| Endwell | 15,999 |
| Fairmount | 15,317 |
| Fairport | 6,474 |
| Fairview | 8,517 |
| Farmingdale | 9,297 |
| Fayetteville | 4,996 |
| Fernwood | 3,659 |
| Firthcliffe | 4,025 |
| Floral Park | 18,422 |
| Flower Hill | 4,236 |
| Fort Edward | 3,733 |
| Frankfort | 3,305 |
| Franklin Square | 32,156 |
| Fredonia | 10,326 |
| Freeport | 40,374 |
| Fulton | 14,003 |
| Garden City | 25,373 |
| Garden City Park | 7,488 |
| Gardnertown | 4,614 |
| Geneseo | 5,714 |
| Geneva | 16,793 |
| Glen Cove | 25,770 |
| Glens Falls | 17,222 |
| Gloversville | 19,677 |
| Goshen | 4,342 |
| Gouverneur | 4,574 |
| Great Neck Plaza | 5,921 |
| Great Neck | 10,724 |
| Green Island | 3,297 |
| Greenlawn | 8,178 |
| Half Hollow Hills | 12,055 |
| Hamburg | 10,215 |
| Hamilton | 3,636 |
| Hartsdale | 12,226 |
| Hastings-on-Hudson | 9,479 |
| Hauppauge | 13,957 |
| Haverstraw | 8,198 |
| Haviland | 3,447 |
| Hempstead | 39,411 |
| Herkimer | 8,960 |
| Herricks | 9,112 |
| Hewlett | 6,796 |
| Hicksville | 48,075 |
| Highland Falls | 4,638 |
| Hillcrest | 5,357 |
| Holbrook-Holtsville | 12,103 |
| Homer | 4,143 |
| Hoosick Falls | 3,897 |
| Hornell | 12,144 |
| Horseheads | 7,989 |
| Hudson | 8,940 |
| Hudson Falls | 7,917 |
| Huntington | 12,130 |
| Huntington Bay | 3,258 |
| Huntington Station | 28,817 |
| Hurley | 4,081 |
| Ilion | 9,808 |
| Inwood | 8,433 |
| Irvington | 5,878 |
| Island Park | 5,396 |
| Islip | 7,692 |
| Ithaca | 26,226 |
| Jamestown | 39,795 |
| Jefferson Valley-Yorktown | 9,008 |
| Jericho | 14,010 |
| Johnson City | 18,025 |
| Johnstown | 10,045 |
| Kenmore | 20,980 |
| Kings Park | 5,555 |
| Kings Point | 5,525 |
| Kingston | 25,544 |
| Lackawanna | 28,657 |
| Lake Carmel | 4,796 |
| Lake Erie Beach | 3,467 |
| Lake Grove | 8,133 |
| Lake Success | 3,254 |
| Lakeview | 5,471 |

**NEW YORK—Continued**

| | |
|---|---|
| Lakewood | 3,864 |
| Lancaster | 13,365 |
| Larchmont | 7,203 |
| Latham | 9,661 |
| Lawrence | 6,566 |
| Le Roy | 5,118 |
| Levittown | 65,440 |
| Lewiston | 3,292 |
| Liberty | 4,293 |
| Lindenhurst | 28,338 |
| Little Falls | 7,629 |
| Liverpool | 3,307 |
| Lloyd Harbor | 3,371 |
| Lockport | 25,399 |
| Locust Grove | 11,626 |
| Long Beach | 33,127 |
| Loudonville | 9,299 |
| Lowville | 3,671 |
| Lynbrook | 23,776 |
| Lyons | 4,496 |
| Mahopac | 5,265 |
| Malone | 8,048 |
| Malverne | 10,036 |
| Mamaroneck | 18,909 |
| Manhasset | 8,541 |
| Manlius | 4,295 |
| Manorhaven | 5,710 |
| Massapequa | 26,951 |
| Massapequa Park | 22,112 |
| Massena | 14,042 |
| Mastic Beach | 4,870 |
| Mattydale | 8,292 |
| Mechanicville | 6,247 |
| Medina | 6,415 |
| Melville | 5,999 |
| Menands | 3,449 |
| Merrick | 25,904 |
| Middletown | 22,607 |
| Mineola | 21,845 |
| Mohawk | 3,301 |
| Monroe | 4,439 |
| Monsey | 8,797 |
| Monticello | 5,991 |
| Mount Kisco | 8,172 |
| Mount Morris | 3,417 |
| Mount Vernon | 72,778 |
| Nanuet | 10,447 |
| Nesconset | 10,048 |
| Newark | 11,644 |
| Newburgh | 26,219 |
| New Cassel | 8,554 |
| New City | 27,344 |
| New Hyde Park | 10,116 |
| New Paltz | 6,058 |
| New Rochelle | 75,385 |
| New Windsor Center | 8,803 |
| New York City | 7,867,760 |
| New York Mills | 3,805 |
| Niagara Falls | 85,615 |
| Nimmonsburg-Chenango Bridge | 5,059 |
| Niskayuna | 6,186 |
| North Great River | 12,080 |
| North Pelham | 5,184 |
| Northport | 7,440 |
| North Syracuse | 8,687 |
| North Tarrytown | 8,334 |
| North Tonawanda | 36,012 |
| Norwich | 8,843 |
| Nyack | 6,659 |
| Oakdale | 7,334 |
| Oceanside | 35,028 |
| Ogdensburg | 14,554 |
| Old Bethpage | 7,084 |
| Olean | 19,169 |
| Oneida | 11,658 |
| Oneonta | 16,030 |
| Orange Lake | 4,348 |
| Orchard Park | 3,732 |
| Ossining | 21,659 |
| Oswego | 23,844 |
| Owego | 5,152 |
| Palmyra | 3,776 |
| Patchogue | 11,582 |
| Pearl River | 17,146 |
| Peekskill | 18,881 |
| Pelham Manor | 6,673 |
| Penn Yan | 5,168 |
| Perry | 4,538 |
| Plainedge | 10,759 |
| Plainview | 32,195 |
| Plattsburgh | 18,715 |
| Pleasantville | 7,110 |
| Port Chester | 25,803 |
| Port Jefferson Station | 7,403 |
| Port Jervis | 8,852 |
| Port Washington | 15,923 |
| Potsdam | 9,985 |
| Poughkeepsie | 32,029 |
| Red Oaks Mill | 3,919 |
| Rensselaer | 10,136 |
| Riverhead | 7,585 |
| Rochester | 296,233 |
| Rockville Centre | 27,444 |
| Roessleville | 5,476 |
| Rome | 50,148 |
| Ronkonkoma | 7,284 |
| Roosevelt | 15,008 |
| Roslyn Heights | 7,140 |

**NEW YORK—Continued**

| | |
|---|---|
| Rotterdam | 25,153 |
| Rye | 15,869 |
| St. James | 10,818 |
| Salamanca | 7,877 |
| San Remo | 8,302 |
| Saranac Lake | 6,086 |
| Saratoga Springs | 18,845 |
| Saugerties | 4,190 |
| Sayville | 11,680 |
| Scarsdale | 19,229 |
| Schenectady | 77,859 |
| Scotia | 8,224 |
| Sea Cliff | 5,890 |
| Seaford | 17,379 |
| Selden | 11,613 |
| Seneca Falls | 7,794 |
| Setauket-South Setauket | 6,857 |
| Shirley | 6,280 |
| Sidney | 4,789 |
| Sloan | 5,216 |
| Solvay | 8,280 |
| Southampton | 4,904 |
| South Glens Falls | 4,013 |
| South Holbrook | 6,700 |
| South Nyack | 3,435 |
| Southport | 8,685 |
| Spring Valley | 18,112 |
| Springville | 4,350 |
| Stony Brook | 6,391 |
| Stony Point | 8,270 |
| Suffern | 8,273 |
| Syosset | 9,970 |
| Syracuse | 197,208 |
| Tappan | 7,424 |
| Tarrytown | 11,115 |
| Thornwood | 6,874 |
| Ticonderoga | 3,268 |
| Tonawanda | 21,898 |
| Troy | 62,918 |
| Tuckahoe | 6,236 |
| Tupper Lake | 4,854 |
| Uniondale | 22,077 |
| Utica | 91,611 |
| Valley Cottage | 6,007 |
| Valley Stream | 40,413 |
| Van Keurens | 3,292 |
| Vernon Valley | 7,925 |
| Vestal-Twin Orchards | 8,303 |
| Viola | 5,136 |
| Walden | 5,277 |
| Walton | 3,744 |
| Wantagh | 21,873 |
| Wappingers Falls | 5,607 |
| Warsaw | 3,619 |
| Warwick | 3,604 |
| Waterloo | 5,418 |
| Watertown | 30,787 |
| Watervliet | 12,404 |
| Waverly | 5,261 |
| Webster | 5,037 |
| Wellsville | 5,815 |
| West Amityville | 6,393 |
| Westbury | 15,362 |
| Westfield | 3,651 |
| West Haverstraw | 8,558 |
| Westmere | 6,364 |
| Westvale | 7,253 |
| Whitehall | 3,764 |
| White Plains | 50,220 |
| Whitesboro | 4,805 |
| Williamsville | 6,835 |
| Williston Park | 9,154 |
| Woodmere | 19,831 |
| Wyandanch | 14,906 |
| Yaphank | 5,460 |
| Yonkers | 204,370 |
| Yorktown Heights | 6,805 |
| Yorkville | 3,425 |

**NORTH CAROLINA**

| | |
|---|---|
| Ahoskie | 5,105 |
| Albemarle | 11,126 |
| Archdale | 6,103 |
| Asheboro | 10,797 |
| Asheville | 57,681 |
| Ayden | 3,450 |
| Balfours | 4,836 |
| Beaufort | 3,368 |
| Belmont | 4,814 |
| Bessemer City | 5,217 |
| Black Mountain | 3,204 |
| Boone | 8,754 |
| Brevard | 5,243 |
| Burlington | 35,930 |
| Butner | 3,538 |
| Camp LeJeune Central | 34,549 |
| Canton | 5,158 |
| Carrboro | 3,472 |
| Cary | 7,430 |
| Chapel Hill | 25,537 |
| Charlotte | 241,178 |
| Cherry Point | 12,029 |
| Cherryville | 5,258 |
| Clinton | 7,157 |
| Concord | 18,464 |

**NORTH CAROLINA—Continued**

| | |
|---|---|
| Conover | 3,355 |
| Dallas | 4,059 |
| Dunn | 8,302 |
| Durham | 95,438 |
| Edenton | 4,766 |
| Eden | 15,871 |
| Elizabeth City | 14,069 |
| Enfield | 3,272 |
| Farmville | 4,424 |
| Fayetteville | 53,510 |
| Forest City | 7,179 |
| Fort Bragg | 46,995 |
| Fuquay-Varina | 3,576 |
| Garner | 4,923 |
| Gastonia | 47,142 |
| Goldsboro | 26,810 |
| Graham | 8,172 |
| Greensboro | 144,076 |
| Greenville | 29,063 |
| Hamlet | 4,627 |
| Havelock | 5,283 |
| Henderson | 13,896 |
| Hendersonville | 6,443 |
| Hickory | 20,569 |
| High Point | 63,204 |
| Jacksonville | 16,021 |
| Kannapolis | 36,293 |
| Kernersville | 4,815 |
| Kings Mountain | 8,465 |
| Kinston | 22,309 |
| Laurinburg | 8,859 |
| Lenoir | 14,705 |
| Lexington | 17,205 |
| Lincolnton | 5,293 |
| Longview | 3,360 |
| Lowell | 3,307 |
| Lumberton | 16,961 |
| Marion | 3,335 |
| Monroe | 11,282 |
| Mooresville | 8,808 |
| Morehead City | 5,233 |
| Morganton | 13,625 |
| Morgantown | 3,547 |
| Mount Airy | 7,325 |
| Mount Holly | 5,107 |
| Mount Olive | 4,914 |
| Murfreesboro | 3,508 |
| New Bern | 14,660 |
| New River-Gieger | 8,699 |
| Newton | 7,857 |
| North Wilkesboro | 3,357 |
| Oxford | 7,178 |
| Plymouth | 4,774 |
| Raleigh | 121,577 |
| Red Springs | 3,383 |
| Reidsville | 13,636 |
| Roanoke Rapids | 13,508 |
| Rockingham | 5,852 |
| Rocky Mount | 34,284 |
| Roxboro | 5,370 |
| Rutherfordton | 3,245 |
| Salisbury | 22,515 |
| Sanford | 11,716 |
| Selma | 4,356 |
| Seymour-Johnson | 8,172 |
| Shelby | 16,328 |
| Siler City | 4,689 |
| Smithfield | 6,677 |
| Southern Pines | 5,937 |
| Spindale | 3,848 |
| Spring Lake | 3,968 |
| Statesville | 19,996 |
| Tarboro | 9,425 |
| Thomasville | 15,230 |
| Wadesboro | 3,977 |
| Washington | 8,961 |
| Waynesville | 6,488 |
| Whiteville | 4,195 |
| Williamston | 6,570 |
| Wilmington | 46,169 |
| Wilson | 29,347 |
| Winston-Salem | 132,913 |

**NORTH DAKOTA**

| | |
|---|---|
| Bismarck | 34,703 |
| Devils Lake | 7,078 |
| Dickinson | 12,405 |
| Fargo | 53,365 |
| Grafton | 5,946 |
| Grand Forks | 39,008 |
| Jamestown | 15,385 |
| Mandan | 11,093 |
| Minot | 32,290 |
| Valley City | 7,843 |
| Wahpeton | 7,076 |
| West Fargo | 5,161 |
| Williston | 11,280 |

**OHIO**

| | |
|---|---|
| Ada | 5,309 |
| Akron | 275,425 |
| Alliance | 26,547 |
| Amberley | 5,574 |
| Amherst | 9,902 |
| Ashland | 19,872 |
| Ashtabula | 24,313 |
| Athens | 23,310 |
| Aurora | 6,549 |
| Austintown | 29,393 |
| Avondale | 5,195 |

**OHIO—Continued**

| | |
|---|---|
| Avon Lake | 12,261 |
| Avon | 7,214 |
| Barberton | 33,052 |
| Barnesville | 4,292 |
| Bay Village | 18,163 |
| Beachwood | 9,631 |
| Bedford | 17,552 |
| Bedford Heights | 13,063 |
| Bellaire | 9,655 |
| Bellefontaine | 11,255 |
| Bellevue | 8,604 |
| Belpre | 7,189 |
| Berea | 22,396 |
| Bexley | 14,888 |
| Blacklick Estates | 8,351 |
| Blue Ash | 8,324 |
| Boardman | 30,852 |
| Bowling Green | 21,760 |
| Brecksville | 9,137 |
| Bridgetown | 13,352 |
| Broadview Heights | 11,463 |
| Brooklyn | 13,142 |
| Brook Park | 30,774 |
| Brookville | 4,403 |
| Brunswick | 15,852 |
| Bryan | 7,008 |
| Bucyrus | 13,111 |
| Cambridge | 13,656 |
| Campbell | 12,577 |
| Canfield | 4,997 |
| Canton | 110,053 |
| Carey | 3,523 |
| Carlisle | 3,821 |
| Celina | 7,779 |
| Centerville | 10,333 |
| Chagrin Falls | 4,848 |
| Chardon | 3,991 |
| Cheviot | 11,135 |
| Chillicothe | 24,842 |
| Churchill | 7,457 |
| Cincinnati | 452,524 |
| Circleville | 11,687 |
| Cleveland | 750,903 |
| Cleveland Heights | 60,767 |
| Clyde | 5,503 |
| Coldwater | 3,533 |
| Columbiana | 4,959 |
| Columbus | 539,677 |
| Conneaut | 14,552 |
| Coshocton | 13,747 |
| Covedale | 6,639 |
| Crestline | 5,947 |
| Crystal Lakes | 5,851 |
| Cuyahoga Falls | 49,678 |
| Dayton | 243,601 |
| Deer Park | 7,415 |
| Defiance | 16,281 |
| Delaware | 15,008 |
| Delphos | 7,608 |
| Dennison | 3,506 |
| Dover | 11,516 |
| East Cleveland | 39,600 |
| Eastlake | 19,690 |
| East Liverpool | 20,020 |
| East Palestine | 5,604 |
| Eaton | 6,020 |
| Edgewood | 3,437 |
| Elmwood Place | 3,525 |
| Elyria | 53,427 |
| Englewood | 7,885 |
| Euclid | 71,552 |
| Fairborn | 32,267 |
| Fairfield | 14,680 |
| Fairlawn | 6,102 |
| Fairport | 3,665 |
| Fairview Park | 21,681 |
| Findlay | 35,800 |
| Forest Park | 15,139 |
| Fort McKinley | 11,536 |
| Fort Shawnee | 3,436 |
| Fostoria | 16,037 |
| Franklin | 10,075 |
| Fremont | 18,490 |
| Gahanna | 12,400 |
| Galion | 13,123 |
| Gallipolis | 7,490 |
| Garfield Heights | 41,417 |
| Geneva | 6,449 |
| Germantown | 4,088 |
| Girard | 14,119 |
| Golf Manor | 5,170 |
| Grandview Heights | 8,460 |
| Granville | 3,963 |
| Greenfield | 4,780 |
| Greenhills | 6,092 |
| Greenville | 12,380 |
| Grove City | 13,911 |
| Hamilton | 67,865 |
| Harrison | 4,408 |
| Heath | 6,768 |
| Hicksville | 3,461 |
| Highland Heights | 5,926 |
| Hilliard | 8,369 |
| Hillsboro | 5,584 |
| Hubbard | 8,583 |
| Huber Heights | 18,943 |
| Hudson | 3,933 |
| Huron | 6,896 |
| Independence | 7,034 |
| Indian Hill | 5,651 |

**OHIO—Continued**

| | |
|---|---|
| Ironton | 15,030 |
| Jackson | 6,843 |
| Jefferson | 3,664 |
| Johnstown | 3,208 |
| Kent | 28,183 |
| Kenton | 8,315 |
| Kenwood | 15,789 |
| Kettering | 69,599 |
| Kirtland | 5,530 |
| Knollwood | 5,513 |
| Lakewood | 70,173 |
| Lancaster | 32,911 |
| Lebanon | 7,934 |
| Lima | 53,734 |
| Lincoln Heights | 6,099 |
| Lincoln | 11,215 |
| Lisbon | 3,521 |
| Lockbourne Base | 5,623 |
| Lockland | 5,288 |
| Logan | 6,269 |
| London | 6,481 |
| Lorain | 78,185 |
| Louisville | 6,298 |
| Loveland | 7,144 |
| Lyndhurst | 19,749 |
| Macedonia | 6,375 |
| Madeira | 6,713 |
| Madison North | 6,882 |
| Mansfield | 55,047 |
| Maple Heights | 34,093 |
| Mariemont | 4,540 |
| Marietta | 16,861 |
| Marion | 38,646 |
| Martins Ferry | 10,757 |
| Marysville | 5,744 |
| Mason | 5,677 |
| Massillon | 32,539 |
| Maumee | 15,937 |
| Mayfield Heights | 22,139 |
| Mayfield | 3,548 |
| Medina | 10,913 |
| Mentor | 36,912 |
| Mentor-on-the-Lake | 6,517 |
| Miamisburg | 14,797 |
| Middleburg Heights | 12,367 |
| Middletown | 48,767 |
| Milford | 4,828 |
| Minerva | 4,359 |
| Mingo Junction | 5,278 |
| Mogadore | 3,858 |
| Monroe | 3,492 |
| Montgomery | 5,683 |
| Montpelier | 4,184 |
| Moraine | 4,898 |
| Mount Healthy | 7,446 |
| Mount Vernon | 13,373 |
| Munroe Falls | 3,794 |
| Napoleon | 7,791 |
| Nelsonville | 4,812 |
| Newark | 41,836 |
| New Boston | 3,325 |
| Newburgh Heights | 3,396 |
| New Carlisle | 6,112 |
| Newcomerstown | 4,155 |
| New Lebanon | 4,248 |
| New Lexington | 4,921 |
| New Miami | 3,273 |
| New Philadelphia | 15,184 |
| Newton Falls | 5,378 |
| Niles | 21,581 |
| North Canton | 15,228 |
| North College Hill | 12,363 |
| North Olmsted | 34,861 |
| Northridge | 10,084 |
| North Ridgeville | 13,152 |
| North Royalton | 12,807 |
| Northwood | 4,222 |
| Norton | 12,308 |
| Norwalk | 13,386 |
| Norwood | 30,420 |
| Oakwood | 10,095 |
| Oberlin | 8,761 |
| Ontario | 4,345 |
| Oregon | 16,563 |
| Orrville | 7,408 |
| Ottawa Hills | 4,270 |
| Ottawa | 3,622 |
| Overlook-Page Manor | 19,596 |
| Oxford | 15,868 |
| Painesville | 16,536 |
| Parma | 100,216 |
| Parma Heights | 27,192 |
| Pepper Pike | 5,933 |
| Perrysburg | 7,693 |
| Piqua | 20,741 |
| Port Clinton | 7,202 |
| Portsmouth | 27,633 |
| Ravenna | 11,780 |
| Reading | 14,303 |
| Reynoldsburg | 13,921 |
| Richfield | 3,228 |
| Richmond Heights | 9,220 |
| Rittman | 6,308 |
| Rocky River | 22,958 |
| Rossford | 5,302 |
| St. Bernard | 6,080 |
| St. Clairsville | 4,754 |
| St. Marys | 7,699 |
| Salem | 14,186 |
| Sandusky | 32,674 |

**OHIO—Continued**

| | |
|---|---|
| Sebring | 4,954 |
| Seven Hills | 12,700 |
| Shadyside | 5,070 |
| Shaker Heights | 36,306 |
| Sharonville | 10,985 |
| Sheffield Lake | 8,734 |
| Shelby | 9,847 |
| Shiloh | 11,368 |
| Sidney | 16,332 |
| Silver Lake | 3,637 |
| Silverton | 6,588 |
| Solon | 11,519 |
| South Euclid | 29,579 |
| Springdale | 8,127 |
| Springfield | 81,926 |
| Steubenville | 30,771 |
| Stow | 19,847 |
| Streetsboro | 7,966 |
| Strongsville | 15,182 |
| Struthers | 15,343 |
| Sylvania | 12,031 |
| Tallmadge | 15,274 |
| Tiffin | 21,596 |
| Tipp City | 5,090 |
| Toledo | 383,818 |
| Toronto | 7,705 |
| Trenton | 5,278 |
| Trotwood | 6,997 |
| Troy | 17,186 |
| Twinsburg | 6,432 |
| Uhrichsville | 5,731 |
| Union | 3,654 |
| University Heights | 17,055 |
| Upper Arlington | 38,630 |
| Upper Sandusky | 5,645 |
| Urbana | 11,237 |
| Vandalia | 10,796 |
| Van Wert | 11,320 |
| Vermilion | 9,872 |
| Wadsworth | 13,142 |
| Walbridge | 3,208 |
| Wapakoneta | 7,324 |
| Warren | 63,494 |
| Warrensville Heights | 18,925 |
| Washington | 12,495 |
| Wauseon | 4,932 |
| Waverly | 4,858 |
| Wellington | 4,137 |
| Wellston | 5,410 |
| Wellsville | 5,891 |
| West Carrollton | 10,748 |
| Westerville | 12,530 |
| Westlake | 15,689 |
| West Milton | 3,696 |
| Wheelersburg | 3,709 |
| Whitehall | 25,263 |
| Wickiffe | 21,354 |
| Willard | 5,510 |
| Willoughby | 18,634 |
| Willoughby Hills | 5,247 |
| Willowick | 21,237 |
| Wilmington | 10,051 |
| Windham | 3,360 |
| Wintersville | 4,921 |
| Woodlawn | 3,251 |
| Woodsfield | 3,239 |
| Wooster | 18,703 |
| Worthington | 15,326 |
| Wright-Patterson | 10,151 |
| Wyoming | 9,089 |
| Xenia | 25,373 |
| Yellow Springs | 4,624 |
| Youngstown | 139,788 |
| Zanesville | 33,045 |

**OKLAHOMA**

| | |
|---|---|
| Ada | 14,859 |
| Altus | 23,302 |
| Alva | 7,440 |
| Anadarko | 6,682 |
| Ardmore | 20,881 |
| Atoka | 3,346 |
| Bartlesville | 29,683 |
| Bethany | 21,785 |
| Bixby | 3,973 |
| Blackwell | 8,645 |
| Bristow | 4,653 |
| Broken Arrow | 11,787 |
| Chickasha | 14,194 |
| Choctaw | 4,750 |
| Claremore | 9,084 |
| Clinton | 8,513 |
| Cushing | 7,529 |
| Del City | 27,133 |
| Dewey | 3,958 |
| Duncan | 19,718 |
| Durant | 11,118 |
| Edmond | 16,633 |
| Elk City | 7,323 |
| El Reno | 14,510 |
| Enid | 44,008 |
| Fort Sill | 21,217 |
| Frederick | 6,132 |
| Guthrie | 9,575 |
| Guymon | 7,674 |
| Henryetta | 6,430 |
| Hobart | 4,638 |
| Holdenville | 5,181 |
| Hugo | 6,585 |
| Idabel | 5,946 |

**OKLAHOMA—Continued**

| | |
|---|---|
| Kingfisher | 4,042 |
| Lawton | 74,470 |
| Lindsay | 3,705 |
| McAlester | 18,802 |
| Mangum | 4,066 |
| Marlow | 3,995 |
| Miami | 13,880 |
| Midwest City | 48,114 |
| Moore | 18,761 |
| Muskogee | 37,331 |
| New Cordell | 3,261 |
| Nichols Hills | 4,478 |
| Norman | 52,117 |
| Nowata | 3,679 |
| Oklahoma City | 366,481 |
| Okmulgee | 15,180 |
| Owasso | 3,491 |
| Pauls Valley | 5,769 |
| Pawhuska | 4,238 |
| Perry | 5,341 |
| Ponca City | 25,940 |
| Poteau | 5,500 |
| Pryor | 7,057 |
| Purcell | 4,076 |
| Sallisaw | 4,888 |
| Sand Springs | 11,519 |
| Sapulpa | 15,159 |
| Seminole | 7,878 |
| Shawnee | 25,075 |
| Spencer | 3,603 |
| Stillwater | 31,126 |
| Sulphur | 5,158 |
| Tahlequah | 9,254 |
| Tecumseh | 4,451 |
| The Village | 13,695 |
| Tonkawa | 3,337 |
| Tulsa | 331,638 |
| Vinita | 5,847 |
| Wagoner | 4,959 |
| Warr Acres | 9,887 |
| Watonga | 3,696 |
| Weatherford | 7,959 |
| Wewoka | 5,284 |
| Woodward | 8,710 |
| Yukon | 8,411 |

**OREGON**

| | |
|---|---|
| Albany | 18,181 |
| Altamont | 15,746 |
| Ashland | 12,342 |
| Astoria | 10,244 |
| Baker | 9,354 |
| Beaverton | 18,577 |
| Bend | 13,710 |
| Burns | 3,293 |
| Canby | 3,813 |
| Central Point | 4,004 |
| City of the Dalles | 10,423 |
| Coos Bay | 13,466 |
| Coquille | 4,437 |
| Corvallis | 35,153 |
| Cottage Grove | 6,004 |
| Dallas | 6,361 |
| Eugene | 76,346 |
| Forest Grove | 8,275 |
| Four Corners | 6,199 |
| Gladstone | 6,237 |
| Grants Pass | 12,455 |
| Gresham | 9,875 |
| Hayesville | 5,518 |
| Hermiston | 4,893 |
| Hillsboro | 14,675 |
| Hood River | 3,991 |
| Keizer | 11,405 |
| Klamath Falls | 15,775 |
| La Grande | 9,645 |
| Lake Oswego | 14,573 |
| Lebanon | 6,636 |
| Lincoln City | 4,198 |
| McMinnville | 10,125 |
| Medford | 28,454 |
| Milton-Freewater | 4,105 |
| Milwaukie | 16,379 |
| Monmouth | 5,237 |
| Newberg | 6,507 |
| Newport | 5,188 |
| North Bend | 8,553 |
| Oakridge | 3,422 |
| Ontario | 6,523 |
| Oregon City | 9,176 |
| Pendleton | 13,197 |
| Portland | 382,619 |
| Prineville | 4,101 |
| Redmond | 3,721 |
| Reedsport | 4,039 |
| Roseburg | 14,461 |
| St. Helens | 6,212 |
| Salem | 68,296 |
| Seaside | 4,402 |
| Silverton | 4,301 |
| Springfield | 27,047 |
| Sweet Home | 3,799 |
| Tigard | 5,302 |
| Tillamook | 3,968 |
| West Linn | 7,091 |
| Woodburn | 7,495 |

**PENNSYLVANIA**

| | |
|---|---|
| Abington | 8,594 |
| Aldan | 5,001 |
| Aliquippa | 22,277 |
| Allentown | 109,527 |

**PENNSYLVANIA—Continued**

| | |
|---|---|
| Altoona | 62,900 |
| Ambler | 7,800 |
| Ambridge | 11,324 |
| Annville | 4,704 |
| Archbald | 6,118 |
| Ardmore | 5,801 |
| Arnold | 8,174 |
| Ashland | 4,737 |
| Ashley | 4,095 |
| Aspinwall | 3,541 |
| Athens | 4,173 |
| Avalon | 7,065 |
| Avoca | 3,543 |
| Baden | 5,536 |
| Bala Cynwyd | 6,483 |
| Baldwin | 26,729 |
| Bangor | 5,425 |
| Beaver | 6,100 |
| Beaver Falls | 14,375 |
| Bedford | 3,302 |
| Bellefonte | 6,828 |
| Bellevue | 11,586 |
| Berwick | 12,274 |
| Bethel Park | 34,791 |
| Bethlehem | 72,686 |
| Blairsville | 4,411 |
| Blakely | 6,391 |
| Bloomsburg | 11,652 |
| Boyertown | 4,428 |
| Brackenridge | 4,796 |
| Braddock | 8,682 |
| Bradford | 12,672 |
| Brandywine | 11,411 |
| Brentwood | 13,732 |
| Bridgeport | 5,630 |
| Bridgeville | 6,717 |
| Bristol | 12,085 |
| Brookhaven | 7,370 |
| Brookville | 4,314 |
| Brownsville | 4,856 |
| Bryn Mawr | 5,737 |
| Butler | 18,691 |
| California | 6,635 |
| Camp Hill | 9,931 |
| Canonsburg | 11,439 |
| Carbondale | 12,808 |
| Carlisle | 18,079 |
| Carnegie | 10,864 |
| Carnot-Moon | 13,093 |
| Castle Shannon | 11,899 |
| Catasauqua | 5,702 |
| Cedarbrook-Melrose Park | 9,980 |
| Cedar Heights | 6,303 |
| Centerville | 4,175 |
| Chambersburg | 17,315 |
| Charleroi | 6,723 |
| Chatwood | 7,168 |
| Chester | 56,331 |
| Churchill | 4,690 |
| Clairton | 15,051 |
| Clarion | 6,095 |
| Clarks Summit | 5,376 |
| Clearfield | 8,176 |
| Clifton Heights | 8,348 |
| Coatesville | 12,331 |
| Collingdale | 10,605 |
| Columbia | 11,237 |
| Connellsville | 11,643 |
| Conshohocken | 10,195 |
| Coplay | 3,642 |
| Coraopolis | 8,435 |
| Corry | 7,435 |
| Crafton | 8,233 |
| Dallastown | 3,560 |
| Danville | 6,176 |
| Darby | 13,729 |
| Derry | 3,338 |
| Dickson City | 7,698 |
| Donora | 8,825 |
| Dormont | 12,856 |
| Downingtown | 7,437 |
| Doylestown | 8,270 |
| Du Bois | 10,112 |
| Dunmore | 17,300 |
| Dupont | 3,431 |
| Duquesne | 11,410 |
| Duryea | 5,264 |
| East Faxon | 4,175 |
| East McKeesport | 3,233 |
| Easton | 30,256 |
| East Petersburg | 3,407 |
| East Stroudsburg | 7,894 |
| Ebensburg | 4,318 |
| Economy | 7,176 |
| Edgewood | 5,101 |
| Edinboro | 4,871 |
| Edwardsville | 5,633 |
| Elizabethtown | 8,072 |
| Ellwood City | 10,857 |
| Emmaus | 11,511 |
| Emsworth | 3,332 |
| Ephrata | 9,662 |
| Erie | 129,231 |
| Etna | 5,819 |
| Exeter | 4,670 |
| Fairhope-Arnold | 3,239 |
| Fairview-Ferndale | 3,723 |
| Farrell | 11,022 |
| Flourtown | 9,149 |

**PENNSYLVANIA—Continued**

| | |
|---|---|
| Folcroft | 9,610 |
| Ford City | 4,749 |
| Forest Hills | 9,561 |
| Forty Fort | 6,114 |
| Fountain Hill | 5,384 |
| Fox Chapel | 4,684 |
| Frackville | 5,445 |
| Franklin | 8,629 |
| Franklin Park | 5,310 |
| Freeland | 4,784 |
| Fullerton | 7,908 |
| Geistown | 3,633 |
| General Wayne | 5,368 |
| Gettysburg | 7,275 |
| Glassport | 7,450 |
| Glen Lyon | 3,408 |
| Glenolden | 8,697 |
| Glenside | 17,353 |
| Greencastle | 3,293 |
| Greensburg | 15,870 |
| Green Tree | 6,441 |
| Greenville | 8,704 |
| Grove City | 8,312 |
| Hamburg | 3,909 |
| Hanover | 15,623 |
| Harrisburg | 68,061 |
| Hatboro | 8,880 |
| Hazleton | 30,426 |
| Hellertown | 6,613 |
| Hershey | 7,407 |
| Highland Park | 5,500 |
| Hillcrest | 3,897 |
| Hollidaysburg | 6,262 |
| Homeacre-Lyndora | 8,415 |
| Homestead | 6,309 |
| Honesdale | 5,224 |
| Hummelstown | 4,723 |
| Huntingdon | 6,987 |
| Indiana | 16,100 |
| Ingram | 4,902 |
| Irwin | 4,059 |
| Jeannette | 15,209 |
| Jefferson | 8,512 |
| Jefferson-Trooper | 13,022 |
| Jenkintown | 5,990 |
| Jersey Shore | 5,322 |
| Jessup | 4,948 |
| Jim Thorpe | 5,456 |
| Johnsonburg | 4,304 |
| Johnstown | 42,476 |
| Kane | 5,001 |
| Kenhorst | 3,482 |
| Kennett Square | 4,876 |
| Kingston | 18,325 |
| Kittanning | 6,231 |
| Kulpmont | 4,026 |
| Kutztown | 6,017 |
| Lafayette Hills | 8,263 |
| Lancaster | 57,690 |
| Lansdale | 18,451 |
| Lansdowne | 14,090 |
| Lansford | 5,168 |
| Larksville | 3,937 |
| Latrobe | 11,749 |
| Laureldale | 4,519 |
| Lawson Heights | 3,844 |
| Lebanon | 28,572 |
| Lehighton | 6,095 |
| Lemoyne | 4,625 |
| Lewisburg | 6,376 |
| Lewistown | 11,098 |
| Liberty | 3,594 |
| Lititz | 7,072 |
| Lock Haven | 11,427 |
| Lower Burrell | 13,654 |
| Luzerne | 4,504 |
| McAdoo | 3,326 |
| McChesneytown-Loyalhanna | 4,283 |
| McKeesport | 37,977 |
| McKees Rocks | 11,901 |
| Mahanoy City | 7,257 |
| Manheim | 5,434 |
| Mansfield | 4,114 |
| Masontown | 4,226 |
| Meadowlands-McGovern | 3,609 |
| Meadville | 16,573 |
| Mechanicsburg | 9,385 |
| Media | 6,444 |
| Merion | 5,686 |
| Middletown | 9,080 |
| Midland | 5,271 |
| Millersville | 6,396 |
| Millvale | 5,815 |
| Milton | 7,723 |
| Minersville | 6,012 |
| Monaca | 7,486 |
| Monessen | 15,216 |
| Monongahela | 7,113 |
| Monroeville | 29,011 |
| Montoursville | 5,985 |
| Moosic | 4,273 |
| Morrisville | 11,309 |
| Mount Carmel | 9,317 |
| Mount Joy | 5,041 |
| Mount Oliver | 5,487 |
| Mount Penn | 3,465 |
| Mount Pleasant | 5,895 |
| Mount Union | 3,662 |
| Munhall | 16,674 |

**PENNSYLVANIA—Continued**

| | |
|---|---|
| Myerstown | 3,645 |
| Nanticoke | 14,632 |
| Nanty-Glo | 4,298 |
| Narberth | 5,151 |
| Nazareth | 5,815 |
| Nesquehoning | 3,338 |
| New Brighton | 7,637 |
| New Castle | 38,559 |
| New Cumberland | 9,803 |
| New Holland | 3,971 |
| New Kensington | 20,312 |
| Norristown | 38,169 |
| Northampton | 8,389 |
| North Ardmore | 5,856 |
| North Braddock | 10,838 |
| North East | 3,846 |
| North Hills-Ardsley | 13,173 |
| Northumberland | 4,102 |
| North Wales | 3,911 |
| Norwood | 7,229 |
| Oak Lane | 6,192 |
| Oakmont | 7,550 |
| Ogontz | 5,463 |
| Ohioville | 3,918 |
| Oil City | 15,033 |
| Old Forge | 9,522 |
| Olyphant | 5,422 |
| Oreland | 9,114 |
| Oxford | 3,658 |
| Palmerton | 5,620 |
| Palmyra | 7,615 |
| Paoli | 5,835 |
| Parkville | 5,120 |
| Pen Argyl | 3,668 |
| Penbrook | 3,379 |
| Pencoyd | 6,650 |
| Penn Square-Plymouth Valley | 20,238 |
| Penn Wynne | 6,038 |
| Perkasie | 5,451 |
| Philadelphia | 1,948,609 |
| Philipsburg | 3,700 |
| Phoenixville | 14,823 |
| Pitcairn | 4,741 |
| Pittsburgh | 520,117 |
| Pittston | 11,113 |
| Plains | 6,606 |
| Pleasant Hills | 10,409 |
| Plum | 21,932 |
| Plymouth | 9,536 |
| Polk | 3,673 |
| Portage | 4,151 |
| Port Vue | 5,862 |
| Pottstown | 25,355 |
| Pottsville | 19,715 |
| Prospect Park | 7,250 |
| Punxsutawney | 7,792 |
| Quakertown | 7,276 |
| Rankin | 3,817 |
| Reading | 87,643 |
| Red Lion | 5,645 |
| Ridgway | 6,022 |
| Ridley Park | 9,025 |
| Rochester | 4,819 |
| Roslyn | 18,317 |
| Royersford | 4,235 |
| Rydal | 5,083 |
| St. Clair | 4,576 |
| St. Marys | 7,470 |
| Sayre | 7,473 |
| Schuylkill Haven | 6,125 |
| Scottdale | 5,818 |
| Scranton | 103,564 |
| Selinsgrove | 5,116 |
| Sewickley | 5,660 |
| Shamokin | 11,719 |
| Sharon | 22,653 |
| Sharon Hill | 7,464 |
| Sharpsburg | 5,499 |
| Sharpsville | 6,126 |
| Shenandoah | 8,287 |
| Shillington | 6,249 |
| Shippensburg | 6,536 |
| Slatington | 4,687 |
| Slippery Rock | 4,949 |
| Somerset | 6,269 |
| Souderton | 6,366 |
| South Greensburg | 3,288 |
| South Williamsport | 7,153 |
| Spring City | 3,578 |
| Springdale | 5,202 |
| State College | 33,778 |
| Steelton | 8,556 |
| Stowe | 3,596 |
| Stroudsburg | 5,451 |
| Sugar Creek | 5,944 |
| Summit Hill | 3,811 |
| Sunbury | 13,025 |
| Swarthmore | 6,156 |
| Swissvale | 13,821 |
| Swoyersville | 6,786 |
| Tamaqua | 9,246 |
| Tarentum | 7,379 |
| Taylor | 6,977 |
| Telford | 3,409 |
| Throop | 4,307 |
| Titusville | 7,331 |
| Towanda | 4,224 |
| Trafford | 4,383 |
| Turtle Creek | 8,308 |
| Tyrone | 7,072 |

**PENNSYLVANIA—Continued**

| | |
|---|---|
| Union City | 3,631 |
| Uniontown | 16,282 |
| Upland | 3,930 |
| Vandergrift | 7,873 |
| Verona | 3,737 |
| Warren | 12,998 |
| Washington | 19,827 |
| Waynesboro | 10,011 |
| Waynesburg | 5,152 |
| Wellsboro | 4,003 |
| Wesleyville | 3,920 |
| West Chester | 19,301 |
| West Hazleton | 6,059 |
| West Homestead | 3,789 |
| West Mifflin | 28,070 |
| Westmont | 6,673 |
| West Newton | 3,648 |
| West Pittston | 7,074 |
| West Reading | 4,578 |
| West View | 8,312 |
| West Wyoming | 3,659 |
| West York | 5,314 |
| Whitehall | 16,551 |
| White Oak | 9,304 |
| Wilkes-Barre | 58,856 |
| Wilkinsburg | 26,780 |
| Williamsport | 37,918 |
| Willow Grove | 16,494 |
| Wilmerding | 3,218 |
| Wilson | 8,482 |
| Windber | 6,332 |
| Wyoming | 4,195 |
| Wyomissing | 7,136 |
| Yeadon | 12,136 |
| York | 50,335 |
| Zelienople | 3,602 |

**RHODE ISLAND**

| | |
|---|---|
| Barrington | 17,554 |
| Bristol | 17,860 |
| Burrillville | 10,087 |
| Central Falls | 18,716 |
| Coventry | 22,947 |
| Cranston | 73,037 |
| Cumberland | 26,605 |
| East Greenwich | 9,577 |
| East Providence | 48,151 |
| Exeter | 3,245 |
| Glocester | 5,160 |
| Hopkinton | 5,392 |
| Johnston | 22,037 |
| Kingston | 5,601 |
| Lincoln | 16,182 |
| Middletown | 29,621 |
| Narragansett | 7,138 |
| Newport | 34,562 |
| North Kingstown | 27,673 |
| North Providence | 24,337 |
| North Smithfield | 9,349 |
| Pawtucket | 76,984 |
| Portsmouth | 12,521 |
| Providence | 179,213 |
| Scituate | 7,489 |
| Smithfield | 13,468 |
| South Kingstown | 16,913 |
| The Anchorage | 3,441 |
| Tiverton | 12,559 |
| Wakefield-Peacedale | 6,331 |
| Warren | 10,523 |
| Warwick | 83,694 |
| Westerly | 17,248 |
| West Warwick | 24,323 |
| Woonsocket | 46,820 |

**SOUTH CAROLINA**

| | |
|---|---|
| Abbeville | 5,515 |
| Aiken | 13,436 |
| Allendale | 3,620 |
| Anderson | 27,556 |
| Avondale-Moorland | 5,236 |
| Bamberg | 3,406 |
| Barnwell | 4,439 |
| Batesburg | 4,036 |
| Beaufort | 9,434 |
| Belton | 5,257 |
| Bennettsville | 7,468 |
| Berea | 7,186 |
| Bishopville | 3,404 |
| Camden | 8,532 |
| Capehart | 4,490 |
| Cayce | 9,967 |
| Charleston | 66,945 |
| Cheraw | 5,627 |
| Chester | 7,045 |
| Clemson | 5,578 |
| Clinton | 8,138 |
| Clover | 3,506 |
| Columbia | 113,542 |
| Conway | 8,151 |
| Darlington | 6,990 |
| Denmark | 3,571 |
| Dillon | 5,991 |
| Easley | 11,175 |
| Florence | 25,997 |
| Forest Acres | 6,808 |
| Fort Mill | 4,505 |
| Fountain Inn | 3,391 |
| Gaffney | 13,253 |
| Gantt | 11,386 |
| Georgetown | 10,449 |
| Goose Creek | 3,656 |
| Greenville | 61,208 |
| Greenwood | 21,069 |

**SOUTH CAROLINA—Continued**

| | |
|---|---|
| Greer | 10,642 |
| Hanahan | 8,376 |
| Hartsville | 8,017 |
| Honea Path | 3,707 |
| Kingstree | 3,381 |
| Lake City | 6,247 |
| Lancaster | 9,186 |
| Laurens | 10,298 |
| Manning | 4,025 |
| Marion | 7,435 |
| Mauldin | 3,797 |
| Mount Pleasant | 6,155 |
| Mullins | 6,006 |
| Myrtle Beach | 8,536 |
| Newberry | 9,218 |
| North Augusta | 12,883 |
| Orangeburg | 13,252 |
| Parris Island | 8,868 |
| Rock Hill | 33,846 |
| St. Andrews | 9,202 |
| Saxon | 4,807 |
| Seneca | 6,027 |
| Shannontown | 7,491 |
| Shaw | 5,819 |
| Simpsonville | 3,308 |
| Spartanburg | 44,546 |
| Summerville | 3,839 |
| Sumter | 24,435 |
| Taylors | 6,831 |
| Union | 10,775 |
| Wade-Hampton | 17,152 |
| Walhalla | 3,662 |
| Walterboro | 6,257 |
| West Columbia | 7,838 |
| Williamston | 3,991 |
| Winnsboro | 3,411 |
| Woodruff | 4,576 |
| York | 5,081 |

**SOUTH DAKOTA**

| | |
|---|---|
| Aberdeen | 26,476 |
| Belle Fourche | 4,236 |
| Brookings | 13,717 |
| Ellsworth | 5,805 |
| Hot Springs | 4,434 |
| Huron | 14,299 |
| Lead | 5,420 |
| Madison | 6,315 |
| Milbank | 3,727 |
| Mitchell | 13,425 |
| Mobridge | 4,545 |
| Pierre | 9,699 |
| Rapid City | 43,836 |
| Sioux Falls | 72,488 |
| Spearfish | 4,661 |
| Sturgis | 4,536 |
| Vermillion | 9,128 |
| Watertown | 13,388 |
| Winner | 3,789 |
| Yankton | 11,919 |

**TENNESSEE**

| | |
|---|---|
| Alcoa | 7,739 |
| Athens | 11,790 |
| Bolivar | 6,674 |
| Bristol | 20,064 |
| Brownsville | 7,011 |
| Chattanooga | 119,082 |
| Clarksville | 31,719 |
| Cleveland | 20,651 |
| Clinton | 4,794 |
| Collierville | 3,625 |
| Columbia | 21,471 |
| Cookeville | 14,270 |
| Covington | 5,801 |
| Crossville | 5,381 |
| Dayton | 4,361 |
| Dickson | 5,665 |
| Dyersburg | 14,523 |
| Eagleton | 5,345 |
| East Ridge | 21,799 |
| Elizabethton | 12,269 |
| Erwin | 4,715 |
| Etowah | 3,736 |
| Fayetteville | 7,030 |
| Fort Campbell South | 9,279 |
| Franklin | 9,404 |
| Gallatin | 13,093 |
| Germantown | 3,474 |
| Greeneville | 13,722 |
| Harriman | 8,734 |
| Henderson | 3,581 |
| Hixson | 6,188 |
| Hohenwald | 3,385 |
| Humboldt | 10,066 |
| Huntingdon | 3,661 |
| Jackson | 39,996 |
| Jefferson City | 5,124 |
| Johnson City | 33,770 |
| Kingsport | 31,938 |
| Kingston | 4,142 |
| Knoxville | 174,587 |
| La Follette | 6,902 |
| Lake Hills-Murray Hills | 7,806 |
| Lawrenceburg | 8,889 |
| Lebanon | 12,492 |
| Lenoir City | 5,324 |
| Lewisburg | 7,207 |
| Lexington | 4,955 |
| Loudon | 3,728 |
| McKenzie | 4,873 |
| McMinnville | 10,662 |

### TENNESSEE—Continued

| | |
|---|---|
| Manchester | 6,208 |
| Martin | 7,781 |
| Maryville | 13,808 |
| Memphis | 623,530 |
| Milan | 7,313 |
| Millington | 21,106 |
| Morristown | 20,318 |
| Mount Pleasant | 3,530 |
| Murfreesboro | 26,360 |
| Nashville | 447,877 |
| Newport | 7,328 |
| Oak Ridge | 28,319 |
| Oliver Springs | 3,405 |
| Paris | 9,892 |
| Pulaski | 6,989 |
| Red Bank | 12,715 |
| Ripley | 4,794 |
| Rockwood | 5,259 |
| Rogersville | 4,045 |
| Savannah | 5,576 |
| Selmer | 3,495 |
| Shelbyville | 12,262 |
| Signal Mountain | 4,839 |
| Smyrna | 5,698 |
| Soddy-Daisy | 7,569 |
| South Pittsburg | 3,613 |
| Sparta | 4,930 |
| Springfield | 9,720 |
| Sweetwater | 4,340 |
| Trenton | 4,226 |
| Tullahoma | 15,311 |
| Union City | 11,925 |
| Waverly | 3,794 |
| Winchester | 5,211 |

### TEXAS

| | |
|---|---|
| Abilene | 89,653 |
| Alamo | 4,291 |
| Alamo Heights | 6,933 |
| Alice | 20,121 |
| Alpine | 5,971 |
| Alvin | 10,671 |
| Amarillo | 127,010 |
| Andrews | 8,625 |
| Angleton | 9,770 |
| Aransas Pass | 5,813 |
| Arlington | 90,643 |
| Athens | 9,582 |
| Atlanta | 5,007 |
| Austin | 251,808 |
| Azle | 4,493 |
| Balch Springs | 10,464 |
| Ballinger | 4,203 |
| Bay City | 11,733 |
| Baytown | 43,980 |
| Beaumont | 115,919 |
| Bedford | 10,049 |
| Beeville | 13,506 |
| Bellaire | 19,009 |
| Bellmead | 7,698 |
| Belton | 8,696 |
| Benbrook | 8,169 |
| Biggs | 4,226 |
| Big Spring | 28,735 |
| Bishop | 3,466 |
| Bonham | 7,698 |
| Borger | 14,195 |
| Bowie | 5,185 |
| Brady | 5,557 |
| Breckenridge | 5,944 |
| Brenham | 8,922 |
| Bridge | 8,164 |
| Bridgeport | 3,614 |
| Brownfield | 9,647 |
| Brownsville | 52,522 |
| Brownwood | 17,368 |
| Bryan | 33,719 |
| Bunker Hill Village | 3,977 |
| Burkburnett | 9,230 |
| Burleson | 7,713 |
| Cameron | 5,546 |
| Canyon | 8,333 |
| Carrizo Springs | 5,374 |
| Carrollton | 13,855 |
| Carthage | 5,392 |
| Castle Hills | 5,311 |
| Center | 4,989 |
| Childress | 5,408 |
| Cisco | 4,160 |
| Clarksville | 3,346 |
| Cleburne | 16,015 |
| Cleveland | 5,627 |
| Clute City | 6,023 |
| Cockrell Hill | 3,515 |
| Coleman | 5,608 |
| College Station | 17,676 |
| Colleyville | 3,368 |
| Colorado City | 5,227 |
| Columbus | 3,342 |
| Comanche | 3,933 |
| Commerce | 9,534 |
| Conroe | 11,969 |
| Copperas Cove | 10,818 |
| Corpus Christi | 204,525 |
| Corsicana | 19,972 |
| Cotulla | 3,415 |
| Crane | 3,427 |
| Crockett | 6,616 |
| Crystal City | 8,104 |
| Cuero | 6,956 |
| Dalhart | 5,705 |
| Dallas | 844,401 |

### TEXAS—Continued

| | |
|---|---|
| Dayton | 3,804 |
| Decatur | 3,240 |
| Deer Park | 12,773 |
| Del Rio | 21,330 |
| Denison | 24,923 |
| Denton | 39,874 |
| Denver City | 4,133 |
| De Soto | 6,617 |
| Devine | 3,311 |
| Diboll | 3,557 |
| Dickinson | 10,776 |
| Dimmitt | 4,327 |
| Donna | 7,365 |
| Dumas | 9,771 |
| Duncanville | 14,105 |
| Eagle Lake | 3,587 |
| Eagle Pass | 15,364 |
| Edinburg | 17,163 |
| Edna | 5,332 |
| El Campo | 8,563 |
| Electra | 3,895 |
| Elgin | 3,832 |
| El Paso | 322,261 |
| Elsa | 4,400 |
| Ennis | 11,046 |
| Euless | 19,316 |
| Everman | 4,570 |
| Fabens | 3,241 |
| Falfurrias | 6,355 |
| Farmers Branch | 27,492 |
| Floresville | 3,707 |
| Floydada | 4,109 |
| Forest Hill | 8,236 |
| Fort Bliss | 13,288 |
| Fort Hood | 32,597 |
| Fort Sam Houston | 10,553 |
| Fort Stockton | 8,283 |
| Fort Wolters | 3,743 |
| Fort Worth | 393,476 |
| Fredericksburg | 5,326 |
| Freeport | 11,997 |
| Friendswood | 5,675 |
| Gainesville | 13,830 |
| Galena Park | 10,479 |
| Galveston | 61,809 |
| Garland | 81,437 |
| Gatesville | 4,683 |
| Georgetown | 6,395 |
| Gilmer | 4,196 |
| Gladewater | 5,574 |
| Gonzales | 5,854 |
| Graham | 7,477 |
| Grand Prairie | 50,904 |
| Grapevine | 7,023 |
| Greenville | 22,043 |
| Groves | 18,067 |
| Haltom City | 28,127 |
| Hamlin | 3,325 |
| Harker Heights | 4,216 |
| Harlingen | 33,503 |
| Haskell | 3,655 |
| Hearne | 4,982 |
| Hebbronville | 4,079 |
| Hedwig Village | 3,255 |
| Henderson | 10,187 |
| Hereford | 13,414 |
| Highland Park | 10,133 |
| Highlands | 3,462 |
| Hillsboro | 7,224 |
| Hitchcock | 5,565 |
| Hondo | 5,487 |
| Houston | 1,232,802 |
| Humble | 3,278 |
| Hunters Creek Village | 3,959 |
| Huntsville | 17,610 |
| Hurst | 27,215 |
| Ingleside | 3,763 |
| Iowa Park | 5,796 |
| Irving | 97,260 |
| Jacinto City | 9,563 |
| Jacksboro | 3,554 |
| Jacksonville | 9,734 |
| Jasper | 6,251 |
| Kaufman | 4,012 |
| Kenedy | 4,156 |
| Kermit | 7,884 |
| Kerrville | 12,672 |
| Kilgore | 9,495 |
| Killeen | 35,507 |
| Kingsville | 28,711 |
| Kleberg | 4,768 |
| Lackland | 19,141 |
| Lake Jackson | 13,376 |
| Lakeview | 3,567 |
| Lake Worth Village | 4,958 |
| La Marque | 16,131 |
| Lamesa | 11,559 |
| Lampasas | 5,922 |
| Lancaster | 10,522 |
| La Porte | 7,149 |
| Laredo | 69,024 |
| Laughlin | 3,458 |
| League City | 10,818 |
| Levelland | 11,445 |
| Lewisville | 9,264 |
| Liberty | 5,591 |
| Littlefield | 6,738 |
| Livingston | 3,925 |
| Lockhart | 6,489 |
| Longview | 45,547 |
| Lubbock | 149,101 |

### TEXAS—Continued

| | |
|---|---|
| Lufkin | 23,049 |
| Luling | 4,719 |
| McAllen | 37,636 |
| McGregor | 4,365 |
| McKinney | 15,193 |
| Mansfield | 3,658 |
| Marlin | 6,351 |
| Marshall | 22,937 |
| Mathis | 5,351 |
| Memphis | 3,227 |
| Mercedes | 9,355 |
| Mesquite | 55,131 |
| Mexia | 5,943 |
| Midland | 59,463 |
| Mineola | 3,926 |
| Mineral Wells | 18,411 |
| Mission | 13,043 |
| Missouri City | 4,136 |
| Monahans | 8,333 |
| Mount Pleasant | 8,877 |
| Muleshoe | 4,525 |
| Nacogdoches | 22,544 |
| Navasota | 5,111 |
| Nederland | 16,810 |
| New Boston | 3,699 |
| New Braunfels | 17,859 |
| North Richland Hills | 16,514 |
| Odessa | 78,380 |
| Olney | 3,624 |
| Orange | 24,457 |
| Palacios | 3,642 |
| Palestine | 14,525 |
| Pampa | 21,726 |
| Paris | 23,441 |
| Pasadena | 89,277 |
| Pearland | 6,444 |
| Pear Ridge | 3,697 |
| Pearsall | 5,545 |
| Pecos | 12,682 |
| Perryton | 7,810 |
| Pharr | 15,829 |
| Pittsburg | 3,844 |
| Plainview | 19,096 |
| Plano | 17,872 |
| Pleasanton | 5,407 |
| Port Arthur | 57,371 |
| Portland | 7,302 |
| Port Lavaca | 10,491 |
| Port Neches | 10,894 |
| Post | 3,854 |
| Prairie View | 3,589 |
| Premont | 3,282 |
| Quanah | 3,948 |
| Randolph | 5,329 |
| Raymondville | 7,987 |
| Refugio | 4,340 |
| Richardson | 48,582 |
| Richland Hills | 8,865 |
| Richmond | 5,777 |
| Rio Grande | 5,676 |
| River Oaks | 8,193 |
| Robinson | 3,807 |
| Robstown | 11,217 |
| Rockdale | 4,655 |
| Rockport | 3,879 |
| Rosenberg | 12,098 |
| Rusk | 4,914 |
| San Angelo | 63,884 |
| San Antonio | 654,153 |
| San Benito | 15,176 |
| San Diego | 4,490 |
| San Juan | 5,070 |
| San Marcos | 18,860 |
| Sansom Park Village | 4,771 |
| Schertz | 4,061 |
| Seabrook | 3,811 |
| Seagoville | 4,390 |
| Seguin | 15,934 |
| Seminole | 5,007 |
| Seymour | 3,469 |
| Sherman | 29,061 |
| Silsbee | 7,271 |
| Sinton | 5,563 |
| Slaton | 6,583 |
| Snyder | 11,171 |
| South Houston | 11,527 |
| Spearman | 3,435 |
| Stamford | 4,558 |
| Stephenville | 9,277 |
| Sugar Land | 3,318 |
| Sulphur Springs | 10,642 |
| Sweetwater | 12,020 |
| Taft | 3,274 |
| Taylor | 9,616 |
| Temple | 33,431 |
| Terrell | 14,182 |
| Terrell Hills | 5,225 |
| Texarkana | 30,497 |
| Texas City | 38,908 |
| Tulia | 5,294 |
| Tyler | 57,770 |
| Universal City | 7,613 |
| University Park | 23,498 |
| Uvalde | 10,764 |
| Vernon | 11,454 |
| Victoria | 41,349 |
| Vidor | 9,738 |
| Waco | 95,326 |
| Waxahachie | 13,452 |
| Weatherford | 11,750 |
| Weslaco | 15,313 |

### TEXAS—Continued

| | |
|---|---|
| West Columbia | 3,335 |
| West Orange | 4,787 |
| West University Place | 13,317 |
| Westworth | 4,578 |
| Wharton | 7,881 |
| White Settlement | 13,449 |
| Wichita Falls | 97,564 |
| Windcrest | 3,371 |
| Woodway | 4,819 |
| Yoakum | 5,755 |

### UTAH

| | |
|---|---|
| American Fork | 7,713 |
| Bountiful | 27,853 |
| Brigham City | 14,007 |
| Cedar City | 8,946 |
| Centerville | 3,268 |
| Clearfield | 13,316 |
| Cottonwood | 8,431 |
| East Millcreek | 26,579 |
| Granger-Hunter | 9,029 |
| Granite Park | 9,573 |
| Heber | 3,245 |
| Holladay | 23,014 |
| Kaysville | 6,192 |
| Kearns | 17,071 |
| Layton | 13,603 |
| Lehi | 4,659 |
| Logan | 22,333 |
| Magna | 5,509 |
| Midvale | 7,840 |
| Moab | 4,793 |
| Mount Olympus | 5,909 |
| Murray | 21,206 |
| North Ogden | 5,257 |
| Ogden | 69,478 |
| Orem | 25,729 |
| Payson | 4,501 |
| Pleasant Grove | 5,327 |
| Price | 6,218 |
| Provo | 53,131 |
| Richfield | 4,471 |
| Riverdale | 3,704 |
| Roy | 14,356 |
| St. George | 7,097 |
| Salt Lake City | 175,885 |
| Sandy City | 6,438 |
| Smithfield | 3,342 |
| South Ogden | 9,991 |
| South Salt Lake | 7,810 |
| Spanish Fork | 7,284 |
| Springville | 8,790 |
| Sunset | 6,268 |
| Tooele | 12,539 |
| Vernal | 3,908 |
| Washington Terrace | 7,241 |
| West Jordan | 4,221 |
| White | 6,402 |

### VERMONT

| | |
|---|---|
| Barre | 10,209 |
| Bellows Falls | 3,505 |
| Bennington | 14,586 |
| Brandon | 3,697 |
| Brattleboro | 12,239 |
| Burlington | 38,633 |
| Colchester | 8,776 |
| Derby | 3,252 |
| Essex | 10,951 |
| Hartford | 6,477 |
| Lyndon | 3,705 |
| Middlebury | 6,532 |
| Milton | 4,495 |
| Montpelier | 8,609 |
| Morristown | 4,052 |
| Newport | 4,664 |
| Northfield | 4,870 |
| Poultney | 3,217 |
| Randolph | 3,882 |
| Rockingham | 5,501 |
| Rutland | 19,293 |
| St. Albans | 8,082 |
| St. Johnsbury | 8,409 |
| Shelburne | 3,728 |
| South Burlington | 10,032 |
| Springfield | 10,063 |
| Swanton | 4,622 |
| Waterbury | 4,614 |
| Williston Road | 5,376 |
| Windsor | 4,158 |
| Winooski | 7,309 |

### VIRGINIA

| | |
|---|---|
| Abingdon | 4,376 |
| Alexandria | 110,938 |
| Annandale | 27,428 |
| Arlington | 174,284 |
| Bailey's Crossroads | 7,295 |
| Bedford | 6,011 |
| Belleview | 8,299 |
| Big Stone Gap | 4,153 |
| Blacksburg | 9,384 |
| Blackstone | 3,412 |
| Bluefield | 5,286 |
| Bon Air | 10,562 |
| Bristol | 14,857 |
| Buena Vista | 6,425 |
| Charlottesville | 38,880 |
| Chesapeake | 89,580 |
| Chester | 5,556 |
| Christiansburg | 7,857 |
| Clifton Forge | 5,501 |
| Collinsville | 6,015 |

**VIRGINIA—Continued**

| | |
|---|---|
| Colonial Heights | 15,097 |
| Covington | 10,060 |
| Culpeper | 6,056 |
| Dale | 13,857 |
| Danville | 46,391 |
| Emporia | 5,300 |
| Fairfax | 21,970 |
| Falls Church | 10,772 |
| Farmville | 4,331 |
| Fort Belvoir | 14,591 |
| Fort Hunt | 10,415 |
| Fort Lee | 12,435 |
| Franklin | 6,880 |
| Fredericksburg | 14,450 |
| Front Royal | 8,211 |
| Galax | 6,278 |
| Groveton | 11,750 |
| Hampton | 120,779 |
| Harrisonburg | 14,605 |
| Herndon | 4,301 |
| Highland Springs | 7,345 |
| Hopewell | 23,471 |
| Huntington | 5,559 |
| Jefferson | 25,432 |
| Lake Barcroft | 11,605 |
| Lakeside | 11,137 |
| Leesburg | 4,821 |
| Lexington | 7,597 |
| Lincolnia | 10,355 |
| Long Branch | 21,634 |
| Luray | 3,612 |
| Lyman Park-Thomason Park | 3,765 |
| Lynchburg | 54,083 |
| McLean | 17,698 |
| Manassas Park | 6,844 |
| Manassas | 9,164 |
| Mantua | 6,911 |
| Marion | 8,158 |
| Martinsville | 19,653 |
| Mechanicsville | 5,189 |
| Newport News | 138,177 |
| Norfolk | 307,951 |
| Norton | 4,001 |
| Petersburg | 36,103 |
| Poquoson | 5,441 |
| Portsmouth | 110,963 |
| Pulaski | 10,279 |
| Quantico | 6,213 |
| Radford | 11,596 |
| Reston | 5,723 |
| Richlands | 4,843 |
| Richmond | 249,621 |
| Roanoke | 92,115 |
| Rocky Mount | 4,002 |
| Rose Hill | 14,692 |
| Salem | 21,982 |
| Seven Corners | 5,590 |
| South Boston | 6,889 |
| South Hill | 3,858 |
| Springfield | 11,613 |
| Staunton | 24,504 |
| Sterling Park | 8,321 |
| Suffolk | 9,858 |
| Tazewell | 4,168 |
| Vienna | 17,152 |
| Vinton | 6,347 |
| Virginia Beach | 172,106 |
| Warrenton | 4,027 |
| Waynesboro | 16,707 |
| Williamsburg | 9,069 |
| Winchester | 14,643 |
| Woodbridge-Marumsco | 25,412 |
| Wytheville | 6,069 |
| Yorkshire | 4,649 |

**WEST VIRGINIA**

| | |
|---|---|
| Beckley | 19,884 |
| Bluefield | 15,921 |
| Bridgeport | 4,777 |
| Buckhannon | 7,261 |
| Charleston | 71,505 |
| Chester | 3,614 |
| Clarksburg | 24,864 |
| Dunbar | 9,151 |
| Elkins | 8,287 |
| Fairmont | 26,093 |
| Follansbee | 3,883 |

**WEST VIRGINIA—Continued**

| | |
|---|---|
| Grafton | 6,433 |
| Hinton | 4,503 |
| Huntington | 74,315 |
| Hurricane | 3,491 |
| Kenova | 4,860 |
| Keyser | 6,586 |
| Logan | 3,311 |
| Martinsburg | 14,626 |
| Morgantown | 29,431 |
| Moundsville | 13,560 |
| Mount Gay | 3,843 |
| New Martinsville | 6,528 |
| Nitro | 8,019 |
| Oak Hill | 4,738 |
| Paden City | 3,674 |
| Parkersburg | 44,208 |
| Point Pleasant | 6,122 |
| Princeton | 7,253 |
| Ravenswood | 4,240 |
| Richwood | 3,717 |
| Ripley | 3,244 |
| St. Albans | 14,356 |
| South Charleston | 16,333 |
| Vienna | 11,549 |
| Weirton | 27,131 |
| Welch | 4,149 |
| Wellsburg | 4,600 |
| Weston | 7,323 |
| Westover | 5,086 |
| Wheeling | 48,188 |
| Williamson | 5,831 |

**WASHINGTON**

| | |
|---|---|
| Aberdeen | 18,489 |
| Anacortes | 7,701 |
| Auburn | 21,817 |
| Bellevue | 61,102 |
| Bellingham | 39,375 |
| Bothell | 4,883 |
| Bremerton | 35,307 |
| Buckley | 3,446 |
| Camas | 5,790 |
| Centralia | 10,054 |
| Chehalis | 5,727 |
| Cheney | 6,358 |
| Clarkston | 6,312 |
| College Place | 4,510 |
| Colville | 3,742 |
| Des Moines | 3,871 |
| Dishman | 9,079 |
| Edmonds | 23,998 |
| Ellensburg | 13,568 |
| Enumclaw | 4,703 |
| Ephrata | 5,255 |
| Everett | 53,622 |
| Fairchild | 6,754 |
| Fircrest | 5,651 |
| Fort Lewis | 38,054 |
| Fruitvale | 3,275 |
| Grandview | 3,605 |
| Hoquiam | 10,466 |
| Issaquah | 4,313 |
| Kelso | 10,296 |
| Kennewick | 15,212 |
| Kent | 21,510 |
| Kirkland | 15,249 |
| Lacey | 9,696 |
| Lakes District | 48,195 |
| Longview | 28,373 |
| Lynnwood | 16,919 |
| McChord | 6,515 |
| Marysville | 4,343 |
| Medical Lake | 3,529 |
| Medina | 3,455 |
| Mercer Island | 19,047 |
| Moses Lake | 10,310 |
| Mountlake Terrace | 16,600 |
| Mount Vernon | 8,804 |
| Normandy Park | 4,208 |
| Oak Harbor | 9,167 |
| Olympia | 23,111 |
| Omak | 4,164 |
| Opportunity | 16,604 |
| Othello | 4,122 |
| Parkland | 21,012 |
| Pasco | 13,920 |
| Port Angeles | 16,367 |
| Port Orchard | 3,904 |
| Port Townsend | 5,241 |

**WASHINGTON—Continued**

| | |
|---|---|
| Pullman | 20,509 |
| Puyallup | 14,742 |
| Quincy | 3,237 |
| Redmond | 11,031 |
| Renton | 25,258 |
| Richland | 26,290 |
| Seattle | 530,831 |
| Sedro-Woolley | 4,598 |
| Shelton | 6,515 |
| Shoultes | 4,754 |
| Snohomish | 5,174 |
| South Broadway | 3,298 |
| Spanaway | 5,768 |
| Spokane | 170,516 |
| Sumner | 4,325 |
| Sunnyside | 6,751 |
| Tacoma | 154,581 |
| Thompson Place-Tanglewilde | 3,423 |
| Toppenish | 5,744 |
| Town and Country | 6,484 |
| Tukwila | 3,496 |
| Tumwater | 5,373 |
| University Place | 13,230 |
| Vancouver | 42,493 |
| Walla Walla | 23,619 |
| Washougal | 3,388 |
| Wenatchee | 16,912 |
| West Clarkston-Highland | 3,797 |
| Yakima | 45,588 |

**WISCONSIN**

| | |
|---|---|
| Algoma | 4,023 |
| Allquez | 13,753 |
| Antigo | 9,005 |
| Appleton | 57,143 |
| Ashland | 9,615 |
| Ashwaubenon | 9,323 |
| Baraboo | 7,931 |
| Bayside | 4,461 |
| Beaver Dam | 14,265 |
| Beloit | 35,729 |
| Berlin | 5,338 |
| Black River Falls | 3,273 |
| Brookfield | 32,140 |
| Brown Deer | 12,622 |
| Burlington | 7,479 |
| Cedarburg | 7,697 |
| Chippewa Falls | 12,351 |
| Clintonville | 4,600 |
| Columbus | 3,789 |
| Cudahy | 22,078 |
| Delavan | 5,526 |
| De Pere | 13,309 |
| Dodgeville | 3,255 |
| Eau Claire | 44,619 |
| Edgerton | 4,118 |
| Elkhorn | 3,992 |
| Elm Grove | 7,201 |
| Fond du Lac | 35,515 |
| Fort Atkinson | 9,164 |
| Fox Point | 7,937 |
| Franklin | 12,247 |
| Germantown | 6,974 |
| Glendale | 13,436 |
| Grafton | 5,998 |
| Green Bay | 87,809 |
| Greendale | 15,089 |
| Greenfield | 24,424 |
| Hales Corners | 7,771 |
| Hartford | 6,499 |
| Horicon | 3,356 |
| Howard | 4,911 |
| Hudson | 5,049 |
| Janesville | 46,426 |
| Jefferson | 5,429 |
| Kaukauna | 11,292 |
| Kenosha | 78,805 |
| Kimberly | 6,131 |
| La Crosse | 51,153 |
| Ladysmith | 3,674 |
| Lake Geneva | 4,890 |
| Lake Mills | 3,556 |
| Lancaster | 3,756 |
| Little Chute | 5,365 |
| Madison | 173,258 |
| Manitowoc | 33,430 |
| Marinette | 12,696 |

**WISCONSIN—Continued**

| | |
|---|---|
| Marshfield | 15,619 |
| Mauston | 3,466 |
| Mayville | 4,139 |
| Medford | 3,454 |
| Menasha | 14,905 |
| Menomonee Falls | 31,697 |
| Menomonie | 11,275 |
| Mequon | 12,110 |
| Merrill | 9,502 |
| Middleton | 8,286 |
| Milton | 3,699 |
| Milwaukee | 717,099 |
| Monona | 10,420 |
| Monroe | 8,654 |
| Muskego | 11,573 |
| Neenah | 22,892 |
| New Berlin | 26,937 |
| New London | 5,801 |
| New Richmond | 3,707 |
| North Fond du Lac | 3,286 |
| Oak Creek | 13,901 |
| Oconomowoc | 8,741 |
| Oconto | 4,667 |
| Onalaska | 4,909 |
| Oshkosh | 53,221 |
| Perry Go Place | 5,912 |
| Pewaukee | 3,271 |
| Platteville | 9,599 |
| Plymouth | 5,810 |
| Portage | 7,821 |
| Port Washington | 8,752 |
| Prairie Du Chien | 5,540 |
| Racine | 95,162 |
| Reedsburg | 4,585 |
| Rhinelander | 8,218 |
| Rice Lake | 7,278 |
| Richland Center | 5,086 |
| Ripon | 7,053 |
| River Falls | 7,238 |
| St. Francis | 10,489 |
| Shawano | 6,488 |
| Sheboygan | 48,484 |
| Sheboygan Falls | 4,771 |
| Shorewood | 15,576 |
| South Milwaukee | 23,297 |
| Sparta | 6,258 |
| Stevens Point | 23,479 |
| Stoughton | 6,081 |
| Sturgeon Bay | 6,776 |
| Sturtevant | 3,376 |
| Sun Prairie | 9,935 |
| Superior | 32,237 |
| Tomahawk | 3,419 |
| Tomah | 5,647 |
| Two Rivers | 13,553 |
| Viroqua | 3,739 |
| Watertown | 15,683 |
| Waukesha | 40,258 |
| Waupaca | 4,342 |
| Waupun | 7,946 |
| Wausau | 32,806 |
| Wauwatosa | 58,676 |
| West Allis | 71,723 |
| West Bend | 16,555 |
| West Milwaukee | 4,405 |
| Weston | 3,375 |
| Whitefish Bay | 17,394 |
| Whitewater | 12,038 |
| Wisconsin Rapids | 18,587 |

**WYOMING**

| | |
|---|---|
| Buffalo | 3,394 |
| Casper | 39,361 |
| Cheyenne | 40,914 |
| Cody | 5,161 |
| Evanston | 4,462 |
| Gillette | 7,194 |
| Green River | 4,196 |
| Lander | 7,125 |
| Laramie | 23,143 |
| Newcastle | 3,432 |
| Powell | 4,807 |
| Rawlins | 7,855 |
| Riverton | 7,995 |
| Rock Springs | 11,657 |
| Sheridan | 10,856 |
| Torrington | 4,237 |
| Warren | 4,527 |
| Worland | 5,055 |

## UNITED STATES POPULATION BY STATES

## FINAL 1970 CENSUS

| | |
|---|---|
| Alabama | 3,444,165 |
| Alaska | 302,173 |
| Arizona | 1,772,482 |
| Arkansas | 1,923,295 |
| California | 19,953,134 |
| Colorado | 2,207,259 |
| Connecticut | 3,032,217 |
| Delaware | 548,104 |
| District of Columbia | 756,510 |
| Florida | 6,789,443 |
| Georgia | 4,589,575 |
| Hawaii | 769,913 |
| Idaho | 713,008 |
| Illinois | 11,113,976 |
| Indiana | 5,193,669 |
| Iowa | 2,825,041 |
| Kansas | 2,249,071 |
| Kentucky | 3,219,311 |
| Louisiana | 3,643,180 |
| Maine | 993,663 |
| Maryland | 3,922,399 |
| Massachusetts | 5,689,170 |
| Michigan | 8,875,083 |
| Minnesota | 3,805,069 |
| Mississippi | 2,216,912 |
| Missouri | 4,677,399 |
| Montana | 694,409 |
| Nebraska | 1,483,791 |
| Nevada | 488,738 |
| New Hampshire | 737,681 |
| New Jersey | 7,168,164 |
| New Mexico | 1,016,000 |
| New York | 18,190,740 |
| North Carolina | 5,082,059 |
| North Dakota | 617,761 |
| Ohio | 10,652,017 |
| Oklahoma | 2,559,253 |
| Oregon | 2,091,385 |
| Pennsylvania | 11,793,909 |
| Rhode Island | 949,723 |
| South Carolina | 2,590,516 |
| South Dakota | 666,257 |
| Tennessee | 3,924,164 |
| Texas | 11,196,730 |
| Utah | 1,059,273 |
| Vermont | 444,732 |
| Virginia | 4,648,494 |
| Washington | 3,409,169 |
| West Virginia | 1,744,237 |
| Wisconsin | 4,417,933 |
| Wyoming | 332,416 |
| Total | 203,184,772 |

# PRINCIPAL FOREIGN CITIES

**Afghanistan**

| | |
|---|---|
| *Kabul | 300,000 |
| Kandahar | 77,000 |

**Albania**

| | |
|---|---|
| *Tirana | 59,887 |

**Algeria**

| | |
|---|---|
| *Algiers | 361,285 |
| Constantine | 149,253 |
| Oran | 299,018 |

**Argentina**

| | |
|---|---|
| Avellaneda | 323,671 |
| *Buenos Aires | 3,703,000 |
| Cordoba | 510,739 |
| General San Martin | 269,514 |
| La Plata | 351,813 |
| Lanus | 244,473 |
| Lomas de Zamora | 125,943 |
| Rosario | 761,300 |
| Santa Fe | 219,620 |
| Tucuman | 244,678 |
| Vicente Lopez | 149,958 |

**Australia**

| | |
|---|---|
| Adelaide | 562,500 |
| Brisbane | 567,000 |
| *Canberra | 43,973 |
| Hobart | 109,200 |
| Melbourne, Gr. | 1,777,700 |
| Newcastle | 192,940 |
| Perth | 389,000 |
| Sydney, Gr. | 2,054,800 |

**Austria**

| | |
|---|---|
| Graz | 231,223 |
| Innsbruck | 102,759 |
| Linz | 185,177 |
| Salzburg | 105,439 |
| *Vienna | 1,667,000 |

**Belgium**

| | |
|---|---|
| Antwerp | 849,432 |
| *Brussels | 1,398,326 |
| Charleroi | 469,259 |
| Ghent | 455,022 |
| Liege | 607,117 |
| Louvain | 343,782 |
| Namur | 225,634 |

**Bolivia**

| | |
|---|---|
| Cochabamba | 87,200 |
| *LaPaz | 339,279 |
| Oruro | 7,500 |
| Sucre | 53,800 |

**Brazil**

| | |
|---|---|
| Belem | 260,600 |
| Belo Horizonte | 501,428 |
| *Brasilia | 75,000 |
| Curitiba | 231,628 |
| Fortaleza | 280,100 |
| Natal | 106,300 |
| Niterol | 221,628 |
| Porto Alegre | 512,951 |
| Recife | 703,726 |
| Rio de Janeiro | 2,940,045 |
| Salvador | 532,619 |
| Santos | 253,629 |
| Sao Paulo | 3,417,208 |

**Bulgaria**

| | |
|---|---|
| Plovdiv | 162,518 |
| *Sofia | 725,756 |
| Varna | 119,769 |

**Burma**

| | |
|---|---|
| Mandalay | 186,000 |
| Moulmein | 103,000 |
| *Rangoon | 740,000 |

**Cambodia**

| | |
|---|---|
| *Phnom-Penh | 550,000 |

**Cameroun**

| | |
|---|---|
| *Yaounde | 38,000 |

**Canada**

| | |
|---|---|
| Calgary | 181,780 |
| Calgary, Gr. | 200,449 |
| Edmonton | 226,002 |
| Edmonton, Gr. | 251,004 |
| Halifax | 93,301 |
| Hamilton | 239,625 |
| London | 101,693 |
| Montreal | 1,109,439 |
| Montreal, Gr. | 1,620,758 |
| *Ottawa | 222,129 |
| *Ottawa, Gr. | 345,460 |

**Canada—Continued**

| | |
|---|---|
| Quebec | 170,703 |
| Quebec, Gr. | 309,959 |
| Regina | 89,755 |
| Saint John, Gr. | 86,105 |
| St. John's, Gr. | 77,991 |
| Saskatoon | 72,858 |
| Sherbrooke | 58,668 |
| Three Rivers | 50,483 |
| Toronto | 667,706 |
| Toronto, Gr. | 1,358,028 |
| Vancouver | 365,844 |
| Vancouver, Gr. | 665,017 |
| Verdun | 78,262 |
| Victoria | 54,584 |
| Victoria, Gr. | 125,447 |
| Windsor | 121,980 |
| Winnipeg | 255,093 |
| Winnipeg, Gr. | 409,121 |

**Ceylon**

| | |
|---|---|
| *Colombo | 426,127 |
| Jaffna | 77,000 |
| Kandy | 57,200 |

**Chile**

| | |
|---|---|
| Concepcion | 158,941 |
| *Santiago | 1,627,962 |
| Valparaiso | 261,684 |

**China**

| | |
|---|---|
| Amoy | 240,000 |
| Anshan | 400,000 |
| Canton | 1,650,000 |
| Changsha | 700,000 |
| Changteh | 300,000 |
| Chengtu | 440,000 |
| Chenteh (Jehol) | 510,000 |
| Chinkiang | 220,000 |
| Chungking | 1,620,000 |
| Dairen | 1,054,000 |
| Fatshan | 450,000 |
| Foochow | 400,000 |
| Hangchow | 600,000 |
| Hankow | 800,000 |
| Hong Kong, Br. | 2,857,000 |
| Hsinking (Changchun) | 420,000 |
| Kowloon | 675,000 |
| Lanchow | 600,000 |
| Macao, Port | 187,772 |
| Nanking | 1,113,972 |
| Ningpo | 218,774 |
| *Peiping | 4,140,000 |
| Pin-chiang (Harbin) | 760,000 |
| Shanghai | 7,100,000 |
| Shenyang (Mukden) | 2,290,000 |
| Sian | 1,500,000 |
| Siangtan | 300,000 |
| Soochow | 260,000 |
| Taiyuan | 500,000 |
| Tientsin | 3,100,000 |
| Tsinan | 472,279 |
| Tsingtao | 850,508 |
| Wenchow | 631,276 |
| Wuhan | 1,800,000 |
| Yanchow | 250,000 |

**China (Taiwan)**

| | |
|---|---|
| Kaohsiung | 371,225 |
| Keelung | 197,029 |
| Taichung | 249,946 |
| Tainan | 287,797 |
| *Taipei | 759,200 |

**Colombia**

| | |
|---|---|
| Barranquilla | 400,000 |
| *Bogota | 1,044,760 |
| Bucaramanga | 163,460 |
| Cali | 404,870 |
| Cartagena | 162,610 |
| Medellin | 545,860 |

**Congo, Rep. of**

| | |
|---|---|
| Elisabethville | 182,638 |
| *Leopoldville | 389,547 |

**Costa Rica**

| | |
|---|---|
| Puntarenas | 15,272 |
| *San Jose, Gr. | 225,000 |

**Cuba**

| | |
|---|---|
| Camaguey | 204,254 |
| *Havana, Gr. | 1,158,203 |
| Holguin | 226,644 |
| Marianao | 229,576 |
| Santa Clara | 144,630 |

**Cuba—Continued**

| | |
|---|---|
| Santiago de Cuba | 166,565 |

**Cyprus**

| | |
|---|---|
| *Nicosia | 82,000 |

**Czechoslovakia**

| | |
|---|---|
| Bratislava | 247,000 |
| Brno | 306,000 |
| Ostrava | 199,902 |
| Pizen (Pilsen) | 134,000 |
| *Prague | 978,000 |

**Denmark**

| | |
|---|---|
| Aarhus | 118,493 |
| *Copenhagen | 786,105 |
| *Copenhagen, Gr. | 1,168,340 |
| Frederiksberg | 118,993 |
| Odense | 105,915 |

**Dominican Republic**

| | |
|---|---|
| *Ciudad Trujillo | 272,769 |

**Ecuador**

| | |
|---|---|
| Guayaquil | 403,184 |
| *Quito | 277,270 |

**Egypt, UAR**

| | |
|---|---|
| Alexandria | 1,400,000 |
| Assiut | 250,000 |
| *Cairo | 2,800,000 |
| Mansura | 101,965 |
| Port Said | 178,432 |
| Suez | 108,250 |
| Tanta | 140,000 |

**El Salvador**

| | |
|---|---|
| *San Salvador | 203,000 |
| Santa Ana | 109,711 |

**Ethiopia**

| | |
|---|---|
| *Addis Ababa | 500,000 |
| Asmara | 132,000 |

**Finland**

| | |
|---|---|
| *Helsinki (Helsingfors) | 453,800 |
| Lahti | 63,800 |
| Tampere | 123,000 |
| Turku (Abo) | 123,000 |

**France**

| | |
|---|---|
| Bordeaux | 257,946 |
| Havre | 165,000 |
| Lille | 194,616 |
| Lyons | 471,270 |
| Marseilles | 661,492 |
| Nantes | 222,790 |
| Nice | 244,360 |
| *Paris | 2,850,189 |
| *Paris Gr. | 6,600,000 |
| St. Etienne | 181,730 |
| Strasbourg | 200,921 |
| Toulouse | 268,863 |

**French Africa Former**

| | |
|---|---|
| Abidjan | 127,000 |
| Bamako | 168,000 |
| Brazzaville | 105,200 |
| Dakar | 230,000 |
| Tananarive | 206,324 |

**Germany, West**

| | |
|---|---|
| Aachen | 159,500 |
| Augsburg | 203,000 |
| Berlin (West) | 2,223,800 |
| Bielefeld | 174,700 |
| Bonn | 141,600 |
| Bremen | 535,100 |
| Bremerhaven | 135,000 |
| Bochum | 356,900 |
| Brunswick | 244,400 |
| Cologne | 749,500 |
| Dortmund | 629,500 |
| Duisburg | 495,600 |
| Dusseldorf | 679,200 |
| Essen | 719,800 |
| Frankfort | 643,100 |
| Freiburg | 134,700 |
| Gelsenkirchen | 387,900 |
| Hagen | 186,300 |
| Hamburg | 1,796,700 |
| Hanover | 558,100 |
| Heidelberg | 125,800 |
| Herne | 116,100 |
| Karlsruhe | 229,900 |
| Kassel | 196,800 |
| Kiel | 263,900 |
| Krefeld | 203,300 |

**Germany, West—Continued**

| | |
|---|---|
| Lubeck | 230,200 |
| Ludwigshaven | 154,700 |
| Mannheim | 297,000 |
| Mulheim (Ruhr) | 177,400 |
| Munchen-Gladbach | 150,000 |
| Munich | 1,016,500 |
| Nurnberg | 436,900 |
| Oberhausen | 253,900 |
| Oldenburg | 119,900 |
| Osnabruck | 132,300 |
| Recklinghausen | 128,400 |
| Remsheid | 121,300 |
| Solingen | 165,000 |
| Stuttgart | 617,800 |
| Wiesbaden | 250,700 |
| Wuppertal | 413,300 |

**Germany, East**

| | |
|---|---|
| *Berlin (East) | 1,200,000 |
| Chemnitz (Karl Marx Stadt) | 289,000 |
| Dresden | 492,000 |
| Erfurt | 186,000 |
| Halle | 285,000 |
| Leipzig | 607,655 |
| Magdeburg | 259,000 |
| Rostock | 114,869 |
| Zwickau | 148,793 |

**Ghana**

| | |
|---|---|
| *Accra | 135,926 |

**Greece**

| | |
|---|---|
| *Athens | 1,378,586 |
| Patras | 109,000 |
| Peiraieus (Piraeus) | 186,014 |
| Thessaloniki (Salonika) | 310,000 |

**Guatemala**

| | |
|---|---|
| *Guatemala City | 385,000 |
| Quezaltenango | 36,209 |

**Guinea**

| | |
|---|---|
| *Conakry | 80,000 |

**Haiti**

| | |
|---|---|
| Aux Cayes | 80,000 |
| Cap-Haitien | 60,000 |
| Gonaives | 75,000 |
| *Port-au-Prince | 200,000 |

**Honduras**

| | |
|---|---|
| *Tegucigalpa | 125,000 |
| San Pedro Sula | 58,931 |

**Hungary**

| | |
|---|---|
| *Budapest | 1,164,963 |
| *Budapest, Gr. | 1,850,000 |
| Debrecen | 130,000 |
| Miskolc | 175,000 |
| Szeged | 136,752 |

**Iceland**

| | |
|---|---|
| *Reykjavik | 73,000 |

**India**

| | |
|---|---|
| Agra | 375,665 |
| Ahmedabad | 788,333 |
| Allahabad | 332,295 |
| Amritsar | 325,747 |
| Benares | 355,777 |
| Bangalore | 778,977 |
| Bombay | 2,840,011 |
| Calcutta | 3,132,114 |
| Delhi | 914,790 |
| Howrah | 433,630 |
| Hyderabad | 1,085,722 |
| Indore | 310,859 |
| Kanpur | 705,383 |
| Lucknow | 496,861 |
| Madras | 1,416,056 |
| Madura | 361,781 |
| Nagpur | 449,099 |
| *New Delhi | 2,000,000 |
| Poona | 480,982 |
| Srinagar | 207,787 |

**Indonesia**

| | |
|---|---|
| Bandung | 931,477 |
| *Jakarta (Batavia) | 2,800,000 |
| Jogjakarta | 428,000 |
| Medan | 410,000 |
| Makassar | 271,364 |
| Palembang | 244,269 |
| Semarang | 337,299 |
| Solo | 500,000 |
| Surabaya | 1,248,300 |

**Iran**

| | |
|---|---|
| Abadan | 283,625 |
| Arak | 352,718 |
| Hamadan | 416,789 |
| Isfahan | 255,000 |
| Meshed | 242,000 |
| Resht | 342,097 |
| Shiraz | 170,000 |
| Tabriz | 290,000 |
| *Tehran | 2,000,000 |

**Iraq**

| | |
|---|---|
| *Baghdad | 1,306,604 |
| Basra | 717,500 |
| Mosul | 502,884 |

**Ireland**

| | |
|---|---|
| Cork | 80,011 |
| *Dublin | 539,476 |
| Drogheda | 17,008 |
| Galway | 21,219 |
| Kilkenny | 10,607 |
| Limerick | 50,886 |
| Waterford | 28,878 |

**Israel**

| | |
|---|---|
| Haifa | 170,000 |
| *Jerusalem | 161,000 |
| Ramat Gan | 71,500 |
| Tel Aviv-Jaffa | 380,000 |

**Italy**

| | |
|---|---|
| Bari | 310,000 |
| Bologna | 418,428 |
| Catania | 355,515 |
| Florence | 421,989 |
| Genoa | 749,580 |
| Messina | 245,450 |
| Milan | 1,434,632 |
| Naples | 1,434,402 |
| Palermo | 582,563 |
| *Rome | 2,100,000 |
| Trieste | 286,965 |
| Turin | 920,789 |
| Venice | 341,761 |

**Japan**

| | |
|---|---|
| Amagasaki | 363,032 |
| Fukuoka | 500,388 |
| Hakodate | 243,783 |
| Hiroshima | 364,677 |
| Kawasaki | 430,543 |
| Kobe | 1,012,192 |
| Kure | 188,000 |
| Kyoto | 1,210,107 |
| Nagasaki | 299,811 |
| Nagoya | 1,387,019 |
| Osaka | 2,632,000 |
| Sapporo | 349,671 |
| Sendai | 383,752 |
| Shizuoka | 292,142 |
| *Tokyo, Gr. | 9,311,774 |
| Yawata | 279,273 |
| Yokohama | 1,182,209 |
| Yokosuka | 274,827 |

**Jordan**

| | |
|---|---|
| *Amman | 70,000 |
| *Amman (district) | 250,000 |

**Kenya (Brit.)**

| | |
|---|---|
| *Nairobi | 186,000 |

**Korea**

| | |
|---|---|
| Inchon | 361,000 |
| Pusan (Fusan) | 1,087,000 |
| Pyongyang (Heijo) | 285,965 |
| *Seoul (Keijo) | 2,093,000 |
| Taegu | 643,000 |

**Laos**

| | |
|---|---|
| *Luang Prabang | 45,000 |
| *Vientiane | 120,000 |

**Lebanon**

| | |
|---|---|
| *Beirut | 450,000 |
| Tripoli | 100,000 |
| Zahle | 40,000 |

**Liberia**

| | |
|---|---|
| *Monrovia | 53,000 |

**Libya**

| | |
|---|---|
| *Bengazi | 70,533 |
| Misurata | 63,000 |
| *Tripoli | 144,000 |

**Liechtenstein**

| | |
|---|---|
| *Vaduz | 3,300 |

**Luxemburg**

| | |
|---|---|
| *Luxemburg | 70,000 |

**Malaya**

| | |
|---|---|
| *Kuala Lumpur | 316,230 |
| Penang | 234,930 |
| Singapore | 1,236,000 |

**Mexico**

| | |
|---|---|
| Aguascalientes | 103,677 |
| Chihuahua | 113,677 |

**Mexico—Continued**

| | |
|---|---|
| Guadalajara | 700,000 |
| Juarez | 187,451 |
| Leon | 165,625 |
| Merida | 181,725 |
| Mexicali | 105,087 |
| *Mexico, Gr. | 4,966,662 |
| Monterey | 615,000 |
| Puebla | 275,667 |
| San Luis Potosi | 168,496 |
| Tampico | 128,428 |
| Torreon | 175,921 |
| Veracruz | 127,286 |

**Mongolian Rep.**

| | |
|---|---|
| *Ulan Bator | 150,000 |

**Morocco**

| | |
|---|---|
| Casablanca | 700,000 |
| Fez | 280,000 |
| Marrakech | 230,000 |
| Meknes | 150,000 |
| *Rabat | 180,000 |
| Tangier | 140,000 |
| Tetuan | 85,000 |

**Nepal**

| | |
|---|---|
| *Katmandu | 175,000 |

**Netherlands**

| | |
|---|---|
| *Amsterdam | 871,577 |
| Arnhem | 121,376 |
| Eindhoven | 159,249 |
| Enschede | 120,480 |
| Groningen | 143,715 |
| The Hague | 606,728 |
| Haarlem | 167,950 |
| Nijmegen | 124,697 |
| Rotterdam | 726,188 |
| Tilburg | 132,877 |
| Utrecht | 249,324 |

**New Zealand**

| | |
|---|---|
| Auckland | 401,500 |
| Christchurch | 205,500 |
| Dunedin | 101,600 |
| *Wellington (incl. Hutt) | 231,900 |

**Nicaragua**

| | |
|---|---|
| *Managua | 176,569 |

**Nigeria (Brit.)**

| | |
|---|---|
| Ibadan | 500,000 |
| *Lagos | 320,000 |
| Ogomosho | 139,000 |
| Oshogobo | 122,000 |

**Norway**

| | |
|---|---|
| Bergen | 115,000 |
| *Oslo | 461,591 |
| Stravanger | 52,000 |
| Trondheim | 59,000 |

**Pakistan**

| | |
|---|---|
| Chittagong | 294,046 |
| Dacca | 411,000 |
| *Karachi | 1,126,417 |
| Lahore | 849,000 |
| Peshawar | 151,776 |
| Rawalpindi | 237,219 |

**Panama**

| | |
|---|---|
| Colon | 55,000 |
| *Panama | 200,000 |

**Paraguay**

| | |
|---|---|
| *Asuncion | 210,000 |
| Concepcion | 28,357 |
| Encarnacion | 33,664 |
| Villarica | 26,000 |

**Peru**

| | |
|---|---|
| Arequipa | 121,896 |
| Callao | 129,365 |
| Cuzco | 68,483 |
| *Lima | 1,186,212 |

**Philippines**

| | |
|---|---|
| Cebu | 167,503 |
| Davao | 111,263 |
| Iloilo | 110,122 |
| Manila, Gr. | 2,022,420 |
| *Quezon City | 107,977 |
| Zamboanga | 103,317 |

**Poland**

| | |
|---|---|
| Bydgoszcz | 216,200 |
| Gdansk (Dansig) | 265,500 |
| Kartowice | 205,500 |
| Krakow | 469,400 |
| Lodz | 687,300 |
| Poznan | 383,300 |
| Szczecin (Stettin) | 244,200 |
| *Warsaw | 1,102,258 |
| Wroclaw (Breslau) | 396,100 |

**Portugal**

| | |
|---|---|
| Funchal | 63,700 |
| *Lisbon | 794,200 |
| Porto | 283,500 |

**Rhodesia, Fed. of**

| | |
|---|---|
| *Salisbury | 260,800 |

**Rumania**

| | |
|---|---|
| Arad | 106,457 |
| Braila | 102,491 |
| *Bucharest | 1,236,905 |
| Cluj | 154,752 |
| Ploesti | 114,560 |
| Timisoara | 142,251 |

**Saudi Arabia**

| | |
|---|---|
| Jedda | 250,000 |
| Hofuf | 120,000 |
| Mecca | 300,000 |
| *Riyadh | 280,000 |

**Somalia Rep.**

| | |
|---|---|
| *Mogadishu | 74,056 |

**So. Africa, Union of**

| | |
|---|---|
| Bloemfontein | 147,900 |
| Cape Town | 729,200 |
| Durban | 634,400 |
| Johannesburg | 1,052,600 |
| *Pretoria | 343,400 |

**Spain**

| | |
|---|---|
| Barcelona | 1,467,000 |
| Bilbao | 268,000 |
| Cadiz | 107,856 |
| Cordoba | 178,973 |
| Granada | 232,054 |
| *Madrid | 2,000,000 |
| Malaga | 299,745 |
| Murcia | 233,239 |
| Palma | 140,000 |
| Seville | 419,000 |
| Valencia | 544,306 |
| Zaragoza | 292,000 |

**Sudan**

| | |
|---|---|
| *Khartoum | 93,103 |
| Omdurman | 132,619 |

**Sweden**

| | |
|---|---|
| Boras | 66,444 |
| Eskilstuna | 58,536 |
| Goteborg | 400,532 |
| Halsingborg | 76,218 |
| Malmo | 225,630 |
| *Stockholm | 807,200 |
| *Stockholm, Gr. | 1,114,903 |
| Upsala | 76,166 |
| Vasteras | 76,167 |

**Switzerland**

| | |
|---|---|
| Basel | 200,700 |
| *Berne | 161,300 |
| Geneva | 168,900 |
| Lausanne | 118,900 |
| Zurich | 428,200 |

**Syria, UAR**

| | |
|---|---|
| Aleppo | 400,000 |
| *Damascus | 395,000 |
| Homs | 293,500 |
| Hamma | 173,000 |
| Lattakia | 109,216 |

**Thailand**

| | |
|---|---|
| *Bangkok | 1,773,318 |

**Togo Rep.**

| | |
|---|---|
| *Lome | 39,200 |

**Tunisia**

| | |
|---|---|
| Bizerte | 46,681 |
| Sfax | 65,635 |
| Sousse | 48,172 |
| *Tunis | 680,000 |

**Turkey**

| | |
|---|---|
| Adana | 172,465 |
| *Ankara | 453,151 |
| Bursa | 131,336 |
| Izmir | 286,210 |
| Istanbul | 1,214,616 |

**U.S.S.R.**

| | |
|---|---|
| Alma-Ata | 455,000 |
| Archangel | 256,600 |
| Astrakhan | 294,000 |
| Baku | 968,000 |
| Barnaul | 320,000 |
| Cheliabinsk | 688,000 |
| Dniepropetrovsk | 658,000 |
| Erivan | 509,000 |
| Gorky (Nizhni Novgorod) | 942,000 |
| Gorlovka | 293,000 |
| Irkutsk | 365,000 |
| Ivanovo | 332,000 |
| Kaliningrad (Koenigsberg) | 202,000 |
| Karaganda | 398,000 |
| Kazan | 643,000 |
| Khabarovsk | 322,000 |
| Kharkov | 930,000 |

**U.S.S.R.—Continued**

| | |
|---|---|
| Kirov Rog | 252,000 |
| Kiev | 1,102,000 |
| Klaipeda (Memel) | 89,000 |
| Krasmoyarsk | 409,000 |
| Krasnodar | 312,000 |
| Krivoy Rog | 386,000 |
| Kuibyshev | 806,000 |
| Leningrad | 3,300,000 |
| Lugansk | 274,000 |
| Lvov (Lemberg) | 410,000 |
| Magnitogorsk | 311,000 |
| Makeyevka | 358,000 |
| Minsk | 509,000 |
| *Moscow | 5,032,000 |
| *Moscow, Gr. | 7,000,000 |
| Murmansk | 226,000 |
| Nikolayev | 224,000 |
| Nizhni Tagil | 338,000 |
| Novosibirsk | 887,000 |
| Odessa | 667,000 |
| Omsk | 579,000 |
| Penza | 254,000 |
| Perm | 628,000 |
| Riga | 605,000 |
| Rostov-on-Don | 597,000 |
| Saratov | 581,000 |
| Sevastopol | 148,000 |
| Stalingrad | 591,000 |
| Stalino | 701,000 |
| Stalinsk | 377,000 |
| Sverdlovsk | 777,000 |
| Tallinn | 280,000 |
| Tashkent | 911,000 |
| Tiflis | 694,000 |
| Tomsk | 249,000 |
| Tula | 345,000 |
| Ufa | 546,000 |
| Vilnius (Vilna) | 235,000 |
| Vladivostok | 283,000 |
| Voronezh | 454,000 |
| Yalta | 40,000 |
| Yaroslavl | 406,000 |
| Zaporozhie | 435,000 |
| Zhdanov | 284,000 |

**United Arab Republic**

See Egypt, Syria

**UNITED KINGDOM**

**England**

| | |
|---|---|
| Birmingham | 1,103,000 |
| Bradford | 287,800 |
| Bristol | 439,600 |
| Coventry | 277,000 |
| Croydon | 249,000 |
| Kingston-on-Hull | 301,100 |
| Leeds | 511,600 |
| Leicester | 281,200 |
| Liverpool | 768,700 |
| *London | 3,225,000 |
| *London, Gr. | 8,222,340 |
| Manchester | 696,700 |
| Newcastle | 275,100 |
| Nottingham | 313,000 |
| Oxford | 104,400 |
| Plymouth | 217,900 |
| Portsmouth | 226,900 |
| Sheffield | 498,800 |
| Stoke-on-Trent | 272,000 |

**Wales**

| | |
|---|---|
| Aberdare | 40,100 |
| Barry | 42,020 |
| Cardiff | 251,300 |
| Merthyr Tydfil | 59,300 |
| Neath | 31,170 |
| Swansea | 162,300 |

**Scotland**

| | |
|---|---|
| Aberdeen | 186,190 |
| Dundee | 179,225 |
| Edinburgh | 465,671 |
| Glasgow | 1,079,364 |

**Northern Ireland**

| | |
|---|---|
| Belfast | 440,100 |
| Londonderry | 51,600 |

**Uruguay**

| | |
|---|---|
| *Montevideo | 722,885 |

**Venezuela**

| | |
|---|---|
| Barquisimeto | 203,000 |
| *Caracas, Gr. | 1,371,875 |
| Maracaibo | 456,000 |
| Valencia | 143,000 |

**Vietnam**

| | |
|---|---|
| Haiphong | 188,600 |
| Hanoi | 297,900 |
| Hue | 96,400 |
| *Saigon | 1,800,000 |
| Vinh | 150,000 |

**Yemen**

| | |
|---|---|
| Hodeida | 40,000 |
| *Sana | 75,000 |
| *Taiz | 25,000 |

**Yugoslavia**

| | |
|---|---|
| *Belgrade | 700,000 |
| Ljubljana | 146,000 |
| Sarajevo | 166,000 |
| Skopje | 156,000 |
| Subotica | 118,000 |
| Zagreb | 441,000 |

# LANDS OF THE WORLD

**Afghanistan,** Const. monarchy, in Southwest Asia. Much of the country is mountainous and arid. Most of the people are Moslems. 250,000 sq. mi. Pop. 15,271,681. Capital: Kabul.

**Albania,** Republic, in Southeastern Europe. Communist regime established in 1945. Large number of the people are Moslems. 11,097 sq. mi. Pop. 1,865,000. Capital: Tirana.

**Algeria,** Republic, in North Africa on the Mediterranean Sea. Belonged to France from 1848 until independence in 1962. 917,537 sq. mi. Pop. 11,500,000. Capital: Algiers.

**Andorra,** Principality, in Europe in Pyrenees Mts. between France and Spain. Nominally under the joint-rule of the President of France and the Spanish Bishop of Urgel but actually governed by elected Council. 191 sq. mi. Pop. 14,408. Capital: Andorra la Vella.

**Angola,** Overseas province of Portugal, on west coast of Africa. 481,351 sq. mi. Pop. 5,154,-000. Capital: Luanda.

**Argentina,** Republic, covering much of southern half of So. America. Second only to Brazil in size among So. American countries. 1,072,700 sq. mi. Pop. 22,691,000. Capital: Buenos Aires.

**Australia,** Commonwealth, on island continent between Pacific and Indian Oceans. The sovereign of Great Britain is also sovereign of this independent member of the Commonwealth of Nations. 2,967,909 sq. mi. Pop. 11,478,703. Capital: Canberra.

**Austria,** Republic, in Central Europe. Most Austrians are German-speaking. 32,376 sq. mi. Pop. 7,255,000. Capital: Vienna.

**Bahamas,** Self-governing British colony of about 700 islands, of which 30 are inhabited, in the Atlantic Ocean off the coast of Florida. 4,404 sq. mi. Pop. 138,700. Capital: Nassau.

**Bahrain,** Arab sheikdom under British protection, on an archipelago in Persian Gulf. 231 sq. mi. Pop. 185,000. Capital: Manama.

**Barbados,** Independent member of the Commonwealth of Nations, in Caribbean Sea. 166 sq. mi. Pop. 245,000. Capital: Bridgetown.

**Belgium,** Const. monarchy, in Northwestern Europe. A highly industrialized nation and important producer of steel. 11,775 sq. mi. Pop. 9,464,000. Capital: Brussels.

**Bermuda,** British possession consisting of 360 islands (20 inhabited), in western Atlantic Ocean. 21 sq. mi. Pop. 47,000. Capital: Hamilton.

**Bhutan,** Semi-independent kingdom in eastern Himalayas, Asia; guided in foreign affairs by India. 18,000 sq. mi. Pop. 700,000. Cap.: Thimbu.

**Bolivia,** Republic, lies on both sides of the Andes Mts. in So. America. More than half of the population are Indians. 416,000 sq. mi. Pop. 3,697,000. Capital: Sucre is legal capital, but La Paz is actual seat of government.

**Botswana,** Republic, in Southern Africa. Formerly British protectorate of Bechuanaland. Member, Commonwealth of Nations. 275,000 sq. mi. Pop. 559,000. Capital: Gaberones.

**Brazil,** Republic in So. America. Largest of the So. American countries. President, elected by Congress rather than popular vote, has great powers. 3,286,473 sq. mi. Pop. 85,655,000. Capital: Brasilia.

**British Honduras,** Self-governing British colony in Central America. 8,867 sq. mi. Pop. 106,-000. Capital: Belize.

**Brunei,** Sultanate under British protection, on northwest side of the island of Borneo. 2,226 sq. mi. Pop. 101,000. Capital: Brunei.

**Bulgaria,** Republic, in Southeast Europe. Communist regime modeled after that of USSR. 42,796 sq. mi. Pop. 8,226,564. Capital: Sofia.

**Burma,** Republic, in Southeast Asia. Full independence of British Empire achieved in 1948. Buddhism is the state religion. 261,789 sq. mi. Pop. 24,732,000. Capital: Rangoon.

**Burundi,** Const. monarchy, in Central Africa. Formerly part of Belgian UN Trusteeship territory of Ruanda-Urundi. 10,744 sq. mi. Pop. 2,600,000. Capital: Bujumbura.

**Cambodia,** Const. monarchy, in Southeast Asia. Formerly part of French Indo-China. 88,780 sq. mi. Pop. 6,200,000. Capital: Phnom Penh.

**Cameroun,** Republic, on west coast of Africa. German colony before World War I. France and Britain held until 1960 and 1961. 183,381 sq. mi. Pop. 5,210,000. Capital: Yaoundé.

**Canada,** Commonwealth in No. America. First of the countries to become independent within the British Commonwealth of Nations. 3,851,-809 sq. mi. Pop. 19,859,000. Capital: Ottawa.

**Canal Zone,** Territory leased by the United States from the Republic of Panama. Canal runs through this strip which is 50 mi. long and 10 mi. wide. 553 sq. mi. Pop. 54,100.

**Canary Islands,** Provinces of Spain, in the Atlantic Ocean off the coast of Northwest Africa. 2,807 sq. mi. Pop. 944,448.

**Cape Verde Islands,** Overseas province of Portugal, in Atlantic Ocean off west coast of Africa. 1,557 sq. mi. Pop. 218,000.

**Carolines, Marianas, Marshalls,** Islands in Western Pacific Ocean administered by the United States as a UN trusteeship.

**Central African Republic,** in Central Africa directly north of the Congo. Formerly part of French Equatorial Africa, now member of the French Community. 238,000 sq. mi. Pop. 1,352,000. Capital: Bangui.

---

KENNETH S. COOPER, B.A., M.A., Ph.D., *Professor of History,* George Peabody College for Teachers.

**Ceylon,** Independent member of the Commonwealth of Nations, island in the Indian Ocean. This country has announced its eventual intention of becoming a republic. 25,332 sq. mi. Pop. 11,232,000. Capital: Colombo.

**Chad, Republic of,** in Central Africa. Formerly part of French Equatorial Africa, now a member of the French Community. 495,000 sq. mi. Pop. 4,000,000. Capital: Fort-Lamy.

**Channel Islands,** British dependency, off northwest coast of France, including islands of Jersey, Guernsey, Alderney, Brechou, Great Sark, Little Sark, Herm, Jethou, and Lihou. 75 sq. mi. Pop. 110,708.

**Chile,** Republic, on west coast of So. America. A long, narrow country consisting of the strip of land between the Andes Mts. and the Pacific Ocean. 286,396 sq. mi. Pop. 8,567,000. Capital: Santiago.

**China, People's Republic of,** occupies large part of East Asia. Communist regime has held Chinese mainland since 1949. The most populous country in the world. 3,746,450 sq. mi. Pop. 760,300,000. Capital: Peking.

**China, Republic of,** on Taiwan (Formosa), an island 110 mi. off the shore of the Chinese mainland. Since 1949 Nationalist government has held only this part of China. 13,886 sq. mi. Pop. 12,819,728. Capital: Taipei.

**Colombia,** Republic, in So. America. Second among world's coffee producing countries. 455,335 sq. mi. Pop. 17,787,000. Capital: Bogota.

**Commonwealth of Nations,** an organization of independent states which were formerly parts of the British Empire and Commonwealth. The 26 full members include in addition to the United Kingdom: Australia, Barbados, Botswana, Canada, Ceylon, Cyprus, Gambia, Ghana, Guyana, India, Jamaica, Kenya, Lesotho, Malawi, Malaysia, Malta, New Zealand, Nigeria, Pakistan, Sierra Leone, Singapore, Tanzania, Trinidad and Tobago, Uganda, Zambia.

**Congo (Brazzaville), Republic of,** Republic, in Central Africa. Formerly French Congo, now independent member of the French Community. 139,000 sq. mi. Pop. 900,000. Capital: Brazzaville.

**Congo, Democratic Republic of,** Republic, in Central Africa. Formerly Belgian Congo. Largest African state south of the Sahara. 904,757 sq. mi. Pop. 15,627,000. Capital: Kinshasa (formerly Leopoldville).

**Costa Rica,** Republic, in Central America, located on the strip which connects No. and So. America. 23,421 sq. mi. Pop. 1,433,000. Capital: San José.

**Crete,** Part of Greece, a large island in the eastern Mediterranean Sea. 3,324 sq. mi. Pop. 482,021.

**Cuba,** Republic, island in the Caribbean Sea. Pro-Communist regime came into power in 1959. 44,206 sq. mi. Pop. 7,631,000. Capital: Havana.

**Cyprus,** Republic, on island in eastern Mediterranean Sea. Formerly British colony, now a member of the Commonwealth of Nations. Most of the people speak Greek; Turkish is the second language. 3,572 sq. mi. Pop. 598,-000. Capital: Nicosia.

**Czechoslovakia,** Republic, in Central Europe. Communist regime took power in 1948. 49,367 sq. mi. Pop. 14,159,000. Capital: Prague.

**Dahomey,** Republic, in West Africa. Formerly part of French West Africa, but has been fully independent since 1960. 44,290 sq. mi. Pop. 2,300,000. Capital: Porto-Novo.

**Denmark,** Const. monarchy, in Northwestern Europe. Smallest in area of the Scandinavian countries. 16,619 sq. mi. Pop. 4,758,000. Capital: Copenhagen.

**Dominican Republic,** in the Caribbean Sea, on the eastern two-thirds of the island of Hispaniola. Santo Domingo, the principal city, founded in 1496, was the first European settlement in the Western Hemisphere. 19,333 sq. mi. Pop. 3,619,000. Capital: Santo Domingo.

**Ecuador,** Republic, on west coast of So. America. The name of the country, Spanish for Equator, indicates its location. 116,270 sq. mi. Pop. 5,084,000. Capital: Quito.

**Egypt** (*see* UNITED ARAB REPUBLIC).

**El Salvador,** Republic, in Central America. Smallest of the Central American states. 8,259 sq. mi. Pop. 2,929,000. Capital: San Salvador.

**England** (*see* UNITED KINGDOM).

**Estonia,** A one-time Republic, on the Baltic Sea in Eastern Europe, now incorporated into the USSR but still recognized by the United States. 17,413 sq. mi. Pop. 1,273,000. Capital: Tallinn.

**Ethiopia,** Const. monarchy, in East Africa. According to ancient tradition, the first king of this country was the son of Solomon and the Queen of Sheba. 398,350 sq. mi. Pop. 22,590,000. Capital: Addis Ababa.

**Federation of South Arabia,** on south coast of the Arabian peninsula. Consists of Aden and 19 other small states. Under British protectorate until Nov. 30, 1967 when it received independence as Republic of South Yemen. 112,000 sq. mi. Pop. 1,220,000.

**Finland,** Republic, in Northern Europe. Ruled by Sweden from 1154 to 1809, by Russia from 1809 to 1917, independence declared in 1917. 130,165 sq. mi. Pop. 4,630,000. Capital: Helsinki.

**France,** Republic, in Western Europe. Present government, established in 1958, is fifth republic since 1793. 212,659 sq. mi. Pop. 49,-157,000. Capital: Paris.

**French Afar Territory,** Overseas territory of France, in East Africa. Formerly known as French Somaliland. 8,880 sq. mi. Pop. 86,000. Capital: Djibouti.

**French Community,** An organization of lands which were formerly French overseas departments or territories. Major members include: France, Central African Republic, Chad, Republic of Senegal, Congo (Brazzaville), Gabon, and Malagasy.

**French Guiana,** Overseas department (or district) of France, in So. America. 35,135 sq. mi. Pop. 35,000. Capital: Cayenne.

**Gabon Republic,** on west coast of Africa. Formerly part of French Equatorial Africa, now a member of the French Community, 102,290 sq. mi. Pop. 4,612,000. Capital: Libreville.

**Gambia,** Independent member of the Commonwealth of Nations, on west coast of Africa. Smallest African country. 4,005 sq. mi. Pop. 330,000. Capital: Bathurst.

**Germany, Federal Republic of,** in Central Europe. Commonly known as West Germany, it includes more than two-thirds of modern Germany. 95,931 sq. mi. Pop. 58,900,000. Capital: Bonn.

**Germany (German Democratic Republic),** in Central Europe. The Communist ruled eastern third of modern Germany. 41,645 sq. mi. Pop. 17,028,000. Capital: East Berlin.

**Ghana,** Republic, in West Africa. Formerly British Gold Coast colony, now member of the Commonwealth of Nations. 91,843 sq. mi. Pop. 7,740,000. Capital: Accra.

**Gibraltar,** British colony, on southernmost tip of Spanish peninsula, Southwest Europe. 2.5 sq. mi. Pop. 24,287.

**Great Britain** (*see* UNITED KINGDOM).

**Greece,** Const. monarchy, in Southeastern Europe. Homeland of the greatest philosophers twenty-five centuries ago. 51,843 sq. mi. Pop. 8,510,000. Capital: Athens.

**Greenland,** Integral part of Denmark, island in North Atlantic. World's largest island, permanent ice cap covers 84% of area. 840,000 sq. mi. Pop. 39,500. Capital: Godthaab.

**Guam,** Territory of the United States, in Pacific Ocean. Acquired from Spain in 1898. 209 sq. mi. Pop. 76,500. Capital: Agana.

**Guatemala,** Republic, in Central America immediately south of Mexico. Site of the oldest Mayan civilization. 42,042 sq. mi. Pop. 4,-438,000. Capital: Guatemala City.

**Guinea,** Republic, on west coast of Africa. Formerly French protectorate. 96,865 sq. mi. Pop. 3,500,000. Capital: Conakry.

**Guyana,** Independent member of the Commonwealth of Nations, on the northern coast of So. America. Formerly British Guiana. 83,000 sq. mi. Pop. 647,000. Capital: Georgetown.

**Haiti,** Republic, on western third of Hispaniola island in Caribbean Sea. French colony before securing independence in 1804. 10,714 sq. mi. Pop. 4,660,000. Capital: Port-au-Prince.

**Honduras,** Republic, in Central America. Spanish colony until 1821. 44,482 sq. mi. Pop. 2,284,000. Capital: Tegucigalpa.

**Hong Kong,** British colony, on South China coast. The main island acquired from China in 1842. 391 sq. mi. Pop. 3,804,000. Capital: Victoria.

**Hungary,** Republic, in Central Europe. Communist regime came into power following World War II. 35,918 sq. mi. Pop. 10,148,000. Capital: Budapest.

**Iceland,** Republic, on island in North Atlantic Ocean. Prior to 1941 King of Denmark was also King of Iceland. Parliamentary assembly is the oldest in the world. 39,758 sq. mi. Pop. 208,000. Capital: Reykjavik.

**India,** Republic, subcontinent of South Asia. Secured independence from Britain in 1947, now member of the Commonwealth of Nations. 1,261,597 sq. mi. Pop. 471,624,000. Capital: New Delhi.

**Indonesia,** Republic, comprising some 3,000 islands in western Pacific Ocean, the principal ones being Sumatra, Java, Madura, Celebes, southwestern Borneo and western New Guinea. Formerly Netherlands East Indies. 735,865 sq. mi. Pop. 160,000,000. Capital: Jakarta.

**Iran,** Const. monarchy in western Asia. At one time more commonly known as Persia. 628,-060 sq. mi. Pop. 23,428,000. Capital: Tehran.

**Iraq,** Republic, in Southwest Asia. Site of earliest civilization, ancient name, Mesopotamia. 172,000 sq. mi. Pop. 8,261,521. Capital: Baghdad.

**Ireland,** Republic, on island in Atlantic Ocean. Ended all ties with Britain in 1948. 27,136 sq. mi. Pop. 2,563,000. Capital: Dublin.

**Isle of Man,** British dependency, island in Irish Sea between Great Britain and Ireland. 227 sq. mi. Pop. 48,151. Capital: Douglas.

**Israel,** Republic, in Southwest Asia. State established in 1948 by modern Jewish Zionists in the ancient Jewish homeland. 7,993 sq. mi. Pop. 2,563,000. Capital: Jerusalem.

**Italy,** Republic, peninsula of Southern Europe. Ancient Romans ruled an empire which extended on all sides of the Mediterranean. Modern Italian state dates from 1861. 116,372 sq. mi. Pop. 52,736,000. Capital: Rome.

**Ivory Coast,** Republic, in West Africa. Formerly a French Overseas Territory. 127,520 sq. mi. Pop. 3,750,000. Capital: Abidjan.

**Jamaica,** Independent member of the Commonwealth of Nations, in Caribbean Sea. World's largest producer of bauxite. 4,411 sq. mi. Pop. 1,800,000. Capital: Kingston.

**Japan,** Const. monarchy, in North Pacific. There are four main islands, many small ones. Leading industrial country of Asia. 142,688 sq. mi. Pop. 98,281,955. Capital: Tokyo.

**Jordan,** Const. monarchy, in Southwest Asia. Largely desert except for irrigated lands near Jordan River. 37,500 sq. mi. Pop. 1,976,000. Capital: Amman.

**Kenya,** Republic, in East Africa. Formerly British colony, now member of the Commonwealth of Nations. 224,960 sq. mi. Pop. 9,365,000. Capital: Nairobi.

**Korea, People's Democratic Republic of** (North), in Northeast Asia. Communist state which occupies northern part of Korean peninsula. 47,858 sq. mi. Pop. 11,790,000. Capital: Pyongyang.

**Korea, Republic of,** (South), in Northeast Asia. The main agricultural part of the Korean peninsula. Allied with U. S. against Communist North during Korean War (1950-1953). 37,427 sq. mi. Pop. 28,647,176. Capital: Seoul.

**Kuwait,** Sheikdom, on Arabian peninsula in Southwest Asia. Land with vast amount of oil and very little water. 5,800 sq. mi. Pop. 468,000. Capital: Kuwait City.

**Laos,** Const. monarchy, in Southeast Asia. Formerly part of French Indo-China. 91,000 sq. mi. Pop. 3,000,000. Capital: Vientiane.

**Latvia,** A one-time Republic, on Baltic Sea in Eastern Europe, now incorporated in the USSR but still recognized by the United States. 24,695 sq. mi. Pop. 2,241,000. Capital: Riga.

**Lebanon,** Republic, in Southwest Asia. About half of the people are Christians, half Moslems. 4,000 sq. mi. Pop. 2,152,000. Capital: Beirut.

**Lesotho,** Const. monarchy, completely surrounded by Republic of South Africa. Formerly British dependency of Basutoland. Member of the Commonwealth of Nations. 11,716 sq. mi. Pop. 858,000. Capital: Maseru.

**Liberia,** Republic, in West Africa. Founded in 1822 as a colony of freed slaves from America. 43,000 sq. mi. Pop. 1,066,000. Capital: Monrovia.

**Libya,** Const. monarchy, in North Africa. Part of the Italian empire before World War II. UN voted to establish independence in 1949. 679,358 sq. mi. Pop. 1,617,000. Capitals: Tripoli and Benghazi.

**Liechtenstein,** Const. monarchy, in Alps between Switzerland and Austria. Since 1924 aligned with Switzerland which handles foreign affairs. 62 sq. mi. Pop. 19,000. Capital: Vaduz.

**Lithuania,** A one-time Republic, on Baltic Sea in Eastern Europe, now incorporated in the USSR but still recognized by the United States. 26,173 sq. mi. Pop. 2,949,000. Capital: Vilnius (Vilna).

**Luxembourg,** Const. monarchy, in Western Europe. The history of this small Grand Duchy dates back more than a thousand years to 963. 999 sq. mi. Pop. 331,000. Capital: Luxembourg.

**Macao,** Portuguese overseas province, at mouth of the Canton River, South China. 6 sq. mi. Pop. 172,000.

**Malagasy Republic,** Island in Indian Ocean off southeast African coast. Formerly French Madagascar, now member of the French Community. 228,000 sq. mi. Pop. 6,262,000. Capital: Tananarive.

**Malawi,** Republic, in Southeast Africa. Formerly British Protectorate of Nyasaland, now member of the Commonwealth of Nations. 49,177 sq. mi. Pop. 3,753,000. Capital: Zomba.

**Malaysia,** Federation of states, in Southeast Asia. Consists of 11 states on Malay peninsula plus Sarawak and Sabah on island of Borneo. Member of Commonwealth of Nations. 128,308 sq. mi. Pop. 9,384,000. Capital: Kuala Lumpur.

**Maldive Islands,** Independent sultanate, islands in Indian Ocean. Formerly British protected state. 112 sq. mi. Pop. 97,000. Capital: Malé.

**Mali,** Republic, in West Africa. Formerly part of French West Africa. 465,000 sq. mi. Pop. 4,576,000. Capital: Bamako.

**Malta,** Independent member of the Commonwealth of Nations, island in the Mediterranean Sea. 122 sq. mi. Pop. 319,000. Capital: Valletta.

**Martinique,** Overseas department (district) of France, in eastern Caribbean Sea. 425 sq. mi. Pop. 303,000. Capital: Fort-de-France.

**Mauritania, Islamic Republic of,** on western coast of Africa. Formerly part of French West Africa. 416,216 sq. mi. Pop. 1,000,000. Capital: Nouakchott.

**Mauritius,** British dependency, an island in the Indian Ocean. 720 sq. mi. Pop. 741,000. Capital: Port Louis.

**Mexico,** Republic, in No. America. Third largest of the Latin American countries. 758,259 sq. mi. Pop. 42,808,600. Capital: Mexico City.

**Midway Islands, Johnson, San, Howand, Jarvis, and Baker Islands,** scattered island possessions of the United States in the Pacific Ocean. 2 sq. mi.

**Monaco,** Const. principality, on French Mediterranean coast. Famous for Monte Carlo Casino. 370 acres. Pop. 22,297. Capital: Monaco-Ville.

**Mongolia,** Republic, in Northern Asia. A Communist ruled state consisting of Outer Mongolia; Inner Mongolia is a part of China. 626,000 sq. mi. Pop. 1,019,000. Capital: Ulan Bator.

**Morocco,** Const. monarchy, in Northwest Africa. French protectorate until 1956. 172,-104 sq. mi. Pop. 13,323,000. Capital: Rabat.

**Mozambique,** Portuguese overseas province, in Southeast Africa. 297,731 sq. mi. Pop. 6,956,-000. Capital: Lourenco Marques.

**Muscat and Oman,** Sultanate, on southeastern coast of Arabian peninsula. Rulers have maintained close ties with Britain. 82,000 sq. mi. Pop. 750,000. Capital: Muscat.

**Nepal,** Const. monarchy, in Central Asia. Site of Mt. Everest, world's highest peak. 54,362 sq. mi. Pop. 9,388,000. Capital: Katmandu.

**Netherlands,** Const. monarchy, in Northwestern Europe. About 20% of land lies below sea level. 15,800 sq. mi. Pop. 12,292,000. Capital: Amsterdam.

**Netherlands Antilles,** Overseas part of the Kingdom of the Netherlands, group of islands in eastern Caribbean Sea. 393 sq. mi. Pop. 207,-000. Capital: Willemstad.

**New Zealand,** Independent member of the Commonwealth of Nations, islands in the South Pacific Ocean. Although first discovered in 1642, settlement did not begin until 1840's. 103,736 sq. mi. Pop. 2,647,282. Capital: Wellington.

**Nicaragua,** Republic, in Central America. Largest of Central American states. 57,145 sq. mi. Pop. 1,655,000. Capital: Managua.

**Niger,** Republic, in West Africa. Formerly part of French West Africa. 490,000 sq. mi. Pop. 3,328,000. Capital: Niamey.

**Nigeria,** Republic, in West Africa. Africa's most populous country. Member of Commonwealth of Nations. 356,669 sq. mi. Pop. 56,400,000. Capital: Lagos.

**Norway,** Const. monarchy, in Northwest Europe. Occupies western half of Scandinavian peninsula. 125,064 sq. mi. Pop. 3,-738,000. Capital: Oslo.

**Okinawa,** Island in western Pacific Ocean. Administered by the United States since World War II. 454 sq. mi. Pop. 738,000. Seat of US Civil Administration: Naha.

**Pakistan,** Republic, in Asia. Consists of two parts divided by nearly 1000 mi. of India. Member of the Commonwealth of Nations. 365,529 sq. mi. Pop. 102,876,000. Capital: Rawalpinda.

**Panama,** Republic, in Central America. Located on the isthmus which connects the Americas. 28,576 sq. mi. Pop. 1,246,000. Capital: Panama.

**Paraguay,** Republic, in So. America. Since country is landlocked, it must depend upon its neighbors' trading facilities. 157,000 sq. mi. Pop. 2,030,000. Capital: Asuncion.

**Peru,** Republic, in So. America. Site of Inca empire in pre-Columbian times. 514,059 sq. mi. Pop. 11,650,000. Capital: Lima.

**Philippines,** Republic, in western Pacific Ocean. Gained independence from the United States in 1946. 115,758 sq. mi. Pop. 32,345,000. Capital: Quezon City.

**Poland,** Republic, in Central Europe. Communist regime established after World War II. 120,359 sq. mi. Pop. 31,496,000. Capital: Warsaw.

**Portugal,** Republic, in Southeastern Europe. World's chief source of cork. 35,466 sq. mi. Pop. 9,167,000. Capital: Lisbon.

**Portuguese Guinea,** Overseas province, in West Africa. 13,948 sq. mi. Pop. 549,000.

**Portuguese Timor,** Overseas province, eastern part of island in Timor Sea. Indonesia holds western half. 5,763 sq. mi. Pop. 536,000. Capital: Dili.

**Puerto Rico,** Commonwealth, between Caribbean Sea and Atlantic Ocean. Self-governing under the United States. 3,435 sq. mi. Pop. 2,349,544. Capital: San Juan.

**Qatar,** Sheikdom, on Arabian coast of the Persian Gulf. British protectorate. 8,000 sq. mi. Pop. 55,000. Capital: Doha.

**Rhodesia,** officially a British self-governing dependency, in Southern Africa. Independence declared in 1965 but not recognized by Britain. 150,333 sq. mi. Pop. 4,260,000. Capital: Salisbury.

**Romania,** Republic, in Southeastern Europe. Communist regime established after World War II. 91,699 sq. mi. Pop. 19,150,056. Capital: Bucharest.

**Rwanda,** Republic, in Central Africa. Formerly part of Belgian protectorate of Ruanda-Urundi. Independent in 1962. 10,166 sq. mi. Pop. 3,000,000. Capital: Kigali.

**Sabah,** Part of Federation of Malaysia, in Pacific Ocean. Formerly British North Borneo. 29,-388 sq. mi. Pop. 498,031. Capital: Jesselton.

**St. Helena,** British possession, island in Atlantic Ocean. Napoleon's place of exile. 47 sq. mi. Pop. 4,634. Capital: Jamestown.

**St. Pierre and Miquelon,** Overseas territory of France, islands in Atlantic Ocean about 15 miles from Newfoundland. 93 sq. mi. Pop. 5,000. Capital: Saint Pierre.

**Samoa,** Possession of the United States, in South Pacific Ocean. 76 sq. mi. Pop. 20,051. Capital: Pago Pago.

**San Marino,** Republic, in the hills of Italy east of Florence. Smallest republic in the world. 23.5 sq. mi. Pop. 17,000. Capital: San Marino.

**São Tomé and Principe,** Portuguese overseas provinces, islands off the west coast of Africa. 372 sq. mi. Pop. 63,676.

**Sarawak,** Part of Federation of Malaysia, on northwest coast of Borneo. 48,250 sq. mi. Pop. 809,737. Capital: Kuching.

**Saudi Arabia,** Monarchy, comprising most of the Arabian Peninsula. Largely a desert country. 870,000 sq. mi. Pop. 8,000,000. Capital: Riyadh.

**Scotland,** (*see* UNITED KINGDOM).

**Senegal, Republic of,** in West Africa. Formerly French Overseas Territory, now member of the French Community. 76,000 sq. mi. Pop. 3,490,000. Capital: Dakar.

**Seychelles,** British possession, in Indian Ocean. 69 sq. mi. Pop. 45,000. Capital: Victoria.

**Sierra Leone,** Independent member of the Commonwealth of Nations, in West Africa. Founded by British in 1787 as a home for freed slaves. 27,925 sq. mi. Pop. 2,200,000. Capital: Freetown.

**Singapore,** Republic, island off the southern tip of Malay Peninsula, in Southeast Asia. For a short time a part of the Federation of Malaysia, now a member of the Commonwealth of Nations. 225 sq. mi. Pop. 1,865,000. Capital: Singapore.

**Somalia,** Republic, in East Africa. Formerly British Somaliland. 262,000 sq. mi. Pop. 2,500,000. Capital: Mogadishu.

**South Africa, Republic of,** southernmost part of Africa. Formerly Union of South Africa, member of the Commonwealth of Nations; independent after 1961. 472,359 sq. mi. Pop. 17,867,000. Capitals: Pretoria and Cape Town.

**South Yemen,** Republic on south coast of Arabian peninsula. Formerly Federation of South Arabia, a British protectorate. 112,000 sq. mi. Pop. 1,220,000. Capital: Aden.

**South-West Africa,** Territory administered by Republic of South Africa, in Southern Africa. One time League of Nations mandate. 317,887 sq. mi. Pop. 574,000. Capital: Windhoek.

**Spain,** Monarchy with no king, in Southwestern Europe. Actually ruled by a Head of State since 1939. 195,504 sq. mi. Pop. 31,604,000. Capital: Madrid.

**Spanish Sahara,** Overseas province, west coast of Africa. 106,409 sq. mi. Pop. 23,700. Capital: El Aaiún.

**Sudan,** Republic, in Northeast Africa. Formerly Anglo-Egyptian condominium. Land of the upper Nile. 967,500 sq. mi. Pop. 13,540,000. Capital: Khartoum.

**Surinam,** Overseas part of the Kingdom of the Netherlands, northern coast of So. America. Also known as Dutch Guiana. 55,400 sq. mi. Pop. 325,000. Capital: Paramaribo.

**Sweden,** Monarchy, in Northwestern Europe. Largest of the Scandinavian countries. 173,378 sq. mi. Pop. 7,773,000. Capital: Stockholm.

**Swaziland,** British Protectorate, in Southeast Africa. 6,704 sq. mi. Pop. 292,000. Capital: Mbabane.

**Switzerland,** Republic, in Central Europe. Mountainous and traditionally free and neutral. Not a member of the U.N. 15,944 sq. mi. Pop. 5,945,000. Capital: Berne.

**Syria,** Republic, in Southwest Asia. Syrians claim that Damascus is the oldest continuously inhabited city in the world. 72,234 sq. mi. Pop. 5,399,000. Capital: Damascus.

**Tanzania,** Republic, in East Africa. Formerly British mandate of Tanganyika and Protectorate of Zanzibar. Member of the Commonwealth of Nations. 363,708 sq. mi. Pop. 10,578,100. Capital: Dar es Salaam.

**Thailand,** Const. monarchy, in Southeast Asia. Known for much of its history as Siam. Important rice producer. 200,148 sq. mi. Pop. 30,561,000. Capital: Bangkok.

**Tibet,** State under rule of Communist People's Republic of China, in Asia. Before 1950 ruled by high priest of the Lamaist religion known as Dalai Lama. 470,000 sq. mi. Pop. 1,300,000. Capital: Lhasa.

**Togo,** Republic, in West Africa. A German colony before World War I, under administration of France from 1922 to 1960. 20,400 sq. mi. Pop. 1,617,000. Capital: Lomé.

**Trinidad and Tobago,** Independent member of the Commonwealth of Nations, islands in the Caribbean Sea. Site of Pitch Lake, world's largest source of asphalt. 1,979 sq. mi. Pop. 975,000. Capital: Port of Spain.

**Trucial States,** Sheikdoms, on Arabian coast of Persian Gulf. Seven states under British protection. 32,300 sq. mi. Pop. 86,000. Capital: Dubai.

**Tunisia,** Republic, in North Africa. Site of ancient Carthage. Became French protectorate in 1881, independent in 1956. 58,000 sq. mi. Pop. 4,675,000. Capital: Tunis.

**Turkey,** Republic, on Anatolian peninsula in Southwest Asia, also called Asia Minor, plus small southeastern tip of Europe. 296,500 sq. mi. Pop. 31,391,000. Capital: Ankara.

**Uganda,** Republic, in Central Africa. Formerly British Protectorate, now member of the Commonwealth of Nations. 91,076 sq. mi. Pop. 7,551,000. Capital: Kampala.

**Union of Soviet Socialist Republics,** in Eastern Europe and Asia. Federation of 15 Communist states, including Russia which has greater population than all the others combined. Total area comprises one-sixth of earth's land surface, making USSR world's largest country. 8,649,498 sq. mi. Pop. 230,000,000. Capital: Moscow.

**United Arab Republic,** in Northeast Africa. In 1958 Egypt and Syria combined to form UAR, but Syria withdrew in 1961 so that state includes Egypt only. 386,198 sq. mi. Pop. 29,600,000. Capital: Cairo.

**United Kingdom of Great Britain and Northern Ireland,** Const. monarchy on British Isles, Northwestern Europe. Great Britain includes England (50,331 sq. mi., Pop. 45,070,000), Wales (8,016 sq. mi., Pop. 2,693,000), and Scotland (30,411 sq. mi., Pop. 5,204,000).

Northern Ireland (5,451 sq. mi., Pop. 1,469,-000) is a part of the United Kingdom but not of Great Britain. 94,209 sq. mi. Pop. 54,-436,000. Capital: London.

**United States of America,** Republic, in No. America. The most populous country and second largest in area in the Western Hemisphere. 3,615,211 sq. mi. Pop. 203,184,772. Capital: Washington, D. C.

**Upper Volta,** Republic, in West Africa. Formerly part of French West Africa, independent in 1960. 105,900 sq. mi. Pop. 4,858,000. Capital: Ouagadougou.

**Uruguay,** Republic, in So. America Smallest of the Republics in So. America. A major producer of livestock. 72,172 sq. mi. Pop. 2,-845,734. Capital: Montevideo.

**Vatican City,** City-state under the rule of the Pope, in Rome, Italy. A remnant of the Papal States which during Middle Ages included much of Central Italy. 108.7 acres. Pop. over 1000.

**Venezuela,** Republic, in So. America. Third largest oil producer in the world and major source of iron ore for the United States. 352,-150 sq. mi. Pop. 8,876,000. Capital: Caracas.

**Vietnam, Democratic Republic of,** in Southeast Asia. The Communist ruled northern part of this land, formerly part of French Indo-China. 62,000 sq. mi. Pop. 16,200,000. Capital: Hanoi.

**Vietnam, Republic of,** in Southeast Asia. The southern half of country divided by Geneva agreement of 1954. 65,000 sq. mi. Pop. 16,-124,000. Capital: Saigon.

**Virgin Islands,** Territory of the United States, consisting of 9 main islands and some 40 smaller ones in the Caribbean Sea. Purchased from Denmark in 1917. 133 sq. mi. Pop. 43,000. Capital: Charlotte Amalie.

**Wake Island,** Island held by the United States, in Pacific Ocean. Stopping place for airplanes. 3 sq. mi. No indigenous pop.

**Wales** (*see* UNITED KINGDOM).

**Western Samoa,** Independent state, in Pacific Ocean. One time German protectorate, administered by New Zealand after World War I, independent in 1962. 1,097 sq. mi. Pop. 135,000. Capital: Apia.

**Yemen,** Republic, in Southwest Asia. Located in the mountainous southern part of the Arabian peninsula. 75,000 sq. mi. Pop. 5,000,000. Capital: Sana.

**Yugoslavia,** Republic, in Southeastern Europe. Created by unifying several southern Slavic lands following World War I. Communist state since World War II. 98,766 sq. mi. Pop. 19,508,000. Capital: Belgrade.

**Zambia,** Republic, in South Central Africa. Formerly British Protectorate of Northern Rhodesia. Member of the Commonwealth of Nations. 290,586 sq. mi. Pop. 3,710,000. Capital: Lusaka.

**Zanzibar** (*see* TANZANIA).

# Civics

## CONSTITUTION OF THE UNITED STATES

THE CONSTITUTION originally consisted of a Preamble and seven Articles, and in that form was ratified by a convention of the States, Sept. 17, 1787. The Government under the Constitution was declared in effect on the first Wednesday in March, 1789. The signers of the original Constitution, by virtue of their membership in Congress, were:

Geo. Washington, President and deputy from Virginia. New Hampshire — John Langdon, Nicholas Gilman. Massachusetts — Nathaniel Gorham, Rufus King. Connecticut — Wm. Saml. Johnson, Roger Sherman. New York — Alexander Hamilton. New Jersey — Wil. Livingston, David Brearley, Wm. Patterson, Jona. Dayton. Pennsylvania — B. Franklin, Robt. Morris, Thos. Fitzsimons, James Wilson, Thomas Mifflin, Geo. Clymer, Jared Ingersoll, Gouv. Morris. Delaware — Geo. Read, John Dickinson, Jaco. Broom, Gunning Bedford jun., Richard Basset. Maryland — James McHenry, Danl. Carroll, Dan. of St. Thos. Jenifer. Virginia — John Blair, James Madison, Jr. North Carolina — Wm. Blount, Hu. Williamson, Richd. Dobbs Spaight. South Carolina — J. Rutledge, Charles Pinckney, Charles Cotesworth Pinckney, Pierce Butler. Georgia — William Few, Abr. Baldwin. Attest: William Jackson, Secretary.

The Constitution was ratified by the thirteen original States in the following order:

Delaware, December 7, 1787 (yeas, 30), unanimous.
Pennsylvania, December 12, 1787, vote 43 to 23.
New Jersey, December 18, 1787 (yeas, 38), unanimous.
Georgia, January 2, 1788 (yeas, 26), unanimous.
Connecticut, January 9, 1788, vote 128 to 40.
Massachusetts, February 6, 1788, vote 187 to 168.
Maryland, April 28, 1788, vote 63 to 11.
South Carolina, May 23, 1788, vote 149 to 73.
New Hampshire, June 21, 1788, vote 57 to 46.
Virginia, June 26, 1788, vote 89 to 79.
New York, July 26, 1788, vote 30 to 27.
North Carolina, November 21, 1789, vote 194 to 77.
Rhode Island, May 29, 1790, vote 34 to 32.

(Vermont, by convention, ratified Jan. 10, 1791; and Congress, Feb. 18, 1791, admitted that State into the Union.)

## *The Constitution*

**PREAMBLE:** We, the people of the United States, in order to form a more perfect Union, establish justice, insure domestic tranquillity, provide for the common defence, promote the general welfare, and secure the blessings of liberty to ourselves and our posterity, do ordain and establish this Constitution for the United States of America.

## ARTICLE I

**Section 1** — (Legislative powers: in whom vested:)

All legislative powers herein granted shall be vested in a Congress of the United States, which shall consist of a Senate and House of Representatives.

**Section 2** — (House of Representatives, how and by whom chosen. Qualifications of a Representative. Representatives and direct taxes, how apportioned. Enumeration. Vacancies to be filled. Power of choosing officers, and of impeachment.)

1. The House of Representatives shall be composed of members chosen every second year by the people of the several States, and the electors in each State shall have the qualifications requisite for electors of the most numerous branch of the State Legislature.

2. No person shall be a Representative who shall not have attained to the age of twenty-five years and been seven years a citizen of the United States, and who shall not, when elected, be an inhabitant of that State in which he shall be chosen.

3. Representatives and direct taxes shall be apportioned among the several States which may be included within this Union according to their respective numbers, which shall be determined by adding to the whole number of free persons, including those bound to service for a term of years, and excluding Indians not taxed, three-fifths of all other persons. The actual enumeration shall be made within three years after the first meeting of the Congress of the United States, and within every subsequent term of ten years, in such manner as they shall by law direct. The number of Representatives shall not exceed one for every thirty thousand, but each State shall have at least one Representative: and until such enumeration shall be made, the State of New Hampshire shall be entitled to choose 3; Massachusetts, 8; Rhode Island and Providence Plantations, 1; Connecticut, 5; New York, 6; New Jersey, 4; Pennsylvania, 8; Delaware, 1; Maryland, 6; Virginia, 10; North Carolina, 5; South Carolina, 5; and Georgia, 3.*

4. When vacancies happen in the representation from any State, the Executive Authority thereof shall issue writs of election to fill such vacancies.

5. The House of Representatives shall choose their Speaker and other officers, and shall have the sole power of impeachment.

**Section 3** — (Senators, how and by whom chosen. How classified. State Executive, when to make temporary appointments, in case, etc. Qualifications of a Senator. President of the Senate, his right to vote. President pro tem., and other officers of the Senate, how chosen. Power to try impeachments. When President is tried, Chief Justice to preside. Sentence.)

1. The Senate of the United States shall be composed of two Senators from each State, chosen by the Legislature thereof, for six years; and each Senator shall have one vote.

2. Immediately after they shall be assembled in consequence of the first election, they shall be divided as equally as may be into three classes. The seats of the Senators of the first class shall be vacated at the expiration of the second year, of the second class at the expiration of the fourth year, and of the third class at the expiration of the sixth year, so that one-third may be chosen every second year; and if vacancies happen by resignation, or otherwise, during the recess of the Legislature of any State, the Executive thereof may make temporary appointment until the next meeting of the Legislature, which shall then fill such vacancies.

3. No person shall be a Senator who shall not have attained to the age of thirty years, and been nine years a citizen of the United States, and who shall not, when elected, be an inhabitant of that State for which he shall be chosen.

4. The Vice-President of the United States shall be President of the Senate, but shall have no vote unless they be equally divided.

5. The Senate shall choose their other officers, and also a President pro tempore, in the absence of the Vice-President, or when he shall exercise the office of President of the United States.

6. The Senate shall have the sole power to try all impeachments. When sitting for that purpose, they shall be on oath or affirmation. When the President of the United States is tried, the Chief Justice shall preside; and no person shall be convicted without the concurrence of two-thirds of the members present.

7. Judgment of cases of impeachment shall not extend further than to removal from office, and disqualification to hold and enjoy any office of honor, trust, or profit under the United States; but the party convicted shall nevertheless be liable and subject to indictment, trial judgment and punishment, according to law.

**Section 4** — (Times, etc., of holding elections, how prescribed. One session in each year.)

1. The times, places, and manner of holding elections for Senators and Representatives shall be prescribed in each State by the Legislature thereof; but the Congress may at any time by law make or alter such regulations, except as to places of choosing Senators.

2. The Congress shall assemble at least once in every year, and such meeting shall be on the first Monday in December, unless they shall by law appoint a different day.

**Section 5** — (Membership, Quorum, Adjournments. Rules. Power to punish or expel.

* See Article XIV, Amendments.

Journal. Time of adjournments, how limited, etc.)

1. Each House shall be the judge of the elections, returns, and qualifications of its own members, and a majority of each shall constitute a quorum to do business; but a small number may adjourn from day to day, and may be authorized to compel the attendance of absent members in such manner and under such penalties as each House may provide.

2. Each House may determine the rules of its proceedings, punish its members for disorderly behavior, and with the concurrence of two-thirds expel a member.

3. Each House shall keep a journal of its proceedings, and from time to time publish the same, excepting such parts as may in their judgment require secrecy; and the yeas and nays of the members of either House on any question shall, at the desire of one-fifth of those present, be entered on the journal.

4. Neither House, during the session of Congress shall, without the consent of the other, adjourn for more than three days, nor to any other place than that in which the two Houses shall be sitting.

**Section 6** — (Compensation. Privileges. Disqualification in certain cases.)

1. The Senators and Representatives shall receive a compensation for their services to be ascertained by law, and paid out of the Treasury of the United States. They shall in all cases, except treason, felony, and breach of the peace, be privileged from arrest during their attendance at the session of their respective Houses, and in going to and returning from the same; and for any speech or debate in either House they shall not be questioned in any other place.

2. No Senator or Representative shall, during the time for which he was elected, be appointed to any civil office under the authority of the United States which shall have been created, or the emoluments whereof shall have been increased during such time; and no person holding any office under the United States shall be a member of either House during his continuance in office.

**Section 7** — (House to originate all revenue bills. Veto. Bill may be passed by two-thirds of each House, notwithstanding, etc. Bill, not returned in ten days, to become a law. Provisions as to orders, concurrent resolutions, etc.)

1. All bills for raising revenue shall originate in the House of Representatives, but the Senate may propose or concur with amendments, as on other bills.

2. Every bill which shall have passed the House of Representatives and the Senate shall, before it becomes a law, be presented to the President of the United States; if he approve, he shall sign it, but if not, he shall return it, with his objections, to that House in which it shall have originated, who shall enter the objections at large on their journal, and proceed to reconsider it. If after such reconsideration two-thirds of that House shall agree to pass the bill, it shall be sent, together with the objections, to the other House, by which it shall likewise be reconsidered; and if approved by two-thirds of that House it shall become a law. But in all such cases the votes of both Houses shall be determined by yeas and nays, and the names of the persons voting for and against the bill shall be entered on the journal of each House respectively. If any bill shall not be returned by the President within ten days (Sundays excepted) after it shall have been presented to him, the same shall be a law in like manner as if he had signed it, unless the Congress by their adjournment prevent its return; in which case it shall not be a law.

3. Every order, resolution, or vote to which the concurrence of the Senate and House of Representatives may be necessary (except on a question of adjournment) shall be presented to the President of the United States; and before the same shall take effect shall be approved by him, or being disapproved by him, shall be repassed by two-thirds of the Senate and the House of Representatives, according to the rules and limitations prescribed in the case of a bill.

**Section 8** — (Powers of Congress.)

1. The Congress shall have power:

To lay and collect taxes, duties, imposts, and excises, to pay the debts and provide for the common defence and general welfare of the United States: but all duties, imposts, and excises shall be uniform throughout the United States.

2. To borrow money on the credit of the United States.

3. To regulate commerce with foreign nations, and among the several States, and with the Indian tribes.

4. To establish an uniform rule of naturalization and uniform laws on the subject of bankruptcies throughout the United States.

5. To coin money, regulate the value thereof, and of foreign coin, and fix the standards of weights and measures.

6. To provide for the punishment of counterfeiting the securities and current coin of the United States.

7. To establish post-offices and post-roads.

8. To promote the progress of science and useful arts by securing for limited times to authors and inventors the exclusive rights to their respective writings and discoveries.

9. To constitute tribunals inferior to the Supreme Court.

10. To define and punish piracies and felonies committed on the high seas, and offences against the laws of nations.

11. To declare war, grant letters of marque

and reprisal, and make rules concerning captures on land and water.

12. To raise and support armies, but no appropriation of money to that use shall be for a longer term than two years.

13. To provide and maintain a navy.

14. To make rules for the government and regulation of the land and naval forces.

15. To provide for calling forth the militia to execute the laws of the Union, suppress insurrections, and repel invasions.

16. To provide for organizing, arming, and disciplining the militia, and for governing such part of them as may be employed in the service of the United States, reserving to the States respectively the appointment of the officers, and the authority of training the militia according to the discipline prescribed by Congress.

17. To exercise exclusive legislation in all cases whatsoever over such district (not exceeding ten miles square) as may, by cession of particular States and the acceptance of Congress, become the seat of Government of the United States, and to exercise like authority over all places purchased by the consent of the Legislature of the State in which the same shall be, for the erection of forts, magazines, arsenals, dry-docks, and other needful buildings.

18. To make all laws which shall be necessary and proper for carrying into execution the foregoing powers and all other powers vested by this Constitution in the Government of the United States, or in any department or officer thereof.

**Section 9** — (Provision as to migration or importation of certain persons. Habeas Corpus. Bills of attainder, etc. Taxes, how apportioned. No export duty. No commercial preference. Money, how drawn from Treasury, etc. No titular nobility. Officers not to receive presents, etc.)

1. The migration or importation of such persons as any of the States now existing shall think proper to admit shall not be prohibited by the Congress, prior to the year one thousand eight hundred and eight, but a tax or duty may be imposed on such importation, not exceeding ten dollars for each person.

2. The privilege of the writ of habeas corpus shall not be suspended, unless when in cases of rebellion or invasion the public safety may require it.

3. No bill of attainder or ex post facto law shall be passed.

4. No capitation or other direct tax shall be laid, unless in proportion to the census or enumeration hereinbefore directed to be taken.

5. No tax or duty shall be laid on articles exported from any State.

6. No preference shall be given by any regulation of commerce or revenue to the ports of one State over those of another, nor shall vessels bound to or from one State be obliged to enter, clear, or pay duties in another.

7. No money shall be drawn from the Treasury but in consequence of appropriations made by law; and a regular statement and account of the receipts and expenditures of all public money shall be published from time to time.

8. No title of nobility shall be granted by the United States. And no person holding any office of profit or trust under them shall, without the consent of the Congress, accept of any present, emolument, office, or title of any kind whatever from any king, prince, or foreign state.

**Section 10** — (States prohibited from the exercise of certain powers.)

1. No State shall enter into any treaty, alliance, or confederation, grant letters of marque and reprisal, coin money, emit bills of credit, make anything but gold and silver coin a tender in payment of debts, pass any bill of attainder, ex post facto law, or law impairing the obligation of contracts, or grant any title of nobility.

2. No State shall, without the consent of the Congress, lay any impost or duties on imports or exports, except what may be absolutely necessary for executing its inspection laws, and the net produce of all duties and imposts, laid by any State on imports or exports, shall be for the use of the Treasury of the United States; and all such laws shall be subject to the revision and control of the Congress.

3. No State shall, without the consent of Congress, lay any duty of tonnage, keep troops or ships of war in time of peace, enter into agreement or compact with another State, or with a foreign power, or engage in war, unless actually invaded, or in such imminent danger as will not admit of delay.

## ARTICLE II

**Section 1** — (President; his term of office. Electors of President; number and how appointed. Electors to vote on same day. Qualification of President. On whom his duties devolve in case of his removal, death, etc. President's compensation. His oath of office.)

1. The Executive power shall be vested in a President of the United States of America. He shall hold his office during the term of four years, and, together with the Vice-President, chosen for the same term, be elected as follows:

2. Each State shall appoint, in such manner as the Legislature thereof may direct, a number of electors equal to the whole number of Senators and Representatives to which the State may be entitled in the Congress; but no Senator or Representative or person holding an office of trust or profit under the United States shall be appointed an elector.

3. The electors shall meet in their respective States and vote by ballot for two persons, of whom one at least shall not be an inhabitant of

the same State with themselves. And they shall make a list of all the persons voted for, and of the number of votes for each, which list they shall sign and certify and transmit, sealed, to the seat of the Government of the United States, directed to the President of the Senate. The President of the Senate shall, in the presence of the Senate and House of Representatives, open all the certificates, and the votes shall then be counted. The person having the greatest number of votes shall be the President, if such number be a majority of the whole number of electors appointed, and if there be more than one who have such a majority, and have an equal number of votes, then the House of Representatives shall immediately choose by ballot one of them for President; and if no person have a majority, then from the five highest on the list the said House shall in like manner choose the President. But in choosing the President, the vote shall be taken by States, the representation from each State having one vote. A quorum, for this purpose, shall consist of a member or members from two-thirds of the States, and a majority of all the States shall be necessary to a choice. In every case, after the choice of the President, the person having the greatest number of votes of the electors shall be the Vice-President. But if there should remain two or more who have equal votes, the Senate shall choose from them by ballot the Vice-President.*

4. The Congress may determine the time of choosing the electors and the day on which they shall give their votes, which day shall be the same throughout the United States.

5. No person except a natural born citizen, or a citizen of the United States, at the time of the adoption of this Constitution, shall be eligible to the office of President; neither shall any person be eligible to that office who shall not have attained to the age of thirty-five years and been fourteen years a resident within the United States.

6. In case of the removal of the President from office, or of his death, resignation, or inability to discharge the powers and duties of the said office, the same shall devolve on the Vice-President, and the Congress may by law provide for the case of removal, death, resignation, or inability, both of the President and Vice-President, declaring what officer shall then act as President, and such officer shall act accordingly, until the disability be removed or a President shall be elected.

7. The President shall, at stated times, receive for his services a compensation which shall neither be increased nor diminished during the period for which he shall have been elected, and he shall not receive within that period any other emolument from the United States, or any of them.

8. Before he enters on the execution of his office he shall take the following oath or affirmation:

"I do solemnly swear (or affirm) that I will faithfully execute the office of President of the United States, and will, to the best of my ability, preserve, protect, and defend the Constitution of the United States."

**Section 2** — (President to be Commander-in-Chief. He may require opinions of Cabinet Officers, etc., may pardon. Treaty-making power. Nomination of certain officers. When President may fill vacancies.)

1. The President shall be Commander-in-Chief of the Army and Navy of the United States, and of the militia of the several States when called into the actual service of the United States; he may require the opinion, in writing, of the principal officer in each of the executive departments upon any subject relating to the duties of their respective offices, and he shall have power to grant reprieves and pardons for offences against the United States except in cases of impeachment.

2. He shall have power, by and with the advice and consent of the Senate, to make treaties, provided two-thirds of the Senators present concur, and he shall nominate and by and with the advice and consent of the Senate shall appoint ambassadors, other public ministers and consuls, judges of the Supreme Court, and all other officers of the United States whose appointments are not herein otherwise provided for, and which shall be established by law; but the Congress may by law vest the appointment of such inferior officers as they think proper in the President alone, in the courts of law, or in the heads of departments.

3. The President shall have power to fill up all vacancies that may happen during the recess of the Senate by granting commissions, which shall expire at the end of their next session.

**Section 3** — (President shall communicate to Congress. He may convene and adjourn Congress, in case of disagreement, etc. Shall receive Ambassadors, execute laws, and commission officers.)

He shall from time to time give to the Congress information of the state of the Union, and recommend to their consideration such measures as he shall judge necessary and expedient; he may, on extraordinary occasions, convene both Houses, or either of them, and in case of disagreement between them with respect to the time of adjournment, he may adjourn them to such time as he shall think proper; he shall receive ambassadors and other public ministers; he shall take care that the laws be faithfully executed, and shall commission all the officers of the United States.

* This clause is superseded by Article XII, Amendments.

**Section 4** — (All civil offices forfeited for certain crimes.)

The President, Vice-President, and all civil officers of the United States shall be removed from office on impeachment for and conviction of treason, bribery or other high crimes and misdemeanors.

## ARTICLE III

**Section 1** — (Judicial powers. Tenure. Compensation.)

The judicial power of the United States shall be vested in one Supreme Court, and in such inferior courts as the Congress may from time to time ordain and establish. The judges, both of the Supreme and inferior courts, shall hold their offices during good behavior, and shall at stated times receive for their services a compensation which shall not be diminished during their continuance in office.

**Section 2** — (Judicial power; to what cases it extends. Original jurisdiction of Supreme Court. Appellate. Trial by jury, etc. Trial, where.)

1. The judicial power shall extend to all cases in law and equity arising under this Constitution, the laws of the United States, and treaties made, or which shall be made, under their authority; to all cases affecting ambassadors, other public ministers and consuls; to all cases of admiralty and maritime jurisdiction; to controversies to which the United States shall be a party: to controversies between two or more States, between a State and citizens of another State, between citizens of different States, between citizens of the same State claiming lands under grants of different States, and between a State, or the citizens thereof, and foreign states, citizens, or subjects.

2. In all cases affecting ambassadors, other public ministers, and consuls, and those in which a State shall be party, the Supreme Court shall have original jurisdiction. In all the other cases before mentioned the Supreme Court shall have appellate jurisdiction both as to law and fact, with such exceptions and under such regulations as the Congress shall make.

3. The trial of all crimes, except in cases of impeachment, shall be by jury, and such trial shall be held in the State where the said crimes shall have been committed; but when not committed within any State the trial shall be at such place or places as the Congress may by law have directed.

**Section 3** — (Treason defined. Proof of. Punishment of.)

1. Treason against the United States shall consist only in levying war against them, or in adhering to their enemies, giving them aid and comfort. No person shall be convicted of treason unless on the testimony of two witnesses to the same overt act, or on confession in open court.

2. The Congress shall have power to declare the punishment of treason, but no attainder of treason shall work corruption of blood or forfeiture except during the life of the person attained.

## ARTICLE IV

**Section 1** — (Each State to give credit to the public acts, etc., of every other State.)

Full faith and credit shall be given in each State to the public acts, records, and judicial proceedings of every other State. And the Congress may by general laws prescribe the manner in which such acts, records, and proceedings shall be proved, and the effect thereof.

**Section 2** — (Privileges of citizens of each State. Fugitives from justice to be delivered up. Persons held to service having escaped, to be delivered up.)

1. The citizens of each State shall be entitled to all privileges and immunities of citizens in the several States.

2. A person charged in any State with treason, felony, or other crime, who shall flee from justice, and be found in another State, shall on demand of the Executive authority of the State from which he fled, be delivered up, to be removed to the State having jurisdiction of the crime.

3. No person held to service or labor in one State under the laws thereof, escaping into another shall in consequence of any law or regulation therein, be discharged from such service or labor, but shall be delivered up on claim of the party to whom such service or labor may be due.

**Section 3** — (Admission of new States, Power of Congress over territory and other property.)

1. New States may be admitted by the Congress into this Union; but no new State shall be formed or erected within the jurisdiction of any other State, nor any State be formed by the junction of two or more States, or parts of States, without the consent of the Legislatures of the States concerned, as well as of the Congress.

2. The Congress shall have power to dispose of and make all needful rules and regulations respecting the territory or other property belonging to the United States; and nothing in this Constitution shall be so construed as to prejudice any claims of the United States, or of any particular State.

**Section 4** — (Republican form of government guaranteed. Each State to be protected.)

The United States shall guarantee to every State in this Union a Republican form of government, and shall protect each of them against invasion; and, on application of the Legislature, or of the Executive (when the Legislature cannot be convened), against domestic violence.

**ARTICLE V**

(Constitution; how amended. Proviso.)

The Congress, whenever two-thirds of both Houses shall deem it necessary, shall propose amendments to this Constitution, or, on the application of the Legislatures of two-thirds of the several States, shall call a convention for proposing amendments, which, in either case, shall be valid to all intents and purposes, as part of this Constitution, when ratified by the Legislatures of three-fourths of the several States, or by conventions in three-fourths thereof, as the one or the other mode of ratification may be proposed by the Congress; provided that no amendment which may be made prior to the year one thousand eight hundred and eight shall in any manner affect the first and fourth clauses in the Ninth Section of the First Article; and that no State, without its consent, shall be deprived of its equal suffrage in the Senate.

**ARTICLE VI**

(Certain debts, etc., declared valid. Supremacy of Constitution, treaties, and laws of the United States. Oath to support Constitution, by whom taken. No religious test.)

1. All debts contracted and engagements entered into before the adoption of this Constitution shall be as valid against the United States under this Constitution as under the Confederation.

2. This Constitution and the laws of the United States which shall be made in pursuance thereof and all treaties made or which shall be made, under the authority of the United States, shall be the supreme law of the land, and the judges in every State shall be bound thereby, anything in the Constitution or laws of any State to the contrary notwithstanding.

3. The Senators and Representatives before mentioned, and the members of the several State Legislatures, and all executive and judicial officers, both of the United States, and of the several States, shall be bound by oath or affirmation to support this Constitution: but no religious test shall ever be required as a qualification to any office or public trust under the United States.

**ARTICLE VII**

(What ratification shall establish Constitution.)

The ratification of the Conventions of nine States shall be sufficient for the establishment of this Constitution between the States so ratifying the same.

OPPOSITION in and out of Congress to the Constitution, in that it was not sufficiently explicit as to individual and State rights, led to an agreement to submit to the people immediately after the adoption of the Constitution a number of safeguarding amendments.

And so it was that the First Congress, at its first session, at the City of New York, Sept. 25, 1789, adopted and submitted to the States twelve proposed amendments — A Bill of Rights as it was then and ever since has been popularly called. Ten of these amendments (now commonly known as one to ten inclusive, but in reality three to twelve inclusive) were ratified by the States as follows — New Jersey, Nov. 20, 1789; Maryland, Dec. 19, 1789; North Carolina, Dec. 22, 1789; South Carolina, Jan. 19, 1790; New Hampshire, Jan. 25, 1790; Delaware, Jan. 28, 1790; Pennsylvania, March 10, 1790; New York, March 27, 1790; Rhode Island, June 15, 1790; Vermont, Nov. 3, 1791; Virginia, Dec. 15, 1791. No ratification by Connecticut, Georgia or Massachusetts is on record. These original ten ratified amendments appear in order below as Articles I to X inclusive.

The two of the original proposed amendments which were not ratified by the necessary number of States related, the first to apportionment of Representatives; the second, to compensation of members of Congress.

## *Amendments to the Constitution of the United States*

**The Ten Original Amendments**

**also called**

**BILL OF RIGHTS**

*(They were declared in force Dec. 15, 1791.)*

**ARTICLE I**

**Religious Establishment Prohibited. Freedom of Speech, of the Press, and Right to Petition**

Congress shall make no law respecting an establishment of religion, or prohibiting the free exercise thereof; or abridging the freedom of speech or of the press; or the right of the people peaceably to assemble and to petition the Government for a redress of grievances.

**ARTICLE II**

**Right to Keep and Bear Arms**

A well-regulated militia being necessary to the security of a free State, the right of the people to keep and bear arms shall not be infringed.

**ARTICLE III**

**No Soldier to Be Quartered in Any House, Unless, Etc.**

No soldier shall, in time of peace, be quartered in any house without the consent of the owner, nor in time of war but in a manner to be prescribed by law.

### ARTICLE IV

**Right of Search and Seizure Regulated**

The right of the people to be secure in their persons, houses, papers, and effects, against unreasonable searches and seizures, shall not be violated, and no warrants shall issue but upon probable cause, supported by oath or affirmation, and particularly describing the place to be searched, and the persons or things to be seized.

### ARTICLE V

**Provisions Concerning Prosecution, Trial and Punishment. — Private Property Not to Be Taken for Public Use, Without Compensation**

No person shall be held to answer for a capital or other infamous crime unless on a presentment or indictment of a Grand Jury, except in cases arising in the land or naval forces, or in the militia, when in actual service, in time of war or public danger; nor shall any person be subject for the same offense to be twice put in jeopardy of life or limb; nor shall be compelled in any criminal case to be a witness against himself, nor be deprived of life, liberty, or property, without due process of law; nor shall private property be taken for public use without just compensation.

### ARTICLE VI

**Right to Speedy Trial, Witnesses, Etc.**

In all criminal prosecutions, the accused shall enjoy the right to a speedy and public trial, by an impartial jury of the State and district wherein the crime shall have been committed, which districts shall have been previously ascertained by law, and to be informed of the nature and cause of the accusation; to be confronted with the witnesses against him; to have compulsory process for obtaining witnesses in his favor, and to have the assistance of counsel for his defense.

### ARTICLE VII

**Right of Trial by Jury**

In suits at common law, where the value in controversy shall exceed twenty dollars, the right of trial by jury shall be preserved, and no fact tried by a jury shall be otherwise re-examined in any court of the United States than according to the rules of the common law.

### ARTICLE VIII

**Excessive Bail or Fines and Cruel Punishment Prohibited**

Excessive bail shall not be required, nor excessive fines imposed, nor cruel and unusual punishments inflicted.

### ARTICLE IX

**Rule of Construction of Constitution**

The enumeration in the Constitution of certain rights shall not be construed to deny or disparage others retained by the people.

### ARTICLE X

**Rights of States Under Constitution**

The powers not delegated to the United States by the Constitution, nor prohibited by it to the States, are reserved to the States respectively, or to the people.

## Later Amendments

### ARTICLE XI

**Judicial Powers Construed**

*The following amendment was proposed to the Legislatures of the several States by the Third Congress on the 5th of March, 1794, and was declared to have been ratified in a message from the President to Congress, dated Jan. 8, 1798.*

The judicial power of the United States shall not be construed to extend to any suit in law or equity, commenced or prosecuted against one of the United States, by citizens of another State, or by citizens or subjects of any foreign state.

### ARTICLE XII

**Manner of Choosing President and Vice-President**

*The following amendment was proposed to the Legislatures of the several States by the Eighth Congress on the 12th of December, 1803, and was declared to have been ratified in a proclamation by the Secretary of State, dated September 25, 1804. It was ratified by all the States except Connecticut, Delaware, Massachusetts, and New Hampshire.*

The Electors shall meet in their respective States, and vote by ballot for President and Vice-President, one of whom at least shall not be an inhabitant of the same State with themselves; they shall name in their ballots the person voted for as President, and in distinct ballots the person voted for as Vice-President; and they shall make distinct list of all persons voted for as President, and of all persons voted for as Vice-President, and of the number of votes for each, which list they shall sign and certify, and transmit, sealed, to the seat of the Government of the United States, directed to the President of the Senate; the President of the Senate shall, in the presence of the Senate and House of Representatives, open all the certificates and the votes shall then be counted; the person having the greatest number of votes for President shall be the President, if such number be a majority of the whole number of Electors appointed; and if no person have such majority, then from the persons having the highest number, not exceeding three, on the list of those voted for as President, the House of Representatives shall choose immediately, by ballot, the President. But in choosing the President, the votes shall be taken by States, the representation from each State having one vote; a quorum for this purpose shall consist of a member or members from two-thirds of the States, and a majority of all the States shall be necessary to a choice. And if the House of Representatives shall not choose a President, whenever the right of choice shall devolve upon them, before the fourth day of March next following, then the Vice-President shall act as President, as in the case of the death or other constitutional disability of the President. The person having the greatest number of votes as Vice-President shall be the Vice-President, if such number be a majority of the whole number of Electors appointed, and if no person have a majority, then from the two highest numbers on the list the Senate shall choose the Vice-President; a quorum for the purpose shall consist of two-thirds of the whole number of Senators, and a majority of the whole number shall be necessary to a choice. But no person constitutionally ineligible to the office of President shall be eligible to that of Vice-President of the United States.

## ARTICLE XIII

### Slavery Abolished

*The following amendment was proposed to the Legislatures of the several States by the Thirty-eighth Congress on the 1st of February, 1865, and was declared to have been ratified in a proclamation by the Secretary of State dated December 18, 1865. It was rejected by Delaware and Kentucky: was conditionally ratified by Alabama and Mississippi; and Texas took no action.*

1. Neither slavery nor involuntary servitude, except as a punishment for crime whereof the party shall have been duly convicted, shall exist within the United States, or any place subject to their jurisdiction.

2. Congress shall have power to enforce this article by appropriate legislation.

## ARTICLE XIV

### Citizenship Rights Not to Be Abridged

*The following popularly known as the Reconstruction Amendment, was proposed to the Legislatures of the several States by the Thirty-ninth Congress on the 16th of June, 1866, and was declared to have been ratified in a proclamation by the Secretary of State, dated July 23, 1868. The amendment got the support of 23 Northern States: it was rejected by Delaware, Kentucky, Maryland, and 10 Southern States. California took no action. Subsequently it was ratified by the 10 Southern States.*

1. All persons born or naturalized in the United States, and subject to the jurisdiction thereof, are citizens of the United States and of the State wherein they reside. No State shall make or enforce any law which shall abridge the privileges or immunities of citizens of the United States; nor shall any State deprive any person of life, liberty, or property without due process of law, nor deny to any person within its jurisdiction the equal protection of the laws.

### Apportionment of Representatives in Congress

2. Representatives shall be apportioned among the several States according to their respective numbers counting the whole number of persons in each State excluding Indians not taxed. But when the right to vote at any election for the choice of Electors for President and Vice-President of the United States, Representatives in Congress, the executive and judicial officers of a State, or the members of the Legislature thereof, is denied to any of the male inhabitants of such State, being twenty-one years of age, and citizens of the United States, or in any way abridged, except for participation in rebellion, or other crime, the basis of representation therein shall be reduced in the proportion which the number of such male citizens shall bear to the whole number of male citizens twenty-one years of age in such States.

### Power of Congress to Remove Disabilities of United States Officials for Rebellion

3. No person shall be a Senator or Representative in Congress, or Elector of President and Vice-President or holding any office, civil or military, under the United States, or under any State, who, having previously taken an oath, as a member of Congress, or as an officer of the United States, or as a member of any State Legislature or as an executive or judicial officer of any State, to support the Constitution of the United States, shall have engaged in insurrection or rebellion against the same, or given aid and comfort to the enemies thereof. But Congress may, by a vote of two-thirds of each House, remove such disability.

### What Public Debts Are Valid

4. The validity of the public debt of the United States, authorized by law, including debts incurred for payment of pensions and bounties for services in suppressing insurrection and rebellion, shall not be questioned. But neither the United States nor any State shall assume or pay any debt or obligation incurred in aid of insurrection or rebellion against the United States, or any claim for the loss or emancipation of any slave; but all such debts, obligations, and claims shall be held illegal and void.

5. The Congress shall have power to enforce by appropriate legislation the provision of this article.

## ARTICLE XV

### Equal Rights for White and Colored Citizens

*The following amendment was proposed to the Legislatures of the several States by the For-*

*tieth Congress on the 27th of February, 1869, and was declared to have been ratified in a proclamation by the Secretary of State, dated March 30, 1870. It was not acted on by Tennessee: it was rejected by California, Delaware, Kentucky, Maryland, and Oregon: ratified by the remaining 30 States. New York rescinded its ratification January 5, 1870. New Jersey rejected it in 1870, but ratified it in 1871.*

1. The right of the citizens of the United States to vote shall not be denied or abridged by the United States or by any State on account of race, color, or previous condition of servitude.

2. The Congress shall have power to enforce the provisions of this article by appropriate legislation.

## ARTICLE XVI

### Income Taxes Authorized

*The following amendment was proposed to the Legislatures of the several States by the Sixty-first Congress on the 12th day of July, 1909, and was declared to have been ratified in a proclamation by the Secretary of State, dated February 25, 1913. The income tax amendment was ratified by all the States except Connecticut, Florida, Pennsylvania, Rhode Island, Utah, and Virginia.*

The Congress shall have power to lay and collect taxes on incomes, from whatever sources derived, without apportionment among the several States and without regard to any census or enumeration.

## ARTICLE XVII

### United States Senators to Be Elected by Direct Popular Vote

*The following amendment was proposed to the Legislatures of the several States by the Sixty-second Congress on the 16th day of May, 1912, and was declared to have been ratified in a proclamation by the Secretary of State, dated May 31, 1913. It got the vote of all the States except Alabama, Delaware, Florida, Georgia, Kentucky, Louisiana, Maryland, Mississippi, Rhode Island, South Carolina, Utah, and Virginia.*

1. The Senate of the United States shall be composed of two Senators from each State, elected by the people thereof, for six years; and each Senator shall have one vote. The electors in each State shall have the qualifications requisite for electors of the most numerous branch of the State Legislatures.

### Vacancies in Senatorships, When Governor May Fill by Appointment

2. When vacancies happen in the representation of any State in the Senate, the executive authority of such State shall issue writs of election to fill such vacancies: Provided, That the Legislature of any State may empower the Executive thereof to make temporary appointment until the people fill the vacancies by election as the Legislature may direct.

3. This amendment shall not be so construed as to affect the election or term of any Senator chosen before it becomes valid as part of the Constitution.

## ARTICLE XVIII

### Liquor Prohibition Amendment

*The following amendment was proposed to the Legislatures of the several States by the Sixty-fifth Congress, December 18, 1917: and on January 29, 1919, the United States Secretary of State proclaimed its adoption by 36 States, and declared it in effect on January 16, 1920.*

*The amendment ultimately was adopted by all the States except Connecticut and Rhode Island. New Jersey ratified on March 10, 1922.*

*Enforcement of the National Prohibition Act was in effect at 12 P. M., January 16, 1920, except as to certain sections of Title II, wherein other dates were specified.*

*Early in 1920, the validity of the Eighteenth Amendment was upheld by the Supreme Court of the United States, in suits to void, brought by the States of Rhode Island and New Jersey, and by various brewers and distillers.*

1. After one year from the ratification of this article the manufacture, sale, or transportation of intoxicating liquors within, the importation thereof into, or the exportation thereof from the United States and all territory subject to the jurisdiction thereof for beverage purposes is hereby prohibited.

2. The Congress and the several States shall have concurrent power to enforce this article by appropriate legislation.

3. This article shall be inoperative unless it shall have been ratified as an amendment to the Constitution by the Legislatures of the several States, as provided in the Constitution, within seven years from the date of the submission hereof to the States by the Congress.

## ARTICLE XIX

### Giving Nation-Wide Suffrage to Women

*The following amendment was proposed to the Legislatures of the several States by the Sixty-fifth Congress, having been adopted by the House of Representatives, May 21, 1919, and by the Senate June 4, 1919. On August 26, 1920, the United States Secretary of State proclaimed it in effect, having been adopted (June 10, 1919-August 18, 1920) by three-quarters of the States. The Tennessee House, August 31, rescinded its ratification, 47 to 24.*

1. The right of citizens of the United States to vote shall not be denied or abridged by the United States or by any State on account of sex.

2. Congress shall have power, by appropriate legislation, to enforce the provisions of this article.

**ARTICLE XX**

**Terms of President and Vice-President to begin on January 20; those of Senators and Representatives on January 3**

*The following amendment was proposed to the Legislatures of the several States by the Seventy-second Congress, in March, 1932, a joint resolution to that effect having been adopted, first by the House, and then, on March 2, by the Senate. On Feb. 6, 1933, the Secretary of State proclaimed it in effect, 39 of the 48 States having ratified. By Oct. 15, 1933, it had been ratified by all of the 48 States.*

**Section 1** — The terms of the President and Vice-President shall end at noon on the 20th day of January, and the terms of the Senators and Representatives at noon on the 3rd day of January, of the years in which such terms would have ended if this article had not been ratified; and the terms of their successors shall then begin.

**Section 2** — The Congress shall assemble at least once in every year, and such meeting shall begin at noon on the 3rd day of January, unless they shall by law appoint a different day.

**Section 3** — If, at the time fixed for the beginning of the term of the President, the President elect shall have died the Vice-President elect shall become President. If a President shall not have been chosen before the time fixed for the beginning of his term, or if the President elect shall have failed to qualify, then the Vice-President elect shall act as President until a President shall have qualified; and the Congress may by law provide for the case wherein neither a President elect nor a Vice-President elect shall have qualified, declaring who shall then act as President, or the manner in which one who is to act shall be selected, and such person shall act accordingly until a President or Vice-President shall have qualified.

**Section 4** — The Congress may be law provide for the case of the death of any of the persons from whom the House of Representatives may choose a President whenever the right of choice shall have devolved upon them, and for the case of the death of any of the persons from whom the Senate may choose a Vice-President whenever the right of choice shall have devolved upon them.

**Section 5** — Sections 1 and 2 shall take effect on the 15th day of October following the ratification of this article (Oct., 1933).

**Section 6** — This article shall be inoperative unless it shall have been ratified as an amendment to the Constitution by the Legislatures of three-fourths of the several States within seven years from the date of its submission.

**ARTICLE XXI**

**Repeal of the Eighteenth (Prohibition) Amendment by Conventions in the States**

*The following proposed amendment to the Constitution, embodied in a joint resolution of the Seventy-second Congress (Senate, Feb. 16, 1933, by 63 to 23; House, Feb. 20, 1933, by 289 to 121), was transmitted to the Secretary of State on Feb. 21 and he at once sent to the governors of the States copies of the resolution. The amendment went into effect on Dec. 5, 1933, having been adopted by 36 of the 48 States — three-quarters of the entire number. The amendment is:*

**Section 1** — The eighteenth article of amendment to the Constitution of the United States is hereby repealed.

**Section 2** — The transportation or importation into any State, Territory, or Possession of the United States for delivery or use therein of intoxicating liquors, in violation of the laws thereof, is hereby prohibited.

**Section 3** — This article shall be inoperative unless it shall have been ratified as an amendment to the Constitution by conventions in the several States, as provided in the Constitution, within seven years from the date of the submission hereof to the States by the Congress.

**ARTICLE XXII**

**Presidents Barred from Serving More than Two Elective Terms**

*The following proposed amendment was approved by the Eightieth Congress on March 26, 1947, and transmitted to the Secretary of State, who sent copies of the resolution to the governors of the States. The amendment went into effect on February 26, 1951, having been adopted by 36 of the 48 States.*

**Section 1** — No person shall be elected to the office of the President more than twice, and no person who has held the office of President, or acted as President, for more than two years of a term to which some other person was elected President shall be elected to the office of the President more than once. But this article shall not apply to any person holding the office of President when this Article was proposed by the Congress, and shall not prevent any person who may be holding the office of President, or acting as President, during the term within which this Article becomes operative from holding the office of President or acting as President during the remainder of such term.

**Section 2** — This Article shall be inoperative unless it shall have been ratified by an amendment to the Constitution by the Legislature of three-fourths of the several States within seven years from the date of its submission to the States by the Congress.

### ARTICLE XXIII

**Citizens of District of Columbia Granted Right to Vote in Presidential Elections**

*The following proposed amendment was approved by the Eighty-sixth Congress on June 16, 1960, and was transmitted to the Legislatures of the 50 States. Ratification by the required three-fourths majority of the States was completed March 29, 1961.*

**Section 1** — The District constituting the seat of Government of the United States shall appoint in such manner as the Congress may direct:

A number of electors of President and Vice-President equal to the whole number of Senators and Representatives in Congress to which the District would be entitled if it were a State, but in no event more than the least populous State; they shall be in addition to those appointed by the States, but they shall be considered, for the purposes of the election of President and Vice-President, to be electors appointed by a State; and they shall meet in the District and perform such duties as provided by the twelfth article of amendment.

**Section 2** — The Congress shall have power to enforce this article by appropriate legislation.

### ARTICLE XXIV

**Poll Tax Barred as Prerequisite in Federal Elections**

*The following proposed amendment was approved by the Eighty-eighth Congress on Jan. 23, 1964, when it was ratified by 38 of the 50 States. It had been submitted to the States by Congress Aug. 27, 1962.*

**Section 1** — The right of citizens of the United States to vote in any primary or other election for President or Vice-President, for electors for President or Vice-President, or for Senator or Representative in Congress, shall not be denied or abridged by the United States or any State by reason of failure to pay any poll tax or other tax.

**Section 2**—The Congress shall have the power to enforce this article by appropriate legislation.

## THE DECLARATION OF INDEPENDENCE

*The Declaration of Independence was adopted by the Continental Congress, in Philadelphia, on July 4, 1776, and was signed by John Hancock as President and by Charles Thomson as Secretary. It was published first on July 6 in the Pennsylvania Evening Post. A copy of the Declaration, engrossed on parchment, was signed by members of Congress on and after Aug. 2, 1776.*

When, in the Course of human events, it becomes necessary for one people to dissolve the political bands which have connected them with another, and to assume among the powers of the earth, the separate and equal station to which the Laws of Nature and of Nature's God entitle them, a decent respect to the opinions of mankind requires that they should declare the causes which impel them to the separation.

We hold these truths to be self-evident, that all men are created equal, that they are endowed by their Creator with certain unalienable Rights, that among these are Life, Liberty and the pursuit of Happiness. That to secure these rights, Governments are instituted among Men, deriving their just powers from the consent of the governed. That whenever any Form of Government becomes destructive of these ends, it is the Right of the People to alter or to abolish it, and to institute new Government, laying its foundation on such principles and organizing its powers in such form, as to them shall seem most likely to effect their Safety and Happiness. Prudence, indeed, will dictate that Governments long established should not be changed for light and transient causes; and accordingly all experience hath shewn, that mankind are more disposed to suffer, while evils are sufferable, than to right themselves by abolishing the forms to which they are accustomed. But when a long train of abuses and usurpations, pursuing invariably the same object, evidence a design to reduce them under absolute Despotism, it is their right, it is their duty, to throw off such Government, and to provide new Guards for their future security. Such has been the patient sufferance of these Colonies; and such is now the necessity which constrains them to alter their former Systems of Government. The history of the present King of Great Britain is a history of repeated injuries and usurpations, all having in direct object the establishment of an absolute Tyranny over these States. To prove this, let Facts be submitted to a candid world.

He has refused his Assent to Laws, the most wholesome and necessary for the public good.

He has forbidden his Governors to pass Laws of immediate and pressing importance, unless suspended in their operation till his Assent should be obtained, and when so suspended, he has utterly neglected to attend to them.

He has refused to pass other Laws for the accommodation of large districts of people, unless those people would relinquish the right of Representation in the Legislature, a right inestimable to them and formidable to tyrants only.

He has called together legislative bodies at

places, unusual, uncomfortable, and distant from the depository of their public Records, for the sole purpose of fatiguing them into compliance with his measures.

He has dissolved Representative Houses repeatedly, for opposing with manly firmness his invasions on the rights of the people.

He has refused for a long time, after such dissolutions, to cause others to be elected; whereby the Legislative powers, incapable of Annihilation, have returned to the People at large for their exercise; the State remaining in the mean-time exposed to all the dangers of invasion from without, and convulsions within.

He has endeavored to prevent the population of these States; for that purpose obstructing the Laws for Naturalization of Foreigners; refusing to pass others to encourage their migrations hither, and raising the conditions of new Appropriations of Lands.

He has obstructed the Administration of Justice, by refusing his Assent to Laws for establishing Judiciary powers.

He has made Judges dependent on his Will alone, for the tenure of their offices, and the amount and payment of their salaries.

He has erected a multitude of New Offices, and sent hither swarms of Officers to harass our people, and eat out their substance.

He has kept among us, in times of peace, Standing Armies, without the Consent of our legislature.

He has affected to render the Military independent of and superior to the Civil power.

He has combined with others to subject us to a jurisdiction foreign to our constitution and unacknowledged by our laws; giving his Assent to their Acts of pretended Legislation: For quartering large bodies of armed troops among us: For protecting them by a mock Trial from punishment for any Murders which they should commit on the Inhabitants of these States: For cutting off our Trade with all parts of the world: For imposing Taxes on us without our Consent: For depriving us in many cases of the benefits of Trial by Jury: For transporting us beyond Seas to be tried for pretended offenses: For abolishing the free System of English Laws in a neighbouring Province, establishing therein an Arbitrary government, and enlarging its Boundaries so as to render it at once an example and fit instrument for introducing the same absolute rule into these Colonies: For taking away our Charters, abolishing our most valuable Laws and altering fundamentally the Forms of our Governments: For suspending our own Legislatures and declaring themselves invested with power to legislate for us in all cases whatsoever.

He has abdicated Government here by declaring us out of his Protection and waging War against us.

He has plundered our seas, ravished our Coasts, burnt our towns, and destroyed the lives of our people.

He is at this time transporting large Armies of foreign Mercenaries to complete the works of death, desolation and tyranny, already begun with circumstances of cruelty and perfidy scarcely paralleled in the most barbarous ages, and totally unworthy the Head of a civilized nation.

He has constrained our fellow Citizens taken Captive on the high Seas to bear Arms against their Country, to become the executioners of their friends and Brethren, or to fall themselves by their Hands.

He has excited domestic insurrections amongst us, and has endeavored to bring on the inhabitants of our frontiers, the merciless Indian Savages, whose known rule of warfare is an undistinguished destruction of all ages, sexes and conditions. In every stage of these Oppressions We have Petitioned for Redress in the most humble terms. Our repeated Petitions have been answered only by repeated injury. A Prince, whose character is thus marked by every act which may define a Tyrant, is unfit to be the ruler of a free people. Nor have We been wanting in attention to our British brethren. We have warned them from time to time of attempts by their legislature to extend an unwarrantable jurisdiction over us. We have reminded them of the circumstances of our emigration and settlement here. We have appealed to their native justice and magnanimity, and we have conjured them by the ties of our common kindred to disavow these usurpations, which would inevitably interrupt our connections and correspondence. They too have been deaf to the voice of justice and of consanguinity. We must, therefore, acquiesce in the necessity, which denounces our Separation, and hold them, as we hold the rest of mankind, Enemies in War, in Peace Friends.

WE, THEREFORE, the Representatives of the United States of America, in General Congress, Assembled, appealing to the Supreme Judge of the world for the rectitude of our intentions do, in the Name, and by authority of the good People of these Colonies, solemnly publish and declare, That these United Colonies are, and of Right ought to be, Free and Independent States: that they are Absolved from all Allegiance to the British Crown, and that all political connection between them and the State of Great Britain is and ought to be totally dissolved: and that as Free and Independent States, they have full Power to levy War, conclude Peace, contract Alliances, establish Commerce, and to do all other Acts and Things which Independent States may of right do. And for the support of this Declaration, with a firm reliance on the protection of Divine Providence, we mutually pledge to each other our Lives, our Fortunes, and our sacred Honor.

# CHIEF LEGAL OR PUBLIC HOLIDAYS

*Each State has jurisdiction over holidays that will be observed in that State. They are designated either by the State legislature or by executive proclamation and, therefore, may be changed with each new State executive or legislature. There are no national holidays in the United States. The President and Congress designate holidays only for the District of Columbia and for federal employees throughout the nation.*

**Jan. 1** — New Year's Day. All the States, District of Columbia, Canal Zone, Guam, Puerto Rico, Virgin Islands.

**Jan. 20** — Inauguration Day. Begun in 1937. It is to be observed every fourth year in the District of Columbia only.

**Feb. 12** — Lincoln's Birthday. All the States except Ala., Ark., Fla., Ga., Ida., La., Me., Mass., Miss., N.H., N.C., Okla., R.I., S.C., Tex., Va. Also observed in District of Columbia and Virgin Islands.

**Feb.** — Washington's Birthday (Third Monday in February). All the States except Okla. Presidents' Day in Hawaii; In Ohio, Washington-Lincoln Day. Observed on Feb. 22 in S. Dakota and W. Virginia).

**March or April** — Good Friday (Friday before Easter). Conn., Del., Fla., Hawaii, Ill., Ind., La., Md., Minn., N.J., N.D., Pa., Tenn., Canal Zone, Puerto Rico, Virgin Islands. In Calif., from 12 noon to 3 P.M. In Ark. and Guam, a Memorial Day.

**May** — Memorial or Decoration Day (Last Monday in May). All the States except Miss., S.C. (In Florida, Memorial Day for Veterans of all Wars.) Observed on May 30 in S. Dakota.

**July 4** — Independence Day. All the States, District of Columbia, Canal Zone, Guam, Puerto Rico, Virgin Islands.

**Sept.** — Labor Day (First Monday in September). All the States, District of Columbia, Canal Zone, Guam, Puerto Rico, Virgin Islands.

**Oct.** — Columbus Day (Second Monday in October). All the States except Alaska, Maine, Miss., N.M., Nev., Okla., Ore., S.C., S.D., Va., Wyo., (Discovery Day in Indiana and North Dakota; Landing Day in Wisconsin. In Arkansas and Oregon, a Memorial Day.) (In Massachusetts on Oct. 12).

**Oct.** — Veterans or Armistice Day (Fourth Monday in October). All the States, District of Columbia, Canal Zone, Guam, Puerto Rico, Virgin Islands. In Okla. and Va., closing of banks and offices is optional.

**Nov.** — General Election Day (First Tuesday after First Monday in November). All the States except Ala., Conn., Ga., Kans., Ky., Me., Mass., Miss., Nebr., N. Mex., N.C., Utah, Vt. Usually observed only when presidential or general elections are held.

**Nov.** — Thanksgiving Day (Fourth Thursday in November). All the States, District of Columbia, Canal Zone, Guam, Puerto Rico, Virgin Islands.

**Dec. 25** — Christmas Day. All the States, District of Columbia, Canal Zone, Guam, Puerto Rico, Virgin Islands.

# PARLIAMENTARY LAW

### Definition

Originally, parliamentary law pertained to a parliament, that of England, and had almost the force of law. Now the expression is used to indicate the forms of procedure used in conducting meetings or debates.

### Model: U.S. Congress

In the United States, rules followed in Congress are generally adopted as a pattern for procedure. There are manuals of parliamentary law which can be obtained at almost any bookstore or public library. Frequently, the constitution of a society names some one particular manual as final resort for settlement of any dispute that may arise.

### Importance

Some acquaintance with parliamentary law should be possessed by everybody. No meeting can have much success in accomplishing its purposes unless conducted by a chairman who knows the rules and with members who are ready to accept them and abide by the rulings of the Chair. Without some standard of procedure, a meeting of citizens to organize a protest against their town's government would resemble a crowd of boys in a field organizing a football game. Everybody would talk at once, and the loudest voice would prevail. To ascertain and express the will of the meeting would be a tedious and disorderly process.

### Special Purpose Meeting

In the case of such a meeting as the one spoken of above, procedure is simple. Someone who is taking the lead will act as chairman in calling the meeting to order. He may occupy so strong a position of leadership as to enable him to assume the chairmanship, or he may call for nominations and take an aye-and-no vote of those present. In such a meeting, it is practically a certainty that the persons who called and organized it will be ready with something in writing, as a petition or protest, upon which the meeting is to act. In all probability, after full and free discussion, a committee would be named to present the paper to the city government. The meeting would adjourn spontaneously rather than formally.

### Formation of a Permanent Organization

A meeting to effect a permanent organization is not quite such a simple matter.

#### TEMPORARY CHAIRMAN

First, a temporary chairman has to be found. As a rule, there is someone among those present to whom the position falls almost automatically. If there are groups or factions in the assembly, it may be necessary to put the choice of a temporary chairman to a vote. On taking the chair, the temporary presiding officer appoints a secretary pro tem., to take minutes of the meeting.

#### CONSTITUTIONAL COMMITTEE

The speed with which matters then move depends upon the definiteness and unanimity of purpose of those assembled. It may be possible to go right ahead with the adoption of a constitution and election of officers; or it may be necessary to appoint or elect a committee to draft a constitution and bylaws, to be submitted at a later meeting, and perhaps to name a committee to present nominations.

#### PURPOSE OF MEETING

If full preparations have been made, and the meeting is ready to proceed with permanent organization, the first step is to have the purpose of the meeting definitely stated, preferably in the form of a motion, declaring it the objective of the meeting that a society for certain purposes is to be formed — athletic, social, political, or whatever it may be.

#### ADOPTING CONSTITUTION

Then if a constitution has already been drafted, it can be submitted for debate leading up to a vote. The temporary chairman engineers the proceedings with what skill he has to keep the machinery running smoothly. It may be possible to vote upon the constitution as a whole and at once, or it may have to be taken article by article, or even clause by clause. Such action may be called for through a motion by any person present. The motion is voted on, and the action called for is taken. After the constitution and bylaws have been voted on, article by article, the chairman asks for further amendments, if any are to be proposed; he then calls for a vote upon the constitution as a whole, and with passage of such a motion, the constitution is declared to have been adopted.

### Constitution

The *constitution* of a society is the statement of its aims and purposes, and the code of rules, by which its members are bound. It may be complete in itself, or it may be supplemented by a set of bylaws. When there are both constitution and bylaws, the former contains the fundamental provisions and the latter embodies the particular rules of action.

#### ARTICLES

Each section of the constitution is called an *article*. The first article usually states the name and object of the association, but sometimes these are separated, the name being given in Article One, the purpose in Article Two. In following articles, the requirements of membership are stated; officers and their duties; committees, meetings, and the method of amending the constitution.

#### BYLAWS

The bylaws would cover such specific details of club government as penalties for non-attendance at meetings, use of library or locker room, and the code of conduct for members.

#### SUPPLEMENTS

Items that might be placed either in the constitution or in the bylaws (but preferably in the former) are:

*Meetings*

under *Meetings*, the quorum required, the order of business to be followed, and the authority to be resorted to in case of disputes as to parliamentary law;

*Members*

under *Members*, the privileges and responsibilities of members, the fees and dues to be paid;

*Officers*

under *Officers*, a full statement of the duties of each;

*Committees*

under *Committees*, a statement of duties, and regulations as to the making of reports.

### Order of Business

The customary order of business is: calling of the roll by the secretary, for the record of attendance; reading of the minutes of the last meeting; reports by committees; unfinished business; new business; adjournment.

### Presiding Officer

The presiding officer is, as the words imply, the one who administers this parliamentary law. It is he who directs the program of a meeting. He rules on all questions of order. He decides who "has the floor," or the privilege of speaking.

When motions are made, it is the presiding officer who puts them; that is, calls for the vote. If a motion is improperly made, it is he who corrects the procedure. He has not only the power and the duty of regulating discussion, but a great trust in keeping the debate on fair grounds. He prevents discussion from rambling inefficiency; he is bound, sometimes, to incur the displeasure of members who think he is restricting their remarks too closely. When two or more members address the chair at once, he accepts the responsibility of recognizing one and holding the others back; and in this way, he can, if he so desires, shape the discussion pretty much his own way. A good presiding officer is firm but absolutely fair; instead of trying to swing the discussion to suit his own ideas, he confines his effort to an impartial direction of the debate so that the true will of the members may be ascertained and executed.

#### MAINTENANCE OF ORDER

A competent presiding officer never interrupts a member who has the floor unless the speaker is out of order — that is to say, violating the rules in some manner. In such a case, he declares the member to be out of order, and states why.

#### RELINQUISHMENT OF CHAIRMANSHIP

He takes no part in the discussion himself unless, wishing to do so, he relinquishes the chairmanship to another officer. After that he moves down to a place on the floor, among the members, and addresses the Chair.

#### IMPORTANCE OF PRESIDING OFFICER

In a club or society, or a board of directors, a good presiding officer is a treasure. It is also important to have a competent substitute to take his place when he is unable to act. The common idea that almost anyone will do for vice-president is bad, because the vice-president takes the president's place when the president is absent, and he should be fully capable of taking over the duties of the presidency.

#### REFERENCE TO "THE CHAIR"

In speaking of the presiding officer, a member refers to him as "the Chair," as in the expression "With the consent of the Chair, I wish . . ."

### Motion

Important motions are often presented to the secretary in writing, so that there may be no mistake as to the terms in which they are made. If the motion is made orally from the floor, the secretary writes it down, so that it may be referred to as need arises. Thus when the presiding officer puts the motion, he may call upon the secretary to read it, and then say: "The motion as read by the secretary has been made and seconded." He then calls for remarks. If amendments are offered, the secretary jots them down. Any member may ask to have the motion read again or to have amendments repeated. The person making a motion or submitting an amendment may withdraw it at any time previous to presentation by the Chair, or presiding officer.

### Vote

When the presiding officer thinks discussion has gone far enough and nothing more is to be forthcoming, he may ask: "Are you ready for the question?" If members are silent, he assumes they are ready to vote, and proceeds to present the question for ayes and noes. If a member rises to make further remarks, the presiding officer gives him the floor. Or possibly members answer: "Ready! Ready," and then the question is promptly put and the meeting proceeds to further business.

#### SUMMARY

Summing up, the procedure on a motion is this: A member addresses the Chair. The Chair recognizes the member. The member says, "Mr. Chairman, I move . . ." Another member addresses the Chair, and the Chair recognizes him, whereupon he says, "Mr. Chairman, I second the motion." Or if two or more members rise and address the Chair simultaneously, the Chair recognizes one or the other, according to his own judgment.

#### DISCUSSION

The chairman then restates the motion or has it read by the secretary, and places it before the meeting for discussion. He may say, "Has anyone any remarks to make upon the motion before the house? If not, we shall proceed to a vote."

#### CALL FOR VOTE

He then calls for the ayes and the noes. Or, if there is discussion, when it begins to lag — or if it gets too hot — he says that, unless there is objection, he shall consider further discussion useless and put the motion to a vote.

### Minutes

The presiding officer also declares the minutes adopted if, after asking, "Has anyone any objection to the minutes as read, or any corrections or alterations to suggest?" there is no reply. He then says, "You have heard the minutes as read by the secretary and as no objections or corrections are offered, I declare them approved as read. The secretary will enter them upon the books."

### Logical Order

There is a fixed, scientific order for all parliamentary action.

When a motion is before the house, these actions are in order:

A motion to amend the motion;
a motion to amend the amendment;
a motion to refer the matter to a committee for report and recommendation;
a motion to postpone action until a stated time;
a call for the previous question;
a vote on the original motion;
a motion to lay the matter on the table, or postpone it indefinitely.

A motion must come to one of these settlements.

An amendment to an amendment is susceptible to no further change. It must be voted down before other amendments can be considered.

**Withdrawal of Motion**

If a member, having presented a motion, asks to withdraw it, and no objection is made, the presiding officer may declare it withdrawn. If objection is made, the request for withdrawal must be debated and finally settled by a vote.

**Refusal of Nomination**

A person nominated for office may refuse the nomination. A member who has made a nomination may withdraw it.

**Point of Order**

Should the Chair be thought to have ruled wrongly or to have been unfair, protest should be made by a member saying, "I rise to a point of order." The Chair says, "You will please state your point of order." The member then explains why he thinks the procedure has been in error. The Chair may yield or deny the point of protest. Appeal from the decision may be made; the presiding officer may himself conduct the discussion of the point or order. For final settlement, a vote may be taken. If the majority votes that the point of protest is well taken, the Chair must yield.

**Committee of the Whole**

Sometimes, to facilitate discussion and conclusion of a matter, a meeting resolves itself into a *committee of the whole*. The entire membership in attendance thus is enabled to debate more freely than in formal meetings. The presiding officer, when a motion to resolve the meeting into committee of the whole is passed, customarily appoints a chairman of the committee to conduct the proceedings. The secretary of the organization, however, acts as secretary of the committee of the whole. A committee of the whole can do no business except to amend or adopt motions. Upon carriage of a motion to rise and report, the meeting resumes its normal course.

**Committee Meeting and Report**

Customarily, the first person named in a list of appointees to a committee is expected to serve as chairman. If he does not call the committee into meeting, a majority of the members may fix a time and place for meeting. For committee meetings, a majority constitutes a quorum. The chairman of a committee makes its report to the organization. Sometimes, two reports are submitted, one for the majority and one for the minority. The minority report is entitled to a reading before the main meeting, and a motion may be made to substitute it for the majority report. The main body has free choice between the two sets of recommendations.

**Motion to Adjourn**

A *motion to adjourn* is in order at any time except when a member is speaking or a vote is being taken. A simple motion to adjourn is not debatable. A motion to adjourn to a specific time or place may be debated. In case of a negative vote, reconsideration may be had.

**Submission of Question to Committee**

When argument over a motion is deadlocked, a motion to submit the question to a committee is in order. If recommendations by a committee are not accepted, a motion to recommit is in order, and upon its passage the committee is charged to prepare new recommendations.

**Appointment of Committee**

Sometimes, to gain speed in disposing of ordinary routine matters, the presiding officer says, "If there is no objection, I shall appoint a committee . . . to do this or that." Then if no member speaks, the presiding officer says, "It shall be entered as the action of this meeting." This is an instance where silence gives consent.

**Question of Privilege**

A *question of privilege* has to do with something apart from the meeting's program or order of business. When a member presents a question of privilege, it outranks all other matters for the time being. It can be brought up when there is disturbance in the meeting room, as by the intrusion of a person not entitled to be present, or in connection with the well-being of members, as to ventilate a stuffy room or to turn on heat.

**Other Privileged Questions**

A question of privilege is a technical subvariety of what are known as privileged questions. The other privileged questions are motions to adjourn or to take a recess, and ask for the orders of the day — that is, to request the Chair to state what particular matters are scheduled for consideration at the time of the present meeting.

**Successful Meetings**

These are fine points of parliamentary procedure that come up in such formal sessions as those of a legislative body rather than in a somewhat informal meeting, as of a club or civic organization. But any meeting is more sure of success in its purpose if conducted by someone who has knowledge of correct procedure and ability to keep things running smoothly and effectively.

# FEDERAL GOVERNMENT ORGANIZATION

**The Democratic Republic**

The Government of the United States is an old government — one of the oldest in the world. Few governments in existence in 1789 when it began still survive. Many countries have changed their form of government several times since that date. The U.S. Government has changed during these years, but these changes have taken place within the original established framework, and the main organs of government remain as they were in 1789.

The Government of the United States is a republic. The term comes from Latin and literally means "public thing," a government which belongs to the public. Supreme power in a republic rests with all the citizens entitled to vote. When citizenship is open to all, a republic is a democracy, but such has not been the case in all republics. The ancient Roman Republic restricted full citizenship to only a part of the population; it was an oligarchy, rule of the few. The U.S. today is a democratic republic since all persons born within the country are citizens and may vote when they reach the legal age. Persons born elsewhere who have lived in the country for 5 years may become citizens through naturalization. Republics were uncommon when the Americans established the Republic of the U.S., but today they are the most common form of government on earth. Some of present-day republics are democratic; some are not. Some states which are republics in title do not in fact permit citizens to exercise power. They may vote but they have no real free choice.

The Americans declared their independence from England in 1776, but they retained much of an English heritage in the Republic which they established 12 years later. The Congress consisted of an upper and a lower house, comparable to the English Parliament. The Federal courts recognized both English Common Law and Equity and used both the grand and the trial juries as in England. The U.S. Constitution also incorporates certain other features of English law, such as the writ of habeas corpus and the law of treason. In framing their government, the Americans did not try to make everything new. They wisely made use of much that they had inherited so that some features of the U.S. Government are in reality older than the Republic.

KENNETH S. COOPER, B.A., M.A., Ph.D., *Professor of History*, George Peabody College for Teachers.

**The Constitution**

An important part of the American inheritance from England was the idea of constitutional government; that is, the idea of having a fundamental law which fixed the structure and limits of government. The Americans not only accepted the idea of a constitution, they tried to include it in a written document. In so doing they attempted what the English had never done, for the English Constitution was not then, nor is it now, a single document; it is rather a tradition expressed in various laws, declarations, and, especially, in history. Perhaps it would seem simpler to have a single written constitution, yet, in fact, it has proved impossible to confine the Constitution to the document. The Americans also have a constitutional tradition that goes beyond the written text. There are basic features of the U.S. Government which are not set forth in the written Constitution. Political parties are fundamental in American government and have been so from the beginning of the Republic, yet the written Constitution does not mention them. In some instances the written text of the Constitution does not really explain the practice. The text describes a method of indirect election for the President and Vice President; the people of the States vote only for electors who in turn actually elect the two chief officials. But, in fact, electors are always pledged to support party candidates nominated in advance so that in practice, the President and Vice President are chosen in a form of popular election. The constitutional tradition on matters of this sort is quite as important as the written Constitution, and the tradition is found not in the document but primarily in the nation's history.

The distinction between the mere documentary Constitution and the tradition is also seen in the ways Americans have changed their fundamental law over the years. Article V of the Constitution describes how changes may be made. An amendment may be proposed either by a two-thirds vote of both Houses of Congress or by a convention called upon application of two-thirds of the States. Once proposed, a measure must be ratified by three-fourths of the States (37 today) before it becomes part of the basic law. Americans have amended the Constitution 24 times in the course of their history, but probably more important than the changes through amendments have been those made by interpretation. As the country has grown and the times have changed, the Federal courts have expanded and reinterpreted the Constitution to fit changing conditions. This capacity to grow and change is, no doubt, one reason why the U.S. Government is one of the world's oldest.

**The Federal Government and the States**

The United States is a Federal Government. It was created by a union of 13 States which has grown to 50. Presumably still other States could be admitted. The Federal system is based upon a division of powers between the Federal and State Governments. The Constitution specifies that certain powers shall be exercised by the Federal Government only. It alone controls foreign relations, raises an army and a navy, declares war and makes peace, coins money, maintains a post office, and regulates commerce among States and with foreign countries. In addition to these exclusive powers, the Federal Government also shares certain kinds of authority with the States. Both State and Federal Governments may tax, borrow money, build public works, charter banks, establish courts, and help agriculture and industry. As stated in the 10th Amendment, powers not delegated to the Federal Government are reserved to the States or to the people. In general the States establish local government, protect law and order, establish and maintain schools, provide care for the needy, and regulate business within a state. But the lines between the two authorities are not as sharply drawn as the 10th Amendment might seem to indicate. The Federal Government, primarily through financial aid, has extended its powers into realms once left entirely to the States, as is shown by the creation of a Federal Department of Urban Affairs and another for Health, Education, and Welfare.

The framers of the Constitution established a Federal system because they did not want to vest all power in any one person or group. They thought that liberty would be more secure if both the Federal and State Governments had limited powers. For the same reason they also divided authority within the Federal Government and created 3 branches, each to exercise one form of governmental power: the Legislative had the power to make laws, the Judicial to interpret them, and the Executive to administer them. The division of authority enables one branch to act as a check and balance on the other two. The idea of checks and balances within the Federal Government, like the division of State and Federal authority, has been somewhat modified by interpretation and usage, but the basic structure still remains.

## LEGISLATIVE BRANCH: THE CONGRESS

The authority to make laws is vested in the Congress which consists of two Houses: the Senate and the House of Representatives. To make a law a member of Congress introduces a bill into the House of which he is a member. The bill is then referred to a committee for study. Sometimes on important matters, a committee will hold hearings at which persons in favor of or opposed to the measure may express their views. A committee may either recommend a bill to the whole House; it may rewrite it; or it may ignore it. If a bill is recommended or brought back in another form, a debate is scheduled in which members discuss the proposal before voting on it. If a House votes in favor of a bill, it is then sent to the other House which follows much the same procedure. After both Houses have passed a bill, it is sent to the President who may either sign it and make it a law or veto it. To pass a bill over the President's veto requires a two-thirds vote of both Houses. If any bill sent to the President is not signed or returned to Congress with a veto within 10 days (Sundays excepted), it becomes a law without his signature unless the adjournment of Congress prevents his return within that time.

The Constitution assigns certain special powers to each of the Houses. The Senate must give its consent to many Presidential appointments. The Senate must also give its consent to any treaty negotiated by the Executive branch. Approval of a treaty requires a two-thirds vote of the members present. The House of Representatives has a special power with regard to raising money since it must originate all revenue bills, that is, measures raising income for the Government. The power of Congress to levy taxes and appropriate money, the "power of the purse," is one of the important checks which it exercises over the Executive branch.

Congress also possesses the power to remove officials and judges — including the President — from office. The House of Representatives may impeach, that is, bring charges against any official guilty of serious misconduct. The Senate sits as a high court to try impeachment charges.

## THE SENATE

### Membership

100 members, 2 elected by popular vote from each of the 50 states for 6 year terms arranged so that one-third of the membership is elected every 2 years. A Senator must be a resident of the State from which he is chosen, at least 30 years of age, and a citizen of the U.S. for at least 9 years.

### Officers

The Vice President of the U.S. is the presiding officer; President Pro Tempore, elected by the Senate from its members, presides in the absence of the Vice President; Secretary of the Senate, elected by the Senate, is custodian of the seal of the Senate and performs a number of formal duties; Sergeant at Arms, elected by the Senate, is the executive officer; Chaplain, elected by the Senate.

## THE HOUSE OF REPRESENTATIVES

### Membership

435 Representatives elected by popular vote from districts within the States for 2 year terms. The number from each State is determined by population, but every State has at least 1 Representative. A Representative must be at least 25 years of age, a resident of the State from which he is chosen, and a citizen of the U.S. for at least 7 years.

### Officers

The Speaker, elected by the House from its membership, is the presiding officer; Clerk of the House, a continuing officer elected by the House whose duties do not end with the adjournment of a session; Parliamentarian; Chaplain.

## CONGRESSIONAL COMMITTEES

Both Houses are organized into standing committees which do much of the actual work of framing and considering legislation. Either standing committees or specially appointed committees may review and investigate the administration of government by the Executive branch or any other matter of national concern.

### Standing Committees of the Senate

Aeronautical and Space Sciences, Agriculture and Forestry, Appropriations, Armed Services, Banking and Currency, Commerce, District of Columbia, Finance, Foreign Relations, Governmental Operations, Interior and Insular Affairs, Judiciary, Labor and Public Welfare, Post Office and Civil Service, Public Works, Rules and Administration.

### Standing Committees of the House

Science and Astronautics, Agriculture, Appropriations, Armed Services, Banking and Currency, Interstate and Foreign Commerce, Merchant Marine, District of Columbia, Ways and Means, Veterans Affairs, Foreign Affairs, Government Operations, Interior and Insular Affairs, Judiciary, Education and Labor, Post Office and Civil Service, Public Works, Rules, House Administration.

## SESSIONS OF CONGRESS

Congress must meet at least once every year. The regular session convenes on January 3. The President may also call special sessions.

## CONGRESSIONAL RECORD

Congress has published a daily record of proceedings in both Houses since March 4, 1873. Members may also insert other materials into the record as well as remarks not delivered on the floor.

## JUDICIAL BRANCH

### The Supreme Court of the United States

The high court of appeal for cases arising under the Constitution and the laws of the U.S. It has original jurisdiction in controversies to which the U.S. is a party, and in cases to which a State is a party, and in all cases affecting foreign ambassadors, ministers, and consuls. The Court consists of the Chief Justice and 8 Associate Justices. A quorum consists of 6. The number of Justices is not fixed by the Constitution but is set by law; the first Court had 6 members. The term of the Court begins the first Monday in October each year and continues as long as required, usually until the middle of June.

### U.S. Courts of Appeal

The U.S. is divided into 11 judicial circuits each with a Court of Appeals which hears cases which the Supreme Court cannot consider. Each Court of Appeals has from 3 to 9 judgeships, a total of 84 in all. Each Court usually hears cases in divisions consisting of 3 judges, but they may sit with all judges present.

### U.S. District Courts

The Federal trial courts in which most actions begin. Each State has at least 1 District Court and some States have several. There are 88 District Courts in the 50 states plus 1 in the District of Columbia and 1 in the Commonwealth of Puerto Rico. Each Court has a clerk, a U.S. attorney, a U.S. marshal, and at least 1 commissioner, 1 referee in bankruptcy, and 1 probation officer.

### Special Courts

Congress has from time to time created special courts to deal with particular types of cases. Included among these: *Court of Claims; Court of Customs and Patent Appeals; Customs Courts; Territorial Courts,* which, except in Puerto Rico, have jurisdiction over local matters which in the States are decided by State Courts.

### Selection and Tenure of Judges

All Federal judges are appointed by the President with the advice and consent of the Senate. Judges hold office for life or until retirement subject to good behavior. Judges may be removed only by impeachment by the House of Representatives and a trial before the Senate.

## EXECUTIVE BRANCH

### The President

The President is the head of state, chief executive officer, commander-in-chief of the armed forces, chief spokesman for the nation in foreign affairs, and partner with Congress in making of laws. The President is the only official chosen by the vote of the whole nation. He is elected for a 4 year term. Since the adoption of the 22nd Amendment in 1951, no person may be elected to the office more than twice. Prior to that date only one President, Franklin D. Roosevelt, had ever broken the 2 term tradition. The President must be at least 35 years of age, a natural born citizen, and 14 years a resident. If the President dies in office or is removed, the Vice President takes his place. After the Vice President the succession follows in this order: Speaker of the House, President Pro Tempore of the Senate, Cabinet members in the order in which the departments were created.

### The Executive Office of the President

A group of agencies and offices which assist the President in carrying out the duties which belong distinctly to his office.

### The White House Office

The staff which aids the President in the performance of various activities incident to his immediate office.

### Bureau of the Budget

Conducts research on the Government's finances, advises the President, and helps prepare the annual budget which the President sends to Congress each year.

### Council of Economic Advisers (CEA)

Advises the President on the state of the national economy.

### National Security Council

Advises President on aspects of foreign, domestic, and military affairs related to national security. *The Central Intelligence Agency* (CIA) is an organ of the Council.

### National Aeronautics and Space Council

Advises the President on space programs and related matters.

### Office of Economic Opportunity (OEO)

Coordinates and directs various programs for the elimination of poverty, the overall authority in charge of the "war on poverty."

### Office of Emergency Planning

Advises the President and coordinates policies in preparation for either military emergencies or natural disasters.

### Office of Science and Technology

Advises the President about the development of scientific and technological programs.

### Office of Special Representative for Trade Negotiations

Advises President and implements trade agreement programs.

## EXECUTIVE DEPARTMENTS

The heads of the 12 major administrative departments form the *Presidents' Cabinet.* The number of departments, and, hence, the Cabinet membership, has been increased from time to time. The Constitution does not mention the Cabinet, but it is in fact the nation's highest executive council. The President appoints Cabinet members with the advice and consent of the Senate. Except for the Attorney General and the Postmaster General, the department heads hold the title of Secretary.

### Department of State

Established July 27, 1789. Primary responsibility for advising the President on foreign affairs and carrying out foreign policies. The department maintains the Foreign Service which represents the U.S. in other countries through Ambassadors, Ministers, and other officers. Included under its authority:

*Agency for International Development* (AID), has responsibility for carrying out non-military foreign assistance programs.

*Peace Corps,* trains and sends American volunteers to work abroad at the invitation of interested countries.

*Mission to the United Nations*

*National Commission for the United Nations Educational, Scientific, and Cultural Organization.*

### Department of the Treasury

Established September 2, 1789, to superintend the national finances, but the Treasury has also come to have a wide range of responsibilities as indicated by its various agencies. Included under its authority:

*Office of the Comptroller of the Currency,* supervises the operation of national banks.

*Bureau of Customs,* administers customs and tariffs.

*Bureau of Engraving and Printing,* produces currency, bonds, stamps.

*Internal Revenue Service,* collects taxes.

*Bureau of the Mint,* produces coins.

*Bureau of Narcotics,* enforces and supervises Federal regulations concerning drugs.

*Secret Service,* among other duties charged with the protection of the President and his family.

### Department of Defense

Established in 1949 to coordinate the activities of the War and Navy Departments which had existed separately since 1798. The separate armed services are designated as the *Department of the Army,* the *Department of the Navy* (includes *Marine Corps*), and the *Department of the Air Force.* The *Joint Chiefs of Staff,* which serves as the immediate military staff of the Secretary of Defense, includes: Chief of Staff, U.S. Army; Chief of Naval Operations; and Chief of Staff, U.S. Air Force. The Commandant of the Marine Corps sits as an equal on matters that directly concern the Corps.

### Department of Justice

The office of Attorney General was created in 1789, but the department of which he is the head was not established until 1870. Provides for the enforcement of Federal laws, furnishes legal counsel in Federal cases, and advises other departments concerning the laws under which they operate. It supervises the Federal penal institutions and represents the Government in legal matters generally. Included under its authority:

*Federal Bureau of Investigation* (FBI), charged with the investigation of violations of Federal laws except those assigned to some other Federal agency.

*Bureau of Prisons*

*Immigration and Naturalization Service*

*Board of Parole,* grants and revokes paroles of Federal prisoners and supervises parolees.

### Post Office Department

The Postal Service was established by the Continental Congress in 1775, but it did not become an executive department under the Postmaster General until 1872. Provides mail services for the nation for the purpose of promoting the general welfare, serving the economy, and advancing education and culture. From 1910 to 1966 the department operated the Postal Savings System.

### Department of the Interior

Established in 1849 to carry on a variety of domestic activities, a general housekeeper for the Federal Government. In recent years the department has become increasingly the custodian of the nation's natural resources although it also retains responsibility for Indian affairs. Included under its authority:

*Fish and Wildlife Service,* concerned with both commercial and sports fisheries.

*Bureau of Mines,* conducts programs for conservation and development of mineral resources and promotes health and safety in the mineral industries.

*Geological Survey*

*Bureau of Indian Affairs,* provides education and other public services on reservations and in general promotes development of the Indian people.

*Bureau of Land Management,* in charge of mineral resources on public lands.

*National Park Service*

*Bureau of Outdoor Recreation*

*Bureau of Reclamation,* develops and manages water resources in dry lands.

*Bonneville, Southeastern, and Southwestern Power Administrations,* operate electric power generating facilities.

**Department of Agriculture**

Established in 1862. Acquires and diffuses information on agriculture, administers various agricultural programs, conducts research, provides consumers' services, and manages national forests. Included among its agencies:

*Commodity Credit Corporation* (CCC) and *Agricultural Stabilization and Conservation Service,* two agencies which work together in administering the price support and production stabilization programs.

*Federal Crop Insurance Corporation,* insures crops against loss from unavoidable causes such as weather, insects, and disease.

*Farm Home Administration* (FHA), provides credit and assistance for purchase and improvements of family farms.

*Forest Service,* manages 186 million acres of national forest and grassland.

*Rural Electrification Service,* provides credit for development of rural electric and telephone systems.

*Soil Conservation Service,* provides surveys and other technical help to locally organized districts.

*Consumer and Marketing Service,* administers consumer protective regulations and distributes surplus commodities.

*Statistical Reporting Service*

*Economic Research Service*

*Agricultural Research Service*

*Federal Extension Service,* the main educational branch of the department.

**Department of Commerce**

Established in 1913 by a reorganization of the Department of Commerce and Labor which had been created in 1903. Develops and diffuses information about manufacturing and shipping industries. Included under its authority:

*Business and Defense Services Administration,* provides information and assistance concerning significant developments in specific industrial areas.

*Office of Business Economics,* provides statistical and other measures of the nation's economy.

*Bureau of the Census,* in addition to a decennial count of the nation's population, it also gathers statistics on many other matters.

*Economic and Development Administration,* plans development of areas which suffer from persistent unemployment.

*Environmental Science Services Administration,* created in 1965 by the consolidation of the Coast and Geodetic Survey and the Weather Bureau.

*Bureau of International Commerce*

*Maritime Administration*

*Patent Office*

*National Bureau of Standards*

*U.S. Travel Service,* encourages travel to the U.S. by people from foreign countries.

**Department of Labor**

A Bureau of Labor within the Department of Interior was created in 1884. A separate executive department was established in 1913 as a reorganization of the Department of Commerce and Labor which had been created in 1903. Administers measures designed to promote the welfare of wage earners. Included under its authority:

*Bureau of Employment Security*

*Labor-Management Services Administration*

*Wages and Hours Public Contracts Division,* gathers information and enforces regulations concerning wages and hours.

*Women's Bureau,* investigates and publishes reports concerning women in industry.

*Bureau of Labor Standards,* promotes standards of health and safety and other improvements in condition of labor.

*Bureau of Labor Statistics*

**Department of Health, Education, and Welfare** (HEW)

Established in 1953. Administers those agencies which deal with these three areas. Included under its authority:

*Public Health Service,* promotes research and distributes information in its area of concern.

*Office of Education,* collects and publishes information concerning education and administers Federal financial assistance to schools and other institutions.

*Social Security Administration*

*Welfare Administration,* administers Federal programs of assistance through the states to people in need.

*Vocational Rehabilitation Administration,* develops and supervises programs for the disabled.

*Food and Drug Administration,* enforces standards for the manufacture and handling of food and drugs.

*Administration on Aging*

**Department of Transportation** (DOT)

Created in 1966 to develop and coordinate a national transportation policy. The department took over a number of agencies and functions which had been placed elsewhere in order to coordinate activities in this area. The office of the Under Secretary of Commerce for Transportation moved into this department. Included under its authority:

*Federal Aviation Agency,* formerly an independent agency.

*Bureau of Public Roads,* formerly in the Department of Commerce, administers Federal aid to the States in the highway building programs.

*The Coast Guard,* formerly under the Treasury, provides rescue service and polices coast and waterways. The service reverts to naval jurisdiction in time of war.

*The Great Lakes Pilotage Administration,* formerly under Commerce, regulates pilots on Great Lakes.

*The Alaska Railroad,* formerly under Interior, an 870 mile line.

## INDEPENDENT AGENCIES

There are a number of special authorities with administrative and regulative powers which are not placed under any of the executive departments. Included among these independent agencies are:

**Atomic Energy Commission** (AEC)

Commission of 5 members appointed by the President with the advice and consent of the Senate. Plans, establishes, and administers programs for the use of atomic energy. Commission has the responsibility for protecting the public health and safety from the use of nuclear materials. Operates atomic energy production facilities and research laboratories.

**Civil Aeronautics Board** (CAB)

Composed of 5 members appointed for 6 year terms by the President with the advice and consent of the Senate. Regulates the economic aspects of air transportation including licensing carriers and fixing rates and fares.

**Commission of Fine Arts**

Composed of 7 persons selected by the President because of their experience in judging the arts. The Commission advises all departments and agencies of the Federal Government and the District of Columbia on matters concerning the arts, such as public buildings.

**District of Columbia**

The municipal government of the District rests with a Commissioner and a 9 member Council appointed by the President. Council may enact city ordinances, but Congress enacts major laws.

**Farm Credit Administration** (FCA)

A 13 member board appointed by the President. Serves as the policy making body which supervises and coordinates a cooperative credit system for agriculture. Under its authority are:

*Federal Land Banks* and *Federal Land Bank Associations,* farmer-owned cooperative banks which supply loans for agricultural purposes.

*Federal Intermediate Credit Banks,* make loans to production credit associations and other financial institutions which supply credit for agricultural purposes.

*Production Credit Associations,* cooperately owned associations which offer short-term credit for all types of farm and ranch operations.

*Banks for Cooperatives*

**Federal Communications Commission** (FCC)

Composed of 7 members appointed by the President with the consent of the Senate for 7 year terms; not more than 4 may be of the same political party. Licenses and regulates radio and television broadcasting and wire communications such as telephones and telegraphs.

**Federal Deposit Insurance Corporation** (FDIC)

Under 3 member board appointed by the President. Insures deposits in banks. More than 97% of nation's banks participate in the plan. Insured banks pay an annual assessment.

**Federal Home Loan Bank Board** (FHLBB)

Composed of 3 members appointed by the President with the advice and consent of the Senate. Provides credit resources for savings and home loan associations. Included under its authority is the *Federal Savings and Loan Insurance Corporation* which insures deposits in the associations.

**Federal Maritime Commission** (FMC)

Composed of 5 members appointed by the President with the consent of the Senate. Licenses, regulates, and sets rates for maritime commerce within the jurisdiction of the U.S. and of carriers engaged in the foreign commerce of the U.S.

**Federal Mediation and Conciliation Service** (FMCS)

Assists in the settlement of labor-management disputes through mediation and conciliation.

**Federal Power Commission** (FPC)

Composed of 5 commissioners appointed by the President with the advice and consent of the Senate. Regulates rates and other aspects of interstate electric power and natural gas industries. Licenses hydro-electric projects on Government lands and on navigable waters.

**Federal Reserve System** (FRS)

The 7 member Board of Governors, appointed by the President with the advice and consent of the Senate, regulates the nation's money supply and credit costs through control of the 12 Federal Reserve Banks which serve as the banks for the nation's commercial banks. Federal Reserve Bank notes make up the bulk of money in circulation.

**Federal Trade Commission** (FTC)

Composed of 5 members appointed by the President with the advice and consent of the Senate for 7 year terms; not more than 3 may be of the same political party. Promotes free and fair competition in interstate commerce by preventing combinations in restraint of trade, such as monopolies and price-fixing agreements, false advertising, and the interstate marketing of certain dangerous products.

**General Services Administration** (GSA)

Under an administrator appointed by the President. Manages property and records of the Federal Government. It secures and distributes supplies, constructs and operates buildings, keeps important records for all departments through the *National Archives and Record Service*.

**Interstate Commerce Commission** (ICC)

Consists of 11 members appointed by the President and confirmed by the Senate. Regulates economic aspects (such as rates) of carriers of interstate commerce, including railroads, pipe lines, motor carriers, and barge lines. Grants permission to operate or abandon service by interstate carriers.

**National Aeronautics and Space Administration** (NASA)

Under an administrator appointed by the President. Plans and administers the nation's space exploration program including its various research and operational centers.

**National Foundation on the Arts and the Humanities**

Encourages and supports a national program in the arts and the humanities (such fields as language, literature, history, philosophy).

**National Labor Relations Board** (NLRB)

Consists of 5 members appointed for 5 year terms appointed by the President with the consent of the Senate. Enforces the Fair Labor Standards Acts designed to enable employees to form labor unions and bargain collectively.

**National Mediation Board**

Consists of 3 members appointed by the President with the advice and consent of the Senate; no more than 2 from the same political party. Deals with labor disputes involving the nation's railroads.

**National Science Foundation** (NSF)

Attempts to strengthen basic research and science education primarily through grants of money.

**Securities and Exchange Commission** (SEC)

Composed of 5 members appointed by the President with the advice and consent of the Senate for 5 year terms, one term ending each year. Regulates trade in the securities and financial markets to protect investors from malpractices as defined in various laws.

**Selective Service System** (SSS)

Headed by a director appointed by the President. Registers and selects men for service in the armed forces under terms of the Universal Military Training and Service Act. Local draft boards make the decisions dealing with individuals which may be appealed to special boards established in each of the Federal judicial districts. A National Selective Service Appeal Board has final authority.

**Small Business Administration** (SBA)

Managed by an administrator appointed by the President with the advice and consent of the Senate. Assists small business concerns by providing information, advice about securing Government contracts, and loans in cases of catastrophes and other special cases.

**Smithsonian Institution**

In 1829 James Smithson of London, England, left his fortune to the U.S. to establish an institution in Washington for the "increase and diffusion of knowledge among men." It now carries on a program of research and operates a series of museums in which it exhibits a part of the 60 million items of scientific, cultural, and historic interest which it possesses.

**Tax Court of the U.S.**

Tries and settles controversies involving tax payments.

**Tennessee Valley Authority** (TVA)

Consists of a 3 member board appointed by the President with the advice and consent of the Senate. Conducts a program of resource development in the Tennessee Valley region. The Authority operates a river control system, recreational facilities, and research laboratories, but it is best known as a supplier of cheap electric power. At one time the power was largely generated in hydro-electric plants, but today most of the power is produced by 10 steam generating plants.

**U.S. Arms Control and Disarmament Agency**

Under a director appointed by the President with the advice and consent of the Senate. Studies problems of arms control.

**U.S. Civil Service Commission** (CSC)

Composed of 3 members who serve 6 years staggered terms. Operates a system for the selection and advancement of government employees on the basis of merit.

**U.S. Information Agency** (USIA)

The purpose of the Agency is to help achieve U.S. foreign policy objectives by influencing public attitudes in other nations. Operates the Voice of America broadcasts.

**U.S. Tariff Commission**

Consists of 6 members appointed by the President and confirmed by the Senate. Investigates tariff matters and reports to the President and Congress.

**Veterans Administration** (VA)

Administers a variety of programs, including hospitals and insurance centers, for the benefit of veterans and their dependents.

# *History*

## FAMOUS AMERICANS

THIS SECTION gives basic information about the most important persons who figure in the study of American history and literature. These are persons who have been important in government, literature, business, science, education, and military affairs of the United States of America. You will find it useful to consult this section for answers to three types of questions: *When* did a man live? *Where* did he live? *What* were his most important achievements?

The names are arranged alphabetically for ready reference, but you may find it interesting to browse among the list; facts about people are fascinating.

**Adams, John.** 1735-1826. 2nd Pres. of the U.S. (1797-1801), *b.* Braintree (now Quincy), Mass. Served in 1st Continental Cong.; signed Dec. of Independence; Vice Pres. during Washington's adm.

**Adams, John Quincy.** 1767-1848. 6th Pres. of the U.S. (1825-29), *b.* Braintree (now Quincy), Mass. Son of John Adams; Sec. of State in Monroe's adm.; served 17 years in H. of Rep. after losing re-election for 2nd term as Pres.

**Adams, Samuel.** 1722-1803. Political leader, *b.* Boston, Mass. Radical leader in Revolution; signed Dec. of Independence; Gov. of Mass.

**Addams, Jane.** 1860-1935. Social worker, *b.* Cedarville, Ill. Established Hull House in Chicago, one of the earliest social settlement centers in the U.S.

**Anthony, Susan.** 1820-1906. Reformer, *b.* Adams, Mass. Lectured, wrote, and organized for the anti-slavery, temperance, and women's rights movements.

**Arthur, Chester A.** 1830-86. 21st Pres. of the U.S. (1881-85), *b.* Fairfield, Vt. Practiced law in N. Y.; held various political appointments; Vice Pres. becoming Pres. after death of Garfield.

**Audubon, John James.** *c.*1780-1851. Artist and naturalist, probably *b.* New Orleans, La. Studied and made drawings of the birds of America.

**Austin, Stephen.** 1793-1836. Colonizer of Tex., *b.* Wythe Co., Va. Carried out his father's (*Moses Austin*) plan to establish colony in Tex., at that time part of Mexico; later played a part in Tex. revolution.

**Bell, Alexander Graham.** 1847-1922. Scientist, *b.* Edinburgh, Scotland. Teacher of the deaf whose experiments led to the invention of the telephone in 1876.

**Boone, Daniel.** 1734-1820. Frontiersman, *b.* near Reading, Pa. Explored and settled Ky., Mo., and other Western lands; "autobiography" ghost-written by John Filson.

**Borah, William E.** 1865-1940. Political leader, *b.* near Fairfield, Ill. Served as Senator from Idaho for 33 years (1907-40). Defended "isolationist" position in foreign affairs.

**Brandeis, Louis.** 1856-1941. Justice of U.S. Sup. Ct., *b.* Louisville, Ky. Served as a liberal on the Court from 1916 to 1939.

**Breasted, James H.** 1865-1935. Historian, *b.* Rockford, Ill. A pioneer in the study of ancient Egypt in the U.S. Director of the Oriental Institute, Uni. of Chicago.

**Bryan, William Jennings.** 1860-1925. Political leader, *b.* Salem, Ill. Unsuccessful Dem. candidate for Pres. in 1896, 1900, and 1908; Sec. of State in Wilson's adm.; advocated free coinage of silver and Biblical Fundamentalism.

**Bryant, William Cullen.** 1794-1878. Poet and editor, *b.* Cummington, Mass. Edited N. Y. *Evening Post;* wrote nature poetry; translated Homer.

**Buchanan, James.** 1791-1868. 15th Pres. of the U.S. (1857-61), *b.* near Mercersburg, Pa. Represented Pa. in H. of Rep. and Senate; served as Minister to Russia and Britain.

**Burr, Aaron.** 1756-1836. Political

---

KENNETH S. COOPER, B.A., M.A., Ph.D., *Professor of History,* George Peabody College for Teachers.

leader, *b.* Newark, N.J. Served in Revolution; Senator from N.J.; Vice Pres. during Jefferson's 1st adm.; political career ended when he killed Alexander Hamilton in a duel.

**Calhoun, John C.** 1782-1850. Political leader, *b.* near Abbeville, S.C. Served in H. of Rep. and Senate; Sec. of War in Monroe's adm.; Vice Pres. during J. Q. Adams' and Jackson's 1st adm.; principal spokesman for states' rights philosophy.

**Carnegie, Andrew.** 1835-1919. Industrialist, *b.* Dunfermline, Scotland. Began as a cotton mill worker but made a fortune in the steel business; gave away much of his fortune for libraries and education.

**Carroll, John.** 1735-1815. Religious leader, *b.* Maryland. Roman Catholic priest who supported American Revolution. Served as the first U.S. Catholic Bishop.

**Carson, Kit (Christopher).** 1809-68. Explorer, *b.* Madison Co., Ky. Served as guide, explorer and Indian fighter in the Southwest and Rocky Mts.

**Carver, George Washington.** *c.*1864-1943. Scientist, *b.* near Carthage, Mo. Negro chemist who discovered new uses for peanuts, cotton, sweet potatoes, and soy beans — crops grown in the South.

**Cather, Willa.** 1876-1947. Writer, *b.* Winchester, Va. Works include: *O Pioneers!* and *Death Comes for the Archbishop.*

**Clark, William.** 1770-1838. Explorer, *b.* Caroline Co., Va. Army officer who served as one of the leaders of expedition which explored La. Terr.

**Clay, Henry.** 1777-1852. Political leader, *b.* Hanover Co., Va. Represented Ky. in Cong. for nearly half a century; framed the Mo. Compromise and that of 1850; Sec. of State in J. Q. Adams' adm.; leader of Whigs.

**Clemens, Samuel.** 1835-1910. Writer and humorist better known as *Mark Twain, b.* Florida, Mo. Boyhood in Hannibal, Mo. provided material for two novels, *Tom Sawyer* and *Huckleberry Finn.*

**Cleveland, Grover.** 1837-1908. 22nd and 24th Pres. of the U.S. (so designated by official State Dept. ruling because his terms were not consecutive: 1st term 1885-89, 2nd term 1893-97), *b.* Caldwell, N.J. Gov. of N.Y.; 1st Dem. to be elected Pres. after the Civil War.

**Cody, William (Buffalo Bill).** 1846-1917. Frontiersman and showman, *b.* near Davenport, Iowa. Hunted buffalo for railway construction crews; entered show business and formed Wild West Show.

**Coolidge, Calvin.** 1872-1933. 30th Pres. of the U.S. (1923-29), *b.* Plymouth, Vt. Gov. of Mass.; Vice Pres. becoming Pres. on death of Harding; re-elected in 1924.

**Cooper, James Fenimore.** 1789-1851. Writer, *b.* Burlington, N.J. Wrote romantic novels dealing with life on the frontier and at sea.

**Cooper, Peter.** 1791-1883. Businessman, *b.* New York City. Built 1st American-made locomotive (Tom Thumb); developed steel and telegraph industries; established Cooper Union for education of working people.

**Crane, Stephen.** 1871-1900. Writer, *b.* Newark, N.J. Most famous work, *The Red Badge of Courage,* is a remarkably realistic war story although the author never saw a battle.

**Custer, George.** 1839-76. General, *b.* near Cadiz, Ohio. Served in Civil War; perished with his men in battle against the Sioux Indians at the Little Bighorn.

**Darrow, Clarence S.** 1857-1938. Lawyer, *b.* Kinsman, Ohio. Won a reputation as defender of unpopular and unorthodox causes and clients. Defended Scopes in Tenn. evolution trial.

**Davis, Jefferson.** 1808-89. Political leader, *b.* near Elkton, Ky. Served in Mexican War; represented Miss. in H. of Rep. and Senate; Sec. of War in Pierce adm.; elected Pres. of Confederacy after secession; confined in Fed. prison for 2 years after Civil War.

**Debs, Eugene.** 1855-1926. Socialist political leader, *b.* Terre Haute, Ind. Ran as Socialist candidate for Pres. 5 times between 1900 and 1920.

**Dewey, George.** 1837-1917. Admiral, *b.* Montpelier, Vt. Served in Civil War; commanded fleet which defeated the Spanish in Manila Bay during Spanish-American War.

**Dewey, John.** 1859-1952. Philosopher, *b.* Burlington, Vt. Established experimental school at Uni. of Chicago; taught at Columbia Uni. for 25 years; his instrumentalist philosophy influenced education.

**Dickinson, Emily.** 1830-86. Poet, *b.* Amherst, Mass. Lived a secluded life, writing poetry which she would not publish; works published after her death have greatly influenced other American poets.

**Dix, Dorothea.** 1802-87. Teacher and reformer, *b.* Hampden, Me. Agitated for special hospitals for the insane.

**Douglas, Stephen A.** 1813-61. Political leader, *b.* Brandon, Vt. Entered politics in Ill.; served in H. of Rep. and Senate; debated Lincoln in 1858 election; unsuccessful Dem. candidate for Pres. in 1860.

**Dreiser, Theodore.** 1871-1945. Writer, *b.* Terre Haute, Ind. Wrote realistic novels of which *An American Tragedy* is probably the best known.

**Earhart, Amelia.** 1898-1937. Aviatrix, *b.* Atchison, Kans. Worked as teacher and social worker in Mass.; made solo flight across Atlantic in 1932; lost in the Pacific during an attempted flight around the world.

**Eddy, Mary Baker.** 1821-1910. Religious leader, *b.* near Concord, N.H. Founded Christian Science Church.

**Edison, Thomas A.** 1847-1931. Inventor, *b.* Milan, Ohio. Rose from railway newsboy to multimillionaire through many inventions which included: phonograph, incandescent light bulbs, and motion pictures.

**Eisenhower, Dwight D.** 1890-1969. 34th Pres. of the U.S. (1953-61), *b.* Denison, Tex. Graduated from West Point; professional soldier rising to Supreme Commander Allied Forces in World War II; Pres. of Columbia Uni.; retired from army to run for Pres.

**Emerson, Ralph Waldo.** 1803-82. Writer, *b.* Boston, Mass. Unitarian minister but he held only one short pastorate; widely known for his essays and lectures.

**Faulkner, William.** 1897-1962. Writer, *b.* New Albany, Miss. Wrote novels which deal with Deep South; won Nobel prize for literature in 1949.

**Field, Cyrus.** 1819-92. Businessman, *b.* Stockbridge, Mass. Organized the companies which laid the 1st Atlantic cable.

**Fillmore, Millard.** 1800-74. 13th Pres. of the U.S. (1850-53), *b.* Locke, N.Y. Represented N.Y. in H. of Rep.; Vice Pres. becoming Pres. after death of Taylor.

**Fitzgerald, F. Scott.** 1896-1940. Writer, *b.* St. Paul, Minn. Wrote novels dealing with the 1920's.

**Ford, Henry.** 1863-1947. Industrialist, *b.* Dearborn, Mich. Worked as a machinist; established company which pioneered in the mass production of automobiles.

**Foster, Stephen.** 1826-64. Composer and song writer, *b.* Pittsburgh, Pa. Wrote Negro dialect songs for minstrel shows that are sometimes regarded as folk music.

**Franklin, Benjamin.** 1706-90. Writer, publisher, scientist, statesman, man of learning, *b.* Boston, Mass. Helped draft Dec. of Independence; represented colonists in France during Revolution; member of the Constitutional Convention.

**Fremont, John C.** 1813-90. Explorer and political leader, *b.* Savannah, Ga. Explored the Rocky Mts. and Cal.; encouraged Cal. to revolt against Mexico; Senator from Cal.; 1st Rep. candidate for Pres.

**Frost, Robert.** 1875-1963. Poet, *b.* San Francisco, Cal. Moved to Mass. as a boy and much of his work dealt with New England; operated a farm that was more famous than profitable; lectured and taught widely.

**Garfield, James.** 1831-81. 20th Pres. of the U.S. (Mar. 4-Sept. 19, 1881), *b.* Cuyahoga Co., Ohio. Represented Ohio in H. of Rep. and Senate; assassinated after 6 months in office as Pres.

**Garland, Hamlin.** 1860-1940. Writer, *b.* near West Salem, Wis. Lived on farms in Iowa and Dakotas; farm experience provided subject matter for most famous works.

**George, Henry.** 1839-97. Economist, *b.* Philadelphia. Wrote *Progress and Poverty* (1879) in which he set forth the idea of the single tax.

**Gershwin, George.** 1898-1937. Composer, *b.* Brooklyn, N.Y. Composed songs for musical shows, symphonic jazz, and a folk-opera, *Porgy and Bess.*

**Gompers, Samuel.** 1850-1924. Labor leader, *b.* London, England. Cigarmaker who helped organize the American Federation of Labor.

**Gorgas, William C.** 1854-1920. Army Medical Officer, *b.* Mobile, Ala. Cleared Isthmus of Panama of Yellow Fever and so made possible the completion of the Canal.

**Grant, Ulysses Simpson.** 1822-85. 18th Pres. of the U.S. (1869-77), *b.* Point Pleasant, Ohio. Professional soldier, serving in Mexican War; became Gen. of the Armies during the Civil War.

**Hamilton, Alexander.** 1757-1804. Political leader, *b.* West Indies. Served in Revolution; helped frame Constitution; Sec. of Treas. in Washington's adm.; leader of the Federalists; killed in duel by Aaron Burr.

**Harding, Warren G.** 1865-1923. 29th Pres. of the U.S. (1921-23), *b.* Blooming Grove, Ohio. Small town newspaper publisher; member of the Senate from Ohio; died in office after 2 years as Pres.

**Harrison, Benjamin.** 1833-1901. 23rd Pres. of the U.S. (1889-93), *b.* North Bend, Ohio. Practiced law in Ind.; represented Ind. in Senate; won majority of electoral votes but not of popular votes in 1888.

**Harrison, William Henry.** 1773-1841. 9th Pres. of the U.S. (Mar. 4-Apr. 4, 1841), *b.* Charles City Co., Va. Military commander in Indian wars; represented Ohio in H. of Rep. and Senate; died after serving 1 month as Pres.

**Hawthorne, Nathaniel.** 1804-64. Writer, *b.* Salem, Mass. First won recognition with short stories; greatest of his novels, *The Scarlet Letter;* lived for a time at Brook Farm.

**Hayes, Rutherford B.** 1822-93. 19th Pres. of the U.S. (1877-81), *b.* Delaware, Ohio. Represented Ohio in H. of Rep.; Gov. of Ohio; chosen Pres. over *Samuel J. Tilden* in disputed election of 1877.

**Hearst, William Randolph.** 1863-1951. Journalist, *b.* San Francisco, Cal. Published a chain of newspapers which featured sensational treatment of the news.

**Hemingway, Ernest.** 1899-1961. Writer, *b.* Oak Park, Ill. Worked as a journalist; fought with Italian troops in World War I; wrote realistic novels.

**Henson, Matthew.** 1867-1955. Explorer, *b.* in Md. Negro who was the only American who accompanied Peary to the North Pole in 1909.

**Henry, Patrick.** 1736-99. Political leader, *b.* Hanover Co., Va. Radical leader during Revolution; Gov. of Va.; opposed Constitution, but worked for first 10 Amendments.

**Holmes, Oliver Wendell.** 1809-94. Writer and physician, *b.* Cambridge, Mass. Taught anatomy at Harvard Uni. and later served as dean of medical school; wrote poetry and informal prose sketches.

**Holmes, Oliver Wendell.** 1841-1935. (*Son of prec.*) Supreme Court Justice, *b.* Boston, Mass. Served in Civil War; taught at Harvard Uni.; member of Mass. Sup. Ct.; served 30 years on U.S. Sup. Ct.

**Homer, Winslow.** 1836-1910. Artist, *b.* Boston. Famous for paintings of sea scenes.

**Hooker, Thomas.** 1586-1647. Founder of Hartford, Conn., *b.* Leicestershire, Eng.

**Hoover, Herbert C.** 1874-1964. 31st Pres. of the U.S. (1929-33), *b.* Cedar Co., Iowa. Mining engineer; administered various world relief programs; Sec. of Commerce in Harding and Coolidge adm.

**Houston, Sam.** 1793-1863. Political leader, *b.* near Lexington, Va. Friend of Andrew Jackson, entered Tenn. politics; migrated to Tex., commanded troops in Tex. revolution; 1st Pres. of Tex. Republic; after Tex. joined U.S., served as Senator and Gov.

**Ingersoll, Robert.** 1833-99. Lawyer and lecturer, *b.* Yates Co., N. Y. Criticized traditional religious beliefs in writings and popular lectures.

**Irving, Washington.** 1783-1859. Writer, *b.* New York City. Wrote essays, satires, and histories which won recognition both in America and Europe; served as U.S. Minister to Spain.

**Jackson, Andrew.** 1767-1845. 7th Pres. of the U.S. (1829-37), *b.* Waxhaw, S. C. Represented Tenn. in H. of Rep. and Senate; commanded troops in War of 1812 at Battle of New Orleans; partisan of democracy.

**Jackson, Thomas (Stonewall).** 1824-63. General, *b.* Clarksburg, Va. (now W. Va.), Served in Mexican War; taught at Va. Military Inst.; became Lee's ablest officer during Civil War; accidentally killed at Chancellorsville.

**James, Henry.** 1843-1916. Writer, *b.* New York City. Brother of William James, the philosopher; lived much of his life in Europe; wrote novels about American and European leisure classes.

**James, William.** 1842-1910. Philosopher, *b.* New York City. Brother of Henry James, novelist; taught at Harvard Uni.; set forth his philosophical views in *Pragmatism: A New Name for Some Old Ways of Thinking.*

**Jay, John.** 1745-1829. Political leader, *b.* New York City. Served on diplomatic missions during and after the Revolution; appointed 1st Chief Justice of the U.S. Supreme Court.

**Jefferson, Thomas.** 1743-1826. 3rd Pres. of the U.S. (1801-09), *b.* Goochland (now Albemarle) Co., Va. Wrote first draft of the Dec. of Independence; Gov. of Va.; Sec. of State in Washington's adm.; Vice Pres. during John Adams' adm.

**Johnson, Andrew.** 1808-75. 17th Pres. of the U.S. (1865-69), *b.* Raleigh, N. C. Represented Tenn. in H. of Rep. and Senate; Gov. of Tenn.; remained loyal to Union in Civil War; Vice Pres. becoming Pres. upon Lincoln's death; impeached by H. of Rep. but acquitted by the Senate.

**Johnson, Lyndon B.** 1908- . 36th Pres. of the U.S. (1963-1969), *b.* near Stonewall, Tex. Taught school in Tex.; represented Tex. in H. of Rep. and Senate; served as naval officer in World War II; Vice Pres. becoming Pres. on death of Kennedy; re-elected in 1964.

**Jones, John Paul.** 1747-92. Revolutionary War naval commander, *b.* Scotland. Won victory in battle between Bon Homme Richard and Seraphis; later served in Russian navy; died in Paris.

**Kennedy, John F.** 1917-63. 35th Pres. of the U.S. (1961-63), *b.* Brookline, Mass. Served as naval officer in World War II; represented Mass. in H. of Rep. and Senate; first Roman Catholic to be elected Pres.; assassinated after 2 years in office.

**La Follette, Robert.** 1855-1925. Political leader, *b.* Dane Co., Wis. Represented Wis. in H. of Rep.; Gov. of Wis.; Senator from Wis.; ran as Progressive candidate for Pres. in 1924.

**Lee, Robert E.** 1807-70. General, *b.* Westmoreland Co., Va. Served in Mexican War; offered field command of U.S. troops in April, 1861, but he would not fight against the South; became Confederate General; after war, he served as pres. of Washington College, later re-named Washington and Lee.

**Lewis, Meriwether.** 1774-1809. Explorer, *b.* near Charlottesville, Va. One of the leaders of expedition to explore La. Terr.; served as Gov. of La. Terr.; died mysteriously — possibly murdered — at inn on Natchez Trace in Tenn.

**Lewis, Sinclair.** 1885-1951. Writer, *b.* Sauk Centre, Minn. Worked as a journalist; wrote novels which satirized middle class life; perhaps best known, *Main Street,* deals with life in small Midwestern town.

**Lincoln, Abraham.** 1809-65. 16th Pres. of the U.S. (1861-65), *b.* Hardin (now Larue) Co., Ky. Practiced law in Ill.; represented Ill. in H. of Rep.; served as Pres. during Civil War; assassinated 5 days after the war's end.

**Lindbergh, Charles A.** 1902- . Aviator, *b.* Detroit, Mich. Made 1st solo transatlantic flight, N. Y. to Paris, in the *Spirit of St. Louis* (1927).

**London, Jack.** 1876-1916. Writer, *b.* San Francisco. Wrote books about life at sea and in the far north which he knew from personal experience.

**Longfellow, Henry W.** 1807-82. Poet, *b.* Portland, Me. Served as Prof. of Modern Languages at Harvard Uni.; wrote poetry which won him wide popularity in his own lifetime.

**Lowell, James Russell.** 1819-91. Writer, *b.* Cambridge, Mass. Wrote poems, satires, and essays; Prof. of French and Spanish at Harvard Uni.; edited *Atlantic Monthly* and *American Review;* served as U.S. Minister to Spain and Britain.

**MacArthur, Douglas.** 1880-1964. General, *b.* Little Rock, Ark. Served in World War I; commanded Allied forces in Southwest Pacific during World War II; in charge of occupation of Japan; commanded U. N. forces in Korean War until removed by Pres. Truman in 1951.

**McClellan, George.** 1826-85. General, *b.* Philadelphia, Pa. Served in Mexican War; held high commands during Civil War; Dem. candidate for Pres. in 1864; Gov. of N. J. 1878-81.

**McCormick, Cyrus.** 1809-84. Inventor and businessman, *b.* Rockbridge Co., Va. Invented mechanical reaper; built factory in Chicago which produced various farm machines.

**McKinley, William.** 1843-1901. 25th Pres. of the U.S. (1897-1901), *b.* Niles, Ohio. Represented Ohio in H. of Rep.; Pres. during Spanish-American War; assassinated 6 months after start of 2nd term.

**Madison, Dolly.** 1768-1849. Wife of Pres. James Madison, *b.* N. C. First husband died; served as official hostess for Thomas Jefferson prior to Madison's adm.

**Madison, James.** 1751-1836. 4th Pres. of the U.S. (1809-17), *b.* Port Conway, Va. Principal drafter of the Constitution; one of the authors of *The Federalist;* represented Va. in H. of Rep.; Sec. of State in Jefferson's adm.

**Mann, Horace.** 1796-1859. Educator, *b.* Franklin, Mass. As 1st Sec. of Mass. State Board of Education, he did much to arouse interest in public schools and the education of teachers; later served as 1st pres. of Antioch College.

**Marshall, John.** 1755-1835. Chief Justice of the Supreme Court, *b.* Fauquier Co., Va. Served in Revolution; Sec. of State in John Adams' adm.; as Chief Justice his decisions supported strong Federal government; had an unequaled influence in shaping the Constitutional tradition.

**Mason, Lowell.** 1792-1872. Composer, *b.* Medfield, Mass. Promoted teaching of music in public schools; composed 1210 hymns.

**Melville, Herman.** 1819-91. Writer, *b.* New York City. Sailed on a whaler in his youth; lived among cannibals in South Pacific; wrote novels which drew from his early experiences at sea.

**Mencken, Henry L.** 1880-1956. Editor and writer, *b.* Baltimore, Md. Caustic critic of American life; edited the *American Mercury;* books include: *The American Language* and *Treatise on the Gods.*

**Monroe, James.** 1758-1831. 5th Pres. of the U.S. (1817-25), *b.* Westmoreland Co., Va. Served in Revolution; member Continental Congress; Gov. of Va.; Sec. of State and Sec. of War in Madison's adm.; issued Monroe Doctrine as Pres.

**Morse, Samuel F. B.** 1791-1872. Inventor and artist, *b.* Charlestown, Mass. Achieved minor fame as a portrait painter; demonstrated practical electric telegraphy to Congress in 1844.

**Nixon, Richard M.** 1913- . 37th Pres. of the U.S. (1969- ), *b.* Whittier, Calif. Practiced law in Calif. Rep. Calif. in H. of Rep. and Senate. Served as Lt. in U. S. Navy. V. Pres. of U.S. (1953-1961).

**Norris, George.** 1861-1944. Political leader, *b.* Sandusky Co., Ohio. Represented Neb. in H. of Rep. and for 30 years in the Senate; an insurgent Republican, he often differed with his party's leaders.

**Oglethorpe, James.** 1696-1785. English military officer and founder of Georgia, *b.* London, England.

**O'Neill, Eugene.** 1888-1935. Playwright, *b.* New York City. Son of an actor; worked as seaman and journalist; wrote psychological tragedies and one popular comedy, *Ah, Wilderness!*

**Peabody, George.** 1795-1869. Businessman and philanthropist, *b.* South Danvers (now Peabody), Mass. Established large fund to promote education in the South after the Civil War.

**Peary, Robert.** 1856-1920. Explorer and naval officer, *b.* Cresson, Pa. Explored Arctic regions; reached North Pole, April 6, 1909.

**Penn, William.** 1644-1718. Founder of Pennsylvania, *b.* London, England. Became a Quaker while at Oxford; established Pa. as a haven for different religions; laid out city of Philadelphia.

**Pershing, John J.** 1860-1948. General, *b.* Linn Co., Mo. Served in Indian campaigns and Spanish-American War; commanded American forces in Europe during World War I.

**Pierce, Franklin.** 1804-69. 14th Pres. of the U.S. (1853-57), *b.* Hillsboro, N.H. Represented N.H. in H. of Rep. and Senate; served as Brig. Gen. in Mexican War.

**Pike, Zebulon.** 1779-1813. Explorer, *b.* N. J. Army officer who explored Miss. and Ark. river valleys; also entered Spanish terr. in Southwest.

**Poe, Edgar Allen.** 1809-49. Writer, *b.* Boston, Mass. Worked as editor for various journals; wrote melancholy poetry, literary criticism, and some classic mystery stories.

**Polk, James K.** 1795-1849. 11th Pres. of the U.S. (1845-49), *b.* Mecklenberg Co., N. C. Practiced law in Tenn.; represented Tenn. in H. of Rep.; Gov. of Tenn.

**Reed, Walter.** 1851-1902. Army officer and surgeon, *b.* Gloucester Co., Va. In charge of experiments which proved that mosquitoes carried yellow fever.

**Revere, Paul.** 1735-1818. Silversmith and Revolutionary leader, *b.* Boston, Mass. Aroused the countryside before the battle of Lexington and Concord, the first clash of the Revolution.

**Riis, Jacob A.** 1849-1914. Writer, *b.* Denmark. Exposed slum conditions in *How the Other Half Lives.*

**Robinson, Edwin Arlington.** 1869-1935. Poet, *b.* Head Tide, Me. Work was unrecognized for many years, but in 1921 he won the first of 3 Pulitzer prizes.

**Rockefeller, John D.** 1839-1937. Industrialist, *b.* Tioga Co., N. Y. Made a fortune through the Standard Oil Trust; gave away much of his wealth; helped establish the Uni. of Chicago.

**Roosevelt, Franklin D.** 1882-1945. 32nd Pres. of the U.S. (1933-45), *b.* Hyde Park, N. Y. Unsuccessfully ran for Vice Pres. in 1920; Gov. of N. Y.; inaugurated "New Deal" program as Pres. and led nation during World War II; only Pres. elected 4 times.

**Roosevelt, Theodore.** 1858-1919. 26th Pres. of the U.S. (1901-09), *b.* New York City. Reformer in N. Y. politics; organized "Rough Riders" in Spanish-American War; Gov. of N. Y.; Vice Pres. becoming Pres. on death of McKinley.

**Ruth, George Herman (Babe).** 1895-1948. Baseball player, *b.* Baltimore, Md. Pitched for Boston Red Sox, but achieved greatest fame as hitter with N. Y. Yankees.

**Sandburg, Carl.** 1878-1967. Writer, *b.* Galesburg, Ill. Served in Spanish-American War; worked as newspaperman; wrote poetry and biographies, including one of Lincoln.

**Scott, Winfield.** 1786-1866. General, *b.* near Petersburg, Va. Served in War of 1812, Blackhawk War, Mexican War, and Civil War; Supreme Commander of U.S. Army from 1841 to 1861.

**Seward, William.** 1801-72. Political leader, *b.* Orange Co., N. Y. Served as Senator from N. Y.; Sec. of State in Lincoln and A. Johnson adm.; arranged for purchase of Alaska.

**Sherman, William T.** 1820-91. General, *b.* Lancaster, Ohio. Served in army during Mexican War; became one of the most effective commanders in Civil War.

**Sitting Bull.** *d.* 1890. Indian Chief. Led the Sioux in war against U.S. forces; won victory over Custer at the Little Bighorn; appeared in Buffalo Bill's Wild West Show.

**Smith, John.** 1580-1631. Explorer and leader of the 1st Eng. colony at Jamestown, *b.* Lincolnshire, Eng.

**Smith, Joseph.** 1805-44. Religious leader, *b.* Sharon, Vt. Founder of the Church of Jesus Christ of Latter-Day Saints based upon the *Book of Mormon;* killed by a mob in Ill.

**Standish, Miles.** *c.*1584-1656. Military leader of Pilgrim colony at Plymouth, *b.* Lancashire, Eng. Longfellow's poem about his courtship is wholly fictitious.

**Steffens, Lincoln.** 1866-1936. Writer, *b.* San Francisco, Cal. Wrote muckraking articles exposing corruption in cities.

**Stevenson, Adlai.** 1900-65. Political leader, *b.* Los Angeles, Cal. Gov. of Ill.; unsuccessful Dem. candidate for Pres. in 1952 and 1956; served as U.S. Ambassador to the U. N.

**Stowe, Harriet Beecher.** 1811-96. Writer, *b.* Litchfield, Conn. Interested in temperance, woman suffrage, and anti-slavery movements; wrote *Uncle Tom's Cabin,* influential anti-slavery novel.

**Sullivan, Louis.** 1856-1924. Architect, *b.* Boston, Mass. Pioneered the idea that the form of a structure should reflect its function; did much of his work in Chicago.

**Sumner, William Graham.** 1840-1910. Scholar, *b.* Paterson, N. J. One of the pioneer sociologists in the U.S.

**Taft, William Howard.** 1857-1930. 27th Pres. of the U.S. (1909-13), *b.* Cincinnati, Ohio. Sec. of War in T. Roosevelt's adm.; appointed Chief Justice Supreme Court in 1921, the only ex-Pres. to hold that office.

**Taney, Roger.** 1777-1864. Chief Justice Supreme Court, *b.* Calvert Co., Md. Attorney General and Sec. of Treas. in Jackson's adm.; Jackson appointed him to Sup. Ct. in 1836 where he generally ruled in favor of pro-slavery forces.

**Taylor, Zachary.** 1784-1850. 12th Pres. of the U.S. (1849-50), *b.* Orange Co., Va. Military hero of Mexican War; died after a year and 4 months as Pres.

**Thoreau, Henry.** 1817-62. Writer, *b.* Concord, Mass. Valued simplicity, self-reliance, and nature; best known work, *Walden,* records an experiment with a simple mode of life.

**Truman, Harry S.** 1884- . 33rd Pres. of the U.S. (1945-53), *b.* Lamar, Mo. Served as officer in World War I; entered politics in Kans. City, Mo.; Senator from Mo.; Vice Pres. becoming Pres. on death of F. D. Roosevelt; led nation during last year of World War II and during Korean War.

**Turner, Frederick Jackson.** 1861-1932. Historian, *b.* Portage, Wis. Developed thesis concerning the influence of the frontier on American life.

**Turner, Nat.** 1800-31. Negro leader of a slave revolt in Aug., 1831, *b.* Southampton Co., Va.

**Tyler, John.** 1790-1862. 10th Pres. of the U.S. (1841-45), *b.* Charles City Co., Va. Represented Va. in H. of Rep. and Senate; Gov. of Va.; Vice Pres. becoming Pres. after death of Wm. H. Harrison.

**Van Buren, Martin.** 1782-1862. 8th Pres. of the U.S. (1837-41), *b.* Kinderhook, N. Y. Served as Senator from N. Y.; Gov. of N. Y.; Vice Pres. during Jackson's 2nd adm.

**Veblen, Thorstein.** 1857-1929. Scholar, *b.* Wis. Taught in several uni.; wrote critical analyses of society of which best known is *The Theory of the Leisure Class.*

**Villard, Oswald Garrison.** 1872-1949. Editor and writer. Worked for liberal causes through the *Nation* which he edited.

**Washington, Booker T.** *c.*1858-1915. Educator, *b.* Franklin Co., Va. Negro who emphasized importance of industrial and technical education; organized Tuskegee Institute (Ala.).

**Ward, Lester F.** 1841-1913. Scholar, *b.* Joliet, Ill. One of America's first sociologists.

**Washington, George.** 1732-99. 1st Pres. of the U.S. (1789-97), *b.* Westmoreland Co., Va. Served in French and Indian War; commanded Continental Army during Revolution; presided at the Constitutional Convention.

**Webster, Daniel.** 1782-1852. Political leader, *b.* Merrimack Co., N. H. Represented N. H. and Mass. in H. of Rep.; Senator from Mass.; Sec. of State in Wm. H. Harrison, Tyler, and Fillmore adm.; leader of Whigs who championed Federal powers against states' rights.

**Webster, Noah.** 1758-1843. Scholar, *b.* West Hartford, Conn. Produced "Blue-backed Speller" and dictionary which did much to standardize American English.

**White, William Allen.** 1868-1944. Writer, *b.* Emporia, Kans. Attracted national attention with editorials in *Emporia Gazette;* wrote short stories, novels, and biographies.

**Whitman, Walt.** 1819-92. Poet, *b.* West Hills, N. Y. Taught school; edited various newspapers in Brooklyn; worked as nurse during Civil War; poetry sang of nature and the common people.

**Whitney, Eli.** 1765-1825. Inventor, *b.* Westboro, Mass. Invented cotton gin from which he realized little profit; built firearms factory which pioneered mass production techniques.

**Whittier, John Greenleaf.** 1807-92. Writer, *b.* near Haverhill, Mass. A largely self-educated Quaker who wrote against slavery; edited newspapers; most famous poems deal with New England.

**Willard, Emma.** 1787-1870. Educator, *b.* Berlin, Conn. Led in the development of collegiate education for women at the Troy (N. Y.) Female Seminary.

**Williams, Roger.** *c.*1603-83. Founder of Rhode Island, *b.* London, Eng. Expelled from Mass. for liberal ideas; established colony where men could have religious freedom.

**Wilson, Woodrow.** 1856-1924. 28th Pres. of the U.S. (1913-21), *b.* Staunton, Va. College Prof.; Pres. of Princeton Uni.; Gov. of N. J.; Pres. during World War I.

**Wolfe, Thomas.** 1900-38. Writer, *b.* Asheville, N. C. Taught at N. Y. Uni.; wrote plays and long autobiographical novels.

**Wright, Frank Lloyd.** 1869-1959. Architect, *b.* Richland Center, Wis. Introduced new ideas of design in building; experimented with new materials.

**Wright, Orville.** 1871-1948. Inventor, *b.* Dayton, Ohio. One of the two brothers who built and flew the first power-driven airplane on Dec. 17, 1903.

**Wright, Wilbur.** 1867-1912. Inventor, *b.* New Castle, Ind. *See* ORVILLE WRIGHT.

## LINCOLN'S GETTYSBURG ADDRESS

*The Battle of Gettysburg was fought on July 1, 2, and 3, 1863. On November 19, 1863, the field was dedicated as a national cemetery by President Lincoln. This two-minute speech was to become immortal. The speech was relegated to the inside pages of the papers. At the same time, a two-hour address by Edward Everett, the leading orator of the time, made headlines. Following is the text of the address.*

FOURSCORE and seven years ago our fathers brought forth on this continent a new nation conceived in liberty and dedicated to the proposition that all men are created equal. Now we are engaged in a great civil war testing whether that nation, or any nation so conceived and so dedicated, can long endure. We are met on a great battlefield of that war. We have come to dedicate a portion of that field as a final resting-place for those who here gave their lives that that nation might live. It is altogether fitting and proper that we should do this. But, in a larger sense, we cannot dedicate, we cannot consecrate, we cannot hallow this ground. The brave men, living and dead, who struggled here have consecrated it far above our poor power to add or detract. The world will little note nor long remember what we say here, but it can never forget what they did here. It is for us the living rather to be dedicated here to the unfinished work which they who fought here have thus far so nobly advanced. It is rather for us to be here dedicated to the great task remaining before us — that from these honored dead we take increased devotion to that cause for which they gave the last full measure of devotion — that we here highly resolve that these dead shall not have died in vain, that this nation under God shall have a new birth of freedom, and that government of the people, by the people, for the people shall not perish from the earth.

## THE MONROE DOCTRINE

*The Monroe Doctrine was proclaimed in President James Monroe's message to Congress, on December 2, 1823. A selection follows.*

IN THE DISCUSSIONS to which this interest has given rise, and in the arrangements by which they may terminate, the occasion has been deemed proper for asserting as a principle in which rights and interests of the United States are involved, that the American continents, by the free and independent condition which they have assumed and maintain, are henceforth not to be considered as subjects for future colonization by any European power. . . . We owe it, therefore, to candor and to the amicable relations existing between the United States and those powers to declare that we should consider any attempt on their part to extend their system to any portion of this hemisphere as dangerous to our peace and safety. With the existing colonies or dependencies of any European power we have not interfered and shall not interfere. But with the governments who have declared their independence and maintain it, and whose independence we have, on great consideration and on just principles, acknowledged, we could not view any interposition for the purpose of oppressing them or controlling in any other manner their destiny by any European power in any other light than as the manifestation of an unfriendly disposition toward the United States.

# PRESIDENTS OF THE UNITED STATES

| | NAME | Birthplace | Year | Paternal Ancestry | Residence | Inaugurated | | Politics | Place of Death | Year | Age |
|---|---|---|---|---|---|---|---|---|---|---|---|
| | | | | | | Year | Age | | | | |
| 1 | George Washington | Westmoreland Co., Va. | 1732 | English | Va. | 1789 | 57 | Fed. | Mt. Vernon, Va. | 1799 | 67 |
| 2 | John Adams | Quincy, Mass. | 1735 | English | Mass. | 1797 | 61 | Fed. | Quincy, Mass. | 1826 | 90 |
| 3 | Thomas Jefferson | Shadwell, Va. | 1743 | Welsh | Va. | 1801 | 57 | Rep. † | Monticello, Va. | 1826 | 83 |
| 4 | James Madison | Port Conway, Va. | 1751 | English | Va. | 1809 | 57 | Rep. | Montpelier, Va. | 1836 | 85 |
| 5 | James Monroe | Westmoreland Co., Va. | 1758 | Scotch | Va. | 1817 | 58 | Rep. | New York City | 1831 | 73 |
| 6 | John Quincy Adams | Quincy, Mass. | 1767 | English | Mass. | 1825 | 57 | Rep. ‡ | Washington, D. C. | 1848 | 80 |
| 7 | Andrew Jackson | Union Co., N. C.* | 1767 | Scotch-Irish | Tenn. | 1829 | 61 | Dem. | Hermitage, Tenn. | 1845 | 78 |
| 8 | Martin Van Buren | Kinderhook, N. Y. | 1782 | Dutch | N. Y. | 1837 | 54 | Dem. | Lindenwold, N. Y. | 1862 | 79 |
| 9 | William H. Harrison | Berkeley, Va. | 1773 | English | O. | 1841 | 68 | Whig. | Washington, D. C. | 1841 | 68 |
| 10 | John Tyler | Greenway, Va. | 1790 | English | Va. | 1841 | 51 | Dem. | Richmond, Va. | 1862 | 71 |
| 11 | James K. Polk | Mecklenburg Co., N. C. | 1795 | Scotch-Irish | Tenn. | 1845 | 49 | Dem. | Nashville, Tenn. | 1849 | 53 |
| 12 | Zachary Taylor | Orange Co., Va. | 1784 | English | La. | 1849 | 64 | Whig. | Washington, D. C. | 1850 | 65 |
| 13 | Millard Fillmore | Summerhill, N. Y. | 1800 | English | N. Y. | 1850 | 50 | Whig. | Buffalo, N. Y. | 1874 | 74 |
| 14 | Franklin Pierce | Hillsboro, N. H. | 1804 | English | N. H. | 1853 | 48 | Dem. | Concord, N. H. | 1869 | 64 |
| 15 | James Buchanan | Cove Gap, Pa. | 1791 | Scotch-Irish | Pa. | 1857 | 65 | Dem. | Wheatland, Pa. | 1868 | 77 |
| 16 | Abraham Lincoln | Larue Co., Ky. | 1809 | English | Ill. | 1861 | 52 | Rep. | Washington, D. C. | 1865 | 56 |
| 17 | Andrew Johnson | Raleigh, N. C. | 1808 | English | Tenn. | 1865 | 56 | Rep. | Carter's Depot, Tenn. | 1875 | 66 |
| 18 | Ulysses S. Grant | Point Pleasant, O. | 1822 | Scotch | D. C. | 1869 | 46 | Rep. | Mt. McGregor, N. Y. | 1885 | 63 |
| 19 | Rutherford B. Hayes | Delaware, O. | 1822 | Scotch | O. | 1877 | 54 | Rep. | Fremont, O. | 1893 | 70 |
| 20 | James A. Garfield | Cuyahoga Co., O. | 1831 | English | O. | 1881 | 49 | Rep. | Long Branch, N. J. | 1881 | 49 |
| 21 | Chester A. Arthur | Fairfield, Vt. | 1830 | Scotch-Irish | N. Y. | 1881 | 50 | Rep. | New York City | 1886 | 56 |
| 22 | Grover Cleveland | Caldwell, N. J. | 1837 | English | N. Y. | 1885 | 47 | Dem. | Princeton, N. J. | 1908 | 71 |
| 23 | Benjamin Harrison | North Bend, O. | 1833 | English | Ind. | 1889 | 55 | Rep. | Indianapolis, Ind. | 1901 | 67 |
| 24 | Grover Cleveland | Caldwell, N. J. | 1837 | English | N. Y. | 1893 | 55 | Dem. | Princeton, N. J. | 1908 | 71 |
| 25 | William McKinley | Niles, O. | 1843 | Scotch-Irish | O. | 1897 | 54 | Rep. | Buffalo, N. Y. | 1901 | 58 |
| 26 | Theodore Roosevelt | New York City | 1858 | Dutch | N. Y. | 1901 | 42 | Rep. | Oyster Bay, N. Y. | 1919 | 60 |
| 27 | William H. Taft | Cincinnati, O. | 1857 | English | O. | 1909 | 51 | Rep. | Washington, D. C. | 1930 | 72 |
| 28 | Woodrow Wilson | Staunton, Va. | 1856 | Irish | N. J. | 1913 | 56 | Dem. | Washington, D. C. | 1924 | 67 |
| 29 | Warren G. Harding | Corsica, O. | 1865 | Scotch | O. | 1921 | 55 | Rep. | San Francisco, Cal. | 1923 | 57 |
| 30 | Calvin Coolidge | Plymouth, Vt. | 1872 | English | Vt. | 1923 | 51 | Rep. | Northampton, Mass. | 1933 | 60 |
| 31 | Herbert C. Hoover | West Branch, Iowa | 1874 | Swiss | Calif. | 1929 | 54 | Rep. | New York City | 1964 | 90 |
| 32 | Franklin D. Roosevelt | Hyde Park, N. Y. | 1882 | Dutch | N. Y. | 1933 | 51 | Dem. | Warm Springs, Ga. | 1945 | 63 |
| 33 | Harry S Truman | Lamar, Mo. | 1884 | English | Mo. | 1945 | 60 | Dem. | | | |
| 34 | Dwight D. Eisenhower | Denison, Tex. | 1890 | German | Pa. | 1953 | 62 | Rep. | Washington, D. C. | 1969 | 78 |
| 35 | John F. Kennedy | Brookline, Mass. | 1917 | Irish | Mass. | 1961 | 43 | Dem. | Dallas, Tex. | 1963 | 46 |
| 36 | Lyndon B. Johnson | Stonewall, Tex. | 1908 | English | Tex. | 1963 | 55 | Dem. | | | |
| 37 | Richard M. Nixon | Yorba-Linda, Calif. | 1913 | Irish | N. Y. | 1969 | 56 | Rep. | | | |
| 38 | | | | | | | | | | | |
| 39 | | | | | | | | | | | |
| 40 | | | | | | | | | | | |

* Jackson called himself a South Carolinian and his biographer, Amos Kendall, recorded his birthplace in Lancaster County, S. C.; but Parton has published documentary evidence to show that Jackson was born in Union County, N. C., less than a quarter mile from the South Carolina line.

† The Democratic party of today claims lineal decent from the first Republican party, and President Jefferson as its founder.

‡ Political parties were disorganized at the time of the election of John Quincy Adams. He claimed to be a Republican, but his doctrines were decidedly Federalistic. The opposition to his Administration took the name of Democrats, and elected Jackson President.

# PRESIDENTIAL VOTES, ELECTORAL AND POPULAR

*Major Parties Only*

Abbreviations of Parties: F, Federalist; D, Democrat; R, Republican; DL, Democratic Liberal; DP, Democratic People's; DR, Democrat Republican; NR, National Republican; W, Whig; P, People's; Pr, Progressive; SR, States' Rights; AI, American Independent.

| Year | President Elected | Popular Vote | Electoral Vote | Losing Candidate | Popular Vote | Electoral Vote |
|---|---|---|---|---|---|---|
| 1789 | George Washington (F) | Unknown | 69 | No Opposition | ... | .. |
| 1792 | George Washington (F) | Unknown | 132 | No Opposition | ... | .. |
| 1796 | John Adams (F) | Unknown | 71 | Thomas Jefferson (DR) | Unknown | 68 |
| 1800* | Thomas Jefferson (DR) | Unknown | 73 | Aaron Burr (DR) | Unknown | 73 |
| 1804 | Thomas Jefferson (DR) | Unknown | 162 | Charles Pinckney (F) | Unknown | 14 |
| 1808 | James Madison (DR) | Unknown | 122 | Charles Pinckney (F) | Unknown | 47 |
| 1812 | James Madison (DR) | Unknown | 128 | De Witt Clinton (F) | Unknown | 89 |
| 1816 | James Monroe (DR) | Unknown | 183 | Rufus King (F) | Unknown | 34 |
| 1820 | James Monroe (DR) | Unknown | 231 | John Quincy Adams (DR) | Unknown | 1 |
| 1824* | John Quincy Adams (NR) | 105,321 | 84 | Andrew Jackson (D) | 155,872 | 99 |
| | | | | Henry Clay (DR) | 46,587 | 37 |
| | | | | William H. Crawford (DR) | 44,282 | 41 |
| 1828 | Andrew Jackson (D) | 647,231 | 178 | John Quincy Adams (NR) | 509,097 | 83 |
| 1832 | Andrew Jackson (D) | 687,502 | 219 | Henry Clay (DR) | 530,189 | 49 |
| 1836 | Martin Van Buren (D) | 762,678 | 170 | William H. Harrison (W) | 548,007 | 73 |
| 1840* | William H. Harrison (W) | 1,275,017 | 234 | Martin Van Buren (D) | 1,128,702 | 60 |
| 1844 | James K. Polk (D) | 1,337,243 | 170 | Henry Clay (W) | 1,299,068 | 105 |
| 1848* | Zachary Taylor (W) | 1,360,101 | 163 | Lewis Cass (D) | 1,220,544 | 127 |
| 1852 | Franklin Pierce (D) | 1,601,474 | 254 | Winfield Scott (W) | 1,386,578 | 42 |
| 1856 | James C. Buchanan (D) | 1,927,995 | 174 | John C. Fremont (R) | 1,391,555 | 114 |
| 1860 | Abraham Lincoln (R) | 1,866,352 | 180 | Stephen A. Douglas (D) | 1,375,157 | 12 |
| | | | | John C. Breckinridge (D) | 845,763 | 72 |
| | | | | John Bell (Const. Union) | 589,581 | 39 |
| 1864* | Abraham Lincoln (R) | 2,216,067 | 212 | George McClellan (D) | 1,808,725 | 21 |
| 1868 | Ulysses S. Grant (R) | 3,015,071 | 214 | Horatio Seymour (D) | 2,709,615 | 80 |
| 1872 | Ulysses S. Grant (R) | 3,597,132 | 286 | Horace Greeley (DL) | 2,834,125 | .. |
| 1876* | Rutherford B. Hayes (R) | 4,033,768 | 185 | Samuel J. Tilden (D) | 4,285,992 | 184 |
| 1880* | James A. Garfield (R) | 4,449,053 | 214 | Winfield S. Hancock (D) | 4,442,035 | 155 |
| 1884 | Grover Cleveland (D) | 4,874,986 | 219 | James G. Blaine (R) | 4,851,981 | 182 |
| 1888* | Benjamin Harrison (R) | 5,439,853 | 233 | Grover Cleveland (D) | 5,540,309 | 168 |
| 1892 | Grover Cleveland (D) | 5,556,918 | 277 | Benjamin Harrison (R) | 5,176,108 | 145 |
| | | | | James Weaver (P) | 1,027,329 | 22 |
| 1896 | William McKinley (R) | 7,104,779 | 271 | William J. Bryan (DP) | 6,502,925 | 176 |
| 1900* | William McKinley (R) | 7,219,530 | 292 | William J. Bryan (D) | 6,358,071 | 155 |
| 1904 | Theodore Roosevelt (R) | 7,628,834 | 336 | Alton B. Parker (D) | 5,084,491 | 140 |
| 1908 | William H. Taft (R) | 7,678,908 | 321 | William J. Bryan (D) | 6,409,104 | 162 |
| 1912 | Woodrow Wilson (D) | 6,293,454 | 435 | Theodore Roosevelt (Pr) | 4,119,538 | 88 |
| | | | | William H. Taft (R) | 3,481,980 | 8 |
| 1916 | Woodrow Wilson (D) | 9,129,606 | 277 | Charles E. Hughes (R) | 8,538,221 | 254 |
| 1920* | Warren G. Harding (R) | 16,152,200 | 404 | James M. Cox (D) | 9,147,353 | 127 |
| 1924 | Calvin Coolidge (R) | 15,725,016 | 382 | John W. Davis (D) | 8,385,586 | 136 |
| | | | | Robert LaFollette (Pr) | 4,822,856 | 13 |
| 1928 | Herbert Hoover (R) | 21,392,190 | 444 | Alfred E. Smith (D) | 15,016,443 | 87 |
| 1932 | Franklin Roosevelt (D) | 22,821,857 | 472 | Herbert Hoover (R) | 15,761,841 | 59 |
| 1936 | Franklin Roosevelt (D) | 27,751,597 | 523 | Alfred Landon (R) | 16,679,583 | 8 |
| 1940 | Franklin Roosevelt (D) | 27,244,160 | 449 | Wendell Wilkie (R) | 22,305,198 | 82 |
| 1944* | Franklin Roosevelt (D) | 25,602,504 | 432 | Thomas E. Dewey (R) | 22,006,285 | 99 |
| 1948 | Harry S Truman (D) | 24,105,695 | 303 | Thomas E. Dewey (R) | 21,969,170 | 189 |
| | | | | J. Strom Thurmond (SR) | 1,169,021 | 39 |
| | | | | Henry A. Wallace (Pr) | 1,156,103 | .. |
| 1952 | Dwight Eisenhower (R) | 33,824,351 | 442 | Adlai E. Stevenson (D) | 27,314,987 | 89 |
| 1956 | Dwight Eisenhower (R) | 35,581,003 | 457 | Adlai E. Stevenson (D) | 25,738,765 | 73 |
| 1960* | John F. Kennedy (D) | 34,221,531 | 303 | Richard M. Nixon (R) | 34,108,474 | 219 |
| 1964 | Lyndon B. Johnson (D) | 43,121,085 | 486 | Barry M. Goldwater (R) | 27,145,161 | 52 |
| 1968 | Richard M. Nixon (R) | 31,770,237 | 302 | Hubert H. Humphrey (D) | 31,270,533 | 191 |
| | | | | George C. Wallace (AI) | 9,906,141 | 45 |

*1800—Thomas Jefferson was elected by the House of Representatives due to a tie electoral vote.

1824—John Quincy Adams was elected by the House of Representatives since no candidate polled a majority.

1840—President Harrison died April 4, 1841, and Vice President John Tyler became President.

1848—President Taylor died July 9, 1850, and Vice President Millard Fillmore became President.

1864—President Lincoln died by assassination on April 15, 1865, and Vice President Andrew Johnson became President.

1876—The election returns of Florida, Louisiana, Oregon, and South Carolina were disputed. A board of Commissioners was created by an act of Congress to settle the dispute. It awarded the 22 disputed electoral votes to Hayes.

1880—President Garfield died by assassination on Sept. 19, 1881, and Vice President Chester A. Arthur became President.

1888—Although Cleveland received more popular votes than Harrison, the 233 electoral votes cast for Harrison against the 168 for Cleveland elected Harrison President.

1900—President McKinley died by assassination on Sept. 14, 1901, and Vice President Theodore Roosevelt became President.

1920—President Harding died Aug. 2, 1923, and Vice President Calvin Coolidge became President.

1944—President Roosevelt died April 12, 1945, and Vice President Harry S. Truman became President.

1960—President Kennedy died by assassination on Nov. 22, 1963, and Vice President Lyndon B. Johnson became President.

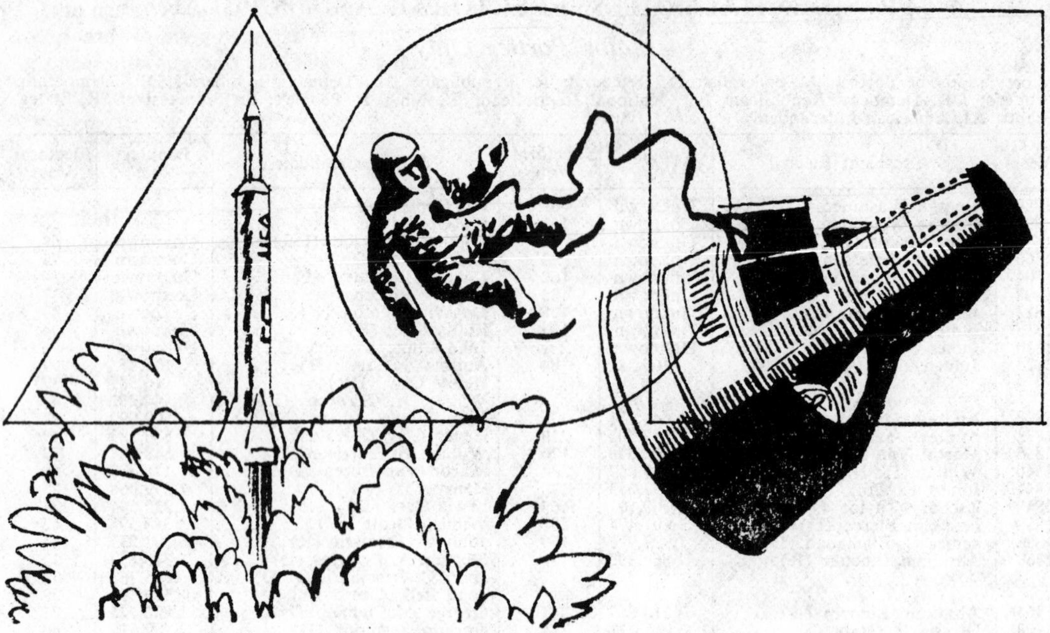

# Physical Sciences

## *Astronomy and Space*

Among the most awe-inspiring spectacles of nature are the rising and setting of the sun, a total eclipse of the sun or moon, the firmament of stars, and the appearance of a brilliant meteor shower. These events and scenes have been observed by man since he first walked the earth.

With the passage of time man's concept of the significance of these sights evolved. A primitive mixture of religious beliefs and practical uses of the stars, sun, and moon to measure the passage of time intervals developed over the eons into a highly sophisticated science embracing many disciplines. The quest to discover the physical nature and constitution of the heavenly bodies continues at an ever increasing rate.

Many civilizations have contributed to the accumulation of knowledge about the universe we live in. Occasionally the introduction of a revolutionary concept such as the heliocentric theory of Copernicus or the invention of a new instrument such as the telescope has enabled a great deal of progress to be made in a comparatively short time. Such a revolutionary trend is now in progress. The use of radio telescopes, satellites, and rockets for investigations and for experiments above the earth's atmosphere is making it possible for us to see in the far ultraviolet and infrared portions of the electromagnetic spectrum for the first time. The information gathered from these experiments has already begun to have an impact on our conception of the size and structure of the universe.

George Corso, *Instructor for the National Science Foundation,* Adler Planetarium, Chicago, Illinois.

### CONSTELLATIONS AND PLANETS

When primitive men first turned their gaze toward the night skies they saw some patterns of stars which reminded them of animals and things around them. After a while some men would begin to make up stories about the pictures in the sky. A few of these stories were passed down from one generation to the next and survived long enough to become a part of our culture.

**Legends of the Constellations**

Those stories, preserved through the ages and passed down to us are known as the legends of the constellations, or star patterns. These constellations are useful to the astronomer because they serve to divide the sky into regions that can be used to specify the approximate position of a star. The astronomers of the world have set down a list of 88 such constellations corresponding to 88 specific areas of the sky. Each constellation has been given a Latin name and each of the brighter stars in a constellation is assigned a letter of the Greek alphabet.

**Names of Stars**

Usually the brightest star of a constellation is designated by the first letter of the Greek alphabet, the next brightest by the second letter, and so on. A few of the stars which are especially bright or are particularly interesting have names as well.

**Zodiac**

The region of the sky in which the sun and planets are to be found at any time of the year is known as the zodiac. Those constellations falling within this region are known as the zodiacal constellations. Their names are Aries, Taurus, Gemini, Cancer, Leo, Virgo, Libra, Scorpius, Sagittarius, Capricornus, Aquarius, and Pisces.

**Circumpolar Constellation**

Those constellations near the celestial poles are referred to as the circumpolar constellations. They appear to revolve about the north and south celestial poles.

**Seasonal Appearances**

Due to the motion of the earth in its orbit about the sun there is an apparent shifting of the sun against the background of the constellations. Because of this, a given constellation will rise two hours earlier each month. The time at which constellations rise varies. Therefore they have been placed into four groups according to the seasons in which they are visible. One who has learned the spring, summer, winter, and fall constellations can use them as a calendar.

**Changing Patterns**

Generally speaking the stars of the constellations are not physically bound together and have different velocities through space. Because of this, over long periods of time the stars change their relative position with respect to each other. As a consequence the star patterns are constantly changing and the patterns we see are not the same as those seen by primitive men nor will they appear the same to our distant descendants.

**Planets**

Besides the true stars which alter their apparent positions only after long periods of time there are also bright starlike objects that are not really stars at all but planets whose positions change relatively rapidly against the background of the fixed stars.

Mercury, Venus, Mars, Jupiter, and Saturn are the only planets visible to the unaided eye. Uranus, Neptune, and Pluto require the use of a telescope to be seen.

**Solar System**

Each of the planets, including the earth, is a member of our solar system and revolves in an orbit about the sun. Some of the planets, like Mercury, have no natural satellites of their own while others, like Jupiter and Saturn, possess a whole family of them.

**Planet Groupings**

Sometimes the planets are grouped according to their similar characteristics. The terrestrial planets, Mercury, Venus, Earth, and Mars, are so called because they are similar to Earth in size and density and are the closest planets to the sun. The Jovian planets, Jupiter, Saturn, Uranus, and Neptune all have a large diameter, rotate rapidly, and possess thick atmospheres. Pluto does not fit into the Jovian group and it is more like the terrestrial planets in size.

## HISTORICAL DEVELOPMENT

When primitive man progressed to the point where he possessed the ability to formulate a lunisolar calendar based upon the motions of the sun and moon the first significant step toward understanding the nature of the heavenly bodies was made.

During the interval from 4,000 to 1,000 B.C. signs of such a level of technical achievement began to appear in Mesopotamia, Egypt, China, and India. The success of agriculture was heavily dependent on the ability to establish an accurate calendar. Planting and harvesting were initiated by rituals of a religious nature. These ceremonies, which had to be performed at definite times pleasing to the gods, could only be predicted by the use of an accurate calendar. Further progress in the accumulation of astronomical knowledge depended upon the belief that the heavenly bodies could be used to foretell the failures and sucesses of men. Events such as an eclipse of the sun or moon, or the appearance of a comet were particularly important to the kings and priests of early civilizations. Great efforts were made by the priests (sometimes facing death for a failure) to predict their appearance and interpret their significance as omens from the gods.

The practice of using the heavenly bodies to tell the future is known as astrology, and it is still practiced today by some primitive and superstitious peoples. However erroneous and primitive such ideas might seem, nevertheless they did stimulate accurate observation of many heavenly bodies which might not otherwise have been studied.

**The Babylonians**

Among the most accurate observers of this era were the Babylonians. They could predict the rising and setting of the planets and the appearance of eclipses; and they constructed an accurate lunisolar calendar. They also formulated the unit of space measurement known as the arc degree and established a time degree equal in duration to four minutes.

**The Greeks (600 B.C.)**

Some of the Babylonian knowledge was passed on to the Greeks, who also possessed a number of thinkers with exceptional ability and acute powers of observation. Such a man was Thales (c. 640-c. 550 B.C.) who established the Ionian school. His teachings included references to the stars' fiery nature, explanations for moonlight, and for the "new moon" phase. He is also reported to have predicted an eclipse that occurred in 585 B.C. which brought an end to a war being waged by his people and the Lydians.

He was succeeded by Anaximander who invented the gnomon, an instrument for determining the solstices and equinoxes.

Another important Greek school of thought was initiated by Pythagoras of Samos (c. 580-c. 500 B.C.). Pythagoras is believed to have identified the morning and evening stars and to have had knowledge of the earth's spherical shape and the relation of the motions of the planets to the ecliptic.

**Plato (c. 429-347 B.C.)**

The Greek philosopher Plato is largely responsible for a concept of the universe in which the earth was placed at the center of a large number of concentric spheres to which the heavenly bodies were fastened and were carried round about the earth as the spheres rotated. One of his followers, Eudoxus of Cnidus (409-356 B.C.) developed Plato's system so that three spheres were needed to produce the motion of the sun and moon, while each of the planets required four such spheres. This system was further modified by Calippus who tried to remove the errors in the representation of the motion of the planets Mars, Mercury, and Venus.

**Aristotle (c. 384-322 B.C.)**

The works of Eudoxus and Calippus were studied by Aristotle who then formulated his own system in which the motive power of the spheres was placed on the circumference of the system and was gradually transmitted to the inner spheres by a complicated linkage of the spheres.

One of Plato's students, Heraclides Pontius, put forth some very important ideas. He held the heavenly bodies to be solid spheres similar to the earth, possessing atmospheres. He is generally credited with being one of the first to suggest the possibility of a heavenly body's moving in an orbit around another heavenly body which is itself moving around the center of the universe.

**Alexandria (332 B.C.)**

A center for Greek astronomical thought arose in Alexandria, built by Alexander the Great about 332 B.C. Alexandria boasted a fine observatory and library as well as several outstanding astronomers. Aristarchus of Samos (280-264 B.C.) was a member of this school. He suggested a heliocentric (sun-centered) system with the earth revolving about the sun. He also wrote a book titled *On the Magnitudes and Distances of the Sun and Moon* in which he showed the sun to be larger than our planet and also to be far away.

About 225 B.C. a system of the universe was proposed by Appolonius of Perga which made use of epicycles and deferent circles to represent the planetary motion. The epicycle was a circle in which a planet could move with constant velocity. A deferent, or eccentric, was a circle having the earth at its center in which the center of the epicycle moved. Hipparchus liked the system and used it to represent the sun and moon's motion. Hipparchus was also the first to detect the precession of the equinoxes.

**Ptolemy (c. 100-200 A.D.)**

The next notable contribution to Greek astronomy was made by Cloudius Ptolemy who wrote a book titled *The Almagest* which was used during the middle ages as a textbook. Unfortunately he preferred a geocentric or earth-centered system which employed eccentrics and epicycles. Because it represented the motions of the heavenly bodies with the accuracy that was attainable with primitive instruments it remained in use until the time of Copernicus.

After Ptolemy Greek astronomy progressed very little and it was not until about the seventh century when new and better observatories began to appear in various parts of the world that further discoveries were possible.

About 100 A.D. the science and thought of the Arabs was rapidly spreading all through Europe and stimulating the formation of great schools. The University of Naples, established about 1224, was one of these great new centers of learning. In 1450 an important source of astronomical work and thought was founded by George Purbach at the University of Vienna.

**Copernicus (1473-1543)**

Astronomy was revolutionized by the work of Nicholas Copernicus who succeeded in establishing a heliocentric theory of the universe which eventually replaced Ptolemy's earth-centered system. Copernicus was born of German descent in a Polish city which is known as Torun. He attended the University of Cracow with the aim of embracing the religious life. He was sent to the University of Bologna, the University of Padua, and the University of Ferrara where he studied law, medicine, theology, mathematics, philosophy, and astronomy.

After completing his studies he went to Heilsburg where he was an adviser to the bishop. While there he formulated a conception of the universe which could offer a simpler and more accurate explanation for the movements of the objects in the sky than was possible with the traditional Ptolemaic theory. According to his theory the planets were all satellites of the sun which was located at the center of the solar system. He published his ideas in a great work titled *De Revolutionibus Orbium Caelestium* in which he attributed many of the apparent motions of the celestial bodies to the motions of our planet.

Although his theory utilized the traditional concept of epicycles and was not capable of a high degree of accuracy it was the best representation of observable phenomena possible in his time. Perhaps even more important, his boldness stimulated other thinkers of the time to cast off traditionally held concepts which could not stand up to critical examination.

**Tycho Brahe (1546-1601)**

Really significant contributions to astronomy's progress were made by Tycho Brahe. Born in Denmark of a Swedish family, he traveled extensively in Germany and was an avid student of astronomy and astrology. In 1572 he observed a new star, or nova, in the constellation of Cassiopeia. He closely followed the changes in brightness and color of this new star. His discovery that a fixed star could change in appearance was contradictory to what had been commonly believed by the thinkers of his day as well as by the ancient astronomers. In 1573 he published his observations in a book that was instrumental in the establishment of a modern view of the heavens.

Tycho was befriended by the king of Denmark, King Frederick, who granted him large sums of money and an island called Hveen so he could found an observatory there. For over 20 years the most accurate and precise observations possible at that time were made at Hveen. Using the information he gathered Tycho compiled a number of books containing many star positions and valuable instrumental data as well as his findings on the precession of the equinoxes.

When his benefactor died, Tycho was forced to leave Hveen and go to Bohemia where he founded a new observatory in the vicinity of Prague. At this new observatory he was assisted by Johannes Kepler who succeeded Tycho after his death.

**Johannes Kepler (1571-1630)**

Kepler used the abundance of observational data gathered by Tycho to formulate extremely powerful and original laws about the nature of planetary motion. In 1609 he published his laws of elliptic orbits and of equal areas. Shortly after, he released the third law which related the periods of revolution of the planets about the sun and the distances of the planets from the sun. Kepler also published a set of tables, begun by Tycho, which are known as the *Rudophine Tables,* in honor of Rudolph II. These tables were the first designed for a heliocentric (sun-centered) theory employing elliptical motion for the planets.

**Galileo (1564-1642)**

The Italian Galileo Galilei, born in the city of Pisa, was destined to play one of the most important roles in the development of astronomy. From his early youth the physical sciences attracted him and he eventually secured a post at the University of Pisa, where he lectured on the Ptolemaic theory. In 1604 he had the opportunity to observe a brilliant supernova and this greatly stimulated his astronomical interests. When, in 1609, he learned of the ability of a lens to magnify distant objects he immediately constructed a small telescope and employed it to make observations of the sky. Using this telescope he discovered four of Jupiter's moons, the phases of Venus, mountains and craters on the moon, and numerous stars too faint to be seen with the eye.

As a result of his observations he came to favor the Copernican theory and when he attempted to publicly support it he ran into much opposition from religious officials and philosophers. He was eventually called before the Inquisition and was forbidden to pursue his investigations of the sky and was made to renounce his belief in the heliocentric theory of Copernicus. However, his impact had been felt and word of his findings was welcomed wherever men sought truth.

**Isaac Newton (1643-1727)**

Born in Woolsthorpe, Lincolnshire, England, Newton's interest in astronomy was linked to his experiments in physics and mathematics. He formulated, among other things, the universal law of gravitation which made it possible for him to determine the masses of a number of celestial bodies, and he was able to explain the planetary motions in terms of gravitational theory. Newton designed and built a new kind of telescope which is now known as a Newtonian reflector. It employed a metal mirror with a parabolic surface to collect light and is free of chromatic (color) aberrations.

**Edmund Halley (1656-1742)**

Newton was assisted for a time by Edmund Halley. Halley was particularly interested in comets and he published an important work on them titled *Synopsis Astronomiae Cometicae.* He is perhaps best known for the successful prediction of the return of the comet which bears his name. He based his prediction of the comet's return upon Newton's gravitational theory and this prediction was one of the first important tests of the validity of the theory. He also was instrumental in the establishment of the new science of geophysics. Halley was the first one to detect the minute changes in the relative positions of the stars which is the result of their motion through space. He accomplished this by comparing the current positions of Sirius, Arcturus, and Procyon with those determined by ancient Greek astronomers.

**Sir William Herschel (1738-1822)**

One of the greatest of the observational astronomers prior to the development of modern astronomical methods was Sir William Herschel. Initially a musician, born in Hanover, he settled in England where he became fascinated by astronomy. He made many important observations with reflecting telescopes he constructed himself. Among other important discoveries, he found the planet Uranus and multiple systems of stars which revolved about their common center of mass. One of his telescopes had a mirror with a diameter of four feet and had a 40 foot focal length. With it he found a previously unknown satellite of the planet Saturn. One of his most impressive achievements was the determination of the direction of motion of our solar system as it is carried through space by the sun.

**Henry Norris Russell (1877-1957)**

One of the greatest of American astronomers was Henry Norris Russell. Educated at Princeton University, he was eventually appointed an instructor of astronomy there in 1905. After advancing to the rank of professor he was made the director of the University's Observatory. Russell did a great deal of work on the masses of stars using the information obtained from a determination of the orbits of multiple stars about their common center of mass. He also determined the distances of many stars and thereby made it possible to get their absolute magnitude.

Russell's investigations of changes in the physical appearance of a star enabled him to formulate a theory of stellar evolution. His researches into the atmospheres of the sun and other stars revealed much about the distribution of density, pressure, and temperature in them. His numerous articles, books, and papers brought him a reputation as one of the leading authorities of astronomical thought.

The first to apply atomic physics to stellar evolution in a systematic and complete manner was Arthur Stanley Eddington (1882-1944). Born in Dendal, Westmorland, England, of Quaker parents he showed an early interest in mathematics and astronomy. He attended Owens' College at Manchester, beginning at the age of 15. In 1902 he went to Trinity College where he distinguished himself in all forms of mathematics. After graduation he performed research at the Cavendish Laboratory but left there when he was offered the chief assistant's position at the Greenwich Observatory. Among his many achievements, perhaps the most notable was his *The Internal Constitution of the Stars,* published in 1926. He was the first to take the effects of radiation pressure inside a star into account when determining the temperature and pressure distribution in a star.

## MODERN TELESCOPES

Shortly after Herschel's time the number of observatories in the world began to rapidly increase. They were also equipped with better instruments for measuring time and position. New mathematical tools became available to speed calculations. Refinement of the spectroscope together with the development of the theory of spectra made it possible to study the physical makeup of the stars and nebulae. Solar astronomy made great strides beginning with the identification of the dark lines in its spectrum as being due to the presence of some of the same elements as are present on the earth.

The largest refracting telescope in the world, at Yerkes Observatory in Williams Bay, Wisconsin, was constructed in 1895 under the direction of George Ellery Hale. In 1918 Hale completed the 100 inch Hooker reflector of the Mt. Wilson Observatory in southern California and in 1948 construction of the world's largest reflector, at Mt. Palomar, also begun by Hale, was finished. This telescope, with a 200 inch mirror, has provided man with the opportunity to see billions of light years into space and probe the deepest secrets of the universe.

The large telescopes, like the one at Mt. Palomar enable us to see far into the universe. They have been joined by a type of telescope designed by the German Bernhard Schmidt that has a large field of view so that larger areas of the sky can be photographed at one time.

Like all the other sciences, astronomy has made great advancements in recent years. Man's space probes, the development of the radio telescope, and new concepts in mathematics and physics have flooded the modern astronomer with information. He is as much concerned with analyzing and formulating themes about his newly won knowledge as he is in seeking out more information.

Radio telescopes give quite a different picture than conventional telescopes. Some bodies are noisy (emit strong radio waves), and some stars that appear bright through reflecting telescopes are not picked up at all by radio telescopes.

A few scientists realized. very early that rockets would enable man to explore space. Although instruments were available for recording phenomena in space, it was not until rockets were more fully developed that experiments could take place. Robert Goddard of the United States was one of the first scientists to work on rocket development. One of the pioneer steps was the launching in 1945 of the WAC Corporal rocket. For some years also, German V-2 rockets were used.

Some years later a committee of the International Geophysical Year suggested that artificial satellites be launched as a part of the year's program. As a result, the Soviet Union launched the first Sputniks and the United States developed the Explorer and Vanguard satellites.

The Van Allen radiation belts were discovered by J. A. Van Allen. Using information received from Explorer I, he suggested that an intense belt of radiation existed around the earth. Later explorations found that two belts of charged particles surround the earth and that these are a potent factor in certain earth phenomena — northern lights, electromagnetic storms, etc.

The first Orbiting Solar Observatory was launched into a 300 mile circular orbit from which it performed many experiments in solar physics and confirmed the origin of solar flare radiation as being confined to a small percentage of the solar surface.

The use of Gemini and Apollo astronauts to perform photographic surveys of stars in the ultraviolet portion of the spectrum and to photograph the sun is yet another step in the program of space exploration and conquest.

**Table 1: SUN, MOON, AND PLANETS***

Diameters, Orbital Periods, Masses, Surface Gravities, and Rotational Periods

| Body | Equatorial Diameter Miles | Orbital Period in Years | Mass Earth — 1 | Surface Gravity Earth — 1 | Rotational Period |
|---|---|---|---|---|---|
| Sun | 864,000[b] | | 332,500[b] | 28[b] | |
| Moon | 2,160[b] | | 0.0123[b] | 0.166[b] | |
| Mercury | 3,100[b] | 0.241[a] | 0.056[b] | 0.37[b] | 88.0[a] days |
| Venus | 7,570[b] | 0.615[a] | 0.82[b] | 0.89[b] | 250[a] days |
| Earth | 7,927[b] | 1.00[a] | 1.00[b] | 1.00[b] | 23.9[a] hrs. |
| Mars | 4,200[b] | 1.88[a] | 0.108[b] | 0.38[b] | 24.6[a] hrs. |
| Jupiter | 88,700[b] | 11.9[a] | 318[b] | 2.54[b] | 9.8[a] hrs. |
| Saturn | 75,100[b] | 29.5[a] | 95[b] | 1.06[b] | 10.2[a] hrs. |
| Uranus | 29,000[b] | 84.0[a] | 14.6[b] | 1.1[b] | 10.8[a] hrs. |
| Neptune | 28,000[b] | 165[a] | 17.3[b] | 1.4[b] | 15.7[a] hrs. |
| Pluto | ? [b] | 248[a] | <1[b] | ? [b] | 6.4[a] days |

* For *The Constellations,* see Table 2 on page 1124.

[a] From *Principles of Astronomy* by Wyatt; Allyn & Bacon, Inc.

[b] From *Introduction to Astronomy* by McLaughlin; Houghton Mifflin.

# DICTIONARY OF SPACE AGE TERMS

## A

**ablation:** the melting or wearing away of layers of material during a space craft's reentry into the atmosphere
**absolute zero:** the temperature at which thermal or molecular motion ceases; approximately 273° below 0° C.
**acceleration of gravity:** the rate of increase in speed as an object moves under the influence of gravity in free fall
**aeroballistics:** the application of the principles of aerodynamics and ballistics; the science of the motion of guided missiles and rockets
**aerodynamic drag:** the slowing down of a body as it moves through the atmosphere; caused by the resistance of the air
**aerodynamics:** the science of the motion of forces as they act upon bodies that move through the air
**aeronautical mile:** air mile; 6080 feet
**aeronautics:** the study of flight and the means of attaining it
**aerospace medicine:** the branch of medicine that is concerned with the well-being of those who fly in the atmosphere and in space
**analog computer:** a computer that measures
**ANNA:** from army, navy, NASA, and air force. A satellite designed to provide information for the study of the earth as a celestial body
**aphelion:** the farthest point from the sun in a planet's elliptical orbit
**astro-:** a prefix from the Greek word *astron;* star
**astrobiology:** the study of the possibilities of life on other planets
**astrochemistry:** the study of the chemical make up of heavenly bodies
**astrocompass:** an instrument used in navigation to determine position by fixing the position of certain heavenly bodies
**astronaut:** a space traveler
**astronomical unit:** a measure of distance equal to the earth's mean distance from the sun, or about 93 million miles
**astronomy:** the study of all the heavenly bodies; includes their distances, as well as their motions
**astrophysics:** the study of the physical nature of the stars and the gas and dust between them
**atmosphere of the earth:** the whole mass of air or the gaseous envelope around the earth
**atmospheric braking:** the process of retarding the motion of a space vehicle; makes use of atmospheric drag
**atmospheric structure satellite:** spacecraft that was equipped with instruments to measure elements in the atmosphere of the earth
**atomic clock:** a device for extremely accurate time measurement which utilizes the vibrations of a molecule or atom

## B

**ballistic missile:** usually refers to a space vehicle that is guided as it ascends into the atmosphere and is allowed to fall freely during descent
**ballistic trajectory:** curved path traveled by a body as it falls freely during descent
**beefed up:** a slang expression that refers to the strengthening of parts or of stress areas; makes them able to withstand forces or pressures stronger than those for which they were originally designed
**bioastronautics:** from biology and astronautics; the study of living organisms as they are affected by space travel
**biomedicine:** the science dealing with human resistance to space travel and methods of protection
**bionics:** the field of science that applies knowledge of biological processes to the planning and building of electronic or mechanical devices and systems
**biopak:** a container for either humans or animals that carries all the equipment necessary to support life during a space flight
**biosatellite:** a satellite that carries live specimens in order to study the effects of space on them
**biosphere:** the portion of the earth and its atmosphere in which living organisms are found
**booster stage:** the first stage in a space vehicle
**braking ellipses:** maneuvers used to slow a space vehicle as it reenters the earth's atmosphere
**break-off phenomena:** the reaction of many pilots who fly at a high altitude; characterized by feelings of detachment from the earth and from humans

## C

**captive firing:** the test firing of a missile in which the missile does not leave the ground; in all other respects the missile is identical to the one that is actually to be fired
**celestial mechanics:** the study of the motions of the planets and other objects in space with the aid of Newton's gravitational theory and relativity
**chromosphere:** an approximately 12,000 km. thick region of the sun's atmosphere which is between the photosphere and the corona
**coronagraph:** a special telescope for observing the sun which uses a metal cone to produce an artificial eclipse
**countdown:** the step-by-step procedure that leads to the launching of a space vehicle
**cut-off:** the point at which the propellant of a missile is shut off

## D

**dark nebulae:** dense clouds of gas and dust which act as a filter to block out the light of the stars behind them
**descent path:** the path that is followed by a space vehicle as it leaves its orbit to land
**descriptive astronomy:** the branch of astronomy that details and describes celestial bodies
**digital computer:** a computer that uses numbers to perform complex calculations through repetitive addition and subtraction; the measurements taken from an analog computer are translated into numbers that can be used by the digital computer
**Doppler effect:** the apparent change in the frequency of sound, light, or radio waves; caused by the relative motion between the source and the observer

## E

**earthlight:** the light of the sun which is reflected from the earth
**echo:** a wave that has been reflected with sufficient intensity or enough delay to distinguish it
**Echo:** the name given to the series of large, balloon-shaped satellites used as communications satellites; they are passive, that is, they do not transmit signals but are used to bounce signals back to the earth
**ecliptic:** the great circle on the celestial sphere which the sun describes in the course of a year; the apparent path of the sun
**electrostatic camera:** used in conjunction with satellites; requires no processing for photographs
**emission nebulae:** large clouds of gas and dust that are near a hot star which excites the clouds to emit radiation that is visible to us
**encode:** the conversion of the information given by an analog computer into information of the kind that can be fed into a digital computer
**environmental space chamber:** a compartment in which the conditions of a space capsule can be duplicated; used for experimental purposes
**escape velocity:** of the earth — the minimum velocity that is necessary for a missile or space vehicle to achieve in order to escape from the gravitational pull of the earth; this is about seven miles per second
**exact orbit:** the planned or intended orbit that a space vehicle must reach in order to get the information for which it was designed
**exobiology:** the study of life in space or the possibilities of life in space

## F

**flying saucers:** a slang expression; refers to unidentified flying objects that are reported to have been seen in many places throughout the world

**fireball:** a meteor that is brighter than any of the planets

**flybys:** satellites launched to record information as they pass by a planet or other body and that do not return to the earth

**free fall:** the motion of an object or missile that is falling through space and is not controlled

## G

**galaxy:** a collection of many millions of stars which are bound together by gravity; the earth is part of the galaxy that is called the Milky Way

**gantry:** shaped like a crane and on wheels, this structure is used for servicing and assembling missiles; before they are launched it is rolled away

**geocentric:** referring to the earth as a center; measuring from the center of the earth

**geodesy:** the study of the shape and structure of the earth

**geodetic satellite:** collects information that permits scientists to study the structure and shape of the earth

**guidance systems:** the methods and instruments that provide continuous flight information and the commands that are based on that information

**guided missile:** an unmanned but guided vehicle; usually the term refers to a missile that is used for military purposes

## H

**heat shield:** the protective covering on a space vehicle that protects the vehicle by absorbing the heat of atmospheric friction

**heliocentric:** uses the center of the sun as a reference point; or it may refer to the sun as the center for reference purposes

**hyperbolic navigation:** the method of navigating or determining position by locating certain celestial bodies

## I

**intercontinental ballistic missile:** a missile that is allowed to go into a ballistic trajectory (or free fall) after an initial stage of controlled thrust; it is capable of reaching other continents

**intergalactic space:** space between the galaxies

**interplanetary dust:** particles that exist in interplanetary space

**Interplanetary Explorer:** a spacecraft that carries equipment for recording information about radiation and magnetic fields

**interpretational astronomy:** the area of astronomy that is concerned with explaining the accomplishments of the science to the layman

**interstellar space:** refers to space between the stars

## L

**LASER:** an acronym from light amplification stimulated by emulsion of radiation

**launch vehicles:** rockets that are used for launching spacecraft into orbit

**law of gravitation:** formulated by Isaac Newton in the seventeenth century it states that each particle of matter in the universe attracts every other particle with a force that is directly proportional to the product of their masses and inversely proportional to the square of the distance between them

**light year:** the distance light travels in a year — about six trillion miles

**lunar probe:** a space vehicle, either manned or equipped with instruments, that is designed to obtain information on the moon or near the moon

**Lunik:** name of the series of Russian satellites used for moon probes

## M

**mass:** the quantity of matter that is contained in a body

**meteor:** a piece of matter from space that is burning and radiating light as it passes through the atmosphere

**meteoric shower:** observable when the earth and a group of meteors are traveling about the sun in a patch which intercepts the earth

**meteorite:** that part of a meteor that finds its way to the earth after passing through the atmosphere

**micrometeorite:** a meteorite with a diameter between a few microns and a millimeter

**microwaves:** high frequency radiation with wave lengths from a few centimeters to a few meters

**Milky Way:** our own spiral galaxy which is made up of a hundred billion stars

## N

**navigational planets:** Venus, Mars, Jupiter, and Saturn; these are usually referred to as the navigational planets because they are used for calculating position in celestial navigation

**nebula:** a vast cloud of gas and dust

**nova:** a violently exploding star whose light may increase a hundred thousand times before declining

## O

**observational astronomy:** the branch of astronomy that deals with the instruments and the data that is collected with those instruments

**orbital period:** the time required for a satellite to make one complete orbit

**Orbiting Solar Observatory:** a spacecraft that is equipped with instruments designed to obtain information about the sun

## P

**parsec:** a unit of measure for space; one parsec equals 3.26 light years

**perihelion:** the nearest point to the sun in a planet's orbit about the sun

**photon:** a massless bundle of energy

**planet** (from the Greek word meaning wanderer): because of their continuously and rapidly changing positions in the sky, this name was attached to the principal bodies of the solar system which orbit the sun

**polar orbit:** refers to the orbit of a satellite or spacecraft that passes near the poles of the earth

**Polar Orbiting Geophysical Observatory** (POGO): a satellite that will record information about the atmosphere and the ionosphere in regions near the poles of the earth

## R

**radar astronomy:** the use of radar to obtain information about celestial bodies

**radio astronomy:** the use of radio telescopes to gather radio waves emitted by celestial bodies

**radio telescope:** large antennas designed to obtain information on the type and amount of radio waves emitted by objects in space

**Ranger:** the first series of American lunar probes; designed to land on the moon

**readied missile:** a missile that is ready to be fired, i.e., after all the steps of the countdown have been completed

**reentry body:** the part of a vehicle that reenters the earth's atmosphere

**reflection nebulae:** clouds of gas and dust that are near a cool star and shine by the reflected light of the star

**regenerative oxygen supply:** oxygen that is purified and breathed over and over again by the astronauts during a flight

**rendezvous maneuvers:** ordinarily the target vehicle is the first to be launched and then the second vehicle is launched into the same orbit that the target is traveling in; through the use of small rockets the astronauts join or dock the two vehicles

**rocket:** a vehicle constructed to travel in the atmosphere and in outer space

## S

**self-guided missile:** a vehicle that is equipped with the instruments that are necessary for its own guidance

**separation rocket:** a rocket that is incorporated into the second or a higher stage of a space vehicle for the purpose of being fired to give extra thrust during separation from the preceding stage

**solar constant:** the total amount of

energy falling on one square centimeter of a surface which is perpendicular to the sun's rays and located at the mean distance of the earth from the sun

**space laboratory:** a space vehicle designed to carry instruments that will record scientific information about space

**Sputnik:** the Russian satellite that was the first artificial satellite

**space probes:** spacecraft that are used to explore the solar system

**space science:** includes all the various disciplines that participate in research in space

**stellar photometry:** the process or procedures involved in determining the brightness of stars

**sunspots:** blemishes on the solar surface which appear dark because they are cooler than the surrounding surface. They are connected with intense magnetic fields

**supersonic aerodynamics:** the study of flight and the problems of flight at speeds above the speed of sound

**T**

**tektites:** small pieces of natural glass which may have originated outside the earth. They are found in only a few locations and range in diameter from a few millimeters to 20 centimeters

**telemetry:** the tracking of a spacecraft and recording of the information that it obtains

**telstar:** active communications satellite; transmits signals

**Tiros:** name given to weather satellites

**two-stage rocket:** a rocket in which each of two separate stages has its own propulsion system

**V**

**Van Allen radiation belts:** two belts of charged particles that surround the earth

**W**

**weather** (meteorological) **satellite:** a satellite that records and transmits information that is valuable in predicting weather

**weightlessness:** condition encountered during space flights in orbit; zero gravity

**Z**

**zero gravity:** the condition of weightlessness; absence of the effects of gravitation

**zodiacal light:** faint band of light along the ecliptic that is caused by sunlight which is scattered by particles in the interplanetary medium

**Table 2: THE CONSTELLATIONS** (From *Principles of Astronomy* by Wyatt; Allyn & Bacon, Inc.)

| Latin Name | English Name | Latin Name | English Name | Latin Name | English Name |
|---|---|---|---|---|---|
| Andromeda[a, c] | Andromeda | Corvus[a] | Crow | Orion[a, c] | Orion |
| Antlia | Air Pump | Crater | Cup | Pavo[a] | Peacock |
| Apus | Bird of Paradise | Crux[a] | Cross | Pegasus[a, c] | Pegasus |
| Aquarius[a] | Water Carrier | Cygnus[a] | Swan | Perseus[a, c] | Perseus |
| Aquila[a] | Eagle | Delphinus[a] | Dolphin | Phoenix[a] | Phoenix |
| Ara[a] | Altar | Dorado[a] | Swordfish | Pictor[a] | Easel |
| Aries[a] | Ram | Draco[a] | Dragon | Pisces[a] | Fishes |
| Auriga[a] | Charioteer | Equuleus | Little Horse | Piscis Austrinus[a] | Southern Fish |
| Bootes[a] | Herdsman | Eridanus[a] | River | Puppis[a, b] | Stern |
| Caelum | Graving Tool | Fornax | Furnace | Pyxis[b] | Mariner's Compass |
| Camelopardalis | Giraffe | Gemini[a] | Twins | Reticulum[a] | Net |
| Cancer[a] | Crab | Grus[a] | Crane | Sagitta[a] | Arrow |
| Canes Venatici[a] | Hunting Dogs | Hercules[a, c] | Hercules | Sagittarius[a] | Archer |
| Canis Major[a] | Larger Dog | Horologium | Clock | Scorpio[a] | Scorpion |
| Canis Minor[a] | Smaller Dog | Hydra[a] | Water Serpent | Sculptor | Sculptor's Tools |
| Capricornus[a] | Goat | Hydrus[a] | Water Snake | Scutum | Shield |
| Carina[a, b] | Keel | Indus[a] | Indian | Serpens[a] | Serpent |
| Cassiopeia[a, c] | Cassiopeia | Lacerta | Lizard | Sextans | Sextant |
| Centaurus[a] | Centaur | Leo[a] | Lion | Taurus[a] | Bull |
| Cepheus[a, c] | Cepheus | Leo Minor[a] | Smaller Lion | Telescopium | Telescope |
| Cetus[a] | Whale | Lepus[a] | Hare | Triangulum[a] | Triangle |
| Chamaeleon | Chameleon | Libra[a] | Scales | Triangulum Australe[a] | Southern Triangle |
| Circinus[a] | Compasses | Lupus[a] | Wolf | Tucana[a] | Toucan |
| Columba[a] | Dove | Lyra[a] | Lynx | Ursa Major[a] | Larger Bear |
| Coma Berenices | Berenice's Hair | Lynx | Lyre | Ursa Minor[a] | Smaller Bear |
| Corona Australis | Southern Crown | Mensa | Table Mountain | Vela[a, b] | Sails |
| Corona Borealis[a] | Northern Crown | Microscopium | Microscope | Virgo[a] | Virgin |
| | | Monoceros | Unicorn | Volans | Flying Fish |
| | | Musca[a] | Fly | Vulpecula | Fox |
| | | Norma | Ruler | | |
| | | Octans | Octant | | |
| | | Ophiuchus[a] | Serpent Carrier | | |

[a] May be found on one or more of the six star maps.

[b] Carina, Puppis, Pyxis, and Vela are modern subdivisions of the original very large constellation Argo Navis, the legendary ship Argo.

[c] In Greek mythology Andromeda was the daughter of Cepheus and Cassiopeia and wife of Perseus; Cassiopeia was the wife of Cepheus; Cepheus was a king of Ethiopia; Hercules was a son of Zeus and celebrated for his great strength; Orion was a hunter who chased the Pleiades and was slain by Diana; Pegasus was a winged horse; and Perseus was a son of Zeus and was the hero who rescued and married Andromeda.

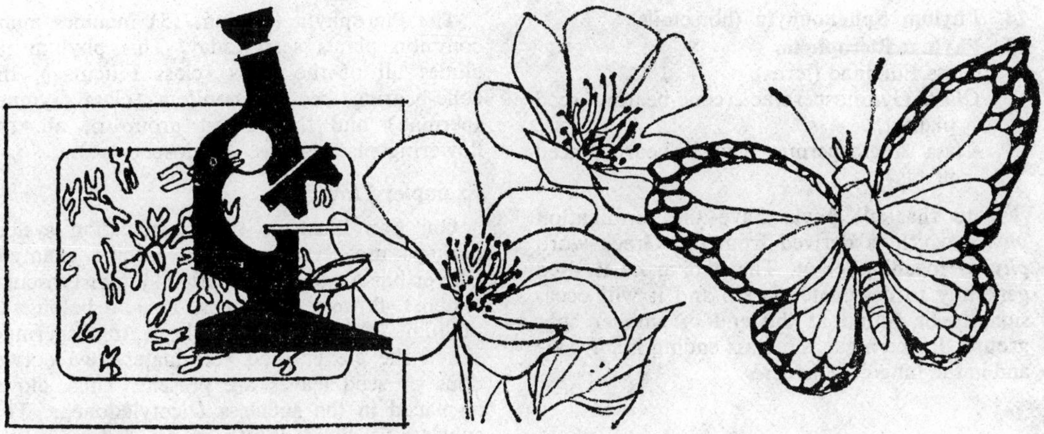

# Biology

## CLASSIFICATION OF PLANTS

THE EFFORTS to classify or group 300,000 or more kinds of plants in the world have been in the direction of arriving at a natural system of classification. Plants have ancestors, just as people do. Some of these have disappeared through the ages and are now said to be extinct. Nevertheless, fossil forms of such plants have been preserved. In any natural system of classifying plants, an attempt is made to express their ancestry.

In making a classification, evidence is derived from many sources: fossils, comparative anatomy or structure, geographical distribution, etc.

Superficial relationships or characteristics (flower color, for example) which vary with each slight change in environmental conditions are not employed.

### WHY DO WE CLASSIFY?

The fundamental rational for classification of plants is to begin with the largest group known and subdivide it into smaller and smaller subgroups. Thus, all plants in the world constitute the plant kingdom.

---

DR. GUS TOMLINSON, *Chairman*, Division of Science and Mathematics, George Peabody College for Teachers. B.S., Peabody College; Ph.D., Vanderbilt University; Postdoctoral, Cancer Research, Swiss Federal Institute, Zürich, Switzerland.

### HOW DO WE CLASSIFY?

The kingdom is then divided into a number of reasonably distinct subgroups called *phyla* (singular, *phylum*). Some phyla are divided into smaller groups called classes. These groups are as follows:

1. **Phylum Schizophyta** (fission plants).
   Class Schizomycetes (bacteria).
   Class Schizophyceae (blue-green algae).
2. **Phylum Euglenophycophyta** (euglenoids).
3. **Phylum Chlorophycophyta** (green algae).
4. **Phylum Charophycophyta** (stoneworts).
5. **Phylum Chrysophycophyta** (diatoms and related forms).
6. **Phylum Pyrrophycophyta** (golden-brown algae).
7. **Phylum Phaeophycophyta** (brown algae).
8. **Phylum Rhodophycophyta** (red algae).
9. **Phylum Myxomycophyta** (slime molds).
10. **Phylum Eumycophyta** (true fungi).
    Class Phycomycetes.
    Class Ascomycetes.
    Class Basidiomycetes.
    Class Imperfecti.
11. **Phylum Bryophyta.**
    Class Hepaticae (liverworts).
    Class Anthrocerotae (anthoceros).
    Class Musci (mosses).
12. **Phylum Psilophyta** (represented chiefly by fossil forms).
13. **Phylum Lycophyta** (clubmosses and quillworts).

**14. Phylum Sphenophyta** (horsetails).
**15. Phylum Pterophyta.**
Class Filicinae (ferns).
Class Gymnospermae (cone-bearing seed plants).
Class Angiospermae (flower-bearing seed plants).

Note that all phyla have the termination *phyta,* which is derived from the Greek word *phyton* meaning plant. The ending *ae* is used generally to designate classes and it will occasionally be found at the end of smaller subgroups. In the algae the class ending is *phyceae* and in the fungi it is *mycetes.*

## CHARACTERISTICS OF PLANT PHYLA

The first ten phyla are often referred to as the *thallophytes* or the "thallus plants", a *thallus* being a very simple plant body lacking true roots, stems, and leaves. The *bryophytes* (phylum 11) or "moss plants" are primitive land plants, like thallophytes in that they have no true roots, stems, and leaves and no specialized system for the conduction of food and water from one part of the plant to another, but unlike thallophytes in that they possess *multicellular reproductive structures.* The last four phyla are often referred to as the *vascular plants* because they possess a vascular or specialized conducting system. Phyla 12, 13, and 14 have been exhaustively studied by plant evolutionists because the living plants belonging to them appear to represent the last examples of an ancient type of vegetation.

Only four species of living Psilophyta are known today and one of these is so primitive that it is devoid of roots and possesses only tiny leaves. The Lycophyta (clubmosses) and Sphenophyta (horsetails) are also vestiges of the past. The living representatives of these two phyla are relatively small and form an inconspicuous part of the present-day flora. Their relative importance was far greater many years ago. There was a time when the earth's vegetation was comprised of extensive forests of these plants. Indeed, a major portion of today's coal supply was formed from the carbonized trunks of representatives of these two phyla.

The Pterophyta (phylum 15) includes many common plants seen today. This phylum includes all of the ferns (class Filicinae), the cone-bearing trees or conifers (class Gymnospermae) and the largest group of all, the flowering plants (class Angiospermae).

**Example: Clover**

One can illustrate the classification system perhaps most vividly *via* a specific example. Clover has a water conduction system (vascular system), flowers, and seeds. Thus, it belongs to phylum Pterophyta and class Angiospermae. When the clover seed germinates, *two* cotyledons or seed leaves are present. Thus, clover is placed in the subclass *Di*cotyledoneae. This subclass is divided into many *orders* on the basis of other characteristics. The order for clover is Rosales which contains at least 14,000 species, all of which share certain selected characters in common. Order Rosales is subdivided into *families,* including the well-known mimosa family (Mimosaceae) and the roses (Rosaceae). Clover is grouped in a family called the legumes (Leguminosae). At least 400 subgroups of the legumes are known and divided into *genera.* Since clovers generally possess three leaves, they belong to the genus *Trifolium.* The final division is into species, of which the genus *Trifolium* contains about 300. Scientists generally specify both the generic and specific names for a plant. This is called the *binomial* system of nomenclature. Thus, the definitive name for white clover is *Trifolium repens.*

In summary, the complete classification for white clover (*Trifolium repens*) is given below:

Phylum — Pterophyta
Class — Angiospermae
Subclass — Dicotyledoneae
Order — Rosales
Family — Leguminosae
Genus — *Trifolium*
Species — *repens*
Scientific name — *Trifolium repens*

The binomial system of nomenclature was first proposed by the great Swedish naturalist, Linnaeus whose monumental work the *Species Plantarum* was published in 1753. The system is complex but it is quickly mastered upon frequent usage.

# CLASSIFICATION OF ANIMALS

THE FUNDAMENTAL RATIONAL for classifying animals is very similar to that described above for the classification of plants. The system is *binomial* and employs *latin* descriptive terminology. Pronunciation of scientific names for animals seems equally distressing to students as those for plants; but both systems become more meaningful when the ambiguities and complexities of common names are considered. Thus a common sparrow of western Europe that is now established throughout the United States is known in different countries as follows:

United States — English sparrow.
England — House sparrow.
France — Moineau domestique.
Spain — Gorrion.
Portugal — Pardal.
Italy — Passera oltramontana.
Germany — Haussperling.
Holland — Musch.
Denmark and Norway — Graspurv.
Sweden — Hussparf.

To scientists all over the world it is simply *Passer domesticus*. Thus, scientific nomenclature strives for universal understanding without ambiguity.

## ANIMAL PHYLA

The major phyla of animals are listed below:

1. **Phylum Protozoa** (microscopic, one-celled animals).
2. **Phylum Porifera** (sponges).
3. **Phylum Coelenterata** (Hydras, jelly fishes, sea corals).
4. **Phylum Ctenophora** (comb jellies).
5. **Phylum Platyhelminthes** (Flatworms, flukes and tapeworms).
6. **Phylum Nemertinea** (Ribbon worms).
7. **Phylum Aschelminthes** (rotifers, "hair snakes", round worms).
8. **Phylum Acanthocephala** (spiny-headed worms).
9. **Phylum Bryozoa** (moss animals).
10. **Phylum Brachiopoda** (lamp shells).
11. **Phylum Echinodermata** (Starfishes, sea urchins, sand dollars, sea lilies, brittle stars).
12. **Phylum Chaetognatha** (arrow worms).
13. **Phylum Mollusca** (chitons, tooth shells mollusks, squids, octopuses).
14. **Phylum Annelida** (segmented worms, leeches, earthworms, sand worms).
15. **Phylum Sipunculoidea** (peanut worms).
16. **Phylum Arthropoda** (lobsters, crabs, insects, spiders, centipedes, mites, ticks, scorpions).
17. **Phylum Chordata** (man, birds, reptiles, frogs, toads, bony fishes, tunicates, lamprey eels, lancelets).

# LAWS, THEORIES AND HYPOTHESES

**Abiogenesis:** Spontaneous generation, life arising from non-living material.
**Aerobic respiration:** oxygen consuming metabolism of glucose or other foods.
**Allen's rule:** Within a species, protruding parts tend to be shorter in cold climates.
**Anaerobic respiration:** Cellular metabolism in the absence of oxygen.
**All-or-none law:** Individual muscle fibers contract and nerves conduct impulses maximally or not at all.
**Alternation of generations:** Alternation of sporophyte and gametophyte generations in plants.
**Antivivisection law:** laws against animal experimentation.
**Antibiosis:** One organism taking the life of another to preserve his own.
**Asexual reproduction:** without fusion of two nuclei from different cells.
**Binomial nomenclature:** naming by specifying the genus and species.
**Biogenesis:** Life arising from preexisting life and in no other way.
**Biological drive:** theory that motivation arises from a need to stabilize the organism as in hunger and thirst.
**Bunsen-Roscoe law:** product law of photoreceptors. Response is proportional to duration of exposure times intensity.
**Cell theory:** The basic structural unit of life is the cell.
**Chromosome theory of heredity:** Sutton's theory that hereditary characters — or genes — are carried on chromosomes.
**Code, genetic:** Theory that hereditary information is carried in the sequence of bases in deoxyribonucleic (DNA).
**Coloration, adaptive:** The theory that organisms acquire in some manner a blending coloration with their environment.
**Competition law of evolution:** If two species compete strongly, the frequent but not inevitable outcome is that one of them becomes extinct.
**Convergent evolution:** Development of resemblance between organisms whose ancestors were less alike.
**Differential reproductive rate:** The relative rate at which organisms of different groups reproduce themselves.
**Divergent evolution:** Divergence of resemblance between organisms whose ancestors were very much alike.
**Dominance, principle of:** An inheritable characteristic may appear in two forms, but a hybrid shows only one of these forms, the dominant.
**Epigenesis doctrine:** A theory of development which states that the fertilized egg holds the characteristics of the species and develops step by step and structure by structure into the adult.
**Eugenics theory:** That human genetics offers

the possibility of improving the inherited characteristics of the race.

**Euthenics theory:** A counterpart of eugenics which emphasizes the effects of environment as a means of improving humans by making fuller use of their potentiality.

**Evolution by natural selection:** change through progressive elimination of the less fit by natural processes.

**Evolution by use and disuse:** Theory that changes have evolved from pre-existing species through modification of their structure depending on the degree of use to which the previously present structure was utilized.

**Feedback, negative:** a stimulus-response system where response is opposite to the initiating stimulus.

**Feedback, positive:** a stimulus-response system in which response is directly related to the eliciting stimulus. For example, the heart normally responds to blood loss by pumping more rapidly.

**First-order reaction:** chemical reactions in which the rate-limiting step depends upon collision of one type of molecule.

**First law of thermodynamics:** Energy is neither lost nor gained when it is converted from one form to another.

**Free energy of reaction:** The change in free energy that occurs when a chemical reaction goes from one state to another.

**Foot candle standard of light measure:** The intensity of illumination on a small area of an object which is placed one foot distant from the candle flame.

**Friedman Test:** "pregnancy test". Induction of ovulation in unmated rabbits by estrogen in the urine of a pregnant human female.

**Geotropic response:** "earth turning response". The growth of roots downward is a positive response in plants. Growth of the shoot of plants upward is said to be a negative geotropic response.

**Germ theory of disease:** Recognition in the late 1870's that many ailments were the result of bacterial infections.

**Gigantism:** Excessive elongation of long bones during the growth period due to over-secretion of growth stimulating hormone. A glandular malfunction among humans.

**Gram-molecular solution:** One gram molecular weight (mole) of a material dissolved in one liter of solution. A measure of the chemical in solution.

**Hardy-Weinberg law:** A mathematical law in genetics which states that the relative frequencies of genes in a population tend to be constant through successive sexually reproduced generations.

**Heredity, multiple factor theory:** That two or more genes can affect one character and that the gene effects can add up without dominance.

**Heredity, transforming principle:** A chemical extract (presumably DNA) from a bacterium (*Pneumococcus*) which is capable of carrying hereditary information.

**Homology theory:** Correspondence between structures of different organisms is due to their inheritance from the same ancestrial line. Such structures may be somewhat dissimilar in spite of their common ancestry.

**Homoplasy and analogy:** Anatomical features may resemble each other in two organisms without such features being inherited *via* a common ancestry.

**Hybrid vigor theory:** Heterosis. Uniting of different hereditary lines of a species may produce offspring whose characteristics are stronger and larger than either parental type. Hybrid corn and animal breeding represent examples or uses of the theory.

**Hypothesis, defined:** A statement of an explanation that a scientist considers possible. It may be only an informed guess which is usually testable by experimental observation.

**Independent assortment principle:** A genetic theory that there is no interference between two characters; each segregates independently of the other.

**Information theory:** A branch of science (cybernetics) which attempts to define the amount of information required to control living processes.

**Innate behavior theory:** Standard responses that are inherited as a part of an animal's evolutionary heritage.

**Irreciprocity of nerve conduction, law:** Nerve impulses in the central nervous system can travel along the nerve axon in only one direction due to unidirectional response of its end plate (synapse).

**Kinetic energy principle:** The energy of motion as opposed to stored (potential) energy.

**Kreb's cycle:** The citric acid cycle. The step by step description of chemical reactions in the mitochondria of cells which are necessary for energy production and food utilization.

**Law, scientific:** A theory or explanation which proves adequate over a long period and is consistent with the most recent scientific data.

**Lamarck, evolution theory:** Great changes in the environment produces a real need for change in a species of animals. This need interacts with the species to produce new traits. First published by the French biologist in his book *Zoological Philosophy* in 1809.

**Learning theory, conditioned response:** Learned responses which involve the substitution of one stimulus for another. That is, assume stimulus A produces response B. If stimulus C can be made to produce response B, then one stimulus has substituted for another and a conditioned response has been formed.

**Malthus population theory:** Reproductive power of a population is much greater than its food supply. Thus, the food supply will become limiting at some point and serve as a check on the increase in population. First stated by the Englishman, Thomas Malthus in 1798.

**Mueller's Law:** The law of specific nerve energies. Generally, that regardless of whether a nerve is stimulated chemically, mechanically, or electrically, the result is always the same; namely transmission of the same impulse.

**Natural selection:** The theory that natural conditions tend to eliminate certain variations in a species and renders other variations distinctly advantageous over a long period of time.

**Negative selection:** elimination of undesirable types among animals to improve the breeding stock.

**Neurohumoral theory:** That nerve impulses as electrical phenomena cease at the end of the nerve fiber. A chemical compound is then produced which excites the next neuron along the pathway.

**Oparin's theory:** A theory published in 1936 which is sometimes referred to as the heterotroph hypothesis. It postulates that the earliest forms of life developed from nonlife through the evolution of very simple organisms over billions of years under special environmental conditions.

**One gene — one enzyme theory:** First postulated by Beadle and Tatum in 1945. It states that a single gene is responsible for the synthesis of a single specific enzyme in living systems.

**Osmotic pressure law:** A solvent moves from a solution of lower solute concentration to a solution having a higher solute concentration when these solutions are separated by a semipermeable membrane.

**Pangenesis theory:** First expounded by the Greek philosopher, Democritus over 2000 years ago. The theory postulated "pangens" which could be transmitted from parent to offspring as a mechanism for the inheritance of acquired characteristics. Thus, the enlarged muscles of a blacksmith were thought to be transmissable to the blacksmith's son by "pangens".

**Parthenocarpy:** The development of seedless fruit by plants.

**Periodicity of population theory:** A cyclic phenomenon in nature whereby the relative proportion of one kind of organism varies in a cyclic pattern which depends on abundance of food and its natural enemies in the wild. Thus a seven-year cycle from maximum to minimum is said to exist for the snowshoe rabbit in its natural habitat.

**Polyclimax hypothesis:** A belief that several "climax communities" may exist in an area. That is, one community of organisms may be limited by climate, another by soil conditions, and others by the topography of the region, etc.

**Principle of recapitulation:** "ontogeny repeats phylogeny". That is, the development of the individual (ontogeny) in successive stages is the same as the development of the species (phylogeny) during its evolutionary descent.

**Principle of Independent Assortment:** (*see* independent assortment).

**Principle of segregation:** The rule that the members of a gene pair separate into different gametes in the formation of germ cells.

**Principles of probability:** **(1)** The results of one trial of a chance event do not affect the results of later trials of the same event. **(2)** The chance that two independent events will occur together is the product of their chances of occurring separately. **(3)** The chance that one or the other of two independent events will occur is the sum of their chances of occurring separately.

**Redi's hypothesis concerning spontaneous generation:** A 17th century discovery by this Italian that maggots did not arise in rotting meat by spontaneous generation but by contamination by flies. He demonstrated that sterilized meat would keep indefinitely without production of maggots.

**Resonance theory** (*sound*): The vibration caused by sound waves falling upon an ear drum (tympanic membrane) in the production of sound detection by animals. Also the vibration of hair cells of differing length in the inner ear (organ of Corti) which enables animals to detect sounds of different wavelength. Also called the Helmholtz or Harp theory.

**Rhodopsin theory of night vision:** The theory that night vision depends on the presence in the rods of a pigment known as rhodopsin or visual purple. This pigment is produced in the dark to account for dark adaptation or the ability of a person to see dimly illuminated objects.

**Sliding filament hypothesis:** The theory that muscular contraction occurs when tiny filaments or fibrils slide over or past one another. It was first proposed by the English scientist, H. E. Huxley.

**Skin color theory:** The skin color of humans depends partly on blood pigments, partly on its light scattering characteristics and partly on definite pigment cells in the skin. Pigmentation that is not lost in ultraviolet-free light is primarily responsible for racial differences.

**Starling's law of the heart:** The initial length of the cardiac muscle fibers determines the strength of the contraction. That is, stretching the fibers by filling the heart with blood causes a contraction proportional to the amount of stretching.

**Swimmer's itch** (*cause*): An American blood

fluke, which normally infests water birds, occasionally enters human skin causing the itch. The scientific name for the fluke is *Schistosome dermatitis.*

**Syncope (*fainting*) theory:** The cerebral cells of the brain are subjected to low oxygen tension or high carbon dioxide tension causing loss of consciousness. The condition is often caused by emotional states which affect heart rate and/or constriction of blood vessels.

**Taste (*Gustatory*) theory:** The sensation of taste is caused by chemical stimulation of sense organs (taste buds) which are bottle-shaped groups of epithelial cells located on the tip, edges and posterior third of the tongue. Insoluble substances have no taste. Thus, if the tongue is dried by a towel and a dry lump of sugar is placed upon it, there is no sensation of taste until some sugar is dissolved.

**Taxonomy, defined:** The field of systematic classification or naming. The name is derived from the Greek word *taxis* which means arrangement.

**Timbre of sound theory:** A violin string and a piano string vibrating at the same intensity and pitch have different sounds. This is because a string not only vibrates as a whole back and forth but each string also vibrates in parts at the same time. This causes other sounds, called overtones to accompany the fundamental sound. The overtones differ for a violin string and causes it to have a different "timbre" from that of a piano string.

**Thirst theory:** A lowering of the water level of the blood, either because of loss of water or too limited intake, increases the osmotic pressure exerted by the blood. As a result water is drawn from the tissue fluids surrounding blood vessels. This stimulates the sense organs of thirst (osmorecepters) located in the carotid arteries. When the impulse is transmitted to the hypothalamus of the brain, the person experiences the sense of thirst.

**Transpiration pull theory:** To raise water to a height of 450 feet, about the height of the Douglas firs or California redwoods, requires a mechanical pressure of 210 pounds per square inch. This force is accomplished in nature by a complex combination of forces called capillary flow, root pressure, diffusion pressure and osmosis.

**Ulcer theory:** The question has often been asked, "Why does the digestive tract not digest itself"? The answer is that it does when the cells that line it die and lose their control over the living permeable membranes which surround them. Local self-digestion of the epithelium of the stomach or duodenum is a primary cause of ulcers.

**Vitalistic theory:** a view where unknown "vital forces" are called upon to explain biological activities. This theory is in contrast to the "mechanistic theory" which holds that living systems obey chemical and physical laws in a predictable manner which may ultimately be understood by the human mind.

**Von Frisch communication theory:** First stated by Karl von Frisch of the University of by Karl von Frisch of the University of Munich on the behavior of honey bees. It states that bees have a "language" which does not include words or sounds but which allows one bee to communicate with others through a series of movements called "dances".

**Weber's law:** A statement of the relationship between our ability to detect an increase or decrease in the intensity of a sensation, especially light detection, and the increase or decrease in the strength of a stimulus.

**Wave theory of light:** The theory that light is propagated as a wave motion often referred to as electromagnetic radiation.

**Zero point energy:** The energy possessed by atoms or molecules of a substance at absolute zero temperature.

# DICTIONARY OF BIOLOGICAL TERMS

**The purpose of this vocabulary is to supplement the word-list of the main dictionary for the specific use of those interested in biology, botany and zoology. Due to the limitations of space, duplications between this vocabulary and the main dictionary had to be avoided. For this reason, it is important for the reader to check entries both in this vocabulary and in the main dictionary, to insure a complete understanding of the term.**

## A

**abdomen,** *n.* in vertebrates, the belly region that contains the viscera; in anthropods, the posterior region of the body.

**abductor,** *n.* a muscle draws a part of the body away from the median line or normal position.

**aboral,** *adj.* refers to the side opposite the mouth.

**abscission,** *n.* in plants, the separation of a part — such as a leaf or fruit — by means of a special layer of cells which are weaker than the stalk, thus permitting it to break off.

**absorption,** *n.* process of taking up water and solutions by cells or tissues.

**accretion,** *n.* growth in size, especially by addition or accumulation.

**acetabulum,** *n.* the cup-shaped socket of the hip bone.

**acetylcholine,** *n.* a chemical substance, thought to be involved in conduction across synapses, liberated at or near nerve endings.

**acoelomate,** *adj.* without a coelom or body cavity.

**acromegaly,** *n.* a permanent enlargement of the bones of the head, hands, and feet, caused by abnormal activity of the pituitary gland.

**acrosome,** *n.* body at apex of spermatozoon; apical body; perforatorium.

**action current,** *n.* an electric current flowing between excited and unexcited regions.

**active center,** *n.* the part of an enzyme protein structure which combines with the substrate where activation and reaction take place.

**adaptation,** *n.* the means by which an organism fits itself to live and reproduce in a particular environment.

**adaptive,** *adj.* enzymes formed when their specific substrates are available.

**adductor,** *n.* a muscle that moves or pulls a part of the body toward the median axis.

**adipose,** *adj.* refers to fat.

**adrenal glands,** *n. pl.* the two small ductless glands on the upper part of the kidneys in mammals.

**adrenalin,** *n.* a hormone produced by the adrenal glands; a drug containing this hormone, used to raise blood pressure, stop bleeding, etc.

**adsorption,** *n.* process by which molecules of one substance attach themselves to the surface of another substance.

**aeciospore,** *n.* a specialized type of spore that occurs in the rust fungi.

**aerenchyma,** *n.* a tissue which, because of its large intercellular spaces, permits air to circulate among its cells.

**aerobic,** *adj.* refers to organisms that can live and grow only where free oxygen is present.

**afferent,** *adj.* leading toward or to a particular region.

**agglutination,** *n.* the formation of clumps or floccules.

**aggregate fruit,** *n.* fruit composed of a number of small, simple fruits, resulting from one flower, such as a blackberry.

**agronomy,** *n.* the art and science of crop production.

**albinism,** *n.* the condition in animals or persons lacking normal coloration; albinos have a white skin, whitish hair, and pink eyes.

**albumen,** *n.* the white of an egg; the nutritive protein substance in germinating plant and animal cells.

**algae,** *n. pl.* a group of plants, one-celled, colonial, or many-celled, containing chlorophyll and having no true root, stem, or leaf: algae are found in water of damp places.

**alimentary canal,** *n.* the passage in the body that food goes through: it extends from the mouth to the anus.

**alkaloid,** *n.* an organic alkaline substance containing nitrogen: some alkaloids taken from plants are used as drugs, as caffeine, morphine, cocaine, and quinine.

**allantois,** *n.* in reptiles, birds, and mammals, this is an extra-embryonic membrane resulting from the growth of the cloaca.

**allele,** *n.* one of a pair of genes affecting inheritance. In genetics, alleles are manipulated as a technique for achieving a desired result.

**alleles,** *n. pl.* alternative forms of a gene, occupying similar loci in homologous chromosomes.

**all-or-none,** — principle that response to a stimulus is either completely effected or is absent.

**alveolus,** *n.* in the lung, a small terminal cavity.

**ambiparous,** *adj.* containing the beginnings of both flowers and leaves.

**amino acid,** *n.* an organic acid, consisting of an amino group and a carboxyl group; an element of proteins.

**amino acids,** *n. pl.* the building blocks of proteins.

**amino acid sequence,** *n.* the linear order of the amino acids in a peptide or protein.

**amitosis,** *n.* simple cell division, without structural change in the nucleus.

**amnion,** *n.* the membrane surrounding the embryos of mammals, birds, and reptiles.

**amniota,** *n. pl.* the group of vertebrates which develop an amnion during their embryonic life.

**amoeba,** *n.* a protozoon in which the shape is subject to constant alterations due to formation and retraction of pseudopodia.

**amoeboid,** *adj.* like an amoeba, as in constantly changing shape.

**Amphibia,** *n. pl.* a class of vertebrates, including frogs, toads, newts, and salamanders, that usually begin life in the water as tadpoles with gills, and later develop lungs: they are cold-blooded and scaleless.

**amylolytic,** *adj.* capable of changing starch into simpler substances such as sugars.

**anabolism,** *n.* refers to the constructive phase of metabolism, during which complex substances are synthesized.

**anaerobic,** *adj.* indicates the absence of free oxygen.

**analogous organs,** *n. pl.* organs with different origins but having similar functions.

**anamniota,** *n. pl.* the group of vertebrates which do not develop an amnion during embryonic life.

**anaphase,** *n.* that phase in cell division when the chromosomes move toward the poles of the spindle.

**anaphylaxis,** *n.* condition of being hypersensitive to a serum or foreign protein, caused by first or sensitising dose.

**anastomosis,** *n.* a connection between parts of a system of vessels, veins, tubes, etc.

**anatomy,** *n.* the science of the structure of plants and animals; the structure of an organism or body.

**androecium,** *n.* the stamens and the parts belonging to them, collectively.

**anemia,** *n.* condition caused by deficiency of hemoglobin in the blood.

**angiosperm,** *n.* any plant that has the seeds enclosed in an ovary.

**angström,** *n.* one ten millionth part of a millimetre, symbol A.

**ankylosis,** *n.* a joining of bones or fibrous parts into a single part.

**annual,** *n.* a plant that lives only one year or season.

**annual ring,** *n.* the ring of wood resulting from one year's growth in a root or stem, as viewed in a cross section.

**annulus,** *n.* any ringlike part or mark, as around the stalk of some kinds of mushrooms.

**antenna,** *n.* a movable sense organ located on the heads of various anthropods.

**antennule,** *n.* a small antenna or feeler, specifically the first pair of antennae in crustacea.

**anterior,** *adj.* refers to the front or head end of an animal.

**anther,** *n.* the part of a stamen that contains the pollen.

**anthocyanin,** *n.* a coloring material in the cell sap of plants which appears red when acid and blue when alkaline or neutral.

**antiobiotic,** *n.* a substance produced by a living organism which will kill, or inhibit the growth, of a parasitic organism.

**antibody,** *n.* a substance produced by an organism to counteract the effect of a foreign substance, usually a protein.

**antigen,** *n.* a substance which stimulates the production of antibodies

when introduced into the body of an organism.
**antipodal cells,** *n. pl.* a group of cells, usually three in number, in the female gametophyte of angiosperms, at the opposite end from the egg.
**antitoxin,** *n.* an antibody, formed to act against a specific toxin.
**antrum,** *n.* a cavity; either of a pair of sinuses in the upper jaw.
**anus,** *n.* the posterior terminal opening of the alimentary tract.
**aorta,** *n.* the main artery of the body, carrying blood from the left ventricle of the heart to all parts except the lungs.
**apical,** *adj.* at the apex or tip, as in a plant.
**aponeurosis,** *n.* a fibrous sheet of fascia or tissue attaching a muscle.
**apogamy,** *n.* the process of reproduction without the production or union of gametes.
**apomixis,** *n.* the formation of an embryo from an unfertilized egglike cell.
**apospory,** *n.* reproduction in plants without the process of spore-production, as in ferns.
**appendage,** *n.* any subordinate or external organ or part, as a leg or tail.
**apterous,** *adj.* having no wings; wingless.
**aquatic,** *adj.* growing or living in or upon water.
**aqueous,** *adj.* watery.
**arboreal,** *adj.* of or like a tree; living in trees or adapted for living in trees.
**archegonium,** *n.* the flask-shaped female reproductive organ in mosses, ferns, etc.
**artery,** *n.* vessel which carries blood away from the heart.
**arthropod,** *n.* any member of a large group of invertebrate animals with jointed legs and a segmented body, as the crustaceans, arachnids, insects, and myriapods.
**ascocarp,** *n.* the fruits in which asci are produced in certain fungi.
**ascomycete,** *n.* any of a class of spore-reproducing fungi, including the mildews, yeasts, etc.
**ascorbic acid,** *n.* pure vitamin C.
**ascus,** *n.* a saclike structure in which the spores of those fungi known as ascomycetes are produced.
**asexual,** *adj.* refers to reproduction without the union of male and female germ cells.
**assimilation,** *n.* the conversion of digested products into protoplasm by an organism.
**asymmetry,** *n.* lack of symmetry; in animals, the condition in which their opposite sides are not alike.
**asymmetrical,** *adj.* structures or organs which cannot be divided into similar halves by any planes.
**atavism,** *n.* resemblance to a remote ancestor in some characteristic which nearer ancestors do not have; reversion to a primitive type.
**atlas,** *n.* the first vertebra upon which the skull rests; that is, the first cervical vertebra.
**atrium,** *n.* an auricle of the heart.
**atrophy,** *n.* a wasting away or failure to grow of an organ, etc., because of insufficient nutrition.
**auditory,** *adj.* of hearing or the sense of hearing.
**auricle,** *n.* one of the heart's chambers which receives blood.
**autecology,** *n.* the biological relations between a single species and its environment.
**autogamy,** *n.* self-fertilization.
**autonomic,** *adj.* autonomous; that is, independent or self-governing.
**autoradiographs,** *n.* when a photographic emulsion is placed in contact with radioactive material (e.g., thin sections of a cell), the radiation exposes the film, revealing details of the location and geometry of the radioactive components.
**autosome,** *n.* any chromosome with the exception of a sex chromosome.
**autosomes,** *n. pl.* refers to chromosomes other than sex chromosomes.
**autotropic,** *adj.* refers to the capacity of organisms to manufacture their own food.
**auxin,** *n.* substances which regulate growth, particularly those which cause increase in the size of plant cells.
**axil,** *n.* the upper angle between a leaf, twig, etc., and the stem from which it grows.
**axilla,** *n.* the armpit.
**axon,** *n.* process of a neuron conducting impulses away from the cell body.

## B

**bacillus,** *n.* a rod-like bacterium.
**backbone,** *n.* the column of bones (vertebrae) along the center of the back; spine.
**back-cross,** *v.t.* to mate a cross or hybrid to a member of one of the parental stocks.
**back-mutation,** *n.* reversion of a mutant gene to its original state.
**bacteriology,** *n.* the science dealing with bacteria.
**bacteriophage,** *n.* a destroyer of bacteria; a bacteriolytic agent; phage.
**basidium,** *n.* a structure shaped like a club, bears four spores externally.
**B-complex,** *n.* a group of accessory food factors comprising thiamine or vitamin $B_1$, riboflavin ($B_2$), pantothenic acid ($B_3$), niacin or P-P factor, pyridoxin ($B_6$), biotin (H), inositol, choline, para-amino benzoic acid, and folic acid (M), and $B_{12}$ anti-pernicious-anaemia factor.
**benthos,** *n.* the flora and fauna found at the bottom of the sea.
**bicuspid,** *adj.* having two cusps or points.
**biennial,** *n.* a plant that lasts two years, usually producing flowers and seed the second year.
**bilateral symmetry,** *n.* refers to the arrangement of body parts in which right and left halves are mirror images of each other.
**bile,** *n.* the bitter, greenish fluid secreted by the liver and found in the gall bladder: it helps in digestion.
**bile duct,** *n.* the tube which transports bile from the gall bladder to the small intestine.
**binary fission,** *n.* a process by which an organism divides into two approximately equal parts; hence, a form of asexual reproduction.
**biochemistry,** *n.* the chemistry of living organisms.
**biogenesis,** *n.* the theory that living organisms come only from other living organisms, and not from non-living matter.
**biology,** *n.* the science that deals with the origin, history, physical characteristics, habits, etc., of plants and animals: it includes botany, zoology, and their subdivisions.
**biosphere,** *n.* the part of the globe containing living organisms.
**biramous,** *adj.* having two branches.
**blade,** *n.* the flat, expanded part of a leaf.
**blastula,** *n.* an early cellular stage of development, during which the cells usually are arranged in the form of a hollow ball.
**blind spot,** — region of retina devoid of rods and cones and where optic nerve enters; optic disc.
**bract,** *n.* a modified leaf, usually small and scalelike, growing at the base of a flower or on its stalk.
**branchial,** *adj.* refers to the upper part of the forelimb of a vertebrate.
**brain,** *n.* the large anterior end of the central nervous system.
**bronchus,** *n.* either of the two main branches of the trachea, or windpipe.
**bryophyte,** *n.* any moss or liverwort.
**buccal,** *adj.* of the cheek or cheeks; of the mouth.
**bud,** *n.* a small swelling on a plant, from which a shoot, cluster of leaves, or flower develops.
**buffer,** *n.* salt solution which minimises changes in pH when an acid or alkali is added.
**bulb,** *n.* an underground bud that sends down roots and has a very short stem covered with leafy scales, as in a lily, onion, etc.
**bulliform cells,** *n. pl.* in grasses and similar plants, special epidermal cells which respond to changes in the air's humidity and cause leaves to fold or roll during periods of rapid transpiration.
**bursa,** *n.* a sac or cavity, especially between joints.
**buttress roots,** *n. pl.* aerial roots that serve as braces at the base of a stem.

## C

**Caenozoid,** *a.* age of mammals, geological era between Mesozoic and Psychozoic.
**callus,** *n.* a growth forming over a cut or wounded area on a plant stem.
**calorie,** *n.* a term used in nutrition and metabolism, this means the amount of heat which would be required to raise the temperature of 1 gram of water 1 degree Centrigrade.
**calyx,** *n.* the outer whorl, or sepals, at a flower's base.
**cambium,** *n.* located between xylem and phloem, this is a layer of meristematic cells.
**cancer,** *n.* the name given to a group of diseases that are characterized by uncontrolled cellular growth.
**capillaries,** *n. pl.* small, thin-walled

blood vessels connecting arteries and veins. Exchanges between the blood and the cells of the body take place through the walls of the capillaries.

**capillarity,** *n.* the property or exertion of capillary attraction or repulsion.

**capsule,** *n.* a case or pod containing seeds or spores; it usually bursts when ripe.

**carbohydrate,** *n.* an organic compound composed of carbon, hydrogen, and oxygen; same proportion of hydrogen and oxygen as in water ($H_2O$).

**carbon dioxide,** *n.* carbonic acid gas, a heavy, colourless gas present in the atmosphere.

**cardiac,** *adj.* of or near the heart.

**carnivorous,** *adj.* flesh-eating.

**carotene,** *n.* a reddish-yellow compound found in carrots and some other vegetables, and changed into vitamin A in the body.

**carpel,** *n.* a simple pistil, regarded as a modified leaf; any of the carpels that unite to form a compound pistil.

**catabolism,** *n.* the breaking down of larger molecules into smaller ones; hence, destructive metabolism.

**catalase,** — an enzyme occurring in plant and animal tissues, which decomposes hydrogen peroxide into water and oxygen.

**catalysis,** *n.* the causing or speeding up of a chemical reaction by the addition of a substance which itself undergoes no permanent chemical change thereby.

**catalyst,** *n.* a substance that can increase the rate of a chemical reaction without being consumed (e.g., enzymes catalyze biological reactions).

**caudal,** *adj.* of or like a tail; at or near the tail.

**cell,** *n.* a small unit of protoplasm, usually with a nucleus and an enclosing membrane: all plants and animals are made up of one or more cells.

**cell-free extract,** *n.* a fluid containing most of the soluble molecules of a cell, made by breaking open cells and getting rid of remaining whole cells.

**cell plate,** *n.* in cell division, the layer of cytoplasm which is formed between the two new nuclei, across the spindle fibers.

**cell sap,** *n.* the water that fills the vacuoles in the protoplasm.

**cellulose,** *n.* a complex carbohydrate which is the chief component of the wall of the plant cell.

**centromere,** *n.* the part of the chromosome located at the point lying on the equator of the spindle at metaphase and dividing at anaphase.

**centrum,** *n.* the body of a vertebra; the central body.

**cephalic,** *adj.* of the head, or skull, or cranium; in, on, near, or toward the head.

**cephalothorax,** *n.* in some anthropods, the fused head and thorax.

**cerebellum,** *n.* a part of the brain immediately in front of the medulla which regulates complex muscular movements.

**cerebrum,** *n.* the anterior part of the brain, large and lobed which functions in learning, memory, and conscious sensations.

**cervical,** *adj.* of the neck or cervix.

**chaeta,** *n.* a seta, or bristle, as of certain worms.

**chasmogamy,** *n.* the opposite of cleistogany, this is the process by which certain flowers open at the time of pollination.

**chemoreceptor,** *n.* a terminal organ receiving chemical stimuli.

**chemosynthesis,** *n.* a process of food manufacturing carried on by certain bacteria; in this process, the bacteria use energy released by the oxidation of inorganic compounds.

**chemotaxis,** *n.* the response which a free-moving organism makes to the presence of chemical substances.

**chitin,** *n.* a horny substance forming the hard outer covering of insects, crustaceans, etc.

**chlorenchyma,** *n.* any chlorophyll-containing tissue.

**chlorophyll,** *n.* the green coloring matter of plants; in the presence of sunlight it converts carbon dioxide and water into carbohydrates.

**chondriosomes,** *n. pl.* rod-shaped or granular bodies found in the cytoplasm; also called mitochondria.

**chordate,** *a.* having a notochord.

**chorion,** *n.* a membrane outside the embryos of reptiles, birds, and mammals; contributes to the formation of the placenta in mammals.

**chromatids,** *n. pl.* the two daughter strands of a duplicated chromosome which are still joined by a single centromere.

**chromatin,** *n.* a granular substance in the nucleus of animal and plant cells that readily takes a deep stain; chromatin contains the genes.

**chromoplast,** *n.* a cytoplasmic structure which contains yellow or red pigment.

**chromosomes,** *n. pl.* composed of chromatin and located in the nucleus, these bodies contain the genes.

**cilia,** *n. pl.* small hair-like bits of protoplasm which move in unison to move cells or particles over its surface.

**cirri,** *n. pl.* small, slender appendages or projections somewhat like tentacles.

**cistron,** *n.* the portion of a chromosome within which a number of mutational entities or loci is integrated for one function.

**cladophyll,** *n.* resembling a leaf in form and function, this is nevertheless a portion of a stem.

**clavicle,** *n.* a small bone connecting the breastbone with the shoulder blade; collarbone.

**cleavage,** *n.* the division of the fertilized egg into multicellular blastula.

**cleistogamy,** *n.* that condition which exists in some plants whereby their flowers never open and in which they are self-pollinated.

**clitellum,** *n.* in the earthworm, a thick glandular region of the body wall which secrets the cocoon.

**cloaca,** *n.* the chamber into which the kidney ducts, the genital ducts, and the intestine all empty.

**clone,** *n,* a group of cells all descended from a single common ancestor.

**clonus,** *n.* a series of muscle spasms.

**coagulation,** *n.* curdling or clotting; the changing from a liquid to a viscous or solid state by chemical reaction.

**coccyx,** *n.* the terminal part of the vertebral column beyond the sacrum.

**cochlea,** *n.* anterior part of labyrinth of the ear, spirally coiled like a snail's shell.

**cocoon,** *n.* the silky case which the larvae of certain insects spin about themselves to shelter them during the pupa stage.

**codon,** *n.* a sequence of three adjacent nucleotides that code for an amino acid (or chain termination?).

**coelom,** *n.* a body cavity lined with mesodermal membrane.

**coenocyte,** *n.* a structure which may contain varying numbers of nuclei in a continuous cytoplasm.

**cohesion,** *n.* a body cavity lined with mesodermal membrane.

**collenchyma,** *n.* a strengthening tissue composed of elongated cells.

**colloid,** *n.* a gelatinous substance made up of insoluble, nondiffusible particles larger than molecules but so small that they remain suspended in a fluid medium.

**colon,** *n.* that part of the large intestine extending from the caecum to the rectum.

**colony,** *n.* a group of contiguous cells, usually derived from a single ancestor, growing on a solid surface.

**combustion,** *n.* the act or process of burning; rapid oxidation accompanied by heat and, usually light; slow oxidation accompanied by relatively little heat and no light.

**commensalism,** *n.* the living arrangement of two species in which one is benefited but in which the other is neither benefited nor harmed.

**companion cell,** *n.* found in the phloem of some plants, this is a long cell associated with a sieve cell, both resulting from the division of a mother cell.

**compound,** *n.* a substance composed of two or more different atoms in chemical union.

**conidium,** *n.* a small asexual spore of certain fungi.

**conjugation,** *n.* refers in plants to isogamous reproduction in which a gamete moves to another gamete through a special tube; in protozoans, to the temporary union of two organisms for the purpose of exchanging micronuclei.

**conjunctiva,** *n.* the mucous membrane lining the inner surface of the eyelids and covering the front part of the eyeball.

**convergence,** *n.* superficial likeness between unrelated organisms which are adapted to live in similar environments.

**coprozoic,** *a.* inhabiting faeces, as some protozoa.

**copulation,** *n.* the joining of a male and female animal sexually, in which sperm cells are introduced into the body of the female by the male.

**corium,** *n.* the derma or inner, sensitive layer of the skin.

**corm,** *n.* the bulblike, scaly under-

ground stem of certain plants, as the crocus.
**cornea,** *n.* the transparent outer coat of the eyeball, covering the iris and pupil.
**corolla,** *n.* the petals, or inner leaves, of a flower.
**cortex,** *n.* the bark or rind of a plant.
**cotyledon,** *n.* a seed leaf; earliest leaf or one of the earliest leaves growing out of a seed.
**cranium,** *n.* the skull; esp., that part containing the brain.
**crenation,** *n.* notched or wrinkled appearance, as of erythrocytes exposed to hypertonic solutions.
**Cretaceous,** *a.* the last period of the Mesozoic era.
**crossing over,** *n.* the process of exchange of genetic material between homologous chromosomes.
**cross-pollination,** *n.* the process of transferring pollen from the anther of one flower to the stigma of another.
**crown,** *n.* a structure composed of a series of appendages of the corolla of a flower, as the tubular part of a jonquil.
**cryptogams,** *n. pl.* plants that bear no flowers or seeds but propagate by means of special cells called spores, as algae, mosses, ferns, etc.
**cutaneous,** *adj.* of or on the skin; affecting the skin.
**cuticle,** *n.* in animals, an external noncellular membrane; in plants, a layer formed on the outer walls of epidermal cells and composed of fatty and waxy materials.
**cutinize,** *v.i. & v.t.* to undergo a process in which the outermost cells of a plant become much thickened and covered with a waxy substance (cutin), making them waterproof.
**cybernetics,** *n.* science of communication and control, as by nervous system and brain.
**cyclosis,** *n.* circulation, as of protoplasm within a cell.
**cyst,** *n.* the inactive stage of some organisms when they are enclosed in a wall or sac.
**cystocarp,** *n.* a structure in the red seaweeds formed after fertilization and later producing spores.
**cytase,** *n.* an enzyme which causes cellulose to be changed into sugars.
**cytology,** *n.* the branch of biology dealing with the structure, function, pathology, and life history of cells.
**cytoplasm,** *n.* the protoplasm of the cell without the nucleus.

## D

**dactyl,** *n.* a finger or toe.
**dalton,** *n.* a unit of weight equal to the weight of a single hydrogen atom.
**decay,** *n.* refers to the breakdown of organic materials which involves microorganisms.
**degenerate codons,** *n. pl.* two or more codons that code for the same amino acid.
**dehiscence,** *n.* the cracking or splitting of a structure when it has reached maturitv.
**dehydration synthesis,** *n.* the chemical combination of molecules that involves the elimination of water.
**deletions,** *n.* loss of a section of the genetic material from a chromosome. The size of the deleted material can vary from a single nucleotide to sections containing a number of genes.
**dendrites,** *n. pl.* those parts of a neuron which carry impulses to the cell body.
**dentary,** *n.* the upper bone in the lower jaw.
**dermis,** *n.* the layer of skin just below the epidermis; derma.
**Devonian,** *a.* palaezoic geological period preceding Carboniferous.
**dew,** *n.* the atmospheric moisture that condenses and appears during the night in little drops on cool surfaces.
**dextrose,** *n.* grape sugar or glucose, the end product of starch digestion, $C_6H_{12}O_6$.
**diagnosis,** *n.* discrimination of a physiological or pathological condition by its distinctive signs.
**dialysis,** *n.* separation of dissolved crystalloids and colloids through semipermeable membrane, crystalloids passing more readily.
**diapause,** *n.* a spontaneous state of dormancy during development, as of insects.
**diaphragm,** *n.* in higher vertebrates, the muscular partition which separates the abdominal and thoracic cavities.
**diastase,** *n.* an enzyme that changes starches into maltose and later into dextrose; amylase.
**diatom,** *n.* a unicellular form of alga with walls impregnated with silica.
**dicentric,** *a.* having two centromeres.
**dichogamy,** *n.* the process by which stamens and carpels mature at different times.
**differentiation,** *n.* refers to the specialization of cells and tissues during development for the purpose of performing particular functions.
**diffusion,** *n.* the movement of particles, both molecules and ions, as a result of their kinetic energy.
**digestion,** *n.* the conversion of insoluble food substances into soluble substances which may be absorbed.
**digit,** *n.* a finger or toe.
**dimorphism,** *n.* the state of having an organ in two forms.
**dioecious,** *adj.* having the male reproductive organs in one individual and the female organs in another; in the gametophyte, having eggs and sperms produced on different plants.
**diploid,** *adj.* refers to the number of chromosomes in the zygote (exactly twice the number of chromosomes in a sperm or egg).
**disaccharides,** *n. plu.* sugars composed of two simple sugars, e.g., lactose, maltose, sucrose.
**disease,** *n.* a particular destructive process in an organism; specific illness or departure from health.
**diuretic,** *a.* increasing the secretion of urine. *n.* any agent causing diuresis.
**Diurnal,** *a.* opening during the day onlv; active in the day-time.
**DNA** (Dioxvribonucleic Acid), *n.* a polymer of deoxyribonucleotides. The genetic material of all cells.
**DNA Polymerase,** *n.* the enzyme that catalyzes the formation of DNA from deoxyribonucleoside triphosphates, using DNA as a template.
**dominant,** *adj.* in genetics, designating or of that one of any pair of opposite Mendelian characters which, when factors for both are present in the germ plasm, dominates over the other and appears in the organism; opposite of the recessive.
**dormancy,** *n.* state of sleep or inactivity, as in buds during winter or the embryos of seeds when stored.
**dorsal,** *adj.* refers to the upper side.
**duct,** *n.* a tube or channel through which secretions or excretions pass through the body; as a bile duct.
**duodenum,** *n.* the first section of the small intestine, below the stomach.

## E

**ecology,** *n.* the branch of biology that deals with the relations between living organisms and their environment.
**ectoderm,** *n.* the outer layer of cells of an embryo in its early stage.
**ectoplasm,** *n.* the outer layer of the cytoplasm of a cell.
**ectosarc,** *n.* in a protozoon, the outer layer of protoplasm.
**effector,** *n.* a gland or muscle.
**efferent,** *adj.* carrying away from; an efferent nerve carries impulses away from a nerve center. *n.* an efferent nerve, duct, or blood vessel.
**electron microscope,** *n.* a microscope which uses electrons instead of light, thus making possible high magnification of selected objects.
**electrophoresis,** *n.* transport of substances, as of colloidal particles, resulting from differences in electrical potential.
**element,** *n.* a substance composed of only one kind of atom.
**embryo,** *n.* an animal in the earliest stages of its development in the uterus.
**embryology,** *n.* the branch of biology dealing with the formation and development of embryos.
**enamel,** *n.* the hard, white, glossy coating of the crowns of teeth.
**endemic,** *adj.* prevalent in or restricted to a certain locality or group; hence, confined to a limited area.
**endocrine,** *adj.* refers to any gland that produces one or more internal secretions that are carried by the blood or lymph to some part whose functions they regulate.
**endoderm,** *n.* the inner layer of cells of the embryo, from which is formed the lining of the digestive tract and other internal organs.
**endoparasite,** *n.* a parasite that lives within the body of its host.
**endophyte,** *n.* a plant that lives inside the tissues of another plant.
**endoplasm,** *n.* the inner part of the cytoplasm of a cell.
**endosperm,** *n.* the nourishment for the embryo, which surrounds the embryo in the seed of a plant.
**endothelium,** *n.* a membrane that lines the heart, blood vessels, and lymphatic vessels.

**enteron,** *n.* the digestive tract.
**entomology,** *n.* that part of zoology which deals with insects.
**enucleate,** *v.* to deprive of a nucleus, as in microdissection of cells. *a.* Lacking a nucleus.
**enzyme,** *n.* an organic substance that is produced in plant and animal cells and causes changes in other substances by catalytic action.
**enzymology,** *n.* the study of enzymes and their functions.
**epicranium,** *n.* in grasshoppers and related forms, the largest sclerite of the head.
**epidermis,** *n.* the outermost layer of the skin in vertebrates; the outermost layer of cells covering seed plants and ferns; the outer layer of the shells of many mollusks.
**epigenesis,** *n.* the theory that all the differentiated parts of the organism arise from an undifferentiated germ cell.
**epigynous,** *adj.* refers to those flowers with perianth and stamen attached above the ovary.
**epiphyte,** *n.* a nonparasitic plant that grows another plant but gets its nourishment from the air, as certain orchids, mosses and lichens; air plant.
**episome,** *n.* a genetic element that can exist either free or as part of the normal cellular chromosome. Examples of episomes are the sex ($F^+$) factor and lysogenic phage DNA.
**epithelium,** *n.* cellular, membrane-like tissue that covers surfaces, forms glands, and lines most cavities of the body.
**erythtopoiesis,** *n.* the production of red blood corpuscles.
**esophagus,** *n.* the passage for food from the pharynx to the stomach; gullet.
**estivation,** *n.* in certain animals, a dormant condition adopted during summer.
**estrogen,** *n.* any of several estrus-producing compounds.
**estrus,** *n.* the sexual excitement, or heat, of female mammals, or the period of such excitement.
**eugenics,** *n.* the science that deals with the improvement of races and breeds, especially the human race, through the control of hereditary factors.
**eumycophyta,** *n.* genuine fungi, as distinguished from bacteria or slime molds.
**euthenics,** *n. pl.* the science that deals with the improvement of races and breeds, especially the human race, through the control of environmental factors.
**eviscerate,** *v.t.* to remove the entralls from; disembowel.
**evolution,** *n.* the development of a species, organism, or organ from its original to its present state; the theory that all species of plants and animals developed from earlier forms by hereditary transmission of slight variations in successive generations.
**excitation,** *n.* act of producing or increasing stimulation; immediate response or protoplasm to a stimulus.
**excretion,** *n.* the process of discharging or eliminating waste products from the body.
**exoskeleton,** *n.* a hard supporting structure developed on the outside of the body; for example, the shell of a crustacean.
**exothermic,** *a.* releasing heat-energy.
**expiration,** *n.* the act of emitting air from lungs; emission of carbon dioxide by plants and animals.
**extensor,** *n.* a muscle that extends or straightens some part of the body, especially in the arm or leg.
**exteroceptor,** *n.* a receptor which receives stimuli from outside the body; a contact receptor, or a distance receptor.
**eye-spot,** *n.* a colored spot, sensitive to light, in certain unicellular algae; usually red in color.

## F

**facet,** *n.* a division of the compound eye.
**fascia,** *n.* a thin layer of connective tissue.
**fat,** *n.* a class of glyceryl esters of fatty acids, insoluble in water.
**fauna,** *n.* the animals of a specified region or time.
**feces,** *n. pl.* waste matter expelled from the bowels; excrement.
**femur,** *n.* the thighbone.
**fermentation,** *n.* the breakdown of complex molecules in organic compounds, caused by the influence of a ferment.
**fertilization,** *n.* the process of making the female reproductive cell fruitful by introducing the male germ cell; the egg nucleus and sperm nucleus together form a zygote.
**fetus,** *n.* the unborn young of an animal while still in the uterus or egg, especially in its later stages.
**fiber,** *n.* a slender, threadlike structure that combines with others to form animal or vegetable tissue; a threadlike root.
**fibrin,** *n.* an elastic, threadlike, insoluble protein formed in the clotting of blood.
**filament,** *n.* in botany, the stalk of a stamen bearing the anther.
**fission,** *n.* a form of asexual reproduction in which the parent organism divides into two or more parts, each becoming an independent individual.
**flagellum,** *n.* a whiplike part serving as an organ of locomotion in bacteria and certain cells.
**flame-cells,** *n.* the terminal cells of branches of excretory system in many worms, with cavity continuous with lumen of duct, and containing a cilium or bunch of cilia, the motions of which give a flickering appearance similar to that of a flame.
**flexor,** *n.* any muscle that bends a limb or other part of the body.
**floriculture,** *n.* the cultivation of flowers or ornamental plants.
**florigen,** *n.* that plant hormone which controls the process of flowering.
**foramen,** *n.* a small opening; esp., a small, natural opening in a bone.
**fossil,** *n.* any hardened remains or traces of plant or animal life of some previous geological age, preserved in the earth's crust.
**free-martin,** *n.* a sterile female twin-born with a male.
**fruit-body,** *n.* the spore-bearing structure, as a sporangiocarp, basidiocarp, condiocarp.
**function,** *n.* the normal or characteristic action of anything; esp., any of the specialized actions of an organ or part of an animal or plant.
**fungus,** *n.* any of a group of plants, including mildews, molds, mushrooms, rusts, etc., that have no leaves, flowers, or green color and reproduce by means of spores.

## G

**galactose,** *n.* a sugar found as a constituent of various carbohydrates in plants.
**gamete,** *n.* a reproductive cell that can unite with another similar one to form the cell that develops into a new individual.
**gametogenesis,** *n.* gamete formation; gametogeny.
**gametophyte,** *n.* the gamete-bearing phase of certain plants.
**ganglion,** *n.* a mass of nerve cells serving as a center from which nerve impulses are transmitted.
**gastric,** *adj.* of, in, or near the stomach.
**gastrocnemius,** *n.* large muscle of calf of leg.
**gastrovascular cavity,** *n.* a body cavity used for both circulation and digestion.
**gastrula,** *n.* an embryo in the early stage of development, consisting of a sac with two layers, the ectoderm and the endoderm.
**gel,** *n.* a jellylike substance formed by a colloidal solution in its solid phase.
**gemma,** *n.* a bud; a budlike outgrowth which becomes detached and develops into a new organism.
**genecology,** *n.* ecology in relation to genetics.
**geneology,** *n.* the study of development of individual and race; embryology and palaeontology combined.
**generative cell,** *n.* that cell in the pollen grain of an angiosperm which has the power of generation or production.
**gene,** *n.* any of the elements in the chromosome by which hereditary characters are transmitted and determined.
**genetic map,** *n.* the arrangement of mutable sites on a chromosome as deduced from genetic recombination experiments.
**genetics,** *n. pl.* the branch of biology that deals with heredity and variation in similar or related animals and plants.
**genital,** *adj.* of reproduction or the sexual organs.
**genotype,** *n.* the genetic makeup of an organism.
**genus,** *n.* a classification of plants or animals with common distinguishing characteristics: a genus is the main subdivision of a family and includes one or more species.

**geotropism,** *n.* movement or growth of a living organism in response to the force of gravity, either toward the center of the earth or away from the center of the earth.

**geratology,** *n.* study of the factors of decadence and old age of populations; cf. gerontology.

**germination,** *n.* the process by which a seed begins to sprout and grow.

**gestation,** *n.* the period during which mammals carry their young in the uterus during pregnancy.

**gibberellins,** *n. plu.* metabolic products of Gibberella fujikuroi, and in flowering plants, which stimulate growth in coleoptiles and shoots, gibberellic acid being a growth factor complementary to auxins.

**gill clefts,** *n. pl.* present in all chordates at some stage in their development, these are paired openings in the sides of the pharynx.

**gizzard,** *n.* the second stomach of a bird: it has thick muscular walls and a tough lining for grinding food.

**gland,** *n.* any organ that separates certain elements from the blood and secretes them in the form of a substance for the body to use, as adrenalin, or throw off, as urine.

**glottis,** *n.* the opening between the vocal cords in the larynx.

**glucose,** *n.* a crystalline sugar, $C_6H_{12}O_6$, occurring naturally in fruits and honey; also called dextrose.

**glycogen,** *n.* an insoluble, starchlike substance produced in animal tissues, especially in the liver and muscles, and changed into a simple sugar as the body needs it.

**glycolipids,** *n. plu.* compound lipids in tissues, particularly in brain, hydrolyzed to galactose and sphingosine; cerebrosides.

**glycoproteins,** *n. plu.* compounds of protein with a carbohydrate, including mucins and mucoids; mucoproteins.

**goblet cell,** *n.* an epithelial cell which secretes mucus.

**gonad,** *n.* a gland that produces reproductive cells; ovary or testis.

**grain,** *n.* a small, hard seed or seedlike fruit, especially that of any cereal plant, as wheat, rice, corn, etc.; the arrangement of fibers, layers, or particles of wood, leather, stone, etc.

**grana,** *n. plu.* minute particles consisting of a pile of thin double platelets, probably containing chlorophyll, in chloroplasts.

**granulocytes,** *n. plu.* granular white blood corpuscles or polymorphs; myeloid cells formed in bone marrow.

**grey crescent,** *n.* crescentic marginal zone of cytoplasm of a fertilized egg before cleavage, inductor of gastrula, as in amphibians.

**growth,** *n.* a growing or developing; increase in size, weight, etc.

**guard cells,** *n. pl.* those cells around the opening of a stoma which are able to make the opening either smaller or larger.

**gullet,** *n.* the tube leading from the mouth to the stomach; esophagus.

**gum,** *n.* a sticky substance given off by certain trees and plants, which dries into a brittle mass soluble in water; any similar plant secretion, as resin.

**gustatory,** *a.* pert. sense of taste; appl. cells, hairs, pores, calyculus, nerves, stimuli, etc.

**guttation,** *n.* the loss of water by plants, usually through special structures under pressure.

**gymnosperm,** *n.* any of a large class of plants producing seeds not enclosed in a seed case or ovary, as certain evergreens.

**gynoecium,** *n.* the female organ or organs of a flower; pistil or pistils.

## H

**habit,** *n.* characteristic growth of an animal or plant; a reflex response that is acquired or conditioned.

**habitat,** *n.* native environment; the place where a person or thing is ordinarily found.

**Haeckel's law,** *n.* biogenetic law, recapitulation theory.

**halophyte,** *n.* a plant which thrives in an environment that contains salt.

**haploid state,** *n.* state of having only one set of chromosomes, as in spores or gametes.

**haustorium,** *n.* that part of a parasitic plant which enables it to absorb food from the host plant.

**hemoglobin,** *n.* the red coloring matter of the red blood corpuscles: it carries oxygen from the lungs to the tissues, and carbon dioxide from the tissues to the lungs.

**hemophilia,** *n.* a hereditary condition in which the blood fails to clot quickly enough, causing prolonged, uncontrollable bleeding from even the smallest cut.

**herb,** *n.* any seed plant whose stem withers away annually, as distinguished from a tree or shrub whose woody stem lives from year to year.

**herbivorous,** *adj.* feeding chiefly on grass or other plants: opposed to carnivorous.

**hereditary disease,** *n.* a pathological condition whose cause is a gene mutation and which can therefore be transferred from one generation to the next.

**heredity,** *n.* the transmission from parent to offspring of certain characteristics; tendency of offspring to resemble parents or ancestors.

**hermaphrodite,** *n.* a person or animal with the sexual organs of both the male and the female; a plant having stamens and pistils in the same flower.

**heterogamy,** *n.* sexual reproduction that involves gametes of different structure, size, and behavior.

**heterocercal,** *adj.* refers to the type of tail that is asymmetrical both internally and externally, as in the shark and sturgeon.

**heterokaryosis,** *n.* presence of genetically dissimilar nuclei within individual cells.

**heterosis,** *n.* the increased vigor or gain in size or function which a hybrid has in relation to its parents.

**heterospory,** *n.* the production of two kinds of spores.

**heterothallic,** *adj.* possessing two distinct types of gametophyte, which function as sexual opposites.

**heterotrophic,** *adj.* refers to organisms which must rely on some outside source for their food, since they cannot manufacture their own.

**high-energy bond,** *n.* a bond that yields a large (at least 5 kcal/mole) decrease in free energy upon hydrolysis.

**hilum,** *n.* a scar on a seed, marking the place where it was attached to the seed vessel.

**histamine,** *n.* an amine discharged by the tissues in allergic reactions: it dilates blood vessels, stimulates gastric secretion, etc.

**histology,** *n.* the branch of biology concerned with the microscopic study of the structure of tissues.

**holophytic,** *a.* obtaining the whole of its food after the manner of a plant; phototrophic.

**holozoic,** *adj.* type of nutrition common to most animals, involving both ingestion and digestion of organic materials.

**homeostasis,** *n.* the balance of nature; maintenance of equilibrium between organism and environment; the constancy of the internal environment of the body, as in birds and mammals.

**homocercal,** *adj.* refers to those tails which are externally symmetrical but internally asymmetrical.

**homologous,** *adj.* corresponding in structure and deriving from common origin: as, the wing of a bat and the foreleg of a mouse.

**homologous chromosomes,** *n. pl.* chromosomes that pair during meiosis, have the same morphology, and contain genes governing the same characteristics.

**homology,** *n.* basic sameness of structures due to genetic relationship.

**homosporous,** *adj.* possessing spores of only one kind, with no apparent differentiation into male and female.

**homothallic,** *adj.* possessing one type of gametophyte which produces sexually-unlike gametes.

**homozygous,** *adj.* describes something produced by the union of gametes similar with respect to the characteristic in question.

**hormogonium,** *n.* the reproductive structure in some algae which consists of a short segment of a filament.

**hormone,** *n.* a chemical substance formed in some organ of the body, as the ovary, adrenal glands, etc., and carried to another organ or tissue, where it has a specific effect; a similar substance in plants.

**horticulture,** *n.* the art or science of growing flowers, fruit, and vegetables.

**humerus,** *n.* the bone of the upper arm or forelimb, extending from the shoulder to the elbow.

**hybrid,** *n.* the offspring of two animals or plants of different species, etc.

**hydrocarbon,** *n.* any compound containing only hydrogen and carbon: benzene and methane are hydrocarbons.
**hydrolysis,** *n.* a chemical reaction in which a compound reacts with the ions of water to produce a weak acid, a weak base, or both.
**hydrophyte,** *n.* any plant growing only in water or very wet earth.
**hymenium,** *n.* that layer in some fungi in which asci or basidia are carried.
**hyoid,** *adj.* designating or of a U-shaped bone at the base of the tongue.
**hypertonic,** *adj.* refers to a solution in which the osmotic concentration is greater than that of the cell contents.
**hypertrophy,** *n.* excessive growth due to increase in size of cells.
**hypha,** *n.* any of the threadlike parts making up the mycelium of a fungus.
**hypocotyl,** *n.* the part of the axis, or stem, below the cotyledons in the embryo of a plant.
**hypoderm,** *n.* the waterproof layer of tissues below the epidermis, as in certain kinds of roots.
**hypophysis,** *n.* the pituitary gland.
**hypopituitarism,** *n.* deficiency of pituitary gland, resulting in a type of infantilism; hypohypophysism.
**hypostome,** *n.* in coelenterates, the region around and just below the mouth.
**hypotonic,** *adj.* opposite of hypertonic; that is, a solution in which the osmotic concentration is less than that of the cell contents.

## I

**ichthyology,** *n.* the study of fishes.
**identical twins,** *n. pl.* a pair of twins of the same sex, developed from a single fertilized ovum.
**ileum,** *n.* the lowest part of the small intestine.
**ilium,** *n.* the uppermost of the three sections of the hipbone.
**imbibition,** *n.* the process by which a solid absorbs a liquid, usually into its molecular structure.
**immunity,** *n.* resistance to a specified disease or toxic substance.
**implant,** *n.* an organ or part transplanted to an abnormal position; a graft.
**implantation,** *n.* the embedding or firm fixing of the ovum in the wall of the uterus in placental mammals.
**inbreeding,** *n.* breeding through a succession of parents belonging to the same stock, or very nearly related.
**inclusions,** *n. pl.* particles of food, nonliving material, etc., in the protoplasm but not a part of it.
**incomplete metamorphosis,** *n.* insect metamorphosis in which young are hatched in general adult form and develop without quiescent stage.
**indehiscent,** *adj.* opposite of dehiscent; describes a structure which does not crack open or split.
**indicators,** *n.* dyes which dissociate to produce a different colour, indicating the range of hydrogen ion concentration of a solution.
**inducible enzymes,** *n. pl.* enzymes whose rate of production can be increased by the presence of inducers in the cell.
**induction,** *n.* act or process of causing to occur; process whereby a cell or tissue influences neighbouring cells or tissues.
**indusium,** *n.* the scale-like growth of a fern leaf that covers a cluster of sporangia.
**inflorescence,** *n.* a flowering; the arrangement of flowers on a stem or axis.
**infracostal,** *a.* Beneath the ribs.
**infundibulum,** *n.* any of several funnel-shaped or dilated parts or organs, such as a calyx of the kidney.
**ingestion,** *n.* the process of taking food into the body for digestion.
**inhibitor,** *n.* any agent which checks or prevents an action or process.
**inoculate,** *v.t.* to implant bacteria, etc., into soil suitable for their growth.
**instar,** *n.* insect at a particular stage between moults.
**instinct,** *n.* an inborn tendency to behave in a way characteristic of a species: natural, unaquired response to stimuli.
**insulin,** *n.* a secretion of the pancreas which helps the body use sugar and other carbohydrates.
**integument,** *n.* an outer covering, as of the body or of a plant.
**interbreed,** *v.* to cross different varieties of plants or animals.
**intermediary metabolism,** *n.* the chemical reactions in a cell that transform food molecules into molecules needed for the structure and growth of the cell.
**internode,** *n.* that portion of a stem between the places where two successive leaves are attached.
**intestines,** *n. pl.* the lower part of the alimentary canal, extending from the stomach to the anus and consisting of a convoluted upper part (the small intestine) and a lower part of greater diameter (the large intestine).
**invertebrate,** *n.* any animal without a backbone (vertebral column).
**in vitro** (*Latin*: in glass), pertaining to experiments done in a cell-free system. Currently, the term is sometimes modified to include the growth of cells from multicellular organisms under tissue-culture conditions.
**in vivo** (*Latin*: in life), pertaining to experiments done in a system such that the organism remains intact, either at the level of the cell (for bacteria) or at the level of the whole organism (for animals).
**ion,** *n.* an electrically charged atom or group of atoms, the electrical charge of which results when a neutral atom or group of atoms loses or gains one or more electrons.
**irritability,** *n.* in physiology, the property of living matter to react when stimulated.
**isogametes,** *n. pl.* gametes that are alike in structure and size.
**isotonic,** *adj.* refers to a solution in which the osmotic concentration is the same as that of the cell contents.
**isotope,** *n.* any of two or more forms of an element having the same or very closely related properties and the same atomic number but different atomic weights.

## J

**jejunum,** *n.* the middle part of the small intestine, between the duodenum and the ileum.
**jugular,** *adj.* refers to the neck or throat; *n.* either of two large veins in the neck carrying blood back from the head to the heart.

## K

**kidney,** *n.* either of a pair of glandular organs in vertebrates, which separate water and waste products from the blood and excrete them as urine through the bladder.

## L

**lachrymal,** *adj.* of, for, or producing tears.
**lacteal,** *adj.* of or like milk; containing chyle, the milky fluid that is a product of digestion.
**larva,** *n.* an insect in the earliest stage after hatching, before it is changed into a pupa; the early form of any animal that changes structurally when it becomes an adult, as the tadpole.
**larynx,** *n.* the structure of muscle and cartilage at the upper end of the human trachea, containing the vocal cords, and serving as the organ of voice.
**latex,** *n.* a milky liquid in certain plants and trees, as the rubber tree, milkweed, etc.: it is the basis of various products, notably rubber.
**layering,** *n.* the process of partly covering a living plant with earth so that it may take root.
**lenticel,** *n.* a pore in the bark of a root or stem which permits the exchange of gases between the internal tissues of the plant and the atmosphere.
**lethal gene,** *n.* a gene capable of causing death.
**leucocyte,** *n.* any of the small, colorless cells in the blood, lymph, and tissues, which destroy organisms that cause disease; white blood corpuscle.
**leucoplast,** *n.* a protoplasmic structure like a chloroplast in shape, size, and origin, but without chlorophyll and hence colorless.
**lichen,** *n.* any of a group of mosslike plants consisting of algae and fungi growing in close association in patches on rocks and tree trunks.
**ligament,** *n.* a band of tough tissue connecting bones or holding organs in place.
**lignin,** *n. a* chemical substance in the walls of the cells of woody tissues such as xylem.
**ligule,** *n.* a tonguelike appendage as of a grass leaf.
**linkage,** *n.* the tendency of genes that are located in the same chromosomes to remain together.
**lipase,** *n.* a fat-digesting enzyme.
**liverwort,** *n.* any of a group of green, red, purple, or yellow-brown plants resembling the mosses.

**lumbar,** *adj.* of or near the loins (small of the back).
**luminescence,** *n.* any giving off of light caused by the absorption of radiant or corpuscular energy and not by incandescence; any cold light.
**lycopsida,** *n.* that group of vascular plants which includes the club mosses.
**lymph,** *n.* a clear, yellowish, alkaline fluid found in the lymphatic vessels of the body; it resembles blood plasma but contains colorless corpuscles.
**lymphatic system,** *n.* in vertebrates, a system of vessels and nodes which lead from the tissue spaces to large veins entering the heart.
**lysis,** *n.* the bursting of a cell by the destruction of its cell membrane.
**lysogenic bacterium,** *n.* a bacterium that contains a prophage.

### M

**macromere,** *n.* in certain animals, the large, yolk-filled cells that are present during the cleavage stages.
**maggot,** *n.* a wormlike insect larva, as the legless larva of the housefly.
**malaria,** *n.* an infectious disease, generally recurrent, caused by protozoa transmitted by the bite of an infected anopheles mosquito: characterized by intermittent chills and fever.
**maltase,** *n.* an enzyme which converts maltose or malt sugar into glucose.
**mandible,** *n.* the jaw, especially the lower jaw; either part of a bird's beak; either of the pair of outermost, biting jaws of an insect or other anthropod.
**mantle,** *n.* the membrane fold of the body wall of a mollusk, etc., containing glands that secrete a shell-forming fluid.
**mastication,** *n.* the act of chewing or grinding food with the teeth.
**matrix,** *n.* in cartilage and bone, the noncellular substance found between the cells.
**maxilla,** *n.* in vertebrates, a jaw or jawbone, especially the upper one; in insects, crabs, etc., either of a pair of jaws just behind the mandibles.
**maxilliped,** *n.* in the crayfish and similar animals, one of the first three pairs of thoracic appendages.
**medulla,** *n.* the inner part of an organ; the widening continuation of the spinal cord forming the lowest part of the brain in vertebrates.
**megaspore,** *n.* sometimes called a macrospore, this is a large spore produced in amegasporangium.
**meiosis,** *n.* the nuclear changes in the maturation of germ cells, in the process of which the chromosome number is reduced from diploid to haploid.
**membrane,** *n.* a thin, soft, pliable layer of animal or plant tissue, that covers or lines an organ or part.
**meninges,** *n. pl.* the three membranes that envelop the brain and spinal cord.
**meningitis,** *n.* inflammation of the meninges, especially as the result of infection.
**meristem,** *n.* tissue in which the cells are actively dividing or capable of dividing, as in the tips of roots and stems.
**mesoderm,** *n.* the middle layer of cells of an embryo.
**mesonephros,** *n.* the vertebrate kidney.
**mesophyll,** *n.* in a leaf, the green parenchyma.
**mesophyte,** *n.* a plant which grows best in a moderately moist environment, neither very wet nor very dry.
**messenger RNA** (mRNA), RNA that serves as a template for protein synthesis.
**metabolic pathway,** *n.* a set of consecutive intracellular enzymatic reactions that converts one molecule to another.
**metabolism,** *n.* the continuous processes in living organisms and cells, comprising those by which food is built up into protoplasm and those by which protoplasm is broken down into simpler substances or waste matter, with the release of energy for all vital functions.
**metacarpals,** *n. pl.* the bones in the hand between the wrist and the fingers.
**metagenesis,** *n.* in the life cycle of some organisms, such as Obelis, the alternation of sexual and asexual reproduction.
**metamorphosis,** *n.* a change in form or function as a result of development; e.g., the physical transformation undergone by various animals after the embryonic state, as of the tadpole to the frog.
**metaphase,** *n.* that stage in the division of a nucleus at which point the chromosomes are in a plane in the middle of the spindle.
**metatarsals,** *n. pl.* bones in the foot between the ankle and the toes.
**Metazoa,** *n. pl.* the large zoological division made up of all animals whose bodies are composed of many cells.
**micron,** *n.* a unit of microscopic measurement, this means one millionth of a meter, or one thousandth of a millimeter.
**micropyle,** *n.* a small opening at the end of a seed or ovule where the internal parts are not completely covered, and through which the pollen grain or tube enters the ovule.
**microspore,** *n.* a small spore which develops into a male gametetophyte.
**migration,** *n.* the movement of a species of animals, birds, fishes, etc., from one region to another.
**mildew,** *n.* a fungus that attacks various plants or appears on damp cloth, paper, etc., as a furry, whitish coating.
**missense mutation,** *n.* a mutation that changes a codon coding for one amino acid with a codon corresponding to another amino acid.
**mitochondria,** *n.* small structures in the cytoplasm in which special chemical activities take place.
**mitosis,** *n.* the indirect method of cell division, in which the nuclear chromatin is formed into a long thread which in turn breaks into chromosomes that are split lengthwise.
**mold,** *n.* a furry growth on the surface of organic matter, caused by fungi, especially in the presence of dampness or decay; any fungus producing such a growth.
**molecular weight,** *n.* the sum of the atomic weights of the constituent atoms in a molecule.
**molecule,** *n.* the smallest particle of an element or compound that can exist in the free state and still retain the characteristics of the substance.
**molt,** *v.i.* to shed the hair, outer skin, horns, etc., prior to replacement by a new growth, as birds, reptiles, etc.
**monocotyledon,** *n.* any plant with only one cotyledon.
**morphology,** *n.* the branch of biology dealing with the form and structure of animals and plants.
**mosaic,** *n.* with reference to leaves, a mosaic is the pattern formed by the leaves as they adjust to the stimulus of light.
**mucous membrane,** *n.* a mucus-secreting membrane lining body cavities and canals, as the mouth, etc., connecting with the external air.
**mucus,** *n.* the slimy secretion that moistens and protects the mucous membranes.
**mushroom,** *n.* any of various rapid-growing, fleshy fungi having a stalk with an umbrellalike top.
**mutagens,** *n. pl.* physical or chemical agents, such as radiation, heat, or alkylating or deaminating agents, which raise the frequency of mutation greatly above the spontaneous background level.
**mutant,** *n.* an animal or plant with inheritable characteristics that differ from those of the parents.
**mutation,** *n.* a sudden variation in some inheritable characteristic of an animal or plant; an individual resulting from such variation.
**mycelium,** *n.* the thallus, or vegetative part, of a fungus, made of threadlike tubes.
**myelin,** *n.* the substance which surrounds the axis cylinder of a medullated nerve.
**myofibril,** *n.* small fibrils found in the protoplasm of the muscle cell or fiber.
**myxomycophyta,** *n. pl.* also known as slime molds, these are organisms which at one period in their life cycle resemble ameboid animals and at another period resemble fungi.

### N

**nares,** *n. pl.* in vertebrates, the external and internal openings of the air passages; the nasal passages, especially the nostrils.
**nephridium,** *n.* the waste-discharging organ of some invertebrates, such as worms, mollusks, etc.
**nerve,** *n.* any of the cordlike fibers carrying impulses between the body organs and the central nervous system.
**nerve fiber,** *n.* the filamentous part of a nerve cell or neuron.
**nerve impulse,** *n.* physicochemical excitation that moves along a nerve fiber.
**neural,** *adj.* of a nerve, nerves, or the nervous system.
**neural canal,** *n.* the canal formed by

the neural arches; the canal through the vertebrae.

**neurocoele,** *n.* the cavity or cavities utilized by the central nervous system, including the ventricles of the brain and the central canal of the spinal cord.

**neuron,** *n.* the structural and functional unit of the nervous system, consisting of the nerve cell body and all its processes.

**node,** *n.* that part of a stem from which a leaf starts to grow.

**nonsense mutation,** *n.* a mutation that converts a codon which specifies some amino acid into one which does not specify any amino acid (a nonsense codon). Nonsense codons may have the function of terminating the polypeptide chain.

**notochord,** *n.* in chordates, the rod-shaped structure which forms a skeletal axis. It is replaced by the vertebrae in vertebrates, after the embryonic stages.

**nucellus,** *n.* the middle part of an ovule in which the megaspore develops.

**nucleolus,** *n.* a conspicuous, spherical body found in the nucleus of most cells.

**nucleus,** *n.* the central, spherical mass of protoplasm in most plant and animal cells, necessary to growth, reproduction, etc.

**nutrient,** *n.* anything nutritious; that is, any substance which a plant can use as food.

**nutrition,** *n.* the series of processes by which an organism takes in and assimilates food for promoting growth and repairing tissue.

## O

**occiput,** *n.* the back part of the skull or head.

**ocular,** *adj.* of, for, or like the eye; by eyesight.

**olfactory,** *adj.* refers to the sense of smell.

**omnivorous,** *adj.* eating any sort of food, especially both animal and vegetable food.

**ontogeny,** *n.* the life cycle of a single organism.

**oocyte,** *n.* an egg before it has reached maturation.

**oogonium,** *n.* a one-celled female sex organ in some thallophytes which produces one or more eggs.

**operon,** *n.* a genetic unit consisting of adjacent genes that function coordinately under the joint control of an operator and a repressor.

**opthalmic,** *adj.* of or connected with the eyes.

**optic nerves,** *n. pl.* nerves running from the brain to the eyes.

**orbit,** *n.* the eye socket.

**organ,** *n.* in animals and plants, a part composed of several tissues, adapted to perform a specific function or functions.

**organelle,** *n.* a specialized part of a cell, such as a cilium, that performs functions similar to those of the organs of many-celled animals.

**orthogenesis,** *n.* evolution in a particular direction, but without external guidance.

**osculum,** *n.* the external opening of the sponge's central cavity.

**osmosis,** *n.* the tendency of fluids to pass through a separating semipermeable membrane, as the wall of a living cell, so as to equalize concentrations on both sides of the membrane; the diffusion of fluids through a porous partition.

**osteology,** *n.* the study of the bones of vertebrates.

**ovary,** *n.* the female reproductive gland, in which ova are formed; in plants, the organ which produces ovules.

**oviduct,** *n.* a duct or tube through which the ova pass from the ovary to the uterus or to the outside.

**oviparous,** *adj.* producing eggs which hatch after leaving the body.

**ovipositor,** *n.* a tubular organ of insects for depositing eggs, usually situated at the end of the abdomen.

**ovulation,** *n.* the process of producing ova and discharging ova from the ovary.

**ovule,** *n.* the part of a plant which develops into a seed.

**oxidases,** *n. pl.* those enzymes which permit cells to utilize free oxygen in producing oxidation.

**oxidation,** *n.* the combination of a substance with oxygen; also, the increase of positive charges, or loss of negative charges, on an atom.

## P

**palpus,** *n.* a jointed organ or feeler for touching or tasting, attached to the mouth of insects, lobsters, etc.

**pancreas,** *n.* a large, elongated gland that secretes an alkaline digestive juice into the small intestine: the pancreas of a calf, etc., when used as food is called sweetbread.

**pappus,** *n.* a downy tuft of bristles on certain fruits, as on the seeds of the dandelion.

**parasite,** *n.* a plant or animal that lives on or within another from which it derives sustenance.

**parathyroid,** *adj.* designating or of any of four small glands located on or embedded in the thyroid gland: their secretions increase the calcium content of the blood.

**parenchyma,** *n.* the functional tissue of an organ, as distinguished from its connective tissue, etc.

**parthenocarpy,** *n.* the process of forming fruit, especially seedless fruit, without fertilization.

**parthenogenesis,** *n.* reproduction by the development of an unfertilized ovum, seed, or spore, as in certain insects, algae, etc.

**pasteurization,** *n.* a method of destroying or checking bacteria in milk and some other liquids by heating the liquid to 142°-145° for thirty minutes.

**pathogenic,** *adj.* causing disease.

**pathology,** *n.* the study of the nature of disease, especially with the structural and functional changes caused by disease; in botany, deals with the diseases of organisms.

**pedicel,** *n.* a small, star-like structure; peduncle.

**pellicle,** *n.* a thin, protective layer on a cell's surface.

**penicillin,** *n.* a powerful antibiotic obtained from the green mold penicillium.

**penis,** *n.* the male organ of sexual intercourse; in mammals, it is also through which urine is ejected.

**pepsin,** *n.* an enzyme secreted in the stomach, aiding in the digestion of proteins.

**perennial,** *n.* a plant with a life cycle of more than two years.

**pericardium,** *n.* the thin, membranous sac around the heart.

**pericarp,** *n.* the wall of a fruit flowering plant, which develops from the wall of the ovary.

**pericycle,** *n.* a layer of parenchyma inside the endodermis of a root or stem.

**periderm,** *n.* in plants, the cork layer covering a root or stem.

**peristalsis,** *n.* the wave-like muscular contractions and dilations of the walls of the alimentary canal and certain other hollow organs, that move the contents onward.

**peristome,** *n.* in a moss capsule, the fringe of teeth around the opening.

**peritoneum,** *n.* the serous membrane lining the abdominal cavity and covering the visceral organs.

**peroneus,** *n.* one of the muscles on the dorsal part of the lower leg.

**petal,** *n.* any of the component parts, or leaves, of a corolla.

**petiole,** *n.* the stalk to which a leaf is attached.

**phagocyte,** *n.* any leucocyte that ingests and destroys other cells, bacteria, etc., in the blood and tissues.

**phagocytosis,** *n.* the process by which a cell ingests solid particles.

**phanerogams,** *n. pl.* all plants with flowers in which pollination can be readily seen.

**pharynx,** *n.* the cavity leading from the mouth and nasal passages to the larynx and esophagus.

**phenotype,** *n.* the visible, measurable characteristics of an organism.

**phloem,** *n.* the cell tissue serving as a path for the distribution of food material in a plant.

**photoperiodism,** *n.* that response which a plant makes to the relative length of periods of light and darkness, day and night.

**photosynthesis,** *n.* the formation of carbohydrates in plants from water and carbon dioxide, by the action of sunlight on the chlorophyll.

**phototaxis,** *n.* the sensitivity to light of a free-moving organism.

**phototropism,** *n.* tropism toward or away from light.

**phycocyanin,** *n.* in the blue-green algae, this is the bluish pigment connected with chlorophyll.

**phycomycetes,** *n.* a group of fungi closely resembling the algae.

**phylogeny,** *n.* the evolutionary development of any plant or animal species.

**phylum,** *n.* any of the broad, basic divisions of the plant or animal kingdom.

**physiology,** *n.* the branch of biology

dealing with the functions and vital processes of living organisms or their parts and organs.

**physique,** *n.* the structure, strength, form, or appearance of the body.

**pigment,** *n.* any coloring matter in the cells and tissues of plants or animals.

**pineal gland,** *n.* a small cone-shaped structure in the brain of all vertebrates having a cranium: it has no known function.

**pistil,** *n.* the seed-bearing organ of a flower, consisting of the ovary, stigma, and style.

**pith,** *n.* the soft, spongy tissue in the center of certain plant stems.

**placenta,** *n.* a vascular organ within the uterus, connected to the fetus by the umbilical cord: it is the structure through which the fetus is nourished.

**plankton,** *n.* the microscopic animal and plant life found floating in bodies of water, used as food by fish.

**plaques,** *n. pl.* round clear areas in a confluent cell sheet which result from the killing or lysis of contiguous cells by several cycles of virus growth.

**plasma,** *n.* the fluid part of blood, without the corpuscles; also the fluid part of lymph or intramuscular liquid.

**plasmolysis,** *n.* the contraction of a cell's protoplasm as a result of its loss of water by osmosis.

**plastid,** *n.* a unit of protoplasm; cell; a granule of specialized protoplasm occurring in some cytoplasm.

**plexus,** *n. a* network of blood vessels, nerves, etc.

**polarity,** *n.* in plants, the condition in which two extremities of a cell or organ are not alike.

**pollen,** *n.* the yellow, powderlike male sex cells on the stamens of a flower.

**pollination,** *n.* the process of placing pollen on the upper tip of the pistil, or from the microsporangium to the gymnosperm's pollen chamber.

**polyp,** *n.* a small, flowerlike water animal having a mouth fringed with tentacles at the top of a tubelike body, as the sea anemone, hydra, etc.; a projecting growth of mucous membrane, as in the bladder, etc.

**polypeptide,** *n.* a polymer of amino acids linked together by peptide bonds.

**posterior,** *n.* the tail end; buttocks.

**predaceous,** *adj.* preying on other animals.

**prickle,** *n.* a small, sharply pointed growth; spine; thorn.

**primordial,** *adj.* existing at or from the beginning; primitive; fundamental; original.

**proboscis,** *n.* an elephant's trunk, or a long flexible snout, as of a tapir; a tubular sucking organ, as of some insects, worms, and mollusks.

**proglottid,** *n.* one of the sections of a tapeworm, capable of living for a time when broken away from the rest of the organism.

**pronephros,** *n.* in vertebrates, the first kidney formed in the embryo.

**prophase,** *n.* that early stage in the division of a nucleus before the spindle is formed.

**protandry,** *n.* that condition in a flower in which the stamen matures before the carpel.

**protease,** *n.* an enzyme which breaks down proteins, resulting in the formation of amino acids.

**protein,** *n.* any of a class of complex nitrogenous substances occurring in all animal and vegetable matter and essential to the diet of animals.

**protoplasm,** *n.* a semi-fluid, viscous, translucent colloid, the essential living matter of all animal and plant cells.

**protoplast,** *n.* the total living part of a cell including cytoplasm, nucleus, plastids, etc.

**protostele,** *n.* a stele that consists of a central core of xylem around which there is a hollow cylinder of phloem.

**protozoan,** *n.* any of a number of one-celled animals, usually microscopic, belonging to the lowest division of the animal kingdom.

**pseudopodium,** *n.* a temporary projection of the protoplasm of certain protozoa, serving as a means of moving about or for taking in food.

**pteridophyte,** *n.* a fern or related plant having no seeds.

**pteropsida,** *n.* a major group of vascular plants, including the ferns.

**pubis,** *n.* either of two bones that, with a third bone between them, make up the front arch of the pelvis.

**pulvinus,** *n.* in some plants, the enlarged joint by means of which the petiole is attached to the stem.

**pupa,** *n.* an insect in the stage between the larval and adult forms.

**pyloric valve,** *n.* a valve at the posterior end of the stomach, opening from the stomach into the duodenum, the first part of the small intestine.

**pyrenoid,** *n.* in some plants, especially algae, a colorless body in the chromatosphore around which grains of starch accumulate.

## Q

**quadruped,** *n.* an animal, especially a mammal, with four feet.

## R

**radical,** *n.* a group of two or more atoms that acts as a single atom and goes through a reaction unchanged, or is replaced by a single atom.

**radicle,** *n.* the lower part of the axis of an embryo seedling.

**radioactive isotope,** *n.* an isotope with an unstable nucleus that stabilizes itself by emitting ionizing radiation.

**radius,** *n.* the shorter and thicker of the two bones of the forearm on the same side as the thumb.

**recapitulation,** *n.* the repetition in the life of a plant or animal of those successive stages which marked the evolution of the race.

**receptacle,** *n.* that part of the stalk from which the flower grows.

**receptor,** *n.* a sense organ; nerve ending specialized for the reception of stimuli.

**recessive,** *adj.* refers to that one of any pair of opposite Mendelian characters which, when factors for both are present, remains latent.

**recombination,** *n.* the appearance in the offspring of traits that were not found together in either of the parents.

**rectum,** *n.* the lowest segment of the large intestine, ending at the anus.

**reflex,** *n.* an involuntary action or automatic response to a stimulus which may or may not cause a conscious sensation.

**regeneration,** *n.* the growing of a new part to replace one that is injured or lost.

**regulatory genes,** *n. pl.* genes whose primary function is to control the rate of synthesis of the products of other genes.

**relative humidity,** *n.* a measurement of the amount of moisture in the atmosphere, in comparison with the maximum amount that it could hold at a given temperature; hence, the degree of saturation.

**rennin,** *n.* a milk-curdling enzyme in the gastric juice of the calf, etc.

**repressible enzymes,** *n. pl.* enzymes whose rates of production are decreased when the intracellular concentration of certain metabolites increases.

**resin,** *n.* a solid or semi-solid organic substance exuded from various plants and trees, as the pines.

**respiration,** *n.* the processes by which a living organism or cell takes in oxygen, distributes and utilizes it in oxidation, and gives off products, especially carbon dioxide.

**retina,** *n.* the innermost coat of the back part of the eyeball, on which the image is formed by the lens.

**rhizoid,** *n.* any of the rootlike filaments in a moss, fern, etc., that attach it to the substratum.

**rhizome,** *n.* a horizontal, rootlike stem under or along the ground, which usually sends out roots from its lower surface and leafy shoots from its upper surface.

**riboflavin,** *n.* a factor of the vitamin B complex, found in milk, eggs, liver, fruits, leafy vegetables, etc.

**ribosomes,** *n. pl.* small cellular particles (~200 A in diameter) made up of rRNA and protein. Ribosomes are the site of protein synthesis.

**RNA (Ribonucleic Acid),** *n.* a polymer of ribonucleotides.

**rotator,** *n.* the type of muscle which produces the rotary motion of one part of an organism on another.

**ruminant,** *n.* any of a group of four-footed, hoofed, even-toed, and cud-chewing mammals, such as cattle, sheep, goats, deer, etc.

**runner,** *n.* a long, trailing stem, as of a strawberry, that puts out roots along the ground, thus producing new plants.

**rust,** *n.* a plant disease caused by parasitic fungi (rust fungi), spotting stems and leaves.

## S

**sagittal,** *adj.* pertaining to the suture between the parietal bones of the skull; hence, pertaining to the median plane of the body.

**saprophyte,** *n.* any organism that lives on decaying organic matter, as some fungi and bacteria.

**sapwood,** *n.* the soft wood just beneath the bark of a tree; alburnum.

**sarcoplasm,** *n.* fluid protoplasmic substance of muscle fibers.

**scapula,** *n.* the shoulder blade.

**scion,** *n.* a shoot or bud of a plant, used for grafting.

**sclereid,** *n.* a short, irregularly shaped cell with a lignified wall, such as make up the shells of nuts.

**sclerenchyma,** *n.* plant tissue of thick-walled cells, as in nut shells.

**sclerite,** *n.* a hard plate, piece, or spicule; a portion of such a form as the locust.

**scolex,** *n.* the head of a tapeworm, either in the larva or the adult stage.

**sebum,** *n.* the semi-liquid, greasy secretion of the sebaceous glands.

**secretion,** *n.* the separation and elaboration of a substance from the blood or sap.

**self-pollination,** *n.* the process by which a flower is fertilized by its own pollen.

**semen,** *n.* the fluid secreted by the male reproductive organs, containing the spermatozoa.

**sense organ,** *n.* any organ or structure, as an eye or taste bud, that receives specific stimuli and transmits them as sensations to the brain.

**sepal,** *n.* any of the leaf divisions of the calyx.

**septum,** *n.* a part that separates; partition: as, the nostrils are divided by a septum.

**serology,** *n.* the science dealing with the properties or use of serums.

**serum,** *n.* any watery animal fluid, especially blood serum, the yellowish fluid which separates from the clot when blood coagulates.

**sessile,** *adj.* attached directly by its base.

**shoot,** *n.* a new growth, sprout; the stem and leaves of a young plant.

**shrub,** *n.* a bushy, woody plant with several permanent stems instead of a single trunk; bush.

**sinus,** *n.* a cavity, hollow, etc.; specifically, any of the air cavities in the skull opening into the nasal cavities; a channel for venous blood; or a narrow channel leading from a pus-filled cavity.

**siphonostele,** *n.* a tubelike stele around a core of parenchyma.

**slime molds,** *n. pl.* simple plants which resemble fungi at one point in their life cycle, and at other times resemble one-celled animals.

**smuts,** *n. pl.* fungi whose spores are black and powdery.

**solvent,** *n.* a substance, usually liquid, used for dissolving another substance.

**soma,** *n.* the body in its entirety, except for the reproductive cells.

**spawn,** *n.* the mycelium of a fleshy fungus, used to propagate that fungus.

**species,** *n.* a single, distinct kind of plant or animal, having certain distinguishing characteristics: a biological classification.

**spectrum,** *n.* a series of colored bands diffracted and arranged in order of their respective wave lengths, from red to violet, by the passage of white light through a prism.

**sperm,** *n.* the male generative fluid, or any of the germ cells in this fluid.

**spermatic,** *adj.* of or having to do with sperm or sperm cells; generative.

**spermatophyte,** *n.* any seed-bearing plant.

**sphincter,** *n.* a ring-shaped muscle that can open or close a natural opening in the body by expanding or contracting.

**spicule,** *n.* a small, hard, sharp-pointed, needlelike piece or process, especially of bony or calcareous material, as in the skeleton of the sponge.

**spindle,** *n.* in plants, refers to a figure made up of cytoplasmic fibers, on which the chromosomes arrange themselves in the division of a nucleus.

**spine,** *n.* any of the short, sharp, woody projections on certain plants, as the cactus.

**spiracle,** *n.* an air hole; specifically, in zoology, an opening through which air or waste is taken in and expelled in respiration, as the blowhole of a whale or one of the tracheal openings of anthropods.

**spleen,** *n.* a large, vascular, ductless organ in the upper left part of the abdomen: it modifies the blood structure.

**sporangium,** *n.* a spore case, as of a fern.

**spore,** *n.* a small reproductive body, usually a single cell, produced by mosses, ferns, etc., and capable of giving rise to a new individual.

**sporophyll,** *n.* a leaf producing spores.

**sporophyte,** *n.* the asexual-spore-bearing phase of certain plants.

**stamen,** *n.* a pollen-bearing organ in a flower, made up of a slender stalk and a pollen sac.

**stele,** *n.* the central cylinder of a root or stem, containing the vascular tissue.

**sternum,** *n.* a thin, flat structure of bone and cartilage to which most of the ribs are attached in the front of the chest in most vertebrates; breastbone.

**stigma,** *n.* the upper tip of the pistil of a flower, receiving the pollen.

**stipule,** *n.* either of two small leaflike parts at the base of some leafstalks, or leaf petioles.

**stoma,** *n.* a breathing pore in plants.

**stomodeum,** *n.* the oral or anterior part of the alimentary canal, lined with extoderm; in embryos, the opening to the digestive tract.

**stratified,** *adj.* arranged in layers or strata.

**streptomycin,** *n.* an antibiotic drug similar to penicillin, obtained from certain molds and used in treating various diseases.

**striated,** *adj.* grooved, streaked with fine lines.

**submucosa,** *n.* the second main layer of the digestive tract's walls.

**sucrase,** *n.* an enzyme which converts ordinary cane sugar (sucrose) into simpler sugars.

**suppressor gene,** *n.* a gene that can reverse the phenotypic effect of a variety of mutations in other genes.

**suspension,** *n.* the condition of a solid whose particles are dispersed through a fluid but not dissolved in it.

**svedberg,** *n.* the unit of sedimentation (S). S is proportional to the rate of sedimentation of a molecule in a given centrifugal field and is thus related to the molecular weight and shape of the molecule.

**symbiosis,** *n.* the living together of two dissimilar organisms in a close association that is advantageous to both.

**synapse,** *n.* the point of contact between adjacent neurons, where nerve impulses are transmitted from one to the other.

**syncytium,** *n.* a mass of protoplasm in which there are many nuclei but which is not divided into separate cells.

**synthesis,** *n.* the formation of a complex chemical compound by the combining of two or more simpler compounds, elements, etc.

## T

**tarsals,** *n. pl.* bones of the ankle.

**taxonomy,** *n.* the science of classification; classification of animals and plants into phyla, species, etc.

**teleology,** *n.* the fact of having a purpose or end, as attributed to natural processes; a belief that natural phenomena are determined not only by mechanical causes but by an over-all design in nature.

**telophase,** *n.* the stage in cell division at which point the chromosomes have reached the poles of the spindle and new nuclei are formed.

**template,** *n.* the macromolecular mold for the synthesis of another macromolecule.

**tendon,** *n.* any of the inelastic cords of tough, fibrous connective tissue by which muscles are attached to bones or other parts; a sinew.

**tendril,** *n.* a threadlike part of a climbing plant, serving to support it by clinging to an object.

**tentacle,** *n.* a long, slender, flexible growth about the head or mouth of some invertebrates, used to feel, grasp, propel, etc.

**testicle,** *n.* the male sex gland; secretes spermatozoa.

**thallophyte,** *n.* any of a primary division of plants including the bacteria, algae, fungi, and lichens.

**thallus,** *n.* the plant body of a thallophyte, showing no clear distinction of roots, stem, or leaves.

**thermotaxis,** *n.* reaction to heat or cold, either positive or negative.

**thigmotactic,** *adj.* sensitive to touch.

**thorax,** *n.* in man and the higher vertebrates, the part of the body between the neck and the abdomen; chest; in insects, the middle one of the three segments of the body.

**thorn,** *n.* a very short, hard, leafless branch or stem with a sharp point.

**thrombin,** *n.* the enzyme of the blood that causes clotting by forming fibrin.

**thymus,** *n.* a ductless, glandlike body, of undetermined function, situated near the throat: the thymus of an animal, when used as food, is called sweetbread.

**thyroid,** *n.* the thyroid gland; a large ductless gland near the trachea, secreting the hormone thyroxine, which regulates growth; malfunctioning of this gland can cause goiter.

**thyroxine,** *n.* a colorless, crystalline compound, the active hormone of the thyroid gland, used in treating goiter, etc.

**tibia,** *n.* the inner and thicker of the two bones of the leg below the knee; shinbone.

**tissue,** *n.* the substance of an organic body or organ, consisting of cells and intercellular material.

**tissue culture,** *n.* the growth and maintenance of cells from higher organisms in vitro, outside the tissue of which they are normally a part.

**toxin,** *n.* any of various poisonous compounds produced by some microorganisms and causing certain diseases; any of various similar poisons secreted by plants and animals.

**trachea,** *n.* in the respiratory tract of vertebrates, that part which conveys air from the larynx to the bronchi; windpipe. In the respiratory system of insects and other invertebrates, any of the small tubules for conveying air.

**transcription,** *n.* a process involving base pairing, whereby the genetic information contained in DNA is used to order a complementary sequence of bases in an RNA chain.

**transduction,** *n.* the transfer of bacterial genes from one bacterium to another by a bacteriophage particle.

**transformation,** *n.* the genetic modification induced by the incorporation into a cell of DNA purified from cells or viruses.

**translation,** *n.* the process whereby the genetic information present in an mRNA molecule directs the order of the specific amino acids during protein synthesis.

**transpiration,** *n.* the process by which vapor and moisture pass through tissue and other permeable substances, especially the pores of the skin or the surface of plant leaves; the giving off of vapor and moisture.

**trichome,** *n.* in plants, a hair or scale growing out of the epidermis.

**tropism,** *n.* the tendency of a plant or animal to move or turn in response to an external stimulus, as light, either by attraction or repulsion.

**trypsin,** *n.* a digestive enzyme in the pancreatic juice: it changes proteins into peptones.

**tuber,** *n.* a short, thickened, fleshy part of an underground stem, as a potato.

**turgor,** *n.* a state of being distended; in cells, a condition of water pressure inside the cell.

## U

**ulna,** *n.* the larger of the two bones of the forearm, on the side opposite the thumb.

**ultracentrifuge,** *n.* a high-speed centrifuge that can attain speeds up to 60,000 rpm and centrifugal fields up to 500,000 times gravity and thus is capable of rapidly sedimenting macromolecules.

**umbilical cord,** *n.* a cordlike structure connecting a fetus with the placenta of the mother and serving to convey food to, and remove waste from the fetus.

**ungulate,** *adj.* having hoofs; of or belonging to the group of mammals having hoofs.

**urea,** *n.* a soluble, crystalline solid, found in the urine of mammals and produced synthetically: it is used in the manufacture of plastics, adhesives, etc.

**uredospore,** *n.* one of the types of spore found in rust fungi; have the capacity to spread the fungus rapidly.

**ureter,** *n.* a duct or tube that carries urine from a kidney to the bladder or cloaca.

**urethra,** *n.* the canal through which urine is discharged from the bladder in most mammals.

**urine,** *n.* in mammals, the yellowish fluid containing urea and other waste products, secreted from the blood by the kidneys, passed to the bladder, and periodically discharged through the urethra.

**uterus,** *n.* a hollow, muscular organ of female mammals in which the ovum is deposited and the embryo and fetus are developed and protected; womb.

## V

**vacuole,** *n.* a bubble-like cavity in the protoplasm of a cell, containing air, water, or partially digested fluid; a small cavity in the tissues of an organism.

**vagina,** *n.* in female mammals, the canal leading from the vulva to the uterus.

**valve,** *n.* one of the segments into which a seed capsule separates.

**variety,** *n.* a group having characteristics of its own within a species.

**vas deferens,** *n.* the convoluted duct that conveys sperm from the testicle to the ejaculatory duct of the penis.

**vaso-motor nerves,** *n. pl.* nerves that regulate the expansion and contraction of blood vessels.

**vein,** *n.* any of the bundles of vascular tissue forming the framework of a leaf blade.

**ventral,** *adj.* of, near, on, or toward the belly or lower side.

**ventricle,** *n.* either of the two lower chambers of the heart which receive blood from the auricles and pump it into the arteries.

**vermiform appendix,** *n.* a small, saclike appendage of the large intestine.

**villus,** *n.* any of numerous hairlike processes on certain mucous membranes of the body, as of the small intestine, serving to secrete mucus and absorb fats, etc.

**vine,** *n.* any plant with a long stem that grows along the ground or climbs a wall or other support by means of tendrils, etc.

**viruses,** *n. pl.* infectious disease-causing agents, smaller than bacteria, which always require intact host cells for replication and which contain either DNA or RNA as their genetic component.

**viscera,** *n. pl.* the internal organs of the body, such as the heart, lungs, liver, intestines, etc.

**vitalism,** *n.* the doctrine that the life in living organisms is caused and sustained by a basic force that is distinct from all physical and chemical forces.

**vitamin,** *n.* any of a number of complex organic substances found variously in foods and essential for the normal functioning of the body.

**viviparous,** *adj.* bearing living young instead of laying eggs: most mammals are viviparous.

**vomer,** *n.* a bone in the skull of most vertebrates, forming part of the nasal septum.

## W

**water table,** *n.* the level below which the ground is saturated with water.

**weed,** *n.* any undesired, uncultivated plant that grows in profusion so as to crowd out a desired crop, etc.

**wild-type gene,** *n.* the form of gene (allele) commonly found in nature.

**wilting,** *adj.* the process of becoming limp because of the loss of water from the cells.

## X

**xanthophyll,** *n.* the yellowish-brown pigment found with chlorophyll in some plants.

**xenia,** *n.* the effect in the endosperm of an angiosperm caused by pollination with pollen from a plant that has a different kind of endosperm.

**xerophyte,** *n.* a plant that thrives in a hot, dry climate.

**xylem,** *n.* the woody tissue of a plant, especially, in higher forms, the firm part that conducts moisture.

## Z

**zoogeography,** *n.* the science dealing with the geographical distribution of animals.

**zoology,** *n.* the branch of biology dealing with the classification of animals and the study of animal life.

**zoospore,** *n.* an asexual spore, as of certain fungi or algae, capable of independent motion usually by means of cilia.

**zygote,** *n.* the result of the union of the male and female sex cells. The zygote therefore has a diploid number of chromosomes.

**zymase,** *n.* an enzyme, present in yeast, which causes fermentation by breaking down glucose and some other carbohydrates into alcohol and carbon dioxide or into lactic acid.

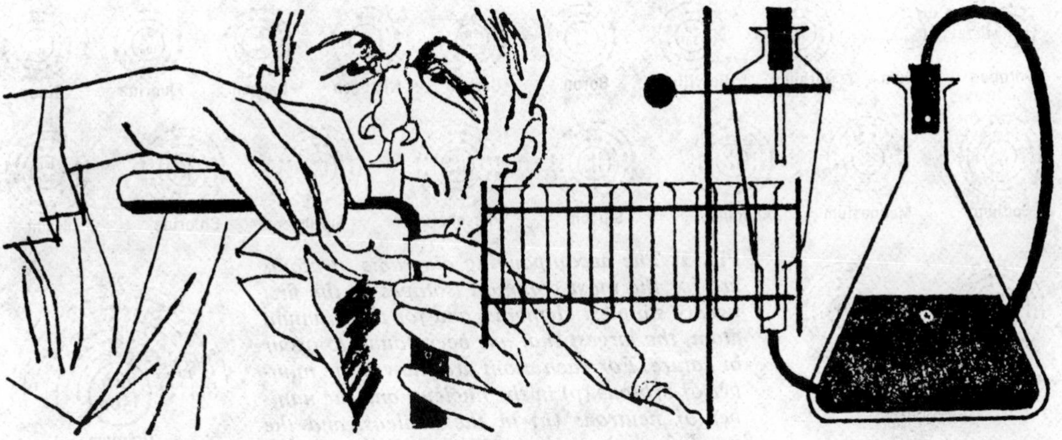

# Chemistry

## DIVISIONS OF CHEMISTRY

The entire field of *chemistry* may be included in two large divisions — *inorganic* and *organic*.

**Inorganic chemistry** includes the study of all the elements, and all of the compounds that do not contain carbon, and a few of the carbon compounds such as limestone ($CaCO_3$), carbon dioxide ($CO_2$), carbon monoxide (CO), etc.

**Organic chemistry** is the study of the carbon compounds. Originally, organic chemistry meant the study of compounds obtained from living organisms.

**Analytical chemistry** is divided into two large divisions — *qualitative analysis and quantitative analysis.*

**Qualitative analysis** is finding out what elements or compounds are contained in any given substance.

**Quantitative analysis** is finding out the percentage of the elements or compounds found in any given substance.

**Physical chemistry** is the study of the laws that govern chemical reactions or chemical phenomena. It is sometimes called *theoretical chemistry*.

**Biochemistry** is the study of the compounds found in living organisms, and of their reactions during the life cycle.

**Agricultural chemistry** deals largely with the chemical composition of soils and fertilizers, and the chemical needs for growing the best crops. It also may include the study of fungicides and insecticides.

---

ROBERT OWENS BEAUCHAMP, B.S., M.A., Ph.D., *Associate Professor of Chemistry and Physics,* Middle Tennessee State University, Murfreesboro, Tennessee.

**Chemurgy** is that branch of applied chemistry devoted to the industrial use of raw organic materials, especially farm products, as the use of Georgia pine for paper, etc.

**Food chemistry** deals largely with the chemical analysis of foodstuffs and the composition of foods needed by animals, particularly human beings, for optimum growth and development.

**Textile chemistry** deals with the chemical composition and properties of the natural and artificial fibers, and also with the chemistry involved in the manufacture of artificial fibers, as well as the chemistry of dyes.

**Thermochemistry** deals with the heat energy changes involved in chemical reactions.

**Nuclear chemistry** deals with the chemical changes that may take place in the nuclei of atoms. This would include radioactivity, and is closely related to nuclear physics.

**Chemical engineering** deals with the industrial applications of any phase of chemistry, and involves the study of the efficiency of chemical reactions and methods of carrying them out. It deals with the selection of raw materials, the location of chemical plants, the design of equipment, the maximum yield, and the economics of producing and marketing chemical products.

## MODERN ATOMIC THEORY, ATOMIC STRUCTURE, AND ISOTOPES

The *modern atomic theory* states that all matter is composed of tiny particles called atoms or molecules, in rapid vibration, with relatively large spaces between.

Although the exact structure of atoms is not definitely known, the "planetary system" theory of atomic structure (with certain modifications)

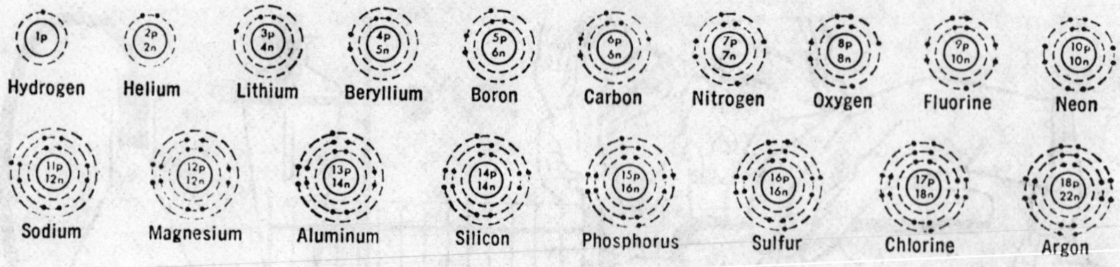


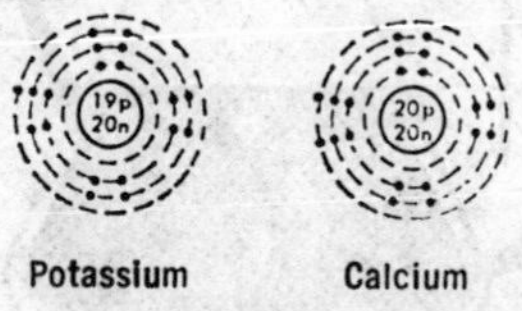

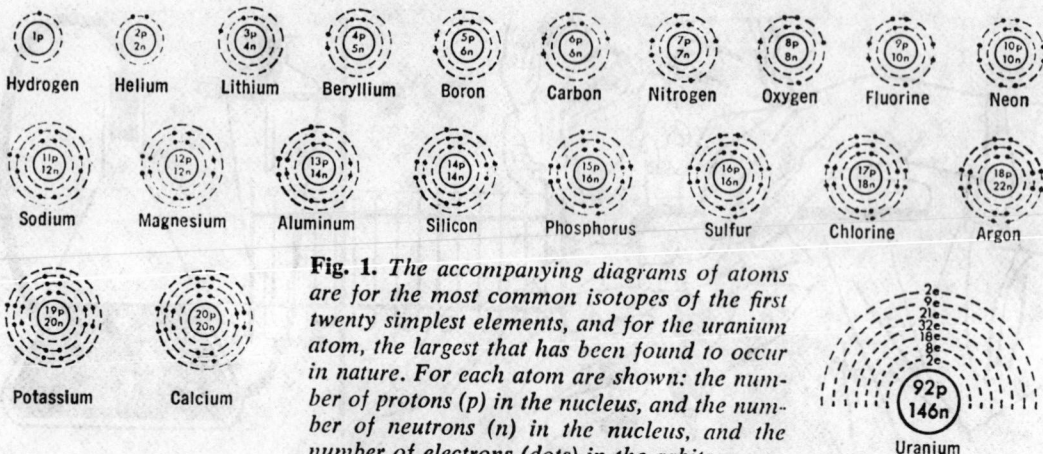

**Fig. 1.** *The accompanying diagrams of atoms are for the most common isotopes of the first twenty simplest elements, and for the uranium atom, the largest that has been found to occur in nature. For each atom are shown: the number of protons (p) in the nucleus, and the number of neutrons (n) in the nucleus, and the number of electrons (dots) in the orbits.*

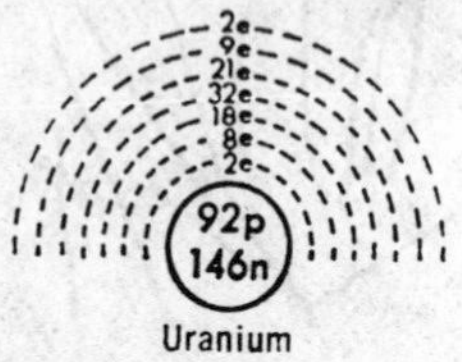


is the one most widely accepted. According to this theory, each atom is composed of a *nucleus* containing all *protons* and *neutrons* present, while the *electrons* revolve in orbits (or shells) around the nucleus. The hydrogen atom is the simplest, and is the only one that has no neutron in the nucleus.

Fig. 1 shows diagrams of the structure of the twenty lightest and simplest atoms. The protons and neutrons in the nuclei are represented by "p" and "n" respectively, and the planetary electrons are represented by dots. In the diagram of the uranium atom, the heaviest atom that has been discovered in nature, the numbers of electrons in the orbits are designated by numbers.

The *atomic weight* of an element is equal to the total number of protons and neutrons in the neucleus of its atom.

The *atomic number* is equal to the number of protons in the nucleus of the atom. It also is equal to the number of planetary electrons in the neutral atom. The atomic number is, in reality, the characteristic that identifies an element, and makes it different from all other elements.

*Isotopes* are different forms of the same element that differ in atomic weights, or the number of neutrons in the nucleus. For example, there are three isotopes of hydrogen, showing atomic weights (mass numbers) of 1, 2, and 3 respectively. See Fig. 2. The number to the upper right of a symbol indicates the atomic weight and the number to the lower left indicates its atomic number.

Fig. 3 shows the diagrams of the three stable isotopes of oxygen with atomic weights of 16, 17, and 18. Most of the elements found in nature occur in the form of two or more isotopes. Some of these isotopes are more stable than others, and occur in larger amounts. The atomic weights given on page 243, however, are the averages of the atomic weights of the elements as they occur in nature. This accounts for the fact that most of the atomic weights given in the table end in decimal fractions.

## WHY ELEMENTS FORM COMPOUNDS — VALENCE

Atoms have a tendency to give up or share the electrons in their outer orbits with other atoms, or to accept from other atoms enough electrons to complete their outer orbits. The first orbit is complete with two electrons, the second with eight, and the seventh normally holds only two electrons. No outer orbit can normally hold more than eight electrons, but the third, fourth, fifth, and sixth orbits can build up to more than eight when they become inner orbits. See the diagram of the uranium atom in Fig. 1, for the final limits of these orbits when they become inner orbits. The inert gases have their outer orbits complete, hence have no tendency to combine with other elements, though they may be made to do so under certain conditions.

*Valence* may be defined as the combining power of atoms (or radicals) compared to the H atom as a positive valence of 1 or the O atom as a negative valence of 2. Elements may combine to form compounds in two ways: *a.* by sharing

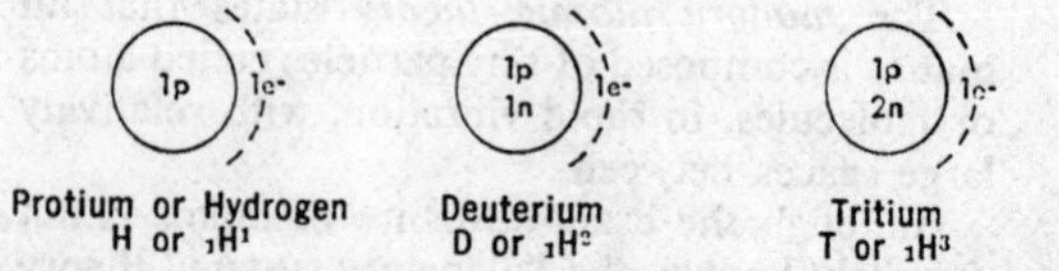


**Fig. 2.** *The isotopes of hydrogen*

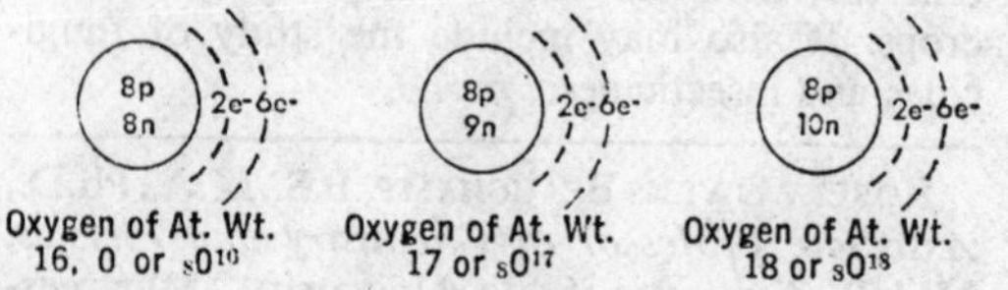


**Fig. 3.** *The stable isotopes of oxygen*

electrons, or *b.* by giving up or taking on electrons.

*Covalence* is the sharing of electrons. Hydrogen and oxygen combine to form water by covalence as follows:

$$\underset{\text{atom}}{H\cdot} + \underset{\text{atom}}{\cdot\ddot{\underset{\cdot\cdot}{O}}\cdot} + \underset{\text{atom}}{\cdot H} \rightarrow \underset{\text{molecule}}{H:\ddot{\underset{\cdot\cdot}{O}}:H} \text{ or } H\text{-}O\text{-}H \text{ or } H_2O$$

The first formula on the right shows how the electrons in the outer orbits are shared to complete the outer orbits of both elements. The second is the usual *structural formula* in which each line (or bond) represents a *pair* of shared electrons. An *empirical formula* (as $H_2O$) shows only the kinds and numbers of atoms in a molecule, and is the one most frequently used.

*Electrovalence* is the giving up or taking on of electrons. Sodium and chlorine combine to form sodium chloride by electrovalence as follows:

$$\underset{\text{atom}}{Na\cdot} + \underset{\text{atom}}{\cdot\ddot{\underset{\cdot\cdot}{Cl}}:} \rightarrow \underbrace{\underset{\text{ion}}{Na^+} + \underset{\text{ion}}{:\ddot{\underset{\cdot\cdot}{Cl}}:^-}}_{\text{molecule}} \text{ or } Na\text{-}Cl \text{ or } NaCl$$

This shows that in the NaCl molecule the Na atom has given up its outer electron to the Cl atom and that the positively charged sodium ion and the negatively charged chlorine ion are held together by electrostatic attraction. The single line (bond) between Na and Cl indicates that Na has given up *one* electron to Cl in this electrovalent compound.

## CLASSIFICATION OF MATTER

There are many ways of classifying matter, but any form of matter will be included in one of the *physical* classes and also in one of the *chemical* classes of matter. See "Dictionary of Chemical Terms" pages 1151 through 1154 for specific definitions of most of the terms used in the following outline:

1. The *physical classes of matter* are: solids, liquids, and gases.
2. The *chemical classes of matter* are: elements, compounds, and mixtures.
3. The *classes of elements* are: metals, nonmetals, metalloids, and the inert elements.
4. The two main *classes of compounds* are: inorganic and organic.

The two main classes of *inorganic compounds* are: electrolytes (acids, bases, and salts, that include most of the inorganic compounds) and some nonelectrolytes.

The two main classes of *organic compounds* are: the aliphatic series (the chain compounds) and the aromatic series (the ring compounds). Both of these series have many subclasses.

## ELECTROCHEMICAL SERIES OR ELECTROMOTIVE SERIES OF COMMON METALS

| | |
|---|---|
| Lithium<br>Potassium<br>Barium<br>Calcium<br>Sodium | Replace hydrogen from cold water and react vigorously with common acids to replace hydrogen |
| Magnesium<br>Aluminum<br>Manganese<br>Zinc<br>Chromium<br>Iron | Replace hydrogen from high temperature steam and from common acids |
| Nickel<br>Tin<br>Lead | Replace hydrogen from common acids |

## HYDROGEN

| | |
|---|---|
| Copper<br>Mercury<br>Silver | React with strong oxidizing agents as nitric acid ($HNO_3$) |
| Platinum<br>Gold | React with aqua regia (HCl plus $HNO_3$) |

Any metal above hydrogen in this series is said to be *active,* because it will replace hydrogen from acids, such as HCl, $H_2SO_4$, and $H_3PO_4$. The metals below hydrogen are said to be *inactive* because they will not replace hydrogen from acids.

Any element in this series will replace any element below it from solutions of its salts, but will be replaced from solutions of its own salts by any element above it in the series. For example:

$$Fe + CuSO_4 \rightarrow FeSO_4 + Cu\downarrow \text{ but}$$
$$Cu + FeSO_4 \rightarrow \text{No reaction}$$

## WEIGHTS AND MEASURES

Since chemistry is an exact science, many of the problems in chemistry involve exact measurements of weights and volumes of the elements and compounds involved in chemical reactions. There are two main systems of weights and measures used in the United States—the *English System* and the *Metric System.* The metric system is the one most widely used in chemistry, and is the system used by all nations in reporting the work done in the scientific fields.

## THERMOMETERS

A thermometer is an instrument for measuring relative intensities of heat on some arbitrary scale. The three most widely used thermometer scales used in this country are the Fahrenheit, the Centigrade, and the Absolute or Kelvin. On the Fahrenheit scale the boiling point of pure water at standard pressure is taken as 212° and the freezing point as 32°. On the centigrade scale the boiling point of pure water at standard pressure is taken as 100° and the freezing point as 0°.

*Heat* is a form of energy due to molecular (or atomic) motion. Theoretically, it is thought that all molecular motion ceases at approximately −273°C, hence there would be no heat in a body at this temperature. For this reason, the absolute scale takes a −273°C as 0.

The following diagrams show the relation of these scales to each other.

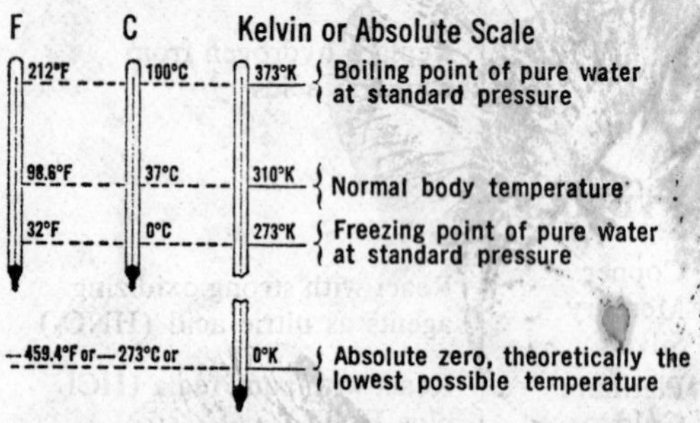


**Fig. 4.** *The Fahrenheit, Centigrade, and Absolute (or Kelvin) thermometer scales*

To change F to C, use the formula:

$$C = \frac{5(F-32)}{9}$$

EXAMPLE: Change 68 degrees F to C. Substituting in the formula:

$$C = \frac{5(68-32)}{9} = \frac{5(36)}{9} = 20°C$$

To change C to F, use the formula:

$$F = \frac{9C}{5} + 32$$

EXAMPLE: Change 20 degrees C to F. Substituting in the formula:

$$F = \frac{9(20)}{5} + 32 = 36 + 32 = 68°F$$

To change C to absolute temperature (K, or usually designated by a capital T), use the formula: $T = C + 273$

EXAMPLE: Change 20 degrees C to absolute temperature. Substituting in the formula:

$$T = 20 + 273 = 293°K$$

## THE BAROMETER

The *barometer* is an instrument used to measure the pressure exerted by the atmosphere. The simple mercury barometer was the first practical instrument used to measure air pressure, and was devised by Torricelli, a student of Galileo. It is sometimes called a Torricelli tube. It may be made by filling with mercury a glass tube

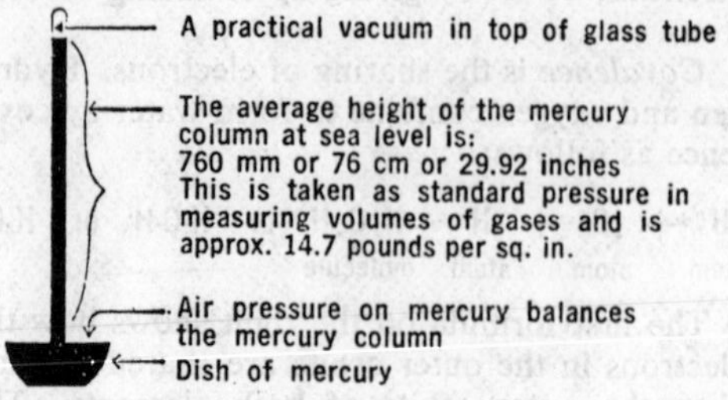


**Fig. 5.** *A simple mercury barometer or a Torricelli tube*

about 32 inches long, sealed at one end, and inverting it in a dish of mercury without admitting any air to the tube. See Fig. 5.

## SOME FUNDAMENTAL LAWS OF CHEMISTRY

The *law of the conservation of mass and energy* states that matter and energy can be neither created nor destroyed, only changed in form. Under certain conditions (as in the atom bomb or the hydrogen bomb) a small amount of matter is changed to energy, but the total amount of matter and energy remains constant. In ordinary chemical changes, the weight of matter that is changed to energy (or vice versa) is infinitesmal, so that for practical purposes we can say that the total weight of the reacting substances in any chemical reaction is equal to the total weight of the products formed. For example, 12 g of carbon combine with 32 g of oxygen to form 44 g of carbon dioxide, as follows:

$$\underset{12g}{C} + \underset{32g}{O_2} \rightarrow \underset{44g}{CO_2} \uparrow \text{(gas)}$$

An arrow pointing upward indicates the product is a gas.

The *law of definite proportions* states that any chemical compound is always composed of the same percentage of its elements by weight. For example, carbon dioxide is always 27.3% carbon and 72.7% oxygen. This may be calculated as follows:

EXAMPLE: If the atomic weight of C is 12 and O is 16, find the percentage composition of carbon dioxide ($CO_2$).

SOLUTION: Determine the molecular weight (mol wt) of $CO_2$ and then calculate what per cent of this weight is due to each element in the compound as follows: (awu stands for atomic weight units).

$CO_2$

$1 \times 12 = 12$ awu due to 1 C atom

$2 \times 16 = 32$ awu due to 2 O atoms

44 awu = mol wt of $CO_2$

$$\text{Per cent of C} = \frac{12}{44} \text{ of } 100\% = 27.3\%$$

$$\text{Per cent of O} = \frac{32}{44} \text{ of } 100\% = 72.7\%$$

Total 100.0%

*Boyle's law of gases* states that, at constant temperature, the volume of a mass of gas is inversely proportional to the pressure upon it, that is: $V_1 : V_2 = P_2 : P_1$ or $V_2P_2 = V_1P_1$

EXAMPLE: A mass of gas has a volume of 500 ml at 740 mm of pressure. Find the volume at standard pressure (760 mm).

SOLUTION: Substituting in the formula:

$$V_2 (760) = 500 \text{ ml } (740) \text{ or}$$

$$V_2 = \frac{500\text{ml} \times 740}{760} = 486.84 \text{ ml}$$

*Charles' law of gases* states that, at constant pressure, the volume of a mass of gas is directly proportional to the absolute temperature, that is:

$$V_1 : V_2 = T_1 : T_2 \quad \text{or} \quad V_2T_1 = V_1T_2$$

EXAMPLE: A certain gas has a volume of 400 ml at 27 degrees C. Find the volume at standard temperature (0 degrees C or 273 degrees absolute).

SOLUTION: Substituting in the formula:

$$V_2 (300) = 400 \text{ ml } (273) \text{ or}$$

$$V_2 = \frac{400 \text{ ml} \times 273}{300} = 364 \text{ ml}$$

*Boyle's and Charles' laws combined.* It is usually necessary to correct volumes of gases for both pressure and temperature, in which case the following formula may be used:

$$V_2 = \frac{V_1 P_1 T_2}{P_2 T_1}$$

EXAMPLE: A certain gas has a volume of 600 ml at 700 mm of pressure and 27 degrees C. Find the volume at standard conditions (760 mm and 273 degrees absolute). Hint: $T_1 = 27 + 273 = 300$ absolute.

SOLUTION: Substituting in the formula:

$$V_2 = \frac{600 \text{ ml} \times 700 \times 273}{760 \times 300} = 502.9 \text{ ml}$$

*Gay-Lussac's law of combining volumes of gases* states that, in any chemical reaction involving gases, the volumes of the gases have the same ratio as their respective coefficients in the balanced equation. This means that in the balanced equation $N_2 + 3H_2 \rightarrow 2NH_3\uparrow$ (gas) *one* volume of nitrogen gas combined with *three* volumes of hydrogen gas to form *two* volumes of ammonia gas.

EXAMPLE: If one has 200 liters of nitrogen in the above equation, find the liters of hydrogen needed to exactly combine with it, and the liters of ammonia formed.

SOLUTION: Write the balanced equation, let $X_1$ be the liters of hydrogen needed, and $X_2$ be the liters of ammonia formed. Place these data around the equation, and solve as illustrated.

$$\overset{200\ l}{\underset{1}{N_2}} + \overset{X_1}{\underset{3}{3H_2}} \rightarrow \overset{X_2}{\underset{2}{2\ NH_3}} \uparrow \text{(gas)}$$

$200\ l : X_1 = 1 : 3$ or $X_1 = 600\ l$ of $H_2$ required

and

$200\ l : X_2 = 1 : 2$ or $X_2 = 400\ l$ of $NH_3$ formed

*Avogadro's law* states that, at equal temperatures and pressures, equal volumes of gases contain equal numbers of molecules. As an outgrowth of this law, it has been found that all gram-atomic weights contain the same number of atoms, and that all gram-molecular weights (g-mol wts) contain the same number of molecules. This number has been found to be $6.02 \times 10^{23}$ or 602 sextillion, and is known as *Avogadro's number.* With this information it is possible to calculate the weight of an atom or molecule of any substance. It also is possible to calculate the space occupied by an atom or molecule if the volume of its formula weight is known.

EXAMPLE 1: If the gram-molecular weight of $H_2$ is 2 g, find the weight of one molecule of $H_2$ (hydrogen gas).

SOLUTION:

$6.02 \times 10^{23}$ molecules of $H_2 = 2$ g

Therefore one molecule of

$$H_2 = \frac{2\text{g}}{6.02 \times 10^{23}} = 3.32 \times 10^{-24} \text{ g}$$

EXAMPLE 2: If a gram-molecular weight of hydrogen ($H_2$) occupies 22.4 liters under standard conditions, find the space occupied by one molecule.

SOLUTION:

Volume of $6.02 \times 10^{23}$ molecules of $H_2 = 22.4$ liters

Volume of one molecule of

$$H_2 = \frac{22.4 \text{ liters}}{6.02 \times 10^{23}} = 3.69 \times 10^{-23} \text{ liter}$$

*Le Chatelier's principle* states that, when a stress is brought to bear upon a system at equilibrium, the system tends to change so as to relieve the stress.

EXAMPLE: Consider the following chemical reaction to be in a state of *equilibrium,* that is, the products formed react to form the original substances at the same rate that the original substances react to form the products.

$$\underset{\text{Sodium Chloride}}{NaCl} + \underset{\text{Potassium Nitrate}}{KNO_3} \rightleftarrows \underset{\text{Sodium Nitrate}}{NaNO_3} + \underset{\text{Potassium Chloride}}{KCl}$$

If more of either of the substances on the left is added or if some of either of the substances on the right is removed, the reaction will tend to go to the right; but if more of either of the substances on the right is added or if some of either of the substances on the left is removed, the reaction will tend to go to the left, until a new state of equilibrium is reached.

*Dalton's law of partial pressures* states that the total pressure in a mixture of gases is the sum of the individual partial pressures. We might add that the pressure exerted by each of the gases is directly proportional to the percentage of the gas present in the mixture.

EXAMPLE: If a mixture of 20% oxygen and 80% nitrogen exerts a pressure of 20 pounds per sq in, what pressure is exerted by each gas?

SOLUTION: Pressure of $O_2 = 20\%$ of 20 lb/sq in $= 4$ lb/sq in. Pressure of $N_2 = 80\%$ of 20 lb/sq in $= 16$ lb/sq in.

*Graham's law of diffusion* states that the

rates of diffusion of two gases are inversely proportional to the square roots of their densities, that is: $r_1 : r_2 = \sqrt{d_2} : \sqrt{d_1}$. However, since the densities of gases are directly proportional to their respective molecular weights, we may substitute molecular weights for densities in the above formula, as follows:

$$r_1 : r_2 = \sqrt{\text{mol wt}_2} : \sqrt{\text{mol wt}_1}$$

EXAMPLE: If 10 liters of methane gas ($CH_4$) diffuses through a certain membrane in one hour, find the liters of sulfur dioxide ($SO_2$) that will diffuse through the same membrane in one hour under the same conditions.

SOLUTION: The mol wt of $CH_4$ is 16 and the mol wt of $SO_2$ is 64. Substituting in the formula:

$$10\ l : r_2 = \sqrt{64} : \sqrt{16} \quad \text{or} \quad 10\ l : r_2 = 8 : 4$$

$$8r_2 = 40\ l \quad \text{or} \quad r_2 = 5\ l \text{ of } SO_2 \text{ per hr}$$

## COMMON TYPES OF CHEMICAL REACTIONS

The *four main types* of chemical reactions are: addition, decomposition, simple replacement, and double replacement. There are many variations of these types, however, such as: complete, reversible, ionization (or dissociation), hydrolysis, neutralization, substitution, and polymerization.

An *addition reaction* is one in which two or more substances combine to form a third substance.

EXAMPLE: $C + O_2 \rightarrow CO_2 \uparrow$

An arrow pointing upward indicates the product is a gas.

A *decomposition reaction* is one in which a compound breaks up into two or more other substances.

EXAMPLE:

$$2\ KClO_3 \rightarrow 2\ KCl + 3\ O_2 \uparrow$$

A *simple replacement reaction* is one in which one element replaces another in a compound.

EXAMPLE:

$$Zn + 2\ HCl \rightarrow ZnCl_2 + H_2 \uparrow$$

A *double replacement reaction* is one in which the metals and nonmetals in two compounds merely swap partners.

EXAMPLE:

$$AgNO_3 + NaCl \rightarrow NaNO_3 + AgCl \downarrow$$

An arrow pointing downward indicates the product is a precipitate.

A *complete reaction* is one in which the products formed do not react (to any appreciable extent) to form the original substances. There are three conditions under which a reaction is usually considered to be complete:

a. If a gas is given off
b. If a precipitate is formed
c. If water is a product

EXAMPLE:

$$2\ NaHCO_3 \rightarrow Na_2CO_3 + H_2O + CO_2 \uparrow$$

A *reversible reaction* is one in which the products formed react to form the original substances.

EXAMPLE:

$$NaCl + KNO_3 \rightleftharpoons NaNO_3 + KCl$$

The arrows pointing in both directions indicate a reversible reaction that is in a state of *equilibrium*, that is, the forward and backward reactions are proceeding at the same rate.

An *ionization reaction* is one in which a molecule breaks up into electrically charged atoms or radicals (usually in water solution).

EXAMPLE:

$$H_2SO_4 \rightleftharpoons 2\ H^+ + SO_4^{=}$$

*Hydrolysis* is a double replacement reaction in which one of the original reacting substances is water.

EXAMPLE:

$$NaCl + HOH \rightleftharpoons NaOH + HCl$$

*Neutralization* is a double replacement reaction of an acid and a base to form a salt and water.

EXAMPLE:

$$NaOH + HCl \rightarrow NaCl + HOH$$

A *substitution reaction* is one in which a certain element will first combine with an atom of a compound, and then add on where the atom was pulled off.

EXAMPLE:

$$CH_4 + Cl_2 \rightarrow CH_3Cl + HCl$$

*Polymerization* is a reaction in which similar molecules combine to form a larger molecule.

EXAMPLE:

$$3\ H_2CO \rightarrow (H_2CO)_3$$

Formaldehyde Trioxymethylene

## STRENGTHS OF SOLUTIONS

**Per cent solutions.** EXAMPLES:

a. 10 g of a solid in 90 g of water is an exact 10% solution by weight.
b. 10 g of a solid in enough water to make 100 ml is an approximate 10% solution.
c. 10 ml of alcohol in 90 ml of water is an exact 10% solution by volume.
d. 10 ml of alcohol plus enough water to make 100 ml is an approximate 10% solution.

*Molar solutions* contain one gram-mol wt of the solute to 1 liter of final solution.

EXAMPLE: If the atomic weight of Na is 23, of O is 16, and of H is 1, the mol wt of NaOH is 40 awu and the g-mol wt is 40 g. Therefore, 40 g of NaOH to 1 liter of final solution is a *molar solution*. Since all g-mol wts contain the same number of molecules, it follows that all molar solutions contain the same number of molecules of solute per liter of solution.

*Normal solutions* contain one *gram-equivalent* of the solute to 1 liter of final solution. A gram-equivalent is the number of g of an element or radical that will combine with or replace 1 g of replaceable hydrogen. To find the gram-equivalent of any element, divide its g-at wt by its valence. For example the g-at wt of Al is 27 g, and its valence is 3, therefore its gram-equivalent is 27g/3, or 9 g.

To find the number of grams of any compound (acid, base, or salt) required to make 1 liter of normal solution:

*First,* determine the g-mol wt of the compound.

*Second,* divide the g-mol wt by the product of the valence of the metal and its subnumber in the formula.

EXAMPLE: If the at wt of Al is 27, of S is 32, and of O is 16, find the g of $Al_2(SO_4)_3$ to 1 liter of normal (N) solution. Valence of Al is 3.

SOLUTION:

$2 \times 27 = 54$ awu for 2 Al
$3 \times 32 = 96$ awu for 3 S
$12 \times 16 = 192$ awu for 12 O
342 awu = mol wt of $Al_2(SO_4)_3$

Therefore 342g = 1 mole of $Al_2(SO_4)_3$

Valence of Al times its subnumber = 6

$$\frac{342g}{6} = 57 \text{ g of } Al_2(SO_4)_3 \text{ to 1 liter of N solution}$$

One of the chief advantages of normal solutions is the fact that 1 ml of any normal acid will exactly neutralize 1 ml of any normal base to form a salt and water. In other words, all normal solutions are exactly the same strength as far as chemical reactions are concerned. This is a great advantage in quantitative analysis involving titration. (See titration problems p 1150.)

*Molal solutions* contain one mole of the solute to 1,000 g of the solvent. One mole of *any* nonelectrolyte to 1,000 g of water raises the boiling point 0.52 degree C and lowers the freezing point 1.86 degrees C. This shows that the effect on the boiling and freezing points is due entirely to the number of dissolved particles per 1,000 g of the solvent, since all moles contain the same number of molecules. Therefore, if ionization were complete, a mole of any electrolyte would have as many times the effect of a mole of a nonelectrolyte on the boiling and freezing points of water as the number of ions into which its molecule dissociates. Since ionization approaches 100% only in very dilute solutions, this offers a method of determining the per cent of ionization of an electrolyte in water solution.

EXAMPLE: Suppose that a 2 molal solution of $CaCl_2$ has a boiling point of 102.6 degrees C. Find the percent of ionization.

SOLUTION: Write the equation for the ionization of $CaCl_2$ and let X equal the moles ionized. Place the proper data under the equation, and work as follows:

$$CaCl_2 \rightleftharpoons Ca^{++} + 2\,Cl^-$$

2 − X moles unionized; X moles forming 3 ions per molecule = 3X mole equivalents

$$\text{Total mole equivs} = 2 - X + 3X = 2X + 2$$

The rise in boiling point is 2.6 degrees C
Since 1 mole (or 1 mole equiv) would raise the boiling point 0.52° C, then:

$$\text{Total mole equivs also} = \frac{2.6°C}{0.52°C} = 5$$
$$\text{and } 2X + 2 = 5 \text{ or } 2X = 3$$
$$\text{and } X = 1.5 \text{ moles ionized}$$

Since the solution is a 2 molal solution, the per cent ionization is:

$$\frac{1.5 \text{ moles}}{2 \text{ moles}} \times 100\% = 75\% \text{ ionization}$$

## BOILING AND FREEZING POINTS OF SOLUTIONS

*Nonvolatile solids in liquids* raise the boiling points and lower the freezing points of the solvents.

A *mixture of liquids* starts to boil at the boiling point of the liquid with the lowest boiling point and continues to rise as this liquid boils off until it reaches the boiling point of the liquid with the highest boiling point. The freezing point of a mixture of liquids is constant, and is somewhere between the freezing points of the liquids, depending on the relative amounts present.

*Gases dissolved in liquids* usually lower both the boiling and freezing points of the solvent.

## SOME TYPICAL PROBLEMS IN CHEMISTRY

In *weight-weight problems,* the actual weights of the substances in any chemical reaction always have the same ratio as the total atomic weight units of these same substances in the balanced equation.

EXAMPLE: In the equation $2KClO_3 \rightarrow 2KCl + 3O_2\uparrow$, if one has 10 g of $KClO_3$, find the weight of KCl formed. Take atomic weight of K as 39, of Cl as 35.5, and of O as 16.

SOLUTION:

$$\underset{245 \text{ awu}}{\overset{10g}{2\,KClO_3}} \rightarrow \underset{149 \text{ awu}}{\overset{X}{2\,KCl}} + 3\,O_2\uparrow$$

$$10g : X = 245 : 149$$

$$X = \frac{10g \times 149}{245} = 6.08g \text{ of KCl}$$

In *weight-volume problems,* one may have the weight of one substance given to find the volume of a gas formed. Since 1 mole of any gas at standard conditions has a volume of 22.4 liters, the following example will illustrate a problem of this type.

EXAMPLE: In the equation $2KClO_3 \rightarrow 2KCl + 3O_2\uparrow$, if one has 10 g of $KClO_3$, find the liters of $O_2$ formed, reduced to standard conditions.

Take atomic weight of K as 39, of Cl as 35.5, and of O as 16.

SOLUTION:

$$\underset{\substack{2\text{ moles}\\=245\text{g}}}{\overset{10\text{g}}{2\,KClO_3}} \rightarrow 2\,KCl + \underset{\substack{3\text{ moles}\\=3\times 22.4\text{ l}=67.2\text{ l}}}{\overset{X\text{ liters}}{3\,O_2\uparrow}}$$

$$\text{Then: } 10\text{g} : 245\text{g} = X : 67.2\text{ l}$$

$$X = \frac{10\text{g} \times 67.2\text{ l}}{245\text{g}} = 2.74\text{ l}$$

In *titration problems,* the strength of the acid times the volume of the acid is always equal to the strength of the base times the volume of the base. The strengths of acids and bases are usually given in terms of *normal* (N) solutions.

EXAMPLE: If it takes 6.4 ml of a 2N base to titrate 10 ml of an acid, find the strength of the acid.

SOLUTION:

$$\underset{10\text{ml}}{\overset{X}{\text{Acid}}} + \underset{6.4\text{ml}}{\overset{2N}{\text{Base}}} \rightarrow \text{Salt} + \text{Water}$$

$$10\text{ml}\ (X) = 6.4\text{ml}\ (2N)$$

$$10X = 12.8\text{ N} \quad \text{or} \quad X = 1.28\text{ N}$$

*Volume-volume problems* are most frequently used when the substances involved are gases. (See Gay-Lussac's law of combining volumes of gases, p. 1147.)

*Other typical problems* that have been given in preceding pages of this article are:

*Thermometer problems* (p. 1146).

*Conservation of mass problems* (p. 1146).

*Percentage composition problems* (p. 1146).

*Problems involving Boyle's and Charles' laws* (p. 1147).

*Problems involving Gay-Lussac's law of combining volumes of gases* (p. 1147).

*Problems involving Avogadro's law* (p. 1147).

*Problems involving Dalton's law of partial pressures* (p. 1147).

*Problems involving Graham's law of diffusion* (pp. 1147-1148).

*Problems involving strengths of solutions* — per cent solutions, molar, normal, and molal solutions, and per cent ionization (pp. 1148-1149).

## RADIOACTIVITY

*Radioactivity* is the spontaneous decomposition of an element by the emission of certain radiations from the nuclei of its atoms. There are three types of radiations emitted by radioactive elements, namely:

1. The *alpha ray* (or particle) is a helium nucleus or helium ion. Its emission lowers the atomic weight by 4 and the atomic number by 2, thus forming another element.

2. The *beta ray* (or particle) is an electron. Its emission from the nucleus increases the atomic number by 1, thus forming another element with approximately the same atomic weight.

3. The *gamma rays* are a form of electromagnetic radiations and are usually emitted when alpha or beta rays are given off.

The *half-life* of a radioactive element is the time that it takes for one-half of any given amount of the element to decompose into the next element in the radioactive series. The half-life of radium is 1620 years and of carbon-14 is 5600 years.

The analysis of ores containing radium to determine what percentage of the original radium remains in the ores offers one means of estimating the age of the earth.

The analysis of archeological remains (such as wood or rope) to determine the percentage of the original carbon-14 that remains, offers a method of estimating the age of these relics. (See any good text on college chemistry for additional information on radioactivity.)

## NUCLEAR ENERGY

*Nuclear energy* (or atomic energy) is the energy that is released by a change in the nucleus of an atom, whereas chemical energy is concerned only with the number and arrangement of the electrons in the orbits, usually the outer ones.

Nuclear energy can be produced in two ways: a. by the *fission* (splitting) of large atoms, and b. by the *fusion* of small atoms. Two of the most important elements for the production of nuclear energy by fission are: uranium-235, used in the first atomic bomb in World War II, and plutonium-239, used in the second one. In the explosion of an atomic bomb the temperature rises to 10,000,000° C, or more.

Nuclear energy is produced by the fusion of 4 hydrogen atoms into one helium atom. In the hydrogen bomb, 0.7% of the mass is converted into energy, whereas in the splitting (fission) of uranium-235 only 0.1% of the mass is converted into energy. (See any good text on college chemistry for additional information on nuclear energy.)

In 1905, Albert Einstein came to the conclusion that mass and energy were not independent of one another, but that a change in energy is always accompanied by a change in mass, and vice versa. He expressed this relationship by his famous equation: $E = mc^2$, in which *$E$ is the change in energy in ergs, $m$ is the change in mass in grams,* and *$c$ is the velocity of light in centimeters per second.* Since the velocity of light is $3 \times 10^{10}$ cm/sec (or 30,000,000,000 cm/sec) it can be seen that when a very small amount of mass is changed to energy, an enormous amount of energy is produced. It is quite probable that in the future more and more of the power used in industry (or even in our homes) will come from the proper harnessing and use of nuclear energy.

# DICTIONARY OF CHEMICAL TERMS

## A

**absolute temperature:** temperature measured from a minus 273 degrees centigrade as zero. Centigrade readings can be changed to absolute temperature by adding 273 to the centigrade readings.

**absolute zero:** the zero point on the absolute temperature scale. At this temperature, theoretically, all molecular motion ceases. It is supposed to be the lowest possible temperature.

**acid:** a compound that yields positive hydrogen ions (protons) in water solution. It is a proton donor.

**acid, strong:** an acid that yields a large percentage of hydrogen ions in water solution.

**acid, weak:** an acid that yields a small percentage of hydrogen ions in water solution.

**adsorption:** a phenomenon in which molecules, atoms, and ions become attached to the surfaces of solids and liquids.

**alchemy:** the chemistry of the Middle Ages, at which time the chief aim was to change the baser metals into gold.

**aliphatic series:** a class of organic compounds in which the molecules occur in chains.

**alkali:** a strong base as sodium hydroxide. Also any compound such as baking soda ($NaHCO_3$) whose water solution will turn red litmus blue.

**allotropic forms:** forms of an element that differ in physical and (or) chemical properties, as oxygen and ozone, red and yellow phosphorus.

**alloy:** a mixture, solid solution, or combination of metals having properties different from those of any one of its constituents.

**alpha particle:** a positively charged helium nucleus expelled from radioactive substances.

**amalgam:** an alloy of mercury and some other metal.

**ammonia:** a light, colorless gas, $NH_3$, with an irritating and pungent odor.

**amorphous:** not having crystalline structure.

**analysis:** the separation of a substance into its constituents.

**Angstrom:** one ten-thousandth of a micron.

**anhydride, acid:** an oxide that combines with water to form an acid.

**anhydride, basic:** an oxide that combines with water to form a base.

**anhydrous:** without water; compounds that contain no water of crystallization.

**anion:** a negatively charged ion that is attracted to the anode or positive pole in electrolysis.

**anode:** the positive pole of an electric system.

**aromatic series:** a class of organic compounds in which the molecules form rings.

**atom:** the smallest particle of an element that is still the element.

**atomic number:** the number of positive charges on the nucleus of an atom or the number of protons in the nucleus of an atom.

**atomic theory:** the theory that all elements are composed of tiny particles called atoms, in vibration, with relatively large spaces between.

**atomic weight:** the weight of an atom compared to the carbon atom as 12. (Formerly the oxygen atom was taken as 16 or the hydrogen atom as 1). It also may be taken as the total number of protons and neutrons in the nucleus of an atom.

**atomic weight unit (awu):** the unit used in determining the weight of an atom or a molecule. It is one-twelfth the weight of the carbon-12 atom. It is approximately the weight of a proton or a neutron.

**atmospheric pressure:** the average pressure exerted by the weight of the air at sea level.

**Avogadro's law:** at constant temperature and pressure equal volumes of gases contain equal numbers of molecules.

**Avogadro's number:** the number of atoms in the gram-atomic weight of any element or the number of molecules in the gram-molecular weight of any element or compound. It is $6.02 \times 10^{23}$ or 602 sextillion.

## B

**babbitt metal:** an alloy, usually composed of tin, antimony, and copper, used for machinery bearings.

**baking soda:** the common name for *sodium bicarbonate*, $NaHCO_3$

**barometer:** an instrument for measuring the pressure exerted by the atmosphere.

**base:** a. the hydroxide of a metal, or positive radical, whose water solution turns red litmus blue and that neutralizes acids. b. a proton acceptor.

**bauxite:** a hydrated oxide of aluminum; one of the chief aluminum ores.

**beta particle:** an electron given off from the nucleus of a radioactive substance. It is thought to be given off by a neutron that then becomes a proton.

**binary compound:** one that consists of two elements as NaCl.

**bleaching powder:** a common name for *chloride of lime*.

**boiling point:** the temperature at which the vapor pressure of a liquid just barely exceeds the atmospheric pressure.

**brass:** an alloy of copper and zinc.

**bronze:** an alloy of copper and tin. Special bronzes may contain other metals.

**Brownian movement:** the haphazard movement of dispersed particles in a dispersion due to the bombardment of the atoms or molecules of the containing phase.

**buffer:** a substance which, in solution, acts to maintain a practically constant hydrogen ion concentration, despite the addition of appreciable amounts of acid or alkali.

## C

**calorie (gram-calorie or cal):** the amount of heat required to raise one gram of water one degree centigrade.

**Calorie (kilogram-calorie or Cal):** the amount of heat required to raise one kilogram of water one degree centigrade. One Calorie equals 1,000 calories.

**carat:** a twenty-fourth part, used to express the fineness of a gold alloy. (In this sense it is sometimes spelled karat and abbreviate as k.) As a unit of weight for precious stones it is 200mg or 1/5 of a gram.

**carbohydrate:** an organic compound composed of carbon, hydrogen, and oxygen, with the hydrogen and oxygen usually in the proportion of 2 to 1. Examples are sugars, starches, dextrines, and celluloses.

**carbolic acid:** an old name for *phenol*, $C_6H_5OH$.

**catalyst (catalytic agent):** a substance that changes the speed of a chemical reaction without itself being permanently changed.

**cathode:** the negative pole of an electric system.

**cation:** a positively charged ion that is attracted to the negative pole or cathode in electrolysis.

**caustic potash:** a common name for *potassium hydroxide*, KOH.

**caustic soda:** a common name for *sodium hydroxide*, NaOH.

**centigrade scale:** the thermometer scale on which the freezing point of water is 0 and the boiling point is 100, at standard pressure.

**centimeter:** one-hundredth of a meter.

**chemical change:** a change in which one or more new substances are formed.

**chemistry:** that science that deals with the composition of matter and the changes that it may undergo.

**chloride of lime:** calcium monochloride monohypochlorite, CaCl(ClO).

**chloroform:** trichlormethane, $CHCl_3$, used as an anesthetic and solvent.

**colloid:** a dispersion in which the dispersed particles are larger than those in true solutions and smaller than those in true suspensions.

**combustion:** a chemical reaction in which appreciable light and heat are given off.

**compound:** composed of two or more elements chemically combined in very definite proportions.

**covalence:** the mutual sharing of electrons between elements when they combine to form compounds.

**critical pressure:** the pressure required to liquefy a gas at its critical temperature.

**critical temperature:** the temperature above which a gas cannot be liquefied.

## D

**decomposition:** the breaking down of a compound into simpler substances or into its elements.
**dehydrate:** to take water from a substance.
**deliquescent:** the characteristic that some solids have of absorbing water from the air until they become wet or even pass into solution.
**density:** weight per unit volume, as the grams per cubic centimeter of a solid, the grams per milliliter of a liquid, or the grams per liter of a gas.
**deuterium:** the isotope of hydrogen with an atomic weight of 2.
**dibasic acid:** an acid that has two replaceable hydrogens in its molecule, such as $H_2SO_4$ (sulfuric acid).
**diffusion:** the mixing of gases, liquids, or solutions, or the dissolving of a solid in a liquid, due to molecular motion only.
**dispersion:** a mixture of two or more substances in which one may be considered as the containing phase and the other one or more as the contained phase or phases.
**dissociation:** the breaking up of a chemical compound into simpler constituents, as in ionization.
**dry ice:** solid carbon dioxide.
**dynamite:** a powerful explosive made by soaking some absorbent material such as wood pulp or wood flour with nitroglycerin. It also may contain other substances such as sodium nitrate, ammonium nitrate, or cellulose nitrate.

## E

**efflorescence:** the loss of water of crystallization by certain hydrates when exposed to air.
**efflorescent substance:** a hydrate that loses water of crystallization on exposure to the atmosphere.
**electrode:** the plate or terminal of an electric system.
**electrolysis:** the decomposition of a substance, melted or in solution, by the use of an electric current.
**electrolyte:** a substance which will conduct an electric current when melted or in solution. A substance that will ionize in water.
**electron:** the unit of negative electricity.
**electrovalence:** the giving up of electrons by metals and the taking on of electrons by nonmetals when they combine to form compounds.
**element:** the simplest form of matter that can be obtained by any ordinary means, such as iron, oxygen, etc. (See the table of elements page 243.) There are 92 elements that occur naturally, and 11 others have been made in the laboratory, making a total of 103 known elements to date.
**energy:** the ability to do work.
**epsom salt (or Epsom salts):** common name for the harsh-tasting purgative, magnesium sulfate heptahydrate, $MgSO_4 \cdot 7H_2O$.
**equation, chemical:** the statement of a chemical reaction in terms of the symbols and (or) the formulas of the substances involved.
**equilibrium, chemical:** a state of balance in a reversible chemical reaction in which the change in one direction is just equal to the change in the opposite direction.
**eutectic mixture:** the alloy of two metals that has the lowest melting point, or the mixture of two liquids that has the lowest boiling point.

## F

**Fahrenheit:** the common thermometer scale on which water freezes at 32 degrees and boils at 212 at standard pressure. It is named after the German scientist, Fahrenheit, who invented the scale.
**filtrate:** the liquid from which suspended particles have been removed.
**formula, chemical:** an expression containing the symbols of the atoms and subscripts showing how many of each kind of the atoms are present in the molecule. The abbreviation for the molecule of an element or a compound. Examples: $O_2$ for oxygen gas or $H_2O$ for the water molecule.
**formula weight:** same as molecular weight. *See* MOLECULAR WEIGHT.
**freezing point:** the temperature at which a liquid changes to a solid.
**fusion:** the changing of a solid to a liquid; melting.

## G

**gamma rays:** electromagnetic rays given off by radioactive substances; similar to x-rays, but with shorter wave lengths than most x-rays.
**gas:** a physical state of matter with indefinite volume and shape. The molecules show little attraction for each other, are in very rapid motion, and distribute themselves uniformly in the space in which they are confined.
**grain alcohol:** common name for ethyl alcohol or ethanol, $C_2H_5OH$. The alcohol in wines and other alcoholic beverages.
**gram:** usually taken as the weight of one cubic centimeter of water at its greatest density, that is 4 degrees C. The international unit of weight in the metric system.
**gram-atomic weight:** the number of grams of an atom that is numerically equal to its atomic weight.
**gram-molecular volume:** the volume of a gas that contains one gram-molecular weight of the gas at standard conditions, that is 0 degrees centigrade and 760 millimeters of mercury pressure. It is equal to 22.4 liters.
**gram-molecular weight:** the number of grams of a molecule that is numerically equal to its molecular weight. It also is called a **mol** or **mole.**
**guncotton:** the highly explosive cellulose nitrates containing 13% or more of nitrogen.
**gypsum:** calcium sulfate dihydrate, $CaSO_4 \cdot 2H_2O$. Heated until it loses three-fourths of its water of crystallization, it forms plaster of Paris.

## H

**Haber process:** an industrial process for making ammonia from hydrogen and nitrogen.
**half-life:** the time that it takes for one half of any radioactive substance to decompose into the next simpler substance of the radioactive series. This may vary from a small fraction of a second to several million years, owing to the substance involved. The half-life of radium is 1620 years while the half-life of carbon fourteen is 5,600 years.
**halide:** a binary compound in which the nonmetal is a halogen.
**halogen:** any element of the chlorine family, that is, fluorine, chlorine, bromine, iodine, or astanine.
**hard water:** *See* WATER, HARD.
**heat:** a form of energy due to the motion of the particles (molecules, atoms, ions, and electrons) that make up the body. Also the infra-red electromagnetic waves whose wave lengths are just longer than red light.
**heat of formation:** the number of calories of heat liberated when one mole of the compound is formed from its elements.
**hydrate:** a compound that contains a definite number of molecules of water of crystallization per molecule of the compound.
**hydride:** a compound of a metal and hydrogen.
**hydrocarbon:** an organic compound composed of carbon and hydrogen only, such as methane ($CH_4$), or ethane ($C_2H_6$).
**hydrogenation:** the addition of hydrogen to the unsaturated molecule of a hydrocarbon or a fat, in the presence of a proper catalyst.
**hydrogen equivalent:** the grams of any element or radical required to combine with or replace one gram of replaceable hydrogen.
**hydrolysis:** a double replacement reaction of a compound with water. The hydrolysis of a salt is the reaction of a salt with water to form an acid and a base.
**hydronium ion:** the positively charged ion ($H_3O^+$).
**hydroxide:** a compound composed of a metal and the hydroxyl radical (OH).
**hydroxyl:** the univalent radical (OH).
**hygroscopic substance:** a substance that will absorb moisture from the air.
**hypo:** sodium thiosulfate, $Na_2S_2O_3$; also called sodium hyposulfite. Used by photographers in "fixing" films.

## I

**indicator:** a substance that is one color in dilute acid solution and another color in dilute basic solution. It may be colorless in one solution and colored in the other.

**inert:** having little or no tendency to react chemically with other substances. The **inert elements** are those whose outer orbits are complete (helium, neon, argon, krypton, xenon, and radon).

**inorganic compounds:** all chemical compounds that do not contain carbon. Some compounds that do contain carbon are usually classed as inorganic, such as limestone ($CaCO_3$), baking soda ($NaHCO_3$), etc. The original meaning was compounds that have no connection with life processes.

**ion:** an electrically charged atom or radical.

**ionization:** the separation (dissociation) of a molecule into electrically charged atoms or radicals called ions, usually in water solution.

**isomers:** compounds that have the same percentage composition of elements, but different properties due to a different arrangement of the atoms in the molecule.

**isotopes:** atoms of the same atomic number but of different atomic weights because of different numbers of neutrons in the nuclei.

## K

**kilo:** a prefix meaning 1,000.

**kilogram:** 1,000 grams.

**kindling temperature:** the lowest temperature at which a substance will catch on fire and continue to burn.

**kinetic energy:** energy that is due to motion.

**kinetic theory:** the theory that all matter is composed of moving atoms or molecules.

## L

**latex:** the milky juice of the rubber tree.

**law:** a statement that summarizes a large number of facts; a generalized statement of some relation in nature.

**limestone:** impure form of calcium carbonate, $CaCO_3$. May be amorphous or crystalline, but will not take a high polish.

**liquid:** a physical class of matter that has definite volume, but indefinite shape.

**liter:** one cubic decimeter; 1,000 cubic centimeters. It is equivalent to 1.06 liquid quarts.

**litmus:** a vegetable indicator that is blue in basic or alkaline solutions and red in acid solutions.

**lunar caustic:** a common name for silver nitrate, $AgNO_3$.

**lye:** sodium hydroxide (soda lye), or potassium hydroxide (potash lye).

## M

**marble:** a crystalline form of calcium carbonate, $CaCO_3$, that will take a high polish. Certain impurities are responsible for the various colors.

**marsh gas:** a common name for methane, $CH_4$. Also called *fire damp*.

**mass:** the actual amount of matter in a substance, independent of gravity.

**matter:** anything that has weight and occupies space.

**melting point:** the constant temperature at which a solid changes to a liquid.

**metal:** an element whose hydroxide is a base and that forms simple positive ions.

**metalloids:** the borderline elements that to some extent exhibit both metallic and nonmetallic properties.

**meter:** approximately one ten-millionth of the distance from the equator to either pole. The distance between two groove marks on a platinum-iridium bar in the International Bureau of Weights and Measures near Paris.

**micron:** one-millionth of a meter or one-thousandth of a millimeter.

**milk of lime:** calcium hydroxide suspended in water.

**milk of magnesia:** magnesium hydroxide suspended in water.

**milli:** a prefix that means one-thousandth.

**millimeter:** one-thousandth of a meter.

**millimicron:** one-thousandth of a micron.

**mixture:** a substance composed of two or more separate substances mingled in any proportion and not chemically combined with one another.

**mole** (or **mol**): a gram-molecular weight.

**molal solution:** a solution containing one mole of the solute to 1,000 grams of the solvent.

**molar solution:** a solution containing one mole of the solute to one liter of the final solution.

**molecular weight:** the sum of the atomic weights of the atoms in a molecule. The weight of a molecule compared to the carbon atom as 12. It is equivalent to the total number of protons and neutrons in the nuclei of the atoms forming the molecule.

**molecule:** the smallest particle of an element or a compound that has the properties of the mass. With the exception of the inert gases, a molecule is composed of two or more atoms chemically combined.

**monobasic acid:** an acid that has but one replaceable hydrogen, as HCl.

**mordant:** a substance used for fixing colors or dyes on cloth.

**"moth balls":** naphthalene, $C_{10}H_8$, a coal tar product, molded into balls.

## N

**nascent state:** the active condition of an atom at the instant it is set free from a compound and before it has time to form molecules with like atoms. An example is monoatomic oxygen.

**negative valence:** the number of electrons needed to complete the outer orbit of an element or a radical.

**neutralization:** the mixing of acid and basic solutions until the mixture has no effect on an indicator.

**neutron:** a very small unit of matter, having no electric charge, and having a mass equal to the hydrogen atom. It is thought to be an intimate combination of a proton and an electron.

**nitroglycerin:** glycerol trinitrate, a powerful explosive.

**nonelectrolyte:** a compound that will not conduct an electric current in water solution or in the molten state. It does not ionize.

**nonmetal:** an element whose oxide is an acid anhydride and which, either as a element or a component of a compound, forms negative ions.

**normal solution:** a solution that contains one gram of replaceable hydrogen, or its equivalent, to one liter of the final solution.

**nutrino:** an uncharged particle having the mass equal to an electron.

## O

**octane number:** the anti-knock value of a gasoline compared with a standard octane taken as 100.

**ore:** any natural rock-like material from which some useful element or compound may be obtained.

**organic chemistry:** the chemistry of carbon compounds.

**organic compound:** a compound in which carbon is the chief constituent. Originally it meant any compound obtained from living organisms.

**oxidation:** in a limited sense it means the combination with oxygen. In a broader sense it means the loss of one or more electrons from an element or a radical, or an increase in positive valence.

**oxidation number:** the number of electrons that an element actually gives to, takes from, or shares with some other element or radical. Numerically, positive oxidation numbers equal positive valences and negative oxidation numbers equal negative valences, except for elements in the free state which are said to have an oxidation number of zero, since they are not actually giving up, taking on, or sharing electrons in the free state.

**oxide:** a binary compound of oxygen with some other element.

**oxidizing agent:** an agent that brings about oxidation. *See* OXIDATION.

**oxyacetylene torch:** a blowpipe that produces a flame of acetylene gas burning in oxygen.

**oxyhydrogen torch:** a blowpipe that produces a flame of hydrogen burning in oxygen.

**ozone:** an allotropic form of oxygen having the formula $O_3$.

## P

**paraffin series:** hydrocarbons having the type formula $C_nH_{2n+2}$.

**Pasteurization:** a process (devised by Pasteur) of partially sterilizing foods, such as milk, by heating for a time to a temperature between 55 and 70 degrees centigrade.

**petroleum:** a natural liquid mixture,

sometimes called "crude oil." Composed mostly of hydrocarbons, and from which we obtain gasoline, kerosene, mineral spirits, mineral oil, fuel oil, lubricating oils, etc.
**phlogiston theory:** the old false theory that burning was due to the escape of a mythical fluid called phlogiston.
**photon:** a unit of radiant energy; the energy emitted by an electron when it jumps from one orbit to the next inner orbit.
**physical change:** any change that does not alter the chemical composition of a substance.
**plaster of Paris:** calcium sulfate monohydrate $(CaSO_4)_2 \cdot H_2O$. Made by heating gypsum. *See* GYPSUM.
**positive valence:** the number of electrons in the outer orbit of an element. The number of its own electrons that an element or radical may give up or share in the formation of chemical compounds.
**positron:** a tiny particle of matter equal in mass to that of an electron, but with a positive charge.
**precipitate:** a solid formed in solution by a chemical reaction, or by the coagulation of a colloidal dispersion.
**producer gas:** a mixture of carbon monoxide and nitrogen obtained by burning coal or coke in a limited supply of air.
**proton:** the ionized nucleus of a hydrogen atom ($H^+$). A tiny particle of matter with a positive charge and a mass of one atomic weight unit.
**pyroxylin:** the soluble nitrates of cellulose containing less than about 13% nitrogen.

## Q

**qualitative analysis:** the analysis of a substance to determine what its components are.
**quantitative analysis:** the analysis of a substance to determine the percentage of each of its component parts.
**quartz:** the common, crystalline form of silicon dioxide. It has the same chemical composition as sand ($SiO_2$).
**quicklime:** common name for calcium oxide, CaO. Sometimes called lime.
**quicksilver:** a common name for mercury. Sometimes called "live silver".

## R

**radical:** a group of two or more elements that act as one in any chemical reaction.
**radioactivity:** the spontaneous emission of alpha, beta, or gamma rays by certain elements.
**reducing agent:** an agent that can bring about a chemical reduction. *See* REDUCTION.
**reduction:** in a narrow sense, the removal of oxygen from a compound; in a broader sense, a decrease in positive valence or an increase in negative valence.
**replaceable hydrogen:** the hydrogen in an acid (or an acid salt) that can be replaced by any metal such as sodium or zinc that is more active than hydrogen. *See* ELECTROCHEMICAL SERIES, p. 1145.
**reversible reaction:** a chemical reaction in which the products formed react to form the original substances.

## S

**sal ammoniac:** common name for ammonium chloride, $NH_4Cl$.
**salt:** a compound formed by the union of the metal of a base with the nonmetal of an acid, as $Na_2CO_3$ or $CaCl_2$.
**salt, acid:** a salt containing one or more replaceable hydrogens, as $NaHCO_3$.
**salt, basic:** a salt containing one or more replaceable hydroxyls, as Ca(OH)Cl.
**salt, normal:** a salt that does not contain any replaceable hydrogens or replaceable hydroxyls, as $Na_2CO_3$ or $CaCl_2$.
**saltpeter:** potassium nitrate. **Chile saltpeter** is sodium nitrate.
**science:** organized knowledge, usually obtained by experiment, accurate observation, and correct interpretation; it comes from the Latin word scio, scire, meaning "to know."
**slaked lime:** common name for calcium hydroxide, $Ca(OH)_2$. Sometimes called lime.
**soaps:** sodium or potassium salts of the higher fatty acids.
**solid:** any substance that has definite size and shape.
**solute:** the contained phase of a solution, as salt dissolved in water.
**solvent:** the containing phase of a solution, as water containing dissolved salt.
**solution:** a clear, uniform dispersion that will not settle on standing. Usually a solid (solute) dissolved in a liquid (solvent).
**specific gravity:** the density of a substance compared to the density of some other substance as a standard. Water is the standard for solids and liquids and air is the standard for gases.
**spontaneous combustion:** combustion caused by slow oxidation that grows faster of itself until the kindling temperature is reached.
**standard conditions:** zero degrees centigrade and 760 mm of pressure, chosen as the standards of temperature and pressure for measuring gas volumes.
**suspension:** a turbid (cloudy), nonuniform dispersion that will settle on standing, such as muddy water.
**symbol:** the abbreviation for the atom of an element, as O for oxygen.
**synthesis:** the formation of a compound from its elements; the artificial production of a substance from its elements.

## T

**temperature:** the intensity of heat in a body as measured by a thermometer.
**ternary compound:** one composed of three different elements, as $KClO_3$.
**theory:** a likely supposition formed in an effort to explain some regularity or relationship in nature.
**tincture:** an alcoholic solution.
**T.N.T.:** symetrical trinitrotoluene; a powerful explosive.
**titration:** finding the strength of an acid (or a base) by exactly neutralizing with a base (or an acid) of known strength, using known amounts of each.
**transmutation:** the changing of one element into another.
**tritium:** the isotope of hydrogen having an atomic weight of three.

## U

**ultraviolet light** (or **rays**): electromagnetic radiations whose wave lengths fall between those of x-rays and violet light (the shortest light waves).

## V

**valence:** the number of electrons that an atom (or radical) can lose, gain, or share with other atoms (or radicals).
**valence electrons:** the electrons in the outermost shell of an atom.
**vapor pressure:** the pressure exerted at any temperature by an evaporating substance.
**volatile:** easily converted into a vapor.
**vulcanized rubber:** rubber hardened by reaction with sulfur.

## W

**water gas:** a mixture of carbon monoxide and hydrogen, made by the reaction of steam with hot coke.
**water, hard:** water containing metallic ions that react with ordinary soap to form insoluble substances.
**water, permanently hard:** hard water that cannot be softened by boiling.
**water, soft:** water that forms no insoluble compounds with ordinary soap.
**water, temporarily hard:** hard water that can be softened by boiling.
**water of crystallization (or hydration):** water that is taken up in definite molecular ratios by certain compounds as they crystallize in water solutions.
**weight:** a measure of the earth's gravitational force upon any body.
**Wood's metal:** a very low-melting alloy of lead, tin, bismuth, and cadmium, used in sprinkler systems. The melting point is 65 degrees C.

## X

**x-rays:** electromagnetic radiations whose wave lengths are longer than most gamma rays and shorter than the ultraviolet rays.

## Z

**zeolite process:** a process whereby metallic ions causing hard water are removed by passing it through a filter containing zeolite (a complex silicate).

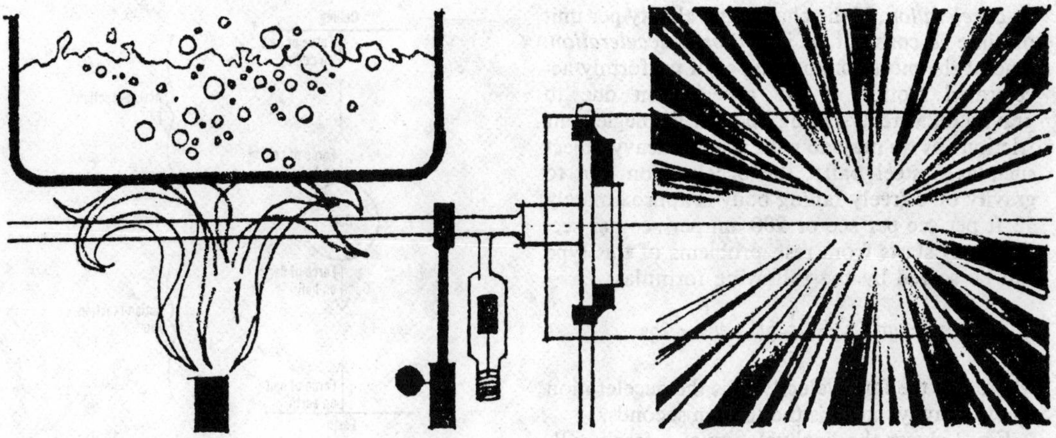

# Physics

## DIVISIONS OF PHYSICS

Physics is primarily concerned with matter and energy as they are used in the world's work. For convenience, it is the custom to divide the study of physics into the following large divisions: (a) mechanics (of solids, liquids, and gases), (b) heat, (c) sound, (d) light, (e) magnetism and electricity, and (f) modern physics, that deals mainly with the structure of the atom and nuclear energy.

## MECHANICS

Since physics is a science based on exact measurements, the student should be familiar with the systems of weights and measures. The English system is most widely used by engineers in industry, while the metric is generally used in laboratory research work.

In the English system, the *fundamental units* are the *foot, pound,* and *second.* This is known as the *foot-pound-second (fps) system* and all other units in the system are derived from these three.

In the metric system the three *fundamental units* are the *meter, kilogram,* and *second.* This is known as the *mks system.* More frequently, however, the metric system uses as the *fundamental units* the *centimeter, gram,* and *second.* This is known as the *centimeter-gram-system (cgs) system.* All other units in this system are derived from these three.

**Types of motion.** Every body in the universe is in motion with respect to most of the other bodies in the universe. There is the motion of our solar system in the galaxy of the milky way; the motion of the earth around the sun; the rotation of the earth on its axis; the motion of a car with a uniform speed of 60 miles per hour; the speed of the car as it slows down for a traffic light and then speeds up again; the motion of atoms in a molecule; the motion of the electrons in an atom; etc., etc. Since we live on the planet earth, we usually think of a body as being in motion only if it is in motion with respect to the earth.

*Uniform motion or uniform velocity* is motion in which the distance (space) covered per unit of time is constant. Problems of this type may be solved by the following formula:

$$s = vt$$

where *s* is the *space* covered, *v* is *velocity,* and *t* is the *time.*

*Variable motion or variable velocity* is motion in which the space covered per unit of time is not a constant. Problems of this type may be solved by the following formula:

$$\text{average velocity} = \frac{s}{t}$$

**Uniformly accelerated motion.** *Acceleration* is the change in velocity per unit of time. If the velocity increases, it is *positive acceleration;* if the velocity decreases, it is *negative acceleration*

---

ROBERT OWENS BEAUCHAMP, B.S., M.A., Ph.D., *Associate Professor of Chemistry and Physics,* Middle Tennessee State University, Murfreesboro, Tennessee.

or *deceleration.* If the change in velocity per unit of time is constant, it is *uniform acceleration.* One of the most common types of uniformly accelerated motion is the acceleration due to gravity on a freely falling body. If we neglect air friction (as we may do with a small heavy object such as a steel ball), the acceleration due to gravity on a freely falling body is approximately 32 ft per sec per sec or 980 cm per sec per sec. If a body starts from rest, problems of this type can be solved by the following formulas:

$$v = gt; \quad s = \frac{1}{2}gt^2; \quad v^2 = 2gs$$

where v is the final velocity, g is the acceleration due to gravity, and t is the time in seconds.

Fig. 1 shows the final velocity of a freely falling body at the end of each of the first four seconds and also the space covered in each of the first four seconds.

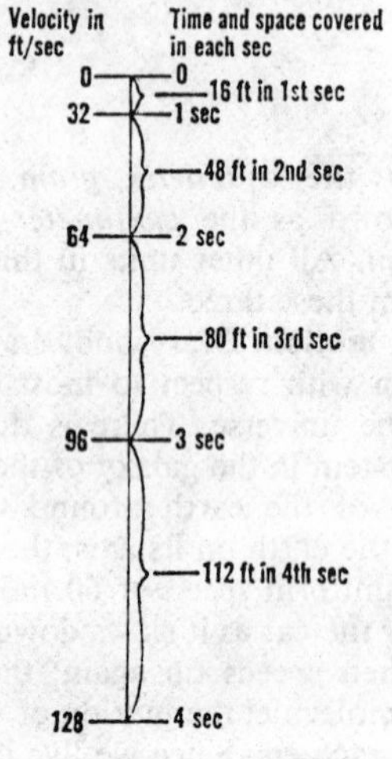


**Fig. 1.** *Increase in speed of freely falling body for 4 sec, neglecting friction. Total space covered = 256 ft.*

*Newton's first law of motion* states that a body at rest remains at rest, or if in motion it continues in uniform motion in a straight line unless acted on by an unbalanced external force.

*Newton's second law of motion* states that the acceleration produced by an unbalanced force acting on a body is directly proportional to the net force, in the same direction as the force, and inversely proportional to the mass of the body.

*Newton's third law of motion* states that when one body exerts a force upon a second body, the second body exerts an equal force upon the first body and that these forces are opposite in direction. In other words, to every action there is an equal and opposite reaction. Fig. 2 illustrates two "action-reaction" pairs.

*Newton's universal law of gravitation* states that any two bodies attract each other with a

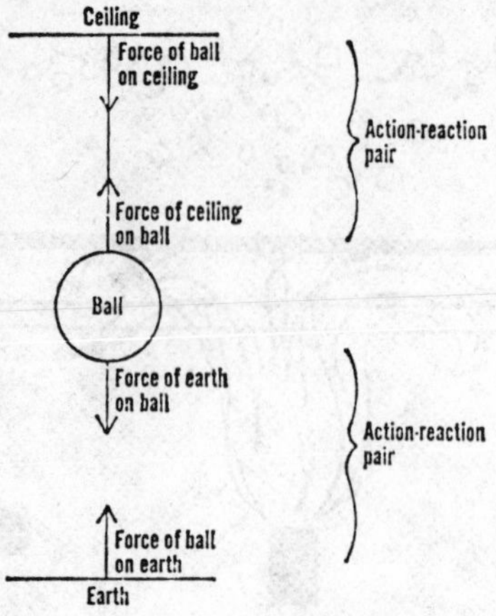


**Fig. 2.** *Two "action-reaction" pairs.*

force that is directly proportional to the product of their masses and inversely proportional to the square of the distance between them.

*Mass* is the actual amount of matter in a substance, whereas *weight* is a measure of the earth's gravitational attraction on a body. In many problems, however, the units of mass and weight are interchangeable.

The *fundamental units of mass* (or frequently called weight) are the *kilogram,* the *gram,* the *pound of weight,* and the *slug* (32 weight-pounds).

The *fundamental units of force* are the *newton,* the *dyne,* and the *pound of force.*

*Work* is force times the distance through which the force acts in the direction it acts. The fundamental units of work are the *joule* (a newton-meter), the *erg* (a dyne-centimeter), and the *foot-pound.*

*Power* is the rate of doing work. The *fundamental units of power* are the *watt* (1 joule per sec), the *kilowatt* (1,000 watts), and the *horsepower* (550 foot-pounds per sec or 33,000 foot-pounds per min).

(For specific definitions of the terms used in the above paragraphs, *see* the DICTIONARY OF TERMS IN PHYSICS, pages 1166-1168).

A *machine* is a device for doing work. The two large classes of simple machines are *levers* and *inclined planes.*

The three *subclasses of levers* are: (a) *simple levers* (1st, 2nd, and 3rd class, depending on the location of the fulcrum), (b) the *wheel and axle,* and (c) the *pulley* (stationary, movable, or the block and tackle).

Neglecting friction, the following formulas may be used:

For *simple levers:*

Force x length of force arm = resistance x length of resistance arm

For the *wheel and axle:*

Force x radius of wheel = resistance x radiux of axle

For any combination of *pulleys:*

Force x distance it moves = resistance x distance it moves

This last formula illustrates the *law of machines,* and may be used for any ideal machine, neglecting friction.

The three *subclasses of inclined planes* are:

(a) *simple inclined plane*
(b) the *screw,* and
(c) the *wedge.*

Neglecting friction, the following formulas may be used:

For the *simple inclined plane:*

Force x length of the plane = resistance x vertical height of plane

For the *jackscrew:*

$$Wp = 2\pi rE$$

where $W$ is the weight (or resistance), $p$ is the pitch of the screw, $r$ is the radius of the circle through which the effort (force) moves, and $E$ is the effort (or force).

There is no practical formula for the wedge, since it is used largely to pry things apart or to hold them together, and friction is one of the chief factors to be considered in problems involving the wedge.

*Friction* is the resistance to motion of surfaces that touch. It is one of the main factors to be considered in all machines. In certain cases it is a great advantage, for example: the efficiency of brakes on a car depends on the friction between the drums and brake linings; and the efficiency of the tires in "holding to the road" depends on the friction (traction) between the tires and the road. In the bearings of a car, however, friction should be reduced to a minimum. This is done by keeping a film of oil or grease between the surfaces of the moving parts. The ratio of the force required to overcome friction to the force pushing the surfaces together is called the *coefficient of friction,* and is expressed by the following formula:

$$\text{Coef. of friction} = \frac{\text{force to overcome friction}}{\text{force pushing surfaces together}}$$

**Hooke's law.** *Elasticity* is the ability of a distorted body to regain its original size and shape. *Stress* is the force that tends to distort a body. *Strain* is the distortion caused by stress. The main types of stress are: *tension* (stretching), *compression, bending, twisting* (torque), and *shear.* If the stress on a body is too great, however, the body will become permanently distorted and will not return to its original size and shape. The smallest stress that will produce a permanent change in a body is called the *elastic limit* of that body. *Hooke's law states that, within the elastic limits of a body, stress is always directly proportional to strain.* That is, twice the amount of stress produces twice the amount of strain.

*Pressure in an unconfined liquid* is directly proportional to the depth (or height) of the liquid times its density. That is:

Pressure = depth x density.

EXAMPLE: Find the pressure at the bottom of a dam 20 ft high if water just reaches the top. (Density of water is 62.4 lbs/ft$^3$.)

SOLUTION: Substituting in above formula:

$$P = 20 \text{ ft} \times 62.4 \text{ lb/ft}^3 = 1248 \text{ lb/ft}^2$$

The *force of any liquid against any surface* is directly proportional to the average pressure against the surface times its area. That is:

Force = average pressure x area.

EXAMPLE: Find the force against a dam that is 20 ft high and 100 ft long, if water just reaches the top.

SOLUTION:

Average pressure = average depth x density.

$$\text{Av. } P = 10 \text{ ft} \times 62.4 \text{ lb/ft}^3 = 624 \text{ lb/ft}^2$$

Force = average pressure x area

$$F = 624 \text{ lb/ft}^2 \times 2000 \text{ ft}^2 = 1{,}248{,}000 \text{ lb}$$

*Pascal's law* (or principle) *states that pressure exerted anywhere on a confined liquid is transmitted undiminished to every portion of the interior of the containing vessel.* This same law applies to gases, and this principle is used in air brakes, hydraulic brakes, and the hydraulic press. The diagram in Fig. 3 illustrates the enormous mechanical advantage of the hydraulic press.

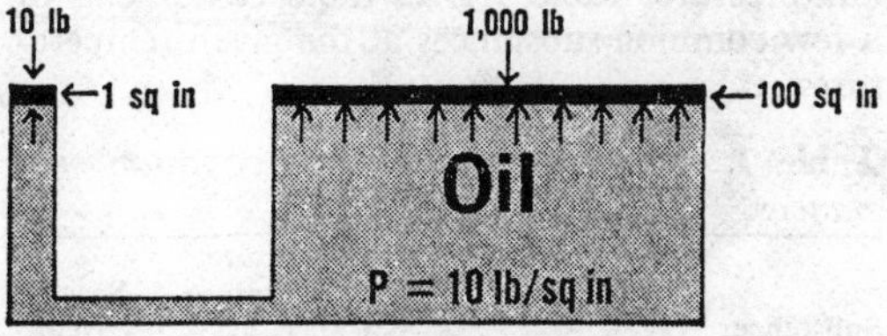


**Fig. 3.** *Pressure on both pistons is the same. Forces on the pistons are directly proportional to their areas.*

*Boyle's law of gases* states that, at constant temperature, the volume of a mass of gas is inversely proportional to the pressure upon it. *See* page 1147 under CHEMISTRY.

*Charles' law of gases* states that, at constant pressure, the volume of a mass of gas is directly proportional to the absolute temperature. *See* page 1147 under CHEMISTRY.

## HEAT

The *modern atomic theory* (also called the *kinetic theory*) states that all matter is composed of tiny particles, called atoms or molecules, in rapid vibration, with relatively large spaces between. Since the study of heat is so closely associated with the movement of the particles that make up matter, it would be well to *see* pages 1143-1144, in the section on CHEMISTRY, for a discussion of the atomic (kinetic) theory of matter.

*Heat* is a form of energy due to the motion of particles (molecules, atoms, ions, electrons, etc.) that make up a body.

*Temperature is a measure of the heat intensity* of a body relative to some fixed point as zero on a thermometer scale. The three thermometer scales most widely used in the United States are the Fahrenheit, the centigrade, and the absolute (Kelvin) scales, *See* pages 1145-1146 under CHEMISTRY for a discussion of these thermometers, and the conversion of temperature from one scale to another.

The *quantity of heat* is measured in *calories* (gram-calories), *Calories* (kilogram-calories), and *British thermal units* (Btu). *See* DICTIONARY OF TERMS IN PHYSICS, pages 1166-1168, for specific definitions of these *heat units.*

*Specific heat* is the *heat capacity* of a substance compared to the heat capacity of water as 1; or the number of calories required to raise 1 g of a substance 1° C; or the number of Btu required to raise 1 lb of a substance 1° F. Since the heat capacity of water is greater than most common substances, the specific heats of practically all common substances are less than 1. Specific heats of solids and liquids vary to some extent with a change in temperature, and specific heats of gases vary with a change in temperature and pressure. Table 1 gives the specific heats of a few common substances at the given temperatures.

**Table 1.** *Specific heats of some common substances.*

| Substance | Temperature or Temperature Range, C | Specific Heat |
|---|---|---|
| SOLIDS | | |
| *Aluminum* | *15-100* | *0.22* |
| *Copper* | *15-100* | *0.093* |
| *Glass* | *20-100* | *0.20* |
| *Ice* | *-3* | *0.50* |
| *Iron or Steel* | *20* | *0.11* |
| *Silver* | *20* | *0.056* |
| LIQUIDS | | |
| *Mercury* | *20* | *0.033* |
| *Water* | *15* | *1.00* |
| GASES | | |
| *Air* | *50* | *0.25* |
| *Steam* | *110* | *0.48* |

**Change of state.** All of the elements, and many of the common compounds, can exist in the *solid, liquid,* or *gaseous state,* depending on the temperature and pressure under which they exist. A change in pressure has a marked effect on the boiling points of liquids; a *decrease* in pressure *lowers* the boiling point of a liquid and an *increase* in pressure *raises* its boiling point. For example, at an altitude of 20,000 ft, the atmospheric pressure is so low that water in an open vessel will boil at 79.6 degrees C, while water in a pressure cooker whose gauge reads 15 lb/in$^2$ (above atmospheric pressure) water boils at 120° C. In a boiler whose gauge reads 100 lb/in$^2$ (above atmospheric pressure) water boils at 170° C, or 338° F. Under an exceedingly high gauge pressure of 3,000 lb/in$^2$, the boiling point of water reaches 369.1° C, or 696.4° F.

*Thermal heat* is heat that changes the temperature of a body. It is absorbed by a body as its temperature rises, and is given off by a body as its temperature drops.

*Latent heat* is the heat required to change the physical state of a substance without a change in temperature. *Heat of fusion* is the latent heat absorbed by a solid changing to a liquid without a change in temperature, and is equal to the latent *heat of solidification* which is the heat given off by the liquid as it solidifies without a change in temperature. *Heat of vaporization* is the latent heat absorbed by a liquid as it changes to a gas without a change in temperature, and is equal to the latent *heat of condensation* which is the heat given off by the gas as it liquefies without a change in temperature. The heat of fusion for ice (or the heat of solidification for water) is 80 cal/g. The heat of vaporization for water (or the heat of condensation for steam) is 540 cal/g. This accounts for the remarkable heating power of steam, since every gram of steam at 100° C that condenses to water at 100° C, gives off 5.4 times as much heat as it would take to raise 1 g of water from 0° C to 100° C.

**Heat transfer.** Heat travels from a region of higher temperature to a region of lower temperature in three ways:

(a) by *conduction,* that is by actual contact, as the steam in contact with a radiator, or an iron rod in a bed of hot coals.
(b) by *convection,* that is by moving currents of a gas or a liquid, as the hot air rising from a steam radiator.
(c) by *radiation,* a method whereby heat travels outward in all directions from any body warmer than its surroundings, such as a hot stove.

Heat radiation takes place more rapidly from rough, dull, and usually dark surfaces and less rapidly from smooth, bright, highly polished, or silvered surfaces.

One of the best heat insulators is the Dewar-flask or "thermos bottle", since it diminishes the transfer of heat by all three methods. See Fig. page 769. The glass and vacuum being poor conductors of heat, reduce heat transfer by conduction. The vacuum also reduces heat transfer by convection, and the silvered surfaces reduce heat transfer by radiation.

## SOUND

In physics, *sound* may be defined as *a series of waves in gases, liquids, or solids produced by some vibrating body. Audible sound* includes those that can be heard by the human ear, and include frequencies from about 16 to 20 per sec to about 20,000 per sec; though an exceptional ear may hear much higher frequencies. *Ultrasonic sound* includes those waves whose frequencies are too high to be heard by the human ear.

Any simple vibrating body such as a tuning fork or a vibrating string produces alternate compressions and rarefactions in air as illustrated in Fig. 4.

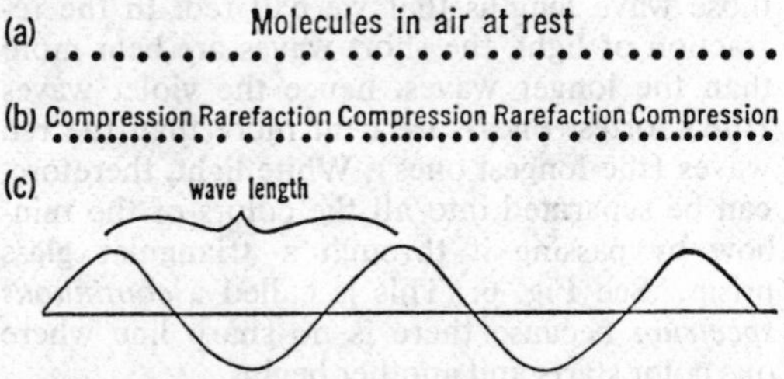


**Fig. 4.** (a) *Relative position of molecules in air at rest.* (b) *Compressions and rarefactions caused by a vibrating body.* (c) *The usual method of showing graphically the compressions and rarefactions in sound waves of a pure single tone. It is a sine wave.*

*Frequency* is the number of sound waves per second in any given tone. *Period* is the time in seconds it takes for any sound wave to pass a given point. *Wave length* is the distance between any two consecutive compressions or the distance between any two consecutive rarefactions.

The *velocity of sound in air* at 0° C is 1,087 ft/sec, and it increases 2 ft/sec for each 1° C rise in temperature. It travels about 4.5 times as fast in water as in air and a little over 15 times as fast in steel as in air.

**Fundamentals and overtones.** Any vibrating body, such as a string, may vibrate as a whole or in segments. The *fundamental* is the lowest tone that any vibrating body can produce when it vibrates as a whole. *Overtones* are the tones produced by a body when it vibrates in segments. *Harmonic overtones* are the overtones whose frequencies are integral multiples of the fundamental. See Fig. 5.

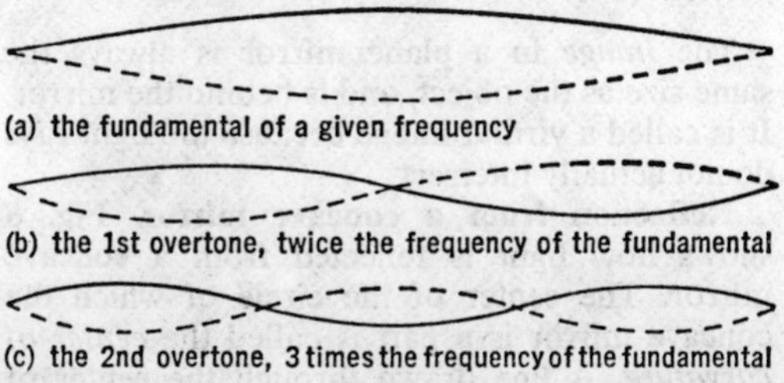


**Fig. 5.** *Vibrating string with its first two overtones.*

**Characteristics of a musical tone.** A string may vibrate as a whole and in segments at the same time, thus producing the fundamental and certain overtones simultaneously, thus giving the characteristic *quality* to the tone. The three characteristics of a musical tone are:

(a) *pitch,* which depends on *frequency*
(b) *loudness* or *intensity,* which depends on *amplitude* (magnitude of vibration)
(c) *quality,* which depends on the number and character of the overtones and their relation to the fundamental

*Superposition* is the ability of gases, liquids, and solids to transmit many different types of sound waves from the same source, or different sources, in the same direction, or in different directions, at the same time.

The *nature of sound waves.* It can be seen from Fig. 4, that the motion of the molecules in sound waves is a "back-and-forth" motion in the same direction that the waves are moving. For this reason, sound waves are said to be *longitudinal waves.* The molecules at the center of a compression or a rarefaction have practically no back-and-forth motion, while the molecules midway between a compression and a rarefaction have a maximum back-and-forth motion.

**Music and noise.** The wave forms of musical tones have a regular, recurring pattern, and are more or less pleasing to the human ear; whereas the wave forms of noise have no regular, recurring pattern, and are usually displeasing to the human ear.

**Reflection of sound.** Whenever sound waves strike an object such as the walls of a room, part of the sound is *transmitted,* part is *absorbed,* and part is *reflected.* A *simple echo* is the reflection of sound waves from a large distant object, such as a mountain, so that the reflected sound is separate and distinct from the original. *Reverberation* is the reflection of sound waves from nearby objects, as the walls and ceiling of a room, so that the reflected sound mingles with and interferes with the original. *Reverberation time* is the time that it takes for a reasonably loud sound in a room to die out, after the original sound ceases. This is a very important factor in the construction of auditoriums and radio studios.

*Diffraction* is the change in direction of sound waves as they bend around an obstacle such as a building.

*Refraction* is the bending of sound waves as they pass from one medium, such as air, into another medium of different density, such as water, at an oblique angle; or as they pass from warm air into cooler air at an oblique angle. On a hot day when the air near the ground is warmer than the upper atmosphere, sound waves tend to curve upward, away from the earth's surface. After the sun goes down on a hot day, and the air near the ground becomes cooler than the upper atmosphere, sound waves tend to curve downward from the warmer, upper layers of air, toward the earth's surface. For this reason, sounds can be heard at a greater distance at night than on a hot day.

*Beats* are caused by the alternate reinforcement and interference of two sound waves of different frequencies. (See definition of *beats*, page 1166.) The number of beats per second is equal to the difference in the frequencies of the two sound waves.

**The Doppler effect.** *See* definition, page 1166.

**The laws of vibrating strings.** There are three important laws that govern the frequencies of vibrating strings.

**First law.** The frequency varies *inversely* as the length of the vibrating string. That is:

$$F_1 : F_2 = L_2 : L_1$$

**Second law.** The frequency varies *directly* as the square root of the tension. That is:

$$F_1 : F_2 = \sqrt{T_1} : \sqrt{T_2}$$

**Third law.** The frequency (or pitch) varies *inversely* as the square root of the weight per unit length of the string. That is:

$$F_1 : F_2 = \sqrt{W_2} : \sqrt{W_1}$$

These three formulas may be combined as follows:

$$\frac{F_1}{F_2} = \frac{L_2 \sqrt{T_1} \sqrt{W_2}}{L_1 \sqrt{T_2} \sqrt{W_1}}$$

## LIGHT

**Nature of light.** In the study of light, there are many phenomena that indicate the "wave theory" of light, and also many phenomena that indicate the "particle theory" of light. Light is usually defined as a form of energy due to electromagnetic radiations (or waves) that vary in wave length from about 0.4 to about 0.7 of a micron. In *ordinary light,* the vibrations are in *every possible direction* at right angles to the direction in which the light waves travel; hence light waves are *transverse waves.*

In *polarized light,* many of the vibrations have been partially absorbed by the polarizing material, so that most of the remaining vibrations are in the *same direction* (or nearly the same direction) at right angles to the direction in which the light travels. The advantage of *polaroid glasses* in reducing glare lies in the fact that polaroid polarizes light in such a manner as to absorb most of the vibrations that cause glare.

The *speed of light* is almost the same in a vacuum, in outer space, and in air, and is approximately 186,000 mi/sec, or $3 \times 10^8$ m/sec. Light would travel around the earth at the equator about 7.5 times per sec; but it takes approximately 8.33 minutes for light to travel from the sun to the earth.

*Refraction of light* is the bending of light rays (waves) as they pass from one medium to another medium of different density, at an oblique angle. *White light* contains all the wave lengths of light in certain definite proportions. Since the color of light depends on its wave lengths, we may say that white light contains all the colors of the rainbow. The color of an object depends on the wave lengths of light it reflects. This means that a white object reflects all colors (or wave lengths), a black object would absorb all wave lengths, and a red object would reflect only those wave lengths that we call red. In the refraction of light, the short waves are bent more than the longer waves, hence the violet waves (the shortest ones) are bent more than the red waves (the longest ones). White light, therefore, can be separated into all the colors of the rainbow by passing it through a triangular glass prism. See Fig. 6. This is called a *continuous spectrum* because there is no sharp line where one color starts and another begins.

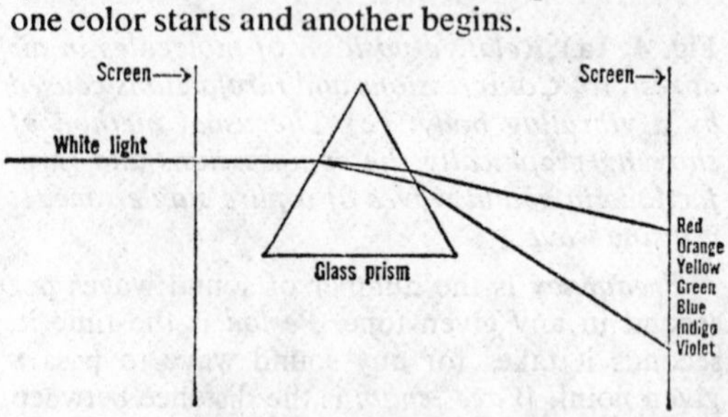


**Fig. 6.** *A continuous spectrum.*

*Reflection from a plane mirror.* When light strikes an object it is either transmitted (as through a transparent substance), or absorbed, or reflected. Fig. 7 shows how light is reflected from a plane mirror.

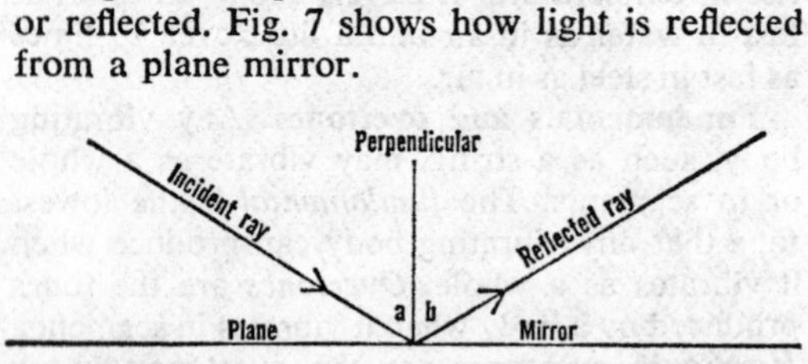


**Fig. 7.** *Reflection from a plane mirror. The angle of incidence* (a) *always equals the angle of reflection* (b).

The *image* in a plane mirror is always the same size as the object, and is behind the mirror. It is called a virtual image because the light rays do not actually intersect.

**Reflection from a concave mirror.** Fig. 8 shows how light is reflected from a concave mirror. The center of the circle of which the concave mirror is a part is called the *center of curvature.* A line drawn through the center of curvature to the center of the mirror is called the *principal axis.* Light rays that are parallel to the principal axis are reflected through a point called the *principal focus* that is midway between the mirror and its center of curvature. Light rays that pass through the center of curvature are reflected back along the same path. The following formula may be used to locate the image in a concave mirror:

$$\frac{1}{Do}+\frac{1}{Di}=\frac{1}{Df}$$

where Do is the distance of the object from the mirror, Di is the distance of the image from the mirror, and Df is the distance of the principal focus from the mirror. This same formula also may be used for convex mirrors and for lenses.

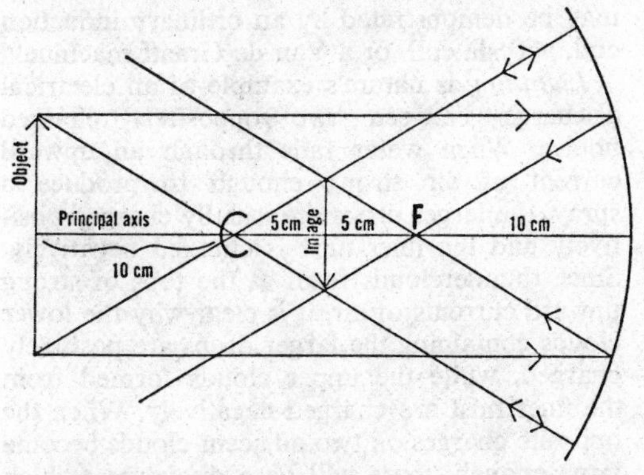


**Fig. 8.** *Reflection from a concave mirror, and location of image. C is the center of curvature and F is the principal focus.*

The following formula may be used for finding the size of the image formed by either mirrors or lenses:

$$\frac{\text{Size of image}}{\text{Size of object}}=\frac{\text{Image-distance}}{\text{Object-distance}}$$

**Types of lenses.** Fig. 9 shows the main types of converging and diverging lenses.

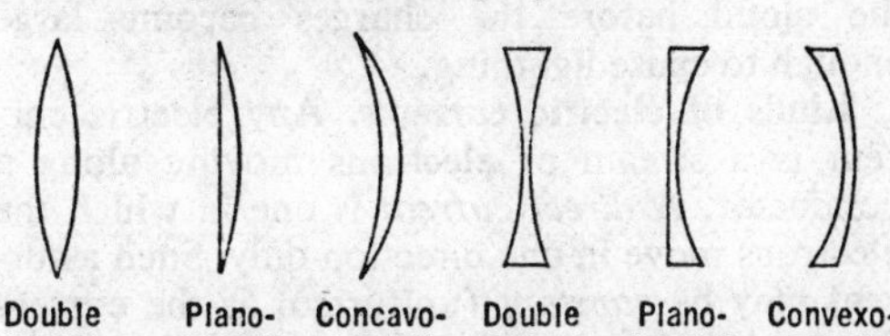


**Fig. 9.** *Types of converging* (convex), *and diverging* (concave) *lenses.*

*Converging lenses* are thicker in the middle than on the edges and bring light that passes through them to a point called the *focus.* The distance from the center of the lens to the focus is called the *focal length* of the lens. See Fig. 10-a.

*Diverging lenses* are thinner in the middle than on the edges and scatter the light that passes through them. See Fig. 10-b.

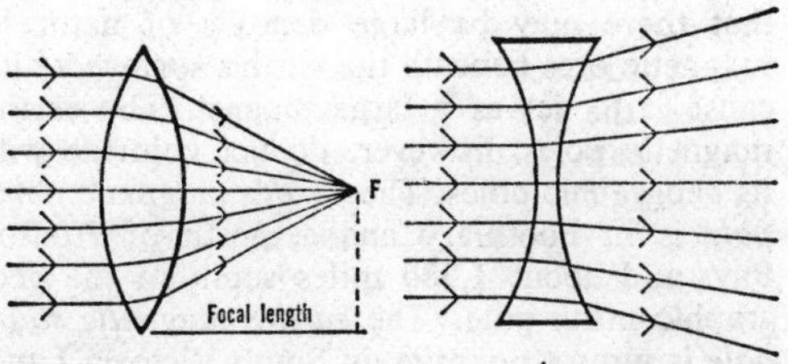


**Fig. 10.** (a) *Showing how a converging lens brings light to a focus.* (b) *Showing how a diverging lens scatters light.*

**Optical instruments.** Single lenses or combinations of lenses are used in many optical instruments, such as: the ordinary magnifying glass, the camera, the motion picture machine, slide projectors, opaque projectors, the compound microscope, telescopes, field glasses, eyeglasses, etc. A detailed discussion of many of these instruments may be found in physics textbooks.

*Concavo-convex lenses* are used to correct *farsightedness;* and *convexo-concave lenses* are used to correct *nearsightedness.*

## MAGNETISM

Almost everyone is familiar with the fact that a magnet will attract objects made of iron, and that an iron object such as a needle, a nail, or a knife blade may be magnetized by stroking it with a magnet.

**Theory of magnetism.** It is thought that any substance, such as iron, that can be magnetized, is composed of atoms or molecules which are tiny magnets. If these atoms or molecules are arranged in a helter-skelter fashion, the material exhibits no external magnetic properties. If, however, a relatively large number of these atoms or molecules are lined up more or less parallel with like ends pointing in the same direction, the substance will become a magnet.

*Magnetic substances* are those that can be magnetized or that are attracted by a magnet. The most common magnetic substances are *iron* (or steel), *cobalt,* and *nickel,* along with some of their compounds (such as magnetic oxide of iron) and some of their alloys. Manganese and chromium are said to be slightly magnetic.

*Magnetic poles* are the points in a magnet where the magnetism seems to be concentrated. The end of a magnetic compass that points in the general direction of north is called the *north-seeking pole* and the end that point in the general direction of south is called the *south-seeking pole.*

The *law of magnets* states that *unlike poles attract each other,* and *like poles repel each other.*

**The earth as a magnet.** The earth itself acts as a huge magnet. The exact cause of the earth's magnetism is not fully known, but one theory is that there may be large deposits of naturally magnetic ores beneath the earth's surface which cause it to act as a large magnet. The earth's magnetic poles, however, do not coincide with its geographic poles. The *earth's magnetic north pole* is in Boothia, Canada, north of Hudson Bay, and about 1,380 miles south of the geographic north pole. The *earth's magnetic south pole* is almost opposite, in South Victoria Land, Antarctica, and about 1,240 miles north of the geographic south pole. For this reason, the north-seeking pole of a compass needle does not always point true north, but points in the direction of the earth's magnetic north pole. The angle between the direction of the north-seeking pole of a compass and true north is called the *angle of declination.* Lines on a map drawn through points that have the same angle of declination are called *isogonic lines.*

**Kinds of magnets.** *Natural magnets* are called *loadstones* (or *lodestones*). *Artificial magnets* may be made in the laboratory. *Permanent magnets* are made by inserting an iron alloy that retains magnetism well in a coil of wire carrying a direct electric current for a short time. They are named according to shape, as: *bar magnets, U-magnets, etc. Temporary magnets* may be made by touching a soft iron bar to a magnet. Since soft iron does not retain magnetism well, it ceases to be a magnet when the contact is broken. *Electromagnets* are temporary magnets, and are made by sending an electric current through a coil of wire surrounding a soft iron core. Electromagnets are most widely used in industry, and are essential parts of many machines and devices, such as: telephone receivers, telegraph sets, lifting magnets, electric bells and buzzers, induction coils, transformers, dynamos, electric motors, dynamic speakers, radio and television transmission and reception, etc.

## ELECTRICITY

*Static electricity* may be defined as *electricity at rest* or *stationary electrical charges.*

The *first law of static electricity* states that whenever two different substances are rubbed together (or even when brought into close contact) one will *lose electrons* and become *positively charged,* while the other will *gain electrons* and *become negatively charged.*

The *second law* states that *unlike* charges *attract* each other, and *like* charges *repel* each other.

If a hard rubber rod is rubbed with a woolen cloth or cat's fur, the cloth (or fur) loses electrons and becomes positively charged, while the rod gains electrons and becomes negatively charged. If this charged rod is touched to the knob of an electroscope, it will give up some of the excess electrons to the electroscope and the charged leaves will separate, showing the repulsion of like charges. *See* illustration of electroscope page 242.

If a glass rod is rubbed with a silk cloth, the rod gives up some of its electrons to the cloth, leaving the rod positively charged. If this charged rod is brought near the knob of a negatively charged electroscope, it will attract the excess electrons to the knob, leaving the leaves neutral and they will come together. This shows that opposite charges attract each other.

When two oppositely charged bodies, carrying very heavy charges, are brought close together, electrons will jump from the negatively charged body to the positively charged body. This is called an *electric discharge.* Such discharges may be demonstrated by an ordinary induction coil, a Tesla coil, or a Van de Graaff machine.

*Lightning* is nature's example of an electrical discharge between two oppositely charged bodies. When water falls through an upward current of air strong enough to produce a spray, the larger drops are usually charged positively and the finer mist is charged negatively. Since thunderclouds form at the tops of strong upward currents of air, it is clear why the lower clouds containing the larger drops are positively charged, while the upper clouds formed from the finer mist are charged negatively. When the opposite charges on two adjacent clouds become large enough, there will be a discharge (which we call lightning) from the negatively charged cloud to the positively charged cloud. When either of these clouds comes near a tall object on the earth (such as a church steeple) an opposite charge is induced in the tall object, and if these charges are large enough, a lightning discharge occurs between the cloud and the object. Since electric discharges occur more easily from sharp objects than from blunt objects, *lightning rods help protect buildings from lightning* by allowing silent discharges between the rods and the cloud before the charges become large enough to cause lightning.

**Kinds of electric currents.** Any electric current is a stream of electrons moving along a conductor. A *direct current* is one in which the electrons move in one direction only. Such a current may be *constant* (uniform), as the current from a battery, or *pulsating,* as the current in a telephone transmitter, or *interrupted,* as the current in the primary of an induction coil.

An *alternating current* is one in which the electrons flow first in one direction and then in the opposite direction. The most ordinary alternating current is a *60-cycle current,* in which the electrons flow in each direction for only 1/120th of a second, making 60 complete cycles per sec. In radio transmission, the carrier wave is an alternating current of very high frequency, usually from about 550 kilocycles per sec to about 1,500 or more kilocycles per sec. These high frequency currents are frequently called *oscillating currents.* Oscillating currents of many million kilocycles per second have been produced.

**Some important electrical terms.** The *coulomb* is the *unit of quantity* in electricity, and is about 6.28 x $10^{18}$ electrons. It also is defined as the quantity of electricity that will deposit 0.001118 g of silver.

The *ampere* is the *unit of electric current,* and is one coulomb per sec. It also is defined as the steady current that will deposit 0.001118 g of silver per sec.

The *ohm* is the *unit of electrical resistance,* and is the resistance offered to the flow of an electric current by a column of mercury that is 106.3 cm long and weighs 14.4521 g, at 0 C. This makes the cross section nearly exactly 1 $mm^2$.

The *volt* is the *unit of electromotive force* (electric pressure), and is defined as the electromotive force required to send a current of one ampere through a resistance of one ohm.

*Electromotive force* (emf) is the force that can send an electric current through a circuit. It is measured in volts.

*Potential difference* is work done per unit charge, and is measured in volts. Two points differ in potential by 1 volt if 1 joule of work is required to move 1 coulomb of charge from one point to the other.

Voltage, electromotive force, and potential difference are all measured in volts, and refer to the same thing, namely, the "push" that moves or tends to move electricity.

*Ohm's law* states that the potential difference between any two points in an electric circuit equals the product of the current and the resistance. That is:

$$E = RI$$

where *E* is *electromotive force in volts, R* is *resistance* in *ohms,* and *I* is *intensity of current* in *amperes.* This is one of the most important laws in electricity, and can be applied to any part of an electric circuit or to the electric circuit as a whole.

**Ammeters and voltmeters.** An *ammeter* measures electric current in amperes, and must always be connected in *series* with the resistance (or resistances) through which the current flows.

A *voltmeter* measures electromotive force in volts, and must always be connected in parallel with the resistance (or resistances) through which the current flows.

Fig. 11 shows the connections and readings of the ammeter and voltmeters in a simple series circuit. The data that immediately follows Fig. 11 shows how Ohm's law applies to this circuit.

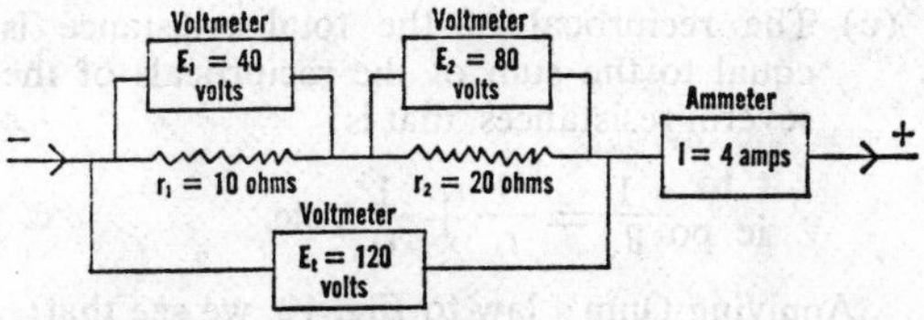


**Fig. 11.** *A simple series circuit.*

In a simple series circuit, as shown in Fig. 11:

(a) The total resistance ($R_t$) is equal to the sum of the several resistances, that is:

$$R_t = r_1 + r_2, \text{ etc.}$$

(b) The current (I) is the same in all parts of the circuit, that is:

$$I = I_t = I_1 = I_2, \text{ etc.}$$

(c) The total voltage ($E_t$) is equal to the sum of the voltages across the several resistances, that is:

$$E_t = E_1 + E_2, \text{ etc.}$$

Applying Ohm's law to Fig. 11, we see that:

(a) $R_t = r_1 + r_2 = 10 \text{ ohms} + 20 \text{ ohms} = 30 \text{ ohms}$

(b) $I_t = \dfrac{E_t}{R_t} = \dfrac{120}{30} = 4 \text{ amps}$

(c) $E_1 = r_1 \times I_1 = 10 \times 4 = 40$ volts, and

$E_2 = r_2 \times I_2 = 20 \times 4 = 80$ volts, and

$E_t = E_1 + E_2 = 40 \text{ volts} + 80 \text{ volts} = 120 \text{ volts}$

Fig. 12 shows the connections and readings of the voltmeter and the ammeters in a simple parallel circuit. The data immediately following Fig. 12 shows how Ohm's law applies to this circuit.

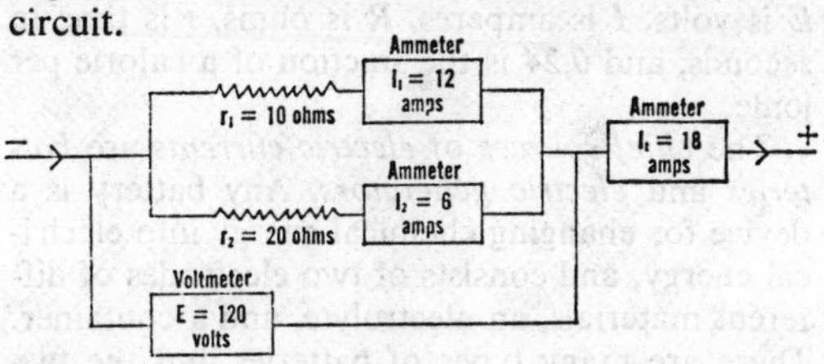


**Fig. 12.** *A Simple parallel circuit.*

In a simple parallel circuit, as shown in Fig. 12:

(a) The voltage (E) is the same for each part of the circuit and for the circuit as a whole, that is:

$$E = E_t = E_1 = E_2, \text{ etc.}$$

(b) In any part of the circuit, the current (I) in that part is equal to the voltage divided by the resistance of the part under consideration, that is:

$$I_t = \frac{E_t}{R_t} \text{ or } I_1 = \frac{E_1}{r_1}, \text{ etc.}$$

Also, the total current equals the sum of the currents in the several resistances, that is:

$$I_t = I_1 + I_2, \text{ etc.}$$

(c) The reciprocal of the total resistance is equal to the sum of the reciprocals of the several resistances, that is:

$$\frac{1}{R_t} = \frac{1}{r_1} + \frac{1}{r_2}, \text{ etc.}$$

Applying Ohm's law to Fig. 12, we see that:

$$\text{(a) } I_1 = \frac{E_1}{r_1} = \frac{120}{10} = 12 \text{ amps, and}$$

$$I_2 = \frac{E_2}{r_2} = \frac{120}{20} = 6 \text{ amps, and}$$

$$I_t = I_1 + I_2 = 12 \text{ amps} + 6 \text{ amps} = 18 \text{ amps}$$

$$\text{(b) } \frac{1}{R_t} = \frac{1}{10} + \frac{1}{20} = \frac{3}{20} \text{ or}$$

$$3R_t = 20 \text{ and } R_t = 6\tfrac{2}{3} \text{ ohms}$$

$$\text{(c) Also: } I_t = \frac{E_t}{R_t} = \frac{120}{6\frac{2}{3}} = 18 \text{ amps}$$

*Electric power* is measured in watts, and may be determined by the following formula:

*Power (in watts)* = *E (in volts) x I (in amperes)*, or $P = EI$.

One *kilowatt* is 1,000 watts. We usually pay for electric power by the *kilowatt hour*, which means 1 kilowatt of power for one hour. One watt for one second (the *watt second*) is also equal to 1 *joule*.

The *heating effect of an electric current* may be found by the formula:

$$H = 0.24\ Pt \quad \text{or} \quad 0.24\ EIt \quad \text{or} \quad 0.24\ I^2Rt,$$

where $H$ is heat in calories, $P$ is power in watts, $E$ is volts, $I$ is amperes, $R$ is ohms, $t$ is time in seconds, and *0.24* is the fraction of a calorie per joule.

The *chief sources of electric currents* are *batteries* and *electric generators.* Any battery is a device for changing chemical energy into electrical energy, and consists of two electrodes of different materials, an electrolyte, and a container. There are many types of batteries, but the two most common are the ordinary *dry cell* and the commercial *lead storage battery.* In this storage battery the negative plates are spongy lead, the positive plates are lead dioxide, and the electrolyte is dilute sulfuric acid. The following chemical equation shows the chemical changes that take place in the discharge and recharge of the lead storage battery:

$$\underset{+\text{ plate}}{PbO_2} + \underset{-\text{ plate}}{Pb} + 2H_2SO_4 \underset{\text{Recharge}}{\overset{\text{Discharge}}{\rightleftharpoons}} 2PbSO_4 + 2H_2O + \text{electrical energy}$$

An *electric generator* is a device for converting mechanical energy into electric energy. Whenever a coil of wire is rotated in a magnetic field, or whenever a magnetic field is rotated around a coil of wire, a current is generated in the coil. This is the principle on which all electric generators work. Small generators that use permanent magnets to produce the magnetic field are called *magnetos,* while the larger generators that use electromagnets to produce the magnetic field are called *dynamos.* The amount of induced emf in any generator depends on three factors, namely: a. the speed of rotation, b. the strength of the magnetic field, and c. the number of turns in the coil.

**Fleming's rule.** The direction of the induced current in a generator may be determined by Fleming's rule which states that if the thumb, forefinger, and center finger of the left hand are extended so as to make right angles with one another, and if the thumb points in the direction of the motion of the wire, and the forefinger points in the direction of the magnetic lines of force, then the center finger will point in the direction of the induced current (the electron flow).

An *electric motor* is a device for changing electric energy to mechanical energy. The physical construction of a motor is practically the same as that of a generator. For this reason, if a dc generator is connected to a battery, it will run as a motor; and if a motor is turned by mechanical means it will generate an emf.

*Lenz's law* states that an induced current has such a direction that its magnetic action tends to resist the motion by which it is produced. This accounts for the fact that it takes so much mechanical energy to turn a generator that is producing a current. It also accounts for the fact that the faster a motor turns, the greater the back emf that resists the flow of current through the motor.

An *induction coil* consists of two adjacent coils, and is a device for changing an interrupted direct current of low voltage in the primary coil to an alternating current of high voltage in the secondary coil. The formula for the induction coil follows:

$$\frac{\text{Turns on primary}}{\text{Turns on secondary}} = \frac{\text{voltage on primary}}{\text{voltage on secondary}} = \frac{\text{current on secondary}}{\text{current on primary}}$$

A *transformer* is a device for changing the voltage (and current) of an alternating current. A simple transformer consists of an iron ring with turns of the primary coil on one side of the ring and turns of the secondary coil on the other side. The formula for a transformer is the same as that for the induction coil given in the preceding paragraph. A *step-up transformer* has more turns on the secondary than on the primary and *raises* the voltage. A *step-down transformer* has fewer turns on the secondary than on the primary, and lowers the voltage.

**Faraday's laws of electrolysis.** *Electrolysis* is the decomposition of a compound by the use of an electric current. Faraday's laws of electrolysis may be summarized in one statement, namely: In electrolysis one faraday of charge (96,500 coulombs) is required to deposit or liberate one gram-equivalent weight of any substance. The *gram-equivalent weight* of any ion is its formula weight in grams divided by the number of charges on the ion. It is also called a *hydrogen equivalent,* which is defined under DEFINITIONS OF CHEMICAL TERMS, page 1152.

**Relationship of magnetism to electricity.** If an electric current is sent through a wire or coil, a magnetic field is set up around the wire or coil; whereas if magnetic lines of force are cut by a wire or coil, a current is set up in the wire or coil. This shows a very close relationship between magnetism and electricity.

**Thumb rule for a straight wire carrying a current.** If one grasps the wire with the left hand with the thumb pointing in the direction of the electron flow, the fingers will point in the direction of the magnetic field.

**Thumb rule for a coil carrying a current.** If one grasps the coil with the left hand so that the fingers curl in the direction of the electron flow, then the thumb will point toward the north-seeking pole of the coil.

## MODERN PHYSICS

*Modern physics* rightfully includes recently acquired knowledge and its applications in all fields of physics. More specifically, however, it is usually considered to be concerned with such topics as the following: atomic structure, subatomic particles, electromagnetic radiations, electronics, rockets and space flights, missiles and antimissiles, orbiting and escape velocities, radioactivity, plasma physics, nuclear energy, etc. Entire books could be written on each of these topics, so that only a few can be mentioned very briefly in the limited space of this article.

The *atomic theory, atomic structure,* and *isotopes* have been briefly discussed in the article on CHEMISTRY. *See* pages 1143-1144.

*Subatomic particles* include such particles as: protons, electrons, neutrons, positrons, nutrinoes, mesons, and many others.

*Electromagnetic radiations* are usually considered to be *waves* produced by *vibrating photons,* although the secondary cosmic rays probably are mainly high speed protons together with some other high speed particles. For convenience, electromagnetic radiations are usually classified into seven types as shown in Table 2, which gives the approximate wave length (or wave length range) for each type in Angstroms. For definition of each type, *see* DICTIONARY OF TERMS IN PHYSICS, pages 1166-1168.

**Table 2.** *Wave lengths of various radiations*

| Type of Radiation | Wave Length in Angstroms |
|---|---|
| Cosmic Rays | 0.0005 |
| Gamma Rays | 0.005-1.40 |
| X-rays | 0.1-100 |
| Ultraviolet, below | 4000 |
| Visible Spectrum (light) | 4000-7000 |
| Infrared (heat), above | 7000 |
| Hertzian Waves, above | $2.20 \times 10^6$ |

*Electronics* is that branch of physics that deals with electronic action in vacuums and gases; and with the use of vacuum tubes, photoelectric cells, etc.

*Radioactivity* is the spontaneous decomposition of an element by the emission of certain radiations from the nuclei of its atoms. It involves *transmutation,* which is the changing of one element into another. *See* the article on CHEMISTRY, page 1150.

*Plasma physics* is a relatively new field and is concerned mainly with the behavior of highly ionized gases.

*Nuclear physics* also is a relatively new field and is one of the most important branches of physics. It is concerned chiefly with the composition of atomic nuclei and the changes that they may undergo. It also involves the study of subatomic particles, radioactivity, transmutation, and the production, control, and application of nuclear (atomic) energy by both fission and fusion. It is, therefore, closely related to that phase of chemistry that deals with these same topics. *See* the article on CHEMISTRY, page 1150.

# DICTIONARY OF TERMS IN PHYSICS

## A

**absolute temperature:** temperature measured from a minus 273 degrees centigrade as zero. Centigrade readings can be changed to absolute temperature by adding 273 to the centigrade readings.

**absolute zero:** the zero point on the absolute temperature scale. At this temperature, theoretically, all molecular motion ceases. It is supposed to be the lowest possible temperature.

**acceleration:** change of velocity per unit of time. An increase in velocity is positive acceleration. A decrease in velocity is negative acceleration or deceleration.

**alpha particle:** a positively charged helium nucleus expelled from radioactive substances.

**alternating current:** an electric current that flows first in one direction and then in the opposite direction.

**ammeter:** an instrument for measuring the intensity of an electric current in amperes.

**ampere:** the steady electric current that will deposit 0.001118 gram of silver in one second.

**amplitude:** the range of a fluctuating quantity from the average to the extreme.

**angle of declination:** the angle between the direction of true north and the direction in which the north-seeking pole of a magnetic compass points.

**angle of incidence:** the angle between a ray of light that strikes a smooth object obliquely and the perpendicular to the object at that point.

**angle of reflection:** the angle between a ray of light that is reflected from a smooth object obliquely and the perpendicular to the object at that point.

**Angstrom:** one ten-thousandth of a micron.

**anode:** the positive pole of an electric system.

## B

**back electromotive force:** the induced electromotive force in an electric motor that tends to oppose the change that causes it.

**bar:** 1,000,000 dynes/cm$^2$. A *millibar* is 1,000 dynes/cm$^2$. *One atmosphere* is the average air pressure at sea level and equals 1013 millibars.

**barometer:** an instrument for measuring the pressure exerted by the atmosphere.

**beats:** a variation in sound intensity caused by the alternate reinforcement and interference of sound waves of different frequencies.

**bel:** the ratio of two sound intensities in which the ratio is 10:1. *See* DECIBEL.

**beta particle:** an electron given off from the nucleus of a radioactive substance.

**betatron:** a machine that uses transformer action to give high energy and high velocity to a stream of electrons.

**British thermal unit (Btu):** the amount of heat required to raise one pound of water one degree Fahrenheit.

## C

**calorie** (gram-calorie or cal): the amount of heat required to raise one gram of water one degree centigrade.

**Calorie** (kilo-gram calorie or Cal): the amount of heat required to raise one kilogram of water one degree centigrade. One Calorie equals 1,000 calories.

**candle power:** originally, the light intensity of a British standard candle, a sperm candle made according to certain specifications.

**cathode:** the negative pole of an electric system.

**cathode rays:** streams of electrons shot off from the surface of the cathode at very high velocity in a highly evacuated tube.

**cell, electric:** an apparatus or device for the production of a direct electric current and whose essential parts are two electrodes of different materials, an electrolyte, and a suitable container.

**center of gravity:** the point at which all the weight of a body may be considered to act; the point around which a freely rotating body will rotate.

**centigrade scale:** the thermometer scale on which the freezing point of pure water is 0 and the boiling point is 100, at standard pressure.

**centrifugal force:** the force that tends to make a rotating body fly outward from the center along a tangent.

**centripetal force:** the force necessary to prevent any body moving in a curved path from flying out from the center along a tangent.

**chain reaction:** a reaction as in the fission or fusion of atoms that is self-perpetuating, and under certain conditions will produce a violent explosion as in the atom bomb or the hydrogen bomb.

**coefficient of friction:** the force required to overcome friction between two bodies divided by the force pushing the bodies together.

**coefficient of linear expansion:** numerically equal to the expansion per unit length for one degree rise in temperature.

**condenser, electric:** an instrument for holding or storing an electric charge; also called a *capacitor*.

**conduction of heat:** the method by which heat travels from one body to another by actual contact, or from one part of a body to another part by the contact of atoms and molecules.

**convection:** moving currents in gases or liquids; a method by which heat travels in gases or liquids by moving currents.

**coulomb:** the unit of quantity in electricity (about 6.28 x $10^{18}$ electrons).

**critical mass:** the mass above which the speed of a chain reaction in certain substances will become explosive.

**cyclotron:** a machine that uses a magnetic field to bend the path of a stream of protons ($H^+$ ions) and thereby increasing their energy and speed.

## D

**decibel:** one-tenth of a bel; usually taken as the unit of sound intensity. One decibel of sound intensity is approximately the faintest sound that the human ear can hear. It also is the smallest difference in sound intensities that the human ear can discern.

**density:** weight per unit volume, as the g/cm$^3$ of a solid, the g/ml of a liquid, or the g/l of a gas.

**dew point:** the temperature at which the water vapor in the air begins to condense, that is, saturates it.

**diffusion:** the mixing of gases, liquids, or solutions, or the dissolving of a solid in a liquid, due to molecular motion only.

**direct current:** an electric current in which the electrons flow in one direction only.

**Doppler effect:** the apparent change in the frequency of a wave due to the relative motion of the source and the observer. A change in pitch is easily observed with sound waves.

**dynamo:** an electric generator that uses electromagnets to produce the magnetic field.

**dyne:** a unit of force that will give an acceleration of 1 cm per sec per sec to a mass of 1 gram.

## E

**efficiency:** the ratio of the output of any machine to the input.

**elasticity:** the property of a distorted body that enables it to recover its original size and shape.

**electric current:** a stream of electrons moving along a conductor.

**electrochemical equivalent:** the mass of an ion deposited by one coulomb of electric current; the mass of an ion deposited in one second by a current of one ampere.

**electrode:** the plate or terminal of an electric system.

**electromagnet:** a soft iron core that becomes temporarily magnetized when an electric current flows through a coil surrounding it.

**electromotive force (emf):** the force that can alter the motion of electricity. It is usually measured in volts.

**electron:** the unit of negative electricity.

**energy:** the ability to do work.

**equilibrant:** a force that can balance two or more other forces.

**equilibrium, physical:** the condition of a body whose velocity is constant in magnitude and direction (including a velocity of zero). A body at rest is in *static equilibrium*. A body in uniform motion in a straight line is in *dynamic equilibrium*.

### F

**Fahrenheit scale:** the common thermometer scale on which pure water freezes at 32 degrees and boils at 212, at standard pressure

**fission, nuclear:** the splitting of the nuclei of large atoms to form smaller ones.

**foot-candle:** the intensity of light at a distance of one foot from a standard candle.

**freezing point:** the temperature at which a liquid changes to a solid.

**friction:** the resistance to motion of surfaces that touch.

**fundamental:** the lowest tone that any vibrating body can produce when it vibrates as a whole.

**fusion, atomic:** the combining of small atoms to form larger atoms of another element, as the combining of 4 hydrogen atoms to form one helium atom.

### G

**galvanometer:** an instrument for detecting and determining the direction of an electric current.

**gamma rays:** electromagnetic radiations given off by radioactive substances; similar to x-rays, but with shorter wave lengths than most x-rays.

**Geiger counter:** an instrument for detecting and counting ionizing particles.

**generator, electric:** a machine used to convert mechanical energy to electrical energy.

**gram:** the weight of one cubic centimeter of water at its greatest density, that is, 4 degrees C.

**gravitation:** the force by which every mass or particle of matter attracts and is attracted by every other mass or particle of matter.

### H

**harmonics:** in music, the overtones whose frequencies are exact integral multiples of the frequency of the fundamental.

**heat:** a form of energy due to the motion of particles (molecules, atoms, ions, and electrons) that make up a body. Also the infrared electromagnetic waves whose wave lengths are just longer than those of red light.

**heat, latent:** heat that changes the physical state of a body without a change in temperature; heat of fusion and heat of vaporization.

**heat of fusion:** heat required to change a solid to a liquid without a change in temperature.

**heat of vaporization:** heat required to change a liquid to a gas without a change in temperature.

**heat, specific:** the calories required to raise 1 g of a substance 1 degree C, or the Btu required to raise one pound of a substance 1 degree F.

**heat, thermal:** heat that changes the temperature of a substance.

**Hertzian waves:** electromagnetic waves longer than the infrared waves and include those waves used in radio, radar, and television.

**horsepower:** a measure of power, or the rate of doing work, and equivalent to 550 foot-pounds per second or 33,000 foot-pounds per minute.

**humidity:** the actual amount of moisture in the air.

**humidity, relative:** the per cent saturation of air with water vapor.

**hydrometer:** an instrument for determining the specific gravity of liquids.

### I

**impedance:** the apparent resistance in an alternating electrical circuit.

**index of refraction:** in optics, the ratio of the velocity of light in a vacuum (or, commonly, in air) to that in some other substance such as glass.

**induction coil:** an apparatus for changing a varying or interrupted direct current of low voltage to an alternating current of high voltage.

**inertia:** the tendency of an object at rest to remain at rest, or of a moving object to continue a uniform motion in a straight line, unless acted on by some outside force.

**infrared rays:** same as heat waves. *See* HEAT.

**inharmonics:** in music, those overtones whose frequencies are not integral multiples of the fundamental frequency.

**input:** the power or energy or work put into a machine.

**insulation:** any material that is a nonconductor of heat, sound, or electricity.

**isobar:** a line on a map drawn through regions of equal barometric pressure.

**isogonic lines:** lines on a map drawn through regions of equal angles of declination.

**isotherm:** a line on a map drawn through points of equal temperature.

### J

**joule:** one joule equals a force of 1 newton acting through a distance of 1 meter. It also equals 10,000,000 ergs.

### K

**kilogram:** 1,000 grams.

**kilowatt:** a unit of electric power equal to 1,000 watts. *See* WATT.

**kilowatt hour:** is one kilowatt for one hour.

**kinetic energy:** energy that is due to motion.

**kinetic theory:** the theory that all matter is composed of moving atoms or molecules.

### L

**laser:** a device that amplifies light waves and concentrates them into a very narrow and intense beam; also called an optical maser.

**lens, concave** or **diverging:** a lens that is thinner in the middle than on the edges and that causes any light passing through it to diverge.

**lens, convex** or **converging:** a lens that is thicker in the middle than on the edges and that causes any light passing through it to converge to a point called the *principal focus.*

**lever:** a rigid bar free to rotate around a fixed point called the *fulcrum.*

**light:** a form of energy due to electromagnetic waves that vary in wave length from about 0.4 to 0.7 of a micron, and that are visible to the human eye.

**light polarized:** light that exhibits different properties in different directions at right angles to the line of propagation.

**liter:** one cubic decimeter or 1,000 cubic centimeters. The unit of volume in the metric system, and equal to 1.06 liquid quarts.

**loadstone** or **lodestone:** a natural magnet; a magnetic variety of magnetite or magnetic oxide of iron.

**longitudinal waves:** waves in which the vibrating particles move in the same direction as that in which the waves move. *Example:* sound waves.

**lumen:** the amount of light that would fall on one square foot of curved surface, all points of which are exactly one foot from a standard candle.

### M

**machine:** a device for doing work.

**magnetic poles:** the points in a magnet around which the magnetism seems to be concentrated.

**magnetism:** the science that treats of magnetic phenomena; the property of a loadstone that causes it to attract iron and some other similar substances; the property of substances such as iron that enable them to be magnetized; the force with which a magnet will attract substances such as iron.

**mass:** the actual amount of matter in a substance, independent of gravity.

**mechanical advantage, actual:** the ratio of the force that performs useful work in a machine to the force that is applied to the machine.

**mechanical advantage, theoretical:** the ratio of the distance that the applied force moves to the distance that the resisting force moves.

**meter:** approximately one ten-millionth of the distance from the equator to either pole. The distance between two groove marks on a platinum-iridium bar in the International Bureau of Weights and Measures near Paris.

**micron:** one-millionth of a meter or one-thousandth of a millimeter.

**mil:** one-thousandth of an inch. A unit used in measuring diameters of wires.

**mil, circular:** the area of a circle that is 1 mil in diameter.

**mil foot of wire:** a wire that is 1 foot long and 1 circular mil in cross section.

**millimeter:** one-thousandth of a meter.

**moment of force:** a measure of the tendency to produce rotation about a point or axis. The product of a force and its perpendicular distance from its line of action to the point of rotation.

**momentum:** the quantity of motion of an object, equal to the product of its mass and its linear velocity.

N

**neutron:** a very small unit of matter, having no electric charge, and having a mass equal to the hydrogen atom.
**newton:** a unit of force that will give a mass of 1 kilogram an acceleration of 1 meter per second per second.
**nuclear reactor:** an apparatus in which nuclear fission can be maintained as a self-supporting, controlled chain reaction. Sometimes called an *atomic pile.*

O

**octave:** in music, the eighth tone above or below a given tone in the diatonic scale.
**ohm:** the resistance offered to an electric current by a column of mercury that is 106.300 cm long and 1 $mm^2$ in cross section at 0 degrees C.
**oscilloscope:** a machine that visually records an electrical wave on a fluorescent screen.
**output:** the total amount of useful work performed by any machine.
**overtones:** the tones produced by a vibrating body when it vibrates in segments.

P

**photoelectric cell:** a small vacuum tube coated with or containing a chemical that emits electrons when exposed to light, and may be used to control the flow of current in an electric circuit.
**physics:** that science that treats of matter and energy as they are used in the world's work.
**pitch:** in music, the highness or lowness of a musical tone, and is determined by the frequency of the tone.
**positive rays:** the positively charged atoms or molecules (ions) in a cathode ray tube that flow from the anode to the cathode. Also called *canal rays.*
**positron:** a tiny particle having the mass of an electron and a positive charge equal in magnitude to the negative charge of an electron.
**pound:** as a unit of force, it is the force that will give an acceleration of 1 foot per second per second to a weight of 1 slug. One slug is equal to 32 pounds of weight. As a unit of weight, one pound (avoirdupois) = 7,000 grains.
**power:** the rate of doing work. *For example,* 550 foot-pounds of work per second is one horsepower.
**pressure:** weight or force per unit area.
**proton:** the ionized nucleus of a hydrogen atom. A tiny particle of matter with a unit positive charge and the mass of 1 atomic weight unit.

Q

**quality:** in music, that characteristic of a musical tone that is determined by the number and character of the overtones and their relation to the fundamental.

R

**radioactivity:** the spontaneous emission of alpha, beta, or gamma rays by certain elements.
**radio waves:** *See* HERTZIAN WAVES.
**rectifier:** a device for converting alternating current to direct current.
**refraction:** the bending of light waves, sound waves, etc., as they pass obliquely from one medium to another of different density.
**resultant:** a single force that would produce the same result as two or more other forces.
**reverberation:** the reflection of sound waves from nearby objects, such as the walls of a room, so that the reflected sound interferes with the original.
**reverberation time:** the time in seconds that a reasonably loud sound can be heard in a room after the source ceases.
**rheostat:** a resistor for regulating an electric current by means of variable resistances.

S

**slug:** a unit of weight in the English system and equal to 32 pounds of weight.
**sound:** physiologically, the sensation produced on the brain caused by certain waves produced by vibrating bodies coming in contact with the hearing mechanism. In physics, sound is considered as the waves produced by vibrating bodies. *See* SOUND WAVES.
**sound waves:** the audible waves produced by vibrating bodies. The frequencies that can be heard by the average human ear are from about 16 or 20 per second to about 20,000 per second.
**specific gravity:** the density of a substance compared to the density of some other substance as a standard. Water is the standard for solids and liquids, and air is the standard for gases.
**standard pressure:** 760 mm of mercury, considered as the average barometric pressure at sea level.
**standard temperature:** 0 degrees C, or 273 degrees absolute.
**strain:** the distortion or deformation of a body produced by a force called stress.
**stratosphere:** that part of the atmosphere which extends from about 6 or 7 miles above sea level to about 64 miles above sea level and in which the temperature is almost constant and clouds do not form.
**stress:** a force that tends to distort or deform a body in size or shape.
**surface tension:** the tendency of the surface of liquids to contract to the smallest possible area.
**sympathetic vibration:** the vibration of a body caused by the vibration of a second nearby body with the same frequency.

T

**temperature:** the intensity of heat in a body as measured by a thermometer.
**thermocouple:** a union of two conductors (wires or bars) joined at their extremities which produces an electric current when heated. Also called a *thermoelectric couple* or a *thermoelectric pair.*
**thermostat:** an instrument for automatically regulating and controlling temperature.
**transformer:** an apparatus for changing the voltage of an alternating current. A *step-up transformer* raises the voltage and a *step-down transformer* lowers the voltage.
**transverse waves:** waves in which the vibrating particles (or vibrations) are at right angles to the direction in which the waves move. *Example:* water waves and light waves.
**transmutation:** the changing of one element into another.
**troposphere:** the part of the atmosphere that extends from the earth's surface to about 6 or 7 miles above sea level and in which clouds form and the temperature varies widely.
**turbine:** an engine driven by the pressure of water, steam, or gases against the curved vanes of a wheel.

U

**ultraviolet rays:** electromagnetic radiations whose wave lengths fall between those of x-rays and violet light.

V

**vector:** (*a*) a quantity having both direction and magnitude; (*b*) an arrow, drawn to scale, that indicates the direction and magnitude of the quantity.
**velocity:** the rate of motion per unit of time.
**volt:** the electromotive force required to send one ampere of current through one ohm resistance.
**voltmeter:** an instrument for measuring electromotive force, or a difference in electrical potential, in volts.

W

**watt:** a unit of electric power, equal to a current of one ampere under a pressure of one volt. Watts = amperes x volts.
**wave length:** the distance between two adjacent wave crests or between two adjacent wave troughs.
**weight:** a measure of the earth's gravitational force upon any body.
**work:** equals force times the distance through which the force acts in the direction that the force acts.

X

**x-rays:** electromagnetic radiations whose wave lengths are longer than most gamma rays and shorter than the ultraviolet rays.

# The Home

## *Foods*

**THE BASIC FOUR FOOD GROUPS**

The eating of a well balanced diet is one key to a healthy, vital body. This task is simple when the Basic Four Food Groups are used as a guide.

**Group I — Enriched or Whole Grain Bread, Flour, Cereals**

Every day, choose *four* servings from the following grain foods:

| | |
|---|---|
| All Enriched Breads | Brown Rice or Converted Rice |
| Whole Wheat Bread | Corn Meal, whole grain or enriched |
| Dark Rye Bread | Macaroni, Noodles, Spaghetti, enriched |
| Rolled Oat Cereal | |
| Whole Wheat Cereal | |
| Other Cereals, whole grain or enriched | |

LALAH GEE, *Home Service Director, Nashville Gas Company.*

**Group II — Meats, Eggs, Dry Beans**

Each day select *two* or *more* servings of meat or other protein-rich foods. Serve at least *one* of these every day:

| | | |
|---|---|---|
| Beef | Veal | Poultry |
| Lamb | Variety Meats | Fish |
| Mutton | Game | Luncheon Meats |

*Other protein-rich food to include:*

| | | |
|---|---|---|
| Eggs | Cheese | Soy Beans |
| Lentils | Peanut Butter | Soya Flour and Grits |
| Nuts | Dried Beans or Peas | |
| Peanuts | | |

**Group III — Milk, Ice Cream, Cheese**

*Daily milk needs:*

| | |
|---|---|
| Adults | 2 or more cups |
| Children | 3 to 4 cups |
| Teen Agers | 1 quart or more |
| Pregnant Women | 1 quart or more |
| Nursing Mothers | 1½ quarts or more |

**Group IV — Vegetables and Fruits**

*Serve at least* four *from this group:*

| | |
|---|---|
| Broccoli | Squash |
| Cabbage (raw) | Spinach |
| Salad Greens | Sweet Potatoes |
| Citrus Fruits | Other greens, including Turnip Greens, Mustard Greens |
| Peppers | |
| Strawberries | |
| Tomatoes | Other Vegetables and Fruits |
| Carrots | |

## TABLE OF MEASUREMENTS

| | |
|---|---|
| 3 teaspoons | 1 tablespoon |
| 4 tablespoons | ¼ cup |
| 8 tablespoons | ½ cup |
| 16 tablespoons | 1 cup |
| 1 cup | 8 fluid ounces |
| 2 cups | 1 pint |
| 4 cups | 1 quart |
| 4 quarts | 1 gallon |
| 8 quarts | 1 peck (dry) |
| 16 ounces | 1 pound |

## SUBSTITUTION OF INGREDIENTS

**1 ounce chocolate** — 3 tablespoons cocoa plus 1 tablespoon fat

**1 cup buttermilk** — 1 tablespoon vinegar or lemon juice plus enough sweet milk to make 1 cup (let stand 5 minutes)

**1 cup milk** — ½ cup evaporated milk plus ½ cup water

**1 tablespoon flour** — ½ tablespoon cornstarch, potato starch, or arrowroot starch

**1 cup cake flour, sifted** — 1 cup all-purpose flour minus 2 tablespoons

**1 cup butter** — 1 cup margarine, ⅞ to 1 cup hydrogenated fat plus ½ teaspeen salt ⅞ cup lard plus ½ teaspoon salt

## CONTENTS OF CANS

| *Can Size* | *Average Contents* |
|---|---|
| 8 ounce | 1 cup |
| Picnic | 1¼ cups |
| Number 300 | 1¾ cups |
| Number 1, tall | 2 cups |
| Number 303 | 2 cups |
| Number 2 | 2½ cups |
| Number 2½ | 3½ cups |
| Number 3 | 4 cups |
| Number 10 | 12 to 13 cups |

## SMART FOOD BUYING

### Selection and Preparation of Meat

Americans are great meat eaters. The average family in this country spends about a third of every food dollar for meat. A smart shopper has several guides to follow when meat shopping. Two important quality guides are:

*Federal Inspection Mark and Label* — The Federal Government inspects all meat which is marketed across State lines. This accounts for over 80 percent of all meat sold in the United States. Meat so inspected and passed carries a stamp saying it has passed the U.S. Department of Agriculture inspection. This stamp tells consumers that the meat came from a healthy animal, that it was processed under sanitary conditions, and that it is honestly labeled. This is *not* an indication of tenderness or flavor.

*Grade Stamp or Packer's Brand* — Unlike the Federal Inspection the U.S.D.A. grade stamp is not required. This grading is paid for by the packer. Some meat packers use brands instead of grades to represent the quality levels of their products. Beef, lamb, mutton, veal, and calf are federally graded and are in most markets. Pork is not usually graded. Beef is the meat most often found with a U.S.D.A. grade stamp. Beef grades are:

*U.S. Prime* — Excellent quality and flavor, may be found in some retail markets, but most of it goes to restaurants.

*U.S. Choice* — Very acceptable quality. This grade is most popular and commonly found in retail markets.

*U.S. Good* — Relatively tender beef with a high ratio of lean to fat.

*U.S. Standard and Commercial* — Little is found in retail markets. Most beef of these grades is acceptable in beef dishes requiring long simmering.

*U.S. Utility, Cutter, and Canner*—Used mostly in processed meat products.

### Meat Cookery

There are six basic methods of meat cookery. The method selected for any one cut depends on the tenderness of the meat, its size and thickness, and cooking facilities.

*Roasting* — This method of cooking is a dry heat method of meat cookery. No water is added and the meat is not covered. Therefore only tender cuts of beef, veal, pork and lamb are used. Some meats suitable for roasting are; beef standing rib, beef sirloin tip, rib eye of beef, veal rolled shoulder, beef rolled rump, veal rib roast, pork Boston butt, pork loin, lamb rolled shoulder, leg of lamb, smoked ham, pork blade loin and lamb rib roast.

*Broiling* — Like roasting this is a dry heat method and only tender cuts of meat are used. Broiling is cooking over or under direct heat for a relatively short period of time. Meats suitable for broiling are; beef steaks, lamb chops, sliced ham, bacon and ground beef or lamb. Steaks and chops should be at least ½-inch thick. Fresh pork and veal steaks or chops are not broiled but pork chops may be. Care should be taken in broiling pork chops to insure that the meat is completely done.

*Panbroiling* — The same tender cuts suitable for broiling when cut 1-inch or less thick may also be panbroiled. A griddle or skillet is used and no fat allowed to accumulate.

*Panfrying* — This differs from the above method because a small amount of fat is added or allowed to accumulate. Thin pieces of tender meat may be fried. Some of these are; beef cube steaks, sausage patties, veal patties, pork tenderloin, pork steak, veal steak and lamb arm and blade chops.

*Deep-Fat Frying* — Meat is cooked floating in hot fat. This method is used for croquettes, sweetbreads and liver. Meat is usually coated with crumbs or batter.

*Cooking in Liquid* — Less tender cuts are prepared by this method. Some of the cuts of meat especially suitable for cooking by this method are; beef brisket, stewing cubes of meat, spareribs, beef heel of round, veal fore shank, pork hocks and pig's feet.

**Selection and Preparation of Poultry**

Most poultry is marketed ready to cook and is sold either chilled or frozen. The class name on poultry suggests the cooking method and help in the right choice for the use intended.

*Chickens* — marked broiler, fryer or frying are good for either broiling or frying and the largest birds of this class are also roasted. Roasting chickens and capons are young birds that have grown to larger size, with full flavor and tender thick meat. Stewing chicken or hens are older, and are good for stewed chicken, casseroles and salads.

*Turkeys* — marked fryer or roaster weigh 4 to 5 pounds and are suitable for frying or broiling as well as roasting. Other turkeys labeled young hen, young tom, or young turkey weigh from 6 to 24 pounds and are roasted. If the word young or yearling is not used on the label the bird may be assumed to be old, and suitable for stewing. Boneless turkey roasts and boneless turkey rolls are popular convenience items.

*Ducks and Geese* — are marketed young. Ducks are usually found in markets frozen and marketed as duckling. Geese generally weigh 6 to 12 pounds.

**Fish and Shellfish**

Look for freshness in the fish. If the fish is frozen be sure it is frozen solid, has little or no odor and no discoloration. Wrapping should be moisture-proof. Keep fish frozen until ready to use. To insure freshness in buying fresh fish observe the following points. *Eyes:* bright, clear, full and bulging. *Gills:* reddish-pink, free from slime or odor. *Scales:* adhering tightly to skin. *Flesh:* firm and elastic. *Odor:* fresh, free from objectionable odors.

Fresh fish market forms are — *Whole:* The natural state of the fish. About 45 percent of a fish is edible when sold whole. *Drawn:* Only the entrails are removed. Almost half of this form is edible. *Dressed:* Scales and entrails have been removed. One pound of dressed fish serves two. *Steaks:* These are slices cut crosswise and ready to cook. A fish steak has a cross-section of the backbone included. One pound serves two.

*Fillets* — The entire side section cut away from the backbone is called a fillet. ¾ to 1 pound serves two.

All fresh whole shellfish except shrimp should be alive when purchased.

**Buying, Storing and Using Eggs**

Remember in buying eggs that quality and size are not related in any way. The three sizes which appear most often in retail stores are — *Large:* most common size and fine for single serving. *Medium:* fine size for general use. *Small:* fine for scrambling and for children's fried or poached egg. These U.S. Department of Agriculture grades indicate quality — *Grade AA:* Thick, high white. Firm, high yolk. Best to fry, poach, or cook in the shell. *Grade A:* Less thick, high white. Firm, high yolk. Good to fry, poach, shell-cook. *Grade B:* Wide spread white. Rather flat, enlarged yolk. Fine for scrambling, general cooking. *Grade C:* Thin, watery white. Flat, easily broken yolk. Good for scrambling, general cooking.

Keep eggs cold and store lightly covered. Shell color does not indicate quality. Egg whites beat better at room temperature. Eggs separate better when cold.

**Vegetables and Fruits**

A variety of vegetables and fruits are now available fresh the year round. In addition the same foods are available canned, frozen and dehydrated.

Fresh vegetables are generally highest in quality and lowest in price when in season. In selecting, look first for freshness. Fruits and vegetables should be comparatively dry; excessive moisture hastens decay. To maintain quality in fresh vegetables and fruits, store them in the refrigerator in the crisper or in plastic bags. Bananas are not refrigerated. Potatoes and onions are stored in a cool dry place.

Canned fruits and vegetables lose quality if stored longer than a year but remain safe to eat indefinitely if the seal is not broken.

For good-quality frozen vegetables buy from a reputable dealer. Select clean, firm packages. Frozen food is safe to eat as long as the package remains frozen, but a storage temperature of 0° F. or lower is necessary to maintain high quality.

**Smart Buying Hints**

Make out a shopping list but be open minded should you spot an unadvertised bargain.

Shop alone if possible — dad and the kids tend to run up the food bill.

Buy in quantity, but only what you need and can use.

Buy in season, but not at first. Prices go down as supply increases.

Shop the ads, shop the special, shop the stores.

When buying meat and vegetables it's the price per serving not the price per pound that counts.

## HIGH ALTITUDE COOKING

Many recipes must be adjusted when elevations are above 3,000 feet. This is most important in cakes. Some cake mixes give these adjustments on the package. In home mixed and baked cakes usually a decrease in leavening or sugar (or both) and an increase in liquid are needed. Recipes vary greatly in balance of ingredients and only repeated experiments can give the most successful proportions to use. Use this table as a starting guide.

| Adjustment in Feet | 3,000 | 5,000 | 7,000 |
|---|---|---|---|
| *Reduce baking powder* | | | |
| For each teaspoon, decrease .. | 1/8 tsp. | 1/8 to 1/4 tsp. | 1/2 tsp. |
| *Reduce sugar* | | | |
| For each cup, decrease ........ | 0 to 1 tbsp. | 0 to 2 tbsp. | 1 to 3 tbsp. |
| *Increase liquid* | | | |
| For each cup, add | 1 to 2 tbsp. | 2 to 4 tbsp. | 3 to 4 tbsp. |

## FOOD PRESERVATION

A bountiful harvest is frequently appreciated even more during the winter's snow when the home canned tomatoes are added to a hearty stew or when the lush strawberries of early spring have been waiting in the freezer.

**Canning**

There are three accepted methods of home canning:

*The Open Kettle Method* — is recommended largely for canning jellies, jams, preserves, pickles, etc., — products in which sugar, vinegar or salt aid in preventing spoilage.

*Boiling Water Bath* — is recommended for canning acid foods, such as fruits and tomatoes.

*Pressure Cooker* — is recommended for canning non-acid vegetables, and for meats, poultry and fish.

The following rules should be followed when examining home canned foods before eating.

1. Never taste before re-heating.
2. Never use contents of a jar that spurts liquid when opened or that shows signs of leakage or fermentation.
3. Never use contents of a jar that is too soft or mushy. Odor should be true to the product.
4. Boil all meats and vegetables, except tomatoes, 15 minutes in an open vessel before tasting or using.
5. Burn all food that does not smell or look right to avoid possible eating by animals.

**Freezing**

The freezing of foods is a relatively easy method of food preservation. The following principles are guides to success.

1. Store food at 0° F. or lower. Freeze food at 0° F. or lower.
2. Do not place a large quantity of unfrozen food in the freezer at once. It will overload the freezing capacity of the freezer and cause the temperature to rise.
3. Package foods properly . . . protect from air.
4. Choose high quality foods.
5. Process foods carefully.
6. Avoid long storage. No food, whether home frozen or purchased frozen products, remains at top quality indefinitely even though frozen. The following chart gives general limits.

**Approximate Storage Life of Some Common Foods**

| | |
|---|---|
| Fruits | 12 months |
| Vegetables | 8 to 10 months |
| Beef | 6 to 12 months |
| Poultry | 3 to 4 months |
| Pies, unbaked | 3 to 4 months |
| Pies, baked | 3 to 4 months |
| Cakes, layer | 6 months |
| Bread and yeast rolls | 2 to 3 months |
| Casserole dishes | 4 to 6 months |
| Fish | 3 to 4 months |
| Sandwiches | 2 weeks |

## TIME TABLE FOR DEFROSTING MEATS AND POULTRY IN THE REFRIGERATOR

Thawing frozen foods in the refrigerator is usually the most satisfactory method. If there is not time to thaw poultry by this method, immerse poultry in its watertight wrapper in cold water. Change water often to hasten thawing. Required time is approximately 1 hour for small chickens and up to 6 or 8 hours for large turkeys.

| | |
|---|---|
| Large meat roast | 4 to 7 hours per lb. |
| Small meat roast | 3 to 5 hours per lb. |
| 1-inch steak | 12 to 14 hours |
| Chickens, 4 lbs. or more | 1 to 1½ days |
| Chickens, less than 4 lbs. | 12 to 16 hours |
| Ducks, 3 to 5 lbs. | 1 to 1½ days |
| Geese, 4 to 14 lbs. | 1 to 2 days |
| Turkeys, 18 lbs. and over | 2 to 3 days |
| Turkeys, less than 18 lbs. | 1 to 2 days |

# CALORIE CHART

| | Amount | Calories |
|---|---|---|
| **Dairy Products** | | |
| Cheese, American | 1 ounce | 105 |
| Cheese, cottage | 1 cup | 240 |
| Cream, whipped | 2 tablespoons | 90 |
| Ice cream, plain | ⅛ quart | 145 |
| Milk, chocolate | 1 cup | 235 |
| Milk, whole | 1 cup | 165 |
| **Poultry and Meats** | | |
| Bacon, fried | 2 slices | 95 |
| Beef roast, lean | 2.5 ounces | 130 |
| Beef steak, broiled | 3 ounces | 330 |
| Beef stew | 1 cup | 185 |
| Chicken, broiled | 3 ounces | 185 |
| Chicken, fried | 3.5 ounces | 230 |
| Chili con carne | 1 cup | 335 |
| Eggs, raw | 1 egg | 80 |
| Frankfurter | 1 frankfurter | 155 |
| Hamburger, broiled | 3 ounces | 245 |
| Lamb, roasted | 3 ounces | 235 |
| Liver, beef, fried | 2 ounces | 120 |
| Pork, chop | 3.5 ounces | 260 |
| Pork, cured, ham | 3 ounces | 290 |
| Pork roast | 3 ounces | 310 |
| Sausage, pork | 4 ounces | 340 |
| Veal roast | 3 ounces | 305 |
| **Fish** | | |
| Fish, broiled | 3 ounces | 150 |
| Fish, fried | 3 ounces | 195 |
| Oysters, raw | 1 cup | 160 |
| Salmon, pink, canned | 3 ounces | 120 |
| Shrimp, boiled | 3 ounces | 110 |
| Tuna, canned in oil | 3 ounces | 170 |
| **Beans and Nuts** | | |
| Beans, dry | 1 cup | 230 |
| Cashew nuts | 1 cup | 770 |
| Peanuts | 1 cup | 840 |
| Peanut butter | 1 tablespoon | 90 |
| Pecans, halves | 1 cup | 740 |
| Walnuts, black | 1 cup | 790 |
| Walnuts, English | 1 cup | 650 |
| **Vegetables** | | |
| Asparagus | 1 cup | 35 |
| Beans, green | 1 cup | 25 |
| Beans, lima | 1 cup | 150 |
| Beets, diced | 1 cup | 70 |
| Broccoli spears | 1 cup | 45 |
| Brussels sprouts | 1 cup | 60 |
| Cabbage, raw | 1 cup | 25 |
| Carrots, raw | 1 carrot | 20 |
| Cauliflower | 1 cup | 30 |
| Celery | 1 stalk | 5 |
| Corn, sweet | 1 cup | 170 |
| Cucumbers | 1 cucumber | 25 |
| Lettuce | 1 head | 30 |
| Mustard green | 1 cup | 30 |
| Okra | 8 pods | 30 |
| Onions, raw | 1 onion | 50 |
| Peas, green | 1 cup | 110 |
| Peppers, sweet, raw | 1 pod | 15 |
| Potato, baked | 1 potato | 90 |
| Potato chips | 10 chips | 110 |
| Potatoes, sweet | 1 sweet potato | 155 |

| Food | Amount | Calories |
|---|---|---|
| Pumpkin | 1 cup | 75 |
| Radishes | 4 radishes | 10 |
| Spinach | 1 cup | 45 |
| Squash, summer | 1 cup | 35 |
| Tomatoes | 1 tomato | 30 |
| Turnips, diced | 1 cup | 40 |
| **Fruits** | | |
| Apples, raw | 1 apple | 70 |
| Applesauce, sweetened | 1 cup | 185 |
| Apricots, canned | 1 cup | 220 |
| Avocados | ½ avocado | 185 |
| Bananas | 1 banana | 85 |
| Cantaloupe | ½ melon | 40 |
| Dates, dried | 1 cup | 505 |
| Fruit cocktail | 1 cup | 195 |
| Grapefruit | ½ grapefruit | 50 |
| Grapefruit juice | 1 cup | 95 |
| Lemons | 1 lemon | 20 |
| Oranges | 1 orange | 60 |
| Orange juice | 1 cup | 120 |
| Peaches | 1 fresh | 35 |
| Peaches, canned | 1 cup | 200 |
| Pears, canned | 1 cup | 195 |
| Pineapple, canned | 1 cup | 205 |
| Pineapple juice | 1 cup | 120 |
| Pineapple, raw | 1 cup | 75 |
| Prunes, dried | 1 cup | 305 |
| Raisins | 1 cup | 460 |
| Strawberries, raw | 1 cup | 90 |
| Watermelon | 1 wedge | 120 |
| **Breads, Cakes and Cereals** | | |
| Biscuits | 1 biscuit | 130 |
| Bread, rye | 1 slice | 55 |
| Bread, white | 1 slice | 60 |
| Bread, whole-wheat | 1 slice | 55 |
| Cake, angel food | 1 sector | 110 |
| Cake, chocolate, iced | 1 sector | 420 |
| Cake, plain, iced | 1 sector | 320 |
| Cake, plain, no icing | 1 sector | 180 |
| Cake, pound | 1 slice | 130 |
| Cookies, plain | 1 cookie | 110 |
| Corn muffins | 1 muffin | 155 |
| Crackers, saltine | 2 crackers | 35 |
| Fruitcake | 1 piece | 105 |
| Macaroni, cooked | 1 cup | 155 |
| Pancakes | 1 cake | 60 |
| Pie, fruit | 1 sector | 340 |
| Rice, cooked | 1 cup | 200 |
| Spaghetti—meat sauce | 1 cup | 285 |
| Waffles | 1 waffle | 240 |
| **Fats** | | |
| Butter or margarine | 1 pat | 50 |
| French dressing | 1 tablespoon | 60 |
| Mayonnaise | 1 tablespoon | 110 |
| **Miscellaneous** | | |
| Beer | 1 cup | 90 |
| Beverage, carbonated | 1 cup | 105 |
| Candy, fudge | 1 ounce | 115 |
| Jelly | 1 tablespoon | 50 |
| Olives, green | 12 large | 65 |
| Sherbet | 1 cup | 235 |
| Sugar, granulated | 1 tablespoon | 50 |

# Household Tips

## A RECIPE FOR WHITE CLOTHES

That white sheet didn't just happen! It took hundreds and hundreds of years for clothes-washing to progress from the banks of a stream to the outdoor wash-pot, and from there to the inside of the house. Good laundering is no longer hard work but it does demand a bit of know-how. Save all manufacturer's instructions accompanying items purchased. Follow those instructions and the basic "recipe" for successful laundering.

1. **Sorting and Loading** — Sort clothes into groups that can be washed together under the same conditions of water, temperature, time, etc.
   Separate white and colorfast fabrics from the non-colorfast fabrics.
   Separate sheer and delicate fabrics from heavy, sturdy fabrics.
   Separate heavily soiled clothes from lightly soiled clothes.
   Wash no more than two large items together. Mix with smaller pieces.
   Don't overload washer.
2. **Proper Washing Temperature** — Laundry experts agree that hot water is essential for most washing.
   *Hot water:* 150 to 160 for white and colorfast cottons and linens. Heavily soiled and greasy clothes.
   *Warm water:* 100 to 120° F. for non-colorfast cottons and linens. Acetates, silks, and woolens. Synthetics, resin-treated fabrics.
   *Cold water:* 40 to 80° F. only to freshen very lightly soiled items or to protect non-colorfast dyes.
3. **Laundry Aids** — Detergents and soaps, bleach, fabric softeners and starch all play a role in good laundry results. Use the right amount for each task. Always measure — don't guess.
4. **Rinsing** — Rinse, rinse, rinse, and rinse. Loosened soil, detergent, or bleach must be removed if clothes are to remain white and bright. If left in, they can "build up" so that clothes will look gray or yellow.
5. **Soft Water** — Soap used in hard water forms a curd that deposits in clothes making them yellow or gray. The water utility in cities can provide this information . . . known as *grains of hardness* in water.

| *Grains per U.S. Gallon* | *Description* |
|---|---|
| 0 | Zero soft water |
| 0 plus to 3 | Fairly soft |
| 3 plus to 6 | Moderately hard |
| 6 plus to 12 | Hard |
| 12 plus to 30 | Very hard |

If the water is hard, soften both wash and rinse with a non-precipitating packaged softener, use a synthetic detergent for washing or install an automatic water softener in the home.

## A RECIPE FOR STAIN REMOVAL FOR WASHABLE FABRICS

1. Treat stains promptly.
2. Use stain removers that suit both stain and fabric. Test remover first on unexposed part of garment.
3. If stain is unknown, avoid hot water.
4. Use most gentle treatment first. Use light, rapid strokes — do not rub into fabric. Rinse thoroughly before washing.
5. Take difficult stains to the dry cleaner.
6. The stain removal aids listed can be purchased at grocery or drug stores. Keep them on hand. Sodium hydrosulphite is a color remover. It is sold under several brand names.

## STAIN REMOVAL CHART

**Blood:** Soak immediately in cold water for 30 minutes or longer. Work detergent into stain and rinse. If stain persists, put a few drops of ammonia on stain and repeat detergent treatment. Bleach if necessary.

**Chocolate or Cocoa:** Soak in cold water 30 minutes, followed by a warm or hot detergent wash, depending on fabric. If brown stain remains, treat with peroxide. If greasy spot remains, use cleaning fluid.

**Foliage and Grass:** Sponge with equal parts of alcohol and water. Then regular hot or warm wash. If yellow stain remains, use liquid bleach.

**Ink:** Some impossible to remove. Others wash out in regular wash, especially if fresh. For all inks, first rub synthetic shampoo into stained area and allow to stand 15 minutes before rinsing. Repeat a number of times if necessary. Ballpoint Ink — Sponge repeatedly with acetone or amyl acetate. Use amyl acetate on acetate, Arnel, Dynel and Verel. Use acetone on all other fabrics.

**Lipstick and Rouge:** Apply undiluted liquid detergent to stain. Or dampen stain and rub in soap or detergent until a thick suds is formed. Work in until outline of stain is gone, then rinse well.

**Perspiration:** Soak for a short time in diluted bleaching solution or in sodium hydrosulphite solution (1 teaspoon to 1 cup water). Hold colored fabrics over open bottle of household ammonia; then sponge with vinegar solution.

**Candle Wax:** Place the stain between clean white blotters or several layers of facial tissues and press with warm iron. To remove remaining stain, sponge with a cleaning fluid.

**Iron Rust:** Dip in hot oxalic acid solution *(1 tablespoon to 1 cup water)*. Rinse immediately. Follow with regular hot wash.

**Grease, Oil and Tar:** Rub spot with lard, then sponge with cleaning fluid over a pad. Follow quickly with regular hot wash.

**Milk and Cream:** Soak in cool or lukewarm water; wash in hot or warm water, depending on fabric.

**Coffee or Tea:** Rub synthetic shampoo on spot; then wash by regular method. If milk or cream is present, see Milk and Cream.

**Soft Drinks:** Sponge immediately with cool water. Soak in cool water before washing. Heat and detergent may set stain.

## CARE AND FIRST AID FOR FURNITURE

Nothing gives a house the cared-for look quite like the glow of beautiful wood furniture. The look does not happen by accident but is the result of persistent effort and that "ounce of prevention". Many finishes are available and vary in their resistance to stains and their needed upkeep. This question is usually answered by the manufacturer or dealer. However, regular dusting and special cleaning and polishing are essential. A few "ounces of prevention" are:

1. Don't put hot dishes on a table without a protective pad.
2. Maintain a good wax finish at all times.
3. Don't put a vase directly on the furniture or pull it across the surface.
4. Don't place furniture too close to radiators or windows.

First aid for furniture can frequently repair accidents to furniture. If the damage has not penetrated the wood itself these suggestions may correct the situation.

**Alcohol Spots:** Check at the hardware store for a scratch-concealing polish . . . use only on dark woods. If the spot is not removed by this treatment mix rottenstone and linseed oil into a paste and apply with a soft cloth. Rub with the grain of the wood. Then polish.

**Burns:** Treat like alcohol stains. When using the rottenstone treatment . . . do not get it into surrounding areas.

**Water Spots:** Place a clean, thick blotter over the rings and press the blotter with a warm, not hot, iron. Repeat.

**Minor Scratches:** Polish with colored wax that matches the furniture finish. Or, rub scratches well with scratch-concealing polish. Or, prepare a paste of linseed oil and a paint coloring. These colorings are available in tubes and in several shades.

## REMOVAL OF HOUSEHOLD STAINS

**Mildew:** Remove mildew spots. Brush off any surface growth outdoors to prevent scattering the mildew spores. Sun and air fabric thoroughly. Wash articles at once with soap and water. On upholstered articles or mattresses, sponge lightly with thick suds of soap or synthetic detergent, and wipe with a clean, damp cloth. If stain remains on washable items, bleach with lemon juice and salt, sodium perborate bleach, or a dilute solution of sodium hydrochlorite or other household chlorine bleach.

**Stains on Upholstery:** Prevent the possibility of staining by buying spot-resistant treated fabric or treat fabric at home. Upholstery stains are difficult to treat because it is not possible to place an absorbent pad beneath. Always test the remover to be used on an inconspicuous section. Follow standard stain removal techniques.

**Animal Stains:** Sponge out immediately with warm water and an absorbent cloth. Old stains are sometimes removed by sponging with a solution of one part soapless lather and five parts water, plus three tablespoonsfuls of white vinegar to each quart water. Repeat if necessary.

## REPLACING FUSES—CIRCUIT BREAKERS

Wiring circuits are protected by either fuses or circuit breakers. When fuses blow or circuit breakers trip the trouble is in the cord, plug, equipment, wiring system, or the circuit is overloaded. *Locate the trouble and correct it before replacing fuse or resetting circuit breaker.*

When replacing a fuse:

a. Stand on dry board or floor.
b. Open main switch.
c. Correct trouble causing fuse to blow.
d. Remove blown fuse.
e. Replace with correct size.
f. Close main switch.

When resetting the circuit breaker:

a. Move handle to "Off" position.
b. Push handle past "Off" position.
c. Return handle to "On" position.

## CONTROL OF HOUSEHOLD PESTS

Modern science has made great progress in the control of household pests. Many insecticides are available for home treatment. The U.S. Department of Agriculture can furnish detailed information about pest control. If desired or if the home is badly infested, a professional exterminator is well trained in pest-control methods. Choose a reliable firm and let their carefully trained specialist take charge.

# Safety Tips

**Check Your Home for Hazards.** It is impossible to list every hazard you could encounter in the home. Most home accidents and fires can be prevented simply by cultivating the habit of being careful. Being careful is a habit and one way to begin this habit is to learn the danger spots. These are *fire hazards:*

1. Faulty insulation. See that all wiring is properly installed and maintained.
2. Check insulation of electric appliances. Never use an electric appliance not in good repair.
3. Always keep a screen in front of the fireplace.
4. Never smoke in bed. Get up if you must smoke.
5. Never allow oily rags to accumulate.
6. In case of fire at night, feel the door. If it seems hot, don't open it. Seek another way of escape.
7. Never leave irons, toasters, etc., turned on when you leave the room.
8. If clothing catches fire, don't run! Stand still and smother the flames by rolling yourself in a rug.
9. If grease catches fire smother it with soda. Never use water.

**Don't Invite Burglars.** Check all these burglary hazards:

1. When you are away on vacation don't tell the world. Tell the milkman and the newsboy to stop deliveries.
2. Leave a light burning in the living room when you are out for the evening.
3. When you plan to be away for some time arrange to have the lawn cut or the paths shovelled.
4. Don't advertise your absence or leave timetables of your activities by leaving notes in the mailbox, etc.
5. Never leave the key under the doormat. Leave it with a neighbor if you must leave it for a member of the family.
6. If your home is burglarized, give the police a complete list of what was stolen, but don't tell the newspapers what the burglars missed.

**The Kitchen** has more "built-in" safety hazards than any room in the house. To think *safety* at all times is the best accident prevention method. Check for hazards:

1. Never mix cleaning aids. Dangerous fumes can be released.
2. Close doors and drawers immediately after use.
3. Wipe up spills immediately.
4. Never leave cooking spoons in pans and always use wooden spoons when working at the range.
5. Use flat-bottomed and well-balanced pots and pans with handles turned away from edge of range or table.
6. Remove lids directed away from body to avoid steam burns.
7. Pick up broken glass with a damp paper towel.
8. Carry pans with pot holders, not dishtowels.
9. Use sturdy stepladders or stepstools for reaching high places.
10. Keep knives sharp; cut with knife edge directed away from body.
11. Wash knives separately from other utensils and store them separately.
12. Follow directions for using pressure cookers and saucepans.

**Check All Wiring for Safety.** Only a qualified electrician can check thoroughly but protection can be increased by following this basic guide.

1. Provide sufficient outlets and circuits to serve all lamps and appliances with safety.
2. Locate switches so they help light the way. For example, at entrances to room and at the head and foot of stairs.
3. Do not overload wiring.
4. Do not place too many small appliances on one circuit.
5. Never touch electrical equipment when any part of the body is in contact with a wet surface.
6. Follow manufacturer's recommendations in using Christmas lighting and use it only where specifically stated.
7. If service line is overhead, check it for signs of wear caused by moving tree limbs or other kinds of friction.
8. Replace frayed and damaged cords and blown fuses. Major repairs and installations should be made by a licensed electrician.

**Fallout Facts:** Most Americans know about the destructive power of atomic and hydrogen bombs and other nuclear weapons. An enemy attack with a nuclear weapon could cause radioactive contamination many miles downwind from the target area. Radioactive material produced by the bomb gives off destructive rays or particles which can injure or kill. The rays or particles when they fall to the earth are called radioactive fallout. The local civil defense authorities can provide detailed information about protection. In the event of such an emergency information will be disseminated to the public in every possible way, including the CONELRAD system, 640 or 1240 on your radio dial. It is wise to keep in mind:

1. If you do not have an underground refuge, at least stay indoors.
2. Remember, fallout is odorless.
3. Obtain a battery radio to be used in emergency power failure.
4. Remain indoors until told by civil defense authorities that the danger from fallout can be tolerated.

# *Sewing*

NOT SO MANY YEARS AGO clothing was made from only three or four different fibers and even fewer finishes were applied. The advent of synthetic fibers and special fabric finishes have greatly increased the ease of care and the versatility of use of many clothing items. It has also added to the complexity of selection. New fabrics and finishes are added so rapidly that no list is ever complete. Fibers can be divided into two categories . . . the *natural fibers* — cotton, linen, silk and wool . . . the *synthetic fibers* — which as the name suggests are man-made fibers.

*Cotton* is used for all types of fabrics from heavy duty work clothes to delicate sheers. Untreated cotton is machine washable in hot water with all-purpose soaps. It can be starched. Treated cottons should be washed at moderate temperature with mild soap or detergent. Do not use chlorine bleach, unless specified on the label. Do not starch. *Linen-Flax* is used for fabrics from sheer to very coarse. It is machine or hand washable according to fabric weight and garment construction. Use hot water, all-purpose detergent or soap for whites. It dampens well. Press with hot iron. *Silk* may be found used for delicate lingerie or heavy rough textured suiting. It should be dry cleaned unless labeled washable. Do not bleach silk. Press with moderately hot iron. Use lukewarm water and very low ironing temperature for white silk to prevent yellowing. *Wool* is used for all types of fabric from sheer wool to heavy fleeced coatings. Wool should be dry-cleaned unless labeled washable. Press on wrong side with steam.

The list of synthetic fibers grows rapidly. Some of the more popular ones are listed. *Nylon* is used for hosiery, underwear and almost all types of fabric, both woven and knitted. It should be washed with mild soap or detergent at moderate temperatures. Wash white nylon alone — it picks up color. Press on low temperature setting. *Rayon* may be found in almost all types of wearing apparel in a variety of weights and textures. It may be washed and ironed like cotton but requires longer to dry and must be handled carefully when wet. *Spandex* is used in foundation garments, swim suits, and other garments where elasticity is required. Avoid exposure to sunlight, heat, oils, fats and greases. Wash frequently. *Acetate* is used in wearing apparel and household textiles. It should be dry-cleaned unless labeled washable. Use low heat setting in drying and pressing. *Polyester* is blended with other fibers and used in men's shirts, women's blouses and other easy care items. It washes easily, dries fast, needs little or no ironing. Pretreat oily stains before washing. *Acrylic* fibers are used in sweaters and knitwear. It is always used in deep pile fur-like coating, blankets, and fabric blends. Acrylic is usually machine or hand washable at moderate temperature. Thorough rinsing is important to prevent yellowing. *Glass* is found in drapery fabric and sheer curtain material. It should be washed by hand and allowed to drip dry. Do not rub, wring, crush or fold. Needs no ironing.

Fabric finishes are many and varied. They have an important role in today's fabric picture. Rely on fabric labels for the finish or finishes used. Always read the labels carefully. Some special finishes are: flame resistant, insulated, mildew resistant, water repellent, shrinkage resistant, spot and stain resistant and minimum care.

Home sewing was once employed strictly as an economy measure. Today home sewing is a creative, interesting and profitable hobby of millions of women.

If sewing is limited to a few necessary repairs or provides clothing for the entire family the essential sewing aids and perhaps a few convenient extras will add pleasure and save time.

**Check Your Sewing Equipment**

1. Properly adjusted sewing machine.
2. Well lighted working area.
3. Sharp scissors.
4. Ruler and flexible tape measure.
5. Sharp pinking shears.
6. Dressmaker type pins.
7. Comfortable fitting thimble.
8. Variety of needles.
9. Threads to suit the task. *Cotton* — for general use. *Silk* — sewing on silk or wool fabrics. *Special* — for sewing on synthetics and stretch fabrics.
10. Beeswax to rub on thread to prevent knotting.
11. Ripping aid.

Sewing, like many skills, is developed by practice. However, a few suggestions to the beginning seamstress and even a few hints to the experienced seamstress will make the job easier and can help eliminate the "homemade" look.

1. Firm, closely woven fabrics are easiest to work with. Very closely woven and very loosely woven fabrics present special problems in handling and cutting.
2. Check body measurements carefully and select the pattern most suitable. Fit and alter pattern.
3. Place pin through materials and pattern vertically with point toward you.
4. Careful pressing is one of the most important phases of clothing construction . . . during the construction and after the gar-

ment is completed. Always press with the grain.

5. Always stitch with the grain, from wide to narrow end.
6. Fullness in set-in sleeves should be eased into the armhole . . . never gathered.
7. Staystitching prevents stretching, and holds the grain in position. Staystitch the neckline, zipper line and armseye.
8. Understitch collar facing.
9. All enclosed seams such as the collar, should be trimmed ¼ inch.
10. All marking should be made on the wrong side of the fabric.
11. Notches should be cut out into the margin away from the pattern.
12. Preserve the grain line of the pattern, no matter what alterations are made.
13. When plaid fabrics are used, the plaid design should be matched carefully at all major seams.
14. Fabric with up and down design or nap must be carefully matched so that the up and down goes in the same direction on all pieces of the garment.
15. Attach facing to outer fabric only at seams.
16. When sewing one full and one flat side together, always have the full side up.
17. Clip diagonally across corner seam allowances, as in collars, to avoid bulkiness.
18. Regulate the machine stitch and tension according to fabric being used.
19. Finish all seams with a finish suited to the material and garment.

Plain seams may be adequate on fabrics that are firm and do not fray easily. Materials that fray, or are bulky, need special seam finishes for durability and professional appearance.

**Double-stitched and pinked seam** — For use on cotton wash clothes made of firmly woven fabrics. These seams are durable, firm and easy to make; they also are easy to iron as they iron straight and smooth from the right side, and the double stitching keeps them from stretching.

**Closed and zigzagged seam** — For use on sleazy, loosely woven, or easily frayed fabrics that need special seam finishing. This seam is also easy to iron from the right side.

**Open and pinked seam** — For use on thick or heavy fabrics, such as embossed or sculptured cottons, and some silks, rayons, and wools that do not fray.

**Opened, stitched, and pinked seam** — For use on wool jersey or on bias seams; the extra rows of stitching helps prevent stretching and also keep jersey seams from rolling.

**Double-stitched and trimmed seam** — For use on laces and eyelet embroideries that require a flat, narrow, inconspicuous, yet durable seam.

**Opened and overcast seam** — For use on heavier fabrics that may fray, such as linen, linen-weave silks and rayons and denim. The edges may be overcast by hand or zigzagged on a machine.

**French seam** — For use on sheer cottons, silks, and synthetics, such as voiles and sheer fabrics, that are likely to fray badly.

**Self-stitched seam** — For use on fabrics that fray too much to be overcast. This seam is also used on unlined jackets or coats of cottons, rayons, and some lightweight wools.

**Zigzagged seam** — For use on lingerie materials. It is stitched on the wrong side, pressed to one side, then zigzagged from the right side over the seam line. It is an elastic seam so is often used on slips. It is hard to wash clean, especially if dark clothes rub against a light-colored seam.

**Flat-fell seam** — For use on men's and boy's shirts and work clothes. This seam with no raw edges is durable, but has a tendency to pucker with laundering and is hard to iron.

**Mock-flat-fell seam** — For use on men's and boy's shirts and work clothes when a flat-fell seam is too heavy. It resembles a flat-fell seam in outside appearance, but is less bulky and easier to make. On the wrong side it has one raw edge which can be pinked or zigzagged if the fabric frays.

**Bound seam** — For use on fabrics that fray badly. Net footing when used to bind seams on colored sheers, such as voile, makes the seams look less heavy than French seams. Rayon binding makes a neat seam finish for unlined jackets and coats of wool; on fabrics of synthetic fibers, binding leaves an imprint on the right side.

# *Miscellany*

## WEDDING ANNIVERSARIES

| | | | |
|---|---|---|---|
| First | Paper | Ninth | Pottery |
| Second | Cotton | Tenth | Tin |
| Third | Leather | Eleventh | Steel |
| Fourth | Silk | Twelfth | Fine Linen |
| Fifth | Wood | Thirteenth | Lace |
| Sixth | Iron | Fourteenth | Ivory |
| Seventh | Copper | Fifteenth | Crystal |
| Eighth | Bronze | Twentieth | China |
| Twenty-Fifth | Silver | Fiftieth | Golden |
| Thirtieth | Pearl | Seventy-Fifth | Diamond |
| Fortieth | Ruby | | |

## LANGUAGE OF GEMS

Marvelous properties were attributed to many precious stones and gems by the ancients, and it is customary among lovers and friends to notice the significance attached to various stones in making birthday, engagement, and wedding presents.

AGATE—Insures health, long life, and prosperity
AMETHYST—Preventive against violent passions
BERYL—Everlasting youth and happiness
BLOODSTONE—Steadfast affection, courage, and wisdom
CARNELIAN—Preventive of misfortune
CATSEYE—Warns against danger and trouble
CHALCEDONY—Drives away sadness
CHRYSOLITE—Frees from evil passions and melancholy
DIAMOND—Signifies purity; maintains peace and disperses storms
EMERALD—Discovers false friends and insures true love
GARNET—Constancy and fidelity
JASPER—Wisdom and courage
MOONSTONE—Good luck
ONYX—Insures conjugal felicity
OPAL—An "unlucky" stone portending injury and mental or physical trouble
PEARL—Signifies purity and innocence
RUBY—Discovers poison, corrects evils resulting from mistaken friendship
SAPPHIRE—Frees from enchantment; denotes repentance
SARDONYX—Married happiness
TOPAZ—Fidelity and friendship; prevents bad dreams
TURQUOISE—Prosperity in love

## BIRTHSTONES

| | |
|---|---|
| GARNET | January |
| AMETHYST | February |
| BLOODSTONE OR AQUAMARINE | March |
| DIAMOND | April |
| EMERALD | May |
| PEARL, MOONSTONE, OR ALEXANDRITE | June |
| RUBY | July |
| SARDONYX OR PERIDOT | August |
| SAPPHIRE | September |
| OPAL OR TOURMALINE | October |
| TOPAZ | November |
| TURQUOISE OR ZIRCON | December |

## BIRTH DAYS

Monday's child is fair of face;
Tuesday's child is full of grace;
Wednesday's child is loving and giving;
Thursday's child works hard for its living;
Friday's child is full of woe;
Saturday's child has far to go;
But the child that's born on the Sabbath day
Is blithe and bonny and good and gay.

# *Medical Information*

## FIRST AID FACTS

An injured person often needs to be treated at once, before the doctor can arrive; or the injured must be taken to a place where proper care can be administered. The number one rule in first aid . . . call a doctor promptly. Another important rule — if a severely injured person must be moved, do so carefully and gently. Never administer food or liquids to an unconscious person. Keep the injured warm to prevent shock. Be familiar with basic first aid facts for specific injuries.

**Poisonings** — 90% of poisoning accidents involve children under 5 years of age. To protect against poisonings:

1. Keep all drugs, poisons, and other household chemical products out of the reach of children and away from food.
2. Read all labels and carefully follow "caution" statements.
3. Be sure all poisons are clearly marked.
4. Do not store poisonous substances in food or beverage containers.
5. Date all drug supplies when you buy them.
6. When medicines are to be discarded destroy them.
7. Never refer to medicine as candy.
8. Don't take medicine in the dark.
9. Know correct counterdoses for poisonings or overdoses of medicine. Some common counterdoses for various poisons and overdoses are:

**Rubbing Alcohol or Overdose of other Alcohol** — Give a glass of milk. Induce vomiting. Give a tablespoon of sodium bicarbonate in quart of warm water.

**Aspirin Overdose** — Follow same remedy as Rubbing Alcohol.

**Food Poisoning** — Induce vomiting. Give 2 tablespoons epsom salt in 2 glasses of water.

**Paregoric Overdose** — Give glass of milk. Give 2 tablespoons epsom salt in 2 glasses of water. Keep patient awake.

**Gasoline or Kerosene Poisoning** — Give water or milk. Give 2 ounces vegetable oil. *Do not* induce vomiting.

**Chlorine Bleach Poisoning** — Give one or two glasses of milk.

**Household Ammonia Poisoning** — Give 2 tablespoons vinegar in 2 glasses of water. Give white of 2 raw eggs or 2 ounces of olive oil. *Do not* induce vomiting.

**Disinfectant Poisoning** — If disinfectant contains chlorine follow counterdose for chlorine bleach.

If it contains carbolic acid, induce vomiting. Then give 2 ounces of castor oil.

Next give glass of milk or whites of 2 raw eggs.

**Sleeping Medicine Overdose** — Induce vomiting. Give 2 tablespoons epsom salt in 2 glasses of water. Then give large quantities of hot coffee or strong tea.

**Barbiturates Overdose** — Follow same treatment as for Sleeping Medicine.

**Wounds** — There are four types of wounds. They are abrasion, tear, cut and puncture. Do not touch wound with anything not clean. Wipe dirt or other foreign particles from wound with sterile gauze pads or cotton, or hold wound under running water. Apply mild antiseptic. To control bleeding and prevent additional infection, cover with sterile gauze pad. Apply bandage over sterile pad, making sure not to bandage too tightly. Anchor with adhesive tape. Do not attempt to clean out deep puncture or badly torn wounds.

**Bleeding** — If bleeding is not severe, it may be controlled by simple elevation of injured part above level of heart; then apply a sterile gauze pad. When bleeding is not controlled in this manner, pressure should be applied over a sterile gauze pad or clean cloth directly to the bleeding site. It may be necessary to hold such a pad in place with a tourniquet. Apply tourniquet only when all other methods fail and life is endangered. A tourniquet improperly used damages nerves, tissues and cuts off blood supply.

**Convulsions** — Lay victim on back to avoid self-injury from thrashing, etc. Turn head sideways, place roll of cloth between teeth to prevent biting of his tongue or your fingers. Lift lower jaw upward to keep tongue from blocking air passage. Sponge neck, head and wrists with cool water.

**Shock** — The victim of severe shock is unconscious or nearly so; the surface of the body is pale, cold and sweaty; the expression is anxious. While waiting for the doctor, keep the injured person absolutely quiet, give him plenty of fresh air, and keep as warm as possible with plenty of loose covering. Remove false teeth, tobacco, etc., and loosen all belts and other tight clothing. If breathing has stopped, perform artificial respiration at once.

**Burns** — There are three types of burns; heat, electrical and chemical. If the burn is caused by fire, hot asphalt, tar or other hot materials do not touch or remove any burned material which may be stuck to the burned area, for if you do, you may remove portions of the burned flesh with the material. Do not open any blisters. The most important first-aid treatment is to prevent infection and lessen the pain by keeping air away from it. A mixture of bicarbonate of soda and vaseline applied to the burned area and covered with a sterile gauze dressing, is the best first-aid treatment. Electrical burns are produced by heat from the electric current. Treat the same as ordinary burns. There are two important things to do when treating acid or alkali burns (except carbolic acid); first, remove all free acid, and second, neutralize the remaining acid. Alkalis neutralize acids. Acids neutralize alkalis. Flood all injured parts with cold water. Then neutralize by bathing with a sodium bicarbonate solution if the burn was an acid burn. Or, if the burn was an alkali burn, a vinegar solution should be used. (1 tablespoonful of vinegar to a cup of clean water).

**Animal Bites and Stings** — Wash wound immediately, using running water and soap to remove animal saliva. Apply sterile dressing. Go to doctor promptly. If dog escapes after biting, try to capture and deliver to health department for observation. A small number of people are unusually sensitive to stings from bees, wasps, yellow jackets, or hornets. If this condition is known or if rapid severe swelling begins rush victim to doctor immediately.

**Electrical Shock** — Follow these instructions, even if the victim appears to be dead. Immediately break the circuit with a single quick motion to free the victim. Do not hold him with bare hand or you may also receive a serious shock. Instantly remove any foreign body from the mouth and throat (tobacco, false teeth, etc.). Loosen clothing and begin artificial respiration at once. Keep up artificial respiration until natural breathing is restored . . . or for at least three hours. Do not give any liquid by mouth until the subject is fully conscious.

**Fainting** — Keep patient flat on back, loosen clothing, lower head or raise limbs, apply cold water to face, and supply fresh, cool air from window or fan. If faint lasts more than a few minutes, keep victim warm, call doctor.

**Nosebleed** — Put victim in chair, tilt head back, apply cold, wet dressing over nose. If bleeding persists, press nostrils together 4 or 5 minutes, or plug with narrow strips of a sterile gauze pad or cotton, leaving end for easy removal.

**Swallowed Objects** — Victims are usually babies and small children. Smooth objects such as buttons and beads are usually not dangerous and will be passed in a few days. Needles and pins are more dangerous and a doctor should be consulted immediately.

**Choking** — Occurring in children should be treated by holding child upside down and slapping him vigorously on the back of his chest. If object is not dislodged and he continues choking and begins to turn blue, rush him to nearest hospital or doctor's office. Have someone else telephone ahead.

**Artificial Respiration or Rescue Breathing** is a vital first aid fact. It is used in the event of electric shock, drowning or asphyxiation.

1. Tilt the victim's head back with victim on his back, neck fully extended.

2. Lift the victim's jaw into jutting-out position by inserting thumb between teeth, grasping lower jaw and lifting it forcefully upward.
3. If air passage is not yet cleared, clear at once with fingers or with several sharp blows between shoulder blades.
4. With lower jaw lifted, open your mouth wide and cover victim's mouth by placing your mouth over his with airtight contact, also closing victim's nose by pinching it between thumb and finger.
5. Blow air into victim's lungs until you see the chest rise; remove your mouth and let him exhale. If chest does not rise check steps above. Repeat step approximately 12 times a minute until victim revives. (20 times a minute for children.)

## COMMUNICABLE DISEASES

### Chicken Pox

*Signs and symptoms* — Slight fever followed by rash which looks like small blisters. Blisters keep developing for 3-4 days and leave crust which falls off in about 14 days.

*Incubation period* — 13-17 days, sometimes up to three weeks.

*Period of communicability* — Usually one day before the rash begins until two days after the last new spots appear.

*Cause* — A virus: Present in secretions from nose, throat, mouth of infected people.

*Protection* — No vaccine available.

*Control* — Exclusion from school for 1 week after eruption appears. Avoid contact with susceptibles. Cut child's fingernails short and keep clean. Immunity usual after one attack.

### Diphtheria

*Signs and symptoms* — Sore throat, fever, patches of grayish membrane on tonsils, in nose and throat. Croup in very young children.

*Incubation period* — 2-5 days.

*Period of communicability* — From about 2 to 4 weeks after onset of disease. Seldom over four weeks.

*Cause* — Present in secretions from nose, throat, and skin of infected people and carriers.

*Protection* — Vaccination.

*Control* — One attack does not necessarily give immunity.

### German Measles

*Signs and symptoms* — A rash like that of measles or scarlet fever or both, slight fever. There are usually swollen glands around the ears, neck and throat.

*Incubation period* — 14-21 days.

*Period of communicability* — From 7 days before to 4 days after onset of symptoms.

*Cause* — A virus: Present in secretions from nose and mouth of infected people.

*Protection* — Gamma globulin may be recommended for women exposed early in pregnancy, but protection of the baby is questionable.

*Control* — Isolation, when necessary, for 5 days after onset. No attempt should be made to protect young girls from this disease. Immunity usual after one attack.

### Measles

*Signs and symptoms* — Sore throat, running nose, inflamed eyes, cough, fever. Rash follows in a few days — blotchy dusky red color starting first on forehead and face.

*Incubation period* — 7 to 14 days.

*Period of communicability* — From 4 days before until 5 days after rash appears.

*Cause* — A virus: Present in secretions from nose and throat of infected people.

*Protection* — Vaccination.

*Control* — Isolation until 7 days after appearance of rash. Immunity usual after one attack.

### Mumps

*Signs and symptoms* — Fever and swelling of glands at the angles of jaw and in front of ears. The swelling may be painful and may start on one side only, later involve both.

*Incubation period* — 2-4 weeks.

*Period of communicability* — A week before the symptoms appear until nine days after.

*Cause* — A virus: Present in saliva of infected people.

*Protection* — A vaccine providing short-term protection is available; recommended after exposure, for special cases only.

*Control* — Isolation until swelling subsides. No attempt should be made to protect boys from this disease before they reach puberty. Immunity usual after one attack but second attacks can occur.

### Poliomyelitis

*Signs and symptoms* — Usually slight or moderate fever, headache, vomiting, muscular stiffness, soreness, weakness.

*Incubation period* — 1-3 weeks.

*Period of communicability* — Usually from the last part of the incubation period through the first week of the disease.

*Cause* — 3 strains of polio virus have been identified: Present in discharges from nose, throat, bowels of infected people.

*Protection* — Vaccination.

*Control* — Isolation for about one week from onset, for duration of fever. Immunity to infecting strain of virus usual after one attack.

### Smallpox

*Signs and symptoms* — Fever, headache, backache. Rash follows — starts on face, arms and wrists. Rash begins as small red spots which fill up with pus. Scabs or pocks form later.

*Incubation period* — 1-2 weeks.

*Period of communicability* — From the first symptoms until scabs and crusts disappear. Most communicable in early stages.

*Cause* — A virus: Present in skin pocks and discharges from mouth, nose, throat, bowels, bladder of infected people.

*Protection* — Vaccination.

*Control* — Isolation until all crusts are gone. Immunity usual after one attack.

**Streptococcal Sore Throat and Scarlet Fever**

*Signs and symptoms* — Sudden fever, sore throat, swollen glands in the neck. Sometimes vomiting. The same symptoms occur in scarlet fever and are followed by a rash. Strep throat and scarlet fever are the same disease except for the rash.

*Incubation period* — 2-5 days.

*Period of communicability* — During incubation and clinical illness. Adequate penicillin treatment will eliminate probability of spread within 24 hours.

*Cause* — Streptococci of several strains cause scarlet fever and "strep" sore throats. Present in secretions from mouth, nose, ears of infected people and carriers.

*Protection* — No vaccine available.

*Control* — Use of antibiotics. One attack does not give immunity.

**Tetanus**

*Signs and symptoms*—Stiffness of neck muscles, painful spasms of jaw muscles (lockjaw). Rigidity is sometimes limited to the part of the body that is injured.

*Incubation period* — 4 days to 3 weeks.

*Period of communicability* — Not communicable from person to person. Tetanus spores may be in the soil, or on the "rusty nail", or whatever caused the injury.

*Cause* — Tetanus bacillus: Present in a wound so infected.

*Protection* — Inoculation with tetanus toxoid.

*Control* — Booster dose of tetanus toxoid for protection after a wound. Antitoxin used in treatment and for temporary protection for child not immunized. One attack does not give immunity.

**Whooping Cough**

*Signs and symptoms* — Irritating cough which sometimes becomes worse at night. Some fever. In about two weeks in typical cases the characteristic "whoop", a spasm of coughing followed by vomiting, usually appears.

*Incubation period* — 7-21 days.

*Period of communicability* — From the first symptoms until about 4th week of the disease. It is often most communicable before a diagnosis has been made.

*Cause* — Pertussis bacillus: Present in secretions from mouth and nose of infected people.

*Protection* — Vaccination.

*Control* — Pertussis immune globulin can lighten attack or give protection after exposure from susceptible children for about 3 weeks from onset of spasmodic cough. Immunity usual after one attack.

## IMMUNIZATION SCHEDULE

The following schedule is a suggested schedule for immunizations during a baby's first year. It is based on recommendations of the American Medical Association and the American Academy of Pediatrics. Your own physician may have a slightly different plan, depending on what he considers best for the child. If the child is past infancy and hasn't yet had all immunizations start them now. Adults, too, need the protections of immunization. They are not necessarily immune to the communicable diseases of childhood — and early immunizations do not last for life. It is necessary to reinforce first doses with booster doses at periodic intervals.

**Diphtheria, Whooping Cough, Tetanus**

| | |
|---|---|
| Age for First Dose | 6 weeks to 2 months. |
| Number of Doses | 3 shots, one month apart. |
| Boosters | At 1 year and again at 4 years; repeated as recommended by physician. |

**Polio**

| | |
|---|---|
| Age for First Dose | 6 weeks to 3 months. |
| Number of Doses | *Salk:* 3 shots, six weeks apart. 4th, after six months or longer.<br>*Sabin:* 3 oral doses, four to six weeks apart. |
| Boosters | Every 2 years, as recommended by physician for *Salk* vaccine.<br>Every year, as recommended by physician for *Sabin* vaccine. |

**Smallpox**

| | |
|---|---|
| Age for First Dose | 15 to 18 months. |
| Number of Doses | 1 vaccination. |
| Boosters | Every 3 to 5 years, and if exposed. |

**Measles**

| | |
|---|---|
| Age for First Dose | 12 months. |
| Number of Doses | "live"-type: 1 shot or "killed"-type: 3 shots, one month apart. |
| Boosters | As recommended by physician. |

# DICTIONARY OF MEDICAL TERMS

*Many medical words and terms not found in this section may be found in the main vocabulary of the Dictionary.*

A

**abdomen** (ab′də-mən, ab-dō′-), *n.* the part of the body between the diaphragm and the pelvis, containing the viscera; the belly.

**abdominal** (ab-dom′ə-n'l), *adj.* of or pertaining to the abdomen.

**abduct** (ab-dukt′), *v. t.* to move or pull (a part of the body) away from the median axis or from another part: as, a muscle that *abducts* the thumb.

**aberration** (ab′ẽr-ā′shən), *n.* 1. mental derangement or lapse. 2. *a*) the failure of the eye to refract light properly so that the light rays from one point do not converge to a single focus. *b*) an error in the lens of the eye that causes this.

**abirritant** (ab-ir′ə-tənt), *adj.* relieving or lessening irritation; soothing. *n.* a medicine or drug that does this.

**ablactation** (ab′lak-tā′shən), *n.* 1. the stoppage of milk secretion. 2. the act or process of weaning.

**ablation** (ab-lā′shən), *n.* the surgical removal of part of the body.

**abort** (ə-bôrt′), *v. i.* 1. to have a miscarriage. 2. to fail to develop. *v. t.* 1. to cause to have an abortion. 2. to check (a disease) before fully developed.

**aborticide** (ə-bôr′ti-sīd′), *n.* 1. the destruction of the fetus within the uterus. 2. any agent or thing capable of destroying the fetus in the uterus.

**abortion** (ə-bôr′shən); *n.* 1. expulsion of the fetus from the womb before it is viable; miscarriage. 2. an aborted fetus.

**abrasion** (ə-brā′zhən), *n.* 1. a spot or area from which the skin or membrane has been rubbed or scraped off. 2. a scraping or rubbing off. 3. the normal wearing away of teeth due to chewing.

**abreaction** (ab′ri-ak′shən), *n.* the act or process of ridding oneself of a repressed or disagreeable emotion by re-enacting it or talking about it.

**abscess** (ab′ses), *n.* a swollen inflamed area in body tissues, in which pus gathers: it is kept from spreading by other tissue surrounding it. *v. i.* to form an abscess.

**abscission** (ab-sizh′ən), *n.* the cutting off of a part by surgery.

**abulia** (ə-bū′li-ə), *n.* loss of will power and the ability to come to decisions.

**acapnia** (ə-kap′ni-ə), *n.* the condition of having a lowered carbon dioxide content in the blood.

**acariasis** (ak′ə-rī′ə-sis), *n.* the condition of being infested with mites or acarids.

**acarid** (ak′ə-rid), *n.* a mite or tick.

**accommodation** (ə-kom′ə-dā′shən), *n.* the self-adjustment of the lens of the eye for focusing on objects at various distances.

**accouchement** (ə-ko͞osh′mənt), *n.* childbirth.

**accoucheur** (a′ko͞o-shũr′), *n.* a medical man who attends childbirth cases; expert in obstetrics.

**accretion** (ə-krē′shən), *n.* 1. accumulation of foreign matter in a cavity. 2. the adding of nourishment to a tissue. 3. the growing together of naturally separate parts.

**acetanilide** (as′ə-tan″'l-īd′), *n.* a drug used to soothe pain and reduce fever.

**acetic** (ə-sē′tik), *adj.* of, like, containing, or producing acetic acid or vinegar.

**acetic acid,** a sour, colorless liquid having a sharp odor: it is found in vinegar.

**acetone** (as′ə-tōn′), *n.* 1. a drug used as an anesthetic and as a remedy for worms. 2. a colorless liquid found in small amounts in normal urine and in larger amounts in diabetic urine.

**acetylcholine** (as′ə-til-kō′lēn), *n.* an alkaloid extracted from ergot and used to lower blood pressure and increase peristalsis.

**acetylsalicylic acid** (as′ə-til-sal′ə-sil′ik), aspirin.

**ache** (āk), *n.* a dull, continuous pain. *v. i.* to have or give such a pain.

**achlorhydria** (ə-klôr-hī′dri-ə), *n.* absence of hydrochloric acid in the gastric juice.

**achromatous** (ā-krō′mə-təs), *adj.* without color or without enough color: as, *achromatous* blood.

**acid** (as′id), *n.* any compound that can react with a base to form a salt: in water solution, an acid tastes sour and turns blue litmus red.

**acidity** (ə-sid′ə-ti), *n.* 1. the condition of being acid or sour. 2. hyperacidity.

**acidosis** (as′i-dō′sis), *n.* a condition in which the alkali reserve of the body is below normal.

**acidulous** (ə-sij′oo-ləs), *adj.* slightly acid.

**aclusion** (ə-klū′zhən), *n.* the condition in which the cusps of the teeth do not fit close together: opposite of *occlusion.*

**acne** (ak′nē), *n.* a chronic skin disease, common in adolescence, characterized by pimples and blackheads on the face, back, and chest.

**acomia** (ə-kō′mi-ə), *n.* baldness.

**aconite** (ak′ə-nīt′), *n.* a drug used as a cardiac and respiratory sedative.

**acoria** (ə-kor′i-ə), *n.* a condition of continual hunger, although the appetite may not be large.

**acoustician** (ak′o͞os-tish′ən), *n.* a person who fits the hard of hearing with hearing aids.

**acrocephaly** (ak′rō-sef′ə-li), *n.* an abnormal condition in which the skull is pointed.

**acromegaly** (ak′rō-meg′ə-li), *n.* a disease marked by abnormal overgrowth of the hands, feet, face, and bones, due to overactivity of the pituitary gland.

**acronyx** (ak′rō-niks), *n.* an ingrowing nail.

**acrophobia** (ak′rə-fō′bi-ə), *n.* fear of high places.

**acrotism** (ak′rə-tiz'm), *n.* absence or imperceptibility of the pulse beat.

**ACTH,** a pituitary hormone used in the treatment of rheumatoid arthritis and certain other diseases.

**actinomycete** (ak′ti-nō-mī-sēt′), *n.* a mold-like parasitic microorganism important in the development of antibiotics.

**actinomycosis** (ak′ti-nō-mī-kō′sis), *n.* a fungus infection that affects the mouth, jaw, skin, bones, and viscera: it is transmitted to man by cattle.

**actinotherapy** (ak′ti-nō-ther′ə-pi), *n.* treatment of disease by the use of actinic light rays.

**active immunity,** immunity (to a disease) due to the production of antibodies in the body tissue.

**acuity** (ə-kū′ə-ti), *n.* sharpness or clearness, as of the vision or hearing.

**acute** (ə-kūt′), *adj.* having a short and somewhat severe duration: said of some diseases.

**Adam's apple,** the projection formed by the thyroid cartilage in the front of the neck.

**addict** (ad′ikt), *n.* a person having a habit or practice; especially, one given to the habitual use of drugs or alcohol.

**addiction** (ə-dik′shən), *n.* habitual inclination; irresistible need for something, especially a drug: as, a morphine *addiction.*

**Addison's disease** (ad′ə-s'nz), a disease of the adrenal glands characterized by anemia, peculiar skin discoloration, low blood pressure, diarrhea, and digestive upset: it is usually fatal.

**adduct** (ə-dukt′), *v. t.* to move or pull (a part of the body) toward the median axis or toward another part.

**adenitis** (ad″n-ī′tis), *n.* glandular inflammation.

**adenoid** (ad″n-oid), *adj.* like or resembling a gland.

**adenoidectomy** (ad″n-oid-ek′tə-mi), *n.* the surgical removal of the adenoids.

**adenoids** (ad″n-oidz), *n.pl.* growths of adenoid tissue in the upper part of the throat, behind the nose: they can swell up and obstruct breathing and speaking.

**adenoma** (ad″n-ō′mə), *n.* a benign tumor of glandular tissue or resembling a gland in structure.

**adhesion** (əd-hē′zhən), *n.* 1. the growing together of normally separate tissues. 2. *pl.* the bands of fibrous tissue by which such tissues are connected.

**adiaphoretic** (ə-di-af′ə-ret′ik), *adj.* causing suppression of perspiration. *n.* that which causes lessening or suppression of perspiration.

**adipose** (ad′ə-pōs), *adj.* fatty. *n.* the fat in the connective tissue throughout the body.

**adiposity** (ad′ə-pos′ə-ti), *n.* the state or condition of being fat.

**adolescence** (ad″l-es′'ns), *n.* the time of life between puberty and maturity; period of development from childhood to adulthood.

**adrenal** (ad-rē′n'l), *adj.* 1. near a kidney. 2. of or from the adrenal glands. *n.* an adrenal gland.

**adrenalectomy** (ad′rē-n'l-ek′tə-mi), *n.* surgical removal of the adrenal glands.

**adrenal glands,** two small ductless glands on the upper part of the kidneys.

**adrenalin** (ad-ren″l-in), *n.* 1. a hormone produced by the adrenal glands. 2. a drug with this hormone in it, used to raise blood pressure, stop bleeding, stimulate the heart muscle, etc.: a trade-mark **(Adrenalin).**

**adrenaline** (ad-ren″l-in), *n.* adrenalin.

**aeration** (ā′ẽr-ā′shən), *n.* the combining of oxygen with the blood in breathing.

**aerophagia** (âr′ə-fā′ji-ə), *n.* an abnormal, spasmodic swallowing of air: often a symptom of hysteria.

**aerophobia** (âr′ə-fō′bi-ə), *n.* an abnormal fear of air, especially of drafts.

**afebrile** (ā-fē′bril), *adj.* having no fever.

**afterbirth** (af′tẽr-bũrth′), *n.* the placenta and fetal membranes expelled from the uterus after childbirth.

**agar-agar** (ā′gär-ā′gär), *n.* a gelatinous preparation obtained from Ceylon moss, a seaweed, and used to relieve constipation, as a base for bacterial cultures, etc.

**agglutination** (ə-glo͞o′t'n-ā′shən), *n.* 1. the clumping together of microorganisms, blood cells, etc., suspended in a fluid. 2. the process of joining together parts in the healing of a wound.

**agnail** (ag′nāl′), *n.* 1. a sore or swelling around a fingernail or toenail. 2. a hangnail.

**agoraphobia** (ag′ə-rə-fō′bi-ə), *n.* a morbid fear of being in open or public places.

**agraphia** (ā-graf′i-ə), *n.* a brain disorder in which the patient's ability to write is partly or wholly lost.

**ague** (ā′gū), *n.* malarial fever or any symptom due to malaria, as regular recurring chills.

**alalia** (ə-lā′li-ə), *n.* loss or impairment of the ability to speak.

**albinism** (al′bə-niz'm), *n.* a condition in which there is abnormal lack of coloration of the eyes, skin, and hair.

**albino** (al-bī′nō), *n.* one affected with albinism: albinos have a white skin, whitish hair, and pink eyes.

**albumen** (al-bū'mən), *n.* 1. the nutritive matter in germinating plant and animal cells. 2. the white of eggs.
**albumin** (al-bū'min), *n.* a protein found in milk, egg, muscle, blood, and in many vegetable tissues and fluids: albumins are soluble in water, coagulated by heat, and consist of carbon, hydrogen, nitrogen, oxygen, and sulfur.
**albuminuria** (al-bū'mi-nyoor'i-ə), *n.* the presence of albumin in the urine, often indicating a diseased condition of the kidneys.
**alcoholism** (al'kə-hôl'iz'm), *n.* a diseased condition caused by habitually drinking too much alcoholic liquor.
**alexia** (ə-lek'si-ə), *n.* inability to read due to lesions of the brain; word blindness.
**algolagnia** (al'gə-lag'ni-ə), *n.* abnormal sexual pleasure derived from inflicting or suffering pain; masochism or sadism.
**algophobia** (al'gə-fō'bi-ə), *n.* an extreme or abnormal fear of pain.
**alienation** (āl'yən-ā'shən), *n.* mental derangement; insanity.
**alienism** (āl'yən-iz'm), *n.* the treatment and study of mental diseases; psychiatry.
**alienist** (āl'yən-ist), *n.* a doctor who specializes in the treatment and study of mental diseases; psychiatrist.
**alimentary canal** (al'ə-men'tə-ri), the passage of the body that food passes through, consisting of the mouth, esophagus, stomach, and intestines.
**alimentation** (al'i-men-tā'shən), *n.* the act of giving or receiving food.
**alkali** (al'kə-lī'), *n.* a base or hydroxide, as soda or potash, that is soluble in water and can neutralize acids: alkalis have an acrid taste and turn red litmus blue.
**alkaline** (al'kə-līn'), *adj.* of, like, or containing an alkali.
**alkaloid** (al'kə-loid'), *n.* an organic alkaline substance containing nitrogen: some alkaloids taken from plants are used in certain drugs, as caffeine, morphine, cocaine, quinine, and strychnine; some are highly poisonous.
**alkalosis** (al'kə-lō'sis), *n.* a condition in which the alkali reserve of the body is higher than normal.
**allantoid** (ə-lan'toid), *adj.* like or resembling the allantois; shaped like a sausage.
**allantois** (ə-lan'tō-is), *n.* a membranous pouch in the embryo that develops into the umbilical cord and the placenta in pregnancy.
**allergen** (al'ēr-jən), *n.* any substance inducing an allergic state or reaction.
**allergy** (al'ēr-ji), *n.* a hypersensitivity to a specific substance (such as food, pollen, dust, etc.) or condition (as heat or cold) which in similar amounts are harmless to most people.
**allopathy** (ə-lop'ə-thi), *n.* treatment of disease by remedies that produce effects different from or opposite to those produced by the disease.
**aloes** (al'ōz), *n.* a bitter, laxative drug made from the juice of certain aloe leaves.
**alopecia** (al'ə-pē'shi-ə), *n.* baldness.
**alopecia areata** (âr'i-ā'tə), baldness in large spots, probably due to a nervous condition.
**alum** (al'əm), *n.* a double sulfate of potassium and aluminum used as an astringent or as an emetic.
**alveolar** (al-vē'ə-lēr), *adj.* 1. of the part of the jaws containing the sockets of the teeth. 2. of the air pockets in the lungs.
**alveolus** (al-vē'ə-ləs), *n.* 1. a small cavity or hollow, as an air cell of a lung, a tooth socket, etc. 2. the ridge of the gums above and behind the upper front teeth.
**amalgam** (ə-mal'gəm), *n.* an alloy of mercury with another metal: silver amalgam is used as a dental filling.
**amaurosis** (am'ô-rō'sis), *n.* partial or total blindness without visible organic change, caused by disease of the optic nerve.
**amblyopia** (am'bli-ō'pi-ə), *n.* the early stage of amaurosis.
**amboceptor** (am'bə-sep'tēr), *n.* a substance present in the blood during infection, believed to help in the destruction of the disease-causing microorganism by connecting it with another substance in the blood.
**amenorrhea** (ā-men'ə-rē'ə), *n.* abnormal absence or suppression of menstruation.
**amentia** (ə-men'shə), *n.* 1. congenital subnormality of intelligence; feeble-mindedness. 2. a type of temporary insanity.
**amino acids** (am'i-nō'), a group of nitrogenous organic compounds that serve as units of structure of the proteins and are essential to human metabolism.
**amnesia** (am-nē'zhi-ə), *n.* partial or total loss of memory caused by brain injury, or by shock, repression, etc.
**amnion** (am'ni-ən), *n.* the innermost membrane of the sac enclosing the embryo.
**amphetamine** (am-fet'ə-mēn'), *n.* a drug used as a nasal spray or inhalant, in sinusitis, head colds, hay fever, etc.
**ampoule** (am-pōōl'), *n.* a small, sealed glass vial containing an exact amount of a medicine for subcutaneous injection.
**amputate** (am'pyoo-tāt'), *v. t.* to cut off; remove surgically.
**amputation** (am'pyoo-tā'shən), *n.* surgical cutting off of a part, as a finger or limb.
**amylase** (am'i-lās'), *n.* an enzyme that helps change starch into sugar: it is found in saliva, pancreatic juice, etc.
**amytal** (am'i-tal'), *n.* a colorless, crystalline compound used as a sedative and narcotic.
**anal** (ā'n'l), *adj.* of or near the anus.
**analgesia** (an'al-jē'zi-ə), *n.* absence or loss of feeling for pain.
**analgesic** (an'al-jē'zik), *adj.* not sensitive to or relieving pain. *n.* a drug which relieves pain.
**anaphrodisiac** (an-af'rə-diz'i-ak), *n.* a drug which represses sexual desire. *adj.* decreasing or repressing sexual desire.
**anaphylaxis** (an'ə-fə-lak'sis), *n.* a condition of hypersensitivity to proteins and other substances in which exposure to or injection of the foreign matter results in attacks, sometimes causing collapse and death.
**anaplasty** (an'ə-plas'ti), *n.* plastic surgery.
**anatomy** (ə-nat'ə-mi), *n.* the science that deals with the form and structure of the body.
**anemia** (ə-nē'mi-ə), *n.* a condition in which there is a reduction in the number of red blood corpuscles or in the amount of hemoglobin in the blood stream or of both.
**anesthesia** (an'əs-thē'zhə), *n.* a partial or total loss of sensation or feeling (i.e., loss of the sense of pain, temperature, touch, etc.) produced by disease or an anesthetic.
**anesthesiology** (an'əs-thē'zi-ol'ə-ji), *n.* the science of anesthesia and anesthetics.
**anesthetic** (an'əs-thet'ik), *adj.* 1. not having the ability to experience sensation. 2. producing anesthesia. *n.* any drug or gas capable of producing anesthesia, or insensibility to pain or sensation.
**aneurysm** (an'yoor-iz'm), *n.* a blood-filled sac formed by dilatation of part of an artery wall, caused by disease or injury.
**angina** (an-jī'nə), *n.* any inflammatory disease of the throat, especially one characterized by spasmodic suffocation, as croup or quinsy.
**angina pectoris** (pek'tə-ris), a heart disease in which there are spasms of pain in the chest, with feelings of suffocation, usually due to an insufficient supply of blood to the heart muscle.
**angioma** (an'ji-ō'mə), *n.* a tumor made up mainly of lymph or blood vessels.
**ankylosis** (aŋ'kə-lō'sis), *n.* stiffening of a joint, caused by fibrous or bony union.
**ankylostomiasis** (aŋ'ki-los'tə-mī'ə-sis), *n.* hookworm disease.
**anociassociation** (ə-nō'si-ə-sō'si-ā'shən), *n.* the prevention of shock in surgery by calming the patient beforehand, and using local anesthetics and sharp dissection, so as to keep pain sensations from reaching the central nervous system.
**anodyne** (an'ə-dīn'), *adj.* soothing; relieving pain. *n.* anything that relieves pain.
**anorexia** (an'ə-rek'si-ə), *n.* loss of appetite for food.
**antacid** (ant-as'id), *adj.* that neutralizes acids; counteracting acidity. *n.* an antacid substance, such as sodium bicarbonate.
**anteversion** (an'ti-vūr'shən), *n.* a displacing of a bodily organ, especially the uterus, in which its axis is inclined farther forward than is normal.
**anthracosis** (an'thrə-kō'sis), *n.* a disease of the lungs caused by inhaled coal dust: it is most common in coal miners.
**anthrax** (an'thraks), *n.* a carbuncle or hard, red swelling containing pus; boil.
**antibiotic** (an'ti-bī-ot'ik), *n.* a chemical substance produced by various groups of microorganisms, specifically bacteria, fungi, and actinomycetes, and having the capacity, in dilute solution, to inhibit the growth of or to destroy bacteria and other microorganisms. Antibiotics are used in the treatment of various infectious diseases.
**antibody** (an'ti-bod'i), *n.* a protein produced in the body in response to contact of the body with an antigen, and having the specific capacity of neutralizing or reacting with the antigen.
**antidote** (an'ti-dōt'), *n.* a remedy to counteract a poison.
**antigen** (an'ti-jən), *n.* a substance which causes the production of an antibody when introduced directly into the body, as into the blood stream.
**antihistamine** (an'ti-his'tə-mēn'), *n.* a drug used to minimize the action of histamine in certain allergic conditions: it is claimed that antihistamines relieve the symptoms in asthma, hay fever, the common cold, etc.
**antipyretic** (an'ti-pī-ret'ik), *adj.* reducing fever. *n.* a remedy to reduce fever.
**antiseptic** (an'ti-sep'tik), *adj.* preventing decay, infection, etc. *n.* an antiseptic substance, as alcohol.
**antitoxin** (an'ti-tok'sin), *n.* 1. a chemical substance in the blood serum which the body manufactures to neutralize toxins. 2. a serum containing an antitoxin: taken from the blood of an infected animal, such a serum is injected into a person to prevent a specific disease, as diphtheria, tetanus, etc.
**antivenin** (an'ti-ven'in), *n.* 1. an antitoxin for venom, as of snakes, formed in the blood by gradually increased injections of the specific venom. 2. a serum containing this antitoxin.
**antrum** (an'trəm), *n.* a cavity, particularly one in a bone, as the sinus in the upper jaw.
**anus** (ā'nəs), *n.* the opening at the lower end of the alimentary canal.
**aorta** (ā-ôr'tə), *n.* the main artery leading from the heart.
**apepsia** (ə-pep'si-ə), *n.* stoppage or failure of digestive activity.
**aperient** (ə-pêr'i-ənt), *adj. & n.* laxative.
**aphasia** (ə-fā'zhə), *n.* loss or impairment of the power to use or understand words, usually caused by brain disease or injury.
**aphonia** (ə-fō'ni-ə), *n.* loss of voice due to organic or psychic causes.
**aphrodisiac** (af'rə-diz'i-ak'), *adj.* arousing or increasing sexual desire. *n.* any aphrodisiac drug, food, or other agent.
**apoplexy** (ap'ə-plek'si), *n.* sudden paralysis with total or partial loss of consciousness

and sensation, caused by the breaking or obstruction of a blood vessel in the brain.
**appendectomy** (ap′ən-dek′tə-mi), *n.* surgical removal of the vermiform appendix.
**appendicitis** (ə-pen′də-sī′tis), *n.* inflammation of the vermiform appendix.
**appendix** (ə-pen′diks), *n.* an outgrowth of an organ; especially, the vermiform appendix, a small saclike appendage of the large intestine.
**aqueous humor,** a watery fluid in the space between the cornea and the lens of the eye.
**Argyrol** (är′jə-rôl′), *n.* a compound of silver and a protein, used as a local antiseptic, especially in treating inflamed mucous tissues: a trade-mark.
**arsphenamine** (ärs′fen-ə-mēn′), *n.* a drug used in the treatment of syphilis: it is a yellowish organic arsenic compound.
**arteriosclerosis** (är-têr′i-ō-skli-rō′sis), *n.* a thickening and hardening of the walls of the arteries.
**arteritis** (är′tə-rī′tis), *n.* inflammation of the arteries.
**artery** (är′tēr-i), *n.* any one of the system of branching tubes carrying blood from the heart to all parts of the body.
**arthritis** (är-thrī′tis), *n.* inflammation of a joint or joints.
**articulation** (är-tik′yoo-lā′shən), *n.* a joint between bones or similar parts.
**ascites** (ə-sī′tēz), *n.* an accumulation of serous fluid in the abdominal cavity; a kind of dropsy.
**asepsis** (ə-sep′sis), *n.* freedom from disease-producing microorganisms.
**aseptic** (ə-sep′tik), *adj.* not putrefactive or infectious.
**asphyxia** (as-fik′si-ə), *n.* loss of consciousness as a result of too little oxygen and too much carbon dioxide in the blood: suffocation causes asphyxia.
**asphyxiate** (as-fik′si-āt′), *v. t.* to cause asphyxia in, as by suffocating.
**aspiration** (as′pə-rā′shən), *n.* 1. act of breathing. 2. the removal by suction of fluid or gas from a body cavity.
**aspirator** (as′pə-rā′tēr), *n.* an apparatus using suction to remove fluid or gas from a body cavity.
**aspirin** (as′pēr-in), *n.* a white crystalline powder used for reducing fever, relieving headache, etc.
**assimilation** (ə-sim′′l-ā′shən), *n.* the change of digested food into part of the living organism.
**asthenia** (as-thē′ni-ə), *n.* lack or loss of bodily strength; bodily weakness.
**asthma** (az′mə), *n.* a chronic disorder characterized by wheezing, coughing, difficulty in breathing, and a suffocating feeling.
**astigmatism** (ə-stig′mə-tiz′m), *n.* a structural defect of the eyes that prevents light rays from an object from meeting in a single focal point, so that indistinct images are formed.
**astringent** (ə-strin′jənt), *adj.* that contracts body tissue and blood vessels, checking the flow of blood. *n.* an astringent substance or drug.
**ataraxia** (at′ə-rak′si-ə), *n.* the state or condition of having a calm or peaceful mind.
**atavism** (at′ə-viz′m), *n.* 1. resemblance to a remote ancestor in some characteristic which nearer ancestors do not have. 2. reversion to a primitive type.
**ataxia** (ə-tak′si-ə), *n.* total or partial inability to co-ordinate voluntary bodily movements, especially muscular movements.
**atherosclerosis** (ath′ər-ō-skli-rō′sis), *n.* a kind of arteriosclerosis in which globules of fat accumulate in the connective tissue of the walls of the arteries.
**athlete's foot,** ringworm of the feet, a contagious skin disease caused by a tiny fungus.
**atrophy** (at′rə-fi), *n.* a wasting away of body tissue, an organ, or other part, or the failure of an organ or part to grow because of insufficient nutrition.
**atropine** (at′rə-pēn′), *n.* a poisonous drug obtained from belladonna: it has many medicinal uses, such as dilating the pupils of the eye and relieving spasms.
**aureomycin** (ô′ri-ō-mī′sin), *n.* an antibiotic drug similar to penicillin, effective against certain viruses and against both Gram-positive and Gram-negative bacteria.
**auricle** (ô′ri-k′l), *n.* 1. the external part of the ear. 2. either of the two upper chambers of the heart, into which the blood flows from the veins.
**auscultation** (ôs′kəl-tā′shən), *n.* a listening, often with the aid of a stethoscope, to sounds in the chest, abdomen, etc. so as to determine the condition of the heart, lungs, etc.
**autoerotism** (ô′tō-er′ə-tiz′m), *n.* 1. sexual sensation arising without external stimulus from another person. 2. self-generated sexual activity directed toward oneself, as masturbation.
**autointoxication** (ô′tō-in-tok′sə-kā′shən), *n.* poisoning by some toxic substance formed within the body.
**autopsy** (ô′top-si), *n.* examination of a body after death to discover the cause of death, damage done by disease, etc.
**autosuggestion** (ô′tō-səg-jes′chən), *n.* suggestion to oneself arising within oneself and having effects on one's thinking and bodily functions.
**avitaminosis** (ā-vī′tə-min-ō′sis), *n.* any disease or disorder due to a vitamin deficiency in the diet.
**axilla** (ak-sil′ə), *n.* the armpit.
**axon** (ak′son), *n.* that part of a nerve cell through which impulses travel away from the cell body.

## B

**bacilliform** (bə-sil′ə-form), *adj.* rod-shaped; shaped like a bacillus.
**bacillus** (bə-sil′əs), *n.* 1. any of the rod-shaped bacteria. 2. *usually* **bacilli**, *pl.*, any of the disease-producing bacteria.
**bacteria** (bak-têr′i-ə), *n.pl.* one-celled microorganisms which have no chlorophyll, multiply by simple division, and can be seen only with a microscope: some bacteria cause diseases such as pneumonia, tuberculosis, and syphilis.
**bacteriophage** (bak-têr′i-ə-fāj′), *n.* an extremely minute agent which destroys disease-producing bacteria in the body.
**balm** (bäm), *n.* any healing or soothing ointment or medicine.
**basal metabolism,** the quantity of energy used by the body at rest; amount of heat produced by the body fourteen to eighteen hours after eating and when at rest for thirty to sixty minutes but not asleep: it is measured by the rate at which heat is given off.
**Basedow's disease** (bas′i-dōz′), overactive thyroid gland causing a rapid pulse, sleeplessness, etc.; hyperthyroidism.
**behaviorism** (bi-hāv′yēr-iz′m), *n.* the psychological theory that objective observation of human behavior provides the only valid data.
**belladonna** (bel′ə-don′ə), *n.* the drug obtained from the leaves and roots of the poisonous deadly nightshade plant: it is used to dilate the pupil of the eye, stimulate the heart, relieve spasms, etc.
**bends** (bendz), *n.pl.* cramps that often attack a person who goes too quickly from a place of abnormal atmospheric pressure to one of normal pressure, as in deep-sea diving.
**benign** (bi-nīn′), *adj.* not malignant.
**Benzedrine** (ben′zə-drēn′), *n.* amphetamine, used as an inhalant to relieve nasal congestion, and as a stimulant of the central nervous system: a trade-mark.
**benzene** (ben′zēn), *n.* a clear, inflammable liquid used as an antiseptic, to kill tapeworms and other parasites, etc.
**benzoic acid** (ben-zō′ik), a white, crystalline organic acid used as an antiseptic.
**beriberi** (ber′i-ber′i), *n.* a deficiency disease, occurring mainly in Asia, caused by lack of vitamin B in the diet: it is characterized by extreme weakness, paralysis, anemia, and wasting away.
**biceps** (bī′seps), *n.* a muscle having two points of origin; especially, the large muscle in the front of the upper arm or the corresponding muscle at the back of the thigh.
**bicuspid** (bī-kus′pid), *n.* any of the eight adult teeth with two-pointed crowns.
**bile** (bīl), *n.* the bitter, yellow-brown or greenish fluid secreted by the liver and found in the gall bladder: it is discharged into the duodenum and helps in digestion.
**biochemistry** (bī′ō-kem′is-tri), *n.* the chemistry of living matter and of life processes.
**biology** (bī-ol′ə-ji), *n.* the science that deals with all forms of life.
**biopsy** (bī′op-si), *n.* the excision of a piece of living tissue for diagnostic examination by a microscope, etc.
**bismuth** (biz′məth), *n.* a metallic element, the salts and compounds of which are useful in the treatment of inflammatory diseases of the stomach and intestines: it is also used in the treatment of syphilis.
**bladder** (blad′ēr), *n.* a bag of membranous tissue capable of inflation to receive and contain liquids: the *urinary bladder* in the pelvic cavity holds urine flowing from the kidneys.
**blastoderm** (blas′tə-dūrm), *n.* the part of a fertilized ovum that gives rise to the germinal disk from which the embryo develops.
**blastula** (blas′choo-lə), *n.* the stage of development at which an embryo consists of one or several layers of cells around a central cavity, forming a hollow sphere.
**blepharitis** (blef′ə-rī′tis), *n.* inflammation of the eyelids.
**blister** (blis′tēr), *n.* a light swelling of the skin, filled with watery matter and caused by burning or rubbing.
**blood** (blud), *n.* the red fluid circulating in the heart, arteries, and veins: it supplies food to all tissues.
**blood count,** the number of red and white corpuscles in a given volume of a person's blood.
**blood group,** any of several (usually four) groups into which a person's blood is classified: also **blood type.**
**blood plasma,** the fluid part of blood, as distinguished from the corpuscles, now used in transfusions.
**blood pressure,** the pressure exerted by the blood against the inner walls of the blood vessels: it varies with age, health, physical exercise, etc.
**bloodshot** (blud′shot′), *adj.* suffused or tinged with blood.
**blood vessel,** a tube through which blood circulates in the body; artery, vein, or capillary.
**blue baby,** a baby born with a bluish tinge due to inherited heart disease or incomplete lung expansion.
**boil** (boil), *n.* a painful, inflamed, pus-filled swelling on the skin: it contains a hard core and is caused by infection.
**bone** (bōn), *n.* any part or piece of the hard tissue forming the skeleton.
**borax** (bôr′aks), *n.* a white, crystalline salt with an alkaline taste, used in antiseptics, etc.
**boric acid** (bôr′ik), a white, crystalline compound with the properties of a weak acid, used as a mild antiseptic.
**boron** (bô′ron), *n.* a non-metalic, chemical element: its compounds are used in the preparation of borax and boric acid.

**botulism** (boch′ə-liz′m), *n.* a type of food poisoning, sometimes caused by poorly canned or preserved foods.
**bowel** (bou′əl), *n.* the intestine.
**brachial** (brā′ki-əl), *adj.* of or pertaining to the arm.
**bradycardia** (brad′i-kär′di-ə), *n.* abnormally slow beating of the heart.
**brain** (brān), *n.* the mass of nerve tissue in the cranium: it is the main part of the nervous system, and is made up of gray matter (the outer cortex of nerve cells) and white matter (the inner mass of nerve fibers).
**breast** (brest), *n.* 1. the front part of the chest. 2. either one of the two rounded, milk-secreting glands protruding from the upper, front part of a woman's body.
**breech presentation,** delivery of a fetus with its buttocks first.
**bridge** (brij), *n.* a fixed or removable mounting for replacing missing teeth: the artificial teeth are fixed to a metal bar which is attached to adjoining natural teeth.
**Bright's disease** (brīts), a kidney inflammation characterized by the presence of albumin in the urine; nephritis.
**bromide** (brō′mīd), *n.* potassium bromide, a white, crystalline compound used as a sedative.
**bronchial** (broŋ′ki-əl), *adj.* of the bronchial tubes.
**bronchial tubes,** the two main branches of the trachea and the tubes branching from them.
**bronchitis** (broŋ-kī′tis), *n.* an acute or chronic inflammation of the mucous lining of the bronchial tubes.
**bronchopneumonia** (broŋ′kō-noo-mō′nyə), *n.* inflammation of the small bronchial tubes accompanied by inflamed, pus-forming patches in the near-by lobules of the lungs: it is generally a secondary disease following an infection of the upper respiratory tract.
**bronchoscope** (broŋ′kə-skōp′), *n.* an instrument used to examine the inside of the trachea or bronchi, or to extract foreign bodies from them.
**bronchus** (broŋ′kəs), *n.* either of the two main air passages from the trachea to the lung.
**bubo** (bū′bō), *n.* an inflamed swelling of the lymph glands of the groin or armpit, often seen after a venereal disease.
**bubonocele** (bū-bon′ə-sēl′), *n.* an incomplete or partial inguinal hernia forming a swelling in the groin.
**bulb** (bulb), *n.* an enlargement of some tissues and organs, as at the root of a hair.
**bunion** (bun′yən), *n.* an inflammation and swelling of the bursa at the base of the big toe, with a thickening of the skin.
**bursa** (būr′sə), *n.* a tiny sac or pocket filled with oily fluid and located between the muscle and bone surface, between joints, etc. to prevent friction.
**bursitis** (bẽr-sī′tis), *n.* inflammation of a bursa.
**buttock** (but′ək), *n.* 1. either of the two fleshy, rounded parts at the back of the hips; either half of the rump. 2. *pl.* the rump.
**Butyn** (bū′tin), *n.* a colorless, crystalline substance used as an anesthetic, especially for surface anesthesia of mucous membranes and in the eye: a trade-mark.

## C

**cadaver** (kə-dav′ẽr), *n.* corpse; especially, one used for experimental purposes or to teach surgery and anatomy.
**caecum** (sē′kəm), *n.* the pouch which is the beginning of the large intestine.
**Caesarean operation,** a surgical operation for delivering a baby by cutting through the mother's abdominal and uterine walls.
**caffeine** (kaf′ēn), *n.* the alkaloid present in coffee, tea, and kola: it is a stimulant to the heart and central nervous system.
**caisson disease,** decompression sickness.
**calamine** (kal′ə-mīn′), *n.* hydrous zinc silicate, a zinc ore: used in skin ointments and lotions.
**calcareous** (kal-kâr′i-əs), *adj.* of, like, or containing calcium, calcium carbonate, or lime.
**calcification** (kal′sə-fi-kā′shən), *n.* the process by which tissue becomes hardened due to deposits of calcium salts within it.
**calcium** (kal′si-əm), *n.* a metallic chemical element present in nearly all tissue, especially tooth and bone tissue.
**calculus** (kal′kyoo-ləs), *n.* a stony mass or other mineral salt concretion formed within the body.
**callous** (kal′əs), *adj.* having a callus or calluses; thick-skinned.
**callus** (kal′əs), *n.* 1. a hardened, thickened place on the skin. 2. a hard substance formed around the ends of a broken bone that helps them to knit.
**calomel** (kal′ə-m′l), *n.* mercurous chloride, a tasteless, white powder used as a purgative, as a remedy in syphilis, and for intestinal worms.
**Calorie** (kal′ə-ri), *n.* the amount of heat needed to raise the temperature of one kilogram of water one degree centigrade: used as the unit for measuring the energy produced by food when oxidized in the body. Also **calorie.**
**camomile** (kam′ə-mīl′), *n.* chamomile.
**camphor** (kam′fẽr), *n.* a volatile, crystalline substance with a strong odor: used as an irritant and stimulant.
**cancer** (kan′sẽr), *n.* a malignant new growth anywhere in the body; malignant tumor: cancers tend to spread and ulcerate.
**canker** (kaŋ′kẽr), *n.* an ulcerated sore that spreads, usually in the mouth.
**capillary** (kap′′l-er′i), *n.* a small, hairlike blood vessel which connects the smaller arteries with the veins.
**capsule** (kap′s'l), *n.* 1. a small, soluble gelatin container for enclosing a dose of medicine. 2. any sac or membrane enclosing a part.
**carbohydrate** (kär′bə-hī′drāt), *n.* any of certain organic compounds of carbon and water, including starches, sugars, and celluloses.
**carbolic acid** (kär-bol′ik), a poisonous acid obtained from the distillation of coal or coal tar and used as an antiseptic and disinfectant.
**carbon dioxide,** a colorless, odorless gas somewhat heavier than air: it passes out of the lungs in respiration.
**carbon monoxide,** a very poisonous, colorless, odorless gas formed by the incomplete combustion of any material containing carbon.
**carbuncle** (kär′buŋ-k'l), *n* a painful, localized, pus-bearing inflammation of the tissue beneath the skin, more severe than a boil and having several openings.
**carcinoma** (kär′sə-nō′mə), *n.* any of several kinds of epithelial cancer.
**cardiac** (kär′di-ak′), *adj.* 1 of or near the heart. 2. relating to the upper part of the stomach. *n.* a medicine that stimulates cardiac action.
**cardiogram** (kär′di-ə-gram′), *n.* a record of the heart's action, traced by a cardiograph.
**cardiograph** (kär′di-ə-graf′), *n.* an instrument designed to record the action of the heart.
**caries** (kâr′ēz), *n.* decay of teeth or bones, or, sometimes, of tissue.
**carminative** (kär-min′ə-tiv), *adj.* expelling gas from the stomach and intestines. *n.* a carminative medicine.
**carotene** (kar′ə-tēn′), *n.* the orange-colored compound in carrots, egg yolk, sweet potatoes, milk fat, and other things, which is changed by the body to vitamin A.
**carotid** (kə-rot′id), *n.* either of the two main arteries in the neck leading from the aorta to the head.
**carpal** (kär′p'l), *adj.* pertaining to the wrist. *n.* a bone of the wrist.
**carpus** (kär′pəs), *n.* 1. the wrist. 2. the wrist bones.
**cartilage** (kär′t'l-ij), *n.* a tough, elastic, whitish tissue; gristle: the skeleton of an embryo is composed largely of cartilage, most of which later turns to bone.
**cascara sagrada** (kas-kâr′ə sə-grādə), a mild laxative made from the bark of the cascara buckthorn tree.
**cast** (kast), *n.* 1. a plaster form for immobilizing a broken arm, leg, etc. 2. a plastic substance formed in the cavities of some diseased organs: as, renal *casts.*
**castor oil,** a colorless or yellowish oil which acts as a strong cathartic.
**castrate** (kas′trāt), *v. t.* to remove the testicles of a male.
**catalepsy** (kat′ə-lep′si), *n.* a condition in which consciousness and feeling are suddenly and temporarily lost, and the muscles become rigid: it may occur in epilepsy, schizophrenia, etc.
**cataract** (kat′ə-rakt′), *n.* 1. an eye disease in which the crystalline lens or its capsule becomes opaque, causing partial or total blindness. 2. the opaque area.
**catarrh** (kə-tär′), *n.* inflammation of the mucous membranes causing excessive mucus secretion, especially from the nose or throat.
**catarrhal** (kə-tär′əl), *adj.* of, like, with, or from catarrh.
**cathartic** (kə-thär′tik), *n.* a medicine for stimulating evacuation of the bowels; laxative.
**catheter** (kath′ə-tẽr), *n.* a narrow tube of metal or rubber, used to insert into a cavity to draw off fluid: it is usually used for drawing off urine from the bladder or to distend a narrow passage or opening.
**catheterize** (kath′ə-tẽr-iz′), *v. t.* to insert a catheter into for the purpose of drawing off fluids.
**cauterize** (kô′tẽr-īz′), *v. t.* to burn with a hot iron or needle, or with a caustic substance, so as to destroy dead tissue, prevent the spread of infection, etc.
**cavity** (kav′ə-ti), *n.* a natural hollow place within the body: as, the abdominal *cavity.*
**cell** (sel), *n.* a microscopic protoplasmic mass of which the tissues of the body are composed.
**cerebellum** (ser′ə-bel′əm), *n.* the section of the brain behind and below the cerebrum: it is regarded as the co-ordinating center for muscular movement.
**cerebral** (ser′ə-brəl), *adj.* of the brain or the cerebrum.
**cerebral palsy,** paralysis due to a lesion of the brain, usually suffered at birth, and characterized chiefly by spasms.
**cerebrospinal** (ser′ə-brō-spī′n'l), *adj.* 1. of or affecting the brain and the spinal cord. 2. designating that part of the nervous system comprising the brain and the spinal cord together with the cranial and spinal nerves.
**cerebrum** (ser′ə-brəm), *n.* the upper, main part of the brain, consisting of two equal hemispheres: it is the largest part of the brain and is believed to control conscious and voluntary processes.
**cerumen** (sə-roo′mən), *n.* a yellowish, waxlike substance secreted by glands in the canal of the external ear; earwax.
**cervical** (sũr′vi-k'l), *adj.* of the neck or any necklike part.
**cervix** (sũr′viks), *n.* 1. the neck. 2. a necklike part, as of the uterus, urinary bladder, etc.
**chamomile** (kam′ə-mīl′), *n.* a drug made from the dried leaves, flowers, and buds of a plant of the aster family: it is used as a carminative and an antispasmodic.

**chancre** (shaŋ′kẽr), *n.* a venereal sore or ulcer; primary lesion of syphilis.
**chancroid** (shaŋ′kroid), *n.* a soft, venereal ulcer of nonsyphilitic origin: it is usually on or about the genitals.
**change of life,** menopause.
**chaulmoogra** (chôl-mōō′grə), *n.* an East Indian tree, the seeds of which yield an oil used in the treatment of leprosy.
**chemotherapy** (kem′ō-ther′ə-pi), *n.* the treatment of infection by the systemic administration of chemicals.
**chicken pox,** an acute, highly contagious, virus disease of childhood, characterized by a slight fever and a skin eruption.
**chilblain** (chil′blān), *n.* a painful swelling and inflamed sore on the hands, toes, feet, or fingers, due to exposure to cold.
**chloroform** (klôr′ə-fôrm), *n.* a sweetish, colorless, volatile liquid used as an anesthetic.
**chloromycetin** (klôr′ə-mī-sē′tin), *n.* a synthesized antibiotic drug effective against certain viruses and rickettsiae as well as against bacteria.
**chloroquine** (klôr′ə-kwin′), *n.* a synthetic drug used in treating malaria.
**chlorosis** (klə-rō′sis), *n.* a type of anemia sometimes affecting girls at puberty: it is characterized by a greenish discoloration of the skin, nervousness, loss of appetite, etc.
**chlorpromazine** (klôr-prom′ə-zēn′), *n.* a synthetic drug used as a sedative and muscle relaxant and experimentally, to control anxiety and agitation in various psychoses.
**cholecyst** (kol′i-sist′), *n.* the gall bladder.
**cholecystitis** (kol′ə-sis-tī′tis), *n.* inflammation of the gall bladder.
**cholelithiasis** (kol′ə-li-thī′ə-sis), *n.* stones in the gall bladder.
**cholera** (kol′ẽr-ə), *n.* an acute infectious disease characterized by violent diarrhea and vomiting, muscular cramps, and collapse.
**cholera infantum** (in-fan′təm), an intestinal disease of infants, characterized by vomiting and diarrhea: it occurs usually in summer.
**cholera morbus** (môr′bəs), a noninfectious, rarely fatal cholera, with diarrhea and cramps: it is usually caused by contaminated foods.
**cholesterol** (kə-les′tə-rōl′), *n.* a crystalline fatty alcohol found in all animal fats and occurring extensively throughout the body: it forms a large part of some gallstones.
**chorea** (kô-rē′ə), *n.* a nervous disease characterized by twitching, jerky movements caused by involuntary muscular contractions: also called *St. Vitus's dance.*
**chromatin** (krō′mə-tin), *n.* a granular protoplasmic substance in the nucleus of cells: chromatin contains the genes.
**chromosome** (krō′mə-sōm′), *n.* any of the microscopic rod-shaped bodies into which the chromatin separates during mitosis: they carry the genes that convey hereditary characteristics, and are constant in number for each series.
**chronic** (kron′ik), *adj.* lasting a long time; also, recurring: said of a disease.
**chyle** (kīl), *n.* a milky fluid composed of lymph and emulsified fats: it is formed from chyme in the small intestine, is absorbed by the lacteals, and is passed into the blood through the thoracic duct.
**chyme** (kīm), *n.* the thick, semifluid mass resulting from gastric digestion of food: it passes from the stomach into the small intestine, where the chyle is formed from it.
**cicatrix** (sik′ə-triks), *n.* a scar or other mark left where a wound or sore has healed.
**circumcision** (sũr′kəm-sizh′ən), *n.* the surgical removal of part or all of the foreskin.
**cirrhosis** (si-rō′sis), *n.* a degenerative disease of an organ, especially the liver, marked by excess formation of connective tissue and the subsequent contraction of the organ.
**claustrophobia** (klôs′trə-fō′bi-ə), *n.* an abnormal fear of being confined in an enclosed or confined place.
**clavicle** (klav′ə-k'l), *n.* a small bone connecting the breastbone with the shoulder blade; collarbone.
**climacteric** (klī-mak′ter-ik), *n.* a period in the life of a person when an important change in health or bodily function occurs, especially the period of the menopause in women.
**clitoris** (klī′tə-ris), *n.* a tiny, erectile organ at the upper end of the vulva: the female equivalent of the male penis.
**clot** (klot), *n.* a thick coagulated mass or semisolid lump of blood.
**clubfoot** (klub′foot′), *n.* a congenital deformity of the foot, characterized by a misshapen or twisted appearance.
**coagulate** (kō-ag′yoo-lāt′), *v. t.* to cause to clot.
**coagulation** (kō-ag′yoo-lā′shən), *n.* a clot or the process of forming one.
**cocaine, cocain** (kō-kān′), *n.* a crystalline alkaloid obtained from dried coca leaves: it is a narcotic and a local anesthetic.
**cocci** (kok′sī), *n.* plural of **coccus.**
**coccus** (kok′əs), *n.* any of the bacteria having a spherical or oval shape.
**coccyx** (kok′siks), *n.* a small triangular bone at the lower end of the vertebral column, formed by the fusion of four rudimentary vertebrae.
**cochlea** (kok′li-ə), *n.* the spiral-shaped part of the internal ear, containing the auditory nerve endings.
**codeine** (kō′dēn), *n.* an alkaloid derived from opium and resembling morphine, but milder in its action and less habit-forming: used for the relief of pain and as a sedative.
**cod-liver oil** (kod′liv′ẽr), a heavy yellowish oil prepared from cod livers, rich in vitamins and used to increase the number of red corpuscles in the blood.
**coition** (kō-ish′ən), *n.* sexual intercourse; copulation.
**coitus** (kō′i-təs), *n.* sexual intercourse.
**cold** (kōld), *n.* an acute inflammation of the mucous membranes of the respiratory passages, especially of the nose and throat, caused by a virus and characterized by sneezing, coughing, etc.; coryza.
**colic** (kol′ik), *n.* a severe pain in the abdomen caused by an abnormal condition in the bowels.
**colitis** (kō-lī′tis), *n.* inflammation of the mucous membrane of the large intestine: the symptoms are cramps, diarrhea, and often mucus and pus in the stool.
**collapse** (kə-laps′), *n.* a sudden breakdown in health; state of extreme physical depression and prostration with failure of circulation, often preceding death.
**collarbone** (kol′ẽr-bōn′), *n.* the clavicle.
**colon** (kō′lən), *n.* the part of the large intestine extending from the caecum to the rectum.
**colostomy** (kə-los′tə-mi), *n.* the surgical operation of making an artificial opening in the colon to serve as an anus.
**coma** (kō′mə), *n.* a state or condition in which there is deep and prolonged loss of consciousness, often caused by injury or disease.
**comedo** (kom′i-dō′), *n.* a plug of dirt and fatty matter in a skin duct; blackhead.
**complex** (kom′pleks), *n.* 1. a group of emotional attitudes associated with a particular object, activity, etc. and remaining partly unconscious but strongly influencing the individual's behavior. 2. an exaggerated dislike or fear.
**complication** (kom′plə-kā′shən), *n.* a disease or abnormal condition that occurs during another disease.
**concretion** (kon-krē′shən), *n.* a hard, inorganic mass deposited in the tissues or in a cavity; calculus.
**concussion** (kən-kush′ən), *n.* a condition of impaired functioning of some organ, especially the brain, as a result of a violent blow or impact.
**congenital** (kən-jen′ə-t'l), *adj.* born with: present at birth; caused by heredity or prenatal environment.
**congested** (kən-jest′əd), *adj.* swollen or filled with too much blood.
**conjunctiva** (kon′juŋk-tī′və), *n.* the mucous membrane lining the inner surface of the eyelid and covering the front part of the eyeball.
**conjunctivitis** (kən-juŋk′tə-vī′tis), *n.* inflammation of the conjunctiva.
**consciousness** (kon′shəs-nis), *n.* 1. state of awareness, especially of what is going on around one. 2. the mind.
**constipation** (kon′stə-pā′shən), *n.* infrequency or difficulty in evacuation of the bowels.
**consumption** (kən-sump′shən), *n.* a disease that causes the body or part of the body to waste away; especially, tuberculosis of the lungs.
**contagious** (kən-tā′jəs), *adj.* spread by direct or indirect contact: said of diseases.
**contraception** (kon′trə-sep′shən), *n.* the artificial prevention of conception; the avoidance of becoming pregnant.
**contraceptive** (kon′trə-sep′tiv), *n.* any device used to prevent pregnancy.
**contusion** (kən-tōō′zhən), *n.* injury in which the skin is not broken; bruise.
**convalescence** (kon′və-les′'ns), *n.* 1. the period of gradual recovery after an illness. 2. such recovery.
**convalescent** (kon′və-les′'nt), *adj.* pertaining to a gradual return to health. *n.* one who is recovering from an illness.
**convolution** (kon′və-lōō′shən), *n.* any of the irregular folds or ridges on the surface of the brain.
**convulsion** (kən-vul′shən), *n.* violent, involuntary muscular contraction or spasm.
**copulation** (kop′yoo-lā′shən), *n.* sexual intercourse.
**corn** (kôrn), *n.* a hornlike hardening of the skin, usually on the feet and toes, caused by pressure or friction.
**cornea** (kôr′ni-ə), *n.* the transparent tissue forming the outer coat of the eyeball and covering the iris and pupil.
**coronary arteries** (kôr′ə-ner′i), the two main arteries supplying blood to the tissues of the heart.
**coronary thrombosis,** the formation of a clot in a branch of either of the coronary arteries, resulting in obstruction of that artery.
**corpuscle** (kôr′pəs-'l), *n.* any of the red cells or white cells that float in the blood, lymph, etc.: red corpuscles contain hemoglobin, which carries oxygen to the body tissues, and certain white corpuscles sometimes kill harmful microorganisms.
**cortex** (kôr′teks), *n.* the outer part or external layers of an internal organ, as of the kidney; especially, the layer of gray matter over most of the brain.
**cortisone** (kôr′tə-sōn′), *n.* an adrenal-gland hormone extracted from ox bile or prepared synthetically from certain tropical plants, used experimentally in the treatment of rheumatoid arthritis and certain other diseases.
**coryza** (kə-rī′zə), *n.* a head cold; acute nasal catarrh.
**counterirritant** (koun′tẽr-ir′ə-tənt), *n.* anything used to produce a slight irritation, as of an area of the skin, to relieve more serious irritation elsewhere.
**cramp** (kramp), *n.* a sudden, painful, involuntary muscular contraction.
**cranial** (krā′ni-əl), *adj.* pertaining to the cranium.

**cranium** (krā′ni-əm), *n.* the upper part of the skull enclosing the brain.
**creosote** (krē′ə-sōt′), *n.* a poisonous, transparent oil obtained by the distillation of wood tar or coal tar: it is used as a local anesthetic and powerful antiseptic.
**crepitation** (krep′ə-tā′shən), *n.* the crackling sound made by the rubbing together of the ends of a fractured bone.
**cretin** (krē′tin), *n.* a person suffering from cretinism.
**cretinism** (krē′tin-iz′m), *n.* a congenital deficiency of thyroid secretion with resulting deformity and idiocy.
**crisis** (krī′sis), *n.* the turning point of a disease when it becomes clear whether the patient will live or die.
**croup** (kro͞op), *n.* an inflammation of the respiratory passages, with labored breathing, hoarse coughing, and laryngeal spasm.
**curettage** (kyoo-ret′ij), *n.* the process of cleaning and scrapping with a curette.
**curette** (kyoo-ret′), *n.* a spoon-shaped instrument for the removal of tissue from the walls of body cavities, especially the uterine cavity.
**cusp** (kusp), *n.* 1. one of the elevations on the chewing surface of a tooth. 2. one of the triangular parts of the heart valve.
**cuticle** (kū′ti-k'l), *n.* 1. the outer layer of the skin. 2. hardened skin, such as accumulates at the base and sides of a fingernail.
**cutis** (kū′tis), *n.* the layer of skin beneath the epidermis.
**cyanosis** (sī′ə-nō′sis), *n.* a state of blueness of the skin due to insufficient oxygen in the blood.
**cyst** (sist), *n.* any saclike structure or pocket, especially if filled with fluid or diseased matter.
**cystitis** (sis-tī′tis), *n.* inflammation of the urinary bladder.
**cystoscope** (sis′tə-skōp′), *n.* an instrument used to inspect the interior of the urinary bladder.
**cystoscopy** (sis-tos′kə-pi), *n.* examination of the urinary bladder with a cystoscope.

## D

**Dakin's solution** (dā′kinz), a mildly alkaline solution of sodium and sulfurous acid, used as an antiseptic in the treatment of wounds.
**dandruff** (dan′drəf), *n.* white, flaky scales of dead skin formed on the scalp.
**debility** (di-bil′ə-ti), *n.* feebleness; extreme weakness of the body.
**decalcification** (dē-kal′sə-fi-kā′shən), *n.* 1. the removal of calcium or lime from bones, etc. 2. the unnatural or morbid softening of the teeth.
**deciduous** (di-sij′o͞o-əs), *adj.* not permanent: said of the first or baby teeth.
**decompensation** (dē-kom′pən-sā′shən), *n.* inability of the heart to compensate for a defect of the heart valves or the heart muscle.
**decompression sickness,** a condition caused by the formation of air bubbles in the blood or body tissues as the result of a sudden lowering of pressure: it is characterized by tightness in the chest, pains in the joints, and convulsions and collapse in severe cases.
**defecate** (def′ə-kāt′), *v. i.* to excrete waste matter from the bowels.
**degeneration** (di-jen′ēr-ā′shən), *n.* biochemical change in tissues or organs, caused by injury or disease and leading to loss of vitality, of function, etc.
**deglutition** (dē′gloo-tish′ən), *n.* the act, process, or power of swallowing.
**delirium** (di-lir′i-əm), *n.* a temporary state of extreme mental excitement, marked by restlessness, confused speech, and hallucinations: it sometimes occurs during fever, and in some forms of insanity.
**delirium tremens** (trē′mənz), a violent delirium resulting from excessive drinking of alcoholic liquor, and characterized by sweating, trembling, anxiety, and hallucinations.
**deltoid** (del′toid), *n.* the large triangular muscle in the shoulder which raises the arm away from the side.
**delusion** (di-lo͞o′zhən), *n.* a false, persistent belief not substantiated by sensory evidence.
**dementia** (di-men′shə), *n.* loss or impairment of mental powers.
**dementia praecox** (prē′koks), a form of dementia, usually beginning in late adolescence, characterized by melancholia, withdrawal, hallucinations, delusions, etc.
**demulcent** (di-mul′s'nt), *n.* medicine or ointment that counteracts the irritation of inflamed surfaces.
**dendrite** (den′drīt), *n.* the branched part of a nerve cell that carries impulses toward the cell body.
**dengue** (deŋ′gi), *n.* an infectious, tropical disease characterized by fever, severe pains in the joints and back, and rash.
**dental** (den′t'l), *adj.* of or for the teeth or dentistry.
**dentifrice** (den′tə-fris), *n.* a powder, paste, or liquid for cleaning the teeth.
**dentine, dentin** (den′tēn, -tin), *n.* the hard, dense, calcareous tissue forming the body of a tooth, under the enamel.
**dentition** (den-tish′ən), *n.* 1. teething. 2. the arrangement, number, and kind of teeth.
**denture** (den′chēr), *n.* a set of teeth, natural or artificial.
**depilate** (dep′ə-lāt′), *v. t.* to remove the hair from (a part of the body).
**depilatory** (di-pil′ə-tôr′i), *adj.* serving to remove hair, especially unwanted hair. *n.* anything that destroys or removes hair.
**depressant** (di-pres′ənt), *n.* anything, as a drug or medicine, that reduces muscular or nervous activity.
**depressor** (di-pres′ēr), *n.* 1. any of various muscles that draw down a part of the body. 2. a nerve the stimulation of which decreases the activity of a part of the body. 3. an instrument that presses a protruding part out of the way during a medical examination or operation: as, a tongue *depressor.*
**derangement** (di-rānj′mənt), *n.* mental disorder.
**derma** (dūr′mə), *n.* dermis.
**dermal** (dūr′məl), *adj.* of the skin or the dermis.
**dermatitis** (dūr′mə-tī′tis), *n.* inflammation of the dermis.
**dermatologist** (dūr′mə-tol′ə-jist), *n.* a physician who specializes in diseases of the skin.
**dermatology** (dūr′mə-tol′ə-ji), *n.* the branch of medicine dealing with the skin and its diseases.
**dermis** (dūr′mis), *n.* 1. the layer of skin just below the epidermis. 2. the skin in general.
**desensitize** (dē-sen′sə-tīz′), *v. t.* to make a person or tissue nonreactive or nonallergic to a substance by removing the antibodies from sensitized cells.
**desmoid** (des′moid), *adj.* 1. like a ligament. 2. of fibrous texture, as certain tumors.
**desquamation** (des′kwə-mā′shən), *n.* peeling of scales from the skin.
**devitalize** (dē-vī′t'l-īz′), *v. t.* to deprive of life or vitality: said of a tooth when the pulp is destroyed.
**Dexedrine** (dek′sə-drin), *n.* an isomer of amphetamine, similar to and used like benzidrine: a trade-mark.
**diabetes** (dī′ə-bē′tis), *n.* a disease characterized by an excessive discharge of urine: there are various types of diabetes.
**diabetes insipidus** (in-sip′ə-dəs), a chronic form of diabetes characterized by the passage of a large amount of urine with no excess of sugar, excess thirst and appetite, loss of strength, and emaciation.
**diabetes mellitus** (mə-lī′təs), a chronic form of diabetes characterized by excess of sugar in the blood and urine, hunger, thirst, and gradual loss of weight: also called *sugar diabetes.*
**diachylon** (dī-ak′ə-lon′), *n.* a plaster consisting essentially of lead oxide, olive oil, and water.
**diagnosis** (dī′əg-nō′sis), *n.* the act or process of finding the nature of a diseased condition by examination.
**diaphoresis** (dī′ə-fə-rē′sis), *n.* perspiration, especially when profuse and artificially induced.
**diaphoretic** (dī′ə-fə-ret′ik), *n.* a medicine, treatment, etc. that produces or increases perspiration.
**diaphragm** (dī′ə-fram′), *n.* the partition of muscles and tendons between the chest cavity and the abdominal cavity.
**diarrhea** (dī′ə-rē′ə), *n.* excessive frequency and looseness of bowel movements.
**diastole** (dī-as′tə-lē′), *n.* the usual rhythmic dilatation of the heart, especially of the ventricles, following each contraction, during which the heart muscle relaxes and the chambers fill with blood.
**diathermy** (dī′ə-thūr′mi), *n.* medical treatment in which heat is produced in the tissues beneath the skin by a high-frequency electric current.
**Dick test,** a skin test to determine susceptibility or immunity to scarlet fever.
**Dicumarol** (dī-ko͞o′mə-rôl′), *n.* an organic compound, a white crystalline powder, used to retard clotting of blood: a trade-mark.
**dietetics** (dī′ə-tet′iks), *n.* the study of the kinds and quantities of food needed for health.
**digest** (di-jest′), *v. t.* to change (food) in the mouth, stomach, and intestines by the action of gastric and intestinal juices, enzymes, and bacteria so that it can be absorbed by the body.
**digestion** (dī-jes′chən), *n.* 1. a digesting or being digested: said of food. 2. the ability to digest food.
**digitalis** (dij′i-tal′is), *n.* a medicine made from the dried leaves of the foxglove plant: used as a heart stimulant.
**Dilantin** (di-lan′tin), *n.* a drug used in the treatment of epileptic attacks: a trade-mark: in full, **dilantin sodium.**
**diphtheria** (dif-thêr′i-ə), *n.* an acute infectious disease characterized by weakness, high fever, and the formation in the air passages of a membrane that interferes with breathing: it is caused by a bacillus.
**dipsomania** (dip′sə-mā′ni-ə), *n.* an abnormal and insatiable desire for alcoholic drink.
**disease** (di-zēz′), *n.* 1. any departure from health. 2. a particular destructive process, with a specific cause and characteristic symptoms; ailment.
**disinfect** (dis′in-fekt′), *v. t.* to destroy or make inactive pathogenic organisms.
**disinfectant** (dis′in-fek′tənt), *n.* anything which destroys or makes inactive pathogenic organisms.
**dislocation** (dis′lō-kā′shən), *n.* abnormal separation of a bone from its usual point of contact in a joint.
**dispensary** (dis-pen′sə-ri), *n.* 1. a room in a hospital, physician's office, school, factory, etc. where medicines are made up and given out. 2. a place where free treatment and medicine may be obtained.
**dissect** (di-sekt′), *v. t.* to cut apart piece by piece, especially for anatomical study.
**dissection** (di-sek′shən), *n.* the cutting apart of tissue, as for study or in surgery.
**distention** (dis-ten′shən), *n.* the state or condition of being enlarged or swollen.

**diuretic** (dī′yoo-ret′ik), *adj.* increasing the secretion and flow of urine. *n.* a diuretic drug.
**diverticulitis** (dī′vẽr-tik-yoo-lī′tis), *n.* inflammation of a diverticulum.
**diverticulum** (dī′vẽr-tik′yoo-ləm), *n.* a small pouch or sac existing as an outgrowth from a tubular organ or main cavity.
**Dobell's solution** (dō-belz′), a solution of baking soda, borax, glycerin, and carbolic acid in water: used as a nose and throat antiseptic.
**douche** (do͞osh), *n.* 1. a jet of liquid applied externally or internally, especially as a bath or treatment. 2. a bath or treatment of this kind. 3. a device for applying a douche.
**Dover's powder,** a preparation of powdered milk, sugar, ipecac, and opium: used to induce perspiration and relieve pain.
**drain** (drān), *n.* a tube or other device for drawing off discharge, as from an abscess.
**drainage tube,** a small tube used for draining pus from an incision or a wound.
**Dramamine** (dram′ə-mēn′), *n.* a drug used to prevent and relieve seasickness, airsickness, etc.: a trade-mark.
**dressing** (dres′iŋ), *n.* materials, as medicine and bandages, applied to wounds.
**Drinker respirator** (driŋ′kẽr), a mechanical apparatus for providing artificial respiration over an extended period: also called *iron lung.*
**dropsy** (drop′si), *n.* the abnormal accumulation of serous fluid in a body cavity or in cellular tissue.
**drug** (drug), *n.* any medicinal substance.
**drum** (drum), *n.* 1. the middle ear. 2. the eardrum.
**duct** (dukt), *n.* a tube in the body for the passage of excretions or secretions, as from a gland.
**ductless gland** (dukt′lis), any of certain glands, as the thyroid and pituitary, which have no excretory ducts and send their secretions directly into the lymph or blood stream.
**duodenal** (do͞o′ə-dē′n'l), *adj.* in or of the duodenum.
**duodenum** (do͞o′ə-dē′nəm), *n.* the first portion of the small intestine, leading from the stomach to the jejunum.
**dura mater** (dyoor′ə mā′tẽr), the outermost, toughest, and most fibrous of the three membranes covering the brain and spinal cord.
**dysentery** (dis′'n-ter′i), *n.* any of various intestinal diseases characterized by inflammation, abdominal pain, toxemia, and diarrhea with bloody, mucous feces.
**dysfunction** (dis-fuŋk′shən), *n.* abnormal, impaired, or incomplete functioning of an organ or part.
**dysmenorrhea** (dis′men-ə-rē′ə), *n.* difficult or painful menstruation.
**dyspepsia** (dis-pep′shə), *n.* impaired digestion; indigestion.
**dysphagia** (dis-fā′ji-ə), *n.* difficulty in swallowing.
**dyspnea** (disp-nē′ə), *n.* difficult or painful breathing.
**dystrophy** (dis′trə-fi), *n.* faulty nutrition: see also *muscular dystrophy.*
**dysuria** (dis-yoor′i-ə), *n.* difficult or painful urination.

## E

**ear** (êr), *n.* the organ of hearing: it consists of *a*) the external ear (pinna and auditory canal); *b*) the inner ear, containing the cochlea and semicircular canals; and *c*) the middle ear (tympanum), a cavity connected to the external ear by the tympanic membrane, to the pharynx by the Eustachian tube, and to the inner ear by a series of three small bones called the *hammer, anvil,* and *stirrup.*
**eardrum** (êr′drum′), *n.* 1. the thin membrane that separates the middle ear from the external ear and vibrates when struck by sound waves; tympanic membrane. 2. the middle ear; tympanum.
**earwax** (êr′waks′), *n.* cerumen.
**ecchymosis** (ek′i-mō′sis), *n.* black and blue discoloration in tissue resulting from the oozing of blood from a blood vessel; bruise.
**eclampsia** (ek-lamp′si-ə), *n.* an attack of convulsions, caused by any of various toxic conditions and occurring especially in the later stages of pregnancy and in childbirth.
**ectoplasm** (ek′tə-plaz'm), *n.* the outer layer of the cytoplasm of a cell.
**eczema** (ek′zə-mə), *n.* an inflammatory skin disease characterized by itching and the formation of scales.
**edema** (i-dē′mə), *n.* the presence of extremely large amounts of fluid in the tissues, cells, and cavities of the body, resulting in swelling; dropsy.
**effluvium** (e-flo͞o′vi-əm), *n.* a disagreeable or noxious odor, as from exhalation.
**effusion** (e-fū′zhən), *n.* 1. an escape of fluid from glands, blood vessels, etc. into body cavities or tissues. 2. the fluid thus escaping.
**ego** (ē′gō), *n.* 1. the conscious part of the mind; the self; I. 2. that part of the psyche which consciously controls the impulses of the id.
**ejaculation** (i-jak′yoo-lā′shən), *n.* a sudden ejection of fluid, especially of seminal fluid, from the body.
**electrocardiogram** (i-lek′trō-kär′di-ə-gram′), *n.* a tracing showing changes in electric potential produced by contraction of the heart muscle: used in diagnosing heart diseases.
**electrocardiograph** (i-lek′trō-kär′di-ə-graf′), *n.* the electrically operated apparatus for making an electrocardiogram.
**electrocautery** (i-lek′trō-kô′tẽr-i), *n.* an electrical apparatus used to cauterize tissue.
**electroencephalogram** (i-lek′trō-en-sef′ə-lə-gram′), *n.* a tracing showing the changes in electric potential produced by the brain.
**electroencephalograph** (i-lek′trō-en-sef′ə-lə-graf′), *n.* an instrument for making electroencephalograms.
**electrograph** (i-lek′trə-graf′), *n.* an X-ray picture.
**electrolysis** (i-lek′trol′ə-sis), *n.* the removal of unwanted hair by destroying the hair roots with an electrified needle.
**electrosurgery** (i-lek′trō-sũr′jẽr-i), *n.* surgery by means of electrically operated instruments used to cut through tissues or destroy them.
**electrotherapy** (i-lek′trō-ther′ə-pi), *n.* treatment of diseases by electricity.
**elephantiasis** (el′ə-fən-tī′ə-sis), *n.* a chronic disease of the skin characterized by the enlargement of certain parts of the body, especially the legs and genitals, and by the hardening and ulceration of the surrounding skin: it is caused by small, threadlike worms which obstruct the lymphatic glands.
**elimination** (i-lim′ə-nā′shən), *n.* the act of expulsion, as of waste products from the body.
**elixir** (i-lik′sẽr), *n.* a medicine made of drugs in alcoholic solution, usually sweetened.
**emaciation** (i-mā′shi-ā′shən), *n.* a wasted condition of the body, caused by starvation, disease, etc.
**embolism** (em′bə-liz'm), *n.* an obstruction of a blood vessel by a blood clot or other foreign matter too large to pass through it.
**embolus** (em′bə-ləs), *n.* any foreign matter, as a blood clot or air bubble, carried by the blood stream from one point of the body to another where it may obstruct a blood vessel and impede circulation.
**embryo** (em′bri-ō′), *n.* a human organism in the earliest stages of its development in the uterus: in the first three months after conception it is called an *embryo,* there after a *fetus.*
**embryonic** (em′bri-on′ik), *adj.* of or like an embryo.
**emesis** (em′ə-sis), *n.* vomiting or the act of vomiting.
**emetic** (i-met′ik), *n.* a medicine or other substance which produces vomiting.
**emetine** (em′ə-tēn′), *n.* an alkaloid obtained from ipecac root, used as an expectorant and an emetic.
**emission** (i-mish′ən), *n.* any discharge of fluid from the body, especially an involuntary seminal discharge.
**emollient** (i-mol′yənt), *n.* preparation or medicine which softens and soothes surface tissues.
**emphysema** (em′fi-sē′mə), *n.* an abnormal swelling of body tissues caused by the accumulation of air; especially, such a swelling of the alveoli or the tissue connecting the alveoli in the lungs.
**empyema** (em′pi-ē′mə), *n.* the accumulation of pus within a cavity, especially in the cavity containing the lungs.
**emulsion** (i-mul′shən), *n.* a preparation of an oily substance held in suspension in a watery liquid by means of a gummy substance: as, an *emulsion* of cod-liver oil.
**emunctory** (i-muŋk′tẽr-i), *n.* any organ or part of the body that gives off waste products, as the kidneys, lungs, and skin.
**enamel** (i-nam′'l), *n.* the white hard layer covering the crowns of the teeth.
**enarthrosis** (en′är-thrō′sis), *n.* a joint in which the head of one bone fits into the socket of another, as the hip joint.
**encephalitis** (en′sef-ə-lī′tis), *n.* inflammation of the brain.
**encephaloma** (en′sef-ə-lō′mə), *n.* 1. a tumor of the brain. 2. a hernia of the brain.
**endamoeba** (en′də-mē′bə), *n.* a type of parasitic amoeba which may cause certain diseases, as dysentery.
**endemic** (en-dem′ik), *adj.* prevalent in or restricted to a particular nation, region, locality, or group: as, an *endemic* disease.
**endocarditis** (en′dō-kär-dī′tis), *n.* inflammation of the inner lining of the heart.
**endocrine** (en′dō-krīn′, -krin), *adj.* 1. designating or of any gland producing one or more internal secretions that are carried by the blood or lymph to some part whose function they regulate or control. 2. designating or of such a secretion. *n.* any such gland or its secretion: the thyroid, adrenal, and pituitary glands are endocrines.
**endocrinology** (en′dō-krī-nol′ə-ji), *n.* the study of the endocrine glands and the internal secretions of the body.
**endoderm** (en′də-dũrm′), *n.* the inner layer of cells of the embryo, from which is formed the lining of the digestive tract and of other internal organs.
**endometritis** (en′dō-mə-trī′tis), *n.* inflammation of the inner lining of the uterus.
**endometrium** (en′dō-met′ri-əm), *n.* the mucous membrane which lines the interior of the uterus.
**endoscope** (en′də-skōp′), *n.* an instrument for examining the interior of a cavity or hollow organ, as the bladder or rectum.
**endoscopy** (en-dos′kə-pi), *n.* the examination of hollow organs by means of an endoscope.
**endothelioma** (en′də-thē′li-ō′mə), *n.* a tumor of the endothelium.
**endothelium** (en′də-thē′li-əm), *n.* the layer of squamous cells lining the inside of blood and lymph vessels, of the heart, and of some other closed cavities.
**enema** (en′ə-mə), *n.* 1. a liquid injected into the rectum to aid bowel movement or as a medicine. 2. such an injection.

**enteritis** (en'tə-rī'tis), *n.* inflammation of the intestine, especially the small intestine.

**enuresis** (en'yoo-rē'sis), *n.* the involuntary discharge of urine: that occurring during sleep is *nocturnal enuresis.*

**enzyme** (en'zīm), *n.* any of various organic substances that are produced in cells and cause changes in other substances by catalytic action: as, pepsin is a digestive *enzyme.*

**ependyma** (ep-en'di-mə), *n.* the membrane lining the central cavities of the brain and spinal cord.

**ephedrine** (ef'ə-drēn', e-fed'rin), *n.* an alkaloid derived from certain plants, used to relieve nasal congestion, as in asthma, hay fever, etc.: it causes constriction of the swollen or inflamed blood vessels.

**epicanthus** (ep'ə-kan'thəs), *n.* a small fold of skin sometimes covering the inner corner of the eye.

**epidemic** (ep'ə-dem'ik), *n.* prevalent and spreading rapidly among many people in a community at the same time, as a contagious disease. *n.* 1. an epidemic disease. 2. the rapid spreading of such a disease.

**epidemiology** (ep'ə-dem'i-ol'ə-ji), *n.* the branch of medicine that investigates the causes and control of epidemics.

**epidermis** (ep'ə-dũr'mis), *n.* the outermost layer of the skin, having no blood vessels and consisting of several layers of cells, covering the rmis.

**epididymis** (ep'ə-did'i-mis), *n.* a long, oval-shaped structure attached to the rear upper surface of each testicle, consisting mainly of the excretory ducts of the testicles.

**epigastrium** (ep'ə-gas'tri-əm), *n.* the upper central portion of the abdomen over and in front of the stomach.

**epiglottis** (ep'ə-glot'is), *n.* the thin, triangular lid of cartilage that folds back to cover the opening of the windpipe during swallowing, thus preventing food, etc., from entering the lungs.

**epilepsy** (ep'ə-lep'si), *n.* a chronic disease of the nervous system, characterized by unconsciousness and convulsions.

**epileptic** (ep'ə-lep'tik), *adj.* 1. of, like, or having the nature of epilepsy. 2. having epilepsy. *n.* a person who has epilepsy.

**epinephrine** (ep'ə-nef'rin), *n.* adrenalin.

**epistaxis** (ep'ə-stak'sis), *n.* nosebleed; hemorrhage from the nose.

**epithelial** (ep'ə-thē'li-əl), *adj.* of, or having the nature of, epithelium.

**epithelioma** (ep'ə-thē'li-ō'mə), *n.* a malignant tumor of epithelial cells, particularly of the skin, mouth, larynx, or urinary bladder.

**epithelium** (ep'ə-thē'li-əm), *n.* cellular tissue that covers surfaces, forms glands, and lines most cavities of the body: it consists of one or several layers of cells.

**Epsom salts** (ep'səm), a bitter, white, crystalline salt, magnesium sulphate, used as a cathartic.

**ergosterol** (ēr-gos'tə-rōl'), *n.* an alcohol prepared from yeast: when subjected to irradiation it becomes a source of vitamin $D_1$: useful in preventing rickets.

**ergot** (ũr'gət), *n.* a dried fungus which grows on certain grains, as rye: it is used as a drug to contract the uterus and to reduce bleeding after childbirth.

**eructation** (i-ruk'tā'shən), *n.* the act of belching.

**eruption** (i-rup'shən), *n.* 1. a breaking out in a rash. 2. a rash.

**erysipelas** (er'ə-sip''l-əs), *n.* an acute infectious disease of the skin or mucous membranes caused by a streptococcus: it is characterized by local inflammation and fever.

**erythema** (er'ə-thē'mə), *n.* an abnormal redness of the skin resulting from the congestion of small capillaries.

**erythrocyte** (i-rith'rō-sīt'), *n.* a red blood corpuscle: it is a very small circular disk with both faces concave, and contains hemoglobin, which carries oxygen to the body tissues.

**esophagus** (i-sof'ə-gəs), *n.* the gullet; the passage for food from the pharynx to the stomach.

**estriol** (es'trī-ōl'), *n.* a female sex hormone used to treat conditions of deficient sexual desire, especially in menopause.

**estrone** (es'trōn), *n.* a female sex hormone injected into the muscles to treat conditions of deficient sexual desire.

**ether** (ē'thēr), *n.* a sweet-smelling, volatile, colorless, highly inflammable liquid used as an anesthetic.

**eucalyptus oil** (ū'kə-lip'təs), an oil derived from the leaves of the eucalyptus tree, used as an antiseptic, astringent, tonic, and deodorant.

**Eustachian tube** (yoo-stā'ki-ən), a slender tube between the middle ear and the pharynx, which serves to equalize air pressure on both sides of the eardrum.

**euthanasia** (ū'thə-nā'zhə), *n.* an easy and painless death.

**exanthema** (ek'san-thē'mə), *n.* 1. a skin eruption or rash occurring in certain infectious diseases, as scarlet fever. 2. an infectious disease characterized by such eruptions.

**excrement** (eks'krə-mənt), *n.* waste matter from the bowels; feces.

**excrete** (iks-krēt'), *v. t. & v. i.* to separate (waste matter) from the blood or tissue and eliminate from the body, as through the kidneys or sweat glands.

**exophthalmia** (ek'sof-thal'mi-ə), *n.* abnormal protrusion of the eyeballs, caused by disease.

**exostosis** (ek'sos-tō'sis), *n.* an abnormal bony projection or outgrowth on the surface of a tooth or bone.

**expectorant** (ik-spek'tə-rənt), *n.* any medicine that causes or stimulates the coughing up and spitting out of mucus or phlegm.

**expectorate** (ik-spek'tə-rāt'), *v. t. & v. i.* to cough up and spit (phlegm, mucus, etc.).

**expiration** (ek'spə-rā'shən), *n.* exhaling; breathing out.

**extensor** (ik-sten'sēr), *n.* a muscle that extends or straightens some part of the body, especially an arm or leg.

**extern** (ek'stērn), *n.* a doctor who is a member of a hospital staff but who does not reside at the hospital.

**exude** (ig-zōōd'), *v. t. & v. i.* to pass out in drops, as through pores, an incision, etc.

**exudate** (eks'yoo-dāt'), *n.* matter exuded.

**eye** (ī), *n.* the organ of sight or vision.

**eyeball** (ī'bôl'), *n.* the ball-shaped part of the eye, enclosed by the socket and eyelids.

**eyebrow** (ī'brou'), *n.* 1. the bony arch over the eye. 2. the arch of hair growing on this.

**eyelash** (ī'lash'), *n.* 1. any of the hairs on the edge of the eyelid. 2. a fringe of these hairs.

**eyelid** (ī'lid'), *n.* either of the two movable folds of flesh that cover and uncover the front of the eyeball.

**eyetooth** (ī'tōōth'), *n.* either of the two pointed teeth in the upper jaw between the bicuspids and the incisors; upper canine tooth.

## F

**faint** (fānt), *n.* a condition of temporary loss of consciousness as a result of an inadequate flow of blood to the brain.

**Fallopian tube** (fə-lō'pi-ən), either of two narrow tubes extending from each ovary to the uterus: they conduct the ova to the uterus from the ovary.

**fascia** (fash'i-ə), *n.* a thin layer of connective tissue covering, supporting, or connecting the muscles or inner organs.

**fasciculus** (fə-sik'yoo-ləs), *n.* a bundle of nerve fibers in the central nervous system.

**fat** (fat), *n.* the oily substance covering connective tissue.

**fatty degeneration,** the abnormal occurrence of fat particles in tissue cells.

**fauces** (fô'sēz), *n.* the passage leading from the back of the mouth into the pharynx.

**favus** (fā'vəs), *n.* an infectious skin disease caused by a fungus and characterized by itching and the formation of yellow crusts about the hair follicles.

**febrifuge** (feb'ri-fūj'), *n.* any substance that removes or reduces fever.

**febrile** (feb'rəl, fē'brəl), *adj.* 1. of or characterized by fever. 2. caused by fever.

**fecal** (fē'kəl), *adj.* of feces.

**feces** (fē'sēz), *n.pl.* waste matter expelled from the bowels.

**fecundation** (fē'kən-dā'shən), *n.* fertilization: *artificial fecundation* is fertilization by injecting live semen into the uterus with a syringe.

**felon** (fel'ən), *n.* a painful, pus-producing infection at the end of a finger or toe, near the nail.

**femur** (fē'mēr), *n.* the thighbone.

**fester** (fes'tēr), *n.* a small sore producing pus. *v.i.* to form pus. *v.t.* to cause the formation of pus in.

**fetish** (fē'tish, fet'ish), *n.* any nonsexual object that excites erotic feelings.

**fetus** (fē'təs), *n.* the offspring in the womb from the end of the third month of pregnancy until birth.

**fever** (fē'vēr), *n.* 1. a disease characterized by rapid pulse, increased body temperature, delirium, etc. 2. a state of abnormally increased body temperature.

**fever sore** or **blister,** an acute infectious disease caused by a virus and characterized by small blisters of the skin and mucous membranes, especially about the mouth.

**fiber** (fī'bēr), *n.* a thin, threadlike structure that combines with others to form tissue.

**fibrin** (fī'brin), *n.* an elastic, threadlike, insoluble protein formed from fibrinogen by the action of thrombin in the clotting of blood, and forming the network of the clot.

**fibrinogen** (fī-brin'ə-jən), *n.* a blood protein that is converted to fibrin by the action of the enzyme thrombin in the clotting of blood.

**fibroid** (fī'broid) *n.* a fibrous tumor, especially one in the uterus.

**fibroma** (fī-brō'mə), *n.* a nonmalignant tumor made up of connective or fibrous tissue.

**fibrous** (fī'brəs), *adj.* containing or composed of fibers.

**fibula** (fib'yoo-lə), *n.* the long, thin outer bone of the leg below the knee.

**filaria** (fi-lâr'i-ə), *n.* a threadlike parasitic worm that lives in the blood and tissues: it is often transmitted by mosquitos.

**filtrable virus,** any virus of ultramicroscopic size, capable of passing through filters that bacteria cannot pass through: some such viruses cause measles, influenza, etc.

**fissure** (fish'ēr), *n.* a groove between lobes or parts of an organ, as in the brain.

**fistula** (fis'choo-lə), *n.* an abnormal hollow passage from an abscess, cavity, or hollow organ to the skin or to another abscess, cavity, or organ.

**fit** (fit), *n.* any sudden, uncontrollable attack: as, a *fit* of coughing.

**flatulence** (flach'ə-ləns), *n.* gas in the intestines or stomach.

**flatulent** (flach'ə-lənt), *adj.* of or having gas in the stomach or intestines.

**fluoroscope** (floor'ə-skōp'), *n.* a machine for examining internal structures by viewing the shadows cast on a fluorescent screen

by objects or parts through which X rays are directed.
**fluoroscopy** (floor-os'kə-pi), *n.* examination with a fluoroscope.
**follicle** (fol'i-k'l), *n.* a tiny sac, cavity, or gland for excretion or secretion: as, a hair *follicle.*
**fomentation** (fō'mən-tā'shən), *n.* treatment of pain or injury by using moist, warm applications.
**fontanel** (fon'tə-nel'), *n.* any one of the soft spots on a baby's head where the bones are separated by membranes: they will be closed up later by the formation of bone.
**forceps** (fôr'seps), *n.* an instrument, like small tongs or pincers, having two blades and handles, used for holding, pulling, or compression.
**foreskin** (fôr'skin'), *n.* the fold of skin that covers the end of the penis and is removed in circumcision; prepuce.
**formaldehyde** (fôr-mal'də-hīd'), *n.* a colorless, pungent gas used in solution as a powerful disinfectant, preservative, and antiseptic.
**fourchette** (foor-shet'), *n.* a small fold of skin connecting the inner lips of the vulva at the lower end.
**fracture** (frak'chēr), *n.* a break in a bone or, occasionally, a tear in a cartilage.
**frenum** (frē'nəm), *n.* a fold of skin or mucous membrane that is attached to a part of the body and checks or controls its motion, as the fold under the tongue.
**fungus** (fuŋ'gəs), *n.* a spongy, granular growth on the body, sometimes malignant.
**funiculus** (fū-nik'yoo-ləs), *n.* a cord; specifically, *a)* the spermatic cord. *b)* the umbilical cord.
**furuncle** (fyoor'uŋ-k'l), *n.* a boil.
**fusion** (fū'zhən), *n.* 1. the merging of the separate images, seen by both eyes, into one. 2. the abnormal growing together of normally separate parts.

## G

**gag** (gag), *n.* a device, used in dentistry, to keep the mouth open. *v.t. & v.i.* to retch or cause to retch.
**galactic** (gə-lak'tik), *adj.* of the flow of milk; helping or increasing the flow of milk.
**gall** (gôl), *n.* bile.
**gall bladder,** a membranous sac attached to the liver, in which excess bile is stored and concentrated.
**gallstone** (gôl'stōn'), *n.* a small, solid mass sometimes formed in the gall bladder: it is formed of cholesterol or, occasionally, of calcium salts, and can obstruct the flow of bile, causing a painful diseased condition.
**ganglion** (gaŋ'gli-ən), *n.* a mass of nerve cells acting as a center from which nerve impulses are transmitted.
**gangrene** (gaŋ'grēn), *n.* decay of tissue in a part of the body when the blood supply is obstructed by injury, disease, etc.
**gas** (gas), *n.* any gas used as an anesthetic, as nitrous oxide.
**gas bacillus,** a rod-shaped microorganism that infects wounds and causes gas to form in them.
**gastric** (gas'trik), *adj.* of, in, or near the stomach.
**gastric juice,** the thin, acid digestive fluid produced by glands in the mucous membrane lining the stomach: it contains enzymes and hydrochloric acid.
**gastric ulcer,** an ulcer of the lining of the stomach.
**gastritis** (gas-trī'tis), *n.* inflammation of the stomach, especially of the stomach lining.
**gastroenteritis** (gas'trō-en'tēr-ī'tis), *n.* inflammation of the lining of the intestines and stomach.
**gastroenterostomy** (gas'trō-en'tə-ros'tə-mi), *n.* the surgical operation of creating an artificial opening from the stomach to the small intestine.
**gastrointestinal** (gas'trō-in-tes'ti-n'l), *adj.* of the stomach and the intestines.
**gastrolith** (gas'trə-lith), *n.* a stony concretion formed in the stomach.
**gastroscope** (gas'trə-skōp'), *n.* an instrument for the examination of the inside of the stomach.
**gastrotomy** (gas-trot'ə-mi), *n.* surgical incision into the stomach, as for removing gastroliths.
**gastrula** (gas'troo-lə), *n.* the embryo in an early stage of development consisting of two layers, the ectoderm and endoderm, enclosing a central cavity.
**gene** (jēn), *n.* any of the elements by which hereditary characters are transmitted and determined, regarded as a particular state of organization of the chromatin in the chromosome.
**genetics** (jə-net'iks), *n.pl.* the science and study of heredity.
**genital** (jen'ə-t'l), *adj.* of reproduction or the reproductive organs.
**genitals** (jen'ə-t'lz), *n.pl.* the organs of reproduction; especially, the external sex organs.
**genitourinary** (jen'i-tō-yoor'ə-ner'i), *adj.* designating or of the genital and urinary organs together.
**germ** (jũrm), *n.* any microscopic organism, especially one of the bacteria, that can cause disease.
**germicide** (jũr'mə-sīd'), *n.* anything that kills germs, especially those causing diseases.
**gestation** (jes-tā'shən), *n.* pregnancy.
**gigantism** (jī-gan'tiz'm), *n.* abnormal overgrowth of the body.
**gingiva** (jin'jə-və), *n.* the gum; tissue surrounding the necks of the teeth.
**gingivitis** (jin'jə-vī'tis), *n.* inflammation of the gums.
**gland** (gland), *n.* any organ that separates certain elements from the blood and secretes them in the form of a substance for the body to use, as adrenalin, or throw off, as urine.
**glandular** (glan'joo-lēr), *adj.* of, like, consisting of, or having a gland or glands.
**glans clitoridis** (glanz klī-tor'ə-dis), the end of the clitoris, corresponding to the glans penis.
**glans penis,** the head, or end, of the penis.
**glaucoma** (glô-kō'mə), *n.* a disease of the eye, characterized by increased tension within, and hardening of, the eyeball: it often leads to blindness.
**gleet** (glēt), *n.* a chronic, urethral discharge due to gonorrhea.
**glossitis** (glo-sī'tis), *n.* inflammation of the tongue.
**glottis** (glot'is), *n.* the space between the vocal cords in the larynx.
**glycogen** (glī'kə-jən), *n.* an insoluble, starchlike substance produced in tissues, especially in the liver and muscles, and changed into simple sugar as the body needs it.
**glycosuria** (glī'kə-syoor'i-ə), *n.* an abnormal condition in which there is sugar in the urine.
**goiter** (goi'tēr), *n.* 1. a diseased condition of the thyroid gland characterized by enlargement of the gland, seen as a swelling in the front of the neck. 2. the enlargement or swelling.
**gonad** (gon'ad, gō'nad), *n.* a reproductive gland; ovary or testis.
**gonococcus** (gon'ə-kok'əs), *n.* the microorganism that causes gonorrhea.
**gonorrhea** (gon'ə-rē'ə), *n.* a venereal disease caused by a gonococcus, characterized by inflammation of the mucous membrane of the genitourinary tract and a discharge of mucus and pus: it is generally transmitted by sexual intercourse and can seriously affect other mucous membranes, especially those of the eye, as in a baby during childbirth.
**gout** (gout), *n.* a disease resulting from a disturbance of the metabolism, characterized by an excess of uric acid in the blood and deposits of uric acid salts in the tissues around the joints, especially of the feet and hands: it causes swelling and severe pain, especially in the big toe.
**Graafian follicle** (grä'fi-ən), one of the small, round sacs in the ovary, each of which contains an ovum.
**graft** (graft), *n.* a piece of skin, bone, or other tissue taken from one body or place on a body and transplanted to another where it may grow to replace a lost or damaged part.
**Gram-negative** (gram'neg'ə-tiv), *adj.* that loses the stain after treatment with alcohol: said of bacteria or tissues.
**Gram-positive** (gram'poz'ə-tiv), *adj.* that retains the stain after treatment with alcohol: said of bacteria or tissues.
**granular** (gran'yoo-lēr), *adj.* containing or consisting of grains: granular eyelids have an inner surface made rough by disease.
**granulation** (gran'yoo-lā'shən), *n.* 1. the formation of small, round, fleshlike masses in wounds that are healing. 2. a mass so formed.
**granuloma** (gran'yoo-lō'mə), *n.* a swelling or tumor composed of granulation tissue.
**granuloma inguinale** (iŋ'gwi-nā'lē), a venereal disease producing chronic enlargement of the external genitals.
**grippe** (grip), *n.* a contagious virus disease like a severe cold, characterized by fever, bronchial inflammation, catarrhal discharge, and intestinal disorder; influenza.
**groin** (groin), *n.* the depressed part or fold where the thigh and abdomen join.
**growth** (grōth), *n.* a tumor or other abnormal mass of tissue developed in or on the body.
**gullet** (gul'it), *n.* the esophagus.
**gum** (gum), *n.* the firm flesh covering the jaws on the inside of the mouth and surrounding the base of the teeth.
**gum boil,** a small abscess on the gums.
**gumma** (gum'ə), *n.* a soft, rubbery tumor occurring in tertiary syphilis.
**gynecologist** (jī'ni-kol'ə-jist), *n.* a specialist in gynecology.
**gynecology** (jī'ni-kol'ə-ji), *n.* the branch of medicine dealing with the study and treatment of women's diseases, especially of the genitourinary and rectal tracts.
**gyniatrics** (jī'ni-at'riks), *n.pl.* the branch of medicine dealing with the treatment of women's diseases.

## H

**halitosis** (hal'ə-tō'sis), *n.* bad-smelling breath.
**hallucination** (hə-lōō'sə-nā'shən), *n.* the false sense impression of seeing or hearing something not actually present: it may occur in certain mental disorders.
**hallucinosis** (hə-lōō'sə-nō'sis), *n.* a mental disorder characterized by hallucinations.
**hallux** (hal'əks), *n.* the great, or big, toe.
**hallux valgus** (val'gəs), displacement of the big toe toward the other toes.
**hammer toe,** 1. a condition in which the first joint of a toe is bent downward in a clawlike position. 2. such a toe.
**hamstring** (ham'striŋ'), *n.* one of the tendons at the back of the knee. *v. t.* to disable by cutting the hamstring.
**hangnail** (haŋ'nāl'), *n.* a bit of torn or cracked skin hanging at the side or base of a fingernail.
**Hansen's disease** (han's'nz), leprosy.
**harelip** (hâr'lip), *n.* 1. a congenital deformity of one or both lips, usually only the upper one, consisting of a cleft like that of a hare's lip: it often results in a speech defect. 2. a lip with such a deformity.

**hay fever,** an acute inflammation of the eyes and upper respiratory tract, characterized by sneezing and sometimes accompanied by fever and asthma: it is an allergic reaction, caused mainly by the pollen of some grasses and trees.
**heart** (härt), *n.* the hollow, muscular organ that receives blood from the veins and sends it out through the arteries by alternate dilation and contraction.
**heartburn** (härt′būrn′), *n.* a burning sensation in the esophagus and stomach, caused by high acidity of the stomach.
**heat exhaustion,** a form of heatstroke characterized by low body temperature, collapse, and, in severe cases, coma and death.
**heatstroke** (hēt′strōk′), *n.* any of several conditions resulting from exposure to excessive heat.
**heloma** (hel-ō′mə), *n.* a corn or callus on the hand or foot.
**hemagogue** (hē′mə-gôg′), *n.* anything that increases the discharge of blood, as in menstruation.
**hematology** (hem′ə-tol′ə-ji), *n.* the study of blood and its diseases.
**hematoma** (hē′mə-tō′mə), *n.* a local tumor or swelling containing blood that has escaped from a blood vessel.
**heme** (hēm), *n.* the nonprotein part of the hemoglobin molecule, containing the pigment.
**hemiplegia** (hem′i-plē′ji-ə), *n.* paralysis of one side of the body.
**hemoglobin** (hē′mə-glō′bin), *n.* the red coloring matter of blood corpuscles: it is a protein that carries oxygen from the lungs to the tissues, and carbon dioxide from the tissues to the lungs.
**hemolysis** (hi-mol′i-sis), *n.* the destruction of the red corpuscles with liberation of hemoglobin into the surrounding fluid.
**hemophilia** (hē′mə-fil′i-ə), *n.* a condition, inherited by males through the mother, in which coagulation of the blood from a wound does not readily take place, causing prolonged, uncontrollable bleeding from even the smallest cuts.
**hemoptysis** (hi-mop′tə-sis), *n.* the coughing up of blood: usually caused by bleeding of the lungs or bronchi.
**hemorrhage** (hem′ēr-ij), *n.* escape of blood from its vessel; bleeding; especially, heavy bleeding.
**hemorrhoid** (hem′ə-roid′), *n. usually in pl.* a painful swelling or tumor of a vein in the region of the anus, often with bleeding.
**hemostat** (hē′mə-stat′), *n.* anything used to stop bleeding; specifically, a clamp-like instrument used in surgery or a chemical applied to a surface wound.
**henbane** (hen′bān′), *n.* a coarse, hairy, foul-smelling plant of the nightshade family: it is used as a narcotic.
**heparin** (hep′ēr-in), *n.* a substance found in various body tissues, especially in the liver, injected into the blood to prevent clotting.
**hepatectomy** (hep′ə-tek′tə-mi), *n.* the surgical removal of all or part of the liver.
**hepatitis** (hep′ə-tī′tis), *n.* inflammation of the liver.
**hermaphrodite** (hēr-maf′rə-dīt′), *n.* a person who possesses both male and female sexual organs.
**hernia** (hūr′ni-ə), *n.* the protrusion of all or part of an organ through a tear in the wall of the surrounding structure; especially, the protrusion of part of the intestines through the abdominal muscles; rupture.
**herpes** (hūr′pēz), *n.* an inflammatory virus disease of the skin, characterized by the eruption of small blisters on the skin and mucous membranes.
**herpes zoster** (zos′tēr), a form of herpes along the course of a nerve; shingles.
**heterosexual** (het′ēr-ō-sek′shōō-əl), *adj.* of or characterized by sexual desire for those of the opposite sex.
**heterosexuality** (het′ēr-ō-sek′shōō-al′ə-ti), *n.* sexual desire for those of the opposite sex.
**hexylresorcinol** (hek′sil-re-zôr′si-nōl′), *n.* a nonpoisonous, pale-yellow, crystalline substance used as an antiseptic and germicide.
**hiccup, hiccough** (hik′əp), *n.* a sudden, involuntary contraction of the diaphragm producing short, sharp sounds and the closing of the glottis at the moment of breathing in.
**histamine** (his′tə-mēn′), *n.* an amine discharged by the tissues in allergic reactions: it lowers the blood pressure by dilating the blood vessels, stimulates gastric secretion, etc.
**hives** (hīvz), *n.* urticaria.
**Hodgkin's disease** (hoj′kinz), a disease characterized by progressive enlargement of the lymph nodes and inflammation of other lymphoid tissues, especially of the spleen.
**homeopathy** (hō′mi-op′ə-thi), *n.* a system of medical treatment based on the theory that certain diseases can be cured by giving very small doses of drugs which in a healthy person and in large doses would produce symptoms like those of the disease.
**homosexual** (hō′mə-sek′shōō-əl), *adj.* characterized by sexual desire for those of the same sex.
**homosexuality** (hō′mə-sek′shōō-al′ə-ti), *n.* 1. sexual desire for those of the same sex. 2. sexual relations between individuals of the same sex.
**hookworm disease,** a disease caused by hookworms in the small intestine, characterized by anemia, fever, weakness, and abdominal pain: the larvae enter the body through the skin of the feet, or in contaminated food or drinking water.
**hormone** (hôr′mōn), *n.* a chemical substance formed in some organ, as the adrenal glands, the pituitary, etc., and carried to another organ or tissue, where it has a specific effect.
**humerus** (hū′mēr-əs), *n.* the long bone in the upper arm extending from the shoulder to the elbow.
**humor** (hū′mēr), *n.* 1. any chronic skin disease. 2. any body fluid.
**hydrocele** (hī′drə-sēl′), *n.* a collection of watery fluid in a cavity of the body, especially in the scrotum or along the spermatic cord.
**hydrocephalus** (hī′drə-sef′ə-ləs), *n.* a condition characterized by an abnormal increase in the amount of fluid in the cranium, causing enlargement of the head, wasting away of the brain, and loss of mental powers.
**hydrophobia** (hī′drə-fō′bi-ə), *n.* rabies.
**hydrotherapy** (hī′drə-ther′ə-pi), *n.* treatment of disease by the use of water.
**hydrothorax** (hī′drə-thôr′aks), *n.* a condition marked by an abnormal amount of watery fluid in the pleural cavity.
**hygiene** (hī′jēn), *n.* the science of health and the preservation of health.
**hymen** (hī′mən), *n.* the mucous membrane which usually covers part of the external vaginal opening in a virgin.
**hyperacidity** (hī′pēr-ə-sid′ə-ti), *n.* an excess of hydrochloric acid in the stomach, causing sourness and heartburn.
**hyperesthesia** (hī′pēr-es-thē′zhə), *n.* an abnormal extreme sensitiveness of the skin or some sense organ.
**hypermetropia** (hī′pēr-mi-trō′pi-ə), *n.* the condition of being farsighted; abnormal vision in which the rays of light are focused behind the retina so that distant objects are seen more clearly than near ones.
**hyperpituitarism** (hī′pēr-pi-tōō′i-tə-riz′m), *n.* 1. underactivity of the pituitary gland. 2. the condition of excessive skeletal growth caused by this.
**hypersensitive** (hī′pēr-sen′sə-tiv), *adj.* abnormally or excessively sensitive.
**hypertension** (hī′pēr-ten′shən), *n.* abnormally high blood pressure, especially in the arteries, or a diseased condition of which this is the chief symptom.
**hyperthyroidism** (hī′pēr-thī′roid-iz′m), *n.* a condition caused by overactivity of the thyroid gland or by taking too much thyroid extract, characterized by a rapid pulse, sleeplessness, etc.
**hypertrophy** (hi-pūr′trə-fi), *n.* abnormal enlargement or increased growth of a part or organ, caused by enlargement of its cellular components.
**hypnosis** (hip-nō′sis), *n.* a sleeplike condition, psychically induced, usually by another person, in which the subject loses consciousness but responds, with certain limitations, to the suggestions of the hypnotist.
**hypnotic** (hip-not′ik), *n.* any drug that produces sleep.
**hypnotism** (hip′nə-tiz′m), *n.* 1. the act or practice of inducing hypnosis. 2. the science of hypnosis.
**hypnotist** (hip′nə-tist), *n.* a person who induces hypnosis.
**hypochondria** (hī′pə-kon′dri-ə), *n.* abnormal anxiety over one's health, often with imaginary illnesses and severe melancholy.
**hypochondriac** (hī′pə-kon′dri-ak′), *n.* a person who has hypochondria.
**hypodermic** (hī′pə-dūr′mik), *adj.* of the parts beneath the skin.
**hypodermic injection,** an injection of a medicine or drug under the skin.
**hypodermic syringe,** a glass syringe attached to a hollow needle (*hypodermic needle*), used for giving hypodermic injections.
**hypogastrium** (hī′pə-gas′tri-əm), *n.* the lower, middle part of the abdomen.
**hypopituitarism** (hī′pō-pi-tōō′i-tə-riz′m), *n.* 1. underactivity of the pituitary gland. 2. the condition caused by this, characterized by excessive fat, loss of the sexual urge, wasting away of the external sex organs, and loss of hair.
**hypotension** (hī′pō-ten′shən), *n.* abnormally low blood pressure.
**hypothyroidism** (hī′pō-thī′roid-iz′m), *n.* 1. underactivity of the thyroid gland, often resulting in sluggishness, goiter, etc. 2. this condition.
**hysterectomy** (his′tēr-ek′tə-mi), *n.* surgical removal of all or part of the uterus.
**hysteria** (his-têr′i-ə), *n.* a psychiatric condition variously characterized by emotional excitability, excessive anxiety, sensory and motor disturbances, and the simulation of organic disorders, such as blindness, deafness, etc.
**hysterical** (his-ter′i-k'l), *adj.* of or characteristic of hysteria.

## I

**ichthyosis** (ik′thi-ō′sis), *n.* a skin disease characterized by a rough, dry scaliness and a thickening of the horny layer of the skin.
**id** (id), *n.* that part of the psyche which is regarded as the reservoir of the libido and the source of instinctive energy: it is dominated by the pleasure principle and impulsive wishing.
**idiocy** (id′i-ə-si), *n.* the state of being an idiot.
**idiot** (id′i-ət), *n.* a mentally deficient person; person mentally equal or inferior to a child two years old.
**ileitis** (il′i-ī′tis), *n.* inflammation of the ileum.
**ileum** (il′i-əm), *n.* the lowest part of the small intestine, opening into the large intestine.

**ileus** (il'i-əs), *n.* an abnormal condition caused by obstruction of the intestines, resulting in severe constipation and pain.
**imbecile** (im'bə-s'l), *n.* a mentally deficient person; person mentally equal to a child between three and eight years old.
**immune** (i-mūn'), *adj.* not susceptible to a particular disease.
**immunity** (i-mū'nə-ti), *n.* resistance to or protection against disease or infection.
**immunology** (im'yoo-nol'ə-ji), *n.* the branch of medicine dealing with immunity to disease.
**impacted** (im-pak'tid), *adj.* pressed tightly together; especially, firmly lodged in the jaw: said of a tooth unable to erupt because of its abnormal position.
**impotence** (im'pə-təns), *n.* lack of ability to engage in sexual intercourse: said of men.
**impotent** (im'pə-tənt), *adj.* unable to engage in sexual intercourse: said of men.
**impregnate** (im-preg'nāt), *v.t.* to make pregnant.
**inanition** (in'ə-nish'ən), *n.* exhaustion from lack of food or an inability to assimilate it.
**incision** (in-sizh'ən), *n.* a cut made into a tissue or organ.
**incisor** (in-sī'zẽr), *n.* any of the front teeth between the canines in either jaw.
**incubation** (in'kyoo-bā'shən), *n.* the phase in the development of a disease between the infection and the first appearance of symptoms.
**incubator** (in'kyoo-bā'tẽr), *n.* an artificially heated apparatus in which premature babies are kept for a period.
**index finger,** the finger nearest the thumb; forefinger.
**indigestion** (in'də-jes'chən), *n.* inability to digest, or difficulty in digesting, food.
**infantile paralysis,** an acute infectious disease, especially of children, caused by a virus inflammation of the gray matter of the spinal cord, often resulting in muscular paralysis; poliomyelitis.
**infarct** (in-färkt'), *n.* an area of dying or dead tissue caused by the blocking of blood vessels normally supplying the part.
**infect** (in-fekt'), *v. t.* 1. to contaminate with disease-producing organisms or matter. 2. to cause to become diseased by bringing into contact with such organisms or matter.
**infection** (in-fek'shən), *n.* a disease resulting from the presence of certain microorganisms or matter in the body.
**infectious** (in-fek'shəs), *adj.* likely to cause infection.
**infectious disease,** any disease caused by the presence in the body of bacteria, protozoa, viruses, or other parasites: it may or may not be contagious.
**inflame** (in-flām'), *v. t.* to cause inflammation in. *v. i.* to become hot, feverish, red, sore, etc.
**inflammation** (in'flə-mā'shən), *n.* a diseased condition of some part of the body, resulting from injury, infection, irritation, etc. and characterized by redness, pain, heat, and swelling.
**influenza** (in'flōō-en'zə), *n.* grippe.
**inguinal** (iŋ'gwi-n'l), *adj.* of or near the groin.
**inhalation** (in'hə-lā'shən), *n.* 1. a medicine to be inhaled. 2. the act of drawing air or other vapor into the lungs by breathing in.
**inhaler** (in-hāl'ẽr), *n.* an apparatus for administering medicinal vapors by inhalation.
**inhibition** (in'hi-bish'ən), *n.* a mental or psychological process that restrains or suppresses an action, emotion, or thought.
**inject** (in-jekt'), *v. t.* 1. to introduce or force (a fluid) into some part of the body by means of a syringe, hypodermic needle, etc. 2. to fill (a cavity, etc.) in this way.
**injection** (in-jek'shən), *n.* 1. an injecting. 2. something injected.
**inlay** (in'lā), *n.* a filling for a tooth, which is first made to fit a cavity and then cemented into it.
**inoculate** (in-ok'yoo-lāt'), *v. t.* 1. to inject a serum, vaccine, etc. into, especially in order to prevent, cure, or experiment with disease, usually so as to make immune. 2. to inject (a disease, virus, etc.) into a person in this way.
**insanity** (in-san'ə-ti), *n.* mental illness or derangement.
**insemination** (in-sem'ə-nā'shən), *n.* fertilization of an ovum by sexual intercourse or by injecting semen into the vagina by artificial means.
**insomnia** (in-som'ni-ə), *n.* prolonged or abnormal inability to sleep.
**inspiration** (in'spə-rā'shən), *n.* drawing in of breath; inhaling.
**instep** (in'step), *n.* the upper surface of the arch of the foot.
**insufflation** (in'sə-flā'shən), *n.* the act of blowing a substance, as powder, air, vapor, etc., into a body cavity, especially the lungs.
**insulin** (in'sə-lin), *n.* 1. a secretion of the islands of Langerhans, in the pancreas, which helps the body use sugar and other carbohydrates. 2. a product extracted from the pancreas of sheep and oxen and used hypodermically in the treatment of diabetes mellitus.
**internal ear,** the part of the ear in the temporal bone, consisting of the labyrinth and semicircular canals: also *inner ear.*
**intestine** (in-tes'tin), *n. usually pl.* the lower part of the alimentary canal, extending from the stomach to the anus and consisting of a convoluted upper part (*small intestine*) and a lower part of greater diameter (*large intestine*): food passes from the stomach into the intestines for further digestion.
**intoxication** (in-tok'sə-kā'shən), *n.* 1. a poisoning or becoming poisoned. 2. the condition caused by excessive use of alcoholic beverages.
**intravenous** (in'trə-vē'nəs), *adj.* into or within a vein or veins, as an injection.
**intubation** (in'tyoo-bā'shən), *n.* the passing of a tube into an opening or organ, as into the larynx to permit breathing when the larynx is obstructed or in severe cases of diphtheria.
**intussuscept** (in'təs-sə-sept'), *v. t.* to telescope (one section of the intestines) into another.
**intussusception** (in'təs-sə-sep'shən), *n.* 1. an intussuscepting or being intussuscepted. 2. the process of taking in food or other foreign matter and converting it into tissue.
**invalid** (in'və-lid), *n.* a sick person; especially, one who is chronically ill or disabled.
**invert** (in'vũrt), *n.* a homosexual person.
**involution** (in'və-lōō'shən), *n.* 1. the return of the womb to its normal size after childbirth. 2. a decline in the normal functions of the body or an organ; especially, the changes occurring at the menopause.
**iodine** (ī'ə-dīn'), *n.* a nonmetallic chemical element of the halogen family, used as an antiseptic.
**iodoform** (ī-ō'də-fôrm'), *n.* a yellow, crystalline compound of iodine, used as a local anesthetic and antiseptic, as a dressing for wounds, and in the treatment of the ulcers of syphilis and tuberculosis.
**ipecac** (ip'i-kak'), *n.* 1. the dried roots of a South American plant. 2. a preparation made from these roots, used as a local irritant, emetic, expectorant, diaphoretic and stomach stimulant, and in the treatment of chronic diarrhea, bronchitis, laryngitis, and some forms of hemorrhages.
**iris** (ī'ris), *n.* the round pigmented membrane surrounding the pupil of the eye, having muscles that adjust the size of the pupil to regulate the amount of light entering the eye.
**iritis** (ī-rī'tis), *n.* inflammation of the iris.
**irradiate** (i-rā'di-āt'), *v. t.* to treat by exposing to X rays, ultraviolet rays, radium, or other forms of radiant energy.
**irradiation** (i-rā'di-ā'shən), *n.* treatment with radiant energy.
**ischemia, ischaemia** (is-kē'mi-ə), *n.* local anemia.
**islands of Langerhans** (laŋ'ẽr-häns), irregular groups of cells in the pancreas that produce the hormone insulin.
**isoniazid** (ī'sə-nī'ə-zid), *n.* an antibacterial drug used in treating tuberculosis.
**issue** (ish'ōō), *n.* 1. a discharge of blood, pus, etc. 2. any incision or artificial ulcer made so that pus may be discharged.
**itch** (ich), *n.* 1. an irritating sensation on the skin that causes a desire to scratch the affected part. 2. a contagious skin disease caused by a parasitic mite and accompanied by intense irritation of the skin.

## J

**jalap** (jal'əp), *n.* the dried root of a Mexican plant, used as a powerful cathartic.
**jaundice** (jôn'dis), *n.* a diseased condition in which the eyeballs, the skin, and the urine become abnormally yellow, caused by the presence of bile pigments in the blood.
**Javelle water** (zhə-vel'), a solution of sodium hypochlorite in water, used as an antiseptic for wounds and for the purification of water.
**jejunum** (ji-jōō'nəm), *n.* the middle part of the small intestine, between the duodenum and the ileum.
**joint** (joint), *n.* 1. a connection between two bones which permits movement between them. 2. the way in which they are connected, or joined.
**jugular vein** (jug'yoo-lẽr), either of two large veins in the neck carrying blood back from the head to the heart.

## K

**Kahn test** (kän), a modified form of the Wassermann test for the diagnosis of syphilis.
**keloid** (kē'loid), *n.* a fibrous tumor arising from connective tissue of the skin, generally an excessive growth of scar tissue.
**keratin** (ker'ə-tin), *n.* an albuminous substance forming the principal matter of the hair and nails.
**keratitis** (ker'ə-tī'tis), *n.* inflammation of the cornea.
**keratosis** (ker'ə-tō'sis), *n.* 1. a wart or callus. 2. any disease characterized by horny growths.
**kidney** (kid'ni), *n.* either of the pair of glandular organs in the upper abdominal cavity, which separate water and waste products of metabolism from the blood and excrete them as urine through the bladder.
**kidney stone,** a hard, mineral deposit formed in the kidney from phosphates, urates, etc.
**kinesthesia** (kin'is-thē'zhə), *n.* the sensation of position, movement, tension, etc. of parts of the body, perceived through the nerve fibers in muscles, tendons, and joints.
**kleptomania** (klep'tə-mā'ni-ə), *n.* an abnormal, persistent impulse or tendency to steal.
**kyphos** (kī'fos), *n.* the spinal hump of kyphosis.
**kyphosis** (kī-fō'sis), *n.* abnormal curvature of the spine resulting in a hump; humpback.

## L

**labia majora** (lā'bi-ə mə-jō'rə), the outer folds of skin on either side of the vulva.

**labia minora** (mi-nō'rə), the folds of mucous membrane within the labia majora.

**labor** (lā'bēr), *n.* childbirth.

**labyrinth** (lab'ə-rinth'), *n.* the cavities of the internal ear.

**laceration** (las'ə-rā'shən), *n.* a jagged wound caused by tearing the flesh.

**lachrymal** (lak'rə-m'l), *adj.* of, for, or producing tears. *n.pl.* the glands which produce tears.

**lactation** (lak-tā'shən), *n.* 1. the secretion of milk by a mammary gland. 2. the period during which milk is secreted. 3. the suckling of young.

**lacteal** (lak'ti-əl), *adj.* containing or carrying chyle, the milky fluid that is a product of digestion. *n.* any of the lymphatic vessels that take up this fluid from the small intestine and carry it to the thoracic duct.

**lance** (lans), *v. t.* to cut open with a lancet.

**lancet** (lan'sit), *n.* a small, pointed, two-edged surgical knife.

**laparectomy** (lap'ə-rek'tə-mi), *n.* the surgical operation of cutting away a part or parts of the abdominal wall in order to provide support and correct sagging.

**laparotomy** (lap'ə-rot'ə-mi), *n.* a surgical incision into the abdomen; abdominal operation.

**laryngitis** (lar'in-jī'tis), *n.* inflammation of the larynx, characterized by hoarseness, sore throat, and, often, a temporary loss of voice.

**laryngoscope** (lə-riŋ'gə-skōp'), *n.* an instrument for examining the larynx, consisting of mirrors attached to a rod.

**laryngotomy** (lar'iŋ-got'ə-mi), *n.* the surgical operation of cutting into the larynx, especially to prevent suffocation in cases of obstruction of the larynx.

**larynx** (lar'iŋks), *n.* the upper part of the windpipe, which contains the vocal cords and serves as the organ of voice.

**laudanum** (lôd''n-əm), *n.* tincture of opium; solution of opium in alcohol.

**laughing gas,** nitrous oxide, used as an anesthetic, especially in dentistry.

**laxative** (lak'sə-tiv), *n.* a medicine used as a mild cathartic.

**leech** (lēch), *n.* a bloodsucking marine worm formerly placed on the skin to draw blood from a part.

**lens** (lenz), *n.* a transparent, biconvex body situated between the iris and the vitreous humor of the eye: its function is to focus upon the retina light rays entering the pupil.

**leper** (lep'ēr), *n.* one having leprosy.

**leprosy** (lep'rə-si), *n.* a chronic infectious disease that attacks the skin, tissues, or nerves: it is characterized by nodules, ulcers, white scaly scabs, deformities, and wasting of body parts, and is apparently communicated only after long and close contact.

**lesion** (lē'zhən), *n.* an injury or other change of an organ or tissue tending to result in impairment or loss of function.

**leucocyte** (lo͞o'kə-sīt'), *n.* any of the small, colorless cells in the blood, lymph, and tissues, which move like amoebae and destroy organisms that cause disease; white blood corpuscle.

**leucocytosis** (lo͞o'kō-sī-tō'sis), *n.* an increase in the number of leucocytes in the blood: it is a normal occurrence in digestion and during pregnancy but a pathological condition in infections, anemia, and certain fevers.

**leucorrhea** (lo͞o'kə-rē'ə), *n.* a morbid, thick, white vaginal discharge, usually resulting from chronic infection.

**leukemia** (lo͞o-kē'mi-ə), *n.* a disease of the blood-forming tissues, characterized by an abnormal and persistent increase in the number of leucocytes and the amount of bone marrow, with enlargement of the spleen and lymph glands.

**libido** (li-bī'dō), *n.* 1. the sexual urge or instinct. 2. psychic energy generally; driving force behind all action.

**ligament** (lig'ə-mənt), *n.* a band of tough tissue connecting bones or holding organs in place.

**ligature** (lig'ə-chēr), *n.* a thread or wire used to tie up an artery or other blood vessel.

**liniment** (lin'ə-mənt), *n.* any liquid medication rubbed on the skin to soothe sore or inflamed areas.

**lipoid** (lip'oid), *adj.* resembling fat.

**lipoma** (li-pō'mə), *n.* a tumor made up of fat tissue.

**lithiasis** (li-thī'ə-sis), *n.* the formation of calculi, or mineral concretions, in the body.

**lithotomy** (li-thot'ə-mi), *n.* the surgical removal of a calculus, or mineral concretion, by cutting into the bladder.

**liver** (liv'ēr), *n.* the largest glandular organ in the body, located in the upper part of the abdomen: it secretes bile, has an important function in carbohydrate, fat, and protein metabolism, and contains a substance essential to the normal production of red blood cells.

**lobar** (lō'bēr), *adj.* pertaining to a lobe or lobes: *lobar pneumonia* is an acute infection of one or more lobes of the lung.

**lobe** (lōb), *n.* 1. the fleshy lower end of the ear. 2. any of the main divisions of an organ separated by fissures or grooves: as, a *lobe* of the brain, lung, or liver.

**lochia** (lō'ki-ə), *n.* the discharge from the vagina for several weeks after childbirth.

**locomotor ataxia,** a chronic disease of the nervous system, usually caused by syphilis: it is characterized at first by intense pain, and later by disturbances of sensations, loss of reflexes and of muscular co-ordination, functional disorders of organs, etc.

**loin** (loin), *n.* the lower part of the back on either side of the backbone between the hipbones and ribs.

**lordosis** (lôr-dō'sis), *n.* forward curvature of the spine, producing a hollow in the back.

**lues** (lo͞o'ēz), *n.* syphilis.

**luetic** (lo͞o-et'ik), *adj.* syphilitic.

**lumbago** (lum-bā'gō), *n.* rheumatic pain in the joints of the lumbar region; backache.

**lumbar** (lum'bēr), *adj.* of or near the loins.

**lumen** (lū'mən), *n.* a cross section of the empty space within a tubular organ.

**lung** (luŋ), *n.* either of the two spongelike respiratory organs in the thorax, that oxygenate the blood and remove carbon dioxide from it.

**lupus** (lo͞o'pəs), *n.* any of various skin diseases: especially, a chronic tuberculous disease of the skin and mucous membranes, characterized by the formation of reddish-brown nodules.

**lymph** (limf), *n.* a clear, yellowish, alkaline fluid found in the lymphatic vessels: it resembles blood plasma but contains only colorless corpuscles.

**lymphatic** (lim-fat'ik), *adj.* of, containing, or conveying lymph.

**lymph gland,** any of the many glandlike structures lying in groups along the course of the lymphatic vessels and producing lymphocytes.

**lymphocyte** (lim'fə-sīt'), *n.* a variety of colorless corpuscle formed in the tissue of the lymph glands and passed from the lymph into the blood.

**lymphoid** (lim'foid), *adj.* of or like lymph or the tissue of the lymph glands.

## M

**maceration** (mas'ə-rā'shən), *n.* the act or process of rendering a solid substance soft by soaking it, as food in the digestive system.

**macrocyte** (mak'rə-sīt'), *n.* an abnormally large red blood corpuscle occurring especially in pernicious anemia.

**magnesia** (mag-nē'shə), *n.* a light, white, tasteless powder, used as an antacid and mild cathartic.

**maladjustment** (mal'ə-just'mənt), *n.* poor adjustment, especially to the environment.

**malady** (mal'ə-di), *n.* an ailment or disease.

**malaria** (mə-lâr'i-ə), *n.* an infectious disease, generally intermittent and recurrent, caused by any of various protozoa that are parasitic in the red blood corpuscles and are transmitted by the bite of an infected anopheles mosquito: it is characterized by severe chills and fever.

**malformation** (mal'fôr-mā'shən), *n.* faulty, defective, or abnormal structure or formation of a body or part.

**malignant** (mə-lig'nənt), *adj.* very dangerous or virulent; causing or likely to cause death: as, a cancer is a *malignant* tumor.

**malnutrition** (mal'no͞o-trish'ən), *n.* faulty or inadequate nutrition; undernourishment resulting from insufficient food, improper diet, etc.

**malocclusion** (mal'ə-klo͞o'zhən), *n.* imperfect meeting of the teeth of the upper and lower jaws.

**mamma** (mam'ə), *n.* a gland for secreting milk in the female; mammary gland.

**mammary** (mam'ə-ri), *adj.* designating or of either of the two milk-secreting glands, or mammae.

**mammilla** (ma-mil'ə), *n.* a nipple.

**mandible** (man'də-b'l), *n.* the jaw, especially the lower jaw.

**mania** (mā'ni-ə), *n.* wild or violent insanity; specifically, the manic phase of manic-depressive psychosis, characterized by abnormal excitability, exaggerated feelings of well-being, excessive activity, flight of ideas, etc.

**manic-depressive** (man'ik-di-pres'iv), *adj.* designating, of, or having a psychosis characterized by alternating periods of mania and melancholia. *n.* a person who has this psychosis.

**marrow** (mar'ō), *n.* the soft, vascular, fatty tissue filling the cavities within most bones.

**masochism** (mas'ə-kiz'm), *n.* the getting of sexual pleasure from being dominated, mistreated, or hurt physically or otherwise by one's partner.

**masochist** (mas'ə-kist), *n.* a person characterized by masochism.

**mastectomy** (mas-tek'tə-mi), *n.* the surgical removal of a breast.

**mastitis** (mas-tī'tis), *n.* inflammation of the breast, or mammary gland.

**mastoid** (mas'toid), *adj.* designating, of, or near a projection of the temporal bone behind the ear. *n.* the mastoid projection.

**mastoiditis** (mas'toid-ī'tis), *n.* inflammation of the mastoid.

**masturbation** (mas'tēr-bā'shən), *n.* genital self-excitation, usually by manipulation; autoerotism.

**maxilla** (mak-sil'ə), *n.* a jaw or jawbone, especially the upper one.

**maxillary** (mak'sə-ler'i), *adj.* designating, of, or near the jaw or jawbone, especially the upper one.

**measles** (mē'z'lz), *n.* 1. an acute, infectious, communicable virus disease, characterized by a skin eruption, high fever, nasal catarrh, etc., and occurring most frequently in childhood. 2. any of various similar but milder diseases; especially, German measles in which the fever is slight.

**meatus** (mi-ā'təs), *n.* a natural opening or passage in the body.

**mediastinum** (mē'di-as-tī'nəm), *n.* 1. a membranous partition between two cavities of the body, especially that separating the lungs or the two pleural sacs. 2.

the space between the pleural sacs, containing the heart and other chest viscera except the lungs
**medulla** (mi-dul'ə), *n.* 1. the marrow in bones. 2. the medulla oblongata. 3. the inner substance of an organ, as of the kidney, adrenal gland, etc.
**medulla oblongata** (ob'lôŋ-gä'tə), the widening continuation of the spinal cord forming the lowest part of the brain and containing vital nerve centers for the control of breathing, circulation, etc.
**megalomania** (meg'ə-lə-mā'ni-ə), *n.* a mental disorder characterized by delusions of grandeur, wealth, power, etc.
**melancholia** (mel'ən-kō'li-ə), *n.* a mental disorder characterized by extreme depression of spirits, brooding, and gloominess.
**membrane** (mem'brān), *n.* a thin, soft, pliable, sheetlike layer of tissue which covers or lines an organ or part.
**meninges** (mə-nin'jēz), *n.pl.* the three membranes that cover the brain and spinal cord.
**meningitis** (men'in-jī'tis), *n.* inflammation of the meninges, especially as the result of infection by bacteria or viruses: the three principal forms are cerebral, spinal, and cerebrospinal.
**menopause** (men'ə-pôz), *n.* the permanent cessation of menstruation, normally between the ages of 45 and 50, or the period during which this occurs; change of life.
**menses** (men'sēz), *n.pl.* the monthly discharge of blood from the uterus, through the genital tract.
**menstruate** (men'stroo-āt'), *v. i.* to have the monthly discharge of the menses.
**menstruation** (men'stroo-ā'shən), *n.* 1. the monthly discharge of the menses: it begins at puberty and occurs each month until the menopause. 2. the period when this occurs.
**menthol** (men'thol), *n.* a white, waxy, crystalline alcohol obtained from oil of peppermint and used externally in skin diseases, colds, and neuralgia.
**mercuric chloride,** a very poisonous compound of mercury, used as an antiseptic.
**Mercurochrome** (mẽr-kyoor'ə-krōm'), *n.* 1. a red, crystalline dye. 2. an aqueous solution of this, used as an antiseptic. A trade-mark.
**Merthiolate** (mẽr-thī'ə-lāt'), *n.* a red or colorless liquid, used as an antiseptic and germicide: it contains over 49 per cent of mercury in organic compound: a trade-mark.
**mesentery** (mes''n-tẽr'i), *n.* a supporting membrane or membranes enfolding some internal organ and attaching it to either the body wall or another organ; especially, a part of the peritoneum enfolding most of the small intestine and attaching it to the rear wall of the abdominal cavity.
**metabolism** (mə-tab'ə-liz'm), *n.* the chemical and physical processes continuously going on in the body and in the cells, comprising those by which assimilated food is built up into protoplasm and those by which protoplasm is used and broken down into simpler substances or waste matter, with the release of energy for all vital processes.
**metacarpal** (met'ə-kär'p'l), *adj.* of the metacarpus.
**metacarpus** (met'ə-kär'pəs), *n.* 1. the five bones extending from the wrist to the fingers. 2. the part of the hand containing these bones.
**metastasis** (mə-tas'tə-sis), *n.* the spread or transfer of disease from one part of a body to another unrelated to it.
**metatarsal** (met'ə-tär's'l), *adj.* of the metatarsus.
**metatarsus** (met'ə-tär'səs), *n.* the part of the foot between the ankle and the toes.
**methylene blue** (meth'ə-lēn'), a bluish-green aniline dye used in staining bacteria and as an antidote in cyanide poisoning.
**Metrazol** (met'rə-zōl'), *n.* a drug used to stimulate circulation and respiration and in the treatment of some mental illnesses: a trade-mark.
**metritis** (mi-trī'tis), *n.* inflammation of the uterus.
**microbe** (mī'krōb), *n.* any of the bacteria that cause disease; germ.
**microorganism** (mī'krō-ôr'gən-iz'm), *n.* any microscopic or ultramicroscopic animal or vegetable organism; especially, any of the bacteria, protozoa, or viruses.
**migraine** (mī'grān), *n.* a type of periodically returning headache, usually limited to one side of the head and often accompanied by vertigo, nausea, etc.
**miliaria** (mil'i-âr'i-ə), *n.* an acute skin disease resulting from inflammation of the sweat glands, accompanied by red, itching patches or pimples, prickly heat.
**miliary tuberculosis** (mil'i-er'i), a form of tuberculosis in which the tubercle bacilli spread through the blood stream from a primary focus of infection to other parts of the body, where multiple tubercles are formed.
**milk fever,** a mild fever sometimes occurring with the first secretion of milk in the breasts after childbirth: it is caused by infection.
**milk of magnesia,** a milky-white liquid preparation of magnesia, used as a mild cathartic and antacid.
**miscarriage** (mis-kar'ij), *n.* the premature birth of a fetus, so that it does not live.
**molar** (mō'lẽr), *n.* one of the back teeth used for grinding food: there are three on each side of both the upper and lower jaws.
**Mongolian idiot,** a person having Mongolism.
**Mongolism** (moŋ'gəl-iz'm), *n.* a type of congenital mental deficiency, accompanied with a flattened forehead, slanting eyes set closely together, etc.
**mononucleosis** (mon'ə-noo'kli-ō'sis), *n.* 1. the presence in the blood of an excessive number of cells having a single nucleus. 2. a disease resulting from this, characterized by fever and enlargement of the lymph nodes.
**morning sickness,** vomiting and nausea occurring in the morning during the first months of pregnancy.
**moron** (môr'on), *n.* a mentally deficient person; person mentally equal or inferior to a child between 8 and 12 years old.
**morphine** (môr'fēn), *n.* a bitter, white, crystalline alkaloid derived from opium and used to induce sleep and relieve pain.
**mucous** (mū'kəs), *adj.* of, containing, or secreting mucus.
**mucous membrane,** a mucus-secreting membrane lining body cavities and canals connecting with the external air, as the alimentary canal and respiratory tract.
**mucus** (mū'kəs), *n.* the thick, slimy secretion of the mucous membranes, that moistens and protects them.
**multiple sclerosis,** a chronic disease in which there is sclerosis in various parts of the nervous system: it is characterized by muscular weakness, tremor, etc.
**mumps** (mumps), *n.pl.* a communicable disease caused by a virus and accompanied by fever and inflammation and swelling of the parotid gland in the neck under the ear: in adults, the external genitals and breasts may become inflamed.
**muscle** (mus''l), *n.* any of the organs consisting of bundles of fibers that can be contracted and expanded to produce bodily movements.
**muscular** (mus'kyoo-lẽr), *adj.* of, consisting of, or accomplished by a muscle or muscles.
**muscular dystrophy,** a chronic, noncontagious disease characterized by progressive wasting of the muscles.
**mutation** (mū-tā'shən), *n.* a sudden variation in some inheritable characteristic, as distinguished from a variation resulting from generations of gradual change.
**mute** (mūt), *adj.* unable to speak; dumb. *n.* one unable to speak.
**myelitis** (mī'ə-lī'tis), *n.* inflammation of the spinal cord or the bone marrow.
**myocarditis** (mī'ō-kär-dī'tis), *n.* inflammation of the myocardium.
**myocardium** (mī'ō-kär'di-əm), *n.* the muscular substance of the heart.
**myopia** (mī-ō'pi-ə), *n.* an abnormal eye condition in which the light rays from distant objects are focused in front of the retina instead of on it, so that the objects are not seen distinctly; nearsightedness.
**myosis** (mī-ō'sis), *n.* prolonged or excessive contraction of the pupil of the eye, resulting from disease or the use of a drug.

## N

**nail** (nāl), *n.* the thin, horny plate covering the ends of the fingers and toes.
**narcissism** (när-sis'iz'm), *n.* arrest at or regression to the first stage of sexual development, in which the self is an object of sexual pleasure.
**narcolepsy** (när'kə-lep'si), *n.* a condition of frequent and uncontrollable desire for sleep.
**narcosis** (när-kō'sis), *n.* a condition of deep unconsciousness produced by a narcotic.
**narcotic** (när-kot'ik), *n.* any drug that induces profound sleep, lethargy, and relief of pain. *adj.* of, like, or capable of producing narcosis.
**nasal** (nā'z'l), *adj.* of the nose.
**nasopharynx** (nā'zō-far'iŋks), *n.* the part of the pharynx lying directly behind the nasal passages and above the soft palate.
**nates** (nā'tēz), *n.pl.* the buttocks.
**nausea** (nô'shə), *n.* a sensation of sickness at the stomach, accompanied by an impulse to vomit.
**navel** (nā'v'l), *n.* the scar in the center of the abdomen caused by the tying off and removal of the umbilical cord at birth.
**necropsy** (nek'rop-si), *n.* examination of a dead body; autopsy.
**Nembutal** (nem'byoo-tôl'), *n.* pentobarbital sodium, used as a sedative, hypnotic, and analgesic: a trade-mark.
**neoarsphenamine** (nē'ō-ärs'fen-ə-mēn'), *n.* a sodium compound of arsphenamine, used instead of arsphenamine because it is less toxic and more soluble.
**neomycin** (nē'ə-mī'sin), *n.* an antibiotic drug similar to streptomycin, used in the treatment of various skin and eye infections and certain systemic infections, and as an intestinal antiseptic.
**neoplasm** (nē'ə-plaz'm), *n.* any abnormal growth of tissue; tumor.
**Neosalvarsan** (nē'o-sal'vẽr-san), *n.* neoarsphenamine: a trade-mark.
**nephrectomy** (ne-frek'tə-mi), *n.* surgical removal of a kidney.
**nephritis** (ne-frī'tis), *n.* an acute or chronic disease of the kidneys, characterized by inflammation, degeneration, etc.: certain types are called *Bright's disease.*
**nephrotomy** (ne-frot'ə-mi), *n.* surgical incision into the kidney, as for removing a renal calculus.
**nerve** (nũrv), *n.* any of the cordlike fibers or bundles of fibers connecting the organs with the brain and spinal cord and parts of the nervous system with each other, and carrying impulses to and from the brain or a nerve center.
**nerve cell,** a cell which with its processes forms the structural and functional unit of the nervous system; especially, a cell of the gray matter of the brain or of a ganglion.

**nerve center,** any group of nerve cells that function together in controlling some specific sense or bodily activity.

**nerve fiber,** any of the threadlike elements making up a nerve: it is the main process of a nerve cell and conducts the impulses.

**nervous** (nũr′vəs), *adj.* 1. of the nerves. 2. made up of or containing nerves. 3. characterized by or having a disordered state of the nerves. 4. emotionally tense, restless, etc.

**nervous system,** all the nerve cells and nervous tissues in the body, including the brain, spinal cord, ganglia, nerves, and nerve centers: it co-ordinates and controls responses to stimuli and conditions behavior and consciousness.

**neuralgia** (noo-ral′jə), *n.* pain along the course of a nerve or in its area of distribution.

**neurasthenia** (noor′əs-thē′ni-ə), *n.* a type of neurosis, usually the result of emotional conflicts, characterized by fatigue, depression, worry, and, often, localized pains without apparent objective causes.

**neuritis** (noo-rī′tis), *n.* inflammation of a nerve or nerves, characterized by pain and muscle tenderness and accompanied by changes in sensory and motor activity in the region of the affected nerve.

**neurology** (noo-rol′ə-ji), *n.* the branch of medicine dealing with the nervous system, its structure, and its diseases.

**neuroma** (noo-rō′mə), *n.* a tumor consisting of nerve cells and fibers: it is derived from nervous tissue.

**neuron** (noor′on), *n.* the stuctural and functional unit of the nervous system, consisting of the nerve cell body and all its processes, as dendrites and axons.

**neurosis** (noo-rō′sis), *n.* a psychic, or mental, disorder characterized by special combinations of anxieties, compulsions, obsessions, and phobias, without apparent organic or structural injury or change.

**neurotic** (noo-rot′ik), *adj.* of, characteristic of, or having a neurosis. *n.* a neurotic person.

**nevus** (nē′vəs), *n.* a colored spot on the skin, usually congenital; birthmark or mole.

**nicotinic acid** (nik′ə-tin′ik), a white, odorless, crystalline substance found in protein foods like lean meat, eggs, wholegrain cereals, etc. and prepared synthetically from nicotine: it is a member of the vitamin B complex and is used in the treatment of pellagra.

**night blindness,** imperfect vision in the dark or in dim light: a sign of vitamin A deficiency.

**nipple** (nip′'l), *n.* the cone-shaped protuberance on the front surface of the breast, which serves as an outlet for milk in suckling the young.

**nitrous oxide** (nī′trəs), laughing gas, a colorless gas used as an anesthetic.

**node** (nōd), *n.* a protuberance; knotty, localized swelling.

**nodule** (noj′ōōl), *n.* a small node.

**novocain, novocaine** (nō′və-kān′), *n.* an alkaloid compound resembling cocaine but less toxic and irritant, used as a local anesthetic: a trade-mark (**Novocain**).

**nux vomica** (nuks′ vom′i-kə), a medicine made from the poisonous seed of an Asiatic tree: it is used as a heart stimulant.

**nyctalopia** (nik′tə-lō′pi-ə), *n.* night blindness.

**nymphomania** (nim′fə-mā′ni-ə), *n.* excessive and uncontrollable sexual desire in a woman.

## O

**obese** (ō-bēs′), *adj.* very fat; plump; overweight.

**obesity** (ō-bēs′ə-ti), *n.* the condition of being very fat.

**obsession** (əb-sesh′ən), *n.* 1. the fact or state of being haunted or troubled with an idea, desire, emotion, etc. 2. such an idea, desire, etc.

**obstetrician** (ob′ste-trish′ən), *n.* a surgeon who specializes in obstetrics.

**obstetrics** (ob-stet′riks), *n.pl.* the branch of medicine concerned with the care and treatment of women during pregnancy, childbirth, and the period immediately following.

**occiput** (ok′si-put′), *n.* the back of the skull or head.

**occlude** (ə-klōōd′), *v. i.* to meet with the cusps fitting close together: said of the upper and lower teeth. *v. t.* to close or block (a passage).

**occlusion** (ə-klōō′zhən), *n.* 1. the contact of the teeth in both jaws when brought together by chewing or closing the mouth. 2. the blocking of a passage.

**ocular** (ok′yoo-lẽr), *adj.* of, for, or like the eye.

**oculist** (ok′yoo-list), *n.* a physician who specializes in diagnosing and treating diseases and abnormalities of the eye.

**odontology** (ō′don-tol′ə-ji), *n.* the science dealing with the structure, growth, and diseases of the teeth; dentistry.

**olfactory** (ol-fak′tẽr-i), *adj.* of the sense of smell.

**omentum** (o-men′təm), *n.* a free fold of peritoneum connecting the stomach to the other visceral organs and supporting blood vessels, nerves, and lymph vessels.

**onanism** (ō′nən-iz′m), *n.* withdrawal in coition before ejaculation.

**oöphorectomy** (ō′ə-fə-rek′tə-mi), *n.* the surgical removal of one or both ovaries.

**operation** (op-ẽr-ā′shən), *n.* any surgical procedure performed with or without the aid of instruments, usually to remedy a physical ailment or defect.

**ophthalmia** (of-thal′mi-ə), *n.* inflammation of the eyeball or of the conjunctiva.

**ophthalmologist** (of′thal-mol′ə-jist), *n.* a doctor who specializes in ophthalmology.

**ophthalmology** (of′thal-mol′ə-ji), *n.* the branch of medicine dealing with the structure, functions, and diseases of the eye.

**ophthalmoscope** (of-thal′mə-skōp′), *n.* an instrument used to examine the interior of the eye.

**opiate** (ō′pi-it), *n.* a medicine containing opium or any of its derivatives, and acting as a sedative and narcotic.

**opium** (ō′pi-əm), *n.* a narcotic drug prepared from the seed capsules of the opium poppy: it is used to relieve pain and induce sleep.

**optic** (op′tik), *adj.* of the eye or sense of sight.

**optical** (op′ti-k'l), *adj.* 1. of or connected with the sense of sight. 2. of the relation between light and vision.

**optician** (op-tish′ən), *n.* one who manufactures and sells eyeglasses and other optical instruments.

**optic nerves,** the pair of nerves connecting the retina of the eye directly with the brain; nerves of sight.

**optometrist** (op-tom′ə-trist), *n.* a specialist in optometry.

**optometry** (op-tom′ə-tri), *n.* examination of the eyes (without the use of drugs or medicine) for defects, as nearsightedness and farsightedness, and the fitting of glasses to correct these defects.

**oral** (ôr′əl), *adj.* of, at, or near the mouth.

**orchitis** (ôr-kī′tis), *n.* inflammation of a testicle.

**organ** (ôr′gən), *n.* any part of the body composed of several tissues, which has a special function or functions.

**organic** (ôr-gan′ik), *adj.* 1. of or having to do with an organ or organs. 2. producing or involving alteration in the structure of an organ.

**orgasm** (ôr′gaz'm), *n.* the climax of a sexual act.

**orifice** (ôr′ə-fis), *n.* an opening, as the mouth or anus.

**orthodontia** (ôr′thə-don′shə), *n.* the branch of dentistry concerned with the correction and prevention of irregular teeth so as to bring about proper occlusion.

**orthodontist** (ôr′thə-don′tist), *n.* a dentist who specializes in orthodontia.

**orthopedics** (ôr′thə-pē′diks), *n.pl.* the branch of surgery dealing with the treatment of deformities, diseases, and injuries of the bones and joints.

**orthopedist** (ôr′thə-pē′dist), *n.* one who is an expert or specialist in orthopedics.

**os** (os) *n.* an opening in the body: as, *os externum,* the opening into the vagina.

**osseous** (os′i-əs), *adj.* composed of, containing, or like bone.

**ossification** (os′ə-fi-kā′shən), *n.* 1. the process of changing or being changed into bone. 2. any bone structure. 3. the pathological or abnormal conversion of soft tissue into bone.

**osteitis** (os′ti-ī′tis), *n.* inflammation of bones or bony tissue.

**osteoarthritis** (os′ti-ō-är-thrī′tis), *n.* chronic arthritis involving a joint and causing thickening, pain, and stiffness.

**osteoclasis** (os′ti-ok′lə-sis), *n.* 1. the breaking of a bone to correct a deformity; especially, the breaking of a bone badly healed after a previous fracture. 2. the breaking down and absorption of bony tissue.

**osteoma** (os′ti-ō′mə), *n.* a tumor composed of bony tissue.

**osteomalacia** (os′ti-ō-mə-lā′shə), *n.* softening of the bones.

**osteomyelitis** (os′ti-ō-mī′ə-lī′tis), *n.* inflammation of the bone marrow.

**osteopath** (os′te-ə-path′), *n.* one who practices osteopathy.

**osteopathy** (os′ti-op′ə-thi), *n.* a theory and system of treating ailments based on the belief that they generally result from the pressure of displaced bones on nerves, etc., and are curable by manipulation.

**osteoplasty** (os′ti-ə-plas′ti), *n.* bone grafting.

**osteotomy** (os′ti-ot′ə-mi), *n.* surgical operation of dividing a bone or cutting out a piece of bone.

**ostosis** (os-tō′sis), *n.* the formation of bone.

**otitis** (ō-tī′tis), *n.* inflammation of the ear.

**otology** (ō-tol′ə-ji), *n.* the branch of medicine dealing with the ear and its diseases.

**otoscope** (ō′tə-skōp′), *n.* 1. an instrument for examining the tympanic membrane and external canal of the ear. 2. a type of stethoscope for auscultating the middle ear.

**outpatient** (out′pā-shənt), *n.* a patient who is not confined in a hospital, but receives treatment from it.

**ovarian** (ō-vâr′i-ən), *adj.* of an ovary.

**ovary** (ō′vẽr-i), *n.* either of the two female reproductive glands in which ova, or eggs, develop at monthly intervals.

**oviduct** (ō′vi-dukt′), *n.* either of the two passages leading from either side of the uterus to the ovaries: it conveys the ovum from the ovary to the uterus or to the outside.

**ovulate** (ō′vyoo-lāt′), *v. i.* to discharge an ovum from the ovary; produce an ovum.

**ovulation** (ō′vyoo-lā′shən), *n.* the process by which a mature ovum escapes from a ruptured Graafian follicle.

**ovum** (ō′vəm), *n.* an egg; a reproductive cell developing monthly in the ovary, from which it passes through the oviduct to the uterus: the union of the ovum and a spermatozoa of the male starts an embryo.

**oxalic acid,** a colorless, poisonous, crystalline acid: it is used as an antiseptic by surgeons.

**oxycephalic** (ok′si-sə-fal′ik), *adj.* designating or having a skull coming to a more or less cone-shaped point on top.

**oxygen tent,** a boxlike enclosure supplied with oxygen, in which a patient is kept to facilitate his breathing: used chiefly in cases of pneumonia and heart disease.

**oxytocic** (ok′si-tō′sik), *adj.* promoting or hastening the process of childbirth by stimulating the contractions of the involuntary muscles of the uterus.

P

**Paget's disease** (paj′its), a chronic bone disease resulting in softening, thickening, and distortion of the bones.

**palate** (pal′it), *n.* the roof of the mouth, consisting of a hard bony forward part (the *hard palate*) and a soft fleshy back part (the *soft palate* or *velum*).

**palliative** (pal′i-ā′tiv), *n.* a medicine or remedy which gives relief but no cure. *adj.* giving relief without curing.

**palpitation** (pal′pə-tā′shən), *n.* a rapid, often irregular, beating of the heart from functional disorder, emotion, etc.

**palsy** (pôl′zi), *n.* paralysis in any part of the body, sometimes accompanied with involuntary tremors.

**pancreas** (pan′kri-əs), *n.* a large, elongated gland situated behind the stomach and secreting pancreatic juice into the small intestine.

**pancreatic juice** (pan′kri-at′ik), the clear, crystalline digestive juice secreted by the pancreas into the small intestine, where its constituent enzymes act on food passed down from the stomach.

**papilla** (pə-pil′ə), *n.* 1. any small nipplelike projection or process of connective tissue, as the small elevations at the root of a developing tooth or hair or the many elevations on the surface of the tongue. 2. the nipple.

**papilloma** (pap′ə-lō′mə), *n.* a tumor of the skin or mucous membrane.

**paralysis** (pə-ral′ə-sis), *n.* (partial or complete) loss of the power of motion or sensation, especially voluntary motion, in some part or all of the body, as the result of injury to the nervous system or to some muscular mechanism.

**paralysis agitans** (aj′i-tənz), shaking palsy.

**paranoia** (par′ə-noi′ə), *n.* a mental disorder characterized by systematized delusions of grandeur or persecution.

**paranoiac** (par′ə-noi′ak), *n.* one affected with paranoia. *adj.* of, like, or having paranoia.

**paraplegia** (par′ə-plē′ji-ə), *n.* motor and sensory paralysis of the entire lower half of the body.

**parathyroid** (par′ə-thī′roid), *n.* any of the four tiny, oval glands lying on or embedded in the thyroid gland but active independently: they secrete a hormone that increases the calcium content of the blood. *adj.* located near or next to the thyroid gland.

**paregoric** (par′ə-gôr′ik), *n.* a medicine that soothes or lessens pain; specifically, a camphorated tincture of opium, used in cough mixtures and to relieve diarrhea.

**parenchyma** (pə-reŋ′ki-mə), *n.* the essential or functional tissue of an organ, as distinguished from its connective tissue, etc.

**paresis** (pə-rē′sis), *n.* 1. partial paralysis. 2. a disease of the brain caused by syphilis of the central nervous system and characterized by inflammation of the meninges, mental and emotional instability, paralytic attacks, etc.

**paresthesia** (par′es-thē′zhə), *n.* an abnormal sensation of tickling, burning, or prickling on the skin.

**Parkinson's disease** (pär′kin-s′nz), shaking palsy.

**parotid** (pə-rot′id), *n.* either of the salivary glands situated below and in front of each ear. *adj.* located near or beside the ear.

**parotitis** (par′ə-tī′tis), *n.* inflammation of a parotid gland; especially, the mumps.

**paroxysm** (par′ək-siz′m), *n.* a sudden intensification or recurrence of the symptoms of a disease.

**patella** (pə-tel′ə), *n.* the kneecap.

**patellar reflex** (pə-tel′ēr), a reflex kick with extension of the leg at the knee, produced by sharply tapping the tendon below the patella: it is a normal reaction in health.

**pathogenesis** (path′ə-jen′ə-sis), *n.* the production or development of disease.

**pathologist** (pə-thol′ə-jist), *n.* one who specializes in pathology.

**pathology** (pə-thol′ə-ji), *n.* the branch of medicine dealing with diseases, especially with the structural and functional changes caused by disease.

**pectoral** (pek′tə-rəl), *adj.* of or located in or on the chest.

**pediatrician** (pē′di-ə-trish′ən), *n.* a physician who specializes in pediatrics.

**pediatrics** (pē′di-at′riks), *n.pl.* the branch of medicine which is concerned with the care and development of children and the diagnosis and treatment of their diseases.

**pediculosis** (pi-dik′yoo-lō′sis), *n.* a skin disorder caused by infestation with lice.

**pellagra** (pə-lā′grə), *n.* a chronic disease caused by a deficiency of nicotinic acid in the diet and characterized by gastrointestinal disturbances, skin eruptions, and nervous disorders: it is endemic in some parts of the world.

**pelvis** (pel′vis), *n.* 1. the basin-shaped, bony structure which supports the spinal column and rests on the tops of the two thighbones. 2. the funnel-shaped part of the kidney leading into the ureter.

**pemphigus** (pem′fi-gəs), *n.* a disease characterized by the formation of watery blisters on the skin.

**penicillin** (pen′ə-sil′in), *n.* a powerful antibiotic obtained from certain fungi growing as green mold on stale bread, decaying fruit, etc.: it is used in the treatment and prevention of some infections due to its ability to inhibit the growth of certain bacteria.

**penis** (pē′nis), *n.* the male organ of sexual intercourse: it is also the organ through which urine is ejected.

**pentobarbital sodium** (pen′tə-bär′bi-tôl′), the soluble sodium salt of barbituric acid, used as a sedative, hypnotic, and analgesic.

**pepsin** (pep′sin), *n.* 1. an enzyme secreted in the stomach, aiding in the digestion of proteins. 2. an extract of pepsin from the stomachs of calves, sheep, etc., used in aiding digestion.

**peptic** (pep′tik), *adj.* 1. of or aiding digestion. 2. of, like, or caused by pepsin or other digestive secretions: as, a *peptic* ulcer.

**percussion** (pēr-kush′ən), *n.* the striking or tapping of the chest, back, etc., with the fingertips so as to determine from the sound produced the condition of any of the internal organs.

**pericarditis** (per′i-kär-dī′tis), *n.* inflammation of the pericardium.

**pericardium** (per′i-kär′di-əm), *n.* the thin membranous sac enclosing the heart.

**perineum** (per′ə-nē′əm), *n.* the region of the body between the thighs, at the outlet of the pelvis; specifically, the small triangular region including the anus and the vulva or the base of the penis.

**periosteum** (per′i-os′ti-əm), *n.* the membrane of tough, fibrous connective tissue covering all bones except at the joints.

**periostitis** (per′i-os-tī′tis), *n.* inflammation of the periosteum.

**peristalsis** (per′ə-stal′sis), *n.* the rhythmic, wavelike motion of the walls of the alimentary canal and certain other hollow organs, consisting of alternate muscular contractions and dilations that move the contents of the tube onward.

**peritoneum** (per′i-tə-nē′əm), *n.* the transparent serous membrane lining the abdominal cavity and reflected inward at various places to cover the visceral organs.

**peritonitis** (per′i-tə-nī′tis), *n.* inflammation of the peritoneum.

**pernicious anemia,** a severe form of anemia characterized by a gradual reduction in the number of red blood cells, general weakness, gastrointestinal and nervous disturbances, etc.: it can be successfully treated by the administration of liver or liver extracts.

**perspiration** (pūr′spə-rā′shən), *n.* 1. sweat. 2. the act of sweating, or perspiring.

**perspire** (pēr-spīr′), *v. i.* & *v. t.* to give forth (a characteristic salty moisture) through the pores of the skin; sweat.

**pertussis** (pēr-tus′is), *n.* whooping cough.

**pessary** (pes′ə-ri), *n.* 1. a device placed in the vagina to support a displaced or weak uterus. 2. a vaginal suppository.

**phalanx** (fā′laŋks), *n.* any of the bones forming the fingers or toes.

**pharyngitis** (far′in-jī′tis), *n.* inflammation of the mucous membrane of the pharynx.

**pharynx** (far′iŋks), *n.* the muscular and membranous cavity of the alimentary canal leading from the mouth and nasal passages to the larynx and esophagus.

**phenol** (fē′nôl), *n.* carbolic acid, a strong corrosive poison used, in dilute solutions, as an antiseptic.

**phenolphthalein** (fē′nôl-thal′ēn), *n.* a white to pale-yellow, crystalline powder used as a laxative.

**phlebitis** (fli-bī′tis), *n.* inflammation of a vein or veins.

**phlebotomy** (fli-bot′ə-mi), *n.* the formerly common act or operation of opening a vein to let out blood as a therapeutic measure.

**phlegm** (flem), *n.* the thick, stringy mucus secreted by the mucous glands of the respiratory tract and discharged from the throat, as during a cold.

**photophobia** (fō′tə-fō′bi-ə), *n.* 1. an abnormal fear of light. 2. an abnormal sensitivity to light, especially of the eyes, as in measles and certain eye conditions.

**phrenic** (fren′ik), *adj.* 1. of the diaphragm. 2. of the mind.

**phthisis** (thī′sis), *n.* a wasting of the body or any of its parts, especially in pulmonary tuberculosis.

**physic** (fiz′ik), *n.* a cathartic.

**physical therapy,** the treatment of disease, injury, etc. by physical means rather than with drugs, as by massage, infrared or ultraviolet light, heat, exercise, etc.

**physician** (fə-zish′ən), *n.* a doctor authorized to practice medicine.

**physiotherapy** (fiz′i-ō-ther′ə-pi), *n.* physical therapy.

**pia mater** (pī′ə mā′tēr), the vascular membrane immediately enveloping the brain and spinal cord.

**piles** (pīlz), *n.pl.* hemorrhoids.

**pimple** (pim′p'l), *n.* a small, reddish swelling of the skin, usually inflamed.

**pink eye,** an acute, contagious form of conjunctivitis in which the eyeball and the mucous membrane lining the eyelid become red and inflamed.

**pituitary** (pi-tōō′ə-ter′i), *n.* a small, oval endocrine gland attached to a stalk at the base of the brain and consisting of an anterior and posterior lobe: it secretes hormones influencing body growth, metabolism, etc.: in full, **pituitary gland** (or **body**).

**pityriasis** (pit′ə-rī′ə-sis), *n.* a scaly skin disease characterized by shedding of flakes of epidermis.

**placenta** (plə-sen′tə), *n.* a vascular organ within the uterus, connected to the fetus by the umbilical cord: it serves as the structure through which the fetus receives nourishment from, and eliminates waste matter into, the circulatory system of the mother.

**plastic surgery**, surgery dealing with the repair or restoration of injured, deformed, or destroyed parts, especially by transferring tissue, as skin or bone, from other parts or from another individual.

**plessor** (ples′ẽr), *n.* a small hammer with a soft head, as of rubber, used in percussion.

**pleura** (ploor′ə), *n.* a thin serous membrane lining each half of the chest cavity and enveloping the lungs.

**pleurisy** (ploor′ə-si), *n.* inflammation of the pleura.

**plexus** (plek′səs), *n.* a network of blood vessels, lymphatic vessels, nerves, etc.: as, the solar *plexus* (of nerves) in the abdomen.

**plumbism** (plum′biz′m), *n.* lead poisoning.

**pneumococcus** (nōō′mə-kok′əs), *n.* the bacterium causing lobar pneumonia and certain other diseases.

**pneumonia** (nōō-mō′nyə), *n.* a disease of the lungs in which the tissue becomes inflamed, hardened, and watery: there are several types of pneumonia, as lobar and bronchial.

**pneumothorax** (nōō′mō-thôr′aks), *n.* the presence of air or gas in the chest cavity, sometimes artificially induced for collapsing and immobilizing the lung in the treatment of tuberculosis.

**poliomyelitis** (pol′i-ō-mī′ə-lī′tis), *n.* inflammation of the gray matter of the spinal cord; especially, infantile paralysis.

**polyp** (pol′ip), *n.* a small, soft, projecting growth in the mucous membranes of the nose, intestines, rectum, vagina, etc.

**polyuria** (pol′i-yoor′i-ə), *n.* excessive urination, as in certain diseases.

**potassium permanganate** (pẽr-maŋ′gə-nāt′), a dark-purple, crystalline compound used as an antiseptic.

**poultice** (pōl′tis), *n.* any hot, soft, moist mass applied to a sore or inflamed part of the body.

**precordial** (prē-kôr′jəl), *adj.* of the precordium.

**precordium** (prē-kôr′di-əm), *n.* the region of the chest over the heart.

**pregnancy** (preg′nən-si), *n.* the condition, quality, or period of being pregnant.

**pregnant** (preg′nənt), *adj.* having a fetus or fetuses growing in the uterus.

**prepuce** (prē′pūs), *n.* the foreskin: fold of skin covering the front part of the penis or clitoris.

**presentation** (prez-′n-tā′shən), *n.* the position of the fetus at the time of delivery with reference to the part which can be touched by a finger inserted into the vagina and which is usually the part first expelled from the uterus.

**prickly heat**, a noncontagious, itching and prickling skin eruption caused by inflammation of the sweat glands.

**probe** (prōb), *n.* a slender, blunt surgical instrument for exploring a wound or the like.

**process** (pros′es), *n.* a projection or outgrowth from a larger structure, as a bone.

**proctoscope** (prok′tə-skōp′), *n.* an instrument used for the direct examination of the interior of the rectum.

**progesterone** (prō-jes′tə-rōn′), *n.* a crystalline hormone secreted by certain tissue in the ovary or prepared synthetically: it serves to prepare the uterus for the reception and development of the fertilized ovum.

**prostate** (pros′tāt), *n.* a muscular gland surrounding the urethra at the neck of the bladder in the male: it aids in the manufacture of seminal fluid.

**prurigo** (proo-rī′gō), *n.* a chronic skin disease characterized by small, pale-red papules and intense itching: the disease usually begins in childhood and remains throughout life.

**pruritus** (proo-rī′təs), *n.* itching.

**psittacosis** (sit′ə-kō′sis), *n.* an acute infectious virus disease affecting birds of the parrot family, often transmitted to man, in whom it is characterized by high fever and pulmonary disorders resembling pneumonia: also called *parrot fever.*

**psoriasis** (sō-rī′ə-sis), *n.* a chronic skin disease characterized by scaly, red patches.

**psyche** (sī′ki), *n.* the mind, especially considered as an organic system serving to adjust the total organism to the environment.

**psychiatrist** (sī-kī′ə-trist), *n.* a specialist in psychiatry.

**psychiatry** (sī-kī′ə-tri), *n.* the branch of medicine dealing with the study and the treatment of disorders of the mind.

**psychoanalysis** (sī′kō-ə-nal′ə-sis), *n.* 1. a method of treating neuroses and some other mental disorders by analyzing emotional conflicts, repressions, etc. through the use of free association, dream analysis, etc. 2. the theory or practice of this.

**psychogenic** (sī′kə-jen′ik), *adj.* caused by mental conflicts.

**psychology** (sī-kol′ə-ji), *n.* the science that deals with the mind and mental processes, feelings, desires, etc.; the study of human behavior.

**psychoneurosis** (sī′kō-nyoo-rō′sis), *n.* a neurosis.

**psychosis** (sī-kō′sis), *n.* any mental disorder in which the personality is very seriously disorganized: psychoses may be functional, as in schizophrenia, or organic, as in paresis.

**psychosomatic** (sī′kō-sō-mat′ik), *adj.* 1. designating or of a physical disorder originating in or aggravated by one's mental or emotional processes. 2. designating the branch of medicine using a psychological approach to such disorders.

**psychotherapy** (sī′kō-ther′ə-pi), *n.* the treatment of nervous and mental disorders by hypnosis, psychoanalysis, etc.

**ptomaine poisoning** (tō′mān), an acute digestive disorder caused by the eating of putrid or rancid food containing certain toxic bacilli.

**puerperal** (pū-ũr′pẽr-əl), *adj.* of or connected with childbirth.

**puberty** (pū′bẽr-ti), *n.* the state of physical development when a person of either sex becomes capable of reproduction.

**pulse** (puls), *n.* the regular, rhythmical beating in the arteries caused by the contractions of the heart.

**pupil** (pū′p′l), *n.* the contractile circular opening, apparently black, in the center of the iris of the eye.

**purgative** (pũr′gə-tiv), *n.* any drug or medicine which acts as a cathartic. *adj.* causing bowel movement.

**purpura** (pũr′pyoo-rə), *n.* a disease characterized by purplish patches on the skin or mucous membranes, caused by the subcutaneous escape of blood from its vessels.

**purulent** (pyoor′ə-lənt), *adj.* of, like, containing, or discharging pus.

**pus** (pus), *n.* the yellowish-white matter produced by an infection, consisting of bacteria, white corpuscles, serum, etc.

**pustule** (pus′chool), *n.* 1. a small inflamed elevation of the skin, containing pus. 2. any small elevation like a blister or pimple.

**pylorus** (pī-lôr′əs), *n.* the opening from the stomach into the duodenum.

**pyorrhea** (pī′ə-rē′ə), *n.* an infection of the gums and tooth sockets, characterized by the formation of pus and, usually, by loosening of the teeth: in full, **pyorrhea alveolaris** (al-vē′ə-lâr′is).

## Q

**quadriceps** (kwäd′ri-seps′), *n.* a muscle with four heads; especially, the large muscle at the front of the thigh, which functions to extend the leg when contracted.

**quartan** (kwôr′t′n), *n.* a type of malaria in which the paroxysms occur every fourth day.

**quickening** (kwik′ən-iŋ), *n.* the stage of pregnancy in which the first fetal movements in the uterus can be felt.

**quinine** (kwī′nīn), *n.* 1. a bitter alkaloid obtained from cinchona bark. 2. a compound of this, used in the treatment of malaria.

**quinsy** (kwin′zi), *n.* an inflammation of the tonsils, accompanied by the formation of pus.

## R

**rabies** (rā′bēz), *n.* an infectious virus disease of dogs, wolves, etc. that can be transmitted to man by the bite of an infected animal and is characterized by choking, convulsions, etc.: it is fatal if not treated immediately: also called *hydrophobia.*

**rachitis** (rə-kī′tis), *n.* rickets.

**radiograph** (rā′di-ō-graf′), *n.* a picture of an internal structure of the body, produced on a sensitized film or plate by X rays.

**radiologist** (rā′di-ol′ə-gist), *n.* a physician who specializes in radiology.

**radiology** (rā′di-ol′ə-ji), *n.* the science dealing with radiant energy and its uses in the treatment of disease, as by X rays.

**radioscopy** (rā′di-os′kə-pi), *n.* the direct examination of internal structures and organs by radiation, as by X rays.

**radiotherapy** (rā′di-ō-ther′ə-pi), *n.* the treatment of disease by the use of X rays or rays from a radioactive substance, as radium.

**radiumtherapy** (rā′di-əm-ther′ə-pi), *n.* the treatment of cancer or other diseases by the use of radium.

**radius** (rā′di-əs), *n.* the long bone in the thumb side of the forearm, extending from the elbow to the wrist.

**râle** (räl), *n.* an abnormal rattling or bubbling sound accompanying the normal sound of breathing, and usually indicating a diseased condition of the lungs or bronchi.

**rash** (rash), *n.* an eruption of red spots on the skin, usually temporary.

**reaction** (ri-ak′shən), *n.* 1. an action induced by resistance to another action. 2. a depression or exhaustion of energy following nervous tension, overstimulation, etc. 3. an increased activity following depression.

**rectal** (rek′t′l), *adj.* of, for, or near the rectum.

**rectum** (rek′təm), *n.* the lower end of the large intestine, usually from six to eight inches in length and ending at the anus.

**reflex** (rē′fleks), *n.* an involuntary reaction, as a sneeze, resulting when a stimulus carried to a nerve center is directly transmitted to the muscle or gland that responds.

**refraction** (ri-frak′shən), *n.* the ability of the eye to bend light rays entering it, so as to form an image on the retina.

**relapse** (ri-laps′), *n.* the recurrence of a disease after apparent recovery.

**renal** (rē′n′l), *adj.* of or near the kidneys.

**renin** (rē′nin), *n.* a protein formed in the kidneys and thought to be associated with some forms of hypertension.

**reserpine** (ri-sũr′pēn), *n.* a crystalline alkaloid extracted from the root of an Indian shrub, used in the treatment of hypertension and in psychotherapy.

**respiration** (res′pə-rā′shən), *n.* breathing.

**respirator** (res'pə-rā'tẽr), *n.* 1. a contrivance, as of gauze, worn over the mouth, to prevent the inhaling of harmful substances, to warm the air breathed in, etc. 2. an apparatus for maintaining breathing artificially.
**resuscitation** (ri-sus'ə-tā'shən), *n.* the act of restoring to life or consciousness.
**retina** (ret''n-ə), *n.* the innermost coat of the back part of the eyeball, a layer of cells sensitive to light: the image formed by the lens on the retina is carried to the brain by the optic nerve.
**retinitis** (ret''n-ī'tis), *n.* inflammation of the retina.
**rheum** (ro͞om), *n.* 1. any watery or catarrhal discharge from the mucous membranes, as of the mouth, eyes, or nose. 2. a cold.
**rheumatic fever** (ro͞o-mat'ik), an infectious disease associated with the presence of streptococci in the body: it most commonly attacks children, and is characterized by fever, pain, and swelling of the joints, inflammation of the heart valves, etc.
**rheumatism** (ro͞o'mə-tiz'm), *n.* any of various painful conditions of the joints and muscles; especially, a disease believed to be caused by a microorganism and characterized by inflammation and pain of the joints.
**rheumatoid arthritis** (ro͞o'mə-toid'), a chronic disease characterized by inflammation, stiffness, and often deformity, of the joints.
**Rh factor,** an agglutinating factor, usually present in the blood, which may cause hemolysis during pregnancy or after transfusion of blood containing this factor into someone lacking it: people who have this factor are *Rh positive;* those who do not are *Rh negative.*
**rhinitis** (rī-nī'tis), *n.* inflammation of the nose, especially of the nasal mucous membrane.
**rib** (rib), *n.* any of the twenty-four arched bones which extend from the backbone to the sternum and enclose the chest cavity.
**rickets** (rik'its), *n.* a disease of the skeletal system, chiefly of children, resulting from a deficiency of calcium salts or vitamin D in the diet, or from lack of sunlight, and characterized by a softening and, often, bending of the bones.
**ringworm** (ring'wũrm'), *n.* any of various skin diseases, as athlete's foot, caused by a fungus and characterized by itching and the formation of ring-shaped, discolored patches covered with scales.
**Roentgen ray** (rent'gən), an X ray.
**rupture** (rup'chẽr), *n.* a hernia; especially, an abdominal or inguinal hernia.

S

**sac** (sak), *n.* a pouchlike part, often filled with a fluid.
**saccharin** (sak'ə-rin), *n.* a white, crystalline chemical compound obtained from coal tar: it is about 400 times sweeter than cane sugar and is used as a substitute for sugar in diabetic diets and under other conditions.
**sadism** (sad'iz'm), *n.* the getting of sexual pleasure from dominating, mistreating, or hurting one's partner, physically or otherwise.
**salicylic acid** (sal'ə-sil'ik), a white, crystalline compound used as a mild antiseptic, and, in the form of its salts, to treat rheumatism, relieve pain, etc.
**saliva** (sə-lī'və), *n.* the thin, watery, slightly viscid fluid secreted by the salivary glands it serves as an aid to digestion by moistening and softening food.
**salivary** (sal'ə-ver'i), *adj.* of or secreting saliva.
**salpinx** (sal'piŋks), *n.* 1. a Fallopian tube. 2. a Eustachian tube.
**sanguineous** (saŋ-gwin'i-əs), *adj.* of or containing blood; bloody.
**sarcoma** (sär-kō'mə), *n.* a malignant tumor that begins in connective tissue or other tissue that is not epithelial.
**satyriasis** (sat'ə-rī'ə-sis), *n.* excessive and uncontrollable sexual desire in a man.
**scab** (skab), *n.* the protective crust formed over a sore or wound during healing.
**scabies** (skā'bi-ēz'), *n.* a contagious skin disease caused by a parasite that burrows under the skin and deposits eggs, causing intense itching.
**scalpel** (skal'pəl), *n.* a small, light, straight knife with a very sharp blade, used by surgeons.
**scapula** (skap'yoo-lə), *n.* the shoulder blade.
**scarlatina** (skär'lə-tē'nə), *n.* scarlet fever.
**scarlet fever,** an acute contagious disease, especially of children, caused by certain streptococci and characterized by sore throat, fever, and a scarlet rash.
**Schick test** (shik), a skin test to determine immunity to diphtheria.
**schizophrenia** (skiz'ə-frē'ni-ə), *n.* a mental disorder characterized by indifference, withdrawal, hallucinations, and delusions of persecution and omnipotence, often with unimpaired intelligence.
**sciatica** (sī-at'i-kə), *n.* any painful condition in the region of the hip and thighs; especially, neuritis of the long nerve passing down the back of the thigh.
**sclera** (skler'ə), *n.* a tough, white, fibrous membrane covering all of the eyeball except the area covered by the cornea.
**sclerosis** (skli-rō'sis), *n.* a hardening of body tissues or parts, as by an excessive growth of fibrous connective tissue.
**scoliosis** (skō'li-ō'sis), *n.* lateral curvature of the spine.
**scopolamine** (skō-pol'ə-mēn'), *n.* a drug used to produce twilight sleep.
**scrofula** (skrof'yoo-lə), *n.* tuberculosis of the lymph glands in the neck.
**scrotum** (skrō'təm), *n.* the pouch of skin containing the testicles.
**scurvy** (skũr'vi), *n.* a disease resulting from a deficiency of vitamin C in the body, characterized by weakness, anemia, spongy gums, bleeding from the mucous membranes, etc.
**sebaceous gland** (si-bā'shəs), any of certain skin glands that secrete sebum.
**sebum** (sē'bəm), *n.* the semiliquid, greasy secretion of the sebaceous glands.
**sedation** (si-dā'shən), *n.* the act or process of reducing excitement, irritation, or pain, especially by means of a sedative.
**sedative** (sed'ə-tiv), *n.* a medicine that lessens excitement, irritation, or pain.
**semen** (sē'mən), *n.* the thick, whitish fluid secreted by the testicles and containing the spermatozoa.
**semicircular canal,** any of the three loop-shaped tubular structures of the inner ear that serve to maintain balance in the body.
**seminal** (sem'ə-n'l), *adj.* of or containing semen.
**senna** (sen'ə), *n.* the dried leaves of certain plants of the pea family, used as a cathartic.
**sepsis** (sep'sis), *n.* poisoning caused by the absorption into the blood of pathogenic microorganisms, as from putrefying material; blood poisoning.
**septicemia** (sep'tə-sē'mi-ə), *n.* blood poisoning caused by the presence of pathogenic microorganisms and their toxic products in the blood.
**septum** (sep'təm), *n.* a thin wall, as the wall of cartilage that divides the nose into two halves.
**sequestrum** (si-kwes'trəm), *n.* a piece of dead tissue, especially dead bone, which has become separated from healthy tissue.
**serous** (sêr'əs), *adj.* 1. of or containing serum. 2. like a serum; thin and watery.
**serous fluid,** any of several serumlike fluids in the body cavities, especially in those lined with serous membrane.
**serous membrane,** a thin membrane that lines most of the closed cavities of the body.
**serum** (sêr'əm), *n.* 1. the clear, yellowish fluid which separates from the clot when the blood coagulates; blood serum. 2. this serum containing agents of immunity, taken from an animal made immune to a specific disease by inoculation: it is used as an antitoxin.
**shaking palsy,** a chronic degenerative disease of the central nervous system, characterized by tremors, muscular rigidity, and a masklike expression.
**shinbone** (shin'bōn'), *n.* the tibia.
**shingles** (shiŋ'g'lz), *n.* herpes zoster.
**shock** (shok), *n.* a condition or disorder of the circulatory system, resulting from injury or a sudden psychic disturbance, and characterized by a decrease in blood pressure, a weak and rapid pulse, and, often, unconsciousness.
**sigmoid flexure** (sig'moid), the lower portion of the colon, shaped like the letter S: it ends in the rectum.
**silicosis** (sil'ə-kō'sis), *n.* a chronic disease of the lungs, caused by the inhalation of silica dust, as in quarrying stone.
**silver nitrate,** a colorless, crystalline salt of silver in various dilutions, used as an antiseptic or cauterizing agent.
**sinew** (sin'ū), *n.* a tendon.
**sinus** (sī'nəs), *n.* any of various cavities, hollows, or passages; especially, *a)* any of the air cavities in the skull opening into the nasal cavities. *b)* a large channel for venous blood. *c)* a dilated part in a blood vessel, etc.
**sinusitis** (sī'nəs-ī'tis), *n.* an inflammation of the sinuses of the skull.
**skeleton** (skel'ə-t'n), *n.* the bony framework of the body, supporting the tissues and protecting the organs.
**sleeping sickness,** 1. an infectious disease, especially of tropical Africa, transmitted by the bite of certain flies: it is characterized by fever, lethargy, and coma, usually ending in death. 2. inflammation of the brain, caused by a virus and inducing drowsiness and lethargy.
**smallpox** (smôl'poks'), *n.* an acute, infectious disease with high fever and a general eruption of blisters and pustules that often leave pitted scars.
**snare** (snâr), *n.* a loop of wire used in surgery to remove tumors and polyps by either cutting them off or tearing them out by the roots.
**solar plexus,** a network of nerves in the upper abdomen behind the stomach.
**spasm** (spaz'm), *n.* a sudden, abnormal, involuntary muscular contraction.
**spastic** (spas'tik), *adj.* of or characterized by spasm; specifically, designating a form of paralysis in which certain muscles are in a state of continuous contraction.
**speculum** (spek'yoo-ləm), *n.* an instrument which opens and enables examination of a passage or cavity.
**sperm** (spũrm), *n.* 1. the male generative fluid; semen. 2. any of the germ cells in this fluid.
**spermatic cord** (spẽr-mat'ik), the cordlike structure suspending a testicle within the scrotum and containing the vas deferens, blood vessels and nerves supplying the testicles, etc.
**spermatozoon** (spũr'mə-tə-zō'on), *n.* the male germ cell, found in semen, which penetrates the ovum of the female to fertilize it.
**sphenoid** (sfē'noid), *n.* the wedge-shaped bone at the base of the skull.
**sphincter** (sfiŋk'tẽr), *n.* a ring-shaped muscle that surrounds a natural opening in the

body and can open or close it by expanding or contracting.

**sphygmomanometer** (sfig'mō-mə-nom'ə-tẽr), *n.* an instrument used to measure arterial blood pressure.

**spinal anesthesia,** local anesthesia of the lower half of the body by the injection of an anesthetic into the lumbar region of the spinal cord.

**spinal canal,** a canal or tube within the vertebral arches, containing the spinal cord.

**spinal column,** the series of jointed vertebrae forming the axial support for the skeleton; spine; backbone.

**spinal cord,** the thick cord of nerve tissue of the central nervous system, extending down the spinal canal from the medulla oblongata.

**spine** (spīn), *n.* the spinal column.

**splanchnic** (splaŋk'nik), *adj.* of the viscera.

**spleen** (splēn), *n.* a large, vascular, ductless organ in the upper left part of the abdominal cavity near the stomach: it has various functions in modifying the structure of the blood.

**spondylitis** (spon'də-lī'tis), *n.* inflammation of the vertebrae.

**sprain** (sprān), *n.* 1. a wrenching or twisting of a ligament or muscle of a joint, as the ankle, without dislocating the bones. 2. an injury resulting from this, characterized by swelling, pain, and disablement of the joint.

**squamous** (skwā'məs), *adj.* 1. formed of, like, or covered with scales. 2. designating or of the thin, scalelike, upper anterior portion of the temporal bone.

**squill** (skwil), *n.* the fleshy scales of a plant of the lily family, used as an expectorant and diuretic.

**staphylococcus** (staf'i-lə-kok'əs), *n.* any of a group of spherical, Gram-positive bacteria that generally occur in irregular clusters or short chains and are the cause of pus formation in boils, abscesses, etc.

**stasis** (stā'sis), *n.* the slowing down or stopping of some fluid, as blood in a blood vessel or feces in the intestines.

**steapsin** (sti-ap'sin), *n.* an enzyme present in the pancreatic juice: it converts fats into glycerol and free acids.

**sterilize** (ster'ə-līz'), *v. t.* 1. to make incapable of producing children by removing the organs of reproduction or preventing them from functioning effectively. 2. to free from living microorganisms, as by subjecting to great heat or chemical action.

**sternum** (stũr'nəm), *n.* a thin, flat structure of bone and cartilage to which most of the ribs are attached in the front of the chest.

**stethoscope** (steth'ə-skōp'), *n.* a hearing instrument used in auscultation, for examining the heart, lungs, etc. by listening to the sounds they make.

**stigma** (stig'mə), *n.* 1. a spot on the skin, especially one that bleeds as the result of certain nervous tensions. 2. any sign characteristic of a specific disease.

**stimulant** (stim'yoo-lənt), *n.* a drug or other agent that temporarily increases the activity of some vital process or of some organ.

**stomatitis** (stō'mə-tī'tis), *n.* inflammation of the mouth.

**strabismus** (strə-biz'məs), *n.* a disorder of the eyes, as crosseye, in which both eyes cannot be focused on the same point at the same time.

**streptococcus** (strep'tə-kok'əs), *n.* any of a group of spherical, Gram-positive bacteria occurring generally in chains: some species cause various serious diseases.

**streptomycin** (strep'tə-mī'sin), *n.* an antibiotic drug similar to penicillin, obtained from certain molds and used in the treatment of various diseases.

**stricture** (strik'chẽr), *n.* an abnormal narrowing of a tube or passage.

**strychnine** (strik'nin), *n.* a white, intensely bitter, poisonous alkaloid used as a stimulant to the nervous system.

**stupor** (stōō'pẽr), *n.* a state in which the mind and senses are dulled, as from the use of a narcotic.

**sty, stye** (stī), *n.* a small, inflamed swelling of a sebaceous gland on the rim of the eyelid.

**styptic** (stip'tik), *adj.* astringent; tending to stop bleeding by contracting the tissues or blood vessels.

**subconscious** (sub-kon'shəs), *n.* that portion of mental activity of which the individual has little or no conscious perception.

**subcutaneous** (sub'kū-tā'nē-əs), *adj.* being, used, or introduced under the skin.

**sudorific** (sōō'də-rif'ik), *n.* a medicine or other substance that causes or increases sweating.

**sulfanilamide** (sul'fə-nil'ə-mīd), *n.* a white, crystalline compound used in treating gonorrhea, septicemia, streptococcus infections, etc.: a synthetic coal-tar derivative.

**sunstroke** (sun'strōk'), *n.* a form of heatstroke caused by excessive exposure to the sun and characterized by high body temperature, convulsions, and, often, coma.

**suppository** (sə-poz'ə-tôr'i), *n.* a small piece of medicated substance introduced into the rectum, vagina, etc., where it is melted and diffused by the body temperature.

**suppurate** (sup'yoo-rāt'), *v. i.* to form or discharge pus; fester.

**suture** (sōō'chẽr), *n.* 1. the joining together, or the line of junction, of two bones, especially of the skull. 2. the act or method of joining together the two edges of a wound or incision by stitching; also, any of the stitches so used.

**synapse** (si-naps'), *n.* the point of contact between adjacent neurons, where nerve impulses are transmitted from one to the other.

**syphilis** (sif'ə-lis), *n.* an infectious venereal disease, caused by a spirochete and usually transmitted by sexual intercourse or acquired congenitally.

**systole** (sis'tə-lē'), *n.* the usual rhythmic contraction of the heart, especially of the ventricles, following each dilatation, during which blood is driven onward through the chambers.

## T

**tabes** (tā'bēz), *n.* locomotor ataxia: in full, **tabes dorsalis** (dôr-sā'lis).

**tachycardia** (tak'i-kär'di-ə), *n.* an abnormally rapid heartbeat.

**taenia** (tē'ni-ə), *n.* 1. a ribbonlike part or structure, as of muscle or nerve tissue. 2. a tapeworm.

**taeniasis** (ti-nī'ə-sis), *n.* infestation with tapeworms.

**talipes** (tal'ə-pēz), *n.* clubfoot.

**tampon** (tam'pon), *n.* a plug of cotton or other absorbent material put into a wound, cavity, etc. to stop bleeding or absorb secretions.

**tannic acid** (tan'ik), a yellowish, astringent substance, especially the kind derived from gallnuts, used locally for burns, and internally as a remedy for diarrhea.

**tapeworm** (tāp'wũrm'), *n.* a long, flat, ribbonlike worm that lives as a parasite in the intestines.

**tarsal** (tär's'l), *adj.* of the tarsus of the foot.

**tarsus** (tär'səs), *n.* 1. the ankle. 2. the seven bones forming the ankle.

**tartar** (tär'tẽr), *n.* a hard deposit on the teeth, consisting of saliva proteins and calcium phosphate.

**teat** (tēt), *n.* the nipple of the breast.

**temple** (tem'p'l), *n.* either of the flat surfaces behind the forehead and in front of the ear.

**temporal bone** (tem'pẽr-əl), either of a pair of compound bones forming the sides of the skull.

**tendon** (ten'dən), *n.* any of the inelastic cords of tough, fibrous connective tissue in which muscle fibers end and by which muscles are attached to bones or other parts.

**terramycin** (ter'ə-mī'sin), *n.* an antibiotic drug derived from an earth, effective against certain viruses, protozoa, bacteria, etc.

**testicle** (tes'ti-k'l), *n.* the sex gland of the male; either of two oval structures that are suspended in the scrotum and secrete spermatozoa.

**testis** (tes'tis), *n.* a testicle. *pl.* **testes** (tes'tēz).

**testosterone** (tes-tos'tə-rōn'), *n.* a male sex hormone produced as a white, crystalline substance by isolation from the testes, or synthesized.

**tetanus** (tet'ə-nəs), *n.* an acute infectious disease, often fatal, caused by the toxins of a specific bacillus which usually enters the body through wounds: it is characterized by spasmodic contractions and rigidity of some or all voluntary muscles. *Lockjaw* is a form of tetanus in which the jaws become firmly closed because of the muscular contractions.

**thalamus** (thal'ə-məs), *n.* a large, ovoid mass of gray matter situated at the base of the brain and involved in the transmission and integration of certain sensations.

**theelin** (thē'lin), *n.* estrone.

**theelol** (thē'lōl), *n.* estriol.

**theobromine** (thē'ə-brō'mēn), *n.* a bitter, crystalline alkaloid extracted from the cacao plant, used as a diuretic and a nerve stimulant.

**therapeutics** (ther'ə-pū'tiks), *n.pl.* the branch of medicine that deals with the treatment and cure of diseases.

**therapy** (ther'ə-pi), *n.* therapeutics.

**thigh** (thī) *n.* the part of the leg extending from the hip to the knee.

**thoracic** (thô-ras'ik), *adj.* of, in, or near the thorax.

**thoracic duct,** the main canal of the lymphatic system, passing along the front of the spinal column and serving to collect lymph from various parts of the body, conveying it into a vein under the left clavicle.

**thorax** (thôr'aks), *n.* the part of the body between the neck and the abdomen; chest.

**throat** (thrōt), *n.* 1. the front part of the neck. 2. the upper part of the passage leading from the mouth and nose to the stomach and lungs, including the pharynx and upper larynx, trachea, and esophagus.

**thrombin** (throm'bin), *n.* the enzyme of the blood that causes clotting by forming fibrin.

**thrombosis** (throm-bō'sis), *n.* coagulation of the blood in some part of the circulatory system, forming a clot that obstructs circulation in that part.

**thrombus** (throm'bəs), *n.* the clot formed in thrombosis.

**thrush** (thrush), *n.* a disease, especially of children, caused by a fungus and characterized by the formation of milky-white lesions on the membranes of the mouth, lips, and throat.

**thymus** (thī'məs), *n.* a ductless, glandlike body, of undetermined function, situated in the upper thorax near the throat: it is most prominent at puberty, after which it disappears or becomes vestigial.

**thyroid** (thī'roid), *n.* 1. a large ductless gland lying in front and on either side of the trachea and secreting thyroxine, which regulates the growth of the body: the malfunctioning or congenital absence of this gland can cause goiter, cretinism, etc. 2. the principal cartilage of the larynx, forming the Adam's apple.

**thyroxine** (thī-rok′sēn), *n.* the active hormone of the thyroid gland, often prepared synthetically and used in treating goiter, cretinism, etc.
**tibia** (tib′i-ə), *n.* the inner and thicker of the two bones of the leg between the knee and the ankle; shinbone.
**tic** (tik), *n.* any involuntary, regularly repeated, spasmodic contraction of a muscle, generally of neurotic origin.
**tic douloureux** (do͞o′lo͞o-ro͞o′), a tic of the facial muscles, accompanied by severe neuralgic pains.
**tinnitus** (ti-nī′təs), *n.* a sound of ringing in the ear, not resulting from external stimulus.
**tongue** (tuŋ), *n.* the movable muscular organ on the floor of the mouth: its movements aid in the formation of speech sounds; it also aids in swallowing, chewing, and tasting.
**tonsil** (ton′s'l), *n.* either of a pair of oval masses of lymphoid tissue, one on each side of the back of the mouth, leading to the pharynx.
**tonsillectomy** (ton′s'l-ek′tə-mi), *n.* the surgical removal of tonsils.
**tonsillitis** (ton′s'l-ī′tis), *n.* inflammation of the tonsils.
**tooth** (to͞oth), *n.* any of a set of hard, bonelike structures (normally 32 in the adult) set in the jaws and used for biting and chewing: a tooth consists of a sensitive, vascular pulp surrounded by dentine and coated on the crown with enamel and on the root with cement.
**torso** (tôr′sō), *n.* the trunk.
**torticollis** (tôr′ti-kol′is), *n.* a condition of involuntary contraction of the neck muscles causing the head to be twisted to an abnormal position.
**tourniquet** (toor′ni-ket′), *n.* any device for compressing a blood vessel to stop bleeding or control the circulation of blood to some part, as a bandage twisted about a limb or a pad pressed down by a screw.
**toxemia** (tok-sē′mi-ə), *n.* any condition of blood poisoning, especially that caused by bacterial toxins transported through the blood stream from a focus of infection.
**toxic** (tok′sik), *adj.* 1. of, affected by, or caused by a toxin. 2. poisonous.
**toxin** (tok′sin), *n.* any of various poisonous compounds produced by some microorganisms and causing certain diseases.
**toxoid** (tok′soid), *n.* a toxin that has been treated, as with chemical agents, so as to eliminate the toxic qualities while retaining the properties of an antigen.
**trachea** (trā′ki-ə), *n.* that part of the respiratory tract which conveys air from the larynx to the bronchi.
**tracheotomy** (trā′ki-ot′ə-mi), *n.* surgical incision of the trachea, as for making an artificial breathing hole.
**trachoma** (trə-kō′mə), *n.* a contagious form of conjunctivitis, characterized by the formation of inflammatory granulations on the inner eyelid.
**transfusion** (trans-fū′zhən), *n.* the transfer of blood from one individual into a blood vessel, usually a vein, of another.
**trauma** (trô′mə), *n.* 1. an injury or wound violently produced; also, the condition or neurosis resulting from this. 2. an emotional experience, or shock, which has a lasting psychic effect.
**traumatic** (trô-mat′ik), *adj.* 1. of, having the nature of, or resulting from a trauma. 2. used in the treatment of wounds.
**trench mouth**, an infectious disease of the mucous membranes of the mouth and throat, caused by a spirochete and commonly affecting troops in trenches.
**trichiasis** (tri-kī′ə-sis), *n.* 1. the abnormal condition of ingrowing eyelashes. 2. the appearance of hairlike filaments in the urine.
**trichinosis** (trik′ə-nō′sis), *n.* a disease caused by the presence of small worms (*trichinae*) in the intestines and muscle tissues and usually acquired by eating insufficiently cooked pork from an infected hog: it is characterized by fever, nausea, diarrhea, and muscular pain.
**trichosis** (tri-kō′sis), *n.* any disease of the hair.
**trismus** (triz′məs), *n.* lockjaw: see **tetanus.**
**trunk** (truŋk), *n.* 1. the body, not including the head, arms, or legs. 2. the main part or stem of a nerve or blood vessel.
**truss** (trus), *n.* an appliance for giving support in cases of rupture and hernia, usually consisting of a pad on a special belt.
**tubercle** (to͞o′bēr-k'l), *n.* 1. a knoblike elevation, as on a bone. 2. any abnormal hard nodule or swelling; especially, the typical nodular lesion of tuberculosis.
**tuberculin** (to͞o-būr′kyoo-lin), *n.* a sterile liquid preparation made from the growth products or extracts of a culture of the bacillus that causes tuberculosis: it is injected into the skin as a test for tuberculosis.
**tuberculosis** (to͞o-būr′kyoo-lō′sis), *n.* an infectious disease caused by a bacillus and characterized by the formation of tubercles in various tissues; especially, tuberculosis of the lungs; consumption.
**tularemia** (to͞o′lə-rē′mi-ə), *n.* an infectious disease of rodents, especially rabbits, caused by a bacterium and transmitted to man in handling the flesh of infected animals or by the bite of certain insects: it is characterized by an irregular fever, aching, inflammation of the lymph glands, etc.: also called *rabbit fever.*
**tumor** (to͞o′mēr), *n.* a swelling on some part of the body; especially, a mass of new tissue growth independent of its surrounding structures, having no physiological function.
**tympanic membrane** (tim-pan′ik), the eardrum.
**tympanum** (tim′pə-nəm), *n.* 1. the middle ear: see **ear.** 2. sometimes, the eardrum.
**typhoid** (tī′foid), *n.* an acute infectious disease caused by a bacillus and acquired through drinking infected milk, water, etc.: it is characterized by fever, intestinal disorders, etc.: also **typhoid fever.**
**typhus** (tī′fəs), *n.* an acute infectious disease caused by a microorganism transmitted to man by the bite of fleas, lice, etc., and characterized by fever, nervous disorders, weakness, and eruptions of red spots on the skin: also **typhus fever.**

## U

**ulcer** (ul′sēr), *n.* an open sore (other than a wound) on the skin or some mucous membrane, as the lining of the stomach (*peptic ulcer*), characterized by the disintegration of the tissue and, often, the discharge of pus.
**ulcerate** (ul′sə-rāt′), *v. t. & v. i.* to form or become affected with an ulcer or ulcers.
**ulna** (ul′nə), *n.* the large, inner bone of the forearm, situated on the side opposite the thumb.
**umbilical cord** (um-bil′i-k'l), a cordlike structure connecting the fetus with the placenta of the mother and serving to convey food to, and remove waste from, the fetus.
**umbilicus** (um-bil′i-kəs), *n.* the navel.
**undulant fever** (un′joo-lənt), a persistent infectious disease caused by a bacterium transmitted to man in the milk of infected cows and goats, and characterized by a recurrent fever, an enlarged spleen, sweating, and pains in the joints.
**urate** (yoor′āt), *n.* a salt of uric acid, present in urine.
**urea** (yoo-rē′ə), *n.* a very soluble crystalline solid found in the urine.
**uremia** (yoo-rē′mi-ə), *n.* a toxic condition caused by the presence in the blood of waste products normally eliminated in the urine: it results from an inadequate secretion of urine.
**ureter** (yoo-rē′tēr), *n.* a narrow tube or passageway that carries urine from the kidney to the bladder.
**urethra** (yoo-rē′thrə), *n.* the membranous canal through which urine is discharged from the bladder: in the male, sperm is also discharged through the urethra.
**urethritis** (yoor′i-thrī′tis), *n.* inflammation of the urethra.
**uric acid** (yoor′ik), a white, odorless, crystalline substance found in urine.
**urinary** (yoor′ə-ner′i), *adj.* 1. of urine. 2. of the organs concerned in the secretion and discharge of urine.
**urinate** (yoor′ə-nāt′), *v. i.* to discharge urine from the body.
**urine** (yoor′in), *n.* the yellowish fluid, containing waste products, secreted from the blood by the kidneys, passed through the ureters to the bladder, where it is stored, and periodically discharged from the body through the urethra.
**urinogenital** (yoor′ə-nō-jen′ə-t'l), *adj.* genitourinary.
**urologist** (yoo-rol′ə-jist), *n.* a physician who specializes in urology.
**urology** (yoo-rol′ə-ji), *n* the branch of medicine which is concerned with the urinogenital system and its diseases.
**urticaria** (ūr′tə-kâr′i-ə), *n.* an allergic skin condition characterized by the eruption of smooth, itching patches; hives.
**uterine** (ū′tēr-in), *adj.* of the uterus.
**uterus** (ū′tēr-əs), *n.* a hollow, muscular organ in which the ovum is deposited and the embryo and fetus are developed and protected, womb.
**uvula** (ū′vyoo-lə), *n.* the small, soft, movable process hanging from the soft palate above the back of the tongue.

## V

**vaccinate** (vak′sə-nāt′), *v. t.* to inoculate with a specific vaccine in order to prevent or lessen the effect of some disease. *v. i.* to perform vaccination.
**vaccination** (vak′sə-nā′shən), *n.* the act or practice of vaccinating.
**vaccine** (vak′sēn), *n.* any preparation of dead bacteria introduced into the body to produce immunity to a specific disease by causing the formation of antibodies.
**vagina** (və-jī′nə), *n.* the passage in the female which leads from the vulva to the uterus.
**vaginal** (vaj′ə-n'l), *adj.* of or for the vagina.
**vaginitis** (vaj′ə-nī′tis), *n.* inflammation of the vagina.
**vagus** (vā′gəs), *n.* either of a pair of cranial nerves, arising in the medulla oblongata and innervating the larynx, lungs, heart, esophagus, and most of the abdominal organs.
**valerian** (və-lêr′i-ən), *n.* a drug made from the roots and dried root-stocks of a European plant: it is used as a sedative and antispasmodic.
**valve** (valv), *n.* a membranous fold or structure which permits body fluids to flow in one direction only, or opens and closes a tube or opening
**varicella** (var′ə-sel′ə), *n.* chicken pox.
**varicocele** (var′ə-kō-sēl′), *n* a varicose condition of the veins of the spermatic cord.
**varicose** (var′ə-kōs′), *adj* abnormally and irregularly swollen or dilated: as, a *varicose* vein.
**variola** (və-rī′ə-lə), *n.* smallpox.
**vascular** (vas′kyoo-lēr), *adj.* designating or of the vessels, or system of vessels, for conveying blood or lymph.
**vas deferens** (vas′ def′ə-renz′), the convoluted duct that conveys sperm from

the testicle to the ejaculatory duct of the penis.
**vasectomy** (vas-ek'tə-mi), *n.* surgical removal of all or part of the vas deferens.
**vasomotor** (vas'ō-mō'tēr), *adj.* regulating the size of blood vessels by causing contraction or dilatation: said of a nerve, nerve center, or drug.
**vein** (vān), *n.* any blood vessel that carries blood from some part of the body back to the heart.
**velum** (vē'ləm), *n.* the soft palate.
**vena cava** (vē'nə kā'və), either of two large veins conveying blood to the right atrium of the heart.
**venereal** (və-nêr'i-əl), *adj.* transmitted by sexual intercourse with an infected person: as, *venereal* disease.
**venous** (vē'nəs), *adj.* 1. of a vein or veins. 2. designating blood being carried in the veins back to the heart and lungs: venous blood has given up oxygen and taken up carbon dioxide and has a dark-red color.
**ventricle** (ven'tri-k'l), *n.* 1. either of the two lower chambers of the heart which receive blood from the auricles and pump it into the arteries. 2. any of the four small continuous cavities within the brain.
**vermiform appendix** (vūr'mə-fôrm'), see **appendix.**
**vermifuge** (vūr'mə-fūj'), *n.* a drug used to expel worms and other parasites from the intestinal tract.
**version** (vūr'zhən), *n.* 1. displacement of the uterus in which it is deflected but not bent upon itself. 2. the turning of the fetus in the uterus to assist in its delivery.
**vertebra** (vūr'tə-brə), *n.* any of the single bones of the spinal column.
**vertigo** (vūr'ti-gō'), *n.* a sensation of dizziness or giddiness.
**vesicle** (ves'i-k'l), *n.* a small, membranous cavity, sac, or cyst; specif., one containing a serous fluid; blister.
**viable** (vī'ə-b'l), *adj.* at that stage of development that will permit it to live and develop under normal conditions, outside of the uterus: said of a fetus or newborn infant.
**Vincent's angina,** trench mouth.
**virulent** (vir'yoo-lənt), *adj.* 1. violent and rapid in its course; highly malignant: said of a disease. 2. highly infectious: said of a microorganism.
**virus** (vī'rəs), *n.* any of a group of ultramicroscopic or submicroscopic infectious agents that cause various diseases.
**viscera** (vis'ēr-ə), *n.pl.* the internal organs of the body, especially of the thorax and abdomen, as the heart, lungs, liver, intestines, etc.
**vitamin** (vī'tə-min), *n.* see **vitamin,** in main vocabulary section.
**vitreous humor** (vit'ri-əs), the transparent, colorless, jellylike substance that fills the eyeball between the retina and the lens.
**vulva** (vul'və), *n.* the external genital organs of a female, including the labia majora, labia minora, clitoris, and the entrance to the vagina.

## W

**wart** (wôrt), *n.* a small, usually hard, tumerous growth on the skin.
**Wassermann test** (väs'ēr-män'), a test for the diagnosis of syphilis by determining the presence of antibodies of syphilis in the blood serum.
**wax** (waks), *n.* earwax.
**wean** (wēn), *v. t.* to train an infant to take food other than its mother's milk; stop suckling.
**wheal** (hwēl), *n.* 1. a pustule. 2. a small itching elevation on the skin, as from the bite of an insect.
**whoop** (hōōp), *n.* the deep-sounding convulsive intake of air immediately following a fit of coughing in whooping cough.
**whooping cough** (hōōp'iŋ), an acute infectious disease, usually affecting children, caused by a bacillus and characterized by catarrh of the respiratory tract and repeated attacks of coughing that end in a whoop.
**windpipe** (wind'pīp'), *n.* the trachea.
**womb** (wōōm), *n.* the uterus.
**wound** (wōōnd), *n.* an injury to the body in which the skin or other tissue is broken, cut, pierced, torn, etc.
**wryneck** (rī'nek'), *n.* torticollis.

## XYZ

**xanthine** (zan'thēn), *n.* a white, crystalline compound resembling uric acid: it is present in blood and urine.
**xeroderma** (zēr'ə-dūr'mə), *n.* a skin disease characterized by roughness and dryness and, often, the formation of scales.
**xiphoid** (zif'oid), *n.* a sword-shaped cartilage at the lower end of the sternum.
**X ray,** an electromagnetic ray or radiation of extremely short wave length produced by the bombardment of metal by a stream of electrons: X rays are used to study internal body structures and to diagnose and treat various disorders.
**yaws** (yôz), *n.pl.* a tropical infectious disease caused by a spirochete and characterized by raspberry skin eruptions followed by destructive lesions of the skin and bones.
**yellow fever,** an acute infectious tropical disease caused by a virus transmitted by the bite of certain mosquitos, and characterized by fever, jaundice, vomiting, etc.
**zinc ointment,** a salve or ointment containing zinc oxide.
**zoster** (zos'tēr), *n.* herpes zoster.
**zygoma** (zī-gō'mə), *n.* 1. a bony arch on either side of the face just below the eye. 2. either of a pair of quadrangular bones of this arch, forming the prominence of each cheek. 3. a process of the temporal bone forming part of this arch.

# INDEX